ISBN 978-0-331-11541-3
PIBN 11015787

FB &c Ltd, Dalton House, 60 Windsor Avenue, London, SW19 2RR.
Company number 08720141. Registered in England and Wales.

For support please visit www.forgottenbooks.com

INDEX TO THE

RECORD AND GUIDE

FOR NEW YORK CONVEYANCES AND PROJECTED BUILDINGS.

Vol. XLVIII.

JULY TO DECEMBER, 1891, INCLUSIVE.

Publication Office,

Nos. 14 and 16 VESEY ST.

NEW YORK.

Subscription Price, $6 Per Year.

THE LAWYERS' TITLE INSURANCE COMPANY

OF NEW YORK.

120 Broadway, New York. Jefferson Building, Brooklyn.
(After May 1, 1892, FRANKLIN TRUST CO. BUILDING.

COMMENCED BUSINESS JULY 18th, 1887.

CAPITAL AND SURPLUS, JANUARY 1, 1892,	$1,443,715.77
Further Security held in aid of liability of the value of	425,000.00
Permanent Guarantee Fund required by law to be invested in Bond and Mortgage, United States, State, City or County Bonds,	750,000.00
TOTAL LOSSES *SINCE THE COMPANY BEGAN BUSINESS,*	2,210.00
LOSSES IN 1891.	*NONE.*

THE LAWYERS' TITLE COMPANY

— IS —

PREFERRED TO OTHER TITLE COMPANIES

— BECAUSE —

1st.—Its *method of examination is the safest.* A comparative statement of losses will show this. The more careful the examination the fewer the losses.

2d.—Its custom of *furnishing abstracts of title and searches* gives the fullest information

An abstract of title *alone* may have little value, and a policy of title insurance *alone* is a mere contract of indemnity; but the *opinion of an expert, examined* and *approved* by this Company, WITH AN ABSTRACT OF TITLE AND A POLICY OF TITLE INSURANCE, furnishes the *fullest* information and most *complete security.*

The only reasons for refusing to furnish an abstract would seem to be where a monopoly was sought to be acquired in the information or some defect was to be concealed.

3d.—Its *method of insurance is the strongest.* It is based on the best *examination* and is issued only after approval by the law department of the Company and the examination of the Committee of Counsel, where questions arise, by *a company that does not insure against admitted defects,* that has the *largest capital employed exclusively in title insurance* and is *managed exclusively by those familiar with the business done.*

4th.—Its policies are universally accepted by *individuals, trustees and corporations,* THE U. S. GOVERNMENT BEING AMONG ITS ASSURED.

There is *very grave doubt* whether an individual trustee or a corporation has a right to take title on purchase or mortgage on a policy of title insurance only, and whether it can do so without *risk of personal liability.*

BUT there is *no doubt* that an individual trustee or a corporation has a right to take a title on purchase or mortgage on the opinion of his counsel, approved by this Company *and a policy of title insurance,* and that by so doing he incurs *no risk of personal liability.*

Out of **$142 000,000** loaned in New York and Kings Counties on bond and mortgage during the six months ending June 30th, 1891, ***all but $8,000,000*** was loaned through the attorneys of lenders.

5th.—It offers peculiar advantages to *parties selling land in parcels* as well as to *builders and brokers.*

COMMITTEE OF COUNSEL.

JOHN H. RIKER, *Chairman.*

E. ELLERY ANDERSON, of Anderson & Man.
CHARLES COUDERT, of Coudert Brothers.
FREDERIC DE P. FOSTER.
JOSEPH H. GRAY, of Owen, Gray & Sturges.
MYER S. ISAACS, of M. S. & I. S. Isaacs, Lecturer on Real Estate Law, N. Y. University Law School.
THEO. F. JACKSON, of Jackson & Burr.
BENJAMIN F. LEE, of Lee & Lee, late Professor of Real Estate and Equity Jurisprudence, Columbia College Law School.
J. LAWRENCE MARCELLUS.
DAVID B. OGDEN, of Parsons, Shepard & Ogden.
THOMAS L. OGDEN, of Ogden & Beekman.
JOHN W. PIRSSON.
J. EVARTS TRACY, of Evarts, Choate & Beaman.
GEORGE WADDINGTON.
SIDNEY WARD.

OFFICERS

President.
EDWIN W. COGGESHALL.

Vice-President.
CHARLES E. STRONG.

Secretary.
WILLIAM P. DIXON.

Treasurer.
JOHN DUER.

General Manager,
DAVID B. OGDEN.

Assistant General Manager.
SAMUEL GREEN.

Assistant Secretary.
EDWARD MORGAN.

DIRECTORS.

EDWIN W. COGGESHALL, of Norwood & Coggeshall.
HENRY DAY, of Lord, Day & Lord.
WILLIAM P. DIXON, of Miller, Peckham & Dixon.
JOHN DUER, of Martin & Smith.
HENRY E. HOWLAND, of Anderson & Howland.
JOHN T. LOCKMAN, of De Witt, Lockman & De Witt.
J. LAWRENCE MARCELLUS.
DAVID B. OGDEN, of Parsons, Shepard & Ogden.
JOHN H. RIKER.
CHARLES E. STRONG, of Strong & Cadwalader.
HERBERT B. TURNER, of Turner, McClure & Rolston.
JAMES M. VARNUM, of Varnum & Harison.
JOHN WEBBER.

INDEX TO THE RECORD AND GUIDE.

VOL. XLVIII. JULY——DECEMBER, INCLUSIVE. 1891.

The following semi-annual Index of the Conveyances and Projected Buildings in New York City, as published in THE RECORD AND GUIDE during the last half of 1891, will be found of great value to those of our subscribers who have preserved all the issues of this paper during that period. Our usual care has been taken to keep the Index up to the same perfect standard which has characterized it in the past. The pages are given on which all the transfers of realty published in Volume XLVIII. can be found, and the streets and avenues are so subdivided that few references are required. For instance, transfers of property on the Bowery appear in nine issues during the six months. The Bowery in the Index is subdivided into five parts, so that the least possible trouble need be incurred, provided it is known between what streets the property is located. In this volume we have continued to arrange the transfers in such a manner that every street affected can be seen at a glance by turning to the pages which the Index calls for. Take for instance page 11 and find thereon:

2d av, Nos. 2055 and 2057 } begins 2d av, w s,
106th st, No. 248 } 50.6 s 106th st,
runs south 50.3 x west 100 x north 100.9 to 106th st, x east 27 x south 50.6 x east 73.

The above applies when a piece of property is on the corner of any street or avenue and runs in depth upon both streets more than 100 feet, or when a plot has buildings fronting on both streets, and also when the property begins on one street and runs to another. Although many of our subscribers have used the Index for years, some of them do not fully understand the completeness of the work. We are frequently told of errors that our readers *think* they have discovered, which, upon investigation, prove to be errors of the searcher—not of the Index. For instance, in the current number appears the following: 76th st, s s, bet 1st and 2d avs, 45, 152, the latter being the pages on which transfers on said street may be found. Now, turning to page 45, the average searcher would fail to find the item referred to, because it does not appear in the alphabetical order of streets. A close search shows the item under the head of Pike st, No. 46, where a contract is made to exchange each for the other. The Index is, therefore, in some cases condemned for a supposed omission which is really the strongest evidence of the thoroughness with which it has been compiled. Where such an omission should occasionally seem apparent to the subscriber, he should search the whole page, and he will then find the item which is referred to. The Projected Buildings are indexed in a similar manner, so that it can readily be ascertained on what streets improvements have been made. Those wishing to keep a file for permanent reference should see that all the numbers are complete and have them bound. A suitable binder can be obtained at the office of THE RECORD AND GUIDE, 14 and 16 Vesey street; price, one dollar.

Annexed will be found a table showing the boundary lines, also the number of blocks contained in each of the thirteen Sections, and under which all property is now indexed in the Register's office by locality on new land maps of New York City, according to law, which went into effect Jan. 1, 1891:

Sec.
1.—South of Grand and Watts sts, between East and North Rivers. Blocks 1 to 315 incl.
2.—From Grand and Watts sts to 14th st, East and North Rivers. Blocks 316 to 660 incl.
3.—From 14th to 40th st, East and North Rivers. Blocks 661 to 992 incl.
4.—From 40th to 96th st, west of 6th av and line drawn parallel thereto. Blocks 993 to 1256 incl.
5.—From 40th to 96th st, east of 6th av, and line drawn parallel thereto. Blocks 1257 to 1592 incl.
6.—From 96th st to Harlem River, east of 6th av, and line drawn parallel thereto. Blocks 1593 to 1819 incl.
7.—From 96th to 155th st, at Harlem River, west of Lenox av, and line drawn parallel thereto. Blocks 1820 to 2104 incl.
8.—From 155th st to Spuyten Duyvil Creek, west of Harlem River. Blocks 2105 to 2259 incl.
9.—From Harlem River to 169th st, west of St. Anns and 3d avs. Blocks 2260 to 2542 incl.
10.—From Harlem River to 169th st, east of St. Anns and 3d avs. Blocks 2543 to 2781 incl.
11.—From 169th st to Pelham av and Kingsbridge road, bet Bronx and Harlem Rivers. Blocks 2782 to 3245 incl.
12.—From Pelham av and Kingsbridge road and city line, bet Bronx River and Broadway. Blocks 3246 to 3401 incl.
13.—From Harlem River and city line, bet Broadway and Hudson River. Blocks 3402 to 3428 incl.

CONVEYANCES.

NOTE.—The figures in extra black type—for instance, pages **217** and **518** under the head of Attorney st, from Broome to Delancey sts—denote that the transaction on the pages given is Leasehold, or a lease running for a long term of years. This explanation is made so that subscribers searching for transfers in fee can at once distinguish between the former and the latter without referring to the page mentioned.

NEW YORK CITY.

STREETS.

Academy....83.
Allen, south of Delancey....183, 268, 345.
  from Rivington to Stanton....45, 81, 151, 403, 516.
  Stanton to Houston....292, 584, 761.
Amity (see West 3d st)....762, 799.
Apthorps lane....9, 216, 517, 550, 689, 762.
Astor lane....800.
Attorney, from Broome to Delancey....**217, 518.**
  Rivington to Houston....403, 404.
Bank....81, 688.
Barclay, from Church st to College pl....**551, 726, 764.**
  College pl to Greenwich st ...320.
Barrow, fm Bleecker to Hudson....584, 655, 762.
Batavia....81.
Baxter, from Park row to Park....**186**, 548.
  Park to Leonard....8, 292, 761.
  Leonard to Franklin....292, **625, 831.**
Bayard, from Forsyth st to Bowery....81, 761.
  Bowery to Elizabeth....8, 292, 474, 584.
Beach, from West Broadway to Varick st....183, 292.
Bedford, from Leroy to Morton....45, 345, 516.
  Morton to Commerce....81, 722.
Beekman, from William to Pearl....81, 374, 548.
Bethune....45.
Bleecker, east of Wooster....403, 761, 762.
  from Wooster st to South 5th av....45, 268, 655, 722, 762, **802.**
  South 5th av to Thompson st....320, 345.
  Thompson to Macdougal....762.
  11th to Bank....**50.**
Bloomingdale road....216.
Bolton road....438.
Boulevard, from 62d to 64th....151, 242.
  64th to 76th....345, 688.
  84th to 88th....346, 474, 517.
  104th to 108th....8, 45.
  112th to 114th....726, 799.
  120th to 123d....403, 761.
  135th to 140th.... 722, 828.
  150th to 155th....516, 801.
Bowery, from Bayard to Canal....**153, 186,** 292, 474.
  Canal to Hester....**764.**
  w s, Broome to Spring....799.
  w s, Bond to Great Jones....45, 183.
  north of 4th....242.
Bridge, from State to Whitehall....436.
Broad, from Wall to Pearl....81, 153, **186, 407,** 655, **802.**
  Front to South....120.
Broadway, south of Morris....215.
  from Cortlandt to Reade....**478, 764.**
  Franklin to Canal....120, 622.
  Spring to Bleecker....**244**, 762, 799.
  Bleecker to 8th....**50**, 374.
  8th to 11th ..**518, 625.**
  11th to 14th....584, 622.
  14th to 17th....**407, 764.**
  23d to 26th....474, **764.**
  26th to 29th....**186**, 268.
  31st to 33d....45, 120.
  41st to 54th....**217**, 403, 584.
  north of 59th (also see Boulevard)....151, 242, 345.
  north of 162d (also see Kingsbridge road)....8, 476.
Broome, from Cannon to Columbia....436, 474, 655.
  Columbia to Sheriff....120, 655.
  Sheriff to Willett....81, 584, 622, 722.
  Pitt to Ridge....584, 722.
  Clinton to Suffolk....45, 403.
  Suffolk to Ludlow....81, 320, 828.
  Eldridge to Forsyth....403.
  Elm to Broadway....268, 436, 722.
  Broadway to South 5th av....436, 517, 584.
  South 5th av to Sullivan st....45, 151, 292, 403, 655.
  Sullivan to Hudson....345.
Burling slip, from Pearl to Water....761.
Canal, from Division to Eldridge....436, 799.
  Eldridge to Centre ...45, 799.
  Varick to Hudson....374.
  Hudson to Greenwich... 548, 799, **802.**
Cannon, from Delancey to Rivington....81, 268.
  Rivington to Stanton....292, 403, 548, 584, 587.
  Stanton to Houston....436.
Carlisle, from Greenwich to Washington....828.
Carmine....8, 799.
Caroline....8.
Catharine....242, 475, 722.
Catharine slip....8, 722.
Cedar....374, 799, 828.
Central Park West, from 83d to 85th....320, 722.
  91st to 94th....183, 403, 436.
  102d to 106th....120, 655, 761.
  106th to 108th....242.
  north of 110th (see 8th av).
Centre....**478**, 762.
Chambers....8, 45, 801.
Charles, east of 4th....45, 403, 436.
Chatham (see Park row)....**761.**
Chatham sq....**321.**
Charlton....45, 215, 475.
Cherry, west of Oliver....45, 268, 345.
  from Market to Rutgers....8, 242, 403, 475.
  Rutgers to Jefferson....242, 584, 655, 799.
  Clinton to Gouverneur....**123**, 688, 722.
  Scammel to Jackson....475.
  Jackson to Corlears....**153, 217, 294, 439.**
  indeft....45.
Chestnut....215, 374.
Christopher, from Greenwich av to Bleecker st....81, 345, 722, 799.
  Greenwich st to West....81, **551.**
Chrystie, from Division to Canal....320, **659.**
  Hester to Rivington....516, 584.
  Stanton to Houston ..242, 268.
Church....8, 655.
Clendenning lane....657, 800.
Clinton, from Houston to Rivington....8, 81, 345.
  Rivington to Delancey....8, 81.
  south of Monroe ...**123**, 345, 374.
Coenties slip, from Front to South....81, 268.
Columbia, from Broome to Delancey....436, 656.
  Delancey to Rivington....45, 436, 548.
  Rivington to Stanton ...45, 292, 722, 799.
  Stanton to Houston....584, 622, 722.
Commerce....81, 762.
Congress....799.
Cooper...548.
Cornelia....242, 268, 320, 584.
Cortlandt....8, 584.
Crosby, from Broome to Houston....151, 436, 762.
Delancey, from Chrystie to Forsyth....120, 151, 689.
  Forsyth to Eldridge....516, 584.
  Ludlow to Essex....183, 437.
  Essex to Norfolk....548, 622, 688.
  Norfolk to Clinton ...374, 436, 475.
  Attorney to Ridge....292, 437, 656, 722.
  Ridge to Pitt....828, **831.**
  Pitt to Willett ...45, 437, 584.
  Willett to Sheriff....81, 403, 437.
  Sheriff to Columbia....45, 345.
  Columbia to Goerck....345, 761.
Division, n s, from Bowery to Chrystie....120, **518.**
  n s, Chrystie to Forsyth....**659.**
  s s, Market to Pike....8.
  n s, Eldridge to Allen....293, **294.**
  s s, Pike to Canal....622.
  n s, Essex to Norfolk....623.
  n s, Norfolk to Suffolk....548.
  s s, Clinton to Montgomery....8, 151, 761.
  n s, Hester to Attorney....8.
  s s, Montgomery to Gouverneur....151, 584.
  n s, Attorney to Ridge....216.

Downing, from Bedford to Varick....403, 437, 761, 799, **802**, 828.
Dry Dock.... 183
Duane, from Rose to Elm....183, 762.
Elm to Hudson....81, 242, 584.
Dutch....**294.**

East Broadway, from Market to Rutgers....183, 403, 799.
Jefferson to Clinton....183, 345.
Gouverneur to Scammel....516.
indeft....**518**
Eastern Boulevard (see Av A).
Edgecombe road (also see Edgecombe av)....48, 243, 624, 725.
Eldridge from Canal to Hester....45, 81, 761.
Hester to Grand....8, 45, 242.
Broome to Stanton....183, 584, 656.
Elizabeth, from Hester to Grand....722.
Grand to Broome....8, 622, 656.
Broome to Spring....475.
Prince to Houston....345, 656, 689, **691.**
Emerson....242.
Elm, from Reade to Duane.... 762.
Howard to Broome....799.
north of Broome....151, 242, 345, 436.
Essex, from Division to Hester....345, 722.
Hester to Grand....151, 183, 656, 829.
Broome to Delancey.... 475.
Delancey to Rivington....8, 215, 292, 475, 516, 584, 656.
Rivington to Stanton....8, 516.
Stanton to Houston....548, 656.

Fletcher....320, 345, 475, 799.
Forsyth, from Division to Canal.... 374, 829.
Canal to Hester....374, 584, 799.
Hester to Grand....584, 799.
Broome to Delancey....**217**, 689.
Delancey to Stanton....584, 722.
Stanton to Houston....8, 45.
Fort Washington Ridge road....45, 81.
Fort Washington Depot road....81.
Frankfort, from Nassau to William....81, 320, 516.
Franklin, from Elm st to Broadway....374, 584, 722.
Front, from Whitehall to Broad....**153**, **831.**
Broad st to Maiden lane....120, 722, 799.
Burling slip to Corlears st....45, 345, 761.
Fulton, from South st to Broadway....622, 656.
Broadway to Greenwich st....320, 622.

Gansevoort....792.
Garden row....46.
Gay.... 120.
Goerck, from Broome to Delancey....45, 151, 292, 403, 656.
Delancey to Rivington.... 584.
Rivington to Stanton....151, 242, 268, 475, 584.
Stanton to Houston....8.
Gold....403.
Gramercy Park....437, 761, 820.
Grand, from Varick to Sullivan....8, 45.
Sullivan to Thompson....656, 689
Thompson to Wooster.... **347**, **764.**
Greene to Mott....120 **659**
Mott to Bowery....**439** 622, 656.
Norfolk to Clinton.... **625** 799.
Clinton to Columbia.... 475 **518.**
Columbia to Lewis....8, 292.
Greene from Houston to Bleecker....762.
Bleecker to 4th....81, 120, 622.
Greenwich, from Cortlandt to Fulton....746.
Duane to Franklin....**587**, 722, **802.**
Barrow to 10th....45, 656, 722.
Perry to 11th....12, 183.
12th to Gansevoort.... 83, 548.
Greenwich lane (see Greenwich av) ..81.
Grove, from Bleecker to 4th....81, 345, 722.

Hague....516
Hamilton....45, 183, 475, 548.
Hamilton terrace....801.
Hammond (see West 11th st) ....120, 763.
Harrison....242.
Henry, from Catharine to Pike....8, 292, 403, 437, 475, 548, **726**, 761, 799.
Pike to Jefferson....292, 345, 510, 548, 584, 656, 722.
Clinton to Montgomery....242, **376**, 404, **587.**
Montgomery to Gouverneur....183, 437.
Scammel to Jackson....45, 437, 722.
indeft....**518**
Hester, from Ludlow to Allen ....8, 268, 689.
Elizabeth to Centre....215, 475, **478**, 548.
Hillside....48, 584
Horatio, from Hudson to Greenwich....45, 120.
Greenwich to Washington 183, 215, 374, 829
Houston, from Cannon to Columbia....**123.**
n s, Sheriff to Av C....242.
s s, Willett to Pitt....242, 516.
n s, Av C to B....242, 292.
s s, Suffolk to Norfolk....374, 722.
n s, Av B to A....45.
Broadway to Greene....**294**, 799.
South 5th av to Sullivan st....122, 151, 183.
Sullivan to Varick ....584, 799, **802.**
Greenwich to West....548.
Hubert 151, 474
Hudson, from Beach to Vestry....**50.**
Broome to Spring....183, 475, **831**
Clarkson to Christopher....374, **376**, 689.
Perry to Jane....8, 320.

Jackson....45, 120.
James....829.
Jane....404, 689.
Jay....45
Jefferson....242, 437, 475, 516.
Jersey....215, 242.
Jones....45, 722.
Jones lane....345.
Jumel terrace....404.

King....45, 215.
Kingsbridge road, south of 165th st....475.
from 177th to 180th.... 8, 10, 45, 375, 376, 437.
180th to 187th....8, 45, 47, 243, 437.
187th to Isham....8, 183, 550
indeft....8, 45, 81, 763.

Leight....215, 437, 474, 475.
Lawrence ....438.
Leonard....345, 548, 799.
Leroy, from Bleecker to Bedford....374, 799.
Bedford to Hudson (also see St. Lukes pl) ....268, 516, 689, 829.
Hudson to Greenwich....120.
Lewis, from Broome to Delancey....345, 404, 548, 584.
Delancey to Rivington....215, 516, 723, 799.
Rivington to Stanton....8, 45, 374, 722, 722, 761.
Stanton to Houston....437, 548, 622, 761, 799.
Houston to 3d....81, 799.
7th to 8th....722.
Leyden....548
Liberty, from Maiden lane to Nassau st....404, 437, 799.
Church to Greenwich....151.
London terrace (see 23d st, bet 9th and 10th avs).
Ludlow, from Division to Hester....45, 437, 584.
Hester to Delancey....45, 268, 404.
Delancey to Rivington....151, 437, 584, **587**, 723.
Stanton to Houston ....475, 516.

Macdougal from Spring to 3d....151, 345, 404.
Madison, from Catharine to Market....81, 656, 799.
Market to Birmingham....8, 151, 183, 723.
Birmingham to Pike....292, 548, 656.
Rutgers to Jefferson....81, 151, 242, 404, 516.
Jefferson to Clinton....374, 723.
Clinton to Montgomery....45, 242, 404, 437, 656.
Montgomery to Gouverneur....45, 475, 622.
Scammel to Jackson....292, 374, 437, 475, 516, 584, 723.
Jackson to Grand....292.
Maiden lane, from Nassau to William....8, 45, 404, 437 **518.**
Pearl to South....320, 345, 475, 799.
Mangin, from Rivington to Stanton....151, 475.
Manhattan (12th Ward, also see Hancock pl).... 10, 47, 216, 624, 690, **764.**
Manhattan road....830.
Manhattan sq (see 77th st s s and 81st st n s, bet Central Park West and Columbus av).
Maria (also see Old Maria st)....216.
Marion, from Broome to Spring....**123**, 151, 242, 345, 516.
north of Prince....215, 242, 762.
Market, from East Broadway to Madison....45, 292, 404, 622, 761.
Madison to Water....345, 723.
Market slip....723.
Mercer, from Broome to 3d.... **294**, **587**, 723.
Minetta....548.
Monroe, from Catharine to Market....120, 183, 475, 516, 622, 829.
Market to Pike....45, 723, 761.
Rutgers to Jefferson.... 81.
Jefferson to Clinton (also see Rutgers pl) ....548, 829.
Clinton to Montgomery....374, 404, 437, 656.
Montgomery to Gouverneur....**659.**
Scammel to Jackson 11, 404, 475, 548, 761, 799
Morris....151, 215.
Morton, from Bleecker to Bedford....656, 829.
Bedford to Hudson....345, 376, 584, 689, 762.
Mott, from Park row to Bayard....723.
Bayard to Canal....81, 215, 320.
Canal to Hester....475, 689, 723.
Hester to Grand....81, **691.**
Broome to Spring....183, 404, 584, 723.
Spring to Prince....**123**, **439.**
Houston to Bleecker....404.
Mulberry, from Park to Bayard....292, 689, 723.
Canal to Hester ....45, 151, 292.
Hester to Broome....**84** 292.
Spring to Prince....8, 404.
Murray....8.

Nassau, from Cedar st to Maiden lane....**802.**
Maiden lane to Fulton st....516, 622, 656.
New, from Exchange pl to Beaver st ....**802.**
(12th Ward) .. 8.
New Bowery, from Roosevelt to James....215, 374, 622.
New Croton Aqueduct....215, 584.
Norfolk, from Hester to Grand....215.
Broome to Delancey....151, 723.
Delancey to Rivington....292, 475.
Rivington to Stanton ....45, 622.
North William....183.

Oak....120, **153**, 183.
Old Bloomingdale road....121, 216, 346, 403, 550, 623, 763.
Old road....586, 657, 763.
Old Boston Post road ....438, 801.
Old Clendening lane....724, 801.
Old Eastern Post road....122.
Old Harlem lane.... 800.
Old Hammond (also see West 11th st)....120.
Old Kingsbridge road (see Kingsbridge road).
Old Manhattan road....801, 830.
Old Maria....81, 215, 216.
Old Stewart....215.
Oliver, from New Bowery to Madison....81.
Madison to Oak....374, 404.
Oak to Cherry....183, 345, 374.
Water to South....799.
Orchard....437, 799.
Otter alley....622.

Park, from Centre to Baxter....320, 345, 374, 622, 723, 761.
Park row, from Ann to Chambers....622.
Chambers to Pearl....81, **294**, **376**, 584.
indeft....**761.**
Pearl, from Broad to Wall....183, **376.**
Fulton to Park row....81, 215, 761.
Park row to Broadway....762, 799.
Peck slip....799.
Pelham....8, 242, 403.
Perry, from Waverley pl to 4th st....81, 242.
4th to Bleecker....8, 292.
Pike, from Division to Henry....8, **217**, 799.
Henry to Monroe....45, 151, 345.
Pitt, from Division to Delancey....81, 345, 404.
Delancey to Rivington.... 45, 183, 215, 374.
Rivington to Houston....584, 723.
Prince, from Crosby to Wooster....81, 762.
Wooster st to South 5th av....345, **625.**

Reade....8, 762, 801.
Renwick....723, 761, 829.
Ridge, from Grand to Broome....45, 242, 723.
Broome to Stanton....**217**, **831.**
Stanton to Houston....183, 584.
Riverside Drive (see Riverside av).
Rivington, from Chrystie to Essex....516, 723.
Suffolk to Attorney....46, 292, 622.
Attorney to Pitt....374.
Pitt to Sheriff ....374, 404, **587.**
Sheriff to Cannon....45, **764.**
Cannon to Goerck....292.
Roosevelt, from Park row to New Chambers st ....516, 622.
New Chambers to South....8, 46.
Rose....46, 81, 215, 320.
Rutgers....656.
Ryder alley....403.

Scammel....46.
Sheriff, from Broome to Delancey....120, 183.
Delancey to Rivington....46, 799.
Rivington to Stanton....46, 404, 516, 761.
Stanton to Houston....292.
Sniffin court....516, 723.
South, south of Old slip 151, 404.
from Wall to Fulton....**659.**
Market to Corlears....45, 799.
South Washington sq (see 4th st)....762.
South William....655.
Spring, from Bowery to Mott st....183.
Mott to Marion....183, 292, 622.
Mercer to Wooster....81, 799.
Wooster to Thompson....8, 120.
Thompson to Macdougal....215, 268, 829.
Spruce....345.
Stanton, from Forsyth to Ludlow....120, 799.
Clinton to Ridge....183, 345, 374, 404, 516, 584.
Ridge to Columbia ....320, 584.
Columbia to Lewis....242, 829.
Lewis to Mangin....120, 404, 723.
Stone ....183.
Suffolk, from Hester to Grand ....46, 81, 292, 437, 475.
Grand to Broome....46, 404, 689.
Broome to Rivington....46, 437, 475.
Rivington to Houston....292.
Sullivan, from Canal to Spring....183, 723.
Spring to Houston....46, 81.
Houston to 3d....268, 762.
Sylvan terrace ....404.

Thompson, from Canal to Grand ....8, 656.
Grand to Broome.... 622, 689.
Broome to Spring ....**153**, 374, 723, **726.**
Spring to Prince....656, 799, 829.
Prince to 4th.... **478**, 584, 762.
Union sq ....**50.**
Vandewater....689.
Varick....**376**, 404.
Vesey ....345.
Vestry ....404.

Walker....799.
Wall, from Pearl to South....345.
Warren....151, **407**, **439**, **478.**
Washington, south of Rector....151, 829.
from Liberty to Dey....**153** 516, 584, **831.**
Vesey to Warren....183, **802.**
Jay to Leight....215, 474.
Watts to Spring....242, 548, 584.
Spring to Houston....215, 374, **376.**
Morton to 10th....81, 656.
10th to Perry....46, 584.
Bank to 12th....46, 584, 622, 829.
Washington sq East (see Wooster st).
North (see Waverley pl).
South (also see West 4th st)....762.
West (see Macdougal st).
Water, from Broad to Old slip....436.
Maiden lane to Fulton st....761, 799.
Fulton to Dover....475, 723, 800, 829.
Dover to Oliver.... 242, 374, 799.
Market st to Gouverneur slip.... **123**, 799.
Gouverneur slip to East st....46, 268, 622.
West, from Cedar to Dey....**153**, 584, 761, **831.**
Dey to Barclay....48, 268, **269** 345, **347.**
Barclay to Beach ....8, **478**, **802.**
Beach to Canal....**11**, 474.
Canal to Houston....216, **802.**
Houston to Barrow....**659**, **802.**
11th to Jane....**153**
West Broadway....242, **625.**
White.... **84**, 516, 799, 829.
Willett, from Grand to Delancey....151, 374.
Delancey to Rivington....46, 292, 320, 345, **518**, **659**, 723.
Stanton to Houston ....81, 120, 242, 516.
William, from Cedar to Fulton....183, 689.
Fulton to Frankfort....**11**, **321.**
Frankfort to Duane....183, 292, 320, 345.

Wooster, from Grand to Prince....374, 632.
Prince to Houston....8, 345, 723, **764**, 799.
Houston to Bleecker....45, 81, 655.
Bleecker to 3d ....8, 634, 655.
3d to 4th....762.
Worth....761.

1st, east of 1st av....**551**.
from 2d to Bowery....**84**, 215, 799.
2d, from Sheriff st to Av C....404.
C to B....8, 320, 723.
B to 2d.... 268, **625**.
3d, from Av C to B....415, **659**.
B to A....**50**, 242, **439**.
A to 2d....**217**, 242.
2d av to Bowery....292, 345.
Greene to Wooster ....8, 268, 762.
Thompson to Macdougal....81, 656.
Macdougal st to 6th av....183, 799.
4th, from Av D to C....404, 584, 723, 761, 799.
C to A....151, 584, **726**
A to 1st....**50**, **217**, **294**, **376**, **691**, **726**.
1st to Bowery....215, 294, 799.
Mercer st to 6th av....46, 764
6th av to Barrow st....120, 183.
Barrow to 10th....81, 829.
10th to Charles....404, 516.
5th, n s, from Av D to C....8, 81, 404, 516, 723.
s s, D to C....404, 548, 689.
C to B. ..81, 120.
n s, A to 1st....**407**.
1st to 2d....584, 723, 829.
2d to Bowery....624.
6th, from Av D to C....46, 183, 345, 404, 584.
C to 1st....8, 183, 345.
2d to Bowery....151, 243, **347**, 437.
7th, from Lewis to Av D....374, 723.
D to B....404, 622, 799.
A to 1st....46, 404, 584.
1st to 2d....516.
2d to 3d....268, 584, 656.
8th, from Lewis to Av D ...9, 723.
C to B....242, 516.
Av B to Broadway (also see St. Marks pl) ....**439**, 548, 762.
west of Broadway (also see Clinton pl).... 81, 120, 374, 656.
9th, from Av C to B ...151, 292, 320.
s s, A to 1st....243, 345, 437.
2d av to Broadway....215, **518**, **625**, 763.
Broadway to University pl....**186**, **407**, **625**.
University pl to 6th av....**294**, 584
10th, from Av D to C....122, 438, 657.
C to A....9, 46.
A to 1st....46, 242, 292, 761.
n s, 1st av to Stuyvesant st....46, 799.
s s, 1st av to Stuyvesant....9, 437, 689.
n s, University pl to 5th av....516, 658.
n s, 5th to 6th. ..151, 404.
s s, 5th to 6th....9, 120.
Greenwich av to Waverley pl....404, 723.
Waverley pl to 4th st....151, 656.
n s, 4th to Bleecker....345, 404, 516.
11th, from n s Av B to A....404, 689, 723.
s s, B to A....9, 46.
1st to 4th....**659**, **726**, **764**
6th av to 4th st....46, 120, 183, 763.
n s, Bleecker to Washington....120, 374, 404, **478**.
12th st, from Dry Dock to Av C....404, **625**.
C to A....215, **691**.
n s, A to 1st....1 , 632.
1st to 2d ...9, 437, 689, 723.
2d to 3d....121, 345, 584, 799.
3d to 4th....584, 723, **726**
Broadway to 6th av....9, 723.
7th av to 4th st....81, 656, **831**.
Hudson to Washington....46, 183, 215.
13th, n s, from Av C to B....**587**.
s s, C to B....81, **269**, 345, 404, **587**, 761.
n s, B to A....215, 632.
s s, B to A.... 183, 4 4.
A to 1st....723, 725, 761.
2d to 5th....9, **321**.
n s, 5th to 6th.. 9, **518**, 689.
6th to 7th....46, 215, 585.
west of 10th....**269**.
14th, s s, from Av B to A....723.
3d av to Broadway....**84**, **726**.
n s, Broadway to 5th av....**50** **153**, **659**.
s s, Broadway to 6th av....242, 292, 320, 437, 474, **551**, **625**
n s, 6th to 7th....215.
n s, 7th to 8th....**478**, 829.
s s, 7th to 8th....81, 183.
s s, 8th av to Hudson st....121.
15th, n s, from Av C to B....81, 340, 404, 623.
1st av to Irving pl....151, 516.
6th to 8th....215, 516.
16th, s s, from Av B to A. ..81, 723, 761.
n s, 3d av to Irving pl....121, **217**, **294**.
5th to 8th....374, **551**, 659.
8th to 9th....83, 516, 761.
n s, 9th to 10th....121.
17th, from Av B to 1st....46, 404.
n s, 1st to 2d....320, 656, 689.
s s, Broadway to 5th av....11, 151, 477.
6th to 8th ...151, 656.
n s, 8th to 9th....46, 48, 183, 374.
s s, 9th to 10th....4 4.
18th, from Av B to A....632.
n s, A to 1st ...248.
s s, A to 1st....8 , 268, 761.
1st to 2d....404, 799, 829.
Irving pl to 6th av....**11**, 81.
s s, 6th to 7th....183, 345.
n s, 7th to 8th....81, 404
n s, 8th to 9th....374, **376**, 475.
s s, 8th to 9th....292, 404.
s s, 9th to 10th....121, 404.
11th to 13th....**625**.
19th st, from Av B to A....**186**, 829, **831**.
Av A to Irving pl....46, 247, 585, 689.
s s, 7th to 8th....658.
n s, 8th to 9th....**11**, 2 5.
s s, 8th to 9th ...**186**, 374.
n s, 9th to 10th....9, 516.
11th to 13th.. **625**
20th, from Av A to 3d....121, **764**.
s s, 3d to 4th....761, 829.
n s, 6th to 7th....475, 689.
s s, 6th to 7th....9, 121, 151.
7th to 9th ...345, 761, 799.
indeft....**659**
21st, from 1st to 3d av....**84**, 404.
n s, 3d to Lexington....185, 723.
Lexington av to Broadway ...404, 723.
5th to 7th ...9, 294, 374.
n s, 7th to 8th....81, 345.
s s, 7th to 8th....151, 374, 375, 404, 723.
8th to 9th....9, 136, **439**, 799.
indeft....**84**
22d, east of 3d av....**50**, 374.
from 3d to 4th....151, 799.
n s, 5th to 6th....**831**
s s, 5th to 6th ...151, 623, 656.
n s, 6th to 7th....46, 659, 723.
s s, 6th to 7th....345.
n s, 8th to 9th....**84**, **186**, 345, **587**.
n s, 9th to 10th... 374, 375, 762.
s s, 9th to 10th....404.
10th to 11th....374, 375.
23d, n s, from 2d to 4th av....81, 632, 799.
s s, 4th av to Broadway....**551**.
s s, 5th to 6th....**347**, **831**.
n s, 6th to 7th....656, 799.
s s, 7th to 8th. ..475, 723.
s s, 8th to 9th....151, 183, **186**, 404, 437.
9th to 10th ...215, **518**, 585.
10th to 11th....**625**.
24th, from Av A to 2d....152, 656.
n s, 2d to 3d....215, 437.
n s, Lexington to 4th....46, 292.
n s, Broadway to 6th....151.
s s, Broadway to 6th....183, 374, 375.
6th to 7th....475, 723.
7th to 9th....84, **691**.
9th to 10th... **123**, 585, 800.
25th, s s, from 1st to 2d av....215, 585.
2d to Lexington ...437, **518**.
s s, Lexington to 4th....800, 829.
n s, 7th to 8th....184, 829.
s s, 7th to 8th....121, 183, 583, 829.
n s, 8th to 9th....**84**, **764**.
10th to 11th....9, 4 4.
26th st, n s, from 1st to 2d av....548, 761, **802**.
s s, 1st to 2d ...293.
n s, 2d to 3d....81.
n s, Lexington to 4th....585, 761, 762.
6th to 7th....345, 437.
s s, 7th to 8th .. 215, 404.
8th to 9th....81, 82, 292, 585, 636.
n s, 9th to 10th....800.
27th, from 3d to 4th av....183, 292, 723.
5th to 6th....84, 153, 800.
6th to 7th....46, 154, 723.
7th to 8th....9, 84, 183, 242.
9th to 10th....46, 183, 268.
10th to 11th....268, 404, 516, 548.
28th, from 2d to 4th av ...656, **726**.
n s, Broadway to 6th....800.
6th to 8th....82, 345.
8th to 9th....**551**, **659**.
10th to 11th... 477, **625**, **659**, 689.
29th, n s, from 1st to 2d av....81, 215, 689.
n s, 2d to 3d....84, 244, 375.
3d to Madison....269, 656, 800.
s s, Broadway to 6th....9, 121, 689.
n s, 6th to 7th....8, 183, 215.
s s, 6th to 7th....82, 184, 586.
7th to 9th. ..404, 656, 723.
11th av to North River ...82, 185.
30th, from 1st to 3d av....632, 762.
3d to 4th ...84, 375.
4th to Madison....656, 723.
5th to 9th....404, 6 6.
31st, n s, from 1st to 2d av....82, 404, 437.
5th to 7th....45, 46, **153**.
7th to 8th... 83, 475.
8th to 9th ...121, 437.
32d, from East River to 1st av....**153**, 829, **831**.
Lexington to 5th....69 , 764, 829.
5th to Broadway ...184, 215, 764, 293.
n s, 6th to 7th....249, **294**, **376**, 659.
7th to 9th....46, **186**, 407, 184.
n s, 9th to 10th....9, 159, **321**, 516, 656.
10th to 11th....415, 244, 268.
33d, from East River to 1st av....**153**, **831**.
1st to 3d....292, 548, 763.
4th to Madison....346, 762.
5th to 7th. . 12 , 516, 656.
7th to 9th....184, 292.
10th to 11th... 84, 268.
34th, from 1st to 2d av....152, 269, 548, 585.
n s, 2d to 3d ..375, 4 7.
3d to Park....46 **294**, 763.
5th to 8th....**294**, 320, 658, 762.
n s, 9th to 10th....46, 121.
s s, 9th to 10th....9, 46.
35th, s s, from 1st to 2d av.. 583, 656.
3d to Lexington....632, **802**.
Lexington to 5th....9, 764.
5th to 6th....375, 723, 764.
Broadway to 8th av....516, 548, 689, 723.
8th to 9th....121, 6 6.
s s, 9th to 10th....375, 585, 829.
36th, from 1st to 3d av....374, 656.
Lexington to Park....583, 689.
s s, 5th to 6th....656.
7th to 8th....242, 585, 689.
8th to 10th....242, 585, **625**.
37th, s s, from Lexington to Park av ...82, 404.
n s, 5th to 6th. . 82, 346.
s s, 5th to 6th....46, 320.
6th to 7th ...121, 624.
s s, 7th to 8th....244, 762, 800.
s s, 8th to 9th....404.
10th to 11th....9, 184, 268, 632, 656, 689.
38th, s s, from 1st to 2d av... 9, 184.
s s, from 5th to 6th ...9, 437, 516.
6th to 8th....121, 548, 723
10th to 11th....639.
39th, from 1st to 3d av....548, 723.
n s, Lexington to Park....656.
7th to 8th....244, 475.
8th to 9th....215, 375, 723.
9th to 11th....761, 800, 829.
40th, from 2d to 3d av....761, 763.
Lexington to 5th....81, 585, 829.
5th to 6th....**50**, 624, 723
7th to 8th ...242, 320, 404, 829.
n s, 8th to 9th....46, 244.
s s, 8th to 9th....46, 475, 800.
41st, n s, from 1st to 2d av....292, 374, 548.
s s, 1st to 2d ..184, 723.
n s, 2d to 3d.. .46
s s, 2d to 3d....242, 320, 548.
n s, 3d to Lexington....**322**, **478**.
Park to 5th....320, 585, 764.
7th to 9th....178, 764.
9th to 11th....46, 292.
42d st, from 1st to Madison av....400, 585, 689.
n s, 5th to 6th ...**478**, **518**.
9th to 11th... 8, 46, 875.
43d st, from East River to 1st av. ..517, 518.
n s, 3d to Lexington. ..830.
s s, Broadway to 6th av....184, 404, 585.
8th to 10th....268, 586, 648.
n s, 10th to 11th....121, 215, 243.
44th, from East River to 1st av....517, 518.
s s, 3d to Lexington....46, 215.
Madison to 8th....437, 585, 659.
8th to 9th. . 9, 585, 656.
n s, 9th to 10th....46, 152, 181.
10th to 11th... 82, 320.
45th st, from East River to 2d av....321, 475.
s s, 2d to 3d ...184, 475.
5th av to Broadway....9, 375, 723.
Broadway to 8th av....**123**, **217**, **244**, **518**, **726**.
n s, 8th to 9th....**659**.
9th to 10th....9, 723, 829.
10th to 11th....656, 723.
west of 11th... 46, 320, 762.
46th, from East River to 3d av....46, 321, 622.
3d to Lexington ...184, 516
n s, Madison to 5th....**269**, **659**.
5th to 6th....215, 800.
6th av to Broadway....292, 585, 656.
Broadway to 8th av....548 **691**.
8th to 9th....**186**, **659**, 800.
n s, 9th to 10th....9, 415.
10th to 11th....346, 656, 763, 820.
47th, n s, from 1st to 2d av....46, 82.
s s, 1st to 2d....215, 375.
n s, 3d to Lexington.. 81, 268.
s s, Madison to 5th....**322**.
5th to 6th....**478**, 689, **764**.
6th to 7th... 345, 437, 585.
9th to 10th....9, 292, 723
west of 10th....**84**, 375, 656.
48th, from East River to 1st av....9, 81, 404.
1st to 2d....268, 724.
2d to 3d....9, **347**, 656.
3d to 5th . 404, 434, 829.
s s, 5th to 6th....**347**, **407**, **727**, **802**.
n s, 6th to 7th ...9, 184, 293, 437.
8th to 10th....82, 292, 516.
10th to 11th....244, 293, **518**.
west of 11th....46, 762.
49th, from East River to 1st av....**153**, 548, **831**.
n s, 1st to 2d....9, 689.
s s, 1st to 2d... 84, 548, 724.
2d to 3d.... 92, 516, 724.
3d to 5th ...215, 404, 548, 656.
n s, 5th to 7th....184, **347**, **802**.
Broadway to 8th....154, 516, 585.
8th to 9th....46, 585
s s, 9th to 10th....82 293.
west of 10th....46, 82, 800.
50th, from East River to 1st av....242.
1st to 2d....82, 404 585.
2d to 3d. ..9, 6 9, 725.
3d to Lexington ...184, 320, 656.
Lexington to Madison ....84.
5th to 6th....**84**, 761, **802**.
s s, 6th to 7th....9, 320.
n s, 9th to 10th....320, 437, 548.
10th to 11th ...46, 82, 152, 437, 516.
51st, from East River to 1st av....346.
1st to 2d....9, 46, 184.
s s, 2d to Madison....46, 764, 829.
n s, 5th to 6th....9.
s s, 5th to 6th....**50**, **84**, **322**, **376**, **802**.
n s, 6th to 7th....242, 585.
n s, 7th to 9th....**376**, 689, **764**.
west of 9th....82, 292, 516.
52d, from East River to 1st av....516, 656.
1st to 2d ...9, 215, 724.
2d to 3d....46, 121, 320.
3d to Park....548, 656.
s s, 5th to 6th....9, 829.
6th to 7th....624, 764.
s s, 7th to 9th....215, **376**, 585.
n s, 9th to 10th....82, 764
s s, 9th to 10th....346, 644, 656.
10th to 11th. ..84, 184, 242, 375, 656, 724.
53d, from 1st to 2d av....46, 84, 549.
Lexington to Madison....46, 724, 829.
n s, Madison to 5th....320.
n s, 5th to 6th .. 346.
s s, 5th to 6th....84, 242, 437.
6th to 7th....320, 656, 800.
7th to 8th....437, 516.
n s, 9th to 10th....121, 215, 585, 689, 724, 800.
s s, 9th to 10th... 9, 583, 724.
10th to 11th....404, 548, 632, 689.
54th, from East River to 2d av....242, 437, 475.
n s, 2d to 3d....404.
s s, Madison to 5th....404.
s s, 5th to 6th....404, 829.

6th to 8th....516, 829.
s s, 9th to 10th....516, 585, 800.
10th to 11th....215, 405, 475.
west of 11th ...624.
55th, from 1st to Lexington av....320, 405, 624.
Park to 6th....320, 475.
s s, 7th to 8th....82, 475.
8th to 10th....184, **407**.
56th, from 1st to 2d av....**764**.
Park to 5th....269, 437, 549.
n s, 6th to 9th....9, 82, 121.
n s, 9th to 10th....9.
s s, 9th to 10th....121, 185, 242, 549, 829.
57th, n s, from Av A to 1st....46, 215, 268, 516.
1st to 2d...**186**, 475, 829.
Park to Madison....475, 829.
Madison to 6th....184, 268, 800.
n s, 9th to 10th...82, 152, 292, 800.
s s, 9th to 10th....829.
west of 10th....121.
58th, n s, from Av A to 1st....152, 375.
1st to 2d....82, 405, 636.
2d to 3d....549.
6th to 7th....121, 689, 724, 800.
7th to 8th ...121, **587**.
n s, 8th to 10th....622, 724, 829.
59th, from East River to 3d av....9, 516, 656.
Lexington to Madison....46, 292, 293, 549.
Madison to 6th....121, 475.
7th to 9th....9, 585.
n s, 10th to 11th....242, 762.
60th, from 1st to Lexington av....46, 724.
Lexington to Madison....46, 656, 724.
8th to 9th....215, 762.
10th to 11th....9, 437, 516, 622.
61st, from Av A to 1st....293.
n s, 1st to 2d....405, 475, 516.
s s, 1st to 2d....762, 829.
2d to Park...9, 762.
Park to Madison....375, 724.
Madison to 5th....622, 762.
n s, 10th to 11th....293
62d, from 1st to 2d av...9, 293, 516.
2d to 3d....9, **152**, **153**.
3d to Park... 762, 800.
s s, 9th to 10th....475, 549, 689.
10th to 11th....46, 242, 724.
63d, n s, from Av A to 1st....268, 655, 829.
s s, 1st to 2d....475, 724.
s s, Park to Madison....9, 656.
8th av to Boulevard....151, 242, 437.
n s, 9th to 10th....585, 623.
s s, 9th to 10th ....9, 293.
s s, 10th to 11th....724.
64th, s s, from Av A to 1st...761.
n s, Park to Madison....762.
9th to 10th....9, 184, 623.
65th, s s, from 3d to Lexington av....585, 623.
Lexington to Madison....152, 375, 725.
8th av to Boulevard ...215, 437, 800.
n s, Boulevard to 9th av....345.
n s, 9th to 10th....345.
s s, 9th to 10th....375, 475, 689.
66th, from Av A to 2d ...46, 516.
Park to 5th...622, 762.
n s, 8th to 10th....152, 405.
n s, 10th to West End....46, 184, 375, 405, 475, 516, 549, 623, 724, 762, 800.
67th, n s, from Madison to 5th av....800.
8th to 9th....9, **439**, 623, 800.
n s, 9th to 10th... 82, 122.
n s, 10th to West End ...9.
s s, 10th to West End ...375, 405, 437, 475, 585, 762.
68th, from 2d to 5th av....9, 184.
8th to 9th....549, 762.
s s, 10th to West End....121, 623.
69th, from 1st to 2d av....375, 405, 437, 762.
n s, 8th to 9th....82, 762, 800.
n s, 9th av to Boulevard....46.
10th to West End... 437, 516, 689.
west of West End....184, 215, 516, 549, 656.
70th, from East River to Av A....121, 242.
A to 2d ... 82, 320, 690.
n s, 8th to 9th...152, 215, 293, 475, 623, 724, 762, 800.
s s, 8th to 9th....829.
west of 1 th....121, 549, 623.
71st, from Av A to 2d....82, 585.
n s, Madison to 5th....689.
8th to 9th....152, 475, 762.
9th to 10th....46, 121, 242.
n s, 10th to West End....121, 475.
72d, n s, from Av B to A....374.
A to 1st....82, 121, 152, 293, 374.
1st to 2d....9, 623.
3d to Lexington....81, 184, 689.
Lexington to Park....121, 215.
s s, Park to Madison....216.
n s, 8th to 9th....184, 346, 437, 585, 623.
s s, 8th to 9th....320.
n s, 9th av to Boulevard....82, 724.
s s, 9th av to Boulevard....320, 475.
s s, Boulevard to West End av....121, 215.
West End to Riverside....121, 585, 800.
73d, n s, from Av A to 1st....405, 724.
s s, A to 1st....82, 152, 184, 405, 475, 585, 762.
s s, 1st to 2d....82, 268.
s s, 2d to 3d....46, 82, 800.
Park to 5th....293, 724.
s s, 8th to 9th....184, 346, 585, 725.
n s, 9th to 10th....243.
Boulevard to West End av....9, 242, 549.
74th, from Av B to A....216, 243, 405, 437.
A to 1st....9, 46, 268.
n s, 1st to 2d....46, 121, 184, 293, 405.
s s, 1st to 2d....293, **691**.
s s, 2d to 3d....9, 152.
3d to Lexington....46, 216, 656.
n s, Park to Madison....669.
n s, 8th to 9th....9, 82, 152, 437, 475, 516, 724.
s s, 8th to 9th....475.
s s, 9th to 10th....437, 585, 689.
n s, Boulevard to West End av....293, 623.
5th, s s, from Av A to 1st....**123**, 346, 475, 762.
1st to 2d....549, 585.
2d to 3d....184, 243, 829.
s s, 3d to Lexington....9, 293.
n s, Lexington to Park....82, 293.
Madison to 5th....184, 293.
n s, 8th to 9th....82, 656, 689, 800, 829.
s s, 8th to 9th....152, 243, 375, 475.
9th to 10th....437, 475, 724.
n s, 10th av to Boulevard....724, 800.
76th, from Av A to 1st... 46, 184, 549.
n s, 1st to 2d....375, 585, 657, 724.
s s, 1st to 2d....45, 152.
2d to Park....46, 152.
Park to Madison....268, 405.
n s, 8th to 9th....9, 243, 293, 320, 346, 405, 585, 724, 761, 829.
s s, 8th to 9th ...475, 585.
n s, 9th to 10th....405, 437, 475.
s s, 9th to 10th....82, 346, 375, 437, 585, 724.
n s, 10th av to Boulevard....475.
n s, west of West End av....657, 724, 800.
s s, west of West End av....293, 475, 476.
77th, n s, from Av A to 1st ...121, 585, 762, 829.
n s, 2d to 3d....152, 405, 476.
Lexington to Madison....46, 689.
8th av to Boulevard....320, **831**.
Boulevard to West End av....438, 516.
78th, from 2d to Lexington av....47, 82.
n s, Lexington to Park....657, 724.
s s, Madison to 5th....437.
s s, 9th to 10th....82, 152, 320.
n s, 10th av to Boulevard....184, 549.
s s, 10th av to Boulevard....216, 293.
n s, West End to Riverside....184, 216, 725.
79th, n s, from Av A to 1st....9, 184, 216.
s s, A to 1st....9, 121, 516, 585.
1st to 2d....184, 293, 623.
n s, 2d to 3d... 82, 121, 829.
s s, 2d to 3d....585.
3d to Park....346, 762, 763.
s s, Park to Madison....516, 549.
n s, 9th to 10th....184, 320, 476, 549.
s s, 9th to 10th...9, 184.
s s, West End to Riverside....725.
80th, from Av A to 2d... 9, 293, 405, 689.
2d to Lexington....47, 152, 293.
n s, Lexington to 5th ..9, 184, 185.
n s, 9th to 10th....405, 623, 762.
s s, 9th to 10th....82, 375, 405, 657.
10th to Riverside ...585, 657, 763.
81st, from Av A to 1st....184, 437, 476, **587**, 724.
1st to 2d....**518**, 724.
n s, 2d to 3d....121, 184.
s s, 2d to 3d....47, 320, 657, 829.
3d to Lexington....585, 622, 689.
s s, Madison to 5th....623.
n s, 8th to 9th...121.
n s, 9th to 10th... 724.
s s, 9th to 10th....516, 517, 585, 657, 829.
82d, from Av B to A ...82, 476, 549.
A to 1st....47, 724, 800.
1st to 2d....405, 437, 549.
2d to 3d ...517, 724, 829.
3d to Lexington....152, 293, 724.
n s, 8th to 9th....623.
s s, 8th to 9th....293, 320, 623, 689, 800.
s s, 9th to 10th....152, 689.
10th to Riverside....122, 623, 724.
83d, from East River to Av B....184.
n s, B to A....47, 375, 405, 437, 476, 549.
s s, B to A....152, 216, 320, 517, 585.
n s, A to 1st .. 82, 152, 216, 268, **269**, 724.
s s, A to 1st....293, 585.
n s, 1st to 2d ...9, 121, 152, 293, 346, 517, 585.
s s, 1st to 2d .. 47, 517.
n s, 2d to 3d... 724.
8th to 9th....82, 405, 762.
n s, 9th to 10th....657, 689.
s s, 9th to 10th....9, 121, 268, 437, 517, 549, 585.
10th to Boulevard....657, 761.
84th, from Av B to A....82, 243, 724.
A to 1st....47, 405.
s s, 1st to 3d. .47, 585, 800.
Lexington to 5th....476, 549.
8th to 9th....243, 549, 585, 829.
9th to 10th....82, 184, 268.
West End to Riverside....47.
85th, from Av B to A....47.
1st to 2d ...152, 184, 549.
n s, 2d to 3d .. 437, 657.
s s, 2d to 3d....293, 405, 476, 800.
Lexington to Madison....268, 292.
Madison to 5th....375, 476, 585.
8th to 9th... 121, 243, 476, 517, 585.
9th to 10th....216, 476, 763, 800.
Boulevard to Riverside... 152, 184.
86th, from Av B to A....47, 184.
s s, 1st to 2d....47, 216, 405, 549.
n s, 2d to 3d....47, 321.
n s, Lexington to Park....82.
s s, Park to Madison....9, 47, 184, 375, 549.
n s, 8th to 9th....47, 320, 437, 476.
n s, 9th to 10th....346, 476, 689.
s s, 9th to 10th....375, 405, 549, 585, 689, 724.
Boulevard to West End....346, 375, 476.
West End to Riverside ...121, 517
12th av to North River....477, 657.
87th, from Av B to A....9, 10, 829.
1st to 3d....47, **376**.
n s, 3d to Lexington...320, 405, **551**, 800.
s s, 3d to Lexington ...346.
Lexington to Madison....293, 657.
8th to 9th....121, 517, 549.
n s, 9th to 10th....346, 689.
s s, 9th to 10th....346, 517, 689.
10th av to Boulevard....474, 517.
n s, West End to Riverside....82, 657.
s s, West End to Riverside....121, 375.
12th av to North River....477, 657.
88th, from East River to Av A....121, 216, 585, 800, 829.
A to 1st av....121, 438, 689.
n s, 1st to 3d....9, 47, 724.
s s, Park to Madison... 800.
8th to 9th... 9, 82.
n s, 9th to 10th....121, 216, 243, 346, 438, 517, 724.
s s, 9th to 10th....47, 121.
10th to West End....762, 800.
n s, West End to Riverside....346, 476, 517.
s s, West End to Riverside....9, 152, 437.
89th, from 1st to 2d av....438, 762.
n s, 2d to 3d av....82, 184.
n s, Park to Madison ...121, 585.
Madison to 5th... 184, 689, 690.
n s, 8th to 9th....549, 585, 800.
n s, 9th to 10th....438.
Boulevard to West End av....152, 268, 476, 623.
West End to Riverside....9, 82, 375, 405, 476, 549, 585, 724.
90th, from 1st to 2d av....47, 346, 585.
2d to 3d....47, 82, **84**.
n s, Lexington to Park....47, 293.
s s, Lexington to Park....405, 643.
Park to Madison....346, 762.
n s, 8th to 9th....689, 800, 829.
s s, 8th to 9th....82, 293, 800.
s s, 9th to 10th....293, 800, 829.
West End to Riverside....47, 82, 121, 375, 476, 517, 689, 724.
91st, from 2d to Park av....**84**, 689, 800.
Madison to 5th....121, 375, 476, 517.
n s, 8th to 9th....724.
92d, from 1st to Lexington av....121, 585, 623.
Lexington to Madison....82, 346.
n s, Madison to 5th....346, 689.
s s, Madison to 5th....216, 346.
8th to 10th....623, 829.
93d, from 1st to 2d av....184.
2d to 3d....375, 585, 800.
n s, 3d to Lexington....405, 438, 800.
s s, 3d to Lexington....152, 657.
s s, Lexington to Park....517, 549.
n s, Park to Madison ...82, 6[illegible].
s s, Park to Madison....47, 82, 268, 724.
n s, Madison to 5th....800.
n s, 8th to 9th....689, 724, 762.
s s, 8th to 9th....82, 293.
n s, 9th to 10th....517.
s s, 9th to 10th....9, 82, 121, 152, 293, 346, 517, 549, 657, 689, 800.
West End to Riverside...320, 405.
94th, from 2d to 3d av. .47, 762.
s s, Madison to 5th ...152.
n s, 8th to 9th....293, 405, 585, 657, 724.
s s, 8th to 9th....184, 405, 438, 724.
n s, 9th to 10th....269, 549, 762.
s s, 9th to 10th....9, 216, 517, 762.
95th, from 1st to Lexington av....293, 346.
n s, Lexington to Park....829.
s s, Lexington to Park....10, 121, 549.
n s, Park to Madison....48.
8th to 9th....243, 689.
n s, 9th to 10th....268, 293.
s s, 9th to 10th....269, 762.
10th av to Boulevard....243, 690, 763.
96th, s s, from 2d to 3d av....269, 585.
n s, 8th to 9th....10, 82, 152, 375, 724, 829.
s s, 8th to 9th....121, 152, 320, 517, 549, 657, 724, 762, 829.
n s, 9th to 10th....184, 405, 438, 623.
s s, 9th to 10th....320, 438, 476.
10th to West End....216, 690.
97th, n s, from 2d to 3d av....762.
3d to Lexington....346, 517, 549, 762.
n s, Park to Madison....83.
n s, 8th to 9th....216, 724.
s s, 8th to 9th....152, 184, 724.
n s, 9th to 10th ...517, 657.
Boulevard to West End....438, 517.
98th, s s, from 1st to 2d av....438.
n s, 2d to 3d....346, 829.
s s, 2d to 3d....346, 549, 762, 829.
3d to 5th....293, 438.
n s, 8th to 9th....216, 829.
s s, 8th to 9th....657, 690.
9th to 10th....438, 657, 762.
10th to West End....268, 517.
99th, n s, from 2d to 3d av....216, 476.
8th to 9th....121, 216, 476.
n s, 9th to 10th....47, 184.
10th av to Boulevard....550.
100th st, from 2d to 3d av... 293, 585.
3d to Lexington....476, 623.
Lexington to 5th....476, 623, 801.
s s, 8th to Manhattan....243.
Boulevard to West End av....320.
101st, from Pleasant to 1st av....184, 185.
n s, 2d to 3d....83, 184, 243.
s s, 3d to Lexington....476, 623.
Lexington to Park....152, 724, 801.
s s, Madison to 5th....829.
n s, Manhattan to 9th .. 47, 438, 623.
9th to 10th....152, 184.
102d, from Pleasant to 1st av....185.
n s, 2d to 3d....47, 375, 405, 657, 690, 724, 800.
s s, 2d to 3d....10, **84**, **153**, 184, 405, 549, 585, 623.
n s, 3d to Lexington....375.
s s, 3d to Lexington....10, 690, 762.
n s, Lexington to Park....375, 476, 623.
s s, Lexington to Park....47, 346.
n s, Manhattan to 9th....690, 725.
s s, Manhattan to 9th....184, 829.
9th to 10th....657, 724.
Boulevard to Riverside....321, 800.

103d, n s, from 2d to 3d av....801.
n s, 3d to Lexington....293.
s s, 3d to Lexington....83, 375, 657, 724.
n s, Park to Madison....476, 549, 623.
Madison to 5th....549.
Manhattan to 9th....10, 184, 690, 725.
9th to 10th....83, 269, 375, 405.
10th av to Boulevard....657, 690, 724, 800, 829
Boulevard to West End av....184, 293, 586.
West End to Riverside....47, 346, 517.
104th, from 1st to 2d av....800.
s s, 2d to 3d....47, 405, 549, 623.
3d to 5th....321, 800, 829.
8th to 10th....216. 800.
10th av to Boulevard....243, 800.
Boulevard to West End av....405, 657, 690, 763.
West End to Riverside....586.
105th, n s, from 1st to 2d av....293, 320, 321, 476, **478**, 829.
2d to 3d....243, 724.
n s, Lexington to Park....153.
n s, Park to Madison....438, 476.
s s, Park to Madison....10, 121, 800, 829.
n s, Madison to 5th....549.
n s, 8th to Manhattan....152.
n s, Manhattan to 9th....184, 216.
9th to 10th....47, 320, 829.
n s, 10th av to Boulevard....10.
106th, from Pleasant to 1st av ...**439**.
n s, 1st to 2d....47, 184, 438, 724.
s s, 1st to 2d....476, 549.
2d to 3d....11, 269, 293.
3d to Lexington....829, 830.
n s, Park to Madison....83, 216, 586.
n s, Madison to 5th....83, 405, 657, 724, 830.
n s, 9th to 10th....243, 800.
s s, 9th to 10th... 48, 517.
10th to Boulevard....375.
107th st, from 1st to 3d av....623, 762.
n s, 3d to Lexington....10, 184, 724.
s s, Lexington to Park....762.
n s, Park to Madison ...184, 269, 517, 800.
s s, Park to Madison....48.
s s, Madison to 5th....83, 405.
s s, 9th to 10th....243.
108th, s s, from 2d to 3d av....346, 657.
s s, 3d to Lexington. .121, 293.
Lexington to Park....47, 405.
Park to 5th....216, 724.
Boulevard to Riverside av....405.
109th, from Pleasant to 1st av....10, 47.
n s, 1st to 2d....549, 801.
2d to Lexington....47, 83, 216.
Lexington to Park....184, **802**.
Park to 5th ...216, 830.
10th av to Boulevard....724.
110th, s s, from 2d to 3d av....10, 83, 293, 405.
s s, 3d to Lexington....293, 690, **831**.
s s, Park to Madison.. 438, 549.
111th st, s s, from 2d to 3d av ...121, 375.
n s, 3d to Lexington....47, 152, 549, 623.
s s, 3d to Lexington....438, 624.
n s, Lexington to Park....216, 476, 549.
s s, Lexington to Park....438.
n s, Madison to 5th....586.
s s, Madison to 5th....185, 243, 438, 517.
112th, from Pleasant to 1st av....152, 762.
1st to 2d....10, 657, 830.
2d to 3d....269, 549, 586.
n s, 3d to Lexington....185.
Park to Madison....586, 724.
Madison to Lenox. .293, 800.
7th av to Boulevard....438, 586, 830.
113th, from Pleasant to 1st av....293, 438, 477, 623.
n s, 1st to 2d....47.
s s, 3d to Lexington....185.
Lexington to Park....243, 724, 830.
Park to Madison....47, 375, 405.
5th to Lenox. ..47, 152, 476, 657.
8th av to Boulevard....586, 657.
114th, n s, from Pleasant to 1st av....586, 623, 724, 830.
s s, Pleasant to 1st av....83, 375, 549, 690, 800.
1st to 2d....47, 549, 724.
n s, 2d to 3d... 10, 83, 152, 346, 405, 586.
n s, 3d to Lexington....83, 269, 762.
s s, 3d to Lexington....47, 83, 438.
n s, Lexington to Park....83, 762.
s s, Lexington to Park....586, 623.
Park to 5th....293, 476, 800, 830.
s s, 5th to Lenox....47. 476, 657, 762.
8th av to Boulevard....47, 657.
115th, from East River to 1st av....690, 724, 830.
n s, 1st to 2d....438, 586.
s s, 1st to 2d....724, 763.
s s, 2d to 2d....152, 405, 517, 724.
Lexington to Madison....47, 690.
n s, Madison to 5th....185, 724.
s s, Madison to 5th....763, 830.
n s, 5th to Lenox....763, 830.
n s, Lenox to St. Nicholas....121, 405, 800.
7th to 8th ...438, 549.
Manhattan to Riverside....517, 763.
116th, from East River to Pleasant av....830.
Pleasant to 1st....185, 476, 586, **587**, 623.
1st to 2d....517, 586, 690.
2d to Lexington....121, 243.
s s, Lexington to Park....10, 476.
Park to Madison....405, 517, 690.
5th to 7th....476, 517, 725.
St. Nicholas to 8th....48, 121, 801.
8th to Manhattan....121, 152, 216.
Manhattan to 9th....83, 830.
9th to 10th....243, 690.
117th, from Pleasant to 1st av....243, 321, 375, 549, 586.
1st to 3d....152, 725.
Lexington to Madison....10, 374.
Lenox to 8th....476, 690.
n s, 8th to Manhattan....321, 346.
s s, 8th to Manhattan....321, 346.
Manhattan to 9th....346.
118th, from East River to Pleasant av....10.
Pleasant to 1st....346, 586, 623, 657, 690.
n s, 2d to 3d....657.
3d to Lexington... 83, 375, 801.
Lexington to Park... 83, 549.
Park to Madison....517, 801.
n s, 5th to Lenox....185, 216, 517, 623.
s s, 5th to Lenox....405.
St. Nicholas to 8th....623, 763.
8th to 10th....321, 725.
119th, from East River to Pleasant av....269, 657.
Pleasant to 1st....405, **478**, 517.
n s, 1st to 2d....185, 243, 725.
s s, 1st to 2d....586.
2d to Park....321, 586.
s s, 5th to Lenox....185, 690, 801.
Lenox to 7th....549, 657.
8th to Manhattan....725, 801.
Morningside to 10th... 216, 243, 690.
Boulevard to Riverside av....121, 216, 346, 623, 763.
120th, from East River to Pleasant av....47, 243.
Pleasant to 2d av .. 549, 586, 763.
n s, 2d to 3d ...47, 405.
Lexington to Park....185, 293, 623.
Park to 5th....438, 476.
5th to Mt. Morris....801, 830.
n s, Lenox to 7th....152, 586, 763.
s s, Lenox to 7th....83, 725, 801.
n s, 7th to St. Nicholas....185, 690.
n s, 10th av to Boulevard....375
121st, from Pleasant to 2d av....10, 405.
n s, 2d to 3d....549, 801.
Park to Madison....10, 47, 243.
n s, Mt. Morris to Lenox....549.
s s, Mt. Morris to Lenox....47, 321, 476.
Lenox to 7th....586, 830.
n s, 7th to 8th....321, 375, 586, 657, 801.
s s, 7th to 8th....122.
8th to St. Nicholas....375, 725.
n s, St. Nicholas to Manhattan....375, 657.
10th to Boulevard....761.
122d, from Pleasant to 2d av....83, 122.
n s, 2d to 3d....438, 549, 623.
s s, 2d to 3d....517.
n s, 3d to Lexington....405.
n s, Lenox to 7th....405, 725.
n s, 7th to 8th....346.
St. Nicholas to Manhattan....10, 243.
s s, Manhattan to 9th....243, 269, 657.
10th to Riverside....405, 761.
123d, from Pleasant to 1st av....10, 476, 725.
n s, 1st to 2d....268, 269.
s s, 1st to 2d....321, 801.
n s, 2d to 3d....152, 185, 293.
3d to Lexington....405, 549.
n s, Lexington to Park....549, 725, **727**.
s s, Lexington to Park....375, 657.
n s, Park to Madison....293, 438.
s s, Mt. Morris to Lenox....725.
n s, Lenox to 7th....438.
s s, Lenox to 7th....10, 47, 801.
s s, 7th to 8th... 185, 243, 476, 586.
8th to 10th....216, 375, 623.
124th, n s, from 1st to 2d av....375, 830.
s s, 1st to 2d....725, 801.
n s, 2d to 3d....83, 216, 725.
3d to Lexington. ..122, 375.
s s, Lexington to Park....185, 517, 623, 724, 763.
Lenox to 7th....293, **764**, **831**.
7th to 8th....405, 725.
St. Nicholas to 9th....10, 216, 624.
125th, n s, from 1st to 2d av....725.
n s, Lexington to Park....**802**.
5th to Lenox....10, 690.
Lenox to 7th....185, 243, **831**.
n s, 8th to St. Nicholas....623.
Manhattan to 10th....47, 83.
10th av to Boulevard....623, 763.
126th, n s, from 3d to Lexington av....657.
Lexington to Madison... 10, 405, 549.
Madison to Lenox....47, 83, 152.
s s, Lenox to 7th....47, 83, 657, 690.
n s, 7th to 8th....216, 346, 375.
n s, 9th av to Lawrence st....438.
127th, s s, from 2d to 3d av....83, 438.
s s, 3d to Lexington....690.
n s, Lexington to Park....438, 725, 763.
Madison to Lenox... 122, 268.
Lenox to 7th....586, 725, 801.
7th to 8th....10, 122, 476, 517.
8th to St. Nicholas....269.
128th, from 2d to 3d av....47, 83.
3d to Madison....185, 321, 438.
s s, Madison to 5th....83.
5th to Lenox....243, 293, 586, 830.
7th to 8th... 269, 725, 763.
n s, 8th to St. Nicholas....47.
129th, from 3d to Park av....152, 243, 586.
5th to 7th....185, 438.
n s, 7th to 8th....725, 763, 801.
s s, 7th to 8th....321.
8th to St. Nicholas....185, 801.
130th, n s, from Park to Madison av....83, 657, 690.
s s, Madison to 5th....321, 517, 801.
n s, 5th to Lenox....47, 269.
s s, 7th to 8th ...185.
Boulevard to Manhattan st....269.
131st, s s, Park to Madison av....375, 549, 657.
n s, Madison to 5th....830.
n s, 5th to Lenox....10, 83, 517, 549, 725.
n s, 7th to 8th....121, 321, 657, 690.
132d, from Park to 5th av....216, 405.
n s, 5th to Lenox ...10, 623, 830.
s s, 5th to Lenox . .47, 517, 657, 763.
n s, Lenox to 7th. ..243, 830.
s s, Lenox to 7th....152, 375.
7th to 8th....346, 405.
133d, from Park to 5th av....152, 293.
s s, 5th to Lenox....152, 549, 623, 763, 830.
n s, Lenox to 7th....10, 83, 152, 346, 476, 517, 801.
s s, 7th to 8th....405, 517, 549, 586, 657.
134th, from Madison to 5th av ...122, 185.
n s, 5th to Lenox....152, 293, 405.
s s, 5th to Lenox... 243.
n s, Lenox to 7th....47, 185.
n s, 7th to 8th....243.
s s, 7th to 8th....405, 586, 801.
135th, n s, from Madison to 5th av....517.
5th to Lenox....152, 185, 293.
Lenox to 7th....185, 476.
n s, 7th to 8th....83, 657, 801.
s s, 7th to 8th....830.
136th, from 5th to 7th av... 47, 83, 517.
7th to 8th....83, 517.
8th to St. Nicholas....152, 725.
n s, St. Nicholas to Convent....10.
137th, n s, from 5th to Lenox av....10, 122.
s s, Lenox to 7th....476, 690, 725.
s s, 8th to St. Nicholas....725.
138th, from 5th to Lenox av....375, 517, 549.
s s, 7th to 8th....726.
139th... 375, 726.
140th....10, 549.
141st, from 7th to 10th av....83, 801.
Hamilton pl to 12th av....375, 549, 586.
142d, from 5th to Lenox av....48, 623, 657.
7th to 10th....243, 762.
143d, n s, from 7th to 8th av....549.
n s, 8th to Convent....346, 657, 763.
s s, 8th to Convent....10, 549, 623.
10th av to Boulevard....801.
144th, s s, from 7th to 8th av....549.
8th to Convent....269, 690, 725.
n s, Convent to 10th....346, 549, 623, 657, 725.
s s, Convent to 10th....47, 476, 517, 830.
145th, s s, from 8th to St. Nicholas av....10, 83, 725, 801, 830.
146th, n s, from 7th to 8th av....763.
St. Nicholas to 10th....47, 549, 801.
147th, n s, from 8th to St. Nicholas av....690.
St. Nicholas to 10th....517, 623, 880.
10th to 12th....47, 586, 693.
148th st, n s, from 7th to 8th av....726.
St. Nicholas av to Boulevard....623, 690.
149th....726.
150th ...375.
151st....83, 438, 725, 763.
152d....476.
155th....48, 657.
156th....405, 657.
157th....346, 657.
159th....10, 549.
160th....83.
161st ...152.
165th... 375, 517.
166th....830.
167th....10, 438, 725.
168th....47, 122.
169th....243.
170th....185, 243
171st....83, 243, 725.
172d....243.
175th....10.
178th. ..10, 47, 243, 725.
179th....10, 243, 321, 657.
180th....10, 47, 83, 185, 243, 657.
181st....10, 152, 293, 321, 549.
182d....47, 83, 243, 517.
183d....185.
184th....47, 476, 763.
185th....549.
186th....321.
187th....321.
188th....321.
189th....405.
209th....550.
210th....550.
214th....321.
215th....321.
223d....518.
227th....518.

AVENUES.

Amsterdam (formerly 10th av, north of 59th st).
from 62d to 64th st....83, 517.
66th to 67th....83, 122, 346, 623, 762.
67th to 69th....216, **478**, 550.
74th to 75th....10, 438.
76th to 79th. ..83, 293, **831**.
80th to 81st....10, 321, 585.
82d to 83d....122, **625**.
85th to 87th....474, 517, 801.
87th to 88th....83, 152.
88th to 89th....185, 405, 438, 762.
91st to 92d....725, 801.
94th to 96th....83, 269, 690, 763.
97th to 98th....152.
98th to 99th....476, 550, 657, 690
100th to 102d....**518**, 623, 689.
114th to 117th....**518**, 690.
120th to 130th....293, 550.
130th to 135th....47, 623.
135th to 145th....47, 725, 726.
145th to 150th....47, 586, **727**.
150th to 160th....**478**, **587**.
160th to 175th....83, 476.
175th to 180th ...8, 10, 241, 375, 376, 437.
180th to 190th....47, 405, 476, 517, 550, 623.
215th to 218th ...185.
Av A, from 2d to 3d st....476, **551**.
6th to 7th....**50**, **625**, **659**, 690.
8th to 14th ...10, 243, 725.
18th to 19th....476, **802**.
54th to 56th....550, 763.
58th to 61th....438, 623.
70th to 73d....476, 623, 725, 801.
73d to 74th ...122, 216, 346, 405.
74th to 75th....216, 243, 495, **802**.
75th to 79th....185, 830.
83d to 85th... 47, 550.

86th to 87th....122, 406.
87th to 88th....550, 586.
north of 100th (see Pleasant av).
Av B, from 5th to 6th st....**625**, **764**.
6th to 7th....550, 586.
10th to 12th....438, 763.
12th to 14th....**551**, 586, 725.
15th to 17th....293, 438, 517.
72d to 83d....374, 623.
87th to 88th....10.
north of 59th (also called East End av).
Av C, from 2d to 6th st....**123**, 623.
6th to 9th....550, **625**, 763.
12th to 16th....10, 346, 623.
Av D, from 4th to 5th st....623, 690.
7th to 9th....346, 725.
9th to 10th....122, 216, 438, 517, 657, 801.
Audubon, from 175th to 178th st....10, 243.
178th to 181st....83, 185, 243.
181st to 183d....152, 243, 549.
185th to 187th....269, 321, 586.
187th to 190th....623, 830.

Bradhurst....438, 657, 763.

Claremont, from 116th to 119th st....121, 216, 346, 623, 763.
Columbus (formerly 9th av, north of 59th st).
from 63d to 64th st....346.
69th to 71st....46, 346, 763.
72d to 73d....346, 725.
74th to 75th....10, 47.
75th to 76th....10, 406, 585.
80th to 81st....**727**.
82d to 83d....83, 476, 657, 725, 801.
83d to 84th....657, 830.
85th to 87th....346, 724, 763.
91st to 92d....47, 48.
92d to 95th....**50**, 122, 550.
95th to 97th....**11**, 376, 623.
98th to 99th....657.
101st to 102d....216, **217**, 657.
102d to 103d....48.
103d to 104th....346, 550, 586.
106th to 107th....142, 185, 243, 586.
123d to 124th....10, 216, 623, 624.
124th to 125th....690.
Convent, from 141st to 145th st....657, 725, 801.
Coogan....763.

Edgecombe, south of 140th st....243, 293.
from 140th to 150th....185, 586, 763.
150th to 160th....48, 83, 725.
north of 170th....243.
indeft....624, 725.
Fort Washington....346.

Greenwich from Christopher to Charles st....269, 691.
Charles to Perry....122, 153.
Bank to 12th....51.

Lenox (formerly 6th av north of 110th st).
from 115th to 117th st....476.
119th to 120th....122, 428, 517, 657.
120th to 123d....624, 725.
126th to 130d....152, 476.
132d to 134th....152, 293, 725.
134th to 137th....185, 269.
137th to 139th....375, 586.
141st to 142d....48, 624.
Lexington, from 21st to 30th st....438, 723, 763.
31st to 35th....122, 243.
47th to 53d....268, 438, 829.
53d to 54th....476, 586, 801.
55th to 56th....586, 690.
57th to 59th....122, 185, 517.
63d to 66th....48, **84**, 476.
70th to 71st....293, 510.
73d to 76th....10, 243, 269, 476.
86th to 87th....84, 346.
89th to 91st....10, 83, 243.
94th to 95th....185, 406, 657.
100th to 102d....763, 801.
102d to 103d....10, 375, 690.
103d to 104th....321.
104th to 105th....10, 83, 476, 725, 801.
105th to 106th....829, 830.
107th to 109th....83, **153**, 406, 690.
110th to 114th....185, 586.
121st to 123d....405, 801.
124th to 128th....375, 690.

Madison, from 27th to 32d st....586, 690.
36th to 42d....48, 406, 438.
54th to 55th....10, 83.
59th to 63d....**11**, 376.
63d to 65th....10, 657.
65th to 67th....763, 830.
67th to 68th....376, 476, 477, 517.
76th to 78th....268, 763.
79th to 80th....9, 48, 517.
84th to 85th....48, 292, **764**.
88th to 89th....690.
91st to 93d....321, 316, 763.
93d to 94th....624, 830.
97th to 98th....84, 763.
98th to 99th....438, 801.
106th to 107th....10, 48, 83, 152, 185, 243.
108th to 110th....216, 549.
110th to 115th....243, 406, 433, 690, 830.
115th to 125th....405, 657.
125th to 130th....152, 269, 624.
130th to 135th....83, 152, 293, 586, 624, 657.
135th to 138th....517.

Manhattan, from 100th to 108th st....690, 725.
114th to 117th....185, 763.
118th to 123d....690, 725.
north of 123d (see Bradhurst av).
Morningside av, from 118th to 119th st....216, 243, 321, 690.
Mt. Morris....83, 346.

New (also see St. Nicholas pl, Bradhurst, Edgecombe, Morningside and Undercliff avs)....48, 761, 763.

Park, from 34th to 35th st....293.
37th to 38th....293, 346, 725.
38th to 39th....690.
49th to 54th....10, 426.
57th to 60th....624, 658.
60th to 72d....84, 152, 293.
78th to 79th....550, 586, 624, 690.
80th to 81st....83, 725.
86th to 87th....293, 321, 406.
91st to 92d....346.
94th to 95th....406, 477, 550.
95th to 98th....48, 83.
100th to 103d....375, 801.
103d to 104th....122, 321.
104th to 107th....48, 374, 801.
109th to 112th....10, **50**, 122, 476.
114th to 115th....122, 830.
115th to 116th....10, 47.
118th to 122d....216, 293, 586.
123d to 124th....185, 293, 517.
128th to 129th....586, 725.
indeft....183.
Pleasant, from 101st to 102d st....185.
112th to 115th....438, 477, 801.
117th to 118th....293, 346, 657.
118th to 119th....517, 550.
121st to 122d....438.
Prescott....438.

Riverside, from 78th to 79th st....153, 725.
81st to 82d....122, 690, 725, 801.
83d to 84th....243.
94th to 95th....550.
105th to 110th....405, 406.

Seaman....83, 438.
St. Nicholas, from 120th to 122d st....243, 550.
122d to 127th....216, 346.
127th to 130th....185, 243.
130th to 143d....243, 376.
145th to 150th....48, 586.
150th to 160th....10, 725.
Sherman....83, 269.
South 5th, from Grand to Broome st....243, 517.
Spring to Prince....10, 293.
Houston to Bleecker....122, 438, 477, 655.
Bleecker to 4th....655, 764.

Terrace View....516, 548.

Vermilyea....48, 83, 122, 517, 586, 690.

Wadsworth, from 177th to 180th st....10, 321, 550.
180th to 190th....405, 550, 763.
West End (formerly 11th av).
from 66th to 67th st....293, 376, 762.
69th to 70th....216, 657.
77th to 80th....438, 763.
80th to 82d....48, 321, 586.
83d to 85th....152, 376, 406, 830.
85th to 87th....48, 406, 657.
87th to 88th....122, 428.
88th to 89th....122, 476, 477, 517, 624, **691**.
89th to 90th....216, 725.
92d to 95th....10, 657, 725.
97th to 98th....10, 438, 477, 517, 586, 830.
101st to 102d....152, 321.
102d to 103d....122, 438, 517.
103d to 105th....10, 624, 763.
north of 106th (see Boulevard and 11th av).

1st, from 5th to 10th st....**186**, **764**.
10th to 11th....**50**, 830.
11th to 12th....152, 216.
15th to 19th....**50**, **84**, **186**.
21st to 24th....293, **294**.
24th to 25th....**153**, **376**.
28th to 29th....**691**, 801.
29th to 32d....477, 690, 725.
34th to 36th....83, 243, 518, 624.
43d to 44th....83, 216, 517, 518.
45th to 48th....10, 11, 48, 321.
51st to 52d....183, 406.
53d to 59th....**186**, **407**, 624.
60th to 63d....10, 477, **625**.
63d to 66th....216, **587**.
69th to 70th....346, 691.
73d to 76th....10, 321, 690, **764**.
77th to 78th....346, 406.
78th to 79th....**439**, 586.
81st to 84th....624, 801.
87th to 89th....269, 624.
91st to 94th....477, 801.
103d to 106th....**217**, **407**, **691**.
108th to 109th....374, 550.
112th to 114th....48, 185, 657, 690.
116th to 117th....321, 586.
117th to 119th....**50**, 550, 725.
119th to 120th....185, **478**, 763.
120th to 124th....**294**, **322**, 586.

2d, from 5th to 6th st....**50**, 477, 550, 586, 801.
6th to 7th....**153**.
20th to 26th....48, 122, 185.
26th to 29th....48, **153**, 550.
30th to 31st....**11**, 477.
32d to 35th....374, 658.
36th to 37th....243, 690.
39th to 41st....83, **376**, 406, 763.
42d to 44th....122, **407**, **478**, 725.
47th to 49th....48, 243, 690.
49th to 50th....586, 725.
53d to 56th....477, 548.
56th to 57th....477, **831**.
58th to 60th....153, 406.
64th to 72d....11, **50**, 406.
73d to 75th....269, 586, 726.
76th to 77th....243, 376.
78th to 81st....243, **587**.
82d to 83d....185, 725.
84th to 89th....48, 293, 518.
96th to 97th....293, **764**.
97th to 98th....183, 658, **659**.
99th to 100th....216, 374, 725.

100th to 101st....11, 48, 216, **551**.
101st to 105th....216, 550, 801.
105th to 107th....11, 48.
108th to 109th....122, 725.
109th to 110th....153, 216.
112th to 113th....293, 586.
113th to 114th....658, 801.
115th to 117th....11, 185.
118th to 120th....321, 376, 550.
123d to 124th....725.
124th to 125th....48, 321, 477, 830.
125th to 126th....518.
3d av, south of 14th st....**50**, **186**, 242.
from 16th to 17th....**217**, **294**.
21st to 27th....83, 185, **347**.
30th to 31st....**551**, 830.
33d to 37th....**294**, **518**.
39th to 41th....**407**, 624, 830.
44th to 45th....518, 586.
47th to 49th....346, 726, **727**.
49th to 51st....477, **518**, 801.
59th to 64th....243, 624.
64th to 66th....**123**, **518**, **551**.
73d to 76th....48, 83, 376.
83d to 88th....321, **551**, **587**.
91st to 92d....690, 726.
92d to 93d....438, 624, 801.
101st to 102d....243, 269, **407**.
103d to 108th....83, 293, 658, **802**.
110th to 111th....624, **691**.
111th to 120th....11, 406.
123d to 130th....**11**, 48, **217**.
north of Harlem River (see 3d av, in 23d and 24th Wards).
4th av, from 16th to 17th....761.
19th to 28th....691, 801.
29th to 32d....762, 799, 829.
north of 34th (see Park av).
5th, south of 11th st....83, 658.
from 16th to 17th....11, 48, 477.
18th to 22d....376, 690, 830.
26th to 29th....153, 185, **478**.
31st to 35th....**153**, 761.
48th to 51st....406, **518**, **764**.
52d to 59th....624, **764**.
61st to 66th....216, 321.
71st to 75th....321, 346, 830.
80th to 83th....185, 406.
85th to 86th....293, 726.
98th to 105th....216, 321, 406.
106th to 109th....83, 216.
114th to 115th....48, 406, 477, 586.
115th to 116th....122, 153, 406.
127th to 131st....376, 406, 690.
131st to 132d....185, 550.
132d to 134th....185, 830.
135th to 136th....216.
6th, from Washington pl to Clinton pl....269, 658.
10th to 12th st....46, 83.
28th to 29th....**551**, 726.
49th to 50th....763.
north of 110th st (is Lenox av).
7th av, from 14th to 15th st....**269**.
21st to 25th....11, 801.
26th to 29th....477, 586.
31st to 32d....586, **587**, 624.
32d to 34th....658.
40th to 41st....**478**, **518**.
41st to 42d....185, **186**, 216.
47th to 52d....**217**, **244**.
53d to 54th....516, 658, 801.
56th to 57th....243, 438, **551**.
117th to 119th....550, 726, 763.
119th to 120th....406, 586.
120th to 121st....185, 438, 586, 763.
124th to 127th....**764**, **831**.
127th to 128th....48, 830.
128th to 129th....316, 546, 801.
129th to 131st....83, 294.
133d to 134th....83, 690, 726.
134th to 140th....726, 830.
140th to 145th....216, 586.
8th av, from 15th to 18th st....48, **347**.
18th to 20th....**269**, **727**.
22d to 28d....185, **186**, **625**, **691**.
37th to 38th....374, 375.
39th to 42d....**691**, 763.
47th to 52d....**376**, **407**, 763.
59th to 110th (see Central Park West).
112th to 117th....48, 550.
117th to 118th....586, 726, 830.
118th to 119th....406, 438, 477.
120th to 126th....216, **294**, 550.
126th to 127th....321, 438, 477, 550, 624.
127th to 133d....121, 243, 550.
135th to 140th....346, 347, 477, 726.
140th to 145th....10, 624, 725.
145th to 155th....243, 321, 428.
9th, from 14th to 17th st....83, **217**.
28th to 33d....48, 658, **802**.
35th to 38th....269, 294, 477.
47th to 49th....244, 658.
49th to 50th....183, 438, 477.
50th to 52d....**376**, 586, **691**.
55th to 56th....85, **269**, **802**.
north of 59th (see Columbus av).
10th, from 27th to 29th st....11, 477, **659**, **727**.
40th to 42d....406, 690.
49th to 51st....**478**, **765**.
54th to 57th....48, **347**, **551**.
north of 59th (see Amsterdam av).
11th, from 18th to 22d st....**407**, **587**, **625**.
39th to 40th....185, **244**, 655.
47th to 52d....243, **478**.
57th to 63d....48, 518, 530, 726.
64th to 106th (see West End av).
108th to 178d (also see Boulevard)....801.
178d to 178th....10, 11, 48, 438.
178th to 181st....10, 11, 48, 321.
180th to 190th....185, 405, 550.
12th....48, 83, **123**, 185, 477, 624, 657.
13th....**625**, 657.
14th....321.

PLACES.

Centre Market....374.
City Hall....799.
Clinton, n s. from Broadway to University pl ....**11, 153, 217, 478, 726.**
University pl to 5th av....**123.**
s s. 5th av to Macdougal st....120, 374.
s s. Macdougal st to 6th av....81.
College, from Barclay st to Park pl....**551.**

Dunscomb....242.

Exchange... 374.

Hamilton....825.
Hancock (also see Manhattan st)....10, 624.

Irving....**84.**

Lafayette, from Great Jones to 4th st....762.
Livingston....151.

Mitchell....548.

Park, from Church st to College pl....**551, 764.**
Prospect, from 40th to 41st....516.

Rutgers (also see Monroe, from Jefferson to Clinton st)....548, 829.

St. Lukes (also see Leroy st)....689, 829.
St. Marks (also see 8th st).
from Av A to 1st av....151, 548.
1st to 2d ...723.
St. Nicholas....761.

Teunissen....516.

Union....**407. 764.**
University, from 13th to 14th st....241, 292, 320, 437.

Waverley, from Broadway to Greene st....584, 723.
Macdougal to Gay....269, 548, 829.
Gay to Perry ...151, 723, 761.
north of Perry....81.

MISCELLANEOUS.

Acre property....321, 376, 406, 518.

Car and Railroad leases....**84.**

Croton Aqueduct....624.

Dyckman property....518.

Hell or Hurl Gate....376, 406.

Highbridge Park....243.

Hudson River Railroad (see New York Central & Hudson River Railroad).

Indeft. Leasehold....**186, 244, 269, 347.**

Interior lots....11, 48, 83, 122, 153, 292, 294, 321, 376, 438, 518, 549, 550, 585, 586, 657, 690, 726, 801, 830.

Kingsbridge....518.

Land of Eliza B. Jumel....376.

Land under water....269, 321, 376, 406, 518, 624, 830.

Mill Rock or Gibson's or Leland's Island....376, 406.

Miscellaneous ..8, 11, 48, 122, 153, 185, 216, 243, 269, 347, 374, 376, 406, 438, 477, 518, 550. 586, 624. 658, 690. 724, 761, 801. 830.

New York Central & Hudson River Railroad....81, 477, 550.

Pier or bulkhead East River. ..**153. 186**, 321.
Pier or bulkhead Harlem River....10, 518, 830
Pier or bulkhead North or Hudson River....48 122, 269, 321, 624, 657.

Spuyten Duyvil Creek or United States Ship Canal....518.

The Hyatt property....518.

TWENTY-THIRD AND TWENTY-FOURTH WARDS.

STREETS.

Ackerman....269.
Ann....216, 802.
Anthony....269, 294.
Ash ...550.
Bayard....439.
Beach or Beech....406. 439, 550.
Beech terrace....83, 216, 217.
Bender (also see 8th av)....550.
Berry....690.
Bettners lane....217, 294.
Bristow....406. 658, 691.
Broadway....153, 518, 802, 830.
Buckhout....321, 347.
Bush....658
Centre....439
Chisholm....321, 726.
Church (also see Church pl and Kingsbridge av) ....321, 477.
Clifton... 518.
Clinton....586.
Cole... 586
College....153.
Columbine....48.
Crotona Parkway....477.

Denman....802.
Donnybrook ....658.
Drive (also see New Drive)....269, 763, 802

Field....406, 439, 624.
Forest....406, 439 477, 518.
Fort Independence....85, 243.
Fox....83, 216, 291, 439, 586, 691.
Frederick....406, 518.
Freeman ..48, 185, 321.

Gambril (also see Suburban st)....439, 550.
Garden....11.
Garfield....49.
George....294.
Gerard....376, 439, 830.
Gouverneur....294.
Gray....269.
Grove (also see Broadway)....625.

Hampden (also see 184th st)....83, 84.
Hawkstone....658.
Hellen. ..830.
Henry....122.
High Bridge....48, 244, 293.
Hill....406, 439, 477, 624
Hoffman....153, 294, 439, 830.
Holly .. 518.
Home....216, 763, 764.

Jacob....294, 518.
Jennings....406
John....185, 376, 550.

Kelly....153, 691, 764.
Kemble....48, 726.
Knowlton ...691.
Knox....48, 123, 726.

Lebanon ...587, 624, 625.
Leggett lane....764
Lorillard. ..659.
Lyon. ..48, 763, 764.

Main....477.
Main st to West Farms....802, 830.
Maple....49. 84.
Maxwell....49, 84.
Mechanic....122.
Monroe... 48
Morris (also see Mount Hope pl) ...269.
Mosholu Parkway ...49, 50, 518, 658, 726
Mott....518.

New (see Proposed).
New Drive, Spuyten Duyvil (also see Drive).... 501, 763, 802.
Niles ...587, 726.
North....11, 48.

Oakley....122, 518, 587.
Oak terrace....48, 216, 624
Old Gerard....376, 830.
Oliver....84.
Opdyke....185.
Orchard. 185, 216.
Orchard terrace....269.

Park View terrace....658, 659, 726.
Penfold....269.
Perot....691, 802.
Pine....321.
Popham....269.
Private lane....726.
Proposed....439.
Public Drive ...152.
Public Parkway....84.
Pyne....243.

Rae....11.
Riverview terrace . 726.
Rockfield....153, 294 321, 406.
Rock....406, 439. 477, 518, 624, 690, 726.
Ryer....84, 376, 624.

Samuel (also see 180th st)....269, 347, 376, 550.
Sidney....216.
Simpson....84 376.
Southern Boulevard, from 3d to Alexander av....**764.**
from 144th to 175th....48, 84.
187th st to Decatur av....48, 347.
Decatur to Jerome....48, 49, 153, 587.
indeft....49, 587, 658.
Spring... 294, 477.
Suburban (also see Gambril st)....49, 84, 406, 439, 550, 691
Summit....518, 624, 830.

Talmadge ...691.
Tiffany, from Westchester av to 169th st....185, 294, 321, 691.
indeft....376, 406.
Topping....49.
Travers....84, 624, 658, 726.

Walker....439.
Walnut....550, 726.
Warren....269, 294.
Waverley.. .477.
Weeks (also see Clinton av)....269, 763.
Wellesley....658, 659.
West... 763.
Wetmore....11.
Willard....185, 518, 550, 691.
Woolf ...518.

1st (also see Vireo av)....153, 321, 518, 830.
2d....439, 477.
3d....48, 84, 153.
6th (see 168th st).
7th (also see 169th st)... 11.
130th....658.
131st... 658.
132d, from Brook to Cypress av....658, 763, 802.
Cypress to Oak....11, 587, 658.
133d (also see Southern Boulevard)....11, 439, 763, **764.**
134th, from 3d to Alexander av....122, 153, 376, 406, 438, 477, 518, 726, 764.
Alexander to Brook....122, 153, 185, 216, 294. 689. 830.
Brook to Cypress....477, 658, 764.
Cypress to Oak....84, 269, 726.
135th, from Railroad to 3d av. . 347.
3d to Alexander... 294, 376, 830.
Alexander to Willis....550, 689.
Brook to Willow....347, 376, 439, 624.
136th, from Alexander to Willis av....347, 764, 802.
Brook to Willow....406, 658, 691.
east of Willow....406.
indeft....122.
137th, from Lincoln to Willis av....122, 294.
east of Willis....294, 406, 439.
indeft....243, 347.
138th, west of 3d av....216.
from Alexander to Willis....123, 185, 216, 477, 550.
Willis av to Brown pl....269.
east of St Anns....269 294, 321, 406, 726.
indeft....243.
139th....11, 49 624.
141st....49, 84, 123, 477, 587. 624.
142d, from Rider to Willis av....**478**, 550.
Willis to Brook....**478**, 587.
indeft....216.
143d, from Alexander to Brook av ...84, 659, 691, 830.
indeft....477.
144th, west of 3d av....477.
Willis to Cypress....185, 269, 830.
145th st. from 3d to Brook av....84, 216, 518.
146th, from 3d to Willis av... 587.
Willis to Brook....49. 216, 244, 269, 294.
indeft....122.
147th, from 3d to Brook av....11, 123, 347.
east of Brook....217, 244, 294.
indeft ...122. 123.
148th, from Railroad to College av....244, 477.
College to Brook av. ..11, 123, 185, 550.
indeft....122, 123, 587.
149th, west of 3d av....185, 658.
indeft....294 477. 478.
150th, west of Walton av....49, **727.**
Walton to Courtlandt ..122, 439.
151st, from Railroad to Courtlandt av....376, 406, 726.
east of 3d....**50**, 658.
indeft....726.
152d, from Mott to Courtlandt av....244, 294, 764.
Courtlandt to 3d....550.
153d, from Railroad to 3d av....84, 764. 802.
154th, from Railroad to Courtlandt av....294, 321, 726.
Courtlandt to Elton....244, 321, 726, 830.
indeft....518.
156th....658
157th....217, 321, 764.
158th, from Railroad to 3d av....11, 153, 244, 269, 764
159th....11, 153, 406, 624, 658, 691.
160th....122, 153, 624.
161st....84, 153, 406, 830.
132d, from Railroad to 3d av....49, 406, 726.
east of 3d....186, 587.
163d, from Railroad to Union av....186, 439, 587, 830.
164th, from Sheridan to Railroad av....406.
Railroad to 3d....49, 84, 658.
indeft....764.
165th, from Jerome to 3d av....11, 518, 587, 658.
east of 3d. ..347, 439.
indeft....347.
166th, east of 3d av ...347.
167th....49, 84. 624. 691.
169th, from Webster to Franklin av....153, 439.
Franklin to Stebbins....153, 406.
east of Stebbins....48, 84, 294, 587, 691.
indeft....11 347, 691.
170th, from 3d to Franklin av....11, 153, 186, 518, 764.
172d....764.
173d ...11, 122, 439, 518, 624, 764.
174th... 376 550.
175th (also see Fairmount av)....84, 217, 587, 764, 802.
176th....49, 123, 217, 439.
177th ...153, 550, 587.
179th....122.
181st....321, 550.
183d ...217. 624.
184th (also see Hampden st)....49, 83, 84, 477.
187th....347, 726.

AVENUES.

Av A....50, 345, 439, 624.
Av B (also see Creston av)....518.
Av C (also see Ryer av; also see Trinity av).... 244.
Alexander, from 134th to 137th st....84, 321.
140th to 143d....49, 477.
Andrews. . 321, 551, 726.
Anthony, from Webster st to Burnside av....122, 152, 269, 347, 376, 477.
Burnside to Van Courtlandt av....347, 439, 518.
indeft .. 269.
Arthur....49, 347, 518, 658.

Babcock....764.
Bailey....84, 122, 153.
Bainbridge (also see 2d av)....49, 186, 439, 658.
Balcom....11.
Bathgate, south of 175th st....153, 186, 217, 376, 477, 726, 764.
from 175th to 179th....84, 186, 691.
179th to 183d....49, 153, 321, 347, 691.
indeft....439, 658.
Beach....294.
Beekman....49, 216, 217, 587.
Belmont....49, 376, 406, 587.
Bergen....49. 122, 764.
Berrian....84, 321, 376, 764.
Boston (also see Boston road)....49, 186, 321, 347, 376, 406.
Bremer.. 764.
Briggs, south of Marion av....84, 186, 439, 830.
from Marion av to Gambril st....49.
indeft ..49, 764.
Bronx....135. 406, 407.
Brook, from 134th to 142d st....186, 406.
142d to 148th....153, 830.
148th to 156th ...185, 244, 658. 802.

156th to 165th....321, 439, 830.
north of 169th....347, 376.
Burnside....347.

Cambreling (also see Jefferson av)....84, 186, 217, 347, 550, 624.
Cauldwell, south of 161st st....186, 269.
from 161st to 165th....347, 587.
indeft ...186, 269, 406.
Central (also see Jerome av)....84, 217, 244, 331, 691, 763, 764.
Clay.. .658.
Clinton (also see Rustic av).
from 175th to Samuel st....406, 550, 587, 624, 658, 802.
indeft....84, 153, 186, 269, 376, 477, 550, 587, 624, 625, 658, 691, 726.
College....49, 122.
Concord....624, 726.
Coster....49, 84.
Courtlandt, south of 153d st....49, 186, 439.
north of 159th....691, 764.
Creston (also see Av B)...186, 376, 406, 624, 658.
Crimmins....49, 84, 550, 587, 624.
Cromwell....727.
Crotona....11, 49, 186, 406, 518, 550, 587, 624, 625, 691, 802.
Cuthbert....802.
Cypress, south of 135th st....658.
north of 145th....691.

Decatur....49, 84, 122, 477, 726.

Eagle....11, 186, 244, 587.
Eastern Bay....49, 84.
Edenwood....122, 185, 244.
Elwood....691.
Elm....122.
Elmwood....84.
Elton, from 155th to 158th st....439, 658.
158th to 161st....11, 84.
north of 161st....84, 439.
indeft....587, 691.

Fairmount (also see 175th st)....217.
Fleetwood (also see 2d av)....11, 294, 321, 438, 477, 550, 624.
Fordham (also see 3d av)....518, 550.
Forest....186, 244, 347, 406, 439, 587.
Forrest....550, 624, 625.
Franklin, south of 170th st....49, 84, 122, 244, 518, 587, 764.
from 170th to Samuel....186, 406, 802.
indeft....122, 347, 477.
Fulton, south of 170th st....84, 186, 269, 726, 764.
from 170th to 175th....658.
indeft....587, 726.

Gardner....764, 802.
Garden....269.
Gerard ...763, 764.
Grant....11, 477, 587, 830.
Grove....550, 625.

Harrison....477.
Highbridge....122.
Hillside. ..49, 84.
Home....122.
Honeywell ...49.
Hull....49, 122, 406, 550.

Intervale, from Westchester av to Lyon st.... 217, 294, 625, 691.
north of Lyon... 764.
indeft....186.
Inwood. ..49, 84, 294, 726, 764.

Jackson....587, 691.
Jefferson (also see Cambreling av). ..244, 439, 518, 550, 587, 625, 726, 830.
Jerome (also see Central av).
from Elliott to 176th st. ..550, 625.
184th st to Southern Boulevard....477, 587, 658, 659.
indeft....**659**, 691.
Johnson (also see Mapes av)....659.

Katonah....49, 122, 726.
Keppler....49, 84, 186, 406, 726.
Kingsbridge (also see Church st and pl)....321.
Kirkside....658, 659.

Lafountaine....122, 477.
Lexington (also see Crane pl and Central and Jerome avs)....49, 269, 376, 406.
Lincoln....550, 659.
Lind....269.
Locust....406, 625.
Loring....186, 764.

Madison....122, 153, 186, 347, 518, 802.
Mali....691.
Mapes (also see Johnson av)....659.
Marion....244, 321, 477, 518, 802.
Meadow....49, 84.
Mohegan....477.
Monroe....406, 439.
Morris, south of 144th st....11.
from 148th to 152d....347, 376, 659, 691.
152d to 165th....217, 376.
174th to Welch....269, 477, 550, 764.
indeft....49, 269.
Morrisania....587, 830.
Morse (see Broadway).
Mott....186, 243.
Mosholu....84.

Nathalie....84, 294, 439.
Northern....152.

Ogden....153.
Old Vanderbilt (see Vanderbilt av).
Old Fordham (also see Fordham av)....550.
Oneida... 185.
Opdyke....11, 84, 122, 153, 186, 376, 439, 518, 625, 726, 830.
Orchard....153.

Palisade....84, 477, 763.
Park View....659.

Pelham....122, 439, 625, 659.
Penfold....439.
Perry....49, 269, 477, 518, 691.
Prospect, from 156th to 167th st....49, 217, 294, 764.
167th to 171st....478, 625, 764.
171st to Tremont av....11, 376, 764.
north of Tremont av....186, 406, 587, 624, 625, 691.
indeft....49, 122, 186, 269, 406, 518, 587, 625, 691.

Railroad (also see Vanderbilt av).
from 160th to 170th st....294, 659.
170th to 176th....11, 49, 153, 439, 625.
north of 176th.. .11.
indeft....294, 321, 439, 659.
Retreat....122, 294, 478.
Rider, from 142d to 144th st....294, 477.
River....477, **727**.
Riverdale....550, 764, 802.
Robbins, north of 150th st....186, 439.
Rustic (see Clinton av).
Ryer (also see Av C)....153, 406, 439.

St. Anns....49, 186.
Scott....439.
Sedgwick....49, 50, 123, 406, 439, 691, 802, 830.
Sheridan....217, 243, 244, 477, 518, 764.
Stebbins, from 165th to 169th st....244, 625, 764.
169th to Freeman....321, 726.
north of Freeman....49, 123, 550, 690.
indeft....49, 691.
Strong....269, 406.

Taylor ...11, 49, 186, 659.
Teller (also see Fleetwood av)....550.
Tinton, from 145th to 154th st....294, 406.
156th to 161st....11, 84, 123, 269, 294, 376, 477, 587, 726, 802.
161st to 168th....439, 518, 625, 691.
indeft....406, 624, 625, 802.
Tiebout....550.
Tremont, from Arthur to Prospect av....49, 518, 550, 587, 625.
Prospect av to Bronx River....406, 550, 625.
indeft....587, 625, 691.
Trinity (also see Av C)....244, 294, 406, 764.

Union, from 154th to 161st st....84, 587.
161st to 167th....153, 269, 550, 659, 764.
north of 167th....153.
indeft....49, 84, 217, 764.

Valentine.. .49, 439, 550, 625, 830.
Vanderbilt av E., south of Samuel st....11, 153, 550, 587, 764.
Samuel to 184th....11, 123, 625.
186th to 188th....11.
indeft ...321.
Vanderbilt av W., south of 179th st....11, 49.
Villa....49, 84, 186, 321.
Vireo, Verio or Veno (also see 1st st). ..11, 49.
Vyse....659.

Wales....269.
Walnut....587.
Walton, from 147th to 155th st....49, 123, 518, 659.
Washington, from 160th to 163d st....244, 726.
163d to 166th....659, 726.
166th to 169th....406, 831.
169th to 172d....11, 123, 153, **153**, 244, 439, 478, 726.
172d to 175th....123, 186, 764.
175th to 179th. ..123, 153, **322**.
179th to 183d....153, 217, 550.
183d to 188th....123, 244, 347.
north of 188th....726.
indeft....49, 84, 550, 551, 625, 691, 764, 831.
Webster, from 169th to 175th st....11, 49, 84, 244, 269, 478, 518, 625, 830.
175th to Oliver....123, 153, 518.
Oliver to Bussing.. .49, 50, 764.
indeft....49, 50, 84, 186, 321, 439, 625, 659, 764.
Western Bay....49, 84.
Westchester, from 3d to St. Anns av....49, 186, 658.
St. Anns av to Fox st....186, 587, 658, 764.
indeft....186.
Wetmore....625.
Willard....84, 122, 153, 186, 269, 321, 518, 691, 726.
Willis, from 134th to 135th st....50, **294**, 347, 587, 689.
137th to 138th....376, **551**.
142d to 144th....50, 347, **587**.
144th to 146th....625, 764, 831.
146th to 148th....764, 831.
Willow....406.
Woodruff....726.
Worth....294, 321, 659.

Yonkers....726.

1st....50, 518.
2d (also see Bainbridge av)....186, 244, 321.
3d, from 141st to 148th st....84, **153**.
151st to 154th....244, 587.
157th to 160th....**659**, 726.
160th to 163d ...376, 691.
163d to 166th....123, 376, 764.
178th to 182d....764.
indeft....11, 84, 123, 217, 269, 376, 518, 802.
6th....153.
8th....50, 518, 550.

PLACES.

Arcularius....518, 586, 690, 726, 763.
Armand....347.

Buchanan....624.
Burnet....406.

Church (see Church st and Kingsbridge av).
Clarke....726, 763.
Cornell....439.
Cordova....294, 439, 477, 763.
Crane (also see Lexington av)....269.
Crotona ...550.

Delancey (also see Washington av)....726.
Denman... 48, 477.

Elmwood....518, 550, 586, 587, 624, 625, 658.
Elsmere....294, 726.
Ernescliff....347.
Evelyn....186, 406.

Fairmount....11, 406, 726.
Findlay....726.

German....11, 153.
Gourverneur....658.
Grove Hill....122.

Hall... 439.
Holly....48.

Lafayette....321.
Lillian... 690.
Lorillard....763.

Marcy....243.
Mount Hope (also see Morris st)....439, 477.
Morton....726.

Oakland....550, 587, 624.
Oakley... 691.

Poe....153.
Pond....518, 587, 802.
Potter....347, 763.
Powell....11.

Ritter.. .726.
Rogers....122, 243, 347, 439, 624, 726.
Ryer....439, 518.

South....185.

Teasdale....11, 726.
Terrace ...122.
Tower....658.

Ursula....518.

Waverley....406.

ROADS.

Boston....84, 153, 376.
Boston Post....153.
Bronx River....406.

Coles (see Boston road or av).

Fordham Landing....726.
Fordham to West Farms....269.
Fordham road (also see 3d av and Highbridge st) ....123.
Fordham to Williamsbridge (also see 2d av).... 244.

Harlem R. R. (see N. Y. & Harlem R. R.).
Harlem River & Portchester R. R....186, 243, 625, 658.
Highbridge....293, 518.
Hudson River (see N. Y. C. & H. R. R. R.).... 152, 764, 802.

Indeft roads....84.

Jerome Park R. R....294, 518, 764.

Kingsbridge, from Broadway to Washington av ....625, 658, 659.
indeft....50, 587, 624, 830.
Kingsbridge to West Farms....84, 217, 321.

Main Post road, from N. Y. to Boston....244.
Macombs Dam (also see Ridge st). ..49, 186, 659, 764.

New roads... 217, 659.
N. Y. C. & H. R. R. R....84, 152, 551, 763, 764, 802.
N. Y. City & Northern R. R ...726.
N. Y. & Harlem R. R....84, 153, 658.
N. Y., N. H. & H. R. R....551.
N. Y. to White Plains road....762.

Old Boston....123, 691.
Old Post, from N. Y. to Albany....186.

Port Morris Branch R. R....186, **691**.
Post....123.
Post, from New York to Albany....153.
Private....802.

Road leading from Mile Square to South Yonkers....439.
Road from West Farms to Hunts Point....551.
Road from West Farms to Kingsbridge....802.

Southern Westchester turnpike (see Southern Boulevard).

Westchester....**691**.
West Farms....153.
West Farms to Hunts Point....153, 294, 659, 726, 802.
Williamsbridge....624.

TOWNS, VILLAGES, ETC.

Berrian Farm (See Fordham).
Barrettos Point....84,

Cedar Hill....406.
Central Morrisania....50.
Central Mott Haven....625.
Crotona Park... 49.

East Morrisania....84.
Eltona....764.

Fordham....269, 321, 551, 625.
Fordham Ridge....269, 478, 764.

Hyatt Farm, near Woodlawn....84, 831.
Hunts Point....406, 407.

Kingsbridge Heights....691, 726.

Morrisania....347, 726.
Morris Heights....11, 50, 659.
Mosbolu....726, 831.

North New York....123, 347.

Powell Farm....406.

Riverdale....217, 726, 831.
Ryer Homestead lots....831.

Springhurst....625.
Spoffords Point ...49.
Spuyten Duyvil....551.

West Farms....321, 406, 407, 439, 691, 726.
Woodlawn....831.
Woodlawn Cemetery....478.
Woodlawn Heights....347, 406, 439, 478, 726, 802.

MISCELLANEOUS.

Acre property....123, 185, 186, 217, 294, 406, 407, 439, 478, 587, 625, 762, 764.

Bronx River....478, 551, 659.
Bronx Kills....658.

Croton Aqueduct....84, 122, 123, 185, 659.

Doughty's Brook....48.

East River (also see Long Island Sound) ...186.

Harlem River....49, 84, 625, **727**.
Hudson River....551, 764, 802.

Interior lots....11, 123, 439, 478, 551, 726.

Land under water....49, 84, 294, 406, 407, 551, 625, 658, **727**, 802.
Leggetts Creek....84.
Long Island Sound....84, 186, 406, 407.

Mill Brook....49, 122, 123, 158, 186, 244, 478, 551, 625, 658, **691**.
Miscellaneous... 50, 186, 551, 659, 691.
Mott Haven Canal ...216, 294.

23d Ward, indeft....186, 376, 478.
24th Ward, indeft....11, 84, 321, 376, 406, 439, 478, 691, 802, 831.

West Farms Creek....478, 551, 659.

PROJECTED BUILDINGS.

NEW YORK.

STREETS.

Academy....280.
Allen ...638, 741.

Bank....24.
Bayard....638, 741.
Bedford ...66.
Beekman ...815.
Bleecker....66.
Bolton road....254.
Boulevard, south of 100th....24, 135.
from 100th to 125th....98, 564.
north of 125th....703, 815.
north of 106th (also see 11th av)....815.
Bowery, south of Grand....165, 741.
Broad....165.
Broadway, from Houston to 14th... 777.
34th to 59th....98.
north of 59th (see Boulevard).
Broome, west of Bowery....455.

Canal, east of Broadway....98.
Central Park West (8th av), north of 100th.... 532.
Centre....455.
Cherry ...532.
Columbia....857.
Cortlandt....490.
Crosby....199, 490.
Delancey....358, 388, 741, 814.

Division....419.
Downing... 135, 564.
Duane....600.
Eastern Boulevard (see Av A).
Edgecombe road (see Edgecombe av).
Eldridge....165.
Elizabeth....741.
Elm....331.

Forsyth....638, 702.
Frankfort....24.
Franklin....98. 279.
Fulton....841.

Goerck....532.
Grand Boulevard (see Boulevard).
Grand, west of Bowery....66, 98.
Great Jones....841.
Greenwich....24, 165, 227.

Hamilton....815.
Henry....279, 358, 638, 841.
Hester....815.
Houston....9, 135, 841.
Hudson, south of Canal....600.
north of 10th....24, 815.

Jersey....305.
Jones....98.

King. ..199.
Kingsbridge road....254, 358.

Lewis....98, 600.
Liberty....777.

Macombs Dam road....532.
Macdougal....135.
Madison....24, 455, 600.
Manhattan....742.
Market....841.
Mercer....24.
Morton....702.
Mott....564, 777.
Mulberry....135, 638.

Nassau....841.
Norfolk....638.

Orchard....490.

Pearl....279.
Pitt....135, 638.

Ridge....358.
Rivington....357.

Sheriff... 66.
Stanton....841.
Suffolk... 490.
Sullivan....532, 841.

Walker....305.
Washington....253, 638.
Watts....638.
West....564, 674.
Willett....279.
William....279, 419.
3d ...9, 135, 358, 388.
4th... 532, 815.
5th....703, 741.
7th....532.
8th (see St. Marks pl).
9th....66, 98, 777.
10th....105, 199, 532.
11th ...253.
12th... 24, 358, 564.
13th... 66, 419.
16th, east of 5th av....66.
west of 5th....564, 702.
17th, west of 5th av....228.
18th, east of 5th av....305, 674.
20th, west of 5th av....638, 841.
21st, from 5th to 8th av....66, 135.
west of 8th....135, 490.
22d ...135, 600.
23d, east of 5th av ...600.
24th, east of 5th av....841.
25th, west of 5th av....66, 388.
26th, west of 5th av....741, 777.
27th, east of 3d av....66.
28th, east of 5th av....358.
west of 5th....98.
29th, west of 5th av....741.
31st... 135, 419.
32d, east of 5th av....66.
34th, east of 5th av....564, 674.
37th, east of 5th av....98.
west of 5th....253, 668.
38th, west of 5th av....638.
39th, east of 5th av....24.
40th, from 5th to 8th av ...841.
41st, east of 5th av....455, 674.
44th, east of 5th av....66.
west of 5th av....98, 165, 702.
45th....98, 253.
47th, west of 5th av....674.
49th, west of 5th av... 199.
50th....490, 600.
51st, west of 5th av....841.
52d, east of 5th av ...532.
54th, west of 5th av....455.
55th....98, 564.
56th, west of 5th av....388, 419.
57th....419, 490.
58th, from 5th to 8th av....778.
59th....200, 600.
60th, east of 5th av....358, 674.
64th, east of 5th av....280.
65th, west of 8th av....67.
66th, west of 8th av....185.
68th, west of 8th av....200, 358, 564, 674, 702, 815.
69th, west of 8th av....228, 358, 703.
70th, west of 8th av....24, 305, 703.
71st....254, 778.
72d, east of 5th av....24, 228.
73d, east of 5th av....279.
74th, east of 5th av....358, 638.
75th....490, 600.
76th, west of 8th av. ..305, 358, 419, 638, 815.
77th, east of 3d av....67.
west of 8th....24, 490.
78th, east of 5th av....600, 815.
west of 10th av....24, 455.
79th....135, 358.
80th, east of 5th av....600.
81st, west of 8th av....564.
83d, east of 3d av....279.
west of 8th av....200, 331.
84th, east of 5th av....67.
west of 8th....135.
85th, east of 3d av....24, 702, 742.
from 8th to 10th. ..135.
87th, east of 5th av....98, 674, 702.
from 8th to 10th....564, 638.
88th, east of 3d av....67, 200, 358, 564, 674.
west of 8th....600.
89th, from 3d to 5th av....200.
90th, from 3d to 5th av....600, 702.
west of 8th....67, 564, 841.
91st, from 3d to 5th av....280.
west of 8th....388, 815.
92d, west of 8th av....98, 490.
93d, west of 8th av....24.
94th, east of 5th av....67.
95th, east of 5th av....98, 532.
west of 8th....815.
96th, east of 5th av....703.
west of 8th....419.
98th, west of 8th av....67, 532.
100th, east of 5th av....490.
101st, east of 5th av....419.
102d, east of 3d av... 419.
west of 8th....24, 67.
103d, east of 5th av ...254, 305, 490, 564, 674, 702.
from 8th to 10th ...98.
west of 10th....67, 419.
104th, east of 5th av....67.
west of 10th....98, 638, 778.
105th, east of 3d av....135.
106th, west of 8th av....564.
107th, east of 5th av....742.
110th, east of 5th av. ..67, 98.
111th, east of 5th av....638.
112th, east of 5th av....200.
113th, east of 3d av....67.
115th, east of 5th av....67, 98, 165, 358.
west of 5th....532.
116th, east of 5th av....254, 564, 600.
from 5th to 8th....815.
117th....419, 600.
118th, east of 5th av....702, 742.
west of 5th ...98, 419, 815.
119th, west of 5th av....455.
120th, east of 5th av....490.
west of 5th....67, 703, 778.
121st, east of Madison av....200.
west of 8th....67, 331.
122d....24, 564.
123d, west of Mt. Morris av....228, 358.
124th, west of 5th av....532.
125th, west of 8th....490.
127th, east of 5th av ....778.
128th, west of 5th av....305.
129th, east of 5th av....388, 564.
130th, west of 5th av....600.
131st, east of Lenox av... 703.
west of Lenox....305, 532.
132d, east of Lenox av....67, 420, 778.
west of Lenox....358.
133d, east of Lenox av....841.
134th, west of Lenox av... 24.
135th....420, 778.
136th, west of Lenox av....254, 564, 600, 742.
138th....24, 388, 455.
139th....455.
141st....24.
142d....600, 674, 703.
143d....490.
144th....305.
147th....778.
151st....674, 778.
152d....532, 600.
154th ...67.
155th....564, 638.
156th.. 564.
157th... 564.
159th....254, 532, 815.
160th....105.
168th. .674.
169th....165.
173d....674.
178th....420.
181st....674.
185th....98, 165.

AVENUES.

Amsterdam (formerly 10th av)....24.

Av A, from 70th to 90th st....358, 564.
north of 100th (see Pleasant av).

Av B, north of 59th st....98, 674.

Bradhurst....600.

Columbus (formerly 9th av north of 59th st).
from 70th to 90th st ...67, 490.
90th to 100th....305, 490, 778.
120th to 140th....742.

Edgecombe....564.

Lexington, from 90th to 109th st....600.
100th to 110th....254, 703.
110th to 120th....490.

Manhattan....98, 815.
Madison, from 59th to 70th st....200.
north of 125th....67.

New (see Bradhurst, Edgecombe and Manhattan avs).

Park (formerly 4th av).
from 75th to 100th st....98, 600, 815.
north of 100th....67, 200, 254, 532.
Pleasant, from 110th to 135th st....135.

Riverside....254.

South 5th, north of Prince st....66.
St. Nicholas, south of 125th....254, 419, 455.
north of 140th....165.

Wadsworth....280.
West End (formerly 11th av, north of 64th st).
from 64th to 80th st ...24, 490, 564.
80th to 90th....135, 200.
north of 100th....67, 98, 419, 778.

1st, from 40th to 80th st....280, 815.
80th to 100th....165, 703.
2d, south of 40th st....66, 600.
from 40th to 50th....331, 778.
north of 100th....254, 419.
3d, south of 60th st .. 165, 742, 777.
from 80th to 100th....419, 778.
4th, south of 25th st....600.
north of 34th (see Park av).
5th, south of 40th st....66.
from 40th to 70th....305, 358.
70th to 100th....24.
6th, south of 40th....258.
7th, south of 59th st....388, 490.
north of 145th ...388, 455, 674.

8th, from 59th to 110th st (see Central Park West).
130th to 160th. .455, 532, 564.

9th, south of 59th st....674, 815.
north of 59th (see Columbus av).

10th, north of 59th st (see Amsterdam av).

11th, south of 50th st....228, 331.
from 64th to 106th (see West End av).
north of 106th (also see Boulevard)....674, 815.

12th... 98, 165, 742.

13th....674.

PLACES.

Exchange....814.

Lafayette....135.

St. Marks (also see 8th st)....600.

Waverley....24.

Pier or Bulkhead North or Hudson River.... 490, 564, 638, 674, 777.

Blackwells Island....280.

TWENTY-THIRD AND TWENTY-FOURTH WARDS.

STREETS.

Ackerman . .99.
Ash....815.

Beech terrace....532.
Bush....331.

Church....358.
College....331.
Columbine....703.

Devoe....703.

Garfield....564.

Hampden ...305.
Home ...200.
Hyatt....455.

Jennings....24, 815.

Kelly....67.

Lowmede....200.

Main....815.

Oak terrace....532.
Orchard ...815.

Ponus....200.

Reservoir Drive....388.
Rockfield....135, 280, 600, 841.

Southern Boulevard....228, 254, 305, 455, 815.
Spuyten Duyvil Parkway .388.
St. George Crescent... 331.
Suburban....388, 532, 674.
Summit....815.

Travers....674, 703.

Woodruff....742.
Wolf ...600.

133d....742.
134th....490, 674.
135th. .455, 778.
137th....254.
138th ...564, 778.
141st... 639.
142d....564.
143d....254, 674.
144th....135, 564.
145th....388.
147th .. 388, 564.
148th....358.
150th....280, 331, 420, 455, 742.
152d....331, 778.
156th....67, 388.
158th....455, 564.
160th....490.
161st....703.
163d ...67
168d....331, 420, 674.
170th... 305.
174th ...639.
176th....67, 200.
179th....254
181st....331, 841.
183d....532.
184th....99, 532.
187th....778.

AVENUES.

Alexander....639.
Aqueduct....67, 165, 532.
Anthony....254, 280, 490.

Bainbridge....165, 564, 703.
Bathgate. south of 175th st....135, 200, 639, 742.
north of 175th....135.
Beekman... 532.
Boston....674.
Boscobel....815.
Brook, north of 140th st....67, 165, 280, 490.
Briggs....67, 532.

Cambreling....455.
Cauldwell....532.
Central (see Jerome av).
Clinton....165, 455.
Commerce....228.
Courtlandt....280, 358
Creston....99, 420, 639, 742.
Crotona....305. 674.
Cromwell ...358, 564.
Cypress....674.

Daley ...331, 600.
Decatur....490.

Eagle....305, 815.
Elton....388.

Fairmont....331.
Fleetwood. ..841.
Forest....420, 674, 742.
Franklin....841
Fulton....331, 639, 674.

Garden....67.
Graud....305.
Grant....490.

Intervale....331.
Iuwood....358, 639.

Jefferson ...24, 532.
Jerome....600. 703, 778, 815.
Johnson....305.

Lafontaine....674.
Locust....388.

Madison....200.
Mapes....254.
Marion....600.
Marmion....532, 778.
Melrose ...778
Morris....24, 99, 420.
Mosholu ...24.
Mott....99, 228.

Nathalie... 639.
North 3d av (see 3d av).

Ogden....165.

Parsons....639.
Perry....388.
Prospect....24, 331, 532.

Railroad....67.
River....331, 420.
Riverdale... 99, 200.

Sedgwick....24. 99. 532, 674.
Stebbins....165, 254, 815.
St. Anns....490.

Taylor....200, 703
Tiebout....420.
Tinton....280. 420, 674.
Trinity....24, 674.

Union....135, 358, 703, 815.

Vanderbilt....135. 228, 358, 490, 674.
Valentine....67, 280, 305, 388, 703.
Villa....67.

Walton... 135.
Washingson, south of 170th st....200, 815.
from 170th to 175th...135, 165, 305.
north of 180th....420.
Webster....99, 200, 228. 280.
Westchester....815.
Willard....703.

1st....674, 703.
3d (also see North 3d av).
south of 150th st....165, 674.
north of 165th... 254, 420, 742.
8th....67.

PLACES.

Arcularius....420.

Dashwood....639.

Elsmere....67. 305.
Elmwood....703.
Ernescliffe....200.

Fairmont....358, 455.

Garfield....280.

Mt. Hope....228.

Poe....67.
Potter....254, 490.
Powell....200.

Ritter....815.

Teasdale....674.

Vanderbilt....742.

ROADS.

Bolton....254.
Boston Post....331.

Kingsbridge....24, 200, 455, 490, 600.

Spuyten Duyvil ...841.

INDEX TO VOLUME XLVIII, OF RECORD AND GUIDE.

Contains Index to New York Conveyances and Buildings, also our Advertisers.

ADVERTISERS IN THE RECORD AND GUIDE CLASSIFIED.

The names given below will be found of value by Bank, Trust and Insurance Companies, Estates, Builders, Owners of Realty, Real Estate Brokers, Architects, etc., who are continually turning to these pages for reference to the official filings recorded during the last half of 1891, and published in Volume XLVIII. of THE RECORD AND GUIDE. *We give below a classified Directory of the yearly advertisers now in* THE RECORD AND GUIDE, *with the address of each, so that further reference is unnecessary. In a sense this forms a complete select Trade Directory, ontaining the names of the principal leading houses in the several trades and professions represented.*

APPRAISERS.

Bennet, O. G ...150 Broadway.
Blackwell, Wilson H., & Co... 67 Liberty and 259 West 125th.
Carreau, Cyrille....Grand st and Bowery.
Fairchild & Yoran... 171 Broadway.
Jayne, S. F., & Co....254 West 23d and 59 Liberty.
Kennelly, Bryan L....66 Liberty.
Phillips, L. J., & Co....149 Broadway, 1195 Columbus av and 149th st and 3d av.
Real Estate Loan and Trust Co....30 Nassau.
White, Wm. A., & Sons....409 Broadway and 115 Broadway.

ARCHITECTS.

Engelhardt, Th....905 Broadway, Brooklyn.
Funk, Hermann E....11 Varet st, Brooklyn.
Hauser, John....1441 3d av.
Herter Bros....191 Broadway.
Huttira, Albert....304 East 70th.
Wennemer, Frank....2?4 East 86th.
Wenz, Edward....1491 3d av.

ARCHITECTURAL PHOTOGRAPHER.

Darling, C. M....122 West 36th.

ASPHALT AND CEMENT PAVEMENTS, SIDEWALKS, ETC.

Hilgers, William....163 West 104th.
Lawrence, F. W....16 Exchange pl.
Matt Taylor Paving Co....15 State.
Tice & Jacobs....510 Pearl.

ATLASES.

Mitchell, J. H....82 Nassau.

AUCTIONEERS.

Blackwell, Wilson H., & Co....65 Liberty and 259 West 125th.
De Walltearss, S....171 Broadway.
Fairchild & Yoran....171 Broadway.
Fogg, W. W ...150 Broadway.
Golding, John N....11 Pine.
Harnett, Richard V., & Co.. .73 Liberty.
*Johnson, Jere., Jr....60 Liberty st, New York, and 189 Montague st, Brooklyn.
Kennelly, Bryan L....66 Liberty.
Kennelly, Wm....47 and 49 Liberty.
Ludlow, E. H., & Co....47 Liberty.
*Mapes, H. C., & Co....59 Liberty st, New York City, and Main st, Westchester, N. Y.
*Muller, A. H., & Son....1 Pine.
Phillips, L. J., & Co....149 Broadway, 1195 Columbus av and 149th st and 3d av.
Smith, Thomas C....111 Broadway.
Smyth & Ryan....111 Broadway.
*Smyth, John F. B....69 Liberty.
*Stearns, J. Thomas....59 Liberty.
*Wells, James L....59 Liberty.

AWNINGS, CANOPIES, ETC.

Skelton, F....1325 Broadway.

BANKERS AND BROKERS.

Jones, Geo. W., & Co....62 Broadway.

BELL HANGERS, ELECTRICAL WORK, ETC.

Haggerty, Geo. A....808 3d av.
Ostrander, W. R., & Co. ;.195 Fulton st.

BOILERS.

Babcock & Wilcox Co....30 Cortlandt.
Franklin, George....142 Centre.
Sheppard, I. A., & Co....Philadelphia or Baltimore.

BRACKETS.

Koch, A. B. Co., Geo. E. Read, agent....90 Nassau st, New York and Peoria, Ill.

BRASS AND BRONZE WORKERS.

Jackson Architectural Iron Works....315 East 28th.
Palmer's Son, J. F....12 East 17th.
Steutzer, H., & Co....474 to 494 Leonard st and 49 to 61 Van Pelt av, Brooklyn, N. Y., and 39 Dey st, New York.
Wagner, J. T....108 Chambers.

BRICKS.

Anchor Brick Co ...Croton Landing, N. Y.
Burns, Russell & Co ...Baltimore, Md.
Boston Terra Cotta Co ...Times Building, New York and 394 Federal st, Boston.
Fleming, Howard....23 Liberty.
Griffen Enameled Brick Co....Times Building.
Hendrickson, I. C., agent....237 Broadway.
Klots, Walter T., & Bros. Sons ...Meserole st and Morgan av, Brooklyn.
Lorillard Brick Works Co....92 Liberty st.
Maurer, Henry, & Son....420 East 23d, and Maurers, N. J.
New York Architectural Terra Cotta Co....38 Park row.
Perth Amboy Terra Cotta Co... 160 Broadway.
Raritan Hollow and Porous Brick Co....115 Broadway.
Sayre & Fisher Co....Bennett Building, Fulton and Nassau sts.
Schermerhorn, J. M ...Times Building.

BRIDLE IRONS AND BUILDING ANCHORS.

McDougal & Potter....55th st and North River.

BUILDERS, CARPENTERS, MASONS AND CONTRACTORS.

Atlas Iron and Construction Co....Times Building.
Lithgow, George W....41 King.
O'Toole, James....165 Western Boulevard.

CABINET MAKERS AND DECORATORS.

American Encaustic Tiling Co....140 West 23d.
Brown, Geo. and Clifford....46 East 14th st.
Buffalo Door and Sash Co. ..Columbus av and 124th st.
Graham, J. R., Jr....30th st and 11th av.
New York Lumber and Wood Working Co....173 Broadway, New York, and Tonawanda, N. Y.
Nimmo, Wilson & Son....8 East 60th st and 336 Columbus av.
Schastey, Geo. A....489 5th av.
Smith, Jarvis B....174 East 116th st.
Wood, Jenks & Co....3 Union sq.

CARPETS, OIL CLOTHS, SHADES, ETC.

Ranch, H., & Son....24 Av B.

CEMENTS.

Camp, Hugh N., & Sons....55 Liberty.
Fisher, Erskine W....18 Broadway.
Fleming, Howard....23 Liberty.
Johnson & Wilson....45 Broadway.
Kanter, Emil....126 Liberty.
Klots, Walter T., & Bros. Sons....Meserole st and Morgan av, Brooklyn.
New York & Rosendale Cement Co....229 Broadway.
Tomkins, Calvin Co....150 Broadway.
Thiele, E. ..78 William.

CHIMNEY TOPS AND CAPS.

Lane, Ira G....207 East 64th.

CLOTHING DEALER.

Shea, D ....Cor Broome and Crosby.

CLOTHES LINE FRAMES.

Price Manufacturing Co....325 East 10th.

COLORS FOR MORTAR.

Fisher, Erskine W....18 Broadway.
Tomkins, Calvin Co....150 Broadway.

COMMISSIONERS OF DEEDS AND NOTARIES.

Adams Bros....482 5th av.
Brown, J. Romaine, & Co....59 West 33d.
Disbrow, Griffin B....56 East 23d.
Kempner, D., & Son....6?2 8th av.
McVay, Geo. P. H....258 West 125th.

CONTRACTING ENGINEER.

Franklin, George....142 Centre.

CORNICES.

Dreyer, Louis....339 West 18th.
Jacob, August ...260 East 78th.
Schwoerer, Jacob....8 2d.
Seton, Jno., & Co....78 and 80 Washington av, Brooklyn, N. Y.
The Architectural Sheet Metal Works... 205 East 99th.

DUMB-WAITERS, DOORS, SASHES, ETC.

Brandt, Fred....169 East 85th.
Matthews, James, & Son....172 East 110th and 510 East 20th.
Murtaugh, James....145 East 42d.

ELECTRICAL ENGINEERS.

Leonard, H., Ward & Co....Electrical Exchange Building.

ELEVATORS.

Graves, L. S., & Son... 92 Liberty, N. Y., and Rochester, St. Louis, Cleveland and Boston.
Murtaugh, Jas.....145 East 42d.
See Mfg. Co., A. B....116 Front st, Brooklyn, N. Y., and 32 West Mitchell st, Atlanta, Georgia.
Sommerville, John....27 Clark.
The D. Frisbie Co....112 Liberty.

FIREPLACES.

American Encaustic Tiling Co....140 West 23d.
Conover, J S, & Co ...28 and 30 West 23d.
Jackson, W. H., & Co....Union sq and East 28th and 29th sts.
Serven & Irwin....1479 Broadway.
Traitel, Bros....409 5th av.

FIRE INSURANCE COMPANIES.

Royal Fire Insurance Co., of Liverpool, Eng.... 50 Wall.

FIREPROOF BUILDING MATERIALS.

Bostwick Metal Lath Co....38 Park row, New York, and Niles, Ohio.
Boston Terra Cotta Co. ..Times Building, New York, and 394 Federal st, Boston.
De Rache, Leonard....West 70th st, bet 10th and 11th avs.
Isaacs, Gustavus....21 Bethune.
Lorillard Brick Works Co....92 Liberty.
Matthews, James, & Son....172 East 110th st and 510 and 512 East 20th.
Maurer, Henry, & Son....420 East 23d, and Maurers, N. J.
New York Architectural Terra Cotta Co....33 Park row.
Perth Amboy Terra Cotta Co....160 Broadway.
Raritan Hollow and Porous Brick Co....115 Broadway.
The Schillinger Co....413 East 91st.
The Van Fire-Proofing Co....92 Liberty.

FLOORING, CEILING, WAINSCOTING, ETC.

Auffermann & Co....211 East 42d.
Bossert, Louis....18-30 Johnson av and 6 and 8 Union av, Brooklyn, E. D., N. Y.
Elterich Art Tile Co....106 Beekman.
Hodson, C. F....738 Water.
Prince, Benj....501 East 70th.
Wood Mosaic Co....Rochester, N. Y., and 315 5th av, New York City.

FURNACES, ETC.

Lane, Ira G....207 East 64th.
Nugent, Thomas....214 East 80th.
The J. L. Mott Iron Works....84 Beekman.

GALVANIZED SHEET IRON, TIN PLATES AND METALS.

Merchant & Co....New York, Philadelphia, Chicago, Kansas City and London.
Merry, John, & Co....535 to 547 West 15th.
The Architectural Sheet Metal Works .... 205 East 99th.
Wagner, J T ...108 Chambers.

GAS FIXTURES, ETC.

Palmer's, J. F., Son....12 East 17th.
Traitel Bros....499 5th av.

GLASS.

Sutphen & Myer....9-13 Desbrosses and 34-38 Vestry.
The Tiffany Glass Co....333 4th av.

HARD WOODS, ETC.

Dannat & Pell....24 Tompkins.
Graham, J. R., Jr....36th st and 11th av.
Hagemeyer, George, & Son....Foot of 10th and 11th sts, East River.
Hermann, H....368 Broome.
Uptegrove, Wm. E., & Bro....Foot of East 10th.
Wood Mosaic Co....315 5th av.

HOIST WHEELS, ETC.

Murtaugh, James....145 East 42d.
Somerville, John....27 Clark.

HORTICULTURAL ARCHITECTS AND BUILDERS.

Hitchings & Co. ..233 Mercer.

HOT WATER FOR WARMING DWELLINGS.

Blake & Williams....197 Wooster.
Franklin, George....142 Centre.
Gillis & Geoghegan....116-122 Wooster.
Hitchings & Co....233 Mercer.

HOT AIR ENGINES.

Rider Engine Co....37 Dey.

HOUSE AGENTS.

Appell, Jacob....277 West 23d.
H. V. Mead & Co....422 8th av.

HOUSE MOVERS.

Drew, J. H., & Bro....431 West 17th.

INSURANCE BROKERS.

Auld, Robert, & Co....8th av, cor 56th st.
Barclay, J. Searle....33 Liberty.
Bennet, O. G....150 Broadway.
Corbit, Jos & Co ...212 9th av.
Disbrow, Griffin B....56 East 23d.
Eckhardt, P. C....693 9th av.
Goodrich & Woodcock....20 8th av and 306 West 12th st.
Holzderber, Wm....155 West 23d.
Hyatt, Geo. E....164 East 84th.
Leist, & Feuerbach....204 East 86th.
Leuly, Jacob....48 Pine.
Livingston & Judson....71 Broadway and Ardsley Park, N. Y.
McKeon, M. J....2312 3d av.
McLaughlin, Thos. F....1252 3d av and 2015 7th av.
Murphy, Agnes K....3d av, n w cor 177th st.
Presdee & Moore....Columbus av, cor 87th st.
Thomas & Eckerson....35 West 30th.
Ward, Beverley....221 West 125th.

INTERIOR TRIM AND FITTINGS.

Buffalo Door and Sash Co....Columbus av and 124th st.
New York Lumber and Wood Working Co.... 173 and 175 Broadway, New York, and Tonawanda, N. Y.
Pritchard, E. M., & Son....138th st and Mott av.
Plasterine Co....295 5th av.

IRON AND STEEL WORK.

Atlas Iron Construction Co....Times Building.
Conover, J. S., & Co....28 and 30 West 23d.
Jackson Architectural Iron Works....315 East 28th.
Jacob, August....260 East 78th.
McDougall & Potter....55th st and North River.
Richey, Brown & Donald....218-224 North 11th, Brooklyn, N. Y.
Seton, John, & Co.. .78 Washington av, Brooklyn, N. Y.
Standard Iron Works....618 West 25th.
Steutzer, H., & Co....474-494 Leonard st and 49-61 Van Pelt av, Brooklyn, N. Y., and 39 Dey st, New York.
Taubert, Albert ...1612 Broadway.
The J. L. Mott Iron Works ...84-90 Beekman.
Traitel Bros....499 5th av.

KINDLING WOOD.

Tripler, Thos. E....532-536 East 18th and 301 Av B.

LAUNDRY, WASH TUBS, SINKS, ETC.

Albemarle Soapstone Co....4 Peck slip.
Bram & Sieg....46-56 Wallabout st. Brooklyn.
Brandt, Fred....169 East 85th.
Empire Granite Works ...509 West 15th.
Lawrence, F W....16 Exchange pl.
O'Neill, Hugh ...Long Island City, L. I.
Penrhyn Slate Co....101 East 17th.
Stewart Ceramic Co....312 Pearl.

LAWYERS, ETC.

Adams, Samuel F....432 5th av.

LINSEED OIL.

Atlantic White Lead and Linseed Oil Co....287 Pearl.

LUMBER MEN.

(See Timber and Lumber Dealers.)

MANAGERS OF ESTATES.

Ashforth & Co....1519 Broadway.
Auld, Robert & Co. ..8th av, cor 56th st.
Brown, J. Romaine, & Co....59 West 33d.
Carreau, Cyrille....Grand st and Bowery.
Corbit, Jos., & Co....212 9th av.
De Walltears, S....171 Broadway.
Fish, Ferdinand....149 Broadway.
Gorsch, Arthur....1444 3d av.
Hollister, Wm H....1475 3d av.
Holzderber, Wm....155 West 25th.
Hunt & Wendell....249 Columbus av.
Hyatt, Geo. E....164 East 84th.
Jayne, S. F., & Co....254 West 23d and 59 Liberty.
Kempner, D., & Son....602 8th av.
Leist & Feuerbach....204 East 86th.
Marling, Alfred E....150 Broadway.
Mead, H. V., & Co....422 8th av.
Merritt, Hiram....53 3d av.
Tanenbaum, L....529 Broadway.
Thomas & Eckerson....35 West 30th.
Zittel, F....1026 3d av and 266 Columbus av.

MANTELS, GRATES, FENDERS, ETC.

Buffalo Door and Sash Co....Columbus av and 124th st.
Conover, J. S., & Co....28 and 30 West 23d.
Jackson, W. H., & Co....Union square and East 28th and 29th sts.
Johnson, E. J....18 Burling slip.
New York Lumber and Wood Working Co.... 173 Broadway, New York, and Tonawanda, N. Y.
Penrhyn Slate Co....101 East 17th.
Pritchard, E. M., & Son....138th st and Mott av.
Smith, Jarvis B....174 East 116th.
Traitel Bros....499 5th av.

MARBLE, ONYX, GRANITE, ETC.

Batterson, See & Eisele....425 11th av.
Fisher, Robert C., & Co....97 to 103 East Houston.
Klaber, A....238 East 57th.
Nichols & Shipway....105 to 111 East 128th st and 104 to 110 East 129th st.
Vermont Marble Co....35 Hancock pl.

MASONS' BUILDING MATERIALS.

Camp, Hugh N., & Sons....55 Liberty.
Canda & Kane... Main office, foot 53d st, N. R.; yards, New York and Brooklyn.
Candee & Smith....Foot 26th and 53d sts, E. R.; 135th st and Mott Haven Canal, and 381 South st.
Fleming, Howard ...23 Liberty.
Klots, W. T., & Bros. Sons....Meserole st and Morgan av, Brooklyn.
Martin & Co....137th st and Madison av.

MATS, MATTING AND ZINC.

Rauch, H., & Son....24 Av B.

MERCANTILE ASSOCIATIONS.

Material Men's Mercantile Association....154 Nassau.

METALLIC LATHING.

Bostwick Metal Lath Co....38 Park row, New York, and Niles, Ohio.
Hayes Metallic Lathing....71 8th av.

METAL SASH CHAINS.

The Smith & Egge Mfg. Co....63 Reade st, New York, and Bridgeport, Conn.

MORTGAGES, LOANS, ETC.

Bennet, O. G ...150 Broadway.
Fitzsimons & Smith....67 Liberty st and 1477 Broadway.
Freedman, Andrew....120 Broadway.
Grening, Paul C....420 Gates av, 1161 Fulton st, and Kingsland av, cor Van Cott av, Brooklyn, N. Y.
Hoffman Bros....4 Warren.
Hunt & Wendell....249 Columbus av.
Kennelly, Wm....47 and 49 Liberty.
Libby, Jas. L., & Sons....79 Cedar.
Magill, J. C., & Co....Madison and La Salle sts, Chicago, Ill.
Maclay, Davies & Co... 120 Broadway.
McLaughlin, A. W., & Co....146 Broadway.
Presdee & Moore....Columbus av, cor 87th st.
Scott Bros....Equitable Building.
Zittel, F....1026 3d av and 266 Columbus av.

NORTH CAROLINA PINE.

Hodsdon, C. F....738 Water.

PAINTING AND PAPER-HANGING.

Oliver, Wm. H....62 University pl.

PAINTS, OILS, ETC.

Atlantic White Lead and Linseed Oil Co....287 Pearl.

PAVING.

Hilgers, Wm....163 West 104th.
Lawrence, F W....16 Exchange place.
Matt Taylor Paving Co....15 State.

PHOTOGRAPHERS.

Darling, C. M....122 West 36th.

PLASTER SLABS.

Curran, Thos....135 Broadway.

PLUMBING, GAS AND STEAM FITTERS.

Backus, Peter, & Son....133 and 135 West 25th.
McShane Co., Henry....625 6th av.

PLUMBERS' SUPPLIES.

Backus, Peter, & Son....133 West 25th.
Colwell Lead Co....63 Centre st and 681 6th av.
Du Bois Manf'g Co....245 9th av.
Huber, Henry, & Co....81 Beekman.
McShane Co., Henry....625 6th av.

RANGES, STOVES, ETC.

Lane, Ira G....207 East 64th.
Sheppard, I. A., & Co....Philadelphia or Baltimore.
The J. L. Mott Iron Works....84 Beekman.

REAL ESTATE AGENTS AND BROKERS.

Adams Bros....432 5th av.
Alden & Sterne....9 East 14th.
Anderson, William S., & Co....1242 3d av.
Appell, Jacob....277 West 23d.
Ashforth & Co....1519 Broadway.
Auld, Robt., & Co ..8th av, cor 56th.
Barclay, J. Searle....33 Liberty.
Bennet, O. G....150 Broadway.
Birdsall, Daniel, & Co....319 Broadway.
Blackwell, Wilson H., & Co....65 Liberty and 259 West 125th.
Borchers, William S....1505 Broadway.
*Brown, Gerald R....120 Broadway.
Brown, J. Romaine, & Co ...59 West 33d.
Cammann, H. H., & Co....51 Liberty.
Carpenter, Leonard J....41 Liberty st and 1181 3d av.
Carreau, Cyrille....Grand st and Bowery.
Cody, John J....1438 3d av.
Corbit, Jos., & Co....212 9th av.
Corwith Bros....309 Manhattan av, Brooklyn.
Cruikshank, E. A., & Co....176 Broadway.
Davis, J. C., & Co....149 Broadway.
De Walltearss, S....171 Broadway.
Disbrow, G B....56 East 23d.
Dreyer, Henry H....Amsterdam av, s e cor 81st st.
*Duff & Conger....1474 3d av.
Eckhardt, P. C....693 9th av.
Ely, Horace S....64 Cedar and 108 West 68th.
Fairchild & Yoran....171 Broadway.
Fish, Ferdinand....149 Broadway.
Fitzsimons & Smith....67 Liberty and 1477 Broadway.
*Foley, John R., & Son....153 Broadway.
Freedman, Andrew....120 Broadway.
Froehlich, L....169 East 61st st and 447 Amsterdam av.
Golding, John N....11 Pine.
Goodrich & Woodcock....20 8th av and 306 West 12th st.
Gorsch, Arthur....1444 3d av.
Grening, Paul C....420 Gates av, 1161 Fulton st and Kingsland av, cor Van Cott av, Brooklyn.
Griffen, C., Field & Co....42d st, opposite Grand Central Depot.
Harnett, Richard V., & Co. ..73 Liberty.
Harrell, C. E....713 Broadway.
*Hegeman, Adrian G., & Co....1321 Broadway.
Hoffman Bros....4 Warren.
Hollister, Wm. H....1475 3d av.
Holzderber, Wm....155 West 23d.
Hoyt, Wm. H., & Co....5 Vanderbilt av.
Hyatt, Geo. E....164 East 84th.
Jayne, S. F., & Co....254 West 23d and 59 Liberty.
Kempner, D., & Son....603 8th av.
Kennelly, Bryan L....66 Liberty.
Kennelly, Wm. ..47 and 49 Liberty.
Kenny, James, & Son... 80 East Houston.
Lawrence, Walter....Columbus av, n w cor 104th st.
Leaycraft, J. Edgar....1544 Broadway.
Leist & Feuerbach....204 East 86th st.
Leuly, Jacob....43 Pine.
Libby, James L., & Son ...79 Cedar st.
Livingston & Judson....71 Broadway and Ardsley Park, N. Y.
Ludlow, E. H., & Co....47 Liberty st.
Maclay, Davies, & Co....120 Broadway.
Magill, J. C., & Co....Madison and La Salle sts, Chicago, Ill.
Mainhart & Lowe....258 West 125th.
*Mapes, Henry C., & Co....59 Liberty st, New York, and Main st, Westchester, N. Y.
Marling, Alfred E....64 Cedar st.
Machette & Kenyon....239 Broadway.
McKeon, M. J ...2312 3d av.
McLaughlin, A. W., & Co....146 Broadway.
McLaughlin, Thos. F....1252 3d av and 2015 7th av.
Mead, H. V., & Co. ..422 8th av.
Merritt, Hiram....53 3d av.
*Muller, A. H., & Son....1 Pine.
Murphy, Agnes K....3d av, n w cor 177th st.
Murphy & Winfield....Mt. Vernon, N. Y.
Pehlemann, R ..171 Broadway and 379 Amsterdam av.
Phillips, L. J., & Co....149 Broadway, 1195 Columbus av and 149th st and 3d av.
Porter & Co....211 West 125th.
Presdee & Moore....Columbus av, cor 87th st.
Read, George R....9 Pine.
Robinson, Douglass, Jr., & Co.....55 Liberty.
Roome, Wm. J....410 6th av.
Scott, Bros....120 Broadway.
Schuyler, Chas. E....288 Columbus av and 80 Broadway.
Seton & Wissmann....11 Pine.
Shaw & Co....109 West 125th st.
Smith, Thomas C....111 Broadway.
Smyth & Ryan....111 Broadway.
Southack, Fred'k....111 and 401 Broadway.
Stacey, Henry B....301½ West 126th.
Swartwout & Co....157 East 125th and 247 West 125th.
Tanenbaum, L....529 Broadway.
Thomas & Eckerson....35 West 30th.
Ward, Beverley....221 West 125th.
Ware, Wm. R....451 Columbus av.
*Wells, James L....59 Liberty.
White, Wm. A., & Sons....111 and 409 Broadway
Zittel, F ...1026 3d av and 266 Columbus av.

ROOFING.

Comins & Evans....81 Fulton st, New York, and 41 Waverly av, Brooklyn.
Dreyer, Louis....339 West 18th.
Jacob, August....260 East 78th.
Johnson, E. J ...18 Burling slip.
Merchant & Co....New York, Philadelphia, Chicago, Kansas City and London.
Merry, John, & Co....535 West 15th.
Penrhyn Slate Co....101 East 17th.
Schwoerer, Jacob....8 2d.
The Architectural Sheet Metal Works....205 East 99th.

ROOFING PLATES.

Merchant & Co... New York, Philadelphia, Chicago, Kansas City and London.
Merry, John, & Co ...535 to 547 West 15th.

SAND.

Goodwin, M... Foot East 29th.

SANITARY SPECIALTIES.

Backus, Peter, & Son....133 West 25th.
Huber, Henry, & Co....81 Beekman st.
McShane Co., Henry....625 and 627 6th av.
Penrhyn Slate Co....101 East 17th st.

SASHES, DOORS, BLINDS, MOULDING, ETC.

Bossert, Louis....18 to 30 Johnson av and 6 and 8 Union av, Brooklyn.
Buffalo Door and Sash Co....Columbus av and 124th st.
Burlington Blind Co....90 Nassau.
Clark, Bunnett & Co....162 and 164 West 27th st.
Morstatt & Son....227 West 29th.
Orr, Wm. G., manager....150 Broadway.
Pritchard, E. M., & Son....138th st and Mott av.
Smith, Jarvis B....174 East 116th.
The New York Lumber and Wood Working Co ....173 Broadway, New York, and Tonawanda, New York.

SECOND-HAND BUILDING MATERIALS, OLD BUILDINGS BOUGHT, ETC.

Hausling, F. M....614 to 622 East 14th and 611 to 623 East 13th.
Macgregor, M. H....160 West 26th.
Perkins, F. E. & Bro....59 to 73 West st, Brooklyn.
Reebers, J., Sons....409 to 431 East 107th.
Seagrist, F. W., Jr., & Co....18th st and Av B.
Southard, C. H....9th av, 14th and 15th sts.
Tripler, Thomas E....Av B, 17th and 18th sts.

SILLS, LINTELS, STEPS, COPING, ETC.

Vermont Marble Co....35 Hancock pl.

SKYLIGHTS.

Bickelhoupt, G ...243 and 245 West 47th.
French, J. C., & Son....452 Canal.
Schwoerer, Jacob....8 2d.
Seton, John, & Co....78 Washington av, Brooklyn.
Stuetzer, H., & Co....71 Van Cott av, Brooklyn, N. Y., and 39 Dey st, N. Y.
The Architectural Sheet Metal Works....205 East 99th.
The Hayes Skylight....71 8th av.

SLATES FOR ROOFING, ETC.

Penrhyn Slate Co....101 East 17th.

SPEAKING-TUBES, DOOR OPENERS, ETC.

Ostrander, W. R., & Co....195 Fulton.
Walsh, Owen.. 105 Walker.

STAINED AND MOSAIC GLASS, ETC.

The Tiffany Glass Co....333 4th av.

STAIR BUILDERS.

Ackerly, E. B....48 West av, Long Island City.
Price, F. R....2 West 129th.

STAIR RAILS, ETC.

Ackerly, E B....48 West av, Long Island City.
Buffalo Door and Sash Co....Columbus av and 124th st.
N. Y. Lumber and Wood Working Co....173 Broadway, N. Y., and Tonawanda, N. Y.

STEAM HEATING APPARATUS, ETC.

Babcock & Wilcox Co....30 Cortlandt.
Backus, Peter, & Son....133 and 135 West 25th.
Blake & Williams....197 Wooster.
Bonner & Van Court....433 and 435 West 42d.
Franklin, George....142 Centre.
Gillis & Geoghegan ...116 to 122 Wooster.
The Hall Steam Power Co....211 Centre.

STEAM PUMPING MACHINERY.

Worthington, Henry R....86 and 88 Liberty st, New York, and Boston, Chicago, St. Paul, St. Louis, Philadelphia.

STEEL, IRON AND WOOD SHUTTERS.

Clark, Bunnett & Co. (Lim.)....162 and 164 West 27th.
Mathews, Jas., & Son....173 East 110th.

STORE, OFFICE FIXTURES, SHELVING, ETC.

(See Second-hand Building Material Men.)

STONE WORKS.

Hilgers, William....163 West 104th.
Moran, John W....Hamilton av, cor Hicks st, Brooklyn, N. Y. (Blue Stone).
Osborne, Thomas, Steam Stone Works... 91st and 92d, East River.
Vermont Marble Co....35 Hancock pl.

SUBURBAN REAL ESTATE.

Griffen, C., Field & Co . 42d st, opposite Grand Central Depot.
*Hegeman, Adrian G., & Co....1321 Broadway.
Hoyt, Wm. H., & Co....5 Vanderbilt av.
Machette & Kenyon....239 Broadway.
Murphy & Winfield....Mt Vernon, N. Y.

TERRA COTTA, FIRE BRICK, ETC.

Baltimore Terra Cotta Co....535 Columbia av, Baltimore, Md. (I. C. Hendrickson, agent, 237 Broadway, N. Y.)
Boston Terra Cotta Co....Times Building, N. Y., and Boston, Mass.
Isaacs, Gustavus....21 Bethune.
Lorillard Brick Works Co....92 Liberty.
Maurer, Henry & Son... 420 East 23d st, and Maurers, N. J.
Mathiasen & Hansen....Perth Amboy, N. J.
New York Architectural Terra Cotta Co....38 Park row.
Perth Amboy Terra Cotta Co....160 Broadway.
Raritan Hollow and Porous Brick Co....115 Broadway.
The Van Fire-proofing Co....92 Liberty.

TILES.

American Encaustic Tiling Co. (Lim)....140 West 23d.
Conover, J. S., & Co....28 and 30 West 23d.
Elterich Art Tile Co....106 Beekman.
Jackson, W. H., & Co....Union square and East 28th and 29th sts.
Serven & Irwin....479 Broadway.
The Schillinger Co....413 East 91st.
Traitel Bros....499 5th av.

TIMBER AND LUMBER DEALERS.

Bell Bros ...11th av and 21st st.
Bossert, Louis....Grand st and Newtown Creek, and 6 and 8 Union av, Brooklyn.
Copcutt, J., & Co....432 Washington.
Crane & Clark....Foot of 30th st, North River.
Dannat & Pell....24 Tompkins.
Decker, A. T., & Co....Foot Bethune st, North River.
Graham, J. R., Jr....30th st and 11th av.
Hagemeyer, George, & Son....Foot of 10th and 11th sts, East River.
Herrmann, H. ..368 Broome.
Hodsdon, C. F....738 to 744 Water.
Johnson, A. B., & Co....Foot of 96th st, East River.
New York Lumber and Wood Working Co.... 173 Broadway, New York, and Tonawanda, N. Y.
Schuyler, G. L., & Co....1st av, bet 97th and 98th sts and East River.
Simonson, T. H., & Son....Foot of 100th st, East River.
Uptegrove, Wm. E., & Bro....Foot of East 10th.
Wilshaw & Co....Foot of 8th st, E. R., and 228 Lewis.

TITLE INSURANCE COMPANIES.

The Lawyers' Title Ins. Co....120 Broadway, New York, and 4 and 5 Court sq, Brooklyn.

TRUST COMPANIES.

Knickerbocker Trust Co....234 5th av, 18 Wall st and 3 Nassau st.
Real Estate Loan and Trust Co....30 Nassau.

VAULT AND SIDEWALK LIGHTS.

French, J. C., & Son....452 Canal.
Tice & Jacobs....510 Pearl.

VENETIAN ROLLING AND SLIDING BLINDS.

Albany Venetian Blind Co., Albany, N. Y. (Wm. G. Orr, manager)....150 Broadway, N. Y.
Burlington Blind Co....90 Nassau.
Clark, Bunnett & Co. (Lim.)....162 and 164 West 27th.
Morstatt & Son....227 and 229 West 29th.
Venetian Blind Co....World Building.

VENTILATORS.

Merchant & Co....New York, Chicago, Philadelphia, Kansas City and London.
Nugent, Thomas....214 East 80th.

WALL PLASTER.

Plasterine Co.....295 5th av.

WATER-TIGHT CELLARS.

Comins & Evans ...81 Fulton st, New York, and 41 Waverly av, Brooklyn.
Lawrence, F. W....16 and 18 Exchange pl.

WHITE AND RED LEADS, OILS, PAINTS, ETC.

Atlantic White Lead and Linseed Oil Co....287 Pearl.

WINDOW SHADES.

Ridley, E., & Sons....Grand, Allen and Orchard sts.

WOOD STAINING.

Auffermann & Co....211 East 42d.

WOOD VENEERS.

Auffermann & Co....211 East 42d.
Copcutt, J., & Co ...432 Washington.
Graham, J. R., Jr....30th st and 11th av.
Hagemeyer & Son, G....Foot 10th and 11th sts, E. R.
Uptegrove, Wm. E., & Bro....Foot of East 10th.

ZINC PLATES.

Rauch, H., & Son....24 Av B.

REAL ESTATE RECORD AND BUILDERS' GUIDE.

ESTABLISHED MARCH 21st 1868.

"Entered at the Post-office at New York, N. Y., as second-class matter."

VOL. XLVIII.---NO. 1,216. NEW YORK, JULY 3, 1891 Price, 15 Cents.

FOR SALE

—AT—

ELMSFORD, WESTCHESTER CO., N. Y.

38 minutes from 125th street; 67 minutes from Wall street; 1-2 mile from New York and Northern RR. Station; 1 1-2 miles from White Plains. Villa plots, high ground, view of Long Island Sound.

One (1) acre, (17 2-5 City Lots) for only $1,000.00.

Easy Terms. —— Judicious Restrictions. —— Exceptionally Desirable.

F. J. STONE, 60 BROADWAY, N. Y.

JOHN F. B. SMYTH, Auctioneer, will sell at Auction
Tuesday, July 7th, 1891,
At 12 o'clock, noon, at the Real Estate Exchange and Auction Room, 59 to 65 Liberty St., New York.
Administrator's Sale
944 Eighth Avenue, bet. 55th and 56th Streets, 5-story and basement, brown stone double flat, with store. Size, 25x100.
S. V. R. COOPER, Att'y for Admr, 52 Broadway. ROBERT AULD, Administrator.

BEVERLEY WARD,
REAL ESTATE AND INSURANCE.
Member Real Estate Exchange. 221 W. 125th St.

MAINHART & LOWE,
Real Estate Brokers,
258 West 125th St., N. Y. Telephone, 355 Harlem

SHAW & CO
REAL ESTATE
109 WEST 125th STREET, Near Lenox Avenue.

GEO. P. H. McVAY,
Commissioner for All the States
— AND —
NOTARY PUBLIC.
Harlem Branch: Uptown Press Office.
258 West 125th St., bet. 7th & 8th Avs.

L. FROEHLICH,
REAL ESTATE, OFFICES.
169 EAST 61ST ST., ADJ. 3d Ave.
1352 AMSTERDAM (10TH Ave.) COR. 81ST ST.
Member of Real Estate Exchange.

S. DE WALLTEARSS,
Auctioneer
and Real Estate Broker,
No. 171 BROADWAY.
Sales of Real Estate and Securities at Excnange.
Entire Charge Taken of Estates.

EDGAR S. BLUNT
REAL ESTATE
183 BROADWAY, NEW YORK

HENRY G. LEIST,
REAL ESTATE AND INSURANCE,
Office, 204 East 86th Street,
Near Third Avenue, NEW YORK.
NOTARY PUBLIC.
Renting and collecting. Entire charge taken of estates

J. SEARLE BARCLAY,
Real Estate and Insurance.
33 and 35 Liberty Street, New York.

M. J. McKEON,
Real Estate and Insurance
2312 THIRD AVENUE,
Near 125th Street, NEW YORK.
RENTS COLLECTED.

AGNES K. MURPHY,
Successor to CAPT. WM. JAY MURPHY)
3d Av., N. W. Cor. 177th St.,
Real Estate and Insurance,
24TH WARD PROPERTY A SPECIALTY.
Member of Real Estate Exchange.
NOTARY PUBLIC. *Telephone, 437 Harlem*

ARTHUR GORSCH,
REAL ESTATE BROKER,
1444 Third Avenue,
Southwest corner of 84d St
ENTIRE CHARGE TAKEN OF ESTATES.

GRIFFIN B. DISBROW,
(Late with the Rhinelander Estate.)
Real Estate and Insurance,
56 EAST 23d STREET N. Y.
Notary Public.

WM. H. HOYT. GEO. W. REEVES.
WM H HOYT & CO.,
Real Estate Brokers
5 VANDERBILT AVE.,
Opposite Grand Central Depot, New York City.
23d and 24th Wards, Westchester County and Suburban property our specialty. Telephone call, 1209 B
Free Catalogues.

JOSEPH CORBIT & CO.,
(ESTABLISHED 1856)
Real Estate and Insurance,
CHARGE OF ESTATES A SPECIALTY.
212 NINTH AVENUE,
Corner 23d Street, NEW YORK.

R. V. MEAD. L. P. VAN RIPER. W. H. SMITH.
H. V. MEAD & CO.,
(ESTABLISHED 1859.)
Real Estate Brokers & House Agents
422 EIGHTH AVENUE,
Bet. 31st and 32d Sts. New York;
Estates Taken in Charge a Specialty.

ISAAC T. MEYER,
REAL ESTATE BROKER,
Money to Loan on Bond and Mortgage.
111 BROADWAY, Room 85, NEW YORK.

McKEAN & KATZENMAYER,
Real Estate and Insurance,
1589 Third Av.,
Branch 45 East 125th Street, NEW YORK
RENTING AND COLLECTING A SPECIALTY.

E. DeF. SHELTON,
The purchase, Sale and Leasing of Factory Properties Negotiated.
Member of New York Rea Estate Exchange.
57 BROADWAY, N. Y.

ELIJAH L. ROAKE,
REAL ESTATE
52 BROADWAY,
Room 78. NEW YORK.

CORWITH BROS.,
REAL ESTATE
309 MANHATTAN AV., BROOKLYN, E. D.
Renting and Collecting a specialty

Telephone, 21st Street, 880.
CITY AND COUNTRY REAL ESTATE,
Condit,
1179 *BROADWAY,*
Near 28th Street. *NEW YORK*

WM. H. HOLLISTER,
Established 1855.
Successor to SAMUEL THOMSON,
REAL ESTATE.
No. 1475 THIRD AVE., Bet. 83d and 84th Sts.
Description of any property which you may have for SALE or to RENT solicited.
ENTIRE CHARGE TAKEN OF PROPERTY.

L. J. PHILLIPS & CO.,
REAL ESTATE BROKERS, AUCTIONEERS AND APPRAISERS,
NO. 149 BROADWAY.
Loans Negotiated. Telephone, 711 John.
Branch Offices, 1196 9th Avenue, 149th St. and 3d Av.

WILLIAM KENNELLY,
(Established July, 1847.)
AUCTIONEER, REAL ESTATE
And Loan Broker,
47 and 49 LIBERTY STREET, - - NEW YORK.
Member of the Real Estate Exchange and Auction Room (Limited).

GUSTAVE HUERSTEL,
Real Estate, Loans & Insurance,
290 BROADWAY, COR. READE STREET, N. Y.
Up-Town office. 3606 Third Ave., near 169th St.
ESTATES MANAGED.
Member of the Real Estate Exchange.

SMYTH & RYAN,
Real Estate Brokers
and Auctioneers,
111 BROADWAY, - - - NEW YORK.
PHILIP A. SMYTH. WM. M. RYAN.

BENJ. P. FAIRCHILD. FRANK YORAN.
FAIRCHILD & YORAN
AUCTIONEERS
And Real Estate Brokers & Appraisers
171 BROADWAY.

GEO. E. HYATT,
REAL ESTATE AND INSURANCE,
164 EAST 84th STREET, NEW YORK.
Personal attention to Renting, Collecting and Management of Property.

Henry B. Stacey,
REAL ESTATE BROKER
301½ West 116th Street New York.

R PEHLEMANN,
Real Estate Broker,
Hours 11 to 2. 171 Broadway.
Branch office: 879 Amsterdam Ave., near 78th Street.

JAMES KENNY & SON,
Real Estate Agents,
80 East Houston St. (near Bowery), N. Y

ROBT. AULD & CO.,
Real Estate and Insurance Brokers,
MANAGEMENT OF ESTATES A SPECIALTY.
Tel. Call, 863—39th. Eighth Av., cor. 57th St.

LUMBER

BELL BROTHERS,
SPRUCE TIMBER
11th AVENUE AND 21st STREET.
Telephone Call, 18th St. Station, 121.

C. F. HODSDON,
DEALER IN
NORTH CAROLINA PINE
Flooring, Ceiling & Wainscoting,
738 to 744 Water St.,
TELEPHONE, 838 SPRING. NEW YORK.

BENJ. PRINCE,
501-505 EAST 70th ST., NEW YORK.

DANNAT & PELL,
MAHOGANY AND LUMBER,
Yards, Broome St., E. R. Office, 24 Tompkins St.
Telephone Call, Spring 164.
CHAPMAN'S DOCKS NEWTOWN CREEK, Near Grand St., BROOKLYN, E. D., N. Y.

T. H. SIMONSON & SON,
Dealers in
LUMBER AND TIMBER,
Foot of 100th Street, East River.
Telephone Call, Harlem 115.

J. COPCUTT & CO.,
Cabinet Woods & Veneers
MEXICAN & ST. JAGO MAHOGANY.
432 to 440 Washington Street,
Cor. Desbrosses St., NEW YORK.
Telephone Call 76 Spring.

G. L. SCHUYLER & CO.,
TIMBER & LUMBER DEALERS
Yards, 1st AVENUE, bet. 97th and 98th STS. AND E. R
Telephone Call, Harlem 163.

CRANE & CLARK,
LUMBER AND TIMBER,
Foot of 30th Street, - North River.
California Red Wood Shingles a Specialty.

VERMONT MARBLE CO.,
35 HANCOCK PLACE, N. Y.
Near 125th St. and 9th Av.
C. T. HULBURT, Agent.
Rear Sills, Lintels, Steps, Roof Coping, Pier Stones, Etc., a Specialty.
Telephone Call—528 Harlem.

THOMAS NUGENT,
Manufacturer of
Moist Warm Air Furnaces
AND VENTILATING APPARATUS.
214 EAST 80th STREET, NEW YORK.

National Chimney Tops.
(Patented.)
The most efficient Chimney Cowl in use. Down drafts and smoky flues cured; a wonderful increase of draft obtained.
WARRANTED "SURE."
The spiral part enlarging as it goes upward, admits the air on all sides, and the wind striking it in any direction is given an upward tendency, thus helping to produce the desired effect.
IRA G. LANE, Patentee.
207 East 64th Street.

ARCHITECTURAL WOOD WORKERS.

THE NEW YORK LUMBER & WOOD WORKING CO.

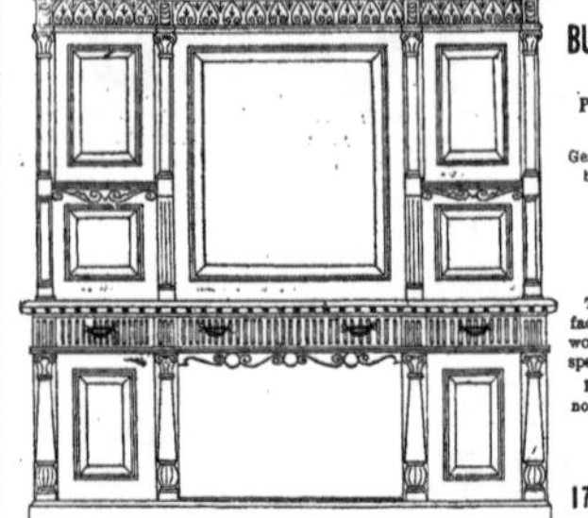

MANUFACTURERS OF
EVERY VARIETY OF
BUILDERS' WOOD WORK
— FOR —
Public and Private Dwellings.

General House Trim, Mantels, Side boards, Hall Frames, Saloon and Bathroom Work, Wainscoting, Door Sashes, Blinds, Shutters, Etc., Etc.

This Company has superior facilities for turning out large work at short notice on either special design or its own.

Estimates furnished on work, not less than for one dwelling.

GENERAL OFFICE,
173 & 175 BROADWAY
NEW YORK CITY.

Factory at BATAVIA, N. Y. Docks at TONAWANDA, N. Y.

HARDWOOD LUMBER in Carload Lots or Quantities to Suit Purchasers.
WALNUT, ASH, OAK, CHERRY, HAZEL and WHITEWOOD.

DIMENSION STOCK
CUT to EXACT SIZES,
KILN DRIED, GLUED, AND PLANED TO ORDER.

For Builders, Frame and Cabinet Makers, Manufacturers of Furniture, Organs and Pianos—in fact all Wood-Workers. Sample order sheet and key to Grading of Dimension Stock, mailed free. Squares Cut to Sizes as Desired.
H. HERRMANN, 368 BROOME ST., NEW YORK, U. S. A.

BUFFALO DOOR AND SASH COMPANY,
Manufacturers of Doors, Sash, Blinds, Mouldings, Mantels. Stair Rails, Brackets, Etc.
CABINET WORK A SPECIALTY.
FACTORY AT BUFFALO, N. Y. OFFICE AND WAREHOUSE, COR. 9TH AV. AND 124TH STREET
James H. Lee. Franklin Lee. Nelson Holland. Chas. S. Kendall.

D. C. NEWELL AND SONS,

Hudson River
Planing Mills.

Yellow Pine, White Pine, Spruce and Hemlock
LUMBER

Foot West 19th Street, New York.

A. B. JOHNSON & CO.,
WHOLESALE AND RETAIL DEALERS IN
TIMBER, PLANK & STEP PLANK, **YELLOW PINE.**
FOOT OF 96th STREET, EAST RIVER,
NEW YORK.
Telephone, 346 Harlem.
A. B. JOHNSON. L. R. BABBITT. H. O. SANDERS.

MAHOGANY,
GEORGE HAGEMEYER & SON,
DEALERS IN SEASONED
HARDWOOD, LUMBER & VENEERS,
WALNUT, CHERRY, POPLAR, ASH, MAPLE, BIRCH, BUTTERNUT,
Plain and Quarter Sawed Oak, Gum and Sycamore.
Office and Yards, Foot of 10th & 11th Sts., E. R., N. Y.

WILLIAM HILGERS,
Artificial Stone and Asphalt Works
163 WEST 104th ST., N. Y.
Concrete and Asphalting for sidewalks, yards, and areas, paving for stables and warehouses.
ARCHES IN CEMENT.

JOSIAH PARTRIDGE,
360 Pearl Street, New York City,
Manufacturer of
CHAIRS OF ALL KINDS,
Chamber Sets and Folding Beds.

ARCHITECTS—SURVEYORS.

JOSIAH A. BRIGGS,
CIVIL ENGINEER & CITY SURVEYOR.
Surveys—Subdivisions—Maps—Plans—Specifications—Estimates—Construction.
4260 Third Avenue, New York City.
Opp. Fordham Station, N. Y. & Harlem R. R.

JOHN HAUSER,
ARCHITECT,
1441 Third Avenue, New York.
Picken & Lilly's Real Estate Office.

J. AVERIT WEBSTER,
ARCHITECT,
Has removed to
No. 250 West 125th St.

THEOBALD ENGELHARDT,
Architect.
No. 905 Broadway, Cor. Wall Street, Brooklyn, E. D.

THOMAS GRAHAM
ARCHITECT,
1269 MADISON AVENUE, cor. 91st St.
Fine Residences and Aparment Houses for sale, and built to order. Appraisement and Expert Examinations of Property a specialty.

Danmar & Fischer
ARCHITECTS.
BROOKLYN OFFICE: No. 2921 Atlantic Avenue, 26th Ward. William Danmar
NEW YORK OFFICE: Room 296 Potter Building, 38 Park Row. Adam E. Fischer.

EDWARD WENZ,
ARCHITECT,
1491 Third Av., northeast cor. 84th st., New York.

Herter Bros.,
ARCHITECTS,
191 Broadway (Mercantile Nat. Bank Building), N. Y.

FRANK WENNEMER,
A R C H I T E C T,
204 East 86th St., Near 3d Av., **New York.**

ALBERT HUTTIRA,
ARCHITECT & SUPERINTENDENT
804 E. 70th St. Elevated Station. NEW YORK.

MISCELLANEOUS

ESTIMATES TO BUILDERS
FOR
CARPETS, OIL CLOTHS, SHADES
MATTING, MATS, ZINC PLATES, Etc.,
CHEERFULLY FURNISHED.
H. RAUCH & SON,
24 AVENUE B., bet. 2d and 3d Sts.

CALVIN TOMKINS CO.
150 Broadway, New York City.
Telephone Call, 1063 Cortlandt.
Tomkins' Cove Blue Crushed Stone
FOR CONCRETE AND MACADAM.
Cement. Brick. Mortar Color. Plaster Paris. Lime.

Price's Patent Fire-Proof Clothes Line Frame.
To Architects and Builders, please specify Price's Improved Frame.
325 East 10th St., Bet. Avs. A and B, N. Y. City.

The frame is built of iron pipe, supported on angle iron which is built into the walls and braced to the same as per cut. In its construction **no screws are put through the roof.** Positively no leakage. This is the lightest, the most durable and the cheapest frame made. Recommended by leading architects, and approved of by Building Department.
PRICE MANUFACTURING CO.,

CEMENT PAVEMENTS
and LAUNDRY TUBS.
F. W. LAWRENCE, 16 and 18 Exchange Place

MISCELLANEOUS.

THE EAST RIVER MILL AND LUMBER COMPANY,
Foot 92d and 93d Streets, East River, New York.
Telephone, 49 Harlem. —DEALERS IN—
LUMBER AND TIMBER,
All Kinds of Rough and Dressed Lumber, and Yellow Pine Flooring and Step Plank.
GEO. H. TOOP, President. GEO. T. CROMBIE, Sec'y and Treas. THOS. J. CROMBIE, Gen'l Manager.

STAMPED METAL ORNAMENTS
FOR CORNICES, FRIEZES, PANELS, ETC., OF BUILDINGS.
Statuary and Large Work in Sheet Metal a Specialty.
W. H. MULLINS, SALEM, OHIO.
J. T. WAGNER, Eastern Agency, 108 Chambers St., New York.

HYDRAULIC ELEVATOR PIPE WORK
GEORGE FRANKLIN,
Mahony Steam and Hot Water House-Heating Boilers,
142 CENTRE ST., NEW YORK.

SAYRE & FISHER CO.
MANUFACTURERS OF FINE FACE BRICK.
Buff, Ochre, Red, Drab, Gray, Old Gold, Bronze and Mottled, both Plain and Moulded.
ALSO HARD BUILDING BRICK. (Produce 500,000 per day.)
Works: Sayreville, on Raritan River, near So. Amboy, N.J. **Office, Bennett Bldg., Fulton & Nassau Sts., New York**

"The Improved Acme Window Blind."
THE ONLY RELIABLE INSIDE BLIND IN THE MARKET.
ARCHITECTS and BUILDERS should not fail to mention these Blinds in their Specifications.
MORSTATT & SON, Patentees and Sole Manufacturers,
Office and Factory, Nos. 227 and 229 West 29th Street, New York.

PASSENGER and FREIGHT ELEVATORS.
THE D. FRISBIE CO., 112 Liberty St., New York.

COMINS & EVANS,
Gravel and Metal Roofing,
WATER-TIGHT CELLARS,
Warren's Natural Asphalt Roofing
41-45 WAVERLY AV., BROOKLYN.
Telephone Call, Brooklyn 366.
MARKET AND FULTON BANK BUILDING
81 and 83 Fulton Street, N. Y. City.

Dwelling Warming by Hot Water Only.
HITCHINGS & CO.,
ESTABLISHED 1844.
233 Mercer Street, - - New York.
Also Horticultural Architects and Builders.

RICHEY, BROWNE & DONALD,
218, 220, 222 & 224 North 11th St.,
BROOKLYN, E. D.
Ornamental Iron a Specialty.
ARCHITECTURAL IRON WORKERS.

J. C. French & Son,
VAULT AND SIDEWALK
LIGHTS
Of every Description.
No. 452 Canal Street, New York.

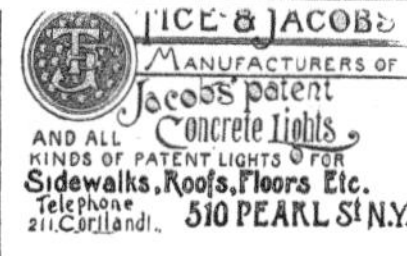

MISCELLANEOUS

STETTIN-GRISTOW PORTLAND CEMENT

Official test for tensile strength; 7 days **654 POUNDS** to the square inch.

This celebrated Cement is of excellent quality, color, extraordinary strength and fineness and is without exception superior to any other Portland Cement manufactured. It is acknowledged by all who have used it to be the best and most reliable Portland Cement in existence, which accounts for its unparalleled success, here and in Europe.

EMIL KANTER,
Sole Agent for the United States.
126 Liberty Street, N. Y.

For Sale in New York and Brooklyn at the yards of Messrs.
CANDA & KANE.

M. GIBBONS & SONS,

M. GIBBONS. R. GIBBONS. M. GIBBONS, Jr.

BUILDING CONTRACTORS

For any work pertaining to Building, sup ly every need in its construction, whether for Dwellings, Public Buildings, Factories or Stores.

Office, 318 and 320 COLUMBIA ST.,
NEAR HAMILTON AVENUE,
BROOKLYN.

Telephone 783. Send for Circular.

Stewart Ceramic Company,

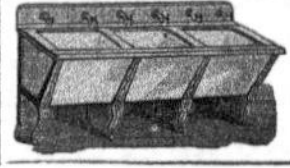

Solid White Crockery
Butler's Pantry, Kitchen,
312 Pearl Street,

Stationary Wash Tubs,
Slop and Corner Sinks.
Corner Peck Slip.

HENRY McSHANE CO.,
(LIMITED.)
Plumbers', Steam & Gasfitters' Supplies
Telephone, 215 39th. 625 AND 627 SIXTH AVENUE.

Sanitary Specialties.

JAMES MATHEWS & SON,

Excelsior, Pat. Dec. 3, 1889.

Sole agents and Manufacturers of
MAX KELLING'S
Patent
FIRE-PROOF
IRON
Dumb Waiter Doors and Casings, Sashes, Windows, Shutters and Wall Closets.

The most durable and cheapest articles in the market.

PRICES:
$3, $4, $6, $7, $8
and upward, according to size and style.

Illustrated catalogue, price list and references sent on application.

Over 5,000 in use in this city.

Main Office & Salesroom,
172 E. 110th St.
Branch & Factory,
510 & 512 E. 20th St.

RAPP SHEET METAL WORKS.

Man'f'rs of
RAPP'S PAT.
IRON
Dumb Waiter DOORS AND FRAMES.

Send for illustrated catalogue and price list.

Indorsed by the leading architects and builders as being the best and cheapest Fire-Proof Door made.

Pat. May 6th, 1890.

J. W. RAPP, Sole Agent,
315-319 E. 94th St., N. Y. City.

LAZZARI & BARTON,
DESIGNERS AND MAKERS OF
Fine Monuments, Vaults, Statuarv, Etc.

Office and Works:
OPPOSITE CEMETERY ENTRANCE,
WOODLAWN, - - NEW YORK CITY.

This cut is from a photograph of a monument built by us, erected in Woodlawn Cemetery February, 1890.

Electric Bells,
Door Openers,
Speaking Tubes, &c.
W. R. OSTRANDER & CO.,
195 AND 197 FULTON ST.,
New York.

O. A. PRICE,
—(STEAM)—
STAIR BUILDER,
415-417 E. 91st St., New York.
Estimates given. All wor promptly attended to.

LIMITED.

Reports and Ratings on
BUILDERS & CONTRACTORS.
Daily Information as to Liens affecting Subscriber's Customers.
A Bureau of Quick and Reliable Information for
MATERIAL MEN.

5?4 NASSAU ST., Tribune Bldg., NEW YORK.

SKYLIGHTS.

MATTHEW C. KERVAN,
SLATE & METAL ROOFER
SKYLIGHTS,
Galv. Iron Cornices, Lintels, Gutters, Leaders, etc.,
106 and 108 West 127th Street, N. Y.
Tin and Slate Roofs and Leaders Repaired and painted. Chimney Tops and Ventilators made and put up.

JACOB SCHWOERER,
(ESTABLISHED 1849.)
Metallic Skylight, Cornice AND ROOFING WORKS,
No. 8 2d St., near Bowery, New York.

A. GERNERT,
SKYLIGHTS
SLATE AND METAL ROOFING.
Galvanized Iron Cornices, Gutters and Leaders, Window Cornices and Sills.
515 West 42d Street, - - - New York.
Orders by Mail promptly attended to.

SOLE PROPRIETOR AND MANUFACTURER OF
THE BICKELHOUPT
SKYLIGHTS,
G. BICKELHOUPT,
243 & 245 WEST 47th STREET,
TELEPHONE, No. 675 38th St. NEW YORK

LOUIS DREYER,
No. 339 WEST 18th STREET,
8th and 9th Avenues. NEW YORK.
MANUFACTURER OF
GALVANIZED IRON CORNICES,
METAL AND SLATE ROOFING, ORNAMENTAL ZINC CASTINGS FOR BUILDINGS.

M. F. WESTERGREN F. L. ANDERSON.
The Architectural Sheet Metal Works
SKYLIGHTS,
Cornice and Roofing.
CORRUGATED IRON WORK.
205 & 207 EAST 99th ST.,
Telephone, 1826, 38th. New York.

The Brooklyn Skylight & Cornice Works

Estimates furnished for Sheet Metal and Wrought Iron Glazed Structures.

John Seton & Co.
78 & 80 Washington Av.
BROOKLYN, N. Y.

HAYES N.Y. 71, 8TH AV. METALLIC SKYLIGHTS

F. SKELTON,

MILDEW PROOF.

1325 Broadway, New York,
Bet. 34th and 35th Streets,
West Side.
MANUFACTURERS OF
AWNINGS, TENTS & FLAGS.
A New Style of Ventilating
AWNING.

Canopies, Dancing Crash, Camp Chairs, Dining Chairs, Round Tables and Extension Tables to let. Invitations delivered—Men to call carriages. Imported and Domestic Canvas and Bunting for Sale.

E. M. PRITCHARD & SON,
Manufacturer of
Window Frames, Wood Mouldings, Interior Trimmings & Wood Mantels
138th Street and Mott Avenue, N. Y.

BUILDING MATERIAL PRICES

Our figures are based upon cargo or wholesale valuations in the main. Due allowance must therefore be made f the natural additions on jobbing and retail parcelsor

BRICK		Cargo afloat
Pale .... ₩ M	—	@ 2 00
Jerseys	$4 00	@ 5 25
Up-Rivers	4 00	@ 5 00
Haverstraws, seconds	4 75	@ 5 00
Haverstraws, firsts	5 12½	@ 5 25
Choice cargoes	5 37½	@ 5 50
Lorillard	5 50	@ 7 50

FRONTS.		
Croton and Croton P'ts—Brown ₩ M	$—	@13 00
Croton do. do.—Dark	—	@14 00
Croton do. do.—Red	—	@14 00
Lorillard	10 00	@15 00
Wilmington	23 00	@24 00
Baltimore	37 00	@41 00
Philadelphia, alongside pier	23 00	@24 00
Trenton, do.	22 00	@23 00
Star	26 00	@ —

Yard prices, 50c. per M higher, or, with delivery added, $2 per M for hard and $3 per M. or N rth River front Brick. For delivery add $5 on Philadelphia, Trenton and Baltimore

FIRE BRICK.

(Usual allowance must be made for store rates:

Welsh, ex vessel	$24 00	@25 00
English	27 00	@30 00
English, choice brands	35 00	@40 00
Scotch	35 00	@40 00
Silica, Lee-Moor	32 50	@33 00
Silica, Dinas	42 50	@45 00
White, Enamelled, English size, ₩ M	100 00	@105 00
do. do. domestic size	90 00	@100 00
American, No. 1	34 00	@35 00
American, No. 2	25 00	@28 00

CEMENT.

Rosendale .... ₩ bbl	$0 90	@ 1 00
Portland, English, general run	2 30	@ 2 60
Portland, German, general run	2 35	@ 2 75
Roman .... ₩ bbl	2 80	@ 3 00
Keene's coarse	4 50	@ 5 50
Keene's fine	7 00	@ 8 25

The following special quotations are furnished by agents of the brands, and they, not we, are responsible for the accuracy of the figures given:

Lafarge	2 90	@ 3 25
Stettin (German) Portland	2 40	@ 2 75
Portland, Saylor's American	2 15	@ 2 45
Portland, Dyckherhoff	2 75	@ 3 00
Portland, Gibbs & Co.	2 60	@ 2 85
Rosendale, Snyders, Bridge brand	1 10	@ —
Valley Improved, H. N. Camp & Sons	95	@ —

Real Estate Record and Builders' Guide.
Established March 21st 1868.
Devoted to Real Estate. Building Architecture, Household Decoration.
Business and Themes of General Interest

PRICE, PER YEAR IN ADVANCE, SIX DOLLARS.

Published every Saturday.

TELEPHONE - - - - CORTLANDT 1370.

Communications should be addressed to

C. W. SWEET, 14 & 16 Vesey St.

J. T. LINDSEY, Business Manager.

VOL. XLVIII JULY 3, 1891. No. 1,216

NOTICE OF REMOVAL.

The publication offices of THE RECORD AND GUIDE *have been removed to Nos. 14 and 16 Vesey street, over The Mechanics' and Traders' Exchange, a few feet west of Broadway.*

NOTICE.

In consequence of many requests from subscribers THE RECORD AND GUIDE *is published this week on Friday, Saturday being a holiday.*

"THE ARCHITECTURAL RECORD."

The first number of the new illustrated quarterly magazine, THE ARCHITECTURAL RECORD, *will be issued within a few days. By sending their names and addresses to the office of publication, Nos. 14 and 16 Vesey street, readers of* THE RECORD AND GUIDE *can become subscribers. The annual subscription price for the four numbers will be $1.00. The magazine will be of the same size as Scribner's, printed on paper similar to what is used by that publication and copiously illustrated. The articles will be contributed by the best-known writers of the day. The purpose of the publishers is to make the magazine the leading architectural publication in this country, and neither expense nor pains will be spared to accomplish it.*

THE stock market during the past week has been dominated by the same cause which has been playing with the long-promised bull "boom" for two months or more. Prices advanced on Tuesday and Wednesday, owing to a fall in the rates of exchange, engineered by one of the largest exchange houses; but on Thursday the rates again went up and more gold exports were threatened—a fact that was sufficient to give stocks another temporary black eye. It is no wonder that operators become anxious and shrink from undertakings in the face of the possible squeeze that these exports may cause. The general situation is somewhat better than it has been; in both America and Europe it is only speculative transactions that show any marked decreases from last year. Owing to the maintenance of rates railway earnings for June were by no means bad; and the shipment of winter wheat will very shortly begin to swell the totals. The dry goods trade, with the exception of print cloths is in a satisfactory condition; the mills are active, and the demand is increasing. Although for many years the price of raw cotton has not been so low as it is at present, yet the manufacturers have not been forced into reducing the price of their goods, something they most assuredly would have been obliged to do if consumption was not following very close on production. Furthermore, if any stringency should take place, our merchants would be in far better condition for the emergency than they were last fall. The liquidation which has been going on ever since has contracted credit very largely, as may be seen from the smaller loans and discounts shown by the bank statement. So that the country is very well prepared for the disaster which may ensue if the gold exports continue. Whether or not they will continue no one seems able to state with any authority; but a prominent financier is quoted as saying that it is to France that we must look for the first signs of a return movement. The Bank of France has never pursued a policy of putting a premium on gold when its exportation was needed in legitimate business.

TRADE in Great Britian maintains the large volume of last year with encouraging persistency. Apparently there are no very marked changes taking place. The earnings of some of the railways show small increases, while those of others exhibit equally small decreases. The statistics of foreign trade show an unimportant falling off; and the crop prospects for the island are considered very fair, the weather having proved remarkably favorable. Money continues to be plentiful and speculation dull. There are rather a larger number of unemployed workmen than there was at the same time last year—due to the fact of an increase in strikes. A similar lack of speculative animation, accompanied by a similar volume of trade, is to be observed in France. The exports for the first half of the year are smaller than for the same period in 1890, while the imports are larger. The market in Berlin is still afflicted by the uncertainty respecting the obligations of foreign countries held so largely in that city. The prospects in Argentina are about as hopeless as could be imagined. Chilian issues are under a cloud owing to the protracted civil strife in that country. Italian bonds are looked upon with a like suspicion by the public, and the financial management of Greece has been subjected to some criticism owing to a recent provisional loan. The condition of the iron and steel trade is far from satisfactory. Business is yielding but narrow profits, due to the shrinkage in the volume of trade and to the inflated prices of raw materials, such as coal, coke and pig iron. Nothing is at present hindering the resumption of specie payments in Austria on a gold standard but the unsafe condition of the international money market; and as soon as the money market improves bills providing for the change will be laid before both the legislative assemblies of Austria and Hungary. The contract entered into between the Hungarian Minister of Commerce and the Austrian State Railway Company for the sale of the Hungarian lines of the company has now been submitted to the Hungarian Reichstag to be sanctioned. In the contract the government promises to pay a yearly rental of about $4,000,000 until the year 1965. The Hungarian government hopes to make a profitable thing out of it by simplyfing the administration, by reducing expenses, by timing the trains more judiciously, and by abandoning those trains which are run merely to compete with the Hungarian lines already in the hands of the State.

UPON the eve of the Fourth of July, the "season" for the first half of 1891, so far as real estate is concerned, may safely be regarded as closed. Next week we shall publish our usual statistics for the past six months, with a review of transactions and the particular lessons and generalizations which they warrant. But there is one fact which may be anticipated, because it lies a little outside of the scope of our statistics—the most noteworthy feature of the market, though perhaps not the most weighty has been the interest which small investors of the tradesman and clerical class have taken in suburban and upper New York real estate. The auction sales of this kind of property have been more than usually numerous and popular. In most cases they have been well attended and successful, though no doubt in the latter particular the statements of interested persons should be accepted with some discount. It is certain, nevertheless, that a great deal of property has been sold, and at profitable prices, to a class of investors which hitherto have cut a very insignificant figure in the market. The advent of this class into the real estate field is the noteworthy fact of the season's business, and upon the success that may happen to attend the ventures of these particular small investors depends how rapidly the market will develop in this new direction. A large part of the capital invested in these suburban lots was withdrawn from the savings banks, so that the question seems to be whether it will pay as well in investments in real estate of small value as in deposits earning three and four per cent. Ultimately in many cases it will; but the immediate prospects are not all encouraging. The conditions surrounding a good deal of the property purchased are of a kind which necessitates a waiting policy if considerable profit is looked for; and that a paying advance over prices paid is expected by investors is shown by the fact that a comparatively small number of them purchased with the intention of improving, and in some cases the new holders are already seeking a market. There is no particular danger so far as things have gone. The property sold has been mostly of sterling worth and has been purchased at figures not exorbitant. Some little caution, however, is necessary. It is so easy to overdo a good thing, and every successful sale is a strong temptation to buyers and sellers to act prematurely.

FOR some time past there has been no little excitement in the Chamber of the Board of Aldermen over a resolution which has been submitted to that body declaring that it is wrong for the Manhattan Railway Company to participate in Battery Park. For a month or more the resolution was bandied about in the Railroad Committee, and public hearings were offered to interested citizens. It seemed at times almost as if Jay Gould had been indulging in his well-known pastime of purchasing elective officials, and one sarcastic newspaper did not fail to hint that the prices of our city fathers had fallen so low that a simple pass, standing for a year of free rides on the pleasant elevated cars, was sufficient to buy the friendly consideration of an Alderman. Never for a moment, however, did the cheap cynicism of this conception of Aldermanic nature commend itself to our intelligence; and for this reason: the Aldermen in considering the resolution were not, properly speaking, transacting business; they were simply weighing well the casting of a "pious opinion" for or against the Manhattan Company; and we do not believe that the pious approval of an Aldermanic body, simply as such, would be worth anything to Mr. Gould—not even one elevated railroad ticket. Hence we never doubted that the Aldermen would throw the weight of their moral influence against the corporation merely as a matter of selecting on which side the weight should be thrown. We think that the Aldermen did not show sound judgment; but this can be overlooked when the full bearing of this departure is considered and appreciated. It has long been apparent that the business utility of our city fathers, like that of the English Crown, had passed, and that their function in the future ought to be mainly a social one. If they wish to discuss public matters they can hold debates and throw their "pious opinions" around as much as they please. But their main utility would not be of a dialectical or legislative order. They ought individually to represent the city at social meetings or scientific gatherings; not a single meeting for a worthy cause, no matter whether it be held for purposes of instruction, purposes of reform, or even for purposes of pleasure, ought to be complete without at least one Alderman. The influence of the body in the moral and social sphere is not large at present; and we fear that they are not any too well equipped for the new sphere; but a competent instructor would, doubtless, soon teach them all that was necessary.

Natural Selection and the Slums.

WHEN a proposal is made to improve and render healthful any portion of the slums of a modern city, the greatest obstacle in the way of the reformers is an apathy begotten of the feeling that when one place is improved some other deteriorates to an equal degree; that slums must needs exist and that we merely change their location by our well-meant and fatiguing efforts. This is the commonest form of resistance to legislative or other measures designed to rid us of a degraded quarter, but from time to time such apathy is reinforced by an intimation that perhaps, after all, such places are positively useful as agents in the removing from the world of the unfit.

Walter Bagehot was one of the first economists to incorporate the idea of natural selection in his political and economic philosophy. He likens the slums to a sewer by means of which society is rid of the unpleasant and unhealthful portions of the population. He even suggests that the great evil of intemperance is not without its compensations in that it removes those of strong appetites and weak wills, and thus makes room for a better race of men. This idea has been much further elaborated in some of the scientific reviews until it would almost seem as though bad habits were, from the standpoint of the species, good. So common is this idea that General Booth, of the Salvation Army, has even suggested that some cynical philanthropist who looked at social questions in this way might give practical application to his theories by endowing a sort of gratuitous groggery where all who had a weakness for intoxicants might, without expense to themselves, demonstrate their unfitness to survive by promptly drinking themselves to death.

At the recent Conference of Charities and Corrections a gentleman was explaining enthusiastically how a new system of providing for foundlings had greatly reduced the death rate of this class of dependents. He was met by the question, "are you not afraid thus to place yourself athwart the path of natural selections?" and could only answer that nature would probably attend to her business, if he attended to his, which was simply to save the babies. The death rate in our cities is much higher among the poor than among the well-to-do, a difference that results largely from the neglect of infants, and the impossibility of properly providing for them under the conditions of tenement house life. It is because of this high death rate in the poorer districts that the heavy drift of population to the cities does not completely overwhelm them. Those who have studied the matter carefully say that there is seldom a third generation of adults in a family living in the poorer class of New York tenements. One who has given the matter careful consideration says that while the cry of "England for Englishmen" may be well enough, it would be impossible to exclude all but Londoners from London, because the city would dwindle at an astounding rate were it not for the reinforcements constantly arriving from the rural districts. As the British population in India can hardly raise boys enough to supply the army with drummers, so in a less degree the crowded life in East London begets such unhealthful conditions that the population cannot perpetuate itself.

It is thus evident that if bad habits and unhealthful slums are nature's chosen and efficient means of eliminating the unfit, then we ought to be on the high road to perfection; even without the assistance of Mr. Booth's cynical philanthropist. The presumably unfit are being eliminated at a tremendous rate, and if this is the cure-all, we ought speedily to be cured. The puny efforts of sympathetic philanthropists have not much impeded the course of natural selection as yet. It is comparatively free to do its perfect work if it can.

But our experience thus far does not indicate an imminent millennium descending upon us by virtue of a high death rate among the unfit. On the contrary, the agents upon which we are asked to rely spread disease among those previously healthy faster than they remove those already diseased. The caustic we are asked to use is itself an unmanageable and diffusive poison. However pleasant it would be to feel that the evils from which society suffers are self-illuminating, it is not a doctrine that accords with the facts of the case. There seems nothing for it but to resume the weary task of making fit conditions, if we wish to be a race fit to survive. Cities may consume the human energy generated in the country districts, but neither Malthus nor Darwin can give them an excuse for conniving at the needless squandering of health and life. For all energy they destroy without an equivalent they are held accountable and suffer for their neglect or perversity. The healthfulness of a city is a prime factor in its ultimate success, whether by success we mean social and political eminence, or merely commercial prosperity.

AMONG the many topics which the winding up of the college year has suggested to newspaper editors there is one, and that a very important one, which, so far as we have been able to observe, has quite escaped their attention. A student in an American college is entirely too prone utterly to cease his college studies with his college year. Vacation to him means the cessation of all book-work, and the glad absorption in the pleasant occupations of conversing with young ladies at summer hotels, playing tennis, camping, fishing, anything in short but mental work. Now, doubtless, in order that a vacation may be a vacation, and not merely a transfer of the location for studying, it is desirable that students should spend their summers more largely than they do winters in the occupations above indicated. But we cannot think that the strain of college work has been so tremendous throughout the year that the tired brain needs full three months of absolute rest. Indeed, we judge that this abrupt change from habits of regular study to habits of regular play rather unsettles them for resuming upon the coming of fall their old bookish ways; and the fact that the students of our colleges are so very willing to dispossess their minds of all those things which have largely occupied their attention for so long shows a lack of serious and settled interest in their studies—the lack of a disposition to make culture play a more than ornamental and perfunctory part in their lives. The function of educated men in a Republic is one of the first importance, and much of the vulgarity and want of distinction in our social life is due to the fact that our college graduates do not assume their rightful responsibilities. They are seekers after culture only while at college, and when the gates of their institution close behind them, no matter whether it be for a few months or for the rest of their lives, they say with a sigh of relief, "There, I am done with the books." Yet, in truth, college education has no meaning apart from what comes after. It is admitted by everyone that during his four years the boy cannot actually learn very much; he can only receive the necessary training, acquire the necessary discipline, and cultivate the larger and greater interests of life. Then when he receives his degree and goes forth into the world with the beginning of his arts and sciences in his head, no matter whether he has to earn his living or not, he can rear some sort of superstructure on this excellent foundation. But, alas! our young men for the most part do nothing of the sort. Just as during their vacation they are occupied solely with play, so the tendency is after their graduation to occupy themselves solely with business. Vacation, in truth, should be the time for seeking knowledge without the constraint which a college course necessarily involves. So it is with the English and German students, and it is a thousand times a pity that our American young men do not follow these excellent examples.

Investments—Good and Bad.

ATCHISON INCOMES.—The prospects for interest on the $80,000,000 of Atchison 5 per cent incomes are very hard to define, and really belong to the results of operations for the months of May and June—for which the report of net earnings has not yet appeared. Still, in view of the fact that interest is computed from results made to June 30th there is a very eager interest in the question, it being of course important to ascertain results as nearly as possible before the official announcement. Atchison officials, though cunningly questioned as to the probabilities, have refused to commit themselves by the expression of an opinion, though in no way averse to bulling their property whenever it can be done. Vice-president Reinhart is quoted by Boston papers as saying that the company will earn about $12,000,000 or $13,000,000 net for the year, and further that from present indications it would earn the whole of the interest on the incomes in the next year. This reference to the future is ominous for the present. The estimate of probable net earnings, if it referred to Atchison as reorganized, would be very satisfactory; but if it included also the net earnings of the properties taken in since the reorganization, it does not afford so much encouragement for the immediate future of the incomes.

It is very probable that Mr. Reinhart's figures are for the system as now created. and that view is supported by an examination of the earnings for the current fiscal year so far as published, being for the first ten months, and of the net earnings of the last two months of the previous fiscal year. The price at which the incomes are selling also confirms the view that the prospects for interest on them are not so good as they were at the end of June last year when the accounts were made up for the previous nine months to permit a change in date of closing the company's fiscal year and when 2¾ per cent. was earned and paid on the incomes. In May of last year these bonds sold as high as 70⅛c, but then prices were booming all along the line and Atchison securities were leading the advance so that that high figure was due as largely to the speculative interest in the bonds as to the increases in earning and the consequent prospects for interest on the incomes, to which the company was reporting about that time. The price slumped in the panic of last November to 45¾, but in January last it was again 53. There was another dip when the Atchison reports of earnings showed such large decreases in February and March, the price touching 38⅝, and recently it has fluctuated between 45 and 47.

Net earnings and the claims upon them are rather difficult to get at from the fact that the Atchison system has been developed by the absorption of the St. Louis & San Francisco, the Colorado Midland, etc., since the reorganization. Current reports do not cover the Colorado Midland's earnings, they being reported separately, probably because the purchase of that property was made during the current fiscal year. These reports, however, do cover earnings of properties taken in prior to the beginning of the fiscal year, and besides include Atchison's proportion of earnings of roads partly owned. Colorado Midland has shown itself to be about self-supporting, and net earnings for the current fiscal year show improvement, and the chances are that Atchison will make directly something by its operation, so that its acquisition should aid the income somewhat. The net earnings of the Atchison system for ten months from July 1, 1890, to April 30, 1891, amount to $10,196,172. In May and June last year Atchison and St. Louis & San Francisco earned together net $1,820,664 and together had income from other sources for the fiscal year ending June 30, 1890, in the neighborhood of $1,000,000. The Atchison system has earned gross from May 1 to the middle of June $5,126,918, or $944,640 less than in the same time last year, so that if net earnings for the last two months of this fiscal year are allowed to be equal to those of the same months of the previous fiscal year the estimate will probably be a generous one. The income from sources outside of operation is a changing quantity made up of interest, commission on bonds, etc., but in this fiscal year it will be very unlikely to exceed the figure of last year. Consequently on this basis the resources would amount to about $13,000,000. The demands on resources cannot be very closely calculated because of the new obligation previously referred to, but they will, as near as can be ascertained, approximate, in round figures, $7,500,000 for Atchison proper and $2,750,000 for St. Louis & San Francisco. The payment of these demands would leave a balance of $2,750,000, about, out of the income previously estimated.

But there are several things to be considered before these two and three-quarters of millions of dollars could be distributed among the income bondholders. Chief of these is Atchison's obligation toward Atlantic & Pacific. Last year the latter showed a small surplus of about $100,000 after payment of fixed charges, but only by reason of a credit of $2,619,498 it received for land sold to Atchison and St. Louis & San Francisco. By the acquisition of St. Louis & San Francisco, Atchison has become practically the sole guarantor of Atlantic & Pacific interest, which the property never earns of itself. Doubtless Atchison will have to provide for a large deficiency, and while it will receive an equivalent in one form or another for any advances it makes, they will make a hole in any surplus Atchison may have from the year's operations after the payment of its own fixed charges. Some additions may be found in interest charges when the statement for the year appears by reason of the new bonds issued by St. Louis & San Francisco to take up its first preferred stock and provide for other things, probably floating debt as well. There may or may not be some increase in miscellaneous income. All these things considered, it is not likely that very much will remain for the income bonds.

The Borings Along Broadway.

The borings along the Broadway Rapid Transit Railroad route which are being made for the Rapid Transit Commission by W. F. Miller, under the supervision of Engineer Wm. Barclay Parsons, were continued during the week, from Howard street to 21st street. In many respects the results were of a surprising character. In several places beds of coarse gravel several feet thick were discovered, and up towards Astor place and 13th street the upper strata were impregnated with clay. The variations in the depth of bed-rock from the street grades indicate as pronounced depressions in the surface of the rock as they were originally in the surface of the earth.

At Grand street rock was struck at 70.8 feet. The formation was of coarse wash sand with here and there small gravel stones running through. At Broome street the drill struck rock at 47.5 feet; at Spring street, at 69 feet; Prince, 70 feet; Houston, 106 feet; Bleecker, 66.15 feet; and Bond, at 68.85 feet, the formation being the same in general as at Grand street. From this point there was a gradual diminution in the quantity and coarseness of the gravel, which continued to be apparent all the rest of the way.

At 4th street rock was struck at 40 feet; Washington place, 34 feet; Waverley place, 48.3 feet, the formation being chiefly fine red sand. At Astor place there was a bed of clay for 12 feet, then coarse gravel for 2 feet, and then fine sand to 49.75 feet, where rock was struck. At Clinton place the formation was nearly all fine red sand for 65.25 feet to rock; at East 9th street rock was struck at 35 feet; 10th street, 42 feet; 11th street, 31 feet; 12th street, 12 feet of clay and then 10 feet of coarse sand—22 feet to bed-rock; 13th street, clay for 13 feet, fine red sand for 7 feet, then coarse sand to bed-rock at 34 feet; 14th street, bed-rock was struck at 13 feet; at 17th street, at 9.33; 19th street, at 10 feet; and 21st street, at 12 feet.

Rapid Transit Schemes.

The Rapid Transit Commission is putting in its final work upon the extension of the Broadway-Boulevard route from Fort George, across the Dyckman meadows, Spuyten Duyvil Creek and through the 24th Ward to the Yonkers line. Engineers Worthen and Parsons with a corps of surveyors were at work getting the topography and exact measurement and description of this portion of the route yesterday. Really, more active work has been done on this extension than on the east side lines. The engineers have prepared two or three schemes for the crossing of the Harlem and the lowlands between Spuyten Duyvil and Fort George and an early selection of a plan is expected.

Apparently much attention has been given to the trans-Harlem extension of the proposed east-side line of rapid transit. On Tuesday a hearing was given to several delegations of property-owners from Tremont, Fordham, Morrisania and other parts of the 23d and 24th Wards. The construction of a rapid transit line branching off from 3d avenue, near 143d street, and following a course about midway between the Harlem road and the Bronx River to Bronx Park was advocated by one speaker. Several of the speakers advocated strongly the proposition to extend the New York Central, Harlem, and New Haven & Hartford systems southward from the Grand Central Station to the Battery or thereabouts. One gentleman living at Tremont said it cost him three hours and 40 cents a day to live in that section of New York City, and he believed if the Harlem road was given the facilities required to enable it to run through cars to the Battery the trip to Tremont would not require over half an hour and would not cost over ten cents.

Another delegate advocated the Gerard or Jerome avenue route through the central portion of the 23d and 24th Wards, alleging that now the residents along these lines had to go from half a mile to a mile to either the Harlem or the New York & Northern road for transit to and from the city. Going out to the theatre or other entertainment after dinner, in the city, was rendered impossible for the resident of the trans-Harlem section of the city for want of transit facilities. No conclusion was reached upon the suggestions of the citizens.

Chauncey M. Depew, who has always been the mouthpiece of the Vanderbilts on the rapid transit question, said on Wednesday that the management of the New York Central & Harlem roads had concluded to have nothing to do with any scheme for rapid transit which the Rapid Transit Commission might devise. It was suggested that the extension of the Central system southward to the Battery might be more cheaply and successfully accomplished than the construction of a new line. Mr. Depew said the company had made no plans, and had no intention of making or presenting any to the commission.

In the City Departments.

Commissioner Louis J. Heintz, of Street Improvements in the 23d and 24th Wards, has awarded contracts for regulating, grading, curbing and flagging Devoe street, from Ogden to Bremer avenue; 138th street, from Rider to Railroad avenue East, and Bristow street, from Stebbins avenue to the Boston road; for regulating, grading, curbing, flagging and paving 145th street, from 3d avenue to 146th street, and for regulating, grading, curbing, flagging and laying of crosswalks, 139th street, from Willis to St. Ann's avenue.

Chief-Engineer Louis A. Risse, of the Department of Street Improvements of the trans-Harlem district, has completed the plans and specifications for sewering the Port Morris district, between the Southern Boulevard and Long Island Sound, and 130th and 138th streets, and will be ready to advertise for proposals within a few days. The work will cost over $100,000.

Plans and specifications for the paving of Brook avenue are nearly ready, and the advertisement for proposals for the work will soon be published. This important piece of paving, over two miles in length, will cost over $150,000, but will add much more to the value of Brook avenue and adjacent property.

There is over a million dollars worth of street improvements in progress now in the section of the city above the Harlem.

Commissioner Heintz is about to advertise for proposals for regulating, grading, curbing and filling Chisholm street, from Jennings street to Stebbins avenue; for curbing, filling and laying crosswalks in Boston avenue, from Jefferson to Tremont avenue, over a mile in length; for sewering Locust avenue, from 139th to 141st street; for regulating, grading, curbing and flagging Hampden street, from Sedgwick to Jerome avenue; and 147th street, from Brook to St. Ann's avenue.

Plans and specifications have been approved, and advertisements for proposals will soon be published for the following street improvements in the 23d and 24th Wards; regulating and grading College avenue, from Morris avenue to 140th street, and 163d street, from 3d avenue to Brook avenue; sewer construction in 161st street, from Sheridan to Mott avenue; 132d street, from Brook avenue to the summit west of Trinity avenue; Wales avenue, from summit east of 149th street to Kelly avenue; 173d street, from Anthony to Morris avenue; the Southern Boulevard, east and west of Willis avenue; 170th street, from 3d to Washington avenue; and for regulating, grading and paving 143d street, from 3d avenue to 144th street.

Surveyors in the employ of the Rapid Transit Commission have been at

— EXAMPLES OF —

Recent Architecture,—at home.

work in the trans-Harlem district, in the vicinity of Mott Haven, during the last week. From indirect sources it is learned that the commission has decided to cross the Harlem at Madison avenue with a bridge and to continue the line past the property of the New York Central & Hudson River Railroad Company, and thence along Sheridan avenue produced, in nearly a straight line to Van Cortlandt Park.

Chief Engineer Risse has adopted the general plan, with the indorsement of Commissioner Heintz, of reforming the map of the 23d and 24th Wards by straightening out and re-establishing the streets and avenues as far as possible on straight lines. Property-owners in general are said to approve of the plan, because the irregular plots and parcels formed by the crooked thoroughfares laid out by the Park Board are found to be of slow sale and costly to improve—there is much waste of land. Some objection to the plan is anticipated; but Mr. Risse said the district should be laid out and improved with reference to the important future it seems destined to fill and not to suit the whims of a few villa-owners.

Building Material Exchange.

The regular monthly meeting of the Building Material Exchange took place on Wednesday, the President, R. P. Chandler, in the chair. Only routine business was transacted, and the following gentlemen were elected members: Frank A. Brockway, Stanley M. Holden, Samuel C. Jones, Robt. A. Kinkele, Frank Malone, Wm. J. Peck, Frank P. Smith and J. H. Symes. A special meeting was also held, at which it was decided to close the Exchange on July 3d. No further meeting has been held of building material dealers, though one is expected to take place next week.

Acting-Secretary Crary, of the Lumber Dealers' Association, said on Thursday that no further meeting of any committee of the association had taken place since our last issue. The yards were all in thorough working trim and everything is proceeding as though no trouble had taken place.

The Opinions of Others.

Joseph D. Smyth said to a reporter: "The trouble with suburban property lately is that every purchaser buys to re-sell instead of to improve. In other words, the small people with a few thousand dollars in the savings banks have got the speculative fever, and it is not doing them much good. If these people only realized that every improvement gave an added value to the land upon which the improvement stood, as well as enhancing the values of adjoining property, they would build houses before trying to sell. If any number of purchasers at these auction sales would improve, it would be all right, but they won't. Everyone is waiting for the land to double of itself"

Notice to Property-Holders

BOARD OF ASSESSORS.

No. 27 CHAMBERS STREET,
NEW YORK, June 30, 1891.

Notice is given to the owner or owners of all houses and lots affected thereby, that the following assessments have been completed and are lodged in the office of the Board of Assessors for examination by all parties interested, who must present their objections in writing, if opposed to the same, within thirty days from date of notice:

SEWERS.

No. 1.—13th av, e s, bet Little West 12th and 13th sts; 13th st, bet 10th and 13th avs.
No. 2.—1st av, bet 45th and 46th sts.
No. 3.—Bridge st, bet Broad and Whitehall sts.
No. 4.—99th st, bet Madison and 5th avs.
No. 5.—99th st, bet Boulevard and West End av.
No. 6.—Madison av, bet 134th and 135th sts.
No. 7.—102d st, bet Boulevard and West End av.
No. 8.—104th st, bet Harlem River and 1st av.
No. 9.—63d st, bet Amsterdam and Columbus avs, extension to sewer.

[The limits embraced by such assessments include all the houses and lots of ground, vacant lots, pieces and parcels of land situated on—
No. 1.—13th st, e s, commencing abt 170 ft. s of Little West 12th st, and extending to 14th st; 13th st, both sides, from 10th to 13th av; Little West 12th st, s s, from 10th to 13th av.
No. 2.—1st av, both sides, from 45th to 46th st.
No. 3.—Bridge st, both sides, from Broad to Whitehall st.
No. 4.—99th st, both sides, from Madison to 5th av.
No. 5.—99th and 100th sts, Boulevard and West End av, the block, including both sides of 99th st, from Boulevard to West End av.
No. 6.—Madison av, both sides, from 134th to 135th st.
No. 7.—102d st, both sides, from Boulevard to West End av.
No. 8.—104th st, both sides, from 1st av to Harlem River.
No. 9.—Columbus av, w s, from 63d to 64th st; 63d st, n s, extending westerly from Columbus av abt 62 feet.]

All persons whose interests are affected by the above-named assessments, and who are opposed to the same, or any of them, are requested to present their objections in writing to the Chairman of the Board of Assessors, at their office, within thirty days from the date of this notice.

The above-described lists will be transmitted, as provided by law, to the Board of Revision and Correction of Assessments for confirmation on the 31st day of July, 1891.

CITY OF NEW YORK, FINANCE DEPARTMENT,
COMPTROLLER'S OFFICE, June 26, 1891.

In pursuance of Section 997 of the "New York City Consolidation Act of 1882," the Comptroller gives notice to all persons, owners of property, affected by the following assessment list, viz.:

ACQUIRING TITLE.

George st, from Boston road to Prospect av.
Railroad av, West from Morris av to East 165th st.

—which were confirmed by the Supreme Court June 19th and entered on the 25th of June, 1891, in the Record of Titles of Assessments, kept in the "Bureau for the Collection of Assessments and Arrears of Taxes and Assessments and of Water Rents," that unless the amount assessed for benefit on any person or property shall be paid within sixty days after the date of said entry of the assessment, interest will be collected thereon at the rate of 7 per cent. per annum, from June 25, 1891. Payments to be made to the Collector of Assessments and Clerk of Arrears, between 9 A. M. and 2 P. M.

Real Estate Department.

The business of the week has been very small, both as to the amount involved and the number of transactions consummated. The short week consequent upon the holiday, which enabled many real estate people who are still in town to get away for a short rest, reduced the number of working days very considerably. This absence of principals, and many of the brokers during the last two or three days of the week, together with the small number of negotiations which were under way, accounts for the scarcity of news. The market generally is very dull and quiet, both as to buyers and sellers, neither class evincing any great anxiety to act. At auction the sales are absolutely featureless, the dullness which accompanies the summer having settled upon the auction room. The money market continues about as it was last week; that is to say, a number of loans have been closed, but the lenders are demanding large margins.

MISCELLANEOUS OFFERINGS ON MONDAY AND TUESDAY.

The auction sales of the first two business days of the week present very little of particular interest. With one or two minor exceptions, all the property was disposed of under legal decrees, and in no case was the bidding active or the results very significant, unless it was in the partition sale of the Hamilton property, at the southwest corner of Central Park West and 94th street, on Tuesday. Here the prices were low, but this fact may be accounted for when it is remembered that there are restrictions on the property. Auctioneer Harnett, who had charge of the sale, said he believed that these restrictions did not prevent the erection of an apartment house, but either this did not reassure the bidders or they did not regard the property very favorably, for the corner lot sold for $18,300 to Hirsh Bros., the building loan operators, and the adjoining lots were purchased at from $11,950 to $12,100 each. On the same day, also in partition, No. 326 West 23d street, just west of 8th avenue, was disposed of. It is a four-story house, 21.10x52x98.9, and it was purchased by Thos. Stokes for $22,250, although the same house sold in 1887 for $23,000, and No. 324 adjoining was transferred in 1885 also at $23,000. In the same sale the four lots on the southwest corner of Amsterdam avenue and 121st street were sold. The lot adjoining the corner was purchased by F. Yoran at $3,600 and the corner itself was purchased by the same gentleman at $9,000. The two other inside lots sold at $3,700 and $3,800. In the foreclosure sale on Monday of Nos. 221 and 223 West 105th street, the plaintiff paid for the flats $28,00C, although the amount due upon them was $39,261. In a similar sale on Tuesday, four 2C-foot unfurnished flats on 85th street east of West End avenue were knocked down to the plaintiff in the action for $5,000 over the amount due, which was about $12,600.

ONE HUNDRED AND TWENTY-FIFTH STREET PROPERTY SOLD.

Two sales constituted Wednesday's business on the Exchange. One of these was a foreclosure, while the other was a public auction sale of Nos. 151 and 153 West 125th street. This latter drew an interested crowd of real estate men who were more concerned in watching the sale than in bidding upon the property. Among those present were Moses Ottinger, I. S. Korn, L. Z. Bach, B. L. Kennelly, Arnold Lustig, J. J. Plummer, J. N. Golding, A. M. Arneberg, L. S. Samuel, Heilner & Wolf and J. E. Leviness. The first bid of $30,000 for each lot was made by Emanuel Heilner, of Heilner & Wolf, and this figure was raised to $34,500 for each lot, or $69,000 for the two, when Auctioneer Jas. Bleecker knocked the property down to Heilner & Wolf, who, it will be remembered, have made some successful deals on this street. S. Magliola, by whose order these vacant lots were sold, purchased them in 1889 for $60,000. The foreclosure sale was of two flats on 106th street, east of Madison avenue, upon which $42,211 was due. They were sold for $42,060.

There were no sales of moment on either Thursday or Friday.

WHAT IS TO BE OFFERED AT AUCTION.

The auctioneers' announçements include little of interest just now, even suburban property being very quiet. As during the past week the sales for some little time to come will be largely of a legal character, and in the case of those parcels which are thus placed upon the market, and which, at the same time, are likely to bring good figures in a more active season, the defendants will secure as many adjournments as possible, so that their property may not be sacrificed as were several parcels sold under foreclosure this week.

On Tuesday, July 7th, John F. B. Smyth will sell the five-story brown stone double flat, No. 944 8th avenue, between 55th and 56th streets.

CONVEYANCES.

	1889. June 28 to July 3, inclus.	1890. June 27 to July 2, inclus.	1891. June 26 to July 1, inclus.
Number	400	445	278
Amount involved	$7,676,241	$11,580,121	$5,218,307
Number nominal	69	85	74
Number 23d and 24th Wards	30	74	35
Amount involved	$523,043	$353,545	$159,602
Number nominal	11	17	5

MORTGAGES.

	1889.	1890.	1891.
Number	373	426	254
Amount involved	$4,948,916	$5,847,885	$3,146,876
Number at 5 per cent	180	230	143
Amount involved	$2,229,208	$3,148,952	$1,938,965
Number at less than 5 per cent.	74	59	20
Amount involved	$1,533,250	$1,095,300	$427,500
Number to Banks, Trust and Insurance Companies	69	76	33
Amount involved	$2,041,500	$2,073,140	$667,262

PROJECTED BUILDINGS.

	1889. June 29 to July 5.	1890. June 28 to July 3.	1891. June 27 to July 2.
Number of buildings	81	54	59
Estimated cost	$1,774,536	$984,750	$1,369,025

Gossip of the Week.

SOUTH OF 59TH STREET.

De Blois, Hunter & Eldridge have sold the "Governor," Nos. 65, 67 and 69 West 12th street, a five-story apartment house, 50x92x104, for Matilda K. Strauss to Theo. A. Havemeyer, on private terms.

T. L. Reynolds & Co. made two peculiarly quick sales of one piece of property during the past week. On Saturday night the contract of sale between E. Jackson and Miss Kate O'Hare was signed, whereby the former transferred to the latter the northwest corner of 6th avenue and 11th street, a four-story flat and store, 25.3x60, for $74,000. On Monday morning the same brokers resold the property for Miss O'Hare to A. M. Bendheim for $75,000. This property, it will be remembered, was sold at auction in 1889 by Auctioneer John F. B. Smyth, after an interesting competition, for $75,000.

Morris B. Baer & Co. have sold for a Mr. O'Brien the four-story, high stoop, brown stone residence No. 45 West 32d street, between 5th avenue and Broadway, size 18x98.9, for about $40,000; and for Mrs. Morgan No. 718 Lexington avenue, between 58th and 59th street, a three-story, high stoop, brown stone residence, 20x69, to a Mr. Bercke for $17,500.

It is reported that Lewis S. Samuel has sold the southwest corner of 6th avenue and 11th street, a plot with a frontage of about 9.6 on the avenue and a depth of 166 feet on one side and 140 on the other.

John D. Hewlett has sold to James Fargo No. 120 East 37th street, a four-story brown stone dwelling, 20x55x98.9, on private terms. Broker, H. S. Ely.

Hiram Merritt has sold No. 615 East 15th street, lot 25x103.3 for Jno. A. Proben for $16,600.

W. B. Taylor & Sons have sold for Wm. G. Robinson, the three-story brick house, No. 109 West 49th street, on lot 25x100, for $20,000.

Peter A. H. Jackson & Sons have sold for Joseph and Margaret A. Kerr to the Welsh Baptist Tabernacle, No. 138 East 27th street, a three-story dwelling, 25x65x98.9, on private terms. The purchasers will alter the building for church purposes.

NORTH OF 59TH STREET.

A. Raymond, the clothier, has sold to H. A. Hutchison, of the Standard Oil Co., the plot, 274x295, on the southwest corner of Broadway and Depot lane, for $92,500.

T. L. Reynolds & Co. have sold for A. M. Bendheim to Miss Kate O'Hare three five-story flats, on plot 50x100, on the east side of Lexington avenue, 25 feet north of 104th street, for $60,000.

Emma Sonn has sold to Samuel Frank, No. 336 East 80th street, a four-story brown stone double flat, 25x65x100, for $14,800.

F. Zittel has sold for Samuel Colcord to Mrs. Mary A. Rich, No. 164 West 88th street, a three-story dwelling, 18x55x102.2, on private terms.

Adler & Herman have sold to A. Meyer, No. 231 East 101st street, a four-story brick flat, 25x65x100, for $14,000.

Barnett & Co. have sold for Donald McLean No. 114 East 129th street, a three-story and basement brick dwelling, 20x50x100, to Wm. G. Rock for the sum of $7,100.

L. J. Phillips & Co. have sold through their 23d Ward office for J. Y. Hallock sixteen lots at 147th street and Tinton avenue for $20,000.

John Armstrong has sold for Radebold & Wenz to John J. Sheehan the five-story double flat, 30x86x100, No. 1414 5th avenue, for $25,000.

Frank L. Fisher & Co. have sold for Gilbert Tompkins to George A. Denig No. 153 West 79th street, a three-story brown stone dwelling, 19x55x102.2, for $25,000.

J. W. Stevens has sold for W. P. Anderson during the past few weeks Nos. 150 and 154 West 93d street, as reported in recent issues of THE RECORD AND GUIDE. The interesting point about these sales is that in both cases the purchasers bought for investment, the broker, Mr. Stevens, securing satisfactory tenants before the closing of the sales. Mr. Stevens thinks from present indications that the investor will become a prominent factor in the West Side private house market during the next twelve months.

Brooklyn.

Corwith Bros. have sold the three-story and basement brick dwelling, 25x40x100, No. 99 Noble street, for John McCort to John Martin for $6,750, and the three-story frame dwelling, 16x50x95, No. 173 Norman avenue, for Chauncey Perry to Martha Doyle for $3,500.

J. P. Sloane has sold for the Kings County Improvement Co. the sixty lots extending from Calyer street to Meserole avenue, and comprising twenty lots on the east side of North Henry street, and an entire block of forty lots between Russell and North Henry streets, to Chas. A. Miller on private terms, and for the Hewitt estate the three-story and basement frame dwelling, 20x40x100, No. 77 Newell street, to George E. Blackball for $3,750.

CONVEYANCES.

	1889. June 27 to July 2, inclus.	1890. June 26 to July 1, inclus.	1891. June 25 to July 1, inclus.
Number	359	312	366
Amount involved	$1,650,250	$1,292,224	$1,196,266
Number nominal	56	72	84

MORTGAGES.

	1889.	1890.	1891.
Number	297	320	287
Amount involved	$1,281,725	$1,407,134	$1,371,716
Number at 5 per cent. or less	185	206	141
Amount involved	$703,685	$983,823	$698,342

PROJECTED BUILDINGS.

	1889. June 28 to July 3, inclus.	1890. June 27 to July 3, inclus.	1891. June 26 to July 2, inclus.
Number of buildings	73	122	67
Estimated cost	$232,100	$757,900	$182,115

Out of Town.

MURRAY HILL, N. J.—F. Payne has sold to Miss Kate O'Hare his residence and twelve acres at this place for $25,000. Miss O'Hare has resold the same to E. Jackson for $26,000. Broker in both sales, T. L. Reynolds & Co.

Out Among the Builders.

Frank Wennemer is the architect for a brick and stone church and parsonage, which the Blinn Memorial Methodist Episcopal Church will build on the southwest corner of Lexington avenue, on a plot 58x100. The fronts will be of Long Meadow stone and Philadelphia brick, the size 45x98, and the cost $60,000. The church will be Gothic in style.

Ed. Wenz has plans on the boards for a five-story brick and stone front flat, 25.2x96, to be built on the northwest corner of Park avenue and 95th street, for N. J. Reville, and three five-story brick and stone flats, 25x88 each, on the north side of 95th street, 100 feet west of Park avenue, for the same owner, the whole to cost about $100,000.

J. C. Burne has plans under way for two five-story brown stone flats, each 24.8x87.6 to be built by Coulon & Gannon on the south side of 84th street, 119 feet west of Avenue B, at a cost of $44,000.

Andrew Spence will furnish the plans for a two-story brick extension to be built by Wm. A. Martin to the Grammar school on the northwest corner of 134th street and Lenox avenue. The size of the extension will be 50x95 and the cost $10,000.

John Hauser has plans under way for three five-story brick and brown stone flats, to be built on the north side of 88th street, 100 feet east of Avenue A. They will be 25x70 with 7x12 extension and will cost the owner, Joseph Schreiner, $50,000.

Richard R. Davis has drawn plans for a four-story brick and stone stable, 50x100.11, to be built by Frederick Hulberg, on the south side of 122d street, 60.1 feet west of St. Nicholas avenue, at a cost of $18,000.

M. V. B. Ferdon has plans under way for a five-story flat, 25x80.0, to be built at No. 331 West 21st street, for Wm. Cumming, Jr., and Robert Ferguson.

Thom & Wilson are preparing drawings for five five-story tenements, the corner 21x96.8, and the others, each 25x70 and extension, to be built by Feehan & Hammer, on the northwest corner of Avenue B and 87th street.

G. A. Schellenger has plans for a five-story flat, 25x89.6, to be built on the north side of 98th street, 150 feet west of Central Park West, for G. A. Kelly.

The first installment in the way of improvements on the property recently sold by the Morgenthau syndicate is in the shape of ten and possibly twelve small private houses, of brick, with stone trimmings, that Messrs. L & K. Ungrich contemplate erecting on 180th street, between Amsterdam (10th) and Audubon avenues.

Out of Town

PUEBLO, COL.—Holly & Jelliff have completed plans for a handsome residence to be built here for J. A. Thatcher. The house will be 75x83 in size and three stories high. It is to be built of Lava stone from the Rocky Mountains and is to have a red slate roof with copper gutters and stone cornice. The interior will be finished in hard woods and the estimated cost is placed at about $100,000.

WESTCHESTER.—Fred. Ebeling is drawing plans for a two-story and attic frame dwelling, 22x40, to be built at this place by F. G. Sheehan; and for a one-story frame dwelling to be built for Mr. Fischer, on Theriot avenue, at a cost of $1,000.

Personal.

James R. Waterlow and family will spend the summer at Deal Beach, New Jersey. Mr. Waterlow will come to town about twice a week.

Simon Adler is at the Atlantic Highlands.

Henry S. Herrman will spend the summer as usual, at the Scarborough Hotel, Long Branch.

Edward Cabot Wilde leaves to-day for a stay at York Harbor, Maine.

Special Notices.

We wish to call the attention of our readers to the card of John Francy's, Son & Co., inserted in another column. The works of this firm are in Toronto, Ohio, and their office and yard at Nos. 608 and 610 West 51st street. They deal in sewer pipes, fluke lining and wall copings. The popularity and excellence of their materials may be judged from the fact that they have the contract to furnish the flue pipes for all the chimneys in the new Hotel Waldorf. Thos. H. Marvin is their agent in this city.

Strong, neat binders, especially made for THE RECORD AND GUIDE, can be obtained at this office. Those of our subscribers who wish to keep a file of the numbers in a compact form and in regular sequence, can have the binder delivered at their office on receipt of order by postal card. Price at office, $1.00, by mail, $1.19.

WANTS AND OFFERS.

(Advertisements strictly in accordance with this title will be inserted at the practically nominal rate of 10 CENTS per line (agate). In figuring for themselves advertisers may count seven words for each line, the address to be taken as one line. The object of this department is to bring buyers and sellers into communication with customers. Advertisements must be marked "Wants and Offers Column," and sent to the office of publication, Nos. 14 and 16 Vesey Street, not later than 8 P. M. Friday.)

WANTS.

ARCHITECT, established in New York City, desires partner to take equal interest; must be a man of ability and experience, capable of taking charge of office; $3,000 required. Address,
ARCHITECT.
July 4-1aw3w. Office of RECORD AND GUIDE.

MASON, BUILDER, ARCHITECT, AND MECHANIC, desires to make himself useful to any one desiring his twenty-five (25) years' experience in the Building Trade, or buying or selling. Address, BUILDER AND ARCHITECT, 81 New st., Room 104; N. Y. C.
May 16—1aw10w.

OFFERS.

Dwellings

SPECULATORS AND INVESTORS.—I have just finished my entire front on 8th av., 118th, 119th; five story, with stores; well rented; prices from $25,000 to $48,000. For particulars. P. BRAKNDER, Owner and Builder, 120 East 86th st (office open till 9 P. M.
July 4-1aw3w.

MODERN DESIRABLE PRIVATE DWELLING on West 22d st.; choice location; good size; $17,000; terms easy. WHITING, 45 Broadway.

A BARGAIN.—For sale or exchange, handsome four-story dwelling on 72d st., close to Lexington av. Particulars, &c.,
S. H. FURMAN & Co., 137 Broadway.

WEST 89TH ST., near Boulevard. Nos. 260, 262 and 264; new three-story brown stone.
CHAS. L. RITZMAN, Owner,
July4-e.o.w.4t 943 Broadway.

FOR SALE—Choicest corner on Riverside Drive, 91st st.; elegant residence to be erected on adjoining plot. Apply to J. R HAY, 7 Wall st.

FOR SALE—2443 8th av.; 26.8½x100: easy terms; commission allowed brokers; apply at
Mar. 28-u-f. ROOM 19, 156 Broadway.

FOR SALE—210 and 212 West 105th st.; five-story apartments; each, 25x80x100; decorated and carpeted; apply at ROOM 19, 156 Broadway.
Mar.28-u-f.

OFFERS.

PEERLESS MANSIONS—Manhattan Square, North (81st Street, between 8th and 9th Aves.); cabinet finish; 25x96; four stories, basement and cellar; classical, original and unique; "L" station at corner; inspection invited; unequaled for beauty and location. Titles will be insured by TITLE GUARANTEE AND TRUST COMPANY, 55 Liberty st., New York. RICHARD DEEVES, Owner and Builder.
Jan.24-u.f 66 West 83d Street.

Improved Property.

FOR SALE.—A first-class business property, which is leased to one party for 10 years at $8,500 a year; 10 per cent on investment; must be sold before July 15, 1891. Address to
H RAWAK, 171 Broadway.

WHITE PLAINS.—Must realize cash at once, on about 40 acres; over 400 city lots; within half-mile from Depot. G. W. KEELER, 51 Pine st.

Vacant Lots.

FOR SALE.—N e cor 116th st and 8th av., 100.11x125; excavated. HYATT, 164 East 84th st.
July 4-11.

FOR SALE.—Four full lots on East 14th st.; suitable for any building purpose; price $90,000; only principals need apply. J. T., REAL ESTATE RECORD.
J. 27-1aw3w.

LEASEHOLD.—For sale—23d st., between 10th and 11th avs., four city lots, 50 feet frontage on 23d st., running through to 22d. Inquire office corner 11th av. and 22d.
GEORGE G. FARNHAM, 65 Broadway.

FOR SALE—Five lots, n e cor Willis av and 137th st, 100x125; easy terms; ead for improvement; splendid location. Apply to
June 27, 1aw4w. JAS. CARNEY, 137 East 52d st.

LARGE FACTORY for sale; price, $28,000; the land itself supposed to be worth the money.
Apr 4-uf FIRST NATIONAL BANK, Brooklyn, N. Y.

OFFERS.

TO BUILDERS—With or without a loan, south side of 81st st., near Amsterdam av., three lots, excavated; terms easy. DA CUNHA, Montclair, N. J.
J 20—1aw5w

Brooklyn Real Estate for Sale.

DESIRABLE INVESTMENT.—Eight-story apartment house; best location in Brooklyn; might exchange equity over $125,000 at 4½ per cent.
J. 20—uf. Apply 60 Broadway, Room 311.

TO LET.—Plot of ground, 100x150; buildings suitable for iron foundry or factory; will be altered to suit tenant. Inquire on premises,
March 28-uf. Quay and West sts., Brooklyn, E. D.

Country Property.

A NEW SEASIDE RESIDENCE at Breezy Point, Far Rockaway, on Jamaica Bay; two acres valuable water front; house has 15 rooms, bath and laundry; fine water supply; views of ocean; Arverne, Coney Island, Brooklyn bridge lights at night; easy terms. Apply, HENRY R. KING, 47 Cedar st, or W. A. TORREY, 6 Wall st, or on premises.

FOR SALE AT YONKERS.—Twenty acres fine land on North Broadway, suitable for villa plots, &c.
Address, 26 East 60th st.

AT MONTCLAIR, N. J.—200 acres for cutting into lots; railroad station on property; number of acres to suit purchaser. DA CUNHA, Montclair.
J. 27-1aw5w.

Miscellaneous.

OWNERS OF PRIVATE HOUSES to sell or lease may find an advantage to send full particulars, as I have a good demand in present dull season to dispose of them. LIONEL FROEHLICH, 169 East 61st st, also 10th av. corner 81st st.

18TH ST., near 6th av., two private stables, can each be altered to accommodate thirty horses; sell or rent; easy terms.
THOMAS KELLY, No. 146 West 18th st.
June 27—July 4.

A PARTY ABOUT TO BUILD A FIVE-STORY factory, 50x98, in Harlem, near water-front, will lease the three upper floors and build to suit tenant. Terms very moderate. Address
May 16 u. f. OWNER, 409 E. 107th St.

SALES OF THE WEEK.

The following are the sales at the Real Estate Exchange and Auction Room for the week ending July 2.

** Indicates that the property described has been bid in for plaintiff's account:*

R. V. HARNETT & CO.

Central Park West, s w cor 94th st, 25.5x100, vacant. Hirsh Bros.......... $18,300
Central Park West, w s, adj, 50x100, vacant. B. Cohen.......... 24,100
Central Park West, w s, 125.8 s 94th st, 25.4 x100, vacant. Owen Fargusson.......... 11,950
23d st, No. 326, s s, 253.1 w 8th av, 21.10x98.9, four-story and basement brown stone dwell'g. Thos. Stokes.......... 22,250
29th st, s s, 600 w 11th av, 50x98.9, vacant.... }
12th av, s e cor 30th st, 49.4x100, vacant...... }
G. A. Muller. (Amt due $25,913).......... 33,000
*85th st, Nos. 252-258, s s, 100 e West End av, 80x102.2, four five-story unfinished brk flats. (Amt due $12,607). Reuben Ross.......... 17,607
*102d st, Nos. 208 and 210, s s, 160 e 8d av, 50x100.11.......... }
102d st, Nos. 212 and 214, s s, 210 e 8d av, 50x100.11.......... }
Four five-story brk tenem'ts, stores in Nos. 212 and 214.......... }
Jonas Weil. (Amt due on Nos. 208 and 210 $18,924 and $18,711 on Nos. 212 and 214).......... 70,100
Amsterdam av, s w cor 121st st, 25x100, vacant. F. Yoran.......... 9,000
Amsterdam av, w s, adj, 25x100, vacant. Same 8,600
Amsterdam av, adj, 25x100, vacant. W. R. Larkin.......... 3,800
Amsterdam av, adj, 25x100, vacant. Geo F. Vengut.......... 3,700

A. H. MULLER & SON.

Front st, Nos. 132 and 134, s w cor Pine st, six-story brk stores.......... }
Water st, No. 133, s e cor Pine st, five-story stone front store.......... }
Leasehold. All right, title and interest.... }
Montgomery Auction and Com. Co.......... 250
Kingsbridge road, at junction private drive to Claflin's, contains 4-5 city lot. Leo. Frank. 650
*114th st, Nos. 302-310, s s, 95 w 8th av, 130x100.11, four five-story brk flats and one vacant lot. David Marx. (Amt due $29,750).......... 30,000
2d av, No 1889, 25x90, five-story brk and stone double flat and store. C. A. Schrouber.......... 17,900
*8th av, Nos. 2099-2105, s w cor 114th st, 100.11x95, four five-story brk stores and flats. David Marx. (Amt due $37,789).......... 51,630

JAS. C. LALOR.

*74th st, No. 315, n s, 200 e 2d av, 25x102.2, five-story brk tenem't with stores. Chas. Wersberger. (Amt due $1,770; prior morts. $15,000).......... 17,100

WM. KENNELLY.

*61th st, No. 140, s s, 397 w 9th av, 18x100.5, four-story stone front dwell'g. Metropolitan Life Ins. Co. (Amt due $18,770).......... 19,500

JOHN F. B. SMYTH.

37th st, Nos. 350-354, s s, 100 e 11th av, vacant. Mary E. Joyce.......... 18,100

OTHER AUCTIONEERS.

Hamilton st, No. 35, n s, 25x55.8x24x50.3. John Cotter.......... 5,800
Sullivan st, e s, 225 n Bleecker st, 25x100. E. Sink.......... 16,100
Waverley pl, s w cor Charles st, 20x75. W. B. Clayton.......... 9,100
*30th st, No. 47, n s, 86.6 w 4th av, runs north 53 x west 2.6 x north 45.9 x west 16.6 x south 98.9 to 30th st, x east 19, four-story brk dwelling. Huntington Richards. (Amt due $708). 18,600
*100th st, Nos. 221 and 223, n s, 200 w Amsterdam av, 50x100.11, two five-story brk flats. Christian Schultheis. (Amt due $39,261).... 38,000
106th st, Nos 59 and 61, n s, 150 e Madison av, 49.6x100.11, two five-story brk flats. (Amt due $4,711; prior morts. on each house $18,750). Chas. Seidler.......... 42,000
7th av, e s, 135.6 n 11th st, 21x68.10. W. B. Clayton.......... 6,900
125th st, Nos. 151 and 153 W., n s, 100 e 7th av, 50x99.11, vacant. Hellner & Wolf.......... 69,000

Total.......... $527,827
Corresponding week 1890.......... $816,540

BROOKLYN, N. Y.

For Week Ending July 3.

T. A. KERRIGAN.

*Chauncey st, s s 325 e Stuyvesant av, 125x100. Josiah Morgans.... $8,250

*Clark st, No. 109, n e s, 95 n w Fulton st, 28.8x90.7 x 29.6 x 91.7, three-story brk dwell'g. Amelia L. Gurlitz 9,000

*Dean st, n s, 100 w Buffalo av, runs west 479.1½ to centre Hunterfly road, x northwest — to e s Rochester av, x north to centre line of block bet Dean st and Pacific st, x east 600 x south 107.2¾, except.......
Dean st, n s, 100 w Buffalo av, runs west 484.8 x north 107.2¾ to centre line of block, x east 484.8 x south 107.2¾ to beginning.....
Henry Weil.... 1,000

*Elton st, s w cor Blake av, 25x88, two-story frame dwell'g. Frederick Middendorf...... 2,000

*Elton st, w s, 50 s Blake av, 25x88, two story frame dwell'g. Margaret C. Reed.... 1,000

17th st, No. 291, n s, 70.4 e 5th av, 14.11½x60, two-story frame building. E. H. Lott...... 1,300

16th av, e s, 375 n Bath av, 53x216 8 to Bay 13th st, x53x216.8, New Utrecht. Anna E. Denyse. 2,050

REFEREE'S SALES AT COUNTY COURT HOUSE.

*Herkimer st, Nos. 757 and 759, n s, 225 w Rochester av, 30.11x102.6½x53.7x100, two two-story frame (brk lined) dwell'gs. Nathan A. Downs.... 6,100

*Herkimer st, Nos. 825–829, n s, 340 e Rochester av, 60x100, three two-story frame dwell'gs. Isaiah S. Corwin.... 6,910

Total.... $37,610

CONVEYANCES.

Wherever the letters Q. C., C. a. G. and B. & S occur, preceded by the name of the grantee they mean as follows:

1st—Q. C. is an abbreviation for Quit Claim deed, i. e., a deed in which all the right, title and interest of the grantor is conveyed, omitting all covenants or warranty.

2d—C. a. G. means a deed containing Covenant against Grantor only, in which he covenants that he hath not done any act whereby the estate conveyed may be impeached, charged or encumbered.

3d—B. & S. is an abbreviation for Bargain and Sale deed, wherein, although the seller makes no express covenants, he really grants or conveys the property for a valuable consideration, and thus impliedly claims to be the owner of it.

NEW YORK CITY.

June 26, 27, 29, 30, July 1.

Baxter st, No. 18, w s, abt 80 s Worth st, 25x116.6x23x116.6, five-story brk tenem't with stores. Abraham Finelite to Alexander Finelite. All title. *Mt.* $16,000. April 25. $4,000

Same property. Alexander Finelite to David Finelite. For life. *Mt.* $16,000. June 25. nom

Bayard st, No. 45, s s, abt 75 w Bowery, 25x50x25.1x50, three-story frame store and tenem't.
Bayard st, No. 47, s s, 100 w Bowery, 25x80.4, four-story brk building.
Frederick Carrard, Flemington, N. J., to John Friedrich. *Mt.* $15,000. June 29. 12,000

Broadway or Kingsbridge road, e s, plot 40 map Isaac Dyckman Fort George property, 50x183.8x58.3x202. Sarah M. Shotts formerly Smith, Yonkers, N. Y., to John C. Hegelein. June 25. 4,600

Boulevard, s w cor 105th st, 106.9x—x100.11x67.5, vacant. Frank L. Smith and Magdalene his wife to Jacob Lawson. *Mt.* $22,000. June 25. nom

Catharine slip, No. 24, s w s, 40.1 n w South st, 20x40.
Catharine slip, No. 22, w s, 60.3 n South st, 20x40.
Two four-story brk tenem'ts with stores.
Jonas Weil and Theresa his wife and Bernhard Mayer and Sophia his wife to William Hennessy. *Mt.* $15,050. June 30. 18,000

Catharine slip, No. 5, e s, 20x67.2x20x65.1. Release mort. The East River Savings Inst. to William T. Black et al. exrs. Joseph C. Appleby and Mary Appleby widow and Alice Horsfield, Josephine H. Black, Emma and Adelaide Smith and James Appleby devisees of Joseph C. Appleby. May 15. nom

Same property. Release mort. Same to same. May 13. nom

Catharine slip, No. 5, e s, 40 s Cherry st, 20x67.2x20x65.1, with use of alley from rear of said lot to Cherry st, three-story frame store and tenem't. James Appleby and Hattie his wife, Houston, Texas, to John W. Arfman. 1-5 part. June 3. 1,100

Carmine st, Nos. 11 and 13. Party wall agreement. Emelia Hoffman with James A. Roosevelt et al. trustees Cornelius V. S. Roosevelt dec'd. May 16. nom

Chambers st, No. 33, 30x151 to Reade st.
29th st, Nos. 151–153 W., n s, 234 e 7th av, runs east 64.7 x north 98.9 x west 30 x south 68.1 to n s of Old lane, x west 50 x south 16.8.
42d st, No. 542 W., s s, 19.7x98.9.
Pew No. 163 in Grace Church and property in Kings and Queens County.
Distribution under trust deed, &c.
William W. Sherman and George P. Wetmore exrs. and trustees and William Man trustee of Annie W. Sherman; allot and set apart above to Georgette W. and Sybil K. W. Sherman in equal shares. Nov. 19, 1890. nom

Cherry st, No. 228 } being Cherry st, n w
Pelham st, Nos. 7 and 8 } cor Pelham st, runs north 135 x west 39.3 x south 38.6 x east 10 x south 100 to Cherry st, x east 29, two six-story brk buildings. Jonas Weil and Theresa his wife and Bernhard Mayer and Sophia his wife to Peter C. Wodzicki and Theodora C. his wife. *Mt.* $35,000. June 26. 70,000

Church st, No. 236. Agreement to accept conveyance as reduction of collateral security for $45,000 between Frederick P. Dimpfel, who accepts above, and Marie L. Kellogg, who conveys. Re-recorded. May 1. val. consid

Clinton st, No. 8–14, e s, 100 s Houston st, 75x100.2, brk synagogue and three-story brk store and dwell'g with one-story frame building on rear of No. 14. Congregation Rodolph Scholom to the Congregation Chasam Sopher. July 1. 72,000

Clinton st, No. 95, w s, 200 s Rivington st, 25.4x100, five-story brk tenem't with stores. Henry Michel and Rebecka his wife to Isaac Schenker. *Mt.* $27,000. July 1. 37,500

Cortlandt st, No. 14, formerly No. 8, also all title trust fund. Edward S. and Olivia B. Walsh exrs. Elizabeth R. Walsh to Louise C. Walsh, Stamford, Conn. All title of Eliz. R. Walsh as a child of Emily M. Walsh and under deed by S. B. Walsh to said Emily R. Walsh. March 16. nom

Same property. Edward S. and Henry B. Walsh legatees Eliz. R. Walsh to same. All title, &c. B. & S. March 16. nom

Cortlandt st, s s, 99 w Greenwich st, 26.3x77.8x24.6x78. Party wall agreement. Henry D. Sedgwick and Henry S. Watts with Archibald McInnes. June 25. nom

Division st, Nos. 241 and 243. Party wall agreement. Morris Margovitz and Morris Weinstein with Andrew J. Smith. June 4. nom

Division st, No. 79, s s, bet Market and Pike sts, 25x66.3x25x66.1, two-story brk store and tenem't. Wolf Bloom and Rachel his wife to Navelle Levin. ½ part. *Mt.* $10,500. June 30. 13,500

Division st, Nos. 234 and 236, n w cor Attorney st, 40.2x95x78x66, two five-story brk tenem'ts with stores. Ascher Weinstein and Annie his wife to Hannah Taylor. *Mt.* $44,000. June 29. See Lexington av. 62,000

Elizabeth st, Nos. 113–117, w s, 51 n Grand st, 74.2x94, three five-story brk tenem'ts with stores. Isabella Labriola and Michelina Mangiere to Salomon Alter. *Mt.* $58,000. July 1. 86,000

Essex st, No. 146, e s, 225 n Rivington st, 25x100, five-story brk tenem't with stores and five-story brk tenem't on rear. Franziska Haupt widow and Louis Haupt to Jacob Wiebe and Magdalena Endholz. *Mt.* $10,000. July 1. See Av A. 36,000

Essex st, No. 128, e s, 35 s Rivington st, 17.6x80, three-story brk store and tenem't. Louis and Adolphus H. Stoiber individ. and as trustee of Felix and Gustavus H. Stoiber, Silverton. Col., to George G. Egler. June 30. 11,750

Eldridge st, No. 78, w s, 100 n Hester st, 25x100, five-story brk tenem't with stores. Isaac Ginsburg and Caroline his wife to Jacob Paskusz and Israel Feldman. *Mt.* $32,000. June 26. 48,000

Forsyth st, No. 204, e s, 175 s Houston st, 24.11x100, five-story brk tenem't with stores. Otto Hamberger and Josephine his wife to Aaron Kaplan. *Mt.* $14,000. July 1. nom

Goerck st, Nos. 139–143, w s, 100 s Houston st, 75x100, two-story brk building and frame sheds, mahogany yard, &c. John L. Daniels and Sarah K. his wife, New York, and John Wilshaw and Sarah E. his wife, Brooklyn, to Julius Dreyfus. June 9. 25,000

Same property. Julius Dreyfus to Jonas Weil and Bernhard Mayer. *Mt.* $18,000. July 1. 25,000

Grand st, No. 546, n s, abt 50 e Cannon st, 25x100, five-story brk tenem't with stores. Sherman Evarts ref. to Alfred R. Conkling. June 25. 32,100

Grand st, No. 10, n s, 122.8 e Varick st, 23x83 to alley, with use of same, three-story frame (brk front) tenem't with one-story frame building on rear. Joseph F. and Harriet A. Piblstrom heirs Joseph F. Piblstrom to Alexander Levett. June 30. nom

Grand st, Nos. 14 and 16, n s, 168.8 e Varick st, 20x83 to alley, x—x72, two three-story frame (brk front) tenem'ts with two-story brk building on rear of No. 14. Michael Scanlon to same. June 30. nom

Henry st, Nos. 86 and 88, s e cor Birmingham st or alley, 38x42, seven-story brk building. Rosanna Rosenfeld to Adolph Cohen and Harry Fischel. *Mt.* $25,000. June 24. 45,000

Henry st, No. 46, s s, 290 w Market st, 25x100, four-story brk tenem't. Samuel Phillips and Rachel his wife to Morris Goldstein. *Mt.* $17,000. June 30. 27,000

Hester st, No. 83, n s, 23.6 w Orchard st, 20.11x63.5x21.1x63.5, two-story frame (stone front) dwell'g. Philip Bernstein and Sarah his wife to Sender Jarmulowsky. *Mt.* $12,000. June 26. nom

Hester st, No. 85, n s, 109.9 e Allen st, 21.2x63.1-x21.2x62.10, six-story brk store and tenem't. Same to same. *Mt.* $22,750. June 26. nom

Hudson st, No. 621, s w cor Jane st, runs south 19 x west 40.3 x south 1.3 x west 14.4 x north 14 x east 55.3, four-story brk store and tenement. Meta J. B. Caldwell formerly Johnson trustee Stacy Pitcher to Calvin C. Church, Brooklyn. *Mt.* $8,000. June 16. nom

Kingsbridge road, w s, adj land William M. Tweed, being lots 34 and 35 map estate Lucius Chittenden at Fort Washington, 61x125x49x125.6. Elliot Smith and Emmeline E. his wife to Frank Koch. *Mt.* $1,400. July 1. nom

Kingsbridge road, n w s, 47.3 n e from boundary bet L. Chittenden and Jos. Potter, 25x281.4 to centre New st, x 25x280 3, with all title to space taken for widening Kingsbridge road, 25x41.4x25x40.3. Cornelius J. Donovan and Lizzie his wife to George H. Sampson, Medford, Mass. *Mt.* $1,000. July 1. nom

Kingsbridge road, s e cor 179th st, 25.6x90.10x25x85.9.
Amsterdam av, s w cor 179th st, 25x100.
Amsterdam av, s w cor 178th st, 25x100.
Kingsbridge road, e s, 25.6 n 180th st, runs east 99.11 x north 50 x east 10 x north 44.6 x west 90.6 to road, x north 96.6.
Isidor Herz and Henriette his wife to Emanuel Heilner and Moses J. Wolf. All liens. June 12. nom

Kingsbridge road, n s, 200 e Academy st, 50x150, with all title to strip in front to present west line of Kingsbridge road. Sarah M. Shotts formerly Smith, Yonkers, to Cornelius J. Donovan. June 26. nom

Kingsbridge road, s e cor 180th st, 25.6x87.6x25x82.4. Pauline Simon to Henry Maibrun. June 10. 5,150

Lewis st, No. 96, e s, 25 s Stanton st, 25x75, two-story brk tenem't. Thomas J. Carleton to Sarah Grozcky. *Mt.* $7,000. July 1. 11,300

Madison st, No. 136, s s, abt 180 e Market st, 25x100, five-story brk tenem't Foreclos. Charles P. McClelland to Samuel Weil. June 30. 4,000

Maiden lane, No. 38, s s, 92.5 e Nassau st, 21.3x62.8x18.5x67.4, five-story stone front store. Foreclos. James B. Lockwood to Sydney J. Colford. June 26. 65,500

Mulberry st, No. 223, w s, abt 115 n Spring st, 24.10x74.3, three-story brk tenem't. Simon Selzer and Annie his wife to Philip Strobel. Mort. $9,000. June 30. 14,500

Murray st, No. 47, n s, abt 170 w Church st, 25x100, five-story stone front store. Jonathan A. Frazee trustee Sara A. Sturtevant dec'd to Nathan Necarsulmer. July 1. 60,200

Perry st, Nos. 80 and 83, s s, 101.8 e Bleecker st, 40x95.1x40x95 2, five-story brk flat. Emma wife of and Nathan Metzger to Fannie O. wife of Charles F. Luiz. *Mt.* $41,000. July 1. 56,000

Pike st, No. 19, e s, 22 n Henry st, 24x44.10, three-story brk tenem't. Anna wife of Savelle Levine to Paulina wife of Harris Levy. *Mt.* $9,000. June 29. 12,000

Roosevelt st, No. 125, w s, 59.8 s Water st, 19x41.6x19x43.6, four-story brk store and tenement. Allan McCulloh ref. to Charlotte E. wife of John C. French. Correction deed. June 30. nom

Spring st, No. 158, s s, 40 e South 5th av, 20x79.11x19.8x79.11, four-story brk store and tenem't. Release mort. First National Bank, Friendship, N. Y., to James Pitts, of same place. June 11. 6,000

Same property. Albert E. Van Beynigen, of Bradford, Pa., and James Pitts, Friendship, N. Y., to Abraham W. Maas. *Mt.* $5,000. June 17. 18,500

Thompson st, No. 16, e s, 72.11 s Grand st, 24.6x93.6x21.9x93.6, two-story frame store and dwell'g with three-story brk building on rear. Rocco Dea and Vittoria his wife to Lewis Z. Bach. *Mt.* $8,000. June 30. 11,000

West st, No. 195 } begins at West st, e s, abt
Caroline st, No. 13 } 58 s Jay st, runs east 79.3 to Caroline st, x south 14.4 x west 36.1 x south 3.8 x west 43.8 to West st, x north 18.1, four-story brk store. George Van Wagenen and Ethelinda his wife to Joseph F. Lippe. *Mt.* $12,500. June 22. 20,000

Wooster st, No. 147, w s, abt 219.4 s Houston st, 25x100, four-story stone front store. Jarvis Slade and Hannah T. his wife to Hyman Sylvester. June 27. 34,000

Wooster st, No. 133, w s, abt 70 n Prince st, 23.9x86.6, two-story brk dwell'g. Clarence A. Van Dyke, Princeton, N. J., to Abraham Beller. 1-5 part. June 11. 3,850

Same property. Mary R. Van Dyke by Charles F. Aukamp guard. to same. 1-5 part. June 11. 3,850

Same property. Samuel A. Blatchford and ano. trustees for and Mary Van Dyke widow to same. C. a. G. 3-5 part. June 11. 11,550

Wooster st, Nos. 232 and 234 } begins 3d st,
3d st, Nos. 40–44 } s e cor Wooster st, 50x46, two three-story brk tenem'ts with store on corner. Bernhard Grunbut and Rachel his wife to Abraham Stern. *Mt.* $40,000. March 21. 10,000

Same property. Louis Grunbut to same. *Mt.* $40,000. April 23. 10,000

Same property. Ascher Weinstein and Annie his wife and Abraham Stern to Michael Carr. *Mt.* $36,000. June 30. 55,000

2d st, No. 251, s s, 97 from Av C, 25x66.6x25.1x64.7, five-story brk tenem't with stores. Margaretha Weisel widow, Margaret wife of John Fritsch, Minnie Fleming widow, Frederick and Jacob Weisel heirs Conrad Weisel to John F. Bauer and Elizabeth his wife. July 1. nom

Same property. Margaretha Weisel and Christian Jager exrs. of Conrad Weisel to same. July 1. 22,000

5th st, Nos. 733 and 735, n s, 264 w Av D, 54x75, two five-story brk tenem'ts with stores. Edwin S. Updike, Sr., and Susan F. his wife to Ernst E. W. Schneider and Henry Herter. *Mt.* $51,000. June 24. nom

6th st, No. 626, s s, 341 w Av C, 21x97, four-story brk tenem't. Henry Kahn and Rosa his wife, Rosa Franklin, Sara Gomprecht and Isabella Noot to Louis Bleier. Q. C. and confirmation deed. June 1. 5,425

8th st, No. 405, s s, 51 w Lewis st, 21.11x22.2, four-story brk store and tenem't. Solomon Frank and Pauline his wife to George Neun. *Mt.* $4,500. June 30. 7,000

10th st, No. 232, s s, 175 w 1st av, 25x92.4, four-story brk tenem't. Moses Jacob and Esther his wife and Joseph Casper to Robert P. Muellenbach and Katharina his wife. *Mt.* $19,000. June 30. 29,000

10th st, No. 68, s s, 78.1 e 6th av, 49.9x92.8x49.7 x94.8, three-story brk dwell'g with one-story brk building on rear. Solomon Sayles and Sarah E. his wife to Janos McClenahan. *Mt.* $18,000. June 23. 42,500

10th st, No. 342, n s, 93 e Av B, 25x94.9, four-story brk tenem't. Adam Moran to Andrew Hansler. July 1. 15,355

Same property. Andrew Hansler and Katharina his wife to Grand Street Free Methodist Church. *Mt.* $6,000. July 1. 15,355

11th st, No. 520, s s, 270.6 e Av A, 25x94.9, four-story brk store and tenem't. Maria wife of Anthony Miller and Joseph Miller and Lena his wife and Charles J. Miller to Henry Timmermann. *Mt.* $6,000. June 30 15,000

12th st, Nos. 65, 67 and 69, n s, 189.6 e 6th av, 50 x103.3, five-story stone front flat. Tillie M. Strouse to Theodore A. Havemeyer, Mahwah, N. J. *Mt.* $100,000. July 1. val consid and 100

12th st, No. 307, n s, 120 e 2d av, 20.6x103.3, three story brk dwell'g. Joseph Gunther and Katharina his wife to Emily M. Wheeler. July 1. 17,000

12th st, No. 309, n s, 140.6 e 2d av, 20x103.3, three-story brk dwell'g. James Muiry and Eliza his wife to same. June 16. 17,000

13th st, No. 18, n s, 250 w 5th av, 16.8x103.3, three-story brk dwell'g. Foreclos. John H. Judge to Ascher Weinstein. July 1. 15,550

13th st, No. 241, n s, 180 w 2d av, 22.6x103.3, four-story stone front dwell'g. Anna Mead to Joseph Gunther. *Mt.* $10,000. July 1. 21,500

19th st, No. 407, n s, 100 w 9th av, 25x76, five-story brk tenem't. George H. Cook et al. exrs. Elisha Bloomer to Thomas C., Gellert, Jr., and John B. H. Oakley. June 12. 27,000

20th st, No. 152, s s, 174 e 7th av, 18x93.10, five-story brk flat. Thomas Monahan and Kate his wife, Brooklyn, to Matilda M. Strouse. *Mt.* $10,000. June 30. nom

Same property. Matilda M. Strouse to John H. Henshaw. *Mt.* $10,000. July 1. 23,150

21st st, No. 163, n s, 120 e 7th av, 20x98.9, four-story stone front dwell'g. William H. Milburn to Harper & Bros. *Mt.* $6,000. June 1. nom

21st st, No. 311, n s, 175.1 w 8th av, —x98 10x 25.1x98.10, five-story stone front flat. Philip Wagner and Anna E. his wife to James B. Gillie. Q. C. June 20. nom

25th st, s s, 100 e 11th av, 125x98 9. Declaration of trust. Thomas E. Sloan owner of 63 439-1000 parts with Margaret H. Rowe owner of 37 561-1000 parts. June 12. nom

27th st, No. 227, n s, 293.3 w 7th av, 25.1x98.9, five-story brk tenem't with stores. Flora wife of and Selim Marks to Thomas H. Harbison. *Mt.* $15,000. June 15. 23,250

Same property. Thomas H. Harbison to Emma L. M. Seaman widow. *Mt.* $15,000. July 1. 25,000

29th st, No. 40, s s, 185 e 6th av, 20.6x98.9, six-story brk store and dwell'g with five-story brk building on rear. Tradesmen's National Bank to Frederick Carrard. June 29. 6,447

Same property. Frederick Carrard to John Friedrich. Sub. to mort. June 29. 16,000

32d st, Nos. 423 and 425, n s, 250.4 w 9th av, 42 10x98.9, two four-story brk tenem'ts with three-story brk tenem't on rear. Joseph L. Harris and Rosa his wife to Gustav Lange. *Mt.* $17,000. June 15. 7,000

34th st, No. 418, s s, 200 w 9th av, 20x98.9, three-story brk dwell'g. Thomas Stokes and Eliza his wife to Elizabeth Eddey. June 25. 15,000

35th st, No. 3, n s, 125 e 5th av, 25x98 9, four-story stone front dwell'g. George H. Francis exr. Mary E. Bird to Eliza M. B. Schenkberg. June 25. 55,000

Same property. Mary K. Bird, Oliver W. Bird and Clara G. his wife to Eliza M. B. Schenkberg. ½ part. June 25. nom

37th st, No 527, n s, 400 e 11th av, 25x98.9, two-story brk stable. James Savage, Jr., and Mary his wife to Julia Callahan. All liens. June 27. nom

38th st, No. 58, s s, 204.2 e 6th av, 20.10x98.9, four-story stone front dwell'g. Caldwell R. Blakeman to Sarah F. V. Blakeman. *Mt.* $21,000. June 25. gift

38th st, Nos. 330-334, s s, 175 w 1st av, 74x95 5 x75x104, three five-story brk tenem'ts. Robert H. Mathews and Fannie C. his wife to Maria N. Winne, Albany, N. Y. *Mt.* $56,000. June 29. 90,000

44th st, No. 328, n s, 300 w 8th av, 25x100.4, four-story brk dwell'g with three-story brk dwell'g on rear. George Sietuon, Sr., et al. exrs. Margaretha Beck to Auguste J. Paris. June 29. 15,200

45th st, No. 426, s s, 350 w 9th av, 25x100.4, five-story stone front flat. Charles D. Shirmer to August Stegmuller. July 1. 25,600

45th st, No. 164, s s, 114.8 e Broadway and 125 e old east line 7th av, 20x100.5, five-story stone front dwell'g. Jennie L. Crawford to William A. Lane. Q. C. *Mt.* $3,000. June 15. nom

46th st, No. 433, n s, 349.8 w 9th av, runs west 26.4 x north 100.5 x east 31 x southwest 13.10 x south 87.1, five-story stone front flat. William H. Gelshenen and Catherine his wife to John P. Ryan. *Mt.* $16,000. June 29. See Columbus av. 25,000

47th st, No. 453, n s, 225 e 10th av, 18.9x100.5, five-story stone front dwell'g. John E. Glimm and Anna E. his wife to Samuel H. E. Jennings and Thomas Welstead. June 29. 13,000

48th st, No. 252, s s, 69.6 w 2d av, 19.2x100.5, four-story stone front dwell'g. Kettchen Putzel to Joseph H. Madden. July 1. 11,615

48th st, Nos. 425 and 427, n s, 325 e 1st av, 50x 100.5, two-story brk stable and wagon yard. George S. Hamlin assignee of Joshua S. Peck, Robert C. Martin and Nathan Peck individ. and as composing the firm of Peck, Martin & Co., to Edwin H. Peck and Walter J. Peck. Sub. to dower of Sarah K. Peck. *Mt.* $5,000, taxes, &c., $327. June 27. 3,100

48th st, No. 149 W., n s, 260 e 7th av, 20x100.5, four story stone front dwell'g. Ada E. wife of Willard P. Reid to George Kitching. Q. C. C. a. G. June 30. nom

48th st, n s, 325 e 1st av, 50x100.5. Release dower. Sarah K. Peck widow to Edwin H. and Walter J. Peck. June 24. nom

49th st, No. 333, n s, 345 e 2d av, 20x100.5, four-story brk dwell'g. Isaac Stiefel and Bella his wife to Isaac Kahn. *Mt.* $3,000. June 25. 11,000

49th st, No. 337, n s, 385 e 2d av, 20x100.5, four-story brk dwell'g. Isaac Kahn and Bertha his wife to Anton Wettach. *Mt.* $5,000. July 1. See 74th st. 12,500

50th st, Nos. 110 and 112, s s, 130 w 6th av, 45x 100.4, four-story brk livery stable. Samuel H. Denton and Caroline F. his wife to Park & Tilford, a corporation. June 29. 59,000

50th st, No. 241, n s, 141 w 2d av, 16x100 5, two-story brk stable. Hugh L. Hood and Sadie his wife to Thomas J. McLaughlin. Sub. to mort. June 10. nom

51st st, No. 61, n s, 94 e 6th av, 20x100 11, four-story stone front dwell'g. William S. Cooper to Meyer L. Sire. *Mt.* 29,000. June 26. 40,000

51st st, No. 314, s s, 185 e 2d av, 15x70.5, five-story stone front tenem't. Charles I. Simonson to Frances W. wife of David Ferguson. B. & S. and C. a. G. *Mt.* $9,000. June 29. nom

Same property. David Ferguson to Charles I. Simonson. B. & S. and C. a. G. *Mt.* $9,000. June 29. nom

52d st, No. 26, s s, 350 w 5th av, 22x100.4, four-story stone front dwell'g. Josephine D. Taylor widow to Grace G. wife of Robert B. Roosevelt, Jr. July 1. 65,000

52d st, No. 327, n s, 306.9 w 1st av, 18.9x100.5, five-story stone front tenem't. Anna R. wife of and Henry Siebert, Jr., to Alexander Pirie. *Mt.* $10,000. July 1. 17,000

53d st, Nos. 408 and 410, s s, 150 w 9th av, 50x 100.5, two five-story brk flats. Foreclos. George B. Newell to Richard P. Lydon. *Mt.* and int. $22,003. June 26. 40,000

56th st, No. 443, n s, 200 e 10th av, 25x100.5, five-story brk tenem't. Foreclos. Henry A. Robinson to Raphael Danziger. June 29. 17,900

56th st, Nos. 109-121, n s, 150 w 6th av, 175x 100.10, seven five-story brk flats, Union. Martha E. wife of and Thomas K. Egbert and Catharine L. wife of and George Lowther and Clara wife of and Charles Greer to Griffen Tompkins. July 1. 205,000

59th st, No. 417, n s, 225 e 1st av, 25x100.5, four-story brk tenem't. Rose wife of Nathan Hyman to Amelia A. Meyers. *Mt.* $10,000. June 30. 13,600

59th st, No. 208, s s, 150 w 7th av, 25x100.5, four-story stone front dwell'g. Joseph Battin to Berachah Orphanage. *Mt.* $20,000. June 26. nom

60th st, No. 231, n s, 350 e 11th av, 25x100.5, four-story brk tenem't. John J. McHugh and Mary A. his wife to Henry Baruch. All liens. June 26. nom

60th st, No. 233, n s, 325 e 11th av, 25x100.5.
60th st, No. 231, n s, 350 e 11th av, 25x100.5.
Two four-story brk tenem'ts, stores in No. 233.
Henry Baruch to Jacob Knecht and Louise his wife. *Mt.* $16,000. July 1. 30,000

60th st, Nos. 243 and 245, n s, 175.1 e 11th av, 49.11x100.5, two four-story brk tenem'ts, stores in No. 243. Wilhelm Busse and Agnes his wife to Henry Strunck. July 1. 23,500

61st st, No. 202, s s, 70 e 3d av, 17x60.5, four-story stone front dwell'g. Partition. Grosvenor S. Hubbard to Mary E. McGovern. *Mt.* $8,500. June 27. 12,750

62d st, No. 249 E. Assign. of rents. Patrick B. O'Mara and Margaret his wife to R. Silverman. June 24. nom

62d st, No. 303, n s, 70 e 2d av, 16x100.5, three-story brk dwell'g. Elizabeth wife of John Morris to Cornelius B. Parker. *Mt.* $3,000. June 26. 8,150

63d st, No. 134, s s, 475 w Columbus av, 25x 100.5, five-story stone front flat. William C. Illig individ. and exr. John G. Illig to William Margerin. June 8. 25,100

63d st, No. 46, s s, 242.11 e Madison av, 14.2x 100.5, four-story stone front dwell'g. Mary S. wife of James A. Rich to Anna Mead. *Mt.* $8,000. July 1. 17,500

64th st, No. 138, s s, 307 w 9th av, 18x100.5, four-story stone front dwell'g. Foreclos. George B. Newell to The Metropolitan Life Ins. Co. June 30. 19,500

64th st, No. 155, n s, 282 e 10th av, 18x100.5.
64th st, No. 153, n s, 300 e 10th av, 18x100.5.
Two four-story stone front dwell'gs.
George de F. Lord and Frances T. his wife to Rachel B. and John C. Brown, Howard Potter and John S. Schultze trustees of George H. Brown. March 5. 38,500

67th st, s s, 175 w 8th av, 50x100.5, vacant. John J. Clancy and Ann J. his wife to William B. Baldwin. June 3. 23,000

67th st, Nos. 215 and 217, n s, 225 w 10th av, 50 x100.5, one-story frame building. Jacob Schlosser and Margaret his wife to Frederick A. Libbey. June 30. See 79th st. 18,000

68th st, No. 50, s s, 100 w 4th av, 20x100.5, four-story stone front dwell'g. Harris C. Childs to Louis Seeberger. June 25. 40,000

72d st, Nos. 315 and 317, n s, 200 e 2d av, 40x 102.2, two four-story stone front flats. Henry D. Harris and Mary E. his wife to Lewis Samuels. *Mt.* $34,000. June 24. 34,000

73d st, No. 272, s s, 100 e West End av, 18x100, four-story brk dwell'g. Release mort. Mary A. Moore, New Brighton, S. I., to James C. Perry exr., &c., Augusta B. Perry. June 29. nom

Same property. James C. Perry exr. and trustee Augusta B. Perry to Walter Lawrence. *Mt.* $20,000. June 29. See 94th st. 39,500

74th st, No. 236, s s, 216.8 w 2d av, 16.8x102.2, four-story stone front dwell'g. Gretchen Rueger to Isidore Stern. *Mt.* $8,000. June 29. 12,500

74th st, No. 480, s s, 275 w Av A, 25x102.2, five-story brk tenem't. Anton Wettach and Lena his wife to Isaac Kahn. *Mt.* $13,000. July 1. See 49th st 19,000

74th st, No. 3, n s, 100 w 8th av, 20x102.2, four-story brk dwell'g. Carrie S. wife of and David T. Kennedy to Harriet C. wife of Frank C. Jones. June 24. 53,000

75th st, No. 182, s s, 225 w 3d av, 18x102.2, four-story stone front flat. Fannie Sichel widow to Joseph Schneider. *Mt.* $8,000. June 30. 15,500

76th st, No. 65, n s, 40 e Columbus av, 20x102.2, four-story stone front dwell'g. Jacob B. Smull and Sarah M. his wife to Marcus Franklin. *Mt.* $24,000. June 29. nom

79th st, Nos. 415 and 417, n s, 225 e 1st av, 53 x102.2.
79th st, Nos. 431-437, n s, 434 e 1st av, 104x 102.2.
Six four-story stone front tenem'ts.
Frederick A. Libbey and Helen I. his wife to Jacob Schlosser. June 30. See 67th st. 102,000

79th st, No. 160, s s, 217 e 10th av, 16x102.2, three-story brk dwell'g. Foreclos. John E. Brodsky to Hennette Blum. June 25. 17,000

79th st, Nos. 438 and 440, s s, 94 w Av A, 50x 102.2, two-story frame dwell'g with one-story frame stable on rear. John M. Conway and Margaret his wife to Sophie Rothschild. July 1. 17,000

80th st, No. 40, s e cor Madison av, 26x66.2, four-story brk dwell'g. The Germania Life Ins. Co. to Mary A. Stokes. July 1. 52,000

Same property. Mary A. Stokes widow to John S., Mary B. and Walter C. Stokes and Lillian S. Holmes. C. a. G. Sub. to mort. June 30. nom

80th st, No. 236, s s, 150 w 1st av, 25x102.2, four-story stone front tenem't. Emma wife of Herman Sonn to Samuel Frank. *Mt.* $10,000. June 15. 14,800

83d st, No. 140, s s, 355 e Amsterdam av, 16x 102.2, four-story stone front dwell'g. Eleanor P. Gage to Susan Murray. *Mt.* $12,500. June 29. See Columbus av. nom

83d st, No. 347, n s, 116.8 w 1st av, 16.8x102.2, three-story stone front dwell'g. Martin Lankenau to Michael Muller. Mort. $7,000. June 25. 12,000

86th st, No. 64, s s, 203 7 w 4th av, 31.11x102.2, five-story stone front flat. William Forster and Maggie E. his wife to Edward Phillips. Mort. $35,000. June 24. 47,000

87th st, n s, 121 w Av B. Party wall agreement. Thomas Moore and John McLaughlin to Charles Laue. June 18. nom

88th st, n s, 175 w 8th av, 75x100.8, vacant. Spencer Aldrich and Harriette H. his wife to Frederick Wood. Mort. $40,000. June 10. 78,500

88th st, No. 50, s s, 242 e 9th av, 20x100.8, three-story stone front dwell'g. Daniel McKeever to Ezekiel Plonsky. *Mt.* $30,000. May 15. 34,000

88th st, No. 308, s s, 163 w West End av, 20x 100.8, four-story brk dwell'g. James B. Gunn and Maggie his wife to Belle F. wife of William V. King. *Mt.* $21,000. July 1. nom

88th st, No. 335, n s, 150 w 1st av, 25x100.8, five-story brk tenem't. Charles H. Michaelis and Emma L. his wife to Augustus Goodman. *Mt.* $15,000. June 30. nom

89th st, Nos. 312-320, s s, 180 w West End av, 102x100.8, five four-story brk dwell'gs. Morris Moses and Minnie L. his wife to Elmore D. Alvard. *Mt.* $18,000. June 30. See 2d av. nom

93d st, No. 154, s s, 274 e Amsterdam av, 17x 100.8, three-story stone front dwell'g. Release mort. Charles G. Judson to Walden P. Anderson. June 30. 2,300

Same property. Release mort. Newburgh Savings Bank to same. June 29. 11,000

Same property. Release mort. Francis M. Jenks to same. June 30. nom

Same property. Walden P. Anderson to Isabella B. wife of Thomas E. Satterthwaite. *Mt.* $12,000. June 30. nom

94th st, No. 102, s s, 30 w Columbus av, 35x98.10 to Apthorp's lane, x35x100, five-story stone front flat. Walker Lawrence and Addie his wife to James C. Perry exr. and trustee Augusta B. Perry. *Mt.* $39,000. June 29. See 73d st. 57,000

95th st, No. 136, s s, 239 e 4th av, 18x100.8, three-story brk dwell'g. Matthew C. Henry and Maria his wife and John Gaykor to Moses Baumgarten. Mt. $12,000. June 30. 17,500

95th st, No. 25, n s, 240 w 8th av, 20x100.11, four-story stone front dwell'g. Edward Kilpatrick and Julia A. S. his wife to Fernando R. Walker. Mt. $22,500. July 1. 33,000

102d st, No. 230, s s, 150 w 2d av, 25x100.11, four-story brk tenem't with stores. Charles Obroek and Katnarina his wife to William Ringe. Mt. $10,000. July 1. 15,000

102d st, Nos. 208 and 210, s s, 160 e 3d av, 50x100.11, two five-story brk tenem'ts. Foreclos. Henry A. Robinson to Jonas Weil and Bernhard Mayer. Mt. $31,878. June 30. 19,000

102d st, Nos. 212 and 214, s s, 210 e 3d av, 50x100.11, two five-story brk tenem'ts with stores. Same to same. Mt. $31,878. June 30. 19,100

102d st, No. 166, s s, 225 w 3d av, 20x100.11, four-story stone front tenem't. Foreclos. Charles W. West to Florence Pomeroy. June 18. 8,000

102d st, No 162, s s, 265 w 3d av, 20x100.11, four-story stone front tenem't. Foreclos. Same to same. June 18. 9,950

103d st, No. 94, s s, 99.6 e 9th av, 20x100.11.
103d st, No. 90, s s, 139.6 e 9th av, 20x100.11.
Two five-story stone front flats.
Morris Mayer to Matthew Hagan. Q. C. June 29. nom

Same property. Matthew Hagan to Charles A. Anderson. Mt. $42,000. June 25. 60,000

105th st, s s, 230 w 4th av, 25x100.11. Release mort. John J. Bell to De Witt Mull and Gotlieb Fromer. June 29. nom

105th st, No. 223, n s, 225 w Amsterdam av, 25x100.11.
105th st, No. 221, n s, 200 w Amsterdam av, 25x100.11.
Two five-story brk flats.
Foreclos. Edgar Ketchum to Christian H. Schultheis. June 30. 28,000

107th st, No. 163, n s, 150 e Lexington av, 17x100.11, four-story stone front dwell'g. Charles Kingwell and Louisa his wife to Abraham Wachtel. Mt $11,250. June 30. 13,000

109th st, n s, 420 e 1st av, runs east to high water mark Harlem River, x north to centre line block bet 109th and 110th sts, x west 193 x south 100.10, vacant. Henry P. McGowan and Mary A. his wife to Julia H. Ryerson. Mt. $5,940. June 27. 8,750

110th st, No 344, s s, 100 w 2d av, 16.8x100.10, four-story brk tenem't with stores. Alice E. wife of William D. Carroll to John J. Herrick. Feb. 13, 1889. nom

Same property. John J. Herrick to William D. Carroll. Feb. 15, 1889. nom

110th st, No. 226, s s, 285 e 3d av, 25x100.11, four-story brk tenem't. Sophie B. Humes to Barbara Krulisch and Mary Hollmann. Mt. $10,900. June 29. 13,200

111th st, No. 97 / Park av, No. 1544 } beings 111th st, n w cor 4th av, runs north 100.11 x west 33 x south 18 x east 15.3 x south 82.11 x east 17.9, three story brk dwell'g on st and two-story brk stable on av. Gustav Lange and Alida his wife to Joseph L. Harris. June 13. 15,500

112th st, No. 306, s s, 100 e 2d av, 25x100.11, two-story frame dwell'g with one-story brk building on rear. Rocco Dia and Vittoria his wife to Lewis Z. Bach. Mt. $4,000. June 30. 7,000

114th st, No. 215, n s, 235 e 3d av. 25x100.11, five-story stone front flat. Sophie Rothschild to John M. Conway. Mt. $17,000. July 1. 26,000

116th st, s e cor Park av, 25x100.11, one-story frame building. Edward Philips and Theodora his wife to William Forster. Mt. $11,375. June 25. 23,000

117th st, No. 126, s s, 239.11 e Park av, 20x100.11, two-story frame dwell'g. Peter C. Carey and ano. exrs. William Carey to C. Cecelia and Amelia Carey. June 9. 7,000

118th st, No. 507, n s, 123.10 e Pleasant av, 24.2x100.11, five-story brk tenem't. Susan M. Thall to John T. Rothmann and Christina his wife. Mt. $8,000 June 29. 16,500

118th st, No. 507, n s, 123 10 e Pleasant av, 24.2x100.11, five story brk flat. John H. Elfers and Catharine his wife and Heinrich Offermann and Mary his wife to Susan M. Thall. Mt. $8,000. June 27. 16,000

121st st, No. 78, s s, 40 w Park av, 20x100.11, four-story stone front flat. Searles Babbitt and Caroline M. his wife to Louis E. Jacobson. Mt. $12,500. June 26. nom

121st st, No. 309, n s, 71 e 2d av, 26x75.8, four-story brk tenem't. Joseph Demmer and Elizabeth his wife to Augusta Fuhr. Mt. $9,000. July 1. 15,700

122d st, s s, 66.1 w St. Nicholas av, 50x100.11, vacant. Adele Hutton, Marquise de Portes, to Frederick Hulberg. June 25, 17,000

123d st, No. 440 E., s s, abt 175 w Pleasant av, 25x100, two-story frame dwell'g. William Austin to Rhoda B. Austin widow and Rhoda A. Austin. July 17, 1889. nom

123d st, s s, 275 e 7th av, 17.6x100.11. Release mort. The German-American Real Estate Title Guarantee Co. to Elizabeth K. Smith. June 30. consid. omitted

125th st, Nos. 47 and 49, n s, 247.6 e Lenox av, 37.6x99.11, two four-story stone front flats with stores. Marx Ottinger and Clara his wife and Moses Ottinger and Amelia his wife to Alfred Jewell. Mt. $35,000. June 22. 33,750

Same property. Emanuel Heilner and Moses J. Wolf and Katie his wife to Alfred Jewell. Mt. $35,000. June 24. 33,750

126th st, No. 47, n s, 215 w 4th av, 20x99.11, three-story stone front dwell'g. Foreclos. Gilbert M. Speir, Jr., to Teresa F. wife of Thomas F. Hayes. June 19 15,100

127th st, No. 220, s s, 172 w 7th av, 18x99.11, three-story stone front dwell'g. Ella I. wife of and Charles R. Shaw to Clara A. Ferdinand. Mt. $12,000. June 30. 20,000

131st st, No. 19, n s, 235 w 5th av, 25x99.11, five-story brk flat. Henry Hawkes and Flora A. his wife, Riverside, Conn., to Paul Eim. Mt. $17,000. July 1. 25,350

Same property. Release mort. Emelina Johnston to Henry Hawkes. July 1. nom

132d st, No. 53, n s, 376.8 e 6th av, 16.8x99.11, two-story frame dwell'g. Andrew C. Reid and Mary C. his wife to John C. Reid, Brooklyn. Q. C. Mt. $1,700. June 11. nom

Same property John C. Reid, Brooklyn, to Mary C. Reid. Q. C. Mt. $1,700. June 11. nom

133d st, No. 167 n s, 125 e 7th av, 25x99.11, five-story brk flat. Carl L. Griesmeyer and Leopoldin his wife to Joseph A. Kennell. B. & S. Mt. $12,500. June 27. nom

136th st, n s, 200 e of Convent av, being a new av bet 10th av and St. Nicholas av, runs north 161.8 x southeast 189.1 x south 86.9 x southwest 35.9 x southwest again 42.6 to 136th st, x west 142.6, vacant. James A. Deering and May his wife to David T. Dean. April 22. nom

137th st, n s, 300 e 6th av, 75x99.11, one-story frame building. George S. Hamlin assignee Joshua S. Peck, Robert C. Martin and Nathan Peck individ. and firm of Peek, Martin & Co. to Edwin H. and Walter J. Peck. C. a G. Sub. to dower of Mrs. Sarah K. Peck widow and taxes and assessm'ts $152. June 27. 9,230

Same property. Release dower. Sarah K. Peck widow to same. June 24. nom

140th st, n s, 150 e Grand Boulevard, 75x99.11, vacant. William E. Parsons, Jr., and Catharine C. his wife to Hugh Brien. Mt. $7,500. June 23. 12,150

140th st, n s, 225 e Grand Boulevard, 50x99.11, three-story frame dwell'g and vacant. William E. Parsons, Jr., and Catharine C. his wife to Henry Maibrunn. Mt. $10,000. June 23. 12,500

143d st, No. 304, s s, 100 w 8th av, 25x99.11, one-story frame building. John C. Sullivan and Juana R. O. his wife to Philip F. Sullivan. July 1, 1889. nom

145th st, Nos. 300–314 / 8th av, Nos. 2719–2725 } begins 8th av, s w cor 145th st, 208x99.11, eight five-story brk flats with stores. Foreclos. William J. Townsend to Horace Ingersoll. Sub. to morts. June 30 180,000

167th st, s s, 139.4 e Amsterdam av, 19.1x109.3x16x120.4. Release mort. George S. Dowley, Brattleboro, Vt., to John E. Cronly. June 26. 250

178th st, n s, 100 w Audubon av, 75x100. Pauline Simon to Samuel McCamman. June 15. 6,150

179th st, s s, 100 w Wadsworth av, 25x100. Pauline Simon to Michael Curley. June 9. 2,375

180th st, s s, 100 w Amsterdam av, 25x100. Pauline Simon to George T. Lorigan. June 12. 2,700

181st st, s s, 100 e Audubon av, 20x119.6. Isidor Herz and Henrietta his wife to Morris Manheimer. Mt. $2,500. June 12. nom

181st st, s s, 25 e 11th av, runs south 100 x west 25 to 11th av, x south 19.6 x east 100 x north 119.6 to 181st st, x west 75. Pauline Simon to Michael J. and Joseph F. Mulqueen. June 11. 22,800

Av A, Nos. 195 and 197 / 12th st, Nos. 441 and 443 } begins Av A, n w cor 12th st, 51.9x100, two four-story brk tenem'ts with stores on av and four-story brk tenem'ts with stores on st. Jacob Wieble and Christina his wife and Magdalena Endholz to Louis and Frauziska Haupt. Mt. $35,000. July 1. See Essex st. 65,000

Av B / 87th st } begins Av B, n w cor 87th st, 100.8x121; also,
All title in strip which is part of Av B, bounded west by w s Av B, south by n s 87th st, east by east line of tract conveyed by Jos. Young to John J. Astor and north by centre line of block extended east, vacant.
Charles Laue and Lena his wife, Brooklyn, to John J. Feenan and Ernest Hammer. Mt. $20,190. June 30. 40,000

Av C, No. 204, e s, 77.6 n 12th st, 25x62.3, four-story brk tenem't with stores. Frederick Bundstein and Louisa his wife to Alexander Erklin. Sub. to morts. and int. July 1. 14,000

Same property. Charles Bundstein to Frederick Bundstein. Q. C. June 30. nom

Amsterdam av, No. 309, e s, 87.4 n 74th st, 17x81, four-story brk dwell'g. Foreclos. Herbert E. Dickson to Annie V. wife of William Bryan. June 23. 15,200

Amsterdam av, No. 420, n w cor 80th st, 27.2x82, five-story brk store and flat. Robert and Joseph Gordon to Ludwig Riederer. Mt. $35,000. June 26. 53,500

Amsterdam (10th) av / 11th av / Audubon av / 175th st } begins 175th st, n s, extends from 10th av crossing Audubon av to 11th av, and being 63 on 10th av and 134 on 11th av. George F. Gantz to James Kearney, Hackensack, N. J. May 26. 100,000

Amsterdam av, w s, 25 n 178th st, 50x100. Isidor Herz and Henrietta his wife to Marcus A. Frank. Mt. $7,000. June 12. nom

Amsterdam av, w s, 25 s 180th st, 25x100.
Kingsbridge road, e s, 25.6 n 178th st, 76.7x81.3x75x96 8
Pauline Simon to Caleb M. Hillman. June 15. 16,600

Columbus (9th) av, Nos. 309 and 311, e s, 51 s 75th st, 51x100, two six-story brk flats with stores. William Smith to John J. Hughes. All liens. June 23. nom

Columbus av, Nos. 313 and 315, s e cor 75th st, 51.2x100, two six-story brk flats with stores. John P. Ryan to William H. Geishenen. Mt. $120,000. June 29. See 46th st. 180,000

Columbus av, No. 323, w s, 25.8 n 75th st, 25.6x100, five-story brk store and flat. Sarah Murray to Eleanor P. Gage. Mt. $36,000. June 29. See 83d st. nom

Columbus av, Nos. 1287–1293 / 124th st / Manhattan st or Hancock pl } begins Columbus (9th) av, s e cor 124th st, runs south 100.11 x east 200 x north 93.11 to Manhattan st, x northwest 15.1 x west 186.7, four five-story brk flats with store in No. 1293 on av, and four five-story brk flats on sts. Foreclos. George B. Newell to Nathan Wise and Adolph M. Bendheim. Mt. $24,500. June 2. 65,000

Lexington av, No. 1368, w s, 84 s 91st st, 16 6x88.3, three-story stone front dwell'g. Louisa wife of Otto Runk to Miron J. Rockwell. Mt. $10,000. June 17. 14,500

Lexington av, No. 1647, e s, 95.2 s 105th st, 15 10x70 to alley, three-story stone front dwell'g. Release mort. The Manhattan Life Ins. Co. to Carrie Meyer. June 22. 9,000

Same property. Carrie wife of Albert A. Meyer to Elise Meyer. June 22. 9,000

Lexington av, No. 1035, s e cor 74th st, 17.2x55, three-story brk (stone front) dwell'g. Hannah wife of and Morris Taylor to Ascher Weinstein. Mt. $10,000. June 29. See Division st. 20,000

Lexington av, s w cor 103d st, 56x100, vacant. William H. Gebhard and Cora his wife to Frederick Willenbrock and Egbert Winkler. June 24. 17,000

Mount Morris av, Nos. 35, 36, 37 and 38, s w cor 124th st, 100.11x100, six-story brk flat. William B. Franke and Anna his wife to Henry Franke. 3-10 part. Sub. to mort. July 1. nom

Same property. Same to Albert Franke. 7-10 part. July 1. nom

Madison av, No. 1584, w s, 50.11 n 106th 25x100, five-story stone front flat. Lizzie F. Brady widow to John A. Wicks and Kate M. his wife, joint tenants. Mt. $20,000. June 30. nom

Madison av, No. 524, w s, 25.5 n 54th st, 25x70, four-story stone front dwell'g. Mary A. Stokes widow to John S. Stokes et al. trustees Henry Stokes. March 11, 1887. 8,928

Same property. Mary A. Stokes et al. exrs., &c., Henry Stokes to Frank R. Lawrence. June 30. 48,500

Madison av, No. 713, e s, 20.5 n 63d st, 22x100, four-story stone front dwell'g. Belle F. wife of and William V. King to Julia A. Chase. June 26. 34,000

Park (4th) av, No. 389, e s, 78.5 s 54th st, 20x90, four-story stone front store and flat. Walter Reid to Robert W. Reid. Mt. $15,000. June 24. nom

South 5th av, No. 136, n w s, 125 n e Spring st, 25x69.6x25x69.4, four-story brk store and tenem't with three-story frame building on rear. Cesare Razzetti and Mary his wife and Guiseppe Razzetti and Marcello Razzetti and Maria M. his wife to William S. Whitman. Mt. $14,000. June 30. 19,500

Same property. William S. Whitman and Mary L. his wife to Denison P. Chesebro. Mt. $14,000. June 30. 19,500

St. Nicholas av / 159th st } begins St. Nicholas av, s e cor 159th st, runs east 163.8 x south 100 x west 50 x north 75 x west 109 to av, x north 25.5, two-story frame dwell'g and vacant. Jacob Vix and Elizabeth his wife to John H. Loos. Mt. $7,965. July 1. 22,000

Wadsworth av, e s, 75 n 178th st, 25x100. Pauline Simon to Mary E. Cowen. June 9. 2,300

Wadsworth av, e s, 75 s 179th st, 25x100. Same to William F. Cowen. June 9. 2,300

Wadsworth av, e s, 50 s 179th st, 25x100. Same to Jane Cowen. June 9. 2,300

West End av, s w cor 104th st, 100.11x100, two-story frame "Boulevard Club" house and vacant. Charles Weinberg to Jane A Brown. Mt. $40,000. June 26. 80,000

West End av, n e cor 93d st, 50.4x100, vacant. Richard V. Harnett and Kate L his wife to Henry W. Donald. June 30. nom

West End av, w s, 75.8 s 98th st, 25.3x100, vacant. Frank L. Smith and Magdalene his wife to Francis M. Jenks. Mt. $4,970. June 9. nom

West End av, s e cor 95th st, 21.4x100x24.1x100, vacant. Frank L. Smith and Magdalene his wife to Francis M. Jencks. Mt. $8,400. June 9. nom

1st av, No. 1097, n w cor 60th st, 25.5x100, five-story brk tenem't with stores. Annie A. Smith widow to Gepke wife of Albert Schulte. June 30. 27,000

1st av, No. 1454, e s, 122.2 n 75th st, 20x78, four-story brk store and tenem't. Morris Heyman and Rose his wife to Fanny Sickel. Mt. $6,000. June 30. 13,250

1st av, No. 837, w s, 22 s 47th st, 26x63, five-story brk tenem't with stores. Philip Levy and Bertha his wife to Barbara Gabrman, Long Island City. Q. C. and confirmation deed. June 29. nom

Same property. Barbara Gahrman, Long Island City, to Elise Laccorn. *Mt.* $6,121. June 30. 16,800

2d av, n w cor 100th st, 100.11x100. Release judgment. Louis Herow to Emil Broggelwirth. March 7. nom

Same property. Release dower. Ann Monaghan widow to same. June 25. nom

2d av, No. 1951, w s, 75.11 n 100th st, 25x100, five-story brk tenem't with stores. Release mort Samuel Weil to same. June 26. 300

Same property. Emil Broggelwirth and Pauline E. his wife to Louis Beer and Michael Shaffner. *Mt.* $16,000. June 26. nom

Same property. Louis Beer and Elisa his wife and Michael Shaffner and Kate his wife to Johanna Behrens. *Mt.* $16,000. June 30. nom

2d av, No. 1351, w s, 25 n 71st st, 25.9x64, five-story stone front tenem't with stores. Catharine Reinhardt, of Worms, Johann Reinhardt and Pauline his wife, of Offenbad, Margarethe Reinhardt, of Giess, Leonhard Reinhardt, of Darmstadt, George Reinhardt and Christina C. his wife, of Wald Michelbach, brothers and sisters of Francis J. Reinhardt to Frank Reinhardt. Q. C. May 15. nom

Same property. Frank and Josephine Reinhardt to Lena Levi. July 1. 23,100

2d av, Nos. 2055 and 2057 } begins 2d av, w s, 106th st, No. 248 } 50.6 s 106th st, runs south 50.3 x west 100 x north 100.9 to 106th st, x east 27 x south 50.6 x east 73, two four-story stone front tenem'ts with stores on av and four-story stone front tenem't on st. William C. Haight and Mary T. his wife to Elmore D. Alvord. All liens. June 30. nom

Same property. Elmore D. Alvord to Morris Moses. *Mt.* $50,500. June 30. See 89th st. nom

2d av, No. 2274, e s, 25.5 s 117th st, 25x84.10, four-story brk tenem't with stores. Thomas McManus and Eliza his wife to Bernard and Theresa F. Niskemper. *Mt.* $12,500. July 1. 19,200

3d av, No. 2103, s e cor 115th st, 26x100, five-story brk (stone front) flat with stores. John H. Hollman to Henry Hollman. *Mt.* $38,000. June 16. 60,000

3d av, No. 2071, e s, 100.11 s 114th st, 25.2x104.6, five-story stone front flat with store. Leopold Yankauer to James G. Patton. *Mt.* $18,000. June 30. 32,000

5th av, No. 95, s e cor 17th st, runs southeast 116.10 to alleyway, x southwest 20 x northwest 54.10 x west — x northwest 60 to av, x north 22.8, five-story brk store with one and three-story brk building on rear. Mary C. wife of and Theodore P. Austin and Rebecca B. Austin widow to W. Jennings Demorest. June 5. 100,000

Same property. W. Jennings Demorest and Ellen L. his wife to Wolf Dazian. June 27. 145,000

7th av, No. 203, e s, 87.3 s 22d st, 18.5x50, four-story stone front dwell'g. Mary A. G. McLochlin to Max Green. July 1. 15,000

10th av, No. 301, w s, 74.1 n 27th st, 24.8x100, five-story stone front tenem't with stores. Henry Meinken and Kate his wife to Rosa Jordan. *Mt.* $20,000. June 3. nom

11th av, w s, 75 s 179th st, 25x100. Benjamin Vollman and Lena his wife to Morris Vollman. ½ part. Sub to ½ mort. $16,000. July 1. 1,625

11th av, n w cor 179th st, 25x100. Pauline Simon to Benjamin and Morris Vollman. June 12. 5,200

11th av, e s, 25 n 173d st, 25x100. Release mort. Emma Berrian to Susan Bunce. June 6. nom

Lot begins at present dividing line bet Nos. 244 and 246 Monroe st, runs east to point 0.6 e from beginning of west wall of No. 246 Monroe st, x south 97.6 x west — x north 97.6 with portion of west wall of No. 246 Monroe st as stands on above. Joseph L. Buttenwieser to John V. Campbell. B. & S. Feb. 26. nom

MISCELLANEOUS.

All real estate, water rights, wharves, &c., in City of New York whereof Robert Kennedy died seized. Frances de Weiler an heir at law and devisee of Robert Kennedy to John G. Kennedy. ½ part. Feb. 17. nom

All title of grantor's interest to the undivided share or interest in residuary estate of Felix Stoiber dec'd. Louis Stoiber and Kate E. his wife, Adolphus H. Stoiber, Gustavus H. Stoiber and Laura M. his wife, Clara M. Stoiber and Louis and Adolphus H. Stoiber trustees of Felix Stoiber to Edward G. Stoiber and Lena his wife. Trust deed. March 16. nom

General assignment. Elijah H. Purdy, William Phyfe and Robert Clenighen, of E. H. Purdy & Co., to Hamilton R. Searles. Jan. 23. nom

General release, especially as to claims against estate of Charles Roth. Frederick Roth to Margarethe Roth. Aug. 9, 1880. 500

General release. Mary H. Trapp formerly Roth to same. May 13. 500

In the matter of David Blumenthal a lunatic. Order appointing Joseph Ullman committee of person and estate. June 25.

23d and 24th WARDS.

Balcom av, e s, 100 s Rae st, 10x24. Release mort. Sarah F. Martin to Joseph Roos. April 17. nom

Fairmount pl, s s, lot 109 map Henry Stoney estate, Tremont, 25x67.7x25x66.1. Release mort. John J. Brady to Charles A. Blair. June 29. consid omitted

Fairmount pl, s s, 372 w Marmion av, 25x66x25x67.7. Caroline A. Blair to John C. Embree. June 29. 650

Garden st, s w s, part lot 278 map Mott Haven, 20x100. Peter A. Hendrick referee to George S. Billings, Brooklyn. *Mt.* $800. July 1. 2,200

North st, n s, lot 388 map Mt. Eden, 50x100 to South Fordham, West Farms. Margarethe Nething widow and extrx. Jacob Nething to John P. Wenninger. June 30. 1,050

Powell pl, s s, 40 w Riverview terrace, 20x98. Mary A. Walker to Mary S. Thompson. June 30. 4,500

Teasdale pl, n s, 366.8 w Delmonico pl, 29.2x100. Louis Krause to Clara Pause. June 29. nom

Wetmore st, s s, 96.7 w Washington av, 100x100. Lucy Wadsworth to Margery Sutcliff. May 9. 3,500

7th st East, n e s, 250 s e Broadway or old Boston road, 50x100. Release mort. Mary A. E. Stewart to Mayor, &c., New York. May 13. nom

133d st, s s, 300 e Cypress av, 50x200 to 132d st. Julia Bradford, Oliver Springs, Tenn., to John H. Clapp, Portchester, N. Y. *Mt.* $2,500. June 25. nom

139th st, s s, 550 e Willis av, 50x100. Alfred B. Hall and Susie his wife to Eliza wife of Nicholas Cotter. *Mt.* $4,000. June 26. 10,500

148th st, s s, 340 w Brook av, runs west 250 x south 200 to 147th st, x east 270.4 x north 199.10. Foreclos. Elliot Sandford to The Bowery Savings Bank. Sub. to easement. June 26. 63,500

165th st, s s, 190 w 3d av, 46.10x100. John J. Wizeman and Eliza his wife to Gustave Ansel. *Mt.* $2,000. June 29. 5,500

170th st, s s, 119.9 w Franklin av, 18.11x123x18.10x124. Marion F. Driver to Arthur Arctander and Jacob Seabold, of Arctander & Seabold. *Mt.* $3,000. June 17. 5,000

Crotona av, n s, 353.6 e Broad st, 25x101.1x25x99. Henry B. Weselman to Mary E. Halley. *Mt.* $720. June 26. 1,500

Eagle av, w s, 50 s 163d st, 50x100. Foreclos. Richard H. Clarke to Myron W. Dow. July 1. 3,020

Elton av, s e cor 159th st, 48x100. Partition. Clarence W. Francis to Moise Geisemann. June 25. 5,050

Fleetwood av late 2d av, w s, lot 265 map Mt. Eden, near Upper Morrisania Depot, 50x100. Charles H. Zeltner and Mary M. his wife to William Urbach. Q. C. June 25. 1,600

Same property. Otto Oertel and Petronella his wife to Charles H. Zeltner. Q. C. May 9. nom

Grant av, e s, 80.6 s 162d st, 50x105. Andrew H. Kellogg and Helen M. his wife to James Noble. Dec. 19, 1889. 2,000

Morris av, w s, 20.5 s 143d st, 87.6x3.10x40x85. Thomas Overington and Mary C. his wife to William W. Burgoyne. June 17. nom

Same property. William W. Burgoyne and Agnes L. his wife to Cecelia Levy. *Mt.* $2,500. June 30. 4,037

Opdyke av, n s, 25 w 2d st, 25x100. Cornelia M. wife of Isaac H. Walker, Bayville, L. I., to Timothy Donovan. June 16. 200

Opdyke av, n s, 50 w 2d st, 25x100. George B. Sealey to same. June 29. 200

Prospect av, w s, 100 n 175th st, 75x100. Henry J. Baach and Eugenia his wife to Mary A. Euler. June 27. 4,500

Railroad or Vanderbilt av, n e cor 187th or Jacob st, 112.6x100. Henry Humphreys and Alice W. his wife to Robert E. Humphreys. July 1. 1,500

Railroad or Vanderbilt av, s e cor 184th or Wetmore st, 25x100. Same to same. July 1. 1,500

Tinton av, e s, 180.11 n Cedar st, 19.1x100. Georgio Narberti and Giovanna De M. his wife to Thomas Hanley and Maria his wife. *Mt.* $1,250. June 29. 3,600

Taylor av, w s, 117.5 s Columbia av, 23x102.9. Ellen Donohue to George Peters and Maggie his wife, joint tenants. June 20. 2,600

Verio or Veno av formerly 1st st, e s, 174.2 s Clifford st formerly Clinton av, 50x100. George W. Oakley and Mary T. his wife to James K. Haslam. Cleveland, Ohio. July 1. 1,600

Vanderbilt av, s e s, 80 n e 178th st, 28x100. Eugene A. Philbin and Jessie H. his wife to David B. Ogden. May 28. other consid. and 100

Vanderbilt or Railroad av, s w cor 176th st, 58x100. James B. Dill trustee to Louis S. Eickwort. June 19. nom

Same property. Partition. William J. Townsend to Louis S. Eickwort. June 20. 6,445

Webster av, s w cor 174th st, 25x86. Margaret wife of Thomas Lusk to Martha wife of Eugene Schaefer. June 15. 1,500

Washington av, e s, 25.1 s 171st st, 50.1x100x50x102.8. Walter J. McIndoe to Israel C. Jones. June 25. 5,400

3d av, w s, lot 24 map Upper Morrisania, 50x90. Patrick Connor and Ellen his wife to Isidore Bloch. June 29. 7,000

Interior lot, 331.4 s e from s e cor 163d st and Washington av and 100 s w 163d st, runs southwest 123 x southeast 40 x northeast 123 x northwest 40. Release mort. Bowery Bank of New York to Frank York. June 10. nom

Same property. Partition. William N. Armstrong to same. June 19. 4,000

Interior lot, 125.11 w 3d av and 100 s 163d st, runs south 123 x west 40 x 123 x 40. Frank Yoran and Lillie T. his wife to Elizabeth Twitchin. B. & S. June 19. 4,000

Lot 45 map 71 lots Kingsland estate at Morris Heights. Hugh N. Camp and Elizabeth D. his wife to Mary Hogan. June 15. 750

Lots 46 and 47 map 71 beautiful lots, Kingsland estate, Morris Heights, 24th Ward. Hugh N. Camp and Elizabeth D. his wife to Mary E. Halley. June 15. 1,500

Lot 24 damage map for acquiring title to East 158th st from Railroad av East to 3d av, 23d Ward. Release mort. Andrew Wengler and Magdalena his wife to same. Feb. 28. nom

Lot 12 damage map for opening German pl from Westchester av to Brook av; also, parcel No. 2 on map for opening Rae st from St. Anns av to German pl. Release mort. Silas D. Gifford to same. May 12. nom

Parcel No. 6 on damage map for acquiring title to German pl from Westchester av to Brook av. Release mort. Harlem Savings Bank to Mayor, &c., N. Y. May 26. nom

Parcel No. 9 on damage map for acquiring title to East 173d st from Weeks st to 3d av. Release mort. Same to same. June 22. nom

Parcel No. 3 on damage map for opening 169th st in 23d Ward. Release mort. The New York and Suburban Co-operative Building and Loan Assoc. to same. May 18. nom

Parcel No. 5 on damage map for opening East 173d st from Weeks st to 3d av, 24th Ward. Release mort. The Mutual Life Ins. Co. New York, to same. May 1. 400

Parcel No. 28 damage map for opening East 169th st from Franklin av to East 167th st, 23d Ward. Release mort. Matthew Rock to same. April 7, 1891. nom

The west ½ of lot 18 damage map for opening 159th st from Railroad av East to 3d av. Release mort. Mary A. Lodge to same. Sept. 23, 1890. nom

LEASEHOLD CONVEYANCES.

Clinton pl, No. 29, n s, 165.11 e University pl, 25x93.11. Assign. lease. Simon Adler and Henry S. Herrman to William G. Vander Roest. 8,500

William st, n e cor Fulton st. Assign. lease. Edward F. Brunjes to John H. Hake. nom

West st, No. 305. Assign lease. Henry Steffens and Frederick Schumacher to The Burr Brewing Co. nom

Same property. Assign. lease. William Meyn and Arnold Schutt to Henry Steffens and Frederick Schumacher. nom

18th st, No. 43 E. Assign. lease. Antonio Viano to Nancy Viano. nom

19th st, n s, 375 e 9th av, 24.9x91.11. Katharine T. Moore to Emilie Revinius. 21 years, from May 1, 1891, per year, taxes and 820

Columbus av, No. 734. Assign. lease. Frederick Wolfe to Sidney Schwab. nom

Madison av, n e cor 59th st, 100x90. Leo Schlesinger and Joseph Hecht to Frederick J. N. Jaeger. 20 years, from Feb. 1, 1892, per year, 25,000, 35,000

2d av, No. 551, store, &c. Assign. lease. George Rossler to Leopold O. Rauser. nom

3d av, No. 2394. Assign. lease. Harry Leopold to Henry J. Robinson and Matilda Seaman. nom

KINGS COUNTY.

JUNE 25, 26, 27, 29, 30, JULY 1.

Ashford st, e s, 200 n Hegeman av, 40x100. Adolph Sussman to Charles H. Ray. $410

Ashford st, w s, 145 s Stanley av, 20x100. Same to Friedrich Rusterholz. 75

Adelphi st, s e cor De Kalb av, runs south 31.1 x east 53.6 x southeast 42.2 x northeast 13.10 x northwest 106.4. John C. Valentine to Ellen Benedict. *Mt.* $8,000. nom

Bayard st, s s, 280.3 w Humboldt st, 20.6x100. Thomas P. Kenna to Savina Desanti. *Mt.* $1,000. 2,450

Same property. Savino Desanti to Gaetani Machia. ½ part. Sub. to morts. $1,450. 1,225

Bradford st, w s, 175 n Liberty av, 75x100. *Mt.* $5,000. Henry Katzmann contracts to exchange above property with Bessie Schneider for farm of 45 acres, at Sweet Hollow, L. I., and pay 2,000

Baltic st, s s, 435 e 4th av, 20.4x55.8. George Bowker trustee Theresa M. Bowker to Carolyn T. Bowker. 3,250

Bergen st, s s, 137.10 e Rogers av, 94.8x132.4x49x125. John P. D. Angus to Asa C. Brownell. 14,000

Bergen st, s s, 100 e Rogers av, 37.10x125x38.10x113.3. William W. Pratt to Asa C. Brownell. *Mt.* $1,000. 5,000

Bergen st, s s, 325 w Howard av, 25x127.9. Patrick Fannon to Morris Riley. Dated 1873. 1,450

Bergen st, n e s, 80 s e Nevins st, 45x100. }
Bergen st, n e s, 125 s e Nevins st, 25x100. }
Partition. James C. Church ref. to Fannie E. Bedell. 7,300

Bergen st, n s, 300 w Rockaway av, 25x107.2. Charles J. Hobe to Rosanna McCormack. Q. C. 85

Same property. Washington Sackmann to same. nom

Bergen st, s s, 145 e Kingston av, 20x100. Sidney V. Lowell to Harriet O. Pettiner. Correction deed. Q. C. nom

Bergen st, s s, 200 w Troy av, 25x127.9. John H. Barnes to William H. Cornell. 50

Berkeley pl, s s, 169 e 7th av, 20x95. Max Goebel to Rosalie J. Goebel. nom

Boerum st, s s, 125 e Ewen st, 50x100. Release judgment. Francis Rausch and Henry Pastorell exrs. Henry Rausch to Ernest Ochs. 250

Boerum st, s s, 125 e Ewen st, 50x100. Jacob Bossert to Bertha Zeisner widow. *Mt.* $9,-000. 17,000

Bond st, s w cor Degraw st, 25x85, h & l. George E. Bellamy to Helena wife of John E. Wulp. 9,150

Broadway, n s, 75 e Hull st, 21x100. James T. Benedict to John W. A. Marsland. *Mt.* $3,-500. 5,000

Butler st, s s, 169.10 e Bedford av, 20x127.9. Peter Ritter to Christian and Magdalena Ritter. 2,200

Butler st, n s, 145 e Howard av, 20x61x20.7x57. Partition. William M. Hoes ref. to Hiram L. Friedlander. 115

Cedar st, s e s, 166.4 s w Myrtle av, 22.7x67.3x18.3x65, h & l. Mary wife of Charles Martin to George Kessel. *Mt.* $2,000. 4,400

Canton st, e s, 67.6 n Myrtle av, runs east 73.8 x northwest 68.4 x southwest 61.9 x west 23.7 x south 20. Eliza D. Heatley to George W. Heatley. *Mt.* $1,800. 4,000

Chauncey st, s s, 211 e Saratoga av, 19x100. Release mort. John W. Phelps to Samuel V. Hyer. nom

Same property. Release mort. Charles D. King and George W. Adams to same. 1,000

Chauncey st, s s, 230 e Saratoga av, 19x100. Release from liens, &c. Daniel and Frank J. Gallagher to Michael McGrath and George Burns. 43

Chester st, s w cor Sackett st, 100x100. Edward E. Bergen to Silas A. Condict. *Mt.* $900. nom

Same property. Silas A. Condict to David Klein. *Mt.* $900. 2,700

Chestnut st, e s, 1,075 n 5th st, 25x150. Adeline B. Smith to Margaret Messner. 550

Cleveland st, e s, 103 n Vienna av, 40x100. Adolph Sussman to Matilda E. Ray. 330

Cleveland st, e s, 270 s New Lots road, 40x100. Adolph Sussmano to Charles W. Tomlinson. 450

Clifton pl, s s, 135 e Bedford av, 15x100, h & l. Alanson Trask to Arthur J. Noonan. B. & S. 5,500

Same property. Fannie W. wife of Rollin E. Beers to same. Q. C. nom

Same property. Fannie W. wife of Rollin E. Beers to same. Q. C. nom

Same property. Arthur J. Noonan, of New York, to Howard McWilliams. In consideration of assuming mort. of 5,000

Columbia Heights, w s, 100.7 s Pineapple st, 25x112. George W. Stetson, of New York, to Winthrop Pond. Q. C. nom

Columbia st, n w cor Carroll st, 20x80, h & l. Alice Regan widow to Adolph Ketchum. *Mt.* $2,500. 10,500

Columbia pl, w s, 90 n Atlantic av, 22.6x75.
Pacific st, n s, 69.10 w Willow st, 25x50.
Thomas, Margaret, Patrick and James Malley children of John Malley to Catharine widow of John Malley. Q. C. nom

Columbia st, w s, 90.4 s Seabring st, 17.11x76. Agostino Dondero, of New York, to Andrew Rosasio. *Mt.* $2,200. 3,000

Conselyea st, n s, 75 e Graham av, 25x100. Oscar Kent one of the devisees under will of Delilah Kent to Evelyn wife of Samuel M. Hull one of the devisees under same will. ½ part. Q. C. 625

Covert st, n w s, 275 n e Evergreen av, 18x100. William H. Barton to Matilda L. Hay. *Mt.* $3,000. 4,200

Dean st, n s, 200 e Nostrand av, 100x100. Jerome S. Plummer to John A. Bliss. 17,000

Dean st, s s, 215 e Rogers av, 60x114.5. Eliot McCormick to Edgar W. Abbot. 15,000

Dean st, s s, 366.8 w Buffalo av, 33.4x107.2. Henry Weil to Joseph D. Clayton. 1,600

Dean st, s s, 337.6 e Hoyt st, 22x100. Margaret McGarry to Charlotte H. wife of Nathan Comstock. *Mt.* $4,000. 7,500

Dean st, n s, 175 w Rochester av, 50x107.2. Mary A. widow, John Harrison to Albert Howard. 1,400

Dresden st, e s, 150 s Arlington av, 50x100. William Clendenning to Phoebe M. Van Buren. 300

Same property. Phoebe M. Van Buren to William Macdonald. 975

Decatur st, n s, 160 w Howard av, 200x100. Foreclos. John Courtney to Joseph P. Puels. 15,000

Same property. Release mort. William Ziegler to Joseph P. Puels. 12,800

Decatur st, n s, 209.8 w Howard av, 275.4x100. John S. Spencer to Thomas H. Radcliffe. *Mt.* $19,200. 25,437

Eastern Parkway, s s, 25 e Osborn st, 25x100. Release mort. Herbert C. Smith to Barnet Frank and Simon Rose. 1,350

Eastern Parkway, s w cor Powell st, 50x100. Henry F. Smith exr. Rosa A. Smith to Leon Weltfish. 1,800

Elm pl, w s, 100 n Livingston st, 75x148.11x75.9x137.6. Release mort. Michael H. Hagerty et al. trustees for Chanly McConvill to Richard Hyde and Louis C. Behman. nom

Essex st, e s, 100 n Ridgewood av, 20x200 to Shepherd av. Thomas Everit to Fred. J. Swift. *Mt.* $800. 1,500

Ewen st, w s, 100 s Jackson st, 25x100. Foreclos. Edward P. Simms to Andrew J. Onderdonk. 1,400

Fleet pl, e s, 225 n Willoughby st, 25x92x27x84. Mary Heery to Abraham Burtis. 3,500

Same property. Abraham Burtis to Stephen P. Cox. 4,500

Floyd st, s s, 230 w Marcy av, 25x100. Margaretha Hermann to John G. Hassler. *Mt.* $3,200. 6,850

Fulton st, n s, 185.8 w Nostrand av, 20x70, h & l. Charlotte M. Carpenter to Thomas Everit. *Mt.* $7,300. exch

Fulton st, s s, 200 e Rockaway av, 100x100. William H. Scott, of New York, to Thomas McDonald. *Mt.* assumed $7,000. 17,500

Fulton st, n s, 50 w Essex st, 25.6x92.6x25x—to beginning. B am Lipsky to Herman Stoff. *Mt.* $1,900enj in 3,500

Fulton st, n s, 180.2 e Bedford av, 20x100. John Adamson to Martin Joost. nom

Garfield pl, s w s, 172.10 n w 8th av, 100x100. Edward H. Moubray to Thorvald and Louis Anderson. 20,000

Garfield pl, n s, 90 w 7th av, 150x100. John H. Styles, New York, to Edward L. Beekman. nom

Glen st, s s, 74 w Crescent st, 26x100. John E. Smith to Harvey W. Fawcett. *Mt.* $2,000. 3,300

Hall st, e s, 84 n Myrtle av, 40x100. Thomas Hanlon to Mary A. wife of Michael F. McGoldrick. *Mt.* $5,000. 8,100

Hall late Elm st, s s, 110 w St. Nicholas av, 40x100.
Greene av, n s, 290 w St. Nicholas av, 20x100.
Louise Wagner, formerly Kraemer, to Otto F. Wagner. nom

Halsey st, s e s, 220 s w Central av, 20x100, h & l. David C. Long, New York, to George Furbeshaw. nom

Halsey st, n s, 365 w Marcy av, 40x87x40.2x93. Susanna E. C. wife of Walter C. Russell to David H. Valentine. 6,400

Halsey st, n s, 67.10 w Lewis av, 17.10x100. Lucy M. wife of and Morris Nunan to Emily F. wife of William Kloth. *Mt.* $3,000. 6,000

Hancock st, s s, 77 e Howard av, 17x80. Anna Liesenberg, of New York, to Max Goebel. *Mt.* $1,200. nom

Hancock st, n s, 145 w Ralph av, 16.8x85. Foreclos. Richard B. Greenwood, Jr., ref. to Israel Meyers. 2,000

Hancock st, n s, 250 e Lewis av, 37.6x100. Carrie L. Gibson to Wesley C. Bush. nom

Hancock st, n s, 287.6 e Lewis av, 37.6x100. Thomas O. Davidson to Wesley C. Bush. nom

Hancock st, n s, 425 e Lewis av, 25x100. Michael Lynan to Wesley C. Bush. *Mt.* $1,000. 2,500

Hanson pl, s s, 40 e Hampden st, 20x90. Sophronia P. wife of and James L. Hodge to Franklin W. Crandell, of Garden City, N. Y. *Mt.* $2,000. nom

Same property. Franklin W. Crandell to James L. Hodge. *Mt.* $2,000. nom

Hart st, s e s, 120 n e Broadway, 20x73.3x20x73.8. Henry Vollweiler to Bertha wife of Levi Kaufmann. *Mt.* $3,000. exch

Hayward st, s s, 54 e Bedford av, 20x80, h & l. Mary B. Riker, Somerville, N. J., to Poline Byk. *Mt.* $7,000. nom

Same property. Poline wife of Morris Byk to Henrietta wife of Alexander Falke. *Mt.* $7,-000. 11,500

Hendrix st, e s, 94.6 s Arlington av, 25x100. Harriet E. Roberts widow to Arthur E. Sumner. *Mt.* $2,500. nom

Henry st, w s, 75 n Huntington st, 50x93. William Mortal to John Caulfield. 2,200

Herbert st, s s, extends from North Henry st to Monitor st, 200x150. John Loughlin to St. Cecilia's Roman Catholic Church. All liens. nom

Herkimer st, s s, 38 e Pleasant pl, 19x90. Foreclos. John Courtney sheriff to Charles Griffen et al. trustees Samuel Willets dec'd. 2,500

Herkimer st, s s, 19 e Pleasant pl, 19x90. Same to same. 2,500

Herkimer st, s s, 76 e Pleasant pl, 19x90. Same to Charles Griffen et al. trustees of the Religious Society of Friends of New York. 2,500

Herkimer st, s s, 57 e Pleasant pl, 19x90. Same to same. 2,500

Hope st, n s, 100 e Keap st, 25x100. Carl J. Emmert to Bertha T. Emmert. nom

Hopkins st, s s, 425 e Marcy av, 25x100. Mary Schwarzwaelder widow to Leopold Michel. 5,300

Same property. Leopold Michel to John Hasselbach. *Mt.* $3,000. 6,500

Hooper st, n s, 105 e Marcy av, runs east 20 x north 96 x west or northwest — x south — to beginning. George R. Kimmel to John Brentano. 7,200

Hooper st, s w cor South 1st st, 45x72.8, hs & ls. John Brown to Henry C. Hearns. *Mt.* $2,000. nom

Java st, n s, 505 e Franklin st, 50x100. William H. Devins, of Whitestone, N. Y., to Margaret J. Devins. Q. C. nom

Same property. Margaret J. Devins to Susan wife of William H. Devins. Q. C. nom

Jerome st, w s, 84.11 n Atlantic av, 25x95. Rudolph C. Wittman to Benjamin Berkovits, New York, and Julie Addis. *Mt.* $7,200. 9,000

Lawton st, s e s, 192.4 n e Broadway, 25x90. George Straub to Peter Weber. *Mt.* $4,500. 9,250

Lawrence st, w s, 100 n Willoughby st, 28x107.6. Thomas Carter, of Boonton, N. J., to George Russell. 9,000

Leonard st, s e cor Johnson av, 25x100. Frederick Zoeller to Isaac, Gustav and Samuel Dreyer. *Mt.* $1,500. nom

Lincoln pl, s s, 237.6 w 6th av, 18.9x100. Edwin D. Phelps to Henry V. Raymond. nom

Livingston st, n s, 497 e Smith st, 20.8x112. William Spence to Lucy E. Stoddard. nom

Lafayette st, s s, 80 w Debevoise st, 20x80. Supreme Council A. and A. Scottish Rite of Freemasonry, &c., to James M. Spear. 5,500

Macon st, n s, 23 w Ralph av, 90x100. Release mort. Bernard Levino, Horatio S. Stewart, Alfred Vanderwerken and George C. Cranford to Benjamin C. Raymond. 1,000

Macon st, s s, 235 w Lewis av, 120x100. John F. Saddington to E. Willard Jones. 16,200

Macon st, No. 741, n s, 290.10 e Ralph av, 18x100. F. Augustus Conkling to George Harper. *Mt.* $4,000 6,600

Madison st, n s, 153.6 e Franklin av, 17.2x100. Esther R. wife of and Alanson H. Tifft to Alexander F. Crichton. *Mt.* $2,500. 4,550

Madison st, n s, 190 e Sumner av, 20x100. Agnes wife of and Fred'k Kraemer to Daniel J. Maujer. *Mt.* $6,000. nom

Same property. Daniel J. Maujer to Isabel Henderson. *Mt.* $6,000. 7,900

Madison st, n s, 300 w Tompkins av, 25x100. Elizabeth F. Driscoll to Mary Brown. 3,000

Marion st, n s, 56.3 e Howard av, 18.9x100. Anna B. wife of Joseph H. McKennee to Thorndyke C. McKennee. *Mt.* $2,000. 3,500

McDougal st, n s, 825 e Tompkins av, 75x100. William Johnston to John O. Whitenack. 4,800

McDonough st, s s, 38.9 w Lewis av, 18.9x100, h & l. Thomas Everit to Charlotte M. Carpenter. *Mt.* $4,500. 7,350

McDonough st, s s, 402.2 e Tompkins av, 20.2x100, h & l. Anna H. Pratt to Fannie W. Peloubet. *Mt.* $8,000. nom

Same property. Fannie W. Peloubet to Spencer T. Pratt and Anna H. his wife, joint tenants. *Mt.* $8,000. nom

McDonough st, s s, 162.6 w Throop av, 20x100. Jennie L. Parsons to Frances C. Thorburn. *Mt.* $7,400. 11,000

Montague st, s s, 26.6 e Henry st, 25x100. Irving Fish, of New York, to Matilda M. Strouse. 40,000

Milford st, e s, 100 n Liberty av, 75x100. John L. Carr to Stephen W. Stoothoff. 1,500

Monroe st, n s, 125 e Marcy av, 100x100. John H. Atwater to George B. Stoutenburg. B. & S. and C. a. G. 11,000

Monroe st, n s, 200 w Tompkins av, 20x100. Frances C. wife of and Frank M. Thorburn to Martin Battle. 5,400

Moore st, s s, 264 e Bushwick av, 25x100. Isaac Gutman to Gottlieb and Margaretha Stumpp. nom

Same property. Gottlieb Stumpp and Margaretha his wife to Ferdinand Feldblum and Kaufmann Fisher. *Mt.* $3,000. 3,550

Moore st, s s, 175 e Leonard st, 50x100.
Moore st, s s, 150 w Ewen st, 25x100.
Jacob Paskusz and Israel Feldman to Isaac Ginsburg, New York. *Mt.* $33,000. 54,000

Moore st, n s, 446.2 e Bushwick av, 25x100. Sigmund Bleyer to Joseph Fein. *Mt.* $4,400. 5,800

Moore st, s s, 100 w Morrell st, 25x100, h & l. John Scherder or Scherter to Jacob H. Werbelovsky and Louis Lurie. 3,850

Montague st, s s, 26.6 e Henry st, 25x100. Foreclos. John Courtney, Sheriff, to Irving Fish, of New York. 23,400

Myrtle st, Myrtle and Bushwick avs, known as Triangular Block, lot 1 block 1059 assessm't map, 18th Ward. John C. McGuire, Registrar Arrears, to Peter and Louis Totans. 75

Morrell st, w s, 25 s Moore st, 25x100. Frank Schaller to Abraham Wishinsky and Harris Rosenberg, of New York. *Mt.* $1,600. 3,600

Nassau st, s s, 284.3 e Jay st, 50x100. *Mt.* $18,000.
Union st, n s, 100 w 4th av, 50x95. *Mt.* $17,500.
Samuel McBride to William A. McBride in trust. In trust to repay Robert P. McBride $15,540. nom

Nassau st, n s, 78.9 w Adams st, —x103x45 x south 15 x west 2.5 x south 85. Gordon L. Ford to James Constable. *Mt.* $14,000. 16,000

Noble st, n s, 145 e Franklin st, 25x100. John McCort to John Martin. *Mt.* $3,800. 6,750

Osborn st late Ocean av, e s, 150 s Duryea av, 25x100. Francis Perry to Johanna Witz. 1877. 130

Ormond pl, w s, intersecting n s land Rem Lefferts, runs north 61.8 to point 250 s Putnam av, x west 145 x south 48.3 x east 145.7; also,
Ormond pl, w s, 268.8 n Fulton st, runs west 10 x west 45.8 x west 44.4 to point 0.3 n Ormond pl, x north 9 x east 100 to beginning.
Delphine S. wife of George Penniman to John Doyle. *Mt.* $2,000. 8,000

Ocean Parkway, w s, 340 n Av N, 60x350 to East 5th st, Gravesend. Thomas Ferguson to Tillie Kyle. 3,000

Osborn st, w s, 25 s Sutter av, 25x100. Chone Lonstein to Anna Wilson, of Wayne Co., Pa. 3,200

Same property. Chone Lonstein to Anna Wilson. *Mt.* $1,600. 3,200

Osborn st, e s, 150 n Eastern Parkway, 25x100. Moritz Blum and Emanuel Schwartz to Joseph Morris. 740

Osborn st, w s, 200 s Belmont av, 25x100. Max Pokalsky and Louis Lebewohl, of New York, to Abram J. Littmann, of New York. *Mt.* $4,280. 6,100

Osborn st, e s, 200 s Sutter av, 75x100. Contract. Henry and I. Jarkowitz to Sophia Blanck. 4,650

Osborn st, e s, 240 s Livonia av, 100x100. Alonzo E. De Baun to Philip Weinreb, of New York. 1,600

Osborn st formerly Ocean av, e s, 150 s Dumont av formerly Duryea av, 25x100. Johanna Witz to Benjamin Hyman. 425

Osborn st, e s, 100 s Livonia av, 100x100. Benjamin Marder to Harris Max. C. a. G. *Mt.* $1,000. 2,050

Pacific st, n s, 36 e Rockaway av, 16x80. Helena wife of and William H. H. Robbins to Edward H. Davidson. *Mt.* $1,850. 1,350

Same property. Edward H. Davidson to George P. and Enoch Jacobs. Sub. to mort. 3,000

Palmetto st, s e s, 184 s w Knickerbocker av, 17x100, h & l. James S. Leonard to Raymond D. and Kate Woodhall. *Mt.* $2,500. 4,000

Pellington pl, e s, 45 s of Cemetery of Evergreens, 20x75. William Metz to Charles Schoene and Mary his wife, joint tenants. *Mt.* $2,000. 2,500

President st, s s, 314.6 w 5th av, 35x100. Albert Matthews to George R. Brown. *Mt.* $12,500. nom

President st, s s, 38 e 7th av, 17.6x100. Foreclos. John Courtney to Samuel Winslow, Worcester, Mass. 7,500

President st, centre line, 169.9 w Kingston av, runs west 174.3 x north 308.1 to centre Union st, x west 77.8 x north 238.1 to s s Sackett st, x east 181.6 x south 238.1 to centre Union st, x east 70.5 x south 308.1 to beginning. Sarah wife of and John T. Walker to Almira F. Pierce, of Providence, R. I. nom

President st, s s, 331.6 w 5th av, 17x100. George R. Brown to William H. Doty, Yonkers. *Mt.* $5,500. exch

Prospect pl, s s, 205 e Franklin av, 18x131, h & l. William O. Hamlin to Julia M. Hamlin. *Mt.* $4,000. nom

Quincy st, n s, 21 e Marcy av, 24x76.3x24.2x72.11, h & l. Charles F. Hunt to Oscar Haviland, Saugerties, N. Y. *Mt.* $8,000. nom

Quincy st, s s, 125 w Nostrand av, 20x100. William H. Hart to Nostrand Av Methodist Episcopal Church. *Mt.* $3,000. 7,000

Quincy st, s s, 275 w Marcy av, 25x100. Mary E Phelps to Elbert C. Martin. *Mt.* $3,500. 4,000

Quincy st, s s, 100 w Stuyvesant av, 90x100. William H. Scott to Rufus L. Scott. B. & S. nom

Scholes st, s s, 50 w Waterbury st, 25x100, h & l. Christian Striffler and Emil Rudolph to John Dittmar. 2,500

Seigel st, s s, 100 w Humboldt st, 75x100, hs & ls. Nicholas Will to David Stern. All title. *Mt.* $15,000. 17,937

Seigel st, n s, 175 e Graham av, 25x100, h & l. Leo H yma to Samuel Parshelsky. *Mt.* $1,800. e n 3,600

Stagg st, n w cor Waterbury st, runs west 50 x north 100 x east 38.8 to Waterbury st, x south 54.3 and 47 to beginning. Mary S. wife of Charles R. Baker to Frederick Zoeller. nom

Suydam st, s e s, 280 n e Broadway, 20x75. Frank J. Miller to Henry Zehner. 4,600

Skillman st, w s, 133.4 s Tillary st, 16.8x100, h & l. Frank Stark to Hjalmer Holm. *Mt.* $1,800. 2,600

Strong pl, e s, 266 n Degraw st, 16.6x106.2. Louis Lehn to Wilhelmine Reiner. 8,000

Tompkins pl, w s, 170 n Degraw st, 20x112.6. Phebe A. Brown to Paul S. Brown. *Mt.* $4,500. nom

Union st, n e s, 346.8 s e Hoyt st, 16.8x75. Christopher Perkins, Maria L. Vaughan, Fannie, Charles, Mary and Harrie Perkins heirs Harriet Perkins to Philip H. Horton. *Mt.* $2,500. nom

Van Sielen st, w s, 304.3 s Av T, runs west 235.5 x southeast to lands of Theodore S. Jenkins, x east 144 to Van Sielen st, x north 124 to beginning, Gravesend. Juliet L. Pinckney widow to Sarah G. Loud. 6,000

Varet st, n s, 100 w Humboldt st, 25x100. Frederick Stroh to Semche Simon, of New York. 3,800

Watkins st, w s, 240 s Livonia av, 100x100. Alonzo E. De Baun to Abram Wolf and Herman Goldstein, of New York. 2,000

Watkins st, w s, 240 s Livonia av, 100x100. Abram Wolf to Louis and Joseph Eisenberg, of New York. ½ part. *Mt.* $1,500. 1,263

Watkins st, e s, 150 n Riverdale av, 150x100. Harriet T. Smith to Mary W. Smith. 1,900

Watkins st, w s, 100 s Livonia late Linington av, 100x100. Alonzo E. De Baun to Samuel Rosenbaum and Charles Faber, New York. 1,700

West st, e s, 620 s Av J, 100x100, New Utrecht. John W. Miller to Ellen Williams, of Sayre, Pa. *Mt.* $600. 1,550

West st, e s, 100 s Av J, 80x200 to Gravesend av; also,
West st, e s, 220 s Av J, 40x100, New Utrecht
Same to same. *Mt.* $1,300. 3,000

Withers st, n s, 140 e Humboldt st, 60x100. Arthur G. Stone to The Faith Mission Assoc. 3,000

Willoughby st, s s, 80 e Grand av, 20x90. Isaac O. Horton, Jr., to Julia E. wife of George W. Bennett. *Mt* $6,000. 8,500

Walworth st, w s, 290 s Willoughby av, 20x100. John R. Woods to Frank H. Tyler. *Mt.* $1,800. exch

Warren st, n s, 450 w Smith st, 20.10x100. Theressa J. Hunt to Berth S. Caccia. 7,400

Willow pl, w s, 173.2 n State st, 24.9x80, h & l. James Foster to Harry E. Sandford. *Mt.* $2,500. 4,500

2d st, n s, 130 e 6th av, 20x100. Nathaniel Niles to Marston Niles. 2,250

2d st, n s, 150 e 6th av, 40x100. Nathaniel Niles, of New York, to Fred'k W. Shrump, of Montclair, N. J. nom

2d pl, n s, 120 w Clinton st, 23.4x133.5. Foreclos. John Courtney to Ranald H. Macdonald. 4,750

East 2d st, e s, 248 n Av P, 188.6x189.9x189.6x190, Gravesend. Elizabeth Stillwell to James M. Saulpaugh. 1,400

South 2d st, n e s, 200 s e Hooper st, 23x46x48x87, h & l. Bird C. Leonard to Belinda E. Leonard Angulo. Q. C. 25

East 2d st, w s, 258 n Greenwood av, 25x100, Flatbush. E. M. Parker to Hiland H. Hervey. 350

3d st, s s, 128 e Smith st, runs south 80 x east 0.8 x south 20 x east 18.4 x north 100 to 3d st, x west 19 to beginning. Vina A. Sumner, of Syracuse, N. Y., to Jeannett Henry. *Mt.* $3,500. 5,000

3d st, n s, 161 e 5th av, 21x90. Foreclos. John Courtney to Amzi Dodd, of Bloomfield, N. J. 6,500

East 4th st, e s, 335.3 n Greenwood av, 25x100, Flatbush. Charles Brady to Mary Silvester, New York. 2,100

5th st, s w s, 97.10 n w 5th av, runs southwest 100 x northwest 300 x southwest 100 to 6th st, x northwest 200 x northeast 200 to 5th st, x southeast 500 to beginning. Charles D. Burwell to Frank A. Barnaby. Sub. to morts. nom

North 5th st, s s, 100 w Roebling st, 25x100. Ann and Bridget Kelly to John Repp. *Mt.* $2,500. 5,200

South 6th st, n s, 126.11 w Wythe av, 25x100. Herman Kahrs to Richard B. Malone. 5,000

North 6th st, n s, 75 w Driggs st, 25x100. Rose widow, Mary, Rose, Jr., Joseph and John Ireland to Thomas H. Ireland. All liens. nom

8th st, n s, 184.4 w 6th av, 18x100. William Brown to Ludwig T. Muench. *Mt.* $4,500. 7,250

8th st, n s, 184.4 w 6th av, 18x100. Release mort. Henry C. M. Ingraham to William Brown. 500

8th st, s s, 166.4 w 8th av, 17x100. Phoebe M. wife of George T. Smith to John W. Barnhart. *Mt.* $1,600. 9,000

South 8th st, s s, 107.2 e Driggs st, 21.5x92.7x21.6x90.10.
Interior lot, 128.7 e Driggs st, at s e cor of land conveyed to H. Cornwell by Meth. Epis. Church on Allen st, &c., runs south 31 x west 21.5 x north 31 x east 21.5, h & l.
Maria wife of Hagaman Cornwell to Hermann J. Oeters. *Mt.* $4,000. 7,500

13th st, s s, 197.10 w 6th av, 25x100. Alexander G. Calder sole devisee Susan Calder to Bertha Clark. *Mt.* $3,000. 6,000

13th st, n s, 272.10 e 4th av, 12.6x100. Mary F. Couzen formerly Owens only heir of Robert F. Owens the only son and heir of Robert Owens to William Scheelye. nom

15th st, s s, 186.4 w 5th av, 16.8x100. Annie McDowell to James Heaney. *Mt.* $600. 3,000

16th st, s w s, 137.10 n w 8th av, 20x100. Esther E. wife of Abraham L. Lamson to Francis Hauretby. 5,100

16th st, n e s, 359.1 s e 4th av, 25.9x14. Anna McDowell to James Heaney. 1,250

17th st, s s, 37 e 8th av, 25.6x83, h & l. Sophronia M. Fickett widow to Charles Burkhardt. *Mt.* $3,500. 6,400

17th st, s s, 37 e 8th av, 25.6x83. Release mort. Ida M. Murphy to Sophronia M. Fickett. 300

17th st, n e s, 350 n w 5th av, 20.4x100.2. Thomas Pitbladdo to The Sixth Methodist-Episcopal Church of Gowanus. 6,500

17th st, s s, 460 e 10th av, 20x100.2. Sarah F. Mead wife of George W. to Peter Curry. 4,000

17th st, n s, 150 w 7th av, 16.8x90. Henry Groth to John B. McCarthy. 2,350

18th st, n e s, 300 s e 8th av, 50x100. James P. Taylor to Alfred A. Fisher trustee. C. a. G. nom

32d st, s w s, 100 n w 5th av, 16.8x100.2. Henry Klee to Ole Christensen. *Mt.* $1,000. 2,725

Bay 38th st, n w s, 240 n e Benson av, 60x96.8, Gravesend. James D. Lynch to Andrew J. McAllister. 900

39th st, n s, 275 e 5th av, 25x80x25.6x73.10. Laura S. Morris wife of and John P. Morris to Isaiah Porter. 725

40th st, n s, 150 e 7th av, 50x100.2. Charles Reckling to Henry J. Chase, Long Island City. 800

45th st, s s, 300 e 3d av, 40x100.2. John P. Cranford and David H. Valentine to Alexander Davidson. 2,100

45th st, s s, 340 e 3d av, 60x100.2. Same to same. 3,150

45th st, n s, 200 e 3d av, 20x100.2. James F. O'Rourke to Peter Kerr and Benjamin Leach. *Mt.* $2,800. 4,700

57th st, s s, 120 e 2d av, 20x100.2. Release mort. Edward T. Hunt to Sarah Maher. consid. omitted

59th st, n s, 180 w 12th av, 20x100.2. Jessie wife of and Henry Thomas to William P. Rae. nom

62d st, s s, 140 w 11th av, 20x123x20x120. Julia A. Sprouls to Elizabeth C. Yake. 160

72d st, n s, 530 w 15th av, 40x100, New Utrecht. William W. Weygandt to Theodore and Louis Krombach. 450

74th st, s s, 450 w 15th av, 60x100, New Utrecht. James V. S. Woolley to Bly Coles Witthaus. 480

85th st, n e s, 120 s e 24th av, 60x100, Gravesend. George E. Schroth, of New York, to Elizabeth Schroth. nom

87th st, s w s, 250 s e 1st av, 100x100, New Utrecht. David D. Field to William H. O'Donnell. 1,200

87th st, n e s, 175 n w 2d av, 35.11x100x32.9x100, New Utrecht. David D. Field to John O'Leary. 460

87th st, n e s, 275 n w 2d av, 33.9x100x29.7x100, New Utrecht. Same to William H. Burroughs. 440

87th st, s w s, 100 s e Narrows av, 25x200 to 88th st, New Utrecht. David D. Field to Charles C. Gutschow. 680

87th st, s w s, 150 s e 1st av, 100x100.
3d av, west cor 87th st, 100x100, New Utrecht.
Same to Harry Held. 3,340

87th st, s w s, 275 n w 2d av, 75x100.
2d av, west cor 88th st, 66.7x107.2x105.3x100, New Utrecht.
David D. Field to Gabriel, Benigno and Miguel Balbin. 2,115

88th st, n e s, 100 n w 2d av, 50x100, New Utrecht. David D. Field to Ernest Sass. 580

88th st, n e s, 150 n w 2d av, 100x100, New Utrecht. Same to William Walsh. 1,160

88th st, n e s, 250 n w 2d av, 100x100, New Utrecht. David D. Field to William Morrison, Minerva T. and Theodore S. Nye. 1,160

88th st, s w s, 250 n w 2d av, 50x182.11x53.8x163.4, New Utrecht. David D. Field to James H. Park. Error. 620

88th st, s w s, 150 s e 1st av, 50x100, New Utrecht. David D. Field to Samuel K. Addoms. 500

88th st, n e s, 100 s e 1st av, 50x100, New Utrecht. David D. Field to William H. O'Donnell. 600

89th st, n e s, 275 s e 1st av, 75x100, New Utrecht. David D. Field to Jacob P. Hardt. 730

89th st, n e s, 225 s e 1st av, 50x100, New Utrecht. Same to Carrie Weishaupt. 490

East 95th st, e s, 150 s Av C, 28x105, Flatbush. John H. Ireland to Pauline Hardy. 225

96th st, s s, 170.2 e Shore road, 25x100, New Utrecht. Richmond Fowler to Charles A. Erickson. *Mt.* $420. 1,200

Alabama av, w s, 100 n Sutter av, 50x100, h & l. Mary H. Blinn to Lena Duchholz. *Mt.* $3,000. 4,000

Albany av, n w cor Butler st, runs west 80 x north 7 x north 152.5 x east 114.4 to Albany av, x south 155.7. John Broad to Charles S. Taber and George C. Case. Sub. to morts. nom

Atlantic av, s s, 365.4 w Utica av, runs south 56.5 x northwest 61.3 to av, x east 23.11, h & l. John B. Marquand to Leonardo Tipedino. 2,000

Atlantic av, s s, 133 e Rockaway av, 16.8x100. Frank T. Loud to John Leadd. *Mt.* $2,000. exch

Atlantic av, s s, 150 e Rockaway av, 16.8x100. Almira McLoud to John Leadd. *Mt.* $2,000. exch

Atlantic av, No. 1909. Contract for property. Clara Stockhohn and P. J. Mahony. 3,200

Bedford av, e s, 20 n Clymer st, 20x90. George E. Barrett to Eleanor J. Barrett. All title. Sub. to mort. 9,000

Blake av, n w cor Sackman st, 25x100. The East Brooklyn Co-operative Building Assoc. to Albert S. Bowne. 700

Same property. Albert S. Bowne to Benjamin Rothbell and Barnet Kreiger. 860

Blake av, s s, 90 e Junius st, 100x500 to Dumont av. A. Judson Palmer to Samuel Cohn, New York. 9,500

Blake av, n w cor Powell st, 100x100. Lewis Hurst to Abraham Rabbi and Aaron Hirsch. Sub. to mort. 2,500

Blake av, n s, 75 e Schenck av, 75x100.
Blake av, n s, 50 e Hendrix st, 25x100.
Blake av, n e cor Hendrix st, 25x100.
Blake av, n s, 75 w Hendrix st, 25x100.
Henry and John Von Glahn to Jared J. Chambers. 3,500

Clinton av, w s, 32 n De Kalb av, 21x112.7x21.5x116.10.
De Kalb av, n s, 132.11 w Clinton av, runs north abt 3 x east 11 x north 21.5 x west 21 x south 21.5 to av x 10.
Anna M. and Samuel C. Payson to Dominick G. Bookin. 15,250

Central av, s w s, 25 n w Eldert st, 25x80, h & l. James Gascoine to John F. Ehlers. ½ part. nom

Same property. Anna E. Cozine widow individ. and with ano. exrs. John G. Cozine to same. ½ part. 750

Christopher av, w s, 175 n Vanderveer av, 100x100. Benjamin Rausch to William Oppenheim, New York. 1,200

Christopher av, e s, 200 s Sutter av, 50x200 to Sackman st. Lewis Hurst to Harry Silberman, Michael Badner and Israel Weg, of New York. Sub. to mort. 2,600

Christopher av, w s, 100 s Belmont av, 50x100. Williamson R. Selover to Lazar Frieder. 1,200

Same property. Lazar Frieder to Meyer Israel, Samuel Applebaum and Abraham Schaffer. 1,640

Christopher av, e s, 100 s Sutter av, 25x200 to Sackman st. Chone Lonstein to Bernard Wilson. Assumes mort. $550. 1,450

Clason av, s w cor Lafayette av, 25x100. Katharine wife of and Henry Ehlers to Meta Bahrenburg. *Mt.* $2,000. nom

Same property. Meta Bahrenburg to Katharina wife of Henry Ehlers. *Mt.* $2,000. nom

Clason av, s w cor Dean st, 73.3x100. Katie L. Donohue an heir of Richard Donohue to John P. Donohue. ½ part. Sub. to mort. $7,000 1,500

Same property. Mary E. wife of Edward Gordon to same. All title. 4,500

Clermont av, e s, 711.11 n Myrtle av, 25.2x100. Charles E., Anna C. and Lester Turner by Charles L. Roe guard. to Mary A. Roe. 817

De Kalb av, s s, 61 w Stuyvesant av, 19.6x85, h & l. Ida M. Treadwell to Valentine Stratton. *Mt.* $3,500. 5,500

De Kalb av, n e cor Spencer st, runs north 108 x east 50 x south 20 x west 30 x south 88 to av, x west 20, h & l. Frank H. Tyler to John R. Woods. *Mt.* $11,000. exch

Evergreen av, s w s, 75.8 s e Palmetto st, 25.3x92.8x25x89.3, h & l. Oscar Hoeftmann, Jonesborough, Ind., to John A. Apelt. 500

Evergreen av, westerly cor Covert st, 25x100. Andrew L. Stulz to Charles F. Lutz. *Mt.* $4,000. 13,300

Flatbush av, e s, 64.3 n Lefferts av, 25x75, Flatbush. Cynthia Lott and Aletta Suydam individ. and Richard J. and John F. Berry exrs. Margaret A. Berry to Paolo Carbonaro. 1,375

Flushing av, s s, 275 e Marcy av, 25x100. Andrew and Jacob Meurer to William B. Boynton. *Mt.* $2,500. 5,500

Gates av, s s, 100 e Stuyvesant av, 25x90. Susanna J. Haubert to Lizzie M. M. Loeffler. *Mt.* $7,500. nom

Gates av, s s, 245 e Marcy av, 40x100, h & l. Leopold J. Lippmann to Adelaide L. Badgley, New York. *Mt.* $8,000. exch

Gates av, s e s, 125 n e Knickerbocker av, 50x100. Matthew Dignan to John Bocker. *Mt.* $6,000. exch and 1,700

Gates av, s e s, 184.1 n e Evergreen av, 25x100. John H. Jerring to Charles Welcher. 1,650

Gates av, s e s, 184 n e Evergreen av, 25x100. Release mort. John Davidson to John H. Jerring. nom

Glenmore av, n s, 100 w Ashford st, 25x100. Release mort. Alexander Matthews, of Huntington, N. Y., to Isabella wife of Stephen D. Mersereau. nom

Same property. Isabella wife of and Stephen D. Mersereau to John Hahn. 750

Greene av, s s, 85.6 w Sumner av, 19.2x100. Thomas B. Bryant to Ferdinand Dalston. *Mt.* $5,000. exch

Greenwood av, n w cor East 7th st, runs north 180.11 x west 100 x south 100.4 x west 30 x south 100 to av, x east 100.
Prospect av, w s, 211 n Greenwood av, 25x180.
Gravesend av, s e Seeley st, 158.6x134.2x150x83, Flatbush.
Catharine B. Aitken widow to Lydia A. and Elizabeth H. Aitken. 15,200

Hamilton av, s w cor Lexington av, 25x102.7x25x102.4, New Utrecht. Frank F. Lisiecki to Herman O. Binninger. 550

Hopkinson av, e s, 75 n Sumpter st, 25x100. Julia R. Kelsey to Isaac Halstead. Sub. to all liens. nom

Howard av, s w cor Macon st, 100x93.6. Release mort. Bernard Levino and Walter F. Clayton individ. and W. F. Clayton trustee to Clarence Lincoln. 2,600

Howard av, s w cor Macon st, 100x100. Release mort. William Ziegler to Clarence Lincoln. 8,500

Hopkins av, e s, 170 s Eastern Parkway, 20x100. Frederick Gottschalk to Joseph P. Smith. 250

Irving av, n e s, 50 n w Stanhope st, 25x100. Caroline wife of and George Creter, of New York, to Adam Keller. 600

Jefferson av, n s, 95 e Stuyvesant av, 80x100. Release mort. William Johnson to Kate Acor. 4,500

Jefferson av, s s, 240 w Nostrand av, 20x100.
Herkimer st, n s, 440 w Albany av, 20x100, h & l.
George W. De Lano to Mary E. Tripp, Jersey City. *Mt.* $11,000. nom

Jefferson av, s s, 90 w Throop av, 20x100. Isaac Colyer to Jane A. Hart. *Mt.* $4,000. 7,525

Johnson av, n e cor Leonard st, 25x100. Barbara, Charles F. E. and Eliza M. Dienst, Emma Waite and Alexander Dienst to Annie A. Klinck. *Mt.* $6,000. 6,800

Same property. Ida Dienst by Edward M. Licht guard. to Annie A. Klinck. 100

Kent av, e s, 74 9 s Willoughby av, 24.11x100. Margaret Shaw widow to Patrick Fitzpatrick. 2,900

Knickerbocker av, southerly cor Stanhope st, 100x100. Release mort. Theodore F. Jackson to Charles A. Wagner. 4,000

Knickerbocker av, east cor Thames st, runs east 100.3 x south 22.8 x southwest 60.6 to av, x northwest 83. Theodore F. Jackson to Ernst Augustin. nom

Knickerbocker av, north cor Thames st, 25x77.3x53.2x61.4. Same to Peter Blank. nom

Lawrence av, s e cor 3d st, 100x100, Flatbush. Oscar L. Steves to Richard W. Steves. nom

Lewis av, e s, 82 n Madison st, 18x100. Foreclos. Michael Furst to William J. Pearson. 5,425

Livonia av, s e cor Osborn st, 20x100. Patrick J. Kenedy, of New York, to James O'Halloran. 350

Livonia av, s e cor Watkins st, 25x75. Max Pokalsky and Louis Lebewohl to Michael Pokalsky. *Mt.* $2,350. 3,350

Lafayette av, s e s, 330 n e Broadway, 20x100. Mary C. Oble to John C. Kluber. 9,000

Lee av, n e s, 50 n w Middleton st, 25x75, h & l. Johannah Behrens to Louis Beer and Michael Schaffner. *Mt.* $2,000. nom

Metropolitan av, s s, 133 e Vandervoort av, runs east 38 to land formerly of the Glendale & East River R. R. Co., x southeast 27.8 x south 53.2 x northwest 96.10. The New York, Brooklyn & Manhattan Beach R. R. Co. and Austin Corbin individ. and as trustee to Theodore R. Chapman. 700

Montauk av, e s, 550 n Liberty av, 18.9x100. William S. Seaman to Alva Seaman, of New York. 1,000

Montauk av, e s, 390 s Blake av, 40x100. Effingham H. Nichols to Elizabeth Seyler. 400

Myrtle av, n e cor Canton st, 19x72.9x33.1x67.6. George Heatley to Patrick Sweeney. 12,000

Myrtle av, s s, 46 e Clason av, 23x71.8x23x71.10, h & l. Christina wife of Joseph Wurzler to Fanny wife of Henry Dreyfuss. *Mt.* $8,000. 9,000

New Jersey av, w s, 100 s Broadway, 50x100. John Kaufman to John G. MacMahon. 1,200

New Utrecht av, w s, 44.9 n 57th st, 22.3x99x20x108.9, New Utrecht. Release mort. Hope H. Colgate to The Blythebourne Improvement Co. 100

Same property. The Blythebourne Improvement Co. to Wilhelmina James. 650

Nostrand av, s e cor Fennimore st, 40x100, Flatbush, hs and ls. John Struss to Christina Struss. Sub. to mort. nom

Norman av, n s, 18 w Jewell st, 18x95, h & l. Henry Roth to William Lynch. *Mt.* $3,100. 3,400

Nostrand av, s w cor Willoughby av, 18x100. Catharine R. Prentiss to Abijah H. Topping. 2,500

Same property. Release mort. Emma Savage to Catharine R. Prentiss. 1,200

Nostrand av, w s, 60 s Lexington av, 20x100. Franklin B. Purdy to John W. Burnhart. Re-recorded. *Mt.* $7,000. 12,500

Ovington av, s w s, lot 1642 block 41 map No. 3 building lots, Bath Junction, adj indeft. right of way. James V. S. Woolley to Margaretha Reichenbach. 250

Ovington av, s w s, 319.4 n w 11th av, 26.8x110.1x34.3x100.3, New Utrecht. Margaretha Reichenbach to Anna B. Sorenson. nom

Paige av, south cor Provost st, centre line, runs southeast to centre line Eagle st, x southwest along same to point 175 s w of Provost st, x northwest —x— to centre Paige av if extended, x east —.
Paige av, west cor Clay st, centre lines, runs southwest to point 100 e of e s Oakland av, x northwest to centre Paige av, x —.
Emma A. Schley widow to Daniel J. Leary. 16,000

Prospect av, w s, 86 n Greenwood av, runs north 50 x west 150 x south 81.9 x northeast 97.7 x east 55.6, Flatbush. Catharine D. Aitken widow to William B. Aitken. 1,500

Prospect av, s s, 300 e 9th av, 25x77x25.4x69.1. Mary Hassou to James Cullen. *Mt.* $450. nom

Ralph av, n w cor Macon st, 100x112. Release mort. William Ziegler to Benjamin C. Raymond. 9,000

Ralph av, w s, 202.11 n Prospect pl, runs west 523.1 to Hunterfly road, x north to land of A. O. Millard, x east to point 650 e from Buffalo av, x south 15 x east 100 to Ralph av, x south 37.8. Annie E. Morrison to John Trecartin. *Mt.* $1,500. 3,900

Reid av, e s, 100 n Greene av, 20x100. Adelina E. F. Praeger heir Gesine Sterling and Hubert F. Praeger her husband to Frederick Stelling. gift

Rochester av, s w cor Dean st, 100x186.7. James M. McNamara and John P. Egan to Edward M. Grout. B. & S. and C. a. G. nom

Rockaway av, e s, 225 n Belmont av, 25x100.1. Samuel Levy to Minna Steinfeld. 1,050

Rockaway av, w s, 132 s Marion st, 16x99.2x19x88 10. John O. Whitenack to Magdalena Fink. *Mt.* $2,500. 3,500

Rockaway av, n w cor Eastern Parkway, 50x100. Henrietta wife of Charles Freyberg to Alexander S. Rosenthal. *Mt.* $4,698. nom

Rockaway av, e s, 101.6 n Hull st, 40x75. Ella M. wife of and F. J. G. Ladd to Nathaniel W. Ladd, of Boston, Mass. *Mt.* $9,750. nom

Schenck av, w s, 225 n Liberty av, 50x100. George Breit as trustee of the New York Classes of the Reformed Church to the German Evangelical Reformed Bethany Church, of Brooklyn, N. Y. *Mt.* $400. 8,000

Snediker av, e s, 200 s Dumont av, 60x100. Joseph P. Puels to Mary J. Wilson. 1,080

Snediker av, e s, 260 s Dumont av, 40x100. Joseph P. Puels to Harrison Willis. *Mt.* $400. 720

Snediker av, w s, 140 n Belmont av, 40x100. Solomon Spaulding, New York, to Michael Rosenthal. *Mt.* $3,500. 4,200

Snediker av, e s, 200 s Dumont av, 60x100. Release mort. Catharine Baird to Joseph P. Puels. 600

Stanley av, n w cor Warwick st, 40x85. William P. St. John, of New York, to James Phillpott. 135

St. Marks av, n s, 350 e Rockaway av, 100x127.9. Charles M. Thompson to Joseph Kreinik. *Mt.* $2,000. 4,400

St. Marks av, s s, 100 w Carlton av, 30x100. Augusta S. wife of and Samuel Crawford to Carrie J. Thompson. *Mt.* $4,000. 8,000

St. Marks av, s w s, 243.6 s e Vanderbilt av, 26.6x131. Release mort. Edwin Packard committee for Henry U. Perry to William B. Martin and Patrick J. Lee. 5,500

Stone av, w s, 150 s Blake av, 50x100. Sarah A. M. Kent to Mary E. Cook, of Newtown, L. I. 1,100

Stone av, s e cor Sumpter st, 11.11x46.9x—x—.
Sumpter st, s s, 58 1 e Stone av, runs east 69.11 x south 78 x northwest 104.8, gore.
Interior lot, 46.6 n of McDougal st, on line which at n s of said st is 200 e Stone av, runs north 40.10 x northwest 50 x south 8.5 x southeast 54.
James T. Benedict to Mary F. Bradford. 2,000

Sutter av, s w cor Essex st, 48x100. John Flood to William A. Northridge. ½ part. *Mt.* $3,775. 2,500

Sutter av, n s, 25 w Smith av, 25x100. Release mort. The Dime Savings Bank to John F. Peterkin. 500

Thatford av, w s, 125 n Belmont av, 25x100.1. Bryce Martin to Samuel and Toby Scheiman. *Mt.* $1,500. 2,550

Thatford av, w s, 175 n Eastern Parkway, 25x100. Silas A. Condict to Rachel Max. *Mt.* $2,200. 2,800

Thatford av, w s, 225 s Belmont av, 25x100.1.
Belmont av, n s, 125 e Thatford av, runs north 100 x west 25 x north 25 x east 52.10 x south 25 x west 2.9 to beginning.
Morris Rosenbloom to Joseph and Dina Davis. *Mt.* $2,800. 5,950

Thatford av, e s, 150 s Glenmore av, 25x100. Andrew R. Culver to Isaac Gingold and Isaac Abrams. Taxes and assessm'ts from Jan., 1888. 400

Thatford av, n w cor Glenmore av, 20x100.1. Patrick Donohue to Joseph Saltzer, of New York. 950

Tompkins av, e s, 80 s Willoughby av, 20x100. Alexander W. and Robert M. Pettit exrs. Robert Pettit, of New Brunswick, N. J., to Anton Braun. 4,700

Utica av, w s, 19.5 s Pacific st, 17.10x75. Ferdinand Walter to Oscar Richter. *Mt.* $2,100. 3,100

Same property. Oscar Richter to Sophie Walter. *Mt.* $2,100. 3,100

Utica av, e s, 84 s Atlantic av, 16x100, h & l. Malechi Finn to Elizabeth M. wife of Stephen J. Heather. 1,800

Washington av, w s, 109.4 n Lefferts av, 27.4x58.4x25x47.8, Flatbush. Cynthia Lott et al. exrs. Margaret A. Berry to Paolo Carbonaro. 1,875

Williamson av, e s, 100 n Blake av, 100x100. Catharine L. Babcock to Elise Danancher. 1,800

Wortman av, n w cor Ashford st, 100x205.
Warwick st, e s, 85 n Wortman av, 120x100.
Adolph Sussman to William C. Hoffman. 805

Wythe av, n w s, 50 s w North 7th st, 25x100. Max S. Levison to Jacob M. Lotto and Jacob Lax, of New York. *Mt.* $2,800. 5,000

Wyckoff av, northerly cor Madison st, 25x95 7x25x95; also,
St. Nicholas av, s w s, 25 s e Jefferson st, 25x90, error.
Eliza A. wife of L. Stewart to James M. McNamara. *Mt.* $300. 200

2d av, e s, 25 s Wakeman pl, 25x100, New Utrecht. Charles A. Erickson to Richmond Fowler. *Mt.* $3,000. 4,400

3d av, southerly cor 87th st, runs southwest 100 x southeast 100 x northeast 90.11 x northwest 41.6 x northwest 59.6, New Utrecht. David D. Field to James P. Farrell. 2,340

3d av, w s, 40 s Wyckoff st, 20x80, h & l. Oscar Haviland to Benjamin Armstrong. nom

4th av, s e s, 60 s w 11th st, 20x97.10. Bertha wife of and Van Brunt Clark to Angelica wife of Charles Delapierre. *Mt.* $500. 1,700

5th av, w s, 25 s 40th st, runs 100.10 x northwest to s s 40th st at point 496.7 w 5th av, x east along st 396 7 x south 25 x east 100. Patrick H. Flynn to Michael J. Coffey. nom

5th av, n e cor 19th st, 25x100. Jane widow and Julia Chapman and Elizabeth J. Read heirs James Chapman to Joseph Dempsey. 5,000

6th av, e s, 20 n 2d st, 60x90; also,
2d st, n s, 130 e 6th av, 120x100.
Joseph N. Tuttle and Henry B Johnson individ. and as trustees to Nathaniel Niles. nom

22d av, southerly cor 85th st, 100x100, New Utrecht. James D. Lynch to Jacob Van Deusen. 4,000

Duryea, Logan, Hegeman and Milford sts—the block. Release mort Jacob Cozine to William H. Jackson. 5,000

Gravesend Bay and Bay 8th st, 16 813-1000 acres, land under water, Bath Beach., People State of New York to Mary A. Young. letters patent

Interior lot, 233 e Buffalo av, 40 s Eastern Parkway, runs west 94 x south 17.9½ x east 3.10 x north 4.2½ x east 90.2 x north 13.7. Mary Hoey to Edwin F. Howell. 450

Interior lot, 142.10 e Buffalo av, 90 n Union av, runs east 38.6 x north 10 x east 73 x north 87 x west 94 x south 77 to beginning.
Eastern Parkway, s s, 139 e Buffalo av, 40x94.
Maria Rotert to Edwin F. Howell. 1,650

Interior lot, 75 n Montrose av and 50 e Leonard st, runs south 5 x west 25x5x25. Franz Pfeiffer to August Bischoff. nom

Lots 182 - 185 map Jacob Snediker property, 26th Ward. Henry Bade to Charles F. Schwing. 800

Lots 267, 268, 484 and 485 map Jacob Snediker property, 26th Ward. Henry Distler to Theodore Kiendl. 580

Lots 1-40 block 181, lots 1-20 block 182, lots 14-18 block 195, map property 17th Ward on which Cornelius N. Hoagland and George L. Kingsland have written their names; also lot 11 block 7 same map. Release mort. Cornelius N. Hoagland to Paul C. Grening. nom

Lot 26 map of plots 12 and 13 lands of James T. Tapscott, Flatbush. James F. Martyn to Patrick Walsh. 130

Same property. Lavinia S. Tapscott to James F. Martyn. 130

Lots 83-87 and 103, 104, 109, 112-114 and 117 map 480 lots of Worth & Strawson, Flatbush. Release mort. Mary and Cath. Vanderveer and Eliza A. Martense to Jacob Worth and Vincent A. Strawson. 1,225

Lots 240-242 and 246-249 and 261, 262 and 264-267 and 272, 273, 276 and 277 same map. Release mort. Same to same. 1,600

Lots 324-327 and 343-346 and 354 and 355 same map. Release mort. Same to same. 725

Lots 156-160 and 188 and 195 same map. Release mort. Same to same. 725

Lots 264-267 and 241 and 242 map 430 lots, Flatbush, owned by Jacob Worth and Vincent A. Strawson. Jacob Worth and Vincent A. Strawson to Frederick Grafelman. 930

Lots 324-327 same map. Same to David Barry. 580

Lots 246 and 247 same map. Same to Joseph P. Smith. 380

Lot 188 same map. Same to William F. Barry. 165

Lots 272 and 278 same map. Same to Thomas Freeman. 280
Lots 156-160 same map. Same to Bridget E. Thompson. 1,075
Lots 261 and 262 same map. Same to Bridget E. Boylan. 330
Lots 343-346 same map. Same to Frederick V. Gillain. 560
Lots 113 and 114 same map. Same to Patrick J. Quinn. 480
Lots 83-87 and 117 same map. Same to Elizabeth F. Lynam. 1,200
Lots 112, 354 and 355 same map. Same to Henriette Block. 550
Lots 103, 109, 195, 240, 248, 249, 276, 277 same map. Same to Philip H. Samilson, of New York. 1,865
Lots 339 and 340 block 12 map 1,197 lots belonging to Wm. Ziegler, Flatbush and New Utrecht. William P. Rae to Jessie wife of Henry Thomas. *Mt.* $1,800. 3,500
Lots 449 and 450 block 8 map 597 lots of W. Ziegler, Gravesend. Frank Pisek to Joseph Beck. 700
Lots 765-780 map No. 2 Abraham Van Wyck property. Louisa A. Van Coperell to Magdalena Specet. Sub. to all morts., taxes, &c. 400
Lots 862-865 and 871-875 inclusive map of C. J. Lott property, each 25x100. Andrew F. Bedell to Lazarus Weil. 3,150
Lots 199-209 block F map Vanderveer homestead, 26th Ward. John H. Vanderveer to Edmund Schissel. *Mt.* $2,000. 4,425
Lots 236 and 237, distinguished as Kings Co., East New York, map B. William Knappmann to Phebe M. Van Buren. Q. C. 435
Lands conveyed from R. Remser to John Ryerson excepting part conveyed to John Ryerson to Jacob Ryerson. Contract. John Ryerson to Samuel Cohn. 36,000
Strip adj roadbed of grantees, being lot 84 map The Brooklyn & Rockaway Beach R. R. Co., being 15x257.8, Flatlands. Emanuel, Jr., and William Holmes and Sarah wife of William H. Kelly children of Emanuel Holmes, Cornelia wife of James H. Moore and Cora Harper children of Susan Holmes heirs, &c., Emanuel Holmes to The Brooklyn & Rockaway Beach R. R. Co. nom
Strip as above, being lot 75 same map. Henry L. Schmeelke to same. nom
Strip adj as above, being lot 69 same map. William H. Murr to same. nom
Strips adj as above, lots 76 and 79 same map. Sub. to right of way. Herman Lohman to same. nom
Strip adj as above, being lot 73 same map. John H. Ireland to same. nom
Strip at Canarsie, adj grantee, 12.6x— to Bay. Hermann Lohmann to Louis Kleinan. 125

WESTCHESTER COUNTY.

JUNE 24 TO 30—INCLUSIVE.

CORTLANDT.

Brown, Southard to Minnie Brown, s s Park st, adj. Elizabeth Brown, 41x126. $200
Radway, Mary J. et al. to Chas. Ammann, part front lot No. 1 Manor, Cortlandt, with 2 acres opposite, also 49 acres adj E. Q. Miller. 6,000

EASTCHESTER.

Dunn, Chas. M. to And. Andersen, lots 80 and 81 w s Jefferson, map Wright property. 250
Hallock, Mary J. to Friederich Buhler, part lot 28 s e s Franklin st, West Mt. Vernon, 45x100. 500
Henneberger, Herman to Mary V. Watts, lots 6 and 7 w s 9th av, map property grantor, 50x105. 900
Same to Mary L. Collins, lots 8 and 9 w s 9th av, 50x105. 1,000
Same to Mary Nolan and ano., lots 23 and 24 e s 10th av, 50x105, also lots 3, 4 and 5 w s same, 75x105. 2,250
Same to Thos. L. Miller, lots 19, 20, 27-33, 51-55, 57-66, 35-42, 67-77, 78, 79, 80 and 81-93. nom
Holler, Margt. to Regina M. Hayes, s e s old Boston road, adj Meade and Howe, 236x127x234x292. 3,000
Koehler, Anna to Henry Lebander, part lot 409 n w s Greenwich st, West Mount Vernon, 30x125. 750
Mapes, Hannah E. to Henry Foster, e s 5th av, 310 s 4th st, 50x105. 8,300
Mulvey, Patrick to Ann Mulvey, n w cor "New" st and old White Plains road, 58x150. nom
Miller, Thos. L. to Mary M. Bock, n e cor 6th st and South 10th av, 50x105. 1,050
Same to And. E. Hanson, lots 29 and 30 e s 10th av, map Henneberger property, 50x105. 900
Proe, Charlotte E. to Daniel J. Ruth, n s "New" st, adj Mary Reed, 29x85. 150
Reid, Mary and ano. exrs. of, to Herman Henneberger, The "Reids Mills" property, 64 acres. 15,000
Underhill, Henry M. to Jas. T. Anderson and ano., s e cor Underhill and Breckinridge sts, 100x100. 1,800
Watts, Mary V. to John J. Crimmins, n ½ lot 692, map Mount Vernon. 500

GREENBURGH.

Beggs, John to Chas. E. Storms, n w cor Haines and Lefurgy avs, 50x100x50x25x100x125. 1,600
Erhardt, Joel B. trustee to John J. Lenehan, w s Western av, 150 n Station sq, 50x100. 700
Smith, Ichabod by John Hart, Freeholder, to Lucinda A. Laviness, 1¼ acres on Central Park av. 2,450

MOUNT PLEASANT.

Durney, Richard and ano. to Edw. Fitzgibbon, s e cor Clinton st and Tompkins av, 50x150. 600
Garrigan, Thos. exr. of, to Arcadius Soltz, ⅛ acre on road from Pleasantville to Unionville, adj railroad. 1,350
Same to same, 14 acres adj Pleasantville Lime Co. 2,800
Purdy, Elisha T. to Henry S. Scott, 81 acres on road from Phebe F. Stoutenburghs to Lewis S. Onderdonks. 16,000
Scott, Henry S. to Isaac N. Cohen and ano., same property. nom
Smadbeck, Louis to Geo. Hankins, lots 353 and 354, Sherman Park. 200

NEW CASTLE.

Cock, Harriet to Phebe A. Murray, e s road from Chappaqua to New Castle, 149 acres. 12,000
Fiero, Alice E. to Edgar S. Werner, plot adj Reuben Birdsall, 3 acres. 1,000

NEW ROCHELLE.

Callanan, Julia A. to Adam Doering, n w cor "New" st and Mayflower av, 50x125. 450
Disbrow, Mary L. to Thos. D. Valentine, lot 117 e s Woodland av, Residence Park, 75x150. 2,000
Downey, Henry B. to Wm. S. Bertine, w s North st, 42 — Burling lane, 40x115. 1,300
Ensinger, Kath. to Ferd. Ensinger, Jr., e s North st, 242 n 5th av, 75x275. 700
Iselin, Adrian J. to Edw. Lambden, Jr., s s Willow Drive, 256 w Leland av, 75x144. 1,075
Lorenzen, Rosina to Columbus O'D. Iselin, n e cor Cedar road and Franklin st, 100x100. 9,000
Manhattan Life Insurance Co. to Helen M. Cobb, lot 19 block B, *Rochelle* Park. 8,500

PELHAM.

Black, Robt. C. to Chas. Whann, 2 plots on Manor Circle, map property grantor and ano, abt 2 acres. 5,200

RYE.

Damon, Carrie N. et al., M. Dillon, ref., to Howard Tingue, lots 73-76 e s Centre st, Mt. Jefferson, 100x200. 5,625
Same to Nancy J. Vaughn, w s Spring st, 130 s Westchester av, 50x100. 520
Same to same, s s Westchester av, 151 e Centre st, 50x130. 3,900
Tingue, Wm. J. to Carrie G. Smack, lot 5 n e s Hawthorne av, Tingue Park, 100x275. 1,500

WESTCHESTER.

Bolton, Lavinia M. to Wm. Astor, s e cor Old Boston road and Pelham Parkway. 15,000
Camp, Hugh N. to Henry Ahles, lots 98 and 99 map McGraw estate. 650
Same to Steph. Butler, lots 127 and 128 same map. 570
Same to Arthur K. Butler, lots 129 and 130 same map. 570
Same to Louisa Burkhardt, lots 143 and 144 same map. 805
Same to Frank Bogenschneider, lots 112 and 215 same map. 605
Same to Jos. Bell, lot 165 same map. 325
Same to Mary A. Casey, lot 115 same map. 300
Same to Michael Casey, lots 119 and 120 same map. 540
Same to Frank S. Ehrgott, lots 147 and 148 same map. 550
Same to Kate Fischer, lots 100 and 101 same map. 650
Same to Otto Freuont, lot 74 same map. 155
Same to Jas. E. Fitzgerald, lot 219 same map. 325
Same to Herman H. Fleddermann, lots 82 and 83 same map. 1,005
Same to Chas. Franz, lots 71 and 72 same map. 470
Same to Jas. L. Fitzpatrick, lot 157 same map. 270
Same to Annie L. Fitzpatrick, lot 158 same map. 270
Same to Jos. H. Fitzpatrick, lots 159 and 160 same map. 540
Same to Harry Randolph, lots 161 and 162 same map. 540
Same to Chas. P. Faber, lots 1 2 and 3 same map. 2,015
Same to Wm. J. Geraghty, lot 73 same map. 285
Same to Bridgett Campbell, lot 56 same map. 400
Same to Adam Hoeppner, lots 78 and 79 same map. 480
Same to Anton Hermany, Jr., lot 23 same map. 280
Same to John Henry, lots 163 and 164 same map. 550
Same to Henry A. Hauck, lots 167 and 168 same map. 480
Same to Frank Hartenstein, lots 26 and 145 same map. 585
Same to Wm. Hanigan, lot 176 same map. 775
Same to Anton Hilkney, lots 177, 201, 203 and 241 same map. 1,565
Same to Martin J. King, lots 131-136 same map. 1,740
Same to John Kinselle, lots 222 and 223 same map. 670
Same to Arthur Du Pree, lots 220 and 221 same map. 660
Same to Henry Koster, Jr., lot 218 same map. 325
Same to Chas. Keeler, lots 45, 125 and 126 same map. 1,020
Same to Charlotte La Coste, lot 142 same map. 300
Same to John Layden, lots 90 and 91 same map. 695
Same to Josiah L. Lindsay, lot 225 same map. 250
Same to Jas. Mahon, lots 154 and 175 same map. 775
Same to Thos. McKenna, lot 183 same map. 295
Same to John H. McGurk, lots 116 and 117 same map. 820
Same to John McQuade, lot 238 same map. 195
Same to Wm. Murphy, lot 155 same map. 410
Same to Peter J. Murray, lot 121 same map. 275
Same to Jas. T. Murray, lots 122 and 123 same map. 550
Same to Thos. A. Murray, lots 42, 43 and 44 same map. 900
Same to Frank Magner, lots 216 and 217 same map. 640
Same to Steph. Mitchell, lot 55 same map. 405
Same to Emma McCaffrey, lots 248 and 249 same map. 440
Same to Wm. Moir, lot 48 same map. 340
Same to Louis Martin, lots 190, 191 and 192 same map. 765
Same to Robertina Kull, lots 193 and 194 same map. 510
Same to Magdalena Busing, lot 195 same map. 255
Same to Michael O'Neill, lot 89 same map. 585
Same to Thos. O'Hair, lots 96 and 97 same map. 670
Same to Patrick O'Connor, lots 197 and 198 same map. 540
Same to Mich. Verstraelen, lot 81 same map. 330
Same to Gustav Rosenberg, lot 188 same map. 275
Same to Jas. Reilly, lots 92 and 93 same map. 680
Same to David A. Ross, lots 140 and 141 same map. 600
Same to John R. Richards, lots 239 and 242 same map. 530
Same to John Rehm, lots 110, 111, 171, 172 and 173 same map. 1,835
Same to Geo. Schilling, lot 124 same map. 280
Same to Jas. Stewart, lot 31 same map. 390
Same to Ann Sheehan, lots 84 and 85 same map. 710
Same to Max Schneckenberger, lots 11 and 12 same map. 690
Same to Anton Sommer, lot 240 same map. 205
Same to Henry Sonnet, lots 32 and 33 same map. 480
Same to Frank A. Bale, lots 34 and 35 same map. 480
Same to Mathew Smith, lot 231 same map. 370
Same to Robt. C. Smith, lot 102 same map. 325
Same to John A. Smith, lots 204 and 205 same map. 610
Same to Henry Wilker, lots 211-214 same map. 1,220
Same to John Wood, lot 27 same map. 280
Same to Geo. Watson, lots 86, 87 and 88, same map. 1,185
Same to Alex. Weir, lots 8, 9 and 10 same map. 900
Same to Edw. Whalen, lots 224 and 230 same map. 650
Same to Abby Ward, lots 46 and 47 same map. 610
Same to Edgar Yeury, lots 18 and 19 same map. 400
Same to John Zinn, Jr., lots 244 and 245 same map. 470
Same to Peter Dascher, Jr., lot 246 same map. 235
Same to Henry Dascher, lot 247 same map. 235
Same to Fred. W. Becker, lots 21 and 22 same map. 460
Griffin, John, Jr., to Thos. R. Thorn, lot 49 s s 4th st, Unionport, 100x108. 400
Jarrett, Geo. F. to Lydia A. Davis, s s Evadna st, 94 e Main st, 50x100. 1,300
Melvin, Bernard to Robt. J. Brady, lot 191 s s 9th st, Unionport. 277

WHITE PLAINS.

Archer, Hannah E. to Daniel Maloney, s s Lake st, adj grantor, 50x200. 1,000
Horton, Abram J. to Orlando J. Smith, the Horton farm, Mamaroneck road, 120 acres. 58,000
Thurston, Franklin A. to Robt. J. Roby, n s Barker av, 50 w Church st, 50x150. 4,000

YONKERS.

Combes, R. Cannan to Marcus Nathan, lots 44-50, Sherwood Park. 15,000
Delavan, Margt. M. B. to Clarence M. Fowler, lot 51, Sherwood Park. 1,500
Devoe, Miriam C. to Nath. B. Valentine, w s Palisade av, 70 s Garden st, 90x100. 4,500
Druid Hill Park Co. to Daniel Wheeler, lot 558, Mohegan Park. 180
Same to Caleb F. Underhill, lot 478 same map. 195
Same to Cath. Goettel, lot 492 same map. 195
Same to Geo. Goettel, lot 493 same map. 195
Same to Cath. Geiler, lots 111 and 112 same map. 440
Same to Mary Goldman, lots 552 and 553 same map. 310
Ellis, Matt. H. to Arthur D. Williams, lot 298 e s Glen av, map Foster Stone property. 250
East Side Land Co. to Martha A. Moore, lots 56 and 57 map Sherwood Hill. 1,400
Herriot, Ann M. to Kate Webb, lot 11 e s Parkhill av, 26x120. 450
Halsey, Geo. A. to Marcus Nathan, lots 39-43, Sherwood Park. 15,000
Jardine, John to Jessie K. Humason, e s North Broadway, adj Cath. H. Fitch, 100x250. 8,000
Jones, Cyrus P. and ano. to Henry Wilson, lots 4 and 5 block E map property grantor. 500

Murphy, Ellen B. to Mary Coombes, s s Myrtle st, 100 e Vineyard av, 25x101. 300

Montague, Charles H. to John Jardine, w s Shonnard terrace, adj Aqueduct, 60x70. 9,000

Sherwood Park Land Co. to Wm. N. Davidson, n s Sherwood av, 114.6 e Crescent pl, 12.6x150. 250

Shonnard, Fred. to Patrick Ahearn, lot 133 Voss av, city map. 350

Smith, Edw. to Mary A. Stack, n s Chestnut st, 525 e Nepperhan av, 25x100. nom

Ware, Mary C. et al. to Elizb. Miller, n s Ware av, 319 w Kimball, 50x125. 375

MORTGAGES.

Note.—The arrangement of this list is as follows. The first name is that of the mortgagor, the next that of the mortgagee. The description of the property then follows, then the date of the mortgage, the time for which it was given, and the amount. The general dates used as headings are the dates when the mortgage was handed into the Register's office to be recorded.

Whenever the letters "P. M." occur, preceded by the name of a street, in these lists of mortgages, they mean that it is a Purchase Money Mortgage, and for fuller particulars see the list of transfers under the corresponding date. Whenever the rate is not given, read as 6 per cent.

NEW YORK CITY.

June 26, 27, 29, 30, July 1.

Agne, George to Louis L. Richman and Mary Berkowitz. Delancey st, No. 197. Receipt on account of principal. June 26. $1,000

Same to George Richman and Mary Berkowitz. Delancey st, No. 195. Receipt on account of principal. June 26. 1,000

Anderson, Charles A. to Matthew Hagan. 103d st, s s, 139.6 e 9th av. P. M. June 29, 2 years, installs, 5 %. 3,000

Same to same. 103d st, s s, 99.6 e 9th av. P. M. June 29, 2 years, installs, 5 %. 3,000

Anderson, Walden P. to Thomas J. Davis and ano. exrs., &c., Elizabeth C. H. Clark. 93d st, s s, 274 e Amsterdam av, 17x100.8. June 30, 3 years, 4½ %. 12,000

Same to The Bradley & Currier Co. 93d st, s s, 325 e Amsterdam av, 100x100.8. Sub. to morts. $97,000. June 15, 6 months. 6,000

Allcot, Edmund C. and Helen J. his wife to Abraham Stoers. Villa av, e s, 375 n Potter pl, 50x100. Sub. to mort $4,000. June 30, due July 30, 1891. 330

Allen, S. Busby to Frederick J. Middlebrook. 124th st, s s, 100 e 1st av, 25x100.11. June 30, 3 years, 5 %. 8,000

Alter, Solomon to Isabella Labriola and Michelina Maugiere. Elizabeth st. P. M. July 1, due Sept. 1, 1892, or sooner. 16,000

Barth, John C. to Louisa Schwegler. 106th st, s s, 125 w Columbus av, 25x100.11. June 29, due July 1, 1892. 4,000

Same to same. 106th st, s s, 150 w Columbus av, 25x100.11. June 29, due July 1, 1892. 4,000

Brosnan, John to Rose C. Newman. Vandam st, No. 22, s s, 259.11 e Varick st, 23x100, with all title in alley on south. July 1, 3 years, 5 %. 5,000

Same to same. Vandam st, No. 23, n s, 230 e Varick st, 20x99.5x19.4x99.5. July 1, 3 years, 5 %. 5,000

Beneke, William to Robert Vollbracht. 2d av, s e cor 70th st, 25.5x74. Jan. 5, 1 year, without interest. 7,000

Brehm, Eugene and Pauline his wife to The German Savings Bank, City New York. 84th st, n s, 210 e 4th av, 25.7x102.2. June 29, due June 30, 1892. 4,000

Bloch, Isidore to Patrick Connor. 3d av. P. M. June 29, due June 27, 1894, or installs, 5 %. 3,000

Bauer, John F. and Elizabeth his wife to Margaretha Weisel. 2d st. P. M. July 1, 5 years or installs, 5 %. 12,000

Beller, Abraham to Samuel A. Blatchford and ano. trustees for Mary Van Dyke. Wooster st. P. M. July 1, 3 years or sooner, 5 %. 11,450

Same to Charles F. Aukamp trustee for Clarence A. Van Dyke. Same property. P. M. Equal lien with last mort. July 1, 3 years, 5 %. 3,550

Bader, Henry to Maria S. Heiser extrx. Christopher Heiser. 70th st, n s, 268 e 1st av, 20x102.2. June 30, 3 years, 5 %. 7,500

Behrens, Johanna to Louis Beer and Michael Shaffner, Brooklyn. 2d av. P. M. June 30, due July 1, 1894, or installs, 5 %. 2,500

Benjamin, Morris to Emily S. Andrews, New York, and Deborah K. Lothrop, Summit, N. J. Broome st, No. 117, s s, 75 e Pitt st, runs south 80 x west 0.8 x south 20.3 x east 25.8 x north 100.3 to Broome st, x west 25. July 1, 3 years, 5 %. 16,000

Brown, James to The Rector, &c., of Trinity Church, New York. 92d st, s s, 400 w Columbus av, 100x100.8. June 30, due July 1, 1894. 43,500

Brown, Jane A. to Charles Weinberg. West End av and 104th st. P. M. June 26, due June 29, 1892. 20,000

Bach, Lewis Z. to Rocco Dia. 112th st. P. M. June 30, due July 1, 1892, 5 %. 3,000

Same to same. Thompson st, P. M. June 30, due July 1, 1892, 5 %. 3,000

Barron, Mary A. wife of and Joseph to Edith Murray. 42d st, n s, 100 e 11th av, 25x100.5. June 30, due July 1, 1896, 5 %. 20,000

Same to Stanley W. Dexter trustee. Same property. Sub. to mort. $20,000. June 30, due July 1, 1892. 3,000

Same to Peter J. Ryan. Same property. Sub. to morts. $23,000. June 30, 1 year. 800

Baldwin, William B. to James J. Clancy. 67th st, s s, 175 w 8th av. P. M. June 3, due Jan. 1, 1892, 5 %. 9,500

Same to same. 67th st, s s, 200 w 8th av. P. M. June 3, due Jan. 1, 1892, 5 %. 9,500

Brennan, Thomas J. to The Mutual Life Ins. Co of New York. 106th st, n s, 100 w 8th av, 75x183. June 26, 1 year. 25,000

Brennan, Thomas and Winifred his wife to David Steinfeld. Water st, s e cor Market slip, 26x80. Sub. to morts. $29,000. June 26, note, 3 months. 2,500

Broggelwirth, Emil, Brooklyn, to Caroline L. Macy. 2d av, n w cor 100th st, 25.11x100. June 26, 3 years, 5 %. gold, 20,000

Same to same. 2d av, w s, 25.11 n 100th st, 25x100. June 26, 3 years, 5 %. gold, 14,000

Same to Eliza L Macy. 2d av, w s, 50.11 n 100th st, 25x100. June 26, 3 years, 5 %. 15,000

Same to William M. Kingsland, Mt. Pleasant, N. Y. 2d av, w s, 75.11 n 100th st, 25x100. June 26, 3 years, 5 %. gold, 16,000

Same to Samuel Weil. 2d av, n w cor 100th st, 100x100.11. Sub. to morts. $65,000. June 26, 4 months. 15,000

Bryan, Annie V. wife of and William to the trustees of the Lenox Library. Amsterdam av. P. M. June 23, due July 1, 1894, 5 %. gold, 11,000

Benjamin, Mary wife of Jacob to Jonas Weil and Bernhard Mayer. Mott st, No. 58, e s, 75 n Bayard st, 25x47. June 29, demand. 490

Same to same. Same property. June 29, installs. 4,500

Same to George M. Miller and ano. trustees Levin R. Marshall dec'd. Same property. June 29, due Dec. 1, 1896, 5 %. 14,000

Campbell, John V. to The Baron De Hirsch Fund. Monroe st, s s, 269.3 e Scammel st, 24.9x97.8. June 26, due June 1, 1896, 5 %. 21,000

Campbell, John V. to Joseph L. Buttenwieser. Monroe st, No. 247, s s, 269.3 e Scammel st, 24.9x97.8. Sub. to mort. $21,000. June 26, demand. 8,700

Colman, Charles H. to Deborah B. Dilleber. Southern Boulevard, w s, 75 n Valentine av, runs west 100 x north 25 x west 20 x north 25 x east 120 to Boulevard x south 50. Mar. 5, 5 years, 5 %. 5,500

Cazenove-Jones, Harriet C. wife of and Frank to Francis H. Weeks and ano. trustees for Helen E. Sedgwick formerly Metcalfe. 74th st. P. M. June 24, 3 years or installs, 5 %. 25,000

Same to Carrie S. Kennedy. Same property. P. M. June 24, 1½ years, or installs. 5,000

Callahan, Cornelius to The Dry Dock Savings Inst. 24th st, s s, 225 w 1st av, 25x98.10. June 30, due July 1, 1892, 4½ %. 6,000

Chisolm, Benjamin O. to John H. Rhoades et al. trustees Benjamin F. Wheelwright. 14th st, No. 50, s s, 225 e 6th av, 22.6x103.3. June 17, due July 1, 1892, 5 %. 25,000

Cushman, Lucy wife of Edward G. to The Mutual Life Ins Co. 38th st, s s, 233.4 w 7th av, 20.8x98.9. June 29, 1 year, 5 %. 10,000

Cohen, Adolph and Harry Fischel to Max Lubetkin. Henry st, s e cor Birmingham st, 38x43. June 24, due June 27, 1894. 7,500

Cavinato, Luigi, Guiseppe, Steffano and Natale to John Bell & Son. Willis av, w s, 25 s 135th st, 50x81.6. May 8, due Dec. 1, 1891, or sooner. 1,500

Cowen, William F. to Henry Morgenthau. Wadsworth av, e s, 75 s 179th st. P. M. June 9, due June 15, 1894, 5 %. 1,600

Cowen, Jane to Henry Morgenthau. Wadsworth av, e s, 50 s 179th st. P. M. June 9, due June 15, 1894, 5 %. 1,600

Cowen, Mary E. to Henry Morgenthau. Wadsworth av, e s, 75 n 178th st. P. M. June 9, due June 15, 1894, 5 %. 1,600

Clark, Matthew to David Mitchell. 74th st, n s 446 w Columbus av, 22x102.2. Sub. to morts. $69,000. Nov. 17, 1 year. 2,600

Same to same. 74th st, n s, 468 w Columbus av, 22x102.2. Sub. to morts. $69,000. Nov. 17, 1 year. 3,000

Same to same. 74th st, n s, 490 w Columbus av, 20x102.2. Sub. to morts. $68,000. Nov. 17, 1 year. 3,000

Same to same. 74th st, n s, 510 w Columbus av, 20x102.2. Sub. to morts. $68,000. Nov. 17, 1 year. 3,000

Same to same. 74th st, n s, 530 w Columbus av, 20x102.2. Sub. to morts. $65,000. Nov. 17, 1 year. 3,000

Same to Alfred C. Oliver. 74th st, n s, 400.3 w Columbus av, 22.9x102.2. Sub. to morts. $20,000. June 25, 1 year. 3,000

Same to The Hardwood Decorative Co. 74th st, n s, 400.3 w Columbus av, 149.9x102.2. Sub. to morts. June 25, due Oct. 15, 1891. 45,000

Same to Thomas Hagan. 74th st, n s, 446 w Columbus av, 104x102.2. Sub. to morts. $176,600. June 25, 1 year or sooner. 2,694

Cronly, John E. to The German Evangelical Lutheran Church of St. Matthew. 167th st, s s, 139.4 e Amsterdam av, 19.1x109.3x10x120.4. June 30, due July 1, 1896, 5 %. 4,000

Church, Calvin C., Brooklyn, to Charles D. Rust. Hudson st, No 621, s w cor Jane st, runs south 19 x west 40.3 x south 1.3 x west 14.4 x north 14 to Jane st, x east 55.3 to beginning. July 1, 1 year. 3,500

Dean, William E. to The United States Life Ins. Co. in City of New York. 125th st, n s, 225 e 7th av, 75x99.11. July 1, 3 years, 5 %. 75,000

Diefenthaler, Henry to Auguste and Katharina Zolvert. 1st av, w s, 124.9 n 21st st, 24x100. Lease. June 30, due July 1, 1896, 5 %. 5,000

Danziger, Raphael to Thomas D. Mason and ano. trustees Sidney Mason. 56th st. P. M. June 29, 3 years, 5 %. 13,000

Donovan, Cornelius J. to Sarah M. Shotts, Yonkers. Kingsbridge road. P. M. June 26, 5 years, 5 %. 3,000

Dazian, Wolf to W. Jennings Demorest. 5th av, s w cor 17th st. P. M. Sub. to mort. $75,000. June 22, due July 1, 1892, 5 %. 25,000

Same to Rector, &c., of the Church of Zion and St. Timothy, New York. Same property. P. M. June 27, 3 years, 4½ %. gold, 75,000

Dennerlein, Julia wife of and John to Abbie H. Wightman. Pelham av, s s, lot 160, map of heirs of Rev. W. Powell, Fordham, 50x117.10, except part taken for widening Pelham av. June 26, 30 days. 750

Dreyfus, Julius to Frederic J. Middlebrook, Brooklyn. Goerck st, w s, 100 s Houston st, 3 lots. 3 P. M. morts., each $6,000. July 1, 1 year or sooner, 5 %. 18,000

Donald, Henry W. to The Mutual Life Ins. Co. of New York. West End av and 93d st P. M. July 1, 1 year. 8,000

Dow, Myron W. to Elizabeth McCleery guard. for Jennie, Posey and Mills McCleery. Eagle av. P. M. July 1, 2 years or sooner. 2,000

Eim, Paul to Henry Hawkes, Riverside, Conn. 181st st. P. M. July 1, installs. 3,400

Eichler, John F. and Maria M. his wife to Michael V. Hutzler. Inwood av, e s, 175 s Wolf pl, 50x130. June 4, 1 year. 225

Egler, George G. to Henry Sturz. Essex st. P. M. June 30, 5 years, 5 %. 7,000

Elliott, Isaac M. to Charles B. Carpenter. 180th st, n s, 100 e 11th av, 25x219.6 to 181st st. June 15, 3 years, 5 %. 5,500

Fielitz, Carrie H. widow to The Manhattan Life Ins. Co. Av A, e s, 50.5 n 58th st, 16.8x75. June 29, 1 year, 5 %. 2,500

Fitzpatrick, John J. and Philip A. to James McCreery. 106th st, n s, 100 w Madison av, 100x100. Building loan. Sub. to mort. $38,000. June 26, due April 3, 1894. 35,000

Fuller, Charles A. to Susan L. Roberts and ano. exrs. and trustees Marshall O. Roberts. 9th av and 82d st. P. M. June 29, 5 years, 5 %. 300,000

Feury, Catharine V. to George W. Kidd. 87th st, No 151, n s, 408.4 w 9th av, 16.8x100.8. June 10. 25,000

Ferdinand, Clara to Edwin A. Whitfield. 127th st, s s, 172 w 7th av, 18x99.11. June 30, 1 year. 3,000

Fairman, Charles F., Brooklyn, to John J. Stiger. Lenox av, No. 423, w s, 24.11 n 131st st, 25x75. June 27, installs. 3,500

Forschner, Charles to Serena Wronkow. 41st st, No. 341, n s, 204.1 w 1st av, 29.4x98.9. July 1, 3 years, 4½ %. 12,000

Feehan, John J. and Ernest Hammer to Charles Laue, Brooklyn. Av B and 87th st. P. M. June 30, due July 1, 1892, or sooner. 19,810

Grasser, Michael to Hartman F. Gundrum, Brooklyn. 35th st, n s, 100 e 3d av, 20x98.9. July 1, 5 years, 5 %. 3,000

Grozcky, Sarah wife of and Abraham J. to Emilio Del Pino. Lewis st, No. 96, e s, 25 s Stanton st, 25x75. Sub. to morts. $7,000. July 1, 3 years. 5,000

Green, Max to Mary A. G. McLochlin. 7th av, e s, 37.3 s 22d st, 18.5x50. July 1, 5 years, 5 %. 11,000

Gallagher, Kate wife of and Joseph F. to Canda & Mathews Mfg. Co. (Lim.) 114th st, s s, 300 w 1st av, 30x100. Sub. to mort. $12,000. June 26, 1 year. 1,900

Gault, Mary wife of James to Sens, Scheubner & Fredrich. 82d st, s s, 157 w 8th av, 18x100. Sub. to mort. $38,000. June 24, 3 months. 2,500

Gaw, Ellen E. wife of and Thomas C. to Hugh W. and Wilson Catherwood, Philadelphia. Pleasant av, n w cor 122d st, 17.11x66. June 25, due July 22, 1892, or installs. 620

Gray, William H. mortgagor with Lehman Bernheimer, Munich, Bavaria, mortgagee. Extension of mort. June 22. nom

Hansson, Christine wife of and Ola to Jessie Alexander. 165th st, s s, 250 e 10th av, 50x63.4x50.6x63.4. June 23, 3 years. 2,500

Hill, Elizabeth E. T. wife of and George A. to Mary Hill. Highbridge or Fordham road. n e cor Croton Aqueduct, 170.7x94.6x133x181.10. June 25, 3 years or sooner, 5 %. 5,000

Hillman, Caleb M. to Henry Morgenthau. Kingsbridge road. P. M. June 15, 3 years, 5 %. 7,350

Same to same. Amsterdam av. P. M. June 15, 3 years, 5 %. 4,270

Hulberg, Frederick to Adele Hutton, Marquise de Portes. 122d st. P. M. June 25, due July 1, 1894, or sooner, 5 %. 12,000

Halley, Mary E. to Hugh N. Camp. Lots 46 and 47 map of 71 lots Kingsland estate. P. M. June 15, due June 25, 1894, 5 %. 900

Hauley, Thomas and Maria his wife to Georgis Narberti and Giovanna De M. his wife. Tinton av. P. M. June 29, installs. 2,050

H.rsen, Henrietta wife of Isidor and Bertha wife of Isidor Schwarzkopf to The Grand Lodge of the United States of the Independent Order Free Sons of Israel. 26th st, No. 441, n s, 417.11 w 9th av, 26.8x98.9. June 29, 5 years, 4½ %. 12,000

Hechinger, Joseph and Bertha his wife to Edward Harmon and ano. trustees Philip Harmon dec'd. Pitt st, No. 12, e s, 125 s Broome st, 25x100. May 15, 3 years, 5 %. 14,000

Same to Harmon and Adele Cozzens. Same property. Sub. to last mort. May 15, 3 years, 5 %. 6,000

Same to Bertha Oppenheimer. Same property. Sub. to morts $30,000. May 15, due Oct. 20, 1891, 5 %. 2,000

Hegelein, John C. to Sarah M. Shotts, formerly Smith, Yonkers, N. Y. Broadway or Kingsbridge road. P. M. June 25, due June 27, 1894, 5 %. 2,760

Hogan, Mary to Hugh N. Camp. Lot 45 map 71 lots Kingsland estate, 24th Ward. P. M. June 15, due June 25, 1894, 5 %. 450

Harris, Joseph L. to Gustav Lange. 111th st, P. M. June 30, due Oct. 13, 1891, 5 %. 8,000

Habes, Gustav to Sophie Beaudel. 2d av, w s, 50.4 n 88th st, 25x75. June 30, due July 1, 1892, 5 %. 2,000

Hausler, Andrew to Adam Moran. 10th st. P. M. July 1, 5 years, 5 %. 6,000

Hayes, Teresa F. wife of Thomas F. to William D. Warden, Burgiss Hill, near Brighton, Eng. 120th st. P.M. June 29, 3 years, 5 %. 13,000

Humphreys, Robert E. to Edward Mitchell and ano. trustees of Effie K. Haight. Railroad or Vanderbilt av and Jacob st. P. M. July 1, 1 year, 5 %. gold, 1,000

Hatton, Elizabeth wife of Jonathan to Martha Foggin. Forest av, w s, 123.9 n 165th st, 75x200. July 1, 5 years or sooner. 6,000

Harbison, Thomas H. to THE TITLE GUARANTEE AND TRUST CO. 27th st. P. M. June 15, due July 1, 1896, 5 %. 15,000

Hughes, Michael to THE GERMAN-AMERICAN REAL ESTATE TITLE GUARANTEE CO. 92d st, n s, 150 w 4th av, 17x100.8. June 29, 3 years, 5 %. 14,000

Jones, Leonora C. to Robert N. Quinn. Webster av, s e cor Tower pl, 25x100. June 29, due Nov. 13, 1893, 5 %. 255

Jennings, Samuel H. E. and Thomas Welstead to John E. Glimm. 47th st. P. M. June 29, installs, 5 %. 11,000

Jewell, Alfred to Frederick A. Constable et al. trustees Richard Arnold. 125th st, No 47 and 49, n s, 247.6 e Lenox av, 37.6x99.11. June 30, 5 years, 4½ %. 35,000

Same to same. Grand st, Nos. 214 and 216, n s, 64.2 w Elizabeth st, 30x51x35.6x50.8. June 30, 5 years, 4½ %. 12,000

Jones, William H. and Maria his wife to Adam Harrmann. 109th st, s s, 66 e 2d av, 17x60.8. June 26, 3 years, 5 %. 1,200

Kahn, Leopold to Frederica W. Trow individ. and guard. of Bertha A. Trow. 134th st, n s, 175 e 7th av, 25x99.11. June 26, installs, 5 %. 18,000

Keller, Theodore with The Grand Lodge of the United States of the Independent Order Free Sons of Israel both mortgagees. Agreement as to priority of morts. made by Henrietta Hirsch and Bertha Schwarzkopf. Dec. 18, 1890. nom

Keller, Pauline to THE CONNECTICUT MUTUAL LIFE INS CO. 1st av, e s, 50.8 n 90th st, 25x94. June 30, 3 years, 5 %. 9,500

Kraus, Maurice J. mortgagor with The New York Association for Improving the Condition of the Poor. Extension of mort. May 18. nom

Kerber, Marks and Morris to Sara L. Cooke. Attorney st, e s, 150 n Stanton st, 25x100.5. June 30, 3 years, 5 %. 20,000

Kerber, Marks and Morris to Alexander Haft and Max Cohen. Attorney st, e s, 150 n Stanton st, 25x100.5. Sub. to mort. $20,000. June 30, due Jan. 1, 1896, or installs. 5,750

Kahn, Isaac to Isaac Stiefel. 49th st. P. M. June 25, due July 1, 1894, 5 %. 5,000

Same to same. Same property. P. M. 2d mort. June 25, due July 1, 1893, 5 %. 3,500

Kaplan, Aaron to THE COMMONWEALTH INSURANCE CO. of New York. Forsyth st. P. M. July 1, 3 years, 5 %. 18,000

Kane, Hugh to THE EMIGRANT INDUST. SAVINGS BANK. 2d av, w s, 86 5 n 36th st, 18.6x105. June 30, 1 year, 4½ %. 1,000

Knecht, Jacob and Louisa his wife to Henry Baruch. 60th st. P. M. July 1, 2 years. 2,000

Laue, Charles to Francis H. Weeks. 75th st, n s, 98 e Av A, 50x102.2. June 30, due July 1, 1896, 5 %. 8,000

Leeder, John to Alfred Storms. 117th st, n s, 127.4 e 1st av, 16.8x100.11. Payable on death of mortgagor. June 30, 5 %. 2,000

Lawrence, Frank R. to James N. Platt trustees John G. Kane. Madison av. P. M. June 30, 1 year, 5 %. 35,000

Levett, Alexander to Catharine A. Taylor et al. exrs. Moses Taylor. Grand st, n s, 2 lots. P. M. June 30, 1 year, 5 %. 15,000

Lewis, Edward to Seth M. Milliken. 160th st, s s, 149.4 e St. Nicholas av, 26x100. June 29, due April 3, 1892. 12,000

Littlefield, Agnes H. wife of and Frederick M. with William A. Booth trustees J. A. Edgar both mortgagees. Agreement as to priority of mort. made by Elizabeth K. Smith. June 30. nom

Levy, Amelia to THE NATIONAL PARK BANK of New York. Madison av, e s, 60.11 n 122d st, 20x100. June 29, installs. 31,262

Lorigan, George T. to Henry Morgenthau. 180th st. P. M. June 12, due June 15, 1893, 5 %. 1,890

Lowen, Charles and Edward F. Halliday to Thomas H. Bauchle trustee for George Y. Bauchle. Rivington st, n w cor Sheriff st, 25x81. June 25, 3 years. 35,000

Same to Thomas H. Bauchle. Sheriff st, w s, 81 n Rivington st, runs north 19 x west 50 x south 21 x east 25 x north 2 x east 25. June 25, 3 years. 10,000

Lynch, Michael and Susanna his wife to W. R. Lamberton, Pelham Manor, N. Y. Tiffany st. P. M. June 24, 3 years or installs, 5 %. 2,200

Langer, Mary wife of and Samuel to the trustees of the Lenox Library. Rutgers pl, n w cor Clinton st, 26.6x131.10. June 26, 5 years, 5 %. gold, 28,000

Laccorn, Elise wife of and Paul Eugene to Barbara Gabrman, L. I. City. 1st av, No. 837. P. M. Sub. to morts. $6,121. June 30, due July 1, 1896, 5 %. 9,800

Lachenbruch, Henrietta to Solomon Tim. 74th st, No. 152, s s, abt 75 e Lexington av, 18.9x88.2. June 30, 5 years, 5 %. 10,000

Labriola, Joseph to Henry de F. Weekes. Mulberry st, No. 85, w s, 150.7 s Canal st, runs south 25.9 x west 55.5 x north 0.6 x west 44.7 x north 25.3 x east 100. July 1, 1 year, 5 %. 8,000

Levi, Lena to Josephine Reinhardt. 2d av. P. M. July 1, 3 years or sooner, 5 %. 1,000

Mulqueen, Michael J. and Joseph F. to Henry Morgenthau. 181st st. P. M. June 11, due June 15, 1894, 5 %. 12,600

Same to same. 11th av. P. M. June 11, due June 15, 1894, 5 %. 3,000

Madden, Joseph H. to Louis Isenburger et al. trustees of Rosina Bluun. 48th st. P. M. July 1, 5 years, 5 %. 6,500

Mass, Abraham W. to THE TITLE GUARANTEE AND TRUST CO. Spring st. P. M. June 17, due July 1, 1894, 5 %. 11,000

Mathews, William J., Yonkers, N. Y., to Fanny L. Korn. 88th st, n e cor Madison av, 36.8x100.8. June 10, 6 months or sooner. 25,000

Michailoff, Alexis and Julianna his wife to William D. Warden, Burgess Hall, Brighton, Eng. 2d av, e s, 20.5 s 43d st, 20x81. June 26, 3 years, 5 %. 9,000

Maibrun, Henry to Henry Morgenthau. Kingsbridge road and 180th st. P. M. June 10, due June 15, 1894, 5 %. 3,600

Murray, Susan to Eleanor P. Gage. 83d st, s s, 355 e Amsterdam av, 16x102.2 Sub. to mort $12,500. June 29, due June 30, 1892. 2,000

Meehan, Peter to Bernheimer & Schmid. 2d av, No. 804. Saloon lease. June 30, 1 year. 2,000

Mapes, Daniel, Jr., to Louisa S. Upson. River road, n w s, adj lands late of heirs Isaiah Golden, now Thomas Munford, 50.3x149.6x50.3x155; Prospect av, s w cor River road, runs northwest 152.5 x southwest 121.8 x northwest 50 x southwest 50 x southeast 71 x northeast 50 x southeast 149.6 to River road, x northeast 87. June 17, 3 years, 5 %. 3,500

Meyer, Elise to THE MANHATTAN LIFE INS. CO. Lexington av. P. M. June 22, 3 years, 5 %. 7,000

Mull, De Witt and Gottlieb Fromer to Ella J. Hennessy, Palmer, Mass. 105th st, s s, 230 w Park av, 25x100.11. June 29, 3 years, 5 %. 20,000

Same to Buffalo Door and Sash Co. 105th st, s s, 180 w Park av, 75x100.11. June 29, due Sept. 10, 1891. 3,500

Muller, Gustav to Eva Bechtel extrx. George Bechtel. Houston st, s e cor Allen st, being No. 169 East Houston st and 206 Allen st. Lease. June 29, demand. 1,955

McGinty, Joseph to Beadleston & Woerz. 4th av, No. 73. Saloon lease. June 22, demand. 2,000

McCamman, Samuel to Henry Morgenthau. 178th st. P. M. June 15, 3 years, 5 %. 4,000

McClenahan, James to Solomon Sayles. 10th st, Nos. 66 and 68, s s, 78.1 e 6th av, 49.9x92.3 x49.7x94.3. June 24, 6 months, 5 %. 44,500

McGrath, Mary J. to Cyrus Lawton, New Rochelle, N. Y. Crotona pl, w s, 199.11 s 171st st, 60x100. June 15, due Mar. 1, 1893. 600

McKenna, Owen E. to James Everard. Chatham sq., No. 23. Assignment of lease as security for mortgage. June 29. nom

Neun, George to Solomon Frank. 8th st. P. M. June 30, 1 year. 1,500

Noble, James to Thomas E. Greacen. Grant av, e s, 98.6 s 162d st, 16x105. June 25, 1 year, 5 %. 2,000

Same to same. Grant av, e s, 114.6 s 162d st, 16x105. June 25, 1 year, 5 %. 2,000

Necarsulmer, Nathan to THE TITLE GUARANTEE AND TRUST CO. Murray st. P. M. July 1, 3 years, 4½ %. 30,000

Opitz, Henry C. to THE KINGS COUNTY SAVINGS INST. 11th st, No. 117, n s, 197 w 6th av, 23x103.3 July 1, 1 year, 5 %. 9,000

O'Neill, John to THE FARMER'S LOAN AND TRUST CO. 6th av, n e cor 22d st, runs east 95 x north 98.9 x west 34 x south 24.8 x east 1 x south 22.4 x west 62 x south 51.9 to beginning. July 1, 3 years, 4½ %. 50,000

Oakley, Thomas C. Gilbert, Jr., and John B. H. to George H. Cook et al. exrs. and trustees Elisha Bloomer. 19th st. P. M. June 12, due June 1, 1896, 5 %. 17,000

Paris, Auguste J. to Charles Wurster, Brooklyn. 44th st. P. M. June 29, 5 years, 5 %. 10,000

Patton, James G. to The Mount Morris Co-operative Building and Loan Assoc. Forest av, w s, 125 n Cedar st, 111.5x175 to Jackson av, x 111.9x175. June 29, installs, 5 %. 5,000

Patton, James G. to Leopold Yankauer. 3d av. P. M. June 30, 2 years, 5 %. 6,000

Parker, Cornelius B. to Elizabeth wife of John Morris. 62d st. P. M. June 26, due June 30, 1892, 5 %. 1,000

Peters, George and Maggie his wife to Ellen Donohue. Taylor av. P. M. June 20, installs, 5 %. 2,300

Purcell, Edward to Charles E. Appleby et al. trustees Leonard Appleby. 80th st, s s, 350 e Amsterdam av, 75x102.2. July 1, 1 year, 5 %. 20,000

Peters, Ella A. to Wilhelmina Mauer, Brooklyn. Spring st, s s, 90 w Hudson st, 20x75. June 30, due July 1, 1893, 5 %. 5,000

Palmer, Sarah J. widow with Clifford A. Hand exr. Charles G. Havens. Agreement as to payment of mort. May 6. nom

Rohrig, William F. to D. Stuart Dodge, Simsbury, Conn. 2d av, No. 2158, e s, 25.11 s 111th st, 25x100. July 1, 3 years, 5 %. 16,500

Reis, Margaretha wife of and Michael A. to Robert I. Murray et al. trustees of Lindley Murray dec'd. Lewis st, No. 55, w s, 175 n Delancey st, 25x100. July 1, 5 years, 5 %. 7,500

Rothschild, Sophie to John M. Conway. 79th st. P. M. July 1, 2 years or sooner, 5 %. 7,000

Roessle, Theophilus mortgagor with THE BANK FOR SAVINGS, New York. Extension of mort. June 25. nom

Same with same. Extension of mort. June 25. nom

Same with same. Extension of mort. June 25. nom

Romano, Rosario to Bernheimer & Schmid. 115th st, No. 231 E. Saloon lease. June 25, note, demand. 2,200

Rosenfeld, Rosanna to Charles Schaper exr. Rebecca M. Coop. Rivington st. P. M. June 26, due March 17, 1892, 5 %. 6,500

Reim, Maggie heir of Barbara Koetzner to August Freutel. 151st st, n s, 200 w Courtlandt av, 25x116.4x25x116.3. June 26, due July 1, 1894. 1,600

Ridal, Annie widow to The Mount Morris Co-operative Building and Loan Assoc. 110th st, n s, 20 w 4th av, 20x100.11. June 29, installs, 5 %. 2,500

Ruff, August to John J. Jones and ano. trustees David Jones. Spring st, No. 192, s s, 25x100. June 29, 5 years, 5 %. 28,000

Rugen, Anna and Charles H. to John Lecron. Bayard st, s s, 150 w Bowery, 25x85. June 24, 1 year. 1,200

Schmeckenbecker, Martin to Merritt Trimble. Av A, No. 1313, n w cor 70th st, 27.8x94. June 29, 5 years, 5 %. 25,000

Same to Zoe D. Underhill guard. of Walter D. and Ruth Underhill. Av A, No. 1315, w s, 27.8 n 70th st, 27.8x94. June 29, 5 years, 5 %. 15,000

Storm, Walton, Edith and Theodora M. and Sarah M. Storm individ. and extrx. Thomas Storm to THE BROADWAY SAVINGS INST. Old slip, Nos. 10 and 12 and No. — Water st, begins Old slip, n e cor Water st, 45.5x47.7x63 8x24.4x22x22.5. June 29, 1 year, 4½ %. 16,000

Sylvester, Hyman to The Baron de Hirsch Fund. Wooster st. P. M. May 27, due July 1, 1894, 5 %. 25,000

Sanchez, Henry and Harriet A. to Martin L. Townsend trustee. 27th st, s s, 300 w 6th av, 80x98.9. June 22, 1 year. 8,500

Schaffmier, Martin J. to William Austin. 121st st, No. 405 E. Lease. June 24, demand. 1,385

Schenkberg, Eliza M. B. widow to THE NEW YORK LIFE INS. AND TRUST CO. 35th st. P. M. June 25, 3 years or sooner, 4½ %. 28,000

Schulte, Albert to John Beckmann. 1st av, s w cor 1st st, 26x58x33.2x57.11. June 1, 5 years, 5 %. 8,000

Schwab, Sidney to Bernheimer & Schmid. Columbus av, No. 734. Saloon lease. June 25, note, demand. 3,500

Sloane, Eliza M. and Helena Hayes and Elizabeth Schwartz mortgagees with Samuel Gleason mortgagor. Extension of mort. June 20. nom

Smith, William W. to THE BANK FOR SAVINGS, New York. Broadway, No. 84, and Nos. 3, 5 and 7 Wall st, begins Wall st, s w cor New st, runs west 24.2 x still west 39.1 x south 32 x west 39.8 to Broadway, x south 30.11 x east 78.11 x north 0.6 x east 26.10 to New st, x north 58.2 to beginning. June 25, due Feb. 14, 1892, 4½ %. 50,000

Smith, Elizabeth K. wife of and Albert E. to Frederick M. Littlefield. 122d st, s s, 174.6 e 7th av, runs south 60 x east 0.6 x south 40.11 x east 100 x north 100.11 to st, x west 100.6. Sub. to mort. $75,000. June 30, due July 3, 1891. 35,000

Smith, Elizabeth K. wife of and Albert E. to William A. Booth trustee James A. Edgar. 123d st, s s, 257.6 e 7th av, 17.6x100.11. June 29, due June 1, 1894, 5 %. 15,000

Sichel, Fanny to Morris Heyman. 1st av. P. M. June 30, 2 years or sooner, 5 %. 3,250

Schaffner, Louis P. to Eva Bechtel extrx. George Bechtel. 3d st, No. 26 W. Lease. June 29. 2,500

Schwoerer, Jacob to THE GERMAN SAVINGS BANK, New York. 1st av, w s, 52 s St. Marks pl, 24.6x50. June 29, 1 year. 15,000

Schulte, Gepke wife of and Albert to Cornelia L. Marshall. 1st av, n w cor 60th st, 25.5x100. June 30, 5 years, 5 %. 15,000

Schaefer, Martha to Margaret Lusk. Webster av, s w cor 174th st, 25x26. June 15, notes. 1,300

Stegmuller, August to Elizabetha Schwarzwalder. 45th st. P. M. July 1, 3 years, 5 %. 15,000

Same to Charles D. Shirmer. Same property. P. M. Sub. to last mort. July 1, installs. 2,600

Schoen, Nickolaus or Nicholas to THE GERMAN SAVINGS BANK. 39th st, No. 314, s s, 175 e 2d av, 25x75. June 30, 1 year. 9,000

Strunck, Henry to Wilhelm Busse. 60th st, n s, 175.1 e 11th av. P. M. July 1, installs, 4½ %. 10,250

Same to same. 60th st, n s, 200.7 e 11th av. P. M. July 1, installs, 4½ %. 10,250

Solomon, Simon to Michael Arnheim. 6th st, s s, 264 e Av C, 24x90. July 1, 5 years, 5 %. 9,000

Simon, Adolph to THE DRY DOCK SAVINGS INST. Av C, w s, 81.4 s 7th st, 20x83. July 1, due June 30, 1892, 4½ %. 7,000

Sutliff, John C. to THE EMIGRANT INDUST. SAVINGS BANK. Hester st, No. 14, s s, 50 w Suffolk st, 25x69x25x70. June 26, 1 year, 4½ %. 6,000

Smith, Margaret E. formerly Phelan wife of and Alfred M. J. to John W. C. Leveridge. Houston st, n s, 25 w Av B, 20x75. July 1, 1 year, 5 %. 1,000

Sampson, George H., Medford, Mass., to Cornelius J. Donovan. Kingsbridge road. P. M. July 1, 1 year, 5 %. 1,000

Stokes, Mary A. to THE MANHATTAN SAVINGS INST. 80th st and Madison av. P. M. June 30, 1 year, 4 %. 30,000

Steffens, John D. to Christian H. D. Steffens. Greenwich st, w s, 18 n Charlton st, 18x54.4. July 1, 2 years or sooner, 5 %. 5,000

Tompkins, Griffen, Brooklyn, to Martha E. wife of Thomas K. Egbert, Catharine L. wife of George Lowther and Clara wife of Charles Greer. 56th st, n s, 150 w 6th av. P. M. July 1, 3 years, 5 %. gold, 28,000

Same to same. 56th st, n s, 178 w 6th av. P. M. July 1, 3 years, 5 %. gold, 21,000

Same to same. 56th st, n s, 199 w 6th av. P. M. July 1, 3 years, 5 %. gold, 28,000

Same to same. 56th st, n s, 227 w 6th av. P. M. July 1, 3 years, 5 %. gold, 21,000

Same to same. 56th st, n s, 248 w 6th av. P. M. July 1, 3 years, 5 %. gold, 28,000

Same to same. 56th st, n s, 276 w 6th av. P. M. July 1, 3 years, 5 %. gold, 21,000

Same to same. 56th st, n s, 297 w 6th av. P. M. July 1, 3 years, 5 %. gold, 28,000

Twitchin, Elizabeth to E. Augusta Tweed. Interior lot, begins 125.10 w 3d av and 100 s 163d st. P. M. June 30, due June —, 1894, 5 %. 3 000

Tileston, Sarah A., Boston, Mass., to THE TITLE GUARANTEE AND TRUST Co. 6th av, No. 610, e s, 24.7 s 36th st, 24.8x62.6. June 23, due July 1, 1896, 4 %. 25,000

Trieber, Frank B. to THE WASHINGTON LIFE INS. Co. Liberty st, No. 98, s e cor Church st, 26.2x54x25.6x54. July 1, due June 1, 1894, 5 %. 75,000

Timmermann, Henry to Maria wife of Anthony Miller. 11th st. P. M. July 1, 3 years or sooner, 5 %. 4,000

The Congregation Chasam Sopher to The Congregation Rodolph Scholem. Clinton st. P. M. July 1, 1 month. 45,000

Same to Julius Lehman. Same property. P. M. 2d mort. July 1, 1 year. 10,000

Taylor, Hannah to Ascher Weinstein. Division and Attorney sts. P. M. June 29, 1 year. 6,000

Ten Eick, Mary E. wife of Cornelius to Helen L. Cilley. 111th st, n s, 124.6 w Park av, 15.8 x100.11. June 25, 3 years, 5 %. 6,000

Thompson, Mary S. to Mary A. Walker, Westfield, S. I. Powell pl. P. M. June 30, 2 years or installs. 1,000

Varker, Thomas to Helenah Kouwenhoven, Long Island City. 80th st, n s, 85 w Lexington av, 20x100.5. June 29, due June 2, 1894, 4½ %. 14,000

Van Nest, Abraham R. to THE SEAMEN'S BANK FOR SAVINGS, New York. 23d st, s s, 175 e 7th av, 25x98.9. June 30, 3 years, 4½ %. 20,000

Vollman, Benjamin and Morris to Henry Morgenthau. 11th av and 179th st. P. M. June 12, due June 15, 1894, 5 %. 8,500

Wallace, James G. to THE MUTUAL LIFE INS. Co. of New York. Rivington st, Nos. 101 and 103, s e cor Ludlow st, 43.9x100. July 1, 1 year, 5 %. 22,500

Wallace, James G. and William J. Smith to THE MUTUAL LIFE INS. Co. of New York. Bowery, Nos. 258, 260 and 26½, w s, 252.7 n Prince st, 37.9x90.5x43.5x91. July 1, 1 year, 5 %. 30,000

Willenbrock, Frederick and Egbert Winkler to William H. Gebhard. Lexington av and 103d st. P. M. June 24, due July 1, 1894, or installs, 5 %. 10,000

Weinstein, Ascher to Frederic J. Middlebrook. 13th st. P. M. July 1, 1 year, 5 %. 10,000

Wenninger, John P. to Frederick Hautau. North st, n w cor Madison st, 50x100, 24th Ward. June 30, 2 years. 1,000

Walker, Fernando R to Edward Kilpatrick. Clinton pl, n s, 323.1 w Broadway, 87.6x93.11. July 1, 2 years, 5 %. 10,000

Warner, Mary P. widow to Elizabeth Gifford. Willard av, s s, 177.9 w Bronx River road, 25x100. July 1, 3 years. 1,500

Weiss, Georg to Katherina Prochazka. 4th st, s s, 100 w 1st av, 25x96.2. July 1, 2 years. 3,000

Winne, Marie N., Albany, N. Y., to Robert H. Matoews. 88th st, No. 334, s s, 175 w 1st av. P. M. June 29, 2 years. 3,000

Same to Elizabeth Diamond. 38th st, No. 332, s s, 200 w 1st av. P. M. June 29, 1 year. 3,000

Same to same. 38th st, No. 330, s s, 225 w 1st av. P. M. June 29, 1 year. 3,000

William R. Beal Land Improvement Co. to Emma L. Van Ness, Cornwall, N. Y. St. Anns av, s e cor St. Marys st, runs south 300 x east 90 x north 319.5 to st, x west 92.1; St. Anns av, e s, 25.4 n 141st st, 250x90; Crimmins av, s w cor St. Marys st, 111.8x58x94.5 to st, x81.10; Crimmins av, s e cor St. Marys st, 91.3x286.1 to Beekman av, x78.5x304.2; Beekman av, n e cor 141st st, 594.9 to St. Marys st, x88.11x601.4 to 141st st, x122.7. June 30, due July 1, 1892, 5 %. 50,000

Wirth, Louis to THE GERMAN SAVINGS BANK, New York. 85th st, s s, 180 e 3d av, 25x100. June 29, 1 year. 15,500

Same to same. 85th st, s s, 155 e 3d av, 25x100. June 29, 1 year. 18,500

Whitman, William S. to Cesare and Guiseppe Razzetti. South 5th av. P. M. June 30, 2 years or sooner, 5 %. 14,000

Wall, Elizabeth M. wife of and Matthew J. to Martha L. Andrews. 122d st, n s, 115.6 w 2d av, 14x100.11. June 27, 1 year. 500

Wodzicki, Peter C. and Theodora C. his wife, Brooklyn, to Jonas Weil and Bernhard Mayer. Cherry st. P. M. June 26, installs. 20,000

Wood, Frederick to Spencer Aldrich. 88th st. P. M. Sub. to mort. $40,000. June 10, due Oct. 1, 1891, or sooner. 58,500

KINGS COUNTY

JUNE 25, 26, 27, 29, 30, JULY 1.

Abbot, Edgar W. to The Title Guarantee and Trust Co. Dean st, s s, 215 e Rogers av, 60x 114.5. June 24, demand. $21,000

Acor, Kate wife of and Lewis to Lucia H. Rider. Jefferson av, n s, 155 e Stuyvesant av, 20x100. June 25, due May 1, 1894. gold, 3,500

Same to same. Jefferson av, n s, 115 e Stuyvesant av, 20x100. June 25, due May 1, 1893. 6,500

Same to Walter Powell, Farmingdale, L. I. Jefferson av, n s, 135 e Stuyvesant av, 20x 100. June 25, due May 1, 1894, 5 %. 6,500

Same to Harriett P. Mulford, Hempstead, L. I. Jefferson av, n s, 155 e Stuyvesant av, 20x 100. June 25, due May 1, 1894, 5 %. 3,000

Acor, Kate wife of and Lewis to Annie T. Jenks, Glen Head, L. I. Jefferson av, n s, 95 e Stuyvesant av, 20x100. June 25, due May 1, 1894, 5 %. 6,500

Ainslie, Elizabeth D. wife of and James to Mary E. wife of John B. Forbes Ross st, n s, 350 e Lee av, 20x100. June 22, due Dec. 19, 1891. 350

Allan, John T. and Nathaniel Proskey to Francis A. Doyle. 4th st, n e s, 277.10 n w 8th av, 20x95. June 25, demand. 2,000

Anderson, Thorvald and Lewis to Edward H. Moubray. Garfield pl. P. M. June 16, demand. 20,000

Same to same. Same property. Builder's loan. June 16, demand. 20,000

Armstrong, Benjamin to William D. Berrian. 3d av, w s, 40 s Wyckoff st, 20x80. June 27, 3 years, 5 %. 3,500

Alt, Joseph to Fannie Fischer. Rocakway av, s e cor Bergen st, 27.9x100. June 30, due July 1, 1894, 5 %. 800

Ames, Sarah E. wife of John H., Jr., to Jane E. Meeker widow. Keap st, No. 252, s s, 150 e Marcy av, 19x100. July 1, 3 years, 5 %. 1,000

Augustin, Ernst to Theodore F. Jackson. Knickerbocker av. P. M. June 15, due June 15, 1894, 5 %. 2,000

Blank, Peter to Theodore F. Jackson. Knickerbocker av and Thames st. P. M. May 15, due June 15, 1894, 5 %. 2,500

Bodkin, Dominick G. to Anna M. and Samuel C. Payson. Clinton av. P. M. July 1, 3 years, 5 %. 7,500

Boynton, William B. to Andrew and Jacob Meurer. Flushing av, s s, 275 e Marcy av, 25 x100, July 1, notes. 2,900

Same to Louis D. Giroux. Same property. P. M. July 1, 3 years, 5 %. 2,500

Brentano, John to George R. Kimmel. Hooper st. P. M. July 1, 3 years, 5 %. 2,200

Brownell, Asa C. to William W. and Jennie B. Pratt Bergen st. P. M. July 1, due Jan. 1, 1892, 5 %. 3,750

Same to John P. D. Angus. Bergen st. P. M. July 1, 3 months, 5 %. 13,500

Burke, John to Brooklyn City Co-operative Building and Loan Assoc. Centre st, n s, 219 e Columbia st, 20x100. March 1, installs. 800

Bard, Frederic B. to William L. Dowling and William S. Anderson. 18th av. P. M, May 15, due Feb. 15, 1892. 9,579

Same to same. Same property. P. M. May 15, due Feb. 15, 1892. 7,116

Battle, Martin to The Daily News Building, Savings and Loan Assoc. Monroe st. P. M. June 29, installs. 3,000

Beardell, John to August Hillmann. East 7th st, e s, 138.5 n Greenwood av, 25x100x23.8x 96.1. June 27, 5 years. 500

Berman, Rosa to Samuel J. Davidson. Atlantic av, n s, 52 w Columbus pl, 16x98.7. June 28, 3 years, 5 %. 228

Bliss, John A. to Jerome S. Plummer. Dean st. P. M. June 25, 2 years, 5 %. 16,500

Bliss, John A. to The Title Guarantee and Trust Co. Dean st, n s, 360 w New York av, 2 lots, each 20x100. 2 morts., each $7,000. June 27, 3 years, 5 %. 14,000

Bloch, Henriette to Jacob Worth and Vincent A. Strawson. Lots 112, 355 and 354 Worth & Strawson property. P. M. June 10, 3 years, 5 %. 275

Bowen, Bridget to Joseph P. Smith. East New York av, s s, 160 e Albany av, 40x100. June 24, 5 years. 800

Bowker, Theresa M. to George Bowker trustee Theresa M. Bowker. Lafayette av, s s, 60 w St. James pl, 20x100. June 30, 3 years, 5 %. 5,000

Brawnrinther, John to The Williamsburgh Savings Bank. Suydam st, n s, 125 e Central av, runs north 100 x west 22 x south 75 x west 2 x south 25 to st, x east 27. June 29, 1 year, 5 %. 1,500

Brosnan, Patrick to The Title Guarantee and Trust Co. Underhill av, e s, 72.2 n Prospect pl, runs east 100 x south 26.11 x east 86.9 to Clinton av, x north 50 x west 159.8 to av, x south 28.7. June 26, 3 years. 1,200

Brown, Mary widow to Elizabeth F. Driscoll widow. Madison st. P. M. June 25, due July 1, 1893, 5 %. 2,000

Bush, Wesley C. to Phineas C. Davidson. Hancock st, n s, 287.6 e Lewis av, 37.6x100. June 25, due July 1, 1893, 5 %. 3,000

Same to Carrie L. Gibson. Hancock st, n s, 250 e Lewis av, 37.6x100. June 25, due July 1, 1893, 5 %. 800

Butterfield, Charles F. and Elizabeth R. his wife to Richard Philpitt. Bushwick av, w s, 51.6 s Devoe st, 25.9x92.6x25x86.4. June 29, 1 year. 800

Carbonaro, Paolo to Cynthia Lott et al. Washington av. P. M. June 19, 3 years, 5 %. 900

Carbonaro, Paolo to The East Side Co-operative Building and Loan Assoc. Flatbush av, e s, 64.8 n Lefferts av, 25x75. May 6, installs. 4,000

Carpenter, Charlotte M. to Thomas Everit. McDonough st. P. M. Sub. to mort. $4,500. June 24, 2 years. 2,000

Case, Mary E. to Marianna H. Moody. 82d st. P. M. June 24, 2 years 700

Caulfield, Thomas to Henry Groge. Hale av, north cor Force Tubes av, 75x100x225x170. June 24, due July 1, 1892. 200

Chambers, Jared J. to Henry and John Von Glahn. Blake av, n e cor Hendrix st. P. M. June 1, 3 years, 5 %. 400

Same to same. Blake av, n s, 50 e Hendrix st. P. M. June 1, 3 years, 5 %. 250

Same to same. Blake av, n s, 75 w Hendrix st. P. M. June 1, 3 years, 5 %. 250

Same to same. Blake av, n s, 75 e Schenck av. P. M. June 1, 3 years, 5 %. 600

Clark, Bertha wife of Van Brunt Clark to Andrew G. Calder. 13th st, s s, 197.10 w 6th av. P. M. Sub. to mort. $4,000. June 25, 2 years, 5 %. 1,000

Same to William Mackenzie, of Bowden Cheshire, Eng. Same property. June 23, due July 1, 1894, 5 %. 4,000

Clayton, Joseph D. to Henry Weil. Dean st, s s, 366.8 w Buffalo av. P. M. June 22, 1 year. 1,600

Same to same. Same property. June 22, 1 year. 2,400

Cohn, Samuel to A. Judson Palmer. Blake av. P. M. June 25, 5 years. 4,900

Collins, Celia to The Brooklyn City Co-operative Building and Loan Assoc. Bridge st, s w cor Talman st, 25x50. June 26, installs. 5,000

Conkling, F. Augustus to Emilie K. Eeks. Macon st, n s, 22 e Ralph av, 18x100. June 25, 1 year. 800

Cook, Mary E to Mary W. Smith. Stone av, w s, 75 s Blake av, 25x100. June 24, 3 years 800

Cook, Mary E. to Sarah A. M. Kent. Stone av, w s, 150 s Blake av, 50x100. June 24, demand. 900

Curry, Peter to Sarah F. Mead. 17th st, s s, 460 e 10th av, 20x100.2. June 27, due May 1, 1894. 4,000

Caccia, Bertha S. to Theressa J. Hunt. Warren st. P. M. July 1, 2 years, 5 %. 2,900

Christensen, Ole to Henry Klee. 32d st, s w s, 100 n w 5th av, 16.8x100.2. June 25, due June 26, 1896. 1,200

Constable, James to Gordon L. Ford. Nassau st. P. M. July 1, 1 year, 5 %. 14,000

Cornwell, Theodore I. W. to Mary P. Hanington, Ridgewood, L. I. Park pl, s s, 100 e Troy av, 250x255.7. June 12. 6,500

Cosgrove, Ellen wife of and James to Agnes H. Davies. 3d av, s e s, 60 n e 27th st, 40x 100. June 29, due May 14, 1892. 2,000

Danancher, Elise to The East New York Savings Bank. Watkins st, e s, 100 n Blake av, 75x100. June 25, 1 year. 1,900

Same to same. Watkins st, e s, 175 n Blake av, 25x100. June 25, 1 year. 3,100

Davidson, Alexander to John P. Cranford and David H. Valentine. 45th st. P. M. June 22, 2 years, 5 %. 2,550

Deats, Edwin O. to Stephen C. Halstead. 18th st, s s, 68 w 6th av, 16x80. June 21, 1 year. 550

Dempsey, Catharine to Daniel S. Arnold. 7th av, n w cor 20th st, 56x80. June 30, due July 1, 1894. gold, 1,100

Dempsey, Joseph to James S. Bearns. 5th av, east cor 19th st. P. M. June 27, due June 30, 1892, 5 %. 2,500

Desanti, Savina to Thomas P. Kenna. Bayard st. P. M. June 2, 2 years, 5 %. 450

Dession, Marie J. E. and Jenny D. to George W. Baker. Elton st, w s, 100 n Arlington av, 25x100. June 15, 3 years or installs. 650

Dittmar, John to Christian Striffler and Emil Rudolph. Scholes st. P. M. June 8, 5 years, 5 %. 1,800

Donohue, John P. to Mary E. Gordon. Classon av and Dean st. P. M. June 26, installs. 8,000

Dresber, Hyman to Mary W. Smith. Watkins st. P. M. June 29, installs. 2,100

Dreyer, Isaac, Gustav and Samuel to Francis E. Clark. Leonard st, s e cor Johnson av, 25x100. June 24, 2 years, 5 %. 1,000

Same to Charles Naeher exr. Louis E. Nicot. Leonard st, s e cor Johnson av, 25x100. June 24, 3 years, 5 %. 4,000

Dickinson, Hattie S. to Mary Bullocke. 2d av, s e cor 84th st, 100x100; 84th st, s s, 100 e 2d av, 100x100, New Utrecht. June 16, 2 years. 2,000

Dreyfuss, Fanny to Joseph Wurzler. Myrtle av. P. M. June 30, due July 1, 1896, 5 %. 5,000

Duckwitz, Julia H. to George T. Duckwitz exr. George F. Duckwith. Henry st, s e s, 325 s w Joralemon st, 25x100. June 30, due July 1, 1896, 5 %. 4,500

Dierking, John to Elizabeth O'Brien. Keap st, s w cor South 4th st, 19.9x69. July 1, 3 years, 5 %. 4,500

Ehlers, John F. to James Gascoine individ. and as exr. of John G. Cozine. Central av, s w s, 25 n w Eldert st, 25x80. June 1, 6 months. 1,500

Same to same. Same property. Building loan. June 1. 2,000

Emich, Louis A. to Jane V. H. Scranton. 14th st, s s, 83.4 e 6th av, 14.6x71. June 25, 3 years. 1,800

Engeman, George H., Passaic. N. J., to The Brooklyn Trust Co. St. Johns pl, n s, 351 8 e 6th av, 69 8x100. June 26, 1 year, 5 %. 22,000

Fagot, August to Charles Naeher exr. Louis E. Nicot. Morrell st, w s, 75 n Moore st, 25x100, June 29, due July 1, 1894, 5 %. 3,000

Fink, Magdalena to John O. Whitenack. Rockaway av. P. M. June 24, 2 years, 5 % 500

Flechsenhaar, Henry to Caroline Broistedt. Van Cott av, s s, 25 w North Henry st, 50x100. 38th st. P. M. June 25, 3 years, 5 %. 6,000

Frank, Barnet and Simon Rose to The East New York Savings Bank. Eastern Parkway, s s, 100 e Osborn st, 25x100. June 26, 1 year. 4,400

Frieder, Lazar to Williamson R. Selover, Jamaica, L. I. Christopher av. P. M. June 27, 3 years. 900

Furbeshaw, George to David C. Long, New York. Halsey st. P. M. May 1, 5 years, 5 %. 4,300

Falke, Henriette wife of and Alexander to Poline Byk. Heyward st. P. M. June 27, 1 year. 1,250

Fein, Joseph to Sigmund Bleyer. Moore st. P. M. June 30, 3 years, 5 %. 900

Gerrety, Anna to Catharine Kenny. Park pl, n s, 155 e Schenectady av, 20x155.7. March 16, 3 years. 340

Ginsburg, Isaac to Jacob Paskusz and Israel Feldman. Moore st. P. M. June 30, 4 months. 2,000

Gilam, Frederick V. to Jacob Worth and Vincent A. Strawson. Lots 343-346 Worth and Strawson property. P. M. June 10, 3 years, 5 %. 280

Good, Kate S. to Joseph Ryan, Bainbridge st, n e cor Saratoga av, 23x100. June 27, 6 months, 5 %. 208

Gutting, George and Charles H. Wagner to James L. Truslow and ano. trustees Gilbert Potter. Knickerbocker av, s w s, 50 s e Stanhope st, 25x80. June 27, due July 1, 1894, 5 %. 3,500

Same to Theodore F. Jackson guard. Emma L., Henry D., Walter and George Klots Knickerbocker av, s w s, 25 s e Stanhope st, 25x80. June 27, due July 1, 1894, 5 %. 4,000

Same to Mary E. Hedges. Stanhope st, s e s, 80 s w Knickerbocker av, 20x75. June 27, due July 1. 1894, 5 %. 2,500

Hardy, Pauline to The East New York Savings Bank. East 95th st, e s, 150 s Av C, 28.1x105 x28.7x105. June 23, 1 year. 1,800

Harper, Jr., George to F. Augustus Conkling. Macon st. P. M. June 26, installs. 12,000

Hasselbach, John to Leopold Michel Hopkins st, s s, 425 e Marcy av, 25x100. June 25, due July 1, 1893, 5 %. 1,500

Hawkins, Mary A. to William K. Mott, Glenwood, L. I. Hart st, s s, 80 e Tompkins av, runs south 75 x east 20 x south 25 x east 11.8 x north 100 to st, x west 31.8. June 26, due June 29, 1896, or installs, 5 %. 4,000

Hay, Matilda L. to William H. Barton. Covert st. P. M. June 24, 2 years. 700

Hedler, Mary wife of and Gustav A. to The South Brooklyn Building and Loan Assoc. 79th st, s s, 140 w 4th av, 20x109.4. June 23, installs. 1,200

Hoffman, William C. to Adolph Sussman. Wortman av, n w cor Ashford st. P. M. June 9, due June 15, 1894, 5 %. 300

Horrigan, James E. to Rosanna Kernan. 5th av, w s, 47 n 21st st, 28x100. June 27, due July 1, 1894, 5 %. 1,500

Hougbland, Margaret E. wife of and William to William F. Corwith. Oakland st, w s, 50 n Freeman st, 25x100. June 15, 1 year. 1,000

Howell, Edwin F. to The Serial Building Loan and Savings Inst. Eastern Parkway, s s, 139 e Buffalo av, runs south 57.9 x east 3.10 x south 72.9 x east 38.6 x north 10 x east 78 x north 87 x east 2.0½ x north 53.7 to Parkway, x west 94. June 29, installs. 2,000

Hoyt, Ella L. to John Harrigan. Van Brunt st. P. M. June 29, due July 1, 1892. 1,000

Hyde, Richard and Louis C. Behman to The South Brooklyn Savings Inst. Elm pl, w s, 100 n Livingston st, 75x148.11x75.9x137.6. June 30, 1 year, 5 %. 25,000

Hanretty, Francis to The New York and Wakefield Co-operative Building and Loan Assoc. 16th st, s w s, 137.10 n w 8th av, 20x100. June 23, installs. 4,250

Hickey, Agnes to The Emigrant Industrial Savings Bank. Hoyt st, e s, 180 s Dean st, 20 x75. June 30, 1 year, 4½ %. 1,850

Hoernlein, Charles J. to Harriet T. Adams. Herkimer st, n s, 200 w Saratoga av, 16.8x100. June 25, 3 years. 2,300

Huber, Otto exr. Otto Huber dec'd mortgagee with Charles F. Lutz mortgagor. Extension of mort. May 26. nom

Hyers, Samuel V. to John M. Stearns. Chauncey st, s s, 211 e Saratoga av, 19x100. July 1, 3 years. 4,000

Same to George W. Adams. Chauncey st, s s, 211 e Saratoga av, 19x100. July 1, 1 year. 850

James, Wilholmina to Joanna C. wife of Albert V B. Voorhies. New Utrecht av, w s, 44.9 n 57th st, 22.3x99x20x108.9, New Utrecht. June 22, 3 years. 1,800

Jones, E. Willard to John F. Saddington. Macon st. P. M. May 28, 1 year, 5 %. 15,200

Joslin, A. Waldo to The Webster Five Cents Savings Bank, Webster, Mass. Madison st, s s, 150 w Franklin av, 20x100. Sub. to life estate Mary C. Joslin. June 16, note. 2,500

Kaiser, Marie wife of and John G. to Jane E. Meeker et al trustees Samuel M. Meeker. Ralph st, s e s, 550 s w Central av, 4 lots, each 25x100. 4 morts., each $3,300. June 25, 3 years, 5 %. 13,200

Kaufmann, Bertha, Newtown, L. I., to Henry Vollweiler. Hart st. P. M. May 29, 3 years. 2,800

Keiser, James R., Montclair, N. J., to Lester D. Berry, Orange, N. J. Lexington av, s s, 165 e Franklin av, 20x100. June 22, due July 1, 1892. 1,000

Kessel, George to Mary wife of Charles Martin. Cedar st. P. M. June 25, 3 years, 5 %. 1,200

Ketchum, Adolph to Alice Regan. Columbia st, n w cor Carroll st, 20x80. June 29, 5 years, 5 %. 8,000

Kelly, Helen to Louise Rose. Lot 570 block 15 map 730 lots at Bath Junction, New Utrecht, Dec. 13, 1890, 1 year. 100

King, George H. to Samuel S. Edmonston. Blake av, s s, 50 e Shepherd av, 25x100. June 30, 1 year, 5 %. 1,200

Klein, David to Silas A. Condict. Chester st, s w cor Sackett st. P. M. June 24, 1 year. 700

Kloth, Emily F. to Lucy M. Nunan. Halsey st. P. M. June 20, 2 years, 5 %. 1,500

Korb, Wenzel to The Williamsburgh Savings Bank. Covert st, n w s, 175 s w Evergreen av, 25x100. June 30, 1 year, 5 %. 3,500

Kreinik, Joseph to Nellie M. Molloy. St. Marks av. P. M. June 25, installs. 900

Kyle, Tillie to Thomas Ferguson. Ocean Parkway, w s, 340 n Av N, 60x250, Gravesend. June 25, 5 years, 5 %. 2,500

Lakeman, Joseph T. to The Fulton Co-operative Building and Loan Assoc. 45th st, s w s, 100 n w 12th av, 50x102.2. June 30, installs. 2,000

Lambias, Joseph G., Fannie T. and John F. to Nellie D. Traphagen. Washington av, e s, 268.5 s Park av, 20x100. April 28, 3 years, 5 %. 500

Lane, George A. to The East New York Savings Bank. Blake av, s s, 75 e Schenck av, 50x100. June 24, 1 year. 2,250

Lang, Max to The National Savings Bank of Albany. Washington av, w s, 110.6 n Fulton st, runs west 38.2 x northeast 13.9 x west 21.11 x northeast 18.11 x west 21.11 x northwest 20 x northeast 8.10 x east 83.4 to av, x south 46. June 26, 1 year, 4½ %. 15,000

Levison, Max S. to Julia A. Blake. Wythe av, n w s, 50 s w North 7th st, 25x100. June 24, due Dec. 1, 1892. 2,800

Lincoln, Clarance to Rudolph and Otto E. Reimer. Macon st, s s, 39.6 w Howard av, 18 x100. April 26, due April 1, 1892. 1,000

Littman, Abram J. to Max Pokalsky and Louis Lebewohl. Osborn st. P. M. June 26, installs. 820

Lotto, Jacob M. and Jacob Lax to Max S. Levison. Wythe av. P. M. June 24, 5 years. 1,400

Loud, Richard H. to Juliet L. Pinckney. Van Siclen st, w s, 304.3 s Av T, 124x144x—x 235.5. June 29, 1 year. 3,000

Lynam, Elizabeth F. to Jacob Worth and Vincent A. Strawson. Lots 83-87 and 117 Worth & Strawson property, Flatbush. P. M. June 10, 3 years, 5 %. 600

Lynch, Mary E. to John C. Benham exr. Sarah Benham. Clinton st, w s, 70 s West 9th st, 30x90. June 24, due July 1, 1894. 6,000

Landesmann, Adolf to William Herod. Eastern Parkway. P. M. June 30, installs. 550

Lutz, Charles F. to Andrew L. Stutz. Evergreen av and Covert st. P. M. July 1, 1 year, 5 %. 3,500

Martin, William B. and Patrick J. Lee to Sarah J. Frasse. St. Marks av, s s, 243 6 e Vanderbilt av, 26.6x131. June 30, due July 1, 1894, 5 %. 6,000

McElwain, Charles R. to Mary A. Knight et al. trustees Henry Knight. Lafayette av, n s, 180 w Stuyvesant av, 20x100. June 26, 5 years, 5 %. 1,500

MacMahon, John G. to John Kaufmann. New Jersey av, w s, 100 s Broadway, 50x100. June 20, 3 years. 600

Mantanus, Susanna to Charles Reinhardt. Stagg st, s s, 50 e Waterbury st, 25x100. June 29, 1 year. 200

Max, Rachel to Silas A. Condict. Thatford av. P. M. June 19. 200

McAllister, Andrew J. to James D. Lynch. Bay 38th st, n w s, 240 n e Benson av, 60x96.8. June 20, due June 23, 1893, 5 %. 473

McCormack, Rosanna to David A. Fithian. Bergen st, n s, 325 e Rockaway av, 16.8x107.2. Collateral. April 6. 300

McCuskin, Michael to Edward J. D. Barnett. Herbert st, s s, 25 e Monitor st, 25x100. June 24, 5 years, 5 %. 1,000

McDonald, Thomas to William H. Scott. Fulton st. P. M. May 1, 1 year. 10,500

Same to same. Same property. Building loan. May 1, 1 year. 30,000

Mead, Joseph to James Rodwell. South 1st st, n e s, 116.6 s e Keap st, 16.6x77. June 18, due July 1, 1894, 5 %. 1,800

Moores, Robert L. and Charles A. Le Quesne to George F. Alexander. Putnam av, n w s, 260 n e Broadway, 20x100. June 15, 1 year. 1,000

Meyers, Israel to The Title Guarantee and Trust Co. Hancock st, n s, 145 w Ralph av, 16.8x85. P. M. June 13, due June 25, 1894, 5 %. 1,500

Michel, Leopold to Maria Schwarzwaelder. Hopkins st. P. M. June 25, 5 years, 5 %. 3,000

Moubray, Edward H. to The Title Guarantee and Trust Co. 3d st, n e s, 297.4 s e 7th av, 100.6x95. June 25, 1 year. 9,500

Murphy, James to Margaretta Remsen, Flushing, L. I. Summit st, n s, 140 w Columbia st, 20x100. June 26, 3 years, 5 %. 600

Myers, Isarel to The Title Guarantee and Trust Co. Flushing av, s s, 25 w Clermont av, 50x79.9x51x90.2. June 25, 1 year, 5 %. 2,000

Noonan, Arthur J., New York, to Alanson Trask. Clifton pl. P. M. Oct. 15, 1890, 3 years, 5 %. 5,000

Norris, Allison V. B. and William C. Turner to Raeburn, Latourette & Co. 8th av, s e cor 11th st, 100x120. June 27, due Sept. 1, 1891. 2,290

Nafis, Margaret A. wife of and George R. to Benjamin C. Leech. Monroe st, s s, 300 w Marcy av, 20x100. July 1, 3 years, 5 %. 3,000

Nelson, Emilie C wife of and Frederick W. H. to Annie K. Richmond. 8th st, n s, 164.6 e 3d av, 18.9x100. July 1, 3 years, 5 %. 1,250

Same to same. 8th st. n s, 145.9 e 3d av, 18.9x100. July 1, 3 years, 5 %. 1,250

O'Connor, Anne to Charles R. Lynde. Watkins st, w s, 100 n Dumont av, 100x100. July 1, 1 year. 900

O'Flaherty, Julia to Richard M. Wyckoff et al. exrs. John S. Andrews. Rockaway av, w s, 100 n Broadway, 50x100. June 26, 5 years. 500

O'Connor, Bridget to Pauline Hahn. Bancroft pl, e s, 98 s Herkimer st, 23x90. June 27, due July 1, 1894. 300

O'Hare, John to William C. Pye. Centre st, n s, 275 e Court st, 25x100. June 20, 3 years. 500

Oppenheim, William to Benjamin Rausch Christopher av. P. M. June 25, due July 1, 1894. 600

Pearson, William J. to Daniel S. Arnold. Lewis av. P. M. June 29, 3 years, 5 %. gold, 4,900

Peterson, Caroline to Catharine Stoothoff. Ashford st, e s, 257.6 s Fulton st, 25x100. June 26, due July 1, 1894. 1,500

Phelan, Gussie L to Rosa Levy. Pilling st, n w s, 87.4 s w Bushwick av, 17x100. June 15, 2 months 200

Phillips, Elisabeth C. to Guy Phillips. 7th av, w s, 20.7 n 2d st, 52.9x90.9. June 24, 1 year. 2,500

Pollacek, Katerina to William Klingler. McDougal st, n s, 25 w Saratoga av, 25x100. Feb. 10, due Jan. 1, 1895, 5½ %. 2,500

Polytechnic Institute of Brooklyn to The Brooklyn Savings Bank. Livingston st, n s, 29.5 e Court st, runs east 241.6 x north 150 x west 222.8 x south 23.4 x west 22.8 x south 126 8. June 29, due July 1, 1892, 4 %. 150,000

Porter, Isaiah to John P. Morris. 39th st. P. M. June 25, 5 years, 5 %. 600

Puels, Joseph P. to The Title Guarantee and Trust Co. Decatur st, n s, 100 w Howard av, 199.8x100. June 25, demand. 37,800

Plazo, Augustus W. to Edwin C. Low. Lewis av, w s, 61 s Putnam av, 19.6x90. May 12, 1 year, 5 %. 2,500

Same to same. Lewis av, w s, 41.6 s Putnam av, 19.6x90. May 12, 1 year, 5 %. 2,500

Same to same. Lewis av, w s, 22 s Putnam av, 19.6x90. May 12, 1 year, 5 %. 2,500

Same to same. Lewis av, w s, 41.6 n Jefferson av, 19.6x90. May 12, 1 year, 5 %. 2,500

Same to same. Lewis av, w s, 61 n Jefferson av, 19 6x90. May 12, 1 year, 5 %. 2,500

Same to same. Lewis av, w s, 80.6 n Jefferson av, 19.6x90. May 12, 1 year, 5 %. 2,500

Same to same. Lewis av, w s, 80.6 s Putnam av, 19.6x90. May 12, 1 year, 5 %. 2,500

Pearson, William J. to The Title Guarantee and Trust Co. 5th av, w s, 20 n Union st, 40 x69. July 1, 1 year, 5 %. 8,000

Pearson, Nils to N. Pendleton Schenck trustee Anna P. Schenck. 4th av, e s, at centre line bet 80th and 81st sts, runs east 102.7 x south 139.4 x west 102.7 x north 139.4. June 30, due July 1, 1894. 3,000

Same to same. 81st st, s s, 102.7 e 4th av, 400x139.4. June 30, due July 1, 1894. 3,000

Poellmann, Daniel to Elizabeth Miller and ano. exrs. Christopher Miller. Monteith st, n s, 50 w Evergreen av, 3 lots, each 25x90. 3 morts., each $3,000. June 22, due July 1, 1892, 5 %. 9,000

Price, Bernard with Christiane Heidenreich. Extension of mort. June 30. nom

Quinn, Patrick J. to Jacob Worth and Vincent A. Strawson. Lots 113 and 114 Worth & Strawson property, Flatbush, P. M. June 10, 3 years, 5 %. 125

Rabbi, Abraham and Aaron Kirsch to Lewis Hurst. Blake av, n w cor Powell st. P. M June 24, 2 years. 1,025

Rafter, Edward to Jaques Van Brunt, New Utrecht. Narrows av and 80th st, New Utrecht. P. M. June 29, due June 1, 1894, 5 %. 2,385

Rapp, John and Hendericka M. his wife to Mary E. Fox. North 5th st. P. M. June 29, 1 year, 5 %. 550

Raymond, Benjamin C. to The Title Guarantee and Trust Co. Macon st, n w cor Ralph av, 22x100. June 27, demand. 4,000

Same to Lucy C. Barron. Macon st, n s, 21 w Ralph av, 5 lots, each 18x100. 5 morts., each $4,500. June 26, 3 years, 5 %. 22,500

Ray, Matilda E. to Adolph Sussman. Cleveland st. P. M. June 9, due June 15, 1894, 5 %. 195

Ray, Charles H. to Adolph Sussman. Ashford st. P. M. June 9, due June 15, 1894, 5 %. 246

Read. Charlotte F. to The Title Guarantee and Trust Co. Washington av, w s, 144 8 s Myrtle av, 16.1x100. June 24, 5 years, 5 %. 4,500

Reis, John and Henry B. Davenport to Theodore D. Dimon exrs. Hannah S. Dimon. Montgomery st, s s, 25 e 18th st, 25x100. June 10, 3 years. 1,000

Rooney, Mary wife of Thomas E. to Nellie C. Van Reypen. Pacific st, n s, 97.1 e Clason av, 34.11x100. June 23, due July 1, 1892. 800

Same to same. Pacific st. n s, 97.1 e Clason av, 34.11x100. June 23, due May 1, 1894, 5 %. 2,500

Rosenbaum, Samuel and Charles Faber, New York, to Alonzo E. De Baun. Watkins st. P. M. June 16, 1 year. 1,000

Rotert, Maria to Bedford Co-operative Building Loan Assoc. Union st, n s, 143 10 e Buffalo av, 38.6x90. June 29, installs. 400

Ruberstein, Israel and Israel Sugalowicz to John S. Junior. Thatford av, e s, 200 s Eastern Parkway, 25x100. June 27, 3 years. 2,000

Radcliffe, Thomas H. to John S. Spencer. Decatur st. P. M. and building loan. July 1, 1 year, 5 %. 6,000

Reilly, Patrick to David A. Fithian. 5th av, w s, 25.2 n 47th st, 50x100; 46th st, s s, 300 w 6th av, 40x100.2. June 30, 1 year. 1,800

Riley, Morris to Hannah P. Littell, Walden, N. Y. Bergen st, s s, 325 w Howard av, 25x127.9. June 13, due June 1, 1894. 300

Rieger, Georgiana wife of and John H. to The Mutual Life Ins. Co., New York. President st, s s, 172.6 e 7th av, 20.4x100. June 17, due June 30, 1892, 5 %. 8,000

Russell, George to Thomas Carter, Boonton, N. J. Lawrence st. P. M. June 25, due July 1, 1893, 5 %. 5,000

Schissel, Edmund to John H. Vanderveer. Lots 199-209 map Vanderveer Homestead. P. M. July 1, 1 year, 5 %. 2,000

Schreiber, Henry W. to Bernhard Davidsburg. Broadway, n w s, 112 s e De Kalb av, 22.6x90. July 1, 5 years, 5 %. 9,000

Searing, Sylvester to William Keegan. 6th st, n s, 117.10 w 5th av, 20x100. July 1, 3 months, 5 %. 1,705

Saltzer, Joseph to Patrick Donohue. Thatford av, n w cor Glenmore av, 20x100. June 25, due Dec. 11, 1891. 650

Samilson, Philip H., New York, to Jacob Worth and Vincent A. Strawson. Lots 103, 104, 109, 195, 240, 248, 249, 276 and 277 Worth and Strawson property. P. M. June 10, 3 years, 5 %. 932

Scheinman, Samuel and Toby to Bryce Martin. Thatford av. P. M. June 25, installs 450

Schurr, Alexander A. A. to Rudolph and Otto E Reimer. Snediker av, e s, 90 n Hegeman av, 40x100. June 25, due July 1, 1892. 250

Schwahn, George to Elizabetha Klein daughter of Peter Klein dec'd and Elizabetha Klein his wife. Ewen st, e s, 75 s Powers st, 25x100. March 25, due Jan. 19, 1894, 4 %. 1,000

Scully, Grace A. to Phebe M. Bergen. Decatur st, n s, 175 w Throop av, 18x100. June 26, 1 year. 1,000

Shrump, Frederick to The Tradesmen's Nat. Bank. 2d st, n s, 150 e 6th av, 40x100. June 17, demand 5,000

Silberman, Henry, Michael Baduer and Israel Weg to Lewis Hurst. Christopher av. P. M. June 22, 2 years. 1,100

Smith, James J and George S. Cahill to Obermeyer & Liebmann. Myrtle av, n w cor Kent av, store and dwell'g. Lease. June 19, demand. 3,000

Smith, Margaret C. to Stephen C. Halstead. 6th st, n s, 137.9 e 5th av, 19.11x100. June 17, 1 year. 800

Smith, Phebe M. wife of and George T. to The Title Guarantee and Trust Co. Nostrand av. P. M. June 25, 3 years, 5 %. 2,500

Spalding, William A. and Elizabeth to Mary P. Wilcox. Atlantic av, n s, 58 w Bond st, 21x80. June 25, 5 years, 5 %. 9,600

Stearns, John M. to The Dime Savings Bank, Brooklyn. Atlantic av, s s, 220 e Rochester av, 40x100. May 26, 1 year, 5 %. 4,000

Stoddard, Lucy E. wife of and John H. to The Mutual Life Ins. Co., New York. Fulton st, s s, 117.8 w Hoyt st, runs west 35.9 x south 73.5 x west 0.2½ x south 103.4 x east 10 6 x south 100 to Livingston st, x east 100.8 x north 95 x east 48.7 to Hoyt st, x north 20 x west 48.8 x south 1 x west 39.1 x north 89.7 x west 20.4 x north 100 to st. June 26, 1 year. 20,000

Stoothoff, Stephen W. to Henry W. Lee guard Milford st, s s, 100 n Liberty av. P. M. June 25, due July 1, 1894. 1,600

Same to Mary E. and Belle Laurence. Milford st, e s, 125 n Liberty av. P. M. June 25, due July 1, 1894. 1,600

Same to Susan J. Norton. Milford st, e s, 150 n Liberty av. P. M. June 25, due July 1, 1894. 1,600

Stoutenburg, George B. to John H. Atwater and ano. exrs. Henry M. Needham. Monroe st. P. M. June 15, due June 1, 1892. 26,000

Stratton, Valentine to Robinson Gill trustee. De Kalb av, No. 1016, s s, 61 w Stuyvesant av, 19.6x85. June 29, note 400

Styles, John H. and Elizabeth R. his wife to Leopold and Benjamin Schwartz, of Schwartz & Co., Buffalo, N. Y. Garfield pl, n s, 90 w 7th av, 150x100. Sub. to mort. June 17, note. 1,442

Stern, David to Nicholas Will. Seigel st, s s, 150 w Humboldt st. P. M. June 30, 5 years or installs. 7,000

Same to same. Seigel st, s s, 125 w Humboldt st. P. M. June 30, 5 years or installs. 6,000

Same to same. Seigel st, s s, 100 w Humboldt st. M. June 30, 5 years or installs. 4,937

Sweeney, Patrick to George W. Heatley. Myrtle av, n e cor Canton st. P. M. Sub. to mort. $8,000. June 20, due June 25, 1892. 1,500

Same to Frank Peterkin. Same property. June 20, due June 25, 1894, 5 %. 8,000

Same to Joseph H. Mabon trustee for creditors. Same property. June 26, demand. 4,220

Sylvester, Mary to The Sun and Evening Sun Building, Mutual Loan and Accumulating Fund Assoc. East 4th st. P. M. June 18, installs, 5 %. 2,817

Shomaker, John H. to Adeline E. Riggs, Rutherford, N. J. 2d av, e s, 40.2 n 55th st, 20x100. June 20, installs. 600

Smith, Phebe M. to The Title Guarantee and Trust Co. Nostrand av. P. M. June 25, 3 years, 5 %. 2,500

Spear, James M. to Louis Hinrichs. Lafayette st, s s, 80 w Debevoise st, 20x80. June 26, 3 years, 5 %. 4,000

Struse, Matilda M. to Charles D. Rust. Montague st, s s, 26.6 e Henry st, 25x100. Sub. to morts. $22,000. July 1, 1 year. 5,500

Same to William A. Spencer et al. trustees Lorillard Spencer. Same property. July 1, 3 years, 5 %. 22,000

Swelt, James and Charles F., James T. and John R. to East Brooklyn Savings Bank. De Kalb av, n s, 100 e Nostrand av, 25x152.2 x26.9x161.9x. June 29, installs, 5 %. 4,000

Thompson, David M. to James W. Smith trustee. Halsey st, s s, 387.6 e Nostrand av, 17.6 x100. June 29, 3 years, 5 %. 5,500

Tomford, Margaretha wife of and John F. to Juliette C. Jeanneret. Fulton st, s o cor Rochester av, 23x80. June 30, 3 years, 5 %. 2,500

Travis, Andrew B, to Benjamin C. Leech. Greene av, n s, 300 e Nostrand av, 20x100. July 1, 3 years, 5 %. 3,000

Tyler, Frank H. to Samuel V. Tunison. Walworth st. P. M. June 29, due July 1, 1894. 2,800

The Sixth Methodist Episcopal Church to Thomas Pitbladdo. 17th st. P. M. June 15, due June 13, 1896, 5 %. 4,500

Thomas, Jessie to William P. Rae. Lots 339 and 340 block 12 map William Ziegler, Flatbush and New Utrecht. P. M. May 1, 5 years. 1,200

Tipedino, Leonardo to John B. Marquand. Atlantic av. P. M., and to secure defects (if any) in title. June 27, due July 1, 1894. 500

Tomlinson, Charles W. to Adolph Sussman. Cleveland st, e s, 270 s New Lots road, 40x100. June 9, due June 15, 1894, 5 %. 270

Tworger, Alicia to Carrie J. Thompson. Bay 7th st, New Utrecht. P. M. June 27, due July 1, 1894. 1,500

Van Deursen, Jacob to James D. Lynch. 2d av, south cor 85th st, 100x100. June 4, due due June 23, 1892, 5 %. 3,500

Same to same. Same property. June 4, due June 23, 1892, 5 %. 2,500

Volckening, Ferdinand F. to The Germania Savings Bank, Kings County. McDougal st, n s, 125.1 w Ralph av, runs north 34 x east 0.1 x north 66 x west 25 x northwest 12.11 x southeast 58.2 x southwest 38.8 to Fulton st, x southeast 19 7 to McDougal st, x east 32.10. July 1, 1 year, 5 %. 7,000

Von Graff, Roderick to Cornelius E. Donnellon. Schermerhorn st, n s, 150 w 3d av, 16.7x100.9. June 30, 5 %. 12,000

Warren, Elizabeth F. to Pauline Hahn. McDougal st, n s, 114 w Howard av, 19.11x—x 16.11x50. June 29, 1 year. 500

Weinreb, Philip to Alonzo E. De Baun. Osborn st. P. M. June 16, 1 year. 1,000

Wells, Fannie E. wife of and Charles W. to Charles E. Sanborn, of Summerville, Mass. Fort Greene pl, w s, 171.6 s Lafayette av, 21.3 x100. June 1, 2 years. 1,200

Whitenack, John O. to William Johnston. McDougal st. n s, 125 e Hopkinson av, 71x100. June 22, due Nov. 1, 1891, 5 %. 10,800

Wittschen, Andrew to Garrett Hartman. Ryerson st, e s, 342.9 s Flushing av, 40x100. June 29, due July 1, 1892, 5 %. 5,000

Wolf, Abram and Herman Goldstein to Alonzo E. De Baun. Watkins st. P. M. June 25, 1 year. 1,005

Woodhall, Raymond D. to Mary E. Gentleman. Palmetto st. P. M. June 27, installs. 1,000

Woolley, Edward A. to Whitehead H Hewlett, Merrick, L. I. Douglass st. n s, 149.8 w 5th av, 20x100. June 25, due May 1, 1894, 4 %. 4,500

Same to same Douglass st, n s, 170 w 5th av, 20x100. June 25, due May 1, 1894, 5 %. 3,500

Waring, William H. to Mary Van Zandt trustee Solomon Solomon N. Henriques. 6th av, n w s, 44.4 n c Prospect av, 18x80. April 19, 1888, 2 years, 5 %. 2,500

Weiber, Lorenz to Lorenz F. J. Weiber. Atlantic av, s s, 68.4 w Clinton st, 21.8x80. June 30, 1 year. 3,000

Werbelovsky, Jacob H. and Louis Lurie to Anna M. Muller. Moore st. P. M. June 29, due July 1, 1894, 5 %. 2,500

Weltfish, Leon to Henry F. Smith exr. Rosa A. Smith. Eastern Parkway, s w cor Powell st, 50x100. June 30, installs. 800

Welton, Henrietta L. wife of R. B. to Patrick J. Prendergast. 4th st. s s, 200 w Bond st, 20 x94 8x20.5x90.4. July 1. 1,000

Wood, Cornelia T. to Juliette M. Jaycox. Ridgewood av, n s, 60 w Essex st, 20x100. April 1, 5 years. 1,000

Wood, Margaretta to Mary E. McDermott. Richmond st, w s, 1,825 n 3d st, 100x150. June 29, due July 1, 1896. 2,000

Zehner, Henry and Elise his wife to John Rupka. Suydam st. P. M. June 24, due July 1, 1896. 2,000

Zeiser, Bertha widow to Jacob Bossert. Boerum st, s s, 125 e Ewen st, 50x100. June 25, installs, 5 %. 6,000

Zoeller, Frederick to Mary S. Baker. Stagg st, n w cor Waterbury st. P. M. June 22, 5 years or installs. 7,000

MORTGAGES----ASSIGNMENTS.

NEW YORK CITY.

June 26 to July 1—Inclusive.

Arendt, Simon to William Cohen. $4,500

Broadbelt, William to The Perth Amboy Terra Cotta Co. 2,500

Broadbelt, William, New Rochelle, N. Y., to Abraham Kaufmann. 6,000

Cameron, Alexander to Sarah J. Murray. nom

Canfield, George F. trustee Albert W. Canfield dec'd to Herman Watjen, Brooklyn. 10,060

Congregation C. M. Rothschild O. B. A. of City of New York to Joseph Wolf. 2,000

Doremus, Cornelius, Ridgewood, N. J., to Martha G. Gray, Elizabeth, N. J. 2,500

Dinkelspiel, Regine et al. exrs. David Dinkelspiel to James Dinkelspiel, Jacksonville, Ill. 13,000

Diamond, Elizabeth, Albany, N. Y., to Abraham Kaufmann. 3,000

Same to same. 3,000

Dick, Robert to John S. Stiger. 5,250

Eveleth, Margaret S. to The New York Life Ins. and Trust Co. 8,000

Eichler, John ano. exrs. William Roth to John Eichler trustee for William Bozenhardt. 6,000

Same to John Eichler trustee for Katie Roth. 4,000

Fish, John to Elkan Kahn. 10,000

Goetz, Samuel to Randolph Guggenheimer and Salomon Marx. 41,500

Same to same. nom

Goldstein, Morris to Louis Lese. 17,000

Same to Sarah Lese. 4,613

Griswold, F. Gray trustee Saul Alley to Lydia A. Griswold. nom

Giles, William O. exr. Elizabeth Giles to Julianna Knorzer, Fort Lee, N. J. 1,000

Hawkes, Henry, Riverside, Conn., to John W. Haaren. 3,400

Hyatt, George E., Brooklyn, to Edward Winslow. 3,500

Same to same. 2 assigns. nom

Hassey, August to Mathilda Weil et al. exrs. Max Weil. 3,000

Harmon, Edward and ano. trustees Philip Harmon dec'd to Annina F. Kingsley. 14,000

Isaacs, Barney to George L. Balheimer. 4,750

Kreuder, Adolf to The Union Square Bank 20,000

Leggett, Francis H. trustee Abraham Leggett dec'd to Rosetta M. Kearney. 1887. 100

Lehmann, Julius to Siegmund B. Steinman. 10,000

Lecrou, John to Paulina Jacobs. 1,200

Levy, Barnett, Louis Gordon and Sophia Gruenstein to Herman Fichter. nom

Lewis, John A. et al. exrs. and trustees Benjamin B. Sherman to Francis Lahey. 13,246

Lamberton, W. R., Pelham Manor, N. Y., to Constance M. L. Miller, Pelham Manor, N. Y. nom

Miller, Jacob, Long Island City, to John Fish. 10,000

Marckwald, Augustus V. to Edward Whitehouse. nom

Middlebrook, Frederick J., Brooklyn, to Paul Ettlinger. 1,600

Milbank, Albert J. to Samuel W. and Albert J. Milbank exrs. and trustees Charles E. Milbank. 3,000

Metzler, John H. to Church E. Gates & Co. 1,500

Morgenthau, Henry to Auguste Steglich. 11,000

Madden, Joseph H. to Jonas Weil. 4,000

Middlebrook, Frederic J., Brooklyn, to Rhoda E. Cochran 9,036

Same to Bernhard Grunhut. 4,100

Pomeroy, William L. to Walter S. Davies, Brooklyn. 10,000

Parker, Margaret K. wife of Willard to Kate Warner. 10,000

Preston, Sarah L. E. formerly Miller to William E. Preston. 5,000

Same to same. 11,000

Rosenbaum, Joseph C. to Raphael Ettlinger. nom

Rogers, J. S. and C. B as trustees of Annie R. Zinn to The Equitable Guarantee and Trust Co. 3 assigns. nom

Same as trustees of Helen Rogers to same. 2 assigns. nom

Russ, Edward admr. John Guyer to M. S. Isaacs trustee. 2,000

Rust, Charles D., Brooklyn, to Maud A. Griswold. 3,500

Sawyer, Merritt E. to Michael Hughes. nom

Steers, Abraham to John S. McWilliam. nom

Stein, Abraham to Sarah and Betsey Dinkelman. 7,000

Sanger, Lillie admrx. Lewis Sanger to Mary L. Kelley. 3,000

Strebeigh, Agnes M. and Lefferts exrs. Robert M. Strebeigh to Barbara J. Vanderbilt, Philadelphia, Pa. 7,500

Searles, Hamilton R. assignee E. H. Purdy & Co. to Nathaniel Niles president. 6,186

Stoppel, Martha to Henry Schumacher. 3,000

Striker, James A. to James W. Smith trustee. 3,000

Title Guarantee and Trust Co. to Atlantic Trust Co. guard. of Eugene S. Reynal. 30,000

Title Guarantee and Trust Co. to Norman Henderson and Edward S. Rapallo trustee. 10,000
Same to The General Theological Seminary of the Protestant Episcopal Church in the United States of America. 30,000
Same to same. 17,000
Title Guarantee and Trust Co. to Frank D Hurtt. 15,000
Same to Henry F. Spaulding and ano. trustees Charles E. Greenough. 20,000
Title Guarantee and Trust Co. to Henry C. West. 12,000
The Murray Hill Bank to The Middlesex Quarry Co., Portland, Conn. 2 assigns. nom
The Knickerbocker Fire Ins. Co. to John W. C. Leveridge. 2,020
Tyson, Henry L., Bay Ridge, L. I., to Isaac N. Hebberd. 7,000
United States Trust Co. to James P. Kernochan and John J. Wysong trustee. 15,112
Von Dreble, Hermann, Ridgefield, N. J., to Carrie C. Moritz. 1,000
Same to same. 4,000
Winslow, Edward to Henry W. Ford trustee of Augustus H. Ward. nom
Weil, Jonas and Bernhard Mayer to Jeanette Adler. 3,900
Same to Max and Jennie Goldstein. 2,900
Wolfenstein, Eve to Franklin N. Billings, Woodstock, Vt. 3,000

KINGS COUNTY.

JUNE 25 TO JULY 1—INCLUSIVE.

Alexander, George F. to Nichols Gas Fixture Mfg. Co. $1,000
Same to Earl A. Gillespie, Woodhaven, L. I. 5 000
Barton, William H. to Melissa Winant. 700
Bossert, Jacob to Hugo Weil. 5,000
Brown, Helen to Charles Brown. nom
Baker, George W. to Thomas Everit. 650
Bennett, Samuel W. admr. Ellan L. Kent to Abel Crook exr., &c., Samuel H. Crook. 6,725
Bardsley, Jane to Mary F. Damerel. 1,500
Behrens, Frederick trustee Frederick Behrens dec'd to Mathias Frank. 2,500
Brundage, James H. to Theodore Kiendl. 731
Canal, Josephine to Salena Lublin. 1,000
Conner, John R. and ano. exrs. Mary Conner to John R. Conner and ano. exrs. George Ricard. 800
Campbell, Hoik D. to Bridget T. McClennen. 1,500
Same to Kate Rockefeller. 1,500
Colcord, Samuel to Amelia S. Sherman. 2,500
Carroll, James G. to Albro J. Newton. 1,100
Condict, Silas A. to Jennie C. B. Reynolds. 275
Conkling, F. Augustus to George R. Ellis. nom
Center, Edward C. to Title Guarantee and Trust Co. 10,000
Doremus, William H. to Mary L. Lawrence. 1,000
Dowling, William L to Lyman D. Calkins. nom
Dowling, William L. to Lyman D. Calkins. 2,375
Elford, Charles E. exr. Cordelia M. Elford to George W. Rumbold et al. exrs. George Elford. nom
Everit, Thomas exr. Valentine Everit to George W. Pearsall. consid. omitted
Ewen, Austin D. exr. George Ricard to Martha A. Losee. 800
Fithian, David A. to Thomas Everit exr. Valentine Everit. 1,000
Fitzgerald, Maurice to Stephen C. Halstead exr. Stephen Halstead. 1,200
Fitzgerald, Maurice to James H. Serene. 500
Fraser, Anna M. to Andreas P. Andresen. 600
Fowler, Mary E. to James D. Rankin and James Ross. 750
Gerdes, Margaretha to Gazina Bohlmann. consid omitted
German-American Real Estate Title Guarantee Co. to Sheltering Arms Nursery. 5,000
Glover, Eva C. to William G. Low and ano. trustees Mott Bedell. 4,233
Godfrey, Phebe H. to Patrick J. Carlin. 1,000
German-American Real Estate Title Guarantee Co. to People's Trust Co. 5,000
Same to same. 5,000
Griffen, Jesse H. and G. J. exrs. of Daniel H. and Amy W. Griffen to Esther H. Barnes, Harrison, N. Y. 4,000
Hart, Frank E. to Edward F. Linton. 1,100
Same to same. 1,340
Halstead, Stephen C. to Anna R. E. Edsall. 500
Hartjen, Herman D. to Joseph Liebmann. 350
Heynen, Ellen F. to John H. Heynen. 1,500
Hurlburt, Lawrence to Maurice Fitzgerald. consid. omitted
Ibert, Frank to Christian Miller and Amelia his wife. 2,000
Jarman, Amanda M. extrx. Zadok H. Jarman to Daniel S. Arnold. 4,142
Knight, Anna F. P. to Mary A. Knight et al. trustees Henry Knight. 1,500
Keppler, Christian A. to Christian C. and Emilia Miller. 700
Klein, David and Solomon Herskovitz to Silas A. Condict. 500
Low, Edwin C. to Frederick Miller. 6 assigns., each $2,500. 15,000
Lewis, Margaretha to George H. Smith. 2,000
Same to same. 2,000
Lublin, Salena to Helen Bissett. 2,532
Mason, Philip D. to Herbert H. Clark. nom
Max, William to Christian Heidenreich extrx. Adolph Heidenreich. 1,000
McKennee, Anna B. to Thorndyke C. McKennee. 1,500
Nelson, John F. to Henry A. Moore. 5,000
Oliver, Paul A., Wilke barre, Pa., to Walter Wheeler. 14,400
O'Neill, Michael to Henry Kordes. 235
Petersen, James to The Germania Savings Bank of Kings County. 8,000
Plummer, Jerome S. to Edwin F. Knowlton. 16,500
Powell, Sarah H. to Harriet E. Kirk, Ivyland, Pa. 7,500
Same to Edward Hopper, Philadelphia, Pa. 8,000
Powell, Sarah H. to Hannah W. Haight. 3,600
Parker, Asa W. to Harriet L. Packard. 45,000
Powell, Sarah H. to George D. Dresser, Yorktown, N. Y. 8,000
Reynolds, William H. to James McLaren. 2,500
Rankin, James D. and James Ross to Lawrence Hurlburt. 2,000
Rumbold, George W. et al. exrs. George Elford to Samuel W. Bennett admr. Ellan L. Elford, otherwise Kent. nom
Rogers, J. S. & C. B. trustees Helen Rogers to The Equitable Guarantee and Trust Co. nom
Stearns, John M. to John T. Runcie. 4,000
Sturgis, Edward B. to Bradley & Currier Co. (Lim.) 1,350
Swift, Fred. J. to Thomas Everit exr. Valentine Everit. 1,500
Sheldon, Mary L. H., Lebanon, Conn., to Mary W. Smith. 4,000
Smith, Mary W. to Samuel J. Underhill trustee Henry Coles. 8,500
Smith, Herbert C. to Agnes H. Davies. 4,500
Switzer, Walter E. to Margaret J. Coles, New York. 1,700
Switzer, John E to Walter E. Switzer. nom
Tandy, Edgar J. exr. John T. Tandy to Jane Armstrong. 2,500
Tandy, Edgar J. to Lewis E. Riggs. 322
Title Guarantee and Trust Co. to Cornelia M. Ten Eyck. 6,000
Same to Mills P. Baker. 4,500
Same to Charles M. Tyler trustee George H. Tyler. 8,000
Same to Brooklyn Trust Co. 4,000
Same to Mary E. Jagger. 2,400
Same to Samuel D. Bussell exr. Charles Bussell. 3,000
Same to Daniel J. Creem. 6,000
Same to Willis R. Goodsell. 1,200
Same to Mills P. Baker. 500
Same to Edward R Keeler. 1,000
Same to John H. Gamgee. 3,000
Same to Brooklyn Trust Co. 2,500
Vaill, Emeline M. to Joseph Liebmann and Theodore Obermeyer. 2,000
Weil, Lazarus to Sarah Dittenhoefer. 2,604
Williams, Esther to Mary E. Lynch. 2,500
Same to same. 2,500
Walsh, A. Stewart to Samuel Riker. 1,500
Williams, Susan to George B. Smith. 1,500
Wickes, William W. to Catharine M. Wilkins. 3,150

JUDGMENTS.

In these lists of judgments the names alphabetically arranged, and which are first on each line, are those of the judgment debtor. The letter (D) means judgment for deficiency (*) means not summoned. (†) signifies that the first name is fictitious, real name being unknown. Judgments entered during the week, and satisfied before day of publication, do not appear in this column, but in list of Satisfied Judgments

NEW YORK CITY.

June and July

27 Allcot, Edmond C—J J Bentz.........$814 81
27 Alt, Adam—E Stanton Riker.........911 33
27 Altieri, Peter; Altieri, Anthony; Altieri, Pasquali; Altieri, Francesco } Fanny Quarants 666 04
29 Atwell, Edwin—W A Sweetser.......74 85
30 Ambler, David A—John Elsey.......106 30
30 Alton, Henry—Hall Steam Power Co. 33 50
30 Alswanger, Hyman—M D Solinger...99 50
30 Archer, John B—Frederick Booss.....584 90
30 Anderson, William C—U S Illuminating Co.......................259 87
30 the same——United Electric Light and Power Co..................340 17
30 Ayres, Marshall, assignee Sawyer, Wallace & Co—Gaetano Aims......7,221 51
1 Andrews, Proctor H—Cyrus Clark...318 66
2 Averell, George W—J L Blauvelt....654 84
2 Anderson, Niles—Frederick Schrayshuen.........................545 62
2 Ackerman, John E—E J Halligan...568 00
2 Adams, Joseph B—N L Cort.........103 96
27 Baer, Selma—J M Bleyer............82 50
29 Boyer, William B—John Wanamaker 30 90
29 Braine, Lawrence F—T R McMann..136 47
29 Bowes, John W—John Murray.......518 71
29 Blake, David—G W McLean, recvr..53 04
30 Barrett, Squire R—Edward Reynolds 390 63
30 Bradley, John—People State N Y....1,000 00
30 Brown, Alexander R—C B Keogh....48 32
30 Barnes, Oliver W—W M Carner......343 76
30 Blair, Henry W—Frederick Booss....584 93
30 Buckhout, Henry—W A Watson, assignee..............................3,230 42
30 Bailey, Samuel H—Charles Siedler, recvr...............................1,012 80
30 Benedix, Gustave—Philip Frank.....31 62
30 Bushman, Henry; Buellesbach, Jacob; Buellesbach, John } William Rosenbush..........67 50
1 Benjamin, Joseph—Jacob Eichhorn..107 49
1 Baumgrass, Julius A—C N Boyd.....119 75
1 Bernsee, Christian D—S E Vernon...310 46
1 Blanchard, Stella—Kate Malloy......227 99
1 Brady, William, Jr—G W Venable...237 26
1 Blake, Frederick D—Hanover Nat Bank.............................2,044 24
2 Brennan, Thomas—A J Donnelly.....48 97
2 Bertin, Paul—R J Hoquet..........15,889 91
2 Brilles, Bernhard—S H Green.......160 19
2 Behrend, Edward—Adolf Kessler, Jr. 1,895 87
2 Burgess, Levi G—H W O Edge.......1,275 30
2 Biggermann, Theodora—C H Reed..1,071 65
27 Crane, Julia M—W & J Sloane......433 84
27 Campbell, Joseph; Campbell, Martha; Campbell, Emma, exrs William Campbell } Nassau Bank.....12,995 36
27 Cohen, Harry L—C R Tice..........98 87
29 Carmiencke, John H—Samuel Colgate 78 35
29 Coombs, John—John Murray........518 71
29 Collins, Frank A—W R Potts.......2,848 93
29 Cater, Henry S—A R Ackert.........377 66
29 Chinnock, Frank R—J R Regan.....211 81
30 Coates, Joseph S—Helen F Baxter...3,238 10
30 Churchill, Henry C—F M Bower.....88 93
1 Cantaluppi, Henry—Augustin Arango 452 43
1 Crawley, William K—Bertha Nonnenbacher..........................206 02
2 Crawford, William H—G S Hamlin, assignee.........................908 09
2 Colleran, John; Colleran, Michael } the same........1,190 64
27*Derbyshire, William H—W G Roome. 733 21
27 Dippel, Frederick—Delamater Iron Works..........................245 60
29 De Forest, Harriet; De Forest, William H, Jr } Samuel Clark...2,475 86
30 Ducy, John M—G W Smith..........268 96
1 Donahue, Daniel J—R C Brown......174 16
1*Duffy, William J—S C Boehm........1,024 05
2†Darcy, William H—J S Barron......82 00
2†Doolittle, Itez C—United Electric Light and Power Co.............211 25
27 Egan, Mary E—C E Lydecker, admr. 108 23
29 Eberspacher, Christian—Leopold Boehm.....................costs 114 77
30 Ehrgoot, Levinia—Moritz Freudenberg...............................28 85
1 Ewing, Justus E—J S Mathews......264 60
1 Eller, Maurice—C T Poore...........93 31
1 Evatt, Sarah K; Evatt, John G } Mary J Bradley....328 20
1 Ehrgott, Levenia—J A Straley.......150 18
2 Emrich, Joseph, Jr—Randolph Guggenheimer.........................359 77
2 Everest, Catharine A—Gertrude Beekman.....................costs 133 34
2 Emanuel, Otto W—Edward Fisher...80 67
27 Fox, Dennis—W E Remy...........770 50
29 Fitzner, Albert—Carl Muller.........247 15
29 Fox, Dennis—W E Remy.............770 50
29 Flynn, Florence B, extrx—Gabriel Schwab...........................1,544 75
30 Feinberg, Jacob—J D K Crook.......491 47
30†Freidenrich, Sarah—George Simon...149 00
30 Fingleton, Henry W—G W Venable..132 43
30 Farrington, John A; Farrington, Jonas S } N Y Small Stock Co...225 22
1 Foster, Elizabeth L—Josias Jones....599 37
1 Franko, Nahan—Leo Schlesinger....324 21
1 Frankel, Mayer—Hulda Schwartz....68 00
1 Ferguson, Daniel F M—Emanuel Pelikan.............................148 14
2 Feltenstein, Amelia—Emanuel Appel. 382 73
2 Feldenstein, Amelia—Thomas Sullivan..............................286 31
29 Graff, Mary Ann, admrx John Graff—W A Lindsay..............costs 150 70
30 Geiger, Usher—Nechе Geiger.........123 60
30 Gilmartin, James—Hermann Hablo..3,865 67
30 the same——G F Vietor..........6,104 66
1 the same——Hermann Hablo....2,256 50
1 the same——G F Vietor..........952 60
1 the same——Peter McGovern.....5,181 54
1 the same——Peter Quinn.........1,070 32
1 the same——Michael Gilmartin...353 22
1 the same——W H Lee..........2,018 65
1 Gedke, Helen—C W Klebisch........79 50
1 Gindon, Gustave—S F Shortland.....223 79
1 Gilmartin, James—W A Hardt.......1,361 65
2 Gibb, Lulu—J L Gibb................240 47
2 Gilmartin, James—James Talcott.... ——
2 Goldfard, Rachel—Emanuel Appel...382 73
2 Greene, Edward C—R J Hoquet....15,889 91
2 Goldberg, Leo; Goldberg, Benjamin; Goldberg, Louis J } S I Mayer......1,062 79
2 Griswold, Margaret D—J R Churchill, trustee........................425 50
2*Goldfarb, Rachel—Thomas Sullivan..286 31
2 Gilmartin, James—W E Tefft........744 21
2 the same——E C Dillingham....3,133 44
2 Germany, Peter A—Nella B Guechsel. ....costs 357 73
27 Hotsch, Julia E—N Y Bank Note Co. 1,140 19
27 Hammerbacher, Paul—Katharine Walter.............................96 66
29 Hayman, Herman—Mary L Standish, admrx...........................71 27
29 Herzfeld, Jeanette—Morris Goldzier..153 76
29 Hauser, G Julius—U S Supply Co (Lim)..............................17 51
30 Hayden, Mortimer M—H F Frasse...103 03
30 Humphreys, Robert Lewis—Melvin Stephens....................costs 69 45
30 Hill, William—Mayor, &c......costs 140 25
30 Horgan, Arthur J—Hattie H Farrell, admrx..........................101 15
30†Hamburg, Bernard—A B King.......42 02
1 Hastings, Joseph—Calvin Tomkins...134 36
1 Hubbard, Henry W—Joseph Beardsley..............................138 53
1 Henigston, Sam—Bernard Branner...535 25
1†Hulburt, Robert—W A Higgins......76 01
2 Hyneman, Julius—Newroder Kunstanstalten Actien Gesellschaft.....2,325 11

2 Hanna, Ellen—Twenty-third Street Railway Co........................ 23 73
2 Herzfeld, Jeannette—Louis Kronthal. 67 29
2 Hirschberg, Gustav / Hirschberg, Simon } J R Doudge.... 222 41
2 Hewitt, Henry S—Lena Werle........ 208 98
2 Immer, Hans—American Champagne Co (Lim)........................ 82 12
29 Irvine, Allen—A R Ackert........... 877 66
30 Ireland, John E—O F Burkart........ 7,082 39
29 Jacobs, Harry C—J T Leavitt......... 502 98
29 Jones, Walter—S B W McLeod....... 46 05
30 Johnston, Coburn H—Otto Frey....... 124 31
2 Jacobson, Selly—Seamless Rubber Co 682 49
2 Johnson, George D / Johnson, Pierrepont E / Johnson, Charles E / Johnson, Edith / Johnson, Edwards, by George D Johnson their guard ad litem } Gertrude Beekman ....costs 133 34
27 Knapp, Walter S—F H Leggett....... 97 29
29 Kramer, Charles—Max Marx......... 36 20
29 Koch, Henry C F—Hattie Siegel.costs 69 25
30 Krakower, Gerson—Isaac Goldstein.. 22 50
30 Kaskel, Paul—Louis Simon.......... 202 80
1 Kreuder, Adolf / Kreuder, Frank F / Kline, Charles } W H Lee....... 8,191 83
1 the same——G F Vietor.......... 899 01
1 the same——J F Johnston 172 81
1 the same——Union Square Bank. 3,994 52
1 the same——Samuel Eiseman....2,821 94
1 the same——Raphael Elias... ...1,976 04
1 the same——Louis Roessel........ 887 80
1 the same——W H H Hull.........3,210 83
1 the same——William Meyer 1,802 53
1 the same——J C Wilmerding.... 781 94
1 the same——A B Knapp.........1,212 59
1 the same——H C Sylvester 1,316 94
1 the same——Engelbert Hardt ... 581 60
1 the same——Julius Franklin.....1,123 81
1 the same——J B Renwick........ 672 58
1 the same——F S Pasavant... .... 825 35
1 the same——Belding Bros & Co.. 311 27
1 the same——Abraham Steinhardt 483 27
1 the same——W E Tefft 5,550 55
1 the same——G D Sweetser........5,952 65
1 Keller, Rudolph—Bernard Branner... 585 25
1 Kiefer, Christian—S C Boehm........ 1,024 05
1*Kensell, William H—F T Parsons.... 146 32
2 Keating, Patrick—William Neely.... 69 68
2 Kreuder, Adolpf / Kreuder, Frank F / Kline, Charles } P R Letson...... 858 17
2 the same——J C Strawbridge.... 967 93
2 the same——The Metropolitan Dry Goods Co........................ 480 03
2 Kneeland, Sylvester H—W H Brown 10,672 29
2 Kelley, Albert—W C Hall......costs. 98 65
27 Leaverett, Alice R—Delamater Iron Works 86 09
27 Lindblom, Robert—W S Williams...63,415 13
27 Ladd, Alfred W—G H Hull........ .. 421 49
27 Leake, Edward C—O W P Westervelt 135 90
29 Lewin, Simon—Jane Hassell.......... 90 50
29 Ladd, Alfred W—G H Hull......... 421 49
29 Linington, Timothy B — Adolph Schwarz.... ... . 229 66
30 Lynch, Sarah—M H Haffey.....costs 186 70
30 Lees, Samuel—W D Wade........ ... 50 08
30 Lovell, Charles W—H F Palmer..... . 93 80
30 the same——Frederick Woehr.... 417 89
1 Levy, Max—Edward Davidow....... 186 35
1 Lustberg, Ignatz—David Brown... . 627 49
1 Lett, William F—H W Haas. 815 87
1 Leeds, William J—F T Parsons. 146 32
2 Lamb, James W—Philips & William Ebling Brewing Co.......... .... 86 00
27 Miller, Nathan G—W S Williams....63,415 13
27 Mackey, Thomas N—John Blakely.... 217 78
29 Morrell, George P—J A Dahn........ 199 20
29 Moses, Dora / Moses, Simon } George Forgotston... 364 39
29 Mahler, Michael—J C de La Mare.... 468 60
29 Myers, Elijah / Moses, I Harby } Faendsticksfabriks Aktiebolaget Nulcan...... .. costs 521 72
29 Macgowan, Robert W—J O Heald, assignee. . ...costs 116 76
29 Matthews, James Brander—Thomas Drummond.............................1,368 45
29 Mueller, William—E J N Stent..... . 72 00
30 Meyer, Sigmund T / Meyer, Arthur L } Twenty-Third Ward Bank... 564 88
30 Morrissy, James W—Francesco Francinlli............... .... 217 50
30 Meitzel, George—Jacob Ruppert.. .. 290 93
30 Mills, Emma D—Leo Von Raven..... 103 75
30 Madigan, Edward—D M Koehler..... 190 50
1 May, S Elwood—H E Bandell....costs 85 70
1 Mordecai, Eugene L—R L Mordecai..2,855 70
1 Moeller, Carl—A B Day 418 13
2 Markle, William—E A Rosenbam.... 376 37
2 Meade, James—C F Imbrie.......... 145 46
2 Morris, Julia—I S Thompson......... 204 45
2 the same——the same.... .... 322 74
2 Merrill, Julian W—Henry Martin ... 142 56
2 Monroe, Robert B / Monroe, George } Jennie Fischer... 922 75
2 Manton, Daniel E / Manton, Maria L } Catherine Cummins............ 49 12
2 Martin, Robert C—E K O'Brien......1,982 89
2 Martin, Robert C—W C Burgess.....1,457 57
2 Mulock, Josephine—Gertrude Beekman... ....costs 133 34
2 Morrison, Mary—C S Storms.......... 70 00
27 Mackey, Thomas N—John Blakely... 217 78
29 McIlhargy, Joseph—Eloise I Chace, extrx 106 34
29 Macgowan, Robert W—J O Heald, assignee..... ....costs 116 76
30 McAnnery, Michael F—Archer & Pancoast Mfg Co.......................... 155 91
1 McLean, Cornelius / MacLean, Charles } Philip Schimel.. 237 34
1 McKenna, Thomas F—August Schieck 44 99
2 McFarlone, John I—Ferdinand McKeige.............................6,096 37
2 McAuliffe, Thomas J admr Sarah A McAuliffe—Eleanor F Bishop......1,988 00
2 McGuckin, Patrick—G S Hamlin..... 168 34
2 McKeon, John H—United Electric Light and Power Co................ 211 25
30 Nagle, Joseph F—People State N Y..1,000 00
30 Nejedly, Joseph—Joseph Kuntz Brewing Co............... .... 437 00
30 Niro, Antonio—Joseph Sussind.costs 108 51
30 Osgood, Harry L—John Elsey........ 106 30
1 Oesterreicher, Ignatz—Richard Meyer ....costs 260 57
2 Oberle, Joseph A—G H Kracht...... 22 87
27 Post, Edward S—Estella Lencioni.... 38 09
27 Peters, William H—F & M Schaefer Brewing Co.. ... . 50 10
27 Pollock, Nathan—Carl Voigt......... 127 30
29 Peck, Edward M—W R Potts.........2,348 93
29 Pollock, Nathan—Carl Voigt......... 127 30
30 Pfluger, Jacob—George Reichardt.... 42 50
30 Palmer, George W—R W Elliott..... 544 55
1 Pray, Edward Everett—John Patterson........... .... 566 41
1 Pearl, Dyer—R L Mordecai....... ..2,855 70
1 Peralta, Reavis J A—C C Rean...... 546 46
1 Portarfield, Charles R—A H Selwyn.. 221 24
2 Pfeiffer, Louis E — Ferdinand McKeige.................................6,096 37
2 Peck, Edward M—A L Fryer. 397 93
2 Pine, Charles H—E V Machette......3,471 16
2 Peck, Nathan—E K O'Brien..........1,992 89
2 the same——W C Burgess.........1,457 57
27 Rennie, Arthur H—M R Muckle..... 216 82
27†Rodda, Robert H — Columbus Nat Bank 39 49
27 Rannow, Rudolph—E C Hazard...... 445 74
29 Reisenburg, Adolph—Hattie Siegel .. .. .costs 69 25
30 Rauzman, Morris—M D Solinger..... 202 66
1 Rubira, Eladio, Jr—George Whitaker 146 61
1 Richardson, Emeline A — H A W Wood................................ 112 50
2 Rice, John—Jennie Fischer.......... 923 75
2 Roberts, Austin J—Mary Brundage.. 199 26
2 Roberts, Joseph—James Talcott...... 695 44
2 Rothschild David—Henry Batjer.... 264 02
2 Rogers, Myron W—Cobansey Glass Mfg Co 5,020 35
27 Shipitiusky, Samuel—Louis Austern. 417 25
27 Salisbury, John, Jr—Edith S Berwin. 137 10
29 Sheridan, John — Christian Erdenbrecher....... .. .. 189 45
29 Seykora, Anton—A L Bullowa....... 53 83
29 Smart, William J—Mary L Standish, admrx................................ 86 26
29 Sykes, Charles P—E F Brown 270 84
29†Selling, John — Helen S Gardner, extrx..................................... 98 94
30 Strauss, Moses / Strauss, Julius } C H Mangels 3,126 23
30 Syska, Adolph G—S L Storer........ 79 32
30 Short, John C—W S Brewster........1,663 61
30 Stiefs, Herman—Elizabeth Meltzer... 614 38
30 Sullivan, Charles P—Robert Forbes.. 337 67
1 Schwarz, Adam—George Lieber...... 171 63
2 Schmidt, Alfred—Newroder Kunstanstalten Actien Gesellschaft.........2,325 11
2 Schwab, Gabriel / Schwab, Nathan / Schwab, Abraham / Schwab, Leo L } Siegfried Rosenberg.......... 425 33
2 Schaeffle, Madelane—Patrick Gallagher....... .... 47 80
2 St John, Cortlandt—H W O Edge....1,275 30
2 Sprague, Charles H / Sprague, Farndon A } W C Hall. ....costs 98 65
2 Scott, John—Adrian Hercq..........4,942 20
30 Smith, Frederick J—John Elsey...... 106 30
1 Smith, Orrin F—Cynthia J Nutting..5,819 28
1†Smith, John—W A Higgins.......... 76 01
27 The Arkansaw & Gulf R R Co—N Y Bank Note Co.................. .....1,140 19
27 American Export & Trading Co—Sackett & Fiske Stationery Co..... 472 79
27 E G Blakslee Sons Iron Works—Charles Whitehead............ .. 222 39
29 Metropolitan Elevated Railway Co—Mary McK. Greenwood, extrx.costs 90 56
29 Belford Co—G A Bell........ .... 328 87
29 The N Y Ice Co—C R Spoerry....... 159 01
29 C C McEwen Co—William Booth..... 369 71
30 The Nat Bank of Commerce—Toronto General Trust Co ....costs 1,496 03
30 The Oregon Pacific R R Co—G J Forrest, exr.... ... . 136 25
30 The Jenness Miller Publishing Co—Eugene Higgins................ ... 326 44
30 The South Publishing Co—Bradley Fertilizer Co...................... 80 36
30 Imperial Buffet Lunch Co (Lim)—F F Vieweg 173 00
30 Lawrence Curry Comb Co—J A Roeblings Sons Co.... .... 257 09
30 the same——W E Dodge......... 389 50
30 The Second Avenue R R Co—Kate Madden 150 00
30 The Mayor, Aldermen, &c—Albert Emmitt.............................costs 105 25
30 Lawrence Curry Comb Co—T H Watson 168 62
30 The Homer Lee Bank Note Co—Shepeng, Litchfield & Northern R R Co 68 47
30 The Mayor, Aldermen, &c—Frank Phelps...............................15,963 33
1 Imperial Buffet Lunch Co (Lim)—Michael Scanlon 177 27
1 the same——N H Snyder......... 108 13
1 The N Y Elevated R R Co / The Manhattan Railway Co. } A D Shepard...costs 83 19
1 The Knickerbocker Lumber Co—H B Shepard.......... ....5,391 15
1 The Southern Boulevard R R Co—P N Spofford. . ...costs 106 65
2 The Associated Lace Makers' Co—Engelbert Hardt.... .... 230 22
2 The Murray Hill Bank—Elizabeth Van Antwerp, exr.............. ..costs 118 15
2 The Lawrence Curry Comb Co—Smith & Griggs Mfg Co 121 78
2 Imperial Buffet Lunch Co (Lim)—W A Shaw............................. 80 07
27 Tessmer, Albert—M J Roth.......... 69 18
27 Taft, Charles S—Addie H Johnston.. 90 81
29 Tobey, Edward H—Geo C Flint Co... 203 24
30 Templeton, Henry / Templeton, Hamilton } John Rudd. 125 85
30 Toper, Ignatz—M D Solinger.. ...... 80 50
30 Tallman, Mary / Tallman, William S } Mutual Benefit Life Ins Co (D)1,681 13
1 Thomas, George C—R L Mordecai...2,855 70
2 Thompson, Joseph R H—Sarah Hogg 377 17
2 the same——W R Creed.......... 433 32
2 Thorne, Arthur—Cobansey Glass Mfg Co..................................5,020 35
1 Uhlig, George M—William Jaenike... 41 50
27*Verrinder, William, Jr / Verrinder, Arnold G } W G Roome 783 21
27 Vernam, Remington—R J Dodge....2,744 03
29 Vooth, Henry W—Samuel Streit..... 418 32
29 Volkmar, Henry G — Metropolitan Telephone and Telegraph Co....... 52 82
1 Valentine, John H E—G F Valentine. 88 20
1 the same——the same............ 117 78
2 Vail, Isaac M—W E Conway......... 204 43
29 Van Siclen, Frank B—J O Heald, assignee............................costs 116 70
27 Wollheim, Aaron—Carl Voigt........ 249 33
27 Walter, William—Katharine Walter ....costs 96 66
29 Wollheim, Aaron—Carl Voigt....... 249 33
30 Wilkes, George / Wilkes, Lizzie T } Twenty-third Ward Bank.... .... 562 88
30†Weiss, John—M D Solinger.......... 171 35
30 Wemple, Phebe J—Pryce Lewis..... 243 28
30 Worsnop, Alfred—J B M Duche...... 269 27
1 Walton, Arthur H, Jr—George Whitaker..... .... 108 36
1†Wood, Albert G—Charles Heckman.. 59 50
1 Wolsky, Mary / Wolsky, Frank } W C Low... ...... 119 70
1 Wittner, Charles—Bernard Branner.. 533 25
1 Waterman, Charles—Hanover Nat. Bank 2,644 24
2 White, Charles J—Bessie Loucheim.. 236 53
2 Wynne, James / Wallach, Caroline } Annie M McIntyre 40 59
2 Wynne, James——the same..........1,162 00
2 Wallach, Caroline——the same...... 374 50
2 Werner, Gottlieb—Samuel Laderer..1,025 46
2 Work, George F—Ferdinand McKeige.....................................6,096 37
2 Wagener, August P—Sarah Lewis, admrx.......................................1,308 08
1 Zugner, Peter J—E D Clark......... 32 08

KINGS COUNTY.

June and July

29 Alcock, Maskelyne—Second Nat Bank of Jersey City........ ....,.... $284 37
29 the same——the same............ 94 71
30 Anderson, Carmen E — E Stevens, extrx.................. .... 170 13
30 Armbruster, Annie—O Armbruster.. 76 69
26 Boyle, Margaret—I Savage........... 32 60
27 Barnum, Stephen C—H Bauendahl...1,027 99
27 the same——the same 614 82
29 Boynton, Edward S—J C Thompson.. 286 16
29 Blum, Louis—Jos Fallert B Co (Lim). 88 71
30 Baker, Henry C—S Simpson......... 615 28
30 Benjamin, Joseph—J Eichorn.... ... 107 49
1 Baumert, Frederick—C Riederer..... 291 23
1 Bolen, George F—Mary A Bolen..... 121 51
2 Bernsee, Christian D—S E Vernon.... 310 46
25 Cole, Ramah—R Knox.............. 194 18
26 Coggeshall, Josephine H—W B Chase 93 01
27*Crosby, George A—H Bauendahl.....1,027 99
27 Crosby, George A——the same....... 614 82
27 Cairns, John M / Cairns, Agnes R } T H McArdle..... 494 92
27 Cairns, John M——the same. 76 67
30 Conkling, August—H C Fischer...... 141 00
30 Coffin, Hannah W—J C C Gatje, exr. 54 05
30 Carmiencke, John H—S Colgate...... 78 35
1 Case, Virgil R—J Gleason.. .... 33 87
26 Donohue, Thomas—C M Marsh 2,578 05
26 Diggs, Charles—Otto Huber Brewery. 77 25
27 De Riesthal, Alphonse / De Riesthal, Gustave E } B B Schneider........1,965 41
29 Devoe, Frederick—S Streit..... ...... 332 09
29 Denley, John B—L L Robbins........ 118 78
30 Dunn, John K—E W Richardson. ... 506 41
2 De Lano, George W—H W Grindal.. 840 03
26 Eisenhart, David S—C S Philips...... 151 46
30 Emerson, Frank H—Jennie Emerson.. 139 38
25 Furgerson, John—M Schriefer.... ... 329 44
26 Flanagan, William—W D Hoag...... 106 71
26 Fleig, A Beatus / Fleig, Elizabeth } H F Gundrum...... 129 41
30†Forley, "Fanny" E—Annie M Agramonte 51 15
2 Fingelton, Henry W—G W Venable.. 132 43
1 Granberry, David W—C T Caufield..2,994 97
26 Hennesy, John—H Hermann......... 165 13
26 Herold, Jr, J George—E V Magee... 363 08
27 Huber, William—D M Koehler....... 204 86
29 Hartmann, Bernhardina, dec'd, estate of—L C Hartmann.................. 74 12

30 Horan, John—G A Drake, assignee... 82 52
1 Hall, Bolton—C T Caulfield.......... 2,994 97
1 †Hanrahan, John J / †Hanrahan, Daniel E } E E V Seyfried........ 168 53
25 Josiah, George—Julia Brandeis 116 27
30 Janes, William D B—J F Smith..... 212 07
25 Klein, Joseph—G Ringler & Co...... 1,375 00
26 Koerner, John—H F Gundrum...... 129 41
27 Krey, Phillip—C Schlesinger......... 135 99
29 Knapp, Walter S—F H Leggett...... 97 29
1 Kuhn, George—J Gleason............ 30 02
26 Lowther, Sarah E / Lowther, John R } A L Katz...... 341 57
27 Lewin, Simon—Jane Hassell......... 90 50
30 Less, Samuel—W D Wade............ 59 03
1 Leifels, Joseph J—H Craft............ 478 55
1 Lincoln, James A—E Tredwell. 120 65
1 Leonard, Robert W—C E Chinnock.. 1,484 59
25 Merrill, Julian W—H Martin........ 204 38
26 Morrell, George P—John A Dahn.... 199 20
26 Menken, John / Menken, Otto } E N Nearing......... 154 60
27 Muller, John—J B Phillips... .... 124 51
27 Marks, Aaron—J Lewy.............. 21 90
29†McArthur, "Edward" H—F O Pierce 194 48
29 Mills, James N—H Walter............ 98 33
30 Meyer, Gesine—E H Richards........ 87 04
30 Monohan, Patrick—Brooklyn Union Publishing Co........................ 44 85
30 Mott, Frank S—C H Morris... ...... 69 95
30 Miller, Frank—G Stewart............ 523 20
1 McCauley, William—C Riederer..... 309 30
2 Meyer, Gesina—E Eising....... ..... 157 04
30 Nallman, Charles U—M Rittenhouse. 961 00
1 Nicoll, Benjamin S T—C T Caulfield. 2,994 97
27 O'Connor, John—W Koeler........... 253 06
30 O'Neil, Dennis—J Callahan........... 777 38
1 Pfohlmann, John G—F A Quintano.. 68 10
25 Renton, John R—M Reynolds........ 410 81
30 Reubl, George—J Arowhold. 109 25
30 Ray, George W—Emma L Deane..... 45 02
26 Sutphen, William—E L Jackson..... 30 69
27 Strumpfter, John—F Ibert... .... 159 25
27 Stephens, Benjamin F—J B Wass.... 145 15
29 Seedorf, Charles—J McEnery........ 125 64
30 Saviero, Frank—H M Day... .... 43 31
30 Schanbacher, Christopher F—D L McDonald.......................... 123 16
30 Schroater, Louis—R Reimer........ 222 22
1 Sickels, George W—J Gleason........ 38 50
26 Townsend, Edward M—B Croner.... 119 29
27 The Clarendon Land Investment and Agency Co (Lim)—L H Carhart..100,052 90
29 The Estate of Bernhardina Hartmann, dec'd—L C Hartmnan.............. 74 12
30 Tallman, Mary and William D—The Mutual Benefit Life Insurance Co .... (D) 1,681 13
1 Thompson, George A—W B Lemmon 109 14
1 The City of Brooklyn—E A Chin..... 5,906 10
1 The J J Nichols Mfg Co—Holmes, Booth & Hayden.................. 669 24
1 The City of Brooklyn—S C Remington 488 62
26 Vernam, Remington—W H Beard.... 4,377 57
26 Viemeister, George A and Edmund C—N H White...................... 212 48
26 the same——Whiting Mfg Co.... 186 77
26 Voss, Claus—E N Nearing............ 577 64
27 Vogel, Henry—J B Phillips.......... 124 51
29 Van Nortwick, Cornelius A—Second Nat Bank of Jersey City, N J...... 284 37
30 Valentine, John H E—G F Valentine. 117 78
26 Woods, William D—A L Katz........ 341 57
27 Wersebe, John H—J V Wilson....... 147 08
30 Whitney, William M—D E Johnson.. 139 79
30 Welton, Isaac W—R Reimer.......... 95 71
1 Willis, Oliver R—Z G Wilson, assignee 132 02
1 Vossick, Henry—N Vinette........... 18 25

SATISFIED JUDGMENTS.

NEW YORK.

June 27 to July 2—Inclusive.

Alden, William H, Jr—Cornelia E Wright. (1887......................... $428 78
Baker, James H—Alexander Thain. (1891).... 175 44
Barrick, William H—A S Ring, exr. (1890)....3,988 61
Bindseil, Herman F—M M Johnson..... (1891) 155 65
Brunner, Adam—Frederick Michel. (1884).... 377 77
Chesebrough, Robert A—Fire Dep't. (1890).. 50 00
Claflin, John—Herman Cantor, assignee. ('90) 1,575 50
Same——same. (1891) 114 12
Same——same. ('891).................. 91 49
Crasto, Frank P—Richard White. (1889)...... 102 74
Contanseau Rapid Foreign Express Co—H H Yard. (1890) 11,784 69
Contanseau, Ludovic——same. (1889).........20,215 58
Columbia Bank—Gospel Tabernacle Church. (1889)........................... 110 57
Same——same. (1889)..................... 580 01
Carey, Peter C—Richard Farrell. (1890)...... 194 63
‖Dean, William E—W J Adler. (1891)......... 252 50
Dennerlein, Julia—H E Hall. (1891) 14 98
Same——same. (1891).................. 182 31
Same——same. (1891)................... 19 28
Eames, Edward E—Herman Cantor, assignee (1890)...............................1,575 50
Same——same. (1891)....................... 114 12
Same——same. (1891)........................ 91 49
Fairchild, Horace J / Force, Dexter N } Herman Cantor, assignee. (1890)..............1,575 50
Same——same. (1891)...................... 114 12
Same——same. (1891)....................... 91 48
Fowler, Mortimer L—A B Purdy. (1882)...... 774 48
Same——J J Lawrence. (1888)................3,523 47
Fox, Sarah J—John McCowan. (1887).......... 56 12
Hurley Stone Co—Sarah J Davidson. (1889)... 294 22
Same——same. (1889)...................... 287 31
Hayes, William B—E S Frink. (1891).......... 51 65
Same——same (1891)...................... 103 50
Horgan, Arthur J—Hattie H Farrell admrx. (1891)................................ 101 15
Same——same. (1891)...................... 78 85
Same——same. (1891)...................... 710 10
‖Henry, Matthew C—G W McLean recvr. (1890)................................ 75 82
Hamburg American Packet Co—Helena Wittebeski. (1891)................................ 324 45

Hill, Benjamin J—People State N Y. (1887)... 91 96
Same——same. (1886)......................... 677 89
Jaquin, Frederick W, Jr—Nason Mfg Co. (1890).................................... 120 69
Kerrigan, Maurice S—Emma A Catterfield. (1880)....................................... 156 57
*Kelly, Thomas P—Murray Hill Bank. (1891) 673 78
Lowe, James A—William Neumann. (1891)... 480 14
Levy, Ferdinand, one of the Coroners of City of N Y—Herman Cantor, assignee. (1891). 91 41
Same——same. (1891).......................... 114 12
Same——same. (1890) 1,575 50
Miller, Edward—Annie R Shinn. (1891)...... 296 80
Munzinger, John C—H J Ehlers. (1891)...... 332 61
Manhattan Railway Co / Metropolitan Elevated Railway Co } Grace Edna. (1891).. 636 90
Manhattan Railway Co—Annie Sinai, admrx. (1891).......................................9,508 78
Mayo, James H—H E Waite. (1890).......... 383 75
Maynard, Edwin C—Blodgett & Orswell Co. (Lim.) (1890) 444 94
Mulry, James—Fire Dep't. (1889)............ 50 00
McGrath, Mary J—L F Brennecke. (1891)..... 262 83
Merrifield, Edward L—E Y Bell, assignee. (1888).. 152 67
Same——same. (1888)..........................17,330 41
O'Hara, Catharine—Elizabeth Christy. (1888). 106 50
Same——same. (1888)........................... 106 50
Prior, Robert J and George B exrs Robert Prior—W H Payne. (1891).................1,316 82
Patron, James G—H J Ehlers. (1891).......... 332 61
Panella, Salvatore—Antonio Buccola. (1891).. 212 18
Robinson, Daniel—Herman Cantor, assignee. (1890) 1,575 50
Same——same. (1891).......................... 114 12
Same——same. (1891).......................... 91 49
Rodamor, John F—E J Halligan. (1891)...... 568 00
Reynolds, Lawrence—John Cosgrove. (1888).. 208 00
Sheehy, John and Ambrose—Samuel Nichols. (1891).. 67 50
Searing, Theodore W—James Linton. (1890).. 94 66
Sweeney, James—John Cosgrove. (1888)...... 208 00
Smith, John H—Julius Somborn. (1891)...... 177 56
Slattery, Vincent J—Hattie H Farrell, admrx (1891).. 710 10
Same——same. (1891) 78 85
Same——same. (1891)........................... 101 15
‡Smith, Elliot—J L Morgan. (1886)...........1,223 09
Roselle, Peter—H J Ehlers. (1891)............. 332 61
Stokes, Mary Ann, John S, Walter C and Henry B, exrs Henry Stokes—N Y Central & Hudson River R R Co. (1889)............ 105 60
Stephens, Richard W—I C Ogden, Jr. (1891).. 852 74
Talbott, Elisha H—Persian Rug and Carpet Co. (1891)....................................... 336 00
Thomson, Alexander N—C W Conrath. ('91) 86 73
Valentine, R H C—L A Ault. (1889)........... 447 78
Williams, Samuel—W R Martin. (1890)....... 350 38

*Vacated by order of Court. †Suspended on Appeal. ‡Released. §Reversal. ‖Satisfied by Execution.

KINGS COUNTY.

June 26 to July 1—inclusive.

Jacqui, Frederick W, Jr—Nason Mfg Co. ('90). $120 69
Jeffrey, Alexander—A T Van Nest. (1890).... 3,261 30
Mannheim, Julius—M Courtney. (1891)....... 77 58
Same——same. (1891)....................... 374 02
McSwyny, Bryan G—H Brown. (1890)........ 2,016 22
Same——M Kearney. (1890).................. 5,016 22
Murphy, Harry E—W H H Childs. (1891)..... 159 48
Nicoll, Donald—M Solomonsky. (1891)........ 566 42
Radner, Louis—E H Richards. (1891) 58 99
Reitz, John—J J Froeblich. (1890)............ 1,010 06
Rockwell, William—N W Burtis. (1890)........ 226 87
Roche, David T—B Newton. (1890)............. 126 08
Samuels, Isaac / Samuels, Leon / Samuels, Emil } L Isenburger. (1891)........ 157 18
Schwalbach Cycle Co—F Baylis. (1891)....... 467 54
Same——same. (1891)........................ 75 47
Stubing, John / Stubing, Annie } C Stubing. (1889)........... 90 00
Sweet, Elnathan, Jr / Young, James R } D Morrison. (1890) ...3,688 59
Sweet, Charles F / Sweet, James } S Bennett, Jr.. (1888)...... 62 40
The National Security Life and Accident Co—M La Manna. (1891) 110 14
Thorn, Robert—A Taylor. (1887) 148 33
Weber, John / Weber, Louis / Weber, Edward / Weber, Hugo } J Gonzales. (1891).......... 242 54
Wissel, Andrew—L Ossman. (1885)........... 274 75

MECHANICS' LIENS.

NEW YORK CITY.

June

27 One Hundred and Thirty-second st, s s, 125 e 5th av, 85x100. Philadelphia Fire Proofing and Brick Co. agt Lizzie T. and George Wilkes, owners and contractors $1,135 22
27 Seventieth st, Nos. 300 and 302, s w cor West End av, 100x—. L. F. Manes agt E. A. Fuller, owner, and Alex. Kani and Conrad Zink, contractor........................ 24 57
27 Park av, No. 567, e s, 75.3 s 63d st, 66.5x—. Hugo Kafka agt Edward J. Woolsey, owner and contractor... .... 165 00
27 One Hundredth st, n s, 150 e 3d av, 50x100. Hoopes & Shipman agt Philip H. Smith, owner, and George Breitenbach, contractor................................... 90 00
27 Macdougal st, No. 9. / Vandam st, Nos. 2-8 } begins Macdougal st. s w cor Vandam st, 60x118. Same agt Charles Downey and George W. Curry, owners, and George Breitenbach, contractor.................. 160 00
27 Seventy-second st, Nos. 414 and 416 E., 50x100. Louis Roller agt Joseph F. and Kate Gallagher, owners and contractors 2,975 00
27 Same property. J. A. Dooner agt Joseph F. Gallagher, owner and contractor...... 739 75
27 One Hundred and Sixty-fifth st, n s, 50.6 e Tiffany st, 25x96.8. C. G. Jorgensen agt Joseph and Edward Sinnott, owners and contractors.................................. 234 75
29 One Hundred and Twentieth st, s s, 125 w 8th av, 75x100.11. Hamann & Brown agt James Thompson, owner and contractor. 1,559 00
29 Thirty-ninth st, Nos. 609 and 611, n s, 175 w 11th av, 50x100. James Slattery agt J. N. Koster, owner, and K. N. Smith & Co., contractor....................................... 171 46

29 Fulton av, Nos. 1237-1241, w s, 129 n 168th st, 52x175. Frank Briener agt Philipp Bunn, owner and contractor.. .... 860 00
29 Seventy-second st, Nos. 414 and 416, s s, 312 e 1st av, 50x100. Louis Roller agt Joseph F. and Kate Gallagher, owner and contractor.... ....2,975 00
29 One Hundred and Eighteenth st, s s, 60 e Madison av, 100x100.11. Bowes & Coombe agt Bernhard Ginsburg, Maria Masche and Samuel Harris, owners, and Marie Masche, contractor........................ 360 00
29 Central Park West, n w cor 104th st, 100.11x100. Malcolm & Taylor agt August Kohn, John J. Carey, Martin J. Barron, Henry Steers and J. F. Menke, owners, and John J. Carey and Martin J. Barron, contractors..2,000 00
29 Eighty-second st, s s, 120 w 8th av, 55x100. Fenn & Braxmar agt Mary Gault, owner, and James Gault, contractor 200 00
30 Ninety-fourth st, n s, 150 w 9th av, 103.8x100. John Rehill agt James B. Brady, owner, and Clegg, Richards & Co., contractors.. 29 70
30 Same property. Thomas Malch agt same.. 28 00
30 Same property. Abraham Dillon agt same 31 95
30 Same property. John Measey agt same... 25 20
30 Same property. James Gunn agt same.... 6 75
30 Same property. Samuel Hanna agt same. 21 37
30 Same property. Patrick Sullivan agt same 30 83
30 Same property. Alexander Renzulli agt same..................................... 8 12
30 Same property. Pasquale Carmeto agt same..................................... 6 87
30 Same property. Dominis Gilliberti agt same..................................... 4 37
30 Same property. Thomas Haney agt same. 27 00
30 Same property. Joseph Carrigan agt same..................................... 15 75
30 Same property. Frank Carrigan agt same. 14 00
30 Seventh av, e s, 50 n 129th st, 25x100. Henry Taylor agt Max Henrich, owner, and Lizzie McComb, lessee and contractor....... 47 50
30 South st, No. 8, n w cor Moore st, 14x105. Nicholas Ryan agt Edward Landers, owner, and William C Turner, contractor.. 108 80
30 Villa av, w s, 375 n Potter pl, 50x100. Gass & Bilhoefer agt Edmund C. Allcott, owner and contractor............................ 264 10
30 Seventy-second st, Nos. 418 and 420, s s, 263 e 1st av, 50x100. Union Stove Works agt Kate and Joseph F. Gallagher, owners and contractors.............................. 798 00

July

1 One Hundred and Third st, s s, 177.5 e Amsterdam av, 150x101.10. Joseph Marren agt James McNiece, owner and contractor..1,558 43
2 One Hundred and Forty-third st, s s, 419 e Boulevard, 58x100. P. J. Ryan agt Hannah M. Halpin, owner and contractor.... 800 00
2 One Hundred and Fifty-fifth st, n s, 185.8 e 8th av, 414x—x305.6x100. J. H. Deeves & Bro. agt Baskin Wood Vulcanizing Co, or its trustees, owners and contractors...3,780 00
2 Inwood av Nos. 24 and 25, e s, 175 s Wolf pl, 50x130. Abrahams Steers agt John F. and Maria M. Eichler, owners, and John Frederick Eichler, contractor.............. 616 38
2 Fulton av, w s, 129 n 168th st, 52.6x100. J. J. Kingston agt Phillip Bunn, owner and contractor.................................. 100 00
2 One Hundred and Thirty-second st, s s, 125 e 5th av, 85x—. Abraham Steers agt Lizzie T. and George Wilkes, owners and contractors.. 500 00
2 Eighth av, n w cor 104th st, 100.11x100. A. G. Pucci agt August Kohn and Steers & Mink, owners, and Carey & Barron, contractors..1,285 00

Editor RECORD AND GUIDE:

The bond to discharge the lien filed June 19th, 1891, by Beers & Kuenster against the Music Hall, Hopper & Co. contractors, has been approved, and the lien will be discharged forthwith.

NORWOOD & COGGESHALL.

KINGS COUNTY.

June

26 Hancock st, n s, 100 w Bedford av, school Building No. 80. Nicholas Ryan agt The Board of Education, Brooklyn, owner, and Daniel F. Blainey, contractor $218 00
26 Seventh av, n w s, 200 n e 58th st, 25x100, New Utrecht. Thomas Robinson agt Robert Carlin, owner and contractor..... 28 00
26 Second st, Nos. 479-485, n s, 90.7 w 7th av, 80x100. The Butler Hardware Co. agt Roderick Von Graff, owner and contractor.... 270 47
26 Eighth av, s e cor 11th st, 118x120x irreg Paul Ayres Co. agt William Turner, owner, and Albert V. B. Norris, contractor...2,437 00
26 Hicks st, n e cor Poplar st, 24x75. John S. Loomis agt Ida W. or Duncan Edwards, owner and contractor.......................... 456 18
26 Patchen av, n s, 20 e Putnam av, 125x30. Edward F. Spear agt Mr. Underhill, owner, and Mr. Yarber, contractor................ 17 50
27 Saratoga av, n w cor Herkimer st, 110x100. Henry McShane & Co. agt George H. Gibby, owner, and John Knox, contractor. 604 10
27 Navy st, e s, 61.7 n Myrtle av, 50x100. Edward T. Nicoll agt Henrietta Fisk, owner, and William H. H. Glover, contractor . 1,450 00
27 Third av, s e cor Bergen st, 25x100. John F. Richartz agt Jacob Goldschmidt, owner and contractor................................ 425 00
27 Eighth av, e s, extends from 15th st to 16th st, —x— (see Lien). John Monahan agt Edwin Berdell, owner and contractor.... 102 83
29 Fifty-third st, s s, 275 w 15th av, 50x100.2, New Utrecht. James Lindsay agt —— Dettmar, owner, and C. F. T. Becker, contractor.. 77 00
29 Second st, s s, 177.10 w 6th av, 80x100. George N. Buchanan and Patrick J. Riley agt Archibald N. McBean, owner and contractor.. 740 00
29 Second st, Nos. 412-416, s s, 437.11 e 5th av, 60x100. Arthur Almstrom agt Archibald N. McBean, owner and contractor........ 100 00
30 Linwood st, e s, 175 n Liberty av, 25x100. George W. Ball agt John Lynch, owner, and Richard Flanigan, contractor........ 40 00

30 Bergen st, No. 1427, n w cor Marcy av, 85.8 x—x28.4, gore. Joseph Cholnocki agt Annie McDonald, owner, and James Downs and Patrick Gilchrist, contractors. 8 00

30 Same property. Lorenz Kaemark agt same owner and contractors. 15 00

30 Court st, s w s, 63.4 s Hamilton av, 20x100. Kenyon & Newton agt Nicholas McCool, Jr., owner and contractor.............. 168 69

30 Second st, n s, 90.7 w 7th av, 80x100. Richardson & Boynton Co. agt Roderick Von Graff, John Halloran, William L. Dowling, Edward O'Brien and George T. Riley, owners, and Roderick Von Graff, contractor.... .... 576 00

July

1 Sixth av, s e cor 1st st, 100x97. Ross & Snyder agt Roderick Von Graff, owner, and Roderick Von Graff and John Halloran, contractors............................1,112 32

1 Fourth st, n s, 297.10 e 7th av, 100x100. Same agt same owner and contractor.... 455 61

1 Fourth st, n s, 297.10 w 8th av, 100x95. Louis Sunders agt same owner and contractor...............................1,415 40

1 Flushing av, No. 695, n s, 100 w Throop av. Max Schoenberg agt Barnett Cohen, owner, and George Ruehl, contractor..... 50 00

1 Chestnut st, w s, 198 s Fulton st, 75x100. 26th Ward. Hodgkiss & Co. agt The Solidarity Watch Case Co., owner, and J. Le Clair & Son, contractors 85 41

2 Fulton st, n e cor Sommers st, 125x45x100, gore. Thomas Sheffield agt Washington T. Bennett, owner and contractor....... 55 00

2 Cropsey av, n e cor Bay 20th st, 100.7x412x100.7x415. New Utrecht. Joel Aronson agt The New York Outing Club of Bath Beach, owner and contractor.................... 848 00

2 Howard av, s w cor Macon st, 100x98.6. Rankin & Ross agt Clarence Lincoln, owner and contractor.......................3,800 00

SATISFIED MECHANICS' LIENS.

NEW YORK CITY.

June

29 Pelham av, s s, 56 e Lorillard st, 50x—. H. E. Hall agt Julia Dennerlein. (Lien filed Nov. 20, 1888)............. .... $325 97

29 Amsterdam av, s w cor 78th st, 100.2x100. W. E. Lyon agt Bernard S. Levy. (June 27, 1891)............ ....1,201 00

29 One Hundred and First st, No. 135 W., n s, 25x—. Standard Hod Elevating Co. agt Gustav Boehm and Owen Donohue and Owen Donohue Sons. (June 13, 1891)..... 26 50

30 Forty-second st, No. 559 W., n s. F. J. Ryan agt Mary Agnes Barron. (June 29, 1891)..................... .. .. 2,300 00

30 One Hundred and Twenty-second st, No. 211 E., n s. Jonson Foundry & Machine Co. agt Elise Thau, John Kerby and J. Feudtner. (Sept. 26, 1888)........... .. .. 158 69

30 Same property. Buffalo Door & Sash Co. agt Henry Thau and John and John E. Kerby. (Sept. 14, 1888)... ....1,823 86

30 Seventh av, Nos. 306-310 / Twenty-seventh st, Nos. 207-211 } begins 7th av, n w cor 27th st. Giuseppe Colletti and 23 others agt W. F. Rohrig and Stephen Colletti. 24 liens. (June 20, 1891)................. 447 39

July

1 Seventy-fourth st, n s, 400.3 w 9th av, 149.9 x102. Thomas Hogan agt Matthew Clark and John Coar. (Jan. 6, 1891)...... 2,100 00

1‡Fifty-sixth st, No. 354, s s, 75 e 9th av, 30x100.5. Peter Keller agt Benjamin and Annie Steinhardt, Berth. Hummel and John & R. C. Best. (Nov. 21, 1890)...... ...... 310 00

1‡Same property. W. H. & J. J. McCaffery agt same. (Nov. 21, 1890) 264 18

1‡Spring st, No. 335, n w cor Washington st, 25x100. Meyer-Sniffen Co. agt Emma S. Olmsted and John R. Miller. (April 13, 1891).. 322 64

1‡Same property. W. A. Barwick agt Emma S. and Cyrus Olmstead. (April 6, 1891)... 217 74

1‡Same property. J. R. Miller agt same. (March 9, 1891)........ .... 600 00

2‡Eighty-eighth st, No. 145 W, n s. International Tile and Trim Co. agt Frank L. Smith and McDowell & Heney. (June 4, 1891) 1,907 20

2 Amsterdam av, s e cor 185th st. F. A. Lang agt Louis W. Duesing. (April 10, 1891)... 75 00

2 Madison av, n w cor 116th st, 100.11x100. John O'Rourke agt Williams & McGowan and Julius Lipman. (April 7, 1891)....... 342 00

2 Fifty-third st, Nos. 406-416 E., s s. Bernhard Voss agt Consumers' Hygien Ice Mfg. Co. (Lim.) (Oct. 7, 1890)........... 578 65

‡Discharged by order of Court on filing bond.

KINGS COUNTY.

June

25 Thirty-second st, n s, 160 w 5th av, —x—. Hyde & Gload Mfg. Co. agt Thomas W. Smith, owner and contractor. (Lien filed June 19, 1891)................. .... $36 00

26 Eighty-second st, n s, 60 e 23d av, 60x10. Michael Caspar agt J. M. Case, owner, and George Stroutman, contractor. (June 24, 1891)... .... 15 00

25 Myrtle av, n s, 100 w Lewis av, 450x100, 18 houses. Philip Dugro agt Max Hallheimer, owner and contractor. (June 11, 1891) 2,006 00

25 Halsey st, s s, 100 e Patchen av, 100x100. Martin D. Walsh agt Hiram Bedell. (June 19, 1891).... .... 250 00

26 Bergen st, s s, 100 w Kingston av, 100x100. Peter A. Blake agt Joseph M. Pilcher, owner and contractor. (June 20, 1891)... 332 25

25 Macon st, Nos. 647 and 649, n s, 300 from Patchen av. E. F. and G. W. Spear agt Mrs. F. Miller. (June 24, 1891)............ 190 00

26 Arlington av, s s, 25 e Linwood st, 29.5x100. D. P. Fielder & Son agt Edward F. Linton and Frank Hart, owners, and Lawrence B. Valk & Son, contractors. (April 23, 1891).... .... 562 50

26 Sixtieth st, s s, bet 12th and 13th avs, 40x150, New Utrecht. Hobby & Doody agt Philip C. and Marie Griesbach, owners, and Frank A. Shulz, contractor. (June 19, 1891.) (Deposit)........................ 143 00

26 Same property. John Dieckmann agt same owner and contractor. (June 20, 1891.) (Deposit) 48 50

26 Sixtieth st, s s, 260 w 13th av, 40x153.7x42.8x 133.10. George W. Harris agt same owner and contractor. (June 22, 1891.) (Deposit.) 27 00

26 Same property. John Gall agt same. (June 23, 1891.) (Deposit)....................... 27 00

26 Same property. Frank A. Schultz agt same. (June 25, 1891.) (Deposit) 176 00

26 Same property. Carl Schaum agt same. (June 25, 1891.) (Deposit).... .... 42 50

29 Cortlandt st, w s, south of New Lots road (see Lien.) Charles Schupf agt Twenty-sixth Ward Land and Improvement Co. and Adolph Sussman, owner and contractor. (June 16, 1891.) (Order of Court).... 175 00

27 Albany av, w s, extends from Park pl to Butler st, 200x100. Hans S. Christian agt James A. Loucks, owner and contractor. (April 16, 1891)........ .... 875 00

29 Sixtieth st, s s, lots 134 and 135 block 7, New Utrecht. Jens C. Jensen agt Philip C. and Marie Griesback, owners, and Frank A. Schultz, contractor. (June 20, 1891).. 80 00

29 Ninety-fifth st, n s, 175 w Av M, 50x— to Brooklyn and Rockaway Beach R. R., Canarsie. R. Cummings Sons agt Mary Cook, owner, and Augustus Wousouski, contractor. (June 23, 1891).... .... 133 41

30 Vanderbilt av, Butler st and Prospect Park Plaza (see Lien). Charles B. Hardick's Niagara Steam Pump Works agt The Brooklyn Riding and Driving Club, owner, and W. Bugbee Smith, contractor. (Jan. 26, 1891)....................... .... 628 18

30 Sixtieth st, n s, 100 e 12th av, 20x100, New Utrecht. Patrick Hussey agt Antonio Parente, owner, and —— Palmer, contractor. (June 20, 1891.) (Deposit) 45 00

July

1 Chauncey st, s s, 211 e Saratoga av, 19x100. George P. Jacobs & Co. agt Adriana Smith, owner, and Scheirmeister Bros, contractors. (Dec. 6, 1890). (Release)..... ..... 70 73

BUILDINGS PROJECTED.

The first name is that of the owner; ar't stands for architect, m'n for mason, c'r for carpenter and b'r for builder.

NEW YORK CITY.

SOUTH OF 14TH STREET.

Greenwich st, e s / Bank st, n s / Hudson st, w s } seven-story brk factory, 117.6x123.3, tin roof; cost, $65,000; P. M. Wilson, 144 West 22d st; ar'ts, D. & J. Jardine; m'n, A. Brown, Jr. Plan 936.

Frankfort st, No. 9, five-story brk building, 28.9 x60, gravel roof; cost, abt $15,000; agent, L. W. Duesing, 1653 9th av; ar't, J. P. Leo. Plan 949.

Madison st, No. 305, five-story brk flat, 26.6x 81.9, tin roof; cost, $23,000; C. Ruff, 228 East 10th st; ar'ts, Schneider & Herter. Plan 953.

Waverley pl, n s, 45 e Christopher st, one-story brk building, 25x25, tin roof; cost, $4,000; W. C. Burmistou, 104 East 12th st; m'ns, Ehreg & Co. Plan 939.

Mercer st, No. 237, six-story brk, iron, stone and terra cotta warehouse, 25x100x93 and 86, tin roof; cost, $45,000; J. Solomon, 51 East Broadway; ar't, F. Wandelt. Plan 959.

12th st, No. 413 E., rear, two-story brk stable, 73x13, gravel roof; cost, $400; Jeannette Weil, 118 1st st; m'n, M. Lang. Plan 960.

BETWEEN 14TH AND 59TH STREETS.

39th st, No. 200 E., one-story brk building, 17x 16, tin roof; cost, $1,250; J. Lynch, 202 East 39th st; ar't, C. Lynch; m'ns, Boehan & Martin; c'r, W. Sexton. Plan 954.

BETWEEN 59TH AND 125TH STREETS, EAST OF 5TH AVENUE.

5th av, s e cor 72d st, five-story brk dwell'g, 35 x125, tin and slate roof; cost, $100,000; J. A. Burden, 139 5th av; ar't, R. H. Robertson. Plan 956.

85th st, n s, 250.10 e 3d av, five-story brk and stone flat, 25.7x80.6, tin roof; cost, $14,000; E. McGinnis, 230 East 85th st; ar'ts, Thom & Wilson. Plan 958.

BETWEEN 59TH AND 125TH STREETS, WEST OF CENTRAL PARK WEST AND 8TH AVENUE.

Boulevard, s w cor 78th st, six five-story brk and stone flats, one 27.2x98, five 25x80, tin roofs; total cost, $175,000; Forster & Livingston, 281 Alexander av; ar't, G. A. Schellenger. Plan 952.

70th st, s s, 125 e Columbus av, ten four-story and basement brk and stone dwell'gs, five 22 and five 23x65, tin roofs; cost, $21,000 each; J. T. and J. A. Farley, 103 West 70th st; ar'ts, Thom & Wilson; m'ns, List & Lennon. Plan 937.

93d st, n s, 200 e 9th av, three-story brk and stone stable, 50x96, tin roof; cost, abt $30,000; H. A. Robbins, 419 5th av; ar't, S. B. Reed. Plan 944.

102d st, n s, 80 w West End av, three-story and basement stone dwell'g, 20x56, tin roof; cost, $16,000; ow'r and b'r, D. Christie, 634 West End av; ar't, M. V. B. Ferdon. Plan 948.

122d st, s s, 66.1 w St. Nicholas av, four-story brk and stone stable, 50x100.11, tin roof; cost, $18,000; F. Hielberg, 265 West 125th st; ar't, R. R. Davis. Plan 938.

Amsterdam av, s w cor 77th st, five-story brk stable, 51x115, tin or gravel roof; cost, abt $20,-000; Euphemia S. Coffin, 13 West 57th st; ar't, B. L. Gilbert. Plan 950.

West End av, n e cor 77th st, one two and three-story brk and terra cotta chapel and school, 175x102.2, tin and slate roofs; cost, $150,000; Reformed Protestant Dutch Church, 14 East 67th st; ar't, R. W. Gibson. Plan 942.

77th st, s s, 104 n West End av, thirteen three-and-a-half-story brk and stone dwell'gs, 20, 21 and 22x55, with extension, tin and tile roofs; cost, $20,000 each; Stewart & Pursell, 5 West 81st st; ar't, C. T. Mott. Plan 955.

NORTH OF 125TH STREET.

134th st, n s, 200 e 7th av, two five-story brk and stone flats, 25x78, tin roofs; cost, $15,000 each; W. J. Gilmore, Berry st, Tremont, N. Y.; ar't, H. Andersen. Plan 947.

138th st, s s, 100 e Lenox av, five-story brk and stone flat, 25x88.6, tin roof; cost, $14,000; P. Farley, 1960 Madison av; ar'ts, Thom & Wilson. Plan 957.

141st st, n s, 175 w 7th av, four-story brk and stone dwell'g, 26x80, tin roof; cost, $30,000; Rev. C. M. O'Keeffe, exr. and trustee, 310 West 141st st; ar't, B. E. Lowe. Plan 961.

23D AND 24TH WARDS.

Jennings st, s s, 280 e Union av, two-story frame dwell'g, 20x30, tin roof; cost, $2,500; F. A. Brohmer, 604 East 83d st; ar't, C. C. Churchill. Plan 945.

Jefferson av, w s, 75 s Columbine av, three-story frame dwell'g, 22x41, tin roof; cost, $3,800; H. J. Johnson, 2733 8th av; ar't, C. C. Churchill. Plan 946.

Mosholu av, n s, 750 w Broadway, two-story frame dwell'g, 22x33, shingle roof; cost, $1,300; ow'r and b'r, J. C. Gaffney, Riverdale, N. Y.; ar't, F. H. Thorne. Plan 943.

Sedgwick av, w s, 500 n Morris Dock, frame shed, 20x30, shingle roof; cost, $75; W. H. Mangels, on premises; b'rs, Wilson & Son. Plan 951.

Trinity av, e s, 196 n 165th st, four three-story brk dwell'gs, 18.9x38 with extension, tin roofs; cost, $4,500 each; ow'r and b'r, J. A. Knox, Marion av, Fordham; ar't, J. De Hart. Plan 940.

Kingsbridge road, s s, 100 w Bathgate av, one-story frame stable, 21x16, shingle roof; cost, $400; ow'r and b'r, same as last. Plan 941.

Morris av, n w cor 152d st, four-story brk and stone flat, 25x75, tin roof; cost, $15,000; F. Habelitz and ano., 309 East 8th st; ar't, A. E. Davis; m'ns, McElroy & Son. Plan 962.

Prospect av, w s, 150 n 175th st, two-story frame dwell'g, 22x49.6, tin roof; cost, $3,000; Mary A. Euler, 944 East 175th st; ar't, D. W. King; c'r, J. H. Euler. Plan 963

Prospect av, w s, 150 n 175th st, two-story frame stable, 26.6x16, tin roof; cost, $300; ow'r, ar't and c'r, same as last. Plan 964.

KINGS COUNTY.

Plan 1228—Livingston st, s e cor Bond st, one four-story brk store and dwell'g, 25x60, tin roof, iron cornice; cost, $16,000; Mrs. Martin Schneider, 16 7th av; ar't, C. Werner; b'rs, M. Gibbons' Sons. (Correction).

1241—St. Marks av, n s, 343 e Clason av, three four-story brk tenem'ts, 25x50, gravel roofs, wooden cornices; cost, each, $10,000; ow'r and ar't, H. Tomlinson, 752 Marcy av.

1242—Flushing av, n s, 181.8 e Porter av, one two-story frame (brk filled) dwell'g, 25.11 and 25 x33.4 and 26.7, tin roof; cost, $2,300; Max Kirchheimer, 34 Moore st; ar't, T. Engelhardt; b'r, D. Kreuder.

1243—Eastern Parkway, e s, 50 e Osborn st, one three-story frame store and tenem't, 25x55, tin roof; cost, $4,500; B. Frank and S. Rose, Belmont av.

1244—3d av, w s, 36 s Degraw st, one two-story frame dwell'g, 18x40, gravel roof; cost, $1,500; Jane Gowdy, 239 6th st; ar't, T. F. Thomas; b'r, R. Martin.

1245—Watkins st, w s, 125 s Eastern Parkway, one three-story frame store and dwell'g, 20x40, tin roof; cost, $3,500; Ada Parmer, 1192 or 1132 Broadway.

1246—Macon st, s s, 290 w Lewis av, two three-story and basement brk and brown stone dwell'gs, 20x45, tin roofs, iron cornices; cost, $7,000 each; E. Willard Jones, 49 Nassau st, N. Y.; ar't, E. S. Coy.

1247—Hudson av, e s, 100 n Fulton st, five four-story brk flats, 32x55, tin roofs, wooden cornices; cost, $10,000 each; Chas. A. Chosborough, Northport, L. I.; ar't and b'r, W. J. Conway.

1248—Luquer st, n s, 102 e Henry st, one one-story brk storage, &c., building, 28.2 and 28.8x 48, gravel roof, wooden cornice; cost, $700; Wm. Littmann, 670 Greenwich st, N. Y.; ar't, J. W. Bailey.

1249—Hancock st, n s, 359 e Lewis av, five two-story and basement sandstone dwell'gs, 18 and 19 x45, tin roofs, iron cornices; cost, $4,250 each; ow'r and ar't, Wesley C. Bush; b'r, day's work.

1250—Chestnut st, e s, 146 n Record pl, one one-story brk engine room, 15.6x30, gravel roof, wooden cornice; cost, $1,100; John J. Lindsay, Chestnut st and Atlantic av; ar't, J. Mumford; m'n, J. Glen; c'r, not selected.

1251—Chestnut st, e s, 178 n Record pl, one one-story frame paper store-house, 20x68, gravel roof; cost, $500; ow'r and ar't, same as last; b'r, not selected.

1252—Hancock st, n s, 250 e Lewis av, six two-story basement and attic sandstone dwell'gs, 19 and 18x45, tin roofs, iron cornices; cost, each, $5,000; ow'r and ar't, Wesley C. Bush; b'r, day's work.

1253—Kent av, s w cor South 11th st, one seven-story brk building for molasses refinery, 76.6x 76.6, gravel roof, brk cornice; cost, $40,000; John Mollenhauer; ar't, T. Engelhardt; b'r, not selected.

1254—3d av, e s, 80 s 53d st, one three-story brk store and dwell'g, 20x45, tin roof, wooden cornice; cost, $4,000; Adam Weise, 192 Degraw st; ar'ts, H. L. Spicer & Son.

1255—54th st, n s, 160 w 4th av, three two-story basement and cellar frame (brk filled) dwell'gs, 20 x40, tin roofs; cost, each, $2,500; Peter Larsen, 54th st, near 4th av; ar'ts, H. L. Spicer & Son.

1256—Rockaway av, e s, 225 n Belmont av, one three-story frame store and tenem't, 25x55, tin roof; cost, $4,200; Mina Steinfeld, Rockaway av.

1257—Court st, n e cor Livingston st, one three-story and basement brk bath annex to Polytechnic Inst., store, offices and apartments with "L" on Livingston st, irreg., tin roof, iron cornice; cost, $25,000; William A. White, 158 Columbia Heights; ar't, W. B. Tubby; b'rs, E. C. Walbridge and Morris & Selover.

1258—Ryerson st, No. 221, e s, 358 n De Kalb av, one three-story and basement brk schoolhouse, 48.4 and 47x81.5, tin roof, copper cornice; cost, $30,000; Trustees Pratt Inst., Pratt Institute, Brooklyn; ar't, W. B. Tubby; b'rs, L. W. Seaman, Jr., & Sons.

1259—Hicks st, w s, 60 s Bush st, one two-story frame stable, 30x20, tin roof; cost, $400; F. C. Malone, 26 South st; ar'ts, H. L. Spicer & Son.

1260—Bedford av, No. 136, one four-story frame (brk filled) store and tenem't, 20.3x55, tin roof; cost, $5,000; W. R. Myers, Bushwick av, near Cooper st; ar't, F. W. Ames; b'r, J. Frazer.

1261—Dumont st, s s, 25 e Thatford av, one two-story frame tailor shop, 20x30, tin roof; cost, $1,500; Isaac Scheerr, on premises.

1262—Essex st, e s, 250 s Ridgewood av, one one-and-a-half-story frame stable, 25x15, shingle roof; cost, $200; Sarah G. O'Donohue, 200 Hendrix st; b'r, W. D. Losee.

1263—Macon st, n s, 270 e Reid av, six three-story and basement stone dwell'gs, 17.6x45, tin and slate mansard roofs, iron cornices; cost, each, $7,000; F. C. Swimm, 358 Putnam av; ar'ts, A. Hill & Son; b'rs, M. J. J. Reynolds Sons.

1264—4th st, s s, 171.10 e 6th av, six three-story and basement brk and brown stone dwell'gs, 19.8 x42, tin roofs and iron cornices; cost, each, $8,000; Moses & Tanton, 176 Broadway, N. Y.

1265—29th st, s s, 175 w 4th av, one one-story frame stable, 25x13, felt roof; cost, $65; William Beyer, 188 29th st.

1266—Ralph av, w s, 98.7 n Atlantic av, one one-story frame shed, 18x20, tin roof; cost, $150; L. Folger, on premises.

1267—26th st, s s, 250 w 5th av, one one-story frame shed 13x20, board roof; cost, $50; John Waller, 228 26th st; b'r, J. Campbell.

1268—Conover st, w s, 75 n Dikeman st, one one-story frame stable, 12x13, tin roof; cost, $150; Fred. C. Barschow, 196 Conover st; b'r, H. H. Rahn.

1269—Stockholm st, s s, 108.2 e Wyckoff av, one one-story frame (brk filled) dwell'g, 25x25, tin roof; cost, $500; ow'r and m'n, August Huber, 900 Flushing av; ar't, H. Vollweiler; c'r, not selected.

1270—Christopher st, e s, 200 n Belmont av, one three-story frame stores and dwell'gs, 20x40, tin roof; cost, $3,600; Berger & Messel, 763 Eldridge st, New York.

1271—Union st, n s, 69 w 5th av, one four-story brk stores and Lodge rooms, 30x85, tin roof, iron cornice; cost, $13,500; John D. Muller, 5th av, n w cor Union st.

1272—Decatur st, n s, 209.8 w Howard av, eight two-story and basement brown stone dwellings, 18.4x43, tin roofs, wooden cornices; cost, $4,000 each; ow'r and ar't, Thos. H. Radcliffe, 826 Fulton st; b'rs, J. Court and J. Andrew.

ALTERATIONS NEW YORK CITY.

Plan 1235—Madison av, No. 532, vault under walk, 15x25.6; cost, $4,000; W. E. Connor, on premises; ar't, D. & J. Jardine.

1236—33d st, No. 1 E., two-story extension, 6.6 x11; cost, $1,000; agent and b'r, J. Downey, 28 East 26th st.

1237—Monroe st, Nos. 188 and 190, walls altered; cost, $500; J. Bohnet, 96 Hewes st, Brooklyn; ar't, B. W. Berger.

1238—27th st, Nos. 440 and 442 W., repair damage by fire; cost, $3,000; P. Fay, on premises; c'r, J. A. Felter.

1239—Greenwich st, Nos. 239-243, repair damage by fire; cost, $3,000; W. H. Hall, 61 West 56th st; b'rs, Clark & Co.

1240—Washington av, No. 2128, move 2 feet and foundation rebuilt; cost, $400; W. Wyand, on premises.

1241—Eldridge st, No. 218, interior alterations and walls altered; cost, $1,000; L. Adelson, 171 Henry st; m'n, C. R. Strevell.

1242—Broadway, No. 1424, new elevator, bath rooms and interior alterations; cost, $15,000; D. S. McElroy, 1514 Broadway; ar't, J. M. Dunn.

1243—33d st, No. 104 W., walls altered; cost, $235; R. Miranda, 54 West 37th st; ar't, T. Commesu.

1244—Crosby st, No. 165, two-story extension, 7x29; cost, $1,000; lessee and m'n, T. Schuerkes, on premises, ar't, G. O'Hanlon.

1245—West Broadway, n e cor Chambers st, boiler chimney altered; cost, $350; lessee, C. F. Wildey, Cosmopolitan Hotel; m'ns, Vassar & Son.

1246—21st st, No. 407 W., one-story extension, 22x19.4, interior alterations and walls altered; new lintels, cornice, &c ; cost, $5,000; J. B. Horner, on premises; ar't, W. W. Howe.

1247—75th st, No. 13 E., interior alterations; cost, $5,000; Julia H. Eldridge, 5 East 43d st; ar'ts, Wood & Palmer; b'rs, Schastey & Co.

1248—117th st, No. 208 E., interior alterations and new front; cost, $300; Mary A. Martin, 1341 Washington av; ar't, John Dey; b'rs, Dey & Somerville.

1249—Av A, Nos. 279 and 281, new fronts; cost, $800; J. Dolguer, 277 Av A; c'r, W. O. Connor.

1250—Ludlow st, No. 91, one-story extension, —x13.9, interior alteration and walls altered; cost, $6,800; City Fire Dep't, 157 East 67th st.

1251—41st st, n s, 190 e 11th av, new roof; cost, $50; Consolidated Gas Co., 4 Irving pl.

1252—14th st, No. 105 E., repair damage by fire; cost, $3,000; J. Cropper and ano., 29 West 17th st; b'r, J. D. Miner.

1253—23d st, No. 14 E., one-story extension, 25 x23.6, interior alterations, walls altered and new front; cost, abt $8,000; lessees, Schwab & Soblesinger, 105 East 60th st; a'rt, R. Berger.

1254—Madison av, n e cor 42d st, interior alterations and rearranged and windows altered; cost, $25,000; Holy Trinity Church, on premises; ar't, C. T. Mathews.

1255—West st, w s, foot of Cortlandt st; interior alterations and bridge over st; cost, $15,-000; Pennsylvania R. R. Co., 2 Exchange pl. Jersey City.

1256—Mercer st, Nos. 187 and 189, one-story extension, 23x50, roof over yard and stairway moved; cost, not given; E. P. Gleason, 118 Kent st, Brooklyn; E. F. Gennert; c'r, A. Leydecker.

1257—Spring st, No. 158, new front; cost, $75; agent, J. H. Meyers, 317 West 50th st; c'r, P. J. Bresnan.

1258—Madison av, No. 535, one-story extension, 14x6; cost, $500; Margaret M. Hoey, for ow'r, on premises; ar'ts, Schickel & Co.

1259—34th st, No. 109 E., two-story and basement extension, 21.6x46, and interior alterations; cost, $3,000; E. L. Keyes, 1 Park av; ar'ts, Thorp & Knowles.

1260—Union sq, No. 19, roof raised 6 ft., extension raised one story, interior rearranged for offices, new elevator, stairs, &c., and new court-yard in n w corner; cost, $30,000; W. Sneckner, 328 West 57th st; ar'ts, Thorp & Knowles.

1261—Mott st, No. 156, new stairs to basement; cost, $15; agent, R. Cohn, 44 Bowery.

1262—49th st, No. 422 W., new front; cost, $75; T. L. Flammer, 901 8th av; c'r, P. J. Bresnan.

1263—10th st, No. 375 E., two-story extension, 20x13; cost, $800; J. Burkhardt, on premises; ar't, A. H. Blankenstein.

1264—1st av, Nos. 771 and 773, two-story extension, 25x100; cost, $4,000; Fegetmeier & Riepe, on premises; ar't, D. E. Graham.

1265—30th st, Nos. 447 and 449 W., elevator walls altered; cost, abt $300; Ferguson Bros., on premises; b'rs, Sheridan & Bryne.

1266—41st st, No. 11 E., extension raised one story, interior alterations; cost, $1,000; W. Jennings, 48 Park av; ar't, W. H. Bussell; m'ns, Conolly & Sons

1267—2d av, No. 790, new show window; cost, $375; Rosa Scheier, on premises; c'r, C. Ziegler.

1268—2d av, No. 560, new front; cost, $300; A. Buse, 402 East 61st st; c'r, F. Beinhauer.

1269—37th st, No. 308 E., raised one story and interior alterations; cost, $6,000; J. M. Farley, rector, on premises; ar't, T. H. Poole.

1270—2d av, n w cor 85th st, walls altered; cost, $300; M. Borger, 387 Park av; m'n, J. Dorsey; c'r, J. Owens.

1271—Horatio st, No. 35, building removed; cost, $100; C. A. Meyer, exr., 41 Horatio st.

1272—49th st, No. 46 W., one-story and basement extension, 18.10x27.5, and interior alterations; cost, $2,000; Annie M. Scott, 27 East 61st st; ar't, G. Robinson, Jr.

1273—27th st, No. 133 W., two-story extension, 25x36.9, interior alterations and walls altered; cost, $2,500; J. Mussel, 163 West 25th st; ar't, J. Wolf.

1274—Lafayette pl, Nos. 49-53, raised one story, new columns, girders, staircases and elevators, other interior alterations and walls altered; cost, $75,000; O. B. Potter, 3 East 57th st; ar't, F. H. Kimball.

1275—30th st, No. 17 W., two story extension, 10x68; cost, $2,500; M. Hardly, 232 Madison av; ar't, C. J. Perry.

1276—Hudson st, Nos. 15-19, repair damage by fire; cost, $2,500; T. Patten, 226 Greenwich st; b'rs, Clark & Co.

KINGS COUNTY.

Plan 609—Rodney st, s s, 100 e Kent av, add one story to building, also a four-story brk extension on front, 31.6x15, and four-story brk extension on rear, 31.6x15, gravel roof; cost, $6,000; J. S. and G. F. Simpson, 26 Rodney st; ar't, B. Finkensieper; b'r, not selected.

610—Freeman st, No. 193, one-story frame extension, 11.6x16, gravel roof; cost, $200; Wm. Smith, on premises; b'rs, G. Smith & Son and L. Gasser.

611—North Elliott pl, No. 70, add two stories; cost, $1,800; ow'r, ar't and m'n, John Thatcher, on premises; c'rs, Oliver & David.

612—Wythe av, No. 572, rebuild front; cost, $1,000; Chas. Richter, on premises; ar't, F. Holmberg.

613—Dean st, s e cor Smith st, one-story brk extension, 10x18, tin roof; cost, $200; Peter McCormac, on premises; b'rs, J. J. Bentzen and H. J. Smith.

614—Clinton st, e s, 50 n Centre st, raised 10 feet on frame story, also two-story frame extension, 6x23, tin roof; cost $500; Peter Donlan, on premises; b'r, P. Watson.

615—Lafayette av, s e cor South Oxford st, interior alterations; cost, $1,300; Lafayette Avenue Presbyterian Church, on premises; ar't, M. W. Morris.

616—St. Felix st, No. 123, three-story and basement brk extension, 19x9, tin roof; cost, $700; Samuel Wright, on premises; ar't and c'r, W. V. Williamson; m'n, J. Wild.

617—Boerum st, Nos. 24 and 26, one brick and one frame building, four-story brk extension on brick house, 25x48, front of frame building altered, also interior alterations; cost, $2,000; J. Wichert & Co., 24 Boerum st; ar't, F. Wunder; b'r, not selected.

618—Hicks st, No. 255, add one-story slate and tin mansard roof; cost, $3,500; A. A. Low; ar't, W. B. Tubby; b'rs, C. Cameron and L. W. Seaman, Jr., & Son.

619—Conover st, No. 190, rebuild rear; cost, $150; Mrs. Larssen, on premises; ar't and b'r, C. M. Detlefsen.

620—Kingsland av, No. 81, add one story of frame, also one-story frame extension, 25x5.6, tin roof; cost, $275; ow'r and b'r, B. Hartman, 81 Kingsland av.

621—Conover st, No. 197, front alterations; cost, $175; Mrs. A. Cassidy, on premises; b'r, C. Kohler.

622—Richards st, s w cor Partition st, one-story frame extension, 16x21, tin roof, wooden cornice; cost, $250; T. Sharkey, on premises; ar't, D. J. Lynch.

623—Henry st, No. 287, two-story iron and brk extension, 25x46, tin roof; cost, $500; Sturgis Coffin, on premises; ar't and b'r, G. Halbert.

624—Kosciusko st, No. 475, one-story and basement brk extension, 18.9x18, tin roof; cost, $600; Edwin Harvey, 55 South 3d st; ar't, R. Von Lehn.

625—North 4th st, n s, 100 w Roebling st, one-story frame extension, 10 6 and 7.6x16.6; cost, $25; Lida E. Teave; b'r, C. A. Teave.

626—Fulton st, Nos. 468 and 470, one-story brk extension, 20x20, tin roof; cost, $1,000; Platt & Conway, on premises; ar't, J. A. Brock; b'r, T. D. Riley.

627—Myrtle av, Nos. 86 and 88, interior alterations, iron column beams, &c.; cost, $1,000; Miss O. Flanagan, Buffalo, N. Y.; ar't, C. Weaver; b'rs, W. & J. Widman.

628—Prospect st, No. 176, flat tin roof; cost, $750; A. Otterson, 97 6th av.

MISCELLANEOUS.

BUSINESS FAILURES.

Schedule of assignments for the four weeks ending July 2, 1891:

	Liabilities.	Nominal Assets.	Real Assets.
Ducey, John M.....	$2,710 62	$2,132 86	$1,492 11
Dritschee, George..	2,408 42	4,018 74	2,672 53
Fowler, James D. and George M ...	572,898 57	996,259 75	22,772 09
Field, John C......	6,217 31	10,613 15	6,156 97
Hyneman, Julius / Schmidt, Alfred..	21,529 27	18,016 01	7,436 94
Lippincott, Jesse H.	1,191,050 47	2,471,938 58	168,950 02
Mahler, Michael....	5,500 52	2,468 96	951 12
Ohannessian, Sarkis	5,577 93	2,116 87	659 04
Thorne, Arthur....	24,928 70	16,209 80	1,952 81

N. Y. ASSIGNMENTS—BENEFIT CREDITORS.

June

27 Morris, Abraham (clothier at No. 478 3d av) to George Nicoll; preferences, $1,125.

29 Gonzalez, Manuel (mfr. of cigars at No. 2590 3d av) to Jose Janquera; without preferences.

30 Bernstein, Philip (retail furniture dealer at No. 85 Hester st) to Louis M. Kommel; preferences, $780.

July

1 Woolman, George S. (optician and dealer in mathematical instruments and drawing supplies at No. 116 Fulton st) to Charles E. Garrison; preferences, $2,744.

2 Schirmer, Edward (surgical instruments and cutlery, at Nos. 31 West 125th st and 307 East 122d st) to Edwin F. Stern; without preferences.

KINGS COUNTY.

GENERAL ASSIGNMENTS.

June

26 Mott, Frank S. to M. L. Towns.

PROCEEDINGS OF THE BOARD OF ALDERMEN AFFECTING REAL ESTATE.

* Under the different headings indicates that a resolution has been introduced and referred to the appropriate committee. † Indicates that the resolution has passed and has been sent to the Mayor for approval. ‡ Passed over the Mayor's veto.

NEW YORK, June 30, 1891.

REGULATING, GRADING, ETC.

Wales av, from n s St. Joseph st to Westchester av.†
Clinton av, bet 169th and Jefferson sts.†

PAVING.

118th st, from Madison to 5th avs; granite block.†

FLAGGING.

11th st, n s / 12th st, s s } bet 2d and 3d avs, at entrance to Stuyvesant alley.†
Amsterdam av, e s, from 72d st to point 100 n therefrom.†

FENCING VACANT LOTS.

144th st, s s, from 8th to Bradhurst av.†

CROSSWALKS.

Chisholm st, at each intersecting st or av from Jennings st to Stebbins av.†
Bristow st, at each intersecting st or av from Boston to Stebbins av.†

CHANGE OF NAME.

Pell st to Harry Howard st.*

APPROVED PAPERS.

Resolutions passed by the Board of Aldermen calling for the following improvements have been signed by the Mayor for the week ending June 27, 1891. *Indicates that the Mayor neither approved nor objected thereto, therefore the same became adopted.

MAINS.

173d st, from Amsterdam av to Kingsbridge road; gas.
181st st, from Amsterdam av to Kingsbridge road; gas.
143d st, bet 8th and Bradhurst avs; water.
76th st, from present line e of Av A to exterior st; Croton.
77th st, from Av A to East River; gas.*

REGULATING, GRADING, ETC.

136th st, from e s Southern Boulevard to w s Locust av.
135th st, from e s Southern Boulevard to w s Locust av.
134th st, from e s Southern Boulevard to East River.
Walnut av, from n line 132d st to s line 138th st.
Locust av, from n line 132d st to s line 138th st.
132d st, from w line Locust av to e line Brook av.
133d st, bet w line Locust av and e line Trinity av.

PAVING.

Bradhurst av, from 142d to 145th st; granite block.
103d st, from 8th to Columbus av; granite block.
108d st, from Boulevard to Riverside Drive.

FENCING VACANT LOTS.

104th and 105th sts, bet Madison and 5th avs.

CROSSWALKS.

138th st, bet R. R. av E. and approach to Madison av bridge.

BROOKLYN BOARD OF ALDERMEN.

BROOKLYN, June 29, 1891.

CULVERTS.

Douglass st, s e cor 3d av. } †
Irving av, n w cor Harman st. }

FENCING VACANT LOTS.

Dean st, n e cor Rockaway av. }
Stockholm st, n s, bet Central and Evergreen avs } †
Pacific st, s s, bet 6th and 7th avs, by request. }

FLAGGING.

Herkimer st, bet Stone av and Sackman st. }
Pacific st, s s, bet Henry and Clinton sts. }
Sackman st, w s, bet Herkimer st and Atlantic av. } †
Bedford av, w s, bet Degraw st and Eastern Parkway. }
Bedford av, w s, bet Butler and Douglass sts. }
Stuyvesant av, s e cor Vernon av.*

GAS LAMPS, ETC.

Butler st, No. 76, in front of. }
McDonough st, bet Howard av and Broadway. } †
16th st, No. 607, in front of. }
Blake av, bet Vesta av and Hinsdale st }

GRADING, PAVING, ETC.

Butler st, bet Brooklyn and Kingston avs.†
Vermont st, bet Atlantic av and Evergreen Cemetery.*
Atlantic av, s s, bet Ashford and Elton sts.†

STREET OPENING.

53d st, bet 3d av and high water mark. } †
Evergreen av, bet Meserole st and Flushing av. }

STREET RENUMBERED.

Laurel st, bet Cleveland st and Noowood av.†

ADVERTISED LEGAL SALES

REFEREES SALES TO BE HELD AT THE REAL ESTATE EXCHANGE AND AUCTION ROOM (LIMITED), 59 to 65 LIBERTY STREET, EXCEPT WHERE OTHERWISE STATED.

July

98th st, Nos. 149-165, n s, 100 e 10th av, 825x113.2x—x129.6, eleven five-story brk unfinished flats and 3 vacant lots, by Richard V. Harnett & Co. (Amt due $41,292; prior mort. $ —) ... 6

Bethune st, No. 53, s s, 163 e Washington st, 22x88.7x22.8x92.10, four-story brk tenem't with one-story brk building on rear, by James L. Wells. (Amt due $3,643) ... 7

Gay st, No. 17, e s, 147.10 n Waverley pl, 19x65, three-story brk dwell'g, by William Kennelly. (Amt due $2,723) ... 7

134th st, Nos. 71-79 { begins 134th st, n s, 197.6 e 6th
135th st { av, original line, 87.6x199.7 to 135th st, x87.6x199.10, five three-story brk dwell'gs on 134th st and five three-story brk dwell'gs on 135th st, by H. Henriques. (Amt due $67,750) ... 7

Madison av, s e cor 107th st, 100.11x400 to Park av, vacant, by Scott & Myers. (Amt due $86,179) ... 7

8th av, No. 944, e s, 25.5 s 56th st, 25x100, five-story stone flat with stores, by J. F. B. Smyth. (Administrator's sale) ... 7

Goerck st, No. 90, e s, 81.3 n Rivington st, 15.4x99.11, five-story brk tenem't, by R. V. Harnett & Co. (Amt due $7,748) ... 8

Horatio st, No. 108, s s, abt 168 w Washington st, 25x87.5, two-story brk stable ... }
Horatio st, No. 101, n s, abt 164 w Washington st, 23x84.8, vacant ... }
by L. J. Phillips. (Partition sale) ... 8

17th st, No. 446, s s, 198.11 e 10th av, 30.4x92, three-story brk dwell'g, by J. L. Wells ... 8

44th st, s s, 100 e Lexington av, 20x100.5 ... }
Washington st, e s, 66.6 n Jay st, 20x80 ... }
2d av, w s, 20.10 n 116th st, 20x70 ... }
by Scott & Myers. (Partition sale) ... 8

120th st, No. 540, s s, 487.6 e Av A, 18.9x100.11, two-story brk dwell'g, by R. V. Harnett & Co. (Dower right, &c.) ... 8

141st st, No. 203, n s, 75 w 7th av, 20x99.11 ... }
141st st, No. 205, n s, 95 w 7th av, 20x99.11 ... }
141st st, No. 207, n s, 115 w 7th av, 20x99.11 ... }
141st st, No. 209, n s, 135 w 7th av, 20x99.11 ... }
141st st, No. 211, n s, 155 w 7th av, 20x99.11 ... }
Five five-story brk flats ... }
by William Kennelly. (Amt due on each $14,133) ... 8

4th st, No. 161, n e s, 86 n w 6th av, runs northwest 20 x northeast 45.4 x north 60.6 x southeast 7.6 x southwest 54 x southeast 4.10 x southwest 19.5 x southwest 40 to beginning, four-story brk tenement with stores, by B. L. Kennelly. (Amt due $5,260) ... 9

137th st, s s, 480 w Lenox av, runs south 99.11 x west 20 x north 48 x west 22 x north 51.11 to 137th st, x east 42, three-story brk dwell'g and vacant, by William Kennelly. (Amt due $15,907) ... 9

145th st, No. 346, s s, 42 e Edgecombe av, 18x99.11, three-story brk dwell'g, by B. L. Kennelly. (Amt due $9,819) ... 9

112th st, n s, 125 w Lenox av, 25x100.11, five-story brk flat, by B. L. Kennelly. (Amt due $2,230; prior morts. $20,000) ... 10

167th st, s w s, 158.4 s e Amsterdam av, 20.7x97.4x17.3x109.8, three-story brk dwell'g, by N. De Waltearss. (Amt due $3,957) ... 10

34th st, No. 316, s s, 228.9 e 2d av, 21.3x98.9, four-story brk tenem't, by R. V. Harnett & Co. (Amt due $3,478) ... 13

38th st, No. 229, n s, 490.1 e 8th av, 20.7x98.9, five-story brk flat, by William Kennelly. (Amt due $10,634) ... 13

54th st, Nos. 427 and 429, n s, 394 e 1st av, 50x100.5, two-story brk stable with one-story frame buildings on rear, by Richard V. Harnett. (Partition sale) ... 13

Amsterdam av, No. 710, w s, 75.8 s 95th st, 25x89.9, five-story brk flat with stores, by Smyth & Ryan. (Amt due $26,654) ... 13

3d av, No. 1070, w s, 50.5 n 63d st, 25x100, five-story stone front store and flat, by R. V. Harnett & Co. (Partition sale) ... 13

KINGS COUNTY.

July

Av B, s w cor East 4th st, 100x100, Flatbush, by James L. Wells, at the Real Estate Exchange, 189 and 191 Montague st ... 6

6th av, s w cor Pacific st, runs south 142.6 x west 125 x north 32.6 x east 25 x north 110 to Pacific st, x east 100 to beginning, three-story brk factory; assessed value $28,000; by T. A. Kerrigan, at 13 Willoughby st ... 6

Cumberland st, No. 390, w s, 376.10 n Atlantic av, 20x100, three-story frame dwell'g; assessed value, $3,500; by T. A. Kerrigan, at 13 Willoughby st ... 7

Bergen st, No 623, n s, 200 w Vanderbilt av, 24.8x110, two-story brk mill; assessed value, $4,200. }
Pierrepont st, No. 61, n s, 129 e Hicks st, 27x132.0½ to Love lane, x27.0½x133.8½, three-story brk dwell'g; assessed value, $21,000 ... }
Howard av, Nos. 299-307, e s, 167 s Herkimer st, runs east 98 x south 69 x west 48 x south 30.6 x southwest 50.11 to Howard av, x north 109.2 to beginning, six two-story frame dwell'g; assessed value, $1,000 each ... }
by T. A. Kerrigan, at 13 Willoughby st ... 8

Devoe st, Nos. 38-42, s s, 139 w Lorimer st, 60x100, saw factory; assessed value, $3,500 ... }
Fulton av, Nos. 2750, 2754 and 2758, s s, 50 w Miller av, 75x100, three two-story frame dwell'gs; assessed value, $1,600 each; partition ... }
by W. Cole, at 7 and 8 Court sq ... 8

Sackett st, No. 178, s s, 57.9 e Hicks st, 19.3x100, three-story brk dwell'g; assessed value, $3,000; partition; by Byran L. Kennelly (through Jere. Johnson, Jr.), at the Real Estate Exchange, 189 and 191 Montague st ... 8

Kings highway, n e cor Ocean Parkway, 434.1x—x—x994.1, contains 10¼ acres, Gravesend ... }
Wythe av, Nos. 508 and 510, w s, 19.8 s South 10th st, 36.1x50, two three-story brk dwell'gs; assessed value, $2,100 each; partition ... }
by Jere. Johnson, Jr., at the Real Estate Exchange, 189 and 191 Montague st ... 9

Vanderbilt st, n s, 260.6¾ e Gravesend av, 75x300.2 to Seeley st, x85.2x300, Flatbush, by W. B. Hill, at County Court House ... 9

Decatur st, No. 47, n s, 247 w Throop av, 18x100, three-story brk dwell'g; assessed value, $6,500, by W. Cole, at County Court House ... 10

Coney Island road, n e cor Van Siclen pl, 40x108x49x107.38 Gravesend ... }
Franklin st, Nos. 117 and 119, w s, 50 n Noble st, 50x70; assessed value, $3,000; all right, title and int.; re-sale ... }
Noble st, Nos. 68 and 63½, n s, 70 w Franklin st, 25x100; assessed value, $1,800; all right, title and int; re-sale ... }
Park pl, No. 102, s s, 191.3 e 6th av, 16.8x100, three-story brk dwell'g; assessed value, $3,300 ... }
3d st, Nos. 160-166, s s, 372.9 e Bond st, 96.9x154.9 to Gowanus Canal, x103.0¾x175.9, coal yard; assessed value, $14,000; re-sale ... }
by T. A. Kerrigan, at 3 Willoughby st ... 10

Oakland st, No. 323, w s, 25 n Huron st, 25x100, two-story frame dwell'g and store; assessed value, $2,000; partition; by W. Cole, at 7 and 8 Court sq ... 10

Atlantic av, Nos. 423 and 425, n s, 250 e Bond st, 50x100, two three-story brk dwell'gs; assessed value, $4,500 each; all right, title and int.; by T. A. Kerrigan, at 13 Willoughby st ... 13

LIS PENDENS, KINGS COUNTY.

June

Hancock st, s s, 120 w Lewis av, 20x100. Pauline Hahn agt James Maly; att'y, H. C. Conrady ... 25

South 2d st, No. 123, n s, 216 e 3d st, 18.9x100. Henry R. Hatfield agt James T. Hatfield; partition; att'y, Wm. L. Whiting ... 26

Herkimer st, n s, 20 w Rockaway av, 20x80. Charles A. Moran trustee Anson Blake agt Eugene H. Wilson; att'ys, Moran & Williams ... 26

Herkimer st, n w cor Rockaway av, 20x80. Drayton Burrill exr. Anna Morris agt Eugene H. Wilson; same att'ys ... 26

Herkimer st, n s, 40 w Rockaway av, 20x80. Mary M. Burrill agt same; same att'ys ... 26

McDonough st, n s, 225 w Tompkins av, 40x100. Garret J. Garretson exr. John J. Ricks agt Cornelia Broach individ. and extrx. John Broach; att'y, George W. Eastman ... 26

Withers st, n s, 38.7 e North 9th st, runs north 50.3 x southwest 61.5 to North 9th st, x southeast 100 to Withers st, x east 38.7. Thomas P. Graham agt Gertrude J. Scaife; att'y, Van Mater Stilwell ... 26

Christopher av, w s, 250 s Sutter av, 150x100 ... }
Christopher av, w s, 100 s Sutter av, 25x100 ... }
Herbert C. Smith agt George A. Remsen; att'y, Herman F. Koepke ... 26

Garfield pl, n s, 262.4 w 9th av, 26x100. Harvey Murdock agt Louis L. Jones; foreclos. mechanic's lien; att'ys, Smith & Martin ... 26

Wyckoff st, s s, 80 e 3d av, 20x100. Annie Fish agt Silas A. Underhill; att'y, Henry B. Johnson. 26

Gravesend av, s w cor 60th st, contains 16 82-100 acres ... }
Gravesend av, n w cor 60th st, contains 1 642-1000 acres ... }
22d av, n w cor of last lot, contains 52-1000 of an acre, 1½ acres of salt marsh or meadow known as Gravesend Neck ... }
Sarah Rice agt Kate L. Hicks; partition; att'y, Wm. H. Stillwell ... 27

Atlantic av, n s, 250 e Bond st, 25x100. Charles Emmons agt Teresa Ennis; att'ys, Campbell & Murphy ... 27

Pennsylvania av, e s, 100.1 s Atlantic av, 25x100. }
Atlantic av, n s, 100.10 e Georgia av, 20.2x80.2x20x80.2 ... }
Pennsylvania av, e s, 75 s Fulton av, 75x110 ... }
Jacob Pirrung agt Rachel Krieger; action to set aside deed; att'ys, Hurd & Grim ... 27

67th st, s s, 100 e 11th av, 40x130. Brooklyn City Co-operative Building and Loan Assoc. agt Gustav Reichenbach; att'ys, McGuire & Low ... 27

President st, s s, 450.8 e 8th av, 25.10x100. Metropolitan Life Ins. Co. agt Franklin P. Gordon; att'ys, Arnoux, Ritch & Woodford ... 27

Garfield pl, n s, 262.4 w 9th av, 26x100. Harvey Murdock agt Louis R. Jones; foreclos. mechanic's lien; att'ys, Smith & Martin ... 27

Saratoga av, s e cor Chauncey st, 100x260. Daniel Gallagher & Son agt Adrianus Smith; foreclos. mechanic's lien; att'ys, Carr & Walsh ... 27

Christopher av, n w cor Dumont av, 100x100. Jacob Cohen agt Johan C. Gottschaldt; action for specific performance; att'ys, J. C. and H. C. Smith & Koepke ... 29

Pennsylvania av, e s, 100.1 s Atlantic av, 25x100. }
Atlantic av, n s, 100.10 e Georgia av, 20.3x80.2x20x80.2 ... }
Pennsylvania av, e s, 75 s Fulton av, 75x110 ... }
Jacob Pirrung agt Rachel Krieger; action to set aside deeds; att'ys, Hurd & Grim ... 29

Jefferson av, s s, 280 w Nostrand av, 20x100. Thomas C. Van Hoesen, exr. Catharine C. Culp agt James C. Rogers; att'y, William A. Crowe ... 29

Garfield pl, s s, 172.4 e 7th av, 19.6x100. Adelaide B. Cromwell agt William B. Martin; att'ys, Sweeney & Cromwell ... 29

Jefferson av, s s, 300 w Nostrand av, 20x100. Elizabeth V. H. Nicholson agt James C. Rogers; att'y, William A. Crowe ... 29

Wyckoff st, s s, 80 e 3d av, 20x100. Annie Fish agt Silas A. Underhill; att'y, Henry B. Johnson ... 29

Howard av, e s, 98 s Herkimer st, 35x98. George R. Haydock agt Ernest D. Yarber; att'y, George R. Haydock, in person ... 30

South 2d st, s s, 161.3 w 6th st, 18.9x120. Mary McIntire agt Alice Douglass; action on attachment; att'y, C. F. Kinsley ... 30

Dumont st, n w cor Christopher av, 100x100. Morris Appelbaum agt Johann Casper; action to compel conveyance by sufficient deed; att'y, Adolph Cohen ... 30

Watkins st, w s, 100 n Dumont av, 100x100. Isaac Haft agt Annie O'Connor; action for specific performance; att'ys, Lindsay & Bacon ... 30

July

Dumont st, n s, 20 e Vesta av, 80x100 ... }
Vesta av, e s, 100 n Dumont av, 299.2x100 ... }
Snediker av, w s, 100 n Dumont av, 24x100 ... }
Snediker av, w s, 280 n Dumont av, 39.10x100 ... }
Dumont st, s s, 20 e Vesta av, 160x100 ... }
Vesta av, e s, 140 s Dumont av, 260x100 ... }
Livonia av, n s, 20 e Vesta av, 160x100 ... }
Snediker av, w s, 100 n Livonia av, 300x10 ... }
Livonia av, Vesta av, Riverdale av and Snediker av—block ... }
Riverdale av, Vesta av, Newport av and Snediker av ... }
Newport av, s e cor Vesta av, runs south 400 x east 100 x north 50 x east 100 to Snediker av, x north 350 to Newport av, x east 200 ... }
Snediker av, e s, 100 s Dumont av, 100x100 ... }
Snediker av, w s, 280 s Hinsdale av, 105x100 ... }
Snediker av, e s, 180 s Livonia av, runs south 300 to Riverdale av, x east 200 to Hinsdale av, x north 350 x west 200 ... }
Riverdale av, s e cor Snediker av, runs south 100 x east 100 x south 300 x east 100 to Hinsdale av, x north 400 to Riverdale av, x west 200 ... }
Snediker av, e s, 180 s Riverdale av, 50x100 ... }
Snediker av, e s, 125 n Newport av, 50x100 ... }
Snediker av, e s, 100 s Newport av, runs south 240 x east 20 x south to New Lots road, x east to Hinsdale av, x north 171.4 x west 100 x north 100 x west 100 ... }
Elihu J. Granger agt Louis H. Irwin; action for specific performance; att'ys, Dailey & Bell ... 1

Halsey st, n s, 300.4 e Reid av, 17.8x100. Stephen C. Halstead agt Elizabeth Tuthill; att'y, G. W. Pearsall ... 1

Lots 369-372 map heirs Whitehead Howard, 26th Ward. John A. Davies agt Frank Crooke; att'y, John H. Ives ... 1

Butler st, No. 947, 16.8x127.6. Granite State Provident Assoc. agt Henry Ellert; att'ys, Carpenter & Hassett ... 1

Lots 54, 55, 69 and 68 map Daniel D. Stillwell, Gravesend. John Lange agt William Sloane; action for specific performance; att'y, S. S. Hemingway ... 1

Fulton st, s s, 200 e Stone av, 50x100. David H. Beyea agt James H. Watson et al.; att'y, James Demarest ... 1

Bergen st, n s, 200 w Kingston av, 100x114.5. Jennie C. B. Reynolds agt Franklin J. Fellows; att'y, Wm. M. Benedict ... 1

7th av, w s, 50 s Lincoln pl, 100x100. William Post committee John Rogers agt William S. Hale; att'y, John J. Leary ... 1

7th av, s e s, extends from 1st to 2d st, 200x97.10. John Adamson agt Joseph E. Rogers; att'y, Charles R. Halsey ... 2

Pacific st, s s, 297.3 e Rochester av, 16.8x107.2 ... }
Pacific st, s s, 313.11 e Rochester av, 16.8x107.2 ... }
William Jervis agt Joseph Hopkins, Jr.; 2 actions; att'ys, S. F., F. H. & H. Cowdrey ... 2

Pacific st, s s, 330.7 e Rochester av, 16.8x107.2 ... }
Pacific st, s s, 347.3 e Rochester av, 16.8x107.2 ... }
Pacific st, s s, 363.10 e Rochester av, 16.9x107.2 ... }
Pacific st, s s, 380.7 e Rochester av, 16.8x107.2 ... }
Pacific st, s s, 430.8 e Rochester av, 16.8x107.2 ... }
Sarah Chauncey agt same; 5 actions; same att'ys ... 2

RECORDED LEASES.

NEW YORK. Per Year

Clinton st, No. 64. Charles F. Lehr to Henry F. Huntemann; 4 10-12 years, from July 1, 1891 ... $900

Delancey st, No. 26, all. Barbara Dudenhoeffer to August Schlag; 5 years, from July 1, 1891 2,606

Houston st, s e cor Allen st, being 169 Houston st and 206 Allen st. Cancellation of lease. Gustav Muller to Norah E. Pearsall et al. exrs. and trustees Elizabeth Pearsall. June 17 .... nom

Same property. Nora E. Pearsall et al. exrs. and trustees Elizabeth Pearsall to Gustav Muller; 6 years, from May 1, 1891 2,000

Marion st, No. 54 .... }
Crosby st, No. 89 .... }
Catharine Bradley to The Herrman Dining Room Furniture Co.; 5 years, from May 1, 1891 3,500

Market st, No. 23, 25x44x irreg. x53 on st. Michael Fay and William Stacom to The Baron de Hirsch Fund; 2 years, from Aug. 1, 1891 1,500

Mott st, No. 36. Michael Minisman to Chang Yot Kee; 7 years, from July 1, 1891 1,320

Washington st, n w cor Houston st, 3 lots. Woodbury G. Langdon to Patrick Coleman; 10 years, from May 1, 1891 2,000

1st st, No. 12, n e cor Extra pl. Samuel D. Barnes to Alfred Blum and Benjamin Stein, of Blum & Stein; 5 1-12 years, from Jan. 1, 1892 1,800

3d st, No. 26 W., s w cor Greene st. Charles T. Cromwell to Louis P. Schaffner; 5 years, from May 1, 1891 .... 2,500, 2,700

21st st, No. 150 E. Frank Krauss to Eliza O'Meara; 5 years, from May 1, 1891, with privilege of renewal for 5 years from May 1, 1896 2,000

23d st, No. 434 W. Rosa Jordan to Abram Besthoff; 2 10-12 years, from July 1, 1891 1,800

59th st, No. 319, n s, 100 e 9th av. Nicholas Henry to George Degenhardt; 6 years, from July 1, 1891 4,400

78th st, Ward No. 46, abt 45.2 e Boulevard, 25x102. Jeremiah W. Dimick to Mrs. Alice Carlin; 5 years, from May 1, 1891 400

114th st, Nos. 440 and 442 E. James Hagerty to Joseph Cappello; 10 years, from June 1, 1891 2,500

117th st, n s, 385 e Pleasant av, runs north 200 to 118th st, x east 75 x south 100 x west 25 x south 100 to 117th st, x west 50. George W. Moore to John F. Crotty and John Lally, of Crotty & Lally; 5 years, from July 1, 1891, with privilege of purchasing said premises for $28,000 900

143d st, No. 732 E. Thomas M. Canton to Charles Nylin; 3 years, from May 1, 1891. 150, 180, 216

Same property. Assign. lease. Charles Nylin to Nils Hanson 300

Av A, No. 1659, store and four a ij rooms and basement. Sigmund Doelafeld to August Lanzig or Zauzig; 5 years, from May 1, 1892 600

Av B, No. 221, store and cellar. Retschel Joseph to Christopher Nirmaier; 5 years, from May 1, 1890 900

Columbus av, No. 1884, store being south ½ ground floor. Margaret Marshall to Edward W. Dee; 3 years, from May 1, 1891 776

Courtlandt av, No. 882. Charles Moritz to John H. Koenig; 10 years, from May 1, 1891 .... 900, 1,200

Elm av, n w cor Southern Boulevard. Kate Hynes to Mary Connors; 3 years, from July 1, 1891 300

Mount Morris av, No. 35, s w cor 124th st, 100.11 x100. Albert and Henry Franke and Eunice R. wife of said Henry to William B. Franke; 10 years, from July 1, 1891, taxes and 16,600

1st av, No. 1663, store. Margaretha F. Rosenberger to Frederick Wisloh; 4 11-12 years, from June 1, 1891 .... 420, 540

1st av, No. 184, store and basement. George Holl to Gustav J. Dohrenwend and Otto A. Leiste; 4 years 10 months and 11 days, from June 20, 1890 1,440

2d av, No. 694, store and bakery. Stanley W. Dexter to Ernest F. Lindenberger; 3 years, from May 1, 1891 780

2d av, No. 804, n e cor 43d st. Edward Rafter to Peter Meenan; 5 years, from May 1, 1891. 1,600

2d av, No. 2274, store floor and rear rooms. Thomas McManus to George Brandan; 3 years, from May 1, 1891 360

3d av, No. 2858, all. Margaret E. Adriance to A. Fletcher; 5 years, from May 1, 1891 1,200

3d av, No. 2894, store and cellar. Margaret, Patrick F., Thomas J. and Jeremiah J. Mullen, of Mullen Brothers, to Harry Leopold; 7 years, 10 months and 22 days, from June 8, 1891 1,200

3d av, n e cor 57th st, 25x85, office on ground floor. Mary M. Davidson to Christian Volzing; 5 years, from May 1, 1891 1,100

4th av, No. 78. Jeannette Goldsmith to Joseph McGinty; 4 10-12 years, from July 1, 1891 2,175

5th av, cor 42d st, Hotel Bristol. William H. Webb to Eugene M. Earle; 10 years, from June 1, 1891 .... 45,000, 75,000

7th av, No. 2268, all. Frederick Beck to L. A. Ware & Co.; 5 years, from July 1, 1891 2,300

12th av, 161st st, Hudson River R. R. land and 160th st and Manhattan st—block. William Dunning to Peter H. Short and William Sheehan; 10 years, from May 1, 1892 5,000

CHATTELS.

Note.—The first name, alphabetically arranged, is that of the Mortgagor, or party who gives the Mortgage. The "R" means Renewal Mortgage.

NEW YORK CITY.

June 26 to July 2—Inclusive.

SALOON AND RESTAURANT FIXTURES.

Abel, Jacob. 735 10th av....G Ehret. (R) $2,500

Adler, Rosa. 242 West....L I Brewery. (R) 2,000

Brown, N. 62 Broome....C and A Berenter. Pool Table. 190

Bennett, Wm. 533 6th av....R A Greacen. 5,000

Buchner, John. 541 1st av....Schmitt & S. (R) 350

Cunnion, D C. 350 2d av....Brunswick-B-C Co. Pool. 350

Cohen, Bennett. 94 Hester....S Green. Restaurant Fixtures. 400

Costello, Mathew. 31 Park ...Beadleston & W. Saloon Pump. 90

Dubuis, Oscar. 206 Wooster....A Van Opstal. Restaurant Fixtures. 100

Drout, John. 122 Varick....J Everard. (R) 1,117

Drucker, Max. 321 Stanton....D Mayer. 5,000

Farnbeimer, Louis. 807 1st av....H Kahn. 160

Feldhaus, Anton. 506 E 5th....Schmitt & S. 200

Fitzpatrick, James. 61 Macdougal....J Hoffman B Co. 370

Gaffney, P T. 640 10th av...Bernheimer & S. (R) 1,500

Same. 667 10th av....same. (R) 4,000

Germann, Jacob. 260 W 41st ...G Ehret. (R) 2,000

Griffin, W T. 411 6th av....F & M Schaefer B Co. 1,000

Griffin & Dowling. 283 7th av....G Ehret. 2,500

Gallagher, M J. 101 Greenwich av....E Tracy. (R) 700

Gardella, Louis. 161 Worth....India Wharf B Co. 800

Geiger, Jacob. 1597 Av A....Williamsburgh B Co. 400

Harnett, John. 175 Av B... G Ringler & Co. 600

Heymann, Leopold. 152 Ludlow....J Eichler B Co. 600

Jones, C A. 141 Av D....O J Bliss. Restaurant Fixtures. 528

Junker, J C. 170 3d av... M Mansfeld. 2,220

King, J & C. 2105 7th av....G Ringler & Co. 900

Knerim, Joseph. 20 North William ...I Roth. 375

Krajicek, Alojisia. 1353 1st av... Schmitt & S. 500

Klein, Jacob 412 W 36th....D Mayer. 500

Kropp, George. 636 E 12th....G Ringler & Co. 500

Keller, John. 636 E 12th....G Ringler & Co. 500

Lohr, Charles. 416 E 34th ...Hirsch & S. (R) 800

Lyon, J A. 2384 3d av....M F Driver. 11,000

Lyon, J A. 3d av and 129th st....Arctander & Seabold. 2,000

Leoparde, Rosa. 54 James....Burger & H B Co. (R) 400

Moeller, George. 1568 1st av....H Elias B Co. (R) 700

Major, Charles. 45 Willett and 230 Delancey.... G Ringler & Co. 500

Mastriaovoco, John. 340 E 110th ...D Mayer. 375

McKenna, O E. 23 Chatham sq .. J Everard. 4,000

Mecke, William. 1666 1st av....G Ringler & Co. 2,000

Meise, William. 191 East Houston....E Ochs. 875

Miller, Louis. 185 Av A... Bachmann B Co. (R) 800

Murphy & Healey. 2211 8th av .. Bernheimer & S. Pool Table. 140

Mafiile, Eugene. 220 Thompson....W H Griffith & Co. Pool Table. 275

Meenan, Peter. 804 2d av....Bernheimer & S. 2,000

Murphy, Patrick. 2395 3d av....G Ehret. 1,000

Neulist, Charles. 641 E 9th....J Eichler B Co. 400

Neumeyer, Andreas. 348 6th ...Welz & Z. 300

O'Connor, G W.... Brunswick-B-C Co. Pool Table. 225

Pyle, Alexander. 216 8th av....H Held. 1,000

Reich, B and L. 50 Essex....D Mayer. 623

Robinson & Seaman. 2894 3d av....H Leopold. Restaurant Fixtures. 1,000

Romano, Rosario. 331 E 115th....Bernheimer & S. Pool Table. 140

Roth, Peter. 442 E 78th ...G Ringler & Co. 600

Ryan, John. 507 3d av....H Clausen & Son B Co. (R) 3,500

Rauser, L O. 551 2d av....G Ehret. 2,000

Redel, John. 205 E 4th....G Ehret. 600

Ruff, Charles. 346 E 9th....G Ringler & Co. 500

Solter, George. 1291 1st av ...W L Flanagan. 500

Scharmgold & Meyerser. 113 Hester....E V Walker. Pool Table. 85

Schmidt, August. 214 E 4th....D Mayer. 418

Schueke, Apollone. 628 E 17th....Burr B Co. 500

Schnitzlein, Charles. 1673 3d av....J Ruppert. (R) 400

Schramm, Peter. 528 W 55th....V Loewers. 500

Schwab, Sidney. 734 Columbus av....Bernheimer & S. 3,500

Same....F Wolfe. 1,000

Singhi, C J and H U. 2039 3d av....G Ringler & Co. 2,752

Stager, Louis. 255 Bowery....D Mayer. (R) 1,900

Strauss, Frederick. 44 Spring....G Ehret. (R) 1,500

Schaffner, L P. 26 W 3d....G Bechtel, exr of. 2,500

Stoerzer, C B. 184 3d av....A Weber. Restaurant Fixtures. 2,000

Vail, I M. 415 6th av....Anna E Vail. Restaurant Fixtures. 1,800

Van Dahl, Henry. 238 E 10th....J P Schuchmann. 500

Walz, Frank 45 Jay....H Zeltner. 250

Wolf, Joseph. 104 1st....C & A Berenter. Pool Table. 140

Woepner, Henry. 103 West Broadway....Bachmann B Co. (R) 700

Walsh, Kate. 19 Grand .. Burr B Co. 1,200

Zeeck, G and S. 198 Av A....F Gruhs. 425

HOUSEHOLD FURNITURE.

Adamo, Domenico. 114 Varick....H Mannes & Son. (R) 192

Albert, Emily. 123 W 15th....J Moriarty. 197

Adams, Hattie. 33 E 27th....H Israel & Sons. (R) 889

Angeloni, Giovanni. 165 Bleecker ...C R Rugger. 119

Brown, Blanch. 228 W 16th... H Israel & Sons. (R) 508

Burr & Parry. 426 W 19th ....P McDowell. 2,000

Bitborn, C H, Mrs. 108 E 86th ...J Moriarty. 285

Blake, E F. 19 E 115th....H Mannes & Son. 126

Brown, Sarah. 208 E 25th....J Moriarty. 238

Boland, Mary E. 386 Park av ...L Baumann. 115

Boughton, Julia. 2216 2d av....A Bollermann & Son. Piano. (R) 71

Bremberg, Gus. 325 E 83d ...Jordan & M. 139

Benton, Frieda. 184 W 10th....W I Blumberg. 175

Conroy, Hannah. 266 W 11th....Jordan & M. 121

Cain, Rose. 108 W 102d....O'Farrell & Co. 201

Cameron, Mary. 228 W 16th....H Israel & Sons. (R) 268

Crandall, Myra. 106 W 40th....H Israel & Sons. 561

Denny, Ella. 1011 Park av ...H Israel & Sons. (R) 101

De Forrest, Mabel. 20 E 12th... McClain, S & Co. 198

Delisser, Esther. 1733 Lexington av....J Moriarty. (R) 226

Donati, Gundela. 47½ E 7th.. .J Moriarty. (R) 152

Evans, L G. 101 W 104th....G Beck. (R) 138

Edwards, Sarah J. 243 W 34th...H Israel & Sons. 197

Erskine, E J. 80 West Washington pl... J Farley. 2,200

Fearon, Rose M. 153 Av A .. W E Wheelock & Co. Piano. (R) 215

Foulkes, Mary. 344 E 82d....S Baumann. 416

Francis, F, Mrs. 159 W 49th....S Knapp & Co. 1,754

Gaffney, Andrew. 5 Vandam....W J Ruddell. (R) 187

Girard, Ethel. 140 W 36th....H Mannes & Son. (R) 144

Goldberg, Rachel. 1930 3d av. ..Philips & B. 114

Gaillard, D A. 418 W 48d....M C Worth. 500

Gerdes, W H. 190 Canal....W E Wheelock & Co. Piano. (R) 188

Grassick, Mrs. 170 8th av....H Israel & Sons. 128

Greenfield, A F. 461 Willis av....J Farley. 142

Harris, Max. 198 Orchard....Fennell & Pye. 172

Hoover, B E. 2750 10th av. ..J Farley. 148

Hart, W J. 143 W 30th....H Mannes & Son. 137

Hays, Louisa. 122 W 123d....S Baumann. 334

Hearn, L A. 2825 2d av....A Romer. 110

Heany, Maggie 548 Broome .L Baumann. 118

Holt, H A & E. 180 W 97th....Harlem Ind and G Assoc. 100

Hudson, Florence. 251 W 29th....L Baumann. 265

Hull, Ella E. 341 W 55th J Moriarty. (R) 109

Isaacs, Ida. 301 Broome . W I Blumberg. 182

Johnston, Mrs L. 439 W 43d....H Thoesen. 158

Johnson, Lottie G. 56 E 114th....W E Wheelock & Co. Piano. 350

Keely, J T. 237 E 107th....Jordan & M. 100

Kiernan, E T. 172 E 96th .. W E Wheelock & Co. Piano. (R) 145

Kimball, May. 1007 6th av....H Israel & Sons. (R) 437

Kaplan, Abraham. 19 Rutgers pl ...W Kaplan. 200

Kladivko, Marie. 126 E 85th....F Krombholz. (R) 560

Kones, L W. 153 W 70th... Lord & Taylor. 246

Konon, T. 268 E 138th A Romer. 181

Kookogey, W P. 97 Pulaski st, Brooklyn.... Mary E Bobrick. 150

Kroft, George. 224 W 18th....L Baumann. 258

Kuphal, Otto. 126 W 83d....L Dolan. 912

Leopold, Joseph. 310 E 51st....S Heyman. 183

Lewis, Mrs M T. 148 E 55th....S Heyman & Co 172

Lipman, Helena. 80 E 109th....W I Blumberg 158

Lorentz, Rosa. 219 E 80th....W I Blumberg. 121

Ludlow, Elizabeth C. 131 E 15th....A R Morris. 1,000

Lanigan, Mark. 30 Henry....S Miles (R) 700

Lehey, Alice J. 219 W 28th....W E Wheelock & Co. Piano. 275

Lester, Julius 39 Essex ...W E Wheelock & Co. Piano. 175

Loewenthal, Max. 256 East Houston....Krakauer Bros. Piano. 275

Maloney, Margaret. 457 W 32d .. O'Farrell & Co. 218

Maning, Mary. 300 W 54th....W E Wheelock & Co. Piano. 150

Masche, Marie. 166th st and Boston av....R Silverman. (R) 100

McManus, Mary E. 242 E 39th ...W E Wheelock & Co. Piano. 500

McNichol, G T. 128 W 63d....Jordan & M. 189

Moskowitz, Bela M. 198 Stanton. . S Hedler. (R) 450

Martinot, Nina. 230 W 43d....W E Wheelock & Co. Piano. 300

Mackintosh, L A. 165 E 83d....Commercial Credit Co. 200

McMichael James. 537 Union av....W E Wheelock Co. Piano. 300

Merritt R and C B. Spuyten Duyvil....M Williams. 600

Metz, Joseph. 316 E 116th....Harlem I and G Assoc. 100

Mannheim, Mamie. 230 E 21st....S Heyman. 190

Mauson, E. 312 W 20th ...A Robertson. 175

Mayer, R W. 158 W 103d....H Mannes & Son. 324

Merrill, Florence. 120 W 63d....O'Farrell & Co. 360

Milliken, Sarah. 335 W 34th ...O'Farrell & Co. 250

Moody, J H. 103 E 88th . L Baumann. 470

Morton, Mamie. 427 W 35th....L Baumann. 177

Nelson, Robert. 231 W 39th....O'Farrell & Co. 441

Ormay, Jeka. 1240 Lexington av... S Heyman & Co. (R) 185

Osborn, Fannie J. 60 W 124th ..W H Moore. 295

Ogg, Sarah. 408 W 34th....C E Pierce. 135

Olbeles, Henry. 142 E 48th....Krakauer Bros. Piano. 190

Pearsall, Mrs Chas. 111 W 58d . .H Israel & Sons. (R) 133

Perkins, Hattie. 211 E 95th....Jordan & M. 100

Page, Frances. 119 W 56th....Rosa B De Casneva. 105

Panza, John. 47 W Little 12th....O'Farrell & Co. 161

Peet, A J. 59 W 45th .. J S Gillies, estate of. 100

Rosenblatt, David. 607 3d av....S Heyman & Co. 100

Ryan, Mrs Wm. 339 E 81st....H Thoesen. 135

Sheldon, Jane. 51 E 106th....W E Wheelock & Co. Piano 375

Smith, Elizabeth. 6 Roosevelt....Mary Lynch. secures rent

Stephens, Herminia. 1697 Madison av....H Israel & Sons. (R) 150

Summer, Frank. 106 Waverley pl .W E Wheelock & Co. Piano. 350

Seifter, Sam. 51 Canal.. .H S Eisler. 103

Stuart, Dora. 1370 Broadway....W & J Sloane. Carpets. 1,400

Sullivan, James. 1020 Av A....Jordan & M. 110

Samuels, Sadie. 142 W 28th....J Moriarty. 378

Sawyer, Carrie M. 314 W 117th....J Moriarty. 177

Sturz, August. 92 E 8th....J Moriarty. 116

Tellier, G and P. 75 Christopher....C R Rugger. 243

Teller, Julius. 683 Broadway....A Bernstein. 315

Thompson, F B. 562 7th av... O'Farrell & Co. 169

Tittell, Mrs M E. 151 W 62d ...H Thoesen. 186

Tuentes, F and M J. 325 W 112th....W H Jackson. (R) 571

Van Heynigan, Jennie. 126 W 47th....L Baumann. 414

Valerio, Nicolino. 377 Broome....Fennell & Pye. (R) 109

Waldstein, Emil. 236 E 57th....A Benesh. 270

Woerner, Ch. 515 E 11th....S Heyman & Co. 110

Wolfe, Grace. 102 W 29th....Degraff & Taylor. 542

MISCELLANEOUS.

Abbott, S A and C B. ..G Dessecker. Coach. 80

Almy & Sulzer....J H Root. Coal Yard Fixtures. 2,500

American Morocco Case Co. 9 Bond....Mosler Safe Co. Safe. 200

Arnsbrey, F M....Perrin, Payson & Co. Coach. 210

Bianco, Raffaele. 520 Hudson....A Schwaab & Son. Barber Fixtures. 39

Blackmore, Robert. 190 7th av....B Rumsby. Butcher Fixtures. 200

Blake, C P. 247 Division....S Rubenstein. Undertaker Fixtures. 400

Bollman, Fred. 522 E 68th....J Urban. Horse, Wagon, &c. 50

Bracco, Alfonso. 14 Prince ...Mosler Safe Co. Safe. 200

Brass Goods Mfg Co. 250-254 State st, Brooklyn ....C Hewlett. Machinery, &c. (R) 2,000

Baer, Caroline. 347 E 92d....E Zimmerle. Grocery Fixtures. 600
Bartholomew, C E. 22 College pl....W H Moore. Press, &c. 3,000
Barry, John... D P Nichols & Co Cab. 400
Baumgartner, A. 104 William....R Rainforth. Barber Fixtures. 126
Boyken, J A. 2296 2d av....B G Amend. Drug Fixtures. 1,000
Bromberg, R B. 525 8th av....L Raunheim. Furniture and Dental Fixtures. 1,300
Belada, V. 1374 Av A....J Blazey. Butcher Fixtures. 125
Casamassa, Angelo. 304 E 34th....G Lordi. Barber Fixtures. 45
Colletti, Matteo. 501½ 10th av....M Azzolino. Barber Fixtures. 40
Cavaliere, Giuseppe. 205 E 30th... G Cavaliere, Sr. Baker Fixtures. 735
Chandler, Joseph. 111 Norfolk....P Reidenbach. Wagon. 99
Childs, E....J W Tufts. Soda Fixtures. 985
Campbell, W F. 326 W 26th....A T Campbell. Horses, Carts, &c. 744
Carello, Michele. 396 Water....A Schwaab & Son. Barber Fixtures. (R) 19
Casey, M S. 441 6th av....Racine Wagon Co. Wagon. 80
Comers, Frank. 701 10th av....A Schwaab & Son. Barber Fixtures. 339
Cornish, W H 25 Cannon....Liberty Machine Works. Press. 225
Couti, J A F. 86 Av D....A Schwaab & Son. Barber Fixtures. 293
De Mattia, Giovanni. 574 11th av....L Desposito. Barber Fixtures. 165
Frankel, Isidor. 5 Av D .M Moses. Butcher Fixtures. 1,000
Freeman, R & Bro. 45-51 Rose....Babcock P P Co. Press. (R) 686
Fuchs, Mayer. 119 Clinton....G Pius. Barber Fixtures. 110
Fina, Carmine. 183 Hester....A Schwaab & Son. Barber Fixtures. 217
Francia, Luca 263½ E 42d....A Schwaab. Barber Fixtures. 591
Fried, Morris. 83 Sheriff .... J Goodman. Butcher Fixtures. 80
Gibb, Lulu. 308 Spring. ..Ann Ford. Store Fixtures. secures rent
Greco, Francesco. 219 Park row....A Schwaab. Barber Fixtures. 491
Greco, Francesco. 2058 1st av....A Schwaab. Barber Fixtures. 110
Guttler, Gustav. 115 Lewis....L Stern. Horse, Wagon, &c. 20
Gallo, James. 419 Broadway....A Schwaab & Son. Barber Fixtures. 628
Gelhaus, August. 1577 2d av .... J Rasche Butcher Fixtures. 500
Griffin & Dowling. 283 7th av....Nat'l Cash Register Co. Register. 175
Goldberg, Lewis. 378 Grand ...Mosler Safe Co. Safe. 130
Goldstein, Barnett. 132 East Broadway....Mosler Safe Co. Safe. 160
Gilmore, J W. 2250 3d av ...A D Puffer & Son. Soda Fixtures. (R) 255
Hammond, George. 82 Reade....G H Sanborn & Sons. Machinery. 300
Harrigan, William. 501 7th av....S Littman. Barber Fixtures. (R) 52
Herzfeld, Jeannette. 365 8th av....B Cohen. Store Fixtures. 500
Hepp, Charles. 134 W 31st....H Ingersoll. Horses. 600
Hotze & Volmer. 2132 3d av....Velte Bros. Grocery Fixtures. (R) 1,900
Jordan, J V. 5th av and 42d st....J H Tremper. Hotel Fixtures. 1,250
Jennings, P J. 733 and 735 1st av....M Miville. Machinery. (R) 500
Jensen & Weltz. 1435 3d av ...E P Gleason Mfg Co. Pump Fixtures. (R) 36
Kallert, John. 1507 1st av....J Schwenn. Barber Fixtures. 100
Kelly, J A 207 W 75th....D B Dunham. Coach. 750
Knoud, W J. 829 West....W Cody. Blacksmith Tools, &c. (R) 850
Kienle, A C. 27 Park pl....W Scott & Co. Press, &c 985
Krikawa, Charles. 403 E 73d....G Schuckman. Furniture Van. 575
Kunath, J B. 841 10th av ...A Kunath. Drug Fixtures. 1,500
Kiley, Michael. 321 E 38th....Bridget Russell. Horses, &c. 2,000
Knickerbocker Print and Pub Co. 108 and 110 Duane....I C Ogden, Jr. Presses, &c. 2,100
Krahmer, A D. 176 and 178 E 105th....J Krahmer. Horses and Express Fixtures. 2,000
Ledermann, Isaac. 12 1st .... I Kaufmann. Bottler Fixtures (R) 1,065
Liguori, Antonio. 43 Washington....L Alfano. Barber Fixtures. 210
Laurent, H A. 919 2d av....B G Amend. Drug Fixtures. (R) 1,237
Ludwig, Louis. 14 Jefferson ...M Solomon. Barber Fixtures. 500
Marcus, Max. 425 E 81st. ..M Mollash. Cigar Fixtures, &c. 500
Markowitz, Max. 318 E 8th ...P Leidesdorf. Machinery. 50
Marose, A. 342 2d av . A Schwaab & Son. Barber Fixtures. 293
Marzullo, Joseph. 164 W 4th....A Schwaab & Son. Barber Fixtures. 388
Monteforte, Aurelio. 188 Canal.. .A Schwaab & Son. Barber Fixtures. 34
Moorhead, Robert, Jr. 1119 1st av....D B Dunham. Coach. 245
Malzman, Pincus. 112 Hester....S Suffer. Barber Fixtures. 925
Marcul, E E. 192 E 125th....A D Puffer & Sons. Soda Fixtures. (R) 515
Nergart, J A. 1215 3d av....C Zimmerman & Co. Bakery Fixtures. 400
North, F J. 618 Tinton av....A D Puffer & Son. Soda Fixtures. (R) 225
Oduberner, H E. 173 Park row....J Matthews. Soda Fixtures. 208
Palmer, W N. 113 Maiden lane....A Fraser. Machinery. (R) 586
Panagrozze, Ferdinando. 2123 1st av .... A Schwaab & Son. Barber Fixtures. (R) 13
Powell, A M. 152 Chambers....Mosler Safe Co. Safe. 250
Quain, Thomas. 16 Washington....J Cunningham S & Co. Coach. (R) 305
Same... same. Coach. (R) 305
Reu, Louis. 114 E 88th....J Rothschild. Horses. (R) 225
Roworth Mfg Co....J W Tufts. Soda Apparatus [illegible] 200

Reiss, A....G Meyer. Coach. 425
Rosenphal, J & A. 224 Broome ...H Lottman. Barber Fixtures. 300
Rosenberg, A & J. 139 and 139½ Madison.... A Cohen. Machines. 500
Rauchfuss, Otto. 106 and 108 Av C....W C Conrad. Drug Fixtures. 2,700
Romain, W G. 156 and 158 W 127th....C B Morris & Co. Livery Stable Fixtures. 2,000
Schneider, Benjamin. 445 W 45th .... Adams Laundry Co. Laundry Fixtures. 200
Schnitzer, Max. 177 Lewis....Singer Mfg Co. Machines. 212
Seaman, C H. 228 E 84th....I R Mayer. Horse and Harness. 20
Schultze, T L. 17 Chatham....Mosler Safe Co. Safe. 145
Skndrna, Holecek & Belsky. 618 5th....S Bauer. Bakery Fixtures. 500
Standard Cell Case Mfg Co. 58 Warren....Mosler Safe Co. Safe. 150
Schaffmeier, M J. 405 E 121st....W Austin. Horses, Trucks, &c. 1,895
Schleimow, Joseph. 172 Rivington....A Kopetowitz. Butcher Fixtures. 100
Schmidt, C H. 133d st and Madison av ...J W Reiss. Horses, Wagons, &c. 100
Sondell, Erlich. 156 Ridge. ..H Hollander. Bakery Fixtures. 47
Stoll, J A. 60 Barclay....C C Bolle. Machinery. (R) 270
Struthers, Servoss & Co. 24-34 New Chambers ....C B Cottrell & Son. Press. (R) 2,478
Toner, Francis. 322 Madison .... J Seaver. Horses, &c. 830
Townsend, Wm C. 138 5th av....Halls Safe Co. Safe. 425
Tracy, G & Co. 143 Liberty....J Matthews Co. Soda Apparatus. 565
"Truth," Newspaper. 140 5th av....Halls Safe Co. Safe. 350
Triton, Geo. 320 1st av....F Hauff. Sausage Fixtures, &c. (R) 1,000
Valentine, J C. 31 and 33 East Houston... Ellen Benedict. Machinery, Presses, &c. 9,000
Vagt, Charles. 229 Monroe .... T Loughran. Butcher Fixtures. 1,200
Wittenberg, Bertha. 539 W 50th....Koenig & Schuster. Grocery Fixtures. 126
Washinsky & Levowitch. 68 Hester....H Silberman. Store Fixtures. 200
Walter, Henry. 243 East Houston....H Krebbiel. Drug Fixtures. (R) 5,000
Weiss, August. 6 City Hall pl . . Elizabeth Weiss. Press. 500
Yarvshefsky, Henry. 33 Canal....S Levy. Machines. 25
Ziegler, John. 883 10th av....S Littman. Barber Fixtures. 102

BILLS OF SALE.

Allers, J A. 338 6th....A Neumeyer. Saloon Fixtures. 150
Arctander & Seabold. 129th st and 3d av ...J A Lyon. Saloon Fixtures. —
Baer, Henry. 347 E 92d... Caroline Baer. Grocery Fixtures. 1,900
Brockwald, Matthew. 520 Pearl....C J Bennewitz. Grocery Fixtures. 180
Cavaliere, G, Sr, and G, Jr. 205 E 30th....G Cavaliere. Barber Fixtures. 735
Christie, Walter. 173 Christopher....Z Jaques. Machinery. 415
Cohen, Moses. 1330 1st av....Sigmund Cohen. Grocery Fixtures. 300
Considine, M J. 211 W 64th....T N Holden. Bakery Fixtures. 110
Doorman, Louise. 658 10th av....L & V Ganther. Fancy Store Fixtures. 300
Garfield, J W....Emeline A Bouton. Furniture. 634
Hill, J M....D K Hill. Scenery of Play "Ship Ahoy." 2,500
Holcroft, Henry. 746 2d av....J Fay. Saloon Fixtures. 211
Hanover, Henry. 502 9th av....J B Hanover. Stove, Store Fixtures, &c. 2,000
Higgins, Thomas. 136 W 4th ...Mary E Higgins. Livery Stable Fixtures, &c. 600
Koenig & Schuster. 539 W 50th....Bertha Wittenberg. Grocery Fixtures. 1
Kahn, Joseph. 1482 1st av....Fannie Kahn. Grocery Fixtures. 1
Krogmann, Aug. 520 Pearl... M Brockwald. Grocery Fixtures. 180
Klie, August. 206 West....J P Purcell. Saloon Fixtures. 2,500
Moloney, R H. 131 3d av....J E Moloney. Dental Fixtures, &c. 200
Schwab, Moritz. 606 8th av....Minna Schwab. Butcher Fixtures. 750
Schwartz, Rosa....L Deutsch. Promissory Notes. 400
Schmits, Charles. 106 South 5th av....Louise S Schmits. Harness Maker Fixtures. 500
Trevisanello, Chas. 40 Grand....C Herzenberg. Drug Fixtures. 700
Vail, I M....Annie E Vail. Launch Elsie V. 1,000
Ward, J F ...Standard Gas Light Co. Iron Pipe. 6,000

ASSIGNMENTS OF CHATTEL MORTGAGES.

Feldman & Weiss to J Feldman. (Mort given by O Unchenstein, Feb 25, 1891.) 1
Same to same. (A Geeb, June 17, 1891.) 1
Same to same. (A Geeb, June 8, 1891.) 1
Hayes, J J to Amelia E Hayes. (E L F Price, April 13, 1891.) 400
Nightingale, James. 437 and 439 W 42d....J Nightingale. Insurance Policies. 2,500
Same....Ellen Nightingale. Silk, &c. 1,100
Same....Ismerie C Nightingale. Insurance Policies. 3,000
Owens, P J to Norton & Christman. (D Black, May 7, 1890.) 1
Riebeschl, H A to P & M McParland. (J P Flynn, Feb 24, 1891.) 50
Shai, Herman to G Wehr. (J Guenther, May 26, 1891.) 25

KINGS COUNTY.

JUNE 25 TO JULY 1—INCLUSIVE.

SALOON AND RESTAURANT FIXTURES.

Agster, J. 113 Withers. ,Williamsburg B Co. $300
Boser, G. 178 Ewen....J Kress B Co. 200
Brix, C. 100 Raymond....Williamsburgh B Co. 500
Behrman, D H. 1083 Halsey....S Liebmann's Sons B Co. 1,650
Berger, F. 18 Lewis av ...F Hower B Co. (R) 650
Beutel, P. 40 Knickerbocker av....Feigenspan B Co. 505
Couly, M F. 91 Boerum pl.... J Everard. 2,547
Clark, B. 108 Kent av....G Ehret. (R) 800
Dolan, J. 50 Gold....Obermeyer & L. (R) 185
Delaney, J. Dresden st, near Jamaica av.... Danenberg & Coles. (R) 566
Dunn, T. 584 3d av....M T Garvey. 500
Ferruggari, Nancy. 23 Union....E Thorp. 450
Forgarty, T. 118 Elizabeth....Abott B Co. (R) 394
Honstrater, F E. 375 9th....A Abel. 600
Same....L I Brewery. 350
Hans, J. 46 Ten Eyck....H Kiefer. Billiard Table. 200
Higgins, E. 290 Columbia....M Seitz. 700
Hogan, W J. 422 7th av....J Gallagher. 1,500
Hunecke, F. 211 Franklin....G Ehret. 2,500
Kaufmann, C A. 35 Walker st, New York....F & M Schaefer B Co. 1,000
Keller, R. 60 Graham av....L Eppig. 700
Keogh, M E. 5 Carroll....Obermeyer & L 400
Krenscher, P. 20 McKibbin .. Danenberg & Coles. (R) 1,000
Kelly, M J. 50 Nostrand av ..F Munch Brewery. 600
Limp, H. 170 Floyd. .W Ulmer. 1,200
McDermott, Cath and T. 157 Myrtle av.... Claus Lipsius B Co. 1,550
McDermott, Cath. 90 Prince....Burr B Co. (R) 600
Murphy, D. 626 Grand av....Williamsburg B Co. (R) 250
McGee, P. 128 Elizabeth....Williamsburgh B Co. 100
Moran, T J. 120 Verona....M Seitz. 250
McDermott, J. 577 Driggs....E Ochs. 1,200
Meyer, J. 165 Graham av....E Ochs. 920
Nugent, T. 197 North 8th st....O Huber Brewery. 2,000
Orthlieb, L. 276 Ainslie....L Eppig. 678
Plunkett, J. 498 3d av....Danenberg & Coles. (R) 300
Patton, R. 69 Herbert....F Ibert. 600
Risnikoff, M. 76 Seigel ...L Eppig. 115
Rode, W. 490 Marcy av ...J Fallert B Co. 609
Sartori, J and L Rossi. 222 Union av .. J Fallert B Co. 600
Schulz, A. 321 Graham av... F Melzer. Pool Table. 115
Schwanenfluegel, F. 357 Pulaski....H B Scharman. 749
Struempfler, P. 125 Melrose... M Seitz. 800
Stroh, J. Sumner av cor Tillary st .. C A Brenter. Pool Table 800
Scherer, P. 141 Montrose av... L Eppig. 400
Schlingplesser, A. 1546 Myrtle av....Feigenspan B Co. (R) 2,400
Smith, J J. 613 Myrtle av....Obermeyer & L. 3,000
Teschmacher, M....G H Wehrenberg. 500
Werner, F. 61 Driggs....Eliz Meltzer. (R) 400
Wolf, J J. 182 Hopkins....F Hower B Co. 675
Zaengle, G. 243 Humboldt....Claus Lipsius B Co. 400

HOUSEHOLD FURNITURE.

Arena, M and P Donato. 7 Union....M Savarese & Bro. 150
Anderson, Martha. 53 Schenck av....M S Hollis. 211
Baldwin, Sophie D. 85 Putnam av....W D Crowell. 110
Brown, Mrs A. 9 Henry. ..Brooklyn F Co. 121
Bell, L L. 150 Lafayette av....Mullins Sons. 137
Bethell, W L....T Taaffe. 178
Bigelow, G W. 6 Van Sielen av....Commercial Credit Co. 150
Cox, G F. Vandeveer st, near Broadway....A Schulz. 183
Crossman, Eliza. 35 Lynch....A Schulz. 193
Canning, Mark. 111 Sands....M S Hollis. 2-2
Crook, F W. 267 Washington ...E A Rorke. 298
Campbell, W J. Hinsdale st and Belmont av.... T Kelly. 214
Durenberg, N J. 599 Flushing av....C T Kendrick & Co. 312
Doten, Anna B. 27 Pierrepont ...A B Stratton. (R) 900
Espada, R. 23 Bond....J McEnery & Co. 225
Fleishmann, J. 182 Varet....C T Kendrick & Co. 302
Flynn, Mary. 90 Havemeyer....T Kelly. 125
Fox, Mary M. 166 Clinton ...D Elston. 374
Few, Jennie. 98 Adelphi ...T F Mulqueen. 176
Fessler, H L. 104 Lincoln pl. . F G Smith. Piano. 400
Guille, G. 155 E 96th st, New York....J Baumann. 200
Hadler, F. 979 Broadway....G W Blauvelt. 326
Haynes, Ellen. 340 Hudson av....E Driscoll & Bro. 135
Heymann, M. 460 Hart... H Israel & Sons. 196
Jewell, Mrs F. 76 Tillery....T Kelly. 159
King, J H. 428 Union....Brooklyn F Co. 237
Lowenstein, Barbara. 250 Stockton ...A Schulz. 185
Lee, D J. 1006 Jefferson av....Caroline Traum. 328
Moran, Mary. 287 Reid av....C T Kendrick & Co. 239
McCarren, Mrs J B. 166 North 6th....I Mason. 475
Moran, J C. 169 Halsey....McEnery & Co. 267
Morris, J. C. 23 Linden....W D Crowell. 140
Myers, G. 57 Stockton....Brooklyn F Co. 115
Neville, Martha. 371 Central av....C T Kendrick & Co. 112
Ordizona, Mrs F. 257½ Wyckoff....E Driscoll & Bro. 100
Owens, P. Av Q, Gravesend....W L Burrill. Piano. 155
O'Neill, M. 191 Atlantic av....F W C Dillon. Upholstery Fixtures and Furniture. 700
O'Connell, Julia F. 103 Willoughby av....C T Kendrick & Co. 155
Peters, Margaret. 441 Sumner av....M Schulz & Bro. 139
Riley, E F. 41 De Kalb av....M Bottstein. 105
Rowland, Mrs J. 297 7th av....T Kelly. 155
Ryan, J. 87 Cooper....T Kelly. 103
Siebert, W M and Louise. 725 Macon....Doris Rausch. 2,000
Schauzenbach, Jessie. 119 Cooper....J Baumann. 493
Shea, J O. 992 3d av....S Heyman. 247
Theuerholz, Marg't L. 15 3d....L Z Murray. 160
Thorne, Mrs G. 78 Sands....E A Rorke. 321
Same....same. 216
Thorne, Mary J. 26 St Andrews pl....I Mason. 110
Tompkins, Agnes E. 724 Union....J McEnery & Co. 123
Valerius, H A. 49 Manhattan av....J Moriarty. 300
Vreeland, Sarah. 249 Lexington av....L G Heshenowitz. 122
Walsh, Mary A. 178 Fulton M Bottstein. 110
Ward, H. 363 14th....Cowperthwait Co. 308
Watson, E. 371 Flatbush av....O'Connor & T. 107
Williams, L 22 St. Andrews pl....J Moriarty. 379
Winans, W. 147 George ...C T Kendrick & Co. 147
Woodbridge, Marg't S. 448 Herkimer....Julia A Condon. 300
Yakel, W. 258 17th....Manges Bros. 188

MISCELLANEOUS.

Aubel, F. 114 Central av....K J Dewald. Cigar Store, &c. 147
Brass Goods Mfg Co. 250-254 State....C Hewlett, Little Neck, L I. Presses, &c. 2,000
Bassen, H. 1399 Broadway....J Matthews Apparatus Co. Soda Water Apparatus. 300
Behrens, I. and A. 142 Graham av....J Behrens. Grocery Fixtures. 1,057
Behrens, R. 677 Herkimer....R Studinger. Bottling Business. 1,000
Best, L. 339 Sumner av ... J Best. Painter Fixtures. 300
Brasse, J M. 616 Fulton....T & G Haag & Co. Barber Fixtures. 460
Collins, H. 120 Livingston....D H Cochran. Printing Fixtures (R) 600
Conklin, H A.. J P Dallimore. Horses, Trucks, &c. (R) 3,000
Crichton, T C. 85 Frankfort....Johnson Peerless Works. Press. 190
Celler & Co. 81 Sumner av....Mosler Safe Co. Safe. 135
Comfort, W B and Ella L and Mary E Sands. Ridgewood av, near Railroad av and in storage at 437-445 Carlton av . . W H Mott. 270
Dede, A. 71 Cook....C Kaiser. Butcher Fixtures. 100
Fleming, T M. 9 Elm pl....C H Evans & Sons. Lease. 687
Froeligh & Middleton. Germania Building.... Mosler Safe Co. Safe. 110
Faust, H M. Vanderbilt st, Flatbush....J Matthews Apparatus Co. Soda Water Apparatus. 102
Gallagher, M. 172 Pacific .... W B Davis. Coach (R) 625
Glasboff, P H. New Utrecht av and 59th st....M Lachner. Market Fixtures and Furniture. 1,500
Green, W. 324-328 Pearl st, New York....Van Allens & B. Press. (R) 2,000
Giglio, C. 349 Van Brunt....A Schwab. Barber Fixtures. (R) 213
Harris, H H. 186 4th av .... G Waterson. Bottling Business. 250
Hassett, E J, and E L Steele. 216 South 8th.... P A Cassidy. Wagon. 140
Henderson, G W. 1068 Bedford av....Johnson Peerless Works Press. 375
Hildebrand, O. 164 Richards....Johnson Peerless Works. Press. 275
Hiltz & Co, L F. 203 Hopkinson av....J Matthews Apparatus Co. Soda Water Apparatus 238
Holly, Anna T. 191 Baltic ...J S Merrian. Furniture. secures rent
Hovell, G W. P Barrett. Furniture Van. 527
Kane, J A. 179 5th av....Mary Robinson. Fixtures. 300
Lohness, A P. 1071 Bedford av....J W Tufts. Soda Fountain. 375
Madadey, W. 200 Tillary....W B Davis. Coach. (R) 350
McDermott, T. 157 Myrtle av....J Roth. Box Fixtures, &c. 1,000
McShane, O....P Barrett. Wagon. 179
Meyers, W. 88 Johnson av....W Hankin, Sr. Machinery. 3,700
Male, T J. 5th av and 18th st....Mosler Safe Co. Safe. 110
Martin & Chase. 188 Ralph av. ..Mosler Safe Co. Safe. 155
Ogilvie, Charlotte E. 1220 Fulton....Johnson Peerless Works. Printing Office. 1,700
Pape, H. 699 Gates av....A D Puffer & Sons. Soda Apparatus. 435
Polhemus, Emily S. 886 Atlantic av....B Fischer. Horses and Wagons. 175
Raeft, E E. 4th av, cor 52d st....Lamson Co. Register. 140
Roche & Hawkins. 348 Fulton....Johnson Peerless Works. Press. (R) 550
Starkey, J and P Braun. 102 Court....E W Bliss. Barber Fixtures. 700
Szparadowski, C J. 290 Wythe av... J Weiss. Barber Fixtures. 168
Simonson, H J. De Kalb av, cor Waverly av ....Cunningham Son & Co. Horses. 1,000
Spillane, P....P Barrett. Horse and Wagon. 211
Stodder, H F. 1659 Fulton ...J A Annin. Tools. 85
Stokes, W H. 574 Court....G E Stokes. Roofing, &c, Business. 500
Sythoff, P and Victoria. 81 Wallabout....J C Collins. Machinery. (R) 198
Thomson, W. 338 Atlantic av....J Downey. Wagon. 100
Terry & Co. 618 Marcy av....R C Addy. Drug Fixtures. (R) 300
Van Court, J H....A W Schmitt. Printing Fixtures. 1,500
Valentine, J C. 31 and 33 East Houston st, New York....Ellen Benedict. Machines, &c. 9,000
Vella, C. 225 Johnson av....A Schwaab & Son. Barber Fixtures. 232
Wolffberg Selma. 57 and 59 Nassau av....J S Drake. Stationery Business. 120
Weigand E. 422 Bushwick av....A Gronert. Bakery Fixtures. 150

BILLS OF SALE.

Bardfski, J. 116 Seigel....S Gollin. Butcher Fixtures. 65
Behrens, J. 142 Graham av....L and A Behrens. Grocery Fixtures. 790
Came, T. 58 Washington av....S L Rowland. Blacksmith Fixtures, &c. nom
Dillon, F W C. 191 Atlantic av ...M O'Neill. One-half of Business. 1,900
Goldberg, A. 29 Moore....S Frankenstein. Grocery Fixtures. 150
Hoffmann, Bertha....E Hoffmann. Dry Goods Fixtures. 2,000
Jenkins, L O. 132 Flatbush av....S C Brooks. Store Fixtures. 700
Mayer, M. 60 Graham av....R Keller. Saloon Fixtures. 1,250
Martens, E W. 502 Myrtle av....A D Martens. Grocery Fixtures. 3,500
McGoldrick, J. Kent av, s w cor Park av....G Malcolm. Saloon Fixtures. 2,431
Struss, J. Nostrand av, cor Fennimore st.... Christiana Struss. Grocery Fixtures. nom
Studley, F J. 214 Freeman... E A Koster. Grocery Fixtures. 400

ASSIGNMENTS OF CHATTEL MORTGAGES.

Long Island Brewery to Williamsburgh Brewing Co. (Mort. given by C Raisch, Jan. 29, 1891.) 500
Thorp, E to M & S Barr. (General assignment of all title in saloon No. 23 Union st.) val. consid
Weidmann, P to Williamsburgh B Co. (Mort. given by C Brix, May 7, 1891). 500

NEW JERSEY.

NOTE.—*The arrangement of the Conveyances, Mortgages and Judgments in these lists is as follows: the first name in the Conveyances is the Grantor; in Mortgages, the Mortgagor; in Judgments, the Judgment debtor.*

ESSEX COUNTY.

CONVEYANCES.

Aschenback, J G—R Sattler, South 14th st......$2,500
Axt, Joseph et al exrs—D Marx, Broome st..... 1
Ballantine, J H et al—Celluloid Co, s s Ferry st cor Westcott st 118x82x100x135x100x15x24x96x80........ 14,497
Bartosch, A F—J N Tuttle, Crawford st......... 1
Bellas, W H—L M Sayre, Oriental st........... 1
Bradley, John—J Kivlehan, Orange 1,800
Breakenridge, J H—L Farley, Clinton.......... 1,200
Same——E D Harrison, Clinton............... 500
Brown, I J—C Desereus, Halsey st.......... 2,800
Burnton, Albert—H Burton et al, Astor st...... 1
Campbell, R C—P E Jacobus, Caldwell.......... 900
Carpenter, H L—M J Burns, South Orange..... 5,000
Carter, K B—H A Smith, Hillside av......... 400
Coe, J A et al exrs—L F Crowell, w s Washington st 101 n Baldwin st 30x118x35x110 7,500
Coe, J A et al exrs—E J Osborne, Washington st........ 1
Same——C B Parker, Governor st......... 1
Coe, J A et al exrs—L F Crowell, Baldwin st.... 1
Coe, J A——same, Marshall pl............. 1
Collyer, W W—J P Mulderick, Oliver st 2,500
Conklin, A W—A Baxter, East Orange.......... 2,700
Crandell, E A W—J L Brown, Eagles st.......... 1
Crowell, L F—J A Coe, w s Washington st 130 n Baldwin st 30x102........ 21,500
Same——C B Parker, n s Governor st 129 w Vine st 25x96x21x96 14,225
Same——J A Coe, Marshall pl.............. 1
Same——E J Osborne, Washington st.......... 2,650
Davis, A V—W D Traphagan, South 9th st 1,400
Depue, Sherrerd—A B Faltoute, Morris & Essex R R av........ 1
De Witt, M J—M D Westfall, Aqueduct st....... 635
Dey, Cornelius—C D Vannus, Caldwell.......... 135
Dodd, G F—J J Rathers, Bloomfield.......... 1
Dodd, R H C—H Knight, East Orange 1
Doland, E J—L Doland, 6th av............. 1
Doland, Lewis—L P Doland, 6th av........... 1
Durand, Allen—W H Rowe, East Orange....... 650
Duryee, A B—J Crow, Howard st 2,400
Eaton, A J—L Smith, Springfield av.......... 1
Everitt, E A—E Johnson, Orange.............. 800
Faltoute, F B—E G Faltoute Coal Co, Railroad av........ 1,500
Same——S Depue, M and E R R Co........... 1
Forest Hill Assoc—G W Huntley, Verona av... 101
Forages, P E—L Smith, 18th av............ 1
Frelinghuysen, Frederick—G Walters, Norfolk st........ 900
Gilland, G H—J Wittkop, Milburn............ 5,820
Gould, C H—D J Edwards, Caldwell 1,356
Gould, G W—T V A Trotter, Caldwell........... 7,000
Green, G R—C F Hinck, Montclair............ 4,250
Hamilton, E P—A Lemassena, Jr, East Orange. 16,000
Harrison, C J et al exrs—J F Hart, West Orange 150
Harrison, E M—N S Colman, Montclair........ 2,150
Hauch, Mary—A Semple, Oxford st.......... 250
Haulenbeck, M S—W C Hadley, North 11th st... 650
Haydon, J H—A Bornstein, High st........... 250
Hedden, C R—J H Worden, East Orange....... 4,000
Henderson, William—E Venino, Orange...... 55
Hesse, J N—L Smith, South 11th st........... 1
Hewitt, J C—C F Huck, Montclair............. 4,250
Hogg, T E—A M Place, Orange............... 18,500
Hinds, O M—G Lane, w s Summer av 385 n 2d av 28x150........ 4,600
Hunt, R E—J Davis, 3d st 550
Jackson, John—H Steudle, e s Nesbitt st cor James st 45x79x37x100........ 8,000
Joralemon, Abram—H M Brison, Poinier st..... 2,500
Keasbey, A Q—P P Ricketts, Clinton 7,000
Same——E Wood et al, w s South 9th st cor 11th av 175x100x25x100x200x200........ 9,750
Kirchlechner, Ignatz—T Maeschle, Clinton...... 700
Kitchel, J T—L M Rudolph, North End terrace.. 200
Knight, Henry—F W Wheaton, East Orange.... 1,870
Ledwith, M J—E Ely, Gothard st 1,000
Lister, J C—J H Dunn, Ogden st........ 800
Lloyd, H M—A B Lloyd, Montclair........ 8,000
Lowenstein, Elizabeth—W J Brehm, Lillie st.... 2,200
Mackin, Francis—F B Manderville, Runyon st... 1,200
Matthews, C B—A H Proffitt, Montclair......... 5,000
Same——same, South Orange............ 7,000
McDowell, Wm—S M Snowden, Norfolk st....... 1
McLoughlin, Ann—J Brunswick, Orange........ 800
McManus, T H—A Maria McManus, Bloomfield.. 1
Miller, J A—A B McGregor, Meadows........ 1,013
Minotaro, Carmine—M Polito, O'Connell st..... 400
Mortland, P B—F Hopper, Bergen st 1
Mucklow, H L—H B Muchlow, Littleton av...... 1
Mullen, John—D Bracken, Orange........ 200
Muller, John—T Joergens, Court st 265
Nevins, Thomas—L Dempsey, East Orange..... 350
Osborne, E J et al—J A Coe, Washington st..... 1
Osborne, J H—W L Douglass Clinton........ 1,000
Parkinson, William—M J Brown, Orange....... 700
Parkinson, Mary—A H McGregor, Emmett st... 600
Pearce, M A E—H J Till, South Orange........ 375
Plume, A G—W H Brown, 3d av........ 2,000
Porter, G S—T Winsor, Bloomfield........ 900
Prieth, L J et al—W Cort, Clinton........ 300
Proffitt, A H—C B Matthews, n s Wright st 218 e Broad st 65x100........ 12,000
Protection B & L Assoc—S Hurd, Dickerson st. 1,900
Protestant Foster Home Society—B H Davis, Summer av........ 1,000
Same——S J Sloan, Summer av........ 1,000
Randall, J M—S L Wyman, East Orange...... 75
Renshaw, C E—C A Renshaw, East Orange.... 1
Redshaw, C A—D Bingham, East Orange....... 700
Renshaw, David—C A Renshaw, East Orange... 1,700
Richardson, H W—M O'Rourke, East Orange... 900
Robison, D A—The N Y & Newark Bay Slip Canal Co., Salt Meadow........ 1
Rowe, J J—E F Rowe, Warren st........ 650
Rudolph, L M—J T Kitchel, n s E Sylvan av 150 e Washington av 25x100 3,000
Sattler, Robert—J A Fritzsche South 14th st.... 2,500
Sayre, H N—W H Bellis, Oriental st. 1
Scheerer, G O—M L Gray, Clinton........ 700
Schmittberger, Magdalena—D Marx, e s Broome st 75 s Montgomery st, 25x80........ 10,000
Schmitt, Lucy—A C Sutton, w s Polk st, 109 w South Market st, 56x108x40x48x58........ 3,900
Smith, F H—W H Mott, South Orange........ 2,500
Smith, J C—J C Smith & Wallace Co, e s Ogden st 118x118x125x191x96........ 37,500
Snowden, S M—E M Nevin, Norfolk st........ 1
Stimis, Henry—S E Burling, River road ....
Sutton, A C—R C Boice Co, n s Polk st, 56x103x40x40x48........ 6,400
Teed, A W et al—G MacAndrew, North 4th st.... 50
Teeling, J J——Kirchlechner, South 19th st... 400
Tichenor, B W et al—W Fagin, Clinton.......... 1
Tuttle, J N—F A Bartosch, Crawford st......... 0
Van Reyper, A E—A Yako, Belleville........ 400
Van Riper, T S—L M Ritter, Belleville. 502
Ward, S S—R C Boice Co, w s Merchant st 165 s Market st 50x100 3,000
Ward, E G—J C Pettit, Bloomfield 6,000
Weis, Charles—A P Wolter, Kossuth st........ 500
Welsh, E A et al—M Lewenthal, e s Broome st 125 s Montgomery st 50x100........ 6,000
Wilson, J C—Manor Real Estate and Trust Co, s s Pionier st 200 e Penna av 30x100........ 6,500
Wheeler, F D—C S Osborne, Columbia st........ 1
Wood, Ebenezer et al—A Q Keasbey, s s Emmet st 36 w Penna av 50x64........ 14,000
Woodruff, J E—M A Wightman, Belmont av.... 1
Woodruff, Frederick et al exrs—S L Wyman, East Orange........ 75
Wright, Mary et al—A C Sutton, s s South Market st 22 w Polk st 100x25x78x30x45x68........ 3,200

MORTGAGES.

Anderson, G F—Newark B and L Assoc, South 7th st........ 1,000
Archer, Elizabeth—M E Archer, Lincoln av..... 4,000
Baum, George—B W Tucker, South 11th st...... 700
Baxter, Alexander—A W Conklin, East Orange. 1,700
Bergschwenger, Johanette—C Biermann, Lawrence st........ 375
Bird, J T—Woodside B and L Assoc, Summer av........ 200
Birkenhaur, Sebastian—W Dorsch, Fairmount av........ 2,500
Bohnert, John—L Leverich, Newton st........ 2,500
Brady, P J—M F Morehouse, West Orange..... 5,000
Brannick, John—A McLoughlin, Orange........ 500
Braun, Katharina—Newark German B and L Assoc, Somerset st........ 2,800
Brison, H M—Fourteenth Ward B and L Assoc, Poinier st........ 2,000
Burns, M J—South Orange B and L Assoc, South Orange........ 3,000
Coe, J A—H F Osborne et al exrs, Washington st........ 8,0 0
Condit, E M—S M Williams, West Orange........ 2,500
Craig, W H—People's B and L Assoc, South 9th st........ 2,900
Crisp, J W—M S Drew, Bloomfield........ 2,100
Crowell, L F—J A Coe et al exrs, Baldwin st... 9,000
Crow, John—C F Gardom, Howard st........ 1,800
Davis, Amelia—E James, Nelson pl........ 9,000
Dean, C G—E L Joy, Walnut st........ 2,500
Dosch, Theresa—C Barkhorn, Fairview av...... 1,300
Douglas, W L—J H Osborne, Clinton 500
Edwards, D J—C H Gould, Caldwell 750
Fitzsche, J H—G Krueger, South 14th st........ 2,500
Foley, Daniel—Howard B and L Assoc, Lake st. 1,680
Frederick, Caroline—Mt Pleasant Cemetery Co, Bergen st........ 2,000
Same——same, Camden st 1,500
Same——same, Camden st........ 2,000
Fried, Isaac—A M Lehlbach, Livingston st...... 2,000
Freeman, C W—F Berg, Orange........ 500
Goskirk, Alexander—G Baker, Summer av..... 1,500
Goskirk, Mary—G Baker et al exrs—Summer av........ 2,000
Gray, M L—G O Schurer, Clinton........ 450
Harrison, E D—C W Harrison, Clinton........ 500
Hopper, Frank—P Waldheim, Bergen st 1,000
Hughes, T J—J J Hubbell, Montclair........ 7,500
Hurd, Stockton—Protection B & L Assoc—Dickerson st........ 1,900
Jacobus, P E—R E Campbell, Caldwell........ 700
Johnson, Ella—J W Condit, Orange........ 2,100
Joralemon, S M—N H Joralemon, Belleville.... 1,000
Keena, A R—B Shephard, Johnson st........ 4,000
Kiersted, M T—I Cairns, East Orange 3,300
Kirchlechner, Ignatz—A Dervine, South 19th st. 2,000
Kitchel, J T—S C Oakley, North End terrace... 2,000
Kosack, Abraham—Fourteenth Ward B and L Assoc, Prince st........ 4,400
Kramer, Anna—E E Coe exr, South 8th st....... 300
Lackey, James—Woodside B and L Assoc, Belleville........ 1,000
Langsworth, T W—G S Porter, Bloomfield...... 200
Leonardis, Vincenzo—First Italian B and L Assoc, River st........ 7,000
Lloyd, A B—E L Hall, Montclair........ 4,400
Marbe, Rieke—M H Raymond, Fairmount av.... 1,200
Mig, O I—T Frelinghuysen exr, Clinton av...... 4,000
McEntee, Mary—C Gallegher, South Orange ... 1,000
McGrath, Patrick—Fidelity Title and Deposit Co, Dickerson st........ 3,500
Miller, A B—S Doughty et al exrs, South 18th st. 100
Miller, Charles—Reliable B and L Assoc, Caldwell........ 1,007
Miller, F W—S Kent, Caldwell........ 650
Miller, H S—C S Stockton, Mt Prospect av....... 18,000
Mueller, Arnold—Security B and L Assoc, Alyea st........ 3,000
Osborne, E J—J A Coe et al exrs, Washington st. 15,000
Owen, R R—E M Dixon, East Orange........ 3,500
Parker, C B—J A Coe et al exrs, Governor st. . 9,000
Perry, Philip—C Lesson, Lentz av........ 1,500
Peterson, John—Montclair B and L Assoc, Montclair 200
Phillips, Nicholas—Security B and L Assoc, Inness st........ 500
Place, A M—Mutual Life Ins Co of New York Orange 10,000
Same — T E Hogg, Orange........ 4,000
Plume, A G—J C Smith, 3d av........ 4,000
Roemer, Louise—C A Feick, South 6th st....... 100
Seewenthal, Morris—J W Welsh, Broom st....... 2,500
Simberg, Golde—J Stein, Baldwin st........ 3,500
Semple, Annie—S A Bonykamper, Oxford st ... 300
Sloan, S J—Protestant Foster Home Society, Summer av........ 500
Smith, P J—Fireman's Ins Co, Jones st 4,000
Stubler, Charles—A Kirschner, Jabez st 1,500
Taylor, S C—F H Jacobus, Caldwell 1,800
Thompson, J M—M Harrison, East Orange..... 700
Trotter, T V A—G W Gould, Caldwell........ 4,000
Tunison, Lydia F—C J Silvers, Nichols st........ 350
Underwood, James—Central av, Orange 1,500
Wallace, S A—T Burnet, East Orange........ 600
Weidenfield, Camille—E Starr, West Orange.... 8,000
Wheaton, F W—East Orange B and L Assoc, East Orange........ 1,600
Wittkop, Julius—G H Gill, Milburn........ 3,000
Yahle, E W—E A Wilkinson, Lang st........ 1,200
Zeh, C A—C Schleeer, South 17th st........ 1,500
Zipfel, John—Firemen's Ins Co, Springfield av.. 1,500

CHATTEL MORTGAGES.

American Drum and Fife Corps—J H Laux, uniforms and instruments........ 275
Anderson, C E—C M Coonyn, furniture and carpets........ 101

Entry	Amount
Beldon, J M—A M Matthews, horses and wagons	2,000
Bell, J T—Hills Union Brewery Co, saloon fixtures	500
Bennett, L L—T S Carley, machinery	981
Callary, Catharine—P Ballantine, saloon and fixtures	200
Chedister & Blanch—L C Blanch, horses, wagon, &c	198
Collins, A W—C Bierman, piano	65
Cooke, G G—B F Strauss, bakery wagon	105
Dienzel, T G—Wilkinson, Gaddis & Co, wagon	125
Farley, Thomas—C Caffrey, horse, harness, &c	1,200
Garrity, James—Hills Union Brewery Co, saloon fixtures	610
Hahr, A C—M S Drake, horse, wagon, &c	330
Halbauer, Albert—F Lisiewski, saloon fixtures	3,500
Heinsinger, John—S Nadel, horse, wagon, &c	125
Hellmer, Gustaf—J Meyer, blacksmith tools	200
Hyman, Regina—J Hyman, factory furniture and fixtures	500
Keefe, D P—B D Robinson, piano and furniture	80
Kridel, A J—Muller & Schmidt, carpet and furniture	616
Koenig, Fred—R Koenig, horse, wagon, &c	700
Kuehnle, George—F Lisiewski, saloon	800
Linnett, Thomas, Jr—L Marbe, laundry fixtures and stock	2,180
Same—J Muir, factory, fixtures and stock	3,000
Marchall, R J—J W Hann, furniture, piano, &c	260
Miller, William—Jesse M Williams, horse, wagon	105
Miller, Herman—J C Reeve, horses, &c	125
National Cash Register Co—M Wheeler, cash register	175
Oliver, Joseph—Hills Union Brewery Co, saloon fixtures	435
Puffer, A D & Sons—C J Lapp, second-hand ice shaver	30
Ransley, J W—J W Tufts, valves and water fixtures	380
Rossodivita, Pasquale—A Di Dio, barber shop fixtures	137
Rothardt, J H—J F Frey, horses, wagons, &c	450
Rothman, Sam'l—E L Segall, grocery store, horse, &c	375
Schilling, William—Hills Union Brewing Co, saloon fixtures	800
Sems, James—P Haas, horse, wagons, &c	950
Simpson, Andrew—Hills Union Brewery, saloon fixtures	500
Sims, Richard—G M Ballard, presses, tools, &c	297
Snyder, David—H Snyder, store fixtures	550
Sommer, Philip—J Dannebaum, horse and carriage	112
Thelen, Charles—J Fisher, saloon fixtures	400
Vols, Theodore—M Raphael, one cutter sleigh	25
White, S J—J M Seymour, horses, wagons, &c	500

HUDSON COUNTY.

CONVEYANCES.

Entry	Amount
Anderson, Thos—A Brook, J City	$475
Barnes, Reon—Mayor and Aldermen, J City	nom
Beltman, E C and Matilda B by sheriff—Mary P Bettman, Bayonne	500
Boyd, Catharine by City Collector—R Davis, J City	1,885
Brown, T C—G T Brown, Bayonne	nom
Same—same, Bayonne	nom
Claus, Emiele—H Ahlers, J City	700
Close, Ellen M—F H Close, Bayonne	nom
Condict, J D—C Prager, J City	3,700
Cox, Geo—E De Groff, Union	500
Crawford, David by exr—H Nederlitz, North Bergen	300
Cumming, W H—G W Deckler, J City	600
Same—Sophia Deckler, J City	600
Decker, C L—Annie Decker, J City	nom
Decker, H S—W P Macrabe, Bayonne	nom
Donaldson, Robert—Mathilda Rothe, J City	4,500
Egbert, T K—W H Vreeland, J City	1,000
Ehrhardt, Catharine—J Birine, West Hoboken	7,700
Eilshemius, H G—G Schiter, Kearney	750
Fereus, J R—J Riechert, North Bergen	475
Fitzpatrick, Eliza—D Gilloon, Hoboken	nom
Foster, J T—W M Foster, Kearney	1,000
Foster, M N—A A Smith, Union	1,000
Gardner, Jno—North Bergen County Railroad Co, Hoboken	5,400
Giblin, Jas, Sr—S McWilliams, West Hoboken	1,800
Gresson, G W—G R Hillier, J City	4,300
Gilloon, Daniel—M Fitzpatrick, Hoboken	nom
Goddard, F M—C Goddard, Bayonne	nom
Goddard, Chas—Susie E Goddard, Bayonne	nom
Gorstang, Hugh—S Worthington, Kearney	300
Goldsmith, Jno—A McCaffrey, J City	800
Hannell, Alex—P Tumulty, J City	950
Hannon, Michael—J Reilley, Weehawken	95
Hetherington, Ann C—Sarah Anderson, J City	800
Hirschberg, Augusta—Anna M F Bucking, Hoboken	9,000
Hoboken Land and Impt Co—Charlotte Thonn, Hoboken	nom
Same—J Gardner, Hoboken	2,460
Horns, Caroline—B M Hall, J City	1,850
Immich, Geo—N Sweeney, Union	600
Johnson, B P and C P, by City Collector—R Davis, J City	610
Jones, Emma A—M Ernst, J City	10,000
Kemp, L S—Eleanor B G Kirkman, Kearney	nom
Kipp, Lincinda—A Hannell, J City	1,900
Kirkman, Eleanor B—Mary E Rubnan, Kearney	nom
Mackin, Thos—B Katz, J City	800
Macrabe, W P—H S Decker, Bayonne	nom
McLaughlin, Dennis—Mary Kennedy, J City	nom
McLean, Shaw D M by City Collector—Mayor and Aldermen, J City	926
Means, Jno—C F Langschmidt, J City	6,500
Murphy, Catharine by sheriff—M J Murphy, J City	300
Mellor, J T, Jr—I J Mellor, J City	nom
Mogridge, Jno—Amelia S Mogridge, J City	2,000
Mount, S C—Emma Siefken, Bayonne	500
Murray, Jas—T Murray, J City	250
Niederlitz, William—H Weinar, West Hoboken	350
Niese, H E—J D Condict, J City	3,500
O'Neill, Jas—D Smith, J City	2,400
Pierson, Susan J—D Mitchell, J City	500
Ranch, Daniel—Marguerite Souariva, North Bergen	nom
Robertson, Jas, Sr—T McDonald, J City	5,375
Roth, Geo—A Knospe, Union	1,700
Rural Homestead Co—J H Pratt, Kearney	nom
Same—same, Kearney	nom
Rutman, G H—Eleanor B G Kirkman, Kearney	nom
Salter, P D—Clarissa Salter, Bayonne	1,000
Salter, A P—A B L Salter, Bayonne	250
Shields, Jno—J McGough, J City	2,500
Salter, D B—A P Salter, Bayonne	nom
Same—A P Salter, Bayonne	nom
Same—same, Bayonne	nom
Same—same, Bayonne	nom
Schmidt, W A—J H Rudiger, Hoboken	475
Schultz, C R—Emil Fietye, Hoboken	850
Seekamp, Hermann—Mary Wintjen, J City	6,000
Sonariva, Anthony—D Rauch, North Bergen	nom
Sullivan, Catharine—J Lee, J City	nom
Symes, J B—J Gardner, Union	584
The Central N J Land and Impt Co—Bergen Neck R R Co, Bayonne	10
The Central R R Co of N J—same, Bayonne	1,000
Tumulty, Philip—C E Reynolds, J City	1,000
Van Buskirk, Dewitt—J V Gibbons, Bayonne	500
Van Duzer, Selah R—Virginia J Cosine, J City	1,000
Van Winkle, Daniel—Barbara Bender, J City	1,200
Van Glahn, H H—G Cox, Union	500
Voyer, Barbara—J Birine, West Hoboken	nom
Vreeland, Marie A—R Staats, Bayonne	700
Whittlesey, Eliphalet—J T Foster, Kearney	1,000
Williams, J B—A B Norden, Union	600
Wintjen, Margaretha—M A Seekamp, J City	6,000

MORTGAGES.

Entry	Amount
Ahlfeld, Carl—Centreville B and L Assoc, Bayonne, installs	2,600
Same—A W Booth, Bayonne, 1 year	500
Armstrong, Francis—People's B and L Assoc, Kearney, installs	1,800
Binkmann, Fred—Provident Inst for Savings, J City, 1 year	4,000
Birnie, Jno—Catharine Ehrhardt, North Bergen, 5 years	6,500
Bour, P A—Provident Inst for Savings, J City, 1 year	10,000
Bowers, Catharine E—Harrison and Kearney B and L Assoc, Harrison, installs	1,400
Butcher, Jas—Pamrapo B and L Assoc, Bayonne, installs	426
Cassidy, Bridget—Provident Inst for Savings, J City, 1 year	2,000
Chambers, Jessie G S—Mutual Life Ins Co, J City, 1 year	9,000
Cole, G B—Henrietta Chesebrough, J City, 3 years	2,000
Dahm, William—Jennina Kemp, North Bergen, 3 years	650
Decker, H S—J A Hassell, Bayonne, 2 years	400
Decker, Sophia—W H Cummings, J City, 2 yrs	575
Dunlop, Jas—D H Baker, J City, 1 year	500
Elzel, J J—P Bauck, Harrison, 1 year	1,400
Fagin, Jas—The Clark Thread Co, Kearney, 1 yr	300
Findekler, Herman—Ann Bose, J City, 5 years	500
Finn, J F—The Provident Inst for Savings, J City 1 year	7,000
Foster, W M—Catherine Hitchcock, Kearney, 1 year	500
Garrabrant, Jesse—T McIntire, Bayonne, 2 yrs	200
Hall, B M—Caroline Horns, J City, installs	1,100
Hall, Jas—G Lincks, Hoboken, 5 years	4,000
Harter, Wilhelmina—P Hauck, Harrison, 1 year	2,800
Helbig, Karoline—same, Harrison, 1 year	3,800
Jordan, T D—The Equitable Life Assur Soc, J City, 2 years	5,900
Kennedy, Mary—D McLaughlin, J City, installs	3,900
Kline, A E—M Long, J City, 3 years	3,000
Kunz, Geo—P J Ullmeyer, North Bergen, 1 year	1,600
Ludlow, J J—A Burley, West Hoboken, 1 year	125
Lynch, Catharine—Harrison and Kearney B and L Assoc, Harrison, installs	900
McDonald, Thos—J Robertson, Sr, J City, 5 years	1,800
McGinnis, Chas—Paulus Hook B and L Assoc, J City, installs	4,000
McMurty, Jno—T Carney, J City, 3 years	2 0
Miehl, Henry—Caroline Roecker, J City, 3 years	1,200
Muendel, Fannie—C M Kramer, West Hoboken, 5 years	6,000
Norden, A B—J B Williams, Union, 3 years	450
Pragler, Chas—J D Condict, J City, installs	1,400
Randall, Jos—P Anderson, West Hoboken, 3 years	1,000
Ricca, Domenica—A Ragaglia, J City, 1 year	425
Roser, Caroline B—J H Cubberly, J City, installs	300
Rothe, Mathilda—R Donaldson, J City, 3 years	1,500
Sanermann, Mary H—T M Hand, Bayonne, 2 yrs	300
Santacose, Salvatore—Hearth Stone B and L Assoc, Harrison, installs	400
Scully, Jno, Jr—Helen Cadmus, Bayonne, 3 yrs	1,100
Smith, C W—J Brady, Bayonne, 1 year	1,000
Sufano, Dominico—Hoboken B and L Assoc, Hoboken, installs	3,000
The New Jersey Bowling Club—A Brannagan, J City, 4 years	1,700
Thies, C E—J Merk, Hoboken, 1 year	500
Vreeland, W H—T K Egbert, J City, 5 years	700
Wolf, Aaron—Emma F Midlege, J City, 3 years	2,500
Young, William—Harrison and Kearney B and L, Harrison, installs	1,500

CHATTEL MORTGAGES.

Entry	Amount
Anderson, Emma, J City—Hoos & Schultz, furniture	278
Bergkamp, H H, West Hoboken—The William Peter Brewing Co, saloon fixtures	600
Bingold, John, Union—Kate Ewen, butcher shop	350
Bondy, Edward, Bayonne—W C Farr, horse and phaeton	125
Boyle, Margaret H, Hoboken—The Burr Brewing Co, saloon stage fixtures	1,500
Brautscheck, August, J City—L G Vogts, machinery, dye stuffs, fur dyeing and dyeing factory	200
Campbell, G K, J City—A D Puffer & Sons, soda water apparatus	1,000
Campbell, Joseph, J City—Hoos & Schultz, furniture	187
Caykewsky, Joseph, J City—India Wharf Brewing Co, saloon fixtures	550
Cooke, Martin, Hoboken—G Schilling, butcher store	70
Dalley, C A, Harrison—L L Carlisle, horse, wagons, harness	600
Darcy, G E, J City—P Ballentine & Son, saloon	500
Deming, Anna, J City—Hoos & Schultz, furniture	226
Eipel, Ludwig, West Hoboken—D Bermes, saloon	300
Fallon, J J, J City—Beadleston & Woerz, saloon, lease	700
Fredericks, B J, Kearney—P H Hanley, furniture	130
Friedemann, Albert, Hoboken—The Rubsam & Hoermann Brewing Co, saloon fixtures	450
Fuller, Mrs S A, New Durham—Jno Matthews Apparatus Co, soda water apparatus	95
Gehn, Diederichs and Maria, J City—Katz Bros, saloon fixtures	235
Hosinger, Nicholas, J City—Mary Viohl, butcher business, horses, wagons	500
Kasmia, August, J City—Lembeck & Betz Brewing Co, saloon	800
Henning, C D, J City—L Bauman, furniture	92
Kimbach, H D, J City—Hoos & Schulz, furniture	136
Khuver, Jno, Hoboken—The F & M Schaefer Brewing Co, saloon fixtures	500
Knapp, Franz, Guttenberg—The William Peter Brewing Co, saloon fixtures	500
Lamb, Peter, J City—P Hauck, saloon fixtures	450
Marcenaro, John, Hoboken—The Consumers Brewing Co, saloon fixtures	450
Maturo, Filippo, Hoboken—M Garone, horses, wagons, harness	300
Olsen, Peter, J City—The Indian Wharf Brewing Co, saloon fixtures	100
Pattberg, J T, Hoboken—D Bermes, saloon and fixtures	1,750
Same—L Budenheuder, saloon fixtures, club-room furniture, &c	1,788
Pflanmer, O T, Hoboken—H L Tinken trustee, furniture	150
Pilewsky, William, J City—Hoos & Schultz, furniture	209
Snow, J J, Weehawken—E B Bishop & Sons, horses, ponies	1,200
The International Grain Elevating Co, State of New Jersey—The Manhattan Trust Co, 26 grain elevators, 10 years	500,000
Thomas, J M C, J City—L Bauman, furniture	445
Tobalker, Clarence, J City—C Birdsall, furniture	115
Travis, James, J City—J Farmer, saloon	300
Turner, Robert, Jr, Bayonne—Beadleston & Woerz, saloon fixtures	300
Verrando, Louis, West Hoboken—The William Peter Brewing Co, saloon and lease	450
Von Teschner, Chas, J City—Emil H P Mehle, butcher and sausage business	50
Wagner, Albert and Josephine, Hoboken—D Bermes, saloon	800
Watt, Maggie, J City—J Mullins & Co, furniture	228

BILLS OF SALE.

Entry	Amount
Brandis, H F and Lisetta his wife, Weehawken—Emma Klotz, florist business	580
Henn, Fredericka, Hoboken—E Wrede, saloon	1,600
Hohmeier, John, J City—J Schroepfer, saloon fixtures	700
Horn, Adolph, Union—J Andres, saloon	900

JUDGMENTS.

Entry	Amount
Becker, Catharine and Henry, firm of Henry Becker & Co—J Osterman	519
Bretzfeld, Morris, Rudolph Bergemann and John Faber—Emile Steger	588
Dunne, Annie—W Dixon	38
Helbing, Max and J Catharine Hinck—P Pfeffer	393
Herche, John—Exr H G D Meschendorf	1,274
McFarland, I E—J E Ketcham	261
Newman, Minnie—The Pavonia Parlor Furniture Co	22
Smith, John—E P Dodge Mfg Co	251
Vickers, William—W Ferguson	208

BUILDING MATERIAL MARKET.

BRICKS.—We do not find receivers in much better humor than last week. They have not had quite so much stock to handle and at the present writing seem to have sold out pretty closely, yet it was only an easy line of valuation that would keep affairs moving and the cost has averaged somewhat lower. Even on the selling side there are now no claims for $5.50 per M., except as a rare piece of good luck under some special influence, and probably the bulk of business has been at about $5.00 per M., with some very fine stock for less. Indeed, the general average of quality continues so good that little opportunity is presented for picking out and making a choice grade to command a premium and it is this attraction of attractive condition that is furnishing the demand, contractors and dealers feeling that there is absolutely no risk at all in handling supplies at the cost and so far as piling room will admit are willing to invest. There has also been some additional incentive for purchasing just at this juncture in view of the fact that the "fourth" is a sort of turning-point of the season, and if manufacturers propose carrying out their threats about stopping shipments, etc., they are quite likely to do so just after the holiday. There does not, however, seem to be any fear of greatly-curtailed supplies for awhile. Pales remain under neglect and nominally unchanged in value. We hear that during the week one or two dealers have found objection made by framers to working on buildings where brick were delivered by non-union drivers, but as they handled timber delivered under similar conditions it is difficult to understand where the fault-finding comes in.

GLASS.—Just now it appears to be a rather quiet sort of market for all kinds of window glass, with local trade in particular dull. It is a seasonable condition, but somewhat intensified by existing doubts and fears regarding the labor question and the effect upon building operations, a feature that will apply at some interior points as well as here. However, rates on both domestic and foreign stock at recent meetings of the trade were reaffirmed, and as most of the fires have been drawn for a two months' suspension of work it is believed the general position can readily be supported. Indeed, some of the jobbers are already talking about an advance in cost and claim to have only about enough stock to carry them to September 1st. Plate is a little slow at the moment, but in a general way promises well enough and rules steady in price.

The following decision has recently been given by the Board of General Appraisers:

Frank L. Davis *vs.* Collector at Chicago, Ill.—Venetian glass and mosaics. Duty assessed at 60 per cent ad valorem under paragraph 108 N. T. The articles in question are small pieces of common opaque glass, 3-16 of an inch thick, 5-16 of an inch square. In the manufacture of these pieces fine gold leaf is attached to the surface intended to be exposed, over which a very fine film of glass is fused to prevent the gold leaf becoming tarnished. The importers claimed that gold is of more value than the glass and that the duty should have been assessed at 45 per cent ad valorem under paragraph 215 N. T. The importers were sustained.

HARDWARE.—The dull conditions of trade to which we some time ago called attention have run into almost a complete suspension of business beyond an ordinary jobbing deal and a stupid sort of market. Operators repeat the complaint about lessened demand for builders' specialties in this neighborhood and say they also notice something of a similar character in other localities, with all explanations attributing the defection to influence of labor difficulties. In a general way prices remain about as for some time quoted on principal specialties, but there is an irregular undertone, with general chances in favor of the buyer.

LATH.—Receivers have scored a point since our last, and made good their prediction of a strengthening tone to the market. Further arrivals came to hand but not in excessive quantity, and found good custom with cost now advanced to $2.10 per M, with the scale of values rather uppish, and a talk of getting very much more money before the month is out. Some demand is of course calculated upon right along; but the main stimulus is found in the prospect of light receipts, all except two small mills having shut down at St. John, for month of July, and others in the Maine district thought likely to follow suit. It is also given out that Ottawa lath are scarce, and even though so inclined agents would find it difficult to bring many lots forward.

LIME.—As we have already intimated, there has been considerable of a racket on the lime market during the past two or three weeks, but just how far the demoralization extended it is pretty difficult to say. Operators who were in it won't tell, sellers in particular showing a fear to have the exact truth known, and all hands seem to be watching each other carefully, if not jealously. Rumors in regard to price are thick enough, and have even intimated 75c. for Rockland, but the lowest substantiated figure is 80c., and that on outside makes, with "regular" stock reported at 85c. and 95c., respectively, for common and finishing. The trouble with the situation has been in miscalculating supplies and running up a big accumulation—at one time 50,000 bbls.—on an unwilling market. The supply is gradually working off, however, and there seems to be a trifle more hopeful feeling at the close.

LUMBER.—More than one operator looked up in surprise, and questioned our representative upon the propriety of a call for information this week. The turn of the month, a holiday at hand, and a natural quiet tone to business were all cited as evidence sufficient that a canvass of the market for news was simply a waste of time, and it soon became evident they had a thorough and complete appreciation of the situation. Even at some of the yards where they ordinarily manage to be doing a little something the dull tone was quite noticeable, and there were a great many admissions that even of the moderate amount of stock moving out a considerable portion of it was simply on booked contracts. It would probably be quite as dull for bulk parcels were trade dependent solely upon naturally developed demand, but between the importunities of agents and the arrivals of stuff seeking an outlet a certain amount of business takes place in some of the staple descriptions of stock, with the circumstances of the negotiation such as to throw weight of advantage in buyers' favor. We find that as a rule dealers entertain very much the same general feeling toward the situation as formerly. They know that considerable work has been postponed temporarily at least, and some entirely abandoned until spring, and are very determined to take matters calmly and understand just what they are most likely to want before investing with some freedom. What they handle now is in the main of goods quite cheap enough to make a thoroughly safe investment, and as near as possible of standard quality only. It is a terrible poor time for manufacturers to attempt marketing any inferior stuff.

Eastern Spruce has lost in a measure the improvement noted one week ago. A peculiar coincidence of frequent development on this market is in the fact of finding receivers reporting supplies expected, as about all at hand and matters ripe for an improving tendency upon the basis of a scant offering and almost immediately thereafter to have an east wind arise and blow into the harbor a fleet more or less difficult to take care of. Such a result occurred just after our last report, and while the number of cargoes would not have been considered by any means large with an ordinary demand they were quite enough as matters are now working. It was therefore necessary to adopt an elastic line of negotiation, and while good luck in some cases secured reasonably full rates, in others there is reason to believe that quite low figures were accepted.

Piling has all sorts of reports, but it does not look as though buyers were losing any advantage and the chances are that stock by cargo has been available just about as low as ever. Some receivers contend that after awhile the supply will all be forward including the raft said to have started at the close of last week and where the better quality of sticks fails to command a full rate the tendency is to put them in chains and wait.

Hemlock remains quiet and nominally unchanged. The scarcity of northern product appears assured, but that does not bother buyers in the present frame of mind, nor do they seem to be much moved by the evidences of a plentiful supply of Pennsylvania stock. There is simply an ordinary moderate demand which does not appear likely to become stirred up for a few weeks to come at least. Advices from Pennsylvania report a good supply of dry stock on hand, and a recent run of logs that about cleans up the principal streams.

White Pine remains only so so. Occasionally reports come from primary sources of sales to this market, but most dealers deny making any important investments and where negotiations have been opened it was only for certain special cuts and assortments to maintain regular yard supplies. Arrivals, however, continue and it looks as though more was bought last fall and early this spring than was generally supposed. Box boards remain tame on value with $13.50@14.00@14.50 quoted and less accepted, and shippers are unsettled owing to continued indifferent attitude of export trade.

Yellow Pine has not come to hand with much freedom of late, but there is enough here so far as consuming wants may be concerned, and dealers are not particularly anxious to add to their stocks at the moment, while on special bills the negotiation is slow and indifferent. Offerings in a quiet way are pretty liberal and, as intimated last week, as manufacturers gradually complete export orders in hand and fail to get renewals they seek the home markets to keep saws employed.

Carolina Pine remains steady and some operators suggest a possible advance in cost. It is hardly likely, however, that the possibility will merge into even a probability for some little time yet, as there is really nothing stimulating in present demand, and buyers' feeling caution about developing a call. It is not the wood, but uncertainty about the quantity likely to be required.

Hardwoods in small lots for manufacturing purposes and occasionally for shipment find some attention, with about the usual variety selected. Some agents claim that they are also contracting with dealers for bulk parcels, mentioning poplar and oak in particular, but are reticent as to terms, and buyers who will acknowledge such deals are by no means easy to discover. A portion of the local trade has representatives quietly looking around at primary points, and while they give no intimation of any great big cut on prices the tenor of their advices is to the effect that there need be no great hurry about investing.

The exports of lumber, exclusive of hardwood, from the port of New York during the month of June were as follows:

	1890. Feet.	1891. Feet.
To West Indies	2,120,000	2,957,000
To South America	2,012,000	1,672,000
To East Indies	661,000	860,000
To Europe	123,000	72,000
Total feet	4,925,000	5,561,000
Previously reported	39,733,000	39,865,000
Total since Jan. 1	44,658,000	45,426,000

GENERAL LUMBER NOTES.

GREAT BRITAIN.

The *Timber Trades Journal* furnishes the following:

In London there is undoubtedly a more hopeful feeling prevailing, and more than one shrewd buyer, influenced probably by the improved statistical position, has during the week shown his confidence in the belief that no further drop in values is likely by purchasing freely at present f. o. b. prices. It is, of course, well-nigh impossible to forecast the position of the market for more than three months, but for at least that period there should be a gradual improvement in prices, and after that the whole position depends on the visible supply during the next two months. A rise in auction values would be very welcome, but it must not be forgotten that every "bid" higher brings them more in accord with f. o. b. figures, and probably another 10s. would make it a matter of indifference to shippers whether they realized their unsold stocks by contract or in the open market through the intervention of the brokers.

At Liverpool auction sale walnutwood, when of good quality and size, was in request, the parcel of 28 logs, per Alex. Elder, going into one hand at 4s. 7d., per foot, but some small and inferior sold as low as 2s. 7d. per foot. The parcel of American whitewood, per Darwin, 89 logs, sold at from 18d. to 23d. per foot, according to size.

At Glasgow there is a lull in the demand for American black walnut, unless for logs of large dimensions, which are in fair request; but small wood, owing to the continuous supplies put on this market for some time past, is difficult of sale meantime, and there have been considerable quantities stored within the part few weeks.

At Greenock some pitch pine cargoes have arrived, and others are reported on the coast and may be looked for immediately. A good many ships have been fixed Quebec to Greenock, but at extremely low rates, the average being about 17s. With the arrival of these ships we have livelier times in the trade here, as numerous parties are holding off, waiting the arrival of new goods. Besides, the stocks of Canadian timber have been so largely reduced here that only a restricted selection is now available.

THE WEST.

The *Northwestern Lumberman* as follows:

Muskegon, Mich., for years the largest single producing point of the white pine lumber industry in the northwest, is falling behind from diminished timber supply. The proportion of stock of good quality coming to Muskegon grows less every year, and considerable lumber is shipped to that point from Menominee and other markets, to fill out assortments and enter into the shipping trade and local consumption, now large and increasing. So manifest is the change in the position of Muskegon, compared with former times, that a dealer of that city expressed the opinion that in fifteen years the growth of the city will have been so large, and the consumption of lumber so great, that more lumber will then be shipped into Muskegon than is now shipped away. This is at a venture, backed by knowledge and observation. Whether the prediction shall be exactly fulfilled or not one fact is emphasized. The important lumber cities of the Northwest are not all ephemeral in their prosperity, nor wholly dependent on lumber manufacture. Time was when they were largely so, but during the years of active lumber production numerous industries, related or otherwise, have been built up and established. Rich agricultural lands have also been cultivated and improved, and such cities as Muskegon have sufficient resources to carry them successfully forward when the immediate pine supply is no longer of great importance. Much of the future prosperity of Northwestern towns will come from the more extensive utilization of hardwoods in diversified manufacture.

At Chicago the market is reported as follows:

There has been no large fleet this week. Wind or no wind, the cargoes this season fail to bunch. No reason is given for this, as has been the case in former years. All that is positively known is that the lumber fails to come on the market in the usual volume. No doubt, however, the decline in product at Muskegon has much to do with the meager supply on the cargo market. Much of that now cut at that point is shipped by rail, and considerable is consumed at home, especially this season, when the burned district of that city is being rebuilt. Probably the failure of the logs to come down rapidly has much to do with the matter, as the disposition of the manufacturers will naturally be to husband their resources. It is evident, too, that lumber this season has not accumulated as in previous years. There is a demand that takes care of it about as fast as it appears in sight. There has been a good deal of buying in blocks at the mills, so that the manufacturers are not so eagerly pressing surplus on the market as in previous seasons. At any rate, the market shows no weakness, but has rather strengthened within a short time. At this season a sag in prices is usually looked for, but the low place is likely to be bridged over this time. If a decline comes at all, it will be later in the season.

All the lumber that has reached the market this week has been readily sold. As heretofore, the special call is for strips and piece stuff. All kinds of stock but coarse boards are in good demand. Long dimension is in meagre supply, and is held very firmly at mill points. Short piece stuff still commands $10.25, slim jims $12.50 to $13, and 2x12 and 3x12 and 14, 20 feet long and upward, sell for an average of $14.50 the range being from $14 to $15.

Cargoes of inch lumber running well to stock width boards and strips are firm.

The *Timberman* as follows:

Speaking of logging matters in the Wisconsin Valley between 400,000,000 and 500,000,000 feet will be driven down the river to the various manufacturing points this season. The boom company was organized about twenty years ago, Wausau being about the only manufacturing point at that time on the stream, but 12,000,000 logs were cut, making the output about 18,200,000 feet. In 1884 118,000,000, were cut, but for the benefit of those not familiar with the figures for the

Wausau Boom Company, of which Secretary Wheeler is somewhat proud, we will state that while there is quite a falling off from the big cut of 1884, the figures for the years since then have maintained a good volume and last year aggregated 86,000,000 feet. This year's crop is approximated at from 65,000,000 to 70,000,000. About two-thirds of the logs cut thus far this year were carried over from last season. The lessening of the volume since 1884 is due to some extent to the cutting out of some of the mills and to the burning of others and the removal by operators of some of the mills to points further north.

And on the Chicago hardwood market as follows:

Oak is still a prime favorite for interior work, but in dwelling houses in particular there seems to be a much greater variety of woods used this year than last. Among others there is a growing demand for selected red birch, and when care enough is taken in the selection of this wood, it makes a finish that cannot be well excelled.

Of the oaks, plain-sawed red is the only variety that is not now in ample supply, although there is no surplus in any of the others. Reports from interior points indicate considerable oak on sticks at the mill, and indications are that the supply will be ample for the balance of the season. Prices paid by dealers are from $1 to $2 per thousand lower than they were the first of the year, while yard prices show an even greater difference.

There is not the activity in cherry that characterized the trade three months ago, but good stock still meets with ready sale. On the lower grades there seems to be a great difference of opinion with regard to values. A certain dealer who had occasion to buy a few thousand feet of cull last week got prices ranging from $13 to $25, while another dealer has been selling some of the same goods at $30. The latter, however, was Pennsylvania stock.

Quarter-sawed sycamore is another wood that is being used more extensively for interior work, but there is still lots of room for the demand to grow.

Walnut is no longer much of a factor in the market.

The monument of logs on the Upper Mississippi is chronicled by the Mississippi Valley *Lumberman* as follows:

The Main river drive is advancing rapidly. Thursday morning its front was reported to be passing St. Cloud and the rear Little Falls. This drive contains logs which are badly needed at the Minneapolis mills and its arrival will enable several of the mills now poorly supplied to resume uninterrupted sawing. On the east side of the river some of the mills are oversupplied. The stage of water is fair and within the next few days is expected to increase in consequence of the heavy rains of the past two days.

The Rum River logs are still picturesquely dispersed along the banks of that river. There is no information from the Rum since the Wednesday rain, but those who are posted on driving conditions there are of the opinion that more rain than that of Wednesday is required to move those logs. They are near enough, however, to render it certain that they will be brought out before long.

It is supposed that the rear Prairie drive is out by this time. There is plenty of water in Prairie, and has been all along, but headwinds have prevented the drives from moving as they should. The bulk of the Prairie River logs are already out.

About 18,000,000 feet of the Swan River logs are out. The driving crews on the Willow have temporarily quit work until a head of water can be raised in the dam. There is no doubt that Willow will come out all right.

E. W. Backus & Co. have advices from the Pine stating that the rear 25,000,000 on that stream arrived in Whitefish Lake Wednesday.

NAILS.—The demand on local account has been limited and the shipping calls could be filled in very short order, business generally having narrow proportions and the market somewhat stupid. Previous valuations are made and stocks are not urged for sale, but figures have a slightly nominal basis at the moment. We quote Cut at $1.65@1.75 per keg for car lots and $1.75@1.85 per keg for parcels from store, for iron, and add 5@10c. per keg for steel. Wire, $2.10@2.15 at mills, and 2.30@2.40 from store.

PAINTS, OILS, COLORS, ETC.—There has been a generally light sort of deal since our last, almost, however, as a matter of course, owing to the turn of month and indisposition among all classes of operators to engage in business, except as a measure of the greatest necessity. A great many of the trade are improving the opportunity for setting their house in order by taking account of stock, writing up books, etc., or running off into the country for a vacation. We learn from most jobbers that collections and settlements have, as a rule, been very successful, and the position therefore is fairly healthy, much of this the result of the previously complained of hand to mouth policy, which has kept the responsibility of a large percentage of custom within the limits of ability. Prices have shown some minor irregularities but, as a rule, regular lists were unchanged. It was thought that cost of White Lead would be revised, but as yet no announcement of new figures has been made. Association Corroders' rates stand as follows: Lead in oil in kegs and dry lead in kegs, in lots of less than 1,000 lbs., 7¼c. net; in lots of 1,000 lbs to 5 tons at one purchase, 6¾c.; 5 tons to 12 tons, one purchase, 6⅝c.; 12 tons and over, one purchase, 6½c.; dry white lead in bbls. ¼c. per lb. less than price in kegs. Lead in oil 12½ lb. in tin pails, add 1c.; in 25 lb. tin pails, add 1½c.; and in 1 to 5 lb. tin cans, assorted (100 lbs. in case) add 2½c. per lb. to keg price. Terms on lots on 1,000 lbs. and over, note or acceptance at sixty days, or 2½ per cent. discount will be allowed for cash paid within fifteen days of invoice date. To make either of the above required quantities any assortment of packages of white lead, red lead and litharge may be counted. The above quotations are free on board cars or boat at corroding point. Linseed Oil has been unsettled and at times more or less nominal with conditions still slack at the close, as a portion of the Western trade appears determined to cut value rather than lose custom. We quote at general range at 47@48c. for Western, and 50@58c. for City. Spirits Turpentine has eased off in price without attracting additional demand and in a general way the market continues dull, with offerings fully equal to outlet. We quote at 37½@38½c. per gallon, according to quality, delivery, etc.

TAR AND PITCH.—Trading continues light and somewhat uncertain, with considerable complaint at times to be heard over the lightness of present sales. The supplies, however, seem to be well in hand and owners steady at former valuations. We quote pitch at $1.70@1.75 per bbl.; Tar at $2.15@2.50, according to quantity, quality and delivery.

BUILDING MATERIAL PRICES

DOORS, WINDOWS AND BLINDS.

DOORS, RAISED PANELS, WITHOUT MOULDINGS.

4.0x6.0	1¼ in.	$ 90	—
2.6x6.6	1¼	1 05	—
2.4x6.8	1¼	1 05	—
2.8x6.8	1¼	1 13	—

DOORS, PANELS AND MOULDED.

Size.	1¼ in.	1½ in.	1¾ in
4.0x6.0	$1 61	—	—
2.0x6.8	1 80	2 18	—
2.6x6.8	2 12	2 59	—
2.6x6.10	2 16	2 65	—
2.6x7.0	2 18	2 71	—
2.8x6.8	2 20	2 72	72
2 8x7.0	2 27	2 89	09
2.10x6.10	2 39	2 98	12
3.0x7.0	2 58	3 12	4 46
Hot Bed Sash Glazed, 3.0x6.0			2 15
Hot Bed Sash Unglazed, 3.0x6.0			85

OUTSIDE BLINDS.

2.0⅝x3.7 to 2.6⅝x6.7,	plain	98	@ 1 71
do. do.	painted	1 58	@ 2 90
7⅝x4.7 to 2.7⅝x6.3,	plain	1 19	@ 1 63
do. do.	painted	2 02	@ 2 75
2.9⅝x4.7 to 2.9⅝x7.3	plain	1 19	@ 1 89
do. do.	painted	2 02	@ 3 19

INSIDE BLINDS.

Per lineal foot, 4 folds, Pine	—	@ 92
Per lineal foot, 4 folds, Ash or Chestn't	—	@ 1 10
Per lin. ft, 4 folds, Cherry or Buttern't	—	@ 1 30
Per lineal foot, 4 folds, Black Walnut	—	@ 1 50

GLASS

Window Glass, Prices Current per Box of 50 feet.

SINGLE.

Sizes.	1st.	2d.	3d.	4th
6x 8—10x15	$12 50	$10 75	$10 00	$9 50
11x14—16x24	14 50	12 75	12 00	11 00
18x22—20x30	19 00	16 50	15 00	14 25
15x36—24x30	20 50	17 50	15 50	—
26x28—24x36	22 00	19 50	17 00	—
26x36—26x44	23 50	20 50	17 50	—
26x46—30x50	26 00	23 00	19 50	—
30x52—30x54	27 00	24 00	20 50	—
30x56—34x56	29 00	25 50	22 00	—
34x58—34x60	30 00	27 00	25 00	—
36x60—40x50	34 00	31 00	27 00	—

DOUBLE.

Sizes.	1st.	2d.	3d.	4th
6x 6— 8x15	17 00	15 00	14 00	13 50
11x14—16x24	21 00	18 50	17 00	—
18x22—20x30	26 50	23 50	21 00	—
15x36—24x30	29 00	25 50	23 00	—
26x28—24x36	31 50	27 50	24 00	—
26x36—26x44	33 00	29 50	25 00	—
26x46—30x50	36 00	32 00	27 00	—
30x52—30x54	38 00	33 50	28 50	—
30x56—34x56	40 00	35 00	31 00	—
34x58—34x60	43 00	39 00	34 00	—
36x60—40x60	47 00	43 00	38 00	—

Sizes above—$15 per box extra for every 5 inches on French, and $10.00 per box extra for every 5 inches on American.

An additional 10 per cent. will be charged for all glass more than 40 inches wide. All sizes above 52 inches in length, and not making more tha 81 united inches will be charged in the 84 united inches Bracket.

Discount 75 and 10 and 5 per cent. single thick on French; 80 and 10 @ 80 and 05 per cent. on American.

HAIR—Duty 12½c. per lb.

Cattle	⅌ bushel of 7 lbs	16@18
Goat		21@23

IRON.

Pig, Scotch, Coltness ⅌ ton	24 50	@ —
Pig, Scotch, Summerlee	23 50	@ —
Pig, Scotch, Eglinton	20 50	@20 75
Pig, American, No. 1	17 00	@18 00
Pig, American, No. 2	15 50	@16 50
Pig, American, Forge	14 00	@15 00

BAR IRON FROM STORE.

Common Iron.		
¾ to 2 in. round and square ⅌ lb	2 00	@ 2 10
1 to 6 in. x⅜ to 1 in.	2 00	@ 2 10
Refined Iron.		
¾ to 2 in. round and square	2 10	@ 2 30
1 to 4 in. x⅜ to 1½ in.	2 10	@ 2 30
4½ to 6 in. x¼ and 5-16	2 30	@ 2 50
Rods—⅝@11-16 round and square	2 20	@ 2 40
Bands—1 to 6x3 16 No. 12	2 40	@ 2 60
Norway nail rods	4	@ 5

Sheet.	Common American.		R. G. American.	
Nos. 10 to 16 ⅌ lb	3 00	@—	3 35	@—
Nos. 17 to 20	3 15	@3 25	3 35	@3 75
Nos. 21 to 24	3 35	@—	3 60	@—
Nos. 25 to 26	3 35	@—	3 60	@—
Nos. 27 to 28	3 50	@3 65	3 85	@4 10

	B. B.		2d quality.	
Galvanized, 14 to 20	4 75	@—	4 60	@—
do. 21 to 24	5 12	@—	5 00	@—
do. 25 to 26	5 50	@—	5 35	@—
do. 27	5 90	@—	5 70	@—
do. 28	6 25	@—	6 10	@—

Patent planished ⅌ lb A, 10c.; B, 9
Russia ⅌ lb 10½@ 11
Rails, American steel — @30 00

LATH—Cargo rate; Eastern, slab

⅌ M 2 10 @ —

LABOR.

Odinary, per hour	$ 28	@ —
Masons, do.	50	@ —
Plasterers, per day	4 00	@ —
Carpenters, do.	3 50	@ 3 75
Plumbers, do.	3 50	@ 4 0
Painters, do.	2 50	@ 2 50
Stonesetters, do.		@ 4 0

LIME.—(Nominal.)

Maine, common	85	@ —
Maine, finishing	95	@ —
State common cargo rate ⅌ bbl	75	@ 80
State, Jointa	1 00	@ 1 05
St. John, common	75	@ 80
Ground	—	@ 75

Add 25c. to above figures for yard rates.

BUILDING MATERIAL PRICES

LUMBER.

Appended quotations are based almost wholly upon prices obtained for goods from first hands. Yard rates necessarily range much higher owing to the expenses attending sorting out and grading cargo and even car lots, besides which must be added the cost of handling and carrying until consumers are ready to invest. Terms of sale also prove important factors and, altogether, it is impossible to give a line of retail quotations thoroughly reliable in character.

SPRUCE—Eastern—special cargoes delivered N. Y.	$15 50	@	16 00
Random cargoes, narrow	12 50	@	13 50
Random cargoes, wide	14 00	@	14 50
PILING—Eastern—cargo rates:			
Ranging 30@40 per cent 12 inch butt, 35 to 40 ft average length	4	@	—
Ranging 45@50 per cent 12 inch butt, 35 to 40 ft average length	4¼	@	4½
Ranging 50@60 per cent One-half 12 inch butt, 38 to 40 ft average length	4¾	@	5
Two-thirds 12 inch butt, 38 to 42 ft average length	5½	@	6
Three-fourths 12 inch butt, 40 to 45 ft average length	5¾	@	6
All 12 inch butt and up, 40 to 45 ft average length	6	@	6¼
Piece stick, 40 feet each	4 00	@	—
do. 45	6 00	@	—
do. 50	8 00	@	—
do. 55	12 00	@	—
Inch spars, per inch	20	@	22
Scaffolding poles, each	60	@	1 00
Clothes poles, 45 to 65 feet, each	3 00	@	5 00
HEMLOCK:			
Penn. joist	12 00	@	12 50
do. boards	13 00	@	13 50
do. timber, 20 ft and under	12 50	@	13 00
do. do. 22 to 24 ft	13 00	@	13 50
do. do. 26 to 28 ft	13 50	@	14 00
do. do. 30 to 32 ft	14 00	@	15 50
do. do. 34 to 36 ft	15 50	@	16 00
do. do. 38 to 40 ft	16 50	@	17 50
WHITE PINE—Good uppers and select, 1 to 2 inch	40 00	@	48 00
Upper and select, 3 to 4 inch	50 00	@	57 00
Shelving	26 00	@	32 00
Ceiling, good to fine	35 00	@	42 00
Ceiling, ordinary	24 00	@	27 00
Moulding	34 00	@	37 00
Siding, bevel	20 00	@	23 00
Box, inch	13 50	@	14 50
Box, thick	15 00	@	15 50
West India shippers	16 00	@	19 00
Rio Janeiro do.	20 00	@	21 00
River Plate do.	29 00	@	30 00
Australia do.	25 00	@	30 00
YELLOW PINE—Random cargoes delivered N. Y.	18 00	@	21 00
Ordered cargoes	22 00	@	23 00
Flooring	21 00	@	22 00
Step plank	26 00	@	28 00
Common siding	13 00	@	14 00
Heart face boards	20 00	@	21 50
Car orders	21 00	@	23 00
At Atlantic ports, f. o. b.	12 50	@	15 00
At Gulf ports, f. o. b.	11 50	@	13 00
North Caroline pine timber	13 50	@	15 00
do. flooring 1 inch	16 00	@	22 00
do. do. 1¼	16 50	@	22 50
do. do. 1½@2 inch.	24 00	@	25 00
do Shipping culls or box	12 00	@	14 00
do Plain and mottled ½@1½ inch.	18 50	@	25 50
Ash, white	36 00	@	43 00
Elm	20 00	@	22 50
Oak, plain	37 00	@	41 00
Oak, quarter sawed	52 00	@	55 00
Oak, quarter sawed, extra thick	56 00	@	60 00
Redwood	45 00	@	52 50
Maple, clear	28 00	@	33 00
Chestnut, clear	33 00	@	35 50
Cypress, clear	30 00	@	32 50
Black Walnut, good to choice	130 00	@	140 00
Black Walnut, ordinary to fair	100 00	@	120 00
Black Walnut, ⅝	78 00	@	83 00
Black Walnut, selected and seasoned	150 00	@	155 00
Black Walnut counters	110 00	@	150 00
Black Walnut, culls	35 00	@	40 00
Black Walnut, rejects	50 00	@	53 00
Cherry, wide	110 00	@	115 00
Cherry, good	85 00	@	100 00
Cherry, ordinary	65 00	@	80 00
Whitewood, inch	30 50	@	32 50
Whitewood, ⅝ inch	24 50	@	26 00
Whitewood, 1¼ to 2½ inch	32 00	@	34 00
Shingles, Pine, 16 inch, extra	2 75	@	3 10
do 18 inch, extra	4 10	@	4 30
do 18 inch, clear butt	2 90	@	3 10
do 16 inch, stocks	4 50	@	4 60
do 18 inch, stocks	5 30	@	5 40
Shingles, Cypress, 6x20	8 00	@	10 00
do larger sizes	11 00	@	16 00
do sawed	6 00	@	9 00
Cedar—Medium to large	6¼	@	7½
do. —Extra large	7¾	@	8
Mahogany—Small	6½	@	7½
do —Medium	8	@	8½
do. —Large	9¼	@	12
do. —Extra Large	12½	@	14

MISCELLANEOUS.

BUILDING MATERIAL PRICES

Rosewood, ordinary to good...	per lb	3¼	@	4
Rosewood, good to fine........	per lb	4½	@	5
Lignumvitæ, 8@12 in......	℘ ton	12 00	@	25 00
Satinwood..................	per foot	15	@	30
Boxwood....................	per ton	15 00	@	19 00
PLASTER PARIS.				
Calcined, ordinary city......	℘ bbl	—	@	1 50
Calcined city casting................		—	@	1 60
Calcined city superfine..............		1 75	@	1 80
Calcined, Eastern		nominal		
PAINTS AND OILS.				
Chalk clock..............	℘ ton	2 57	@	2 75
China clay........................	℘ ton	10 00	@	12 00
Whiting, gilders, &c.............	℘ lb	50	@	55
Whiting, common		35	@	40
Paris White, English...............		80	@	1 10
Lead, white, American, dry..........		6½	@	7¼
Lead, white, American, in oil pure..		6½	@	7¾
Lead English B. B., in oil...........		9	@	10
Lead, red		6½	@	7¼
Litharge		6½	@	7¼
Ochre, French, dry		1⅝	@	7½
Venetian red, American..............		1	@	1¾
Venetian red, English, per 100 lbs....		1½	@	1¾
Tuscan red..........................		9½	@	11
Indian red..........................		5½	@	7
Vermilion, American, lead		11½	@	13
Vermilion, English..................		64	@	77
Carmine, American, No. 40		3 10	@	3 20
Orange Mineral......................		8½	@	10
Paris green.........................		14	@	15¾
Sienna, lump........................		1¾	@	3½
Sienna, powdered....................		5	@	6½
Umber, Amer., raw and powdered...		1¼	@	1½
Umber, Turkey, lump................		2¼	@	3
Umber, Turkey, powder..		3¼	@	4
Drop Black, English.................		12	@	13¾
Drop Black, American................		8	@	11
Prussian blue		30	@	35
Ultramarine blue		7	@	25
Chrome green		8	@	25
Oxide zinc, American................		4¾	@	5
Oxide zinc, French..................		7½	@	8¾
Glue, low grade....................	℘ lb	8	@	10
Glue, cabinet		12	@	14
Glue, medium white..................		13	@	15
Glue, extra white...................		17	@	20
Glue, French........................		10	@	21
Glue, English.......................		10	@	15
Glue, Irish.........................		12	@	15
Colors in oil as follows:				
Blue, Chinese		35	@	40
Blue, Prussian......................		30	@	45
Blue, ultramarine...................		12	@	18
Brown, Vandyke......................		7	@	12
Green, chrome.......................		8	@	13
Green, Paris........................		16	@	18½
Sienna, raw.........................		7	@	14
Sienna, burnt.......................		7	@	14
Umber, raw..........................		7	@	10
Umber, burnt........................		7	@	10
SLATE	Delivered at New York			
Purple roofing slate.........	℘ square	$7 00	@	7 50
Green slate.........................		7 00	@	7 50
Red slate...........................		12 00	@	15 00
Black Slate, Pennsylvania (at Jersey City)............		4 25	@	5 50
STONE—Cargo rates, delivered at New York.				
Amherst freestone, in rough,	℘ C ft.	$ 80	@	90
Berlin freestone, in rough..........			@	90
Berea freestone, in rough...........		—	@	85
Longmeadow freestone...............		80	@	75
Brown stone, Portland, Ct...........		1 00	@	1 10
Brown stone, Belleville, N. J.		—	@	1 00
Granite, rough......................		45	@	75
Lime stone, buff....................		—	@	1 00
Lime stone, blue....................		—	@	1 05
NATIVE STONE.				
Common building stone.......	℘ load	2	@	3 00
Base stone, 2½ ft in length,	℘ lin. ft.		@	50
Base stone, 3 ft in length			@	75
Base stone, 3½ ft in length			@	75
Base stone, 4 ft in length...........			@	00
Base stone, 4½ ft in length..........		1	@	1 25
Base stone, 5 ft in length...........		1 00	@	1 50
Base stone, 6 ft in length.		2 50	@	3 00
SOLDERS.				
Extra		14¾	@	15
Half and half.......................		14	@	14½
No. 1...............................		12	@	12½
No. 2...............................		11½	@	11¾
TIN PLATES.				
I C charcoal, ½ cross ass't, Melyn grade		6 30	@	6 35
Each additional X, add $1.50.				
C charcoal, ½ cross ass't, Allaway grade		5 90	@	6 00
Each additional X add $1.				
Charcoal terne, M F grade, 14x20 ...		7 37½	@	7 40
M F grade, 20x28.....		15 20	@	15 30
Worcester, 14x20.....		5 75	@	5 80
Worcester, 20x28.....		11 60	@	11 65
Dean grade, 14x20....		5 15	@	5 20
Dean grade, 20x28....		10 15	@	10 50
D. R. D grade, 14x20.		4 85	@	4 90
D. R. D. grade 20x26.		9 85	@	10 00
I C coke, Penlan grade..............		5 30	@	5 35
J B grade, 14x20...........		5 42½	@	5
C Bessemer steel squares......	basis	5 75	@	5 45
I C Siemens steel squares......	basis	5 90	@	5 90
ZINC.				
Sheet, cask	℘ lb	6½	@	7
Sheet, open		7½	@	7¾

STEAM & WATER HEATING
BLAKE & WILLIAMS,
197 WOOSTER STREET,
Telephone. Spring "840." NEW YORK.

HYDRAULIC, STEAM AND POWER
FREIGHT AND PASSENGER
ELEVATORS
L. S GRAVES & SON,
ROCHESTER. CLEVELAND.
ST. LOUIS. BOSTON.
92 and 94 Liberty Street.
FRANK M. REYNOLDS, Manager,
NEW YORK OFFICE.

A. B. SEE MANF'G CO.,
PASSENGER AND FREIGHT
ELEVATORS,
116, 118 & 120 FRONT STREET, BROOKLYN, N. Y.
Telephone 1097, Brooklyn. Southern office,
ALONZO B. SEE. 32 West Mitchell Street,
ELI S. GODFREY. Atlanta, Ga.

WORTHINGTON
STEAM PUMPING MACHINERY
Send for General Catalogue
HENRY R. WORTHINGTON
86 and 88 Liberty Street
NEW YORK
Boston Philadelphia
Chicago St. Louis St. Paul

JOHN SOMMERVILLE,
ELEVATORS,
27 CLARK STREET, Near Spring St.,
7 blocks west of Broadway, NEW YORK.
All kinds of Elevators and Hoist Wheels put up and Repaired.

M. H. MACGREGOR,
Second-Hand
Building Materials.
Old Buildings Bought and Promptly Removed.
Yards and Office,
160 WEST 26th STREET, - - NEW YORK.

GEO. A. HAGGERTY,
ELECTRIC-MECHANICAL
BELL HANGER
No. 803 THIRD AVENUE, N. Y.

J. F. PALMER'S SON,
GAS FIXTURES.
Brass Goods and Ornamental Metal Work.
No. 12 East 17th Street, New York.

J. ROMAINE BROWN & CO.,
REAL ESTATE
59 WEST 33D STREET, Northeast cor. B'way.
Telephone Call 381—39th St.
Entire charge taken of Estates.
Notary Public and Commissioner of Deeds.
J. ROMAINE BROWN. A. P. W. KINNAN.

WILLIAM S. BORCHERS,
(Successor to TIMPSON & PEET.)
REAL ESTATE.
No. 1500 BROADWAY,
Southwest cor. 44th Street

BATTERSON, SEE & EISELE,
(Successors to A. L. FAUCHERE & CO.)
Importers and Workers of
MARBLE, ONYX & GRANITE
425, 427, 429, 431 and 433 ELEVENTH AV. N. Y.

J. H. DREW & BRO.,
HOUSE MOVERS,
Office and Yard, 431, 433 and 435 WEST 17TH STREET
Bet. 9th and 10th avenues, New York.
Telephone Call. 337—21st Street

MACHETTE & KENYON,
REAL ESTATE,
239 BROADWAY, NEW YORK (Room A),
Opposite Post Office. Elevator on Park Place.
Telephone No., 2402 Cortlandt.
Subdivision and sale of Suburban Property a specialty.

JOHN M. CANDA. JOHN P. KANE.
CANDA & KANE,
MAIN OFFICE, YARDS,
Foot West 52d St., N. Y. New York and Brooklyn.
MASONS' BUILDING MATERIALS.

PRIZE MEDALLISTS.
Exhibitions of 1862, 1865, 1867, 1872, 1873, and only Award and Medal for Noiseless Steel Shutters, at Philadelphia, 1876; Paris, 1878, and Melbourne, 1881.
CLARK, BUNNETT & CO. (LIMITED)
(Late CLARK & COMPANY.) ORIGINAL INVENTORS AND SOLE PATENTEES OF
NOISELESS, SELF-COILING REVOLVING STEEL SHUTTERS, FIRE & BURGLAR PROOF.
Improved Rolling Wood Shutters and Patent Metallic Venetian Blinds.
OFFICE AND MANUFACTORY, 162 and 164 WEST 27th STREET, . . . NEW YORK.

C. H. SOUTHARD,
OFFICE AND STORE FIXTURES,
Buildings bought and promptly removed.
Telephone call, 21st St. "678."
YARDS—9th AVENUE, 14th to 15th STREETS, N. Y.
SECOND-HAND
BUILDING
MATERIAL.

STEAM AND HOT WATER HEATING APPARATUS.
GILLIS & GEOGHEGAN,
Nos. 116, 118 and 120 and 122 WOOSTER STREET, NEW YORK.
THIRTY YEARS' EXPERIENCE.

F. W. SEAGRIST, JR., & CO.,
F. W. SEAGRIST JR.
B. W. GREENE, JR.
SECOND-HAND BUILDING MATERIALS.
GRANITE, IRON BEAMS, FLAGGING.
Yards, 18th Street and Avenue B. TELEPHONE CALL, 496, 21st STREET

F. M. HAUSLING,
SECOND-HAND
BUILDING MATERIALS.
Lumber, Stone, Iron, Etc.
Office, Store Fixtures, Etc.
HIGHEST CASH PRICES PAID FOR OLD BUILDINGS.
QUICK AND CAREFUL REMOVAL GUARANTEED
Yards { 614 TO 622 EAST 14TH STREET, 611 TO 623 EAST 13TH STREET, Between Avenues B and C, NEW YORK. } TELEPHONE CALL, 920—21st STREET.

J. REEBERS' SONS,
OLD BUILDINGS BOUGHT AND REMOVED AT SHORT NOTICE.
SECOND-HAND BUILDING MATERIALS, STONE & IRON
OF EVERY DESCRIPTION. STORE OFFICE FIXTURES AND SHELVING.
YARDS, 409 TO 431 EAST 107TH STREET, EAST OF 1st AVENUE, - NEW YORK.
G. A. REEBER. Telephone, 431 Harlem. ESTABLISHED 1870. W. C. REEBER.

THOMAS E. TRIPLER,
SECOND-HAND
BUILDING MATERIAL.
BUILDINGS REMOVED ON SHORT NOTICE.
Yards and Office,
AVENUE B, 17th to 18th STREETS,
Established by S. H. BESSEY, 1835. } NEW YORK. { Succeeded by T. E. TRIPLER, 1855.
Telephone Call 474—21st Street.

THOS. E. TRIPLER.
KINDLING WOOD,
FACTORY,
Nos. 532-536 E. 18th St.
OFFICE, 301 AVENUE B,
Telephone Call 474—21st Street.
Orders Received by Mail, Telegraph or Telephone.

ESTIMATES FURNISHED AND YEARLY CONTRACTS
MADE FOR THE ENTIRE CARE OF STEAM PLANTS, INCLUDING LABOR, SUPPLIES AND REPAIRS. COMPETENT MEN ONLY EMPLOYED. SATISFACTORY SERVICE GUARANTEED
THE HALL STEAM POWER CO.,
211 CENTRE STREET, NEW YORK.

SUTPHEN & MYER,
J. S. SUTPHEN, JR.
CHAS. R. MYER.
POLISHED AND ROUGH PLATE GLASS,
BEVELED PLATES AND MIRRORS A SPECIALTY.
STORE FRONTS, STRIPS AND SASH SIZES OF POLISHED PLATE
NEW YORK. { 9, 11, 13 DESBROSSES STREET. 34, 36, 38 VESTRY STREET. } TELEPHONE CALL, 862 SPRING.

JOHN W. MORAN,
Blue Stone Dealer
HAMILTON AV., COR. HICKS ST., BROOKLYN.

C. M. DARLING,
ARCHITECTURAL PHOTOGRAPHER,
122 West 36th Street,
Second door West of Broadway, NEW YORK

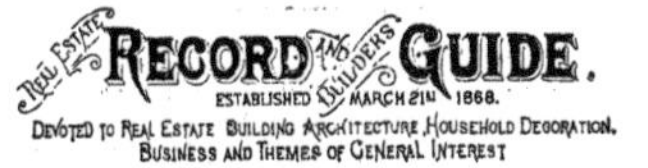
REAL ESTATE RECORD AND BUILDERS' GUIDE.
ESTABLISHED MARCH 21st 1868.
DEVOTED TO REAL ESTATE BUILDING ARCHITECTURE HOUSEHOLD DECORATION. BUSINESS AND THEMES OF GENERAL INTEREST

PRICE, PER YEAR IN ADVANCE, SIX DOLLARS.

Published every Saturday.

TELEPHONE - - - - - CORTLANDT 1370.

Communications should be addressed to

C. W. SWEET, 14 & 16 Vesey St.

J. T. LINDSEY, Business Manager.

VOL. XLVIII JULY 11, 1891. No. 1,217

The publication offices of THE RECORD AND GUIDE *have been removed to Nos. 14 and 16 Vesey street, over The Mechanics' and Traders' Exchange, a few feet west of Broadway.*

THE Stock Market retains the features which have characterized it for so long. There are movements within certain limits engineered by professional operators; the decline is limited because lower prices do not frighten holders, and the advance because higher prices do not induce new buyers into the market. All the ordinary stock in trade news of bulls and bears has been threshed threadbare, including crop prospects. It seems as if the public is waiting for substantial results before entering on any pronounced buying movement. Still the outlook is in the main not unsatisfactory. If the last advance does not exceed the former every decline stops at a figure a little higher than the preceding one, indicating a growing bullish feeling. Just at the moment the market is very strong, news being favorable; how far it will advance on the turn will depend on the disposition of the "Room" as much as anything, and the Room in its turn is largely controlled by a few big operators. Judged by recent experience, there ought to be a slight reaction, but a departure from this course would be a better indication of a substantial advance than any we have seen for some time. At the meeting of the Louisville and Nashville directors this week a report was read by the Secretary, showing that the foreign holdings of this stock had increased 37,000 shares compared with the same date in 1890. The St. Paul showed also a large increase of shares held abroad; and these two facts about such representative railroads do not at all harmonize with the repeated statements made by financial writers that Europe has been selling our securities and taking the gold away. Crop prospects continue extremely favorable, and it still looks as if we were certain of a good market for our grain, but it must not be forgotten that our greatest crop—corn—is yet two months away. We have often had good crops since 1879, but never big crops with good markets abroad and at home. The last conjunction of these two things was a great factor in the speculation of 1880. General business is gradually improving and there are signs that the wheel is again beginning to turn, and let it once get to going it will be as difficult to stop as it was to start.

A TABLE was recently published in the *Economist* giving the prices of Argentine securities in the London market since the beginning of the year, which shows that since January 1st Argentine 5s have fallen from 77 to 67; Cedulas, from 29 to 19, after having been sold as low as 15; Buenos Ayres 1882-6 are down from 69 to 40; Chilian 4½ per cent, from 101 to 83; and Portguese 3 per cent, from 58 to 46, after having sold at 38¾. These prices look very tempting and show why the British speculator feels timid, and until these securities take on a better look it is unlikely that he will care to buy many railroad shares in this market. In comparison with this take our securities dealt in at the London Exchange and we find that since January 1st Atchison has advanced 3 points, St. Paul 13, Wabash 5, Union Pacific 1, with Louisville, Erie and others about stationary, and the only railroad shares showing a marked decline is Denver, which has a loss of 8 points. The British home railways show declines fully as great if not greater than the South Americans: For instance, Great Northern A is down from 92 at the beginning of the year to 72; London and Brighton A from 160 to 140, while North British Deferred is from 52 to 38, and South Eastern A's from 96 to 84, with nearly everything else showing losses from 3 to 10 points. These figures tell why gold was wanted in England, and further show that the British investor has held on to his American shares more tenaciously than to his home securities. In Germany business matters still wear a very unfavorable look. In most lines stagnation is spreading and the market for stocks and funds is paralyzed. The only things which are rising in price are bread and meat, and this is a powerful ally to discontent. Wages are declining and must continue to do so until they reach a point where the export trade will be resumed. Berlin continues to look to London for relief, and the business in foreign loans, which at one time was done independently of London and Paris, is now dependent on these cities for quotations. It would seem as if the first trouble showed itself in these two cities, and it is to them we must look for the first signs of relief.

THE "great popular uprising" for the removal of the Elevated road from the Battery Park, which the New York *Times* has been working up so assiduously in its own altitudinous office, is as frothy a bit of "fake" journalism as has made its appearance lately. In its virtuous determination to secure the public parks against unscrupulous grabbers, the *Times* reminds one of the patriotic footman who sat up at night to keep watch over the British Constitution. The whole business is a silly proceeding, quite unworthy of the newspaper. The "public sentiment," etc., etc., exists in no real sense, and as to the petitions and the letters addressed to the Aldermen, they amount to nothing. We could probably get up as strong a "popular" movement for the demolition of the Times Building as exists to-day for the removal of the elevated railroad structure from Battery Park. The *Times* is simply running amuck against Jay Gould. Few people, from a public point of view, either love or respect that gentleman. There is no doubt that the elevated roads are a disfigurement to our streets and an inconvenience to people who live on and pass through the thoroughfares they occupy. There is no doubt, moreover, that they meet only in a very inadequate way this city's necessities for comfortable and rapid transportation. It may even be admitted that the Battery Park would be a somewhat pleasanter and much sightlier public place if the iron structures were removed from it; but with sensible people it does not follow from these admissions that the best thing to do under present circumstances is to lock up Jay Gould, tear down the elevated roads from one end of the line to the other and leave our citizens in full and untrammeled possession of Battery Park and all the thoroughfares through which the elevated road passes. Even disagreeable circumstances have to be met with common sense; and but for this necessity the position which the *Times* has taken would be an excellent one. That it is not common sense is, we think, fatal. Rapid transit, other than that which can be obtained from the elevated roads, is yet a long way off. It is still some years away from us. In the meantime people must move up and down town as comfortably and speedily as possible. Consequently anything within reasonable limits that will improve *the service we have* is desirable; and anything that will curtail or hamper it, undesirable—indeed, in our present condition, intolerable. To bid the elevated roads purchase the land they need at the Battery "reads easily," but it is doubtful whether it would work quite so well as it reads. A large real estate purchase in that part of the city might not pay. The Manhattan Company consequently, if removed from Battery Park, might refuse to make an unprofitable investment, preferring that people should use some other means of conveyance than theirs below Battery place. Then, even if they were willing to purchase the land it might take a considerable time to obtain it, as the proceedings in the case of the United States Government to acquire land for the new Custom House in the neighborhood of Battery Park show. There is no likelihood, however, that the Manhattan Road will be disturbed at present. The little agitation in the *Times* office will soon go the way of all silly mental perturbations. Public common sense is a barrier to any flighty and extravagant action. The Manhattan Company is not an alien corporation in whose affairs the people of this city have no interest. On the contrary, its system performs perhaps the most important function in maintaining and promoting the general vitality and growth of the city. To check or thwart it means to check and thwart our own prosperity, our own growth, our own advancement. By and by things may be different. Then we may be able to act differently, with wisdom. We are now in the position of the lame man on the blind man's shoulders; It is to our advantage to sit as lightly as possible upon him, and to guide his feet so that he does not slacken his pace nor stumble by the way.

THE tax budget for 1891 has been presented to the Board of Aldermen. Among other things it shows that real estate valuations in the metropolis have increased about $66,000,000, or, to be precise, $65,957,813. Almost without exception the press of the city has set up a howl about this. They declare that the wicked set of politicians who were intrusted at the last election to run the city for us have inflated the valuation for the purpose of deceiving the innocent taxpayer with a low tax rate. This may be all very well as a political cry; it may be, indeed, that it represents Tammany's motives accurately enough, but we have nothing to do, neither have good citizens anything to do in this particular matter with "politics" or with Tammany's motives. The real question, in which we ought to be interested is: Have real estate valuations increased as much as the tax budget says they have? If the tax budget is right there is no good reason for criticising the figures, and as to Tammany's motives they have nothing to do with the case. The Commissioners of Taxes and Assessments are doing only their duty in setting down the value of the real estate in the city as they find it; and if, for campaign purposes, Tammany by and by tries to gull people with talk about a low tax rate, they are only following one of the commonest practices in "politics" as at present understood in this country.

HAVE real estate values increased in round figures $66,000,000? We think that a glance at the records of the Building Department as published from week to week in this paper shows that they have. Let us take the cost of the new buildings projected between January and December 1890. During that period plans were filed for new structures estimated to cost $74,676,373. Not all of these plans resulted in building, it is true; but, on the other hand, there were a number of plans carried over from the year previous into this period. A million or two, one way or the other, does not affect our conclusions, particularly as in the foregoing figures no account is taken of the amount expended in altering and improving old buildings, an amount which probably does not fall very much short of $10,000,000. Accepting, then, $74,676,373 as representing in a rough and general way the amount added during 1890 to the real estate values of the city, and omitting as unnecessary to the calculation any deduction for the value of the old buildings replaced by the new ones, it is shown clearly enough that there is ample justification for the increase in real estate valuations of $65,957,813 exhibited in the tax budget. In discussing this matter it is necessary also to take into account the fact that during the past year property generally has acquired some of that "unearned increment" which has been so much deplored in certain quarters. For the sake of comparison and the emphasizing of our argument we have compared the increase in the assessed valuation of property south of 14th street as shown in the tax budget with the estimated cost of the new buildings and alterations planned for in that section during the year. The increased valuation is in round figures $20,000,000. The cost of the new buildings and alterations projected (nearly all of which have been finished) is about $19,500,000. In view of these facts, we believe that a conscientious investigation would completely justify the so-called "Tammany figures."

THE logic of events is pushing hard to the wall those people who oppose the municipalization of gas and electric light plants. Kansas City is the last important town to question the advisability of paying to private corporations for its electric light service from between 300 to 400 per cent more than the cost of performing the same service for itself. From the taxpayer's point of view—though this point of view does not always prevail—there is only one answer to the question, so Kansas City is now negotiating for the acquisition of the plant of the Consolidated Electric Light and Power Co. In the course of their investigations the committee found that seventeen cities, owning and operating their own electric light works, supplied themselves with light at an average cost of $58 per lamp per annum; whereas, out of seventy-eight cities that depended upon private corporations, fifty-nine paid more than $100, and twenty-eight more than $125 for the same service. The difference in the matter of cost between municipal and private ownership cannot be better exemplified than by comparing what Boston pays for its light, to private corporations, and what Chicago pays for its light, obtained from its own plant. The cost in Boston is $180 per annum, and in Chicago $36.50. Hitherto Kansas City has paid 55 cents per lamp per night—the number of lights used is 114, the candle power 2,000. In the town of Little Rock, which owns its own plant, 110 lights, also of 2,000 candle power, are in operation, and the cost is only 13⅓ cents. Again, Lowell, Mass., has 180 lights and pays a private corporation for them 50 cents per night. Topeka has 184 lights, operated by its own plant, and the cost of the same service is 28 cents. There was a time when it was but justifiable conservatism to doubt, or at any rate suspend judgment upon the advisability of turning over a commercial enterprise like that of supplying electric light to the municipal authorities. The advisability of so doing cannot now be questioned. Experiment after experiment in large cities like Chicago and in smaller cities all over the country has demonstrated, we believe, in every case the advisability of the municipality operating all natural monopolies.

ALBERT SHAW is performing a most excellent and needed task in laying before American readers the results accomplished by good administration in foreign municipalities. His article on Paris in the current *Century* is fully up to the level of those which have preceded it, and contains matter which every New Yorker, interested in the economical and intelligent expenditure of his taxes, would do well to read carefully. In a number of respects the conditions of the two cities are similar, but particularly in respect to the density of its population. New York and Paris are pre-eminently the two cities of the world given over largely to flats, apartment houses and tenements. This density of population makes the evil the worse and the good the more beneficent, on the one hand by simplifying the tasks of the mal-administrators, on the other by simplifying that of the good administrators. The expenditures and the debt of both cities per capita are very large, the public franchises are of enormous value, and the scale of improvements, constantly being undertaken, gigantic yet growing. The case of London cannot be compared to them, because, until recently, the administration of that city was in the hands of the local vestries; and though the tendency is towards centralization, and though the County Council has already assumed many important functions, yet in many respects it remains a juvenile. Berlin, by its surprising growth and great energy, is continually approximating to the conditions of Paris and New York; but it is not yet so much of a city as either.

ONE conclusion of a very general character may reasonably be drawn from the recent descriptions of the forms of municipal government in the various successfully administered cities; and this is that these forms apparently make very little difference. In New York our vain efforts at reform have always taken the shape of some tampering with the methods of administration. We have gradually shorn our City Fathers of the many functions, which they fulfilled so badly, and concentrated responsibility in the hands of the Mayor, of the chiefs of departments and of many-headed boards appointed, as a rule, by the Mayor. The principle underlying these changes is, that a city corporation should be administered like any business corporation, the responsibility being concentrated, and the forms such as are conducive to executive activity and freedom of movement within a rigorously defined sphere. Of course the governmental forms of the Metropolis are far from realizing this ideal in its simplicity—the many-headed "non-partisan" boards being as little business-like as possible, but compromises of this kind with the pure principle were inevitable, and were made and have been maintained in the interests of the politicians. The typical French system is the same with some differences. The people elect a Council varying in numbers according to population upon a scale fixed by general law. The Council names the Mayor and also his executive assistants from its own membership, and the business of the Commune is administered by this "corps executif." The Mayor though a creature of the Council is a fully empowered executive officer. He is a less responsible functionary than a Mayor of one of our own cities who has been emancipated from the Board of Aldermen by reform legislation, but more responsible than the Mayor generally of our cities, who is continually checked by the local deliberative body. Yet the old system worked ill in this country, and the new has worked no better. In England a government by Council simply has worked well. Paris at the present time is suffering from the same lack of autonomy that New York is. It is actively governed by the Prefect of the Seine and his colleague, the Prefect of Police, both of whom are appointed by the general government and are responsible directly to the Minister of the Interior. Ever since 1871 the Municipal Council, which has large discretionary control over finances and taxation, has been clamoring for a restoration of its central mayoralty and a release from its position of tutelage. And no wonder, for the Prefect is the representative of the government of the day, and is principally its political agent. French ministries are too short-lived and too busy with interests more vitally affecting themselves to permit the Minister of the Interior to hold the Prefect of the Seine to a frequent and careful accounting for the ordinary administration of the affairs of Paris. Yet anomalous and seemingly antagonistic of good government as such a division of responsibility ought to be, the affairs of the city continue to be excellently administered, because in spite of the changes in the Prefect and his irresponsible position, the sub-officials are so competent and their organization so complete that the machine to a large extent runs itself. We may safely say that no amount of autonomy for this city, desirable as autonomy is, and no concentration of responsibility, desirable as this concentration is, will give New York good government, so long as our voters are blind to the present waste and indifferent to the present degradation.

HOW the vitality of laws depends upon public sentiment is very clearly demonstrated by the recent electrical executions. One of the wholesomest enactments in the law changing the mode of capital punishment was that which prohibited the presence of a horde of reporters on a search for the horrible. Yet the new law has created a direr affliction; for now decent people, that read the papers, have to undergo a week of ghastly head-lines, surmises, speculations and column after column of coarse sensational detail which common minds love to gloat over. Formerly we got through with the affliction in one day. The reports of executions had become almost as stereotyped in form and phraseology as the reports of weddings. There was a change of names in each new case; that is all. Now we have sixty reporters on the outside of the jail, spying and dodging, questioning and concocting. It would be far better to make executions public, have ready-made scaffolds or other appliances at hand and hurry the direful business through as rapidly as possible. An "execution week," like the one we have just got through, is a public disgrace. If people must know all about these affairs, it is better to repeal the present law in this particular, than have it deliberately and overtly defied.

Municipal Self-Government.

SOME weeks ago we spoke of the city government of Washington as an example of local self-government as a failure, and remarked that the representation of the citizens in the management of its municipal affairs was an unregretted thing of the past. Since then the ghost of a desire for local autonomy has risen, one of the daily papers of the city acting as medium and doing its best to give form and substance to the spirit it has called up. The cause of this apparent reaction is found in the course pursued by the District Commissioners, who have been very vacillating as to the Health Officer and the Chief of Police, and who have exasperated the public by refusing to explain their tortuous procedure. How much of the exasperation is really felt by the public and how much of it is manufactured by newspaper men who have been snubbed it is not easy to determine.

But, at any rate, a certain amount of dissatisfaction with the existing form of government has been manifested, and one might think that a vigorous demand for the representation of local interests in the government was to be made. When ex-Senator Ingalls made his first appearance as a lecturer before a summer Chautauqua assembly, convened near the city, he seemed to appreciate the fact that such a feeling existed, and in his opening remarks threw out some feelers to test its strength.

After stroking all the local prejudices the right way and assuring the delighted audience that the capital would never be removed, he touched on the matter of the municipal govesnment. "There is no territory," he said, "in the realms of the Czar, there is no area in the dominions of the Sultan, the Khan of Tartary and the Khedive of Egypt from which the last shred and vestige of local self-government has been so absolutely eliminated as here. The people are dumb, and have no voice in the selection of the executive officers by whom the functions of the municipality are exercised. They are taxed without being either represented or consulted. Their rights are enforced and their wrongs redressed in courts and tribunals appointed by the President without their consent. Their children are taught in schools over which their control is nominal. The police, public health, street improvements, parks, and the protection of life, property and liberty, all are under exterior supervision."

The speaker, who it should be remembered had been, while in the Senate, chairman of the committee on the District of Columbia, added much more in the same strain, but said that strange as it might seem the people appeared to be contented and happy under this despotism. This statement was greeted by cries of both "no" and "yes" from all parts of the auditorium. He commented on the fact that they were not decided among themselves, and then declared, "I have no doubt that if the question were to be submitted to the people, whether they should resume the old system of popular suffrage or retain the present form of government, the present would be sustained by an overwhelming majority." This confession of faith was greeted with loud and continued applause.

The speaker further admitted that it is discouraging and discreditable to free popular institutions, that Washington with popular suffrage and self-government abrogated should be "the best governed city on this continent;" and he concluded this portion of his address by propounding the conundrum, "If it works well in Washington why should it not work well everywhere else in this country?"

We have already asked those who are so fond of governing great cities from the state capitals why they do not point to Washington as the last possibility in the way of ideal government for American cities. Probably one reason is that they have not thought of it, and another may be that it is easier to plead for an abstract ideal than to apologize for the shortcomings of some actual example.

One thing that forced Washington to accept without remonstrance her present frame of government was the fact that Congress was bound to interfere with her administration from time to time. Owning about half the real estate within the old city limits, and taking with a high hand anything that it happened to want, the federal government could not be left out of the accounting in local affairs. But the federal power was so huge and awkward that it could not co-operate efficiently with the local authorities, and the result was the customary stagnation of all municipal affairs. This gave the usual opportunity for rascality, which was made use of in the usual thorough manner. The way out of the difficulty was to make either the one party or the other entirely responsible for the city government. As already indicated the influence of the federal government could not be eliminated, and therefore the only alternative was to make the federal authorities supreme.

The experiment at Washington also had greater chances of success because it was in the hands of men with national reputations to lose in case scandals were discovered in connection with it. Its finances are looked after by the Secretary of the Treasury or his subordinates, and no likelihood of misappropriation of funds exists. The despotic board of commissioners are appointed by the President and he is not likely to imperil his reputation by selecting corrupt men from a population that will have nothing to do with his re-election. No other city is so circumstanced that it could secure the attention of equally eminent men in the management of its affairs.

But, on the other hand, no other city of the United States is so situated that it is out of the question to allow it to manage its own affairs. The same conflict of local with superior authorities that played havoc with the government of Washington exists in all the States where the legislature continually interferes in municipal affairs. But a solution that was not possible in Washington is possible elsewhere; the city may be left to work out its own municipal salvation or damnation and let its citizens take the consequences. The whole drift of events appears to be away from trying this even experimentally; but the suggestion of the Governor of Ohio that a constitutional convention or something like it should be called to draft a form of government for Cincinnati is in this line. We at least hope that the self-government of American cities will not be considered impossible until it has been tried.

Six Months of Real Estate.

AT the beginning of the year few well-informed persons expected that the Spring real estate market would be as active as it was in 1890. To dampen the speculative ardour there was the financial stringency begotten of the serious monetary difficulties of the Fall; and co-operating with this stringency to curtail the solider sort of investments in the upper part of the city there was the intense doubt and darkness surrounding the interminable Rapid-Transit problem which then had not been illuminated by the gentle light which the legislators at Albany have since thrown upon it.

The figures which we publish to-day for the past six months consequently will not be disappointing. They are not as large as those for the same period of 1889 and still smaller are they than those of 1890. But the first part of 1890 was exceptionally active in the New York real estate market and the results of a six months' trading could fall considerably below those of the earlier half of that year without betokening dullness. Between Jan. 1st and the last day of the month that has just closed 8,119 conveyances were recorded with an expressed consideration of $142,002,130, and these totals can hardly be regarded as indicating "inactivity." But these figures do not reveal the tone of the market, and it was the tone as much as any other thing—the halting, sluggish, doubtful tread of transactions—which created the feeling which undoubtedly exists, that business has been dull and results unsatisfactory. To a certain extent they have been, but hardly to the extent that popular impression runs. Compared with 1890 the number of conveyances recorded this year were 966 fewer and the amount involved $26,169,677 less, while along with these figures goes the further fact that the average amount involved in each conveyance was in round figures only $17,500 this year against about $18,500 last year. The decline in this latter particular is partly to be accounted for by the larger proportion of 23d and 24th Ward property transferred this year, the proportion to the whole number of transfers being about 4.2 per cent against about 3.8 in 1890. No doubt there has been some slight curtailment of prices, and our tables show it; no doubt, moreover, a somewhat cheaper grade of property has formed a larger part of the transactions than a year ago, and these facts, each in a degree not exactly calculable, have been the cause of the lower average—amount of the conveyances. Still, in these figures there is nothing indicative of any particular weakness, and when we say real estate has felt the depression which has touched more or less every trade, the market for the past six months has been adequately described.

One matter in our conveyance tables worth noticing is the increase in the proportion of nominal deeds compared with 1889 and 1890. This year the proportion is about 28 per cent., last year it was 25 per cent, and in 1889, 22 per cent of the whole number of deeds recorded.

The mortgage tables reveal some financial weakness on the part of purchasers and holders of real estate. During the six months 7,982 mortgages were filed for $99,188,254, against 8,346 for (deducting certain corporation mortgages specified in our tables) $106,336,743 in 1890, and 7,739 for $99,345,462 in 1889. Here, again, to interpret these figures properly, we must convert them into statements of proportion. This year the proportion which the amount of mortgages bears to the purchase-value expressed in the conveyances is about 69 per cent, in 1890 it was 63 per cent and in 1889 62 per cent. Of the $99,188,254 loaned on real estate mortgage this year $16,627,264 was at a rate of interest less than 5 per cent. $51,745,264 was at 5 per cent. and $30,815,726 at more than 5 per cent. Compared with 1889, when about the same amount of money was loaned, a somewhat larger proportion has been furnished this year by the Savings Banks and Trust Companies and a considerably smaller proportion was loaned at rates less than 5 per cent. At the 5 per cent rate a larger proportionate sum was loaned. Conservative judges would hardly consider a general equity of 31 per cent in real property purchased too small unless in times of very severe disturbance, so that the mortgage tables may be regarded as not unassuring.

In all sections of the city there has been during the past six months, when compared with 1890, a falling off in building operations. Instead of plans being filed for 2,025 buildings, costing $45,698,511, the figures of last year, only 1,589 buildings were projected, estimated to cost but $34,500,816. The only district that shows an advance over last year is the 23d and 24th Wards, and there fewer buildings were planned for, but at a greater cost per building, so that the monetary total is larger than in 1890. The figures are for 1890, 422 buildings to cost $2,225,288; for 1891, 393 building to cost $2,256,718. In the other sections of the city the decline in operations is pretty evenly distributed, so that it is plain that some common cause has been at work producing a curtailment of buildings. This robs the tables of any particular significance. The East Side and West Side of the city, south of 14th street, and north of 14th street, have all alike shared in the depression for which, undoubtedly, the financial stringency and the labor troubles are responsible. The falling off in activity may be regarded in general as a good thing. In the upper sections of the city there were unmistakable signs, as we have shown in our East and West Side Supplements, of over-building, which nothing short of a financial disaster would check. The monetary stringency called a halt to much ill-considered work and caused not a little property to pass into stronger hands.

SIX MONTHS OF REAL ESTATE.

NEW YORK CONVEYANCES.

	No. Conveys.	Amount.	No. Nom.	No. 23d & 24th W.	Amount.	No. Nom.
1891.						
January	1,072	$16,5?7,0?6	344	214	$758,507	61
February	1,009	17,862,630	310	161	738,700	41
March	1,316	25,411,524	364	222	1,093,110	67
April	1,844	31,679,981	536	256	1,400,333	73
May	1,432	26,644,170	417	214	1,?93,657	55
June	1,426	23,876,549	322	284	924,769	56
Total	8,119	$142,002,130	2,293	1,355	$5,949,076	358
1890.						
January	1,234	$22,416,586	370	174	$689,545	59
February	1,167	22,289,285	334	177	725,680	56
March	1,301	27,119,325	333	209	924,958	54
April	2,151	35,797,732	467	241	1,517,291	75
May	1,725	35,729,268	438	227	1,60?,669	49
June	1,447	24,819,611	365	293	1,096,555	59
Total	9,085	$168,?71,8?7	2,307	1,324	$6,555,698	350
1889.						
January	1,212	$20,877,405	325	207	$754,225	54
February	1,185	22,169,835	288	172	665,331	41
March	1,413	25,937,167	385	274	1,092,734	71
April	1,889	26,012,316	305	271	1,081,177	55
May	1,725	33,587,799	288	298	2,146,114	77
June	1,276	31,106,161	324	256	1,329,641	58
Total	8,700	$159,740,683	1,915	1,478	$7,069,202	356

MORTGAGES.

	No Morts.	Amount.	No. at 5 p. c.	Amount.	No. at less than 5 p. c.	Amount.	No. to B. T. & I. Cos.	Amount.
1891.								
January	1,172	$12,656,066	546	$6,446,187	93	$1,912,030	145	$3,616,800
February	948	12,055,307	440	5,6?4,014	102	2,197,450	154	3,508,469
March	1,316	17,065,964	617	8,428,567	142	3,295,024	243	6,101,259
April	1,579	21,496,817	832	11,175,016	164	3,998,818	244	7,341,671
May	1,474	21,251,337	7?2	11,709,299	154	3,219,067	217	5,516,768
June	1,498	14,662,764	914	8,354,231	101	2,004,885	176	3,529,499
Total	7,982	$99,186,254	4,111	$?1,743,264	756	$16,627,264	1,179	$29,614,461
1890.								
January	1,294	$16,728,539	619	$9,511,809	165	$3,011,699	185	$4,842,600
February	1,162	‡55,788,071	535	10,171,151	126	‡42,809,285	183	‡45,698,779
March	1,333	†21,352,332	572	†12,348,394	174	3,385,300	178	†8,334,401
April	1,552	19,488,431	839	9,439,630	176	3,478,396	244	4,047,746
May	1,506	21,027,775	738	10,265,276	183	4,28?,750	231	6,028,200
June	1,410	16,951,595	722	9,601,463	147	3,014,400	182	4,219,840
Total	8,346	$151,336,748	4,025	$61,487,698	971	$59,589,680	1,203	$73,166,566
1889.								
January	1,146	$15,511,299	467	$5,491,671	140	$3,588,020	163	$4,474,461
February	1,101	13,910,257	560	7,160,758	107	2,542,325	150	4,075,000
March	1,288	16,140,125	569	7,684,381	144	2,594,847	151	3,102,900
April	1,567	19,620,823	801	9,745,845	208	4,355,787	210	4,949,000
May	1,489	20,528,6?6	714	9,339,302	227	4,560,250	242	5,650,807
June	1,133	13,634,932	537	6,108,975	146	2,827,469	172	3,677,800
Total	7,739	$99,341,462	3,6?8	$45,450,882	972	$20,478,668	1,078	$25,636,968

‡Includes mortgage given by the Manhattan and Metropolitan Elevated Railway Companies on real and personal property to The Central Trust Co. for $40,000,000.

†Includes mort. given by the Edison Illuminating Co. to The Central Trust Co. for $5,000,000.

NEW YORK BUILDINGS PROJECTED DURING SIX MONTHS, GIVEN BY DISTRICTS.

	1889. Jan. to June, inc.	1890. Jan. to June, inc.	1891. Jan. to June, inc.
Total No. of plans filed	1,187	1,168	948
Total No. of buildings projected	2,170	2,025	1,589
Estimated cost	$41,084,072	$45,698,511	$34,500,816
No south of 14th st	300	279	246
Cost	$10,246,045	$12,558,650	$9,069,200
No. bet 14th and 59th sts	191	248	196
Cost	$4,850,875	$9,572,390	$6,830,245
No. bet 59th and 125th sts, east of 5th av	355	346	290
Cost	$5,578,540	$6,272,865	$4,278,698
No bet 59th and 125th sts, west of 8th av	520	464	374
Cost	$12,13?,?50	$11,079,500	$9,541,600
No. bet 110th and 125th sts, 5th and 8th avs	59	67	37
Cost	$1,613,550	$1,390,000	$755,000
No. north of 125th st	271	201	128
Cost	$3,755,935	$2,293,518	$1,769,360
No. 23d and 24th Wards	469	422	393
Cost	$2,859,557	$2,225,288	$2,256,718

NEW YORK BUILDINGS PROJECTED DURING JUNE, GIVEN BY DISTRICTS.

	1889. June.	1890. June.	1891. June.
Total No. of buildings projected	380	323	230
Estimated cost	$7,793,967	$8,492,493	$5,087,998
No. south of 14th st	56	46	37
Cost	$1,983,800	$1,922,800	$1,464,100
No. bet 14th and 59th sts	24	42	18
Cost	$681,100	$2,810,700	$1,210,400
No. bet 59th and 125th sts, east of 5th av	63	44	39
Cost	$1,083,?0?	$616,690	$695,063
No. bet 59th and 125th sts, west of 8th av.	115	93	66
Cost	$2,945,550	$2,029,050	$1,410,000
No. bet 110th and 125th sts, 5th and 8th avs	18	10	....
Cost	$215,500	$356,000	....
No. north of 125th st	21	25	8
Cost	$255,600	$313,350	$57,?00
No. 23d and 24th Wards	83	61	65
Cost	$629,21?	$448,903	$251,184

	1889 No. b'ld'gs.	1889 Cost.	1890 No. b'ld'gs.	1890 Cost.	1891 No. b'ld'gs.	1891 Cost.
January	250	$4,040,390	228	$5,473,700	141	$3,267,953
February	298	5,477,475	316	7,087,675	219	3,922,620
March	397	6,753,975	350	6,709,438	313	5,607,920
April	434	8,988,790	384	8,743,980	370	7,784,178
May	411	8,029,475	424	9,191,225	316	8,760,150
June	380	7,793,967	323	8,494,493	230	5,087,998
Total	2,170	$41,084,072	2,025	$45,698,511	1,589	$34,500,816

FOR THE MONTH OF JUNE, 1891, CLASSIFIED.

	Flats and Tenem'ts No.	Flats and Tenem'ts Cost.	Private Dwell'gs No.	Private Dwell'gs Cost.	Hotels, Stores, Churches, Office Build'gs, &c. No.	Hotels, Stores, Churches, Office Build'gs, &c. Cost.	Miscellaneous, Stables, Shops, &c. No.	Miscellaneous, Stables, Shops, &c. Cost.
South of 14th st	23	$337,000	..	....	7	$832,000	7	$95,100
Bet 14th and 59th sts	3	65,000	1	$65,000	6	868,000	8	$212,400
Bet 59th and 125th sts, east of 5th av.	24	451,000	5	99,000	5	134,353	5	10,700
Bet 59th and 125th sts, west of 8th av	10	217,000	44	911,500	3	205,000	6	76,500
Bet 110th and 125th sts, 5th & 8th avs	..	....	..	....	.	....	..	....
North of 125th st	2	30,000	2	7,900	.	....	4	19,360
23d & 24th Wards	4	58,000	42	129,550	3	39,500	16	19,035
Total for June 1891.	66	$1,253,000	94	$1,223,050	24	$2,078,853	46	$433,095
Total for June 1890.	136	$2,856,500	104	$1,259,250	37	$4,096,523	46	$270,220

THE COSTLIEST BUILDINGS.

Location and Character.	Owners.	Cost.
Nassau st, e s, 78.11 n Ann st, seven-story office building	John Petrit	$400,000
William st, No. 64, eight-story office building	Germania Fire Ins. Co.	200,000
40th st, Nos. 113-119 W., five-story club-house	A. C. Clark	200,000
51st st, n s, bet Broadway and 7th av, seven-story factory	H. A. C. Taylor	150,000
56th st, No. 3 E., five-story dwelling	J. T. Woodward	65,000
60th st, s s, 311 w 9th av, five-story school	Paulist Fathers	50,000
Riverside av, n e cor 90th st, two-story dwelling	J. Matthews, Brooklyn	80,000
West End av, n e cor 77th st, one, two and three-story chapel and school	Reformed Protestant Dutch Church	150,000
4th av, e s, bet 33d and 34th sts, one and three-story armory	Mayor, &c.	350,000
7th av, n e cor 56th st, seven-story hotel	B. Mortimer	175,000
Ten buildings, to cost		$1,820,000

FLATS AND DWELLINGS IN ROWS.

Location and Character.	Owners.	Cost.
Pike st, n e cor Madison st, two six-story flats	Herter Bros	$84,000
70th st, s s, 125 e Columbus av, ten four-story dwellings	J. T. & J. A. Farley	210,000
88d st, n s, 150 w 8th av, nine four-story dwellings	C. H. Lindsley	198,000
67th st, s s, 350 w 8th av, five four-story dwellings	G. Edgar	125,000
87th st, n s, 121 w Av B, seven five-story flats	Moore & McLaughlin	126,000
88th st, s s, 125 e Av A, nine five-story flats	Same	162,000
102d st, n s, 100 w West End av, five three-story dwellings	C. G. Judson	75,000
Riverside av, n e cor 78th st, seven three and four-story dwellings	C. R. Robert, Oakdale, L. I.	178,000
West End av, s w cor 85th st, eight three and four-story dwellings	R. G. Platt	99,000
Sixty-two buildings, to cost		$1,257,000

KINGS COUNTY CONVEYANCES.

	1890. Number.	1890. Am't involved.	1890. Nom.	1891. Number.	1891. Am't involved.	1891. Nom.
January	1,342	$5,816,828	341	1,429	*$7,878,196	412
February	1,293	5,187,587	344	1,219	4,704,985	390
March	1,685	7,6?8,870	423	1,602	6,245,195	475
April	2,176	11,587,703	49?	1,998	9,042,227	490
May	1,882	9,317,276	437	1,802	7,230,963	482
June	1,515	5,920,270	357	1,731	6,233,014	405
Total	9,893	$45,388,532	2,392	9,781	$41,334,580	2,654

KINGS COUNTY MORTGAGES.

	1890 No.	1890 Am't involved.	1890 No. at 5 per cent. or less.	1890 Am't involved.	1891 No.	1891 Am't involved.	1891 No. at 5 per cent. or less.	1891 Am't involved.
Jan.	1,264	$4,994,740	798	$3,455,240	1,182	†$14,007,748	620	$2,417,480
Feb.	960	4,117,787	553	2,639,475	1,082	4,123,056	615	2,802,984
March	1,272	5,643,729	780	3,916,105	1,229	5,147,777	682	3,072,420
April	1,679	6,575,719	1,067	4,586,146	1,581	6,871,680	917	4,165,699
May	1,516	6,042,149	917	4,233,752	1,272	5,059,614	680	2,941,829
June	1,332	5,488,301	772	3,937,174	1,460	5,654 829	792	3,727,914
Total	8,013	$32,862,415	4,892	$22,737,892	7,806	$40,864,729	4,306	$19,138,386

*Includes seven deeds at a total of $1,560,000 given by the various sugar companies in Brooklyn to The American Sugar Refining Co. of New Jersey.

†Includes mortgage given by The American Sugar Refining Co. of New Jersey to The Central Trust Co. of New York, for $10,000,000.

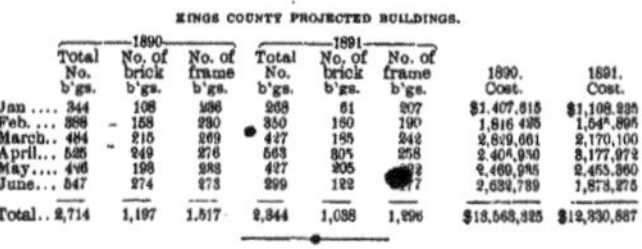

KINGS COUNTY PROJECTED BUILDINGS.

	1890 Total No. b'gs.	1890 No. of brick b'gs.	1890 No. of frame b'gs.	1891 Total No. b'gs.	1891 No. of brick b'gs.	1891 No. of frame b'gs.	1890. Cost.	1891. Cost.
Jan....	344	108	236	268	61	207	$1,407,615	$1,108,235
Feb....	388	158	230	350	160	190	1,816,425	1,548,895
March..	484	215	269	427	185	242	2,829,661	2,170,100
April...	525	249	276	563	305	258	2,408,930	3,177,972
May....	496	198	298	427	205	[illegible]	2,469,985	2,453,360
June...	547	274	273	299	122	[illegible]77	2,632,789	1,873,275
Total..	2,714	1,197	1,517	2,344	1,038	1,296	$13,563,325	$12,330,887

Investments—Good and Bad.

PAST, PRESENT AND FUTURE.—An ingenious calculator has caused a great deal of talk in the last week by showing how and by what means the prices of Trunk line stocks, Easterns and Westerns, have fallen off in the last decade, and it is argued therefrom that the causes which brought about those declines will still continue to operate with similar results in future. This is as much as to say that railroad managers are an exception to the rule, that one learns from experience. It also overlooks the fact of the severe discount that has been made of whatever unfavorable conditions previously prevailed. It is always in times of low prices and uncertainty that such statements and arguments are most prevalent. Their influence appears to be larger than it really is, no credit being given to the blue pill which accompanies them. The times have been exceedingly unpropitious to purchase operations, both investment and speculative, in the stock market and have not the best of promise for the very immediate future, but for one not very near nor so very distant there is much promise. This country suffers periodically from a limited capital being allied to unlimited enterprise. When this faculty of unlimited enterprise has full swing large loans are made abroad, mostly in the form of sales of securities with which a guarantee of repurchase goes; when guarantee is presented it has to be honored, and results in repressing the enterprise for long or short periods, during which a most aggravating chafing is kept up from one ocean to the other as business declnes on all sides. Being a luxurious nation it is an immense importer, by which reason it increases its foreign obligations. Moreover, being a producer of gold in excess of its requirements, this country is largely drawn upon for that metal whenever and wherever it is urgently needed.

The causes adverse to the industry of this country have been operating for some years now, during which railroad extensions have been curtailed and railroad managers have been learning a lesson which has stood them in good stead and which everybody hopes they will continue to profit by. A few years ago such a dispute as Alton has had with the Western Passenger Association would have disorganized and probably would not have been confined to passenger rates. That is a sign that the railroad managers are benefiting by the results of a too belligerent policy in the past and are now willing that reason shall even guide their disputes. They have been severely disciplined by the banks which at one time raised the money for railroad extensions and had to take most of the odium for their failure which naturally arose in the mind of the investor. The roads are being consolidated into great systems which tends to reduce the expenses of operation and to promote harmony among the managers. Chief of all the causes to which an improvement of affairs may be looked for is the growth of the country and the increasing adequacy of the population and business, (to reverse the usual order of things,) to the railroad facilities. So it is only looking very narrowly at the situation to see what has gone before and to prophecy therefrom only what will come. To argue that because prices have declined 30 per cent in ten years the opening of the next century will find them correspondingly declined shows a want of reasoning and a weakness of arithmetic. After what the country has gone through every argument a bear can drag out of the past is really a bull point on stocks to-day. The values of securities are not made by their past, but by their futures. New York, New Haven & Hartford first 4s, to quote a railroad bond which makes about the least return on the investment of any, does not sell on a 3½ per cent basis because of the guarantee for principal and interest given by the property in the past, but because all the facts taken together makes them certain for the future. It is the same with everything on the list. The past has been reducing prices to their proper level, where their future may be seen and where it can be decided whether or not it will be profitable to buy them. If any will take the trouble to refer to the bonds mentioned in this column for some time past they will see how prices have resisted recent adverse influences, some of them very remarkable, particularly one, the immense amount of gold that has been shipped to Europe, which if it had occurred in a time of inflated values must have had a disastrous result. The influence of these shipments, taking the time from the beginning of April, when they began to be heavy, has not been much more than sufficient to curtail business and prevent advances in prices, as will be easily seen from the figures quoted hereafter.

The more severe the sickness the slower the recovery. The perils and alarms and disasters to which the financial world has been subjected for a year and more have been many and severe. The fact that it does not recover from them quicker is improperly taken to be a bear point on the situation, whereas a steady progress toward recovery is the most satisfactory that could be had. Failures and liquidations are having their effect in freeing funds for more profitable uses; money is becoming cheap, both at home and abroad, with more confidence on the part of the banks in making time loans, always a sign of getting to bottom and a prospect of a rebuilding. The unfavorable features relate more to currency questions and to fears of what next Congress may do in the matter of silver coinage at home and to the unsettled condition of foreign markets. That American railroad securities are held with confidence is shown by the course of prices for the first half of the year. To make this clear the following table has been prepared, showing the point from which the start was made and the great movements since. Nine stocks which have been most active during the year have been taken and their prices given on certain days when an upward or downward movement culminated, though they are not necessarily the highest or lowest prices seen in all cases, though nearly so:

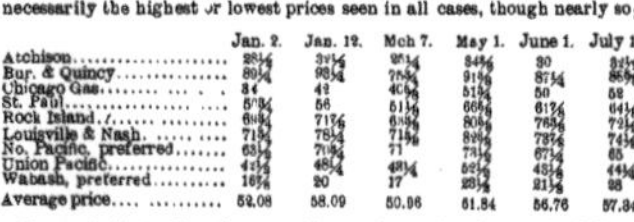

	Jan. 2.	Jan. 12.	Mch 7.	May 1.	June 1.	July 1.
Atchison	28½	31½	25¼	34⅝	30	31½
Bur. & Quincy	89¾	95¾	75⅝	91⅝	87¼	86⅝
Chicago Gas	34	42	40⅝	51¼	50	58
St. Paul	57¾	56	51⅛	66⅝	61⅞	64⅛
Rock Island	68¾	71⅞	68⅝	80⅝	76⅝	72½
Louisville & Nash	71¾	78¼	71⅝	82⅝	78⅞	74⅝
No. Pacific, preferred	63½	70¾	71	73½	67¼	65
Union Pacific	41½	48¼	48¼	52½	43⅛	44¼
Wabash, preferred	16⅝	20	17	23½	21⅛	23
Average price	52.08	58.09	50.96	61.84	56.76	57.34

Now, notwithstanding the many blows the market has received from time to time and the special causes which have operated to make great declines in individual cases, the average price of these nine stocks on July 1st was 5.26 higher than at the opening of the new year, though not so high as they were on January 12th or May 1st. Another important feature brought out by these figures is the time the movements either way consumed. In ten days there was an average advance of 6.01, but an average decline of 7.13 occupied almost two months, and in about the same time there was an average advance of 10.88; the decline in a further month's time was only 4.08, at which there has been an almost steady maintenance of price, July 1st figures showing an average increase of .58. These facts, considering all the circumstances of the case, show the confidence with which stocks are held. How far this confidence is deserved, looking but a little way ahead, is a question dependent upon a great many uncertain things, but there is no doubt in the long run it will find its reward.

The Assessed Valuations for 1891.

A LARGE INCREASE IN ASSESSMENTS AND A PROSPECTIVE SMALL DECREASE IN THE TAX RATE.

The assessed valuation of real and personal estate for the year 1891, just confirmed, gives evidence that we have been on the up-grade in the worth of our possessions in realty and personalty during the past year. When the figures of the current year's assessments were published in July, 1890, showing an increase of $66,711,716 in real estate and $26,427,561 in personal estate, there was a general feeling, in real estate circles particularly, that the party in power was "rushing" up valuations with the object of reducing the tax levy, and so gaining a fictitious credit for accomplishing what its predecessors were unable to achieve. Whatever truth there may have been in this assumption, it was offset by the fact that the increased building in that year alone would have accounted for the large increase in the real estate valuations, and this being the case, it was felt that, after all, values had not been advanced outside of these improvements one iota, and that the large increase was justified.

This year the increase is well maintained, being $65,957,813, only $753,903 less than the increase of last year. In personal estate the increase is $3,506,426 less. The total increase for 1891 is $88,878,948, and this will suffice to reduce the tax levy by a few cents for every $100 of valuation.

A review of the figures shows that there is an increase in every ward. The largest advance is, as has been usual for many years past, in the 12th Ward, which takes in the vast section between 86th street and the extreme northern boundary of the city bounded by the Harlem, East and North Rivers. The increase in this ward, which takes in the centres of building activity, including part of the West Side, is $19,244,525, as against $20,163,165 last year. The 22d Ward comes next, with an increase of $7,079,060, as against $6,979,229 last year. The 21st and 23d Wards come next, with an unusul evidence of prosperity in the latter, namely, $4,462,075, as against $2,668,570 last year, the increase in the former ward also making a strong showing, being $4,473,050 as against $2,298,200 last year. The 19th, 15th and 1st Wards come next in succession, while the increases in the other wards are comparatively small, their areas being considerably less, the building activity within their boundaries being also much smaller.

Of the total increase this year the 12th Ward shows over 29 per cent and the 12th, 21st, 22d and 23d together a total of $35,258,710, over 53 per cent.

An analysis of the several sections of New York City shows that in the fifteen wards south of 14th street, and bounded by the East and North Rivers, there is an increase of only $21,155,751. These are the 1st, 2d, 3d, 4th, 5th, 6th, 7th, 8th, 9th, 10th, 11th, 13th, 14th, 15th and 17th Wards. In the section between 14th and 40th streets and North and East Rivers there is an increase in the four wards within those boundaries of only $8,318,500. These are the 16th, 18th, 20th and 21st Wards. Thus, in the nineteen wards comprising the whole of Manhattan Island, south of 40th street, there is an aggregate increase in the assessed valuations of realty of but $29,474,251, which is a little under 45 per cent of the total increase for the whole twenty-four wards, the remaining five wards, namely, the 12th, 19th, 22d, 23d and 24th, showing an increase of over 55 per cent.

The personal estate of residents, non-residents and shareholders of banks shows an increase of $22,921,135 over 1890. The last-named are assessed at $4,061,268 more. In speaking of this item to a reporter of THE RECORD AND GUIDE the Secretary of the Tax Commission said:

"The tax on shareholders of banks is heavier, proportionately, than on owners of realty. In taxing such shareholders we take the statement of the Clearing House, as made from their quarterly reports. We add the amounts of the capital stock and the net profits, and then deduct therefrom the real estate owned by banks; the tax on the previous year's assessment, which has to be paid out of the net profits shown in the Clearing House statement, and the next quarterly dividend. We also deduct 4 per cent from the amount of the loans and discounts as an allowance for bad debts and other losses. After all these deductions we get the net total value of the capital stock and profits, and these we tax, dividing the amount by the number of shares and taxing each share whatever the tax levy may be. Corporations are better off than banks, because their debts, legal tenders, government bonds and stocks of other corporations which they may be holding, are deducted from the gross assets."

The figures are given in the following tables:

RELATIVE ASSESSED VALUATION OF NEW YORK REAL AND PERSONAL ESTATE FOR 1890 AND 1891.

REAL ESTATE.

Wards.	Assessed valuation 1890.	Assessed valuation 1891.	Increase.
First	$84,844,558	$88,646,169	$3,801,694
Second	35,680,850	36,908,147	1,227,297
Third	39,696,570	41,247,910	1,552,340
Fourth	14,076,503	14,882 104	805,600
Fifth	47,640,220	48,599,920	979,700
Sixth	25,312,300	26,062,900	750,000
Seventh	20,175,357	22,096,507	1,921,150
Eighth	40,158,088	41,138,988	980,900
Ninth	32,521,090	34,510,640	1,989,550
Tenth	20,791,132	21,618,232	827,100
Eleventh	20,400,587	21,074,237	673,650
Twelfth	208,335,125	227,579,650	19,244,525
Thirteenth	18,263,229	18,888,229	625,000
Fourteenth	25,796,092	26,366,892	570,800
Fifteenth	59,174,880	62,984,970	3,810,090
Sixteenth	40,603,435	41,223,285	624,850
Seventeenth	41,022,808	41,663,158	640,350
Eighteenth	82,139,600	83,599,550	1,459,950
Nineteenth	225,647,570	229,533,330	3,885,760
Twentieth	49,587,900	51,350,550	1,762,650
Twenty-first	93,539,300	98,012,850	4,473,050
Twenty-second	133,512,299	140,591,359	7,079,060
Twenty-third	28,559,831	31,021,906	4,462,075
Twenty-fourth	15,836,703	17,648,855	1,812,152
Total real estate	$1,398,290,007	$1,464,247,820	$65,957,813

PERSONAL ESTATE.

	1890.	1891.	Increase.
Resident	$217,439,160	$233,184,137	$15,744,977
Non-resident	11,740,041	14,854,931	3,114,890
Shareholders of banks	69,509,182	73,570,450	4,061,268
Total personal estate	$298,688,383	$321,609,518	$22,921,135

Total real and personal estate for 1890, $1,696,978,390; total real and personal for 1891, $1,785,857,338; total increase, $88,878,948.

THE TAX WILL BE ABOUT $1.90 PER CENT.

The reporter tried to ascertain what the tax levy would be for the forthcoming year. This is to be calculated, very approximately, by getting at the cost of running the city government for the ensuing year and dividing the amount by the total assessed valuation of real and personal estate.

Thus, the expenditures for the forthcoming year will be $35,960,891.22. From this must be subtracted $2,821,610.88, the city's expected income from various sources grouped under what is known as the "General Fund." This leaves $33,139,280.34. To this must be added an allowance not to exceed 3 per cent. of the total amount of expenditure, which is to provide against unforeseen expenses that may be required and which have not been included in the total appropriations. Last year these expenses amounted to about $710,000. Allowing a similar amount for such additional expenses next year, the total cost of running the city government for the forthcoming twelve months will be $33,849,280.34. This sum divided by $1,785,857,338, the total amount of the assessed valuation of real and personal estate, gives us an average of a fraction over $1.89 per cent. But, as the city levies a smaller tax on certain corporations (this was $1.69 last year), and will thus receive less than the proportion raised on other property, it will make the rate about two cents higher.

Comptroller Myers was seen, and he said: "The tax rate next year will be between $1.90 and $1.91." Deputy-Comptroller Storrs was also seen. He said: "The tax rate will be about $1.91, possibly a shade less." This tallies very closely with the calculation made above.

The tax rate for the current year is $1.97. The year before it was $1.95, and the year before $2.22. In 1885 it was $2.40. The highest tax levy since 1868, the year in which THE RECORD AND GUIDE was published, was in 1875, when it was $2.94 per cent.

The Commissioners of Taxes and Assessments hereby give notice that the assessment rolls of real and personal estate for the year 1891 have been finally completed and have been delivered to the Board of Aldermen and will remain open to public inspection in the office of the Clerk of the Board for fifteen days, from July 7, 1891, the date of this notice.

The Broadway Improvements.

Property-owners and business men along Broadway are complaining about what they term the dilatory and obstructive tactics pursued by Contractor John D. Crimmins, who is engaged in the reconstruction and improvement of that main arterial business thoroughfare. Beginning early in the spring (they say) his men have torn the street open in patches and sections time after time, blockading the sidewalks with paving stones and planking, and obstructing the street traffic in a manner which has for the time put an effectual embargo on business traffic.

In anticipation of several months of this sort of interference with their business many merchants last winter deserted Broadway and went into the side streets for business quarters. They foresaw that with the condition of things in prospect and that has existed since early spring, it would often be impossible for trucks and wagons to call for or deliver merchandise at their Broadway doors, the only means of approach to their stores. While they would have given Broadway the preference, under normal conditions, it was necessary that access by wagon to their stores should be unobstructed, and as this was not to be had in Broadway, it had to be sought elsewhere. This fact, according to Folsom Brothers, large real estate agents, accounts in an important measure for the present depression of Broadway rents. Owners of property had to submit for a season, they saw, to this effect upon their income. They felt sure that the work of repairing, relaying and readjusting the mains, conduits and other sub-surface works, laying the cable for the railroad and repaving the street, would be accomplished during the favorable weather of the summer and early fall, and that they could look forward to the advent of a more auspicious renting season in February, with the street in first-class shape for unobstructed traffic.

Now they are alarmed and indignant. The work on the cable conduit is proceeding they say at so slow a pace from 33d street southward and from Morris street northward that it begins to appear as if the contractor will remain in possession of the thoroughfare far into another year. The promise that the entire work—the readjustment of the sub-surface works, the construction of the cable conduit and the repavement of the street—would be proceeded with simultaneously has not been fulfilled they say. First, the street was torn open, and remained open for weeks while the pipes were being reconstructed; then it was reopened to permit of the conduit construction, and after this is done the entire street will be placed under an embargo while the repaving is being done. Commissioner Gilroy has had these matters called to his attention, and has promised to do his best to keep Mr. Crimmins to the letter of his contract to complete the work upon the street before winter sets in. He has had occasion to call the contractor to terms in the matter heretofore, and has not hesitated to do it. Property-owners believe that Crimmins should be required to push his work with more expedition, and if necessary to put on two or three more gangs of conduit builders at different points along the line. They would like to know why, for instance, not a thing is being done on the cable between 23d and Chambers streets. Is Crimmins waiting for the busy mercantile season of September, October and November in order to give merchants as much trouble and annoyance as possible with his work?

Borings in Broadway.

Engineers Wm. E. Worthen and Wm. Barclay Parsons have completed their subterranean survey of Broadway throughout the business district, from the South Ferry to 33d street, begun about a month ago for the purpose of ascertaining what character of earth formation they would have to deal with in the construction of the Broadway-Boulevard Rapid Transit Railroad.

THE RECORD AND GUIDE has presented the results of the work done from week to week, and now reproduces the figures in tabular form, with the results of the last week's work. The record is from an official source, is reliable and complete. It will be found of value to property-owners, present and prospective, since it will afford them the information not heretofore procurable without great expense, of the character and depth of the soil upon which the foundations of their buildings rest.

On Whitehall street:

Corner of	Bed rock at feet.	Corner of	Bed rock at feet.
Front street	20.	Rector street	63.1
Water street	23.	Wall street	60.1
Pearl street	16.	Pine street	70.
Bridge street	20.	Cedar street	70.75
Stone street	21.	Liberty street	70.9
Beaver street	34.	Cortlandt street	70.3
On Broadway:		Dey street	76.85
Morris street	85.25	Fulton street	83.25
Exchange alley	51.5	Houston street	105.6
Vesey street	81.5	Bleecker street	66.15
Barclay street	101.15	Bond street	68.85
Park place	112.5	Third street	53.
Murray street	113.5	Fourth street	40.1
Warren street	109.2	Washington place	34.55
Chambers street	100.75	Waverley place	48.85
Reade street	116.	Astor place	49.75
Duane street	163.5	Clinton place	65.25
Thomas street	138.5	Ninth street	35.25
Worth street	147.5	Tenth street	40.33
Leonard street	96.55	Eleventh street	31.15
Franklin street	88.45	Twelfth street	22.
White street	103.5	Thirteenth street	34.
Walker street	107.2	Fourteenth street	13.35
Lispenard street	68.25	Seventeenth street	10.15
Canal street	87.65	Twenty-first street	17.
Howard street	50.	Twenty-third street	21.50
Grand street	70.8	Twenty-fifth street	24.
Broome street	47.75	Twenty-seventh street	19.90
Spring street	70.1	Thirtieth street	15.
Prince street	70.	Thirty-third street	4.

The formation throughout the entire course is clear sand impregnated with gravel, thickly at Canal street, and from there to Bond street, and thickly all the way from Duane to 33d street. In the lower portion of the route the sand is generally very fine and red, and there are streaks of it at intervals in the district above Duane street; but generally above Duane street the sand is of a coarser cleaner grit. The results from the underground railroad point of view are in the highest degree satisfactory. They indicate that through the important business section of the city, from South Ferry to 11th street, the shield by means of which the excavation will be made can be pushed rapidly without rock obstruction or necessity for blasting, and without in the slightest degree affecting the foundation of buildings along the line.

Street Opening Proceedings.

Application will be made to the Supreme Court, at a Special Term on August 4, 1891, for the appointment of a Commissioner of Estimate and Assessment, in the place of Henry A. Gildersleeve, resigned, in the matter of acquiring title to lands for a public park at or near Corlear's Hook, in the 7th Ward.

The Commissioners of Estimate and Assessment in the matter of opening Woodruff street, from the Southern Boulevard to the centre of Bronx River, in the 24th Ward, give notice that they have completed their estimate and assessment, and that the same, together with damage and benefit maps, etc., will be deposited with the Commissioner of Public Works, at No. 31 Chambers street, there to remain till August 17, 1891.

The Commissioners in the matter of opening Cauldwell avenue, from Boston road to East 163d street, and from Clifton street to Westchester avenue, in the 23d Ward, give notice that they have completed their estimate and assessment and that the same, with damage and benefit maps, etc., have been deposited with the Commissioner of Public Works, there to remain till August 12, 1891.

Notice is given that the bill of costs, etc., incurred in the matter of opening East 162d street, from Vanderbilt avenue East to 3d avenue, in the 24th Ward, will be presented for taxation at the Supreme Court, in Chambers, on July 14, 1891, at 10:30 A. M., in the County Court House.

Noice is given that the Board of Street Opening and Improvement propose to close that part of Rutgers slip between the south side of Cherry street and the north side of Water street, and between the south side of Water street and the north side of South street, in the 7th Ward. The proceedings will be taken under authority of Chapter 410 of the Laws of 1882.

Contractors' Notes.

Bids will be received at the office of the Department of Public Works, No. 31 Chambers street, until 12 M., Tuesday, July 21st: For furnishing, delivering and laying 12-inch cast-iron water-pipe in 106th street, between 1st avenue and Harlem River, across Harlem River to Ward's Island and across Harlem River; for furnishing cast-iron water-pipes, branch-pipes and special castings; for alteration and improvement to sewer in 18th street, between East River and Avenue A, connecting with outlet sewer to be built by Department of Docks; new sewer in Avenue C, between 16th and 18th streets, and connections with existing sewers in Avenue B at 18th street, and in 17th street at Avenue C; for sewer in Astor place, between Broadway and Lafayette place; for sewer in 103d street, between Harlem River and 1st avenue; for sewer in 119th street, between St. Nicholas and 8th avenues, connecting with present sewer east of St. Nicholas avenue, and for sewer in 65th street, between property of New York Central & Hudson River Railroad and West End avenue.

Bids will be received at the Department of Public Charities and Corrections, No. 66 3d avenue, until Wednesday, July 22, 1891, for material and work required in the reconstruction and additions to South Hospital, Randall's Island, N. Y.

Sealed proposals will be received by the Board of School Trustees for the 19th Ward, at the Hall of the Board of Education, No. 146 Grand street, until 9.30 A. M., Monday, July 13, 1891, for new wings, alterations, etc., at Grammar School No. 18.

Bids are invited for the masons', carpenters, plumbing, steam-heating, electrical and bowling alley work, for the erection of Columbia Club-house, Hoboken, N. J. Plans and specifications, and all other matters appertaining thereto, can be found with the architects, Messrs. French, Dixon & De Saldern, 57th street and Broadway, New York. Sealed bids must be handed in on or before July 25, 1891, at office of the architects, or to Columbia Club, Box No. 244, Hoboken, N. J.

Our Letter Bag.

Editor RECORD AND GUIDE:

B, desiring a loan on first mortgage on city property, obtained the same through a broker and is paid his commission in full for obtaining same by B. Six months afterwards B, desiring a loan on some other city property, applies directly to the broker's principal, at the request of the principal himself, who acts as a broker in the matter, and is paid a brokerage for the loan. Has the party who was the broker in the first case any right, legal or moral, to a commission for obtaining the loan in the second case?

A SUBSCRIBER.

The broker is not entitled to a commission on the second or subsequent loans. His agency terminated on the obtaining of the first loan, and thereafter the dealings were directly between B and the principal. There is no rule which prevents the owner and principal from so dealing directly in subsequent transactions, and in such case the agent or broker is not entitled to commission.

Law Editor RECORD AND GUIDE:

Can you inform your subscriber to what depth the owner of a plot of land controls. It has been said that he owns above to the sky. If this is so, does he control to the centre of the earth?

Yes. The rule is that he is the owner to the centre of the earth.

Editor RECORD AND GUIDE:

I would be obliged to you if you could enlighten me in regard to a contract. I signed and paid a deposit on a plot of ground one week after the contract was signed and settled on. The agent came to me and said the plot of ground was sold to another party one week before I signed the contract and paid the deposit. I wish you would post me some way as what to do about it, as I don't want to be cheated out of it with my eyes open. Hoping to hear from you soon, I remain. ROB'T TATE.

The making of the first contract does not relieve the seller from liability to the purchase in the second contract. It may be that because of performance of that first contract the purchaser of the second contract will be unable to obtain a specific performance of the latter contract. But that will not prevent him from obtaining damages from the seller for failure to perform the contract. The notice given will operate to lessen the damages. The purchaser in the second contract, if the seller refuse or be unable to perform, will be entitled to damages; and in case the first contract be not completed, or that the equities of the purchaser on second contract be sufficient, a specific performance may be obtained.

New Brooklyn Buildings.

Several important buildings have just been commenced in Brooklyn. One is on the south side of Flatbush avenue and the north side of Livingston street, 104.2 and 87.2x152 and 96. It is to be a four-story brick store, costing $100,000, the architect of which is C. B. Fish. Work on the excavation is now under way.

Another building for which excavations are being made is for the apartment house, to be built on the plot, 160x100, on the north side of Schermerhorn street, 150 feet west of 3d avenue, for which Richard M. Upjohn is the architect. The building, it is said, is to be of brick, terra cotta and iron-work, and will cost, with the land, about a quarter of a million dollars.

The six-story building for the Young Women's Christian Association will be built, from designs by J. C. Cady & Co., on the south side of Schermerhorn street, near Flatbush avenue. It will also be constructed of brick and terra cotta.

J. Graham Glover is the architect for the new Twenty-sixth Wark Bank which will be built on the corner of Georgia and Atlantic avenues. The materials used will be granite, Indiana limestone, buff brick and terra cotta.

The First Baptist Church on the corner of Clinton and Pierrepont streets have determined to sell their property to the Concord Street Savings Bank, and upon the site the bank intend erecting a handsome structure. The plans have not yet been selected, although it is said several architects are endeavoring to secure the commission.

A New Saf Deposit Company for Brooklyn.

The Franklin Safe Deposit Company has been incorporated with a capital of $100,000, to carry on a deposit and storage business in the city of Brooklyn. The trustees are: Alexander E. Orr, Edwin Packard, William H. Wallace, George M. Olicott, George B. Southard, John B. Woodward, Cromwell Hadden, Felix Campbell, George M. Coit, E. A. Daly, Darwin R. James, Martin Joort and Whitman W. Kenyon.

New Incorporations.

The Metropolitan Realty Company filed a certificate of incorporation in the County Clerk's office, on July 9. The objects of this company are the purchase and improvement of real estate. The capital stock is $150,000, divided into 1,500 shares of $100 each. The names of the directors are Manly A. Ruland, William Duryea, Lucius H. Biglow, Andrew Little, James W. Pratt, Thomas Russell, James McGee, Frederick A. Ringler and William H. McCord.

The West Side Index.

A few copies of the Ten Years' Index to Conveyances of West Side real estate can be had at the publication office of THE RECORD AND GUIDE, Nos. 14 and 16 Vesey street, at $5 per copy. The index is most valuable to brokers, lawyers and others who are desirous of keeping a list of the ownerships of property on the West Side. It is neatly bound, and is arrayed in the order of streets and avenues consecutively in such a simple manner that owners of property can easily be traced.

Newark News.

W. Frank Bower has plans for a two-story double brick flat, to be built on South 11th street, for Albert Straddling, at a cost of $7,000; a three-story brk flat and storehouse for John A. Blatt & Bro., 30x100 in size, to cost $8,000; a two-story brick stable, at No. 78 Academy street, for the same firm, to cost $3,500; and an addition to the store at No. 111 Academy street, also for the same firm, to cost $1,800.

The following are the latest plans filed: W. J. Paine, 2½-sty fr dwg, 21x42, 201 and 203 North 3d st; J. C. Pfister, 3-sty fr dwg, 25x52, 331 Waverly av; Fred. Andlauer, 3-sty fr dwg, 22x52, 19 Somerset st; Peter Petry, 3-sty fr tenem't, 22x42, 241 Bergen st; Adam Turkes, 1½-sty fr barn, 16x25, 388 South 6th st; Mrs. E. L. Dodd, 3-sty brk dwg, 50x20, 5 Warren st; Helmuth Shumaher, 2-sty fr photo gallery, 16x40, 14 West st; Jaenecke-Ulman Printing Ink Co., 2-sty brk factory, 68x302, cor Av B and Wright st; S. A. Smith, 1-sty fr extension dwg, 13x23, 39 Nelson pl; John Cunack, 2-sty fr shop, 25x100, 33 Chapel st; Ernest Coe, 2-sty fr dwg, 22x26, 160 14th av; F. B. Allen, 2½-sty fr dwg, 18x40, 727 South 14th st; Peabody Land and Loan Co., 2½-sty fr dwg, 22x30, 765 Mt. Prospect av; John G. Aschenbach, 3-sty fr dwg, 21x39, 102 Waverly pl; Henry Spellmeyer, 2-sty fr flat, 22x35, rear, 112 Oraton st; Gus Elwert, 2-sty fr dwg, 21x42, 269 Lafayette st; Mrs. E. Stout, 2-sty fr dwg, 18x36, 139 North 11th st; Patrick O'Brien, 2-sty fr tenem't, 44x46, Lentz av; Mrs. McCurdy, 3-sty fr extension, 17x15, 25 Belleville av; H. C. Alward, 2-sty fr carpenter shop, 16x30, 74 Summer av; Paul H. Brangs, two 2-sty fr dwgs, 20x28, 151 North 9th st; R. W. Pryor, 2½-sty fr dwg, 36x55, cor Roseville and 6th avs; Gegenheimer & Eisele, 3-sty fr dwg, 25x58, 220 Prince st; R. Sattler, 1-sty fr extension, 18x20, South 16th st and Montgomery av; A. Pittman, 1½-sty fr dwg, 22x38, 470 Gotthard st; Robt. F. Maier, two 2-sty fr tenem'ts, 16x30, 120 and 122 Clifford st; Mulford & Vreeland, 2-sty fr extension, 17x72, 265 Mt. Pleasant av; F. Fiuter, 3-sty brk boiler room, 40x134, cor Market and Congress sts; John F. Fields, 2½-sty fr dwg, 22x22, 18 Hunterdon st; C. B. Pruden, four 2-sty brk dwgs, 25x36, 283 to 289 North 7th st; Hannah Levy, 4-sty fr store and tenem't, 25x57, 228 Kinney st; Jennie Clinchard, 2½-sty fr tenem't, 22x42, 112 Gotthardt st.

The Largest Mortgage Lender.

The mortgage records of the past six months show that by far the largest lender on mortgage, both in New York and Brooklyn, has been the Title Guarantee and Trust Company. The aggregate loaned by the company in the two cities exceeded $8,000,000. This is more than has been loaned by any three of the life insurance companies or of the savings banks combined.

These mortgages the company has turned over to investors with its guarantee of title without any delay or expense to the investors. These facts are full of significance to the real estate interests. They mean that the company is bringing borrower and lender together, and is becoming in effect a mortgage exchange, where the borrower can borrow with ease and economy, and where the lender can invest his money with safety and get it at interest as soon as he has selected his mortgage, without waiting for thirty or forty days while the title is being investigated.—*Advt.*

Real Estate Notes.

Judge Beach has granted the application of the Colonial Club for leave to execute a second mortgage of $160,000 on their new club house, under course of erection at the corner of Boulevard and 72d street. The house will cost $250,000, and the first mortgage is for $50,000.

The Polytechnic Institute, of Brooklyn, have borrowed $150,000 at 4 per cent. from the Brooklyn Savings Bank. The mortgaged property is on Livingston street, north side, 29.5 east Court street, size 241.6x150x irreg.

William Astor has leased the Hamilton hotel property on the west side of 8th avenue, extending from 124th to 125th street, running back on each street 150 feet to Peter Doelger the brewer. The lease recorded is for 1½ years at $24,000 per annum, with privilege of renewal for 18½ years at same rent.

The five lots on the southwest corner of Columbus avenue and 75th street has been sold at an expressed consideration in deed of $145,000 or at the rate of $29,000 a lot.

Notes from Mount Vernon.

[COMMUNICATED.]

THE GREAT REAL ESTATE AND BUILDING MOVEMENT IN THAT TOWN—THE PROPOSED ELECTRIC ROAD—THE NEW FAIRFAX BUILDING DESCRIBED.

The remarkable changes which are taking place in the character of our suburban towns and cities are hardly realized by New Yorkers. We are so much preoccupied with our own affairs that we have little time or inclination to consider what our neighbors north of the city boundary are doing.

The metropolis is ever increasing in population—increasing in such proportions that our people find it difficult to get houses at any reasonable figures within easy distance of the great business centres. Private houses are, it is true, to be rented as low as from $800 to $1,000 in Harlem, and at $1,200 to $1,800 in the streets south of 59th street and in some parts of the West Side. But there are thousands of families whose income makes it impossible for them to live in the city with any degree of comfort and this has brought them to places near New York, like Mount Vernon, where fine houses can be had with all improvements at from $50 to $75 per month. On the other hand a large number of well-to-do New Yorkers, pleased with the beauty of the scenery in the vicinity, as well as the healthfulness of the locality, have built handsome houses in Mount Vernon and the neighborhood. Many of these houses are situated in parks, which were created by capitalists who saw the advantages of the locality, and each of these parks contains specimens of domestic architecture that vie in cost and beauty with many larger towns. The surrounding country is very richly settled and takes in Westchester, Bartow-on-Sound, City Island and Pelham Manor, and the drives are delightful.

THE GROWTH OF MT. VERNON.

There is probably no town in Westchester County that can boast of such rapid progress as Mt. Vernon has made during the last four or five years. The population has nearly doubled since the last census, and is now about 15,000. Hundreds of families have moved up from New York each year. The increase in population has, of course, brought with it an advance in the value of land. Lots which sold for $800 to $1,000 each four years ago now bring from $700 to $1,500 and more. Building has been quite active, as may be attested by the fact that there are now seventeen architects in Mt. Vernon. Nearly 300 new buildings were erected last year, and others are under way. Among the latest of these is the Mt. Vernon Bank Building and the "Fairfax," the latter being situated on the southeast corner of 1st street and 1st avenue.

THE "FAIRFAX" DESCRIBED.

This building is undoubtedly one of the handsomest—probably the handsomest—architecturally and structurally, of any building of its kind in Westchester County.. It partakes somewhat of the character of the Opera House, Yonkers, though it is superior in point of construction.

The "Fairfax" has a frontage of 183 feet on the avenue and 104 feet on the street. The first floor contains five stores, the corner of which is 25x104 in size, while the others average about 20x75 each. They have large plate-glass windows covering their entire fronts. Above the store there is an office floor containing twenty offices, capable of being thrown together in suites of two or more.

The floor above contains an assembly room. This is not only the most important feature of the building, but a most valuable and useful hall for the citizens of Mount Vernon. That thriving place has long needed just such a room for assemblies, high-class concerts and balls. The room is about 25 feet high and covers about 7,200 square feet of floor space. It has a seating accommodation for about 750 people and will have a stage for amateur theatricals, as well as ladies' and gentlemen's reception rooms. The floor is large enough to permit of thirty-five sets of lancers, and a hundred couples can dance on it without the slightest overcrowding. The room has four exits and is descended by two easy flights of stairs. There is considerable social life in Mount Vernon and this hall will no doubt be in frequent demand, especially during the winter season. The decorations are to be of an unusually high order and are to be done by the Tiffany Company.

The building is within a few moments' walk of the New York, New Haven & Hartford Depot, and from its upper windows commands a view of some of the finest residences in the town. The journey to Mount Vernon, from the Central Depot, at 42d street, is twenty-five minutes by schedule time and is to be accomplished in twenty minutes as soon as the Harlem Road lays four tracks to the town, which will be within a few months.

The "Fairfax" is owned by Frank X. Radley, of Radley & Greenough, New York. Architecturally the building has some strong points. It is in modern Colonial style. The body brickwork is of flat Colonial-shaped brick, 1½x10 in size, trimmed with rock-faced bull-nosed work of the same brick, with Lake Superior stone laid in irregular ashlar. All the arched windows of the second story are laid up with brick in the same kind of work. There is a gable roof, with a tower on the corner and a balcony overlooking Chester Hill and North Mount Vernon, both "swell" residence sections.

A strong feature of the "Fairfax" is the excellent character of the construction. The writer does not exaggerate in saying that it is equivalent to some of the best work done in New York City, and gives the impression that the builder, as well as the owner, was in search of reputation as well as profit. Well, it no doubt pays to do things well.

An interesting feature is the door on the street side, from which the upper floors are entered. It is an arched entrance laid up with four row-locks of bull-nosed, rock-faced brick, similar to the brick described above. This work has been done extensively on both the street and avenue fronts and enhances the exterior appearance. The door is 6 feet wide and is a fine piece of masonry work.

The building is to be steam heated throughout, and will also be lighted by electricity. Every room opens on the direct light, and thorough ventilation has evidently been provided for in the designs. The architect, W. H. Stickles, late of New York, has done a very creditable piece of work. The owner, Frank X. Radley, has displayed considerable courage and enterprise in erecting so costly a building, and he has given Mount Vernon a piece of architecture which will be one of the ornaments of the town.

It is not generally known that Mount Vernon is soon to have an electric surface railway. A company has been incorporated and capital subscribed for constructing a road joining that place with Yonkers, via New Rochelle.

WANDERER.

The Opinions of Others.

D. Y. Swainson said: "THE RECORD AND GUIDE should endeavor to reform the water meter department of its bad habits. Only agents who do a large renting business know the loss and trouble that this department causes both owners and their representatives. The bills which are due the first of May are not delivered to us until the first of September. In the meantime tenants have moved and very often we have the greatest trouble in finding them, and when found it is often hard to collect such old bills. When you go to the department to inquire as to the cause of the delay you are told that the office force is too small, that they are so pressed with work that to get bills out on time is an impossibility. Now, if the force is really too small why not enlarge it? and if the trouble is that the clerks are indolent, let them be discharged, but let us get our bills on time in a business-like way and not be kept waiting six months until the people who are really in debt to the city are beyond our reach. It is not fair to make the owner of a house pay for the inefficiency or carelessness of a public department."

"In going over the conveyances for the past six months," said an experienced broker, "I found more transfers which had been made to put a fictitious value on the property transferred or to get a mortgage on a 'straw' bond than I think I ever noticed before. A speculator buys a piece of property and immediately transfers it to a 'dummy' at an advanced consideration. The dummy subsequently conveys it back to the original owner at a still higher figure. The consequence is that the original purchaser holds it at from 25 to 50 per cent—and sometimes even more—than what he paid for it. These 'fake' conveyances help to swell the year's totals considerably, although they represent no actual business. Another thing which induces men to use 'dummies' are the State mortgage laws, which permit the holder of mortgages to come back for payment of any deficiency on the original maker of the mortgage, although the property may have passed out of his hands long since. The number of men who give 'straw' bonds being very large, therefore, on account of this law, it will be seen that the number of conveyances to and from 'dummies' must be a very important factor in the totals. This year this conveyancing, which does not convey, has been larger, I think, than I ever remember it before, so that the figures showing the number and amount of transfers must not be taken as representing the actual amount of business consummated."

"The newspapers," said Wm. H. Hollister, "give as the reason for the present summer dullness the fact that so many people are out of town. Now, of course while this has something to do with it, it is not, I think, the main cause. The real reason is that prices are so high that no one can buy, and so soon as they come down to a reasonable basis there will be activity and not before."

"Several people have spoken to me about the scheme proposed by me, in THE RECORD AND GUIDE, to establish a labor exchange," said John J. Brierly to a reporter. "Among them was a carpenter in my employ who tells me that some years ago the carpenters had such an exchange, down in 8th street. It seems though, that the man employed by the union to take charge of the office was or was reported to be corrupt, often showing favoritism to one carpenter over another. This bred jealousy among the men and the exchange was discontinued, although with the exception of the charge of favoritism everything worked smoothly enough."

Special Notices.

Personal.

A. G. C. Fletcher sailed on Thursday on the Nebraska for a three-month's absence in Europe.

"The Fairfax."

Frank X. Radley, Owner.— —Walter F. Sickles, Architect.

Real Estate Department.

The market this week shows the dullness so usual at this season of the year and this stagnation is even emphasized by the long period of quiet which real estate has so lately been through. In some parts of the city there are signs which seem to indicate that owners are making concessions—larger concessions than they were willing to make during the past spring and winter seasons—but still not great enough to secure purchasers. During the past eight months or so owners have been so afraid to take their money out of real estate, fearing that equally desirable investments would not be found, that they have held off from negotiations, demanding that the purchaser make all the advances. This the latter has not always been willing to do and so deals, which under more favorable conditions would have been closed, have remained unconsummated. This feeling of hesitancy on both sides has been carried on into the summer months and it has succeeded in making real estate about as dull as it well can be. That matters will not improve until the fall seems very likely and real estate men hope for little better; but the fall, they expect will present a very different market. With the new outside money which has never been in real estate before, and which it is fully expected will leave stocks and other securities for real property, and with the general prosperity consequent on what promise to be good crops, they look for an active and entirely successful season, with prices perhaps even a little higher than those now prevailing.

THE SALES OF THE WEEK.

The sales at auction during the past week developed very little of interest or importance to the market in general. With the exception of three or four offerings of out-of-town property nearly all the sales were held under the auspices of referees, and these legal sales seemed only to attract those who were more or less directly interested. The auction market is now so dull that it affects even the forced sales where bidders are sure that there is no protection, and where the highest bid must be the selling price. The plaintiffs in the legal actions who are generally the active bidders at the foreclosure sales have been securing great bargains of late, the selling price often falling below the amount of mortgages and costs due, as has been frequently pointed out in this column. Two striking instances were afforded this week of this inability to dispose of property for the amount of the mortgage. On Tuesday five three-story dwellings on the north side of 134th street, east of Lenox avenue, and five similar dwellings in the rear on 135th street, on a plot 87.6x200, were offered under foreclosure to satisfy claims of $67,750. The ten houses were knocked down to the plaintiff for $60,000. On the same day the block front, south side of 107th street, between Madison and Park avenues, 400x100.11, vacant, was offered also under foreclosure. In this case the amount due on the property was $85,175, while the selling price was only $74,800. The country property offered has fared little better than the city holdings. Some of the parcels were withdrawn from sale, while others were bid in, and the price for that sold was in no case high.

THE OFFERINGS AT AUCTION NEXT WEEK.

The announcements for next week discourage all hope that the auction market will revive until fall. Each week now the sales become fewer in number and generally less important in character. Suburban business, so far as the exchange, at least, is concerned, is at an end for the year, and although a number of auctioneers will hold sales on the premises to-day, the indications are that the season is fast drawing to a close. The city property announced to be sold next week is offered in nearly every instance by order of the courts. The exception is a sale which Auctioneer Richard V. Harnett will conduct and the result of which will indicate very well the prevailing feeling in the market at present. The property to be offered covers most of the block bounded by Washington, King, West and Charlton streets. It has a frontage on Washington street of 69.5, on King street of 93.6, on West street of 30, and on Charlton street of 38.9 feet.

On Thursday, July 16th, Richard V. Harnett & Co. will sell the following properties, valuable for improvement: The southeast corner of West and King streets, 30x70 feet; three lots, with building, 69.5x120 feet, on Washington street; four lots, 93.6x104.1, on King street; and two lots on Charlton street, 38.9x100 feet, the whole comprising 22,955 square feet, nearly nine and one-fifth city lots.

On Thursday, July 16, Richard V. Harnett & Co. will sell the lot on the northwest corner of 11th avenue and 30th street, 31.6x100, now leased as a lumber yard.

On Saturday, July 18th, Jere. Johnson, Jr., will sell, on behalf of Wm. Ziegler, some very desirable cottage property and villa sites at Babylon, L. I., surrounding the well-known Argyle Hotel and Casino. The property comprises some fourteen cottages, all fully furnished and built in different styles of architecture, and supplied with water, gas, sewer connections, telephones, etc., and containing from nine to thirteen rooms each. Argyle Park, in which this property is situated, is rigidly restricted, and Argyle Lake abounds with tropical flowers and shrubs and is the home of many song-birds. The sale will also comprise 300 villa sites in the park, adjoining the hotel. The property is located within easy distance of the Great South Bay and is accessible to Fire Island. It can be reached in a comparatively short time from New York City. Those who will attend the sale should come prepared for the pleasant accessories of a clam bake and music by the Twenty-third Regiment Band.

Fred. J. Stone, of No. 60 Broadway, offers for sale, in one acre plots of 17 2-5 lots each, a tract of land at Elmsford, N. Y., within a few minutes' drive of the depot. The property is on high ground overlooking the hills at White Plains and the Sound on the one side and the Palisades on the other side. It is within 20 minutes' drive of White Plains and is 67 minutes from Wall street, via the Northern Road and Manhattan Road express. The ground is offered at $1,000 per acre for choice plots.

CONVEYANCES.

	1889. July 5 to 11, inclus.	1890. July 3 to 10, inclus.	1891. July 2 to 9, inclus.
Number	267	378	417
Amount involved	$4,565,323	$5,839,197	$5,309,901
Number nominal	56	98	93
Number 23d and 24th Wards	96	108	137
Amount involved	$289,398	$433,678	$429,147
Number nominal	16	20	24

MORTGAGES.

	1889.	1890.	1891.
Number	262	244	406
Amount involved	$3,451,407	$3,749,587	$8,729,758
Number at 5 per cent	128	116	216
Amount involved	$1,268,724	$1,069,618	$1,837,759
Number at less than 5 per cent	25	27	39
Amount involved	$549,500	$578,500	$675,450
Number to Banks, Trust and Insurance Companies	35	43	51
Amount involved	$847,600	$1,050,000	$1,015,250

PROJECTED BUILDINGS.

	1889. July 6 to 12, inclus.	1890. July 3 to 10, inclus.	1891. July 3 to 10, inclus.
Number of buildings	74	49	91
Estimated cost	$1,697,815	$1,056,000	$1,128,317

Gossip of the Week.

SOUTH OF 59TH STREET.

E. A. Cruikshank & Co. have sold for Mrs. C. L. O'Conor Jones and the Cruger Estate, the north half of pier 23 and the south half of pier 24, North River, with the bulkhead between, to the City of New York.

Otto Pullich has sold for a Mr. Ritterbasch the four-story flat and store, No. 729 9th avenue, for A. Buxbaum, on private terms.

NORTH OF 59TH STREET.

We hear that L. J. Phillips & Co. have sold for the estate of Christopher Meyer the northwest corner of the Boulevard and 65th street, on private terms. The plot fronts 116 on the Boulevard x164 on 65th street x100.5x106.6, and it will be improved probably by the erection of flats.

David T. Kennedy, it is reported, has purchased four lots on the north side of 71st street, 100 feet west of Central Park West, on private terms. The seller is Andrew Scher.

W. B. Taylor & Sons and F. Zittel have sold for J. C. Umberfield to Frank Tilford, of Park & Tilford, the four-story brown stone house No. 41 West 75th street, size 20x60x102.2, with butler's pantry extension, 10x14, for $42,000.

J. H. Hunt & Co. have sold for McKinley & Gunn to A. B. Hepburn No. 414 West End avenue and No. 304 West End avenue, both of them four-story brick and stone dwellings. Terms private.

Jas. T. Hall has sold one of his handsome four-story, box stoop, light stone front residences on the north side of 75th street, between Central Park West and Columbus avenue, 22x60 and three-story extension, for about $46,000.

J. B. Johnson, it is reported, has sold for the owner the three five-story brick (25-foot front) flats Nos. 19, 21 and 23 East 114th street for $19,000 each.

Wilson H. Blackwell & Co. have sold for Frank M. Tichenor No. 63 West 126th street, a three-story brown stone dwelling, 17.10x50x100, to A. H. Brummell on private terms.

Henry J. Carr has sold for the estate of H. B. Helmke the five-story brick flat and store, No. 646 Columbus avenue, to Arthur Wehrmann for $29,000.

Potter Bros. have sold to James T. Berry for improvement the plot 100 x100 on the south side of 142d street, 100 feet west of 3d avenue, for $20,000.

Gutwillig Bros. have purchased from Scott & Bowne the five lots on the south side of 90th street, 200 feet west of Central Park West, on private terms.

H. H. Dreyer has sold his five-story improved flat, 27x87x100.11, No. 316 West 116th street, to a Miss Ettenheimer, on private terms.

J. W. Stevens has sold for C. Kirkland to D. D. Lawson the three-story Queen Anne dwelling, 17x50x70, on the northwest corner of Manhattan avenue and 105th street, for $18,500.

L. Froehlich has sold for John Casey to Leopold Goldberg No. 64 West 85th street, a four-story dwelling, 19x56x100.11, for $31,000.

Adler & Herrman have sold to H. Hader No. 229 East 101st street, a four-story brick building, 25x65x100, for $14,000. The sale of this house is the last of four which Adler & Herrman have made on this street within the past month.

Mainhart & Lowe have sold for Sarah M. Shotts two lots on Kingsbridge road, near Elwood street, 50x202, to Peter C. Hegelin for $4,600; for Mrs. John Gribbel the three-story and basement brown stone house, No. 495 Manhattan avenue, 15x60x80, to a Mr. Lesser for 16,000; for the Genet Lumber Co. the four-story and basement dwelling, No. 43 West 130th street, 20x50x100, to Wm. R. Lowe for $22,500.

LEASES.

H. Rinaldo & Bro. have leased for Fay & Stacom the store and basement on the southwest corner of Market and Henry streets to the Baron de Hirsch Fund for five years, for $1,500 per annum. The lessees will spend $10,000 in altering the premises for bath purposes.

Brooklyn.

Corwith Bros. have sold the three-story and basement frame dwelling, 25 x43x100, No. 153 Oakland street, for Wm. H. Port to Susan Covert for $8,350; and the lot, 20x75, on the northwest corner of Lorimer and Calyer streets with temporary buildings thereon for Rorden & Kohlmann to Harriet Port for $3,750.

J. P. Sloane has sold for Mrs. Ann Lewis the three-story and basement frame dwelling house, 22x45, lot 25x100, No. 686 Leonard street, to Mortimer W. Price for $5,850.

Mainhart & Lowe, of New York, have sold for Wm. R. Lowe the four-story double flat No. 70 Carlton avenue, 25x75x100, for $21,500.

CONVEYANCES.

	1889. July 3 to 10. inclus.	1890. July 2 to 9, inclus.	1891. July 2 to 8, inclus.
Number	399	486	471
Amount involved	$1,656,670	$2,889,327	$1,807,583
Number nominal	71	97	101

MORTGAGES.

	1889.	1890.	1891.
Number	386	433	381
Amount involved	$1,223,672	$1,902,459	$1,252,116
Number at 5 per cent. or less	247	296	218
Amount involved	$816,468	$1,313,604	$788,795

PROJECTED BUILDINGS.

	1889. July 4 to 11, inclus.	1890. July 3 to 10, inclus.	1891. July 3 to 9, inclus.
Number of buildings	68	103	47
Estimated cost	$297,580	$841,035	$221,400

Out of Town.

HEMPSTEAD, L. I.—Lee Witty, one of the executors of the estate of Morris R. Williams, has sold the Williams residence containing twenty-six rooms together with five acres of ground for $20,000. The purchaser is August Belmont, Jr., who has occupied the house for six years.

Out Among the Builders.

Wood & Palmer have completed plans for remodeling the first and second stories of the private residence at No. 13 East 75th street, for Mrs. T. P. Eldridge. The wood-work of these two stories will also be changed to oak and mahogany, and $5,000 will be spent on the improvement.

J. C. Burne has plans under way for alterations to the four-story building on the northwest corner of 2d avenue and 83d street, and for a five-story tenement house and store, to be built on the north side of 83d street, about 80 feet west of 2d avenue, size 27x94. The cost of both jobs will be $32,000, and the name of the owner is P. Sheehy.

James T. Berry will build four five-story flats, 25x72, on the south side of 142d street, 100 feet west of 3d avenue, at a cost of $64,000.

The northwest corner of the Boulevard and 65th street, 116x164x100.5x 106.6 in size, sold this week by the Christopher Meyer estate, will be improved probably by the erection of flats. The name of the purchaser is not known.

Frederick Ebeling is drawing plans for a five-story flat and store, 25x40, to be built by Jacobson & Margovitz at No. 133 Willett street, at a cost of $14,000. The front will be of buff brick and brown stone.

Buchman & Deisler have plans for a three-story and basement fire-proof extension, 40x55 in size, to be built to the Manhattan Hospital on 131st street, west of Amsterdam avenue, at an estimated cost of $30,000.

Out of Town.

ASHVILLE, N. C.—G. E. Wood has completed plans for a five-story and basement stone and cement-faced frame hotel, to be built upon one of the most commanding sites in this section. The building will be irregular in size, having a frontage of 300 feet and an average depth of 60 feet. It will contain 150 rooms, arranged in suites, each suite having a connecting bath-room, open fire-place, and opening upon a small balcony. The interior finish is to be of oak and native woods, and one of the chief features of the hotel will be the dining-room. This room has been most advantageously placed, in view of the attractive scenery from this point, and its interior has been made doubly pleasing by having its sides and one end extended in large bay windows. The hotel has been abundantly supplied with piazzas and balconies for out-of-door life, and in all its appointments will be of first-class description. The estimated cost is placed at $150,000.

BERWICK, PA.—F. C. Merry has completed plans for a three-story stone and half-timber dwelling, to be built for C. R. Woodin. The house will be 40x64, with a two-story L extension, 24x23. It will be finished in hard woods and is to cost $25,000.

NEW ROCHELLE, N. Y.—Trinity Church congregation will build, from plans drawn by F. C. Merry, a one and two-story parish house, 79x75 in size. The building will be of frame construction, with shingle-finished exterior and will cost $15,000.

BRIDGEPORT, ALA.—G. E. Wood is the architect of a four-story and basement brick and stone hotel, to be built here by the Hoffman estate, of New York. The building will be 125x40 in size, having 125 rooms, finished in yellow pine, and will cost $40,000.

BELLE HAVEN, CONN.—W. W. Richards will build a two-story and attic frame cottage, 36x45, with shingle exterior, to cost $5,500. F. C. Merry is the architect.

WANTS AND OFFERS.

(Advertisements strictly in accordance with this title will be inserted at the practically nominal rate of 10 CENTS *per line (agate). In figuring for themselves advertisers may count seven words for each line, the address to be taken as one line. The object of this department is to bring buyers and sellers into communication with customers. Advertisements must be marked "Wants and Offers Column," and sent to the office of publication, Nos. 14 and 16 Vesey Street, not later than 3 P. M. Friday.)*

WANTS.

WANTED.—$25,000. first mortgage, four-story corner brick building, three stories, eleven flats; all improvements; rents, $4,344.
R. Z. 91, RECORD office.

A GENTLEMAN OF EXPERIENCE AND EDUCAtion desires a position in a real estate office; acquainted with New York and Brooklyn; best of references as to ability. Address,
July 11—18 G. W., RECORD AND GUIDE.

DRAUGHTSMAN, four years in an architect's office, wishes situation in same or with builder; A1 reference. C. A., 1888 Park av.

WANTED.—Position as salesman to hardwood trim mill; thoroughly practical.
EXPERIENCE, RECORD office.

ARCHITECT, established in New York City, desires partner to take equal interest; must be a man of ability and experience, capable of taking charge of office; $3,000 required. Address,
ARCHITECT,
July 4-1aw3w. Office of RECORD AND GUIDE.

MASON, BUILDER, ARCHITECT, AND MEchanic, desires to make himself useful to any one desiring his twenty-five (25) years' experience in the Building Trade, or buying or selling. Address, BUILDER AND ARCHITECT, 81 New st., Room 104; N. Y. C.
May 16—1aw10w.

Real Estate Wanted.

WANTED.—For special customer—dwelling; Washington Heights preferred; limit, $30,000; owners and brokers address.
H. F. SCHELLHASS, 171 Broadway.

WANTED.—Improved property on 9th av. in exchange for plot, avenue lots; equity $55,000.
H. F. SCHELLHASS, 171 Broadway.

OFFERS.

Dwellings

FOR SALE OR TO LET at Woodlawn, 24th Ward, city, new frame house, nine large rooms and bath, suitable for two families. Inquire by letter to
C. S., 533 East 116th st.

FOR SALE.—Brick tenements, front and rear building lots, 25x100, near my office; $18,000.
WM. S. BORCHERS, 1505 Broadway, corner 44th st.

DESIRABLE CITY EQUITIES TO EXCHANGE for country property and vice versa; particulars here. WHITING, 45 Broadway.

OFFERS.

GOOD, ESTABLISHED PROFITABLE BUSINESS to exchange for income producing equity, tenement or flat. WHITING, 45 Broadway.

BUY THE BEST.
72D ST., THE PARK DRIVEWAY.
SEVERAL 25-FOOT PALATIAL RESIDENCES.
ONE SUPERBLY DECORATED.
NONE MORE ELEGANT AND SPACIOUS.
The best judgment of long experience has been given to their construction. The most critical will be satisfied in the taste displayed and the excellent character of the workmanship and material; prices reasonable.
F. CRAWFORD, 114 West 72d st.
July 11-1aw8w.

DESIRABLE 19-FOOT DWELLING ON WEST 22D st. for sale to close estate; $17,000.
WHITING, 45 Broadway.

SPECULATORS AND INVESTORS.—I have just finished my entire front on 8th av., 118th, 119th; five story, with stores; well rented; prices from $25,000 to $48,000. For particulars, P. BRAENDER, Owner and Builder, 120 East 86th st (office open till 9 P. M.
July 4-1aw3w.

FOR SALE—2443 8th av.; 26.3½x100; easy terms; commission allowed brokers; apply at
Mar. 28-u-f. ROOM 19, 156 Broadway.

FOR SALE—210 and 212 West 105th st.; five-story apartments; each, 25x89x100; decorated and carpeted; apply at ROOM 19, 156 Broadway.
Mar. 28-u-f.

Improved Property.

PLANING MILL FOR SALE.—Is located at 24th st. and 11th av., on four or five city lots, leased ground, and consists of two and three-story brick buildings and adjoining sheds; also 90 horse-power engine and boiler, planers, moulders, saws, etc., all in good running order and now in operation; owner will leave a portion of value on bond and mortgage three years; this offers splendid opportunity to enlarge wood-working industry or to secure good mill business to add thereto. For further particulars, etc., apply to
July 11-18. EBEN PECK, 24th st. and 11th av.

Vacant Lots.

100TH ST., between 2d and 3d avs; ten lots, cheap; all mortgage if improved.
July 11-1aw8w. EDWIN A. ELY, 108 Gold st.

40 CHERRY ST., between Roosevelt and Franklin sq., 32x64, vacant; $14,000; accommodating terms. EDWIN A. ELY, 108 Gold st.
July 11-1aw8w.

OFFERS.

FOR SALE.—Four full lots on East 14th st.; suitable for any building purpose; price $90,000; only principals need apply. J. T., REAL ESTATE RECORD.
J. 27-1aw3w.

FOR SALE—Five lots, n e cor Willis av and 137th st, 100x125; easy terms; ready for improvement; splendid location. Apply to
June 27, 1aw4w. JAS. CARNEY, 137 East 53d st.

LARGE FACTORY for sale; price, $28,000; the land itself supposed to be worth the money.
Apr 4-uf FIRST NATIONAL BANK, Brooklyn, N. Y.

TO BUILDERS—With or without a loan, south side of 81st st., near Amsterdam av., three lots, excavated; terms easy. DA CUNHA, Montclair, N. J.
J 20—1aw5w

Brooklyn Real Estate for Sale.

FOR SALE.—A corner store on a business av., finally situated for a grocery; needs only to be seen to be appreciated. Call and examine same.
ALEX. SMEDES, 415 Central av.

DESIRABLE INVESTMENT.—Eight-story apartment house; best location in Brooklyn; might exchange equity over $125,000 at 4½ per cent.
J. 20—uf. Apply 60 Broadway, Room 811.

16½ PER CENT.—Best I can do on investment of $15,000 in plate glass store property on leading business thoroughfare of 17th Ward of Brooklyn; the plot is 140x90; consists of seven two-story buildings; rents for $1,592 per annum, and mortgage of $27,500 can remain for long term. Examine this gilt edge investment. J. P. SLOANE,
July 11—1aw4w. 348 Manhattan av., Brooklyn.

Country Property.

AT MONTCLAIR, N. J.—200 acres for cutting into lots; railroad station on property; number of acres to suit purchaser. DA CUNHA, Montclair.
J. 27-1aw5w.

Miscellaneous.

MONEY TO LOAN in any amounts on good real estate; security at 5 %.
16 East 42d st.

A PARTY ABOUT TO BUILD A FIVE-STORY factory, 50x98, in Harlem, near water-front, will lease the three upper floors and build to suit tenant. Terms very moderate. Address
May 16 u. f. OWNER, 409 E. 107th St.

SALES OF THE WEEK.

The following are the sales at the Real Estate Exchange and Auction Room for the week ending July 10.

* *Indicates that the property described has been bid in for plaintiff's account:*

R. V. HARNETT & CO.

Goerck st, No. 90, e s, 81.3 n Rivington st, 15.4x99.11, five-story brk tenem't. Henry Frohwitter. (Amt due $7,748)	$10,000
*93th st, Nos. 149-165, n s, 100 e Amsterdam av, 85x113.8x—x129.6, eleven five-story brk unfinished flats and 3 vacant lots. Julius Lipman. (Amt due $41,292; prior mort. $ —)	163,810
120th st, No. 540, s s, 437.6 e Av A, 18.9x100.11, two-story brk dwell'g. (Dower right, &c.) Jas. Monahan	4,400

JAMES L. WELLS.

Bethune st, No. 53, s s, 163 e Washington st, 22x88.7x22.8x92.10, four-story brk tenem't with one-story brk building on rear. Bradley & Currier Co. (Amt due $3,643)	25,500
17th st, No. 446, s s, 198.11 e 10th av, 30.4x92, three-story brk dwell'g. J. C. Cady	10,500

WM. KENNELLY.

Gay st, No. 17, e s, 147.10 n Waverley pl, 19x65, three-story brk dwell'g. Eleanor McMahon. (Amt due $2,723)	3,035
*141st st, Nos. 203-211, n s, 75 w 7th av, 100x99.11, five five-story brk flats. Robert C. Watson et al exrs. (Amt due $70,665)	71,000

J. F. B. SMYTH.

11th st, No. 111 E, 25x100, four story brk building and store. M. J. Fox, party in interest. (Leasehold)	9,100
8th av, No. 944, e s, 25.5 s 56th st, 25x100, five-story stone flat with stores. Peter Farley	39,400

B. L. KENNELLY.

*4th st, No. 161, n e s, 86 n w 6th av, runs northwest 20 x northeast 45.4 x north 60.6 x southeast 7.6 x southwest 54 x southeast 4.10 x southwest 19.5 x southwest 40 to beginning, four-story brk tenem't with stores. Isaac Mannheimer. (Amt due $5,260)	12,000
74th st, No. 59, n s, 100 e Columbus av, 20x102.2, four-story stone front dwell'g. J. P. Campbell	35,000
74th st, No. 57, adj, 20x102.2, similar dwell'g. Same	41,000
74th st, No. 53, n s, 160 e Columbus av, 20x102.2, four-story stone front dwell'g. W. B. Baldwin	43,900
145th st, No. 326, s s, 42 e Edgecombe av, 18x99.11, three-story brk dwell'g. Ann C. Brown. (Amt due $9,819)	9,500

L. J. PHILLIPS & CO.

Horatio st, No. 76, s s, 144.5 w Greenwich st, 25x87.5, four-story brk flat. Mitchell A. C. Levy	13,500
Horatio st, No. 33, n s, 90.9 e Washington st, 23x84.3, three-story brk dwell'g. Ottinger Bros	9,350

OTHER AUCTIONEERS.

Washington st, e s, 66.6 n Jay st, 20x80. John H. Newtown	25,600
44th st, s s, 100 e Lexington av, 20x100.5. Abram E. Moore	15,000
*134th st, Nos. 71-79 / 135th st — begins 134th st, n s, 197.6 e 6th av, original line, 87.6x199.7 to 135th st, x87.6x199.10, five three-story brk dwell'gs on 134th st and five three-story brk dwell'gs on 135th st. Wm. H. Vredenburgh. (Amt due $67,750)	60,000
167th st, s s, 158.4 e Amsterdam av, 20.7x97.4x17.3x109.8, three-story brk dwell'g. J. E. Crouly. (Amt due $3,957)	5,200
Madison av, s e cor 107th st, 100.11x400 to Park av, vacant. Isaac H. Smith. (Amt due $85,179)	74,800
2d av, w s, 20.11 n 116th st, 20x70. Abram E. Moore	11,200
Total	$572,895
Corresponding week 1890	$71,847

BROOKLYN, N. Y.

FOR WEEK ENDING JULY 9.

JERE JOHNSON, JR.

54th st, n s, 90 e 16th av, 2 lots. Thos. Hogan	$760
54th st, adj, 2 lots. —— Harmon	340
54th st, adj, 2 lots. H. Bradley	350
54th st, adj, 3 lots. —— Morgan	495
54th st, s s, 90 e 16th av, 3 lots. F. Holland	495
54th st, adj, 4 lots. S. Wicant	800
55th st, n s, 130 e 16th av, 6 lots. A. W. Tonjes	990
55th st, n s, 80 w 17th av, 3 lots. —— Downe	465
55th st, s s, 80 w 16th av, 3 lots. —— Hawes	600
55th st, adj, 4 lots. —— Tucker	800
55th st, s s, — w 16th av, 3 lots. H. Keenan	570
55th st, adj, 4 lots. —— Cleary	780
56th st, n s, 100 w 16th av, 4 lots. —— Schwarke	760
56th st, adj, 2 lots. E. D. Spear	400

57th st, n s, 120 w 16th av, 8 lots. C. J. Kinsey. 1,440
57th st, adj, 2 lots. Louis Olsen........ 390
57th st, adj, 4 lots. Thos. Hogan.... 740
57th st, adj, 2 lots. Wm. Hunt.......... 850
*Wythe av, Nos. 508 and 510, w s, 19.8 s South 10th st, 36.1x50, two three-story brk dwell'gs. Mary M. More.......... 6,450
16th av, s e cor Cowenhovens lane, 3 lots. L. Moody 600
16th av, n e cor 54th st, 5 lots. Thos. Hogan.. 1,025
16th av, e s, 56th to 57th st, 10 lots. L. Moody. 2,000

JOHN F. B. SMYTH.

48th st, No. 275, n s, 100 e 4th av, 20x100, two-story frame dwell'g. Isaac Donald........ 3,850
48th st, No. 277, adj, 20x100, similar dwell'g. Jos. Miller.......... 3,925
Van Cott av, n e cor Manhattan av, 50x100. J. Manheim 8,475

JAMES L. WELLS.

*Av B, s w cor East 4th st, 100x100, Flatbush. The Brooklyn and New York Arcanum Building, Loan and Savings Assoc.......... 2,000

BRYAN L. KENNELLY.

Sackett st, No. 178, s s, 57.9 e Hicks st, 19.3x100, three-story brk dwell'g. Anna M. Roes.... 4,050

OTHER AUCTIONEERS.

Cumberland st, No. 390, w s, 376.10 n Atlantic av, 20x100, three-story frame dwell'g. M. Lang 4,225
Devoe st, Nos. 38-42, s s, 139 w Lorimer st, 60x100, saw factory. R. Eldridge.......... 5,000
Fulton st, Nos. 2750, s s, 100 w Miller av, 25x100, two-story frame dwell'g. D. Rosenberg..... 1,730
Fulton st, No. 2754, s s, 75 w Miller av, 25x100, two-story frame dwell'g. J. A. Davies...... 1,700
Fulton st, No. 2758, s s, 50 w Miller av, 25x100, two-story frame dwell'g. Q. A. Parker..... 1,550
*Vanderbilt st, n s, 260.6¾ e Gravesend av, 75x300.2 to Seeley st, x85.2x300, Flatbush. W. C. Dornin.......... 2,650
Howard av, Nos. 293-307, e s, 167 s Herkimer st, runs east 98 x south 69 x west 48 x south 30.6 x southwest 50.11 to Howard av, x north 109.2 to beginning, six two-story frame dwell'gs. German-American Real Estate Title Guarantee Company, W. J. C. Miller and N. Kaplan 10,510

Total.......... $70,815
Corresponding week, 1890.......... $78,856

CONVEYANCES.

Wherever the letters Q. C., C. a. G. and B. & S occur, preceded by the name of the grantee they mean as follows:

1st—Q. C. is an abbreviation for Quit Claim deed, i. e., a deed in which all the right, title and interest of the grantor is conveyed, omitting all covenants or warranty.

2d—C. a. G. means a deed containing Covenant against Grantor only, in which he covenants that he hath not done any act whereby the estate conveyed may be impeached, charged or encumbered.

3d—B. & S. is an abbreviation for Bargain and Sale deed, wherein, although the seller makes no express covenants, he really grants or conveys the property for a valuable consideration, and thus impliedly claims to be the owner of it.

NEW YORK CITY.

JULY 2, 3, 4, 6, 7, 8, 9.

Allen st, No. 175, w s, 25.1 s Stanton st, 25x64.11x25x65.2, three-story frame (brk front) store and tenem't. Contract. Betsey Wolf to Michael J. Adrian. July 3. $14,000

Bedford st, No. 55, w s, 100.1 n Le Roy st, 21.2x75.6, two-story brk dwell'g. Mary J. wife of Abram Hull to Frederick and Marie Haldy, joint tenants. July 1. 9,000

Bethune st, No. 19, s s, 163 e Washington st, 23x88.7x23.8x92.10, five-story brk tenem't. Foreclos. Frank Schaeffler to Francis M. Wilmurt. July 8. 3,500

Bleecker st, No. 124 | Wooster st, Nos. 185-189 } begins Bleecker st, s w cor Wooster st, 25x100, two-story frame (brk front) store and tenem't on Bleecker st and three two-story brk stores on Wooster st. Philip Sammet to Abraham Stern. ½ part. *Mt.* $50,000. Dec. 10. nom

Boulevard, e s, 26.1 s 108th st, 77.5x88x75.6x105.4, vacant. George W. Thedford and Charlotte H. his wife to George O. Curtiss. June 30. 25,000

Same property. George O. Curtiss to Oscar T. Mackey. *Mt.* $20,000. July 6. 27,000

Bowery, No. 340, w s, 79 s Great Jones st, runs west 98.6 x south 24.10 x east 60.4 x south 0.6 x east 45.11 to Bowery, x north 26.1, four-story brk tenem't with stores. Max and Clarence Hartman, Therese wife of Ludwig Baumann, Bessie wife of David Auerbach, Eva wife Henry Hoffbeimer, Rose wife of Samuel Milius, Martha wife of Joseph C. Wolff heirs Isaac Hartman to Ignazio Mercadante. June 24. 37,000

Broome st, No. 192, n s, abt 25 e Suffolk st, 25.1x75.1x24.11x75.5, five-story brk store and tenem't with three-story brk tenem't on rear. Sigmund Kurtz and Hannah his wife to Morris Shapiro. *Mt.* $18,250. July 1. 26,000

Broome st, No. 525, s s, 90 e Sullivan st, 20x60.6 to alley, with use of same, three-story frame (brk front) store and tenem't. George J. McFadden to Lizzie Donovan. June 15. nom

Broadway, No. 1240, n e cor 31st st, 22x74.2x20.6x66.9.
31st st, Nos. 43-47, n s, 66.9 e Broadway, 54.6x98.9.
Four, five, eight and nine-story brk hotel and stores.
Mary E. Hanley widow to Robert and Ogden Goelet. *Mt.* $190,000. June 23. 600,000

Canal st, No. 203, n w cor Mulberry st, 26.7x72.5x25.3x80.10, five-story brk store. Florence Geery, Brooklyn, to Anna S. wife of Isaac J. Geery, Stamford, Conn. ⅓ part. *Mt.* $2,812. Re-recorded. March 31, 1890. 5,625

Chambers st, No. 77, n s, 119 w Broadway, being lot 555 Church farm, 25x75, five-story iron front store. Sarah A. Peddie widow, Newark, N. J., to The First Baptist Peddie Memorial Church, of Newark, N. J. Trust deed. March 7. nom

Charles st, No. 42, s s, 241.7 e 4th st, 20x95, three-story brk dwell'g. Ann A. S. wife of and Cornelius R. Blauvelt, Nyack, N. Y., to Louis Gompper. June 25. nom

Charlton st, No. 42, s s, 133.7 e Varick st, 23x100, three-story brk tenem't. Marietta L. and Sheridan S. Norton by Anthony Barnett guard. to John McGinn. July 3. 20,000

Same property. Release dower. Marietta Norton widow to Marietta and Sheridan S. Norton. Nov. 5. nom

Cherry st, bet J. Hamilton's and Thos. Ellison's lots, 16.8x100, excepting portion taken off rear for Chambers st extension, being 16.8x20x—x40. Ann wife of William Swanton, Brooklyn, to Ann Finn. Reserves life estate. June 30. nom

Columbia st, No. 55, w s, 125 n Delancey st, 25x100, four-story brk stable. Jacob Scharf to Atga Scharf. June 13. nom

Columbia st, No. 87, w s, 175 s Stanton st, 27x100, four-story brk stores and tenem't with four-story brk tenem't on rear.
Columbia st, No. 91, w s, 125 s Stanton st, 25x100, four-story brk store and tenem't with three-story brk tenem't on rear.
August Buermann and Sophie his wife and Charles Buermann and Sophia E. C. his wife to Henry Buermann. B & S. July 3. nom

Delancey st, No. 218, n s, 50 e Pitt st, 26.3x76.3, five-story brk tenem't with stores. Samuel Davis and Dora his wife to Henry Michel. *Mt.* $18,000. June 30. 26,500

Delancey st, No. 264 | Columbia st, Nos. 49 and 51 } begins Delancey st, n w cor Columbia st, 24.8x80x25x80, a three-story brk tenem't with stores on each st. Helena C. wife of J. Peter Mochus, Mt. Vernon, N. Y., heir of Heinrich Lingelbach to Elizabeth E. wife of William H. Kottman, also heir Heinrich Lingelbach. July 2. 4,000

Eldridge st, No. 39, w s, 50 n Canal st, 25x100, five-story brk tenem't with stores. Jeannette Bleistift to William Mathis. *Mt.* $21,000. July 1. 33,500

Eldridge st, No. 73, w s, 100 n Hester st, 25x100, five-story brk tenem't with stores. Israel Feldman and Anna his wife, Brooklyn, to Jacob Paskusz. All title. *Mt.* $32,000. June 30. nom

Forsyth st, No. 204, e s, 175 s Houston st, 24.11x100, five-story brk tenem't with stores. Aaron Kaplan and Rachel his wife to Augusta Steffens. *Mt.* $18,000. July 1. 28,000

Fort Washington Ridge road, e s, 150 n Fort Washington Depot road, 50x100. Partition. John A. Deady to Charles Fleischmann. July 2. 3,000

Front st, No. 365 | South st, No. 384 } begins Front st, s s, 125 w Jackson sq, 25x140 to South st, two-story brk stable on Front st and vacant lot on South st. Lyman Tiffany and Edward Wood exrs., &c. Charlotte L. Fox to John W. Sullivan, Brooklyn. May 1. 12,000

Same property. Mary L. Tiffany daughter of Charlotte L. Fox to same. Q. C. June 24. nom

Goerck st, No. 41, w s, 75 s Delancey st, 25x100, five-story brk tenem't with stores and four story brk tenem't on rear. Isaac Cohn and Tillie his wife and Leo Katz to Haris Kosinsky. *Mt.* $18,750. June 30. 23,500

Grand st, n s, 145.8 e Varick st. Agreement modifying party wall agreement. Jennie wife of Robert Spriggs formerly Allen to Alexander Levett. June 4. nom

Grand st, No. 12, n s, 145.8 e Varick st, 22x83, three-story frame (brk front) store and tenement with two-story brk stable on rear. Jennie wife of and Robert H. Spriggs, formerly Allen, to Alexander Levett. July 8. nom

Hamilton st, No 3, n s, abt 50 e Catharine st, 20.4x51.5x20.4x52.4, three-story frame store and tenem't. John Cotter and Catherine his wife to Mary Haggerty. June 30. 5,000

Houston st, No. 270, n e s, 253.5 n w Av B, 20x106.6, four-story brk store and tenem't with two-story brk stable on rear. Katharine Hoffmann to Mary Goodman. July 1. nom

Same property. Mary Goodman to Henry Friedman and Amelia his wife. *Mt.* $14,500. July 2. nom

Horatio st, No. 60. All real estate of Peter Van Natter dec'd. Release legacy. Anna M. Finch to Thomas J. Van Natter. July 7. 300

Henry st, No. 311, n s, 288.1 e Scammel st, 23.6x70.8x23.6x71.4, five-story stone front tenem't. Isidor Obstbaum and Paulina his wife to Julius Robinson. *Mt.* $15,000. July 1. 27,500

Jackson st, No. 34, e s, 100 n Cherry st, 25x100, five-story brk store and tenem't with four-story brk tenem't on rear.
Jackson st, No. 32, e s, 125 n Cherry st, 25x100, three-story frame stores and tenem't with four-story brk tenem't on rear.
Louis Lese and Sarah his wife, Morris Deutsch and Morris Goldstein and Pauline his wife to Charles H. Reed and William Schmohl. *Mt.* $24,000. July 1. See 87th st. 40,000

Jones st, No. 23, n s, abt 148 e Bleecker st, 25x100, one and two-story frame buildings. Samuel Kempner to Theodore Van Eupen. *Mt.* $6,000. June 30. 17,500

Jay st, No. 7, n e cor Staple st, 22.9x58.7x22.3x58.6, two and three-story brk and frame buildings. The American Bible Soc. and The American Home Missionary Soc. to Julius Wolff and Herman Reessing. June 30. 25,000

King st, Nos. 23 and 25, n s, 84 w Congress st, 60x75x66x75.2, two-story brk stable. Alois Gutwillig to Michael McCormick and Henry Madden. *Mt.* $15,500. July 8. 42,000

Kingsbridge road, w s, 25.3 s 184th st, if extended, runs north 55.6 to point opposite centre line 184th st, x west 110.5 to centre 12th av as formerly laid out, x south along same 55 x east 118.5. Arnold Lustig to Helen F. Ducey. July 8. 7,000

Kingsbridge road, e s, 25.6 s 179th st, 76.7x106.8x75x90.10. Pauline Simon to Robert McGarity and Mary A. his wife. June 11. 10,350

Kingsbridge road, w s, lots 34 and 35 map Lucius Chittenden, 61x125x49x125. Frank Koch and Isabella his wife to George Reubert. *Mt.* $1,400. July 2. 5,000

Lewis st, No. 78, e s, 124.9 n Rivington st, 25x99, five-story brk store and tenem't with five-story brk tenem't on rear. Louis Lese and Sarah his wife, Morris Goldstein and Pauline his wife to Barnett and Louis Levy. *Mt.* $21,000. July 1. 27,250

Ludlow st, No. 94, e s, 138 s Delancey st, 24.6x87.6, five-story brk tenem't with stores. Foreclos. William H. Leonard to Lewis Friedman. Re-recorded. April 27, 1878. 15,500

Same property. William H. A. and Joseph C. Rubino and ano. exrs. and trustees of Frederick H. Rubino to Jacob and Lippman Katz. ½ part. July 1. 13,250

Same property. William H. A. Rubino and Charlotte M. his wife to same. ½ part. July 1. 13,250

Same property. Release dower. Anna E. Rubino widow to same. ½ part. July 1. nom

Ludlow st, No. 5, w s, 50 n Canal st, 25.3x87.6, five-story brk tenem't with stores. Morris Goldstein and Sarah his wife to Samuel Phillips. *Mt.* $29,000. June 30. 40,250

Madison st, No. 305, n s, 75 e Montgomery st, 26.6x93, three-story frame (brk front) tenem't with four-story brk tenem't on rear. William A. C. Dougherty and Catharine his wife to Charles Ruff. *Mt.* $8,000. July 6. 18,000

Madison st, Nos. 278-282, s s, 115 w Montgomery st, 69x100, one and two-story frame and brk buildings, coal yard, &c. Israel Minor, Jr., Brooklyn, exr. Jane V. C. Cooper to James E. Dougherty. July 9. 33,500

Maiden lane, Nos. 51 and 53, n e s, abt 235 s e Nassau st, runs northeast 139 x southeast 49.4 x southwest 6 x southeast 15.6 x southwest 40.3 x northwest 24.1 x southwest 93.9 to Maiden lane, x northwest 39.2, six-story stone front store. John Pettit and Alida R. his wife, East Orange, N. J., to Edward Mahoney, Norfolk, Va. *Mt.* $140,000. June 25. nom

Maiden lane, Nos. 53 and 55. Release party wall agreement. John G. Wendel, Irvington, N. Y., to John Pettit. June 24. nom

Monroe st, No. 69, n s, abt 157 w Pike st, 25x100, three-story brk tenem't with six-story brk building on rear. Barnet Levy and Lieba his wife to Samuel Goldfarb. *Mt.* $17,450. July 8. 26,000

Market st, No. 40, n e cor Madison st, being front and rear 1-9 part of the distance bet Madison and Henry sts, x 87 and 86.11, three-story brk store and tenem't. Sophia L. Schroeder widow, Brooklyn, to Maggie Reilly. *Mt.* $7,500. July 2. 27,500

Mulberry st, No. 121, w s, 100 s Hester st, 25x100, five-story brk store and tenem't with four-story brk tenem't on rear. Ida Michalesky to Nicola Mangier. *Mt.* $18,000. July 6. 31,000

Norfolk st, No. 154, e s, 50 s Stanton st, 25x100, five-story brk store and tenem't. Samuel First and Theresa his wife to Bernhard Silberstein and David Moss. *Mt.* $33,000. July 1. 43,000

Pike st, No. 46, e s, abt 50 s Madison st, 25x87, five-story brk tenem't. Contract to exchange for 76th st, No. 332 E., s s, abt 125 e 2d av, 25x100.2, four-story stone front tenem't. Louis Gewirz to Hayman Wallach. Equality of exchange. July 6. 11,000

Pitt st, No. 57, w s, 168.8 n Delancey st, 18.7x63, three-story brk store and tenem't. Ignatz Gluck and Hannah his wife to Ignatz Kaufman. *Mt.* $9,000. July 3. 12,000

Ridge st, No. 24, e s, 126.2 n Grand st, 25x100, three-story brk tenem't with four-story brk tenem't on rear. Marks Levin and Betsie his wife to Louis Levy. *Mt.* $16,000. July 1. 24,125

Rivington st, No. 271, s s, abt 28 e Columbia st, 18.1x58.10x18.1x58.10, three-story frame (brk front) store and tenem't. Charles Schaper exr. Rebecca M. Coop to Rosanna Rosenfeld. June 25. 7,200

Rivington st, n s, 75 e Clinton st, 0.6x57. Henri Strasbourger and Rachel his wife to George Riehl. Q. C. July 9. 300

Rivington st, No. 188, n s, 50.6 e Clinton st, 25x57, five-story brk tenem't with stores. George Riehl and Helene his wife to Levy Sobol. July 9. 22,000

Roosevelt st, No. 90, e s, abt 140 n Cherry st, 20x63.6x20x62, two-story frame (brk front) store and tenem't. Bridget Diffley to James F. McCarthy. Mt. $4,000. July 6. 8,500

Rose st, No. 61, s s, 74 4 w Pearl st, runs south 81.2 x west 44.3 x north 27.1 x east 18.2 x north 57.9 to Rose st, x east 26 3, three-story brk store and tenem't. Lyman Tiffany and Edward Wood exrs. and trustees Charlotte L. Fox to Esther A. Wheaton. June 12. 26,500

Scammel st, Nos. 36 and 36½, e s, abt 25 n Monroe st, 27x95, five-story brk tenem't. Samuel Weil and Rachel his wife to Julius Dreyfus. June 23. 39,000

Same property. Julius Dreyfus to Samuel Weil. Mt. $19,000. July 8. nom

Sheriff st, No. 48, e s, 75 n Delancey st, 25x25, three-story frame tenem't. Frederick Kotta and Louisa his wife, Jersey City, N. J., to Heiman M. Kaplan. July 7. 6,250

Sheriff st, No. 87, w s, abt 173 s Stanton st, 25x100, five-story brk tenem't. Michael Fay and Mary his wife, William Stacom and Catharine his wife to Louis W. Preger and Oscar Dobroczynski. Mt. $22,000. July 2. 36,000

Suffolk st, No. 13, w s, 100 n Hester st, 25x100, five-story brk tenem't with stores. James E. Sullivan and Alice his wife, Charles R. and Walter C. Sullivan to Dora Landsberger. ½ part. July 6. 15,500

Same property. Mary A. and Clara M. and Georgiana F. Sullivan by James E. Sullivan guard. to same. ½ part. July 6. 15,500

Suffolk st, No. 55, w s, 75 s Broome st, 25x75, five-story brk tenem't with stores. Ernestine Kiwi to Lewis Solinsky and Morris W. Monsky. Mt. $15,000. July 1. 28,300

Suffolk st, No. 116, e s, 100 s Rivington st, 25x100, five-story brk tenem't with stores. Joseph Oberle and Annie his wife to Edward Hillenbrand. Mt. $10,000. July 2. 27,500

Same property. Edward Hillenbrand and Theodore Schloerb and Barbara his wife to Joseph Oberle. Mt. $10,000 and taxes, &c., from 1869. July 1. 17,500

Sullivan st, No. 154, w s, 145 s Houston st, 25x100, four-story brk tenem't with four-story brk tenem't on rear. Clarence A. Van Dyke to Charles F. Aukamp. 1-5 part. June 12. nom

Washington st, No. 701, s e cor Perry st, 24.9x79.5x42 6x70.7, five-story brk store, with alley across rear.
Washington st, No. 699, e s, 25.7 s Perry st, 23x85x23 2x79.4, five-story brk tenem't.
Partition. John A. Deady to Charles Fleischmann, Cincinnati, Ohio. July 2. 91,062

Washington st, Nos. 740 and 742, w s, 128.5 s Bethune st, 42.9x81; No. 740, one-story frame front and rear buildings; No. 742, three-story brk tenem't. Partition. Frederick P. Forster to Cornelius M. Demarest and Rachel S. Hutton. July 9. 16,200

Water st, No. 684, n w cor Jackson st, 25x100, two-story frame (brk front) store and tenem't with one-story frame buildings on rear. George F. Frick and Auguste E. his wife to Jacob Frick. Mt. $8,000. July 1. 4,000

Willett st, No. 64, e s, 175 s Rivington st, runs north — x east 100 x south 25x100, four-story brk tenem't with stores and four-story brk tenem't on rear. Jacob Larchan and Rebecca his wife to Nathan Scheib. Mt. $14,000. July 1. 25,000

Willett st, No. 49, w s, 44 8 n Delancey st, 25.1x88, four-story brk tenem't with three-story brk tenem't on rear. Joseph Davis and Dina his wife to Morris Rosenbloom. Sub. to mort. June 25. 19,900

4th st, Nos. 18 and 20, s s, 25 w Mercer st, 50x91x50x91.1, six-story brk store. Albert Wagner and Katie F. his wife to Samuel Hirsh. Mt. $115,000. May 29. 166,750

6th st, No. 721, n s, 278 11 e Av C, 25.5x90.10, five-story brk tenem't. Marks Levin and Betsie his wife to Jacob Hacker and Anna his wife. Mt. $19,000. July 1. 32,000

7th st, No. 100, s s, 162.11 e 1st av, 25x90.10, three-story brk tenem't. Siebrand Niewenhous and Elizabeth his wife to Sophia Bissert. July 1. 21,000

10th st, No. 317, n s, 295.6 e Av A, 25x94.8, four-story brk tenem't. Maria Singer to Rudolph F. Singer and Maria his wife, joint tenants. Correction deed. Mt. $15,000. June 30. nom

10th st, No. 261, n s, 344 w Av A, 25x94.8, five-story brk tenem't with stores. Rachel Levy to Annie Rosenthal. Mt. $20,000. July 1. 36,750

Same property. Annie Rosenthal to David Leventritt. Sub. to ½ mort. $23,000. July 1. 13,375

10th st, No. 213 E., n s, abt 260 e 2d av, three-story brk tenem't; also property in Fairfield Co., Conn. Archibald M. Pentz to Mary E. Pentz. All title. Oct. 31, 1887. 10,000

11th st, No. 522, s s, 295.6 e Av A, 25x94.8, four-story brk tenem't with stores and four-story brk tenem't on rear. Herman Schnepel and Annie his wife to Katie Jaecker. Mt. $8,000. July 1. 17,625

11th st, Nos. 102 and 104 / 6th av, No. 149½ / Garden row, Nos. 1-5 } begins 11th st, s w cor 6th av, runs west 56 10 x southwest 140.6 x south 50.6 x east 166.7 to 6th av, x north 9.6 to beginning, one and two-story frame and brk stores on 11th st and 6th av, and five three-story brk dwell'gs on Garden row. Lewis S. Samuel to John Glass. Mt. $35,000. July 8. nom

12th st, No 337, n s, 64.10 w Greenwich st, 18x79.10x7x38.4x9.7x41.6, three-story brk dwell'g.
34th st, No. 431, n s, 400 e 10th av, 25x98.9, five-story stone front flat.
William Salomon to Hannah wife of Henry Adler. July 3. 1,200

13th st, No. 156, s s, 120.6 e 7th av, 20x103.3, three-story brk dwell'g. Andrew Devlin to Samuel Devlin. ½ part. July 1. 8,000

17th st, Nos. 309 and 311 W. Agreement as to beam rights. Harriet F. Howe to John J. Coffey. July 2. nom

17th st, No. 508, s s, 143 e Av A, 23.9x92, five-story brk store and tenem't. Peter Borst and Magdalena his wife to Thomas Krekeler. Mt. $4,758. July 6. 15,200

19th st, No. 225, n s, 279 w 2d av, 23x92, three-story brk tenem't. Clarence C. Rice and Jennie D. his wife to The New York Post Graduate Medical School and Hospital. B. & S. Mt. $10,000. May 28. 14,200

22d st, No. 167, n s, 60 e 7th av, 20x49 4, three-story stone front dwell'g. Robert W. Hall to William S. Cooper. Mt. $8,000. April 27. 14,000

Same property. William S. Cooper to Edward Holland. Mt. $11,000. July 3. 15,250

24th st, Nos. 125 and 127, n s, 80 w Lexington av, 45x98.9, six-story brk flat. Peter N. Ramsey and Hartense his wife to Samuel G. Revans. Mt. $110,000. June 30. nom

27th st, No. 451, n s, 260 e 10th av, 25x98.9, three-story brk tenem't with three-story brk tenem't on rear. Edith H. wife of and Robert S. Simmons to Caleb D. Gildersleeve. Mt. $7,000. July 1. 10,550

27th st, No. 159, n s, 106.3 e 7th av, runs north 50 x west 0.6 x north 48.9 x east 25.2 x south 25.7 x east 3 6 x south 73.1 to st, x west 28.2.
27th st, No. 157, n s, 134.5 e 7th av, runs north 73.1 x west 3.6 x north 25.7 x east 24.6 x south 25.6 x west 1.4 x south 73.2 to st, x west 19.10.
Two five-story brk tenem'ts with stores and two four-story brk tenem'ts on rear.
James F. Ellison to Benjamin Sire. Sub. to morts. July 3. nom

31st st, No. 113, n s, 141.8 w 6th av, 20.10x98.9, four-story stone front dwell'g. Partition. John W. Boothby to Edmond O. Mancier. June 12. 23,300

32d st, No. 350, s s, 412 6 w 8th av, 19x98.9, four-story stone front dwell'g.
40th st, No. 304, s s, 150 w 8th av, 25x98.9, four story brk store and tenem't with five-story brk tenem't on rear.
Marie M. Martin, Philadelphia, Pa., to William G. McCrea. June 11. 1,000

32d st, s s, 412.6 w 8th av, 19x98.9.
40th st, No. 304, s s, 150 w 8th av, 25x98.9.
Henry A. Hefferan and Mary J. his wife to Henry Allen. C. a. G. All liens. March 26. 1,200

34th st, No. 450, s s, 258.4 e 10th av, 20.10x98.9, four-story brk dwell'g. Mary L. Asten to Annie T. Murray. July 1. 12,500

34th st, No. 109, n s, 120.6 e Park av, 20x98.9, four-story stone front dwell'g. Maria W. Livingston, Islip, L. I., to Edward L. Keyes. July 6. 41,000

37th st, No. 18, s s, 288.8 w 5th av, 19.6x98.9, four-story brk dwell'g. Frances S. Shepard admrx. Francis N. Shepard to Anna C. McCreory. July 1. 31,000

40th st, No. 357, n s, 100 e 9th av, 20x97.6, five-story brk store and tenem't. Joseph R. Black and Julia C. his wife to William B. Pope. Mt. $18,913. June 29. 21,500

41st st, No 548, s s, 150 e 11th av, 25x98.9, five-story brk tenem't with two-story brk and frame buildings on rear. Daniel Orth and Maria C. his wife to John J. Breudlin. Mt. $12,500. July 1. 15,500

41st st, Nos. 223-227, n s, 255 e 3d av, runs east 50 x north 98 10 x west 25.2 x north 5.9 x southwest 41 x south 71.9, three four-story brk tenem'ts. Karl M. Wallach and Samson Wallach and Hannah his wife to Peter Albert. Mt. $16,000. July 1. 26,700

42d st, No. 430, s s, 325 e 10th av, 25x98.9, five-story brk tenem't with stores. Philip L. Runkle to Siegfried W. Mayer. Mt. $15,000. July 6. 25,500

44th st, No. 138, s s, 140 e Lexington av, 15x100.5, three-story brk dwell'g. Foreclos. Elliot Sandford to John T. Nagle. July 1. 10,275

44th st, No. 449, n s, 200 e 10th av, 20x100.4, four-story brk tenem't. John H. and Thomas Nesbitt exrs. Charles Nesbitt to Edwin Bellman. July 2. 12,400

45th st, No. 608, n s, 75 w 11th av, 25x75, one-story frame building on rear of lot. Robert Dick and Katie his wife to Charles Groll. June 26. 4,600

46th st, No. 237, n s, 127 w 2d av, 25x100.4, five-story brk tenem't with stores. Maria Heine to Theodore Degenhardt trustees for Charles, Anna, Helene and George Koelish children Caroline Koelish. June 30. nom

46th st, No. 239, n s, 100 w 2d av, 27x100.4, four-story brk tenem't. Same to Josephine Degenhardt. Oct. 15, 1889. nom

47th st, No. 329, n s, 400 e 2d av, runs north 100.5 x east 25 x south 39.2 x west 0.2 x south 61.3 to st, x west 24.10, four-story brk store and tenem't with three-story brk tenem't on rear. Terence McManus to Emanuel S. Kahn. Mt. $8,000. July 1. 11,500

49th st, Nos 606-619. / 48th st, No. 613. } begins 49th st, s s, 125.2 w 11th av, runs south 44 x east 0.2 x south 56.5 x west 100 x south 100.5 to 48th st, x west 25 x north 71.5 x northwest 9.4 x west 17 x north 123.7 to 49th st, x east 149.10, three five-story brk buildings and one-story frame building and vacant lot on 49th st and vacant lot on 48th st. Emila W. wife of Chester W. Chapin to George W. Vultee. Mt. $58,000. July 1. See 51st st. other consid. and 100

49th st, No. 340, s s, 200 e 9th av, 25x100.5, five story brk store and tenem't. Edgar Conover and Josephine L. his wife to Henry Tonyan. Mt. $18,000. July 9. 29,000

50th st, No. 504, s s, 100 w 10th av, 25x100.5, four-story stone front tenem't. Augustus Hoelze and Caroline F. his wife to Julius E. W. Bendt and Adeline D. his wife. Mt. $19,500. July 1. 17,500

51st st, No 312, s s, 165 e 2d av, 20x70.5, five-story stone front tenem't. Jacob Gladke and Rachel his wife to Samuel Weiss. Mt. $8,000. July 1. 16,000

51st st, Nos. 40-44, s s, 75 w 4th av, 75x100.5, three five-story brk flats. George W. Vultee to Emilia W. wife of Chester W. Chapin. Sub. to mort. $131,250. July 2. See 49th st. other consid. and 100

52d st, No. 219, n s, 208 e 3d av, 16x110.10, three-story stone front dwell'g. Joseph H. Whitehead and M. Elizabeth his wife to Elizabeth Bohmfalk. July 1. 10,000

53d st, No. 59, n s, 66.8 w 4th av, 16.8x100.5, four-story stone front dwell'g. Almira Greer to George F. Putnam. May 16. 30,500

Same property. George F. Putnam to Sarah B. Putnam. June 16. 30,500

53d st, No. 332, s s, 275 w 1st av, 25x100.5, five-story stone front tenem't with stores. Julie Rich widow to Moses Mayer and Daniel Nathan. Mt. $13,000. July 1. 21,000

57th st, No. 417, n s, 139 9 e 1st av, 16.8x100.4, three-story stone front dwell'g. Henrietta Wimpfheimer to Caroline Ehrle. July 2. 13,000

59th st, Nos. 53 and 55, n s, 190 e Madison av, 33 4x100.5, two four-story stone front dwell'gs. David L. Newborg and Caroline his wife to Albert Wagner. Mt. $35,000. July 7. 55,000

60th st, No. 27 on map 37, n s, 149 e Madison av, 20x100.5, four-story stone front dwell'g. Margaret L. Salisbury widow to Ann E. Everitt. July 2. 4,000

60th st, No. 169, n s, 115 w 3d av, 20x100.5, four-story stone front dwell'g. Samuel M. Gross an heir of Henry Gross and Daisy his wife to Rebecca Gross. 1-6 part. Sub. to rights of other heirs. July 2. 1,000

62d st, No. 218, s s, 275 w 10th av, 25x100.5, five-story brk tenem't. Christian Williams and Lizzie his wife to George Alston. Mt. $18,000. July 1. 20,000

66th st, Nos. 239 and 241, n s, 200 e West End av, 50x100.5, two five story brk and stone tenem'ts. Eugene C. Potter and Margaret S. his wife to Mary E. wife of Henry D. Harris. Mt. $30,000. June 30. nom

66th st, No. 348, s s, 133.4 w 1st av, 16.8x100.5, three-story brk dwell'g. Albert Wagner and Katie F. his wife to Emma and Frederick Behrens. Mt. $4,000. June 29. 6,700

69th st, No. 101, n w cor Columbus av, 25x100.5; five-story brk flat with stores. Charles F. E. Vogler and Olga his wife to Mary A. O'Reilly. Mt. $34,500. July 8. 68,000

71st st, No. 69, n s, 570 w 9th av, 20x102.2, four-story stone front dwell'g. O. William Whitaker exr. Eliza Chester to William A. Downing. July 1. 17,100

73d st, No. 207 n s, 110 e 3d av, 27.6x102.2, four-story stone front flat. Maria Heine to Emelia Herlex. Oct 15, 1889. nom

73d st, No. 205 E., n s, 82.6 e 3d av, 27.6x102.2, four-story stone front flat. Same to Josephine Degenhardt trustee Maria Degenhardt. April 4, 1890. nom

74th st, No. 429, n s, 250 w Av A, 25x59.10x25x55.10, three-story frame store and tenem't. Andreas Gerin to Caroline Gerin. ½ part. July 8. nom

74th st, No. 315, n s, 200 e 2d av, 25x102.2, five-story brk tenem't with stores. Foreclos. Richard H. Clark to Charles Weisberger. Mt. $15,000. July 8. 2,100

Same property. Charles Weisberger and Mary his wife to Max C. Baum. Sub. to ½ mort. $15,000. July 8. 10,050

74th st, No. 148, s s, 37.6 e Lexington av, 18.9x68.2, three-story stone front dwell'g. Albert King and Isabella his wife to Isaac Rinaldo. Q. C. and correction deed. April 28. nom

76th st, No. 229, n s, 350 e 3d av, 25x102.2, four-story stone front tenem't. Albert Steindler and Therese his wife to Daniel Meder and Annie his wife, joint tenants. Mt. $12,000. July . 16,200

76th st, No. 419, n s, 268 e 1st av, 20x102.2, five-story brk store and tenem't. Henry Bader and Julia his wife to Simon Abrahams and Lena his wife. Mt. $9,000. July 1. 11,500

77th st, No. 61, n s, 162.6 e Madison av, 18.9x102.2, three-story stone front dwell'g. William L. Jaques to Emma J. Jaques. ½ part. Mt. $12,000. Nov. 14, 1890. nom

Same property. Henry B. Jaques to same. ½ part. Mt. $12,000. Nov. 14, 1890. nom

78th st, No. 176, s s, 120 w 3d av, 30x102.2, five-story stone front flat. Michael Meyer to Catharine Pierre widow. *Mt.* $7,800. June 15. nom

Same property. Catharine Pierre widow to Charles J. Hennelly. *Mt.* $7,800. July 3. 27,000

80th st, No. 172, s s, 159 w 3d av, 19x102, four-story stone front dwell'g. Katti wife of and Max H. Raubitschek to Henry M. Bendheim. *Mt.* $16,000. July 3. nom

81st st, No. 236, s s, 104.1 w 2d av, 23x102.2, five-story brk tenem't. George Wurst and Marie his wife to Malvina A. Levy. June 30. 24,400

82d st, No. 423, n s, 256.6 w Av A, 25x102.2, five-story brk tenem't. August Ganzenmueller and Louisa his wife to Justus Schneider. *Mt.* $10,000. July 2. 19,500

83d st, No. 338, s s, 100 w 1st av, 25x102.2, five-story stone front tenem't. Mary L. Collins to Henry Maas and Elizabeth R. his wife. July 3. 22,250

83d st, No. 527, n s, 398 e Av A, 25x102.2, five-story brk tenem't. George Schreiner and Virginia his wife to Louis Lese. *Mt.* $16,000. July 6. See 115th st. 24,000

84th st, No. 222, s s, 330.5 e 3d av, 25.5x102.2, five-story brk tenem't. Gottlieb Jetter and Matilda his wife to Adolph E. Rauch. *Mt.* $15,000. July 2. 25,500

84th st, No. 218, s s, 279.7 e 3d av, 25.5x102.2, five-story stone front tenem't with stores. Helena C. wife of and J. Peter Moebus and Elizabeth E. Kottmann heirs Heinrich Lingelbach to William H. Kottmann. July 2. 4,000

84th st, No. 346, s s, 452.1 w West End av, 22.11 x102.2, three-story stone front dwell'g. John R. MacArthur to Pauline A. MacArthur. *Mt.* $18,000. July 2. nom

84th st, No. 446, s s, 119 w Av A, runs south 184.10 x northwest 69.3½ x northeast — x east — x north — to 84th st, x east 49.6, three-story frame dwell'g with two two-story frame buildings on rear. Nathan Frank, St. Louis, Mo., to Michael Conlan and Terence Gannon. July 6. 24,000

85th st, No. 530, s s, 323 e Av A, 25x102.2, five-story brk tenem't. Charles Schafer and Maria his wife to David Y. Disbrow and Josephine his wife. *Mt.* $7,000 and assessm't for Park. July 1. 20,500

86th st, No. 211, n s, 200 e 3d av, 25x100.8, five-story brk store and flat. Anna M. wife of and William J. Frost to Frank E. Wise. July 5. nom

Same property. Frank E. Wise and Emma F. his wife to Mary Pearson. July 1. See below. 40,000

86th st, No. 542, s s, 148 w East End av, 25x 102.2, five-story stone front tenem't. Jacob Johann and Margaretha his wife to Emma Bohnig. *Mt.* $17,500 and assessm't for park. July 2. 28,000

86th st, No. 71, n s, 114.6 e Columbus av, 20.6x 100.8, four-story brk dwell'g. John G. Prague to Thomas Reid. July 2. other consid. and 50,000

86th st, No. 76, s s, 70 w Park av, 17.10x102.2, four-story brk dwell'g. Mary Pearson to Frank E. Wise. July 2. See above. 27,000

86th st, No. 308, s s, 122 e 2d av, 18x102, three-story stone front dwell'g. Henry Spies and Mary his wife to Melchior Noser. July 8. 15,000

87th st, Nos. 336-340, s s, 320.2 e 2d av, 84.9x 100.8, three four-story stone front flats. Charles Reed and Elizabeth his wife and William H. Schmohl and Elizabeth his wife to Louis Lese, Pincus Loweufeld, Morris Goldstein and Sarah F. Deutsch. *Mt.* $40,000. July 1. See Jackson st. 74,000

88th st No. 237, n s, 75 w 2d av, 25x100.8, five-story stone front flat. Margaretha Hoffman to Philipp Stuernagel. *Mt.* $12,000. June 29. 22,200

88th st, No. 164, s s, 252 e Amsterdam av, 18x 100.8, three-story stone front dwell'g. Samuel Colcord and Alice B. his wife to Mary S. Rich. *Mt.* $16,000. June 29. 21,300

90th st, No. 306, s s, 145 w West End av, 15x 100.8, four-story stone front dwell'g. Charles T. Barney, Francis M. Jencks and William E. D. Stokes to Frank L. Smith. June 24. nom

Same property. Same to same. June 24. nom

90th st, No. 330, s s, 175 w 1st av. 25x100.8, five-story stone front tenem't. Frederick W. Sauer and Magdalena his wife and Conrad Gross and Lena his wife to Henry Schadowsky. *Mt.* $12,500. July 1. consid. omitted

90th st, No. 206, s s, 135 e 3d av, 25x100.8, five-story brk tenem't. Margaretha Hoffmann widow to Henry Bader. *Mt.* $13,000. June 29. 24,000

90th st, No. 137, n s, 375 e 4th av. 25x100.8, three-story frame dwell'g with two-story frame building on rear. Mathias McCabe, Fall River, Mass., to Michael McCabe, Rhode Island. Q. C. July 5, 1890. other consid. and 500

93d st, Nos. 68-72, s s, 105 w Park av, 63x100.8, three five-story stone front flats. Nicholas J. Reville and Theresa A. his wife to Francis J. Schnugg. *Mt.* $57,000. June 25. See Park av. nom

94th st, n s, 285.6 w 2d av, 39.6x100.8, vacant. Mayor, &c., New York, to Sarah B. Brainerd. Q. C. June 16. 350

99th st, n s, 100 e Amsterdam av, 50x100.11, vacant. Henriette Blinn individ. and extrx. Christian Blinn to Bernard Mooney and John Connor, of Mooney & Connor. June 26. 14,000

101st st, n s, 150 e Columbus av, 25x100.11, Release mort. William D. Murphy to William M. Walsh, Williamsbridge, N. Y. July 1. 7,333

102d st, No. 215, n s, 230 e 3d av, 25x100.11, five-story brk tenem't. Augusta Steffens to Aaron Kaplan. *Mt.* $12,500. July 1. 19,600

102d st, No. 124, s s, 75 w Lexington av, 25x 100.11, five-story brk tenem't. William J. Hendrick and Mattie H. his wife and Robert B. Cotter and Anna R. his wife to Louis Michaelis. *Mt.* $16,000. June 16. 20,000

103d st, n s, 100 e Riverside Drive, 100x100.11, vacant. Alexander Walker and Margaret A. his wife and Judson Lawson and Martha A. his wife to John J. Egan and Daniel Halleey. *Mt.* $20,000. July 1. nom

104th st, No. 236, s s, 212.6 w 2d av, 18.9x100.11, three-story stone front dwell'g. Babette Geib widow to Henry Aronson. *Mt.* $4,000. July 2. 10,500

105th st, Nos. 146 and 148, s s, 325 e 10th av, 50 x100.11, two five-story brk flats. Henry T. Bunn to Mary A. Scutt. *Mt.* $52,000. May 30. 61,000

106th st, No. 307, n s, 150 e 2d av, 25x100.11, four-story brk tenem't. Fanny Bach and Jacob Berlinger exrs. Alexander Bach to David Reggel. *Mt.* $6,000. July 1. 14,000

Same property. Fanny Bach widow to David Reggel. *Mt.* $6,000. July 1. nom

106th st, No. 319, n s, 300 e 2d av, 25x100.11, four-story brk tenem't with stores. Paul Gantert and Rebecca his wife to Louis Molia. *Mt.* $10,500. July 2. 15,000

108th st, No. 105, n s, 53 e Park av, late 4th av, 26x73.11, four-story brk tenem't. Dietrich W. Wehrenberg and Sophie his wife to John Ott. *Mt.* $8,660. July 8. 13,000

109th st, No. 159, n s, 100 e Lexington av, 25x 100.11, four-story stone front tenem't. Maria Holthausen to Rachel Haltenbach. *Mt.* $9,500. July 1. 13,200

109th st, s s, 95 e 1st av, 20x100.11x25x100.11 (?), two-story frame building. Ida wife of Philip E Haag to Herman Kahrs and Peter Stribhei. May 25. 8,500

109th st, s s, 95 e 1st av, 25x100.11, two-story frame building. George Bradish and Elizabeth J. his wife, Flushing, to Ida wife of Philip E. Haag. Q. C. This release is contingent upon legal ownership of Ida Haag as grantee of Eliza Taylor. June 12. nom

111th st, No. 177, n s, 120 w 3d av, 25x100.11 four-story stone front tenem't. Hugh O'Rorke to Moses May and Yetta his wife. *Mt.* $10,000. July 1. 18,000

113th st, No. 77, n s, 124.6 w 4th av, 26.4x100.11, five-story brk flat. Herman Reisner and Henriette his wife to Celia Weil and Ida Ulrich. *Mt.* $16,000. June 22. 23,500

113th st, No. 337, n s, 233.4 w 1st av, 16.8x100.10, three-story brk dwell'g. Herman Wronkow and Serena his wife to Lena wife of Marcello St. Barilati. *Mt.* $3,000. July 7. 6,500

114th st, s s, 475 e Lenox av, 25x100.11. }
113th st, n s, 475 e Lenox av, 25x100.11. }
Samuel J. Joyce individ. and as exr. Lydia A. Joyce and Lillie A., Hattie L. and Martha J. Joyce heirs Lydia A. Joyce to Jeremiah C. Lyons. July 1. nom

114th st, s s, 450 e Lenox av, 75x100.11, two-story frame building and vacant. }
113th st, n s, 450 e Lenox av, 75x100.11, vacant. }
Jeremiah C. Lyons and Susie T. his wife to Henry Franke. *Mt.* $25,000. June 15. nom

114th st, No. 170, s s, 196 w 3d av, 24x100.11, brk church with one-story brk building on rear. Elizabeth Lahr to Esther Goldman. June 30. nom

Same property. The German Methodist Episcopal Emanuel Church of Harlem, New York City, to same. June 30. 11,500

114th st. No. 319, n s, 228 e 2d av, 22x100.11, two-story frame dwell'g. Michael Carroll and Margaret A. his wife to Herman J. Rohrich. *Mt.* $2,200. July 1. 4,550

114th st, Nos. 302-310, s s, 95 w 8th av, 130x 100.11, four five-story brk flats and one vacant lot. Foreclos. Somerville P. Tuck to David Marx. *Mt.* $16,000. July 3. 12,750

115th st, n s, 126 e 4th av, runs east 29 x north 100.11 x west 75 x south 25.3 x east 46 x south 75.8 to beginning, vacant. Kieran Egan and ano. exrs. Joseph L. Gerety to Louis Lese. July 6. 9,000

115th st, No. 115, n s, 126 e 4th av, runs east 29 x north 100.11 x west 75 x south 25.8 x east 46 x south 75.8, vacant. }
Park (4th) av, e s, 75.8 n 115th st, 25.3x80, vacant. *Mt.* $3,150. }
Louis Lese and Sarah his wife to George Schreiner. July 6. See 83d st. 17,250

115th st, s s, 80 e 4th av, runs north 100.11 x south 100.11 to st, x west 0⅛ in., gore. Edmond Dwyer to Truman H. Baldwin. Q. C. July 1. nom

115th st, No. 112, s s, 80.0⅛ e 4th av, 24.11¾x 100.11x25x100.11, five-story brk flat. Edmond Dwyer to Truman H. Baldwin. *Mt.* $12,000. July 1. 20,000

Same property. Mary E. Gerety widow to same. Q. C. July 8. nom

Same property. John Foley, Jr., to same. C. a. G. July 6. nom

120th st, Nos. 506 and 508, s s, 100 e Pleasant av, 50x100.11, two three-story frame dwell'gs with one-story frame building on rear. August Meyer and Louise his wife to Jacob Schloeder. June 27. 10,500

120th st, No. 213, n s, 156.3 e 3d av, 18.9x100.10, three-story brk dwell'g. Caroline Hockenberry widow to Minnie W. Carsen. *Mt.* $7,500. June 8. nom

121st st, No. 74, s s, 80 w Park av, 20x100.11, four-story stone front flat. Margaret A. wife of George McGrath to Hermann C. Junker. *Mt.* $11,500. July 8. 18,000

121st st, No. 76, s s, 60 w 4th av, 20x100.11, four-story stone front flat. Michael Elias and Johanna his wife to Searles Babbitt. July 2. nom

Same property. Searles Babbitt and Caroline M. his wife to Emilie Bohne. *Mt.* $12,000. July 2. 17,200

121st st, No. 4, s s, 100 w Mt. Morris av, 20x 100.11, four-story stone front dwell'g. Release mort. Reuben Ross to Samuel O. Wright, Rockville Centre, L. I. July 1. nom

Same property. Samuel O. Wright and Maria T. his wife to Carrie A. Taylor. *Mt.* $25,000. July 2. 40,000

123d st, s s, 240.6 e 7th av, 17x100.11. Release mort. German-American Real Estate Title Guarantee Co. to Elizabeth K. Smith. June 30. nom

123d st, s s, 223.6 e 7th av. 17x100.11. Release mort. Same to same. June 30. nom

123d st, s s, 190.6 e 7th av, 16x100.11. Release mort. Same to same. June 30. nom

123d st, s s, 206.6 e 7th av, 17x100.11. Release mort. Same to same. June 30. nom

125th st / Manhattan st } begins 125th st, n s, 100 e 10th av, runs north 59.1 x southeast 0.6⅛ x northeast 81 to Manhattan st at point 155.6 e of 126th st, x east 25 x southwest 81 x southeast 67.10 x southwest 16 to 125th st, x west 79, vacant. James A. Deering and Mary his wife to John C. Barth. *Mt.* $20,000. June 29. See 136th st. exch

126th st, No. 34, s s, 56 w Madison av, 18x83, three-story stone front dwell'g. Carrie A. Taylor to Samuel O. Wright. *Mt.* $10,000. July 7. 22,000

126th st, No. 172, s s, 20 e 7th av, 18x80, four-story stone front dwell'g. Robert L. Harrison to Julia S. Valentine. July 8. nom

128th st, n s, 100 w 8th av, 50x99.11. Release mort. Annie R. Bauerdorf to John S. Conaheer. May 18. nom

128th st, No. 219, n s, 224.7 e 3d av, 19.5x99.11, four-story brk tenem't. George F. Johnson and Emma his wife to George L. Loutrel. *Mt.* $10,000. July 1. See 132d st. 18,000

130th st, No. 43, n s, 375 e 6th av, 20x99.11, four-story stone front dwell'g. Callie F. wife of L. Franklin Genet to The L. F. Genet Lumber Co. New York. *Mt.* $16,500. June 26. nom

132d st, s s, 460 w 5th av, 50x99.11, vacant. George L. Loutrel and Annie L. his wife to George F. Johnson. July 1. See 128th st. nom

134th st, n s, 200 e 7th av, 50x99.11, vacant. Ethelbert Wilson and Adelaide his wife to William J. Gilmore. *Mt.* $11,000. July 8. 17,500

136th st, s s, 225 w Lenox av, 75x99.11, vacant. John C. Barth and Mary G. his wife to James A. Deering. *Mt.* $12,500. July 1. See 125th st. exch

144th st, No. 476, s e cor Amsterdam av, 30x 99.11, five-story brk flat with stores. John R. Agnew to Thomas McBride. *Mt.* $32,500. July 1. See St. Nicholas av. nom

146th st, No. 466, s s, 200 e Amsterdam av, 20x 99.11, four-story brk flat. Jane C. wife of James C. Boyle to James C. Boyle. June 30. nom

147th st, n s, 25 w New Croton Aqueduct, 50x99.11. Milton See and Sarah R. his wife to John J. McEvoy. *Mt.* $6,862. June 9. 10

147th st, n w cor New Croton Aqueduct, 25x 99.11. Truman H. Baldwin and Lesa L. his wife to same. *Mt.* $4,406. June 29. nom

168th st, Nos. 510 and 512, s s, 200 w 10th av, 50 x95. John D. Halleren and Mamie E. his wife to Philip Becker. All morts. July 1. nom

168th st, s s, 120 e Audubon av, 50x95. Caroline Schalk, Newark, N. J., to John D. Halleren, Brooklyn. Q. C. All liens. May 25. exch

178th st, n s, 100 e Wadsworth av, 50x100. Pauline Simon to John Yates. June 15. 4,550

178th st, n s, 150 w Wadsworth av, 25x100. Pauline Simon to Amos M. Lyon. June 15. 2,525

180th st, s s, 95 e Audubon av, 25x100. Pauline Simon to Alfred H. Taylor. June 15. 2,425

182d st, n s, 345 w 10th av, 20x99.11. Clara Fairchild to John L. Davis. *Mt.* $2,920. July 6. nom

184th st, s s, 480 w 11th av, 50x99.11. }
Kingsbridge road, s e cor 184th st, 50.5x96.3x 49.11x108.2. }
Emma Darling, Plainfield, N. J., to Frederick Adler. July 1. 9,500

Amsterdam (10th) av, e s, 25 s 131st st, 74.10x 125. Release mort. Henry W. Ford trustee Augustus H. Ward to Thomas Moloney. June 29. 35,000

Amsterdam (10th) av, s e cor 185th st, 79.11x 100. Louis W. Duesing and Mary H. his wife to Michael J. Callahan. *Mt.* $12,250. June 22. 19,000

Amsterdam (10th) av, w s, 99.11 n 149th st, 75x 100, vacant. Mary E. Field widow, Rome, Italy, to Byron L. Strasburger. July 1. 19,000

Av A, No. 1575, w s, 52.2 s 84th st, 25x79, five-story brk tenem't with stores. Josephine Kretschmer widow to Adolphus Reimann. *Mt.* $15,000. July 8. 25,800

Columbus av, s w cor 75th st, 127.8x100, vacant. Jacob Rothschild and Regina his wf to Simon Banner. July 6. 145,000

Columbus av, No. 646, w s, 75.8 n 91st st, 25x 80, five-story brk store and flat. Henry B. Helmke, Gesine M. H. Ahrens and Henrietta M. H. Montross legatees Behrend Helmke to Arthur Wehrmann. *Mt.* $16,000. July 1. 30,000

Same property. Henry B. Helmke admr. will annexed of Behrend Helmke to same. *Mt.* $16,000. July 1. 30,000

Columbus av, No. 869, w s, 25.11 n 102d st, 25x75, five-story brk store and flat. Henry D. Sedgwick and Henrietta E. his wife, Stockbridge, Mass., to Simon Adler and Henry S. Herrman. *Mt.* $17,000. July 6. 25,000

Edgecombe av or road, n e cor 155th st, —x101 x100x114.8. Release mort. The New York Life Ins. Co. to Sarah Lynch. June 30. nom

Lenox av, s e cor 142d st, 99.11x175, vacant. Contract to exchange for
106th st, Nos. 106 and 108, s s, 150 w Columbus av, 50x100.11.
Two five-story brk flats.
Thomas R. Hughes, Weehawken, N. J., to John C. Barth. Equality of exchange. July 4. 3,000

Lenox av, s e cor 142d st, 99.11x100, vacant.
142d st, s s, 100 e Lenox av, 75x99.11, vacant.
Margie B. Lacy extrx. Frederick Lacey to Peter J. Brady. May 20. nom

Lexington av, No. 880, w s, 120.5 n 65th st, 20x70, four-story stone front dwell'g. James S. McGovern and Frances his wife to Louisa Schulz. *Mt.* $10,000. July 2. 16,000

Lexington av, No. 886, s w cor 66th st, 20.5x70, four-story brk (stone front) store and dwell'g. Frederick Bucker and Margaretha his wife to Marie A. wife of Albin Wibom. *Mt.* $21,500. July 2. 28,000

Madison av, No. 272. Juliu H. Billings to James A. Billings and Irving H. Brown. Trust deed to secure $4,000, &c. April 17. val. consid

Madison av, No. 1035, e s, 22.2 n 79th st, 20x77, four-story stone front dwell'g. Mary E. wife of Henry D. Harris to Thomas R. Hughes. *Mt.* $16,000. June 30. nom

Same property. Thomas R. Hughes, Weehawken, N. J., to E. Clifford Potter. *Mt.* $29,500. June 30. 40,000

Madison av, No. 1133, e s, 84.2 s 85th st, 20x75, five-story brk flat. Frank Reynolds and Annie his wife to Charles R. Gregor. April 15. 23,000

Madison av, s e cor 107th st, 100.11x100.
Park (4th) av, s w cor 107th st, 100.11x100.
107th st, s s, 100.11 e Madison av, 200x100.11.
All vacant.
Foreclos. J. Sergeant Cram to John B. Smith. *Mt.* $70,000 and int. July 8. 1,000

New av immediately east of Kingsbridge road, e s, 25 n 175th st, 25x100. Partition. John A. Deady to Charles Fleischmann. July 2. 2,000

New av immediately east of Kingsbridge road, n e cor 175th st, 25x100. Partition. Same to same. July 2. 5,000

Park av, n w cor 95th st, 25.2x100.
95th st, n s, 100 w Park av, 75x100.8.
Vacant.
Esther A. Wheaton to Francis J. Schnugg. Sub. to morts. June 11. nom

Same property. Francis J. Schnugg and Carrie H. his wife to Nicholas J. Reville. *Mt.* $20,500. July 1. See 92d st. 42,000

St. Nicholas av, No. 746, e s, 229.11 s of centre line of 148th st if extended, 25x100, two-story brk dwell'g. Thomas McBride and Mary A. his wife to John R. Agnew. *Mt.* $10,000. July 1. See 144th st. nom

Vermilyea av, e s, bet Hawthorne and Academy sts, being lots 161–166 map estate Isaac Dyckman. Joseph H. Godwin and Phoebe A. his wife to Julius J. Lyons. June 29. 4,050

West End av, No. 453, w s, 69.8 s 87th st, 20x100, four-story brk dwell'g. Jacob Lawson, Brooklyn, to Frank L. Smith. July 1. nom

Same property. Frank L. Smith and Magdaline his wife to Michael Tanner. *Mt.* $25,500. July 7. 35,500

West End av, w s, 50.8 s 87th st, 30x100. Release mort. George Williamson admr. Margaret Williamson to Jacob Lawson. July 3. nom

West End av, No. 345, w s, 42 n 81st st, 20x66, three-story brk dwell'g. Foreclos. George B. Newell to John Hennessey. July 2. 20,050

Same property. John Hennessey and Kate his wife to Isaac C. Ogden, Jr. *Mt.* $15,000. July 2. consid. omitted

1st av, No. 849, w s, 50.3 n 47th st, 25.1x100, five-story brk tenem't with stores. Frederick Berg and Dora his wife to Michael Johannes and Christina his wife. *Mt.* $15,000. July 1. 22,000

1st av, No. 2211, w s, 75 n 113th st, 25x100, five-story brk store and tenem't. Teresa wife of and Matthew Coogan to Pasquale Venturieri. *Mt.* $14,000. July 2. 23,000

Same property. Release mort. Edwin A. Bradley and George C. Currier to Teresa wife of Matthew Coogan. July 3. nom

Same property. Release mort. The Murray Hill Bank to same. July 6. nom

1st av, w s. Party wall agreement. Stephen H. Thayer to same. Aug. 25, 1884. nom

2d av, No. 509, n w s, 74.1 n e 28th st, runs northwest 52.11 x southwest 18.8 x southeast 16.6 to old boundary line bet Rosehill farm and Kips Bay farm x north — x nearly south to av, x 18.10, five-story brk store and tenement. Stephan Baust to Ella C. Riker, Woodside, L. I. *Mt.* $5,000. Re-recorded. Sept. 1, 1890. 14,500

2d av, No. 352, e s, 78 n 20th st, 20.3x90, three-story brk tenem't. John Bickmann and Elizabeth his wife to Maria Sharkey. *Mt.* $10,000. July 1. 19,000

2d av, No. 1767, w s, 75.4 n 88th st, 25x75, five-story stone front flat with stores. Jacob Levy and Susie his wife to Jacob Gruner. *Mt.* $15,000. July 1. 24,500

2d av, No. 2075, w s, 25.11 s 107th st, 25x75, four-story brk tenem't with stores. Isaac Brown and Sophia his wife to Louis H. Morris. Reserves right of action against Elevated R. R. July 1. 16,000

2d av, No. 2419, w s, 20 n 124th st, 27x80.6, five-story stone front tenem't with stores. Emily wife of Milton L. Dorland to George Bendheim. *Mt.* $12,000. July 2. 21,500

2d av, w s, 25.11 n 100th st, 25x100. Release mort. Samuel Weil to Emil Broggelwirth. July 3. 4,000

2d av, w s, 50.11 n 100th st, 25x100. Release mort. Same to same. July 3. 3,000

2d av, No. 1947, w s, 25.11 n 100th st, 25x100, five-story brk tenem't with stores. Emil Broggelwirth and Pauline E. his wife, Brooklyn, to Elise Lotze. *Mt.* $14,000. June 26. 24,000

2d av, No. 1949, w s, 50.11 n 100th st, 25x100, five-story brk tenem't with stores. Same to Elizabeth Klein. June 26. 100

2d av, No. 914, e s, 75.4 s 49th st, 16.9x100, four-story brk store and tenem't. Joseph F. Blaut to Hannah Straus. Q. C. Sept. 4, 1885. nom

3d av, No. 1275, e s, 51.1 n 73d st, 25.6x80, five-story stone front tenem't with store. Same to Elizabeth Bastian. Oct. 15, 1889. nom

3d av, No. 2277 and 2279. Agreement as to fire escape. Harlem Savings Bank to John and Jacob Spies. June 25. nom

5th av, w s, 91.6 n 16th st, 0.6x89. Robert Goelet and Henriette W. his wife and Ogden Goelet and Mary R. his wife to William Ziegler, Brooklyn. Q. C. March 20. 1,057

5th av, No. 1393, e s, 58.3 s 115th st, 17.8x100, five-story brk flat. Foreclos. Henry A. Robinson to Henry A. Jordan. Sub. to mort. $17,500. June 30. 1,000

7th av, No. 2147–2151, n e cor 127th st, 99.11x100, three five-story brk flats. Lansing Hoteling, Albany, N. Y., to George F. Johnson. *Mt.* $113,000. July 1. 163,000

8th av, No. 143 }
17th st, Nos. 303–309 } n w cor 17th st, 25x103, three and four-story brk and frame stores and tenem'ts. Margaret J. Howe to John J. Coffey. Q. C. June 24. nom

Same property. Charles W. and Harriet F. Howe exrs. John W. Howe to same. July 2 49,000

8th av, Nos. 2099–2105, s w cor 114th st, 100.11x95, four five-story brk flats with stores. Foreclos. Somerville P. Tuck to David Marx. *Mt.* $20,000. July 3. 30,000

8th av, n e cor 116th st, 100.11x100.
116th st, n s, 100 e 8th av, 25x100.11.
One-story frame store and vacant.
George E. Hyatt and Margaret W. his wife to Edward T. Smith. *Mt.* $85,000. June 16. nom

9th av, No. 323, w s, 74.1 s 29th st, 24.8x100, three-story brk store and tenem't. John H. Lucken and Sarah his wife to Joseph Corbit. July 6. 17,000

10th av, No. 825, w s, 50.5 s 55th st, 25x100.
10th av, No 823, w s, 75.5 s 55th st, 25x100.
Two five-story brk tenem'ts with stores.
Partition. Wilbur Larremore to William Salomon. June 28. 40,400

Same property. William Salomon to Hugo S. Mack. *Mt.* $26,000. June 28. 40,400

11th av, n e cor 62d st, 100.5x100. Release covenant. Julia A. Low individ. and devisee Susan Low to John B. Smith. Feb. 2, 1891. nom

11th av, n w cor 173d st, 25x100. Partition. John A. Deady to Charles Fleischman. July 2. 5,000

11th av, w s, 25 n 173d st, 25x100. Partition. Same to same. July 2. 3,000

11th av, w s, 125 n 173d st, 25x100. Partition. Same to same. July 2. 3,000

11th av, w s, 150 n 173d st, 25x100. Partition. Same to same. July 2. 3,000

11th av, w s, 175 n 173d st, 25x100. Partition. Same to same. July 2. 5,000

11th av, w s, 75 n 173d st, 25x100. Partition. Same to same. July 2. 3,000

11th av, w s, 50 n 173d st, 25x100. Partition. Same to same. July 2. 5,000

11th av, w s, 100 n 173d st, 25x100. Partition. Same to same. July 2. 3,000

11th av, w s, 75 s 180th st, 25x100. Pauline Simon to August H. Fitschen. June 10. 3,850

Interior lot, 73.9 s 33d st and 325 e 2d av, runs east 25 x south 25x20x25. William Byrne to Margaret Byrne. C. a. G. June 29. 2,000

Interior lot, begins at point in centre line bet 47th st and 48th st, at point 424.10 e 2d av, runs east 0.2x39.2. Release mort. Thomas C. T. Crain, Chamberlain, New York, to Terence McManus. July 7. nom

Interior lot, begins at point 424.10 e 2d av and 59.6 n 47th st, runs north 40.11 x east 0.2 x south 40.11 x west 0.2. Joseph Loeb and Rachel his wife to Terence McManus. Sub. to morts. and on this adjoining property. July 2. 350

15 lots, of which John R. McCann died seized, more particularly described in judgment of Supreme Court in action of Elizabeth Patterson agt Mary Hettrich, two of said parcels being in block 720 section 3, one in block 693, one in block 770, one in block 761, and ten in block 825 section 3 land map of New York. Elizabeth Patterson to Mary Hettrick. C. a. G. ½ part. July 9. nom

Same lots. Mary Hettrich to William Patterson. C. a. G. ½ part. July 9. 25,000

All title in Pier old No. 28 North River commonly called Vesey st Pier and Pier old No. 24 with 109.4 of bulkhead connected therewith on west side of West st next south of Barclay st ferry, with land under water, &c. James Cruikshank trustee for and Cath. Louise O. and C. Jones to the Mayor, &c., New York. All title. June 29. 100,000

Same property. Bertram de N., Violet D. and Frederick H. Cruger by Robert Sewell guard. to same. All title. July 6. 16,667

Same property. Eugene C. Cruger and Meta K. his wife to same. B. & S. April 24. 16,667

Same property. William J. Cruger and May his wife to same. All title. April 29. 33,333

Same property. James P. Cruger and Amy N. his wife, Newburg, to same. B. & S. All title. April 29. 33,333

Same property. Release dower. Blanche E. Cruger to Bertram de N., Violet D. and Frederick H. Cruger. July 1. nom

Same property. Release dower. Blanche E. Cruger to Eugene G. Cruger. July 1. 1,000

Same property. Release dower. Same to Mayor, &c., New York. July 1. nom

MISCELLANEOUS.

All title of grantor in estate of Samuel B. H. Judah, dec'd. Celestine A. Burchell to George B. and Samuel A. Goldschmidt and John A. Burchell. Trust deed. June 22. nom

Release legacy. John H. Clearwater to Edward Clearwater exr. John H. Clearwater and individ. as residuary devisee. April 12, 1890. 600

Similar release. Eliza A. Clearwater to same. Feb. 18, 1889. 600

Similar release. Henry E. Vaughan to same. Nov. 1, 1890. 600

Similar release. John H. Vaughan to same. Feb. 15, 1889. 600

23d and 24th WARDS.

Columbine st, s s, 25 w Jefferson av, 50x75. Charles V. Lamb to George Meyer. *Mt* $500. July 6. 1,500

Denman pl, n e s, if extended, lot 5 map Woodstock, 100x48.10. John P. White to John McGeehan. July 2. 1,500

Freeman st, n s, 100 e Stebbins av, 97.8x101.11 x62.6x91.4. Mary wife of Wenzel Wavra to Frank Belsky. July 2. 4,500

Highbridge st, n w cor 1st av, 171.10x102.11 to Doughtys Brook, x191x100. Partition. William N. Armstrong to William and Elizabeth Knight. July 3. 2,000

Hillside st, centre line, plot 139 I. Dyckman's Fort George property, 50x227.6x50x226.9. Edward Stroud and Elizabeth A. his wife to Henry Battermann. July 2. 3,125

Holly pl, n s, 140 w Katonah av, 40x100. Ephraim B. Levy to David H. Lenox, Plainfield, N. J. July 2. nom

Kemble st, n s, 250 e Keppler av, 40x100. Jacob J. Blauvelt and Eliza A. his wife, Jersey City, N. J., to Joseph Ullmer. July 6. 825

Knox st, s s, 160 w Katonah av, 60x100. Ephraim B. Levy to Ellen F. Harkin. July 2. 1,125

Lyon st, s s, 174 w Fox st, runs south 68.9 x southwest 55.11 to n e s 169th st, x northwest 30 x northeast 44.3 x west 32.2 x north 45.5 to Lyon st, x east 60. Henry D. Tiffany and Caroline C. his wife to Peter J. Stumpf and Catherine J. his wife. July 2. 1,400

Monroe st, w s, 100 n Spring st, 25x100. James A. Flack, late Sheriff, to James G. and Robert A. Powers and Allen B. Potter. June 26. 1,100

North st, n s, lot 385 map Mount Eden, 50x100. Eleanor M. Bell to Martha P. and Alice L. Woodall. Q. C. June 18. nom

Same property. Mary A. T. Moore formerly Turner admrx. Malcolm C. Turner to same. Q. C. and release tax sales. Nov. 29, 1889. 52

Same property. William H. Foster and ano. exrs. James T. Foster to same. April 14. 700

Same property. Thomas O. Woolf and John A. Woolf and Mary E. his wife to same. Q. C. Jan. 24. nom

Oak terrace, n s, 100 w Beekman av, 25x100. William R. Beal Land Improvement Co. to Henry Uhl and Barbara his wife. July 8. 1,975

Oak terrace, s s, 36 e Crimmins av, 25x100. Same to Charles Hasenbalg. July 8. 2,000

Oak terrace, n s, 125 w Beekman av, 25x100. William R. Beal Land Impt. Co. to Babette Schmidt. July 8. 1,975

Oak terrace, s s, 61.1 e Crimmins av, 25x100. Same to Charles Hacker and Elizabeth M. his wife. July 8. 1,975

Southern Boulevard, e s, 254.6 n Lyon st, 37.6x100. William S. Whitman and Mary L. his wife to Denison P. Chesebro. *Mt.* $2,500. July 2. nom

Southern Boulevard, s e cor Briggs av, 25x100 x34.3x100.5. Twenty-fourth Ward R. E. Assoc. to Kate wife of John J. Cullen. June 15. 1,800

Southern Boulevard, s w cor Bainbridge av proposed, 30.7x100x50x101.11. Same to Charles F. Wetzel. June 15. 2,400

Southern Boulevard, n s, 96 w Webster av proposed, 25x100. Same to James Hynes. June 15. 1,625

Southern Boulevard, s s, 50 e Briggs av, 25x100. Same to Jacob F. Keyser. June 15. 1,400

Southern Boulevard, s s, 30.7 w Bainbridge av proposed, 50x100. Same to Matilda B. Toussaint. June 15. 2,700

Southern Boulevard, s s, 80.7 w Bainbridge av proposed, 50x120. Same to James Thomas. June 15. 3,150

Southern Boulevard, s s, 25 e Briggs av, 25x100.
Briggs av proposed, e s, 50.3 n Garfield st, 25.1x99.5x25x101.9.
Garfield st proposed, n s, 106.4 e Briggs av, runs north 100 x east 25 x north 25 x east 50 x south 125 to st, x west 75.
Same to Zabdiel S. Sampson. June 15. 5,350

Southern Boulevard, s w cor Berrian av, 172.7x100.5x172.7x99.6. Sub. to any right of way over gore at Southern Boulevard and Corsa av, as shown on map. Therese wife of Frederick Toussaint and Julius F. Toussaint and Matilda B. his wife to Abby wife of Frederick Runk. Sub. to morts. July 1. 15,000

Suburban st, s w s, 97 s e Decatur av, 50x90.11x51.7x103.7. Twenty-fourth Ward Real Estate Assoc. to Edward Ehrlich. June 15. 2,850

Topping st, s w cor 174th st, 100x100. Sarah J. Elsey, Brooklyn, to John Gallagher. July 2. 5,000

3d st, n e cor 1st av, 40x100, 24th Ward. Caroline wife of Benjamin W. Cole, West New Brighton, to Joseph Ullmer. July 6. 800

139th st, n s, 106.6 e Alexander av, 25x100. Partition. John A. Deady to Charles Fleischmann, Cincinnati, Ohio. July 2. 6,105

141st st, n s, 200.6 w Beekman av, 25x104.4x25x106.1. William R. Beal Land Imp m Co. to Robert Schwend. July 8. rove [illegible]

141st st, n s, 225.6 w Beekman av, runs north 104.4 x west 61 to Crimmins av, x south — to 141st st, x 139.8. Same to George Garlan. July 8. 5,700

146th st, s s, 400 e Willis av, 50x100. Sarah A. Williamson to Anna T. Dale. July 1. See Alexander av. 6,750

146th st, No. 719, n s, 265 w Brook av, 24.6x100. Elizabeth wife of and George Ross to Elizabeth Reilly. *Mt.* $4,500. June 30. 100

146th st, s s, 250 e Willis av, 25x100. Theodore Baumbach and Amalie his wife to Elizabeth wife of John Elterich. *Mt.* $4,400. July 3. 8,200

150th st, s s, 200 w River av, runs south 206.4 x west 451.2 to pier and bulkhead line on e s Harlem River, x north 24.11 x 241.9 x east 547.10, also lease of same. Release mort. Mary J. Lyon to Abbie L. and Anna J. Sturges. June 10. consid. omitted

162d st, s w s, 186 s e Courtlandt av, 54x100. Joseph E. King to Mary King. June 18. nom

164th st, s w s, 90 n w Washington av, 30x100. Henry Bischoff to Mary wife of John H. Lammers. *Mt.* $4,000. June 20. 7,900

167th st, s e s, 63.10 s w Fox st, 63.10x62.2x46x40. John De Hart and Chattie his wife to Francis D. Bale. July 6. nom

176th st, s w s, 100 s e Fleetwood av, 100x125. Elizabeth C wife of Emil Slayton to William McNabb. *Mt.* $5,500. July 1. 7,000

184th st, n s, 100 e Vanderbilt av, 25x100. Mary J. wife of John J. Barry to Margaret Geary. B. & S. and C. a. G. July 1. 1,250

Arthur av, lot 435 map S. Cambreleng et al., Fordham, 25x87.6. Release mort. Andrew Weiser to James O'Neill and Annie his wife. May 5. nom

Alexander av, e s, 115 n 142d st, 60x106.6. Anna T. wife of James Dale to Henry L. Morris trustee Mary M. Ostrander. Q. C. July 1. nom

Alexander av, e s, 95 n 142d st, 20x106.6, excepting portion taken for av, h & l. Anna T. wife of James Dale to Sarah A. Williamson. *Mt.* $15,000. July 1. See 146th st. 21,000

Alexander av, e s, 95 n 142d st. Party wall agreement. Henry L. Morris trustee for Mary M. Ostrander to same. July 1. nom

Bainbridge av proposed, w s, 76.5 n Garfield st, 25.6x100x25x104.10. Twenty-fourth Ward Real Estate Assoc., New York, to Charles Uihlein. June 15. 1,250

Bainbridge av, n w cor Garfield st proposed, 76.5x104.10x75x119.5. Same to Mary L. Knox. June 15. 4,110

Bainbridge av proposed, w s, 101.6 s Southern Boulevard, runs west 100 x south 20 x east 8.9 x south 25 x east 100 to av, x north 45.10. Same to Michael Redmond. June 15. 2,430

Bathgate av, No. 2075, w s, 159.7 s 180th st, 21.1x94.8. Jarvis B. Smith to Eliza T. Carey. *Mt.* $2,500. July 6. 4,500

Beekman av, w s, 25 n Oak terrace, 50x100. William R. Beal Land Improvement Co. to John A. Keane. July 8. 4,000

Beekman av, s w cor Oak terrace, 25x100.
141st st, n s, 175.5 w Beekman av, 25x106x25x107.10.
Same to John Kolter. July 8. 4,500

Beekman av, n w cor Oak terrace, 25x100. Wm. R. Beal Land Improvement Co. to Margaret Scallion. July 8. 2,500

Belmont av, s e s, 150.5 n e John st, 35.1x163.11x35x159.5. Henry V. Walsh and Cathrine C. his wife to George Widmer. July 7. 900

Bergen av, s e cor Grove st, 85x82.6 to Mill Brook, x100.6x44. Eliza Prescott widow to Anna P. Brown. April 24. 6,000

Same property. Anna P. Brown to John L. Mead. *Mt.* $5,000. July 2. 6,000

Boston av, n w s, adj Thomas Minford, runs north 322 to Crotona Park, x west 121.4 x southeast 354.4 to av, x east 52.4. Julia wife of Gustave Huerstel, Matilda wife of George J. Grossman, Annie wife of Albert F. Brugman formerly Wilkens, Walter Wilkens and Florence his wife and Henry P. De Graaf and Amanda M. his wife to William G. Watt. July 1. 5,000

Same property. William G. Watt to The Suburban Land Impt. Co. Q. C. July 1. nom

Briggs av, n e cor Garfield st proposed, 25.1x104x25x106.4. Twenty-fourth Ward Real Estate Assoc., New York, to William W. Walker. June 15. 1,175

Briggs av, e s, 120.6 s Southern Boulevard, runs east 119.10 x south 25 x west 25 x south 25 x west 99.5 to av, x north 50.3. Same to George E. Debevoise. June 15. 2,100

Briggs av proposed, e s, 100.5 s Southern Boulevard, 20x111x20x109.3. Same to Ann Vion. June 15. 1,000

College av, s e s, 85 n e Powell pl, 20x95. Release mort. John Schneider to Joseph Shea. June 29. nom

Same property. Joseph Shea and Louisa D. his wife to Michael Hicks. July 1. 4,000

Courtlandt av, w s, 25 s 149th st, 28.3x100. Bernerdt Joost to Christopher Seeker and Rebecca his wife, Brooklyn. Sub. to mort. July 8. 10,996

Courtlandt av, e s, 75 n 149th st, 25x100. Andrew W. Gerlach to Wanda Gerlach. *Mt.* $3,000. July 6. nom

Courtlandt av, e s, 95.5 n 150th st, 23x100. Mary Mantel, Wilhelmina and Herman H. Sichling to Catharine C. Twomey. July 1. 4,250

Courtlandt av, e s, 72.5 n 150th st, 11.6x100. Catharine C. Twomey to Thomas Falvey. July 9. nom

Crimmins av, w s, 312.4 n 141st st, 25x80. William R. Beal Land Improvement Co. to John McCann. July 8. 1,725

Crimmins av, w s, 27 n 141st st, 21.4x80.
Crimmins av, w s, 287.4 n 141st st, 25x80.
William R. Beal Land Improvement Co. to Catharine A. Gibney. July 8. 3,325

Crimmins av, w s, 337.4 n 141st st, 50x80. Same to William H. Wright and William J. Pragnell. July 8. 3,350

Crotona av, n s, 358.6 e Broad st, 25x101.1x25x99. Mary E. wife of Charles V. Halley to Catherine A. Ferguson. *Mt.* $720. July 1. 5,000

Decatur av, w s, 150 s Ozark st, 25x100. Edward J. O'Gorman to Margaret J. Canning. July 6. 700

Decatur av, w s, 325 s Ozark st, 100x100. Edward J. O'Gorman to George B. Corsa. July 6. nom

Decatur av, w s, 216.6 n Southern Boulevard, 75x110. The Twenty-fourth Ward Real Estate Assoc. to The Crescent Real Estate Assoc. June 15. 4,500

Eastern Bay av, e s, 285 s from n e cor Maple st, runs west 1,796.4 to west exterior line of land under water, x southeast along same 190.3 x east 1,679.8 to av, x north 159.
Coster av, centre line, 175 n from centre Maple st, runs west 1,213.11 to w s Western Bay av, x south 72.3 to w s of exterior line of lands under water, &c., x south along same 189.2 to centre Maple st, x east 1,070 to centre Coster av, x north 175.
Hillside av, centre line, 405 n of centre line of Maxwell st, runs east 183.6 to Spoffords land, x south 27.2 x southeast still along Spoffords 234.9 x south 98.9 x southeast 145.2 all along Spoffords to Maxwell st, x west 106.9 to Meadow av, x north 30 x west 290 along centre Maxwell st to centre Hillside av, x north 405.
William O. Giles and Kate his wife individ. and exr. Elizabeth Giles to Florence M. and Murray, George W. and Helen E. Giles. B. & S. and C. a. G. ⅓ part. nom

Same property. Same to Bessie, Marquise de Talleyrand Perigord nee Curtis, Paris, France, and Mary J. Ruspoli. 2-9 part. B. & S. and C. a. G. June 19. nom

Same property. Same to Bessie Marquise de Talleyrand Perigord nee Curtis as trustee George W. L. Curtis. 1-9 part. B. & S. and C. a. G. June 17. nom

Franklin av, s e s, 110 s w 169th st, 32x137. Nellie E., William A., David C. Sinclair and Mabel E. his wife and Annie H. S. Lobingier widow heirs David Sinclair to Salina C. Sinclair widow. Q. C. June 29. nom

Honeywell av, e s, 95 s Samuel st, 25x100. Laphelia Bowman to Eugene M. Bowman. June 30. nom

Hull av, e s, 376.7 s Gun Hill road, 25x100. Edward J. O'Gorman to Charles Haider. July 6. nom

Hull av, w s, 21.1 s Mosholu Parkway, 25x113.6. The Twenty-fourth Ward Real Estate Assoc. to Nellie M. Brown. June 15. 1,325

Hull av, s w cor Mosholu Parkway, 21.1x113.6x49.1x123.5. Same to William Gallagher. June 15. 1,675

Hull av, w s, 46.1 s Mosholu Parkway, 50x113.6. Same to Eva wife of David Graham. June 15. 2,600

Inwood av, w s, 325 s Goble pl, runs south 8.3 x southwest — x west 150 to Macombs Dam road, x north 30.5 x east 173.5. Berthold Hehre to Massillon F. Rhoades. Sub. to mort. July 6. 3,400

Katonah av, s w cor Holly pl, 60x100. Ephraim B. Levy to Adelbert J. Howe. June 16. nom

Katonah av, w s, 60 s Holly st, 40x100. John W. Earle and Victoria F. his wife to Myron C. Burton. April 14. nom

Kepler av, s w cor Oakley st, 50x100. Release mort. Annie R. Weeks to Andrew Arvidson. July 6. 333

Kepler av, s w cor Oakley st, 50x100. Andrew Arvidson and Augusta his wife, South Mount Vernon, N. Y., to Heinrich Hofmann. July 6. 1,000

Lexington av, s w cor Spring st, 50x100. Devinia wife of and James Dorgan to Charles F. and Elizabeth Schropp. *Mt.* $3,500. July 7. 7,500

Morris av, e s, 206 s Highbridge road, 24x131. Sarah A. Lisk to Charles E. Schoder. *Mt.* $3,000. July 1. 5,000

Perry av, e s, 56.4 s Mosholu Parkway, 100x110. Twenty-fourth Ward Real Estate Assoc. to Andrew J. Dalton. June 15. 4,200

Perry av, s e cor Mosholu Parkway, 56.4x110x—x123.4, probable error. Same to Mary A. Kiely and Thomas J. Clarke. June 15. 1,400

Prospect av, n e cor Westchester av, 38.10x112; also strip in front extending from old e s line to new e s line, 17.7x134.2. Hartwig I. Phillips to Harry L. Phillips. *Mt.* $3,700. July 6. 5,500

Same property. Julia wife of and Gustave Huerstel, Matilda wife of and George J. Grossman, Annie wife of and Albert F. Brugman formerly Wilkins, Walter Wilkins and Florence his wife to Hartwig I. Phillips. July 6. 5,400

Prospect av, n w s, 125 s w John st, 25x66. Maria S. Simpson to William J. Reynolds. July 9. 500

Sedgwick av, west cor Perot st, 25x99. Benjamin T. Fairchild to Robert Scrimgeour. July 2. 1,600

St. Anns av, e s, 275.4 n 141st st, 75x90. William R. Beal Land Impt. Co. to Herman Oetjen. July 8. 8,175

St. Anns av, n e cor 141st st, runs north 25.4 x east 90 x south 10.4 x east 80 to w s Crimmins av, x south 27 to 141st st, x west 170.5. William R. Beal Land Impt. Co. to James Fulton. July 8. 7,625

Stebbins av, s e s, 83.9 n e Freeman st, runs southeast 170 x north 169.2 x southwest 138.1 x northwest 126 to av, x southwest 25. Wenzel Wavra and Mary his wife to Frank Belsky. July 2. 1,250

Stebbins av, e s, 584.11 n Freeman st, 51.6x102.7x51.6x100.1. Denison P. Chesebro and Harriet P. his wife to John Kubes. July 2. 1,900

Stebbins av, e s, 55 s Home st, runs east 89 x north 22 x east 59 x south 50 x west 48 to av, x north 28. Maria A. wife of and Adolph J. Wuytack to John H. Hahn and Elizabeth his wife. *Mt.* $6,000. July 1. 7,400

Taylor av, n w s, south ½ lot 146 map Belmont Village, 50x100. James Pettit and Elizabeth his wife to Clarence W. Gaylor. July 6. 800

Tremont av proposed, n s, 96.1 e proposed e s Franklin av, 50.8x117.6x50.10x117.6. Release mort. Abraham B. Tappen and John B. Haskin to Lucy A. Mason. May 5. 3,000

Union av, w s, 133.3 n Clifton st, 16.9x137.6. Mary wife of Frederick A. Kessel to James Kelly. July 8. 3,100

Valentine av, n s, 240 e Southern Boulevard, 126.2x169.6x113.1. Emma C. Cromwell to Thomas Cunningham. June 30. 2,025

Vanderbilt or Railroad av, s w cor 176th st, 58x100. Henry C. Broas and Mary A. his wife to The Suburban Club, New York. *Mt.* $6,000. June 30. nom

Same property. Louis Eickwort and Anna H. his wife to Henry C. Broas. June 30. nom

Vanderbilt or Railroad av, n w s, 58 s w 176th st, 25x100. William J. Townsend referee to Benjamin C. Bent. June 20. 1,900

Same property. James B. Dill trustee to same. Q. C. June 19. nom

Villa av, e s, 375 n Potter pl, 50x100. Edmond C. Allcot and Helen J. his wife to Alfred C. Hunker. July 3. 9,000

Verio av, all of lot 220 and 15 feet of lot 222 map No. 1, partition of Hyatt farm, near Woodlawn, 24th Ward, being together 40x153. Alexander Forsyth and Josephine his wife to Antoinetta M. Ghetti. July 1. 1,000

Westchester av, n e cor Bergen av, runs east 69.11 x north 85.1 x northwest 10.5 to Bergen av, x southwest 107.3. Jonas Weil and Theresa his wife and Bernhard Mayer and Sophia his wife to Samuel Weil. ½ part. Sub. to mort. $2,500 and encroachment and assessments if any. May 6. nom

Walton av, w s, 210 s 150th st, 35x101.9x35x100.1. Release mort. Henry L. Morris to Anna T. Dale. July 2. 1,500

Washington av, n e cor Fletcher st, 148x100. John Jefferson and Ellen his wife to Thomas Carroll. July 2. 10,000

Washington av, e s, 180 n Bathgate pl or 10th st, 50x120. Foreclos. John H. Hull to George D. Hilyard. July 6. 2,000

Webster av, e s, 22.1 n 171st st, 25x97.11 to Mill Brook, x25x96.6. Louis Eickwort and Anna his wife to Bertha Unger. July 7. 1,550

Webster av, e s, 47.1 n 171st st, 25x99.3 to Mill Brook, x 25x97.11. Same to Thomas P. Hicks. July 6. 1,425

Webster av, s e cor Tower pl, 25x100. Robert N. Quinn and Charlotte F. his wife to Leonora C. Jones. *Mt.* $435. June 29. 1,300

Webster av proposed, w s, 25 n Southern Boulevard, 25x96.
Southern Boulevard, s s, 75 e Briggs av, 25x100.
Briggs av proposed, e s, 25.1 n Garfield st, 25.1x101.9x25x104.
Twenty-fourth Real Estate Assoc. to Alice M. Mullen. June 15. 4,575

Webster av proposed, w s, 225 n Southern Boulevard, 50x121.
Decatur av, s w cor Mosholu Parkway, 50x159.6x65.5 to Hull av, x122.6 to Parkway, x246.10.
Same to Michael J. Callahan. June 15. 11,575

Webster av proposed, w s, 375 n Southern Boulevard, 25x121. James P. Sonneborn and Harriet L. his wife and Thomas J. Clarke and Adelia L. his wife to Charles F. Hallam. July 1. 1,800

Webster av proposed, w s, 450 n Southern Boulevard, 50x112.11x32.6 and 17.6x121.

Twenty-fourth Ward Real Estate Assoc. to Albert Wiggins. June 15. 3,350

Webster av proposed, w s, 350 n Southern Boulevard, 25x121. Same to Frederick Allen and Sarah his wife. June 15. 1,525

Webster av proposed, w s, 125 n Southern Boulevard, 50x121. Same to Joseph A. Booth. June 15. 3,450

Webster av proposed, w s, 275 n Southern Boulevard, 50x121. Same to Samuel E. Duffy. June 15. 3,100

Webster av proposed, w s, 175 n Southern Boulevard, 50x121. Same to Elizabeth C. Elliott. June 15. 3,150

Webster av proposed, w s, 400 n Southern Boulevard, 50x121. Same to Carl R. Eberth. June 15. 3,350

Webster av proposed, w s, 325 n Southern Boulevard, 25x121. Same to Josie N. Glass. June 15. 1,525

Webster av proposed, w s, 100 n Southern Boulevard, 25x121. Same to Anna P. wife of Herman Gunther. June 15. 1,675

Webster av proposed, w s, 375 n Southern Boulevard, 25x121. Same to James P. Sonneborn and Thomas J. Clarke. June 15. 1,500

Webster av proposed, s w cor Suburban st, 46.1 x113x58.6x100.9. Same to Peter Seery. June 15. 4,200

Webster av proposed, n w cor Southern Boulevard, 25x96. Same to Felix Grimly. June 15. 3,950

Webster av proposed, n w cor Suburban st, 95.4 to Mosholu Parkway, x79.6x109.10 to proposed Suburban st, x101. Same to Mary E. Moulton. June 15. 7,025

Webster av proposed, w s, 50 n Southern Boulevard, 50x96. Twenty-fourth Ward Real Estate Assoc., New York, to Julius Levy, Louis r d im and Lippman Altmayer. Jun 15 F ie he 3,600

Williss av, No. 153, s w cor 135th st, 25x81.6. Release judgment. William and Hannah Kunn to Luigi Guiseppi, Natale and Steffano Cavinato. July 1. 200

Willis av, e s, 25 n 143d st, 25x90.6. George F. Johnson and Emma his wife to George L. Loutrel. *Mt.* $13,000. July 1. 23,000

1st av, n s, 180 e 3d st, 40x100, 24th Ward.
Av A, s s, lots 11 and 12 map of new village of Jerome, 50x100.
All real estate or property in New York and Westchester Counties of which Newton S. Briggs died seized or was entitled to.
Newton Van Derzee to Amos D. Briggs and ano. exrs. William S. Briggs dec'd. Q. C. Aug. 15. nom

1st av, n s, 180 e 3d st, 40x100, 24th Ward. Amos D. Briggs and Elizabeth B. Van Derzee exrs. William S. Briggs to Alexander Forsyth, Aug. 20, 1890. 700

8th av, near Walnut st, w s, lot 21 map Mt. Eden, 50x100. Caroline Stern to Betsey Libman. June 20. 500

Kingsbridge road, e s, 75 s Nathalie av, runs northeast 106.4 x southeast 25.7 x southwest 14.11 x southeast 40 x southwest 100 to road, x75.
Sedgwick av, w s, Villa Sites D and E map Anthony estate, 146.10x104.1x144.10x168.8.
Arthur B. Claflin and Minnietta A. his wife to Hugh N. Camp. Oct. 29, 1890. 16,000

Lots 48 and 49 map 71 lots Kingsland estate at Morris Heights, 24th Ward. Hugh N. Camp and Elizabeth his wife to Emilie Coletti. June 15. 2,700

Lot 116 map Central Morrisania. James L. Parshall to Francesca C. Nesbitt. March 1, 1889. nom

Lots 1, 2, 3 and 20 map 71 lots of Kingsland estate, situate at Morris Heights, 24th Ward. Hugh N. Camp and Elizabeth D. his wife to Henry A. Dewey. June 15. 5,600

Lots 10 and 11 same map. Same to William L. Saulpaugh. June 15. 2,800

Lots 68 and 69 same map. Same to Charles Van Riper. June 15. 1,500

LEASEHOLD CONVEYANCES.

Broadway, No. 717. Assign. lease. Valentine H. Muller to Hyman Hein. nom

Bleecker st, No. 413. Assign. lease. William F. Schneider to William F. Schneider, Jr. nom

Hudson st, No. 179, s w cor Vestry st. Assign. lease. James McCauley and John J. McGuire to Thomas Curran. nom

Union sq, No. 2. Assign. lease. James W. Carroll to Thomas P. Flynn. nom

3d st, n s, 127 w Av B, 24x96.2. Assign. lease. Joseph Henning individ. and exr. Elizabeth Henning to Robert F. Teuchtler. 6,750

3d st, s s, 367.6 e Av A, 24x105.11. Assign. lease. Leopold and Maria Gerber to Gottfried Vetter. 9,400

Same property. Consent to assign. lease. Lewis M. Rutherfurd and Rutherfurd Stuyvesant exrs., &c., John W. Chandler to Leopold and Maria Gerber. June 30. nom

4th st, n s, 87.11 e 1st av, 25x96.2. Assign. lease. Caroline Kiefer and Georgine D. Braun to Catharine Langguth. 12,050

14th st, No. 17 E. Assign. lease. The Demorest Fashion and Sewing Machine Co. to Mills W. Barse. 10,000

22d st, No 223 E. Assign. lease. Michael Collin to Christian Bode. nom

49th st, No. 46 W., n s, 568.4 w 5th av. Consent to assign. lease. Trustees of Columbia College to Emilia M. Peters. nom

51st st, No. 12 W. Bill of sale of buildings. Henry J. and John J. Burchell exrs. James G. Burchell to Elias C. Benedict. July 9. nom

Same property. Assign. lease. Same to same. July 9. 24,000

151st st, No. 928 E. Assign. lease and bill of sale. Joseph Schaub to Ignatz Kinderman. 300

Av A, w s, 68.2 n 6th st, 22.8x100. Charles A. Bristed to Peter Doelger. 20 years, from Nov. 1, 1891, per year, taxes and 625

Columbus av, No. 715. Assign. lease. Patrick Lynch, Brooklyn, to Martin Considine. nom

Park (4th) av, s e cor 110th st. Assign. lease. James Devine to James Connelly. nom

1st av, No. 163. Cancellation of lease. Solomon Rosenthal to J. Hooker Hamersley. nom

1st av, No. 2276, n e cor 117th st, 25.2x64. William Austin to Christopher Von Bergen and Adeline M. Von Bergen. 15 years, from May 1, 1891, per year, 900

1st av, e s, 51.9 n 15th st, 25.9x94. Assign. lease. Max Rosenthal to Solomon Rosenthal. 1,750

2d av, No. 94. Assign. lease. Louis Hoffmann to Mary Goodman. nom

2d av, w s, 100.5 n 64th st, 25x105. Abraham B. Cox et al. exrs. Abraham B. Cox to Ferdinand Reinert. 20 years, from May 1, 1891, per year, gold, 400

3d av, No. 112. Assign. lease. Frederick Scharmann to Hermann B. Scharmann. 3,250

KINGS COUNTY.

JULY 2, 3, 4, 6, 7, 8.

Ashford st, w s, 122.7 n Atlantic av, 25x100. Release mort. Thomas Monahan to Edward F. Linton. $1,200

Same property. Edward F. Linton to Henry Oberbeck. *Mt.* $3,200. 4,750

Ashford st, e s, 245 s Stanley av, 40x100. Adolph Sussman to Henry Heinstadt. 104

Ainslie st, n s, 216.10 w Lorimer st, 20x100.3. Willi m H. Pruden to Elmira M. Rich. Q. C. a nom

Bainbridge st, n s, 150 e Reid av, 100x100. Peter Langan to Edward E. Gorman. nom

Bayard st, n s, 235.8 e Graham av, 20.7x100. Abraham A. Bates to James T. Bates. 700

Bergen st, n s, 250 w Classon av, 25x110. Partition. Theodore Burgmyer to Catharine A. Clancy. 6,100

Bergen st, s s, 125 w Grand av, 25x110. Patrick Coates to James Dougherty. 3,000

Bergen st, n s, 175 w Brooklyn av, 16.8x107.2. Martin Joost to Emily M. Charles, Florence Hamilton and Henry and Grace Salmon, Alice M. Cooper and Mirriam S. Tooker. *Mt.* $4,500. 7,850

Bergen st, s s, 386.7 w Franklin av, 20x—x19.6x 131. Francis Plunkett to Patrick Coates. All liens. 3,500

Bergen st, n s, 150 w Rockaway av, 20.11x107.2, h & l. Joseph Lang to Samuel and Max Mallinger. *Mt.* $1,750. 2,500

Berkeley pl, n s, 184 e 8th av, runs east 45.10 to w s Plaza st, x north 91.1 x south 78.9 to beginning. Charles N. Peed to Albert Steiner. 8,500

Bleecker st, s e s, 275 n e Evergreen av, 25x100. Erhard Ingold to Samuel Gluck, of New York. *Mt.* $4,500. 8,400

Boerum st, n e cor Leonard st, 25x90.9, h & l. Catharina Lipsius to William C. Gluck. 1886. 9,000

Boerum st, n e cor Leonard st, 25x90.9, h & l. William C. Gluck to Anna Gluck. 9,000

Boerum st, s s, 474.9 e Bushwick av, 25x87.6. Criszentia M. Treubig widow to Martin Lang. *Mt.* $2,000. 6,300

Boerum pl, w s, 50 s Dean st, 25x80. John Boyle to Conrad Kapp. 3,000

Boerum st, s s, 75 e Humboldt st, 25x100. John Newman, of New York, to Semche Simon. *Mt.* $4,325. 5,525

Butler st, s s, 374.8 e Nostrand av, 16.8x100.
Butler st, s s, 391.4 e Nostrand av, 16.8x100.
John Anderson to Jennie S. Conklin, Cold Spring, L. I. *Mt.* $4,500. 10,800

Bond st, w s, 50 s Douglass st, 50x100. Elizabeth L. wife of and Joseph A. Davidson to Elizabeth wife of Charles Zimmer. *Mt.* $1,500. 3,000

Broadway, n e s, 60 n w Van Buren st, 20x90, h & l. Abraham and Aaron Kodzeisen to Franz Scharf. *Mt.* $6,000. 9,850

Broadway, n e s, 112 s e De Kalb av, 22.6x90. Henry W. Schreiber to George Schreiber. ½ part. nom

Same property. Bernhard Davidsburg to Henry W. Schreiber. 13,000

Broadway, n e s, 25 n w Gates av, 25x80. Phebe E. Leverich extrx., &c., Augustus A. Leverich to Charles J. Nielsen. 15,000

Broadway, s s, 494.7 e Brooklyn av, 120x100, Flatbush. Bertha M. wife of and Edward F. Taber, of Patchogue, to Joseph Swesey, of Patchogue, N. Y. exch

Broadway, s s, 50 w Brooklyn av, 20x100, Flatbush. Edward Egolf to Goetano Guaranto. 225

Broadway, n e s, 75 n w Covert st, 25x88.10, h & l. Peter Johnson to Abraham and Aaron Kodziesen. *Mt.* $11,000. nom

Broadway, n e s, 50 n w Covert st, 25x88.10, h & l. Peter Johnson to same. *Mt.* $10,000. nom

Canton st, e s, 149.9 n Myrtle av, runs east 48.2 x northwest 62.2 to point in Canton st, 49.0½ from Auburn pl, x south 39.6 to beginning. William O'Flaherty to Annie wife of Thomas A. Blaney. *Mt.* $2,300. nom

Carroll st, s w s, 90 s e 3d av, 76x69. Esther R. wife of Charles H. Parsons to Edward E. Bergen. *Mt.* $8,000. 12,000

Same property. Edward E. Bergen to Silas A. Condict. *Mt.* $8,000. nom

Carroll st, n s, 90 w 6th av, 20x100. Mary T. wife of Edward W. Parsons to John A. Boyle, of New York. 7,725

Carroll st, s w s, 126 s e 3d av, 38x69. Silas A. Condict to Otto Heidelklang. *Mt.* $2,000. 6,500

Carroll st, s w s, 90 s e 3d av, 38x69. Silas A. Condict to Thomas Williams. *Mt.* $4,000. 6,500

Caton pl, n w cor Coney Island plank road, 238.3x267.2x111.6 to w s grand entrance to Prospect Park, x south in circular line 240 to road, x south 92.8, excepting portion taken for Franklin av extension and widening Coney Island plank road, &c., Flatbush. William Graham, Paterson, N. J., to George D. Bader. *Mt.* $14,000. 30,000

Central pl, n e s, 201.5 s e Greene av, runs southeast 18.5 x northeast 11 x northeast 40 x northwest 20 x northeast 29.6 x northwest 15.2 x southwest 80.6. Michael Mulvihill to Eugene Muller. *Mt.* $2,800. 6,050

Charles pl, e s, 200 n Myrtle av, 23.2x100x7.4x 101.8. Elizabeth Byrnes to Charles Witzel. 1,550

Chauncey st, s s, 78 e Saratoga av, 38x100. Margaret McDowell to Carrie E. Elmore. 50

Chester st, e s, 325 n Eastern Parkway, 25x100. Emil Remcking to Herman Markowitz and Hyman Krantz. *Mt.* $2,700. 4,400

Collins st, n s, 400 e Albany av, 40x100, Flatbush. Jessie Fenton to Thomas Little. 300

Conover st, n w s, 25 n e Partition st, runs northwest 80 x southwest 25 to Partition st, x northwest 20 x northeast 50 x southeast 100 to Conover st, x southwest 25 to beginning. Frederick T. Aldridge special guard. Magdalena E. Schmadeke to Heinrich Finkeldey. 7,000

Cook st, n s, 307 e Bushwick av, 22x100. Anton Kiesel to Christian Schleyermacher. 1,200

Cooper st, s e s, 84 s w Knickerbocker av, 16x 80. Michael Sullivan to Charles S. Taber. *Mt.* $2,100. 3,000

Cooper st, n w s, 338 n e Bushwick av, 16x110. Augustus H. Levy, of New York, to Joseph Lilienthal. *Mt.* $1,900. nom

Cooper st, n w s, 418 n e Bushwick av, 16x100. Carrie Blyn to Emil H. Bach. *Mt.* $400. 3,200

Covert st, n w s, 130 n e Broadway, 20x100. Peter Johnson to Salome wife of Peter Johnson. nom

Covert st, s e s, 180 s w Bushwick av, 20x100. Thomas Purcell to Philip Mehling. *Mt.* $4,000. 5,600

Cleveland st, w s, 240 n Hegeman av, 40x100. Christian Nicklaus to Augusta Boehm. 530

Cleveland st, w s, 280 n Hegeman av, 20x100. Same to same. 265

Cleveland st, e s, 246.10 n Atlantic av, 50x100. Julia J. wife of and William H. Whitlock. to Arthur E. Sumner, of New York. nom

Dean st, n s, 25 e Kingston av, 35x107.2. David Taylor to Martha and Mary W. Waldron, joint tenants. *Mt.* $5,000. 1880. 8,500

Dean st, s s, 100 w Schenectady av, 16x107.2½. Sophronia M. Fickett widow to Frank B. Waterman. *Mt.* $1,600. 2,800

Dean st, s s, 116 w Schenectady av, 16x107.2½. Same to same. *Mt.* $1,600. 2,800

Dean st, s s, 165 w Brooklyn av, 20x107.2. John A. Bliss to John C. Simmons. *Mt.* $7,500. 13,000

Dean st, n s, 100 w Buffalo av, 479.1 to centre Hunterfly road, x northwest along same to e s Rochester av, x north to centre of block bet Dean and Pacific sts, x east along same 600 x south 107.2, excepting as follows
Dean st, n s, 100 w Buffalo av, runs west 484.8 x north 107.2x484.8x107.2.
Foreclos. John Courtney to Henry Weil. 1,000

Debevoise st, n s, at line bet Gilbert and Cook estates, 16th Ward, 25x100. Elisa Sondericker to Isidor Mock. 5,000

Debevoise st, n s, on line bet Gilbert and Cook estates, 16th Ward, 25x100, h & l. Katharina wife of and Peter Horn to Elisa Sondericker. nom

Decatur st, n s, 90 e Lewis av, 16.8x100, h & l. Catharine A. Walton, Ridgewood, L. I., to The Union Trust Co., New York. *Mt.* $4,500. consid. omitted

Degraw st, n s, 200 w Rogers av, 40x127.9½. Noah Tebbets to Alois Lazansky. 1,200

Degraw st, s s, 240 e Smith st, 20x100, h & l. Catherine Scanlon widow to Elizabeth C. Scanlon. nom

Dikeman st, n s, 150 e Ferris st, 125x100.
Wolcott st, s s, 150 e Ferris st, 225x100.
Mary L. Libby to The Lidgerwood Mfg. Co. 16,800

Dodworth st, s e s, 121.1 s w Bushwick av, 25x 91. Louise wife of Sebastian Hoh to Henry Rockel and Elizabeth his wife. 5,000

Dodworth st, n w s, 95.8 n e Broadway, 25x90. Seraphine Levine widow to Fanny wife of Lewis Jacobs. 4,250

Same property. Lewis Jacobs to Seraphine Levine. 4,250

Eagle st, s s, 220 e Franklin st, 25x100. Sarah J. wife of and Rutsen Rhinehart to John Morgan. 5,800

Eastern Parkway, s w cor Warwick st, 50x100. Charles H. Lohr to Charles J. Clements. 2,500

Eastern Parkway, n s, 25.1 e Rockaway av, 25x 100, h & l. William Herod to Adolf Landesmann. *Mt.* $2,050. 2,350

Eastern Parkway, s e cor Christopher av, 100x 100. James G. Roberts to Adolph Pasternack. *Mt.* $1,200. 3,100

Eastern Parkway, n e cor Montauk av, 20x90.
Montauk av, e s, 90 n Eastern Parkway, 20x 100.
Adolph Osberg to Abbie E. Coffin. nom

Eckford st, e s, 211.8 s Norman av, 16.8x100, h & l. Hazel Banker, Hartford, Conn., devisee Euphemia M. Davis to Edwin J. Sutphin. *Mt.* $1,500. 2,500

Eckford st, e s, 246.8 s Norman av, 16.8x100. David M. Davis, Alva E. Abrams and Effie

M. Turnbull to Edwin J. Sutphin. Q. C. nom

Eldert st, s s, 275 e Evergreen av, 18x100. Helen M. Buttle to Juan B. C. Phillips. Mt. $3,250. nom

Eldert st, s e s, 300 n e Bushwick av, 20x100, h & l. Peter Johnson to Salome wife of Peter Johnson. Mt. $4,000. nom

Ellery st, n s, 225 e Throop av, 25x100, h & l. Ernst Emlaut to Samuel Leff and Adolf Moskowitt. Mt. $5,000. 6,475

Ellery st, n s, 306.6 e Broadway, 25x100. Karl Enderle to Frederick Stroh and Christiana his wife. 6,450

Ellery st, s s, 250 w Throop av, 25x38.4x38.4x52.7, h & l. Isaac Horowitz to John Steffens. 3,500

Elton st, s w cor Blake av, 25x83. Sheriff's deed on foreclos. John Courtney, Sheriff, to Frederick Middendorf. 2,000

Essex st, e s, 360 n Arlington av, 40x100. Contract. John O'Donohue to Dennis J. McCarthy and William F. Gallagher, Jr. 4,200

Freeman st, n s, 195 e Franklin st, 71.1x—x24.3x100. Chauncey M. Depew, New York, et al. exrs. Robert J. Niven to The Brooklyn Wire Nail Co. 2,500

Frost st, n s, 504.2 w Kingsland av, 19.4x98 to Manhattan Beach Railroad, x 20.10 x 100. James Gascoine to John H. McKenna. 900

Fulton st, s s, 231.3 w Schenectady av, 18.9x100. Lewis Jacobs to Seraphine Levine. 4,000

Same property. Seraphine Levine widow to Fanny wife of Lewis Jacobs. 4,000

Fulton st, n e cor Rockaway av, 26 8x123 to Somers st, x7x26x117.8, h & l. Thomas Haggerty to Samuel E. Harris. Mt. $3,600. exch

Fulton st, s e s, 50 n e Essex st, 48.9x86.1x west 23.4 x southeast 25 6 x west 24.6. Gilliam Schenck to Frederick, Richard and Otto Kampfe. 2,100

Fulton st, s s, 20 w Albany av, 20x100. Margaret Bossong to George E. Schroeder. Mt. $6,000. 8,000

George st, n w s, 200 s w Knickerbocker av, 25x80, h & l. Jakob Klumpp to Charles Boelkow and Louise his wife. 6,300

Grand st, n s, 304 11 s e Driggs st, 19.10x85.5x19.11x83.9. Frances W. Blackwell, Maria L. wife of and John H. Mathews, Emma K. wife of and Samuel B. Tisdale, Gertrude B. Wiley widow and Thomas G. Evans to Frederick W. Ehrlich. 10,500

Grand st, No. 116, s s, 25x100. Partition. Stephen B. Jacobs to Frederick Scholtz. 9,800

Greene st, s s, 195 e Franklin st, 75x100. J. Edward Ogden to Charles L. Rowland. nom

Greene st, n s, 375 e Manhattan av, 25x100. John McKeegan to Michael Quinn. Mt. $3,000. 5,050

Grove st, n s, 110 w St. Nicholas av, 40x100. Henrietta Hager widow to Frederick Erhardt. nom

Grove st, n s, 110 w St. Nicholas av, 40x100. Elizabeth wife of and James H. Allan to Henrietta Hager. 1,500

Harrison st, n e cor Henry st, 20x83. William Abeles to Michael Wynne. Mt. $4,000. 7,750

Halsey st, s s, 317.4 e Nostrand av, 17 6½x100. Catherine V. Chevallier to Clement E. Chevallier. Mt. $6,000. nom

Halsey st, n s, 135 w Stuyvesant av, 20x100. Matilda L. Bolles, of Bayport, Conn., to Katherine Dunn. Mt. $4,500. exch

Hancock st, n s, 100 w Marcy av, 20x100. Sarah M. wife of and William Young to John J. Dowd. Q. C. nom

Hart st, s s, 335 e Throop av, 20x100. Frederick Hauck to Minnie Gehrhardt. 8,250

Hawthorne st, s s, 95.6 w Nostrand av, 45x106, Flatbush. Release mort. Asa W. Parker, Hempstead, L. I., to John F. Hart. nom

Same property. John F. Hart to Alexander Cooper. 7,000

Herbert st, s e s, 214.3 s w North Henry st, runs southeast 124 x west 50.4 x 101 x northeast 30.4. Mary wife of and Henry Miller, of Sonth Orange, N. J., to Edward Cassidy. 1,325

Herbert st, n s, 261 w Humboldt st, 24x80. James Meakim to Louis Seitz, of New York. Mt. $900. 2 800

Herkimer st, n s, 64 w Kingston av, 56x100. Henry J. Brown to Julia B. F. wife of John D. Fish, of Hempstead, L. I. Mt. $12,500. exch

Herkimer st, n s, 64 w Kingston av, 18x100. Julia B. F. wife of John D. Fish to Mary C. Comfort. Mt. $3,000. exch

Herkimer st, n s, 145 e Troy av, 20x100, h & l. Joseph H. Butler, Augustus F. Butler, Lydia M. wife of Henry E. Tuthill and Grace E. wife of Alonzo D. Kittle to Dorcas E. wife of William H. Randolph. Mt. $3,100. 400

High st, s w cor Gold st, 23x97.6x23x97.10. Thomas McCarthy to Mary A. wife of Robert F. Cranford. 10,500

Hooper st, n s, 172.6 e Bedford av, 20x100. Isabella C. Starr to Nellie E. C. Furman. 9,000

Hopkins st, s s, 100 w Tompkins av, 20x100, h & l. Frank Lenz to John Schellhaasz. Mt. $4,500. 5,500

Hull st, n w cor Stone av, 30x100. Margaretha Lewis to George H. Smith. Mt. $6,000. nom

Huntington st, s s, 80 e Hicks st, 20x100. Joseph Foley to George T. Hay. 650

Huron st, n s, 70 w Franklin st, 25x50. Susan Covert to Catherine Foley. 3,000

Ingraham st, n s, 125 w Morgan av, 25x100. Helena wife of Joseph Abt to Charles Werner. Mt. $3,500. 6,100

Ingraham st, n s, 175 w Morgan av, 25x100, h & l. Marie wife of Leonhard Erk to Creszentia Treubig. Mt. $3,500. 6,100

Imlay st, e s, 25 n William st, runs east 90 x north 25 x east 20 x north 125 x west 110 x south 150. Salem H. Wales exr. Sarah N. Clayton to Warren E. Smith as trustee, &c. Mt. $4,500. nom

Imlay st, e s, 25 n William st, runs east 90 x north 25 x east 20 x north 125 x west 110 to st, x south 150. Warren E. Smith trustee Sarah N. Eagleton to Henry Franke. Mt. $4,500. 9,000

Irving pl, e s, 160 s Putnam av, 20x100. John F. Withers to John Moeller. Mt. $3,000. 5,200

Java st, s s, 225 e Manhattan av, 25x100. John C. Provost to Frances E. wife of David H. Valentine. Mt. $1,250. 3,000

Jefferson st, s e s, 176.3 n e Bremen st, 18.9x100, h & l. Elizabeth Decker to Caroline Fritschler. 4,800

Jefferson st, e s, 400 s w Irving av, 50x100. Caroline O. wife of John B. Sabine to John and Anton Amann. 2,200

Joralemon st, s s, 84.9 w Court st, 25.1x128.4 in two courses, x25x132.3 in two courses. Adolphina wife of Joseph Huhn to Joseph Huhn. Mt. $11,000. 10,000

Kane pl, e s, 121.7 n Atlantic av, 46x105. Foreclos. John Courtney sheriff to Mary A. Taylor. 100

King st, n e s, 190 s e Van Brunt st, 25x60.6x31.9x40.9. Mary E. and John, Jr., Hegarty to Thomas Owens. nom

King st, n e s, 190 s e Van Brunt st, 25x40.9x31.9x60.6. Foreclos. Samuel S. Hemingway to Mary E. Hegarty. 1,305

Kosciusko st, n w cor Lewis av, 23x98.6. John O. White, of Camden, N. J., to Amos D. Highfield, of Sharon Hill, Pa. Mt. $17,000. 7,000

Kosciusko st, s s, 100 w Stuyvesant av, 25x100. William Jung exr. John Roessle to Frank Roessle. Sub. to mort. nom

Kosciusko st, n s, 200 e Reid av, 25x100. Henry Ruthmann to Michael Hoch. Mt. $7,000. 12,500

Lake st, e s, 285.2 n Av U, 40x75, Gravesend. George W. Bennett to Martha A. McCabe. Q. C. nom

Lawrence st, w s, 275 n Willoughby st, 25x107.6.
Louis pl, w s, 98 s Herkimer st, 46x98.6.
Jacob Widmann to Frederick Widman. Q. C. nom

Little Nassau st, s s, 175 e Kent av, 27x100, h & l. Christopher Million to Catherine Burns. Mt. $600. 2,600

Lorimer st, n w cor Calyer st, 20x75. Henry Borden and Martin Kohlmann to Harriet wife of William H. Port. Mt. $1,500. 3,750

Lorimer st, n w s, 57 n e Devoe st, 18x91.6, h & l. Elise Mueller to Louis A. Bartholdt. Mt. $800. 2,850

Lorimer st, e s, 70 n Norman av, 25x80. Sarah L. S. Guernsey et al. to Henry Harrje. 4,000

Lorimer st, n w cor Ten Eyck st, 25x100. Sarah M. wife of William R. Morgan to Mary L. wife of Thomas J. Summond, Rockville Centre, L. I., Edith A. wife of George W. White and Ella V. wife of Andrew Spence, Jr., and Eliza C. Spender. All title. B. & S. 1,000

Logan st, w s, 1,625 n 2d st, 25x150. Eliza and William N. Strong to Frederick Grob. 800

Macon st, s s, 22 w Howard av, 17.6x100. Clarence Lincoln to Emily C. Gilfoy, of New York. Mt. $5,500. 6,800

Macon st, s s, 75.6 w Howard av, 18x100. Same to Thomas Purcell. Mt. $4,500. 6,800

Macon st, s s, 39 6 w Howard av, 18x100. Same to Grove M. Harwood. Mt. $5,500. 6,800

Macon st, s s, 57 6 w Howard av, 18x100. Same to Mary Leonhardt. Mt. $4,500. 6,800

Macon st, s w cor Howard av, 22x100. Same to Morris Isaacs. Mt. $12,000. 19,000

Madison st, n s, 371 e Patchen av, 18x100. Charles W. Denike to Charles A. Farrington. 3,700

Madison st, No. 235A. Contract. Sarah E. wife of William W. Hanold to Gesine Larkenau. 6,000

Madison st, n w s, 400 s w Central av, 20x100. James W. and Albert J. Lamb to Susan wife of Benjamin Cook. 5,000

Madison st, n w s, 420 s w Central av, 20x100. James W. and Albert J. Lamb to Guy S. Frazey. Mt. $2,500. 5,200

Maujer st, No. 266, s s, 411.7 e Bushwick av, 24.7x95x95.7x95. Vincenz Robesch to Catharine Robesch his wife. Mt. $1,000. nom

McDougal st, n s, 166 w Stone av, 16x100. Anne F. Case to Lillie Cohen. nom

McDougal st, n s, 182 w Stone av, 16x100. Sanford D. Case to Lillie Cohen. nom

McDonough st, s s, 268.9 e Ralph av, 18.9x100. Thomas H. Radcliffe to Isaac Colyer. Mt. $4,500. 6,800

McDonough st, s s, 212.6 e Ralph av, 18.9x100. Same to Ernest A. W. Soppett. Mt. $4,500. 6,800

McDonough st, n s, 205 w Tompkins av, 60x100. Cordelia Broach to John H. Broach. All liens. gift

McDonough st, s s, 193.9 e Ralph av, 18.9x100, h & l. Thomas H. Radcliffe to Charles E. Silkworth. Mt. $4,500. 6,800

Melrose st, s e s, 250 n Evergreen av, 25x100. Philip Auer to John Scherer. Mt. $2,500. 5,900

Meserole st, n s, 25 e Graham av, 25x100. Franz Scharf to Michael Brunn. Mt. $2,600. 9,000

Meserole st, n s, 125 w Lorimer st, 25x100. Bella Jonas to Michael Sellner. Mt. $5,000. 7,700

Middleton st, s e s, 100 n e Harrison av, 30x100. Catharine Kassebaum to John Bettfreund. Mt. $3,000. 8,800

Milford st, w s, 90 s Belmont av, 40x100. John White to Aminda W. Post. 400

Minna st, s s, 100 w Chester st, 50x100, Flatbush. Mary Chesebrough, of New York, to Mary G. Hanly. nom

Monitor st, e s, 210 n Norman av, 100x100. The Kings Co. Improvement Co. to Henry A. Purdy. 2,000

Monmouth st, n w s, 100 n e Lexington av, 50x125, New Utrecht. Maria A. Gelston widow, George S., Maria A. and Mary S. daughters and Thos. S. son of George S. Gelston to Owen Brady. 700

Montague st, s s, 100 w Hicks st, 25x100, h & l. Deidrich H. Schult to John M. and William H. Schult. Mt. $15,000. 30,000

Monroe st, s s, 150 e Stuyvesant av, 16.8x100. Theodore W. Swimm to Caroline E. Swart. Mt. $3,500. 6,150

Montieth st, n s, 75 e Bremen st, 25x75. Adam Kreuscher to Lina Dinstman. Mt. $4,800. 5,400

Montieth st, n s, 150 e Bremen st, 25x90. John Steffens to Isaac Horowitz Mt. $4,300. 6,000

Montgomery st, n s, 150 e 18th st, 50x100, Flatbush. Garret, Kate and Mary E. Cowenhoven and Garret and Mary E. Cowenhoven exrs. Jacob V. D. Cowenhoven to Henry B. Davenport and John Reis. 500

Moore st, s s, 175 w Morrell st, 25x100, h & l. Eva Fleckenstein widow to Friederich Ott. Mt. $3,000. 7,300

Moore st, s s, 461 e Old Bushwick av on old map, 25x100. Margaretha Zaebelein to Simeon Siminowetche. Mt. $3,200. 6,500

Moore st, n s, 100 w Graham av, runs north 50 x east 20 x south 47 x southwest 8 x west 17. Isack Wolpert to Sara Freund. Mt. $2,000. 2,900

Myrtle st, n w s, 100 n e Hamburg av, 50x100. Adelgunda M. Piel and George Schneider to Philip Brandmeier. 2,800

Newell st, w s, 241.5 n Van Cott av, 25x100, h & l. Eliza McAteer widow to Philip Kelly. 3,000

North Elliott pl, w s, 141.8 s Flushing av, 16 8x80.7x16.8x81.10. Thomas Doyle to James Boggs. 2,275

Oakland st, w s, 100 s Meserole av, 25x100. William H. Port to Susan Covert. Mt. $4,000. 8,350

Ocean Parkway, w s, 824 s Sheepshead Bay and Coney Island plank road, 50x200 to West 1st st, Gravesend. Jacob Knecht, of New York, to Henry Baruch. Mt. $1,500. exch

Osborn st, e s, 100 n Eastern Parkway, 25x100. Elizabeth C. wife of John Power to Louis Weintraub. 2,500

Osborn st, e s, 125 n Eastern Parkway, 25x100. Same to Jacob Lewis. Mt. $1,600. 2,500

Osborn st, e s, 100 n Glenmore av, 100x100. Release mort. Claus Luehrs to Herbert C. Smith. 2,000

Osborn st, e s, 150 n Glenmore av, 50x100. Herbert C. Smith to Louis Stoiber. 1,700

Osborn st, w s, 150 s Dumont av, 50x100. Sarah A. Brewster to Jacob W. Erregger. 2,200

Palmetto st, s e s, 117 s w Knickerbocker av, 16x100.
Palmetto st, s e s, 201 s w Knickerbocker av, 17x100.
Cooper st, s s, 52 w Knickerbocker av, 16x50.
James S. Leonard to Norman B. Neiley. Mt. $5,900. nom

Pacific st, s s, 194 w Henry st, 25x100. William Meynor to Albert Morrow. 8,700

Pearl st, w s, 177 n Tillary st, 20.3x102.11x20 3x102.11; also,
4th av, s w cor 34th st, 100x106.2.
Adolph Ketchum to E. Sinnamon Calvert. Mt. $6,000. exch

Prince st, w s, 489 s Willoughby st, runs south 13.6 to Fleet st, x southwest 14 x northwest 30.9 x west 51.4 x north 11 x east 85 to beginning. Lewis Jacobs to Seraphine Levine. 4,040

Same property. Seraphine Levine widow to Fanny wife of Lewis Jacobs. 4,040

Partition st, s w s, 150 s e Richard st, 25x100. John McCormack, New Haven, Conn., to Charles H. and Frances S. Wright. 1,300

President st, s s, 38 e 7th av, 17.6x100. Samuel Winslow, of Worcester, Mass., to Ellen J. Lewis. 8,000

President st, s w s, 394 s e 8th av, 19x100, h & l. Patrick Sheridan to Abraham M. Stein. Mt. $12,000. nom

Quincy st, s s, 220 w Patchen av, 20x100. Rachel M. Sellers to Erastus N. Root and Mary W. his wife, joint tenants. 6,900

Quincy st, s s, 287.6 w Throop av, 187.6x100. Release mort. William H. Beard et al. exrs. and trustees William Beard to Albert Sibley. 12,500

Same property. Release mort. Andrew D. Baird to same. 14,000

Same property. Release mort. Same to same. 8,600

Raymond st, w s, 100 s Bolivar st, 25x75. Jacob Hartwig to Bernard Vogel. Mt. $6,100. 7,350

Rodney st, n w s, 100 n e South 3d st, 40x125. John Drescher, Jr., to Clara Schoning. Mt. $6,000. 5,500

Rodney st, n s, 175 e Lee av, 20x100. Catherine Ropke to Jacob Herrmann exr. and Catherine Ropke extrx. Jacob Hermann. nom

Same property. Catherine Ropke extrx. and Jacob Hermann exr. Jacob Herrmann to Mary E. Neale. 6,750

Rush st, s s, 231 8 e Wythe av, 16.8x100. Adelaid Ballin widow and devisee Jacob Ballin to Franz Krieger. 6,525

Russell st, e s, 155 s Norman av, 20x100. William F. Corwith to Albert A. Lydecker. Mt. $1,800. 3,600

Sackett st, n s, 383.4 w Smith st, 16.8x100. Josephine wife of Joseph H. Hammill to Willard S. Pladwell. Mt. $2,500. nom

Schaéffer st, n w s, 252 s w Hamburg av, 16x91 x16x91.1. Edwin O. Phelps to Robert S. Neely. *Mt.* $1,600. nom

Same property. Robert S. Neely to Sophie wife of John Graf. *Mt.* $1,600. nom

Seigel st, n s, 225 w Leonard st, 25x100.
Seigel st, n s, 100 w Leonard st, 25x100.
Jacob Paskusz to Israel Feldman. All title. nom

Seigel st, s s, 100 e Leonard st, 25x100. Simon Simon and Jacob Harris to Benjamin Wolf and David Stein. *Mt.* $6,500. 10,500

Sherman st, e s, 140 s Greenwood av, runs east 135 x south 10 x southwest 31.8 x west 127 to st, x north 40, Flatbush. Anna M. Ferris and Jennie V. Wilbur to Henry Rudloff. 1,050

Skillman st, w s, 100 n Park av, 25x100. Partition. Samuel Walker ref. to Rosanna Woodworth. 2,505

Stagg st, n s, 43.7 w Bogart st, runs north 87.4 x north 7.1 x west 24.6 x south 87.11 to st, x east 25, h & l. Joseph Maurer to Anna Schultz. *Mt.* $3,000. 5,600

Stagg st, n s, 150 w Lorimer st, 25x100. Charles Ross to Mary Kiefer. 3,300

Stanhope st, n w s, 350 n e Hamburg av, 25x 100. Theodore F. Jackson to John Eich. 1,300

Stanhope st, n w s, 325 n e Hamburg av, 25x 100. Wilhelmina Schwenck to Peter Eisemann. *Mt.* $3,000. 5,800

State st, n s, 120 e Furman st, runs east 20 x north 58 x west 4 x north 12 x west 6 x south 9 x west 10 x south 61. Susan L. Kenney to John Casey. *Mt.* $2,000. 5,250

Steuben st, e s, 286.8 s De Kalb av, 23x100. Carrie A. Bushnell to Emma A. Van Saun. ½ part. Sub. to mort. $8,000. nom

Stockholm st, s e s, 200 s w Evergreen av, 16.8x 100. Henry Roth to August Petry and Margaretha his wife, joint tenants. *Mt.* $2,000. 3,000

Stockholm st, s e s, 300 n e Knickerbocker av, 250x100. Theodore F. Jackson to Anna Weber. 10,000

Suydam st, s e s, 250 n e Hamburg av, 25x100, h & l. Frank Spaeth and John Senger to Henry Bescher and Sarah his wife, joint tenants. *Mt.* $3,500. 6,500

Suydam st, s s, 350 w Evergreen av, 25x95. Andrew Boegel to William Kaiser. *Mt.* $1,500. 4,500

Suydam st, s s, 350 e Central av, 25x100. Ernestine widow Andreas Stahl to Elisa Sondericker. *Mt.* $3,000. nom

Taylor st, n s, 153.7 e Kent av, 20.1x80. Abigail Farrelly to Thomas Wallace. *Mt.* $2,000. 4,800

Thames st, n s, 340 e Bogart st, 27x100. Julius Buttschardt to Sophia C. wife of August Zimmermann. *Mt.* $1,000. 1,002

Thames st, n s, 33 w Morgan av, 1x—x19.2x 100. August Zimmermann to Julius Buttschardt. nom

Thames st, n s, 340 e Bogart st, 26x101.8x7.10x 100. Sophia C. wife of August Zimmermann to same. *Mt.* $1,000. 1,001

Union st, s s, 225.6 e 8th av, 20x95. James and E. Sinnamon Calvert to Adolph Ketchum. *Mt.* $8,000. exch

Union st, s s, 91.3 e Smith st, 17.6x98. John C. Koehler to Veronica wife of John C. Koehler. ½ part. nom

Verona st, s w s, 140 s e Van Brunt st, 25x100. Mary Malone individ. and extrx. James Malone and John E., Michael J., William F. and Mary A. Malone to William Malone and Anastasia his wife, joint tenants. ½ part. 1,000

Verona st, s w s, 115 s e Van Brunt st, 25x100, h & l. William Malone to Mary, John E., Michael J., William F. and Mary A. Malone. ½ part. exch

Van Brunt st, n w s, 75 s w King st, 25x90. Maria A. Hartung to Solomon Steiner. *Mt.* $4,000. 10,250

Van Brunt st, n w s, 50 s w King st, 25x90. Wolf Ashman to Adele Kurtz. nom

Van Voorhis st, n s, 150 w Evergreen av, runs west 51 x north 100 x east 2 x north 100 to Schaeffer st, x east 50 x south 100 x west 1 x south 100 to beginning. Bessie H. Dauley to Virginia A. Kleine. *Mt.* $4,000. nom

Van Voorhis st, n w s, 100 s w Evergreen av, 51x100.
Van Voorhis st, n w s, 202 s w Evergreen av, 83x100.
Edwin J. Bedell to Robert H. Irish, Hempstead, L. I. All liens. nom

Varick st, n e s, 175 n w Meeker av, 43 10x26.4x 103.9x97.5. The Kings Co. Improvement Co. to George Ackerman. 1,100

Wallabout late River st, s s, 150 e Harrison av, 25x100. Jacob Sapiro to Fannie Freiberger. *Mt.* $6,000. 6,900

Walton st, s s, 250 w Harrison av, 25x100. John Schmidt to Peter Herbert. *Mt.* $4,000. 6,675

Warwick st, e s, 230.7 s Fulton st, 25x95. Edward F. Linton to Clara wife of Henry Turner. 4,700

Warwick st, w s, 200 s Sutter av, 25x100. Philip Altsott to Frank Hess and Ernestine his wife. 475

Warwick st, w s, 143.2 s Fulton av, 25x95. Thomas Krekeler to Peter Borst. nom

Willow st, Nos. 108 and 110, n w s, 115 s w Clark st, 35.5x100. Spencer Trask to William L. and Charles F. Burrill. 28,000

Woodbine st, s e s, 160 s w Knickerbocker av, 200x100. Albert Berckmeier to Samuel Ray. nom

Watkins st, w s, 240 s Livonia av, 100x100. Herman Goldstein, of New York, to Louis and Joseph Eisenberg. *Mt.* $1,500. 1,263

Waverly pl, easterly cor Forest pl, runs southeast 60.7 x northeast 100 x northwest 7.2 to Forest pl, x west 113.4, New Utrecht. Owen Brady to Jane Atkinson. 700

Winthrop st, s s, 142 6 w Nostrand av, 50x122.6, Flatbush. Franz Kannengieser to George Fenton. 2,750

Withers st, n s, 300 e Graham av, 30.10x69.2x 82x15.9x78. Release dower. Bridget Kelly widow to James S. Kelly. nom

Same property. James S. Kelly heirs Richard Kelly to James McNally. 2,300

2d st, n s, 426.9 e 5th av, 18x100. James H. McKenna to Nathaniel Roe. *Mt.* $4,500. 6,350

East 2d st, w s, 160.4 s Greenwood av, 25x125, Flatbush. Frederick G. Handley to Joseph Kirschner. 300

Same property. Release mort. Jennie V. Wilbur to Frederick G. Handley. 250

South 2d st, s s, 103.6 e Bedford av, 19.1x95. Sarah W. Nicholson to Samuel W. Nicholson. *Mt.* $6,000. 6,000

3d st, s s, 142 e Smith st, 33x100. Edward M. Townsend individ. and as exr. Belma R. Townsend to Vina A. Sumner, of Syracuse, N. Y. 8,875

South 3d st, n e s, 125 n w Hewes st, 25x120. Maria A. wife of and Jacob L. Deem, of Colona, Ill., to Henry May. *Mt.* $500. 3,700

South 4th st, No. 292, s s, 104.3 w Rodney st. 19.10x104.6x19.10x104.3. Adrienne I. wife of James Stevenson to Louis and Martin Kirsch. *Mt.* $3,000. 4,500

North 4th st, n s, 104 e Roebling st, 25x121.6x 23.3x113. Mary wife of Michael O'Connell to Eugene O'Connell. nom

South 5th st, n e cor Roebling st, 40x73, hs & ls. Mary A. Manjer trustee Daniel Manjer dec'd to Ambrose M. Morgan. 11,000

South 6th st, s s, 20 w 2d st, 23x82.4x23.1x84.6. Maria Otterbeck to Julius G. Otterbeck. gift

South 8th st, s s, 194 w 2d st, 24x132. Walter E. Brigham, of Desplaines, Ill., to Mary D. Cook. 1-30 part. 200

9th st, s w cor 7th av, 19.10x72.6. Albro J. Newton to John Maxwell. Q. C. nom

South 9th st, s s, 206.9 e Havemeyer st, 23x 128x23x124.
South 4th st, s s, 146.6 e Driggs st, 21x100.
Havemeyer st, n e cor South 3d st, 18.9x100.
South 1st st, n s, 100 e Kent av, 29.2x100x32.9 x100.
Edwin A. and Albert E. Martin and Addie F. wife of William H. Vogel heirs Samuel S. Martin to Emma L. Martin widow. All title. nom

North 10th st, n s, 25 e Kent av, 25x100. Francis J. Lynch, of Thorndike, Mass., to Ellen Flood. 7,000

11th st, s s, 391.6 s e 5th av, 37x100. Andrew Suydam to William F. Wing. nom

Same property. William F. Wing to Rebecca Suydam. B. & S. nom

11th st, n e s, 39.6 s e 6th av, 19x63.6x19x63. James Jack to Mary L. Piper. *Mt.* $3,500. 6,250

13th st, n e s, 60 n w 5th av, 18.11x50.
13th st, n e s, 78.11 w 5th av, 18.11x50.
Lewis Jacobs to Seraphine Levine. 4,925

Same property. Seraphine Levine widow to Fanny wife of Lewis Jacobs. 4,925

13th st, n s, 272.10½ e 4th av, 12.6x100. William Scheelje, Jr., to Mary F. wife of Lawrence Conzen. nom

13th st, s s, 427 e 3d av, 20.10x100. Ann Cosgrove to Ann Many. 2,600

14th st, n s, 142.4 e 8th av, 18.6x100. William Hawkins to John H. Clark. *Mt.* $3,500. 6,250

15th st, n s, 335.11 e 6th av, 16x100. William A Consall to Louis Prosch, Jr. *Mt.* $2,300. 4,300

16th st, s s, 241.3 e 4th av, 17x100. Charles L. Prindle to Alice L. Carpenter. *Mt.* $2,000. 3,300

17th st, s s, 403 e 7th av, 16x100.2. Martha A. Van Sielen, of Jamaica, N. Y., to George A. Moeckel. 2,750

17th st, n s, 176.4 w 4th av, 16.8x100. Thomas Pitbladdo to Matilda Will. 5,000

20th st, n e s, 283.8 s e 5th av, 24.8x100. Ralph Kirkman to Louis Brilliant and Isaac Tarshis. 8,500

20th st, n e s, 240.7 w 8th av, 15.7½x100.2. Henry C Bull, of New Utrecht, to John L. Olson. *Mt.* $1,500. 2,600

24th st, n s, 450 e 3d av, 25x100. Martin Erickson to August L. Schultz. *Mt.* $3,500. 5,550

24th st, n s, 240 e 3d av, 20x100. Edward E. Bergen to Silas A. Condict. nom

Same property. Silas A. Condict to Robert Stewart. 3,200

28th st, s s, 475 e 3d av, 25x100.2. Walter L. Suydam and Helen S. wife of R. Fulton Cutting to Anders J. Anderson. 800

Bay 35th st, s e s, 80 n e of J. B. Denyse, 4x 97.11, Gravesend. Harmon W. Cropsey to Edward P. Abearn. 80

41st st, s w s, 120 n w 3d av, 300x100.2. Franz Franz to Philip H. Schoeing. *Mt.* $4,905. exch

45th st, s w s, 250 n w 13th av, 50x100.2, New Utrecht. West Brooklyn Land and Improvement Co. to John W. Force, Waterbury. Conn. 2,500

46th st, n s, 180 e 5th av, 20x100.3. Francesca wife of Alessandro Alessi to Mary wife of Felix Carrao. *Mt.* $3,200. 4,000

48th st, s s, 200 w 4th av, 32x100. Release mort. Julia M. Budlong extrx. William Menck to William McMonegal. 228

48th st, n s, 260 e 4th av, 20x100.2. William F. Costello to Maud A. wife of Charles W. Tomlinson. 800

48th st, s s, 200 w 4th av, 16x100.2. William McMonegal to Henry Groth. 2,700

49th st, s s, 360 e 3d av, 20x100.2, h & l. William Clemett to Jacques Van Brunt. *Mt.* $3,000. 6,250

49th st, s s, 420 e 8th av, 60x100.2, New Utrecht. James V. S. Woolley to John J. Downey. 575

52d st, s w s, 180 s e 3d av, 20x100.2. Margaretta wife of and Frederick Ritterbush to William H. Shepard. 3,500

52d st, s s, 260 e 6th av, 40x100.2.
6th av, e s, 25.2 n 53d st, 50x100.
Mary J. Foley to Honora R. Sweeny. nom

Same property. Honora R. Sweeny to John C. Foley and Mary J. his wife, joint tenants. nom

53d st, n s, 135.6 w 2d av, 17.9x100.2.
54th st, s w s, 120 n w 8th av, 60x100.2, New Utrecht.
Mary A. Kirby to Margaret I. Conlan. All liens. 4,800

54th st, s s, 100 e 3d av, 50x100. John J. G. Sanger to Jaques Van Brunt. *Mt.* $2,100. 5,500

54th st, n s, 260 e 6th av, 40x100. William T. Guy to Ellen M. Hart. 600

54th st, n e s, 125 n w 15th av, 50x100.2, New Utrecht. West Brooklyn Land and Improvement Co. to George Gaskell. 700

54th st, n e s, 225 n w 15th av, 100x100.2, New Utrecht. William Dittmar, Jr., to William R. Abbott. *Mt.* $2,250. 5,500

57th st, n e s, 260 s e 12th av, 60x100.2, New Utrecht. Belinda L. Bergen to Frank P. Herig. *Mt.* $2,000. 4,000

59th st, s s, 220 e 11th av, 40x100.2, New Utrecht. John H. and William Doherty to Jacob S. Merkert. 400

63d st, s s, 140 w 14th av, 20x107.1x20x107.4, Bath Junction. James V. S. Woolley to Robert McIntyre. 200

63d st, s s, 160 w 14th av, 20x106.11x20x107.1, Bath Junction. Same to Elizabeth McGahey. 200

63d st, s w s, 100 s e 10th av, 20x100.
63d st, s w s, 140 s e 10th av, 20x100, New Utrecht.
Claus Doscher to Emelyn wife of Charles Lange. B. & S. and C. a. G. 210

65th st, n s, 440 w 14th av, 40x100, New Utrecht. Effingham H. Nichols, of New York, to Martin T. McMahon. 460

66th st, n e s, 313 n w 18th av, 40x100, New Utrecht. Deed on execution. Clark D. Rhinehart, Sheriff, to George W. Gilbert. All title. 50

67th st, s s, 340 e 14th av, 40x120, New Utrecht. Effingham H. Nichols to Alfred Luckhurst. 550

67th st, s s, 200 e 13th av, 40x125, New Utrecht. Same to Franklin E. Vail of Norwalk, Conn. 370

71st st, n s, 210 w 15th av, 40x100, New Utrecht. James V. S. Woolley to Thomas E. Brown. 460

79th st, s s, 100 w 1st av, 120.8x124.8x120.3x 118.5, New Utrecht. Jaques Van Brunt to John J. Granger. 3,200

87th st, s w s, 100 s e 1st av, 50x100, New Utrecht. David D. Field to Jennie Lahey. 640

87th st, s w s, 100 n w 2d av, 175x100, New Utrecht. David D. Field to Louis Nova. 2,100

89th st, s w s, 275 n w 4th av, runs southwest 86.10 x northwest 327 to 89th st, x southeast 313.11 to beginning. David D. Field, of New York, to Anna Reynolds. 1,100

Albany av, w s, 69.10 s Prospect pl, 16.7x80. John F. Dettmar to Annie K. Dettmar his wife. nom

Arlington av, s s, 75 w Essex st, 16.8x80. Benjamin T. Coray to Mary C. Keach. *Mt.* $1,000. 3,250

Arlington av, s s, 75 w Linwood st, 16.8x90. B. T. Corey to E. G. Freeman, of New Jersey. 3,700

Arlington av, s s, 91.8 w Essex st, runs south 80 x west 8.4 x south 10 x west 8.4 x north 90 x east 16.8 to beginning. Same to John Meyn. 3,700

Arlington av, s w cor Warwick st, 115x100.
Arlington av, s e cor Jerome st, 40x100.
Fred. J. Swift to William H. Baker. *Mt.* $9,100. 27,000

Atlantic av, s e cor Warwick st, 35x113x35x103. Anna Schmidt widow to Anna K. Than. 3,150

Atlantic av, s s, 163 e Bond st, 22x80, h & l. Ezekiel H. Miller, Orangetown, N. Y., to Joseph Wolf. 7,250

Atlantic av, n e s, 25 s e Court st, 25x100. Nette Wider, of Jersey City, to Henry Seidensticker. 9,000

Belmont av, s s, 25 e Osborn st, 25x100. Solomon Wolff to Harris Schwartz, of New York. *Mt.* $3,000. 5,950

Belmont av, n e cor Van Sielen av, 100x100. Caroline Bick to Theodore M. Le Beau. 3,700

Belmont av, s s, 25 e Van Sielen av, 25x100. J. Wyckoff Van Siclen to Thomas Meredith. 800

Belmont av, s w cor Powell st. 100x300. Robert L. Woods, Jr., to James G. Roberts. *Mt.* $2,500. 6,500

Belmont av, s e cor Thatford av, 25x100. Louis Rosenblatt and Nathan Zwetschkenbaum to Michael Rosenthal. 1,425

Bedford av, w s, 257.9 n Myrtle av, 50x100. Samuel Allen to Robert Allen. C. a. G. nom

Benson av, westerly cor Bay 25th st, 96.8x100, New Utrecht. Augustus Meyers, of New York, to Josephine L. Ketcham. 3,125

Blake av and Junius st, Powell st and Dumont av—the block, 500x200.
Junius st, s e cor Blake av, 500 to Dumont av, x90.
Dwight E. Rogers to Herbert C. Smith. 27,000

Bushwick av, s w s, 80 n w Weirfield st, 20x75. Agnes, Josephine, William H. and Charlotte Duffy by John Petrie, Jr., guard. to William Ruthmann. 5,500

Same property. Louisa Duffy widow to same. Release dower. 521

Bushwick av, n e s, 20 n w Halsey st, 20x80. Lonny Schroeder to George M. Peper. *Mt.*, $5,000. 10,000

Central av, s w s, 75 s e Palmetto st, 25x100. Barbara Beisel formerly Kirsch to Clarence R. and Gerhard Hashagen. *Mt.* $3,000. 6,600

Christopher av, w s, 250 s Sutter av, 150x100.
Christopher av, w s, 100 s Sutter av, 25x100.
George A. Remsen to Bridget Barrett. *Mt.* $14,850. nom

Christopher av, e s, 125 s Blake av, 25x100. The National Bank of Rondout to J. Woolley Shepard. Q. C. nom

Same property. Elizabeth and James J. Sweeney indivivid. and as surviving partners of E. Sweeney & Sons, Kingston, N. Y., to same. 2,000

De Kalb av, n w cor Evergreen av, runs north 125 x west 100 x south 50 x east 75 x south 75 to De Kalb av, x east 25, hs & ls. Philip H. Schoeing to Franz Franz. *Mt.* $12,000. exch

De Kalb av, s s, 80 e Reid av, 19x100. Margaret Mulvihill wife of and Nicholas to Herman Hamel. *Mt.* $4,500. 8,000

Division av, s s, 87.2 w Wythe av, 20.1x133.7x21.7x142.6. William A. Roberts to Henry F. Roberts. 10,000

Division av, n w cor Miller av, 50x50. Joseph Sosa to Margaret Sosa wife of Joseph. *Mt.* $1,500. 2,100

Dumont av, n w cor Thatford av, 25x100. Hyman Goldstein to Abraham Wolf. 1,000

Dumont av, s s, 50 w Watkins st, 25x100. Louis Davidson and Louis Berman, of New York, to Isaac Haft. *Mt.* $700. 1,420

Same property. Isaac Haft to Adolph Fischman. *Mt.* $700. 1,600

Flushing av, s s, 100 e Marcy av, 25x100. Patrick W. English to Leopold Michel. *Mt.* $1,980. 4,200

Fort Hamilton av, n w cor 65th st, runs north 143 to Cowenhovens lane, x west 107.6 x south 115.2 x east 89.10; also,
Fort Hamilton av, n w cor 67th st, 101.8x163.6x100x181.1, New Utrecht.
Phebe M. and Eleanor F. Clarke and Geo. H. Houghton exrs., &c., Henry L. Clarke to Mary Delorac, of Cincinnati, Ohio. *Mt.* $2,807. 401

Furman av, n s, 117 e Bushwick av, 17.6x100. Anna E. wife of Frederick N. Riggs to Elizabeth F. Driscoll. *Mt.* $1,500. 2,000

Gates av, n s, 255.6 w Stuyvesant av, 19.6x100, h & l. Charles J. Clements to Charles H. Lohrs. *Mt.* $7,000. nom

Gates av, n s, 220 w Sumner av, 20x100. Release mort. Frederick W. Jaqui to Frederick W. Jaqui, Jr. nom

Same property. Frederick W. Jaqui, Jr., to George C. Ihrig. *Mt.* $7,800. 10,000

Gates av, n s, 250 e Lewis av, 37.6x100, h & l. Nathaniel W. Burtis to John W. A. Marsland. *Mt.* $6,200. 9,000

Glenmore av, s s, 75 w Jerome st, 25x100. Lorenz Schweitzer to John Moeller. 2,300

Graham av, w s, 154.9 s Van Cott av, 24x100, h & l. Amalia Harris and Amalia Wechsler to David Kesper, New York. *Mt.* $3,550. 4,525

Graham av, e s, 25.9 s Varet st, 24.3x100. Martin Mayer to Isaac Horowitz. 7,000

Gravesend av, e s, 25 s lands of Barnard Doyle, 25x86.
Gravesend av, n w cor lands of Barnard Doyle, 25x100, Gravesend.
Martha A. McCabe wife of Charles to George W. Bennett. Q. C. 1,800

Greene av, n w s, 90 s w Central av, 20x100. Frank L. Singer to Julius Ackernecht, Henry Manny and Clementina Herb. 4,500

Hamburg av, w s, 25 s Greene av, 25x90, h & l. George Covert to Gottlob Weber. 6,800

Hamburg av, north cor Stanhope st, 100x100. Robert H. Barry to John Klein and Frank Elles. nom

Hamilton av, south cor Hicks st, 38x19.10x13.2x40.2.
Carroll st, s s, 146 e Clinton st, 22x100.
Ann wife of William Swanton to Ann Finn. Reserves life estate. nom

Hancock av, s w cor Patchen av, 20x75, h & l. Joseph A. Cross to Bernhard Davidsburg. *Mt.* $7,500. 15,000

Howard av, e s, 130.4 n St. Marks av, runs northeast 356.1 x south 32.2 x southwest 356.1 x north 32.2. James O. Carpenter to William Goetz. 1,200

Hegeman av, s s, 60 w Junius st, 20x90. Edwin B. Lilly to Sarah F. Barton. 175

Irving av, east cor Greene av, 25x90. John Bayer, Joseph Weidner and Serafin W. Turner to Martin Mayer. *Mt.* $4,500. 9,800

Jefferson av, s s, 340 w Nostrand av, 20x100. Harry H. Spengeman, of Jersey City, to Augustus Haviland. *Mt.* $7,000. nom

Jefferson av, No. 454, s s, 306.8 e Throop av, 16.8x100.
Jefferson av, No. 456, s s, 323.4 e Throop av, 16.8x100.
Louise O. Wheeler, Middletown, N. Y., to Samuel D. Horton. *Mt.* $9,000. 14,500

Jefferson av, s e s, 293.6 n e Evergreen av, 18x100. Timothy G. Sellew to Rose Pedrosa. nom

Jefferson av, s s, 280 e Nostrand av, 20x100. Mary A. Maujer to Mary A. wife of James R. Davies. 14,000

Johnson av, s s, 143 e Bushwick av, 50x100. Christian A. Keppler to Esther Sweet. *Mt.* $4,000. 9,150

Kingston av, n e cor Pacific st, 80x96. Franklin J. Fellows, of Central Islip, N. Y., to Benjamin F. Hobby and Daniel Doody. *Mt.* $31,500. nom

Knickerbocker av, s w s, 75 s e Harman st, 48.3x57.3. Philipp Duerkes to Philipp Weisgerber. 1,250

Knickerbocker av, southerly cor Stanhope st, 25x80. George Gutting and Charles A. Wagner to John Herlich. *Mt.* $5,500. nom

Knickerbocker av, w s, 80 s w Cooper st, 120x100. Orson W. Sheldon, of Fort Ann, N. Y., to Isabella Pettit. nom

Knickerbocker av, s s, 40 s e Grove st, 60x100. Hannah F. wife of Herman E. Street, of Rockville Centre, to Michael J. Hand. 2,100

Lee av, n w cor Middleton st, 26.8x80. Margaret wife of Nicholas Mulvihill to John Horigan. *Mt.* $7,500. 14,000

Lexington av, n s, 240 w Marcy av, 20x100. Frank Bond to George E. White. nom

Lexington av, s s, 137.6 e Reid av, 17x100. The East Brooklyn Co-operative Building Assoc. to George Jahn. 4,225

Lexington av, n s, 126 e Patchen av, runs north 100 x west 40 x north 20 x west 86 to Patchen av, x south 120 to Lexington av, x east 126. Alice B. wife of and Smith Cox to John B. Altmann. *Mt.* $13,000. 15,500

Lexington av, s s, 50 w Throop av, 50x100. David S. Beasley to Marietta Rich. *Mt.* $12,500. 20,500

Liberty av, s w cor Hemlock st, 25x100. John Cain, Jersey City, N. J., to Caroline Peterson. 700

Manhattan av, w s, 250 s Meserole av, 75x100. Charles W. Preston to John J. Randall and William G. Miller. 21,000

Maspeth av, s s, 200 e Bushwick av, runs south 89.4 x east 16.6 x northeast 38.7 x north 54.5 x west 25. James Kelly, of Danbury, Conn., to Gaetano Manganaro. 2,950

Meeker av, s s, 165 e Graham av, 24x100. George W. Sammis to Otto Hoske. 2,000

Metropolitan av, s s, 250 e Catharine st, 25x100. Christian Bott to Frederick Kekut. Sub. to morts. 6,500

Meserole av, n e cor Russell st, runs north 400 to Calyer st, x east 200 to North Henry st, x south 400 to Meserole av, x west 200 to beginning; also,
Meserole av, n e cor North Henry st, extends along st 400 to Calyer st, x 100.
The Kings County Improvement Co. to Charles A. Miller. nom

Nassau av, n s, 75 w Newell st, 25x100. Sarah M. Disbrow widow to Edward and Charles Schwindt. 2,125

Nassau av, n s, 75 e Oakland st, 25x100. Same to Philip Schwindt. 2,125

New York av, s e cor Degraw st, runs south 32.11 x northeast 145 to Degraw st, x west 140 to corner. Mary wife of Walter W. Berck, Amelia Vredenburg widow, Phebe E. Willis widow, Rebecca Bowlby widow, Robert Miller, Elizabeth Scott and Elmira wife of John S. Bogart heirs Mary Bennett to William H. Murr. 700

Norwood av, w s, 1,475 n 1st st, 50x150. John Liddy to Mary A. wife of Louis J. Kaufman. 1,300

Norman av, n s, 20 e Diamond st, 16x95. Chauncey Perry to Martha wife of John Doyle. 3,500

Park av, s s, 215.8 w Broadway, 22x100. Frederick J. Greifenstein to Joseph Graf and Mary M. his wife. nom

Same property. Mary M. wife of Joseph Graf to Frederick J. Greifenstein. nom

Patchen av, w s, 75 s Hancock st, 15x100. William M. Evans to Alice M. Foss. *Mt.* $3,000. 5,350

Reid av, w s, 50 n Halsey st, 50x100. Release mort. Charles Emmons, of New York to George W. McCormick. 4,000

Rochester av, s w cor Dean st, 100x186.7. Robert A. Wason, of Delphi, Ind., heir Sarah E. and Frances A. Wason and sole devisee under will Ellen B. Wason and Gertrude L. wife of Robert A. Wason to Edward M. Grout. 1,200

Rochester av, e s, 103.3 s Pacific st, 32.4x80, hs & ls. Giulia Brandies to Henry Weil. 75

Rockaway av, e s, 150 s Glenmore av, 25x100.1. Morris and Joseph Lubliner, of New York, to Jacob Manheim. *Mt.* $1,850. 2,400

Rockaway av, e s, 131.6 s Sutter av, 18.6x110.2. Gilbert S. Thatford to Fannie wife of Hyman Shapiro. 4,112

Rockaway av, e s, 75 s Belmont av, 50x100.1. Harris Fein to Meyer Wolinsky and Isaac Bernstein. *Mt.* $400. 1,800

Saratoga av, e s, 70 n Marion st, 30x78. Margaret McDowell to Wilhelm Straus. nom

Schenck av, w s, 125 n Union av, 25x100. Andrew Sullivan, of New York, to George Dehn. 1,000

Schenectady av, w s, 25 s Bergen st, 25x75, Henrietta wife of William J. Douglass to William Herod. 2,150

Schenectady av, w s, 207 s Montgomery st, 50x100, Flatbush. Cornelius Donovan to Peter Dervan. Sub. to taxes and sales for same. 425

Sheffield av, e s, 100 n Liberty av, 50x100. Clara Steinhardt formerly Wiesenbach to Lottie Strasser. 6,000

Shepherd av, e s, 25.6 s Gay st, 25.6x100. Mary wife of and Thomas Smith to Peter Mullen and Mary A. his wife. 2,900

Skillman av, n s, 22.5 e Lorimer st, 25x100. Jacob O. Steinberg to Louis Riechers. 2,325

Skillman av, s s, 175 w Ewen st, 25x100. Alonzo E. De Baun to Sarah A. and Mary E. Neil. 4,000

Snediker av, w s, 155 n Sutter av, 15x100. John P. Free to Emma Langdon. *Mt.* $1,500. 3,000

St. Marks av, n s, 175 w Vanderbilt av, 25x131. Joseph Hackett to Margaret Hecker. gift

St. Marks av, n s, 275 w Underhill av, 25x131. Lawrence W. Clark to Erick Soderstrom. 1,300

St. Marks av, n s, 250 w Underhill av, runs north 114.10 x north to centre line bet St. Marks av and Bergen st, x west to point 275 of Underhill av, x south 131 to av, x east 25. Charles A. Clark, New York, to same. 1,300

Stone av, w s, 300 s Blake av, 25x100. Release mort. John C. and Herbert C. Smith and Herman F. Koepke to Mary E. Cook, of Newtown, N. Y. 100

Same property. Mary E. Cook to Frank Rosenberg, of New York. *Mt.* $2,000, and taxes 1891. 3,500

Stone av, w s, 43 n Blake av, 23x100. Mary A. L. wife of William H. Baker to Isaac and Jacob Goldberg. *Mt.* $1,700. 2,357

Stone av, w s, 150 s Dumont av, 25x100. Brani Zwikel to Benjamin Epstein. *Mt.* $1,220. 2,800

Stone av, n w cor Hull st, 100x90. George H. Smith to Margaretha Lewis. B. & S. C. a. G. 29,000

Stone av, w s, 112 n Blake av, 23x100. William H. Baker to Boozy Spevack. *Mt.* $1,700. 2,278

Sumner av, w s, 125 s Decatur st, runs west 99.8 x southeast 101.5 x east 81.11 to av, x north 100. Julia B. F. wife of John B. Fish to Henry J. Brown. *Mt.* $7,500. exch

Sumner av, n e cor Myrtle av, 75x100, hs & ls. Marion Dickie to Susannah A. Dickie. 27,000

Thatford av, w s, 100 n Glenmore av, 100x100.1. James J. Christopher to Charles Goldstein, of New York. *Mt.* $1,500. 2,500

Thatford av, e s, 100 s Eastern Parkway, 25x100. Jacob and Davis Axelrod to Morris Brodoosky. *Mt.* $2,200. 4,050

Same property. Morris Brodoosky to Bernhard Weinberger. *Mt.* $3,050. 3,850

Thatford av, e s, 150 n Rapelje av, 25x100. William Hartman to Jacob Ehrenzweig. Sub. to mort. 1,675

Thatford av, e s, 175 n Rapelje av, 25x100. Pauline wife of William Hartman to Nathan Ellerstein. *Mt.* $1,500. 2,700

Thatford av, e s, 150 s Union av, 100x100. Elizabeth Augusty widow to Hannah Gottehrer. 4,000

Thatford av, e s, 50 s Sutter av, 25x100. Joseph Morris to Louis and Harris Lembik. *Mt.* $1,800. 3,300

Thatford av, e s, 225 s Livonia av, 50x100. Hirsch Wickenfeld and Nathan Rittermann, of New York, to Samuel Goldstein and Lipman Bubrofsky. *Mt.* $350. 1,225

Thatford av, w s, 150 150 s Belmont av, 25x100.1. Louis Bellar to Wolf Kaplan. *Mt.* $1,400. 2,300

Throop av, e s, 25 n Wallabout st, 25x59.2x26.9x68.8. Emilie Loch to Rosa N. Geis. 4,300

Throop av, s w cor Whipple st, 20x110. John F. Batterman to John Schmitt. *Mt.* $6,000. 7,825

Vanderbilt av, w s, 355 n Gates av, 20x100, h & l. Henrietta G. wife of John F. Brush to Jane E. Williams. nom

Same property. Jane E. Williams to Anna F. P. wife of Henry C. Knight. 9,000

Van Sielen av, n e cor Belmont av, 100x100. Theodore M. Le Beau to Elias Helgaus. 3,800

Vernon av, n s, 350 e Tompkins av, 18.9x100. Benjamin T. Valentine to Julius Dippel. *Mt.* $4,000. 6,750

Washington av, w s, 342.1 s Fulton st, 18x130.9 Cora C. Russell to Abram B. Wyckoff. *Mt.* $10,000. exch. and 1,000

Washington av, n w cor St. Marks av, 32x60.7x30.7x4.11x89.1. Philip Sullivan to Charles D. King. *Mt.* $6,500. 1,000

Willoughby av, n s, 100 e Evergreen av, 25x121.6 x 25.4 x 125.11. George Schoner to George Schoner, Jr., and Maggie his wife. *Mt.* $2,000. 5,000

Willoughby av, n w s, 225 n e Central av, 25x100, h & l. George Cellers trustee to Philip Schneider. 2,300

Willoughby av, n w s, 100 n e Central av, 25x100. Maria Hoffmann to Frederick Davis. *Mt.* $3,000. 5,000

Willoughby av, n w cor Grand av, runs west 24 x north 94 x east 14.1 x south 7.1 x east 9.8 to Grand av, x south —. Release judgment. Brooklyn Door and Sash Co. to Edward Judson. nom

1st av, w s, 20 n 80th st, 100x100, New Utrecht. Jaques Van Brunt to William Clemett. exch and 500

2d av, n e cor 40th st, 100.2x350; also,
40th st, n s, 100 w 3d av, 250x100.2.
Percy R. Pyne, Jr., to M. Bayard Brown. nom

3d av, n w cor 40th st, 25.2x100. J. Archibald Murray, of New York, to M. Bayard Brown. nom

3d av, s e s, 59.7 s w 11th st, 19.9x65; also,
3d av, s e s, 39.10 s w 11th st, 19.9x65; also,
3d av, s w cor 11th st, 20x80.
John J. Voorhees to Albert V. B. Voorhees. Sub. to an annuity, nom

3d av, w s, 17 s 14th st, 25x75. James H. McKenna to Christopher Butz. *Mt.* $4,000. 6,550

3d av, east cor 70th st, 107.2x190, New Utrecht. John T. Clark to George T. Hay. *Mt.* $5,000. nom

3d av, westerly cor 95th st, 25x110, New Utrecht. Edward I. Horsman to Jane Atkinson, of New York. 1,350

3d av, south cor 97th st, 41.7x108.8x40x120.1, New Utrecht. Maria Antoinette, Maria A. and Mary S. Geiston and Thomes H. Geiston widow and heirs George S. Geiston to Jane wife of Henry J. Atkinson. 1,750

3d av, n w s, 50 s w 88th st, 50x100, New Utrecht. David D. Field to Otto F. Eichberg. 1,270

4th av, west cor 58th st, 129x102.6x106.5x100,

New Utrecht. David D. Field to Michael Fitzgerald. 2,200
4th av, north cor 77th st, 59x100, New Utrecht. Release mort. Eleanor C. Townsend, South Orange, N. J., to Anna Martin. 1,000
4th av. n w cor 44th st, 100.2x100. Ira O. Miller to Warren S. Burt. *Mt.* $4,000. 7,700
Same property. Warren S. Burt, of New York, to Louis B. Gorgeis. *Mt.* $6,000 nom
4th av, n w cor 14th st, 30x86 10. Richard J. Murphy to Charles Obroek. *Mt.* $10,000. 18,000
4th av, southerly cor 87th st, runs southwest along av 85.8 x southeast 71 x northeast 80 x northwest 101.10, New Utrecht. Joseph H. Yauch to Anna wife of Christian Ellmers. 1,600
4th av, s e s, 85.8 s w 87th st, runs southwest 34.11 x southeast 58.10 x northeast 25.9 x northwest 71, New Utrecht. Same to Christian Ellmers. 275
4th av, n e cor 48th st, 25.2x100. James Dunn to Frank Roenbeck. 3,000
5th av, s e cor Berkeley pl, 95x87.2. Lawrence V. Cortelyou and ano. exrs., &c., Jaques Cortelyou to Thomas Brown. 19,000
6th av, s e cor 1st st, 100x90. Roderick Von Graff to John D. Hallaren. *Mt.* $25,000. nom
7th av, w s, 30.7 s Carroll st, 108.4x100. Stephen Buckingham Sturges to John F. Hart. 52,000
8th av, n w s, 80 n e Windsor pl, 20x97.5. The Nassau Land and Improvement Co. to Eleonora Sasse, of Union Hill, N. J. 6,500
8th av, s e cor 15th st, runs east 160 x south 200 to 16th st, x west 18 x north 100 x west 18 x south 100 to 16th st, x west 124 to 8th av, x north 200 to beginning. Edwin J. Bedell to Thomas McCann, William J. Fitzpatrick and William Martin. Sub. to liens, &c. nom
13th av, e s, 20 n 67th st, 20x100, New Utrecht. Effingham H. Nichols to Edmund W. Stillwell. 2,130
13th av, n e cor 67th st, 20x100, Lefferts Park. Effingham H. Nichols to Edward Peterson. 375
19th av, north cor Cropsey av, 287.6x107.7x 286.6 to Cropsey av, x93.1x93.1, New Utrecht. Tillie M. Strouse to Irving Fish. *Mt.* $4,500. 23,500
Interior lot, 14.6 s Putnam av and 349.6 w Reid av, runs south 58 x west 0.6 x north 58 x east 6. Miranda L. Mitchell to Charles Isbill. nom
Interior lot, 275 e Franklin av and 85.11 n Prospect pl, runs south 43 thence along Old Kent av 10.10 x northeast 67.6 x north 54.11 x southwest — to beginning. Robert W. Gleason to William E. Cox. Q. C. 500
Interior lot, 275 e Franklin av, 85.11 n Prospect pl, runs north 42.7 x east 65.6 x south 12.9 x southwest — to beginning. Robert W. Gleason to William E. Cox. 500
Interior gore, on farm line, bet Meserole and Calver, at s e cor of lot 2 on J. A. Meserole map, runs south at right angle to Greenpoint av, 24.2 x east 3.4 x northwest 24. Thomas Gunn to Mary Roach. 40
Lots 1, 8-17, 34-45, 74-78, 87-90, 96-100, 103-106, 112-116, 119-123, 139-143, 148 and 149, 167-170, 176-190, 193-197, and 923-932 all inclusive map 221 lots Michael J. Bergen, New Utrecht. Michael J. Bergen to James V. S. Woolley, of New York. 7,000
Lots 14-18, inclusive, block 195, and 11-22 block 7 map of property upon which Hoagland and Kingsland have written their names, 17th Ward. Release mort. Elbert Snedeker to Paul C. Grening. nom
Lots 59-61 map Gilbert S. Thatford, New Lots. Francis J. Taylor, of New York, to Adolph Blumenkrantz. 1,500
Lots 232-235; also lots 247-249 block 7 map Jacob Snediker property, 26th Ward. Fritz Breitenstein to Michael and Caspar Scheen. 1,200
Lot 420 block 13 map Jacob Snediker, 26th Ward. Anna Leinfelder to Eliza Taylor. 100
Lots 289 and 290 map Worth & Strawson, map Flatbush. Jacob Worth and Vincent A. Strawson to Thomas Farrell. 300
Lots 291 and 295 same map. Same to Joseph Farrell. 300
Lot 294 same map. Same to Mary Nolan. 155
Lots 320 and 321 same map. Same to Thomas S. Elliott. 280
Lot 288 same map. Same to Robert J. Dunn. 150
Lots 292 and 293 same map. Same to Henry Devlin. 300
Lots 322 and 323 same map. Same to Eugene McCarthy. 280
Lots 243 and 244 same map. Same to Delia Gibbons. 300
Lot 312 same map. Same to William Hood. 135
Lot 115 same map. Same to Mary E. Keiser. 240
Lot 116 same map. Same to Susanna Clark. 240
Lots 318 and 319 same map. Same to Joseph P. Smith. 300
Lots 75 and 76 same map. Same to H. Theodore Meyer. 400
Lot 77 same map. Same to William Barb. 215
Lots 418, 419, 420 same map. Same to Gustav M. Koppel. 500
Lots 427 and 428 same map. Same to William Howard. 240
Lots 270 and 271 same map. Same to Charles Baker. 290
Lots 115 and 116 same map. Release mort. Mary and Catharine Vanderveer and Eliza A. Martense to Jacob Worth and Vincent A. Strawson. 250
Lots 34-36 and 75-77 inclusive same map. Release mort. Same to same. 975
Lots 243, 244, 270 and 271 same map. Release mort. Same to same. 350
Lots 288-295 and 312, 314-323 and 350 and 351 and 418-421 and 427 and 428 same map. Release mort. Same to same. 2,250
Lots 314-317 map 430 lots Jacob Worth and Vincent A. Strawson, Flatbush. Jacob Worth and Vincent A. Strawson to James Slattery. 560
Lots 350 and 351 same map. Same to George Breher. 290
Lots 198, 220 and 221 block F map of Vanderveer Homestead, 26th Ward. John H. Vanderveer to Emil Reineking. *Mt.* $500. 1,070
Lots 564 and 565 "block L" map Zabriskie Homestead, Flatbush. William J. Kaiser, John H. Vanderveer and George W. Dalton to Eibe H. Itjen. 1,000
Lincoln road (East New York av), n s, 283.6 e Washington av, 100.3x205 to Lefferts av. Cordelia Broach to John H. Broach. All liens. gift
Old Plank road, s e s, 100 s w Bath av, runs southeast 154.4 x southwest to point 128.3 southwest Bath av, x northwest to Old Plank road, x northeast 28.3; also,
Bay 16th st, n w s, 500 s 86th st, 50x96.8, New Utrecht.
William G. Morrisey to Minnie J. Morrisey. Sub. to morts. nom
All lands of grantor in Kings County. John I. Voorhees to Albert V. B. Voorhees. B. & S. nom

WESTCHESTER COUNTY.

JULY 1 TO 7—INCLUSIVE.

BEDFORD.

Parent, Mary A. to Benj. J. Thom, s w s road from Cherry st to Katonah, 243x105. $875

CORTLANDT.

Brown, Southard to Wm. Valentine, n s Lincoln terrace, adj Leila S. Frost, 37x125. 163
Cole, Emma to Daniel Conklin and ano., s s Oil Cloth Factory road. 47x105. 450
Conkling, Daniel and ano. to Aurillia Lounsbury, same property. 450
Mandeville, Harriet T. to Thos. S. Brennan, w s Depew st, 110 n Elm, 40x100. 800
Simpson, John exr. of. to Sarah F. Herrick and ano., lot 7 w s Washington st, 65x130. 3,275

EASTCHESTER.

Darby, Wm. J. to Chas. A. Tier, e s Rich av, 135 n Primrose, 100x100. nom
Darling, Alfred B. et al. to Viola W. Jordan, s s Prospect av, 175 e Park, 50x100. 3,400
Doremus, Morton R. et al., Jas. H. Moran, referee, to The Willson & Adams Co., lot 74 n s Urban st, Villa Park, 50x100. 3,775
The Willson & Adams Co. to Lulu F. Andrews, same property. 4,500
Eltz, Kath. to Wm. Goyke and wife, lot 388 w s Union st, West Mt. Vernon, 25x100. 1,800
Forrest, Wm. H. to Emma J. Cushman, n s Willow pl, 184 e Rich av, 52x110. nom
Gundlach, Caroline to Veronica Clark, w s 4th av, 75 s Bridge st, 25x100. 1,500
Phipps, Edw. L. E. to Wm. Van Buren, part lot 80 s e s Railroad av, West Mt. Vernon, 25x130. 2,750

GREENBURGH.

Berthel, Emily C. to Moses W. Courtwright, tract on Central av and Hartsdale road, abt 20 acres. 30,000
Bliss, Albert E. to Mary Armar, lot 6 Dixon st map Bliss Bros.' property, 33x100. 1,000
Ehrhardt, Joel B. trustee to Sarah Harney, n e cor Danforth and Maple avs, 75x100. 900
Elmsford Improvement Co. to Thos. P. Newman, lot 11 Goodwin av, 25x100. 50
Same to Sherman Evarts, lots 1-16 block 63 Elmsford Park. 960
Murray, Sarah to John H. McCullagh, lots 1 and 7 Park av, Sunnyside Park, 7½ acres. 8,000
Winne, Maria W. to Robt. H. Mathews, tract on Tarrytown road, adj And. Martine, 38 acres. 26,500

MOUNT PLEASANT.

Hunter, Mary E. et al. to Louis Smadbeck, tract adj Steph. Hammond and Aaron Hall, 40 acres. 6,175
Smith, Ann M. to Bridget Martin, w s Cortlandt st, adj John Fallon, 30x95. 700

NEW ROCHELLE.

Bartnett, Robt. to Cath. Cordial, lot 6 Lorenzen map, abt 50x175. 1,800
Downey, Henry B. to Gerhard H. Blume, n w cor Burling lane and North st, abt 42x120. 1,800
Same to Albert M. Kreitler and wife, w s May st, 141 n Burling lane, 90x88. 1,800
Fiske, Phillip M. to Henry T. Grant, lots 167, 168 and part 166, map Residence Park. nom
Gregg, Jas. A. S. to John Loughlin, s s Mayflower av, 50 e Gloucester pl, abt 50x150. 450
Iselin, Adrian, Jr., to Harriet L. Sweet, s s Willow Drive, 481 w Leland av, 75x143. 960
Same to John A. Bowers, lot 19 e s Neptune av, Neptune Park, 70x135. 1,300
Same to John J. Kerwin and ano., lot 29 e s same av, 70x135 1,500
Same to Thos. R. Ebert, lots 33 and 34 e s same av, 148x135. 4,100
Lane, Albert W. to Chas. A. Tier, lot 151 s w s Laurel pl, Residence Park, 74x150. 1,550
Reid, Thos. J. assignee of, to J. Albert Mahlstedt, e s Rose st, adj Jos. Lambden, 20x—. 5,000

NORTH SALEM.

Whitlock, Aaron B. to Odle Close, lot adj grantee, 100x105. 250

OSSINING.

Robinson, Josephine A. to Rich'd P. Barnes, e s Spring st, 99 s William st, 50x122.4. 1,350
Schneider, Jacob, by John Gibney ref., to Lena Schneider, s e s Main st, 19.6x123. 6,600
Washburn, Chas. H. to Gilbert H. Davis, n e cor Edward and James sts, 40x100. 3,075

PELHAM.

Hunter, John, Jr., to Horace H. Chittenden, e s Pelham road, adj Caleb Pell, 98 acres. 47,350
King, Elizb. R. B. exr. of, to Jas. W. Brady, lots 544 and 545 e s King av, map estate grantor. 1,700
Shoebottom, Wm. to Normen A. Lawlor, lot 251 map Pelhamville, 100x100. 600

RYE.

Damon, Carrie M. et al., M. Dillon ref., to Harvey Clark, w s Spring st, 180 s Westchester av, 50x100. 275
Same to John Leonard, s s Westchester av, 100 e Centre st, 50x140. 3,625
Same to Geo. C. Wright, s s Westchester av, 46 e Centre st, 54x140. 3,750
Same to Nellie Mertz, e s Centre st, 451 s Westchester av, 100x198. 1,450
Same to John Ryan, e s Centre s, 501 s Westchester av, 50x197. 770
Same to same, lots 91, 92, 97 and 98 map Mt. Jefferson. 3,550
Same to John F. Mills, lots 88 and 101 same map. 1,525
Kelenen, Jane E. extrx. of, to Louis Keller, n s Central av, 83 w Clinton av, 100x163. 300

WESTCHESTER.

Arnow, Thos. S. to Chas. Thorne and ano., part lot 421 e s Jackson st, Unionport, 50x108. 600
Same to Geo. Herold and ano., part same lot, 50x108. 600
Burlando, Emanuel to And. McKee, west ½ lot 365 w s 2d av, Wakefield. 3,000
Same to Giovani Cantalupi, part lot 351 n s 9th av, same map, 50x114. 700
Same to Ira S. Angevine, west ½ lot 364 s s 3d av, same map, 50x114, 4,000
Camp, Hugh N. to John Hansel, lot 189 map McGrau estate. 270
Same to Jacob F. Liebler and ano., lot 207 and 208 same map. 600
Same to Sidney G. Law, lots 107 and 108. 650
Same to Ellen Traynor, lots 113 and 114. 600
Same to Alfred Crook, lots 36, 37 and 57-65. 2,820
Same to Philip H. Smith, lots 226-229. 1,000
Same to Edward Murray, lots 40 and 41. 600
Same to Selena McCarthy, lot 210. 305
Same to Edw. M. McCormick, lot 118. 295
Same to Daniel Krueger, lots 169 and 170. 520
Hughes, Rachel to Morris H. Powers, n w cor Av B and 6th st, Unionport, 108x205. 1,800
Lyon, Dore to Cornelius Vought, e s Glebe av, 361 n Westchester, 25x—. 575
Lamphear, Wm. H. to Annie D. Buchanan, e s 2d av, 140 n 1st st, 40x100. 3,250
Same to Maggie E. Buchanan, e s 2d av adj above, 40x100. 2,650
Mace, Levi H. et al. to Theresa M. Carroll, lots 74-81 and 127-134, Lacoma Park. 3,200
O'Brien, Margt. to John C. Starks, s s 2d st, 100 e 3d av, Olinville, 50x100. 3,000
Sanders, Joshua C. to Sarah C. Ombony, w s Newell av, 400 s Elizabeth st, 111x—. 1,800
Strachan, Jas. R. to John Young, lots 295 and 296 s s 1st av, Wakefield.
exch. for property and 1,500
Shirmer, Chas. D. and ano. to Florence E. Kubele, lots 21-24 n s Ash av, Lacoma Park. 100x100. 800
Troman, Annie to Wm. Grassing, n s 11th av, 505 e 2d st, Wakefield, 50x114. 2,500
Young, John to Jas. R. Strachan, east ½ lot 394 s s 6th av, Wakefield, 50x114. 5,000

WHITE PLAINS.

Nicolas, Isabella to Merwin Sniffin, w s Grove st, 50x120. 1,650
Ryan, Wm. to Wm. H. Albro, n w cor Broadway and Evergreen av, 140x1,048. 8,000
Smith, Orlando J. to The Longview Co., 17 acres s end Lexington av. nom
Same to same. The Horton farm, Mamaroneck road, 120 acres. nom

YONKERS.

Ackerman, John W. to Eva L. Fairchild, s s Quincy pl, 184 e Warburton av, 28x116. 2,550
Bell, Jas. L. to Simon Strauss, s w cor Nepperhan av and Terrace pl, abt 115x145. 6,000
Cain, Jos. H. to Wm. Allen Butler, block 14 map property Lowerre station. 12,000
Same to same. Lots 5-8 block 16½, 2-5, 7 and 8 block 8. nom
Delacroix, Amelia to Daniel G. Terry, s s Hudson st, 100 e Buena Vista av, 19.5x95. 5,000
Druid Hill Park Co. to John Feldhusen, lots 386-389 Monegan Park. 675
Same to Cath. Leighton, lots 370 and 371. 360
Doty, Wm. H. to Esther A. Hastings, e s, Riverdale av, 100 n Riverdale pl, 25x100. nom
Edie, Jas. to Richard Edie, lot No. 71 w s School st. nom
Fowler, Clarence M. to Sherwood Land Co., plot 51 Sherwood Park. 4,500
Hazen, Josephine to Charlotta Borcher, s e cor Jerome av and Park pl. 7,500
Jones, Cyrus P. and ano. to Frauois X. Routier and wife, lots 2 and 3 block C. 500
Lowerre, Seaman to Charlotte E. Courtney, w s Van Cortlandt Park av, 146 s McLean, 50x 116. 800

Same to Auguste J. Paris, lots 6-10 block 14 map lots Lowerre Station. 775

Lawrence, Fannie E. to Wm. A. Poulton, s ½ lot 231 map Hyatt farm. 250

Knox, C. Gorden to Elizabeth W. Wilson, w s Highland av, 497.6 n Ludlow st, 102x312. 7,000

Nathan, Marcus to Sherwood Land Co., plots 39-50, Sherwood Park. 40,000

Roys, Chas. S. to John Carey, s e cor Poplar and Willow sts, 25x100. 3,600

Shonnard, Fred. to Thos. F. Coyle, No. 153 Lake av, city map. 600

Same to Mary E. Frabel, No. 247 Vineyard av, city map. 150

Venn, Isaac H. to Edw. R. Holder, e s Woodworth av, 300 n Wells, 27x100. 2,444

Ware, Enoch R. trustee of to Reuben M. Cramer, s w cor Richmond and Linsly av, 300x125. 1,650

Washburn, Wilbur F. to Wm. W. Scrugham, lot 11 w s Greystone terrace map property grantor, 60x198. 5,000

Waring, Jeannette P. to Jeremiah P. Lyons, e s Nepperhan av, 150 n Lake, 50x100. 600

MORTGAGES.

NOTE.—*The arrangement of this list is as follows. The first name is that of the mortgagor, the next that of the mortgagee. The description of the property then follows, then the date of the mortgage, the time for which it was given, and the amount. The general dates used as headings are the dates when the mortgage was handed into the Register's office to be recorded.*

Whenever the letters "P. M." occur, preceded by the name of a street, in these lists of mortgages, they mean that it is a Purchase Money Mortgage, and for fuller particulars see the list of transfers under the corresponding date. Whenever the rate is not given, read as 6 per cent.

NEW YORK CITY.

JULY 2, 3, 4, 6, 7, 8, 9.

Abrahams, Simon and Lena his wife to Henry and Julia Bader. 76th st. P. M. July 1, 3 years, 5 %. $1,500

Andrews, John H. to THE EMIGRANT INDUST. SAVINGS BANK. 120th st, No. 448, s s, 85 w Av A, 20x100.5. July 6, 1 year, 4½ %. 4,000

Arnheim, Louis mortgagor with Michael Pfrommer mortgagee. Extension of mort. at reduced int. July 1. nom

Baldwin, Truman H. to Edmond Dwyer. 115th st. P. M. July 1, 2 years, 5½ %. 4,500

Same to same. Same property. P. M. July 1, 1 month, 5½ %. 1,000

Barbee, Clifford to Elizabeth A. Jenness, Brooklyn. 142d st, n s, 547.1 w 11th av, old line, 48.6x99.11x48.7x99.11. June 26, 1 year. 3,500

Baylis, Isaac W. mortgagor with Emma D. Van Vleck and ano. trustees Patrick Dickie dec'd mortgagees. Extension of mort. June 23. nom

Barilati, Lena wife of Marcello to Herman Wronkow. 113th st. P. M. July 7, installs., 5 %. 1,500

Beaudet, Homer J. to Joseph M. De Veau. Boulevard, s w cor, 85th st, 102.5x93.7x102.2x100.10. July 6, 3 months or sooner. 10 000

Baum, Max C. to Charles Weisberger. 74th st. ½ part. P. M. July 8, 1 year or sooner. 500

Bellman, Edwin to Thomas Nesbitt. 44th st. P. M. July 2, 1 year, 5 %. 3,000

Same to Gertrude O. Snyder. Same property. P. M. July 2, 1 year, 5 %. 5,000

Booth, Joseph A. to The Twenty-fourth Ward Real Estate Assoc. Webster av. P. M. June 15, due July 1, 1894, 5 %. 1,725

Banner, Simon to Jacob Rothschild. Columbus av and 75th st. P. M. July 6, 1 year or installs, 5 %. 120,000

Brohmer, Frederick A. to The New York and Suburban Co-operative Building and Loan Assoc. Jennings st, s s, 245.2 e Union av, 28.11x abt 100x abt 32x100. July 3, installs, 5 %. 2,500

Baker, Joseph F. to Mary F. Baker. 3d av, No. 1418, w s, 80.6 n 80th st, 19.6x70. Sub. to mort. $14,000. July 3, 1 year, 4½ %. 10,000

Babbitt, Searles to Michael Elias. 121st st. P. M. July 2, 3 years or sooner, 4½ %. 12,000

Bader, Henry to Margaretha Hoffmann. 90th st. June 29, due July 1, 1893, or sooner, 5 %. 3,500

Bambach, Henry W. and Sophia M. his wife to John Kopp. Essex st, No. 108, e s, 150.3 n Delancey st, 25x100. July 1, 5 years, 5 %. 15,000

Bendheim, George to Emily Dorland. 2d av. P. M. July 2, 5 years or installs, 5 %. 5,000

Boettcher, Emil W. to Johanna McMorris, Perth Amboy, N. J. Tinton av, e s, abt 127.9 s 166th st, 16.5x100. June 30, 3 years, 4 %. 2,500

Bohmfalk, Elizabeth to Charles W. Bohmfalk. 52d st, n s, 208 e 3d av, 16x110.10. July 2, 1 year, 5 %. 3,000

Bowman, Eugene M. to Frank B. Proffen. Honeywell av, e s, 95 s Samuel st, 25x100, 24th Ward. July 2, 3 years. 2,000

Braender, Frederick to Catharine Irvin. Park or 4th av, s e cor 95th st, 20.8x60. Sub. to mort. $19,000. June 8, 1 year. 3,000

Brady, Peter J., Brooklyn, to Margie B. Lacey extrx. Frederick Lacey. 142d st. P. M. May 20, 2 years or sooner, 5 %. 9,000

Same to same. 6th av, s e cor 142d st. P. M. May 20, 2 years or sooner, 5 %. 18,000

Brettell, Frederica wife of George to Lavinia H. Montross. 120th st, n s, 156.3 e 1st av, 18.9x100.11. July 1, 5 years, 4 % 6,000

Bollenbacher, Adam and Barbara mortgagors with Emma D. Van Vleck and ano. trustees Patrick Dickie mortgagees. Extension of mort. June 23. nom

Brenneman, Mary to Waldemar Franze. Rider av, w s, 380 n 138th st, 100x125 to Mott Haven Canal. July 1, 3 years, 5 %. 7,000

Bross, Henry C. to Lillie Sanger admrx. Lewis Sanger. Vanderbilt or Railroad av, s w cor 176th st. P. M. June 30, due July 1, 1894. 6,000

Butler, James H. to Augusta H. Leypoldt and ano. trustees for Emilie H. Christern. 120th st, s s, 100 w Amsterdam av, runs south 99.11 x west 15.9 x northwest 17.2 x southwest 8.10 x west 46 x southwest — x north 49.3 x northeast 5.10 x southeast 50 x northeast 90.7 to st, x east 10.10 to beginning. June 30, due July 1, 1896. gold, 8,000

Byrnes, Patrick to Annie E. Dyer. 187th st, n s, plot 15 partition map heirs of Thomas Bassford, 24th Ward, 50x112.6. July 1, 3 years. 1,000

Byk, Poline, Brooklyn, to Clara M. Parkhurst. Lexington av, w s, 75.11 s 56th st, 24.6x90. July 2, 1 year. 10,000

Burchard, Samuel D. to THE SEAMEN'S BANK FOR SAVINGS, New York. 48th st, n s, 151 e 5th av, 24x100.5. June 29, 1 year, 5 %. 5,000

Backer, Jacob and Annie his wife to Marks Levin. 6th st. P. M. July 1, 1 year, 5 %. 5,750

Burke, Patrick J. to THE EMIGRANT INDUST. SAVINGS BANK. 60th st, s e cor 9th av, 60x75.5. July 9, 1 year, 4½ %. 20,000

Battermann, Henry to Edward Stroud. Hillside st. P. M. July 2, due July 7, 1894, or sooner, 5 %. 1,800

Baylies, Nathalie E., Taunton, Mass., to William H. Phillips trustee Charles C. Hastings. 9th av, n e cor 28th st, 98.9x91.8. July 6, due Nov. 6, 1894, 4½ %. 40,000

Bruening, William, East Orange, N. J., to Henry Sturz. 32d st, No. 248, s s, 193.9 e 8th av, 21.10x98.9. July 9, due May 28, 1893. 2,000

Cavinato, Luigi, Guiseppe, Steffano and Natale to Julius Weill, Titusville, Pa. Willis av, s w cor 135th st, 25x81.6. Sub. to mort. $21,500. June 30, 1 year. 2,500

Clare, William J. to James R. Haney. Frederick st or St. Johns av, w s, 253 s Pelham av, 25x87.6. July 2, 1 year. 100

Cohn, Rowena H. wife of and Albert L. to Hibbert B. Masters, Brooklyn. 81st st, n s, 133.11 w Columbus av, 17x102.2. May 20, 1 year, 5,000

Considine, Martin to Bernheimer & Schmid. Columbus av, No. 715, s e cor 95th st. Saloon lease. July 6, note, demand. 4,000

Connelly, James to H. Koehler & Co., a corporation. 110th st, No. 100, s e cor Park av. Saloon lease. July 7, demand. 1,800

Christie, David to Frederic de P. Foster. West End av, n w cor 102d st, 100.11x100. May 1, 1 year. 45,000

Coulter, Arthur H. and Pauline M. his wife to Charles B. Coulter. Water st, No. 396, n s, 58.10 e Catharine slip, 16.8x60.3x16.8x61.7. July 7, due Aug. 1, 1893. 1,000

Conway, Patrick to THE EMIGRANT INDUST. SAVINGS BANK. 130th st, n s, 100 w Amsterdam av, 33x11x—x—. July 7, 1 yr, 4½ %. 1,000

Cohn, Amalie to Henry R. Beekman trustee for Margaret L. Slosson. Willett st, No. 121, w s, 103.9 n Stanton st, 18.9x75.4x18.9x75.2. July 8, 3 years, 5 %. gold, 8,000

Cohn, Rowena H. wife of Albert L. to Samuel Adams and John Flanigan individ. and of Adams & Co. 81st st, n s, 133.11 w Columbus av, 17x102.2. May 9, due Sept. 12, 1891. 5,000

Cromwell, Albert, Boonton, N. J., to William Man as trustee. Grand st, n s, 50 e Eldridge st, 50x87.6. July 2, 3 years. 7,500

Camp, Hugh N. to Arthur B. Claflin. Kingsbridge road. P. M. Oct. 29, due Jan. 30, 1893, 5 %. 3,000

Same to same. Sedgwick av. P. M. Oct. 29, due Jan. 30, 1893, 5 %. 3,300

Crescent Real Estate Assoc. to The Twenty-fourth Ward Real Estate Assoc. Decatur av. P. M. June 15, due July 1, 1894, 5 %. 2,250

Chesebro, Denison P. to William S. Whitman. 2d av, s e cor 64th st, 50.5x100. Lease. July 6, 3 years. 6,500

Curtiss, George O. to George W. Thedford. Boulevard. P. M. June 30, due July 1, 1894, or sooner, 5 %. 20,000

Cowles, Edmund B., Meridan, Conn., mortgagor with Charles Hendricks mortgagee. Extension of reduced mort. July 1. nom

Corsa, George B. to David Webster exr. Caroline Webster. Decatur av. P. M. July 6, 1 year, 5 %. 1,500

Cahill, Mary E. wife of John M. to Rose A. wife of Daniel E. Reilly. 143d st, s s, 225 e Boulevard, 16.8x99.11. July 1, due July 2, 1894, 5 %. 5,000

Carpenter, Francis O. to Blanche B. wife of Adelbert Ames. Valentine av, n w cor 184th st, 50x150. July 2, 5 years. 3,500

Combes, Mary L. wife of George E. to George A. Siller and Rose his wife, Brooklyn. Briggs av, n w s, 127.4 n e Travers st, 25x100. July 1, 3 years. 1,400

Coffey, John J. to THE TITLE GUARANTEE AND TRUST CO. 8th av and 17th st. P. M. July 2, 3 years, 5 %. 27,000

Conabeer, John S. to THE WASHINGTON LIFE INSURANCE CO. 128th st, n s, 100 w 8th av, 50x99.11. July 2, due June 1, 1896. 20,000

Cottek, Herman to Adelheid Tscheiller. Lewis st, No. 56, e s, 175 n Delancey st, 25x101; Lewis st, No. 58, e s, 200 n Delancey st, 25x100. July 1, due June 1, 1893. 6,000

Chandler, Austin C. to Clara A. M. wife of Charles Greer. Coenties slip, w s, 57 s Front st, 27x45. July 6, 3 years, 5 %. gold, 10,000

Carey, Eliza T. to Jarvis B. Smith. Madison or Bathgate av. P. M. July 6, 1 year. 200

Cooper, William S. to Catharine A. F. Casanova. 22d st, No. 167 W. P. M. June 2, 3 years, 5 %. 11,000

Cotter, Eliza wife of and Nicholas to Edward and Henry Hirsh. 139th st, s s, 550 e Willis av, 50x100. July 1, 1 year, or sooner. 4,000

Crawford, John J. to Joseph L. Buttenwieser. 4th st, No. 226, w s, 52.11 s West 10th st, 26.5x101. July 1, demand. 3,500

Cudlipp, Mary A. widow to Abby S. Tuttle, Demarest, N. J. 124th st, s s, 193 w 7th av, 16x100.11. July 2, 2 years, 5 %. 2,000

Cunningham, Thomas to John Claflin. Valentine av, 24th Ward. P. M. June 30, due July 1, 1894, 5 %. 1,012

Dougherty, William A. C. mortgagor with Rose C. Newman mortgagee. Agreement as to time of payment of mort. July 1. nom

Dunn, John and David to Theodore M. Bertine. 53d st, No. 362, s s, 100 e 9th av, 25x100.5. July 1, 6 months. 5,000

Same to same. 53d st, No. 360, s s, 125 e 9th av, 25x100.5. July 1, 6 months. 5,000

Same to same. 96th st, No. 124, s s, 250 w 9th av, 25x100.8. July 1, 6 months. 5,000

Same to same. 96th st, No. 126, s s, 275 w 9th av, 25x100.8. July 1, 6 months. 5,000

Dale, Anna T. wife of James to Sarah A. Williamson. 146th st, s s, 400 e Willis av. P. M. July 1, 3 years, 5 %. 1,200

Same to same. 146th st, s s, 425 e Willis av. P. M. July 1, demand, 5 %. 1,800

Dale, Anna T. wife of James S. to Morton D. Bogue guard. for children of Alma T. Hatch. Walton av, w s, 110 s 150th st, 17.6x101.11x17.6x100.10. July 2, 3 years. 5,500

Same to same. Walton av, w s, 227.6 s 150th st, 17.6x102.8x17.6x101.11. July 2, 3 years. 5,500

Debevoise, George E. to The Twenty-fourth Ward Real Estate Assoc. Briggs av. P. M. June 15, due July 1, 1894, 5 %. 1,050

Duffey, Samuel E. to The Twenty-fourth Ward Real Estate Assoc. Webster av. P. M. June 15, due July 1, 1894, 5 %. 1,550

Dooley, James and Mary to THE DRY DOCK SAVINGS INST. Lexington av, No. 668, w s, 55.5 s 56th st, 20.6x90. July 8, 1 year, 4½ %. 8,000

Dreyfus, Julius to THE GERMAN SAVINGS BANK, New York. Scammel st. P. M. July 1, due July 2, 1892. 19,000

Dobler, Anton to Charles A. Schieren. 44th st, s s, 320 w 9th av, —x100.4x25x100.4. July 2, due July 1, 1892, or sooner. 1,000

Doering, Mary A. wife of and John to Frances M. O'Connor. 32d st, n s, 119 e 10th av, 31x98.9. July 1, 5 years, 4½ %. 12,000

Devlin, Samuel to Andrew Devlin. 13th st, No. 156, s s, 120.6 e 7th av, 20x103.3. July 1, 10 years, 5 %. 8,000

Dewey, Henry A. to Hugh N. Camp. Lots 1, 3 and 20 map of 71 lots of Kingsland estate, Morris Heights, 24th Ward. P. M. June 15, due June 25, 1894, 5 %. 2,850

Disbrow, David Y. and Josephine to Charles Schafer. 85th st. P. M. July 1, 3 years, 5 %. 10,000

Dougherty, James E. and Mary A. his wife to THE EMIGRANT INDUST. SAVINGS BANK. Willis av, n w cor 144th st, 50x106. June 24, 1 year, 4½ %. 15,000

Dougherty, James E. to Michael J. Newman et al. trustees John H. Hughes dec'd. Madison st. P. M. July 9, 1 year, 5 %. 19,000

Dunne, Thomas P. to Joseph Crawford. 116th st, s s, 125 w Manhattan av, 25x100.11. July 2, 5 years, 5 %. 21,000

Same to same. 116th st, s s, 150 w Manhattan av, 25x100.11. July 2, 5 years, 5 %. 21,000

Same to same. 116th st, s s, 175 w Manhattan av, 25x100.11. July 2, 5 years, 5 %. 21,000

Dufort, Charles and Victor Francis to Beadleston & Woerz. 6th av, No. 474. Saloon lease. July 2, demand. 1,500

Demarest, Cornelius M., Brooklyn, and Rachel S. Hutton, Nanuet, N. Y., to THE EMIGRANT INDUST. SAVINGS BANK. Washington st. P. M. July 8, 1 year, 4½ %. 7,500

Dexter, Levi to Mary E. Tappenbeck, Brooklyn. 91st st, n s, 80 e Columbus av, 27x100.8. July 9, due July 1, 1896, 4½ %. 18,000

Downing, William A., Brooklyn, to Marietta L. and Sheridan S. Norton. 71st st, n s, 570 w 9th av, 20x102.2. July 6, due Jan. 2, 1894, 5 %. 9,000

Donovan, Lizzie to George J. McFadden. Broome st. P. M. June 15, due July 9, 1894, or sooner, 4½ %. 6,500

Dean, Elizabeth widow to THE MUTUAL LIFE INS. CO. of New York. Hudson st, Nos. 643-649, s w cor Gansevoort st, 88.9x62x87.10x71.2. March 11, demand, 5 %. 35,000

Elterich, Elizabeth wife of and John to Herrmann Wischebrink and Theotor Sauer. 146th st, s s, 250 e Willis av, 25x100, 23d Ward. July 3, due May 1, 1894, 5 %. 1,000

Elliott, Elizabeth C. to The Twenty-fourth Ward Real Estate Assoc. Webster av. P. M. June 15, due July 1, 1894, 5 %. 1,575

Ehrlich, Edward to The Twenty-fourth Ward Real Estate Assoc. Suburban st. P. M. June 15, due July 1, 1894, 5 %. 1,425

Eberth, Carl R. to The Twenty-fourth Ward Real Estate Assoc. Webster av. P. M. June 15, due July 1, 1894, 5 %. 1,675

Egan, John J. and Daniel Halleey to Alexander Walker and Judson Lawson. 103d st. P. M. July 1, 7 months. 25,000

Same to same. Same property. July 1, 7 months. 9,000

Eggers, George W. to George P. Upham, Nahant, Mass. 100th st, n s, 100 w Central Park West, 99.6x100.11. July 7, 3 years, 5 %. 50,000

Eggers, George W. and Margaretha his wife to Joseph Fox. 100th st, n s, 100 w Central Park West, 175x100.11. Sub. to morts. $86,000. July 7, due Oct. 9, 1891, or sooner. 15,000

Ehrle, Caroline wife of and Edward to Henrietta Wimpfheimer. 57th st. P. M. July 2, 5 years or installs, 5 %. 9,000

Fairman, Charles F. mortgagor with Charles Meyerhoff. Assignment of rents to secure mortgage. July 2 nom

Farrell, Michael J. to George C. Reisenweber. Av A, n e cor 20th st, 23x70. July 1, 3 years, 5 %. 6,000

Fay, Patrick H. to THE TITLE GUARANTEE AND TRUST CO. Broadway, e s, 241 s n Spring st, 35x100. July 3, 1 year, 4½ %. 65,000

Feld, Anna M. wife of George A. to Louis Pfingstag. 129th st, s s, 160 w 3d av, 25x99.11. July 1, 4 years, 5 %. 5,000

Finke, Frederick to George Schramm. 1st av, No. 1513. Store lease and chattel mortgage. March 6, 1891, notes. 4 500

Fitschen, August H. to Henry Morgenthau. 11th av. P. M. June 10, due June 15, 1892, 5 %. 1,000

Fitzgerald, Thomas to Bridget and Patrick Ducey. Av A, e s, 25 s 56th st, 25.5x100; 56th st, s s, 100 e Av A, 25x100.5. May 25, note 2,000

Fitzgerald, Martha J., Tarrytown, N. Y., to Leonora A. Arnold, Brooklyn. Amsterdam av and 181st st. P. M. Jan. 10, demand, 5 %. 5,000

Fairchild, Clara to E Augusta Tweed. 3d av, w s, 136.7 n 183th st, runs northwest 200.10 x west 97.11 to e s Vanderbilt av, x south 99.1 x east 99.4 x southeast 77.5 x east 76.11. July 1, 1 year, 5 %. 5,000

Friedrich, Maria wife of Conrad to Anna M. Michels. 3d av, w s, lot 33 map of Morrisania, 25x100. July 3, due July 1, 1896, 5 %. 5,000

Frick, Jacob mortgagor with Friedrich Seibel. Extension of mort July 3. nom

Frick, Jacob to George F. Frick. Water st, No. 684, n w cor Jackson st, 25x100. July 1, 1 year or sooner, 4½ %. 1,200

Fulton, James to William R. Beal Land Improvement Co. St. Anns av and 141st st. P. M. July 8, 3 years or sooner, 5 %. 3,812

Frame, James A. to Edward Oppenheimer and Isaac Metzger. 87th st, s s, 250 w Central Park West, 100x100.8. May 9, due May 1, 1892, or sooner. 50,000

Geary, Margaret to David Beckman. 184th st, n s, 100 e Vanderbilt av East, 25x100. July 1, 2 years. 800

Goetz, Christian to John L. Fabie, Bay Ridge, L. I. 2d av, No. 494, e s, 49.5 s 28th st, 24.8x75. July 2, due July 1, 1894, 5 %. 6,000

Goldman, Esther wife of and Harris B. to Oscar T. Marshall. 114th st. P. M. July 1, 5 years, 5 %. 10,000

Gompper, Louis to William Dann. Charles st. P. M. July 2, due 60 days after demand, 5 %. 6,000

Graham, William J. and Mary E. to Elizabeth M. Bolger. 86th st, No. 151, n s, 62.2 e Lexington av, 25.7x100.8. July 1, 2 years 1,000

Graves, Elizabeth wife of James and Margaret McCluskey to Frederick A. Constable. Boston av, ss, 217.11 e Jefferson st, 25x100. June 18, 1 year, 5 %. 1,266

Gilmore, William J. to Ethelbert Wilson. 134th st, n s, 200 e 7th av, 50x99.11. P. M. June 8, 1 year or sooner. 6,500

Gill, Charles R., West Park, N. Y., to Donald Mackay exr. and trustee Elizabeth R. B. King. Liberty st, No. 122, and Cedar st, No. 125. June 4, due July 6, 1894, 5 %. 3,000

Gillies, Anna E. wife of and James W. mortgagors with Emily A. Thorn. Extension of mort. Feb. 21. nom

Gunst, Jacob mortgagor with Julius Goebel mortgagee. Extension of mort. July 8. nom

Geery, Anna S. wife of and Isaac J., Stamford, Conn., to THE CITIZENS' SAVINGS BANK. Canal st, No. 203, n w cor Mulberry st, 26.7x72.5x25.3x80.10 July 2, 1 year, 5 %. 40,000

Glass, John to Charles A. Peabody, Jr. 11th st. P. M. July 8, due Jan. —, 1892. gold, 19,000

Garlan, George to William R. Beal Land Impt. Co. 141st st. P. M. July 8, 3 years, 5 %. 3,990

Glass, Josie N. to The Twenty-fourth Ward Real Estate Assoc. Webster av. P. M. June 15, due July 1, 1894, 5 %. 762

Grunley, Felix to The Twenty-fourth Ward Real Estate Assoc. Webster av. June 15, due July 1, 1894, 5 %. 1,975

Goodman, Mary to Katharine Hoffmann. Houston st, n s, 253.5 w Av B. P. M. July 1, 10 years or installs, 5 %. 14,500

Same to Louis Hoffmann Houston st, n s, 273.5 w Av B. Lease. P. M. July 1, 10 years or installs, 5 %. 14,500

Heidenfeld, Theodore E. to Alfred C. Corning guard. of Robert S. Clark 1st av, No. 1502, e s, 102.2 s 79th st, 25x94. June 30, 3 years, 4½ %. 9,000

Haider, Charles to David Webster, exr. Caroline Webster. Hull av. P. M. July 6, 1 year, 5 %. 325

Hasenbalg, Charles to William R. Beal Land Impt. Co. Oak terrace. P. M. July 8, 3 years, 5 %. 1,400

Hicks, Thomas P. to Louis Eickwort. Webster av. P. M. July 6, 3 years, 5 %. 423

Hirsch, Leon M. to Evelina Hartz. 104th st, s s, 155 w 4th av, 25x100.11. July 7, due July 1, 1893, 5 %. 3,000

Hermanny, Caroline wife of Anton to Margaret O'Leary widow. Robbins av, e s, 180 s Westchester R. R. st, 25x230. July 7, due July 1, 1894, 5 %. 2,500

Hirsh, Samuel to Lily W. Churchill et al. trustees Louis C. Hamersley. West 4th st. P. M. May 20, 5 years, 4½ %. 100,000

Hassinger, Peter to THE GERMAN-AMERICAN REAL ESTATE TITLE GUARANTEE CO. 65th st, n s, 100 e 2d av, 25x100.5. July 7, 1 year, 4½ %. 12,500

Hoffstadt, Mary wife of and J. Henry to George F. Bristow. Rockfield st, n s, 500 e Marion av, 25x126.11. July 1, 3 years. 2,500

Herrick, Bauman L., Stamford, Conn., to THE MANHATTAN LIFE INS. CO. 26th st, No. 9, and 27th st, No. 4, begins 26th st, n s, 130.6 e 5th av, 27x197.6 to 27th st. July 6, 1 year, 5 %. 70,000

Haggerty, Mary to John Cotter. Hamilton st. P. M. June 30, due July 2, 1896, or installs, 5 %. 3,000

Hahn, John H. and Elizabeth his wife to Silas D. Gifford and ano. exrs. and trustees Charles Bathgate. Stebbins av, s e s, 33 s w Home st, 50x148. July 1, 4 years, 5 %. 6,000

Haldy, Frederick and Marie to THE WEST SIDE SAVINGS BANK. Bedford st. P. M. July 1, due Nov. 1, 1892, 4½ %. 5,250

Herter, Peter and Frank W. to John J. Jones and ano. trustees David Jones dec'd. Rivington st, n e cor Cannon st, 50x89. July 9, 5 years, 5 %. 70,000

Hacker, Charles and Elizabeth M. his wife to William R. Beal Land Improvement Co. Oak terrace. P. M. July 8, 3 years or sooner, 5 %. 1,382

Higgins, James and James King to Frederic J. Middlebrook. 90th st, s s, 275 e 2d av, 24.6x100.8. July 8, due July 9, 1894, 5 %. 12,500

Horan, Thomas to The J. Chr. G. Hupfel Brewing Co. Indefinite lease made by John H. Meyer to William Berner and John Hamard. July 3, demand. 1,500

Halfman, Hermine wife of Louis to John Bohlken. 153d st, s s, 70 w Elton av, 75x100. July 2, 5 years, 5 %. 6,000

Hartung, George C. to Bernheimer & Schmid. 1st av, No. 67, n w cor 4th st. Saloon lease. July 3, note, demand. 3,500

Haltenbach, Rachel to Maria Hotthausen. 109th st. P. M. July 1, 1 year, 5 %. 700

Hendrick, William J. and Robert B. Cotter mortgagors with Harry A. Grant mortgagee. Extension of mort. June 13. nom

Hennessey, John to Emily V. Satterlee wife of Clarence, New Hamburgh, N. Y. West End av. P. M. July 2, 2 years, 5 %. 15,000

Hensle, George L. mortgagor with George Grossmann mortgagee. Extension of mort. July 2. nom

Hillenbrand, Edward to THE CITIZEN'S SAVINGS BANK. Suffolk st, e s, 100 s Rivington st. 25x100. July 2, 1 year, 5 %. gold, 16,000

Hillebrand, Isidor and Gertrude his wife to Elizabeth Bernhard. 148th st, n s, 200 e Courtlandt av, 25x106.6. July 2, 5 years, 5 %. 1,000

Hoffman, Cornelius Q. to Eugene D. Miller. 140th st, s s, 575 e 6th av, runs south 184 x northeast 29.11 x southeast 51.5 x north — to 140th st, x west 75. June 10, 1 year. 1,500

Howe, Adelbert J. to Ephraim B. Levy. Katonah av and Holly pl. P. M. June 16, due July 2, 1894, 5 %. 750

Hughes, Thomas R., Weehawken, N. J., to Sarah R. Van Duzer, Newburgh, N. Y. Madison av. P. M. July 3, due July 1, 1894, 5 %. 24,000

Hughes, Thomas R., Weehawken, N. J., to Frederick G. Potter. Madison av, No. 1035, e s, 22.2 n 79th st, 20x77. June 30, due Oct. 1, 1892. 5,500

Isaac, Emanuel to Isaac and Pauline Goodman. Clinton st, No. 99, w s, 250.8 s Rivington st, 25.4x100. July 1, 3 years, 5 %. 5,000

Jacobs, Solomon mortgagor with William M. Kingsland, Mt. Pleasant, N. Y., mortgagee. Agreement as to priority of mortgages made by Solomon Jacobs. July 1. nom

Jordan, Henry W., Hoboken, N. J., to The Bradley & Currier Co. (Lim.) 5th av. P. M. June 30, due July 1, 1893, or installs. 5,000

Jones, Leonora C. to George A. Briggs. Arthur av, e s, 168.6 s Pelham av, 25x87.6. July 2, 2 years. 1,500

Jordan, Henry W. to Augustus E. Butts. 142d st, n s, 250 w 8th av, 64.11 to Bradhurst av, —x100.6x54x99.11. June 6, due July 6, 1893. 1,000

Kirkup, Charles O. to Babette Geib. Myrtle av or Vanderbilt av West, w s, part lot 72 map of Upper Morrisania, runs west 312 to Webster av, x south 40 x east 159 x north 0.8 x east 150 to Myrtle av, x north 41.4 to beginning. July 3, 3 years, 5 %. 4,000

Kahn, Emanuel S. to Terence McManus. 47th st. P. M. July 1, 1 year, 5 %. 1,000

Kolter, John to William R. Beal Land Improvement Co. Beekman av; also 141st st. P. M. July 8, 3 years, 5 %. 3,150

Keane, John A. to William R. Beal Land Improvement Co. Beekman av. P. M. July 8, 3 years, 5 %. 2,800

Knox, Mary L. to The Twenty-fourth Ward Real Estate Assoc. Bainbridge av and Garfield st. P. M. June 15, due July 1, 1894, 5 %. 2,055

Keyser, Jacob F. to The Twenty-fourth Ward Real Estate Assoc. Southern Boulevard. P. M. June 15, due July 1, 1894, 5 %. 700

Kiely, Mary A. and Thomas J. Clarke to The Twenty-fourth Ward Real Estate Assoc. Perry av and Mosholu Parkway. P. M. June 15, due July 1, 1894, 5 %. 700

Klett, Caroline M. wife of John C. to Katharina Menninger widow. Emerson st, e s, 25 n Vermilyea av, 75x100. July 3, due July 1, 1896, or sooner, 5 %. 1,900

Kremm, Paul to Peter Doelger. Essex st, No. 149. Store lease. July 7, demand. 1,000

Knight, William and Eliza, Brooklyn, to Phebe A. Holman, Clayville, N. Y. 1st av, n e cor Highbridge st, 100x191 to Doughty's Brook, x 102.11x171.10. July 3, 5 years. 1,000

Kubes, John to Denison P. Chesebro. Stebbins av, e s, 584.11 n Freeman st, 51.5x102.7x51.6x100.1. July 3, 3 years, 5 %. 1,800

Kleinknecht, Catharine to Mrs. A. Fiegel widow. 146th st. n s, 225 w St. Anns av, 25x100. July 1, 5 years, 5 %. 3,500

Kahn, Leopold to Flamen B. Candler and ano. trustees Joshua Brookes dec'd. 134th st, n s, 150 e 7th av, 25x99.11. June 30, 3 years, 5 %. 18,000

Kahrs, Herman and Peter Stribbel to Ida wife of Philip E. Haag. 109th st, s s, 95 e 1st av. P. M. June 25, due July 2, 1894, or sooner, 5 %. 4,000

Kaplan, Aaron to Bernhard Silberstein. 102d st, n s, 230 e 3d av, 25x100.9. July 2, installs. 3,500

Katz, Jacob and Lippman to Babette Siedenbach. Ludlow st. P. M. July 1, 3 years, 5 %. 15,000

Same to William H. A. Rubino. Same property. P. M. Sub. to last mort. July 1, 2 years, 5 %. 2,000

Kaysser, Louis to George Barth. Webster av, n e cor Anna pl, 25x90. July 2, 3 years, 5 %. 4,500

Same to Louis Vath. Same property. Sub. to last mort. July 2, 3 years, 5 %. 1,500

Ketchum, Edgar to The Good Samaritan Dispensary. 125th st, s s, 125 e 7th av, 25x100.11. July 2, 3 years, 5 %. 37,500

Same to same. 125th st, s s, 150 e 7th av, 25x100.11. July 2, 3 years, 5 %. 37,500

Same to William A. Martin. Same property. Sub. to last mort. July 2, 1 year. 2,500

Same to same. 125th st, s s, 125 e 7th av, 25x100.11. Sub. to mort. $37,500. July 2, 1 year. 2,500

Kilpatrick, Thomas to Mary M. Stewart widow. 92d st, s s, 125 e 9th av, 99.8x100.8. July 3, 1 year. 7,500

King, Mary to Joseph E. King. 162d st. P. M. June 18, 5 years, 5 %. 2,500

Kitching, George, Orange, N. J., to Elward Smith. 61st st, No. 138, s s, 222.8 e Amsterdam av, 22.2x100.5. July 2, due July 1, 1896, 5 %. 10,000

Klinger, John and Margarethe his wife to Andreas Kolb. 15th st, s s, 88 e Av B, 25x103.3. July 1, 3 years, 4½ %. 2,000

Knirim, Joseph to Eva Bechtel extrx. George Bechtel. North William st, No. 20, Store lease. July 1, demand. 1,200

Kopta, Antony and Tony his wife to George P. Herrmann. 3d st, s s, abt 263.9 e Av B, 24.9x105.11. Lease. July 1, 5 years or installs, 5,500

Kosinsky, Haris to Isaac Cohn and Leo Katz. Goerck st. P. M. June 30, due July 15, 1896. 1,750

Kuhn, Louise to Sigmund Cohn. 16th st, No. 618, s s, 280 e Av B, 25x103.3. July 3, due July 1, 1894. 1,000

Keyes, Edward L. to Maria W. Livingston, Islip, L. I. 34th st. P. M. July 6, due Jan. 8, 1893, 4½ %. 20,500

Kelley, James to The Daily News Building, Savings and Loan Assoc. Union av. P. M. July 8, installs, 5 %. 3,000

Katz, Lippman to Fanny Jacobs. East Broadway, No. 114, 20x75. July 1, 6 months, 5 %. 3,000

Levy, Julius, Louis Friedheim and Lippman Altmayer to The 24th Ward Real Estate Assoc. Webster av. P. M. June 15, due July 1, 1894, 5 %. 1,800

Laughlin, Robert to George Ebret. 6th av, No. 465, s w cor 28th st. Lease. July 2, demand. 4,000

Landsberger, Dora wife of Solomon to Stephen O. Lockwood, Brooklyn. Suffolk st. P. M. July 6, 5 years, 5 %. 20,000

Lyon, Anna M. to Henry Morgenthau. 178th st. P. M. June 15, 3 years, 5 %. 1,760

Levy, Maurice to Yetta Rosenberg. Mott st, No. 18, e s, 204.8 n Park row, 23.3x100.2x23.4x103.4. Sub. to mort. $20,000. July 6, 3 years. 4,000

Lorch, H. Charles and Sophie L. his wife to Emily wife of William Momberger. Fulton av, e s, part lot 99 map of Morrisania, 30x211. July 3, 3 years, 5 %. P 1,000

Lyons, Julius J. to Joseph H. Godwin. Vermilyea av. P. M. June 29, due July 1, 1896, or installs, 5 %. 4,050

Lilianthal, Louis mortgagor with John B. Schmaus and Stephanie his wife mortgagees. Extension of mort. June 25. nom

Lammers, Mary wife of John H. to Josephine L. Horton, Brooklyn. Fulton av, e s, 412 n 169th st, 25x211. July 1, 5 years or installs, 5 %. 4,000

Leamy, Joseph F. to Francis Bourne. Simpson st, w s, 146.8 n 169th st, 25x74.11. July 2, 5 years. 1,500

Lehr, Charles F. to Gustav A. Fischer. Clinton st, e s, 100 n Rivington st, 25x100. July 1, due May 1, 1896, 5 %. 11,000

Same to Philip Bolender. Same property. July 1, 5 years or sooner. 4,500

Larchan, Jacob and Rebecca his wife to Philip Bolender. Willett st, No. 64, e s, 150 s Rivington st, —x100x25x100. July 1, 3 years, 5 %. 14,000

Lenox, David H., Plainfield, N. J., to Ephraim B. Levy. Holly pl. P. M. July 2, 3 years or sooner, 5 %. 400

Lent, Elmira S. wife of Whitman S. and Charlotte C. wife of William H. Rogers and Henry Sleight and Mary L. Sleight widow heirs of Barnet Sleight to Cornelia L. Marshall. Waverley pl, No. 202, w s, 20 s Charles st, 18.10x75. July 1, 5 years, 5 %. gold, 7,000

Levy, Louis to Marks Levin. Ridge st. P. M. July 1, due May 1, 1896, or installs. 5,000

Levy, Dora to Benjamin Kaiser. Broome st, Nos. 220, 220½ and 222, n s, 44.2 e Essex st, runs north 75 x east 21.3 x north 27.9 x east 35.1 x south 102.6 to st, x west 56.5. July 1, due Oct. 30, 1891. 3,500

Levy, Malvina A. to George Wurst. 81st st, s s, 104.1 w 2d av, 23x102.2. June 30, 5 years, 5 %. 17,000

Same to same. Same property. Sub. to last mort. June 30, 6 years or installs., 5 %. 5,000

Lese, Louis, Pincus Lowenfeld, Morris Goldstein and Sarah F. Deutsch to Charles H. Reed and William H. Schmohl. 87th st, s s, 320.2 e 2d av. P. M. July 1, 3 years, 5½ %. 4,000

Same to same. 87th st, s s, 376.7 e 2d av. P. M. July 1, 3 years, 5½ %. 4,000

Same to same. 87th st, s s, 348.7 e 2d av. P. M. July 1, 3 years, 5½ %. 4,000

Lipman, Henry to Adele Kneeland exr. Charles Kneeland. Madison av, n w cor 116th st, 100.11x110. July 1, 1 year. 15,000

Same to Henry A. Bogert trustee for Frances S. Draper. Same property. Equal lien with last mort. July 1, 1 year. 12,000

Same to Mary A. wife of Henry A. Bogert, Flushing, L. I. Same property. Equal lien with last 2 morts. July 1, 1 year. 15,000

Littman, Selig to THE FRANKLIN SAVINGS BANK. 41st st, n s, 400 w 8th av, 25x98.9. June 30, 1 year, 5 %. 12,000

Littlefield, Agnes H. wife of and Frederick M. with Mary Barteld widow all mortgagees. Agreement as to priority of morts. made by Elizabeth K. Smith. July 2. nom

Same with John J. Freedman all mortgagees. Agreement as to priority of morts. made by Elizabeth K. Smith. July 2. nom

Same with Hanna V. Deshler all mortgagees. Agreement as to priority of morts. made by Elizabeth K. Smith. July 2, nom

Same with Margaret Ingliss all mortgagees. Agreement as to priority of morts. made by Elizabeth K. Smith. July 2. nom

Levett, Alexander to Catharine A. Taylor et al. trustees for Albertina S. Pyne, Kate W. Winthrop, Mary Lewis and George C. and Henry A. C. Taylor. Grand st, n s, 122.8 e Varick st, 66x83x66x72. July 8, due June 30, 1893, or sooner, 5 %. 30,000

McCormick, Michael and Henry Madden to Alois Gutwillig. King st. P. M. July 8, due March 1, 1892. 42,000

Same to same. Same property. P. M. Building loan. July 8, due March 1, 1892. 27,000

Mullen, Alice M. to The Twenty-fourth Ward Real Estate Assoc. Southern Boulevard. P. M. June 15, due July 1, 1894, 5 %. 700

Same to same. Briggs av. P. M. June 15, due July 1, 1894, 5 %. 537

Same to same. Webster av. P. M. June 15, due July 1, 1894, 5 %. 1,050

Mahoney, Edward, Norfolk, Va., to John Pettit, East Orange, N. J. Maiden lane. P. M. June 26, due Nov. 1, 1893. 50,000

Muller, Conrad, Jr., and Anna wife of Hermann Hauff to Victor P. P. and Bertha M. Erslev. 115th st, s s, 275 e 8th av, 175x100.11. Sub. to morts. May 29, demand. 9,175

Same to Bertha M. wife of Victor P. P. Erslev, Broooklyn.. Same property. Sub. to morts. March 14. 3,500

Same to Oline Erslew and Elof Nielsen. 115th st, s s, 275 e 8th av, 25x100.11. Sub. to morts. Feb. 12, due Aug. 1, 1891. 750

Myers, Charles F. to THE EMIGRANT INDUST. SAVINGS BANK. 33d st, No. 411, n s, 162.6 w 9th av, 12.6x98.9. July 8, 1 year, 4½ %. 4,000

Myers, Charles F. and Alice E. his wife to Joseph I. West. Same property. July 8, 1 year, 5 %. 1,750

Murray, Annie T. to Mary L. Asten, Brooklyn. 34th st, No. 450, s s, 258.4 e 10th av, 20.10x98.9. July 1, 3 years, 5 %. 5,500

Mayer, Moses and Daniel Nathan to Marianna Knecht, Brooklyn. 53d st, s s, 275 w 1st av, 25x100.5. July 1, 5 years, 5 %. 13,500

Mancier, Edmond O. to Frederick P. Olcott and ano. trustees for Arthur and Howard Corlies. 31st st. P. M. June 12, due July 1, 1894, 5 %. gold, 15,000

Manheim, Jacob to Marks Jacobs and Israel M. Cohen. Broome st, No. 86, n s, 25 w Columbia st, 25x85.10. July 7, due Oct. 7, 1892, note. 3,000

Morgan, William H. to THE TITLE GUARANTEE AND TRUST CO. 81st st, No. 227, n s, 305 e 3d av, 25.5x102.2. July 7, 3 years, 5 %. 2,000

Moores, Robert L. and Charles A. Le Quesne to George F. Alexander. 106th st, s s, 300 e 3d av, 25x100.10. July 1, 2 years. 5,000

Mangiere, Nicholas to Henry de F. Weekes. Mulberry st. P. M. July 6, due July 1, 1892. 5,000

Mooney, Bernard and John Connor, of Mooney & Connor, to Henriette Blinn extrx. Christian Blinn. 99th st. P. M. June 26, due June 1, 1892, 5 %. 9,800

Maas, Henry and Elizabeth R. to Mary L. Collins. 83d st. P. M. July 3, 5 years, 5 %. 16,000

Maguire, John to THE EMIGRANT INDUST. SAVINGS BANK. Hubert st, n s, 100 e Greenwich st, 25.7x100.6x25.3x100.6. July 1, 1 year, 4½ %. 2,000

Martin, Erwin P. H. to Dorothea Hartwig. 6th st, s s, 225 e Av A, 25x97. June 15, 3 years. 4,000

Mathis, William to Philipp Bobner, Brooklyn. Hester st, n s, 24.4 n Eldridge st, 18.3x50. July 1, 5 years, 5 %. 10,000

Same to same. Eldridge st, w s, 50 n Canal st, 25x100. July 1, 2 years, 5 %. 2,000

Same to Jeanette Bleistift. Same property. July 1, 2 years. 2,000

Mead, John L. to Anna P. Brown. Bergen av, s e cor Grove st, 85x82.6 to centre Mill Brook, x100.6x44. July 2, 1 year, 5 %. 1,000

Meder, Daniel and Annie his wife to Albert Steindler. 76th st. P. M. July 1, installs, 5½ %. 2,200

Mehrtens, Henry W. to THE GERMAN SAVINGS BANK, New York. 11th av, w s, 100.5 n 44th st, 25.1x100. June 30, 1 year. 6,500

McCann, John to William R. Beal Land Improvement Co. Crimmins av. P. M. July 8, 3 years or sooner, 5 %. 650

Mayer, Siegfried W. to Hoffman Miller admr. Robert C. Townsend. 42d st, No. 436, s s, 325 e 10th av, 25x98.9. July 9, due Aug. 1, 1896, 5 %. 15,000

McKenney, Elijah, Liberty Falls, N. Y., to THE NEW YORK SAVINGS BANK. 19th st, n s, 125 w 9th av, 21.5x80. July 8, due June 1, 1894, 5 %. 7,500

Mercadante, Ignazio to John H. Rhoades et al. trustees Benjamin F. Wheelwright. Bowery, No. 340. P. M. June 24, due July 1, 1896, or installs, 5 %. 25,000

Same to Max Hartman. Same property. P. M. Sub. to last mort. June 24, due July 1, 1892. 5,000

Merritt, Robert B. to Jacob Bickes. 3d st, s s, 313.4 e Av B, 24.9x105.11. Lease. July 2, due July 1, 1890. 4,500

McGarity, Robert and Mary A. to Henry Morgenthau. Kingsbridge road. P. M. June 11, due June 15, 1894, 5 %. 7,245

McGinn, John to THE TITLE GUARANTEE AND TRUST CO. Charlton st. P. M. July 3, 1 year, 4½ %. 6,000

Michel, Henry to Samuel Davis. Delancey st. P. M. June 30, due July 1, 1893. 1,000

Michel, Christiane mortgagee to George Oestreich present owner. Statement that amount due on mort. made by George Oestreich dated May 14, 1889, is 8,000

Minsky, Louis to William M. Kingsland, Mt. Pleasant, N. Y. Madison st, n s, 216 e Scammel st, 23.10x96. July 1, 5 years, 5 %. gold, 13,000

Moller, Christian to THE GREENWICH SAVINGS BANK. 56th st, s s, 100 e 8th av, 20x100.5. July 2, due July 1, 1892, 5 %. 3,000

Moloney, Thomas to The Greenwood Cemetery, Brooklyn. Amsterdam av, e s, 74.10 s 131st st, 25.1x125x25.1x125. July 2, due Aug. 1, 1896, 5 %. 17,500

Same to same. Amsterdam av, e s, 50 s 131st st, 24.10x125x25x125. July 2, due Aug. 1, 1896, 5 %. 16,500

Same to Paulina A. Morgan. Amsterdam av, e s, 25 s 131st st, 25x125. July 2, due Aug. 6, 1896, 5 %. 16,500

Morris, Louis H. to Isaac Brown 2d av. P. M. July 1, 5 years, 5 %. 10,000

Mott, Isabella T. wife of and John C. to Agnes W. Seaton. 8th av, n w cor 87th st, 25x100. June 26, due June 30, 1894. 5,000

Monsky, Morris W. and Louis Solinsky to Ernestine Kiwi. Suffolk st. P. M. Sub. to mort. $15,000. July 1, installs. 8,000

Nesbitt, Francesca C. widow to THE EAST RIVER SAVINGS INST. Washington av, e s, 150 s 174th st, 50x120; Bathgate av, w s, 100 s 174th st, 50x120. July 2, 1 year, 5 %. 7,500

Noser, Melchior to Henry Spies. 80th st. P. M. July 8, 5 years or sooner, 5 %. 8,000

Nagle, John T. to THE EMIGRANT INDUST. SAVINGS BANK. 44th st. P. M. July 1, 1 year, 4½ %. 5,000

Newman, Lewis and Rachel his wife to Lucas Glockner. 7th st, 241.11 e Av C, 18.5x90.10. July 1, 3 years, 5 %. 6,000

Nixon, Ann to Edward H. Moeran. 3d av, w s, 29 n 178th st, 25x100. July 1, 5 years. 1,000

O'Gorman, Edward J. to David Webster exr. Caroline Webster. Decatur av, w s, 175 s Ozark st, 50x100. July 6, 1 year, 5 %. 750

Same to same. Hull av, e s, 401.6 s Gun Hill road, 25x100. July 6, 1 year, 5 %. 420

O'Neil, Margaret widow to THE WEST SIDE SAVINGS BANK. Christopher st, Nos. 154 and 154½, s w cor Washington st, runs south 94.5 x west 29.1 x north 10.10 x east abt 20 x north 72.3 to Christopher st, x east 40.5 to beginning. July 1, due Nov. 1, 1892, 4½ %. 10,000

Oetjen, Herman to William R. Beal Land Improvement Assoc. St. Anns av., P. M. July 8, 3 years, 5 %. 5,722

Pearson, Mary to THE INSTITUTION FOR THE SAVINGS OF MERCHANTS' CLERKS. 86th st. P. M. July 1, 5 years, 4½ %. 12,500

Pendergast, William C. to Peter Doelger. Av A, No. 1546. Lease. June 30, demand. 1,000

Perrier, Marguerite to Frederic R. Coudert et al. admrs. Dumas N. Bunel. 45th st, No. 9, n s, 170 w 5th av, 15x100.5. June 29, due July 1, 1894, 5 %. gold, 18,000

Price, Charles R., Woodsburgh, L. I., to Susan A. Luce, Brooklyn. 55th st, Nos. 337 and 339, n s, 214.11 w 1st av, 35.8x100.5. June 25, due June 30, 1892, 5 %. 4,000

Preson, Jette to Francis H. Ross. 102d st, s s, 75 e 2d av, runs south 100.11 x west 25 x north 35.11 x east 0.4 x north 65 to st, x east 24.8. June 30, 1 year. 2,000

Pohaski, David to Abraham Rothstein. Madison av, w s, 67.11 n 113th st, 16.6x70. July 2, 1 year. 4,000

Phillips, Hartwig I. to Julia Huerstel, Matilda Grossman, Annie Brugman formerly Wilkens and Walter Wilkens. Prospect and Westchester avs. P. M. July 6, 3 years or sooner, 5 %. 2,700

Prager, Louis W. and Oscar Dobroczynski to Michael Fay and William Stacom. Sheriff st. P. M. July 3, installs. 6,750

Primrose, Emma J. wife of and George H., Mt. Vernon, N. Y., to Oliver G. Barton. 131st st, No. 246, s s, 325 e 8th av, 16.8x99.11. July 8, due July 9, 1892, 5 %. 5,000

Peetsch, Henry C. L. to William J. Gardiner, Newark, N. J. 114th st, n s, 95 e 1st av, 50x100.10. July 7, 2 years, 4½ %. 5,000

Revans, Samuel G. to THE METROPOLITAN LIFE INS. CO. of New York. 24th st, Nos. 112 and 114, n s, 80 w Lexington av, 45x98.9. July 9, due Oct. 1, 1896, 5½ %. 105,000

Same to Joseph F. Stier. Same property. Sub. to mort. July 9, demand. 10,000

Ritter, Margaretha wife of and Jacob to Ambrose Schiller. 97th st, n s, 125 e 11th av, 25x100.11. June 30, due July 1, 1892, 5 %. 2,200

Rosenthal, Annie to Herman Joseph. 10th st, No. 261, n s, 344 w Av A, 25x94.8. Sub. to morts. $23,000. July 1, 2 years, 5 %. 6,875

Rinaldo, Isaac to Eliza Wiener trustee Heinrich Wiener dec'd. 74th st, No. 148, s s, 37.6 e Lexington av, 18.9x68.2. July 7, 5 years, 4 %. 8,000

Radley, William P. to Ellen M. Harlow. 27th st, No. 429, n s, 349.6 w 9th av, 18.6x88.9, with all title to alley 10 ft. wide in rear. July 1, 1 year or installs. 800

Rauch, Adolph E. to Gottlieb Jetter. 84th st. P. M. July 9, due July 1, 1894, or installs, 5 %. 4,500

Reckhardt, Conrad W. to John Wolf and Anna M. his wife. 10th av, n w cor 31st st, 24.8x100. July 2, due July 1, 1893, 5 %. 10,000

Reilly, Maggie to THE EMIGRANT INDUST. SAVINGS BANK. Market st, No. 40, n e cor Madison st. P. M. July 2, 1 year, 4½ %. 5,500

Reggel, David to Fanny Bach and Jacob Berlinger exrs. Alexander Bach. 106th st. P. M. July 1, installs. 5,000

Reeves, William to James B. Smith. Church st late Kingsbridge av, w s, 68 n of lands of Spuyten Duyvil & Port Morris R. R. Co., 37.6x200. July 3 3 years. 4,000

Rice, Rosa wife of and Peter to Francis J. Schmid. Washington av, n w cor 163d st, 22.3x100. July 3, 3 years, 5 %. 4,500

Robinson, Julius and Rebecca to Isidor Obstbaum. Henry st. P. M. July 1, installs. 7,500

Robinson, Eleanor J. to THE TITLE GUARANTEE AND TRUST CO. 24th st, No. 41, n s, 262.6 e 6th av, 20.10x98.9. July 2, 1 year, 5 %. 20,000

Rohrich, Michael J. to Michael Carroll. 114th st. P. M. July 1, due July 2, 1892, 5 %. 200

Rohrs, Frederick to Hewlett Scudder, Northport, L. I. 102d st, n s, 177 e Park av, 50.6x100. July 1, due Oct. 2, 1891. 12,500

Same to Matilda B. Brown. Same property. July 1, due Nov. 2, 1891. 13,500

Rosenthal, Annie to Rachel Levy. 10th st. P. M. July 1, 2 years, 5 %. 3,000

Runk, Abby wife of and Frederick to John Schneider. Southern Boulevard and Berrian av. P. M. July 1, 3 years. 3,750

Same to Adolph G. Hupfel. Same property. P. M. Sub. to morts. July 1, 3 years. 5,250

Runkle, Philip L., Paris, France, to THE UNITED STATES TRUST CO. of New York. 3d av, w s, 51.2 s 75th st, 51x100. June 12, due July 1, 1896, or sooner, 5 %. 45,000

Rinschler, Anton to Paul Dannhauser. 164th st, n s, 200 w Trinity av, 25x120; 164th st, n s, 225 w Trinity av, 25x120. All title. July 2, 2 years, 5 %. 4,000

Rippe, Nathan and Sarah his wife to Louis Levy and Morris W. Monsky. Division st. P. M. July 1, installs. 3,250

Riker, Ella C., Woodside, L. I., to the trustees of Levy Lodge, No. 5, Independent Order Free Sons of Israel. 2d av, w s, 74.1 n 28th st, runs northwest 52.11 x southwest 18.8 x southeast 16.6 x north — south to 2d av, x — 18.10 to beginning. July 8, due July 1, 1894, 5 %. 8,000

Reynolds, Lawrence to THE EMIGRANT INDUSTRIAL SAVINGS BANK. Edgecombe av, e s, 159.7 s 145th st, 19.1x79.7x18.11x82.3. July 2, 1 year, 4½ %. 5,000

Same to same. Horatio st, s s, 150 w William st, 25x87.8. July 2, 1 year, 4½ %. 4,000

Schneider, William F., Jr., to Anthony Eickoff. Bleecker st, e s, 65.11 s Bank st, 20.7x50. July 7, due July 1, 1891, 5 %. 10,000

Schreiner, George to George M. Miller as trustee. 115th st. P. M. July 6, due Aug. 1, 1892, or sooner, 5 %. 6,000

Schneider, Charles A. to Herman Schneider. 10th st, No. 287, n s, 37.6 w Av A, 18.9x71. July 1, 2 years, 5 %. 6,000

Smith, Frank L. to Jacob Lawson, Brooklyn. West End av. P. M. July 1, 3 years, 5 %. 20,000

Same to same. Same property. P. M. Sub. to last mort. July 1, 3 years, 5 %. 5,500

Schroeder, Henry W. to Frank Schroeder. Marion st, No. 17, 25x100. July 1, 1 year, 4½ %. 12,000

Smith, Elizabeth K. wife of Albert E. to Margaret Inglis. 123d st, s s, 190.6 e 7th av, 16x100.11, error. July 2, due July 1, 1894, 5 %. 14,000

Same to Mary Barteld widow. 123d st, s s, 223.6 e 7th av, 17x100.11. July 2, 3 years, 5 %. gold, 15,000

Same to Hannah V. Deshler, Hightstown, N. J. 123d st, s s, 206.6 e 7th av, 17x100.11. July 2, 3 years, 5 %. 15,000

Same to John J. Freedman. 123d st, s s, 240.6 e 7th av, 17x100.11. July 2, 3 years, 5 %. gold, 15,000

Smith, Frank L. to Harriet A. Phelps, trustee George D. Phelps. 90th st, s s, 145 w West End av, 15x100.8. June 25, 3 years, 5 %. gold, 14,500

Smith, Andrew J. to Mary Valentine, Brooklyn. Madison st, s s, 56.2 w Montgomery st, 18x75. Lease. July 1, 2 years, 5 %. 2,300

Schulz, Louisa wife of Eugen to James S. McGovern. Lexington av. P. M. July 2, due Nov. 5, 1891. 2,000

Schumann, Gustav to Elizabeth Laux, Brooklyn. 18th st, s s, 244 e 2d av, 20x78. July 1, 5 years, 5 %. 8,500

Scrimgeour, Robert to Benjamin T. Fairchild. Sedgwick av and Perot st. P. M. July 2, 1 year, 5 %. 600

Seiffert, Franciska wife of Charles to The Union Dime Savings Inst., New York. Melrose av, s w cor 158th st, 98x99. July 2, due May 1, 1896, 5 %. 5,000

Same to Charlotte Mentzer. Same property. July 2, 3 years, 5 %. 500

Siedenburg, Diedrich to Adelheid Peters. Av B, e s, 76.8 s 84th st, 25.6x59. July 30, due July 1, 1893, 5 %. 2,000

Saulpaugh, William L. to Hugh N. Camp. Lots 10 and 11 map of 71 lots of Kingsland estate. P. M. June 15, due June 25, 1894, 5 %. 1,000

Schadowsky, Henry to Frederick W. Sauer and Conrad Gross. 90th st. P. M. July 1, due April 21, 1894. 4,000

Schappert, Dorothea to Mary Corsa. Railroad av, w s, lot 157 map of Morrisania, 30x183x—x180. May 28, 3 years, 5½ %. 800

Scheib, Nathan to Jacob Larchan and Rebecca his wife. Willett st, No. 64, e s, 150 s Rivington st, 25x100. July 1, installs. 9,000

Schlamp, Elizabeth to Henry W. Meyer. 87th st, s s, 321.4 e 4th av, 17.6x100.8. June 25, 3 years. 3,000

Schreyer, John to The Mutual Life Ins. Co., New York. Bank st, No. 117, n s, 201 w Greenwich st, 26x109.1 x east 10.1 x south 12.10 x east 18.6 x south 95. July 2, 1 year. 15,000

Same to same. Bank st, No. 119, n s, 227 w Greenwich st, 25.8x114.2x26.3x109.1. July 2, 1 year. 15,000

Same to same. Bank st, No 121, n s, 252.8 w Greenwich st, runs west 16.5 x north 95 x east 8.11 x north 21.10 x east 7.8 x south 114.2. July 2, 1 year. 10,000

Spaulding, Thomas A. to The New York Life Ins Co. 90th st, n s, 180 w Central Park West, 20x100.8. June 1, 3 years. 20,000

Same to same. 90th st, n s, 160 w Central Park West. 20x100.8. June 1, 3 years. 20,000

Same to same. 90th st, n s, 140 w Central Park West, 20x100.8. June 1, 3 years. 20,000

Same to same. 90th st, n s, 120 w Central Park West, 20x100.8. June 1, 3 years. 20,000

Same to same. 90th st, n s, 200 w Central Park West. 20x100.8. June 1, 3 years. 20,000

Same to same. 90th st, n s, 100 w Central Park West, 20x100.8. June 1, 3 years. 20,000

Same to The Murray Hill Bank of New York. 90th st, n s, 100 w 8th av, 120x100.8. Sub. to 6 morts. $120,000. June 1, 1 year. 24,000

Same to same. 90th st, n s, 100 w 8th av, 80x100.8. Sub. to morts. $104,000. June 1, 1 year. 22,500

Same to Patrick Ryan and Rawden Rawnsley, of Ryan & Rawnsley. 90th st, n s, 200 w 8th av, 20x100.8. Sub. to morts. $44,000. June 1, 1 year. 4,100

Same to John M. Canda and John P. Kane, of Canda & Kane. 90th st, n s, 180 w 8th av, 26x100.8. Sub. to morts. $44,000. June 1, 1 year. 1,895

Same to Frederick Haas. 90th st, n s, 200 w 8th av, 20x100.8. Sub. to morts. $44,000. June 1, 1 year. 5,000

Seitz, Frank A. to Lily W. Churchill et al. trustees Louis C. Hamersley dec'd. Prince st, n s, 50.8 e Wooster st, 3 lots, together in size, 99.4x95. 3 morts., each $60,000. July 8, 5 years, 4½ %. 180,000

Sampson, Zabadiel S. to The Twenty-fourth Ward Real Estate Assoc. Garfield st, n s, 106.4 e Briggs av. P. M. June 15, due July 1, 1894, 5 %. 487

Same to same. Garfield st, n s, 131.4 e Briggs av. P. M. June 15, due July 1, 1894, 5 %. 488

Same to same. Garfield st, n s, 156.4 e Briggs av. P. M. June 15, due July 1, 1894, 5 %. 487

Same to same. Briggs av, e s, 50.3 n Garfield st. P. M. June 15, due July 1, 1894, 5 %. 525

Same to same. Southern Boulevard. P. M. June 15, due July 1, 1894, 5 %. 687

Schwend, Robert to William R. Beal Land Improvement Co. 141st st. P. M. July 8, 3 years, 5 %. 1,400

Sedgwick, Henrietta E. wife of Henry D., Stockbridge, Mass., to The Inst. for the Savings of Merchants' Clerks. 102d st, n s, 75 w 9th av, 25x100.11. July 6, due Aug. 15, 1896, 4½ %. gold, 13,000

Sharkey, Patrick to John Bickmann. 20th st, No. 239, n s, 150 w 2d av, 25x92. Lease. July 1, 4 years. 4,000

Sharkey, Maria to Lena Jaeck. 2d av, No. 852, e s, 78 n 20th st, 20x90. July 2, 2 years. 2,000

Silverberg, Sarah wife of Solomon to Alexander D. Wilson. Eldridge st, No. 15, w s, 150 s Canal st, 25x100. July 7, due July 1, 1893. 3,000

Seery, Peter to The Twenty-fourth Ward Real Estate Assoc. Webster av and Suburban st. P. M. June 15, due July 1, 1894, 5 %. 2,100

Schmidt, Babette to William R. Beal Land Improvement Co. Oak terrace. P. M. July 8, 3 years or sooner, 5 %. 1,382

Sullivan, John W. to Lyman Tiffany and ano. exrs. and trustees Charlotte L. Fox. Front st. P. M. July 9, 3 years or sooner, 5 %. 8,000

Simon, Marks to Theresa Nathan. Rutgers pl (Monroe st), n s, 104.6 w Clinton st, 26x110. July 9, due Jan. 1, 1895, or installs. 5,000

Simon, Theodore to Emilie A. wife of Alexander Nones. 3d av, n e cor 83d st, 23.1x77. July 9, due Dec. 31, 1893, 5 %. gold, 4,000

Sobol, Levy to Nancy L. Sherwood and Mary E. Blodgett. Rivington st. P. M. July 9, 3 years, 5 %. 16,000

Storey, Frederick D. to The Harlem Savings Bank. Washington av, south cor 174th st, 100x120. July 9, 1 year, 5 %. 7,500

Strasburger, Byron L. to The United States Trust Co. of New York. 10th av. P. M. June 1, due July 1, 1894, 5 %. 10,000

Toayan, Henry to George Scott. 49th st, s s, 200 e 9th av, 25x100.5. July 9, 3 years or installs, 5 %. 8,500

Teuchtler, Robert F. to Charles Thyson. 3d st. Leasehold. P. M. July 8, due July 1, 1892. See Conveys 1,500

Tilden, Lilian E. F. widow to Aime Pellorce and Emile Brenet, Paris, France. Fulton st, s e cor Pearl st, runs east 100 x south 80 x west 60 x north 10 x west 58 x north 75 to beginning, United States Hotel; Pearl st, No. 258, e s, 75 s Fulton st, 20x58; 17th st, No. 136, s s, 230 e Irving pl, 20x92. All title. June 19, 1 year, 5 %. 1,000

Twomey, Catharine C. to Herman M. Sichling. Courtlandt av. P. M. July 1, due July 2, 1892, 5 %. 4,000

The Roman Catholic Church of The Holy Name in the City of New York to The Emigrant Indust. Savings Bank. Bloomingdale road, Amsterdam (10th) av, 97th and 96th sts, 203.8x154.10x201.10x175.1. July 6, 1 year, 4½ %. 70,000

Thomas, James to The Twenty-fourth Ward Real Estate Assoc. Southern Boulevard. P. M. June 15, due July 1, 1894, 5 %. 1,575

Toussaint, Matilda B. to The Twenty-fourth Ward Real Estate Assoc. Southern Boulevard. P. M. June 15, due July 1, 1894, 5 %. 1,350

Toussaint, Therese wife of Frederick and Julius F. Toussaint to John Schneider. Berrian av, n w cor Walton av, 99.6x172.8x101.8x172.8. July 1, 3 years, 5 %. 3,000

Taylor, Alfred H. to Henry Morgenthau. 180th st. P. M. June 15, 3 years, 5 %. 1,700

Thompson, James to Henry Brown and G. Herman Hainann. 120th st, s s, 125 w 8th av, 75x100.11. Sub. to morts. July 6, 9 mos. 1,089

Unger, Bertha to Louis Eickwort. Webster av. P. M. July 7, 3 years, 5 %. 930

Uihlein, Charles to The Twenty-fourth Ward Real Estate Assoc. Bainbridge av. P. M. June 15, due July 1, 1894, 5 %. 625

Umberfield, John C. to Gideon Fountain. 75th st, s s, 400 e Columbus av, 40x95. July 8, 1 year. 10,000

Venturiere, Pasquale to Teresa Coogan. 1st av. P. M. July 2, due July 8, 1893, or sooner. 3,000

Vanderbilt, John mortgagee to Laura Leaman and Edith de L. Woolsey formerly Southwick, present owners. Statement that amount due on mortgage made by Agnes and Thomas Auld, dated Dec. 30, 1868, is 4,000

Van Riper, Charles to Hugh N. Camp. Lots 68 and 69 map of 71 lots of Kingsland estate, Morris Heights, 24th Ward. P. M. June 15, due June 25, 1894, 5 %. 1,080

Van Eupen, Theodore to Samuel Kempner. Jones st. P. M. June 30, due Oct. 1, 1891. 11,500

Same to same. Same property. June 30, due Jan. 1, 1892, or sooner. 10,000

Vetter, Gottfried to Friederich Vetter. 3d st, s s, 342.9 e Av A, —x105.11x24.9x105.11. Lease. July 6, 5 years, 4 %. 6,500

Wright, Samuel O., Rockville Centre, L. I., to Reuben Ross. 126th st, s s, 56 w Madison av, 18x83. July 7, due Jan. 2, 1892, or sooner. 4,000

Wheaton, Esther A. to Lyman Tiffany and ano. exrs. and trustees Charlotte L. Fox. Rose st. P. M. June 30, due May 1, 1892, 5 %. 20,000

Wilson, Mary to Patrick Cassidy. 31st st, No. 215, n s, 175 w 7th av, 25x98.9. Sub. to morts. July 2, 2 months. 1,000

Weber, Henry to Nicholas Winkler. 161st st, s s, 150 e Courtlandt av, 25x100. July 6, due July 1, 1894, 5 %. 1,400

Wiggers, Albert to The Twenty-fourth Ward Real Estate Assoc. Webster av. P. M. June 15, due July 1, 1894, 5 %. 1,675

Wright, William H. and William J. Pragnell to William R. Beal Land Improvement Co. Crimmins av. P. M. July 8, 3 years or sooner, 5%. 2,345

Walsh, William M. to Adele Kneeland individ. and extrx. and trustee Charles Kneeland dec'd. 101st st, n s, 150 e Columbus av, 25x100.11. June 25, 3 years, 5 %. 20,000

Same to William H. Scott. Same property. July 2, due July 1, 1892. 8,634

Watt, William G. to Henrietta S. wife of Conrad D. Orth. Boston av. P. M. July 1, 3 years, 5 %. 2,500

Webb, Thomas to Alexander Forsyth. Lots 12 and 13 map of Charles Darke, Yonkers, on n w s of a lane 365 n e from Kingsbridge to Williamsbridge road, 50x86x50x87.9. June 30, due July 1, 1893. 800

Weiss, Samuel to Jacob Gladke. 51st st. P. M. July 1, 1 year, 5 % 2,000

Wallach, Eleonora wife of Abraham to Alfred C. Clark guard. of Robert S. Clark. Columbus av, n e cor 91st st, 25.3x80. July 9, 5 years, 5 %. 27,000

Wagner, Albert to David L. Newborg. 59th st. P. M. July 7, 2 years. 10,000

Washburn, Wilbur F. to William W. Scrugham, Yonkers, N. Y. 138th st, s s, 767.9 e Willis av, 19.7x50; 138th st, s s, 450 e Willis av, 16.8x100. June 30, 1 year. 6,125

Yates, John to Henry Morgenthau. 178th st. P. M. June 15, 3 years, 5 %. 3,185

Zuelch, Henry to George T. Vingut trustee for Henry K., Augusta F., Elizabeth K. and Benjamin V. H. Vingut. 35th st, n s, 175 w 9th av, runs west 24.11 x north 71.2 x west 0.2½ x north 27.7 x east 25 x south 98.9. July 2, 3 years, 5 %. 12,000

KINGS COUNTY.

July 2, 3, 4, 6, 7, 8.

Acker, Howard N. to Frederick Behrens trustee Frederick Behrens. Elton st, e s, 215.2 s Fulton st, 25x100. July 1, 3 years. $2,800

Ach, Christopher mortgagor with Sibyl Shaw. Extension of mort. at 5 %. July 8. nom

Ackerknecht, Julius, Henry Manny and Clementina Herb to Frank L. Singer. Greene av. P. M. July 1, 4 years, 5 %. 3,500

Acor, Kate wife of and Lewis to The Title Guarantee and Trust Co. Pulaski st, s s, 293.9 w Marcy av, 18.9x100. July 2, 3 years, 5 %. 3,000

Addy, Richard C. to Hester Studwell. Willoughby av, s s, 80 e Marcy av, 20x75. July 1, due July 6, 1894, 5 %. 3,000

Arena, Maria T. to William J. Costigan. Clinton av, lot 202 sectional map No. 5, village of Fort Hamilton. June 29, 1 year. 250

Altmann, John B. to Smith Cox. Lexington av, n s, 95 e Patchen av. P. M. July 1, 5 years, 5 %. 3,000

Same to same. Lexington av, n e cor Patchen av. P. M. July 1, 5 years, 5 %. 10,000

Atkinson, Jane wife of Henry T. to Maria A., Maria Antoinette, Mary S. and Thomas S. Gelston. 3d av, 97th st. P. M. May 21, 5 years, 5 %. 875

Abbott, William H. to William Dittmar, Jr. 54th st, New Utrecht. P. M. Sub. to mort. $2,250. July 1, installs. 1,750

Allen, Robert to Daniel K. Hall, Jr. Bedford av, w s, 282.9 n Myrtle av, 25x100. July 2, 3 years, 5 %. 2,500

Bates, James T. to Abraham A. Bates. Bayard st, n s, 235.9 e Graham av, 20.7x100. July 3, 1 year, 5 %. 300

Bromell, Thomas to Christopher Haug. Sullivan st, s s, 200 w Richards st, 25x100. July 1, 5 years. 850

Burrill, William L. and Charles F. to Washington Trust Co. committee Martha Green. Willow st, n w s, 115 s w Clark st. P. M. June 10, 3 years, 4¾ %. 7,000

Same to same. Willow st, n w s, 133 s w Clark st. P. M. June 10, 3 years, 4¾ % 7,000

Same to Sarah H. Powell. Same property. P. M. June 10, installs, 5¾ %. 2,000

Same to same. Willow st, n w s, 115 s w Clark st. P. M. June 10, installs, 5¾ %. 2,000

Bailey, James S. and Charles H. Parsons exrs. Solomon Freeman mortgagees to Grace and John Carr mortgagors. Certificate of amount due on mortgages. July 1. nom

Same to Edward E. Bergen mortgagor. Certificate of amount due on mortgages. July 1. nom

Bailey, James S. and Charles H. Parsons exrs. Solomon Freeman and Charles H. Parsons individ. mortgagees with Edward E. Bergen mortgagor. Certificate as to amount due and extension of mort. June 24. nom

Baker, William H. to Hannah Hitchings. Arlington av, s e cor Jerome st. P. M. June 27, due June 1, 1894, 5 %. 4,500

Same to Hannah Hitchings extrx. Charles F. Hitchings. Arlington av, s w cor Warwick st. P. M. June 27, due July 1, 1894, 5 %. 4,500

Same to same. Arlington av, s s, 75 e Jerome st. P. M. June 27, due July 1, 1894, 5 %. 3,500

Same to same. Arlington av, s s, 40 w Warwick st. P. M. June 27, due July 1, 1894, 5 %. 3,500

Barton, William E. to Hezekiah S. Archer. North Elliott pl, w s, 46 s Auburn pl, 20x65. July 3, due July 1, 1896, 5 %. 2,500

Bettfreund, John to Catharine Kassebaum. Middleton st. P. M. July 1, 1 year, 5 %. 2,800

Blumenkrantz, Adolph to Frances I. wife of Thomas C. Taylor. Thatford av, w s, lots 59, 60 and 61 map Gilbert S. Thatford, 75x100. July 1, 1½ years or installs. 1,200

Bogart, Elvira E. to George E. Nostrand. Stewart av, n w s, at intersection with centre line 77th st, 130.8x289x130x276.3. July 3, 3 years. 500

Borikow, Charles and Louise his wife to Jacob Klumpp. George st. P. M. July 1, 5 years, 5 %. 4,000

Bossert, Margaretha wife of and Henry to The German Savings Bank of Brooklyn. Harrison av, n e s, 20 s e Lynch st, 26.8x79.11. June 30, due Dec. 1, 1892, 5 %. 3,000

Same to same. Stanhope st, s e s, 424.6 n e Evergreen av, 19.6x100. June 30, due Dec. 1, 1892, 5 %. 2,000

Bennett, George W. and Mary A. his wife to Martha A. McCabe, Troy, N. Y. Gravesend av, e s, 25 s of B. Doyles land, 25x86; Gravesend av at n w cor of B. Doyles land, 25x86, Gravesend. July 3, 5 years. 675

Brandmeier, Philip to Karl J. Dewald. Willoughby av, n w s, 100 n e Hamburg av, 50x100. July 1, 1 year. 800

Brennan, Patrick to Michael Kavanagh. 5th av, west cor Union st, 23x92. *Mt.* $10,000. July 2, due July 1, 1898, 5 %. 7,000

Same to Hannah E. Miller. Same property. July 2, due July 1, 1894, 5 %. 10,000

Bruns, Agnes M. to John V. Van Pelt. Bay 22d st, n w s, 370 s w 86th st, 40x96.8, New Utrecht. July 2, due May 1, 1896. 2,200

Burns, Catherine to Christopher Million. Little Nassau st, s s, 175 e Kent av, 27x100. July 1, 5 years, 5 %. 600

Bach, Emil H. to Carrie Blyn. Cooper st. P. M. June 8, 1 year. 400

Bertram, Frederick to Frederick Homeyer. Gates av, s e s, 325 s w Central av, 50x100. July 1, 5 years. 3,500

Block, Julie wife of and Jules to The Bowery Savings Bank. Broadway, east cor Myrtle av, runs east along av 100.2 x south 41.3 x southwest 41.8 to Broadway, x northwest 100.2. July 3, 1 year, 4½ %. 25,000

Boggs, James to The Equitable Co-operative Building and Loan Assoc. North Elliott pl. P. M. June 29, installs. 2,500

Braun, Julia A. to Adolph Manuel. Bushwick av, s w s, 22.6 n w Lawton st, 22.6x70.5. July 1, 3 years, 5 %. 2,500

Buck, Henry to Anthony D. Kaufmann. 3d av, w s, 40.2 s 45th st, 40x100. July 1, 3 years, 5 %. 1,200

Bader, George D. to William Graham, Paterson, N. J. Caton pl, Coney Island road. P. M. June 30, due July 1, 1891, 4 %. 11,000

Same to Charlotte E. Findlay. Same property. P. M. June 30, due July 1, 1894. 14,000

Boehm, Augusta to Christian Nicklaus. Cleveland st. P. M. July 1, 3 years, 5 %. 500

Brophy, Elizabeth to John J. Campbell and ano. exrs. Mary A. Campbell. Lewis av, e s, 66 s Hart st, 17x80. July 7, due July 2, 1894, or installs, 5 %. 2,500

Same to same. Lewis av, e s, 32 s Hart st, 17x80. July 7, due July 2, 1894, or installs, 5 %. 2,500

Brown, Thomas to Lawrence V. Cortelyou and ano. exrs. Jaques Cortelyou. 5th av, s e cor Berkeley pl. P. M. May 11, due May 15, 1892, 5 %. 19,000

Brodoosky, Morris to Jacob and Davis Axelrod. Thatford av. P. M. given in place of another mortgage containing error in description. June 9, installs. 850

Brownell, Asa C. to The Title Guarantee and Trust Co. State st, n s, 250 e Hoyt st, 100x100. July 2, demand. 10,000

Burchell, George W. to The Mutual Life Ins. Co., New York. Greene av, n s, 300 w Nostrand av, 20x100. July 2, 1 year. 7,500

Burt, Warren S. to Ira O. Miller. 4th av, n w cor 44th st. P. M. June 20, due July 1, 1896. 2,000

Butz, Christopher to James H. McKenna. 3d av. P. M. July 2, 3 years or sooner, 5 %. 1,000

Bertina, Joseph to Williamsburgh Savings Bank. Flushing av, s s, 175 w Throop av, 25x100. July 7, 1 year, 5 %. 2,800

Clark, Melissa to Alfred S. Miles. Gates av, s e s, 175 n e Knickerbocker av, 50x100. July 7, 1 year, 5 %. 1,500

Crane, Bridget wife of Henry to Mary wife of William Schnoor. Williamson av, w s, 200 n Linington av, 50x100. July 6, 2 years. 200

Clancy, Catharine A. to Elizabeth F. Dougherty. Bergen st. P. M. July 1, 3 years, 5 %. 2,000

Cook, Mary E. to Florence E. Twibell. Stone av, w s, 175 s Blake av, 25x100. July 6, 3 years. 800

Chauncey, George W. trustee Mary L. Kirby to Mary E. Van Auten trustee Mary L. Kirby. nom

Chinnock, Elizabeth L. to John Molander. Waverly av. P. M. July 3, 1 year, 5 %. 500

Same to same. Waverly av, s e cor Gates av, 25x72. July 3, 1 year, 5 %. 3,000

Clark, Ellen wife of John T. to Mary B. Van Tuyl. 14th st, s w s, 197.10 n w 4th av, 40x100x10x40x101.3. July 2, 3 years. 2,600

Cook, George H. mortgagor with The Title Guarantee and Trust Co. Extension of mort. July 1. nom

Cooper, Alexander to John F. Hart. Hawthorne st. P. M. July 1, 3 years. 2,000

Same to Annie E. Turrell. Hawthorne st. P. M. July 1, 3 years, 5 %. 4,000

Cornell, William H. to Isaac Halstead. Bergen st, s s, 200 w Troy av, 25x127.9. July 2, 5 years or installs. gold, 5,000

Cowenhoven, Samuel V. D. to Emma L. Streeton. Norwood av, e s, lot 81 map 995 lots Rapalje property, 25x150. July 2, due July 1, 1894. 900

Cutler, Robert N. to Cornelia A. Kneeland. Grand av, e s, 357.5 n Gates av, 20x59.11 to old road from Brooklyn to Bedford, x27.8x78.11. July 1, 3 years, 5 %. 4,500

Carpenter, Alice L. to Charles L. Prindle, Sharon, Conn. 16th st. P. M. June 26, due July 1, 1893. 800

Carlile, Susan wife of and James to The Union Dime Savings Inst., New York. 5th av, n w s, 50 n e 14th st, 25x97.10. June 29, due Nov. 1, 1894, 5 %. 5,000

Cornell, William H. to Isaac Halstead. Bergen st, s s, 200 w Troy av, 25x127.9. Sub. to mort. $5,000. July 2, demand. 1,800

Callaghan, Francis and Lawrence E. O'Bryan. Sands st, No. 109, n s, 81.7 e Jay st, 18.4x111. July 2, due Nov. 1, 1896. gold, 6,500

Coffin, Elizabeth R. to Harriet M. Coffin. Monroe st, n s, 100 e Reid av, 20x100. July 1, 3 years, 5 %. 3,500

Collins, Charles H. to The Title Guarantee and Trust Co. 4th av, w s, 100 n 9th st, 30x60. July 7, 3 years, 5 %. 6,000

Connors, Patrick to Mary Meehan. Van Brunt st, n w s, 75 s w Sullivan st, 25x90. July 1, 2 years, 5 %. 400

Crawford, Mary A. to Thomas McCarty. High st, Gold st. P. M. July 2, 5 years, 5 %. 6,500

Delorac, Mary, Cincinnati, O., to Phebe M. Clarke et al., exrs., &c., Henry L. Clarke. Fort Hamilton av, n w cor 65th st; Fort Hamilton av, n w cor 66th st; Fort Hamilton av, n w cor 67th st, New Utrecht. P. M. July 2, due June 4, 1896, 5 %. 2,807

Dierking, John to William J. G. Bearns. Keap st, s w cor South 4th st, 19.9x69. Sub. to mort. $4,500. July 1, 3 years. 500

Dowd, John J. to James S. Barclay trustee Eliza B. Howell. Hancock st, n s, 100 w Marcy av, 20x100. July 1, due July 1, 1894, 5 %. 6,500

Doyle, Martha wife of John to Chauncy Perry. Norman av. P. M. July 1, 5 years, 5 %. 2,500

Davies, Mary A. wife of James R. to Mary A. Maujer. Jefferson av. P. M. July 6, 5 years, 5 %. 11,000

Davis, Frederick to Maria Hoffmann. Willoughby av, n w s, 100 n e Central av, 25x100. July 3, 3 years, 5 %. 1,900

Dinstman, Lina to Adam Kreuscher. Montieth st, n s, 75 e Bremen st, 25x75. Sub. to mort. $1,700. July 1, 5 years, 5 %. 3,100

Dorsey, John J. to Anna M. Ferris. East 4th st, w s, 105.8 s Greenwood av, 47x100x12.10x106.6. June 23, 3 years, 5 %. 1,300

Ehlers, Frank to William H. Beadleston. 3d av, east cor 42d st, 20x80. July 1, due July 2, 1894, 5 %. 5,500

Epstein, Benjamin to Brany Zwickel. Stone av, w s, 159 s Dumont av, 25x100. July 7, installs. 400

Eich, John to Severin Linsenmeyer and Katharina his wife. Stanhope st, n w s, 350 n e Hamburg av, 25x100. July 2, installs, 5 %. 3,500

Eagan, John J. to Charles Engert. Van Pelt av. P. M. Sub. to mort. $3,000. July 1, installs, 5 %. 1,500

Same to The Kings Co. Savings Inst. Same property. July 1, 1 year, 5 %. 3,000

Ellerstein, Nathan to Pauline wife of William Hartman. Thatford av. P. M. July 1, installs. 900

Erhardt, Frederick to Frederick C. Erhardt, New York. Grove st. P. M. July 2, due July 1, 1894, 5 %. 700

Faron, Mary E. to William M. Prichard and ano. exrs. and trustees George Z. Foster. 21st av, west cor Bath av, 102.6x96.8x108.9x96.10. July 3, 3 years. 7,500

Fenton, George to Franz Kannengieser and Louise his wife. Winthrop st, Flatbush. P. M. July 1, 5 years or installs, 5 %. 2,250

Fischman, Adolph to Isaac Haft. Dumont av, s s, 50 w Watkins st, 25x100. July 1, installs. 700

Finkeldey, Heinrich to Frederick T. Aldridge guard. Magdalena E. Schmadeke. Conover st. P. M. July 1, 4 years, 5 %. 3,500

Fishkoufski, Harris to Ellen Gillner. Riverdale av, s w cor Stone av. P. M. July 6, 4 years or installs. 500

Foss, Alice M. to William M. Evans. Patchen av, w s, 75 s Hancock st, 15x100. July 1, installs. 1,850

Foster, Catherine A. to George W. Pearsall. 8th st, n s, 225 w 5th av, 21.6x100. June 23, 1 year. 100

Fowler, Mary E. wife of Levi to Elizabeth H. Taylor. St. Marks av, n s, 320 e Franklin av, 20x128x20x128.6. July 6, due July 1, 1894. 6,000

Flood, Ellen to Francis J. Lynch. North 10th st, n s, 125 e Kent av, 25x100. July 1, 5 years, 5 %. 4,000

Flood, John and William A. Northridge to Charlotte E. Northridge. Sutter av, s w cor Essex st, 25x100. July 3, 3 years. 3,000

Foley, Catherina to The Long Island Building and Loan Assoc. Huron st. P. M. July 1, installs. 3,250

Farrington, Charles W. to Gertrude Schoonmaker, Mount Clair, N. J. Madison st. P. M. July 2, due July 6, 1894, 5 %. 2,500

Freiberger, Fannie to Jacob Sapiro. River st, s s, 150 e Harrison av, 25x100. Sub. to mort. $5,400. July 1, 4 years or installs. 600

Folsom, Mary A. to Lena G. Roney. Fort Hamilton av, n s, 75 w 92d st, 25x116.3x25x116.8; Fort Hamilton av, n s, 100 w 92d st, 50x232.6 to Gelston av, New Utrecht. July 7, due Sept. 1, 1891. 190

Force, John W. to The West Brooklyn Land and Impt. Co. 45th st, New Utrecht. P. M. June 24, due Sept. 24, 1895, 5 %. 420

Frick, John and Louis and Frederick to Bertha Kolb. Irving av, n e s, 25 n w Himrod st, 3 lots, each 25x100. 3 morts., each $3,500. July 1, 3 years, 5 %. 10,500

Same to same. Irving av, n e cor Himrod st, 25x100. July 1, 3 years, 5 %. 4,500

Fuchs, Wilhelmina to Frederick, Otto and Richard Kampfe. Elton st, e s, 150 n Arlington av, 25x100. June 25, due June 1, 1893, 5 %. 2,000

Frasey, Guy S. to James W. and Albert J. Lamb. Madison st. P. M. July 8, installs. 1,700

Gaskell, George to The West Brooklyn Land and Improvement Co. 54th st, New Utrecht. P. M. June 22, due Sept. 22, 1895, 5 %. 400

Gengler, Gabriel to Philip Gengler. Powers st, s s, 275 w Olive st, 25x100. July 1, 3 years, 5 %. 2,000

Good, Samuel R. to Cross, Austin & Co. Bainbridge st, n s, 137.6 w Ralph av, 18.9x100. June 29, 1 year. 450

Granger, Ellen to Margaret H. and Lizzie Dunn exrs. Patrick J. Dunn. Bergen st, n s, 325 e Grand av, 20x110. July 1, 3 years. 1,300

Gilfoy, Emily C. to Clarence Lincoln. Macon st. P. M. July 3, 3 years, 5 %. 700

Goldstein, Hyman and Abraham Wolf to The East New York Savings Bank. Dumont av, n w cor Thatford av, 25x100. July 6, 1 year. 3,250

Goldstein, Joseph to Abram Rankin, Jersey City. Thatford av. P. M. July 2, due Oct. 2, 1891. 300

Goldstein, Joseph to The Title Guarantee and Trust Co. Union st, s s, 500.6 w 5th av, 16.8x95. July 3, 3 years, 5 %. 2,500

Gorse, Tine wife of Christopher to Henry Legenhausen. Floyd st, s s, 275 e Sumner av, 25x100. July 1, 3 years, 5 %. 2,000

Gsanger, John J. to Jaques Van Brunt. 79th st, New Utrecht. P. M. June 23, due July 2, 1894. 1,000

Gentzlinger, Henry to Peter Otten. Graham av, s e cor Richardson st, 44x75. July 1, 5 years, 5 %. 6,000

Georg, John and Minnie his wife to Charles Engert. North Henry st. P. M. Sub. to mort. $1,700. July 1, installs, 5 %. 1,200

Same to The Kings County Savings Institution. Same property. July 1, 1 year, 5 %. 1,700

Gerhardt, Minnie to Frederick Hauck. Hart st, s s, 335 e Throop av, 20x100. June 15, 5 years, 5 %. 2,000

Gluck, Samuel to Edward Ingold. Bleecker st. P. M. July 2, installs, 5 %. 2,400

Graves, Robert J. to The Title Guarantee and Trust Co. Park pl. P. M. June 23, due July 1, 1894, 5 %. 5,500

Glover, Josephine to John Levis. Driggs st, n e cor South 5th st, 20.1x75. July 1, 3 years. 1,200

Goldberg, Jacob to Mary A. L. wife of William H. Baker. Stone av. P. M. July 1, installs, 5 %. 450

Groh, Friederich mortgagor with Carl Gross mortgagee. Extension of mort. June 30. nom

Graf, Sophie to Edwin O. Phelps. Schaeffer st. P. M. June 27, due July 1, 1893. 225

Green, Caroline A. wife of John D. to Catharine A. Bleecker. Union st, n s, 305 w Hoyt st, 15x90. July 6, 1 year, 5 %. 3,000

Hoske, Otto to William Bedford. Meeker av. P. M. July 1, 5 years, 5 %. 1,000

Hand, Michael J. and Catharine his wife to Hannah F. Street, Rockville Centre, L. I. Knickerbocker av. P. M. July 1, 1 year, 5 %. 1,000

Hanold, Sarah E. wife of and William W. to Terence Jacobson. Madison st, n s, 216.8 e Nostrand av, 16.8x100. June 30, due Nov. 1, 1891. 1,000

Harrje, Henry to Frederick Borghard. Lorimer st. P. M. March 27, due July 1, 1894, 5 %. 2,500

Hay, George T. to Joseph Foley. Huntington st. P. M. March 20, 2 years. 250

Hayward, William to Whitman W. Kenyon. Union st, n s, 290 w Hoyt st, 15x90. June 18, 3 years, 5 %. 3,500

Herbst, Peter to Emma C. wife of A. M. Webb. Scholes st, n s, 225 w Waterbury st, 25x100. July 1, 5 years, 5 %. 2,200

Herlich, John to George Gutting and Charles A. Wagner. Knickerbocker av and Stanhope st. P. M. July 1, 2 years, 5 %. 1,500

Hopfer, John J. to Amalie Gesele widow. Throop av, n w cor Willoughby st, 25x100. July 1, 5 years. 3,000

Harwood, Grove M. to Clarence Lincoln. Macon st. P. M. July 3, due July 1, 1892. 350

Hayman, Richard M. to Philip Nies. Mill road, s s, 49.6 e of land of John Hayman dec'd, 39.6x330.4; Indeft. right of way, w s, 17.3x156 to Gravesend Bay, x44.9x east 156, Gravesend. July 2, 3 years. 1,700

Hein, Ferdinand R. to Maria T. Hein. Rodney st, No. 234, s s, 100 w Marcy av, 25x100. July 2, 1 year, 5 %. 2,000

Heinemann, Barbara to Phebe E. Sharp. Stockholm st, s s, 200 e Willow av, 25x100. July 6, 3 years. 1,000

Herold, Fanny and Ida Friedrich and Emil Landcraf to Clemens and Philipp Wocker. 3d av, e s, 75 s Prospect av, 25x100. July 1, 3 years, 5 %. 1,700

Hiepe, Julius and Augusta his wife to Theodore Kiendl. Sutter av, n s, 50 e Van Sielen av, 25x100. July 1, 1 year. 125

Herod, Josephine wife of William to Richard Mayes. Albany av, w s, 155 n Butler st, 48.5x—121.2x—x114.4. June 30, due July 1, 1893, 5 %. 1,000

Herod, William to same. Schenectady av, w s, 25 s Bergen st, 25x75. June 30, due July 1, 1893, 5 %. 1,150

Hopkins, William F. to Starr Co-operative Building and Loan Assoc. 55th st, n e s, 200 s e 14th av, 50x100.2, New Utrecht. June 16, installs. 4,327

Harrison, J. Rodman to Katharine H. Taber extrx. Samuel T. Taber. 55th st, n e s, 250 s e 14th av, 50x100.2. July 8, due July 1, 1898. 3,000

Hart, John F. to Stephen B. Sturges. 7th av, P. M. June 8, demand. 52,000

Hennenlotter, Frances M. wife of Joseph to Frank Lambrecht. 3d av, s w cor 52d st, 20.2x80. July 2, 3 years, 5 %. 2,500

Haussner, Bernhardt mortgagee with Charles F. Pundt mortgagor. Extension of morts. July 7. nom

Herig, Frank P. to Belinda L. Bergen. 57th st, New Utrecht. P. M. June 12, 3 years, 5 %. 850

Herskovitz, Solomon to Martha A. Vogt. West st. P. M. July 7, installs. 1,000

Horowitz, Isaac to Conrad Meis. Graham av, P. M. July 7, due July 1, 1896, 5 %. 4,500

Hughes, Henry J. to Samuel Cary. 55th st, s w s, 240 n w 6th av, 60x100.2. Nov. 21, 1890, 1 year, 5 %. 1,000

Judson, Edward to Ida F. Dumont and ano. exrs. Theodore S. Dumont. Grand av, n w cor Willoughby av, runs west 24 x north 94 x east 14.1 x south 7.1 x east 9.8 to av. x south 87. July 6, due July 1, 1894. 13,000

Jenkins, Frank mortgagor with Sarah E. wife of William T. De Nyse. Extension of mort. June 25. nom

Johnson, Sven to The Nassau Co-operative Building and Loan Assoc. Schenck av, w s, 300 n Blake av, 25x100. July 3, installs. 1,500

Jones, Richard to George G. B. Irish. Calyer st, n s, 50 w Oakland st, 25x75. July 1, 5 years, 5 %. 1,800

Juhren, Didrich to Joseph Hartman, Woodbury, L. I. Gates av, s s, 290 e Reid av, 30x100. July 3, due July 1, 1894, 5 %. 3,000

Kane, Sarah M. to Charles Collins. Grand av, e s, 184.6 s Flushing av, 25x100. 2d mort. July 3, 1 year. 230

Same to Charles M., Horace A. and Frederic B. Pratt. Same property. July 2, installs. gold, 1,300

Kekut, Frederick to Michael Seitz. Metropolitan av, s s, 250 e Catharine st, 25x100. July 1, 3 years, 5 %. 3,300

Kiefer, Mary to The Title Guarantee and Trust Co. Stagg st, n s, 150 w Lorimer st, 25x100. June 26, due July 1, 1892. 500

Kopp, Conrad to John Dill, Jr. Boerum pl. P. M. July 1, 2 years, 5 %. 1,000

Kraus, Peter to Susanna Simon. Stagg st, n s, 630 w Waterbury st, 23.5x123.5x54.6x119.4. July 1, 2 years, 5 %. 3,000

Kuhn, Maria A. widow, John A., Caroline L. and Frederick W. Kuhn heirs Joseph Kuhn to George Kaiser. Graham av, 50 s Seigel st, 25x75. July 1, 4 years, 5 %. 4,000

Kaufman, Mary A. wife of Louis J. to John Liddy. Norwood av. P. M. June 30, due July 1, 1894. 800

Knight, Anna F. P. to Mary A. Knight et al. trustees Henry Knight. Vanderbilt av, w s, 355 n Gates av, 20x100. July 1, 1½ years, 5 %. 700

Knorr, Barbara to Gottlieb Hartmann. Scholes st, n s, 350 w Waterbury st, 75x100. July 1, 5 years, 5 %. 2,000

Kodziesen, Abraham and Aaron to Peter Johnson. Broadway, n e s, 50 n w Covert st. P M. July 1, due April 1, 1893, 5 %. 1,500

Same to same. Broadway, n e s, 75 n w Covert st. P. M. July 1, due April 1, 1893, 5 %. 1,500

Same to The Title Guarantee and Trust Co. Boerum st, s w cor Bushwick av, 25x60. July 2, due July 3, 1894, 5 %. 5,000

Kelly, Philip to The Greenpoint Savings Bank. Newell st, w s, 341.5 n Van Cott av. P. M. July 1, 1 year, 5½ %. 1,000

Kirby, Joseph I. to Edwin Beers. Lexington av, s s, 113 e Grand av, 25x83. July 6, 1 year. 2,000

Kissam, Edward H. mortgagee to Shepherd J. and Theodore E. Raymond mortgagor. Receipt for $500 on account of mortgage against premises in Hancock st. July 1.

Krackon, Marx to Wolf Finkelstein. Boerum st, n s, 125 e Graham av, 25x100. July 2, 6 months. 200

Kupfer, Sophia widow, Karolina Dittrich, formerly Kupfer, and Josephina Moehringer, formerly Kupfer, to Albert Voltz. Boerum st, s s, 150 w Ewen st, 25x100. July 3, due July 1, 1894, 5 %. 500

Kenny, John to Williamsburgh Savings Bank. Evergreen av, s w s, 75 s e Greene av, 25x100. July 7, 1 year, 5 %. 2,000

Loughran, Michael to Emilie Huber. Broadway, s e cor 5th st, 21x77.8x20.2x82.5; 5th st, e s, 82.5 s Broadway, 18x60.7x18x60.7. July 6, 10 years, 5 %. 31,000

Lyons, Susan T. to The Williamsburgh Savings Bank. Lewis av, e s, 60 n McDonough st, 20x90. July 8, 1 year, 5 %. 1,200

Lewis, Margaretha to Title Guarantee and Trust Co. Hull st, n w cor Stone av. P. M. July 7, 3 years, 5 %. 6,000

Lang, Joseph to Guernsey Sackett, Frank C. Lang, Charles A. Reed and James B. McKewan. Bergen st, n s, 150 w Rockaway av, 20x107.2x20.11x107.2. July 1, 5 years. 1,095

Lang, Martin and Elizabeth his wife to Crescentia M. Treubig. Boerum st, s s, 474.9 e Bushwick av, 25x87.6. June 29, due July 1, 1894, 5 %. 1,300

Lahey, Thomas M. to The South Brooklyn Savings Inst. Smith st, n w cor Bergen st, 20x65. July 6, 1 year, 5 %. 2,000

Lange, John to Maria Sauer. Bushwick av, courtyard line, w s, 48 s Troutman st, runs west 67.10 x south again 9.5 x southeast 38.6 x east 61.6 to courtyard line of Bushwick av, x north 46.10, with all title in courtyard. July 1, 5 years, 5 %. 4,000

Leff, Samuel and Adolf Moskovits to Ernst Eenlaut. Ellery st. P. M. June 27, installs, 5 %. 5,000

Lang, Martin and Elizabeth his wife to Jacob Zimmer. Boerum st, s s, 474.9 e Bushwick av, 25x87.6. June 29, due July 1, 1892, 5 %. 1,000

Lifsbitz, Abram to Fanny wife of Hyman Shapiro. Sutter av. P. M. June 16, installs. 1,112

Loew, Martin to The German Tailors Union No. 2, Brooklyn, E. D. Varet st, s s, 150 w Morrell st, 25x100. July 1, 3 years, 5 %. 4,000

Lydecker, Albert A. to William F. Corwith. Russell st. P. M. July 1, 5 years or installs. 1,300

Lyons, Henry B. to Caroline A. Rushmore. Berkeley pl, s s, 87.2 e 5th av, 54.3x95. July 3, 1 year, 5 %. 1,500

Laing, Donald to Louisa W. Taylor, Boston, Mass. Belmont av, n s, 20 w Montauk av, 20x90. July 2, 3 years. 2,000

Lembik, Louis and Harris to Joseph Morris. Thatford av. P. M. July 1, installs. 900

Lewis, Ellen J. to The Title Guarantee and Trust Co. President st. P. M. June 26, due Nov. 1, 1891. 4,000

Lewis, Jacob to Elizabeth C. wife of John Power. Osborn st. P. M. July 1, installs. 600

Lincoln, Clarence to James D. Rankin and James Ross. Macon st, s s, 22 w Howard av, 12.6x100. June 30, 1 year. 1,000

Same to same. Macon st, s w cor Howard av, 22x100. July 2, 1 year. 2,000

Michel, Leopold to The Title Guarantee and Trust Co. Flushing av. P. M. July 3, due July 7, 1892, 5 %. 2,000

Michel, Leopold to John A. Bachmann. Flushing av, s s, 250 e Nostrand av, 25x100. July 1, 3 years, 5 %. 5,000

Same to Charles Kiehl. Varet st, s s, 225 e Graham av, 25x100. July 1, 3 years, 5 %. 5,000

Same to John A. Bachmann. Flushing av, s s, 225 e Nostrand av, 25x100. July 1, 3 years, 5 %. 5,000

Mallinger, Samuel and Max to Guernsey Sackett, Frank C. Lang, Charles A. Reed and James B. McKewan. Bergen st. P. M. July 1, installs. 500

Mason, Mary E. to Charles A. Thorpe. Thatford av, e s, 148 n Glenmore av, 16x100. June 13, 6 months. 250

McCormick, George W. to Mary E. Dorian. Reid av, w s, 50 n Halsey st, 25x100. July 2, 3 years, 5 %. 8,500

McCormick, George W. to Charles Emmons. Reid av, w s, 50 n Halsey st, 50x100. Sub. to morts. July 2, demand. 6,000

Same to Mary E. Dorian. Reid av, w s, 75 n Halsey st, 25x100. July 2, 3 years, 5 %. 8,500

McMormick, John J. to Theodore Brouwer. Devoe st, s s, 150 w Leonard st, 25x100. July 1, 5 years, 5 %. 5,500

Meredith, Thomas to J. Wyckoff Van Siclen. Belmont av, s s, 25 e Van Sielen av, 25x100. July 1, 1 year. 1,200

Minto, Robert F. to Ellen Connolly. Central av, e s, 95 s Linden st, 19x78.2x13.4x78. Sub. to mort. $4,000. June 25, due July 1, 1892. 700

Moores, Robert L. and Charles A. Le Quesne to George F. Alexander. Broadway, s w s, 74.11 s e Madison st, runs southwest 80.4 x south 30.6 x east 9 x northeast 95.4 to Broadway, x northwest 28. July 6, 2 years. 3,500

Same to same. Broadway, s w cor Madison st, runs west 21.10 x south 48.2 x northeast 49.5 to Broadway, x northwest 18.11. July 6, 2 years. 3,500

Moores, Robert L. and Charles A. Le Quesne to The Henry McShane Mfg. Co. Madison st, s s, 140 e Howard av, 80x100. July 2, notes. 4,421

Same to George F. Alexander. Putnam av, n s, 140 e Howard av, 40x100. July 1, 2 years. 1,000

Many, Ann to Ann Cosgrove. 13th st. P. M. July 1, 5 years, 5 %. 1,000

Martin, Frank P. to Henry Weil. Bergen st, n s, 250 w Buffalo av, 65x107.2. July 2, 1 year. 4,800

Same to same. Same property. July 2, due Jan. 1, 1892. 2,800

Mathis, William to Philip Bohner. 7th st, s w s, 372.10 n w 6th av, 50x100. July 1, 3 years, 5 %. 2,000

Maxwell, John to The Title Guarantee and Trust Co. 9th st, s w cor 7th av, 19.10x72.6. June 26, 2 years, 5 %. 9,500

McCarthy, Bridget wife of Justin J. to The Title Guarantee and Trust Co. Canton st, w s, 93.6 n Willoughby st, 16.5x79.7x17x83. July 2, 3 years. 1,500

Mehling, Philip to Thomas Purcell. Covert st. P. M. July 1, 3 years or installs, 5 %. 1,800

Mentz, Joseph to The German Savings Bank. Flushing av, n e cor Lee av, 25x82.1x51.3x68.10. June 29, due Dec. 1, 1892, 5 %. 1,500

Same to John Auer. Same property. July 1, 3 years, 5 %. 6,500

Meyer, Ludwig to Charles Engert. North Henry st. P. M. Sub. to mort. $1,750. July 1, installs, 5 %. 1,250

Same to Kings County Savings Inst. Same property. P. M. July 1, 1 year, 5 %. 1,750

Miller, Charles A. to Cornelius N. Hoagland. Meserole av, n e cor Russell st; Meserole av, n e cor North Henry st. P. M. July 1, 7 years, 5 %. 12,000

Mills, Margaret wife of James J. to Wilton G. Beny guard. Sophia Beny. 3d av, s w cor 78th st, 54.7x110. June 26, 5 years. 10,000

Morgan, John and Ann his wife to The Greenpoint Savings Bank. Eagle st, s s, 220 e Franklin st, 25x100. July 1, 1 year, 5 %. 2,750

Morrison, Annie M. to Susan Hutchinson. Eckford st. P. M. June 9, due July 1, 1894, 5 %. 1,000

Morrow, Albert and Lizzie R. his wife to William Meynor. Pacific st. P. M. July 3, 3 years, 5 %. 3,000

Moeller, John and Elizabeth his wife to Henry Moeller. Glenmore av. P. M. July 2, 5 years, 5 %. 2,000

Mullen, Peter and Mary A. his wife to Mary wife of Thomas Smith. Shepherd av, e s, 400 s Gay st. P. M. June 10, 5 years, 5 %. 1,000

Markowitz, Herman and Hyman Krantz to Emil Reineking. Chester st. P. M. July 1, installs. 750

Malone, William to Ellen Brady. Verona st. P. M. July 6, 2 years. 400

Martin, Anna wife of Levi V. to Leffert L. Bergen. 4th av, north cor 77th st, 59x100. July 1, 3 years. 5,000

Maass, Carl to William Max. Barbey st, e s, 320 n Hegeman av, 20x100. July 1, 3 years. 1,000

McNamara, John to Henry H. Adams, County Treasurer of Kings. Franklin st, e s, 50 s Oak st, 20x70. July 3, 1 year, 5 %. 3,000

Middleton, Angeline I. wife of Benjamin P. to The Brooklyn Savings Bank. 55th st, n s, 150 w 2d av, 27x100.2. July 1, 1 year, 5 %. 2,000

Meyer, Emma wife of and Henry A. to Theresa H. Baker. Nevins st, e s, 141.3 s Dean st, 18.9x80. July 1, 5 years, 5 %. 2,000

Neil, Sarah A. and Mary E. to Alonzo E. De Ba . Skillman av. P. M. July 8, 1 year, 5 %un 1,500

Same to William E. Valentine. Same property. P. M. July 8, 5 years, 5 %. 2,000

Nicholas, Samuel W. to Sarah N. Nicholson. South 2d st, s s, 103.6 e Bedford av. P. M. July 7, 10 years or installs, 5 %. 2,600

Nielsen, Charles J. to Phebe E. Leverich extrx. Augustus A. Leverich. Broadway. P. M. July 1, 5 years, 5 %. 14,000

Natelson, Abraham to Henry Kinn. Judge st. P. M. July 1, 5 years or installs, 5 %. 6,000

Newland, Sarah C. to Mary E. Fox. Sumner av, e s, 40 s Hart st, 20x100. July 1, 2 years. 215

Nason, Mary E. wife of and Leonard to Louis Wolferz. Lots 37 and 38 plot No. 1 map Garrett Stryker, Gravesend. July 1, 2 years. 2,000

Northridge, William A. and John Flood to Elizabeth Taber et al. exrs. Franklin W. Taber. Sutter av, s s, 25 w Essex st, 28.7x100. July 3, 5 years. 1,800

Oberbeck, Henry to Edward F. Linton. Ashford st. P. M. Sub. to mort. $2,200. July 1, installs. 1,550

Obroez, Charles to Richard J. Murphy. 4th av. P. M. July 2, 1 year. 2,000

Owens, Thomas to Mary E. Hegarty. King st. P. M. July 1; 2 years, 5 %. 500

O'Connell, John A. to Mary E. Little, Washington, D. C. Bay Ridge av, n s, 8 e 1st av, —x—x56x150. July 1, due Dec. 15, 1895. 500

Otterbeck, Julius G. to Christian Hild, New York. South 6th st, s s, 20 w 2d st, 23x84.6x23.1x82.4. July 3, due July 1, 1894, 5 %. 2,500

Opitz, John G. to Hermann Peltz. Hoyt st, e s, 60 s Baltic st, 40x78. July 1, 5 years, 5 %. 9,000

Olmstead, Hannah E. to Jennie S. Conklin. Butler st, s s, 391.4 e Nostrand av, 16.8x100. Building materials. June 15. 900

Olsen, John L. to Henry C. Bull. 20th st, n e s, 240.7 n w 8th av, 15.7x100.2 P. M. Sub. to mort. $1,500. July 4, installs. 900

Peyton, Richard to Rachel M. Gilsey and ano. extrxs. John C. C. Gilsey. Lots 50 and 51 map of land trustees Reformed Dutch Church, Flatbush. July 3, 3 years, installs. 1,600

Pedrosa, Rose to Timothy G. Sellew. Jefferson av, s e s, 293.6 n e Evergreen av, 18x100. July 15, installs, 5 %. 3,300

Peper, George M. to Henry Wessel. Bushwick av. P. M. July 6, 1 year, 5 %. 1,000

Phelan, Mary J. to Leah Hughes. Van Voorhis st, s e s, 412.6 n e Bushwick av, 18.9x100. July 1, 5 years, 5 %. 2,000

Powlson, Peter to Cornelia M. Cammann and ano. exrs. William Cammann. South 1st st, s w s, 25 s e Havemeyer st, 25x100. July 6, 2 years, 5 %. 1,200

Purcell, Thomas to Clarence Lincoln. Macon st. P. M. July 3, due July 1, 1892. 200

Papps, Israel to John Jones. Leonard st, w s, 100 s Nassau av, 19.7x100; Leonard st, w s, 119.7 s Nassau av, runs west 100 x south 5.4 x west 17.9 x east — to 4th st, x north 27.1 to beginning. July 1, 5 years, 5 %. 4,500

Parkhill, Mary wife of and James to Susan Vanderveer. Pulaski st, n s, 87.6 e Nostrand av, 18.9x100. July 1, 2 years, 5 %. 1,000

Paye, Emeline wife of and William I. to The Dime Savings Bank of Brooklyn. Fulton st, s s, 60 w Hanover pl, 20x71.4x20x71.1. July 2, 1 year, 5 %. 20,000

Peterson, Caroline to Catharine Stoothoff. Liberty av, s w cor Hemlock st. P. M. June 29, due July 1, 1894. 2,200

Pettit, Isabelle to Orson W. Sheldon. Knickerbocker av. P. M. April 20, demand. 6,200

Same to same. Same property. P. M. April 20, demand. 7,000

Ray, Samuel to The Title Guarantee and Trust Co. Woodbine st, s e s, 160 s w Knickerbocker av, 20x100. June 29, due July 7, 1892, 5 %. 800

Rehn, Theodor to Catharine Huff. Smith st, n w s, 66.8 n e Dean st, 21.1x100.7x21x100.7. July 7, due July 1, 1894, 5 %. 5,000

Reilly, Patrick F. to George W. Pearsall. 5th av, w s, 25.2 n 47th st, 50x100; 46th st, s s, 300 w 6th av, 40x100.2. June 30, 1 year. 200

Rafferty, Michael mortgagor with William H. Chapman exr. Sam'l Wanser. Extension mortgage. June 24. nom

Rhinehart, Sarah J. wife of and Rutson to The Greenpoint Savings Bank. Eagle st, s s, 245 e Franklin st, 25x100. July 1, 1 year, 5 %. 2,250

Same to The Greenpoint Savings Bank. Graham av, n w cor Sandford st. P. M. June 10, 1 year, 5½ %. 2,500

Roach, Mary widow to Susan Hutchinson. Greenpoint av, s s, 93.9 e Eckford st, runs east 25 x south 35.10 x again south 24 x west 29.6 x north 67.8 to beginning. July 1, 5 years, 5 %. 3,500

Roberts, Henry F. to William A. Roberts. Division av, s s, 87.2 w Wythe av, 20.1x142.6x21.7x132.7. June 17, due July 1, 1901, 5 %. 7,000

Roberts, James G. to Jeremiah Mullen. Eastern Parkway, s e cor Christopher av, 109x100. July 1, due Nov. 6, 1892. 1,200

Same to same. Christopher av, e s, 100 s Eastern Parkway, 50x100. July 1, due Nov. 6, 1892. 1,100

Roberts, James G. to Robert L. Woods, Jr. Belmont av. P. M. July 6, 2 years, 5 %. 2,000

Robertson, Mary L. wife of and Alexander to Mary A. and J. A. Smith and ano. exrs. Dan'l C. Silleck in trust for Cath. J. Silleck. 52d st, s w s, 320 s e 4th av, 40x100.2. June 30, due July 1, 1896, 5 %. 300

Raiesky, Michael to Charlotte Wills. Sumpter st, n s, 25 e Patchen av, 25x100. July 2, 1 year, 5 %. 900

Raymond, Benjamin C. to Lottie N. Palmer. Macon st, n w cor Ralph av, 22x100. July 2, 2 months. 1,000

Same to Bernard Levino, Horatio S. Stewart, Alfred Van Derwenken and George C. Cranford. Same property. July 2, 2 months. 1,550

Same to The Title Guarantee and Trust Co. Same property. July 6, demand. 8,000

Rosenberg, Frank to Mary E. Cook, Newtown, L. I. Stone av. P. M. June 10, installs. 1,000

Ross, Jennie L. to Robert Morgan. 2d st, s w s, 197.10 n w 7th av, 19.8x100. Sub. to mort. $24,000. June 25, demand. 800

Rockel, Henry to Maria Tag. Dodsworth st. P. M. July 1, 5 years, 5 %. 2,500

Same to Louise Hoh. Same property. Sub. to last mort. July 1, 6 years, 5 %. 1,700

Randall, John J. and William G. Miller to The Greenpoint Savings Bank. Manhattan av, w s, 250 s Meserole av, 3 lots, each 25x100. 3 morts., each $10,000. July 1, 1 year, 5 %. 30,000

Rehfeldt, Catherine to Sarah Valentine. Vesta av. P. M. July 1, 3 years. 500

Ringler, Frederick A. to Joseph Shasser. 53d st, n s, 300 w 3d av, 200x100.2. July 1, 3 years, 5 %. 2,000

Rohrs, Wilhelmena to Henry Rohrs. Union st, Nos. 683-689, n s, 237.6 w 4th av, 84x95. Jan. 1, 5 years, 5 %. 6,000

Ross, Jennie L. to Albert G. C. Hahn. 2d st, s w s, 117.10 n w 7th av, 8x100x80x100 (?). Sub. to morts. July 6, 3 months. 1,000

Ruth, Abraham to James G. Roberts. Sackman st. P. M. July 1, 2 years. 1,800

Reineking, Emil to John H. Vanderveer. Lots 193, 220 and 221 map Vanderveer homestead. P. M. July 7, 3 years, 5 %. 500

Rich, Marietta to David S. Beasley. Lexington av. P. M. July 7, 1 year, 5 %. 3,700

Ritterband, Margaretha wife of Frederick to Albert W. Lemcke and John Doscher. 52d st, s w s, 160 s e 3d av, 20x100.2. July 6, due July 1, 1894, 5 %. 1,000

Rudloff, Henry to Mary Powell. Sherman st, Flatbush. P. M. June 15, 3 years, 5 %. 2,000

Scheen, Caspar to Fritz Breitenstein. Hegeman av and Williams av. P. M. July 1, installs, 5 %. 1,000

Schmitt, John to John F. Battermann. Throop av, s w cor Whipple st. P. M. July 1, installs, 5 %. 6,000

Schneider, Philip to George Collins. Willoughby av, n w s, 225 n e Central av, 25x100. July 1, 3 years or installs. 1,000

Schoenig, Philip H. to Franz Franz. 41st st. P. M. July 1, installs, 5 %. 2,000

Schultz, Anna to Joseph Maurer. Stagg st. P. M. July 1, 3 years, 5 %. 1,600

Schwindt, Philipp to Robert J. Whittemore. Oakland st, e s, 125 s Nassau av, 25x100. July 1, 3 years, 3,000

Sibley, Albert to Andrew D. Baird. Quincy st, s s, 287.6 w Throop av, 187.6x100. Builder's loan. July 3, demand. 36,000

Same to Joseph P. Puels. Same property. July 3, demand. 25,000

Siminowetche or Simonavetcke, Simeon to Margaretha Zoebelein. Moore st. P. M. July 1, 4 years, 5 %. 1,300

Simon, Semche to Friederich Stroh. Varet st. P. M. June 30, 5 years, 5 %. 2,400

Same to James A. Ross. Moore st, s s, 275 e Graham av, 25x100. July 1, 3 years, 5 %. 7,000

Smith, Herbert S. to Dwight E. Rogers. Blake av. P. M. July 3, 2 years, 5 %. 9,500

Smith, Maurice W. to The Flatbush Co-operative Savings and Loan Assoc. Lot 9 map Linden terrace, Flatbush. June 22, installs. 11,500

Spencer, Albert E. to The East Brooklyn Savings Inst. Bleecker st, n w s, 250 n e Evergreen av, 25x100. June 29, installs. 4,000

Staats, Jacob, Jr., to Jacob Staats, Sr. Park av, s s, 225 e Sumner av, 25x100. July 1, 5 years, 5 %. 2,300

Stewart, Robert to Silas A. Condict. 24th st. P. M. July 1, 1 year. 250

Stoiber, Louis to Herbert C. Smith. Osborn st, e s, 150 n Glenmore av. P. M. June 29, installs. 350

Same to same. Osborn st, n s, 175 n Glenmore av. P. M. June 29, installs. 350

Stroh, Frederick to Karl Enderle. Ellery st, n s, 306 6 e Broadway, 25x100. July 2, due July 1, 1896, 5 %. 3,000

Sumner, Vina A. to Edward M. Townsend exr. Belinda R. Townsend. 3d st, s s, 142 e Smith st. P. M. June 30, due July 1, 1894, 5 %. 3,250

Same to same. 3d st, s s, 161 e Smith st. P. M. June 30, due July 1, 1894, 5 %. 3,250

Sweeney, Elizabeth A. wife of and Job L. to Mary D. Nicot. South 1st st, n e s, 138 s e Keap st, 17x77. June 29, 3 years. 1,700

Sweet, Esther to Christian A. Keppler, Johnson st. P. M. July 1, 3 years, 5 %. 3,000

Scheuing, Clara to John Drescher, Jr. Rodney st. P. M. June 30, 5 years, 5 %. 5,000

Seidenstacker, Henry to Nette Wider, Jersey City. Atlantic av. P. M. July 3, installs, 5 %. 7,000

Shepard, William H. to Margaretta wife of Frederick Ritterbush. 52d st. P. M. Sub. to mort $2,000. June 6, due July 1, 1894. 1,000

Same to Elizabeth Stillwell. 52d st. P. M. June 26, due July 1, 1894, 5 %. 2,000

Steffens, John to John N. Wirth. Ellery st, s s, 250 w Throop av, 25x38 4x38.4x52.8. July 1, 5 years, 5 %. See Conveys. 1,800

Stern, Hannah to Leopold Michel. Bushwick av, e s, 44.11 n Varet st, 29.10x110.9x25.2x127.7. July 6, 5 years, 5 %. 2,350

Struse, Christina wife of and John to Heissenbuttel, Nearing & Co. Nostrand av, s e cor Fennimore st, 40x100, Flatbush. July 2, 1 year, 5 %. 548

Sutphin, Edwin J. to Hazel Banker. Eckford st. P. M. June 15, due July 3, 1893, 5 %. 1,500

Schadowsky, Henry A. to Bertha Schmitt. Narrows av, w s, 120 n 74th st, 80x100. July 1, 2 years 1,000

Schoner, George, Jr., and Maggie his wife to George Schoner. Willoughby av, n s, 100 e Evergreen av, 25x121.6x28.4x125.11. July 1, 8 years, 4 %. 2,500

Schork, Karolina to Michael Fritz. East New York av, n s, 149.2 w Rockaway av, 25x— to Prospect pl, x 25x93.11. June 30, due July 1, 1894, 5 %. 200

Schwartz, Harris to Solomon and Dora Wolff. Belmont av. P. M. Sub. to mort. $3,000. July 1, installs. 1,400

Scott, James to John Jones. Norman av, s s, 25 w Diamond st, 25x95. July 1, 5 years, 5 %. 5,000

Sellner, Michael to Bella Jonas. Meserole st, n s, 125 w Lorimer st. P. M. 1,000

Simons, Orrin W., Sarah K. and Kittie R. to Cyrus D. Reid. Nostrand av, w s, 46 n Park pl, 20x100. Feb. 24, 1 year. 300

Simmons, John C to John A. Bliss. Dean st, s s, 165 w Brooklyn av, 20x107.2. July 6, 2 years. 3,500

Sittig, Lena wife of Frank to Christiana V. Henry. Putnam av, s s, 390 e Marcy av, 20x100. July 1, 1 year. 2,500

Shapiro, Fanny wife of Hyman to Gilbert S. Thatford. Rockaway av, e s, 131.6 s Sutter av. July 1, installs. 900

Same to same. Same property. July 1, installs. 2,000

Slattery, James and Margaret his wife to Jacob Worth and Vincent A. Strawson. Lots 314-317 inclusive Worth & Strawson property. P. M. July 3, 3 years, 5 %. 280

Spor, Minnie to John Brunnemer and James L. Bennett. Stockton st, s s, 175 w Lewis av, 25x100. June 24, due May 1, 1893, 5 %. 675

Squires, Anson to The Citizen's Co-operative Building and Loan Assoc. Stillwell av, south cor 86th st, runs south 233.4 to Av N, x east 111.3 x northeast 83 to 86th st, x northwest 221.10, Gravesend. June 15, installs. 2,250

Stackhouse, Elizabeth wife of Charles R. to Sarah A. Baum. Atlantic av, s s, 250 w Stone av, 50x100. July 1, 3 years. 1,500

Steiner, Solomon to Maria A. Hartung. Van Brunt st. P. M. Sub to mort. $4,000. July 2, installs, 5 %. 4,000

Steiner, Albert to Charles N. Peed. Berkeley pl. P. M. May 1, 3 years, 5 %. 5,000

Stryker, Gerrit to John B. Meyenborg, Jr. Main road, n e cor Stryker av, 230.7x312.6x218.5x304.6, Flatbush. July 1, 2 years, 5 % 1,500

Sutter, Frank to The East New York Savings Bank. Liberty av, n w cor Schenck av, 74.7x100. July 1, 1 year. 8,000

Scott, Niels S. to Robert Hunter. Halsey st, n s, 463 5 w Reid av, 17.9x100. July 6, 3 years, 5 %. 4,000

Sherwood, Samuel T. to Sarah R. Hubbard. 47th st, n s, 100 e 4th av, 20x100.2. July 3, 3 years, 5 %. 3,000

Same to Jane A. Bennett and ano. exrs. Cornelius Bennett. 47th st, n s, 120 e 4th av, 20x100.2. July 3, 3 years, 5 %. 2,500

South Brooklyn Railroad and Terminal Co. to Jonathan K. Gapen trustee. 38th st, s s, 333.7 w 8th av, runs west to city line, x south or southwest to 39th st, x west to point 249 w 8th av, x north or northwest to beginning. Agreement that above property is included in mortgages to parties of 2d part. June 30. nom

Steingotter, Phillip to Jacob Kiefer. Bushwick av, s w s, 107 n w Van Voorhis st, 18x75. July 1, 3 years. 4,000

Sutherland, Andrew M. to Mary W. Smith. Thatford av, w s, 100 s Eastern Parkway, 25x100.1. July 8, 1 year. 250

Totten, Gilson J. to The Williamsburgh Savings Bank. Kent av, e s, 92 n South 8th st, 23.8x102.1x22.10x98.1. July 8, 1 year, 5 %. 8,000

The Lidgerwood Mfg. Co. to Mary L. Libby. Dikeman st. P. M. June 27, due July 1, 1896. gold, 14,000

The Reformed Protestant Dutch Church of Bushwick to The Williamsburgh Savings Bank. Bushwick av, w s, 125.9 n North 2d st, runs north 368 6 x west 199.11 to Humboldt st, x south 27 9 x again south 125.6 x southeast 207.6; Humboldt st, e s, 122.1 n Maspeth av, runs northeast to point 204 n North 2d st, x northwest 119.2 x north 6 x southwest 6.11 to st, x south 124.5. July 3, 1 year, 5 %. 5,000

Thurber, Julia C. widow to The Mutual Life Ins. Co. of New York. Cumberland st, e s, 397 n Lafayette av, 25x100. Already mortgaged to party of 2d part. July 1, 1 year. 500

Tritschler, Caroline to Elizabeth Decker. Jefferson st. P. M. July 1, 5 years. 3,800

Teale, Mary E. widow to Mary F. wife of Charles W. Morro. Bridge st, e s, 25 s Myrtle av, 25x75.2. July 3, 1 year, 5 %. 2 600

Turner, Clara to Edward F. Linton. Warwick st. P. M. Sub. to mort. $2,200. July 1, installs. 2,000

Vincent, Ladowick H. to Alice R. Skidmore, Jamaica, L. I. Lewis av, e s, 40 n Hancock st, 20x80. July 6, due Nov. 1, 1894. 1,600

Same to same. Lewis av, e s, 60 n Hancock st, 20x80. July 6, due Nov. 1, 1894. 1,600

Von Hasseln, John to Louise Kroger widow. Sumpter st, n w cor Howard av, 25x100. July 1, 5 years, 5 %. 2,500

Van Saun, Emma A. to Carrie A. Bushnell. Steuben st, e s, 108 s De Kalb av, 22.4x100. July 1, 1 year, 5 %. 1,500

Vollmer, Edward R. to William Arrowsmith. Elton st, w s, 250 n Dumont av, 150x84. June 27, due July 1, 1893. 725

Volk, Aaron B. to Thomas H. Rodman trustee Eleanor Kip. Moore st, n s, 125 w Ewen st, 25x100. July 3, 3 years, 5 %. 5,500

Von Graff, Roderick to The Hardwood Decorative Co. 2d st, n s, 90.9 w 7th av, 20x100. June 20, 3 months. 2,000

Weilbrenner, Philip to Adam Schneider. Elm st, s s, 150 w St. Nicholas av, 20x100. July 3, due July 1, 1894, 5 %. 300

Wolf, Benjamin and David Stein to Jacob Harris. Seigel st. P. M. July 6, installs. 1,500

Wright, Charles H. to Mary Grogan. Partition st, s w s, 150 s e Richards st, 25x100. June 30, due July 1, 1894. 1,000

Weber, Anna to Theodore F. Jackson. Stockholm st. P. M. May 15, due July 1, 1894, 5 %. 7,500

Weber, Gottlob to George Covert. Hamburg. av. P. M. June 22, due July 1, 1896, 5 %. 4,100

Weintraub, Louis to Elizabeth C. wife of John Power. Osborn st. P. M. July 1, installs. 600

Widmann, Frederick to Frederic B. Elliott trustee for Pauline. Lawrence st, w s, 275 n Willoughby st, w s, 25x107.6. July 1, 5 years. 8,400

Will, Matilda to Thomas Pitbladdo. 17th st. P. M. July 1, 5 years, 5 %. 4,000

Witzel, Charles to Ellen McLaughlin. Charles pl. P. M. July 2, 3 years, 5 %. 1,000

Wolf, Joseph to The Germania Savings Bank. Atlantic av, s s, 185 e Bond st, 22x80. July 2, 1 year, 5 %. 3,500

Wolff, Solomon to The East New York Savings Bank. Belmont av, s s, 25 e Osborn st, 25x100. July 1, 1 year. 3,000

Wehmhoefer, John H. to Jacob Waldeck. Frost st, n s, 400 w Kingsland av, 62.6x100. July 1, 3 years, 5 %. 2,400

Wehr, William G. to Henry Waterman. Evergreen av, w s, 75 s Schaeffer st, 25x100. July 1, 3 years, 5 %. 3,500

Same to same. Evergreen av, w s, 50 s Schaeffer st, 25x100. July 1, 3 years, 5 %. 3,500

Weidmann, Paul to Margaretha S. Hulsberg. Wythe av, s w cor North 1st st, 50x83.5x40x85.1. July 6, 2 years, 5 %. 10,000

Weinberger, Bernhard to Morris Brodoosky. Thatford av. P. M. June 30, 4 years. 300

Wilson, Arthur H. to Kunigunde Buhn. Livonia av, n s, 50 e Osborn st, 25x100. July 1, 3 years. 1,300

Same to same. Livonia av, n s, 25 e Osborn st, 25x100. July 1, 3 years. 1,300

White, George E. to William Grandy. Lexington av, n s, 240 w Marcy av, 20x100. July 1, 1 year. 1,500

Yolleberer, Hannah to Elizabeth Augusty. Thatford av. P. M. July 2, 3 years. 2,000

Zahn, George to The East Brooklyn Savings Inst. Lexington av. P. M. June 30, installs. 5,000

MORTGAGES---ASSIGNMENTS.

NEW YORK CITY.

JULY 2 TO 9—INCLUSIVE.

Alexander, George F. to James H. Watson and James H. Pittinger, of Watson & Pittinger, Brooklyn. $5,000

Auld, Thomas to Thomas E. McLaughlin, Anthony M. Clegg and Jerome E. Richards, of McLaughlin, Clegg & Co. nom

Barth, John C. to James A. Deering. 5,000

Same to same. 3,000

Browning, Edward F. to Alexander Maitland. 2,000

Blinn, Henriette extrx. Christian Blinn to The Blinn Memorial Methodist Episcopal Church of the City of New York. 9,800

Beer, Louis and Michael Schaffner to Louis Schaffner & Kunigunda his wife. 2,500

Bannen, John to Emilio J. Murray. 3,000

Barnard, Hannah to Julia Whitchurch. nom

Beinecke, Bernhard to Joseph Hesdorfer. 12,615

Brennan, Thomas S. exr. and trustee Patrick Brennan to Catharine Brennan. 2,045
Bridge, John to William F. Bridge. 2,500
Bridge, William F. to Virginia R. Prime, Brandon, Vt. 1,500
Briggs, Amos D. exr. William S. Briggs to Alexander Forsyth. nom
Buttenwieser, Leah to Jonas Weil and Bernhard Mayer. 25,000
Becker, Jacob and Anna his wife to Marks Levin. 4,250
Cullen, Stratford J. to Thomas J. Falls. 2 assigns. nom
Cain, Joseph H. and Lillie T. Yoran to Benjamin F. Gerding. 800
Cochran, William F., Yonkers, N. Y., to The St. Johns Riverside Hospital. 10,153
Connoly, Alice I. to Mary wife of Christian Betz. 2,500
Cohen, Israel M. to Solomon Bachrach. 3,500
Dingfelder, Peter and Adolf Libko to Francis P. Kurtz, Jersey City, N. J. 800
Davis, Eugene H., Montreal, Can., to Cecil A. Marks. 7,000
Erslew, Oline and Elof Nielsen to Edwin S. Updike, Sr. 750
Franklin, Morris to Sarah F. wife of Albert Deutsch. 3,300
Frank, Herman to Pietro Altieri. nom
Francis, Isabella G. to Adeline I. Phillips. 8,122
Graham, Malcom to The Equitable Life Assur. Soc. of United States. 9,000
Geier, John J. and Martharetha his wife to George Wiegand. 2,050
Gerding, Benjamin F. to David Webster exr. Caroline Webster. nom
Giles, William O. exr. Elizabeth Giles to Florence M. Giles, Paris, France. nom
Same to Helene E. Giles, Paris, France. nom
Gorsch, Sophia to James Gribble. 2,000
Gruenstein, Heyman and Esther to Henry W. Berg. 5,000
Goodrich, Cornelia P. to John L. Hamilton. 4,000
Guerber, Emma, Nyack, N. Y., to Frank A. Wilcox. 2 assigns. nom
Gerry, Elbridge T. exr. Robert J. Livingston to Louisa M. wife of Elbridge T. Gerry. 2 assigns., each $4,000. 8,000
Same to same. 2 assigns., each $3,500. 7,000
Gusthal, Leopold and ano. exrs. and trustees Edward Ridley to Frederic J. Middlebrook. 9,047
Hickey, John to The Mount Morris Bank. 5,500
Hall, Elise B., Santa Barbara, Cal., to Anna H., Ella P. and John R. Wilde. 22,122
Hershfield, Levi N. to Henry M. Leipziger. 3,500
Harris, Sigmund and Albert, of Harris Bros., to Lippman Toplitz. 27,500
Jackson, Jerome A. to Edwin Shuttleworth. nom
Same to same. nom
Johnson, Eliza J. to John A. Aspinwall and ano. trustees of Katharine A. Kingsland. 9,500
Jencks, Francis M. to Alexander and Robert L. Maitland trustees for Eliza L. Dwight. 5,100
Jarmulowsky, Sender to Samuel Weil. 3,080
King, Letitia to Hyman Schnitzer. 3,000
Kerr, Samuel to Samuel K. McGuire. 19,000
Kuppenheimer, Sophia to Jonas Weil and Bernhard Mayer. consid. omitted
Kearney, Rosetta M. to Dennis M. Moran. nom
Key, Fanny D. formerly Jones, Colorado, to William K. MacLaury. 13,750
Landon, Charles G. and ano. exrs. and trustees Benjamin H. Hutton to Adele Hutton, Marquise de Portes. 19,000
Levy, Barnett and Louis to Louis Lese and Morris Goldstein. 3,250
Levy, Louis and Morris W. Monsky to Louis Wisansky. 3,250
Libman, Meyer to Charles Thomson. 3,067
Lyon, Wesley G. exr. Gilbert A. Lyon to Emma F. Flanagan. 2,576
Mayer, Sophia to Fanny Bach. 5,000
Middlebrook, Frederic J., Brooklyn, to B. Anna R. Seymour. 2,512
Same to Sarah E. Woodbury, Bayside, L. I. 24,696
Middlebrook, Frederic J., Brooklyn, to Thomas C. T. Crain. 6,019
Miller, Eugene D. to Smith Ely. 1,500
Moore, William exr. Henry S. Moore to Marietta Norton. 5,000
Morrison, David M. exr. James M. Morrison to David M. Morrison, Brooklyn. 15,097
MacLaury, William K. to Harriet D. Potter. 13,750
Mount Morris Bank to Russell Sage. 6,000
Mochrie, Robert to Robert Deely & Co nom
Mayer, Fredericke to Eliza Guggenheimer. nom
Martin, John J. to David Stern. 5,068
Newman, Jacob M. to William Hall's Sons. 2 assigns. nom
Nicoll, William G., Babylon, L. I., to John W. Somarindyck, Glen Cove, L. I. 8,640
Newman, Adolph to Theodore Bittermann. 2,050
Norton, Marietta to Anthony Barrett, Brooklyn. 9,000
Oothout, Edward trustee Maria J. Bowen dec'd to Julia C. Oothout. 5,000
Orr, Alexander E., Brooklyn, to Agnes W. Inness. 4,000
Redmond, Margaret F. to Michael Redmond. nom
Rosendorff, Morris to Isaac Shiman. nom
Ryer, Samuel and ano. admrs. of Mary J. Ryer to Abbie E. Wille. 716
Rothstein, Abraham to Mitchell Hershfield. 4,000
Ryan, Martin exr. Catharine Maher to Patrick Maher legatee of Catharine Maher. nom
Roosevelt, James trustee of Rebecca H. Roosevelt to J. Roosevelt Roosevelt, Hyde Park, N. Y. nom
Schreyer, John to William J. Fields. 2,000
Smith, William W., Oyster Bay, L. I., to Henry de F. Weekes. 3,000
Smith, Mary B., Brooklyn to Mary T. Thain. 1,500
Striker, Mary H. extrx. George W. Striker to George W. Striker. 8,000
Schaeffler, Peter to Catherine Springer. 14,500
Same to same. 8,500
Schlotterbeck, Philip J. exr. Veronicka Graf to George Grossmann. 4,000
Schmidt, Elizabeth to Sophia Beaudel. 2,200
Shapiro, Morris to Sigmund Kurtz. 3,000
Sherwood, Charlotte, Weehawken, N. J., to James H. Alexander. 4,000
Spellissey, Anne, Union, N. J., to Charlotte Sherwood, Weehawken, N. J. 4,000
Stiger, John S. to Charles Meyerhoff. consid omitted
Stone, Sumner R. and ano. trustees Jesse Stone dec'd to Nannie S. Heacock, Ilion, N. Y. 9,075
Same to Mary M. Stone. 8,067
Seifert, Annette C. to Randolph Guggenheimer and Isaac and Samuel Untermyer. 8,337
Tyson, William H. H. admr. Susan M. Tyson to Susan M. Pooley, Brooklyn. 3,183
The Farmers' Loan and Trust Co. to George J. Schermerhorn. nom
The Equitable Life Assurance Soc. of the United States to Charles F. Wildey admr. Jane A. Wildey. 17,000
The Equitable Life Assur. Soc. of the U. S. to Walter D. Stuart, Brooklyn. 12,000
The Lawyers' Title Insurance Co. of New York to Frank T. King and ano. trustees Katharine A. Rockwell dec'd. 17,066
Title Guarantee and Trust Co. to Martha Nordlinger. 27,000
Same to The National Savings Bank of Albany. 65,000
Same to The Excelsior Savings Bank. 20,000
Same to Mary T. and Elisabeth V. Cockroft. 10,000
Same to The National Savings Bank of Albany. 20,000
Title Guarantee and Trust Co. to John W. Somarindyck and ano. admrs. Jarvis Frost. 7,000
Title Guarantee and Trust Co. to The American Employers' Liability Ins. Co. 6,000
Valentine, Moses and Jacob Rabinowitz to Marks Rinaldo. 6,134
Van Dyke, Clarence A., Princeton, N. J., to Charles F. Aukamp. nom
Van Reypen, Nellie C. to Willard S. Clark, Brooklyn. 1,500
Williamson, Smith to Mary A. and Mary E. Van Zandt. 3,500
Wolf, Abraham et al. exrs. and trustees Schaul Bach to Deborah and Benjamin Bach. 2,019
Same to same. 5,169
Wechsler, David to Isaac Bitterman. nom
Weil, Jonas and Bernhard Mayer to Sophia Kuppenheimer. consid. omitted
Wall, Charles to John Claven. 1,750

KINGS COUNTY.

JULY 2 TO 8—INCLUSIVE.

Amann, Anton to Anthoney Klein. $1,400
Alexander, George F. to Maud P. Nelson. 3,500
Same to Maud P. Nelson. 3,500
Alderton, Marion F. to John Williamson. 10,750
Brodoosky, Morris to Hannah Friedlander. 150
Baldwin, Fanning J. to Stephen Baldwin. 200
Barclay, James S. trustee Eliza B. Howell dec'd to Richard L. Howell. 2,521
Bogart, Peter S. and Charles A. Clark exrs. Elizabeth Bogart to Mary S. Clark. 6,000
Baas, Wilhelmine to Augusta Tarnow. 500
Baas, Bernard, Jr., to same. 500
Baas, Lena to same. 500
Bond, Charles F. to James Lane. 300
Brown, Herbert R to Jennie L. Brown. 5 000
Bryan, Mary A. to D. P. Fielder. 200
Bailey, Frank to Julia Young. 15,000
Beasley, David S. to George McLeon. consid. omitted
Berg, Josephine to Adolph and Carrie Berg. 900
Boelkow, Charles to Martin F. Lindhorn. 3,700
Brunn, Michael to Amalie Gesele. 1,400
Conlon, John to Charles Nelson. 600
Cooke, William G. to Fream Lorillard guard. Francis D. Sheldon. 410
Casternack, Adolph to James G. Robents. 1,500
Doering, Philip to Charles Hoyler. 875
Denyse, William T. to Harriet D. Denyse. 1,500
Same to William T. Denyse. 1,500
Drake, John J. to George S. Ingraham. 150
Eden, Frederick F. to Eva Wiegel. 1,200
Feldman, Israel to Jacob Paskusz. nom
Finkeldey, Henry guard. Eliza Finkeldey to Eliza Finkeldey. nom
Fuchs, Joseph to Edward J. Hauck. 2,000
Ferris, Morris P. to Elizabeth M. Mills extrx. William Mills. 2,020
Garrettson, Francis T. trustee Elizabeth A. Gloucester to Adelaide Rice. 6,884
Gately, Catharine C. and John Smith, of Gately & Smith, to John C. Provost. 1890. 400
German-American Real Estate Title Guarantee Co. to Augelina A. Henderson. 5,000
Heatley, George W. to Josephine Canal, Astoria. 500
Hein, Ferdinand R. to Maria T. Hein. 1,500
Hutchinson, Horace F. to Catharine Hollmann. 3,000
Halstead, Isaac to Levi A. Fuller. 5,000
Hoagland, Cornelius N. to Ella Collins. 2,500
Hansell, Elizabeth A. to Harriet V. Groat. 155
Ingraham, William M. to Julia E. Brick. 8,000
Jelliffe, William M., James Cruikshank and Charles E. Tuthill to The Brooklyn Teachers' Aid Assoc. nom
Johnson, Peter to Virginia A. Kleine. 3,000
Kathe, Louise to Clemens and Philipp Wecker. 2,500
Same to same. 2,000
Kidd, Adelaide L. to Rebecca Stemmermann. 3,000
Kurtschinsky, Haris to Isaac Cohn and Leo Katz. 1,500
Kouwenhoven, Geoege committee Freelove J. Corteiyou to Thomas Edwards. 900
Kent, Richard W. individ. and exr. Ellan L. Kent to Abel Crook exr., &c., Samuel H. Crook. 6,725
Lockwood, Mary E. to George R. Lockwood and ano. trustess Roe Lockwood. 2,749
Lawrence, Jane B. to Nannette Marks. 1,000
Libby, Mary L. to Amos R. Eno. 14,000
Lincoln, Clarence to Morris Isaacs. 500
Leonard, James S. to Anna G. Welton, Boston, Mass. 1,175
Lowell, Sidney V. to William M. Dean. 3,500
McNally, James to Marie E. L. Werner. 1,010
Morgan, Ann to Alfred Stuckey. 1,500
Martin, Robert exr. and trustee Daniel Marley to Robert Martin. 13,000
McLoughlin, Edmund, Jr., exr. Edmund McLoughlin to Samuel Blume. 3,000
Montague, George exr. William Underhill to trustees of the Fund for Aged and Infirm Clergymen of the Protestant Episcopal Church, New York. 4,829
Mowbray, Edward H. to James McLaren. 1,200
Nevins, Louise K. to Title Guarantee and Trust Co. 2,000
Nelson, Charles to David E. Meeker. 600
Perry, Chauncy exr. Jabez Williams to Albert L. Perry. 1,517
Puels, Joseph P. to Thomas T. Barr. 25,000
Parsons, Charles H. to James S. Bailey and ano. exrs. Solomon Freeman. 12,500
Pilcher, Joseph M. to Nora V. D. wife of John S. Griffith. 575
People's Trust Co. to German-American Real Estate Title Guarantee Co. 5,000
Payson, Samuel C. to Anna M. Payson. nom
Roberts, James G. to Emma Buckley. 1,500
Reid, Cyrus D. to Louisa A. Crane. 300
Reeve, Catherine to Edward Claussen. 1,250
Robinson, Catherine to Wilhelmine Wils. 2,000
Robinson, David L. to John Dill, Jr. 150
Smith, Mary W. to Herman F. Koepke. 800
Smith, Mary W. to Lucy L. Chapman. 1,600
Schreiber, Charles and Herman Kinzler to John N. Greiner. 1,500
Sedlmeir, August to Karl J. Dewald. 2,000
Same to same. 2,000
Stewart, Horatio S. and Bernard Levino to Grace Hunter. 800
Stroh, Friederich to Karl Enderle. 2,400
Schmidt, Catharine E. to Eva and John Kramer. 412
Shapiro, Fanny to Gilbert S. Thatford. 1,112
Stearns, John M. exr. Sarah I. Stearns to Charles B. Davis. 1,000
Stuchfield, Armstrong to Walter A. Stuchfield. 600
Schafer, John to Emma Brickman. 1,450
Stone, Sumner R. and ano. trustees Jessie Stone to Elizabeth G. Walker. 6,050
Same to Seth G. Heacock. 2,722
Same to same. 2,622
The Board of Education of the Reformed Church in America to Giles H. Mandeville. 5,000
The Blythebourne Improvement Co. to William C. Pye. 400
Thorpe, Charles A. to Henry H. Thorpe. 550
Thorpe, Henry H. to The East River Lead Co. nom
Title Guarantee and Trust Co. to Charles Emmons. 3,500
Same to same. 2,750
Same to Robert A. Ryons. 2,000
Same to The Franklin Trust Co. trustees for Ellen M. Blackwell. 450
Same to Catharine Colvill. 5,000
Same to Edwin P. Selpho. 5,000
Same to Sarah MacPherson. 3,000
Same to Zacheus Bergen et al. exrs., &c., Robert A. Robertson. 10,000
Same to Charles F. W. Aukamp. 1,500
Same to Christina Wackerhagen. 2,000
Same to Michael J. Garvey. 3,000
Same to Horatio G. Meriok exr. Edward A. Whaley. 7,000
Same to William M. Ingraham. 9,500
Tower, Elizabeth C. wife of John to Herbert C. Smith. 600
Underhill, Benjamin T. to Phebe Carpenter. 2,500
Van Dyke, Clarence A. to Charles F. Aukamp. nom
Van Tuyl, Mary B. to Herbert C. Smith. 1,400
Van Winkle, Charles B. exr. Susan H. Campbell to Sarah E. Bussell. 4,000
Von Glan, Henry to Henrietta G. Von Glahn. 1,500
Voorhees, Jane B. to Ella Collins. 2,000
Van Brunt, Amelia to Julius and Martha Noll. 1,000
Voorhees, Cornelia et al. exrs. Jacobus I. Voorhees to John A. Lott, Jr. 300
Whiting, Clara and ano. exrs. Howard Whiting to Franklin Whiting. 6,500
Weisgerber, Phipp to Robert Plant. 1,000
Wyckoff, William F. exr. Jacob S. Wyckoff to Edward F. Linton. 500
Same to same. 600

West Brooklyn Land and Improvement Co. to A. C. Bournonville, Philadelphia, Pa. 2,000
Willets, John T. admr. Lydia T. Post to Edward Claussen. 2,000
Wils, Andrew to Henry Schoenbals. 2,500
Williamsburgh Savings Bank to Adelaid L. Kidd. nom
Young, William to Theodore E. and George W. Green. 1,000

JUDGMENTS.

In these lists of judgments the names alphabetically arranged, and which are first on each line, are those of the judgment debtor. The letter (D) means judgment for deficiency (*) means not summoned. (†) signifies that the first name is fictitious, real name being unknown. Judgments entered during the week, and satisfied before day of publication, do not appear in this column, but in list of Satisfied Judgments.

NEW YORK CITY.

July

7 Allen, William S—Hempstead Bank. $398 03
8 Ackerman, John E—A E Hoffman... 107 59
8 Aims, Alfred C—Louis Bergdoll Brewing Co... 329 67
8 Allison, Nathaniel—O H Meyer... 1,030 22
9 Allen, William S—F L Moore... 550 00
9 Anglim, Thomas A—Francis Higgins, recvr... 734 13
10 Alcott, Edmond C—Gilbert Morrison. 269 38
10 Ambs, John—Simon Hatch... 336 65
3 Buchanan, William C—A C Haynes.. 760 02
6 Baum, Louis—Joseph Fallert Brewing Co (Lim)... 88 71
6 Barnes, Jacob John—J W Binney.... 19 75
6 Bloomingdale, Joseph F—C W Logeling... 137 98
6 Boughton, Edward De R—Metropolitan Telephone and Telegraph Co... 28 50
6 Bennett, James P—Eppens, Smith & Wilmann Co (Lim)... 2,114 46
6 Bates, Charles R—F W Devoe... 142 33
7 Baur, August—Susan D Roberts..... 1,217 64
7 Blauvelt, Howard E—Hemstead Bank 398 03
7†Bell, Clara—William De Mott... 76 72
7 Brown, Ezra—N Y Press Co (Lim)... 136 30
7 Brady, James B—Edward Behrendt.. 26 82
8 Bocock, John Paul—John Wannmaker... 183 99
8 Behlmer, John F—Bradley & Currier Co (Lim)... 438 67
8 Brooks, Julius—Albert Blumenthal.. 2,337 36
8 the same——Julius Stein... 694 35
9 Burbank, Samuel—M J Biggane..... 344 09
9 Babcock, Edward B—Schuylkill & Lehigh Valley Railroad Co... costs 101 23
9 Betts, Frederick W—R E Leavitt.... 95 55
9 Barratt, George G—John Bernard.... 368 43
9 Brand, Segmund—Michael Smart ... 383 73
9 Buxton, William H—People State N Y 7,500 00
10 Burr, Osmer S—Howard Thornton.... 260 43
10 Barnes, Oliver W—Edward Vaugham 167 27
10 Byk, Morris—E G Byrnes... 427 25
10 Biesinger, Charles—Charles Wood.... 106 07
10 Brush, Thomas H—E H Raynolds.... 327 88
3 Cohen, Charles—H I Durbach, exr... 354 44
3 Clark, Joseph—J T McDowell... 115 00
3 Cooper, William—G H Stetson... 1,733 06
3 Cusack, John H—Francis Higgins, recvr... 136 61
3 Curry, George W—Mark Goodwin... 173 70
6 Camp, W Stanley—Anna Goetzel.... 43 17
6 Cook, George—Annie E Otto... 96 01
6 Coogan, Matthew—Thomas Farrell... 155 43
6 Caguey, William T—J J Martin, comm'r... costs 104 85
6 Conkling, John R—A H Colver... 261 61
7 Coles, Charles N—J C Nugent... 148 56
7†Carl, Adam—Frederick Sturz... 75 11
7 Clear, John—T C Lyman... 303 55
7 Cutter, Chester G—Hammond Type Writer Co... 31 70
7 Conlan, James F—R H Howard... 93 98
7†Cole, James A—S M Riker... 518 52
8†Carter, Mary—Henry Wagner... 117 50
8 Corey, Edwin H—R C Rudd... 4,628 42
8 Collins, Samuel—J S Underhill 80 45
9 Carle, James—Lizzie M Barnett... 150 19
9 Conlon, John J—D D Brinckerhoff... 86 54
9 Clemens, F M—F T Hempstead... 159 50
9 Curtis, John J—Francis Higgins, recvr... 734 1°
9 Cummings, John—J J Mathews. ... 197 74
9 Clay, William F—S T Knapp... 122 57
9 Cohen, Bryon W—People State N Y.. 7,500 00
9 Carroll, Robert F—John Alburger.... 297 36
9 Carey, John J—J H Heroy... 325 86
10 Craighead, John P—Brooklyn City R R Co... 642 82
10 Collins, Samuel—J S Underhill... 1,448 21
10 Cantaluppi, Henry—Elbano Spinnetti. 443 67
10 Coleman, Robert H—Beals Railway Brake Co... 333 31
3 Dowd, William B—Joseph Park. 498 36
3 Davis, Alva E—G H Stetson... 1,738 06
3 Downey, Charles—Mark Goodwin.... 173 70
6 Donovan, Nora—Margaret Nix... 450 36
6 Degener, Frederick L—Mary B Harmon... 203 87
6 Downey, Charles—August Jacob..... 164 06
6 Donnell, Raymond L—M Crane Electrotyping and Stereotyping Co..... 207 09
7†Darling, William H—John Baehr.... 120 00
7 Duff, John S—Mayor, Lane & Co.... 175 24
8 Diamond, Lazarus—William Ulmer.. 867 00
8 De Forest, William H, Jr—C B Keogh Mfg Co... 535 28
9 Dorschel, Fritz O—Gustave Erichsen. 171 87
9 Delany, Patrick B—P W Latham... costs 92 33
9†Day, Owen W—Angelo Myers... 166 80
9†Dreste, Christian M—Angelo Myers.. 98 56
10 Dovale, Ricot J—B L Ackermann... costs 280 76
10 Dilhan, Joseph—A H Fridenberg ... 2,102 83
3 Ehrlich, Abraham / Ehrlich, Hymen } Joseph Kaufmann... 147 80
3 Evatt, Sarah K—William Hatfield... 138 08
7 Evatt, Sarah K / Evatt, John G } P C Esler... 497 89
7 the same——Henry McDougall... 1,143 45
7 Evatt, John G——the same... 1,319 95
7 Emmerich, William J—Elizabeth Emmerich... 5,146 15
9 Evatt, Sarah K—Frank Becker... 425 02
10 Eckstein, Frank / Eckstein, Philip } Mary Siebold... 507 84
10 Elias, William M—W J Demorest.... 91 69
10 the same——the same... 91 69
10 Emile, Rohaupt—A H Fridenberg... 2,102 83
10 Eppinger, Louis—Simon Hatch... 336 65
7 Fleron, William—Alfred Von Beuren. 223 41
8 Farrington, John A / Farrington, Jonas S } Hugo Josephy.. 408 71
8 Fisig, Joseph—M D Solinger... 77 13
8*Fowler, William—J H Eagan... 639 39
9 Fuller, Edgar C / Fuller, Waldo E / Fuller, Mary E } W G Schuyler.. 2,659 10
9 Freud, Karl—George Lester... 243 50
10 Fogg, John C—L R Millen... 9,002 76
10 French, Alonzo—Angelina Johnson.. 81 71
2 Gilmartin, James—James Talcott.... 291 78
3 Gilmartin, James—S J Nowell... 1,809 47
3 Goodwin, Wendell—E B Lawrence... 279 34
3 Gore, Calvin—J L Morgan... 449 60
3 Gibb, Lulu—Aaron Rosenzweig... 158 00
3 the same——Joseph Goldstein.... 133 63
3 Giegerich, Philipp—Herman Struss... 111 91
3 Gilmartin, James—Joseph Strauss.... 274 84
3 the same——W J Adams... 2,881 62
3 the same——S J Weaver... 908 93
3 Garczynski, Caroline R—G F Gilman, exr... 3,284 78
6 Galligan, Henry—Knickerbocker Ice Co... 78 26
6 Gore, Calvin—Michael Meyberg... 1,133 58
6 Gilbert, Sarah E / Gilbert, Eliakim W } C F Kelly... 181 11
6 Gilmartin, James—Emil Oelbermann. 1,363 70
6 Griswold, Harriet E—Harriet D Green... costs 116 12
7 Gilmartin, James—Maria O'Donohue. 1,257 82
7 Griswold, Clarence—Edwin Wallace. 243 04
7 Gardinier, Adelbert—N Y Engraving & Printing Co... 115 22
7 Garvey, Isaac E / Garvey, Isadore E } Gutta Percha Rubber Mfg Co... 597 32
7 Gray, Frank De F—D M Kinnear... 34 94
7†Gibbs, Lena—Anna Goldstein... 90 78
7 Gantz, Cornelia A—J L Toch, assignee... 150 99
7 the same——the same... 167 89
7 Gilmartin, James—E B Weed... 468 07
8 Gunn, John G—Cornelius Van Cott, admr... 126 38
8 Grossman, Maurice—W F Smith..... 134 91
8 Goldthwaite, William M—W P Raynor... 117 18
8 Goldstein, Harris—M D Solinger..... 75 63
8 Garrison, George F / Garrison, William D } W E Perry.. 1,313 14
9 Graham, James H—H Clausen & Son Brewing Co... 183 21
9 Goldberg, Nathan—Jacob Rubenstein. 266 64
10 Guhring, John M—Leonhardt Hilsenbeck... costs 110 10
10 Gibb, Lulu—James Rorke... 107 82
10*Gardiner, Edward M / Gardiner, Charles R } George Bleistein, as president.. 304 52
10 the same——the same... costs 20 48
10 Gardiner, Charles R——the same.... 8,142 10
10 Goldman, Abraham J—Joseph Oshinsky... 192 13
3 Hennesy, John—Henry Hermann.... 165 13
3 Hooper, Rachel A—J L Morgan... 449 60
3 Hennessy, Frederick—T F McLaughlin... 137 50
3 Hartung, Lorenzo R—P & F Corbin.. 109 15
3 Hefter, Louis—William Schwab... 103 14
3 Holmes, Edward—I C Kiggins, as President... 342 38
6*Hooper, Rachael A—Michael Meyberg 1,133 58
6 Holsted, Augustis M—Orange Judd Co... 160 87
6 *Hall, Mary E / *Humphreys, Dolly / Humphreys, Robert L } Robert McNaughton 223 02
6 Hart, Patrick F—T W Todd... 132 87
6 Herzog, Sigmund—Alfred Sharp..... 2,511 17
7 Honce, Charles A—E P Dodge Mfg Co... 479 34
7 Hyneman, Julius—Edward Wolf..... 6,140 77
7 Happ, August—Williamsburg Brewing Co (Lim)... 213 95
7 Hauff, Herman / Hauff, Anna } Moritz Weiss... 227 37
7 Heagney, Eugene F—John Reilly..... 45 50
7 Horstmann, Richard—Henry Huber.. 110 84
7 the same——the same... 641 88
8 Harned, William B—J S Whiteside... 122 73
8 Hamilton, Adelaide A / Hamilton, William B } M J McKeon.. 550 00
9 Hartung, Lorenzo R—Rathbun Co... 1,529 00
9 Hartman, Ernest—Henry Goldberger, assignee... 19 78
9 Heyerdahl, William—Moross Jenkins Flour Co... 108 31
9*Haughey, Edward—H Clausen & Son Brewing Co... 183 21
9 Hymes, Isidore / Hymes, Julius } A H Cohen, admx.. 34,077 82
9 Harris, Jacob—Isaac Levy... 74 01
10†Hewitt, Henry S—L M Cronk... 104 15
10 Herrenschmidt, Marie / Herrenschmidt, Gustave } E G Byrnes 427 25
10 Hersh, Ephraim—D S Walton... 261 81
10 Harding, Charles N—L M Cronk..... 161 47
8 Ives, Margaret Seaman—O J Cuthbert... costs 117 27
9†Inslie, John H P—J L Reynolds... 103 38
3 Jones, George, as Treasurer of New York Times—V A Witcher... 1,146 37
6 James, Michael—Albert O'Loughlin.. 343 88
6 the same——Rebecca Simon... 517 88
6 the same——the same... 517 88
6 Johnson, Mary—Lorillard Brick Works Co... (D) 3,508 89
7 Jenkins, Margaret—James Hetherington... 79 25
7 Junior, William—William Smith..... 219 29
3 Kiley, Michael—G O Heffter... 40 50
3 Kreuder, Adolf / Kreuder, Frank F / Kline, Charles } C H Langdon.... 392 89
3 the same——T G Hood... 462 22
7 Kley, Anna C—Michael Moloughney. 84 59
7 Kahn, Samuel—M L Stieglitz... 697 80
7 Kan, Charles I—H W Dunlap... 39,109 77
7 Kirk, Henry M / Kirk, Mary C } J L Toch, assignee. 150 99
7 the same——the same... 167 89
7 Kreuder, Adolf / Kreuder, Frank F / Kline, Charles } E D Jordan..... 696 17
8†Ketchum, William—Angelo Myers... 131 97
9 Kearney, Edward R—G W Smith.... 630 33
9 Kitsell, William T—Knickerbocker Ice Co... 248 09
9 Kelly, Thomas P—F T Hempstead... 159 50
9 Keinper, Charles—Eva Bechtel, extrx 907 00
10 Krafft, John C—Commercial Bank of St Louis... 366 90
3 Lawton, J Warren—Kate F Brown... costs 122 78
3 Lawrence, Henry C—W E Conway... 233 25
6 Locurto, Giovanni Battista—Marianna Carretta... 76 18
6 Lehmaier, Ludwig—Alfred Sharp.... 2,511 17
6 Lovejoy, John F—F W Devoe... 142 33
7 Lovejoy, John F—James Taylor..... 265 89
7 Locke, Charles E—N W Strobridge.. 226 59
7 Lincoln, Lowell, assignee John F Plummer & Co—F C Linde.... costs 176 50
7 Laughlin, Joseph—Phillip Heipershausen... 3,553 83
7 Lowenstein, Benjamin / Lowenstein, Moses } J P Walther. 124 09
8 Le Barbier, Charles E—Augustin Arango... 452 43
8 Le Bowski, George—Charles Simon.. 191 89
8 the same——Abraham Unger.... 83 31
8 Leyrer, Christian—F G Moore... 92 64
9 Legendre, Mary—James Dalton..... 42 57
10 Levin, Louis—Sarah Cohen... 469 36
3 Marshall, William H—J E Overtons.. 5,016 59
3 Myers, Charles A—Gerda Lefran..... 420 59
3 Mills, Sarah T—Diamond Paste Co... 83 86
3 Muller, John—F W Mertens... 314 13
3 Meyer, Maurice—Mary F Winant.... 2,567 61
3 Milair, Gustave A J—Nat Bank of Republic... 173 11
3 Martin, Robert C—Brockway Brick Co... 1,419 91
3 the same——the same... 789 72
6*†Morris, John—Anna Goetzel... 43 17
6 Muldoon, William H—William Wilkenning... 42 90
6 Mackey, William D—Benjamin Rausch, exr... costs 86 00
6 Morgan, George P—Martin Schrenkeisen... 165 27
7 Martin, Robert C—John Paye... 2,032 14
7 the same——the same... 2,053 41
7 the same——the same... 2,064 08
7 the same——the same... 1,201 78
7 the same——the same... 1,877 31
7 the same——the same... 1,924 03
7 the same——the same... 2,066 89
7 the same——the same... 1,821 99
7 Morris, Ellis—G W Price... 78 33
7 Miller, Conrad, Jr—Moritz Weiss.... 227 37
7 Martin, Robert C—Robert Main..... 2,012 42
7 the same——the same... 1,535 93
7 the same——the same... 2,020 79
8 Murphy, George W—F G Moore... 1,376 15
8 Magill, Henry U W—Thomas Parry.. 156 04
8 Martin, Lawrence—Henry Stellman. 554 35
8 Muhlker, Charles F—William Hatfield 144 89
8 Martin, Robert C—Robert Main..... 2,031 35
8 the same——the same... 1,118 02
8 the same——the same... 1,261 70
8 the same——the same... 486 47
8 the same——the same... 1,336 01
8 the same——the same... 1,073 46
8 the same——the same... 1,972 09
9 Morse, John T / Miller, Benjamin F } N Y Central & Hudson River R R Co... 137 61
9 Maguire, William—Germania Bank.. 475 62
9 Mayers, Isaac—J W Farmer... 155 92
9 Masche, Marie—James Murray... 233 43
9 Morgan, Gwendolen—John Aburger.. 297 36
9 March, James E—James Cunningham Son & Co... costs 135 47
10 Morris, James—Patrick Cassidy..... 2,260 52
10 Miller, Frederick—J P Boyd... 120 83
10 Mason, James H—Elijah Cabble, exr. 244 50
10 March, James E—James Cunningham Son & Co... costs 135 47
10 Metzger, August / Metzger, Charles } W J Demorest.... 116 69
10 the same——the same... 106 39
10 Moore, William L, admr Harriet Gross—Margaret A Oliver... 83 43
10*Macdonald, James D—E G Byrnes... 427 25
10 Meyer, Arthur L—Elbano Spinnetti.. 443 67
10 Masche, Marie—Karl Mathiasen..... 435 10

10 Michel, Frederick—J B Colegrove.......costs 773 97
10 Martin, Robert C—William Lahey... 1,264 85
10 the same——the same............1,337 06
10 the same——the same. 1,320 65
10 the same——the same.... .... 1,306 59
3 McKenzie, Alexander C—Michaelis Kaliski.............costs 124 18
3 McGrath, Timothy W—A J Auchterlonie.......... 97 34
3 McCarthy, Daniel J—N A Merritt... 78 05
3 McDonald, Curran E—Keuffel & Esser Co... .... 93 50
3 McGovern, Charles H—Kosting Gas Engine Co (Lim)..........costs 66 64
6 McGrath, Mary J—William Clarke.. 86 21
6 McKenna, Patrick; McKenna, Margaret } Louis Cooper. 99 50
6 Mackey, William D—Benjamin Rausch, exr...........costs 86 00
7 McGuire, Barney J; McGuire, William } Edwin Wallace. 248 04
8 McDonald, William H—Twelfth Ward Bank 1,030 34
9 McGrath, Mary Jane—Kate Wilson. 117 50
9 McEvoy, James J—Rebecca Edwards 269 90
10 McMurray, Gerald—Andrew McMurray 179 50
10 McClelland, Elizabeth A—Thomas Moore.......... 159 41
10*Macdonald, James D—E G Byrnes.... 427 25
10 McMullen, Archibald C—May Davies.......... 107 95
6 Nordhoff, John—J T Huner.......... 85 52
7 Nichols, John H—H C Henderson.... 5,055 38
8 Newhall, Richard W—A R Page.. . 475 07
3 O'Brien, Thomas—J F Couch......... 164 76
7 O'Loughlin, Mary—John Baehr...... 794 27
8 O'Connor, John—William Koller..... 253 06
9 Owen, Robert J—D D Brinckerhoff.. 205 94
10+Orirgoni, Raymond—Elbaro Spinnetti 443 67
10 Obert, William P—Charles Wood.... 106 07
3 Peck, Nathan—Brockway Brick Co.. 1,419 91
3 the same——the same............. 789 72
6*Pfifferling, Benjamin—Louis Cooper. 99 50
6 Pool, Richard N—C R Brown........ 879 48
7 Peck, Nathan—John Faye...... . ...2,032 14
7 the same——the same............2,053 41
7 the same——the same............2,064 08
7 the same——the same. 1,201 78
7 the same——the same......... .1,877 31
7 the same——the same 1,924 03
7 the same——the same........... 2,066 89
7 the same——the same... ....1,821 99
7 Pride, George H—N Y Insulated Co.. 540 09
7 Plaut, Isaac S; Plaut, Ralph } M L Stieglitz........ 697 80
7 Peck, Nathan—Robert Main..........2,012 42
7 the same——the same.... ....1,555 93
7 the same——the same.... .... 2,020 79
8 Perry, Andrew J—William Fullerton 301 36
8 Perry, J Hazen—W E Perry......... 1,313 14
8 Peck, Nathan—Robert Main..........1,261 70
8 the same——the same.............1,073 38
8 the same——the same.............2,031 35
8 the same——the same.............1,118 02
8 the same——the same.. ....1,972 09
8 the same——the same............ 486 47
8 the same——the same.............1,336 01
9 Pendleton, Walter—George Whitaker 195 19
9 Price, Oscar A—C H Willson........ 392 57
9 Piser, Abraham—Isaac Levy......... 74 01
10 Porr, Louis J—Mary Siebold......... 507 84
10*Parkhurst, George A—E G Byrnes... 427 25
10 Peck, Nathan—William Lahey. 1,264 85
10 the same——the same.... ...... 1,337 05
10 the same——the same............ 1,320 65
10 the same——the same............ 1,306 59
10 Price, Rodman M, Jr—Adolph Altman........... 126 16
7 Quinn, Peter—C W Moelrus.......... 454 00
8 Reynolds, Jessie; Reynolds, William M } John Dobson. 928 97
8 Ross, William H—F R Biedler........ 5,303 94
3 Ross, J Stewart—W D Murray........ 219 49
6 Roberts, Anna M—John Davidson.... 192 55
6 Rice, Adelbert D—Metropolitan Telephone and Telegraph Co..... ...... 31 89
6 Riley, James—Thomas Farrell........ 155 43
6 Ripinski, Charles; *Ripinski, Morris } American Hosiery Co.............. 944 97
7 Rognon, Blanche—Charles Rattier.... 250 60
7 Reichardt, Fritz—John Nuth......... 718 12
7 Robinson, Charles—C A Parsons. s 77 38
7 Radesky, Samuel—Morris Spiegelbaum 1,144 05
7 Reiness, Israel—Frederick Kaffeman. 45 50
8 †Rousseau, John P; †Rousseau, John E } Amelia Westheimer.......... 200 55
8 Reynolds, Agnes—J M Sprague. 155 17
8 Raynor, George A—C C Shayne...... 448 07
8*Rodarmor, John F—A E Hoffman.... 107 59
8 Rubino, Eugene—O H Meyer 1,030 22
8 Ryan, Hattie T—W A Miles & Co.... 526 90
9 Rognon, Blanche—Carl Schefer...... 470 55
9 Reilly, Michael—J B Smith......... 85,697 26
9 Robbins, Eliza T—Charlotte P Robbins.......................costs 74 25
9 Redmond, Vincent—F C Martin...... 189 83
10 Richardson, Leander—W. F Rochester.............................. 104 15
10 Reichardt, Fritz—Isaac Simon...... .. 909 74
10 Roberts, Stephen M—L D Bulkley. .. 825 59
3 Solifrey, Samuel—Gerda Lefran...... 420 59
3 Salisbury, Amos M—Williams & Clark Co......................... 112 58
3 Schumacher, William—F W Mertens. 314 13
3 Salisbury, John L—Mary E Norton.. 514 22
3 Sotscheck, Carl—S B Solomon.......2,240 04
6 Small, Cyrus K—Benjamin Rausch, exr.................... ....costs 86 00
6 Schniewind, Max A—Metropolitan Telephone and Telegraph Co....... 28 50
6 Schirmer, Gustave—F S Myers....... 242 44
6 Streifer, Jacob—G F Norton.......... 172 51
7 Schmidt, Alfred—Edward Wolf..... 6,140 77
7 Stevens, John A—Strobridge Lithographing Co........................2,380 21
7 Senior, Mendez D—Milan Hulbert.... 874 85
7 Samuels, Julius—Rudolph Hormann. 288 09
7 Sotscheck, Carl—Julia A Sotscheck.. 2,003 14
7 Siebert, Joseph E; Stewart, Peter... } N Y Veal and Mutton Co.......... 92 37
7 Smith, John W—P S Bennett......... 187 36
7 Selling, Joseph—J S Langley........ 170 76
8 *Steenworth, Charles C; †Steenworth, Francis J } J G Phelan.. 165 00
8 Streeter, William H—C W Packard.. 526 61
8 Singer, Markus—Adolph Goldsmith.. 101 79
8 Stern, Samuel—W F Smith.......... 134 91
8 Sears, R Thatcher—Marie Pfauder.. 5,404 96
8 Stillwell, John W—Michael Quigley. 419 31
8 Schermerhorn, Antoinette Lucinda—O J Cuthbert..................costs 118 70
9*Squier, Albert C—John Pirkl........ 1,780 42
9 the same——W R Creed.......... 1,078 01
9 Senior, Mendez D—Marcellus Hartley.............................. 804 99
9 *Sonn, Julius; Sonn, Herman } Sutro Bros Braid Co. 167 52
9 Sylvester, Lewis; Sylvester, Allie L } Max Eckman.... 105 09
9 Sherwood, John W; Schwartz, Abraham } Jacob Macher 481 20
9 Snow, Tristain B—C R Weeks........ 2,768 00
10 Scribner, Gilbert H, Jr—L R Millen. 9,002 76
10 Schmidt, Konrad—Henry Henrici.... 798 69
10 the same——Henry Siebert, Jr... 297 89
10 Senior, Mendez D—F W Blossom..... 147 34
10 Sparling, Thomas—George Mackenzie 195 70
10 Sommer, Moritz—Raritan Woolen Mills.................. .... 247 52
3 The Lawrence Curry Comb Co—J A Griffiths..................... 117 61
3 Mechanics' and Traders' Bank—W S Kieley, recvr.................costs 100 70
3 The Mayor, Aldermen, &c—Jerome Brady.......................... 272 59
3 Cary & Moen Co—Cleveland Rolling Mill Co.......................... 199 26
3 The Imperial Buffet Lunch Co (Lim)—T O Smith, Jr....... .... 400 96
3 Joseph B Tiffany & Co—Robert Graves Co...................... .. 134 82
3 The N Y Book Depository—E M Perbaes.............................. 342 58
2 Bridgeport Knitting Co—W J Tingue 1,304 28
3 The Pneumatic Dynamite Gun Co—Richmond Kingman............... 19,696 43
3 the same——O E Abraham....... 8,763 34
3 the same——De Borden Wilmot.. 1,904 66
3 the same——G H Graham........ 1,057 94
3 the same——W W Gage.......... 688 10
3 the same——D W McWilliams.. 12,577 47
3 the same——William Cramp & Sons' Ship and Engine Building Co. 124,597 61
6 The N Y Elevated R R Co; The Manhattan Railway Co } W P Abendroth 8,017 41
6 American Export and Trading Co—Metropolitan Telephone and Telegraph Co........................ 16 19
6 Belford Magazine Co—Mary F Bates.. 39 47
6 Nat'l Phototype Co—H G Allen.......1,139 49
6 The Brooklyner Merkur Publishing Co—Philip Heinrich............... .. 223 37
6 Pneumatic Dynamite Gun Co—F W Devoe............................ . 82 40
6 Joseph B Tiffany & Co—F W Devoe & Co............................. 330 28
7 Pneumatic Dynamite Gun Co—J N Raymond........ .... 286 44
7 Joseph B Tiffany & Co—William Hannam............................. 598 46
7 Lawrence Curry Comb Co—A J Hopper... .... 218 69
7 Pneumatic Dynamite Gun Co—J A Stewart..........................40,283 84
7 the same——Osgood Welsh..... 13,576 48
7 the same——First Nat Bank.... 40,283 84
7 the same——A J F Leith...... 40,283 84
7 The N Y & Brooklyn Suburban Investment Co—Samuel Schurr.. .... 640 39
7 The Mayor, Aldermen, &c—F J Keenan.............................. 108 47
7 The Facer Refrigerating and Ice Co—J C Davis......................... 153 39
7 Pneumatic Dynamite Gun Co—J H Bunnell...........................1,201 22
8 The Murphy & Potts Mfg Co—F G Moore.......................... 1,376 15
8 The N Y Steamship Co—S M Nelson. 101 11
8 Lawrence Curry Comb Co—Edward Ely.............................. 174 06
8 N. Y, New Haven & Hartford R R Co—G T Shambon.... .... costs 100 70
8 The Dexter Stock Indicator and Telegraph Co—William Courtenay 668 42
8 Belford Co—Photo-Electrotype Engraving Co.... .... 333 35
9 Rapid Printing Co—A D Farmer..... 146 36
9 Harlem Lighting Co; Manhattan Electric Light Co (Lim) } Thomson-Houston Electric Co...... 35,466 31
9 Imperial Buffet Lunch Co (Lim)—Percy Rockwell..................... 525 24
9 The Manhattan Railway Co; The Metropolitan Elevated Railway Co } B S Suarez ....costs 111 04
9 the same——P S Suarez.....costs 152 39
9 Pyrogravure Co—Siegfried Gruner... 1,008 01
9 Variety Iron Works—H J Bracker... 496 01
9 Joseph B Tiffany & Co—G F Allen... 436 66
9 The Second Av R R Co; The Houston, West st & Pavonia Ferry R R Co } Frederick Schneider ....costs 101 61
9 Taconic Marble Co—Jacob Macher... 481 20
9 The Lawrence Curry Comb Co—E D Griggs.......................... 216 31
9 The J J Nichols Mfg Co——the same. 155 97
10 Richard Thomson Co (Lim)—A R Whitney..................... 748 48
10 The N Y Elevated R R Co; The Manhattan Railway Co } Aaron Buchsbaum..costs. 188 52
10 Chicago Wire Goods Co—Harry O'Neill............................. 2,126 45
10 The N Y Elevated R R Co; The Manhattan Railway Co } Margaretha Rupp.... 184 98
10 Pneumatic Dynamite Gun Co; The Excelsior Dynamite Co } Washington Nat Bank 110 34
10 Central Iron Works—L N Lukens.... 439 12
10 North American Relief Society for the Indigent Jews in Jerusalem, Palestine—Sampson, Simson Leo....costs 80 59
10 The Hub Publishing Co—J H Eggers. 1,903 38
10 the same——Barker & Eggers Co ....costs 246 09
10 Belford Co—Photo Engraving Co.... 224 03
10 Ackerly & Gerard Co—George Hagemeyer............................. 533 63
3 Terry, Julia A—J E Overton 5,016 59
6*Tiffany, Joseph B—Anna Goetzel.... 43 17
6 Talmadge, Hiram E—Caroline A Ketchum............................. 152 82
7 Thwaite, Amanda A—W R Comfort. 83 97
8 Tode, Adolph—Frederick Reiset 406 98
10 Tallman, Mary; Tallman, William D } Jacob Hays, trustees...(D) 87 83
10 Townsend, Walten—J B Colgrave... ....costs 773 97
3 Volkmer, Henry G—Charles Scheideller............................ 67 15
3 Viemeister, George A; Viemeister, Edmund C } Joseph Lassner........ 410 35
6 *Vroman, Sanford; Vroman, Peter } J H Hubbell..... 414 75
6 the same——William Affleck..... 395 54
6 the same——Samuel Titus........ 259 61
6 the same——Henry Dusenbery... 259 97
6 the same——Joseph Volkommer.. 280 22
6 the same——James Rozell........ 99 50
6 the same——J J Devitt.......... 1,609 97
6 the same——Jacob Knight....... 125 21
6 the same——Thomas Fonda...... 309 94
6 the same——G E Van Vorst...... 1,132 82
6 the same——E D Dusenberry..... 624 74
6 the same——Oscar Kent......... 185 98
7 Vogel, Robert—George Ringler & Co. 567 26
8 *Vroman, Sanford; Vroman, Peter } J H Ostrum...... 271 48
10 Vassiliades, Constantine D—George Whitaker.......................... 223 75
7 Van Riper, Josiah P—Henry Huber... 122 48
7 Vanderbeck, Henry A—Jackson Architectural Iron Works............ 260 37
10 Van Steenberg, Berhans—F T Russell. 162 28
3 Warner, John W—Mutual Life Ins Co..... ....1,801 25
3 the same——the same 1,787 30
3 the same——the same............1,787 30
3 the same——the same............1,787 30
3 Warmington, William—W B Warmington......... ....costs 67 25
3 Wolcott, Erastus G—W A Higgins... 74 10
6 Winant, George W—Nathan Simon.. 77 15
7 Waldron, Robert H—Michael Moloughney........................ 84 59
7 Walsh, John E—M J Coffey..........2,068 05
7 Wavra, Wenzel—Beadleston & Woerz 841 38
7 Whipple, Nelson M—James Murray.. 302 87
8 Wulling, John—Frederick Reiset..... 406 98
8 Weile, Ernest—Jacob Stuber. 4,695 00
8 Wilkinson, Daniel F—Angelo Myers.. 105 67
8 Whyard, William W—J S Aitken.... 150 17
8 Warmington, William—J H Eagan... 639 39
8 Walker, George W—L E Wilmerding. 164 73
8 White, John J—F G Moore.......... 92 64
9 Watson, William A, assignee—G E Atwood.......... ....costs 29 27
9+Walters, John N—Alfred Pearson.... 132 50
9 Whipple, Nelson M—John Pirkl......1,780 42
9 the same——W R Creed.........1,078 01
9 Ward, William T, admr—G L Prentiss, guard........ ....3,140 30
9 Weinberg, Perry—Julia Hess....costs 25 55
9 Wolff, Oscar—Ernest Dreber.......... 173 35
9 White, William H—J M Canda....... 352 69
9 Walton, Joseph—Edwin Rider........ 182 63
9 Waddell, James A—German-American Bank........ ....4,441 62
9 Werdenschlag, Abraham, Jr—Michael Smart. 333 78
9 Ward, William T, admr—Theresa Dosot................ ....,......... 150 00
10 Ward, Henry—C H Jacobus......... 258 67
10 Wood, George—Elijah Cabble, exr... 244 50
10 Wood, George E—T J Robinson.costs 96 00
10 Woods, Jane—Simon Katzenstein.... 74 50
10 Wellwood, John H—Butler Hardware Co.................................1,184 46
7+Young, Albert V—T P Kelly......... 67 02

KINGS COUNTY.

July

3 Averell, George W—J L Blauvelt.... $654 84
3 Abbe, Charles C—G E Knowles 366 15
3 Ames, Eliza J—A W Frisbie.......... 349 94
7 Allen, Barnabas H, exr, &c, Julia M Babcock, dec'd—C B Babcock......6,865 14
7 Alexander, Morris—M Mayer.. .... 104 29
7 Ahrens, Christian R—J W Johnson .. 538 60
8 Allison, Nathaniel—O H Meyer......1,030 22

2 Burtiss, Nathan W—J A Cross & Co. 391 61
3 Bell, Francis W—W Reeves 760 06
3 Baldwin, Sophie—H Adickes 76 13
7 Babcock, Julia M, dec'd, exr of—C B Babcock 6,865 14
7 Barratt, George—G Hofer 669 72
8 Bruns, Henry—J F Gerlach 234 67
8 Burgess, Levi G—H W O Edye 3,541 29
8 the same——the same 1,275 30
8 the same——J E Brett 5,687 81
9 Brooks, Julius—J Stern 694 35
9 the same——A Blumenstein 2,337 36
2 Cimbar, Pietro—Emma Cimbar 95 12
2 Crawley, William K—Bertha Nonnenbacher 206 02
2 Conradi, William—Leibinger & Oehm B Co 117 22
2 Conway, Agnes T / Conway, James J } C H Randall...(D) 228 17
2 the same——the same 95 38
3 Case, V R—N Y Stove Works 220 72
6 Custer, Fannie—W Beni 86 92
7 Close, Edwin H / Clark, John } Casco Nat Bank, of Portland, Me 8,271 75
8 Carlson, Mary—L Kastz 15 72
8 Chinnock, Frank R—J R Regan 211 81
8 Collins, Samuel—J S Underhill 80 45
9†Cole, "James A"—S Riker 518 52
7 Dexter, Andrew J—J W Johnson 538 60
7 Dietz, Jacob Y—A J Dexter 79 47
7 Ennis, Thomas A—C Falleson 154 13
2 Folkes, Louis—W Battermann 573 27
8 Fowler, Warren C—J Duane 203 26
3 Felix, Edward—M Mayer 51 58
7 Fellows, Franklin J—P L Bonalds 421 35
8 Farrell, Michael J——the same 93 30
8 Fleig, William / Fleig, Mary } F E Weber 103 69
2 Goldsmith, Benjamin—W A Sherman 260 88
3 Grant, Frederick R—J McCarthy 760 06
7 Gill, William P—A W Blazo 2,418 38
7 Grabau, Gerd—J F Ebrgott 282 56
8 Gore, Calvin—M Meyberg 1,133 58
7 Henjes, Gerd H—H W Thomas, admr 2,815 89
8*Hooper, Rachel A—M Meyberg 1,131 58
8 Hawley, Oscar F—P Van Rensselaer 1,431 77
8 Honce, Charles A—E P Dodge Mfg Co [illegible]9 34
9 Hill, Catharine H and Patrick—Mary A Taylor 5,163 50
9 Hennessy, William—H E Kane 71 97
9 Hill, George W—P Stout 2,186 09
7 Ivins, William—A J Dexter 79 47
3 Kirchner, Louis—Burger & Hower B Co 32 65
7 Kenny, Patrick—J Stetson 424 45
8 Kehoe, Eunice—A C Hallam 105 54
9†Kelly, "Joseph"—T W Lucas 53 12
9 Kenny, Edward J—H E Kane 133 78
3 Lynch, John—W R Lemmon 75 67
3 Lord, Byington—C T Austin 149 06
3 Loser, David—J Q Maynard 34 55
8 Longhlin, John—T C Lyman & Co 1,312 40
6 Lindner, John—Hobby & Doody 421 20
8 Leonard, Lewis H—Caroline Nerini 188 08
2 Merrill, Julian W—H Martin 142 56
2 Marsland, John W—J A Cross & Co. 391 61
3 McFarlone, John J—F McKeige 6,096 37
8 Myers, Charles A—G Lefran 420 59
3 Miller, Fred—J Q Maynard 46 96
3 McKenzie, Alexander C—M Kaliski 124 18
6 McAveney, John A—P Boben 121 92
6 Merkert, Joseph B—P Koch 17 93
7 McGovern, Charles H—Korting Gas Engine Co (Lim) 66 64
7 Meyer, Gazina—R H Wright 211 36
7 McGilliwie, Alexander—A Pearson 165 10
7 Magee, Francis—A J Dexter 79 47
8 Mason, George N—J H Hull 81 32
8 Mason, James H—E Cabble et al 244 50
8 Martin, Christopher F—R S Leighton 258 58
7 Nordhoff, John—J T Huner 85 52
8 Newman, William D—J T Story 392 58
8 Newhall, Richard W—A R Page 475 07
8 Newman, John—J W Wilde 83 54
8 Olney, George—D L McDonald 71 49
9 O'Neill, Dennis—A H Curtis 196 86
9 the same——the same 90 85
9 the same——O Goerke 199 41
8 Pfeiffer, Louis E—F McKeige 6,096 37
8 Persch, William—M Stal 258 94
7 Poole, Mary A—C Molten 13 11
7 Palmer, John—Mayor, &c, N Y 116 65
7 Post, Harry G—J Leffler 118 62
7 Parr, Robert A—J Sloan 136 47
6 Ropke, Henry—M Hawkins 1,266 06
8 Rubino, Eugene—O H Meyer 1,030 22
8 Russell, Samuel—L M Holton 118 81
9 Reilly, John—J Schmulbeiser 144 25
8 Rollfrey, Samuel—G Lefran 420 59
6 Squier, Albert C—Z West 793 50
6 Shoffer, B K—M Bramley 164 08
7 Stockschlaeder, Joseph—F P Scudder 126 46
8 St John, Cortlandt—J E Brett 5,687 81
8 the same——H W O Edge 1,275 30
8 the same——H W O Edge 3,541 29
8 Shaw, Jerome B—R S Leighton 258 58
9 Selling, Joseph—J S Langley 170 76
3 The admr of John Wiegand—A E Schreiber 100 00
7 The Clark & Chaplin Ice Co—Casco Nat Bank of Portland, Me 8,271 75
7 The Hunt Engineering Co—W S Hill 96 31
7 The exrs Julia M Babcock, dec'd—C B Babcock 6,865 14
7 The Brooklyner Merkur Publishing Co—P Heinrich 223 37
7 The Allgemeine Arbeiter Kranken und Sterbe Kasse—P Joehmann 171 25
6 Uhlig, George M—W Jaenike 41 50
7 Ullman, Max—R Bookman & Co 78 80
7 Viemeister, George A / Viemeister, Edmund C } J Lassner 410 35
9 Van Riper, Josiah P—H Huber 122 48
2 Wagener, August P—Sarah Lewis 1,308 08
3 Work, George F—F McKeige 6,096 37
3 Wisbauer, George / Wisbauer, Lena } J J Budd 55 43
3 Wiegand, Jacob, admr of John Wiegand, dec'd—Anna E Schrieber 100 00
6 Whipple, Nelson M—Z West 793 50
7 Wingert, Charles—P McCarthy 41 04
7 Walsh, John E—M J Coffey 2,068 05
7 Wanser, Frank—B A Beal 86 52
8 Wood, George—E Cabble et al 244 50
8 Warshaw, Louis—J A Strauss 212 38
9 Weinhandler, Max—L Kronenberg 43 42
9 Walker, George—L E Wilmerding 164 73

SATISFIED JUDGMENTS.

NEW YORK.

July 3 to 10—Inclusive.

Alcorn, Wm W and Samuel—A A Brush. (1891) $786 08
Auld, Thomas—J A Benson. (1891) 261 40
§Ackermann, Bernard L, Sr and Jr—R J Dovale. (1890) 5,827 18
Bachrach, Abraham M—Harry Lehr. (1891) 81 17
Bowen, Henry C—W L Bull, as pres't. (1891) 97 27
Same——same. (1891) 85 12
Same——same. (1889) 572 20
Barnes, Henry W, assignee—E H Coffey. (1891) 419 19
Bendheim, Henry M—J A Nesbit. (1890) 91 50
Same——same. (1889) 922 90
Same——same. (1891) 74 24
*Bickman, John—G C Flint Co. (1888) 89 16
Same——Thomas Larkin. (1889) 110 36
Clemens, James R—C H Pleasants. (1891) 156 07
Same——Union Gas and Oil Stove Co. (1891) 112 15
Same——D H Shipman. (1891) 291 61
Same——Louis Hoopes. (1891) 235 92
Coyle, Bernard D—Mayor, &c. (1889) 100 00
‡Dillingham, Charles T—Mary G Pinkney. (1891) 3,551 83
Davis, Ralph and Frank—J N Koster. (1891) 146 30
Eberspackle, Christian—Leopold Bohm. ('91) 114 77
Friend, Julius—Abraham Ettinger. (1885) 413 27
Fowler, Mortimer L—Loeb Hess. (1882) 125 24
German Evangelical Church of Yorkville—Martin Lahm. (1890) 1,880 85
Gray, Robert J—John Scott. (1891) 333 08
Greene, William B / Geise, Albert L } Memphis City Bank. (1891) 124 63
Same——same. (1891) 194 84
Same——same. (1891) 175 18
Grabau, Gerd—J F Ehrgott. (1891) 282 56
Glueckmann, Joseph—Alfred Greenebaum. (1891) 188 07
Gaylord, Don A—Citizens Nat Bank. (1890) 1,087 84
Hall, Marcus W—F H Stege. (1881) 729 94
Hazard, Hazard & Co—J B Bertrand. (1891) 1,424 80
Hines, Eide H—A R Matthage. (1890) 72 87
‡Jones, James A—Julius Baehr. (1890) 2,349 24
Kafferman, Frederick—Israel Reiness. (1891) 69 26
Klein, Bella—Abram Losey. (1891) 1,106 91
Kempson, St George—Exchange Printing Co. (1888) 166 67
Kanter, Frederick A—J W Fox. (1891) 292 27
Lowe, James A—U S Illuminating Co. (1890) 168 91
Lindemann, Anton W—Herrmann Weiller. (1891) 28 70
‡Laux, Jacob—Percival Knauth. (1890) 698 47
McAnnery, Michael F—D H Shipman. (1891) 291 61
Same——Union Gas and Oil Stove Co. ('91) 112 15
Same——C H Pleasants. (1891) 156 07
Same——Louis Hoopes. (1891) 235 92
Same——Archer & Pancoast Mfg Co. ('91) 155 91
Manhattan Railway Co / Metropolitan Elevated Railway Co } J A Frazee, trustee. (1891) 1,722 88
Murray Hill Bank—Elizabeth Van Antwerp. (1891) 118 15
Mars, Henrietta A—E M Van Buren. (1890) 1,390 91
McElwee, James G—Citizen's Nat Bank. ('90) 1,087 84
McIlbargy, Joseph—Eloise J Chase, extrx. (1891) 106 34
Mayer, Ellenore, Paul A, Bruno E, Elinor M, Charles E and Rudolph M—Henry Seibert. (1891) 623 18
Manhattan Railway Co / Metropolitan Elevated Railway Co } Joseph Campbell. (1891) 1,130 60
Moore, Herbert W—T E Greacen. (1891) 254 48
McEachen, James C—E G Byrnes. (1891) 427 25
Nooney, Mary—Lydia R Notman. (1885) 104 64
Nat Union Bank of Dover, N J—M T Reed. (1891) 187 75
Same——L S Howard. (1891) 142 49
Neuberger, David M—F A Fais. (1891) 62 87
Oherle, Joseph—Frank Shulte. (1890) 26 00
Pitz, John—S J Berry. (1887) 224 06
Rinaldo, Louis—Joseph Brown. (1891) 552 42
Ridal, Anne—Henry Batzer. (1890) 385 46
Salisbury, Estella L—Henry Seibert. (1891) 623 18
Sleight, Henry—N Y County Nat Bank. (1888) 500 81
Schwartz, Max—Herman Langenhop. (1891) 1,386 00
Stein, Abraham—Abram Losey. (1891) 1,106 91
Scholes, Mary J—Ephens, Smith & Wieman Co. (1890) 297 01
Same——William Nixon. (1890) 506 34
Same——same. (1890) 499 59
Sternheimer, Bella—A D Rockwell. (1891) 748 54
Stengel, Margaret—Erwin Fery. (1891) 109 86
Wilkinson, Alfred and J Forman—Jennie B Kelley. (1885) 388 64
Wolff, Robert—A J Bedell. (1891) 68 00

*Vacated by order of Court. †Suspended on Appeal. ‡Released. §Reversal. ‖Satisfied by Execution.

KINGS COUNTY.

July 3 to 9—inclusive.

Armstrong, John L—F J Ward. (1891) $189 78
Burns, Elizabeth—T Hand. (1890) 110 95
Day, Olive S—Mary L Mathies. (1879) 363 34
Same——same. (1879) 87 53
Grace, William H—F C Vrooman. (1884) 225 58
Same——D O'Brien. (1884) 79 24
Horrigan, James E—N Y & Brooklyn Casket Co. (1891.) (Execution) 1,175 19
Same——same. (1891.) (Execution) 69 30
Judson, Edward—J May. (1891) 331 94
Jones, Whitfield E—F W Devoe. (1891) 74 00
Lincoln, Jonas A—Ella Tredwell. (1889) 97 04
Same——same. (1891) 120 65
Same——same. (1888) 4,479 08
Lindemann, Anton W—H Weiller. (1891) 28 70
Miller, Ira O—W R McLaughlin. (1889) 98 71
Same——same. (1891) 108 76
Same——same. (1890) 79 57
Mayer, Ellenore / Mayer, Paul A / Mayer, Bruno, I / Mayer, Ellenore M / Mayer, Charles E / Mayer, Rudolph M / Salisbury, Estella L } H Seibert. (1891) 623 18
Preston, Albert I and Charles W—T H Bradley. (1890) 3,676 87
Same——J Van Dervater. (1891) 118 59
Pitz, John—S J Berry, Jr. (1887) 224 05
Reitz, John—S T Maddox. (1889) 56 50
Same——G Schwab. (1889) 70 04
Sprole, Mary—G S Townsend. (1890) 84 91
The New York Condensed Milk Co—J Oelerich. (1889) 97 38
Same——same. (1889.) (Execution) 898 48
Wingerter, Jacob—F A Perdue. (1891) 340 23

MECHANICS' LIENS.

NEW YORK CITY.

July

8 One Hundred and Fourteenth st, No. 342, s s, 300 w Av A, 30x100. Scully & Moran agt Joseph F. and Kate Gallagher, owners and contractors $65 00
3 Ninth av, Nos. 702-706, e s, 29 n 48th st, 75x100. Holbrook Bros. agt —— Lewis, owner, and Kenzie & Lasuroe, contractors 175 48
3 One Hundred and Fifth st, n s, 75 e Madison av, 50x100. Thomas Tracy agt John O'Connor, owner and contractor 800 01
3 Seventy-second st, Nos. 414 and 416, s s, 213 e 1st av, 50x102.2. Culbert Bros. agt Joseph F. Gallagher, owner and contractor 437 62
3 Crotona pl, e s, 100 s 171st st, 21x100. Thomas Farrell agt Mary J. McGrath, debtor and owner 35 00
3 Fifth av, n w cor 119th st, 45x50. Patrick O'Connell agt John or Isabella V. Hogan and Catharine Murphy, owners, and John H. Summerhays, contractor 27 00
3 Twenty-fourth st, Nos. 407, n s, 125 e 1st av, 25x100. Martin Smith agt John P. Bants, owner and contractor 525 00
6 Riverside av or Drive, s e cor 82d st, 100.8x122.4x102.2x161.1. G. F. Werner agt Squier & Whipple, owners and contractors 1,311 00
6 One Hundred and Fifteenth st, n w cor Madison av, 80x100. Mary A. Chancellor agt J. Dillon and William F. McEntee, owners, and William F. McEntee, contractor 490 00
6 Villa av, w s, 375 n Porter pl, 50x100. Jesse Reynolds agt Edmund C. Allcott, owner and contractor 58 80
6 Same property. A. D. Knapp agt same 596 38
6 One Hundred and Eighteenth st, Nos. 64-64, s s, 60 e Madison av, 100x100. August Kissling agt Lipmann Kingsburg, owner, and Marie Masche, contractor 647 00
6 Ninety-ninth st, No. 173, n e cor 10th av, 100x25. Steinman & Hoffman agt M. Celler, owner, and I. Sackman, contractor 75 00
6 One Hundred and Sixth st, No. 54, s s, 100 w Manhattan av, 25x85. Same agt J. Coyle, owner, and I. Sackman, contractor 58 77
6 West End av, s w cor 103d st, 100.11x166. J. J. Brown agt Elizabeth Steinmetz, owner and contractor 600 00
6 Same property. James McLaughlin agt same 777 38
6 Same property. Charles Hillemeier agt same and Welcome R. Steinmetz, owner and contractor 8,250 00
6 Forty-second st, No. 559, n s, 100 e 11th av, 25x100. William Spearing agt Mary A. Barron, owner and contractor 1,036 00
6 Crotona pl, w s, 100 s 171st st, 21x100. Thomas Farrell agt Mary J. McGrath, debtor and owner 35 00
6 Kingsbridge road, e s, 351 n Coles lane, 56.8x—. C. W. Vreeland agt Fannie Chambers, owner and contractor 408 40
7 One Hundred and Forty-fifth st, s s, 84 w 10th av, 116x—. John Leyes agt Henry and William Niebbuhr, owners, and Joseph Haas, contractor. (Continued from July 8, 1890) 39 00
7 Same property. Ludwig Maus agt same. (Continued from July 8, 1890) 33 00
7 Villa av, e s, 375 n Potter pl, 50x100. J. M. Cantwell agt Edmund C. Alcott, owner and contractor 521 00
7 One Hundred and Eighteenth st, s s, 60 e Madison av, 125x100. Kelly & Costello agt John Doe, owner, and Herman Masche, contractor 4,900 00
7 Freeman st, No. 1099, n s, 100 e Stebbins av, 75x125. S. B. Leary agt Mary and Wenzl Wavra, owners and contractors 747 00
7*Fourth st, Nos. 226, w s, 53 s 10th st, 26.6x101. Kertscher & Co. agt John J. Crawford, owner, and William H. Crawford, contractor 378 67
7 Second av, No. 160, n e cor 10th st, 25x100. F. M. Hausling agt Daniel C. Potter, owner and contractor 200 00
8 Thirty-fourth st, Nos. 126 and 128, s w cor Lexington av, 90x117.6. S. G. Bull & Son agt Lexington Improvement Co., owners and contractors 1,975 25
8 Same property. Archer & Pancoast Mfg. Co. agt same 4,597 99
8 Seventy-sixth st, No. 339, n s, 200 e 2d av, 25x100. John Sheehy & Son agt Mortimer M. Menken, debtor and owner. (Continued from July 10, 1890) 6,460 00
One Hundred and Fortieth st, n s, 400 w 7th w 7th av, 75x100 / One Hundred and Forty-first st, s s, 400 w 7th av, 75x100 }
8 One Hundred and Forty-first st, n s, 400 w 7th av, 75x100 / One Hundred and Forty-second st, s s, 400 w 7th av, 75x100 }
Patrick Guilfoyle agt Charles M. O'Keefe, owner, and McGowan & Heaton, contractors 11
8 West End av, s w cor 103d st, 100.11x159.10. James McLaughlin agt Elizabeth and Welcome Steinmetz, owners and contractors 717 18
8 Thirty-ninth st, Nos. 609-617, n s, 125 w 11th av, 125x100. K. N. Smith & Co. agt John N. Koster, owner and contractor 5,886 78
8 Villa av, Nos. 16 and 17, e s, 50x100. Richard Cassidy agt Edward Allcock, owner and contractor 83 00

8 Thirty-fourth st, No. 157, n s, 165 e 7th av, 16.8x98.9. James Ross agt Mrs. V. M. and Annie C. Hallett, owners and contractors.................. 108 75

9 One Hundred and Twentieth st, n s, 125 w 8th av, 75x100. Louis Roller agt James Thompson, owner and contractor........ 8,338 50

9 Henry st, No. 57, n s, 140 w Market st, 20x100. L. A. Burke agt Catharine C., Rose A. and Elizabeth L. Allen, owners, and Thomas Allen, contractor.......... 6,087 71

9 Convent av, n w cor 143d st, 100x100. J. M. McArdle agt Louise M. Hartwell, owner and contractor.................. 2,400 00

9 Eighth av, n w cor 104th st, 100.11x100. N. F. Vought agt August Kohn, John J. Carey, Martin J. Barron, Henry Steers and John F. Menke, owners, and August Kohn and John J. Carey, contractors.... 595 00

10 Davidson av, w s, 185 n Fordham Landing road, 50x100. T. W. Ringrove and Forester Chandler agt Adelaide Yeandle, owner, and George W. Yeandle, contractor...... 310 00

10 One Hundred and Forty-fifth st, s s, 84 w 10th av, 110x—. Louis Anderson agt Joseph Haas, debtor, and Henry and William Niebbur r, contractor. (Continued from July 11, 1890).................. 90 75

10 Same property. Joseph Cashin agt same. (Continued from July 11, 1891)......... 28 00

10 Sixty-third st, n s, 300 w Central Park West, 75x100.5. J. F. Pease Furnace Co. agt Richard Everett, Robert Carey and Esther E. Barron, owners, and Robert Carey, contractor.................. 500 00

10 One Hundred and Thirty-second st, s s, 125 e 5th av, 85x100. W. H. Brandt agt George and Lizzie T. Wilkes, owners, and George Wilkes & Co., contractors........ 827 50

10 Madison av, Nos. 1835–1839. John Dempsey agt Mrs. James Gault, owner, and Nicholas L. Demorast, contractor.............. 150 00

10 One Hundred and Twentieth st, No. 14 E., s s. Same agt same.................. 150 00

10 Kingsbridge road, n s, 100 w Arthur av, 75x—. J. G and C. T. Colwell agt Margaret Stonebridge, owner, and Emil Weiser, contractor.................. 850 00

*Editor Record and Guide:

The lien put on record on July 7, 1891, against the building known as No. 225 West 4th street, by the firm of Kertscher & Co., was entirely unbusinesslike and evidently the result of a misunderstanding.

Their contract to furnish mantels in the building was not completed and hence, according to our agreement, they were in no position to expect or demand the money which would only become due them on the performance of said contract.

Wm. H. & J. J. Crawford.

KINGS COUNTY.

July

2 Wooden Walkway, s s, known as New Bowery, Coney Island (see Lien). Samuel Anderson agt Ellen Tilyou and Joseph Brosseau, owners, and Joseph Brosseau, contractor.................. $75 00

2 Prospect av, s w s, 254 n w 8th av, runs southwest 90.4 x north west 46 x northeast 10 x northwest 50 x northeast 80 to av, x southeast 96. N. H. and B. C. Raymond agt Fannie Fielding, owner, and Robert W. Fielding, contractor.................. 250 00

2 McDonough st, s s, 175.6 e Sumner av, 100x100. John Garrahan and George Burke agt Michael Rofano, owner and contractor.................. 275 00

3 Twelfth av, n w cor 58th st, 100.2x100. Frank D. Creamer agt Martha J. Gue, owner, and Emil Kehler, contractor.................. 489 95

3 Montague st, n s, 175 w Court st, 50x200 to Pierrepont st. C. B. Keogh Mfg. Co. agt The Real Estate Exchange (Lim.), Brooklyn, owner, and James J. Garland, contractor.................. 6,751 00

3 Schenck av, e s, 162 n Arlington av, 75x100.1. Danmar & Fischer agt Mrs. Thomas F. Parker extrx, Thomas F. Parker dec'd and Elizabeth J. Rapalje, owners, and Thomas F. Parker, contractor... 100 00

3 Hicks st, No. 25, n e cor Poplar st, 25.3x75. Washington Bulkley agt Ida Edwards, owner and contractor.................. 507 50

6 North 4th st, s s, 116 e Wythe av, 50x100. Joseph H. Colyer agt —— Wiskittel, owner, and Thomas McDonald and Jabez Burns & Sons, contractors.................. 188 70

6 Hicks st, n e cor Poplar st, 25.3x75. Sheehy & McGarry agt Ida M. Edwards, owner, and John Edwards, contractor........ 120 00

6 Same property. Joseph H. Colyer agt same owner and contractor.................. 585 83

7 Bergen st, s s, 150 w Schenectady av, 25x127. Michael Lynch agt A. & M. McGarvey, owners and contractors.................. 225 00

7 Chestnut st, w s, 198 s Fulton av, 75x100. Ernst Kubnla agt The Solidarity Watch Co., owner, and John Gibbs and John Le Clair, contractors.................. 62 00

7 Montague st, n s, Nos. 189 and 191 .... }
Pierrepont st, s s, Nos. 148 and 150........ }
South Brooklyn Saw Mill Co. agt The Brooklyn Real Estate Exchange (Lim.) and J. J. Garland.................. 1,509 77

7 Seventh st, n s, 160 w 4th av, 60x100...... }
Fourth av, n w cor 7th st, 50x60.......... }
Central G. and Elect. Fixture Co agt Charles H. Collins, owner and contractor. 198 94

7 Atlantic av, No. 2761, n s, 25 w Miller av, 25x100. August Hensinger agt Christian and Catharina Gumpert owners, and William Howard, Jr., contractor.......... 75 00

8 Sixth st, s s, 180 w 4th av, 115x100. Becker & Moloney agt Emil Lindburg, owner, and O. M. Olsen, contractor.................. 1,000 00

8 Same property. Andrew Johnson agt same owner and contractor........ 100 00

8 Fifty-third st, s s, 240 w 15th av, 100x100, New Utrecht. Henry McShane Mfg. Co. agt William Dittmir, owner, and C. F. F. Becker, contractor.................. 245 00

8 Van Voorhis st, Nos. 77–88, n s, 100 w Evergreen av; also.................. }
Van Voorhis st, Nos. 91–95 .... }
George W. Morton agt Edwin J. Bedell, owner and contractor.................. 105 00

8 Patchen av, s e cor Halsey st, 100x200. Rudolph Reimer & Co. agt Hiram Bedell, owner and contractor.................. 92 16

8 Fourteenth st, n s, 217.10 w 8th av, 100x100. James Briscoe agt George F. and Catharine Beatty, owners and contractors.... 75 00

8 West av, s s, 40 w West 2d st, 40x100, Gravesend. William Rubien agt Mary B. Rosenbaum, owner and contractor ... 782 29

9 Second st, n s, 90.7 w 7th av, 80x100. George W. Jones agt Roderick Von Graff, John Halloran, William L. Dowling, Clara O'Brien and George T. Riley, owners and contractors.................. 820 00

9 Macon st, s w cor Howard av, 200x100. Rudolph and Otto E. Reimer agt Clarence Lincoln.................. 1,965 00

9 Second st, s s, 177.10 w 6th av, 80x100. T. B. Willis & Bro. agt Archibald F. McBean, owner and contractor.................. 553 85

9 Macon st, s w cor Howard av, 93.6x100. Friedlander & Green agt Clarence Lincoln. 382 00

9 Second st, n s, 90.7 w 7th av, 80x100. John J. Campbell agt Roderick Von Graff, owner and contractor.................. 200 00

9 Linwood st, n s, 175 w Liberty av, 25x100. John C. Creveling agt John Lynch, owner, and Richard Flanagan, contractor.... 218 57

9 Elton st, s w cor Ridgewood av, 84x100. Danmar & Fischer agt Thomas F. Parker exr., &c., Thos. F. Parker dec'd and E. F. Linton, owner.................. —

SATISFIED MECHANICS' LIENS.

NEW YORK CITY.

July

3 Ninetieth st, n s, 100 w 8th av, 100x100.8. Frederick Haas agt Thomas A. Spaulding. (Lien filed Nov. 14, 1890).................. $1,300 00

3 Same property. Thomas Hagan agt same. (Feb 11, 1891).................. 1,692 00

3 Same property. Same agt same and Bernard Spaulding. (Feb. 3, 1890).......... 610 00

3 Same property. P. H. Kerwin agt same. (Nov. 1, 1890).................. 400 00

3 Fulton av, w s, 129 n 168th st. J. J. Kingston agt Phillip Bunn. (July 2, 1891)...... 100 00

3‡ Seventh av, s e cor 57th st, 175x25........ }
Fifty-sixth st, n s, 100 e 7th av, 25x—..... }
J. D. Beers and Edward Kuenstner agt Andrew Carnegie and Isaac A. Hopper & Co. and Kelly Bros. (June 19, 1891)...... 5,512 00

6 One Hundred and Twentieth st, s s, 125 w 8th av, 75x100.11. Hamann & Brown agt James Thompson. (June 29, 1891)........ 1,589 00

6 Fifty-seventh st, No. 154, s e cor 7th av, 150x175. John Kaser agt Andrew Carnegie, Charles Pollock & Co. and Adolph Scherer, (May 8, 1891).................. 39 37

6 Same property. Harry Fenwirth agt same. (May 8, 1891).................. 51 75

6 Seventy-fourth st, Nos. 435 and 437 E., n s, 25x102. Thomas Gilligan agt Harriet B. and Thomas Webster. (May 26, 1891).... 254 58

7 Thirty-ninth st, No. 410 W., s s. Herman Ehrhardt agt —— Messmer and —— Tamor. (Oct. 24, 1890).................. 19 00

7 Fulton av, w s, 129 n 168th st, 3 lots. Fischer & Helbig agt Philip Bunn. (June 25, 1891) 220 00

7 One Hundred and Fifteenth st, s s, 275 e 8th av, 175x100. G. B. Robbins & Co. agt Muller & Hauff. (April 28, 1891).............. 281 12

7 Ninety-fourth st, n s, 150 w Columbus av, 108.6x100. Thomas Haney and seven others agt James B. Brady and Clegg, Richards & Co. 8 liens. (June 30, 1891)...... 202 43

7* West End av, s w cor 87th st, 125x100. Fuller & Warren Co. agt Squire & Whipple and W. E. D. Stokes. (March 6, 1891).... 700 00

8 One Hundred and Sixteenth st, Nos. 356-362 W., s s, 75x100. Central Gas & Electric Fixture Co. agt Charles E. Moore. (May 14, 1891).................. 480 49

8 Same property. Same agt same. (April 13, 1891).................. 480 49

9¶ Thirty-eighth st, No. 342 E., s s. Lawrence Fagan agt Rachel Jacoby and John Kelleher. (July 7, 1891).................. 140 00

9‡ Twenty-sixth st, Nos. 226–232, s s, 140 w 2d av, 110x98.9. G. B. Christman agt Christopher Lochmann and Morris Grosner. (May 29, 1891).................. 1,081 05

9 Twenty-third st, n s, 200 w 6th av, 25x98.9. Frederick Klingman agt R. Rosalia Pizer Mendes. (July 9, 1891).................. 5,000 00

*Discharged by depositing amount of lien and interest with County Clerk.

‡Discharged by order of Court on filing bond.

¶Editor Record and Guide:

The filing by Lawrence Fagan against Rachel Jacoby and John Kelleher, of a mechanic's lien, July 7, 1891, was through a misunderstanding.

Lawrence Fagan.

KINGS COUNTY.

July

2 Prospect av, s e cor 8th av, 20x80.2....... }
Prospect av, s s, 46 e 8th av, 50x80.2...... }
Albany Venetian Blind Co agt Henry E. Murphy. (Lien filed Dec. 18, 1890). (Release).................. $810 00

2 Prospect av, s s, 46 e 8th av, 52x82. Herman J Hoff agt Henry J. Murphy. (Dec. 15, 1890). (Release).................. 448 16

2 Same property. John Q. Maynard agt same owner and contractor. (Jan. 16, 1891). (Release).................. 350 00

2 Prospect av, Nos 426-438, s e cor 8th av, 175x100. Charles E. Ring agt Henry E. Murphy, owner and contracror. (Dec. 18, 1890).................. 500 50

2 Madison st, No. 87, n s, 153.6 e Franklin av, 17.2x100. Daniel Fuchs agt —— wife of Alanson H. Tifft. (June 20, 1891)......... 35 00

2 Pacific st, n e cor Kingston av, 80x96. Charles H. Rice agt Franklin J. Fellowes, owner, and Bernard Marrow, contractor. (June 24, 1891).................. 405 40

3 Linden st, s e s, 219.9 n e Evergreen av, 20x100. Frederick Bertram agt Aaron Kaplan, owner and contractor. (June 9, 1891) 190 00

3 Bay 28th st, w s, 223 s Bath av, 80x96, New Utrecht. Andrias Riendian agt R. C Lane, owner, and Anson Squires, contractor. (June 2, 1891).................. 28 95

3 Macon st, s w cor Howard av, 93.6x100. Rankin & Ross agt Clarence Lincoln, owner and contractor. (July 2, 1891) .. 3,800 00

6 Sixtieth st, s s, bet 12th and 13th avs, 40x150, New Utrecht. Carl Schaum agt Philip C. and Mary Griesbach, owner, and Maria Schultz, contractor. (June 25, 1891)..... 42 50

6 Hancock st, n s Public School No. 80. Nicholas Ryan agt Board of Education, Brooklyn, owner, and Daniel F. Blainey, contractor. (June 26, 1891).......... 218 00

6 Seventh av, n w s, 200 n e 58th st, 25x100. Thomas Robinson agt Robert Carlin, owner and contractor. (June 26, 1891).... 28 00

6 Essex st, e s, 200 n Ridgewood av, 40x100. William J. Battersby agt George Josiah, owner and contractor. (July 1, 1890).... 60 00

6 Sackett st, Nos. 41-49. Benjamin R. Sage, Jr., agt Daniel Ferry, owner, and John F. Tilman, contractor. (July 2, 1891). ... 84 10

6 Same property. Andrew Deas agt same owner and contractor. (July 2, 1891)..... 77 00

6 Same property. Same agt same owner and contractor. (July 2, 1891).......... 45 75

6 Sixth av, e s. Patrick O'Hara agt Roderick Von Graff. (June 20, 1891).......... 390 00

6 Floyd st, No. 68, s s, 100 w Marcy av, 80x abt 100. Christian Konig agt Charles Armbruster, owner, and Casper Waehlen and Hermann Casper, contractor. (June 8, 1891.) (Deposit).................. 13 50

6 Same property. John Maier agt same. (June 8, 1891.) (Deposit).................. 17 80

6 Same property. Balthasar Dilgert agt same. (June 8, 1891.) (Deposit).................. 18 12

6 Same property. George Pflumm agt same. (June 9, 1891.) (Deposit).................. 21 50

8 Willoughby av, n w cor Grand av, 25x100. Charles M. White & Co. agt Edward Judson. (March 5, 1891).................. 54 08

8 Same property. Butler Hardware Co. agt same owner and contractor. (March 11, 1891).................. 410 07

8 Same property. R. G. Phelps agt same owner and contractor. (March 18, 1891).. 381 71

9 Prospect av, s e cor 8th av, 175x100. Manquis Bros. agt Harry E. Murphy. (Dec. 10, 1890).................. 52 58

9 Fourth st, n s, 297.10 e 7th av, 100x100. Ross & Snyder agt Roderick Von Graff and John Halloran, owners ond contractors. (July 1, 1891).................. 455 61

9 Fourth st, n s, 297.10 e 8th av, 100x96. Louis Sunders agt Roderick Von Graff, owner and contractor. (July 1, 1891).......... 1,415 40

10 De Kalb av, s s, 150 w Marcy av, 100x100. Johnson & Phelan agt Elizabeth S. Maitland, owner, and Charles H. Collins, contractor. (July 2, 1889.) (Deposit)........ 167 57

BUILDINGS PROJECTED.

The first name is that of the owner; ar't stands for architect, m'n for mason, c'r for carpenter and b'r for builder.

NEW YORK CITY.

SOUTH OF 14TH STREET.

Bleecker st, s s, 72.5 w Mercer st, eight-story brk and stone building, 56.1x189, gravel roof; cost, $190,000; L. Schlesinger, 128 East 74th st; ar't, Buchman & Deisler. Plan 972.

Grand st, Nos. 182 and 184, six-story brk and iron building, 51.6x85, tin roof; cost, $50,000; lessee, L. M. Hirsch, 170 East 61st st; ar't, R. Berger. Plan 967.

Sheriff st, No. 48, six-story brk building, 25x49 and 53, tin roof; cost, $12,000; H. M. Kaplan, 252 Delancey st; ar't, C. Rentz. Plan 991.

South 5th av, Nos. 33 and 35, six-story and basement brk and iron building, 50x90, metal roof; cost, $50,000; Matilda W. Bruce, 39 East 23d st; ar'ts, Jordan & Giller. Plan 981.

2d av, No. 120, five-story brk flat, 26.8x110, tin roof; cost, $25,000; L. T. Schmalholz, 93 2d av; ar't, B. W. Berger; m'n, G. Staiger. Plan 971.

Bedford st, Nos. 51 and 53, two five-story and basement brk and stone flats, one 25x89 and one 25x65 and 89.6, tin roofs; total cost, 38,000; J. L. Buttenweiser, 227 East 60th st; ar't, G. F. Pelham; m'n, J. Van Dolsen. Plan 1002.

9th st, s s, bet Avs C and D, four iron closets, irreg., tin roofs; cost, $1,000 each; Mayor, &c., City Hall; ar't, G. W. Debevoise. Plan 996.

13th st, s s, near 7th av, three iron closets, irreg., tin roofs; cost, $1,000 each; ow'r and ar't, same as last. Plan 997.

BETWEEN 14TH AND 59TH STREETS.

21st st, No. 331 W., five-story stone flat, 25x86.6, tin roof; cost, $20,000; ow'rs and b'rs, Cumming & Ferguson, 436 West 46th st; ar't, M. V. B. Ferdon. Plan 970.

25th st, Nos. 551–555 W., six-story brk shop, 75x90, tin roof; cost, $75,000; J. M. Cornell, 29 East 37th st. ar't, G. B. Cornell. Plan 983.

16th st, No. 415 E., two iron closets, irreg., tin roof; cost, $1,000 each; Mayor, &c., City Hall; ar't, G. W. Debevoise. Plan 998.

25th st, Nos. 532–534 W., three-story brk factory, 50x93.9, gravel roof; cost, $10,000; W. M. Merrill, 548 West 25th st; ar't, J. G. McMurray. Plan 1000.

27th st, n s, near 2d av, three iron closets, 26x17, 31x8.6 and 35x5, tin roof; cost, $1,000 each; Mayor, &c., City Hall; ar't, G. W. Debevoise. Plan 994.

32d st, Nos. 211–217 E., one-story iron closet, 33x6, tin roof; cost, $1,000; ow'r and ar't, same as last. Plan 995.

44th st, No. 224 E., five-story brk factory, 25x100.5, gravel roof; cost, abt $12,000; Sebastian Mfg. Co., 217 East 43d st; ar'ts, Weber & Drosser. Plan 1007.

5th av, No. 114, seven-story brk, stone, iron and terra cotta building, 46.6x150, cement and gravel roof; cost, $150,000; W. Ziegler, s w cor 5th av and 50th st; ar't, G. H. Edbrook; m'ns, Carlin & Co.; c'r, J. Lee's Sons. Plan 1011.

BETWEEN 59TH AND 125TH STREETS, EAST OF 5TH AVENUE.

94th st, n s, 330 e 3d av, three-story brk stable, 17.6x63.6 with extension, tin roof; cost, $12,000; J. H. Parker, 1459 Lexington av; ar't, G. A. Schellenger. Plan 965.

84th st, s s, 119 w Av A, two five-story stone flats, 24.8x87.6, tin roofs; cost, $22,000 each; Conlan & Gannon, 131 East 111th st; ar't, J. C. Burne. Plan 979.

110th st, Nos. 418-422 E., frame platform, 10x97, no roof; cost, $850; R. Bunke, 325 East 111th st; ar't, H. Cording. Plan 990.

113th st, No. 408 E., frame shed, 10x50, tin roof; cost, $20; H. McNally, 161 East 118th st. Plan 974.

77th st, Nos. 412 and 414 E., frame shed, 13x70, tin roof; cost, $350; lessee and b'r, G. F. Werner, 408 East 77th st. Plan 1001.

88th st, s s, 100 e Av A, three five-story brk and stone flats, 25x77, tin roofs; cost, $17,000 each; J. Schreiner, 110 West 121st st; ar't, J. Hauser. Plan 1003.

104th st, No. 307 E., frame shed, 20x8, tin roof; cost, $30; lessee, A. Floris, on premises; c'r, J. J. Corbin. Plan 1008.

Park av, e s, 75.8 n 115th st, five-story brk and stone flat, 25.2x77, tin roof; cost, $18,000; Geo. Schreiner, 104 West 121st st ar't, J. Hauser. Plan 1004.

115th st, n s, 126 e Park av, five-story brk and stone flat, 29x77, tin roof; cost, $20,000; ow'r and c'r, same as last. Plan 1005.

BETWEEN 59TH AND 125TH STREETS, WEST OF CENTRAL PARK WEST AND 8TH AVENUE.

65th st, Nos. 132 and 134 W., two three-story and basement stone dwell'gs, 18 and 18.5x56, with extensions, tin roofs; cost, $10,000 each; L. McCabe, 145 West 63d st; ar't, R. H. Robertson. Plan 989.

90th st, s s, 100 e 10th av, four five-story brk and stone flats, 25x85, tin roofs; cost, $20,000 each; L. M. Muller, 241 Union st, Brooklyn; ar't, G. A. Schellenger. Plan 986.

98th st, n s, 150 w 8th av, five-story brk and stone flat, 25x89, tin roof; cost, $25,000; E. J. Kelly, 69 East 100th st; ar't, G. A. Schellenger. Plan 985.

121st st, No. 307 W., four-story brk, stone and terra cotta building, 25x72, tin roof; cost, $17,442; M. A. Stone, chairman, 20 East 66th st; ar'ts, D'Oench & Simon. Plan 980.

West End av, n w cor 102d st, five three and four-story and basement stone dwell'gs, one 20.11, and four 20x51 with extensions, tin roofs; total, cost, $83,000; ow'r and b'r, D. Christie, 634 West End av; ar't, M. V. B. Ferdon. Plan 969.

103d st, n s, 100 e Riverside Drive, five three-story and basement stone dwell'gs, 20x55, with extension, tin roofs; cost, $16,000 each; ow'rs and b'rs, Egan & Hallecy, 273 West End av; ar't, M. V. B. Ferdon. Plan 1009.

Columbus av, No. 462, one-story brk, frame and g a store, 25.6x90, tin roof; cost, $4,000; F. H. Walker, 1 West 81st st; ar't, T. E. Thomson. Plan 1006.

110TH TO 125TH STREET, BETWEEN 5TH AND 8TH AVENUES.

120th st, s s, 410 w 5th av, four-story and basement stone dwell'g, 20x56, with extension, tin roof; cost, $20,000; O. Hammerstein, 2323 7th av; ar't, G. A. Schellenger. Plan 988.

NORTH OF 125TH STREET.

154th st, n s, 100 e 8th av, frame shed, —x50, tin roof; cost, $500; sub-lessee, C. Eiseman, 462 West 146th st; ar't, A. Spence; c'r, A. Revekes. Plan 982.

Madison av, s e cor 132d st, six five-story brk flats, two 27x75.6, two 25x70 and 75.6, one 25x92, and one 24 11x70 and 75.6, tin roofs; total, cost, abt $81,000; F. Rohrs, 302 East 126th st; ar't, W. H. C. Hornum. Plan 999.

23D AND 24TH WARDS.

Elsmere pl, n s, 400 w Marmion av, three-and-one-half-story frame dwell'g, 21x32, shingle roof; cost, abt, $3,000; J. Cappolo, Monroe av, Belmont; ar't, C. S. Clark. Plan 968.

Kelly st, s s, 50 e Tinton av, two-story brk building, 50x50, tin roof; cost, $2,500; D. Robitzek, Forest av and 156th st; ar't, A. Pfeiffer. Plan 975.

162d st, s s, 387 w Elton av, four two-story frame dwell'gs, 18.9x47, tin roofs; cost, $2,600 each; L. V. Conover, 692 East 162d st; ar't, C. C. Churchill; c'r, E. G. Ward. Plan 973.

176th st, s s, 175 w Franklin av, two-story frame dwell'g, 18x28, tin roof; cost, $1,500; Alice Titus, 946 East 176th st; b'r, A. Livingston. Plan 987.

Aqueduct av, w s, 250 n Hampden st, three-story frame dwell'g, 28.11x43.2, shingle roof; cost, $7,000; F. S. Moore, 342 East 69th st; ar't, J. W. McKecknie. Plan 984.

Brook av, n w cor 156th st, four five-story brk flats, 25x89 and 96, tin roofs; cost, $12,000 each; G. F. Johnson, 36 West 92d st; ar't, A. S. Hait. Plan 976.

Railroad av, e s, 744 s 144th st, one-story frame shop, 12x30, plank roof; cost, $75; ow'r and b'r, W. H. Hand, Mott av, n e cor 138th st; ar't, J. Wolf. Plan 992.

Valentine av, w s, 25 n Garfield st, two-story and attic frame dwell'g, 22x47, slate and metal roof; cost, $3,000; G. Schweppenhauser, 2512 8th av; ar't, G. Robinson, Jr. Plan 977.

Villa av, e s, 460.3 n Southern Boulevard, two-story frame dwell'g, 20x30, with extension, tin roof; cost, $2,000; Christina Pierce, 46 Willow terrace, Hoboken, N. J.; ar't, M. Hensel. Plan 978.

8th av, s w cor 174th st, one-story frame stable, 25x12, gravel roof; cost, $100; T. Back, on premises. Plan 966.

Poe pl, e s, 205.5 n Coles lane } ten two-
Briggs av, e s, 150 n Sherwood st } story and
attic frame dwell'gs, 20x39, slate roofs; cost, $3,000 each; W. Wicke, 34 East 68th st; c'r, G. Armstrong. Plan 1010.

Garden av, s s, 300 w Southern Boulevard, two-story frame stable, 17x25, tin roof; cost, $400; M. Ross, 82 Garden av; ar't, T. Keller. Plan 993.

KINGS COUNTY.

Plan 1273—18th st, No. 373, n s, 172.10 w 7th av, one four-story brk tenem't, 25x60, tin roof, wooden cornice; cost, $6,000; Lavinia E. Blott, 328 15th st; ar't, J. A. Hoffman; b'rs, Blott & Hoffmann.

1274—Sands st, n w cor Jay st, one five-story brk store and tenem't, 30.4x72, tin roof, iron cornice; cost, $20,000; J. T. Taaffe, Concord and Liberty sts; ar't, C. F. Eisenach; b'rs, T. Donlon and J. Lee's Sons.

1275—Henry st, s w cor Nelson st, seven four-story brk stores and tenem'ts, 25x50, tin roofs, wooden cornices; cost, each, $6,000; ow'r and b'r, John Caulfield; ar'ts, H. L. Spicer & Son.

1276—Glenmore av, n e cor Osborn st, four three-story frame stores and tenem'ts, 25x50, tin roofs; cost, each, $3,000; Feidberg & Barusch, 95 Seigel st; ar't, H. Smith; m'n, H. Schlacter; c'r, not selected.

1277—53d st, s s, 160 w 5th av, two two-story and attic frame (brk filled) dwell'gs, 20x32, single roofs; ow'r and b'r, C. B. Spicer, 3d av and 53d st; ar'ts, H. L. Spicer & Son.

1278—Withers st, n s, 225 w Graham av, one three-story frame (brk filled) tenem't, 25x55, tin roof; cost, $4,800; Elizabeth Thompson, 147 Withers st; ar't and c'r, W. A. Sloan; m'n, J. Tench.

1279—Stone av, e s, 150 n Sutter av, one three-story frame store and dwell'g, 20x36, tin roof; cost, $4,500; Jacob Axelrod, Osborn st.

1280—Linwood st, w s, 225 s Ridgewood av, 22x45, tin roof; cost, $3,500; George Purdy, 169 Linwood st; ar't, J. Wanmaker; b'r, P. G. Kerr.

1281—Broadway, e s, 162 s Greene av, one one-story frame carpenter shop, 20x15, tin roof; cost, $50; Henry Smith, 1025 Gates av.

1282—Bergen st, s s, 325 e Rochester av, one two-story frame dwell'g, 18x36, tin roof; cost, $1,500; Henry Schreiber, Rochester av, near Dean st; b'rs, P. Schubart and J. Yonder.

1283—Willoughby av, s s, 200 w Central av, one one-story frame wagon shed, 30x13, tar paper roof; cost, $75; ow'r, ar't and b'r, John Stevens, 23 Cook st.

1284—Williams av, w s, 100 n Atlantic av, one two-story frame (brk filled) dwell'g, 23x38, tin roof; cost, $3,000; Mary McCook, Atlantic av, near Essex st; ar't, C. Mainz; b'rs, J. Bennett and H. Cook.

1285—Stanhope st, n s, 100 e Hamburg av, two three-story frame (brk filled) tenem'ts, 25x56, tin roofs; cost, $4,000; ow'r and b'r, Geo. Gess, 183 Stanhope st; ar't, H. Vollweiler.

1286—Varet st, No. 103, one four-story frame (brk filled) tenem't, 25x80, tin roof; cost, $6,060; S. Simon, 85 East Broadway, New York; ar't, H. Vollweiler; b'r, not selected.

1287—South 1st st, s s, 100 e Driggs st, one one-story brk dwell'g, 38x14, gravel roof, iron cornice; cost, $650; ow'r and ar't, W. H. Sanford, on premises; b'rs, M. Smith and G. Layton.

1288—Halsey st, s s, 350 e Reid av, three two-story and basement brk and brown stone dwellings, 16.8x45, tin roofs, wooden cornices; cost, each, $3,500; F. C. Swimm, 358 Putnam av.

1289—Bedford av, No. 177, one three-story frame dwell'g, 20x40, tin roof; cost, $4,300; Alfred Fox, 184 Bedford av; ar't, M. J. Morrill; b'r, P. F. Fitzgerald.

1290—49th st, n s, 100 e 6th av, one two-story frame dwell'g, 20x45, tin roof; cost, $2,200; James Dunlevy, 469 Atlantic av; ar't, J. Quesenburg; b'rs, Edwards Bros.

1291—Suydam st, No. 246, one-story frame wagon shed, 25x12, tar-paper roof; cost, $75; ow'r and b'r, Henry Ruhl, 723 Hart st.

1292—Myrtle av, s s, 50 e Hart st, one one-story frame carpenter shop, 20x25, tin roof; cost, $300; Engel & Zimmermann, 79 Myrtle av; ar't, F. Holmberg.

1293—Hale av, e s, 24 s Ridgewood av, one two-story frame store and dwell'g, 17x25, tin roof; cost, $2,500; Peter Lawrence, 2921 Atlantic av; ar'ts, Danmar & Fischer; b'r, not selected.

1294—Weirfield st, n s, 81 w Central av, one three-story frame (brk filled) dwell'g, 20x64, tin roof; cost, $4,500; ow'rs, ar'ts and b'rs, L. J. Lippmann & Co., 142 Eldert st.

1295—Atkins av, w s, 230 s Sutter av, one one-story frame dwell'g, 20x20, tin roof; cost, $1,000; Fr. Franks, Hinsdale st and Atlantic av; ar'ts, Danmar & Fischer; b'r, not selected.

1296—Carroll st, No. 459, one three-story brk machine shop, 25x65, tin roof, brk cornice; cost, $6,000; H. F. L. Holbrook, 265 Pearl st; ar't, G. H. Wundram.

1297—7th st, No. 365, one story brk stable, 24.6x22, tin roof, wooden cornice; cost, $2,000; ow'r and b'r, O. Wiesner, 367 7th st; ar't, G. M. Miller.

1298—Hicks st, w s, 30 s Harrison st, one four-story brk store and tenem't, 40 and 37.3x41.2, tin roof, iron cornice; cost, $7,000; P. Pollard, on premises; ar't, W. N. Cook; b'rs, J. F. Nelson and D. J. Lynch.

1299—Clason av, e s, 60 s Lexington av, two four-story brk and red stone tenem'ts, 20x68, tin roofs, wooden cornices; cost, $24,000; John Crawley, 1059 Jefferson av; ar't, J. L. Young.

1300—Jay st, w s, 50 s Plymouth st, one five-story brk storehouse, 75x75 and 90, gravel roof, iron cornice; cost, $25,000; John W. Masury & Son, 45 Pearl st; ar't, P. Faust; b'rs, G. H. Stone & Son.

1301—28th st, s s, 475 e 3d av, one three-story frame tenem't, 25x52, tin roof; cost, $3,500; ow'r and b'r, D. Anderson, 152 28th st.

1302—Bleecker st, n s, 300 w Central av, one three-story frame (brk filled) store and tenem't, 25x57, tin roof; cost, $4,500; ow'r and b'r, Adam Metz, 177 Stanhope st; ar't, H. Vollweiler.

1303—Watkins st, w s, 100 s Dumont av, one one-story frame tailor shop, 18x20, tin roof; cost, $250; John Monsees, on premises; b'rs, McMurray Bros.

1304—Spencer st, e s, 80 n De Kalb av, one one-story brk stable, 20x45, gravel roof, brk cornice; cost, $500; John R. Woods, 573 De Kalb av; ar't, E. S. Selover; b'r, J. Thatcher.

1305—Liberty av, n e cor Hemlock st, one two-story frame store and tenem't, 25x50, tin roof; cost, $2,000; ow'r and c'r, Fred. Peterson, 171 Ashford st; ar't, C. Meins; m'n, K. A. Murphy.

ALTERATIONS NEW YORK CITY.

Plan 1277—3d av, n e cor 74th st, repair damage by fire; cost, $4,800; P. J. Curry, 216 East 73d st; ar'ts, Schneider & Herter.

1278—32d st, No. 205 E., walls altered; cost, $200; J. Everard, 29 East 32d st; ar't, M. V. B. Ferdon; b'r, E. Mallon.

1279—150th st, No. 541 E., one-story extension, 15x15; cost, $500; H. Klein, on premises; ar't, A. F. A. Schmidt; c'rs, Kramer Bros.

1280—Broome st, No. 25, new front; cost, $200; M. Jolien, 121 East 113th st; ar't, A. F. A. Schmidt; c'r, J. S. Wirsing.

1281—78th st, No. 48 E., two-story extension, 30.6x14.7, interior alterations and walls altered; cost, abt $9,500; Maria S. Gibbs, 157 Clinton st, Brooklyn; ar't, W. Hull.

1282—41st st, Nos. 247 and 249 W., interior alterations and walls altered; cost, $500; Mahony Bros., 52 New Bowery.

1283—3d av, s w cor 126th st, three-story extension, 24.11x42, walls altered and new show window; cost, $10,000; W. T. & J. H. Purdy, 40 East 126th st; ar't, C. A. Millner, Jr.; b'r, A. Arctander.

1284—Lorillard st, w s, 140 s 187th st, two-story extension, 24x17, and interior alterations; cost, $1,000; P. McBride, 2381 Lorillard st; ar't, W. Guggolz.

1285—Lawton av, Nos. 7-11, Grace av, Nos. 34 and 36, walls altered; cost, $200; City of New York; ar't, J. W. Crawford; m'n, G. Crawford.

1286—Norfolk st, No. 166, interior alterations and new front; cost, $350; W. Borosheck, 149 East 56th st; ar't, W. Graul.

1287—5th av, No. 130, windows cut in wall; cost, $180; Chickering & Son, on premises; c'r, R. McGregor.

1288—68th st, No. 50 E., one-story and basement extension, 10.2x14, interior alterations, walls altered and plumbing changed; cost, $7,000; L. Seeberger, 52 East 61st st; ar't, A. Zucker.

1289—5th av, s w cor 37th st, southern portion on av to be raised, four-story extension, 21.6x97, and front wall rebuilt; cost, $75,000; R. & O. Goelet, 9 West 17th st; ar'ts, McKim, Mead & White; m'ns, Reid & Co.; c'rs, Hamilton & Sons.

1290—47th st, No. 453 W., one-story and basement extension, 18.9x45, interior alterations and walls altered; cost, $1,000; ow'rs and c'rs, Jennings & Welstead, 922 9th av; ar'ts, Hubert, Pirsson & Hoddick; m'ns, Mahoney & Watson.

1291—162d st, n s, 120 w Elton av, foundation rebuilt, raised one story, windows altered; cost, $3,500; G. N. Reinhardt, 1110 Washington av; ar't, P. Weiler.

1292—Columbus or 9th av, s w cor 99th st, windows altered; cost, $100; Sonu Bros., 1038 5th av; ar't, J. C. Burne; b'r, P. Drommeshausen.

1293—11th av, w s, 25 n 25th st, front and roof altered; cost, $1,000; I. T. Williams, 18 West 36th st; b'r, A. Balschun.

1294—5th av, No. 288, interior alterations, new front; cost, $2,000; lessee, J. L. Myers, 1277 Madison av; ar't, C. B. J. Snyder; m'n, F. L. Wingent.

1295—Crosby st, Nos. 13-17, rear, new boiler, foundation and stack; cost, $500; lessee, V. Thurkauf, 342 East 43d st; m'n, C. Dinger.

1296—Webster av, n e cor 178th st, moved and new foundation; cost, $200; A. Van Bensen, 224 East 123d st; m'n, W. W. Taylor.

1297—28th st, No. 40 W., walls altered for new front; cost, $1,000; lessee, J. Ulber, on premises; ar't, J. Hauser; m'ns, Priebe & Co.

1298—115th st, No. 344 E., interior alterations and walls altered; cost, $500; F. Caparino, 108 Mulberry st; ar't, H. Dudley; m'n, P. Integlia.

1299—Lexington av, No. 198, interior alterations and walls altered; cost, $450; H. Bohlen, 200 Lexington av; ar't, W. Graul.

1300—3d av, Nos. 1310-1320, new show windows and doors; cost, $1,800; Vogel Bros., 111 East 80th st; c'r, P. Haughey.

1301—120th st, No. 513 E., windows altered; cost, $100; Mayor, &c., City Hall; ar't, G. W. Debevoise.

1302—32d st, No. 23 W., one-story extension, 13x25; cost, $2,000; agents, S. V. R. Cruger & Co., 187 Fulton st; b'rs, Spearing & Son.

1303—36th st, Nos. 226 and 228 E., interior alterations; cost, abt $5,000; P. T. O'Brien, 118 East 56th st; ar'ts, Snook & Sons.

1304—41st st, Nos. 45 and 47 E., eight-story extension, 25x90; cost, abt $130,000; Lincoln Safe Deposit Co., 32 East 42d st; ar'ts, Harney & Purdy; m'n, McCabe Bros.; iron, A. J. Campbell.

1305—Pitt st, No. 137, interior alterations, walls altered and new front; cost, $1,500; E. Jacobs, 57 East 88th st; ar'ts, Kurtzer & Rohl.

1306—South st, No. 261, repair damage by fire; cost, $2,500; agent, T. Hitchcock, 8 East 29th st; m'n's, W. A. & F. E. Conover; c'rs, Hoe's Sons.

1307—Broadway, No. 1289, new chimney; cost, $50; lessee, J. Trainor, 1291 Broadway; m'n, J. Curran.

1308—Delancey st, No. 206, interior alterations, walls altered, new front; cost, $800; P. Neuville, on premises; ar't, H. Horenburger.

1309—43d st, Nos. 217-233 E., interior alterations, walls altered; cost, abt $500; Sebastian Mfg. Co., on premises; ar'ts, Weber & Drosser.

1310—3d av, n e cor 99th st, one-story extension, 25x20; cost, $1,500; Louise Ellis, 38 West 34th st; ar't, E. Wenz.

1311—Sedgwick av, No. 1767, interior alterations and chimneys altered; cost, $1,300; H. H. Caigill 2d, 233 West 135th st; ar't, J. S. Post; m'n, —— Hargrave; c'r, —— Kennedy.

1312—Delancey st, No. 126, repair damage by fire; cost, $2,000; T. Harris, 135 East 54th st; b'rs, Clark & Co.

1313—Morris av, No. 697, raised to grade; cost, $300; C. Bauer, on premises; art, F. J. Miller.

1314—23d st, No. 118 W., first and second stories altered for stores, walls altered and extensive interior changes; cost, $13,000; agent, J. R. Brown, 152d st, bet 11th and 12th avs; ar'ts, D. & J. Jardine.

1315—23d st, No. 49 W., new elevater; cost, $3,000; W. C. Schermerhorn, on premises; ar't, H. J. Hardenbergh.

1316—Broome st, No. 415, building on lot No. 417 moved next to No. 415, extended four stories, 25.1x60.6, buildings connected, party wall underpinned, &c.; cost, $23,000; New York Catholic Protectory, on premises; ar't, L. J. O'Connor.

1317—5th av, No. 235, walls altered; cost, $400; agent, J. M. Martin, on premises; m'n, J. V. Myers; c'rs, Crockett & Weeks.

1318—Delancey st, No. 188, raised one story, four-story and basement extension, 19.6x47.3, interior alterations, new store front, walls altered and chimneys rebuilt; cost, $10 000; Jetta Brokowsky, 69 Henry st; ar't, F. Ebeling.

1319—13th st, No. 124 E., one-story extension, 24.6x34, interior alterations and walls altered; cost, $1,500; E. Kearney and ano., 16 East 30th st; m'n, B. W. Brown; c'r, E. Marden.

1320—Columbus av, w s, bet 67th and 68th sts, new gallery; cost, $3,000; City of New York; ar't, J. Guy.

1321—53d st, No. 3 E., repair damage by fire; cost, $10,000; W. S. Pyle, 557 Madison av; ar'ts, Romeyn & Stever.

1322—1st av, Nos. 185 and 187, interior alterations; cost, $100; C. H. Reed, on premises; ar't, C. Rentz; c'r, F. Bochert.

1323—Delancey st, No. 252, walls altered and new front; cost, $3,000; H. M. Keplan, on premises; ar't, C. Rentz.

1324—West st, w s, foot Cortlandt st, shelter shed removed and covered balcony erected; cost, $2,000; Pennsylvania Railroad Co., 233 South 4th st, Philadelphia, Pa.

1325—River av, e s, 150 s 182d st, walls altered; cost, $1,000; Mrs. M. Murphy, on premises; ar't, J. C. Kerby.

1326—36th st, No. 39 W., repair damage by fire; cost, $1,835; att'y, R. L. Stanton, on premises; ar't, R. W. Gibson; c'r, E. Smith.

1327—5th av, No. 321, one-story and basement extension, 26x31; cost, $2,500; lessees, Baumgarten & Co., 25 West 73d st; ar'ts, Schiesel & Co.

1328—3d av, No. 2375, walls altered and front rebuilt; cost, $1,000; lessee, J. H. Knoop, 2113 Lexington av; ar't, M. Gerstt; b'r, P. Suhr.

1329—Ogden av, n e cor Union st, basement raised 4 feet, three-story extension, 18x16, interior alterations, and walls altered; cost, $1,500; T. F. Kennedy, on premises; ar't, A. Spence.

KINGS COUNTY.

Plan 629—Greene st, No. 216, flat tin roof; cost, $400; Joseph Wey, on premises; ar't, C. Dunkhase; b'r, —— Mulhearn.

630—McKibbin st, n s, 640 e Bushwick av, one-story frame extension, 71x25 and 10.4, gravel roof; cost, $1,000; Williamsburgh Flint Glass Co., on premises; ar'ts, D. Acker & Son.

631—Willoughby av, No. 1005, brk foundation; cost, $100; Mrs. L. Rheinhardt, on premises; b'r, W. Boyle.

632—Powers st, No. 113, two-story frame extension, 22x15, tin roof; cost $700; John Harrington, on premises; ar't and c'r, C. Flood; m'n, A. Huber.

633—Evergreen av, e s, 105 s Noll st, raised 10 feet on stone foundation; cost, $500; ow'r and ar't, J. Becker, 12 Central av; b'r, A. Sachs.

634—5th av, n e cor 11th st, roof raised 3 feet, tin roof; cost, $450; M. Kavanagh, on premises; b'r, T. J. Smith.

635—Broadway, Nos. 1143 and 1145, one-story brk extension, 25x34.6, tin roof; cost, $1,800; M. Blonsky, 1145 Broadway; ar't, F. Holmberg; b'r, not selected.

636—3d av, w s, 25 n 18th st, flat tin roof; cost, $600; L. S. Batterson; b'r, H. Miller.

637—Sands st, No. 93, underpin east wall, lay foundation and brk wall; cost, $500; lessees, J. O. Zobst & Son; ar't, C. F. Eisenach; b'r, T. Donlon.

638—Van Buren st, No. 139, one-story and basement brk foundation, 12.6x16, tin roof; cost, $400; Mr. Preston, on premises; ar'ts, I. D. Reynolds & Son; b'r, D. S. Beasley.

639—Sumner av, No. 474 raised 6 feet on brk wall, also one-story brk extension, 15x12, tin roof; cost, $500; Joseph B. F. Hodgson, on premises.

640—Wythe av, No. 172, inclose first story of extension; cost, $120; J. M. Lotts, on premises.

641—Sutter av, n s, 151 e Van Sielen av, two-story frame extension, 15x12, tin roof; cost, $200; Julius Heipe, 374 Sutter av.

642—New York av, n e cor St. Marks av, two-story and basement brk extension, 7.9 and 3.9x13.9, tin roof; cost, $600; Henry Bentz, on premises; ar't, G. P. Chappell.

643—Keap st, No. 193, three-story and basement brk foundation, 20x14, tin roof; cost, $2,000; Wm. H. Knight, on premises; b'rs, W. & T. Lamb and R. B. Ferguson.

644—Court st, e s, 36 n Livingston st, walls underpinned with brk wall, &c.; cost, $800; Williamson Parker, Court st; ar't, W. B. Tubby; b'rs, A. C. Walbridge and Morris & Selover.

645—Eckford st, No. 218, one-story frame extension, 8x8, tin roof; cost, $200; ow'r and c'r, Geo. Robbins, on premises; m'ns, G. Smith & Son.

646—Evergreen av, n w cor Covert st, raised 18 inches on brk wall; cost, $250; M. Sutz; b'r, E. Loerch.

647—Maspeth av, No. 34, add one story, also new cellar and front alteration; cost, $2,500; G. Manganaro, 21 Marion st, New York; ar't, H. Vollweiler; b'r, not selected.

648—St. Felix st, No. 42, add one story, flat tin roof; cost, $125; ow'r, ar't and b'r, Wm. H. Cottrell, on premises.

649—De Kalb av, No. 751, add one story, flat tin roof; cost, $700; August Tanguerey, on premises; ar't and b'r, J. H. Smith.

650—Broadway, e s, 75 s Ditmars st, interior alterations; cost, $100; ow'r, ar't and m'n, Fr. Luke, on premises; c'r, J. Rueger.

651—Fulton st, cor Hopkinson av, take out part of party wall, insert girder; cost, $100; M. Pabst & Son, on premises; b'r, C. Baur.

652—Suydam pl, No. 22, two-story frame extension, 13 and 16x25, tin roof; cost, $500; Ellen Bolton, on premises; ar't and b'r, E. J. Bedell.

653—Reid av, s e cor Halsey st, three-story brk extension, 23.6x13.6, tin roof; cost, $1,400; Herman Hartjen, on premises; ar't, A. Herbert; b'r, J. H. Smith.

654—Tompkins pl, No. 37, interior alterations and balcony fire escapes; cost, $3,500; R. C. Layton, 64 South st, New York; ar't, J. W. Bailey; b'r, not selected.

655—Melrose st, s s, 200 w Knickerbocker av, dig away hill and lower church, also one-story frame extension, 8.3x45, shingle roof; cost, $2,000; Emanuel German Evangelical Church; ar'ts, Danmar & Fischer; b'r, not selected.

656—Jamaica av, s w cor Bradford st, brk wall east end and interior alterations; cost, $500; ow'r, ar't and b'r, R. Given, 55 Canton st.

657—Stone av, w s, 40 n Bergen st, add one story to extension; cost, $100; Henry T. Gregory, 11 Somers st.

658—Broadway, n e cor Ditmars st, repair damage by fire; cost, $300; Anton Figelino.

659—Centre st, No. 63, flat tin roof; cost, $100; John M. Smith, on premises.

660—Flushing av, No. 364, repair damage by fire; cost, $750; T. B. Ryrie, Flushing and Kent avs; ar'ts and b'rs, Holmes Bros.

MISCELLANEOUS.

BUSINESS FAILURES.

N. Y. ASSIGNMENTS—BENEFIT CREDITORS.

July

3 Andrews, Proctor H. (dealer in hardware and house-furnishing goods, at No. 334 West 125th st), to William C. Reddy; preferences $2,050

6 Salomon, William and Michael Frank (composing the firm of Salomon & Frank, wholesale tobacco business, at No. 85 Maiden lane), to Louis H. Rascover; without preferences.

7 Bureton, Albert (bookseller and stationer, at No. 49 8th av), to William Z. Snyder; without preferences.

7 Arnold, Brainerd T. (hotel keeper, at No. 825 Broadway), to Ensign O. Beale; without preferences.

8 Keiler, Raphael (retail dealer in children's clothing), to Nathan Lewis; without preferences.

8 Butler, Morris (doing business under name of Joseph Butler, jewelry dealer, at No. 1107 2d av), to Max A. Kreielsheimer; without preferences.

8 Harmer, Mary (retail boot and shoe dealer, at No. 2249 3d av), to Thomas H. Bartindale; without preferences.

8 Engel, Leopold and Rachel Stern (Stern & Engel, wines and liquors, at No. 168½ Attorney st), to Michael E. Goodhart; without preferences.

9 Pearce, John, Jr., and Henry M. Leverich (Pearce & Co., engineers' supplies, at 681 1st av), to Edmund T. Oldham; without preferences.

PROCEEDINGS OF THE BOARD OF ALDERMEN AFFECTING REAL ESTATE.

* Under the different headings indicates that a resolution has been introduced and referred to the appropriate committee. † indicates that the resolution has passed and has been sent to the Mayor for approval. ‡ Passed over the Mayor's veto.

New York, July 6, 1891.

PAVING.

122d st, from Av A to Harlem River; granite block.†
101st st, from 3d to Lexington av; granite block.†
122d st, bet Manhattan and Columbus avs; asphalt.†
90th st, from crosswalk near westerly intersection of 1st av to crosswalk near easterly intersection of 2d av; granite block.†
19th st, from westerly crosswalk of Av A to easterly crosswalk of 1st av; granite block.†
121st st, from Av A to Harlem River; granite block.†
115th st, from Av A to Harlem River; granite block.†
101st st, from 1st to 2d av; granite block.‡
119th st, from 7th to Lenox av; granite block.†
116th st, from Av A to Harlem River; granite block.†
58th st, from a point abt 360 feet w 11th av to Hudson av; granite block.†
117th st, from 8th to Columbus av; asphalt.†
100th st, from 3d to Lexington av; granite block.†
96th st, from Lexington to 4th av; granite block.†
117th st, from Madison to 5th av; granite block.†

FLAGGING.

6th av, s w cor 32d st, 30x100; relaid and reset.†
2d av, n w cor 101st st, 110x110.†
94th st, s s, from 2d av to point abt 135 w therefrom; relaid and reset.†
5th av, n w cor 85th st, —x150.†
34th st, from 10th av to North River.†
10th av, e s, from 29th to 30th st.‡
30th st, s s, from 9th to 10th av.†
19th st, from Av A to 1st av.†
Riverview terrace, e s, from Sedgwick av to point 508 ft. therefrom.†
Riverview terrace, w s, from Sedgwick av to Dock st.†
Madison av, both sides, from 71st to 72d st.†

FENCING VACANT LOTS.

98th st, n e cor 5th av.†
92d st, n s, from Central Park West to Columbus av.†
144th st, s s, bet 8th and Bradhurst avs.†

MAINS.

86th st, from Av B to East River; gas.†
146th st, from Boulevard to Hudson River R. R.; water.†
146th st, from Boulevard to Hudson River R. R.; gas.†
Albany Post road, from Dash lane to Riverdale lane; gas.†
Creston av, from Kingsbridge road to St. James st; gas.†
Coles pl, from Kingsbridge road to Poe pl; water and gas.†
Poe pl, from Coles pl to point 450 n therefrom; water and gas.†

REGULATING, GRADING, ETC.

Amsterdam av, from s s 194th st to Fort George av.†
Bronx River road, bet Grand av and Eastchester st.†

APPROVED PAPERS.

Resolutions passed by the Board of Aldermen calling for the following improvements have been signed by the Mayor for the week ending July 4, 1891. *Indicates that the Mayor neither appoved nor objected thereto, therefore the same became adopted.

REGULATING, GRADING, ETC.

152d st, bet Courtlandt av and east curb line Railroad av East.

PAVING.

53d st, from e s 12th av to Hudson River.

CROSSWALKS.

Jennings st, at each intersecting st or av, from Union to Stebbins av.
7th av, at n and s s 134th st.

FLAGGING.

7th av, n w cor 120th st, 100x100.
Church st, w s, bet Vesey and Fulton sts.
East st, Nos. 11, 13 and 15, in front of.
5th av, e s, from 116th to 117th st.
131st st, s s, from 5th to Lenox av.

FENCING VACANT LOTS.

77th st, south cor Columbus av, 150x100.

BROOKLYN BOARD OF ALDERMEN.

Brooklyn, July 6, 1891.

CULVERTS.

Wyckoff st, s w cor Nevins st.†

CROSSWALKS.

Manhattan av, at Meserole av.†

ELECTRIC LIGHTING.

Washington av, s e cor De Kalb av.†

FENCING VACANT LOTS.

Pennsylvania av, bet Fulton st and Atlantic av.†

FLAGGING.

Ashford st, e s, bet Atlantic and Arlington avs.
Ashford st, w s, bet Fulton st and Arlington av.
Elton st, bet Atlantic av and Fulton st.
Fulton st, bet Dresden and Crescent sts.
Fulton st, bet Warwick and Dresden sts.
Linwood st, bet Atlantic av and Fulton st.
Linwood st, s s, bet Ridgewood st and Arlington av.
Albany av, w s, bet Butler and Douglass st, by request. } †
Arlington av, bet Cleveland and Fulton sts.
Arlington av, bet Jamaica and Van Siclen avs.
Arlington av, s s, bet Warwick and Ashford sts.
Arlington av, n s, bet Ashford and Cleveland sts.
Ridgewood av, bet Elton and Linwood sts.
4th av, bet 39th and 50th sts.

GAS LAMPS, &C.

Ashford st, bet Glenmore av and Eastern Parkway.
Christopher st, bet Glenmore and Sutter avs.
Eastern Parkway, bet Powell st and Stone av.
Eastern Parkway, bet Stone and Rockaway avs.
Folsom pl, bet Essex and Linwood sts.
Moffat st, bet Central and Knickerbocker avs.
Osborn st, bet Glenmore and Sutter avs.
Sackman st, bet Eastern Parkway and Sutter av.
Thatford st, bet Liberty and Sutter avs.
Warwick st, bet Glenmore av and Eastern Parkway. } †
Watkins st, bet Eastern Parkway and Sutter av.
Atlantic av, bet Railroad av and Enfield st.
Belmont av, bet Christopher st and Rockaway av.
Liberty av, bet Berriman and Enfield sts.
Liberty av, bet East New York and Christopher avs.
Stone av, bet Glenmore and Sutter avs.
St. Marks av, bet East New York and Rockaway avs.
Sutter av, bet Christopher and Rockaway avs.

GRADING, PAVING, ETC.

Moffat st, bet Central and Knickerbocker avs.†
Pilling st, bet Broadway and Bushwick av.*
Scholes st, bet Waterbury st and Morgan av. }
13th st, bet 8th and 9th avs. } †
St. Marks av, bet Buffalo and Saratoga avs, by request. }

SEWER.

Moffat st, bet Central and Knickerbocker avs.†

STREET OPENING.

Moffat st, bet Central and Hamburg avs. } †
Moffat st, bet Knickerbocker av and City line. }

ADVERTISED LEGAL SALES

REFEREES SALES TO BE HELD AT THE REAL ESTATE EXCHANGE AND AUCTION ROOM (LIMITED), 59 to 65 LIBERTY STREET, EXCEPT WHERE OTHERWISE STATED.

July

34th st, No. 316, s s, 228.9 e 2d av, 21.3x98.9, four-story brk tenem't, by R. V. Harnett & Co. (Amt due $8.478) 13

38th st, No. 229, n s, 490.1 e 8th av, 20.7x98.9, five-story brk flat, by William Kennelly. (Amt due $10,684) 13

54th st, Nos. 427 and 429, n s, 394 e 1st av, 50x100.5, two-story brk stable with one-story frame buildings on rear, by Richard V. Harnett. (Partition sale) 13

Amsterdam av, No. 710, w s, 75.8 s 96th st, 25x89.9, five-story brk flat with stores, by Smyth & Ryan. (Amt due $26,854) 13

3d av, No. 1070, w s, 50.5 n 63d st, 25x100, five-story stone front store and flat, by R. V. Harnett & Co. (Partition sale) 13

11th st, No. 328, n s, 163 w Greenwich st, 23x95, three-story brk tenem't with three-story brk tenem't on rear, leasehold, by Smyth & Ryan.. 14

19th st, No. 319, n s, 200 w 8th av, 21.4x92, three-story brk dwell'g, by D. P. Ingraham & Co. (Partition sale) 14

22d st, No. 44, s s, 257 e 6th av, 23x98.9, four-story stone front dwell'g, by William Kennelly. (Amt due $28,960) 14

50th st, No. 120, s s, 250 w 6th av, 25x100.5, three-story brk stable, by D. P. Ingraham & Co. (Amt due $20,114) 14

75th st, No. 222, s s, 270.10 e 3d av, 19.7x102.2, four-story brk tenem't, by B. L. Kennelly. (Partition sale) 14

3d st, s s, 190 s e Av A, 24.9x105.11x24.4x105.11 ....
18th st, s s, 244 e 1st av, 25x92 ....
2d av, e s, 50.3 s 48th st, 50.2x100 ....
6th st, s s, 82.8 e 3d av, runs south 44.3 x southwest 4.6 x west 0.9 x south 49 x east 25 x north 97 to 6th st, x west 22.6 to beginning, except portion on west side ....
48th st, Nos. 309 and 311, n s, 125 e 2d av, 50x100.5 ....
3d st, s s, 98 e Av A, 22x88.6 ....
3d av, e s, 24.4 s 6th st, runs southeast 60.1 x northeast 24.4 to 6th st, x southeast 19.11 x southwest 48.6 x northwest 80 to 3d av, x northeast 24.2 to beginning ....
6th st, s s, 82.8 s e 3d av, runs southwest 44.3 x southwest 4.6 x northwest 0.9 x northeast 18 to 6th st, x southeast 2.6 to beginning ....
Av A, s w cor 9th st, 27x86.6 ....
by William Kennelly. (Partition sale) 15

Carmine st, No. 79, n s, abt 300 w Bedford st, 24 x—, three-story brk store and tenem't ....
Houston st, No. 228 } begins Houston st, n s, 68.6
Downing st, No. 64 } e Varick st, 25x81.5 to Downing st, x25x71.3, five-story brk tenem't with stores ....
Downing st, Nos. 57 and 59, n s, 240.9 w Bedford st, 39.1x90, three and five-story brk tenem'ts with stores and two-story brk building on rear ....
by Samuel W. Bower, recvr., at City Hall. (Receiver's sale) 16

Av A, Nos. 1314–1320, n e cor 70th st, 100.4x98, four and five-story brk planing mill, &c., by R. V. Harnett & Co. (Amt due $54,984) 16

137th st, s s, 430 w Lenox av, runs south 99.11 x west 20 x north 48 x west 22 x north 51.11 to 137th st, x east 42, three-story brk dwell'g and vacant, by William Kennelly. (Amt due $15,947) 16

112th st, n s, 125 w Lenox av, 25x100.11, five-story brk flat, by B. L. Kennelly. (Amt due $4,230; prior morts. $20,000) 16

54th st, No. 542, s s, 300 e 11th av, 26x156x25.3x152.6, three-story brk store and tenem't, by William Kennelly. Amt due $1,450) 17

50th st, Nos. 35 and 37, n s, 150 w Park av, 50x100.5, two five-story brk flats, by J. N. Goldjug. (Amt due $95,175) 20

50th st, No. 589, n s, 500 w 10th av, 25x100.5, five-story brk tenem't with stores, by R. V. Harnett & Co. (Amt due $3,548; prior morts. $7,000) 20

Amsterdam av, Nos. 641–649, n e cor 91st st, 136.5 x100, five five-story brk flats with stores, by R. V. Harnett. (Amt due $39,139; prior morts. $120,000) 20

KINGS COUNTY.

July

6th av, s w cor Pacific st, runs south 142.6 x west 125 x north 32.6 x east 25 x north 110 to Pacific st, x east 100 to beginning, three-story brk factory; assessed value $28,000; by T. A. Kerrigan, at the Real Estate Exchange, 189 and 191 Montague st 13

Bushwick av, n e cor Flushing av, 17.8x115x15x100; assessed value, $500; partition; by F. W. Rebhann, ref., at County Court House 14

Repose pl, n s, 120 w Jerome st late John st, 60x—, vacant; assessed value, $270; by T. A. Kerrigan, at County Court House 15

Pierrepont st, No. 61, n s, 120 e Hicks st, 27x132.0½ to Love lane, x27.0½x133.8½, three-story brk dwell'g; assessed value, $21,000 ....
St. Marks av, Nos. 976–984, s w cor Albany av, 100x105, four three-story and basement brk dwell'gs; assessed value $3,500 each, and one four-story brk flat with store, assessed value $6,000 ....
by T. A. Kerrigan, at 13 Willoughby st 15

Furman av, Nos. 19–25, n w s, 180 n e Broadway, 80x100, four two-story frame dwell'gs; assessed value, $2,500 each; by F. W. Keller, ref., at County Court House 16

Georgia av, w s, 175 s Fulton av, 50x100, two two-story frame tenem'ts; assessed value, $6,000; partition ....
Jefferson av, No. 444, s s, 228.4 e Throop av, 16.8 x100, three-story brk dwell'g; assessed value, $4,200 ....
by T. A. Kerrigan, at 13 Willoughby st 16

St. Marks av, No. 279, n s, 150 w Underhill av, 25 x131, four-story brk tenem't; assessed value, $7,000 ....
St. Marks av, No. 281, n s, 125 w Underhill av, 25 x131, four-story brk tenem't; assessed value, $7,000 ....
Lot at Coney Island known as No. 4 on map of Wyckoff tract of common lands of Gravesend, begins at intersection of south line of lot 3 on same map and lot hereby described, runs south along w s of a road 50 ft wide — x west to e s of 10-foot way, x north — x east to beginning, except ....
West 5th st, w s, 43.4 s of W. Thompsons land, runs northwest along land of Coney Island Elevated Railroad 52.7 x northeast 134.11 to st, x south 43.4 ....
by T. A. Kerrigan, at 13 Willoughby st 17

LIS PENDENS, KINGS COUNTY.

July

7th st, s s, 402.1 w 8th av, 20.9x100. George A. Minasian agt Mary J. Harvey; att'y, George A. Minisian in person 8

Prospect av, n e s, 515 s e 3d av, 20x62.11x29.10x61.3. Peter McKiernan agt Marilla Goodwin; att'y, A. R. Thompson, Jr 8

Grove st, n w s, 225 n e Central av, 22x100. Virginia A. Kleine agt Charles Lohrentz; att'y, William H. Ingraham 8

Palmetto st, n w s, 320 n e Central av, 90x100. Thomas Berkeley agt Julius A. M. Mosby; att'y, Bolton Hall 8

1st st, s w s, 386 n w 1st av, 53.11x100. Cornelius E. Donnellon agt Francis A. Constant; att'y, Marion A. Vintch 8

Eldert st, s e s, 75 s w Evergreen av, —x75. Richard Goodwin agt Abby J. Bills; att'y, Frederick Cobb 8

Saratoga av, n w cor Herkimer st, 120x100. Noah Tebbetts agt George H. Gibby; att'y, Noah Tebbetts, in person 6

Saratoga av, s w cor Fulton st, 60x100. Same agt same; same att'y 6

7th av, w s, 20.9 s 1st st, 105.11x90.9. Thomas Roberts Stevenson Co. agt Emily Reeves; foreclos. mechanic's lien; att'ys, Phillips & Avery. 6

Fleet st, n w s, 184.9 n e De Kalb av, runs northwest 42.10 x west 12.2 x north 19.2 x east 20.8 x southeast 42.10 to st, x southwest 22 ....
Bergen st, s s, lot 32 map Nehemiah Denton, 25x94.9x25x112.7 ....
Pacific st, s s, 150 w 6th av, runs south 110 x east 23 x north 104 to Flatbush turnpike road, x northwest 11 to st, x west 17 ....
Isabella Aitken agt Margaret A. Aitken; partition; att'y, Daniel B. Thompson 6

Cooper st, s s, 52 w Knickerbocker av, 19x80 ... }
Palmetto st, s s, 117 w Knickerbocker av, 50x100. }
Palmetto st, s s, 201 w Knickerbocker av, 17x100. }
Isaac W. Welton agt James S. Leonard; action for dissolution of partnership; att'y, James P. Philip 6

14th st, n e s, 149.6 n w 6th av, 16.8x100. Townsend C. Willis agt Edwin A. Austing; att'ys, Garretson & Eastman 6

Bedford av, s w cor Rodney st, 133x100. James Floy agt Mary Tallman; att'y, George W. Ellis. 6

Graham av, e s, 50 n Scholes st, 25x100. East New York Savings Bank agt Jacob J. Seelbach; att'ys, Sackett, Lang, Reed & McKewen 6

Van Voorhis st, n w s, 134 s w Evergreen av, 17x100. Julian Lucas agt Edwin J. Bedell; att'ys, Hirsh & Rasquin 6

Van Voorhis st, n w s, 258 s w Evergreen av, 17x100. Same agt Mary N. McLaren; same att'y ... 6

Greene av, s s, 80 e Carlton av, 41.10x100. Gustav H. Haman agt Joseph Welbier; foreclos. mechanic's lien; att'y, Frank Schaeffler 7

Varet st, s s, 175 w Ewen st, 25x100. Theodor Fraundorf agt August Fraundorf et al.; partition; att'y, C. L. Suardi 8

Lee av, No. 164, w s, 121 n Rutledge st, 15x81.8. Jonathan B. and J. M. Rider exrs. Frebon Rider agt Marie wife of Richard Treu; att'y, J. M. Rider 8

Elton st, w s, 175 n Liberty av, 25x90. Benjamin Evdon agt Israel Ivdan; partition; atty's, E. & K. Thornton 8

5th av, w s, 130 n Pacific st, 32.7x14.4x28.11x1x14.11 to 5th av, x 30. Mary S. Clark agt William Curry et al.; att'y, C. A. Clark 8

Macon st, s s, 272.6 w Stuyvesant av, 17.6x100. Arthur Taylor agt Mary E. Winters; att'y, J. H. H. Blauvelt 9

Bay 14th st, n w s, 150 s w 86th st, 25x108.4. Town New Utrecht Co-operative Building and Loan Assoc. agt Anna White; att'y, J. C. Church 9

Cumberland st, w s, 303.10 n Atlantic av, 17x100. John R. McDonald agt Caroline A. Henry et al.; att'y, A. G. McDonald 9

McDonough st, n w cor Reid av, 25.6x100. Charles G. Reynolds agt Jennie S. wife of John A. Sinclair; att'y, D. Barnett 9

Van Voorhis st, n w s, 258 s w Evergreen av, 17x100. Julian Lucas agt Mary N. McLaren et al.; att'ys, Hirsh & Rasquin 9

Van Voorhis st, n w s, 134 s w Evergreen av, 17x100. Same agt Edwin J. Bedell et al.; same att'ys 9

Old Clove road, centre line, at s s Prospect pl, which point is 345.6 e Rogers av, runs south along road 100 x south still along Old road 28.3 x west 161.1 x north 28 x east 137 x north 100 to Prospect pl, x east 20.6. Patrick and Kate C. Ledwith agt Peter McDonough; action to cancel deed; att'y, J. F. Foley 9

Glenada pl, w s, 200 s Decatur st, runs north 100 x west 100 x south 87.11 x east 24.11 x south 6.10 x east 77.2. Barstow Stove Co. agt William W. Reynolds and Walter V. Burcher; attachment. 9

RECORDED LEASES.

NEW YORK. Per Year

Bayard st, No. 88. August Lindemann to John C. Felten; 10 years, from May 1, 1884. $1,500

Bayard st, No. 88. Barney Isaacs to Charles Davis; 8 years, from May 1, 1894 1,500

Bayard st, No. 10, store and basement. Michael Harrison to Samuel Juskowitz; 3 years, from May 1, 1891 1,080

Baxter st, No. 144. Magdalena Baumann to Mrs. Charles Roth; 8 years, from May 1, 1891 324

Broadway, No. 826, store floor and basement. Samuel D. Folsom to Louis Klopsch; 4 11-12 years, from June 1, 1891 .... 800, 1,000

Broadway, No. 826, n e cor 12th st. J. Waldron Gillespie to Alva Owen; 5 years, from May 1, 1891 7,250

Essex st, No. 149, store floor and basement. William Schnelle to Paul Kremm; 2 10-12 years, from July 1, 1891 840

Fulton st, No. 256, store floor and basement. John H. Meyer to William Berner and John Hamald; 5 years, from Dec. 1, 1889 1,300

Henry st, No. 84, first floor. Moses Zerwich to Congregation Beal Zion Anshe Jerusalem; 1 year, from May 1, 1891 576

Little West 12th st, No. 48 and sometimes known as No. 51, being 100 w Washington st. John Fleming to William Kolloge; 7 10-12 years, from June 1, 1891 3,500

Mulberry st, Nos. 114 and 116. Don Felice Morelli to Marino Rettagliata; 5 years, from Jan. 1, 1893 4,800

Same property. Assign. lease. Rettagliata Carlo to Peratta Pietro 675

Spring st, No. 210. Peter Mullen to Fanny Bressant; 5 years, from May 1, 1890 850

Washington st, No. 770, front and back store and cellar. Emma D. Warner to John J. Danahan; 2 years 10 months and 8 days, from June 22, 1891 900

4th st, No. 253, store floor. Helene C. Schmidtmann to Philip Nehrbass; 5 years, from May 1, 1891 600

4th st, No. 61 E. Ida M. Fish Woburn to Theodora Fichtner; 10 years, from May 1, 1891. 1,600

10th st, No. 249 E., store. Ludwig Heck to Richard Krafft; 3 years, from May 1, 1891 ... 320

13th st, Nos. 51 and 53 W., first floor and basement. Benjamin O. Chisolm to Matthew Callahan and Thomas Morrissey, of Callahan & Morrissey; 3½ years, from Nov. 1, 1891 2,500

Same property } Same to same; 5 years,
14th st, No. 50 W. } from May 1, 1895 12,250

51st st, Nos. 167 and 169 E. Abiel M. Hawkins and Margaret M. Hayward exrs. Peter Asten to Charles, Solomon and Mayer Bickart, of Charles Lederer & Co.; 3 years, from May 1, 1891 2,640

52d st, No. 218 E. Max Koch to Henry M. Rath. 4 10-12 years, from July 1, 1891 1,200

151st st, No. 292 E. Mary Silver to Joseph Schaub; 3 years, from July 15, 1890 300

Av A, No. 1546, store. Stephen Pendergast to William C. Pendergast; 5 years, from May 1, 1891 .... 1,200, 1,500

Av B, No. 157, corner store. Gustav Salomon and Salomon Salomon to Daniel Gillespie, 4 10-12 years, from July 1, 1891 1,950

Av C, No. 145, store floor and part cellar. Charlotte J. Gregory and Euphemia Steventon exrs. Robert Gregory to Daniel Gillespie, 4 11-12 years, from June 1, 1891 900

Lexington av, No. 740. J. Trumbull Smith, agent for Normand Smith, to Charles A. Richter; 2 years, from Oct. 1, 1890 1,600

Park av, s e cor 110th st, store and part cellar. George B. Robinson to James Devine; 3 years, from May 1, 1893 900

2d av, s e cor 84th st, 50.5x100. James G. Sanders to Denison P. Chesbro; 10 years, from May 1, 1891 850

2d av, No. 1103, n w cor 58th st. Simon Herman to Commerford & Murphy; 4 10-12 years, from July 1, 1891 1,000

2d av, w s, 100.5 n 64th st, 25x80. Ferdinand Reinert to George Guttroff; 6½ years, from Nov. 1, 1891 1,650

3d av, e s, near 180th st, 25x100, store and dwell'g. Bridget Curry to Martin Meagher; 5 years, from May 1, 1890 .... 360, 504

3d av, No. 2558. Joseph H. Bearns to Philip Wagner; 4 10-12 years, from July 1, 1891 480

3d av, No. 3225, store and basement. Otto H. Georgi guard. Lisette Georgi to William Hayes; 1 year, from May 1, 1891 300

5th av, n w cor 16th st, Judge Building, fifth floor. The Judge Publishing Co. to Sackett & Wilhelms Lithographing Co.; 10 years, from May 1, 1889 6,000

Same property, third floor. Same to same; 8 years, from May 1, 1891 2,750

Same property, portions of building. Same to same; extension of leases for 10 years, from May 1, 1899, on original terms .... —

5th av, No. 426. Edgar B., Mary D. and Elizabeth S. Van Winkle to Sidonie C. wife of Leopold F. Thurn; 10 years, from May 1, 1891 .... 6,250, 7,000

6th av, No. 474, store. Georgina E. B. Lear to Charles Dufort and Victor Frances; 4 10-12 years, from July 1, 1891 1,500

8th av, w s, extends from 124th to 125th st and to line 150 w of 8th av. William Astor to Peter Doelger; 1½ years, from May 1, 1892, with privilege of renewal for 18½ years, from Nov. 1, 1893, at same rent 24,000

10th av, No. 503, store and cellar. Daniel R. Currin to William Price and Dennis O'Brien, of Price & O'Brien; 8 10-12 years, from July 1, 1891 2,700

CHATTELS.

NOTE.—The first name, alphabetically arranged, is that of the Mortgagor, or party who gives the Mortgage. The "R" means Renewal Mortgage.

NEW YORK CITY.

JULY 3 TO 9—INCLUSIVE.

SALOON AND RESTAURANT FIXTURES.

Arnstein, A. 419 E 70th.... Beadleston & W. Saloon Taps, &c. $55
Same....same. Saloon Ice House. 90
Same....same. Saloon Pump, &c. 90
Allport, J G. Sedgwick av.... Morrison & Kennedy. 1,000
Brodawsky, Morris. 214 Broome.... M & Griffith & Co. Pool. 300
Byrne, Joseph. 15 Madison.... T C Lyman & Co. (R) 920
Boehm, Isaac. 500 E 115th st and 278 Pleasant av.... Bernheimer & S. 2,500
Bode, Christian. 223 E 22d.... H Elias B Co. 1,800
Boylan, Lizzie. Broome and Goerck s's.... V Loewers. (R) 200
Barthune, Jacob. 84 Cannon.... M Seitz. (R) 550
Berndtson, Edward. 250 8th av.... Bernheimer & S. (R) 1,800

Bub, George. 161 Av B ..G Bechtel exr of. 2,000
Bernius & Huger. 600 11th av....Bernheimer & S. (R) 140
Block, Eliza. 70 E 4th....J Ruppert. (R) 1,000
Blum, Ernest. 1756 10th av....Bernheimer & S. (R) 1,500
Boulanger, Edward. 791 Washington... Bernheimer & S. (R) 200
Boymann, Hermann. 1463 Av A....Schmitt & S. 250
Bechtold, Geo. 1691 3d av. ..G Ehret. (R) 400
Bell, Charles. 88 4th av....J Eichler B Co. 2,600
Bock, George. 234 E 102d....P Doelger. (R) 500
Carney, James. 526 E 13th....S Liebmann's Sons B Co. 481
Clundt, Christian. 117 Av A....G Ehret. (R) 600
Cooper, John. 2525 8th av....G Ehret. (R) 3,500
Capizzuto, George. 81 Baxter....J Ruppert. (R) 763
Cooney, M J and P H. 1644 3d av....J Wallace. (R) 1,250
Callahan, T J. 503 W 61st....Williamsburgh B Co. (R) 500
Connelly, James. 100 E 110th....H Koehler & Co. 1,300
Considine, Martin. 715 Columbus av....Bernheimer & S. 4,000
Conway, Michael. 538 W 47th....D Mayer. 400
Cronley, Edward. 306 W 60th....D Stevenson. (R) 300
Culhane & Costello. 141 Amsterdam av....Beadleston & W. 500
Cardulli, Pasquale. 420 E 113th....Burr B Co. 500
De Simone & Di Palma. 397 E 11th....Bernheimer & S. Pool. (R) 125
Deyerberg, H H. 27 10th av....C Iba. 4,150
Dorsch, H G. 159 Boulevard....Wagner & S. Pool. (R) 330
Dote, Henry. Kingsbridge road and Southern Boulevard....H Zeltner. 250
Driscoll, J J. 132 Chrystie....Anchor B Co. (R) 1,775
Dubois, Oscar. 206 Wooster....Restaurant Furniture Co. Restaurant Fixtures. 49
Doughney, J J. 39 Attorney....V Loewers. 392
Doerr, G P. 228 1st av ..G Ehret. (R) 750
Daubermann, Gottfried. 526 E 116th ...W Danz. (R) 400
Dufort & Francis. 474 6th av....Beadleston & W. 1,500
Eisenberg, Frederick. 203 Stanton....F Oppermann, Jr. (R) 1,000
Eibsen, Louis. 45 West....H Kroger & Co. 1,956
Feeley, F A. 168 9th av....J Kress B Co. (R) 2,406
Ferretti, Frank. 7 Baxter....J Kress B Co. (R) 600
Fay, W J. 164 Madison....Wagner & S. Pool Table. 125
Flynn, T P. 2 Union sq... J Ahles B Co. 2,000
Farley, T H. 812 10th av .. Beadleston & W. (R) 1,500
Flynn, P L. U S Custom House....W Thompson. Restaurant Fixtures (R) 300
Gillespie, Daniel. 145 Av C....S Liebmann's Sons B Co. 1,000
Same. 157 Av C....same. 3,000
Graham, John. 19 2d av....P Doelger. (R) 1,000
Gerstle & Geiger. 1642 3d av....J Ruppert. 1,880
Giles, Patrick. 880 8th av. .M Groh's Sons. (R) 1,500
Gort, Louis. 317 5th. ..G Ringler & Co. 1,150
Grau, Alois. 202 E 76th....J Kress B Co. (R) 682
Heidelberg, Morris. 215 E 28th.. .J Kress B Co. (R) 800
Hitchcock, Frederick. 622 E 142d....J Everard. (R) 250
Hartung, G C. 67 1st av . .Bernheimer & S. 8,500
Hildebrand, John. 55 Rutger....M Eckstein B Co. 400
Hesselschwert, John. 216 E 98th....J Kuntz B Co. 300
Higgins, John. 2432 1st av....D G Yuengling, Jr, B Co. 800
Hogan & Dempsey. 1597 2d av .. G Ehret. 1,750
Horan, Thomas. 266 Fulton....J C G Hupfel B Co. 1,400
Kennedy, Minnie. 143 Spring....C H Evans & Sons. 500
Kakerbeck, Gustav. 45 Chrystie. H Schwartz. 600
Keris, Herman. 835 3d av....F & M Schaefer B Co. 2,500
Kopta, Anthony. 228 E 3d....F Oppermann, Jr. (R) 900
Kremm, Paul. 149 Essex ...P Doelger. 1,000
Kuirim, Joseph. 20 North William....C & A Bereuter. Pool Table. 875
Laughlin, Robert. 465 6th av....G Ehret. 4,000
Lungershausen, August. 114 E 3d....J A Allers. 1,300
Lieb, John. 16 Bond... Burr B Co. 1,500
Loehr, Joseph. 624 Courtlandt av....J & M Haffen. (R) 100
Ledermann, Isaac. 750 5th....G Ringler & Co. (R) 1,341
Lehmann & Monsees. 18 Little West 12th....S Liebmann's Sons B Co. (R) 400
Leahy & Turner. 571 3d av....J Ruppert. (R) 600
Maher, W J. 174 Henry....G Ehret. (R) 1,000
McGuire, J J. 1489 4th av....F & M Schaefer B Co. (R) 1,000
McHugh & Flynn. 148 Washington....J Kress B Co. (R) 400
Muhlhan, Frederick. 748 E 148th....D Stevenson. 386
Mohl, Christian. 194 10th av ...F & M Schaefer B Co. 1,000
Morgenweck, William. 545 9th av....C Morgenweck. 1,000
Makay, Frank. 38 Sheriff....V Loewers. 300
Matulewicz, Wladislaw. 135 Chrystie....W Peter B Co. 800
McCarren, Michael. 552 Water....J & M Haffen. (R) 268
Mack, James. 212 Broadway....J Everard (R) 1,141
McCarthy, John. 4 Bleecker....G Ringler & Co. 800
McCloskey & Slavin. 588 Greenwich.. J Kress B Co. (R) 500
McHugh, Patrick. 683 1st av....D Stevenson. 400
Meitzel, George. 1572 1st av....F Hower B Co. 500
Merzweiler, George. 226 E 22d... G Ringler & Co. 1,500
Meyer, J F. 1601 2d av. . J Everard. (R) 2,867
Moser, Frederick. 2466 8th av....Bernheimer & S. (R) 2,000
Murphy, P J. 144 E 14th....E M Govern. 3,000
Neuman, E and H. 237 Sullivan....M Van Rensselaer, Jr. 1,500
Newman, Charles. 407 3d av.... —— Bereuter. Pool Table. 135
Nenna, Raphael. 405 E 112th....Bernheimer & S. (R) 400
Neville, J J. 545 3d av....J Ruppert. (R) 1,000
Noonan, Michael. 348 Bowery .. J Everard. 5,085
Noon, Michael. 515 1st av... D Stevenson (R) 1,500
Nunziorto, Ferdinando. 89 Mulberry....J Kuntz B Co. (R) 500
Noonan, J E. 875 Brook av....D Mayer. (R) 1,475
Nugent, James. 470 3d av....J Everard. 1,000

O'Connor, Daniel. 208 Monroe....W H O'Connor. (Corrects error in May 23d as to Bernheimer & Schmid.) 3,000
O'Connor, John. 9 Rector....M T Garvey. 100
O'Connor, James. 1690 Madison av....Burr B Co. (R) 100
O'Connor, Patrick. 147 E 113th....P & W Ebling B Co. 2,076
O'Keefe, P J. 212 3d av....J Everard. 3,055
O'Brien, Patrick. 1505 3d av....Bernheimer & S. (R) 1,500
O'Neill, William. 194 Bleecker....Bernheimer & S. (R) 1,500
O'Reilly, Thomas. 1548 2d av....Bernheimer & S. (R) 1,800
Same. 1897 2d av Bernheimer & S. (R) 2,000
Orsat, Marie C. 124 W 27th....J Groh. (R) 1,000
Pendergast, W C. 1546 Av A....P Doelger. 1,000
Prendeville, J E. 46th st and 1st av....Bernheimer & S. Saloon Ice House. 115
Same....same. Saloon Ice House. 85
Price & O'Brien. 505 10th av....J Kress B Co. 2,000
Plate, Hermann. 1637 Lexington av....Bernheimer & S. (R) 2,500
Puckhaben, Henry. 88 South....Burr B Co. 1,089
Pflugi, Edward. 130 Greenwich....P Suess. 4,000
Reimann, Adolphus. 119 Bowery....G Ehret. (R) 5,000
Roubaud, Robert. 92 9th av .. J C G Hupfel. 1,700
Richter, Adolph. 239 Pearl....P Ballentine Son. 3,000
Roche, T L. 121 East Broadway....O Huber Brewery. (R) 868
Ryan, Jeremiah. 139 Washington....Knickerbocker B Co. 200
Ruckert, W H. 60 East Houston ...K Kleinhenz. Restaurant Fixtures. 600
Ruggiero, Cesare. 141 Mulberry....H Elias B Co. 1,400
Rapp, Anna. 217 E 37th....G Bechtel, exr of. 500
Rosenthal, Max. 134th st and 4th av....Bernheimer & S. Pool Table. 150
Scharmann, Frederick. 112 3d av....H B Scharmann. Restaurant Fixtures. 3,250
Scinto, Frank. 119 Mulberry ...India Wharf B Co. 600
Segner, Gustav. 164 Orchard....India Wharf B Co. 400
Shutts, C F. 190 West....Bernheimer & S. (R) 1,500
Solner, John. 449 E 78th....F Hower B Co. 650
Sullivan, John. 2457 3d av....D G Yuengling, Jr, B Co. (R) 1,472
Sasserath, K and S. 1481 9th av....Bernheimer & S. (R) 5,000
Schaentzler, John. 23 Prince....J Eichler B Co. (R) 600
Schurter, Richard. 528 W 47th....F & M Schaeffer B Co. (R) 300
Smith, J H. 34 Bond....Anchor B Co. Saloon Ice House. 48
Steffens & Schumacher. 305 West....Burr B Co. 4,200
Sarmoria & Lermo. 134 Sullivan... E Arreca. Restaurant Fixtures. 75
Schalkenstein, Elias. 119 Chrystie .... F Glazier. 450
Schoen, Nic. 56 Av D....O Huber Brewery. (R) 1,200
Schulte, Richard. 114 Mott....S Liebmann's Son B Co. 1,896
Schumann, Hermann. 969 1st av....J Ahlers B Co. (R) 800
Sherman, Hannah. 152 and 154 E 42d....G Ehret. (R) 1,565
Seman, George. 1325 Av A....F Hower B Co. 400
Skudrus, Aug. 1121 1st av....Beadleston & W. Saloon Pump, &c. 125
Spitz & Graeber. 70 2d av....S Reitmann. Restaurant Fixtures. 1,500
Schaefer, Frank. 17 Crosby....G Winter B Co. (R) 300
Shine, J B. 1792 3d av....P Buckel. (R) 150
Silberstein, Salomon. 225 Rivington....J Hoffmann B Co. 400
Sweeney, J F and J J. 37 Beaver....Mary A Sweeney. Restaurant Fixtures. 300
Sweeney, Michael. 355 3d av....G Ehret. (R) 1,000
Thompson, J H. 490 Hudson....F & M Schaefer B Co. (R) 1,000
Tremer, Andrew. 452 W 38th....Knickerbocker B Co. 250
Thaden, J W. 356 Broome....F & M Schaeffer B Co. (R) 1,500
Thom, Sr, D R. 86 Pine....C F Thom. 2,500
Trimborn, Christian. 2069 2d av... F Hower B Co. 860
Wendel, Louis. 109th st and 9th av....Bernheimer & S. (R) 7,500
Woeslick, Adolph. 209 E 40th....D Stevenson. 250
Wickbiller, Conrad. 2910 3d av .. J Eichler B Co. 1,200
Wendel, Louis, Jr. 182d st and Amsterdam av ....J Ruppert. 2,500
Willis, J J and W S. 144 W 26th....M Van Rensselaer, Jr, trustee. 732
Weiss, Herman. 328 East Houston....W H Griffith & Co. Pool Table. 350
Wertheimer & Zitron....F Melzer. Pool Table. 115
Whitford, James. 430 Pearl....S Liebmann's Sons B Co. (R) 200
Same....same. (R) 400

HOUSEHOLD FURNITURE.

Abraham, Sarah. 828 E 3d....Simpson & P. Piano. (R) 110
Anderson, A C. 168 E 88th ....J Baumann. 357
Anderson, Etta. 168 E 88th....J Baumann. 357
Babcock, N H. 1978 Vanderbilt av....Dreisacker & Co. 113
Bingham, L K. 509 E 143d....S Bingham & Son. 4,290
Bourgeous, E A. 74 Grove .... Commercial Credit Co. 100
Boyer, E H. 321 W 85th....Commercial Credit Co. 200
Bucken, T L. 1 E 3d.... C E Rhinelander. 3,000
Bunel, Alfred. 140 W 10th....J Baumann. 129
Begemann, Ella. 10 Beach ...F Hoppe. 575
Brown, M. 221 W 40th....J Early. 453
Burke, T P. 61 Grove....J J Coogan. 388
Butler, James. 681 E 13th ...J J Coogan. 222
Boehm, Jenny. 323 E 13th....Manges Bros. 488
Betts, C H. Nutuchen, N J....L Wolf. 1,354
Brown, Ellen A. 44 W 128th....A Barlow. (R) 2,000
Cannon, Annie. 12 Amsterdam av....J Baumann. 162
Conklin, Laura B. 101 W 43d.. .O'Farrell & Co. 228
Conlon, J M and M. 446 Lexington av... Hannah Sullivan. 200
Constant, Mary A. 502 E 136th....Laura Veritz. 828
Cook, Edward. 25 Jones....L Baumann. 128
Cleary, Margaret M. 2216 2d av....R M Walters. Piano. (R) 125
Cornwell, Mrs. C M. 2028 Lexington av....H Thoesen. (R) 598
Carroll, Alice. 50 E 18th....F Morel. 1,000

Cashman, J J, Jr, Mrs. 548 Broome....J J Coogan. 132
Cline, Jennie. 154 W 50th....Brooklyn F Co. (R) 182
D'Esplen, Agnes. 160 W 53d....M Hurwich. 1,000
Dickson, J B. 78 W 94th ...J Baumann. 547
Donati, Gundela. 47½ E 7th. ..J Moriarty. (R) 145
Dautsch, Martin. 237 Stanton....L Baumann. 121
Devine, Mary. 173 Hudson....C E Pierce. 100
Eschbach, Rebecca V. 307 W 123d....T Leonard. (R) 176
Fink, Abram. 121 Allen....S I Herschmann. 188
Fisher, R. 1714 1st av....Brooklyn F Co. 260
Foran, Margaret. 132 E 127th....American Guar Assoc. 8,0
Fargo, Olivia D. 2096 3d av....F G Underhill. 75
Same S A Underhill. 687
Fellows, Annie. 311 E 4th....L Baumann. 110
Fisher, O N. 521 E 83d....F G Smith. Piano. (R) 235
Foster, S J. 221 W 61st....Jordan & M. 110
Fullen, J A. 318 W 44th....F T Higgins. (R) 150
Gage, J S, Mrs. 3344 3d av....J McCormack & C. 227
Gavagan, Nora. 140 W 39th....J Early. 206
Gale, E H and S H. 122 and 124 Lexington av ....G S Dixon. (R) 3,000
Glanding, Mary J. 233 Newark av, Jersey City, N J....J Baumann. 153
Geiger, Antonie. 120 W 47th....L Baumann. (R) 286
Gormand, M J. 1883 3d av....B M Cowperthwait & Co. 182
Godfrey & Hall. 124 W 49th ...T Leonard. 160
Gonzales, Javier. 122 W 63d....J Baumann. 197
Harris, Aaron. 149 Clinton ...S I Herschmann. 110
Harbeck, Howard. St Anns av and 136th st ... J J Gaffney. 350
Hunagen, Ida. 222 E 84th .. H Israel & Sons. 104
Hahn, L C. Fordham....Krakauer Bros. Piano. 350
Harrington, Emma. St Anns av and 155th st.... J Baumann. 252
Hazeltine, M W & S D. 44 W 76th....T Mathews. 800
Heinle, Matheas. 155th st and Amsterdam av.... J Baumann. 197
Henderson, Jane. 695 Greenwich... J Baumann. (R) 150
Howell, H C. 48 W 73d....E C Hinsdale. 500
Halpenn, Charlotte. 257 E 72d....F J Brechtel. (R) 163
Hickman, R N. Winona Flats....L Baumann. 854
Howland, B F. 316 W 36th.. O'Farrell & Co. 126
Hunter, E. 116 E 122d....C E Pierce 130
Koehler, Lillie. 248 W 16th....L Baumann. 147
Keating, Annie. 542 E 17th....Jordan & M. 161
Kelly, W J. 244 W 30th....J S Rice. 111
Kiernan, Maria M. 693 E 114th ...J Baumann. (R) 118
Kipp, Carrie. 121 E 47th....J Moriarty. (R) 115
Kauzelbaum, Louis. 153 E 163d....H S Eisler. 131
Kane, Dora. 219 E 77th....S I Herschmann. 109
Kauffman, Maurice. 122 W 31st....J Moriarty. 125
Latimer, Ettie. 220 E 27th .. J Moriarty. 215
Leahy, Nellie. 407 W 19th....S I Herschmann. 183
Little, Mrs T G. 43 E 41st....H Thoesen. 120
Little, W P. 101 W 82d... J Gregg & Co. 133
Lanther, John. 2 W 14th....J Baumann. 161
Lloyd, W G. 312 W 42d....J Baumann. 226
Lynch, John, Mrs. 402 Madison ...D M Brown. 125
Latimer, F L. 61 W 105th ...L Baumann. 187
Laughlin, Michael. 226 W 61st....L Baumann. 176
Lindholm, Rosa. 342 W 39th....O'Farrell & Co. 219
Maroux, Nellie S. 612 7th av....E S Simmons. 5,000
Moses, Max. 521 E 82d.... Krakauer Bros. Piano. (R) 235
Mabbett, Annie E. 144 W 103d....L Baumann. 184
Mears, A. 101 W 104th....J J Coogan. 141
Miller, A R. 95 E 10th....J Gregg. 289
Morse, Carrie E. 10, 12 and 14 W 125th....Harlem I and G Assoc. 500
Mount, Charles. 237 E 80th ...J J Coogan. (R) 106
Mulligan, Mary. 2476 8th av....L Baumann. 171
Madden, Kate. 323 E 80th ...J Baumann. 168
Malosse, Frank. 43 E 9th....G Hellrung. 500
Maloney, D H. 904 E 166th....Dreisacker & Co. 163
Martin, R W. 734 E 138th....J P Van Orden. Piano. 150
McGovern, J A. 408 W 36th .. J Baumann. 142
Meigs, C B. 180 5th av . J Baumann. 137
Melvin, J K and J F. 52 W 10th....T B Harms. (R) 170
Mittenzwei, Elizabeth. 230 E 80th....Mary A Birtles. 250
Morse, Carrie E. 10-14 W 125th....American Guar Co. 500
Mandel, Mary. 17 1st....Meirowitz & Altman. 241
Markus, Ida....J Moriarty. 202
Miller, Augustus. 158 W 132d....J Baumann. (R) 175
Moore, Emma. 152 W 103d....H Israel & Son. 485
Narew, S W. 74 Christopher....Rosa B De Casanova. 130
Neville, Michael. 328 Henry ...J J Coogan. 165
Nihis, Mrs Henri. 317 E 48th... H Thoesen. 168
O'Brien, J. 100 Henry....J J Coogan. 167
O'Hare, Mrs Jos. 218 E 44d... G Renbel. 131
O'Keefe, Elizabeth. 1765 Park av ...J Early. 121
Ott, Philip. 241 Madison....J J Coogan. 216
O'Brien, James. 500 W 55th....J Baumann. 118
Okkerse, John. 239 W 32d....J Baumann. (R) 194
O'Reilly, J F. 131st st and 10th av....J Baumann. 155
Prince, A P....J Moriarty. 230
Parker, M. 225 W 40th....J Kabatchnick. 143
Parrier, G. 201 W 61st....D M Brown. 129
Pearce, Mrs G. 226 W 17th....Alexander Bros. (R) 320
Parsons, T E and S D. 128 W 129th....Sloan & Hastings. (R) 1,275
Porter, L D. 171 W 95th ...C E Pierce. 190
Parsons, Elizabeth. 479 E 144th....W Reubel. 125
Pauszky, Henry. 62 E 108th ...American Guar Assoc. 150
Phillips, Mary. 19 W 38th....M E Hewitt. 875
Quigley, Felix. 325 W 44th ...J J Coogan. 176
Rankins, Adaline F. 266 W 24th....F T Higgins. (R) 300
Robinson, M C. 2061 7th av....J G Loeser. 1,500
Read, Harry. 210 E 10th....J Moriarty. (R) 147
Rice, Anna. 204 E 11th....J Baumann. 317
Riordan & Smith. 436 E 50th....Alexander Bros. (R) 300
Russell, Mary A. 10th av and 153d st....McDowell, Pierce & Co. 400
Rosenzweig, J. 139 Delancey....S I Herschmann. 106
Sachs, Marx. 82 Eldridge... J Moriarty. 206
Simonson, Henry. 488 W 52d....T Leonard. (R) 146
Seabrook, Fanny. 977 6th av....J Baumann. 376
Schlottmann, Herman. 677 E 134th....Fennell & Fye. 108
Silberstein, Adolph. 317 E 9th....L Amolsky. 225
Steenburgh, Rosa. 246 W 18th....J Baumann. 111

Spaulding, E and I. Storage ...Commercial Credit Co. 500
Stebbins, E H. 76 E 115th....L Applegate. 150
Stone, H G, Jr. 238 E 12d....Alexander Bros. (R) 121
Strund, Joseph. 5 Chrystie...Alexander Bros. (R) 139
Silverstein, Adolph. 817 E 9th....L Deutsch. 150
Specht, Clara. 109 W 130th....American Guar Assoc. 150
Springer, Jr, G. 431 W 35th ... J Early. 268
Stafford, E B and A G. 8 E 27th....J P Stafford. 2,2C
Schroeder, Peter. 160 W 11th ...L Baumann. 166
Sullivan, Sadie. 211 9th....L Baumann. 142
Simson, Max. 206 E 49th....A Dinkelmann. 75
Thomson, C C. 265 W 124th....C E Pierce. 130
Thronson, August. 127 W 58th....H S Eisler. 168
Trube, Clara. 584 Robbins av....S Krahmes. 230
Tramasure, P A. 9 Christopher....J Baumann. (R) 122
Troy, Kate. 226 W 4th....J Gregg & Co. 124
Uishofer, Lina. 500 E 82d .. J Baumann. 460
Van Tine, W and M L. 622 Columbus av ... Commercial Credit Co. 200
Van Vleit, Jas L. 236 W 144th....Fennell & Pye. 178
Van Note, G W. 467 Grove....J Baumann. 215
Vidal, Gabriel. 118 W 42d ...E C Hinsdale. 250
Velez, Ramon. 48 W 26th....J Baumann. (R) 105
Von Gildern, Max. 211 E 11th....H S Eisler. 168
Vosburgh, Mary. 171 E 109th....L Baumann. 179
Walton, Mrs Ray. 200 W 41st....R Thoesen. 1,113
Washinsky, M. 166 6th av....H Thoesen. 210
Wilhelm, Anna. 1191 3d av....American Guar Assoc. 200
Walsh, Mary. 454 E 10th ...F G Smith. Piano. (R) 178
Williams, Mamie. 126 W 27th....J S Rice. 121
Woodman, Anna. 217 W 24th....J Baumann. (R) 400
Wood, Mary. 227 E 47th ....Krakauer Bros. Piano. (R) 109
Wood, M A. 178 W 102d ...R M Walters. Piano. 27
Young, T A. 250 W 31st....J S Rice. 230

MISCELLANEOUS.

Asmus, Charles. 1484 2d av....W Sussman. Paint Store Fixtures. 250
Barry, John....D P Nichols. Cab. 750
Bock, Lizzie. 1685 2d av ...C Rieges. Confectionery Fixtures. 225
Bockell, O B. 454 W 146th....Smith, Worthington & Co. Machinery. 225
Breakstone, Abe. 155 Madison....P Reidenbach. Wagon. 175
Byrne, J and A. 74 Irving pl....D Pike. Machinery. (R) 100
Byrne, John. 74 Irving pl....D Pike. Machinery. (R) 110
Bendix, August. 12 Centre....A Dias & Co. Cigar Fixtures. 500
Berndtson, Edward. 2509 8th av....Lamson Consol S S Co. Register. (R) 210
Blayer, S H. 74 Canal ...Liberty Machine Works. Press. 160
Calena, Antonio. 132 Bleecker....A Schwaab. Barber Fixtures. 260
Cornish, W N. 261 Division....Liberty Machine Works. Press. 275
Casper, Samuel. 78 Bayard....M Shedlowfsky. Butcher Fixtures. 200
Clark & Dolan. 82d st and Av B ...P H Neary. Stone Yard Fixtures. (R) 500
Carroll, Michael. 14 and 16 Catharine slip....J Jennings. Store Fixtures. 5,000
Cavanagh, J J. 528 1st av....Lamson Consolidated S S Co. Register. 165
Coari, Louis. 59th st and 9th av... Lamson Consolidated S S Co. Register. 450
Condon & Hickey. 61 Ann....Van Allens & B. Press. (R) 541
Crow, Margaret. 853 W 38th....F Allen. Horses, Coaches, &c. 700
Dampf, C J. 201½ E 89th... G Gennert. Photo Fixtures. 233
De Saxe, H J. 162-178 E 125th....A Gibbons. Scenery, &c. (R) 13,229
Di Matteo, Salvatore. 140 Mott....A Schwaab. Barber Fixtures. 481
Dirndourian, Asadour. 57 Washington....E H Matigian. Store Fixtures. 400
De Angelis, O. 218 Canal....A Galella. Barber Fixtures. 100
Donohue, John. 416 E 16th....W B Davis. Coach. (R) 300
Dowell & Lancaster. 68 and 70 Wooster....M Dowell. Machinery. 5,000
Eberhardt, Geo. 150th st and 8th av....J W Tufts. Soda Fixtures. (R) 267
Eichler, Charles. 154 1st av....L Eichler, admr of. Tools, &c. 40
Eisenberg, H. 124 Ludlow....W Ginsberg. Grocery Fixtures. 65
Ettinger, Henry. 132d st and 5th av....J W Tufts. Soda Fixtures. (R) 640
Esberg & Lauppe. 701 E 6th....M Katz. Horse, Wagon, &c. 204
Edwards, W E and A M. 624 Washington....T F Jones. Horse and Milk Wagon. 180
Felter, F L. 88 and 90 Walker....D J Carroll. Machinery. (R) 1,200
Fox, Edward. 10 Wall .. A Fox. Cigar Fixtures, &c. 700
Fuchs, Henry. 21 7th....G Landan. Grocery Fixtures. 150
Greenstein & Zuker. 130 Wooster....L Thompson & Co. Machines. 121
Greenfeder & Cohn. 17 Rutger pl....J Koerner. Express Fixtures. 142
Giardino, Antonio. 352 E 17th... S Panarello. Shoe Store Fixtures. 300
Giorgi, Domenico. 547 W 59th... R Cortese. Barber Fixtures. 90
Gunther & Bayr. 428 E 19th....J Matthews Co. Soda Apparatus. 1,317
Gunther, Herman. 1079 10th av....T De Sieghardt. Cigar Fixtures. 400
Gibbs, F S. 427 W 22d....J H Gould. Pictures, &c. (R) 1,000
Gottschalk, S. 177 Eldridge....Liberty Machine Works Press. 225
Greenbaum, Maurice. 170 Division ...R Rainfurth. Barber Fixtures. 30
Gennaro, Salvatore. 2341 3d av....B Gennaro. Barber Fixtures. 80
Gibson, Fred. 537 W 37th. ..J Hickin. Hansom. 120
Green, Munson and Merrill. 116 Lincoln av.... P A Cassidy. Wagon. 72
Gunther & Bayr. 428 E 19th....A D Puffer & Sons. Soda Fixtures. (R) 130
Habe, Christian. 103d st and West End av.... A Sperr. Garden Fixtures. 250
Hoyt & Weller. 37 E 17th ...Marvin Safe Co. Safe. 300

Handville, Mansfield. 12 E 23d....W J Lamm. Optical Fixtures. 1,500
Icke, Caroline. 1692 Park av....Caroline Puckhafer. Grocery Fixtures. 150
Julien Electric Traction Co ...Mercantile Trust Co. Cars, Motors, &c. (R) 215,270
James, Michael. 146 Bowery ...D Vigdor. Window Fixtures. 250
Kalmuk, Leo. 35 Norfolk....J H Lippe. Coach. (R) 611
Karrer, Frank. 874 6th av....J G Wacker. Store Fixtures, &c. 400
Kleinburg, Joseph. 54 Norfolk....R Rainfurth. Barber Fixtures. 84
Kelly Bros....M Armstrong & Co. Coaches. (R) 1,400
Krum, J S. Cortlandt and West sts....Lord & Taylor. Hotel Furniture, &c. 602
Kappes, Mary. 441 W 40th av....J Herweg. Butcher Fixtures. 200
Karp, Otto. 1732 Madison av....J W Tufts. Soda Apparatus. (R) 40
Kauffman, Hermann....P Barrett. Truck. 617
Kavanagh, Thomas. 134 W 49th....C Murray. Horses, Cabs, &c. 1,100
Kelly, John....W H Davis. Coupe. 62
Kent, John. 69 Varick....L Hurst. Machines. (R) 330
Krohnengold, Philip. 30 Stuyvesant and 217 E 9th....F Weiler. Barber Fixtures. 150
Kellogg & McMullen.... G B Newton. Press, &c. (R) 3,292
Klein, Ernst. 247 W 41st....D B Dunham. Coach. 450
Lizzio, Nicola. 201 E 107th....M Cosumano. Barber Fixtures. 90
Lowe, Isaac. 432 5th av....W C Schmidt. Tailor Fixtures. 65
Lussen, G L. 502 and 504 E 133d....P Blass. Horses, Wagon, &c. 200
Lewinsohn, Sigfried. 419 Willis av....J Wornes, exr of. Store Fixtures. 500
Lus, Sigmund. 233 E 74th....C Dieter. Express Wagon 110
Levin, Hyman. 12 Essex ...J Blumberg. Bakery Fixtures. 250
Lewis, Ignace. 3 Dutch....A Dewes. Press. 113
Lombard, Edward. 745 6th av....A Schwaab. Barber Fixtures. 163
Lus, Sigmund. 202 E 74th....Seligman & Hahn. Horse. 105
Mahoney & Reid. 98 Henry and 42 South....J Reid. Horses, Trucks, &c. 1,000
Mauer, Frank. Cherry and Clinton sts....Roberts & Collins. Bakery Fixtures. (R) 200
Miller, William....M Armstrong & Co. Coach. (R) 110
McKenna, M and P. 259 nd 261 W 123d....H Israel. Horses, &c. 375
Marquardt, Henriette. 109 1st av....C Paxmann. Confectionery Fixtures. 200
McGeorge, P A. 220 and 222 William....Van Allens & B. Press. (R) 2,025
McVay, G P H. 258 W 125th....Manhattan Type Co. Press. 175
Merritt, E H. 581 9th av... J W Tufts. Soda Fixtures. (R) 189
Moriarty, Michael. 1 Commerce, 4th and Barrow sts ...L E Muller. Furniture, Horses, Trucks, &c. (R) 573
McSherry, James....J Gottsleben. Coach. 140
Murphy, A A. 238 and 240 W 50th....S Nelson. Horse, Wagon, &c. 2,000
Netz, Charles. 232 Mulberry ....A Brucker. Butcher Fixtures. 350
New York Industrial Assoc. 219 and 221 E 97th ...W Spencer. Store Fixtures. 150
Nowak, C J. 695 6th av....E Jost. Store Fixtures. 150
Neumann, Michael. 16 Forsyth....E Bachman. Cigar Fixtures and Furniture 2.775
Neumann Bros....Campbell P P Co. Press. (R) 2,200
Oliviri & Dibella. 981 10th av....A Schwaab. Barber Fixtures. 136
O'Connell, William. 185 W 125th....Lamson Consol S S Co. Register. 165
O'Leary, A J. 159 E 110th .. J J White. Plumber Fixtures. 280
O'Connor, Catharine. 938 E 168th....National Casket Co. Undertaker's Fixtures. 981
Palmisano, Leonarde. 749 3d av....A Bollino. Barber Fixtures. 739
Post, E S. 1354 Broadway and 619 6th av... Elizabeth L Post. Horses, Vans, &c. 4,000
Pfister Bookbinding Co. 428 W 14th ...Montague & Fuller. Press, &c. 1,567
Same....Smyth Mfg Co. Machines. 2,048
Pizza, Salvatore. 214 Canal....A Schwaab. Barber Fixtures. 38
Prescott, H S. 4 Duane....C E Pierce. Machinery. 130
Reich, Charles. 99 Norfolk....P Reidenbach. Wagon. 160
Rabinowitz, Isaak. 65 Chrystie....M Shub. Machinery. 180
Rapid Printing Co. 220 William....E Seymour trustee. Printing Fixtures. 10,000
Same....Remington Paper Co. Printing Fixtures 13,000
Rieders, Joseph. 553 9th av....F Kwieschinski. Cigar Fixtures, &c. 200
Riggs, G H. 791 8th av....A Llerena. Cigar Fixtures. 2,729
Same...same. Tobacco. 2,729
Rohkohl, Mary. 315 W 145th....Lang & Co. Bakery Fixtures. 437
Ruck, F H. 1088 2d av ..F A Reiss. Butcher Fixtures. 1,000
Rohde, Adolph, 177 Allen....W Bayrhaff. Drug Fixtures. (R) 221
Sheehan, J L. 247 and 249 W 41st....H A Pine. Horse, &c. 363
Schoenberger, Louis. 21 and 23 Centre....Liberty Machine Works. Press. 375
Schurer, Emil. 2555 8th av....P Westphal. Barber Fixtures. 120
Scott & Reynolds. 50 W 22d....C F Cornelius. Store Fixtures, &c. 65
Simon, Theodore. 1471 3d av....H Kiehbiel. Drug Fixtures. 500
Simpson, S W. 39 W 14th....Liberty Machine Works. Press, &c. 3,700
Sudovitz, Max. 85 Monroe....G Bechtel. Horse, &c. 50
Schick, Thomas. 123 Cannon....J Weiss. Barber Fixtures. 70
Steinecke, W D. 13-17 Crosby ...E Siegman. Machinery. (R) 2,000
Sullivan, D B. 650 Water....C F Schmale. Horses, Trucks, &c. 500
Schrader, J W. 735 Washington....National Cash Register Co. Register. 200
Schneider, Adolph. 501 E 72d....P A Cassidy. Wagon. 116

Stagg, F S....R E Wilcox. Horses and Ice Wagon. 250
Stodder Bros. 182 William....R Hoe & Co. Press. (R) 658
Tropical American Telephone Co.... J H Howard. Telephone Fixtures. 4,000
Tumpovsky, Emanuel. 81 Essex....M Steenbuck. Drug Fixtures. 500
Townsend, Thomas. 810 W 49th....M Armstrong. Cab. (R) 113
Trube, F A. 208½ E 93d....J Redegeld. Machinery. 600
Tschaler, Clementine. 1339 3d av....H Rice. Bakery Fixtures. 500
Tyson, Nettje. 813 Amsterdam av....J Messener. Machines, &c. 350
Varallo, Salvatore. 1432 Av A....A Schwaan. Barber Fixtures. 153
Walker, John....M Armstrong & Co. Coach. (R) 350
Weller, E G. 488 6th av....L Roth. Barber Fixtures. 247
Wilson, Robert. 1018 E 128th....W H Sage. Furniture and Horse. (R) 125
Wood, Susan A. 142 W 39th....M Armstrong. Horse, Wagon, &c. (R) 900
Workingmen Co-operative Assoc. 434 and 436 E 72d....J Kovar. Printing Fixtures. 1,000
Weingarten, Gustav. Pelham and Arthur avs ....H Weyl. Horses, Butcher Fixtures, &c. 150
Weil, J H. 145 Av A....Magdalena Weil. Drug Fixtures. 4,000
Weller, E G. 488 6th av ...E F Bachmann. Barber Fixtures. 120
Wolpert & Greenberg. 192 Broome....J L Gottlieb. Barber Fixtures. 142
Wolpert, Max. 87 Allen ...J L Gottlieb. Barber Fixtures. 142
Wilts, William exr of. 439 Lenox av....A D Puffer & Son. Soda Fixtures. (R) 500
Wm G Martin Printing House. 111 John.... Leila R Martin. Presses, &c. (R) 3,500
Zierbut, Peter. 5 2d av....P Wurster. Harness Shop Fixtures. 50
Zelenko, Harry. ....S Wolman. Machines. 87
Zirinsky, Max. 172 Division .... S Zirinsky. Jewelry Store Fixtures. 200
Zweifel, Henry. 2409 2d av .... J Zweifel. Bakery Fixtures. 300

BILLS OF SALE.

American Trust Co. 173 Broadway ..Munger, Thomas & Co. Office Fixtures. 1
Arnold, Brainerd T. 825 Broadway and 45 and 47 E 12th st....R Mortimer, exr of. Hotel Fixtures. 1
Ash, W H. 355 W 42d....Phebe A Ash. Machinery. 1
Baumgarth, J G. 249 Willis av....Chas Baumgarth. Saloon Fixtures. 10
Bergman & Hertzberg. 42 Division ...B Eilenberg. Machinery. 200
Boylan, Hugh. 724 10th av....R Hill. Grocery Fixtures. 650
Bowen, William. 322 E 89th....R Bowen. Grocery Fixtures. 100
Catarsi, Argia. 134 Sullivan....Catarse & Stefanini. Saloon Fixtures. 280
Carroll, P J. 531 East Houston....J J Carroll. Grocery Fixtures. 600
Copeland, L P. 2153 3d av....H W Stearns. Bakery Fixtures. 850
Glacermeyer, August. 532 E 12th ..Sida De Brunner. Store Fixtures. 50
Herzheimer, Leopold. 1430 2d av....Marie M Spatthoff. House Furnishing Goods. 1
Hoffmann, S L. 166 Suffolk....J Zeisler. Saloon Fixtures. 100
Icke, Anna. 1692 Park av ...Caroline Icke. Grocery Fixtures. 300
Kraus, Adele. 232 Mulberry....C Netz. Butcher Fixtures. 5
Krewit, Elizabeth. 145th st and Southern Boulevard....Krewit & Peters. Furniture. 1
London Toilet Bazar Co. 38 W 23d ...Isabel Cassidy. Fixtures. stock, 7,500
Leo, Paolo. 301 E 33d....A Geardino. Shoe Store Fixtures. 75
Lewis, Theodore. 543 1st av ...R Halpern. Furniture, Store Fixtures, &c. 1,700
McDonald & Taylor. 1441 Broadway...Rider and Driver Pub Co. Newspaper. cash, 1,000; stock, 9,000
Mahoney, Daniel. 98 Henry and 42 South ... Mahoney & Reid. Horses, Trucks, &c. 1,600
Mundbenk, Albert. 2191 3d av....C Dukek. Butter and Egg Fixtures. 100
New Amsterdam Stamm No 33, U O R M....M Stutzbach. Regalias, &c. 1
Perry, Jeremiah exr of. 98 Henry and 42 South ....D Mahoney. Horses Trucks, &c. 1,600
Pike, Daniel. 12 E 23d....M Handville. Optical Fixtures, &c. 3,000
Seldner, Henry. 150 Nassau....J Flock. Office Fixtures. 100
Spatthoff, W A. 1430 2d av....L Herzheimer. House Furnishing Goods. 1
Thom, D R, Sr. Inwood....Rachel R Thom. Frame House, Furniture, &c. 3,000
Wynne, H G....S M Stilwell. Oil Painting. 1
Wynne, H G....S M Stillwell Oil Painting. 1
Zeisler, Jakob. 166 Suffolk....Theresia Hoffmann. Saloon Fixtures. 85

ASSIGNMENTS OF CHATTEL MORTGAGES.

Arnold, Eliza F to W W Macbean. (Mort given by Brainerd T Arnold, April 27, 1891.) 1,685
Brucker, Albert to Emma Netz. (Chas Netz, July 2, 1891). 350
Gilsey, Peter exr of to J H Rodgers. (Pearson & Fife, Aug 2, 1890.) 1
Hayes, J J to Amelia E Hayes. (W G Romaine, Nov. 12, 1890.) 1,504
Schwartz, Rosa to L Deutsch. (H Sommer, Jan 5, 1891.) 400
Tierney, Kate. 203 E 26th....O'Farrell & Co. 125
Trowbridge, E E. 140 W 33d....L Baumann. (R) 113
Watkins, Delia. 180th st and Webster av....L Baumann. (R) 110
Wendel, A. 47 Allen....H S Eisler. 120

KINGS COUNTY.

[JULY 2 TO 8—INCLUSIVE.

SALOON AND RESTAURANT FIXTURES.

Behill, F. 216 Bedford av....Liebmann's Sons B Co. $850
Berris, Mike. 201 Kent av....S Liebmann's Sons B Co. (R) 400

Byrnes, G. 718 Hicks... Claus Lipsius B Co. 250
Baumgarten, K A. 192 Troutman....L Eppig. 300
Cusick, M E. 110 Wythe av....T C Lyman & Co. 487
Carhart, C, and T Hanold. 496 5th av....Anna Kornemann. 2,000
Dallman, D. 87 Division av....L Eppig. (R) 1,407
Dill, C J. 154 Bridge....J Dill. 1,000
Devoe, F. 720 Hancock....Claus Lipsius B Co. 500
Diehl, W. 2679 Atlantic av....Leibinger & Oehm B Co. 800
Donnelly, W. 207½ Willoughby....Claus Lipsius B Co. 400
Dooley, Mary. 148 Sackett....M Seitz. (R) 246
Fagan, M. Baltic st, cor Columbia st....Malcom B Co. 1,000
Finn, D S. 130 Patchen av....W & D Shields. (R) 2,000
Fogarty, J J. 328 Columbia....Scharmann & Sons. 1,500
Fowler, W C. 95 Columbia....W Ulmer. 900
Frising, O. 63 Bushwick av. ..J H Bereuter. Billiards. 200
Fengler, H. 97 Franklin....Burger & H B Co. (R) 600
Fingleton, H W. Fulton, s e cor Manhattan Crossing....H Vogel. 150
Fiola, N. 80 Maspeth....Welz & Z. 120
Fitzgeral, G. Columbia st, n e cor Warren st ....O Huber Brewery. (R) 220
Gifford, H. 1288 Myrtle av... J Eppig. 650
Gildea, H H. 489 3d av....M Seitz. 510
Grotz, W F. 152 and 154 Ewen ...O Huber Brewery. 3,300
Helfrich, M. 14 Throop av....S Liebmann's Sons B Co. (R) 800
Higgins, M. 593 5th av....Danenberg & Coles. (R) 425
Hoffmann, G. 131 George....Eliz Meltzer. 457
Hunecke, O. 481 Manhattan av... P Doelger. 2,000
Hahnle, M. 238 Hopkins....G Bechtel. (R) 300
Heck, L. 1156 Myrtle av....M Seitz. 200
Heinrich, C. 261 Floyd.. J Eppig. 500
Huber, F. 790 Grand....O Huber. (R) 900
Jud, J. 58 Graham av....S Munch and ano, exrs. (R) 350
Kaas, J D. 45 Jay....R Kent. Restaurant Fixtures. 116
Kane, P F. 652 Clason av....L I Brewery. 550
Kruse, G. 216 Norman av....P Doelger. 500
Kuhlkan, J. 220 McDonough....S Liebmann's Sons B Co. (R) 1,500
Kekul, F. 118 Metropolitan av....M Seitz. 304
Laurer, G. Fresh Pond, L I J Eppig. (R) 800
Lewis, J. 263 Johnson av....L Eppig. 1,182
Lauber, C. 99 Boerum pl ...Liebmann Sons B Co. (R) 700
McEwen, F F. 3126 Atlantic av....Williamsburgh B Co. 715
McKenna, J. 740 4th av ...Danenberg & Coles. 567
Moran, Kate. 251 Myrtle av....H Koehler & Co. 600
Muhs, H F. 186 Monroe... J Eppig. (R) 500
Muller, H. 816 Broadway....W Ulmer. 1,000
Nubling, R. 200 Wyckoff av....Feigenspan B Co. 500
Qualy, D S. 353 Kent av....Burger & Bower B Co. (R) 806
Raport, A. Sutter av, cor Blake av....C Iba. 50
Reese, Wilhelmina. 217 Court....C Wegman. 2,500
Smith, P. 159 Franklin ...C Stein. 700
Streck, G and L. 829 Manhattan av....O Huber Brewery. 1,300
Schillinger, L F. Liberty av, cor Barbey st ... Danenberg & Coles. (R) 300
Schlumpf, G. De Kalb av, s e cor Wyckoff av ....S Liebmann's Sons B Co. (R) 500
Schroeder, J. 393 Central av... M Seitz. 425
Schwaner, F. 181 Wyckoff av....G Feigenspan. 350
Seeler, K W. 406 7th av....M Seitz. (R) 585
Sullivan, D B. 358 Van Brunt ...C A Marotzki. 400
Sullivan, F P. 873 5th av....Abbott B Co. 500
Switbenbeck, R. 181 Pearl ...P Doelger. (R) 1,200
Taylor, E. 51 Wolcott....S Liebmann's Sons B Co. (R) 200
Trusheim, J. 48 Sackett .. S Liebmann's B Co. (R) 395
Vonsars, J. 76 Morrell....O Huber Brewery. 400
Vidt, G. 52 Throop av....J Eppig. 800
Wildbrett, F. 165 Throop av....W Ulmer. (R) 800
Winters, H. 563 Kent av....J Kress B Co. (R) 687
Wilber, L A and D T Hoag. 1031 Gates av.... Williamsburg B Co. 1,100
Wilkens, B. 97 Cedar ...S Liebmann's Sons B Co. (R) 600
Wohlke, E. 454 Ralph av.. Burger & Hower B Co. 400
Wolf, E. 101 Knickerbocker av....Leibinger & Oehm B Co. 500
Zeygardt, F. 1056 Myrtle av....Leibinger & Oehm B Co. (R) 500

HOUSEHOLD FURNITURE.

Alingren, A. 741 Bedford av....O'Connor & Treacy. 116
Berry, W. 87 Utica av....E Driscoll & Bro. 141
Bosworth, Mrs P. 201 Java ...R M Walters. Piano. 155
Bahman, T H. 260 52d....Brooklyn F Co. 151
Baninger, G. 781 Macon....Brooklyn F Co. 406
Beck, Charlotte A. 9 Decatur ...Nau & Helm. 1,046
Bell, G. 87 Hicks....Brooklyn F Co. 251
Byrnie, Mary. 270 Washington....Brooklyn F Co. 174
Conroy, J H A. 184 Luquer....O'Connor & Treacy. 236
Ennis, Margaret. 11 Lawrence ....W D Crowell. 100
Ford, R E. 110 Waverly av....Jordan & M. 429
Girady, W 329 Maujer....L Frank. 100
Giffin, M. 78 Carroll....Brooklyn F Co. 335
Hall, Lizzie D. 483 Herkimer....J Hegeman & Co. 117
Heymans, C. 710 4th av....L Baumann. 206
Hyatt, Mary. 172 Nassau....L Baumann. 169
Jones, E and Eliz. 462 Putnam av....E C Hinsdale 375
Kastendieck, J T W. 488 Bedford av ...L Baumann. 762
Knoedler, C. 296 Ellery....C T Kendrick & Co. 177
Leroy, Phebe C. 18th av....Du Vivier & Co. 165
Loeffler, Lizzie M M. 730 Gates av....J Fischer. 200
Lovell, C W. 167 Prospect pl .. G Scott. 1,000
Lovely, P. 686 6th av ...H Vogel. 1,700
Mathews, E J. 618 McDonough ...G E Guerrier. 175
McMurray, Lizzie C. 97 Oxford ...Jordan & M. 114
McGlaskey, W. 14 Ocean pl....Eliza Drew. 200
McCutcheon, Mrs F. 1654 Atlantic av....Brooklyn F Co. 465
McKeever, J. 99 Dupont....Brooklyn F Co. 166
O'Connell, C J. 286 Lexington av....O'Connor & T. 289
Rapraport, S. Osborn st .. H S Eisler. 110
Reese, H P. 498 Herkimer....Brooklyn F Co 291
Reilly, Mrs E. 110 Vanderbilt av....Brooklyn F Co. 212
Roth, A E. 211 McDougal....H S Eisler. 137
Seaman, J. 157 Skillman....J McEnery & Co. 213
Schaefer, A. 396 18th....Julia Scherer. 400
Tucker, C H. 111 Lynch....J J Coogan. 227
Thom, J F. 830 St Marks pl....L Baumann. 167
Van Pelt, T C. 805 6th ...J Coyne & Co. 178
White, S. 499½ 8th... Brooklyn F Co. 105
White, R T. 818 Myrtle av....W Weed. 125
Willemin, O. 69 Clermont av....C T Kendrick & Co. 184
Zepine, Anne. 1652 Fulton....S J Roe. 100
Zittlosen, J. 205 Grand....J Baehr & Co. 179

MISCELLANEOUS.

Ackermann, H W. 689 5th av ...Lamson Co. Register. 140
Bassemir, J. 43 Centre....Eliza D Griggs. Machinery. (R) 1,000
Bayly, D Y. 1881 Fulton....B S Bayly. Drug Fixtures. 775
Berger Bros....Hodge & Davis Machine Tool Co. Lathe. 150
Brooklyn Cycle Repair Co. 822 Gates av... Frasse & Co. Lathes, &c. 79
Bistramb, C H. 703 3d av... A D Puffer & Sons. Soda Apparatus. 190
Campbell, J T and M H. 287 Marion....P A Cassidy. Wagon. 92
Davidov, S H. 410 Atlantic av....H Davidov. Store Fixtures. 1,100
Donner, Elizabeth. 280 Ellery....M F Lindhorn & Co. Bakery Fixtures. 275
Davis, W W. 6 and 8 Front....Brooklyn Union Publishing Co. Press. (R) 61
Equity Gas Light Co....Farmers Loan and Trust Co. All Property Real and Personal. issues bonds. 1,000,000
F Hower Brewing Co (Lim). 239-269 Pulaski ....M O'Keeffe. Ice Machines. 43,600
Felty, A J. Atlantic av, s s, 100 s e Clason av, 40x70....G W King. Machinery. 400
Friedlem, Annie. 390 Marcy av....Roberts & Co. Bakery Fixtures. 500
Graver, W. 177 Atlantic av....J E Parnell. Fixtures. 500
Gunther, J. Fulton near Chestnut st....R A Holcke. Barber Fixtures. 105
Gerham, B H. 402 Court....H Kern. Butcher Fixtures. 200
Halper, V. 406 5th av ...Marvin Safe Co. Safe 110
Harris, Mary A. 322 9th....P G Shakers. Chop House Fixtures. 150
Heath & Co. 117 John....Walker & Bresnan. Printing Office. (R) 599
Jones, O F. 1341 Fulton....Mary E Jones. Drug Fixtures. 2,600
McGuire, Margt. 357 Baltic .... W B Davis. Coach. (R) 400
Ortlieb, M. 280 Nevins....M W Hart. Machinery. 115
Pierce, J J. 207 Franklin av....Mary E Lambert. Horse, &c. 100
Pasarello, P. 96 Walworth....F Ciancimano. Grocery Fixtures. 130
Price, J. 63 Rutgers slip, New York....T D Hurst. Presses. 2,062
Pye, R H. 740 Fulton....A L Reid, Jr. Shoe Store. 200
Reynolds, J. 407 and 409 Court....T C Lyman & Co. Saloon Fixtures. (R) 1,000
Schneider, H. Brooklyn av and Malbone st.... C Hart. Horses, &c. 150
Squire, F J. 267 Flatbush av ...G H Squire. Painters Fixtures. 210
Verney, J....W B Davis. Coach. 800
Walker, C. 62 Fleet pl....W B Davis. Coach. (R) 400
Walther, J. 748 Park av....Gaus & Miller. Bakery Fixtures. 511

BILLS OF SALE.

Batz, A. 185 Throop av... G Batz. ½ part of Grocery. 700
Bruswitz, E. 412 Bedford av....E Bruswitz. Painter's Fixtures. 1,900
Boyle, A. 263 Hamilton av....P Kilgallen. Saloon Fixtures. 1,200
Fowler, W C. 495 5th av....C Carhart and ano. Saloon Fixtures. 2,500
Gronwoldt, Emma. 1041 Fulton... B Fischer & Co. Grocery Fixtures. 425
Hausmann, F. 424 Degraw....H W Hausmann. Grocery Store. 1,456
Kammenzind, M. 949 Grand....G Schaefer. Restaurant Fixtures. 800
Le Bowsky, G. 467 Grand ...M Michael. Hat Store. 850
Petti, S. 60 Flushing av ...G Aurolone. ½ of Barber Fixtures. 300
Schlaweedt, H. 298 and 300 Flushing av....J H Krogmann. Horses, Wagons, &c. 1,200
Schaefer, G. 949 Grand....Kate Hammenzind. Restaurant Fixtures. 800
Seedorf, C. 329 Washington....J F Tribcken. Saloon Fixtures. 1,000
Shaffer, B K. 1584 Broadway and 153 Buffalo av ....Annie M Shaffer. Produce Store Fixtures, &c. 2,000
Tribcken, J F. 329 Washington....Cath Seedorff. Saloon Fixtures. 1,000
Walter, F. 701 Atlantic av....F Bones. Lumber and Tools. 800

ASSIGNMENTS OF CHATTEL MORTGAGES.

Ford, D M to Alex McDonald. (Mort given by C J Dietz, Oct 6, 1890). nom
Knox, R to Etta G Felty. (A J Felty, March 9, 1891). 204
Scharmann, H B to E Ochs. (A Barth, May 3, 1886.) 1,000

NEW JERSEY.

NOTE.—*The arrangement of the Conveyances, Mortgages and Judgments in these lists is as follows: the first name in the Conveyances is the Grantor; in Mortgages, the Mortgagor; in Judgments, the Judgment debtor.*

ESSEX COUNTY.

CONVEYANCES.

Atwater, Samuel—W G Jacobus, Caldwell....... $1
Ballantine, J H et al—F Fichel, n s Springfield av adj D Harrison's land 27x50x27x53x47x73... 18,000
Ballantine, I L—same, Springfield av......... 1
Baker, T C—J Throssell, South Orange.......... 56
Barnett, Timothy—C J Barrett, South Orange.. 450
Barth, Catharine—H Newman, w s Barclay st 378 Waverley pl 25x97....................... 3,900
Beach, S H—A E Niven, Bloomfield.................. 5,500
Bernz, J A—Otto Bernz, South Orange av...... 1,000
Boehlmann, Christina—J Kopf, Morton st....... 2,800
Breintnall, J H H et al—C A Martin, Breintnall pl 2,150
Brown, R M—G Remesnick, Darcy st 1,860
Brown, E L—M J Cannon, East Orange......... 4,000
Butterfield, E T—J E March, East Orange...... 1
Campfield, M E—E White, Orange............. 800
Campfield, M E—A B Finan, Orange............ 2,000
Carter, K B—C D Halstead, Hillside av.......... 500
Central N J Land and Imp Co—R C Boice, Salt Meadows.................................. 200
Coe, Theodore et al exrs—C F Seitz, South 8th st. 650
Condit, E A—E Geach, Orange 850
Connor, Patrick—S E Connor, Chatham st...... 1,000
Cooper, H J—A E Van Gieson et al, Montclair... 100
Coyt, Julius—W Brookes, South Orange 150
De Hart, H M Le—S S Gross, Orange.......... 1
Devine, Arthur—W Michenfelder, Clinton 180
Dewitt, W H—J Taylor, Montclair............... 1,100
Dey, J W—H Cook, East Orange 360
Dike, F B—J C Crevier, Caldwell.............. 6,000
Dobbins, S S—Caldwell Land Co, Caldwell....... 6,000
Dodd, B L—F Wackenhuth, Cortlandt st........ 1,000
Dodd, Amzi—C A Martin, Breintnall pl......... 2,150
Dyer, R N—C J Franklin, East Orange 1,500
Eberle, Addie—M J Sliker, West Orange........ 650
Edwards, R R—A J McManus, e s Clifton av 161 Drift st 28x100............................ 3,000
Floim, F L—J W Till, South Orange............. 1,250
Gaston, G H—M M Ellithrope, e s North 7th st 500 6th av 50x100.............................. 4,900
Gifford, S V—C F Ray, Nutley.................. 2,000
Giegenbeimer, J P—H Schwarz, e s Prince st 575 Montgomery st 25x100..................... 5,900
Glennon, James—E D Roche, South Orange..... 500
Gotthainer, Louis—J J Haag, Orange 1,500
Graham, Susan—M J Peters, Montclair.......... 2,750
Haas, Christian—R Gracie, Bloomfield.......... 3,200
Harris, N B—J S Rice, West Orange.............. 15,000
Harrison, C J et al exrs—M West, West Orange. 125
Hartshorn, Stewart—C L Conover, Milburn..... 7,400
Same——A G Winter, Milburn................ 9,000
Haug, J C—R Blechschmidt, Somerset st....... 1,150
Hebring, Mary—Rose Gaughren, Hunterdon st. 1
Horwitz, Moritz—J Isaacs, e s Bedford st adj S Hayes land 30x99.......................... 6,000
Jacobus, Ella—C F Wettyen, Caldwell......... 600
Same——same, Caldwell.................. 2,950
Jimmerson, N S—T Varly, North 2d st. 25
Keasbey, A Q—M B Schott, South 10th st....... 660
Kirby, J I et al exrs—C T Hornecker, Central av................................ 833
Klose, Gustave—H Gilbert, Rutgers st.......... 1,150
Lane, Isaac—J A Hayden, Caldwell 5,000
Lehlback, E A—S A Lennon, Jefferson st 900
Lindsley, Ogden W—P McCormack, East Orange 175
Lister, J C—J Levy, s s Lafayette st cor Monroe st 48x100x65x25x108x125 9,000
Lord, J F—A L Conway, South Orange......... 20,000
Lum, C M—E S Vreeland, James st. 1
March, J E—I M Butterfield, East Orange....... 1
Marquet, J B—F E Bataille et al, Washington st. Release................................ 1
Marvin, E B—J R Cuming admr, Montclair...... 1
Matthews, C B—M I Matthews, s s Ferry st cor Union st 38x38 3,500
McKay, William—V Mehl, East Orange......... 250
Same——J C Thomas, East Orange........... 250
Same——T Buffsmith, East Orange 250
Miller, H J—M Kalisch, n s Ferry st 29 Jackson st, 28x96 4,000
Mitchell, A P et al—C T Hornecker, Central av. 1,555
Morris, Charlotte—C F Seitz, South 8th st....... 550
Morfitt, J A—J S De Revoise, East Orange...... 4,500
Munn, J L—F W Coolbaugh, East Orange...... 1,750
Nesler, C L—C A Ward, Chadwick av........... 300
O'Farrell, M J—P Leonard, e s Belleville av 24 Clark st 28x75.......................... 3,000
Peck, Cyrus—H A Crone, 4th st................ 750
Plume, A G—E S White, 3d av................ 450
Porter, T W—J Porter, Montclair.............. 375
Powles, Henry et al exrs—C Force, West Orange 125
Same——S J Sayre, West Orange 250
Redden, Jane—J E Connolly, Wakeman av...... 1,000
Richards, M S—F W Smith, Vincent st.......... 800
Rickert, Louis—J E Stagg, North 3d st........ 1
Robinson, E P—Essex County Electric Co, Orange.............................. 8,000
Robley, James—P Finerty, Montclair........... 1,600
Rowe, E F et al—M Rowe, Dawson st........... 1
Russell, Nathan—J Connolly, East Orange...... 350
Scheiner, Leonhardt—W Schoenamsgruber, w s Bedford st, 406 s Dark lane, 30x115........... 5,200
Schierer, G O—F Strickfuss, Clinton........... 300
Scott, J S—A E Trusdell, East Orange.......... 200
Shipman, Daisy—A E Ryerson, w s Garside st 312 South 5th av 25x99......................... 3,250
Simonson, George—A E Van Gieson et al, Montclair.............................. 1
Smith, B R—Tenth Ward B and L, Clinton...... 1
Smith, Luman—M C Kuhn, 18th av. 750
Stewart, H C—E J Smith, East Orange.......... 1,350
Szymanowitz, Maria—Peter Merkel, e s Rankin st, 261 Springfield av, 27x100................. 3,650
The Wickliffe Presby Church—W M Rankin, n s Orange av 25 w Wickliffe st 17x32x77x59x71 3,600
Same——W Rankin, South Orange av......... 1,800
The Protestant Foster Home of Newark—H A Cozzens, Summer av............................ 1,000
Turrell, G B—The Morris & Essex R R Co, South Orange.................................. 900
Turnbull, Alexander—D Schmitt, Humes st..... 500
Turnbull, Alexander et al——same, Humes st... 500
Underhill, Eugene—T L Smull, Caldwell...... 1
Van Gieson, H O—C F Rhinehart, Montclair.... 200
Same——W Witz, Montclair................ 200
Van Gieson, A E et al—T H Bird, Montclair..... 100
Van Riper, Theodore et al—F M Van Riper, Belleville.................................. 1
Same——G Van Riper, Belleville............. 1
Same——same, Belleville................... 1
Varick, John—F L Flohn, South Orange......... 1
Vreeland, J H—C M Lum, James st............. 1
Vreeland, E S—M Hapler, s s Central 101 w High st 25x80...................................... 6,250
Wakeman, E P—R D Brower, Milburn.......... 1
Ward, D B—A W Osmun, w s Washington st adj W R Ward's land 200x200.................. 20,000
Ward, W C—A Miller, Chadwick av............. 550
Same——A M Hughes, Chadwick av........... 550
Wilson, J C—N Y Bay R R Co, Salt Meadows.... 960
Winzer, Bertha—M Jones, w s Liberty st, adj O Baldwin's land 25x100................... 5,200

MORTGAGES.

Entry	Amount
Bird, C M—M J Flynn, Sheffield st	1,800
Brower, H A—E Alcock, Columbia st	500
Butterfield, E S—G W Blackwell, East Orange	3,050
Caldwell Land Co—S S Dobbins, Caldwell	5,000
Cannon, P V W—E L Brown, East Orange	2,000
Cassidy, J C—O H Bowers, East Orange	2,000
Clinchard, J E—Marion B and L Assoc, Gotthardt st	2,400
Collins, Stephen—The Orange B and L Assoc, Orange	200
Condit, E A—F T Johnson, guard, Orange	1,50[illegible]
Conover, C L—S Hartshorne, Milburn	7,150
Conway, A L—J T Row, South Orange	15,000
Corbelly, James—J S Bigbie, Norfolk st	500
Del Guercio, Alfonso—W S Brown, Sheffield st	4,000
Edgar, William—E H Snyder, East Orange	200
Essex County Electric Co—E P Robinson, Orange	7,000
Finan, A B—M E Campfield, Orange	1,500
Fischel, Frederick—J H Ballantine, Springfield av	16,500
Frink, Andrew—M B Conover, Montclair	3,000
Fronappel, Joseph—G A Oakes, Bloomfield	2,300
Gaughren, Rose—P Reilly, Hunterdon st	500
Geib, Levi—Fidelity Title and Deposit Co, Jelliff av	200
Gwalter, L L—S Rordorf, East Orange	4,839
Same—S Rordorf-Gwalter, East Orange	8,050
Grover, S R—W C Ward, Clinton	550
Halstead, C D—K B Carter, Hillside av	800
Hassinger, Peter—S Doughty, Alpine st	1,500
Hass, William—Standard B and L Assoc, Clinton	1,600
Hebring, Mary—P Reilly, Warren st	500
Hedden, C P—S E Buster, Clinton	600
Heller, Leopold—Savings B and L Assoc, Prince st	6,000
Herser, S W—Fidelity Title and Deposit Co, Mt Prospect av	6,000
Heywood, J T—R Shepherd, North 3d st	2,400
Hill, William—G T Casebolt, South 2d st	3,000
Holly, J I—G A Dowden, East Orange	3,300
Hornecker, C T—J I Kirby et al exrs, Central av	1,500
Isaacs, Joseph—M Rechner, Bedford st	600
Same—Simon Lowy, Bedford st	3,500
Jeffrey, A B—Ross C Browning, South Orange	5,000
Johnson, E G—H Glorieux, Miller st	580
Jones, Maria—B Wurzer, Liberty st	3,000
Kopf, Joseph—A Kaufmann, Morton st	1,800
Krautheim, R J—A E Speedling, South 7th st	2,500
Kuhn, M C—N Axt, 18th av	5,000
Kummer, Valentine—A Behrendt, Mercer st	1,000
Lau, Adolph—P M Clayton, Quitman st	1,200
Mackin, Francis—S S Ward, Komorn st	1,300
Same—same, Komorn st	1,300
Same—same, Komorn st	1,300
Marianni, Antonio—H W Smith, Orange	2,000
Marvin, C M—The American Ins Co, Montclair	1,000
McCormick, Patrick—N Deroxtro, East Orange	200
McLagan, J T—E Adams, Summer av	2,500
McManus, A J—D Daley, Clifton av	1,500
Merkel, Peter—W Una, Rankin st	2,000
Niven, A E—S H Beach, Bloomfield	4,000
O'Leary, Winifred—P Reilly, Crane st	500
O'Neill, A D—The Orange Savings Bank, Orange	500
Osmun, A W—D B Ward, Washington st	5,000
Peaget, P T—R Hart, Montclair	2,400
Pidgeon, Edward—The Washington B and L Assoc, Bank st	200
Ponto, John—P Wirth, Charlton st	2,000
Quinn, Rosanna—J M Williams, Orange	2,000
Raleigh, Thomas—A P Lawrence, Monroe st	500
Roche, E D—J Glennon, South Orange	800
Rowe, Mary—Newark Fire Ins Co, South st	400
Russell, C E—T Oakes, East Orange	2,500
Schaeffer, William—C D Hayes, Charlton st	150
Schwarz, Herman—J P Gegenheimer, Prince st	450
Same—Lincoln B and L Assoc, Prince st	5,000
Schoenamsgruber, William—G Schoenamsgruber, Bedford st	1,800
Schott, M B—A Q Keasby, South 10th st	200
Stevens, C A—Howard Savings Inst, Roseville av	500
The Wickliffe Presbyterian Church—W Rankin, 13th av	1,400
Van Vess, S H—W C Ward, Chadwick av	500
Van Vleck, Joseph—Mutual Benefit Life Ins Co, Montclair	30,000
Winter, Augustus G—S Hartshorne, Milburn	9,000

CHATTEL MORTGAGES.

Entry	Amount
Anderson, David et al—A Anderson, machinery	2,000
Angell, Edith—C Bierman, furniture	400
Axtell, F C—L Baumann, furniture	628
Burns, James—P Ballantine & Sons, saloon	810
Campbell, George—C Feigenspan, saloon	200
Carr, J F—The Brunswick-Balke-Collender Co, pool table	225
Day, Edward—J M Hann, furniture	100
Dill, Sebastian—F J Kastner, saloon	265
Foley, Luke—J M Hann, furniture	130
Gordon, Jacob—A Schulman, bottlers fixtures	774
Greenberg, Charles—B Berman, furniture	500
Grock, S J—J W Hann, furniture	180
Hernandez, Florence—W C Dodd, furniture	6[illegible]0
Johnson, Agnes—L Bloomer, furniture	30
Kleb, John—F J Kastner, saloon	150
Klein, J N—A D Puffer & Sons, soda apparatus	315
Korte, Margaret—L Baumann, blankets	72
Krueder, George—Hills Union Brewery Co, saloon	310
Lapp, C J—F A D Smith, stock of drugs	1,500
McHenry, A L—C Bierman, piano	180
McNamara, J J—P Ballantine & Sons, saloon	211
Moran, J J et al—H Koch, groceries	1[illegible]0
Nowazluski, Ludwig—F J Kastner, saloon	600
Totten, James—same, saloon	500
von Oertzen, Hans—K Strack, carriages and furniture	1,260
Wells, Ida—Brooklyn Furniture Co, furniture	108
Wings, E L—J M Hall, saloon	80

JUDGMENTS.

Entry	Amount
Agens, F G—A M Agens	785
Esch, F W—W H Nagel	613
Same—same	545
Lauber, Emanuel—G P Gamble	209
Hoffman, Louis—J S Chambers	400
Malloy, J J—L R Barnard	514
Man, Frederick—R Struller et al	231
McNally, Bernard—J J Murphy	284
Neill, James—J E Denise	285
Romine, J W et al—J J G Mcshane	505
Rowbotham, James—D George	852
Same—H L Gans	740
Shapiro, Jacob—J Borofski	12,096
The Electric Power Co—The Newark Schuyler Electric Light Co	993
Trefz, Charles et al—W N Trusdell	167
Wurster, Catharine et al—C Burgy	459

HUDSON COUNTY.

CONVEYANCES.

Entry	Amount
Alsworth, H B—A Jaeger, J City	$650
Bammesberger, Annie—Catharine Desque, J City	nom
Bennett, Rob—New York B and L and Banking Co, Bayonne	3,300
Benny, Jas—G W Conklein, Bayonne	350
Bille, Sarah A—H Heere, J City	5,000
Booraem, Cornelia W by exr—T V Eaton, J City	800
Brady, Ellen A—M Flemming, Bayonne	400
Bramhall, Eliza A—J R Smith, Bayonne	5,600
Braunagan, Andrew—The New Jersey Bowling Club, J City	2,200
Browning, J H—B Callagher, J City	1,900
Browning, J H—Ellen Farley, J City	2,800
Budke, G H—T Kelly, Hoboken	2,500
Bumsted, W G—Ed Irvine, J City	3,000
Cadmus, Helen—T Fitzsimmons, J City	2,500
Central N J Land and Impt Co—J Mulligan, Bayonne	425
Congdon, H R—H B Alsworth, J City	nom
Conklein, G W—C E Powell, Bayonne	4,700
Corbett, Frances M—C Welsohn, J City	3,000
Crowin, Elizabeth I—J Matthews, J City	nom
Cubberly, J H—Caroline H Rorer, J City	800
Deublein, Andreas—C Schlesier, Union	8,000
Donohue, Peter—A Grobholz, J City	4,000
Doyle, G C, Jr—Eliza Killen, J City	nom
Dumnont, Augustus by sheriff—B Dumont, J City	500
Eagan, Thos—Trustees of Young Men's Assoc of St Bridget's Church, J City	2,000
Eberhard, F N—S Berry, Hoboken	335
Everitt, Ada J—W E Everitt, J City	nom
Everitt, W E—J R Everitt, Jr, J City	nom
Field, A L—Sarah G Wauters, Bayonne	—
Filan, Martin—Town of Union, Union	1,000
Fitzsimmons, Thos—Sebastian Bradt, J City	3,000
Fox, Chas, by sheriff—Paulena Wufern, J City	1,675
Froehlich, Louis—J F Sexton, J City	3,100
Frost, William—D Van Winkle, J City	600
Gardner, John—G Wirth, West Hoboken	210
Givori, Antonio—J Raffo, Hoboken	237
Godfrey, Joseph—M Schmidt, J City	675
Grub, Philip—F Reuther, Kearney	nom
Hamilton, W A—Louise F Hamilton, Bayonne	nom
Hanson, J G—C Parker, Jr, Bayonne	2,000
Harrison, Henry, by exrs—H Walker, Union	2,000
Hawes, G R—D W Armstrong, J City	5,000
Heath, Mary E—F R Crowell, Kearney	2,000
Hermann, Henry—Sophie L Herrmann, J City	1,370
Hinman, Elizabeth—B S Schoonover, Kearney	11
Hitzelberger, James—H Muntzer, West Hoboken	250
Hobson, Eliza—A Hey, Harrison	4,750
Hoboken Land and Impt Co—I Mansfield, Hoboken	10,800
Same—Martha Steljes, Hoboken	2,886
Hohm, Albert—A Hehman, Jr, J City	nom
Horns, Caroline—Emil Schoenstein, J City	4,400
Horns, Claus—W Freitag, J City	1,300
Howard, Eleanor S—J S Byers, Bayonne	800
Humphreys, Solon—Ellen Wynn, Bayonne	2,500
Hunt, Jno—Sarah McGovern, J City	1,500
Jones, D M—B Max, J City	nom
Kent, William—G Savage, J City	3,500
Killen, Martin—G C Doyle, Jr, J City	nom
La Tourette, David—H D Fuller, Bayonne	nom
Lembeck, Henry—F E McGrehan, J City	1,700
Linn, Clarence—W D Salter, Bayonne	nom
Loeffler, Joseph by sheriff—D G Yuengling, Jr, Brewing Co, Guttenberg	1,400
Lueck, Cath—Paulina Wright, Union	700
Macauley, Robt—G Ogibie, J City	4,000
Mager, Henry—W Mager, Guttenberg	1,000
Maguire, Jas—J Edelstein, J City	500
Martin, Milton—G Donzilli, West Hoboken	700
Matthews, John—Elizabeth I Crowin, J City	nom
Max, Bernard—D M Jones, J City	nom
McQuoid, William by exr—J H Erbert, Bayonne	1,800
Menzel, Christian—Henry R Congdon, J City	800
Newkirk, Elizabeth and J D et al—H H Hackmann, J City	1,842
O'Gara, Michael—Catharine Gilcher, J City	2,300
Paoli, John—F Lemerie, Hoboken	2,800
Praet, Annie—J Broadley, J City	500
Relter, M K—S Santacroce, Kearney	2,200
Reuther, Frank—P Grub, Kearney	nom
Rice, W W—D M Auld, J City	1,449
Robinson, Priscilla, by trustee—North Hudson Driving Park Assoc, North Bergen	4,000
Rothermung, Anna—Maria Mueller, Union	1,050
Russell, Mary A—J F Russell, J City	nom
Salter, D B—C Linn, Bayonne	3,000
Same—D Salter, Bayonne	3,100
Same—P D Salter, Bayonne	7,500
Salter, P D—D Salter, Bayonne	8,000
Same—same, Bayonne	2,000
Sasse, Eleonore—P Laux, Union	5,000
Scharfenberger, Jacob—Town of Union, Union	3,000
Schoonover, B S—Julius H Pratt, Kearney	nom
Schultz, C S—A Busch, J City	4,5[illegible]0
Schumann, Robert—C H Weller, J City	nom
Schwartz, J G—Town of Union, Union	3,600
Siegfried, Adam—G J McEwan, West Hoboken	1,800
Same—J V Shelley, West Hoboken	900
Slop, A F by guard—Catharine E Lighte, J City	600
Sip, R G—H Heen, J City	1,000
Smith, Anna by sheriff—P McCauley, J City	2,000
Smith, Philip—A J Goodman, Kearney	3[illegible]0
Sohn, Henry—F C Hansen, Guttenberg	1,380
Spies, W A—J W Dickinson, West Hoboken	1,300
Staehle, Katharine—Pauline Schaller, Union	nom
Stearns, A C by exr—J M Knox, Jr, Bayonne	40,000
Steincke, Mathilda H—T Freichle, J City	1,300
St John, C E—W G Bumsted, J City	50
Storrs, Chas by exrs—A Storrs, Kearney	nom
Tappan, J E C—P W Morris, J City	900
Taylor, Thos—W Wood, J City	2,250
Tay, Owen—M Tierney, J City	50
Thacher, T A by exrs—B S Schoonover, Kearney	200
Thacher, C H—B S Schoonover, Kearney	11
Thacher, Elizabeth B—B S Schoonover, Kearney	166
Thomsen, Peter—H Ropers, J City	2,800
Tierney, Myles—D O'Connell, J City	1,140
Toffey, J J—W Jex, J City	2,000
Tuttle, G F—Matilda A Gardine, J City	6,000
Van Buskirk, Dewitt—Mary J See, Bayonne	1,880
Same—P Guy, Bayonne	975
Same—P Illensworth, Bayonne	nom
Van Reipen, Anna H—Sarah E Dutchen, J City	1,400
Van Winkle, Elizabeth—A A Van Winkle, J City	nom
Vill, J A—J F Finn, J City	2,000
Vogel, Catharine—H Kornah, J City	1,500
Vogler, Otto—W C Collins, J City	700
Vreeland, Marie A—Sarah A Maguire, Bayonne	850
Vreeland, Clarence by special guard—M O'Neil, J City	550
Wallace, Doretta—L Qual, Jr, J City	4,500
Wedmeyer, C H—J Hertner, Union	3,000
Weller, C H—Marie Schumann, J City	nom
Weimar, Henry—P W Brett, West Hoboken	450
Wicucke, R G—G Weiss, Union	500
Wolf, Aaron—Matilda Drachmann, J City	4,500
Wynn, Ellen—P Rosenthal, Bayonne	1,200

MORTGAGES.

Entry	Amount
Alsberg, Zelina—G Bruek, J City, 3 years	6,000
Anglesey, J J—The Provident Inst for Savings, J City, 1 year	1,500
Armstrong, D W—G A Hawes, J City, 6 months	2,200
Bergemann, Elizabeth B—C Spierling, J City, 1 year	1,000
Bertram, Chas—The Jersey City B and L Assoc, J City, installs	3,4[illegible]0
Bloom, W E—Maria L Rooth, Bayonne, 5 years	600
Boll, Martin—A C Hesse, J City, 5 years	1,500
Bradt, Sebastian—F Dubel, J City, 3 years	1,200
Breetz, William—F Posser, J City, 3 years	5,100
Bunning, Jno—C Pfenning, J City, 3 years	2,000
Casper, Henry—J Hecht, North Bergen, 3 years	800
Chandless, Maria L—The Industrial M B and L Assoc, J City, installs	2,000
Coffey, Agnes—Angeline M Barrett, J City, 5 years	4,000
Conway, Mary J—Exr Naomi C E Wright, J City, 3 years	800
Copertine, Josephine—Exr A B Dayton, J City, 1 year	8,000
Crone, A W—S Newberger, J City, 3 years	1,500
Datz, Elizabeth—New Jersey Title Guarantee and Trust Co, J City, installs	2,000
Dominick, Isabella—Excelsior M B and L Assoc, J City, installs	7,000
Downes, Jas—Hudson City Savings Bank, J City, 1 year	800
Eichner, Ferdinand—Hoboken Bank for Savings, Hoboken, 3 years	10,000
Eicke, A H—G Von Drehle, Union, 3 years	2,500
Eltringham, Hannah E—Provident Inst for Savings, J City, 1 year	2,000
Faber, Jno—J Heumel, West Hoboken, 1 year	1,075
Farley, Ellen—J H Browning, J City, 3 years	1,600
Farmer, W W—Jersey City Gas Light Co, J City, 3 years	15,000
Fisk, W C—N Williamson, J City, 1 year	2,000
Freitag, Wilhelm—Mary J Von Greiff, J City, 5 years	900
Fuchs, Jos—Phoenix L & B Assoc, J City, installs	2,200
Gemmet, William—Hudson City Savings Bank, Hoboken, 1 year	2,000
Gilcher, Catharine—M O'Gara, J City, 5 years	1,000
Same—same, J City, installs	800
Goodman, A J—W O Woost, Kearney, 1 year	90
Grieff, Rudolph—Lafayette M B and L Assoc, J City, installs	600
Grove, F H—Columbia B and L Assoc, J City, installs	1,500
Guy, Prudence—D Van Buskirk, Bayonne, 3 years	175
Same—same, Bayonne, 3 years	300
Hall, Susan—Jersey City B and L Assoc, J City, installs	600
Hertner, Jacob—Guard of S Ball, Union, 1 year	1,400
Same—C H Wedemeyer, Union, 5 years	1,000
Hey, Alfred—Eliza Hobson, Harrison, 1 year	3,000
Same—P Hauck, Harrison, 1 year	2,000
Irvine, Ed—W G Bumsted, J City, 1 year	300
Jaeger, Herman—A Dewblein, Weehawken, 3 years	2,500
Jensen, Anna M—F Schmidt, Hoboken, 5 years	500
Jex, William—J J Toffey, J City, 2 years	1,500
Kirk, E R—Hoboken Bank for Savings, Hoboken, 1 year	2,500
Kornahrens, Herman—Hoboken Bank for Savings, J City, 1 year	4,000
Koutnick, Geo—Hudson Trust and Savings Inst, West Hoboken, West Hoboken, 5 years	900
Krebs, C F—E Kimball, J City, 5 years	2,500
Kuhlen, William—D Bermes, J City, 3 years	1,200
Lagomarsine, Ann—Frances Cavagnari, Hoboken, 5 years	3,000
Lamb, Peter—P Hauck, J City, 1 year	450
Leidner, Nikolaus—G Troister, J City, 5 years	1,500
Lemerie, Ferdinand—J Paoli, Hoboken, 3 years	1,000
Malloy, J E—The Provident Inst for Savings, J City, 1 year	1,800
Mansfield, Isaac—Hoboken Bank for Savings, Hoboken, 3 years	16,000
May, Adam—Theresa Melchior, J City, 3 years	100
McEwan, Mirian A—J Belle, J City, 1 year	1,800
McEwen, A C—Elisa J Eveland, J City, 1 year	4,000
McGearghty, Bridget—C V Shaddle, J City, 3 years	1,500
McLane, Jane—J Sheehan, J City, 2 years	200
Meiss, Anthony—H Martels, J City, 5 years	400
Mohl, Louis—Eva Maier, J City, 3 years	1,500
Morgan, J L—G Hunlock, J City, 1 year	400
Mulligan, Jas—C P Vreeland, Bayonne, 3 years	600
Ogilvie, Geo—R Macauley, J City, 5 years	2,000
Phelan, J W—Town of Union B and L Assoc, Union, installs	1,000
Powell, C E—G W Conklein, Bayonne, 1 year	3,160
Qual, Louis, Jr—Doretta Wallace, J City, 1 year	4,000
Reinhardt, Igo—The Rising Sun Brewing Co, Bayonne, 1 year	85[illegible]
Reinemann, Mary—J Pratt, J City, 4 years	3,000
Saladin, John—J Gonzales, Hoboken, 1 year	350
Sasse, G W—Helen Cadmus, Bayonne, 3 years	1,[illegible]00
Schelhorn, C W—Igo Reinhardt, Bayonne, 3 years	300
Schmidt, Moritz—J Godfrey, J City, 5 years	575
Schumann, Marie—Greenville B and L Assoc, J City, installs	1,460
Segner, Gustav—The India Wharf Brewing Co, J City, 1 year	400
Sexton, J F—Excelsior M B and L Assoc, J City, installs	2,800
Sheller, J V—A Siegfried, West Hoboken, 3 years	2,300
Shervin, Thos—Exrs H V Shaddle, J City, 1 year	1,500
Same—Security B and L Assoc, J City, installs	1,400
Smith, W B—Howard Savings Inst, Kearney, 1 year	1,000
Stanaway, Catharine—D Van Winkle, J City, 2 years	458
Stretz, Chas—C Ott, J City, 3 years	2,500
Sullivan, Jesse—L Cramer, Kearney, 1 year	961
Taylor, N D—D Baumann, J City, mortgage on lease	1,014
Thompson, A D—The Mutual Life Ins Co, J City, 1 year	10,000
Viehwey, F E—Town Union B and L Assoc, Union, installs	1,400

Vietmeyer, Carl—J Loewer, J City, 1 year	1,000
Weiss, Geo—A Deublein, Union, 3 years	1,600
Wieland, Etta—Sarah A Ross, J City, 2 years	400
Witsohm, Chas—H G Fried, J City, 4 years	1,000
Winser, Emma L—C T Meyer, J City, 4 years	500
Wright, Paulina—Mathilda Schmidt, Union, 3 years	500
Wulpenie, Paulena—H Pusten, J City, 3 years	800
Wunneburg, J A—Exr N S Hibbler, Bayonne, 3 years	1,000
Wurth, Geo—J Gardner, West Hoboken, 5 years	500

CHATTEL MORTGAGES.

Andres, Jno, Union—The William Peter Brewing Co, saloon	500
Beal, Albert, J City—The Burton Brewing Co, saloon fixtures	500
Cornell, Eva O, J City—F G Smith, piano	325
Curhart, C M and H F Otis—J Wallace & Son, saloon fixtures	200
Cosgrove, Joseph, J City—J Hetherington, saloon fixtures	100
Fehr, George, Hoboken—C Birdsall, furniture	125
Ferris, Madison, J City—C Birdsall, furniture	190
Garbs, D H, J City—Bernheimer & Schmid, saloon and lease	700
Green, Margaret, Bayonne—F G Smith, piano	450
Healy, Patrick, J City—The Home Brewing Co, saloon fixtures	450
Kettler, Henry, Hoboken—D Bermes, saloon fixtures	400
Kolley, Jacob, J City—W Gaddis, grocery and meat store	91
Kull, George, J City—A Hohman, horse, wagon	62
Latimer, Annie, J City—F G Smith, piano	192
Lattman, Emil, West Hoboken—Lembeck & Betz Eagle Brewing Co, saloon	800
Meyer, Herman, Union—L Fuss, saloon fixtures	550
McCullough, Frank, J City—Lembeck & Betz Eagle Brewing Co, saloon	200
Oesman, Theodore and Rudolph, West Hoboken—R Murray, silk mill	1,557
Peloubet, J H, J City—E C Leonard, truck	25
Pennycook, J T and Robert Hoy, partners as Pennycook & Co, J City—J Hay, 10,000 sq ft prismatic glass	2,000
Plump, L H, J City—J Wilson, horse, wagon and harness	400
Racioppi, Dominick, Hoboken—Lembeck & Betz Eagle Brewing Co, saloon fixtures	300
The A Kremer Brewing Co, Guttenberg—The De La Vergne Refrigerating Machine Co, refrigerating machine and plant	15,700
Van Brunt, George, J City—Jordan & Moriarty, furniture	152
Von der Linden, Maria, Hoboken—Jordan & Moriarty, furniture	60
Wandler, H F, J City—G Schmidt et al, saloon fixtures	400
Watson, Harriet, J City—Eliza Ehrich, furniture	1,200
Wright, Stephen, J City—Jordan & Moriarty, furniture	71

BILLS OF SALE.

Elzkorn, Wilhelmine, J City—A C Lembech, saloon	100
Fried, Henry, J City—Winifred Horlbech, saloon	2,500
Fuss, Ludwig, Union—H Meyer, saloon fixtures	1,550
Horlbech, Herman, J City—H Fried, saloon	2,500
Izza, Pietro, J City—C Dampra, barber shop	95
Keller, Minnie, J City—Lizzie J Kimble, bakery, wagon, &c	100
Nasser, Frederick, Union—J F Ihensen, bakery	700
The Pneumatic Dynamite Gun Co, J City—D W McWilliams, Spezia gun	465

JUDGMENTS.

Frank, Philip—G Schaumloeffel, who sues for the use of Adam Wick & Co	180
Gerlach, J W and Pauline—A Engelbrecht	91
Grimm, Herman—J Geayer	4,804
Seckamp, Herman—J Knight et al	204

MECHANIC'S LIEN.

Neibank, C D, builder and owner; Lorenz Pfeffer, claimant, J City	768

BUILDING MATERIAL MARKET.

BRICKS.—The position of Common Hards does not as yet change for the better, and it remains practically a buyers' market. Arrivals have not been quite so liberal, yet gave a plentiful supply for the outlet and daily left a reserve surplus of anywhere from two to three millions, under which it was probably needless to add prices failed to gain a better position, and some of the trade call the tone easier. On the general range we allow about former quotations to stand, but as sellers have to open the negotiations and keep them up continually it is natural they should occasionally ease off a fraction in order to expedite matters. On open market and in the ordinary way probably nothing exceeds $5.25, and some call that a full quotation, but occasionally goods go quite a fraction higher where custom insists upon some peculiar color or special brand. We hear of a little washed stock turning up this week, but as a rule the run of quality is very good. There are no Keyports coming forward, and Hackensacks are only sold on orders. As before advised few, if any, buyers object to current cost of brick and the indifferent attitude is the result of absence of necessity for more animated movement. In fact, based on consumptive requirements alone, the market would be even less active, as considerable of the buying is for accumulation on the belief that rates can go no lower. Pales are still without a direct demand and $2.00 seems to be about all that can be obtained for them. There is not much information to be obtained from primary sources, though the evidences generally point to a continuation of production at pretty much all yards and a steady reiteration of grumbling. As one of our receivers put it, in referring to manufacturers, "they cuss, and cuss, and keep on making still," and there seems to be no probability of an immediate suspension of work.

LATH.—The advantage has remained with sellers, and a further strengthening on values is advised. Some few arrivals are noted, with now and then a cargo tendered to arrive, but everything found custom out of town, dealers coming in to help swell the demand, and at the close we have business reported at $2.30 per M. Moderate production and small shipments form the basis of improvement, and receivers appear very confident regarding the situation and look for higher rates, though from an occasional expression dropped it might be inferred that there was some fear of Northern stock.

LIME.—The market is in somewhat better shape, it is said. The heavy surplus accumulation has by hook and by crook finally become pretty well-worked down, the arrivals are smaller, and receivers seem more determined to make a stand on basis of figures ruling before recent break, or say 90c. for Common and $1 for Finishing. Rates, however, are still occasionally cut, even on the best goods, and the poor stuff sells pretty low. Dealers are naturally well stocked, and for some little time the strength of the market will depend upon the supply offering.

LUMBER.—To a certain extent conditions on the general market may still be considered tame, and it would unquestionably prove a difficult matter to place any considerable quantity of stock just now, no matter how attractive, unless some allowance was made on the line of valuation. There are, however, evidences of an improving undertone, and we commence to hear expressions of a more hopeful character regarding the general outlook. Dealers see to feel strong in the unity of action recently attained, and consequently able to cope with any ordinary labor difficulty that may arise, and hence the timidity and hesitation based upon that issue are gradually wearing off. There is, of course, a certain amount of work entirely lost from this year, but considerable that was merely postponed to await events is gradually being taken up and prepared for, and there are new enterprises projected that, if carried, must add materially to consumption. Buyers, therefore, commence to give greater attention to offerings of a staple and attractive character, and agents feel encouragement in consequence, especially as there are very few, if any, kind of stock upon which the accusation of overdrawn valuation can be placed. There is one difficulty thought likely to arise through the chances of a better trade, in the shape of too much anxiety to take advantage of it, and it will certainly be a great mistake if sellers from any section or of any grade of stock overload the market with an excess of offering in the effort to make up for lost time.

Eastern Spruce, while commented upon in a somewhat irregular manner, has on the whole shown a tendency to secure a better market. Not many buyers show any real anxiety to obtain stock, but they are more attentive to the chances of getting something to suit their respective wants, and have to bid slightly fuller rates on desirable specifications. Receivers feel supported and encouraged by the diminution of the cut as a basis upon which to build up a firmer tone, and are very hopeful that by the time manufacturers are ready to resume shipments the market will be much better prepared to receive their product. It is thought that at the other side of the bridge yards are in want of a considerable quantity of stock. Northern Spruce still promises to rule scarce, and comparatively high in cost. It is reported that there is danger of labor trouble at St. Johns about the middle of present month.

Piling remains plenty enough to keep the price low, but stock is not being sacrificed to any extent at the moment. Dealers seem to have much faith in the fall and winter consumption, and will put into chains anything standard size that may not happen to find a quick and ready sale. The large quantity by raft has had no influence upon the general market, as probably none of the stuff in the tow will be offered for sale.

Hemlock is meeting with only a fair present demand, and there are some signs of dissatisfaction among sellers. It is, however, claimed that no stock of importance is pressing into notice from any locality, and agents are commencing to feel hopeful and confident over the chance ahead, especially for the better qualities. On the primal market a steady tone is preserved and manufacturers endeavor to keep the production down as much as possible.

White Pine retains practically the former general run of features, embracing a slowish, uncertain trade and a feeling of sufficient confidence among sellers to induce them to combat the adverse influences by offering moderately and making careful valuation. This keeps a balance, permitting a steady tone, and the chances are against any further decline, though an advance is doubtful unless the outlet greatly broadens. There is too much stuff on hand and no special desire to carry it over into next season. Exporters show a little interest, but mainly in cheap stuff.

Yellow Pine meets with very little inquiry and more or less complaint may still be heard over the condition of market. At the price, however, there is no pressure to realize and the effort is directed to keeping the offering within a narrow compass and preventing too much competition for the few orders extant. Not much promise is found in the export trade at the moment.

Carolina Pine will pick up trade in unison with other kinds of stock, and there is a natural hopeful feeling over the situation. It is a market, however, upon which buyers can afford to be quite particular in matters of selection, and the successful sellers will be those who steadily maintain a high standard of quality in their offerings.

Hardwood meet at the moment a moderately active demand and have an indifferent sort of market, but it is no worse than a week ago. On the contrary, the same promising feeling to which we have referred as prevailing in other sections of the market is gaining ground here also, and there seems little doubt that in two or three weeks there will be a better opportunity to place standard stock with greater freedom than at present. There is a firmer tone on mahogany, especially large sizes, of which supply is small.

GENERAL LUMBER NOTES.

STATE.

The Albany market is reported by the *Argus* as follows:

There is no improvement in the lumber situation as far as this market is concerned and from present indications it looks very much like a very quiet summer. Receipts of pine during the last few days have been heavy and there was quite a string of canal boats awaiting this morning to get to their berths in various parts of the district, while many more were unloading cargoes. The stock of pine on hand is large and is more than sufficient for the demand now prevailing, which as a whole is very moderate. Comparatively few orders are coming in and very little shipping is being done. Hemlock is also moving moderately, and while Spruce culls are in fair request the wants of the trade, particularly in New York, are not up to the average. Hardwoods are inactive, while shingles and lath do not seem to be doing much. In prices no change can be reported. Pine is not particularly firm in many grades, while Spruce remains firm and higher than usual on many sizes of culls.

THE WEST.

Referring to the Chicago yard trade the *Northwestern Lumberman* says:

Piece stuff is worrying the local wholesalers somewhat. They find stiff prices at the mills, with no sign of weakening there. The manufacturers are in fact holding their stock at figures which make it impossible to get out more than even after paying lake rates and handling charges here if sold at the current price list. This condition, together with the prospective big local demand from current building and the World's Fair construction, makes it seem necessary that prices should advance. But right here comes an obstacle in the shape of competition from the North. It is alleged that interior Wisconsin points are shipping lumber, and particularly piece stuff, right by Chicago, having a through rate that is less than the sum of the locals, and delivering it at Illinois, Indiana and Ohio points naturally tributary to this market at lower prices than can be made from here. The conclusion is that manufacturers along the lakes are asking too much for their piece stuff or that the Wisconsin mills too little. As the former are encouraged in their views by the Eastern demand, and as the local dealers think the outlook for the future of this class of material is good, it must be concluded that the Wisconsin people are selling too cheap.

A feature of the market is the demand for all grades of siding and ceiling. This is largely from the east, and dealers say their chief trouble is that they cannot get enough of this stock to supply the requirement. Fencing flooring No. 1 is also in particular request. In fact, almost all the better kinds of lumber are firm, with a tendency to an advance on many kinds. Common and cull boards are also scarce and in demand.

The *Timberman* as follows:

This being the "heated term," the increase in activity does not make itself apparent in the larger cities so much as in an increase in the volume of orders received at producing points and shipment of stock therefrom. During the past week the improved condition has made itself apparent in this manner at a number of Michigan and Wisconsin producing points and a great tide of forest products is now making its way from the west to the east.

The stocks of dry pine lumber in Wisconsin have been very much broken all the spring and have only been on the mend in the last few weeks. Shipments have been large, which of course has kept things in fair shape. However, nearly every manufacturer has his yard piled with green lumber and when August 1st comes around there will be a fine lot of dry lumber, unless the "boom" comes before that date.

June has been a much better month in the hardwood trade than May, although dealers say there is still much to be desired in the way of improvement. Prices have kept up very well, but there has not been that rush of demand which is necessary before the average yard dealer will admit that trade with him is even fair.

In regard to the situation among manufacturers the month has brought little change. Prices are somewhat weaker, perhaps, the natural result of freer offerings, but a ready market is still found for all dry stock, and it is not often the mill man has trouble in disposing of anything offered, provided only that it is up to grade and well manufactured.

Oak has been accumulating to some extent, and in most sizes and grades the supply is now well up to the requirements of the market. If any scarcity remains it is in dry plain-sawed red oak, for which demand is very active. The call for quarter-sawed white oak also continues to be quite pronounced, but the yards are in a position to readily supply all demand. Oak plank and timber sell fairly well, some quite heavy orders for both being reported recently. Prices at the mills are not a good deal lower than they were when dealers were scouring the country for oak, the difference being not more than $2 per thousand, except on an occasional lot where circumstances have rendered it necessary for the holder to sell.

Selected red birch continues to grow in favor among local manufactures, both for furniture and interior work.

Quartered sycamore is another wood that is becoming quite extensively used for interior work, but as it is only in a room or two in a house, the orders placed are small. For quarter-sawed firsts and seconds dealers are paying $22 to $25.

Demand for maple flooring shows no abatement locally, while the shipping trade is increasing. Selling prices will average about $28.50 for carloads, and $30 for smaller lots. With strips bringing $21 to $22, this does not leave much margin over the cost of manufacture, and in fact there is nothing in it for the yard dealer.

GREAT BRITAIN.

The *Timber Trades Journal* as follows:

LONDON.

The small stock at the docks and the scarcity of new goods compared with other seasons attract considerable attention at the present time. A few gaps have been filled up, but the quantity brought into London so far is nothing like what it has been in former years, and if the importation continues on its present moderate scale prices are pretty certain to harden still further. It must not, however, be forgotten that the financial position is not so good as in 1890, and any attempt to bring in goods in anticipation of demand will inevitably bring about a reaction. We believe that there is no intention on shippers' part to send forward consignment cargoes, and if the policy of waiting until buyers are ready to purchase is steadily adhered to, both shippers and buyers will benefit, as the consuming powers of London and district cannot be doubted.

GLASGOW.

There is little change to note in the position of the trade here. The Glasgow imports of wood goods for the week are light, not comprising any full cargo, and as regards parcels of deals coming forward per the regular steam liners from Quebec and Montreal, they are in very moderate quantities, and make no material addition to stock, when current deliveries are taken into account.

There is the likelihood of a quiet season in imports of deals, and this is generally anticipated, so far as we can learn from those conversant with the importing trade.

A public sale of deals was held here on 24th inst., the catalogue comprising several of the new season's imports of Quebec pine deals, besides a variety of other goods.

There was a fair attendance, but the bidding was rather slow, and not many lots out of the extensive catalogue submitted changed hands, but some business was done privately at the close of the auction. Some old lots, which the exposers were desirous to close, were cleared out without reserve.

For broad 1st yellow pine deals, of which the catalogue contained a few lots, there were one or two offers, as 2s. 9d. for 15 ft. 12-18x8, and 2s. 10d. for 14 ft. 12-14x8, but the goods were held for higher figures.

METALS.—COPPER—Ingot has undergone very little change, and there is practically nothing new to suggest in regard to general conditions of the market. Speculative feeling appears dormant at the moment, export orders few and far between, and the home trade confined mainly to small odd lots adapted to immediate wants, with value about as before. On an average range of valuations we quote at 12⅞@13c. for Lake, and 11¾@12¼c. for casting brands. Manufactured Copper has found a somewhat irregular trade, but on the whole the movement is said to be quite as full as could be expected at this season, and no special complaint is made. Prices generally rule about steady. We quote as follows: Sheet, not above 30x72 in., 16 oz. and over, 25c.; do. 14 to 16 oz., 23c.; do. 12 to 14 oz., 24c.; do. 10 to 12 oz., 26c.; do. 8 to 10 oz., 28c.; do under 8 oz. 30c. Sheets longer than 72 inches add 1c. for 12@14 oz., 2c. for 10@12 oz. and 3c. for 8@10 oz. Sheets, not above 36x96 in., 16 oz and over, 22c.; do. 14 to 16 oz. 24c.; do. 12 to 14 oz. 26c.; do. 10 to 12 oz. 30c.; do. 8 to 10 oz. 33c. Sheets longer than 96 inches 22c. for over 32 oz. and add 1c. for 16 to 32 oz.; 3c. 14 to 16 oz.; 5c. 12 to 14 oz., and 13c. for 8 to 10 oz. Sheets, not above 48x96 32 to 64 oz., 22c.; do. 16 to 32 oz., 25c.; do. 14 to 16 oz., 27c.; do. 12 to 14 oz. 29c.; do. 10 to 12 oz. 33c. Sheets wider than 48x96 and longer, 22@25c. for 32 to 64 oz. and over. 27@30c. for 16 to 32 oz. 30c. for 14 to 16 oz and 34c. for 12 to 14 oz. All bath tub sheets, per lb., 16 oz. 27c.; 14 oz. 29c.; 12 oz. 31c.; and 10 oz. 35c. Bolt copper ¾ inch diameter and over, 23c. Circles, 60 diameter and less, 3c. above price of sheets of same thickness; circles, 60 to 96 do do, 5c. do; circles, 96 do and over 6c. do. Segment and pattern sheets, 3c. above price of sheets required to cut them from. Cold or hard rolled copper, 1@2c. per lb. above the foregoing prices. Copper bottoms, 26@32c. per lb. IRON—Scotch Pig has secured a few special orders, but chances for the stock are not plentiful, and it secures only a small rating in the structure of the metal market. We quote more or less nominally at $22.00@24.50 per ton, according to brand. American Pig shows a somewhat irregular market, according to quality. The choice makes of foundry have secured an excellent demand and are closely sold up to production with full rates readily obtained, while of No. 2 there is an abundance against the rather indifferent inquiry and now and then a showing on value is made to hasten the movements of buyers. We quote at $17.00@18.00 per ton for No. 1 X foundry; $15.50@16.50 for No. 2 X do., and $14 00@15.00 for Gray Forge. Old material not very active at the moment, and the market somewhat uncertain. As a rule, however, offerings are made with moderation, and holders are asking former rates steadily. We quote at about $20.50@22.50 for old rails; $20.00@21.00 for No. 1 wrought scrap; $17.00@18.00 for cast scrap, and $17.00@17.50 for car wheels. Manufactured Iron has no unusual animation and the market seems barren of new or interesting features at the moment. Prices on standard products, however, are sustained and the position is a steady one throughout. We quote Common Merchant Bar ordinary size, at 2.00@2.10c. from store, and refined at 2.30@2.60c; Rods, round and square, 2.30@2 40c.; Bands, 2.40@2.60c.; Norway Nail Rods, 4@5c., and domestic sheet on the basis of 3.00@3.05c. for common Nos. 10@16. Other descriptions at corresponding prices, with 1-10c. less on large lots from cars. Steel rails up to the present writing have found no very extensive deal, but a fair number of orders are being booked for lots of 1,500 tons and less and reasonably well divided among the principal mills. Manufacturers have remained firm and persistently refused to make any modification on line of cost. We quote standard sections $30 per ton at mill, with usual advance for delivery at tide water. Pig Lead finds fair trade occasionally and, while a few minor irregularities on value occasionally develop, the general tendency appears to be toward firmness and a comparatively moderate offering. We quote at 4.45@4½c. per lb. The manufactures of lead are quoted at 7c. for Pipe, 7¾c. for Sheet, 15c. for Tin-lined Pipe, and 37½c. for Block Tin Pipe. Pig Tin finds only moderate call from consumers, even less than ordinary at this season, and with the speculative feeling limp, under adverse accounts from abroad, prices are easier. We quote at about 20.30@20.35c. for round lots, and 20½@20⅝c. for jobbing parcels. Tin Plate as a rule is firmly held, but buyers stand off and in many cases entertain a hope that the large supply will eventually act as a weight to depress the line of value. Actual consumption, however, will be fuller this season than last. We quote prices as follows: I. C. Charcoal, ½ cross assortment, Melyn grade, $6.30@6.35, each additional X add $1.50; I. C. Charcoal, ½ cross assortment, Allaway grade, $5.90@6.00, each additional X add $1; Charcoal terne, M. F. grade, 14x20, $7.37½@7.40; M. F. grade, 20x28, $15.25@15.30; Worcester, 14x20, $5.75@5.80; Worcester, 20x28, $11.50@11.55; Dean grade, 14x20, $5.15@5.20; Dean grade, 20x28, $10.15@10.50; D. R. D. grade, 14x20, $4.85@4 90; D. R. D. grade, 20x28, $9.95@10.00; I. C. Coke, Penlan grade, $5.30@5.35; J. B. grade, 14x20, $5.42½@5.45; I. C. Bessemer steel, squares, $5.75@5.80 basis; I. C. Siemens steel, squares, $5.90@6.00 basis. Spelter has retained a firm market and indeed seems to be gaining strength on later deliveries which are held above spot valuation. We quote 5.03@5.10 for Common Western, according to brand.

NAILS.—Some improvement in demand is claimed, but the deal is not full enough to create any animation and readily met from supplies in hand. Prices have in some cases shaded a trifle, but of late appear inclined to a firmer position. We quote Cut at $1.65@1 75 per keg for car lots and $1.75@1.85 per keg for parcels from store, for iron, and add 5@10c. per keg for steel. Wire, $2.10@2.15 at mills, and 2.30@2.40 from store.

PAINTS, OILS, COLORS, ETC.—So far as it goes the market is good enough, but it does not go very far, and the volume of business makes no rapid expansion. It is a seasonable feature, however, and one for which most operators are prepared, so that no special fault finding is to be heard, and there is a considerable measure of faith expressed in general prospects. Dependent trade has at no time been calling for supplies beyond early consumptive wants, or at least that was the claim, and it is therefore assumed that as fall requirements commence to pick up jobbers will have to bring prompt reflection upon bulk lots. Prices generally are well sustained and a feeling of firmness prevails regarding staple goods. The impression in matter of revision of White Lead was correct and actually made before our last report, but only now given out. It shows an advance in price pretty much all around and some changes in quantity allowance, the latter in buyers' favor. Association Corroders' rates stand as follows: Lead in oil in kegs and dry lead in kegs, in lots of less than 500 lbs., 7½c. net; in lots of 500 lbs to 5 tons at one purchase, 7c.; 5 tons to 12 tons, one purchase, 5¾c.; 12 tons and over, one purchase, 6¾c.; dry white lead in bbls. ½c per lb. less than price in kegs. Lead in oil 12½ lb. in tin pails, add 1c.; in 25 and 50 lb. tin pails, add ½c.; and in 1 to 5 lb. tin cans, assorted (100 lbs. in case) add 2½c. per lb. to keg price. Terms on lots on 500 lbs. and over, note or acceptance at sixty days, or 2½ per cent. discount will be allowed for cash paid within fifteen days of invoice date. To make either of the above required quantities any assortment of packages of white lead, red lead and litharge may be counted. The above quotations are free on board cars or boat at corroding point. Linseed Oil meets with fair average demand, but the market retains an unsettled tone and valuations range a little wide at times. We quote at general range at 45@48c. for Western, and 50@58c. for city. Spirits Turpentine meets with only about the ordinary trade demand, and in a general way the market rules somewhat tame. About former rates are ruling, with conditions just a trifle nominal at the moment. We quote at 37½@38½c. per gallon, according to quality, delivery, etc.

TAR AND PITCH.—Buyers generally are unwilling to invest except as a matter of necessity, and business is uncertain. Supplies, however, seem to be under control, and owners' views steady at about old rates. We quote pitch at $1.70@1.75 per bbl.; Tar at $2.15@2.50, according to quantity, quality and delivery.

MISCELLANEOUS.

MISCELLANEOUS.

BIDS ARE INVITED FOR THE MASONS', CARPENTERS', PLUMBING, STEAM-HEATING, ELECTRICAL AND BOWLING ALLEY WORK, for the erection of Columbia Club House in the City of Hoboken, N. J. Bidders will be expected to furnish satisfactory bonds for full amount of contract. Plans and specifications, and all other matters appertaining thereto, can be found with the architects, Messrs. FRENCH, DIXON & DE SALDERN, 57th Street and Broadway, New York. Sealed bids must be handed in on or before July 25th, 1891, at office of the architects, or to Columbia Club, Box No. 241, Hoboken, N. J. Club reserves the right to reject any or all bids.

By order of the Building Committee.

G. PERCY ESKENBRACH, Chairman.

ARTHUR SEITZ, Secretary.

BLINDS.

MISCELLANEOUS.

Devoted to Real Estate, Building Architecture, Household Decoration, Business and Themes of General Interest

PRICE, PER YEAR IN ADVANCE, SIX DOLLARS.

Published every Saturday.

TELEPHONE - - - - CORTLANDT 1370.

Communications should be addressed to

C. W. SWEET, 14 & 16 Vesey St.

J. T. LINDSEY, Business Manager.

VOL. XLVIII JULY 18, 1891. No. 1,218

The publication offices of THE RECORD AND GUIDE *have been removed to Nos. 14 and 16 Vesey street, over The Mechanics' and Traders' Exchange, a few feet west of Broadway.*

The index to Volume XLVII of THE RECORD AND GUIDE *is issued with this number of the journal, and subscribers who may not receive a copy should report the fact to the office of publication, Nos. 14-16 Vesey street.*

THE NEW MAGAZINE.

Within a few days now will be issued the first number of the new illustrated quarterly magazine, THE ARCHITECTURAL RECORD. *Readers of* THE RECORD AND GUIDE, *and those who have received our circular letter, who desire to become subscribers to the new magazine should lose no time in sending in their names and addresses to the offices of publication, Nos. 14 and 16 Vesey street, New York City. The reception which has been given to the new enterprise by the architectural profession, the builders of this country and the general public has been most encouraging. The new magazine will start with thousands of readers in every State in the Union, and the large cities have shown an unexpected interest in the new periodical. We are desirous, of course, of having the subscription list as large as possible for the first number, and in order that delivery may be prompt, all intending subscribers are requested to send us a postal card at once. The first number of the magazine will contain "The Revival of Romanesque," by Montgomery Schuyler, with thirty full-page illustrations; "An 'American Style' of Architecture," by Barr Ferree; "Architectural Fads," by George Keister; the "New York Building Law," by William J. Fryer, Jr.; "Terra Cotta," by Jas. Taylor; "Byzantine Architecture," by Prof. Aitchison, and other articles, editorial departments, etc., with numerous illustrations of recent designs for office buildings, residences, clubs, churches, country houses, electrical fixtures, furniture, interiors, etc. The magazine will be printed on the finest paper, and no expense or pains have been spared to make it the leading architectural paper in the country. The annual subscription price is $1.*

THE present market for stocks may be very aptly described as a brokers' market, inasmuch as its movements are about sufficient only to pay the brokers' commissions. Whatever characterizing tendency there may be in it is towards lower prices. A narrow market is not the one the public like, and business cannot be attracted towards it until its movements are guided by strong hands which give some life and excitement to it. While it drifts in this fashion quotations are likely to be lower, and whatever business must be done on the Exchange is likely to be done at lowering figures. Louisville & Nashville and Burlington & Quincy have pressed on the market somewhat, and if any large selling movement can be induced into those two issues a considerable decline all round is sure to follow. There are, too, stories afloat that all is not right with some of the Villard Specialties and some of Inman-Brice-Thomas issues; the latter are certainly selling at figures which proclaim that some time friends are treating them with marked neglect; nor are quotations for the former the most satisfactory. Reports from London are gloomy, and that fact, coupled with a new shipment of gold, even though of a small amount, while Exchange rates are so low, has anything but a reassuring effect. We are, too, approaching the time when this centre is likely to feel the effects of the movement of money to the interior. These effects may not be serious, because of the long-time warning everyone has had. Most bankers have availed themselves of the ample opportunities given them to secure their money sufficient to supply such of their needs as they could foresee for the next few months; but there is likely to be great caution in undertaking new business and hesitation in advising any large expansion of old for a little time to come.

IF the increase of the revenue of a country is an index to prosperity, Great Britain ought at the present time be in a fairly satisfactory condition. The total collections for the last quarter aggregated £21,914,100, against £21,468,600 in the corresponding period in 1890—an increase of £445,500. This is a far better showing than Mr. Goschen anticipated; but it is not likely that the rate of increase will be continued. The condition of trade is not improving, and it is possible that before the end of the year the revenue will lose the impetus it received during the past two years of speculative business activity. On the whole, the best authorities are inclined to believe that the character of the half year has not been such as to encourage anything but great caution. The prices of the principal commodities during that period has been downwards. The "Index Number" of the *Economist* representing the combined prices of twenty-two leading commodities now stands at 2,187. This is lower not only than at the beginning of the half-year, but also than at this time last year; and it is necessary to go back to July, 1889, to find prices at a lower level than at present. The result of movements in prices during the last half-year has been to reduce the "Index Number" by a little over 17 per cent. It is noticeable, however, that while most commodities have fallen in value, food stuffs on the whole have risen—a change due, of course, to the threatened scarcity of European harvests. The French government has come forward with an elaborate and complicated scheme for creating a Workmen's National Pension Fund—similar to that already created in Germany. The basis of the project is a daily contribution of five to ten centimes by workers of either sex, to which the employer must add a like sum, and in addition the State would contribute two-thirds of the total subscribed by the worker and employer. Payment is to begin at the age of 25, and is to continue to the age of 55. It is calculated that the payment of 5 centimes per day by the workman and as much by the master, with the addition of two-thirds of 10 centimes by the State, invested at 4 per cent with compound interest, would produce at the end of thirty years a capital representing the value of a life annuity of 300 francs from the age of 55. With a daily payment of 10 centimes the annuity would be 600 francs, the maximum contemplated by the bill. The calculation is made on the supposition that workmen are employed on 290 days in the year. The Berlin market is sinking into a rather depressing dullness, the changes being but few and for the most part for the worse.

THERE is something illusive about a "popular movement," or else the New York *Times* has been deceiving us. In reading those articles about "public indignation" and the "stern determination of outraged taxpayers," everyone must have felt that the tenancy of the Elevated Road in Battery Park had at last become a matter of an hour or two, and the moment might arrive at any time when popular feeling, thitherto kept in restraint by the sleepy decorum of the *Times*, would no longer feel satisfied in expressing itself in fabricated anonymous letters and fake mass meetings, but would burst into revolutionary activity, tear down the elevated structure in the park and vindicate the inalienable right of a few score of tramps, servant girls and time-burdened individuals to an unobstructed view of the architectural marvels of State street. Trivial, fortuitous circumstances have before this proved fatal to great schemes. An inopportune storm played havoc with the Armada, and the recent hot weather and the humidity must have enervated the feelings of the multitude as to the Battery Park "grab," so that they have left Jay Gould a little longer in his ill-gotten position;—and, concurrently, several hundred thousand travelers in the enjoyment of somewhat more comfortable, and somewhat speedier, transportation facilities than would be theirs if the park were wholly given up to the tramps. Even the Aldermen back-slid into a favorable attitude towards the elevated railroad Ogre, and it seems that nothing is now left to the few individuals in the *Times* office who have charge of the Public's indignation, but to bottle up the winds for a time—Ulysses-like—and make for the sea-shore for their summer vacation. In the Fall there may be a better opportunity for their slightly cheeky operations.

THE failure of this last onslaught upon the Elevated Road illuminates that somewhat vague subject which we hear of from time to time—the "power of the press." For several weeks past all the daily newspapers of the city, with the exception of the *Sun*, have been foaming at the mouth about the terrible iniquity committed against the 1,700,000 people of this city because the Elevated Road uses a few feet of the border land of Battery Park for the benefit of its patrons. From the "scare lines" one might reasonably suppose that a little revolution was on foot against the Manhattan Company. Petitions were displayed, mass meetings concocted, indignation poured forth by the column. Readers were assured that the popular feeling would no longer tolerate the usurpation of valuable public land by a monopolistic and dark-minded corporation. The Day of Judgment for the Grabbers was announced; and what came of it? A ridiculous fiasco. There was not only too little powder for a report, but what there was of it was wet. The whole affair was a demonstration of newspaper impotence and public common sense.

AFTER all the nonsense we have had about the Public and the Manhattan road isn't it time that the newspapers took a really public view of the position which this city and that corporation hold to one another? Years ago this unrestrained antagonism to the elevated roads first showed itself; since then all common sense and all reasonableness have been thrown aside to give place to a narrow and what would be a disastrous prejudice if its full effects were permitted. No one who knows anything of the growth and development of New York in the last decade will hesitate for a moment to assign to the elevated roads the place of one of the chief factors in the progress. The city now has considerably outgrown the capacity of the system which has done so much for it; but the city is in this position to-day: the elevated roads furnish the *only* rapid transit facilities which it possesses. A new and a better system we know is in the process of construction, or it would be more correct to say is in the process of being planned for; but that better system is yet a long way off, and the old adage recommending the keeping of dirty water until the clean is obtained is applicable to this case. The underground railroad which the Rapid Transit Commissioners promise us will not be in running order for some years to come. In the meantime, what is the best thing for New York to do? To oppose all and every improvement of the present elevated system and submit to a condition of affairs that grows more and more intolerable every day, or would it be better to assist as far as possible the Manhattan Co. to improve their system, enlarge their stations, run longer trains, and develop a third-track service. Any additional privileges needed by the company might be given, not in a reckless manner, but with proper safeguards, and for a just and equitable public consideration. Surely this is a policy wiser than the one of newspaper spite and public prejudice, willing to do anything that hampers the company, even though everybody suffers by it.

CHAUNCEY M. DEPEW, after an annoying delay, has again set sail for Europe. There he will meet his many friends in the upper circles of society, among whom we may not fail to mention the Prince of Wales. Europe's gain is America's loss. We are growing accustomed to Mr. Depew's absence during the summer months, but we cannot grow reconciled to it. Our only consolation under his afflicting absence is a sturdy confidence, based on the experience of past years, that Mr. Depew will not fail to tell us on his return many amusing anecdotes of the ways of aristocrats and the impressions that these curious doings make upon the cultured American gentleman, the finest product of civilization. There is a rare savor to the thought that this representative of republicanism hob-nobbing with dukes and lords, and listening to the feeble drippings of their circumscribed and caste-bound intellects, is well aware that he is gathering rich feast for the fine palates of his republican brethren. It is as if the American people sent their "brightest" and "brainiest" reporter to interview the classes of Europe. Delightful, however, as are the pictures which his departure calls to mind and the anticipations which his much-to-be-desired return stimulates, it is not particularly of these to which we wish to draw attention at the present juncture. It is only Mr. Depew's relation to rapid transit that we desire to touch upon, and we regret to say that this relation is not so commendable or so promising of product to his fellow-citizens as his relations to the foreign aristocracies. The cloak of illusion and romance with which the papers surround Mr. Depew falls to the ground when he becomes simply the president of a Vanderbilt corporation. He must ever be happiest as an after-dinner speaker and as a subject for interviews.

A SHORT time before he departed he stated to a reporter in his prosaic capacity as president of the Central that his corporation would have nothing to do with any east side rapid transit line. The statement has caused but little comment, not because there is any doubt as to the truth of the interview, but because of some doubt as to the sincerity of the speaker; for it is sometimes part of the duty of the presidents of great corporations to conceal their intentions from the public, and, if necessary, to lie for the sake of so doing. Consequently the declaration forms a basis for interesting speculation. What does Mr. Depew mean when he says the Vanderbilts will have nothing to do with an east side rapid transit line? In endeavoring to answer this question we do not pretend to any telepathic insight into the workings of Mr. Depew's mind, such as some morning journals have of the devious processes of Mr. Gould's intelligence; yet the city's past experience with the Vanderbilt corporations constitutes a key for one plausible reading of this most perplexing asseveration. Perplexing is the word to describe it, because superficially the Vanderbilts have every interest in controlling a rapid transit line which would bring the lower wards into convenient connection with their trans-Harlem tracks. These tracks drain a large part of the most desirable suburban property to be found in the vicinity of the city—territory which under anything like equal conditions of accessibility would far more popular for residences than either Long Island or New Jersey can ever be. Yet with the southern terminus at Forty-second street their growth must ever be hampered. In the past the Central, the New Haven and the Harlem have not been able to secure anything like the number of commuters which the Pennsylvania and the Jersey Central have secured, for their local service even within the severe restrictions imposed by their southern terminus has been most inadequate. But with a terminus for local service at the Battery, the Vanderbilt corporations could within five years obtain a large and remunerative traffic. If, however, it is desirable for the Vanderbilts to control a rapid transit system from Forty-second street south, the property-owners, not only on the line of the roads north of the Harlem, but also along the proposed route south of Forty-second street will obtain an equal if not a greater benefit therefrom. In the past the Vanderbilts under such circumstances have forced the property-owners to share with them the cost of such improvements. The owners along 4th avenue paid half of the cost of the open cut in that avenue, just as the owners along the Harlem road are paying half the outlay attending the open cut for that road in the 23d and 24th Wards. May not the Vanderbilts be seeking similar assistance on this new proposed route? And may they not be determined to hold off until they get it? When the route of the Belmont Commission was announced, Mr. Depew took a very different tone as regards this matter, and on several occasions the Vanderbilts have evinced their willingness to seek for plums in the New York rapid transit pie. The explanation of the present stand would seem to be that they intend to hold out for very good terms.

Municipal Lodging Houses.

RECENTLY the Board of Estimates and Apportionment gave a hearing to representatives of the various charitable societies of the city in advocacy of the establishment of a municipal lodging house, and the abandonment of the police station lodging rooms, the disgraceful condition of which has been a matter of notoriety these years. Those in favor of this project claim that it will be a means of reducing trampery and vagrancy, and will at the same time afford decent shelter to respectable men temporarily destitute. In support of this claim the experience of Boston is instanced. We give the facts as gathered by a representative of one of these societies.

Twelve years ago Boston established what is known as the Wayfarer's Lodge, and in connection with it a Wood Yard, utilizing for the purpose an abandoned school building and playground. Cots were put in the large and well-ventilated upper rooms, while the lower stories and basement were fitted up as office, kitchen and dining rooms, back rooms, carpenter shops, etc., and a shed put up in the yard for the protection of the workers and the wood against the weather.

It was then arranged that persons applying for shelter at the police station should be furnished, if not disorderly or suspicious, with a card of admission to this lodge. On entrance here every man is obliged to take a bath. His clothes, if "animated," are subjected to a heat which exterminates the vermin; he is given a clean night shirt and a good cot bed. In the morning he is obliged to do a certain amount of labor in return for what he receives. This labor is either sawing wood or splitting or carrying or piling it when sawed. The work requires from one to three hours. After it is done the lodger is entitled to a breakfast of warm soup and bread. This is practically the whole scheme, though dinners and suppers are furnished to "out of works," usually very few in number, for work rendered. The lodgers are under strict discipline. Any one who refuses to submit to the rules may be taken before a magistrate and sent to the workhouse.

Now, what has been the result? Prior to 1879 there were lodged in the Boston station houses, according to the statement of one of the overseers of the poor of Boston, from 200 to 600 persons per night. Now, the total number of lodgings given yearly is under 30,000, or less than 100 per night. This is exclusive of women, who are sent to another lodging house. And as to the character of those who now apply for the city's shelter, the overseers say: "The crowds that have always thronged the station houses, disturbing their discipline, tainting their atmosphere, and interfering with the more legitimate duties of the department, have disappeared. Tramps who shirk work no longer infest the street by day and night, and the applicants, as a rule, are for the most part persons seeking honestly for employment." The Lodge and Wood Yard have been carried on at a net cost of between $7,000 and $8,000 per year, the latter paying into the treasury annually above expenses about $2,000. A part of the wood is disposed of to the city, the remainder to the public at market prices.

What should we have to expect of the experiment in New York City? First of all, the cleaning out of those foul holes of contagion in the station houses. Second, the provision of decent shelter to those who under the stress of misfortune need it, and under such conditions as not to destroy self-respect. Third, a decrease in the number of tramps in New York City, and the end of the "revolver" system; and lastly, the removal of the cause of much imposition upon householders under the plea of shelter for the night. There is now no decent place to which the citizen can send the penniless man, and as a result he is either passed or intrusted with a coin which nine times out of ten, perhaps, goes for drink and not for shelter. The establishment of a city lodging house such as proposed would doubtless save to the citizens much more than the amount required for its establishment and maintenance.

Investments—Good and Bad.

LOUISVILLE & NASHVILLE.—The ten per cent. addition to its capital which the Louisville & Nashville Railroad Company is now asking its stockholders to subscribe to at 70 does not seem to be received with unqualified favor. This increase of capital is somewhat calculated to take off the edge of the stockholders' pleasure at receiving a cash dividend. The influence on the market for the stock has been bad, weakening the price, if not causing any great decline, and it seems inevitable that with the market as narrow as it is, the portion of the new stock which has to find purchasers must bring the price of all down to its own figure and perhaps lower. This is the only reasoning from experience that can be had. Last year this company issued stock in a similar manner, but at 85, and although there was a broad and buoyant market the price of Louisville & Nashville had, there is every reason to believe, to be supported at the subscription figure and broke that as soon as the new stock was out and the support withdrawn. The company made a good showing for the last fiscal year, having a surplus of $482,340. It has authority to issue $2,200,000 of stock besides the $4,800,000 for which it is now asking subscriptions, and whether all is issued or not, it must keep up the rate of its earnings in order to maintain its dividends of 5 per cent per annumu, and have the balance in hand over and above dividends necessary in the management of so large a property. There are some other reasons beside the narrowness of the market which make the wisdom of this new issue of stock questionable. Net earnings per mile show a tendency to decrease while operating expenses increase. It has been computed that as a result of the issue of $4,800,000 new stock surplus earnings after paying fixed charges will be increased only about $16,000, but that estimate is based on the dangerous theory of what has been will be. Still it is singular that the company has chosen a time like the present to ask stockholders to subscribe to its stock, and it will be remarkable if it does not meet the same experience as the Norfolk and Western Railroad Company which some months ago, when its preferred stock was selling at about 55 or 56, offered a block of that stock to its stockholders at 52 only to see the quotations drop to a point below that at which the new stock was offered, at which figure it has not again sold, and it is now quoted between 50 and 51, with very little business done in it. It is singular, too, that if Louisville & Nashville is the good property it seems to be on the showing of the annual reports and has a fair prospect of continuing to be prosperous, the Kentucky Central would not have been bought with stock, as the C. B. & Q. acquired the C. B. & Northern, and as the Atchison acquired the San Francisco and the Colorado Midland, instead of asking the stockholders to go down and into the pockets to pay for the property with cash. The paying of a cash divi end on the outstanding stock, and at the same time making so large an issue of new stock creates suspicion and looks very much like sugaring a disagreeable pill. Still, while looking at the worst features of the case, it is only fair to take the better into consideration and not to forget the remarkable record Louisville & Nashville has made in the last six years, at the beginning of which it only saved itself from bankruptcy by the issue of bonds at almost ruinous rates, which bonds it has since retired, and having worked itself first into a stock dividend payer is now a cash dividend payer.

NEW ISSUES.—Whoever may cast a gloomy look on the financial situation the promoter of new enterprises does not, but comes to the front with all the cheerfulness so characteristic of him. The promoter and his optimism both have their uses, especially in times of doubt and gloom, as the sun to disperse clouds, but it is not necessary to take them too readily any more than to expose oneself to sunstroke. There are quite a number of offers of fortune from the promoter. There are, to say nothing—and perhaps it is best that nothing be said—of the Georgia-Alabama Investment and Development Company, the stock of the Standard Chemical Company, the bonds of the Railway Equipment Company of Minnesota and the stocks of the Trow Directory, Printing and Bookbinding Co. The advantages of the first seem to be based on a theory similar to that of Alnascar, the unfortunate glass merchant of the Eastern story. The Equipment Company, through a well-known house, offers bonds issued at about two-thirds of the value of what appears to be some very expensive equipment. This equipment is leased by the Chicago, St. Paul and Kansas City Railway Company, which is an amalgamation of some other companies which have not had a very satisfactory experience, though lately, in the amalgamated form, making a very good showing. The Equipment Company is said to have a capital of $1,000,000, "of which $995,500 has been subscribed and paid in cash," at what rate is not stated. The Trow Directory, Printing and Bookbinding Company make an offer of $750,000 8 per cent Cumulative Preferred stock and $250,000 general stock, and accompanies the offer with statements which, if examination verify them, as it most probably will, would make these issues very desirable to investors. The details consist of the nature of the business, the property acquired and its value, and the result of the examination of the books with a view to show the profits for the last five years, made by a firm of accountants of standing and repute. The Board of Directors of the Trow Company is composed of representative business men.

MINING.—The promoter and capitaliser of mines is to the fore. Paragraphs, not by any means brief, are appearing in newspapers and news sheets, asking why speculators and investors neglect mines for railroad stocks and whether mining stocks are to start the boom! The profits which have been made in mining are strongly brought out. Boston people are particularly anxious that the world should know how much they have made in, or perhaps it would be more proper to say out of, mines. All this is very nice and ingenious, but the object is too apparent. If any one wants to know why mines have, to use the expressive slang of the streets, a black eye, they can be informed that it is because more money has been sunk in them than taken out, and if the speculative and investive world continues in its right mind, the optical discoloration of this line of business will only be removed when mining enterprises can be tested by the same rules as other enterprises, and that whatever may be said to the contrary by those having stocks to sell is not the case now.

ADVANCE CALCULATIONS.—The danger of placing a too implicit reliance on expert calculations was illustrated last week by the Bank Statement. The temptation to forecast results is very great and the endeavors made in that direction are often very laudable, but liable to create disappointment. According to one authority the statement should have shown an increased reserve of about $1,800,000, and according to another a similar sum, while in scattering opinions the amount varied, but all were for an increase. The fact, therefore, of a decrease of over $900,000 created much disgust when announced. The moral of this is, take all such statements with a grain of salt, not excepting those made in this column. A wise man has said, "figures are facts, but there is nothing so deceptive as facts."

Rapid Transit Schemes.

A crowd of indignant Washington Heights and West End property-owners left the rooms of the Rapid Transit Commission yesterday afternoon. A week before they had been told that they would be given a hearing at a meeting which would convene at 1.45 P. M. But when they got there they found no meeting. The solitary messenger informed them that the meeting had adjourned nearly an hour before. The indignant citizens suppressed their feelings and went their way, without having been heard. Later it came out that because Commissioners John H. Inman and Samuel Spencer could not attend an afternoon session, the hour for meeting had been changed too late for public notice, to 10.45 o'clock A. M. Commissioner Inman had come on especially from Atlanta, and Commissioner Spencer from the West, to attend the meeting, but found so many other meetings relating to their private affairs awaiting them that they had to change the hour of the Rapid Transit meeting.

As it was, nothing definite was accomplished. Over an hour and a half was given to the comparison of two plans of construction for the Broadway-Boulevand route. One of them is for a double-decked tunnel with two tracks on a level, one above the other, which will take up comparatively little of the roadway, and the other is for a roadway with all four tracks on a level, which would in some places take up all the roadway to the house line and would require the use of the sidewalk vaults for station purposes. The commissioners found it difficult to decide between them. Another perplexing question is where to locate the extension of the proposed east side line through the 23d and 24th Wards. As President Steinway said: "On the west side are the New York Central and Northern roads, and on the east side are Harlem and Suburban roads. These already pretty well supply the residents along their respective lines, as least as far south as 42d street. But there is a lovely section of country about a mile and a quarter wide, and seven miles long, lying between the Harlem and Northern roads, altogether without transit facilities, and without a soul to use them if they were there. We could locate the new line parallel with and close to either the Harlem or Northern road and make it pay at once, and the question is whether to do so, or to locate the route along the line of Jerome avenue and help develop this region. Another difficulty is this: The law specifically prohibits the construction of a surface road. Now a surface road could be built for a tenth of what a viaduct or underground would cost, and it seems to be a waste of money to require either of these where there is so much vacant territory to fill up." He said that the commissioners were now considering the propriety and feasibility of providing for a slightly depressed road, and thus getting around the expensive limitations of the law.

He said, also, that in view of the fact that two of the commissioners would have to be away through August it had been resolved to meet next Tuesday and hold long and continuous sessions through Wednesday and Thursday, if necessary, to reach a conclusion with respect both to the plan of construction of the Broadway Boulevard line and the route of the East Side line.

The Condition of Broadway.

The contractor for the cable construction and paving of Broadway scouts the idea that the street will be unfinished when winter comes. He says all the serious obstructions have been overcome, and that from the present forward all his forces have comparatively smooth sailing. In earnest of his statements work was begun yesterday upon two new sections—from 14th to Bleecker street, and from 23d to 17th street. South of 14th street the excavation is being made two-track wide, and while the work is being done the Broadway cars are running through Bleecker and Wooster streets and University place, from Broadway and Bleecker to 14th and Broadway. Traffic is of course seriously interfered with, and shopkeepers and merchants in Broadway are scanning mournfully the scant showing of profits on their current business; but it is a sort of summer tonic they are taking now, which is expected to do them a world of good when the winter holiday trade sets in. Therefore, though with wry faces, they are swallowing their medicine gracefully.

Upper Ward Improvements Delayed.

One way in which the Tammany members of the Board of Street Opening end Improvement can punish the citizens of the Twenty-third and Twenty-fourth wards for electing Commissioner Heintz in violation of their wishes, is to ignore their demands for improvements—and this they appear to be doing. There was to have been a meeting of the board yesterday, and a large number of trans-Harlem property-owners were in attendance, expecting to get a hearing on the subject of improvement, of which there were several branches. The Brook avenue improvement; the Third avenue sewer, and several street opening matters needed the consideration and action of the board—but there was no meeting. The visitors waited until it became apparent that there would not be a quorum, and then they left. One of tnem remarked: "If Purroy had been elected there would never have failed a quorum of the board."

Notice to Property-Holders.

BOARD OF ASSESSORS.

No. 27 CHAMBERS STREET,
NEW YORK, July 16, 1891.

Notice is given to the owner or owners of all houses and lots affected thereby, that the following assessments have been completed and are lodged in the office of the Board of Assessors for examination by all parties interested, who must present their objections in writing, if opposed to the same, within thirty days from date of notice:

PAVING.

No. 1.—89th st, from 10th av to the Western Boulevard; granite blocks and laying crosswalks.

No. 2.—151st st, from 10th to St. Nicholas av; granite blocks and laying crosswalks.

No. 3.—95th st, from 10th av to the Boulevard; granite blocks and laying crosswalks.

No. 5.—166th st, from 3d to Vanderbilt av; trap blocks.

CROSSWALKS.

No. 4—5th av, at the northerly and southerly sides of 113th, 114th, 115th, 116th, 117th and 118th sts.

SEWERS.

No. 6.—College av, bet 142d and 143d sts.

No. 7.—Lincoln av, e s, bet 136th and 137th sts.

[The limits embraced by such assessments include all the houses and lots of ground, vacant lots, pieces and parcels of land situated on—

No. 1.—89th st, both sides, from 10th av to the Boulevard, and to the extent of half the block at the intersecting avs.

No. 2.—151st st, both sides, from 10th to St. Nicholas av, and to the extent of half the block at the intersecting avs.

No. 3.—95th st, both sides, from 10th av to the Boulevard, and to the extent of half the block at the intersecting avs.

No. 4.—To the extent of half the block, from the northerly and southerly intersections of 113th, 114th, 115th, 116th, 117th, 118th sts and 5th av.

No. 5.—166th st, both sides, from 3d to Vanderbilt av, and to the extent of half the block at the intersecting avs.

No. 6.—College av, both sides, from 142d to 143d st.

No. 7.—Lincoln av, e s, from 136th to 137th st.]

All persons whose interests are affected by the above-named assessments, and who are opposed to the same, or any of them, are requested to present their objections in writing to the Chairman of the Board of Assessors, at their office, within thirty days from the date of this notice.

The above-described lists will be transmitted, as provided by law, to the Board of Revision and Correction of Assessments for confirmation on the 17th day of August, 1891.

CITY OF NEW YORK, FINANCE DEPARTMENT,
COMPTROLLER'S OFFICE, June 26, 1891.

In pursuance of Section 997 of the "New York City Consolidation Act of 1882," the Comptroller gives notice to all persons, owners of property affected by the following assessment list, viz.:

ACQUIRING TITLE.

Birch st, from Wolf st to Marcher av.

East 157th st, from Railroad av East to 3d av.

—which were confirmed by the Supreme Court, June 29th and July 3, 1891, and entered the 3d and 9th of July, 1891, in the Record of Titles and Assessments kept in the "Bureau for the Collection of Assessments and Arrears of Taxes and Assessments, and of Water Rents," that unless the amount assessed for benefit on any person or property shall be paid within sixty days after the date of said entry of the assessment, interest will be collected thereon at the rate of 7 per cent per annum, from July 3d for Birch street, and July 9th for East 157th street. Payments to be made to the Collector of Assessments and Clerk of Arrears, between 9 A. M. and 2 P. M.

Special Notices.

W. R. Ostrander & Co., of Nos. 195 and 197 Fulton street, have just issued the eighth edition of their catalogue, which is revised to date. This book contains 111 pages of illustrations and descriptions of the various materials manufactured by them. These include their patented speaking-tube hardware, speaking-tubes, elbows, mouthpieces, bell alarms, etc., gongs, bell-bangers' hardware, electric bells and supplies, pneumatic call-bells; oval, electric, mechanical and pneumatic annunciators, etc. The catalogue contains about 250 cuts of various articles of manufacture, with elaborate price lists, etc., including an index to all the articles named. It can be obtained on application to their office, or at their factory, Nos. 1461 and 1463 De Kalb avenue, near Knickerbocker avenue, Brooklyn.

Street Opening Proceedings.

Notice is given in the matter of opening Lowell street, from 3d to Rider avenue, 23d Ward, that application will be made at a Special Term of the Supreme Court, August 11th, 1891, for the appointment of Commissioners of Estimate and Assessment in the matter.

Application will be made at a Special Term of the Supreme Court, August 4th, 1891, for the appointment of Commissioners of Estimate and Assessment. In the matter of the application of the Board of Street Opening and Improuement to acquire title to certain lands required for a Public Park at or near Corlears Hook, in the 7th Ward.

Trow's City Directory.

Messrs. John H. Davis & Co., Messrs. S. V. White & Co. and Messrs. Connor & Co. offer for subscription 7,500 shares of 8 per cent cumulative preferred stock and 2,500 shares of common stock of the Trow Directory, Printing and Bookbinding Company, organized under the laws of New Jersey. This corporation has been formed to take over and carry on the business established in 1786 of the Trow City Directory Company of New York, and also that of Trow's Printing and Bookinding Company established in 1826, the two businesses having hitherto been conducted as separate concerns. The capital of the new company consists of $1,500,000, divided into 7,500 shares of 8 per cent cumulative preferred stock, and 7,500 shares of general common stock, of which one-third is included in the present subscription. People interested in the old companies and their associates retain the residue of the common stock. The statement of the vendors shows that for the five years ending December 31st, the net profits of the two companies have been $661,411.30, or an average of $132,282.26 yearly. A sum equivalent to 8 per cent. on the preferred stock, and more than 11 per cent. on the common stock. The preferred stock will be entitled to cumulative preferential dividends of 8 per cent. per annum, which will be payable out of the earnings of the company before any payments are made upon the common stock. All shares issued will be full-paid stock and non-assessable. Stockholders will have no personal liability. The subscription lists will be open at 10 o'clock on Tuesday, July 21st, and close on or before Thursday, July 23d. The prospectus published in another column of this issue gives all additional details.

Real Estate Notes.

Judge P. Henry Dugro and Frederick Wagner have borrowed for one year at 6 per cent $425,000 from The Mutual Life Insurance Company. The property mortgaged comprises the five lots on the southeast corner of Fifth avenue and 59th street, upon which an eleven-story hotel is being completed.

The Temple Beth-El, at 5th avenue and 76th street, has been given leave by Judge Truax, in the Supreme Court, to borrow $350,000 upon mortgage from the Manhattan Life Insurance Company. Mortgages aggregating $240,000 are to be paid, and the remainder of the money is to be used in finishing the synagogue building.

Edward H. Van Ingen, the Broadway woolen merchant, has mortgaged for $400,000 the plot on the northeast corner of Broadway and 40th street, size 128.1 on Broadway x 203.10 feet on 40th street. This plot adjoins the Hotel Vendome, and perhaps may have been securod for an addition thereto.

John M. Ruck has traded the sixteen vacant lots on Madison avenue, Park avenue and 97th street, at $160,000, with John Casey, for the two five-story brick flats with stores, Nos. 1313 and 1315 3d avenue, at $150,000.

$290,000 is the consideration mentioned in a deed conveying the six-story brick store Nos. 197 to 201 Greene street.

The three two and four-story brick stores and stables Nos. 40 to 53 West 188th street were transferred during the week at $150,000.

Josephine H. Coggeshall has taken title to the four-story stone front dwelling No. 1 East 40th street, size 27.6x93. The consideration in the deed is $110,000.

Notice.

On July 11th, the firm of Ketcham & Butler, real estate brokers, was dissolved by mutual consent. J. B. Ketcham will alone sign in liquidation and continue the business at the old stand, No. 58 West 125th street.

New Incorporations.

The East New York Land Company filed a certificate of incorporation in the County Clerk's office, on July 16th. The company is organized to purchase and improve real estate. Its capital stock is $50,000, divided into 500 shares of $100 each. The names of the directors are: Samuel Cohen, Marcus Nathan, Leon M. Hirsch, Julius Crossman and Charles Strauss.

Contractors' Notes.

Bids will be received by the Commissioner of Street Improvements of the 23d and 24th Wards, at his office, No. 2622 3d avenue, corner of 141st street, until 3 P. M., Thursday, July 23, 1891: For regulating and grading, setting curb-stones, laying flagging and crosswalks and building culverts in 138th street, between Rider and Railroad avenues East; for regulating, grading, setting curb-stones and flagging the sidewalks on Chisholm street, from Jennings street to Stebbins avenue; in Hampden street, from Sedgwick to Jerome avenue; and on 147th street, from Brook to St. Ann's avenue; for setting curb-stones, flagging the sidewalks and laying crosswalks on the north side of Boston avenue, from Jefferson street to Tremont avenue, and laying crosswalk across Boston avenue, at the southerly side of Bristow street; for constructing sewer and appurtenances in Locust avenue, between 139th and 141st streets; and for constructing sewer and appurtenances in German place, between Westchester avenue and 156th street, with branches in Rae street and in Carr street, between German place and St. Ann's avenue.

Personal.

Byam K. Stevens has ordered THE RECORD AND GUIDE mailed to London, England, where he will stay during the warm months.

Alex. Walkers will eschew building operations for some weeks and will stay at Windsor Lake House, Greenfield, Ulster County, N. Y., until the fall.

C. S. Kennedy is spending his time under the athletic shades of Southampton, L. I.

W. F. Corwith, who never allows a week to pass by without chronicling a sale or two in THE RECORD AND GUIDE, is vacating at the Chester House, Chestertown, N. Y.

L. K. Fries is summering near yachting quarters at New Rochelle.

S. J. Silberman asks to have this paper mailed to him at Long Branch, where he will stay during July and August.

Miss A. Falibee, who is a regular reader of THE RECORD AND GUIDE, is at the Delaware Water Gap.

Bryan L. Kennelly and family are spending the summer at Whitestone, L. I., Mr. Kennelly coming to the city daily. He will later on go on a vacation to Black Rock, Conn., making his headquarters at the George Hotel.

Readers of THE RECORD AND GUIDE *may subscribe to the new illustrated quarterly magazine,* THE ARCHITECTURAL RECORD, *by sending their names and addresses to the office of publication, Nos.* 14-16 *Vesey street. The annual subscription is* $1.

Real Estate Department.

The market this week has, on the whole, been dull. The offerings are decreasing in number as the season advances, and what with the intense heat and the departures for the country the attendance on 'Change has been small and the bidding uninteresting, while the general report in brokers' offices is that few customers are on hand to purchase. It is evident that during the remainder of the current month and during August there will be comparatively little doing. One or two prominent dealers seen appear to think that we shall have a good fall business, due to the large grain crop and the possibility of unusually large exports this year and a return of gold in the fall, all of which will help the stock market, and so reflect itself upon the real estate market.

THE SALES THIS WEEK.

Only two or three sales attracted any attention this week. By far the most important of these was that of the fine block of property offered by Richard V. Harnett & Co., comprising the unimproved parcels, with old buildings thereon, at No. 331 West street, corner King street; Nos. 132 to 138 King street, Nos. 536 to 540 Washington street, and Nos. 133 and 135 Charlton street. The whole occupies an area equivalent to about 9 1-5 full city lots and it was bought on Thursday in one parcel, by Jas. T. Pyle, the soap manufacturer, for $155,060.

Another parcel of interest sold on Monday. It comprised the five-story flat and store, No. 1070 3d avenue, the purchaser being Anthony Clincby. A Bowery parcel, on the east side of that thoroughfare, 24.4 feet south of 6th street, with a plot 60.1 x irregular, was sold by Wm. Kennelly for $38,000 to Mary Sanders. There is a five-story building on the site. The sale of the southwest corner of Avenue A and 9th street also elicited some interest. It is a five-story building, on a lot 27x60, and was purchased by E. Jacobs for $37,550. The latter also bought the adjoining five-story building on 9th street, on a lot 27x26, for $11,200. Other sales were unimportant and were adjourned or withdrawn or under foreclosure proceedings.

Fred. J. Stone, of No. 60 Broadway, offers for sale, in one-acre plots of 17 2-5 lots each, a tract of land at Elmsford, N. Y., within a few minutes' drive of the depot. The property is on high ground, overlooking the hills at White Plains and the Sound on the one side and the Palisades on the other side. It is within 20 minutes' drive of White Plains and is 67 minutes from Wall street, via the Northern Road and Manhattan Road express. The ground is offered at $1,000 per acre for choice plots.

On Thursday, July 23d, Richard V. Harnett & Co. will sell, by order of the Supreme Court in partition, the five-story brick building, lot 24.9x100, No. 263 5th avenue, on the southeast corner of 29th street.

On Tuesday, July 28th, the Receiver of the Middlesex Company, will sell on the premises, near Sayville, Middlesex County, N. J., the valuable brick manufacturing plant of the said company, consisting of a farm of 282 acres.

CONVEYANCES.

	1890. July 11 to 17 inc.	1891. July 10 to 16 inc.
Number	272	278
Amount involved	$3,876,815	$4,763,586
Number nominal	62	93
Number 23d and 24th Wards	93	66
Amount involved	$230,856	$225,386
Number nominal	13	19

MORTGAGES.

	1890.	1891.
Number	341	278
Amount involved	$4,773,257	$3,578,490
Number at 5 % or less	192	127
Amount involved	$3,628,101	$1,517,161
Number at less than 5 per cent	88	25
Amount involved	$1,369,800	$769,675
Number to Banks, Trust and Ins. Cos	34	34
Amount involved	$1,292,000	$1,184,000

PROJECTED BUILDINGS.

	1890. July 12 to 18 inc.	1891. July 11 to 17 inc.
Number of buildings	102	56
Estimated cost	$1,443,080	$697,400

Gossip of the Week.

SOUTH OF 59TH STREET.

Knox McAfee has sold for Mrs. Gertrude V. C. Hamilton the lot on the northwest corner of 11th avenue and 30th street, 31.6x100, to John Jordan for $14,000.

Levy and Daniel Rothstein have sold to Faust D. Malzone No. 126 Mulberry street, a five-story brick tenement, for $15,000. Andrew Kopple, broker.

Harris Mandelbaum has purchased from James Dougherty a plot, 70.2x100, with the old buildings thereon, now used as coal yard, Nos. 278 to 282 Madison street.

NORTH OF 59TH STREET.

Samuel McCamman has sold for Thomas Smith to Peter Conlin, No. 127 West 120th street, a three-story and basement brown stone dwelling, 21x55, with an extension of 10 feet, lot 100 feet, on private terms.

J. H. Hunt & Co. have sold for McKinley & Gunn to A. B. Hepburn the four-story house, No. 264 West 88th street, not 304 West End avenue, as reported last week.

Picken & Lilly have sold for F. J. Schnugg the two single flats at Nos. 70 and 72 East 93d street, each on a lot 21x100.8½, at $28,000 each; No. 70 to Henry Meyer and No. 72 to Henry Waters.

LEASES.

Gonon & Macdonald have leased for ten years for Edward P. Dicke the five-story dwelling, No. 32 West 28th street, at an average rental of $5,000 per annum. The tenant will alter the building for business purposes.

L. J. Froehlich has leased for J. M. Ruck, the two-stores, first floors and basements of the buildings, Nos. 1313 and 1315 3d avenue, to the furniture house of Baumann Bros. for three years, at $4,000 per annum, with the privilege of renewal at $5,000 per annum.

Brooklyn.

J. P. Sloane has sold for Timothy Brennan the three-story and basement frame dwelling, 25x36x100, No. 195 Huron street, to Martha H. Kavanagh for $3,950.

Corwith Bros. have sold the two-story frame dwelling, 25x36, on lot 25x100, No. 35 Newell street, for Eliza McAleer to Philip Kelly for $3,000, and the two-story frame dwelling, 20x40, on lot 20x100, No. 182 Russell street, to A. A. and M. S. Lydecker for $3,600.

CONVEYANCES.

	1890. July 10 to 16 inc.	1891. July 9 to 15 inc
Number	400	392
Amount involved	$1,737,067	$1,250,741
Number nominal	69	101

MORTGAGES.

	1890.	1891.
Number	328	336
Amount involved	$1,192,988	$1,159,275
Number at 5 per cent. or less	202	176
Amount involved	$777,284	$724,151

PROJECTED BUILDINGS.

	1890. July 10 to 17 inc.	1891. July 10 to 16 inc.
Number of buildings	74	52
Estimated cost	$354,090	$183,583

Out of Town.

MORRISTOWN, N. J.—Bryan L. Kennelly has sold at private sale the premises known as No. 20 High street, Morristown, N. J., to Mr. L. O. Stiles, at $8,575. This place was the residence of Dr. T. B. Flagler, late owner of Flagler's Mills, and also the Morris County race track at this place.

RED BANK, N. J.—B. L. Kennelly, of New York, has sold the residence and grounds owned by Bryan Lawrence, consisting of ninety acres of land on the Shrewsbury River, on private terms.

Out Among the Builders.

Some weeks since D. W. King filed plans for a two-story frame dwelling to be built on the east side of Sedgwick avenue, near 161st street. For reasons these plans have been abandoned, the architect being now engaged in others for a two-story frame cottage, 20x43, to be built upon the same plot for J. P. Bailkhe, at a cost of $6,000.

L. J. O'Connor has plans under way for alterations to be made in the Cathedral parish school building in 50th street. The entire building will be raised one story in brick and stone with fire-proof furring and slate steps. Yellow pine will be used for the interior wood-work, while the new roof will be of tin. $17,000 will be spent on the improvement which is to supply a larger number of class-rooms.

Charles Rentz has plans under way for two five-story and basement brick, stone and terra cotta flats, 24.6x77, to be built at Nos. 196 and 198 Orchard street. Mrs. E. Hartsfelder is the owner, and the cost is estimated at $35,000.

James T. Pyle will build a twelve-story factory on a plot covering 22,955 square feet, nearly 9 1-5 full city lots, and situated at No. 331 West street, southeast corner King street; Nos. 132 to 138 King street; Nos. 133 and 135 Charlton street, and Nos. 536 to 540 Washington street.

John Hauser has plans prepared for six five-story brick and brown stone front tenements, 25x77 each, to be built on the north side of 88th street, 96 feet west of Avenue B, by Joseph Schreiner, to cost $90,000; and three similar buildings, two 25x65 each, and one 16x65, to be built on the north side of King street, 84 feet west of Congress street, by Michael McCormick and Henry Madden, at a cost of $50,000.

Thomas F. Cook has had plans drawn for the erection of two five-story tenement houses, 25x65 each, on the south side of 79th street, 150 feet west of Avenue A. John C. Burne is the architect.

Thom & Wilson have plans on the board for a five-story tenement house, 27x87, to be built on 138th street, south side, 100 feet east of Lenox aveuue, by Patrick Farley.

A five-story tenement house, 25x88, is to built at No. 211 West 21st street, by Drought & Carew. The architect is M. V. B. Ferdon.

Thom & Wilson are drawing plans for five four-story and basement private houses, each to bo 20 feet wide, to be built on the north side of 69th street, 125 feet east of Columbus avenue.

Brooklyn

The Memorial Baptist Church Society will build a washed brick and Indiana limestone church, on the corner of 8th avenue and 16th street. It is to 60x80 in size, Romanesque in style, finished with stained glass windows and natural wood interior, costing $25,000. Charles G. Jones is the architect.

Out of Town.

ROSEVILLE, N. J.—Frank F. Ward has plans on the boards for a two-and-a-half-story stone and frame dwelling, 36x55, to be built here for R. W. Pryor. The frame portion of the house will be shingle-finished and the roof of slate. The interior finish is to be of hardwood in part. A two-story frame stable, with stalls for five horses, carriage rooms, coachman's quarters, etc., is included in the plans, and the estimated cost is placed at about $19,000.

NORFOLK, CONN.—Stephenson & Green have drawn plans for a two-and-a-half-story frame cottage, 50x80, shingle-finished, to be built for Dr. Peaslee, at a cost of $6,000.

WARWICK, N. Y.—D. W. King will draw plans for a three-story frame dwelling, 40x40, cabinet trim, to be built here for M. N. Kane, at a cost of $6,000.

PORT HENRY, LAKE CHAMPLAIN, N. Y.—Stephenson and Greene have completed plans for a three-story stone and frame club house, to be 108x85 in size. The frame portion of the building will be shingle finished and the interior wood-work of yellow pine. The estimates put the cost at $22,000.

ORANGE, CONN.—E. E. Gandolfo will draw plans for a two-story and basement frame building, 30x40, with shingle finished exterior, to be built here for the Yale Field Corporation. The building is to be used as a toilet-house and will be arranged with lockers, shower-baths, toilet and sitting-rooms, and is to cost between $8,000 and $10,000.

BLOOMFIELD, N. J.—Charles G. Jones has drawn plans for a two-story and attic frame dwelling, 27x32, with extension 18x15, to be built here at a cost of $5,000, for H. P. Dodd.

RUTHERFORD, N. J.—Schweitzer & Diemer have drawn plans for a two-story and attic frame dwelling, 28x50, to be built for S. H. Rhodes; and for a similar dwelling, 26x35, with extension 20x23, to be built for W. E. Carter. These houses will cost $5,000 each.

FREEHOLD, N. J.—John R. Hinchman has plans on the boards for a three-story factory, to be built here for V. Henry Rothschild & Co. The building will be a brick and stone structure, 50x120 in size, with tin roof, and heavy factory finished interior.

HOBOKEN, N. J.—John A. Hamilton has drawn plans for a four-story frame tenement, 25x60, to be built at No. 64 Grand street, at a cost of $10,000, f6r A. Ramsey.

WANTS AND OFFERS.

WANTS.

WANTED.—For a term of years, an unfurnished house; must be in first-class condition and locality, betwe n 25th and 40th sts., Madison and 6th avs. Address, J. W. D. D., 427 4th av.

WANTED.—In a private real estate office, young man who thoroughly understands taking charge of tenement property; salary $10 per week. References required. Address, ARTHUR, RECORD AND GUIDE office, 14 Vesey st.

ARCHITECT, established in New York City, desires partner to take equal interest; must be a man of ability and experience, capable of taking charge of office; $3,000 required. Address, ARCHITECT, Office of RECORD AND GUIDE.
July 4-1aw3w.

MASON, BUILDER, ARCHITECT, AND MECHANIC, desires to make himself useful to any one desiring his twenty-five (25) years' experience in the Building Trad, or buying or selling. Address, BUILDER AND ARCHITECT, 81 New st., Room 104; N. Y. C.
May 16—1aw10w.

OFFERS.

Dwellings and Flats

A NEWLY-BUILT DOUBLE FLAT in Essex st., now fully tenanted and returning 7 per cent on price asked, or 9½ per cent on investment required; full particulars and accounts. FULLER & FROTHINGHAM, 945 Broadway, cor 22d st.

A SMALL THREE-STORY HOUSE, on west side of Harlem, about $12,000. PURCHASER, RECORD AND GUIDE office.

TENEMENTS.—Bargain; must be sold. GEO. C. GOELLER, 3d av and 134th st.

WEST 88TH ST., near Boulevard. Nos. 260, 262 and 264; new three-story brown stone. CHAS. L. RITZMAN, Owner, 943 Broadway.
July4-e.o.w.4t.

SPECULATORS AND INVESTORS.—I have just finished my entire front on 8th av., 118th, 119th; five story, with stores; well rented; prices from $25,000 to $48,000. For particulars, P. BRAENDER, Owner and Builder, 120 East 86th st (office open till 9 P. M.
July 4-1aw3w.

OFFERS.

FOR SALE—210 and 212 West 105th st.; five-story apartments; each, 25x99x100; decorated and carpeted; apply at ROOM 19, 156 Broadway.
Mar.28-u-f.

BUY THE BEST.
72D ST., THE PARK DRIVEWAY.
SEVERAL 25-FOOT PALATIAL RESIDENCES.
ONE SUPERBLY DECORATED.
NONE MORE ELEGANT AND SPACIOUS.
The best judgment of long experience has been given to their construction. The most critical will be satisfied in the taste displayed and the excellent character of the workmanship and material; prices reasonable. F. CRAWFORD, 114 West 72d st.
July 11-1aw8w.

FOR SALE—2443 8th av.; 26.8½x100; easy terms; commission allowed brokers; apply at ROOM 19, 156 Broadway.
Mar. 28-u-f.

Improved Property.

PLANING MILL FOR SALE.—Is located at 24th st. and 11th av., on four or five city lots, leased ground, and consists of two and three-story brick buildings and adjoining sheds; also 80 horse-power engine and boiler, planers, moulders, saws, etc., all in good running order and now in operation; owner will leave a portion of value on bond and mortgage three years; this offers splendid opportunity to enlarge wood-working industry or to secure good mill business to add thereto. Advertiser intends to continue his lumber business now carried on at above address. For further particulars, etc., apply to EBEN PEEK, 24th st. and 11th av.
July 11-18.

Vacant Lots.

BARGAIN.—At Tremont, two blocks from station. Lot, 18x78, on Bathgate av, $1,500; on 179th st, 25x6x100, gore, $750. G. W. BRIGGS, 45 Powers st., Brooklyn.

FOR SALE.—Choicest corner on Riverside Drive, 91st st.; elegant residence to be erected on adjoining plot. Apply to J. R. HAY, 7 Wall st.

100TH ST., between 2d and 3d avs; ten lots, cheap; all mortgage if improved. EDWIN A. ELY, 108 Gold st.
July11-1aw8w.

40 CHERRY ST., between Roosevelt and Franklin sq., 32x84, vacant; $12,000; accommodating terms. EDWIN A. ELY, 108 Gold st.
July11-1aw8w.

OFFERS.

FOR SALE—Five lots, n e cor Willis av and 137th st, 100x125; easy terms; ready for improvement; splendid location. Apply to JAS. CARNEY, 137 East 52d st.
June 27, 1aw4w.

TO BUILDERS—With or without a loan, south side of 81st st., near Amsterdam av., three lots, excavated; terms easy. DA CUNHA, Montclair, N.J.
J 20—1aw5w

Brooklyn Real Estate for Sale.

DESIRABLE INVESTMENT.—Eight-story apartment house; best location in Brooklyn; might exchange equity over $125,000 at 4½ per cent. Apply 60 Broadway, Room 311.
J. 20—uf.

LARGE FACTORY for sale; price, $28,000; the land itself supposed to be worth the money. FIRST NATIONAL BANK, Brooklyn, N. Y.
Apr 4-uf

16½ PER CENT.—Best I can do on investment of $15,000 in plate glass store property on leading business thoroughfare of 17th Ward of Brooklyn; the plot is 140x90; consists of seven two-story buildings; rents for $1,592 per annum, and mortgage of $27,500 can remain for long term. Examine this gilt edge investment. J. P. SLOANE, 343 Manhattan av., Brooklyn.
July 11—1aw4w.

Country Property.

AT MONTCLAIR, N. J.—200 acres for cutting into lots; railroad station on property; number of acres to suit purchaser. DA CUNHA, Montclair.
J. 27-1aw5w.

Miscellaneous.

EVERGREEN CEMETERY LOT.—High ground, near the office; a bargain. JAMES GARITY, 18 West 14th st.

SECOND MORTAGAGES on improved New York City property, centrally located; small amounts; $2,450, $4,000, $2,450; short time to run; second mortgages equal 20 per cent, subject to first mortgage of 45 per cent leaving margin of 35 per cent. Address, MORTGAGEE, P. O. Box 62, White Plains, N. Y.

A PARTY ABOUT TO BUILD A FIVE-STORY factory, 50x98, in Harlem, near water-front, will lease the three upper floors and build to suit tenant. Terms very moderate. Address OWNER, 409 E. 107th St.
May 16 u. f.

SALES OF THE WEEK.

The following are the sales at the Real Estate Exchange and Auction Room for the week ending July 17.

** Indicates that the property described has been bid in for plaintiff's account:*

R. V. HARNETT & CO.

Charlton st, Nos. 133 and 135, n s, 120.2 w Washington st, three-story buildings and plot, 38.9x100.
King st, Nos. 132-138, s s, 69.11 e West st, 93.6 x irreg., vacant.
Washington st, Nos. 536 and 538, w s, 101.1 s King st, two three story buildings and lots, 24.2x120.6 each.
Washington st, No. 540, w s, 80.1 s King st, three-story building and lot., 21x80.
West st, No. 331, southeast cor King st, 50x 69.11x30.1x70.8, vacant.
James T. Pyle $155,000

34th st, No. 316, s s, 228.9 e 2d av, 21.3x98.9, four-story brk tenem't. Lincoln W. McLeod. (Amt due $3,478) 9,200

54th st, Nos. 427 and 429, n s, 394 e 1st av, 50x 100.5, two-story brk stable with one-story frame buildings on rear. Daniel Herbert 17,200

3d av, No. 1010, w s, 50.5 n 63d st, 25x100, five-story stone front store and flat. Anthony Clinchy 41,000

WM. KENNELLY.

3d st, s s, 120 s e Av A, 24.9x105.11x24.4x105.11, two five-story brk buildings, front and rear. Henry J. Mahr 23,500

3d st, s s, 98 Av A, 22x88.6, five story brk buildings, front and rear. Same 27,800

6th st, s s, 60 e 3d av, 22.5x48.5, four-store brk building. Mary Sanders 15,400

6th st, s s, 82.8 s e 3d av, runs southwest 44.3 x southwest 4.6 x northwest 0.9 x northeast 48 to 6th st, x southeast 2.6 to beginning, four and five-story brk front buildings. Same 26,100

9th st, No. 440 E., s s, 60 w Av A, 27x26, five story brk building. E. Jacobs 11,900

18th st, s s, 244 e 1st av, 25x92, five-story brk tenem't. Mary Sanders 13,900

*38th st, No. 229, n s, 490.1 e 8th av, 20.7x98.9, five-story brk flat. Virginia W. Baldwin, (Amt due $10,684) 20,500

48th st, No. 309, n s, 125 e 2d av, 25x100.5, five-story brk tenem't. Chas. Helm 16,500

48th st, No. 311, adj, 25x100.5, five-story brk tenem't. Mary Sanders 16,000

54th st, No. 542, s s, 300 e 11th av, 25x156x25.3x 152.6, three-story brk store and tenem't. Andrew Doerrschuck, party in int. (Amt due $1,450) 2,535

137th st, s s, 430 w Lenox av, runs south 99.11 x west 20 x north 48 x west 12 x north 51.11 to 137th st, x east 42, three-story brk dwell'g and vacant. Patrick Farley. (Amt due $15,967) 17,000

Av A, s w cor 9th st, 27x60, five-story brk building. E. Jacobs 37,550

Bowery, e s, 24.4 s 6th st, runs southeast 60.1 x northeast 24.4 to 6th st, x southeast 19.11 x southwest 48.6 x northwest 80 to 3d av, x northeast 24.2 to beginning, five-story stone front building. Mary Sanders 38,000

2d av, Nos. 894 and 896, e s, 50.3 s 48th st, 50.2x 100, two five-story stores and tenements; No. 894, $23,000; No. 896, $22,400. J. Korn 45,400

SMYTH & RYAN.

Amsterdam av, No. 710, w s, 75.8 s 96th st, 25x 89.9, five-story brk flat with stores, F. H. Weeks. (Amt due $26,654) 27,330

D. P. INGRAHAM & CO.

19th st, No. 319, n s, 200 w 8th av, 21-4x92, three-story brk dwell'g. Sarah J. Miller 17,000

R. L. KENNELLY.

75th st, No. 222, s s, 270.10 e 3d av, 19.7x102.2, four-story brk tenem't. M. L. Wallach 10,600

*112th st, n s, 125 w Lenox av, 25x100.11, five-story brk flat. (Amt due $2,230; prior morts, $20,000). Geo. N. Manchester 21,275

Total $609,040
Corresponding week, 1890 ..... $191,200

BROOKLYN, N. Y.

For Week Ending July 16.

Coney Island road, n e cor Van Siclen pl, 49x108x49x107.38. Gravesend. John Y. McKane ... $3,500

*Decatur st, No. 47, n s, 247 w Throop av, 18x100, three-story brk dwell'g. R F. Welles, trustee ... 7,600

*Franklin st, Nos. 117 and 119, w s, 50 n Noble st, 50x70; all right, title and int.; re-sale..
Noble st, Nos. 63 and 63½, n s, 70 w Franklin st, 25x100; all right, title and int; re-sale..
John C. Orr and Henry Steers ... 100

Jerome st, w s, 110 s New lots road, 60x52.3, vacant. Dr. H. F. Praeger ... 200

Oakland st, No. 323, w s, 25 n Huron st, 25x100, two-story frame dwell'g and store. Patrick Kelly ... 3,400

*Park pl, No. 102, s s, 191.3 e 6th av, 16.8x100, three-story brk dwell'g; all right, title and int. Anna Thien ... 570

Atlantic av, Nos. 423 and 425, n s, 250 e Bond st, 50x100, two three-story brk dwell'gs; all right, title and int. John A. Roebuck ... 1,000

*Bushwick av, n e cor Flushing av, 17.8x115x15x100. Henry Irwin ... 1,900

*Furman av, No. 19, n w s, 180 n e Broadway, 20x100, two-story frame dwell'g. John J. Colgan ... 2,500

Furman av, No. 21. Same ... 3,000

Furman av, No. 23. Same ... 3,100

Furman av, No. 25. Same ... 3,350

Jefferson av, No. 444, s s, 223.4 e Throop av, 16.8x100, three-story brk dwell'g. Max Lang ... 5,135

*St. Marks av, Nos. 976-984, s w cor Albany av, 100x105, four three-story and basement brk dwell'gs and one four-story brk flat with store. Richard Goodwin ... 24,000

Total ... $66,445

Corresponding week 1890 ... $128,407

CONVEYANCES

Wherever the letters Q. C., C. a. G. and B. & S occur, preceded by the name of the grantee they mean as follows:

1st—Q. C. is an abbreviation for Quit Claim deed, i. e., a deed in which all the right, title and interest of the grantor is conveyed, omitting all covenants or warranty.

2d—C. a. G. means a deed containing Covenant against Grantor only, in which he covenants that he hath not done any act whereby the estate conveyed may be impeached, charged or encumbered.

3d—B. & S. is an abbreviation for Bargain and Sale deed, wherein, although the seller makes no express covenants, he really grants or conveys the property for a valuable consideration, and thus impliedly claims to be the owner of it.

NEW YORK CITY

July 10, 11, 13, 14, 15, 16.

Allen st, No. 165, w s, 150.6 s Stanton st, runs west 46 x north 0.6 x west 41 6 x south 25 x east 87.6 to st, x north 24.6, five-story brk store and tenem't with three-story brk tenem't on rear. Lena Cohn to Simon Sigel. *Mt.* $16,500 July 15. $24,000

Bank st
Greenwich av or lane
12th st
Waverley pl
} the block.

Bedford st, Nos. 75½ and 77, s w cor Commerce st, 40x184.6x40x171.

Bedford st, Nos. 73 and 75, w s, 35x169x36.6x182.

Broad st, s e cor Stone st, 20.4x—.

Mott st, No. 130, w s, lot 370 map Bayards farm, 25x100.

Bank st, No. 7
12th st, No. 240 W
} all title.

Edwin Gomez and Margaret his wife to Edwin, Jr., Louis and Rosalie Gomez and Madeline wife of Henry Steinbach, tenants in common. Conveys life estate in 1-6 part. July 13. nom

Batavia st, Nos. 18-22, n s, 50.6½ w James st, 57.3x75, three two and three-story brk tenements. John M. Knox and Maria L. his wife to Martin Tuohey. May 25. 9,000

Bayard st, No. 14, n s, 31.3 e Chrystie st, 18.9x50x18.9x49 10, four-story brk store and tenem't. Isaac Natelsohn and Julia his wife to Jenny Diamant. *Mt.* $10,000. July 10. See Eldridge st. 17,000

Beekman st, No. 56, n e s, 47.1 n w Gold st, 24.6x87.6x24 2x87.11, five-story stone front store. Charles D. Towl et al. exrs. John W. Towl to Stephen F. Shortland, Brooklyn. July 15. 53,000

Broome st, No. 99, s s, abt 75 w Sheriff st, 25x75, five-story brk tenem't with stores. Kaufman Marks and Jennie his wife to Philip Cohen and Yetta his wife. *Mt.* $17,000. July 14. 21,250

Broome st, No. 196, n w cor Suffolk st, 25x52, two-story frame stores and dwell'gs. Clara J. wife of William T. Brown, Stamford, Conn., to Samuel Kempner. July 9. nom

Cannon st, No. 52, e s, abt 100 n Delancey st, 25x100, four-story brk store and tenem't. Conrad Kuhling and Ida E. his wife to Alter Gottlieb. *Mt.* $14,000. July 15. 16,850

Christopher st, Nos. 149 and 151, old Nos. 139 and 141, n s, 129 3 e Washington st, 40.1x95.

Washington st, No. 659, s e s, 83.8 s w West 10th st, runs southeast 88.1 x northwest 7.10 x east 14 x southwest 95 to Christopher st, x northwest 20.1 x northeast 58.6 x northwest 90.3 to Washington st, x northeast 30.

Christopher st, No. 155, n s, 89.3 e Washington st, 20x57.7x20.8x62.11.

Brk church on Christopher st and three-story frame store and dwell'g on Washington st.

John F. Fitzharris to Church of Saint Veronica. *Mt.* $60,000. July 16. nom

Same property. Release covenant. Charles Perceval to Joseph S. Carreau. July 16. nom

Clinton st, No. 84, e s, 100 n Rivington st, 25x100, one, two and three-story brk building. Charles F. Lehr and Amelia his wife to Philip A. Decker. All liens. July 8. 19,500

Clinton st, No. 93, w s, 175 s Rivington st, 25x100, five-story brk tenem't with stores. Karl M. Wallach to Lena wife of Solomon Karansky. *Mt.* $20,000. July 15. 34,000

Clinton pl, No. 133, n s, 77.7 e 6th av, 25x93.11, four-story brk store and tenem't. Joseph S. Carreau to Charles Perceval. *Mt.* $15,000. July 16. 30,000

Coenties slip, No. 31, w s, 36 6 n South st, 27.6x45, four-story brk store and tenem't. Susan T. wife of Charles Dunlap an heir of George H. Rice to Austin C. Chandler. Q. C. June 8. nom

Same property. Nettie wife of Henry G. Dieffenbach and heir of George H. Rice to same. Q. C. June 8. nom

Same property. John Q. Burnett individ and exr. Susan Rice and Helen M. his wife and Charles Pitcher and Harriet C. wife of Archibald M. Rice and Woodbridge C. Rice and Elizabeth his wife heirs Susan Rice to same. C. a. G. June 8. 20,000

Delancey st, No. 233, s s, 26 6 e Willett st, 23.6x87.6, two-story frame dwell'g with two-story frame building on rear. Clara J. wife of William T. Brown, Stamford, Conn., to Samuel Kempner. July 9. nom

Duane st, Nos. 131, 133, 135, n s, 125.2 w Church st, 75.1x75x75x75, five-story stone front stores. William A. Brewer, Jr., and ano. exrs. Thomas Hope to Eugene A. Hoffman. July 9. 175,000

Eldridge st, No. 36, e s, abt 75 n Canal st, 25x109, four-story brk store and tenem't with five-story brk tenem't on rear. Jenny Diamant to Isaac Natelsohn. *Mt.* $23,000. July 10 See Bayard st. 34,000

Fort Washington Ridge road, e s, 150 n New road, 60 feet wide, extdg. from Kingsbridge road to N. Y. Central & Hudson R. R. R. Co.'s Station, near Fort Washington Point, 25x100. Charles Fleischmann and Henrietta his wife to James McGuire. July 6. 2,000

Fort Washington Ridge road, e s, 175 n above named road, 25x100. Same to Ellen wife of James McGuire. July 6. 2,000

Frankfort st, No. 9, s s, abt 108 w William st, 28.8x103.9x32x104 3, two, three and four-story brk and frame buildings. Charles L. Heins to Excelsior Steam Power Co. 1-12 part. C. a. G. Nov. 22, 1884. 2,500

Greene st, Nos. 197-201, w s, 175.1 n Bleecker st, 73.9x100x73.7x100, six-story brk store. Ferdinand H. Mela and Fannie his wife to Julius Loewenthal. *Mt.* $165,000. July 14 290,000

Grove st
Christopher st
} begins Grove st, n w cor 4th st, 56x77.6 to Christopher st, x 59.8x66.2. *Mt.* $100,000.

Grove st, No. 69, n s, 83 w 4th st, 27x88.10 to Christopher st, x 26x82.2. *Mt.* $34,000.

Grove st, No. 67
Christopher st, No. 70
} being Grove st, n s, 56 w 4th st, 27x82.2 to Christopher st, x 26x77.6. *Mt.* $32,000.

29th st, n s, 52.2 e 2d av, runs north 35.6 to centre of former old Maria st, x east 50 x south 29 6 to 29th st, x west 50. *Mt.* $14,000

47th st, No. 125, n s, 67 e Lexington av, 17x80. *Mt.* $13,000.

48th st, s s, 225 e 1st av, 25x100.5. *Mt.* $7,380.

72d st, No. 153 and 155, n s, 210 w 3d av, 39.5x102.2x39.10x102.2. "The Orienta." *Mt.* $77,500, and liabilities, $25,000.

Monroe st, No. 139, n s, 261.1x½ block. *Mt.* $26,000

Philip Goerlitz and Lizzie his wife to Anthony J. Dittmar and John Goerlitz trustee for creditors. July 16. nom

Kingsbridge road, s w cor Fort Washington Depot road, 295x274x296x274. Aaron Raymond and Sarah E. his wife to H. A. Hutchins. *Mt.* $70,000. July 15. 92,500

Lewis st, No. 143, w s, 146 n 2d st, 21.2x100x21.4x100, three-story frame store and tenem't. Anton Kuster to William Henne and Fanny his wife. July 15. 12,500

Madison st, No. 105, n s, 163 w Market st, 25x100, five-story brk tenem't with stores. Flora Rubenstein and Flora Pohalski to Saffarus D. Gebhard, Brooklyn. Mort. $25,000. July 11. 35,850

Madison st, No. 214, s s, abt 130 w Jefferson st, 26.1x100, five-story brk tenem't. Robert F. Campbell and Ellen his wife to Kevy Friedman. *Mt.* $26,000. July 10. 45,000

Madison st, No. 214, s s, 26 1x100. Release mort Joseph L. Buttenwieser to Robert F. Campbell. July 1. nom

Mott st, No. 58, e s, 75 n Bayard st, 25x47, five-story brk store and tenem't. Mary Benjamin to Barnet Levy. *Mt.* $19,559. July 9. 21,500

Oliver st, No. 27, w s, abt 100 s New Bowery, 21x77.5x21.11x77.2, three-story brk store and tenem't. Ann wife of Jeremiah Murphy to the Church of St. James. Mort. $5,000. July 14. 16,500

Park row, Nos. 147 and 149, s s, 117.7 w Pearl st, 30.1x64.6x30.6x64.6, two two-story frame (brk front) stores. Jarvis Mason trustee for children of Stephen G. Fotterall and remaindermen and Sarah A. Harriman, Annie E. McMichael and Frederick W. Fotterall heirs Stephen G. Fotterall to Bernhard Gutter. June 29. 35,000

Pearl st, No. 421
Rose st, Nos. 63 and 65
} begins Pearl st, s w cor Rose st, 16.5x74, three three-story brk stores and tenem'ts. Jarvis Mason substituted trustee Stephen G. Fotterall, The Pennsylvania Co. for Insurance on Lives and Granting Insurances, original trustee of S. G. Fotterall, with consent of Sarah A. Harriman, Annie E. McMichael and Frederick W. Fotterall, heirs Stephen G. Fotterall to Esther A. Wheaton. June 29. 27,000

Perry st, No. 37, n s, 167 e 4th st, 17x74, four-story brk dwell'g. Jeremiah Pangburn and Margaret B. his wife, Jeremiah Pangburn, Jr., and Elizabeth S. his wife to George H. Budke, Clarkstown, N. Y. June 1. 10,000

Pitt st, No 15, w s, 80 s Broome st, 20x100, two-story frame (brk front) dwell'g with six-story brk building on rear. Saville Levin and Anna his wife, Wolf Blum and Rachel his wife to Max Cohen. *Mt.* $16,500. July 15. See 73d st. 24,000

Prince st, Nos. 113-121, n s, 50.8 e Wooster st, 99.4x95, three six-story brk stores. Frank A. Seitz and Barbara his wife to Richard Sidenberg. Morts. $180,000. July 13. nom

Spring st, Nos. 131-137, n s, 48.2 w Greene st, runs north 95.6 x west 17.10 x southwest 8 x north 7 x west 27.3 x north 3 6 x west 46.2 x south 100 to st, x east 98.2, with use of passage or alleyway adjoining, four two and three story brk stores and tenem'ts. Phillip Goerlitz and Lizzie his wife to John Goerlitz. ½ part. *Mt.* $149,500. July 16 nom

Sullivan st, No. 113, e s, 175 s Prince st, 25x100, five-story brk store and tenem't with five-story brk tenem't in rear. Catharine and John A. Cooper exrs. and trustees William Cooper to John H. and Emma M. Cooper. July 15 nom

Suffolk st, No. 12, e s, abt 75 n Hester st, 25x50, five-story brk tenem't with stores. Tobias Berman and Rachel his wife to Mary Schlomberg, Washington, D. C. *Mt.* $21,500. July 7. 12,500

Willett st, No. 121, w s, 193 5 n Stanton st, 18.9x75, four-story brk store and tenem't. Amalie Cohn to Louis Cohen. *Mt.* $8,000. July 10. nom

Wooster st, Nos. 186 and 188, s e s, 100 s w Bleecker st, 50x100, two and three-story brk and frame stores with five-story brk factory on rear. Jeremiah C. Lyons and Susie T. his wife to Alois Gutwillig. *Mt.* $50,000. July 15. nom

3d st, No. 105, n s, 100 e Macdougal st, 25x100, three-story brk tenem't. Marcus Rosen and Rachel his wife, Jacob S. Rosen and Hene his wife and Rachel L. Epstein to Julius Dreyfus. *Mt.* $7,000. July 11. other consid. and 100

5th st, No. 727, n s, 324 8 e Av C, 16.5x83x17 5x83, three-story brk tenem't. Frieda wife of Charles Rosenthal to Max Landesmann. July 14. 10,000

5th st, No. 647, n s, 134.7 w Av C, 19.10x97, four-story brk store and tenem't with four-story brk tenem't in rear. Marianne Moses to Louis Bleier. July 15. 15,000

8th st, No. 109, n s, 531.5 w 5th av, 23x93.11x20x93.11, three-story brk tenem't. Janet Rudd widow to Janet, Eliza M. and Mary F. Rudd trustees George Rudd dec'd. Q. C. July 9. nom

13th st, No 640, s s, 158 w Av C, 25x103.3, five-story brk store and tenem't. Moses Schloss and Hannah his wife to Abraham Katz and Louis Maier. *Mt.* $10,000. July 11. 17,500

14th st, No. 232, s s, 325 e 8th av, 25x103.3, five-story stone front dwell'g. Bernhard Freund and Rebecca his wife to Emil J. Constam. *Mt.* $16,000. June 23. 28,000

15th st, No. 615, n s, 438 w Av C, 25x103.3, five-story brk tenem't. John A. Proben to Permelia A. Quackenboss, Brooklyn. *Mt.* $9,000. July 15. 16,600

16th st, Nos. 514 and 516, s s, 220.6 e Av A, 50x103.3, two five-story brk stores and tenem'ts with two and three-story brk buildings in rear. Kaufman Henschel and Julia his wife to Mitchell A. C. Levy. Sub. to mort. July 14. See 124th st. 55,000

18th st, No. 53, n s, 160 e 6th av, 25x92, two and four-story brk store and dwell'g.

18th st, No. 51, n s, 185 e 6th av, 25x92, two-story brk stable.

18th st, No. 49, n s, 210 e 6th av, 25x92, three-story brk stable.

Isabella A. wife of J. Henry Lane to John W. Sterling. *Mt.* $50,000. May 11. 150,000

18th st, No 235, n s, 325 e 8th av, 25x92, five-story brk flat. William Rankin and Elizabeth his wife to John Rankin. July 13. nom

18th st, No. 418, s s, 269 e 1st av, 25x92, five-story brk tenem't with stores Henry Kelling and Mary his wife to Mary Kelling. ½ part. *Mt.* ½ $7,000. July 10. gift

21st st, No. 211, n s, 150 w 7th av, 25x98 9, three-story stone front dwell'g. Jane wife of Abraham Besthoff to Charles J. Carew and William Drought. July 16. 23,000

Same property. General release, especially as to location and character of westerly wall of above. Charles J. Carew and William Drought to Jane Besthoff. July 16. nom

23d st, No. 215, n s, 2.9 7 e 3d av, 24.5x98.8, four-story brk store and tenem't with two-story brk building on rear. Martha J. Stark, Lena and Margaret A. Murray, Denver, Col., devisees of Thomas Murray to Robert B. and James D. Powell. *Mt.* $8,894. June 29. 22,250

26th st, No. 353, s s, 130 e 9th av, 20x98.9, two-story brk store and dwell'g with three-story brk dwell'g on rear. Augusta L. Hempt widow to Maria L. Graff. July 9. 11,000

Same property. Charles F. Schellenberg and Louisa his wife to Maria L. wife of Jacob Graff. Q. C. July 9. nom

26th st, No. 239, n s, 100 w 2d av, 25x98.8, five-story brk tenem't with stores. Friederich

Weber and Caroline his wife to Mary wife of Ferdinand Eidman. *Mt.* $18,000. July 16. 30,500

26th st, No. 322, s s, 550 e 9th av, 18.2x98.9x18.2 x—, five-story brk tenem't. Mary Walsh to Mary A. McDermott, Brooklyn. July 15. nom

27th st, No. 210, s s, 166.8 w 7th av, 24.10x98.9, four-story brk store and tenem't with three-story brk tenem't on rear. David S. Walton and Mary A. his wife, East Orange, N. J., to William R. Wilson, Elizabeth, N. J. *Mt.* $14,000. July 15. 21,000

27th st, No. 18, s s, 450 e 6th av, 25x—.
27th st, No. 20, s s, 425 e 6th av, 25x—.
27th st, No. 22, s s, 400 e 6th av, 25x—.
27th st, No. 24, s s, 375 e 6th av, 25x—.
Mutual agreement releasing buildings. Henry Amy, The Catholic Club, George C. Foster and Fitz Gibbons Foster and Frances M. Dibblee with each other. July 12. nom

28th st, No. 152, s s, 150.6 e 7th av, runs south 73.5 x east 1.9 x south 24.6 x east 24.9 x north 24.6 x west 3.10 x north 73.5 to st x west 22.7, five-story brk store and tenem't with four-story brk tenem't on rear. James F. Ellison to William S. Cooper. May 26. 24,000

28th st, No. 152, s s, 150.6 e 7th av, runs south 73.5 x east 1.9 x south 24.6 x east 24.9 x north 24.6 x west 3.10 x north 73.5 to st, x west 22.7, five-story brk store and tenem't with four-story brk tenem't on rear. William S. Cooper to Benjemen Sire. *Mt.* $16,300. May 26. nom

29th st, Nos. 237 and 239, n s, 100 w 2d av, 50x98.9, two five-story brk tenem'ts. Jacob Miller, Long Island City, and Ida his wife to John Fish. ½ part. *Mt.* $25,060. Jan. 3. 31,000

29th st, s s, if continued, 600 w 11th av, 50x98.9, vacant. Foreclos. Martin T. McMahon to Nathalie E. Baylies. July 10. 10,700

29th st, No. 132, s s, 330 w 6th av, 20x98.9, three-story brk dwell'g. Pauline wife and Joseph Rimoldi to Herbert M. Kinsley, Chicago, Ill. *Mt.* $12,000. July 6. 16,200

30th st, No. 235, n s, 230 w 2d av, 20x98.9, three-story brk tenem't. Lina S. Hoff, formerly Steffan, to Babette wife of William L. Titus. *Mt.* $7,000. July 11. 14,500

31st st, s s, 100 e 8th av, 25x36.11x25.2x39.2. William Waters and Annie his wife to Mary E. Campbell. Q. C. July 8. nom

31st st, No. 256, s s, 100 e 8th av, 25x98.9, four-story brk tenem't with stores. Mary E. Campbell to John J. Herbert. July 6. 22,500

31st st, No 337, n s, 230 w 1st av, 20x98.9.
31st st, No. 347, n s, 190 w 1st av, 20x98.9.
Two four-story brk tenem'ts, stores in No. 337.
Barron Davis exr. and trustee of Isabella Woolf to Bernard Galewski. July 10. 15,750

33d st, Nos. 553-557, n s, 63 e 11th av, 75x98.9, one and two-story brk and frame iron foundry. John E. Browning and Harriet O. his wife to Andrew J. Campbell. July 2. 16,000

37th st, No. 120, s s, 100 w Lexington av, 20x98.9, four-story stone front dwell'g. John D. Hewlett and Emma E. his wife, Cold Spring Harbor, L. I., to James C. Fargo. July 10. 37,000

37th st, No. 63, n s, 55 e 6th av, 20x58.8, three-story stone front dwell'g. Francis Lawton to William T. Bull. *Mt.* $16,000. May 29. nom

40th st, No. 1, n s, 95 e 5th av, 27.6x92.7x27.6x93.8, four-story stone front dwell'g. Martha A. wife of and Henry S. Leavitt to Josephine H. Coggeshall. July 9. 110,000

44th st, No. 504, s s, 100 w 10th av, 25x100.5, four-story brk tenem't. John Hoersch to Margaret B. Hoersch. July 13. nom

44th st, No. 528, s s, 375 e 11th av, 25x100.5, three-story brk store and tenem't with two-story frame storage house on rear. John Hoersch to Margaret B. Hoersch. July 13. nom

44th st, No. 539, n s, 275 e 11th av, 25x100.5, five-story brk tenem't. Simon Mayer and Augusta his wife to Louis Grunig. *Mt.* $15,-000. July 15. 20,100

47th st, No. 329, n s, 400 e 2d av, runs north 100.5 x east 25 x south 39.2 x west 0.2 x south 61.3 x west 24.10, four-story brk store and tenem't with three-story brk tenem't on rear. Emanuel S. Kahn and Bertha his wife to German, Jacob and Isaac Kahn. *Mt.* $9,000. July 8. nom

48th st, No. 437, n s, 275 e 10th av, 25x83.5, five-story brk tenem't. Babetta Regel to Eva Korzendorfer. *Mt.* $18,000. July 15. 27,250

49th st, No. 308, s s, 125 e 2d av, 25x100.5, four-story brk store and tenem't. Louis M. Rosenthal and Julia his wife to Sarah Kahn, Trenton, N. J. *Mt.* $8,500. July 15. 14,150

49th st, No. 546, s s, 150 e 11th av, 25x100.4, one-story frame store with two-story frame dwell'g on rear. Francis B. Kineke and Mary A. his wife, Newark, N. J., to Philip Wagner. July 14. 7,750

49th st, No. 460, s s, 81.6 e 10th av, runs south 20 x east 0.6 x south 80.5 x east 18.6 x north 100.5 to st, x west 19, five-story stone front tenem't. Nicholaus Joost and Mary M. his wife to Charles Konig. June 18. 19,500

50th st, Nos. 550, 552 and 561 W. Agreement that conveyance of above premises is intended to secure performance of contract to deliver raw silk of value of $12,000. John Rioichiro and Rosalie Steinhardt with Richard V. Briesen. Recorded as mort. July 9. nom

50th st, No. 550, s s, 158.3 e 11th av, 15x112.6 x18.1x102.5, five-story brk store and tenement.
50th st, No. 552, s s, 128.2 e 11th av, 30.1x102.5x34.9 in two courses, x93.6, three-story brk silk ribbon factory.
50th st, No. 561, n s, 23 e 11th av, 25.8x48.11, five-story brk tenem't with stores.
Rosalie wife of Lesser Steinhardt to Richard V. Briesen trustee. *Mt.* $32,661. July 9. nom

50th st, No. 328, s s, 274.6 e 2d av, 20.6x100.5, four-story stone front dwell'g. Jonas Stolts to Morris Blum. *Mt.* $6,000. July 15. 15,000

51st st, Nos. 517 and 519, n s, 525 e 11th av, 40x100.5, two four-story stone front tenem'ts. Ernest B. Herb and Elizabeth his wife to Katherina Karl. July 15. 29,000

52d st, No. 433, n s, 425 w 9th av, 25x100.5, five-story brk tenem't. Daniel J. O'Conor and Katherine D. his wife to Flora wife of Selim Marks. *Mt.* $10,000. July 11. 21,000

52d st, No. 541 and 543, n s, 300 e 11th av, 52x100.5, two five-story brk stores and tenem'ts. Contract to exchange above sub. to morts. $39,500 for out-of-town property. G. Julius Hauser to David L. Kellam. July 9. nom

53d st, No. 318, s s, 200 e 2d av, 18.4x100.5, four-story stone front dwell'g. Mary F. Donegan widow to Hannah A. Donegan. *Mt.* $4,-500. July 14. nom

53d st, No. 46, s s, 252.8 e 6th av, runs south 90.5 x west 7.6 x south 10 x east 25 x north 100.5 to st, x west 17.6, four-story stone front dwell'g. Lucinda H. Cornish to Joseph L. McBirney, Chicago, Ill. *Mt.* $32,000. June 30. 47,000

53d st, No. 322, s s, 236.4 e 2d av, 18x100.5, four-story stone front dwell'g. Henry Bank to Henriette Straus. *Mt.* $8,000. July 15. 13,000

55th st, No. 232, s s, 92.3 w Broadway, 20x100.5, three-story brk dwell'g. Thomas Auld and Agnes his wife to John Downey. *Mt.* $16,000. July 15. 27,000

56th st, s s, 70 e 9th av, 30x100.5. Release mort. August M. Weil to Berthe Hummel and Annie Steinhardt. July 8. nom

56th st, Nos. 109-121, n s, 150 w 6th av, 175x100.10, seven five-story brk flats. Griffen Tompkins and Bertha E. his wife, Brooklyn, to Herman Wronkow. *Mt.* $175,000. July 1. 275,000

57th st, No. 467, n s, 115 e 10th av, 20x100.5, four-story stone front dwell'g. Anna C. wife of Otto Wessell to Henry Schweckendick. *Mt.* $8,000. July 15. 19,000

58th st, No. 331, n s, 326.6 e 2d av, 23.6x100.5, five-story stone front tenem't. Ada K. Reid formerly Kitching, Babylon, N. Y., to George Kitching, Orange, N. J. Q. C. and correction deed. July 11. nom

67th st, s s, bet 9th and 10th avs, lot 476 map David Cargill not in Register's office. Judgment of Supreme Court in Fox agt Warner, setting aside deed and amending grantee's name so as to read John J. Wanner instead of Warner. July 13. nom

69th st, n s, 125 e Columbus av, 200x100.5, vacant. Peter J. McCoy and Anna R. his wife to Arthur M. Thorn and James W. Wilson. *Mt.* $87,000. June 29. 108,000

70th st, No. 415, n s, 288 e 1st av, 25x100.4, one-story frame building. John Byrne and Jane T. his wife to Charles Koch. *Mt.* $1,000. July 13. 4,500

71st st, No. 404, s s, 85 e 1st av, 28x75.3, four-story stone front tenem't. Thomas Columb to Mary A. Columb. July 13. nom

72d st, No. 165, n s, 136 e Amsterdam av, 20x102.2, four-story stone front dwell'g. Stephen V. White and Eliza M. C. his wife to Ida M. Murphy. *Mt.* $15,000. July 10. nom

72d st, Nos. 414-416, s s, 213 e 1st av, 50x102.2, two five-story brk tenem'ts. Joseph F. Gallagher to Kate Gallagher. July 10. nom

73d st, No. 322, s s, 300 w 1st av, 25x102.2, five-story brk store and tenem't. Albert Steindler and Therese his wife to Anton Kotzum and Katharine his wife. *Mt.* $15,000. July 1. 23,000

73d st, No. 218, s s, 285 e 3d av, 25x102.2, four-story stone front tenem't. Caroline Green to Frank Gass. *Mt.* $12,000. July 16. See 128th st. 18,000

73d st, No. 434, s s, 100 w Av A, 25x102.2, five-story brk tenem't. Max Cohen to Wolf Bloom and Saville Levin. *Mt.* $17,600. July 13. See Pitt st. 23,450

74th st, No. 53, n s, 160 e Columbus av, 20x102.2, four-story stone front dwell'g. Foreclos. Edward C. O'Brien to William B. Baldwin. *Mt.* $25,000. July 3. 43,900

75th st, Nos. 111 and 113, n s, 196.4 e 4th av, 53.3x102.2, two five-story stone front flats. Alois Gutwillig to Samuel W. Bowne. *Mt.* $49,000. July 15. See 90th st. nom

75th st, No. 41, n s, 263 e 9th av, 20x102.2, four-story stone front dwell'g. Release mort. Charles T. Barney and Helen T. his wife to John C. Umberfield. July 10. 2,000

Same property. John C. Umberfield and Mary W. his wife to Charles E. Tilford. *Mt.* $26,900. July 16. nom

76th st, No. 180, s s, 25 e Amsterdam av, late 10th av, 18x77.2, four-story stone front dwell'g. Silas B. Brown and Elizabeth E. his wife, Brooklyn, to Frank Hyde, Brooklyn. B. & S. *Mt.* $17,250. July 7. exch

78th st, No. 250, s s, 180 w 2d av, 18.9x102.2, three-story brk dwell'g. Jacob Zurneider and Fanny his wife to Martin Bosong. *Mt.* $6,000. July 15. 10,750

78th st, No. 156, s s, 220 e 10th av, 20x102.2, four-story stone front dwell'g. Sarah J. Lozier to Ellen A. Slaven. *Mt.* $22,000. July 15. nom

79th st, No. 235, n s, 425 e 3d av, 25x105.7x31.5 x124.8, four-story stone front flat. Oscar T. Marshall to Anna E. Nehrbas July 1. 23,000

80th st, s s, 250 e Amsterdam av, 20x102.2. Release mort. Charles E. Rhinelander to George J. Cohen. July 6. nom

Same property. Release mort. Leopold Gusthal to same. July 7. consid. omitted

Same property. Release mort. James N. Platt, James G. K. Lawrence and Cornelia Von Klenck exrs., &c., William B. Lawrence to same. July 2. nom

Same property. Release mort. Frank L. Fisher to same. July 6. 8,000

82d st, No. 548, s s, 138 w Av B, 13.4x102.2, two-story brk dwell'g. Jacob Gronbach and Lena his wife to Margaretha Helmecke. July 1. 5,300

83d st, No. 415, n s, 150 e 1st av, 16.8x102.2, three-story stone front dwell'g. George W. Wager and Laura B. his wife to Lassa Lazarus. July 10. 7,575

83d st, No. 431, n s, 300 e 1st av, 25x102.2, four-story stone front tenem't. Paulina Breivogel to Sophia Endlich. *Mt.* $10,000. July 15. 17,250

83d st, n s, 110 w Central Park West. Party wall agreement. Ferdinand B. Hauck with Charles H. Lindsley. July 14. nom

84th st, No. 504, s s, 123 e Av A, 25x102.2, five-story brk tenem't. August Ganzenmuller and Louisa his wife to Heinrich Roth. July 15. 21,600

84th st, No. 155, n s, 150 e Amsterdam av, 25x102.2, five-story stone front flat. William L. McCreery to Patrick Prendergast. *Mt.* $20,000. July 15. See below. nom

84th st, No. 159, n s, 100 e Amsterdam av, 25x100, five-story stone front flat. Patrick Prendergast and Rosie M. his wife to William L. McCreery. *Mt.* $23,000. July 15. See above. nom

86th st, n w cor Lexington av, 90.6x100.8. Arthur J. Marshall and Dora A. his wife to Mary E. Dwinelle. Q. C. and correction deed. July 1. nom

86th st, No. 127, n s, 60.6 w Lexington av, 30x100.8, four-story stone front flat. Mary E. Dwinelle to Paulinem Brehm. *Mt.* $27,600. July 1. 30,500

87th st, n s, 325 w West End av, 62x100.8, vacant. Charles De H. Brower and Mary B. his wife to Frank L. Smith. July 2. 25,250

Same property. Frank L. Smith and Magdalene his wife to Francis M. Jencks. *Mt.* $19,-250. July 11. nom

87th st, n s, 325 w West End av, 100x100.8. Agreement restricting buildings. Frank L. Smith with Charles De. Hart Brower. July 2. nom

88th st, No. 58, s s, 164 e 9th av, 19x100.8, three-story stone front dwell'g. The Equitable Life Assurance Society of the United States to Thomas D. Jordan. July 16. nom

89th st. Nos. 303 and 305, n s, 90 w West End av, 40x100.
89th st, Nos. 309 to 319, n s, 150 w West End av, 120x100.
Eight three-story stone front dwell'gs.
Frank L. Smith and Magdalene his wife to William E. Lanchantin. *Mt.* $151,500. July 11. 200,000

89th st, No. 221, n s, 250 w 2d av, 25x100.8, five-story brk tenem't. Henriette wife of Jacob Harris to Heinrich Giese and Louis Friedrich. *Mt.* $12,500. July 16. 20,050

90th st. No. 306, s s, 130 w West End av, 15x100.8, four-story stone front dwell'g. Frank L. Smith and Magdalene his wife to Arthur B. Chase. July 16. nom

90th st, No. 281, n s, 375 e 3d av. 25x100.8, two-story frame building. Michael McCabe to Emma G. Coutoy. Q. C. July 11. nom

90th st, s s, 200 w 8th av. 125x100.8, vacant. Alfred B. Scott and Ella F. his wife to Samuel W. Bowne. *Mt.* $22,500. July 7. nom

Same property. Samuel W. Bowne and Nettie his wife to Alois Gutwillig. *Mt.* $28,500. July 14. See 75th st. nom

90th st, s s, 90 w West End av, 20x100.8. Release mort. The New York Lumber and Wood Working Co. to Frank L. Smith. July 15. 2,000

Same property. Release mort. Charles T. Barney, Francis M. Jencks and William E. D. Stokes to same. July 15. nom

Same property Release mort. Same to same. July 15. nom

92d st, No. 106, s s, 55 e 4th av, 17x80, three-story stone front dwell'g. Stephen Ballard and Abby his wife, Brooklyn, to Frank Hyde, Brooklyn. B. & S. *Mt.* $12,500. July 6. exch

93d st, No. 68, s s, 147 w Park av, 21x100.8, five-story stone front flat. Francis J. Schnugg and Carrie H. his wife to August Ganzenmuller. *Mt.* $19,000. July 8. 28,000

93d st, No. 65, n s, 161 w Park av, 30x100.8, five-story stone front flat. Patrick McMorrow and Katie E. his wife to William J. Johnston, Stamford, Conn. *Mt.* $26,000. July 6. 48,000

93d st, s s, 325 e Columbus av, 75x100.8, vacant. Nathan Clark to Edward Hirsh. Confirmation deed and release from covenants. June 19. nom

93d st, s s, 325 e Amsterdam av, 19.10x100.8. Release mort. The Bradley & Currier Co. (Lim.) to Walden P. Anderson. July 14. nom

Same property. Release mort. Francis M. Jencks to Walden P. Anderson. July 15. nom

Same property. Release mort. Same to same. July 15. nom

Same property. Release mort. Charles G. Judson to same. July 15. nom

96th st, No. 27, n s, 260 w Central Park West, 20x100.11, four-story stone front dwell'g. Edward Kilpatrick and Julia A. S. his wife to Frank Lugar. *Mt.* $22,500. July 10. 35,000 st, Nos. 233 and 235, n s, 100 w 2d av, 50x .11, two four-story brk tenem'ts. Simon ler and Emma his wife, Henry S. Herrn and Jennie his wife to Bertha Marks. $20,000. July 10. 28,000

st, No. 231, n s, 150 w 2d av, 25x100.11, ur-story brk tenem't. Same to Abraham Meyer. *Mt.* $10,000. July 10. 13,250

st, No. 105, n s, 125 w Columbus av, 25x 11, five-story brk flat. Charles F. E. gler and Olga his wife to Hattie Frank. ly 15. nom

st, No. 103, n s, 100 w Columbus av, 25x .11, five-story brk flat. Same to same. ly 15 nom

st, No. 145, n s, 366.6 w 9th av, 16.6x100.11, ree-story stone front dwell'g. Release dgment. Albert P. Chase, West Sumtt, N. J., to Gottlieb Gennert. July 9 nom

e property. Gottlieb Gennert, Jersey City, J., to James W. Vannett and Elizabeth s wife. June 13. 15,840

st, s s, 102.6 w 3d av, 108x100.11, two-story ame dwell'g and vacant Margaretta H. ard to Lewis Z. Bach. July 13 20,800

h st, Nos 59 and 61, n s, 150 e Madison av, .6x100.11, two five-story brk flats. Foreclos. alter M. Rosebault to Charles W. Kleich. July 13. 4,000

h st, No. 237, n s, 180 w 2d av, 20x100.10, o-story frame dwell'g. Foreclos. Rufus Livermore to John Wilsbusen. July 8. 5,175

h st, No. 250, s s, 100 w 2d av, 16.8x100.10, o-story brk dwell'g. William D. Carroll d Alice E. his wife to Randolph F. Mcord. July 10. 7,000

h st, Nos. 420 and 422, s s, 270 e 1st av, 55.2 00.11, two four-story brk tenem'ts. Annie cobs to Lydia Friedberg. *Mt.* $20,000. ne 27. 27,000

h st, No. 139, n s, abt 78.7 w Lexington av d being 573.7 w 3d av, 17.10x100.10, threeory frame dwell'g. John A. Yglesias to lizabeth Yglesias. C. a. G. June 16. nom

h st, No. 164, s s, 253.4 w 3d av, 16.8x 0.10.
h st, No. 168, s s, 220 w 3d av, 16.8x 0.10.
wo three-story brk dwell'gs.
arah A. Terrett widow to Julia A. wife of udley B. Holbrook, Sarah L. wife of Willm H. C. Holt, Harriet M. and Lillian R. errett heirs Dudley R. Terrett. 16-27 part. ub. to same proportionate part of all liens. ly 1. nom

e property. Julia A. Holbrook and Sarah . Holt, Harriet M. and Lillian R. Terrett to arah A. Terrett. All liens. July 1. nom

h st, No. 161, n s, 293.8 w 3d av, 26.4x100.11, our-story brk flat. Margaret A. Murphy o Herman H. and John F. Ries. *Mt.* $9,000. uly 14. 20,250

h st, No. 237, n s, 175 w 2d av, 25x100.11, ve-story brk tenem't. Martin Bossong and redericka his wife to Jacob Zurnieden and anny his wife. *Mt.* $15,000. July 15. 23,500

h st, No. 368, s s, 175 w Manhattan av, 25x 0.11, five-story brk flat. Thomas P. Dunne nd Maria D. his wife to Eliza J. Ritchie. *Mt.* $21,000. July 11. nom

th st, No. 364, s s, 125 w Manhattan av, 25x 0.11, five-story brk flat. Same to Henry J. onnolly. *Mt.* $21,000. July 11. nom

h st, No. 157, n s, 260 w 3d av, 25x100.11, ve-story stone front flat. John D. Mennie nd Mary O. his wife to Bertha Altman. Sub. mort. July 13. 25,000

th st, Nos. 110 and 112, s s, 90.6 e 4th av, uns south 50 x west 0.6 x south 50.11 x east x north 100.11 to st, x west 49.6, two fivetory brk flats. Katharina Ziegler to Henry nd Karolina Stender. ½ part. July 15. nom

th st, No. 150, s s, 491.8 w Lenox av, 16.8x 1.6, three-story stone front dwell'g. Anony McReynolds to Minna Lissner. *Mt.* 8,000 June 30. 10,600

d st, No. 305, n s, 80 e 2d av, 29.6x100.11, ve-story brk flat. Mary E. Barry to Conad Thonges and Gertrude his wife. July . nom

th st, No. 205, n s, 100 e 3d av, 40x100.11, ve-story brk flat. Mitchell A. C. Levy to Kaufman Henschel. *Mt.* $38,000. July 15. ee 16th st. 55,000

th st, Nos. 426-432, s s, 375 e 10th av, 100x 00.11, four five-story brk stores and tenements. Henry M. Bendheim and Clara his wife to William H. Scott. Q. C. Correction eed. March 1, 1890. nom

th st, No. 172, s s, 20 e 7th av, 18x80, fourtory stone front dwell'g. Julia S. wife of nd Robert H. C. Valentine to Howard T. Montgomery, White Plains. July 9. nom

th st, No. 63, n s, 213.7 e Lenox av, 17.10x 9.11, three-story stone front dwell'g. Frank . Tichenor and Josephine B. his wife to Adonijah H. Brummell. *Mt.* $12,000. June 0. 14,600

th st, No. 218, s s, 180 e 3d av, 40x99.11, three-story frame dwell'g and vacant. Mary A. Dunn to Eliza Aldhous. *Mt.* $13,000. June 25. nom

th st, No. 218, s s, 217.6 e 3d av, 18.9x99.11, three-story stone front dwell'g. Frank Gass and Katharina his wife to Caroline Green. *Mt.* $4,500. July 16. See 73d st. 9,850

th st, No. 8, s s, 130 e 5th av, 20x99.11, three-story stone front dwell'g. Release mort. Reuben Ross to Samuel O. Wright, Rockville Centre, L. I. July 7. nom

me property. Samuel O. Wright and Maria T. his wife, Rockville Centre, L. I., to Marie E. De Novellis. *Mt.* $15,000. July 6. 20,000

131st st, No. 21, n s, 260 w 5th av, 25x99.11, five-story brk flat. Release mort. Emeline Johnston to Henry Bawkes, Riverside, Conn. July 11. nom

Same property. Henry Bawkes and Flora A. his wife to Albert Schonberr. *Mt.* $17,000. July 11. 25,000

133d st, No. 163, n s, 175 e 7th av, 25x99.11, five-story brk flat. Carl L. Griesmeyer and Leopoldine his wife to Emil W. Gerber. *Mt.* $12,500. July 13. 22,000

133d st, No. 165, n s, 150 e 7th av, 25x99.11, five-story brk flat. Same to same. *Mt.* $12,500. May 30. 22,000

135th st, No. 285, n s, 250 e 8th av, 25x99.11, five-story brk flat. Foreclos. Thomas H. Lee to Emilie F. Wallace et al. exrs. William L. Wallace. June 30. 1,900

136th st, Nos. 6-14, s s, 110 w 5th av, 125x99.11, five five-story brk flats. John W. Hasren to Andrew T. Judge. *Mt.* $70,000. July 15. 110,000

136th st, No. 243, s s, 319.2 e 8th av, 17.6x99.11, three-story brk dwell'g. Release mort. Alfred C. Cheney trustee to Thomas C. Van Brunt. July 6. 1,500

Same property. Thomas C. Van Brunt and Lizzie M. his wife to Annie Murphy. July 8. 17,500

141st st, No. 211, n s, 155 w 7th av, 20x99.11, five-story brk flat. Foreclos. James J. Nealis to Robert C. Watson et al exrs. and trustees of William Watson. July 16. 14,500

141st st, No. 209, n s, 135 w 7th av, 20x99.11, five-story brk flat. Foreclos. Same to same. July 16. 14,000

141st st, No. 207, n s, 115 w 7th av, 20x99.11, five-story brk flat. Foreclos. Same to same. July 16. 14,000

141st st, No. 205, n s, 95 w 7th av, 20x99.11, five-story brk flat. Foreclos. Same to same. July 16. 14,500

141st st, No. 203, n s, 75 w 7th av, 20x99.11, five-story brk flat. Foreclos. Same to same. July 16. 14,500

145th st, No. 326, s s, 42 e Edgecombe av, 18x 99.11, three-story brk dwell'g. Foreclos. Edward L. Patterson to Robert I. Brown. July 15. 9,500

160th st, s s, 137.4 e St. Nicholas av, runs west 26 x south 50 x east 1 x south 50 x east 25 x north 100, one-story frame building. Thomas S. Van Volkenburgh and Mary P. his wife to Seth M. Milliken. July 16. nom

160th st, s s, 147.4 e St. Nicholas av, runs west 36 x south 50 x east 1 x south 50 x east 35 x north 100. Seth M. Milliken to Edward Lewis. July 1. 9,360

180th st, s s, 100 w 11th av, 25x100. Pauline Simon to Hermine Haan. June 10. 2,550

182d st, s s, 100 e Audubon av, 20x70. Pauline Simon to Joseph H. Cain. July 11. 2,200

Amsterdam av, Nos. 565 and 567, e s, 50.8 n 87th st, 50x100, two five-story brk stores and tenem'ts. Leo Dinkelspiel to Sarah Hess. *Mt.* $50,000. July 13. 67,000

Amsterdam av, No. 728, late 10th av, w s, 75.8 s 96th st, 25x89.9, five-story brk tenem't with stores. Foreclos. John H. V. Arnold to Andrew T. Doyle. July 16. 27,330

Amsterdam (10th) av, n w cor 171st st, 20x 100.
171st st, n s, 100 w Amsterdam av, 25x95, vacant.
R. Clarence Dorsett to John Reneban. C. a. G. July 9. 10,000

Amsterdam av, s w cor 79th st, 102.2x100. Release mort. Sarah M. Sandford, widow, Plainfield, N. J., to Susanna V. Hagen. July 9. 39,000

Amsterdam av, No 1003, w s, 25.5 s 64th st, 25x 100, five-story stone front flat with stores. Josephina Schuck to William L. Dippel. *Mt.* $20,000. July 1. 25,700

Amsterdam (10th) av, No. 1055, w s, 50.5 n 66th st, 25x90, five-story stone front store and flat. Frank C. Rack and Katharina his wife to Theodore H. Mulch. *Mt.* $19,000. July 10. 29,000

Audubon av, e s, 25 s 180th st, 25x95. Pauline Simon to Albert E. Miller. July 15. 2,000

Columbus av, No. 462, w s, 25.8 n 82d st, 25.6x 100, vacant lot. Clifford A. Hand exr. Charles G. Havens to Frederick H. Walker. July 15. 17,000

Edgecombe av, s e cor 151st st if laid out, 143.6 x118.7x—x112.6, vacant. Catharine B. Aitken widow to William B. Aitken. July 10. 2,800

Lexington av, No. 1716, w s, 20.11 s 108th st, 20x75, three-story brick dwell'g. David Sullivan and Margaret his wife and David A. Sullivan and Anna F. his wife to Ann O'Hagan. *Mt.* $1,800. July 7. 8,750

Lexington av, Nos. 1639-1643, e s, 25 n 104th st, 50x70, three five-story stone front flats. Adolph M. Bendheim and Henriette his wife to James J. Ryan. *Mt.* $12,500. July 13. nom

Lexington av, No. 1356, w s, 40.6 s 90th st, 20x 81, four-story brk tenem't. Raphael Ettinger and Jennie his wife to Julia Cunningham. *Mt.* $10,000. July 15. 15,750

Madison av, No. 534, w s, 25.5 n 54th st, 25x70, four-story stone front dwell'g. Mary A. Stokes widow, John S. and Henry B. Stokes and Walter C. Stokes and Adele W. his wife and Lillian S. Holmes to Frank R. Lawrence. C. a. G. June 30 nom

Madison av, n e cor 97th st, 100.10x100.
Park (4th) av, n w cor 97th st, 100.10x100.
97th st, n s, 100 e Madison av, 200x100.10.
Vacant.
John M. Ruck and Clara A. his wife to John Casey. *Mt.* $100,000. July 1. See 3d av. 160,000

Madison av / 5th av / 106th st / 107th st } the block. Mary A. B. wife of and Alfred Wagstaff, Alice Barnard, George G. Barnard and Lillie G his wife, Francis A B wife of and Raymond L. Ward and John C. Barnard the heirs and devisees of George G. Barnard to James McCreery. Q. C. June 15. nom

Mt Morris av, No. 12, w s, 25.11 n 121st st, 25x 78, four-story brk dwell'g. James V. S. Woolley and Emma J. his wife to William Cauldwell *Mt.* $23,000. July 13. 40,000

Park av, s w cor 72d st Agreement as to easement for light and air. Richard W. Buckley to Robert McCafferty. May 25. nom

Park av, No. 754, w s, 67 s 72d st, runs west 24 x south 6 x west 23 x south 1 x west 4 x southwest 7 x west 16 x south 23.3 x east 72 x north 35.2, four-story brk dwell'g. Richard W. Buckley and Josephine G. his wife to Robert McCafferty. *Mt.* $20,000. May 4. nom

Park (4th) av, No. 9262 w s, 83.2 n 80th st, 20x 80.6, four-story brk dwell'g. Francis Cronin and Martha his wife to William P. Lynch. *Mt.* $25,915. July 9. 40,000

Seaman av, n s, 525 w Emerson st, 50x174.4x 50.7x182. Bertha Goldbacher widow to Thomas W. Busche. July 9. 3,000

Sherman av, e s, 125 s 173d st, 25x100 Johanna Nittke to John T. Nittke. May 12. gift

Sherman av, e s, 100 s 173d st, 25x100. Same to Frederick W. Nittke. May 12. gift

Vermilyea av / Academy st } begins Vermilyea av, n e cor Academy st, 150x150. Joseph H. Godwin and Phoebe A. his wife to Cornelius J. Donovan. July 8. val. consid. and 6,300

1st av, No. 659, s w cor 36th st, 20.10x75, four-story brk store and tenem't. Nicholas G. Geraty to Henrietta A. Hunt. *Mt.* $10,000. July 15. 23,500

1st av, No 771, w s, 100.5 n 43d st, 25x100, vacant. Release mort. Cecilia A. Pulleyn to Dennis Harrington. July 15. 5,000

Same property. Dennis Harrington and Mary his wife to August I. Tegetmeier and Ignatz A. Riepp. July 15. 10,000

2d av, No. 729, n w cor 39th st, 20x83, four-story brk store and tenem't. Mary Looram to Catharine Looram. March 7. nom

3d av, No. 361, e s, 24.8 n 26th st, 24.8x110, five-story stone front store and tenem't. Mary C. Nooney to Robert B. Nooney. Q. C. May 27. nom

Same property. John H. Nooney and Susan S. his wife to same. Q. C. July 10. 3,000

Same property. Robert B. Nooney to Charles Dorn. *Mt.* $30,000. April 29. 45,000

3d av, Nos. 1871-1875, e s, 50.6 n 103d st, 50.10x 100.10, three four-story brk stores and tenem'ts. Richard Hennessy and Mary A. his wife to Robert McCafferty. *Mt.* $22,000. July 10. 43,000

3d av, e s, 50.5 n 103d st, 0.3x110. Simon Haberman and Rosie his wife to Richard Hennessy. Q. C. July 7. 100

3d av, Nos. 1313-1315, e s, 27.2 n 75th st, 56.3x 105, two five-story brk flats with stores. John Casey and Kate his wife to John M. Ruck. *Mt.* $90,000. June 30. See Madison av. 150,000

5th av, No. 10, n w cor Clinton pl, 28.6x100, four-story brk (stone front) dwell'g. Jane C. Work widow and devisee John C. Work to Henry W. Jesup, Orange, N. J. C. a. G. July 2. nom

6th av, No. 151, n w cor 11th st, 25.3x60, four-story brk store and tenem't with one-story brk stable on rear. Edward N. Jackson and Julia M. his wife, Jersey City, N. J., to Adolph M. Bendheim. *Mt.* $42,000. July 14. nom

7th av, Nos. 2208 and 2210, w s, 50 s 131st st, 50.5x75, two five-story brk flats. Contract to exchange for
130th st, n e cor Madison av, 35x99.11, vacant.
George C. Currier to Elizabeth Foley. Equality of exchange. May 1. 81,000

7th av, Nos. 2271 and 2273, e s, 24.11 s 134th st, runs east 75 x south 47.4 x southwest 4.5 x west 71.5 to av, x north 50, two five-story brk flats with stores. James Riley and Margaret his wife to The Murray Hill Bank. *Mt.* $46,000. Dec. 18, 1889. nom

9th av, Nos. 88-92 / 16th st, Nos. 361-365 } begins 9th av, n e cor 16th st, 78.10x100, three four-story brk tenem'ts with stores on av and one and two-story brk provision house on st. John H. Dresler and Charles T. Bartlett exrs. and trustees of Filibena Keller to Caroline wife of Frederick Keller. July 11. 85,100

12th av, s e cor 30th st if continued, 49.4x100, vacant. Foreclos. Martin T. McMahon to Nathalie E. Baylies. July 10. 22,800

Interior lot, 121 e 6th av and 94.10 n West 10th st, runs south 4.2 x west 49.10 x east 49.8, gore. Release mort. The Society for the Relief of Half Orphan and Destitute Children to Solomon Sayles. June 30. nom

23d and 24th WARDS.

Beech terrace, s s, 86 e Crimmins av, 25x100. William R. Beal Land and Improvement Co. to Alice L. wife of Samuel C. Thompson. July 8. 1,975

Fox st, w s, 62.2 s 167th st, 41.9x29.3x47.3x46, h & ls. Dora wife of and John Brockman to Bessie Butler. *Mt.* $1,200. July 8. nom

Hampden st formerly East 184th st, s s, at intersection west line of land conveyed by Alf. J. Taylor to Helen L. Willis, 52.2x145.3x8.8x 42.3x133.6. Alfred J. Taylor and Kathleen K. his wife to William D. Peck. ⅜ part. Sub. to mort. Oct. 15. nom

Same property, all of. William D. Peck to Laura A. Cadwell. July 14. 11,000

Hampden st late 184th st, s s, 100 w Andrews av, runs south 70.6 x west 114 to east side Hampden st, x northeast along said east and southerly side of Hampden st 141.9. William D. Peck to Laura A. Cadwell. July 14. 4,500

Oliver st, s e cor Berrian av, 116.2x123x91.2x121. John E. Connolly Company to Ephraim C. Gates, John F. Steeves, Henry H. Barnard and Bradley L. Eaton. *Mt.* $6,000. April 30. See Bathgate av. nom

Same property. John E. Connolly and Margaret his wife, Harry J. Hunter and Hattie his wife to same. Q. C. April 30. nom

Public Parkway, s w s, lot 646 map George F. and Henry B. Opdyke, adj New York City private park, except portion taken for parkway, —x35.5x25x57.3. William S. and Charles W. Opdyke to James M. J. Lynch. March 21, 1889, taxes, &c., since May 15, 1886. 36

Ryer st, e s, 177 s from north line of Charles Berrian farm, lot 405 map said farm, 25x148.10x25x147. John J. Herrick to Rudolph Kubel and Bridget his wife. July 11. 700

Simpson st, w s, 96.7 n 169th st, runs north 25 x west 62.1 x southwest 62.1 to 169th st. x southeast 25 x northeast 49.4 x east 49.4. Kathleen P. wife of George W. Wilton to James F. Neill, Savannah, Ga. May 28. nom

Southern Boulevard, w s, 50 n 144th st, 50x100. Elizabeth W. wife of and Thomas Lester to Edward E. Higgins, Cleveland, Ohio. June 9. 4,975

Suburban st, w s, 312.1 s Bainbridge av, 38x147 x—x150 Mary wife of Edward J. Kiely to Drake V. Smith. June 16. 450

Travers st, n e s, 77.7 n w Briggs av, 25.10x104.1x25x97.5. Isabel Merritt to John C. Bennett. July 13. 800

3d st, e s, 25 s Opdyke av, 75x100. Mary E. Monaghan to Caroline wife of Nickolaus Schwarz. July 13. 1,500

134th st, s w s, 304 n w Willow av, 12.6x100. Jacob H. Johnson and Mary A. his wife to Lena Muller, Greenpoint, L. I. ½ part. July 11. 250

143d st, s s, 200 w Brook av, 25x100. Edward F. Doyle exr. Julia Brennan to George Connor. *Mt.* $1,500. July 11. 4,000

145th st, s s, 74 e Willis av, 25x50. Gottlob Volz to Theodore Ebeling. *Mt.* $2,000. July 15. 3,000

153d st, s s, 550 e Courtlandt av, 25x100. Joseph Kolb and Anna his wife to Regina Nieland and Margaretha Stadta. July 14. 3,125

161st st, s s, 250 w Forest av, 50x95.2. Julius Heiderman exr. Kathrine Niggeschmidt to John A. Kaiser. July 13. 6,500

164th st, n s, 262.9 w Washington av, runs north 100 x east 20 x north 100 x west 50 x south 100 x east 20 x south 100 to 164th st, x east 10. James J. Fitzpatrick and Margaret D. his wife to Conrad Troxler. Sub. to mort. $1,500, and right of way over premises. July 18. 5,000

167th st, n e cor Simpson st, 25x90. John W. Hyland and Harriet J. his wife and Wm. J. Corcoran heirs Thomas J. Hyland to F. A. Pfister. *Mt.* $350. July 15. 800

175th st, s s, 100 w Vanderbilt av, 50x168. Andrew Wynn and Bridget his wife to Mary F. wife of Joseph P. O'Donnell. July 10. 2,000

Alexander av, e s, 40 s 135th st, 20x75. Thomas H. Cooper and Anna R. his wife to Stephen Miller. *Mt.* $4,500. July 8. 7,500

Bathgate av, Nos. 1978 and 1980, s e s, part lot 18 map Upper Morrisania, 36x88x36x88. Ephraim C. Gates and Vashti R. his wife to John E. Connolly Company. *Mt.* $1,500. April 30. See Oliver st. nom

Bailey av, e s, lot 80 map Wm. O. Giles at Kingsbridge, 50x98.11x55.4x87. Jane Wallace, Hoboken, N. J., to Elizabeth Duettmann July 14. 4,250

Same property. Release mort. Jane Wallace, Hoboken, N. J., widow to same. July 14. nom

Briggs av, n s, 302.4 e Travers st, 25x100. Charles L. Starbuck and Imogene W. his wife and G. Fred. Starbuck to Teresa M. wife of William H. McCormick. July 15. 3,550

Clinton av, n s, 275 w 2d st, 25x200 to Willard av, 24th Ward. Edward K. Willard to Emma A. Willard. July 14. nom

Cambreling av, s e s, 100 n e Columbia av, 25x100. Release mort. Thomas J. Phelan to Edward Donohoe. June 24. nom

Same property. Edward Donohoe to Patrick I. or J. Phelan and Julia his wife. July 11. 700

Crimmins av, w s, 48.4 n 141st st, 239x80. William R. Beal Land Improvement Co. to William E. Wheelock, Brooklyn. July 8. 16,800

Crimmins av, s e cor Beech terrace, 100x86.
141st st, n s, 50 w Beekman av, 50.1x88.1x50x91.7.
William R. Beal Land Improvement Co. to Charles T. Wills. July 8. 11,475

Decatur av proposed, w s, 175.4 s proposed Travers st, 25x85x25.2x86.4. Twenty-fourth Ward Real Estate Assoc. to Thomas Wilson. June 1. 625

Eastern Bay av, e s, 285 s Maple st, runs west 1,796.4 to exterior line of lands under water granted to Baretto by People of the State of New York. x southeast 190.3 x east 1,679.8 to av, x north 150.
Coster av, centre line, 175 n Maple st, runs west 1,213.11 to Western Bay av, x south 72.3 to said exterior line, x southeast 189.2 to centre Maple st. x east 170 to centre Coster av, x north 175.
Hillside av, centre line, 405 n Maxwell st, runs east 183.6 x south 27.9 x southeast 234.9 x south 98.9 x southeast 145.2 to Maxwell st, x west 106.9 to Meadow av, x north 30 to centre Maxwell st, x west 290 to centre Hillside av, x north 405, with land under water in Long Island Sound and Leggets Creek.
William O. Giles exr. Elizabeth Giles to Madeline Pierce. ½ part. July 2. nom

Same property. William O. Giles and Kate his wife to same. ½ part. July 2. 13,500

Same property. Madeline Pierce to The East Harbor of New York Land Co. B. & S. C. a. G. ½ part. July 15. nom

Elmwood av, w s, 187.9 n St. James st, 50x106 to Croton Aqueduct. Elmer A. Allen and Mary E. his wife to Henry S. Fuller. July 15. 2,100

Elton av, n e cor 161st st, 70x33.5x33.5x70. Foreclos. Thomas W. Donnelly to Myron W. Dow. July 1. 2,600

Elton av, e s, 73 s 159th st, 25x100. Partition. Clarence W. Francis to George Peters. July 10. 4,650

Franklin av, w s, 52 n 168th st, runs west 100.4 x north 49.10 x west 80.8 x north 43.2 x east 209 to av, x southwest 97.7, h & l. Jesse Smith to Samuel W. B. Smith. All liens. July 6. 17,000

Fulton av, e s, 100 n 168th st, 43x100x41x100. Jessie Smith to Samuel W. B. Smith. All liens. July 6. nom

Inwood av, e s, 129.11 n Girard av, 100x112.5.
Central av, w s, lots 289, 290, 291 and 292 map of Inwood, 101.2x142.2x100x126.11.
William J. Davison to Morris M. Budlong. ½ part. Sub. to ½ of mort. July 7. nom

Inwood av, e s, 129.11 n Girard av, 100x112.5.
Central av, w s, lots 289–292 map Inwood, 101.2x142.2x100x126.11.
Morris M. Budlong and Julia M. his wife to James Harden. ½ part. B. & S. July 7. nom

Keppler av, s w cor Opdyke av, 125x100. Carlos Warner, New York, and Charles D. Smith, Londonderry, Vt. to James H. See and Rudolph Schaefer. July 6. nom

Mosholu av, n s, 344.2 w Old Post road, 100x100.
Mosholu av, n s, 244.2 w Old Post road, 25x100.
Thomas E. Thorn and Margaret E. his wife, William F. Thorn and Margaret his wife, John H. Thorn and Carrie H. his wife, William E. Thorn and Amelia A. his wife to Francis Cox. June 11. 1,900

Nathalie av, e s, villa site "P" on map of 80 lots and 16 villa sites map of part Anthony estate, Kingsbridge Heights, 24th Ward, 29.7x125x64.9x129.10. David McClenahan and Martha J his wife, Parkville, L. I., to Amasa T. Day. *Mt.* $1,200. July 15. 2,150

Opdyke av, s e cor 3d st, 25x100. Alphonsus L. Smith and Mary E. his wife to Caroline wife of Nicholaus Schwarz. July 13. 750

Palisade av, w s, adj Peter O. Strang, 96x95.7 along private drive, x387.9 to N. Y. Central and Hudson River R. R., x 57.8x473.11. Joseph W. Teets and Minnie W. his wife to Jennie F. Des Brisay. *Mt.* $6,000. June 25. 7,800

Tinton av, e s, 101.6 n Denman pl, 20.8x92. Release mort. Isabella McCormack to John W. Decker. June 13. 1,500

Same property John W. Decker to Niels P. F. Nielsen and Emma his wife. *Mt.* $3,500. July 13. 5,800

Union av, w s, 170.9 n Cedar st, runs west 169.1 x south 20.6 x east 64.9 x southeast 14.7 x east 90 to av, x north 25.6. John W. Decker to Lena B. wife of George W. Boskowitz. July 10. 6,500

Union av, e s, n w ½ of lot 77 map of Woodstock, 46.5x176. James S. McKenzie and Catherine his wife, Woodside, L. I., to Franz A. Pacher. Q. C. July 8. nom

Union av, e s, n w ½ lot 77 map of Woodstock, 46.5x166.2. Same to same. July 8. 4,500

Villa av, e s, 370 s Van Courtlandt av. Agreement as to easement for light and air. Frank Pistone and Charles W. Vreeland trustees to Board of Health, New York. July 10. nom

Villa av e s, 535.3 n Southern Boulevard, 50x83.8x50x86.2. Edward W. Parsells and Leonora his wife to Adalbert Voss. *Mt.* $460. July 10. 1,700

Webster av, w s, 150 n Scott av, 25x100.
Webster av, w s, 200 n Scott av, 25x112.6.
Edward W. Parsells and Leonora his wife to Adalbert Voss. *Mt.* $570. July 9. 2,000

Webster av, e s, 59.10 s 173d st, 29x90. Charles E. Appleby, recvr. Metropolitan Ins Co. to Emma J. Crocheron. April 15. 1,575

Webster av, w s, 125 n Scott av, 25x100. Edward W. Parsells and Leonora his wife, Jersey City, to Nicholas J. Comerford. July 10. 1,000

Washington av, n w s, part lot 46 map Upper Morrisania, 54 to grantees land, —x150x54x150, h & l. Mary C. wife of Thomas Macfarlan to Sarah J. Wyckoff. July 15. 7,200

Webster av, e s, 50 n Signal pl, 25x100. Edward W. Parsells and Leonora his wife, Jersey City, to Delia R. Borden. *Mt.* $275. July 15. 1,000

3d av, e s, 140.1 n 145th st, 28x97.7x25x109.11. Nicholas or Nicolaus Thiel and Katharina his wife to Josiah Jones and John Reidenbach. *Mt.* $10,500. July 14. 13,000

3d av, lot 47 block 1113 map 342. Consent to easement. Ellen L. Kellaher to Suburban Rapid Transit Co. Feb. 19. nom

3d av, lots 83 and 85 block 1116 same map. Consent to easement, James Thatcher to same. Aug. 7, 1890. nom

Boston road, n e cor 144th st, 28x91.9x25x104.5. Michael Faulhaber and Kate his wife to Christina Knoeppel. *Mt.* $10,000. July 9. 23,

Kingsbridge to West Farms road, e s, 201 Bayard st, 1x117. Patrick Byrnes and Mary his wife to Thomas W. Strong. Q. C. and correction deed. June 27.

Kingsbridge to West Farms road, e s, 183 Powell pl, 61x117x50x148. Thomas W. Strong, Metuchen, N. J., and Esther his wife to Mary W. Washburn. March 23.

New York and Harlem Railroad, s w cor 17 st, 24.5x100. Thomas Falvey and Kate wife to John Brady. July 3.

Plot 26 map of Harlem River fronts divided plots of 5 lots and upwards situated in 2 Ward belonging to G. A. Sacchi and E. Burling, &c., excepting parts conveyed A. J. Taylor to Cath. R. Appleton, and sa to C. Augusta Golderman and same to R. Ely. Alfred J. Taylor and Kathleen wife to William D. Peck. ⅜ part. Nov. 1888.

Lot 828 map East Morrisania, east of Bra Railroad, &c. Assign. tax sale. John Clarke to Natalie Cambeis. July 13.

All title to road or highway to centre ther in front of 15 feet of lot 222 and in front all lot 220 on map No. 1 in Valentine ver Brady, part of Hyatt farm. Michael N bauer and Anna C. his wife to Antoine M. Ghetti. Q. C. July 10.

LEASEHOLD CONVEYANCES.

Irving pl, s w cor 15th st.
14th st, No. 111 E.
Assign. lease. Gu tav Amberg Leo Von Raven.

Mulberry st, Nos. 139 and 141. Assign. lea Ceasare Ruggiero to Henry Elias Brewi Co.

Same property. Assign. lease. Catharine C nato to Ceasare Ruggiero.

Same property Assign. lease. Rosa Fu to same.

White st, No. 34. Assign. lease. Simon Go lieb to Henry Handrich.

1st st, No. 12. Assign. lease. Alfred Bl and Benjamin Stein to The Blum & Stein C

21st st, lot 603 map Peter G. Stuyvesant (lo Assign. lease. Ferdinand A. O'Hagan, divid. and exr. Ferdinand O'Hagan and A O'Hagan widow to Charles F. Murphy.

21st st, s w s, 340 n w 1st av, 20x93. Ruth furd Stuyvesant to Ferdinand O'Hagan. years, from March 1, 1887, per year, tax and

22d st, No. 317, n s, 114.8 w 8th av, 14.8x98.9 Leasehold interest. Sarah G. Davis to Caroline M. Conner, Brooklyn. C. a. G. May 9 1885. 6,

25th st, n s, 250 w 8th av, 50x98.9. Consent to assign. lease. David D. Field to Patrick H McManus. n

47th st, n s, 100 w 10th av, 25x100.5. Assign. lease. Franz Chwatel and Maria his wife to Michal Merklen. 20,

50th st, n s, 731 w 5th av. Consent to assign lease. Trustees of Columbia College to Orim St. J. wife Lawrence D. Alexander. n

51st st, No. 12 W., s s, 250 w 5th av, 22x100.5 Trustees of Columbia College to James G. Burchell. 21 years, from April 1, 1888, per year, taxes and 1,

90th st, n s, 100 w 2d av, 25x100.8. Assign lease. Anton Hoffmann to Jacob Ruppert n

91st st, s s, 100 w 2d av, 25x100.8. Assign. lease. Anton Hoffmann to Jacob Ruppert. n

102d st, No. 234 E. Assign. lease. George Bock to Peter Doelger. n

Lexington av, s w cor 64th st, 20.5x90. Consent to assign. lease. Gerard and James W Beekman, individ and trustees James W Beekman to Robert McCafferty. n

Same property. Assign. lease. Robert Mc Cafferty to Richard Hennessy. 15,

1st av, n e cor 18th st, 18x70. Henry Parish exr. &c, Mary Griffin to Catharine J. McGuire 21 years, from May 1, 1889, per year, taxes and

Locomotives (16) and rolling stock. Car lease. W. Emlen Roosevelt lessor and trustee to The Buffalo, Rochester and Pittsburgh Railway Co. May 1. 120,

KINGS COUNTY.

JULY 9, 10, 11, 13, 14, 15.

Adelphi st, e s, 124 s Myrtle av, 25x123.10x25x123.11. Frederick W. Rowe to Elizabeth L Chinnock. *Mt.* $6,000. ex

Ashford st, e s, 430 n Hegeman av, 20x100 Adolph Sussman to Bridget Macdonald. $

Ashford st, w s, 225 s Stanley av, 40x100; also.
Wortman av, n e cor Warwick st, 100x85.
Same to James Philpott.

Ashford st, e s, 100 n Eastern Parkway, 25x90. George Schade to August H. Dahl. 2,

Baltic st, s s, 164 e 3d av, 54x100. John Hart of Newark, N. J., to William B. Stretch, of Jersey City, N. J. *Mt.* $5,500. n

Barbey st, e s, 175 n Sutter av, 25x100. August H. Dahl to William Nolan, of New York. 2,

Barbey st, w s 100 s Wortman av, 136.6x61.6x136.6, gore.
Ashford st, w s, 160 s Wortman av, runs west 100 x south to M. S. Duryea farm line, x east along same to st, x north —.
Adolph Sussman to Mary F. Brown.

Bergen st, n s, 117.4 e Ralph av, 17x107.2. Re

lee mort. George G. Reynolds to Mary E. M on. nom

er n st, n s, 100 e Ralph av, 220x107.1. Paul W Ledoux and Orson W. Sheldon to Mary E wife Isaac D. Mason. Taxes, &c. 1

..a property. Alexander K. Ingraham to sa e. B. & S. nom

..ecker st, s e s, 283.4 s w Knickerbocker av, 16x100.
..ecker st, s e s, 266.8 s w Knickerbocker av, 16x100.
..ecker st, s e s, 233.4 s w Knickerbocker av, 33x100.
F..eclos. John Courtney to Hannah F. S..et, Rockville Centre, L. I. *Mt.* $7,167. 1,000

..ecker st, e s, 425 n Evergreen av, 25x100. J..ph Pender to Paul H. Gottschald. 1,450

..m st, s s, 200 w Graham av, 25x100. Hon..e Pibet to Jacob H. Werbelovsky. 3,800

..e property. Jacob H. Werbelovsky to A..aham Greenstone. 1,900

..m st, n s, 472.9 e Bushwick av, 25x61.2 x..59.5. Thomas Lynn, of New York, to C..rles F. Fleckenstein. *Mt.* $3,000. 5,000

..st, No. 30, n w cor Livingston st, 20x63. A..ert T. Wyckoff to John Gibb. other consid. and 1,000

..ford st, w s, 300 s Fulton av, 25x100. Fred..k W. Hearn, Jr., to Henry Ries. 2,850

..ord st, w s, 225 n Fulton st, 24.6x100, h & l. D..id Rosenberg to Morris Klein. 2,000

..ide st, w s, 74 n Concord st, 23.11x50. Peter S..ck to Thomas J. Carroll. 5,000

..way, s s, 100 w Macon st, 40x100. Franz F..z to Benjamin Olbricht. *Mt.* $4,500. 18,000

..way, n e s, 50 n w Locust st, 25x100. T..odore L. Schneider to Henry Schneider. ..$5,000. 16,000

..t st, n s, bet Rochester and Buffalo avs, ..g lot 51 block 178 assessm't map, 24th W..d. John C. McGuire, Registrar of Ar..es, to John J. Lynes. 38

..t st, s s, bet Rochester and Buffalo avs, ..g lot 12 block 174, 24th Ward. Same to ..e. 40

..t pl, s w cor Poplar st, 100x75.4x100x75.6, h..s & ls. Thomas Heffernan to Catherine ..dermott. *Mt.* $1,000. nom

..t st, s s, 81.9 e Columbia Heights, 20.7x75.6 x..4x75.6. Martins T. Lynde to Harriet B. w..f of Alexander H. Broadway. 12,500

..wand st, e s, 246.10 n Atlantic av, 50x100. A..hur E Sumner, of New York, to Emma S..mner. 4,000

..n pl, s s, 82.6 e Franklin av, 22 6x50. ..e under forclos. by advertisement. M. H..ell Topping, auctioneer certifies to pur..e of above property on June 5, 1884, to ..ert E. Topping for 2,000

..nt st, w s, 100 s Weldon st, 25x100. Eliz..th Taber to Eleanor M. Davidson. *Mt.* ..109. 2,000

..dyea st, r s, 94 w Graham av, runs north 50 west 5.11 x north 50 x west 24.2 x north..t 2.5 x south 102 3 to st, x east 31. Au..a Wirman widow and Emil A. Kraatz ..d Emma wife of and Rudolph Brummer.. heirs Herman Kraatz to Ernest Hoepp..e 3,400

..property. Release dower. Augusta K..tz to same nom

..r st, s e s, 265 s w Knickerbocker av, 10x 10.. Minne S. Cornell to Gordon Dunn, Pas..c N. J. Any assessm'ts. nom

..r st, s s, 335 w Knickerbocker av, 20x100. J..ph W. B. Rose to Kate Rose. *Mt.* $2,000. 2,000

..r st, s s, 315 w Knickerbocker av, 20x 10.. Same to Ole Harrison. *Mt.* $2,000. 4,000

..t, n s, 250 e Ewen st, 25x100. Conrad ..bing to Leopold Michel. 3,100

..ia st, w s, 50 n Evergreen av, runs north t..entre line old Bushwick road now closed, x ..., gore. Adrian M. Suydam to John ..ahan. 1

..st, No. 84, w s, 71.9 n Schermerhorn st, ..x100, h & l. Sarah O. and Cath. F. O. L..kletter formerly Onderdonk to Mark Ro..al. 18,000

..tle in any additional land in rear of ..ve. Same to same. Q. C. nom

.. st, No. 84. Release mort. Andrew J. O..erdonk et al. exrs. Horation G. Onder..k to Sarah O. and Cath. E. O. Linklet.. nom

..t st, n w s, 311 n e Evergreen av, 18x100, h..l. William H Barton to John Butterly. ..$3,000. 4,200

..nhoven lane, lot begins 500 s e 4th av and ..h w 67th st, runs southwest 105 to Cowen..en lane, x east along lane 40.4 x northeast ..x northwest 40, New Utrecht. James W. ..phy and Michael McCormack to Thomas K..elly. 900

..t, n s, 64.6 w Smith st, 18x67.6x18x67.5, ..l. Deborah W. Merritt widow to Mary ..wife of John Carroll. 3,200

..t, n s, bet Schenectady and Troy avs, ..g lot 46 block 156 assessm't map 24th ..rd. John W. McGuire, Registrar of Ar..s, to Leopold Gusthal. 182

..t, n s, 200 e Albany av, 20x80. Mary C. .. of George C. Comfort to Julia B. F. .. of John D. Fish, Hempstead, L. I. exch

..t, n s, 70 e Vanderbilt av, 25x110. John ..g exr. and trustee Bridget Gill to St. ..phs Roman Catholic Church. 6,000

..r st, n s, 247 w Throop av, 18x100, h & l. ..eclos. Robert Merchant to Frederick R. ..les. 7,600

..ass st, s s, 310 w 5th av, 16.8x100, h & l. ..elius J. Bergen to Elizabeth M. Bing..m. *Mt.* $3,000. 3,500

Douglass st, n s, bet Rochester and Buffalo avs, being lot 54 block 174 24th Ward. John C. McGuire, Registrar of Arrears, to John J. Lynes. 31

Dumont st, s s, 50 e Thatford av, 25x100. Bridget wife of John Barrett to Abraham Shiff, of Albany, N. Y. 2,600

Dumont st, s s, 25 w Watkins st, 25x100. John Miller to Jacob Robinson and Morris Greenberg. Mort $1,900. 2,000

Dumont st, Powell st, Livonia av and Junius st—block, 200x500. A. Judson Palmer to Jacob Manheim. *Mt.* $5,100. 20,000

Eastern Parkway, n w cor Osborn st, 25x100. Herbert C. Smith to John Power. 1,100

Eldert st, n w s, 278 n e Evergreen av, 19x100. Release mort. Anna E. Cozine extrx. and James Gascoine individ. and as exr. John G. Cozine to Leopold J. Lippmann. 2,387

Same property. Leopold J. Lippmann to Katherine Kelly. nom

Erasmus st, s s, part of sections 36 and B map G. L. Martense properly, Flatbush, 50x130. Ella J. Williamson to William A. Schmid. *Mt.* $1,500. 2,450

Folsom pl, s s, 100 w Essex st, 25x100. Paul D. Nelson to Bryce Martin. 1,700

Fulton st, s w cor Nostrand av, 100x70. Walter S. Brewster to Charles A. Betts. nom

Fulton st, Nos. 1454 and 1456, s s, 320 e Brooklyn av, 40x100. Katie M. wife of Ferdinand C. Bamman to Mary D. Blauvelt. *Mt.* $18,000. exch

Fulton st, e s, 46 7 n Nassau st, runs east to point 34.3 w from alley running through from Nassau to High st, x south 2 x east 8.3 x north 9 x east 26 x north 37.7 x west 96 to Fulton st, x south 44.6. Release mort. Henry Day et al. trustees will Edwin D. Morgan to The Kings Co. L. R. R. nom

Same property. Daniel Lord, Jr., to same. Release from damages. 1,200

Fulton st, s w s, 102.4 s e Navy st, 20x78.5x12.7 x17x71. William Johnston to Alexander Campbell. nom

Fulton st, s s, 200 w Stone av, 100x100. William H. Scott to Jennie L. Ross. Sub. to morts. 7,500

Grove st, n w s, 225 n e Central av, 22x100. Jacob H. Walters to Mary E. Koster 150

Halsey st, n s, 110 e Bedford av, 20x100. M. Beatrice King to Ella E. Hall. *Mt.* $9,000. 10,700

Same property. Ella E. Hall to Walter P. Denslow. B. & S. C. a. G. *Mt.* $9,000.

Halsey st, n s, 343.9 w Tompkins av, 18.9x100, h & l. Emma wife of Charles Klamburg to Emily wife of Arthur Pratt. *Mt.* $6,000. 4,400

Hancock st, n s, 325 e Lewis av, 100x100. Henry Weil to Wesley C. Bush. 10,000

Hancock st, n s, 255 e Sumner av, 40x100, h & l. Leonard D. Hills, Amherst, Mass., to Winston H. Hagen. *Mt.* $13,000. nom

Hancock st, n s, 200 e Reid av, 50x100. George Schoenewald to Joseph H. and William J. Burkart. 9,000

Hawthorne st, n s, at point which at n s of Winthrop st is 1,530.7 e Main road or Flatbush av, 25x100, Flatbush. Louisa S. Lennox an heir of L. A. H. Lennox to Charles S. S. Lennox. 1-6 part. nom

Hendrix st, e s, 150 s Blake av, 25x100. Jacob T. Van Sielen to Wolf Rosentall. 400 taxes, &c. 9,500

Herkimer st, n s, 481 e Nostrand av, 40x100, h & l. Charles A. Betts to George Brewster. *Mt.* $15,000. nom

Herkimer st, s s, 97 w Ralph av, 22x98. Catharine Scheidt to Maria A. Scheidt widow. nom

Herkimer st, n s, 200 w New York av, 20x100, h & l. Charles A. Betts to George H. and Henry M. Olney. *Mt.* $7,500. 13,000

Herkimer st, n s, 200 w Rockaway av, 40x100. The General Synod of the Reformed Church in America to Joseph Kellow. 12,500

Heyward st, n w s, 195 s w Harrison av, 25x100. Marie A. Steitz to George H. Steitz. Sub. to mort. nom

Same property George H. Steitz to Theresa Stietz. ½ part. Sub. to mort. nom

High st, s s, 75 e Jay st, 25x103.6, h & l. Benjamin Fisher to Anne M. Fisher. *Mt.* $3,745. 4,114

Himrod st, s e s, 80 n e Evergreen av, 20x100. George Hussenuetter to William E. Berge. *Mt.* $3,000. 6,500

Hubbard st, n w s, 193 from road leading to Flatlands Neck, contains 486-1,000 acres, Flatlands. Smith Watts to Rebecca S. Williamson and Joanna and Sarah D. Kouwenhoven. 600

Hull st, s s, 131.3 w Hopkinson av, runs west 56.8 x south 79.10 x southeast 56.7 x north 86.1. Frederick C. Urban to George H. Chinnock. *Mt.* $12,850. exch

Hull st, n s, 275 e Rockaway av, 37.6x100. Hiram Bedell, East Orange, N. J., to Michael J. Boylan. *Mt.* $8,900. nom

Ingraham st, n s, 150 e Bogert st, 25x100. Charles W. Truslow admr. William Wall to Mary wife of Leonhard Erk. 1,300

Ingraham st, n s, 200 w Morgan av, 25x100. Theodore F. Jackson to Helena wife of Joseph Abt. 1,300

Jerome st, w s, 375 s Sutter av, 25x100. Louis Fisher to Caroline Koerner. 450

Johnson st, s e cor Lawrence st, 28x100.
Hanson pl, n s, 120 w St. Felix st, 20x85.
Pacific st, n s, 151.10 w 4th av, 21x90.
Margaret S. Lawrence to Samuel N. Garrison. B. & S. nom

Same property. Samuel N. Garrison to Margaret S. and Helen W. Lawrence, joint tenants. B. & S. nom

Johnson st, s s, 89 w Lawrence st, runs south 106 x west 18.6 x north 6 x west 3.6 x north 100 to Johnson st x east 22. Release mort. Clara M. Edmonds et al. heirs James Edmonds to John Robinson. nom

Johnson st, s s, 89 w Lawrence st, 22x100.6x 18.6x100.6. Catherine Donohue widow to Mary A. Robinson. Reconveyance of property conveyed to secure debt. 4,000

Same property. John Robinson to Mary A. Robinson. B. & S. nom

Judge st, e s, 181.2 n Powers st, 24.6x111.10x 24.6x110.6. Henry Kinn to Abraham Natelsen. 7,500

Kosciusko st, n w s, 381.8, s w Bushwick av, 18 x98.9. John R. Gullen, of Torrington, Conn., to Emily M. wife of John Herbold. 3,050

Same property Samuel L. Caverley to John R. Gullen, of New Haven, Conn. nom

Lawton st, s e s, 217 4 n e Broadway, 25x90. George Straub to Peter and Berman Sturcke. *Mt.* $4,500. 9,250

Leonard st, n e cor Richardson st, 100x100. John Lewis and William Egginton to The United States Foundry Co. 10,000

Leonard st, e s, 125 s Culver st, 25x100. Anne widow Robert Lewis to Mortimer W. Price. 5,850

Linden st, e s, 215.11 n Evergreen av, 20x100. Aaron Kaplan to Simon Friedman. *Mt.* $1,500. 4,300

Livingston st, n e s, 58.4 s e Nevins st, 16.8x80. John S. Williamson to Jesse C. Woodhull. *Mt.* $5,000. 6,500

Livingston st, s w s, 270 s e Bond st, 22.6x100.9. Sheriff's deed on execution. Charles B. Farley to George M. Hard. 2,000

Same property George M. Hard to Adaline F. Annin. *Mt.* $6,000. 9,000

Same property. Assignment of sheriff's certificate of sale. Stephen R. Pinckney to George M. Hard. nom

Logan st, w s, 130 n Sutter av, 20x100. Effingham H. Nichols to John W. Kelly. 200

Logan st, w s, 150 s Glenmore av, 20x100. Robert T. Maujer to Richard Gaskell, Jr. 375

Main st, No. 47, e s, 116.8 s Water st, 16.8x75.2. Release dower. Mary widow of Edward McCarthy to Patrick Nolan. nom

Same property. Harris Salit to Jacob Frank, of New York. *Mt.* $2,100. 3,650

Macon st, s s, 250 w Reid av, 50x100. Adam S. Pratt, of Washington, D. C., trustee estate of Sophia M. Pratt and children to Mary A. Bellows. 3,600

Macon st, n s, 185 w Howard av, 90x100. Release mort. Frank Bailey to Calvin W. Raymond and Michael Dowley. 12,600

Same property. Release mort. Bernard Levino to same. 1,510

Same property. Release mort. Bernard Levino, Horatio S. Stewart, Alfred Vanderwerken and George C. Cranford to same. 1,800

Macon st, s s, 293 e Reid av, 18x100, James G. Roberts to James N. Harris. *Mt.* $5,500. 8,750

Macon st, n s, 490 e Ralph av, 90x100. Joseph A. Cross to Richard Mullowney. *Mt.* $16,435. nom

Macon st, s s, 210 w Ralph av, 18x100. Walter F. Clayton to Newton Cannon. *Mt.* $5,000. 8,500

McKibbin st, s s, 100 e Leonard st, 24.6x100. Albert Beck to Morris Alexander. *Mt.* $4,000. 7,000

Monroe st, s s, 518.9 w Marcy av, 18.9x100. Laura A. wife of William R. Bell to Louise A. wife of James A. Belford. *Mt.* $5,000. exch. and 500

McDonough st, n s, 100 w Sumner av, 20x 100; also,
McDonough st, s s, 215 w Lewis av, 20x100.
McDonough st, s s, 135 w Lewis av, 20x100.
McDonough st, s s, 155 w Lewis av, 20x100.
Lewis av, w s, 80 n Macon st, 30x95.
Julien T. Davies assignee Grant & Ward to Walter S. Johnson recvr. Marine Nat'l Bank of New York. 20,400

McDonough st, s s, 205 w Tompkins av, 40x135, hs & ls Charles A. Betts to George Brewster. *Mt.* $20,000. nom

Melrose st, s e s, 375 s w Hamburg av, 25x100. Barbara Kalb to Konrad Brantigan, New York. 6,425

Milford st, e s, 150 n Blake av, 40x100. Effingham H. Nichols to Richard T. Short. 500

McDougal st, s s, 164.7 w Hopkinson av, 160.5x 100. Release judgment. Nath'l H. Clements to Susie D. wife of Peter L. Brokaw. 10,000

Newell st, w s, 60 n Nassau av, 20x75. Isabella G. wife of James S. Knecht formerly Hewitt and Archibald E. Hewitt by John A. Jenkins guard. to George E. Blackball. Infants' shares. 1,875

Same property. Margarette E. wife of Samuel T. Dunn and William T. B. Hewitt to same. ½ part. 1,875

Newell st, w s 60 n Nassau av, 20x75. George E. Blackball to Joseph Blackball. ½ part. Sub. to mort 1,875

Newton st, s s, 275 e Union av, runs east 275 to Lorimer st, x south 200 to Bayard st, x west to point 275 e Union av, x north 200. Susanna wife of Paul Weidmann to The Brooklyn Transportation Co. (Lim.) 35,000

Newport st, n s, 100 e Stone av, 75x100.
Christopher av, w s, 100 n Newport av, 25x 100.
Eliza A. Dunning widow, New York, to Ascher Schiff. 1,040

Oakland st, w s, 295 s Norman av, 25x100. Matthias Duke to John McCort. 3,175

Osborn st, e s, 150 s Dumont av, 25x100. Benjamin Hyman to Wolf Lewis, of New York. 600

Osborn st, e s, 200 s Eastern Parkway, 1.6x100. Herbert C Smith to Charles Shapiro and Davis Nichol. 40

Osborn st, e s, 149.9 n Eastern Parkway, 0.3x 100. Jacob Lewis to Joseph Morris. Q. C. nom

Osborn st, w s, 150 n Belmont av, runs west 100 x north 50 x east 53.1 x south 1.6 x east 46.11 to st, x south 48.6. Jacob V. Smith to Josef Friedman. Mt. $2,000. 3,000

Same property. Josef Friedman to Wolf Lewis. Mt. $2,500. 3,500

Osborn st, e s, 175 s Eastern Parkway, 25x100. Herbert C. Smith to Abraham Ruth. 700

Pacific st, n s, 210 w Albany av, 20x100, h & l. Amanda M. wife of Harry Diver to Charles F. Hubbs and William T Lyons. 6,000

Pacific st, n s, 328 e Rochester av, 16x100. Frederick Dhuy to Christian A. Neuber. Mt. $1,700. 2,800

Pacific st, n s, 312 e Rochester av, 16x100. Frederick Dhuy, Jr., to Solomon Newdoll. 2,800

Pacific st, n s, 166 8 w New York av, 16.8x100. Clarence Dickerson to Ann E. and Sarah G. Dickerson. Mt. $4,000. 8,750

Plymouth st, Nos. 321 and 323, n e s, 200.1 s e Hudson av, 28.3x100 Amos S. Lamphear to Eugene H. Vanderbilt. Mt. $11,000. 18,500

Same property. William S. Cooper, New York, to Amos S. Lamphear. Mt. $9,000. 15,000

Pineapple st, s w s, 70 n w Willow st, 31x26.4. Nathaniel W. Burtis to Mary L. Burtis. B. B. & S. Mt. $7,400. nom

President st, s s, 263.6 w 5th av, 34x81.7. David J. Ramsdell to George R. Brown. Mt. $9,000. nom

President st, s s, 263.6 w 5th av, 34x81.7. George R. Brown to William H. Doty, Yonkers, N. Y. Mt. $9,000. exch

President st, n e s, 278.2 s e 5th av, 17.9x95. Herbert R. Brown to Jennie L. wife of Herbert R Brown. Mt. $6,000 nom

Quincy st, s s, 212 6 e Tompkins av, 12.6x100. William J. Spence to Albert Sibley. 1,600

Same property. Release mort. Alonzo E. De Baun to William J. Spence. nom

Ralph st, n w s, 200 s w Central av, 50x100. John Sjanken to William Schmidt and Mary his wife, joint tenants. Mt. $1,700. exch. and 500

Ralph st, s e s, 190 s w Central av. 140x100. Release mort. The Williamsburgh Savings Bank to John Rapp. 1,500

Roebling st, n s, 80 n South 9th st, runs west 75 x north 21 x east to Roebling st, x south 14. John McAleer to Ann wife of John McAleer. nom

Richardson st, n s, 100 e Union av, 25x100. John Turner to John M. Amory. 305

Sackett st, s s, 304 w Clinton st, 57x100. Release mort. Hamilton Trust Co. to John Murphy. 14,000

Sackman st, e s, 100 s Sutter av, 225x100. Jacob W. Erregger to Samuel Polly, Rachel Sacks, Harris Goldberg and Philip Rothlein. Mt. $5,435. 6,435

Sackman st, w s, 100 n Eastern Parkway, 50x 200 to Christopher av. James G. Roberts to Abraham Ruth. 2,800

Schaeffer st, s e s, 275 n e Broadway, 25x100. Mathies Wardzinski to Louis Hahnenburger. Mt. $3,500. 6,600

Seigel st, n s, 275 w Leonard st, 25x100, h & l. Joseph Zirinsky to Jacob Shapiro. Mt. $6,000. 7,500

Senator st, part of st lying bet n e s of proposed Senator st and n e s of Cowenhovens lane, in front of premises heretofore conveyed to grantees herein. Michael McCormack and James W. Murphy to Elizabeth L. Fox and Richard A. Larke. nom

Skillman st, w s, 125 n Willoughby av, 25x100. James V. B. Hammond to Mary Spencer. 5,100

Skillman st, w s, 18 s Willoughby av, 18x66. John C. Kane to Margaret Rafferty. 3,000

State st, s s, 200 e Smith st, 50x90. Charles D. Towt, Louis L. Robbins and Howard Van Buren exrs. John W. Towt to Addie C. wife of Edgar S. Gregory. 13,850

Stagg st, n s, 50 w Morgan av, 175x100.
Stagg st, n s, 250 w Morgan av, 50x100.
Mary S. wife of Charles R. Baker to Francis E. Clark. nom

Stagg st, n s, 50 w Morgan av, 175x100. Francis E. Clark to Jacob Bossert. nom

Stockholm st, n w s, 225 n e Irving av, 25x100. Partition deed. Samuel Walker, referee to Alois Lazansky. 900

Sumpter st, n s, 350 e Ralph av, 25x100. Paul Hahn to Albert Otto. Mort. $500. 1,425

Sumpter st, n s, 427.11 e Hopkinson av, runs east 22.1 x north 40.10 x northeast 35.3 to Brooklyn and Jamaica turnpike road, x northwest 50 x south 99 to Sumpter st; also right, title, &c.
Brooklyn and Jamaica pike, s s, lot begins centre line bet Sumpter and Marion sts at point 427.11 e Hopkinson av, runs south to s s Brooklyn and Jamaica pike, x southeast 50 x north — x west —.
Albert Otto to Josephine Pletsch. Mort. $1,000. 2,200

Stanhope st, n w s, 100 n e Hamburg av, 50x 100. Theodore F. Jackson to Wilhelmina Schwenk. 2,400

Stanhope st, n w s, 125 n e Hamburg av, 25x 100. Wilhelmina Schwenk to Josephine wife of Peter Eiseman. 1,400

Suydam st, n w s, 250 n e Hamburg av, 25x100. August Sedlmeir to Jacob Becker and Maria his wife, joint tenants. Mt. 3,000. 6,300

Troutman st, s s, bet Wyckoff and St. Nicholas avs, being lot 12 block 1161 assessm't map 18th Ward. John C. McGuire, Registrar Arrears, to John H. Van Thun. 15

Troutman st, n s, 276.9 e Bushwick av, 50x100. Catharina Shellwald to Henriette wife of Emily C. Bauer. Mt. $2,700. nom

Union st, n e s, 346.8 s e Hoyt st, 16.8x75. Philip H. Horton to Theresa J. Greenlund. Mt. $1,500. 2,800

Union st, s s, 142.6 w Columbia st, 20.6x100. Katy Seery to Mary Murnane. ½ part. 2,000

Vanderveer st, s s, 80 w Bushwick av, 16.10x 100. Edwin J. Bedell to Robert H. Irish. Sub. to mort. nom

Vanderveer st, s e s, 96.10 s w Bushwick av, 16.8 x100. Charles H. Reynolds to Isabella wife of John C. Rogers. Mt. $1,900. 2,620

Van Voorhis st, s e s, 431.3 n e Bushwick av, 0.4x100. Release mort. John Kempton to Mary J. Phelan. nom

Van Brunt st, east cor Delevan st, 25x90. Mary Looram, New York, to Catharine Looram. B. & S. nom

Vanderbilt st, s e cor Short st, 50x104, Flatbush. Levi Shults, Johnstown, N. Y., to John Beardall. 1,500

Vermont st, e s, 100 n Belmont av, 25x106. Mary wife of Henry C. Heyser to Thomas F. Vaughan and Bridget his wife. Mt. $2,000. 2,925

Vermont st, w s, 141.8 n Liberty av, 33.4x100. Release mort. Charles F. Wildridge to Mary H. Sopher. 300

Warren st, n e s, 225.9 n w Hicks st, 25x99.10. Grace A. wife of Francis V. Lindon to John Hegarty, Jr. 500

Same property. John Hegarty, Jr., to Thomas Sharkey. 3,700

Warren st, n s, 25 e 3d av, 25x100. William H. Bierds to Jennie A. Ives. Mt $7,500. exch

Warren st, n s, 50 e 3d av, 25x100. Same to Frank Hyde. Mt. $7,500. exch

Walworth st, e s, 232.7 n Myrtle av, runs east 46 x north 0.2½ x east 54 x north 25 x west 100 to Walworth st, x south 25.1, h & l. Robert Wilson to Eliza W. Christopher. C. a. G. 2,733

Washington Park, e s, 223 n De Kalb av, 22x 100. Alonzo E. Wemple to Pauline Paradis. Mt. $9,000. 15,000

Watkins st, e s, 200 s Sutter av, 50x100. Peter Ostraszewski, of New York, to Harris Max. 1,275

Watkins st, w s, 125 s Belmont av, 25x100. Abraham Silberman to Harris Silberman. Mt. $1,825. 1,350

Watkins st, e s, 75 s Dumont av, 25x100. Henry S. Ahrens to Jacob Hubel. ½ part. Sub. to mort. 325

Watkins st, e s, 150 n Glenmore av, 50x100.
Stone av, w s, 200 n Glenmore av, 50x100
William Schwartz to Nathan Schlussel and Philip Rosenthal. 3,000

Same property. Nathan Schlussel and Philip Rosenthal to Isaac Axelrod, Wolf Horwitz and Solomon Sindenband, of New York. Mt. $12,000. 3,200

Watkins st, e s, 100 n Glenmore av, 50x100. William Schwartz to Meyer Pincus and Bonceret Helfann. Mt. $12,000. 1,500

Watkins st, e s, 300 n Glenmore av, runs east 200 to Stone av, x south 300 to Glenmore av, x west 200 x north 300. Bentley F. Adams to Wm. Schwartz. 17,000

Watkins st, e s, 100 n Riverdale av, 50x100.
Rockaway av, e s, 180 n Glenmore av, 80x 100.1.
Rockaway av, e s, 20 n Glenmore av, 60x 100.1.
Tulip st, n s, 169.1 w Troy av, 100x100, Flatbush.
John Rabbits to Michael Sullivan. Sub. to mort. nom

Same property. Michael Sullivan to John Rabbits. Sub. to mort. nom

West st, e s, 100 s Broadway, 50x100. Martha A. wife of Ernst Vogt to Solomon Herskovitz. Mt. $700. 2,600

Willow st, s s, 392.3 e Pierrepont st, 35.5x100x 35.1x100. Louisa S. Lennox an heir of Louisa A. H. Lennox to Charles S. S. Lennox. 1-6 part. nom

Windsor pl, s s, 211 6 e 7th av, 13.8x100. Mary wife of John S. Edwards to Thomas Sloan and Susan Mullin. Mt. $1,200. 1,900

Wyona st, w s, 175 s Eastern Parkway, 25x100. Daniel McCallen to Cordt Gerken. 700

Woodhull st, n e s, 122 n w Henry st, 22x100. Statira A. wife of Jeremiah C. Murphy to Margaret O'Neil. 6,400

1st st, n s, 387.6 w 6th av, 18.9x100. Herbert R. Brown to Jennie L. wife of Herbert R. Brown. Mt. $5,450. nom

North 2d st, s e cor Roebling st, runs south 110 x east 75 to North 1st st, x north 21 x east 6 x north 88.6 to North 2d st, x west 38. Margaret J. Maurice, Maspeth, L. I., to James Cavanagh. Q. C. nom

4th st, n e s, 97.7 n w 6th av, 17.4x95, h & l. John Miner to John H. Hunter, Orangetown, N. Y. Mt. $4,000. 8,500

South 4th st, s s, 213.6 e Driggs st, 23x100, h & l. Adolph Obrig exr. and trustee G. J. Obrig to John Keresey. 7,000

South 4th st, s s, 213.6 e Driggs st, 23x100.
Grand st, s s, 20 e Leonard st, 20x100.
Release dower. Anna widow Gerhard J. Obrig to Adolph Obrig exr., &c., Gerhard J. Obrig. nom

South 5th st, s w s, 50 s e 12th st, 24.6x100. Johann Marshall to John A. Bachmann. 575

South 5th st, s s, 75 e Hewes st, 25x100, h & l. Catharine Miller devisee Ludwig Speck to Catharine Matthes formerly Speck. Q. C. nom

Same property. Louisa F. Gaensle heir Karl L. Speck to same. Q. C. nom

Same property. Louis Hempfling devisee Karl L. Speck to same. Q. C. nom

Same property. Christine Keller heir of same to same. Q. C. nom

Same property. Christine Stiefel heir, &c., of same to same. Q. C. nom

Same property. Louisa Schmidt devisee of same to same. Q. C. nom

South 5th st, n e s, 75 n w 11th st, 25x—x25x—. Henry G. Zyfers to John J. and William Graber. 4,50[illegible]

6th st, n e s, 357.10 n w 5th av, 40x100. Release mort. Edward H. Litchfield to Erwin G. Gollner. 1,[illegible]

6th st, s s, 180 w 4th av, 115x100. Emil Lindberg to Patrick Mahoney. All liens. [illegible]

East 7th st, e s, 120 w Av E, 40x241 to East 8th st, Flatbush. Joseph Wechsler to William Barbor. 1,[illegible]

8th st, n s, 220.7 w 6th av, 18.2x100. William Brown to Hugh J. Kennelty. 7,[illegible]

North 8th st, n e s, 200 s e Bedford av, 25x100. August C. Diestelhorst to John Abt. 5,[illegible]

Same property. Release mort. Henry C. W. Ingraham to William Brown. [illegible]

10th st, s w s, 280.8 s e 4th av, 17.4x100. William C. O'Keeffe to Mary E. wife of Edward Murtagh. Mt. $3,000. 4,[illegible]

12th st, s s, 135 w 4th av, 18x100. Margaret Cullen to John Anderson. Mt. $1,000. 3,[illegible]

13th st, s s, 522.10 e 5th av, 0.2½x100. William S. Hassan to Elizabeth A. Lundequist. [illegible]

18th st, n e s, 100 n w 10th av, 60x100.2.
Prospect av, s w s, 320 s e 10th av, 60x92.2.
Mary J. Scholes to Henry F. Risch. Mt. $540. 2,[illegible]

20th st, s s, 132 n w patent line bet Flatbush and Brooklyn, 25x100. George S. Wheeler exr. Nancy B. Wheeler to Margaret Jennings. [illegible]

Bay 20th st, n w s, 425 s w 85th st, 25x96.8, New Utrecht. Elizabeth Grenier to William G. Gasson. [illegible]

21st st, s s, 247.6 e 4th av, 27.6x100.2. Charles Tokonauer to John Tokonauer. 2,5[illegible]

Same property. John Tokonauer to Amelia Tokonauer. 2,5[illegible]

21st st, n s, 200 e 4th av, 25x100, h & l. Ellen Gilmartin widow to Francissek Lewandowski and Victoria his wife 2,5[illegible]

Bay 22d st, n w s, 225 n e Bath av, runs northwest 96.8 x southwest 6.8 x east 96.11 to beginning, New Utrecht. Mary F. Zundt to Joseph Stehlin. no[illegible]

24th st, n s, 250 e 3d av, 20x100. Henry F. Sammis, Huntington, L. I., to Edward E. Bergen. 2,8[illegible]

28th st, s w s, 225 n w 5th av, 25x100.2. Foreclos. Samuel M. Hubbard, referee, to William Cruikshank. [illegible]

30th st, s s, 125 e 3d av, 25x100.2; also,
30th st, s s, 150 e 3d av, 25x100.2.
Michael Fleich to Flora C. Fleico. n[illegible]

33d st, n s, 217 6 w 5th av, 64x100.2. William E. Kay to William Dittmar, Jr. Mt. $8,000. 14,4[illegible]

41st st, n s, 200 e 3d av, 25x100.2 Cornelius Duffy to William A. W. Wettergreen. Mt $2,000. 1,[illegible]

45th st, s s, 240 e 3d av, 20x100.2. James G. Carroll to Otto Vockmer. Mt. $2,300. 4,[illegible]

48th st, n s, 260 e 4th av, 20x100.2. Maude A. Tomlinson to Louis Bossert. [illegible]

51st st, n s, 360 e 8th av, 20x100.2, New Utrecht. Michael J. Bergen to Ira L. Bursley. [illegible]

53d st, s w s, 275 n w 15th av, 50x100.2, h & l. New Utrecht. William Dittmar, Jr., to Matilda Meyer. 4,[illegible]

54th st, n s, 180 e 5th av, 20x100.2. John J. Byrne to George A. Comer. n[illegible]

54th st, s s, 314 w 3d av, 18x100.2. Margaret wife of and Thomas Ostick to James T. Derby. Mt. $2,500. 4,[illegible]

56th st, n e s, 420 n w 3d av, 80x100.2. Henry Siebert, of Bayonne, N. J., to Elizabeth Cuming. 3,[illegible]

65th st, s s, 420 e 12th av, 40x100, Bath Junction. James V. S. Woolley to Eric O. Strom. [illegible]

66th st, n e s, 313 n w 18th av, 40x100. Mattie J. Perkins to George W. Gilbert. Q. C. n[illegible]

66th st, n e s, 313 n w 18th av, 40x100, New Utrecht. Edward R. Johnes to George W. Gilbert. Q. C. n[illegible]

71st st, n s, 550 w 15th av, 60x100, Lefferts Park. James V. S. Woolley to Sarah Aroua. [illegible]

72d st, s s, 270 w 15th av, 60x100, New Utrecht. James V. S. Woolley to William Twiddy. [illegible]

75th st, n e cor 18th av, runs northeast to land of Jane Roberts, x northeast to 20th av, x southwest to 76th st, x northwest to 19th av, x northeast to 75th st, x northwest to 18th av, place beginning, New Utrecht. Frederic E. Bard to William D. Barnes. Sub. to mort. n[illegible]

75th st, n s, 340 w 18th av, 40x100, New Utrecht. John H. Hanley to Annie Hogan. [illegible]

75th st, n s, 380 w 18th av, 40x100, New Utrecht. John H. Hanley to Thomas Hogan. [illegible]

77th st, s s, 170 w 3d av, 40x109.4, New Utrecht. John R. Fraser, of New York, to Adolph Brymer. 1,[illegible]

83d st, n e s, 280 s e 21st av, 60x100, New Utrecht. James D. Lynch to Charles B. Barnum. 1,[illegible]

83d st, s w s, 80 s e 24th av, 60x100, Bensonhurst. Thomas Johnston to Henry F. Lippold. [illegible]

84th st, n e s, 60 n w 24th av, 60x100, Gravesend. James D. Lynch to Addie Legate. [illegible]

86th st, n e s, 65 s e Bay 16th st, 25x100, New Utrecht. William G. Morrissey to Mary Agrill. 2[illegible]

87th st, s w s, 100 n w 3d av, runs southwest 2[illegible] to 88th st, x northwest 140.1 x northeast 178[illegible]

x southeast 150, New Utrecht. Daniel D. Field to Kate A. Righter. 3,100

88th st, s w s, 200 n w 1st av, 75x100; also, 89th st, n e s, 225 n w 1st av, 25x100, New Utrecht. David D. Field, of New York, to Ambrose W. Whittelsey. 1,295

88th st, easterley cor Narrows av, 100x100, New Utrecht. Same to Margaret wife of Thomas H. Harper. 2,500

Av A, s s, 100 e East 19th st, 50x150, Flatbush. James A. Hamblin, John McElvery and Robert Getty to Emma G. wife of Morrison Hoyt. 10,750

Av B, n s, 551.7 w Ocean av, runs north 401.1 x southwest 291.6 x south 91.3 x east 140 x south 200 to Av B, east x 130, Flatbush. Phebe A. Henderson to Emeline Gallup. Q. C. nom

Av D, n e cor East 9th st, 80x100, Flatbush. William T. Fruin to Mary De C. widow of Richard De Courcey and Margaret Doheny. 1,400

Albany av, w s, 120 s Herkimer st, runs west 80 x north 20 x west 195 x south 85.6 x east 195 x north 45.6 x east 80 to Albany av, x north 20. James E. Granniss to John Fitzgerald. B. & S. and C. a. G. *Mt.* $3,500. nom

Same property. John Fitzgerald to Alexander E. Guerringue. B. & S. and C. a. G. *Mt.* $3,500. 4,500

Atlantic av, s s, 20.4½ w Williams av, 20.4½x89.5x20x93.3; also, Atlantic av, s s, 61.1 w Williams av, 40.9x97.1 x40x104.11. Edwin Beers to Harvey Fawcett. 10,500

Atlantic av, n s, 300 e Smith st, 25x90. Charles D. Towl et al. exrs. John W. Towl to Philipp Bohner. 7,000

Atlantic av, n s, 264.10 w Utica av, 16.6x99.1, h & l. Emily L. E. Weineman to Agnes wife of William G. Hoople. C. a. G. nom

Atlantic av, n s, 300 e New York av, 60x149.1. Walter S. Brewster to Charles A. Betts. nom

Blake av, s e cor Stone av, 20x100; also, Stone av, e s, 45 s Blake av, 5x100. Francis Ullrich and Louise his wife to Samuel Lemberg. 800

Bedford av, s e s, 60 n e North 5th st, 20x80. Josephine Hamilton to Henry Hamilton. nom

Brooklyn av, n e cor Fennimore st, 100x200, Flatbush. Thomas H. Robbins to William J. Penoyer, of Chester, N. Y. *Mt.* $1,500. 3,500

Buffalo av, w s, 20 s Pacific st, 16.8x85. George F. Stults to John Mitchell. *Mt.* $2,000. 3,500

Central av west cor Weirfield st, 100x341. Alexander Taylor to Leopold J. Lippmann. Sub. to mort. nom

Carlton av, w s, 117.7 s Fulton st, 25x100. Almira Jenks to Edward J. Fearon. Upon trust. nom

Christopher av, e s, 125 s Blake av, 25x100, h & l. J. Woolsey Shepard to Jacob Cohen. *Mt.* $1,700. 2,050

Clason av, e s, 59 n Madison st, 19.6x92. Walter Dickinson to George W. Wager. 8,100

Clason av, w s, 125 n De Kalb av, 25x198.5x25x197.11. William C. and Melissa P. Benedict to Louise J. Johnson and Kate Mackenzie. 1,200

Clason av, w s, 75 s Gates av, 25x100. Hester A. wife of George W. Montgomery, New York, to James E. Sleight. *Mt.* $6,000. 7,250

Clason av, w s, 197.11 s Myrtle av, 50x150. Partition. John A. Deady to Charles Fleischmann, Cincinnati, Ohio. 27,996

De Kalb av, s s, 50 e Evergreen av, 25x79.6. Jacob Frey, Long Island City, to Anna Frey. 7,000

Evergreen av, westerly cor Covert st, 125x100. Charles F. Lutz to Frances J. wife of Charles F. Lutz. All liens. nom

Flatbush av, n e s, 120.7 s e Carlton av, 38.6x75. Josephine C. wife of John Downie to Maria K. wife of William Siebert. *Mt.* $11,000. 18,000

Flushing av, s s, 25.5 w Spencer st, 25x93x25x100. Annie L. wife of Patrick Myers, Mary wife of and John Nagel, and Annie wife of and John Keefe to Mary A. Oliver. Q. C. nom

Flushing av, No 128. Contract. Georgianna McIlvain to Margaret Brennan. 7,500

Flushing av, s s, 375 e Nostrand av, 25x100. Saja Guttmann, of N. Y., to Bernhard Breithart, of N. Y. 3,300

Flushing av, s s, 100 e Marcy av, 25x100. Leopold Michel to Nathan Rosenthal. *Mt.* $2,000. 4,800

Gates av, s e s, 225 n e Knickerbocker av, 25x100. Leopold Heymann to Silas C. Edwards. nom

Gates av, n s, 262 e Nostrand av, 20x100, h & l. Louis A. wife of James A. Belford to Laura A. Bell. *Mt.* $2,500. nom

Gates av, n s, 44.6 w Clason av, 43.6x82x44.6x79. John M. Holder exr. John B. Holder to Charles D. Rust. 10,650

Glenmore av, s e cor Alabama av, 75x100. Gustav Korner, Huntington, L. I., to Ernst F. Sutterlin. 3,500

Glenmore av, s w cor Snediker av, 25x100. Magdalena Dupignac to Annie A. Olson. Mort. $1,200. 3,000

Glenmore av, n w cor Berriman st, 50x85. John Meehan to Mary wife of Thomas Smith. 3,000

Greenwood av, s w cor East 5th st, 80x100x45.10x105.8, Flatbush. Anna M. Ferris to John F. Cunningham. 1,150

Graham av, e s, 29.5 s Varet st, 24.3x100, h & l. Isaac Horowitz to Moses Sussmann, New York. *Mt.* $4,500. 8,000

Gravesend av, w s, adj late Court Stillwells, 85 x190 to centre Lake st, x 93x190, Gravesend, h & l. Adam Moran to James Mullen. nom

Gravesend av, w s, 75 n 2d pl, 50x110, Gravesend. Henry Dolle, Anna, Charles and Looff Rudolph and Emma Dolle to Charles Kies. 2,500

Gravesend av, e s, 374.6 s Av Q, 82.4x224.2 to East 2d st, and 82.4x224.2, Gravesend. Nellie S. wife Richard L. Van Kleek to Adam Moran. 3,500

Gravesend av, w s, adj late Court Stillwells, 85 x190 to centre Lake st, x 93x190, Gravesend, h & l, John C. Van Siclen to Adam Moran. 3,500

Hegeman av, n w cor Ashford st, 100x100. Adolph Sussman to George Niebling. 935

Hopkinson av, s w cor Decatur st, 100x100. John W. Harman to Joseph P. Puels. 10,000

Hopkinson av, n w cor Decatur st, runs west along st 295 x north 100 x east 200 x north 100 to McDonough st, x east 95 to av, x south 200 to beginning. Joseph P. Puels to William McClenahan. *Mt.* $25,000. 31,500

Hopkinson av, w s, extends from Bainbridge st to Decatur st, 200x100. Contract. John W. Harman to Frank McMahon. 20,000

Hopkinson av, e s, 75 n Hull st, 25x100. Partition. Philip L. Balz, referee, to Jacob and Valentine Guthy. 1,600

Jamaica av, n s, 225 e Barbey st, 25x114.3x25x114.1, h & l. George Leybold to Emil Boehme. *Mt.* $1,200. 3,250

Jamaica av, s w cor Elton st, 80.5x129.2x75x100.2. Edward F. Linton to Alfred W. Houchin. 4,800

Jefferson av, s s, 100 e Throop av, 36x100. Frank Hyde to Charlotte A. Bierds. exch

Jefferson av, No. 154, s s, 320 w Nostrand av, 20x100. Sub. to mort. $8,500. Jefferson av, No. 160, s s, 260 w Nostrand av, 20x100. Sub. to mort. $8,500. Jefferson av, Nos. 164 and 166, s s, 200 w Nostrand av, 40x100. Sub. to mort. $17,000. James C. Rogers to William E. Ross. nom

Jefferson av, s s, 200 w Nostrand av, 40x100, h & l. William E. Ross to E. J. Churchill, of New York. nom

Kent av, e s, 133 n Flushing av, 25x75. Ellen Hanlon to Thomas Hanlon. B. & S. nom

Kent av, s w cor North 7th st, 50x100. Amelia wife of William J. Finn individ. and as extrx., &c., of John Davison to The Brooklyn Cooperage Co. 27,000

Knickerbocker av, s w s, 107 n w Flushing av, runs northwest 8.4 x south 21.3 x east 25 x north — x 21.8. Sigmund Bleyer to Rudolph Bleyer. 500

Livonia av, n e cor Junius st, runs east 189 to land of N. Y. & Manhattan Beach R. R. Co., x north 500 to Dumont av, x west 24 x south 100 x west 80 x south 100 x east 10 x south 80 x west 95 to Junius st, x south 220 to beginning. A. Judson Palmer to Scheyer Nathan, of New York. 13,520

Livonia av, s e cor Osborn st, 20x100. James O'Halloran to Abraham Seidenbergh and Rochmiel Abramovitz. 550

Miller av, e s, 229.6 n Liberty av, 20.6x100. Samuel Lubinsky to Rachel Sunshine. *Mt.* $2,100. 4,000

Montauk av, e s, 140 n Blake av, 30x100. Hyman Kaplan to Louis Cohen, of New York. 500

Montauk av, w s, 240 s New Lots road, 40x100. William H. Jackson, of New York, to Conrad Blass. 400

Myrtle av, n s, 175 w Marcy av, runs north 96.1 x northwest 10 x southwest 27.2 x south 82.11 to Myrtle av, x east 25. Martha J. W. Campbell to Emile Loch. *Mt.* $4,000. 7,800

New Jersey av, w s, 100 s Broadway, 50x100. John G. MacMahon to Corah Gerken. 1,400

New Jersey av, w s, 100 s Glenmore av, 25x100. John W. Pitkin, of Englewood, N. J., to George and Mary Scherer. 800

Ocean av, s w cor The Neck road, runs south along av 70 x west 125 x north 25 to s s Neck road, x northeast 125 to beginning, Gravesend. Oscar E. Shaul to Sophia Tepe. 400

Park av, s s, 75 e Spencer st, 25x82.3. William B. Davenport, public admr. and as admr. John Gordorn to Isaac O. Horton, Jr. 2,500

Prospect av, s s, 79.6 e 5th av, 119.6x40.2, hs & ls. J. Trumbull Smith to Jane H. Cowdrey, Ridgefield, N. J. Q. C. nom

Prospect av, n e s, 34.4 n w 7th av, 16.4x76x16x76. Partition. Jacob New ref. to Michael Hanrahan. 2,100

Putnam av, n s, 300 e Broadway, 20x100. Robert L. Moores and Charles A. Le Quesne to Charles E. Ring. *Mt.* $4,500. nom

Putnam av, n s, 65 e Sumner av, 20x100. Letitia Holmes to A. Stewart Walsh. *Mt.* $7,250. nom

Putnam av, n w cor Bedford av, 80x200 to Madison st; also, Fulton st, s s, 40 w South Oxford st, runs west 40 x south 60 x southeast 29.10 to Hanson pl, x east 33 x northwest 26.2 x northeast 14 x north 35.1; also, South Portland av, n e cor Hanson pl, runs north along av 69.1 x east 31 x northeast 68.3 to Fulton av, x southeast 40 x southwest 39.5 x south 72.2 to Hanson pl, x west 80 to beginning; also, Fulton st, s w s, 68.5 s e Portland av, runs southwest 59.1 x west 20 to av, x south 20 x east 31 x northeast 68.3 to Fulton st, x northwest 20 to beginning; also, Franklin av, e s, 80 s Madison st, 20x90. Franklin av, w s, 46 s Madison st, 60x80. Lexington av, n s, 234.5 w Franklin av, 30x121.7. Julius A. Holbrook, Sarah L. Holt, Harnet M. and Lillian R. Terrett to Sarah A. Terrett. nom

Same property. Sarah A. Terrett widow to Julia A. wife of Dudley R. or B. Holbrook, Sarah L. wife of William H. C. Holt, Harriet M. and Lilliau R. Terrett, each 4-27 part. nom

Putnam av, s s, 172 w Howard av, 17x100, h & l. Margaret H. wife of Charles H. Murch to Emilie wife of John Mayer. *Mt.* $5,000. 5,400

Putnam av, s s, 217 e Reid av, 19.6x100. Putnam av, s s, 275.6 e Reid av, 39x100. Release mort. Title Guarantee and Trust Co. to John Hennessy. nom

Same property. Release mort. Same to same. Q. C. and 13,500

Reid av, e s, 60 n Hancock st, 57.6x100. William H. Scott, of New York, to John S. Willdridge. Sub. to mort. $4,175. 8,750

Riverdale av, s w cor Osborn st, 150x100. Valentine Green to Thomas Goldstein. 2,350

Rockaway av, w s, 300 n Eastern Parkway, 50 x100. William Schwartz to Samuel Levy. 1,750

Rockaway av, w s, 50 n of line bet Ames and Kowenhovens Flatlands, 25x100. George F. Secor to Mary L. wife of William H. Pink. 1873. nom

Rockaway av, w s, 450 n Eastern Parkway, 25x100. Robert Smith to Michael Rosenthal. 850

Schenck av, e s, 162 n Arlington av, 213x100. Elizabeth M. wife of Williamson Rapalje to Sebastian T. Hollister. 7,200

Shepherd av, e s, 530 s Ridgewood av, 20x101.7. Release mort. Williamsburg Savings Bank to Edward F. Linton. 350

Shepherd av, e s, 100 n Arlington av, 20x101.7. Edward F. Linton to Elizabeth Henkel. 650

Skillman av, n s, 150 w Lorimer st, 25x100. Release mort. The Williamsburgh Savings Bank to Margaret Lynch. 1,500

Same property. Margaret wife of and John Lynch to Frederick C. Budden. *Mt.* $2,750. 300

St. Marks av, n s, 98 e Rogers av. 18x80.7x18.5 x76.6. Florence A. wife of Frederick J. Ashfield to Mary E. Sandford. *Mt.* $4,000. 8,500

Stanley av, s s, 40 e Jerome st, 20x85. William E. Sudlow to Herbert J. Knapp. Sub. to mort. 72

Stewart av, e s, lot 1 partition map Simon Denyse, runs east 90 x north 80 x east 582.10 x south 328.4 to a point 100 south of 76th st, x west 638.1 to av, x north 110.1, contains 3 7003-10000 acres, New Utrecht. Peter S. Bogart and ano. exrs. Elizabeth C. Bogart to Julius W. Copmann. 6,000

Stone av, w s, 20 n Blake av, 69x100. Maria E. Jones to Mary A. L. Baker. *Mt.* $5,500. 8,400

Stone av, e s, 11.11 s Sumpter st, runs south 13.1 x east 77.10 x northwest 33.9 x southwest x southwest again 46.9 to av. Samuel M. Carr, of New York, to Elizabeth Carr. 800

Stone av, e s, 150 s Rapalje av, 50x100. Newport st, n s, 25 w Christopher av, 75x100. Christopher av, w s, 100 n Newport av, 25x100. Release mort. Sarah M. Mygatt and ano. trustees Jacob A. Robertson to Eliza A. Dunning. nom

Stone av, w s, 100 s Belmont av, 25x100. Charles E. Maguire to Sam Barkin. *Mt.* $2,350. 400

Stone av, w s, 18 s Livonia av, 32x100. Michael Sullivan to Barnet Goldstein and Jacob Schwartz. *Mt.* $2,500. 3,600

Stone av, Riverdale av and Christopher st, 22 lots, all 25x100, excepting 2 lots of 20x100 each. Contract. Thomas McGee to Abraham Simon, Haska Silverman and Simon Alker. 8,360

Stone av, w s, 50 s Belmont av, 25x100. Hyman Goldberg to Morris Winer and Samuel Joseph. *Mt.* $2,850. 3,550

Stone av, e s, 175 s Belmont av, 25x100. Rosa Rudderman to Joseph Scharar and Samuel Hackboth. *Mt.* $200. 825

Stone av, s w cor Livonia av, 18x100. Michael Sullivan, of Flatbush, N. Y., to Louis Wemglass. *Mt.* $2,200. 3,600

Stone av, e s, 150 n Sutter av, 25x100. Herbert C. Smith to Jacob and Davis Axelrod and Isaac Levinson. 650

Stone av, w s, 135 n Blake av, 23x100, h & l. Henry C. Soop, Kingston, N. Y., and Frank M. Andrus, Roxbury, N. Y., to Harris Ponstein. *Mt.* $1,700. 2,525

Sumner av, n w cor Lexington av, 20x75, h & l. Mary J. Quin to Edward P. Shields. *Mt.* $11,500. nom

Surf av, n s, part of lot 24 common land of Gravesend, 20x157.6, Coney Island. Ellen Tilyou to Ellen Fliedner. Sub. to assessm'ts. 1,200

Sutter av, n w cor Watkins st, 25x100. Bernhard Silberstein to Baer Schiller and Simon Jacobs. *Mt.* $120. 1,285

Thatford av, e s, 200 s Eastern Parkway, 25x100. Israel Rubenstein and Israel Sugalowicz to Marks Yudelowitz and William Walcoff. *Mt.* $2,000. 3,800

Thatford av, w s, 250 s Belmont av, 25x100.1. Contract. Moritz Blum and Emanuel Schwartz to Moritz Weintraub. 2,435

Thatford av, w s, 100 n Glenmore av, 100x100.1. Charles Goldstein to Simon Silverstein and Louis Goldstein. *Mt.* $1,500. 2,000

Thatford av, e s, 125 s Glenmore av, 25x100. Aaron Grabosh to Morris Handler, Newark, N. J. *Mt.* $300. 250

Thatford av, e s, 225 s Glenmore av, 25x100. Moses and Louis Stern to Nathan Berman. *Mt.* $1,950. 2,650

Same property. Max Landesmann, of New York, to same. *Mt.* $1,600. 2,525

Thatford av, w s, 100 n Riverdale av. 50x200 to Rockaway av. Goodman Shapiro et al. to Isaac Nathan and Israel Lippmann. 1,600

Same property Isaac Nathan and Israel Lippmann to Harris Friedman and Ida Lippmann. 1,800

Thatford av, e s, 175 s Duryea av, 75x100. Solomon Seligman and Isaac Cohen to Sarah Seligman and Dora Cohen. *Mt.* $2,100. 2,000

Union av, e s, 50 s Skillman av, 25x100; also, Union av, e s, 75 s Skillman av, 25x100. Thomas Shaw and Michael Dubigg exrs. and C. Annie O'Brien to Julia A. Whittaker and Catharine Taylor. 1,900

Union av, e s, 84 s North 2d st, 22x107. Sale under foreclosure by advertisement. R. Howell Topping, auction certifies to purchase of above property on Dec. 15, 1888, by M. Howell Topping for 800

Van Sielen av, e s, 200 n Dumont av, 75x100. Catharine Quin to Matilda Bolles, Bayport, Conn. *Mt.* $2,250. exch

Van Sielen av, e s, 150 s Arlington av, 25x100. Lucy A. Dixon to Arthur S. Dixon. *Mt.* $1,800. nom

Vernon av, n s, 185 e Lewis av, 40x100, h & l. Isabella B. wife of John N. Booth to Joseph A. Cross. *Mt.* $14,750. nom

Waverly av, s e cor Gates av, 22x70. Elizabeth L. wife of George H. Chinnock to Frederick C. Urban. *Mt.* $8,500. 9,000

Washington av, w s, 71.8 n Bergen st, 24x88.4x25.2x85.9. Ann wife of John Parkinson to Berno Fischer. 1,900

Willoughby av, n s, 393.9 w Marcy av, 18.9x100. John H. Graham to John O. Graham. *Mt.* $4,500. 7,600

Wyckoff av, west cor De Kalb av, runs southwest 89.9 x northwest 100 x southwest 5 x northwest 50 x northeast 101.5 to Wyckoff av, x southeast 150.8. Benjamin Olbricht to Lisette Siegfried. *Mt.* $3,000. 8,700

2d av, n e cor 88th st, 100x100, New Utrecht. David D. Field to Augustus C. Fischer. 1,960

2d av, s e s, 80 s w Bennetts lane, 80x120, New Utrecht. James Van Brunt to Simon Stiner. exch

3d av, w s, 40 s Wyckoff st, 20x80. Benjamin Armstrong to Charles F. Hunt. *Mt.* $3,500. nom

3d av, n w s, 60 n e 56th st, runs northeast 40 x northwest 160 x southwest 100 to 56th st, x southeast 60 x northeast 60 x southeast 100.
2d av, east cor 56th st, 100x200.
Elizabeth Cuming to Mari A. Cuming. 11,600

3d av, northerly cor 81st st, 109.4x110, New Utrecht. Jaques Van Brunt to James A. Townsend. exch

3d av, s w cor 81st st, runs south along av to farm line of grantees, x northwest to 81st st, x east — to beginning, New Utrecht. Jaques Van Brunt to Anna C. Hegeman, Elizabeth Bennett, Rebecca B. Lott and Jennie Cropsey. nom

3d av, e s, 109.4 n 8th st, 21.9x95.9. Frederick Olmstead, of Redding, Conn., to Ida V. Higgins. 800

3d av, w s, 70 s Bay Ridge av, 20x97, New Utrecht. George Self to Charles and Benjamin Martin. 2,000

4th av, w s, 25.2 n 52d st, 50x100. Jane E. Haight to Henry Kettelhodt. *Mt.* $1,500. 2,600

4th av, w s, 58 s 13th st, 28x86.10. Release mort. Hamilton Trust Co. to William Bowers. 8,000

5th av, w s, 43.9 s Carroll st, 21x100.2x21.1x98.2. Michael O'Keeffe to James M. Baker. 14,000

6th av, s w cor 52d st, 25.2x100.
6th av, w s, 25.2 n 54th st, runs east 100 x south 25.2 to 54th st, x east 100 x north 200.4 to 53d st, x west 200 to 6th av, x 175.2 to beginning.
6th av, e s, 75.2 n 53d st, runs east 100 x north 25 x east 120 x north 100.2 to 52d st, x west 220 to 6th av, x south 125.2.
52d st, s s, 300 e 7th av, runs south 100.2 x east 200 x south 100.2 to 53d st, x east 100 x north 200.4 to 52d st, x west 300.
6th av, n e cor 52d st, 112.6x100x116x100.
52d st, n s, 240 e 6th av, runs north 100.2 x east 360 x north 25 x east 100 to 7th av, x south 125.2 to 52d st, x west 460.
48th st, s s, 100 w 7th av, 200x100.2.
Tertullus G. Matthews to Stewart McDougall. ½ part. *Mt.* ½ of $7,000. nom

9th av, e s, 60.2 n 18th st, 20x100. Charles Hart to Denis McAuliffe. *Mt.* $1,300. 1,500

9th av, s w cor 49th st, 100.2x100.5, New Utrecht. Michael J. Bergen to Ira L. Bursley. 2,155

11th av, west cor 56th st, 186.5 to Cowenhovens lane, x 43.3 to 57th st, x 472.9x184x72.5 to 56th st, x 391.4.
56th st, s w s, at s e line of L. D. Aymar's land, 64.1x72.5x20.10, gore, New Utrecht.
Frank Hyde to Stephen Ballard. *Mt.* $3,500. exch

12th av, s e s, extends from 76th to 77th st, 200x340; also,
12th av, northerly cor 76th st, 100x120, New Utrecht.
Holk D. Campbell to Horace E. Bailey. 8,750

12th av, n w s, 50.2 s w 44th st, 50x100, New Utrecht. West Brooklyn Land and Improvement Co. to William F. Spencer. 1,100

13th av, s w cor 65th st, 60x90.9x64x68.6, Bath Junction. James V. S. Woolley to Frederikka C. Rasmussen. 600

15th av, s w cor Bay Ridge av, 80x90, New Utrecht. James V. S. Woolley to Montague S. Child. 1,325

18th av, 20th av, bet 74th and 76th sts, New Utrecht. Agreement as to releases of mortgages. Aletta Suydam, William L. Dowling and William S. Anderson with Frederick B. Bard. nom

Brooklyn and Jamaica pike, n e cor Barbey st, 50x113.1x50x112.10. Kate Foster widow, Hoboken, N. J., to Caroline O. wife of John B. Sabine. ½ part. Sub. to ½ of mort. $700. 750

Receipt of legacy and release. Catharine Scheidt to Peter Scheidt 1,650

Road or highway, s s, bet lands of Johannes Vanderveer and Jacob Snediker and extending to Fresh Kill or Creek, with all title in New Lots road and creek, but except land taken for New York & Manhattan Beach R. R., 26th Ward. Ulpian and Adrian Van Sinderen to A. Judson Palmer. 24,150

Shore road, e s, 72.6 s 79th st, 69.8x144.10x60x109.2, New Utrecht. Simon Stiner to Jaques Van Brunt. exch

Shore road, s e cor 79th st, 72.6x109.6x—, New Utrecht. James A. Townsend to Jaques Van Brunt. exch

Lots 375–382 Worth and Strawson property, Flatbush. Jacob Worth and Vincent A. Strawson to Frederick V. Gillam. 1,040

Lots 352, 353 and 375–382 inclusive Worth and Strawson property, Flatbush. Release mort. Mary and Cath. Vanderveer and Eliza A. Martense to Jacob Worth and Vincent A. Strawson. 750

Lots 34 to 36, Worth and Strawson map, Flatbush Jacob Worth and Vincent A. Strawson to Owen Lynam. 885

Lots 352 and 353 map 430 lots, property of Worth and Strawson, Flatbush. Jacob Worth and Vincent A. Strawson to B. Sydney Law. 800

Lots 64–68 block 4 map Jacob Snedeker property, 26th Ward. Release mort. John M. Stearn to Catharine Molloy. 350

Same property. Catherine Molloy to Rebecca F. Forman. 375

Interior lot, 50 n e Evergreen av and 100 n w Cornelia st, runs southeast 88.6 to Old Bushwick road now closed, x northwest along old road to point 100 n w from Cornelia st, x northeast — to beginning. John Menahan to Adrian M. Suydam. exch. and 240

Interior lot at centre line between Pulaski st and De Kalb av, at point 293.9 e Nostrand av, runs east 31.3 x south 24.4 x northwest 33.10 x north 11.9. Elizabeth Eagleston, Staten Island, to Thomas Orr. 175

Interior lot, 100 e Thatford av and 150 s Glenmore av, runs south 75 x east 53.11 x north 75 x west 54.1½. Andrew R. Culver to Simon Green. 400

Interior plot, 196 n Tillary st and 221.6 e Jay st, runs north 52.4 x east 155 x south 55.5 to Lawrence pl, x west 155, with use of alley. John J. Hennessy to James Burrell. nom

Brooklyn and Jamaica plank road, s w cor Elton st, 80.4x100.2x75x129.2. Release mort. Williamsburgh Savings Bank to Edward F. Linton. 1,050

Parcel of 14 acres, 42d, 43d and 44th sts, partly in Brooklyn and partly in New Utrecht, adj Van Duyne et al.
8th av, east cor 44th st, 180.2x170x— to st, x 116.
6th av, n w cor 43d st, lots 33 to 46 block 13 Delaplaine property.
Tertullus G. Matthews to Stewart McDougall. ½ part. *Mt.* ½ of $11,000. nom

Acceptance of provision in will of Chas. D. Oatman and release dower. Emma S. Oatman to Emma S. Oatman, Edwin W. and Robert E Bullinger exrs., &c.

Strip along e s of Brooklyn & Rockaway Beach R. R. in Flatlands, contains 24,165 sq. feet. Helen W. Schenck to The Brooklyn & Rockaway Beach R. R. ½ part. 808

Strip along same road, 20x201.10, reserving right of way. Richard L. Baisley to same. nom

Strip along same, 15 feet wide. Same to same. nom

Strip along same, 15 feet wide, x1,611. Charles Jantzen to same 200

Strip on e s of said road, 15x1,611. Lawrence V. De Foreest to same 435

Similar strip, 15x1,611. Release dower. Julia M. Schenck to same. 127

Same strip. Lawrence V., Jr., and Lillie P. De Foreest by Union Trust Co. guard. to same. Infant's share. 367

WESTCHESTER COUNTY.

JULY 8 TO 14—INCLUSIVE.

BEDFORD.

Hoyt, Armenia et al. to Nellie McBeth, 112 acres on Cross River, adj John Jay. $5,000

Palmer, Bryant S. to Ida J. Westcott, part lots, 28x29, w s Palmer av, map property grantor. 350

Same to same, lot 30 and part 29, adj above. 250

Richards, Lewis B. to Samuel F. Howland, e s North Castle road, adj Jas W. Raymond, 114 acres. 8,000

CORTLANDT.

Depew, Martha M. exr. of et al. to Mary A. Tate, w s Fremont st, 150 s Elm, 50x160. 600

Same to Mary J. Sherwood, w s same st, 100 s Elm, 50x160. 600

Finch, Winifred K. to Bridget Gallery, n s Brown st, 171 e James, 45x100. 2,500

Larkin, Francis to Edw. White, s e s New Post road, adj Friends Meeting House. 2,000

Rose, Phebe A. to Alfred Reynolds, lot 2, map property Cath Reynolds, Montrose. 250

EASTCHESTER.

Roe, John, assignee of, to Ernest Simons, part lot 361 e s 5th av, Mt. Vernon, 25x105. 500

Crary, Chas., exr. of, to Henry Deike, n s Willow pl, 130 e Rich av, 61x110. 7,000

Cudlipp, Edw. F. to Thomas H. Mulch, n w cor Broad st and Westchester av, 140x143. 1,500

Darling, Alfred B. et al. to Mary G. Turner, w s Cottage av, 100 n Prospect. 1,550

Same to same, n s Prospect av, 175 w Cottage, 25x100, and also e s Park av, 300 s Sidney. 6,450

Doolittle, Mary C. to Wm. P. Montague, lot 302 e s 4th av, Mt. Vernon, 100x105. 2,700

Dodge, Henry C. to Edw. L. E. Phipps, w s Marion st, 241 n Kossuth av, 29.8x—. 500

Henneberger, Herman to Chas. F. Putney, lot 56 w s 10th av, grantors map. 500

Hebert, Maurice to Martha P. Ford, w s Rich av, 255 n Prospect. 65x125. 3,250

Johnston, Wm. J. to Patrick McMorrow, lot 429 e s 5th av, Central Mt. Vernon, 50x100. nom

Miller, Thos. L. to Ida M. Milligan, lots 41 and 42 w s 10th av, Henneberger map. 900

Mulch, Theo. H. to Fred. Muller, n w cor Broad st and Westchester av, 140x143. 5,500

Noyes, Samuel St. J. to Baldwin F. Strauss, s s Prospect av, 100 w Rich, 50x145.9. 9,300

Powers, Michael to Clifford J. Mathews, lot 68 w s Jefferson st, map Wright property. 400

Philip, Wm. G. to Chas. Reehl and ano., w s 10th av, 337.6 s 3d st, 87.6x105. 1,230

Pierce, Chas. W. to Norah Gage, part lot 468 e s 6th av, Mt. Vernon, 50x105. 2,500

Roberts, Mary E. to Wm. Specht, lots 28 and 29, Vernon Park. 875

Same to John Eosinger, lots 30 and 31 same map. 875

Simons, Ernest to The Washburne Machine Co., part lot 361 e s 5th av, Mt. Vernon, 25x105. 500

Staab, Christina K. to Gert. H. Staab, lot 3, Dusenberry map. 50x100. 250

Slawter, Howard D. to Henry D. Hubbell, lot 10 Chester Hill, Forster map. 750

Smith, Isaac E. to Dennis W. Griffin, G 13, s w White Plains road, Wakefield. 700

Tiers Jennie L. to Chas. A. Tier, s s Prospect av, 133.4 e Park, 41.8x—. nom

Same to Hannie L. Van Demark, lot 16 n s Valentine st, Central Mt. Vernon, 50x100. 6,500

Ven Demark, Hannie L. to Jennie L. Tier, n e cor Stevens av and White Plains road, 114x79x88.8x97.6. 11,000

GREENBURGH.

Erhardt, Joel B. trustee to Henry Eibel, s s Station Square, 50 w Western av, 50x100. 700

Gillender, Aug. T. to Ezekiel Fixman, 170 acres on Tarrytown road. 35,000

Fixman, Ezekiel to Aug. F. Gillender et al, same property. 35,000

Hatch, Warren D. exr. of, to Garrett R. Hasbrouck, e s Broadway, adj Steph. Archer, ¼ acre. 1,200

Leviness, Solomon W. to Hadley A. Clark, plot on road from Scarsdale depot to Greenville, 1 acre. 1,900

Slocum, Wm. E. to Patrick E. Haley, lot at Ardsley adj D. O. Bradley. 1,300

HARRISON.

Allen, Eleanor T. to Wm. Young, n w cor Harrison av and Davenport st, 100x150 1,900

MAMARONECK.

Hoffman, Arthur T. to Jos. Hoffman, n w s Manik av adj Alex. Taylor, Jr., 165x314. 400

MOUNT PLEASANT.

Smadbeck, Louis to Genie Chapman, lot 893, Sherman Park. 150

Same to J. H. Borman, lots 483 and 673. 300

Same to Richard Burge, lot 1208. 150

Same to Lena Martin, lots 1174 and 5. 300

Same to Mathew J. Coggey, lot 528. 100

NEW CASTLE.

Quinby, Wm. H. to Jennie Hunter, lot 1, cor Sing Sing road and Croton av, map Merritt farm. 2,900

Quinby, Willett J. to same, lots 115, 116 and 117 e s Croton av, same map. 600

Hunter, Annie C. to Henry R. Pratt, w s road from Chappaqua to Levi Hunts, 100x—. 300

NEW ROCHELLE.

Bradley, And. R. to John F. Coffin, n s Morris st, 532 w North st, 50x150. nom

Coffin, John F. to Mary A. Dingwall, part same lot, 20x150. 500

Noxon, Olive M. to same, n s Morris st, adj above, 50x150. 3,500

Disbrow, Susan W. exr. of, to Fred O. Simpson, lot 21, map plot 1, Huguenot Park. 350

Hudson, Alex. B. to John H. Monroe, s e s Birch st, 150 n e Boston road, 50x150. 1,400

Iselin, Adrian, Jr., to Leonard H. Goldsmith, lot 14 e s Neptune av, Neptune Park, 65x135. 1,500

Same to Edwin C. Smith, lot 60 w s same av, 75x150. 2,700

Levison, Solomon to Frank Levison, w s av, 300 s Union av, 30x100. 375

Miller, Mary E. to Wm. L. Sanders, n w cor Centre av and Bancker pl, 50x150. 2,600

Sanders, Wm. L. to Fred. E. St. John, part lot 154 n s Linden pl, Residence Park, 25x155. 800

OSSINING.

Carpenter, Arthine A. to Thos. Mapelsden exr. of, n w cor Ellis pl and Churchill st, 36x107. 3,800

Lobb, Marcius L. exr. of, to Francis Larkin, n s Lincoln pl, cor Underhill lane. 14,500
Hitchcock, Eugene S. to Chas. Lewis, n e cor Spring and William sts, 50.10x123. 8,000
Thompson, Mary E. to Jas A. Volker, n w cor Highland and Everett avs, 50x148. 1,800

PELHAM.

Horton, Margt. A. to Pierre J. L. De Rache, s s Washington av, adj the Bay, abt 27.8x100. 2,980
King, Eliz'h R. B. exrs of, to John H. Ripley, lots 536-539 e s King av. 3,700
Same to Henry Bischoff, lots 406-409 e s Minneford av. 4,300

RYE.

Brooks, John to Henry L. Phillips, s w cor Davis and Manursing av, abt 112x112. 300
Same to Edwin V. Osborne, s w cor Goldwin and Meadow sts, abt 144x244; also n w cor same, abt 144x142. 800
Same to Patrick Kelly, lots 9 and 10 w s Davis av, map Hayward. 470
Same to John A Gwynne, lot 18 e s Centre st, same map. 51
Cosgrove, Marg't to Chas. W. Landen, n e cor Main and Bond sts, abt 126x315. 950
Damon, Carrie M. et al., M. Dillon ref., to Wm. J. Tingue, e s Centre st, 762 s Westchester av, 100.5x —. 1,735
Same to Francis M. Osborne, e s Centre st, 151 s Westchester av, 104x100. 890
Same to Richard T. McCarty, e s Centre st, 651 s Westchester av, 100x195; also 351 s same, 50x198. 2,360
Foskey, Robt. to Margt. Foskey, n w cor Willett av and Grove st, 50x125; also w s Willett av, 100 n Cleveland st, 100x125. 2,000
Peck, Edw. H. to Elliott Smith, lot 21 n s Alto av, map Grace Church st lots, 50x140. 750
Same to Ella J. Wishart, lot 20 adj, 50x138. 750
Sherwood, Gardiner W. to Chris. Walker, lot 27 n s William st, map Auser property, abt 96x100. 500
Taylor, Maria L. and ano. Jas. H. Moran ref. to Valeria P. Taylor, s s Purdy av, adj Byram River, 210x218. 5,000
Wells, Marianna P. to Aug. Y. Van Amringe, lots 29-33 w s Union av, Rye Neck. 3,745

SCARSDALE.

Palmer, Esther D. to Sarah A. Willetts, n s New Rochelle road, adj Daniel Dusenberry, 35 acres. 5,000

WESTCHESTER.

Arnow, Thos. C. to Michael Stenger, lot 473 e s Washington st, Unionport, ½ acre. 1,200
Camp, Hugh N. to Bridget Curley, lots 24 and 25 McGraw estate. 725
Clock, G. Dewitt to Emma J. Carter, e s Barker av, 166 n Julianna st, 34x125. 705
Dalbe, Jos. F. to Wm. H. Morse, n e cor 4th st and 14th av, Wakefield, 100x114. 5,000
Dawson, John to Terrance Greene, w s 2d av, 240 s 1st st, Olinville, 25x100. 500
Lamphear, Wm. H. to And. Dey and wife, e s 2d av, 260 n 1st st, Olinville, 40x100. 2,500
Lyon, Dore to Cecelia B. Cross, e s Glebe av, 286 n Westchester av, 25x80. 600
Mahon, Jas. to Cath. Walls, lot 175 map McGraw estate. 415
Mealy, Marg't A. et al. to Levi H. Mace, lot 1083 s s 14th av, Wakefield. 800
Mussing, Louis et al. to Christian Kastner, s s 10th st, 300 w Av B, Unionport, 100x216. 2,100
Newcomb, Herbert M. to Alfred Haines et al., n w cor 2d av and 5th st, Wakefield, 105x114. 1,200
Ovens, John to Christian A. Schmidt, n w cor Bronx and Pelham Parkway and Boston road. 1,500
Same to John Klockemeyer, s w cor Thwaites pl and Boston road, 25x107. 600
Schuh, Eliz'h to Fred C. Fischer, lots 1-6 St. Pauls av, map property grantor. 1,700

WHITE PLAINS.

Albro, Wm. H. to John Philips, e s Grove st, adj grantee, 50x95. 500
Mangles, Henry to Maria O. Hubbell, 13 acres road to Mt. Pleasant, adj Wm. Fisher. 4,150
Oezine, John to Walter E. Sniffin, lot e s Horton av, 50x100. 800
Sutton, Chas. D. to Geo. W. Campbell, n s Clinton st, 60 e Stewart pl, 58x—. 3,750

YONKERS.

Armour Villa Park Assoc. to Henry M. Clarke, lots 70 and 71. nom
Same to Herman E. Van Horne, lots 13-16 and 24. nom
Beall, T. Ashby to Frank S. Palmer, lots 311-318 and 400-402, Armour Villa Park. nom
Cohn, Samuel to Marcus Nathan, lots 127 and 128, Sherwood Park. 1,000
Same to same, lot 2, Sherwood Hill. 500
Druid Hill Park Co. to Walter L. Cree, lot 372, Mohegan Park. 180
Same to Giles N. Cree, lot 373. 180
Same to Wm. Noble, lot 383. 185
Same to Henry A. Koelsch, lots 560, 561, 562, 563, 378 and 379. 1,210
Gramatan Park Co. to Wm. Bloodgood, lots 117-121, Mohegan Park. 1,075
Jones, Cyrus P. and ano. to Noe Trahan, lots 3-6 block G map property grantor. 1,000
Same to Wm. Hodgkins, lot 9 block E. 250
Kingsbury, Jos. A. and ano. to Fred. B. Mee and ano., No. 143 w s Orchard st, 25x125. nom
Lawrence, Fannie E. to Margt. J. Alexander, part lot 255 map Hyatt farm. 500
Lowerre, Fannie M. to Amos P. Dunn, lots 31 and 32 block map property Lowerre Station. 5,000
Miller, Eliz'h. to Jas. Pease, n s Ware av, 320 w Kimball, 50x125. 600
Powers, Michael to Cyrus Cleveland, exr. of, e s Alder st, 70 s Elm, 25x100. 1,529
Reardon, Michael to Maggie Reardon, lot 50 ft. e of a point 225 s Ash st, abt 37.6x95. 700
Same to Anna T. Reardon, lot adj, 37.6x90. 500
Shonnard, Fred. to Mary Kay, lots 699 and 703 Nepperhan av, city map. 470
Sullivan, Peter J. to Margaret Buckley, w s Midland av, 150 s Summerfield st, 50x100. 700
Valentine, Nath. B. to Clara M. Valentine, w s Palisade av, 70 s Garden st, 90.4x100. —

MORTGAGES.

NOTE.—*The arrangement of this list is as follows. The first name is that of the mortgagor, the next that of the mortgagee. The description of the property then follows, then the date of the mortgage, the time for which it was given, and the amount. The general dates used as headings are the dates when the mortgage was handed into the Register's office to be recorded.*

Whenever the letters "P. M." occur, preceded by the name of a street, in these lists of mortgages, they mean that it is a Purchase Money Mortgage, and for fuller particulars see the list of transfers under the corresponding date. Whenever the rate is not given, read as 6 per cent.

NEW YORK CITY.

JULY 10, 11, 13, 14, 15, 16.

Allen, Elmer A. to Gustav H. Schwab and ano. exrs. Gustav Schwab. Edenwood av, s e cor Primrose st, 300x200 to Davidson av. July 13, 3 years or sooner, 5 %. gold, $5,500
Same to same. Edenwood av, n e cor Primrose st, 580.8 to Kingsbridge road, x — to Davidson av, x 566.3 to st, x 200. July 13, 3 years or sooner, 5 %. gold, 11,000
Same to same. Davidson av, n e cor Primrose st, runs north 483.10 x south in two courses 505.6 to st, x west 143 7; Davidson av, s e cor Primrose st, runs south 376.7 x northeast 418.7 to st, x west 144.7. July 13, 3 years or sooner, 5 %. gold, 6,000
Altman, Bertha to John D. Mennie. 118th st. P. M. July 15, 3 years or sooner. 3,000
Anderson, Walden P. to Frances E. Holt. 93d st, s s, 325 e Amsterdam av, 19.10x100.8. July 15, 3 years, 5 %. gold, 22,000
Same to Charles G. Judson. Same property. Sub. to last mort. July 15, demand. 1,500
Same to The Bradley & Currier Co. (Lim.) Same property. Sub. to morts. $23,500. June 15, 3 months. 2,000
Alt, Adam to Sophie F. Gobel. Sheriff st, e s, 81.9 n Rivington st, 18.3x75. July 16, 3 months, 5 %. 950
Backer, Jacob and Louisa mortgagors with Marks Levin mortgagee. Agreement increasing rate of interest. July 14. nom
Bach, Lewis Z. to Margaretta H. Ward. 108d st, s s, 102.6 w 3d av, 4 lots. 4 P. M. morts., each $4,000. July 13, 1 year, 5 %. 16,000
Boyce, Charles to THE EMIGRANT INDUST. SAVINGS BANK. Southern Boulevard, No. 577, n e cor Alexander av, 24x80. July 15, 1 year, 4½ %. 10,000
Barron, Esther E. to Theodore Westing. 63d st, n s, 300 w Central Park West, 37.6x100.5; July 10, 1 year or sooner. 1,000
Bach, Alice H. wife of and Albert to Rosina Feuchtwanger. 76th st, n s, 398 w 9th av, 17x102.2. May 26, due Sept. 14, 1891. 2,500
Bannen, John to Emilie J. Murray. 120th st, n s, 110 w 2d av, 75x100.11. June 30, 1 year or sooner 10,000
Beall, John A. to Frank L. O'Neil. 97th st, n s, 281 w Central Park West, 19x100.3. Sub. to mort. $12,500. July 1, 1 year. 1,900
Bergen, John H. to Harry Overington. Lot 5 map of 155 building lots of Charles A. Stádler, 23d Ward. July 9; 1 year. 400
Boskowitz, Lena B. wife of George W. to John W. Decker. Union av, w s, 179.9 n Cedar st, runs west 169.1 x south 20.6 x east 64.9 x southeast 14.7 x east 90 to av, x north 25.6. July 10, due Dec. 1, 1896, 5 %. 3,250
Same to same. Same property. July 10, installs. 2,750
Bouhan, Jane E. to Edward M. Cameron and ano. trustees A. M. Cameron dec'd. 19th st, s s, 162.7 e 2d av, 20.11x92. July 10, due July 1, 1894, 5 %. gold, 7,600
Same to Edward M. Cameron trustee Marie L. Cameron dec'd. Same property. Equal lien with last mort. July 10, due July 1, 1894, 5 %. gold, 3,400
Buttlar, Robert A. K. to THE NEW YORK SAVINGS BANK. Hudson st, n w cor Jane st, 25x52.10x31.6x50. July 10, due June 1, 1894, 4½ %. 10,000
Behrens, Emma wife of and Frederick to Randolph Guggenheimer. 66th st. P. M. July 1, installs, 5 %. 3,000
Bennett, John C. to Isabell Merritt. Travers st. P. M. July 13, 3 years, 5 %. 500
Bleier, Louis to Marianne Moses. 5th st. P. M. July 15, 5 years, 5 %. 8,000
Blum, Morris to THE NEW YORK SAVINGS BANK. 1st av, e s, 76.6 n 75th st, 25.7x88. July 14, due June 1, 1894, 4½ %. 12,000
Bock, John W. to Emilie Trepp. 3d av, No. 294. Store lease. July 14, demand. 3,500
Bculger, Sarah T. widow to Esdor Jacobson. 60th st, n s, 200 w 10th av, 25x100.5. July 14, installs. 1,400
Baker, Mary F. to THE EMIGRANT INDUST. SAVINGS BANK. 3d av, No 1412-1416, w s, 22 n 80th st, 3 lots, each 19.6x70. 3 morts., each $10,000. July 15, 1 year, 4½ %. 30,000
Brady, John to Ann O'Reilly. N. Y. & Harlem R. R., s w cor 170th st, 24.5x100 to Brook av. July 3, 3 years or sooner, 5 %. 1,200
Cadwell, Laura A. wife of and Warren W. to Alfred J. Taylor and William D. Peck. Hampden st, s s, adj Helen L. Willis. P. M. July 14, due Aug. 1, 1894. gold, 4,300
Same to same. Hampden st, s s, 100 w Andrews av. P. M. July 14, due Aug. 1, 1894. gold, 3,500
Cain, Joseph H. to Henry Morgenthau. 182d st. P. M. June 11, due June 15, 1894, 5 %. 1,540
Campbell, Andrew J. to John E. Browning. 83d st. P. M. July 2, due July 14, 1892, or sooner, 5 %. 8,000
Chesebrough, Robert A. to John T. Lord trustee. Southern Boulevard, s s, 383.10 e 149th st, runs east 389.5 x south 471.5 to centre line of Leggett's lane, x— to lands of Harlem River branch of N. Y., N. H. & H. R. R. Co., x west 363.5 x north 864.8, with all title to strip marked "proposed railroad" on diagram in deed. July 13, 2 years, 5 %. 25,000
Cohen, Philip and Yetta his wife to Kaufman Marks, Brooklyn. Broome st. P. M. July 14, installs. 2,250
Cone, Joesephine M. widow, Larchmont, N. Y., to THE SEAMEN'S BANK FOR SAVINGS. 39th st, s s, 489.7 e 8th av, 20.7x98.9. July 14, 3 years, 4½ %. 11,000
Connolly, Henry J. to Thomas P. Dunne. 116th st, No, 364, s s, 125 w Manhattan av, 25x100.11. July 11, 1 year or sooner 2,500
Clark, Serena B. wife of Orlando R. to Eden Bryant. Union av, e s, 330 s 165th st, 60x175. July 15, 1 year. 1,000
Corporation of the Memorial Baptist Church of Christ in New York to THE UNITED STATES TRUST Co. of New York. Washington sq or 4th st, s w cor Thompson st, 65.5x100.2x62.10x100.2. July 16, due July 1, 1898, 5 %. 50,000
Cohen, George J. to Esther W. Byers et al. trustees John Byers dec'd. 80th st, s s, 250 e Amsterdam av, 20x102.2. July 8, 3 years, 5 %. 24,000
Carew, Charles J. and William Drought to Jane Besthoff. 21st st. P. M. July 16, due May 1, 1892, or sooner, 5 %. 20,000
Cambeis, Natalie to Charles Furcht. Robbins av, east cor Westchester av, 100x218x76x168 to Westchester av, x 54.5. July 1, 2 years or sooner. 1,200
Campbell, Robert F. to Alexander Maitland and ano. trustees for Eliza L. Dwight. Madison st, No. 214, s s, 26.1x100. July 10, 5 years, 5 %. 26,000
Same to Joseph L. Buttenwieser. Same property. July 10, demand. 13,337
Connick, Andrew J. to The Farmer's Loan and Trust Co. 73d st, s s, 121 w Columbus av, 18x102.2. July 10, 3 years, 5 %. 18,000
Cooper, William S. to Thomas C. T. Crain, as Chamberlain of the City of New York. 28th st, s s, 150.6 e 7th av, runs south 73.5 x east 1.9 x south 24.6 x east 24.9 x north 24.6 x west 3.10 x north 73.5 to st, x west 22.7. May 26, 2 years, 4½ %. 13,800
Same to William Rankin. Same property. Sub. to last mort. July 10, due Feb. 17, 1892. 2,500
Cordes, Henry to John A. Lewis et al. trustees for Cornelia L. Fowler. 2d av, n e cor 88th st, 25.8x100. July 10, 3 years, 5 %. 20,000
Same to Cordt Gerken, Brooklyn. Same property. Sub. to last mort. July 10, 2 years. 11,450
Crawford, John J. to Joseph L. Buttenwieser. 4th st, No. 226, w s, 52.11 s w 10th st, 26.5x101. July 10, demand. 3,500
Crocheron, Emma J. to Edgar S. Appleby. Webster av. P. M. July 13, 3 years. 700
Crockett, Arthur W. to Metropolitan Co-operative Building and Loan Association. 35th st, s s, 166.10 w 2d av, 16.4x98.9. July 1, installs, 5 %. 2,000
Delabarre, Elizabeth M. to C. Talbot Belt. 22d st, s s, 257 e 6th av, 23x98 9. Feb. 19, 1 year or sooner. 15,000
Dennerlein, John to HARLEM SAVINGS BANK. Washington av, s w cor 185th st, 100.5x95.6x100x87.6. July 15, 1 year, 5 %. 3,000
Dow, Myron W. to Joseph O. Brown. Elton av and 161st st. P. M. July 1, due July 10, 1892, 5 %. 2,000
Duffy, James to George J. Bernhard. 102d st, s s, 100 e 3d av, 35x100.11. July 15, due Aug. 17, 1891. 1,000
Day, Anna M. wife of and Charles H. to Mary A. Berry, Rye, N. Y.. Edenwood av, centre line, 375.6 n of Fordham Landing or High Bridge road, 50x132.3 to Croton Aqueduct. July 3, 3 years 5,000
Same to the Campbell Sash, Door, and Moulding Co. (Lim). Same property. July 9, 1 year. 187
Des Brisay, Jennie F. to Joseph W. Teets. Palisade av. P. M. June 25, installs., 5 %. 6,000
Devine, Thomas F. to John E. and Christian F. Glimm exrs. Christian Glimm. 11th av, e s, 100.5 s 65th st, 25.1x100. July 10, 3 years, 5 %. 9,000
Donovan, Cornelius J. to Joseph H. Godwin. Vermilyea av and Academy st. P. M. July 8, due July 9, 1896, or installs., 5 %. 6,300
Dreyfus, Julius to Joseph L. Buttenwieser. West 3d st. P. M. July 11, demand. 11,000
Same to Marcus and Jacob S. Rosen and Rachel L. Epstein. Same property. P. M. July 11, due Nov. 1, 1892, or sooner, 5 %. 2,000

Dugro, P. Henry and Frederick Wagner to THE MUTUAL LIFE INS. CO., New York. 5th av, s e cor 59th st, runs east 150 x south 100.5 x west 50 x north 25 x west 100 to av, x north 75.5. July 13, 1 year. 425,000

Doyle, Andrew T. to Francis H. Weeks. Amsterdam av, s w cor 96th st, 100.8x171.9x100.9 x175.6. July 16, due Feb. 1, 1892. 5,000

Same to Thomas Stokes and ano. trustees Elizabeth C. Stokes. Amsterdam av, w s, 75.8 s 96th st. P. M. July 16, 3 years, 5 %. 20,000

Dailey, Frank C., Chicago, Ill., to Morris R. Thompson. West st, Nos. 403 and 404, s e cor Charles st, 44.9x70x43.1x81.11. ¼ part. July 15, 2 years or sooner, 5 %. 2,500

Delabarre, Elizabeth M. wife of Walter E. to Edward Delabarre, Conway, Mass. 22d st, s s, 257 e 6th av, 23x98.9. Sub. to all liens. July 13, 3 years. 13,000

Diefenthaler, Henry to Adele Lyra et al. exrs Carl Lyra. 6th st, s s, 150 e 1st av, 25x97 6th st, s s, 175 e 1st av, 25x97. Lease. July 16, due July 1, 1894, 5 %. 4,000

Endlich, Sophia to Paulina Breivogel. 83d st. P. M. July 15, 5 years, 5 %. 1,250

Eidman, Mary to John Brummer. 26th st. P. M. July 16, 1 year. 2,500

Eckert, Thomas T. to Mary E. Hanley. 58th st. P. M. July 15, 5 years or sooner, 5 %. 15,000

Fischer, George and Valentine to THE SEAMEN'S BANK FOR SAVINGS in the City of New York. Forsyth st, w s, 117 s Houston st, 26x68.10. July 13, 1 year, 4½ %. 5,000

Friederichs, Ernest H. to Mary H. Mahan. 2d av, No. 182, e s, 82.7 s 12th st, 20.8x100. July 10, 1 year, 5 %. 5,000

Farley, Patrick to Henry and Annie R. Spratley guard. of Girard A. Whitney. 76th st, s s, 125.1 w Columbus av, 20x102.2. July 15, 3 years, 5 %. 25,000

Same to Annie R. wife of Henry Spratley. 76th st, s s, 145.1 w Columbus av, 20x102.2. July 15, 3 years, 5 %. 25,000

Same to Henry Spratley. 76th st, s s, 165.1 w Columbus av, 20x102.2. July 15, 3 years, 5 %. 25,000

Same to same. 76th st, s s, 185.1 w Columbus av, 20x102.2. July 15, 3 years, 5 %. 25,000

Same to Horace P. Witney, Yonkers, N. Y. 76th st, s s, 205.1 w Columbus av, 20x102.2. July 15, 3 years, 5 %. 25,000

Frank, Hattie to Charles F. E. Vogler. 103d st, No. 103 W. P. M. July 15, 5 years or installs, 5 %. 21,000

Same to same. Same property. P. M. July 15, 3 years or installs. 2,500

Same to same. 103d st, No. 105 W. P. M. July 15, 5 years or installs, 5 %. 21,000

Same to same. Same property. P. M. July 15, 3 years or installs, 5 %. 2,500

Fitzharris, John F. to THE EMIGRANT INDUST. SAVINGS BANK. Christopher st, n s, 89.3 e Washington st, runs east 80.1 x north 95 x west 54.1 x south 7.10 x northwest 88.1 to Washington st, x southwest 30 x southeast 69.7 x south 64.11. July 16, 1 year, 4½ %. 60,000

Same to Margaretha Dumpel. Same property. Sub. to last mort. July 16, 3 years, 5 %. 3,500

Fuller, Henry S. to Frederick W. Devoe. Edenwood av, w s, 187.8 n St. James st, 50x106, to Croton Aqueduct. July 16, 2 years, 5 %. 3,000

Fisher, Joseph to Henry Zeltner. 3d av, No. 3309. Store lease. Collateral. July 14. 1,035

Friedman, Kevy to Robert F. Campbell. Madison st. P. M. July 10, installs. 11,000

Same to same. Same property. P. M. Collateral to another mort. July 10, demand 2,750

Gibney, Thomas to James Flanagan. 9th av, No. 230, n e cor 24th st, 24.8x100. July 1, installs, 5 %. gold, 50,00

Gallup, Albert to Randolph Hurry trustee. 12th st, No. 5 E., n s, 25x114x26x107. July 1, 1 year. 2,000

Goldfarb, Samuel to Sarah Lese. Monroe st, No. 69, n s, 25x100. July 15, due Feb. 19, 1894. 2,500

Gebhard, Saffarus D. to Jacob Rubenstein and Flora Pohalski. Madison st. P. M. July 11, installs 3,850

Grasse, Louis to Hugh Sieberg. Morris st, s s, 375 e Madison av, runs south 125 x east 50 x north 121.8 to st, x west 10.6 x west 40. June 30, 5 years, 5 %. 3,000

Gutwillig, Alois to THE MUTUAL LIFE INS. CO. of New York. 90th st. P. M. July 14, due July 15, 1894. 40,000

Gallagher, Joseph F. to Louis Roller individ. and as trustee for creditors. 72d st, s s, 213 e 1st av, 50x102.2. Sub. to morts $36,000. July 11, due July 10, 1892. 7,826

Gallo, Angelo and Rosa his wife to Wilber A. Bloodgood and ano. trustees for William B. Trowbridge. King st, s s, 213 w Macdougal st, 21x75. July 10, 3 years, 5 %. 2,500

Gaus, Carrie mortgagor with Miriam J. Andrews mortgagee. Extension of mort. July 9. nom

Gilmore, William J. to Ethelbert Wilson. 134th st, n s, 200 e 7th av, 50x99.11. July 11, demand. 10,000

Gloeckner, John and Rosana his wife to Herman W. Hildebrand. Johnson av, n w s, part lot 122 map of East Tremont, West Farms, 25x100. July 1, 3 years or sooner, 5 %. 500

Goss, Charles C. to THE MANHATTAN SAVINGS INST. Varick st, w s, 42.6 n Watts st, 21.3x 65.6, with use of alley adj. July 3, 1 year, 5 %. 5,000

Graff, Maria L. formerly Schellenberg wife of and Jacob to THE RIVERHEAD SAVINGS BANK. 26th st, s s, 130 e 9th av., 20x98.9. July 10, 3 years, 5 %. 5,500

Gutter, Bernhard to Jarvis Mason trustee Stephen G. Fotterall. Park row. P. M. July 10, 3 years, 5 %. 21,000

Haan, Hermine to Henry Morgenthau. 180th st. P. M. June 10, due June 15, 1894, 5 %. 1,785

Hagan, Susanna V. to GERMAN-AMERICAN REAL ESTATE TITLE GUARANTEE CO. Amsterdam av, s w cor 79th st, 102.2x100. July 10, 4 months. 50,000

Same to Julius Lipman and William Cohen. Same property Building loan. July 10, due May 1, 1892. 60,011

Hagan, Susanna V. to Julius Lipman and William Cohen. Amsterdam av, s w cor 79th st, 102.2x100. Building loan. July 10, due May 1, 1892. 71,321

Helbig, Henriette formerly Burguiere to Louis Muller. 156th st, s s, 325 w Courtlandt av, 25x100. July 8, due July 1, 1894, 5 %. 600

Helmcke, Margaretha to Jacob Gronbach. 82d st, s s, 138 w Av B, 13.4x102.2. July 1, installs., 5 %. 3,500

Herbert, John J. to Mary E. Campbell. 31st st. P. M. July 6, due July 1, 1896, 5 %. 17,500

Higgins, Edward E., Cleveland, O., to Mary A. Brugman. Southern Boulevard, w s, 50 n 144th st, 50x100. June 9, 2 years or installs, 5 %. 2,500

Hogan, Lawrence F. and James H. Dempsey to George Ehret. 2d av, No. 1597, s w cor 83d st. Store lease. July 2, demand. 1,750

Holahen, Mary A. to Mary McGill. 163d st, s s, 465 e Courtlandt av, 25x100. July 8, due Feb. 18, 1894. 500

Hutton, John W. to Richard Wallack. 98th st, n s, 268.6 e Amsterdam av, runs north 33x northwest 15 x north 75.7 x east 42 x south 73.6 x southwest 15 x southwest 33 to st, x west 27. Sub to morts. $169,548. June 7, due Dec., 1891. 4 000

Hall, James T. to Walther Luttgen, Linden, N. J. 75th st, n s, 112 e Columbus av, 88x 102.2. July 15, 1 year. 25,000

Henne, William and Fanny his wife to Anton Kuster. Lewis st. P. M. July 15, 5 years, 5 %. 8,000

Same to Rosa Weiler. 3d st, Nos. 364 and 366, s s, 55.5 w Lewis st, 55.4x59x50.2x58.4. July 14, due July 1, 1894, 5 %. 2,000

Herter, Peter to John J. Jones and ano. trustees David Jones. Rivington st, n w cor Suffolk st, runs west 34 x north 75 x west 44 x north 25 x east 78 to Suffolk st, x south 100. July 14, 6 months, 5 %. 45,000

Hoffman, David L. to Herman Heinemann. 28th st, s s, 222 e 3d av. 22x98.8. July 14, 3 years. 5,000

Buck, William to James J. Fitzpatrick. 164th st, n s, 272.10 w Washington av, 20x100. Feb. 3, 1891, due Feb 4, 1893 657

Hummel, Berthe and Annie Steinhardt to William H. Lane. 56th st, No. 354, s s, 70 e 9th av, 30x100.5. June 23, 1 year. 4,000

Hummel, Berthe and Annie and Benjamin Steinhardt to THE HOMESTEAD BANK. 9th av, e s, 49.4 s 56th st, 25.4x70. July 10, installs, note. 3,500

Same to same. 9th av, e s, 74.8 s 56th st, 25.9x 70. July 10, installs, note. 4,500

Same to same. 56th st, s s, 90.11 e 9th av, 30x 100.5. July 10, installs, note. 7,500

Hunt, Henrietta A. to Nicholas G. Geraty. 1st av, No. 627, s w cor 36th st, 20.10x75. July 15, 1 year, 5 %. 2,000

Hutchins, H. A. to Aaron Raymond. Fort Washington Depot road, s w cor Kingsbridge road. P. M. July 15, 3 years, 5 %. 10,000

Horton, Lotou to George L. Slawson. 77th st, s s, 165 w 10th av, 25x102.2. July 10, 3 years or installs, 5 %. 12,000

Herrmann, Henry to MUTUAL RESERVE FUND LIFE ASSOC. Mott st, w s, 100 s Spring st, 50x100. June 26, due July 1, 1894, or sooner, 5 %. 35,000

Judge, Andrew T. to John W. Haaren. 136th st, s s, 110 w 5th av. 5 lots. 5 P. M. morts. each $4,500. July 15, installs. 22,500

Same to Emeline Johnston. 136th st, s s, 110 w 5th av, 125x99.11. Sub. to mort. $92,500. July 15, 1 month 10,000

Jordan, Thomas D. to THE EQUITABLE LIFE ASSUR. SOC. of U. S. 88th st. P. M. July 16, due January 1, 1893, 4 %. gold, 18,000

Jessup, Henry W., South Orange, N. J., to George E. Hyatt, Brooklyn. 5th av, n w cor Clinton pl, 28.6x100. July 13, 1 month. 35,000

Jones, John J. exr. David Jones mortgagee with Berthe Hummel and Annie Steinhardt present owners. Agreement apportioning mortgage. July 6. nom

Jackson, Lewis D. and Mary E. Murphy to Eliza Worthington. College av, s e cor Cross st, 100x100. July 7, 2 years. 1,000

Kaiser, John A. to August Treutel. 161st st. P. M. July 13, 3 years. 3,000

Keller, Caroline wife of Frederick to Charles E. Strong and John L. Cadwalader as trustees. 9th av and 16th st. P. M. July 11, 3 years, 5 %. 50,000

Kotzum, Anton and Katharine his wife to Albert Steindler. 73d st. P. M. July 1, installs, 5½ %. 5,000

Kunde, William to Henry Ranken, Hoboken, N. J. South st, No. 60, or 120 Wall st. Lease. July 1, notes. 12,600

Karl, Katherina to Ernest H. Herb. 51st st. P. M. July 15, 5 years or installs., 5 %. 19,000

Konig, Charles to Nicolaus Joost. 49th st. P. M. July 15, 5 years or installs, 5 %. 9,000

Kelaher, Ellen L. wife of and Thomas F. to Charles A. Silliman guard. for Harper Silliman. 8d av, lot 24 map of Upper Morrisania, 25x162 to Bathgate av. July 14, 5 years, 5 %. 6,000

Kempner, Samuel to Carsten H. Meyer, Brooklyn. Broome st. P. M. July 15, 1 year, 5 %. 9,000

Kenn, Jane wife of and James to Ann Dowd. Creston av, e s, 318.7 s Donnybrook st, 40x 75.3x40x75.1. July 15, 5 years, 5½ %. 4,000

Kilpatrick, Edward to Harriet Overhiser. West End av, n e cor 97th st, runs east 125 x north 100.11 x west 25 x north 100.11 to 98th st, x west 100 to av, x south 201.10. July 13, 1 year or sooner. 25,000

Kitching, George, Orange, N. J., to THE TITLE GUARANTEE AND TRUST CO. Bond st, No. 43, s s, 25x94.7x—x89.7. July 14, due July 15, 1896, 5 %. 15,000

Same to same. 52d st, No. 345, n s, 130.6 w 1st av, 20x100.5. July 14, due July 15, 1894, 5 %. 6,500

Same to same. 58th st, No. 331, n s, 326.6 e 2d av, 28.6x100.5. July 14, due July 15, 1894, 5 %. 7,000

Krug, Florian to William Mertens. 41st st, n s, 210 e 5th av, 22x98.9. July 8, due Sept. 1, 1891. 15,890

Kaufman, Ignatz to Ignatz Gluck. Pitt st, No. 57, w s, 108.8 n Delancey st, 18.7x63. July 3, 4 years or installs. 2,000

Karansky, Lena wife of Solomon to Karl M. Wallach. Clinton st. P. M. July 15, installs. 8,500

Lissner, Minna to Anthony McReynolds. 120th st, s s, 491 8 w Lenox av, 16.8x81.6. July 6, due Oct. 10, 1891, or sooner. 6,000

Lambe, John to Peter Doelger. Bedford st, No. 22, n e cor Downing st. Store lease. July 11, demand. 4,500

Lazarus, Lassa to Anna M. Braun. 83d st. P. M. July 10, 5 years or sooner, 5 %. 5,000

Levy, Mitchell A. C. to Alfred B. Dunn. Bleecker st, No. 125, n s, 50 w Wooster st. 25x100. July 11, 1 year. 3,000

Loonie, Daniel to Wilhelmina Albert. 48th st, n s, 150 w 1st av, 25x100.5. June 30, due July 2, 1896, 5 %. 5,000

Lowenstein, Albert L. to Bertha Worms. Webster av, e s, 88.10 s 173d st, 29x90. July 2, 1 year. 1,000

Labatat, Mary E. to Mary E McDermott, Brooklyn. West Washington pl, No. 108, s w s, 101 n w 6th av, 21x75, July 13, due Jan. 1, 1894. go'd, 500

Lambert, Alexander to Frederic J. Middlebrook. 58th st, s s, 182 w Lexington av, 19x 100.5; 58th st, s s, 106 3 w Lexington av, 37.4 x100.5. Sub. to morts. $39,000. July 15, 1 year. 6,000

Landesmann, Max to Charles Rosenthal. 5th st. P. M. July 15, 5 years, 5 %. 8,000

Lawrence, Eunice C. wife of and Sarle G to Johanna Doyle. Lots 24, 25 and 26 map of 87 lots at Bedford Park, 24th Ward. Sub. to mort. $4,600. July 14, due Jan. 14, 1894. 400

Levy, Mitchell A. C. to Kaufman Henschel. 16th st, s s, 220.6 e Av A. P. M. July 14 1 year. 2,000

Same to same. 16th st, s s, 245.6 e Av A. P. M. July 14, 1 year. 2,000

Lewis, Edward to Seth M. Milliken. 160th st P. M. July 1, 1 year. 9,360

Martin, Robert P. to Thomas H. Messenger exr. Harry Messenger. West End av, e s, 47 s 74th st, 17.6x54. July 15, 3 years, 5 %. 12,000

McBirney, Joseph L., Chicago, Ill., to Lucinda H. Cornish. 53d st. P. M. Sub. to mort. $22,000. June 30, due July 1, 1894, or sooner, 5 %. 10,000

McCormack, Teresa M. wife of William H to Charles L. and G. Fred Starbuck. Briggs av. P. M. July 15, 3 years or installs., 5 %. 2,250

Mela, Ferdinand H. to "The Baron de Hirsch Fund." Greene st, Nos. 197, 199, 201, w s, 175.1 n Bleecker st, 73.9x100x73.7x100. July 14, due April 14, 1894, 5 %. 165,000

Merrill, Frederick J. H., Albany, N.Y., to TITLE GUARANTEE AND TRUST CO. Sedgwick av, e s, 199.10 n 184th st. 75x136.5x74.4x126.3. July 13, due July 14, 1894, 5 %. 3,000

Metzger, Frank B. to Martha Foggin. Morris av, n e cor Ash st, 46.8x100x45.6x100. July 15, 3 years or sooner. 1,500

Meyer, Abraham E. to Simon Adler and Henry S. Herrman. 101st st. P. M. July 10, installs. 2,250

Mintz, Solomon mortgagee to Solomon Wrubel present owner. Statement that amount due on mortgage made by Solomon Wrubel, dated June 18, 1891, is 800

Mulholland, James to Mary J. wife of Garret A. Wanmaker, Mt. Vernon, N. Y. Washington av, s w cor Jacob st, 100x150. July 13, 3 years. 6,000

Murray, Ann to Mary Smith. Suburban st, s w cor Valentine av, 98x129.6x85x80.6. July 1, 5 years, 4½ %. 3,000

Mulshine, Dennis to THE EMIGRANT INDUST. SAVINGS BANK. 59th st, s s, 100 w 1st av, 25x100.4. July 16, 1 year, 4½ %. 7,000

Mayer, Charles to NEW YORK LIFE INS. CO. 122d st, n s, 221.3 e 1st av, 16.8x100.11. July 10, 3 years, 5 %. 1,500

Mull, De Witt & Gotlieb Fromer to Greenwood Cemetery, Brooklyn. 105th st, s s, 205 w Park av, 25x100.11. July 16, due Aug. 1, 1896, 5 %. 18,000

Same to same. 105th st, s s, 180 w Park av, 25x 100.11. July 16, due Aug. 1, 1896, 5 %. 18,000

Same to Buffalo Door and Sash Co.. 105th st, s s, 180 w Park av, 75x100.11. Sub. to morts. $56,873. July 16, due Sept. 10, 1891. 3,525

Same to John Bell & Son. 105th st, s s, 180 w 4th av, 25x100.11. *Mt.* $18,000. July 16, due Sept. 10, 1891. 873

Maher, William J. to George Ehret. Henry st, No. 174. Store lease. July 3, demand. 1,000

Murphy, Ida M. wife of and Charles C. to THE MANHATTAN SAVINGS INST. 72d st. P. M. Secures bond of mortgagors and Stephen V. White. July 10, 1 year, 4½ %. gold, 10,000

McCauley, Catharine wife of and John to James Flanegan. 10th av, n w cor 28th st, 24.8x100. July 7, 2 years, 5 %. 24,000

McCormack, Francis to Peter Doelger. 10th av, No. 637, n w cor 45th st. Store lease. July 11, demand. 1,500

McGuiness, Edward to George E. Hyatt, Brooklyn. 85th st, s s, 255 e 3d av, 49.10x102.2. July 9, due Jan. 1, 1892. 2,000

McNally, Ellen widow to John C. Arfmann. 85th st, n s, 537.6 w 9th av, 23.3x95.9. July 8, 3 years, 5 %. 3,000

Myer, William H. to Hoffman Miller admr. of Robert C. Townsend. 54th st, s s, 137.6 e 7th av, 18.6x100.5. July 10, due Aug. 1, 1896, 5 %. 15,000

Myers, Sarah J. to Alice E. Worthington. Garden av, n s, lot 85 map of South Belmont, 50x100. July 4, 3 years. 200

Natelsohn, Isaac to Jenny Diamant. Eldridge st. P. M. July 10, due June 3, 1894, or installs. 4,000

Nielsen, Niels P. F. and Emma his wife to John W. Decker. Tinton av. P. M. July 13, installs. 1,800

Nolan, John J. to Frank D. Carley, Tuxedo, N. Y., and Daniel G. Brown, Newburgh, N. Y. Intervale av, w s, 318 10 n Westchester av, 25x100. June 16, 5 years, 5 %. 2,000

Nebrbas, Anna E. widow to Oscar T. Marshall. 79th st. P. M. July 1, 5 years or installs, 5 %. 16,000

Nieland, Regina and Margaretha Stadta to Julius Rauter. 155th st. P. M. July 14, due July 1, 1894. 1,700

Ouderdonk, William M. to Henry Naylor. 74th st, n s, 121.8 e 10th av, 21.3x102.2. March 3, 1890, demand. 6,000

Ockershausen, Lillie V. to Andrew R. Robinson. 113th st, s s, 125 e Grand Boulevard, 25x100.11. June 28, due May 2, 1892. 500

O'Donnell, Mary F. to Andrew Wynn. 175th st. P. M. July 10, 3 years or installs, 5 %. 1,000

O'Halloran, Edward to Ida A. W. Siney. Market st, No. 36, e s, bet Madison and Henry sts indeft., x 86.10x—x86.9. July 13, due Jan. 1, 1892. 1,250

O'Halloran, Edward to Sarah A. Bergen. Market st, No. 36, e s, bet Madison and Henry sts, —x86.10x—x86.9. July 10, due Jan. 1, 1892, or sooner. 7,000

Pacher, Franz A. to John Wilson and ano. trustees David Gibson. Union av. P. M. July 9, due July 6, 1892. 3,000

Pentz, Margaret C. wife of George B. to Rachel P. Shannon. Grand st, n s, 50 e Forsyth st, 25x87.6. 1-6 part. July 9, 1 year, 5 %. 1,000

Peters, George to Andreas Wrede. Elton av. P. M. July 10, 3 years. 1,800

Pollock, Georgianna wife of Edward H., Brooklyn, to Hugh O'Neill. Warren st, No. 45, s s, 25x75. Lease. May 1, note. 7,000

Perceval, Charles to Joseph S. Carreau. Clinton pl. P. M. July 16, due July 1, 1896, 5 %. 15,000

Pendleton, Francis K. to THE TITLE GUARANTEE AND TRUST CO. 35th st, No. 105, n s, 105 e Park av, 18.9x100.5. July 15, 3 years, 5 %. 15,000

Pierce, Madeline to William O. Giles. Eastern Bay, Coster and Hillside avs. P. M. July 2, due July 15, 1892, or sooner, 5 %. 6,500

Rankin, John to THE GERMAN SAVINGS BANK, New York. 18th st, No. 235, n s, 345 e 8th av, 25x92. July 14, due July 15, 1892. 18,000

Rogers, Jane wife of and Abel to THE UNION DIME SAVINGS INST. Independence av, n e cor Warren av, 172.5x200x121.2x—. July 15, due May 1, 1895, 5 %. 6,000

Rohrig, William F. to George E. Hyatt, Brooklyn. 7th av, n w cor 27th st, 34.8x68.8x34.8x68.2. July 14, due Jan. 1, 1892. 36,000

Same to same. 7th av, w s, 34.8 n 27th st, 54x69.4x52.3x68.8. July 14, due Jan. 1, 1892. 55,000

Same to same. 27th st, n s, 68.2 w 7th av, runs north 86.11 x west 25.5 x north 127 x west 50 x south 98.9 to st, x east 75. July 14, due Jan. 1, 1892. 60,000

Roth, Heinrich to August Gauzenmuller. 84th st, No. 504, s s, 123 e Av A, 25x102.2. July 15, 5 years or installs, 5 %. 12,000

Russak, Benjamin to The Good Samaritan Dispensary. Madison av, e s, 26 n 114th st, 27x91. July 14, 3 years, 5 %. 18,000

Same to Julia E. Cameron. Madison av, e s, 53 n 114th st, 27x91. July 14, 3 years, 5 %. 18,000

Same to same. Madison av, e s, 80 n 114th st, 20.11x91. July 14, 3 years, 5 %. 14,000

Rogers, Lilian wife of George W. to William McShane. Amsterdam av, s w cor 99th st, 40x82.2 to e s of late Bloomingdale road, x40x77.6. July 10, 4 months. 2,006

Rothwell, P. John to THE MANHATTAN SAVINGS INST. 51st st, s s, 91 e 1st av, 18x100.5. July 9, 1 year, 5 %. 2,000

Renehan, John to R. Clarence Dorsett. Amsterdam (10th) av, n w cor 171st st. P. M. Sub. to prior morts. July 9, due June 1, 1894, or installs. 3,000

Same to same. Same property. P. M. July 9, due June 1, 1894, 5 %. 6,000

Rohrs, Frederick to The Bradley & Currier Co. (Lim.). Park av, n e cor 102d st, 100.11x227.6. Sub. to morts. $121,000. June 7, 4 months. 20,000

Schaefer, Christian and Mary his wife to Carl Kurz and Christine his wife. 161st st, s s, lot 34 map Melrose, 25x100. July 15. 3,500

Smith, Frank L. to Adelaide A. Hillyer guard. George H. Hillyer. 90th st, s s, 90 w West End av, 20x100.8. July 15, 3 years, 5 %. 17,500

Smith, Cora A. widow, Nyack, N. Y., to Timothy G. Sellew. 18th st, No. 305, n s, 84 e 2d av, 20x54. Sub. to morts. $8,500. July 1, 1 year. 2,000

Smith, Terence to James Gribble. 88th st, s s, 210 e 4th av, 25.7x100.8. July 1, 5 years, 5 %. 2,000

Smith, Frank L. to Charles De H. Brower. 87th st. P. M. July 2, due July 9, 1892, or sooner. 19,250

Sayles, Solomon to THE EQUITABLE LIFE ASSUR. SOC. of the U. S. 6th av, e s, 90 8 n West 10th st, 64.6x121. June 30, due Jan. 1, 1893. 110,000

Schmidt, Henry W. to Henry Stoeber and Anna C. his wife. 9th av, s w cor 49th st, 25.1x100. July 1, 5 years, 4½ %. 8,000

Simon, Theodore mortgagor with Emilie A. wife of Alexander Nones mortgagee. Extension of mort. July 9. nom

Skinner, Elizabeth P. to Simon Rothschild. 76th st, s s, 200 w West End av, 20x102.2. Sub. to mort. $18,000. July 11, due July 13, 1892, or sooner. 3,000

Spaulding, Catharine M. to Edgar M. Gordon. 90th st, n s, 100 w 8th av, 20x100.8. Sub. to morts. $44,000. Secures building material. July 10. 3,150

Same to same. 90th st, n s, 120 w 8th av, 20x100.8. Sub. to morts. $44,000. Secures building material. July 10. 3,150

Stricker, William and Henrietta his wife to The John Eichler Brewing Co. Arthur av, No. 2023, w s, lot 92 map of Monterey, Upper Morrisania, 50x100. July 11, 1 year, 5 %. 1,650

Schachtel, Michael, Jr., to Nicholas Schachtel. 16th st, n s, 236.8 e 7th av, 28.8x92.1x24.8x92. Lease. Jan. 2, 3 years, 5½ %. 6,000

Schlesinger, Joseph to George Ehret. 2d av, n w cor 128th st, 83x42. Lease. July 12, demand. 2,500

Schmeckenbecker, George and John G. mortgagors with Charles Scholle mortgagee. Extension of mort. June 26. nom

Schneider, Henry to Charles H. Pinkham, Jr. Manhattan av, e s, 64 n 121st st, 36x95. Sub. to all liens. July 14, 6 months. 3,000

Schwarz, Caroline wife of Nickolaus to Sarah E. Fairbanks. 3d st, 24th Ward. P. M. July 13, 1 year, 5 %. 750

Same to Henry C. Schaefer. 3d st and Opdyke av. P. M. July 13, 1 year, 5 %. 600

Schweckendick, Henry to Anna C. wife of Ottos Wessell. 57th st. P. M. July 15, 3 year, 5 %. 4,000

Shortland, Stephen F. to THE TITLE GUARANTEE AND TRUST CO. Beekman st. P. M. July 15, 1 year, 4½ %. 30,000

Sigel, Simon to Lena Cohn. Allen st. P. M. July 15, installs. 4,500

Stanfield, Hope G. to Oliver G. Wells. 76th st, No. 43, n s, 82.6 e Madison av, 12.6x102.2; 17th st, No. 394, s s, 208.3 e 7th av, 16.7x100.2. All title. July 14, due Jan. 1, 1892. 1,000

Stender, Henry and Karolina to Katharina Ziegler. 118th st, s s, 92.6 e 4th av, runs south 50 x west 0.6 x south 50.11 x east 25 x north 100.11 to st, x west 24.6. July 15, 1 year, 5 %. 15,000

Same to same. 118th st, s s, 115 e 4th av, 25x100.11. July 15, 1 year, 5 %. 15,000

Tilden, Lilian E. F. widow to Mary A. Evans widow. ½ part or share of mortgagee in real or personal estate of William Tilden. March 16, due June 24, 1891, 4 %. sterling, £135

Tegetmeier, August I. and Ignatz A. Riepe to Cecilia A. Pulleyn. 1st av. P. M. July 15, due Aug. 1, 1893, 5 %. 5,000

Thompson, James and Jessie M. his wife to Louis Roller. 120th st, s s, 125 w 8th av. 75x100. Sub. to morts. $65,250. July 13, demand. 3,338

Thornton, William M. to Nathaniel Wise, 105th st, n s, 200 e 5th av, 100x100.9. July 13, demand. 3,500

Tober, Owen to John Armstrong. Arthur st, n e cor Jacob st, 25x87.6. July 14, 5 years. 1,000

Tompkins, Sophia H. and Mary A. and Johnson Knight, all of New Jersey, to THE TITLE GUARANTEE AND TRUST CO. 30th st, No. 349, n s, 213 e 9th av, 13.6x98.9. July 14, 2 years. 2,000

Toumey or Toumey, William and Mary F. wife of John Meade to Mary and Patrick Cashman. 135th st, n s, 325 w 3d av, 25x100. July 10, 3 years, 5 %. 500

Troxler, Conrad to James J. Fitzpatrick. 164th st, n s, 262.10 w Washington av, runs north 100 x east 20 x north 100 x west 50 x south 100 x east 20 x south 100 to st, x east 10. July 14, due Aug. 1, 1896, or sooner, 5 %. 3,500

Thom, Arthur M. and James W. Wilson to Peter J. McCoy. 69th st. P. M. June 9, due July 13, 1892. 18,500

Thompson, Alice L. wife of Samuel C. to The William R. Beal Land Improvement Co. Beech terrace. P. M. July 8, 3 years, 5 %. 1,382

Tscheppe, Adolph and Carl Schur mortgagors with Emma L. Van Ness, Cornwall, N. Y., mortgagee. Extension of mort. at 4½ %. June 3. nom

Vannett, James W. and Elizabeth his wife to THE TITLE GUARANTEE AND TRUST CO. 103d st. P. M. June 13, due July 10, 1894, 4½ %. 7,000

Van Ingen, Edward H. to Catharine A. Taylor et al. trustees for Albertina S. Pyne, Kate W. Winthrop, Mary Lewis, George C. and Mary A. C. Taylor. 40th st, n s, 279.6 w 6th st, runs west 203.10 to Broadway, x north 128.1 x east 92.8 x south 24.8 x east 59.10 x north 98.9 to 41st st, x east 65.1 x south 98.9 x east 20.6 x south 98.9. June 30, 3 years, 4½ %. 400,000

Washburn, Mary B. to Thomas W. Strong, Metuchen, N. J. Kingsbridge to West Farms road. P. M. May 23, 5 years, 5 %. 6,500

Same to same. Same property. P. M. Sub. to last mort. May 23, 2 years, 5 %. 500

Wheaton, Esther A. to Jarvis Mason trustee Stephen G. Fotterall. Pearl st, No. 421; Rose st, Nos. 63 and 65. P. M. July 13, due July 14, 1892, 5 %. 16,200

Williams, Hattie E. to THE BANK FOR SAVINGS, New York. 119th st, n s, 100 w 1st av, 50x201.10 to 120th st. July 14, 1 year, 5 %. 40,000

Wilsbusen, John to Charles H. Tyson exr. James M. Tyson. 109th st. P. M. July 13, 3 years, 5 %. 3,000

Wilson, Thomas to 24th Ward Real Estate Assoc. Decatur av. P. M. June 1, due June 10, 1894, 5 %. 312

Wood, William G. to Katie T. Schermerhorn and ano. admrs. Amos Cotting. 3d av, n w cor 118th st, runs north 151.4 x west 185 x south 50.5 x west 5 x south 100.11 to st, x east 190. July 15, 3 years, 4½ %. gold, 125,000

Wahlers, Frederick to Beadleston & Woerz, a corporation. Vesey st, No. 66. Lease. July 10, demand. 1,500

Wehner, Ernest and Joseph Schafer to Frances Beckman. Arthur av, w s, 208 s Pelham av, 25x117.8x25x117.6. July 1, 3 years. 2,000

West, Joseph I. to THE EQUITABLE LIFE ASSUR. SOC. of U. S. 62d st, n s, 250 e 5th av, 20.6x100.5. July 10, due Jan. 1, 1893, 5 %. gold, 25,000

Wheelock, William E., Brooklyn, to William R. Beal Land Improvement Co. Crimmins av. P. M. July 8, 3 years, 5 %. 11,760

Wills, Charles T. to William R. Beal Land Improvement Co. Beech terrace, s e cor Crimmins av; 141st st, n s, 50.1 w Beekman av. P. M. July 8, 3 years, 5 %. 8,032

Wolff, Abraham to Max Wolf. Broome st, s s, 80 w Pitt st, 20x60. July 7, 2 years. 2,000

Walker, Frederick H. to Clifford A. Hand exr. Charles G. Havens. Columbus av. P. M. July 15, due July 23, 1894, or sooner, 5 %. 12,000

Zeller, Julius to Bertha V. Zeller. 122d st, No. 352, 170 w Manhattan av, 16x100.11. July 7, 3 years, 4½ %. 6,900

Same to Marie L. Hollerith. Same property. Equal lien with last mort. July 7, 3 years, 4½ %. 2,400

KINGS COUNTY.

JULY 9, 10, 11, 13, 14, 15.

Acor, Kate wife of and Lewis to Sarah Lee. Jefferson av, n s, 195 e Stuyvesant av, 20x100. July 1, 1891, due May 1, 1894, 5 %. $6,000

Same to Hannah K. Van Vranken. Jefferson av, n s, 175 e Stuyvesant av, 20x100. July 1, due May 1, 1894, 5 %. 6,500

Same to Charles W. Mulford. Jefferson av, n s, 215 e Stuyvesant av, 20x100. July 7, due May 1, 1894, 5 % gold, 6,000

Adler, Albert A. to Title Guarantee and Trust Co. Grand st, s s, 250 Lorimer st, 24.1x110. July 13, 1 year, 5 %. 3,000

Alexrod, Jacob and David and Isaac Levinson to Herbert C. Smith. Stone av. P. M. July 7, due Aug. 18, 1891. 350

Anderson, John to Margaret Cullen. 12th st. P. M. June 16, installs. 800

Abt, John to August C. Diestelhorst. North 8th st. P. M. July 14, due July 1, 1896. 350

Alexander, Morris to Albert Beck and Paulina his wife. McKibbin st. P. M. July 14, 4 years, 5 %. 1,200

Bailey, Horace E. to Frank Bailey. 12th av and 76th st, New Utrecht. P. M. April 14, 1 year. 3,000

Beardall, John to Levi Shults and Rebecca W. his wife. Vanderbilt st, south cor Short st, 50x100, Flatbush. July 6, 5 years. 700

Bergen, Jacob D. H. with Theresa J. Greenlund mortgagor. Agreement to accept principal before maturity. June 26. nom

Bossert, Jacob to The German Savings Bank, Brooklyn. Stagg st, n s, 175 e Bogart st, 175x100. July 8, due Dec. 1, 1893, 5 %. 2,800

Brown, Mary F. to Adolph Sussman. Barbey st and Ashford st. P. M. June 9, due June 15, 1894, 5 %. 276

Bulger, Julia widow to Abram Cooke. Grand st, n s, 125 w Ewen st, 25x100. July 15, 5 years, 5½ %. 7,000

Burhart, Joseph H. and William J. to Justus Schoenewald. Hancock st, n s, 200 e Reid av, 50x100. July 14, 8 years, installs., 5 %. 8,000

Bursley, Ira L. to James V. S. Woolley. Lots 136 and 55 to 59 and 28 to 33 and 155 map of 221 lots of M. J. Bergen property, New Utrecht. P. M. June 8, 1 year, 5 %. 1,100

Baker, James M. to Michael O'Keeffe. 5th av, w s, 43.9 s Carroll st. P. M. Sub. to mort. $10,000. July 10, 3 years, 5 %. 3,450

Same to Mary Brown. Same property. P. M. July 10, due July 1, 1894, 5 %. 10,000

Barnewold, William J. to William Ulmer. Bergen st, s s, 24 e Rochester av, 25x77.9. July 10, 1 year, 5 %. 4,000

Beck, Albert to The Williamsburgh Savings Bank. McKibbin st, s s, 100 e Leonard st, 24.6x100. July 9, 1 year, 5 %. 4,000

Berge, William E. to George Hussennetter. Himrod st. P. M. July 9, 3 years, 5 %. 2,000

Bauer, Maria A. to Barbara Kalb. Melrose st, s e s, 350 n w Hamburg av, 25x100. July 1, 3 years 5 %. 3,000

Beasley, Lester W. to The South Brooklyn Savings Inst. Willoughby av, n s, 85 e Tompkins av, 20x100x50x15x95. July 8, 1 year, 5 %. 4,500

Bergen, Cornelius J. to Lulu H. Bissell. Douglass st, s s, 310 w 5th av, 16.8x100. June 17, 3 years, 5 %. 3,000

Bergen, Edward E. to Carrie Haldeman. 24th st, P. M. May 15, 3 years or installs. 2,200

Same to James Dunn. 24th st, n s, 230 e 3d av, 20x100. July 10, 1 year. 500

Bethelship Norwegian Methodist Episcopal Church to The Board of Church Extension of the Methodist Episcopal Church. 58th st, s w s, 140 n w 12th av, 40x100.2, New Utrecht. May 20. 500

Blackball, George E. to The Long Island Building and Loan Assoc. Newell st. P. M. July 1, installs, 5 %. 4,500

Boehme, Emil and Emma his wife to George Leybold. Jamaica av. P. M. July 11, 3 years, 5 %. 1,800

Boye, Nettie to Frederick Boye and Mary his wife. Clark st, s s, 61 w Stewart av, 39x69, New Utrecht. July 10, 3 years or installs, 5 %. 1,800

Brown, Thomas to Lawrence V. Cortelyou and Caroline A. Rushmore 5th av, s e cor Berkeley pl, 95x87.2. July 9, due Oct. 1, 1891, 5 %. 3,447

Brokaw, Susie D. wife of and Peter L. to Sarah C. Savage trustee Elihu Chauncey. McDougal st, s s, 164.7 w Hopkinson av, 4 lots, each 16x100. 4 morts., each $3,250. June 1, 3 years. 13,000

Same to Charles H. Reynolds. McDougal st, s s, 244.9 w Hopkinson av, 80.2x100. Sub. to $3,250. July 9, due Sept. 1, 1891. 2,500

Same to same. McDougal st, s s, 100 w Hopkinson av, 64.7x100. Sub. to mort. $3,250. July 9, due Sept. 1, 1891. 2,200

Same to Charles H. Reynolds. McDougal st, s s, 164.7 w Hopkinson av, 16x100. Sub. to mort. $3,250. July 9, due Sept. 1, 1891. 550

Same to Amelia P. Clement. McDougal st, s s, 100 w Hopkinson av, 64.7x100. July 9, due Sept 1, 1891. 12,000

Same to same. McDougal st, s s, 164.7 w Hopkinson av, 160.5x100. July 9, due Sept. 1, 1891. 10,000

Same to Samuel Hart, Hartford, Conn. McDougal st, s s, 308.11 w Hopkinson av, 16x100. June 6, 3 years. 3,250

Same to Annie B. Bedell. McDougal st, s s, 292.11 w Hopkinson av, 16x100. July 9, 3 years. 3,250

Same to Sarah C. Savage. McDougal st, s s, 260.10 w Hopkinson av, 16x100. June 1, 3 years. 3,250

Same to same. McDougal st, s s, 276 10 w Hopkinson av, 16x100. June 1, 3 years. 3,250

Same to Samuel F. Cowdrey trustee. McDougal st, s s, 244.9 w Hopkinson av, 16x100. June 19, 3 years. 3,250

Same to same. McDougal st, s s, 228.9 w Hopkinson av, 16x100. June 1, 3 years 3,250

Budden, Frederick C. to Margaret Lynch. Skillman av, n s, 150 w Lorimer st, 25x100. Sub. to mort. $1,500. July 9, installs, 5 %. 1,250

Same to The Williamsburgh Savings Bank. Same property. July 9, 1 year, 5 %. 1,500

Bullwinkel, Henry to Beadleston & Woerz. Gates av, No. 885. Lease. July 7, demand, 3 %. 3,000

Burke, John to William O. Moore et al. exrs. Abraham Underhill. Oakland st, e s, 25 s Eagle st, 25x75. July 10, 3 years. 2,000

Burrell, James to The Title Guarantee and Trust Co. Lawrence pl, interior lot. P M. July 8, 1 year, 5 %. 4,000

Burrows, Mary A. to Margaret A. Chappell. Macon st. P. M. July 8, due July 1, 1893, 5 %. 2,500

Bush, Wesley C. to Henry Weil. Hancock st. P. M. July 10, 3 years, 5 %. 10,000

Buttle, Helen M. to James H. Watson and James H. Pittinger, of Watson & Pittinger. Eldert st, s s, 311 e Evergreen av, 18x100. Sub. to morts. $3,250. July 2, 11 months, 5 %. 545

Barber, William to Joseph Wechsler. East 8th st, Flatbush. P. M. July 14, 3 years, 5 %. 230

Bannerman, Francis to Francis Bannerman, trustee for Frank, Jr., David B., Walter and Thomas Bannerman. Butler st, s s, 90 e Brooklyn av, 40x120.3. July 13, demand 3,157

Barkin, Sam to Charles E. Maguire. Stone av. P. M. July 13, installs. 650

Barnum, Charles K. to James D. Lynch. 83d st, n e s, 280 s e 21st av, New Utrecht. P. M. July 9, due July 13, 1892, 5 %. 1,050

Same to same. Same property. July 9, due July 13, 1892, 5 %. 2,250

Betts, Charles A. to Hamilton Trust Co. Nostrand av. s w cor Fulton st. P. M. July 14, 1 year, 5 %. 14,000

Same to same. Atlantic av. P. M. July 14, 1 year, 5 %. 2,500

Birdsall, Anna E. wife of and Henry D. to John T. Runcie. Taylor st, s e s, 184 n e Bedford av, 21x100. Nov. 19, 1 year. 1,000

Bleyer, Sigmund to Gustav Reinhardt. Flushing av, n s, 90.7 w Knickerbocker av, 25x71.10x27.10x84.1. June 26, due July 1, 1894, 5 %. 4,000

Brautigan, Konrad to Barbara Kalb. Melrose st. P. M. July 1, 3 years, 5 %. 4,000

Browne, Julia E. to Jane E. Meeker et al. exrs. Samuel M. Meeker. Schenck av, e s, 80 n Repose pl, 82.6x100x31.1x100; Repose pl, n s, 120 e Schenck av, 20x100; New Lots road, s w cor Schenck av, 40x90; Montauk av, n e cor New Lots road, 41.4x—x9x105.1. July 13, 3 years. 500

Broadway, Harriet B. wife Alexander H. to Martius T. Lynde. Clark st. P. M. July 7, due Aug. 1, 1896, 5 %. 7,500

Carroll, Thomas J. to Peter Strack. Bridge st. P. M. July 14, due Aug. 1, 1896, 5 %. 2,000

Clark, Francis E. to Mary S. Baker. Stagg st. P. M. July 13, 1 year, 5 %. 2,000

Conway, Bridget to Bedford Co-operative Building and Loan Assoc. Baltic st, n s, 135 e Schenectady av, 20x155.7. July 6, installs. 100

Creighton, Edwina S. and Elizabeth W. mortgagors with Joseph O. Brown exr. Extension of mort. July 7. nom

Calder, Alexander G. to The Williamsburgh Savings Bank. 19th st, s w s, 72 n w 7th av, 18x100. July 9, 1 year, 5 %. 2,000

Same to same. 7th av, west cor 19th st, 25x72. July 9, 1 year, 5 %. 4,000

Same to same. 7th av, n w s, 25 s w 19th st, 4 lots. each 25x72. 4 morts., each $4,000. July 9, 1 year, 5 %. 16,000

Camp, Calvin B. to The Mutual Life Ins. Co., New York. Park pl. n s, 120 e Rogers av, runs north 127.7 x east 193 to Old Clove road, x south 91.1 x southeast 42.5 to Park pl, x west 289.1. Already mortgaged to party of 2d part. July 9, due July 10, 1892. 1,000

Christopher, Eliza W. to Robert Wilson. Walworth st, e s, 233.7 n Myrtle av, runs east 46 x north 0.2½ x east 54 x north 25 x west 100 to Walworth st, x south 25.1. July 11, 3 years. 2,021

Carlen, Reinbold to Isaac Trimble. Atlantic av, n s, 50 e Buffalo av, 16.8x98.7. July 9, 1 year. 3,000

Carroll, Mary A. wife of and John to The South Brooklyn Savings Inst. Dean st, n w cor Smith st. P. M. July 10, 1 year, 5 %. 1,600

Clinch, James to Anna C. Van Pelt. Bay 13th st, s e s, 200 s w Benson av, 75x108.4, New Utrecht. July 1, 3 years. 2,000

Creamer, Frank D. to Hester J, Hunter. 6th av, s e s, 100.2 s w 50th st, 25x100. July 2, due July 1, 1894. 1,200

Cunningham, John T. to Anna M. Ferris, Flatbush, L. I. Greenwood av, s w cor East 5th st, Flatbush. P. M. July 24, 3 years, 5 %. 950

Cummings, Mary G. wife of and Thomas to Julia D. Harris. Bushwick av, e s, 127.2 n Maujer st, runs east 95.4 x south 50 x east 75 to Agate st, x north 72.2 x west 86.10 x north 26.8 x west 85 to av, x south 50.4; Union av, s e cor Amslie st, 25x107.1x25x108.6. July 10, 3 years. 1,000

Child, Montague S. to Stephen C. Halstead. 15th av, s w cor Bay Ridge av, New Utrecht. P. M. July 9, due July 1, 1893. 500

Churchill, Edward J. to John E. Currie. Jefferson av, Nos. 164 and 166, s s, 200 w Nostrand av, 40x100. July 9, 6 months. 1,150

Coleman, Catharine widow and sole devisee Patrick Coleman to William F. Corwith. Ewen st, e s, 25 s Withers st, 25x100. July 13, 3 years. 900

Collins, Charles H. to James H. Watson and James H. Pittinger, of Watson & Pittinger. 4th av, w s, 120 n 9th st original line, 30x60. Sub. to mort. $6,000. July 7, demand. 4,500

Costello, Catharine to Augustus Schaffel. Hicks st, w s, 105 s Rapelye st, 20x76.11x28.7x97 3. June 29, due July 1, 1894, 5 %. 2,600

Crane, Jennie F., San Antonio, Texas, to Joseph C. Taylor. Putnam av, s s, 51 e Nostrand av, runs south 80 x east 13.2 x again east 3.2 x north 79.8 to av, x west 16.4. May 1, 3 years, 5 %. 1,500

Davidson, Eleanor M. to Elizabeth Taber. Cypress av. P. M. May 1, installs. 491

Dahl, August H. and Caroline his wife to George Schade. Ashford st. P. M. July 11, installs, 5 %. 2,050

Dahn, John A. and A. August to The Dime Savings Bank, Brooklyn. Oxford st, e s, 158.5 s Flushing av, 50x100. July 9, 1 year, 5 %. 10,000

Derby, James T. to Thomas Ostick. 54th st, s s, 314 w 3d av, 18x100.2. July 8, 3 years, 5 %. 1,300

Dhuy, Jr., Frederick to Sophia Loffler. Pacific st, n s, 472 e Rochester av, 3 lots, each 16x100. 3 morts., each $1,600. July 1, 3 years, 5 %. 4,800

Same to same. Pacific st, n s, 408 e Rochester av, 2 lots, each 16x100. 2 morts., each $1,200. July 1, 3 years, 5 %. 2,400

Same to Wilhelmine Goepel. Pacific st, n s, 328 e Rochester av, 16x100. July 1, 3 years, 5 %. 1,200

Dittmar, Jr., William to William E. Kay. 33d st. P. M. July 8, installs. 3,200

Doherty, Frances to Jane A. Vanderveer, Flatlands, L. I. Portland av, w s, 570 s Hanson pl, 20x100. May 1, 1 year. 800

De Revere, John J. to Randolph H. Cole. Putnam av, s s, 392 e Reid av. 3 lots, each 19.4x100 3 morts., each $4,000. July 6, due Nov. 1, 1894, 5 %. 12,000

Same to John Leach. Putnam av, s s, 372.8 e Reid av, 19.4x100. July 6, due Nov. 1, 1894, 5 %. 4,000

Same to Elizabeth S. Schenck. Putnam av, s s, 353.4 e Reid av, 19.4x100. July 6, due Nov. 1, 1894, 5 %. 4,000

Same to Cornelius S. Stryker, Gravesend, L. I. Putnam av, s s, 334 e Reid av, 19.4x100. July 6, due Nov. 1, 1894. 4,000

Devlin, James to Mary C. Goldrick. Pacific st, s s, 296 e Rockaway av, 24x107.2. July 15, 3 years. 1,750

Erlanger, Max to The Williamsburgh Savings Bank. Duffield st, e s, 175.2 s Concord st, runs south 28.1 x east 32 x again east 68 x north 28 x west 100. June 22, 1 year, 5 %. 8,000

Essig, Wilhelm and Hedwig mortgagors with John Dressel and Friedericke his wife. Extension of mort. July 9. nom

Ersler, Victor P. P. to Edwin S. Updike, Sr., New York. Lexington av, n s, 326 e Reid av, 34x100. June 1, due July 10, 1891. 5,500

Fitzgibbons, William P. to Thomas J. Shea. Leonard st, e s, 80 s Withers st, 20x75. July 1, 3 years, 5 %. 1,800

Frank, Jacob to Harris Salit. Main st, No. 47. P. M. July 14, 1 year. 600

Fischer, Dora wife of and August to The South Brooklyn Savings Inst. Columbia st, s e cor President st, 20x75. July 10, 1 year, 5 %. 1,250

Flegenheimer, Marcus to The German Savings Bank. Ewen st, w s, 50 n Johnson av, 25x100. July 11, due Dec. 1, 1892, 5 %. 10,000

Friedman, Simon to Aaron Kaplan. Linden st. P. M. July 1, due Nov. 1, 1891. 1,500

Friedman, Josef to Gilbert S. Thetford. Osborn st. P. M. March 24, 5 years or installs. 500

Fawcett, Harvey to The Williamsburgh Saving Bank. Atlantic av, s s, 90.6 w Williams av, 20.4x104 11x20x101. July 14, 1 year, 5 %. 4,000

Same to same. Atlantic av, s s, 61.2 w Williams av, 20.4x101x20x97.1. July 14, 1 year, 5 %. 4,000

Same to same. Atlantic ay, s s, 20.5 w Williams av, 20.4x98.3x20x89.5. July 14, 1 year, 5 %. 4,000

Forrester, William O. to John Cassidy. Putnam av, n s, 100 e Reid av, 100x100. July 14, 6 months. 5,000

Goldstein, Barnet and Jacob Schwartz to Michael Sullivan. Stone av. P. M. July 8, installs. 400

Graber, John and William to Henry Zyfers. S t 5th st. P. M. July 14, 3 years, 5 % h 3,000

Goldstein, Thomas to Valentine Green. Riverdale av, s w cor Osborn st. P. M. July 14, due July 1, 1894. 200

Same to same. Riverdale av, s s, 25 w Osborn st, 5 lots. 5 morts., each $200. P. M. July 14, due July 1, 1894. 1,000

Genither, Frederick to Elsie M. Blewitt. McDougal st, n s, 95 e Howard av, 80x100. July 9, 1 year. 500

Gianini, Giosno to Francis T. Johnson. 87th st, &c. P. M. June 25, 2 years. 480

Golding, Thomas F. to Julia Crez. Bay 16th st, n w cor 86th st, 125x106. July 4, 5 %. 5,850

Goldstein, Jacob to E. Christian Korner. Christopher av. P. M. July 10, 2 years. 800

Gottschald, Paul H. to Joseph Pender. Bleecker st. P. M. July 11, due July 1, 1892, 5 %. 875

Gregory, Addie C. wife of and Edgar S. to Charles D. Towl et al. exrs. John W. Towl. State st, Nos. 300 and 302. P. M. July 10, due May 1, 1892, 5 %. 7,500

Graeber, Jacob and Christian to Mary Graeber. Central av, e s, 50 n De Kalb av, 25x100. June 20, 5 % 1,000

Graebeduenkel, Josephina to Louis Froehlich. Linwood st, w s, 225 n Liberty av, 25x90; Linwood st, w s, 200 n Liberty av, 25x90. July 1, due Dec. 1, 1893, 5 %. 300

Harrison, Ole to Kate Rose. Cooper st. July 14, 2 years. See Conveys. 1,000

Hertlin, Mary to Andrew Ginter. McDougal st, n s, 350 e Saratoga av, 25x100. July 8, due July 1, 1894, 5 %. 2,500

Heyser, Mary wife of and Henry C. to Mary C. McGoldrick. Arlington av, s s, 25 w Linwood st, 25x100. July 15, 3 years. 3,250

Houchin, Alfred W. to The Williamsburg Savings Bank. Jamaica av, s w cor Elton st, 80.5x100.2x75x129.2. July 14, 1 year, 5 %. 5,500

Same to Edward F. Linton. Same property. P. M. Sub. to mort. $5,500. July 14, installs. 1,400

Haesloop, John to S. Liebmann's Sons Brewing Co. Broadway, south cor Kosciusko st, runs west 47.2 x south 100 x east 25 x north 7.9 x northeast 30.7 to Broadway, x northwest 50. July 13, due July 1, 1898, 5 %. 16,000

Hahnenberger, Louis and Katie his wife to Mathias Wardinski. Schaeffer st. P. M. July 1, 3 years, 5 %. 800

Hanlon, Thomas to William A. De Long and ano. exrs., &c., Charlotte A. Schlim. Kent av, s e cor Wallabout st, 100.1x75. July 10, 3 years, 5 %. 9,000

Hay, George T. to Frederick H. Lawrence exr. George C. Tallman. 1st pl. P. M. July 3, 3 years, 5 %. 8,000

Heinz, Philip to George P. Moller. Suydam st, n w s, 492.11 s w Wyckoff av, 25x100. July 10, 3 years. 700

Henning, Valentine to John Schaefer. Georgia av, s w cor Belmont av, 97.1x100. July 19, 3 years, 5 %. 2,000

Herbold, Emily M. wife of and John to John R. Gullen, Torrington, Conn. Kosciusko st. P. M. May 19, 3 years, 5 %. 2,000

Hoyt, Emma G. wife of Morison to James A. Hamblin and John McElvery and Robert Getty. Av A. P. M. July 13, installs, 5 %. 8,000

Huggins, Catharine widow, Mary J. Gallagher, Robert J. and James T. Huggins heirs John Huggins to John Davis. Jefferson st, s s, 95 e Washington st, 25x100. July 13, due May 1, 1894. 500

Hollister, Sebastian T. to Elizabeth M. Rapalje. Schenck av. P. M. July 6, 1 year. 6,250

Same to W. Frederick Middendorf. Schenck av. P. M. July 6, demand. 2,400

Hubbs, Charles F. and William T. Lyons to Amanda M. Diver. Pacific st. P. M. July 10, 5 years, 5 %. 500

Isbill, Charles to Margaret Hendrickson, Jamaica, L. I. Jefferson av, s s, 249.10 e Stuyvesant av, 16.11x100. July 11, due Nov. 1, 1894, 5 %. 4,500

Same to same. Hancock st, n s, 250 e Stuyvesant av, 16.10x100. July 11, due Nov. 1, 1894, 5 %. 4,500

Jacobs, James C. to Lydia Van Cleaf. Warren st, s s, 200 w Hoyt st, 25x100. June 30, 1 year, 5 %. 2,000

Jennings, Margaret to George S. Wheeler exr. Nancy P. Wheeler. 20th st. P. M. April 21, 5 years. 500

Johnson, Louise J. and Kate Mackenzie to Nellie C. Van Reypen. Poplar st, No. 68, also Clason av, w s, 125 n De Kalb av, 25x197. June 30, due Nov. 1, 1893. 1,300

Johnson, George F. to William T. Graff and ano. trustees for Mary J. Markham. Fulton st, s s, 60.5 w Franklin av, 20x117. June 30, 1 year, 5 %. 5,500

Same to Augustus Rapelye, Newton, L. I. Fulton st, s s, 40.5 w Franklin av, 20x117. June 30, 1 year, 5 %. 7,000

Same to Henry W. McMann. Prospect pl, s s, 328.10 e 5th av, 25x100. July 2, 2 years. 12,500

Same to Henry W. McMann. Prospect pl, s s, 308.10 e 5th av, 25x100. July 2, 2 years. 12,500

Same to same. Fulton st, s s, 596.4 e Clason av, 21.4x117. July 2, 2 years. 3,500

Judson, Edward to Charles S. Kendall. Willoughby av, n w cor Grand av, 24x94x14.11x7.1x19.8 to Grand av, x south 87. Sub. to mort. $13,000. July 6, due July 15, 1891. 215

Same to Leopold and Benjamin Swartz. Same property. Sub. to mort. $13,000. July 7, demand. 136

Same to Charles E. Lovejoy. Same property. Sub. to mort. $13,000. July 7, demand. 312

Same to George Alexander. Same property. Sub. to mort. $13,000. July 7, demand. 500

Same to Richard G. Phelps & Co. Same property. Sub. to mort. $13,000. July 7, demand. 382

Same to Jennie W. Brown. Same property Sub. to mort. $13,000. July 7, demand. 1,000

Same to Stephen B. Sturges. Same property. Sub. to mort. $13,000. July 7, demand. 1,300

Jaeger, Charles W. F. to The State Executive Committee Young Men's Christian Assoc., New York. Lynch st, s s, 100 w Lee av, 20x100. July 14, 3 years, 5 %. 1,000

Kellow, Joseph to The General Synod of the Reformed Church in America. Herkimer st, n s, 200 w Rockaway av. P. M. July 13, due July 1, 1894, 5 %. 4,500

Same to same. Herkimer st, n s, 220 w Rockaway av. P. M. July 13, due July 1, 1894, 5 %. 4,500

Same to same. Atlantic av, s w cor Hinsdale av, 102.3x109.1x100x87.6. July 13, due July 1, 1893, 5½ %. 32,000

Kidd, Bridget wife of and John to The Bedford Co-operative Building and Loan Assoc. Baltic st, n s, 100 e Schenectady av, 35x155.7. July 6, installs. 460

King, Timothea A. to The Williamsburgh Savings Bank. Bradford st, w s, 125 n Fulton st, 25x100. July 8, 1 year, 5 %. 1,600

Klein, Morris to David Rosenberg. Bradford st, w s, 225 n Fulton st. P. M. July 14, due July 17, 1894, 5 %. 1,500

Same to same. Same property. Sub. to mort. $1,500. July 14, installs. 500

Kaiser, Frederick to Elizabeth Decker. Gates av, n w s, 200 s w Central av, 25x100. June 29, 5 years, 5 %. 3,000

Kloster, Anton to William F. Corwith. Eckford st, w s, 150 s Meserole av, 25x100. July 13, 5 years. 5½ %. 2,500

Kennelty, Hugh J. to William H. Beadleston. 8th st. P. M. June 23, due July 10, 1894, 5 %. 5,000

Kelly, Thomas F. to James W. Murphy and Michael McCormack. Cowenhovens lane. P. M. July 11, 1 year. 200

Kelly, Katharine to William O. Moore et al. exrs. Abraham Underhill. Eldert st. P. M. July 1, 3 years, 5 %. 2,500

Same to John Haas. Eldert st. P. M. Sub. to mort. $2,500. July 6, 3 months. 1,000

Kellow, Joseph and Matilda his wife to The Twenty-sixth Ward Bank. Fulton st, s s, 40 e Rockaway av, 20x100; Fulton st, s s, 80 e Rockaway av, 20x100; Fulton st, s s, 120 e Rockaway av, 40x100. July 13, advances not to exceed $15,000, present debt 10,156

Kinney, Patrick to The South Brooklyn Savings Institution. Bond st, e s, 50 n Douglass st, 50x100. July 11, 1 year, 5 %. 2,000

Kirby, J. Mason to Joseph P. Fuels. Decatur st, n s, 100 e Howard av, 260x100. Sub. to mort. $39,434. June 30, demand. 7,500

Koch, George to Virginia A. Kleine. Greene av, n s, 20 e Stuyvesant av, 30x100. July 11, demand. 2,000

Same to Sarah M. Striker, Tribes Hill, N. Y. Same property. July 11, 2 years or installs. 2,000

Koechler, Joseph to Mary E. Brush. Fulton st, s s, 102 w Ashford st, 25.5x94x25x99.4. July 4, due April 9, 1894. 500

Koerner, John to Katharina Grubel. Seigel st, s s, 175 w Graham av, 25x100. July 1, 3 years, 5 %. 1,800

Lamphear, Amos S. to Georgianna Galloway. Plymouth st, Nos. 321 and 323. July 10, 1 year or installs. See Conveys. 2,000

Laing, Donald to Caroline M. Brown. Glenmore av, s s, 80 w Milford st, 20x90. July 10, 3 years. 1,000

Same to Jane Brown. Same property. Equal lien with last mort. July 10, 3 years. 1,000

Laird, Daniel and Elizabeth his wife to Eliza G. and Mary Hampton and John C. Creveling, of Hampton & Creveling. Lots 22, 23, 24 and 29-34 inclus. July 10, due Jan. 10, 1893. 850

Lemberg, Samuel to Francis and Louise Ullrich. Stone av, s e cor Blake av, 20x100. July 6, 5 years. 550

Levy, Samuel to Stephen B. Sturges. Rockaway av. P. M. July 8, demand. 7,000

Lewandowski, Francissek and Victoria his wife to Martha F. Gray. 21st st. P. M. July 7, 3 years. 1,000

Livingston, Jr., William to The Williamsburgh Savings Bank. North 3d st, n e cor Berry st, 86x122. July 13, 1 year, 5 %. 8,000

Lord, Isabella S. wife of George S., New Haven, Conn., to Augusta H. Wyand. Nassau st, s w cor Duffield st, 25x88.9. July 1, 3 years 500

Luger, Charles to The Williamsburgh Savings Bank. Kent av, south cor North 10th st, 100x100. July 11, 1 year, 5 %. 9,000

Lyons, Henry B. to Lawrence V. Cortelyou and Caroline A. Rushmore. Berkeley pl, s s, 87.2 e 5th av, 54.3x95. July 9, due Oct. 1, 1891, 5 %. 2,500

Lehmann, Nathilde to James W. Crawford. Fulton st, n e cor Elton st. P. M. July 11, 1 year. 500

MacDonald, Bridget to Adolph Sussman. Ashford st, e s, 420 n Hegeman av, 20x100. July 9, due June 15, 1894, 5 %. 138

Mahon, Stephen W. to Archibald Young. Bay 16th st, n w s, 550 s w 86th st, 50x96.8, New Utrecht. Jan. 19, 3 years, 5 %. 600

Murtagh, Mary E. wife of Edward to William C. O'K . 10th st. P. M. July 6, installs, 5 %. eefe 900

Maul, Frances M. wife of and Frederick W. to Hugo J. Panzer. 2d av, s e s, 40.2 s w 4th st, 20x80, error. July 8, due Jan. 1, 1895, 5 %. 2,000

McAuliffe, Denis to Charles Hart. 9th av. P. M. July 9, 5 years, 5 %. 1,300

McCarthy, Bridget to George W. Pearsall. Canton st, w s, 93.6 n Willoughby st, 16.8x79.7x17x83. July 11, installs. 100

McClenahan, William to Joseph P. Fuels. Hopkinson av, n w cor Decatur st. P. M. Sub. to morts. $25,000. June 27, due Jan. 1, 1893. 5 %. 5,500

McCormick, Maria to Timothy Perry. Franklin st, w s, 50 s Freeman st, 25x95. July 9, 3 years. 400

McLean, Mary to David A. Fithian. Lots 42, 43, 52 and 53 map Theodore Sedgwick, New Utrecht. July 11, due July 10, 1894. 650

Mock, Isidor to Joseph Fuchs. Debevoise st. P. M. July 1, 2 years, 5 %. 3,000

Moritz, Gustav and Marie his wife to Lucy F. Ronyon extrx. Alphonse Ronyon. 47th st, n s, 100 w 4th av, 20x100.2. June 14, 3 years. 3,000

Mullen, James to Adam Moran. Gravesend av, w s, adj land of Court Stillwell, runs north 85 x west 190 to centre Lake st, x south 93 x east 190, Gravesend. June 27, 5 %. 3,500

Murnane, Mary to South Brooklyn Savings inst. Union st, s s, 142.6 w Columbia st, 20.6x100. July 11, 1 year, 5 %. 2,000

Manheim, Jacob to A. Judson Palmer. Dumont av, s e cor Powell st. P. M. July 13, 3 years or sooner, 5 %. 10,900

Martin, Bryce to Paul D. Nelson. Folsom pl. P. M. July 7, 3 years. 800

May, Bernard to Kate V. Amerman. Van Buren st, s s, 311.9 w Throop av, 20x100. July 10, 3 years, 5 %. 4,500

Monaghan, Phillip to The South Brooklyn Savings Inst. Harrison st, s s, 150 w Henry st, 27.3x100. July 13, 1 year, 5 %. 1,000

Moores, Robert L. and Charles A. Le Quesne to Adelia Burr. Putnam av, n s, 100 e Howard av, 40x100. July 11, due July 13, 1896, 5 %. 17,000

Morris, William H. and William Bowers to Charles Griffen et al. trustees Samuel Willets. 4th av, w s, 58 s 13th st, 28x86.10. July 13, due June 13, 1894, 5 %. 9,000

Manning, Ellen wife of and John to Emeline Davison, Rockville Centre, L. I. Conover st, west cor Vandyke st, 20x80. July 14, due July 1, 1894. 5,000

Mason, Mary E. wife of Isaac D. to Walter Barnes trustee James Barnes. Bergen st. P. M. June 29, due March 1, 1896. 2,000

Same to Orson W. Sheldon. Same property. P. M. Sub. to last mort. June 30, due Dec. 15, 1891. 300

Same to Paul W. Ledoux. Same property. Sub. to mort. $2,000. June 30, demand. 800

Same to same. Same property; also, Bergen st, n s, 134.4 e Ralph av, 185.8x107.2. July 15, demand. 21,000

Same to same. Same property. July 15, demand. 8,600

McGovern, James J. to Mary W. Smith, Glenmore av, s s, 125 e Thatford av, 29.5x100x29.3x100. July 13, 2 years. 300

Menahan, John to The Williamsburgh Savings Bank. Cornelia st, n w s, 70 n e Evergreen av, 20x100. July 14, 1 year, 5 %. 2,000

Same to same. Cornelia st, n w s, 50 n e Evergreen av, 20x100. July 14, 1 year, 5 %. 2,000

Miller, William M. to Lucretia Miller. Nichols av, w s, 225 n Union av, runs north 125 x west 200 x south 150 x east 100 x north 25 x east 100. July 14, 3 years. 2,000

Murphy, John to Margaret C. Eyre and ano. exrs. Jane C. Moore. Sackett st, s s, 121 e Henry st, 28.6x100. July 13, 3 years, 5 %. 9,000

Same to same. Sackett st, s s, 149.6 e Henry st, 28.6x100. July 13, 3 years, 5 %. 9,000

Nathan, Scheyer to A. Judson Palmer. Livonia av and Junius st. P. M. July 10, due August 15, 1896, 5 %. 10,370

Natelson, Abraham to David Stern. Judge st. P. M. July 1, 4 years. 1,000

Neuber, Christian A. to Frederick Dhuy, Jr. Pacific st. P. M. July 1, 5 years or installs. 1,200

Newdoll, Solomon to Joseph Furman. Pacific st, n s, 312 e Rochester av. P. M. July 1, 3 years, 5 %. 1,200

Same to Frederick Dhuy, Jr. Same property. 2d mort. July 1, 6 years. 1,200

Niebling, George and Barbara his wife to Adolph Sussman. Hegeman av, n w cor Ashford st. P. M. June 9, due June 15, 1894, 5 %. 561

Nolan, William to August H. Dahl. Barbey st. e s, 175 n Sutter av, 25x100. July 1, 7 years or installs, 5 %. 1,300

Norris, Daniel B. to Williamsburgh Savings bank. Macon st, n s, 195.9 w Lewis av, 3 lots, each 19.9x100. 3 morts., each $4,200. July 9, 1 year, 5 %. 12,600

Olbricht, Benjamin to Franz Franz. Broadway, s s, 100 w Macon st. P. M. July 1, 4 years, 5 %. 2,900

Same to same. Broadway, s s, 120 w Macon st. P. M. July 1, 4 years, 5 %. 2,900

Ogden, Alfred to Title Guarantee and Trust Co., New York. Atlantic av, s s, 150 e Saratoga av, 100x100. July 12, demand. 5,000

Same to Frank Reynolds. Pacific st, n s, 100 e Saratoga av, 100x100; Atlantic av, n s, 80 e Russell pl, 30x98.7; Bergen st, n s, 325 e Saratoga av, runs north 5.7 x southwest to n s Bergen st at point 295 e Saratoga av, x east 80; Bergen st, s s, 32.5 w Saratoga av, runs southwest 341.1 x south 32.2 x northeast to Saratoga av, x north 26.1 to st, x west 32.5. July 7, 1 year. gold, 2,500

O'Neil, Margaret to Statira A. Murphy. Woodhull st. P. M. April 2, 5 years, 5 %. 3,400

Oluey, George H. and Henry M. to Charles A. Betts. Herkimer st, n s, 209 w New York av, 20x100. July 10, installs. 2,800

Olson, Annie A. to Magdalena Dupignac. Glenmore av, s w cor Snediker av. P. M. July 13, 1 year, 5 %. 1,300

Pink, Bernhard J. to The Long Island Loan and Trust Co. trustee John A. Cross. Rockaway av, w s, 400 n Eastern Parkway, 25x100. July 14, due Dec. 1, 1894, 5 %. 3,000

Same to same. Rockaway av, w s, 425 n Eastern Parkway, 25x100. July 14, due Dec. 1, 1894, 5 %. 3,000

Palmer, A. Judson to Ulpian and Adrian Van Sinderen. Road or highway. P. M. July 10, 5 years, 5 %. 14,000

Parmer, Ada wife of Lewis to Mary W. Smith. Watkins st, w s, 100 s Eastern Parkway, 51.6x100. July 10, 10 days. 400

Philpott, James to Adolph Sussman. Ashford st; Warwick st, n e cor Wortman av. P. M. June 9, due June 15, 1894, 5 %. 229

Picard, Sarah wife of and Isaac to Rosa Rosenheim. Ten Eyck st, n s, 175 w Ewen st, 25x100. July 10, 3 years. 1,000

Pletsch, Josephine to Albert Otto and Madeline his wife. Sumpter st, n s, 400 e Hopkinson av, 27.11x76 to Old Jamaica plank road, x 50.10x54.3. July 8, 3 years or sooner, 5 %. 500

Polley, Samuel, Rachel Sachs, Harris Goldberg and Philip Rothlein to Jacob W. Erregger. Sackman st. P. M. July 9, 3 years. 5,435

Pomstein, Harris to Henry C. Soop, Kingston, N. Y., and Frank M. Andrus, Roxbury, N. Y. Stone av. P. M. July 3, installs. 625

Price, Mortimer W. to Title Guarantee and Trust Co. Leonard st, e s, 125 s Calyer st, 25x100. June 24, 1 year, 5 %. 2,000

Fuels, Joseph P. to John W. Harman. Hopkinson av, s w cor Decatur st, 100x100. July 9, demand, 5 %. 24,000

Power, John to Mary W. Smith, Eastern Parkway, n w cor Osborn st, 25x100. July 13, 5 years. 3,500

Raymond, Calvin W. and Michael Dowley to Horatio S. Stewart. Macon st. P. M. Sub. to mort. $4,000. July 15, 1 year. 1,250

Reuss, William to Heinrich W. F. Schulz, Hoboken, N. J. Fulton av, s s, 76.7 w Linwood st, 25.6x85.9x25x90.11. June 9, 5 years. 4,000

Robbins, Thomas H. to William J. Pennoyer, of Chester, N. Y. Patchen av, w s, extends from McDonough to Macon st, 200x80. Sub. to morts. $51,000. July 10, due Oct. 1, 1891. 5,000

Rogers, Isabella wife of John C. to Charles H. Reynolds. Vanderveer st. P. M. July 10, due July 1, 1892, 5 %. 400

Rosenthal, Mark to Andrew J. Onderdonk et al. exrs. Horatio G. Onderdonk. Court st. P. M. July 13, due May 1, 1896, or installs. 5 %. 12,000

Same to Sarah O. and Cath. E. O. Linkletter. Same property. P. M. July 13, due May 1, 1896, or sooner, 5 %. 4,000

Rafferty, Margaret to East Brooklyn Savings Bank. Skillman st. P. M. July 9, 1 year. 1,500

Raymond, Calvin W. and Michael Dowley to Elizabeth M. Rapalje. Macon st, n s, 203 w Howard av, 18x100. July 6, 3 years, 5 %. 4,500

Same to Elizabeth Wilson. Macon st, n s, 221 w Howard av, 18x100. July 6, 3 years, 5 %. 4,500

Same to Elizabeth M. Price. Macon st, n s, 239 w Howard av, 18x100. July 6, 3 years, 5 %. 4,000

Same to same. Macon st, n s, 257 w Howard av, 18x100. July 6, 3 years, 5 %. 4,000

Same to Lottie N. Palmer. Macon st, n s, 436 e Ralph av, 18x100. Sub. to mort. $4,500. July 9, due June 24, 1892. 800

Same to Lucy E. Barron. Macon st, n s, 185 w Howard av, 18x100. July 6, 3 years, 5 %. 4,500

Rust, Charles D. to Sarah F. wife of Edgar B. Mangam. Gates av, n s, 66 w Clason av, 22x81.8x22x80.11. June 22, 3 years, 5 %. 5,000

Same to same. Gates av, n s, 44.6 w Clason av, 21.6x80.11x21.7x79.9. June 22, 3 years, 5 %. 5,000

Ries, Henry to Frederick W. Hearn, Jr. Bradford st. P. M. July 1. 1,800

Robinson, Mary A. wife of and John to John Bisco. Johnson st, s s, 89 w Lawrence st, 22x100x6x18.6x106. July 10, 3 years, 5 %. 2,000

Roessle, Frank to Christina Roessle. Kosciusko st, s s, 100 w Stuyvesant av, 25x100. July 2, 3 years, 5 %. 625

Rosse, Augusta to Isaac Embree. Adams av, s w cor Sheridan av, 50x100. July 10, 1 year. 350

Ross, Jennie L to William H. Scott. Fulton st, s s, 200 w Stone av. P. M. April 21, 1 year. 10,500

Same to same. Same property. April 21, 1 year. 30,000

Ruyl, Barbara to Fredericka Nicklaus. Ashford st, e s, 275 s Ridgewood av, 25x100. July 8, 3 years, 5 %. 2,500

Rosenthal, Nathan to Leopold Michel. Flushing av. P. M. July 8, due July 1, 1894, or installs. 1,400

Reiff, Gottfried to William H. Dill. Greenwood av, s s, 50 e Sherman st, 25x104.10x26.5x96.4; Greenwood av, s e cor Sherman st, runs south 100 x east 132.4 x north 25 x west 51 x north 96.4 to av, x west 50; Hawthorne st, centre line, s s, on line which at n s Winthrop st is 2,955.7 e of Flatbush av, 50x136, Flatbush. June 20, due July 1, 1893. 450

Roth, Henry to The Williamsburgh Savings Bank. Ralph st, s e s, 190 s w Central av, 100x140. July 6, 1 year, 5 %. 4,000

Schiff, Ascher to Eliza A. Dunning. Newport av, Christopher av. P. M. July 9, installs. 840

Smith, Andrew H., Elberon, N. J., to Alexander E. Orr. Broadway, s w s, 54.5 n w Van Buren st, runs southwest 55.2 to Van Buren st, x west 66.11 x north 64.7 x northwest — x north 27 x northeast 64.8 to Broadway, x southeast 150. July 15, 1 year, 5 %. 30,000

Smith, Henry T. to Richard Conklin. Broadway, No. 152, s s, 55 w Driggs st, 23.2x41.9x22.2x48. July 13, 1 year. 500

Same to Ernest G. Stache. Same property. July 13, due July 1, 1894. 3,000

Spencer, William F. to West Brooklyn Land and Improvement Co. 44th st. P. M. May 23, due Nov. 1, 1895, 5 %. 660

St. Joseph Roman Catholic Church, Brooklyn, to The People's Trust Co. Pacific st, s s, 70 e Vanderbilt av, runs south 220 to Dean st, x east 320.6 x northeast 5.4 x north 217.3 to Pacific st, x west 325. July 14, 1 year, 4½ %. 16,000

Sturcke, Peter and Herman to George Straub. Lawton st. P. M. July 15, 1 year, 5 %. 500

Scherer, George and Mary his wife to Kunigunde Buhn. New Jersey av. July 1, 5 years. See Conveys. 1,600

Schlueter, Edward H. to The Title Guarantee and Trust Co. Meserole av, s s, 25 e Oakland st, 25x100. July 13, 1 year, 5 %. 1,000

Schmidt, John to Solomon May. Grand st, n s, 168 e Kent av, 25x129x25x131. July 8, 2 years, 5 %. 1,500

Schneider, Henry to Theodor L. Schneider. Broadway. P. M. July 8, 3 years, 5 %. 5,000

Schneider, John E to Henry Schneider. Harrison av, e s, 75 n Wallabout st, 25x100. July 8, 5 years, 5 %. 1,550

Schroff, Louisa wife of and Max to The Union Square Permanent Co-operative Building and Loan Assoc. Spencer st, w s, 58 n De Kalb av, 12.6x100. July 2, installs. 2,000

Schultheis, John to The German Savings Bank, Brooklyn. Debevoise st, s s, 200 w Humboldt st, runs south 141.7 x west 13.1 x south 11.1 x northwest 102.7 x north 60 to st, x east 50. July 8, due July 1, 1892, 5 %. 11,000

Schwenk, Wilhelmina to Josephine Eisemann. Stanhope st, n w s, 100 n e Hamburg av, 25x100. July 9, due July 1, 1894, 5 %. 3,006

Schwartz, William to Bentley F. Adams. Williamson av. P. M. July 8, 1 year. 12,000

Shapiro, Charles and David Nicbol to Meyer Vesell. Osborn st, e s, 175 n Bay av, 25x100. May 25, 3 years, installs. 3,000

Shapiro, Jacob to Joseph Zirinsky. Seigel st. P. M. Sub. to morts. $4,650. July 9, due July 1, 1894. 1,350

Shiff, Abraham, Albany, N. Y., to Bridget wife of John Barrett. Dumont av. P. M. July 8, installs. 2,000

Sleight, James E. to George W. Montgomery. Clason av, w s, 75 s Gates av, 25x100. March 27, due May 1, 1889, 5 %. 6,000

Smith, Elwood M. to Charles R. Cornell. Richmond st, e s, 775 n 4th st, 25x150. July 9, installs. 2,750

Smith, Peter to Conrad Stein. Franklin st, No. 159. Lease. July 6, demand. 700

Spencer, Mary to James V. B. Hammond. Skillman st, w s, 125 n Willoughby av, 25x100. July 1, 5 years, 5 %. 3,100

Stern, Moses and Louis to Max Landesmann and Max Friedlander. Thatford av. P. M. July 10, installs. 350

Stiner, Simon to Jaques Van Brunt. 2d av. P. M. July 9, due June 1, 1894, 5 %. 1,345

Sullivan, Michael to Joseph Seitz. Rockaway av, e s, 25 n Glenmore av, 25x80. July 7, 1 year. 4,000

Susmann, Mores to Isaac Horowitz. Graham av. P. M. July 7, installs, 5 %. 2,500

Sutterlin, Ernst F. to Gustav Korner, Huntington, L. I. Glenmore av, s e cor Alabama av. P. M. June 20, 1 year. 2,900

Sweet, Charles F., John R., James T., Jr., James and Mary A. to Francis Feely. De Kalb av, n s, 100 e Nostrand av, 25x152.2x26.9x161.9. June 29, due July 10, 1891. 1,500

Siebert, Maria K. wife of and William to Benoit Massermann. Flatbush av. P. M. Sub. to mort. $4,000. July 1, installs. 1,500

Same to Josephine C Downie. Same property. P. M. July 1, due Oct. 29, 1894. 4,000

Sharkey, Thomas to The Title Guarantee and Trust Co. Warren st. P. M. July 13, 1 year, 5 %. 1,000

Taylor, Arthur to Henry Albers, Jersey City. Macon st, s s, 255 e Stuyvesant av, 20x100. July 14, 3 years, 5 %. 4,000

Tuozzo, Antonio to Samuel Mosbacher and Sigmund Herzfelder, of Mosbacher & Co. Carroll st, No. 39, n s, 200 w Columbia st, 20x100. July 13, 1 year, 5 %. 800

Tabel, Emma to Barbara Tabel. 14th st, n s, 356.2 e 5th av, 16.8x100. July 1, 3 years, 5 %. 1,500

Terpenning, Irving B. to The Hamilton Trust Co. 10th st, s s, 160.3 w 4th av, 18x100. July 9, 3 years, 5 %. 2,000

The United States Foundry Co. to John Lewis and William Egginton. Leonard st, n e cor Richardson st. P. M. July 1, 5 years, 5 %. 6,000

Townsend, James A. to Jaques Van Brunt. 3d av and 81st st. P. M. July 9, due July 1, 1894, 5 %. 1,400

Vaughan, Thomas F. and Bridget his wife to George Brutscher, Franklin, N. J. Vermont st. P. M. July 8, 5 years. 400

Volckmer, Otto to James G. Carroll. 45th st, s s, 240 e 3d av, 20x100.2. July 1, 3 years. 1,300

Wagner, George W. to Walter Dickinson. Clason av. P. M. July 13, due July 1, 1892, 5 %. 500

Woodhull, Jesse C. to The Brooklyn Savings Bank. Livingston st, n e s, 58.4 s e Nevins st, 16.8x80. July 13, 1 year, 5 %. 5,000

Washburn, Wilford W. to James W. Elgar. 71st st, n s, 330 w 15th av, 40x100, New Utrecht. July 3, 6 months. 750

Weinglass, Louis to Michael Sullivan. Stone av, s w cor Livonia av, 18x100. July 8, installs. 800

Wey, Joseph J. to William F. Corwith. Greene st, s s, 75 w Oakland st, 25x50. July 7, due July 1, 1894. 500

Willdridge, John S. to William H. Scott, New York. Reid av, e s, 60 n Hancock st. P. M. April 29, 1 year. 4,575

Same to same. Same property. April 29, 1 year. 16,500

Williams, Edgar D. to Fanny Hohorst. Clinton st, s e cor Baltic st, 17.4x91.11x15.10x92.2. July 9, 3 years, 5 %. 1,500

Whittaker, Julia A. and Catharine Taylor to John Davies. Union av, e s, 50 s Skillman av, 25x100; Union av, e s, 75 s Skillman av, 25x100. July 9, 3 years. 2,600

Willets, Sarah J. to The Ninth Street Savings and Loan Assoc. Nostrand av, w s, 80 s Kosciusko st, 20x80. May 16, installs. 3,500

Yudelowitz, Marks and Philip Walcoff to Israel Rubenstein and Israel Sugalowicz. Thatford av, e s, 200 s Eastern Parkway, 25x100. July 9, installs. 650

Zipprian, Margaretta wife of and George to Jacob Hack. Warwick st, e s, 106 s Glenmore av, 22x90x34.2x90.10. July 8, 1 year. 300

MORTGAGES----ASSIGNMENTS.

NEW YORK CITY.

JULY 10 TO 16—INCLUSIVE.

Aymar, Herbert R., East Orange, N. J., to Frederic J. Middlebrook, Brooklyn. $5,534

Bayer, Minnie guard. of Stephen A. and Edwin M. Bayer to Henry Stiehl guard. of Annie, Minnie and Henry Stiehl, Jr. 10,304

Bussing, Amanda admrx. Susan Valentine to Amanda Bussing. 2,000

Same to same. 1,000

Bossert, Louis, Brooklyn, to Leon Cohen. nom

Bernins, George D. to Alice S. A. Whitney. 18,000

Coogan, Teresa to Pasquale Caponigri. 3,000

Cruger, S. Van Rensselaer trustee of Mary E. Field to James S. Clarke trustee Benjamin M. Clark dec'd. 5,281

Crane, Sarah H. to Mary E. Braun. 3,000

Cooper, Catharine and ano. exrs. and trustees William Cooper to John H. and Emma M. Cooper. 3 assigns. nom

Cohen, Leon to Eugene Mehler. nom

Campbell, Robert F. to Laemmlein Buttenwieser. 2 assigns. nom

Decker, John W. to R. Clarence Dorsett. nom

Same to same. nom

Same to Annie Ormiston 3,250

Delano, Franklin H. to F. H. Delano et al. trustees for Laura A. Delano. 15,000

Same to same. 12,000

Same to same. 15,000

Ehrmann, Julius to Babette Scholle et al. exrs. and trustees Abraham Scholle. nom

Floy, James, Elizabeth, N. J., to Almira J. Brown, Milburn, N. J. 1,000

Friedman, Kevy to Robert F. Campbell. 2,784

Fisher, Frank L. and Isabella H. his wife to The Hudson River Bank. Re-recorded. 20,000

Garrettson, Francis T. exr. Lucie J. Preterre to Charles O. Livingston, Kingston, N. Y. 7,034

Goodman, Louis to Samuel Valentine. nom

Goldstein, Aaron to Morris Waterman. 1,000

Gottlieb, Aaron to Moses Solomon. nom

Guggenheimer, Randolph to Wilhelmina Albert. 1,000

Same to Sophia Ruhl. 1,000

German-American Real Estate Title Guarantee Co. to Russell Sage. 50,000

Green, Ashbel to Douglas Campbell. nom

Habnenberger, Louis to Mathias Wardzinski, Brooklyn. 2,000

Hoffman, Daniel to Isaac Marx. nom

Hahn, Max to Jacob Schwarz. nom

Henning, Joseph to Elizabeth Henning his wife. nom

Holland Trust Co. to Edgar S. Appleby. 14,606

Home Life Ins. Co. of Brooklyn to Frank A. Seitz. nom

Herman, Simon to Alois Gutwillig. 3,000

Jacobs, Elias to Herman Watjen, Brooklyn. 7,250

Same to same. 4,000

Same to same. 6,000

Jacob, August to Gustav Lange. 1,500

James, John A., London, Eng., to Morton D. Bogue guard. for children of Alma T. Hatch. 18,000

Jones, Susan M., Huntington, L. I., to John J. Brady. 150

Kreuter, Ferdinand to John Beckmann and Anna his wife. 3,000

Kepes, Joseph to Arthur Fishmann. 2,000

Lee, Rosa W. to Martin J. Fleming. 2,500

Lockwood, Stephen O., Brooklyn, to Ella D. Goodrich extrx. and trustee John W. Schmidt. 20,000

Langbein, J. C. Julius to Thomas H. Cook. 1,530

Luyster, Peter, Jr., exr Peter Luyster to Mary L. Woodward, Brooklyn. 10,000

Lyding, Peter to Adam Happel. 751

Marks, Bertha to Simon Adler and Henry S. Herrmann. 2,500

Merritt, Rushanna, Westchester, N. Y., to Albert B. Marshall 900

Marks, Jeannette to Jacob Friedlander. 10,201

March, Mary L. extrx. and trustee John P. March to Louisa Minturn, Lenox, Mass. 22,000

Same to The Nursery and Child's Hospital. 22,000

Middlebrook, Frederic J., Brooklyn, to Leopold Gusthal and ano. exrs. Edward Ridley. 10,011

Same to same. 6,007

Same to Archibald Rogers, Hyde Park, N. Y. 9,887

Moore, William I. to Emanuel Emmerich. 2,041

Morgan, Edwin D., Newport, R. I., to John T. Terry et al. trustees Edwin D. Morgan, dec'd. 13,000

Same to same. 15,000

Man, William trustee to William W. Sherman guard. of Georgette W. and Sybil K. W. Sherman. 10,000

Michel, Andrew and ano. exrs. Andreas Michel to Elizabetha W. Michel widow. 5,500

Middlebrook, Frederic J., Brooklyn, to Leopold Gusthal. 4,087

Same to Walter N. De Grauw, Jr., and ano. exrs. and trustees Samuel Aymar. 12,576

McClenahan, James to Viola Hill. 10,000

Neubauer, Elizabetha individ and admrx. John Neubauer to William Sutorius. nom

Nesbitt, John H. and ano. exrs Charles Nesbitt to Mary E. Birrell guard. of Susan A. Sarles. 5,000

Platt, William O., Brooklyn, to William Man trustee. 10,000

Rentz, Charles to Louisa Nuhn. 1,667

Same to same. 2,359

Regan, Evelyn G. wife of James, formerly Munson, to Lizzie A. Otis. 3,000

Redmond, Margaret F. to Michael Redmond. nom

Rinaldo, Louis to Samuel Weil. 5,135

Sands, Benjamin A. guard. of Thomas Barron to Thomas Barron. nom

Same to same. nom

Solomon, Moses to Joseph Wittner. 3,000

Steinhardt, Lewis to Theodore Sattler. nom

Storke, Henry L., Auburn, N. Y., to Adolph M. Bendheim. 8,800

Salter, William H. to John Schreyer. nom

Sanger, Adolph L. to Morris and Julius Valenstein. 1,850

Schumann, Gustav to Philipp Bohner, Brooklyn. 3,056

Schuyler, Philip and ano. trustees Gertrude L. Lowndes dec'd to Mary L. March extrx. and trustee John P. March. 66,000

Seaman, Mary A., North Tarrytown, N. Y., to Amalia Heider. 5,500

Stix, Louis to Rosa Rice. 3,045

Smith, James W. trustee for Elizabeth A. Draper to James W. Smith trustee. 10,000

Sigel, Simon to Lena Cohn. 1,250

Tucker, John A. and ano. exrs. and trustees Margaret A. Tucker to Allen Tucker and Mary A. Synge and John A. Tucker and ano. trustees for Samuel A. Tucker. 20,000

The Hudson River Bank to Frederic J. Middlebrook. 10,000

The Lawyers' Title Ins. Co. of New York to Walter N. De Grauw Jr., and ano. exrs. and trustees Samuel Aymar. 16,078

Title Guarantee and Trust Co. to Emma R. Riblet. 2,000

Same to Home Life Ins. Co. 30,000

Same to Julia M. Hurtt 8,000

Title Guarantee and Trust Co. to Eugene A. Lane, Ridgewood, N. J. 3,000

Same to Atlantic Trust Co. guard. of Nathaniel C. Reynal. 30,000

Same to Atlantic Trust Co. as trustee. 6,500

Same to Hennah Griessman. 7,000

Title Guarantee and Trust Co. to Henrietta Swartz et al. exrs. Solomon M. Swartz. 15,000

Townsend, Adaline D. to Mary A Sinnott. 1,500
Tweedy, Oliver B. exr. Joseph N. Lord to Central Trust Co. of New York, trustee Joseph N. Lord, dec'd. consid. omitted
Valenstein, Morris and Julius to Leonard and Adolph Lewisohn. nom
Walsh, Walter, admr. Teresa Welch to Stephen Ward, Sing Sing, N. Y. 2,500
Weil, Jonas and Bernhard Mayer to Sophie Bertram. 5,061
Weill, Julius, Titusville, Pa. to Max Cohen. 10,000
Williamson, Sarah A. to John Entwistle and ano. exrs. Joseph Horridge. 1,200
Wray, Julia to Max Bernstein. 4,557
Wallach, Leopold to August M. Weil. 3,000
Wells, Grace T., Franklin, N. J., to Lucretia S. Jones. 20,000

KINGS COUNTY.

JULY 9 TO 15 INCLUSIVE.

Alfred, Richard to William S. Wood. $1,500
Alexander, George F. to Charles R. Weeks & Brother. 1,000
Bailey, Frank to Julia E. Brick. 3,000
Bardsley, Joseph to Jane Moir. 3,000
Same to Mary Wright. 2,000
Belford, Louise A. to Reuben Ross. 500
Bliven, William W. et al. exrs. Louisa Bliven to William M. Evarts. 7,000
Bliven, William W. and Edward M. to Louisa Bliven. 7,000
Bonnell, J. H., & Co. (Lim.) to Robert H. C. Valentine. nom
Burr, Andrew E. to Theodore F. Jackson exrs Guy C. Hotchkiss. 100
Barrett, Bridget wife of and John to John Christian, Bound Brook, N. J. 1,500
Booth, Edwin, Boston, Mass., to William Post, Hempstead, L. I. 3,000
Buhmer, John K. to Julius H. and Gertrude Goetze. 2,000
Clement, Jesse B. and Leander W. Stockwell to Erastus N. Root and Mary W. his wife. 2,000
Corning, Ephraim L. to Sarah A. D. Lewis. 6,037
Same to Ephraim L. Corning admr. Ephraim Corning. 4,025
Cole, Randolph to Mamie E. Park, Flushing, L. I. 800
Condict, Silas A. to James Dunn. 250
Cook, Mary E. to William M. Miller. 1,000
Cox, James W. to Celia A. Cox. nom
Cole, Randolph H. to Sarah D. Allen. 500
Same to John and J. Adrian Ditmis. 4,500
Same to William A. Skidmore, Manhasset, L. I. 4,500
Dillmeier, Conrad to Peter Kaufman and Gertrude his wife, Greenburg, N. Y. 850
Dill, Jr, John to Bridget Powers. 1,000
Diver, Amanda M. to William Moir. 5,000
Embury, Philip to Benjamin T. Kissam. nom
Eastman, Henry M. W. to Mary S. wife of Calvin S. Denman, Madison, N. J. 2,000
Fleich, Michael to Flora C. Fleich. nom
Gutting, George and Charles A. Wagner to William De Nyse. 4,000
Heinson, John S. to Jacob Rapp. 550
Hurlburt, Lawrence to Maurice Fitzgerald. 1,250
Heatley, George W. to Edmund A. Gearon. 1,500
Hendrickson, Charles and ano. exrs. Banardus Hendrickson to Elsie Hendrickson widow. 600
Jackson, Theodore F. to Emma Weeks, Glen Cove. 5,000
Jackson, Theodore F. exr. Maryett Hodgetts to Charlotte Leavens. 2,562
King, Theophilus, Quincy, Mass., to Richard Long. nom
Kaplan, Elias to Louis Bossert. 935
Laing, Mary E. to Emma E. Brown. 1,063
Lambert, Patrick and James H. Mason to John W. Gildersleeve. 3,000
Lamphear, Amor S. to Jose E. Pidgeon. 2,500
Lefferts, John to Catharine Byrne. 750
Leopold, Lorenz to Herman Weber. 1,000
Lewandowski, Francissek to Bernard Cruise, Jr. 1,225
Lott, John A., Jr., to Catharine L. Williamson. 3,000
Lott, Phebe A. to John A. Lott, Jr. 3,000
Lovett, George E. to William C. Ryon. 757
Lyon, Caroline A., White Plains, N. Y., to John Abberley. 1,800
Leary, Mary C. to Emma A. Schley. 24,000
Levin, Barnet to Rudolph and Otto E. Reimer. 500
Linton, Edward F. to John Thomas. 308
Same to same. 1,960
Morrissy, William P. to Matilda and Mary E. Calder. 1,500
Macvey, Sarah H. admrx. George W. Macvey to Isabella Cuming guard. Bessie J. Cuming. 1,826
Max, Harris to Herbert C. Smith. 735
McGowan, Lawrence to John and Frederick Dressell. 1,500
Meyer, Henry H. L. to Thomas H. Cook. nom
Morris, Joseph to Louis Bossert. 675
Mullins, John to Daniel Garvy. 10,000
Mulligan, Michael to Robert E. Topping. 500
Meehan, Christopher to Martha H. Beers widow. 3,500
Molineux, Maria to Anna Molineux. 4,500
Northridge, William A. to Thomas H. Northridge. 375
Newlin, Margaret M., Fishkill-on-Hudson, to Samuel S. Stillwell, Gravesend, L. I. 5,046
Noon, Phebe E. to Lucretia A. Noon. nom
Osborne, Carrie A. to Lydia Winant, Rossville, S. I. 915
Pearsall, George W. to Mary Fitzgerald. 100
Phillips, Guy, Yonkers, N. Y., to Sally W. Lovell. 2,500
Packard, Josiah S. to Elizabeth C. Smith. 2,521
Parmly, Ehrick et al. trustees Anna R. Adams and Ehrick K. Rossiter to Samuel S. Stillwell. nom
Pidgeon, Jose E. to George C. Case, Flatbush, L. I. nom
Power, Elizabeth C. to Theodore Kiendl. 600
Phillips, Emma J. to Julius B. Davenport. 1,600
Powell, Sarah H. to Jeremiah, &c., V. Wintringham exrs. Elizabeth V. Wintrinham. 5,000
Rosenthal, Nathan to Leopold Michel. 950
Rankin, James D. and James Ross to David Gowans. 1,000
Simon, Semche to Jacob Manheim. 162
Sceneider, Henry to Theodore L. Schneider and Carolina his wife. 1,530
Shapiro, Jacob to Joseph Zirinsky. 600
Suydam, Adrian M. to John Davies. 1,200
Title Guarantee and Trust Co. to Gustave T. Kreppel, 2,500
Same to Hamilton Trust Co. 4,000
Same to Henry Dickinson et al. trustees Nathaniel Smith Fund of New York Yearly Meeting of Friends. 2,000
Same to Charles Byrne. 2,500
Same to Charles Holt. 5,500
Same to Robert C. Reeves. 7,000
Same to Nelson B. Simon. 500
Same to Eleanor M. Kearney. 5,000
Same to Charles F. Aukamp guard. Mary R. Van Dyke. 3,500
Same to Pacific Fire Ins. Co., New York. 3,750
Same to Eliza Ross. 6,000
The Mutual Life Ins. Co., New York, to Board of Domestic Missions of the Ref. Church in America. 6,000
Topping, Robert E. to Coleb H. Corwith and ano exrs. Charles W. Corwith. 2,000
Townsend, James A. to Eleanor C. Townsend, South Orange, N. J. 350
Same to same. 375
Same to same. 200
Upward, Bensie V. to Catharine L. Williamson. 2,000
White, Janette F. to Edward Egolf. 250
Williamsburgh Savings Bank to James D. Leary. 3,091
Worth, Jacob and Vincent A. Strawson to Adolph Vanrein. 113
Wygand, John to Herrmann Wischebrink and Theodor Sauer. 2,500

JUDGMENTS.

In these lists of judgments the names alphabetically arranged, and which are first on each line, are those of the judgment debtor. The letter (D) means judgment for deficiency (*) means not summoned. (†) signifies that the first name is fictitious, real name being unknown. Judgments entered during the week, and satisfied before day of publication, do not appear in this column, but in list of Satisfied Judgments.

NEW YORK CITY.

July

11 Amberg, Gustav—John Wanamaker. $80 80
13†Ackerman, John—Nicholas Chapins.. 345 62
14 Abeles, Edmund—Thomas Sullivan... 101 55
14 Allen, Harry—Henry Cranston 568 69
14 Arnold, Nathan; Arnold, Benjamin; Arnold, Walter C } G S Bowdoin.... 136 28
15 Asmus, Charles—David Morgan...... 231 50
15 Arnold, Hobart G—H L Morehouse.. 201 76
15 Allen, Harry; Allen, Harry } Franklin Allen, exr. 284,895 00
16†Abrahams, Morris—Joseph Rubenstein 142 29
16 Allen, Harry—Marie L Vanderbilt, extrx.......... 79 48
11 Brown, Levi L—Third Nat Bank of Springfield, Mass..........10,275 20
13 Bierhoff, Joseph—Emil Oelbemann... 192 05
13 Bell, George H—John Moore......... 419 36
13 the same——Nat Bank of Cortland.......... 383 66
14 Baldwin, Theron—Georgiana I. Hotchkiss.......... 744 14
15 Bell, George H—A B Nelson......... 328 94
15 Bentley, Frederick—H S Miller...... 318 97
16 Brooks, Julius—Moritz Freedman.... 1,016 88
16 Bowles, Benjamin L—Montgomery Armstrong.......... 851 82
16 Brainerd, Charles A—A E Chasmar.. 918 47
16 Bradner, Julia E—A J Skinner....... 533 60
16 Byrne, William J—H H Cammann... 210 81
16 Betts, Langley—William Berger...... 79 75
17 Balch, George T—Ordelia M Hillman. 300 50
17 Blackman—A M Woodward........ 128 94
17 Brush, Thomas H—G B Germond.... 194 24
11 Cohn, Bernard—John Tonyes........ 89 18
11 Carmiencke, John H—Adolph Amend 78 80
13 Collins, Frank A—C H Ryan......... 919 18
13 Costello, James A—C F MacLean ....costs 69 90
14 Campbell, Frank—Andrew Mullen.... 273 08
14 Cox, William—James Chambers (Lim) 177 80
14 Cole, Ramsh—Richard Knox 194 18
14 Carmichael, Alexander R—Julius Gruber.......... 281 61
14 Cobbs, Stanhope F—W G Taylor..... 143 41
15 Clendenning, Teresa—Joseph Beck... 188 77
16 Callahan, Thomas F—Goold Hoyt.... 486 60
16 the same——the same.......... 329 85
16 the same——the same.......... 325 40
16 Curry, George W—D H Shipman.... 302 14
16 Conly, Catherine—Wright, Gillies & Bros.......... 106 82
16 Cunningham, Robert—P J Claassen.. 130 83
17 Canovan, Michael—Patrick Dougherty.......... 75 34
17 Condit, Frederick A—Bank of Jamaica 155 69
17 Cashin, Thomas J—Conrad Doersch.. 108 54
17 Catarsi, Dionisio—Achille Starace.... 171 91
11 Donnelly, Thomas W—G M Miller.... 110 51
13†Doe, John—Nicholas Chapins...... 345 62
13*Duffy, William J—William Ottmann 744 11
13 Dunn, J Halstead—W F Lennon..... 100 17
14†Demong, William J—Levi Spear..... 270 51
14*Doe, John—George Mackenzie....... 167 18
14 Dooley, William—S Liebmann's Sons Brewing Co.......... 101 40
14†Doe, John—G A Phelphs............ 238 82
15 Downey, Charles—Bernard Kaskell.. 62 30
15 Deane, Bertha A—S C Croft........ 626 13
15 Dunham, David W—H L Morehouse 201 76
15 Delabarre, Elizabeth M—W A Washington.......... 483 36
16 Douglass, Margaret K—Mary Monell. 186 23
16 Devine, John C; Devine, Michael J } S P Tregoning ....costs 75 48
16 Dumabaut, Delia Ann—Ann C Brown ....(D) 850 87
16 Downey, Charles—D H Shipman..... 302 14
16 De Forest, William H, Jr—Mary A Martin.......... 177 34
16 Dempsey, John—E J Knauer......... 142 10
11 Evatt, John O; Evatt, John G } Herman Glass Co... 43 25
15 Elias, Michael A—Davis Rubin 31 47
16 Edelson, Abraham—W T Hance. 1,296 94
17 Elster, Charles M—W A Jacobson.... 672 39
11 Futorausky, Samuel—Aaron Goodman 82 00
11 Farley, Henry—J L Devoe........... 136 32
11 Fischer, Frederick W—Marvin Safe Co..........costs 51 33
11 Foran, Thomas E Jr—T E Foran.costs 47 93
13 Farrington, Jonas S—Hugo Josephy 1,188 90
14 Fraley, John W—G S Bowdoin....... 136 28
15 French, Lyman P—Brush Swan Electic Light Co. of New England..costs 87 31
15 Field, John C—Marshall Field....... 96 41
15 the same——the same.......... 254 33
15 Finley, Henry T—J T Scott 318 16
15 Franklin, Edward M—Marten Doscher.......... 953 43
16 Fogg, John C—W P Greenlie......... 2,004 31
16 Friedman, Jacob—Herman Hirsch ....costs 121 85
16 Friedman, Benjamin Z——the same ....costs 116 75
16 Flynn, James P—Mary Flynn........ 352 17
16 Flynn, Peter H—Anthony Fischer.... 149 44
16*Fox, Henry E—E L Mooney......... 117 92
16 Feigenblum, Aaron—Moritz Horwitz. 279 65
17 Folger, Thomas—J M Griggs......... 374 00
17 Felt, George H—W M Fuller........ 103 59
11 Gould, Frederick H—Lucius Moses...3,691 09
11 the same——the same. ....costs 251 46
11 the same——H S White and Giles Everson..........1,295 90
11 the same——the same..........3,755 47
11 the same——the same. 300 05
11 the same——J S Crouse, assignee..1,701 09
13†Gough, Mary—Helen Franc.......... 25 50
13 Gardner, Joseph A—C F Mac Lean commr..........costs 59 40
14 George, William R—Aaron Raymond 134 93
14 Griswold, Margaret D—Georgiana I Hotchkiss.......... 744 14
14 Gasser, August—Emil Heller......... 358 46
14 Gade, Ernst—Henry Schwoon........ 74 15
14 Godfrey, Lincoln—G S Bowdoin 138 28
15 Greer, Elizabeth A—J R Cady....... 351 28
15 Gerdes, William H—George Ringler & Co.......... 378 77
15 Gottscho, Herman; Gottscho, Isaac } H E Frankenberg.......... 89 15
15 Geisenheimer, Edward G—Jacob Ruppert.......... 453 63
16 Gartlan, James H—Goold Hoyt...... 436 60
16 the same——the same.......... 329 85
16 the same——the same.......... 325 40
16 Graham, Harry—Ehrman & Simon Mfg Co.......... 324 47
16 Greve, William M—Henry Meier..... 34 18
17 Greenleaf, Amos C—G S Cox......... 1,494 00
11 Hodges, Amory G—Lucius Moses.. .. 3,691 06
11 the same——the same........costs 251 49
11 the same——H S White and Giles Everson..........1,295 90
11 the same——the same.......... 3,755 47
11 the same——the same.......... 300 05
11 the same——J S Crouse, assignee 1,701 09
11 Hiller, George—Max Lehmann....... 160 30
11 Hubbard, Thomas W—H H Spies.... 159 29
11 Husted, Charles B—F G Swartwout.. 80 65
13 Hume, Charles E—James Shaw...... 45 30
13 Hazard, George R—Samuel Kessler.. 169 45
13 Hayman, Charles—C C Rice.......... 32 80
14 Higgins, Charles S—Benjamin Altman 699 67
14 Haas, Bertha—Thomas Sullivan..... 101 55
44 Hamilton, Walter—Harry Rice...... 165 95
14 Hume, Charles E—Nat. Barrow and Truck Co.......... 165 86
14 Henderson, Juliette C—C T Barney.. 548 73
16 Hevenor, William G—E S Jaffray.... 9,294 75
16 Hill, Charles M—Marcus Starlight... 271 85
16 Hartigan, Dennis J—H H Cammann. 210 31
16 Haire, Robert J—R M De Leew 32 87
16 Harper, William D—T B Hidden.....1,393 76
17 Haak, Frederick—Bank of Jamaica.. 155 69
17 Haas, Francis—A J Clark............ 170 67
17 Horton, Charles G—Delamater Iron Works.......... 488 48
17 Heiser, John A—H B Claflin Co......3,136 10
13 Joyce, Thomas; Joyce, Maurice J } W H Van Tassel 1,337 37
14 James, Edward F—Frederick Rode... 587 71
17 Johnson, Alexander G Jr—G M Miller 110 51
13 Kiefer, Christian—William Ottmann & Co.......... 744 11

13 Kornhauser, DeWitt H—Emil Oelbemann.... 192 05
13 the same——J B McKeon, recvr.. 749 51
14 Keubler, Christian admr William Keubler—Mayor, &c ....costs 134 60
14 Katz, Leah—H B Claflin Co.... 187 07
14 Kingsland, Janet. admrx Henry F Topping—G W Murray.... 259 46
14 Kotzenberg, Gustav—G S Bowdoin.. 136 28
15*Kelsey, James—A B Nelson.... 388 94
15 Kreuder, Adolph; Kreuder, Frank F; Kline, Charles } Louis Levi.... 895 76
15 Kelly, Thomas P—William Fiss.... 699 04
15 Kessell, Charles L—M W Cortwright. 38 00
15 Kennedy, Charles S—I P Martin.... 11,469 04
16 Krausch, Theodore—Brewers' Journal 428 63
17 Karliner, Morris—Jacob Cohen.... 105 46
17 Keiler, Raphael—Manhattan Electric Light Co (Lim).... 671 81
17*Kastor, Adolph—G S Cox.... 1,494 00
11 Lynam, Peter J—Langdon & Granger Brewing Co.... 112 04
13 Loewenstein, Samuel; Loewenstein, Henrietta; Loewenstein, Ida; Loewenstein, Jennie } Emil Oelbermann.... 192 05
13 Loewenstein, Ida—J B McKeon, recvr. 500 00
13 Loewenstein, Jennie——the same....1,500 00
13 Lett, William F, Jr—Beinecke & Co.. 646 76
14 Lau, Rudolph—N Y, N Haven & Hartford R R Co.... 58 50
14*Leverich, Henry M — Patterson, Gottfried & Hunter (Lim).... 103 85
14 Ladd, Alfred W—R L Rees.... 32 87
15 Loritz, Nicholas—John McClave.... 786 78
15 Lenk, Peter; Lenk, Carl P; Lenk, Rudolph; Lindenmeyer, John } W J Farrell.... 2,113 22
15 Lewis, Daniel C—Robert Morrison.... 154 80
15 Lynch, Patrick—Bensinger Self-Adding Cash Register Co.... 137 18
15 Levy, Max—Charles Simon.... 194 06
15 Lissberger, Lazarus — Pennsylvania Steel Co....57,871 38
16 Lawrence, William C—J F Miller.... 109 84
16 Luhrs, Ernest A—Park & Tilford.... 228 30
17 Lawrence, William C—The Fourteenth Street Bank.... 224 56
17 Lippmann, Israel—Jacob Barnett.... 923 71
11 Mabie, Edgar W—M M Smith.... 79 50
11*Minzesheimer, Moses; Minzesheimer, Benjamin; *Minzesheimer, Milton } Thurber, Whyland Co.... 805 60
11 Munn, Archibald B—C E Johnson.... 201 63
13 Moller, August—Henry Hahn.... 178 23
14 Markstone, Isador D—T E Greacen.. 385 97
14 Mosby, Julius A—W D Starr.... 290 77
14 Menken, Mortimer M—H W Benedict. 131 57
14 Maxwell, Charles M—John Ratzer.... 575 06
14 Meyer, Arthur L; Meyer, Siegmund T } George Mackenzie.... 167 18
14 Miller, George A—Max Freund.... 180 68
14 Mann, W D—Henry Cranston....4,374 62
14 the same——the same....1,232 74
14 Molitl, Francesco—G A Phelpbs.... 838 81
14 Milair, Gustave A J—Herman Ebmeier.... 871 22
14 Meierdiercks, George—Emil Heller.... 358 46
14 Miller, William—A J Eusyn....1,048 20
14 Meyer, Anton; Meyer, Heinrich } G S Bowdoin.... 136 28
15 Meyer, William—Murray Hill Bank.. 25 81
15 Mathews, George—Jacob Stahl, Jr.... 157 25
15 Miner, John B—Jane M Evans....2,194 16
15 Martin, George C—I P Martin....11,469 04
15 the same——the same....2,558 04
16 Macnaughtan, Francis J—Samuel Cocking.... 115 13
16 Mascord, Edward W—W J Quinlan, trustee.... 375 88
17 Marvin, Julius S—Maria B Marvin.... 287 41
17 Mignore, Dincenzo—John Baehr.... 83 00
17 Mallett, Edwin A—Sheppard Knapp.. 246 29
17 Meyer, Gesene—George Gennerich.... 455 76
17 Moisan, Delphis F—Delamater Iron Works.... 438 48
17 Merritt, George B—H B Claflin Co...3,136 10
17*Miller, Albert W W—G S Cox....1,494 00
13 McQuade, Mary—Isaac Boehm.... 63 75
14 McDonald, Francis—James Chambers (Lim).... 177 80
16 Macnaughtan, Francis J—Samuel Cocking.... 115 13
16 McQuade—Andrew Beacom.... 243 01
16 McCormick, George W—L H Gentles. 115 28
17 McCormick, John—Monroe Eckstein Brewing Co.... 535 00
13 O'Neill, Samuel M—E M Reilly.... 86 83
14 Oppenheimer, Jacob; Oppenheimer, Bertha } H A Mott.... 98 75
16*O'Hanlon, Phillip F—H W Jordan.... 28 80
13 Pease, Charles G, exr Clara E Pease—Clara M Eagan, individ and extrx. 88 92
13 Potter, Daniel C—W R Romain.... 83 20
13 Peper, John H—Elizabeth E Stack.... 136 57
13 Peck, Edward M—C H Ryan.... 919 98
13 Prince, Simeon H—H D Prince....2,027 34
14*Payne, Elmer E—Andrew Mullen.... 273 68
14 Perine, Christine F—Joseph Sawyer.. 625 56
14 Pearce, John—Patterson, Gottfried & Hunter (Lim).... 103 85
14 Pierson, Edgar L—Harry Rice.... 91 18
14 Passavant, Herman—G S Bowdoin.. 136 28
14 Potter, Edward H—Henry Cranston.10,698 88
14 Pollock, Louise A; Pollock, William J; Pollock, Thomas C } First Nat Bank of Elizabeth..1,563 27
16 Pool, Herbert W—J C Brown.... 84 50
16 Pavleny, Richard—James Lynch.... 140 60
17 Peck, Edward M—Bank of Jamaica.. 155 69
17 Pfohlmann, George—J J Froelich.... 125 00

17 Pascale, Nicola—George Funchard.... 90 11
17 Payne, Randolph—P F Munde.... 179 29
17 Pomeroy, Lemuel—Tiffany & Co.... 696 49
11 Read, William G—Lucius Moses....3,691 09
11 the same——the same....costs 251 46
11 the same——H S White and Giles Everson....1,295 90
11 the same——the same....3,755 47
11 the same——the same.... 300 05
11 the same——J S Crouse, assignee. 1,701 09
13 Roe, Richard—Nicholas Chapins.... 345 62
13 Russell, Washington—Nehemiah Andrews.... 309 53
14 Romeyn, Vermilye W—Elizabeth R Henderson.... 243 84
14*Roe, Richard—George Mackenzie.... 167 18
15 Richter, Ludwig H—J H Jackson.... 325 09
16 Roberts, Thomas—H N Cornett.... 86 92
16 Roberts, Walter—E L Mooney.... 117 92
17 Ramsey, Peter A—Vanderbeck Iron Work Co....2,531 18
17 Rapp, Frank B—E H Wootton.... 322 33
11 Seidenberg, Abraham—Phillip Leidesdorf.... 77 50
13 Simons, Leopold; Shulmann, F; Sandrowitz, Herman; Sandrowitz, Philip; Sandrowitz, David } Emil Oelbermann.... 192 05
13 Sandrowitz, Herman—J B McKeon, recvr....6,000 00
13 Simons, Leopold——the same....9,584 04
13 Stanley, John—Michael Shanley.costs 83 38
13 Saxe, Simon P—John Hartmayer.... 818 86
13 Salant, Solomon—Asher Salwen.... 123 36
13 Seward, Charles H—Nathaniel Waterbury.... 267 50
13 Stafford, E F—Nat Bank of Cortlandt 383 66
13 Saehr, Gottlieb—F E McAllister.... 89 03
13 Sayles, Whipple O; Stabler, Charles M } Metropolitan Telephone and Telegraph Co.. 43 74
13 Smyth, Margaret C—Mayor, &c.costs 181 80
13 Strauss, Samuel—Harlem Lighting Co 85 61
14 Sotscheck, Carl—Charles Weinberg..1,642 06
14 the same——C P Rogers.... 416 21
14 Stemmetz, Elizabeth—J L Mott Iron Works.... 450 06
14 Schwartz, Samuel—Tenenbaum Davis. 419 47
14 Syska, Adolph G, Jr—Hudson River Beef Co (Lim).... 196 32
14 Schlesinger, Oscar L—W J De Rivera. 73 55
14 Sutton, George W; Sandhagen, William; Simpson, William; Simpson, William, Jr. } G S Bowdoin.... 136 28
14 Stephens, Richard W—I C Ogden, Jr. 938 97
15 Senior, Mendez D—Manhattan Brass Co.... 231 09
15 Sayles, Whipple O—S E Goodwin.... 178 18
15 Stockhoff, Herman—Moise Geissmann. 166 80
15 Stovenel, Kate A—N B Cohen.... 180 30
15*Stead, Charles M—Franklin Allen..284,895 00
15 Schutz, Bernard—Pennsylvania Steel Co....57,871 38
15 Straus, Louis—F A Hamilton....10,713 23
16 Scribner, Gilbert H, Jr; Scribner, Howard } W P Greenle....2,004 31
16 Stanbrough, Rufus G—John Powers.. 36 63
16 Simmons, James A—Benjamin Altman 825 64
16 Schlicht, Paul J—E S Mayo.... 281 10
16 Sinclair, William—R Q Bowers.... 115 07
17 Suther, Otto—Sophie Kobler.... 59 50
17 Streat, George, Jr—F W Devoe.... 841 23
17 Street, James—Ettie B Slote.... 234 66
17 Styles, Frederick W—A J Campbell.. 155 65
17 Sterling, Georg C—D W Bogert.... 420 26
17 Stefanini, Luigi—Achille Starace.... 171 91
17 Schofield, Joseph L—Jacob Loewenthal.... 758 66
14 Smith, Edward—H W Benedict.... 131 57
16 Smith, Stephen T—E S Mayo.... 281 10
11 The Conant Mfg Co—Florence Elliott.5,928 28
11 Boston Car Spring Co—Charles Loewenthal....8,738 53
13 The Mayor, Aldermen, &c—Peter Larkin admr....2,000 00
13 The Metropolitan Gas Light Co of Elizabeth, N J—American Meter Co. 544 44
13 The N Y Elevated R R Co; The Manhattan Railway Co } E M Sloane.. 352 77
13 The Broadway & Seventh Av R R Co—Mary Heath....costs 97 81
14 Lawrence Curry Comb Co—New Haven Wire Mfg Co.... 140 30
14 Belford Co—Peter Adams Co.... 519 81
14 The Lyons Medicine Mfg Co—James Whitall.... 263 14
14 The First Hungarian Congregation Poal Zedek—Adolph Berkowitz.... 336 31
14 Prentiss Tool & Supply Co—F G Moore....costs 83 30
14 Assabet Mfg Co; The John Haslam (Lim) } G S Bowdoin.... 136 28
14 Belford Co—International Art Publishing Co.... 290 25
15 Pneumatic Dynamite Co—Alexander Pollock.... 808 26
15 The Medford Fancy Goods Co—People State N Y....costs 75 00
15 The N Y Elevated R R Co; The Manhattan Railway Co } Augusta L Jones 824 40
15 The Lawrence Curry Comb Co—John Merry.... 130 06
15 The N Y Elevated R R Co; The Manhattan Railway Co } Caroline A Benjamin.... 804 69
15 the same——Lewis Seasongood trustee....5,457 92
15 the same——Lewis Seasongood, exr....1,304 10

15 Loos Mfg Co—F W Devoe.... 272 18
15 The American Export and Trading Co—G E Guerrier.... 808 09
16 The Mayor, Aldermen, &c—T E Senior.... 100 00
17 The Lexington Improvement Co—Thomas Hagan.... 524 34
17 United Electric Traction Co—Illinois Electric Material Co.... 102 29
17 Joseph B Tiffany & Co—W & J Sloane Co.... 656 14
17 The N Y Chemical Co—C D Levey.... 355 18
17 J H Bonnell & Co (Lim)—Western Nat Bank....1,55 48
17 the same——the same....1,555 84
17 the same——the same....1,645 67
17 the same——the same....2,035 18
17 the same——the same....1,272 86
17 the same——the same....1,129 01
17 The Facer Refrigerating and Ice Machine Co—T E Hogg....1,831 38
17 Lawrence Curry Comb Co—The Fourteenth St Bank.... 224 56
17 J H Bonnell & Co (Lim)—Western Nat Bank....1,222 42
14 Tangemann, Richard — Anthony Fischer.... 106 73
14 Thayer, Stephen H, individ; Thayer, Horace H; exrs Stephen W Thayer } A S Webb 2,627 22
14 the same——the same.... 584 28
14 the same——the same.... 628 92
15 Taaffe, Matthew J—F & M Schaefer Brewing Co.... 384 38
16 Thomas, John—Ernest Ohliger.... 87 50
16 Tutty, John—D M Koehler.... 436 01
17 Tode, Adolph—John Guth.... 368 36
11 Underwood, John T; Underwood, Frederick W } F L Degener....3,733 34
16 Uhrie, George—T F Gilroy, comm'r....costs 258 30
16 Ulber, John—Nat Ice Co.... 104 27
13 Van Valkenburg, Theodore—Charles Schlesinger.... 238 22
15 Vandenburg, Peter T—J T Scott.... 318 16
11 Willard, Edward K—Lucius Moses....3,691 09
11 the same——the same....costs 251 46
11 the same——H S White and Giles Everson....1,295 90
11 the same——the same....3,755 47
11 the same——the same.... 300 05
11 the same——J S Crouse, assignee. 1,701 09
11 Webster, Thomas—J B Smith.... 79 50
11 Whiting, Antonia V—Gardner Wetherbee....1,265 13
11 Woolsey, Edward J—G H Smith.... 169 50
13 Westlonton, Albert E—C F MacLean, comm'r....costs 68 95
14*Wilkes, George—George Mackenzie.... 167 18
14 Welles, Alfred K—H G Ratine....1,173 56
15 Welch, Deshler; Welch, Marie Adelaide } Edmond Clark.... 240 18
15*Walker, Joseph—P F Ferrigan.... 139 50
16 Weisberger, Nathan—Anna Richter.. 25 41
16 Washburn, Henry L—P J Claassen.... 130 83
17 Wallach, Julius; Wallach, Joseph G } Rosa Kind.... 71 83
17 Wulling, John—John Guth.... 363 36
17 White, Johanna—P H McManus....1,024 71
17 Wilson, Louis—Joseph Mass, assignee 78 13
17 Yorke, William C—A G Hupfel.... 124 30
15 Yost, Abram—P F Ferrigan.... 139 50
15 Yesky, Arthur—Frederick Beiermeister 499 68
16 Zorn, John—C H Kelly.... 54 50

KINGS COUNTY.

July
9 Aims, Alfred C—Louis Bergdoll Mfg Co.... $329 67
15 Arbuckle, Andrew—Thurber, Whyland & Co.... 46 34
15 Adams, Frank E—J N Willard.... 121 26
16 Altenbrand, Albert — Geneva Nat Bank....1,147 75
9 Baker, Henry C—G P Jacobs.... 444 57
9 Brooks, Julius—J Stein.... 141 59
10 Becker, Christian F T—Bay Ridge Mfg Co....3,156 28
10 Bedell, Edwin J—T G Chamberlain.. 194 38
10 the same——C H Nichols.... 44 75
10 the same——T G Chamberlain.... 212 51
11 Benedict, Elizabeth—Annie E Schinzel....(D) 4,786 90
11 Bailey, William T—J McGroarty.... 300 00
13 Bell, George H—National Bank of Cortland.... 383 66
13 Brush, Thomas H—E H Raynolds.... 327 88
13 Baron, Bernhard—L C Miner, Jr.... 81 77
14 Bernstein, Julius—Brooklyn Varnish Mfg Co.... 89 97
15 Bunce, Charles—J J White, Jr.... 71 83
15 the same——T Stratton.... 216 88
15 Bahlen, John Baumann—H Bennett.... 121 22
16 Brooks, Julius—M Freedman....1,016 88
16*Bruswitz, "Edward"—Rebecca A R Barefield.... 109 25
16 Brown, Theodore N—Behrens Bros.... 99 77
9 Craighead, John P—Brooklyn City R R Co.... 641 82
11 Cornell, William—P McCauley.... 63 89
13 Carman, Thomas D—E H Reynolds.. 327 88
14 Conkling, John B—F W Beers.... 30 46
14 Crawley, William K—Empire Moulding Works.... 203 59
16 Cochran, Alexander—Amelia L Gurlitz....(D).2,739 80
10 Dalton, Matthew—Emma Dalton.... 193 74
13 Day, William H—H F Martens.... 220 87
14 Daul, Magdalena—Commissioners of Charities and Corrections.... 91 36
15 Doyle, Thomas—Rector, &c., Trinity Church, N. Y.... 76 21
15 Devoe, Fred—L Lang.... 297 12

13 Delgardo, Joseph A—Annie E Delgardo.......... 98 14
16 Dooley, William—S Liebmann's Sons B Co.......... 101 40
16 Dubigg, Michael, exr Annie O'Brien, dec'd—Catharina Taylor.......... 175 00
14 Engelhardt, William F } Claus Lipsius
Engelhardt, Albert F } B Co.......... 148 28
14 Eddy, George B—R Pontlarge.......... 80 23
13 Finken, Elizabeth—Margarethe Rederle.......... 88 69
14 Flood, Catherine—W Haaker Co.......... 33 03
16 Finan, James—Third Nat Bank of Buffalo.......... 296 01
10†Gamble, A L—Catherine Kaufmann.. 127 20
11 Gubriog, John M—L Hilsenbeck.......... 110 10
14 Green, Peter—Claus Lipsius B Co.... 118 36
15 Gottscho, Herman } H E Frankenberg
Gottscho, Isaac } 89 15
15 Gilman, Thesplilius—M Smith.......... 149 14
10 Hollsberg, William C—J Vollkommer 223 84
10 Happ, August—Williamsburgh Brew-Co.......... 213 95
10 Hamilton, Adelaide E } M J McKeon. 550 00
Hamilton, William B }
11 Hewer, Henry—Thurber, Whyland & Co.......... 28 75
11 Hyde, Albert D—T W Cummings.. 170 77
13 Haviland, Lizzie—Margarethe Rederle 88 69
13 Hill, Harry—R Vom Hofe.......... 295 08
14 Homeyer, Christopher D—Claus Lipsius B Co.......... 115 50
14 Harrison, John—E W Richardson.. 207 08
14 Harberger, Frederick — Comm'rs Charities and Corrections.......... 91 36
16 Higgins, Charles S—B Altman.......... 699 67
16 Higgins, Patrick—J Nickels.......... 77 85
13 Kraus, Henry—L C Miner, Jr.......... 81 77
15 Kirkland, William—J N Willard.... 121 28
11 Ledwith, Patrick—J Behrens.......... 167 47
11 Luhrs, Elizabeth—A E Schinzel...(D) 4,766 90
13 Lynan, Peter J—Langdon & Granger Brewing Co.......... 112 04
14 Lett, William F, Jr—Beinecke & Co. 646 76
10 Miller, Frederick—J P Boyd.......... 120 83
10 McCarron, James—Obermeyer & L.. 134 37
10 Mitchell, Charles H—S T Birdsall.... 81 85
11 McBean, Andrew N—H Miles.......... 104 63
11 Moncrief, Calleb—J B Peck.......... 1,037 33
13 Mott, Frank S—Broadway Bank.... 348 62
13 McCracken, Henry B—A Tompkins.. 180 10
15 Mosby, Julius A—W D Starr.......... 200 77
16 Mascord, Edward W—W J Quinlan.. 375 88
16 McGovern, Charles H—N Langler.... 328 62
16 Mehl, John W—C Fullesen.......... 79 58
13 Newman, John—J V Wilson.......... 47 87
14 Neidig, Edward—Claus Lipsius B Co. 113 32
14 Olney, George—Laura L Preston.... 159 79
16 O'Reilly, Annie E—Ada Aller.......... 54 24
10 Palmer, George W—R W Elliott.... 544 55
13 Pavieng, Richard—J Lynch.......... 140 60
16 Peper, John H—Elizabeth E Stack... 136 57
11 Quantin, Edward H—F & M Schaeffer B Co.......... 37 44
15 Quick, David M } H C Wright.......... 89 99
†Quick, "Mary" }
10 Redmond, Vincent—F C Martin.......... 189 83
13 Richter, Emil—F Roth.......... 98 10
13 the same—the same.......... 93 10
14 Reilly, Thomas—P Flynn.......... 78 64
15 Ross, William H—F R Biedler.......... 5,303 94
16 Rogers, Joseph E—T McCann.......... 174 60
10 Shanley, Mary T } B Katz........(D) 3,098 86
Shanley, John }
10 *Steenworth, Charles C } J G Phelan.. 165 00
†Steenworth, Francis J }
10 Schlotter, Killian—A Dietzel.......... 441 02
13 Stafford, E F—Nat Bank of Cortland. 383 66
14 Steinherz, Leon, also called Leo and Otto Steinherz—Claus Lipsius B Co. 117 78
14 Sagar, Alonzo M } United States Foun-
Sagar, Edgar E } dry Co.......... 111 32
15 Sanford, James A—H H Frost.......... 100 00
15 Smith, Ulysses G—Mary E Smith.... 85 25
16 Shaw, Thomas, exr of—Catharine Taylor.......... 175 00
11 Thwaite, Amanda A—W R Comfort. 83 97
13 The guard Francis Ward—M Smock. 37 31
13 The Citizens' Ins Co—P P Baldwin... 89 11
13 Timmerman, Charles—D H Houghtaling.......... 121 06
16 Thornberg, Edgar D—H F Nieber.... 85 89
13 Underwood, John T } F L Dege-
Underwood, Frederick W } ner.... 8,738 04
10 Wheeler, Henry F—S Wendelin.......... 36 60
10 Ward, Henry—C H Jacobus.......... 258 67
13 Ward, Francis, by William Ward, guard—M Smock.......... 37 31
13 Willdridge, John S—Margaret Willdridge.......... 54 10
14 Wegmann, John—W Klein.......... 06
15 Webster, Thomas—J B Smith.......... 79 50
15 Welles, Alfred K—H G Ristine.......... 1,173 56
14 Young, Thomas—E I Hampton.......... 181 66

SATISFIED JUDGMENTS.

NEW YORK.

July 11 to 17—Inclusive.

Alury, Frederick—New Britain Nat Bank. (1889).......... $5,080 49
Alury, Frederick—First Nat Bank of Hazleton (1889).......... 5,061 36
Same—First Nat Bank of Rockville. (1889). 5,064 90
Same—Rockville Nat Bank of Rockville. (1889).......... 5,067 02
Alt, Adam—E S Riker. (1891).......... 907 32
Armstrong, William A—C R Hickox. (1884)... 597 31
Bien, Julius—J H Springer. (1891).......... 2,721 79
Bernhardt, Frances D—G W Smith. (1888). .. 783 50
Brewer, Daniel R—T W Lord. (1891).......... 693 55
Brush, Thomas H—E H Raynolds. (1891)..... 327 88
Barr, William J—Patrick Sharkey. (1887).... 154 90
Carman, Thomas D—E H Raynolds. (1891)... 327 88
Cleveland, Delancey—Benjamin Altman. ('91). 705 48
Cambies, Natalie—W F Redlich. (1891).......... 384 92
Central Park, North and East River R R Co—Mary O'Toole. (1891).......... 90 19
Same—same. (1890).......... 1,203 29
Same—same. (1891).......... 112 87
Diebolt, Charles S—James Chambers (Lim). (1891).......... 293 37
Dimond, William H—H M Hitchings. (1886).. 322 14
Ernest, Max G—Richard Friedlander. (1891). 325 73
Ewing, Justus E—T W Lord. (1891).......... 638 55
Franklin, William M—J H Springer. (1891).. 2,721 79
*Facer Refrigerating and Ice Co—J C Davis. (1891).......... 158 39
Fitzwilson, George H—V A Krepps. (1888)... 253 74
Gilbert, Sarah E and Eliakim—C F Kelly. ('91) 181 11
Geery, David R—Alfred Geery. (1890).......... 220 18
Husted, Peter V—L J Finch. (1889).......... 105 82
Husted, Sabina E—John Williams. (1891)..... 550 02
‡Same and Peter V—Hyman Israel. (1890).. 573 57
Hoffman, Isaac—C I Schampain. (1891)...... 207 50
Holly, John I—W B Smith. (1890).......... 31,440 97
Holmer, John—Henry Zeimer. (1891).......... 280 82
Haskin, John B—Health Department. (1890). 209 87
†Hagenbuchle, John B—Sabina F Kernes. (1891).......... 5,143 70
†Same—F W Kerns. (1891).......... 3,694 70
Johnson, Edward S and Martin—George Boyce. (1891).......... 162 79
Kennard, Edward P—W B Smith. (1890)..... 31,440 97
Lamson, Theodore—Rockville Nat Bank of Rockville. (1889).......... 5,067 02
Same — First Nat Bank of Rockville. (1889). 5,064 90
Same First Nat Bank of Hazleton. (1889).. 5,061 36
Lees, Samuel—W D Wade. (1891).......... 59 03
Lowenstein, Benjamin & Moses—J P Walther. (1891).......... 124 09
Lippman, Moritz—Thomas Meehan. (1891). . 166 06
Lamson, Theodore—New Britain Nat Bank. (1889).......... 5,080 49
Morrison, Edward—G T Tutney. (1891). 178 10
Mills, George H—G E Atwood. (1891).......... 29 77
Manhattan Railway Co—George Garlan, admr. (1891).......... 3,500 00
N Y Flexible Wood Flooring Co—Louis Eickwort. (1891).......... 2,041 47
Same—same. (1891).......... 1,002 74
‡N Y Steamship Co—S M Nelson. (1891)....... 120 47
Nooney, Mary—Eliza Sullivan. (1884)....... 72 83
Ripley, George H....G H Wilson. (1886)...... 851 76
Reed, Emma A—Photo Gravure Co. (1891)... 315 98
Roberts, Anna M—John Davidson. (1891)..... 192 55
Smith, Curtis—James Rose. (1891).......... 4,322 01
Southwick, John C—First Nat Bank of Memphis. (1881).......... 1,152 51
Smith, Albert H—C E Atwood. (1891).......... 29 77
Sloane, John }
South Brunswick Terminal R R Co } W B Smith. (1890).. 31,440 97
Smith, William Bigbie—S B Potter. (1894)... 709 92
Samuels, Julius—Rudolph Hermann. (1891). 288 09
Turner, William C—C F Nagel. (1890)...... 73 04
Thomson, Francis J—Mount Morris Bank. (1884).......... 1,211 40
Unverzagt, Charles H—Charles McGreevy. (1890).......... 59 50
Union Iron Co, of Buffalo—Ario Pardee. ('79) 285,788 28
*Vetter, Michael—Whitson Oakley. (1887).... 184 52
Von Armim, Otto F—First Nat Bank of Hazelton. (1889).......... 5,061 36
Same—First Nat Bank of Rockville. (1889) 5,064 90
Same—Rockville Nat Bank of Rockville. (1889).......... 5,067 02
Von Armin, Otto F—New Britain Nat Bank. (1889).......... 5,080 49
Vrasda, Ignace—F M Zimmermann. (1891).. 508 50
Whiting, Holland S, and Jean Noble—George Whitaker. (1891).......... 846 63
Watson, William A, assignee Wm P Robeson—G E Atwood. (1891).......... 29 77
Youle, John D—Mutual Life Ins Co. (1888).... 223 40

KINGS COUNTY.

July 10 to 16—Inclusive.

Grabau, Gerd—J F Ehrgott. (1891).......... $282 56
Mayer, Daniel A—H F Hutchinson. (1887) ... 174 43
Perhacs, Emil M—same. (1887).......... 174 43
Scholes, Mary J—W Nixon. (1890).......... 499 59
Same—Elphens Smith & Wiemans Co. (1890).......... 297 01
Same—W Nixon. (1890).......... 506 24
Townsend, George S—C F Field. (1887)...... 230 53

MECHANICS' LIENS.

NEW YORK CITY.

July

11 One Hundred and Fifteenth st, Nos. 252-264, s s, 275 e 8th av, 175x100. Charles Lindemann and six others agt Miller & Hauff, owners, and Erslew & Nielson, contractors $204 75
11 Ninety-fifth st, No. 68, s e cor Columbus av, 80x25. James Murray agt Mrs. Platho, owner, and Frank Leimeister, contractors 60 00
11 Madison av, n w cor 115th st, 100.11x85. H. Kunn & Co. agt M. E. and William N. McEnttee, owners and contractors.......... 570 00
11 Seventy-fourth st, No. 323 E., n s. Minna Mueller agt —— Federgreen, owner and contractor.......... 48 49
11 Ninety-fourth st, n s, 100 w Columbus av, 50x100.8. Morton Bros. & Co. agt Francis J Hillenbrand, owner and contractor.... 1,900 00
13 Eighty-sixth st, n s, 100 e Riverside Drive, 125x100.......... }
Eighty-sixth st, s s, 200 e Riverside Drive, 125x100.......... }
Seventy-second st, n s, 100 e West End av, 150x100.......... }
West End av, s e cor 72d st, 100x125.......... }
Philip Biershenk agt W. E. D. Stokes, owner, and Squire & Whipple, contractors.......... 4,000 00
13 Eighty-second st, s e cor Riverside Drive, 109.5x—. Same agt Squire & Whipple, owners and contractors.......... 1,550 00
13 Home st, s s, 175 e Stebbins av, 75x100. Bengt Bengtson agt Triffler H. Allard and Alexander McCone, owners and contractors.......... 125 00
13 One Hundred and Fifteenth st, s s, 275 e 7th av, 175x100.11. Mary L. Halpin agt Conrad Muller, Jr., and Anna Hauff, debtors and owners.......... 2,200 00
13 Park av, s w cor 93d st, 105x100.8. P. McDowell & Co. agt Downey & Curry, owners, and Standard Mantel and Slate Works, contractor.......... 500 00
13 Sixty-third st, Nos. 33 and 35, n s, 400 w 8th av, 75x100.5. White Rock Lime and Cement Co. agt R. Everett and Robert Carey, owners, and Donald Frazer, contractors.......... 585 68
14 Park av, s w cor 93d st, 100.5x100.8. John Heany agt Charles Downey and George W. Curry, debtors and owners.......... 68 00
14 One Hundred and Thirty-second st, s s, 200 w Madison av, 75x100. Patrick Moran agt George Wilkes, owner and contractor.... 59 00
14 Central Park West, n w cor 104th st, 100.11x100. James McNally agt August Kohn, John J. Carey, Martin J. Barron, Henry Steers and J. F. Menke, owners, and John J. Carey and Martin J. Barron, contractor.......... 100 00
14 Eleventh st, Nos. 310 and 312, s s, 225 e 2d av, 50x—. Ferdinand Ehrhart agt Moses, Sophie, Joseph, Sarah, Carrie, Minnie and Julia Weil and Hannah Schuster, owners. (Continued from July 9, 1891).......... 532 33
14 Vandam st, s w cor Macdougal st, 86x92. Joseph Marren agt Charles Downey and George W. Curry, owners and contractors.......... 898 20
14 One Hundred and Sixtieth st, s s, 183.4 e St. Nicholas av, 36x100. G. B. Robbins & Co. agt J. S. Dale, owner and contractor...... 16 00
14 Gramercy Park, No. 40, s e cor 21st st, 19.8x80.......... }
Twenty-first st, No. 148, s s, 80 e Gramercy Park, 22.9x78.10.......... }
M. H. Spelman's Sons agt Eliza O'Meara, owner and contractor.......... 248 00
14 Vandam st, s w cor Macdougal st, 87x118.4. L. C. Bochert agt Downey & Curry, owners and contractors.......... 775 00
14 Park av, s w cor 93d st, 100.8x105. Same agt same.......... 20 00
15 West End av, s w cor 103d st, 100.11x159.10. William Hilgers agt Welcome R. Steinmetz, owner and contractor.......... 1,450 00
15 Fifty-third st, No. 518, s s, 275 w 10th av, 25x85. George Mungo agt —— Glory, owner and contractor.......... 75 00
15 Fourth st, No. 60, s s, 299.10 w 2d av, 25x100. Same agt —— Silvester, owner, and Divinney & Cannon, contractors.......... 50 00
15 Bayard st, No. 59, s s, 248.4 w Bowery, 25x100. Same agt same.......... 100 00
15 Clinton st, n w cor Delancey st, 75x100. August Bornholz agt Weil & Mayer, owners and contractors.......... 171 00
15 Villa av e s, 375 n Potter pl, 50x100. C. E. Gates & Co. agt E. C. Allcot, owner and contractor.......... 112 29
15 Seventy-sixth st, No. 339, n s, 200 e 2d av, 25x—. Same agt Mortimer M. Menken, owner, and John Sheehy, contractor. (Continued from July 17, 1890).......... 534 63
16 Park av, s w cor 93d st, 100.8x175. A. J. Finkle agt Downey & Curry, debtors and owners.......... 150 00
16 Seventy-eighth st, s s, 100 w Amsterdam av, 100x100. August Kassassa and three others agt John Doe, owner, and John McLaugulin, contractor.......... 96 00
16 Park av, s w cor 134d st, 100x100. Charles Lein agt Edward Broome, owner, and John Dixon, contractor.......... 140 00
16 Central Park West, n w cor 104th st, 100.11x100. J. E. Quick agt John J. Carey, Martin J. Barron, J. F. Menke, August Kohn and Henry Steers owners, and John J. Carey and Martin J. Barron, contractors 3,703 50
16 Ninth st, No. 11, n s, 200 e 5th av, 25x92.3. Morton & Chesley agt Charles Burrall Hoffman, owner and contractor...... 4,308 80
16 Fifth av, n w cor 119th st, 28x55x40x58. John Bell & Son agt Kate J. Murphy, debtor and owner.......... 202 00
16 One Hundred and Fifty-fourth st, s s, 125 w Courtlandt av, 25x100. Jas. W. Colwells' Sons agt Catharine Twomey, owner, and Frank Lotz, contractor.......... 221 35
16 Home st, s s, 176 e Stebbins av, 75x100. Weber & Strom agt Triffle H. Allard, Frederick Rouseau and Albert McCone, owner, and Frederick Rouseau and Albert McCone, contractor.......... 78 39
16 Ninth st, No. 30, s s, 456 1 w 5th av, 25.4x93.11. Morris Eschwege agt Rosalie Schoenberg, trustee, owner and contractor.......... 412 00
16 Second av, s w cor 96th st, 100x200. G. B. Robbins & Co. agt F. A. Clark, owner and contractor.......... 541 59
16 One Hundred and Tenth st, s s, 100 w Madison av 50x100 N. Y. Anderson Pressed Brick Co. agt John O'Connor, owner and contractor.......... 387 00
16 Eighty-sixth st, s s, 200 e Riverside Drive, 100x100. H. C. and G. S. Bailie agt William E. D. Stokes, owner, and Squire & Whipple, contractors.......... 775 00
16 Eighty-sixth st, n s, 200 e Riverside Drive, 100x100. Same agt same.......... 775 00
16 Eighty-sixth st, s s, 200 e Riverside Drive, 100x—. Same agt William E. D. Stokes, owner, and J. N. Franklin, contractor.... 1,400 00
16 Eighty-sixth st, n s, 200 e Riverside Drive, 100x100. Same agt same.......... 1,200 00
16 West End av, n w cor 86th st, ½ block x 100. Same agt same owner, and Squire & Whipple, contractors.......... 1,260 00
16 West End av, n e cor 87th st, ½ block x 100. Same agt William E. D. Stokes, owner, and Squire & Whipple, contractors....... 1,200 00
16 West End av, s w cor 87th st, ½ block x 100. Same agt Francis M. Jencks, owner, and Squire & Whipple, contractors.......... 1,000 00
16 Seventy-second st, n s, 100 e West End av, 125x100 Same agt Wm. E. D. Stokes, owner, and Squire & Whipple, contractors.......... 750 00
16 West End av, s e cor 72d st, 100x100. Same agt same.......... 500 00
16 Seventy-second st, n s, 100 e West End av, 125x100. Same agt Wm. E. D. Stokes, owner, and John N. Franklin contractor, 1,860 69
16 Central Park West, n w cor 104th st, 100x100. John Lenehan agt John Doe and Richard Roe, owners, and John J. Carey and George E. Kroas, contractors.......... 50 00
16 One Hundred and Thirty-second st, Nos. 26 to 30, s s, 235 w 5th av, 100x100. Albert Taubert agt Henry C. Adams, owner and contractor.......... 2,200 00
16 Thirty-second st, No. 117, n s, 175 w 6th av, 25x50. F. J. McKeon agt Carrie Baker and F. W. Leek, owners and contractors. 90 95
16 West End av, s w cor 103d st, 100.11x465. Valentine Moeslein agt Elizabeth and Welcome R. Steinmetz, owners, and Elizabeth Steinmetz, contractor.......... 982 50

17 Thirtieth st, No. 44, s s, 211 e 6th av, 34.5x—. J. H. Glander agt Howard Moody, owner, and C. V. Moore, contractor 20 00

17 Thirty-first st, No. 215, n s, 175 w 7th av, 25x—. James O'Shea agt Mary Wilson, owner, and John Wilson, contractor 218 00

17 Lexington av, s w cor 34th st, 100x75. Emil Rattey agt The Lexington Improvement Co., owner and contractor 2,859 95

17 Park av, n w cor 133d st, 100x100. J. J. Brady agt Edward Bromme, William and William R. Bell, owners, and William and William R. Bell, contractors 575 00

West End av, n e cor 87th st, 100x100 .... }
17 West End av, w s, extends from 86th to 87th st, 200x100 .... }
William Wilkenning agt William E. D. Stokes, owner, and Squires & Whipple, contractors 1,862 40

17 Seventy-eighth st, Nos. 164-170, s s, 150 w 3d av, 100x100. P. J. Dingnan agt William C. Burne, owner and contractor 2,900 68

17 One Hundred and Tenth st, s s, 100 w Madison av, 50x100. Frederick Brandt agt John O'Connor, owner and contractor... 871 00

KINGS COUNTY.

July

10 Ocean Parkway, s w cor Av E, 200x300, Flatbush. D. Lewis Grant agt Helen and James F Graham, owner, and John Erickson and James F. Graham, contractors $188 80

11 Patchen av, s e cor Halsey st, 100x250. Long Island Brick Co. agt Hiram Bedell, owner and contractor 1,611 20

11 Cooper st, e s, 175 s Central av, 175x100. Brooklyn Slate Mantel Co. agt Thomas J. Allen, owner and contractor 178 00

11 Twelfth av, s s, 75 e 5-th st, 25x50, New Utrecht. Henry McShane Mfg. Co. agt Ida Hofler, owner, and Emil Kehler, contractor 179 79

11 Howard av, s w cor Macon st, 100x98.6. T. B. Willis & Bro. agt Clarence Lincoln, owner and contractor 650 57

13 Ocean Parkway, w s, 100 s Av E, 25x100, Flatbush. John Williams agt Mrs. Graham, owner, and John Erickson and Richartz Bros., contractors 875 00

13 Flushing av, Nos 695 and 697, n s, 90.10 w Thornton st, abt 40x83.7x irreg. George Ruebl agt Samuel Conen and Abraham Simon, owners and contractors 1,600 00

13 Forty-fifth st, n s, 300 e 5th av, 40x100.2. Hobby & Doody agt John L. Parish, owner, and A. D. Hyde, contractor 177 74

14 Seigel st, No. 72, s s, 150 e Ewen st, 25x100. Alois Flohl agt —— Beshadsley, owner and contractor 112 73

14 Kingston av, n e cor Pacific st, 96x80. Ronalds & Co. agt Hobby & Doody, owner, and Franklin J. Fellows, contractor 398 38

15 Central av, n e cor Ralph st, 25x100. John McCormack agt Mary Cooney, owner and contractor 87 50

15 Sixth av, s e cor 1st st, 100x90. W. F. Fisher & Co. a corporation, agt Roderick Von Graaf, owner and contractor 1,040 63

16 Cropsey av, n s, 100 e 21st av, 25x100, New Utrecht. Conrad Gans agt Catharine F. Monjo, owner and contractor 157 89

16 Forty-fifth st, n s, 300 e 5th av, 40x100. Thomas and Robert Edgerton agt John L. Parish, owner, and A. D. Hyde & Co., contractors 200 00

16 Bath av, s s, 50 w Bay 19th st, 25x100, New Utrecht. Charles Stauche agt M. Simonson, owner, and Joseph Trautman and Mr. Laiser, contractors 18 00

16 Hancock st, n e cor Bedford av, 30x92. Robert W. Starr agt John Doe, owner, and Washington L. Baker, contractor 6 25

16 Somers st, n s, 90 e Stone av, 20x100. Same agt M. Chorinski, owner, and Washington L. Baker, contractor 6 25

SATISFIED MECHANICS' LIENS

NEW YORK CITY.

July

11 One Hundred and Fourteenth st, No. 332 E., s s, 30x100 W H Simonson & Son agt Joseph F and Kate Gallagher. (Lien filed June 27, 1891) $809 53

11 Same property. Scully & Moran agt same. (July 3, 1891) 65 00

11 Seventy-second st, Nos. 414 and 416 E. 100x—. Louis Roller agt same. (June 27, 1891) 2,975 00

11 Same property. Same agt same. (June 29, 1891) 2,975 00

11 Same property. W H Simonson & Son agt same. (June 26, 1891) 1,928 63

11 Same property. J A Dooner agt same. (June 27, 1891) 739 25

11 Same property. Culbert Bros agt same. (July 3, 1891) 437 82

13 Forty-eighth st, Nos. 322 and 324 W, s s. James Taylor agt Mary Callaher. (Dec. 16, 1889) 155 00

13 West End av, e s, 75 n 64th st, 25x100. Perth Amboy Terra Cotta Co. agt Thomas F. Devine. (June 22, 1891) 423 23

14‡Madison av, n w cor 116th st, 100x100. Nicola Sarina and 17 others agt John Doe and George Williams. (April 8, 1891) 692 98

14 One Hundred and Thirteenth st, No. 124 E., s s, 16.9x100.10. J M Fielder agt Caroline Marvin Lawrence. (May 2, 1891) 112 30

14 One Hundred and Twenty-second st, No. 303 E, n s. Oscar Klemfuss agt Ludwig Guenkal and James Harry. (March 18, 1891) 18 60

14 Same property. John Zulch agt same. (March 18, 1891) 28 75

14 Same property. Peter Reimschach agt same. (March 18, 1891) 11 75

14 Forty-second st, No. 559 W, n s, 25x100.5. G. E. Tilford agt Mary A. Barron and William Spearing. (June 22, 1891) 239 30

14 Same property. O. D. Person agt William Spearing. (June 15, 1891) 85 45

15 Decatur av, e s, — s Scott st. C. E. Gates & Co. agt H. R. Knoop and E. Goeb. (June 22, 1891) 709 98

15 One Hundred and Fifty-third st, n s, 194 e 10th av, 26x99.11. J. B. Robinson agt Mary Frances Disbrow and William Baker. (July 11, 1891) 739 00

15 One Hundred and Twentieth st, s s, 125 w 8th av, 75x100. Louis Roller agt James Thompson. (July 9, 1891) 3,338 50

16‡Seventy-second st, Nos. 414-420 E., s s, 100x102.2. Pauline B. Blumenthal agt Joseph Gallagher. (June 24, 1891) 513 75

16 One Hundred and Eighteenth st, s s, 240 w Park av, 100x100.11. Bowes & Coombs agt Bernhard Ginsburg and Marie Masche and Samuel Harris. (June 29, 1891) 360 00

16 Fulton av, Nos. 1237-1241, w s. E. T. Hawkins agt Philip Bunn and Frank Breiner. (July 14, 1891) 131 78

17 Thirty-first st, No. 215 W, n s. Morton Bros. & Co. agt Mary Wilson and John Sheridan. (July 11, 1891) 616 00

17 Fulton av, w s, 129 n 168th st, 57x—. Wm. Eppinger & Son agt Phillip Bunn. (July 14, 1891) 40 50

17 Fourth st, No. 226 W., s s. Herman Kertscher agt John J. and Wm. H. Crawford. (July 7, 1891) 378 67

17 Fifty-sixth st, Nos. 405 and 407 W., n s, 96x100. N. Y. Anderson Pressed Brick Co. agt James Adams. (Aug. 12, 1890) 332 00

17 Same property. John Thompson agt same and Felix Adams. (Sept. 9, 1890) 2,000 00

17 Same property. Same agt same. (Sept. 9, 1890) 2,000 00

17 Same property. Canda & Kane agt James A. and Felix Adams. (Aug. 11, 1890) 3,132 55

17 Same property. Tait & McWhirter agt Felice and John A. Adams and Solomon Prell. (Aug. 14, 1890) 2,400 00

17 Same property. W G. & J. E. Schuyler agt Felice and J. A. Adams. (Aug. 15, 1890). 1,299 98

17 Same property. Antonio Scerbo agt same and William Prell. (Aug. 15, 1890) 1,000 00

17 Same property. Murray & Hill agt James A. Adams. (Aug 16, 1890) 240 00

17 Same property. Vermont Marble Co. agt same and Felice Adams. (Aug. 21, 1890). 225 00

17 Fifty-sixth st, Nos. 405-409 W., n s, 75x100. William Simms agt Felice Adam, Adams or Adamo and John Thompson. (Sept. 11, 1890) 61 50

17 Same property. Michael Kiely agt same. (Sept. 11, 1890) 21 75

17 Same property. James McGann agt same. (Sept. 11, 1890) 5 90

17 Same property. John Cahill agt same. (Sept. 11, 1890) 29 25

17 Same property. James Bruen agt same. (Sept. 12, 1890) 19 86

17 Same property. Robert Thompson agt same. (Sept. 15, 1890) 35 00

17 Same property. P. J. Algie agt same. (Sept. 15, 1890) 37 50

17 Same property. William Keating agt same. (Sept. 15, 1890) 50 85

17 Same property. Rasmo Basilio agt same. (Sept. 16, 1890) 26 40

17 Same property. William Zann agt same. (Sept. 11, 1890) 50 00

17 Same property. Joshua B. Thompson agt same. (Sept. 18, 1890) 8 50

17 Same property. Charles Ellis agt same. (Sept. 19, 1890) 18 50

17 Same property. Michael Speed agt same. (Oct. 6, 1890) 18 12

17 Same property. Patrick McSweeney agt same. (Sept. 16, 1890) 27 50

17‡Seventieth st, n s, 110 e 9th av, 100x—. Vincenzo Roba and ten others agt P. W. Gallaudet and John Johnson; 11 liens. (Jan. 30, 1828) 179 39

‡Discharged by order of Court on filing bond.

KINGS COUNTY.

July

9 Hopkinson av, s w cor Decatur st, 100x100. Jeremiah Hackett agt John W. Harman, owner, and Frank McMahon, contractor. (Lien filed May 19, 1891) $1,800 00

9 Twelfth av, n w cor 58th st, 100.2x100. Frank D. Creamer agt Martha J. Gue, owner, and Emil Kehler, contractor. (July 8, 1891) 489 95

10 Dergen st, s e cor 3d av, 25x40 John F. Richartz agt Jacob Goldschmidt, owner and contractor. (June 27, 1891) 425 00

10 Schneck st, e s, 162 n Arlington av, 213x100. Long Island Brick Co. agt Elizabeth Rapelje, owner, and Thomas F. Parker, contractor. (April 30, 1891) 450 00

10 Fifty-third st, s s, 275 w 15th av, 50x100.2, New Utrecht. James Lindsay agt —— Dettmar, owner, and C. F. T. Becker, contractor. (June 29, 1891) 77 00

10 Macon st, n s, 185 w Howard av, 90x100. Bertha Horwitz to Calvin W. Raymond and Michael Dowley. Release lien agt E. J. Ames, owner and contractor. (May 11, 1891) 50 00

10 Same property. Salvator McCue to same. Release lien agt same owner and contractor. (May 27, 1891) .... nom

10 Fifty-third st, s s, 240 w 15th av, 100x100, New Utrecht. Henry McShane Mfg. Co. agt William Dittmir, owner, and C. F. T. Becker, contractor. (July 8, 1891) 245 00

10 De Kalb av, s s, 150 w Marcy av, 100x100. Johnson & Phelan agt Elizabeth S. Maitland, owner, and Charles H. Collins, contractor. (Dec. 2, 1891). (Deposit) 167 57

11 Willoughby av, n w cor Grand av, 24x100. John Seton & Co. agt Edward Judson, owner and contractor. (March 7, 1891)... 146 00

11 Saratoga av, s s, extends from Decatur st to Bainbridge st, 200x12?. King & Adams agt Kate S. Good, owner, and Samuel R. Good, contractor. (June 20, 1891) 1,912 75

15 Sixtieth st, s s, bet 12th and 13th avs, New Utrecht. John S. Loomis agt Philip and Mary Greesbach, owner, and Frank Shultz, contractor. (June 25, 1891) 176 00

Bay 34th st, s s, 260 e Benson av, 120x96.8. }
15 Bay 34th st, s s, 200 e Benson av, — x96.8, Gravesend .... }
C. E. Hartelius agt Ronal, Edward and Mathew Desvernine, owners, and Henry J. Dudley, contractor. (Sept. 22, 1890).. 80 00

15 Bay 34th st, s e s, 100 n e Benson av, 180x96, Gravesend. E. W. Voorhies & Bro. agt same owner and contractor. (Oct. 4, 1890) 216 30

16 Fourteenth st, n s, 217.10 e 8th av, 100x100. James Briscoe agt Catharine Beatty, owner, and John F. and Catharine Beatty, contractors. (July 8, 1891). (Deposit)... 75 00

BUILDINGS PROJECTED.

The first name is that of the owner; ar't stands for architect, m'n for mason, c'r for carpenter and b'r for builder.

NEW YORK CITY.

SOUTH OF 14TH STREET.

Franklin st, No. 185, six-story brk factory, 20x64, tin roof; cost, $11,500; J. W. Dimick, 67 Madison av; ar't, M. A. Ryan; b'rs, Ryan & Bros. Plan 1032.

Grand st, Nos. 10, 12 and 14, six-story brk building, 74.6x83, gravel roof; cost, $60,000; A. Levett, 33 West 73d st; ar't, J. Roth. Plan 1031.

Jones st, No. 23, five-story and basement brk flat, 25x88.8, tin roof; cost, $22,000; T. Van Eupen, 307 Bowery; ar't, W. Graul. Plan 1017.

Lewis st, No. 25, five-story brk flat, 25x88.6, tin roof; cost, $23,000; M. Conferti, 2265 1st av; ar'ts, Schneider & Herter. Plan 1015.

Canal st, No. 78, iron fence in yard; cost, $700; M. L. Goldman, 27 Eldridge st; ar't, W. Graul. Plan 1041.

9th st, No. 323 E., rear, one-story brk shop, 84x11.4, tin roof; cost, $200; A. Kraemer, on premises; ar't, H. Horenburger; m'n, I. C. Walter. Plan 1039.

BETWEEN 14TH AND 59TH STREETS.

Broadway, s e cor 43d st, one-story frame shed, 20x50, fire-proof paint roof; cost, $300; agents, Richards & Sause, Liberty and Nassau sts. Plan 1033.

28th st, No. 527 W., two-story brk and iron dwell'g and store, 25x45, tin roof; cost, $3,000; lessee, F. Farrell, 525 West 28th st; ar't, J. H. Collins. Plan 1016.

44th st, Nos. 437 and 439 W., five-story brk flat, 40x90, tin roof; cost, $28,000; W. G. Jordan, 199 2d av; ar't, J. W. McKecknie. Plan 1029.

55th st, n s, 275 w 10th av, one-story brk shop, 25x100.5, gravel roof; cost, $2,000; lessee, M. Ward, 518 West 52d st; ar't, J. W. Cole. Plan 1026.

37th st, No. 120 E., five-story brk, stone, and terra cotta dwell'g, 20x51.4 and 28.8, tin roof; cost, $35,000; J. C. Fargo, 56 Park av; art's, Romeyn & Stever. Plan 1038.

45th st, n s, 75 w 11th av, four-story brk building, 25x75, tin roof; cost, $7,000; ow'r and b'r, C. Groll, 548 West 40th st; art's, M. V. B. Ferdon. Plan 1040.

BETWEEN 59TH AND 125TH STREETS, EAST OF 5TH AVENUE.

110th st, No. 332 E., frame shed, 11x40, tin roof; cost, $200; R. K. Grace, 64 East 106th st. Plan 1034.

115th st, Nos. 204 and 206 E., brk and stone church, 41.8x100.11, tin and slate roof; cost, $25,000; St. Bartholomew's wardens and vestry, 348 Madison av; ar't, W. H. Russell. Plan 1021.

Park av, n w cor 95th st, five-story brk and stone flat, 25.2x96, tin roof; cost, $28,000; N. J. Reville, 425 East 61st st; ar't, E. Wenz. Plan 1036.

95th st, n s, 100 w Park av, three five-story stone flats, 25x87.4, tin roof; cost, $18,000 each; ow'r and ar't, same as last. Plan 1037.

Av B, n w cor 87th st, five-story brk and stone flat, 21x96.8, tin roof; cost, $18,000; Feeban & Hammer, 1113 2d av; ar'ts, Thom & Wilson. Plan 1043.

87th st, n s, 21 w Av B, four five-story brk and stone flats, 25x70, with extension, tin roofs; cost, $16,000 each; ow'rs and ar'ts, same as last. Plan 1044.

BETWEEN 59TH AND 125TH STREETS, WEST OF CENTRAL PARK WEST AND 8TH AVENUE.

Boulevard, n e cor 104th st, brk, stone and terra cotta church, 73.6x105, slate and tin roof; cost, $50,000; Southern New York Baptist Assoc., Times Building; ar't, H. F. Kilburn. Plan 1012.

Manhattan av, n w cor 103d st, six three-story brk and stone dwell'gs, 17.7 and 16.8x48, tin roofs; cost, $8,500 each; W. J. Davenport et al., 319 West 22d st; ar't, W. Howe; b'r, E. D. Garnsey. Plan 1019.

92d st, Nos. 54-62 W., five three-story and basement brk and stone dwell'gs, 20x54, tin roof; cost, $15,000 each; T. Kilpatrick, 75 West 94th st; ar't, A. E. Barlow. Plan 1020.

West End av, s w, cor 104th st, one three-story and basement stone dwell'g, 20.11x55, tin roofs; cost, $20,000. Jane A. Brown, 124 Manhattan av, ar't R. S. Townsend. Plan 1045

West End av, w s, 20.11 s 104th st, four three-story and basement stone dwell'gs, 20x55, tin roofs; cost, $15,000 each; ow'r and ar't same as last. Plan 1046.

110TH TO 125TH STREET, BETWEEN 5TH AND 8TH AVENUES.

118th st, s s, 109 w St. Nicholas av, four-story and basement brk and stone dwell'g, 22x65, tin roof; cost, $18,000. Rev. J. J. Keogan, 247 West 121st st; ar't, Thom & Wilson; m'n J. Fish. Plan 1042.

NORTH OF 125TH STREET.

185th st, s s, 125 e 11th av, two-story frame dwell'g, 18x45.6, tin and shingle roof; cost, $3,000; H. Doscher, 144 Reade st; ar'ts, Co-operative Building Plans Assoc.; b'r, O. Hansson. Plan 1035.

12th av, s w cor 133d st, brk freight house, 81.6x60, gravel roof; cost, $7,000; N. Y. C. & H. R. R. Co., Grand Central Depot. Plan 1023.

23D AND 24TH WARDS.

147th st, s s, 40 e Prospect st, two two-story frame dwell'gs, 20x35, tin roofs; cost, $1,200 each; W. Ryan, 147th st and Southern Boulevard; ar't, E. R. Will. Plan 1027.

184th st, n s, 175 w Washington av, one-and-a-half-story frame stable, 25x20, shingle roof; cost, $400; O. Tober, Cambrelling av and Bayard st; ar't, W. Guggolz. Plan 1018.

Creston av, w s, 30.9 s Welch st, four two-and-a-half-story frame dwell'gs, 20x49.6, shingle roofs; cost, $2,000 each; T. C. Lisk, n s Sherwood st, near Marion av; ar't, J. S. O'Meara. Plan 1030.

Morris av (87 west of), 200 s 161st st, frame shed, 288.10x30, gravel roof; cost, $12,000; N. Y. C. & H. R. Railway Co., Grand Central Depot. Plan 1022.

Mott av, No. 220, one-story frame stable, 18x36, sand roof; cost, $200; lessee, S. M. Saunders, 680 East 142d st; ar't, J. H. Valentine. Plan 1025.

Sedgwick av, e s, 749 n Jerome av, two-story frame dwell'g, 20x18, tin roof; cost, $2,000; G. & W. Reber, 243 East 113th st; ar't, J. H. Valentine; c'r, P. Berenger. Plan 1024.

Riverdale av, 90 w Ackerman st, one-and-a-half-story frame stable, 27x65, shingle roof; cost, $1,800; I. M. Dyckman, Kingsbridge, N. Y.; b'r, S. L. Berrian. Plan 1013.

Ackerman st, e s, 260 n Riverdale av, two-story frame dwell'g, 16x26, shingle roof; cost, $1,250; ow'r and b'r, same as last. Plan 1014.

Webster av, n w cor Tower pl, two-story frame building, 20x30, tin roof; cost, $3,500; agent, T. Gannon, College av, n s, near Pelham av; m'n, T. Wilson; c'r, C. B. Jones. Plan 1028.

KINGS COUNTY.

Plan 1220A—Seigel st, No. 83, one three-story frame (brk filled) dwell'g and two tailor shops, 25x30, tin roof; cost, $2,000; J. Gollin, on premises; a'rt, H. E. Funk; c'rs, Wheeler Bros.; m'n, not selected.

1306—Jay st, w s, 50 s Plymouth st, one five-story brk store house, 75x75 and 90, gravel roof and iron cornices; cost, $25,000; John W. Masury & Son, 45 Pearl st; ar't, P. Faust; b'rs, G. H. Stone & Son.

1307—28th st, s s, 475 e 3d av, one three-story frame tenem't, 25x52, tin roof; cost, $3,500; ow'r and c'r, D. Anderson, 152 25th st.

1308—Knickerbocker av, w s, 107 n Flushing av, one two-story frame stable, 12x15, tin roof; cost, $300; ow'r and b'r, R. Bleyer, 134 Throop av; ar'ts, D. Acker & Son.

1309—Ingraham st, n s, 225 w Morgan av, two three-story frame (brk filled) tenem'ts, 25x56, tin roof; cost, $4,000; ow'r, ar't and b'r, Leonard Erk, Prospect st near Hamburg av.

1310—Cook st, No. 23, one four-story frame (brk filled) tenem't, 25x60, tin roof; cost, $6,500; Leopold Michel, Graham av; ar'ts, D. Acker & Son.

1311—Penn st, s s, 110 e Wythe av, one four-story brk apartment house, 21x66, tin roof, wooden cornices; cost, $5,000; Thomas B. Saddington; ar't, J. L. Young.

1312—20th st, s s, 275 w 4th av, one two-story frame shop and stable, 25x35, tin roof; cost, $800; ow'r, ar't and b'r, George G. Melch, 149 21st st.

1313—Belmont av, n s, 50 w Osborn st, one two-story frame tailor shop, 20x30, tin roof; cost, $1,500; A. Stone, Belmont av.

1314—Stone av, w s, 150 n Fulton av, one one-story frame tailor shop, 18x27, tin roof; cost, $400; Harris Forocesky, Rockaway av; b'r, J Fletcher.

1315—Madison st, n s, 260 e Hamburg av, five two-story and basement frame (brk filled) dwellings, 20x45, tin roofs; cost, $3,000 each; Adolphus Gload, 38 Eldert st; ar'ts and b'rs, Francisco Bros.

1316—Atlantic av, n w cor Van Sielen av, one two-story frame stable, &c., 24x40, tin roof; cost, $2,000; E. F. Linton, on premises; ar'ts, Danmar and Fischer; b'r, not selected.

1317—Glenmore av, s s, 60 e Milford st, two two-story frame dwell'gs, 20x30, tin roofs; cost, $4,400; ow'r and c'r, Donald Laing, Belmont av, cor Atkins av.

1318—3d av, e s, 75 n 22d st, one two-story brk stable, 22x48, tin roof, brk cornice; cost, $1,200; Fred. Herbst, 695 3d av; ar't, R. Dixon; b'r, J. Kolle.

1319—Sumner av, n w cor Fulton st, one one-story and cellar brk stores, 25 and 12x90, gravel roof; cost, $2,000; J. O'Sullivan, 144 Decatur st; ar't, J. D. McAuliffe; b'rs, King Bros. and P. Brady.

1320—Hart st, s s, 210 w St. Nicholas av, one one-story frame chicken house, 20x8, tar paper roof; cost, $35; Ed. Skerett, on premises.

1321—Railroad av, w s, 75 s Griffin pl, two two-story frame dwell'gs, 18x30, shingle roofs; cost, $2,200; Christina A. Lorentz, 1308 Herkimer st; b'r, not selected.

1322—Cleveland st, w s, 125 n Eastern Parkway, one two-story frame dwell'g, 20x30, tin roof; cost, $2,500; David Hopkins, New Lots road and Berriman st; ar't, L. F. Schillinger; b'r, F. Gundermann, Jr.

1323—Franklin st, Nos. 260 264, n e cor Eagle st, three four-story brk stores and tenem'ts, 24 and 24.6 and 31.6x53, tin roofs, iron cornices; cost, total, $22,000; F. Heneke, 71 Freeman st; ar't, C. Dunkhase; b'r, not selected.

1324—Belmont av, n s, 75 e Osborn st, one one-story frame stable, 20x18, tin roof; cost, $150; ow'r and c'r, Solomon Wolf, on premises; ar't, A. J. Warren.

1325—Warwick st, w s, 175 s Eastern Parkway, one two-story frame dwell'g, 18x30, tin roof; cost, $2,200; George Schade, Ashford st, near Eastern Parkway; ar't, L. F. Schillinger; b'rs, F. Gundermann, Jr., and A. Reuter.

1326—Livonia av, s e cor Osborn st, one three-story frame store and tenem't, 20x60, tin roof; cost, $3,000; ow'rs and b'rs, Sidenberg & Abramowitz, on premises; ar't, A. J. Warren.

1327—Apollo st, e s, 200 s Nassau st, one one-story frame dwell'g, 20x20, 17th Ward, felt roof; cost, $150; ow'r, ar't and b'r, James Bergen, 526 East 14th st, New York.

1328—Varet st, No. 76, one four-story frame (brk filled) tenem't, 25x60, tin roof; cost, $5,200; J. F. Kuhn, on premises; ar'ts, D. Acker & Son.

1329—Buffalo av, w s, 52 n Butler st, three two-story frame dwell'gs, 16.8x40, tin roof; cost, total, $5,000; John Robinson, 190 Buffalo av; b'r, not selected.

1330—Richardson st, n s, 175 e Lorimer st, one three-story frame (brk filled) tenem't, 25x55, tin roof; cost, $4,500; Patrick Kane, 376 Lorimer st; ar't, C. Buchheit; b'r, F. Hanweber.

1331—McKibbin st, n s, 50 w Leonard st, one four-story frame (brk filled) tenem't, 25x60, tin roof; cost, $5,000; ow'r and b'r, D. Kreuder, 47 McKibbin st; ar'ts, D. Acker & Son.

1332—Stockholm st, s s, 350 e Evergreen av, one three-story frame (brk filled) store and tenement, 25x58, tin roof; cost, $4,500; A. Dillmann, on premises; ar'ts, D. Acker & Son.

1333—Broadway, n e cor Park st, one one-story frame furniture shipping room, 26x25, tin roof; cost, $175; D. S. Traum, 154 Vernon av; ar't and b'r, W. C. Stark.

1334—Thatford av, e s, 150 s Glenmore av, one three-story frame store and dwell'g, 25x55, tin roof; cost, abt $5,000; Isaac Abrahams and Isaac Gingold, 106 East Broadway, New York, and Max Bernstein, 241 East Broadway, New York; ar't, Michael Bernstein.

1335—Park av, n e cor North Oxford st, rear, one two-story brk stable, 20x28, gravel roof, brk cornice; cost, $800; H. Hohn, on premises; ar't and b'r, S. Rippingale.

1336—Monroe st, s s, 100 w Stuyvesant av, four two-story and basement brown stone dwell'gs, 17.6x45, tin roofs, wooden cornices; cost, $5,000 each; ow'r, ar't and b'r, H. Grasman, 840 Hancock st.

1337—Seigel st, No. 40, one four-story frame (brk filled) tenem't, 27x75, tin roof; cost, $6,500; ow'r, ar't and b'r, C. Buhrow, on premises.

1338—Jerome st, e s, 80 s Dumont av, one two-story frame dwell'g, 18x30, tin roof; cost, $1,800; ow'r and b'r, J. H. Brundage, Jerome st.

ALTERATIONS NEW YORK CITY.

Plan 1330—10th and 11th avs, 176th and 178th sts, one-story extension, 33x40, interior alterations and walls altered; cost, $5,000; E. N. Carpenter, sup't, 176th st and 10th av; ar't, I. D. Clarke; m'n, J. D. Murphy; c'rs, Sneith & Ball.

1331—3d av, No. 612, one-story extension, 24x22.10, walls altered and new cornice; cost, not given; M. Greenbaum, 230 East 38th st; ar't, F. Prochazka.

1332—Park row, No. 231, new store windows and doors; cost, $300; agent, H. Sterume, 313 East 20th st; ar't, W. Graul.

1333—156th st, n s, 300 w Courtlandt av, one-story extension, 22x21; cost, $500; J. Hortzel, 549 East 156th st; ar't, C. F. Lohse.

1334—German pl, s e cor Rea st, moved to rear; cost, $600; F. Schuessler, 312 East 146th st; ar't, C. F. Lohse.

1335—Washington st, No. 8, repair damage by fire; cost, $2,556; Trustees of U. S. Trust Co. of N. Y., 45 Wall st; c'r, E. Smith.

1336—45th st, Nos 505 and 507 W., new bridge; cost, $250; W. C. Smith, exr., 71 Perry st; ar'ts, F. & W. E. Bloodgood.

1337—51st st, No. 15 E., interior alterations; cost, $175; Miss S. Dyckman, on premises; m'n and c'r, P. J. Ryan.

1338—56th st, No. 33 W., one-story extension, 11x10; cost, $1,000; Mrs. R. Schell, on premises; ar'ts, Rose & Stone.

1339—Av B, s w cor 80th st, excavation, 16.2x16.2x10.4, cemented; cost, $150; Manhattan Electric Light Co., on premises; m'n, O. N. Eaton.

1340—25th st, Nos. 146 and 148 W., interior alterations; cost, $300; W. B. Conklin, secretary, 249 West 54th st; ar't, J. E. Terbune.

1341—South st, No. 383, one and two-story extension, 25x60.8; cost, $2,000; J. W. Sullivan, 156 Hewes st, Brooklyn; ar't, G. R. Madden.

1342—14th st, Nos. 14 and 16 W., interior alterations and repairs; cost, $3,000; agent, H. H. Cammann, 43 West 38th st; ar't, F. S. Schlesinger; c'r, J. C. Klett.

1343—27th st, No. 6 E., raised one story and walls altered; cost, $5,000; F. Kernochan, attorney, 11 Madison sq; ar't, B. Jones.

1344—Park av, No. 33, two-story extension, 8x10.6, and window altered; cost, $1,500; agent and b'r, P. Walsh, 501 West 34th st.

1345—Howard st, No. 12, interior alterations and walls altered; cost, $1,500; lessees, J. P. Friedhoff et al., 400 5th st; ar't, B. W. Berger.

1346—6th av, s e cor 21st st, chimney rebuilt; cost, $200; lessee, J. L. Wall, Harrison, N. Y.; ar't, J. Kastner.

1347—7th av, s e cor 57th st, frame platform; cost, abt $1,500; Music Hall Co. of New York, on premises; ar't, W. B. Tuthill; m'n, I. Hopper; c'r, J. Elgar.

1348—17th st, No. 508 E., roof raised in front, new cornice and gutter; cost, $500; T. Krekeler, 100 Jerome st, Brooklyn.

1349—3d av, e s, 75 n 113th st, extension to be raised, interior alterations and walls altered; cost, $1,000; J. G. Patton, 208 East 110th st; ar't, R. E. Rogers.

1350—Fulton av, No. 1385, two-and-a-half-story extension, 10x16; cost, $300; H. Zeltner, on premises; m'n, J. M. Wilson; c'r, L. Chartrand.

1351—81st st, No. 165 W., walls altered; cost, $300; ow'r and b'r, O. T. Mackey, on premises.

1352—10th st, No. 22 E., raised one story and walls altered; cost, $2,000; J. Otis, on premises; ar't, W. W. Howe; b'r, A. Ravekes.

1353—22d st, No. 543 W., walls altered; cost, $100; agent and m'n, J. H. Slocum, 76 Rodney st, Brooklyn.

1354—Centre st, No. 116, one-story extension, 25x20, interior alterations and walls altered; cost, $4,500; lessee, L. Dittenheimer, 214 East 75th st; ar'ts, Kurtzer & Rohl.

1355—New st, Nos. 45 and 47, portion of front rebuilt; cost, $7,000; N. Y. Improved Real Estate Co., 44 Broadway; ar'ts, Carrere & Hastings; b'rs, Hoffman & Co.

1356—Mt. Morris av, s w cor 124th st, one-story extension, 9.8x18.8, door and window alterations; cost, $300; W. B. Franke et al., 35 Mt. Morris av.

1357—55th st, Nos. 147 and 149 W., extension raised one story and walls altered; cost, $1,000; C. T. & H. T. Barney, 7 Wall st; ar't, M. Grimes.

1358—8th av, No. 878, one-story extension, 20x15, and interior alterations; cost, $1,700; H. P. Smith, 269 West 52d st; b'r, J. Murphy.

1359—106th st, No. 202 E., interior alterations and roof altered; cost, $150; I. & M. Steinberg, on premises; ar't, J. H. Lynch.

1360—50th st, n s, 100 w Lexington av, rear raised one story, interior alterations and walls altered; cost, $17,000; trustees St. Patrick's Cathedral, 120 East 21st st; art, L. J. O'Connor; m'n, L. Burns; c'r, P. K. Lantry.

1361—12th st, No. 506 E., walls altered, new front; cost, $700; Anna K. Ihlenburg, 512 East 76th st; b'r, J. D. Eggero.

1362—Hudson st, No. 531, interior alterations and walls altered; cost, 675; J. Dimick, 67 Madison av; b'rs, Ryan & Bros.

1363—10th av, Nos. 823 and 825, interior alterations and repairs, new roof, new store front and door; cost, $5,500; H. S. Mack, 69 West 46th st; c'r, F. Rouke.

1364—59th st, No. 319 W., doorway altered; cost, $75; lessee, W. M. Thomas, 303 West 59th st; b'rs, List and Lennon.

1365—Christopher st, No. 177, walls altered; cost, $250; H. C. and J. H. Calkin, 192 Lenox av.

1366—Eldridge st, No. 165, interior alterations, walls altered and new show window; cost, $1,500; O. Schmidt, 62 Rivington st; ar't, F. Ebeling; c'r, C. T. Schukraft.

1367—7th st, No. 13, new show window; cost, $400; agent, G. T. Ernst, on premises; ar'ts, Kurtzer & Rohl; c'rs, Thies & Folz.

1368—3d av, No. 19, interior alterations, walls altered and new front; cost, $5,000; lessee, F. Buse, 43 East 7th st; ar'ts, Kurtzer & Rohl.

1369—Attorney st, No. 96, interior alterations and walls altered; cost, $1,500; B. Friend, 217 East Broadway; ar't, H. Horenburger.

1370—1st av, No. 555, door and window cut in wall; cost, $50; W. & P. Ebling, 760 St. Ann's av; c'r, F. Graham.

1371—Mott st, No. 110, interior alterations and walls altered; cost, abt $750; W. H. Cooper, 25 Catharine st; ar't, T. S. Godwin.

1372—23d st, No. 159 W., one-story and basement extension, 25x43.9, interior alterations and walls altered; cost, $8,000; G. W. Van Nest, att'y, 345 5th av; ar'ts, Constable Bros.; m'ns, B[illegible]ma[illegible] & Sullivan; c'rs, Springstead & Moekabeen.

1373—5th av, No. 424, new elevator shaft with iron skylight; cost, $4,500; Margaret Switzer, on premises; ar'ts, Hubert, Pirsson & Hoddick; c'rs, Mandeville & Son.

KINGS COUNTY.

Plan 661—10th st, No. 78, raised 6 feet on brk wall; cost, $75; Johannah Schicker, 116 9th st; b'r, H. Rahn.

662—Schermerhorn st, No 193, flat tin roof; cost, $800; James Beckett, on premises; b'r, A. C. Hendrickson.

663—Lafayette av, No. 666, one-story brk extension, 8x12, tin roof; cost, $173; John H. Graham, on premises; ar't and c'r, E. W. Phillips; m'n, J. Softy.

664—Hart st, No. 545, three-story brk and frame extension, 8.6x12, gravel roof, interior alterations; cost, $1,000; Mary McDonald, 547 Hart st; art's, Langston & Dahlander.

665—McDonough st, s s, 200 w Stuyvesant av, one-story brk extension, 10.6x58, tin roof; cost, $7,000; Church Good Shepherd; ar't, G. P. Chappell.

666—3d av, n w cor 53d st, two buildings, add one story, interior alterations, steel beams, &c.; cost, each, $1,000; George H. Parshall, on premises; ar't, T. Burnett; b'rs, Kelly & Fryer.

667—Ashford st, No. 173, two-story frame extension, 17x27, tin roof; cost, $250; John G. Schreiner, on premises; ar'ts, Danmar & Fischer; b'r, not selected.

668—Fulton st, No. 1347, two-story brk extension, 20x30, gravel roof; cost, $1,500; C. I. Sundstrom, on premises; ar'ts, Langston & Dahlander.

669—Pacific st, No. 933, front and interior alterations; cost, $200; Philip Cloak, 939 Pacific st.

670—Clinton av, No. 249, doorway and windows, &c.; cost, $500; Fred A. Schroeder, on premises; ar't, C. F. Eisenach; b'rs, T. Donlon and Long & Barnes.

671—Columbia st, No. 171, rebuild front wall; cost, $825; Wm. Walsh, 90 2d pl; b'r, C. E. Sherman.

672—Court st, n e cor Baltic st, walls rebuilt and strengthened; cost, $50; Mrs. Burk, 480 Hicks st; b'rs, Burns & McCann.

673—Fulton st, No. 309, add one attic story, tin roof; cost $1,250; W. A. Husted, 338 Clinton av; ar't, J. G. Glover; b'r, not selected.

674—Boerum st, No. 167, new store front; cost, $275; Joseph Herte, on premises; ar't, F. Herte.

675—Myrtle av, No. 169, interior alterations; cost, $1,000; Joseph Dempsey, on premises; ar't, M. J. Morrill; b'r, not selected.

676—Broadway, No. 851, one-story brk and frame extension, 8x20, tin roof; cost, $50; Henry Schneider, 851 Broadway.

677—Belmont av, s w cor Vermont av, add one story to extension; cost, $400; Frank Kunz, on premises; ar't, L. F. Schillinger; b'r, R. H. Obenauer.

678—Belmont av, n s, 75 w Osborn st, add one story, flat tin roof, also three-story frame extension, 20x5, tin roof; cost, $700; Joseph Davies, 26 Essex st, New York; b'r, A. Stone.

679—Tompkins av, No. 330, one-story brk extension, 12x9, tin roof, front basement wall removed; cost, $400; J. Smith, 541 Putnam av; b'r, W. L. Vrooman.

680—Bergen st, No. 1131, two-story brk extension, 17x24, tin roof; cost $1,000; George G. Brooks on premises; ar't, J. G. Glover.

681—Emmett st, w s, 1'0 s Atlantic av, front alterations; cost, $500; Mrs. Henrietta Martin, Pierrepont st; b'rs, J. Demott & Sons.

682—Oakland st, No. 186, three-story frame extension, 8.4x5.6; cost, $60; Michael Murphy, on premises; b'r, T. Brayshaw.

683—Debevoise pl, No. 7, two-story and basement brk extension, 16.8x13, tin roof; cost, $400; I Burk, on premises; ar't, W. Kane.

MISCELLANEOUS.

BUSINESS FAILURES.

N. Y. ASSIGNMENTS—BENEFIT CREDITORS.

July

11 Romain, Stephen M. (retail grocer, at No. 338 West 125th st) to Charles W. Pinckney; without preferences.

11 Black, Joseph R. (plumbers', steam and gasfitters' supplies, also dealer in high and low pressure steam heating, &c., at No. 357 West 40th st and 511 and 513 East 137th st) to William B. Pope; preferences, $6,800.

11 Byrne, William J. and Dennis J. Hartigan (Byrne & Hartigan, merchant tailors, at No. 248 4th av) to Richard Jerome Lyons, Jr.; preferences, $580.

14 Adelman, Amelia A. F. (liquor store keeper, at No. 618 9th av) to Jacob Karch; preferences, $267.

14 Brencher, Conrad (retail furniture dealer, at No. 705 Columbus av) to Conrad Weiler; preferences, $920.

14 Russell, Mary A. (dealer in groceries, at n e cor 153d st and Amsterdam av), to Charles F. Adams; without preferences.

16 Crossley, Charles A. (steam heating, at No. 82 Church st), to John W. Bartram; preferences, $10,273.

KINGS COUNTY.

GENERAL ASSIGNMENTS.

July

13 Adams, Frank E. to Frederick Cobb.

13 Foale, H. James to Joseph F. Nightingale.

13 Kirkland, William to Frederick Cobb.

PROCEEDINGS OF THE BOARD OF ALDERMEN AFFECTING REAL ESTATE.

* Under the different headings indicates that a resolution has been introduced and referred to the appropriate committee. † Indicates that the resolution has passed and has been sent to the Mayor for approval ‡ Passed over the Mayor's veto.

New York, July 14, 1891.

FLAGGING.

132d st, s s, from Lenox to 7th av; relaid and reset.†

PAVING.

141st st, from e s Alexander av to w s Willis av; trap block.†

114th st, bet Manhattan and Columbus avs; asphalt.†

119th st, from 7th to Lexington av; granite block.†

MAINS.

Daly av, from Samuel st to Tremont av; water.†

APPROVED PAPERS.

Resolutions passed by the Board of Aldermen calling for the following improvements have been signed by the Mayor for the week ending July 11, 1891. *Indicates that the Mayor neither appoved nor objected thereto, therefore the same became adopted.

FLAGGING.

72d st, n s, from Amsterdam av to point 100 e therefrom.

11th st, n s / 12th st, s s } bet 2d and 3d avs at entrance to Stuyvesant alley.

Amsterdam av, e s, from 72d st to point 100 n therefrom.

ADVERTISED LEGAL SALES.

REFEREES SALES TO BE HELD AT THE REAL ESTATE EXCHANGE AND AUCTION ROOM (LIMITED), 59 to 65 LIBERTY STREET, EXCEPT WHERE OTHERWISE STATED.

July

50th st, Nos. 35 and 37, n s, 150 w Park av, 50x100.5, two five-story brk flats, by J. N. Golding. (Amt due $95,175) 20

50th st, No. 539, n s, 500 w 10th av, 25x100.5, five-story brk tenem't with stores, by R. V. Harnett & Co. (Amt due $4,548; prior morts. $7,000) 20

Amsterdam av, Nos. 641–649, n e cor 91st st, 136.5 x100, five five-story brk flats with stores, by R. V. Harnett. (Amt due $29,132; prior morts. $120,000) 20

41st st, No. 306, s s, 92.6 e 2d av, 16.8x67x17.10x59.9, four story brk dwell'g, by Scott & Meyers. (Amt due $5,600) 21

52d st, No. 521, n s, 275 w 10th av, 25x100.5 ....
52d st, No. 523, n s, 300 w 10th av, 25x100.5 ....
Two five-story brk tenem'ts ....
by Wm. Kennelly 21

59th st, No. 547, n s, 200 e 11th av, 25x100 ....
59th st, Nos. 535 and 537, n s, 325 e 11th av, 50x 100 ....
Three four-story brk tenem'ts with stores ....
by William Kennelly. (Amt due $3,428; prior morts. $35,000) 21

73d st, Nos. 177–181, n s, 28 e 10th av, 54x76.8, three four-story brk and stone dwell'gs, by Richard V. Harnett. (Amt due $43,983) 21

101st st, Nos. 311–325, n s, 150 w West End av, 100 x100 11, three-story brk dwell'g, two-story frame dwell'g and vacant ....
102d st, s s, 150 w West End av, 25x100.11, vacant ....
by William Kennelly. (Amt due $7,977) 21

Amsterdam (10th) av, No. 585, e s, 53.10 n 88th st, 28.4x100, five-story brk flat with stores, by R. V. Harnett & Co. (Amt due $22,400) 21

Bailey av, w s, known as plot 103 map of land at Kingsbridge, belonging to Wm. O. Giles, 50x131 2 x30x128.5, by William Kennelly. (Amt due $2,234) 21

Lenox av, No. 470, e s, 79 11 n 134th st, 20x84, five-story brk store and flat, by R. V. Harnett & Co. (Amt due $18,352) 21

West End av, No. 519, s w cor 95th st, 24x90, four-story brk dwell'g, by R. V. Harnett & Co. (Amt due $33,152) 21

11th st, No. 328, n s, 163 w Greenwich st, 25x95, three-story brk tenem't with three-story brk tenem't on rear, leasehold, by Smyth & Ryan 21

96th st, No. 58, s s, 200 e 9th av, 20x100.8, four-story brk dwell'g, by William Kennelly. (Amt due $5,644; prior morts. $20,000) 22

101st st, No. 203, n s, 90 e 3d av, 20x100.11, four-story brk store and tenem't with two-story brk building on rear, by B. L. Kennelly 22

126th st, No. 265, n s, 145 e 8th av, 20x99.11, two-story brk dwell'g ....
3d av, No. 2191, e s, 25 s 120th st, runs east 90 x north 20 x east 10 x south 25 x east 25 x south 26 x west 125 to 3d av, x north 31 to beginning, four-story brk store ....
by J. F. B. Smyth. (Partition sale) 22

122d st, No. 421, n s, 254.7 e 1st av, 16.8x100.11, three-story stone front dwell'g, by B. L. Kennelly. (Amt due $6,101) 23

Lenox av, Nos. 467–471, w s, 25 s 134th st, 99.10x100, three five-story brk flats with stores, by William Kennelly 23

5th av, No. 263, s e cor 29th st, 24.9x100, five-story brk store, by R. V. Harnett & Co. (Partition sale) 23

Av A, Nos. 1314–1320, n e cor 70th st, 100.4x98, four and five-story brk planing mill, &c., by R. V. Harnett & Co. (Amt due $54,234) 23

KINGS COUNTY.

July

Kingsland av, No. 105, w s, 125 s Herbert st, 25x 100, two-story frame dwell'g; assessed value, $800 ....
Lot in 26th Ward, begins at intersection of w s of The Road leading to the Mill and south line of lands of Jacob L. Van Wicklen, runs northwest 971 3 to centre of a brook, x along curves of same —, x northeast 89 x southeast 46.10 x — to n s of a road, x southeast 696.8 to w s road leading to mill, x northwest 385.10 x northeast 208.7 to beginning, contains 14 59–100 acres; partition ....
by T. A. Kerrigan, at 13 Willoughby st 21

Bergen st, No. 623, n s, 200 w Vanderbilt av, 24.8 x110, two-story brk mill; assessed value, $4,000 ....
Franklin st, No. 120, e s, 75 s Milton st, 25x70, two-story frame dwell'g; assessed value, $3,000 ....
Lefferts pl, Nos. 124 and 126, s s, 132.1 w Clason av, 40x138, three-story frame dwell'g on plot; assessed value, $9,500 ....
President st, s s, 363.4 w Columbia st, 16.8x100, three-story brk tenem't; assessed value, $2,000
Atlantic av, Nos. 995 and 997, n s, 238 8 w Clason av, 30x100, vacant; assessed value, $900 ....
by T. A. Kerrigan, at 13 Willoughby st 22

Putnam av, Nos. 1183 and 1185, n s, 90 w Evergreen av, 40x100, two three-story frame tenem'ts; assessed value, $3,800 each; all right, title and int. which David H. Scott had on March 24, 1890; by Taylor & Fox, at 45 Broadway 22

6th av, No. 592, n w s, 41.4 n Prospect av, 18x80, four-story frame tenem't and store; assessed value, $3,300; by T. A. Kerrigan, at 13 Willougby st 23

LIS PENDENS, KINGS COUNTY.

July

Howard av, n w cor Butler st, 127.9x100. Albert N. Monroe agt The Merchants Bank of Lockport; action to determine title; atty'y, John Winslow. 10

Livingston st, n e s, 100 s e Hanover pl, 20x125 to Grove pl. United States Trust Co. agt William H. Noe; att'ys, Stewert & Sheldon 10

26th st, n s, 325 w 5th av, 25x70. Virginia P. Kent agt Mary H. Downing; att'y, Charles Unangst 10

Kingston av, n w cor Bergen st, 40x100 ....
Bergen st, 100 w Kingston av, 60x114 5 ....
Lawrence Hurlburt agt Silas A. Condict; att'y, George W. Pearsall 10

Washington av, e s, 160 s Willoughby av, 20x200 to Hall st. James McK. Graeff agt Robert Otto; notice of attachment; att'ys, Hatch & Warren 10

Pacific st, s s, 75 w Utica av, 298 8x107.2. Henry Weil agt Joseph Hopkins, Jr.; att'y, R. Murray. 10

Leonard st, e s, 100 s Boerum st, 25x100. Isaac Greenblatt agt Karl Renz; action for specific performance; att'ys, J. M. & T. B. Seaman 11

Herkimer st, s s, 200 w Nostrand av, 50x186.6 to Herkimer pl. Stephen P. Sturges agt Sarah L. Smith; action for specific performance; att'ys, Sturges & Roby 11

South 2d st, s s, 161.3 w 6th st, 18.9x12; attachment. John P. Hoffman agt Alice Douglass; att'y, C. T. Kinsley 11

Lorimer st, s e cor Withers st, 50x100. Mary J. Cannon and Margaret Frazier agt Robert Smullen et al; suit to reject; att'ys, Rudd, Hunt & W 11

Montgomery st, n s, 382.11 e 8th av, 20x83.5x20x87. Maillard M. Canda agt Alfred J. Andrews, Daniel Doody, A. G. Spalding & Bros and the Brooklyn Citizen; att'y, N. J. O'Connell 11

President st, s s, 375 e 8th av, 80x100. Marvin Cross et al. agt Rudolph S. Timper and Pat. Sheridan; foreclos. mechanic's lien; att'ys, Fisher & V 11

5th av, n w cor 23d st, 100x175. Robert Scrimgeour agt Philip Zeh et al; att'y, E. S. Fowler 11

Bergen st, s s, 119.7 e Clason av, 24x131. Marvelle W. Cooper agt Henry Dundas; att'ys, Norwood & Coggeshall 11

Bergen st, s s, 143 7 e Clason av, 24x131. Same agt same; same att'ys 11

Bergen st, s s, 167.7 e Clason av, 24x131. Same agt same; same att'ys 11

Bergen st, s s, 191.7 e Clason av, 24x131. Same agt same; same att'ys 11

Raymond st, w s, 175 s Bolivar st, runs west 75 x south to Willoughby st, x east to Raymond st, x north 26. Lula P. McGarry agt Frank N. O. Brien; att'y, Charles H. Winslow 13

Raymond st, w s, 150 s Bolivar st, 25x75. Same agt same; same att'y 13

Dresden st, w s, 270.5 n Atlantic av, 75x103. Jane L. Smith agt William H. Bowlsby; att'y, John H. Ives 13

Putnam av, s s, 213 e Reid av, 114x90. Goodwin & Polley agt John Hennesy; foreclos. mechanic's lien; att'y, George F. Elliott 13

Lots 369, 370, 371, 372 map Whitehead Howard, 26th Ward. John A. Davies agt Frank Crooke; amended foreclos.; att'y, John H. Ives 14

Van Siclen av, e s, 125 s Blake av, 25x100. Charles W. Osborne and ano. exrs. Peter B. Schoonmaker agt Josephine Quinn et al.; amended notice; att'ys, Rolfe & Snedeker 14

Glen st, s w cor Crescent st, 25x100. Same agt same; amended notice; same att'ys 14

Ocean Parkway, w s, 1,024 s Sheepshead Bay and Coney Island road, 100x250 to roadway. John L. Voorhees, commissioner, &c., agt Bernard Bighn; att'ys, Hubbard & Rushmore 14

Throop av, s e cor Hancock st, 23x81. American Baptist Home Mission Society agt Ervin G. Gollner et al.; att'y, E. S. Clinch 14

Lafayette av, s s, 302.6 w Lewis av, 20x100. Ferdinand Sloat agt Mary A. Wildey et al.; att'ys, Garretson & Eastman 14

21st st, n s, 814.3 e 5th av, 71.5x100. Michael J. Newman et al. exrs. John H. Hughes agt William H. Kennagh; att'y, James F. Swanton 15

Fulton st, n s, 85.4 e Clinton av, 16.8x63.2x15x62.9. Theodore Bossbard agt Anna C. Bossbard; action for conveyance; att'y, H. F. Lawrence 15

Sandford st, w s, 283 n De Kalb av, 25x100. Albert G. McDonald agt James Hopkins; att'y, Michael Furst 15

Union st, n s, 227.6 w Clinton st, 140x100. Spencer Aldrich agt Charles W. Andress; att'y, Spencer Aldrich, in person 15

3d av, n e cor 77th st, 25x100, New Utrecht. Edward H. Parsons agt James Mills; foreclos. mech. lien; att'y, John C. Kinkel 15

Prospect av, s e cor 8th av, 150x80.2. Patrick Keegan agt Henry E. Murphy; foreclos. mechanic's lien; att'ys, Johnson & Lamb 15

65th st, s s, 375 e 6th av, 25x100.2, New Utrecht. Hamilton Co-operative Building and Loan Assoc. agt Thomas K. Robinson; att'ys, Tredwell & Catlin 15

Columbia Heights, No. 204, w s, 248.1 n Pierrepont st, 37.6x150 to Furman st, x27.9x151. Charles H. Collins agt Mary S. Bewsey; foreclos. mechanics' lien; att'ys, Rochfort & Stantou 15

36th st, n s, 104 w 4th av, 21x100.2. Phebe V. Kent agt Catharina S. Svenlin et al.; att'y, C. Unangst 16

Hull st, n s, 375 e Rockaway av, 18.9x100. John F. Edwards agt Hiram Bedell et al.; att'y, J. F. Nelson 16

Hull st, n s, 393.9 e Rockaway av, 18 9x100. Same agt same; same att'y 16

6th st, s s, 75 w 4th av, 105x100. Title Guarantee and Trust Co. agt Charles H. Collins et al.; att'y, C. R. Halsey 16

Bedford av, s w cor Rodney st, 133x100. Bradley & Currier Co. (Lim.) agt Charles W. Andress et al.; att'y, E. H. Moeran 16

RECORDED LEASES.

NEW YORK. — Per Year

Bowery, No. 53. Simon Herman to Turner & Timberman; 11 years, from May 1, 1891. $4,000, 4,500

Canal st, No. 154. Peter Kraeger to Jacob Davidson; 5 years, from May 1, 1892 2,000

Canal st, No. 130, basement store. Charles Plath to Henry Hartmann; 2 years, from May 1, 1891 570

Carmine st, No. 49, all. William H. Terry exr. Joseph H. Terry to James J. Larkin; 3 years, from May 1, 1891 1,800

Gansevoort st, No. 98. Marie K. R. Thumann to Henry K. Meyer; 6 years, from May 1, 1891 1,800

Hamilton st, No. 3, store and basement. Mary Haggerty to Christopher D. Sullivan; 4 years, 11 months and 15 days, from July 15, 1891 300

Henry st, No. 174, store and cellar. John Fish to William J. Maher; 5 years, from May 1, 1891 .... 1,300, 1,500

Hester st, No 84 / Allen st, No. 37½ } James R. Griswold to Pauline Cohen; 5 years, from July 31, 1891 3,200

Jefferson st, No. 56, all. Teresa H. wife of James Hickey to William Meyn; 5 years, from July 31, 1891 1,900

Peck slip, No. 7. John P., Richard W. and Edward Block to John Wiechmann; 5 years, from May 1, 1891 800

Pitt st, No. 62, basement floor. Annie Kasner to Isidor I. Hirsch; 5 years, from May 1, 1891 420

South st, No. 60 / Wall st, No. 120 } n w cor. Henry Ranken to William Kunde; 6 years, from July 1, 1891 7,000

Stanton st, No. 122, ground floor, second floor and cellar. Anna M. Fett widow to Peter Brickelmaier; 5 years, from Aug. 1, 1891 .... 720, 780

9th st, No. 743 E. William Winans to John C. Bonn; 3 years, from May 1, 1890 900

14th st, No. 6 E., room or office in front of east

side. Sophia Schwab and Nathan Schwab, att'y. to Mrs. Eliza Kallage; 4 years, from May 1, 1891 .... 420, 480
Same premises, photograph gallery on top floor and other portions of premises. Same to Rudolph Bachmann; 5 1-6 years, from March 1, 1891 .... 1,200, 2,000
27th st, Nos. 207 and 209 E. Catharine A. Smith, Purdy Station, N. Y., to George Maughan; 9¾ years, from Aug. 1, 1891 .... 2,000, 2,500
44th st, Nos. 218-222 E. George and William Newschafer to Henry Bunke; 6 years, from May 1, 1892 1,800
71st st, No. 304 E. Margaret Dunn to Joseph Kregci; 5 years, from May 1, 1891 .... 790, 840
85th st, No. 534 E, store floor on east side. William Kirchhof and Charlotte his wife to Balzer Danner; 4 11-12 years, from June 1, 1891 420
85th st, No. 106 E., all. Nettie McGowan to Samuel Kahn; 3 years, from May 1, 1891 ... 900, 1,000
111th st, Nos. 204-208 E. George W. Bryant to Jonas Kolb; 5 years, from July 15, 1891 2,700
169th st, No. 842 E. Charles M. Julian to Fritz Reinhardt; 4 years, from May 1, 1890 400
Av A, No. 117, store floor and basement. Heinrich Vollmar, Clanetville, S. I., to Concordia Clund; 5 years, from May 1, 1891 .. 1,380
Av B, No. 205. Karl Hense exr Margaretha Hense to Adolph Steiner; 4¾ years, from Aug. 1, 1891 1,740
2d av, n w cor 128th st, 83x42. William Hayes to Joseph Schlesinger; 4 10-12 years, from July 1, 1891 1,500
2d av, No. 2217, s w cor 114th st, store and part cellar. Henry Gieschen to Hermann Eggers; 5½ years, from Jan. 1, 1891 1,500
2d av, No. 1404, store and part cellar. Anton Schwartz to Jacob and Sigmund Katz, of Katz Bros.; 4 years, from May 1, 1891 1,600
3d av, No. 2045, store and cellar. Lueder Pieper to John W. Thaden; 3 years, 8½ months, from July 15, 1891 1,200
3d av, No. 2750. Frank Faulhaber to Herman Schomburg; 4⅚ years, from Aug 1, 1891 600
3d av, No. 3309, basement floor, first floor and cellar. Lidmila Sobischek to Joseph Fisher; 5¾ years, from Aug. 1, 1891 900
4th av, No. 320, all. Elizabeth Larkin to Francisco de Luesada; 3 years, from May 1, 1891. 1,000
5th av, No. 288, all. Georgiana M. Payne to Joseph L. and Arthur J. Myers; 5 years and 7 days, from June 23, 1891 .... 7,000, 8,000
10th av, No. 491, store and bakery. Henry W. Leonard exr. Conrad W. Frey to Wiegand Frey; 10 years, from May 1, 1891 600

CHATTELS.

Note.—The first name, alphabetically arranged, is that of the Mortgagor, or party who gives the Mortgage. The "R" means Renewal Mortgage.

NEW YORK CITY.

JULY 10 TO 16—INCLUSIVE.

SALOON AND RESTAURANT FIXTURES.

Arnold, Andrew. 328 E 11th ... G Bechtel. (R) $3,500
Baum, A K. 434 11th av... D Stevenson. 200
Bayer, Lisete. 428 W 39th... D Stevenson. (R) 350
Bellocchio & Amecro. 133 3d av.... D Stevenson. (R) 554
Bernius, J G. 92 Prince V Loewers. 600
Blank, Henry. 162 East Broadway.... Burger & Hower B Co. (R) 631
Blind, Fr. 421 5th.... J Hoffmann B Co. (R) 235
Bock, J W. 294 1st av .. E Trepp. 3,500
Bock, George. 234 E 102d ... P Doelger. 200
Bolte, William. 323 E 26th .. J Ruppert. (R) 750
Bonnard, P A ... F Arnault. 500
Buggeln, John. 29th st and 1st av.... W L Flanagan. (R) 600
Cartellano & Zugio. 115 Elizabeth .... India Wharf B Co. 500
Cervante, Annie. 114 6th av.... D H Rohrs. 3,000
Christ, Dorothea R. 181st st and Kingsbridge road.... G Ehret. 1,875
Clark, C F. 1435 Amsterdam av.... G Ehret. 3,288
Connolly, B A. 575 1st av.... D Stevenson. 1,500
Cole, A O. 107 Canal ... F Kopp. 250
Corrodi, J W. 551 Pearl ... Rubsam & H B Co. 1,000
Danner, Balzer. 182 Orchard.... Bernheimer & S. (R) 400
Daudorph, H E. 442 W 39th.... D Stevenson. (R) 373
Day, F M. 1983 7th av.... J Miller. 750
Dettinger, Frank. 212 6th .... G Ringler & Co. 400
Donnellan, John. 862 2d av.... W L Flanagan. 1,500
Dougherty, James. 122 Mott.... A Hupfel's Son. 500
Donnelly, J J. 2311 3d av ... H Becamore. (R) 517
Dorrhofer, Jacob. 428 E 82d.... Burr B Co. 800
Dougherty, John. 55 Great Jones.... D Mayer. (R) 500
Downing, J M. 822 2d av.... J Everard. (R) 1,000
Dunn, Edward. 371 E 62d.... Bernheimer & S. (R) 1,200
Duppler, Charles. 45 3d av ... G Ehret. (R) 1,500
Drummond, Angus. 152 W 52d.... E W Larner. 500
Eppler, Adam. 92 Av A.... A Finck & Son. 5,000
Fegundio, Billy. 102 Mott.... J Wallace & Son. 300
Flanigan, Joseph. 597 3d av.... P Doelger. (R) 5,000
Fleich, Albert. 832 1st av.... F Oppermann, Jr. 250
Fraenkle, Karl. 331 and 333 Bowery.... G Ringler & Co. 2,000
Froelich, F L. 102 Av A.... J Eichler B Co. 1,000
Fisher, Joseph. 3309 3d av.... H Zeltner. 1,035
Gluck, Moritz. 285 2d.... J Doelger's Sons. 450
Guido, Alfonco. 77 Mulberry.... H B Scharmann & Sons. 150
Getzoff, Eliza. 170 Elm.... I Johnson. Restaurant Fixtures. 100
Goold, Michael. 231 E 111th ... F & M Schaefer B Co. (R) 350
Hann, Jacques. 1420 Av A.... F Oppermann, Jr. 700
Heidelberg, Morris. 215 E 28th.... J H Conway. (R) 700
Hempel, John. 93 1st av.... J Ruppert. 650
Hesse, Charles. 2184 8th av.... Bernheimer & S. (R) 1,500
Hirsch & Friend. 729 E 177th.. .India Wharf B Co. (R) 1,200
Horan, J J. 442 2d av.... P Buckel. (R) 3,000
Houlihan, Daniel. 150th st and 12th av.... O'Reilly, Skelly & Fogarty. Ale Pump. 105
Hunt, J F. 11 James.... S Liebmann's Sons B Co. 500
Herzog & Eberth. 8 Barclay...., R Von Hofe. (R) 1,50
Hilficker, Rudolf. 157 Forsyth ... J & M Haffen. (R) 250
Hirsch, Isidor I. 171 Eldridge.... H B Scharmann & Sons. (R) 400
Hodes, Regina. 159 Rivington.... H B. Scharmann & Sons. 200
Jacobs, Aron. 71 Suffolk.... H B Scharmann & Sons. 500
Jefferds, E L. 382 8th av.... G Ehret. (R) 2,000
Jakubovics, L. 243 E 3d... Bernheimer & S. 250
Jensen & Harenburg. 188 and 190 Greenwich .... J N Crusius. (R) 12,325
Kelly, John. 184 Cherry.... F Oppermann, Jr. (R) 463
Keely, Timothy. 861 1st av.... E Poin. 200
Kirchherr, Jacob. 200 Allen.... G Ringler & Co. (R) 400
Kitsell, W T. 613 and 615 3d av.... C Iba. 475
Knaebel, Louis. 174 Wooster.... G Baltzll. 400
Knirim, Joseph. 20 North William ... G Bechtel, exr of. 1,200
Knittel, Frank. 1323 2d av.... Bernheimer & S. (R) 700
Kunde, William. 120 Wall.... H Ranken. 12,600
Kowalewski, Hugo. 162 E 4th... Budweiser B Co. 800
Landthaler, John. 218 Chrystie .. P Doelger. (R) 700
Lynch, M D. 2080 2d av.... Budweiser B Co. 1,000
Lahm, Philip. 17 Cannon .. G Ringler & Co. 1,500
Laier, Anton. 242 6th.... J Ruppert. 450
Lambe, John. 22 Bedford ... P Doelger. 4,500
Laugheinz, Edward. 11-15 East Broadway.... A Horn. 5,000
Landsmann, A 263 Stanton ... V Loewers. (R) 325
Lefebvre, Jules. 76 West Houston.... F. Boucherz. 500
Lesser, Philip. 139 Madison ... Burr B Co. 1,500
Leun, Philip. 666 St Anns av.... H Zeltner. (R) 700
Livingston, S C. 518 Lexington av.... J Everard. 1,116
Lopez, S. 81 New ... J H Bereuter. Pool Table. 180
Mariano, John. 288 Mulberry.... Burr B Co. (R) 400
Mayers, Mark. 2402 3d av... Bernheimer & S. (R) 3,500
Meyn, William. 56 Jefferson.... Consumers' B Co. 4,000
Muhs, H F. 186 Monroe.... J Eppig. (R) 500
Moran, Bridget. 1724 3d av.... J Everard. 1,025
McCormack, Francis. 687 10th av.... P Doelger. 1,000
McCarthy, John. 205 Madison.... F Bachmann. (R) 200
McShane, P. F. 2339 3d av ... J Wallace & Son. (R) 933
McMahon, Bernard. 27 9th av.... G Ringler & Co. 1,000
McSorley, B J. 456 11th av.... D Stevenson. (R) 1,300
McElroy, James. 439 W 32d ... Budweiser B Co. 500
McWilliams, John. 924 9th av.... H Elias B Co. (R) 675
Monahan, E J. 511 6th av.... W L Flanagan. (R) 1,000
Moskowitz, A and Bro. 118 Delancey ... Budweiser B Co. 1,500
Mrozynski, Anton. 628 E 150th .. J & M Haffen. (R) 547
Mustard, John. 2248 10th av.... D D Yuengling, Jr. B Co. 1,300
Newman, Charles. 407 3d av. .. A B Marx. Pool Table. 100
O'Brien, John. 1133 1st av.... D Sullivan. 850
O'Toole, James. 411 10th av.... Bernheimer & S. (R) 1,500
Overbaugh, Cyrus. 75 Greenwich av.... J Ruppert. 800
O'Neill, J P. 757 8d av... P Doelger. (R) 1,200
Parker, G W. 412 Grand.... D Stevenson. (R) 400
Payne, Robert. 788 11th av.... H Ferris & Son. Ale Pump. 78
Rousseau, J P and J E ... G D Pohalski. Restaurant Sideboard. 300
Ruhl, Henry. 135 Essex.... G Ehret. 900
Ranft, Bernhardt. 7 Chambers.... J Hoffmann B Co. 1,700
Rosenhain, Max. 235 E 107th.... G Ringler & Co. 868
Sannwald, Peter. 170 Hester.... India Wharf B Co. (R) 600
Saroni, Nicola. 278 Mulberry.... Feigenspan B Co. 769
Sarvicki, Anna. 215 Eldridge.. .J Hoffmann B Co. (R) 275
Schildknecht, Magdalena. 28 Stanton .... J Kress B Co. (R) 213
Schlag, August.... 26 Delancey.... J H Berenter. Pool Table. 140
Schuttheis, J F. 68th st and Av A.... G Ehret. (R) 40,000
Schwartz, Magdalena. 821 3d av.... P & W Ebling B Co. (R) 400
Schwerkolt, Adolph. 56 9th av.... G Ehret. (R) 1,000
Seekamp, Richard. 496 2d av.... Clausen & Price B Co. 2,400
Singer & Klein. 154 Attorney.... Bernheimer & S. Ice House. 110
Same.... same. Pump. 101
Same .. same. Ice House. 115
Smith, J J. 61 West End av.... Benheimer & S. Pool Table. (R) 140
Sommers, Hattie. 5 St Marks pl.... Hirsh & S. 425
Stadelmann, J G. 28 2d av.... S. Liebmann's Sons B Co. 750
Steinhardt, S I. 6 Clinton.... J Ruppert. 800
Stern, Nathaniel. 78 W 3d.... J Everard. 2,040
Stoehr, Charles. 89th st and 3d av.... Brunswick B C Co. Pool Table, &c. 350
Straub, Louis. 918 8th av .. J Eichler B Co. 1,394
Sheridan & Eagan. 271 Av C.... Budweiser B Co. 500
Tismer, Berthold. 502 Brook av.... G Ringler & Co. 625
Traziadio, Giacinto. 406 E 113th.... Bernheimer & S. Pump. 81
Same.... same. Ice House. 130
Same.... same. Pump &c. 24
Twenty-second Regiment Veteran Club. 144 w 62th.... Brunswick B C Co. Pool Table. 312
Tobias, Theresa. 108 Allen.... H B Scharmann. (R) 500
Von der Lieth, John. 183 William.... D Stevenson. (R) 2,500
Wais, Carl. 246 Rivington.... H B Scharmann. (R) 200
Weber, Adolph. 654 E 154th.... H Zeltner. 400
Winters, Theodore. 93 Oliver.... Budweiser B Co. 800
Wahlers, Frederick. 66 Vesey.... Beadleston & W. 1,500
Weik, William. 86 Willett.... S Liebmann's Sons B Co. 870
Weil, Emanuel. 923 3d av .. P Buckel. 800
Werner, Wm. 335 Madison.... S Liebmann's Sons B Co. 800
White, C E. 167th st and Jerome av.... Ada H Southwick. Hotel Fixtures. (R) 2,500
Williams, James. 100 E 125th st and 2295 and 2297 4th av.... Julia R Foley. 2,000
Same.... J Everard. 5,075
Wosslick, Ad. 209 E 43d ... J Hoffmann B Co. 350
Young, Bertha. 1345 1st av ... E Jacobson. 1,400
Zimmermann, Ernest. 183 Lewis.... Eagle B Co. Pump. 10

HOUSEHOLD FURNITURE.

Adams, Carrie. 293 W 12th.... D M Brown. (R) 140
Adams, Maggie. 402 2d av.... J Moriarty. (R) 101
Allen, George. 1752 Madison av.... J H Little. 193
Alvers, P. 1798 3d av ... J S Rice. 154
Ahrens, Randolph. 1703 Lexington av.... R M Walters. Piano. 130
Arthe, J C. 2258 7th av.... J Moriarty. 136
Arnheim, Charles. 16 E 13th.... S I Herschmann. (R) 174
Barenburg, Phillip. 137 Essex... L Baumann. 116
Bartley, Sarah J. 59 W 98th.... F G Smith. Piano. (R) 173
Barton, Richard. 301 E 102d.... L Baumann. 227
Baumeister, Ida. 435 E 57th,.... Fanny Adler. 3,000
Becker, Maud B. 531 E 144th .. F Hartenstein. Piano. 285
Belton, S I. 151 W 133d... J H Little. 262
Berger, Mrs J A. 41 E 22d... J Mullins. (R) 708
Bischoff, A H. 62 E 3d.... H F Kasschau & Co. 307
Bithoun, Harriet. 108 E 86th.... J Moriarty. 303
Blair, William. 68 W 99th.... J Mullins & Co. (R) 212
Bleck, William. 416 Pleasant av.... H F Kasschau & Co. 123
Blodgett, W C. 658 Broadway.... L Baumann. 239
Boehm, Maggie. 406 E 14th ... J Steinbugler J. 215
Bogardus, Nettie. 118 Charles.... B M Cowperthwait & Co. 138
Boire, Eugene. 227 W 43th.... O'Farrell & Co. (R) 175
Boyle, Kittie. 1524 1st av ... Lincoln I and G Assoc. 110
Burns, John. 111 W 62d.... J Moran. 114
Carney, Tom. 2748 8th av.... J S Rice. 177
Civelette, Stephen. 330 3d av ... Krakauer Bros. Piano. 80
Collins, Margaret C. 406 W 57th.... C H Brown. Paintings, &c. 1,000
Comrad, Thomas. 334 E 64th.... L Baumann. 130
Constant, Mary A. 592 E 136th ... American G Assoc. 150
Conway, J W. 360 W 30th.... B M Cowperthwait Co. 134
Crone, Kate. 314 W 27th.... L Baumann. 149
Cummings, William. 1383 Lexington av.... J R Cooper. 200
Clement, J C. 1046 Franklin av.... S Heyman & Co. (R) 104
Cozzens, S D. 240 W 135th ... S Knapp & Co. 1,316
Donaldson, Chester. 113 W 71st.... American Loan Assoc. 250
Delgado, Mary A. 332 E 81st... H S Eisler. 120
Demarest, P A. 230 W 17th.... H Thoesen. 152
Deutschberger, Frederick. 108 W 42d.... Leah Deutschberger. 3,000
Donaldson, Mrs E L. 29 E 46th.... H Thoesen. 1,258
Donnelly, Mrs M. 37 King.... J A Luddy. 200
Dudley, W G. 234 E 85th ... J Moriarty. 174
Eareckson, V O. 142 W 28th.... J Moriarty. 288
Ernest, J S. 32 W 31st.... J H Little. 123
Ernst, Max. 1046 2d av .. C E Pierce. 130
Esterman, Isaac. 234 7th av.... O'Farrell & Co. 143
Fish, Marion E. 349 W 4th ... Cowperthwait & Co. 141
Flaherty, Mrs J. 73 W 83d.... J Moriarty. 102
Foster, Mrs J W. 56 E 4th. H S Eisler. 162
Frank, Alexander. 198 Orchard.... H Israel & Sons. 162
Foster, J E. 852 E 170th .. American Guarantee Assoc. 100
Gallagher, Kate. 112 E 113th.... L Baumann. 121
Gerstel, Augusta. 346 E 13th.... J Moriarty. 141
Gilmore, Bart. 214 E 73d.... J Moriarty. 130
Gistedt, Carl. 118 Christopher ... L Baumann. 185
Gleason, T J. 856 E 88th ... J Moriarty. 113
Goodrich, G G. Storage.... American G Assoc. 200
Gordon, G and R A. 183 8th av.... R B De Cosanora. 105
Graham, Elizabeth. 258 E 128th.... Fennell & P. (R) 277
Griffin, S H. 414 E 89th.... J Moriarty. 138
Halovtschuer, G A. 1 Bespert alley.... H S Eisler. 111
Hamilton, G W. 1674 Madison av.... J H Little. 219
Hastings, S L and C A. 16 W 24th.... Commercial Credit Co. 400
Hickey, Josephine. 214 Madison.... B M Cowperthwait & Co. 136
Hommedieu, Mrs E L. 50 Greenwich av.... J Moriarty. 110
Hughes, J B. 161 E 30th.... J Moran. 128
Hazen, Edith. 124 E 52d ... E Von Kattengell. 1,266
Heyman, Benjamin. 107 Sheriff.... S I Herschmann. (R) 113
Johnson, F, Mrs. 77 W 52d.... E Doring. 332
Jacobs, S L. 39 E 60th.... S M Blun. (R) 1,400
Jennette, Louise. 260 W 122d.... L Baumann. 168
Johnson, Gustav. 341 E 80th.... Jordan & M. 106
Joyce, Mrs M. 339 W 59th.... J H Little. 367
Kolb, Maggie. 235 E 26th. Manges Bros. 162
Kruger, R G. 1584 Madison av.... Manges Bros. 121
Kelsey, Mary H. 303½ E 33d.... L Baumann. 113
Kieley, Mamie. 329 E 24th.... J Steinbugler, Jr. 112
Klauer, C A. 159 W 68th.... A Ballin. 142
Klein, Julius. 337 E 23d.... J Rubenstein. 247
Lages, Paul. 309 W 44th.... L Baumann. 163
Laughran, Patrick. 245 E 127th.... L Baumann. 196
Lewis, M R Mrs. 118 W 25th.... J H Little. 136
Lissenden, Jennie. 456 W 20th . A Ballin. 141
Lowber, Martha. 56 E 4th ... H S Eisler. 169
Maccabe, T J. 1714 Lexington av.... Jordan & M. 170
Markham, Annie C. 1282 Columbus av.... J F Markham. 200
Masterson, A C. 68 E 109th.... S Heyman & Co. 138
McCarthy, Bessie. 19 Cherry.... B M Cowperthwait & Co. 156
McCauley, C F. 131 E 30th.... J H Little. 277
McCarthy, Samuel. 610 E 142d.... Krakauer Bros. Piano. 250
McCormick, Mary Mrs. 509 W 42d.... W E Wheelock & Co. Piano. 350
McDonnell, John. 654 8th av.... A Hahn. Piano. 135
McDonell, Mary. 276 W 38th.... J Moriarty. (R) 154
McDonald, Mary. 419 E 15th.... J Moriarty. 112
MacDonald, W A. 420 E 72d. .. H Thoesen. 138
McGann, Mary. 146 Madison.... Jordan & M. 328
McGrath, James. 130 43d st, Brooklyn.... J A Luddy. 238
Monroe, Annie F. 50 W 12th ... C A Wentz. 1,200
McKenna, Patrick. 261 W 123d ... Fennell & Pye. 149
McNulty, Michael. 438 10th av.... J S Rice. 163
Meade, Susannah P. 201 W 43d.... W H Meade. 3,000

Michael, Cora B. 267 W 40th ...B M Cowperthwait & Co. 179
Nay, Victorine. 101 E 80th....O'Farrell & Co. (R) 146
Needham, J T. 18 E 111th . American G Assoc. 105
Neues, Clara. 962 Fleetwood av....Fennell & Pye. 147
Nicholl, G O F. 70 W 88th....F G Smith. Piano. (R) 240
Odell, Amelia M. 231 E 115th....J H Little. 214
O'Donnell, John. 43 Whitehall....B M Cowperthwait & Co. 289
O'Malley, John. 303 10th av. . J S Rice. 163
Oppermann, Miss A E. 140 W 103d ...J H Little. 146
Page, Frances. 119 W 56th....C E Pierce. 186
Palmero, Antonio. 426 W 27th....O'Farrell & Co. 150
Palmer, William. 134 W 20th ..J Moran. 226
Peaulejeune, H and H. 12 Charles....E C Hinsdale. 130
Peters, Anna. 282 W 144th.. Fennell & Pye. 127
Pierce, Mary R. 221 E 126th....Fennell & Pye. 134
Potwyn, Belle. 910 6th av....J Moriarty. 297
Poll, John. 118 Charlton ...S Heyman & Co. 150
Power, Mary. 84 E 119th....J Moriarty. 152
Rixa, Johanna....S Heyman & Co. (R) 163
Rasteiter, Mary. 645 E 16th....J Steinbugler, Jr 126
Raymond, Florence. 39 W 60th....O'Farrell & Co. 302
Reichert, J and F. 226 Rivington and 112 3d... J Goldstein. 180
Robertson, W F. 890 Western Boulevard... D Laughlin. 364
Rohrs, Fred. 306 and 308 E 71st....J J Dobson. Carpets. 156
Rosen, F E. 214 Henry....R M Walters. Piano. 170
Ryerson, Hattie. 1926 3d av....Fennell & Pye. 216
Sappe, Antony. 316 Pleasant av....Jordan & M. 161
Sauch, J W. 64 6th av and 178 1st av....H S Kisler. 309
Schmidt, Otto. 263 E 10th....J Steinbugler. 140
Schwartz, J, Mrs. 265 E 10th....A Ballin. 112
Sheridan, Hattie. 314 E 90th....B M Cowperthwait & Co. 195
Silsby, Sarah. 138 W 20th... J Moriarty. 425
Simpson, Catharine A. 162 E 37th....T B Hand. 585
Sinclair, Margaret. Williamsbridge....Krakauer Bros. Piano. 225
Smith, J P. 88 W 89th... H F Kasschau & Co. 834
Snedicker, William. 893 Elton av....W Reubel. 130
Steele, E G & E A. 183 E 93d....R Lathers, Jr. Paintings. 96
Stern, Esther. 90 W 134th....Dreisacker & Co. (R) 136
Stevenson, Mary. 265 W 41st....J Moriarty. 408
Schacht, Joseph. 1425 Av A....S Heyman & Co. (R) 138
Siegel, Hattie. 239 E 126th ...G C Flint Co. 264
Solomon, C N. 165 E 77th. ..S Heyman & Co. 293
Spaeth, Sophie. 15 Broome....Krakauer Bros. Piano. 170
Taillard, E B & P. 220 Thompson....E Laporte. 200
Termien, Sarah. 134 W 83d....J Moriarty. 197
Thibouet, Annie. 128 E 10th....B M Cowperthwait & Co. 126
Thropp, Emma L. 260 W 38th....J Foulks, Jr. 180
Topp, Gresuenz. 39 Clinton pl ...M Gebhard. 500
Tarbell, W N V. 11 E 29th....N B Farrar. 1,000
Towie, F S. 134 E 112th ...S Heyman & Co. 816
Uockenstein, O & A. 211 W 14th....E W Ashley. 295
Walker, David. 101 W 97th....L Baumann. 156
Walsh, Mrs Maggie. 50 Downing ...Krakauer Bros. Piano. 180
Watson, Euphemia 2044 Madison av....Dreisacker & Co. (R) 122
Weidmann, Mrs C. 799 2d av... J Steinbugler, Jr. 156
Weiss, Nicolol....J Moriarty. 295
Wellhausen, Herman. 280 6th... J M Anderson. 180
Wendel, A. 29 Attorney....H S Eisler. 150
Wolf, Mary. 285 Bleecker....R M Walters. Piano. 175
Watson, Emma. 227 E 70th....S I Herschmann. 225
Webster, A. 222 and 224 W 133d....S Knapp & Co. 313
Whelan, Michael. 140 W 63d....S Heyman & Co. 117
Younghans, E H. 501 W 50th....S Heyman & Co. 210
Yavanitzky, Anton. 62 Stanton....J Rubenstein. 192
Zimmer, Louis. 320 W 39th....L Baumann. 215

MISCELLANEOUS.

Allen, George. 880 3d av....Bramhall, Deane Co. Range, &c. 50
Banks, M F. 148 E 93d....Hincks & Johnson. Coach. 270
Baruc, B S & G. 712 Broadway....American G Assoc. Office Fixtures 100
Barry, John. 178 E 83d....D P Nichols & Co. Horse. 100
Baumel, Morris. 972 2d av....Lamson Consol S S Co. Register. (R) 210
Behrmann, H J. 69 Ludlow .... C Geerdes. Bottler Fixtures. 900
Beth Eden Baptist Church. 187th st and Lorillard pl .. Henrietta C Dingee. Organ. 235
Bingel, Charles. 469 and 471 E 146th....S Gampert. Horses, &c (R) 1,000
Blumenthal, Bertha. 1101 1st av .... Jersey City Packing Co. Butcher Fixtures. 285
Brower, W E. 521 3d av .... Lamson Consol S S Co. Register. (R) 210
Bodenburg, John. 207 E 85th....H Heins.... Horses, Trucks, &c. 300
Cars, W H ...Story & Fox. Machinery. 300
Caulfield, E J. 642 8th av .... F G Minshall. Horse, &c. 350
Camp, J T. 22 and 26 Howard .... J P Leo. Machinery. (R) 568
Carolan, Nicholas....M Armstrong & Co. Coach. 400
Churchill, J W. 205 E 86th....P A Cassidy. Carts, &c. 154
Collins, J J. 2810 3d av....T F Baur. Machinery. 150
Congregation Menachim Zion. 71 Sheriff.... Amelia Deutsch. Church Fixtures. 200
Cregio, C A and T....L E Miner. Dredging Machines, &c. 2,800
Cronk, L M. 9th av and 11th st....Lamson C S S Co. Register. (R) 225
Cucci, Luciano. 162 Greenwich....G Lordi. Barber Fixtures. 110
Cusco, Giovanni. 649 and 883 3d av....G Eufenri. Barber Fixtures. 900
Davidson, A and J. 196 Grand....S Blaut. Bakery Fixtures. 700
Drewes, Ernst. 632 9th av....A Koenig. Grocery Fixtures. 659

Dubin, S and S. 44 Clinton....J Chrystal. Cigar Fixtures. 250
Dunkly, E P. Cottage pl....C Meyer. Horse, Wagon, &c. 200
Fanghenel, Louis. 418 6th....Martha R Fanghenel. Grocery Fixtures. 500
Feldman, B M. 170 E 79th and 170 E 83d....Julia Feldman. Horses, Furniture, &c. 2,000
Finan, James. 1507 1st av....J Cunningham. Coach. (R) 848
Finkelstein, Arthur. 364 and 366 E 3d....E Reiss. Machines. 250
Federhart, Albert. 167th st and Amsterdam av ... H Vogel. Cabinet Fixtures. 400
Fitzgerald, James. 2190 8th av....Marvin Safe Co. Safe. 130
Goldsmith, L H. 910 Broadway....Mosler Safe Co. Safe. 137
Goldthwait, J C. 130 Fulton....S Goldthwait. Office Fixtures. 2,800
Grady, F E. 393 Pearl ...D J Lynch. Machinery. (R) 2,000
Grecco, Angelo. 865 10th av....V Lombardi. Barber Fixtures 90
Gaetano, A & C C. 241 Mulberry....F Grecca. Grocery Fixtures. 75
Halbach & Welsh. 433 E 12th....J Everard. Wagon. 204
Haldane, Charles. Pulitzer Building....Financial Credit Co. Office Fixtures. 100
Hart, P F. 57 8th av....S Baillie & Son. Tools. 300
Heiter, J G. 136 W 52d ...B H Meyer. Butcher Fixtures. 750
Higgins, J F. 501 W 56th....J Creighton. Machinery. 110
Jackson, David. 520 7th av....Mary A Kelly. Drug Fixtures. 200
Jarboe, Catharine. 321 E 19th ...E P Ide. Machinery. (R) 55
Joiner, Walter. 476-480 E 139th....S A Woods Machine Co. Machinery. 700
Keifer, Henry. 2520 8th av....Hudson River Beef Co. Butcher Fixtures. (R) 750
Kennedy, W J. 217 W 26th....H Killam Co. Coach. (R) 1,828
Kennedy & Pringay. 50 Wooster....Financial Credit Co. Horse, Wagon, &c. 200
Krueger, Henry. 248 East Houston....C Stegeler. Horses, Trucks, &c. (R) 298
Kerr, Thomas. 43d st and 1st av....D B Fayerweather, Machinery. (R) 720
Same....Fayerweather & Ladew. Machinery. (R) 70
Loewenstein, J E. 813 5th....E Katz. Horses, Wagons, &c. (R) 8,000
Lustig, Paul. 16 E 8th....W H Butler. Safe. 183
Lawrence, H C. 39 Monroe and 69 Baxter....M T Rosenberg. Butcher Fixtures. 283
Lines, W L. 406 Greenwich and 23, 25 and 27 Hubert....G W Millar & Co. Machinery. 9,927
Lippoldt, Louis. 1722 3d av....Weeks & Parr. Bakery Fixtures. 300
Locklin, Thomas....W Hunter. Coupe. 550
Lopez, Gaetano. 433 W 56th....S Cerniglia. Barber Fixtures. 275
Losewsky, Peter. 174th st and Fleetwood av.... S Jacobs Garden Fixtures. 900
Lowenthal, Adolph. 41 Delancey....A Sametz. Bakery Fixtures. 500
Maclay, A E .. W P Chase. Electrotype Plates, &c. (R) 115
Marvin, T H....P Barrett. Trucks. 150
McKenna, R M. 2321 3d av....Lamson Consol S S Co. Register. (R) 210
Meier, C U. 1303 and 1305 Lexington av....Popp & Hasberg. Barber Fixtures and Pool Table. 1,000
Molloy, John. 241 W 41st....D B Dunham. Coach. 450
Morsch, Henry. 137 Grand....Lamson Consol S S Co. Register. 250
Maniaci, Nunzio. 336 E 74th....S Ribando. Barber Fixtures. 50
McIntyre, John. 536 Morris av....P McIntyre. Grocery Fixtures. (R) 500
Muller & Wetzel. 510-514 W 56th....Nuffer & Lippe. Coach. (R) 566
N Y Recorder Co....Knickerbocker Trust Co Newspaper Fixtures. 200,000
Noll, Theobald. 1644 Columbia av and 164 Av D .. C Edeler. Grocery Fixtures, &c. (R) 559
Noonan, Michael. Bowery and Great Jones st ..Lamson Consol S S Co. Register. 210
N Y Industrial Assoc. 219 and 221 E 97th....C Gordon. Fixtures, &c. 400
O'Connor, Margaret .... Hincks & Johnson Coach. (R) 360
O'Neill, Owen. 333 W 40th....W E Devlin. Horses. 393
Osterndorff, Henry. 150 W 100th....J Boehm. Horses, Carts, &c. 1,000
Onderdonk, W M & Co. 1 and 3 Beaver....H Naylor, exr of. Office Fixtures. 1,007
Pelham Hod Elevating Co... J J McCabe. Machinery. 2,090
Pincus, Sam. 150 Ridge .... L Heinsfurter. Butcher Fixtures. 500
Presdee & Moore. 87th st and 9th av....Marvin Safe Co. Safe. (R) 135
Prucha, Frank. 532 E 68th....J Kubes. Horses, Ice Wagon, &c. 900
Quandt, Paul. 943 E 166th....A D Puffer & Son. Soda Fixtures. (R) 455
Rock, Stephen. 75 Av B....Mosler Safe Co. Safe. 120
Roberts, Samuel. 369 Pearl and 3, 5 and 7 Hague ....Hans Rees' Sons. Machinery. (R) 3,780
Rohrs, Henry 639 Greenwich....J Kennedy. Cab. (R) 250
Romain, W G. 156 and 158 W 127th....Asbury Park Nat Bank. Stable Fixtures. 1,400
Roy, Elizabeth. 264 W 116th....Cheywidden & Thomas. Grocery Fixtures. 28
Rugen, Herman. 801 Willis av....Korner & S. Store Fixtures. 300
Russell, H A. 298 West Houston....H McNeelly. Grocery Fixtures. 590
Schneider, J and C F. 45 West 44th....J Everard. Bottler Fixtures. 2,440
Sebastian, William. 1316 1st av....W Sprenger. Cigar Fixtures. 100
Sickles, G G. 180 Pearl....M S Maley. Machinery. 250
Silverstein, Davis. 243 Division....B Silverstein. Machines. 75
Smith, G C....Gas Engine and Power Co. Launch, &c. 2,100
Spizzoca, Vincenzo. 43 Madison....M Rega. Barber Fixtures. 635
Sonnenberg, Max. 153 Bowery....A Levy. Machines. 250
Straut, J J. 343 E 85th....J W Scott. Horses, Ice Wagon, &c. (R) 600

St John Burial Society....M Armstrong & Co. Coach. 150
Streesemann, J F. Riverdale av, Kingsbridge .. C Markert. Butcher Fixtures. 1,000
Schomburg, Herman. 2750 3d av....A Baukauf. Bakery Fixtures. 1,000
Simpson, Abraham. 82 Church....C R Merwin. Press, &c. 1,500
Teller, Julius. 683 Broadway....Duparquet, H & M Co. Range, &c. 302
Tilden, Lilian E F....Mary Ann Evans. Interest in estate of William Tilden. £135
Table, Harris. 29 Pitt....A Grinspan. Bakery Fixtures. £
Thistleton, Frederick....D P Nichols & Co. Coach. 375
Tim, David. 280 Broadway....S Tim. Office Fixtures. (R) 1,008
Umbey, Frederick. 20 2d av. ..T Katz. Barber Fixtures. 100
Vogel, Jonas, 141 Essex....P Beidenbach. Wagon. 160
Volkmar, H G ....J McCollom. Wagon. 115
Volkmar, H G....R A Randell & Son. Harness 165
Same. 307 W 75th....R A Randell & Son. Harness. 125
Wagner, H F, 101st st and Amsterdam av.... P Doelger. Butcher Fixtures. 300
Waibel, George. 634 Courtlandt av....Roberts & Collins. Bakery Fixtures. 71
Warr, H A. 355 Greenwich....O W Van Campen. Grocery Fixtures. 151
Weichselbaum, Tobias. 79 Suffolk....C Leib. Bakery Fixtures. 400
Weiss & Co. 399 Broadway....J Matthews. Soda Fixtures. (R) 1,451
Wilson, H P. 7 Murray....G E Todd. Boots and Shoes, &c. 350
Witte, Heinrich & Frenz. 175 1st av .. E Burger. Van. 225
Wood, F E. 146 W 39th....Hincks & Johnson. Coach. (R) 45
Wasserman, H. 165 Attorney ... C Mayer. Butcher Fixtures. 55
Wiederspiel, Adolph. 252 Stanton ...F & G Haag & Co. Barber Fixtures. 48
Werdenshlag, A, "Agent." 466 6th av ...H Israel & Sons. Horses, Wagon, &c. 300
Wennies, W & A. 12 and 14 Peil ...C Stevens. Machinery. (R) 2034
Zipris, Samuel. 155 Division and 19 Canal.... Dubin & Carroll. Drug Fixtures. (R) 510
Zodikow & Lewinthan. 148-152 Goerck....P Pryibil. Machinery 271

BILLS OF SALE.

Ackermann, C L. Washington Market ...F F Waller. Fixtures, &c. 1
Amberg, Gustav....Amberg Theatre and Terrace Garden ...L Von Raven. Theatre Fixtures. 1
Bryant, G W. 204-208 E 111th .. J Kolb. Horses, Coaches, &c. 2,500
Carroll, J F. 501 East Houston ...Annie Carroll. Grocery Fixtures. 600
Erbert, F F. 695 2d av....W Robertson. Machinery, Fixtures, &c 210
Frankel, Justus. South Beach....A Trum. Fixtures, &c. 250
Geis, W L....P Conlon. Theatrical Fixtures, Horses, &c. 100
Gottlieb, Simon. 34 White....H Handrich. Saloon. 5,000
Grossman, Moritz. 1606 and 1636 3d av....S Grossman. Hardware, &c. 1,500
Heusel, Diedrich. 56 Jefferson....W Meyn. Saloon. 5,000
Jacobs, Solomon. 174th st and Fleetwood av.... P Losewsky. Garden Fixtures. 1,825
Kriete, Henry. 315 E 77th....Huntenberg & Flathmann. Horse, Ice Wagon, &c. 300
Krobling, C L. 86 Willett.. .C. Griese. Saloon Fixtures. 1,000
Ledermann, Moritz. 139 Delancey....H Jacobins. Butcher Fixtures. 150
Montani, Philippo. 2131 1st av....P Montani. Drug Fixtures. 105
Same. 188 Mulberry .. P Montani. Drug Fixtures. 105
Munz, David. 214 West Houston....A Langwasser. Machinery. 300
Nieman, H. 2576 Amsterdam av....A E Otto. Butter and Egg Fixtures. 28
Neuman, Herman. 228 and 230 Stanton....J Newman. Hat Store Fixtures. 200
Pieper, L F. 2005 3d av....J W Thaden. Grocery Fixtures, &c. 2,500
Prodgers & Treharne, ... Mary A Ferris. Share of an estate of R Treharne. (R) 1,700
Robertson, William. 698 2d av....Rosa Erbert. Machinery Fixtures, &c. 210
Ryan, Hannah T. 131 and 133 E 124th....H Freudenthal. Saloon Fixtures. 1,985
Schoen, Alexander. 48 Manhattan....B Fischer & Co. Grocery Fixtures. 101
Stoeber, H and A. 719 9th av....H W Schmidt. Building, ½ int. 6,000
Thaden, J W. 2005 3d av .. Louise Thaden. Grocery Fixtures 2,500
Volkmer, Joseph 1393 3d av....Mary B Volkmer. Boots, Shoes and Furniture. 1,115
Waller, F F. Washington Market....Laura P Ackermann. Fixtures. 1
Winter, J F. 2143 3d av....G A Winter. House Furnishing Fixtures.

ASSIGNMENTS OF CHATTEL MORTGAGES.

Cathelin, George to L Chevanney. (Mort given by A Guinet, July 6, 1891.) 40
Eibsen, Louis to Burr B Co. (J Lange, May 19, 1890). 1,282
Haas, Ryttenberg & Co to J E Ryttenberg. (C E White, July 14, 1890). 2,500
Kepes, Joseph to S Zipser. (F X Haas, Feb. 3, 1891). 500
Same to same. (K Steinhardt, Feb. 21, 1891). 100
Lewin, Julius to C H Rosenham. (C H Rosenham, Sept. 1, 1890). 12
Larner, E W to P & W Ebling B Co. (A Drummond, July 15, 1891.) 1

KINGS COUNTY.

JULY 9 TO 15—INCLUSIVE.

SALOON AND RESTAURANT FIXTURES.

Arfmann, J. 237 Manhattan av .... G Ebret. (R) $1,500
Armstrong, G. 43 Meeker av....J Fallert B Co (Lim). (R) 1,400
Barth, A. 329 Evergreen av....H B Scharmann. 1,000

Laluka, A. 119 Furman....Otto Huber Brewery. 600
Bernard, J. 70 Hamburg av....J Eppig. (R) 700
Beron, A. 100 Debevoise....Claus Lipsius B Co. 600
Beutel. P. 40 Knickerbocker av....Jacobina Beutel. 1,500
Bonner, A. 469 North 2d ...E Ochs. 600
Bullwinkel, H. 717 Gates av....Beadleston & W. 3,000
Bouquet, F. 308 Wallabout ...J Kress B Co. (R) 500
Buonomo, J and A Mangini. 42 Front....M & D Colicchio. 400
Coleman, D. 54 Union ...T C Lyman & Co. (R) 250
Donovan, J H. 261 Court....M Seitz. (R) 1,500
Duerkes, P. 1081 Myrtle av F Ibert. 700
Endres, T. 132 Throop av....J Kress B Co (R) 800
Franken, H. 91 Hull ...B B Scharmann. (R) 675
Frising, O. 63 Bushwick av....J Eppig. 400
Gabbraith, J. 131 Seigel....E Ochs 900
Gehrling, L. 185 Harrison av....J Fallert B Co. 800
Grow, D. 69 Conover ...M Seitz. 300
Haag, C. 8 Harrison av....Liebmann's Sons B Co. (R) 400
Hartman, Ida. 155 Lawrence....Beadleston & Woerz. (R) 1,200
Hirt, W. 87 Johnson av....J Eppig. (R) 500
Holn, N. 4th av, cor 64th st....Welz & Z. 150
Joyce, J....M Seitz. (R) 950
Krafft, W C. 188 Broadway ...W Ulmer. (R) 1,700
Kunkel, G. 217 and 219 Maujer....M Seitz. 550
Kohn, J. 836 6th.... J Eppig. 600
Krebs, A. 47 Throop av....M Seitz. (R) 1,105
Leichter, C. 640 Broadway....M Seitz. 900
Lorenz, R. 47 Meserole....Welz & Zerweck. 2,000
McDermott, T. 157 Myrtle av....Burr B Co. 1,500
McLoon, P. J. 927 Fulton....J Eppig. 400
McVey, P. 311 Van Brunt....M Seitz. (R) 1,968
Meagher, T. 186 Richards....M Seitz. (R) 340
Maderer, G. 7 Leonard....J Kress B Co. 430
Marr, C H. 2549 Atlantic av....P H Reid. Restaurant Fixtures. 125
Meagher, J. 127 9th....Long Island Brewery. 2,000
Mertz, L G. 28 Johnson....W Ulmer. 3,000
Meyer, W and A F Geerben. 12-16 Fulton . P Ballantine & Sons. (R) 2,275
Morey, D P....G Mason. 1,000
Mueller, J T. 1018 3d av....Danenberg & Coles. (R) 800
Mulligan, M E. 185 Nassau av....P Weidmann. 400
Murphy, M L. 441 Keap....H Elias B Co. (R) 800
Neumann, J. 295 Floyd . Claus Lipsius B Co. 600
Olifiers, B J. 106 Diamond....J Ruppert. (R) 759
Oechsner, J. 266 Floyd....J Eppig. 300
O'Connor, E A. 194 Court ...S Wilson. 300
Pfretzschner, E. 458 Broadway....M Seitz. 931
Puckhaber, J H W. 47 Grand....P Weidmann. 1,500
Robke, F. 951 Herkimer ...W Craft. 1,050
Schoeffel & Fleck. 56 Moore ...Burger & Hower B Co Lim. 400
Schurr, G. 243 Devoe....M Seitz. 300
Seibert, A. 223 Cook....J Fallert B Co. 600
Snediker, J. 1006 Broadway....Fred Hower B Co. 425
Saake, F W. Marcy av, cor South 2d st....G Graban. 800
Voege, H. 7 Tillary....Beadleston & W. (R) 1,100
Welton, D. 110 Dwight....M Seitz. 500
Wilshusen, C. 2208 Fulton ...W Ulmer. 3,500
Wise, W. 931 3d av .. Liebman's Sons B Co. 275
Wolf, T. Leonard, cor Moore... J Kress B Co. 300
Wolf, T. 21 Tompkins av....J Kress B Co. 800
Zettlein, G. 1191 Myrtle av....Obermeyer & L. (R) 300

HOUSEHOLD FURNITURE.

Baker, A S. 527 Lafayette av....Fennell & Pye. 232
Baulsier, M C. 62 Harman....Kendrick & Co. 118
Buys, G L. 167 Waverly av....H Manne. 150
Byrns, Maggie. 688 Wythe av ...W E Wheelock. Piano. 325
Batista M. 618 7th av....I Mason. 130
Burke, J. 91 Nevins....T F Mulqueen. 318
Copeland, R I. 478 Pacific....Cowperthwait Co. 331
Doherty, M. 223 High....I Mason. 146
Dickneider, F. 52 Covert ...I Mason. 109
Egeln, C. 338 Vernon av ...Krakauer Bros. Piano. 190
Erickson, C. 620 President ...C S Lacey. 115
Evarts, A J. 68 North Portland av....J McEnery & Co. 287
Fleming, Eliz E. 445 State....C H Evans & Sons. (R) 600
Green, W E. 77 Lexington av....Commercial Credit Co. 100
Gregory, Mrs Jessie. 571 Leonard....Jordan & M. 234
Hogan, P F. 641 3d av....I Mason. 359
Haerter, C 75 Nassau... T F Mulqueen. 121
Hagen, C. 122 Middleton . J McEnery & Co. 263
Hoepfner, F. 141 Palmetto....Kendrick & Co. 198
Hurley, E. 76 Georgia av....Kendrick & Co. 147
Jackson, Josie. 466 Clermont av ...L Baumann. 164
Kattenbach, J. 11 Stewart....M Bottstein. 140
Kelly, Mrs J. 163 Carroll... I Mason. 190
Kelly, J W. 41 South 6th....Kendrick & Co 154
Kettner, L G. 1081 Myrtle av....Kendrick & Co. 120
Leonard, Winifred. 53 North 6th.. Brooklyn F Co. 221
Lynes, Maria. 9 Montague terrace... F Shaw. 300
Lund, O. 628A President ...J McEnery & Co. 265
Mattson, Marie. 46 South 3d....A Schulz. 124
Magonigle, Lucy. 478A 16th....H B Marchbank. Piano. 140
O'Keefe, J A. 419 Union....I Mason. 268
Pell, S D. St Marks av, cor Bedford av....Cowperthwait Co. 522
Ries, Emma. 131 Debevoise....L Baumann. 141
Riley, F. 624 Wythe av....Commercial Credit Co. 100
Seaver, A H. 49th st near 1st av....L Baumann. 155
Street, Charlotte....A L Martin. 125
Sullivan, Sadie. 214 9th st....L Baumann. 148
Salbach, Clara. 101 Norman av....Krakauer Bros. Piano. 225
Sturgberg, Charlotte. 83 Tompkins pl .. A Jones. 350
Whallon, S S. 391 6th av. ..Financial Credit Co. 125
Wilcox, Ida M. 211 Adelphi....E M Lloyd. 250

MISCELLANEOUS.

Alt & Downing. 273 Tompkins av ...National Cash Register Co. Register. 175
Ahlers, L F. Montague st....Lamson C S S. Co. Register. 140
Ash, Jr, J H. 418 Tompkins av....Mary Kinahan. Horse and wagon. 110
Bell, G H.....S C Beckwith. Wagon. 500
Bohack, H C. 1648 Broadway....Lamson C S S Co. Register. 210
Brownson, J M....Campbell P P and Manufacturing Co. Press. 668
Clark, F H. 316 Bedford av....National Cash Register Co. Register. 175
Christian, J H. Railroad av, cor Hunterfly road....S Strauss. Horses. 140
Coleman, F. 373 Myrtle av .. W H Tomford. Jewelers' Fixtures. (R) 303
Condon, J and J J Hickey. 61 Ann st, New York....Van Allens & B. Press. (R) 850
Connelly, R. 75 Van Sicklen av....J H Henn. Barber Fixtures. 100
Daley, P J. 189 Pacific....A M Stein & Co. Horses, Carts, &c. (R) 120
Devlin, W E. Wallabout Stable....B Weill. Horses. 145
Diauby, V A K. 1591 Bushwick av...J D Wright. Machiney, &c. 1,000
Domenico, D. 272 North 2d....V Cirolla. Barber Fixtures. 154
Donnelly, J B. 89 Parker....L Weil. Cows. 557
Everett, Susan M. 327 Washington ...Estella M Quantin. Machinery. 500
Same....G F Rogers. Machinery. 1,300
Ferchland, C. 215 23d....D B Dunham & Son. Coach. (R) 225
Gorman, T. Coney Island road, near Caton pl ....Underhill, Clinch & Co. Horses, &c. 100
Grafton, J T. 361 Court....H W Coates. Drug Fixtures. 3,000
Guida, P. 101 York....Maria Femminella. Barber Fixtures. 200
Harvey, E. Logan st, near Atlantic av....Brussels Tapestry Co. Looms, &c. 609
Heinsohn, P. 408 Central av....Nat Cash Register Co Register. 225
Hildenbrand, J. 1130 De Kalb av....L Abrahams. Blacksmith Fixtures. 100
Harrison, Ann. 1738 Fulton....Sprague Nat Bank of Brooklyn. Grocery Fixtures. (R) 4,000
Hart, P....M & B Kraus. Horses and Trucks. 130
Hassenstein, E. 149 Maujer ...E Hoeninghaus. Horse and Wagon. 150
Ideal Rubber Co. Kent av....Birmingham Iron Foundry. Machinery. 1,550
Johnson, J P....Teresa Johnson. Horse and Wagon. 100
Lewry, W J. 270 Flatbush av. . Wallace & Keeney. Fish Store. (R) 200
Lutz, V F. 276 Tompkins av....C Buermann. Tools, &c. 600
Mahl, E. 128 Union....H Kahn. Store Fixtures. 285
Moran, J C. 169 Halsey....M Moran. Store Fixtures. 1,500
Massa, L. 7 President....R Rainforth. Barber Fixtures. 125
McGuckin, J E. 125 Oakland....J Cunningham Son & Co. Undertaker's Wagon. 450
McIntire, H E. Fulton and Hendrix sts....A F Snelling. Fixtures. 1,500
Mertz, L G. 28 Johnson....Lamson Consol S S Co. Register. 165
Mott, F S. 80 Vernon av ...M Armstrong. Coaches, Horses, &c. 1,150
Mott, F S. 80 Vernon av....B Weill, Horse. 150
O'Brien, John. 58 and 60 North 1st....Joseph O'Brien. Machinery. Secures Indorser. 2,200
Petit, M E....W Conrady. Wagon. 120
Rock, M. 246 Loraine....T Rheims. Horse. 200
Reid, T. 39 South st, New York ...J Reid. Horses, &c. (R) 2,000
Robinson, M. 1896 Fulton....F & G Haag & Co. Barber Fixtures. 182
Scheuring, G. 11 Gates av....A A Kloster. Confectionery Store. 300
Slater, J. 10 Meeker av....J Hirstins. Horses and Wagons. 1,000
Smith, S. Coney Island ...W H Butler. Safe. 110
Snedeker, G V D. 39 Grand av....J Husing. Horse, &c. 400
Sanford, J A. 87 Atlantic av . .H H Frost. Fish Store. 100
Union Elevated R R Co....Central Trust Co. Railroads, Structures, Rights and Franchises. 2,500,000
Wollman, E. 333 Central av... P Crook. Horse and Wagon. 215
Weil, M. 9 Floyd....Fannie Leabmann. Butcher Fixtures. 500

BILLS OF SALE.

Bauer, A. 37 Bushwick av....L A Stecher. Paint Store. 100
Bruns, V. Central av, cor Jefferson st .. P Heinsohn. Grocery Fixtures. 2,350
Dauber, L H. 1116 Bedford av. ..H C Dauber, Grocery. 2,500
Farrenkopf, J. 70 Central av .. Louisa Farrenkopf. Cigars, &c. 200
Fullerton, W. 73 Kent av....M Reynolds and ano. Brass Foundry. nom
Hanley, J. 25-27 Atlantic Market....H Deventhal. Stands and Fixtures. 500
Holbrook, Julia A, Sarah L Holt and Harriet M and Lilian R Terrett to Sarah A Terrett. All personal property of D R Terret dec'd. nom
Holtz, E F....G Lotz Saloon. 3,950
Karcher, J....C Karcher. Shoe Store Fixtures. 500
Lehrer, F W. 194 Smith....Louise Braun. Barber Fixtures. 250
Orthlieb, L and O. 8 Myrtle av....Eliza Orthlieb. Restaurant Fixtures 1,000
Quirk, A. 441 Hicks ...M Stern. Butcher Fixtures. 275
Rametta, F. 8 Bedford av....G A Rametta. Dressmaking Establishment. nom
Same. 165 Calyer....same. Shoe Store. nom
Robbins, W. 866-870 Grand....J Cooke, Jr. Frame Buildings. 300
Rosenberg, H E....L Arensberg. Horses, &c. 150
Terrett, Sarah A to grantors above, same property; to each 4-27 part. nom
Weigel, J. 835 Gates av....H Bullwinkel. Saloon Fixtures. 5,900
Wieland, C. 41 State....J Buchlager. Butcher Fixtures. 125
Wortman, S. Liberty av, cor Hendricks st....A McNeil. Frame Building. 250

NEW JERSEY.

NOTE.—*The arrangement of the Conveyances, Mortgages and Judgments in these lists is as follows: the first name in the Conveyances is the Grantor; in Mortgages, the Mortgagor; in Judgments, the Judgment debtor.*

ESSEX COUNTY.

CONVEYANCES.

Allen, Frank B exr—J J Ehmann, Moreland st.. $175
Allen, F B exr—Wheeler & Russell Hat Co, s l Miller st cor N J R R av 103x231x103x178.... 10,007
Atwater, Samuel—J Eastwood, Broad st........ 1
Atwater, Samuel assignee—J Eastwood, Broad st........ 1
Anderson, Emily et al—A McKenzie, Sherman av........ 1,500
Armstrong, E R—Paul Merz et al, Lillie st........ 1,800
Babbit, Charlott E—H L Munster, Orange........ 3,300
Baker, J E—C E Lyon, North 18th st........ 500
Bizzolo, Antonio—V Ippolito, s s 8th av 233 e Nesbitt st 23x65x20x90x20........ 4,600
Bowes, J J—B T Madden, 6th av........ 1,500
Same—M E Madden, Prospect av........ 1,500
Breakenridge, J R—E H Grauff, Clinton........ 300
Brewster, E M—E A Raymond, East Orange.... 1
Brous, H W—T McGuire, Broome st........ 1
Causse, M L—L H Farmer, South Orange........ 2,600
Clark, D T—S E Dodd, South Orange........ 1
Clark, Jacob—P McCaffrey, Summer av........ 1,000
Coe, Abby dec'd by exrs—S E Parkhurst, South 9th st........ 2,250
Coolbaugh, F W—A Reasoner, East Orange.... 1,750
Connaughton, Ellen—C C O'Connor, South 11th st........ 1
Conover, W H—J Breen, North 4th st........ 600
Cooper, H J—P Cockefair, Montclair........ 700
Corcia, Ginseppe—V A Bagnulo, North 3d st.... 2,500
Cornwall, G R—A B De Camp, Montclair........ 2,800
Corwin, C R—E P Hand, 10th av........ 1
Croscup, G E—L C Goodrich, Milburn........ 12,000
Davis, A S—I McIlree, New st........ 1
De Jonge, Solomon—F Schaaf, Clinton........ 90
Dike, F B—R E Cogan, Montclair........ 1,450
Same—W B Dodd, Montclair........ 1,450
Dodd, Amzi et al exrs—W Schaub, Bank st.... 1,800
Earle, J E—Wm Crane, 7th av........ 2,200
Earl, J K—J P Jube, s e cor Clinton av and Wright........ 13,000
Essex & Hudson Land Imp Co—N Y Bay R R Co, Salt Meadow........ 3,300
Forest Hill Association—W T Bishop, Parker st.. 400
Garrabrant, C R—M E Burgess, Polk st........ 1
Garrabrant, E R—A Divine, Clinton........ 1,000
Garrabrant, Sarah—Mayor and Common, Council, South 14th st........ 160
Gracie, Richard—H J Cooper, Bloomfield........ 3,200
Gray, T J—A Devine, Clinton........ 1,000
Hall, P M—J C Crevier, Montclair........ 4,200
Health, W C—A E La Valla, n s cor Miller and Brunswick sts, 27x100........ 3,000
Hill, G R—E M Work, Franklin........ 4,500
Hills, T R—W Terriberry, Roseville av........ 10
Hoffman, Adolph—F W Shrump, West Orange.. 3,550
Hopkins, H A—F Niebuhr, Prince st........ 1,500
Hotz, Herman—W P Rommell, Ridgewood av.. 700
Hunt, R E—A J Pain, 3d st........ 550
Same—W J Pain, 3d st........ 1,100
Jacklin, Harrison—F Mackin, Jacob st........ 1
Jerolaman, Henry—R P Conlon, Peddie st........ 300
Joergens, Charles—T Joergens, Court st........ 150
Kamlah, Charles—P Kling, Belleville........ 1
Keller, C G—L Peter, n e cor Darcy and Niagara sts 50x105........ 5,000
Kellet, James—A Smith, Academy st........ 1
Knapp, F W dec'd by exrs—G Hoyt, East Orange........ 2,700
Kremeutz, George—C W Clayton, Kinney st.... 1
Laine, C E—F Amodis, s s South Orange av 75 e Broome st 25x100........ 4,500
La Valla, A C—W C Heath, n e cor Miller and Brunswick sts 27x100........ 3,000
Lindsley, J N—O S Wood et al exrs, Orange.... 1
Lister, J C—R Wyatt, e s Belleville av 295 s Harvey st 23x100........ 5,500
Lister, J C—W P Dunn, Market st........ 2,000
Lockwood, L G et al. trustee—F W Lestrade, Caldwell........ 267
Same—G V Morgan, Caldwell........ 260
Lombard, L L—D C Lyon, Salt Meadow........ 10
Lux, B E—J Lux, Montclair........ 1
Lux, Joseph—J E Huestis, Montclair........ 3,864
Mackin, Francis—C Wild, Bremen st........ 55
Masi, Vincenzo—G Rita, M & E R R av........ 2,500
McGuire, J F—H W Brous, Broome st........ 1
McKone, Bernard—W Hill, Ridge st........ 500
Mead, E R—L A Farmer, South Orange........ 1
Munn, J L master—Wm Ward, Chapel st........ 2,000
Murray, Catherine—M Murray, Orange........ 1
Mussen, J C—H Betzler, Elizabeth av........ 1,550
Mutual B & L Assoc—P Clark, Hunterdon st.... 2,500
Nevins, Thomas—H Griffith, East Orange........ 3,750
Same—F J Griffith, East Orange........ 30,000
O'Brien, James—T J O'Brien, South Orange.... 1
O'Connor, C C—J Conor et al, South 11th st.... 1
Pain, W J J G Fotheringhame, 4th st........ 4,200
Parkhurst, A L—A M Jacobus, Caldwell........ 150
Parkinson, William—J E Fleming, West Orange. 682
Peck, Cyrus—E R Coffin, 4th st........ 900
Same—G Weyrauch, 4th st........ 800
Reilly, John—Mayor & Common Council, Emmett st........ —
Riker, William—H Durand, Clinton........ 2,200
Rommel, August—Newark Sanitary and Mfg Co, Old River road, adj Van Rensselaer land, 90x540x175x600........ 15,000
Rusby, H B—S E M Rice, e s Mt. Prospect av, adj Scharff property, 48x248........ 4,560
Schaeffer, Joseph—C Linder, South 10th st........ 2,550
Schoenfeld, Flora—L Bucholtz et al, w s Norfolk st 276 n South Orange av, 30x100........ 6,775
Sedille, E D—P Reiff, w s 2d st, 510 South 7th av, 25x89........ 4,000
Sims, Richard—J S Crone, e s Summer av, 200 s Nursery st, 25x110........ 4,500
Sindle, T H—I L Sindle, Caldwell........ 1,000
Same—T H Sindle, Caldwell........ 1
Smith, Rachel—P Schulz, Bloomfield........ 650
Stein, Joseph—M J De Witt, Aqueduct st........ 550
Sturges, M I—C R Garabrant, Polk st........ 1
The Manufacturers' Nat Bank—G Fletcher, North 7th st........ 750
The Orange Savings Bank—J Bradley, West Orange........ 1,000
The Peabody Land and Loan Co—H W Dobbins, Mt Prospect av........ 562
Trefz, Charles—H Seutt, Livingston st........ 700
Trench, M R—G E Croscup, Milburn........ 16,000
Tuers, David—L R Trimble, Montclair........ 1,500
Van Camp, J G—E S Sayers, South Orange........ 1,550
Van Duyne, Harrison—R McQueen, North 8th st 2,000
Van Riper, J G—H L Rowan, Belleville........ 3,000
Ward, William—D Dunn, e s Chapel st, 200 s Lister av, 25x100........ 3,000
Wettyen, C F—E Jacobus, trustee, Caldwell.... 10
Wightman, M A—F Schoenfeld, e s Belmont av, 450 s Montgomery st, 50x100........ 6,500
Wort, H E—T J Gray, Walnut st........ 1

MORTGAGES.

Amodio, Francesco—W S Brown, South Orange av........ 3,500
Arnold, Charles—Reliable B and L Assoc, East Orange........ 800

Baum, E T—The 8th Ward B and L Assoc, Parker st 8,400
Betzler, Henry—S Doughty et al. exrs, Elizabeth av 1,000
Birrell, H W—The 8th Ward B and L Assoc, Summer av 1,200
Bishop, W T—The Woodside B and L Assoc, Parker st 2,000
Brown, H A—E N Crane, Calumet st 1,300
Clark, Patrick—The Mutual B and L Assoc, Hunterdon st 2,500
Cogan, R E—F R Dike, Montclair 1,050
Croscup, G E—M R French, Milburn 7,000
Davis, Joseph—G G Hardy, 3d st 2,400
Dealing, W H—W R Ward, East Orange 500
Dennis, C P—E Matthews, East Orange 5,000
Dodd, W B—F B Dike, Montclair 1,050
Dow, J W—A L Dow, Milburn 2,000
Dunn, Dennis—The Enterprise B and L Assoc, Chapel st 2,200
Same—C Feigenspan, Chapel st 1,000
Fleming, J E—W Pierson, West Orange 2,800
Gegenheimer, J E—C J Shaer, Orange 2,200
Goodrich, L C—M R French, Milburn 6,000
Same—G E Croscup, Milburn 3,000
Griffith, F J—T Nevins, East Orange 20,000
Same—T Nevins, East Orange 3,000
Hagemann, A J—C Libel, South 10th st 600
Harbeck, M A—M A Johnson, South Orange 2,000
Hill, William—J de Jianne, Ridge st 250
Hoyt, George—M A Knapp, East Orange 2,090
Hughes, J E—J Lux, Montclair 3,000
Ippolito Vitale—Reliable B and L Assoc, 8th av 2,400
Jacobus, W G—F T Johnson, Caldwell 700
Johnston, A S—S Shannon, East Orange 1,000
Koegel, Christian—L F Crowell, Bruce st 1,000
Kull, Albert—John Frank, 7th av 2,700
Linder, Christina—J Schaeffer, South 10th st 1,500
Lyon, D M—The Mutual Benefit Life Ins Co, Washington st 35,000
Mackin, Francis—L Leverich, Komorn st 1,800
Same—same, Komorn st 1,800
Maltempo, Frank—Howard Savings Inst, South st 5,000
McDavit, Harry—J Wills, Clinton 2,000
McIlree, Isabella—A S Davis, New st 500
McNulty, Bernard—J McCrickaw, Orange 200
Merz, Paul et al—E R Armstrong, Lillie st 1,800
Miller, J G—J J Brown, Bergen st 550
Mucklow, H B—Fourteenth Ward B and L Assoc, Littleton av 600
Munn, J L—C Rayner, Bloomfield 1,500
Munster, H L—E Babbitt, Orange 2,000
Navatier, E C—J H Breakenridge et al, Clinton 60
Neuman, Heyman—Standard B & L Assoc, Prince st 1,400
Newman, Harriet—G Kuhnle, Barclay st 2,500
Same—C Barth, Barclay st 500
O'Brien, T J—T Burnet, South Orange 500
Parker, M A—Orange Savings Bank, East Orange 2,500
Picco, Louis—A H Campfield, East Orange 436
Price, W H—P T Lewis, Mt Pleasant av 1,000
Reiboldt, Bertha—L F Crowell, 14th av 500
Rice, S E M—H H Busby, Mt Prospect av 1,517
Robb, W L—The Mutual Benefit Life Ins Co, Clinton av 4,000
Rommel, W P—Lincoln B & L Assoc, Ridgewood av 700
Schaub, Wm—John Jelliff, Bank st 2,600
Same—John Kocher, Jr, Bank st 1,500
Schloss, Sarah—E Schloss, William st 1,000
Schlund, Fidel, Jr—J E Terhune, Hanover pl 1,000
Schoenfeld, Flora—The Newark B & L Assoc, Belmont av 4,500
Same—M A Wightman, Belmont av 600
Schulz, Peter—The Essex B & L Assoc of Bloomfield, Bloomfield 550
Serbe, A F—W T Serbe, Bergen st 700
Spagnuolo, Irena—The 14th Ward B & L Assoc, Adams st 5,000
Spoerri, A F—E M Dixon, Orange 4,000
Squier, F C—M E Campfield exr, East Orange 4,000
Shrump, F W—E Venino, West Orange 1,800
The Newark Sanitary Mfg Co—A Rommel, Old River road 12,000
Thieme, George—J J Brown, Newton st 2,100
Trimble, J M—American Ins Co, Montclair 1,000
Van Horn, Abraham—S F Niblo, Woodside av 1,700
Van Riper, J G—C P Cullmann, Belleville 300
Wheeler & Russell Hat Company—F B Allen exr, Miller st 17,000
Same—same, Miller st 10,000
Wolf, George—C Wolf, Spruce st 1,300
Wiebuhr, Friedrich—H A Hopkins, Prince st 1,200

CHATTEL MORTGAGES.

Babendrier, Gustav—W H Marcell, horses and wagon 119
Buchanan, William—J Ketcham, furniture 195
Ehehalt, F H—A Stiep, butcher fixtures 800
Hermery, C E—J Ketcham, furniture 195
Horey, Harriet—J W Hann, furniture 42
Kaiser, Wm—A R Denman, furniture 150
Karp, Jacob—Wilkinson, Gaddis & Co, stock groceries 100
Kunstlich Alexander—Muller & Schmidt, furniture 207
Larcbe, Joseph—F Larche, rifle gallery fixtures 100
Menagh, H P—C Bierman, furniture 100
Rennie, R T—J G Vermilye, furniture 1,200
Rizzolo, Feliz—P Ballentine & Sons, saloon 225
Scott, L D—P H Hanley, furniture 65
Sellick, Robert—C E Cannon, furniture 213
The Fisher Varnish Company—A M King, varnish tanks, &c 1,090
Tillyer, J W—O Bernz, machinery 150
Tiplin, H B—F H Tiplin, brick buildings 3,323
Wells, Ida—Brooklyn Furniture Co, furniture 108

JUDGMENT.

Conlon, Julia—Wm A Leggett et al 384

HUDSON COUNTY.

CONVEYANCES.

Allen, Robert, and Michael M Forrest—Amelia A Gray, Kearney $300
Same—C K O'Neill, Kearney 1,100
Astarita, Amilcare—Annie E Shaffer, J City ..... nom
Same—D Shaffer, J City 5,200
Astley, Horatio—J McArthur, Kearney 1,250
Barden, Rich—Lizzie Fagan, J City ..... nom
Barnickel, C A—F N Eberhard, Hoboken 500
Bayonne Impt Co—W J Hardy, Bayonne 1,400
Bell, H P—L Goldsmith, Kearney 650
Black, Jannett E—H Pfizenmaier, Harrison 950
Bramhall, Esther A—J Lloyd, J City 800
Brett, P W—Mary J Houston, West Hoboken ..... nom
Broeg, Adeline—J Weiss, Union 425
Brown, T C—J C Bouton, Bayonne 2,000
Browning, J H—P Anglesey, J City 1,100
Same—T O'Reilly, J City 2,500
Burns, H W—W Crowell, Kearney 2,800
Cadmus, J R—Mary E Duke, Bayonne 430
Caulfield, C H—Irene Hopkins, J City 300
Central N J Land and Impt Co—The Central R R Co, Bayonne ..... nom
Same—D Van Buskirk, Bayonne ..... nom
Clausen, Christian—J Spendler, West Hoboken 5,000
Condict, Fillmore—F Greathead, Kearney 150
Same—W T Wilkinson, Kearney 275
Condict, H V—W W Rice, J City 3,800
Cottier, C C—Amanda M Cottier, J City ..... nom
Cubberly, J H—E Y Allison, J City 760
Dueber, Gottlieb—Minna Diana, Union 1,550
Dunne, Annie—Mary E Burke, J City 1,000
Eaton, Mary S—Emma E Tillman, J City 4,000
Edge, Isaac—Ada E Atkins, J City 5,600
Emmons, E F—Alma Kestner, J City 2,800
Fischer, Susan L—W D Edwards, J City 3,000
Foster, Kate—J B Sabine, J City 1,000
Frambach, Julia—H Schmidt, West Hoboken 700
Gardner, Jno—F Copin, North Bergen 5,000
Gerlach, Pauline—F Steeger, Hoboken 7,000
Greenleaf, S H—The Trustees of School District No 3, North Bergen 1,900
Hamilton, Jas, Jr—W R Muirhead, J City 2,800
Hilliard, C V T—J McCarthy, West Hoboken 565
Hobson, Eli by exrs—H Pfizenmaier, Harrison 950
Houston, Mary J—Mary E Brett, West Hoboken ..... nom
Howell, G P—A L McDermott, J City 5,800
Illensworth, W P—D Van Buskirk, Bayonne ..... nom
Immich, Washington—E P Stils, J City 2,400
Johnston, Caroline W—H Astley, Kearney 475
Same—J Hood, Kearney 630
Kedder, Elizabeth—J F Marion, J City ..... nom
Kiernan, Francis—D Daly, Bayonne 1,500
Krollmann, Andrew—A L McDermott, Hoboken 6,800
Lamb, James—C Schnelweiss, Hoboken 3,000
Leidner, Nichols—F Kuhlsen, J City 2,525
Lessey, Emile—E Hostmann, J City 4,400
Lienan, Michael—A Siegfried, J City 20,800
Loenenstein, Marie—J Schmidt, West Hoboken 2,700
Malone, Pat—E Perry, J City 1,090
Mannion, John—S C Ecb, J City 2,000
Marion, J F—J Kedder, J City ..... nom
Meagher, Jeremiah—P Semler, J City 930
Mehl, Jno—E A Brickwedel, J City 1,200
Mezger, Margaret—F Mezger, J City 2,500
Murphy, Cath—Jessie K Vreeland, Bayonne ..... nom
Newham, C E—Hudson City Savings Bank, J City 300
Nichols, E H—C H Caulfield, J City 500
Nolan, T D—Greenville B & L Assoc, Bayonne ..... nom
Nordenholtz, Anna—H L Petersen, Hoboken 9,000
Nuce, Nicholas—A Berenaro, J City 7,500
Ogden, W B by exrs—C Vietmeyer, J City 1,000
O'Halloran, P D—C Diercksen, J City 2,000
Piaget, H V—Anna Morris, J City 6,150
Pierson, Susan J—S J Young, J City 500
Prigge, Henry J—C Deiber, Jr, J City 500
Prigge, Henry—J Lloyd, J City 150
Provident Inst for Savings—W Talcott, J City 12,000
Rademan, Peter—J Regan, J City 800
Reilly, Andrew—T McGuiness, J City ..... nom
Reilly, J G by special guard—Jesse K Vreeland, Bayonne 3,700
Roberts, Harriet—W Morten, J City 2,400
Rudiger, J H—F Cathcart, West Hoboken 700
Russ, Edward—Hoboken Land and Impt Co, Hoboken 18,000
Schneider, Chas—H Koehler, J City 2,000
Schuyler, Mary A—J H Dobson, Bayonne 600
Schuyler, R V R by trustee—W Kelly, Bayonne 450
Semler, Peter—Louis Meyer, Jr, J City 500
Shotwell, J B—Henrietta Van Benschoten, J City 1,900
Siedler, Chas—West Side Connecting R R Co, J City 11,815
Siegfried, Adam—J C Peterson, J City 900
Steeger, Frederick—Pauline Gerlach, Hoboken 6,000
Stewart, Chas—R Allen, Kearney 3,000
Stratford, Geo—Geo Stratford Oakum Co, J City ..... nom
Symes, J H—T Wiseman, Union 500
Same—D Tortorelli, Union 1,600
Tappan, Dewitt—E Tappan, J City 1,000
Tappan, Eugene—D Tappan, J City 3,500
Tappan, Dewitt—Eliza C Tappan, J City 8,500
Tenny, Ann E—O Lyons, Bayonne 1,400
Thacher, Elizabeth B—B S Schoonover, Kearney 400
Thachee, J H—B S Schoonover, Kearney 11
The Delta Co—The Jersey City Printing Co, J City ..... nom
The Hudson City Savings Bank—J F Taylor, J City 1,900
The Indian Spring Land Co—J H Hoffman, West Hoboken 500
Tierney, Myles—R Barnes, J City 1,200
Torney, Judith—T McGuiness, J City ..... nom
Van Buskirk, Dewitt—Fannie Evans, Bayonne 4,625
Same—J G Hanson, Bayonne 1,495
Von Diehle, Herman by exrs—Matilda Lorentz, West Hoboken 3,300
Van Emburg, J D—Mary Murray, Kearney 100
Same—same, Kearney 600
Walker, Herman and Emmerick Louis—J Schatzler, Union 575
Wegner, Henry—E Wegner, North Bergen 100
Weiss, Geo—A Ragadi, Guttenberg 2,100
Wescott, W R—W H Cook, Bayonne 3,000
Williams, I F—E F Emmons, J City 2,900
Williams, Jas—E Russ, Hoboken 18,000
Winters, Jeno, by City Collector—J B Niblett, J City 127
Woods, R M—Engene Schonseegel, Kearney 1,000
Same—J A Dorman, Kearney 400
Same—L N Hanover, Kearney 675

MORTGAGES.

Allison, Elmira Y—J A Allison, J City, 5 years 760
Alsberg, Irving—G Bruck, Hoboken, 3 years 8,000
Arnold, Nicholas—G Wilkinson, J City, 1 year 150
Atkins, Ada E—J De Vries, J City, 3 years 6,000
Bantz, F J—Hudson Trust and Savings Inst, West Hoboken, 3 years 1,800
Barclay, W A—Susan J Wortendyke, J City, 3 years 1,150
Bech, Pauline—D Bermes, Union, 3 years 8,000
Betts, Lucy A—C Linn, J City, 3 years 1,000
Bouton, J C—T C Brown, Bayonne, 2 years 1,500
Brown, Jane A—Exr J Brown, Hoboken, 2 years 3,500
Same—Hudson Trust and Savings Inst, Hoboken, 3 years 4,000
Cannon, Peter—C J Cronan, J City. To secure payment of promissory note 1,500
Chapman, Anna—Mary M Finke, J City, 1 year 3,000
Cother, Amand M—F Luxton, J City, 3 years 2,500
Cook, W H—Security B & L Assoc, Bayonne, installs 2,800
Same—W P Wescott, Bayonne, 1 year 200
Copin, Frances—J Gardner, North Bergen, 3 years 4,800
Croghan, Johanna—E Gleeson, Bayonne, 3 years 200
Cuinkshand, Will—Mary M Cunkshank, Bayonne, 1 year 100
Daly, Daniel—Greenville B and L Assoc, Bayonne, installs 2,190
Dormann, J A—R M Woods, Kearney, 1 year 225
Eck, S C—J Marnion, J City, 5 years 1,500
Emmons, E F—T S Bloodgett, J City, 1 year 1,200
Evans, Fannie—D Van Buskirk, Bayonne, 3 years 3,400
Same—J E Andrus, J City, installs 1,600
Same—same, J City, installs 1,600
Funcken, G C—H Plate, J City, 1 year 110
Furey, Catti E—The Knights of Pythias B and L Assoc, J City, installs 5,000
Hanover, L N—R M Woods, Kearney, 1 year 550
Hearney, Kate—Greenville B and L Assoc, J City, installs 3,650
Heere, Henry—Excelsior M B and L Assoc, J City, installs 1,000
Kaehler, Henry—H Stueck, J City, 5 years 1,200
Kehr, Phil—C Steltmann, J City, 3 years 2,000
Kendall, Chas—R Allen, Kearney, 3 years 537
Kerr, E J—Mary O Seaman, J City, 1 year 3,000
Kestner, H A F W—T S Bloodgett, J City, 3 yrs 1,300
Same—E F Emmons, J City, 4 months 400
Klausmeier, Fred—E J Veraismes, Guttenberg, 1 year 100
Lauer, G H—W Burrows, Bayonne, installs 3,800
Livingston, Will—W G Bumsted, J City, 3 years 2,100
Logan, Martin—J Cummings, Bayonne, 1 year 50
Mac, Mary E—A Stayert, J City, 3 years 3,000
McDermott, Allan L—E L Corbin, J City, 2 yrs 25,000
McGrehan, Frances—H Lembeck, J City, 3 yrs 1,000
McLean, King Will—W J Daly, J City, 2 years 5,000
Mezger, Fred—Margaret Mezger, J City, 3 years 1,000
Miller, E J—J Noe, West Hoboken, 3 years 2,000
Mohr, Henry—J Moylan, West Hoboken, 1 year 100
Morecraft, Isaac—Hudson County Land and Improvement Co, J City, 2 years 185
Morris, Anna—H V Piaget, J City, 1 year 600
Same—same, J City, 3 years 2,800
Muirhead, W R—Union B and L Assoc, J City, installs 1,800
O'Reilly, Thos—J H Browning, J City, 5 years 2,100
Pederson, J C—A Siegfried, J City, 3 years 400
Rehm, Ernst—Hoboken Bank for Savings, Hoboken, 3 years 1,800
Reichling, C W—J B Stratton, J City, 3 years 600
Rice, W W—Ella M Partridge, J City, 3 years 2,000
Ricker, H A—A Dutnken, J City, 1 year 1,500
Schnsiegel, Eugene—R M Woods, Kearney, 1 year 700
Siegfried, Adam—W Lienau, J City, 2 years 14,500
Skerry, Ann—Starr M B and L Assoc, J City, installs 1,800
Sherry, Felix—J Gallagher, J City, 5 years 2,500
Slavin, Sarah F—Geo K Camp, J City, 2 years 500
Smith, Sarah J—Highland M B and L Assoc, J City, installs 1,000
Sortorelli, Domenico—Exr A Schleicher, Union, 3 years 750
Spindler, Jno—C Clauser, West Hoboken, 3 yrs 3,500
Sturgis, Margaret A—Marg A Walter, J City, 1 year 375
Talcott, Will—Provident Inst for Savings, J City, 1 year 9,000
Same—same, J City, year 1,000
Taylor, J F—Hudson City Savings Bank, J City, 1 year 900
The Evangelical Lutheran St Paul's Church—Dorothea Och, J City, 5 years 7,000
Tognatti, Antonio—Hudson Trust and Savings Inst, West Hoboken, 1 year 1,200
Van Benschoten, Henrietta—Sun and Evening Sun B M L and Accumulating Fund Assoc, J City, installs 1,848
Van Riper, C R—I Cadmus, Bayonne, 3 years 2,500
Vreeland, Jesse K—J E Young, Bayonne, 3 yrs 4,800
Weigele, Helena—J G Morgan, Union, 2 years 1,000
Weissett, Jas—Maria Schneider, Union, 5 years 700
Wesseling, Anna—M G Usidel, Union, 3 years 2,000
Wiseman, Thos—J H Symes, Union, 3 years 1,500

CHATTEL MORTGAGES.

Asendorf, Catharine E and I H, Bayonne—The Consumer's Coal and Ice Co, butcher shop 300
Bixler Emma, Bayonne—F G Smith, organ 85
Bromley, E D, Kearney—P Hauck, saloon 250
Campana, Vincenzo, J City—M Bruno, barber shop 220
Cloke, William, J City—F G Smith, piano 200
Coriell, T a, J City—A Hohman, horse, wagon, harness 40
Cronin, M T, J City—Wm Peter Brewing Co, ice box 125
Donop, Leopold, Union—Wm Peter Brewing Co, saloon 1,500
Duggan, J P, J City—Elizabeth Finck, saloon 200
Durant, Philip, J City—L Bauman, furniture 84
Ellenberg, Carl, Hoboken—D Bermes, saloon 1,200
Ellend, Leopold, J City—Hill's Union Brewing Co, saloon, grocery fixtures 250
Etzkorn, Wilhelmine, J City—G Stanacker, furniture and safe 50
Fallon, J J, J City—J H Lippe, coach 784
Griswold, G L, J City—Bridget Moran, furniture 100
Hoffman, Madeline, Hoboken—G Dompeirre, furniture 170
Hinst, C D, J City—Lembeck & Betz Eagle Brewing Co, saloon 600
Hunter, J H, Harrison—P Hauck & Co, saloon 319
Jacobsen, Antonio, West Hoboken—J G Symes, wagon, violins, &c 485
Kelly, Mary, J City—F G Smith, piano 200
King, G F, J City—Lembeck & Betz Eagle Brewing Co, saloon 585
Levy, Morris, J City—A Kohn, dry goods business, &c 1,000
Madden, S C, Bayonne—B M Cowperthwait, furnithre 510
McIver, George, J City—Peter Hauck & Co, saloon 500
McKecknie, Robert, Hoboken—F G Smith, piano 157
McKeon, John, J City—The Burton Brewing Co, saloon 500
Meyer, John, J City—The Bachman Brewing Co, saloon 600
Meyer, Mina, Hoboken—Ludwig Bauman, furniture 73
Mittner, John, J City—William Peter Brewing Co, saloon 450
Mohr, Henry, West Hoboken—C Steinel, piano 165
Moebus, Peter and John, firm Moebus Bros, J City—F Lisiewski, saloon 485
Montrose, J H, J City—F G Smith, piano 180

Murphy, John, Union—Wm Peter Brewing Co, ice box ... 139
Murray, J F, J City—Commercial Credit Co, furniture ... 195
Nutzhorn, F B, Hoboken—B F Nutzhorn, grocery store ... 500
Peterson, John, West Hoboken—J G Symes, coal yard ... 500
Pitt, John, J City—L Bauman, furniture ... 90
Poeschen, Herman and John Unger, West Hoboken—Wm Peter Brewing Co, saloon ... 140
Prenzel, Anton, West Hoboken—R Oehme, furniture ... 50
Randall, C J, J City—J Randall, canal boat ... 300
Reilly, Patrick, J City—M Culihan, horse and cart ... 65
Schaefer, Charles, J City—The Burton Brewing Co, saloon ... 350
Snow, G W, J City—L Bauman, furniture ... 96
Staib, C F, J City—Josephine Staib, cigar store. 500
Stover, H D, Hoboken—J D Storer, grocery store, horse and wagon ... 1,500
Wehrenberg, George, J City—William Peter Brewing Co, saloon ... 1,898
Weissman, Peter, J City—Hills Union Brewing Co, saloon ... 850
Whittle, William, Harrison—P Hauck, saloon. . 420
Williams, C M, Bayonne—A Hohman, merry-go-round, &c ... 16
Wisch, Alvin, J City—Lembeck & Betz Brewing Co, saloon ... 448

BILLS OF SALE.

Lawson, M F—Mrs Sarah A Mariner, furniture.. 5
Nutzhorn, B F, Hoboken—F B Nutzhorn, horse, wagon, &c ... 1 000

JUDGMENTS.

Bauer, William—Wm D and T Henry ... 189
Bombach, George, Jr—C Turk ... 205
Etzkorn, Sebastian and Wilhelmina—H Thompson et al, partners ... 490
McCabe, C J—D Stein ... 1,492
Murphy, M V—Blau & Quaife ... 126
Petike, Frank—Bore & Brandt ... 88

MECHANIC'S LIEN.

Maddigan, Annie, builder and owner; James Connelly, claimant, J City ... 172

BUILDING MATERIAL MARKET.

BRICKS.—The usual weekly canvass of the market for Common Hard brings to light nothing of an improved character, so far as values are concerned, at least. On the contrary, the tone seems to be a trifle easier, if anything, than one week ago, and $5.00 per M is now practically the top figure. Some exceptional lots of stock, possessing special merit in the eyes of buyers, do upon occasion sell higher, but are few and far between, and form no basis for a legitimate valuation, while the majority of buyers are looking for something a little under $5.00, and are getting a great deal of stock at the shading. Of course, the rates are disgustingly low, and create a feeling of much dissatisfaction on the part of both makers and receivers, but almost the entire body of the trade are frank enough to admit the unpleasant fact, the very few exceptions being found in that unhappy class of individuals, who imagine the contemptible trick of furnishing false quotations for publication is calculated to help the market.

Demand seems to have been good enough and indeed it is understood that the amount of stock actually handled this season to date, in this city, is greater than for the same time last year, but supplies keep coming along and there is always enough and to spare for available custom, with a fine line of quality maintained, and it is the latter feature that keeps values condensed to such narrow compass and robs many makes of the premium or extra full rate they ordinarily command. Considerable stock is still being piled away, though the bulk of purchases are for consumption in one form or another. Just a little more demand for Pales developed this week and fine stock sold as high as $2.25 per M., but as a rule $2.00 is all buyers care to pay. There seems to be no let up in the production, good weather keeping matters rushing in full swing and, notwithstanding the quantities forwarded, accumulations at yards are increasing. It is even predicted that as matters are now progressing the sheds will soon be full and shipments made direct from the kilns. That will save one handling and some breakage.

HARDWARE.—Dealers who make a specialty of the various kinds of builders' hardware are still complaining over the dull character of trade. So much work has been delayed, voluntarily postponed or practically abandoned under the adverse influences of the season, as to greatly curtail the consumption, and the chances are against any revival until fall. It is claimed, however, that production has become adjusted to the outlet and acts as a balance to keep the market steady. No changes in lists at least are announced, and it is said none are contemplated.

LATH.—Receivers are managing to hold their position in first-rate form, and it has proven a strong market, with further gain made on values. Moderate arrivals have turned up, and some few cargoes afloat were reported, for all of which custom could be found, and sales were expeditious, with probably a chance for a little more stock, the final rate standing at $2.25 per M., and some salesmen claiming to ask more. The strike at St. John, of course, is used for all it is worth as an argument in favor of the situation, and is a good one for the present, but the current price is also pretty full, and conservative operators suggest that it may before long prove an attraction to bring in Northern-made lath.

LIME.—A good steady position is claimed and former rates quoted. According to current report, buyers are reappearing in search of stock who were thought to be pretty well supplied, and with arrivals now moderate enough to be controlled without much difficulty, there seems to be a hope of keeping the market in position.

LUMBER.—Generally the pitch of the market appears to be toward a somewhat better tone. A great many yards find business still dragging, and now and then the complaint from dealers is of very pronounced character, but in other cases reports are heard of a considerable improvement in business and exceptionally there are instances where operations were upon a really liberal scale. This improvement is of a cheering character naturally and there is a natural hope that it will continue and expand, but as yet there has been no marked influence upon the market for bulk lots outside of exceptional cases where supplies are temporarily scarce. Dealers do not refuse to negotiate in quite so general and persistent manner as a short time ago but abandon none of the spirit of caution and as yet refuse to raise the line of bids, more particularly on goods from interior sources, which have been tendered here by an army of agents, and all acting as though fully determined to secure custom. From some sections come reports of probable material shortage in the cut, and the determination of manufacturers to make a contest for fuller rates, etc., etc., but without appearing to care much whether the stories be true or otherwise dealers express a determination to simply take their own time for entering upon fresh investments. All in all, however, the tendency is toward somewhat greater animation, as the evidences point to greater consumption this fall than was expected a short time ago; and in any case there must soon be some move made toward accumulating winter stocks. The $1 per car per day demurrage imposed by the Car Service Association is causing some complaint among receivers, and it is thought will have the effect to almost entirely shut off the practice of consigning parcels by rail.

Eastern Spruce, in all general particulars, favors the sellers, so far as immediate trading is concerned. In some of the yards there is a fair stock, but the majority are only scantily supplied, and if they want renewals they want them quickly. That in conjunction with small offerings of course gives sellers much advantage, and rates can, for the time being, be sustained without difficulty, while there is evidently hope of a further gain. The strike of the laborers at St. John, and consequent curtailment of work, together with shutting down of mills in other localities, will probably for some time keep supplies in limited proportion, but many dealers think that eventually the offering will be ample, and they are inclined to wait wherever they can do so without discomfort. The action of manufacturers in comparing prices with last year is simple rot, as no one forgets that the full figures then ruling were the result of abnormal circumstances entirely independent of natural market influences.

Piling has inclined to a somewhat better tone. No raft stock is expected upon the market, regular arrivals have been moderate, and receivers are certainly talking with greater confidence. They have, as a test, plenty of work already planned and under way, with chances of considerable more, and claims that the accumulation in chains is by no means as full as might have been expected.

Hemlock is not spoken of with much enthusiasm, and some of the ordinarily most cheerful and sanguine operators are considerably given to complain. Quite a large amount of stock, however, was turned into dealers' hands just after the strike, and except in way of placing a few odd contracts, there has not been much done since. Reflecting the attitude of manufacturers, however, agents are asking about former rates, and refusing to urge negotiations.

White Pine is still without any direct or special tendency to become active, but there has been a little more business done under the temptation of low prices. Especially does that hold good on box boards of which Western operators have made free offerings, and in some cases again accepted as low as $13 per M. Agents, however, are offering other grades comparatively cheap, and buyers who have opportunity to secure parcels suited to their special trade do not object to occasionally picking up an odd lot, especially when delivery will be somewhat distant. Representatives of the Canadian interest are not offering much stock, and insist that the curtailment of make creates a certainty that no extensive supply can become available during balance of the season, and some of them predict higher rates before the close of navagation.

Yellow Pine, so far as can be learned through the look-wise and say-nothing form of reporting adopted by so many operators, is without much animation. Some few special orders have been boxed on home account, and a little f. o. b. export trade done, but generally buyers are not plenty and demand is that of necessity rather than of choice. Prices remain about as before, possibly somewhat steadier, but all quotations just now might fairly be considered nominal. There seems to be some hope of fuller call from the railways.

Carolina Pine, according to some reports, might be considered active up to the palmiest days of the market. As a matter of fact, however, there has simply been an increase in the volume of demand sufficient to break the previous dull tone, and sellers reflect their encouragement in making reports in a more pronounced tone of cheerfulness. Rates ruling about as before and pretty steady on standard quality and cut.

Hardwoods, all things considered, are doing fairly well and there seems to be no greater ground for complaint than on the coarser grades of stuff. There is, however, the same general experience regarding the caution and indifference of operators and actual wants; the temptation of some very nice stock at very low rates, or some other special attraction is required to create a showing of interest among buyers. First-class goods are firmly held in pretty much all cases, but without tendency to buoyancy at the moment. From most accounts there will be a pretty good supply of all standard stuff, but some operators predict a scarcity of good plain oak owing to the universal craze for quartering.

NAILS.—The demand has shown no special improvement, indeed, on the whole, the actual deal since our last fell away somewhat, if anything, and of course there was the usual grumble. On cut nails the tone is easy, but for wire somewhat greater strength is shown, owing to reduced stock at the mills We quote Cut at $1.65@1.75 per keg for car lots and $1.75@1.85 per keg for parcels from store, for iron, and add 5@10c. per keg for steel. Wire, $2.10@2.15 at mills, and 2.30@2.40 from store.

PAINTS, OILS, COLORS, ETC.—Some little improvement in trade is reported, apparently simply a natural recovery from the suspension of demand at the turn of month, and there must be a great deal more doing to bring affairs up to a condition of animation. It is, however, hardly likely that buyers will show an inclination to take hold with much greater freedom until toward fall, when the necessity for making accumulations in second hands ordinarily becomes more urgent. In the meanwhile manufacturers, importers and agents are gradually getting their stocks into shape to the end that they may be prepared for calls made upon them as the interest among buyers commences to expand. Zincs are firm, and at the recent advance in cost White Lead and kindred pigments are well held and selling readily. Association Corroders' rates stand as follows: Lead in oil in kegs and dry lead in kegs, in lots of less than 500 lbs., 7¼c. net; in lots of 500 lbs to 5 tons at one purchase, 7c.; 5 tons to 12 tons, one purchase, 6¾c.; 12 tons and over, one purchase, 6½c.; dry white lead in bbls. ¼c. per lb. less than price in kegs. Lead in oil 12½ lb. in tin pails, add 1c.; in 25 and 50 lb. tin pails, add ½c.; and in 1 to 5 lb. tin cans, assorted (100 lbs. in case) add 2½c. per lb. to keg price. Terms on lots on 500 lbs. and over, note or acceptance at sixty days, or 2½ per cent. discount will be allowed for cash paid within fifteen days of invoice date. To make either of the above required quantities any assortment of packages of white lead, red lead and litharge may be counted. The above quotations are free on board cars or boat at corroding point. Linseed Oil has been selling fairly well, but the condition of the market is unsettled. City crushers have suddenly and unexpectedly dropped the line of cost, and while that action was said to be due to lower rates on material, it is much more likely the outcome of competition from Western makers. We quote at general range at 42½@44c. for Western, and 44@56c. for City. Spirits Turpentine has been fairly active on average trade orders, but the offerings ample and with a decline at primary points the market is easier all around. We quote at 37@38c. per gallon, according to quality, delivery, etc.

TAR AND PITCH.—To fill in on contract work there has been some little call for stock, but generally the demand ran moderate and the market somewhat stupid. Offerings fair. We quote Pitch at $1.70@1.75 per bbl.; Tar at $2.15@2.50, according to quantity, quality and delivery.

MISCELLANEOUS

STETTIN-GRISTOW PORTLAND CEMENT

Official test for tensile strength ; 7 days **654 POUNDS** to the square inch.

This celebrated Cement is of excellent quality, color, extraordinary strength and fineness and is without exception superior to any other Portland Cement manufactured. It is acknowledged by all who have used it to be the best and most reliable Portland Cement in existence, which accounts for its unparalleled success, here and in Europe.

EMIL KANTER,
Sole Agent for the United States.
126 Liberty Street, N. Y.

For Sale in New York and Brooklyn at the yards of Messrs.
CANDA & KANE.

M. GIBBONS & SONS,

M. GIBBONS. R. GIBBONS. M. GIBBONS, Jr.

BUILDING CONTRACTORS

For any work pertaining to Building, supply every need in its construction, whether for Dwellings, Public Buildings, Factories or Stores.

Office, 318 and 320 COLUMBIA ST.,
NEAR HAMILTON AVENUE,
BROOKLYN.
Telephone 783. Send for Circular.

Stewart Ceramic Company,

Solid White Crockery Butler's Pantry, Kitchen, Stationary Wash Tubs, Slop and Corner Sinks.

312 Pearl Street, Corner Peck Slip.

HENRY McSHANE CO.,

(LIMITED.)

Plumbers', Steam & Gasfitters' Supplies

Telephone, 215 39th. 625 AND 627 SIXTH AVENUE.

Sanitary Specialties.

JAMES MATHEWS & SON,

Sole agents and Manufacturers of **MAX KELLING'S** Patent **FIRE-PROOF IRON** *Dumb Waiter Doors and Casings, Sashes, Windows, Shutters and Wall Closets.*

The most durable and cheapest articles in the market.

PRICES:
$3, $4, $6, $7, $8 and upward, according to size and style.

Illustrated catalogue, price list and references sent on application.

Over 5,000 in use in this city.

Main Office & Salesroom,
172 E. 110th St.
Branch & Factory,
510 & 512 E. 20th St.

Excelsior, Pat. Dec. 3, 1889.

RAPP SHEET METAL WORKS.

Pat. May 6th, 1890.

Man'f'rs of **RAPP'S PAT. IRON** Dumb Waiter **DOORS AND FRAMES.**

Send for illustrated catalogue and price list.

Indorsed by the leading architects and builders as being the best and cheapest Fire-Proof Door made.

J. W. RAPP, Sole Agent,
315-319 E. 94th St., N. Y. City.

LAZZARI & BARTON,

DESIGNERS AND MAKERS OF

Fine Monuments, Vaults, Statuary, Etc.

Office and Works:
OPPOSITE CEMETERY ENTRANCE,
WOODLAWN, - - NEW YORK CITY.

This cut is from a photograph of a monument built by us, erected in Woodlawn Cemetery February, 1890.

Electric Bells,
Door Openers,
Speaking Tubes, &c.

W. R. OSTRANDER & CO.,
195 AND 197 FULTON ST., New York.

O. A. PRICE,

—(STEAM)—
STAIR BUILDER,
415-417 E. 91st St., New York.
Estimates given. All work promptly attended to.

Material Men's Mercantile Association,

LIMITED

Reports and Ratings on BUILDERS & CONTRACTORS.

Daily Information as to Liens affecting Subscriber's Customers.

A Bureau of Quick and Reliable Information for **MATERIAL MEN.**

154 NASSAU ST., Tribune Bldg., NEW YORK.

SKYLIGHTS.

MATTHEW C. KERVAN,

SLATE & METAL ROOFER
SKYLIGHTS,
Galv. Iron Cornices, Lintels, Gutters, Leaders, etc.,
106 and 108 West 127th Street, N. Y.
Tin and Slate Roofs and Leaders Repaired and painted.
Chimney Tops and Ventilators made and put up.

JACOB SCHWOERER,

(ESTABLISHED 1849.)

Metallic Skylight, Cornice AND ROOFING WORKS,

No. 8 2d St., near Bowery, New York.

A. GERNERT,

SKYLIGHTS
SLATE AND METAL ROOFING.
Galvanized Iron Cornices, Gutters and Leaders, Window Cornices and Sills.
515 West 42d Street, - - - New York.
Orders by Mail promptly attended to.

SOLE PROPRIETOR AND MANUFACTURER OF THE BICKELHOUPT **SKYLIGHTS,**

G. BICKELHOUPT,

243 & 245 WEST 47th STREET,
TELEPHONE, No. 675 38th St. NEW YORK

LOUIS DREYER,

No. 339 WEST 18th STREET,
8th and 9th Avenues. NEW YORK.
MANUFACTURER OF
GALVANIZED IRON CORNICES,
METAL AND SLATE ROOFING, ORNAMENTAL ZINC CASTINGS FOR BUILDINGS.

M. F. Westergren F. L. Anderson.

The Architectural Sheet Metal Works

SKYLIGHTS,

Cornice and Roofing.
CORRUGATED IRON WORK.
205 & 207 EAST 99th ST.,
Telephone, 1826, 38th. New York.

The Brooklyn Skylight & Cornice Works

Estimates furnished for Sheet Metal and Wrou g Iron Glazed Structures.

John Seton & Co.
78 & 80 Washington Av.
BROOKLYN, N. Y.

HAYES N.Y. 71 8TH AV. METALLIC SKYLIGHTS

F. SKELTON,

MILDEW PROOF.

1325 Broadway, New York,
Bet. 34th and 35th Streets,
West Side.
MANUFACTURERS OF
AWNINGS, TENTS & FLAGS.
A New Style of Ventilating
AWNING.

Canopies, Dancing Crash, Camp Chairs, Dining Chairs, Round Tables and Extension Tables to let. Invitations delivered—Men to call carriages. Imported and Domestic Canvas and Bunting for Sale.

E. M. PRITCHARD & SON,

Manufacturer of
Window Frames, Wood Mouldings, Interior Trimmings & Wood Mantels
138th Street and Mott Avenue, N. Y.

ESTABLISHED MARCH 21st 1868.

DEVOTED TO REAL ESTATE, BUILDING, ARCHITECTURE, HOUSEHOLD DECORATION, BUSINESS AND THEMES OF GENERAL INTEREST

PRICE, PER YEAR IN ADVANCE, SIX DOLLARS.

Published every Saturday.

TELEPHONE - - - - - CORTLANDT 1370.

Communications should be addressed to

C. W. SWEET, 14 & 16 Vesey St.

J. T. LINDSEY, Business Manager.

VOL. XLVIII JULY 25, 1891. NO. 1,219

The publication offices of THE RECORD AND GUIDE *have been removed to Nos. 14 and 16 Vesey street, over The Mechanics' and Traders' Exchange, a few feet west of Broadway.*

THE NEW MAGAZINE.

Within a few days now will be issued the first number of the new illustrated quarterly magazine, THE ARCHITECTURAL RECORD *Readers of* THE RECORD AND GUIDE, *and those who have received our circular letter, who desire to become subscribers to the new magazine should lose no time in sending in their names and addresses to the offices of publication, Nos. 14 and 16 Vesey street, New York City. The reception which has been given to the new enterprise by the architectural profession, the builders of this country and the general public has been most encouraging. The new magazine will start with thousands of readers in every State in the Union, and the large cities have shown an unexpected interest in the new periodical. We are desirous, of course, of having the subscription list as large as possible for the first number, and in order that delivery may be prompt, all intending subscribers are requested to send us a postal card at once. The first number of the magazine will contain "The Revival of Romanesque," by Montgomery Schuyler, with thirty full-page illustrations; "An 'American Style' of Architecture," by Barr Ferree; "Architectural Fads," by George Keister; "The New York Building Law," by William J. Fryer, Jr.; "Terra Cotta," by Jas. Taylor; "Byzantine Architecture," by Professor Aitchison, and other articles, editorial departments, etc., with numerous illustrations of recent designs for office buildings, residences, clubs, churches, country houses, electrical fixtures, furniture, interiors, etc. The magazine will be printed on the finest paper, and no expense or pains have been spared to make it the leading architectural paper in the country. The annual subscription price is $1.*

THE conditions adverse to the stock market which we pointed out last week are still in the ascendant. Business is limited and more directed to selling than to buying; Louisville & Nashvile and Burlington & Quincy remain attractive spots for the aim of operators on the short side; there is more talk of trouble in London; the gold movement continues under such anomalous conditions that it is impossible to calculate where the end will be; finally, the Richmond Terminal issues continue to sustain the anxiety of their holders. The disfavor with which the new issue of Louisville & Nashville has been received is shown by the quotations for the rights, worth at the time of their announcement from twenty-five to thirty-five dollars, which yesterday sold for four dollars. Burlington & Quincy is weak because the payment of dividends at the rate of 4 per cent per annum is sailing very closely to the extreme limit of the company's earnings. There is no doubt the management is relying on an unusually large fall business to carry it through and with good reason. The grain movement even now is very great, but meantime the stock finds few supporters, and unless the expectations of an increase of earnings this fall are realized, the selling will be justified by the action the directors will find themselves compelled to take on the dividend. The main trouble in London, the River Plate Bank having been disposed of so far as to suspend, is with a house that has been more than once the subject of similar talk since last November, and anything which could happen to it now would not be so very injurious, probably a collapse would be less prejudicial to the general market than these periodic relapses. More serious is the engagement of a million and a-half of dollars gold for shipment to-day with exchange at about three and a-half cents lower than the cost of the gold to the European buyer. And no explanation, whether it be to meet drafts to be made later on or to relieve the necessities of an embarrassed foreign market can remove the anxiety which the continuation of gold exportations causes. For these reasons there is little prospect of change in the attitude of the stock market in the near future. There are some features favorable to American securities, however, which should not be lost sight of, and which at a time like this it is particularly important to bear in mind. For instance, London confidence in them is displayed in over-subscribing the $5,000,000. Manitoba 4 per cent loan and the grain movement in Chicago has already begun to be heavy, which must benefit all the lines converging at that point.

THE security of the obligations of many governments, both in this country and abroad, has lately been so continuously impugned that a summary of the present position and prospects of these obligations by a well-informed correspondent of the London *Economist* will prove interesting and instructive. This writer premises that strong governments in great and wealthy countries can always find money by loans if they choose to adapt their conditions to the wants of the public and the interest of the bankers. With a clever, energetic Minister of Finance the credit of a strong and well-administered empire seems inexhaustible. Everything is a question of skill, convenience and adaptation. When the Old Regime broke down the French Government could find no money, and it was thought that the country could not bear its debts. After passing through a period of complete disorganization the French Empire, under Napoleon, was again on the top of prosperity, although the debt of France had risen to many times the amount it stood at during the last days of the Old Regime. This was simply the effect of good administration, political and economical prosperity, military strength, and the organization of credit. This example shows how impossible it is to put a limit on the extent to which a country may incur obligations. No one can say that Russia, France or Germany could go beyond a certain sum in their loans and expenses only by destroying their credit. If they can discover new fountains of income, create new resources, maintain or increase their political prestige, they may go to almost any length. It is, therefore, absolutely impossible to say anything definite about the probable course of the market for the loans issued by the strongest countries on the Continent. The case is somewhat different as regards the securities of the weaker nations. Austrian finances have never been regarded as being administered in a way that could serve for a model—a fact that is not due to lack of financial genius among her statesmen, but to the political composition of her empire. To centralize is very difficult here. Yet the more steadily and the more efficiently the administration in Austria and Hungary works, the greater credit the monarchy will enjoy in the market. And from this point of view Austro-Hungary undoubtedly shows herself in a most advantageous position. About Italian loans there is an unmistakable conflict between opinions and wishes. German financiers, because of the feeling engendered by the Triple Alliance, would like to help Italian loans; but all efforts in this direction are thwarted by the present unfortunate economic position of the country. Similar observations may be made in regard to Portugal, Turkey, Greece and Spain, and it does seem probable that the public will adopt any very hopeful views in respect to these countries. Of late the renewal of the Triple Alliance for six years is referred to as an element of strength, and the alleged addition of England to that alliance is also made a strong point. But everybody is aware that, in spite of treaties, Europe is an armed camp, and though the views referred to may be attractive to one-half of Europe and consequently to tend to an improvement in business, the impression on the other half of Europe is just the contrary. There is yet another view to take. In some of the European nations tariff questions are now, or are about to become the order of the day. In others the prices of breadstuffs give rise to all sorts of discussions, which indirectly bear on the causes influencing the market for loans. In Germany it is proposed to reduce considerably the Customs tariff for cereals. This question has already had a serious effect on operations in rouble notes and Russian loans. They rose when the reduction was credited, and fell when the hopes therefor were temporarily disappointed. It is not improbable that the German politicians and economists will in the course of time have to approach other tariff questions, besides those concerning grain. The coal trade and consequently the iron and steel trades cannot be left in their present suffering condition. The conclusion is inevitable that the political and economical prospects of the continental countries are fraught with uncertainty, and obviously this must detract from the value of funds in the market, coupled with the fact that values have at present a natural tendency to fall.

THE Rapid Transit Commissioners have again commended themselves to the traveling public of this city by the selection of the second route, one with novel elements not before suggested in the newspapers. It was generally supposed that the route selected would be that of the Belmont Commission as far north as 42d street, but the Commissioners have made what is under the circumstances a wise variation from the plan of the earlier body. The utilization up to 14th street of the route already selected for the West Side is a wise measure. The island narrows as it goes south and the same number of tracks are not needed south of 14th street as north. If, indeed, expense were less of a consideration than it is, the running of tracks on the line of Elm street would not of itself have been a bad thing, for that part of the city between Broadway and the Bowery is sadly in need of some leavening influence. If it were only more accessible, and had a street system that was not a hindrance to traffic, it might well be covered with handsome warehouses in place of the present rookeries. But the aim of the Commissioners has manifestly, and most judiciously, been to provide a maximum of accommodation at a minimum of expense; and the saving of two or three miles of costly tunneling and many stations is a wise and necessary economy. The line along Broadway itself will do much to open the stale and arid region to the east of that thoroughfare, provided the Board of Street Opening and Improvement has enough sense and energy to order that long-discussed and much-needed Elm Street Improvement. The remainder of the route runs very much as expected. Even if the Vanderbilts have nothing to do with it, the station at 42d street will be a great convenience to the patrons of the Central and the New Haven and Harlem roads. Express trains ought certainly to shorten by one-half the time required at present to get down town from the 42d street depot. North of 42d, running as it will under Madison avenue, the route will attract many of the present customers of both the Third and Sixth Avenue Elevated roads, and it is a class of people who travel a great deal. Above 59th street and as far up as 90th there is a good deal of traffic to be had. We are not so sure, however, whether above 90th street—a district at present very little improved—the class of inhabitants will be of a character that will originate many passengers. It is, however, a section that is sadly in need of transit facilities. If the route is extended above the Harlem, parallel to the Vanderbilt lines, and any other corporation can be found that is willing to build and operate it, we do not see that the Vanderbilts will have any alternative but to control it. Furthermore, it must be remembered that this middle line has a far more intimate connection with the West Side line than any one supposed it would have, and that both are certain to be under one management. Speculations, however, on these matters can be left until the financial and controlling parts of the scheme are clearer than at present.

THE property-owners on Washington Heights who ventured to come down town last week in order to recommend to the Rapid-Transit Commissioners that the elevated roads be extended into their district have been stigmatized by the "smart" newspaper reporters as emissaries of Jay Gould. THE RECORD AND GUIDE must confess, however, to a certain sympathy with them, if only because they are victims of newspaper villification. A man could not go very far wrong nowadays if, after seeking the consensus of newspaper opinion, he formulated an opinion diametrically opposed, and then declared that he had discovered a law. That these property-owners had a certain amount of sense on their side is shown sufficiently by a few facts and interviews, to be found in another column of this issue. Some difference of opinion has been expressed of late as to the strength of real estate values in Harlem round about 125th street. Some people have declared that there was a shading off all around, while others thought that prices remained firm. The inquiry instituted tends to establish the truth of the former position. While no marked weakness or general slump of values is to be observed, still concessions are undoubtedly being made, and a slightly lower plane of values has been established. The reason for this is sufficiently obvious. If overbuilding has existed there has certainly been none of it just in that region. The one cause is that people find the journey to 125th, over the elevated road under present conditions to be longer and more uncomfortable than they can tolerate. Hence the surplusage is going to Long Island and New Jersey, which are continually being made more accessible by the improvement and extension of facilities already existing. The consequence will be a permanent loss of population and a delay in the improvement of the upper wards that put them back at least two or three years. Indeed, unless the new rapid transit routes are constructed with a relatively greater degree of speed than they have been planned, we may expect a couple of summers hence to find the residents of the New Jersey suburbs coming to spend the hot weather in the delightful and healthy country districts situated in the northern part of New York City. The keeping of summer boarders may become as great an industry in the metropolis as the keeping of winter boarders. This, we say, may be one consequence of the dense stupidity of those people who will not accept the existing facts of transit, but, disregarding them, rush off to occupy two or three years in building a perfect system, meanwhile leaving the need for immediate action entirely out of account. Our readers may think that we have preached enough on this text; but so important do we deem this aspect of the matter, and so inadequate a representation does it receive elsewhere that we shall continue to point this moral, even at the expense of becoming tiresome. We believe, indeed, that property-owners on Washington Heights are foolish to wish to have any extension of the Manhattan structure through their district, provided the plan of the Commission is financially feasible; but they and their brethren to the south and east have a right to more recognition than they have received from newspapers or officials. The fact of it is that the great newspaper offices, or rather the great offices of the newspapers, are so convenient to the Bridge that we suspect that a large number of the influential members of the staff live in Brooklyn. They certainly write about New York affairs as if they lived in Kalamazoo.

696-702 Broadway.

THIS is the most conspicuous building in that part of Broadway in which it is situated, and which is very much in need of any architectural improvement that can be bestowed upon it. The buildings of this region are not only for the most part pretty bad in themselves, but they do not make even a pretense of forming an ensemble, and they do not conform to each other in style or in lines or in material. So loudly, indeed, do they swear at each other that a front which is merely dull and stupid, like that of the Metropolitan Hotel or that of the New York Hotel takes on a positive distinction among these vulgar and riotous edifices. There is a respectable warehouse at the corner of Broome street and another at the corner of Bond street, and these are almost the only peaceful oases we recall in the howling wilderness from Canal street to Astor place. The state of things is so bad indeed, architecturally, that a single good building, or even a dozen good buildings unless they were continuous, could do nothing to redeem the general aspect, but could only serve as an emphatic protest against the general proceedings.

The building we are considering is thus unfortunate in its surroundings, though otherwise it would be fortunately placed, having an unusually ample frontage on Broadway, and ample depth on the side street. It is evidently enough by the author of the Times building and the Union Trust Company, or an imitation of his work, and employs the same main motive that has been used in each of those edifices. It seems to us less successful than either.

The materials are a very red sandstone for the basement of two stories, and for the superstructure yellow brick, used in conjunction with a terra cotta as nearly as may be of the same tint as the stone. The central division is virtually that of the Times building, though this consists of but six stories above the basement, and ought, therefore, to be more tractable than the eleven stories of the older building. There are four bays in the front, of which one is devoted in the basement to the entrance, while each of the other three consists of a tall flat-arched opening between slightly projecting piers in the lower story, the stone being here rough faced while in the second story each bay has a pair of lintelled openings divided by a mullion, and treated with absolute plainness though the stone is here dressed smooth, the piers only continuing rock-faced. The entrance is itself a very admirable piece of Romanesque modeling. An arch of three orders is carried on an equal number of shafts, the moulding corresponding to each shaft being confined to the intrados instead of being a continuance of the shaft itself, as is perhaps the more strictly Romanesque fashion. These large rolls, however, must be covered with carving or subdivided to avoid the look of heaviness and clumsiness, although in the present instance they are perhaps too light to be fully effective. The detail of the entrance, nevertheless, is in general very good, and it is the most effective feature of the building, being projected from the face of the wall, bounded at the sides by polygonal piers and above by a cornice repeating the capitals of the piers of the basement, while the spandrils are richly carved.

The middle division is of four stories—or three stories and a mezzanine—the openings running through and closed by round arches above the sixth story. The jambs are decorated with a roll moulding in terra cotta treated as a shaft with a capital at the spring of the arch. This is a mistake, since the decoration of the jamb ought evidently to be a modeling of the mass. In stonework the treatment adopted here would be legitimate and might be effective, as it is highly effective in the building of the Union Trust Company. But with brick piers a mere recession of the piers by offsets with square arrises would be more constructional than the insertion of a great moulding of another material. This does not prevent this central part of the building from being impressive. The main difficulty of the composition arises with the attic, which is here of two stories, grouped by pairs of openings running through them and closed by round arches, each pair corresponding to one of the single arches below. The effect is undoubtedly awkward and ineffective, and it is not immediately clear why this should be so. A basement of two stories and an attic of two, including a central division of four, seems to be an appropriate and promising composition for an eight-story building, but here it does not turn out well. It is to be observed that the upper story of the basement is an intermediate story and effects a transition between the first and second member of the composition, while there is no transition at all between the second and third. There is a feature very similar to this attic in the Times building, but there it is introduced as a transition between the central mass and the roof-division, while here it is itself the upper division. What the composition needs is an intermediate feature here, such as is supplied with great success by the arcade of equally spaced openings, disregarding the division into bays below, of the Union Trust Company—an arcade that owes much of its effectiveness to its recalling the design of the fourth story. The arcade is there a preparation for a visible roof, but here there is no visible roof. Its absence is the misfortune of the architect and not his fault, but it is not his misfortune that he has made no effort to compensate for its absence. If the lower of these two attic stories had repeated the upper story of the basement, of course with such variations as were called for by its position and its material, and the upper had been united in treatment with the cornice, and the cornice itself had been very much more emphatic, the harmonious relation between the parts which the building now altogether lacks would have been supplied, and the building would have come nearer than it now comes to being a work of architectural art.

There are seven bays on the side treated like those of the first, and showing the same defect of composition, but impressive from their extent.

Fashions in Finance.

SPECULATIVE dealings in Wall Street have apparently reached the low water-mark of dullness, and financial writers have been exercising their wits to explain away this ever-recurring phenomenon with a degree of success that has scarcely equalled the valiancy of the effort. Times for some years past have certainly been hard with brokers. With expenses that have remained very nearly constant, receipts, particularly from commissions, have shown so sustained and marked a tendency to decrease that many small firms have been weeded out and many large ones have been obliged to depend on other sources of income for their profit. Indeed a salient feature of the stock market, ever since the ending of the "boom" times of 1880, has been a greater or less degree of absence on the part of the public. Ten years or more ago the exchange of 400,000 shares a day was only an average amount of business, while on days of excitement the total of business ran up to a million shares. At present if 300,000 shares are exchanged the market is called active. Yet during this period the railway mileage of the country has increased by fully two-thirds, and securities representing the increase have been listed on the New York Stock Exchange. In addition to this a number of large mercantile concerns have assumed a corporate form, and their stock and bonds are dealt in on the Exchange. Thus, although the area of speculation has enormously enlarged, the lack of assiduous and enthusiastic farmers has led to a shrinkage of the yield. It should be added that much of the enlarged area has proved to be far from fertile ground, in such wise that any attempt to cultivate it by adventurous agriculturists has brought discouragement and threatened bankruptcy. The old fields also, once so productive, would seem to need renewal. The prices of the stocks of the main trunk lines both east and west have undergone severe depreciation.

Some of the causes of this continued lack of speculative dealing in the market have been sufficiently pointed out, and our purpose does not demand any re-statement thereof. It is well known that the movement of finance and business, like every other kind of movement, has its rhythm, and that there are recurring periods of low prices and high prices, of depression and excited speculation. Thus economists have shown that for the last 150 years a panic has taken place about every ten years, and this generalization, crude, empirical, and untrustworthy within limits, as it is, nevertheless represents about the length of the financial cycle. Every panic is, of course, preceded by a period of expansion and inflation, which, in turn, is preceded by a more or less prolonged period of dullness and comparative depression. Now it would be untrue to say that since 1885 the United States has lacked business prosperity, for, taking all in all, the second half of the decade has been a period of profitable business and some speculative activity outside of the Stock Exchange; but, as we have pointed out, never since the last few months of 1881 has anything like a "boom" prevailed in Wall street, and it is full time that the spirit of speculation which has been scampering around the country should return to what is and ever must be its favorite home and fitting couch.

On all the exchanges there are, in addition to the legitimate traders, a certain number of people who make speculation a business. They may be taken as the great equalizers of prices. With a tolerably penetrating eye for the value of a security, with a quick and not too insistent judgment, and with a ready ability to sail in the eye of the wind, they pounce upon any inequality in prices not due to powerful manipulation and soon put the stock in its proper place. Such men do not, however, make a market; they only take advantage of one. For, a pronounced movement Wall street must depend on attracting that surplusage which remains with business men all over the country after the books for the year are balanced. This surplusage, the investment increment of the people, is also the speculative powder; and, while a certain share of it is always distributed, one man coveting a house, another a good bond, another some more perilous venture, yet a very large share flows in some one popular direction. There are fashions in finance as in dress. A certain kind of investment is always in the air; one man confides to you the result of a successful "deal;" another button-holes you to share with him in some promising enterprise, all redolent of promise of profit. The newspapers spread the intelligence rapidly, and before you know it your surplus is swept off to take the chances of the prevalent speculation. Of late years the popular gamble has been real estate. In certain parts of the country, such as lower California, in 1886, the speculation degenerated into the foolishest and emptiest kind of inflation; but as a rule the speculation has been orderly, sensible in a measure, and not too enthusiastic. On the one hand large sums were invested in Western farm mortgages, with results to the investor that have varied in the different States. On the other, heavy blocks of capital were put into building in the big cities. The years 1889 and 1890, alike in New York, Chicago, Brooklyn, Philadelphia and in many of the smaller cities, were marked by an activity in building far exceeding that of any previous years. Then real estate speculation has been rampant in the New South.

Now this interest in real estate has been checked all over the country. The failure of many of the Western mortgage investment companies, the widespread foreclosures which Eastern lenders have been obliged to undertake, the belligerency of the Alliance have all tended to lessen the flow of money to the Western states. There are some indications also that the South has been "boomed" rather too quickly, and that for the next few years there is likely to be a subsidence of the investment of capital in Southern enterprises. As to the building in the large cities, it has probably been to some extent overdone—not to so large an extent that any collapse is to be feared, but sufficiently to make lenders and investors cautious. Building always follows so close upon general prosperity that it cannot be inactive when people are making money; but in New York, certainly, and in the other large cities, the supply of office buildings, warehouses and hotels, and to a smaller extent that of dwellings is somewhat ahead of the demand. We may expect in consequence rather less activity for the next few years. The building filings in all these cities for the first half of this year do not compare favorably with those of the same period in 1890.

These facts tend to show that the speculative surplus of the country will probably be deflected into some other channel in the near future—that is, if the money market does not interfere with speculation. Thus far in 1891, with the exception of the flurry in wheat, there cannot be said to have been any speculation. People have been drawing their breaths and testing their financial bones after the troubles of last Fall. They have very well discovered by this time that no bones were broken in that memorable crisis; and the speculative spirit which is always latent in the human breast, will be sure again to come to the surface, stronger for its temporary dormancy. To predict that this speculation will, after its long absence, return to its proper home in Wall street would be going altogether too far.

> "Thou hast not wit enough
> To sound the bottom of the after times,"

says Shakespeare; and the financial writer should paste this legend in his cap. But there are reasons which need not be too carefully rehearsed, which give a certain plausibility to this opinion. Walter Bagehot, after a careful analysis of the sources of prosperity, came to the conclusion that the two essential prerequisites of a "boom" were good crops and cheap money. The former we have, the yield of corn being the only one which is yet in doubt. The money market is an uncertain factor, for it is easy at present, only because of the lack of speculation. Other conditions are, however, to be considered. Speculation always means inflation, that is the conduct of business on credit. In order to produce the confidence necessary to the extension of credit the financial body must, in the first place, be compact and sound. So it is with us at the present time. We have brought back large amounts of our own securities from abroad, and consequently have a good basis for future borrowing. Our merchants and manufacturers are making money, which is, of course, the precondition of there being any large speculative surplus at all. Demand is equal to supply in all lines of dry goods, with the exception of print cloths. The first effect of a probably increased demand will be to make merchants increase their basis of supplies which will give a sudden impetus to general trade of all kinds. Then our securities are likely to find more favor abroad. And to cap these conditions it is possible, as we have pointed out, that it may again become the fashion to speculate in Wall street. The large financiers with interest in the market (there are plenty of them) will be glad to aid such a speculative movement.

Investments—Good and Bad.

RICHMOND TERMINAL BONDS.—A sarcastic reference to Richmond Terminal as strong around 13 made recently, pretty accurately express a just opinion of the estimation in which Richmond Terminal and the bonds issued by it are held. Still there are a good many people who, beguiled by the long-time talk of the immense growth and development of the South, believe in Richmond Terminal on the theory that where the improvement and consequent growth of wealth are so general some cannot fail to attach to Richmond Terminal. Doubtless the Argentine Republic is a much richer country than it was ten years ago, yet it is unable to pay its debts; that being the case its wealth in a general sense gives very little comfort to the people who poured their savings into its lap. It might be going too far, though not so very much too far, to say that the South is the Argentine of the North. It is not going too far, however, to say that, as in the case of the Argentine, a great deal of Northern money has gone into the South which will never come out again. The parallel may be drawn still closer. It may be said confidently that this money can no more be recovered to the original investor than to the first buyer of Argentines for the same reason—so much stopped on the way to the enterprises for which it was intended in the shape of discounts, commissions, fraudulent valuations, etc.

Now mark what has been the case in Richmond Terminal. Its stock has never been issued by the company at less than 20 and is now, as has been before remarked, "strong" around 13. It has issued $5,500,000 6 per cent collateral trust bonds which are selling down at 93 and $11,065,000 collateral trust 5 per cent bonds issued at from 85 to 80, which are quoted around 61. The cause for these declines is simply that these securities lack backbone. Among the stacks of rattletraps deposited to secure the two loans, there is not one first mortgage bond; that is a bond being in every sense a first lien on the property on which it is issued. The last annual report says that the 6s are secured by stocks and bonds whose par is $17,996,900, and which are valued at $14,541,300. Among these securities is one, and one only that can be tested by the only fair test, market quotations, viz., $6,000,000 East Tennessee first preferred. The company values this at par. The Stock Exchange quotation is from 42 to 45. At the latter figure, to use the most favorable one, this stock is worth $2,700,000. Another item of the collateral is $1,325,000 Western North Carolina first consols. There is among the quotations somewhere a bid of 99 for these bonds, but no transaction recorded for so long a time as makes the quotation valueless. There is also the item of 17,609 shares Richmond & Danville at 200, making $3,521,800. The rest of the collateral has no apparent value. The three items of value make together $7,546,800, cutting the original valuation of the collateral nearly in half, and that depended on three very doubtful things: 1. That Richmond & Danville is worth 200, while its 5 per cent. bonds sell at 80. 2. That Western North Carolina 1st consols are worth 99, and that East Tennessee first preferred will not sell below 45.

The 5 per cent bonds are secured by stocks and bonds of a par value of $40,845,300 and valued at $15,195,560. They are comprised mostly of the stocks of companies which have been absorbed into the different systems making up the Richmond Terminal property and valueless inasmuch as the loan issues of the several companies more than cover their value, so many having made deficiencies on fixed charges from year to year. The marketable securities seem to be 7,081 Richmond & Danville, $3,447,000 Ga. Co. Collateral Trust 5s, 22,832 East Tennesse First preferred, 2,200 Central R. R. and Banking Co. of Ga. and 42,250 East Tennessee Second preferred. The East Tennessee First preferred appears in the estimate at 80 and the Second at 25. At 45 the First is worth $1,027,440 and at 12 the Second preferred $507,000 instead of $1,826,560 and $1,056,000 at which amounts they severally appear in the company's valuation. Given anything like a similar depreciation in the other collateral, the bonds at 61 are dear. The 5s are a second lien on the collateral of the 6s and an additional lien on $2,500,100 Richmond & Danville stock wholly required for other purposes.

Earnings of the Richmond Terminal properties, as far as can be ascertained, do not show favorably. That goes without saying almost, seeing the decline in its securities. East Tennessee earned net from July 1, 1890, to June 1, 1891, $2,824,809. June earnings are expected to be light. Its charges, based on the bonds outstanding and taxes the same as last year, would amount to $2,317,255. Central of Georgia earned net from July 1, 1890, to April 30, 1891, $1,924,149, compared with $1,974,227 in the same ten months of the previous year. These figures do not include the operations of auxiliary lines, without which it is impossible to estimate the probable standing of the Richmond Terminal Company. Net earnings of the Richmond & Danville are not published yet. Gross for the year from June 1, 1890, appear to be $13,393,886 against $12,536,695 in the previous year, a gain of $857,191. Without a knowledge of the cost of operation the gross figures may gratify curiosity but cannot be of much value in determining the benefit, if any, the Richmond Terminal Co. is to receive from its holdings of Richmond & Danville, and in such a case, in the face of falling securities it is well to take nothing for granted. In the last fiscal year, which ended Nov. 30, 1890, the Richmond Terminal Co. reported a surplus of $210,330, after paying 5 per cent on its preferred stock. Its fixed charges, however, included interest on $8,253,000 5s; in the current year it must pay on $11,065,000, which will make a difference of $140,600 in interest charges.

These are the facts relating to these bonds so far as some considerable industry can gather them and they are given for what they are worth, to satisfy, as far as possible, the demand for information the movement of the Richmond Terminal bonds and stock has aroused. It only remains to add that interest has been regularly paid on the bonds hitherto and official assurance is given that the next coupon will be honored.

The Condition of Harlem Real Estate.

Harlem real estate has never quite recovered from the boom which accompanied the World's Fair agitation in the summer of 1889—the boom which started the great speculation on 125th street and brought to the attention of the residents of the lower wards the importance of Harlem as a part of the City of New York. Outside the almost phenomenal activity on 125th street, Harlem real estate has been very quiet since that time, although prices have remained high—so high, many shrewd judges say, that it has been impossible to buy and sell it with any good chance of immediate profit.

The history of the World's Fair boom is like that of so many other booms, with the exception that the site for the World's Fair, upon securing which property-owners depended to justify the rise in values, was located in Chicago, not in New York. Harlem had everything settled in its own mind as to the Fair. The Site Committee of the Local Board of Commissioners even went so far as to designate the boundaries of the site, and these were in and about Harlem, as our readers doubtless remember. No wonder then that holders of up-town property advanced their prices. A great World's Fair was to be held in their neighborhood and nearly all of the immense business would be transacted on or near their property. Consequently prices went up 25, 50, even 100 per cent, and transactions in Harlem real estate were very generally at an end, although it was thought there would be a resumption of activity as soon as Congress settled definitely just where the Fair was to be held. But the stagnation continued even after the decision of Congress had been announced and there was no large business such as had been expected and as had been interrupted by the unfortunate boom. Harlem real estate is still very quiet.

This dullness is attributable partly to the causes which have been common to real estate in all parts of the city; but in addition to this there seems to be a very general impression that the main reason lies in prices which are too high. Such an assertion is of course very hard to verify. If owners know that business is dull because prices are too high they keep the fact to themselves, hoping either that a general prosperity will take their property off their hands without loss, or that at least they may get out before the real truth becomes known and prices drop to their true level. Below this level they cannot go, for investors and speculators are quick to find out the truth about property, and they are no more ready to believe false reports that are bad than false reports that are good. Real estate has nothing to fear from the truth, concealment of the facts alone injures it and destroys confidence in it. At this time, too, real estate men should be particularly careful not to either over or understate the facts. Many investors whose money has previously been placed in stocks and bonds have had their confidence shaken in those securities, and would gladly place their capital in real property if they felt that its value was real and true, not inflated and fictitious.

Realizing this THE RECORD AND GUIDE could not overlook reports that prices were too high up town, and that the figures demanded for property were not warranted either by the rent rolls or by the prices obtained for neighboring holdings. Only during the last week a local real estate agent told a reporter that flat property in Harlem was not averaging 2 per cent. on the investment. This statement is probably exaggerated, but it is a well-known fact that two to four months' free rent is quite common up town; the object being to secure a large income on paper, and so dispose of the property with as small a loss as possible. That this practice of giving free rent has done the greatest injury to real estate no one who is cognizant of the facts can doubt. It leads poor families to assume obligations that they cannot meet, and as soon as the free rent period is over they are forced to move to other quarters often not less expensive, but with more free rent. This evil is teaching its lesson, and doubtless before long there will be a reaction against the practice and owners will refuse to accept tenants who will not pay for their accommodation. The day of reform will be a red letter day for real estate everywhere, but especially for sections of the city now in course of development and improvement.

In selling and transferring property it is such a common thing for owners to misstate or entirely conceal the real consideration that the recorded transfers have been of little help in endeavouring to find out whether or not Harlem property was really weak. We have therefore had recourse to two sources, the most reliable under the circumstances, and we print below a few foreclosure sales, together with some facts gleaned from brokers, in relation to other property where they could have no object in painting the facts in dark colors. The foreclosure sales at least are beyond dispute. They are selected from the sales held on the Real Estate Exchange since May 1st of this year, and they include all the foreclosure sales north of 100th street and south of the Harlem River, in which the amount due for mortgages and costs exceeded the total selling price. The list is rather a surprising one for such a short time, and it will be perused with interest by up-town owners, brokers, and speculators:

101st st, No. 131, n s, 75 w Lexington av, 25x100.11, five-story brk flat. (Amt due $1,330; sold April 7, 1890, under foreclos. for $18,500) $16,700

*102d st, Nos. 208 and 210, s s, 160 e 3d av, 50x100.11 ....
102d st, Nos. 212 and 214, s s, 210 e 3d av, 50x100.11 ....
Four five-story brk tenem'ts, stores in Nos. 212 and 214 ....
(Amt due on Nos. 208 and 210 $18,924 and $18,711 on Nos. 212 and 214) 70,100

*102d st, No. 166, s s, 225 w 3d av, 20x100.11, four-story stone front tenem't. (Amt due $10,082) 8,000

*105th st, Nos 221 and 223, n s, 200 w Amsterdam av, 50x100.11, two five-story brk flats. (Amt due $39,261) $28,000

106th st, Nos. 59 and 61, n s, 150 e Madison av, 49.6x100.11, two five-story brk flats. (Amt due $4,711; prior morts. on each house $18,750) 42,000

*105th st, No. 225, n s, 250 w 10th av, 25x100.11, five-story brk flat. (Amt due $15,967) 15,000

*Madison av, Nos. 1570-1576, w s, 24 11 s 106th st, four five-story brk flats, each 19x100. (Amt due $106,094) 80,000

Madison av, s e cor 107th st, 100.11x400 to Park av, vacant. (Amt due $85,179) 74,800

*112th st, n s, 125 w Lenox av, 25x100.11, five-story brk flat. (Amt due $2,230; prior morts. $20,000) 21,275

*5th av, No. 1395, e s, 41.1 s 115th st, 17.2x100, five-story brk flat. (Amt due $6,017; prior morts. $17,500) 18,500

*5th av, No. 1397, e s, 23.11 s 115th st, 17.2x100, five-story brk flat. (Amt due $8,626; prior morts. $15,000) 16,000

*5th av, No. 2147, e s, 25 n 131st st, 25x99, five-story brk flat. Amt due $3,104; prior morts. $16,000; sold Aug. 15, 1890, for $27,000). 20,600

*5th av, No 1393, e s, 58.3 s 115th st, 17.8x100, five-story brk flat. (Amt due $5,960; prior morts. $17,500) 18,500

*118th st, Nos. 302–308, s s, 100 w 8th av, 100x100.11, four five-story unfinished flats. (Amt due $13,761; prior morts. $20,000) 29,000

*119th st, No. 533 on map No. 534, s s, 462.3 e Av A or Pleasant av, 17.10x100,11, three-story stone front dwell'g. (Amt due $6,395) 6,250

*Madison av, No. 2119, s e cor 133d st, 19.11x80, three story brk (stone front) dwell'g. (Amt due $16,492) 10,000

*134th st, Nos. 71–79 } begins 134th st, n s, 197.6 e 6th av, original
135th st } line, 87.6x199.7 to 135th st, x87 6x199.10, five three-story brk dwell'gs on 134th st and five three-story brk dwell'gs on 135th st. (Amt due $67,750) 60,000

*144th st, No. 462, s s, 141 e Amsterdam av, 47x99.11, three-story brk dwell'g. (Amt due $13,774) 13,000

145th st, No. 326, s s, 42 e Edgecombe av, 18x99.11, three-story brk dwell'g. (Amt due $9,819) 9,500

* Indicates that the property described has been bid in for plaintiff's account.

Numerous reports have reached us, all seeming to show the weakness of up-town property. We give them for what they are worth.

On the north side of 125th street, just east of 7th avenue, are two lots, which were sold at auction on July 1st for $69,000. We are assured by a broker that he offered $70,000 for the property last October, and that his offer was refused.

The northeast corner of 7th avenue and 127th street, four flats on a plot 100x100, and now owned by a savings bank, were offered, it is said, to a reliable buyer for $162,000; only $2,000 cash required.

Nos. 208 and 210 East 107th street, near 3d avenue, two four-story tenements, each 21.10x60x100, fully rented, and near the 106th street station, are offered at $9,000 each, and there are no buyers. The land on which each house stands must be worth at least $6,000, and the houses would cost to build $8,000 or thereabouts.

A plot of lots on the north side of 118th street, east of Lenox, have been held stiffly at $8,000 each, the owner is quite willing to sell now at $6,000 each.

The corner of Columbus avenue and 117th street, 100x100, was strongly held by the owner a year ago at $45,000. He would take $38,000 for it now.

Of course, the facts stated above may not mean all that they appear to. It may be, as one of the most prominent brokers up-town stated to a RECORD AND GUIDE reporter recently, that sacrifices are being made only in isolated cases, and that as a general rule Harlem real estate is well and strongly held. It is far from our object to create any distrust of real estate in Harlem, or anywhere else, but it is our desire to have the truth known, and with that object alone in view, we have gathered together the facts stated above, believing that our readers will be able to judge truly the state of the case from the evidence furnished them.

The Latest Goelet Purchase.

A BROADWAY CORNER THAT BROUGHT A HIGH FIGURE—OTHER HIGH-PRICED REALTY IN NEW YORK—AN IMPORTANT LEASE.

The property on the northeast corner of Broadway and 31st street, to which the Goelet estate has just taken title, and the sale of which was reported in THE RECORD AND GUIDE a few weeks ago, is one of the most valuable parcels of real estate on Manhattan Island.

The Goelet purchase is known as the "San Carlo." It comprises an eight and nine-story building, which contains stores on the first floor and an apartment hotel above, with a four and five-story building adjoining on the street, known as the "San Carlo Cafe." It comprises No. 1240 Broadway and Nos. 43 to 47 West 31st street. The "San Carlo" proper occupies the corner lot, 22x74.2x20.6x66.9 in size, as well as Nos. 45 and 47 West 31st street, which covers 36x98.9. The cafe takes in 18.6x98.9. The price paid by the Goelet estate was $600,000 for the whole property.

The price paid for No. 43 West 31st street, November 30, 1888, was $30,000. The property is now worth about $45,000, allowing for improvements, increased value, etc. Deducting $45,000 from $600,000, we have a balance of $555,000 as the price practically paid for the "San Carlo" proper.

This latter building, with ground, covers an area of 5,052.6 square feet. Taking $555,000 as the actual price paid for the property it would give an average of $109.84 per square foot.

A subscriber to THE RECORD AND GUIDE, however, argues that the corner sold for the highest price ever attained for real estate in New York. His argument is that this corner, which occupies 22x74.2x20.6x66.9, or 1,497.6 square feet, sold for $334 per square foot. He gets at this result in the following way: He states that Nos. 43 to 47 West 31st street comprise 54.6x98,9, and as two city lots thereabouts are worth about $50,000 each, or about $100,000 together, it leaves $500,000 for the corner comprising 1,497.6 feet. This gives an average of $334.28 per square foot, which is a few dollars per square foot higher than the highest price ever previously paid for any New York property, as will be seen from the table of high-priced real estate which is given below.

Such a mode of calculation is both fallacious and misleading. As a matter of fact the San Carlo stands not only on No. 1240 Broadway, comprising 1,497.6 square feet, but also where the two houses once stood, known as Nos. 45 and 47 West 31st street, which covers 3,555 square feet. In a word, the eight and nine-story building known as the "San Carlo," now occupies a site which covers 5,052.6 square feet. It would be inaccurate, therefore, to count in the 36x98.9 on which part of an eight and nine-story building now stands, and the 18.6x98.9 now occupied by the four and five-story cafe, the whole covering 54.6x98.2, a little over two city lots, and then, throwing them in together at a valuation of $100,000, divide the balance of $500,000 by 1,497.6. This is clearly a sophism to obtain a high valuation per square foot, but it is unreasonable on the face of it.

Not only that, but in calculating the amount per square foot which the San Carlo property brought, it would be equally unreasonable to do so on the same basis as the other properties in the table given below. Those properties were all what is known as "unimproved;" that is, the buildings were old and valueless and were torn down to make way, in nearly every instance, for a handsome structure which was to form the permanent improvement. Now, in the case of the San Carlo, the old buildings which stood on the site have long since been torn down and the permanent improvement has been reared in their place. Thus, instead of about $109.84 per square foot, which, as is shown above, the San Carlo proper actually sold for, it would be more proper to subtract the cost of the permanent improvement, which is said to have been about $275,000, from the $555,000 practically paid by the Goelet estate. This would leave $280,000 as the value of the 5,052.6 square feet unimproved, which would be $55.41 per square foot. The actual cost of the ground and the old buildings which stood on the site of the San Carlo Hotel and cafe was $205,000, and $280,000 would show an advance of $75,000 in from three to four years.

ABOUT THE SELLER.

Mary E. Hanley, who figures in the deeds as the seller of the property to the Goelets, is the widowed sister of Daniel A. Loring, of Western and Eastern "bucket-shop" fame. Mrs. Hanley signs all the contracts in Mr. Loring's transactions, which are altogether conducted by her brother. Some comment has been made about the shrewdness of this lady in making such a profitable real estate transaction, but the shrewdness is that of "Dan" Loring. His sister acts in what is known in real estate parlance as a "dummy."

WHAT THE PROPERTY COST D. A. LORING.

A reference to the files of THE RECORD AND GUIDE shows that No. 1240 Broadway was transferred to Mary E. Hanley, June 9, 1887, for $120,000. It then had on it a five-story brick store and dwelling. No. 47 West 31st street was transferred June 7, 1888, for $45,000. It then had on the site a five-story stone front dwelling, the lot being 18x98.9. No. 45 West 31st street was transferred July 10, 1858, the consideration named being nominal, but the price is understood to have been $40,000. It comprised a lot 18x98.9, on which there stood a four-story stone front dwelling. No. 43 West 31st street, now the San Carlo cafe, on a lot 18.6x98.9, was transferred for $30,000 November 30, 1888. All these parcels were conveyed to Mary E. Hanley. The cost of the San Carlo proper is said to have been about $275,000. Thus the entire property cost Mr. Loring about $485,000. On this sum he obtained from the Goelets an advance of $115,000.

AN IMPORTANT LEASE.

In conjunction with this sale an important lease has been consummated. The Goelets have leased the property for nineteen years, the rent commencing from August 1, 1891, to Messrs. Robt. Stafford and H. P. Whitaker, the present lessees of the Hotel Imperial, on the southeast corner of Broadway and 32d street. In conjunction therewith the Goelets are also building a nine-story addition at No. 44 West 32d street, 21x98.9 in size, adjoining the Imperial, from plans by McKim, Mead & White, and this is to be ready in the fall. In the meantime the San Carlo is to be used as an annex to the Imperial, and when the addition on 32d street is finished the entire property will be joined to the Imperial and thrown into one.

WHAT THE LESSEES SAY.

Mr. Whitaker, one of the lessees, was seen. He said: "Yes, we have been successful beyond our anticipations, and this is why we have leased more property. We are already in possession of the San Carlo and our rent for that property and the 32d street addition will be nearly $50,000 per annum."

At the office of the Goelet estate the actual terms of the lease could not be learned.

It may be remembered that in the fall of 1889 the Imperial was leased for twenty years, from September 1, 1890, by Robert and Ogden Goelet to Messrs. Stafford & Whitaker, at a total of $1,900,000, the rent for the first year being $60,000, for the second year $70,000, for the third year $80,000, for the fourth year $90,000, and for the remaining sixteen years $100,000 per annum. Thus, when the lessees take possession of the San Carlo property and the 32d street extension in the fall, they will be paying a rental of about $130,000 per annum for the years 1891-2.

POINTS.

The rent roll of the San Carlo is reliably reported to have been about $45,000 per annum.

It is whispered that the Goelet estate may purchase the "Winchester" from the Hurry estate. The Winchester is the only building between the Imperial and the San Carlo, and, if acquired by the Goelets, would give them an uninterrupted parcel taking in the entire Broadway front between 31st and 32d streets. The Winchester has a frontage on Broadway of 83.9 feet, being 78.2½ feet in the rear, with a depth of 104.2 on the north side and 74.2 on the south side.

HIGH-PRICED REAL ESTATE.

The following is a list of the figures paid for the highest priced realty on Manhattan Island. All these properties may be said to have been unimproved, as they contained only old or unimportant buildings when they were purchased, and, with one or two exceptions, have since been torn down and replaced by handsome modern office buildings:

Location.	Date sold.	Purchaser.	No. of sq. feet.	Cost.	Price per sq. foot
S w cor Wall and Broad sts..........	April, 1882..	M. Wilkes	508	$168,000	$330.70
No. 149 Broadway and No. 83 Liberty st, n w cor........	Mar. 14, 1890	Singer Mfg. Co.....	3,006.6	544,500	181.12
No. 7 Wall st, s w cor Wall and New sts.	May 1, 1882..	W. W. Smith......	1,525	240,000	157.37
N e cor Broadway and Pine st......	Jan. 2, 1885,	Eq. Life....	4,896	762,500	155.75
No. 137 Broadway..	Mar. 15, 1887	Niagara Fire Ins Co	2,525	356,200	141.10
N e cor Liberty and Broadway........	May 31, 1882	W'msbg Fire In. Co	3,070	356,000	115.96
Nos. 8 and 10 Pine..	Mar. 8, 1884.	Eq. Life	....	400,000	115.00
No. 12 Wall st.......	Nov. 1, 1882.	J. J. Astor........	2,695	300,000	111.31

No. 135 Broadway, s e cor Cedar st, extending to Temple st....	Mar. 15, 1887	Horace Waldo......	3,283	351,000	106.94
Nos. 4 and 6 Pine st.	Mar. 8, 1884	Eq. Life	2,506	267,500	106.74
Nos. 8 and 10 Wall st	Jan. 22, 1881	J. J. Astor..........	5,709	500,000	87.58
S e cor Cedar and Nassau sts.........	July 31, 1882	Ger. Life Ins. Co....	5,494	462,000	84.18
No. 19 Nassau st....	May 10, 1882	Julia F. Ludlow.....	2 050	170,000	82.92
No. 11 Broad st......	Mar. 11, 1881	D. O. Mills..........	2,486	200,000	80.44
Nos. 17 and 19 Broad st, and 55 Exch. pl.	April 27, 1881	D. O. Mills..........	8,655	637,500	73.65
Nos. 35 Wall and 13 and 15 Broad sts..	May 2, 1882	D. O. Mills..........	8,622	625,000	72.48
No. 9 Pine st........	Mar. 17, 1881	J. J. Astor....... ..	1,752	100,000	57.07
S e cor Broadway and Exchange pl.	Jan. 1883....	J. J. Astor..........	19,115	1,000,000	52.31

Letter Bag—The Newspaper Curse.

Editor RECORD AND GUIDE :

Amid a great deal that is hasty, sketchy, flimsy, and altogether ridiculous, there is one passage in a recent article by Hamilton Aide on "Social Aspects of American Life" which deserves a wider currency than it has received. The reason that it has not received such publicity is sufficiently apparent from the nature of the passage. Mr. Aide says that after a dinner, at which he was the only stranger present, given evidently in New York City with no reporters present, one speaker after another rose and denounced in "scathing terms the corruption, the neglect, the incompetence that reigned throughout" the government of this city. "The last speech," he continued, "contained a charge the truth of which was so borne home to me during my sojourn in the States that I have never forgotten the gist of it, though, of course, I cannot pretend to reproduce the words."

"What lies at the root of all this evil? The press. 'Which of us here present would be willing to undertake the duties of any prominent post in this city, knowing to what he and all his family would be immediately exposed! His secrets dragged to light, his honor impugned, his buried past unearthed—no slander too foul to be fastened on his name—and all without redress. You may shoot the editor of a paper in which your wife or daughter has been traduced, and a jury will acquit you of murder; but if you bring an action against them for libel you will never obtain a conviction, or, if you do, the penalty imposed will be a mockery. And whose fault is this? It is yours, gentlemen—yours, who do not resolve to put down with a strong hand this crying infamy, this disgrace to your country. In no other land would such outrages on private individuals be tolerated. We boast of being a free people. I tell you that the Czar of all the Russias is not so great a tyrant as this press of ours. No man's house is safe from its intrusion. No man's character secure from its attacks. Until we resolve to cut out this plague-spot on our civilization, which is eating into the heart of the nation, corrupting what is purest in the young, poisoning the daily draught of those who have lived and suffered, until we do this the best citizens among us will stand aloof. Only those who have 'squared' the newspapers, or are callous to obloquy, will get into the pillory to be pelted with rotten eggs."

This vituperative attack was made, remember, by some prominent citizen of New York, and the Englishman is only reporting the speech. I will assume that he has reported it correctly.

Here is a cause of municipal misgovernment which, very naturally, we do not read very much about. The morning papers have been taken to task for directly abetting Tammany during elections; but, so far as I know, no one one has ever insisted on the fear of the journalistic consequences of publicity as the main reason for the avoidance of politics by the "better element." Indeed, I think that this view is rather fanciful. Our respectable citizens cannot evade responsibility in that way. At any rate, whatever may be the effect of the journalistic parade of personalities, trivialities and filth, the fact is sufficiently apparent, sufficiently significant and sufficiently degrading. As an evening newspaper of the better class recently said, the only restriction put upon the diffusion of prurient nastiness was, and is, measured by the law forbidding indecencies; and it would not be strange to find some of them agitating for the repeal of that law. It is not, however, their grosser faults of sensationalism, pruriency, etc., to which I particularly wish to draw attention. Their conduct is as indefensible from an intellectual as from a moral standpoint or any standard of taste, and more of them are open to attack for sins against intelligence than for sins against morals or taste. They are, I have no doubt, one efficient cause for persistency of Tammany rule; but this is so rather because they cultivate intellectual irresponsibility, shiftiness, coarseness, confusion, irrelevance, vulgarity, and density of thought, than because they help to exclude our better class from politics by holding over them the threat of distasteful publicity. Nine out of every ten newspapers of the present day are simply festering coagulations of clap-trap. Even when they attack Tammany, they do in a spirit of petty unfairness, which revolts any one not as silly and hide-bound as themselves.

Ex-Mayor Hewitt, when in office, used to have a fashion of calling the reporters of the daily newspapers into him and asking them when they and their editors were going to stop lying. That is just the difficulty. In the sanctum, that a statement is untrue is nothing against it. The average American newspapers are the most inveterate, the most incorrigible, the most blatant liars on the face of the earth. The headlines lie because they are "catchy" instead of descriptive. The reporters lie, distort, misrepresent with measureless audacity, this being partly the result of gross ignorance and partly the result of a deliberate intention to mangle the news. The editorial writers lie in the same way, and for the same reason as the reporters. The whole sheet is what I may call a general lie, in that instead of presenting the history of a day they present to a large extent only the pathology of a day. And what a mass of this pestilential stuff is poured on the public every day. A short while since I drove one Sunday morning some twenty miles through the New Jersey suburbs. The houses on either side of the road were as a rule those of people in comfortable circumstances; they must have represented the average middle-class American in tastes, habits and intelligence. Yet almost without exception the father of the family was to be found sitting on the porch with his feet on the railing pouring over his newspaper as if it was the word of God. And I asked myself: What can be the effect of the universal attention granted to this mass of print? What is there in those bits of paper that would appeal to a sensible right-minded man? After excluding from each of the journals all misrepresentation, irrelevance, foolishness, sloppiness, vulgarity, indecency and fustian, how much would remain? And if in spite of the preponderance of this kind of writing, these sheets are still read, what effects will they have on the mental and moral qualities of the reader and what deficiency does absorption in them imply in him?

These effects and deficiencies are not very far to seek. Americans do not seem to be able to keep small things small and great things great; an appalling lack of seriousness is to be observed in their characters. The almost exclusive devotion of their time to business, and the perpetual nervous strain that such a life entails seems to leave no energy for a deep, wholesome, careful, intelligent interest in artistic or scientific matters. This does not mean, of course, that such an interest is entirely lacking. On the contrary a small, but I think, growing minority possess it and put it to good use, but it does mean that such people are outside of the mass of their countrymen, and alien to them. Theodore Watts has lately spoken of the cultivated classes of America as being "hopelessly divided from the most prejudiced and narrow-minded class in the civilized world—America's illiterate mob." These are strong words, but they have this much truth. I do not believe that the "illiterate mob" of other countries are any more intelligent than that of America; but then nobody claims intelligence for them, and they are certainly more serious. Our own "illiterate mob" has an amount of nauseating and fulsome flattery stuffed down their throats by their "leaders of public opinion" which would suffocate a people who took it seriously. "Illiterate," however, is not the word to describe the "mob" of this country. They can read, most of them, but what do they read, and how do they read it? Anything outside of business is a pastime. Reading is a pastime; theatre-going is a pastime; politics is a pastime—except to those who make it a business. And is religion anything more?

The effects of this may be illustrated in various ways. We congratulate ourselves on our humor, but too often it is only a cheap flippancy, which conceals ignorance by pert assurance. No other country in the world has so many comic papers; and the mass of drivel that they print is in its implications one of the most solemn facts in our national life. Again, how often do you hear people say that they go to a theatre in the evening merely as a rest from the weariness of a day's work. And a mental rest most theatres are. The auditors have every encouragement to be passive; but what porous sponges they must be to absorb what they hear. In the forty weeks of the dramatic season, how many of the twenty theatres in New York produce anything but sloppy and slangy swash. The late P. T. Barnum used to advise young men, in case they had only thirteen dollars, to buy something with two and advertise it with eleven. This counsel has some chance of success in America. In what other country would such a master-humbug be able to accumulate a fortune of four or five million dollars? Our public is the most guillible in the world. Barnum's proper place was that of a traveling showman at farmer's fairs. He would have ranked no higher in a country the people of which were better able to distinguish between a mere "fake" and something that is honest. And so it is in everything that is not business. Americans rush after them in a loose, idle, frivolous, superficial way; and the consequence is that they pay higher for things that are worth less, and are more frequently deceived than are people of other nationalities and less restricted lives.

Every extreme contains the seeds of its own dissipation. We Americans are certainly going to an extreme. The people who are preaching the gospel of wealth inveigh loudly against the nationalists, hayseed economists and other cranks, who are followed so largely all over the country. If they had eyes they could see that the predominant importance they give to money making in their theories has for its consequences in practice a crushing and flattening of the intelligence, which makes our people legitimate prey for all the hair-brained extremists which emotional insanity can produce. So sensitive are Americans to public opinion, and so little is public opinion rectified by reason, that it is quite possible that the country will some day be swamped by some utterly wild and foolish craze. As it is we are afflicted by childishness, by partial insanity, and by down-right lack of honesty among the people who hold the public ear. Does any one suppose that the silly froth and the puerile clap-trap which passes for editorial in our daily newspapers has a bit more worth than the craziest outgivings of any Wiggins or any latter-day prophet. But the trouble is that one is read as if it were something sensible, while we smile when we take up aught of Wiggins. That such a journal as the *Mail and Express* could have more than five hundred circulation would be simply incredible were it not that sad experience forces on one the limitlessness of human unintelligence. It is no one wonder, when integrity is supposed to end when debts are paid, that Tammany and Hills and Quays are flouted in our faces; and all our protests are as useless as a boy's pop-gun. And just because the newspapers most clearly illustrate this prevailing departure from sound intellectual standards, and perpetuate it by their popularity that I consider them to be a curse to the country.

JOHN EMBERT.

[In the main we agree fully with what our correspondent says; The Press of this country is a curse. But the evil condition of the Press is an effect as well as a cause, and both sides of the matter need to be looked at. The low intellectual tone of newspapers to-day is due in part to the low intellectual tone of the nation, and in its turn the Press reacts upon the character of our national life by fostering, extending, perpetuating, and accentuating the intellectual deficiency, the morbid tastes and unenlightened tendencies of people. It is very difficult to set forth with due measure yet clearly and convincingly the deficiencies of the Press. Indeed, it is almost as hard to draw up an indictment against the Press as it is to do so against a nation, there are so many exceptions to be made, and so many little qualifications which ought to be considered pop up around every fact, that the candid critic finds it difficult to formulate a precise and thorough judgment which will at once strike home to the centre of the reader's conviction along all the directions in which the latter views the matter. To say that the newspapers are a curse may seem at first glance a statement too strong and too sweeping, and before it is possible to gain acceptance for it people must recognize the validity of some reasonable standard to which a newspaper should conform. To hold that its mission is to reflect in any or every sort of way anything or everything that happens would be to give to the Press a roving commission which would end in a very short time in being a serious matter for Civilization. The difficulty is to get the public to accept a really reasonable, intellectual and moral standard for the Press. It is hard to get people to see that all the miserable stuff that is published about the doings and sayings of the great army of political tricksters, which our party method of government quarters on the country; all the sensational gossip and stories about crimes and scandals, hangings and accidents, all the silly twaddle of a personal character about millionaires, actresses, and notable nobodies, should have no place whatever in the interest which an intelligent person takes in his day and generation. Yet, if from the contents of our leading morning papers we abstract political twaddle, sensational stories and the reports of criminal or quasi-criminal events, how much would be left? Two Sundays ago, on the first page of one of the New York "dailies," there was only one "item" that was not a story of some crime, accident, or piece of folly. As the human body can withstand, without apparently deleterious effects, a certain amount of unwholesome food, so it is perhaps possible for the mind to absorb a small amount of literary miasma from [the newspapers without impairing and vitiating its healthy activity. But newspaper reading is practically the only reading done by a very large proportion of the population. Morning, evening, and Sunday, the little leisure-time which hundreds of thousands have is spent in running through columns of stuff which neither creates an impression, stirs an emotion, nor gives to the memory a single fact of any real value to a serious life.—Ed.]

Proposing to Close the Harlem.

The New York Central camel is poking its nose into the Harlem River bridge question again. Defeated in Congress in its efforts to have this important waterway closed to commerce, the company has begun a quiet and insinuating campaign against the natural development of commerce on the river. Some weeks ago it filed a petition with the Park Board to have the Madison and 3d avenue bridges kept closed between the hours of 7 and 10 in the morning and 4 and 7 in the evening, so that its railroad bridge at 4th avenue could be kept closed during the same hours, and the running of trains across it uninterrupted during those hours.

There was a hearing upon this question before the Park Board on Wednesday. Frank Loomis, attorney for the Central road, was the only advocate of the scheme present. He enlarged upon the growing traffic and suburban travel on the road and the increasing interference with the running of trains by the opening of the bridge for the passage of boats, many of which were mere tramp pleasure craft, whose captains seemed to take especial delight in requiring the bridge to be swung at all hours and as often as they could make it necessary. He argued in favor of the jurisdiction of the Park Board of the subject, saying, that although the Harlem was a navigable stream it had not been accepted by the General Government, who therefore had no jurisdiction over it or the bridges which spanned it.

Several persons appeared in opposition to the petition. The New York & Northern Railroad Company, represented by Sherman Evarts, took a strong position against the Central's demand. The closing of the bridge would seriously injure the business of the Northern road and would hamper and interfere with the upbuilding of commerce and business on and along the river. He argued that the General Government had acquired superior jurisdiction of the river and the bridges over it when it took possession of the land under water. Henry Lewis Morris, on behalf of himself and other property-owners along the river, protested against the granting of the petition of the Central company. He pointed out that large outlays had been made for the improvement of the docks and wharves along the Harlem, that the population of the North Side was rapidly on the increase, and that with the increase of population the commerce of the river and the demand for dock facilities had largely increased. All this would be arrested if the demands of the New York Central Railroad Company should be granted. This petition was only the forerunner of another and stronger effort which the company would make to have the bridges made permanent and the river "macadamized."

Albert Rogers, appearing in behalf of owners of the tow-boats, and John Winthrop, representing the Freight Handlers' Association, also addressed the board in opposition to the scheme. Mr. Winthrop said he represented 7,000 'longshoremen, freight-handlers and tug-boat operatives, whose business would be very detrimentally affected by keeping the bridges closed. If the petition should be granted it would only leave six hours in the middle of the day, during which commercial craft could navigate the stream. And if by any chance a vessel, a coal-laden barge, a lumber-laden schooner, or a brick-laden sloop should get to the bridge a few minutes too late, it would have to tie up for the rest of the day or night. The company was better able to stand the cost of raising its tracks to a level which would permit of a bridge spanning the river at 50 feet above high tide, under which nearly all the craft of commerce could clear, or to lower its tracks and build a tunnel under the river for them, than the owners of property on the Harlem could afford to have the value of their property destroyed or the thousands of hard-workers engaged in commerce on the Harlem could afford to have their means of livelihood taken away. Mr Winthrop asked that a time be set for another hearing, and the time was fixed for Wednesday, August 5th.

The New Rapid Transit Route.

Another rapid transit railroad route was laid out by the commissioners at their meeting on Tuesday. It is a central route, branching off from the proposed Broadway-Boulevard route at 14th street, under the south-east corner of Union square in nearly a direct line into 4th avenue, which is followed to within a short distance of 42d street. From this point the route diverges to the westward under the business buildings at the southwest corner of 42d street and 4th avenue and under the blocks between 42d and 44th streets, just west of the Grand Central Station, to Madison avenue at 44th street. Thence the proposed road is to follow Madison avenue to 96th street, where there is a sharp declivity to the broad level of the Harlem plains. Up to this point from 14th street the road is to run underground through solid rock all the way.

From 96th street the line diverges again through private property to "a point not less than 100 feet east of and parallel to Madison avenue;" thence it follows a direct line parallel with Madison avenue to 135th street, whence it diverges to the east and crosses the Harlem River by an iron bridge intended by the engineers to be 50 feet above high tide. From 96th street to the Harlem River the road is to be a viaduct. Necessarily, it will be higher at all points than the New York Central viaduct, for it will cross 125th street at a height above the grade which will not interfere with the traffic of the street, and will preserve as nearly a level grade as may be to the crossing of the river. An investigation made by the engineers showed them that under a span 50 feet above the level of the river, nearly all the craft that ply upon the Harlem could clear without making it necessary to swing the bridge open. All the excursion steamers, lumber schooners, brick barges and sloops that make up the ordinary traffic of the Harlem could pass without finding the bridge, at such a height, any obstruction. It would be only when some larger seagoing masted vessel had to pass that the bridge would have to be swung.

That the commissioners, in laying out the new route, did not bring it straight down 4th avenue and through Lafayette place and Elm street to the proximity of the Brooklyn Bridge was a surprise to most people, but has appeared to be a disappointment to but few. The reason given by the commissioners for making the connection with the main line at Broadway is the economical one—it saves the cost of a line from 14th street to the Battery. It will also serve the very important and appreciable purpose of increasing the relative earning capacity of the Broadway line, and by minimizing investment and expenses, and maximizing income, will make the whole rapid transit project much more attractive to investors than it would otherwise have been. Besides, the plans thus far enunciated have been made with relation to a future plan for an East Side route from the Battery to the northern city line, somewhere along the line of the Bowery and 3d or 2d avenue, which will probably tap the Bridge traffic at either William street or Park row, and which would be made to connect with the Central and West Side systems by a shuttle or branch through 14th street. But with the Broadway—Boulevard and Madison avenue lines as projected, and as illustrated on another page of this issue of The Record and Guide, once completed and in operation, it is believed, the strain on the Third Avenue Elevated road would be so relieved that any extension of East Side facilities of transit would not be necessary for several years. The East Side populace is not of the car-fare paying kind. The large majority of its toiling population is of the unskilled class, employed in factories, yards, mills, shops, or on the streets in the vicinity of their ever-shifting homes. They walk long distances to and from their work to save the expense of riding; indeed, when a man gets a "steady job" in some given locality, it is cheaper for him to move into a near-by tenement than to attempt to pay car fares. Though much less densely populated, the district between 4th avenue and Broadway affords the transit companies much better patronage than the district east of 3d avenue—a statement which is proved by the fact that the Second Avenue Elevated road has only just begun to pay something more than the fixed charges.

From 75th street to the Harlem River the Madison avenue route will traverse a district at present too sparsely populated to afford a sustaining traffic to the road; but that it is sparsely populated is only because it has not been supplied with the recessary means of travel, and it goes without question that when work is once actively begun upon the Madison Avenne rapid transit line, the enterprising builder will contrive to be in advance of the running of trains with habitations for a hundred thousand people—of the traveling species. Beyond the Harlem things are still left in a conjectural shape. The commissioners have before them a plan for the extension of the Madision Avenue line northward through Sheridan avenue to a point east of Jerome avenue and thence through private property parallel with Jerome avenue to the northern city line. This plan is viewed with general favor by the residents and owners of property in the trans-Harlem district—or North Side, as the denizens prefer to have it called. It is remarked that the transit facilities for the villages and settled portions of the North Side are already better than they are south of the Harlem. But for the beautiful region between the Harlem and the New York and Northern roads there are no means of travel except by private conveyance. Here, in the region traversed by Jerome avenue, there is room for a vast population, which will undoubtedly be invitingly prepared for by the builder of houses and suburban villas. The property is already quoted at respectable prices and will undoubtedly increase rapidly in value from the time of the beginning of the new road.

Another plan for the extension of rapid transit lines through the North Side, which the commissioners have before them, is for a viaduct structure over Highbridge, connecting the Boulevard line with the contemplated Jerome Avenue line, as shown by the dotted line on the map. Still another scheme is for the spanning of the Harlem ship canal, near Kingsbridge,

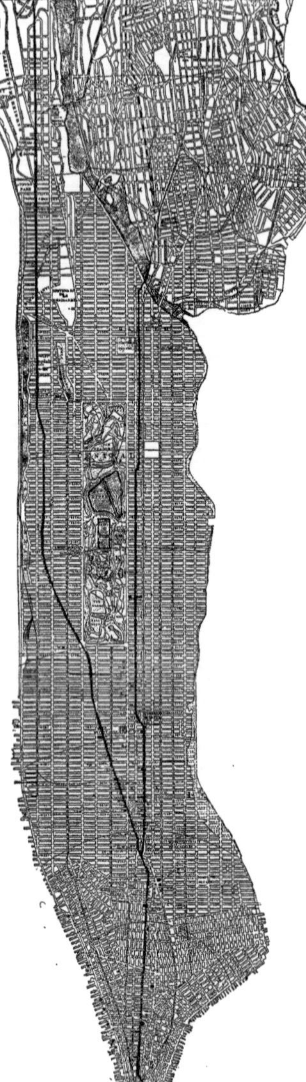

with an iron bridge also 50 feet above high-water mark. This would be for the continuation of the line from 11th avenue by viaduct across the Dyckman meadows and north of the Harlem along the line of Spuyten Duyvil Parkway. The design of all these North Side extensions is not to provide transit facilities in response to any present pressing need, but to open up for settlement the vast regions within the city limits that have hitherto been inaccessible. There appears to the commissioners to be no good reason why there should not be another Brooklyn across the Harlem.

Having disposed of the questions of route for the time being in a manner which will approve itself to practical people, the commissioners are now confronted with the critical question of plan of construction. On this point more has leaked out about their plans than they are pleased to discover, and not enough to afford a satisfactory basis for criticism. In a general way the commissioners have decided to have the underground roads as near to the surface of the street as is practicable. This point was settled for them by the revelations of the borings in Broadway, a horizontal sectional view of which is presented on another page. In Austin Corbin's deep tunnel plan for a tunnel through the solid rock, it was assumed that with the possible exception of Canal street, rock would be found all along the line at within 90 feet of the surface and for most of the distance within 40 feet. If this assumption had been found correct some of the commissioners have said they would undoubtedly have settled upon a tunnel through the solid rock, as by all odds the most acceptable for the purpose for which it was intended. But the borings effectually settled the deep tunnel scheme, and what is of still more importance, showed the commissioners that they had a far less difficult formation to deal with in Broadway than had ever been supposed. In fact, they are satisfied that the conditions against which they have got to contend are less difficult than they would be with any other formation. The "quick sands" to which one of the papers has alluded in its effort to discredit the work of the commissioners is the same formation upon which Trinity Church, the Standard Oil Trust Building, the Union Trust Company Building, Aldrich Court, the Equitable, the Post-office, the Potter, the *Times* and the Pulitzer and many other massive architectural structures have been built, and which affords as perfect foundations as could be desired.

In the Rapid Transit Act provision is made for the construction, incidentally with the railway, of a conduit for all the sub-surface mains, pipes, tubes and conductors of every character. This is involved in the question now before the commissioners: whether to build close up to the surface of the street and construct a pipe gallery through the middle of the street between two double-decked railway tunnels, or to go 6 or 8 feet deeper down under the sub-surface works and build a single tunnel, taking up the entire width of the street between curbs, laying all four tracks on a level, and ignore the mains, pipes, tubes and conductors entirely. The first proposition means the reconstruction of the roadway of Broadway on a permanent and abiding basis, with a tunnel for underground works, accessible at all times through iron traps between the cable railroad tracks, for repairs, connections or alterations, with a railway tunnel on each side of this pipe gallery, and between it and the curbwalls, each tunnel containing two tracks, one above the other, accessible from stations under the sidewalks, without the necessity of elevators, the stairways shorter by several feet than those leading to the elevated railroad stations; with a massive iron roof extending from curb to curb over the railway tunnels and the pipe-galleries, supporting the cable conduits and a permanent granite pavement laid in concrete, which there will never be any occasion for disturbing until it has worn down to the concrete; and finally, with the abomination of tearing up the street pavement everlastingly done away with. It will not be disputed that such a reconstruction of Broadway would more than double its traffic facilities, and would be a greater benefit to property-owners, to the cable railroad company, and to the people generally, than would a magical doubling of the width of the thoroughfare. The street thus improved would be a model for all generations.

The cost, which is the important thing to be considered, the engineers declare, would be but slightly greater, if at all, in original outlay, than for the construction of the rapid transit railroad on the other plan. It will require in indirect outlay, however, the practical surrender of the thoroughfare, not all at once, but in sections, to the contractors, for another entire season. The road would have to be opened to the surface of the street, one-third at a time, in several sections working toward each other until the entire gigantic task was completed. Engineer Wm. Barclay Parsons is willing to be quoted as authority for the statement that the interruption to traffic would not be as great as it is by the present cable construction. The cable railroad would not be disturbed, but could be operated without interruption. Neither would the interruption be continuous along any one block for more than a few weeks in the aggregate; but as soon as a block was completed it would be restored to surface traffic without further interruption. The commissioners are manifestly predisposed in favor of this plan. They declare that it involves no disturbance of or encroachment upon private property or vested rights, but would add so immensely to the value of property along the line that it ought to be welcomed by and receive the enthusiastic support of every property-owner.

If the other plan of construction is adopted the work can be done, though with difficulty and additional expense, without disturbing the surface of the street. In order to do it some sort of shield would have to be employed to sustain the super-imposed weight of the roadway while the tunnel proper was being constructed. Then, too, the road would at a few points overlap on private property, which would have to be condemned, together with property for the stations. The descent to the station platforms would be in the neighborhood of 28 feet, which is almost as deep a stairs as any of those of the elevated roads, and deeper than most of them. Then the permanent roadway would not be secured. And there can be no doubt but that if the pipe gallery is not provided for, the old nuisance of frequently breaking into the pavements in order to get at the pipes will be continued in the future as it has in the past. The 5th avenue pavement was laid in massive and enduring manner, at an expense of over $5 per

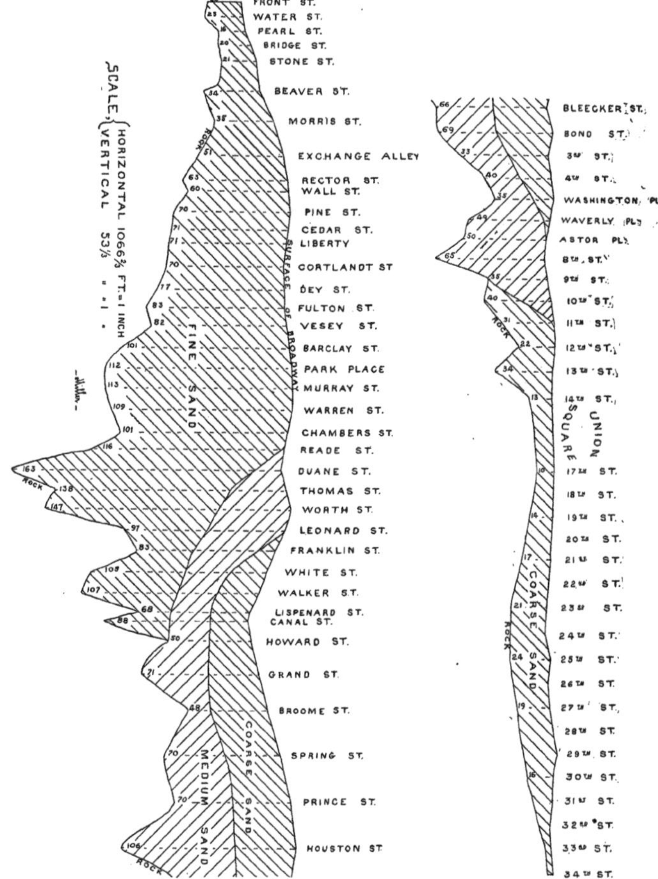

Diagram of the Borings along Broadway.

square yard, and yet it was not down a month before it was torn open in a score of places for the purpose of getting at the sub-surface works. The time for the summer vacations of the commissioners is coming on and they have declared their intention of deciding this question of construction within the next few days, so as to get their engineering and executive forces at work preparatory to an early report of the routes and plans of construction to the Common Council.

New Incorporations.

On Tuesday last the Metropolitan Realty Company filed a Certificate of Incorporation with the County Clerk. The president is Lucius H. Biglow, and the treasurer is William H. Whiting.

On the same day Articles of Association were filed by The East River Building and Loan Association for the purpose of loaning moneys by co-operation to members for the purchase and improvement of real estate, within a radius of twenty-five miles of the City Hall. Isaac Goodman is the president and Morris Cukor attorney.

Real Estate Notes.

The Supreme Court has confirmed the report of commissioners awarding $11,000 to John P. Nathaniel and Samuel J. Huggins, as damages to the fee of the Cosmopolitan Hotel at Chambers and Hudson streets, from the construction and operation of the elevated railroad.

Judge Barrett has appointed Eugene S. Ives, Robert Maclay and John Connolly commissioners to appraise property in connection with the new Cathedral Parkway. The property is that part of 110th street, between 7th avenue and Riverside Park.

The mortgage from the Temple Beth El to the Manhattan Life Insurance Company for $350,000 was recorded on Wednesday.

Manufacturing Fire-proof Building Material at Perth Amboy.

[COMMUNICATED.]

A VISIT TO THE FACTORY OF GUSTAVUS ISAACS—ONE OF THE FINEST CLAY DEPOSITS IN NEW JERSEY—ACRES OF FIRE-PROOFING MATERIAL DESTINED FOR IMPORTANT BUILDINGS—KILNS WHERE THREE THOUSAND DEGREES OF HEAT IS EMPLOYED—THOUSANDS OF TONS OF CLAY WITHIN TWO HUNDRED YARDS OF DEEP WATER—THE PROCESS OF MANUFACTURE DESCRIBED.

The manufacture of fire-proofing material has assumed enormous proportions. Not only in the East, but in the West, it has become distinctly recognized that the era of combustible building material is passing away, and that the structures of the future must, wherever possible, be of a fire-proof character.

Not only is this realized by owners of buildings for the safety of their own and their neighbors' property, but it is recognized as of extreme importance on account of the diminution in fire risks, which enables property owners to obtain much easier terms from fire insurance companies than if their buildings were not incombustible. This is by no means a small item, especially in large and costly buildings.

Not only this, but there are other advantages connected with the use of fire-proof material, when composed of fire clay. In case of conflagration it will stand the greatest heat. Iron will bend itself into a shapeless mass, while stone will crack and melt. Everyone remembers how the granite in the Western Union building on Broadway and Dey street cracked and sizzled under a temperature which was not half as severe as that to which fire-brick is subjected, while other instances of a similar character are fresh in our memories, notably in Chicago, where entire blocks of buildings of granite and stone, both natural and artificial, were destroyed. The additional stories of the Western Union building are now being constructed of brick, the experience of the fire having proved a convincing argument in favor of the baked material.

The processes used in the manufacture of fire-proofing brick have undergone many improvements during the last decade or two.

Better machinery, greater economy in production, more care and watchfulness in the manufacture, new designs, the capacity for making brick of different patterns to fit ironwork of all sorts and shapes—all this has tended to make fire-proof material both useful and popular.

Naturally, the clay deposits from which this material is made are not all uniform in grade. On the contrary, they are extremely variable. Some brick brought to the New York market will melt at a heat of less than 2,000 degrees, whereas other brick is subjected to a heat of 3,000 degrees and over. So I was informed by John H. Mulchahey, graduate of Columbia College, who manages the works of Gustavus Isaacs at Perth Amboy.

I found Manager Mulchahey a very useful man for my purposes. I had come over to see the works with the intention of learning something about the manufacture of fire brick and I was not disappointed.

Mr. Mulchahey showed me the clay deposits. "Here," he said, "we have what is pronounced by experts the finest clay deposit, with the greatest depth of face, which is now in use for the manufacture of fire-proofing material, in the neighborhood of New York. We have thus the advantage of not requiring to dig pits and pump water. We have forty acres of ground composed entirely of this deposit. It is now eight years since we began to take clay from here and we have so far only exhausted about 100 square feet of superficial area. At the same rate it would take us 1,392 years to use up the forty acres which Mr. Isaacs owns; but," he added, with a smile, "I don't think you or I will be here when the last ton is used up."

My attention was then called to a fact which must be of considerable economical importance to a manufacturer of brick—the unusual nearness of the clay deposit to navigation. The point where the clay was being digged out to the point where I saw the brick being shipped on barges is only about 150 yards. "This clay is the nearest from the point of primary production to the point of shipment that is to be found anywhere," remarked the manager. "Then, you will also notice," he added, "that our clay deposit is almost in a direct line with our dock, and that our machinery is also in this direct line." This is true to such an extent that one may stand at the spot overlooking the clay deposits and see almost every process of manufacture before one's eyes, including the stacking of the material and its shipment.

This process is very interesting to an outsider, and every stage of manufacture is to be seen under way. The process may be briefly described as follows: The clay is taken from the bank and is brought on cars, which are worked by cable, into a soak-pit. This pit is in the clay-house, which is covered in, so that clay deposited there in winter will not freeze, and so be unfit for use. The clay-house contains about 2,000 tons of clay, and this quantity can be extended indefinitely, there being adequate room for the storage of enough clay to last for many weeks, either in summer or winter. Thus, the manufacture of the material is uninterrupted during all seasons of the year, cold weather forming no detriment, as is the case in many brick factories.

When the clay leaves the soak-pit it enters a pugmill, which cuts it up into smaller pieces. It then runs along a belt and is tempered and passed through another pugmill, whence it issues in smaller and harder shape. It then passes through another pugmill and from this it emerges on to the other "cut-off" table. Here several men are engaged in cutting the brick or blocks or whatever material the pattern in the pugmill may bring the clay out in. This cutting process is done by a machine so constructed that brick can be cut of any desired length by placing wires at the necessary distances apart. These wires slice the hard clay material into pieces of any size. These pieces, whether in the form of bricks, slabs or pipes, are then placed on pallets, which are carried upstairs by machinery into the different storerooms, where they are deposited until required to be placed in the various kilns. The next process is to place these bricks, etc., in their raw state, into the kilns. The kilns are then closed hermetically and a slow fire is kindled and kept up for nearly three days, the heat becoming more intense each hour, until about 3,000 degrees Fahrenheit is reached. Then the material is allowed to cool for three or four days, till capable of being handled. It is then taken out, stacked up and stored in the yard and wharves and shipped to various points of destination, as required.

THE BUILDINGS DESCRIBED.

The factory comprising the works, which are owned by Gustavus Isaacs, is situated on the Perth Amboy side of the Raritan River, and it is within a few minutes' drive of the Jersey Central and Pennsylvania depots at Perth Amboy. The buildings cover a total frontage of 600 feet and a maximum depth of 200 feet. They are three and four stories in height, the ground floor being used for the main machinery and kilns, and the floors above being utilized for drying, surface and lighter machinery, such as belting, etc. Some of this machinery contains improvements, in one or two cases of a very novel kind. "We have about 136,000 square feet of surface room, excluding our yard storage area of about 600x200 feet," said the manager. And here, at a glance, I saw acre upon acre of ground covered with fire-proofing material of all kinds, including buff and common brick, stacked from six to seven feet high. This vast quantity of material, he informed me, was nearly all ordered or sold. I asked in what buildings it would be used, and he replied: "The H. B. Claflin Co.'s building on the southeast corner of Thomas street and West Broadway; the addition to the Museum of Art in the Central Park; the Boston Library; the Criminal Courts building; the eight-story building for the Alexander Hayes estate at Nos. 21 and 23 Maiden lane; the addition to the State House, Trenton, N. J.; the ten-story building for the Edison Electric Light Company on Elm and Pearl streets; the Bank of Paterson, N. J., and other buildings.

In speaking of completed buildings for which Gustavus Isaacs has supplied fire-proofing material, Manager Mulchahey named the following: The Washington, Welles, Columbia and Astor office buildings, the Cotton Exchange, Aldrich Court, the Edison building on Broad street, the Dakota and Vancorlear apartment houses, the extension to Columbia College, some of the Navarro apartment houses on 59th street, the Goelet and Havemeyer residences on 5th avenue, the Havemeyer sugar refinery at Greenpoint, L. I.; the Providence Bank, Philadelphia; the Court House, Hanover, Me.; and residences in Hartford, Newport, etc.

On leaving the works the manager said: "We have both the means and the capacity for manufacturing all sorts of fire-proof building material. We have a great advantage over other manufacturers in the nearness of our clay deposit to our works and to deep water, which is right on the spot. This enables us to produce cheaply. We are about to erect more buildings, so as to increase our capacity about 50 per cent, and this, with improved machinery, in combination with our natural facilities, will make our plant and material second to none in the country."

WANDERER.

Contractors' Notes.

Bids will be received at the office of the Department of Public Works until 12 M., on Tuesday, July 28, 1891, for regulating and grading 127th street, from Boulevard to Riverside Drive, and setting curb-stones and flagging sidewalks therein, and for furnishing materials and performing work in repairing Clinton Market.

Bids for constructing a highway, retaining walls, appurtenances, etc., at Croton Dam, in the town of Yorktown, Westchester County, New York, as called for in the approved forms of contract and specifications on file in the office of the Aqueduct Commissioners, will be received at Room 209, Stewart Building, No. 280 Broadway, until 3 P. M., Wednesday, July 29, 1891.

Bids will be received by the Commissioner of Street Improvements of the 23d and 24th Wards, at his office, No. 2622 3d avenue, corner 141st street, until 3 P. M., Thursday, July 30, for regulating, paving with granite blocks, curbing and flagging and laying crosswalks in Brook avenue, from a line 487 feet south of the southerly line of 132d street to the southerly curb line of 156th street; for regulating, grading, setting curb-stones, flagging the sidewalks and building culverts in and paving with granite-block pavement the roadway of 138th street, between Railroad avenue East and the Madison Avenue Bridge; and for regulating and grading, setting curb-stones, flagging the sidewalks and laying crosswalks in 169th street, from Franklin avenue to 167th street.

Bids will be received at the Department of Public Charities and Correction, No. 66 3d avenue, until July 29th, at 10 A. M., for materials and work required for steam heating a pavilion for alcoholic patients at Bellevue Hospital, New York City.

Notice to Property-Holders.

CITY OF NEW YORK, FINANCE DEPARTMENT,
COMPTROLLER'S OFFICE, July 17, 1891.

In pursuance of Section 997 of the "New York City Consolidation Act of 1882," the Comptroller gives notice to all persons, owners of property affected by the following assessment list, viz.:

ACQUIRING TITLE.

127th st, bet Boulevard and Manhattan st.

—which were confirmed by the Supreme Court, July 8, 1891, and entered the 15th of July, 1891, in the Record of Titles and Assessments kept in the "Bureau for the Collection of Assessments and Arrears of Taxes and Assessments, and of Water Rents," that unless the amount assessed for benefit on any person or property shall be paid within sixty days after the date of said entry of the assessment, interest will be collected thereon at the rate of 7 per cent per annum, from July 15. Payments to be made to the Collector of Assessments and Clerk of Arrears, between 9 A. M. and 2 P. M.

Unpaid Water Rates.

Commissioner Gilroy gives notice that, according to law, 5 per cent will be added on August 1st to all unpaid Croton Water Rates.

Street Opening Proceedings.

Notice is given in the matter of the application for opening Manhattan street, from 12th street to the established bulkhead line in the Hudson River, that the bill of costs, etc., will be presented for taxation at the Supreme Court, in Chambers, August 4, 1890, at 10.30 A. M., and that the said bill of costs, etc., has been deposited in the Department of Public Works for ten days from July 22, 1891.

In the matter of opening Intervale avenue, from the Southern Boulevard to Wilkins place, 23d Ward, notice is given that an application will be made, at a Special Term of the Supreme Court, on August 15th, for the appointment of Commissioners of Estimate and Assessment in the matter.

Readers of THE RECORD AND GUIDE *may subscribe to the new illustrated quarterly magazine,* THE ARCHITECTURAL RECORD, *by sending their names and addresses to the office of publication, Nos. 14-16 Vesey street. The annual subscription is* $1.

A Big Improvement.

A solid block of dwelling houses and flats of light buff brick, white terra cotta and Euclid stone on 138th and 139th streets, 7th and 8th avenues, attracts the attention and engages the interest of every passer-by. The improvement is that undertaken by David H. King a couple of months ago, and the work has advanced so rapidly that many of the houses have already been roofed in, and the others are all above the third tier of beams. As matters stand now the houses, both flats and dwellings, will be ready for occupancy in the late fall. The exteriors are plain but handsome, and the block will be a decided addition to the neighborhood. Two entrances on each street and one on each avenue give access to an interior court, which will be used by tradesmen and others for the delivery of goods. As soon as Mr. King has finished his present undertaking he will commence work on a similar block of houses, to be built just north of those he is now engaged on.

These improvements on lots held by the Equitable Life Assurance Society have long been expected, so that the present movement does not come at all as a surprise. Neighboring owners and residents, however, seem to believe that at present a waiting policy is the best one, and consequently, although those in the vicinity of Mr. King's improvements believe that these blocks of houses will be of the greatest benefit to surrounding property, they prefer to wait until the houses are put upon the market and they have a chance to judge of their success before making investments.

This cautious policy is induced by a trouble which is common to many parts of the city at the present time—that of making apartment house property yield a fair return on the investment. One, two, three and even four months free rent is given to families who will engage a flat, the object being to secure a large rent roll on paper and by means of this to dispose of the property. This practice has had the effect of making every buyer mistrustful, and it accounts in some measure for the dullness of the market during the past eight or nine months.

One effect which may, perhaps, be laid to this building activity in the neighborhood of 135th street is the work which has been done by property-owners on that street to have it opened to 10th avenue. The success of 125th street has led them to believe that, with proper facilities, 135th street may be made a very important thoroughfare. Already 135th street has been declared open to Convent avenue, and a petition signed by all the property owners, which will shortly be submitted to the Board of Street Opening and Improvements, asks to have the street opened to Amsterdam or 10th avenue. When this is accomplished it is hoped that the railroad company, the route of whose projected road starts at 129th street and 3d avenue, running through that street to Madison avenue, and up Madison avenue to 135th street, and thence through 135th street to St. Nicholas avenue, will see the wisdom of continuing on through 135th street to 10th avenue, instead of turning up St. Nicholas avenue. As matters stand now, we are assured by a reliable authority, the road will never secure the consent of 135th street property-owners to run through that street, unless the railroad follows 135th street to at least Amsterdam avenue. On the other hand, as soon as the road agrees to do this, the consents of adjoining property-owners are ready for them.

Property-owners in the neighborhood of 131st street and the Boulevard are somewhat agitated over the prospect of having a large gas storage tank located in the immediate vicinity of their holdings. The Standard Gas Co. has already laid a circular concrete floor for the tank on the north side of 131st street, just west of the Boulevard, for the purpose, the company says, of storing gas to be used on the west side. The tank, it is said, will be hermetically sealed and no manufacturing of gas is to be done in the neighborhood. Notwitstanding these reassuring statements by the company, the property-owners and residents fear that the tank will be a menace to the public health, and the attorneys for the Manhattan College, whose building is located close to the site of the proposed tank, have entered into correspondence with the gas company with a view to preventing the completion of the tank.

Personal.

J. Jay Smith moves his offices to-day to Room 31, third floor, No. 171 Broadway.

A Report Denied.

THE MUTUAL LIFE HAS NOT RAISED ITS RATES.

The New York *Herald* stated on Monday that the Mutual Life Insurance Company had held a meeting last week, at which it was decided to raise the rate of interest on mortgages from five to six per cent.

The attention of an officer of the company was called to this important statement, which he denied in the following terms: "There has been no such resolution passed at any meeting of the company. Our mortgages have always varied from five to six per cent., according to the character of the security. We have made absolutely no such change as the *Herald* states."

Law Quesions.

Law Editor RECORD AND GUIDE:

We desire a little information regarding the preper form of seal for a corporation; also the effect of omitting small words in signing the name of a corporation to instruments. With several other old subscribers we are interested to know your decision. J. P. & E. J. MURRAY.

[A corporation can select and use any form or design of seal. The statute permits it to impress the seal on the paper without using any wafer or wax or other substance, and this form is quite generally adopted. It can also, if so desired, use such a form impressed on wax, wafer or other substance affixed to the paper. The omission of a word or letter in the signing of the corporate name will not affect the validity of the instrument subscribed, provided it was the intention to affix the corporate name to the instrument, and the party affixing or subscribing it had power so to do. The same rule will apply in such a case as in the execution of papers by individuals. If a party intend to subscribe his name to an instrument, but make a mistake or leave out a letter in the signing of his name, he is still bound, the signature he subscribed being his signature for that purpose.]

By a New Name.

West Sider.—"Where are you living now?"

North-Sider.—"Up on the North Side."

W. S.—"North Side! Where do you mean—in Chicago?"

N. S.—"Not at all. I mean the North Side of New York—the biggest part of the city outdoors."

W. S.—"Where is the North Side, and where in it do you live?"

N. S.—"The North Side is all that part of the city above the Harlem River; formerly known by several ridiculous titles—the 'annexed district,' the '23d and 24th Wards,' the 'trans-Harlem district,' 'neber der Rhein,' and several village appellations. But we are a large and thriving part of New York city now, and have taken the North Side for a descriptive title in contradistinction to the East and West Sides. 'It is easier spoken and written, takes up less space on paper, and is more descriptive of our identity as a part of the city. I live in Bedford Park, on the North Side, and am nearly as accessible from the *Times* building as I would be in Riverside Park, on the West Side, or in East River Park, on the East Side."

A Point in Title Insurance.

A point of some interest to property-owners was settled in the Philadelphia Court of Common Pleas recently in the case of Ganler *vs.* The Solicitors' Loan and Trust Co.

The circumstances were as follows: The plaintiff purchased a yearly ground rent issuing out of a lot numbered 618 Lombard street, and the defendant insured his title. The deed, however, conveyed a ground rent issuing out of 614 Lombard street.

The plaintiff made sale of his ground rent as issuing out of No. 618 Lombard street, but his title was rejected by counsel. He brought suit against the Title Company, who interposed the defense that as the conveyancing was done by the plaintiff's conveyancer the insurance company was not liable.

Judge Arnold, in deciding the case, said:

"This defense is based on the motion that not only may title insurance companies do conveyancing, but that they must be employed to do it in order to hold them on their policies. This is a great mistake. They have no right whatever to do conveyancing, draw deeds, write wills, or the like. * * * The argument that unless they are permitted to draw deeds and convey titles they will have none to insure, is as specious as would be an argument that a fire insurance company should be allowed to make contracts to build houses in order to insure them. * * * If the defendant had made a proper examination of the title and required a certificate of no defense from the tenant of No. 618 this loss would not have happened. As it is the loss was caused by its own neglect."

Real Estate Department.

There has been a sort of midsummer spurt in the real estate market this week as unaccountable as it was unexpected. Several of the large transactions which are just consummated represent several months' previous work, and it is doubtful if any of the negotiations which terminated in important sales were commenced within the month. The increase of news therefore must not be taken as an indication of a revival of activity; it has no such significance. If it means anything, it is that the season's work is being cleared up, and that for a month or so there will be very little doing. Many, if not the majority, of the real estate fraternity will spend that month out of town, and they will come back to town refreshed and invigorated for the large fall business which many are expecting, and apparently every one predicting. The general condition of things is unaltered. Prices generally are firm, moving neither up or down, although in parts of the city there are signs of weakness which may or may not be significant. Money does not seem to be quite as easy as it has been, but there are no signs of stringency, and so no cause for alarm.

THE AUCTION SALES OF THE WEEK.

In the Auction Room sixteen sales have been held during the week, and every one of these has been by order of the courts in either partition or foreclosure suits. These sales present little of particular or general interest. The southeast corner of 5th avenue and 29th street, sold in partition by Auctioneer Richard V. Harnett, furnished none of the interesting features that were anticipated, although it brought a good price. There was an upset price on the property of $165,000, and this figure was the first bid. A rather indifferent competition ensued until $178,200 was reached, when Philip L. Runkle, a party in interest, became the purchaser. The property, which is a five-story building on lot 24.9x100, rents for $7,000 per annum, and a 3-10 interest in it was purchased in December of last year by Philip L. Runkle, Sr., for $48,000; assuming that the rest of the building was held at the same figures proportionately, then the price would have been $160,000. Another partition sale, that of No. 2191 3d avenue. showed a rise in values that was highly satisfactory. There is a frontage on the avenue of 31 feet by an irregular depth of 125. The property was sold on Wednesday by Auctioneer John F. B. Smyth for $60,400. It was transferred last, May, 1884, for $25,000. The remaining sales were quite ordinary in character.

THE ANNOUNCEMENTS.

Each week the list of offerings becomes smaller and next week the announcements, almost entirely of a legal character, are even fewer in number than those of the week just passed. Among these legal sales there is practically nothing that will attract or interest real estate men generally, so that the Exchange is likely to be a very dull place for some time to come. The suburban business, like city real estate, becomes quieter each week, and if there is any substantial revival it will not show itself for a month or more.

CONVEYANCES.

	1890. July 18 to 24 inc.	1891. July 17 to 23 inc.
Number	308	146
Amount involved	$3.686.412	$2,203,543
Number nominal	49	49
Number 23d and 24th Wards	74	49
Amount involved	$256,145	$176,721
Number nominal	12	10

MORTGAGES.

	1890.	1891.
Number	258	221
Amount involved	$3,194,830	$3,034,712
Number at 5 % or less	140	103
Amount involved	$1,021,501	$1,759,596
Number at less than 5 per cent	14	12
Amount involved	$622,250	$167,200
Number to Banks, Trust and Ins. Cos	25	21
Amount involved	$955,000	$1,227,500

PROJECTED BUILDINGS.

	1890. July 19 to 25 inc.	1891. July 18 to 24 inc
Number of buildings	99	33
Estimated cost	$1,668,025	$606,525

Gossip of the Week.

SOUTH OF 59TH STREET.

Geo. R. Read and Richard V. Harnett & Co. have sold for the estate of Charles H. Marshall No. 40 East 14th street, running through to and forming an L with No. 79 University place, for a sum in the neighborhood of $250,000. The plot contains 4.368 square feet and it is covered by a five-story building, which is leased for a period of ten years, the rental for the first five years being $16,500 per annum, and for the second term of five years $18.000 per annum. It was reported that the Astors were the purchasers, but this rumor could not be confirmed. This property, it may be remembered, was offered at auction in the early part of last June, and subsequently withdrawn at a bid of $247,000.

Dr. Edward L. Keyes, who has this week purchased James McCreery's house on 5th avenue, has sold his old dwelling, No. 1 Park avenue, northeast corner of 34th street, for about $100,000. The house is a four-story dwelling. on lot 25x80 feet.

Amos R. Eno has sold the plot, 50x100, Nos. 101 and 103 Wooster street, on the West Side, between Spring and Prince streets, for $57,000; three-story old buildings at present cover these lots, but these will probably be torn down and an improved warehouse erected in their stead. The name of the purchaser could not be ascertained.

L. J. Adams has sold a plot, 50x159, on Greenwich street, running through to Washington street, rear Charlton street, for $60,000 for improvement.

Mrs. Captain J. P. Levy has sold No. 118 West 3d street, a five-story building, on lot 25x100, for $32,000.

Ascher Weinstein has sold to John McSweeney for improvement the two three-story buildings, on plot 50x92, Nos. 313 and 315 West 17th street, for $35,000.

D. Kempner & Son have sold for the Brodeck estate the five-story double apartment house, 25x72x100, No. 307 West 39th street, for $25,000 to a Mr. Mitchell.

NORTH OF 59TH STREET.

It is reported on very good authority that the Vyse estate, containing seventy-five acres on the Southern Boulevard, at 167th street, in the 23d Ward, has been sold by the Ninth National Bank for $525,000 to a wealthy syndicate who will commence at once to improve the same by opening up streets and regulating and grading the same. The property will be ready by the fall and will be sold at auction. We learn that Miss Agnes K. Murphy was the only broker connected with the sale.

Chas. A. Seymour & Co. have sold for Jas. McCreery the four-story dwelling, on the northeast corner of 5th avenue and 74th street, to Dr. E. L. Keyes for $150,000.

Bellamy & Winans have sold for J. A. Bostwick No. 802 5th avenue, a five-story stone front dwelling, 20.5x100, for $140,000. The purchaser is said to be Mrs. Marshall Allen. The same brokers have sold for Dr. Franklin E. Robinson to a Miss Hough No. 303 West 72d street, a four-story dwelling, on lot about 21x100, for $60,000.

Hugh Stevenson, the lawyer, has made a trade with McCloud & Mahoney whereby he transfers to the latter the northeast corner of Riverside Drive and 83d street, 57.4x100, for about $50,000, and receives in exchange the forty-six lots on Edgecombe and 10th avenues, at the intersection of 160th street, for a consideration of $137,500.

John B. Hibbard has sold for James Duffy to George Bernhard & Son Nos. 204 and 206 East 102d street, a plot 35x100, with a four-story brick factory and stable thereon, for $29,000.

It is reported that John Hickey has sold No. 10 East 111th street, a five-story brown stone single flat, for $17,250.

Morris B. Baer & Co. have sold for E. D. Pohalski, No. 29 East 73d street, a four-story brown stone dwelling, 15x60x80, for $23,000.

Jesse C. Bennett has sold for the Misses Beekman to Mrs. B. P. Flanagan No. 217 West 78th street, a three-story brown stone dwelling, 20x55x100, on private terms. Mr. Bennett sold this house to the late owners about thirty days ago, and the sale this week, it is said, was made at a profit on that investment.

It is reported that Herman Wronkow has purchased Nos. 257 to 261 West 128th street, two five-story double flats and one five-story single flat, on private terms.

Ames & Co. have sold for Robt. J. McGirr the five-story brown stone and brick double flat, No. 188 West 101st street, size 25x85x100.11, to Edward Karsch for $24,000.

W. B. Taylor & Sons have sold for Dr. A. W. Lozier the four-story Euclid stone front house, No. 158 West 78th street, size 20x55x butler's pantry extension, 10x12x102.2, on private terms; for the same owner, the four-story brown stone house, No. 168 West 78th street, size 20x55x butler's pantry extension, 10x12x102.2, on private terms; and for Mrs. Slasen the three-story house, size 16.8x55x99.11, No. 313 West 136th street, for $15,250.

Goodman & Stern have sold for Jacob Schlosser to Wm. Fritzel the four houses, Nos. 431-437 East 79th street, for $66,500; and for Wm. Fritzel to Mr. Schlosser the house No. 413 East 81st street, for $21,500.

Ascher Weinstein has sold to M. S. Kauffman and others the four-story brown stone dwelling, 17.4x45x60, No. 1055 Lexington avenue, southeast corner of 75th street, on private terms.

Brooklyn

J. P. Sloane has sold for Timothy Brennan the two-story and basement frame dwelling, 25x33x100, No. 193 Huron street, to Claus Dunkhase for $2,875.

J. R. Cruikshank has sold for H. G. Baker to P. Hemmer the two four-story brick apartment houses on Hopkinson avenue, between Herkimer street and Atlantic avenue, 56x97.6, for $20,000.

Corwith Bros. have sold for Eliza Duke the two-story and cellar frame dwelling, 21x30x100, No. 83 Oakland street, to John McCort, for $3.175.

CONVEYANCES.

	1890. July 17 to 23 inc	1891. July 16 to 22 inc
Number	365	325
Amount involved	$1,406,796	$1,106,913
Number nominal	77	74

MORTGAGES.

	1890.	1891.
Number	275	328
Amount involved	$1,014,076	$1,109,795
Number at 5 per cent. or less	155	167
Amount involved	$662,942	$640,348

PROJECTED BUILDINGS.

	1890. July 18 to 24 inc.	1891. July 17 to 23 inc.
Number of buildings	64	88
Estimated cost	$336,050	$424,850

Out of Town.

LOWERRE, YONKERS, N. Y.—Charles Henry Butler, of Holt & Butler, has sold to a syndicate composed of Richard V. Harnett, Juben T. Davies, Marcellus Hartley and Wm. Allen Butler, Jr., the remaining 100 lots of the plot which the Holt & Butler syndicate purchased and developed last year. The majority of the lots were disposed of at auction last July and October, many of the purchasers being employes of the elevated roads. Already the purchasers have commenced to build, and about twenty-five improvements are now under way. The City of Yonkers, too, is laying sewers and grading and curbing streets through the property.

FREEPORT, L. I.—J. P. Sloane has sold for Elbert Cox a tract of land comprising eighteen acres for $3,500.

ERASTINA, S. I.—George F. Edwards has sold for H. G. and H. M. Sequine one lot, unimproved, for $500 to Mary Frawley.

Out Among the Builders.

The old Merchant's Hotel, at No. 41 Cortlandt street, is being torn down to make way for an eleven-story office building to be erected by J. Monroe Taylor.

Charles C. Haight has completed plans for a four-story stone residence to be built for Henry O. Havermeyer on the east side of 5th avenue, 50 feet north of 66th street. The house will be 25x70 with extension, and completed with every appointment for modern luxury and comfort.

John Hauser is the architect for four five-story brick and brown stone flats and stores, 25x77, to be built on the north side of 88th street, 175 feet east of Avenue A, at a cost of $70,000. John Schreiner, Jr., owner.

G. A. Schellenger has plans on the boards for a six-story and basement brick and stone warehouse to be built on the west side of Greenwich street, 25 feet north of Franklin. The building will be 25x90, completed with all modern improvements and is to cost $40,000. Mrs. Amalie Coon is the owner.

Some of the largest building operations going on at this season are alterations and improvements of buildings for residence and business purposes.

Plans have been prepared by Thayer & Robinson for extensive changes to be made in the two 20-foot houses at Nos. 19 and 21 East 54th street, converting them into one dwelling, for Gen'l John Watts Kearney. The only changes to be made in the front consist of making a window of one entrance and building a new stoop and steps at the other. The interior of both houses will be thoroughly remodeled throughout. The plumbing, decorating and woodwork will be entirely new and of the finest description. The houses will be extended at the rear first by a 9-foot extension, same height and size as the old buildings, to which will be added a three-story brick and stone extension, 17 feet square. The cost has not been estimated, but no expense will be spared to make of these two houses a model dwelling of first-class description.

Andrew Spence has plans on the boards for a two-story and cellar brick stable to be built by August F. Schwarzgler on the northwest corner of Pleasant avenue and 120th street. The size will be 74x125 and the cost $30,000.

John McSweeney will build two five-story flats, on plot 50x92, at Nos. 313 and 315 West 17th street. The flats will accommodate two families on a floor and will have all improvements.

Richard R. Davis will furnish the plans for two five-story brick and brown stone flats, 25x82, to be built by Elizabeth K. Smith on the south side of 123d street, 200 feet west of 7th avenue, at a cost of $44,000.

Brooklyn.

A seven-story building, from plans by Carl F. Eisenach, is to be erected on the northwest corner of Fulton and Jay streets, for J. Rothschild, the milliner. The estimated cost is $200,000, the material brick and stone, and the style Romanesque. The land which it will occupy has 112 feet on Fulton street and 130 feet on Jay street.

The negotiations for the purchase by the Brooklyh Savings Bank of the property of the First Baptist Church, Clinton and Pierrepont streets, have been completed. The bank pays $200,000 for it. It intends to erect a very handsome building on the site. The church people will move up town.

Flatbush avenue promises to receive new character now that two of the leading establisments in the city, Journeay & Burnham and Ovington Bros. are to move up there. It is said that property values are already in the ascendancy. The former firm will have built for them a four-story brick structure, suitable for dry-goods. It will cost $200,000. The Ovington Bros., who are dealers in china and fragile articles, will rent the store adjoining, which was finished recently.

John C. Burne will furnish plans for five three-story and basement brown stone dwellings to be built on the south eastcorner of Carroll street and Fiske place, by Wm. Irvine, at a cost of $80,000. They will be each 20x52 in size with extensions of 14x18 feet.

William Grant has drawn plans for two five-story tenements, 20x85 each, for Mrs. Emilie Talbot and Mrs. Mary L. Bishop. The sites are Nos. 1624 and 1628 1st avenue.

Out of Town.

BAY RIDGE, L. I.—S. B. Reed is the architect for a two-story frame dwelling, 30x41, to be built here for Mme. E. Ravin d'Elpeux at a cost of $3,000.

BEDFORD PARK, N. Y.—J. F. Klein has commissioned S. B. Reed to draw plans for a two-story and attic frame dwelling with tower. It is to be 26x30, with shingle exterior, and will cost $4,000.

BRIDGEFIELD, N. J.—A part of the De Groot property is about to be improved by the erection of a station for the Northern Railroad Company of New Jersey, and twelve or more two-and-one-half-story frame cottages, which will contain eight to twelve rooms and are to average in size about 20x32 and 38. This property has a frontage on Overspeck creek, and among the features of improvement under consideration are a dock and factory on the water front. D. T. Atwood is the architect.

CARLTON HILL, N. J.—Ward & McKenzie will build a one-story and basement brick and stone warehouse, 50x100, of fire-proof construction, from plans drawn by S. B. Reed. The building will cost $10,000.

CHARLOTTESVILLE, VA.—Jefferson M. Levy, the owner of the Thomas Jefferson place, "Monticello," near this town, will build in the grounds a marble stairway and balustrade connecting two terraces. Plans have been drawn by Charles H. Israels, and the estimated cost is about $4,000.

CORONA, L. I.—Frank Wickham, M. D., will build a two-story frame building, to be used as a dwelling and store. It will be 20x40 in size and cost $3,500. S. B. Reed has drawn the plans.

CEDARHURST, L. I.—A two-and-one-half-story frame dwelling, 30x60, to cost $9,500, is to be built here for G. H. Adams, from plans by Sibell and Miller.

DUNDEE, N. J.—A frame church, 45x80, with tower 75 feet high, is to be built here for the Presbyterian congregation, and for which S. B. Reed will draw plans. The building will be finished with slate roof, stained glass windows and shingle finished exterior at a cost of $8,000.

FLUSHING, L. I.—J. J. Wright will build a two-story frame dwelling, 26x40, to cost $4,500, from plans by S. B. Reed.

FOREST HILL, N. J.—Sibell & Miller have drawn plans for a three-story stone and frame house to be built for E. G. Heller. It will be 48x55 in size, finished with slate and tile roof and the frame portion of exterior of shingles. The interior will be done in oak, white and gold and natural cherry. The estimates place the cost at $20,000.

LAWRENCE, L. I.—Supt. William Murray has ordered plans from Sibell & Miller for a two-story and attic frame dwelling, 65x70, shingle finished in part, to cost $13,000.

MADISON, N. J.—Stanley S. Covert has drawn plans for a two-story and attic frame dwelling, 40x60, the exterior of which will be shingle-finished in part, and the interior done in hard woods. J. W. McGraw is the owner, and the cost will be $11,000. The same architect has completed plans for another two-story and attic frame dwelling, 35x48, to be built here at a cost of $9,000 for C. E. Whittlesey.

NEWBURGH, N. Y.—S. B. Reed has completed plans for a two-and-a-half-story brick dwelling to be built here for Judge M. H. Hirschberg. The house will be 42x60 in size, with slate roof, cabinet trim, parquet floors and all modern improvements. The cost is placed at $15,000.

PASSAIC, N. J.—A. F. Rice will build a two-story and attic frame dwelling, 38x52, a portion of exterior to be shingle finished, and to cost $7,000, from plans by Stanley S. Covert, who is the architect for a similar house, 38x41, to be built for T. M. Moore at a cost of $9,000.

RIDGEWOOD, N. J.—A two-story and attic frame dwelling, 40x55, shingle finished exterior, and a two-story frame stable, 23x40, will be built here at a cost of $8,000 for F. H. White, from plans by S. B. Reed.

ROSE BANK, S. I.—Mrs. E. Dunshee has ordered a $3,000 frame cottage, to be 22x35 in size and two stories high, with attic. S. B. Reed is the architect.

ROSELLE, N. J.—William Howe has plans under way for a two-story and attic frame dwelling, 32x43, with slate roof, to be built here for J. H. Childer, at a cost of $5,000.

WOODLAWN HEIGHTS, N. Y.—A frame dwelling and stable are to be erected here for Mrs. I. L. Senior, from plans by S. B. Reed. The house will be two stories and attic, 28x45, while the stable, also two stories in height, will be 20x28. The estimated cost is $4,500, and J. B. Roberts is the builder.

WOODSIDE, N. J.—H. B. Hills will build, from plans by Sibell and Miller, a two-story and attic frame dwelling, 22x40, to cost $4,000.

A number of Brooklyn citizens have formed a taxpayers' league for the regulating of assessments and other reforms relating to the problem of taxation. They think that the Legislature should pass a bill to permit Counties of the State to collect taxes from different classes of property.

WANTS AND OFFERS.

(Advertisements strictly in accordance with this title will be inserted at the practically nominal rate of 10 CENTS *per line (agate). In figuring for themselves advertisers may count seven words for each line, the address to be taken as one line. The object of this department is to bring buyers and sellers into communication with customers. Advertisements must be marked "Wants and Offers Column," and sent to the office of publication, Nos. 14 and 16 Vesey Street, not later than 3 P. M. Friday.)*

OFFERS.

Vacant Lots.

100TH ST., between 2d and 3d avs; ten lots, cheap; all mortgage if improved.
July11-1aw8w. EDWIN A. ELY, 103 Gold st.

40 CHERRY ST., between Roosevelt and Franklin sq., 32x64, vacant; $12,000; accommodating terms. EDWIN A. ELY, 103 Gold st.
July11-1aw8w.

Brooklyn Real Estate for Sale.

FOR SALE.—A fine three-story brown stone house; all improvements; 13 rooms; Pacific st., near Flatbush av.; a bargain if sold at once. S. H. NEWBY, room E, Cotton Exchange Building, New York.

DESIRABLE INVESTMENT.—Eight-story apartment house; best location in Brooklyn; might exchange equity over $125,000 at 4½ per cent.
J. 20—uf. Apply 60 Broadway, Room 311.

LARGE FACTORY for sale; price, $28,000; the land itself supposed to be worth the money.
Apr 4-uf FIRST NATIONAL BANK, Brooklyn, N. Y.

OFFERS.

FLATS, 93 Concord st., Brooklyn, near the Bridge; five-story double flat property, in perfect order and always rented for $2,300 per year, paying easily 15 per cent per annum on investment; terms easy. Apply to owner.
R. J. KELLEY, 377 Broadway, New York.

16½ PER CENT.—Best I can do on investment of $15,000 in plate glass store property on leading business thoroughfare of 17th Ward of Brooklyn; the plot is 140x95; consists of seven two-story buildings; rents for $4,592 per annum, and mortgage of $27,500 can remain for long term. Examine this gilt edge investment. J. P. SLOANE,
July 11—1aw4w. 343 Manhattan av., Brooklyn.

Country Property.

FREE AND CLEAR COUNTRY PROPERTY or business for city; also city for country.
WHITING, 45 Broadway.

AT MONTCLAIR, N. J.—200 acres for cutting into lots; railroad station on property; number of acres to suit purchaser. DA CUNHA, Montclair.
J. 27-1aw5w.

OFFERS.

A DESIRABLE COTTAGE PROPERTY.—Large house and stable; over 1¾ acres land; finest location at West End, Long Branch, N. J.; all city conveniences; valued at $35,000; will exchange for lots in 23d or 24th Ward, or acreage property in Westchester, on cash basis. Apply to
T. D. O'CONNOR, 16 Exchange pl., New York.

Miscellaneous.

TO LET FOR BUSINESS PURPOSES.—Corner store, 81st st. and (10th) Amsterdam av.; also, adjoining avenue stores; part of store, desk room for architect, surveyor, insurance; in real estate office of L. FROEHLICH, 447 Amsterdam av., near 81st st.

A PARTY ABOUT TO BUILD A FIVE-STORY factory, 50x98, in Harlem, near water-front, will lease the three upper floors and build to suit tenant. Terms very moderate. Address
May 16 u. f. OWNER, 409 E. 107th St.

FIVE YEAR LEASEHOLD on lower Broadway for sale; will renew for 20, 40 or 60 years to party who will build. GRANITE, 318 World, uptown.
July 25—1aw3w.

SALES OF THE WEEK.

The following are the sales at the Real Estate Exchange and Auction Room for the week ending July 24.

** Indicates that the property described has been bid in for plaintiff's account:*

R. V. HARNETT & CO.

*73d st, Nos. 177–181, n s, 28 e 10th av, 54x76.8, three four-story brk and stone dwell'gs. First Nat'l Bank of Sing Sing. (Amt due $43,983)........ $79,500

*Amsterdam av, No. 585, e s, 53.10 n 88th st, 28.4x100, five-story brk flat with stores. N. Y. Life Ins. Co. (Amt due $22,400)........ 28,200

Lenox av, No. 470, e s, 79.11 n 133d st, 20x84, five-story brk store and flat. Wm. McElroy. (Amt due $18,852)........ 18,900

West End av, No. 519, s w cor 90th st, 24x90, four-story brk dwell'g. Eugene Mehler. (Amt due $33,152)........ 37,900

5th av, No. 263, s e cor 29th st, 24.9x100, five-story brk store. Philip L. Runkle........ 178,200

SMYTH & RYAN.

11th st, No. 323, n s, 163 w Greenwich st, 25x95, three-story brk tenem't with three-story brk tenem't on rear, leasehold. Wm. Deans........ 4,100

WM. KENNELLY.

*59th st, No. 547, n s, 200 e 11th av, 25x100....
59th st, Nos. 535 and 537, n s, 325 e 11th av, 50 x100....
Three four-story brk tenem'ts with stores.
Edith H. Simmons. (Amt due $3,428; prior morts. $35,000)........ 39,930

*96th st, No. 58, s s, 200 e 9th av, 20x100.8, four-story brk dwell'g. Wm. Rankin. (Amt due $5,614; prior morts. $20,000)........ 23,250

Bailey av, w s, known as plot 103 map of land at Kingsbridge, belonging to Wm. O. Giles, 50x131.2x50x128.5. Chas. J. Silleck. (Amt due $2,234)........ 2,335

Lenox av, Nos. 467–471, w s, 25 s 134th st, 99.10x 100, three five-story brk flats with stores. Wm. Livingston........ 135,000

J. P. & SMYTH.

126th st, No. 263, n s, 145 e 8th av, 20x99.11, two-story brk dwell'g. Jos. Dierhoff........ 8,800

3d av, No. 2191, e s, 95 s 120th st, runs east 90 x north 20 x east 10 x south 25 x east 25 x south 26 x west 125 to 3d av, x north 31 to beginning, four-story brk store. Richard Weber........ 60,400

B. L. KENNELLY.

*122d st, No. 421, n s, 254.7 e 1st av, 16.8x100.11, three-story stone front dwell'g. (Amt due $6,001.) Ann E. Morris........ 7,000

Total........ $618,515
Corresponding week, 1890........ $550,800

BROOKLYN, N. Y.

FOR WEEK ENDING JULY 23.

T. A. KERRIGAN.

*Bergen st, No. 623, n s, 200 w Vanderbilt av, 24.8x110, two-story brk mill. Kings Co. Co-operative Building Assoc........ $4,000

Franklin st, No. 130, e s, 75 s Milton st, 25x70, two-story frame dwell'g. Christian Fedder. 4,130

*Lefferts pl, Nos. 124 and 126, s s, 132.10 w Clason av, 40x138, three-story frame dwell'g on plot. Joseph Schuetter........ 9,000

President st, s s, 383.4 w Columbia st, 16.8x 100, three-story brk tenem't James Usher.. 775

*Kingsland av, No. 105, w s, 125 s Herbert st, 25x100, two-story frame dwell'g. George W. Sammis........ 1,500

*St. Marks av, No. 279, n s, 150 w Underhill av, 25x131, four-story brk tenem't. William J. Hart........ 7,800

*St. Marks av, No. 281, n s, 125 w Underhill av, 25x131, four-story brk tenem't. Same........ 8,000

6th av, No. 592, n w s, 41.4 n Prospect av, 18x80, four-story frame tenem't and store. A. H. Henriques........ 4,321

Lot in 26th Ward, begins at intersection of w s of The Road leading to the Mill and south line of lands of Jacob L. Van Wicklen, runs northwest 921.3 to centre of a brook, x along curves of same —, x northeast 89 x southeast 46.10 x — to road, x northwest 385.10, contains 14 59-100 acres; partition. H. W. Rozell........ 9,475

TAYLOR & FOX.

*Putnam av, Nos. 1183 and 1185, n s, 90 w Evergreen av, 40x100, two three-story frame tenem'ts. Geo. F. Chapman. (All right, title and interest)........ 400

Total........ $49,404
Corresponding week 1890........ $60,170

CONVEYANCES.

Wherever the letters Q. C., C. a. G. and B. & S occur, preceded by the name of the grantee they mean as follows:

1st—Q. C. is an abbreviation for Quit Claim deed, i. e., a deed in which all the right, title and interest of the grantor is conveyed, omitting all covenants or warranty.

2d—C. a. G. means a deed containing Covenant against Grantor only, in which he covenants that he hath not done any act whereby the estate conveyed may be impeached, charged or encumbered.

3d—B. & S. is an abbreviation for Bargain and Sale deed, wherein, although the seller makes no express covenants, he really grants or conveys the property for a valuable consideration, and thus impliedly claims to be the owner of it.

NEW YORK CITY.

JULY 17, 18, 20, 21, 22, 23.

Broadway, No. 1272 } begins Broadway, e s,
33d st, No. 60 } 68.3 s 33d st, 23.3x65.10 x north 75.6 to 33d st, x west 22.3 x south 60 x west 51.3 to beginning, three-story brk store on Broadway with four-story brk building with store on 33d st. John Downey to Mary E. Hanley. July 15. nom

Broadway, No. 402, e s, 30 n Walker st, runs south 25 x east 100 x south 19 x west 10 x south 6 x west 90, five-story stone front store. Peter Lorillard and Emily T. his wife to Mary L. Barbey. C. a. G. June 26. nom

Same property. Sherman Evarts ref. to Mary L. Barbey. June 25. $100,000

Same property. Release dower. Louis L. and Katherine B. Lorillard to same. July 8. nom

Broome st, No. 86, n s, 25 w Columbia st, 25x 85.10, four-story brk store and tenem't with one-story brk building on rear. Jacob Mauheim to Mayer Lewin. *Mt.* $14,375. July 21. 17,930

Central Park West (8th av), Nos. 426–430, s w cor 103d st, 100.11x100, three five-story brk flats. Joseph O'Connor and Annie G. his wife, Newark, N. J., to James Stevenson, Boston, Mass. *Mt.* $120,000. April 14. nom

Clinton pl, No. 90, being West 8th st, s s, 72.10 e Macdougal st, 24.3x100 to alleyway, x24.3x 100, with right to alley, three-story brk dwell'g. Mayer Kahn and Henrietta his wife to Thomas D. Day, Jr. June 22. nom

Delancey st, No. 33, s s, 20 w Forsyth st, 20.3x 75, three-story brk store and tenem't. Augusta wife of Adolph Heinrich, of Neustadt, Germany, to Mary Herr, Huntington, Pa., all heirs of George Zahn. ½ part. Sub. to ½ morts. for $7,000. May 6. nom

Same property. Mary Herr, Huntington, Pa., to Michael Englert. *Mt.* $7,000. May 21. 14,000

Division st, No. 44, n w cor Chrystie st, 26.4x 48.4x24.8x36.5, four-story brk store and tenement. Peter Lorillard and Emily T. his wife to Aaron Herzberg. C. a. G. July 8. nom

Same property. Sherman Evarts ref. to same June 25. 19,000

Same property. Mary L. Barbey to same. C. a. G. July 8. nom

Same property. Release dower. Louis L. and Katherine B. Lorillard to same. July 8. nom

Front st, No. 27, s s, abt 48 e Broad st, 28.5x 65.4x28.4x74.6, also 7 ft. sq. on n e cor of lot on which stands No. 117 Broad st and adj s e cor of above.
Broad st, Nos. 113 and 115, s e cor Front st, 62.7x47x65.4x48.
Three four-story brk stores.
Lewis A. Mitchell to Jefferson M. Levy. Sub. to morts. April 24. nom

Grand st, No. 184–186. Agreement as to beam rights. Annie W. Van Rensselaer to Leon M. Hirsh. June 27. 2,500

Greene st, Nos. 204 and 206, e s, 100 s 3d st, 50x 100, five-story brk stores. Partition. James Flynn to Louis Schultz. July 17. 147,500

Greenwich st, No. 791, e s, abt 93.10 s 12th st, runs east 66.5 x north 30 x west 11 x north 4.5 x west 55.5 to Greenwich st, x south 34.6, four-story brk tenem't. Du Bois Smith and Fannie E. his wife, Smithtown, L. I., to Anton Tittels. *Mt.* $18,000. July 15. 26,500

Gay st, No. 17, e s, 147.10 n Waverley pl, 19x65, three-story brk dwell'g. Foreclos. Wilbur Larremore to Eleanor Mulvany. July 22. 3,035

Horatio st, No. 66, s e cor Greenwich st, 18.8x 50, four-story brk store and tenem't. Jessie Williams widow to Benjamin F. Elgar. *Mt.* $6,000. July 16. 16,125

Jackson st, Nos. 3 and 5, w s, 35 s Henry st, 50 x100, two five-story brk tenem'ts with stores. Richard D. Jewett and Elisa M. his wife, Nyack, N. Y., and Sarah Jewett heirs Elizabeth H. Jewett to John Judd. ½ part. B. & S. and confirmation deed. July 7. nom

Leroy st, No. 107, n s, 80 w Hudson st, 20x75, two-story brk dwell'g. Mary A. Newcomb to John S. Lyle, Tenafly, N. J. *Mt.* $7,500. July 22. 3,500

Monroe st, Nos. 19–23, n s, abt 280 e Catharine st, three five-story brk tenem'ts and stores.
Contract to exchange for
Stanton st, No. 326, n s, abt 32 e Goerck st, 28x70, five-story brk tenem't and store, and $79,000.
Joseph Wittner to S. Jones. July 20. nom

Oak st, No. 37, s s, 60 e James st, 17x50.9x17 x51.4, three-story brk tenem't with stores. Charles Upthur to Catharine Upthur his wife. Q. C. All joint rights. July 17. nom

Sheriff st, No. 35, w s, abt 130 e Delancey st, 21.10x100, three-story brk tenem't and six-story brk building on rear. Israel M. Cohen and Harriet his wife to Karl M. Wallach. *Mt.* $17,500. July 15. 22,500

Same property. Karl M. Wallach to Sam Halpern and Amale his wife. *Mt.* $15,000. July 15. 22,125

Sheriff st, No. 35, w s, 21.10x100. Sam Halpern to Amali Halpern. *Mt.* $20,125. July 20. nom

Spring st, Nos. 170–174, s s, 62 e Thompson st, 63.8x66.6x63.6x64.4, three three-story brk stores and tenem'ts. Henrietta A. Colt widow and Sarah A. Colt to Richard Hennessy. 1-9 part. July 15. 4,722

Same property. Sarah W. Sheppard to same. ⅙ part July 20. 14,667

Same property. William P. Colt and Abigail his wife, Stockton, Col., to same. All title. June 10. 2,500

Same property. Mary C. and Olcott C. Colt by George W. Morton guard. to same. Infant's share. July 15. 9,444

Same property. Sarah A. Colt widow, Samuel S. Colt and Ida M. his wife, Thomas C. Colt and Maud M. his wife, Mary S. Colt and Edward Geach, Orange, N. J., children of Thomas A. Colt dec'd to same. 4-5 part. July 14. 11,667

Stanton st, Nos. 101 and 103, s w cor Ludlow st, 42.6x50, two six-story brk stores and tenem'ts. Kassel Oshinsky and Esther his wife, Chicago, Ill., to Louis Rubenstein. *Mt.* $30,000. July 14. 47,000

Willett st, No. 121, w s, 193.5 n Stanton st, 18.9 x75, four-story brk store and tenem't. Louis Cohen to Amalie Cohn. All liens. July 21. nom

4th st, No. 161 W., n e s, abt 86.1 n w of 6th av, 20x45.4 and 60.6 x southeast 7.6 x southwest abt 54 x southeast abt 4.10 x southwest 19.5 x southwest 40, four-story brk tenem't with stores. Foreclos. Jefferson M. Levy to Isaac Mannheimer. *Mt.* $8,000. July 16. 12,000

5th st, No. 625, n s, 293 e Av B, 21.5x97, four-story brk tenem't with stores. Jacob S. and Columbus B. Rogers trustees Theodore Rogers to Theodore B. Rogers. B. & S. Feb. 19. 10,000

10th st, No. 54, s s, 235.11 e 6th av, 21.6x91.9. *Mt.* $5,000.
10th st, No. 52, s s, 257.5 e 6th av, 21.6x92.3 *Mt.* $7,500.
No 52, two-story frame and brk dwell'g; No. 54, three-story brk dwell'g.
Frederick Geller to William Evens and Alice his wife. C. a. G. July 17. nom

Same property. William Evens and Alice his wife to Frederick Geller. C. a. G. Sub. to same morts. July 17. nom

West 11th st or old Hammond st, No. 127. Jane Westervelt, Hackensack, N. J., to Sophia wife of John W. Banta. Made in pursuance of a partition. Nov. 13, 1850. 2,000

West 11th st, late Hammond st, No. 127, n s, adj land of Andrew Van Buskirk, 22.9x20x23x15. Isaac Haring and Mary his wife to Abraham A. Campbell. May 2, 1827. 125

11th st, No. 337, n s, 266.6 w Greenwich st, 22.6 x62.2x22.9x—, three-story brk tenem't. Rachael Durie and Henry J. Banta and

Sarah his wife, Englewood, N. J., to Josephine L. Peyton. July 18. 8,000

12th st, Nos. 205 to 213, n e s, 385 n w 2d av, 125 x103.3, five-story brk factory. Trow's Printing & Bookbinding Co., a corporation of New York, to Trow's Printing & Bookbinding Co., a corporation of New Jersey. *Mt.* $80,000. July 21. nom

14th st, No. 314, s s, 200 w 8th av, 25x103.1x 25.6x98, four-story brk dwell'g. Rachel L. Epstein to Florence Pohalski. C. a. G. ½ part. July 17. nom

16th st, No 137 E. Agreement as to building of extension. Emma A. Marson to John P. Schmenger. July 20. 1,250

16th st, No. 413, n s, 150.3 w 9th av, 25x92, three-story frame building with two two-story frame buildings on rear. Elihu Ayres to Patrick H. Quirk. July 17. 10,500

18th st, No. 428, s s, 313.6 w 9th av, 20.5x92, three-story brk dwell'g. Margaret Wilson, John Wilson and Marion G. his wife and William Wilson to Theodore A. L. Davis. July 20. 7,333

Same property. James Thompson trustee John Wilson dec'd to same. ½ part. July 20. 3,667

Same property. William Ives exr. and trustee John Wilson at request of John and William Wilson to Margaret Wilson. July 20. nom

20th st, Nos. 414 and 416, s s, 199.6 e 1st av, 40 x92, two four-story brk tenem'ts with store in No. 414. Daniel Lonergan and Margaret M. his wife to Catharine Sinnott. June 30. 15,500

20th st, No. 128, s s, 353.8 w 6th av, 25x92, three-story brick stable. Samuel J. Powers and Caroline M. his wife, Carmel, N. Y., to Marie Von Bothmer and Charles J. Platt. July 15. 19,000

25th st, Nos. 226 and 228, s s, 250 w 7th av, 50x 117.6 two five-story brk flats. Abraham Quackenbush and Louisa his wife and John Farrell and Jane E. his wife to The Bush Company (Lim.) *Mt.* $60,000. July 17. 95,000

29th st, No. 46, s s, 125 e 6th av, 20x98.9, three-story brk store and dwell'g. Louis L. Todd to John E. Kaughran. *Mt.* $18,000. July 14. 28,000

31st st, No. 365, n s, 137.6 e 9th av, 18.9x98.9, four-story brk dwell'g. Mary widow and Edward J. and Michael F. Loughman heirs Simon Loughman to Margaret J. Plant. *Mt.* $15,000. July 11. 15.000

34th st, No. 435, n s, 350 e 10th av, 25x98.9, five-story stone front flat. Jacob Pizer and Laura his wife to James McCun. B. & S. July 21. 26,500

35th st, No. 310, s s, 100 w 8th av, 12.6x98 9, three-story brk dwell'g. Samuel Middleton to Mary J. Middleton his wife. June 24. nom

37th st, No. 138, s s, 210 e 7th av, 17x98.9, four-story stone front dwell'g Frank B. Treiber to Jefferson M. Levy. Sub. to mort. April 18. nom

38th st, No. 229, n s, 490.1 e 8th av, 20.7x98.9, five-story brk dwell'g. Foreclos. Edward Jacobs to Virginia W. Baldwin. *Mt.* $15,500. July 17. 5,000

43d st, No. 547-551, n s, 100 e 11th av, 75x100.5, sheds and two-story brk and frame buildings. Samuel P. Jones and Mary J. his wife, Black River Falls, Wis., to Sarah J. Rice. ½ part. July 20. 6,000

52d st, No. 218, s s, 220 e 3d av, 20x82.5, three-story brk dwell'g. Marcus Koch and Celia his wife to William Hanning and Elizabeth his wife. *Mt.* $7,000. July 21. 12,625

53d st, n s, 250 w 9th av, 25x100.5. Release mort. Marx and Moses Ottinger to Luigi, Steffano, Natale und Giuseppe Cavanato. July 21. 7,167

Same property. Release mort. Same to same. July 21. nom

Same property. Release mort. The Bradley & Currier Co., (Lim) to same. July 21. nom

Same property. Release judgment. Thomas C. Ennever to same. July 20. nom

56th st, Nos. 422 and 424 W., s s, abt 325 w 9th av, 50x69.2x50x75.5, two five-story brk tenements. Contract. Edward J. Bannon and Catherine his wife to Joseph M. Ledwith. July 20. 30,000

56th st, No. 133, n s, 433.4 w 6th av, 20.10x100.5, five-story stone front flat. Frank L Smith and Magdalene his wife to Mortimer P. Thain. *Mt.* $25,000. March 9. nom

57th st, No. 561, n s, 66.8 e 11th av, 16.8x100.5, three-story brk dwell'g. John Burchill to Mary Burchill. *Mt.* $3,500. July 17. 6,500

58th st, No. 132 W., s s, abt 315 w 6th av, 16.1x 100, four-story stone front dwell'g. James S. Lee and Mary H. his wife to William H. Lee. C. a. G. Re-recorded. Aug. 16, 1889. 3,650

58th st, s s, 200 w 7th av, 50x57.10, vacant. Release mort. John M. Laing and Mary F. McKibben, Leavenworth City, Kan., to American Fine Arts Society. July 13. 50,000

58th st, s s, 175 w 7th av, 75x57.10, vacant. The American Fine Arts Society to George W. Vanderbilt. July 13. 45,000

59th st, No. 20, s s, 225 w 5th av Plaza and 425 w 5th av, 25x100.5, three-story brk school. Dennis Beach and Minnie O. his wife to Alfred T. Leward. *Mt.* $30,000. July 13. 47,500

Same property. Agreement as to terms of contract to sell between owner and mortgagee. Dennis Beach to John R. Platt et al. exrs. and trustees Samuel R. Platt. July 9. nom

Same property. Bill of sale or assignment of interest under party wall agreement. Mary E. Gibbens individ. and extrx. Edwin A. Gibbens to Alfred T. Leward. July 10. nom

68th st, Nos. 232 and 234, s s, 375 w Amsterdam av, 50x100.5, one-story frame buildings. Clara wife of and Richard L. Leggett to James Butler. *Mt.* $7,000. July 13. 15,250

70th st, No. 328, s s, 329 4 w West End av, 23.2 x100.5, three-story brk stable. Hubert Van Wagenen and Cornelia his wife to Margaretha Card. B. & S. and C. a. G. Oct. 15. nom

70th st, n s, 223 e Av A, 25x100.5. Release mort. Henry W. Ford trustee Augustus H. Ward to Frederick Rohrs. July 17. consid. omitted

Same property. Release mort. The Bradley & Currier Co. (Lim.) to Frederick Rohrs and Louisa his wife. July 16. nom

71st st, n s, 173 9 w Boulevard. Party wall agreement. Terence J. Duffy to Christ Protestant Episcopal Church. July 18. nom

71st st, n s, 550 e West End av, 54x102.2, vacant. Daniel J. Dineen to Terence J. Duffy. July 18. nom

72d st, No. 303, n s, 115 w West End av, 22x 102.2, four-story stone front dwell'g. Franklin E Robinson and Lillie L. his wife to Ida M. Hough. *Mt.* $30,000. July 16. 60,000

72d st, No. 118, s s, 218.9 w Lexington av, 18.9x 102.2, four-story stone front dwell'g. James Boyce and Sallie K. his wife, Baltimore, Md., to Harry H. Seabrook. *Mt.* $18,000. May 21. 27,500

72d st, No. 258, s s, 125 e West End av, 25x112.2, four-story stone front dwell'g. Foreclos. James M. Varnum to Lydia R. Coffin. *Mt.* $22,250. June 26. 54,100

72d st, No. 260, s s, 100 e 11th av, 25x112.2, four-story stone front dwell'g. Foreclos. James M. Varnum to William H. Gray. *Mt.* $22,-250 June 26. 50,000

72d st, No. 424, s s, 363 e 1st av, 25x102.2, five-story brk tenem't. Foreclos. Henry W. Sackett to Morris Franklin. *Mt.* $29,456. June 30. 13,650

72d st, No. 422, s s, 338 e 1st av, 25x102.2, five-story brk tenem't. Foreclos. Same to same. *Mt.* $29,456. June 30. 13,700

72d st, No. 420, s s, 313 e 1st av, 25x102.2, five-story brk tenem't. Foreclos. Same to same. *Mt.* $29,456. June 30. 13,300

72d st, No. 426, s s, 388 e 1st av, 25x102.2, five-story brk tenem't. Foreclos. Same to Robert Garcewich. *Mt.* $29,456. June 30. 13,600

74th st, No. 345, n s, 175 w 1st av, 25x98, five-story brk tenem't and stores. Elizabeth Neubauer to Daniel Kilian and Elizabeth his wife. *Mt.* $16,800. July 20. 21,500

77th st, No. 407, n s, 144 e 1st av, 25x102.2, five-story stone front tenem't. Mary wife of and Michael Hannan to Samuel Stark. *Mt.* $20,-000. July 15. 30,000

Same property. Samuel Stark and Gussie his wife to David and Jacob Finelite. *Mt.* $21,-900. July 15. nom

79th st, No. 239, n s, 110 w 2d av, runs north 102.2 x west 45 x southeast 25.2 x south 86.6 to st, x east 25, five-story brk flat. David Moss and Annie his wife to Sarah Feiner. *Mt.* $18,000. July 15. 26,000

79th st, Nos. 438 and 440, s s, 94 w Av A, 50x 102.2, two-story frame dwell'g and one-story frame stable on rear. Sophie Rothschild to Thomas F. Cooke. *Mt.* $7,000. July 1. 17,000

81st st, No. 215, n s, 178 e 3d av, 25.4x102.2, five story brk tenem't. Mary F., Thomasena V., Thomas N., Cora M., Owen L. and Oscar Smith by the Farmers' Loan and Trust Co. guard. to Mary L. Tynan. Infants' share. *Mt.* $18,000. July 14. 15,803

Same property. Margaret C. Smith widow, Andrew A. and John J. Smith and Annie R. Pack to Mary L. Tynan. All title. *Mt.* $18,000. July 9. 9,197

81st st, No. 43, n s, 250 e Columbus av, 25x104.4, vacant. Alice B. wife of Samuel Colcord to Mary E. Hanley. July 14. nom

81st st, No. 221, n s, 254.1 e 3d av, 25.6x102.2, five-story brk tenem't. Margaret C. Smith widow, Andrew A. and John J. Smith, Annie R. Pack to John F. Heil. All title. *Mt.* $18,000. July 9. 9,197

Same property. Mary F., Thomasena V., Thomas N., Cora M., Owen L. and Oscar Smith by The Farmers' Loan and Trust Co. guard. to same. All title. July 14. 15,803

81st st, Nos. 217 and 219, n s, 203.4 e 3d av, 50.9 x102.2, two five-story brk tenem'ts. Mary F., Thomasena V., Thomas N., Cora M., Owen L. and Oscar Smith by The Farmers' Loan and Trust Co. guard. to Anna M. Hoch. All title. July 14. 31,606

Same property. Margaret C. Smith widow, Andrew A. and John J. Smith and Annie R. Pack to same. All title. July 9. 18,394

83d st, No. 339, n s, 200 w 1st av, 25x102.2, five-story stone front tenem't. Thomas Moore, Annie his wife and John McLaughlin to Henry Struckhauser and Lena M. his wife. *Mt.* $15,000. July 15. 28,000

83d st, Nos. 164-168, s s, 80 e Amsterdam av, 70x111.3x70.3x105.8, three five-story brk flats. Foreclos. William J. Townsend to Henry J. Burchell. *Mt.* $57,000. July 20. 4,150

85th st, No. 64, s s, 175 e Columbus av. 19x102.2, four-story stone front dwell'g. John Casey and Kate his wife to Leopold Goldberg. *Mt.* $21,000. July 10. 31,000

86th st, No. 314, s s, 219.6 w West End av, 21.7x102.2, four-story stone front dwell'g. Mary F. wife and Woolsey R. Hopkins, Stamford, Conn., to William Y. Wilson. *Mt.* $21,000. July 17. 33,000

87th st, s s, 350 w Central Park West. Party wall agreement. George Edgar to James A. Frame. May 27. nom

87th st, s s, 100 w West End av, 100x100.8, vacant. Francis M. Jencks and Elizabeth P. his wife to John C. Heney. C. a. G. May 1. 47,750

87th st, s s, 450 w Central Park West. Party wall agreement. Same to Charles Buek. May 25. nom

88th st, n s, 100 e Av A, 75x100.8, vacant. Lambert Suydam to Joseph Schreiner. Sub. to assessm't for East River Park. June 30. 22,000

88th st, No. 429, n s, 257 w Av A, 25x100.8, four-story brk tenem't. Wilhelm Gundlach exr. Arnolde Gundlach to Friedrich Meyer and Julie his wife. *Mt.* $8,000. July 14. 15,000

88th st, No. 118, s s, 162.6 w Columbus av, 15.6x 100.8, three-story brk dwell'g. Ariel N. Barney and Harriet E. his wife to J. Wesley Rosenquest. *Mt.* $18,000. July 17. 18,000

88th st, No. 149, n s, 374 e Amsterdam av, 17 x100.8, three-story stone front dwell'g.
88th st, No. 145, n s, 408 e Amsterdam av, 17 x100.8, three-story stone front dwell'g.
Frank L. Smith and Magdalene his wife to John C. Heney and Hugh McDowell. July 1. 40,000

89th st, No. 67, n s, 184.5 w Park av, 25.7x 100.11.
89th st, n s, 184.5 w Park av, runs east — x north — x west 2,2 x south 100.11.
One-story frame buildings.
Contract. Sarah S. Runge to rector, &c. of the Church of the Beloved Desciple. June 26. 12,000

90th st, Nos. 302 and 304, s s, 90 w West End av, 40x100.8.
90th st, Nos. 306 and 308, s s, 145 w West End av, 35x100.8.
Four four-story stone front dwell'gs.
Frank L. Smith and Magdalene his wife to Theodore A. Squier. July 20. nom

91st st, n s, 175 e 5th av, 25x100. vacant. Henry Hirsh and Barbara his wife and Seligman Oppenheimer and Theresa his wife to Thomas Graham. C. a. G. July 7. 16,500

92d st, No. 346, s s. 100 w 1st av, 25x100.8, five-story brk tenem't and store. Deborah wife of Samnel L. Lewis to Susette J. Lewis. B. & S. July 21. nom

93d st, No 150, s s, 308 e Amsterdam av, 17x 100.8, three-story stone front dwell'g. Walden P. Anderson to Marc Klaw and Abraham L. Erlanger. July 21. nom

Same property. Release mort. Charles G. Judson to Walden P. Andrews. July 23. nom

Same property. Release mort. Francis M. Jencks to same. July 23. nom

Same property. Release mort. Newburg Savings Bank to same. July 23 11,000

95th st, No. 158, s s, 307 e 4th av, 18x100.8, three-story brk dwell'g. Matthew C. Henry and Maria his wife and John Gaynor to Ivan Frank. *Mt.* $12,000. July 22. 16,500

96th st, No. 58, s s, 200 e 9th av, 20x100.8, four-story brk dwell'g. Foreclos. William M. Hoes to William Rankin. *Mt.* $20,000. July 23. 750

99th st, Nos. 26 and 28, s s, 225 w 8th av, 50x 100.11, two five-story stone front flats. John L. Brewster to Hugh McDowell. C. a. G. July 20. 23,000

105th st, Nos. 62-66, s s, 180 w 4th av, 75x100.11, three five-story stone front flats. De Witt Mull and Amy A. his wife and Gottlieb Fromer and Selma his wife to Annie E. Wilsey. *Mt.* $60,398. July 17. 84,000

108th st, No. 168, s s, 203 w 3d av, 17x100.11, four-story stone front flat. Louis Heyman and Eva his wife to Patrick B. Burns. *Mt.* $7,000. July 23. 13,000

111th st, No. 244, s s, 100 w 2d av, 20x100.11, three-story frame building on rear of lot. Clara A. wife of William De la Huerta to Patrick McGrath. *Mt.* $3,000. July 23. 5,500

115th st, n s, 525 w Lenox av, 25x100.11, vacant. Anna M. Purdy, Syracuse, N. Y., to Jerusha C. McClelland. Q. C. June 19. nom

116th st, No. 219, n s, 220 e 3d av, 20x100, three-story stone front dwell'g. Mary C. Worster to Grace and Julia L. Worster. B. & S. Aug. 10, 1882. 1,000

116th st, Nos. 309 and 311, n s, 150 w 8th av, 50 x100.11, two five-story brk flats. Marx Ottinger and Clara his wife and Moses Ottinger and Amelia his wife to Thomas P. Dunne. *Mt.* $12,000. July 16. other consid. and 100

116th st, s s, 200 e 8th av. Party wall agreement. J. Allen Townsend to Harry C. Horton. May 23. nom

119th st, s s, 9.4 w Claremont av, and being at the w s of Old Bloomingdale road, runs south along said w s to line 300 south of 119th st, x east to Claremont av, x north to 119th st, x west —, vacant. Anna P. wife of Edward L. Short to Charles C. and Henry M. Taber. Q. C. June 24. nom

Same property. Emily M. wife of Edward C. Lord to same. Q. C. June 16. nom

Same property. Eliza L. De P. Clarkson, Henry, Wilson, Edgar, and Emily M. Depeyster, and Beekman Depeyster and Annie G. his wife to same. Q. C. May 28. nom

Same property. William W. Greene and Richard H. Greene and Mary G. his wife to same. Q. C. May 21. nom

Same property. Anna De P. Hunt to same. Q. C. June 18. nom

Same property. Anna H. Livingston widow to same. Q. C. June 16. nom

Same property. Theodore W. Todd and Emma L. his wife, and Charles H. Todd and Fanny M. his wife to same. Q. C. May 4. nom

Same property. Cornelius R. Duffie and Lillian A. his wife to same. Q. C. May 18. nom

121st st, No. 212, s s, 158 w 7th av, 15x100.11, three-story stone front dwell'g. Sinclair Myers to May L. Myers his wife. *Mt.* $11,500 and all liens. July 18. nom

121st st, No. 240, s s, 391.8 w 7th av, 16.8x100.11, three-story brk dwell'g. Mary wife of and Michael Hannan to Samuel Stark. *Mt.* $15,000. July 15. 25,000

Same property. Samuel Stark and Gussie his wife to David and Jacob Finelite. *Mt.* $16,900. July 15. nom

122d st, No. 421, n s, 254.7 e 1st av, 16.8x100.11, three-story stone front dwell'g. Foreclos. Royal S. Crane to Ann E. Morris. July 23. 7,000

124th st, No. 154, s s, 339.8 w 3d av, 21.4x100.11, three-story brk dwell'g. Moses Foltz and Henriette his wife to Aaron Hoffman. Dec. 1. 11,110

127th st, No. 257, n s, 477 w 7th av, 16x99.11, three-story stone front dwell'g. Hubbard H. Upham and Harrie M. his wife to Louis I. Haber. All liens. July 13. nom

Same property. Louis I. Haber and Carrie J. his wife to Harrie M. Upham. All morts. July 14. nom

127th st, No. 62, s s, 228 9 e Lenox av, 18.9x99.11, three-story brk dwell'g. Frederick Clinch and Ina his wife to Edward S. Clinch. All title. July 10. nom

131st st, No. 211, n s, 176 w 7th av, 15.8x99.11, three-story brk dwell'g. John Tully and Etta V. S. his wife to Louis I. Haber. All liens. July 13. nom

Same property. Louis I. Haber and Carrie J. his wife to Etta V. S. Tully. All liens. July 14. nom

134th st, Nos. 15 and 17, n s, 250 e 5th av, 50x99.11, two four-story brk tenem'ts and stores. Caroline A. and Henry A. Bereuter exrs. John H. Bereuter to Emelie B. Westermann. *Mt.* $18,000. July 23. 32,000

134th st, Nos. 11 and 13, n s, 200 e 5th av, 50x99.11, two similar tenem'ts. Same to Henry A. Bereuter. *Mt.* $16,000. July 23. 32,000

137th st, Nos. 59 and 61, n s, 200 e Lenox (6th) av, 50x99.11, two-story frame dwell'g with one-story stone building on rear. Hugh Colwell to Margaret Colwell. All liens. July 23. nom

168th st, n s, 120 e Audubon av, 25x95. James Flynn to Rosetta McKenna. Q. C. July 16. nom

Same property. Rosetta wife of James McKenna to Matilda V. Roof. July 16. 3,550

Av A, No. 1642, e s, 80 n 86th st, 20x75, four-story stone front dwell'g. John V. May and Maggie his wife to Frederick Abendschein. *Mt.* $7,000. July 20. 14,250

Av A, No. 1640, e s, 60 n 86th st, 20x75, four-story stone front dwell'g. Same to same. *Mt.* $7,000. July 20. 14,250

Av A, Nos. 1374 and 1376, e s, 52.2 n 73d st, 50x98, two five-story brk tenem'ts with stores. Henry Neus ahd Bernhardina his wife to Louis Kreulewitch. *Mt.* $40,000. July 20. 49,000

Av D, Nos. 143 and 145, s w cor 10th st, 50x93, four and five-story brk cigarette factory.
10th st, No. 444, s s, 93 w Av D, 25x92.3, four-story brk cigar factory.
Interior lot, 72 s 10th st and 73 w Av D, runs west 25 x south 22 x east 20 x north 22.
10th st, No. 442, s s, 118 w Av D, 21x92.3, with all title to strip adj, and distant on s s of 10th st 139 w Av D, and being 1.4x92.3. Four-story brk cigar factory with two-story brk building on rear.
Also title to interior lot, 93.3 s 10th st and 93 w Av D, runs south 1.9 x west 25 x north 1.9 x east 25.
Foreclos. La Roy S. Gove to Elias Spingarn. *Mt.* $65,000. June 24. 1,000

Amsterdam (10th) av, No. 1064 } begins Amster-
67th st, No. 144 } dam av, s e
cor 67th st, 25x100, three-story brk tenem't and store on av and two-story brk stable on st. Herman Fox and William A. Klinger exrs., &c., Helena Smith to James E. Branigan. July 14. 26,000

Amsterdam av, No. 477, s e cor 83d st, 25x80, five-story brk flat and store. Foreclos. William J. Townsend to George Peper and Anna his wife. *Mt.* $26,000. July 20. 16,400

Columbus av, n e cor 92d st, 100.8x100, vacant. Hamilton A. Gale, Baltimore, Md., by Edwin Baldwin guard. to Charles Gahren. Infant's share. July 23. 37,625

Same property. Susan J. Gale widow, Baltimore, Md., to same. ⅛ part. July 15. 37,625

Columbus av, No. 952, w s, 25 s 107th st, 25.5x100, five-story brk tenem't and store. Peter Mitchell and Lucy B. his wife to Henry Strunck. *Mt.* $22,900. July 17. 25,000

Greenwich av, No 39, n w cor Charles st, 26.10x77.1x12x82.2, five-story brk store and tenement. Rosina Vollbart widow to Michael Sullivan. July 15. 33,700

Lexington av, No. 718, w s, 20.5 s 58th st, 20x68.9, three-story stone front dwell'g. Paulina A. Morgan widow to Gustav Bercke. July 22. 17,500

Lexington av, No. 246, w s, 104.6 n 34th st, 20.6x81.6 to centre of former Eastern Post road, x 20.6x82, four-story stone front dwell'g. Daniel S. McElroy and Linda L. his wife to Francis L. Ogden. *Mt.* $15,000. July 10. 40,000

Lenox av, No. 185, w s, 43.11 n 119th st, 19x75, four-story brk dwell'g. Esther A. Hastings to John O. Hoyt, Jr., Brooklyn. All liens. June 1. nom

Park av, Nos. 1613-1615, e s, 25.11 s 115th st, 50x80, two five-story brk tenem'ts and stores. Mathilde Von Ellert, mother, to Mathilde Von Ellert, daughter. *Mt.* $29,000. July 15. gift

Park av, No. 1540, w s, 75.11 s 112th st, 25x78.9, five-story stone front flat. Jessie M. wife of James Thompson, Yonkers, to Daniel and Joseph Kramer. *Mt.* $15,000. July 20. 20,000

Park av, n w cor 103d st, 100.11x80, vacant. J. Allen Townsend and Viola H. his wife to De Witt Mull and Gotlieb Promer. July 6 26,000

Riverside av, Nos. 92-100 } begins Riverside av,
82d st, Nos. 318-326 } s e cor 82d st,
109.3x122.4x102.2x161.1, five four-story brk and stone dwell'gs on av, and four four-story stone front dwell'gs on st. Albert C. Squier and Louise his wife to the Squier & Whipple Co. *Mt.* $204,893. July 18. 300,000

South 5th av, Nos. 68 and 70 } begins South 5th
Houston st, No. 88 W. } av, n w cor
Houston st, 98x18. Assignment of judgment and release. Augustus F. Kinnersley to Adeline M. Logan and David V. Johnson. July 21. nom

Vermilyea av, n s, 100 w Isham st, 75x125. Bennett Hymes and Jennie his wife, Savannah, Ga., to Morris Happ, Macon, Ga. ⅛ part. ⅛ of all liens. May 4. 500

West End av, e s, 62.8 s 89th st, runs south 19 x east 82 x north 14 x west 18 x north 5 x west 64. Release mort. Alfred M. Hoyt et al. trustee Mary I. Hoyt to Frank L. Smith. May 5. nom

Same property. Release mort. Armintha Merritt to same. July 9. nom

Same property. Release mort. Charles T. Barney, Francis M. Jencks and William E. D. Stokes to same. July 15. nom

West End av, s e cor 103d st, 25.11x100, vacant. Sophia R. C. Furniss et al. trustees for Clementina Furniss to Alexander Walker and Judson Lawson. July 8. nom

West End av, e s, 25.11 s 103d st, 75x100, vacant. Sophia R. C. and Clementina Furniss and Margaret E. Zimmerman to same. July 8. nom

West End av, Nos. 470-478, s e cor 88th st, 100.8x100, five four-story brk dwell'gs. Frank L. Smith and Magdalene his wife to Jacob Brandt. All liens. July 1. nom

1st av, Nos. 189 and 191, w s, 46.1 s 12th st, 45.10x100, two five-story brk tenem'ts with stores. Sarah wife of Solomon Feiner to David Moss. *Mt.* $51,000. July 15. 69,000

2d av, No. 423, w s, 24 n 24th st, 24x97.7, three-story brk tenem't and store. Catherine, Julia, Maria and James Ryan to Eugene Philippe. July 10. 18,500

Same property. Release dower. Sarah E. wife of James Ryan to same. July 15. nom

2d av, No. 2118, s e cor 109th st, 17x66, three-story frame brk front store and tenem't. Michael D. Coyle to Rose M. Coyle. July 8. nom

2d av, No. 788, e s, 20.5 n 42d st, 20x80.6, four-story stone front tenem't and store. Eliza Morang to Bernard Laguna and Rachael Laguna. Sub. to mort. July 22. nom

5th av, w s, 80.11 s 116th st, 20x100, five-story stone front flat. Release mort. Morris Steinhardt to William Radebold and Edward Wenz. July 20. 2,000

Same property. William Radebold and Albertina his wife and Edward Wenz and Anna his wife to Bridget Casey. July 18. 24,000

8th av, No. 352, e s, 24.11 s 128th st, 25x75, five-story brk flat. John G. Lampe and Catharine M. his wife to Henry Heuer. July 13. nom

Same property. Henry Heuer and Ottilie his wife to John G. Lampe and Catharine M. Lampe as tenants in common. B. & S. July 13. nom

Pier No. 23 (old number), known as Vesey st pier, and pier No. 24 (old number), North River, including all the 109.4 of bulkhead or wharf property connected therewith on w s of West st, with all riparian rights, land under water, &c. James P. Cruger and Amy M. his wife, Newburg, N. Y., to The Mayor, &c., New York. All title. July 6. 33,333

MISCELLANEOUS.

Real estate mortgages on property in Brooklyn, Orange, N. J., and St. Paul, Minn.; also various railroad bonds, &c. Deed of trust. Lowell Mason and John or John B. Mason and Marion M. his wife to James Hollyer, Brooklyn. July 17. nom

23d and 24th WARDS.

Grove Hill pl, s w s, 123.2 s e Av C, 23.2x75, h & l. Elizabeth Berner, Long Island City, to Clarence E. Horn. July 20. 2,550

Mechanic st, being the most n e cor now or late of Joseph Peets, 24th Ward, 25x137. Mary E. Byrne to Bernard Byrne. July 9. nom

Oakley st, n s, 100 e Keppler av, 40x100. Release mort. Mary L. wife of William G. Word, formerly Randell, to Henry Y. Chubb, Staten Island. July 17. 400

Same property. Henry Y. Chubb, New Brighton, S. I., to Alexander Forsyth. July 17. 800

Rogers pl, s e s, 672.3 n e Westchester av, 30x74x23.9x79. Jeremiah Healy and Mary his wife to John Schell. *Mt.* $600. July 21. 1,500

Terrace pl, n e cor Elton st, 54.3x113.10x50x134.11. John Schultz and Anna his wife to Nicholas Thiel and Catherine his wife. July 1, 1886. 2,000

134th st, No. 722, s s, 617.7 e Willis av, 17x100. Anna M. wife of and William P. Roberts to John Van Gelden. July 20. 7,500

134th st, n s, 125 w Alexander av, 25x100. Release mort. M. Dasher Wylly, Bayonne, N. J., to Frederick Rohrs. June 30. nom

Same property. Release mort. M. Taylor Pyne to same. June 30. 1,552

137th st, s s, 125 e Lincoln av, 25x100. John Bell and Frances E. his wife and John J. Bell and Carrie M. his wife to Eliza M. wife of William H. Monks. *Mt.* $14,000. July 20. 19,350

138th st, n s, 25.3 w Willis av, 26.3x100. John Cotter and Sarah his wife and Nicholas Cotter and Eliza his wife to Margaret A. and Mary C. Cain. *Mt.* $15,000. July 21. nom

141st st, n w cor Beekman av, 50 1x91.7x50x95.3. William R. Beal Land Improvement Co. to Martha S. wife of T. Hamilton Burch. July 8. 4,900

146th st, n e s, lot 182 map Mott Haven, 50x— to Public School, x44.8x152. Caleb M. Hynard to Mary C. Perine. July 21. other consid. and 4,000

150th st, s s, 100 w Courtlandt av, 50x100. Michael Vetter devisee of Felliphine or Philepena Vetter and Benedicta his wife to Annie M. wife of Joseph J. Nimphius. *Mt.* $1,500, and assessm't. ⅛ part. July 21. 3,400

160th st, s s, lot 63 map village Melrose South, 50x100. August Schluter and Augusta his wife to Elizabetha Stahl. Dec. 17, 1890. 3,500

173d st, n s, 110 e Washington av, 38x100. Sereno D. Bonfils and Anna D. his wife to C. Adelbert Becker. *Mt.* $2,250. July 20. 3,800

179th st, n s, 64 w 3d av, 26x84.6x25x108.5. Charles E. Chapple and Sarah E. his wife to Michael J. Keane. July 21. 3,700

Anthony av, e s, 5.9 n 175th st prolonged, 25x113.5x26x106.3. Release mort. E. Augusta Tweed to Fannie E. Lawrence. July 17. 900

Same property. Fannie E. Lawrence to Henry Humphreys. July 21. 1,350

Bailey av, w s, lot 103 and part lot 104 map William O Giles, West Farms, 50x131x50x126.5. Foreclos. George B. Newell to Charles D Silleck. July 21. 2,335

Bergen av, s e s, 248.8 n e Westchester av, 25x100. Charles Reim and Fredericka his wife to Philipp Aiker. *Mt.* $1,400. July 20. 3,300

College av, s s, lots 197 and 182 map Union Hill Powell estate, 50x183 to Pelham av, x50x183. Mary B. and William O'Donnell to Julia Dennerlein. July 20. 4,200

Decatur av, lot 36 map village of Fordham, 50x100. George W. Hill and Dora E. his wife to Joseph A. Goulden. *Mt.* $1,200. July 23. 2,000

Edenwood av, w s, 237.8 n St. James st, 75x106 to Croton Aqueduct. Elmer A. Allen and Mary E. his wife to Ella wife of Edward Baker. July 15. 3,150

Elm av, s w s, lots 21, 22 and 23 map South Belmont, 150x100, hs & ls. John Hahn and Barbara his wife, Westchester, to George Metzger and Sophia his wife. Q. C. July 2. nom

Franklin av, w s, 73.5 s 170th st, 20x100. Amelia D. wife of J. Henry Whitney to Susanna J. wife of James Cowan. *Mt.* $5,000. July 22. 1,600

Franklin av, s e s, part of lot 125 map of village of Morrisania, 20x100. Susanna J. wife of James Cowan to Amelia D. wife of J. Henry Whitney. *Mt.* $1,000. July 22. 2,500

Highbridge av, s e s, part of parcel 28 map of Highbridgeville, 25x125. George W. Robinson and Mary E. his wife to John J. Byrne. July 17. 1,750

Home av, w s, 52 6 n 136th st, 53.6x100.
136th st, n w cor Home av, 50x100.
Q. C. deed of 2.6x100 between above 2 parcels.
Thomas W. Strong and John McLoughlin exrs. Robert H. Elton to Rosetta B. Marston. Q. C. and confirmation. July 16. nom

Hull av, n w s, 150 n e Mosholu Parkway, 50x110.
Hull av, n w s, 200 n e Mosholu Parkway, 31.11x110x28.4x110.
Mary A. Thompson to Mary A. McCahill. July 17. 2,650

Katonah av, s w cor Knox st, 100x120. Ephraim B. Levy to Carlos Warner and Charles D. Smith, Londonderry, Vt. July 6. nom

Lafontaine av, w s, 600 s Pine st, 200x250. L. Napoleon Levy to Jefferson M. Levy. July 21. nom

Madison av, w s, 189 n Fitch st, 27x120. Mary J. Fraser to C. Adelbert Becker. July 21. 4,500

Opdyke av, s s, 150 w 3d st, runs south 200 to Willard av, x west 50 x north 100 x east 25 x north 100 to Opdyke av, x east 25. Richard Delmage and Annie his wife, Bayonne, N. J., to Abram G. More. July 1. 1,050

Prospect av, e s, 179 n of north line of lot 67 map Gouverneur Morris known as Woodstock, 21x100. Release mort. John Bussing, Jr., to Caroline Mihm. July 16. nom

Same property. Caroline wife of Theodore Mihm to Louisa A. Merce. July 16. 5,500

Retreat av, at intersection with n e line of Lewis Morris farm, runs southeast 171 x again southeast 87 to centre Millbrook, x southwest 46 x southwest 117.5 x southwest again 92 x northwest 57 x northwest again 214 x northeast 25, except portion taken for 147th st.
Retreat av, south cor Henry st, runs south 221 to n edge of Millbrook, x west 40 x northwest 258 to s s Retreat av, x east 175, except portion taken for 148th st.
Millbrook (so called) at s s of 148th st, runs east 95 x south 200 to 147th st, x west 191 to Millbrook, x —, except plot of nearly 21 city

lots conveyed to Theodore C. Shell, the east boundary line of which is 340 w Brook av and extends 250 on 148th st and 270 on 147th st and 0.5 to a line at right angles to 148th st.
Edward H. Pirsson to Sarah J. Pirsson. B. & S. C. a. G. ½ part. Dec. 11, 1890. nom

Sedgwick av, n w s, plot D map of villa sites and plots, being part Anthony estate, Kingsbridge Heights, 24th Ward. 98.7x144.10x44.7 x142.3. Hugh N. Camp and Elizabeth D. his wife to Samuel L. Berrian. July 20. 5,000

Stebbins av, e s, 756.4 n Freeman st, 125x116.10 x125.2x110. Margaret A. Sheridan to Richard McLaughlin. July 7. 1,050

Tinton av, e s, 83.4 s Cedar st or pl, 16.8x100. Clarence L. Horn and Isabella his wife to Francis Volz and Katharine his wife. *Mt.* $2,500. July 2. 3,450

Vanderbilt av, e s, 200 s 182d st, 25x150. Sereno D. Bonfils and Anna D. his wife to C. Adelbert Becker. *Mt.* $850. July 20. 1,250

Walton av, w s, 245 s 150th st, 17.6x103.7x17.7x 102.8. Release mort. Henry L. Morris to Anna T. Dale. July 21. 700

Washington av, w s, 50.2 s 184th st, 50.2x115x 50x119.6. John Seidel and Annie his wife to Joseph Wodicka. *Mt.* $800. July 2. 3,200

Washington av, n w s, 200 n e 170th st, 50x150.6 x47.8x150.6. Betsey M. Garey extrx. Leander Garey to Z. S. Sampson. July 10. 5,000

Same property. Z. S. Sampson and Evelyn A. his wife to Philip Smith. July 10. 8,000

Washington av, e s, 50 n 176th st, runs north 58 x east 105 x south 108 to 176th st, x west 25 x north 50 x west 80. C. Adelbert Becker and Margaret G. his wife to Ellen S. Ward, Brooklyn. July 20. 27,750

Washington av, w s, 50 s 173d st, 50x105. Sereno D. Bonfils and Anna D. his wife to C. Adelbert Becker. *Mt.* $5,000. July 20. 12,500

Webster av, s e cor 179th st, 33x60x43x40. Mary A. Hyland to Sereno D; Bonfils. ½ part. July 22. 594

3d av, w s, 150.9 s 165th st, 25.1x147.2x25x144.5. John Sobischek and Dorethea his wife and Emma S. Bures otherwise Boresh heirs Emanuel Sobischek, Sr. and Jr., to Lirdmila Sobischek. B. & S. July 1. nom

Fordham road or 3d av, lot 18 map Upper Morrisania, 54x100. George Neuffer and Maria his wife to Henry Peffer. *Mt.* $5,000. July 23. nom

Old Boston road, s s, centre line, 3.6 s Locust Tree marked with a blaze and three notches, runs southeast 80 to Croton Aqueduct, x southwest 504.9 x southwest 1,673 to brook, x northwest 353 to Old Boston road at crossing of brook, x irreg., 37 49-100 acres. A. D. Lawrence Jewett and ano. exrs. Richard W. Dickinson to Hugh N. Camp. May 11. 25,000

Same property. Richard D. Jewett and Eliza M. his wife and Sarah Jewett heirs Elizabeth Jewett to same. ½ part. May 11. nom

Post road, e s, adj lands Isaac Cooper and Thomas Walker dec'd, 24th Ward, 56x107x19 x25x75x130. Mary E. Byrne to Bernard Byrne. July 9. nom

Lots 10 and 11 block 24 sections A and B map North New York. Edward H. Pirsson to Sarah J. Pirsson. Q. C. Jan. 12. nom

Lot begins at division line bet lands of Suburban Land Improvement Co. and Marion Bathgate at point 159.11 w Boston av as widened and 55.7 n of said av, runs west 103.11 x northwest 28.3 to point 130 n Boston av, x east 149.3 x south 74.5, contains 2 736-100 city lots. Release mort. Moses Schloss and Herman Goldman to The Suburban Land Improvement Co. July 22. 1,642

Mill Brook, former centre line, at intersection of s s 147th st, runs south 29 x northwest 70 to st, x east 57 to beginning. Edward H. Pirsson to Christian Vorndran. Q. C. April 16. nom

LEASEHOLD CONVEYANCES.

Clinton pl, n s, 158.11 w University pl, 25x93.11. Trustees Sailors' Snug Harbor to Edward Schell. 21 years, from May 1, 1876, per year, taxes and 500

Cherry st, s e cor Clinton st, runs south along Clinton st 115 to Water st, x east 88.3 x north 114.5 to Cherry st, x west 88.3. Robert G. Remsen to Robert M. Jarvis. 21 years, from May 1, 1891, per year, taxes and 2,500

Cherry st, s e cor Clinton st, runs south 115 to Water st, x east 88.3 x north 114.5 to Cherry st, x west 88.3.
Cherry st, s s, abt 163.4 e Clinton st, 23.4x 113.10 to Water st, x 23.4x114.
Cherry st, s s, abt 140 e Clinton st, 23.4x abt 114.1 to Water st.
Clinton st, e s, extends from Water st to Front st, 147.3x88x145.8x88.
Assign. leases. Victoria S. wife of Orville Oddie to Robert M. Jarvis. nom

Same property. Assign. lease. Nathalie Jarvis to same. nom

Same property. Release of rights to re-assignment. Algernon S. Jarvis to same. April 19, 1891. nom

Same property. Victoria S. wife of Orville Oddie to Angeline Davis. As to 1st parcel, from May 27, 1878, to April 20, 1898; as to 2d parcel, from May 27, 1878, to April 20, 1892; as to 3d parcel, from May 27, 1878, to April 20, 1892; as to 4th parcel, from May 27, 1878; to April 21, 1892. May 27. gross rental, 700

Same property. Assign. leases. Angeline Davis to Nathalie Jarvis. July 12, 1878. nom

Houston st, n s, 273.5 w Av D, 38.7x111. Assign. lease. Mary Goodman to Henry Friedman and Amalia his wife. July 2. nom

Mott st, No. 227. Henry Keteltas trustee John Gardner and Malvina Keteltas ratifying to Henry J. and William Wirth. 20½ years, from July 11, 1891, per year, taxes and 600

Marion st, Nos. 7, 9 and 11. Assign. lease. Thomas Gill to George Heyman. 2,000

24th st, s s, 90 e 10th av, 18x80. Casimir De R. Moore and Catharine Van C. Moore to Kate Green. 21 years, from May 1, 1887, taxes, &c. 160

24th st, s s, 54 e 10th av, 18x80. Mary E. Moore to Kate Green. 21 years, from May 1, 1887, per year, taxes, &c., 160

45th st, n s, 150 e 8th av, 20x100.5. Charles F. Southmayd and James F. Chamberlain trustees Henry Astor to Charles B. Perry and Henry D. Tiffany exrs., &c., Isabel T. Perry. 21 years, from Aug. 1, 1891, per year, taxes and 480

75th st, Nos. 433-439 E. Assign. lease. Robert Flemming to Walter E. and Sydney A. Phillips. nom

Same property. Consent to assign. lease. Peter Ablass to Robert Flemming. nom

Same property. Assign. lease. Walter E. and Sydney A. Phillips to William Texter. nom

Av C, e s, 100 n 2d st., 25x92.10. Augustus W. and Sarah B. Reynolds to Marks Harris. 35 years, from May 1, 1891, per year, taxes and 560

3d av, No. 1123. Assign. lease. Charles A. Steuerwald to William E. Lucas. nom

12th av, w s, 114.11 n 131st st, 31.11x83x69.3x 79.9. Assign. lease. Daniel Katz to The Sioux City Dressed Beef and Canning Co., of Sioux City, Iowa. nom

KINGS COUNTY.

JULY 16, 17, 18, 20, 21, 22.

Adams st, s s, 726.1 w Coney Island plank road, 12.6x103.4x12.6x103, Flatbush. Frederick B. Traviss to Charles Winkler, Portchester. *Mt.* $800. $2,000

Bainbridge st, n s, 41.6 e Saratoga av, 18.6x 100. Victor J. Dowling, of New York, to William H. Good. B. & S. nom

Bainbridge st, n s, 115.6 e Saratoga av, 18.6x100. Victor J. Dowling to William H. Good. B. & S. nom

Same property. William H. Good to William S. and Thomas Ross. nom

Barbey st, e s, 60 s Dumont av, 40x100. Catherine Cummings to Nora A. Cashen. 650

Bergen st, n s, 100 e Stone av, runs north 138.8 x southeast 37.10 x south 101.1 x west 25. Frederick Heddesheimer to John Bergman. 3,300

Bergen st, n s, 202 e Ralph av, 68x107.2. Release mort. Paul W. Ledoux to Mary E. Mason nom

Bergen st, s s, 180 w Clason av, 20x100. Margaret Antisell, Middletown, Md., to Jemima Magrath. 1,250

Bergen st, s s, 400 e Albany av, runs south 2 x east 3 to st, x west 2, gore. Julia wife of Peter A. Young to Thomas Cahill. 38

Berriman st, e s, 150 s Belmont av, 20x100. Charles H. Smith and Theordore Kiendl to Abbie E. wife of Edward H. Coffin. nom

Bleecker st, s e s, 150 n e Irving av, 20x100. James M. Shourt to James F. Gillen. 900

Bleecker st, n s, 309 w Central av, 50x100. Adam Henrich to Adam Metz. 2,900

Boerum st, s s, 200 w Ewen st, 25x100. John A. Loehr to Lazer Lurie. *Mt.* $2,500. 5,500

Broadway, n e s, 20 n w Cornelia st, 25x100. Adam Kaiser, Charles Rissler and August Todebusch to Simon Hutter. *Mt.* $8,000. exch

Broadway, s w s, 66.2 n w Putnam av,, runs northwest 28 x southwest 62.1 x south 23.5 to Putnam av, x east 28 x north 11.8 x northeast 50.4, hs & ls. Robert L. Moores and Charles A. Le Quesne to Samuel G. Richards. *Mt.* $11,000. nom

Broadway, w s, 186.11 s Madison st, runs west 62.1 ff south 23.5 to n s Putnam av, x east 28 x north 11.8 x east 50.4 to Broadway. Stephen B. Sturges to Robert L. Moores and Charles A. Le Quesne. nom

Broadway, n e s, 21 n w Moffat st, 19x80.
Broadway, n e s, 99.6 s e Covert st, 25.6x100.
Rudolph Reimer to Bernhard Davidsburg. *Mt.* $15,500. 27,250

Broadway, northerly cor Cornelia st. 20x100. Adam Kaiser to Learnore Agricolo. ¼ part. *Mt.* $14,000. 3,000

Bradford st, w s, 175 n Liberty av, 75x100. Henry Katzmann to Bessie Schneider. *Mt.* $5,000. exch

Clinton st, e s, 82.9 n 2d pl, 17.3x76.6. James J. Ferry to John McGahie. *Mt.* $4,240. 6,500

Cleveland st, w s, 160 n Hegeman av, 40x100. Christian Nicklaus to Theresa Seitz. 500

Cooper st, s e s, 250 n e Evergreen av, 19.6x 100, h & l.
Cooper st, s e s, 289 n e Evergreen av, 136x 100, hs & ls.
Thomas J. Allen to Hannah M. Rose. *Mt.* $20,432. nom

Columbia st, w s, 18 n Commerce st, 17.10x79.5 x16.8x72.10. Release mort. Pasquale Capongiri, of New York, to Giovanni Tiscornia. 250

Same property. Agostino Dondero to same. *Mt.* $2,400. 3,000

Cumberland st, w s, 687.3 s Park av, 25x100.
Cumberland st; w s, 712.3 s Park av, 25x100.
Alonzo E. De Baun to William Spencer and Jennie M. Wallace. *Mt.* $7,000. 8,500

Cedar st, n s, 400 e Evergreen av, 25x125 to Myrtle av, x29x139.10. Martena G. Peterson, Adeline E. Koebler and Anna M. Schaus devisees Marg't Tietjen to Betty Simon. *Mt.* $8,000. 6,475

Same property. Franklin Koehler and ano. exrs. Marg't Tietjen to same. *Mt.* $3,000. 6,475

Dean st, n s, 200 e Albany av, 20x80. Julia B. F. wife of John D. Fish to William Hughes. 3,200

Degraw st, n s, 363 n e Schenectady av, 6.10 x127.9x32.1x130.3.
Degraw st, n s, 390 e Schenectady av, 20x 127.9.
Degraw st, s s, 380 e Buffalo av, 59.1x65.7x 70.10x78.
Susie E. wife of Melvin Brown to L. R. Reynolds. nom

Degraw st, n s, 363.2 e Schenectady av, runs east 6.10 x north 127.9 x west 32.1 x southeast 130.3.
Degraw st, n s, 390 e Schenectady av, 20x 127.9.
Degraw st, s s, 380 e Buffalo av, 59.1x65.7x 70.10x78.
L. K. Reynolds, Stockport, N. Y., to Eugene H. Vanderbilt. Taxes, &c. nom

Same property. Eugene H. Vanderbilt to Amos S. Lamphear. Taxes, &c. 2,500

Driggs st, east cor North 5th st, 100x100. John D. Walsh to Christopher W. Wilson, ½ part. *Mt.* $3,000. 2,050

Dwight st, n w cor King st, runs west 24x83 in crooked line to Dwight st, x — to beginning; also,
Dwight st, s w cor King st, runs west 23.3 x south 58.4 to Dwight st, x north — to beginning; also,
Bush st, s s, east from Otsego st, where an old water line crosses Bush st, runs south 33 x east 96 x north — to Bush st, x west 152 to beginning.
Joseph Foley to James L. Bearney. nom

Dwight st, n w cor King st, runs west 24 x 83 in crooked line to Dwight st, x — to beginning; also,
Dwight st, s w cor King st, runs west 23 3 x south 58 4 to Dwight st, x north to beginning; also,
Bush st, s s, east from Otsego st, where an old water line crosses Bush st, runs south 33 x east 96 x north to Bush st, x west 140 to beginning.
John M. Bettman, North Plainfield, N. J., to Joseph Foley. nom

Eastern Parkway, s e cor Christopher av, 100x 100. Adolph Pasternack to Wolf Potashinski, of Wooster, Mass. *Mt.* $1,200. 3,330

Eastern Parkway, n s, 75 e Thatford av, 25x 100. Mary Maguire to Ike Kapolowich, Abraham Goldstein and Harris Becher, New York. *Mt.* $1,500. 2,725

Eastern Parkway, s e cor Milford st, 40x90. Effingham H. Nichols to Julia E. Browne. 700

Elton st, w s, 75 s Blake av, 25x83. Bridget Sinot to Henry Kruse. 1,775

Elton st, e s, 278.5 n Atlantic av, 25x100. Frederick Eiermann to George C. Hatterer. *Mt.* $2,000. 3,600

Elton st, e s, 190.2 s Fulton st, 25x100. Julia J. wife of and Wilbur H. Whitlock to Mary Parkhill. 350

Essex st, w s, 200 s Ridgewood av, 30x100, hs & ls. Theodore M. Le Beau and John Fensch to Christian H. W. Lueders. 3,800

Ewen st, w s, 100 s Jackson st, 25x100. Andrew J. Onderdonk to David Michel. 1,600

Fulton st, n s, 25.6 w Cleveland st, 25.6x109.9 x25x104.7. Louis Ilsemann to Frank Ehlers. 6,000

Same property. Release mort. Williamsburgh Savings Bank to Louis Ilsemann. 4,000

Fulton st, n e cor Elton st, 25.6x103.4x25x108.6. James W. Crawford to Mathilde Lehmann. Sub. to assessm't. 1,975

Fulton st, s s, 180 w Troy av, 20x100. Walter S. Davies exr. of James Pilling to James Pilling. 6,000

Same property. James P. Rappelyea and Susan E. Collins and Agnes D. Davies to same. Q. C. nom

Furnald st, n s 114.6 w Hudson av, 20x100, Flatbush. Luke Mahon to Emideo Furfind. 770

Gerry st, s s, 150 e Harrison av, 25x100, h & l. Abraham Arndt to Isaac Newman. *Mt.* $9,000. 10,000

Grand st, s s, bet Morgan av and Newtown Canal Interior, lot 19 block 927 assessm't map, 18th Ward. John C. McGuire, Registrar Arrears, to Charles R. Smith. 458

Same property. Same to same. 400

Same property. Charles R. Smith to Martin Kalbfleisch's Sons Co. nom

Grand st, n e s, 143 s e Kent av, 25x134.8x25.6x 131.10. Henry W. Junge to Henry Distler. All liens. nom

Same property. Henry Distler to Henry W. Junge and Anna M. his wife. All liens. nom

Hall st, e s, 124.6 n Myrtle av, 25x100. Thomas Hanlon to Ellen Hanlon. B. & S. nom

Halsey st, s e s, 100 n e Evergreen av, 20x100. Ernestine Gastmeyer to Mary J. Hunter. 4,500

Halsey st, s e s, 200 s w Central av, 20x100. James Gascoine to Joseph R. Platt and Julia his wife. nom

Harman st, s s, 300 e Central av, 50x100. Adam Henrich to William Berlinger. 2,800

Hendrix st, w s, 125 n Fulton av, 25x100. John Hahn to Thomas Bloomer. 1,300

Herkimer st, s s, 365 e Utica av, 20x135.6. Harvey H. Thompson to Irene C. wife of Harvey H. Thompson. B. & S. nom

Same property. Irene C. wife of Harvey H. Thompson to James Kiely. *Mt.* $2,750. 4,000

Herkimer st, s s, 155 w Albany av, 26.3x100, h & l. Rosita H. Davis to James P. Philip. *Mt.* $4,500, &c. 40

Hull st, w s, 90 s Bushwick Boulevard, 120x100. Edward B. Sturges to Rebecca C. Brooks. *Mt.* $13,500. exch

Hull st, n s, 60 w Stone av, 30x100. Margaretha Lewis to Ida E. Stratton. *Mt.* $8,000. nom

Hull st, s s, 206.3 w Hopkinson av, 18.9x75.8x18.10x77.9. Mary C. Donohue to Spencer Aldrich, New York. *Mt.* $4,250, taxes, &c. exch

Hull st, s s, 150 w Hopkinson av, 37.6x79.1x37.8x84.10, h & l. George H. Chinnock to John O. Hoyt. *Mt.* $8,500. nom

Humboldt st, e s, 447 s Newtown Pike, 22x100, h & l. Arabella Kingsland individ and extrx. John A. Kingsland to Joseph A. Ganzke and Wladislawa his wife, joint tenants. 2,000

Huron st, n s, 350 e Manhattan av, 25x100, h & l. Timothy Brennan to Murtha H. Kavanagh. 3,950

Same property. Release mort. John H. W. Viemeister to Timothy Brennan. nom

Jerome st, e s, 160 s Dumont av, 20x100. Charles Johnson to James H. Brundage. 300

Jerome st, e s, 180 s Blake av, 20x100. Charles F. Duryea to George H. Cook. 350

Junius st, e s, 120 s Dumont av, 40x85. A. Judson Palmer to Fanny B. Perkins. 2,500

Logan st, e s, 625 n Liberty av, 25x100, h & l. Israel T. Cochran to Edward F. Miller. 2,850

Lawrence st, e s, 100 s Tillary st, 25x106.6. James Gibbs to Charles Disch. 6,060

Macon st, n s, 200 e Patchen av, 90x100. Release mort. William Ziegler to Jane Mieler. 6,750

Macon st, s s, 90 e Ralph av, 90x100. Release mort. William Ziegler to John R. Pitt. 6,750

Macon st, No. 747, n s, 344.10 e Ralph av, 18x100. F. Augustus Conkling to Isaac G. Merritt and Margarete Ve B. his wife. *Mt.* $4,000. 6,600

Macon st, n s, 203 w Howard av, 18x100, h & l. Calvin W. Raymond and Michael Dowley to Mary E. wife of Geo. W. Brown and Sarah E. Stainburn. *Mt.* $4,500. 6,400

Madison st, s s, 225 w Howard av, 25x100. Andrew L. Dalton to Charles and Frederick Marquart. 1,800

Madison st, s e s, 98 s w Knickerbocker av, 18x100. George A. Craig to Annie L. Covert. *Mt.* $2,000. nom

Madison st, n s, 350 w Ralph av, 18x100. Wilhelmine Lembert widow to Margaret Bossert. exch

McDonough st, s s, 234.4 e Reid av, 16.8x100, hs & ls. Henry B. Hill to Ella Burtis. *Mt.* $4,000. 6,300

McKibbin st, n w cor Leonard st, 25x100. John Ketterle to Samuel Parshelsky. 14,000

McKibbin st, n s, 150 w Bushwick av, 25x100. Michael and John Bohleber to August Gomer and Jacob Wollpert. Q. C. and confirmation deed. nom

Middagh st, n s, 178 w Henry st, 22.5x100.8. Stephen Miller to The New York World Cooperative Building and Loan Assoc. nom

Moffat st, n w s, 200 n e Hamburg av, 100x100. Release mort. Alfred J. Pouch to Minnie S. Cornell. 1,000

Monroe st, s s, 365 e Bedford av, 40x83.6x40x87.6. Joseph W. Alsop, Middletown, Conn., to Mary O. Alsop, of New York. *Mt.* $6,000. 7,500

Monroe st, s s, 337.6 e Stuyvesant av, .04x100. Release mort. Joseph McMurray to Mary J. McMurray. nom

Same property. Mary McMurray to A. Stewart Walsh. 100

Monroe st, w s, 200 s Clark st, 25x100. Cornelia M. Peabody to Frederick W. Peabody, New York. Sub. to morts. nom

Newport st, n w cor Watkins st, 50x100. Henry Luhrsen to James O'Halloran. *Mt.* $500. 1,500

Same property. James O'Halloran to Catherine Dilzer. *Mt.* $500. 2,300

Newport st, extends from Stone av to Watkins st, 200x200.
Watkins st, e s, 200 n Newport st, 50x100.
Robert L. Woods to William H. Mount. *Mt.* $1,000. 7,200

North Elliott pl, w s, 166 n Auburn pl, 32x100. Alexander Brown to Catherine M. Brown. nom

North Henry st, e s, 152.3 n Van Pelt av, 17x100. Charles Engert to John W. Johnson. 3,500

North Henry st, e s, 118.3 n Van Pelt av, 17x100. Same to John H. Keppelman. 3,500

Osborn st, w s, 225 s Belmont av, 25x100. Max Pokalsky to Herman Graff and Solomon Michael. *Mt.* $4,400. 5,950

Osborn st, w s, 225 n Blake av, 25x90. Mary Zimmerman widow Andrew to Annie Zwerdling. 1,450

Osborn st, w s, 225 n Blake av, 25x90, h & l. Annie Zwerding to Henry Arkowitch and Davis Barow. *Mt.* $700. 1,650

Osborn st, e s, 175 n Belmont av, 25x100, h & l. Charles Shapiro and Davis Nichol to Pesak Midonsky. *Mt.* $1,800. 3,775

Osborn st, w s, lot 139 map No. 2 G. S. Thatford property, East New York, 25x90. Henry Dove to Jacob Greenberg and Israel Lewis. *Mt.* $700. 1,725

Pacific st, n s, 80 e Brooklyn av, 20x100. Sarah A. wife of and Andrew Miller to Frances O. Drisler. *Mt.* $7,000. nom

Powell st, w s, 150 s Glenmore av, 25x100. Alvina Buechner widow to Lucinda H. Jones. 600

President st, n e s, 320 s e Nevins st, 20x100, h & l. Thomas Dunn to Joseph Sisto and Raphael Sanseverino. *Mt.* $3,300. 4,000

President st, s s, 142 e Henry st, 25x100. Elizabeth W. Lewis, Hempstead, L. I., to Elizabeth W. Lewis. *Mt.* $3,500. 9,000

Palmetto st, s e s, 117 s w Knickerbocker av, 16x100.
Palmetto st, s e s, 201 s w Knickerbocker av, 17x100.
Cooper st, s s, 52 w Knickerbocker av, 16x80.
Norman R. Neiley to James S. Leonard. Sub. to morts. nom

Park pl, s s, 191.3 e 6th av, 16.8x100. Foreclos. John Courtney, sheriff, to Anna E. Thien. 570

Parkway, n s, 129 e Schenectady av, runs north 220.7 to Degraw st, x east to point 184.3 from Schenectady av, x south and east 225.10 to Parkway, x west 100 to beginning. William M. Evarts, of New York, to Charles Fabr. 6,400

Partition st, n e s, 100 n w Richards st, 25x100. Partition deed. William J. Carr ref. to Joseph M. Foley. 5,000

Plymouth st, Nos. 321 and 323, n e s, 200.1 s e Hudson av, 28.3x100. Eugene H. Vanderbilt to Lizzie R. Reynolds. *Mt.* $11,000. 21,000

Powell st, w s, 182 n Liberty av, 18x100. John F. Vrooman to Annie C. Carpenter. *Mt.* $2,000. 3,300

Quincy st, s s, 100 e Reid av, 72x110. Charles H. Doremus to Catharine Schard, Amityville, L. I. *Mt.* $7,500. 15,000

Roebling st, n w s, 80 s w North 7th st, 20x100. Daniel Springsteel, Greenburgh, N. Y., to Elizabeth T. and William V. Schilling. 2,300

Ross st, southerly cor Marcy av, 20x69.10. Ada L. Smith to Sarah E. Wilson. *Mt.* $1,000 nom

Ross st, n w s, 255.1 n e Bedford av, 19.11x100. Release mort. The Taylor & Fox Realty Co. (Lim.) to George C. Mahon, of Plainfield, N. J. no consid

Same property. George C. Mahon to John W. Sullivan. *Mt.* $5,000. 10,000

Rush st, s s, 150 w Wythe av, 20x100. Jacob Danman and Solomon Scheikowitz to Joseph Newborg, of New York. *Mt.* $5,000. 10,000

Same property Joseph Newborg, of New York, to Jacob Danman. *Mt.* $5,000. 10,000

Ryerson st, w s, 604.5 n Myrtle av, 20x100. Robert Gabriel to Heymann Hecht. ½ part. *Mt.* $2,800. nom

Sackett st, n s, 75 w Smith st, 19x100. Rachel wife of and John Faulkner to Albert and Martie Bonk. 4,900

Schaeffer st, s e s, 200 s w Bushwick av, 25x100. Margaret wife of Philip Bossert to Wilhelmine Lembert widow. *Mt.* $4,250. exch

Schermerhorn st, s s, 24.10 w Nevins st, 18.9x100. Herman Posbergh to Frank Andemars 8,500

Seigel st, n s, 9.7 e Broadway, 20x50, h & l. Eva wife of Henry Freedman to Henry Freedman. nom

Sherman st, e s, 180 s Greenwood av, 40x115.4x41.8x126.11, Flatbush. Henry Rudloff to Theresa L. Haskins. *Mt.* $1,500. 3,400

Stanhope st, n w s, 250 n e Hamburg av, 25x100, h & l. Adam Metz to Karl Enderle and Augusta his wife. *Mt.* $3,000. 5,900

Stewart st, n w s, 236.5 n e Broadway, 21.4x113.6x75.11x100. Charles Ebel to Tobias Hermann. 4,000

Sumpter st, n s, 450 e Howard av, 25x100. Gottlieb Keller to John North. 3,000

Troutman st, s e s, 167.1 n e Wyckoff av, 25x100. John H. Van Thun to Edmund Stein. Sub. to assessm't. $12. 350

Union st, n s, 175 w 4th av, 25x95. David J. Ramsdell to George R. Brown. *Mt.* $10,000. nom

Union st, n s, 175 w 4th av, 25x95, h & l. George R. Brown to David J. Ramsdell. 18,000

Van Siclen st, w s, 124.3 s Av T, 80x98x82.6x118.4, Gravesend. Sarah A. wife of Harmin V. Storm to Dora E. Rice. ——

Vanderbilt st, n s, 260.7 e Gravesend av, 75x300 to Seeley st, x85.2x300.2, Flatbush. Foreclos. William B. Hill ref. to William C. Dornin. *Mt.* $987. 2,650

Varet st, n s, 50 w Humboldt st, 25x100, h & l. Leonhard Schneider to Louise wife of Sebastian Hoh. 1,000

Varet st, n s, 75 w Humboldt st, 25x100, h & l. Heinrich Langlois to Joseph Zirinsky. 3,350

Vermont st, w s, 141.8 n Liberty av, 33.4x100, hs & ls. Mary H. Sopher to James Gilchrist. Sub. to morts. exch

Wallabout st, s e cor Kent av, 75x100, 3 hs & ls. Thomas Hanlon to Ellen Hanlon his wife. B. & S. nom

Warren st, s s, 275 w Flatbush road, 50x85x52.2x100.1. John Kennedy to Mary E. Humphrey. Sub. to mort. 2,500

Warwick st, w s, 105.6 n Fulton st, 25x95. John C. Schenck to James H. Hart. 760

Same property. James H. Hart to Peter G. Kerr. 875

Weirfield st, s e s, 75 s w Bushwick av, 20x100, h & l. Barbara Seitz to William Schwencke. *Mt.* $3,000. 6,650

Weirfield st, n w s, 221 s w Central av, 20x100. Leopold J. Lippmann to John Haas. nom

West st, e s, 50 s Broadway, 50x100. Albert A. Gerlach to Charles E. Cloud. 762

Watkins st, w s, 225 s Belmont av, 50x100. Hyman Kaplan to Isaac Marx, New York. 1,550

Watkins st, e s, 25 n Riverdale av, 25x100. Mary E. Cook, Newtown, L. I., to Sarah Burstein. *Mt.* $1,300. 2,400

Watkins st, e s, 125 s Dumont av, 200x100. Catharine L. Babcock widow to Jacob Manheim. *Mt.* $2,000. 4,000

Watkins st, w s, 100 s Dumont av, 25x100, h & l. John Monsees to Rubin Robinson. *Mt.* $1,950. 2,900

Watkins st, w s, 175 n Livonia av, 25x100. Catharine Dilzer widow to James O'Halloran. *Mt.* $2,150. 2,550

Same property James O'Halloran to Piser and Abram Germansky, of New York. *Mt.* $1,200. 3,100

Windsor pl, n s, 223.3 e 9th av, 38x100. John Assip and Timothy J. Buckley to Gita Kohnstamm. *Mt.* $2,500. 8,000

Wolcott st, n e s, 165 s e Van Brunt st, 25x100. John Kelbride to Mary wife of Francis Mullady. nom

2d st, s s, 437.11 e 5th av, runs east 8 x south 95 x west 76.11 x south 5 x west 3.1 x north. Release from covenant. Charles Hagedom to Archibald McBean. nom

North 2d st, s s, 150 w Leonard st, 25x100, h & l. Jacob Nelson to Valentine Becker. 3,500

3d st, s s, 104 e Smith st, 19x80. Vina A. Sumner, of Syracuse, N. Y., to Mary Hefner. *Mt.* $3,500. nom

South 5th st, s s, 19.6 e Berry st, 20x50. Alvira Gutgesell to Alfred Brett. 6,000

6th st, n s, 114.6 w 6th av, 16.8x100. Samuel G. Richards to Andrew Peck. *Mt.* $4,000. 7,000

South 8th st, n s, 220 e Bedford av, 0.6x101.6. Henry C. Wright to William E. Horwell. 130

10th st, No. 350, s s, 271.9 w 5th av, 18.6x100, h & l. Delia A. Jerome to Minnie E. wife of James B. Day. *Mt.* $4,000. 6,250

14th st, n e s, 197.10 s e 8th av, 20x100. William H. McDonald to William Hawkins. *Mt.* $650. 1,800

14th st, n s, 217.10 e 8th av, .04x100. Catharine Beatty to William Hawkins. 175

Bay 16th st, n w s, 550 s w 86th st, 50x96.8, New Utrecht. Release mort. Archibald Young to William G. Morrissey. 750

16th st, n s, 347.10 e 10th av, 12.6x100, hs & ls. James Mackiverkin to Catherine Wilkie. 1,550

16th st, n s, 322.10 e 10th av, 37.6x100. Release mort. Patrick J. McGlinchy to James Mackiverkin. 4,500

16th st, n s, 322.10 e 10th av, 25x100. James Mackiverkin to Charles Williams. 3,150

19th st, s s, 250 e 3d av, 25x100. Ellen wife of Edwin Parsons to Frances F. wife of C. Fleuter. *Mt.* $1,200. 75

Bay 20th st, s e s, 260 s w 86th st, 165x96.8, New Utrecht. John V. Van Pelt to Leopoldina M. Chaves. 2,800

20th st, n s, 150 e 3d av, 125x100. Jeremiah O. Mahoney to John Andrews, Jr. Correction deed. nom

Same property. Release judgment. John Andrews to John Andrews, Jr. nom

20th st, n s, 200 e 3d av, 25x100. John Andrews, Jr., to Walenty Kaczmarek. *Mt.* $2,500. 4,650

22d st, s s, 300 e 6th av, 25x100. Eliza Donelly widow to Daniel Connelly and Ellen his wife. 1,000

22d st, n s, 275 w 5th av, 16.8x100; also,
Hamilton av, n e s, 106.9 n w Prospect av, runs northeast to Prospect av, x northwest to Hamilton av, x southeast to beginning.
Winant H. Bennett heir of Peter W. Bennett to Van Brunt W. Bennett. 1-6 part. 235

22d st, n s, 275 w 5th av, 16.8x100. Amanda B. Hotchkiss, Harmanus and Van Brunt W. Bennett, Catharine M. wife of A. V. W. Tandy and Emma B. wife of Daniel Dunlop heirs Peter W. Bennett to George B. Hall. 2,100

24th st, n s, 220 e 3d av, 20x100. Edward E. Bergen to Silas A. Condict. *Mt.* $2,700. nom

24th st, n s, 220 e 3d av, 20x100. Silas A. Condict to William F. Taylor. *Mt.* $2,200. 5,200

Bay 29th st, n w s, 100 s w Benson av, 100x96.8, New Utrecht. George A. Domminey to Robert Main. *Mt.* $1,200. nom

Bay 34th st, s e s, 80 s w 86th st, 60x96.8, Bensonhurst. James D. Lynch to Amos Nichols. 1,200

42d st, s w cor of the Driveway as shown on map of the International Docks, &c., 150x100, with half of the 100-foot slip, &c. The Brush Co. (Lim.) to Frank D. Creamer. 12,000

Same property. Sarah M., Wendell T. and Irving T. Bush to same. Q. C. nom

48th st, n s, 120 e 4th av, 20x100.2. Stephen Hazzard to Joseph Muller, of New York. *Mt.* $2,600. 4,600

56th st, s w s, 100 n w 12th av, runs northwest along st 26 x west along Cowenhovens lane 14.9 x southwest 95.7 x southeast 40 x northeast 100.2, New Utrecht. The Blythebourne Improvement Co. to Edwin Sands. 800

56th st, n e s, 140 s e 11th av, 40x100.2, New Utrecht. Holk D. Campbell to Ludwig Merklein, of New York. 600

59th st, s w s, 260 n w 17th av, 40x100.2; also,
60th st, n e s, 110.2 n w 18th av, 80x100.2, New Utrecht.
Release mort. William A. Copp exr. Mary M. Warner to Hans C. Pfalzgraf. 500

59th st, s w s, 260 n w 17th av, 40x100.2, New Utrecht. Hans C. Pfalzgraf to Johann G. Schanz. 600

60th st, n e s, 110.2 n w 18th av, 80x100.2, New Utrecht. Hans C. Pfalzgraf to John Tedd. 1,600

61st st, n s, 220 w 14th av, 20x100, Bath Junction. James V. S. Woolley to Plasido Bombaci. 225

66th st, s s, 200 w 12th av, 80x100, New Utrecht. John Miotk to Erik Carlson, New York. 800

67th st, n s, 140 w 13th av, 53.8x100.1x57.11x100, Lefferts Park. Effingham H. Nichols to George E. Gansmann. 500

70th st, n s, 110 w 15th av, 20x100, New Utrecht. James V. S. Woolley, of New York, to Joseph Wallak. 260

72d st, s s, 235.10 w 18th av, 40x100, New

Utrecht. John H. Hanley to James McClelland. 380

73d st, s w s, 310 s e 3d av, 40x100, hs & ls. Daniel E. Driscoll to William C. Hale. 5,000

73d st, s w s, 250 s e 3d av, 60x100, New Utrecht. Thomas Gillespie to Gesche Gerken. *Mt.* $4,000. nom

76th st, n s, 470 w 15th av, 20x100, Lefferts Park. James V. S. Woolley to Sidney L. Harrigan. 150

78th st, n e s, 280 n w 19th av, 60x100, New Utrecht. John Lott Nostrand to George R. Lindley. 825

78th st, n e s, 220 n w 19th av, 60x100. Same to George R. Lindley. 825

80th st, n e s, 220 s e 12th av, 60x100.
11th av, west cor 77th st, 60x100, New Utrecht.
Hoik D. Campbell to Benjamin F. Antrim, Pittstown, Pa. 1,350

80th st, s w s, 180 s e 12th av, 40x100, New Utrecht. Same to Frank H. Antrim. 400

83d st, s w s, 200 s e 23d av, 60x100, Bensonhurst. James D. Lynch to Henry H. Robertson. 900

88th st, north cor Shore road, 361.3 to bulkhead line, x 102.10x368.3 to road, x 101.5, with land under water, &c., New Utrecht. David D. Field to Louis H. Schenck. 6,800

88th st, n w s, 175 n e 1st av, 50x100, error.
88th st, n w s, 100 s e 3d av, 50x191x51.3x 179.9, New Utrecht.
David D. Field, of New York, to John W. Porter. 550

East 94th st, s w s, 100 s e Flatlands av, 52.7x½ block x52.3x—, Flatlands. Hermann Lohmann to Clara E. Wilde. 400

Atlantic av, s w cor Buffalo av, 75x138.4x76.3x 124.6. Eugene A. Lachaise to Alfred Ogden. *Mt.* $5,900. 6,000

Atlantic av, s s, 260 e New York av, 20x100. Mary C. Skelly to William J. Skelley. nom

Atlantic av, s s, 240 e New York av, 20x100. Alice M. Lynes to William J. Skelley. 2,000

Atlantic av, s s, 200 e Hoyt st, 25x100. Ellis H. Lubry to Ester Krotosky. *Mt.* $4,000. nom

Same property. Ester Krotosky widow of Simon, of Scranton, Pa., to Augusta Lubry. *Mt.* $2,500. nom

Atlantic av, s w cor Buffalo av, 75x138.4 x west to point 100 w Buffalo av and 56.8 n of Pacific st. x south 21.8 x east 100 to Buffalo av, x north 165. Alfred Ogden to Thomas S. Denicke. Sub. to mort. 8,250

Atlantic av, s s, 200 e Utica av, 25x200 to Pacific st. Clemence G. Bates to Edmund Bates. 1,000

Atlantic av, n s, 143 w Grand av, 19x70. James P. McGarry to Margaret McGarry. *Mt.* $2,000. 3,000

Atlantic av, s s, 278.11 w Crescent st, known as lot 5 block 603 assessm't map 26th Ward. Catharine McCarty to Rebecca F. Forman. 475

Atlantic av, n s, 122.10 w Franklin av, runs west 60 x north 84.2 x again north 10.3 to Clove pl (closed), x east 52.6 x south 40 x again south 78.4, with all title to Clove pl. John Riley to Almira B. Smith. All title. Q. C. nom

Same property, excepting so much as lies within limits of any old road, railroad or highway. Same to same. *Mt.* $4,750. 5,750

Atlantic av, s s, 166.8 e Rockaway av, 16.8x100. Ella Patterson, New York, to Jessie M. Thompson, Yonkers, N. Y. *Mt.* $2,500. exch. and 4,000

Atlantic av, No. 2276, s s, 216.8 e Rockaway av, 16.8x100. Louis H. Myers, Jr., to Jessie M. Thompson. *Mt.* $2,000. 4,000

Bay Ridge av, at s e cor land of Charles H. Little, 40x100, New Utrecht. Frederick Vonderlehr to Rudolph F. Emmerich. 1,000

Buffalo av, w s, 75.6 n Pacific st, runs west 100.8 x south 31.1 x east 50.4 x east 50 to av, x north 40.6. James T. Kinney to Alfred Ogden. nom

Buffalo av, n w cor Pacific st, 35x100. Alfred Ogden to John Gibbons and Ellen his wife. Q. C. nom

Bushwick av, e s, 133.6 s Devoe st, 25x100. Franciska Ibert widow and Martin Ibert exr. of Anthony Ibert to Charles Stehlin. Correction deed. nom

Same property. Charles Stehlin to Philipp Rudmann. *Mt.* $4,000. 7,000

Bushwick av, w s, 50 s Halsey st, 20x79.4. George Koch to William Devermann. *Mt.* $5,500. 7,500

Carlton av, e s, 150 n Lafayette av, 26.6x100. James H. Oliphant trustee, &c., Elizabeth H. Bowman to Mary P. Morris. 9,000

Carlton av, w s, 308 n Lafayette av, 22x100. George Gravenhorst to Christopher G. Kinkel. C. a. G. nom

Same property. Christopher G Kinkel to Katharina D. Gravenhorst. C. a. G. nom

Central av, s w s, 25 s e Ralph st, 25x100. Simon Hutter to Adam Kaiser, Charles Rissler and August Todebusch. exch

Christopher av, w s, 150 n Lott av, 25x100. William Mitchell to Edmund Beardsley. 160

Clinton av, No. 97. William Baird, Riverhead, L. I., to Arietta Baird. ½ part. 1,681

Clason av, e s, 150 s Myrtle av, 25x100. Charles Collins to Frederick Niclas. *Mt.* $1,500. 3,000

Clason av, e s, 61 n Douglass st, 20x100. Warren Foote to George H. Roberts. Q. C. 600

Same property. George H. Roberts, Jr., to Warren Foote. Q. C. 650

Same preperty. Warren Foote to The Sisters of St. Joseph of the Brooklyn Diocese. 900

Clason av, e s, 61 n Douglass st, 20x100. Warren Foote to Sisters of St. Joseph of the Brooklyn Diocese. 900

De Kalb av, s s, 300 e Reid av, 25x100. Robert S. Neely to Margaret Costello widow. nom

De Kalb av, s s, 200 w Reid av, 50x100. Flora C. Enrich to Henry Battermann. 4,500

De Kalb av, s s, 415 w Nostrand av, 29x100. Leo Kohnstamm to John Assip and Timothy J. Buckley. *Mt.* $2,500. 4,500

East New York av, n w s, 121.10 s w Van Sinderen av, runs northwest 87.8 x west 26.2 x south 104.8 to Pacific st, x east 14.11 to East New York av, x northeast 70.11 to beginning. Release dower. Elizabeth widow of Whitson Colyer to Le Roy E. Bunker. nom

Same property. Elizabeth Colyer and John D. Brownell exrs. Whitson Colyer to same. 5,000

Flushing av, n s, 100 e Vandervoort pl, runs east 25 x north 119.2 x northwest 25.11 x south 125 11, h & l. Lazer Laurie to John A. Loehr and Anna M. his wife, joint tenants. *Mt.* $4,550. 7,500

Fountain av, Logan st, Eastern Parkway and Glenmore av, 400x200. William T. Gonndie and Charles M. Bellows to Henry J. Robinson, of New York. *Mt.* $6,500. 14,000

Fort Hamilton av, s e s, intersection n s 73d st, runs southeast 160 x north 100 x northwest 60 x southwest 75 x northwest 95.6 to av, x southwest to beginning, New Utrecht. Mary Schweitzer to Lena J. Meht. 4,000

Gates av, n s, 125 e Marcy av, 20x105, h & l. Hannah C. Somers to Sarah E. Butler. *Mt.* $7,600, taxes 1890, &c. 10,100

Gates av, n s, 100 w Tompkins av, 27x100. Mortimer E. Weldon, of Bristol, Conn., to Mary E. wife of Rowland Sweet. *Mt.* $4,000. nom

Gates av, Nos. 199 and 201. Charles D. Rust to John M. Holder exr. &c. Receipt of money deducted from bid in settlement of covenants, &c. 400

Gates av, s s, 135.1 w Evergreen av, 20x100. Release mort. Isaac and Abraham Rosenthal to Henry Roth. 1,000

Gates av, s e s, 100 s w Hamburg av, 25x115.6 x25.8x109.5. Henrietta Obst to Otto Singer and William Mogt. 1,275

Glenmore av, s s, 25.7 w Essex st, 25x100. Agnes West, New York, to James Mulroy. 400

Glenmore av, n w cor Christopher av, 25x100. John Herckes to Charles and Diederich Baecker. *Mt.* $500. 4,550

Graham av, e s, 41 s Maujer st, 20x54.9. Edward Hechinger to Barbara Berker. 3,650

Greene av, n s, 100 w Lewis av, 100x100. Isaac C. De Bevoise to Thomas B. Bryant. 11,500

Georgia av, w s, 275 n Liberty av, 50x100. Frederick A. Reid to Samuel Samelson and Pincus Ronginsky. *Mt.* $1,800. 3,200

Gravesend av, w s, 542 n 86th st, runs west 336 x south 333 to st, x northwest 143 x north 251 x west 194 x northeast 265 x east 118.6 to Van Sielen st, x south 58 x east 44.6 to Gravesend av, x south 120 to beginning, Gravesend. Rebecca E. Brooks widow to Edward B. Sturges. *Mt.* $4,800. exch

Hegeman av, n e cor Warwick st, 40x100. Annie E. wife of George Stelzenmuller to John B. Spiegel. 425

Hamburg av, east cor Moffat st, 100x100. Gordon Dunn, Passaic, N. J., to Minne S. Cornell. *Mt.* $2,500. nom

Harrison av, e s, 25 n Wallabout st, 25x100. Mary wife of John Haas to Sarah Taylor. nom

Hudson av, e s, 104.2 s Myrtle av, 50x100.5. Silas A. Condict to William H. Ferguson. 10,000

Hudson av, e s, 246 s Water st, runs east 50 x north 21 x east 60.6 to U. S. Navy Yard wall, x southwest 63.3 x west 73 to av, x north 29 to beginning. John G. Collins, Margaret E. wife of George Clark, Ann M. wife of James F. Donohue, children and devisees of Thomas Collins, to Constant Le Blanc, of New York City. 1,000

Jefferson av, n s, 255 e Stuyvesant av. Party wall agreement. William Johnston with Kate Acor. 200

Kingston av, n e cor Pacific st, 96x80. Benjamin F. Hobby to Daniel Doody. Q. C. *Mt.* $31,500. nom

Lee av, e s, 68.8 s Wallabout st, runs east 78.7 x south 15 x southeast 35.6 x north 81.3 to Lee av, x north 50, hs & ls. Jacob Bossert to Francis E. Clark. *Mt.* $8,000. nom

Same property. Francis E. Clark to Henry Roth. *Mt.* $8,000. exch

Lewis av, e s, 60 s Lexington av, 20x80. Eugenia H. Campbell to Hardy H. Dignan, New York. *Mt.* $6,700. nom

Lexington av, s s, 230 e Stuyvesant av, 20x100. Catherine Thompson to Cyrus L. Scottron. *Mt.* $3,000. 4,500

Lincoln av, e s, 100 s Adams av, 25x100. Luther L. Kellogg to Franklin A. Baltz. 2,000

Marcy av, e s, 36 n Gwinnett st, 18x85. John Van der Clute, of Woodhaven Junction, N. Y., special guard. of Kurt, George, Charles, Rosa, John, Samuel and Esther Winkel to John Fehrs. *Mt.* $1,900. 500

Marcy av, w s, 17 n Vernon av, 33x82, h & l. Conrad Dickel to Eleanor Firth. *Mt.* $6,000. 9,600

Marcy av, n w cor Vernon av, 17x82x18x50x 100. Release mort. Robert A. Mackenzie to Conrad Dickel. 3,000

Narrows av, east cor 68th st, 146.10x535.7x 146.7x518.
Narrows av, north cor 68th st, 146.10x458.9x 146.3x446.3, New Utrecht.
Henry H. Cochran to Eliphalet W. Bliss. *Mt.* $43,500. nom

Ovington av, n s, 108 6 w Stewart av, 30x170.2, Bay Ridge. George Self to Abraham A. De Groff. 660

Patchen av, w s, 105 s Hancock st, 15x100. Margaret Van Ostrand to John W. Gasteiger. *Mt.* $4,000. 5,500

Patchen av, s e cor Halsey st, 100x200. Hiram Bedell, of East Orange, N. J., to William E. Valentine. Sub. to morts. nom

Putnam av, s s, 179 e Ralph av, 49.6x100. Alfred L. Beasley and Charles Lewis to Charles Lewis. nom

Putnam av, s s, 230 e Marcy av, 20x100. Lydia F. Gale widow to Martha J. Paul. 6,000

Rockaway av, e s, 50 n Belmont av, 25x100.1. Samuel Levy, New York, to David Greenstein, New York. *Mt.* $3,500. 6,400

Rockaway av, e s, 125 s Glenmore av, 25x100. Jacob Bluestein, of Newark, N. J., to Marcus Lehman. *Mt.* $1,850. 2,660

Rockaway av, e s, 150 s Glenmore av, 25x100.1. Jacob Manheim, of New York, to Kalman Flamanhaft and Samuel Shissel, of New York. *Mt.* $1,850. 2,590

Rockaway av, w s, 225 n Eastern Parkway, 25 x100. Nicoline Andersen to Benjamin Hyman. *Mt.* $2,000. 2,500

Saratoga av, e s, 22 n Marion st, 19x78. Samuel V. Hyers to Eva Hyers. All liens. 10,000

Schenck av, w s, 100 s Blake av, 25x100. Albert H. W. Van Sielen to John C. Uhl. Taxes, &c., from April, 1890. 450

Shepherd av, e s, 305.9 n Atlantic av, 100x101. Sarah E. wife of and William R. Wasson to Philip Mehl. *Mt.* $1,000. 1885. 2,300

Shepherd av, w s, 120 n Ridgewood av, 20x100. Daniel P. Morse to Peter C. Kerr. *Mt.* $400. 600

Shepherd av, e s, 353 s Ridgewood av, 17x101. Zipporah L. Hollister to Anna Leinfelder. *Mt.* $1,775. 2,900

Snediker av, e s, 100 s Dumont av, runs east 100 x south 60 x east 100 to Hinsdale st, x south 40 x west 200 to Snediker av, x north 100.
Hinsdale st, w s, 295 s Dumont av, 105x100.
Riverdale av, n s, extends from Hinsdale st to Snediker av, 200x300.
Riverdale av, s w cor Hinsdale st, runs south 400 x west 100 x north 25 x west 100 to Snediker av, x north 50 x east 100 x north 100 x west 100 to Snediker av, x north 50 x east 100 x north 75 x west 100 to Snediker av, x north 100 to Riverdale av, x east 200.
Newport st, n e cor Snediker av, 25x100.
New Lots road, n w cor Hinsdale st, runs north 171.4 x west 100 x north 100 x west 100 to Snediker av, x south 240 x east 20 x south 94.1 to road, x east 190.7.
Snediker av, w s, 100 n Dumont av, runs west 100 x south 100 to Dumont av, x west 80 x north 100 x west 20 to Vesta av, x north 299.2 x east 200.8 to Snediker av, x south 35.10 x west 100 x south 40 x east 100 to Snediker av, x south 240.
Dumont st, s s, 20 w Snediker av, runs south 100 x east 20 to Snediker av, x south 300 x west 20 x south 100 to Livonia av, x west 160 x north 100 x west 20 to Vesta av, x north 260 x east 100 x north 40 x west 80 x north 100 to Dumont av, x east 160.
Snediker av, Livonia av, Vesta av, Riverdale av, 200x500, block.
Riverdale av, Snediker av, Vesta av, Newport st, 200x500, block.
Snediker av, s w cor Newport av, runs south 350 x west 100 x south 50 x west 100 to Vesta av, x north 400 to Newport av, x east 200. Reserving rights of the Brooklyn & Rockaway Beach R. R. Co. in Vesta av.
Louis H. Irwin to Albert Scott. *Mt.* $30,000. 112,500

Same property. Albert Scott to Elihu J. Granger. *Mt.* $82,500. 112,500

Snediker av, n w cor Vienna av, runs northwest 20 x west 100 x north 130 to Hegeman av, x west 100 to Vesta av, x south 550 to Vienna av, x east 200.
Snediker av, s w cor Vienna av, runs south 290 to n s of proposed Fresh Creek Canal, x west and south along same to Stanley av, x west to Vesta av, x north 300 to Vienna av, x east 200.
Release mort. The Peoples' Trust Co. to Louis H. Irwin and Henry J. Robinson. 10,000

South Portland av, w s, 160 n Lafayette av, 20x 100, h & l. Annie F. Edwards to Emil M. Perbacs. *Mt.* $4,000. 7,600

Same property. Emil M. Perbacs to Alexander Hengstler, of New York. *Mt.* $4,000. 8,500

South Portland av, w s, 180 n Lafayette av. 20x 100. Same to same. 3-5 part. *Mt.* $4,000. 5,500

Same property. Harriet A. Purdy to Emil M. Perbacs. 1-5 part. Sub. to mort. 1889. 700

Same property. Annie F. Edwards and Lizzie Brand to same. 2-5 part. 1,400

Stewart av, e s, intersection south line land formerly occupied by the Methodist Episcopal Church, runs east 90 to land of R. Van Brunt, x north 80 to land of same, x east 582.10 x south 328.4 to point 100 south from 76th st, x west 638.1 to av, x north 110.1 to beginning, contains 3.7003 acres, New Utrecht. Julius W. Copmann to Peter S. Bogart. 6,000

Stone av, e s, 175 n Sutter av, 25x100. Barnet Levin and Max Gittelsohn to Betsie Siedenfried. 800

Stone av, w s, 66 n Blake av, 23x100. Mary A. L. Baker to Harris Fordnisky. *Mt.* $1,900. 2,300

Stone av, e s, 100 s Sutter av, 75x100. Oscar W. Velsor to Louisa wife of Nicholas Kaufold. 10,625

Stone av, e s, 150 s Belmont av, 25x100. Williamson R. Selover, of Jamaica, New York, to Herman Schneider and Abraham Blauferb. *Mt.* $2,300. 2,730

Stone av, n e cor Dumont av, 50x100. Mary E. Cook to Chauncey J. Hastings, all of Newtown, L. I. *Mt.* $800. 1,600

Stone av, e s, 125 s Liberty av, 50x200 to Christopher av. A. Judson Palmer to Louis Regenbogen. 3,000

Stone av, e s, 125 s Belmont av, 25x100. Williamson R. Selover, of Jamaica, New York, to Rosa Rudderman. *Mt.* $300. 700

Stone av, w s, 200 s Duryea av, 25x100. Thomas Cochran to William T. Evans, of Belman, N. J. exch

Stone av, e s, 300 n Newport av, 50x100. Eliza A. Dunning widow to Wolf Beller, Joseph Adam and Abraham Fischman. 530

Stuyvesant av, e s, 41.6 n Lexington av, 19.6x75, h & l. Eliza wife of Charles W. Smith to Ellen Haring. *Mt.* $1,000. 8,000

Stuyvesant av, w s, 119 2 n Madison st, 19.6x100. Maggie A. Cornell to Elizabeth L. Stokes. *Mt.* $4,500. exch

Stuyvesant av, n e cor Hart st, 16x60. Annie F. B. Ely to Mary J. Colyer and Emma E. Hill. nom

Stuyvesant av, e s, 61 n Macon st, 19.6x82. Robert Main, of Rondout, N. Y., to George A. Domminey. *Mt.* $4,000. 250

St. Marks av, No. 126, s s, 177.6 w Carlton av, 19x131. Daniel F. M. Class to George W. R. Class. ½ part. 3,333

St. Marks av, s s, 79.6 e Utica av, 38x127.10. Henry Smith to George F. Van Doorn. 1,350

Sutter av, s e cor Atkins av, 60x90. Mary wife of Thomas Smith to John Meehan. 1,100

Sutter av, n w cor Logan st, 100x90. Jay Nova and Felix Hessberg to Abbie E. wife of Edward H. Coffin. nom

Sunnyside av, s s, 225 w Miller av, 25x100. Peter N. Lammers to William H. Smith. 687

Sunnyside av, s s, 200 w Miller av, 25x100. Same to Charles Pfeiffer. 687

Sunnyside av, n s, 100 e Barbey st, 50x200 to Laurel st. Charles Corey to Henry Farrer. 2,875

Thatford av, s, 225 s Glenmore av, 25x100. Nathan Berman to Moses Tischler. *Mt.* $1,950. 1,375

Thatford av, e s, 100 s Glenmore av, 25x154.2x25x154.3. Andrew R. Culver to Moriz Handler, of Newark, N. J., and Samuel Balsam. 583

Thatford av n w cor Belmont av, 50x100.1. Andrew R. Culver to Louis Ratner. Taxes and assessm'ts from 1887. 800

Thatford av w s, 225 s Belmont av, 25x100.1. Joseph Davis to Tobie Eimann widow. *Mt.* $1,200. 2,700

Tompkins av, e s, 75 s Hopkins st, 25x75. Bernhard Levy to Jacob H. Bernkopf. *Mt.* $3,800. nom

Same property. Jacob H. Bernkopf to Theresa Levy New York. *Mt.* $3,800. nom

Tompkins av, w s, 58.4 s Kosciusko av, 16.8x100. Mary J. wife of William T. Evans, Monmouth, N. J., to Thomas Cochran. *Mt.* $2,500. other consid. and 500

Troy av, s e cor Malbone st, 60x100, Flatbush. Mark D. Knight to Margaret Farrell. 600

Utica av, w s, 142 s Pacific st, 17.4x75. Release mort. Henry Weil to Frank W. and Arthur J. Robbins. 200

Utica av, s w cor Earl st. extends from Utica av to Furnald st, 200x284.1, Flatbush. Jirah I. Foote and Mary E. Bradford exrs. Horatio N. Otis to Jacob Strauss. 2,000

Van Cott av, s s, 250 w Humboldt st, 25x99.4, h & l. Bernard Buchenholz and Solomon Blatteis to William Morris. *Mt.* $4,800. 6,200

Van Cott av, n e s, 25.11 s e Eckford st, 25.11x92.10x25x99.8. David Michel to Bernard Buchenholz. *Mt.* $4,000. 8,700

Vernon av, s s, 287 w Sumner av, 18x95. Henry Roth to Francis E. Clark. *Mt.* $5,500. nom

Same property. Francis E. Clark to Sigmund Eisenbach. *Mt.* $5,500. 8,000

Washington av, w s, 91.3 s Lafayette av, 35x185.11. Robert C. Embrer exr. Elizabeth L. Smith to Blanche M. wife of Clarence Creighton. 16,100

Wyckoff av, e s, bet Troutman and Starr sts, being lot 2 block 1161 assessm't map 18th Ward. John H. Van Thun to Edmund Stein. Assessm't $165. 700

3d av, e s, 80.2 n 55th st, 20x100. William Hunt to Henry G. A. Lamb, of New York. 7,400

3d av, s w cor Bay Ridge av, 50x97, New Utrecht. George Self to Copley H. Self. nom

4th av, w s, 40 n Carroll st, 20x100. George S. Wheeler to Antonio Christia. 1,500

5th av, s e cor 6th st, 28x97.9. Mary wife of and Herman Henken to Margaret wife of Alexander J. Rooney. *Mt.* $8,000. 13,000

6th av, n w cor 6th st, 20x79.10. Elizabeth wife of and Thomas Butler to Elizabeth wife of Henry Hartly. *Mt.* $8,000. 12,000

6th av, east cor 18th st, 20.2x70. William Rose to John H. Bahrenburg and Elizabeth his wife. *Mt.* $2,400. 6,250

7th av, west cor Lincoln pl, runs southwest 30 x northwest 90 x southwest 20 x northwest 20 x northeast 50 to pl, x southeast 100. Charles H. Collins to Thomas E. Warman, North Plainfield, N. J. Sub. to mort. $15,000 and to encroachment. nom

13th av, w s, 60 n 67th st, 20x100, New Utrecht. Effingham H. Nichols to Daniel H. Cranmer. 250

Lots 105-110 inclusive map Van Pelt manor, New Utrecht. Release mort. Townsend C. Van Pelt to John L. Nostrand. nom

Lots 110 and 123 map Linden terrace, Flatbush. Archibald Crawford, Philadelphia, Pa., to George Harper and Alfred W. Simpson. 900

Lots 163 and 164 map land John J. Voorhies, New Utrecht. Peter B. Brackin to Johann Klebbe. Q. C. nom

Lots 163-167 inclusive block F map of Vanderveer Homestead, 26th Ward. John H. Vanderveer to Anna Leinfelder. 2,800

Lots 69 and 70 map 430 lots Worth & Strawson, Flatbush. Release mort. Mary and Catharine Vanderveer and Eliza A. Martense to Jacob Worth and Vincent A. Strawson. 250

Same property. Jacob Worth and Vincent A. Strawson to Maria Donovan. 390

Lots 164 and 165 map 186 lots, Bay Ridge, J. Evarts Tracy property, 20x146.3, New Utrecht. Frank F. Brown, of Buffalo, N. Y., to Henry H. Cochran. 2,800

Lots 52-78 and 141-162 inclusive same map. Release mort. Jeremiah E. Tracy to Henry H. Cochran. nom

Same property. Frank F. Brown to Henry H. Cochran. *Mt.* $43,500. 64,225

Interior lot, 78.5 n Atlantic av, on line which at said n s Atlantic av is 222.10 w Franklin av and at centre Old Brooklyn and Jamaica pike, runs northeast 39.2 x northwest 38.6 x southwest 39.2 x southeast 33.6, being part of old road. Alanson Tredwell to William Waterworth. Q. C. 350

Interior lot, 25 s South 1st st, x108.6 e Bedford av, 3x18.9. Jane C. wife of Alfred Hobley to Robert B. Stokes. Q. C. nom

Appointment of trustees to care for their interests. E. J. Tyler and Anna E. La Pierre to H. H. Webb and J. J. Boworn, all of Georgia.

Brooklyn & Rockaway Beach Railroad, e s, lot 86 map by N. F. Palmer of lands of said R. R. Co., 15x1,110. Nicholas W. Schenck to The Brooklyn & Rockaway Beach R. R. Co. 1-24 part. nom

Declaration of trust. Ferdinand A. E. Hen to Edward Hen. 1862. nom

Flatbush to Canarsie Landing road, s w s, adj n Schenck, Canarsie, 165.3x211x164x211.5. Gevert Wendelkin to Albert P. Fisher. 1,300

Gravesend to New Utrecht road, s s, adjoins land of S. S. Strykers property, 23 3-100 acres, Gravesend. David S. Jones to Samuel W. Bowne. 39,000

Release guardian. Caroline wife of John Fenske formerly Rummel an heir of Edward Rummel to Michael Danzglock. 209

Release of all rights of dower, &c. Hannah L. Clayton to Ransom F. Clayton from whom she was divorced. nom

WESTCHESTER COUNTY.

JULY 15 TO 21—INCLUSIVE.

CORTLANDT.

Crane, Rachel B. to Chas. E. Ames, w s High st, 40x96. nom

Same to Seth Taber, w s High st, 40x96. nom

Field, Cortlandt de P. to Mary S. Underwood. lots 1, 7 and part 6, s e cor South and Requa sts, Catlin & Lent map. nom

Underwood, Mary S. to Nathan L. Ely, lot 1, same map. nom

Tompkins, Leander et al., Robert McCord ref., to James C. Ward, n s Academy st, 65x—; also s s Brown st, 30x150. $1,100

Wilson, Clemence R. to Sarah A. Hobby, s e cor Main and Field sts, 88x—. 1,760

EASTCHESTER.

Bard, William H. to Herman A. D. Hollman, lot 201, Washingtonville. 229

Brady, Hugh to Ferd. R. Elder, lots 10 and 12, Dunham Park. 400

Bates, George W. to Alfred K. Montgomery, part "Bates Farm," White Plains road, 63 acres. 25,000

Montgomery, Alfred K. to The North End Land Co., same property. 25,000

Bishop, Agnes to Gilbert F. Archer, lot 234 w s 7th av, Mt. Vernon, 50x100. 1,700

Bussing, John J. to Wm. D. Thurber, part lot 235 n w s Union st, West Mt. Vernon, 33.4x100. 933

Brush, Edw. F. to New York and Westchester Water Co., tract on Hutchinson River, 16 acres. 16,000

Fuller, Carrie W. by N. A. Lawlor ref., to Madeline Pierce, part lot 745 w s 8th av, Mt. Vernon, 37.6x105. 3,000

Gundlach, Karoline to Elizabeth A. Sackett, part lot 736 w s 8th av, Mt. Vernon, 50x105. 2,250

Henneberger, Herman to Owen O'Rourke, lots 43-46 w s 10th av, grantor's map, 100x105. 1,950

Knebel, Fred to Emily Thompson, e s Union st, 410 s Bridge st, 44x113.6. 2,900

Miller, Thos. L. to Jos. Mathern, lots 53 and 54 w s South 10th av, Henneberger map. 900

McGrath, Margery to Martha Wilson, part lot 35 e s 1st av, Mt. Vernon, 50x105. 4,000

Owen, Daniel to Sarah A. Stearns, lot 938 s s 16th av, Wakefield, 100x105. 1,600

Wells, Walter to Geo. H. Story, e s Union av, West Mt. Vernon, 64x100. 992

GREENBURGH.

Cunningham, Mary R. and ano. to Theo. M. Lochowic, lot 124 ft. s Dobbs Ferry road and 50 w R. R., Ardsley, 25x100. 300

Erhardt, Joel B. trustee to Mary A. Fleming, n s Station sq, 50 w Western av, 100x100. 1,400

Same to same and ano., s e cor Stanley av and Station sq, 50x100; also e s Stanley av, 25x100. 1,150

Fargo, Jas. C. and ano. to Chas. Worthington, s s Sunnyside road, adj Aqueduct, 4¼ acres. 12,972

Field, Laura B. to Peter J. Carpenter, e s Broadway, 50 n Belden road, 50x160. nom

Meeks, Robt. F. to Fannie E. Lawrence, n s Ashford road, 100 w Railroad, 39 acres. 28,057

Lawrence, Fannie E. to Cyrus P. Jones and ano., same property. 30,960

Vollmer, Wm. to John Culleton, lots 289-299 map Uniontown. 1,700

MAMARONECK.

Black, Alex. G. to John F. Black, w s Weaver st, adj Larchmont Water Co., 51 acres. 12,495

Kane, Michael A. to Mary C. Figuer, s w cor Beach and Oak avs, 100x125. 8,000

Spencer, Jas. C. to And. R. Bradley, lots 1, 22, 23 and 24 map property grantor. 5,700

Sidell, Phebe A. to Caroline M. Greve, w s Addison av, 100 s Chatsworth, 50x125. 3,800

Young, Chas. H. to same, w s Addison av, adj above, 50x125. 600

MOUNT PLEASANT.

Smadbeck, Louis and ano. to John Cameron, lots 17-20 and 52 Lakehurst Villa Park. 500

Smadbeck, Louis to Robert J. Gray, lots 1198 and 1199 Sherman Park. 300

Same to Lincoln Gray, lots 1176 and 1177. 300

Same to Ida Starke, lots 627 and 628. 200

Same to Rose Levy, lot 851. 100

Same to Pauline A. Palmer, lots 1098 and 1099. 400

Same to Rose Fraissinet, lots 896-899 and 1118. 400

Same to Leonce Fraissinet, lots 875, 876, 894, 895 and 1119. 400

Same to Fred. Nauds, lot 1090. 250

Same to Henry C. Schaeffer, lot 135. 175

Same to Gilbert B. Keeler, lot 604. nom

Same to Bernard P. Kernan, lot 263. nom

Same to C. F. Howland, lot 780. 100

NEW ROCHELLE.

Armstrong, Wm. A. to Fred. L. Merriam, lots 31 and 33 Park View av, map Park View. 400

Gregg, Jas. A. S. to Sarah L. Kendall, lot 10 Highland Park, 103x200. 3,000

Howe, Wm. H. I. to Sheldon B. Bruce, lot 37 s s Guion st, grantor's map, 50x162. 900

Same to Wm. A. Arnolds, lot 38, adj above, 50x160. 900

Levison, Solomon to Edw. Piering, w s Av A, 250 s Union av, 50x100. 1,000

NORTH CASTLE.

Purdy, Esther A. to Wm. K. Haviland, s s New road, adj grantee. 250

Smith, David W. et al., Wilson Brown, Jr., ref., to The Westchester Fire Ins. Co., The David W. Smith farm, 142 acres. 10,000

OSSINING.

Contant, Richd. W. et al., R. V. Boyd ref., to Mary C. Ryme and ano., w s McCord road, 6 acres. 5,000

Tompkins, Josephine M. to Herschell Smith, s s Croton av, 40 w Belleview av, abt 44x135. 500

PELHAM.

Daggett, Ezra to Aug. Godfrey, lot 313 w s 3d av, Pelhamville, 100x100. 800

Same to same, lot 11 e s 2d av, 100x100. 800

King, Elizh. R. B. exr. of, to Philip Flynn, lot 342 e s Main st, map estate grantor. 450

POUNDRIDGE.

Robertson, Wm. H. to Cecil C. Higgins, the "Chichester Farm," 79 acres. 8,625

RYE.

Damon, Carrie M. et al., M. Dillon ref., to Robt. K. Clark, e s Centre st, 551 s Westchester av, 50x196. 860

Kingsley, Kate J. to Eloise Eusko, s e s Locust av, part "Anna Lyon Farm." 4,800

Drew, George F. to Adelaide A. Wishart and ano., n w cor Olivia and Regents st, 50x130. 275

Same to same, lots 1 and 2, e s Regent and lot 4 n s Olivia st., map Drew property. 450

Same to John L. Thompson, lot 26 s s Olivia st, 50x110, same map. 170

Same to Louis Degnin, n s Olivia st, 205 e Regent, 100x100. 280

Same to Luke Reeney, s s Olivia st, 221 e Regent, 100x100. 425

Sands, Purdy G. to George H. Simpson, s s Sands st, 235.6 w Grace Church st, 85x70. 785

Graves, Ellen to John Ryan, n s Mill st, adj Abendroth Bros., 77.2x—. 6,200

WESTCHESTER.

Baumann, John C. to Michael Zentgraf, part lot 285 s s 12th st, Unionport, 25x108. 325

Camp, Hugh N. to Elizabeth Kyle, lot 300 map McGraw estate. 235

Same to Wm. Keleher, lot 327. 320

Same to Chas. Kuber, lot 270. 220

Same to Patrick Considine, lots 272 and 273. 460

Same to Joel Hull, lot 275. 215

Same to Chas. Hahn, lot 252. 310

Same to Valentine Gies, lots 260 and 261. 450

Same to And. Gray, lots 259, 285 and 286. 865

Same to Jas. L. Fitzpatrick, lot 359. 140

Same to Annie Engleson, lot 263. 225

Same to Ignatz Weisberg, lots 333-337. 965

Same to Samuel W. Davis, lot 355. 210

Same to Michael Casey, lots 328 and 329. 515

Same to Bernard Clark, lot 352. 210

Same to Patrick F. Brady lot 325. 175

Same to Jos. J. Cowan, lots 186 and 187. 560

Same to Geo. H. Taylor, lots 94 and 95. 680
Same to John B. Livingston, lot 156. 280
Same to Angelina Bale, lots 287, 313 and 314. 820
Same to Henrietta T Frielingsdorf, lots 305 and 306. 575
Same to Chas. Ward, lot 349. 200
Same to Wm. Muller, lot 281. 195
Same to Geo. J. Walker and ano. lots 291 and 292. 460
Same to Louis Wechsler, lots 322, 323, 347 and 348. 810
Same to Robt. A. Wier, lots 268 and 269. 450
Same to Margt. Snyder, lots 290, 264 and 265. 675
Same to Thos. Sweeney, lot 343. 140
Same to Henry Hickman, lot 288. 280
Same to Edw. Sherwood, lots 276 and 277. 450
Same to Geo. A. Springsteel, lots 266 and 267. 450
Same to Louis F. Silbereisen, lot 350. 205
Same to Dora Silbereisen, lot 351. 205
Same to Stiph. B. Provost, lots 356 and 357. 440
Same to Wm. H. Peters, lot 342. 140
Same to Franz Visata, lots 256 and 257. 500
Same to Finbar M. O'Brien, lot 284. 200
Same to Edw. O'Neil, lot 271. 405
Same to Steph. Mitchell, lots 295 and 296. 450
Same to Terence Murtha, lots 311 and 312. 480
Same to John J. Miller, lot 321. 200
Same to John McQuade, lot 70. 225
Same to Lawrenc McCarty, lot 326. 180
Same to Thos. Murtha, lot 297. 235
Same to Franz O. Dietze, lot 283. 195
Same to Patrick J. McManus, lot 315. 365
Same to Robertina Kuil, lot 278. 335
Ferris, Vincent to John L. Grennan, lot 169 s s 8th st, Unionport, 50x100. 500
Grube, Rosa exr of and ano. to Johan G. Maihofer, lot 44 n s 2d st, Unionport, 100x108. 1,525
Haines, Alfred and ano. to Richard Bray and ano., lot 329 s s 3d av, Wakefield, 100x105. 1,500
Haines, Alfred to Chas. F. Zimmer, part lot 865 n s 7th av, Wakefield, 75x114. 3,300
Jarrett, Geo. F. to Wm. H. Springsteel, e s Main st. 50 s Evadna st, 50x95. 2,500
Mapes, John S. to John M. Kuhbauth, e s Cornell av, 250 n Mapes av, 25x100. 215
Same to Fred. R. Morris, n s Maitland av, 175 w Mapes av, 50x100. 410
Same to Henry Herwig, s s Middleton road, 100 e Mapes av, 50x112. 625
Same to Tiburt Strassle, n s Zulette av, 150 w Mapes av, 100x100. 800
Mace, Levi H. and ano. to Herbert M. Newcomb, lots 17-20, 27 and 28, Laconia Park. 1,200
Same to Solomon Jimmerman, lots 25 and 26, Laconia Park. 400
Myers, Mary A. to Wm. Gillard, n s Maitland av, 178 e Old road, 25x100. 240
Macklin, John J. to Lula D. Coakley, s w cor Fowler pl and Van Cortlandt st. 600
Springstead, Wm. to Wilhelmina Lappe, lot 177 s s 8th st, Unionport, 200x216. 2,500
Sheil, Denis R. to And. Braun and ano., s w cor 13th av and 5th st, Wakefield, 165x114. 5,650
Tinagero, Josie A. to Wm. H. Sage, e s 3d av, 200 n 2d st, Olinville, 100x150. 100
Vail, Sarah W. to Chas. E. Knoll, e s 3d av, 300 n 1st st, Olinville, 50x100. 3,500

WHITE PLAINS.

Barnes, Samuel J. to Alicia H. Harkins, e s North st, adj. Solomon Haviland, 10 acres. 6,300
Faile, Samuel to Frank W. Pierce, s w cor Mamaroneck and Rutherford avs, 100x190. 1,600

YONKERS.

Davidson, John exr. of, to Leslie M. Saunders, w s Waverly st, 22.10 s Maple, 70x99. 6,500
Saunders, Leslie M. to Margt. M. Gorton, ½ int. same property. 3,250
Duff, Matilda admrx. of, to Elizb. B. Ulrich, w s New st. past School House, adj. Ethan Flagg, 40x100. 2,350
Duden, Herman to And. J. Mackay, blocks 32, 23 and 22 map Sunnyside Park. 1
Same to Jas. M. Simpson and ano., n w cor Bronxville and Texas avs, 203x326x45x215x180. 3,517
Druid Hill Park Co. to Bertha De Lancy, lots 495, 496 and 497, Mohegan Park. 1,500
Same to Chas. Duffy, lots 401 and 402. 1,000
Same to Victoria Bessunger, lots 547, 548 and 549. 1,500
Same to Mary Alcorn, lots 404 and 405. 1,000
Foote, Hannah W. to Michael McGrath, w s St. Josephs av, 223 s High st, 25x100. 750
Fowler, Clarence M. to Cornelia A. Sherwood, e s Crescent pl, 225 n Sherwood av, 50x100. 1,000
Gramatan Park Co. to Bertha De Lancy, lots 101, 102 and 103, Mohegan Park. 1,500
Same to Annie Duffy, lots 91 and 92. 1,000
Same to Charlotte Duffy, lots 89 and 90. 1,000
Same to Victoria Bessunger, lots 93 and 94. 1,000
Herriot, Ann M. to Thos. Derivan and ano., e s Willow st, 175 s Oak pl, 75x100. 825
Same to Fannie M. Lowerre, part plot 3 e s Park Hill av, map No. 1, Herriot property. 21,500
Morrison, Emma to John Allen, e s Fort Hill av, adj grantee, 7 acres. 1,363
Shearwood Hill Land Co. to John H. Corwin, lots 136, 137 and 138. 1,600
Shonnard, Fred. to Cornelius Heffernan, lot 190, Woodland av, City map. 175
Same to Patrick McDonald, lots 709 and 725, Nepperhan av, City map. 455
Schulz, Otto to Caroline Girardin, n s Maple st, 100 w Linden, 25x—. 5,800
Yonkers North End Land Co. to Jas. Cloughly, tract adj grantor and Northern R. R. 1

YORKTOWN.

Flewellin, Wm. H. to Cath. A. Covert, tract adj Abram Ryder, 84 acres. 3,000

MORTGAGES.

NEW YORK CITY.

JULY 17, 18, 20, 21, 22, 23.

Anderson, Elizabeth formerly Bauerlin wife of and Charles to The Henry Elias Brewing Co. 147th st, s s, 365 w Brook av, 75x100. July 16, demand. $1,600
Anderson, Walden P. to Robinson Gill, Brooklyn. 94th st, s s, 100 e Amsterdam av, 225x101.2 to centre line Apthorps lane, x—x91.8, with all title to lane. Sub. to morts. $162,250. July 17, note. 15,600
Ammon, Marie to Mary L. Fiegel. 88th st, s s, 217 e Amsterdam av, 17x100.8. July 10, due July 1, 1894, 5 %. 6,000
Adler, Ignatz to A. Hupfel's Sons. 2d av, No 2172. Lease. July 18, demand. 2,000
Aiker, Phillipp to John Corbett. Bergen av, s e s, 248.7 n Westchester av, 25x100. June 26, 1 year, 5 %. 400
Abraham, Adelaide with Josephine Taylor both mortgagees. Agreement as to priority of mortgagees made by William Watson. July 14. nom
Briggs, Thomas A. mortgagor with The American Baptist Home Mission Soc. mortgagee. Extension of mort. at 5 %. July 16. nom
Bereuter, Henry A. to Carolina A. Bereuter. 134th st P. M. July 23, due Aug. 1, 1895. 2,000
Byrne, John J. to THE NORTHERN BUILDING SAVINGS AND LOAN ASSOC. Highbridge av. July 18, installs. See Conveys. 3,000
Benziger, Nicholas C. to Lily W. Churchill et al. trustees Louis C. Hamersley. Edgecombe av, n w cor 150th st. 62.6x100. July 18, 3 years, 4½ %. 22,000
Brotherton, William to The Union Building Loan and Savings Inst. Fort Independence st, w s, south ½ plot 69 map W. O. Giles, Kingsbridge. July 20, installs, 5 %. 1,600
Bleier, Sigmund H. to Benjamin F. Reynolds. 123d st, s s, 260 w 3d av, 25x100.11. July 20, due Dec. 3, 1892, 5 %. 16,000
Becker, C. Adelbert to Katie M. Conklin. Madison av. P. M. July 21, 3 years, 5 %. 3,000
Buese, John to THE BOWERY SAVINGS BANK. 151st st, s s, 250 w Courtlandt av, 100x118.5. July 21, 1 year, 5 %. 12,000
Blumenthal, August to THE MUTUAL LIFE INS. Co. of N. Y. 88th st, s s, 125 w Central Park West. 150x100.8, July 20, 1 year, 5 %. 50,000
Bartels, Gustav and Sophia his wife to Silas D. Gifford and ano. exrs. and trustees Charles Bathgate. Courtlandt av, s e cor 157th st, 50x100. July 11, 3 years, 5 %. 2,500
Bauer, Moritz to William A. Darling pres't. 8th av, McDam road, 153d st and 154th st, block. May 8, 1 year. 10,000
Becker, C. Adelbert to Caroline Weiner. Washington av, e s, 372.9 n old Quarry road, 23.9x100x22.4x100. July 16, 3 years, 5 %. 3,500
Branigan, James E. to THE GERMAN-AMERICAN REAL ESTATE TITLE GUARANTEE Co. Amsterdam av and 67th st. P. M. July 14, due July 17, 1892, 5 %. 17,000
Same to Herman Fox and William A. Klingler. Same property. July 17, 1 year. 3,500
Brendlin, John J. to Anne M. Donnell, Newberne, N. C. 41st st, s s, 150 e 11th av, 25x98.9. July 17, 5 years, 5 %. gold, 10,000
Burch, Martha S. wife of T. Hamilton to William R. Beal Land Improvement Co. 141st st and Beekman av. P. M. July 8, 3 years, 5 %. 3,430
Bloom, Wolf and Saville Levin mortgagor, with Robert R. Willets as treasurer of N. Y. Monthly Meeting mortgagee. Extension of mort. July 21. nom
Bercke, Gustav to Paulina A. Morgan widow. Lexington av. P. M. July 22, 3 years, 5 %. 11,000
Brennan, Michael to William D. Manning. Central Park West, s w cor 75th st, 153.2x100. Sub. to mort. $400,000. July 21, due Dec. 31, 1891. 30,000
Cohen, Samuel and Bertha his wife to The Society Chebra Bnai Jischre Lef, a corporation. Houston st, s s, 90 w Goerck st, 20x50. July 20, due July 21, 1896, 4½ %. 6,000
Coffin, Lydia R. to George H. Byrd. 72d st, s s, 125 e West End av, 25x112.2. July 21, installs, 5 %. gold, 35,000
Cavinato, Luigi, Guiseppe, Steffano and Natale, of Cavinato Brothers to Daniel J. Carroll. South 5th av, No. 65, s e s, 100 n e Houston st, 24x100. June 25, 1 year or sooner. 655
Cohen, George J. to THE METROPOLITAN TRUST Co. trustee William R. Garrison. 80th st, s s, 330 e Amsterdam av, 20x102.2. July 22, 3 years, 5 %. 22,500
Same to same trustee William A. Seaver. 80th st, s s, 310 e Amsterdam av, 20x102.2. July 22, 3 years, 5 %. 22,500
Same to same. 80th st, s s, 270 e Amsterdam av, 20x102.2. July 22, 3 years, 5 %. 22,500
Same to same as trustee William R. Garrison. 80th st, s s, 290 e Amsterdam av, 20x102.2. July 22, 3 years, 5 %. 22,000
Camp, Hugh N. to A. D. Lawrence Jewett and ano. exrs. and trustees Richard W. Dickinson. Old Boston road. P. M. May 11, due July 2, 1893, 5 %. 96,816
Cohn, Amalie to Morris Smoley. Willett st. P. M. July 21, 3 years. 2,100
Cornet, William H. to George E. Hyatt. 21st st, n s, 425.2 e 9th av, 24.10x98.9. July 18, due Jan. 1, 1892. 22,000
Christman, George B. to Elizabeth Weimar. 64th st, s s, 100 e 2d av, 25x100.5. July 20, 3 years, 5 %. 11,000
Casey, Michael J. and Thomas F. to Fanny Maginn. 48th st, s s, 225 w 10th av, 25x100.5. Lease. July 20, 5 years 7,000
Cooke, Thomas F. to Sophie Rothschild. 79th st. P. M. Sub. to mort. $7,000. June 30, due July 1, 1892, 5 %. 10,000
Same to same. Same property. Sub. to morts. $17,000. June 30, due July 1, 1892. 16,000
Card, Margaretta wife of James V. D. to "Isabella Heimath," a corporation 70th st, s s, 239.4 w West End av, 23.2x100.5. July 21, 3 years, 4½ % 10,000
Cavinato, Luigi, Steffano, Guiseppe and Natale to James A. Billings trustee James F. Seymour. 53d st, n s, 250 w 9th av, 25x100.5. July 21, due July 15, 1894, 5%. gold, 20,000
Same to Marx and Moses Ottinger. Same property, July 21, due Aug. 20, 1891. 2,000
Same to The Bradley and Currier Co. (Lim.) Same property. Sub. to mort. $20,000. July 21, 1 month. 3,236
Collins, Michael C. to THE TITLE GUARANTEE AND TRUST Co. 77th st, No. 421, n s, 394 w Av A, 25x102.2. July 23, 3 years, 5 %. 8,000
Cimino, Vito to A. Adler & Co. Mulberry st, No. 58, e s, 125 s Bayard st, 25x92.9x25x93.11. July 23, 3 years, 5 %. 10,000
Cregan, James to William R. Mason. 37th st, n s, 325 e 8th av, 25x98.9. July 23, due Aug. 1, 1892. 3,000
Cowman, Thomas to Flamen B. Candler and ano. trustees Joshua Brooks. 119th st, s s, 150 e 8th av, 25x100.11. July 23, 3 years, 5 %. 19,200
Same to same. 119th st, s s, 125 e 8th av, 25x100.11. July 23, 3 years, 5 %. 18,700
Same to John R. M. Heruz trustee Ramon M. Heruz. 119th st, s s, 100 e 8th av, 25x100.11. July 23, 3 years, 5 %. 19,000
Donohoe, Edward to Patrick Conway, Brooklyn, N. Y. Cambreling av, s e s, 100 n e Columbine st, 100x100. Oct. 11, 1889, demand. 150
Dale, Anna T. wife of James S. to Mortimer F. Porter guard. Victor E. Francire. Walton av, w s, 245 s 150th st, 17.6x103.6x17.6x102.8. July 21, 3 years, 5 %. 5,000
Dunne, Thomas P. and Maria D. his wife to John B. Quinlan. 116th st, s s, 150 w Manhattan av, 25x100.11. July 22, 1 year. 2,500
Dieterich, August to Susan H. Geissenhainer. 10th av, e s, 75.5 n 51st st, 25x75. July 21, 3 years, 5 %. 2,000
Donovan, Lizzie to Cornelius J. Donovan. Broome st, s s, 90 e Sullivan st, 20x60.6. July 21, 1 year, 5 %. 1,000
Day, Thomas D., Jr., to Percy R. and Moses T. Pyne and Thomas H. Barber. West 8th st, s s, 72.10 e Macdougal st, 24.3x100. July 21, 5 years, 4½ %. 17,100
Dexheimer, Albert and Julia widow to John C. Boettner. West Houston st, n s, 18 e Thompson st, 19.2x62. July 20, 2 years, 5 %. 11,000
Dunne, Thomas P. to Marx and Moses Ottinger. 116th st. P. M. July 16, due Dec. 19, 1891. 22,500
Dennerlein, Julia to Mary B. and William O'Donnell. College av. P. M. June 26, 3 years, 5 %. 2,000
Davis, Theodore A. L. to TITLE GUARANTEE AND TRUST Co. 18th st. P. M. July 20, 3 years, 5 %. 7,500
Dow, Myron W. to William J. Light. Eagle av, w s, 50 s 163d st, 50x100; Elton av, n e cor 161st st, 33x70. July 15, demand. 3,500
Davall, Reuben J. to Mary A. D. Lange. Webster av, e s, 100 n 179th st, 75x100. July 13, due July 15, 1894. 5,000
Denmark, William S. mortgagor with Mabel Sands, London, Eng. Agreement extending reduced mortgage at 5 %. Feb. 13, 1889. nom
Egan, John J. and Daniel Hallecy to THE GERMANIA LIFE INS. Co. 103d st, n s, 166 e West End av, 3 lots, each 17x100.11. 3 morts., each $13,500. July 17, due Nov. 30, 1894, 5 %. 40,500
Same to same. 103d st, n s, 183 e West End av, 17x100.11. July 17, due Nov. 30, 1894, 5 %. 14,000
Elderd, William E. to THE HARLEM SAVINGS BANK. Edsall st, s w s, at n w cor of George Greene's lot, 30x100. July 17, 1 year, 5 %. 3,000
Elgar, Benjamin F. to Jessie Williams. Horatio and Greenwich sts. P. M. July 16, 1 year. 2,500
Fay, John G., Eastchester, N. Y., to Cornelia A. Shearwood, Yonkers, N. Y. Hudson st, w s, 50 n Franklin st, 25.3x100.2. July 1, 1 year. 1,000
Fay, Joseph J. to Conrad Stein. Amsterdam av, No. 160. Saloon lease. July 20, note, demand. 3,000
Fitzgerald, James to George Ehret. 8th av, No. 2190, n e cor 118th st. Saloon lease. July 20, demand. 2,225
Friedhoff, John P. and Henry C. Meyer to John C. Oscar. 1st av, s e cor 5th st, 21.9x67.2. Lease. July 1, 3 years. 8,000
Fuller, Henry S. to Elmer A. Allen. Edenwood av, w s, 137.8 n St. James st, 50x106 to Croton Aqueduct. July 16, 1 year, 5 %. 1,500
Feiner, Sarah wife of and Solomon to David Moss. 79th st. P. M. Sub. to mort. $18,000. July 15, 4 years. 6,000
Farrington, Georgie E. wife of John A. to Deborah A. Haviland. 133d st, s s, 166.8 e 8th av, 16.8x99.11. July 21, due July 1, 1894, 5 %. 1,000

Flanagan, Mary A. widow to Charles Kinken, Brooklyn. Av B, s w cor 14th st, 23x95. July 15, due July 1, 1896, 5 %. 12,000

Frank, Jacob A. to Philipp Hill and Katie his wife. 150th st, s s, 450 w Courtlandt av, 25x 100. July 1, 3 years, 5 %. 1,200

Farrington, Isabella D. to The Mutual Life Ins. Co. 20th st, n s, 290 e 2d av, 20x92. Already mortgaged to party of second part. July 20, due July 21, 1892, 5 %. 500

Franklin, Morris to Thomas D. Mason and ano. trustees Sidney Mason. 72d st, s s, 363 e 1st av. P. M. July 23, 3 years, 5 %. 15,500

Same to Caroline L. Macy. 72d st, s s, 313 e 1st av. P. M. July 23, 3 years, 5 %. 16,000

Same to same. 72d st, s s, 338 e 1st av. P. M. July 23, 3 years, 5 %. 16,000

Gahren, Charles to Susan J. Gale widow. Columbus av, n e cor 92d st. P. M. July 23, 1 year, 5 %. 32,625

Same to Edwin Baldwin guard. Hamilton A. Gale. Same property. P. M. July 23, 1 year, 5 %. 32,625

Garcewich, Robert to Ernestine and Louise Day. 72d st, s s, 338 e 1st av. P. M. July 23, 5 years, 5 %. 15,000

Same to Pincus Lowenfeld. Same property. P. M. Sub. to mort. $15,000. July 23, 2 years, 5 %. 1,000

Graham, William J. and Mary E. to Edwin Baldwin exr. John Hardman. Madison st, s s, 239.11 e Scammel st, 23.6x94.10x23.6x95 1. July 23, 3 years, 5 %. 12,000

Gray, William H. to The Mutual Life Ins. Co. 72d st. P. M. July 13, due July 23, 1892. 5 %. 32,500

Gaddis, Mary T. wife of David E. to The Teachers' Mutual Benefit Assoc. 132d st, n s, 260 w Lenox av, 16x99.11. July 13, due July 1, 1896. 5 %. 7,500

Goerlitz, John to Samuel Untermyer. Greenwich av, Nos. 17 and 19, w s, 26.2 s West 10th st. 50x90.6x50.6x81.8. July 17, 6 months. 10,000

Gough, Edward to George Ehret. 120th st, No. 219 E. Lease. Demand. 500

Galway, Harry to Andrew Ewald. Columbus av, w s, 75.9 n 97th st, 25.1x100. Secures bond of mortgagor and Elias T. Hatch. July 23, due June 1, 1892, 5 %. 10,000

Greenberg, David to Magdalena Mixsell. Columbia st. w s, 100 n Stanton st, 25x100. July 1, 5 years, 5 %. 10,000

Giese, Heinrich and Emma his wife to Adolph Mansen and Elise his wife. 84th st, n s, 348 e Av A, 25x102.2. July 14, due July 1, 1893, 5 %. 3,000

Graham, Thomas to Randolph Guggenheimer. 91st st. P. M. July 20, 1 year. 4,250

Same to Seligman Oppenheimer. Same property. P. M. July 7, due July 20, 1892. 14,000

Gault, Mary wife of James to Thomas Hagan. 82d st, s s, 120 w 8th av, 19x100. Sub. to mort. $38,000. July 8, 3 months or sooner. 1,000

Giese, John, Sr., to The Harlem Savings Bank, Brook av, w s, 50 n 148th st, 50x90. July 17, 1 year, 5 %. 12,000

Gordon, Robert and Joseph to William Hall's Sons. Amsterdam av, s w cor 82d st, 102.2 x125. July 20, due Dec. 31, 1891. 35,000

Goldsmith, Pauline to Emilie Wallach. 10th st, n s, 328 e 1st av, 24x92. July 22, 3 years, 5 %. 8,000

Heney, John C. to Francis M. Jencks. 87th st, s s, 100 w West End av, 100x100.8. May 1, demand. 45,000

Herzberg, Aaron to Thomas S. Ollive committee Edwin O. Brinckerhoff. Division st, No. 44. P. M. July 22, 3 years, 4½ %. 15,000

Harris, Joseph L. to Sarah K. Cowdin guard. Elliot C. Cowdin. 111th st, n w cor Park av, runs north 100.11 x west 33 x south 18 x east 15.3 x south 82.11 to st, x east 17.9. July 22, due July 1, 1896, 5 %. 10,000

Helmke, Henry B. to The United States Life Ins. Co., New York. Central Park West, n w cor 83d st, 55.6x110. July 22, due Aug. 1, 1894, 5 %. 110,000

Same to William Hall's Sons. Same property. Sub. to last mort. July 22, 2 years or sooner. 25,000

Heil, John F. to Frederick Correll. 81st st. P. M. July 14, 1 year. 3,000

Hyde, Ellen wife of and John M. to William Dempsey and John Smith. 124th st, s s, 125.11 w 3d av, 27.1x100.11. Sub. to morts. $26,000. July 16, due Feb. 1, 1892. 1,450

Harris, Marks to John Metzger. Av C. July 22, 5 years. See Leasehold Conveys. 5,000

Heyiman, Harriet A. to The United States Savings Bank. 3d av, No. 2011, e s, 75.1 n 110th st, 25.10x110. July 16, due July 17, 1892, 5 %. 5,000

Horn, Clarence E. to Elizabeth Berner, Long Island City. Grove Hill pl. P. M. July 20, 3 years or installs, 5 %. 1,500

Hyde, Ellen wife of John M. to The Bradley & Currier Co. (Lim.) 124th st, s s, 125.11 w 3d av, 27.1x100.11. Sub. to morts. $27,450. June 22, 3 months. 2,636

Halpern, Sam. and Amali his wife to Karl M. Wallach. Sheriff st. P. M. July 15, installs. 5,125

Harlow, Ellen M. wife of and George J. to The Germania Life Ins. Co. 104th st, s s, 100 e West End av, 3 lots, each 19x100.11. 3 morts., each $14,500. July 17, due Aug. 1, 1894, 5 %. 43,500

Same to same. 104th st, s s, 156 e West End av, 19x100.11. July 17, due Aug. 1, 1895, 5 %. 14,000

Heins, Henry G. and Frederick H. Stahlhut to Bachmann Brewing Co. Gold st, No. 96. Saloon lease. July 13, demand. 3,000

Hassey, Anna C. S. wife of and Edward to The New York Life Ins. and Trust Co. 75th st, s s, 220 e Columbus av, 20x102.2. July 10, 5 years, 4½ %. 15,000

Hennessy, William P. to Bachmann Brewing Co. Prince st, No. 31. Saloon lease. July 17, note. 700

Hough, Ida M. to Franklin E. Robinson. 72d st. P. M. Sub. to mort. $30,000. July 16, installs, 5 %. 25,000

Heney, John C. to Francis M. Jencks. 87th st. P. M. May 1, demand. 47,750

Hennessy, Richard to The Emigrant Indust. Savings Bank. Spring st, Nos. 170-174, s s, 62 e Thompson st, 63.8x66.6x63.6x64.4. July 21, 1 year, 4½ %. 20,000

Hall, James T. to Walther Luttgen, Linden, N. J. 75th st, n s, 112 e Columbus av, 88x102.2. Sub. to mort. $70,400. July 18, due July 15, 1892. 25,000

Johnson, John P. to Bradley L. Eaton. 142d st, n s, adj Suburban R R, bet Willis and Alexander avs, 25x100. Lease. July 21, demand. 507

Jones, Solomon to Samuel Valentine. Stanton st, n s, 32 e Goerck st, 27.5x70. Sub. to morts. ——. July 1, due June 1, 1892. 4,000

Klaw, Marc and Abraham L. Erlanger to Richard M. Harison. 93d st. P. M. July 21, 3 years, 5 %. 14,500

Keckeissen, Margaret wife of and Frank to Peter Schupp. 70th st, No. 231, n s, 72 w 2d av, 28x100.5. July 20, due July 1, 1893. 2,000

Kramer, Daniel and Joseph mortgagors with John J. Schwartz mortgagee. Extension of mort. July 21. nom

King, Mary, Bellville, N. J. to Martha King. All title in estate of Jerome B. King dec'd. Sept. 28, 1880, notes. 10,000

Kane, John P. with James H. and Franklin Lee, Nelson Holland and Charles S. Kendall, of the Buffalo Door and Sash Co. mortgagees. Agreement that morts. made by Felice Adams shall be equal liens. July 3. nom

Kaughran, John E. to Louis L. Todd. 29th st, s s, 145 e 6th av. P. M. July 14, due Nov. 1, 1893, or sooner. 5,000

Kusche, Harriet to The Harlem Savings Bank. Willis av, w s, 75 s 140th st, 25x106. July 17, 1 year, 5 %. 6,000

Keane, Michael J. to The Murray Hill Co-operative Building and Loan Assoc. 179th st, n s, 64 w 3d av, 26x108.5x25x108.5. July 21, installs. 3,250

Lewin, Mayer to Jacob Manheim. Broome st. P. M. July 21, installs. 2,355

Lenz, Catharine F. to Tremont Building and Loan Assoc. Prospect av, e s, north ½ lot 79 map of East Tremont, 33x150. July 17, installs. 3,000

Laccorn, Elise mortgagor with Barbara Gahrman guard. Emilie Steiert. Extension of mort. at reduced int. June 30. nom

McDowell, Hugh to John L. Brewster. 99th st. P. M. June 20, demand. 23,000

Mars, Henrietta A. wife of James W. to Edward Davis. Willow st, n s, lots 23 and 24 map East Morrisania, contains 6 72-100 acres. July 20, 5 months. 1,500

Meyer, Friedrich and Julie his wife to Helena B. Jockel. 88th st, No. 429, n s, 257 w Av A, 25x100.8. July 21, due July 1, 1894, 5 %. 500

Meder, Daniel and Annie his wife to Dorothea Meder. 76th st, No. 229, n s, 355 e 3d av, 25x 102.2. July 9, 3 years, 4 %. 500

Mathews, Robert H. to James E. Sullivan. 128th st, n s, 140 w 4th av, 25x99.11. Collateral to another mortgage. July 20, 1 month. 1,000

McCun, James to John A. Lewis et al. trustees for Cornelia L. Fowler. 34th st, n s, 350 e 10th av. P. M. July 21, 3 years, 5 %. 15,000

Same to Frederic J. Middlebrook. Same property. P. M. July 21, 1 year or sooner. 1,000

McCahill, Mary A. to Mary A. Thompson. Hull av, n w s, 150 n e Mosholu Parkway; Hull av, n w s, 200 n e Mosholu Parkway. P. M. July 17, 3 years or sooner, 5 %. 1,000

McKinstry, Isabel A. wife of Robert and Victorine E. P. Bowles to James McLean trustee Mary H. Echoes. Madison av, w s, 50.10 s 130th st, 16.5x75. July 13, 3 years, 5 %. 10,000

Merce, Louisa A. to Caroline Mihm. Prospect av, e s, 179 n lot 67 map Woodstock, 21x100. Sub. to mort. $2,500. July 16, 2 years, 5 %. 500

Same to John Bussing, Jr. Same property. July 16, installs. 2,500

Meyer, Siegmund T. to Joseph Wallach. 75th st, No. 24, s s, 25.7 w Madison av, 25x102.2. July 1, 1 year. 1,500

Mulford, Mary, Jersey City, N. J., to Patrick H. Gilhooly. Greenwich st. n e cor Jane st, 50x96. 1-17 part. July 14, due July 31, 1891. 300

Mulligan, James to James Murtagh. Pyne st, w s, 175 s Pyne st, 25x100. July 15, 3 years, 4 %. 500

Murray, Thomas E. to Elizabeth S. Jones. 53d st, No. 430, s s, 425 w 9th av, 25x100.5. July 17, 3 years, 5 %. 16,000

McQuade, Thomas to The Bradley & Currier Co. (Lim.) 17th st, n s, 250 w 9th av, 50x92. Sub. to morts. $38,500. July 16, 3 months. 5,030

Metzger, George and Sophia his wife to Hugo Weil. Elm av, s w s, lots 21, 22 and 23 map of South Belmont, 150x100. July 20, 3 years. 1,000

McLaughlin, Richard to Margaret A. Sheridan. Stebbins av, e s, 786.5 n Freeman st. P. M. July 7, 3 years, 5 %. 850

McDowell, Hugh to John L. Brewster. 99th st, s s, 225 w 8th av, 50x100.11. Sub. to mort. $23,000. July 20. 22,000

Moore, Hiram M. and Ida E. his wife to Frederick P. Foster. Manhattan av, n w cor 114th st, runs north 100.11 x west — to e s Morningside av, x south 118.9 to 114th st, x east 68.3. May 2, demand. 12,000

Morelli, Felix to Gaetano Croce. 109th st, s s, 225 e 2d av, runs east 257 x south 100.11 x west 34.9 x north 0.11 x west 222 3 x north 100. July 20, due June 30, 1894, 5 %. 1,000

Mehrtens, Bernard mortgagor with Julianna Knorzer mortgagee. Extension of mort. July 10. nom

Muldoon, William H. to Henry M. Bendheim. 14th st, s s, 88 w Av C, 250x103 3. June 17, d Sept. 1, 1891. 63,000

Same to same. Same property. June 17, due Oct. 1, 1891. 33,000

Same to Peter H. Walsh. 14th st, s s, 304.6 w Av C, 27x103.3. Sub. to mort. $33,000. July —, due Jan. 1, 1892. 800

Same to William Rankin. Same property. Sub. to mort. $33,000. June 30, due June 1, 1892. 800

Monks, Elizabeth M. wife of and William H. to John Bell & Son. 137th st. P. M. July 20, 2 years. 2,689

Munch, Margarethe to William H. Simonson. Henry st, s s, 135 w Pike st, 25.4x100. Lease. Sub. to morts. $14,900. July 21, 4 months. 2,000

Mull, DeWitt and Gotlieb Fronier to Richard H. L. Townsend. 103d st, n w cor Park av. P. M. July 6, demand. 18,000

Same to same. 103d st, n s, 27 w Park av. P. M. July 6, demand. 13,000

Same to same. 103d st, n s, 53 w Park av. P. M. July 6, demand. 13,000

Same to same. Park av, w s, 75.11 n 103d st. P. M. July 6, demand. 12,000

Nimphius, Annie M. wife of and Joseph J. to Gustav Horst. 150th st, s s, 100 w Courtlandt av, 50x100. July 21, 5 years, 5 %. 2,000

Same to Charles Schledorn. Same property Equal lien with last mort. July 21, 5 %. 1,500

Panse, Clara to Matthaus Gress. Teasdale pl, n s, 366.8 w Delmonico pl, 29.2x100. July 13, 2 years. 1,500

Philippe, Eugene to Mary A. and Andrew W. Smith exrs. Samuel Smith. 2d av, No. 423, w s, 24 n 24th st, 24x97.7. July 17, 3 years, 5 %. gold, 12,000

Prell, Solomon to John P. Kane. 56th st, n s, 100 w 9th av, 75x106.2x75.7x96 5. Sub. to mort. $26,000. July 16, 6 months. 5,000

Same to J. Woolsey Shepard trustee. Same property. Sub. to mort. $26,000. July 16, installs. 7,030

Same mortgagor to Mitchell Valentine, John P. Kane and J. Woolsey Shepard trustees. Agreement extending mort. so as to cover 56th st, n s, 99.9 w 9th av, 0.3x75. July 16. nom

Quirk, Patrick H. to Elihu Ayres. 16th st. P. M. July 17, 3 years, 5 %. 7,000

Raab, Friedrich W. and Katharina to The Phenix Ins. Co. 27th st, n s, 143.2 w 7th av, 20x96. July 13, 1 year, 5 %. 1,000

Rohrs, Frederick to Anna M. Romer, Ridgewood, N. J. 134th st, n s, 125 w Alexander av, 25x100. July 16, due July 15, 1892. 1,800

Roof, Matilda V. wife of Stephen W. to Percival C Smith. 168th st, n s, 120 e Audubon av, 25x95. July 16, 3 years, 5 %. 1,750

Redler, Joseph mortgagor with Edward Whitehouse mortgagee. Extension of mort. June 26. nom

Riley, Eleanor B. wife of William to Benjamin N. Rhodes. 81st st, n s, 325 e 10th av, 18.9x 102.2. July 20, 1 year. 10,000

Rohrs, Frederick to Paul G. Decker. Westchester av, n e cor Eagle av, runs east 102.4 x north 116.5 x east 15 x north 75 x west 115 to Eagle av, x south 212.9 to beginning. July 15, 1 year, 5 %. 5,000

Rohrs, Frederick to Frederick H. Wiggin and ano. trustees Catherine Lawrence and others. 70th st, n s, 223 e Av A, 25x100.5. July 21, 5 years, 5 %. 13,000

Same to Mary M. Post, Hoboken, N. J. Same property. Sub. to last mort. July 20, 4 months. 1,500

Rohrs, Frederick to Bradley & Currier Co. (Lim.) 70th st, n s, 223 e Av A, 25x100.5. Sub. to morts. $14,500. July 16, 3 months. 2,500

Rubenstein, Louis to Kassel Osthiusky, Chicago, Ill. Stanton st, s w cor Ludlow st. P. M. Sub. to morts. $30,000. July 14, installs. 7,000

Rain, William H. to Charles Frazier. 115th st, n s, 200 e 8th av, 25x100.11. July 23, 6 months. 1,500

Robinson, Gilbert, Jr., to James Rogers. 133d st, n s, 240 w 7th av, 20x99.11. Sub. morts. $20,500. July 20, 6 months. 1,500

Ruggles, James F. to John C. Vanden Heuvel. 18th st, n s, 180 w 3d av, 18.10x92. July 8, 1 year, 5 %. 5,000

Reinert, Ferdinand to George Guttroff. 2d av, w s, 100.5 n 64th st, 25x100. Lease. July 7, due July 1, 1897, or installs. 5 %. 3,000

Stark, Samuel to Mary wife of Michael Hannan. 121st st, 127th st. P. M. July 15, installs. 1,900

Samelson, Moses to George E. Hyatt, Brooklyn. 117th st, s s, 100 e Columbus av, 100x 100.11, error. July 21, due Aug. 15, 1892. 4,000

Sinnott, Catharine to Nancy Crozier. 20th st, s s, 219.6 e 1st av. P. M. June 30, due July 1, 1894, 5 %. 4,250

Same to Mary Harrison. 20th st, s s, 199.6 e 1st av. P. M. June 30, due July 1, 1894, 5 %. 4,250

Schwed, Mayer to Charles A. Peabody, Jr. 2d av, No. 1036, e s, 60.5 s 55th st, 20x64. July 22, due Jan. 18, 1892. 1,000

Struckhausen, Henry and Lena his wife to Thomas Moore and John McLaughlin. 83d st. P. M. July 22, 3 years, 5 %. 2,500

Schreiber, Joseph to Lambert Suydam. 88th st, n s, 100 e Av A. P. M. July 13, due Aug. 1, 1892. 20,000

Same to same. Same property. July 13, due Aug. 1, 1892. 20,000

Sullivan, Michael to Rosina Vollbart. Greenwich av, n w cor Charles st. P. M. July 15, 1 year, 5 % 25,000

Same to Meyer L. Sire. Same property. July 15, installs., 5 %. 7,000

Silleck, Charles D. to Adeline C. Arnold guard. Ursula S. Arnold. Bailey av. P. M. July 21, 3 years, 5 %. 2,000

Shampansky, Harris to Israel Bloch. Madison st, n s, 125 e Jackson st, 25x79 to Grand st, x 28x92.9. July 20, 2 years. 3,000

Smith, Frank L. to Francis M. Jencks. 88th st, n s, 408 e Amsterdam av, 17x100.8; 88th st, n s, 374 e Amsterdam av, 17x100.8 July 2, 6 months. 5,500

Stanton, Agnes wife of and Peter B. to Jacob Ruppert. Tinton av, s w cor 165th st, 90x 49.10. July 21, 1 year, 5 %. 1,600

Steinert, Maria A. widow to Margaretha Dennerlein. Courtlandt av, n w s, 50 n e 158th st, 50x100. July 10, 3 years, 5 %. 500

Schultz, Louis to THE EMIGRANT INDUSTRIAL SAVINGS BANK. Greene st, e s, 100.2 s West 3d st, 50x100. July 17, 1 year, 4½ %. 60,000

Smith, Frank L. to Edwin B. Meeks exr. and trustee Joseph W. Meeks. West End av, e s, 62.8 s 89th st, runs south 19 x east 82 x north 14 x west 18 x north 5 x west 64. July 17, due May 1, 1896, 5 %. 17,000

Same to Armintha Merritt, Springfield, Mass. Same property. Sub. to last mort. July 17, demand. 5,000

Smith, Philip to Ada A. Entz. Washington av. P. M. July 17, 3 years, 5 %. 5,000

Sobischek, Lirdmila to HARLEM SAVINGS BANK. 3d av, w s, 150.9 s 165th st, 25.1x147.2 x25x144.5. July 7, 1 year, 5 %. 6,500

Satteustein, Reuben and Fanny his wife to Jacob Hecht. Broome st, No. 212 and 214, and Norfolk st, No. 71, begins Broome st, n w cor Norfolk st, 42x75. June 15, due July 22, 1894. 10,000

The Colonial Club (formerly Occident Club) to THE EQUITABLE LIFE ASSURANCE SOC. Boulevard, s w cor 72d st, runs west 44.11 x south 97.7 x southeast 88.8½ to Boulevard, x north 115.3 to beginning. June 11, due June 1, 1893. 190,000

The Colonial Club of New York to THE MANHATTAN TRUST Co. trustee. 72d st, s w cor Boulevard, 44.11 x 97.7 x 88.8x115.3, and all rights, privileges and franchises. July 1, due Jan. 1, 1893, 5 %. Secures 2d mort. bonds. 160,000

Thurston, Franklin A. to Isabella McCormack. 133d st, s s, 250 w 7th av, 150x99.11. July 20, demand. 50,000

Same to Elizabeth F. Geery. 133d st, s s, 292 w 7th av, 2 lots, each 27x99.11. 2 morts., each $24,250. July 20, due Dec. 1, 1894. 48,500

Same to Margaret Green. 133d st, s s, 346 w 7th av, 2 lots, each 27x99.11. 2 morts., each $24,000. July 20, due Dec. 1, 1894. 48,000

Same to Mary A. Bennet. 133d st, s s, 250 w 7th av, 42x99.11. July 20, due Dec. 1, 1894. 35,000

The Temple Beth-El to MANHATTAN LIFE INS. Co. 5th av, s e cor 76th st, 102.2x150. July 22, 5 years or installs, 5 %. 350,000

Tiffany, George F. to Lyman Tiffany and ano., exrs., &c., Charlotte L. Fox. Fox st, north cor 169th st, 82.5x54.4x34.11x92.4. July 15, 1 year. 500

The Merchants' Refrigerating and Ice Mfg. Co. to Charles E. Appleby, Glen Cove, L. I. Beach st, No. 30 and 32, and North Moore st, No. 35 and 37, begins Beach st, s s, 135 e Hudson st, 54x175 to North Moore st. July 23, due Sept. 15, 1892. 150,000

Voege, John H. to Peter Doelger. 1st av, No. 427, s w cor 25th st. Lease. Demand. 2,000

Van Vechten, Jessie L. wife of and Cuyler to Emily J. Phillips, Piermont, New York. Canal st, No. 172½, s s, 93.1 e Mott st, 15.11x 50.2. Mar. 26, 3 years, 4½ %. 12,000

Von Bothner, Marie and Charles J. Platt to Samuel J. Powers, Carmel, N. Y. 20th st. P. M. July 15, due July 1, 1901, or installs., 5 %. 16,000

Walker, Alexander and Judson Lawson to THE TITLE GUARANTEE AND TRUST Co. West End av, s e cor 103d st. P. M. July 20, due July 21, 1892. 27,500

Walsh, Thomas to The John Kress Brewing Co. Arthur st or av, w s, 25 s 187th st, 25x62. March 11, demand. 900

Walter, Frederick to John Schickling and Katharina his wife. Southern Boulevard, w s, 25 n Penfold av, 25x100. July 17, due July 20, 1893, 3 %. 500

Warner, Carlos and Charles D. Smith to Ephraim B. Levy. Katonah av, s w cor Knox st. P. M. July 6, due July 17, 1894, 5 %. 1,500

Willcox, Edwin C. to Edward C. Center. Cherry st, No. 407, s s, 247.3 e Scammel st, 25 x86.8x25x85.9. July 16, 1 year, 5 %. 3,500

Wilson, Elizabeth J. wife of and Alexander to James Mehaffey. 41st st, s s, 64 e 10th av, 36 x98.8. May 18, 1 year. 1,600

Wagner, Katie T. wife of and Albert to German Liederkranz. Grand st, s s, 25 e Clinton st, runs south 75 x east 25 x south 25 x east 25 x north 100 to st, x west 50. June 29. Secures performance of contract to extent of 3,000

Ward, Ellen S. to C. Adelbert Becker. Washington av, e s, 64.6 n 176th st. P. M. July 20, due July 22, 1894, or sooner, 5 %. 3,000

Same to same. Washington av, e s, 86 n 176th st. P. M. July 20, due July 22, 1894, or sooner, 5 %. 10,300

Same to same. 176th st. P. M. July 20, due July 22, 1894, or sooner, 5 %. 3,500

Walker, Mary A., Westfield, S. I., to William H. Hewlett, Manhasset, L. I. Dock st, n s, 45 w Riverview te a e, 20x100. Collateral security. July 23.rr c 4,450

Westermann, Emelie B. to Caroline A. Bereuter. 134th st. P. M. July 23, installs. 4,000

Watson, William to Josephine T. Coit. 96th st, s s, 127.8 e 3d av, 27x100.8. July 1, 3 years, 5 %. 15,000

KINGS COUNTY.

JULY 16, 17, 18, 20, 21, 22.

Addoms, Samuel K. to David D. Field. 89th st, s w s, 150 s e 1st av, 50x100, New Utrecht. May 28, 5 years, 5 %. $800

Aichmann, Charles to The Williamsburgh Savings Bank. Bleecker st, s e s, 133.4 s w Knickerbocker av, 4 lots, each 25x100. 4 morts., each $3,000. July 16, 1 year, 5 %. 12,000

Allan, John T. and Nathaniel Proskey to Theresa A. Cannon. 4th st, n e s, 235.10 n w 8th av, 21x95. July 16, demand. 1,200

Same to same. 4th st, n e s, 197.10 n w 8th av, 20x95. July 16, demand. 2,800

Anderson, Thorvald and Lewis and Edward H. Mowbray with The Title Guarantee and Trust Co. Agreement as to priority of mort. made by said Thorvald and Lewis Anderson. July 17. nom

Antrim, Benjamin F. to Frank Bailey. 80th st, 11th av, west cor 77th st, New Utrecht. P. M. May 25, 1 year. 450

Same to same. 80th st, s w s, 180 s e 12th av. P. M. May 25, 1 year. 150

Axelrod, Jacob and Isaac Levingson to Herbert C. Smith guard. Alice E. and William P. Field. Thatford av, w s, 75 s Belmont av, 25 x100. July 13, 5 years. 1,950

Anderson, Anders J. to Charles Swanfors. 28th st, s s, 450 e 3d av, 25x100.2. July 18, due Nov. 20, 1892, 5 %. 1,000

Assip, John and Timothy J. Buckley to Gila Kohnstamm. De Kalb av. P. M. July 15, 3 years, 5 %. 2,500

Allen, Patrick to Henry Kettelhodt. 6th av, n w cor 51st st, 25.2x100. July 20, 2 years. 100

Anderson, John R. to Thomas Anderson. Park av, n e cor Washington av, 20x100. July 21. 3,000

Arkowitch, Henry and Davis Baron to Annie Zwerdling. Osborn st. P. M. July 21, installs. 450

Beller, Wolf, Joseph Adam, and Abraham Fischman to Eliza A. Dunning. Stone av. P. M. July 16, 2 years. 330

Bridge, M. Palmer to The Hamilton Trust Co. President st, n s, 217 e 6th av, 62.6x95. July 20, 3 years, 5 %. 5,000

Burstein, Sara, New York, to Mary E. Cook, Newtown, L. I. Watkins st. P. M. July 1, installs. 900

Badger, William O. to John Lind. Henry st, e s, 115.7 n Pineapple st, 22x92.6. July 18, 1 year. 2,300

Bates, Edmund J. to The Harlem Co-operative Building and Loan Assoc. Atlantic av, s s, 200 e Utica av, 25x200 to Pacific st. July 14, installs. 1,000

Berlinger, William to Adam Henrich. Harman st, s s, 300 e Central av, 25x100. July 2, due July 1, 1892. 1,000

Buchenholz, Bernard to David Michel. Van Cott av. P. M. July 18, due Aug. 1, 1896, or installs, 5 %. 3,350

Burtis, Ella to Adelaide R. Hill. McDonough st. P. M. July 18, installs. 1,800

Bailey, Horace E. to Frank Bailey. 12th av and 76th st, New Utrecht. P. M. April 14, 1 year. 1,000

Baltz, Franklin A. to Luther L. Kellogg. Lincoln av. P. M. July 14, 2 years. 2,000

Beatty, Catharine wife of and George F. to Henry C. M. Ingraham trustee Elizabeth K. Underhill. 14th st, n s, 287.10 e 8th av, 20x 100. July 17, due July 1, 1894, 5 %. 4,200

Becker, Valentine and Caroline his wife to The German Savings Bank, Brooklyn. North 2d st, s s, 150 w Leonard st, 25x100. July 17, due Dec. 1, 1892, 5 %. 1,500

Behre, John H. to Gretje Behre. Manhattan av, e s, 75 n Meserole av, 25x65. July 14, 3 years, 5 %. 4,000

Same to Gretje Behre et al. exrs. August Behre. Manhattan av, e s, 100 n Meserole av, runs east 65 x north 11 x east 35 x north 14 x west 100 to av, x south 25. July 14, 3 years, 5 %. 5,000

Berlinger, William to Phebe E. Leverich extrx. Augustus A. Leverich. Harman st, s e s, 300 n e Central av, 25x100. July 17, 3 years, 5 %. 3,500

Same to same. Harman st, s e s, 325 n e Central av, 25x100. July 17, 3 years, 5 %. 3,500

Bershadsky, Nathan to Nellie C. Van Reypen. Seigel st, No. 72, s s, 100 e Ewen st, 25x100. July 14, due July 1, 1896, 5 %. 4,000

Bleha, Francis to Albert V. B. Voorhies. 67th st, s s, 460 e 14th av, 40x120, New Utrecht. July 16, 3 years. 1,800

Bonk, Martin and Albert to Rachel Faulkner, Gravesend, L. I. Sackett st. P. M. July 15, 5 years or installs, 5 %. 3,900

Bergman, John to Fred. Heddesheimer. Bergen st. P. M. July 15, 5 years, 5 %. 2,900

Brown, Frank F., Buffalo, N. Y., to Joseph H. Choate. Bay Ridge av, north cor Bay av, runs northeast 220 to centre 68th st, x northwest — x north 176.4 x northwest 21.1 to high-water mark, New York Bay, x southwest along same to n e s Bay Ridge av, x southeast — to beginning, with land under water, dock, &c., New Utrecht. July 16, 3 years or sooner. 35,000

Brooks, Rebecca C. widow to James Williamson. Hull st. P. M. July 15, 6 months. 3,300

Bowne, Samuel W. to David S. Jones. Gravesend to New Utrecht road, Gravesend. P. M. June 22, due July 16, 1896, 5 %. 29,000

Baecker, Charles and Diedrich to Anna M. E. Schroeder. Glenmore av and Christopher av P. M. July 18, due July 1, 1894, 5 %. 4,000

Bahrenburg, John H. and Elizabeth his wife to William Rose. 6th av, east cor 18th st, 20.2x 70. July 17, 1 year, 5 %. 2,400

Ball, Walter to Isaiah Smiles. Marion st, s s, 100.7 w Ralph av, 24.5x100. July 20, 3 years. 1,000

Berker, Valentine and Caroline his wife to Catharina Lipsius. North 2d st, s s, 150 w Leonard st, 25x100. July 20, 1 year, 5 %. 1,000

Becker, Barbara to Edward and Christina Hechinger. Graham av. P. M. July 20, due July 1, 1896, 5 %. 2,500

Brown, George R. to Robert F. Rhodes. President st, s s, 314.6 w 5th av, 17x100. July 1, 1½ years, 5 %. 1,250

Bryant, Thomas B. to Isaac E. De Bevoise. Greene av. P. M. April 1, 1 year. 10,500

Bunker, Le Roy E. to Elizabeth Colyer extrx. Whitson Colyer. East New York av. P. M. July 15, 3 years, 5 %. 8,900

Carpenter, Annie C. to John F. Vrooman. Powell st. P. M. July 17, installs, 5 %. 750

Cloud, Charles E. to Albert A. Gerlach. West st, w s, 50 n Broadway, 50x100. July 14, 1 year. 362

Cochran, Henry H. to Frank F. Brown. Narrows av, e cor 68th st; Narrows av, n cor 68th st, New Utrecht. P. M. July 16, 3 years, 5 %. 12,000

Same to same. Narrows av, New Utrecht. P. M. July 16, 3 years, 5 %. 21,000

Same to same. 68th st, New Utrecht. P. M. July 16, 3 years, 5 %. 10,500

Corrigan, William to Agnes H. Davies. 12th st, n s, 97.10 w 5th av, 20x100. June 24, due July 1, 1896, 5 %. 4,500

Same to same. 12th st, n s, 117.10 w 5th av, 20x 100. June 24, due July 1, 1896, 5 %. 4,500

Same to Peter B. Koechlein, Bound Brook, N. J. 12th st, n s, 137.10 w 5th av, 20x100. July 10, due July 1, 1896, 5 %. 4,500

Same to same. 12th st, n s, 157.10 w 5th av, 20 x100. July 10, due July 1, 1896, 5 %. 4,500

Same to Hannah E. Miller, Philadelphia, Pa. 12th st, n s, 177.10 w 5th av, 20x100. July 17, due July 1, 1894, 5 %. 4,500

Same to Hannah E. Miller trustee of Hannah M. Lovett. 12th st, n s, 197.10 w 5th av, 20x 100. July 17, due July 1, 1894, 5 %. 4,500

Same to same. 12th st, n s, 217.10 w 5th av, 20 x100. July 17, due July 1, 1894, 5 %. 4,500

Creamer, Frank D. to James W. McDermott et al. exrs. Ellen M. Murray. 42d st. P. M. July 16, due Jan. 1, 1897, 5 %. 10,000

Creighton, Blanche M. to Robert C. Embree exr. Elizabeth L. Smith. Washington av. P. M. March 24, due April 15, 1894, 5 %. 11,000

Chaves, Leopoldine M. widow, New York, to John V. Van Pelt. Bay 20th st. P. M. July 22, 5 years, 5 %. 2,300

Clark, John H. to Catharine Dempey. 14th st, n s, 142.4 e 8th av, 18.6r100. July 21, 5 years. 1,000

Cohen, Harris and Nathan Plimack to Jacob and David Axelrod. Riverdale av. P. M. Sub. to mort. $1,700. July 3, installs. 300

Comollo, Angelo to The East New York Savings Bank. Sutter av, s s, 48 w Essex st, 48x 100. July 18, 1 year. 1,700

Christia, Antonio and Lucia P. his wife to John Zipp. 4th av, w s, 40 n Carroll st, 20x100. July 20, 2 years. 2,500

Clarke, John to Emigrant Indust. Savings Bank. Bedford av, n w cor De Kalb av, runs west 75 x north 33 x west 25 x north 25 x east 100 to Bedford av, x south 58. July 15, 1 year, 4½ %. 14,000

Collyer, Mary A., Wappingers, N. Y., to Robert S. and Lillie E. Collyer and Helen Mahaney. Clinton st, No. 505, e s, 16.8 n 4th pl, 16.8x75. May 7, 1 year, 5 %. 1,950

Connolly, Ellen wife of and Daniel to Anna Uttley. 22d st. P. M. July 1, 3 years. 500

Cook, Mary E., Newtown, L. I., to Mary W. Smith. Stone av, w s, 150 s Blake av, 50x 100. July 14, demand. 1,100

Costello, James J. to Robert Wilson. Moffat st, s s, 200 e Central av, 16x100. July 15, 4 years. 1,500

Creed, Camilla to Rulef J. Van Brunt. 81st st, s s, 260 e 2d av, 80x109, New Utrecht. July 15, 3 years, 5 %. 3,000

Dickover, William M. to Bernard Larzelere. 54th st, s w s, 200 n w 15th av, 50x100.2. Oct. 22, 1891, due Oct. 22, 1891. (?) 1,500

Davidson, Alexander to Elizabeth Bergen and ano. exrs. John G. Bergen. 45th st, s w s, 300 s e 3d av, 20x100.2. July 20, 3 years, 5 %. 2,500

Denike, Thomas S. to Alfred Ogden. Atlantic av, Buffalo av. P. M. July 17, due Nov. 17, 1891. 8,250

Deuell, Joseph to Ella Burr. Gold st, e s, 78 s Willoughby av, 22x86. July 20, 3 years, 5 %. 2,000

Disch, Charles to Robert Ferguson. Lawrence st. P. M. July 20, due July 1, 1896, 5 %. 4,500

Dolan, Bridget formerly Clark to Thomas Dolan. 49th st, n s, 120 w 4th av, 20x100.2, Dec. 20, 1890, 5 years. 1,000

Duffy, James G. to The Brooklyn City Co-operative Building and Loan Assoc. Coney Island plank road, w s, 253.9 n Greenwood av, 23.5x150.1x22x148.8, Flatbush. March 1, installs. 3,350

Davidsburg, Bernhard to Rudolph Reimer. Broadway. P. M. July 16, due July 19, 1892, 5 %. 5,750

Doody, Daniel to Charles Frazer. Kingston av, n e cor Pacific st, 96x80. July 17, 1 year, 5 %. 5,000

Danman, Jacob to Joseph Newborg, New York. Rush st. P. M. July 17, installs. 3,300

Same to Sander Hollender. Same property. Sub to morts. $8,860. July 17, due May 25, 1883. 200

Dilzer, Catharine widow to James O'Halloran. Newport st and Watkins st. P. M. July 16, installs. 1,419

Drummond, Robert W. to The Co-operative Building Bank. 40th st, n s, 116.8 e 3d av, 16.8x100.2. July 6, installs. 1,500

Same to same. 40th st, n s, 133.4 e 3d av, 16.8x100.2. July 6, installs. 1,500

Ehlers, Frank to The Williamsburgh Savings Bank. Fulton st, n s, 25.6 w Cleveland st, 25.6x109.9x25x104.7. July 16, 1 year, 5 %. 3,800

Eichberg, Otto F. to David D. Field. 3d av, n w s, 50 s w 88th st, 50x100, New Utrecht. May 12, 1890, 6 years, 5 %. 762

Eimann, Tobie widow to Joseph Davis. Thatford av. P. M. July 1, installs. 1,100

Endom, Henry T. to Long Island Brewery. Ovington av, n e cor 11th av, 100x94.9x100x93.5. July 6, demand. 600

Emerson, Nora E wife of and Charles F. to Sophronia E. Barton, Chicago, Ill. Park pl, n s, 315.5 w 7th av, 20x100. July 18, 3 years. 2,500

Engelbrecht, Charles P. to Leonard Eppig. Liberty av, s w cor Hendrix st, runs south 40 x west 20 x south 5 x west 20 x north 10 x east 20 x north 35 to av, x east —. July 11, due July 15, 1894, 5 %. 1,500

Enrich, Conrad to Martha E. Durban. 67th st, s s, 180 e 11th av, 40x130, New Utrecht. July 15, 5 years. 600

English, Matthew H. to Hary E. Hobart. Monroe st, n s, 407 e Bedford av, 18x100. July 20, 3 years. 1,000

Fahr, Charles, Jersey City, N. J., to William M. Evarts. Eastern Parkway, n s, 129 e Schenectady av. P. M. July 10, 5 years, 5 %. 5,000

Fineilite, David and Jacob mortgagors with Carsten H. Meyer. Extension of mort. June 26. nom

Same to Lena Finelite. Willow pl, n w s, 100.7 n e State st, runs northwest 150 to Columbia pl, x northeast 25.3 x southeast 70 x northeast 22.11 x southeast 80 to Willow pl, x southwest 47.5. July 10, due Jan. 1, 1892. 2,000

Fredrickson, Erick and Maria his wife to Charles Swanfors and John Nelson. 32d st, n s, 240 w 5th av, 20x100.2. July 20, 4 years. 5 %. 2,000

Farrer, Henry to Charles Corey. Sunnyside av. P. M. July 15, 5 years, 5 %. 2,000

Ferguson, William H. to John and Rosa Zipp exrs. George Zipp. Hudson av, e s, 129.2 s Myrtle av. P. M. July 20, 3 years. 3,000

Same to same. Hudson av, e s, 104.2 s Myrtle av. P. M. July 20, 3 years. 3,400

Ficken, George H. to Beadleston & Woerz. Broadway, No. 839. Lease. July 14, demand. 4,000

Flamanbaft, Kalman and Samuel Shissel to Jacob Manheim. Rockaway av, e s, 150 s Glenmore av, 25x100.1. July 15, 4 months. 155

Forman, Rebecca F. to Edward J. McCarty. Atlantic av. P. M. July 1, 1 year, 5 %. 250

Fowler, Mary E. wife of and Levi to Jesse B. Clement. St. Mark's av, n s, 300 e Franklin av, 20x128.6. July 14, due July 1, 1894, or sooner. 7,500

Same to John Ludlam. St Marks av, n s, 280 e Franklin av, 20x128.6. July 10, 3 years, 5 %. 7,500

Same to Robert V. N. Ludlam. St. Marks av, n s, 260 e Franklin av, 20x128.6. July 10, 3 years, 5 %. 7,500

Farrell, James P. to David D. Field. 3d av, south cor 87th st, 100x100x90.11x466x59.6, New Utrecht. May 28, 5 years, 5 %. 1,404

Fitzgerald, Michael to David D. Field. 4th av, west cor 87th st, 129x102.6x106.5x100, New Utrecht. May 12, 1890, 6 years, 5 %. 1,320

Fienter, Frances formerly Parsons to Nellie A. Hiers. 19th st, s s, 250 e 3d av, 25x100. July 15, 1 year. 100

Foley, Joseph M. to Caroline and Charlotte Hewlett, East Rockaway, L. I. Partition st. P. M. June 17, due July 1, 1894, 5 %. 3,000

Farrell, Margaret to Mark B. Knight, Flatbush, L. I. Troy av, s e cor Malbone st, Flatbush. July 20, 5 years, 5 %. 530

Fisher, Albert P. to Gevert Weedelken. Flatbush to Canarsie Landing road. P. M. July 17, 1 year. 1,300

Gaw, Elizabeth A., Hoboken, N. J., to The Title Guarantee and Trust Co. Olive pl, No. 29, e s, 38 n Atlantic av, 18.6x79. July 20, 3 years. 5 %. 1,000

Gerrity, Anne wife of and James to Bedford Co-operative Building and Loan Assoc. Baltic st, n s, 155 e Schenectady av, 20x155.7. July 8, installs. 200

Good, William H. to Henry Miles. Bainbridge st, n s, 41.6 e Saratoga av, 18.6x100. July 11, 1 year, 5 %. 400

Greenwood, John to Harriet H. Petty. East 27th st, e s, adj land of James McCormick, —x—x—x155, Gravesend. July 14, 5 years. 5 %. 1,500

Germann, Charles P. to Greenpoint Savings Bank. Manhattan av, e s, 67 s Norman av, 28x50. July 16, 1 year, 5½ %. 3,500

Germansky, Piser and Abraham to James O'Halloran. Watkins st. P. M. July 16, installs. 1,500

Graver, William to Harry A. Gubner, Atlantic av, No. 177. Lease. July 16, 1 year. 1,100

Greenstein, David to Samuel Levy. Rockaway av. P. M. July 18, installs. 1,400

Grund, Peter and Katharina his wife to John H. Scheidt. Stanhope st, n w s, 300 n e Irving av, 25x100. July 9, due July 1, 1896, 5 %. 800

Geyer, Mary J. W. wife of and Horace to The Title Guarantee and Trust Co. Park pl, n s, 445.10 w Vanderbilt av, 20.10x131. July 15, 3 years, 5 %. 5,000

Gomer, August and Jacob Wollpert to Edward Hopper, Philadelphia, Pa. McKibbin st, n s, 150 w Bushwick av, 25x100. July 20, 3 years, 5 %. 6,000

Same to Phebe B. Field, Greenwich, Conn. McKibbin st, n s, 125 w Bushwick av, 25x100. July 20, 3 years, 5 %. 6,000

Grill, August, Charles Gorman and Frederick Haggerty mortgagors with Albert Voltz, Sr., mortgagee. Extension of mort. July 7. nom

Harper, Margaret wife of Thomas H. to David D. Field. Narrows av, east cor 88th st, 100x100, New Utrecht. May 12, 5 years, 5 %. 1,500

Held, Harry to David D. Field. 87th st, s w s, 150 s e 1st av, 100x100; 2d av, west cor 87th st, 100x100, New Utrecht. May 28, 5 years, 5 %. 2,004

Hack, Henry o Franz Wedeke. McKibbin st, s s, 175 w Morrell st, 25x100. July 18, due July 1, 1894, 5 %. 3,100

Handler, Moritz and Samuel Balsam to Herman F. Koepke. Thatford av. P. M. July 14, due Jan. 1, 1892. 500

Harvey, Mary M. wife of and George S. to Louisa M. Aukamp. Navy st, s w cor Willoughby st, 29.8x58x38x57.7. July 18, 1 year. 800

Heatley, George W. to Robert S. Naylor. Canton st, e s, 67.6 n Myrtle av, runs east 73.8 x northwest 68.4 x southwest 61.9 x west 23.7 to st, x south 20. July 18, 3 years, 5 %. 2,100

Hefner, Charles and Mary his wife to William J. G. Bearns and Jacob Brenner, of Bearns & Brenner. Huntington st, n s, 130.1 e Clinton st, 20.3x100. July 18, 1 year, 5 %. 500

Heyne, Paul O. and Deocara F. his wife to August Hillmann. Prospect av, w s, 311 n Greenwood av, 25x150; East 5th st, e s, 421.6 n Greenwood av, 25x100, Flatbush. July 15, 3 years. 1,700

Hillebrand, Theodore to Mary Preston. Huron st, s s, 397.11 e Franklin st, 32.1x100. June 1, 5 years, 5 %. 4,500

Hunter, Mary J. to The Title Guarantee and Trust Co. Halsey st. P. M. July 18, 1 year, 5 %. 2,000

Same to Ernestine Gastmeyer. Same property. P. M. Sub. to last mort. July 18, 2 years. 1,200

Hall, George B. to The South Brooklyn Co-operative Building and Loan Assoc. 22d st. P. M. July 7, installs. 2,250

Hamilton, Mary J. to John P. Moore. 87th st, s w s, 300 n w 4th av, 40x67.1x41x76, New Utrecht. June 30, due July 1, 1894, 5½ %. 1,000

Haskins, Theresa L. to Henry Rudloff. Sherman st. P. M. June 25, due July 24, 1895, or installs, 5 %. 900

Hatterer, George C. to Frederick Eiermann. Elton st. P. M. July 15, installs. 700

Hennings, Alfred F. to Pasquale Caponigri. Bath av, s w s, extends from Bay 25th st to Bay 26th st, 193.9x82.6, New Utrecht. July 15, 1 year. 1,000

Howard, Coe F. mortgagee with John Monsees mortgagor. Extension of mort. July 9. nom

Herrmann, Tobias and Elizabeth his wife to Emile Jacok. Stewart st, n w s, 236.5 n e Broadway, 21.3x113.6x75.11x100. July 17, due July 15, 1894. 2,000

Hornet, John J., Mary W., Thomas V. and Annie Hornet by Mary E. Hornet guard. and Mary E. Hornet widow to George E. Nostrand. Bay 13th st, w s, 250 n Bath av, 50x108.4, New Utrecht. July 15, 3 years, 5 %. 500

Hughes, William to The Fort Green Co-operative Building and Loan Assoc. Dean st. P. M. July 18, installs, 5 %. 2,500

Hutter, Simon to Adam Kaiser, Charles Rissler and August Todebusch. Broadway. P. M. July 16, 2 years. 2,750

Harper, George and Alfred W. Simpson to Archibald Crawford, Philadelphia, Pa. Lots 110 and 123 map Linden terrace, Flatbush. P. M. July 11, 2 years, 5 %. 400

Humann, Caspar to Ann E. Buckley. Glenmore av, s w cor Jerome st, 25x100. July 18, 3 years, 5 %. 3,000

Hyer, Julia F. to William H. C. Brown. South 3d st, s e cor Havemeyer st, 25x95. July 21, due Jan. 1, 1894. 500

Ives, Jennie A. to Julius Dietz, Jr. Macon st, s s, 355 e Sumner av, 20x100. July 16, due Oct. 15, 1892, 5 %. 1,000

Isaacs, Amelia wife of and Harry to Rebecca S. Monfort, Oyster Bay, L. I. 3d av, w s, 79.11 n 13th st, 20.1x97.10. July 20, due Aug. 1, 1893, or sooner. 400

Jacobs, George P. and Enoch to Jane E. Collins. Degraw st, s s, 159 e 4th av, 16.4x100. June 12, due July 1, 1894, 5 %. 2,500

Judge, Annie wife of and Francis W. to Andrew D. Baird. Herkimer st, n s, 242.6 e Albany av, runs north 120 x east 22.6 x south 20 x east 4.8 x south 100 to st, x west 27.2. June 1, 1 year, 5 %. 1,250

Johnston, John W. to Kings Co. Savings Inst. N r h Henry st. P. M. July 1, 1 year, 5 %. 1,750

Same to Charles Engert. Same property. 2d mort. Installs. 1,250

Junge, Henry W. to Alfred Hodges. Grand st, n e s, abt 143 s e Kent av, 25x131.10x25.6x134.8. July 16, due July 1, 1894. gold, 1,000

Same mortgagor with same. Extension mort. July 16. nom

Jones, Lucinda H. to David A. Fithian. Orient st, w s 175 s Baltic av, 25x100. July 16, 3 years. 1,000

Kane, Julia widow to Patrick J. Kenedy. Nostrand av. P. M. July 17, due July 18, 1894. 700

Kissane, William to James L. Jensen. Van Cott av, n s 24 w Lorimer st, 25x92.7x25.11x85.10. July 1, 1 year. 300

Keppelman, John H. to The Kings County Savings Inst. North Henry st. P. M. July 1, 1 year, 5 %. 1,750

Same to Charles Engert. Same property. 2d mort. July 1, installs. 1,250

Kaczmarek, Walenty to John Andrews. 20th st. P. M. July 10, installs, 5 %. 650

Kaufold, Louisa wife of and Nicholas to Mary W. Smith. Stone av, e s, 100 s Sutter av, 4 lots, each 18.9x100. 4 morts., each $1,650. July 15, 3 years. 6,600

Kavanagh, Martha H. to The Title Guarantee and Trust Co. Huron st. July 15, 3 years, 5 %. 2,000

Kenney, Mary F. wife of and William to Jane A. Voorhies. Hubbard st, n w s, 525 s w Mill road, 50x129.1, Gravesend. July 15, 10 years. 1,634

Klebbe, Johann to John A. Voorhies. 74th st, n e s, 275 s e 15th av, 52.11x100.4x50.2x100. July 7, 3 years. 600

Kaiser, Adam and August Todebusch and Charles Rissler to The Kings County Savings Inst. Broadway, north cor Cornelia st, 20x100. July 9, 1 year, 5 %. 14,000

Same to same. Central av, s w s, 25 s e Ralph st, 25x100. July 16, 1 year, 5 %. 3,000

Same to same. Broadway, n e s, 20 n w Cornelia st, 25x100. July 9, 1 year. 8,000

Keily, James to Irene C. wife of Harvey H. Thompson. Herkimer st. P. M. July 15, due Jan. 1, 1892. 750

Koenig, Francis H. to The John Street Methodist Episcopal Church Trust Fund Soc. Essex st, w s, 350 s Ridgewood av, 20x100. July 18, due July 1, 1894. 2,500

Knowles, Charles C. to Ellen W. Hubbard. Jefferson av. P. M. Sub. to *Mt.* 2,500. July 15, due May 15, 1896. 2,200

Kracke, Henry to David D. Field. 2d av, north cor 87th st, 41.3 x 85.6 x 38.4 x 100, New Utrecht. May 12, 5 years, 5 %. 600

Lonis, Mary to David D. Field. 88th st, n e s, 150 s e 1st av, 100x100, New Utrecht, error. May 28, 5 years, 5 %. 684

Lehrian, Emil to The German Savings Bank, Brooklyn. South 3d st, s w s, 100 n w Hooper st, 25x95. July 14, due Dec. 1, 1892, 5 %. 6,500

Same to same. South 3d st, s w s, 125 n w Hooper st, 25x95. July 14, due Dec. 1, 1892, 5 %. 6,500

Levy, Bernard to Williamsburgh Savings Bank. Tompkins av, e s, 75 s Hopkins st, 25x75. July 16, 1 year, 5 %. 3,800

Levy, Samuel to Nellie K. Rabney. Rockaway av, e s 50 n Belmont av, 25x100.1. July 16, due July 15, 1894. 3,500

Livingston, William, Samuel L. Matthews and Leon Weltfisch to Hitel Waxberg. Rockaway av. P. M. July 14, 3 years. 663

Leinfelder, Anna to John H. Vanderveer. Lots 163–167 map Vanderveer homestead. P. M. July 7, 3 years, 5 %. 1,350

Levy, Davis, Jacob Jackerson and Frank Glasser to Mary W. Smith. Rockaway av, e s, 100 s Eastern Parkway, 25x100.1. July 17, 2 months. 800

Lindley, George R. to John L. Nostrand. 78th st, New Utrecht. P. M. July 20, 5 years, 5 %. 1,400

Lewis, Margaretha to George H. Smith. Hull st, 60 w Stone av, 30x100. July 16, installs. 4,000

Same to The Title Guarantee and Trust Co. Same property. July 16, 3 years, 5 %. 4,000

Lamb, Henry G. A. to Charles H. and William Langdon exrs. Thomas B. Langdon. 3d av, e s, 80.2 n 55th st, 20x100. July 15, 1 year. 4,500

Same to William Hunt. Same property. July 15, 2 years. 500

Larsen, Peter to The Title Guarantee and Trust Co. 1st st, n s, 197.4 w 6th av, 77.8x100. July 18, demand. 20,000

Levy, Gerson with Nellie C. Van Reypen mortgagees. Agreement as to priority of morts. made by Nathan Bershadsky. July 16. 250

Lucke, Caspar to The Church of All Saints. Herkimer st, s s, 50 e Howard av. 2 lots, each 16x98. 2 morts., each $2,350. July 1, 1 year, 5 %. 4,700

Same to same. Herkimer st, s s, 82 e Howard av, 16x98. July 1, 1 year, 5 %. 2,300

Max, Harris to Peter Ostraszewski. Watkins st. P. M. July 1, 3 years. 1,075

Merritt, Isaac G. to F. Augustus Conkling. Macon st, No. 747. P. M. July 18, installs. 20,000

Metz, Adam to Adam Henrich. Bleecker st, n s, 325 w Central av, 25x100. July 17, 1 year. 800

McBean, Archibald N. to James Jack. 2d st, s s, 437.11 e 5th av, runs south 100 x east 3.1 x north 5 x east 76.11 x north 95 to 2d st, x west 80. July 16, demand. 7,500

Miller, Jane to Rudolph and Otto E. Reimer. Macon st, n s, 200 e Patchen av, 18x100. Sub. to mort. $4,500. June 30, due July 1, 1892. 1,000

Malz, Jacob to Nathan Hyman. Thatford av. P. M. July 18, installs. 1,500

Manheim, Jacob to Annie O'Connor. Watkins st. P. M. Sub. to mort. $1,000. Feb. 27, 1890, due July 15, 1894. 1,500

Same to Catharine L. Babcock. P. M. Feb. 27, 1890, due July 15, 1894. 1,000

Mason, Mary E. wife of and Isaac D. to Paul W. Ledoux. Bergen st, n s, 202 e Ralph av, 4 lots, each 17x107.2. 4 morts., each $300. July 15, due Jan. 1, 1892. 1,200

Same to same. Same 4 lots. July 15, demand. 4,300

Same to George G. Reynolds. Same 4 lots, 4 morts., each $2,000. July 15, 3 years, 5 %. 8,000

McBean, Archibald N. to A. S. Nichols & Co. 2d st, s s, 237.10 w 6th av, 20x95. July 20, 1 year. 472

Same to George R. Lockwood and ano. trustees Rose Lockwood. 2d st, s s, 487.11 e 5th av, 30x95. July 13, 3 years. 11,000

Same to same. 2d st, s s, 437.11 e 5th av, runs east 20 x south 95 x west 16.11 x south 5 x west 3.1 x north 100. July 13, 3 years. 8,000

Same to same. 2d st, s s, 457.11 e 5th av, 30x95. July 13, 3 years. 11,000

Same to Samuel G. Richards. 2d st, s s, 207.10 w 6th av, 30x95. July 20, 1 year. 700

Metzger, Felix to Stephen T. Rushmore. Bridge st, e s, 73.2 n Nassau st, 21.10x50 to alley. Sub. to morts. $3,000. July 9, 1 year, 5 %. 1,200

Miller, Edward F. to Albert Brons. Logan st, e s, 625 n Liberty av, 25x100. July 14, 3 years. 450

Martin, Charles A. and Benjamin to William Silberman. 3d av, w s, 70 s Bay Ridge av, 20x97. July 3, 1 year or sooner, 5 %. 1,000

Maul, Frances A. and Frederick W. to Lawrence Hurlburt. 3d av, s e s, 40.2 s w 41st st, 20x80. July 9, due July 8, 1892. 500

McClenahan, William to Williamsburgh Savings Bank. McDonough st, n w cor Hopkinson av, 21x80. July 16, 1 year, 5 %. 6,000

Same to same. McDonough st, n s, 21 w Hopkinson av, 4 lots, each 19.9x90. 4 morts., each $4,000. July 16, 1 year, 5 %. 16,000

McIntyre, Robert to David H. Field. Interior lot on centre line of block (?) 400 s e 3d av, runs northeast 23.11 x southeast 69.8 to centre block, x northwest 107.4, New Utrecht. May 12, 1890, 6 years, 5 %. 66

Meht, Lena I. to Henry Manne admr. Fort Hamilton av, east cor 78d st, New Utrecht. P. M. July 15, 6 months. 3,000

Michel, David to Andrew J. Onderdonk. Ewen st. P. M. July 20, due Nov. 1, 1892, 5 %. 1,000

Miller, Jane wife of and Abel to Horatio S. Stewart. Macon st, n s, 290 e Patchen av, 110x100. July 3, demand. 2,000

Same to Virginia E. Carver. Macon st, n s, 272 e Patchen av, 18x100. June 24, 3 years, 5 %. 4,500

Same to Ann Charman. Macon st, n s, 254 e Patchen av, 18x100. June 24, 3 years, 5 %. 4,500

Same to Bernard Levino, Horatio S. Stewart, Alfred Van Derwerken and George C. Crawford. Macon st, n s, 290 e Patchen av, 110x100. Sub. to mort. July 3, demand. 1,900

Same to Hope H. Colgate. Macon st, n s, 200 e Patchen av, 3 lots, each 18x100. 3 morts., each $4,500. June 24, due July 1, 1892, 5 %. 13,500

Moores, Robert L. and Charles A. Le Quesne to Edward North exr. Joseph T. Burr. Broadway, s w s, 66.2 n w Putnam av, runs northwest 28 x southwest 62.1 x south 23.5 to Putnam st, x east 28 x north 11.8 x northeast 50.4. July 11, due July 13, 1897, 5 %. 11,000

Morrison, William and Minerva T. and Theodore S. Nye to David D. Field. 88th st, n e s, 250 n w 2d av, 100x100, New Utrecht. May 28, 5 years, 5 %. 696

Mullin, Patrick to Harry Loomis. Seige av, w s, 600 s Division av, 50x104.2. June 2, 3 years. 2,000

Moors, Joseph to P. Ballantine & Sons. Jay st. No. 182. Lease. July 20, note. 1,000

Morgan, Ambrose M. to Thomas Guille. South 5th st, n e cor Roebling st, 40x78. July 16, 1 year, 5 %. 1,000

Manning, Rachel O. to Augusta L. Potter. Gates av, s s, 322 w Nostrand av, 19x100. July 17, due July 21, 1896, 5 %. 2,000

McCormick, James to Sarah C. Cann. Skillman st, e s, 211.10 s Myrtle av, 25x100. July 21, 3 years, 5 %. 1,000

Mount, William H. to Robert L. Woods, Jr. Newport st, n e cor Watkins st. P. M. July 16, 1 year, 5 %. 5,000

Myers, Louis H., Jr., to Daniel and Joseph Kramer, Johnstown, Pa. Dean st. P. M. July 20, due June 30, 1892. 1,000

Nasel, Jacob to Charles S. Cutter. Wyckoff av, n e s, 50 n w Starr st, 25x95.4x25x96. July 1, 2 years, 5 %. 1,200

Newman, Isaac and Sarah his wife to Abraham Arndt and Sarah his wife. Gerry st. P. M. July 1, installs, 5½ %. 4,000

Nova, Louis to David D. Field. 87th st, s w s, 100 n w 2d av, 175x100, New Utrecht. May 28, 5 years, 5 %. 1,260

Newman, Olof A. to The F. & M. Shaefer Brewing Co. Atlantic av, No. 329. Saloon lease. July 18, 1 year. 1,000

Norris, William H. and William Bowers to Charles Griffin et al. trustees Samuel Willets, dec'd. 4th av, w s, 30 s 13th st, 28x86.10. July 21, 3 years, 5 %. 9,000

Same to Lester A. Lewis. 2d st, s s, 207 e 6th av, 90.10x95; 4th av, w s, 30 n 14th st, 112x86.10. July 16, 1 year. 14,943

O'Brien, John J. to John F. Horie. Douglass st, n s, 310 w 5th av, 20x100. July 1, 2 years, 5 %. 300

O'Donnell, Jane wife of and Hugh to Herman B. Scharman. Atlantic av, n s, 155.1 w Nostrand av, 16.8x50. July 7, 3 years, 5 %. 3,000

O'Donnell, William H., New York, to David D. Field. 88th st, n e s, 100 s e 1st av, 50x100, New Utrecht. May 28, 5 years, 5 %. 360

Same to same. 87th st, s w s, 250 s e 1st av, 100x100, New Utrecht. May 28, 5 years, 5 %. 720

Ogden, Alfred to Eugene A. Lachaise. Atlantic av, s w cor Buffalo av, 75x138.4x—x124.6. July 2, due Oct. 17, 1891. 5,500

O'Halloran, James to Maria B. Linington. Watkins st, w s, 100 n Livonia av, 25x100. July 15, due Nov. 1, 1894. 1,200

O'Connell, Matthew and Christopher to Almira Delaplaine extrx. John Delaplaine. North 10th st, s w s, 300 s e Roebling st, 72x200 to North 9th st. July 1, 3 years, 5 %. 2,000

Ordronaux, John mortgagee with Alice L. Carpenter mortgagor. Extension of mort. July 10. nom

O'Donnell, James to Brooklyn Savings Bank. Hudson av, n e cor Evans st, 23.4x75. July 15, 1 year. 500

Olsen, Elizabeth widow to John A. Latimer and ano. trustee Hosea Webster. Navy st, e s, 85 s Lafayette av, runs south 1.2 to Flatbush av, x southeast 39.5 x northeast 64.4 x east 46.5 x north 11 x west 0.6 x north 1.8 x west 120.6; Flatbush av, n e s, 39.5 s e Navy st, runs southeast 0.6 x northeast 66 x west — x southwest 64.4. July 16, 3 years, 5 % gold, 10,000

Prosser, John to Jacob S. E. Litchfield. Sackett st, n s, 319.8 e 4th av, 47.6x100. July 17, demand. 2,000

Parshelsky, Samuel to John Ketterle. McKibbin st, n w cor Leonard st. P. M. July 1, 10 years, 5 %. 8,000

Perkins, Fanny B. to A. Judson Palmer. Junius st. P. M. July 18, 5 years, 5 %. 2,000

Peterson, Martena G., Adelina E. Koehler and Anna M. Schanz mortgagors with Robert A. B. Dayton trustee for Mary M. Martin mortgagee. Extension of mort. at 5 %. July 13. nom

Picard, Sarah mortgagor with Carl Goedel mortgagee. Extension of mort. July 10. nom

Peabody, Frederick W. to Cornelia M. Peabody exr., &c., Charles A. Peabody and James Myers exr. Enoch W. Peabody. Monroe pl or st, w s, 200 s Clark st, 25x100. July 10, 1 year, 5 %. 2,000

Pfeiffer, Lorenz or Lorence to The Title Guarantee and Trust Co. 5th av, s e s, 135 n e 7th st, 18x75. July 22, 3 years. 5 %. 2,200

Quaid, Jeremiah to Emigrants' Indust. Savings Bank. 5th av, north cor 10th st, 50x95.9. July 16, 1 year, 4½ %. 7,000

Ratner, Charles and Israel Zagalovitz to C. Theresa Davison. Eastern Parkway, s s, 25.1 w Thatford av, 25x100. July 21, 3 years 3,500

Ratner, Louis and Lottie his wife to Ella H. Davison, New York. Eastern Parkway, n s, 25 e Thatford av, 25x100. July 21, 3 years. 3,500

Raymond, Benjamin C. to Hall Sash and Door Co. Macon st, n s, 40 w Ralph av, 18x100. Sub. to mort. $4,500. July 13, 1 year. 1,200

Reid, David C. to John Konvalinka. St. Marks av, s s, 182.6 e Rogers av, runs south 95 x west 17 x south 55.7 x east 52.2 x north 150.7 to St. Marks av, x west 35.2. July 22, 3 years, 5 %. 10,000

Rose, Kate to William Nolte and Frank W. Koch. Cooper st, s s, 335 w Knickerbocker av, 20x100. Sub. to mort. $2,000. July 15, 2 years. 800

Ross, Jennie L. to George A. and Robert Miller, Jr., of G. A. and R. Miller. 2d st, s s, 19.3 w 7th av, 19.8x100. July 1, 1 year. 2,500

Raymond, Benjamin C. to Lottie N. Palmer. Macon st, n s, 76 w Ralph av, 18x100. Sub. to mort. $4,500. July 13, due Sept. 15, 1891. 1,000

Regenbogen, Louis to A. Judson Palmer. Stone av and Christopher av. P. M. July 15, 3 years. 2,500

Rothaug, Adam to German Savings Bank. McKibbin st, n s, 125 e Graham av, 25x100. July 17, due Dec. 1, 1892, 5 %. 1,500

Robertson, Henry H. to James D. Lynch. 83d st, s w s, 200 s e 23d av, 60x100. July 13, due July 14, 1893, 5 %. 630

Rowland, Mary O. wife of and James to The Irving Savings Inst. Taylor st, s e s, 323.6 s w Bedford av, 16.6x100. July 13, 1 year, 5 %. 4,500

Ramsdell, David J. to Eva S. wife William F. Cochran. Union st, n s, 175 w 4th av, 25x95. July 16, due July 1, 1894, 5 %. 7,500

Same to Robert T. Rhodes. Same property. July 16, due Jan. 16, 1893, 5 %. 2,500

Richards, Samuel G. to Robert L. Moores and Charles A. Le Quesne. Broadway. P. M. July 17, due Aug. 6, 1893, 5 %. 2,000

Robinson, Franklin to Alfred J. Robinson, Fennimore st, s s, 525 e Rogers av, 40x86.5x40x86.4, Flatbush. July 1, 5 years, 4 %. 300

Rooney, Mary G. wife of and Thomas E. to Marie E. Jacobson. Pacific st, n s, 529.8 w Franklin av, 40x100. July 16, installs. 5,000

Robinson, Rubin to John Monsees. Watkins st. P. M. July 9, installs. 700

Rudderman, Rosa to Williamson R. Selover. Stone av. P. M. July 15, 3 years. 300

Ruwe, Anna M. to The Williamsburgh Savings Bank. Ross st, n w s, 346.8 s w Bedford av, 16.8x100. July 17, 1 year, 5 %. 2,000

Ryan, John to John N. Eitel. Nassau st, s w cor Navy st, 25x75. July 15, 3 years, 5 %. 6,000

Sands, Edwin to Otto Gubner. 56th st, s w s, 100 n w 12th av, runs northwest 26 to Cowenhoven's lane, x west 14.9 x southwest 95.7 x southeast 40 x northeast 100.2, New Utrecht. July 7, 3 years. 2,000

Seitz, Theresa to Christian Niclaus. Cleveland st, w s, 150 n Hegeman av, 40x100. July 18, 2 years. 400

Spencer, William and Jennie M. Wallace to Alonzo E. De Baun. Cumberland st. P. M. July 15, due Aug. 1, 1893, 5 %. 500

Stabler, Elisabetka wife of and John to John Kolle. 21st st, s s, 225 e 3d av, 75x100. July 15, notes. 830

Samelson, Sam. and Becky Ronginsky to John S. Junior. Thatford av, e s, 150 n Belmont av, 25x100. July 16, 3 years. 3,000

Samelson, Samuel and Pincus Ronginsky to Frederick A. Reid. Georgia av. P. M. July 20, 4 years or installs. 900

Schilling, Elizabeth T. wife of and William V. to Daniel Springsteel, of Ardsley, N. Y. 6th st. P. M. July 1, 5 years, 5 %. 1,100

Schneider, Bessie wife of and Philip to Henry Elias Brewing Co. Bradford st, w s, 175 n Liberty av, 75x100. July 20, due Aug. 1, 1892, 5 %. 1,000

Schneider, Herman and Abraham Blauferb to Rosa Rudderman. Stone av. P. M. Sub. to mort. $2,000. July 15, installs. 300

Same to Williamson R. Selover. Same property. P. M. July 15, 3 years. 2,000

Scholl, John B. to William J. Cosby. Linwood st. P. M. July 11, due Dec. 21, 1895. 800

Schultz, August L. and Marie H. C. his wife to L d Seebeck. Extension of mort. July 15u er nom

Stein, Edmund to Karl J. Dewald. Wyckoff av, n e s, 25 n w Starr st, 25x96; Troutman st, s e s, 167.1 n e Wyckoff av, 25x100. July 16, 3 years, 5 %. 2,500

Sass, Ernest, New York, to David D. Field. 88th st, n e s, 100 n w 2d av, 50x100, New Utrecht. May 28, 5 years, 5 %. 348

Scottron, Cyrus L. to Catherine Thompson. Lexington av. P. M. July 15, installs. 700

Sharrot, Annie M. to Anna A. Schmeelk, Canarsie, L. I. Lot at Canarsie, begins at n e cor of lands of James Lawrence, runs east 66 x south 114 x west 66 x 114, with right of way on south. July 1, 3 years. 1,000

Schildwachter, Otto to Phillip Schildwachter. President st, n s, 282.5 e Smith st, 17.7x98. July 15, 1 year, 5 %. 1,100

Scott, Albert to Louis H. Irwin. Snediker av, &c. P. M. July 21, 3 years, 5 %. 52,500

Simonson, Charles H and Ida C. his wife to Edward, Gustav and Leonard Friend, of E. and G. Friend & Co. Bay 26th st, n w s, 100 n e Benson av, 60x96.8, Bensonhurst. July 17, 6 months. 5,709

Skillman, Caroline to The Dime Savings Bank of Williamsburgh. Broadway, n e s, 25 s e Ellery st, 50x100. July 17, 1 year, 5 %. 17,000

Snyder, Nicholas H. individ. and exr. Emily I. Snyder to Thomas F. Smith. Monroe st, n s, 232.3 w Sumner av, 17.9x100. July 11, 2 years. 1,000

Straub, John G. to Peter Bertsch exr. William Broestedt. Cook st, s s, 325 e Morrill st, runs south 100 x east 101.2 to Bushwick av, x north 25.4 x west 75 x north 75 to Cook st, x west 25. July 21, 1 year, 5 %. 1,000

Thompson, William G. to Susan E. Hoyt et al. trustees for Willard E. Hoyt. Quincy st, s s, 292 w Sumner av, 28x100. July 21, due July 1, 1896, 5 %. 6,000

Taber, Elizabeth to Elizabeth Taber et al. exrs. Eleanor Davidson. Crescent st, w s, 75 n Magenta st, 25x100. April 1, 1887, demand. 1,109

Taylor, William F. to Siles A. Condict. 24th st. P. M. July 15, due July 1, 1892. 300

Terhune, Julia A. to Julia J. Whitlock. Hendrix st, e s, 150 n Blake av, 25x100, 1 year, 5 %. 400

Uehlinger, Bertha to Mary Rohr widow. Moffat st, s e s, 134.6 n e Broadway, 18x75. July 1, 3 years, 5 %. 2,000

Vanderbilt, Eugene H. to Amos S. Lamphear. Degraw st, n s, 363.1 e Schenectady av, 6.10x127.9x32.1x130; Degraw st, n s, 390 e Schenectady av, —x127.9x20x127.9; Degraw st, s s, 380 e Buffalo av, 59x65.7x70x78. July 18, 1 year, 5 %. 1,500

Vanderbilt, Eugene H. to L. K. Reynolds, Columbia Co., N. Y. Degraw st, n s, 363.2 e Schenectady av, runs east 6.10 x north 127 x west 32.1 x southeast 130.3; Degraw st, n s, 390 e Schenectady av, 20x177.9x20x127.9; Degraw st, s s, 380 e Buffalo av, 59.1x65.7x70.10x78. July 16. 600

Van Doorn, George F. to Henry Smith. St. Marks av. P. M. April 17, due July 17, 1892, 5 %. 1,100

Van Orden, George O. to Charles F. Schweinfurth. 5th st, s s, 78 w 6th av, 19.10x100. July 11, 1 year. 7,500

Walsh, William, New York, to David D. Field. 88th st, n e s, 150 n w 2d av, 100x100, New Utrecht. May 28, 5 years, 5 %. 696

Watt, James E. to Mary W. Smith. Sunnyside av, n s, 300 w Miller av, 50x248.6x50x250. July 15, 2 years. 500

Weisbaupt, Carrie to David D. Field. 89th st, n e s, 225 s e 1st av, 50x100, New Utrecht. May 28, 5 years, 5 %. 294

Wilson, Sarah E. to Frederick V. L. Smith. Ross st, south cor Marcy av, 20x69.10x20x69.10. July 11, 1 year, 5 %. 1,000

Wendelken, Gevert to Katherine Niesterman. Surf av, n s, at centre line West 8th st proposed, 100x232.4x100x170, Coney Island. July 2, 2 years, 5 %. 5,000

Wilkins, Anna M. to Emilie Huber. Norman av, s w cor Newell st, 25x67. July 14, demand. 1,000

Wittschen, Andrew to Andrew Icken. Sackett st, n e s, 300 n w 6th av, 25x100. July 15, 1 year, 5 %. 4,500

Young, Peter and Joseph to The Title Guarantee and Trust Co. Gold st, e s, 75 n Concord st, runs north 50 x east 106.8 x south 125.3 to Concord st, x west 48.10 x north 75 x west 49. July 20, 3 years, 5 %. 6,500

Same to same. Adelphi st, e s, 333.4 s Park av, 16.8x100. July 20, 3 years, 5 %. 2,000

Same to same. Clermont av, e s, 136.11 n Myrtle av, 50x120. July 20, 3 years, 5 %. 4,000

Same to same. North Portland av, e s, 109.6 s Flushing av, 25x104.3x25.6x109.5. July 20, 3 years, 5 %. 2,000

Same to same. Myrtle av, s s, 98 w Adelphi st, 25x85x25.6x85. July 20, 3 years, 5 %. 3,500

Young, Peter and Joseph to The Title Guarantee and Trust Co. Carlton av, e s, 808.3 s Park av, 50x100. July 20, 3 years, 5 %. 2,500

Same to same. Carlton av, w s, 342.5 s Park av, 49x100. July 20, 3 years, 5 %. 4,500

Same to same. Carlton av, e s, 502.3 s Park av, 50x100. July 20, 3 years, 5 %. 3,000

Same to same. Vanderbilt av, w s, 594.2 n Myrtle av, 33.4x100. July 20, 3 years, 5 %. 3,500

Young, Nicholas P. and Peter to The Title Guarantee and Trust Co. Willoughby st, n s, 100 w Hudson av, runs north 41.4 x northeast 26 8 x northwest 4.6 to Fleet st, x southwest along same 78.1 to Willoughby st, x east 35. July 20, 5 years, 5 %. 4,000

Same to same. Carroll st, n s, 70 w 6th av, 20x100. July 20, 3 years, 5 %. 4,500

Zirinsky, Joseph to Heinrich Langlos and Mary his wife. Varet st. P. M. July 15, 5 years, 5 %. 2,300

Zwerdling, Annie to Mary Zimmermann widow. Osborn st. P. M. July 15, 5 years. 700

MORTGAGES----ASSIGNMENTS.

NEW YORK CITY.

JULY 17 TO 23—INCLUSIVE.

Arnaud, Petrin to William Tilden exr. William Tilden. $13,606

Bach, Lewis Z. to Gideon Fountain. nom

Bormann, William H. to Louisa Widder. 3,000

Brown, Joseph O. exr. James Munson and trustee for Lavainia C. Roof to Bridget C. wife of Thomas Sullivan. 2,400

Becker, C. Adelbert to Isabella G. Francis, Bridgehampton, L. I. 3,500

Bliven, William W. et al. exrs. Louisa Bliven to Emma P. Yergens. 4,000

Bythiner, Bertha to Philip Bouton. 5,000

Banks, David S. to Real Estate Loan and Trust Co., New York. 6,000

Bendheim, Henry M. to Adolf Kerbs. nom

Same to same. nom

Cruger, James P. to trustees of St. Stephen's College. 21,000

Casey, Bridget to William Radebold and Edward Wenz. 1,000

Cohen, Barnett to Meyer Cohen. nom

Canda & Mathews Manufacturing Co. (Lim.) to Simon Adler and Henry S. Herrman. $1,200

Devoe, Frederick W. to Joanna C. Jones. 3,000

Dunne, Thomas P. to Henry Leute. 2,500

Ehret, Frank A. to George Ehret. 13,000

Freeland, Isabella and Alfred Jaretzki to Mary M. Sullivan. 2,225

Fay, Michael and William Stacom to William Hall's Sons. 6,000

Gebhardt, Lena to Canda & Mathews Mfg. Co. (Lim.) 1,500

Goebel, Max to John J. Bowes, Passaic, N. J. nom

Hyatt, George E. to Edward Winslow. nom

Same to The Lawyers Title Ins. Co. of New York. 34,992

Hand, Clifford A. exr., &c., Charles G. Havens to The Havens Relief Fund Society. 12,000

Hagemeyer, Garetta P. admrx. F. E. Hagemeyer who was trustee for Alwina A. C. Hagedorn to Guarantee Trust and Safe Deposit Co. substituted trustee. nom

Hamming, William and Elizabeth his wife to Isaac Reinheimer. 3,500

Hall, Thomas R. A. and William H., of William Hall's Sons, to George S. Hall. consid. omitted

Hubener, Christian to Louis P. Mahler. 4,000

Louis, Amelia E., Brooklyn, N. Y., to Randolph Guggenheimer. 5,000

Lawrence, Frazier & Co. to Wilbur F. Washburn. 3,750

Monks, William H. to John Bell & Son. 2,000

Middlebrook, Frederic J. to James N. Platt et al. trustees William B. Lawrence. 6,018

Same to same. 16,136

Same to same. 10,043

Middlebrook, Frederic J., Brooklyn, to Bernard Grunhut. 10,082

Same to same. 3,025

Marks, Cecil A. to Bernard Cohen. val. consid. and 100

Middlebrook, Frederic J., Brooklyn, to Bernhard Grunhut. 2,017

Same to same. 4,020

Middlebrook, Frederic J., Brooklyn, to Leopold Gusthal. 6,000

McGuire, Emma L. wife of Francis to William S. Denmark. nom

Nally, Christopher to Cassidy & Adler. nom

O'Connor, Eleanor K. to Thomas H. O'Connor exr. and trustee John F. O'Connor. nom

Pettit, Elizabeth to James Pettit. 4,000

Putnam, James D. to Orlando B. Potter. 125,000

Randell, Charles H. exr. Betsey A. Randell to Mary L. Randell, Westchester, N. Y. 4,400

Schneider, Louis exr. Anna Schwarz to Jacob Siegel. 9,000

Saxton, Alanson H. et al., exrs. Thomas Kenworthy to Martha J. Kenworthy widow, Stapleton, S. I. 7,037

Schwarzwaelder, Rachel extrx. Christian Schwarzwaelder to The Germania Bank. nom

Sink, Mary C., Brooklyn, to Alfred Roe. 1,000

Smith, Frank L. to Mary B. Smith, Brooklyn. nom

Same to same. 4,000

Scheider, Joseph to Ambrose K. Ely. 4,443

Smith, Frank L. to Mary B. Smith, Brooklyn. 500

Sire, Meyer L. to Edward F. Browning. 7,000

Title Guarantee and Trust Co. to Harvey J. Ubert. 2,000

Title Guarantee and Trust Co. to Giles R. Dart. 7,500

Same to E. Eliot Harris exr. Abraham Harris. 12,000

Title Guarantee and Trust Co. to The Mercantile Trust Co. guard. of Adelaide S. Washburn. 7,000

The Lawyers' Title Ins. Co. of New York to Eliza M. Sloane. 15,927

Same to same. 22,082

Wilde, John and A. Ward Brigham exrs. Sarah Wilde, Brooklyn, to Emma J. wife of A. Ward Brigham. 10,000

Wallach, Joseph to Rosa Cohn, San Francisco, Cal. nom

Washburn, Wilbur F., Yonkers, N. Y., to The First National Bank of Yonkers, N. Y. nom

Widder, Louisa to William H. Bormann. 1,590

Wilson, John T. trustee of John Wilson dec'd to Morton D. Bogue guard. for the children of Alma T. Hatch. 6,000

Walker, Mary A., Westfield, S. I., to William H. Hewlett, Manhasset, L. I. 4,501

Young, George to Thomas H. Bauchle trustee for George Y. Bauchle. 15,000

KINGS COUNTY.

JULY 16 TO 22—INCLUSIVE.

American Steam Boiler Ins. Co. to Francena B. Partridge. $4,067

Benjamin, Joseph to Leopold Michel. nom

Bicker, Frederick to Elizabeth Bicker his wife. 1,500

Bissell, West to William Saville. 1,000

Briggs, Benjamin F. to James White. 500

Brunnemer, John and James L. Bennett to Caspar Huwer. 575

Barth, Emilia to Nuns of Order St. Dominick. 15,000

Brouwer, Theophilus A. trustee Margaret M. Brouwer to Charles A. Vermilyea. 4,083

Buckley, Charles P. exr. Ella A. P. Buckley to Ellen A. Buckley. 2,000

Buchenholz, Bernard to David Michel. nom

Colyer, William T. to Cornelius R. Colyer. nom

Cose, Elizabeth to Samuel M. Terry, Southold, L. I. 1,050

Cozine, William H. to John H. Cozine. 600

Denike, Thomas S. to Alfred Ogden. 1,200

Enderle, Augusta to Leonhardt Martin. 500

Fithian, David A. to Lawrence Hurlburt. 650

Gallagher, Bridget to Mary A. Dunigan. 300

Hagemeyer, Garretta P. admrx. of F. E. Hagemeyer trustee of Alwina A. C. Hagedorn under will of Bohl Bohlen to Guarantee Trust and Safe Deposit Co. of Philadelphia, trustee of said A. A. C. Hagedorn, &c. 17 assigns. of morts. nom

Haight, Gilbert L. to Caleb D. Gildersleeve. 7,500

Hoag, John, County Treasurer of Westchester County, to Sarah A. Masten, Kingston, N. Y. 3,000

Jackson, Theodore F. to David and Grahams Polley. 7,500

Same to same. 2,500

Jackson, William H. to Samuel Levy. 745

Lebohner, George C. to Emma Brickman. 1,600

Lott, Rebecca B. to Richard J. and John F. Berry exrs. Margaret A. Berry. 2,000

Lynes, John J. to Susan Ward, Farmingham, Conn. 987

Livingston, Charles O. to Helen J. Garrettson. 2,035

Lamb, James W. and Albert J. to Janet H. wife of William H. Sleeper. 1,700

Lincoln, Clarence to Rudolph Reimer & Co. consid. omitted

Linton, Edward F. to Hannah D. White. 500

Same to same. 500

Same to same. 900

Same to same. 500

Same to John Beach. 1,420

Maher, Daniel to William Schindele. 2,250

Michel, Leopold to Joseph Benjamin. nom

Same to same. 500

Miller, Hannah E., Philadelphia, Pa., to Robert J. Miller. 2,000

Mowbray, Edward H. to The Title Guarantee and Trust Co. nom

Parker, Asa W. to Emily F. von Bernuth. 1,132

Rankin, James D. and James Ross to Clark T. Hamilton. 1,000

Rankin, James D. and James Ross to Lawrence Hurlburt. 2,700

Reynolds, William H. to Charles D. King. 1,500

Roth, Henry to John L. Gaus and Charles Miller. 1,000

Ruth, Abraham to Hall Sash and Door Co. 800

Smith, Herbert C. to Herman F. Koepke. 1,000

Suydam, Aetta, New Utrecht, to Henry R. Read. 2,500

Sampson, Rebecca L. to Solomon Tim. 1,500

Sarles, Mary S. M., Little Silver, N. J., to Kate A. wife of William J. Fruin. 5,500

Smith, Mary W. to Ellen J. Quackenbush. 800

Schneider, Doris D. to Christian G. Moritz. 1,000

Smith, Mary to John Meehan. 1,000

Smith, William H. to Louis Bossert. 800

Simonson, William B. to Warren C. Hubbard, Rochester, N. Y. 3,000

Thomas, Mary wife of Solomon to Albert Davis, Oyster Bay, L. I. 503

The City Savings Bank of Brooklyn to William Spence. 8,500

Title Guarantee and Trust Co. to John C. Ager and ano. trustees Wealthea A. Neale. 12,000

Same to Thomas T. Barr. 8,000

Same to John S. Pollard. 5,000

Same to Mary D. Green. 3,000

Same to Mary Vigelius. 5,000

Same to Mary S. Brown. 2,000

Same to George R. Lockwood and ano. trustees Roe Lockwood. 29,854

Same to James Sullivan. 1,000

Same to Edward de Witt Mason. 4,000

Same to Charles Holt. 5,000

Same to Chauncey J. Hastings. 6,000

Same to Julia Young. 3,000

Same to same. 4,000

Thompson, Catherine to James Williamson. 700

Wolff, Lee to Rebecca L. Sampson. 1,500

Wandel, Sarah J. to Ella M. Mooney, Plainfield, N. J. 4,250

Williamson, James to Sarah E. Dunderdale. 3,000

Waters, James to George E. Nostrand. consid. omitted

Wenz, Sarah E. to John Hoagland. nom

Winant, Lydia to Edward F. Linton. 1,600

JUDGMENTS.

In these lists of judgments the names alphabetically arranged, and which are first on each line, are those of the judgment debtor. The letter (D) means judgment for deficiency (*) means not summoned. (†) signifies that the first name is fictitious, real name being unknown. Judgments entered during the week, and satisfied before day of publication, do not appear in this column, but in list of Satisfied Judgments

NEW YORK CITY.

July

20 Ahern, Dennis—J H White.......... $314 60

20 Ammann, John C—H W. Jordan..... 20 00

21 Ascher, Solomon, treas. of the Ladies' Uptown Aid Society of N Y—Severin Norman Jouette.......... 77 92

22 Anhalt, Jacob—Harriet A Case...... 2,239 10

22 Aschcroft, John—American Photo-Engraving Co.......... 45 50

18 Barker, Ralph P—D G Yuengling, Jr, Brewing Co.......... 442 54

18 Boehm, Emil P—Mari A Cumiug.... 76 46

18 Brady, Terence—Empire State Brewing Co.......... 231 36

20 Baltz, Edward F—Chas A Page. ....costs 34 06

20 Briggs, George E—C A Briggs........ 252 81

20 Baum, David—Bernard Goldfinger... 368 00

21 Braune, Joseph—Guiseppe Matai.... 221 16

21 Breinig, Revere M—Ruleman Muller 176 33

21 Bernstein, Philip—Louis Rosen...... 1,392 77

21 Bennett, John R—Jas. S Conover.... 735 03

21*Baptiste, Benjamin F—E W Fisher... 269 03

22 Blumenthal, Hanchen—Chas Moebus, assignee.......... 61 20

22 Beardsley, Homer S—Melvin Stephens 569 22

22 Bowne, Harrison, Percy—A L Knight. ....costs 58 60

22 Beardsley, Charles S—Twenty-third Ward Bank.......... 253 27

22 Bonnell, John Harper—The Chatham Nat Bank.......... 899 53

22 Belvin, Mary—H M Kaminski........ 436 61

22†Benson, Michael / Beaudet, Homer J } David Marx...(D) 9,993 19

22† the same——the same.........(D) 9,714 16

23*Beardsley, Charles—D C Foster...... 287 57

23 Brennan, John—Coleman Brewing Co 191 74

24*Bunting, James H—Theodore Diebold 98 68

24 Biershenk, Peter F—Wm Rankin..(D) 5,452 03

24 Bonny, Frederick C—Chas J Warren. 125 00

24 Baruth, Henry—Edwin Wallace..... 616 03

24 the same —— James Chambers (Lim).......... 359 57

24 Bernstein, Philip—Mendel Singer.... 330 51

24 Buckhout, Henry—J Edward Simmons, as recvr of the American Loan and Trust Co..........17,987 65

20 Commings, Lawrence H—H F Lord.. 120 20

20 Cimmino, Maria—J and M Haffen... 120 00

20 Curran, Mary Ann—C W Schwarting 106 04

21 Cox, William—James Chambers (Lim) 143 00

21 Cameron, Allan J / Cameron, Letitia } C A Spalding...... 126 78

21 Coggeshall, Edward C—B G Gliddon, 89 50

21 Crawford, Abram—R F Chapman...... 91 98

21 Cory, Enos W—E W Fisher.......... 209 03
21 Crary, William P—Lillie S Crary.... 274 34
23 Copeland, L P—J R Couper.......... 197 89
22 Cadman, Charles P—C H Lottridge.. 107 36
23 Cleary, John—C V Fornes........... 285 02
23*Clemens, Harold—J H Middendorf... 1,522 72
23 Cassidy, Mary F—Marvin Safe Co ....costs 52 33
23 Clark, Heman—D E Donovan 108,987 39
24 Chapman, Charles P—Theodore Diebold.......... 93 08
24 Collins, Richard M—Ludwig Baumann 78 53
24 Cox, Henry E—G L Wood 356 09
24 Collins, Jeremiah J—Bernard French. 110 56
17 Donnelly, Thomas W—Geo M Miller. 110 51
20 Doyle, Andrew T—James Nunan.... 1,237 34
20 Dobler, Anton, *Dobler, Charles } The Gutta Percha Rubber Mfg. Co. 96 00
21 de Murguiondo, Carter—Fourteenth Street Bank.......... 211 25
21 de Varona, Salvador—E P Jenkins... 29 87
23 Davis, John C—D C Foster.......... 287 57
23 Daly, James—Coleman Brewing Co.. 129 50
24 Delury, Robert F—Ludwig Baumann 35 00
24 Driggs, W Lincoln—S D Bond....... 148 36
20 Esselborn, Edward—G F Swift....... 204 71
20 Emery, Franies F—Adolph Scheftel.. 1,621 44
21 Ellsler, Effie—Ernest Horchheimer... 201 70
21 Ehrlich, Hiram—Stephen G Patterson 94 00
22 Edler, Jacob, Jr—Smith Clift, exr.... 135 37
23 Ellis, William H—Henry Henjes..... 257 17
24 Eckstein, Frank—Mary Siebold...... 2,632 00
24 Everett, Susan M—P J Hickey....... 191 21
20 Finer, Jacob—William Fieder....... 93 49
20 Ferriter, James—The Windsor Lime Co.......... 270 56
20 Fitz, Charles R—George Smith, Jr, admr.......... 1,031 01
21 Franke, Louis—C A Joslyn.......... 3,202 93
21 Farrington, John A, Farrington, Jonas S } C H Cone.... 529 39
21 Fogg, John C—Thomas Monahan.... 3,927 87
21 Frank, Michael—Max Hartman, admr 2,030 77
21 the same——the same.......... 1,506 00
22 Freely, Alfred—T K Miller.......... 100 35
22 Fere, Fernand—Marie Babin, admrx. 624 08
23 Fay, Anna Bam—D C Foster......... 287 57
23 Foley, Thomas P—Nathaniel Waterbury.......... 202 57
23 Flagg, Jared—Elise A H Kimball.... 4,360 00
23 Faulkner, Henry N—C H K Curtis... 123 71
24 Fronk, Edwin C—J R Byrne......... 106 32
24 Frey, Pauline—Henry Wirth........ 212 54
18 Gibson, John F—G N Percey...... 94 50
18 Gottscho, Isaac, Gottscho, Herman } Emil Dieckerhoof 283 56
18 Gilson, Lottie—B J Falk.......... 45 50
21 Guggenheimer, Newton S—Julia Exstein.......... 324 42
21*Gutmann, Nathan—James Barrett... 75 11
22 Gibb, Lulu—Oscar Goerke.......... 493 80
22 Gregor, John—Helen R Russell..... 272 80
22 Gilmartin, James—J M Valentine.... 1,502 55
23 Gaffney, James—W J Lynam........ 267 50
23 Gordon, Hannah — The Manhattan Railway Co.......... 162 53
23 Glaeser, Emanuel—Martin Bentz..... 698 28
23 Gilmartin, James—Wm Stursberg... 901 12
23 Grant, Hugh J, as Sheriff—Jette Grunberg, admrx 4,339 66
23 Groht, Lucy M—Stephen Underhill.. 97 97
24 Gallo, Antonio—James Maloney..... 258 13
18 Hunsicker, Jacob—Enyard & Bain... 1,980 71
18 Harper, William D—The Western Nat Bank.......... 741 25
20 Halstead, Augustus M—Manhattan Brass Co.......... 74 66
21 Hayman, Charles—John Condon..... 284 22
21 Hinaman, Emily J—O L Hinds....... 128 55
21 Huber, Anton—Geo Ringler & Co.... 668 00
21 Hill, James M—Herman Kubnast.... 434 10
22 Hogg, Julia D—Samuel Lord........ 369 38
21 Hauff, Annie—J S Haft.......... 272 96
22 Hanmer, Albert S—C F Claflin....... 126 29
22 Hicks, James—D G Gautier.......... 206 00
22 Harper, William D—The Chatham Nat Bank.......... 844 09
22 Healey, Charles—Albany Brewing Co 368 80
23 Hall, William F—J S R Byrne....... 174 67
24 Haigh, Joseph L—Thomas Brennan.. 512 06
24 Hayman, Charles—M H Moses & Co. 69 38
24 Hannegan, John J—W H Hussey.... 588 98
23 Infeld, William—Samuel Schlesinger. 71 12
20 Johum, Joseph A—Johan Kaudutsch. 274 45
24 Jones, Edwin T—S C Beckwith...... 358 28
18+Krakow, Max—Joseph Goldstein..... 39 55
18 Kahn, Aaron—John Koenig.......... 192 01
20 Kacensky, Abraham, *Kadin, Eva } Wm Fieder... 261 91
20 Katz, David—Siegmund Raduziner... 269 59
20 Klein, Henry—Taylor Jelliffe 282 00
20 Kandel, Jacob—Bernard Goldfinger.. 368 01
21 Krakauer, David—James Barrett.... 75 12
21 Klenen, Martin—The Boynton Furnace Co.......... 38 94
22 Kirkham, Henry A—Frances S Naylor, extrx.......... 1,010 12
23 Kinsey, Benjamin D—John Hancock Mutual Life Ins Co.......... 160 11
23 Kayser, Alfred S—Lewis Lyon....... 173 57
23 Koransky, Salomon, Koransky, Lina } Morris Levenson.......... 593 81
23 Kareski, Leo—Mason, Au and Margenheimer Confectionery Mfg Co.... 280 53
23 Kenney, Margaret—Chas Lane....... 205 28
23*Keller, Amos E—Stephen Underhill.. 97 97
18 Lotterhos, Lottie—The N Y Veal & Mutton Co.......... 146 14
18 Lavelle, Henry E—G W Martin...... 582 62
20 Leverich, Henry M—Eaton Cole and Burnham Co.......... 469 62
21 Lecuyer, Charles G—Alphonsine Lecuyer.......... 1,138 67

21 the same——John Rogers......... 267 07
21 the same——Wm Neely.......... 561 88
21 the same——the same.......... 2,635 12
21 Linch, Patrick—Empire State Brewing Co.......... 485 93
21 Loewenstein, Henry—H E Williams.. 81 00
21 Leseman, Sully O—George Forbes.... 1,719 71
22 Lawless, Michael—R V Lawless...... 8,179 49
22 the same——the same.......... 8,226 99
22 Lyon, Lansing D, Lyon, Clarence W, Lyon, Clara M } Union Mutual Life Ins Co of Maine... costs 107 81
22 Logan, Sidney S—H W Hill......... 375 34
22 Littlefield, Milton S—Melvin Stephens 569 22
22 Lawson, Louise—Thomas Graham.... 320 83
23 Laviada, Antonio—J O Ward......... 3,763 28
23 Luyster, James R—Wm R Potts, exr. 926 27
23 Lawson, Louise—Geo M. Miller....... 236 06
24 Locke, Kate—Ludwig Baumann...... 60 63
24 Lennon, William F—David Conover.. 1,799 08
24 Lane, James R—C J Warren..... 402 70
24 Luhrs, Johan—Isaac Manheimer..(D) 2,764 74
24 Landrock, John G—The N Y Life Ins Co.......... 105 99
24 Leonard, John S—Lyonce Langer.... 423 39
18 Martin, Robert C—J J Fitzgerald.... 1,670 45
18 the same——Alva S Staples....... 6,149 83
20 Meyers, Nathan—Isaac Levy......... 194 25
20 Miltner, Peter—Campbell Sash, Door and Moulding Co (Lim).......... 91 00
20 Meyer, Herman—John Wilde........ 110 00
20 Moe, Ira W—The Ansonia Brass and Copper Co.......... 283 44
20 Munz, David—Auguste Noel......... 161 00
21 Mathews, Elizabeth A—C S Spaes.... 408 01
21 Martin, Robert C—F A Norton...... 11,259 66
22 Muller, Conrad, Jr—J S Haft........ 272 96
22 Moore, Charles V—Frances S Naylor, admr.......... 1,010 12
23 Moonelis, Adolph — Elias Spingarn ....(D) 15,592 78
24 Mooney, Henrietta R—The National Butchers and Drovers' Bank....(D) 832 84
24 Mayers, Isaac—C B Abbott.......... 129 36
24 Marchi, Jules J—Antonio Lombardi.. 93 86
24 Mills, Sarah T—Thomas Dempsey.... 45 60
24 Mangham, John H—W C Sheldon.... 1,238 24
24 Marvin, William Bradbury—A J Connick.......... 209 91
24 Mueller, William—Henry Walter..... 95 38
18 McEwen, Edson H—L E Ransom..... 185 39
18 the same——the same.......... 349 60
18 the same——the same.......... 193 80
21 McDonald, Francis—James Chambers (Lim).......... 143 00
21 McHugh, Peter Harry—R T Chapman.......... 107 55
22 McKenzie, John, *McPherson, Duncan } David Schuldner.......... 92 67
23 McDonald, William P—P S Colomeno. 1,592 47
23 McDonald, Philip F—Wm Johnston, Jr.......... 284 62
23 McLean, Cornelius—F F Gunther.... 352 10
23 McDonald, Wm H — The Twelfth Ward Bank.......... 1,529 82
18+Norton, Jane L C—Sophie Kraker... 194 15
20 Nevelle, James J—Anthony Fischer.. 226 55
21 Nisbet, Henry T—C H Amsden...... 266 23
21 the same——F J Amsden.......... 607 58
21 Nordenschild, Elijah—S F Hart...... 1,047 98
22+North, Frank J—G H Bartholf....... 74 70
22 Onderdonk, William M—Frances S Naylor, extrx.......... 1,050 94
22 the same——the same.......... 1,010 12
23 Owens, David S—John Hancock Mutual Life Ins Co.......... 160 11
18 Peck, Nathan—Jas J Fitzgerald...... 1,670 45
18 the same——Alva S Staples...... 6,149 83
20 Pearce, John—Eaton Cole and Burnham Co.......... 469 62
21 Pierce, John—H W Strikeman....... 248 95
21 Peters, Philip—Rubsam & Horrmann Brewing Co.......... 95 52
21 Prager, Jacob E—Hannah Abrahams 168 50
21 Palmer, George W—Edward Thompson Co.......... 38 87
21 Prince, Simeon H—C & J Falkenberg 253 77
21 Pryor, Samuel Morris—F S Rook.... 249 79
21 Peck, Nathan—F O Norton.......... 11,259 66
21 Pfister, Theophile—Louis Wahl...... 395 19
22 Pfeiffer, Charles—J M C Martin...... 157 69
22 Purdy, Jonathan S—F E Ga Nun.... 94 33
22 Pulver, Frank—Elias Bach.......... 219 71
23 Pfieffer, Elizabeth—The Manhattan Railway Co..........costs 163 63
23 Pearson, Eugene—E S Jaffray........ 541 10
24 Porr, Louis J—Mary Siebold......... 2,632 00
18 Quigley, Hugh J—Empire State Brewing Co.......... 400 01
18 Ross, J Stewart—E Louis Akin..... 389 12
18 Ross, Ivisen M—M H Moses & Co. .. 377 00
20 Rubin, Carl, Rubin, Morris } Wm Frieder.......... 123 65
20 Rider, Charles W—G F Swift 85 67
20 Read, Cassius H—Geo Haseltine 546 17
20*Rossell, John—The Windsor Lime Co 270 56
20 Raduziner, Adolph—Arnold Kohn... 1,269 62
20 the same——Alois Kohn.......... 952 67
20 Rossbach, Frederick—F V Mayforth. 17 50
20 Raduziner, Adolph—Frederick Kaffeman.......... 819 91
21 Rich, William, Rich, Henry B } Emil Weil.......... 432 12
21 Ross, George, *Ross, Elizabeth K } Joseph Bierhoff.. 168 73
21 Rich, William, Rich, Henry B } John F Rich.......... 123 55
21 Rollins, George M—M A Sutherland. 793 75
21 Reilly, Bryan—Edward Connaughton 30 50
21 Rogers, Joseph E—W R Dougherty.. 324 46
21 Reinhardt, Josephine, *Reinhardt, Frank } M V Freund.. 251 79
23 Rogers, Myron W—W H Magoffin... 693 41
23 Russel, George D—A S Odell........ 162 00

23+Riker, John—Ferdinand Greenbaum. 101 75
23 Reynolds, Victor S—M C Byrnes..... 101 08
23 Reynolds, John M—John Fleming.... 255 91
23 Richardson, Charles A—Joseph Brugger.......... 140 25
24 Reamer, Job M—Daniel Gould 6,122 16
18 Sullivan, James E—G N Percey...... 94 50
18 Stern, Benjamin—The N Y Veal & Mutton Co.......... 77 30
18 Sotscheck, Carl—E F Faulkner...... 336 93
18 Saunders, Sarah J—Tarrant & Co.... 193 47
20 Schwarz, Laser—Henry Blank....... 292 70
20 Sotscheck, Carl—W C McGibbon..... 79 23
20 Silverman, Joseph—Wm Fieder...... 89 77
20 Silverman, Michael——the same...... 93 49
20*+Solwedel, Joseph—Campbell Sash, Door and Moulding Co (Lim)...... 91 00
20 Siebert, Frederick—Abraham Berliner.......... 73 00
20 Sidell, Ferdinand—N Y Life Ins Co.. 145 70
20 Steinschneider, Malvina E—Workingmen Co-operative Assoc 29 35
20 Soutter, Agnes Gordon, individ and as extrx of James T Soutter, Sr—Lewis Sanders.......... 3,784 96
20 Sanford, Mary D—The Fourth Nat Bank.......... 75 72
21 Struss, Henry W—C S Joslyn........ 3,202 93
21 Swan, William J—Jabez Burns....... 117 86
21 Scully, John J—Florence Frazee..... 394 52
21 Steinberger, Solomon—Edward Weinberger.......... 26 50
21*Siniscalco, Carmine—Guiseppe Matai. 231 16
21 Simons, Joseph—The Norton Can Co.. 188 51
21 Scribner, G Hilton, Jr—Thomas Monahan.......... 3,927 87
21 Salomon, William — Max Hartman, admr.......... 2,080 77
21 the same——the same.......... 1,506 00
21 Sistare, William H M—J R Adams... 7,371 43
22 Sparks, Alfred M, Sparks, Alfred A } R Wallace & Sons Mfg Co.......... 275 66
22 Schlansky, Moses—The J L Mott Iron Works.......... 234 55
22 Sparks, Alfred M, Sparks, Alfred A } The Meriden Britanica Co...... 791 51
22 Scott, George H—Francis Smith...... 259 50
22 Singer, Marcus—P A Jeannaret 292 34
22 Strunck, Herman—Henry Eggers.... 71 15
22 Sotscheck, Carl—Martin Worn....... 238 23
23 Silver, Horatio N—The Manhattan Railway Co..........costs 107 27
23 Serrell, Mary E—Lewis Gold......... 440 15
23 Scott, Charles B—E S Jaffray........ 541 10
23 Stevenson, Vermon K—L H Jauvrin. 171 84
23 Sistare, William H M—J W Middendorf.......... 1,522 72
23 Southerland, William—Wm Fiss..... 101 49
24 Schuck, Philip, Jr—Max D Stern.... 84 52
24 Searing, Theodore W—C F Lawrence. 104 33
24 Sinnot, Amos J—Mount Morris Electric Light Co.......... 266 14
24 Schiffmann, Max—Henry Seelig..... 450 83
24 Stoerger, Babette, Stoerger, Henry } S Strauss........ 71 50
24 Squier, Albert C—E F Keating...... 303 00
24 Seekamp, John H—J F Hembockel.. 2,115 00
21 Smith, Albert E, *Smith, Elizabeth K } Joseph Bierhoff. 168 73
22 Smith, William Dolsen, admr de bonis non of William Dolsen, dec'd—Joseph Husson.......... 242 27
24 Smith, Frank L—W Rankin......(D) 5,452 03
24 Smith, Edward—C H Richter... .... 157 44
18 Lawrence Curry Comb Co—Chas C Gordon.......... 1,056 91
18 J H Bonnell & Co (Lim)—The Western National Bank.......... 741 25
20 Ulster & Delaware R R Co—Alice S Vandercooke.......... 859 01
20 J H Bonnell & Co (Lim)—Thos B Hidden.......... 1,394 56
22 Wemple Litho Printing Co — The Tradesmen's Nat Bank.......... 537 97
22 Abbe Engine Co—J Q Maynard...... 213 50
22 The John Ashcroft Patent Grate Bar and Furnace Door Mfg Co—C T Quintard.......... 358 67
22 The Metropolitan Elevated Railway Co, The New York Elevated Railroad Co, The Manhattan Railway Co } Charles Buek. 556 40
23 J H Bonnell & Co (Lim)—The Western Nat Bank.......... 1,738 99
23 Metropolitan Elevated Railway Co—Louisa A Siefke.......... 2,400 00
23 Washington Cold Storage Co—Anton Beberdick.......... 73 88
23 Lawrence Curry Comb Co — The Fourteenth St Bank.......... 120 26
23 Corona Tile Mfg Co—Margaret Maidhof.......... 3,034 28
24 The Mayor, Alderman, &c—J H Strahan.......... 5,000 00
24 The Hudson River Boot and Shoe Mfg Co—Clinton Bank.......... 2,024 79
24 New York Refrigerating Construction Co—McNab & Harlin Mfg Co...... 3,157 36
24 Lawrence Curry Comb Co — The Fourteenth St. Bank.......... 211 50
21 Trisdorfer, Henry—H K Thurber.... 538 63
21 Tuttle, Emmet—Phillips & Avery.... 47 66
21 Tremper, Seymour—Anchor Brewing Co.......... 102 06
22 Thompson, James—C H Briggs....... 112 42
23 the same——Lenox Hill Bank.... 525 61
23 Thorne, Arthur—W H Magoffin..... 693 41
23 Treulieb, Allen C—Marvin Safe Co.. ....costs 44 83
23 Tolk, Berel—Mason, Au & Magenheimer Confectionery Mfg Co...... 280 53
23 Thorne, Edwin—Edward Kearney... 395 24

Thayer, Stephen H, Jr, individ; 24 Thayer, Horace H, as exr and trustee of Stephen H Thayer } Emma Wood 593 90
24 the same——the same 1,102 16
22 Vernam, Remington; *Vernam, Florence G } J W Clowes 578 61
23 Valentine, Robert H C—The Chatham Nat Bank 964 68
20 Weed, Addison P—Mary A Weed 217 38
20 the same——W P Hurlbutt 223 69
21 Wallace, Mrs I R—The United States and Brazil Mail Steamship Co 143 58
22 Wemple, Henry Y; Wemple, Charles E } The Tradesmen's Nat Bank 587 97
22 Wasdell, Leonard S—J F Kaiser 63 90
22*Weil, Isidor—H M Kaminski 436 61
23 Walsh, William B—Annie Kurtz 125 64
23†Woolsey, Edward J—Richard Webber 67 50
23 Walters, Julius W—The Delamater Iron Works 49 68
23 Wright, Arthur—William Fiss 101 49
24 Williams, Benson J—Carl Voght 218 00
24 Waldman, Aaron R—The National Butchers' and Drovers' Bank of N Y 832 84
24 Whitestone, David—Henry Seelig 450 83
24*Whipple, M—E F Keating 302 00

¶ *Editor* Record and Guide:

The two judgments in favor of David Marx for $9,993.19 and $9,714.16 respectively, entered July 22, 1891, against Homer J. Beaudet for deficiencies on foreclosures, were not intended to be entered against him, but only against Michael Benson. The judgment will be released as against Mr. Beaudet at once.

J. H. V. Arnold, Att'y for David Marx.

KINGS COUNTY.

July
17 Augustine, John—F Kuckuk $49 75
20 Adams, Frank H—A Lazansky 177 92
17 Brainerd, Charles A—A E Chasmar 918 47
17 Burns, Hugh—P J Carlin 1,047 58
17 Brooks, Julius—S F Rothschild 67 44
18 Brush, Thomas H—G B Germond 214 24
20 Bigelow, Georgianna—N H Davol 101 47
20 Bennett, William J—B Fischer 294 72
20 Bennett, Henry D and wife—M Fierebrendt 20 91
21 Bedell, Edwin J—C B Leet 320 92
22 Bretsch, Sophie—H Goodstein 58 85
23 Butler, S B—G T Homan 130 00
16 Cochran, Alexander—Amelia L Gurlitz (D) 2,749 20
16 Campbell, James—B Garvey 143 06
20 Cosby, James—Catherine Cosby 736 82
21 Chapman, Hawley—H Cranston 126 90
21 Crary, William P—Lillie S Crary 274 34
23 Cohn, Henry L—H Baljer 253 13
18 Dillon, Frank—L W Lamberson 107 55
22 Dukeshire, Pharus C; Dukeshire, William } M B Morrin 142 96
18 Elster, Charles M—W A Jacobson 672 39
16 Finan, James—Third Nat Bank, Buffalo 296 01
18†Feely, "Mary"—B Hertzog 59 45
18 Franklin, Edward M—M Doscher 953 43
20 Fogg, John C—T Monahan 3,927 87
20 Flanagan, John A—P Booden 94 50
20 Forrester, Thomas G—W E Bryant 74 95
21*Ferris, Robert R—J Dresh 647 83
17 Grimes, Michael F—P Backus 195 73
17 Good, Samuel R—J L Armitage & Co 168 28
21 Green, Henry—Edison Electric Illuminating Co. of Brooklyn 31 84
21 Gottscho, Isaac; Gottscho, Herman } E Dieckerhoff 283 56
22 Greve, William M—H Meier 34 18
17 Horton, Joseph H—T J Preston & Co 87 83
17 Hayman, Charles—J Condon 284 22
17 Hillenbrand, John—F A Doyle 77 60
18 Hamilton, Louis D—T T Lines 119 64
20 Holtz, Edwin F—L Blumgart 187 11
20 Hegeman, Kate L—B A Beal 49 10
21 Henderson, Frederick D—W M Connor 244 52
22 Hamilton, Adelaide A—C H Payne 200 00
23 Hnutley, William; Huntley, George W } E M Travis 226 78
23 Huber, Anton—George Ringler & Co 668 00
20 Kennell, Joseph A—W H Shipman 480 70
20 Kirkland, William—A Lazansky 177 92
21 the same——C B Leet 320 92
21†Krakow, Max—J Goldstein 39 55
17 Lansdell, Henry—J Q Maynard 196 35
17 Levenstein, Bernhard—J Esever 258 01
20 Lowther, Sarah E; Lowther, John R } Cross, Austin & Co 282 67
21 Lemine, Francis—Julia Lemine 68 86
21 Ledwith, Patrick J—J Dresh 647 83
23 Levy, Julius; Levy, Augustus H; Levy, Moses D } N May 20,482 09
23 Loewenstein, Henry—H E Williams 81 00
16 Mulligan, John—J Nickels 67 60
17 Meyer, George; Meyer, Gesine } Caroline Traum 92 08
17 Merribew, Aaron B—T J Preston & Co 87 83
17 Morrison, Catherine; Morrison, John } Richardson & Boynton Co 53 70
17 McCormick, George W—L H Genties 115 28
17 Meyer, Gesene—G Gennerich 455 76
17 Manning, Michael J—The Syndicate Watch Co 256 96
18 Meyer, Gazina—F H Leggett 288 79
20 Mignore, Dincenzo—J Baehr 83 00
21 Meyer, Gesine—R Reimer 84 71
21 McDonough, Peter—J Dresh 647 83
20 Neilson, Hans J and Elizabeth his wife—M C Sorenson 200 25
23 Newman, Isador—G Weiber 82 50
16 O'Brien, Annie, exrs of—Catharine Taylor 175 00
18 Pearson, Eugene—S B Solomon 826 51
20 Pfohlmann, George—J J Froelich 125 00
23 Peters, Philip—Rubsam & Horrmann B Co 95 52
17 Raynor, George A—C C Shayne 448 07
17 Risenkopf, Max—Mary Bullowa 35 50
18 Ross, J Stewart—E L Akin 389 12
20 Reilly, John H—Alice Reilly 86 22
20 Rogers, Joseph E—W R Dougherty 324 46
17 Squire, Frank J—Mary A Grey 119 85
18 Scott, Charles P—S B Solomon 826 81
18 Seidenberg, Abraham—P Leidesdorf 77 50
18 Sheldon, Cevedra B — International Tile & Trim Co 707 25
18 the same——the same 593 19
20 Scribner, Jr, G Hilton—F Monahan 3,927 87
20 Seaman, Jamison C—W H Shipman 480 70
20 Smith, Richard T; Smith, Charles H } S T Valentine 234 57
21 Sanders, Sarah J—Tarrant & Co 192 47
22 Steinberger, Solomon—E Weinberger 26 50
22 Schlensky, Moses—J L Mott Iron Works 234 55
16 The exrs, &c, Annie O'Brien, dec'd—Catharine Taylor 175 00
17 The Metropolitan Gas Light Co, Elizabeth, N J—J D Walsh 796 56
17 Tutty, John—D M Koehler 436 01
16 Walton, Arthur—Ann M Miles 58 60
17 Wenman, Richard N—W Munford 43 15
20 Wallace, John W—Alice Tombo 78 08
21 Wilkius, William R—W E Clark & Bro 111 98
23 Wohlfarth, Charles—R Caspary 13 35
16 Zeh, Charles—County of Kings 125 00

SATISFIED JUDGMENTS.

NEW YORK.

July 18 to 24—Inclusive.

Barnecott, John F—Robert Manson. (1891) $528 24
Bradley, Moses H—H L Potter. (1891) 1,251 77
Broeckx, Eugenie—Emma L Toplitz. (1891) 274 18
Buttell, John J—The American Champagne Co (Lim). (1891) 76 78
Booth, Henry P—Jose Tanco, Jr. (1890) 132 60
Booth, Henry P—Jose Tanco, Jr. (1891) 67 88
§Bowler, Richard R—W D Wilson Printing Ink Co. (1891) 394 68
Bradley, Andrew J—G W Venable. (1891) 73 65
Beach, Alfred E—R B Harris. (1891) 2,368 92
Cohen, Byron A—W S. Carver. (1890) 931 99
Central Lithographing and Engraving Co—Julius Bien & Co. (1890) 417 36
Cassidy, Asa R——same. (1890) 417 36
Cane, Henry W, Abraham and George—Jas B Case. (1884) 2,090 04
Doe, John—Jose Tanco, Jr (1890) 132 60
De Kay, Minna C and Sidney—Eliza A Partridge. (1890) 206 39
Evan, John—Denis L Henessy. (1884) 89 01
Same——James Carstairs. (1884) 731 48
Same——Alfred Mamcffe. (1884) 145 59
Same——Wm Sullivan. (1885) 136 97
Same——Frank A Hall. (1884) 230 18
Friel, Lehman—Horace Galpen. (1880) 72 97
Fiels, Annie—Wm Nelson. (1886) 102 15
Goettmann, Albert, as exr Wm Schreiber—Isidor Alkus. (1891) 1,797 43
Hughes, William H T—Jose Tanco, Jr. (1891) 67 88
Hughes, William H T—Jose Tanco, Jr. (1890) 132 60
Heisenbuttle, Herman—Louis Runkel. (1889) 105 51
Ingersoll, James H, Ida M and John E—The Germania Bank. (1887) 7,649 05
John, Evan—W & H McShane. (1885) 108 06
Jennings, James—Jacob B Carpenter, exr. (1882) 222 69
*Kelsy, Frederick W—John F Gunther. (1887) 81 46
Laguna, Bernard and Rachel—Wm Dugan. (1891) 696 70
Miner, Henry C and Henry C, Jr—Julius Bien & Co. (1890) 417 36
Mulry, William P—Geo W Post. (1891) 90 70
Murray Hill Bank—Eliz Van Antwerp. (1889) 89 46
Same——same. (1887) 312 33
McCaffery, James W—James B Case. (1884) 2,090 04
*Murray Hill Bank—Theo V A Trotter. (1887) 199 27
*Meyer, Siegmund T and Arthur L—Twenty-third Ward Bank. (1891) 569 88
Minto, Robert F—Sarah C Minto. (1889) 526 49
McDonald, Roderick J——same. (1889) 526 49
‡Same——Wm H Brandt. (1889) 72 59
New York Ice Co—Chas R Spoerry. (1891) 105 01
Pendergast, Stephen—John Byrne. (1891) 689 98
Power, Richard—Mary Anderson. (1890) 75 59
Pfarrius, Minna—Geo Fennell. (1891) 77 36
Post, Edward S—Estella Lencioni. (1891) 38 00
Roe, Richard—Jose Tanco, Jr. (1890) 132 60
Ryan, William—W & H McShane. (1885) 108 06
Ryan, William—Denis L Henesey. (1884) 89 01
Same——James Carstairs. (1884) 731 48
Same——Alfred Mamcffe. (1884) 145 59
Same——Wm Sullivan. (1885) 136 97
Same——Frank A Hall. (1884) 230 18
Springer, John H—Julius Bien & Co. (1890) 417 36
Starbuck, Wm H—Thomas C Avery. (1889) 3,411 25
Strobel, Caspar—F R Miller. (1886) 30 00
Smith, Eugene—J L Butterly. (1891) 78 50
Tausick, Mitchell E—Laflin & Rand Powder Co (E Greenfield Son & Co, by assign.) (1891) 4,182 16
*The Harlem Lighting Co; *The Manhattan Electric Light Co } The Thomson-Houston Electric Co. (1891) 35,466 31
The Metropolitan Elevated Railway Co—Francis C Lawrence. (1891) 134 18
Same——same. (1889) 2,431 18
Same——same. (1891) 213 70
The Manhattan Railway Co——same. (1891) 134 18
Same——same. (1889) 2,431 18
Same——same. (1891) 213 70
Urias, Alexander—Manasses Oppenheimer. (1885) 400 35
United States Stamping Co—The Germania Bank. (1887)‖ 7,649 35
*Wilkes, George and Lizzie T—Twenty-third Ward Bank. (1891) 562 88
Waldron, Dyckman—J R Potts. (1891) 192 74
Woolsey, Edward I—James Donnelly. (1889) 103 43
Ziegfeld, Hugo—Julius Bien & Co. (1890) 417 36

*Vacated by order of Court. †Suspended on Appeal ‡Released. §Reversal. ‖Satisfied by Execution

KINGS COUNTY.

July 17 to 23—Inclusive.

Bierds, William H; Bierds, John T } Cross, Austin & Co. (1891) $385 23
Brush, Thomas H; Carman, Thomas D } E H Reynolds. (1891) 327 88
Finken, Elizabeth—M Renderle. (1891) 154 17
Same——same. (1891) 88 69
Fields, Annie—W Nelson. (1885) 1,021 15
Haviland, Lizzie—M Renderle. (1891) 154 17
Same——same. (1891) 88 64
Hoddison, A Edward—M Kieselbach. (1891) 190 16
Lees, Samuel—W D Wade. (1891) 59 03
O'Mahoney, Jeremiah—P L Ronalds. (1886) 254 32
Same——T Burke. (1886) 96 09
Prout, Hannah M—M P Prout. (1891) 102 59
Ryder, James; Ryder, Catharine } J D Ronnie. (1869) 663 82
The Ocean Navigation and Pier Co—W H Lewis. (1891) 1,350 69
Zeh, Philip; Zeh, Philip, Jr, of; Zeh, Philip & Son } M Dalton. (1890) 388 57
Same——A Wollmers. (1891) 116 55
Same——Bath & Hayward. (1891) 90 90
Same——P Henderson. (1889) 171 11

MECHANICS' LIENS.

NEW YORK CITY.

July
18 Eighty-third st, s s, 175 w Columbus av, 25x102.2. James Thomson agt John Chisholm, owner and contractor $1,150 00
18 Park av, s w cor 93d st, 100x105.8. Geo. B. Robbins & Co. agt Downey & Curry, owners and contractors 36 11
18 Vandam st, s w cor Macdougal st, 118.4x87. Same agt same 54 04
18 One Hundred and Twentieth st, s s, 125 w 8th av, 75x100. Frederick Eichler agt James Thompson, owner and contractor 290 00
20 Seventy-eighth st, Nos. 164-170, s s, 150 w 3d av, 100x100. Rider Engine Co. agt Wm. C. Burne, owner and contractor 340 00
20 First av, No. 1743; Ninetieth st, Nos. 329-341 } begins 1st av, n w cor 90th st, 50.8x250. John Dahlmeyer agt T. J. Jenkins & Bro., owners and contractors 95 00
20 Eighty-eighth st, Nos. 203-209, n w cor Amsterdam av, 100x100. Thomas Dixon agt John A. Amundson, owner, and Wm. Bell, contractor 578 55
20 Ninety-eighth st, n s, 375 e Columbus av, 25x100.11. Ryan & Rawnsley agt Gregory Leahy and Frank Reynolds, owners and contractors 600 00
20 Forty-second st, No. 559, n s 100 e 11th av, 25x100. Barr, Thaw & Fraser agt Mary A. Barron, owner, and Wm. Spearing her agent, as contractor 324 00
20 Southern Boulevard, s w cor Decatur av, 50x200. Wm. Clarke agt ——Katz, reputed owner, and H. Rosenbaum, debtor 379 70
21 Park av, n w cor 133d st, 100x85. Thomas Dixon agt Amelia Bell, owner, and Amelia and Wm. Bell, contractors 570 00
21 West End av, n e cor 87th st, 5 houses. Benjamin Prince agt W. E. D. Stokes, owner, and Squier & Whipple, contractors 2,527 25
21 Fourteenth st, Nos. 624-640, s s, 88 w Av C, 244x100. Charles L. Andrews as pres't of Central Iron Works (W. S. Anderson, by assign.) agt Wm. H. Muldoon, owner and contractor 1,014 40
21 Eighty-third st, s s, 175 w 9th av, 25x100. Thomas Normoyle agt John Chisholm, owner, and M. Normoyle, contractor 35 00
21 Same property. John Normoyle agt same. 28 00
21 Same property. Morton Bros. & Co. agt John Chisholm, owner and contractor 1,150 00
21 Waverley pl, No. 175, e s, 60 n Christopher st, 25x40. James Garvey agt Wm. C. Burmiston, owner, and Wm. Campbell and Julius Ehrig, contractors 276 00
21 Same property. Wm. F. Campbell agt Wm. C. Burmiston, owner, and Julius Ehrig, contractor 394 00
21 Columbus av, w s, 127 n 80th st, 25.6x119; Eightieth st, n s, 100 w Columbus av, 25.10x117.10 } Robert Lorzing agt Wm. Eisenberg, owner and contractor 201 12
22 Fifth av, No. 124. R. J. Chapman Co. agt Richard De Logerot, owner and contractor 812 75
22*One Hundred and Forty-first st, n s, extends from Convent av to Hamilton terrace, 200x70. Wm. G. Leeson agt St. Lukes Episcopal Church, owner, and Jones & Co. contractors 1,822 60
22 One Hundred and Thirty-third st, n s, 80 w Park av, 50x100. Thomas Dixon agt Addison Brown and Amelia Bell owners, and Amelia and William Bell, contractors 125 15
22 Ninety-fifth st, s s, 100 w Columbus av, 50x100. Joseph O. Clement agt Francis J. Hillenbrand, owner and contractor 250 00
22 Ninety-fourth st, n s, 150 w Columbus av, 50x100. Same agt same 250 00
22 Ninety-fourth st, n s, 150 w Columbus av, 100x100. The United States Dynamite and Chemical Co. agt James T. Blanchard, owner, and Clegg & Co. contractors 108 35
22 Seventy-eighth st, s s, 100 w Amsterdam av, 75x100. Same agt Arthur Boehmer, owner, and Clegg & Co., contractors 143 95
22 Eightieth st, Nos. 170-182 W., s s, 105 e Amsterdam av, 145x102.2. James Hartley agt Morris and Abraham Schneider, owners and contractors 545 00
22 Amsterdam (10th) av, s w cor 96th st, 25x100; Ninety-sixth st, s s, 100 w Amsterdam av, 78x100 } Wm. Hilgers agt Andrew T. Doyle, owner and contractor 151 40
22 Vandam st, s w cor Macdougal st, 118.4x87. Wm. R. Williams agt Charles Downey and Geo. W. Curry, owners and contractors 208 00
23 Waverley pl, No. 175, e s, 50 n Christopher st, 25x40. Gass & Edsall Co. agt Wm. C. Burmiston, owner, and Julian Ehrig, contractor 75 00
23 Fifty-seventh st, s e cor 7th av, 125x175; Fifty-sixth st, n s, 100 e 7th av, 25x— } John D. Beers and Edward Kneustner agt The Music Hall Co. (Lim.), owner and contractor 2,012 00

23 Same property. Same agt same as owner and Charles Schneider, Hopper & Kelly and Kelly Bros., contractors ... 6,980 00

23 Ninety-fourth st, n s, 100 w Amsterdam av, 100x102.2. John Coleman agt James Brady, owner, and A. M. Clegg, contractor ... 11 95

23 Seventy-eighth st, s s, 100 w Amsterdam av, 75x100. John Walsh agt Arthur Boehmer, owner, and McLoughlin, Clegg & Co., contractors ... 82 62

23 Same property. Michael Powers agt same. 12 37

23 Same property. Daniel Singleton agt same ... 23 62

23 Same property. Morris Linehan agt same. 18 88

23 Same property. Thomas Kennedy agt same 29 25

23 Same property. John Flanagan agt same. 21 00

23 Same property. George Snuddeck agt same ... 6 75

23 Same property. Patrick Reilly agt same. 16 87

23 Same property. Peter Cheever agt same.. 31 50

23 Same property. Thos. Costello agt same.. 3 50

23 Same property. John Donohue agt same.. 28 00

23 Same property. Frank Reilly agt same... 10 00

23 Same property. Matthew King agt same. 10 12

23 Same property. Bernard McHugh agt same ... 7 88

23 Same property. John Coleman agt same.. 42 00

23 Seventy-eighth st, s s, 100 w Amsterdam av, 75x100. John Burchell agt Arthur Boehmer, owner, and McLoughlin, Clegg & Co., contractors ... 50 00

23 Ninety-fifth st, Nos. 106 and 108, s s, abt 100 w Columbus av, 50x100. Albemarle Soapstone Co. agt Francis J. Hillenbrand, owner and contractor ... 252 00

24 Seventh st, No. 243, s s, 150 w Av D, 25x100. Rollin E. Gilbert agt S. Reinhardt, owner, and John Kurtz, contractor ... 78 80

24 Arthur av, w s, 7th building south of Pelham av, 25x100. Church E. Gates & Co. agt Ernest Wehner, reputed owner, and D. Kent, contractor ... 150 00

24 Honeywell av, e s, 125 s Samuel st, 25x100. Same agt E. M. Bowman, reputed owner, and L. A. Soule and D. Kent, contractors. 74 00

24 Briggs av, w s, 50 n Travis st, 25x100. Same agt W. H. Hall, reputed owner, and D. Kent, contractor ... 40 00

24 Honeywell av, e s, abt 100 s Samuel st, 25x100. Edward Welsh and Chas. Bennett agt Daniel Kent, owner and contractor... 115 00

24 Ninety-fourth st, Nos. 113-121 W., n s, bet 9th and 10th avs. Francesco Gianlo agt Thomas Brady, owner, and G. Craig, contractor ... 9 00

24 Same property. Guardia Ventura agt same ... 12 00

24 Same property. Guisseppe Santore agt same ... 24 00

24 Same property. Corlo Ciambanelli agt same ... 18 00

24 Same property. Michele Bucca agt same.. 24 00

24 Same property. Marco Marino agt same... 21 00

24 Same property. Giovanni Grecco agt same. 8 25

24 Same property. Guiseppe Patnano agt same ... 6 75

24 Same property. Giovanni Piedimonte agt same ... 18 40

24 Same property. Gennairo Petrarco agt same ... 20 00

24 Eighty-third st, s s, 175 w 9th av, 25x100. John M. Canda agt John Chisholm, owner and contractor ... 1,142 35

24 One Hundred and Sixty-ninth st, s w cor Vanderbilt av, 81x98. John Diehl agt Jacob Pfeiffer, owner and contractor ... 2,600 00

24 Madison av, e s, extends from 129th to 130th st, 199.10x110. New York Architectural Terra Cotta Co. agt The Roman Catholic Church of All Saints, owner and contractor ... 1,466 85

*Editor RECORD AND GUIDE:

The above lien filed by Wm. G. Leeson is unjust. He has been fully paid according to his contract with us, which is not yet completed. We will at once bond the lien and contest the claim. JONES & Co.

KINGS COUNTY.

July

17 Montague st, n s, 17 w Court st, 50x200. Watson & Pittinger agt The Brooklyn Real Estate Exchange (Lim.), owner, and J. J. Garland, contractor ... $88 37

17 Howard av, n e cor Macon st, 100x93.6. Adelbert S. Nichols agt Clarence Lincoln, owner and contractor ... 900 00

17 Eighth av, s w cor 11th st, 120x100. Adelbert S. Nichols agt Allen Norris and William Turner, owners and contractors ... 168 00

17 Eighty-second st, n s, 80 e 23d av, 40x100, Gravesend. L. F. Dennis agt Mary E. Case, owner, and Henry Case, contractor. 50 00

18 Patchen av, s e cor Halsey st, 100x200. John Connelly agt Hiram Bedell, owner and contractor ... 417 50

18 Eighty-second st, n s, 80 e 23d av, 40x100, Gravesend. W. T. Cowenhoven agt Mary E. Case, owner, and Henry Case, contractor ... 58 02

18 Same property. Samuel H. Case agt same owner and contractor ... 53 95

20 Patchen av, s e cor Halsey st, 100x200. R. G. Phelps agt Hiram Bedell, owner and contractor ... 444 45

20 Eighty-second st, n s, 80 e 23d av, 40x100, Gravesend. Gerd H. Henjes agt Mary E. Case, owner, and Henry Case, contractor ... 225 00

20 Bergen st, n s, 100 e Ralph av, 220x107.1. Potts Bros. agt Mary E. Mason and Isaac D. Mason, contractors ... 285 45

21 Fourth st, n s, 297.10 e 7th av, 100x95. James Monroe agt Roderick Von Graff, owner and contractor ... 105 00

21 Linwood st, e s, 175 n Liberty av, 25x100. John Gans agt John J. Lynch, owner, and Richard Flanagan, contractor ... 300 36

21 Second st, n s, 90.7 w 7th av, 80x100. John H. Mellor agt Roderick Von Graff, John Halloran, Wm. L. Dowling, Edward O'Brien and George T. Reilly, owners, and Roderick Von Graff, contractors ... 74 00

21 Bond st, No. 248, w s, 100 s Butler st, 40x50. Thomas McLaughlin agt Patrick Kenney, owner and contractor ... 250 00

21 Hart st, n s, abt 70 w Sumner av, 20x100. Abram Remsen agt Barney or Bernard Kilduff, owner, and William H. Colson. 46 25

22 East 31st st, w s, lots 50 and 51 block 3, Reformed Dutch Church property, Flatbush, 40x100. Peter J. Heffron agt Richard Payton, owner, and George J. Craigen, contractor ... 49 99

22 Stuyvesant av, s e cor Jefferson av, 120x95. Lewis R. Harsha agt Grace Presbyterian Church ... 2,765 65

22 Dresden st, w s, 95.7 n Atlantic av, 30x150. James B. Wood & Co. agt P. Mullen, owner and contractor ... 52 25

22 Prospect av, No. 394-404, s s, abt 250 w 8th av, 96x60. Adelbert S. Nichols agt Mrs. R. W. Fielding, owner and contractor ... 270 00

22 Sumner av, n w cor Decatur st, 100x140x90x140. Martin Wilkison agt The Calvary Baptist Church, owner, and James M. Mandeville, contractor ... 275 00

22 Pacific st, No. 1091. Owen McDonald agt James Connolly, owner and contractor... 40 00

22 Ridgewood av, n s, extends from Hemlock st to Railroad av, 200x100, 10 houses. Hall Sash and Door Co. agt William H. Baker ... 416 02

23 Av E, s w cor Ocean Parkway, 200x200, Flatbush. George Schmidt agt Helen and James F. Graham, owner, and Reichartz Bros., contractors ... 20 00

23 Hinsdale st, w s, 275 s Dumont st, 20x100. John O'Donoghue agt F. Weil, owner, and Alfred D. Hyde & Co., contractors ... 92 50

23 Ocean Parkway, w s, 150 s Av E, 50x100, Flatbush. John Williams agt Mrs. Leslie, owner, and Richartz Bros., contractors.. 330 00

23 Schaeffer st, n s, 300 e Central av, 32x88.6. Henry H. Thorpe agt Robert S. Neeley, owner and contractor ... 151 00

23 Howard av, n e cor Macon st, 100x93.6. C. W. Williams & Son agt Clarence Lincoln ... 1,900 00

SATISFIED MECHANICS' LIENS.

NEW YORK CITY.

July

18 Eleventh and 12th avs, 27th and 28th sts. P. P. & J. H. Staats agt Wm. W. Rossiter. (Lien filed April 11, 1891) ... $51,288 41

20 Twenty-third st, No. 129 W. F. Klingman agt R. Rosalia Pizer Mendes. (July 9, 1891) ... 4,175 00

20 Park av, e s, 75.3 s 63d st, 66.5x100x60x100. Hugo Kafka agt Edward J. Woolsey. (June 27, 1891) ... 163 00

20‡Seventieth st, n s, 110 e Columbus av, 100x100. Vincenzo Roba et al. agt Peter W. Gallaudet et al. (Jan 30, 1888.) (11 liens) ... 800 00

20 One Hundred and Sixtieth st, s s, 188.4 e St. Nicholas av, 36x100. Geo. B. Robbins & Co. agt J. S. Dale. (July 14, 1891) ... 16 00

21 Fort Independence st, w s, at Kingsbridge, known as south ½ of plot No. 69 map of Giles estate. S. L. Berrien agt Wm. Brotherton. (May 26, 1891) ... 1,060 00

22 Ninth av, Nos. 702-706. Holbrook Bros. agt Kerzie & Laaune. (July 3, 1891) ... 175 46

22 One Hundred and Sixteenth st, s s, 125 w Manhattan av, 25x100.11. Joseph P. Donnigan agt Thos. P. Dunne and Chas. E. Moore. (April 20, 1891.) (Released) ... —

22 Twenty-eighth st, Nos. 218 and 220 E. Joseph Marreu agt James A. Trimble and Thomas Sauderson. (Feb. 16, 1891) ... 910 41

23 One Hundred and Fourteenth st, n e cor Morningside av, being 70 feet on 114th st, 110 on Morningside av and 96 on Manhattan av. Richard Cummings agt Hiram M. Moore. (July 20, 1891) ... 7,000 00

24*Tenth av, w s, extends from 132d to 133d st, 200x100. Frederick Speth agt John Sullivan and John Fallon. (July 21, 1891)... 24 75

24 Willett st, No. 32. Isaac Haft agt Christian Eberspacker and Plowden Stevens. (Aug. 7, 1888) ... 116 20

24 One Hundred and Eighteenth st, s s, 60 to 185 e Madison av, 125x100. Kelly & Costello agt Herman Mascha. (July 7, 1891) ... 4,900 00

*Discharged by depositing amount of lien and interest with County Clerk.

‡Discharged by order of Court on filing bond.

KINGS COUNTY.

July

18 Fifty-third st, s s, 240 w 15th av, 100x100, New Utrecht. Henry McShane Mfg. Co. agt William Dittmir, owner and C. F. T. Becker, contractor. (July 8, 1891).. $245 00

20 Sixtieth st, s s, 260 w 13th av, 40x150, New Utrecht. Hobby & Doody agt Philip C. Griesbach and Marie his wife, owners, and Frank A. Schulz, contractor. (June 19, 1891) ... 143 00

20 Same property. John Gall agt same owners and contractor. (June 23, 1891) ... 27 00

20 Same property. George W. Harris agt same owners and contractor. (June 22, 1891) ... 27 00

20 Same property. John Dieckmann agt same owners and contractor. (June 20, 1891) ... 48 50

22 Fifty-eighth st, s s, 110 e 12th av, 40x100.2, New Utrecht. Adaline A. Newman agt Anne Van Wart, owner and contractor. (Oct. 25, 1890) ... 366 09

22 Essex st, e s, 250 n Ridgewood av, 60x100. Spear & Bartholomew agt Minnie Josiah, owner, and George Josiah, contractor. (Feb. 7, 1891) ... 31 00

22 Myrtle av, n s, 100 w Lewis av, 450x100. Butler Hardware Co. agt Max Hallheimer, owner and contractor. (May 26, 1891).... 506 05

22 Twenty-first av, n e cor Cropsey av, 75x100. New Utrecht. Gustav Reichenbach agt Kate F. Monjo, owner and contractor. (May 14, 1891) ... 134 00

22 Same property. Same agt same. (April 29, 1891) ... 80 00

23 Forty-fifth st, n s, 300 e 5th av, 40x100.2. Frank D. Creamer agt John L. Parrish, owner, and James Crouch and A. S. Hyde, contractor. (July 21, 1891). (Deposit) ... 150 00

23 Cooper st, s s, 125 w Evergreen av, 50x100. William Foley agt Edward Davidson, owner, and Henry Cortis, contractor. (July 22, 1891). (Deposit) ... 24 00

17 Shepherd av, e s, 280 n Ridgewood av, 120x102.7x120x102.5. Henry McShane Mfg. Co. agt Sebastian T. Hollister, owner and contractor. (July 16, 1891.) (Deposit)... 274 51

23 Forty-fifth st, n s, 300 e 5th av, 40x100. Thos. and Robert Edgerton agt John L. Parish, owner, and A. D. Hyde & Co., contractors. (July 16, 1891.) (Deposit) ... 200 00

BUILDINGS PROJECTED.

The first name is that of the owner; ar't stands for architect, m'n for mason, c'r for carpenter and b'r for builder.

NEW YORK CITY.

SOUTH OF 14TH STREET.

Downing st, No. 44, five-story and basement brk and stone flat, 20.10x81, tin roof; cost, $16,000; ow'r and m'n, S. W. B. Smith, 1236 Fulton av; ar't, C. H. Israels. Plan 1051.

Lafayette pl, No. 55, seven-story brk and terra cotta factory, 27.6 and 68.8x43.2 and 189.4, tile roof; cost, $120,000; O. B. Potter, 3 East 57th st; ar't, F. H. Kimball. Plan 1050.

Mulberry st, No. 32, five-story brk and stone flat, 20x70.6, tin roof; cost, $15,000; L. Peirano, 31 Mulberry st; ar't, J. K. James. Plan 1048.

3d st, No. 68 W., five-story brk and stone flat, 25x90 and 100, tin roof; cost, $20,000; J. L. Buttenweiser, 227 East 60th st; ar't, G. F. Pelham; m'n, J. Van Dolsen. Plan 1060.

Houston st, No. 264 E., rear, four-story and basement brk shop, 17.8x30, tin roof; cost, $4,000; L. Kohlmann, 263 East Houston st; ar't, F. Ebeling. Plan 1068.

Macdougal st, Nos. 24 and 26, two five-story brk flats, 25x88.8, tin roofs; cost, $18,000 each; A. Ruff, 73 East 4th st; ar'ts, Kurtzer & Rohl. Plan 1069.

Pitt st, No. 66, rear, six-story brk shop, 25x45, tin roof; cost, $8,000; H. Przeworsky, 59 Suffolk st; ar't, H. Horenburger. Plan 1067.

BETWEEN 14TH AND 59TH STREETS.

22d st, No. 61 W., seven-story brk building, 26x98.9 and 88.9, plastic slate roof; cost, $18,000; J. O'Neil, 328 5th av; ar'ts, Danmar & Fischer. Plan 1052.

31st st, No. 112 W., rear, two-story brk shop, 20.10x28, tin roof; cost, $1,000; N. B. Beam, 167 West 92d st; ar'ts, Lienau & Nash. Plan 1058.

21st st, No. 211 W., five-story stone flat, 25x88, tin roof; cost, $20,000; Drought & Carew, 465 West 47th st; ar't, M. V. B. Ferdon. Plan 1070.

21st st, No. 306 W., five-story and basement brk flat, 25x82.6, tin roof; cost, $20,000; H. C. Hoerle, 690 6th av; ar't, G. H. Griebel. Plan 1073.

BETWEEN 59TH AND 125TH STREETS, EAST OF 5TH AVENUE.

79th st, s s, 96 w Av A, two five-story brk and stone flats, 25x88, tin roofs; cost, $22,000 each; T. F. Cook, 351 East 87th st; ar't, J. C. Burne. Plan 1061.

105th st, No. 315 E., frame shed, 9x10; cost, $25; J. Dooley, on premises. Plan 1056.

Pleasant av, n w cor 120th st, three-story brk building, 26.11x96, tin roof; cost, $20,000; lessee, A. F. Schwarzler, 445 East 120th st; ar't, A. Spence. Plan 1062.

Pleasant av, w s, 26.11 n 120th st, two-story brk stable, 74x125, tin roof; cost, $30,000; lessee and ar't, same as last. Plan 1063.

BETWEEN 59TH AND 125TH STREETS, WEST OF CENTRAL PARK WEST AND 8TH AVENUE.

Boulevard, n e cor 84th st, six-story brk and stone stable, 80.5x86.2 and 75, tin roof; cost, $50,000; Crawford & McMillan, 252 West 73d st; ar't, C. Fox, Jr. Plan 1049.

85th st, s s, 150 e Columbus av, four-story and basement stone dwell'g, 25x58, with extension; cost, $25,000; J. Bannon, 104 West 77th st; ar't, G. A. Schellenger. Plan 1054, substituted for plan No. 38, New Building, 1891.

West End av, e s, 27.2 n 85th st, three four-story and basement stone dwell'gs, 25x60, tin roofs; cost, $20,000 each; E. Kilpatrick, 1234 Madison av; ar't, G. A. Schellenger. Plan 1053.

78th st, s s, 150 e 10th av, two five-story stone flats, 25x89, tin roof; cost, $40,000 each; Powers & Welcker, 228 West 105th st; ar't, M. V. B. Ferdon. Plan 1071.

23D AND 24TH WARDS.

Rockfield st, s s, 316 e Anthony st, two-story and basement frame dwell'g, 21x30, tin roof; cost, $1,500; Rosanna Torrance, 1 18th st, Hoboken, N. J.; b'r, J. J. McMillan. Plan 1055.

144th st, n s, 115 w Brook av, two-story brk and stone church, 50x73.8, slate roof; cost, abt $25,000; pastor and trustee, H. Richter, 705 East 142d st; ar't, P. W. Roos. Plan 1057.

Bathgate av, e s, 300 s 183d st, two-story frame dwell'g, 20x45, tin roof; cost, $4,500; J. Fitzpatrick, 772 Amsterdam av; ar't, W. Guggolz. Plan 1047.

Union av, e s, 175 s 165th st, three-story frame dwell'g, 22.6x35, with two-story extension, 20.6x14.6; tin roof; cost, $5,500; C. Schiedorn, 582 East 148th st; ar't, A. Pfeiffer. Plan 1059.

Bathgate av, e s, 40 n 172d st, two-story frame dwell'g, 17x35, tin roof; cost, $2,400; E. Gibb, 1638 Bathgate av; ar't, J. M. Fisher. Plan 1072.

Vanderbilt av, e s, 351 n 180th st, one-and-a-half-story frame dwell'g, 20x26, wooden roof; cost, $600; W. R. Miller, 323 East 8th st; ar't, J. Robinson; c'r, D. Sullivan. Plan 1066.

Walton av, Nos. 555-559, three three-story and basement brk dwell'gs, 17.6x50, tin roofs; cost,

$8,000 each; att'y, J. S. Dale, 641 Walton av; ar't, W. L. Dale; m'n, J. B. Martin. Plan 1064.

Washington av, e s, 25 s 171st st, three-story and attic frame dwell'g, 22x50, shingle roof; cost, $6,000; I. C. Jones, House of Refuge, Randalls Island, N. Y.; ar't, R. E. Rogers. Plan 1065.

KINGS COUNTY.

Plan 1339—Buffalo av, s w cor Prospect pl, one three-story frame store and dwell'g, 20x38, tin roof; cost, $8,000; ow'r and m'n, W. L. Beers, 215 Monroe st; ar't and c'r, N. A. Taylor.

1340—Buffalo av, w s, 20 s Prospect pl, two two-story frame dwell'gs, 16.4x38, tin roofs; cost, total, $5,000; ow'r, ar't and b'r, same as last.

1341—South 8th st, s s, 28 w Berry st, one four-story brk tenem't, 25x56, tin roof, wooden cornice; cost, $7,500; John Kriete, Astoria, L. I.; ar't, B. Finkensieper; b'rs, S. Parker and J. Trevor.

1342—Clinton av, s e cor Myrtle av, four four and five-story brk and red stone tenem'ts, 20x39 and 40x80 and 72.10 and 75.8, tin roofs, iron cornices; total cost, $75,000; John Englis, Jr., Clinton av; ar't, F. Jacobson.

1343—Stagg st, n s, 175 w Bushwick av, one three-story frame (brk filled) tenem't, 25x52.6, tin roof; cost, $8,800; Fred Weiland, 212 Ten Eyck st; ar't, H. Vollweiler; b'r, not selected.

1344—Bergen st, s s, abt 175 from Rockaway av, one two-story and basement frame (brk filled) dwell'g, 20x40, tin roof; cost, $2,000; Rosa Rosenfeld, Christopher and Blake avs; ar't and b'r, Chas. M. Thompson.

1345—Boerum st, n w cor Lorimer st, two four-story frame (brk filled) stores and tenem'ts, 25x55, tin roofs; total cost, $10,000; George Hilderbrand, 31 Boerum st; ar't, H. Vollweiler; b'r, not selected.

1346—Barbey st, w s, 364 11 s Fulton av, one two-story frame (brk filled) dwell'g, 22x36 6 and one-story extension, 13x15, tin roof; cost $1,500; Lizzie Stimis, adj premises; ar't, H. Vollweiler; b'r, not selected.

1347—48th st, n s, 160 e 4th av, one two-story basement and attic frame (brk filled) dwell'g, 20x38, tin roof; cost, $4 000; ow'r and c'r, Wm. R. Rogers, 314 48th st; ar't, G. Walkenshaw.

1348—Hart st, No. 990, one two-story frame (brk filled) dwell'g, 20x35, tin roof; cost, $3,500; —— Campler, 307 Evergreen av; ar't, H. E. Funk; b'r, —— Rossteusher.

1349—Cleveland st, e s, 330 s New Lots road, one two-story and attic frame dwell'g, 20 and 26x26, shingle roof; cost, $600; o'wr, ar't and c'r, Frank W. Phillips, Cleveland st and New Lots road.

1350—Hamilton av, w s, 175 n Atlantic av, two two-story and attic frame dwell'gs, 18 and 22x30, tin roofs; cost, $1,600 each; Augusta Rosse, Sheridan and Lincoln avs; ar't, L. Rosse; b'r, not selected.

1351—Scholes st, s s, 300 w Waterbury st, one one-story frame coppersmiths shop, 25x50, tin roof; cost, $1,200; Metzger Bros, on premises; ar't, T. Engelhardt; m'ns, U. Maurer Sons; c'r, not selected.

1352—Park pl, s s, 180 w Kingston av, one three-story brk dwell'g, 38x40, tin roof, wooden cornice; cost, $12,000; Miss Alla Otis, 823 Prospect pl; ar'ts, A. L. Brockway and A. W. Lord.

1353—Howard av, n w cor Madison st, one four-story brk store and halls, 40x80, tin roof, iron cornice; cost, $25,000; East Brooklyn Building and Loan Assoc., 1361 Broadway; ar'ts, I. and D. B. Hutton; b'r, T. B. Rutan.

1354—McDonough st, n s, 300 e Tompkins av, three three-story and basement brown stone dwell'gs, 20x46, tin roofs, wooden cornices; cost, $10,000 each; John Fraser, 44 Rochester av; ar'ts, A. Hill & Son.

1355—North 6th st, n s, 75 w Roebling st, one three-story frame (brk filled) tenem't, 25x65, tin roof; cost, $5,200; Frank Parks, on premises; ar't, T. Engelhardt; b'r, not selected.

1356—Greene av, s w cor Hamburg av, two two and three-story frame (brk filled) stores, offices and dwell'gs, 30 and 40x65 and 20, tin roofs; cost, $9,000; C. Heinbockel & Co., 17 Harman st; ar't, T. Engelhardt; b'r, J. Auer.

1357—Marion st, s s, abt 350 e Howard av, four two-story frame (brk filled) dwell'gs, 18.8x50 and 55, tin roofs; cost, abt $3,000 each; Elizabeth P. McNab, 310 Livingston st; ar't, S. B. Bowles.

1358—Schaefer st, No. 184, s s, 200 w Hamburg av, one one-story frame show room, 20x14.6, felt roof; cost, $3,500; Jno. M. Shea, Bangor, Pa.; c'r, C. Merritt.

1359—Menjer st, n s, 125 e Humboldt st, three four-story frame (brk filled) tenem'ts, 25x65, tin roofs; cost, $6,200; ow'r and b'r, Joseph Frisse, 19 Ten Eyck st; ar't, T. Engelhardt.

1360—Woodbine st, n s, 25 w Knickerbocker av, one three-story frame (brk filled) tenem't, 20x50, tin root; cost, $4,000; ow'r, ar't and c'r, A. Buchmeier, 101 Ralph st; m'n, J. Miller.

1361—Eastern Parkway, n s, 25 e Osborn st, one three-story frame store and dwell'g, 20x40, tin roof; cost, $3,500; John Powers, Van Siclen av and Eastern Parkway.

1362—Jerome st, w s, 240 s Blake av, one two-story frame dwell'g, 17.6x28, tin roof; cost, $2,000; ow'r and b'r, Fredk. Eiermann, Ridgewood av.

1363—Osborn st, w s, 150 n Glenmore av, one three-story frame store and tenem't, 25x55, tin roof; cost, $4,500; A. Ruth, Osborn st.

1364—Partition st, n s, 80 w Conover st, one two-story frame wagon shed, 20x40, tin roof; cost, $600; H. Finkeldey, Conover st, cor Partition st; ar't and b'r, C. M. Detlefsen.

1365—43d st, n s, 100 e 4th av, one one-story frame stable, 31x14; cost, $100; Mr. Berge, New York; ar't and b'r, L. H. Raymond.

1366—Eastern Parkway, s s, 50 w Sackman st, two three-story frame stores and tenem'ts, 25x55, tin roof; cost, each, $3,000; ow'r and b'r, Wolf Patashunk; ar't, A. J. Warren.

1367—Stone av, e s, 250 s Sutter av, two three-story frame stores and tenem'ts, 25x55, tin roofs; cost, each, $4,500; Regenbogen & Davis, 150 Varet st.

1368—14th st, n s, 197.6 e 8th av, one two-story and basement brk dwell'g, 20x45, tin roof, wooden cornice; cost, $4,000; ow'r and b'r, Wm. Hawkins, 461 14th st; ar't, H. B. Hawkins.

1369—Lewis av, w s, 75 s Floyd st, one four-story brk tenem't, 25x65, tin roof, iron cornice; cost, $9,500; ow'r and b'r, Math. Beck, 264 Rutledge st; ar't, T. Engelhardt.

1370—Prospect av, s s, 175 w 8th av, two three-story brk tenem'ts, 20x45, tin roofs, wooden cornices; total cost, $10,000; Simon Henschel, 8 Jackson pl; ar't, C. Braun.

1371—Harman st, s s, 100 e Central av, two three-story frame (brk filled) tenem'ts, 25x60, tin roofs; cost, $4,500; Hahn Bros., 286 Central av; ar't, A. Berckmeier.

1372—Garden st, Nos. 29 and 31, rear, one one-story frame (brk filled) tailor shop, 40x19.4 and 13, tin roof; cost, $500; Mayer Greenfelder, on premises; ar't, H. Vollweiler.

1373—Watkins st, e s, 100 s Dumont av, one three-story frame store and dwell'g, 20x45, tin roof; cost, $3,000; P. O'Halloran, Watkins st; ar't, A. J. Warren.

1374—Thatford av, e s, 75 s Livonia av, one three-story frame store and tenem't, 25x55, tin roof; cost, $3,000; Solom Wolfe, Belmont av; ar't, A. J. Warren.

1375—Meeker av, n s, 125 e Varick av, one two-story frame shed, 40x100, tin roof; cost, $2,000; Alfred Brumme, 411 East 22d st; ar't, H. Vollweiler; b'r, not selected.

1376—McDougal st, s s, 75 e Saratoga av, one three-story frame tenem't, 25x60, tin roof; cost, $3,500; E. H. Blinn, 77 Cooper st; ar't, A. J. Warren

1377—Osborn st, e s, 150 s Liberty av, two three-story frame stores and tenem'ts, 25x55, tin roofs; cost, $4,200 each; Cohen & Simon, Blake av and Sackman st; ar't, A. J. Warren.

1378—Bushwick av, n w cor Hull st, one one-story frame shed, 20.6x29.4, gravel roof; cost, $100; Jos Payez, 1573 Bushwick av.

1379—Stone av, e s, 125 s Belmont av, one three-story frame store and tenem't, 25x55, tin roof; cost, $3,000; Elias Retterman, Rockaway av; ar't, A. J. Warren; b'r, not selected.

1380—Pacific st, n s, 101 w Utica av, twelve two-story and basement frame dwell'gs, 16 4x42, gravel roofs; cost, each, $2,000; T. S. Denike, 724 Herkimer st; ar't, A. Hull; b'rs, R. Stultz and Stultz & Smith.

1381—50th st, s s, 100 6 w 3d av, two two-story and basement brk dwell'gs, 20x40, tin roofs, wooden cornices; cost, $3,500 each; Lorenzi Guli, 232 3d av.

1382—3d st, s s, 150 s e 3d av, two six-story granite tin plate works, &c., 50 and 56x100, tin roofs, stone and tile cornices; cost, $30,000; Somers Bros., 3d st; ar't, O. M. Somers; b'rs, M. Cooney and Mr. Johnson.

1383—Lafayette av, n s, 225 w Reid av, six two-story and basement brk and brown stone dwellings, 16.8x40, tin roofs, wooden cornices; cost, $4,500 each; George Fletcher & Sons, 38 Grove st.

1384—Humboldt st, e s, 75 s Van Cott av, one one story frame store and shed, 20x25, gravel roof; cost, $450; Mr. Mead; ar'ts and c'rs, Randall & Miller; m'ns, I. & J. Van Riper & Co.

1385—Skillman av, s s, 64 w Leonard st, two three-story frame (brk filled) tenem'ts, 18 and 18 and 20x55, tin roofs; cost, $7,080; Louis Reicher, 78 Skillman av; ar'ts, D. Acker & Son; b'rs, M. Armendinger and K. Schneider.

1386—Herbert st, n s, 53 e North Henry st, one three-story frame (brk filled) dwell'g, 20x43, tin roof; cost, $4,500; Peter Delap, 1622 Fulton st; ar't, O. E. Hofses; b'r, J. A. Decamp.

1387—42d st, s s, on pier at foot of street, one one-story frame coal shed, 150x60, pine roof; cost, $2,000; The Bush Co. (Lim.), 202 Columbia Heights; c'r, J. Bulk.

1388—Albany av, w s, 120 s Herkimer st, one one-and-a-half-story brk stable, 25x60, gravel roof, wooden cornice; cost, $600; Alex. E. Gueringue, 438 Herkimer st; ar't, W. H. Birck.

ALTERATIONS NEW YORK CITY.

Plan 1374—Broadway, No. 63, repair damage by fire; cost, $1,656; agent, W. H. Spear, 366 Adelphi st, Brooklyn; c'r, E. Smith.

1375—Jane st, No. 165, repair damage by fire; cost, $635; G. E. Green, Nyack, N. Y.; c'r, E. Smith.

1376—127th st, Nos. 50 and 52 W., raised one story, three-story extension, 50x25, interior altered and repaired; cost, $4,500; Mary A. McCormack, on premises; ar't, J. H. Valentine.

1377—Frankfort st, No. 7, one-story extension, 30x27, and rear rebuilt; cost, $2,400; lessees, N. Y. Zeitung Publishing and Printing Co., on premises; ar't, F. T. Camp; b'r, J. G. Porter, agent.

1378—Riverdale av, 1350 s of. w of Delafield lane, three-story and basement extension, 23x25.6, and interior alterations; cost, $15,000; W. E. Dodge, s w cor Madison av and 39th st; ar'ts, Renwick, Aspinwall & Russell; m'ns, J. & G. Stewart; c'r, S. F. Quick.

1379—9th st, No. 138 W, four-story extension, 20.3x49.2, interior alterations and walls altered; cost, $8,500; Kinsley & Baumann, Holland House; ar'ts, Harding & Gooch.

1380—Broadway, Nos. 877 and 879, tank on roof; cost, $325; Loeb L. Scheff, 37 East 38th st; m'n, P. H. Murphy.

1381—14th st, No. 608 E, interior alterations and repairs, new fire escapes, cornice, sills, caps, &c, walls altered and new front; cost, $1,100; agent, L. H. Kircher, 145 Av B; ar't, W. Graul.

1382—58th st, n s, 200 w 6th av, six-story extension, 25x90.2; cost, $65,000; R. Lo Forte, 127 West 58th st; ar'ts, D. & J. Jardine.

1383—11th st, No. 16 W., rear raised one story, two-story extension, 7x8, and interior alterations; cost, $2,500; Mrs. A. S. Sullivan, on premises; b'r, W. Bloodgood.

1384—Trinity pl, Nos. 6-12, front alterations; cost, $100; C. Spiess, 230 South 3d st, Brooklyn; c'rs, McEnerny & Hilton.

1385—1st av, No. 323, walls altered and new front; cost, $800; Marie Kiefer, on premises; ar't, L. F. Heinecke; b'r, C. Leigh.

1386—Hudson st, No. 577, show windows changed; cost, $50; lessee, W. F. White, 35 Charles st.

1387—3d av, e s, 150 s 183d st, interior alterations; cost, $100; Home for Incurables, 182d st and 3d av; ar't, R. E. Rogers; m'n, J. Spears.

1388—60th st, Nos. 162 and 164 E., one-story and basement extension, 40x5.1; cost, $5,000; Bloomingdale Bros., 59th st and 3d av; ar't, A. Wagner.

1389—Chrystie st, Nos. 55-59, four-story portion raised one story, one-story extension, 21.6x —, windows altered; cost, $3,000; W. A. Niles & Co., on premises; ar't, W. B. Tubby; b'r, W. S. Miller.

1390—2d av, s e, cor 26th st, cut opening in chimney; cost, $30; P. Gaffney, 235 East 32d st; m'ns, Spellman & Sons.

1391—5th av, No. 549, bay window extended to second story, walls altered for that purpose; cost, abt $3,000; C. F. Eckert, on premises; ar't, H. J. Hardenbergh; b'r, J. B. Smith.

1392—12th av, s e cor 26th st, raised one story; cost, $250; G. B. Cornell, 141 Centre st.

1393—14th st, No 34 W., three-story extension, 25x31, interior alterations and walls altered; cost, abt $7,000; Ludwig Bros., 36 West 14th st; ar't, C. J. Perry.

1394—Franklin st, Nos. 9 and 11, repair damage by fire; cost, abt $4,000; agent and c'r, G. A. Burggroff, Jr., 465 West 47th st.

1395—148th st, n s, 75 e 12th av, to be moved; cost, $70; Mrs. M. Talbert, 149th st, s s, 75 e 12th av.

1396—6th av, n e cor 22d st, walls altered; cost, $400; J. O'Neill, on premises; ar'ts, Daumar & Fischer; m'ns, Brennan & Sullivan.

1397—18th st, No. 401 E., front wall rebuilt; cost, $165; Mrs. J. L. Lissner, 15 Livingston pl; ar't, M. Lally; m'n, H. Gebhard.

1398—27th st, No. 138 E., two-story extension, 25x36, interior alterations, walls altered and new bay window; cost, $5,000; N. Williams, sec'y, 301 West 51st st; ar't, C. Rentz.

1399—22d st, No. 360 W., four-story extension, 16.6x13, interior and front alterations; cost, $3,5 0; Ella C. Lamb, Alpine, N. J.; ar't, M. N. Cutter.

1400—Stanton st, No. 88, one-story extension, 14.8x22, and interior alterations; cost, $400; lessee, A. Bernhard, on premises; ar't, H. Horenburger.

1401—122d st, No. 237 W., interior alterations; cost, $1,000; C. A. Cowen, on premises; ar't, G. Keister.

1402—4th av, No. 240, interior alterations and area enlarged; cost, $450; D. Weismantle; ar't, A. Wagner.

1403—3d st, Nos. 27-29 W, interior alterations; cost, $1,000; agent, E. Leaycraft, 129 West 82d st; ar't, B. W. Berger.

1404—Cherry st, Nos. 187-189, repair damage by fire; cost, abt $16,000; P. Young, 235 Berkeley pl, Brooklyn; a'rt, F. Lyons, Jr.

1405—Lexington av, n w cor 48th st, one-story extension, 12x25; cost, $175; American Express Co., 65 Broadway; ar't, E. H. Kendall; c'rs, Bogert & Bro.

1406—Spring st, No. 258, interior alterations; cost, $100; P. L. Schell, exr., 260 Spring st; c'r, M. J. Crosbie.

1407—Broadway, No. 957 and No. 185 5th av, third story removed, building repaired and painted; cost, $450; lessees, N. Y., L. E. & W. R. R. Co., 21 Cortlandt st; c'rs, Gilbert & Sweeney.

1408—52d st, No. 64 W., two-story extension, 6x18; cost, $1,600; J. M. Diven, Elmira, N. Y.; ar't, G. H. Budlong; b'r, J. T. Hall.

1409—39th st, No. 24 W., one-story and basement extension, 9.3x13; cost, $1,500; B. Tuckerman, 106 East 36th st; m'ns, W. A. & F. E. Conover; c'rs, Hoe's Sons.

1410—164th st, n s, 500 w Washington av, interior alterations and new front; cost $500; C. Troxler, 880 Courtlandt av; ar't, C. F. Lohse.

1411—Elton av, No 814, raised 8 inches and repaired; cost, $500; G. Peters, 536 Courtlandt av; ar't, C. F. Lohse.

1412—Vesey st, Nos. 41 and 43, five-story and cellar extension, 25x71.6, interior alterations, elevator and stairs put in extension, west wall of old building removed and iron columns substituted; cost, $16,000; L. J. Callanan, 68 West 11th st; ar'ts, Thom & Wilson; m'ns, List & Lennon; c'r, T. J. Duffy.

1413—92d st, No. 3 E., wall altered; cost, $750; A. H. Gross, 46 East 76th st; ar't, W. Reid, Jr.; m'ns, See & Conover.

1414—Lawrence st, Nos. 112 and 114, lightshaft cut through floors, new skylights and closets; cost, $200; G. W. Geitz, on premises; ar't, F. Jacobsen.

1415—Mulberry st, No. 223, one-story extension, 24.10x33, interior alterations, walls altered; cost,

$8,000; P. Strobe, 23 East 127th st; ar't, A. Wagner.

1416—Fulton st, No. 118, and No. 15 Dutch st, walls altered and buildings connected; cost, $8,000; C T. Naething, 118 Fulton st; ar't, C. M. Disosway; m'n, J. Allen; c'r, C. Wendt.

1417—41st st, n s, 40 e 7th av. interior alterations and walls altered; cost. abt $500; W. H. Cooper, 25 Catharine st; a'rt, T. S. Godwin.

KINGS COUNTY.

Plan 684—Grand st, No. 138, new store front and interior alterations; cost, $900; Fred Scholtz, 93 South 4th st; ar't, B. Finkensieper; b'rs, A. Hayes and S. L. Hough.

685—9th st, No. 114, raised 4 ft. on brk foundation; cost, $175; John F. Nolan, on premises; m'n, T. Buckley.

686—Devoe st, No. 185, two-story frame extension, 18x12, tin roof; cost, $650; ow'r and ar't, —— Ferris, on premises; b'r, G. W. Williams.

687—Park av, No. 201, repair damage by fire; cost, $557; A. Yates, on premises; b'r, A. McKnight.

688—Grand st, Nos. 273 and 275, alteration to walls; cost, $350; D. B. Livingston, on premises; b'r, M. Smith.

689—Adams st, No. 248, add one story, flat tin roof; cost, $500; A. Winter, on premises; b'r, W. Winter.

690—Water st, No. 262, excavate rear part of basement to level of front basement, shore up and underpin west wall, &c.; cost, $1,600; Benjamin Moore & Co., 262 Water st; b'r, J. Allen.

691—Rockaway av, e s, 125 n East New York av, one-story frame extension, 14x16, tin roof; cost, $200; Gertrude Schroeder, on premises.

692—Manhattan av, e s, 175 s Greenpoint av, one-story brk extension, 10.6x15 8, tin roof; cost, $300; St. Anthony's R. C. Church, Greenpoint; ar't, F. Weber; b'r, J. Rooney.

693—Enfield st, e s, 200 s Dumont av, one-and-a-half story frame extension, 20x18, shingle roof; cost, $500; Wm. Torborg, on premises; ar't, L. Rosse.

694—Scholes st, s s, 275 w Waterbury st; posts set under trusses, &c.; cost, $50; Metzger Bros., on premises; ar't, T. Engelhardt; m'ns, Maurer Bros; c'r, not selected.

695—Madison st, No. 563, one-story brk extension, 8x10, tin roof; cost, $150; Mary E. Peek, on premises; b'rs, J. Dickinson and F. Woodhouse.

696—Wyckoff st, No. 172, interior alterations; cost, $800; Mr. Kaiser, on premises.

697—39th st, n s, 200 e 3d av, raised 10 feet on frame story, also deeper cellar; cost, $700; Percy Watkins, 179 39th st; ar't, H. Stafford.

698—Myrtle av, No. 1321, raised 11 feet on frame story; also two-story frame extension, 9.6 and 11x12 and 18, tin roof; cost, $1,400; Henry W. Walter, on premises; ar't, E. Dennis; b'r, B. J. Dennis & Son.

699—Verona pl, No. 8, add one story to main building and extension; cost, $1,350; C. Schleges, on premises; ar't and b'r, J. I. Kirby.

700—Hanson pl, No. 81, interior alterations; cost, $500; Columbian Club, on premises; ar't, T. F. Houghton; m'n, not selected; c'rs, Long & Barnes.

701—Prospect st, No. 161, flat tin roof; cost, $500; Abraham Knight, on premises; b'r, M. Knight.

702—5th av, s w cor 9th st, add two stories to extension; cost, $500; John McCormick, on premises; b'rs, W. Corrigan & Sons.

703—Atlantic av, No. 505, repair damage by fire; cost, $400; Mrs. C. Mannie, 346 Union st; b'r, Wm. Mahler.

704—Scholes st, No. 35, new store front; cost, $600; John Fisher, on premises.

705—South 3d st, No. 222, flat tin roof; cost, $750; Wm. A. Spiess, on premises; b'rs, M. Smith and Marinus & Gill.

706—Moore st, No. 132, front altered; cost, $500; —— Friedmann, on premises; H. E. Funk; b'rs, Wechler Bros.

707—Fulton st, No. 400, partition wall set upon girder; cost not decided; John French, Clinton av, cor Gates av; ar't, J. Mumford; b'rs, Morris & Selover and C. Cameron; iron, Howell & Saxton.

708—15th st, No. 28, raised 6 feet on stone foundation; cost, $150; Michael Quinn, on premises; b'r, A. Gildersleeve.

709—Grand av, Nos. 147-153, add two stories of brk, also two-story brk extension, 15x22, &c.; cost, $10,000; John Underwood & Co., 30 Vesey st, New York; ar't, E. A. Sargent.

710—Prospect pl, n s, 170 e Rogers av, three one-story brk extensions, 40x40, tin roofs; cost, $3,000; Lewis Ward, on premises; b'rs, Powderly & Murphy.

711—Fulton st, Nos. 481 and 483, one-story brk extension, 19 and 13x32, felt roof, front alterations, &c.; cost, $2,400; M. Rosenberg, 481 Fulton st; b'r, A. C. Hendrickson.

712—Graham av, No. 42, new store front; cost, $250; Mrs. Bell, on premises.

713—Decatur st, No. 271, add one story to extension; cost, abt $75; L. M. Stone, on premises.

714—43d st, n s, 275 e 2d av, raised 9 feet to grade of st on stone foundation; cost, $300; E. H. Conklin, 117 43d st; b'r, O. Heron.

715—Madison st, s s, 75 e Patchen av, add one story; cost, $1,000; Leo Prange, on premises.

716—Hart st, No. 679, one-story frame extension, 15x16, tin roof; cost, $250; Catharine Braun, on premises; b'rs, Bremeis & Hanold.

717—Lee av, Nos. 27-31, one-story brk extension, 20x30, gravel roofs; cost, $1,000; Berger & Price, Bedford av; ar't and c'r, T. Chaffers; b'r, M. Smith.

MISCELLANEOUS.

BUSINESS FAILURES.

N. Y. ASSIGNMENTS—BENEFIT CREDITORS.

July

20 Bessey, Frederick A. (box manufacturer, at Nos. 455 and 457 West 26th st), to George H. Bessey; preferences, $5,500.

20 Riker, Carroll L. (publisher, at 101 Park pl), to John F. Maxfield; without preferences.

22 Bigganum Manufacturing Corporation of Haddam, Conn., to Phineas C. Lounsbury and Clement S. Hubbard as trustees; without preferences.

23 Walter, John, and Joseph M. Crane (composing firm of Walter & Crane, dealers in fruit at No. 13 West 42d st), to Edward H. Willis, preferences, $1,000.

APPROVED PAPERS.

Resolutions passed by the Board of Aldermen calling for the following improvements have been signed by the Mayor for the week ending July 18, 1891. *Indicates that the Mayor neither appoved nor objected thereto, therefore the same became adopted.

MAINS.

86th st, from Av B to East River; gas.
146th st, from Boulevard to Hudson River R. R.; water.
146th st, from Boulevard to Hudson River R. R.; gas.
Creston av, from Kingsbridge road to St. James st; gas.
Coles pl, from Kingsbridge road to Poe pl; water and gas.

REGULATING, GRADING, ETC.

Amsterdam av, from s s 194th st to Fort George av.
Wales av, from n s St. Joseph st to Westchester av.

PAVING.

118th st, from Madison to 5th av; granite block.
122d st, from Av A to Harlem River; granite block.
101st st, from 3d to Lexington av; granite block.
90th st, from crosswalk near westerly intersection of 1st av to crosswalk near easterly intersection of 2d av; granite block.
19th st, from westerly crosswalk of Av A to easterly crosswalk of 1st av; granite block.
121st st, from Av A to Harlem River; granite block.
115th st, from Av A to Harlem River; granite block.
101st st, from 1st to 2d av; granite block.
119th st, from 7th to Lenox av; granite block.
116th st, from Av A to Harlem River; granite block.
58th st, from a point abt 380 feet w 11th av to Hudson av; granite block.
100th st, from 3d to Lexington av; granite block.
96th st, from Lexington to 4th av; granite block.
117th st, from Madison to 5th av; granite block.

FLAGGING.

6th av, s w cor 32d st, 30x100; relaid and reset.
2d av, n w cor 101st st, 110x110.
94th st, s s, from 2d av to point abt 135 w therefrom; relaid and reset.
5th av, n w cor 85th st, —x150.
34th st, from 10th av to North River.
10th av, e s, from 29th to 30th st.
19th st, from Av A to 1st av.
Madison av, both sides, from 71st to 72d st.

FENCING VACANT LOTS.

86th st, n e cor 5th av.
92d st, n s, from Central Park West to Columbus av.
144th st, s s, bet 8th and Bradhurst avs.

CROSSWALKS.

Chisholm st, at each intersecting st or av from Jennings st to Stebbins av.
Bristow st, at each intersecting st or av from Boston to Stebbins av.

BROOKLYN BOARD OF ALDERMEN.

* Under the different headings indicates that a resolution has been introduced and referred to the appropriate committee. † Indicates that the resolution has passed and has been sent to the Mayor for approval ‡ Passed over the Mayor's veto.

BROOKLYN, July 13, 1891.

CULVERTS.

Graham av, s w cor Van Pelt av.†

FENCING VACANT LOTS.

Dean st, bet Underhill and Washington avs.
Pacific st, n s, bet Washington and Grand avs.
Park pl, n s, bet Clason and Franklin avs.
Prospect pl, s s, bet Clason and Franklin avs.
7th st, s s, bet 3d and 4th avs.
7th st, s w cor 4th av.
Washington av, w s, bet Pacific and Dean sts.
4th av, w s, bet 7th and 8th sts. } †

FLAGGING.

Fulton st, n e cor Throop av.*
Fulton st, n w cor Throop av.*
Clason av, w s, bet Douglass and Degraw sts.†

GAS LAMPS, &C.

Sutter av, bet Vesta and Alabama avs.†

GRADING, PAVING, ETC.

Bayard st, bet Union av and Ewen st.*
Pilling st, bet Broadway and Bushwick av.
Richmond st, bet Fulton st and Jamaica av.
29th st, 30th st, 31st st } at owners' expense. } †
Saratoga av, 167 s Herkimer st to Butler st.*

SEWERS.

Hicks st, bet Hamilton av and Lorraine st.†
29th st, 30th st, 31st st } at owners' expense.†

STREET OPENING.

Ralph st, bet Hamburg and Knickerbocker avs.†

ADVERTISED LEGAL SALES.

REFEREES SALES TO BE HELD AT THE REAL ESTATE EXCHANGE AND AUCTION ROOM (LIMITED), 59 to 65 LIBERTY STREET, EXCEPT WHERE OTHERWISE STATED.

July

50th st, Nos. 35 and 37, n s, 150 w Park av, 50x100.5, two five-story brk flats, by J. N. Golding. (Amt due $95,175) 27

42d st, No. 25, n s, 354.2 w 5th av, 20.4x100.5, four-story stone front store and dwell'g, by R. V. Harnett. (Leasehold; action No. 1; amt due $5,420).......... 28

Same property, by R. V. Harnett. (Leasehold; action No. 2; amt due $10,650).......... 28

76th st, n e cor Madison av, 48x102.2, vacant, by Wm. Kennelly. (Amt due $32,699).......... 28

84th st, No. 36, s s, 435 w 8th av, 20x102.2, three-story brk dwell'g, by Wm. Kennelly. (Partition sale).......... 29

106th st, Nos. 63-69, n s, 200 e Madison av, 100x100.11, four five-story brk flats, by R. V. Harnett & Co. (Amt due $74,228).......... 29

100th st, Nos. 63-67, n s, 199.6 e Madison av, 75.6x100, three five-story brk flats, by R. V. Harnett & Co. (Amt due $2,728; prior morts. $70,750).......... 29

Clinton av, s e cor Spring st, 100x100, by Smyth & Ryan. (Amt due $2,765).......... 29

101st st, No. 203, n s, 90 e 3d av, 20x100.11, four-story brk store and tenem't with two-story brk building on rear, by B. L. Kennelly.......... 29

Av A, Nos. 1314-1320, n e cor 70th st, 100.4x98, four and five-story brk planing mill, &c., by R. V. Harnett & Co. (Amt due $54,234).......... 30

100th st, Nos. 155-169, n s, 95 e Lexington av, 200x100.11..........
101st st, Nos. 154-168, s s, 95 e Lexington av, 200x100.11..........
Sixteen five-story brk tenem'ts.......... } by D. P. Ingraham; 2 actions. (Amt due on each action $22,300; prior morts. ——.).......... 30

Evelyn pl, s s, 175 w Jerome av, 50x100, by Wm. Kennelly. (Amt due $1,229; sub. to prior mort. $3,000).......... 30

33d st, No. 372, s e cor 9th av, 22x67.6, five-story brk tenem't with stores, by R. V. Harnett. (Amt due $3,625).......... 31

Park av, Nos. 565-569, e s, 75.3 s 63d st, 66.5x100x60x100, five-story brk flat, "Lonsdale," by Wm. Kennelly. (Amt due $11,077; prior mort. $90,000).......... 31

KINGS COUNTY.

July

Elton st, w s, 25 s Blake av, 25x23, two-story frame dwell'g..........
Troutman st, No. 17, n w s, 86.2½ s w Bushwick av, 25x100, three-story frame dwell'g; assessed value, $4,300..........
Hudson av, No. 36, w s, 58.4 s John st, 16.8x90, three-story brick tenem't and store; assessed value, $2,100..........
Voorhees av, centre line, at intersection with centre line of East 27th st, runs east 232 x south 132 x west 69.9 x north 13.4 x west 152 to centre East 27th st, x north 130 to beginning, Gravesend.......... } by T. A. Kerrigan, at 13 Willoughby st.......... 29

Atlantic av, No. 2288A, s s, 333.4 w Stone av, 16.8x100, three-story frame dwell'g; assessed value, $1,600; by J. Cole, at 389 Fulton st.......... 29

6th av, s w cor Pacific st, runs south 142.6 x west 125 x north 32.6 x east 25 x north 110 to Pacific st, x east 100 to beginning, three-story brk factory; assessed value $28,000; by T. A. Kerrigan, at the Real Estate Exchange, 189 and 191 Montague st.......... 30

Lot at Gravesend, begins at Atlantic Ocean at division line bet old lots 22 and 23 on one side and old lots 20 and 21 on the other side, as shown on Kowolski's map of common lands of Gravesend, Coney Island, runs north — x west — x south to ocean, x east to beginning, except strip 40 ft. wide condemned for use of New York & Coney Island R. R. Co., and part lying south of centre of Surf av; partition.......... } by T. A. Kerrigan, at 13 Willoughby st.......... 30

Evergreen av, No. 316, w s, 25 n Stanhope st, 25x100, two-story frame dwell'g; assessed value, $2,500..........
Flushing av, No. 590, s w cor Marcy av, 25x100, three-story frame (brk lined) building and three-story frame dwell'g in rear known as 453 Marcy av; assessed value, $6,000; partition.......... } by Taylor & Fox, at 45 Broadway, E. D.......... 30

Fenimore st, s s, 615.72 e Flatbush av, 100x125, Flatbush, by T. A. Kerrigan, at 13 Willoughby st.......... 31

Aug.

Cumberland st, No. 140, w s, 177.3 n Myrtle av, 25x100, three-story frame dwell'g; assessed value, $2,500; by G. F. Elliott, ref., at County Court House.......... 3

McDonough st, No. 333, n s, 280 w Stuyvesant av, 20x100..........
McDonough st, No. 331, n s, 300 w Stuyvesant av, 20x100..........
Two three-story brk dwell'gs; assessed value, $7,000 each.......... } by Michael Furst, ref., at County Court House.. 3

Prince st, No. 99, e s, 238.9 n Myrtle av, 21.3x55, three-story frame dwell'g; assessed value, $2,500; by T. A. Kerrigan, at 13 Willoughby st.. 3

LIS PENDENS, KINGS COUNTY.

July

Union st, s s, 145 w Bond st, 20.4x100. Phebe R. Kissam agt Abram P. Fardon; att'y, W. Ryerson Kissam.......... 17

India st, n s, 245 e Franklin st, 25x100. Charles E. Rolston agt Mary A. Rolston; partition; att'ys, C. & T. Perry.......... 17

Putnam av, s s, 236.6 e Reid av, 39x100..........
Putnam av, s s, 314.6 e Reid av, 19.6x100.......... } Title Guarantee and Trust Co. agt John Hennessy; att'y, Charles R. Halsey.......... 17

West av, s s, 40 w West 2d st, 40x100, Coney Island. William Rubien agt Mary B. Rosenbaum; foreclos. mechanic's lien; att'y, George C. Eldridge. 17

Lot at Gravesend, being on West Meadow Bank known as No. 38 on map thereof, begins at edge of salt meadows, runs southwest 400 Brooklyn, Bath & Coney Island R. R., x 200 to Creek, x southeast 100 x northeast 620 x northwest 87.9.
Lots 35 to 37 same map, adj above.......... } Frank W. Bover agt Henry Hohenstein; action to set aside deeds; att'y, S. S. Hemingway.......... 18

Graham av, e s, 25 n Scholes st, 25x100. Ferdinand M. Thieriot exr. Marie T. Marsh agt Jacob J. Seelbach; att'y, E. Louis Lowe 18
17th st, n e cor 6th av, 20x75. Mutual Life Ins. Co., New York, agt Magdalena Zenner; att'y, Robert Sewell........ 18
Madison st, No. 789, n s, 278 w Ralph av, 18x100. Same agt Catharine Cushing; same att'y........ 18
South Oxford st, e s, 99.10 s De Kalb av, 22x91.8. Same agt John D. Fish; same att'y........ 18
Carroll st, n s, 445.2 e 5th av, 17.4x100. Same agt James C. Jewett; same att'y........ 18
Carroll st, n s, 427.11 e 5th av, 17.8x100. Same agt same; same att'y........ 18
Bergen st, n s, 240 e 6th av, 20x100. Same agt Joseph F. Brush; same att'y........ 18
Bergen st, n s, 260 e 9th av, 20x100. Same agt same; same att'y........ 18
Pennsylvania av, w s, 150 s Glenmore av, 16.8x100. William H. Baker agt Catharine F. Maguire; att'y, A. W. Baker........ 18
Pennsylvania av, w s, 166.8 s Glenmore av, 16.8x100. Same agt same; same att'y........ 18
Pennsylvania av, w s, 183.4 s Glenmore av, 16.8x100. Frederick E. Pitkin agt same; same att'y. 18
Av X, n s, extends from East 14th st to East 15th st, —x—, Gravesend. John Lange agt William Sloan; action to set aside deeds; att'y, S. S. Hemingway........ 18
Van Voorhis st, s s, 100 e Evergreen av, 200x200. Catherine M. Trimble agt Gilbert Haynes; action to recover real estate; atty, Arthur P. Carlin........ 18
Raymond st, w s, 50 s Bolivar st, 25x75. Lula P. McGarry agt Frank N. O'Brien; att'y, Charles H. Winslow........ 20
Raymond st, w s, 25 s Bolivar st, 25x75. Same agt same; same att'y........ 20
Raymond st, w s, 75 s Bolivar st, 25x75. Same agt same; same att'y........ 20
Bedford av, s w cor Rodney st, 133x100. Elizabeth W. Aldrich agt Mary Tallman; att'y, Spencer Aldrich........ 21
Decatur st, n s, 229 w Throop av, 18x100. Moses Sahlein agt John C. Bushfield; att'ys, Boardman & Boardman........ 21
Decatur st, n s, 211 w Throop av, 18x100. Same agt same; same att'ys........ 21
Prospect pl, s s, 250 e Rogers av, 33.4x100. James H. Watson and James H. Pittinger agt James E. Jenny or Jenney; att'y, J. Herbert Watson.. 21
Putnam av, s s, 236.6 e Reid av, 39x100........ }
Putnam av, s s, 314.6 e Reid av, 19x100........ }
Title Guarantee and Trust Co. agt John Hennessy; att'y, Charles R. Halsey........ 21
Decatur st, s s, 48.9 w Ralph av, 18.9x100. Same agt Samuel R. Good; same att'y........ 21
Utica av, w s, 19.5 s Pacific st, 17.10x75. Cornelius C. Colgate trustee Hannah Colgate agt Louis Kraus; att'ys, S. F., F H. and H. Cowdrey........ 21
Kingston av, w s, extends from centre line of Earl st to centre of Furnald st —x40, Flatbush. William H. Beadleston agt Louis Kerz; att'ys, Guggenheimer & Untermyer........ 22
Gold st, w s, 479.4 s Willoughby st, 16.2x115.6. Stephen B. Sturges agt Henry de Zavala; att'ys, Sturges & Roby........ 22
Bainbridge st, n s, 150 e Howard av, 18x100. Watson & Pittinger agt Elizabeth Higginson; att'y, J. Herbert Watson........ 22
7th av, n w s, 20.9 s w 1st st, 108.11x90.9. Joseph H. Swift agt Lewis M. Muller; att'ys, Sutphen & Sutphen........ 22
Freeman st, n s, 225 w Oakland st, 25x100. Ada M. Chapman agt Peter Hughes; att'ys, Garretson & Eastman........ 22
King st, s w s, 252 n w Richards st, 23x100 x southeast 5 x southwest 30 x southeast 20 x north 61.8 x northwest 2 x northeast 64.4. Nellie Morgan agt Francis J. Smith; action for specific performance; att'ys, Tredwell & Catlin........ 22
Navy st, No. 70, w s, 60 n Park av, 20x80x27x1.6x65. Jane Lane agt George S. Wheeler et al; action to bar any claim to inheritance in above property; att'y, J. P. Philip........ 22
Raymond st, w s, 175 s Bolivar st, 26x75. Lula P. McGarry agt Frank N. O'Brien; att'y, C. H. Winslow........ 22
Flatbush to Canarsie road, s s, 100 e of N. Cummins land, runs south to land of L. Cornell, x northwest to N. Cummins, x north 504.10 to road, x east 100, Flatbush. Frederick H. Smith, Jr., agt Charles Hallock et al.; att'ys, Dennison & Hall........ 22
Jefferson av, e s, 300 n Broadway, 18x100. Elizabeth L. Studwell et al. exrs. John J. Studwell agt George Walker; att'y, George W. Mead........ 23
Bainbridge st, s s, 205.3 w Reid av, 16.8x100. Lawrence Hurlburt agt Edwin C. Schaffer; att'y, G. W. Pearsall........ 23
Decatur st, n s, 340 w Throop av, 18.9x100. Ida A. W. Siney agt Mary A. Poole; att'y, Benjamin Wright........ 23
Decatur st, n s, 358.9 w Throop av, 18.9x100. Same agt same; same att'y........ 23
Tompkins av, n w cor Willoughby av, runs north 77.6 x west 80 x north 22.6 x west 45 x south 100 to Willoughby av, x east 125. George Silver and ano. trustees Hugh B. Scott agt The Church of the Covenanters, Brooklyn; att'ys, Cohen & McWilliams........ 23
Ashland pl, e s, 90 n Hanson pl, 15x79.6x15x80.2. Charles and Sarah E. Dennis agt Leonard L. Johnson; att'y, George A. Black........ 23

RECORDED LEASES.

NEW YORK. Per Year

Bowery, No. 1; part of. Daniel Casey to Raffaele Rosso; from July 17, 1891, to May 1, 1894........ $720
Broadway, No. 45, basement room, 11.9x29.6x16.4x29.6, used as barber's shop. Western Union Telegraph Co. Henry Koch; 5 7-12 years, from July 1, 1890........ 1,200
Broadway, No. 641, inner store. John J. Harkin to Samuel H. and Edward C. Stone; 2 years, from August 1, 1891, per year $1,500, with privilege of renewal for 3 years at........ 1,800
Canal st, No. 25. Joseph Kassel to Elias Dubin; 4¾ years, from Aug. 1, 1891........ 2,100
Hudson st, No. 93. The New York Mercantile Exchange to John P. G. Dornheim; 5 years, from May 1, 1891........ 8,000
Lewis st, Nos. 179-183, front part of top floor. Simon Strauss to Henry Harris; 2 years, from May 1, 1891........ 720
Mulberry st, No. 113, front and rear buildings. John Ward to Pasquale Levaglio; 2 years, from May 1, 1892........ 2,700
Peck slip, No. 10, basement and cellar. Pauline A. Brooks to Samuel S. Toombs; 5 years, from May 1, 1891........ 700
Warren st, No. 113, store, building and premises. Anthony Fischer and Charles Heinrichs, of Fischer & Heinrichs, to Frederick C. Padecken and William Raap, of Padecken & Raap; 5 years, from May 1, 1890........ 2,500
9th st, No. 229. Catharine Broberick widow to Thomas Fletscher; 5 years, from May 1, 1891........ 1,000
20th st, No. 426 W., cellar, store and five rooms. Archey Crossman to John Pfisterer; 5 years, from May 1, 1891........ 1,200
22d st, No. 433 W. Gertrude V. C. Hamilton to David C. Westervelt; 4 years, from May 1, 1891........ 900
45th st, No. 601 W. Karl Groll to Theodore H. Mulch; 10 years, from Oct. 1, 1891........ 1,260
51st st, No. 141 W. Mary C. Fash agent for Frank Shephard to Amy Douglass; 5 years, from Aug. 1, 1891........ 2,400
68th st, s s, 498 e Av A, 25x150.8. James H. Jones to Patrick Dean; 9 years, from May 1, 1891........ 150
129th st, No. 219 E., store floor and basement. George W. Rennert to Edward Gough; 5 years, from Aug. 1, 1891........ 420
130th st, No. 106 W. Annie E. Valentine to Emanuel Wallach; 2 years, from May 1, 1890. 1,000
Amsterdam av, No. 183. James E. Branigan to Curan & Buckley; 5 years, from July 1, 1891........ 480
Brook av, No. 509, store and part first floor. John Diehl to Berthold Tismar; 8¾ years, from August 1, 1891. 240, 300
Courtlandt av, No. 815, and stable in rear. Hasbrouck Du Bois to August Lichtenau; 5 years, from May 1, 1891........ 1,020
Lexington av, No. 2028, store and basement or cellar. Webster White and Stephen P. Anderson to Albert Kuehn; 3 years, from Jan. 1, 1892........ 1,300, 1,400
Morris av, No. 530, store floor. Anne Miller to Michael J. Broderick; 5 years, from Aug. 1, 1891........ 300
1st av, No. 1432, store and basement. George Muhler to Vaclav Jarkoosky; 5 1-6 years, from Aug. 1, 1891........ 1,152
2d av, No. 2172, store and front cellar. Mary Otten to Ignatz Adler; 2¾ years, from Aug. 1, 1891........ 780
7th av, Nos. 926-934. }
58th st, Nos. 205 and 207 W. }
59th st, Nos. 204 and 206 W. }
Sigmund Cohn and Siegfried and Gustav Heinemann, of Cohn & Heinemann to Central Park Riding Academy; 8 years, from May 1, 1893........ 10,000
8th av, No. 596. Lewis Ash to Isaiah Mayers; 3 years, from May 1, 1889........ 1,104
Same property. Assign. lease. Isaiah Mayers to John Friedrich........ nom

CHATTELS.

NOTE.—*The first name, alphabetically arranged, is that of the Mortgagor, or party who gives the Mortgage. The "R" means Renewal Mortgage.*

NEW YORK CITY.

JULY 17 TO 23—INCLUSIVE.

SALOON AND RESTAURANT FIXTURES.

Adler, Ignatz. 2172 2d av....A Hupfel's Sons. $2,000
Albert, Harris. 46 Essex....D Mayer. (R) 819
Amsler, J J. 1564 3d av.... G Ringler & Co. (R) 700
Beik, George. 1208 2d av....G Ehret. 900
Biedermann, Eberhardt 272 Spring .... V Loewers. 250
Bockelmann, Frederick. 446 W 50th....P Doelger. 500
Broche, Albert. 1883 Park av. ..D G Yuengling. Jr, B Co. 750
Bley, Henry. 131 E 3d....Budweiser B Co. (R) 800
Broderick, M J. 1145 1st av . Knickerbocker B Co. 500
Bolger, Martin. Riverdale av....D Mayer. (R) 255
Cole, A O. 117 Canal....Bernheimer & S. 650
Carr, John. 90 South....J Everard. (R) 1,228
Dietz, Lina. 116 Ludlow....J Ahles B Co. 300
Doris, James. 400 E 82d....P Doelger. (R) 300
Durkin, James. 19 Roosevelt....Budweiser B Co. (R) 1,000
Dorschel, Oscar. 1086 1st av....F Oppermann, Jr. 500
Efinger, Bernhard. 535 3d av....Bernheimer & S. Pool Table 140
Eisler, L C. 378 7th av....R Kessler. (R) 400
Ernst, Louis. 55 E 4th....Budweiser B Co. (R) 1,000
Engel, Joseph. 168½ Attorney....D Mayer. 2,500
Falvey, D D. 106 Mulberry....E W Ashley. (R) 1,500
Feeley, Michael. 1907 2d av ...G Ehret. 150
Fitzgerald, James. 2190 8th av... G Ehret. 2,225
Fowley, J J. 350 West .. Shook & Everard. (R) 1,590
Francez & Dupont. 474 6th av....A B Marx. Billiard Saloon. 480
Fay, J J. 160 Amsterdam av....C Stein. 3,000
Goldstein & Wasser. 92 Hester....V Loewers. 1,179
Greenbaum, A and F. 8 Bond and 140 E 34th ....C E Butler. Restaurant Fixtures. secures rent
Gough, Edward. 219 E 120th....G Ehret. 500
Gatti, Riccardo. 242 Washington....J C G Hupfel B Co. 2,300
Grun, J H. 305 E 6th....J Hoffmann B Co. 600
Heiser, Engel. 35 John....J N Grimm. 1,500
Huners & Lebers. 1945 2d av....G Ehret. 2,500
Heins & Stahlbut. 96 Gold....Bachmann B Co. 3,000
Hennessy, W P. 31 Prince....Bachmann B Co. 700
Hughes, Joseph. Broadway and 53d st ...H. Hughes. (R) 2,635
Hahn, F L. 2229 1st av....F & M Schaefer B Co. (R) 400
Hernberg, Emilie. 338 E 81st ...J & A Doelger. 900
Ihle, Rosa. 332 W 40th....V Loewers. 300
Kelly, M B. 1356 2d av....Burr B Co. 600
Kennedy, Minnie. 143 Spring....H Elias B Co. (R) 2,000
Knoll, Joseph. 422 W 40th....V Loewers. (R) 438
Kabatchnick, Philip. 88½ Orchard....Burger & H B Co. 625
Kaelble, Ernest. 45 W 125th....India Wharf B Co. 800
Keller, Caroline. Rivington st....Elizabeth Meltzer. (R) 1,000
Koch, Theresa. 1275 1st av....P. & W. Ebling B Co. 600
Kammitter, Frank. 250 10th av ...S Liebmann's Sons B Co. 350
Kohn, Julius. 336 6th....J Eppig. 600
Krother, Richard. 1700 2d av.... G Ehret. (R) 600
Leary, Timothy. 623 9th av....J Fullam. (R) 1,264
Lies, Frank. 78 West Broadway....Restaurant F Co. Restaurant Fixtures. 47
Lamphere, G W. 457 Washington....P. Ballentine & Sons. 114
Lux, Moritz. 119 Essex....Burger & H B Co. 500
Lipshitz, Hyman. 36 Eldridge ...S Spielberg. Restaurant Fixtures. 100
McCormick & Mundorf. 620 and 622 Grand ... D Fincke. (R) 12,000
McGirr, Peter. 281 7th av....O'Reilly, Skelly & Fogarty Co. 715
McGloin, Michael. 2069 1st av....J Ruppert. 1,000
Meurer, Peter. 327 Spring....V Loewers. 700
Miller, Edward. 69½ 1st..Bernheimer & Schmid. Ice House. 100
Same....same. Pump. 87
Same....same. Ice House. 93
Madigan, Edward. 71 Montgomery....Rubsam & H B Co. (R) 600
Mai, Louis. 820 Cortlandt....P & W Ebling B Co. 725
Mayer, Charles. 153 W 27th....D G Yuengling B Co. (R) 1,400
McGrew, John. 157 Bleecker....G Ringler & Co. (R) 668
Morsch, Henry. 137 and 139 Grand....G Ehret. 1,000
Martin, Henry. 489 1st av.... J Ahles B Co. 862
Murphy, W H. 326 1st av....Shook & Everard. (R) 2,669
Mangels, William. 314 E 41st....J C G Hupfel B Co. (R) 350
Mansmann, George. 1905 10th av....J Wenner. (R) 2,000
Mannkopf, Dora. 81 4th av ...S Liebmann's Sons B Co. 1,870
McCauley, John. 683 11th av....V Loewers. 2,300
Neumeyer, Andreas. 388 6th....P Weidmann. 300
Nooney, Christopher. 2102 3d av....Knickerbocker B Co. 2,500
O'Brien, James. 1805 Park av .. P McCann. 800
Pause, Max. 45 Exchange pl....G Ehret. 1,010
Pasdolfi, Gaetano. 301 E 107th....Bernheimer & S. Pool Table. 140
Rappolt, Franz. 96th st and 11th av....F Bachmann. 500
Reimer, W A. 63 Sullivan....M Eckstein B Co. (R) 1,829
Rogers, Lawrence. 342 7th av....Shook & Everard. (R) 2,537
Reimers, Martin. 2761 Amsterdam av....J Ruppert. (R) 700
Rodding, Bertha. 500 1st av....H Koehler & Co. 2,000
Rueinish, J H. 760 Tremont av....A Hupfel's Sons. 2,000
Schwarz, John. 334 E 54th....J Hoffmann B Co. (R) 750
Slattery & Hanley. 11 3d av....P O'Toole. (R) 1,222
Sugerman, William. 83 Eldridge....Eva Walker. Pool Table. 85
Scherer, Frank. 1574 2d av....F Oppermann, Jr. 1,500
Schillo, John. 20 Stanton....P Doelger. 800
Schmann, William. 101 Allen.. Anchor B Co. 500
Stein, Charles. 341 E 47th....F Oppermann, Jr. (R) 300
Swan, J L. 107 E 125th....S H Bleier. Restaurant Fixtures. 250
Sachs, Solomon. 200 East Broadway...D Dundes. Restaurant Fixtures. 500
Sauer, F A. 283 William .G Ehret. 800
Sullivan, J F. 90 Roosevelt....India Wharf B Co. 500
Salolovsky & Linsky. 97 Chrystie....J H Berenter. Pool Table. 130
Slosson, G F. 940-948 Broadway....J W Kearney Billiard Table. (R) secures rent
Smith, Mathew. 1001 3d av....G Ringler & Co. 2,697
Staiger, Friedrich. 217 Av A... J & M Haffens. 573
Stimmel, Francis. 1219 3d av....G Ringler & Co. (R) 400
Stipek, John. 1397 and 1399 Av A....P Weidmann. 1,200
Sullivan, Mortimer. 819 Bowery....H Vogel. 1,150
Sullivan, T O. 341 W 40th....P & W Ebling B Co. 400
Takach, M and R. 236 E 2d....H B Scharmann & Sons. 700
Terk, Pesach. 115 Hester....F Ibert. 900
Tietjen, John. 448 1st av....J Eichler B Co. (R) 1,700
Underhill, W. G. ..Jerome av and 184th st....A Huffel's Sons. (R) 500
Urban, Joseph. 1340 1st av....H Vogel 950
Voege, J H. 427 1st av ...P Doelger. 2,000
Walsh, Hugh. 617 1st av....Bernheimer & S. Ice House. 100
Walter, Leopold. 112 Av D. ..G Ehret. 2,000
Willet, R P. 530 8th av....M Kelsey. Restaurant Fixtures. 400

HOUSEHOLD FURNITURE.

Ackerson, G N. 410 W 36th....H Mannes & Son. 133
Aiello, Thomas. 460 6th av....O'Farrell & Co. 144
Atwood, Marion E. 258 W 43d....H Thoesen. (R) 124
Ackerman, Laura. 107 W 104th ...D Schwarzkopf. 412
Ahles, Otto. 309 E 69th....L Baumann. 310
Bajorath, Minna. 428 E 92d ...Krakauer Bros. Piano. (R) 135
Benalu, Jacob. 289 E 106th....J Moriarty. (R) 146
Bker, Anna. 206 St Nicholas av....A Bellermann. Piano. 225
Breman, Mrs M. 2363 1st av....A Bollermann. Piano. (R) 140
Breen, Rosie. 389 E 21st....S Goldschmidt. 160
Briggs, G E. 239 E 31st....Friel & Hand. 109
Burton, Arthur Wilmont. West Farms.....W Reubel. 112
Becker, G and J. 255 E 10th....Commercial Credit Co. 100
Burgis, T C. 228 W 44th....S Knapp & Co. 1,458
Barton, A E. 217 E 25th.. .J Moriarty. 102
Binch, E J. 691 E 145th....H Mannes & Son. 155
Brown, Ellen A. 44 W 128th Annie J Barlow. 2,000
Buckley, C S. 314 W 133d....J Baumann. 457
Corliss, W E. 1656 9th av ...B M Cowperthwait & Co. 155
Comery, Mary. 163 Varick....H Thoesen. (R) 116
Chiperio, Archille. 71 Thompson ...J Moriarty. 103
Clonan, Mary. 85 Madison....J Moriarty. 179
Crone, Kate. 314 W 27th.. .L Baumann. 140
Daggett, William. 228 E 6th ...L Baumann. 228
Dwyer, Honora. 364 W 11th....H S Eisler. 124
Del Pino, R and L. 35 E 9th....W J Ruddell. 385
Deumler, Leonard. 161 Orchard....F J Brechtel. 126
Diosey, Josie. 126 W 47th ..J Moriarty. (R) 467
Donnolly, Ellen. 242 E 23d....H Thoesen. 263
Ehrlich, David. 160 E 66th....Commercial Credit Co. 200
Endy, C W. 536 W 50th....W J Ruddell. 114
Erlanger, G S. 1964 7th av... J Guinevan. (R) 101
Friedrich, H and J. 97 Rivington....Am G Assoc. 100

Flynn, Kate. 619 E 141st....D Schwarzkopf. 477
Feilding, Lydia....H Wilber. 100
Fondevila, C S. 221 E 18th....B Gorgoll. 2,140
Friedberg, Charlotte. 442 W 24th....M Bayersdorf. (R) 1.100
Flagg, Jared. 414 W 23d....J Baumann 700
Foley, Mrs W. 76 Willett....D M Brown. 101
Frank, Rosa. 222 E 52d....J Baumann. 117
Fromkess, Delia. 548 Broome....J Baumann. 218
Gallagher, Edward. 286 9th av....H Mannes & Son. 123
Goldstein, Amelia. 249 Delancey....R M Walters. Piano. 300
Goldstein, W Morris. 29 Attorney....D M Brown. 125
Gorman, S J. 51 New....B M Cowperthwait & Co. 220
Grandon, Jennie. 36 E 4th....F J Brechtel. 245
Gravel, Adilaid. 58 E 4th....O'Farrell & Co. (R) 143
Gurschke, Ernestine. 147 E 89th....H Gursche. 500
Ganey, Ellen. 409 E 52d....L Baumann. 174
Gotthold, E S. 55 E 11th ...W A Taylor. (R) 135
Geary, Mary. 800 2d av....H Thoesen. 175
Gehr, Martin. 783 E 146th....D Schwarzkopf. 122
Hawkins, Florence. 156 E 122d....D Schwarzkopf. 206
Hickey, Maria L. 7th av, bet 124th and 125th sts ....L Baumann. 240
Hodges, Alice M. 119 W 56th....C H Ten Eyck. 147
Hopkins, Francis. 157 Bleecker....J Moriarty. 286
Horan, Mary. 263 Henry....D M Brown. 177
Hine, Caroline S. 320 W 58th....J Baumann. 165
Herrick, Nettie. 65 W 95th....T Kelly. (R) 289
Same....same. (R) 250
Horton, Mary G. 73 E 114th....Jordan & M. 201
Isaacs, Clara. 506 E 83d ...L Baumann. 127
Johnson, Frank. 5 Rivington....J Moriarty. 117
Jones, Mrs A... J Moriarty. 499
Kaliski, Rachael. 50 Greenwich....D M Brown. 120
Keegan, Ellen. 786 11th av....J Baumann. 139
Killalea, James. 518 E 83d....J Moriarty. (R) 126
Lambert, C L. 94 E 114th....W Weed. 195
Lawrence, Mary. 304 W 11th....J Baumann. 142
Lewin, J. B & A. L. 1687 Madison av....American Guar. Assoc. 100
Loria, Henrietta. 22 Sutton pl....Krakauer Bros. Piano. 285
Lacekel, Tony. 1451 1st av. ..S I Herschmann. 107
Leckie, William. 396 3d av....J Baumann. 142
Lynch, Fannie M. 70 Charles....D Schwarzkopf. 219
Marwell, Ellen. 301 10th av....L Baumann. 171
McCloy, Fred. 82 W 20th....D Schwarzkopf. 232
McNichol, John. 500 W 49th... T Leonard. 302
Meyer, Henry. 220 E 20th. Selma Lenox. 1,500
Mahen, Daniel. 168 W 22d....J J Gorman. 120
Mantes, Cloudice. 146 Macdougal... H S Eisler. 170
McGee, Mary. 833 10th av....L Baumann. 123
Metzger, John. 414 W 39th....L Baumann. 144
Mace, Maria. 400 W 46th....J. Foulke, Jr. 400
Mackin, W, P. 508 E 83d .. Jordan & M. 152
Meyer, Joseph. 108 Clinton pl....Maria D. Favier. 800
Murphy, James. 690 9th av....J. Baumann 241
Musket, Jacob.....J. Moriarty. 124
Nitzert, Auguste. 165 Forsyth....D. M. Brown. 168
Nobles, Grace. 959 6th av....H Israel & Sons. 1,125
O'Brien, Timothy, 25 Sutton pl ...J, Moriarty. 119
O'Reilly, J. F. 131st st and 10th av....J. Baumann. 319
O'Neill, K. 206 E 105th....D Schwarzkopf. 171
Palmer, Kittie. 171 E 116th ...American Guar Assoc. 165
Pierson, Anna. 126 W 124th .. D Schwarzkopf. 550
Ruch, Fritz. 447 W 37th....J Guinevan. 117
Rombeld, W. & A. 345 E 46th....Commercial Credit Co. 150
Rowland, Ella. 229 W 16th....J. Baumann. 432
Reilly, Mary A. 349 E 41st....L Baumann. 143
Ricca, Louis. 208 E 14th....Krakauer Bros. Piano. (R) 250
Rice, Henry. 520 E 83d....American Guarantee Assoc. 250
Roos, N. 131 E 86th....Lincoln I and G Assoc. 200
Sachs, N. 1 Canal ...Krakauer Bros. Piano. 180
Schaefer, Emma. 93 Suffolk....J Moriarty. 217
Simon, Louis. 1754 Madison av ...J Moriarty. 252
Sklover, Rosalia. 163 E 108th....Krakauer Bros. Piano. 303
Stampfer, Josephine. 156 2d av... I Grinstein. 139
Schmidt, John. 227 E 52d....Commercial Credit Co. 125
Sturtevant, Kate. 236 E 27th... Jordan & M. 157
Saldim, M. 262 Spring....H Thoesen. 100
Sturges, Susie M. 364 W 23d .Mary A Birtles. 480
Trowbridge, E E. 140 W 83d....L Baumann. (R) 110
Toipfer, William. 106th st and 1st av....L Baumann. 138
Vogel, D. 15 2d... S I Herschmann. 110
Walcome, Lilla B. 330 W 21st....L Sternberg. 189
Woodman, Anna. 217 W 24th....J Baumann. 140
Woodruff, H S. 218 Produce Exchange....J Baumann. 150
Wright, Mrs L. 150 W 128th....D Schwarzkopf. 411
Welch, P H. Mount Vernon, N Y....Rosa B De Casanora. 167
Wheeler, T M. 571 Park av ...Fidelity I & G Co. 265
Wognum, J H. 215 Washington .. W J Brunner. 300
Wade, Jane. 157 E 107th ...Spies Bros. 232
Weiss, Nicolai. 312 E 5th....J. Moriarty. 314
Whitford, Louise H, 8 E 113th....J. Baumann, 239
Whykoff, Tillie. 201 W 30th....L. Baumann. (R) 353
Woolsey, Estella. 184th st and Morris av....J. Baumann. 295
Ziemann, F. & L. 128 E 4th....L. Baumann. 280

MISCELLANEOUS.

Alber, Godfrey. 220 Chrystie....A Eppinger. Butcher Fixtures. 100
Alty, William. 87 Washington....Weeks, Douglass & Co. Bakery Fixtures. 833
American Cigar Label Co... Campbell P P Co. Press. (R) 2,400
Amsbry, F M....Perrin, Payson & Co. Carriages. 220
Arsen, Sohak. 39 Maiden lane....M M Mangasanan. Tools, &c. 300
Ahrens, Ellen, 406 10th av....Lamson Consol S S Co. Register. 165
Bizinsky, Gussie. 131 Clinton....C Dierking. Butter Ice Box. 110
Blumenberg, Shema. 146 Attorney....F Maurer. Machines. 50
Boyd & Co. 2269 7th av....Marvin Safe Co. Safe. 120
Bradley, Enoch. 620 W 52d....L S Keller. Horses, &c. (R) 535
Bowles, Lizzie. 215 Lexington av....D B Dunham & Son. Harness. 145
Cranston, T L....Campbell P P Co. Press. (R) 12,500
Conklin, H A. 154 Rodney st, Brooklyn....J P Dallimore. Horses, Trucks, &c. (R) 3,000
Cornell, Mary E....T L Coles. Grain Elevator, "George Albert." (R) 3,000
Cornish, L H. 54 Beekman....E F Kenyon. Machinery. 1,000
Dimond, W H. West 13th....Josephine W Stephenson. Horse, Truck, Lighter. 3,000
Dondero, Charles. 192 Wooster... Catharine Rossi. Grocery Fixtures. 600
Dimond, W H. 424 W 13th....G Vandenhove. Horses, Trucks and Lighter. 986
Dolcenascolo, Vincenzo. 202 E 108th....Ribando & de Palermo. Barber Fixtures. 150
Dambro, Louis. 286 8th av ..Archer Mfg Co. Barber Fixtures. (R) 466
Davidson & Peruren. 1931 3d av....A Hekoch. Barber Fixtures. 500
Dinnerstein, S & B. 151 Attorney....N Weismann. Grocery Fixtures. 180
Di Tore, Giovani. 225 W 27th....Schwaab & Son. Barber Fixtures. (R) 40
Dobler, Anton. 333 and 335 W 30th....J G Flammer. Machinery. 953
Egninion, Haigag. 12 Frankfort....Denig & Grant. Machinery. 350
Eisler, Mary. 2916 and 2918 3d av....J M Lean. Butcher Fixtures. 134
Everitt, Susan M, 215 Washington....Bramhall Deane & Co. Range, &c. (R) 250
Freligh, M. McDougall alley....G T Reeves. Horse and Express Fixtures. 225
Freund, O & Co. 11 Lispenard... J Stewart. Machinery. 1,440
Farina, Pietrina. 1084 Park av....P A Cassidy. Wagon. 75
Fagio, Constantino. 513 Hudson....Archer Mfg Co. Barber Fixtures. 33
Frey, Daniel. 530 6th....G Grau. Horses, Trucks, &c. 175
Goldstein, Nathan. 24 Norfolk.. Archer Mfg Co. Barber Fixtures. 111
Green, Eva A. 1455 3d av....J Rummel and others. Fixtures, &c. 375
Gross, Gus. 774 2d av....Archer Mfg Co. Barber Fixtures. (R) 118
Garrety, John....Rothschild Bro. Horse 60
Guberman & Kruvitz. 190 East Broadway ... Manhattan Type Co. Press, &c. 235
Gertenbach, Theresa. 377 W 125th....Hudson River Beef Co. Butcher Fixtures. (R) 500
Gluck, Samuel. Attorney, bet Stanton and Houston sts I Gluck. Horses, Vans, &c. 2,500
Granie, Oscar. 916 9th av....J N Heubner. Bakery Fixtures, &c. 300
Greenberg & Einbinder. 144 Orchard.. .I Baumann. Horse, Wagon, &c. 100
Groth, C A. 1622 and 1624 Broadway, 58 and 60 W Houston and 33 Lispenard....M J Lichtenstein. Express Fixtures. (R) 7,500
Harlem Reporter Co. 203 E 124th....J C Graff, Presses, &c. 8,000
Hodes, Simon. 35 Sheriff....R Spahn. Machinery. 60
Hall, William .. P Barrett. Truck. (R) 238
Harlem Lighting Co....Farmers' Loan & T Co. Franchises, &c. (R) 300,000
Hawison, Robert. 113 W 125th ... National Casket Co. Undertaker Fixtures. 650
Haase, Charles....J A Hyland. Lighter, Nangatuck. security as bondsman
Horn & Nowak. 24 Delancey....Roberts & Collin. Bakery Fixtures. 50
Horton, G M S "trustee." 243 Greenwich st.... Babcock P P Co. Press. (R) 1,083
Horowitz, M. Bleecker st and Broadway.... Archer Mfg Co. Barber Fixtures. 245
Humbert, Nicholas. 239 Bowery....G F Humbert. Hats, &c. 500
Jung, Jacob. 319 8th av....M Buddendick. Machinery. 350
Jenkens & McCowan....Campbell P P Co. Press. (R) 2,000
Jerufsky, Max. 287 Broome ...R Spahn. Machine. 75
Kaldenberg, F J. Nassau & Beekman sts....Marvin Safe Co. Safe. 225
Kropp, J and W. 902 Amsterdam av....Couper, Zimmerman & Co. Bakery Fixtures. 300
Kee, Wing. 10 Catharine....G Chong. Laundry Fixtures. 150
Knowlton, Willis. 335 4th av; 246 5th av....J L Breese. Photo Fixtures. (R) 1,270
Katz, M. 124 East Broadway....Archer Mfg Co. Barber Fixtures. 100
Kuntzburg, John. 557 Grand....Archer Mfg Co. Barber Fixtures. 215
Lawrence, Reuben. 85 Baxter....Elizabeth Hulton. Butcher Fixtures. 200
Same. 131 Mott....Elizabeth Hulton. Butcher Fixtures. 350
Learneg, Michael. 65th st and 1st av....J Rothschild. Horses. 225
Levin & Malkiel. 264 Division....M Nusberg. Machines. 110
Luckas & Lucas. 1294 3d av and 164 E 87th st.... E C Komer. Undertaker Fixtures. (R) 2,500
Lascheri, Antonio. 156 Forsyth ...L Frenna. Barber Fixtures. 185
Laurowitz, Louis. 41 and 43 Willett....J Gottlieb. Machinery, Horse, &c. 500
Macgowan, D E. 7th av and 28th st. . Campbell P P Co. Press. 5,533
Massoth, Frederick. 1823 Amsterdam av....C Massoth. Butcher Fixtures. 500
Mayer, E A. 512 E 137th....J Cunningham Son & Co. Coach. 700
McCauley, John. 49th st and 11th av....I Roth. Bar Fixtures. 1,900
McGeorge, P A....Campbell P P Co. Press. (R) 620
McPeck, Hugh. 436 E 77th ...D P Nichols & Co. Horse. 25
Meier, Pauline. 73 Forsyth....Anna Adams. Grocery Fixtures 350
Molner, Ignatz. 120 Av D....H. Spiegel. Machines, &c. 325
Moore, J J. 153 E 118th....J Cunningham Son & Co. Coach. 2,080
Mulstein, Adolf. 344 Hudson....C E Paice. Barber Fixtures. 100
Municipal Statistics Co. 55 Liberty....R Smith and ano. trustees. Books, Records, &c. (R) 45,000
Mahr, Richard. 130th st and 8th av....Archer Mfg Co. Barber Fixtures. (R) 287
Martin, Herman. 1104 Lexington av....Archer Mfg Co. Barber Fixtures. 830
McDougall, A S. 133 W 42d....American Guar Assoc. Dental Fixtures. 100
Mele, Poalo. 1255 9th av... Archer Mfg Co. Barber Fixtures. (R) 360
Moons, Margaret. 508 11th av....S Dorfmuller. Butcher Fixtures. 75
Musta, Carmine. 29 Mulberry....Schwaab & Son. Barber Fixtures. 478
Nilnenberg, L. 106 Ridge....Archer Mfg Co. Barber Fixtures, (R) 28
Nebewzchal, Abraham. 88 Pitt .. M Goldstein. Machines. 70
O'Brien, W E. West End av and 79th st....S A Smith. Horses, Wagons, &c. 638
Ochs, Henry. 1218 3d av....A and H Smith. Tools, &c. 120
Otto, Wilhelm. 148 Orchard....J Weiss. Barber Fixtures. 40
Pall, A S. 947 and 949 Marcy av, Brooklyn, N Y ...Stein Mfg Co. Undertaker Fixtures. (R) 705
Poto, Felice A. 211 Mulberry....A Carracia. Tailor Fixtures 100
Price & Lewis. 186-194 Lewis... J C Price. Machinery. 150
Paradouski, J E. 16 Stanton....J C Hess. Barber Fixtures. (R) 150
Paynter, W R & Bros. 210 Fulton....J A Lowe. Presses, &c. (R) 7,000
Picker, Chas. 1756 3d av....Lamson Consol S S Co. Register. 140
Passananti, Sam. 168 Orchard ...Schwaab & Son. Barber Fixtures. (R) 105
Patera, Salvatore. 1639 3d av....Archer Mfg Co. Barber Fixtures. (R) 100
Quigley, James W F O'Rourke. Horse, &c. 200
Ritter, W B. 445 W 45th....B F Kenney. Machinery. 750
Radwziner, Adolph 832 Grand....State of Bank New York City. Store Fixtures. 2,000
Ramsey, P N....Buffalo Refrigerating Machine Co. Machinery. 4,500
Reres, Paola. 115 Pitt....F Carozza. Barber Fixtures. 55
Riding Club. 58th st and 5th av....Cadwalder & Lanier. Franchises, &c. (R) 85,000
Reutlinger, Caroline....E Reutlinger. Horses, Wagons, &c. 650
Reynolds, C T. 35 Frankfort....J T Hendrickson. Machinery. 250
Rocco & Marone. 27 Baxter....A Schwaab & Son. Barber Fixtures. (R) 168
Roma, Frank. Electric Ex Building....Archer Mfg Co. Barber Fixtures. 588
Rosenberg, L. 53 Willett....Archer Mfg Co. Barber Fixtures. 111
Rossi, Louis. 297 Av A... Archer Mfg Co. Barber Fixtures. (R) 170
Schippel, A. 14th st and Broadway....Archer Mfg Co. Barber Fixtures. (R) 566
Schwaiting, C W. Ogden av and Union st....R Uffelmann. Grocery Fixtures. 648
Schwarzler, Joseph. 1073 5th av....B Doblin. Horse, Truck, &c. 1,000
Spaulding, Frank....P Barrett. Truck. 295
Salm, Jacob. 157 7th av....D M Priest. Drug Fixtures. 2,500
Schneider, Peter. 501 E 72d....P A Cassidy. Wagon, &c. 106
Smith, J E. 347 Washington....F Akers. Horses, Trucks, &c. 250
Schenck, Anna M. 289 Greenwich....J Pyle. Barber Fixtures. 400
Scheuerman, Edward. 405 5th....F Mayer. Grocery Fixtures. 125
Schonberg, L. 28 Elm....J P Rathbun & Co. Machinery. 98
Schultheis, J F. 205-217 E 67th....G F Krumm. Saloon Fixtures, &c. 3,000
Same....same. Saloon Fixtures, &c. 2,500
Smith, Henry....G Dessecker. Coupe. 150
Slarace, Michael. 897 3d av....S Klingler. Barber Fixtures. (R) 100
Schwartz, Max. 181 South 5th av. . P Schwartz. Horse, Truck, &c. 200
Scott, John. 15 Spruce and 13 Frankfort....G H Morrill et al. Press, &c. (R) 14,720
Stutz, Frederick. 44 Sullivan....J Hassinger. Butcher Fixtures. 250
Tedford, Adelina M. 231 W 38th....E C Schoonmaker. Piano and Jewelry. (R) 200
Tiger, Moritz. 160 Stanton .S Kemler. Barber Fixtures. (R) 100
Townsend, W A....G P Putnam's Sons. Piano, Books, &c. 150
Vincent & Villone. 56 W 30th....S Littman. Barber Fixtures. 334
Ventrice, Jos. 31 6th av....Archer Mfg Co. Barber Fixtures. (R) 126
Vinti, Ed. 88 Wall....Archer Mfg Co. Barber Fixtures. (R) 320
Williams, W R. 101st st and E River....R H Conner. Personal Property, all kinds. 2,000
Walsh, Mathew. 61 South 5th av.. .J Souvay. Barber Fixtures. 59
Wardwell Sewing Machine Co....J W Simpson and ano. Franchises, &c. (R) 215,000
Weinstock, Jacob. 1098 2d av....P A Cassidy. Wagon. 100
Werdenshlag, Gertrude. 466 6th av....R L Epstein. Butcher Fixtures. 300
Williams, C. 1865 2d av ...Lamson Consol S S Co. Register. 210
Zanger, Emma. 116 Broome....H Oppenheim. Drug Fixtures. 600
Zaborowski, Meyer. 176 Clinton....S Littman. Barber Fixtures. 145
Zuckertrod, Morris. 127 E 108th....J Stein. Machines. 100

BILLS OF SALE.

Binning, John. 2312 1st av....P Muller and wife, New Jersey. Grocery Fixtures. 525
Binning, Lena. 2312 1st av... J Binning. Grocery Fixtures. 1
Bleibler, Martin. 421 E 5th....G Schebik. Grocery Fixtures. 450
Colwell, Hugh. 61 W 137th....Margaret Colwell. Horses, Trucks, &c. 1
Cellio, Vincenzio. 319 E 115th ...Caterina Cellio. Grocery Fixtures. 150
Ehrmann, Yette. 34 Jones....L Simon. Butcher Fixtures. 50
Gilnsman, C H. 96 Gold....Heins & Stahlhut. Saloon Fixtures. 3,500
Heim, Herman. 427 W 37th ...J Zeman. Toys. 350
Kent, Martin. 39 and 41 Suffolk....L Theil. Restaurant Fixtures. 60
Knief, Henry. 149th st and Walton av....D Bultman. Grocery Fixtures. 2,000
Kenny, B F. 445 W 45th....W F Ritter. Machinery. 1.500
L[illegible], Louis. 359-363 W 59th....L Coari. Restaurant Fixtures, &c. 10,000
Morang, Eliza. 788 2d av....B & L Laguna. Stationery and Cigar Fixtures. 1
Nathanson, Isidor. 89 Av A....Peppi Nathanson. Restaurant Fixtures. 300
Spivak, Baruch. 187 Eldridge....Ciarna Spivak. Saloon Fixtures. 600
Schellhaas, Ferdinand. 25 Rivington....J Grassenauer. Barber Fixtures. 500

Schulhoff, Henry. 157 Ridge....S Balles. Crockery Store Fixtures. 500
Vollmar, Dorothea P. 2812 1st av...Lena Binning. Grocery Fixtures. 600

ASSIGNMENT OF CHATTEL MORTGAGES.

Mayer, Jenny R to M Brand. (Mort given by E Stoessel. April 6, 1891.) 50
Weil, Samuel to F B Downing. (J Dwyer, Jr, April 17, 1890.) 325

KINGS COUNTY.

JULY 16 TO 22—INCLUSIVE.

SALOON AND RESTAURANT FIXTURES.

Beverly, J. 219 Navy....M Seitz. $900
Bongartz, A. 983 3d av....Elizabeth Bongartz. (R) 5,000
Brand, J M. 591 Bushwick av....Danenberg & C. (R) 500
Baldwin, G and Sarah E Swift. Main st, s e cor Plymouth st...P Buckel. 1,450
Bleichner, M and E. 249 Hopkins....W Ulmer. 600
Botte, A. 377 Graham av....W Ulmer. 1,500
Boylan, J P. Vesta av....Obermeyer & L. 325
De Filbro, C. 1771 Atlantic av ...J Noll. 550
Dugan, M. 78 Sandford....Danenberg & C (R) 406
Dunn, T. 532 3d av...H B Scharmann & Sons. 600
Ebel, W. 412 Bushwick av....Claus Lipsius B Co 700
Ellmore, W. 36 Tompkins av ...Claus Lipsius B Co. 604
Ficken, G H. 839 Broadway....Beadleston & W. 4,000
Fitzgerald, J E. 51 Raymond....Budweiser B Co. 1,090
Flanagan, J P. 287 5th av...Financial Credit Co. Restaurant. 100
Fleischer, Theressia. 133 Leonard....F Ibert. (R) 400
Fowler, W C. 5th av. cor 12th st....F Hower B Co. 600
Graham, J M 146 Columbia.....Malcolm B Co. 2,750
Graver, W. 177 Atlantic av....H A Gubner. 1,100
Giacomino, R. 30 Maspeth av....Budweiser B Co. 300
Hollwedel, C H. 290 Washington....G Ringler & Co. 3,000
Harrison, Ann. 8 Utica av....Budweiser B Co. (R) 500
Hilburger, J. 993 Flushing av ...Claus Lipsius B Co 450
Hartman, Ida. 155 Lawrence....Beadleston & W. (R) 1,500
Heffernan, T. 157 Myrtle av....Burr B Co. 1,500
Herriot, T M. 214 Flatbush av....M Seitz. 450
Herold, G. 1057 Flushing av.....C Frese. 568
Kenna, M. 399 Van Brunt....H B Scharmann. (R) 300
Kenny, C E. 195 Franklin......S Liebmann's Sons B Co. 1,000
Kerrigan, E F & J P. 149 4th av.... P Doelger. 600
Kelaher, J. 1446 Bergen....Budweiser B Co. (R) 250
Kinnally, C. 639 Clason av....Claus Lipsins B Co. (R) 500
Lane, C. 66 Sumner av....Weiz & Zerwick. 1,000
McGeehin, B. Underhill av and Dean st....Budweiser B Co. (R) 400
Morgan, Sarah. 163 Hudson av....G Ringler & Co. (R) 1,000
Moors, J. 182 Jay....P Ballantine. 1,000
Maloney, J. 144 Grand.....H B Scharmann & Sons. (R) 2,000
Martin, L. 141 Montrose av ....L Eppig. 500
McKeever, C. 614 Myrtle av.....E Ochs. 3,041
Morehouse, S R.....Brunswick-B-C Co. Pool Table. 250
Mueller, P. 456 Central av....Danenberg & C. 242
Neuman, O A. 329 Atlantic av....F & M Schaefer B Co. 1,000
Peach, G H. 59 39th....Budweiser B Co. (R) 300
Ruege, H. 1089 De Kalb av....Obermeyer & L. (R) 300
Schaeffer. 375 De Kalb av ...Eliz Metzler. 300
Sangster, J M & Co. 589 Park av....Johanna Correy. Horses, &c. 500
Stein, E. 41 Wyckoff av....J Eppig. (R) 600
Schaefer, J. 93 Tompkins av... Obermeyer & L. (R) 1,700
Seivenspinner, C. 95 Lorimer....Obermeyer & L. 800
Sharkey, D. 512 4th av....Budweiser B Co. (R) 1,000
Smith, P. 364th....Budweiser B Co. (R) 210
Sutton, Charlotte J. 794 Fulton . Budweiser B Co. (R) 400
Senz, C. 96 Meserole ...J Fallert B Co. 650
Siefert, A. Knickerbocker av, cor Ingraham st ....W Ulmer. (R) 575
Silber, E. 111 Varet ...Abbots B Co. 500
Smith, P. 159 Franklin....Wagner & Sandford. Billiards. 140
Spengler, F. 49 Morrell....P Weidmann. 600
Theissing, H W. 257 Johnson av....C Frese. 500
Voege, G. 1507 Broadway ...W. Ulmer. 2,000
Wasiak, A... L Eppig. 1,182
Weber, D. 138 Harrison av....S Liebmann's Sons B Co. 500
Wilkens, Anna M. Norman av, s w cor Newell st....Emilie Huber. 1,000

HOUSEHOLD FURNITURE.

Angevine D. 12 Little Hull....O'Connor & Tracy. 134
Bolio, Virginia. 278 10th....J Moriarty. 151
Bowne, Jennie. 214 9th....L Baumann. 132
Charles, Mrs H. 203 Hull O'Connor & T. 135
Conrad, J. 204 Nostrand av....C T Kendrick & Co. 195
Cobb, J H. 205 Grand av....C E Pierce. 100
Doyle, J J. 580 18th....Cowperthwait & Co. 225
Duane, T M. 542 4th av D M Brown. 168
Deonis, G B. 352 Lafayette av... E C Hinsdale. 190
Duryea, A. Sunnyside av....C H Ten Eyck. 109
Gibson, Mrs T. 1777A Broadway....H Israel & Sons. 315
Haessig, H T. 146½ Concord....L Z Murray. 123
Hagar, Jessie G. 59 Park pl....E C Hinsdale. 190
Harris, W L. 288 and 290 Court ...F B Lattimer. 143
Iriam, Mrs C B. 223 Lexington av....Platt & C. 666
Johnson, Mrs. M A. 757A Union....Cowperthwait & Co. 373
Kingston, Mary. 40 Eldert....A Schulz. 185
Levin, T. 141 4th av....E Driscoll & Bro. 114
Langdon, Julia. 284 Nostrand av....J Michaels. 183
Lukes, W J. 201 Smith....J Michaels. 186
Mainland, Louisa. 162 Decatur .. L Z Murray. 371
McCarthy, E. 78 Henry ... Cowperthwait & Co. 129
Megonigle, Lucy. 478A 16th....C R Armstrong. 200
McGuire, T. 2004 Atlantic av....A Pearson. 118
Meftelberger, N. 89 North 4th....H S Eisler. 187
Molinghini, E. 360 Wythe av .... Cowperthwait & Co. 100
Morse, Mary H. 272 Schermerhorn....E H Howell. 200
McKee R. Myrtle av and Skillman st....C T Kendrick & Co. 140
Mooney, J F. 65 Rutledge....W O'Neill. 247
Roy, G. 1015 Bedford av....C T Kendrick & Co. 182
Schoenberg, J. 204 Moore....M Lesslau. 172
Shields, S. 451 Halsey... M Bottstein. 105
Sheldon, Eveline. 136 State....Bertha A Hausmann. (R) 500
Sugarman, L. 24 2d....East New York Furniture Co. 193
Stevens, Eugenie. 176 Levis av....J Baumann. 260
Von Graff, R. 164 7th av....Platt & Co. 640
Watt, J C and Eliz. 737 Myrtle av....E C Hinsdale. 126
Wekerle, Emma A. 444 W 58th st, New York....J Baumann. 127
Warner, C. 375 Gates av...D Richardson. 751
Yonkers, T. 351 Stockholm....J A Schwarz. 293

MISCELLANEOUS.

Angevine, J F. 912 Gates av....Martha C Angevine. Butcher Fixtures. 300
Adriance & Curtis. Machine Works, 174 and 176 Worth st, New York....S W Balch. One Shaper. (R) 1,000
American Cigar Table Co....Campbell Press and Mfg Co. Press. (R) 2,400
Banta, S. 458 3d av....J Fulton. Barber Fixtures. 145
Bedell, W A....P Barrett. Truck. (R) 125
Brousseau, J. Coney Island...I Brousseau. Theatre. 2,772
Cianciminio, P. New York Harbor....Elizabeth G Cianciminio. Two Scow Barges. 250
Conklin, H A. 154 Rodney....J P Dallimore. Horses and Trucks. (R) 3,000
Crawford, J C....W Conrady. Wagon. 106
Cornell, Mary E. New York Harbor....T L Coles. Grain Elevator. (R) 3,000
Connolly, P. 1061 Atlantic av....J J Newbury. Machinery, Tools, &c. 488
Covert, W J.....P Barrett. Truck. 200
Dittmann, J H....204 Reid av....Juliane Bingel. Butcher Fixtures (R) 800
De Arrastia, M....A C Gonzalez. Horse and Truck. 200
Dukeshire, P C & Son. Foot 19th....J Ruppert. Horse, &c. 300
Dukeshire, C C & Son. Foot 19th st... J A Hart. Frame Building. 1,000
Elliott, J M. 25-27 Ralph av....D B Dunham. Horses, Coaches, &c. 1,634
Foerster, E. 679 Bedford av....J W Tufts. Soda Fountain. 750
Grafton, J T. 361 Court... J Matthews Apparatus Co. Soda Water Fountain. 360
Hanlon, J J. 80 Wallabout....J T Hanlon. Machinery &c. 2,500
Hutchinson, G E. 52 Harrison av....Financial Credit Co. Milk Store. 125
Hall, A T. 2056 Fulton. . H Bramwell. Store Furniture. 250
Hawkhurst, D W E. 91 Greenpoint av. ..R E Silverbrandt. Baker Fixtures. (R) 118
Jenkins, H C and A McCowan....Campbell Press and Mfg Co. Press. (R) 2,000
Johnston, S. 2 Liberty st, N Y....Dennison & Brown. Printing Office, 2,00
Kelly, A. 413 Broadway....Puffer & Sons Mfg Co. Soda Fountain. (R) 135
McSorley, M. 1031-1033 De Kalb av....J Cunningham, Son & Co. Coach. 865
Nelson, E. 316 Columbia....N Olsen. Printing Office. 300
Ortlieb, M. 280 Nevins....Acme Glue Co. Horse and Wagon. 91
Oppenheimer, L. 254 8th....J Schwab. Horse and Wagon. 200
Pfaff, F. 391 Myrtle av....R C Fuller. Tobacco Store. 600
Russell, J H....P Barrett. Wagon. 118
Robinson, A. Guernsey st, near Norman av....J C Hendrickson. Machinery. 100
Ruoff, L & Son. 109 Bushwick av....G L Brownell. Hearse. 900
Robinson, J D. 1091 De Kalb av....J Conners' Sons. Printing Office Fixtures. (R) 200
Schweng, W. 484 Central av ...Maggie Roth. Butcher Fixtures. 150
Schuler, L. 51 Meserole....Couper, Zimmermann & Co. Bakery. 180
Schwicker, L. East New York av, near Sackman st....W Deterling. Butcher Fixtures. 150
Schwenaker, A....P Barrett. Horses, Trucks. (R) 850
Simpson, A. 32 Church st, New York City....C B Merwin. Printing Office. 1,500
Thomas, S E. 5th av and 31st st....L M Doup. Horse and Wagon. 400
Van Sickle, A. Amity, N Y....J Ellnor. Milk Farm. 3,000
Same. Goshen, N Y....Same. Farming Stock. 700
Same. South Bay, L I....Same. Schooner Antelope. 500
Van Sickle, A. 560 Vanderbilt av....J. Ellnor. Milk Business, &c. 150
Wilkenhoh, H. 45 and 47 Myrtle av....C Hohorst. Grocery. 3,000
Woehr, R F. 180 Atlantic av....Mary C Woehr. Picture and Frame Store. 500
Wrightington, F. Franklin st....F H Lindner. Horses, Coaches, &c. secures rent
Zoeller, L E. 251 Hopkins....L Ewing. Sewing Machines, &c. 230

BILLS OF SALE.

Brousseau, Joseph. Coney Island....F P Budden. Machinery. 500
Carsten, W G 138 Division av .. D S Stewart. Butcher Fixtures. 225
Brady, T J. 557 5th av....Mary J Brady. Saloon. 2,000
Carroll, J T. 501 East Houston....Annie Carroll. Grocery Store, Horse and Wagon. 600
Fickeissen, G. 1102 De Kalb av....L Best. Barber Shop. 325
Herring, C. 30 Schaeffer....B and S Spiegler. Barber Shop. 200
Riesterer, C. 383 Fulton....N Burner. Shoe Business. 3,572
Schwartz, H. 91 Graham av....B Greenberg. Fixtures. 350
Syre, F. 232 10th ...Madeleine Syre. Provision Store. 400
Weidhorn, C A. 313 Evergreen av... W Ulmer. Saloon. nom

ASSIGNMENTS OF CHATTEL MORTGAGE.

Claus Lipsius Brewing Co to The Budweiser B Co. (Mort given by C Kinnally, Aug 21, 1890.) 500

NEW JERSEY.

ESSEX COUNTY.

CONVEYANCES.

Adams, C T et al.—J A Frothingham, South Orange $1
Abbe, Christian—C A E Friedlaender, n s Sterling st, 100 e Howard st, 25x64.......... 6,950
Archbold, A M—S H Richards, East Orange.... 14,250
Ballantine, J H et al—F Fischel, Springfield av. 1
Ball, N C—C N Hayes, Bloomfield 3,000
Bassini, Charles et al—G Ditzel, Clinton.......... 250
Same——R Beck, Clinton.......... 250
Billhofer, C C—C P Hedden, Clinton.......... 4,500
Bloodgood, Augustus—S A Tyler, East Orange. 1,500
Booth, Ella—L J Dodd, Montclair.......... 1
Bower, S W—J H Pratt, Montclair.......... 1,500
Breakenridge, J H—J Helmbrecht, Clinton..... 300
Coe, Theodore et al—J P Gegenheimer, Prince st.......... 800
Comstock, L J—P B Delaney, South Orange.... 1,050
Condit, E A—E W Hine, Orange.......... 3,500
Condit, Stephen—J A Cunningham, West Orange 1,000
Connor, John et al—C C O'Connor, South 11th st 1
Cooper, Henry—F Gehring, Johnston st.......... 500
Coruin, C R—T A McEntee, 18th av.......... 1
Crane, Mary et al—A H Kingman, Orange.... 15,000
Del Guercio, Alfonso—L Russomanno, 8th av... 1,750
De Tornos, Manuel—M De Tornos, Montclair.... 1
Dobinson, Bridget—H Dobinson, East Orange.. 150
Same——H McNulty, East Orange.......... 450
Dodd, L J—E Booth, Montclair.......... 1
Dotzer, A J—G Kitching, West Orange.......... 6,000
Doup, T V—J R Bryan, East Orange.......... 1,500
Dreher, Antonia—F J Scheller, South 15th st.... 500
Fish, C J—E Plaut et al, Broad and Cedar sts 30x104.......... 3,500
Same——E Plaut, s s Cedar st, 148 w Broad, 30x104.......... 3,500
Fish, Delia J—E Plaut, Cedar st.......... 1
Fischer, Fridolin—J Hallbauer, Railroad av..... 1
First African Methodist Episcopal Church—F A Schlosstein, Arlington st.......... 2,200
Firth, John—A A Stryker, East Orange.......... 1
Gegenheimer, J P—J C Eisele, Prince st.......... 400
Guenther, J U—J W Sipp, South 14th st.......... 1,200
Hallbauer, John—F Fischer, Railroad av.......... 1
Harrison, M A—B H B Sleght, n s Clinton av, 100 s Halsey st, 31x180.......... 23,000
Hearn, M O—A Kaiser, South 9th st 550
Honiss, John, exr—Peabody Land and Loan Co, South st.......... 2,500
Hunter, Deephina—S E Sayre, East Orange.... 12,000
Jacobus, C H—M Smith, Caldwell.......... 500
James, J C—T Spencer, South Orange.......... 1,605
Jerolaman, Henry—R P Conlon, Peddie st...... 85
Same——same, Peddie st 350
Kipp, J H—J J Freese, 1st st.......... 900
Lighthipe, C A—City of Orange, Orange.......... 1
Mackin, Francis—F Scheck, Bremen st.......... 1,250
Same——R Buhl, Bremen st.......... 50
Same——W Muller, Bremen st.......... 50
McCracken, J H—C E Reeves, Oraton st.......... 240
Meeker, Samuel—Drexel Improvement Co, Montclair.......... 6,912
New Jersey Zinc Co—J Cusick, Chapel st....... 700
Same——same, Chapel st.......... 700
O'Connor, C C—E Connaughton, South 11th st.. 1
Osborne, J H et al—E Shepard, Clinton.......... 1,000
Osborne, J H—G W Conn, Clinton.......... 1,000
Orr, James—C Smith, Franklin.......... 11,000
Same——G Ely, Franklin.......... 15,000
Pfefferle, J F—A Radel, w s Essex st, 191 w Orange st, 117x177x80x149x30.......... 2,800
Powell, R M—H S Lesser, w s Myrtle av, 190 n Sussex av, 50x81x64x81.......... 5,500
Radel, Andrew—J F Pfefferle, s s South Orange av, cor South 14th st, 182x498x512.......... 18,000
Reilly, Mary—J Lentz, Hamburg pl.......... 1,600
Rowe, Francis—H M De Kolt, East Orange...... 2,700
Rust, Frederick—M Schmitz, w s Prince st, 75 n Montgomery st, 25x100.......... 3,000
Russell, S A—B Farley, Houiss st.......... 1
Sandford, G W—A H Kingman, Orange 3,776
Scheel, R L—D Kellner, s s Elm st 150 e Mulberry st 25x91.......... 3,900
Schreck, Franz—E Yaneh, Bremen st 2,525
Schneider, Justus—F Voigt, Newton st.......... 1
Sellew, T G—E Booth, Montclair 1
Same——same, Montclair.......... 1
Same——same, Montclair.......... 1
Same——same, Montclair.......... 1
Shaw, W J—C B Morris, Montclair.......... 1,000
Stapff, Julius—E Schickhans, Hamburgh pl..... 1
Taylor, A H—C Strasser, Av L 1
Torrey, H F—J H Pratt, Montclair.......... 6,000
Tunis, Nehemiah—O E Herold, Van Buren st ... 900
Voigt, Frank—J Schneider, Newton st.......... 1
Wardell, M B—H G McFadden, East Orange.... 12,000
Weber, Joseph—G Lapp, South 6th st.......... 950
White, N H—Fitz Gerald, w s Burnett st 131 w James st 28x102.......... 11,000
Wood, Alexander—S Mickens, Sylvan av 1,500

MORTGAGES.

Arnold, T L—M E Arnold, Montclair.......... 8,000
Barrett, E A—E E Moran, Belmont av.......... 1,800
Berg, Henry—R C Browning, Orange.......... 4,500
Berry, J J—J P Berry, South Orange 1,800
Beyer, Dora—Mt Pleasant Cemetery Co, Morton st.......... 2,000
Blackwood, George—American Ins Co, South Orange.......... 2,000
Booth, Ella—T G Sellew, Montclair.......... 4,000
Same——same, Montclair.......... 4,000
Same——same, Montclair.......... 4,250
Same——same, Montclair.......... 4,250
Brown, August—J Buckrens, Peshine av.......... 1,000
Carr, Michael—P Ballantine, Railroad pl.......... 4,300
Cleveland, F M—Mutual Life Ins Co of N Y, Short Hills.......... 10,000
Cook, G W—J H Osborne, Clinton.......... 700
Conniff, Bernard—Essex Co B & L Assoc, Bloomfield.......... 1,300
Cort, Thomas, Jr—West B and L Assoc, 7th st... 3,000
Cozzens, H A—L Cozzens, Summer av.......... 3,000
Crane, Clara—H T Brumley, Columbia st.......... 1,400
Cueman, M L—Bloomfield Savings Inst, Bloomfield.......... 2,000
Cunningham, J A—S Condit, Fairmount av... 800
Cusack, John—N Y Zinc and Iron Co, Chapel st 600
Denman, S B—B D Denman, Milburn 2,500
Drexel Impt Co—S Meeker, Montclair.......... 5,412
Ely, George—D B Luckey, Clinton.......... 7,000
Fennessy, Wm—E L Richards, Joseph st.......... 800
Fengar, W M—C Porter, Johnson av 2,400
Fischel, Frederick—J H Ballantine, Springfield av.......... 16,500
Fitz Gerald, W H—N H White, Burnett st....... 10,000

Friedlaender, C A E—C Abbe, Sterling st. 1,600
Griffin, J J—W L Rhodes, 7th st. 800
Humphrey, Rosamond—W R French, Milburn. 3,500
Hanschka, R M—R F Ballantine, North 3d st. 3,100
Hedden, C P—W Stockman, Clinton. 1,500
Same——Same, Clinton. 2,000
Hein, Hermann—Lincoln B & L Assoc, South 7th st. 400
Hoffman, Adolf—Half-Dime Savings Bank, Orange. 2,500
Ippohto, Vitale—M Napotiello, 8th av. 1,000
Kane, E E—J H Stewart, Orange st. 2,500
Kingman, A H—C C Dechert, Orange. 3,681
Same——G W Sandford, Orange. 3,681
Same——M Crane, Orange. 4,686
Kitching, George—A J Datger, West Orange. 3,000
Klink, John—A Hirt, Lewis st. 1,400
Lesser, H S—R M Powell, Myrtle av. 1,100
Lister, H S——Same, Myrtle av. 2,750
Lothar, Sigmund—W Hill, Belleville av. 2,800
Mabey, T D—American Ins Co, Montclair. 2,500
Same——F B Baldwin, Montclair. 1,000
Mackinson, M E—M Gounley, East Orange. 1,100
Mahoney, John—Essex Co Brewing Co, Crane st 600
Maurer, Frederick—M D Mitchell, East Orange. 500
McGuire, Theresa—C A Feick, Broome st. 400
McLagan, J F—J Honiss exr, Cedar pl. 1,600
McNelis, Annie—H A Smith, Montclair. 1,500
McNulty, Hugh—B Dobinson, East Orange. 200
Meyler, S M—J R Sayre, Clay st. 370
Momberger, W H—L Mayer, Montclair. 855
Osborn, G H—M L Gray, Astor st. 1,500
Peabody Land and Loan Co—J Honiss exr, South st. 2,000
Pierson, A R—J C Beach, Bloomfield. 5,000
Pfeiffer, Nanette—G A Richards, Darcy st. 800
Plaut, Emma et al—C J Fish, Broad st. 30,000
Pierson, H S—C M Forrie, Greene st. 3,500
Raebler, Margaretha—Prudential Ins Co, Prince st. 800
Radel, Andrew—J F Pfifferle, Essex st. 10,000
Reeve, L S—A F Tillon, South Orange. 1,600
Richardson, S H—A M Archbold, East Orange. 10,000
Riker, Frederick—Otto Fentztaff, Montclair. 350
Roussell, Maria—W S Canon, Court st. 2,500
Rowan, H L—J G Van Riper, Belleville. 375
Rowan, H L—N J B and L Assoc, Stephens st. 2,500
Russomanno, Lorenzo—A Del Guercio, 8th av. 1,250
Ryan, D J—Mt Pleasant Cemetery, High st. 3,000
Schlosstein, F A—M J Carr, Arlington st. 1,500
Same——same, Arlington st. 3,500
Schuetz, Charles—N Booth, East Orange. 2,000
Senft, Henry—C Trefz, Waverly pl. 500
Sipp, J W—J U Guenther, South 14th st. 600
Shepard, Edwin—J H Osborne, Clinton. 700
Sleght, B H S—M A Harrison, Clinton av. 2,000
Same——same, Clinton av. 17,000
Slingerland, Isabella—T Burnet, Astor st. 3,800
Smith, Caroline—D O Hulse, Franklin. 5,000
Smith, E J—H C Stewart, East Orange. 750
Smith, J B—E Ziehr, Bloomfield av. 3,750
Snow, S M—Half-Dime Savings Bank, Orange. 900
Strasser, Christian—F Millerring, Av L. 1,000
Ten Eyck, M G—Howard Savings Inst, Belleville. 2,300
Tyler, S A—A Bloodgood, East Orange. 1,000
Van Houton, F W—M Doremus, North 6th st. 1,800
Walsh, Martin—J C McDonald, Morris av. 900
Weeks, E W—R Martin, East Orange. 2,500
Webb, Annie—Howard Savings Inst, Montclair. 750
Williams, G W—J H Baldwin, Montclair. 1,000
Yaneh, Engelbert—Security B and L Assoc, Bremen st. 2,100
Young, J C—The Newark Firemen's Relief Assoc, Broad st. 1,000
Zarra, Nicola—A Del Guercio, 8th av. 1,600
Zipfel, John—J Zipfel, Jr, Springfield av. 4,900

CHATTEL MORTGAGES.

Aspinwall, S D—G B Badgley, furniture. 270
Basile, Nicolo—G Krueger B Co, saloon. 92
Bermhein, W G—J M Hann, furniture. 48
Berry, Harold—P H Hanley, furniture, &c. 190
Byrne, Michael—A Walter, cows and horses. 185
Ceicer, Nicolo—G Krueger B Co, saloon. 75
Del Guercio, Alphonso——same, ice box. 55
Del Tufo, Pasquale——same, saloon. 160
Denton, A W—J M Hann, carpet and furniture. 100
Eppolito, Vitale—G Krueger B Co, saloon. 113
Fitz Patrick, Rudolph—McManus Bros, carpet and furniture. 445
Furchello, Frank—G Krueger, saloon. 128
Haworth, M A—G Krueger, saloon. 297
Hess, Franz J, Jr—F J Hess, Sr, barber shop fixtures. 210
Hirschfield & Co—R A McCabe, one safe. 70
Julianno, M A—G Krueger, saloon. 70
Karp, Jacob—Wilkinson, Gaddis & Co, store fixtures. 100
Keller, Nicholas—E Ziehr, saloon. 425
Kert, M E—J Ketcham, carpet and furniture. 180
Levis, Jacques—G Krueger Brewing Co, saloon. 1,000
Marion, Martha—L Bloomer, furniture. 80
Matebie, L D—J L Armitage, cylinder press. 900
Miller, Anthony—O Hoernlein, horses and wagon. 25
National Cash Register Co—F Domians, cash register. 200
National Cash Register Co—J I Monsky, cash register. 225
Pallatsiluck, Adolf—A Golden, sewing machine. 35
Post, Mary—M Kane, furniture. 40
Presdee, John—A Bernhardt, furniture. 315
Racioppo, Gaetono—G Krueger Brewing Co, saloon. 100
Ramsley, W R—C Trefz, saloon. 600
Schull, C L—L Baumann, furniture. 113
Scott, L D—P H Hanley, furniture. 65
Simpson, Robert—C Bierman, furniture. 130
Snyder, J A—F Frelinghuysen, wagons, &c. 5,260
Spagnuolo, Irena—14th Ward B and L Assoc, flour, &c. 5,000
Spirati, Alfonso—G Krueger Brewing Co, saloon. 165
Stern, John——same, saloon. 125
Sweet, M J—G Minchin, office fixtures, &c. 1,000
Tamburro, Ornato—G Krueger, ice box, &c. 170
Ulrich, F G—W E Bovet, machinery and fixtures 11,050
Wendel, N H—C Bierman, barber shop fixtures. 65
Winkler, C—Prentiss Tool and Supply Co, machinery. 115
Zarro, Nicolo—G Kreuger Brewing Co, ice box. 60

HUDSON COUNTY.

CONVEYANCES.

Arlington Homestead Assoc—D Eastman, Kearney. $1,250
Arlington Homestead Assoc—C Valentine Schuyler, Kearney. 700
Archibald, A B—S A Archibald, J City. nom
Arndt, Theresa—E K May, J City. 2,400
Bernhard, Anna—Anna Goeger, Union. 575
Bishop, Rachel A—J Giblin, Hoboken. 750
Bramhall, W E—P Holst, J City. 900
Butz, C T—G Butz, Union. 5,000
Cahill, Phillip—A D White, Harrison. 500
Connolly, John—Geo M Severance, Kearney. 2,200
Conrod, P T—L Rosa, West Hoboken. 650
Corbin, W H—W G Bumsted, J City. 900
Crevier, Alice—F N Eberhard, Hoboken. 1,000
Crookall, Isabella—Ellen Cunliff, Kearney. 3,100
Cuppinger, Emma—Madeline Greviellot, North Bergen. nom
Currey, Annette—Katie Forster, West Hoboken 1,300
Deutsch, I S—Jeanette Bernhard, J City. nom
Dieffenbach, Fred—W H Dieffenbach, J City. 5,000
Same——H Hollstein, J City. 1,200
Drayton, J W—W B Drayton, J City. 50
Drescher, Chas by exr—Anna Markins, West Hoboken. 900
Same——Pauline Doerfer, West Hoboken. 400
Ermisch, Louis—W Wagner, Hoboken. 6,250
Same——same, Hoboken. nom
Estenfelder, Barbara—A Trautmann, Guttenberg. 480
Feldhures, Henry—F C Hansen, Union. 100
Fitch, Harriet—R Bain, J City. 1,800
Fry, Ann W—Eliza A Fry, J City. nom
Fry, Asa W—E W Fry, J City. 4,500
Gallagher, Jno—F Sherry, J City. 5,150
Garagan, Jas—P Cahill, Harrison. nom
Gardner, John—Emma F Ahrens, Union. 600
Same——W Paulus, Union. 700
Gibney, J B—Margaretha Muller, J City. 500
Goldbeck, Fred—Susanna Hoedt, Union. 2,600
Greenfield, Ernst by exr—E F Emmons, J City. 1,500
Hennessey, Patrick—Margaretha Muller, J City 300
Hicks, Mary J—Mary Rudolph, Kearney. 2,500
Hoboken Land and Impt Co—Pauline C Brown, Hoboken. 5,094
Same——C A Dieck, Hoboken. 3,380
Isbills, William—C A Steurer, J City. 2,200
Kelly, Will—G W Conklin, Bayonne. 500
Kreutzkamp, Chas—C A Sterling, Bayonne. 5,500
Maguire, Rose—A Loorl, J City. 1,550
Mathey, J L—H Erxmeyer, Hoboken. 6,500
McCarthy, Will by sheriff—J Mullins, J City. 2,400
McClane, B B—Anna Lindgrien, Kearney. 1,600
McCoy, Emile—A F Mount, J City. nom
Metcalf, Mary—Margaretha Muller, J City. 200
Miller, Ed—J J Heuster, West Hoboken. 200
Morris, T F—P Sheehan, J City. 3,000
Mount, A F—J F McCoy, J City. nom
Muller, Ferdinand—W Von der Leith, Hoboken. 4,400
Muller, Richard—Maria Muller, J City. 2,000
Nichols, E H—F Brandt, J City. 300
Same——H Lauterbach, J City. 900
Oesman, Theo—W H Harper, West Hoboken. nom
Osborg, Adolf by master—A Osborg, Hoboken. 29,000
Parnickel, C A—Cscar Frommel, Hoboken. 400
Phillips, G H—F Ott, Harrison. 1,600
Podesta, Jno—Angelo Podesta, Hoboken. nom
Podesta, Angelo—J Podesta, Hoboken. nom
Prentiss, F H—Mary J Leonard, Bayonne. 1,550
Prevots, A A—T Brown, J City. 4,000
Reid, Lyle—W Davidson, J City. 5,350
Reilly, Ellen—Rose Maguire, J City. nom
Robinson, Mary—P T Neafsey, Union. 900
Saint Patrick's Catholic Church—Margaretha Muller, J City. 500
Schepeler, C A—Caroline D Dorr, J City. nom
Schutte, Alfred—Charlotte Thomas, J City. nom
Semrad, August—C Junge, Hoboken. 4,500
Siegfried, Adam—Emma Carlewitz, J City. 1,650
Same——C Keitz, North Bergen. 1,200
Sisson, Mary E by guard—A Wolf, J City. 22,001
Slapp, Catharine—Jacob Dunnick, J City. 1,400
Stingham, M V—G D Allen, Bayonne. 1,150
The Bergen Hall Assoc—D Wegman, J City. 12,200
Van Buskirk, Rebecca L—Lizzie M Thomas, Bayonne. 3,700
Same——H Kern, Bayonne. 600
Van Buskirk, De Witt—W E Elsworth, Bayonne. 717
Same——H C Elsworth, Bayonne. 1,887
Same——Mary A Doyle, Bayonne. 1,300
Van Riper, C R—Rachel C Van Riper, Bayonne. 300
Van Tassell, Mary A—J Frisch, Hoboken. 6,550
Van Wagenen, Albert—C E Geibel, Bayonne. 830
Van Winkle, Eliza—Mary F Van Winkle, J City. 480
Vreeland, N S by exr—Trustee of Sophia S Baylor, J City. nom
Same——Anna H Freeland, J City. nom
Same——same, J City. nom
Vreeland, N S—P Sheehan, J City. nom
Vreeland, Anna M—G Tompkins, J City. 1,926
Vreeland, Anna H—P S Baylor, J City. nom
Walker, Herman—A Ziegler, Guttenberg. 445
Same——Cath Umbach, Guttenberg. 400
Same——H Frecken, Guttenberg. 150
Wenner, C W—Anna Wilbrandt, J City. nom
Wilbrandt, Christian—C W Wenner, J City. nom
Young, T E—Jesse K Vreeland, Bayonne. nom

MORTGAGES.

Adams, Jas—The Washington B and L Assoc, J City, installs. 500
Allen, G D—The Centreville B and L Assoc, Bayonne, installs. 1,000
Bambach, Maria—A Courtrel, J City, 5 years. 3,000
Bernhard, Jeanette—The Provident Inst for Savings, J City, 1 year. 800
Brown, Pauline C—Martha B Stevens, Hoboken, 5 years. 20,000
Calamari, Angelo—The Italian Co-operative B and L Assoc, J City, installs. 1,600
Carlenitz, Ed—The Provident Inst for Savings, J City, 1 year. 6,500
Connery, Rosa—The Hoboken B and L Assoc, J City, installs. 1,400
Connor, Arthur—T J Loughlin, Harrison, 1 year 200
Cunliffe, Ellen—The Harrison and Kearney B and L Assoc, Kearney, installs. 2,500
Same——Isabella Cookall, Kearney, 1 year. 600
De Plasse, Louis—Marie E Laporte, J City, 3 years. 1,000
Dieck, C C F—The Hoboken Bank for Savings, Hoboken, 1 year. 5,000
Dummik, Jacob—Catharine Slapp, J City, 5 years. 1,000
Eastman, David—The Arlington Homestead Assoc, Kearney, 1 year. 600
Ely, E B—The Bayonne B Assoc No 2, Bayonne, installs. 3,000
Same——same, installs. 3,000
Same——same, installs. 3,000
Same——same, installs. 2,800
Erxmeyer, Henry—Mutual Life Ins Co, Hoboken, 1 year. 5,000
Fresch, Jno—Hudson Trust and Savings Inst, Hoboken, 1 year. 4,000
Same——same, Hoboken, 1 year. 800
Fritchie, Theo—A Lany, J City, 1 year. 550
Garrison, W V—Cartaret Mutual B and L Assoc, J City, installs. 800
Same——same, J City, installs. 800
Same——same, J City, installs. 800
Hordt, Susanna—Henrietta Bull, Union, 3 years. 900
Holst, Peter—F G Stricken, J City, 3 years. 500
Hortman, Ed—Emile Lessey, J City, 5 years. 1,900
Hurar, Thos—W C Farr, Bayonne, installs. 1,000
Junge, Claus—A Semral, Hoboken, 5 years. 3,500
Kiehnel, Anton—A A Stroever, Guttenberg, 2 years. 850
Knoebel, P F R—R Knoebel, Union, 5 years. 1,200
Krumm, Martin—J H Merendierch, Hoboken, demand. 989
Kuehne, Richard—Gussie Grossman, J City, 5 years. 1,700
Same——F Uldrick, J City, 5 years. 1,100
Matthews, Jane E—New Jersey Title Guarantee and Trust Co, J City, installs. 1,000
May, E K—Hudson Co Caledonian B and L Assoc, J City, installs. 1,832
McGlynn, Timothy—V Ruthart, Union, 4 years. 1,800
Morse, Laura T—J Wilkinson, J City, 3 years. 5,000
Muller, Fred—Lizzie Schoppinger, Hoboken, 3 years. 3,000
Nolan, Michael—Ann S W Small, J City, 3 years 800
Oelman, Reinhardt—G Schmidt, Jr, Union, 3 years. 2,000
Osborg, Adolph—Hoboken Bank for Savings, Hoboken, 1 year. 4,000
Same——Margaretha Webur, Hoboken, 3 yrs. 4,000
Osborn, Mary E—J E Andrus, J City, installs. 8,000
Osmer, Anna M—S A Besson, Union, 3 years. 1,270
Otting, Henry—W Keruse, J City, 1 year. 400
Roberts, Hugh—The Indian Spring Land Assoc, West Hoboken. 4,500
Schissler, Adaline—Hudson Trust and Savings Inst, West Hoboken, demand. 250
Schmidt, A T—Greenville United B and L Assoc, J City, installs. 2,198
Shaffer, De Witt—Communipaw B and L Assoc, J City, installs. 4,600
Sheeran, Patrick—T F Morris, J City, 3 years. 1,500
Smith, Fannie F—M V Stringham, Bayonne, 1 year. 4,000
Switzer, Christian—A Salzman, Kearney, 1 year. 700
Terry, Grace I—Equity B and L Assoc, Kearney, installs. 4,500
Thomas, Lizzie M—Bayonne B Assoc No 2, Bayonne, installs. 2,000
Van Reiper, Rachel C—Helen Cadmus, Bayonne, 1 year. 600
Vauthier, Jules—H Stueck, West Hoboken, 5 years. 1,500
Wagner, William—Hoboken Bank for Savings, Hoboken, 1 year. 3,500
Same——same, J City, 1 year. 3,500
Walters, Hannah E—Equity B and L Assoc, Kearney, installs. 400
White, A D—Mary Stumpf, Harrison, 1 year. 500
Wolf, Aaron—Guard Mary E Sisson, J City, 6 years. 18,000

CHATTEL MORTGAGES.

Ammermann, E D, Hoboken—C Kuhnapfel, horse, wagon. 111
Angelo or Teatorsbio, Will, J City—Lembeck & Betz Eagle Brewing Co, saloon. 180
Bouker, G W, J City—A D Puffer & Son, soda water apparatus, &c. 125
Braun, Karl, Union—D Bermes, saloon. 650
Carabacher, A F, Hoboken—C Feigenspan, saloon. 500
Crowley, J J, J City—C Birdsall, furniture. 130
Donop, Leopold, Union—W Fetterer, saloon. 1,000
Ebet, Julins and Annie, J City—J Franz, barber shop. 250
Eelis, S S, J City—Eadley Winterbottan, printing press, steam fixtures, &c. 255
Favor, I P, Kearney—C Birdsall, furniture. 130
Garbo, D H, J City—Carolina Schmidthauser, saloon. 425
Gebhard, J N, Union—William Peter Brewing Co, pool table. 125
Gizang, Herman, J City—Bernheimer & Schmidt, pool table and fixtures. 140
Glaab, Geo, J City—F Heismeyer, saloon. 1,000
Haase, Chas, Hoboken—J A Hyland, Lighter Narrgatuch. 1,750
Kane, Samuel, J City—John Matthews Apparatus Co, soda water fountain. 575
Kohlbund, Mrs C, North Bergen—William Peter Brewing Co, ice box. 115
Konig, Fris, J City—William Peter Brewing Co, ice box. 120
Kuehne, A E, North Bergen—W Siebrecht, horse, wagon, harness. 500
Leery, Patrick, J City—G Dompierre, furniture. 274
Marher, W H, Hoboken—H Thoeser, furniture. 110
McCaffrey, Ed, Weehawken—William Peter Brewing Co, saloon fixtures. 500
Morrissey, John, J City—F Kimmerly, horses, trucks, harness. 500
Muller, Adolph, J City—William Peter Brewing Co, ice box. 147
Muller, Nicholas and Margaretha, Guttenberg—Margaret Meyer, furniture. 100
Municipal Statistics Co of New Jersey—C R Smith, books, abstracts, records, &c, now at Rooms 15 and 16, No 55 Liberty st, New York. 45,000
Murphy, W J, Union—William Peter Brewing Co, saloon fixtures. 704
Niehaus, C F—William Peter Brewing Co, saloon fixtures. 385
Paupon, Geo, Union—Caroline G Schmidt, undertaking business. 1,000
Racioppi, Frank, Hoboken—Lembeck & Betz Eagle Brewing Co, saloon. 500
Rizzo, Michael, Hoboken—Lembeck & Betz Eagle Brewing Co, saloon. 250
Ross, Michael, Hoboken—Bernheimer & Schmidt, saloon and lease. 500
Scott, J J, J City—William Peter Brewing Co, ice box. 140
Simon, Will, West Hoboken—Mary Kuehler, silk business and machinery. 200
Smith, John, Passaic—P Hauck, saloon. 700
Travis, James, J City—Lembeck & Betz Eagle Brewing Co, saloon. 300
Tully, James and Fanny, J City—Beadleston & Woerz, saloon. 845
Verrander, Louis, and Domenico Recchi, West Hoboken—William Peter Brewing Co, saloon fixtures. 450
Walton, James, J City—R A Washburn, horses, wagon, harness. 537
Wenz, Daniel, J City—F Niestermann, horses, wagons, trucks. 3,600
Westling, Richard, J City—F J Kastner, saloon and dining-room. 300

BILL OF SALE.

Dreyer, Ellen, J City—J Wallis, saloon........ ....other val consid and nom

JUDGMENTS.

Groux, Arthur, Philip Oesman and Theo Oesman—F Hall........................ 188
Grimm, Herman—G L Brownell 433
Lauster, Ed and Geo Schwoerer—G C Lizker.... 109
Lepanowich, Stephen—The William Peter Brew Co.............................. 394
Roth, John—E Ruhlmann & Co................ 327
Sullivan, Jesse—Wilkinson, Gaddis & Co........ 192
Telfer, James and J G Hutchinson—J Huggins & Bro................................ 87

MECHANIC'S LIEN.

Jones, Mary J and W H Jones, owners; W J Foote, builder; C H O'Neill, claimant, J City 338

BUILDING MATERIAL MARKET.

BRICKS.—In all essential features the market for Common Hards remains just about the same as for the past two or three weeks, and operators who attempt o review the situation do not seem able to demonstrate anything that is new or interesting. The majority of business continues to be done at from $5.00 per M downward, with a few choice cargoes as usual ranging up 12½@25c. per M more, and some of the specials at even a still greater fractional premium, but as these latter do not count in making up quotations when the market is in better general condition there is no reason why they should be run in now. The demand has been pretty good, covering actual consuming wants as well as investments to lay away at a cost that seems absolutely safe, but there was the usual plentiful supply with something to spare and an excellent average of quality under which buyers have retained the advantage as noted, and there does not appear to be a hope of any immediate change for the better. It was quite a relief to find dealers in Pales reporting a better business and firmer market, with sales of the best as high as $2.50 per M. The demand, however, was less pronounced at the close. So far as can be learned there is practically nothing new at primary points, work going along without interruption, and the product coming forward in search of a market with no clear idea current as to when operations will cease. There are quite a number of manufacturers enjoying quite a picnic in delivering brick under early season engagement at $6.00 per M, but when they hang around the village store and post-office and boast of the rate to their less fortunate neighbors they ought to tell the grounds upon which it is obtained. The customers to whom they deliver are naturally not over-well pleased, and some of them by delaying unloading and detaining boats have entertained a hope that it might induce the breaking of contracts, but manufacturers have too good a bargain to resort to that measure.

LATH.—Moderate arrivals have again been quickly snapped up, with most of the cargoes offering to arrive placed under engagement, and an outlet for more had they been offered. Naturally values ruled firm, and $2.25 per M may fairly be called an inside figure as there is no doubt receivers could have forced a much higher price if so disposed. Consumption continues good, the strike at St. Johns is not settled with, mills standing idle in consequence, and the competition from Northern stock does not materialize as some had feared. Some of the latter we know to have been sold, but not a sufficient quantity to be felt.

LIME.—Some moderate arrivals coastwise have come in and found ready custom and the same will apply to offerings from the interior, all commanding full rates. In fact, so far as can be ascertained upon this peculiar market, most conditions at the moment are healthful and cheerful, and receivers seem to think the market is all right.

LUMBER.—No important changes for better or for worse have developed on the local market since our last. Some dealers report a further slight gain in business, others a loss, showing that trade fluctuates to some extent, but on the whole the tendency is toward growth, and after a while the movement will be of a more general character. Selections are principally from standard goods and against early well-marked requirements, though now and then manufacturers invest to a moderate extent for stock. With the exception of coastwise supplies the tenders from first hands have continued full, and made in a manner calculated to keep dealers in a more or less easy frame of mind regarding chances for obtaining stock, though in very few cases do they appear to expect much, if any, easier terms. Indeed, quite a number are making contracts, as from time to time they find parcels to suit them, with deliveries to be made later on, and in that way business may be considered as gradually growing into larger proportions.

Eastern Spruce has retained a firm position up to the present writing and upon the same basis as before noted. The curtailment of production through the shutting down of mills, voluntary in some cases and forced in others by the labor strikes, insures light shipments for some time from some of the best localities, and buyers understanding that are better disposed to negotiate for supplies against well assured wants and it has increased the calls for specials. Naturally sellers are working advantages for all they may be worth, and as a rule expect to retain fair control of the market until fall. The very strength shown, however, will act as a stimulus for production and may eventually lead to a reaction. At about present prices and ruling freight charges manufacturers can do well enough, and the continuation of talk about the much lower level as compared with last year, when shippers almost had to buy a vessel to get a cargo forward, is absurd and deceives no one.

Piling is meeting with a fair demand, and has a pretty steady market throughout. Cargoes have been coming in much less freely, the consumption of supplies is in accord with expectations, and growing steadily, and there is an evident inclination to take a firmer view of valuations on all attractive goods.

Hemlock has been applied for to a moderate extent, mainly on a sort of special call, and the market fails to reach a point of real animation, to the evident disgust of some of the agents. On the whole, however, the position seems to be managed very well, the Pennsylvania manufacturers maintaining a steady attitude, and Northern supplies not offering to any noticeable extent. Better trade is expected as fall approaches, but with every probability that there will be stock enough available.

White Pine does not develop greatly improved conditions, and about the best that can be said of the market is to note a gain in business of moderate volume. None of the increase of demand is of a hurry character, but simply such as might naturally be expected on the attractions tendered by the traveling salesmen, who are so plentiful, and without obtaining really lower cost buyers manage to hold about former advantages. The export trade fails to offer encouragement for the finer qualities, but is taking a little of the coarser stuff all the while.

Yellow Pine has been called for on specials to some extent, but the demand still fails to broaden out, and the market as a whole is slow and hesitating. About former quotations are named, but buyers who apply for terms and seem to really want supplies are quite likely to obtain a little easing off from regular figures, on the quiet. The shutting down of mills at the South is an indication of the condition of trade, but the action must eventually strengthen the position.

Carolina Pine is meeting with a demand quite up to the ordinary relative proportion in the general movement and sustaining a steady position. Now and then someone talks about an advance, but that is not the idea of the principal operators who evidently see the impropriety of any such attempt for the present.

Hardwoods are getting a little more attention from the furniture men, but no great force or anxiety shown in demand and an absence of stimulus to values. Indeed, on the contrary, there are rumors of some cutting on both poplar and oak, and, while no one admits the soft impeachment, the manner of denial in some cases carries an impression that the story has some foundation. Agents are making some fair offerings, but the chances are against many commission lots, owing to the danger of being caught for demurrage charges against cars not unloaded within forty-eight hours after arrival.

GENERAL LUMBER NOTES.

GREAT BRITAIN.

The *Timber Trades Journal* gives reports of recent auction sales as follows:

LONDON.

Now came on again goods "without reserve." American walnut lumber, and bullet tree logs, the price for the last being from 2s. 1d. to 2s. 4d., followed by several parcels of American walnut logs, ex "divers ships," for absolute sale. For these there was good bidding, the price varying considerably up and down, from 1s. 6d. to 3s. 7d. per foot cube.

LIVERPOOL.

The auctioneer commenced the sale by offering several parcels of American black walnutwood, but the bidding for most of it was only languid. There was some competition for the shipment ex Mathew Bedlington, a fair parcel of New Orleans wood, and out of this fifty-eight logs were sold at prices ranging from 3s. 5d. to 5s. 3d. per foot, averaging 4s. 1¼d. per foot. Eleven logs ex Rossmore, from Baltimore, realized from 3s. 6d. to 4s. 3d. per foot, averaging 3s. 7¾d. per foot. A few logs of whitewood, fair quality, sold at from 1s. 10d. to 2s. per foot. There was no disposition to buy satin walnut.

GLASGOW.

At Dundee and Aberdeen advantage is being largely taken of the great cattle trade carried on there, from Canada, for the consignment of deals from Montreal by the steamers. Last season several lots were brought in by these steamers, and so suitable was it found that this year almost every steamer is taken advantage of, for the shipment of parcels of deals, and this medium is likely to become the chief one for the conveyance of this class of shipments; every advantage is derivable from the new method.

THE WEST.

Speaking of the business in cargo lots on Chicago market, the Northwestern *Lumberman* says:

The demand has been equal to the supply. The market is moving along easily this season, with prices steady and firm, there being a notable absence of excitement. The expectation on the part of the yard men that prices would drop about July 4 was not realized. The commission men now think that the pinch of the season has been passed. There is no crowding of piece stuff or medium and good grades. No. 1 lumber has been generally bought at the mills. The yards have scarcely begun in earnest to stock up with piece stuff. Should prices continue to hold firm, and there is no reason why they should not, they are likely to advance rather than recede. There is plenty of coarse inch, and such lumber sells slower than any other and at prices comparatively less than for the better classes of lumber. The urgent call is for piece stuff and inch lumber that sells at $13 a thousand and upwards, strips being in especial request.

Short piece stuff is firm at $10.25 a thousand, with an expectation on the part of the commission men that $10.50 will be realized for it later on. Slim jims are selling at $12.50 to $13, and long wide joists at $14 to $15. There is a good call for timbers both short and long.

At the yards the dealers are beginning to figure on the effect that hung-up logs will have on the market. The season is getting along toward the last half, and some of the mill managers are contemplating the probable necessity of shutting down their mills at an early day in the season. This is especially the case with reference to the Menominee region and the upper peninsula generally. The shortage, if there be any, is likely to affect the piece stuff supply, and that, as has been said, is not in excess. All that is available would be wanted to meet the ordinary demand.

The *Timberman* says:

Speaking of the present stocks of hardwoods in Chicago, one of the oldest dealers in the city said to the *Timberman* the other day that he thought most of the yards here and at other wholesale points were carrying more than an average stock, but that this was only the natural result of last season's scarcity. Dealers who found it almost impossible to secure dry stock a year ago, were evidently determined not to be caught in the same way again, and therefore bought quite heavily of shipping dry stock during the spring months, piling the same in their yards until it should become dry enough to place on the market. Manufacture was also greatly stimulated, especially in oak, by the scarcity of last year, and in the opinion of the dealer above quoted, unless there should speedily be a largely increased demand from the furniture trade, there will soon be a heavy surplus, with consequent lower prices.

With regard to the future outlook for hardwoods, opinions differ, but no one questions the fact of there being plenty of stock this fall. Evidence of this is already found in the manner shipments are made. A few months ago the manufacturer calmly sat back in his office chair, waiting for the buyer not only to come to him, but to come to his terms as well. Now the conditions are reversed, and dealers who have no buyers out claim to be receiving more lumber than they did a year ago, when they were hustling for lumber. And in many cases these shipments are made without a question as to price, nor is there any grumbling regarding "Chicago inspection." These shipments come from all sections, many from localities that ordinarily send very little lumber to this market. For instance one dealer was this week receiving considerable oak and whitewood from points in Ohio and Pennsylvania. This affords evidence that the eastern markets are at least fully as well supplied with stock as Chicago, even were this not indicated by correspondence from those markets. Whether or not this ample supply of stocks will seriously affect prices or not remains to be seen. There will certainly be a decline unless demand shows material increase, and regarding this one can only express an opinion. Quotations have not changed much as yet but prices are naturally somewhat weaker at the mills than they were. Wisconsin manufacturers being about the only ones who yet stand firm, the greater part of Wisconsin oak being in strong hands.

METALS.—COPPER—Ingot has found comparatively moderate and indifferent demand, and the tone of the market was dull throughout. Offerings have been ample and free in all ordinary forms, and the run of prices rather inclined in favor of buyers. On an average range of valuations we quote at 12¾@13c. for Lake, and 11¾@12¼c. for casting brands. Manufactured Copper meeting with a reasonable call and showing steady rates, but the market barren of particularly noteworthy features at the moment. We quote as follows: Sheet, not above 30x72 in., 16 oz. and over, 26c.; do, 14 to 16 oz., 23c.; do, 12 to 14 oz., 24c.; do, 10 to 12 oz., 26c.; do, 8 to 10 oz., 28c.; do under 8 oz., 30c. Sheets longer than 72 inches add 1c. for 12@14 oz., 2c. for 10@12 oz., and 3c. for 8@10 oz. Sheets, not above 36x96 in., 16 oz and over, 22c.; do, 14 to 16 oz, 24c.; do, 12 to 14 oz, 26c.; do, 10 to 12 oz, 30c.; do, 8 to 10 oz, 33c. Sheets longer than 96 inches 22c. for over 32 oz, and add 1c. for 16 to 32 oz.; 3c. 14 to 16 oz.; 5c. 12 to 14 oz, and 13c. for 8 to 10 oz. Sheets, not above 48x96 .32 to 64 oz, 22c.; do, 16 to 32 oz, 25c.; do, 14 to 16oz, [illegible] do, 12 to 14 oz, 29c.; do, 10 to 12 oz, 33c. Sheets wider than 48x96 and longer, 22@25c. for 32 to 64 oz. and over, 27@[illegible]c. for 16 to 32 oz, [illegible]c. for 14 to 16 oz and 34c. for 12 to 14 oz. All bath tub sheets, per lb., 16 oz, [illegible] 14 oz, 29c.; 12 oz, [illegible]; and 10 oz, 35c. Bolt copper ¾ inch diameter and over, 23c. Circles, 60 diameter and less, 3c. above price of sheets of same thickness; circles, 60 to 96 do do, 5c. do; circles, 96 do and over 6c. do. Segment and pattern sheets, 3c. above price of sheets required to cut them from. Cold or hard rolled copper, 1@2c. per lb. above the foregoing prices. Copper bottoms, 26@32c. per lb. IRON—Scotch Pig secures no regular or important attention and has a somewhat nominal market, though about former rates are as a rule quoted, and there is no stock here. We quote more or less nominally at $22.00@24.50 per ton, according to brand. American Pig meets with more or less demand, but only from regular sources, and the outlet is so overlapped by production as to steadily add to the accumulation. According to recently published data there are now in blast in this country 298 pig iron furnaces with a total weekly capacity of 171,000 tons. This indicates a heavier output than at any previous time this year, and an increase of over 59,700 tons per week over the output four months ago. On the first of July, 1890, the capacity was about 175,700 tons per week, or only 4,700 more than it is at the present time. Anthracite furnaces, it is shown, are turning out more iron now than they did a year ago, but coke and charcoal furnaces less. On p[illegible] the position is about steady for best makes and [illegible] on poor stock We quote at $17.00@18.00 per ton for No. 1 X foundry; $15.50@16.50 for No. 2 X do. and $14.00@15.00 for Gray Forge. Old material selling slowly and irregular, and there seems to be nothing in the market at the moment of a noteworthy character. We quote at about $20.50@21.50 for old rails; $20.00@21.00 for No. 1 wrought scrap; $17.00 @18.00 for cast scrap and $17.00@17.50 for car wheels. Manufactured Iron is getting some custom on contracts now and then, but the open market trade is slow and indifferent, with prices nominally unchanged. We quote Common Merchant Bar ordinary size at 2.00@2.10c. from store, and refined at 2.30@2.60c; Rods, round and square, 2.20@2.40c.; Bands, 2.40@2.60c.; Norway Nail Rods, 4@5c., and domestic sheet on the basis of 3.00@4.05c. for common Nos. 10@16. Other descriptions at corresponding prices, with 1-10c. less on large lots from cars. Steel rails have been held steadily at the combination price, and no intimations of "cutting" given. Demand, however, proves light and apparently is a little disappointing to some manufacturers. We quote standard sections $30 per ton at mill, with usual advance for delivery at tide water. Pig Lead has been very well held and offered with moderation, but did not find much more than the ordinary demand, and the market was complained of by sellers. We quote at [illegible] c. per lb. The manufactures of lead are quoted at 7c. for Pipe, 7¾c. for sheet, 15c. for Tin-lined Pipe, and 37½c. for Block Tin Pipe. Pig Tin meets with fair average jobbing demand, but as a rule the market lacked animation, and holders gained no advantage beyond such as could be extracted from the cable advices. We quote at about 20¼@20.30c. for round lots, and 20⅜@20½c. for jobbing parcels. Tin Plate attracts some attention when cheap lots can be picked up, but those are not very plenty, and business is moderate. Holders generally are looking for old rates on all grades. We quote prices, as follows: I. C. Charcoal, ½ cross assortment Melyn grade, $6.50@6.55, each additional X add $1.50; I. C. Charcoal, ½ cross assortment, Allaway grade, $5.90@6.00, each additional X add $1; Charcoal terne, M. F. grade, 14x20, $7.50@7.55; M. F. grade, 20x28, $15.50@15.55; Worcester, 14x20, $5.75@5.80; Worcester 20x28, $11.40@11.45; Dean grade, 14x20, $5.25@5.30; Dean grade, 20x28, $10.50@10.55; D. R. D. grade, 14x20, $4.85@4.90; D. R. D. grade, 20x28, $10.00@10.05; I. C. Coke, Penlan grade, $5.20@5.25; J. B. grade, 14x20, $5.35@5.40; I. C. Bessemer steel, squares, $5.75@5.80 basis; I. C. Siemens steel, squares, $5.85@6.00 basis. Spelter has, as a rule, sold slowly, but offerings somewhat scant and prices firm for all the more popular brands. We quote $5.05@5.15 for Common Western, according to brand.

The bulletin of the American Iron and Steel Association, published this week, contains the exact figures of the production of pig iron in the United States in the first half of 1891. The total production was 3,871,925 gross tons, against 4,560,513 gross tons in the first half of 1890, a decrease of 1,188,588 gross tons, or 26 per cent.

The decline in our production of pig iron in the first six months of 1891 affected the pig iron producing States very unequally. Some States actually increased their production in the first half of 1891 as compared with the first half of 1890. The States which increased their production were Massachusetts, Connecticut, Georgia, Texas, Michigan, and Colorado. Four of the States produced only charcoal pig iron.

NAILS.—A moderately active line of trade is reported, mostly in regular form, and the market presents no really new feature of a pronounced character. Supplies are liberal enough, with fair offerings as to quantity and assortment, and values sustained all around. Talk of reduced production does not materialize. We quote Cut at $1.65@1.75 per keg for car lots and $1.75@1.85 per keg for parcels from store, for iron, and add 5@10c. per keg for steel. Wire, $2.10@2.15 at mills, and 2.30@2.40 from store.

PAINTS, OILS, COLORS, ETC.—Demand has not expanded to any extent and generally the market is dull. Such goods as buyers think they can use to immediate advantage are taken, but beyond that there is a very general refusal to invest, and an attempt to realize or urge business just now must of necessity result in allowing concessions. Some hope had been entertained of a little steadier position and a possible advance in Mixed Paints, Oil Colors, etc., but the low price of Linseed Oil unquestionably tend to tip the tone in opposite directions, and buyers really have the greatest advantage. Block Chalk is now comparatively plenty and rates easy, and competition among manufacturers presents much strength on the market for Whiting. Zincs all around are firm and selling well. White Lead is finding an outlet about up to average for the season, and rules firm at the late advance. Association Corroders' rates stand as follows: Lead in oil in kegs and dry lead in kegs, in lots of less than 500 lbs., 7⅛c. net; in lots of 500 lbs to 5 tons at one purchase, 7c.; 5 tons to 12 tons, one purchase, 6⅞c.; 12 tons and over, one purchase, 6¾c.; dry white lead in bbls. ½c. per lb. less than price in kegs. Lead in oil 12½ lb. in tin pails, add 1c.; in 25 and 50 lb. tin pails, add ½c.; and in 1 to 5 lb. tin cans, assorted (100 lbs. in case) add 2½c. per lb. to keg price. Terms on lots on 500 lbs. and over, note or acceptance at sixty days, or 2½ per cent. discount will be allowed for cash paid within fifteen days of invoice date. To make either of the above required quantities any assortment of packages of white lead, red lead and litharge may be counted. The above quotations are free on board cars or boat at corroding point. Linseed Oil retains an unsettled position, though on the general range former figures are quoted. Reduced cost, however, it is expected will stimulate consumption and gradually infuse a stiffer body to the market as the surplus stock becomes cleared out. We quote at general range at 40½@44c. for Western, and 44@56c. for City. Spirits Turpentine meets with only a moderate uncertain demand, and the market rules tame. Stocks not excessive, but quite full enough for present wants. We quote at 36½@37½c. per gallon, according to quality, delivery, etc.

TAR AND PITCH.—Business moderately active, with no very new feature in the market at the moment. Supplies keep well together, and owners' ideas are steady enough, but buyers invest only as absolute necessity may arise. We quote Pitch at $1.70@1.75 per bbl.; Tar at $2.15@2.50, according to quantity, quality and delivery.

MISCELLANEOUS.

MISCELLANEOUS

BUILDING MATERIAL PRICES

LUMBER.

Appended quotations are based almost wholly upon prices obtained for goods from first hands. Yard rates necessarily range much higher owing to the expenses attending sorting out and grading cargo and even car lots, besides which must be added the cost of handling and carrying until consumers are ready to invest. Terms of sale also prove important factors and, altogether, it is impossible to give a line of retail quotations thoroughly reliable in character.

SPRUCE—Eastern—special cargoes delivered N. Y.	$16 00 @	17 00
Random cargoes, narrow	13 50 @	14 50
Random cargoes, wide	14 50 @	16 00
PILING—Eastern—cargo rates:		
Ranging 30@40 per cent 12 inch butt, 35 to 40 ft average length	4 @	—
Ranging 45@50 per cent 12 inch butt, 35 to 40 ft average length	4¼@	4½
Ranging 50@60 per cent One-half 12 inch butt, 38 to 40 ft average length	4¾@	5
Two-thirds 12 inch butt, 38 to 42 ft average length	5½@	6
Three-fourths 12 inch butt, 40 to 45 ft average length	5¾@	6
All 12 inch butt and up, 40 to 45 ft average length	6 @	6¼
Piece stick, 40 feet each	4 00 @	—
do. 45	6 00 @	—
do. 50	8 00 @	—
do. 55	12 00 @	—
Inch spars, per inch	20 @	22
Scaffolding poles, each	60 @	1 00
Clothes poles, 45 to 65 feet, each	3 00 @	6 00
HEMLOCK:		
Penn. joist	12 00 @	12 50
do. boards	13 00 @	13 50
do. timber, 20 ft and under	12 50 @	13 00
do. do. 22 to 24 ft.	13 00 @	13 50
do. do. 26 to 28 ft.	13 50 @	14 00
do. do. 30 to 32 ft.	14 00 @	15 50
do. do. 34 to 36 ft.	15 50 @	16 00
do. do. 38 to 40 ft.	16 50 @	17 50
WHITE PINE—Good uppers and 1 to 2 inch	40 00 @	4° 00
Uppers and select, 2½ to 4 inch	50 00 @	18 00
Shelving	26 00 @	31 0'
Pickings, 1 inch	33 00 @	15 00
Cutting-up, 1 inch	25 00 @	28 00
Bracket plank	30 00 @	35 00
Dressing-boards	18 00 @	22 00
Box, inch	13 50 @	14 0
Box, thick	14 50 @	15 50
West India shippers	16 00 @	19 00
Rio Janeiro do.	21 00 @	21 00
River Plate do.	29 00 @	30 00
Australia do.	25 00 @	30 00
YELLOW PINE—Random cargoes delivered N. Y.	18 00 @	21 00
Ordered cargoes	22 00 @	23 00
Flooring	21 00 @	22 00
Step plank	26 00 @	28 00
Common siding	13 00 @	14 00
Heart face boards	20 00 @	31 50
Car orders	21 00 @	23 00
At Atlantic ports, f. o. b.	12 50 @	15 00
At Gulf ports, f. o. b.	11 50 @	13 00
North Caroline pine timber	13 50 @	15 00
do. flooring 1 inch	16 00 @	22 00
do. do. 1¼	16 50 @	22 50
do. do. 1½@2 inch.	24 00 @	25 00
do Shipping culls or box	12 00 @	14 00
do Plain and mottled ½@1½ inch.	18 50 @	25 50
Ash, white	36 00 @	43 00
Elm	20 00 @	22 50
Oak, plain	37 00 @	41 00
Oak, quarter sawed	52 00 @	55 00
Oak, quarter sawed, extra thick	56 00 @	60 00
Redwood	45 00 @	52 50
Maple, clear	28 00 @	33 00
Chestnut, clear	33 00 @	35 50
Cypress, clear	30 00 @	32 50
Black Walnut, good to choice	130 00 @	140 00
Black Walnut, ordinary to fair	100 00 @	120 00
Black Walnut, ⅝	78 00 @	83 00
Black Walnut, selected and seasoned	150 00 @	155 00
Black Walnut counters	110 00 @	150 00
Black Walnut, culls	35 00 @	40 00
Black Walnut, rejects	50 00 @	53 00
Cherry, wide	110 00 @	115 00
Cherry, good	85 00 @	100 00
Cherry, ordinary	65 00 @	80 00
Whitewood, inch	30 50 @	32 50
Whitewood, ⅝ inch	24 50 @	26 00
Whitewood, 1¼ to 2½ inch	32 00 @	34 00
Shingles, Pine, 16 inch, extra	2 75 @	3 10
do 18 inch, extra	4 10 @	4 30
do 18 inch, clear butt	2 90 @	3 10
do 16 inch, stocks	4 50 @	4 60
do 18 inch, stocks	5 30 @	5 40
Shingles, Cypress, 6x20	8 00 @	10 00
do larger sizes	11 00 @	18 00
do sawed	6 00 @	9 00
Cedar—Medium to large	6½@	7½
do. —Extra large	7¾@	8
Mahogany—Small	6½@	7½
do —Medium	8 @	8½
do. —Large	9¼@	12
do. —Extra Large	12½@	14

REAL ESTATE RECORD AND BUILDERS' GUIDE.
ESTABLISHED MARCH 21st 1868.
DEVOTED TO REAL ESTATE, BUILDING ARCHITECTURE, HOUSEHOLD DECORATION, BUSINESS AND THEMES OF GENERAL INTEREST

PRICE, PER YEAR IN ADVANCE, SIX DOLLARS.

Published every Saturday.

TELEPHONE . . . . CORTLANDT 1370.

Communications should be addressed to

C. W. SWEET, 14 & 16 Vesey St.

J. T. LINDSEY, Business Manager.

VOL. XLVIII AUGUST 1, 1891. NO. 1,220

The publication offices of THE RECORD AND GUIDE *have been removed to Nos. 14 and 16 Vesey street, over The Mechanics' and Traders' Exchange, a few feet west of Broadway.*

THE bears had and seem to have control of the stock market and have worked it to their own interest—truly it would be strange if they worked it to any others' interest—with great vigor and success. All the old-time depressive measures have been resorted to, even to the most pernicious of all, the unfair handling of reputations. It is extraordinary that in the midst of success this most cowardly tactic cannot be left alone. However, it is useless to talk of it, because Wall street has no bowels, consequently no compassion. The course of the market has indicated that there were people hard pressed and battling against the tide, and a mere suspicion of trouble was sufficient excuse for dragging in some of the best names in the street, the better the name the more effective the rumor. With the declines seen in some special issues, that there were no failures is a matter for congratulation and induces the hope that we may still escape them, although the market does not evince very great strength. The buying yesterday following the raid on Burlington & Quincy, Rock Island and Atchison had a healthier appearance than any seen for some days and may augur a substantial rally. Recent advances have generally been on buying to cover shorts, and consequently the improvement occasioned thereby from time to time has been very short-lived indeed. This buying, however, appeared to come from organized support to the stocks attacked, and its influence may be beneficial for a little while. Outside conditions do not favor a permanent change in the course of prices. Loaners of money are refusing to make time contracts even on good collateral, and mortgage issues of standing and worth can only find a market by making concessions in prices. The management of Burlington & Quincy continue to discount the future in the declaration of the usual quarterly dividend of 1 per cent. only two days after publishing a statement showing a gain of net earnings made from economies in operation. At home and abroad there are fears of tight money, to realize which nothing could be more effective than an active and extensive buying movement, if in the present condition of affairs such a movement was possible. The best that can be hoped from the market is a maintenance of such strength as it has at present, though that is not what happens when there is a prospect of money becoming scarce and, as a consequence, commanding high rates.

THE distribution of the English railways in dividends almost without exception show for the first six months of this year a falling off from the rate prevalent in 1890. The Great Eastern has decreased from 2 to 1½, the London & Brighton from 4¼ to 3¼, the South Eastern from 3¼ to 2¼, and so on. This is not so much due to a decrease of traffic as to an increase of working expenses. It is also interesting to note that the scare which the English banks suffered last fall, and the consequent demand on the part of Mr. Goschen and the press that they should increase their cash reserves has been promptly responded to, although the percentage of cash liabilities is still far below that which is deemed necessary in this country. The large joint stock banks vary among themselves in a quite inexplicable way. The City bank is content with a reserve amounting to 7½ per cent of its liabilities, and the Alliance with one of 9.9 per cent, while the London and Westminster now holds as much as 16¼ per cent, and the Union maintains a proportion of upwards of 15 per cent. The returns of the Bank of England show that the bankers' balances with that institution have increased during the past year by from £8,000,000 or £9,000,000; and it is considered that this addition imposes a duty on the Bank of adding about 3½ millions to its own reserve. Hitherto it has been the custom to look upon a bank reserve of £10,000,000 as a minimum, but the standard must now be raised, and instead of £10,000,000, between £13,000,000 and $14,000,000 must now be regarded as a minimum. In Paris speculation is a little heavy. It is remarked that while the dividends of the great French railway companies remain stationary, or are decreasing, their working profits have continued to increase. During the last twenty-five years the net annual earnings of the Eastern Company have advanced from 45 million francs to 56 millions; the Lyons from 91 to 191 millions; the Southern from 21 to 43 millions; the Northern from 51 to 99 millions; the Orleans from 53 to 83 millions, and the Western from 35 to 63 millions. The interest on bonds have risen with the receipts, and in some outstripped them. In Berlin the market for funds has continued subject to adverse influences. Russian notes, loans and bonds are still falling. This slow and steady decline is chiefly due to harvest reports which represent Russia as in a state approaching famine. Some observers are of opinion that these reports, although correct in foundation, are exaggerated, but the public at large do not indorse this view, and think it safer to sell Russian securities. Dullness, rather than depression, pervades the rest of the market. The state of financial affairs in Berlin is very well indicated by the decrease in new companies started. In the first six months of 1891, eighty-six of them were founded with a capital of 45.60 million marks; during the same period of 1890 the number was 123, and the capital 134.95 million marks.

THE scandalous exposure of the Oregon Pacific Railroad has led to a committee being formed to take charge of the foreclosure and reorganization of the property. This function should properly belong to the Farmers' Loan and Trust Company, trustee under the mortgage; but the bondholders justly feel under the circumstances that it is safer to take the business in their own hands. The exhibition made in recent years of the pernicious effect of pitching great railroad trusts indiscriminately into Trust Companies finds a most striking example in this scandal. The bondholders through their committee object that the lien on the land grant has not been paid and that only about 140 miles of road are completed, the entire $15,000,000 of bonds, nevertheless, having been issued and being in the hands of the purchasers or pledged for loans. Mr. Herbert B. Turner, counsel for the Farmers' Loan and Trust Company, is reported to have made the following statement:

"The bond contains a provision that the bonds shall be issued not exceeding $25,000 per mile; it does not say of completed road. The mortgage states that the bonds are to be issued to the extent of $15,000,000—equal to $25,000 a mile for the full extent of the projected road. Now, the mortgage contains a provision that the trustees shall certify bonds and deliver them to the railroad company on receiving certain certificates from the Executive Committee that the bonds are needed for certain specified purposes. The Trust Company, on receiving such certificates, certified all the bonds from time to time and delivered them to the railroad company. The question is probably made as to the right of the railroad company to sell bonds at the rate of more than $25,000 per mile of finished road. I presume the railroad officials claim that the limit in the bond of $25,000 per mile did not mean completed road, because if it did then the provisions of the mortgage as to issuing bonds on these certificates would be meaningless, and that reading the mortgage and the bond together the only construction that would reconcile them both is that the bond means $25,000 a mile of projected railroad. As to the lands, the Trust Company holds that it has tendered the amount due on the lands, and that the lands, therefore, have been saved for the bondholders."

Is this not perfectly in the line with the performances of Trust Companies generally, as trustees? How much had their fee of one dollar a bond for certifying to do with their view of the construction of the terms of the bond? Mr. Turner and the Farmers' Loan and Trust Company knew perfectly well that every purchaser of the bonds, reading the provisions of the bond, expected that he was buying a security issued at the rate of $25,000 per mile of road; that is to say, of completed road; nobody invests in bonds on projected roads secured by mortgages on air. The evil of the matter is that in theory the Trust Company is employed as trustee to take care of the bondholder, but it receives the employment from the railroad company whom it is always, therefore, ready and anxious to oblige and meet in all questions of construction, etc., while as to its beneficiary, the bondholder, widow, orphan or what not, why—the deuce take them. If anybody can point to a Trust Company having ever taken any steps to protect bondholders, except perfunctorily or as an incident to make a show of activity so as to give color to a big claim for services, we would like to see it. The *Chronicle* says: "A gentleman representing some of the dissatisfied bondholders, said that 'out of the whole issue of $15,000,000 bonds, outstanding, from $9,000,000 to $10,000,000 worth have been sold, and between $7,000,000 and $8,000,000 cash has been realized. What has become of this cash? Five millions of the bonds have been pledged to secure a debt of about $3,000,000."

NINE times out of ten "public good" spells "private advantage." The talk of the newspapers at present about the sacred "freedom of the press" in connection with the recent prosecutions for publishing illegal particulars about the electrocutions at Auburn is well among the nine. Indeed the editorial indignation over a law which makes for decency and refinement is conspicuously hypocritical. The pretense made is that the columns of sickening details and flaring head-lines were published and in future similar cases should similarly be published solely because the public had and ever will have a serious scientific interest in the new method of capital punishment and is and will be anxious to guard against the inhuman cruelty of prison officials; the implication being that the only and the proper way to guard against said cruelty is to have one hundred or more reporters prying, dodging and hunting for the sensational outside the prison walls. The cant of all this is obvious enough. According to the newspapers even, the last executions were "successful;" there was no hitch; no cruelty; nothing that a society solicitous that criminals should have a comfortable ending to a murderous career could not learn from a short paragraph written strictly in accordance with the law. Was it scientific interest that necessitated the big head-lines and gave importance to the details of how the criminal was dressed; what he eat and said; whether he trembled upon seeing the "fatal chair," and spent his last night on earth in singing ribald songs or in saying his prayers? Away with all this nonsense! The editorial objection amounts just to this: the law stands in the way of the publication of a rich sensational story with plenty of "gore" in it, and as such stories sell papers and put money in publishers' pockets the law is an iniquitous and damnable infringement of the "public's rights."

THE application of the New York Central Railroad to have the Madison and 3d avenue bridges kept closed between the hours of 7 and 10 in the morning and 4 and 7 in the afternoon, so that its railroad bridge at 4th avenue could remain undisturbed during the same hours, indicates a laudable wish on the part of that corporation to bring its suburban traffic up to a higher standard of efficiency; but as this purpose can be accomplished only at the expense of interests that demand encouragement rather than repression, the Park Board will in all probability deny the petition. It is a pity that this corporation will not look squarely in the face the obstacle it is obliged to overcome in the Harlem River. The decision has been finally taken that this river is necessary to the water front of New York. Large sums have already been spent in endeavoring to make it navigable by vessels of heavy draught; and still more will be spent in the future. All this is being done on the supposition that the available water front around New York harbor is rapidly becoming occupied; and that this additional frontage is required for certain local purposes. It is surely sound policy on the part of the Central to recognize these facts. The company cannot retain the prevailing system of draw-bridges for many years more. As soon as the river commerce develops, the draws would practically have to be open perpetually. The quicker, then, some other method of getting over or under the Harlem is adopted, the better it will be for the Central and its passengers. A tunnel or a high bridge is doubtless a matter of large expense; but the postponement of the outlay does not decrease its amount. On the contrary, the longer the corporation waits before undertaking the comprehensive and permanent improvement needed, the more expensive that improvement will be. For while the river commerce is growing, the number of suburban trains will be growing also, and the local service will be continually hampered by the draws over the Harlem—a fact which cannot fail to have its effect on the settlements of the districts along the line of the roads. It would of course be far more economical for the Central, and somewhat helpful for its service, to fill in the Harlem; but the balance in favor of making it a waterway is so enormous that the public of the city will rightly insist on its being so improved. And this is quite compatible with an excellence of local service which would soon build up a valuable traffic—that is, if the Central will only meet the situation and take some more effective means of passing the river. Perhaps, after its usual fashion, it is waiting for some opportunity to distribute the expense. The Pennsylvania is wiser. It has boldly gone to work and is spending many millions in an improvement of its facilities through the New Jersey towns that will in time largely increase its revenue and build up the area tributary to its lines.

AFTER having been praised on all sides for their evidently thorough understanding of the conditions of the rapid transit problem in New York, and the efficient method in which they are meeting its exacting requirements, the Commissioners have during the past week come in for some little criticism. The engineering editors of some of the daily journals have settled that the best method of construction that the Commission can possibly adopt is that known as the Greathead system. Consequently when Commissioner Steinway announced that the Board had decided not to employ this system, these editors felt that there must be some mistake and they gave expression to a kind of wounded yet sceptical amazement that such a thing could be. Later Mr. Steinway denied that the Commission had any intention of leaving the Greathead system out of account, and the papers consequently uttered a sigh of heartfelt relief. The incident has a slightly ludicrous flavor to it. We are far from denying the advantages of the Greathead system of tunneling, but the assumption of its friends that it is the one system adapted to the transit needs of this city cannot be admitted for an instant. It has some manifest disadvantages—the elevator, for instance—and there is nothing impossible about the supposition that a tunnel might be constructed nearer the surface and still be rendered bearable by the use of the electric traction. This premature criticism and hasty decision of disputed points, with only half the evidence in, can do no good, and it is unfair to the Commission, which has so far proved itself to be worthy of every confidence. Unfair, also, in a slightly different way is the impatience displayed by the residents of the "North Side" because the Commission does not accelerate its speed in dealing with the difficult rapid transit problems north of the Harlem. This impatience, like the impatience which has been exhibited by all the residents of upper New York since the Commission began its work, is natural without being justifiable. Difficult as it has been to deal with the matter south of the Harlem, it will be still more difficult to provide for the sparsely settled region to the north. The lines of population have not as yet been determined; and the traffic will not be such as to pay immediately for a very costly route. The doubt whether capitalists will consider it profitable to supply the money for construction and operation is much stronger as regards these divisions of the system than any other. They will have to be built ahead of the growth in population, because they are necessary to that growth; consequently for some time they may have to be operated at such a loss that the company would need to be reimbursed by the more valuable franchises of the Island itself.

AN increased tendency towards intoxication among its population can, under no circumstances, be considered as an indication of a nation's growth in vitality and power; but it becomes particularly deplorable when the people so changing have hitherto been considered models of sobriety. The French peasant has long been a subject for much praise. His thriftiness, abstemiousness, his steadiness, and his ability to bear enormous burdens courageously, have been particularly remarked by English economists, and all these virtues have been laid to the beneficent system of peasant proprietorship, which makes every farm laborer a responsible capitalist, and gives him the best encouragement to save. But, according to facts and statistics now published, the French Hodge seems to be forsaking the old narrow path and treading on the treacherous roads of sensual indulgence. Every one who has lived in a French city knows that the citizens thereof are very much given to the comsumption of the strongest spirits—this being true not only of the middle class citizens, but of the common laborers. That the peasantry would follow suit has always been a cause for apprehension. These apprehensions have been realized. The craving for eau-de-vie is spreading into every hamlet of France. In the villages, says one writer, the women are obliged like the wives of the working men in the cities to hang about the public houses on pay-days in order to fight for their children's bread with their besotted husbands. Of old the peasant only regaled himself with a stoup of liquor on high days and holidays; but now he treats not only himself but his friends and acquaintances every day in the week. What is worse, the wives of married peasants frequently imitate the bad habits of their husbands, and the whole family goes off regularly into stupefaction. Being very cheap the stuff that is drunk is of course noxious and deleterious to the last degree. What may be the cause of this change from habits of sobriety to those of intemperance we do not learn; but it is reasonable to suppose that the immense burdens that the peasantry have to bear are responsible for it. Individuals may by continued indulgence in liquor cultivate a taste for spirits which is simply a matter of habit, but classes of people are not driven to intemperance from custom. When such a phenomenon arises it means that the people are drinking to stupefy and deaden their senses, to get rid of themselves and their woes. So it is in Russia at the present time, where intoxication is more general, more continuous and more brutal than in any European nation. And so it probably is in France, where the peasantry are groaning under an enormous load of taxation. The consumption of spirits is increasing all over the world, but in this country it is not increasing any more rapidly than the population. But the demand for beer is growing at a wonderful rate. Americans are somewhat frivolous in their drinks as in all their amusements.

THE London County Council apparently feels none of the indisposition to assume new responsibilities to the public which we find among our local authorities in New York. It has been doing its best to obtain control of the water supply of London, and is considering the purchase of the franchise of the gas companies. Undaunted by the magnitude of these undertakings, the same body is now preparing to buy its share of the transit service of the city,

In 1870 Parliament passed a bill requiring the tramway companies to sell their franchises to the local authorities, if the latter so desired, after the expiration of twenty-one years of operation. Under the terms of this act the County Council will be able to purchase, after August 11th next, all the tramway systems which were laid down in 1870. Every disposition exists, apparently, to take advantage of the provisions of this measure, and in this the local authorities are supported by the public press. The authorities have no intention of working the tramways themselves; they are expressly debarred from so doing by the terms of the act in question; but the duty of the councillors to their constituents and to the traveling public demands (so it is held) the exercise of their power of purchase. The franchise can then be leased to a company under stipulations that will cheapen the service. The task will be complicated and difficult, for two reasons. The local authorities have the power to purchase only such tramways as have been constructed twenty-one years. Many of the companies which were in existence previous to 1870 have since made many additions to their systems. In the second place, there is some doubt as to the legal method of estimating the value of the tramways to be purchased, the wording of the statute being far from explicit. The interesting aspect of the whole matter is, however, the unanimity of opinion as to the desirability of the County Council making the purchase, and so securing to the public what increase ensued in the value of the franchise. We do a great deal of talking about rapid transit in New York, but if any proposition is advanced for the municipality to own a system of transit, it is stigmatized by officials and editors as "undemocratic," a practice which unnecessarily and foolishly makes Democracy inseparable from the exploitation of the public by private companies. We are shortly about to sell in this city a franchise that ultimately will be one of the most valuable in the world. The terms under which the Commissioners will offer have not as yet been divulged, even if they have been decided upon; but for all it is said about the matter this valuable function may be sold in perpetuity without any voice being raised in very loud and strenuous objection.

Fashions in Finance—and Real Estate.

WE spoke last week in these columns about "Fashions in Finance," pointing out the tendency which speculation has to perambulate among the many different securities and commodities that are within easy touch for the investing public. At one time it may be railroad bonds and shares that are the fashion, "industrials" at another, or it may be petroleum certificates or mining shares. Western mortgages were the "rage" for a time, and real estate for some years past has held a prominent place in public favor.

This fact of the flow and ebb of speculation from point to point raises an important question for our readers, who are particularly interested in discerning how far it may reasonably be expected that just as investment drifted from the Stock Exchange, forsook the giddy allurement of pipe-line certificates and the plump percentages of Western mortgages so will the recent fat years in real estate be followed by lean ones. Indeed there are not a few who believe that already we are on the verge of meagre and unsatisfactory times.

This question cannot be answered fully in a word. Confining our remarks to New York City we find that there has been this year a marked but not a remarkable decline in activity in real estate, compared with either 1890 or 1889, a decline attended by characteristics which enforce the admission that in the present outlook there is nothing that confidently promises immediately brisker times. Now, no doubt some part of the enormous transactions in real estate of the past few years has been the result of one of those "fashions in finance" of which we have spoken. Speculation has been allured by ample promises, kept abundantly at first. But the fulfillment of each brought disappointment for others nearer, so that to-day in certain sections of the city speculation has been much overdone. Confidence and capital have been sown broadcast in an imprudent and not seldom a reckless manner, and as fortunes cannot be grown like crops it would not be at all wonderful if some of the speculative ventures now at sea turn out to be unprofitable, or suffer disaster on a "reef of visionary gold," and if, consequently, the financial fashion which hitherto has favored real estate should depart for a time for the Stock Exchange again, or for the oil market, the far West, or for any other promising field.

In what condition will this departure leave us? In the stagnant state of the Stock Exchange; or the hopeless condition of the oil market? With many, fear hovers about this point; but it ought to be obvious that nothing of the kind is to be anticipated, for real estate is differently circumstanced from Stock Exchange and other similar securities. In the first place, speculation pure and simple—and that it is that follows most closely the "financial fashions"—has nothing like the same predominance in real estate that it has in dealings on the Stock Exchange. There is as constant a demand, apart from all speculation, for realty as for butcher's meat; because every year there is a certain increase in population which holds pretty steady despite the temporary ups and downs of business; and this additional population has not only to be housed, but provided for in factories, stores, municipal buildings and school houses. The builder comes as surely as the doctor in the increment of population. And more than speculation, more than financial fashion, it is this increment which is the foundation of activity in real estate. About the constancy of this increment in the metropolis no one is likely to have doubts.

There is still another fact to be considered: New York is now a pretty big place, too big to move like a wheel—all together. Of late years we have seen that activity in one section does not mean activity in all other sections, nor, conversely, that dullness affects all parts at the same time. For a few years it is the East Side that is "booming;" property there is in demand, prices advance, building becomes active. By the time the "movement" has spent itself another has commenced, it may be on the West Side, in Harlem, "down town" among the old office buildings, or it may be a new section is developed, as in the case of the Mercantile District. There is always some section of the city that offers opportunities to the wide-awake speculator, whose footsteps are soon followed by the "crowd." New York is really a congeries of cities, and nothing short of a serious national depression can so affect real estate that there will be dead dull times in every part. Relatively dull times we may have, but there will always be a steady demand for real estate such as does not obtain with any other commodity that financial fashion has so far taken hold of.

Our Newspapers.

A CORRESPONDENT asks us whether we are not greatly mistaken in saying that the first page of one of the leading New York dailies was recently given up almost entirely to news about criminal and quasi-criminal events. He affirms that he reads the papers a great deal, but has not observed any such dire condition of affairs. Well, our correspondent cannot be very observant, or his memory is at fault. Let him turn for example of the truth of what we said to the *Sun* of Monday last. The *Sun* surely is one of our "leading dailies." It is edited by a gentleman who holds a no insignificant place in American scholarship, and the paper lays some stress in a modest way upon the purity of the English printed in its columns and upon its circulation. Certainly, it is read daily by tens of thousands of our "best people." Let us see what news this editor thinks his readers are interested in; and for the purpose of discovery we will glance at the head lines on the first page of Monday's issue.

The first column and a-half is given to "Cable news from Germany—Debts of the Emperor William and his son—Frederick was generous, but William II. was extravagant—Both in the hands of usurers—Herr Paasch to be sent to an asylum—Rupture in the Social Democratic Party—In Heligoland—Abs the champion wrestler—Krautz wants to be the official executioner again." Abs and Krautz! What would an intelligent nation do if it did not have the cable to keep it informed about these worthies? The head lines on the remainder of the second column read: "Fifty excursionists killed—The talk of Paris—Anarchists begin a fight;" "Special favors to the Harrison family." The third column is devoted to: "Death faced him each way—Lawyer Newcombe chose to risk it by the surgeon's knife," wherein an operation for cancer in the stomach is minutely described. In a measure, the reader is prepared for the fourth column, the head lines on which are: "Reuter forgot to—He won't say what—his dog bit into a cop's check trousers"—"Dead in an empty coal-bin—Suicide because he put the savings of a life time in a poor business"—"Who killed Frankeloso—Suspicions that Cotta did it, and intended to elope with his victim's wife"—"Shot himself in the breast"—"Identified by Mrs. Brigham"—"Upset of a stolen boat"—"Almost killed by a mastiff." Ghastlier yet is the fifth column, which begins with big letters: "He hacked them to death." After this come: "She said she shot him; a wife's attempt to shield her husband, who killed a man over five cents"—"An Ocean Grove arrest"—"Lost his life in a land slide"—"A suicide's body identified"—and "Died on a load of hay." Following this mass of bloody, or perhaps we should say putrid news, what is given on the sixth column is an unsatisfactory descent toward decency: "A sailing party missing"—"Col. Conger at Bar Harbor"—"Blaine holds the reins; the Secretary takes a drive of an hour over the country roads"—"Miss Warden's assassin"—"Earthquake in Indiana"—"He snapped the unloaded gun"—"Strikers threaten"—"Mr. Gould at church in the Rockies"—"President Harrison's callers." The news on the seventh and last columns is more of a family character—reflections as it were from the fireside: "Mrs. Mackey has left him; but the Rev. Joseph Mackey says he has done no wrong"—"Eloped on a sloop; it was the plan of the young woman, who thought it would be inexpensive"—"A steeple struck during church service"—"Inspector Cohen in hard luck."

Now, we would like the *Sun* or our correspondent to inform us what there is in this mass of gutter news and trivial personalities worth one second's attention of intelligent, not to speak of educated, refined and cultured people. What purpose can it be printed for except to pander to a coarse and brutal appetite for the lowest and dirtiest facts of social life. One can understand costermongers reading the stuff—and the decent part of society instantly organizing literary Sanitary and Disinfecting Societies to save the intellectual lives of the unfortunates and guard against the creation of a pestiferous epidemic—but it is very difficult to apprehend the fact that tens of thousands of respectable people in an important community rub such filth into their lives daily. It is as hard to comprehend as the custom that certain savage peoples have of rubbing their bodies with asafetida and regarding themselves as deliciously perfumed.

At least three-fourths of the intellectual life of this nation centers in the newspapers. Outside of business what is it the majority of people talk of? Newspaper facts. What are the opinions that nine-tenths of the public bandy about? Newspaper opinions. Indeed, our public school system is a preparation not for a sympathetic interest in the literature of the world, the science of the time, the large public questions of the day, for a keen appreciation of the warmth and light of life, but for newspaper reading. There may be books in the farm house, a few of which may have been read once, and some may be glanced at occasionally; but they are for the greater part as unproductive as unsown seed; it is the newspapers filled with the details of the crimes and nastiness of the cities and the petty politics and gossip of the county that is persistently read, and read with avidity and an active spirit. In the city home, the book-shelf or the library has a place it is true, but it is even seldomer turned to than the "show" furniture. Night and morning the newspapers are read by nearly every inmate in the house from the mistress to the cook, each perusing a journal after its kind, but all these journals alike are replete with nastiness and triviality. On the railroad car, the street car, the ferry, night and morning, morning and night, every man's face is hidden behind a newspaper. So much reading never has been done before under the sun—and all of it is of the same general, despicable, unhealthy character. Is there not reason for deploring this "newspaper curse." Is not the "newspaper" responsible for the fact that we are to-day, speaking in the highest sense of the word, the least educated of the advanced nations? It is not the matter of mere literacy we have in mind. Facility in reading and writing is general enough amongst us; but what do we read and write? What are we interested in? The newspapers answer the question. No nation on earth would tolerate the stuff.

Investments—Good and Bad.

CROPS AND STOCKS.—Wall street has been heedless of the good old saw, "Don't count your chickens before they are hatched." Before the corn was in the ground estimates were made of the crop and of its effect on stocks. Too little heed was given to the time which must elapse before the market could benefit from the crops which are now being harvested, and what responsibilities lay on the financial world in the interim. This has generally been the case in years of large crops. Those who remember what took place in 1879 need not be reminded of this. The largest crops of wheat and corn in ten years were harvested. But stock exchange prices were depressed until everything looked dirt cheap and it was not until late in the year, and then under the success which attended the resumption of specie payments, that the substantial advance came. Money flowed into New York and the advance was remarkably rapid. This movement continued through 1880 and culminated in the summer of 1881. There was a larger crop in 1880 than in 1879, the success of the one year having led to an enlargement of the agricultural industry. In 1881 the yield on a still more largely increased acreage was much less, and bad times followed for the farmer. Again in 1884 the cereal crop was very large. That year brought disaster in commercial circles, involving panic, failures and shameful exposures, which were followed by heavy declines in values. Again was one good year of agricultural prosperity followed by another, and in 1885 people once more awoke to the fact that railroad securities had a higher value than was indicated by the quotations, and under the incentive of the West Shore settlement there was quick and substantial advance. Lake Shore, which was 50¾ just before the Trunk Line settlement, moved up to 75 without a break; Lackawanna sold at about 88 and was 129⅝ in the following December. There were similar advances all through the list. This movement also continued about a year and a-half, reaching its limit in December, 1886. But while the signal for buying stocks came from some event more particularly affecting them, the beginning of the bull movement in each case was the quiet absorption of bonds which had been going on for some time before. Those sanguine people who have predicted a bull movement this summer on the strength of a large crop have overlooked the process by which the stock market receives its benefit from the crops and the time it takes in its operation. Consequently, instead of now seeing prices advance, they see them decline because of the heavy calls on this centre for means with which to move the grain to the point where it can be turned into money. How heavy these calls are may be seen if any one will pause for a moment and think of it. Suppose New York had been called upon to loan only one-tenth of a cent per bushel to move the crop of wheat, corn and oats of last year, to say nothing of rye, barley and buckwheat, amounting to many millions of bushels, the amount of that loan would be $2,412,853. Of course the actual amount per bushel was very much more and spread over the long period the grain was moving. This is sufficient to show how heavy the demands from the interior may become. The farmer must realize on his product before he can purchase in other directions; the merchant must be prepared to supply the farmer when he is ready to make his purchases, and both are using their credit in the centres of money before in order to be able to trade. Meantime the money centres suffer more or less and can only recover their advances by the operation of trade when the merchant has redeemed the credit extended to him to enable him to meet the purchasing requirements of the farmer. All this takes time, and it is not to be wondered at if negotiable securities decline in selling if not in intrinsic value, though this is the case also sometimes, and aggravates the hardness of the times in the money market. Fortunately, business on the Stock Exchange has been very dull this year. Had an advance been possible and brought about, the decline recently seen would have been much more rapid and severe. As it is, declines of from seven points down to one point in the active list has occupied nearly three weeks, and the heaviest declines have been due as much to special causes as to the general one of the need of money. Louisville & Nashville, for instance, owes a large part of its decline to an untimely increase of its capital, and Burlington & Quincy owes it to its financial condition. The causes of the decline in Richmond Terminal securities have already been noticed. It is also unnecessary to again refer to the serious consequences of the gold exportations of this year. That is another matter that has been treated too lightly, though the published opinions of Secretary Forster and the President of the Chemical National Bank are opening the eyes of the public to the fact that there is also in this case a lengthy process to be undergone before an adequately compensating import movement can set in. Should money command high rates here this fall gold will come to avail itself of those rates, but only in amounts sufficient to relieve a stringency, but not sufficient to remove it. That was seen last year, when in the period of tight money only a part of the gold which had been shipped to Europe in the summer returned in the fall to lighten the pressure on the money market. It is as certain as the recurrence of day and night that an immense amount of wealth coming out of the ground will in due time raise the value of investment and speculative issues, but it will take its own time, and meanwhile the holder of those issues must be patient if he can.

NEW LOANS.—The public is offered $2,000,000 of $2,500,000 of the stock of the Enterprise Mining Company. The owners of this stock are willing that the public shall have it, although it is said to represent property, which they already have the means to develop, capable of producing $1,000,000 profit in the first year of operation. A rare piece of disinterestedness. The owners seem really anxious to confer this valuable privilege on the public, as witness the advance articles we noticed a fortnight ago extolling the wonderful results of mining operations. An offer is also announced of $500,000 of the preferred stock of the Demorest Publishing and Sewing Machine Company entitled to 8 per cent. preferential accumulative dividends. The capital is represented by $500,000 common stock in addition to the preferred stock offered to the public. The property represented, outside of good-will, etc., is valued at about $930,000. Of the $500,000 the public is expected to subscribe, $100,000 is to be set aside as a working capital. Sixteen months' profits ending April 30th, 1891, amounted to $104,782.43, according to an accountant's certificate, and the company is said to be now earning at the rate of $100,000 per annum. Briefly the vendors take $400,000 cash and $500,000 common stock for their business and property and the subscribers to the preferred stock have first lien on the property and future profits. This may be a good opportunity for the subscribers; it certainly is a good arrangement for the vendors. It would have been well had the accountant's examination for profits gone farther back.

RICHMOND TERMINAL.—It is to be regretted that the management of Richmond Terminal has failed to make any reassuring statement to its security-holders. If the property is in the satisfactory condition its stock and bondholders are apparently wanted to believe, judging from the vague and general remarks that have been obtained and are put forward by newspapers friendly to the management, it would be no difficult task to make the assurance positive from figures and resources at the command of the management. In default of a statement embodying these and in the face of the decline of its issues, the inference is naturally drawn that the company is not in a healthy condition.

The New Appraiser's Stores Site.

The condemnation proceedings undertaken by the Treasury Department against Patrick J. Roon and Ida L. Pryor, owners of four lots on the block bounded by Barrow, Washington, Christopher and Greenwich streets, the site selected for the new appraiser's stores, were continued before Judge Wallace in the United States Circuit Court during the week. The testimony produced by the defendants is corroborative of the facts reported in THE RECORD AND GUIDE some time ago. This evidence shows that John Lindley, a lawyer, made a contract with the Treasury Department to convey to the Government the block above named for $500,000, although at the time he owned none of the land. He succeeded in purchasing two lots at $45,000, and these he conveyed to the Government for $99,000. Trinity Church Corporation also conveyed sixteen lots for about $321,000, leaving a balance of $80,000 for the four lots owned by Mr. Roon and Mrs. Pryor. These owners refused to convey the property for the sum stated, alleging that their proportion of the money remaining out of the $500,000, after Trinity Church had been paid, should be equal to Lindley's. The latter maintains that under his contract with the Government he had the right to convey only a portion of the property, receiving therefor an amount in proportion to the whole area of the site for which the Government was to pay $500,000. Mr. Lindley notified the Treasury Department before January 1, 1891, according to contract, that Mr. Roon and Mrs. Pryor would not convey their land, and the present suit is the result. Judge Wallace has not yet rendered his decision in the case.

Readers of THE RECORD AND GUIDE *may subscribe to the new illustrated quarterly magazine,* THE ARCHITECTURAL RECORD, *by sending their names and addresses to the office of publication, Nos. 14-16 Vesey street. The annual subscription is $1.*

Rapid Transit Problems.

A partial exposition of the lines upon which the Rapid Transit Commission is working, having drawn down upon it a blast of criticism from the *Times* and *Evening Post*, the commissioners have announced their determination to talk no more to reporters until their plans are completed and prepared for presentation to the public judgment with all the details sufficiently explained to afford an intelligent conception of the whole scheme. President S. William Steinway was reported as saying that the so-called Greathead system of construction would not be used, and that the commissioners had determined to have the tunnels constructed as near to the surface of the street as possible. In the accompanying description of the plan of construction it was given out that it would be necessary to open the street surface.

An effort to correct the first interview has only resulted in an apparently worse misunderstanding of the facts. Mr. Frank J. Sprague, having misconstrued Mr. Steinway's remarks, wrote that gentleman a letter, in which he entered a protest against "the summary disposal of the claims made for the Greathead system, and the shutting out from bidding on construction this action would necessitate." He contended that with the Greathead shield the lower Broadway tunnel could be more rapidly, cheaply and safely constructed than in any other way; that the resulting tunnel would be stronger and less disturbing to existing foundations and pipe systems, and that the work could be carried on without disturbance of the streets. He suggested that opportunity be given for the submission of alternative plans before the commission submitted its plans to the common council for approval, and in further support of his claims for the Greathead system, stated that it had been employed in the construction of the St. Clair River tunnel, and that its use on the Hudson River tunnel work had been made a prerequisite to the subscription of capital by British lenders.

It appears upon investigation that the "Greathead system" has in reality never been employed on any of the works in this country. In fact there is an entirely erroneous impression as to what the Greathead system consists of. On the St. Clair River tunnel a shield was used, but it bore no greater resemblance to the Greathead shield than it did to any one of a dozen shields which had been used in the construction of great public works in various parts of the world since its invention away back in the 30's. Before the St. Clair tunnel was built a shield was used in Broadway by the Beach Pneumatic Tube Company for the construction of the short section of tunnel built by it just opposite the City Hall, and which is there yet. On the Hudson River tunnel work a shield designed by Sir Samuel Baker, which was a substantial modification of Mr. Greathead's shield, was used, and the requirement of the British money-lenders was not that the Greathead shield should be employed, as stated by Mr. Sprague, but was that the work should be done under the supervision of Sir Samuel Baker and his associate.

The only exclusive features of the "Greathead system," and the features upon which the Greathead Subway and Tunnel Company has been organized to exploit, are the patented devices for grouting and for excavating loose or saturated headings by a flushing machine. The grouting machine was experimented with on the Hudson River Tunnel and every effort was made that could be made to have it perform the work for which it was invented, but it proved an absolute failure and had to be abandoned. The loose silt through which the tunnel is being constructed flowed in upon the tunnel so quickly after the shield had been set forward that the cement merely mixed with it as it would with so much semi-liquid mud. The flushing machine there was no use for, and it has never been tried. The interest of the owners of the Greathead patents in the Broadway Rapid Transit line is to have a deep tunnel system of construction adopted so that the methods they pretend to have patented would be practically indispensable and they could command a royalty for their use if they did not actually obtain the contracts for the construction of the road. The public may undoubtedly expect to hear a great deal about the danger to the foundations of Broadway property from any other method of construction except the "Greathead system."

As has already been stated in the columns of THE RECORD AND GUIDE, the Rapid Transit Commission is busily engaged in an effort to ascertain the best possible system of construction for all the projected lines; it has under consideration two plans of construction, one providing for a tunnel down only deep enough to escape contact with the sub-surface pipes; but so wide as to take in the entire roadway, and in some places a little more, so as to provide room for all four tracks on a single level. This tunnel would not require the tearing up of the pavement for its construction; but it would leave the old nuisance of tearing up the pavements for every little house connection or repair of pipes or mains to go on for time indefinite as it has in the past, a nuisance that is more expensive every year than the cost of everlastingly doing away with it.

The other plan contemplates two tunnels in Broadway, one on each side of the street close to the curb line and about 10 feet wide, containing each two tracks, one above the other. It contemplates also a subway in the middle of the street, between the two tunnels, into which all the pipes and mains in the street would be placed, and above it a solid roadway in which the only works of any kind would be the cable railroad conduit and cable; the rest of the roadway would rest on a massive iron roof and would be constructed of concrete for a foundation for a permanent granite pavement that would never thereafter be broken into or disturbed. For this method of construction the engineers of the commission have emphatically declared that it would not be necessary to disturb the pavement any more than was done in the construction of the electric subway; less than a quarter of the roadway would be open at any time and at no point along the line would it be open for any great length of time. If a perfect street, with a solid and permanent pavement, and a subway for the pipe systems that is always accessible without tearing up the pavement, is desirable and is ever to be had, it can never be had on any better terms than the present. The street is about to be torn up for repavement anyway, and with but a slight continuation of the necessary disorder the Rapid Transit Tunnel can be built on the plan above described. The commission has decided nothing in relation to these two plans as yet, but is still at work in consultation with its engineers upon their almost interminable details. As to either of them in any manner endangering the foundations of Broadway buildings, the assertion is ridiculed by everybody who knows anything about building. If the foundations of buildings were so easily unsettled there could be no excavation for foundations for new buildings, and yet almost every day one can see somewhere along Broadway the foundations of some big building laid bare to the lowest stone, and a deep trench dug alongside to take the foundation of some still larger structure.

If the commission shall ultimately decide in favor of the double-decked tunnel plan of construction, there will be ample time for criticism when the plans of the commission are officially made known. Criticism at that time will at least be enlightened by some knowledge of the facts.

North Side Street Improvements.

North Side Commissioner Heintz, on Thursday, opened and awarded contracts for three important public improvements, viz.: The regulating, grading, curbing, flagging and laying of crosswalks in East 169th street, between Franklin avenue and East 167th street.

The regulating, grading, building culverts and paving the roadway with granite blocks of East 138th street, from Railroad avenue East to Madison Avenue Bridge.

The regulating, grading and paving of Brook avenue, from a point 487 feet south of the southerly line of East 132d street to the southerly line of East 156th street. This last contract is expected to start an activity in building along the line of Brook avenue that will soon transform the appearance of the entire district. The time allowed for the completion of the contract is 150 days, or substantially five months, but the work is not expected to be finished much before another year, because the winter weather will make it necessary to suspend work for several months.

The people of the North Side are waiting with ill-concealed impatience for the action of the Board of Street Opening and Improvements to act upon several important items of street improvements. They want 3d avenue, above 175th street, sewered, a stretch of nearly two miles. The Suburban rapid transit road is now open and running to 177th street, and the company is ready to extend it up the avenue to the city line as rapidly as the avenue is improved, so that property-owners would be justified in proceeding with their building operations. The North Siders also want Brook avenue, from East 165th street to Wendover avenue, opened. The section to be opened is 4,700 feet long, and the cost is estimated at $85,000. It will be necessary to condemn a hundred lots for the roadway, all but four of which will have to be paid for at full value. The Board of Street Opening and Improvements is hesitating about this work because, although less than a mile in length in actual fact, it is held that it can only be considered in connection with that portion of the avenue south of 165th street, which has already been improved, and with which the avenue would be over a mile long, and would therefore impose upon the city the statutory requirement to pay for the entire work. But the Board of Street Opening and Improvement has in every instance of importance thus far held that it was not justified in standing in the way of the proper development of any section of the North Side for the mere sake of avoiding an obligation imposed by law, and especially in which the city would be gaining more than it would lose by the improvement. It is confidently expected therefore that when the Board reaches the decisive point that it will order the improvement.

The Westchester Electric Railway Company has been granted a franchise by the proper authorities to construct a Trolley road from the Hudson to the Sound, from Yonkers to New Rochelle. The Company promises to have the road completed and running by Jan. 1, 1893.

Notice to Property-Holders.

CITY OF NEW YORK, FINANCE DEPARTMENT,
COMPTROLLER'S OFFICE, July 29, 1891.

In pursuance of Section 997 of the "New York City Consolidation Act of 1882," the Comptroller gives notice to all persons, owners of property affected by the following assessment list, viz.:

ACQUIRING TITLE.

John st, from Brook to Eagle av.

—which were confirmed by the Supreme Court, July 20, 1891, and entered the 28th of July, 1891, in the Record of Titles and Assessments kept in the "Bureau for the Collection of Assessments and Arrears of Taxes and Assessments, and of Water Rents," that unless the amount assessed for benefit on any person or property shall be paid within sixty days after the date of said entry of the assessment, interest will be collected thereon at the rate of 7 per cent per annum, from July 28. Payments to be made to the Collector of Assessments and Clerk of Arrears, between 9 A. M. and 2 P. M.

Contractors' Notes.

Bids will be received at the Department of Public Works, until 12 M., Tuesday, Aug. 11, 1891: For flagging 8 feet wide and reflagging, curbing and recurbing the sidewalks on south side of Rivington street, from Mangin street to East River; on east side of Park avenue, between 117th and 118th streets, and north side of 117th street, east of Park avenue; on northwest and southwest corners of 122d street and Mount Morris avenue, and on both sides of 38th street, from 10th to 11th avenue; for flagging and reflagging, curbing and recurbing the sidewalks on block bounded by 75th and 76th streets, Columbus avenue and Central Park West; on north side of 103d street, from Central Park West to Columbus avenue, and on west side of Central Park West, from 103d to 104th street; on south side of 120th street, from Madison to Lenox avenue, and on south side of Rivington street, from Norfolk to Suffolk street; for regulating and grading 106th street, from the Boulevard to the Riverside Drive, and setting curbstones and flagging sidewalks a space 5 feet wide therein; 138th street, from 5th to Lenox avenue, and setting curbstones and flagging sidewalks therein, and 140th street, from Amsterdam to Convent avenue, and setting curbstones and flagging sidewalks therein; for flagging full width and reflagging, curbing and recurbing the sidewalks on 125th street, from 8th to Columbus avenue, and on north side of 125th street, west of 7th avenue, and on west side of 7th avenue, from 125th to 127th street, and on 126th street, west of 7th avenue.

Street Opening Proceedings.

Notice is given that application will be made on August 25th, at a Special Term of the Supreme Court, for the appointment of Commissioners of Estimate and Assessment in the matter of opening St. Nicholas terrace, from Academy place, near 129th street, to Convent avenue, opposite 140th street; also, on the same date, for the appointment of Commissioners of Estimate and Assessment in the matter of opening 179th street, between Amsterdam avenue and Kingsbridge road; 180th street, between Amsterdam avenue and Kingsbridge road; 182d street, between Amsterdam avenue and Kingsbridge road, all in the 12th Ward.

The Commissioners of Estimate and Assessment in the matter of opening Decatur avenue, from Brookline street to Mosholu Parkway, 24th Ward, give notice that they have completed their estimate and assessment, and that objections thereto in writing must be presented on or before September 12th; parties so objecting to be heard within ten week-days after that date at 3 P. M. each day. The abstracts, with damage and benefit maps, affidavits, etc., have been deposited with the Commissioner of Public Works, where they will remain until September 14th.

The Harlem River.

Editor RECORD AND GUIDE :

SIR—Congress should be requested to change the law in respect to Harlem River canal, which passes through the largest city in our country, and abate the growing nuisance of delays by the frequent opening of the many city drawbridges, to the great delay of the country's mails as well as of the laboring and business men.

Let the freight vessels yield to the greater interest of the whole community by having low smoke pipes to pass under bridges 25 feet above the water. Let masted sailing vessels land above or below the bridges, as the many have rights as well as the few.

A canal with drawbridges in the centre of any great city should be wholly controlled by the city and not by the national government. The city should offer to restore to the national government the small outlay already expended to remedy this great unforeseen mistake caused by the city's growth northward. Congress would, if petitioned by the people, remedy this great and growing blunder. GEO. W. DEAN.

Editor RECORD AND GUIDE :

One insuperable objection to the closing and filling in of the Harlem River appears to be overlooked, viz., its sanitary aspect. This river receives the natural drainage from many miles of land on its borders, and to disturb this would inevitably result in disease-producing miasma.

W. T. VAN ZANDT.

Newark News.

The following plans for new buildings were filed here this week : St. Augustine R. C. Church, 2-sty fr dwg, 12x17, 166 Sussex av; St. Augustine R. C. Church, 1-sty fr hall, 40x80, 55 and 57 Norfolk st; St. Augustine R. C. Church, 3-sty brk flat, 25x88, Clay st, near High st; Hemming & Thielman, 3-sty fr store and tenem't, 30x52, 69 Norfolk st; R. E. Cogan, 3-sty fr dwg, 36x46, 335 Clinton av; Mrs. W. H. Slingerland, 2-sty fr dwg, 22x31, 91 Astor st; J. H. Hesse, 3-sty brk store and dwg, 20x44, cor North 1st st and 7th av; Jaenceke-Ullman Printing Ink Co., two 1-sty brk factories, 70x246, Av B and Miller st; Joseph Hensler, 3-sty brk store and dwgs, 44x85, Ferry and Prospect sts; Harriet Pearson, 1-sty fr dwg, 18x22, 11 Coes pl; Mr. Gilbert, 2-sty fr dwg, 20x44, 57 Rutgers st; E. C. Burling, 2-sty fr dwg, 28x28, Riverside av; W. F. Fengar, 2-sty fr dwg, 20x26, 168 Johnston av; Winslow Zeliff, 2-sty fr store and dwg, 22x42, 350 Belleville av; Jacob Weber, Jr., 2-sty brk flat, 20x38, 13 Alyea st; Chas. Brown, 3-sty fr dwg, 22x52, 823 South Orange av; Thos. Varley, 2½-sty fr dwg, 20x40, 185 North 2d st; Frank Burkard, 1½-sty fr stable, 16x22, 38 Bremen st; W. T. Bishop, 2-sty fr dwg, 20x28, 823 Parker st; Sarah Sheldon, 3-sty fr dwg, 21x32, 276 Parker st; Nietzer & Charick, 2-sty fr shop, 16x24, 26 Kipp st; Mrs. Hill, 2-sty brk dwg, 18x20, 899 Broad st; Laycala Giovanni, 2-sty brk dwg, 13x39, rear 176 8th av; D. Kelly, 3-sty fr store and dwg, 38x39, Bergen and Warren; H. Bedell Crane, 3-sty fr dwg, 24x34, 205 Elwood av; H. Bergfels, 1½-sty fr stable, 20x24, 168 Elizabeth av; A. McKinzie, 3-sty fr flats, 25x63, 59 Sherman av; C. C. Streeter, 2-sty fr dwg, 17x25, Chester av; Emil Eyrich, 3-sty fr dwg, 59x48, 14th av; Geo. Scheider, 2-sty fr dwg, 22x36, Lentz av; William A. Pruden, 3-sty fr dwg, 43x44, 141 Clinton av; Thos. Manhaffy, 2-sty fr dwg, 22x39, 262 Summer av; R. Ledig, 2-sty fr shop, 25x50, 628 South 14th st; R. B Sutphen, 3-sty fr dwg, 22x32, 398 South 10th st; A. Zicore, 3-sty fr dwg, 23x46, 18th av; Cogswell, Boulter & Co., four 2-sty brk flats, 18x27, 99-103 8th av; H. B. Wills, 2-sty fr dwg, 22x35, 222 Lincoln av; Gottfried Krueger, 3-sty fr store and dwgs, 25x54, 44 4th st; J. G. Ehehalt, 2-sty fr dwg, 23x44, cor 12th st and 9th av.

In consequence of a judgment entered against him Philip Goerlitz, the builder, of No. 125 East 47th street, has placed his property in the hands of John Goerlitz and Anthony J. Dittmar, as trustees for his creditors. His embarrassment dates from a contract to build the flats at the corner of Lexington avenue and 48th street, and for which it is said he was not paid. The amount of Mr. Goerlitz's debts is about $50,000, while his trustees think his equity in the property which he owns amounts to $200,000. This property consists of Nos. 153 and 155 East 72d street, against which there are mortgages and claims of $102,500; the big flats at the corner of Grove and 4th streets, mortgaged for $100,000; No. 69 Grove street, mortgaged for $34,000; Nos. 67 Grove street and 70 Christopher street, mortgaged for $32,000; No. 139 Monroe street, mortgaged for $26,000; No. 125 East 47th street, mortgaged for $13,000; property on 29th street, between 1st and 2d avenues, mortgaged for $14,000, and on 48th street, between 1st avenue and Avenue A, mortgaged for $7,300.

The Opinions of Others.

Henry Lewis Morris said to a reporter: "There is one matter that I would like to see THE RECORD AND GUIDE take up, and that is the attempt which the New York Central is making to keep their bridge over the Harlem River closed during certain hours of the day. The excursion and business traffic on the Harlem River just now is quite extensive and it is growing larger every year, and yet the New York Central people want to close their bridge and blockade the river during what are some of the most important hours of the day. Such a step would injure property above the bridge more than most people appreciate and make the river practically useless for a large amount of business that is now transacted on it. I don't think that the New York Central Company has been entirely frank in the bridge matter. They have gone to work and made such expensive improvements both north and south of the Harlem that to build a tunnel, which is the best solution of the problem, is practically out of the question. In order to construct a tunnel now they would have to alter the grade of their road from about 82d street up, for the grade is now so steep at 99th street that trains have some difficulty in mounting it. For this reason a tunnel is not to be considered. A bridge is the only thing that is practical now, but that bridge can be built with a height of 24 feet above high tide, and the rise of the bridge, according to a report made some years ago by the Chief Engineer of the War Department, need not commence until just past 127th street. If they built such a structure 128th street would have to be closed, but that street is not used very much at Park avenue, and 129th street, too, would be useless except for pedestrians. In the case of the latter street there is at present a rise of about six feet in the bridge which crosses the railroad cut so that that street is only available for light traffic. To close it altogether for vehiclar traffic therefore would not be a very great hardship under the circumstances. These difficulties disposed of, nothing stands in the way of the railroad company erecting a bridge 24 feet above high tide, and I think that I can safely say that if they did build such a bridge property-owners along the Harlem would not object to having it closed during the busy hours of the day, for such a bridge would not interfere with the passage of any but very large craft, and only a small proportion of the business is done by these vessels with high spars and smoke stacks. My plan, you see, is an entirely different one from that suggested in the bill introduced into the Legislature last session, and which proposed to commence the necessary viaduct at 125th street. This bill did not pass, and now the Central Railroad Company wants to know what it is going to do. Build the bridge, but build it with as little cost and trouble to adjoining property-owners as possible, and this can be done by commencing at 127th street instead of 125th street."

In talking of the abuses in some of the city departments, Cyrille Carreau said: "It has always been my idea that the present undesirable state of affairs in our municipal departments will only be changed when the actual taxpayers, the real estate owners, take a hand in the government of the city. I do not mean by that to make them paid office-holders, we have too many of that class already, but rather a sort of board of supervisors, with sub-committees having charge of special departments. For instance, a thousand taxpayers might be chosen and these might be divided up into boards having special supervision over one department of the city government. It should be the duty of these boards to report on and correct abuses in the special branch of the municipal government that they had charge of. These taxpayers would be quite willing to give up a small part of their time each week to such good work, and the results would, I am sure, be truly astonishing. No more sinecures, no more politics, but business pure and simple in the municipal administration. The saving in the city expenses would probably be one-third, and taxpayers would at least be sure to receive the full value for their money, instead of paying it out to saloon-keepers or men with other private business who hold positions in the city departments and who give an hour or two's work for a day's pay."

D. Y. Swainson said : "I was glad to see THE RECORD AND GUIDE call attention to some of the abuses in the Water Department and I sincerely hope that the exposure will have the effect of bettering matters a little. The water bills due last April and which should have been paid by the tenants last May have not yet been received, and from many of those tenants who have left their last year houses nothing will be heard and the owners will have to stand the loss all because of delay and carelessness in the Water Department. Another trouble that we frequently have is with the meters. They get out of order and in one month register more water than has been used in the whole preceding year. When this occurs and you complain the Water Department "averages" your bill and it is reduced, but of course the result is not satisfactory, for they have no way of telling how much water you have used and the best result they can obtain is by a bad guess."

Personal.

Leonard Scott is at White Plains.

Geo. H. Henry's summer address is Seabright, N. J.

L. M. Thorn has left Southampton, L. I., where he has been staying for some time past, and has gone to Normandie-by-the-Sea, N. J.

Louis De Bebian is staying at Dobb's Ferry.

Thomas Crawford will read THE RECORD AND GUIDE at Mount Kisco, N. Y.

Theo. Dieterlen will spend a vacation in the Catskill Mountains.

John Noble Golding, late of Brown & Golding, made his debut as an auctioneer on Monday when he sold a couple of flats on 50th street, just west of Park avenue, in foreclosure proceedings. It was impossible to judge whether his voice was strong enough for ordinary occasions when six or seven other auctioneers are all going at the same time and the room itself is packed to its utmost capacity by a talking, jostling crowd; but the indications are that Mr. Golding will be able to hold his own in the new department of real estate he has just entered.

John Hauschild is at Saranac Lake, in the Adirondacks.

Special Notices.

A. W. McLaughlin & Co. have been instrumental in placing many of the largest and most important loans made during the past year on down-town business buildings, as well as on properties on the East and West Sides up town, and in all sections of New York City. This enterprising firm, by their integrity and careful and correct business methods, have won the confidence of both borrowers and lenders. Their business with the leading loaning institutions and capitalists is already extensive, and it is rapidly increasing.

F. E. Perkins & Bro., long known as dealers in scrap iron and metals, have secured a block bounded by West, Milton and Noble streets, in Brooklyn, where they propose to deal in second-hand building materials. T. C. Candee, Jr., who has been engaged in this business for over ten years in New York, will have charge of this branch and will give it his personal attention. Estimates for tearing down and removal of old buildings given and all work executed with safety and dispatch. With long experience in the business, ample means and facilities, they assure our patrons that all work will be executed to their satisfaction.

Real Estate Department.

The pronounced dullness of the real estate market this week comes as a corroboration of the view advanced in this column last week that the unexpected activity then reported was significant only of the clearing up of the season's work. Little or nothing has been done this week, although the brokers who are now in town have been busy enough. The fruitlessness of their work only goes to show the futility of attempting to bring negotiations to a close at the present time when none of the speculators and investors care to do anything unless they see large and immediate profits ahead of them. In the present market of high and steady prices such opportunities do not present themselves, and consequently the moneyed men are treating offers of property with comparative indifference, preferring to wait and see what the fall market has in store for the real estate world.

All the talk just now has to do with the fall prospects, and certainly the weight of opinion seems to be on the side of good prices and an active season. Already many of the best brokers have orders on hand for houses in good localities, which their clients are desirous of either renting or purchasing, but it is doubtful if any of these orders will be filled for a month or more. In the meantime it is a hopeful sign that the outside public, with whom the fate of the real estate market largely rests, so early evidences a desire to invest, and this fact will doubtless give an added tone and strength to negotiations in the coming fall.

Down-town investments and other classes of real estate in the more settled parts of the city are as firm as possible, with no indications at the present time that prices will weaken; and while in those districts where speculation is and has been general there is a tendency to weed out weak holders, and especially weak builders, there are no positive signs pointing to a decline in prices except in isolated cases. Exceptions to this statement may be found in various parts of the city, and they may be accounted for by the fact that values in the sections of the city referred to are not on a true level, and prices will continue to fall until the fault has been remedied. In the money market there is little new to report. Loans are not difficult to obtain, although large margins are demanded by the lenders.

THE SALES OF THE WEEK.

The auction room has been rather a deserted place during the past week. The list of sales, all of them of a legal character, were not attractive or numerous enough to draw the moneyed men from out of town, so that the competitors for property offered at auction have been generally the interested parties. As a consequence the selling price has been low—so low that plaintiffs in foreclosure suits have entered deficiency judgments against defendants of $15,000 and $20,000. It was with one such deficiency that the business of the week opened. The sale was of two flats on 50th street, west of Park avenue, upon which there was due $95,175. The plaintiffs purchased the property for $75,000. Another sale where a large deficiency occurred was that of four flats on 106th street, east of Madison avenue, sold for $61,500, although the amount due was nearly $77,000. Auctioneer John F. B. Smyth held a successful sale of what is technically known as a blind or interior lot on Wednesday. The sale was by order of the veteran speculator, Joseph I. West, acting as trustee, and the irregular lot, 58.2 feet at one end and 8.9 at the other, with an irregular depth of about 46.10 feet, is located on the block bounded by 29th and 30th streets, 7th and 8th avenues. It was sold after some competition to Francis E. Johnson, who, it is said, owns adjoining property, for $3,000.

WHAT IS TO BE OFFERED NEXT WEEK.

The announcements in the auction market for next week show very decidedly the business depression always noticeable in the month of August. The season has been gradually growing duller, and within the next two weeks or thereabouts the tide of business will reach its lowest ebb. After that the market will brighten up, and auction, as well as private, sales will become both more numerous and more important. Until the turn, however, nothing more than the commonplace run of foreclosure and partition sales, such as make up next week's list, can be expected.

On Wednesday, August 5th, Jere. Johnson, Jr., will sell 300 desirable lots on the celebrated Cowenhoven Farm, New Utrecht, situated on 54th, 55th, 56th, 57th, 58th, 59th and 60th streets and 16th and 17th avenues. The property is near Blythebourne, Bath Beach Junction and Lefferts Park, and opposite the lands of the West Brooklyn Improvement Company. A free excursion will be afforded on the Brooklyn, Bath Beach and West End Railroad. This line runs to the Union Depot, 36th street and 5th avenue, where it connects with the 5th avenue elevated. The lots may be paid for in monthly installments, or a discount will be allowed for all cash.

CONVEYANCES.

	1890. July 25 to 31 inc.	1891. July 24 to 30 inc.
Number	244	184
Amount involved	$3,956,367	$2,304,591
Number nominal	39	60
Number 23d and 24th Wards	36	33
Amount involved	$204,105	$244,995
Number nominal	15	12

MORTGAGES.

	1890. July 25 to 31 inc.	1891. July 24 to 30 inc.
Number	266	234
Amount involved	$3,013,587	$1,916,174
Number at 5 % or less	122	108
Amount involved	$1,387,722	$891,215
Number at less than 5 per cent	27	11
Amount involved	$652,500	$135,000
Number to Banks, Trust and Ins. Cos	27	25
Amount involved	$870,500	$288,000

PROJECTED BUILDINGS.

	1890. July 26 to Aug. 1 inc.	1891. July 25 to 31 inc.
Number of buildings	72	31
Estimated cost	$1,024,515	$672,575

Gossip of the Week.

SOUTH OF 59TH STREET.

t tenem't and store.
rge Dudenhoeffer to $15,500. July 24. 28,000
y and Ridge sts, 19.5
dolph Raduziner to
7th July 24 1,700

Same property. Sherman Evarts to Henry and Hyman Sonn. Referee's deed. June 25. 23,250

St. Marks pl, No. 109, n s, 250.6 w Av A, 12.6x94, five-story stone front tenem't. Christian Rothemund to Maria Rothemund. July 18. nom

Daniel S. McElroy has purchased from Charles H. Steinway the four-story dwelling No. 51 Park avenue, adjoining the northeast corner of 37th street, on private terms.

Andrew Coppela and Henry Wise have sold Nos. 110 and 112 Mulberry street, 50x100, for Abraham Kassel to Victor Gomino for $76,000.

It is reported that No. 119 Maiden lane has been sold for about $40,000. The size is 26x86.2x—x85, and the name of the owner Ellis Potter.

Wm. R. Mason has sold for Mary L. Asten the three-story brick dwelling, No. 450 West 34th street, 20.10x45x98.9, for $12,500, and for Annie T. Harris the three-story brick dwelling, No. 241 West 36th street, 18.6x42x98.9, for $12,500.

NORTH OF 59TH STREET.

Seton & Wissman have sold the four-story high stoop brown stone dwelling, No. 306 West 86th street, 21x65x ½ block, to John T. Robeson on private terms.

A. L. Brudi has sold for Mrs. Henrietta Harris No. 21 East 90th street, a five-story brick flat, 25x83x100, to Henry Friedrich for $20,050, and for the same owner to George Geise No. 23 East 90th street, a similiar flat, for $20,100. Mr. Brudi has also sold for his brother, Wm. Brudi, to a Mr. Judelsohn, a plot, 50x100 feet, on the west side of 3d avenue, 250 feet south of 167th street, for $7,000.

Frederick Reed has sold for a Mrs. Currie to a Mrs. Sullivan the brown stone dwelling, No. 210 West 123d street, for $16,500.

Ogden & Clark have sold for a Mrs. Summers to Jacob Fromann, No. 339 East 75th street, a four-story brick and stone apartment house, 28x80x100.5, on private terms.

Goodman & Stein have sold for Jacob Schlosser to Moritz Weisskopf Nos. 415 and 417 East 79th street for $35,000, and for Pauline Weisskopf to Jacob Schlosser No. 1209 1st avenue for $24,000.

LEASE.

It is reported that J. W. Goddard & Sons, manufacturers of tailors' trimmings, have leased the new building to be erected at Nos. 98 and 100 Bleecker street.

Brooklyn

J. P. Sloane has sold for Albert Morlock the four-story brick double store property, 25x56x100, situate No. 93 Eagle street, to Christopher Huss for $8,750.

Corwith Bros. have sold for the Platt estate the house and lot, 33x50, on the north side of Eagle street, 66.7 west of Oakland street, to Matilda Weinberger and Lena Herskowics for $1,600, and the house and lot, 16.8x40x100, No. 81 India street, for James E. Brown to Michael Toomey for $5,000.

CONVEYANCES.

	1890. July 24 to 30 inc.	1891. July 23 to 29 inc.
Number	291	300
Amount involved	$962,457	$962,051
Number nominal	57	76

MORTGAGES.

	1890.	1891.
Number	233	260
Amount involved	$958,623	$853,559
Number at 5 per cent. or less	128	122
Amount involved	$555,039	$462,726

PROJECTED BUILDINGS.

	1890. July 25 to 31 inc.	1891. July 24 to 30 inc.
Number of buildings	103	46
Estimated cost	$787,965	$177,600

Out of Town.

ARLINGTON, N. J.—H. G. and F. E. Eilshemius have sold two Queen Anne cottages, situated on Grand avenue, on the Eilshemius tract, near Private Park, to R. Davidson and William F. Clemmens, of New York; consideration, over $10,000. Also a building site on west side of Grand avenue, for $1,600 to a Brooklyn party, for immediate improvement.

SPARKILL, N. Y.—Taliaferro & Foutz have leased to Hannibal Price, Haytian Minister to the United States, the "Ferdon Place," for two years and three months from August 1, 1891.

Out Among the Builders.

Lorenz F. J. Weiher, Jr., has about completed plans for a seven-story apartment house, to be built on the north side of 72d street, 30 feet west of Lexington avenue. The building will be 125x90 in size, with front of Tiffany brick, brown stone and terra cotta. The main entrance will be in the centre of the building and will be 25 feet wide. The interior will be arranged to accommodate forty-nine families, and in all its appointments is to be strictly first class; $375,000 will be spent on this improvement by Lorenz Weiher, Sr., the owner.

The Trustees of the Protestant Cathedral of St. John the Divine have selected the plans of Heins & La Farge.

J. C. Burne has plans on the boards for a five-story brick and stone flat, 25x75, to be built on the north side of 112th street, 150 feet east of 5th avenue, at a cost of $20,000; owner, John Shields.

Boring, Tilton & Mellen have about completed plans for four three-story, high stoop English basement houses to be built on the west side of Boston avenue, between 165th and 166th streets for the Equitable Life Assurance Society. The houses will be of stone, brick and terra cotta with slate roofs and hardwood interior finish. They will be 18x55 in size and are to cost about $30,000.

Charles Rentz has plans on the boards for a five-story and basement brick and stone flat, 31x96, to be built for M. Solomon, at No. 266 Henry

and abate the growing nuisance of delays by the frequent opening of the many city drawbridges, to the great delay of the country's mails as well as of the laboring and business men.

Let the freight vessels yield to the greater interest of the whole community by having low smoke pipes to pass under bridges 25 feet above the water. Let masted sailing vessels land above or below the bridges, as the

five-story and basement apartment house, which G. J. McLoughlin will erect, at Nos. 104 and 106 Bedford street, and for alterations which Mrs. E. B. Grannis will make to the house, No. 88 East 22d street.

Charles H. Israels has plans under way for two five-story brick and stone flats, 25x77, to be built at Nos. 313 and 315 West 17th street, for John McSweeny, at a cost of $17,000 each.

Out of Town.

CALDWELL, N. J.—A two-and-a-half-story frame cottage, 27.6x45.6, containing nine rooms, is to be built here for a Mr. Backus at a cost of $3,000. C. P. Karr is the architect.

COLORADO.—Boring, Tilton & Mellen have plans under consideration for a four-and-a-half-story stone hotel, 295x260 in size, with accommodations for 300 guests. This hotel is to be built for an English and American company which is not as yet ready to make the exact location public. The rooms will be arranged in suites with bath-room attached. In finish and appointments the building will be complete and of the highest order, costing something like $350,000.

MADISON, N. J.—A Mr. Felch, of this place, has ordered from C. Powell Karr plans for a two-story frame cottage, 24x36, to cost about $2,800.

MONMOUTH BEACH, N. J.—Jeremiah O'Rourke, of Newark, has plans for a frame church for the Church of the Precious Blood, size 40x120, to cost $10,000.

NEWARK, N. J.—Peter Charles has plans for a two-and-a-half-story frame flat for Mr. Weyrauch on 11th street, near Sussex avenue, size 21x50, to cost about $3,500.

NEW UTRECHT, L. I.—Wm. Ditmar, Jr., will build a two-story and attic frame Colonial dwelling, 28x46, to cost $5,000, for which P. F. Higgs is the architect.

RYE, N. Y.—C. Powell Karr has drawn plans for changes to be made in the dwelling of Mrs. Emma Munsell. The house will be raised one story and a new bath-room added, all to cost $1,200.

WEST BROOKLYN, N. Y.—P. F. Higgs has drawn plans for a two-story and attic frame cottage, 25x35, to be built at a cost of $4,000 for Wm. Dickover; also for a like cottage, 28x28, for W. F. Hopkins to cost $3,000, and for a two-story frame store and lodge building, 60x60, to cost $5,000, and owned by J. A. Pfalsgraf et al.

WANTS AND OFFERS.

(Advertisements strictly in accordance with this title will be inserted at the practically nominal rate of 10 CENTS *per line (agate). In figuring for themselves advertisers may count seven words for each line, the address to be taken as one line. The object of this department is to bring buyers and sellers into communication with customers. Advertisements must be marked "Wants and Offers Column," and sent to the office of publication, Nos. 14 and 16 Vesey Street, not later than 3 P. M. Friday.)*

WANTS.

FACTORY PROPERTY WANTED.—A manufacturing site outside of New York, but within easy reach of the city, with suitable buildings if possible, ready for immediate occupancy, to be purchased or leased on favorable terms by a manufacturing company employing five hundred hands; will require one machine-shop 30,000 square feet, a second building for brass-finishing and assembling, a foundry and a power-house, a total of about 100,000 square feet; enough land to be reserved in the neighborhood to allow plenty of room for additional buildings when required. In replying please state fully railroad facilities, dimensions of tract at disposal, condition of buildings if already erected, whether or not willing to alter buildings to suit tenants if taken on long lease.

If buildings are not erected on what terms would build for tenants or purchasers.

Address, W. A. L., 83 Madison av, New York.

Aug. 1—8

WANTED.—For special customers, lots with builder's loans, New York or Brooklyn. Also medium-sized plots, 23d or 24th Wards (on Boston road preferred). Owners and brokers address,
H. F. SCHELLHASS, 171 Broadway.

LOTS, FLATS, PRIVATE HOUSES AND TENEMENTS wanted for free and clear Farms, Country seats and cash.
H. B. FANTON, 176 Broadway.

Real Estate Wanted.

WANTED TO PURCHASE.—Dwelling, 43d or 44th sts., Broadway and 6th av. Particulars.
CREVIER & WOOLLEY, 1512 Broadway, 44th st.

OFFERS.

Dwellings and Flats

FOR SALE.—At a sacrifice, new five-story double flats, near 125th st. L station. Address,
Aug. 1—1aw-9w. BUILDER, 319 East 125th st.

SINGLE FLAT for double flat, oil paintings and cash. 415 West 57th st. Also boarding house to let: vacant; twenty-one rooms; in fine order.

BUILDERS TAKE NOTICE—50x100, between 5th and 6th avs., 10th st.; $50,000.
CREVIER & WOOLLEY, 1512 Broadway, 44th st.

A BARGAIN FOR SOMEBODY.—The three-story 20-foot front brown stone, 124th st., between 1st and 2d avs; perfect order; all improvements; $11,500; no less; terms easy; don't miss this if you want a home cheap. J. B. KETCHAM, 58 West 125th st.

THE DESIRABLE BRICK VILLA, 403 Lenox av., near 130th st.; must be seen to be appreciated; will sell at a bargain; terms easy.
J. B. KETCHAM, 58 West 125th st.

BUSINESS PROPERTY, corner 124th st. and 2d av., 20x80: will sell cheap and terms to suit.
J. B. KETCHAM, 58 West 125th st.

FOR SALE.—A newly-built double flat in Essex st., now fully tenanted and returning seven per cent net on price asked or 9½ on investment required; full particulars and accounts. FULLER & FROTHINGHAM, 945 Broadway, corner 22d st.

FOR SALE.—West 47th st., near Broadway, a very desirable four-story high stoop brown stone house, 20x52x100; price $32,000. Apply to FULLER & FROTHINGHAM, 945 Broadway, corner 22d st.

FOR SALE OR TO RENT.—East 85th st., near Lexington av., a very desirable English basement house in perfect order; rent $1,600. Apply to FULLER & FROTHINGHAM, 945 Broadway, corner 22d st.

WEST 89TH ST., near Boulevard. Nos. 260, 262 and 264; new three-story brown stone.
CHAS. L. RITZMAN, Owner,
July4-e.o.w.4t. 943 Broadway.

FOR SALE—2443 8th av.; 26.8½x100; easy terms; commission allowed brokers; apply at
Mar. 28-u-f. ROOM 19, 156 Broadway.

BUY THE BEST.
72D ST., THE PARK DRIVEWAY.
SEVERAL 25-FOOT PALATIAL RESIDENCES.
ONE SUPERBLY DECORATED.
NONE MORE ELEGANT AND SPACIOUS.
The best judgment of long experience has been given to their construction. The most critical will be satisfied in the taste displayed and the excellent character of the workmanship and material; prices reasonable.
F. CRAWFORD, 114 West 72d st.
July 11-1aw8w.

FOR SALE—210 and 212 West 105th st.; five-story apartments; each, 25x89x100; decorated and carpeted; apply at ROOM 19, 156 Broadway.
Mar.28-u-f.

Improved Property.

PLANING MILL FOR SALE.—Is located at 24th st. and 11th av., on four or five city lots, leased ground, and consists of two and three-story brick buildings and adjoining sheds; also 80 horse-power engine and boiler, planers, moulders, saws, etc., all in good running order and now in operation; owner will leave a portion of value on bond and mortgage three years; this offers splendid opportunity to enlarge woodworking industry or to secure good mill business to add thereto. For further particulars, etc., apply to
EBEN PECK, 24th st. and 11th av.
Advertiser intends to continue his lumber business now carried on at above address. July25-Aug1

Vacant Lots.

BROADWAY LOTS.—Riverside fronts and lots with loan.
J. ALBERT GRANGER, Mills Building.

LOT ON 76TH ST., near 4th av., for sale.
W. W. KIRBY, Room 63, World Building, New York.

PLOT OF TEN valuable lots on prominent corner; 23d Ward, will be sold very cheap; need money, rare chance. K. CHISHOLM, 89 Nassau st.

100TH ST., between 2d and 3d avs; ten lots, cheap; all mortgage if improved.
July11-1aw8w. EDWIN A. ELY, 108 Gold st.

40 CHERRY ST., between Roosevelt and Franklin sq., 32x64, vacant; $12,000; accommodating terms. EDWIN A. ELY, 108 Gold st.
July11-1aw8w.

Brooklyn Real Estate for Sale.

FOR SALE.—Frame house; two story; brick cellar and basement; nine rooms; all improvements; on Lewis av., near seminary; good order.
Particulars, 9 Ann st., New York, or 683 Lafayette av., Brooklyn.

DESIRABLE INVESTMENT.—Eight-story apartment house; best location in Brooklyn; might exchange equity over $125,000 at 4½ per cent.
J. 30—uf. Apply 60 Broadway, Room 311.

LARGE FACTORY for sale; price, $68,000; the land itself supposed to be worth the money.
Apr 4-uf FIRST NATIONAL BANK, Brooklyn, N. Y.

OFFERS.

16½ PER CENT.—Best I can do on investment of $15,000 in plate glass store property on leading business thoroughfare of 17th Ward of Brooklyn; the plot is 140x90; consists of seven two-story buildings; rents for $4,592 per annum, and mortgage of $47,500 can remain for long term. Examine this gilt edge investment. J. P. SLOANE, July 11—1aw4w. 343 Manhattan av., Brooklyn.

Miscellaneous.

FOR SALE.—East River water front; deep water; 400 feet long; Long Island City. EXECUTOR, 100 East 49th st.

OFFERS.

REAL ESTATE, 23D AND 24TH WARDS.—We offer for sale nice cottages, houses, stores and building lots; choice sites; easy terms. Also, three double five-story brown stone flats, elegantly decorated, six rooms and bath, cellars and janitor's apartments; $5,000 to $7,000 cash; balance 5 per cent. AGNEW & BARLOW, 2973 3d av., 153d st.

A PARTY ABOUT TO BUILD A FIVE-STORY factory, 50x98, in Harlem, near water-front, will lease the three upper floors and build to suit tenant. Terms very moderate. Address May 16 u. f. OWNER, 409 E. 107th St.

OFFERS.

FIVE YEAR LEASEHOLD on lower Broadway for sale; will renew for 20, 40 or 60 years to party who will build. GRANITE, 818 World, uptown. July 25—1aw8w.

Country Property.

HOBOKEN PROPERTY.—Factory site for sale; is located on the east side of Bloomfield st., commencing 25 ft. north of Ferry st.; the plot of ground is about 55 ft. 6 in. front by about 75 ft. deep, with two-story unfinished brick building thereon about 55.6x30 deep; this property is only four blocks from New York ferries. For further particulars, etc., apply to CHAS. A. MANSFIELD, 101 Hudson st., Hoboken, N. J.

SALES OF THE WEEK.

The following are the sales at the Real Estate Exchange and Auction Room for the week ending July 31.

** Indicates that the property described has been bid in for plaintiff's account:*

R. V. HARNETT & CO.

106th st, Nos. 63-69, n s, 200 e Madison av, 100x100.11, four five-story brk flats. S. M. Cohen. (Amt due $76,956) $61,500

SMYTH & RYAN.

Clinton av, s e cor Spring st, 100x100. L. Ryan. (Amt due $2,765) 4,100

WM. KENNELLY.

76th st, n e cor Madison av, 45x102.2, vacant. Dix & Fhyfe. (Amt due $32,669) 39,150

*84th st, No. 36, s s, 435 w 8th av. 20x102.2, three-story brk dwell'g. Elizabeth F. Haud. 15,000

*Evelyn pl, s s, 175 w Jerome av, 50x100 John S. McWilliam. (Amt due $1,229; prior mort. $3,000) 3,500

J. N. GOLDING.

50th st, Nos. 35 and 37, n s, 150 w Park av, 50x100.5, two five-story brk flats. Equitable Life Assurance Society. (Amt due $95,175). 75,000

J. F. B. SMYTH.

Interior lot, centre line of block, 29th and 30th sts. 306.8 w 7th av, 46.10x8.9x32.1x14.9x58.2 to beginning. Francis E. Johnson 3,900

Total $202,150
Corresponding week. 1890 .... $235,850

BROOKLYN, N. Y.

FOR WEEK ENDING JULY 30.

TAYLOR & FOX.

Evergreen av, No. 316, w s, 25 n Stanhope st, 25x100, two-story frame dwell'g. Peter Feely. $1,500

Flushing av, No. 590, s w cor Marcy av, 25x100, three-story frame (brk lined) building and three-story frame dwell'g in rear, known as 458 Marcy av. Jos. Ryan, 2d deed 9,900

OTHER AUCTIONEERS.

*Elton st, w s, 25 s Blake av, 25x23, two-story frame dwell'g. Hermann Boehme $900

*Lefferts pl, Nos. 124 and 126, s s, 132.10 w Clason av, 40x138, three-story frame dwell'g on plot. Joseph Schuetter. (Correction) 9,000

*Troutman st, No. 17, n w s, 86.2½ s w Bushwick av, 25x100, three-story frame dwell'g. Charlotte Willis 7,550

Atlantic av, No. 2488A, s s, 333.4 w Stone av, 16.8x100, three-story frame dwell'g. Thomas Everett 2,250

*Hudson av, No. 36, w s, 58.4 s John st, 16 8x90, three-story brick tenem't and store. Emilie W. Dana 3,000

*St. Marks av, No. 279, n s, 150 w Underhill av, 25x131, four-story brk tenem't. William J. Hart 7,800

*St. Marks av, No. 281, n s, 125 w Underhill av, 25x131, four-story brk tenem't. Same 8,000

*Voorhees av, centre line, at intersection with centre line of East 27th st, runs east 232 x south 132 x west 69.9 x north 13.4 x west 152 to centre East 27th st. x north 130 to beginning, Gravesend. James W. Birkett 1,500

6th av, No. 592, n w s, 44.4 n Prospect av, 18x80, four-story frame tenem't and store. A. H. Henriques. (Correction) 4,821

6th av, s w cor Pacific st, runs south 142.6 x west 125 x north 32.6 x east 25 x north 110 to Pacific st. x east 100 to beginning, three-story brk factory. E. S. Leaycraft 50,310

Total $106,081
Corresponding week 1890 .... $8,500

CONVEYANCES.

Wherever the letters Q. C., C. a. G. and B. & S occur, preceded by the name of the grantee they mean as follows:

1st—Q. C. is an abbreviation for Quit Claim deed, i. e., a deed in which all the right, title and interest of the grantor is conveyed, omitting all covenants or warranty.

2d—C. a. G. means a deed containing Covenant against Grantor only, in which he covenants that he hath not done any act whereby the estate conveyed may be impeached, charged or encumbered.

3d—B. & S. is an abbreviation for Bargain and Sale deed, wherein, although the seller makes no express covenants, he really grants or conveys the property for a valuable consideration, and thus impliedly claims to be the owner of it.

NEW YORK CITY.

JULY 24, 25, 27, 28, 29, 30.

Allen st, No. 175, w s, 25.1 s Stanton st, 25x64.11x25x65.2, three-story brk front and frame dwell'g with store and three-story brk extension. Betsey wife of Max Wolf to Michael J. Adrian. *Mt.* $10,000. July 30. 14,000

Boulevard (Broadway), s e cor 63d st, runs east 123 4 x south 84 11 x west 25 x north 62 x west 85 to Boulevard, x north 25.
Boulevard, e s, 25 s 63d st, 24x73x20x85.
Boulevard, e s, 49 s 63d st, 20x62x17x73, vacant.
Sarah M. Storm widow individ and extrx., &c., of Thomas Storm to George W. Vultee. ½ part. Sub. to taxes, &c. July 1. 35,717

Same property. Walton Storm and Leila S. his wife, Edith and Theodora M. Storm to same. ½ part. Sub to taxes, &c. July 1. 71,433

Broome st, No. 527, s w s, 72.2 e Sullivan st, 18.1x68.0½x19 1½x62.11, three-story brk flat and frame dwell'g with store, with use of alleyway to Thompson st. Simon Simon to Julius J. Lyons. July 28. nom

Crosby st, No. 49, e s, abt 190 n e Broome st, 25x100, two-story brk building with stores. Arthur J. Horgan and Martha W. his wife and Vincent J. Slattery and Fannie G. his wife to Jacob Korn. *Mt.* $12,500. July 17. 23,000

Same property. Richard J. Mahoney and Emma M. his wife to Arthur J. Horgan and Vincent J. Slattery. *Mt.* $12,500, taxes, &c. Sept. 30, 1890. nom

Delancey st, No. 26, n s, abt 75 e Chrystie st, 25x100, four-story brk tenem't and store. Barbara wife of and George Dudenhoeffer to Nathan Hutkoff. *Mt.* $15,500. July 24. 28,000

Division st, s s, bet Attorney and Ridge sts, 19.5x93x17 4x101, indeft. Adolph Raduziner to John Ambacher. *Mt.* $1,700. July 24. 1,700

Elm st, No. 207, e s, 20x41 to Marion st, x21x35.2, two-story brk front and frame dwell'g. Henry Lesoine and Helena M. his wife, Louis Lesoine and Lizzie his wife, John Lesoine and Katie his wife, Leonard Lesoine and Catharine his wife, David Lesoine and Tressa E. his wife, George Lesoine and Frederick Lesoine and Laura his wife to Albert Etzel and Emanuel Kronacher. July 27. nom

Same property. Louis and George Lesoine extrs. Leonard Lesoine to same. July 27. 8,000

Essex st, No 30, e s, abt 75 n Hester st, 24.11x75x25x75, five-story brk tenem't and store. Israel Krakower and Rachel H. his wife, Brooklyn, N. Y., Abraham Kraner and Yetta his wife to Jacob Loeb. *Mt.* $21,000. July 27. 33,000

Goerck st, e s, Nos. 104-108 } begins Goerck
Mangin st, Nos. 95, 97 and 99 } st, e s, 246.7 n Rivington st, runs east 100 x north 34 10 x east 100 to Mangin st, x north 65.9 x west 100 x south 26 x west 100 to Goerck st, x south 75, three five-story brk tenem'ts and stores on Goerck st and vacant lots on Mangin st. Foreclos. Charles A. Jackson to Moses Weinman. *Mt.* $50,800. July 23. 12,500

Goerck st, No. 36, e s, 100 s Delancey st, 25x100, three-story frame tenem't and five-story brk tenem't in rear. Robert B. Merritt and Margaret F. his wife to Katharine wife of Bernhard Schaeffel. *Mt.* $12,425. July 29. 16,800

Houston st, Nos. 100 and 102, n s, 37.2 e Thompson st, runs north 62 x east 19.1 x north 9.10x east 19 x south 71.10 to st, x west 38.1, six-story brk building. Philip Kotlowsky and Hannah his wife and Barnet Levy and Libby his wife to Nicholas Foller. *Mt.* $30,000. July 30. 60,250

Hubert st, No 10, n w cor Collister st, 25.1x88.5x25 11x88.6, two-story brk dwell'g with two-story brk dwell'g on rear. Michael Murtha and Frances his wife to Joseph H. Bearns *Mt.* $13,000. July 22. 25,250

Liberty st, No. 98, s e cor Trinity pl, 26.2x54x25.11x53, five-story stone front building and store. Frank B. Treiber to Jefferson M. and L. Napoleon Levy. Sub. to mort. July 15. nom

Livingston pl, Nos. 2 and 3, e s, 27.6 n 15th st, 50x97, two four-story stone front dwell'gs. Susan E Le Roy widow to New York Infirmary for Women and Children. July 15. 60,000

Ludlow st, No. 116, e s, 175 n Delancey st, 25x87.6, five-story brk tenem't and store. Max S. Korn to Joseph Fuchs, Mary Fuhrken and Frank and Lina Kohlsdorf tenants in common. All taxes, assessments, &c. July 30. other consid. and 100

Macdougal st, No. 128, e s, bet Bleecker st and 3d st, old Amity st, 25x100, three-story brk front and frame dwell'g. Daniel Coffey and Bridget his wife to Benedict A. Klein. *Mt.* $10,000. July 29. 16,400

Same property. Benedict A. Klein and Karoline his wife to Laemmlein Buttenwieser. *Mt.* $12,000. July 29. nom

Madison st, No. 213, n s, abt 155 w Jefferson st, 26.1x100, four-story brk tenem't and five-story brk building on rear of lot. Abraham Schlesinger and Pauline his wife and Aline Coshland to Morris Breslauer. *Mt.* $21,700. July 25. 28,000

Madison st, No. 125, n s, abt 85 e Market st, 25.4x100, five-story brk tenem't. Michael Fey and Mary his wife and William Stecom and Catharine his wife to Samuel Prager. *Mt.* $25,000. July 18. 43,000

Mulberry st, No. 148, e s, 50 s Hester st, 16x50, five-story brk tenem't and store. Levy Rathstein and Rosa his wife to Faust D. Malzone. *Mt.* $10,000. July 30. 13,750

Norfolk st, No. 78, e s, 125 n Broome st, 25x100, three-story brk front and frame dwell'g with laundry in basement. Philip Hilger, Hudson City, N. J., to Julius Ruff. Re-recorded. C. a. G. *Mt.* $12,000. April 10, 1883. 100

Pike st, No. 46, w s, 50 s Madison st, 25x86, five-story brk tenem't. Louis Gewiez and Lizzie his wife to Hayman Wallach. *Mt.* $30,600. July 29. See 76th st. 39,000

South st, No. 29, n w cor Cuyler's alley, 19.1x85.3x19.2x84.7, five-story brk building Peter Lorillard and Emily T. his wife to Hyman and Henry Sonn. C. a. G. June 6. nom

Same property. Mary L. Barbey to same. C. a. G. July 8. nom

Same property. Release dower. Louis C. Lorillard and Katharine B. his wife to Hyman and Henry Sonn. July 8. nom

Same property. Sherman Evarts to Henry and Hyman Sonn. Referee's deed. June 25. 28,250

St. Marks pl, No. 109, n s, 250.6 w Av A, 12.6x94, five-story stone front tenem't. Christian Rothemund to Maria Rothemund. July 18. nom

Warren st, No. 59, s s, 25 e College pl, 25x70.4x24.9x70.6, four-story brk building. Elizabeth Bennet widow, Greenwich, Conn., to Charles Lesinsky. Q. C. June 18. nom

Washington st, No. 43 } begins n e cor Morris
Morris st, No. 12 } st, 25x79, five-story brk building and store on Washington st and five-story brk building and store on Morris st Mahlon Buckman to Joshua C. Sanders. *Mt.* $10,000. July 28. nom

Waverley pl, No. 184 } begins Waverley pl, s w
10th st, Nos. 154-158 } cor 10th st, 23.5x83.8, three story brk dwell'g. James W. Ketcham and Appolonia his wife to Albert L and Meyer L. Sire. *Mt.* $25,000. April 4. 57,000

Willet st, No. 32, e s, 168.9 n Broome st, 25x100, five-story brk tenem't. William E. Burkhardt and Elise his wife to Solomon Goldstein. *Mt.* $24 000. July 14. 35,000

4th st, No. 252, s s, 115 e Av B, 25x96, three-story brk dwell'g. Charles Boss and Anna M. his wife to Joseph Herrmann and Josephine his wife. July 9. 17,250

6th st, No. 222, s s, 280 w 2d av, 25x97, three-story brk tenem't. Pierce and Richard Maloney to Margaret Maloney. *Mt.* $2,000. July 18. nom

9th st, No. 624, s s, 313 e Av B, 20x76, four-story brk tenem't and stores. Jacob Kleinhans and Phillipina his wife to Jane, Eliza and Alice Carberry, joint tenants. July 30. 10,600

10th st, No. 9, n s, 151.10 w 5th av, 25x94.10, three-story stone front dwell'g. Harriet V. Ogden widow to Henry L. Slade. July 28. 39,000

15th st, No. 136, s s, 168 w 3d av, abt 22x84, four-story brk dwell'g. Marx Ottinger and Clara his wife and Moses Ottinger and Amelia his wife to Berta Lopez. B. & S. *Mt.* $14,700. June 30. 19,700

17th st, No. 256, s s, 152 e 8th av, 17 4x74.6x17 4x72.6, three-story brk dwell'g. John McLellan and Euphemia his wife to Jessie Griffin. *Mt.* $7,500. July 29. 1,000

17th st, No. 20, s s, 200 w Union sq, 25x93, four-story stone front dwell'g and store. William Bryce, Jr., Madison, N. J., to Mary T. Bryce. ½ part. July 15. nom

20th st, s s, 236 e 7th av, 20x92. Release mort. New York Savings Bank to Mayor, &c., New York. July 15. 4,000

21st st, No. 236, s s, 419.5 w 7th av, 19.7x109x19.7x108.6, three-story brk dwell'g. James E. Connor to James E. Connor, Jr. *Mt.* $8,000. July 29. gift

22d st, No. 14, s s, 256.3 w 5th av, 27x98.9, four-story stone front dwell'g.
22d st, No. 146, s s, 190 w 3d av, 20x98.9, two-story brk building; also,
Land at Irvington, N. Y.
Ellen, Jane H. wife of Theodore Haight, Irvington, N. Y., to Robert B. Coutant, Tarrytown, N. Y. ½ part. July 29. nom

23d st, No 326, s s, 253 1 w 8th av, 21.10x98.8, five story stone front dwell'g. Partition. Leicester Holme to Thomas Stokes. July 30. 22,250

24th st, n s, 475 e 6th av, 25x98.9, four-story stone front dwell'g. Edith and Theodora M. Storm heirs John G. Storm to Andrew J. Bastine. Q. C. June 30. nom

24th st, n s, 125 e 1st av, 25x98.9. John P. Ranta and Annie his wife to Belle P. wife of Samuel H. Huxford. July 23. nom

27th st, No. 121, n s, 266.8 w 6th av, 16.8x98.9. Release judgment. Dennis D. McKoon to M. Emile de Gilbert and Blanche his wife. July 30. nom

27th st, No. 121, n s, 266.8 w 6th av, 16.8x98.9, three-story stone front dwell'g. M. Emile de Gilbert and Blanche his wife to Ellen Eagen. *Mt.* $6,000. July 29. 12,000

32d st, No. 437, n s, 400 w 9th av, 25x98.9, four-story brk tenem't and store and three-story brk building on rear. John Merkel and Katie his wife to James Shanney. *Mt.* $6,000. July 30. 15,000

34th st, s s, 65.4 w 1st av, 34.8x31.3, one-story frame stable. Thomas Murtha to Annie M. wife of said Thomas Murtha. C. a. G. July 30. nom

44th st, Nos. 535 and 537, n s, 300 e 10th av, 40x100.4, two five-story brk tenem'ts. Samuel Hirsh and Eugenie his wife to William G. Jordan. *Mt.* $16,000. July 2. 25,000

49th st, No. 225, n s, 328.6 e 8th av, 21.6x100.5, four-story stone front dwell'g. William H. Munn and Rebecca his wife and Frances Bovie widow to Mary W. Munn. B. & S. C. a. G. July 25. nom

50th st, s s, 158.3 e 11th av, 15x112.6x18.1x 102.5.
50th st, s s, 128.2 e 11th av, runs south 93.6 x east 17.4 x southeast 15.5 x north 102.5 to st, x west 30.1.
50th st, n s, 23 e 11th av, 25.8x48.11.
Release mort. A. C. Cheney trustee to Rosalie Steinhardt. June 30. nom

57th st, No. 445, n s, 505 w Columbus (9th) av, 20x100, five-story stone front flat. Charles Wise and Helen B. his wife to Leopold Wise. *Mt.* $15,000. July 20. nom

58th st, No. 431, n s, 267.8 w Av A, 18.1x100.4, three-story stone front dwell'g. Edward G. Jardine and Margaret R. his wife to John C. Heidingsfelder. *Mt.* $6,000. July 29. 10,700

62d st, s s, 161.3 e 3d av, 18.9x100.9. Catharine D. Blair to Sarah C. Blair. Q. C. July 21. life lease and nom

65th st, No. 127, n s, 130 w Lexington av, 20x 100.5, three-story stone dwell'g. Mayer Goldsmith and Theresa his wife to Jacob Goldberg. July 20. 20,250

66th st, n s, 525 w Central Park West (8th av), 50x100.5, vacant. Effingham H. Nichols and Caroline R. his wife to Nicholas Leibrock. *Mt.* $8,000. July 1. 15,500

Same property. Nicholas Leibrock and Frieda his wife to Charles E. Miller. *Mt.* $8,000. July 24. 17,450

70th st, No. 71, n s, 180 e Columbus av, 22.6x 100.5, four-story brk dwelling. Charles Buek, Westport, Conn., and Abbie B. his wife to Petera B Worrall. *Mt.* $26,000. July 16. 38,000

70th st, n s, 180 e Columbus av, 22.6x100.5. Release mort. Harriet Overbiser to Charles Buek. July 14. 3,000

71st st, s s, 125 w Central Park West, 100x100.5, vacant. Andrews Sober and Minnie his wife to Carrie S. wife of David T. Kennedy. July 21. 64,000

72d st, Nos. 422-426, s s, 313 e 1st av, 75x102.2, three five-story brk flats. Morris Franklin and Henrietta his wife to Michael Dimand, of Laredo, Texas. ½ part. *Mt.* $47,500. July 23. 32,141

73d st, Nos. 414 and 416, s s, 238 e 1st av, 50x102.2, two five-story brk flats
73d st, Nos. 422 and 424, s s, 225 w Av A, 50x102.2, two five-story brk flats.
Adolph S. Jaeger and Carrie his wife and Morris S. Jaeger and Frances his wife to Aaron J. Bach. B. & S. C. a. G. All title. July 23. nom

Same property. Adolph S. Jaeger and Carrie his wife and Frances Jaeger to Morris S. Jaeger. B. & S. All title. July 23. nom

74th st, Nos. 213 and 215, n s, 160 e 3d av, 50x 100, two four-story brk tenem'ts, and store in No. 213. James Kiernan and Mary his wife, Richmond Hill, L. I., Major J. Kiernan and Margaret his wife and Patrick F. Kiernan and Catharine his wife to John McArdle. Q. C. May 6. 3,000

74th st, No. 59, n s, 100 e Columbus av, 20x102.2, four-story stone front dwell'g. Foreclos. Edward C. O'Brien to Ambrose F. Travers. *Mt.* $25,000, int. from July 18, 1890, taxes, &c. July 3. 35,000

74th st, No. 57, n s, 120 e Columbus av, 20x102.2, four-story stone front dwell'g. Foreclos. Same to same. *Mt.* $25,000, int. from July, 1890, taxes, &c. July 3. 41,000

74th st, Nos. 244 and 246, s s, 133.4 w 2d av, 33.4x102.2, two four-story brk dwell'gs Gerson Siegel and Jenny his wife to Mary Schott. *Mt.* $14,000. Feb. 1. 20,750

75th st, No. 42, s s, 260 e 9th av, 20x102.2, four-story stone front dwell'gs. Ida Ehrich to James T. Hall. *Mt.* $30,000. July 9. nom

75th st, No. 54, s s, 140 e Columbus av, 22x102.2. James T. Hall and Helen M. his wife to Ida Ehrich. *Mt.* $30,000. July 9. nom

76th st, No. 116, s s, 154 e Park (4th) av, 16x 102.2, three-story stone front dwell'g. Ella Sugden widow to Mathilde wife of Nathan Wolff. *Mt.* $12,000. July 24. 16,750

76th st, No. 332, s s, 125 e 2d av, 25x102.2, four-story stone front dwell'g. Hayman Wallach and Rose his wife to Louis Gewirz. *Mt.* $11,000. July 29. See Pike st. 18,000

77th st, No. 233, n s, 305 e 3d av, 12.6x102.2, three-story brk dwell'g. Homer J. Beaudet and Eliza his wife to Edward Oppenheimer and Edward Hirsh. *Mt.* $4,500. July 29. nom

78th st, No. 158, s s, 200 e Amsterdam av, 20x 102.2, four-story stone front dwell'g. Sarah J. Lozier to Ellen A. Slaven. *Mt.* $22,000. July 27. See 136th st. nom

78th st, No. 168, s s, 100 e Amsterdam av, 20x 102.2, four-story stone front dwell'g. Same to same. *Mt.* $22,000. July 27. See 136th st. nom

80th st, No. 173, n s, 183.4 w 3d av, 16.8x100, three-story stone front dwell'g. John Schiff and Rachel his wife to Solomon H. Aaron. *Mt.* $8,000. July 30. 14,500

82d st, No. 166, s s, 177.9 w 3d av, 25.2x102.2, five-story brk flat. Philipp Diehl and Margaret his wife to Herman Ruschmeyer. *Mt.* $15,000. July 30. 28,150

82d st, Nos. 170-174, s s, 100 e Amsterdam av, 50x 102.2, three three-story stone front dwell'gs. James Bradley and Lillian M. his wife to John H. Wessel. ½ part. *Mt.* $45,000. July 28. 6,000

83d st, No. 508, s s, 148 e Av A, 25x102.2.
83d st, No. 449, n s, 76.6 w Av A, 20x102.2.
Contract. Joseph Schneider to George Herbener. July 25. 36,250

83d st, No. 339, n s, 200 w 1st av, 25x102.2, five-story stone front flat. John McLaughlin and Margaret his wife to Henry Struckhausen and Lena M. his wife. *Mt.* $15,000. July 29. nom

85th st, No. 333, n s, 325 e 2d av, 25x102.2, four-story stone front flat. Louis Ascher and Mina his wife to George Solomon. *Mt.* $7,000. May 19. nom

Same property. Same to Mina Ascher. *Mt.* $19,000. May 19. nom

85th st, s s, 325 w 11th av, 50x102.2. Partition. John Whalen to Timothy Donovan. July 23. 10,900

89th st, s s, 100 e West End av. Party wall agreement. Charles T. Barney, Francis M. Jencks and William E. D. Stokes to Frank L. Smith. July 16. 300

93d st, No. 156, s s, 316.8 w 3d av, 16.6x100.8, three-story brk dwell'g. James G. Bennett, Paris, France, to Charles A. Du Bois. July 16. 10,000

93d st, No. 158, s s, 316.8 w 3d av, 16.6x100.8, three-story brk dwell'g. Charles A. Du Bois to Hattie wife of Henry D. Greenwald. *Mt.* $8,000. July 28. 14,500

93d st, s s, 325 e Amsterdam av, 100x100.8. Release mort. Charles G. Judson to Walden P. Anderson. July 28. nom

94th st, s s, 178.5 e 5th av, 0.6x100.8. Release mort. Mutual Life Ins. Co. to John H. Gray. July 24. nom

97th st, s s, 168 e Columbus av, 19x100.11.
96th st, n s, 204 e Columbus av, 21x100.11.
96th st, n s, 141 e Columbus av, 42x100.11.
96th st, s s, 220 e Columbus av, 80x100.8½.
Frank L. Smith and Magdalene his wife to The Squier & Whipple Co. All liens. July 20. nom

101st st, No. 136, s s, 300 w Columbus av, 25 x100.11, five-story brk flat. Henry S. Cates and Anna A. his wife to William Broadbelt. *Mt.* $22,600. July 29. See 113th st. 29,600

101st st, No. 131, n s, 75 w Lexington av, 25x 100.11, five-story brk flat. Foreclos. Robert L. Redfield to Don A. Gaylord. July 30. 10,700

101st st, Nos. 137 and 139, n s, 350 w Columbus av, 50x100.11, two five-story stone front flats. William Smith to John J. Hughes. April 10. 200

105th st, No. 113, n s, 100 e Park (4th) av, 25x 100.11, five-story brk flat. Maria L. wife of William McGinnis to Adolph Grabowski. *Mt.* $13,000. July 24. 19,500

105th st, No. 45, n e cor Manhattan av, 17.3x70, three-story brk dwell'g. Consuela wife of William A. Kirkland to Daniel D. Lawson. *Mt.* $15,000. July 27. nom

111th st, No. 171, n s, 199.6 w 3d av, 30x100.11, four-story stone front flat. Joseph H. Bearns and Selena his wife, Brooklyn, to Hugh O'Rorke. July 28. 22,500

112th st, Nos. 415-425, n s, 268 w Pleasant av, 100x100.10, one-story brk and frame factory. Henry Maguire and Catherine his wife to Pietro Altieri. *Mt.* $7,000. July 23. 18,000

113th st, No. 2, s s, 100 w 5th av, 17.9x100.11, three-story stone front dwell'g. William Broadbelt and Jane L. his wife, New Rochelle, N. Y., to Anna A. Cates. *Mt.* $11,-000. July 29. See 101st st. 18,000

114th st, No. 217, n s, 260 e 3d av, 25x100.11, five-story stone front tenem't. Sophie Rothschild to Lizzie Horwitz. *Mt.* $17,000. July 30. 24,000

115th st, Nos. 242 and 244, s s, 100 w 2d av, 20x 61.8x20x82.5, two two and three-story frame dwell'gs. John F. Monks to Frederick Schuck. *Mt.* $2,000. July 28. 5,500

116th st, No. 316, s s, 87 e Manhattan av, 27x 100.11, five-story brk flat. Henry H Dreyer and Margaret his wife to Henry and Rebecca F. Ettenheimer. *Mt.* $25,000. July 16. 35,000

117th st, Nos. 330 and 332, s s, 375 e 2d av, 50x 100.11, two four-story brk dwell'gs. Bertha wife of Louis Picus to Lena Schwartz. *Mt.* $20,000. July 27. nom

120th st, No. 127, n s, 350 w Lenox av, 21x100.11, three-story stone front dwell'g. Release mort. Henry Weil to Edward T. Smith. July 22. nom

Same property. Edward T. Smith to Peter Conlin. *Mt.* $16,000. July 24. nom

123d st, Nos. 221-223, n s, 218 e 3d av, 33.3x 100.11, two five-story stone front flats. William J. Mathews and Mary A. his wife to Robert H. Mathews. July 15. nom

126th st, No. 18, s s, 197.6 e 5th av, 13.9x99.11, three-story stone front dwell'g. Walter F. McConnell to Siebrand Niewenhous. Re-recorded. April 20. 16,500

129th st, No. 114, s s, 200.2 e 4th av, 19.9x99.10 x20x99.11, three-story brk dwell'g. Jane A. Mead, Elizabeth, N. J., to William G. Rock. July 15. 7,100

132d st, No. 104, s s, 91.8 w Lenox av, 16.8x99.11, three-story stone front dwell'g. Roderick J. Kennedy to Thomas A. Briggs. *Mt.* $9,500. July 27. 16,500

133d st, No. 14, s s, 210 w 5th av, 25x99.11, five-story brk flat. Morris S. Thompson to Nelson S. Cubberley. B. & S. Sub. to mort. July 28. 24,000

133d st, No. 155, n s, 275 e 7th av, 25x99.11, five-story brk flat. Thomas A. Briggs and Deborah T. his wife to Roderick J. Kennedy. *Mt.* $20,000. July 27. 32,000

133d st, No. 17, n s, 200 e 5th av, 17.6x99.11, two-story brk dwell'g. John B. Carss and Marion his wife and John Carss to James Everard. *Mt.* $2,500. July 30. 6,250

134th st, Nos. 71-77, n s, 197.6 e Lenox (6th) av, before widening, 87.6x99.11, five three-story brk dwell'gs and vacant.
135th st, Nos. ——, s s, 197.6 e Lenox (6th) av, before widening, 87.6x99.11, five three-story brk dwell'gs and vacant. This property sub. to mort. $20,000.
Foreclos. John H. Judge to William H. Vredenburgh. July 29. 40,000

136th st, No. 313, n s, 168.4 w 8th av, 16.8x99.11, three-story brk dwell'g. Ellen A. Slaven to Sarah J. Lozier. July 28. See 78th st. 15,250

161st st, n s, 350.6 w Amsterdam (10th) av, 50x 100, three-story frame dwell'gs. William R. Knapp and Alice M. his wife and Charles B. Knapp and Alice S. his wife to Hamilton Pomeroy. July 29. 10,000

Amsterdam av, Nos. 768-770, w s, 50.5 s 98th st, 50.6x92.6, two five-story brk flats and stores. Charles S. Kohler and Katie his wife to John H. Wittpenn. *Mt.* $36,000. July 7. 52,250

Amsterdam av, e s, 125.8 n 87th st, 25x100. Release mort. Elizabeth Buch extrx. Charles Buch to Timothy J. Shea. July 27. 1,417

Anthony av, e s, 28.5 s 175th st, runs east 51.11 x again east 45.2 x north 35.2 x west 106.2 to av, x south 34.1.
Anthony av, e s, 225.8 n 175th st, 95x142.5x 98.11x170.
Louis Adler and Benjamin L. Wertheimer assignees Monroe Eckstein and Leopold Wertheimer to Timothy Donovan. Feb. 25. 7,300

Audubon av, n e cor 181st st, 100x170, vacant. Pauline Simon to Joseph Beran. June 9. 36,850

Lenox av, No. 423, w s, 24.11 n 131st st, 25x75, five-story stone front flat. Charles F. Fairman and Fenella his wife to John S. Gaffney. *Mt.* $23,000. July 17. 24,500

Lenox av, Nos. 467-471, w s, 25 s 134th st, 99.10 x100, three five-story brk flats. Foreclos. Henry R. Beekman to William Livingston. Sub. to morts. *Mt.* $25,600. July 23. 72,000

Madison av, No. 2120, s w cor 133d st, 99.11x80, three-story stone front dwell'g. Sarah J. Collins widow to Samuel A. Thompson. May 27. 13,000

Madison av, No. 2050, w s, 50.10 s 130th st, 16.5 x75, three-story stone front dwell'g. Victorine E. P. Bowles to Isabel A. McKinstry. ½ part. *Mt.* $10,000. July 25. 8,500

Madison av, No. 1588, w s, 75.11 s 107th st, 25x 100, five-story stone front flat. Lizzie F. Brady to Isaac Mayer. *Mt.* $20,000. July 30. 27,000

Northern av, w s, at n e cor of irregular piece of land of Thompson N. Hollister, runs northwest 300 x again northwest 329 to lands of Hudson River R. R. Co., x northeast 262.6 x southeast 530.9 to av, x southwest 366.5, except portion taken for Public Drive. Charles Cronkright, Fairview, N. J., to Hugh N. Camp. B. & S. C. a. G. July 24. nom

Northern av, as laid out on map, w s, at n e cor of irregular piece conveyed by J. A. Haven to T. N. Hollister formerly of Isabella S. Connolly, 366.5x530.9 to Hudson River R. R., x262.6x629, excepting part taken for Public Drive. Philip F. Olwell exr. Philip Malone to Hugh N. Camp. ½ part. Sub. to mort. $10,000. July 22. 14,000

Same property. Charles Cronkright, Fair View, N. J., to same. ½ part. *Mt.* $10,000. July 20. 14,000

Same property. Bianca Connolly by Louise I. Connolly guard. to same. All title. July 23. 1,000

Same property. Patrick Malone, Philip F. Olwell and Patrick J. Olwell and Margaret his wife to same. B. & S. and C. a. G. All title. July 23. nom

Same property. Washington A. and Marie L. Connolly to Charles Cronkright. 2-15 part. B. & S. and C. a. G. July 14. 2,000

Park av, w s, 67 s 72d st, runs west 24 x south 6 x west 23 x south 1 x east 23 x north 6 x east 24 to av, x north 1. Release mort. The New York Life Ins. Co. to Robert McCafferty. July 17. nom

West End av, s w cor 102d st, 25.11x100, vacant. Mary E. wife of Alfred B. Church, Elgin, Ill., to Thomas B. McGovern. July 7. 18,000

West End av, No. 414, e s, 23.2 s 85th st, 19x 80, four-story brk dwell'g.
88th st, No. 304, s s, 121 w West End av, 21x 100.8, four-story brk dwell'g.
James B. Gunn and Maggie his wife to Alonzo B. Hepburn, Canton, N. Y. *Mt.* $44,000. July 24. nom

2d av, No. 1128, e s, 50.2 n 59th st, 25.3x76.7, four-story frame tenem't and store. Lewis Z. Bach to John J. Reilly. *Mt.* $8,000. July 15. 15,500

2d av, No. 2134, e s, 25.8 s 110th st, 25x75, four-story stone front tenem't and store. David Lese to Simon Cohen. *Mt.* $9,500. July 30. 14,400

5th av, No. 234 / 27th st, Nos. 1–11 } begins n w cor 27th st, runs north 28.6 x west 100 x north 30 x west 25 x south 58.6 to 27th st, x east 125, five-story brk building and store on av and five-story brk building and store on st.
Broad st, No. 51, e s, 80.3 n Beaver st, 28.2x58.7x25.5x58.7, four-story brk building. } Tammisin H. Bonnell to Margaret C. Bonnell, Middletown, S. I. 1-5 part. All liens. May 29. 30,000

5th av, w s, 51 s 116th st, 29.11x100, five-story stone front flat. Release mort. Morris Steinhardt to William Radebold and Edward Wenz. July 28. 2,000

Same property. William Radebold and Albertine his wife and Edward Wenz and Anna his wife to John J. Sheehan. *Mt.* $28,000. July 27. 34,000

9th av, No. 729, w s, 75.4 n 49th st, runs west 80.6 x north 29 x east 12.4 x south 2.6 x east 2.6 x south 5.6 x east 65.8 to av, x south 21, four-story brk dwell'g and stores. William Ritterbusch to Aaron Buchsbaum. Reserves rights agt Elevated roads. *Mt.* $4,500. July 29. 20,500

New York & Harlem Railroad lands, w s, part lot 157 map Morrisania, runs south 28 x east 3.7 x south 42 x west 196.8 to centre Mill Brook, x north 27.1 x north 25x25.3x54.10 x east 124 x south 55 x east 100.11. Horace D. Hufcut, Poughkeepsie, N. Y., admr. Jacob P. Giraud, Jr., to Mary E. Monaghan. July 16. 3,465

Post road from New York to Albany, s e s, lots 19 and 21 map Mary C. P. Macomb, Kingsbridge, 150x323x150x325. Foreclos. John H. Judge to George G. Guion. *Mt.* $7,500. July 23. 6,200

Lot begins at point in centre line bet 78th st and 79th st, 400 w West End av, runs north 19.11 to Riverside Drive, x southwest 22.8 x east 3.4. Therese widow Louis, Victor, Nellie and Harry Falkenau and Arthur Falkenau and Emily his wife to Christopher R. Robert, Islip, L. I. June 29. 2,500

MISCELLANEOUS.

Appointment of new trustee under deed of trust. Emily H, wife of Henry Cauncey appoints Charles H. Russell new trustee in place of Robert S. Hone. April 29, 1891. nom

General release, especially as to claims for injuries. George Balken to Nicholas Geiger and estate of Francis Geiger dec'd and Elias J. Pattison trustee. July 23. nom

23d and 24th WARDS.

Broadway, e s, begins at north cor of lot 50 map Mary C. P. McComb, Kingsbridge, 25x100x24.4x100, 24th Ward. Partition. Franklin Bien to Allen Taylor, Yonkers, N. Y. *Mt.* $475. July 29. 970

College st, s w s, 100 s e Hoffman st, 29x100. John Hanna and Catherine his wife to Warren J. Mitchell. July 23. 2,300

Hoffman st, e s, part lot A K map Cedar Hill plot, Powell farm, 1x118.3. Cara S. wife of and William H. Coffin to Robert Jeffcott. July 24. 100

Hoffman st, e s, lot A K same map, 25x118.5x25x118.3. Philip Duffey exr. Ellen Kane to Robert Jeffcott. July 25. consid. omitted

Hoffman st, e s, part lot A K map Cedar Hill plot on Powell Farm, Fordham, 1x118.3. Release mort. Andrew J. Dalton to Carra S. Coffin. July 24. nom

Poe pl, e s, 151.1 n Coles pl, 54.3x130.10x54.10x130.4. Henry C. Peters and Babette his wife to James E. Hodgson, Newport, Ky. July 30. nom

Rockfield st, n s, 675 e Marion av, 25x126.7. Berthold Heim and Ettienette his wife to George C. Engel. July 29. 600

Southern Boulevard, e s, 100 s Bainbridge av, 25.2x104x25x101. William H. Freystadt and Anna S. his wife to Mary E. Moulton. *Mt.* $552. July 28. 1,500

3d st, e s, 100 s Willard av, runs east 100 x south 100 to Clinton av, x west 36.3 x northwest 67.9 to 3d st, x north 76.10. Charles F. Williams and Eliza C. his wife to Adelbert J. Howe. June 17. nom

Same property. Edward Lucas and Julie E. his wife to Charles F. Williams. Q. C. July 20. nom

134th st, No. 545, n s, 125 w Alexander av, 25x100. Frederick Rohrs and Louise his wife to Bertha wife of Herman Schmuck. *Mt.* $15,800. July 29. 22,000

134th st, n s, 375 e Willis av, 50x100. Eliza wife of Randolph Guggenheimer to Moses Weinman. July 16. nom

Same property. Moses Weinman to Fredericke Mayer. *Mt.* $30,100. July 10. 39,000

158th st, s s, 250 w Elton av, 50x100. Gyulo Armeny to Deutsch Amerikanischer Turn Verein. Q. C. *Mt.* $3,000. July 27. 5,200

160th st, s s, lot 63 map Melrose, 50x100, hs & ls. Elizabetha Stahl to Elizabeth Stahl her daughter. July 23. 3,250

161st st, s e cor William st, 147.6x99.1x101.6. Elizabeth Driscoll exr., &c., Ellen Short to Charles E. Rhinelander. July 29. 4,300

170th st, s s, 111 e Fulton av, 100x118x100x109.11. Release mort. Russellana Purdy admrx. Charles A. Purdy to Fernando Wood. July 20. nom

177th st, n s, 82.6 e Bathgate av, 37.6x81x37.10x75. Christian Schulze and Magdalena his wife to L. Napoleon Levy. July 23. nom

Bailey av, w s, plot 103, and part plot 104, map W. O. Giles' property, Kingsbridge, 24th Ward, 50x131x50x128.6. Charles D. Silleck and M. Josephine his wife to Charles T. George. *Mt.* $2,000. July 22. 2,400

Bathgate av, e s, 40 s 182d st, 20x90. William J. Pragnell and Agnes M. his wife to Charles R. Ford. July 24. 4,250

Bathgate av, No. 2069, w s, 199.4 s 180th st, 21.2x94.5x21.2x94.8. Jarvis B. Smith to Marie L. Striebel. *Mt.* $2,500. July 6. 4,653

Bathgate av, e s, 40 n 172d st, 20x120. Henry J. Behrens, Jr., to Edward Gibb. July 27. 1,750

Bathgate av, e s, 60 n 172d st, 20x120. Same to George L. Hurd. July 27. 1,750

Brook av, w s, 75 s 143d st, 25x90. Andrew Martin to Jacob Scheuer. July 25. 3,500

Same property. Jacob Scheuer to Caroline Katchen and Sarah Scheuer. *Mt.* $2,500 July 28. nom

Greenwich av, No. 39, n w cor Charles st, 26.10x77.1x12x82.2. Michael Sullivan to Albert I. and Meyer L. Sire. *Mt.* $33,000. July 21. 40,000

Madison av, w s, 153 n Kingsbridge road, 25x60. Louise Meyer to Jacob Arm. June 28. 500

Ogden av, w s, 52.4 n Birch st proposed, 16.8x100. William Crafts trustee and George I. Crafts to Peter Catella. July 17. 1,800

Ogden av, w s, 35.8 n Birch st proposed, 16.8x100. Same to Amelia wife of A. Judson Demarest. July 17. 1,800

Opdyke av, s w cor 1st st, runs south 82.7 x west 117.7 x south 25 x west 25 x north 100 to av, x east 177.8. Fannie E. Lawrence to Henry Franz. *Mt.* $1,600. July 28. 2,800

Orchard av, s e s, part lot 287 map East Tremont, 22x112.6. Thomas Doud, Jr., to Paul H. Holmer. July 25. 500

Railroad av, s e s, 239 n e 170th st, 25x150. John Kilgour, Baltimore, Md, heir Martha Kilgour and individ. to Betsey M. Garey extrx. Leander Garey. Correction deed. July 20. nom

Ryer av, e s, lot 404 map part farm Charles Berrian, 25x144. John J. Herrick to William D. Carroll. July 22. 700

Ryer av, e s, lot 417 same map, 25x168. Mary wife of John F. Melia to same. July 22. 700

Union av, No. 1173, w s, 203.8 s 168th st, 19.4x141.5x17.6x141.5. Julia C. Hendrickson to Byron A. Beale, Brooklyn. Trust deed to secure indebtedness of grantor on note made by The Investment Association of New Jersey. April 10. 40,000

Union av, e s, 274 n 165th st, 50x175. Katharina Volcker widow, Katharina the younger and Elizabeth Volcker heirs of John Volcker to Carolina wife of Philip Eckstein. July 29. 6,200

Vanderbilt av, e s, 204 n 170th st, 25x110.6x40x150.6. Betsey M. Garey exr. Leander Garey to James W. Mortimer. July 24. 2,100

Vanderbilt av, e s, 229 n 170th st, runs southeast 110.6 x northeast 3 x southeast 40 x northeast 22 x northwest 150.6 to av, x southwest 25. Betsey M. Garey extrx. Leander Garey to August Berbert. July 22. 1,450

Washington av, n w s, 25– s w 170th st, 25x150.6x23.10x150.6. Betsey M. Garey extrx. Leander Garey to August Berbert. July 25. 1,975

Washington av, w s, 200 n 180th st, 50x100. Ernest Sass to James Burns and Mary his wife. *Mt.* $2,044. July 24. 4,000

Washington av, e s, 50 n 176th st, runs north 58 x east 105 x south 108 x west 25 x north 50 x west 80. Ellen S. Ward widow to Sereno D. Bonfils. *Mt.* $16,800 on this and other property. July 21. nom

Webster av, e s, 33 s 179th st, 27x62 to Mill Brook. Agnes Reed to Sereno D. Bonfils. July 28. 4,500

Willard av, s s, 186.11 w 1st st, 50x100. Ann wife of Peter Dolan to Thomas W. Dolan. *Mt.* $4,000. July 27. nom

6th av, w s, lot 67 map Mount Eden, 50x100. Benjamin Kerr to Thomas Fawcett. July 23. 1,700

Boston Post road, s w cor Mechanic st, 41.10x57.5x38.9x57.5. Mary A. Rice to Patrick Rice her husband. B. & S. July 20. gift

New York & Harlem R. R. land, w s, 53 s of division line between lots 157 and 158 map Morrisania, runs south 28 x east 3.7 x south 42 x west 196.9 to centre Mill Brook, x north 27.1 x again north 25 x along same course 25.3x54.10 x east 124 x south 55 x east 110.10. Mary E. Monaghan to William Urbach. *Mt.* $2,079. July 28. 5,000

West Farms road, s e s, 523.7 n e Lyon st, runs south 257.1 x east 50.2 x north 291.8 x southwest 64. Charlotte I. wife of William Nagle, Jr., to Arabella Hyland. July 27. nom

West Farms to Hunts Point road, lots 13 and 14 map Hedges Farm, runs south 100 x northwest 197 x northeast 82.6 x southeast 193, except right of way over strip 3 feet wide on north side. William H. Oakley exr. Dennis Valentine to Amanda Bussing. July 1. 1,750

Parcels 3 and 4 on damage map for opening German pl, from Westchester av to Brook av. Release mort. Sarah L. Cook extrx. Mary Cooke to Mayor, &c., New York. June 23. 3,495

Parcels 3 and 4 on damage map for opening Kelly st, from Westchester av to Wales av. Release mort. David Robitzek to Mayor, &c., New York. June 10. nom

Parcel 7 same map. Release mort. Same to same. June 10. nom

Parcel 9 on damage map for opening East 160th st, from Railroad av East to Washington av. Release mort. Frederick Schwab to Mayor, &c., New York. Feb. 19. nom

Parcel 15 on damage map for opening East 169th st from Franklin av to East 167th st. Release mort. Jane E. Losee, Greenburgh, N. Y., to John F. Marlow. April 30. nom

Parcel 19A on damage map for opening East 159th st from Railroad av East to Washington av. Release mort. Maggie Dennerlein to Mayor, &c., New York. April 21. nom

LEASEHOLD CONVEYANCES.

Bowery, No. 30, store. Assign. lease. Michael Sweeney to Diederich Otteman. nom

Same property. Assign. lease. Richard and John Harms to Ferdinand R. Minrath. nom

Cherry st, No. 448, n s, 100 e Jackson st, 25x100. Mary C. wife of John A. King, North Hempstead, L. I., to William Chapman. 16 1-3 years, from July 1, 1891, per year. 200

Clinton pl, No. 11. Assign. lease. Simon Adler, Henry S. Herrman and Simon Herman to William G. Vander Roest. 12,300

Front st, Nos. 13 and 17. / West st, No. 118. / Washington st, Nos. 174 and 176. / Thompson st, Nos. 57–61. } Agreement modifying leases. New York Steam Co. to Standard Gas Light Co., New York. July 22. nom

Oak st, Nos. 30 and 32. Assign. lease. Annie Bertie to Minnie Gregory. nom

West st, n w cor Bank st, 22.1x101.2x23.5x101.4. Assign. lease. Eloise I. Chase extrx. Charles T. G. Chase to Frank L. Froment. 1,500

Same property. Consent to assign. lease. Charles T. Hoffman to Eloise I. Chace extrx. Charles T. G. Chace. nom

Same property. Same to Charles T. G. Chace. 10 years, from May 1, 1889, per year, 800

14th st, n s, 42 e 5th av, 50x129. Assign. lease. Frederick S. Howard to Florence G. Vernam, Woodsburgh, L. I. nom

14th st, No. 3 E. Assign. lease. Remington and Florence G. Vernam to The Garfield National Bank. 15,000

31st st, No. 114 W. Assign. lease. Emile Regnier to Raphael Israel. 5,000

31st st, No. 116 W. Assign. lease. Same to same. 5,000

32d st, n s, 275 e 1st av, 25x98.9. The New York Steam Co. to The Standard Gas Light Co. 100 years, from Aug. 1, 1888. 625

33d st, 4 lots on water front on the East River, extending to centre of block. / 49th st, s s, 225 e 1st av. } Agreement modifying leases. New York Steam Co. to Standard Gas Light Co., New York. July 22. nom

62d st, s s, 161.3 e 3d av, 18.9x100.5. Sarah C. Blair by Sarah C. Blair guard. to Catharine D. Blair. Life lease. July 22. nom

102d st, No. 234 E. Assign. lease. George Bock to Peter Doelger. nom

Lexington av, No. 1740. Assign. lease. Frederick Ahlers to The J. Chr. G. Hupfel Brewing Co. 1,000

Washington av, No. 1394. Assign. lease. Jacob Schappert to William and Henrietta Stricker. nom

1st av, No. 427. Assign. lease. Louis H. M. Luhrs to John H. Voege. nom

2d av, n e cor 6th st, 25.10x87. Surrender lease. Ferdinand Ehrhart to Matilda C. Jantzen. nom

2d av, No. 515, store. Dora Bauer to Patrick Kiernan. 5 years, from May 1, 1890, per year, 900

2d av, No. 515. Assign. lease. Patrick Kiernan to Patrick J. Cribbin. nom

3d av, s w cor 143d st. Martin Norz admr. Elizabeth Norz to Henry Schraeder. 15 years, from May 1, 1892, per year, 1,500, 1,800

5th av, No. 303. Assign. lease. William B. Keiley assignee Henry S. Aspinwall to Margaret A. Walsh. 500

KINGS COUNTY.

JULY 23, 24, 25, 27, 28, 29.

Adelphi st, e s, 232.5 n Lafayette av, 25x126, h & l. Margaret E. Gage to Elizabeth A. Hays, New York. *Mt.* $5,000. $5,900

Bainbridge st, n s, 156.3 w Ralph av, 18.9x100. Victor J. Dowling, of New York, to Orville D. Lankford. *Mt.* $3,500. 5,500

Bancroft pl, w s, 90 n Atlantic av, 30x90x30.10x90. Christopher P. Skelton to Louisana I. Gleason. Taxes, &c. 750

Bennett st, s s, 125 w Banzett st, 25x100, h & l. Florentine Jacobi to Emanuel Faust and Mary G. his wife. 2,100

Bergen st, n s, 100 e Stone av, runs north 138.8 x southeast 37.10 x south 101.11 x west 25. John Bergman to Alexander Spitzer and Solomon Beck, of New York. *Mt.* $2,900. 3,550

Bergen st, n s, 200 w Stone av, 25x107.2. Frederick Heddesheimer to Alexander Spitzer and Solomon Beck, of New York. 2,700

Bradford st, e s, 175 n Fulton av, 25x100. William M. Scott, of Jamaica, N. Y., to Charlotte T. Brinsley. 2,200

Bridge st, e s, 177.5 n Tillary st, 22x100. Charles L. Behlert to Samuel Less. *Mt.* $4,000. 7,800

Bristol st, e s, 275 n Eastern Parkway, 25x100, h & l. John M. Linz to Albert W. Van Siclen. 2,000

Bush st, n s, 100 e Columbia st, 20x100. John A. Johnsen to Gimhilde P. Johnson. Sub. to mort. nom

Butler st, n s, 225 w Howard av, 25x256 6 to Park pl. Catharine Allen, of New York, to Medora J. wife of Salmon H. Long, of San Francisco, Cal. gift

Butler st, n s, 250 w Howard av, 25x256 6 to Park pl. Same to Kate M. wife of Thomas P. Stoney, of San Francisco, Cal. gift

Carroll st, n s, 220 w Columbia st, 20x100 Angelo Gatino to Giuseppe Cinque. 4,200

Carroll st, s s, 276 w 7th av, 16.6x137.10x16.7x139 5. John Burns and James V. Johnson to William Morris. Mt. $5,000. 6,500

Chauncey st, s s, 192 e Saratoga av, 19x100. Samuel V. Hynes to Charles D. King and George W. Adams. Sub. to mort. 6,000

Chauncey st, s s, 211 e Saratoga av, 19x100. Samuel V. Heyes to Christian F. Hammel. All liens. 6,000

Chester st, e s, 350 s Eastern Parkway, 50x100. Hilda Anderson to Abram Plotkin. Mt. $2,100. 2,600

Clark st, n e s, 95 n w Fulton st, 28.3x90.7x20.6x90.7. Foreclos. John Courtney to Amelia L Gurlitz. 9,000

Clementina st, s s, 375 w Chester av, 100x100, Flatbush. Thomas F. Walsh heir Thomas Walsh to Mary A. wife of John Sexton. ½ part. 150

Crescent st, w s, 89.7 n Fulton st, 60x105. Marenus J. Goodenough to Charles H. Smith. 1,575

Dean st, s w s, 60 s e Bond st, 20x95. Mary J. wife of and William S. Banker to Nelson J. Botsford. Mt. $3,500. Deed dated 1865. 6,500

Same property. Jennie wife of Nelson J. Botsford, of New York, to Bertha Steinbart. Mt. $3,000. 6,500

Dean st, n w cor Buffalo av, 27.8x100. Margaretha Koehl to John Koehl. gift

Dean st, s s, 150 w Clason av, 50x110, hs & ls. Daniel and Joseph Kramer, Johnstown, Pa., to Louis H. Myers, Jr. Mt. $6,500. 12,500

Dean st, n e cor Kingston av, 25x107.2. David Taylor to John D. Taylor. C. a. G. Mt. $5,500, 1880. 3,000

Same property. John D. Taylor to St. Martha's Sanitarium and Dispensary. Mt. $5,500. 7,550

Dean st, n s, 25 e Kingston av, 75x107.2. Mary W. Waldron to St. Martha's Sanitarium and Dispensary. Mt. $5,000. 9,500

Dean st, n s, 140 e Stone av, 20x107.2. James Golden exr. Ellen T. Golden to Erastus D. Benedict. 1,200

Same property Erastus D. Benedict to Sarah C. Golden. Mt. $1,250, taxes, &c. 1,200

Dean st, n s, 83 4 e Utica av, 84.11x ½ block. Henry Weil to Charles A. Martin. 4,000

Decatur st, n s, 208 w Stuyvesant av, 0.6x100. Release mort. Mary H. Powers to James A. Lawrence. nom

Diamond st, n s, 1639.7 e Flatbush av, 70x200, Flatbush. Alfred H. Olena to Rudolph G. Berger. 15,000

Same property. Rudolph G. Berger to Ella Bender. Mt. $7,555. 15,000

Diamond st, n s, 1,639.7 e Flatbush av, runs east 20 x north 300 x west 70 x south 50 x east 50 x south 150, Flatbush. Theophilus Olena to Alfred H. Olena. 1,500

Douglass st, n s, 375 w Smith st, 22x100. Elizabeth Armstrong to Sarah E. Armstrong. nom

Dresden st, e s, 100 n Arlington av, 25x100. John McColloch to William Bedford. 1,200

Eastern Parkway, s e cor Watkins st, 100x100. Byron W. Clarke to Ada wife of Lewis Parmer. 4,400

Eastern Parkway, s s, 40 e Hendrix st, 20x100. Gilbert B. Strang to Moritz Feldmann. 2,400

Eagle st, n s, 560 w Manhattan av, 25x100. Eliza widow of John Kienle to Albert Morlock. Q C. 350

Same property. Albert Morlock to Catherine Stockhofer and Christopher Huss. Mt. $4,000. 8,600

Eldert st, n w s, 95 s w Evergreen av, 140x100.
Eldert st, s e s, 95 s w Evergreen av, 140x—x 95x—.
Highland Nat Bank, Newburgh, to Abram S. Cassedy. nom

Eldert st, n w s, 95 s w Evergreen av, 140x100. Abram S. Cassedy to Virginia A. Kleine. nom

Essex st, w s, 250 s Ridgewood av, 20x100.
Essex st, w s, 290 s Ridgewood av, 20x100.
Release mort. Williamsburgh Savings Bank to Edward F. Linton. 700

Ewen st, e s, 75 n Skillman av, 21.10x51.8x18.5x64.7.
Skillman av, n s, 25.2 e Ewen st, runs north 56 6 x west 14.3 x southeast — to beginning.
Thomas Gibbons to Charles Frazier. Q. C. nom

Fulton st, n s, 280.6 w Rockaway av, runs north 40.4 to Somers st, x west 22.11 x south 35.2 to Fulton st, x east 23.6, h & l. Nathaniel F. Jones to Spencer Aldrich. Mt. $5,200, taxes, &c. nom

Fulton st, s s, 20 w Albany av, 20x100, h & l. George E. Schroder to Charles Miller. Mt. $6,000. exch

Freeman st, n s, 295 e Franklin st, 25x100. Philipp Bierschenk to Charles Bierschenk. 3,500

Floyd st, n s, 340 e Nostrand av. Party wall agreement. Louis Beer and Michael Schaffner to Joseph Hoegerle. nom

Frost st, s s, 200 w Humboldt st, 25x154.6x25x140. John Rueger to Henrietta Cronacher. Mt. $4,000. exch

Frost st, s s, bet Lorimer and Leonard sts, being lot 87 block 24 assessm't map 15th Ward. John C. McGuire, Registrar of Arrears, to Mary Carroll. 84

Grand st, s s, 88 e Havemeyer st, 12x77. John H. Ahrens to Frank M. Eldredge. Mt. $3,500. nom

Gerry st, s s, 125 e Harrison av, 25x100. Julianna Ferber to Henry Hessner and Kate his wife. 3,450

Graham st, e s, 229.7 s Little Nassau st, 25x85. Coro Vannvarato to Gerrado Ferando. 800

Halsey st, s e s, 140 n e Evergreen av, 20x100. Ernestine Gastmeyer to Charles Seifert and Louise his wife. 4,500

Halsey st, n s, 250 w Howard av, 16 8x100. Lauretta Gill to James H. Loper. Mt. $2,400. 638

Halsey st, s s, 300 e Lewis av, 20x100. Phebe Smart to William S. Fair, of New York. Mt. $3,000. 8,500

Hancock st, n s, 431.3 e Reid av, 18.9x100. Asa W. and Sophie G. Parker, of New Hamburg, N. Y., to James H. Doremus. Mt. $3,000. 5,800

Hall st, No. 127, e s, 144 6 n Myrtle av, 20x100, h & l. Thomas Hanlon to Ellen Hanlon. nom

Hart st, s s, 210 w Sumner av, 19.6x100. Charles Miller to George E. Schroeder. Mt. $5,000. nom

Heyward st, No. 74, s s, 114.10 e Bedford av, 19x100, h & l. Amanda H. Brown to Asahel F. Mitchell. 4,300

Hendrix st, w s, 225 s Blake av, 75x100. Jacob T. Van Sielen to Daniel A. Weber, Illion, N. Y. Taxes, &c., from 1889. 1,200

Hopkins st, s s, 80 w Throop av, 20x100. Gertrude Schmidt individ. and as extrx. Christian Schmidt to John C. Krumminauer and Mary S. his wife. 5,000

Hopkins st, s s, 275 w Throop av, 25x100. Max Gottlieb and Bemath Tangeir to Simon Solomon and Peter Hertz. Mt. $4,500. 5,850

Hull st, n s, 50 w Stone av, 30x100. Margaretha Lewis to Letitia Holmes. Mt. $3,500. nom

Hull st, n w s, 166 n e Bushwick av, 16.6x100, h & l. John C. Rogers to Alexander S. Stott. Mt. $1,800. 2,800

Hull st, n w s, 182.6 n e Bushwick av, 16.8x100. John C. Rogers to George W. White. Mt. $1,800. 2,800

Huron st, n s, 325 e Manhattan av, 25x100. Timothy Brennan, Morris Park, L. I., to Claus Dunkhase. 2,875

Junius st, w s, 131.7 s New Lots road, 40x100.
Hinsdale st, w s, 205.5 s New Lots road, 80x100.
Hinsdale st, e s, 86.5 s New Lots road, 60x100.
Williams av, w s, 214.2 s New Lots road, 60x100.
Frank Forman to John H. Forman. nom

Junius st, e s, extends from Sutter to Blake av, 500x90. Andrew Peck to Joseph H. Van Winkle, Hempstead, L. I. 10,000

Jerome st, w s 140 s Dumont st, 40x100. Emma L. Clayton to Nora A. Casben. 640

Johnson st, s e cor 18th st, 100x100, Flatbush. Ann M. wife of John Y. Dunn to Henry B. Davenport and John Reis. 800

King st, n w cor Dwight st, 24x— in irregular line to Dwight st, x83.
King st, s w cor Dwight st, 23.3x—to Dwight st x 58.4.
Bush st, s s, where an old water line crosses Bush st, near Otsego st, runs south 33 along irregular line x east 60 to another old water line, x north along same to Bush st, x west 152.
Joseph Foley to James L. Kearney. (Correction.) nom

Keap st, n s, 60 e Wythe av, 20x100. John Brennan to Louis and Martin Kirsch. 4,600

Linwood st, e s, 120 n Ridgewood av, 20x110.11x20x110.10, h & l. William J. Crosby to John B. Scholl. Mt. $1,700. 3,300

Logan st, w s, 150 s Belmont av, 20x100. Harry C. H. Robinson to George H. Spring. 150

Lefferts pl, s s, 132.10 w Clason av, 40x138. Mt. on this $7,000.
Atlantic av, n s, 238.8 w Clason av, 30x100.
Foreclos. Adolph L. Sanger to Joseph Schuetter, New York. 2,000

Macon st, n s, 165 w Howard av, 18x100. Calvin W. Raymond and Michael Dowley to Fred. W. Dowley. Mt. $4,500. Q. C. nom

Same property. Fred. W. Dowley to Mary H. Dowley. Mt. $4,500. Q C. nom

Macon st, n s, 221 w Howard av, 54x100. Calvin W. Raymond to Michael Dowley. Q. C. Mt. $14,550. nom

Macon st, No. 711, n e cor Ralph av, 22x100, h & l. Andrew D. Baird and F. Augustus Conkling to Fredericka Gosenholz. Mt. $6,500. 16,000

Macon st, n s, 130 w Ralph av, 18x100. Benjamin C. Raymond to James D. Rankin and James Ross. Mt. $5,500. 6,800

Macon st, n s, 220 e Reid av, 16.8x100. Frank C. Swimm to Delia F. Louvet. Mt. $3,800. 6,300

Madison st, No. 1248, s e s, 332 s w Knickerbocker av, 15x100. Sophie wife of and Louis Gelb to George A. Craig. Sub. to mort. 1

Malbone st, s s, 220 w New York av, 40x100, Flatbush. Adam Scheiff to John and William Williams. 600

Market st, w s, 1,075 n Record pl, 25x150. Adaline wife of Samuel I. Smith, of Port Washington, N. Y., to Alexander S. Cook. 625

Monroe st, s s, 215 e Bedford av, 20x100. Frank B. Beers exr. Huldah A. Powell to Mary A. wife of and James J. Wood. 8,250

Monroe pl, w s, 200 s Clark st, 25x100. Frederick W. Peabody to Cornelia M. Peabody. nom

Monroe st, n s, 179 w Sumner av, 17 9x100. Thomas Charlton, Tonawanda, N. Y., to Maurice L. Hanan. Mt. $4,000. 6,500

Melrose st, n s, 84 w Bremen st, 50x100. Michael Renner to Philip H. Renner. nom

Same property. Release mort. Asa A. Spear to Thomas Charlton. 600

Nassau st, s w cor Pearl st, 26x100 to Gothic alley. George E. Wheeler to Samuel and John H. Burling. Mt. $3,000. 10,000

Newport st, n e cor Watkins st. runs north 250 x east 100 x south 50 x east 100 to Stone av, x south 200 to Newport av, x west 200. William H. Mount to James G. Roberts. Mt. $6 000. nom

North Henry st, e s, 230.3 n Van Pelt av, 17x100. Charles Engert to William A. and Permillie Smith. 3,500

Osborn st, w s, 75 n Blake av, 25x100. Livi Gross to Max Green. Mt. $1,500, taxes. 3,100

Osborn st, w s, 175 s Blake av, 50x100. George B. Horne to Isaac M. Cohen and Marks Jacobs. 1,100

Osborn st, e s, 150 s Eastern Parkway, 25x100. Abraham Ruth to Max Blumenkranz and Samuel Faske, of New York. Mt. $3,000. 5,850

Osborn st, w s, 200 s Livonia av, 75x100. Lewis Rapps to Solomon Kassel. Mt. $800. 1,800

Pacific st, s s, 94 w 3d av, 13.6x100. Arthur Koch to Antonio Lopes. 4,000

Pacific st, n s, 100 e Albany av, 108x100. Julia wife of Peter A. Young to William V. Young. 5,000

Same property. Release mort. Henry Ringsbauser to Julia wife of Peter A. Young. 1,500

Palmetto st, n w s, 225 n e Knickerbocker av, 75x100. Constantine Reichert to Anton Weinig, of New York. 6,100

Powell st, w s, 150 s Liberty av, 25x100. James H. Hart to Maria B. Day. Sub. to morts. 3,500

President st, No 187, n s, 135.6 e Henry st, 16x100, h & l. Mary A. wife of William H. Hammond and Ann L. Baker, Pleasantville, N. Y., to Artemas S. Cady. Mt. $5,168. 6,300

President st, s s, 309.8 e 5th av, 17 6x100. Julia A. Van Vleck, of Hudson, N. Y., to Ann E. Gray. Mt. $6,000. nom

President st, s s, 3:7 e 5th av, 35x100.
President st, s s, 379 e 5th av, 35x100.
Also strip .06x100 belonging to No. 704 President st.
Ann E. Gray, of Hudson, N. Y., to Julia A. Van Vleck. Mt. $26,250. 15,000

President st, s s, 314.6 w 5th av, 17x100, h & l. George R. Brown to N. Denison Morgan, New York. Mt. $6,250 and taxes 1890. exch. and 250

President st, n s, 217 e 6th av, 62 6x95. M. Palmer Bridge to William L. Perkins. Mt. $5,000. 15,000

Pulaski st, n s, 260 w Tompkins av, 20x100. Charles Wise to Leopold Wise. ½ part. Mt. $3,000. nom

Pulaski st, n s, 257 e Nostrand av, 18x100. Edwin Arden, of Castleton, N. Y., to Margaret A. Eagleson, of same place. Mt. $2,800. 2,400

Pulaski st, s s, 150 w Tompkins av, 28x100, h & l. Lizzie M. wife of Frederick W. Hayward to Robert Ernst. Mt. $13,000. nom

Same property. Frederick C. Jeandheur to Lizzie M. wife of Frederick W. Hayward. ½ part. Sub. to mort. $13,000. nom

Quincy st, n s, 158 4 e Throop av, 16 8x100. Margaret P. and Louis A. Troisi, of Boston, Mass., heirs of Gaetano A. Troisi to Willard S. Pladwell. Mt. $3,000. nom

Quincy st, n s, 158 4 e Throop av, 16.8x100. Willard S. Pladwell to John Molander. Mt. $3,000. nom

Ralph st, n s, 355 w Central av, 20x100. Franklin Phillips to Eliza Phillips. Mt. $1,800. nom

Ralph st, n s, 130 w St. Nicholas av, 20x100. Max Schumann to Anna wife of Max Schumann. nom

Richards st, n w s, 60.10 s w Rapelye st, 19.4x60. Bridget and John H. Canfield and Ellen Clark to Ellen F. Canfield. nom

Richards st, s cor Sullivan st, 20x80. Timothy Gill to William Dempsey. B. & S. nom

Same property. William Dempsey to Caroline Gill. B. & S. nom

Richardson st, n s 137.8 w Humboldt st, 24x65x20 6x52. Ann A. Allen widow and devisee George C. Allen to James Meakim. 700

Richardson st, s s, 150 w Lorimer st, 25x100.
Interior lot, 100 n Frost st and 175 w Lorimer st, runs north 95 x southwest 68.6 x southeast 55 x southwest 31 x east 47.
Patrick Smith to Herrmann Rhein. Mt. $300. 2,100

Sanford st, e s, 432.3 s Park av, 25x100. Release dower. Maria Happ widow to Charles H. Dilthey. 500

Same property. Mathilda Steinbauer, Bertha and Jennie Happ heirs Leonard Happ and Theodore Speth to same. Mt. $5,500. 8,500

Schaeffer st, n w s, 100 n e Knickerbocker av, runs northeast 294 6x northwest 165 9x northwest 34 4 to Covert st, x southwest 50 x southeast 110 x southwest 224 x southeast 100. August C. Feigenspan, Newtown, L. I., to Charles Guudlich. Mt. $5,100. 9,000

Seigel st, s s, 175 w Ewen st, 25x100. Lazarus Weil to Joseph Rosenberg and Jacob Feinberg. 9,500

Same property. Joseph Rosenberg and Jacob Feinberg to Jacob H. Werbelovsky. Mt. $8,500. 500

Seigel st, s s, 125 w Graham av, 25x100. Julius Lewy to Louis Rosenthal. Mt. $1,900. 5,000

Sackett st, n s, 388.4 w Smith st, 16 8x100. Willard S. Pledwell to Alfred R. Wigg, of New York. 4,900

Skillman st, e s, 161.10 s Myrtle av, 25x100. John P. Officer to Bruno and Henry C. Mattfield. 4,500

Stagg st, n s, 100 e Lorimer st, 20x100. Elizabetha Grob widow Philipp to Charles G. Hoerner. nom

Same property. Charles G. Hoerner to Rosa Wilhelm. 5,400

Stagg st, n s, 200 e Lorimer st, 20x100. Louis Wrede, North Hempstead, L. I., to Henry Schulz. *Mt.* $1,500. 3,000

Stanhope st, n s, 200 w Evergreen av, 20x100. Augusta wife of Henry C. Bauer to Henry Goetz. *Mt.* $1,600. 4,000

Same property. Henry Goetz to Ella E. Hall. nom

Same property. Ella E. Hall to Henry Goetz. nom

Stanhope st, s s, 170 w St. Nicholas av, 20x100. Max Schumann to Anna wife of Max Schumann. nom

Stanhope st, s s, 125 e Evergreen av, 25x131.9 x25x131. Annie Fickeissen and Lena Koller to Louis Koller. ⅜ part. 2,000

Same property. Louis and Emma Detering by Martha Detering guard. to same. 1-8 part. 1,000

Same property. Release dower. Martha Detering widow to same. nom

Suydam st, n w s, 300 n e Hamburg av, 25x100. August Sedlmeier to Heinrich Horner. *Mt.* $3,000. 6,200

Suydam st, n w s, 275 n e Hamburg av, 25x100. Same to same. *Mt.* $3,000. 6,200

Suydam st, n w s, 150 s w Knickerbocker av, 25x100, h & l. August Sedlmeir to George Dumser and Margaretha his wife, joint tenants. *Mt.* $3,000. 6,300

Tompkins pl, w s, 142 s Harrison st, 21x119.6. Susie C. wife of Joseph Bates to Kate Muller. 7,500

Varet st, n s, 260.7 e Bushwick av, 25x100. Benedict Vogt to Moritz Zimmerman. 3,400

Same property. Moritz Zimmerman to Leon Gerstenfeld, of New York. nom

Vermont st or av, w s, 50 n Belmont av, 25x100. Agnes Fitzpatrick widow to Katherine Ochs. 700

Union st, n s, 293.8 w Smith st, 15.8x100. Edmond W. Allen legatee under will of Mary E. Parker formerly Allen to Daniel W. Parker. nom

Same property. Daniel W. Parker to Patrick McNamara. *Mt.* $2,800. 4,250

Walton st, n s, 95 e Harrison av, 25x103.1x24.1 x105.1. Jennette wife of William Johnston to Stephen Hamilton. 3,400

Warwick st, w s, 125 s Arlington av, 25x95. Francis H. Koenig to George Adler. *Mt.* $2,750. 4,450

Watkins st, e s, 100 s Broadway, 100x100. Byron W. Clarke to Abram Simon and Haskel Silberman. 3,200

Watkins st, e s, 75 n Dumont av, 25x100. Charles R. Lynde, of New Jersey, to Markus Paul. *Mt.* $15,000. nom

Same property. Markus Paul to James O'Halloran. 450

Weirfield st, s e s, 440 n e Bushwick av, 20x100. Elizabeth M. Hoffmann to August H. T. Hoffmann. *Mt.* $1,400. nom

Woodbine st, s e s, 138 n e Hamburg av, 18x100. Release mort. Anna E. Cozine and James Gascoine exrs. Jno. G. Cozine and James Gascoine individ. to George W. and Charles H. Francisco. 2,331

Same property. George W. and Charles H. Francisco to James H. Little. nom

Woodbine st, n w s, 25 s w Knickerbocker av, 200x100. James Gascoine to Albert Berckmeier. ½ part. nom

Same property. Anna E. widow John G. Cozine individ. with James Gascoine as exrs., &c., John G. Cozine to same. ½ part. 5,250

1st st, s w s, 386 n w 5th av, 58.11x100. Francis A. Coutant to Ezra D. Bushnell. *Mt.* $5,600. nom

3d pl, s s, 190 e Henry st, 17x133.5. Albert Most to Pauline Most. nom

South 4th st, s s, 213.6 e Driggs st, 23x100. John Keresey to William F. Guilfoyle. 7,800

South 5th st, n e cor Roebling st, 40x76. Ambrose M. Morgan to Mary A. Maujer trustee Daniel Maujer. B. & S. 11,000

6th st, s s, 228.10 e 6th av, 17x100, h & l. Thomas H. Robbins to Absalom W. Dieter. All liens. 500

East 7th st, w s, 230.11 n Greenwood av, 25x100, Flatbush. Henry J. Cullen, Jr., ref. to William E. Murphy. 395

East 7th st, w s, 230.11 n Greenwood av, 12.6x100, Flatbush. Sophronia M. Fickett widow to William J. Guy. 1,700

East 9th st, centre line, lots 29 and 30 block 27 map Ocean Parkway and Park lots extending to Coney Island av, Flatbush. Peter H. McNulty to Charles Gold. 600

East 9th st, w s, 160 n Av C, 40x100, Flatbush. Benjamin J. Conroy to Annie Fox. *Mt.* $215. 590

9th st, s s, 218.1 w 8th av, 20.5x72.6x20.4x72.6.
9th st, s s, 277.6 w 8th av, 18.8x72.6x18.10x 72.6.
9th st, s s, 335.4 w 8th av, 40.3x82.6.
9th st, s s, 415.8 w 8th av, 40.6x82.6x40.5x82.6.
John F. Hart to John Moore. 20,000

10th st, s s, 114 w 7th av, 18.6x100. Francesco Romeo to Annita Romeo. nom

14th st, s w s, 145 n w 3d av, 15x90. Mary M. Stevens widow to Henrietta L. wife of R. B. Welton. *Mt.* $800. nom

16th st, n s, 302.10 w 7th av, 26.8x100. Sophia L. wife of and George O. Van Orden to Thomas Calvert. *Mt.* $2,800. exch

17th st, No. 316, s w s, 70 s w 6th av, 15x100.10. Edward P. Day to J. Godfrey Schutz. 1,800

19th st, s w s, 275 s e 3d av, 16 8x100. Charles A. Parsons to Jochein M. Bening. 2,150

20th st, s s, 300 e 4th av, 25x100.2. Release mort. Susan M. Barclay to Carl Thorstensen. 600

22d st, s w s, 550 s e 6th av, 25x100. James More, New York, to Joseph S. Iverson. Sub. to mort. nom

Same property. Joseph S. Iverson to Frank W. Wagner. *Mt.* $600. nom

23d st, n e s, 250 s e 5th av, 25x100. Bertha Boerner to William Moore. ⅛ part. 1,200

44th st, s s, 452 e 3d av, 20x100.2. William Bihl to Rudolph Reller. ⅛ part. 537

54th st, n s, 380 w 3d av, 17.6x100. Release mort. Lawrence Hurlburt to Levi V. Martin. 200

60th st, n s, 260 e 12th av, 20x100.2, New Utrecht. James V. S. Woolley, of New York, to Ganaro Uliano. 300

63d st, s w s, 120 s e 10th av, 20x100. Claus Doscher to Emelyn Lange. 105

67th st, n e s, 280 n w 12th av, 40x100.
12th av, east cor 75th st, 100x100.
75th st, n e s, 200 s e 12th av, 100x100, New Utrecht.
Hoik D. Campbell to George B. Adams, Middletown, N. Y. 2,650

70th st, n s, 130 w 15th av, 20x100, Lefferts Park. James V. S. Woolley to Joseph Kunczal. 260

73d st, s s, 99.6 w 18th av, 40x100, New Utrecht. John Hanley to Catherine Hanlon, of New York. 500

75th st, n e s, 220 n w 4th av, 40x100, New Utrecht. William V. Williamson to Amanda Miller. *Mt.* $2,500. 5,000

76th st, s s, 270 w 15th av, 40x80.9x40x79.9 Lefferts Park. James V. S. Woolley to Frank R. Mattoon, West Summerville, N. J. 250

76th st, s w s, 411 n w 18th av, 80x100, New Utrecht. James A. Townsend to James W. Johnstone. 800

76th st, n e s, 220 n w 12th av, 60x100, New Utrecht. Hoik D. Campbell to John H. Bradner, of Middletown, N. Y. 600

76th st, n e s, 120 n w 12th av, 100x100, New Utrecht. Hoik D. Campbell to F. Louise Butler, of Olean, N. Y. 1,000

84th st, s w s, 100 s e 23d av, 20x200 to 85th st, New Utrecht. James D. Lynch to St. Mary's Roman Catholic Church at Bensonhurst. 400

84th st, easterly cor 29th av, 60x100, Gravesend. George Sibley to Emma S. Lathrop wife of David P. Winne. 825

Atlantic av, Nos. 2528 and 2530, s s, 61.2 w Williams av, 40.8x104.11x40x97.2.
Atlantic av, No. 2584, s s, 20.6 w Williams av, 20.4x93.4x20x89.5.
Harvey W. Fawcett to Matilda L. Bolles, Bayport, Conn. *Mt.* $12,000, taxes, &c. 25,000

Atlantic av, n e cor Ocean pl, 18.6x80. Release mort. Nelson Hamblin to James A. Hamblin. 1,600

Bay Ridge av, n w cor Bay st, runs northeast 320 to centre 69th st, x northwest — x north 176.2 x northwest 21.6 to high-water mark of New York Bay, x southwest to Bay Ridge av, x southeast —, with all title to land under water and dock extending from said premises into the bay. Frank T. Brown, Buffalo, N. Y., to Mary H. Brown. 1¼ part. B. & S. nom

Belmont av, s s, 50 w Barbey st, 50x100. Hannah L. Kenney to James F. Kenney. B. & S. nom

Belmont av, n w cor Montauk av, 20x90. James D. Lynch to Annie Flynn. 350

Belmont av, n s, 60 w Montauk av, 20x90. James McMurdo to Thomas J. McLaughlin. *Mt.* $1,800. 2,825

Bushwick av, s w s, 69 s e Dodworth st, 22.6x 71.2. Charles J. Hauck to Carrie J. wife of Joseph Probst. *Mt.* $3,600. 6,800

Bushwick av, n e cor Flushing av, 17 8x115x15x 100, comprising portion of old Newtown & Flushing road. Foreclos. Frederick W. Rebhann to Anna M. Irwin and George W. Conselyea. 1,900

Bushwick av, n w cor Van Voorhis st, 30x75. Philip Steingotter to Otte Velter, of New York. *Mt.* $7,000. nom

Bushwick av, w s, 60 n Van Voorhis st, 29x75. Same to Augusta Stumm. *Mt.* $5,000. nom

Christopher av, w s, 175 n Lott av, 25x100. Thomas E. McRae to Edmund Beardsley. 275

Central av, westerly cor Weirfield st, 100x341. Release judgment. Equitable Co-operative Building and Loan Assoc. to Leopold J. Lippmann. 2,022

Central av, e s, 15 n Hart st, 15x70. Francis S. Cronk to Andreas Ruegamer. *Mt.* $1,500. 2,250

Central av, e s, 180 s Noll st, 30x100. Jacob Lauth, of New York, to Pauline Frank. *Mt.* $7,000. 9,300

Clinton av, No. 97. Frank S. Laird to Arietta Baird. ¼ part. Sub. to a dower right, &c. 1,681

De Kalb av, s s, 90 e Knickerbocker av, 10x25. Release mort. Andrew Ginter to Christian A. Keppler. nom

Flushing av, s w cor Clermont av, 25x79.9x40.7 x75, h & l. Georgianna wife of William S. McIlvain formerly Dickson to Margaret wife of John Brennan. C. a. G. 7,000

Fort Hamilton av, s e cor 66th st, runs south along av 101.8x272.2x100x254. Phebe M. individ. and as extrx. Eleanor F. Clarke and George H. Roughton exrs., &c., Henry L. Clarke to John R. Weir. 1,840

Franklin av, e s, abt 116 8 n Park av, 16.8x100. Anne Conway widow to Susan Doonan. B. & S. gift

Gates av, n s, 44.6 w Classon av, 43.6x82x44 6x 79, h & l. Charles D. Rust to George H. Chinnock. *Mt.* $6,000. exch and 10,750

Glenmore av, n e cor Watkins st, 100x100. William Schwartz to Joseph Levin. *Mt.* $12,000 on this and other premises. 3,200

Gravesend av, s w cor 60th st, contains 16 62-100 acres, Gravesend. Kate L. wife of Albert D. Hicks, of Newark, N. J., to Sarah Rice, Amelia A. Stillwell, Jennie M. Read, Sarah G. Loud, Dora E. Rice and Catharine R. Ward. Q. C. 1,200

Gravesend av, n w cor 60th st, contains 1 642-1,000 acres; also.
22d av, n w s, adj north line of above if extended northwesterly 52-1,000 acres, Gravesend.
Sarah and Dora E. Rice, Amelia A. Stillwell, Jennie M. Read, Sarah G. Loud and Catharine R. Ward to Kate L. wife of Albert D. Hicks. Q. C. nom

Greene av, s s, 290 w Hamburg av, 25x100, h & l. George Covert to Ernest Reichardt and Wilhelmina his wife. 6,500

Greene av, n s, 500 e Grand av, 25x100. William H. Tunison to The Dennison Mfg. Co. *Mt.* $4,000. 9,500

Harrison av, w s, 50 s Wallabout st, 25x100, h & l. August Achterrath to Morris Jablin. 8,350

Hamburg av, n e s, 25 n w Madison st, 75x80.
Hamburg av, n e s, 100 n w Madison st, 75x100.
James Gascoine to Jacob Manneschmidt. nom

Hamilton av, s w s, 211.4 n e Henry st, runs southwest 56.6 x northeast 63.1 to Luquer st, x southeast 16.7 to av, x south 32.4. Ella wife of and Charles Benner to Theophilus Olena. *Mt.* $4,000. exch

Howard av, e s, 184 s Herkimer st, 16.10x98. Foreclos. John Courtney to William J. C. Miller. 1,800

Irving av, n e s, 25 s e Greene av, 25x90. John Bayer, Joseph Weidner and Serafin W. Turner to Margarethe Fusekbr. *Mt.* $3,500. 6,575

Knickerbocker av, s w s, 107 n w Flushing av, 8.4x21.3x25x21.8. Rudolph Bleyer to Sigmund Bleyer. 800

Knickerbocker av, n s, 25 e De Kalb av, runs west 25 x north 10 x east 50 x south 100 to Knickerbocker av, x west 25. Christian A. Keppler to Nathan F. Munz. *Mt.* $3,500. 7,400

Livonia av, n s, 50 w Thatford av, 25x100. Davis Rosinovitz to Guta Meyer. *Mt.* $1,300. 2,000

Livonia av, n w cor Stone av, 175x100. Constant Leigeois to David Rosing. *Mt.* $2,500. 4,200

Lafayette av, n s, 137.6 e Sumner av, 18 9x100. William Conselyea to Martha S. Gray. *Mt.* $4,000. 6,400

Lexington av, n s, 250 e Reid av, 16.8x100. William A. Hughes to Mary J. wife of Daniel B. Furry. *Mt.* $2,250. 5,000

Linnington av, n e cor Thatford av, 100x100. Bessie Naughton to Adolf Mandel. 2,500

Marcy av, s e s, 25 s w South 1st st, 25x100, h & l. George H. Schauer, Frank Kessler, Barbara Dumproff individ. and exr. of Andreas Dumproff and John M. Dumproff to James Monaghan. *Mt.* $8,000. 14,550

Marcy av, w s, 40.6 n Division av, 18.2x100x south 17.5 x east 100. Thomas Shepherd to William H. Meyers. 7,600

Myrtle av, s s, 60 e Bleecker st, 100x80.
Knickerbocker av, e s, 80 s Bleecker st, 60x80.
Stephen P. Sturges to Edward Thompson, Yonkers. nom

Myrtle av, n s, 58.7 w Pearl st, 22.2x80. Edward J. Harvey to Augeline E. Darling, Utica, N. Y. *Mt.* $7,000. 12,500

Meeker av, s s, 141 e Graham av, 24x100. John H. Hall to Rachel Baschwitz. 2,300

Montrose av, s s, 80 w Humboldt st late Smith st, 20x100. Emil Rauth, Joseph Meyer and Anna M. Scheertl to Samuel Cohau or Coban. 5,200

Montauk av, e s, 650 n Liberty av, 75x100. Robert Plowright, Freeport, L. I., to Charles Hancock. 1,650

Narrows av, west cor 88th st, 100x125.
Narrows av, south cor 88th st, 148.8x842 8 x south 15.9 x southeast 10.5 x northeast 100 to 88th st, x northwest 330, New Utrecht.
David D. Field to Lizzie Poulson. 9,820

Park av, n s, 86 w Franklin av, 22.6x90.1x23.11 x 90.1, excepting 2.3 taken for Park av. Anne Conway widow to Margaret Meurer. B. & S. gift

Park av, n s, 60.10 w North Elliott pl, 20.7x49.5 x14.10x45.3. Release mort. Harriet F. Post, of Quogue, N. Y., to William McKeon. 2,000

Same property. William McKeon to George W. Heatley. *Mt.* $2,000. 3,175

Patchen av, e s, 75 n Monroe st, 25x100, h & l. William Storm to Mary Gregory. 3,500

Prospect av, n s, 273 w 3d av, 44.1x43x44x47.10. Elizabeth L. wife of George H. Chinnock to Frederick W. Rowe. *Mt.* $2,000. exch

Prospect av, n s, 141 w 3d av, 22x62.6x22x64. Deborah C. Topping, of South Glastonbury, Conn., to Gustaf V. Waeberg. 2,500

Putnam av, n w s, 180 s w Central av, 60x100. Leopold J. Lippmann to James W. and Albert J. Lamb. *Mt.* $1,800. nom

Putnam av. Party wall agreement. John D. Miller with Leopold J. Lippmann.

Putnam av, s s, 130 e Ralph av, 49x100. Alfred L. Beasley and Charles Lewis to Alfred L. Beasley. *Mt.* $14,400. nom

Putnam av, s s, 40 w Broadway, runs west 19 x south 91.10 x northeast 30.7 x north 67.10. James W. Lamb to Charles T. Corby. *Mt.* $4,500. 8,900

Putnam av, n w s, 100 s w Central av, 100x100. Frederick Hauschildt, of New York, to James W. and Albert J Lamb. 4,050

Putnam av, n s, 90 w Evergreen av, 20x100. Russell Benedict ref. to George F. Chapman. 200

Putnam av, n s, 110 w Evergreen av, 20x100. Same to same. 2,000

Putnam av, n s, 310 e Lewis av, 20x100, h & l. Theodore W. Swimm to Mary E. Fox and Catherine I. Menihan, New York. *Mt.* $6,000. 10,500

Ralph av, n e cor Chauncey st, runs north to centre Brooklyn and Jamaica turnpike, x100 x— to st, x—. Mary F. Riley et al. to Margaret Riley. Q. C. nom

Rochester av, w s, 36 s Herkimer st, 18x74. Charles J. Warren to Amanda L. Farnquist, of New York. 2,500

Rockaway av, w s, 125 s Eastern Parkway, 25 x100. Sabra E. wife of Howard Gregg to Herman Markowitz. nom

Same property. Herman Markowitz to Marcus Lehmann. *Mt.* $800. 1,650

Rockaway av, e s, 100 s Duryea av, 125x100. Hilel and Beckey Waxberg to William Livingston ⅓ part, Samuel L. Matthews ⅓ part a d Leon Weltfisch ⅓ part. Sub. to mort. $900. 2,563

Rockaway av, w s, 150 s Eastern Parkway, 75x 100. Sabra E. wife of Howard Gregg to Jacob Jackerson, Davis Levy, Mary Aaronson and Harris Meyer. 4,700

Schenectady av, w s, 67.2½ s Dean st, 40x100. Lilian Ward to Frederick Hauschildt. *Mt* $4,500. 8,550

Schenectady av, w s, 94.2 s Dean st, 13x100. Sophronia M. Fickett widow to Lilian Ward. *Mt.* $1,500. 2,850

Schenectady av, w s, 67.2 s Dean st, 14x100. Same to same. *Mt.* $1,500. 2,850

Schenectady av, w s, 81.2½ s Dean st, 13x100. Same to same. *Mt.* $1,500. 2,850

Scott av, centre line, intersection centre line Townsend st, runs north 233 to s s Newtown Creek, x southeast to Townsend st, x southwest 247 to Scott av, also land under waters of creek adj; also,
Scott av, at intersection high-water line Newtown Creek, runs on said line being a curved line to Townsend st, x northeast 64 to exterior bulkhead line of creek along said line northwest 403 to centre line of Scott av if extended x south 22, contains 11,570 sq. ft.
Partition. George W. Fisher ref. to Thomas G. Evans. 4,000

Sheffield av, s e cor Glenmore av, 25x100. Clara Lehmann to Lucas Glokner, of New York. 2,500

St Marks av, n s, 250 w Rockaway av, 100x 127.9, h & l. Alexander Gordon to Ferdinand F. Volckening. 2,100

Sutter av, n s, 75 e Van Siclen av, 25x100, h & l. Clara H. Ives to William T. Ashford. *Mt.* $500. 2,200

Stone av, e s, 125 s Belmont av, 25x100. Rosa Rudderman to Sarah Cohen. ½ part. Sub. to mort. $300. 400

Stone av, w s, 350 s Blake av, 25x100. Mary E. Cook, Newtown, L. I., to Rosa Lisansky. *Mt.* $2,000. 3,000

Thatford av, e s, 100 s Blake av, 50x100. Samuel Grodginsky, New York, to Reuben Goldstein. 2,700

Thatford av, e s, 125 n Duryea av, 50x100. Charles H. Dietze to Emil Dietze and Anna his wife. nom

Thatford av, n e cor Livonia av, 100x100. Adolf Mandel to Aaron Lankay. 3,600

Thatford av, w s, 175 s Belmont av, 25x100.1. Moritz Stern to Josephine Lefkowitz. ½ part. 1,400

Throop av, n e s, 25 s e Bartlett st, 25x95, h & l. Charles Halbe to Frank Krashes. *Mt.* $4,250. 5,800

Throop av, w s, 40 s Stockton st, 60x100. William Hoffman and Valentine Bruckhauser to Deutsche Evangelische Prot. Volks Kirche, &c. 7,100

Union av, e s, 84 s North 2d st, 22x107. Theodore D. Dedeiks to M. Howell Topping. nom

Union av, e s, 84 s North 2d st, 22x107. M. Howell Topping to Ellen M. wife of Peter McGovern. *Mt.* $2,000. 2,900

Utica av, w s, 142 s Pacific st, 17.4x75, h & l. Frank W. and Arthur J. Robbins to Harris L. Litke. *Mt.* $2,100. 3,000

Vernon av, n s, 225 e Nostrand av, 114x100. Susan Vanderveer to John Parkin. 13,400

Van Siclen av, e s, 100 s Livonia av, 25x100. Jacob T. Van Siclen to Sarah A. Brewster. 550

Warehouse av, lots 2 to 5 inclusive, and 68 to 75 inclusive, and parts of lot 6 map Asa W. Parker, Bath Beach, and land under water in front of said lots. Gustav Feigenspan to Charles Gundlich. 13,000

Williams av, w s, 175 s Bay av, 25x100. George Schadt to John Miller. 175

Wortman av, s w cor Elton st, 40x100.
Cleveland st, w s, 265 s Vienna av, 40x100.
August Niemann to Katharina Niemann. nom

Wythe av, e s, 20.8 n South 1st st, 48x77x49x 75.5. Elizabeth L. Stokes to Michael and John J. Reilly. *Mt.* $7,250. 10,550

2d av, south cor 88th st, 35.8x99.1x92.5, gore, New Utrecht. David D. Field to Phillip J. Connel. 280

3d av, n w cor President st, 20x75. Max Klein to Arthur Newman. B. & S. nom

4th av, n w s, 80.2 n e 17th st, 20x60. John Keaveny, of Port Deposit, Maryland, to Andrew Kavanaugh. Dated 1876. 5,000

4th av, n w s, 20.2 s w 35th st, 40x82. Release mort. Charles E. Rogers to Mary A. Kenny, of Spring Valley, N. Y. 320

Same property. Mary A. Kenny to Sarah J. wife of Andrew J. Powell. *Mt.* $3,000. 9,000

5th av, n w cor 21st st, 25x100. James E. Horrigan to Mary J. Horrigan. Sub. to morts. nom

5th av, w s, 47 n 21st st, 28x100. Same to same. nom

5th av, easterly cor 7th st, runs northeast 19.10 x southeast 34 x northeast .06½ x southeast 18.2 x northeast .02 x southeast 17.10 x southwest 20.6 to 7th st, x northwest 70 to beginning. John Miner to Margaret Rooney. 18,000

6th av, w s, 159.6 s 12th st, 15.6x80. Theodore B. and Henry A. Willis to Martin Mehrtens. *Mt.* $2,800. 4,050

8th av, south cor St. Johns pl, 13x100x5x95.2. John Lefferts and Gertrude L. Vanderbilt to Maria L. Sweeney. Q. C. nom

11th av, s w cor Sherman st, 87.7 x south 100 x west 121.6 x south 355 to city line, x east along same to Sherman st, x north 610. Foreclos. James C. Bergen to William O. Platt. 2,995

12th av, southerly cor 79th st, 120x100.
11th av, easterly cor 77th st, 100x100.
12th av, northerly cor Kings Highway, 72.4x 100x47.3x103.1.
75th st, s w s, 100 s e 12th av, 40x100.
75th st, s w s, 320 s e 12th av, 40x100.
75th st, n e s, 300 s e 12th av, 80x100, New Utrecht.
Hoik D. Campbell to William S. Brazier, of New York. 5,100

13th av, e s, 40.2 s 57th st, 40x100, Bath Junction. James V. S. Woolley to Aline Ortel. 500

13th av, e s, 80.2 n 59th st, 20x100, New Utrecht. James V. S, Woolley, of New York, to Martin Erickson. 275

18th av, w s, 40 n e 73d st, 40x98.1x40x98.8, New Utrecht. John H. Hanley to Frank McDermott, of New York. 800

25th av, east cor 85th st, 100x136.2 to Hillside av, x145.7 to 85th st, x242, Bensonhurst. James D. Lynch to Teresa B. Ross. 3,300

Shore road, south cor 88th st, 123x90.1x100x 109.5.
1st av, east cor 86th st, 200 to 87th st, x100.
1st av, s e s, extends from 88th st to 89th st, 200x100.
89th st, n e s, 100 s e 1st av, 125x100.
1st av, south cor 89th st, 129.5x218 to 89th st, x200, New Utrecht.
David D. Field to Lizzie Poulson. 16,290

Clove road, e s, 27.3 n Malbone st, 30.3x107.4x 20x84.7. Timothy C. Conklin to Anna E. wife of Martin Zimmerman. 300

Lot at Canarsie adj R. L. Baisley's and Chas. and Lizzie Boestelmann, 50x100. George Knoth to Henry A. Zahn. 300

Lot 256 map No. 2 Manufacturing District, East New York. Edward Wemple, State Comptroller to Lewis Hurst. Tax deed. nom

Lot 208 map 2 of G. S. Thatford property, East New York. Same to same. Tax deed. nom

Lot 143 same map. Same to same. Tax deed. 10

Lots 25–28 inclusive map Williamson Homestead, 26th Ward. Release, &c. Frank C. Lang trustee to Elise Danancher. nom

Lot at Coney Island, on line bet J. P. Cranford and J. M. Voorhies and 52 from s e cor Phoebe Voohies property, runs south 12 to land of Phoebe Voorhies, x northwest 95 x north 8 x east 96. John P. Cranford to Phoebe Voorhies. B. & S. nom

Lot begins at stake on the second division line of New Utrecht woodlands adj George Van Brunt, —x—, New Utrecht. Ella E. Hall to Hoik D. Campbell. *Mt.* $6,407. nom

Same property. Ira O. Miller to Ella S. Hall. 14,202

Lots 119, 120, 121 and 122 block 2 map 221 lots of M. J. Bergen property, New Utrecht. James V. S. Woolley to Richard Murphy. 800

Lot 716 block N map Vanderveer homestead. Cancellation of covenants. John H. Vanderveer to William Sinclair. nom

Plot of land bounded west by Old Canarsie road, north by land formerly Richard Remsen, Sr., and Bernard B. Remsen, south by Manhattan Beash R. R. and land formerly John A. Voorbees, contains 5 7,453-10,000 acres, Flatlands. Richard Remsen, Jr., to Herbert C. Smith. 6,888

Right of way, w s, 626 s East New York av, 50 x80, Flatbush. Thomas Rogers to George Shanley. 400

Same property. John Kane to Thomas Rogers. 330

Strip 15 ft. wide, adj n e s road of party second part, Flatlands. Release mort. James W. Voorhies to Brooklyn & Rockaway Beach R. R. Co. nom

Strip adj n e s of roadbed of party second part, Flatlands, 15x—. Mary S. Eglinton to Brooklyn & Rockaway Beach R. R. Co. nom

All title of grantor in and to land under water of Coney Island Creek, Gravesend. Phebe Voorhies to John P. Cranford. Q. C. nom

Parcel begins on centre line bet New York and Brooklyn avs, being 350 e New York av and 14.8 s from n s Sackett st, runs southwest 552.10 to e s of H. Schoonmaker's land, x south along same to centre Crown st, x southeast 207.3 to centre Brooklyn av, x southwest 808.5 to patent line, x east 206.10 x north 2,188.8 x west 101.11 except as follows: Sackett st, centre line, 350 w Brooklyn av, runs south to centre of Union st, x east to land of J. Skillman, x north to centre Sackett st. x west 110. Foreclos. Clark D. Rhinehart late Sheriff to Edward Schell trustee of Mary P. Cargill. 1889. 15,000

WESTCHESTER COUNTY.

JULY 22 TO 28—INCLUSIVE.

CORTLANDT.

Banker, Alfred to Augusta M. Banker, n s Crompond road, adj Gilbert Ferris, 40x126. $1,000

Brown, Leila S. et al. F. Couch ref. to Minnie B w , n e cor Elizabeth and Academy sts, 60x150. 4,500

Brown, Southard to Abr. Cohn, s s Lincoln terrace, 28x125. 196

Frost, Leila S. to Wm. Valentine, n s same, 37 x125. 175

Same to Jos. Snidamann, s s same, 25x125. 125

Same to Harriet E. Querean, n s Crompond road, 103x125. 100

Hyatt, Elizh. exrs. of to Robt. McCord, s s Bay st, cor Frederick, abt 160x140. 300

McCord, Robt. to Southard Brown, e s Frederick st, 40 n s Franklin, 40x120. 240

Same to Wm. Underwood, 1½ acre. 500

Nelson, Thos. to Jas. W. Husted, n w cor Decatur and Paulding sts, abt 447x385. 4,500

Taylor, Susan to John R. Lancaster, n s Lincoln terrace, adj grantee, 50x—. 700

EASTCHESTER.

Bulmahn, Fred C. et al. F. N. Glover ref. to Fred. Johnson, s w s Howard av, n w Greenwich st, 40x52. 1,705

Brown, Ann M. et al. to Chas. Dusenberry, Jr., e s Lake av, adj Hodgman, ½ acre and other property. 15,000

Booker, John to Emma K. Dutcher, part lot 9 Lake av map Gould lots, 50x100. 4,000

Bonnett, Wm. L. to Palmer Brundage, lots 146 and 147 map Findlay lots. 1,550

Bullard, John E. et al. to Clinton S. Loveland, lot 30 e s Johnson st, grantors map, 25x100. 275

Cassel, Cecilia to Hartwig L. Phillips, e s lane on Old Fowler farm, 10 acres. 16,000

Eggers, Henrietta to Edw. L. E. Phipps, lot 695 and part G 10 n w cor 21st av and Kingsbridge road, Wakefield. 4,400

Fowler, Clarence M. et al. to Jos. W. Archer, part lot 242 s e s Greenwich st, West Mt. Vernon, 33.4x100. 4,250

Ferry, Harvey S. to Bridget Akins, part lots 5 and 6 e s 7th av, grantor's map 36.6x100. 525

Gay, Margt. C. to Carl Stange and ano., w s 2d st, 50 n 20th av, Wakefield, 50x105. 800

Grove, Geo. W. to Henrietta Eggers, part lot 115 n w s Railroad av, West Mt. Vernon, 45 x—. 2,250

Ham, Alfred G. to Benj. A. Vantassel, Jr., w s Glen av, 180 n Sidney, 60x—. 5,750

Mayer, Fred. to Jas. W. Irwin, part lot 900 w s 11th av, Mt. Vernon, 25x105. 4,100

Miller, Thos. L. to Kath. Eisler, s e cor 6th st and South 11th av, 50x105. 1,050

Same to Lawrence Dooling, lot 55 w s South 10th av, Henneberger property, 25x105. 450

McBride, Laura R. to Ralph D. P. Brown, s s Bronxville road, adj Harlem R. R., 6 acres. 3,175

Nordman, Margaretha to Mary L. Goldbeck, lot 168 w s 8th av, Central Mt. Vernon, 50x 105. 1,900

Smeallie, Jas. A. to Ada V. Smeallie, lot 215 e s 8th av, Central Mt. Vernon, 50x100. nom

Seder, Richard to Fred. G. Luhr, lot 78 s e s Railroad av, West Mt. Vernon, 78.8x128. 1,800

Treuer, Wm. H. to Edw. W. Storms, part lot 58 w s Union av, Mt. Vernon, 50x105. 1,000

Same to Margt. L. Nesbitt, n s Monroe st, 309 e Franklin av, 40x91. 505

Same to Benj. de F. Curtiss, n s Monroe st, 259 e Franklin av, 50x91. 710

GREENBURGH.

Blake, Ann et al., S. H. Thayer ref., to Geo. Munson exr. of, lots 26–31 s w cor Warren and High sts, Uniontown. 500

Munson, Geo. exr. of, to Geraldine W. Morgan, same property. 1,000

Erhardt, Joel B. trustee to Willis Gaylord and ano., e s Stanley av, 150 n Station sq., 50x 100. 700

Storms, Chas. E. to Owen Devlin, n e cor Haines and Lefurgy avs, 50x125. 1,800

MAMARONECK.

Jordan, Theresa to Merritt Sands, w s Boston road, adj School lot. 1,500

Same to same, w s same, adj grantee, 60x114. 2,000

Boyd, Richard V. to John W. Chapman, Jr., s s Sands st, 150 w Florence, 50x100. 300

MOUNT PLEASANT.

Bogen, Jas. C. to Arcadius Soltz, 10 acres adj Harlem R. R. and the Peak Co. 4,000

Hall, Chas. H. to Harriet M. Calver, e s Washington av, Pleasantville, 50x150. 450

Smith, Wm. R. to Wm. Glenning, lots 14 and 15 block 10 map Lake Kensico. 100

Smadbeck, Louis to Hugh M. Byron, lots 661 and 662, Sherman Park. 200

Same to Finlay W. Howell, lots 1243 and 1244. 200

Same to Georgietta Beale, lots 1114 and 1115. 250

Same and ano. to Alfred Pellet and ano., lots 203 and 204 Lakehurst Villa Park. 500

Same to Gustave A. Kerker, lots 193–196 and 207–210. 1,600

Same to Harry Green, lots 121-124. 750

Same to John W. Hinton, lots 1081, 1082, 1172 and 1173. 900

Same to And. Rauh and ano., lots 384, 385, 386, 933, 934 and 935. 750

NEW ROCHELLE.

Briggs, John W. to Geo. W. Bard, 1A on Hutchinsons Creek, North Union Corners road. 1,100

Emmet, Richard S. et al. to Robt. T. Emmet, lot adj Jane E. Edgar and Burling Brook, 50 x100. 500

Lorenzen, Fred to Thos. Hutchinson, s s Morgan st, 200 from Mayflower av, 50x75. 150

Manhattan Life Ins. Co. to Sarah Kemble, lots 6 and 7 block F. Rochelle Park. 4,200

Same to N. Malon Beckwith, lot 11 block F. 1,450

Whelan, Jas. to Wm. L. Virrill and ano., n e cor Grove av and Charles st, 50x100. 1,200

OSSINING.

Brandreth, S. Louise to Hugh N. Curtis, lots 82, 83 and 84 3d map Clark estate. 300

Cobb, Annie G. to Virginia Ellegood, n e cor Lincoln pl and Highland av, 50x125. 454

RYE.

Drew, Geo. F. to Sarah Kaiser, s e cor Regent and Olivia sts, abt 121x118. 485

Ford, Wm. H. to Geo. Henderson, 2 acres on West. turnpike and gore bet Old and New Boston roads. 5,150

Henderson, Geo. to John A. Gwynne, w s Milton av, 889 n Rye Beach av, 181x157. 3,000

Same to John H. Whittemore, w s same av, adj Anna M. Corning, 125x188. 2,000

WESTCHESTER.

Curry, John L. to Wm. J. Elliott, lot 7, map School House plot. 2,150

Cobb, Marcius L. exr. of, to Henry Ruhl and ano., part lot 2, map Pugsley farm. 26,458

Camp, Hugh N. to Karl Perina, lots 258 and 262, map McGraw estate. 535

Same to Victor W. Baumbach, lot 69. 225

Same to Max Selig, lot 289. 289

Same to Bridget Ward, lot 324. 180

Duval, Jos. R. S. to Peter Polchinski, s e cor Elliot av and B st, 25x100. 450

Gerdes, Chas. H. to Levi H. Mace, lot 458 s s 9th av, Wakefield, 105x114. 1,900

Lamphear, Wm. H. to Maggie E. Buchanan, lot 1133 w s 2d av, Wakefield, 109.6x105. 2,000

Mace, Levi H. and ano. to Jacob Kalisher and ano., lots 172 and 258, Laconia Park. 400

Same to Wm. Roberts, lots 47 and 48. 400

McCormack, Thos. J. et al. to Steph. Honore, lot 284 n s 11th st, Unionport, 50x108. 1,750

Schuh, Eliz'h to Anna M. Cornely, lots 67 and 68 n e s St. Pauls av, grantor's map, 50x102. 600

WHITE PLAINS.

Young, Jackson exr. of, to Cornelius P. Young, coal yards n s Railroad av, W. R. R., ½ int. 12,000

YONKERS

Archer, Jos. W. to Eleanor H. Almond, n s Dunwoodie st, 225 e Yonkers av, 54x100. 5,000

Beall, T. Ashby to Ellen C. Ewing, lots 350 and 351 Armour Villa Park. nom

Brown, Ann M. et al. to Charles Dusenberry, The "Abram Lent Farm," w s Valley road, 67 acres, and other property. 15,000

Duden, Herman to Chas. F. Mayer, block 10 map Sunnyside Park. 4,475

Same to Ernest Machenbach, block 7 same map. 4,552

Druid Hill Park Co. to Annie E. Strang, lots 489 and 490, Mohegan Park. 400

Gramatan Park Co. to And. Andersen, lots 113 to 116, Mohegan Park. 820

Herriot, J. Groshon exr. of, to Robert Wilson, lot 71 w s Beech st, 25x100. 860

Hodgman Rubber Co. to Chas. A. Hodgman, n s Tuckahoe and Scarsdale roads, about 5 acres. 10,000

Redington, Lyman W. to The National Homestead Co., e s Riverdale av, 75 n Riverdale pl, 25x100. 4,500

Trenchard, Henry S. to Cyrus P. Jones and ano., e s Mile Square road, cor Midland av, 9 acres. 12,000

MORTGAGES.

NOTE.—*The arrangement of this list is as follows. The first name is that of the mortgagor, the next that of the mortgagee. The description of the property then follows, then the date of the mortgage, the time for which it was given, and the amount. The general dates used as headings are the dates when the mortgage was handed into the Register's office to be recorded.*

Whenever the letters "P. M." occur, preceded by the name of a street, in these lists of mortgages, they mean that it is a Purchase Money Mortgage, and for fuller particulars see the list of transfers under the corresponding date. Whenever the rate is not given, read as 6 per cent.

NEW YORK CITY.

JULY 24, 25, 27, 28, 29, 30.

Adams, Julia B. to THE MUTUAL LIFE INS. CO., New York. Madison av, e s, 60.6 s 124th st, 20x80. Already mortgaged to mortgagee. July 23, 1 year, 5 %. $1,000

Adler, Bertha to Gad Widow and Orphan Benevolent Assoc., New York. 49th st, s s, 356.6 e 2d av, 18.6x100.5. July 23, due July 1, 1896, 4½ %. 4,000

Altieri, Pietro to Henry Maguire, Eastchester, N. Y. 112th st. P. M. July 23, due Jan. 27, 1893, 5 %. 10,000

Anderson, Walden P. to Horace S. Ely and ano. exrs. Alexander M. Ross. 93d st, n s, 415 w Columbus av, 20x100.8. July 28, due Aug. 1, 1896, 5 %. gold, 21,000

Same to same. 93d st, n s, 435 w Columbus av, 20x100.8. July 28, due Aug. 1, 1896, 5 %. 21,000

Same to Martha G. Farish. 93d st, n s, 395 w Columbus av, 20x100.8. July 28, due Aug. 1, 1896, 5 %. 21,000

Same to same. 93d st, n s, 375 w Columbus av, 20x100.8. July 28, due Aug. 1, 1896, 5 %. 21,000

Same to Charles G. Judson. 93d st, s s, 375 w Columbus av, 4 lots, each 20x100.8. 4 morts., each $2,125. Sub. to mort. of $21,000 on each. July 28, demand. 8,500

Same to The Bradley & Currier Co. (Lim.) 93d st, s s, 325 e 10th av, 100x100.8. Sub. to morts. $118,125. July 28, due Sept. 15, 1891. 6,000

Adelson, Lewis to Selah R. Van Duzer, Newburg, N. Y. Eldridge st, No. 220, e s, 25 s Stanton st, 24.6x87.6. July 21, 5 years, 5 %. 18,000

Same to Jonas Weil and Bernhard Mayer, Same property. July 30, 2 years. 1,500

Babbitt, Searles mortgagor with Julius J. Lyons. Agreement reducing interest to 5 %. July 21. nom

Barron, Esther E. to Martin Cullen, Albany, N. Y. 63d st, n s, 300 w Central Park West, 37.6x100.5. July 27, 3 years. 8,000

Barstow, John E. and Eliza C. Barstow and Kate A. Williams heirs Eliza Barstow to Jane C. Gulick. 165th st, n s, extends from Prospect av to Union av, 350x108. July 27, due Aug. 1, 1894. 1,000

Bonnell, Margaret C. wife of and J. Harper to Charles Coudert. Broad st, No. 51, e s, 80.3 n Beaver st, 28.2x58.7x26.5x58.7. 1-5 part. July 30, 5 years. 8,500

Breslauer, Morris to Abraham Schlesinger and Aline Coshland. Madison st, No. 213. P. M. Sub. to mort. $21,700. July 25, due Aug. 1, 1893, or sooner. 2,300

Burns, William to The J. Chr. G. Hupfel Brewing Co. Christopher st, No. 154. Lease. June 12, demand. 800

Bonfils, Sereno D. to Anna J. Randell extrx. Ebenezer B. Belden. Webster av, s e cor 179th st, 60x60.11 to Mill Brook, x 70x60. July 24, 3 years. 4,500

Boymann, Herman to Bernheimer & Schmid. Av A, No. 1453. Saloon lease. July 29, demand. 800

Bussing, Amanda to William H. Oakley exr. Dennis Valentine. West Farms to Hunts Point road. P. M. June 1, 3 years, 5 %. 875

Boyce, Charles to THE EMIGRANT INDUSTRIAL SAVINGS BANK. Southern Boulevard, n s, 24 e Alexander av, 22.6x80. July 27, 1 year, 4½ %. 5,000

Same to same. Southern Boulevard, n s, 46.6 e Alexander av, 22.6x80. July 27, 1 year, 4½ %. 5,000

Berger, Elizabeth S. to Andrew J. Dwiuelle. Clifton st, n s, 35.8 e Tinton av, 19.2x100. July 27, 1 year. 500

Baker, La Fora S., Chicago, Ill., to Selah R. Van Duzer. Park av, w s, 50.8 s 94th st, 19x80. July 21, 5 years, 5 %. 16,000

Same to same. Park av, w s, 69.8 s 94th st, 31x80. July 21, 5 years, 5 %. 26,000

Beran, Joseph to Henry Morgenthau. Audubon av, n e cor 181st st. P. M. June 9, due June 15, 1892, 5 %. 25,800

Budde, Christiana A. to John G. Dautel. Courtlandt av, e s, 25 n Gouverneur st, No. 153, 25x100. July 23, due July 1, 1894, 5 %. 2,400

Cates, Anna A. wife of and Henry S. to William and Thomas Morton and David Brown, of Morton Bros. & Co. 113th st, No. 2 W. P. M. Sub. to mort. $2,500. July 29, 6 months. 300

Cates, Anna A. to William Broadbelt. 113th st, No. 2 W. P. M. July 29, 1 year. 2,500

Cogswell, Edna M. wife of William L., Huntington, L. I., to Maria R. Shaffer. Mott st, No. 282, e s, 75.8 s Houston st, 25x86.11; Mott st, No. 280, e s, 101.4 s Houston st, 25x81.3x25x81.2; Mott st, No. 278, e s, 125.8 s Houston st, 25x87.1x25x87. July 30, 1 year, 5 %. 5,500

Cohen, Simon to David Lese. 2d av, No. 2134. P. M. July 30, installs, 5 %. 500

Cooper, Howard to THE MANHATTAN SAVINGS INST. Bowery, No. 281, n e cor Houston st, 23x70.1. July 30, 1 year, 4½ %. 35,000

Cruger, S. Van Rensselaer to MUTUAL LIFE INS. CO., New York. 35th st, s s, 146.8 e Park av, 33.4x98.9. July 21, due July 30, 1892, 5 %. 32,000

Cambreleng, Stephen C. to Maurice Stack. Madison av, e s, 50.8 s 96th st, 25x80. July 24, due July 24, 1892. 225

Campbell, John B., R. H. Thompson, E. S. Mower, T. H. Wheeler, S. E. Hyde and J. H. Wheeler, John H. Poggenburg, John G. Hannah, E. H. Allen and Joseph Heinberger, ⅔ of stockholders of The Fibrone Mfg. Co. Consent to a mortgage by Company to Thos. H. and J. H. Wheeler, S. E. Hyde, R. H. Thompson and E. S. Mower. July 23. nom

Cone, Adelbert J. to Charles F. Williams. 3d st. P. M. July 17, due July 15, 1894, or sooner. 1,500

Cohen, Betsey and Harris to Charles Laue, Brooklyn. Delancey st, No. 44, n s, 100.6 e Forsyth st, 25x100. July 24, due Nov. 2, 1891, 5 %. 5,000

Catella, Peter to William Crafts trustee. Ogden av. P. M. July 17, due July 17, 1894, 5 %. 800

Civill, Acton T., Bovina Centre, Del., to Josephine Wandell. Monroe st, No. 96, s w cor Pelham st, runs west 36 x south 25 x southwest 23.2 x east 47.7 to Pelham st, x north 44.11. ½ part. July 24, due July 28, 1892. 2,500

Corr, Patrick to THE GREENWICH SAVINGS BANK. 26th st, No. 212, s s, 185 e 3d av, 28x98.9. July 27, due Aug. 1, 1892, 4½ %. 2,000

Cubberley, Nelson S. to Morris S. Thompson. 133d st. P. M. July 28, 6 months, 5 %. 3,450

Coffin, Edmund, Jr., to THE TITLE GUARANTEE AND TRUST CO. Bradhurst av, No. 39, w s, 209.6 s 145th st, 18.1x72.9x18.2x75.2. July 22, due July 29, 1892, 5 %. 5,500

Same to same. Bradhurst av, No. 37, w s, 227.7 s 145th st, 18.1x70.2x18x72.9. July 22, due July 29, 1892, 5 %. 5,500

Same property. Bradhurst av, No. 35, w s, 245.9 s 145th st, 18.1x67.9x17.11x70.2. July 22, due July 29, 1892, 5 %. 5,000

Same to same. Bradhurst av, No. 33, w s, 263.11 s 145th st, 18.1x65.2x18.2x67.9. July 22, due July 29, 1892, 5 %. 5,000

Same to same. Bradhurst av, No. 31, w s, 282 s 145th st, 18.2x62.9x18.1x65.2. July 22, due July 29, 1892, 5 %. 4,500

Decking, Bernhard J. to Henry Frey trustee Henry W. Sparnicht. Lexington av, s w cor 108th st, 20.11x75. July 29, 1 year. 2,000

Duncan, William H. to THE GERMAN-AMERICAN REAL ESTATE TITLE GUARANTEE CO. Tiebout av, w s, 50 s Clark st, 25x100. July 28, 3 years, 5 %. 3,500

Same to Minna Bresler. Same property. Sub. to mort. $3,500. July 24, due July 27, 1892. 1,275

Demarest, Amelia wife of A. Judson to William Crafts trustee. Ogden av. P. M. July 17, 3 years, 5 %. 1,080

Dowling, John W. to The Sheltering Arms. 43d st, s s, 158 e 5th av, 20.6x100.5. July 17, 1 year, 5 %. 2,500

Downes, William and Charles W. Downes to James L. Willis, Eastchester, N. Y. Pitt st, e s, 204.9 n Stanton st, 22.5x75. July 1, 2 years, 5 %. 1,000

Dunbar, James to David J. Steinhardt. Vyse av, lot 27 map Thomas Walker, West Farms, 25x143.3x25x143. July 22, due July 22, 1896. 750

Dow, Myron W., New Castle, N. Y., to THE METROPOLITAN LIFE INS. CO. 39th st, n s, 90 w 3d av, 19x94.4x19.2x91.8. July 27, due Oct. 1, 1892, installs. 24,000

Same to same. 39th st, n s, 109 w 3d av, 27.3x98.2x27.6x94.4. July 27, due Oct. 1, 1892, installs. 33,000

Dow, Myron W. to William J. Light. 39th st, n s, 90 w 3d av, 46.3x98.2x46.9x91.8. July 27, demand. 2,500

Same to THE MURRAY HILL BANK. Same property. July 27, demand. 24,000

Dunne, Thomas P. to Marx and Moses Ottinger. 116th st, n s, 150 w 8th av, 50x100.11. July 21, due Dec. 19, 1891. 10,000

Donohue, Mary wife of Patrick to Johannes Bagger. 160th st, s s, 275 e Courtlandt av, 25x100. July 25, due Dec. 30, 1893. 800

Duffy, James to George J. Bernhard. 102d st, s s, 100 e 3d av, 35x100.11. July 23, due Aug. 17, 1891. 1,800

Demarest, Henry H. to Francis B. Chedsey. Sullivan st, Nos. 119-123, e s, 60.4 s Prince st, runs east 75 x south 41.2 x east 25 x south 25 x west 100 to Prince st, x66.2; Sullivan st, e s, 126.6 s Prince st, 25x100. Collateral to another mortgage on property in Sullivan county. July 22, due Oct. 1, 1891. 1,316

Du Bois, Charles A. to Alina B. wife of Edward L. Young. 93d st, s s, 316.8 w 8d av. P. M. July 28, 3 years, 5 %. 4,000

Same to Frances E. Bates. Same property. P. M. Equal lien with last mort. July 28, 3 years, 5 %. 4,000

Eagan, Ellen to M. Emile and Blanche de Gilbert. 27th st, No. 121, n s, 266.8 w 6th av, 16.8x98.9. July 30, 2 years. 3,000

Eckstein, Caroline to Katharina and Katharina, Jr., and Elizabeth Volcker. Union av. P. M. July 29, due Aug. 1, 1899, or sooner, 5 %. 4,000

Etzel, Albert and Emanuel Kronacher to Adaline D. Townsend. Elm st, No. 207. P. M. July 27, 3 years, 5 %. 5,000

Earley, William to Elbert T. Bailey et al. exrs. Abraham C. Baylis. 65th st, s s, 225 e West End av, 25x100.5. July 28, 3 years, 5 %. 2,500

Frohwein, Otto T. to Margaret Frohwein. Rivington st, No. 268, n e cor Columbia st, 25x75. July 1, 5 years, 5 %. 14,000

Foster, Scott lessee to THE EQUITABLE LIFE ASSUR. SOC. of the United States mortgagee. Agreement subordinating lease to mortgage. July 27. nom

Feder, Cacilie wife of and Julius to Sara Sichel widow. 80th st, No. 206, s s, 100 e 3d av, 25x102.2. July 30, due Aug. 1, 1894, 5 %. 6,000

Frank, Abraham to Harris M. Fischer. 50th st, n e cor 1st av, 19.8x80. Sub. to mort. $15,000. March 16, installs. 4,000

Fuchs, Joseph, Mary Fuhrken, Frank and Lina Kohlsdorf to Joseph Korn and ano. admrs. Max Holzman. Ludlow st, No. 116. P. M. July 30, installs, 5 %. 18,000

Galway, Harry to Elias T. Hatch trustee for Segonia Hatch. Columbus av, w s, 75.9 n 97th st, 25.1x100. Sub. to morts. *Mt.* $26,000. July 24, due Dec. 1, 1892. 3,500

Gerber, Emil W. to Philip Fuchs. 133d st, No. 163, n s, 175 e 7th av, 25x99.11. July 30, due Sept. 15, 1891. 275

Gaylord, Don A. to Mary R. Bennett. 101st st P. M. July 30, 3 years, 5 %. 13,000

Grabowski, Adolph to Maria L. McGinnis. 105th st. P. M. Sub. to mort. $1,800. July 24. installs. 5 %. 1,800

Goldstein, Solomon to Abraham Stein. Willett st P. M. July 28, 1 year. 1,500

Goldberg, Jacob to Mayer Goldsmith. 65th st. P M. July 20, due Jan. 1, 1892, 5 %. 18,000

Graff, George to Martin Norz. Courtlandt av, w s, 25 n 156th st, 25x100.4. July 20, 3 years, 5 %. 2,500

Gilmore, William J. to Marston Watson, West Orange, N. J. 134th st, n s, 200 e 7th av, 50x99 11. July 28, 3 months. 16,000

Gibb, Edward to New York and Wakefield Co-operative Building and Loan Assoc. Bathgate av, e s, 40 n 172d st, 20x120. July 27, installs, 5 %. 3,000

Gray, John H. to THE MUTUAL LIFE INS. CO., New York. 94th st, s s, 238.5 e 5th av, 17 2x100.8. July 23, due July 27, 1893. 16,000

Same to same. 94th st, s s, 198 5 e 5th av, 20x100.8. July 23, due July 27, 1892. 18,000

Same to same. 94th st, s s, 218.5 e 5th av, 20x100.8. July 23, due July 27, 1892. 18,000

Same to same. 94th st, s s, 178.5 e 5th av, 20x100.8. July 23, due July 27, 1892. 18,000

Graham, James M. to Marx and Moses Ottinger. 51st st, n s, 376 8 e 3d av, 33.4x100.5, *Mt.* $30,000. July 23, due Aug. 22, 1891. 4,955

Graham, James M. to Edward M. Cameron, trustee Marie L. Cameron. 51st st, n s, 300 w 2d av, 33.4x100.5. July 22, due July 1, 1894, 5 %. 30,000

Graham, James M. to Bradley & Currier Co. (Lim) 51st st, n s, 376.8 e 3d av, 33.4x100.5. Sub. to morts. $34,955. July 23, due Jan. 1, 1892. 1,262

Same to Domenico Peloso. Same property. Sub. to morts. $36,217. July 23, due Jan. 1, 1892. 1,534

Goldstein, Solomon to Harriet A. Phelps, trustees George D. Phelps. Willett st, No. 32. P. M. July 14, due July 20, 1894, 5 %. gold, 20,000

Hyland, Arabella to Alida J. Woolley. West Farms road, s e s, 523.7 n e Lyon st. P. M. July 27, 5 years, 5 %. 2,600

Hummel, Abraham H. to Henry C. Miner. 9th av, s w cor 56th st, runs northwest along st 125 x southwest 100.7 x southeast 25.2 x northeast 3.8 x southeast 100 to 9th av, x northeast 100.5, being Nos. 855 and 861 9th av and 402 and 404 West 56th st. May 22, 2 years. 6,950

Habelitz, Francis to Stephen Duncan, Natchez, Miss. Morris av, north cor 152d st, 25x110. July 24, due Aug. 1, 1896, 5 %. 12,000

Hughes, John to Peter Doelger. 39th st, No. 508 W. Lease. July 23, demand. 750

Hutkoff, Nathan to Barbara Dudenhoeffer. Delancey st. P. M. July 24, due Jan. 1, 1895, 5 %. 7,000

Hellman, Myer to George G. De Witt and ano. trustees Sarah Talman dec'd. 74th st, n s, 275 e 2d av, 25x102.2. July 21, due July 24, 1896, 5 %. 3,000

Same to same. Same property. Equal lien with last mort. July 21, due July 24, 1896, 5 %. 8,000

Herrmann, Joseph and Josephine his wife to Charles Boss. 4th st. P. M. July 28, due July 1, 1896, 5 %. 9,000

Hurd, George L. to The New York and Wakefield Co-operative Building and Loan Assoc. Bathgate av, e s, 60 n 172d st, 20x120. July 27, installs, 5 %. 3,000

Hoeland, Magdalena H. D. to Sarah L. Myers. 3d av, s w cor 163d st, 51.4x97.11x50.11x99. July 28, 3 years, 5 %. 7,000

Healy, Mary wife of and Thomas to Patrick Ryan. 89th st, s s, 166 e 1st av, 40x100 8. Sub. to mort. $33,000. July 29, 1 year. 2,000

Hyatt, John G. to Edith Kane. West st, No. 175, e s, 26.6 s Warren st, 26.6x88.1x26.6x88.4. July 27, due Aug. 1, 1896. 29,000

Hyatt, John G. to George D. L. Harison. West st. No. 175, e s, 26 6 s Warren st, 26 6x88.1x26.6x88.4. *Mt.* $21,000. July 27, due Jan. 1, 1892, 5 %. 1,000

Hackett, Martin J. to William H. McWhirter trustee for creditors. 85th st, n s, 70 w 4th av, 65x102.2. Sub. to mort. $59,000. July 7, 6 months. 12,472

Hall, James T. to Abraham Goldsmith. 75th st, s s, 100 e Columbus av, 40x102.2; 75th st, s s, 162 e Columbus av, 38.6x102.2; 75th st, s s, 260 e 9th av, 20x102 2. Sub. to morts. $140,000. July 30, 1 year. 28,000

Same to Charles Weinberg. 75th st, s s, 100 e Columbus av, 40x102.2; 75th st, s s, 162 e Columbus av, 38.6x102 2. Sub. to morts. $160,000. July 30, due Jan 1, 1892. 10,000

Same to THE NEW YORK LIFE INS. CO. 75th st, s s, 162 e Columbus av, 20x102.2. July 15, 3 years, 5 %. 26,000

Same to same. 75th st, s s, 120 e Columbus av, 20x102.2. July 15, 3 years, 5 %. 26,000

Same to same. 75th st, s s, 100 e Columbus av, 20x102.2. July 15, 3 years, 5 %. 25,000

Same to same. 75th st, s s, 182 e Columbus av, 18.6x102 2. July 15, 3 years, 5 %. 23,000

Howe, Adelbert J. to Charles F. Williams, 3d st, e s, 100 s Willard av. P. M. June 17, due July 15, 1894. 1,500

Huners, Friedrich and George Lebers to George Ehret. 2d av, No. 1945. Lease. July 22, demand. 2,500

Jordan, William G. to Samuel Hirsch. 44th st, n s, 300 e 10th av, 40x100.4. July 2, due Feb. 1, 1893. 15,000

Same to same. Same property. P. M. July 2, due Feb. 1, 1892. 9,000

Jantzen, Matilda C. individ. and extrx. Joseph Jantzer to Baron de Hirsch Lund. 2d av, Nos. 104 and 106 and Nos. 303 and 305 6th st, begins 2d av, s e cor 6th st, 51.9x125. July 27, 5 years, 5 %. 72,000

Jeffcott, Robert to Philip Duffey exr. Ellen Kane. Hoffman st. P. M. July 25, 3 years, 5 %. 1,250

Jenkins, Thomas J. and George to George E. Hyatt, Brooklyn. 118th st, s s, 200 e 8th av, 100x100.11. July 21, due Oct. 1, 1891. 2,500

Same to same. 118th st, s s, 100 e 8th av, 100x100.11. July 21, due Oct. 1, 1891. 2,500

Jacob, Emma L. wife of and Leonard to Charles G. Moller. Broadway, No. 635, w s, bet Houston st and Bleecker st, 34x200 to Mercer st. July 27, due Aug. 10, 1894, or sooner. 4½ %. 25,000

Jefferson, John mortgagor to THE UNITED STATES TRUST CO, New York. Certificate of amount due and acceptance of notice of assignment. July 28. nom

Koplik, Rosalie wife of and Abraham S. to THE MUTUAL LIFE INS CO. 32d st, n s, 81 w 2d av, 19x74.1. Already mortgaged to party of second part. July 29, 1 year, 5 %. 1,000

Kennedy, Thomas F. to John M. Lyon. Ogden av, n e cor Union st, 59x100. Sub. to mort. $1,500. July 20, 1 year. 1,000

Kennedy, Carrie S. wife of and David G. to Andrews Sober. 71st st. P. M. July 21, due Feb. 10, 1892. 61,000

Klein, Benedict A. to Daniel Coffey. Macdougal st. P. M. July 29, 2 years or installs., 5 %. 2,000

Lange, Edward to Horace K. Thurber. 107th st, s s, 265 w 9th av, 60x100.11; 84th st, s s, 100 w 9th av, 100x100.2; 116th st, Nos. 169 and 171, n s, 173.6 w 9th av, 34.6x100.11. Secures amount advanced to Trows Printing and Book Binding Co. Feb. 14.

Lange, Margaret J. to same. 104th st, n s, 125 w 10th av, 25x100 11; 104th st, n s, 175 w 10th av, 25x100.11; 106th st, n s, 245 w 9th av, 20x201.10 to 107th st. Secures credits of Edward Lange and Trows Printing and Book Binding Co. Feb. 14.

Levy, Abraham to Samuel Samter, Maurice Levy and Benjamin Samter. Tremont to Fordham road, s e s, adj land Thomas W. Ludlow, 10 acres. ½ part. July 24, demand. 6,000

Levy, Dora wife of and Isaac to Alexander D. Wilson. Columbia st, No. 50, e s, 120 n Delancey st, 20x100; Broome st. Nos. 216 and 218, n s, 42 w Norfolk st. 58.1x75.2x58.1x75 3. Sub. to mort. $9,000. July 23, due July 1, 1894. 1,850

Same to Josephine W. Johnson trustee. Columbia st, e s, 120 n Delancey st, 20x100. July 23, due Aug. 1, 1896, 5 %. 9,000

Levy, L. Napoleon to THE TWELFTH WARD SAVINGS BANK. 177th st, n s, 120 e Bathgate av, 37.6x81x37.10x75. July 24, 1 year, 5 %. 5,000

Livingston, William to Edward Oppenheimer and Isaac Metzger. 35th st, n s, 100 w 10th av, 50x98 9; Jane st, No. 21, n s, 26x80. July 24, due Oct. 1, 1891. 69 000

Same to same. Lenox av, w s, 25 s 134th st, 99.10x100. July 24, due Oct. 1, 1891. 69,000

Lopez, Berta to Marx and Moses Ottinger. 15th st. P. M. June 30, installs, 5 %. 3,700

Same to Mount Sinai Hospital. Same property. P. M. June 30, due July 24, 1894, 5 %. 11,000

Lyons, Julius J. to Simon Simon. Broome st. P. M. July 28, 5 years, 5 %. 9,000

Lawson, Daniel D. to Cousue'a Kirkland. Manhattan av, n e cor 105th st. P. M. Sub. to morts. $15,000. July 27, 4 months. 3,000

Linscott, John A. to Michael Cain. 52d st, n s, 375 e 11th av, 75x100.5. July 28, note. 1,000

Lee, Mortimer C. to John N. Lanthier. 122d st, n s, 154.7 e 1st av, 16.8x100.11. July 21, due July 22, 1896, 5 %. 6 000

Leipziger, Moritz to Elizabeth F. Hand. 51st st, n s, 175 w 2d av, 25x100.5. July 27, 5 years, 5 %. 15,000

Loeb, Jacob to Abraham Kraner and Israel Krakower. Essex st, No. 30. P. M. Sub. to mort. $21,000. July 27, installs. 5,000

Loughran, Thomas to THE EMIGRANT INDUSTRIAL SAVINGS BANK. 140th st, n s, 250 w Amsterdam av, 84 to Hamilton pl, x108.6x99.11. July 29, 1 year, 4½ %. 8,000

Metzler, John H. to Magdalena Schulze. Elsmere pl, s s, 202.4 e Prospect av, 20x100. July 22, 3 years. 1,500

Metzler, John H. and Annie M his wife to Lena Seiferd. Elsmere pl, s s, 202.4 e Prospect av, 20x100. July 25, 3 years. 1,600

Mortimer, James W. to THE HARLEM SAVINGS BANK, New York. Vanderbilt av, e s, 204 n 170th st, runs east 150.6 x north 28 x west 40 x south 8 x west 110.6 to av, x south 25. July 29, 1 year, 5 %. 1,000

Mayer, Fredericke widow to THE COMMONWEALTH INS. CO., New York. 134th st, n s, 408.4 e Willis av, 16.8x100. July 27, 3 years, 5 %. 7,000

Same to same. 134th st, n s, 391.8 e Willis av, 16.8x100. July 27, 3 years, 5 %. 7,000

Same to same. 134th st, n s, 375 e Willis av, 16.8x100. July 27, 3 years, 5 %. 7,000

Merkel, Henry to THE GERMAN SAVINGS BANK, New York. 37th st, No. 404, s s, 100 w 9th av, 25x98.9. July 23, 1 year. 2,500

Maloney, Mary A. wife of William H. to THE EQUITABLE LIFE ASSUR. SOCIETY of the U. S. 5th av, s e cor 125th st, 19.11x80. Recorded June 11, 1891. June 11, due Jan. 1, 1898, 5 %. 10,000

Monaghan, Mary E. to Horace D. Hufcut admr. Jacob F. Geraud, Jr. New York & Harlem Railroad lands. July 18, 3 years, 5 %. See Conveys. 2,079

Moran, Robert to Alice Carroll. Wooster st. w s, 56.5 s 4th st, 19.6x52.3; Wooster st. No. 243, w s, 19.6x52. July 25, demand, 4½ %. 7,000

Monell, Mary mortgagor with Gideon Fountain. Extension of mort. July 28. nom

Same mortgagor with same. Extension of mort. July 28. nom

Monell, Mary widow to Gideon Fountain. Madison av, s w cor 32d st, 24.9x94.8. July 28, due Aug. 1, 1896. 8,250

Monell, Mary widow to Gideon Fountain. Agreement as to management of mortgaged premises. July 28. nom

Meckel, Johann to Silas D. Gifford and ano. exrs., &c., Charles Bathgate. Fordham av, w s, 50 n 166th st, 24x100. July 28, 3 years, 5 %. 3,000

McGovern, Thomas B. to Marie A. Sherman, London, Eng. West End av, s w cor 102d st. P. M.; West End av, w s, 25.11 s 102d st, 25x100. July 7, due July 28, 1892. gold, 16,000

Moores, William to Bella J. Sutton. 125th st, n s, 361.3 w 6th av, 19 9x99.11. Sub. to mort. $15,000. July 29, 1 year. 1,000

McKinlay, Duncan C. to The Bradley & Currier Co. (Lim.) 76th st, n s, 200 e Amsterdam av, 75x102.2. Sub. to morts. July 24, due Oct. 24, 1891. 3,400

Miller, Charles E. to Nicholas Leibrock. 66th st. P. M. Sub. to mort. $8,000. July 24, installs. 6,450

Muller, Michael to Simon E. Bernheimer and Josephine Schmid. 83d st, n s, 116.8 w 1st av, 16.8x102.2. July 24, demand. 2,500

Milliken, David to Russell H. Hoadley trustee. 7th av, w s, 99.11 n 143d st, 25x75. July 10, due July 15, 1893. 2,500

Mitchell, Warren J. to Frank B. Proffen. College st. P. M. July 23, due July 1, 1894. 1,260

Niebuhr, Henry P. to Nathan Wise. 145th st, s s, 84 w Amsterdam av, 116x199.10 to 144th st. July 14, due Feb. 1, 1892. 3,000

Nicolai, Curt E. H. to Rudolph Engehardt. 119th st, n s, 320 e 3d av, 20x100.10. July 28, 2 years, 5 %. 2,500

O'Rorke, Hugh to Joseph H. Bearns. 111th st. P. M. July 28, 5 years, 5 %. 14,000

O'Brien, James to H. Koehler & Co. Park av. No. 1805. Saloon lease. July 29, demand. 850

Ogden, Harriet V. to David B. and Gouverneur M. Ogden exrs. Cadwalader E. Ogden. 10th st, No 9, n s, 151.10 w 5th av, 25x94.10. Nov. 14, 1888, demand, 5 %. (Discharged of record) 3,621

Perry, James C. exr. Augusta B. Perry to Mary A Moore, New Brighton, S. I. 75th st, s s, 350 e 11th av, 81.2 to Boulevard, x50.5 x95.11x48.6. Sub. to morts. $64,000. June 29, due May 1, 1891. 10,000

Pomeroy, Hamilton to William R. and Charles B. Knapp. 161st st. P. M. July 29, 5 years, 5 %. 8,000

Pope, Lauretta W., Miriam E., Irving W. and Anna E. heirs John H. Pope to Anna T. Pope. Norfolk st, No. 64, e s, 25x100. June 8, note. 2,089

Purnhagen, Henry to Frank W. Robb. 85th st, n s, 376 6 e 2d av, 24.3x102.2. July 28, due Aug. 1, 1896, 5 %. 6,000

Peck, Wallace mortgagor with James McFeeter and John J. Matheson mortgagees. Extension of mort. and agreement to pay principal in gold coin. June 29. nom

Pohlmann, Hans to A. Hupfel's Sons. Courtlandt av, No. 820. Lease. July 28, demand. 1,000

Prime, Henry to James A. Scrymser trustee estate of N. Birne. 38th st, n s, 327.3 w 9th av, 27x98.9. July 24, 3 years, 5 %. 1,000

Prager, Samuel to Michael Fay and William Stacom. Madison st, No. 125. P. M. Sub. to mort. $25,000. July 16, installs. 11,600

Same to Larry B. Rosenstein. Same property. P. M. Sub. to mort. $36,600. July 29, 1 year, 5 %. 1,000

Quinn, Elizabeth to THE FRANKLIN SAVINGS BANK, New York. 79th st, s s, 194 e 1st av, 25x102.2. July 24, 1 year, 5 %. 5,000

Reilly, Mary F. wife of and Charles to THE EQUITABLE LIFE ASSURANCE SOCIETY of the U. S. Water st, No 666, n s, 225 w Jackson st, 25x100. July 28, due July 24, 1891. 5,000

Rheinish, Joseph H. to A. Hupfel's Sons. Tremont av, No. 761; Bathgate av, No. 1901, Lease. July 23, demand. 2,000

Riley, James G. to William Burke. Lincoln av, w s, 50 n 135th st, 25x100. July 7, due July 1, 1896, 5 %. 10,000

Ryan, Thomas to Bernheimer & Schmid. Chatham sq, No. 20. Lease. July 23, demand. 850

Roth, Heinrich mortgagor with Isaac Wallach et al. exrs. Samson Wallach mortgagee. Extension of mort. July 10. nom

Reinheimer, Isaac to Joseph Priest, Brooklyn, N. Y. 2d av, w s, 78.9 s 76th st, 25x105. July 28, 3 years, 5 %. gold, 16,000

Reinhardt, Henry mortgagor with Francis Hein mortgagee. Extension of mort. July 27. nom

Reilly, John J. to Lewis Z. Bach. 2d av. P. M. Sub. to mort. $16,000. June 15, due June 1, 1892. 7,500

Same to George E. Hyatt, Brooklyn. Same property. June 15, 1 year. 16,000

Roch, William G. to The New York Co-operative Building and Loan Assoc. 129th st, s s, 200.2 e 4th av, 19.11x99.11x20x99.11. July 27, installs. 7,100

Rohrs, Frederick to Charles S. Longhurst, Brooklyn. 126th st, No. 314, s s, 250 e 2d av, 25x100. June 18, 1 month. gold, 763

Schaeffel, Katharina wife of and Bernhard to Frederick Baker. Goerck st. P. M. July 29, instal's. 2,775

Schwab, Noah to Henry Ungrich. Lenox av, w s, 56 n 124th st, 19.8x75. July 23, due Sept. 1, 1893, 5 %. 5,000

Siemering, John and Friederika his wife to Eleanor Shearwood, New Rochelle, N. Y. 153d st, n s, 125 e Morris av, 25x100. July 15, 5 years, 5 %. 2,100

Slade, Henry L. to Albert N. Hallgarten. 10th st. P. M. July 23, due July 30, 1894, 4½ %. 25,000

Smith, Roby A. wife of and J. Henry to Anna H. Wilde and ano. trustees Caroline M. Wilde. 109th st, n s, 225 e Boulevard, 50x100. July 30, 1 year. 7,000

Sternfels, Bernard mortgagor with John E. Lockwood mortgagee. Extension of reduced mortgage. June 1. nom

Stoker, Charlotte M. wife of Richard to THE HARLEM SAVINGS BANK, N. Y. 2d pl, s s, 350 w Grove av, 75x100. July 3, 1 year, 5 %. 6,000

Stokes, Thomas to Leicester Holme ref. 23d st. P. M. July 30, 5 years, 5 %. 14,460

Sturtz, Morris, otherwise Moritz, to THE GERMAN SAVINGS BANK, New York. Broome st, No. 158, n s, 25x60. July 29, due July 30, 1892. 2,000

Scheuer, Jacob to Andrew Martin. Brook av. P. M. July 25, 3 years, 5 %. 2,500

Selfridge, John to The New York Lumber and Wood Working Co. 75th st, s s, 175 e Amsterdam av, 100x100. Sub. to mort. $69,000. Secures carpenter and cabinet work. July 21. 20,683

Smith, Ormond G., George C. and Anne K. to Merritt E. Sawyer exr. Francis S. Smith. Moore st, Nos. 11-19, e s, extends from Water to Front st, 139.5x16x139.10x13.8. July 24, due Aug. 3, 1892, 5 %. 10,000

Same to THE MERCANTILE TRUST CO. admr. Jules R. Gimbernat. Same property. July 10, due July 13, 1894, 5 %. 30,000

Schwarting, Henrietta R. to Christina Goess. 4th av n w s, part plot 10 map Claremont, near Highbridge, begins at south cor of land of Patrick McCann, 30x135x35x140. Jan. 1, 3 years, 5½ %. 1,800

Schonberr, Albert to Henry Hawkes. 131st st, n s, 260 w 5th av, 25x99.11. P. M. July 11, due July 15, 1894, or sooner, 5 %. 1,000

Schott, Mary to William R. Rose. 74th st, s s, 183.4 w 2d av, 33.4x102.2. June 1, 5 years. 5 % 5,750

Schwartz, Lena wife of John to Josephine W. Johnson trustee. 117th st, No. 330, s s, 375 e 2d av, 25x100.11. July 28, due Aug. 1, 1896. 5 %. 8,000

Same to Paulina A. Morgan. 117th st, No. 332, s s, 400 e 2d av, 25x100.11. July 28, due Aug. 1, 1896, 5 %. 8,000

Sims, Lillian M. wife of H. Marion Sims to THE EQUITABLE LIFE ASSUR. SOCIETY. 72d st, s s, 343 w West End av, 22x102.2. July 7, due Jan. 1, 1893, 5 %. 30,000

Southard, Charles H. to Fernando C. Candee, Jr. 135th st. P. M. Sub. to mort. $19,000. July 27, 1 year. 1,600

Solomon, George to Louis Ascher. 85th st, n s, 325 e 2d av, 25x102.2. July 19, demand. 12,000

Sonn, Hymann and Henry to Waldron P. Brown and Anson W. Hard trustees for Julia E. Brown. South st, No. 29. P. M. June 25, 3 years, 4½ %. gold, 15,000

Striebel, Marie L. to Jarvis B. Smith. Bathgate av, No. 2069. P. M. July 6, installs. 1,153

Stokes, Kate B. wife of and John W. to MUTUAL LIFE INS. CO., New York. 32d st, n s, 150 w 5th av, 25x98.9. July 14, 1 year, 5 %. 16,000

Thorp, Carrie A. V. to Charles S. Van Loon. 71st st, n s, 207 e 11th av, 18x93.2. Sub. to mort. $12,500. July 15, 8 months. 500

Tiffany, Charles L. mortgagee with Mary A. Walker and Andrew Powell. Agreement to accept payment of principal by installs. June 24. nom

Thompson, Samuel A. to Sarah J. Collins widow. Madison av, s w cor 133d st. P. M. May 27, 2 years, 5 %. 9,000

Trillich, Adam to Adolph Wallach. St. Marks pl, n s, 75 w 1st av, 25x55.11. July 30, 2 years. 1,500

Tripler, Thomas E. to Rosa Mayer. 17th st, No 542, s s, 126 w Av B, 26x92. July 30, 2 years. 3,000

Same to same. 17th st, No. 540, s s, 152 w Av B, 26x92. July 30, 2 years. 3,000

Same to same. 17th st, No. 544, s s, 100 w Av B, runs south 90 x west 3 x south 2 x west 23 x north 92 to st, x east 26. July 30, 2 years. 3,000

Vultee, George W. to Walton Storm et al., trustees Thomas Storm. Broadway Boulevard and 63d st. P. M. July 1, 1 year. 71,433

Vander Roest, William G. to Mary A. Booth. Certificate that $11,000 has been paid on mortgage. July 24. nom

Vogel, Louis and Jacob mortgagors with BANK FOR SAVINGS in the City of New York, mortgagee. Extension of mort. July 23. nom

Volkening, Bertha to Jessie Clark, Cornwall-on-the-Hudson. 53d st, n s, 475 w 10th av, runs north 44.10 x northwest to point 300 w 10th av, and 48.4 n 53d st, x north 51.8 x west 50 x south 46.8 x northwest to point 150 e 11th av, and 69.4 n 53d st, x south 69.4 to 53d st, x east 175. July 21, 1 month. 15,000

Willett, Sarah E. wife of and Wallace P. to Harriet I. Cruger. Taylor av, n w s, lot 157 map Belmont village, 100x100; Taylor av, n s, lots 122 and 123 same map, runs north 100 to Webster av, x northwest 200 to Washington av, x southwest 200 x southeast 100 x northeast 100 x southeast 100. July 14, due Aug. 1, 1894. 5,000

Wilsbusen, John and Dora his wife to Charles H. Tyson exr. John Tyson. 109th st, n s, 180 w 2d av, 20x100.10. July 13, 3 years, 5 %. 3,000

Wallach, Hayman to Louis Gewirz. Pike st. P. M. July 29, due Aug. 1, 1896. 1,800

Wise, Frank E. to Henry de F. Weekes trustee. 86th st, s s, 70 w Park av, 17.10x102.2. July 27, due May 1, 1896, 5 %. 20,000

Wall, Emma Van D. wife of Henry P. to Artlissa V. wife of Miles Gearon, Brooklyn. 54th st, No. 261, n s, 62.6 e 8th av, 18.9x62.11. July 25, 1 year. 300

Ward, Thomas to Johanna Garvey. 104th st, s s, 21.8 e Boulevard, 15.11x70.2. July 24, 3 years, 4 %. 4,000

Webster, Georgiana F. to Thomas Mackellar. Boston av, s e cor 164th st. 107.5x115x100x76.5. July 24, due Oct. 1, 1891. 3,000

Wittpenn, John H. to Charles S. Kohler. Amsterdam av, w s, 50.5 s 95th st. P. M. July 7, due July 30, 1894, 5 %. 2,000

Same to same. Amsterdam av, w s, 75.5 s 98th st. P. M. July 7, due July 30, 1894, 5 %. 2,000

KINGS COUNTY.

JULY 23, 24, 25, 27, 28, 29.

Ashford, William T. to Clara H. Ives. Sutter av. P. M. July 24, installs. $1,200

Barlow, Clinton W. and Edward M. to Maria L. Spring. Monroe st, n s, 319 w Franklin av, 17.9x85. July 28, due July 1, 1894, 5 %. 4,500

Beierlein, Josephine to Otto Gubner. 18th av, w s, 407 n Bath av, 75x96.5. July 24, 1 year. 1,000

Benziger, Adebrich and Maria his wife to John Gratzer. Greene av, w s, 100 s Irving av, 15x80.6x15x81.2. July 24, due Aug. 1, 1892, 5 %. 700

Brown, Julius S. to A. Judson Palmer. Dumont av, n w cor Powell st. P. M. July 21, due July 6, 1894. 2,000

Buckley, Signor A. to Mary A. Kouwenhoven, Gravesend, L. I. 12th st, s s, 117 w 4th av, 18x100. July 1, 1 year, 5 %. 2,500

Butler, Thomas B. to Jane H. wife of William M. Gibson. Lafayette av, s s, 467 e Lewis av, 17x100. Sub. to mort. $3,500. May 1, 5 years. 700

Berckmeier, Albert to James Gascoine individ. and with Anna E. Cozine exrs. John G. Cozine. Woodbine st, n w s, 25 s w Knickerbocker av, 200x100. June 1, demand. 15,000

Same to same. Same property. P. M. June 1, 6 months. 10,500

Berger, Rudolph G. to Alfred H. Olena. Diamond st. P. M. July 23, 3 years, 5 %. 7,550

Baschwitz, Rachel to John H. Hall. Mecker av. P. M. July 24, due Aug. 1, 1896, 5 %. 1,800

Blumenkranz, Max and Samuel Faske to Abraham Ruth. Osborn st. P. M. July 23, installs. 1,550

Bossert, Margaretha to The German Savings Bank of Brooklyn. Myrtle av, s s, 325 e Evergreen av, 25x100. July 24, due Dec. 1, 1892, 5 %. 2,000

Bower, Julia S. to William C. Kennedy and ano. exrs. Thomas Kennedy. Hewes st, s s, 80.6 e Wythe av, 19x100. July 22, 1 year, 5 %. 350

Brennan, Margaret wife of John to Georgianna wife of William S. McIlvain. Flushing and Clermont avs. P. M. July 23, 5 years. 4,000

Same to same. Same property. July 23, installs. 1,000

Bryant, Thomas B. to The Title Guarantee and Trust Co. Greene av, n s, 100 w Lewis av, 100x100. July 9, demand. 25,000

Bening, Jochen M. to Charles A. Parsons. 19th st, s w s, 275 s e 3d av, 16.8x100. July 23, 5 years. 1,150

Bull, Henry C. to Phebe Carpenter. 19th st, s s, 287.6 w 8th av, 15.6x100. July 23, due Aug. 1, 1896, 5 %. 1,500

Same to Elbert T. Bailey, Oyster Bay, L. I. 19th st, s s, 272 w 8th av, 15.6x102.2. July 23, due Aug. 1, 1896, 5 %. 1,500

Same to Gussie R. Eastman, Roslyn, L. I. 19th st, s s, 334 w 8th av, 16x102.2. July 23, due Aug. 1, 1896, 5 %. 1,500

Same to same. 19th st, s s, 303 w 8th av, 15.6x100.2. July 23, due Aug. 1, 1896, 5 %. 1,500

Same to Sarah Van Cott, Oyster Bay, L. I. 19th st, s s, 318.6 w 8th av, 15.6x102.2. July 23, due Aug. 1, 1896, 5 %. 1,500

Same to Elizabeth R. Van Cott. 19th st, s s, 225 w 8th av, 16x102.2. July 23, due Aug. 1, 1896, 5 %. 1,500

Same to J. Clifton Monfort, North Hempstead, L. I. 19th st, s s, 241 w 8th av, 15.6x100.2. July 23, due Aug. 1, 1896, 5 %. 1,500

Same to Caleb Mott. 19th st, s s, 256.6 w 8th av, 15.6x100.2. July 23, due Aug. 1, 1896, 5 %. 1,500

Burns, James to The Title Guarantee and Trust Co. Carroll st, n s, 215 w Hicks st, 20x100. July 24, 3 years, 5 %. 3,000

Beers, William L. to Lucy O. Embury, Plainfield, N. J. Buffalo av, w s, 20 s Prospect pl, 16.4x52. July 27, due Nov. 1, 1894. 1,750

Same to Helen Embury. Buffalo av, s w cor Prospect pl, 20x52. July 27, due Nov. 1, 1894. 2,500

Same to Milton Sherwood, Round Hill, Conn. Buffalo av, w s, 36.4 s Prospect pl, 16.4x52. July 27, due Nov. 1, 1894. 1,750

Capazolli, Cirello to Catharine Cowenhoven, New Utrecht. Bay 38th st, s e s, 300 s w 86th st, 100x96.8, Gravesend. July 27, 2 years. 1,700

Cronacher, Henrietta widow to John Rueger. Frost st. P. M. July 28, 10 years, 5 %. 5,000

Cappe, Grace R. to The Brooklyn Trust Co. Greene av, n s, 370 w Patchen av, 20x100. July 23, 1 year, 5 %. 2,000

Cohan, Samuel to Emil Rauth, Joseph Meyer and Anna M. Schaertl. Montrose av. P. M. July 22, 5 years, 5 %. 1,500

Cohan, Samuel to Geraldine B. Bertuch. Montrose av, s s, 80 w Humboldt st, 20x100. July 22, 1 year, 5 %. 3,000

Collins, Charles H. mortgagor with The Title Guarantee and Trust Co. mortgagee. Two Extensions of morts. July 21. nom

Collins, Ellen T. to John H. Riechers. Rapelye st, s s, 100 w Hicks st, 25x100. July 23, 5 years, 5 %. 2,000

Cosgrove, Catharine with Rachel M. Gilsey mortgagees. Agreement as to priority of mort. made by John Stapleton. July 22. nom

Costello, Margaret to The Homestead Co-operative Building and Loan Assoc. De Kalb av, s s, 300 e Reid av, 25x100. July 24, installs, 5 %. 3,600

Crowley, James F. to The South Brooklyn Savings Inst. 6th av, w s, 80 n Carroll st, 19.6x70. July 28, 1 year, 5 %. 2,000

Carlin, Patrick and Thomas to Edward Eastment. Quincy st, No. 834, s s, 200 w Ralph av, —x—. July 24, installs. 325

Cinque, Guiseppe and Teresa his wife to Angelo Gabino. Carroll st. P. M. July 25, 1 year, 5 %. 2,500

Chinnock, George H. to Charles D. Rust. Gates av, n s, 44.6 w Clason av. P. M. July 17, 6 months. 1,875

Same to same. Gates av, n s, 66.3 w Clason av. P. M. July 17, 6 months. 1,875

Dumler, George to August Sedlmeir. Suydam st, n w s, 150 s w Knickerbocker av, 25x100. July 24, 5 years, 5 %. 1,900

Davidson, Alexander to Aletta Suydam. 45th st, s w, 320 s e 3d av, 20x100. July 22, 3 years, 5 %. 2,500

Day, Maria B. to James H. Hart and Margaret his wife. Powell st. P. M. April 1, installs, 5 %. 1,390

Dunkhase, Claus to The Greenpoint Savings Bank, Brooklyn. Huron st. P. M. July 27, 1 year, 4½ %. 1,500

Deinhardt, Maggie wife of and Henry T. to John Lefferts. Washington av, e s, 145.2 n Lefferts av, 32.5x25x21.3x27.5. July 24, due July 1, 1894, 5 %. 100

Doremus, James H. to William De Nyse. Hancock st. P. M. July 23, due Jan. 1, 1895, 5 %. 2,300

Deinhart, Martin to Annie Reynolds and Samuel Feather trustees Thomas Reynolds. Hart st, s e s, 200 n e Hamburg av, 25x100. July 29, 3 years, 5 %. 3,300

Embrick, John H. to Charles Shaw. Putnam av, n s, 118 w Lewis av, 19x100. June 1, 10 years, 3 %. 8,000

Faust, Emanuel to Maria Bindrim. Bennett st, s s, 125 w Banzett st, 25x100. July 22, 3 years, 5 %. 500

Feldmann, Moritz and Annie his wife to Irene Strang. Eastern Parkway. P. M. July 23, installs. 7,050

Feldmuller, Aaron to Sarah J. Morris. Bergen st, n s, 200 w Underhill av, 50x105.7. July 22, 3 years, 5 %. 1,000

Folger, Louisa E. to Germania Savings Bank, Kings Co. Ralph av, w s, 98.7 n Atlantic av, 46x105. July 23, 1 year, 5 %. 2,500

Fox, Annie to Benjamin J. Conroy. East 9th st. P. M. July 18, 1 year, 5 %. 315

Franke, Henry to Albert Franke. William st, n e cor Imlay st, runs north 175 x east 110 x south 125 x west 20 x south 50 to William st, x west 90. July 23, 1 year, 5 %. 12,000

Friedel, I. H. Gustav to Julius Lehrenkrauss. Shepherd av, e s, 100 s Blake av, 100x200 to Berriman st. June 1, due July 1, 1892. 400

Fehling, Hugh to The Dime Savings Bank of Williamsburgh. South 4th st, s w s, 145.6 n w Hooper st, 25x95.10x25x95.7. July 25, 1 year, 5 %. 6,500

Fuselehr, Margarethe widow to John Bayer, Joseph Weidner and Serafin W. Turner. Irving av. P. M. July 27, 3 years or sooner, 5 % 1,100

Farnquist, Amanda L. to Charles J. Warren, Jr. Rochester av. P. M. July 24, 5 years, 5 %. 1,500

Finck, Amelia wife of and Daniel to Rosa Schoeffel. Halsey st, n w s, 160 n e Evergreen av, 80x100. July 24, 2 years, 5 %. 2,000

Faust, Helena and Michael Reif to Frederick Hackmann. McDougal st, n s, 400 e Hopkinson av, 25x100. July 27, 5 years. 500

Fowler, Mary E. wife of and Levi to Adolph Vaurein. St. Marks av, n s, 200 e Franklin av, 60x128.6. July 28, due Dec. 1, 1891. 7,500

Fox, Mary E. and Catharine I. Minehan to Theodore W. Swimm. Putnam av, n s, 310 e Lewis av, 20x100. June 1, due May 1, 1893, installs. 3,500

Grauer, John G. to Frederick Wagner, Newtown, L. I. Greene av, s s, 90 w St. Nicholas av, 140x100; Bleecker st, n s, 130 w St. Nicholas av, 60x100. Error. July 24, due June 9, 1896, 5 %. 15,000

Grinnon, Mary wife of John to John Englis, Jr., et al. exrs. John Englis, Sr. Manhattan av, e s, 100 n India st, 20x100. July 24, 3 years, 5 %. 4,000

Guilfoyle, William F. to John Keresey. South 4th st. No. 186, s s, 213.6 e Driggs st, 23x100. July 25, due Aug. 1, 1894, or installs, 5 %. 3,000

Guy, William J. to Sophronia M. Fickett. East 7th st. Flatbush. P. M. July 23, installs. 600

Same mortgagor with Thomas McCracken. Extension of mort. July 24. nom

Goetz, Henry to Augusta wife of Henry C. Bauer. Stanhope st. P. M. July 22, due July 1, 1897. 2,000

Grace, Lizzie T. mortgagor with Alice M. Osborn mortgagee. Extension of mort. June 1. nom

Gregory, Mary to Rosalie T. Slade, Riverhead, L. I. Patchen av, e s, 100 s Gates av, 25x100. July 16, due July 1, 1894. 3,000

Hack, Henry to The Joseph Fallert Brewing Co. (Lim.) McKibbin st, s s, lot 180 map Williamsburgh by Alexander Martin, 25x100. July 18, demand. 700

Hagedorn, Charles to William M. Ingraham. 16th st, s s, 168.9 e 3d av, 113.1. July 25, demand. 9,000

Haigh, William H. to Elizabeth W. Robb. 43d st, n e s, 350 s e 12th av, 50x100.2. July 22, 3 years. 1,800

Hamblin, James A. to Richard J. Godwin. Ocean pl, n e cor Atlantic av, 18.6x80. July 22, 3 years. 3,500

Hanan, Maurice Z. to Asa A. Spear. Monroe st. P. M. July 16, installs. 1,500

Hartmann, Pauline to James S. Reynolds. Thatford av, e s, 150 n Livonia av, 25x100. July 24, due Aug. 1, 1894. 1,500

Haviland, Edward T. and Annie B. his wife to Elsie A. Martin extrx. Isaac Martin. 18th av, n w s, 350 s w 86th st, 50x96.8. July 15, 5 years, 5 %. 2,500

Hays, Elizabeth A. mortgagor with John S. Lott mortgagee. Extension of mort. July 21. nom

Heatley, George W. to William McKeon. Park av, n s, 60.10 w North Elliott pl. P. M. July 23, 1 year. 500

Hess, Leonhard to John J. Hassinger. Greene av, s e s, 200 s w Irving av, 25x100. June 25, 3 years, 5 %. 3,000

Same to Jacob N. Herrle. Greene av, s e s, 170 s w Irving av, 30x100. July 24, 1 year, 5 %. 750

Holsten, John D. to Joseph H. Bearns. 3d av, east cor 49th st, 50x100. July 23, 5 years, 5 %. 15,000

Howard, Joseph C. to George A. Hughes. Barbey st. e s, 140 s Duryea av, 40x100. July 23, 5 years. 1,200

Hyers, Samuel V. to King & Adams. Cedar st, s s, 221.9 e Evergreen av, runs southeast 117.3 x east 14.6 x southeast 34.9 x east 53.3 x northwest 79.9 x west 39.6 x northwest 82.7 to Cedar st, x southwest 20. July 1, due July 1, 1896, 5 %. 2,500

Hall, Ella E. to Ira O. Miller. Lot begins at stake on the 2d division line of New Utrecht Woodlands, New Utrecht. P. M. July 24, 3 years, 5 %. 6,407

Holmes, Letitia to Margaretha Lewis. Hull st. P. M. July 22, installs 4,200

Hallaren, John D. to G. A. and R. Miller. 6th av, e s, 40 s 1st st, 20x90. Sub. to mort. $7,000. July 21, 1 year or sooner. 1,500

Hamblin, James A. to Austin Abbott trustee James Rowe dec'd. Ocean pl, e s, 18.6 n Atlantic av, 5 lots, together 80.1x80. 5 morts., each $2,200. July 27, due Nov. 1, 1894. 11,000

Hamilton, Stephen to Jennette wife of William Johnston. Walton st. P. M. July 25, 5 years or installs, 5 %. 1,900

Hancock, Charles to Alfred Hancock. Snediker av, e s, 25 s Glenmore av, 25x100. July 28, 1 year. 1,400

Henshaw, Frances M. mortgagor with Ellen M. McGovern mortgagee. Extension of mort. July 13. nom

Hessner, Kate wife of and Henry to Andrew Wissel. Gerry st. P. M. July 28, 5 years. 3,000

Hunecke, Frederick to Peter Doelger. Eagle st, n s, 72 e Franklin st, runs north 80 x east 34.7 x northwest 24 x east 47.8 x south 100 to st, x west 73. July 25, 5 years, 5 %. 6,000

Huss, Christopher to Charlotte T. Perry. Eagle st, n s, 275 w Manhattan av, 25x100. July 28, 2 years or sooner. 1,300

Jackerson, Jacob, Davis Levy, Mary Aaronson and Harris Meyer to Sabra E. Gregg. Rockaway av, w s, 150 s Eastern Parkway. P. M. July 15, 3 years. 3,000

Jablin, Morris, New York, to August Achterrath. Harrison av. P. M, July 27, installs., 5 %. 7,300

Johnson, Christian to Virginia A. Kleine. Eldert st, n w s, 95 s w Evergreen av, 140x100. July 23, demand. 10,000

Johnstone, James W. to James A. Townsend. 76th st, s w s, 411 n w 18th av, New Utrecht. P. M. July 21, 1 year, 5 %. 400

Kennedy, Annie A. to Lydia W. Giroux. 4th av, s e s, 96 n e 37th st, 20x81. July 23, due Aug. 1, 1894, 5 %. 1,700

Kerr, Peter G. to James H. Hart. Warwick st. P. M. July 21, due Aug. 15, 1891. 400

Kilian, Sabina to John N. Wirth. Hopkins st, s s, 75 e Tompkins av, 25x100. July 1, 5 years, 5 %. 2,000

Koch, Henry F. to John L. Speroni. Schaeffer st, n w s, 300 n e Evergreen av, runs northwest 50 x northeast to centre old Bushwick road, x southeast to Schaeffer st, x southwest —. Collateral mortgage deed. July 15. 8,500

Krashes, Frank to Charles Halbe. Throop av, n e s, 25 s e Bartlett st, 25x95. July 22, due Aug. 1, 1896, 5 %. 1,550

Kirby, Joseph I. to Margaret Hendrickson. Grand av, e s, 377.5 n Gates av, runs north 18 x east 80 x south 15 x southwest 6 x west 76. July 17, due Nov. 1, 1892, 5 %. 500

Kenny, James F. to The Nassau Co-operative Building and Loan Assoc. Bay av, s s, 50 w Barbey st, 25x100. July 28, installs. 3,500

Klee, Minnie E. wife of Henry W. to Aaron Levy. Gates av, n s, 20 w Tompkins av, 20x100. July 27, 3 years, 5 %. 1,398

Kaplan, Elias to Sophie G. Parker, New Hamburgh, N. Y. Watkins st, late Williamson av, w s, 275 s Bay av, 25x100. July 24, demand. 500

Kerr, Peter to Jacob Cozine. Shepherd av, w s, 120 n Ridgewood av, 20x100. July 25, due July 1, 1894. 2,000

Krenig, Joseph to Catharina Lipsius. Ten Eyck st, s s, 175 e Ewen st, 25x100. July 24, 1 year, 5 %. 2,900

Kuhn, Maria A. widow and John A., Caroline L. and Frederick S. Kuhn heirs Joseph Kuhn to Louis Braun. Graham av, s e cor Seigel st. 50x75. July 1, 5 years, 5 %. 9,000

Kenny, Catharine with Bedford Co-operative Building Loan Assoc. mortgagees. Agreement as to priority of mortgages made by Anne and James Gerrety. July 8. nom

Kernan, John A. to James C. Foley. 4th av. P. M. July 27, due July 28, 1896, 5 %. 700

Kirsch, Louis and Martin, of Kirsch Brothers, to The Sandy Hook Pilot's Charitable Fund. Keap st, n s, 60 e Wythe av. P. M. July 27, due July 1, 1896, 5 %. 3,000

Kraus, Morris and Benjamin to Catharine Luhn. Union st, n s, 335 e Van Brunt st, 32x100. July 28, 3 years, 5 %. 3,000

Lamkay, Aaron to Adolph Mandel. Thatford av, n e cor Livonia av. P. M. July 27, due Aug. 1, 1894. 1,500

Lawrence, James A. to The Long Island Loan and Trust Co. as trustee of John A. Cross dec'd. Decatur st, n s, 96.6 w Stuyvesant av, 6 lots, each 18.8x100. 6 morts., each $7,000. July 27, 1 year, 5 %. 42,000

Lisansky, Rosa to Mary E. Cook, Newtown, L. I. Stone av. P. M. July 25, installs. 700

Laner, Edward W. and Charles J. Kissel to Jacob Cozine. Blake av, s s, 50 w Barbey st. 25x100. July 25, due July 1, 1894. 1,500

Leonhardt, Anna C. wife and John to The Dime Savings Bank, Brooklyn. Broadway, w s, 109.4 s Walton st, 24x74x25x northeast 27 x again northeast 33; also all title to strip adj. begins at point 33 s w Broadway, runs southwest 27 x northwest 1.7 x northeast 29. July 25, 1 year, 5 %. 5,500

Laing, Mary E. and Donald to Charles H. Maclim. Ashford st, e s, 185 s Hegeman av, runs south 60 x east 100 x north 20 x east 100 to Cleveland st, x north 40 x west 200. July 21, 1 year. 600

Louvot, Delia F. to Frank C. Swimm. Macon st. P. M. July 24, 3 years. 800

Lefkovitz, Josephine to Moritz Stern. Thatford av. P. M. ½ part. July 15, installs. 250

Lewis, Alfred G. to Elizabeth W. Robb or Bobb. 96th st, n s, 210.5 e Marine av, 25x100. New Utrecht. July 22, 3 years. 700

Leverich, Henry M. to Mary E. Oldham. Pierrepont st, s s, 52 e Hicks st, 26x100. 1-6 part. July 20, demand. 1,000

Lewis, Margaretha to The Title Guarantee and Trust Co. Hull st. P. M. July 7, due July 22, 1894, 5 %. 3,500

Little, James H. to The Title Guarantee and Trust Co. Woodbine st. P. M. July 8, due July 24, 1894, 5 %. 2,000

Same to Joseph Ryan. Same property.. July 8, installs. 1,000

Same to same. Same property. July 8, installs. 1,310

Lopes, Antonio to John Phraner, Hempstead, L. I. Pacific st. P. M. July 15, due Nov. 1, 1893, 5 %. 1,000

Ludder, Betty S. to Oscar J. Chase. Vandeveer st. P. M. July 20, due Sept. 15, 1893, 5 %. 500

Maguire, Dennis to George B. Forrester. Glenmore av, s s, 50 e Wyona st, 50x100. July 21, due July 1, 1892. 1,000

McAdam, Grace A. to Susan J. Mortimore. Hart st, n s, 160 e Stuyvesant av, 20x100. July 28, 3 years, 5 %. 1,500

McKeon, William to Harriet F. Post, Quogue, L. I. Same property. July 23, due May 1, 1894, 5 %. 2,000

McLaughlin, Thomas J. to Robert Forrest and James McMurdo. Belmont av. P. M. July 23, installs. 425

McNamara, Mary A. to Joseph Ruppert. Park av, s e cor Schenck st, 138x26x138x76. July 23, 1 year, 5 %. 500

McNeely, Anthony to David D. Field. 3d av, north cor 88th st, New Utrecht. P. M. May 12, 5 years, 5 %. 1,704

Same to same. 3d av, west cor 87th st New Utrecht. P. M. May 12, 5 years, 5 %. 780

Midonsky, Pesak to Charles Shapiro and Davis Nichol. Osborn st. P. M. July 21, installs. 975

Mitchell, Charles F. S. to The East Brooklyn Co-operative Building Assoc. Pulaski st, s s, 205 w Lewis av, 20x100. July 25, installs. 250

Molloy, William and Maria his wife mortgagor with David D. Field mortgagee. Extension of mort. May 8. nom

Morris, Joseph to Edward L. Snyder and ano. exrs. Samuel F. Engs. Osborn st, e s, 149.9 n Eastern Parkway, 25x100. July 10, 2 years. 3,500

Mullady, Mary to Caroline and Charlotte Hewlett. Wolcott st, n e s, 165 s e Van Brunt st, 25x100. July 23, 3 years. 2,000

Miller, William J. C. to Sophia L. Schroder. Howard av. P. M. July 8, 1 year. 1,500

Murray, John to Ernest Ochs, a corporation. Manhattan av, s w cor Nassau av, 24x75. Sub. to mort. $5,000. July 22, 1 year. 2,500

Markowitz, Herman to Sabra E. Gregg. Rockaway av. P. M. July 15, 3 years. 800

McBean, Archibald N. to Henry McShane Mfg. Co. 2d st, s s, 207.10 w 6th av, 30x95. Sub. to mort. $700. July 20, demand. 712

McDermott, Luke to The Title Guarantee and Trust Co. Gates av, n s, 85 e Sumner av, 20x100. July 22, 3 years, 5 %. 5,000

Miller, Kate wife of and Jacob to The Title Guarantee and Trust Co. Tompkins av. P. M. July 15, due July 27, 1894, 5 %. 4,500

Moore, John to John F. Hart. 9th st. P. M. July 25, demand. 4,200

Same to Daniel Doody. Same property. July 25, demand. 27,000

Most, Albert and Pauline his wife to John Lind and Francisca his wife. Sackett st, s s, 96 w Van Brunt st, 100x95. July 25, due July 1, 1894, 5 %. 4,000

Manneschmidt, Jacob and Margaretha his wife to James Gascoine. Hamburg av. P. M. April 1, 6 months. 16,000

Martin, Charles A. to Henry Weil. Dean st. P. M. July 20, 1 year. 4,000

Same to same. Same property. July 20, 1 year. 6,000

McNeely, Michael to Michael Dowd. 2d st, s s, 20 e Bond st, 20x80. July 27, 2 years. 200

Mendenhall, Sarah M. to Gustav Dessecker. Rogers av, No. 80, s s, bet Park av and Prospect pl. July 27, note. 555

Meyer, Henry and Emma L. his wife to Magdalena Hornung. St. Marks av, n s, 166.3 w Rochester av, 75x127.9. July 1, 5 years or installs., 4 %. 2,000

Miller, Amanda to William V. Williamson. 75th st, New Utrecht. P. M. July 27, 3 years. 1,350

Mulvihill, Margaret wife of Nicholas to The Dime Savings Bank of Williamsburgh. Bedford av, s e cor Rutledge st, 20x95. July 28, 1 year, 5 %. 14,500

Same to same. Bedford av, e s, 20 s Rutledge st, 5 lots, each 26x100. 5 morts., each $9,700. July 28, 1 year, 5 %. 48,500

Munz, Mathaus F. and Anna to Christian A. Keppler. Knickerbocker av. P. M. July 23, due Jan. 23, 1894. 2,300

McGovern, Ellen M to M. Howell Topping. Union av. P. M. July 13, 3 years, 5 %. 200

Nimmo, George to The Union Savings Inst. Myrtle av, n s, 65 w Greene av, 29.3x67.10x39.9x39.9. July 28, due Nov. 1, 1892. 2,500

O'Neil, John to Michael D. Kelly. Columbia st, w s, 21 s Congress st, 21x80. July 13, 3 years, 5 %. 2,000

Powell, Sarah J. to Mary A. Kenney. 4th av, n w s, 40.2 s w 35th st. P. M. July 22, due Nov. 1, 1892, 5 %. 500

Same to same. Same property. July 22, due Nov. 1, 1892, 5 %. 500

Perry, Nellie T to Anthony R. Dyett. St. Marks av, n s, 120 w Bedford av, 20x128.6. July 23, due Sept. 17, 1891. 500

Philips, Fanny W. wife of and James mortgagor with Henry T. Meyer mortgagee. Two Extensions of morts. July 5. nom

Phillips, George to The Title Guarantee and Trust Co. Pacific st, s s, 200 e Brooklyn av, 5 lots, each 20x107.2. 5 morts., each $7,500. July 25, 3 years, 5 %. 37,500

Peterson, Frank O. to Margaret M. Easton. 11th st, n s, 343.6 e 8th av, runs south 100 x east 19.5 x south 48.10 x south 51.2 to st, x west 18.11. July 24, 3 years, 5 %. 4,000

Same to same. 11th st, n s, 324.7 e 8th av, 18.11 x100. July 24, 3 years, 5 %. 4,000

Parmer, Ada wife of Lewis to Byron W. and Helen E. Clarke. Broadway and Watkins st. P. M. July 23, 1 year. 3,850

Parkin, John to Susan Vanderveer. Vernon av, n s, 225 e Nostrand av, 6 lots. 6 morts., each $4,000. P. M. May 4, 3 years, 5 %. 24,000

Phelan, William J. and Annie M. Malone to The Long Island Brewery. Court st, No. 144. Lease. July 22, note. 1,500

Reilly, John to John and Thomas Charlton, of Tonawanda, N. Y. Bainbridge st, s e cor Ralph av, 25x100. July 10, 6 months. 2,416

Robinson, William to Richard Goodwin. Jefferson av, s e s, 264 n e Broadway. P. M. Sub. to mort. $3,000. July 27, 1 year. 850

Same to same. Same property. P. M. Sub. to morts. $3,850. July 27, 6 months. 400

Rooney, Margaret wife of Alexander J. to John Miner, 5th av, east cor 7th st. P. M. July 25, due July 28, 1894, 5 %. 10,000

Reichardt, Ernst to George Covert. Greene av. P. M. July 27, due July 1, 1896, 5 %. 5,000

Rosenberg, Joseph and Jacob Feinberg to Lazarus Weil. Seigel st. P. M. July 27, installs, 5 %. 8,500

Reis, John and Henry B. Davenport to Catharine J. Bergen. Montgomery st, s s, 200 e 18th st, 25x100. July 16, 3 years. 1,000

Reynolds, Charles H. with Amelia P. Clement, both mortgagees. Agreement as to priority of morts. made by Susie D. and Peter L. Brokaw. July 23. nom

Radcliffe, Thomas H. to John C. Schenck. McDonough st, s s, 62 e Ralph av, runs south 90 x east 38 x south 10 x east 75.4 x north 100 to McDonough st, x west 113.4. July 24, demand, 5 %. 3,000

Radford, William to John McColloch. Dresden st. P. M. July 22, 5 years, 5 %. 600

Reller, Rudolph to Abraham Mandeville. 42d st, s s, 425 w 3d av, 25x100.2. July 24, due July 1, 1893. 1,000

Raymond, Benjamin C. to James D. Rankin and James Ross. Macon st, n s, 94 w Ralph av, 18x100. Sub. to mort. $4,500. July 28, 1 year. 1,000

Reilly, Louisa F. wife of and John to James H. Watson and James H. Pittinger. Bushwick av, south cor Aberdeen st, runs southwest 90 x southeast 200 to Hull st, x northeast 79 to land of Manhattan Beach R. R. Co., x north 22.1 to av, x northwest 180.6. July 6, due July 15, 1891. 2,000

Same to same. Same property. May 21, demand. 4,500

Reynolds, Charles H. mortgagee to Susie D. Brokaw. Declaration that mortgage held by party of first part is a second mortgage. July 9. nom

Rhein, Hermann to Thomas Connoy. Richardson st, s s, 275 e Union av, 25x100. July 1, 3 years. 2,000

Ross, Teresa B. to James D. Lynch. 25th av, east cor 85th st, New Utrecht. July 18, due July 21, 1892, 5 %. 2,400

Schnebel, Nicholas to The East Brooklyn Savings Bank. Throop av, n e cor Kosciusko st, 100x100. July 27, 1 year, 5 %. 4,000

Smith, Charles H. to Marenus J. Goodenough. Crescent av. P. M. May 7, due May 15, 1892, 5 %. 787

Stoll, Alexander S. to John C. Rogers. Hull st. P. M. July 25, 5 years, 5 %. 550

Sweizer, John J. to The F. & M. Schaefer Brewing Co. East Broadway, s s, 120 e Main road, Flatbush. Saloon and bottling business. Lease. July 24, 1 year. 2,500

Sexton, Mary A. wife of John to Annie E. De Groff. Clementina st, s s, 375 w Chester av, 100x100. July 27, due July 1, 1896. 800

Seifert, Charles to Ernestine Gastmeyer. Halsey st. P. M. Sub. to mort. $2,000. July 22, installs. 1,800

Same to The Title Guarantee and Trust Co. Same property. July 22, 1 year, 5 %. 2,000

Simon, Abram and Haskel Silberman to Byron W. Clarke and Helen S. his wife. Watkins st. P. M. July 1, 1 year. 2,400

Spencer, William, Jr., to The Title Guarantee and Trust Co. 1st st, n s, 212.10 w 7th av, 100 x100. July 24, 1 year. 6,000

Spitzer, Alexander and Solomon Beck to Frederick Heddesheimer and Maria his wife. Bergen st. P. M. July 25, due Aug. 1, 1896, 5 %. 2,200

Stapleton, John to Catharine Cosgrove. Union st, s s, 100 e Lott st, 50x150, Flatbush. July 13. 500

St. Martha's Sanitarium and Dispensary, Brooklyn, to Mary W. Waldron, New York. Dean st. P. M. July 23 due July 23, 1896, 5 %. 4,500

Same to John D. Taylor New York. Kingston av and Dean st. July 20, due July 23, 1892, 5 %. 1,000

Strembel, George to Balthaser Strembel. Norman av, n e cor Oakland st, 50x95. July 1, 1 year, 5 %. 4,000

St. Martha's Sanitarium and Dispensary, Brooklyn, which is to assume mortgage with Mary E. Bissell, Litchfield, Conn. Extension of mort. July 18. ——

Stumm, Augusta to Philip Steingotter. Bushwick av, s w s, 60 n w Van Voorhis st, 29x75. July 22, 3 years or installs, 5 %. 700

Schroeder, George E. to Charles Miller. Hart st. P. M. July 27, due July 1, 1892. 1,000

Schultz, J. Godfrey to Edward P. Day. 17th st, No. 317, s w s, 70 s e 6th av, 15x100.2. July 29, installs. 1,600

Sedgwick, Robert B. to The Serial Building Loan and Savings Inst. 13th av, north cor 55th st, 55.8 to Cowenhoven lane, x108x14.10x 100, New Utrecht. July 21, installs. 2,600

Smith, Herbert C. to Richard Remsen, Jr., Flatlands, L. I. Old Canarsie road, Flatlands. P. M. July 22, due June 24, 1894, 5 %. 4,500

Smith, William A. to Charles Engert. North Henry st. P. M. Sub. to mort. $1,750. July 1, installs, 5 %. 1,250

Same to The Kings County Savings Inst. Same property. July 1, 1 year, 5 %. 1,750

Taber, Charles S. and George C. Case to The Hyde & Gload Mfg. Co. Albany av, w s, 22.3 n Butler st, 16.8x100. July 3, due July 20, 1892. 600

Thompson, Jessie M. wife of and James, Yonkers, to Emma T. Coleman. Atlantic av, s s, 166.8 e of w s of Rockaway av, 16.8x100; Atlantic av, s s, 216.8 e of w s of Rockaway av, 16.8x100. July 15, 1891, due July 16, 1891. 2,000

Thompson, Edward, Yonkers, to Stephen B. Sturges. Myrtle av, Knickerbocker av. P. M. Secures debt of Edward and James Thompson. July 22, demand. 33,900

Thorstensen, Carl to William P. Hillmann. 20th st, s w s, 300 s e 4th av, 50x100. July 25, 3 years. 3,100

Ullinger, Anna E. wife of Anton formerly Pflanz to Martha Betz. Bushwick av, s w s, 20 n w Dodworth st, 20x74. July 27, due July 1, 1894, 5 %. 1,000

Van Wart, Anne to Adaline A. Newman. 58th st, s s, 140 e 12th av, 40x100.2, New Utrecht. May 20, 6 months. 266

Van Winkle, Joseph H., Hempstead, L. I., to Andrew Peck. Junius st. P. M. July 21, 1 year. 7,500

Van Siclen, Albert W. to John M. Linz and Pauline R. his wife. Bristol st. P. M. July 22, 3 years. 1,500

Vega, Mary A. widow to Adelheid Hasenkamp, New York. Greene av, n s, 175 w Bedford av, 20x108.1x20x108.3. July 22, due July 1, 1894, 5 %. 2,000

Voltz, Albert, Jr., and Katharina L. his wife to Albert Voltz, Sr. Myrtle av, east cor Harman st, 86.6x71.4x11.7x111.6. July 24, due July 1, 1892, 5 %. 2,000

Wierk, John P. to The Greenpoint Savings Bank. Cleson av, n e cor Bergen st, 20x80. July 16, 1 year, 5½ %. 7,000

Wrieden, John to John Finken. De Kalb av, s w cor Sumner av, 20x100. July 1, 3 years. 5 %. 3,000

Walker, Thomas A. to John Dill, Jr. Gates av, n s, 265.3 e Marcy av, 20x100. July 24, due July 1, 1892, 5 %. 150

Waterman, Alice G. wife of and Daniel M. to Title Guarantee and Trust Co. 2d st, n e s, 259.9 n w 7th av, 18x100. July 24, 1 year, 5 %. 2,000

Webber, Mary A., formerly Nolan, to Samuel B. Richardson. 16th st, s s, 273 w 3d av, 22 x46x22x48.11. July 20, 5 years. 700

Wegmann, John to Peter P. Boschert. Myrtle av, n s, 113 w Harman st, 25x94.10x35.1x70.3. July 1, 1 year, 5 %. 1,750

Wilhelm, Rosa wife of and Wilhelm to Josephine K. Stone. Stagg st. P. M. July 13, due July 1, 1894, 5 %. 2,000

Wilkinson, John W. to William M. Tebo. 53d st, s w s, 260 n w 8th av, 40x100.2. July 16, 6 years, 5 %. 3,100

Wingerath, William to Daniel Doody. 16th st, n s, 135.9 w 8th av, 76.4x100. July 23, due Oct. 22, 1891. 675

Wood, Mary A. wife of and James J. to The Title Guarantee and Trust Co. Monroe st. P. M. July 15, due July 25, 1894, 5 %. 4,600

Walberg, Gustaf V. to Deborah C. Tepping, South Glastonbury, Conn. Prospect av. P. M. July 25, due July 1, 1894, 5 %. 1,300

Wingerath, William to James H. Watson and James H. Pittinger, of Watson & Pittinger. 16th st, n s, 135.9 w 8th av, 76.4x100. July 25, demand. 694

Wall, Thomas to Mary Geary. 20th st, n e s, 125 s e 8th av, 50x100. July 27, 3 years, 5 %. 2,000

Wigg, Alfred R. to The Assured Building Loan Assoc. Sackett st, n s, 383.4 w Smith st, 16.8 x100. July 27, installs. 4,900

Wilkie, Catharine to Patrick J. McGlinchey. 16th st, n s, 347.10 e 10th av, 12.6x100. July 8, due April 8, 1894, 5 %. 1,050

Williams, Charles to Patrick J. McGlinchey. 16th st, n s, 322.10 e 10th av, 25x100. July 8, 3 years, 5 %. 2,550

Zimmerman, Moritz to Benedict Vogt. Varet st. P. M. July 25, 5 years, 5 %. 3,000

Zahn, Henry A. to George and Katarina Knoth, Canarsie, L. I. Lot at Canarsie adj land of Richard L. Baisley, 50x100, Flatlands. April 2, 2 years. 100

Zepp, William to Williamsburgh Savings Bank. Stockton st, s s, 124 w Tompkins av, 41x100. July 24, 1 year, 5 %. 4,500

Zimermann, Anna E. wife of Martin to Timothy C. Conklin. Clove road. P. M. July 22, installs. 250

MORTGAGES----ASSIGNMENTS.

NEW YORK CITY.

JULY 24 TO 30—INCLUSIVE.

Asinari, Helena L. G. to Augustus T. Gillender trustee Washington F. Benjamin and Lilly M. S. Wood. $11,209

Blair, Sarah R. guard. Sarah C. Blair to Catharine D. Blair. 14,000

Blackwell, Samuel to Benjamin Steinhardt. 15,000

Baruch, Henry to David Weisburger. 2,000

Bendheim, Henry M. to George W. Galinger. nom

Cohen, Morris and John Morrisey to Henry Wittgowski. 6,000

Davis, Eugene H. to Cecil A. Marks. ——

Downer, Frederick W. to Samuel A. York trustee Samuel R. Downer. 10,500

Same to same. 20,000

Downing, George S. guard. John W. and Garret W. Nostrand to The Glen Cove Mutual Insurance Company of Glen Cove, L. I. nom

Fichter, Herman, Barnett Levy, Louis Gordan and Sophia Gruenstein to Jacob Rieser. consid. omitted

Fay, Michael and William Stacom to John J. Geier and Margaretha his wife. 3,764

Frazier, Charles to James McCurrach. 1,500

Frisbee, Anna G. to The Mutual Life Ins. Co. 5,000

Frank, Solomon to Jacob Lauth. nom

Folz, Frederick to Bertha Mennel. 1,500

Same to same. 2,500

Geismann, Moise to Elizabeth Wright. 8,100

Goldstein, Solomon to Solomon Bachrach. 1,500

German-American Real Estate Title Guarantee Co. to Hamilton Trust Co. 68,000

Gillender, Augustus T. trustee Washington F. Benjamin and Lilly M. S. Wood to Louise L. Williams. 15,612

Gross, Charles to Jeremiah Tuohey. 26,000

Hayden, Henry W. guard. Marion J. Tuttle to Elizabeth wife of John H. Bloodgood. nom

Hein, Frances to Henry Robert. 4,000

Hawkes, Henry to Emeline Johnson. 1,000

Hamann, G. Herman to Peter Graber. 527

Kennedy, Carrie S. to Elizabeth A. Kennedy. 5,000

Lahnstein, Herman to Abraham H. Berrick. nom

Loew, Sarah L. wife of William L. to Thomas H. Cook. 2,000

Laundrie, J. Russell to William McShane. nom

Leszynsky, Albert H. trustee to Moses Adler nom

Leland, Francis L. to William Fletcher. 10,000

Leibrock, Nicholas to Charles T. Krauss and August C. Hassey. 6,450

Lowenfeld, Pincus to Emma Arnstein. 500

Mason, Edith to Hetty H. R. Green trustee Hetty S. A. H. R. Green. 6,089

Mason, John to same. 20,297

Mills, Andrew and ano. exrs. William T. Blair to Sarah R. Blair guard. Sarah C. Blair. 14,000

Same to same. 30,000

Same to Catharine D. Blair. 14,000

Mott, Henry A. trustee Valentine Mott to Alexander B. Mott. 1885. 9,000

Mott, Henry A. and ano. exrs. Valentine Mott to Alexander B. Mott. 4,690

Moore, formerly Andariese, Amanda E. wife of Frederick D. to Mary A. A. Woodcock, Bedford, N. Y. 5,000

Monheimer, Isidor to Charles Dexheimer. 2,500

Maring, Elba A. and ano. exrs. Susan A. Maring to Mary A. Brown, White Plains, N. Y. 800

New York Infirmary for Women and Children to John T. Willets, Treasurer of Endowment Fund of the Schofield Normal Av Industrial School of Aiken, S. C. 8,000

Schmuck, Bertha wife of Herman to Babette Blumenthal. 3,000

Steiner, David to Joseph Steiner. nom

Shiman, Isaac to Abraham Stern. 4,000

Schneider, Charles to Henry Schneider. nom

Scott, Julius admr. Caroline S. Scott to Julius Scott, Caroline A. Hamilton and Clara J. Zehner. nom

Shedlinsky, Harris, Julius and Isidore Schweitzer to Bessie Schweitzer. nom

Schreiber, Pauline to Joseph Larchan. 500

Title Guarantee and Trust Co. to John R. Platt et al. trustees Samuel R. Platt. 5,000

Same to Lawrence H. Schwab. 5,000

The trustees of St Stephens College of Annandale, New York, to The United States Trust Co. 3,055

The Dry Dock Savings Inst. to Gideon Fountain. nom

The McElwee Mfg. Co. to Gottfried Schultz 2,000

Wittkowski, Henry to Andrew H. Mickle, Flushing, L. I. 6,000

Wenz, Edward and William Radebold to Bridget Casey. 950

Weil, Jonas and Bernhard Mayer to Auguste Veit. 3,000

Same to Henry De F. Weekes. nom

Wetmore, Benjamin C. and ano. exrs. Francis McKernan to Daniel M. K. Simpson. 5,026

Wittner, Joseph to Emanuel Glauber. ——

Zittel, Frederick and ano. exrs. William S. Blair to Catharine D. Blair. 7,000

KINGS COUNTY.

JULY 23 TO 29—INCLUSIVE.

Altenbrand, Katharina to Charles W. Schluchtner. $2,436

Bannigan, Joanna E. widow to Ann M. Fisher. 2,541

Brown, Mary E. to Calvin W. Raymand and Michael Dowley. nom

Bedell, Hiram to Henry S. Wells. 750

Berry, Lillian to W. Ryerson Kissam. 7,500

Brown, James C. to James W. Lamb. 1,800

Barth, Emilia to The Nuns of the Order of St. Dominick. 2,500

Same to same. 2,000

Same to same. 1,400

Same to same. 4,000

Same to same. 4,000

Same to same. 3,000

Cole, Randolph H. to Elias J. Hendrickson, Jamaica. 4,500

Collins, Sarah W. to Phebe T. Sutton. 1,000

Same to Elnathan Carpenter. 1,000

Cox, Emma C., North Hempstead, L. I., to Rebecca S. Monfort, Oyster Bay, L. I. 2,000

Cropsey, James to The Long Island Bank. 1,500

Cohn, Isaac and Leo Katz to Julius Lewy. 1,500

Collins, Richard S. to William H. and Stephen W. Collins. 2,000

Davis, Joseph to Herman F. Koepke. 950

Elliot, Phoebe F. to The East River Savings Inst. 5,056

Faber, Wilhelmina to Welcome S. Jarvis. 800

Gallagher, Bernard guard. of and Margaret M. McConnell to George W. Blauvelt. 1,525

Green, Marcus to James Bolton. 1,150

Goodnow, Jane M. to Lois R. Hastings. 2,250

Griffen, Jesse H. and Geo. G. exrs. Daniel H. Griffen to Jesse H. Griffen. 900

Same to Mary A. Carpenter, of Harrison, N. Y. 2,000

Same to Jesse H. Griffen, 1,200

Same to same. 1,200

Hart, John F. to Asa W. Parker, New Hamburg, N. Y. 4,200

Hauck, Frederick to The German Savings Bank, Brooklyn. 2,000

Huntting, John B. exr. James M. Huntting to James M. Huntting, Andover, N. J. 1,000

Same to same. 2,800

Same to same. 1,000

Same to same. 500

Halstead, Stephen C. to David A. Fithian. 550

Jarvis, Welcome S. to Niels O. Olsen. 800

Koenig, August and Carl Schuster to Emilie Huber. 1,000

Loomis, John S. to Robert A. Davison. 2,000

Litchfield, Henry C. to Elizabeth Fullagar, Newburg, N. Y. 200

Litchfield, Jacob T. E. to same. 200
Livingston, Charles O. trustee for R. M. Livingston to Eliza H. Livingston, Glenham, N. Y. 1,007
Martindale, Mary M. and Annie A. Moran to Virginia Clark. 2,000
McGill, Joseph to Emilie Huber. 2,000
Martin, Levi V. to Lawrence Hurlburt. 540
Parmer, Ada to Byron W. and Helen E. Clarke. 550
Roth, Henry to Jacob H. Werbelovsky. 3,041
Radford, William and Hannah to Wilhelm and Mary Schnoor. 300
Rhodes, George R., Jr., to Robert F. Rhodes. 1,250
Rich, David individ. and exr. Solomon Rich to John E. Lovell. 650
Rogers, Charles E. to Rebecca F. Forman. 200
Ryan, Joseph to Manufacturers' National Bank. 1,310
Raymond, Calvin W. and Michael Dowley to Blanche E. Raymond. nom
Stewart, C. James et al. exrs. James Stewart to Gilla A. Gates. nom
Same to Charles Gates. nom
Sayres, Phebe H. to James M. Huntting. 3,000
Slocum, Louis W. and Eliza S. admrs. of Charles L. Slocum to Emma L. Peckham. 2,507
Title Guarantee and Trust Co. to James Sullivan. 1,500
Same to Mary L. Brown. 2,500
Same to same. 2,500
Same to Mary A. Littlewood. 3,5 0
Same to same. 3,750
Same to Adelia K. Broome. 7,500
Same to same. 7,500
Same to Bernard Cruse, Jr. 500
Same to August P. Rockwell and ano. trustees for Annie C. Decker. 4,000
Same to Mary Vigelius. 4,800
Same to Henry F. Sammis. 6 000
Same to James Hembury. 6,000
Same to Kings County Trust Co. 2,200
Same to same. 2,000
Same to Jeremiah L. Zabriskie. 3,000
Same to Sarah A. Johnson extrx. 3,500
Same to Riverhead Savings Bank. 2,000
Same to same. 2,000
Same to Brooklyn Trust Co. 7,500
Same to same. 7,500
The People's Trust Co. to People's Trust Co. trustee Margarethe Herrmann. 5,000
Underhill, Mary K. to Elias H. Underhill. 250
Waldorf, John F. to James S. Bearns. 5.000
Wilde, John and ano. exrs. Sarah Wilde to Emma J. wife of A. Ward Brigham. 6,900
Werbelovsky, Jacob H. to The Broadway Bank of Brooklyn. 3,000

JUDGMENTS.

In these lists of judgments the names alphabetically arranged, and which are first on each line, are those of the judgment debtor. The letter (D) means judgment for deficiency (*) means not summoned. (†) signifies that the first name is fictitious, real name being unknown. Judgments entered during the week, and satisfied before day of publication, do not appear in this column, but in list of Satisfied Judgments

NEW YORK CITY.

July
25 Andrews, Charles S—W E Stewart... $678 89
25 Aymar, Jose—Frederick Ringler costs 78 50
27 Allen, Rudolph—Peter Lauckhardt... 344 89
27 Alger, Byron—J A De Camp.......... 125 86
27 Aspinwall, Lloyd—Thomas Mathews. 1,164 91
27 Andres, Henry / *Andres, Thomas, as copartners. / Andres, Henry, individ. } Caspar Mahr.. 382 59
28 Arnheimer, David—Marcus Sommerfield.......... 1,637 53
30 Ash, William H—L B Lynch........ 3,125 19
30 Arkinsburg, Robert H—H R Gordon. 174 05
31 Aspinwall, Lloyd—Charlotte M Goodridge.......... 525 75
25 Batynsky, John—Matthias Yodyszus. 215 20
25 Bixby, Frank M, Jr—Axel Lindstrom 52 85
25 Brennan, James—J T Rider.......... 132 67
25 Bailey, James J—Siegfried Rosenberg 217 79
25 Buchanan, Robert D—Cady & Nelson Co (Lim).......... 227 01
27 Barstow, Jacob P—Christian Jourgeson.......... 39 84
27 Burke, Richard—J H Jackson... .... 215 85
27 Brooks, John E—Columbus Market Co 109 50
28 Boylan, Michael J—I C Odgen, Jr.... 1,011 67
28 Baringer, Harvey C—N Y Veal and Mutton Co.......... 133 12
29 Beyer, Conrad—Mineralized Rubber Co.......... 30 00
29 Bechter, Conrad—Frank Gass... .... 124 18
29*Bostwick, John O—Columbia Downing, Jr.......... 283 55
29 Beck, Francis E—Simonds Mfg Co... 129 20
29 *Borrmann, William / Borrmann, Louis } J F Heinbockel. 465 00
29 Bassett, George F—G S P Stillman... 71 37
29 Bensel, Rebecca / *Bensel, Frank O } James Grimes...... 113 90
30 Butler, William J—D G Ryer........ 340 33
30 the same——W H Wulling....... 249 36
30 Benjamin, Mary—Samuel Lord...... 632 09
30 Brown, Charles S—Meriden Britannia Co.......... 292 80
30 Bornstein, Morris—Jewellers' Weekly Publishing Co.......... 61 88
30 Beck, Francis E—Mayor, Lane & Co. 183 38
30 Bellmer, Abrend—Conrad Stein...... 2,022 94
30 Bostwick, Charles B — Baltimore & Ohio R R Co.......... 21,997 96
31 Belvin, Mary—Henry Abegg....... 837 59
31 Butler, William J—F F Lowenfels... 153 95
31†Brady, Peter A—G I Grossman....... 89 67
31 Burki, Frederick—Elizabeth Humes.. 796 86
31 Brown, Levi L—Charter Oak Nat Bank.......... 5,159 23
31 Bressant, Andrew—People State N Y. 3,000 00
24 Carroll, Thomas G — W L Bevan, admr..........costs 158 33
25 Craus, Henry S—J L Reynolds........ 1,087 10
25 Clark, Heman—John Seton.......... 1,272 77
25 Cahill, John—Maria W Dittmar..... 739 73
25 Casey, James—Mayor, Lane & Co... 1,853 04
27 Conaghan, Hannah—J B Ryan...... 118 84
27 Carroll, George—G W Venable..... 92 34
27 Caul, James——the same............ 73 77
27 Cohen, Moses—M S Kauffman....... 1,310 50
27 Carpenter, Robert B—Durland's Riding Academy Co.......... 140 42
28 Cohen, Moses—Benjamin Siegel...... 324 62
28 the same——Samuel Grodzinsky. 167 97
28 Collins, Frank A—F C Boynton...... 391 64
28 Carr, Thomas—John Brosen.... ..... 118 44
28 the same——Heman Renken .. . 101 10
28 Church, Afton—R S Hudspeth....... 93 50
28 Cornish, Charles E / Cornish, Louis M, exrs / Charles L Cornish } Lavinia D Cornish. ......costs 494 89
28 the same——Aaron Butler......... 65 75
28 Corbitt, James R—People State N Y. 2,000 00
29 Carroll, Carroll F—Ludwig Renn.... 155 00
29 Cleveland, Henry W—S R Ten Eyck. 1,037 38
30 Cohn, Julius—M S Wise.... .... 72 27
30 Clark, Francis A—Nat Ice Co......... 491 81
30 Clark, Nathaniel E / Corn, Abraham } Sol Lindenborn. 440 68
31 Crosby, Oliver M—A A Clough..costs 40 80
31 the same —the same.... .... 40 80
31†Considine, Michael F—R S Riddell... 121 11
31 Corcoran, John B—O L Hinds....... 379 43
24 Donner, Conrad N — Henry Herrmann.......... 342 62
25 Doran, S Gregor—Jasper Nichols..... 46 39
25 Doyle, Patrick J—Siegfried Rosenberg 217 79
25 Deane, William E, admr Theresa M Deane—Ellen Fegan.......... 955 46
27 Dunham, Sumner T—J E Heller...... 339 67
27 Devlin, James—Moses Weiss.......... 45 50
27 Davis, Edward A—J J Frank......(D) 3,092 20
28 Davidson, Ephraim—F W Devoe & Co.......... 160 72
28†Doe, John—L S Chase 42 37
29 Donovan, John, Jr—P A Welch. 1,339 80
29 the same——the same.... .... 1,170 87
30 Doremus, Morton R — German Exchange Bank. 2,262 25
30 Dempsey, John—J H Giles........... 107 15
31 Delaney, William H—John Patterson 187 41
31 Dilaberto, Anton—Lucy M Copeland. 111 32
27 Ehrlich, Abraham / Ehrlich, Hyman } Sigmund Kraus 176 81
28 Eldridge, John S—W P Wentworth.. 171 68
28 Eickhoff, Frederick—L S Chase...... 40 37
28 Eldridge, John S—W P Wentworth.. 99 53
29 Earle, Ellen M / Earle, James } N Y Life Ins Co. (D) 305 39
30 Ernst, Frank—F A Martin........... 17 50
30 the same——Henry Andre....... 25 00
30 Eustace, Mary V—Albert Russmann. 5,515 00
31 Edelson, Abraham—People State N Y 500 00
31 Evatt, Sarah K / Evatt, John G } Henry McShane Co (Lim).......... 1,478 07
25 Fortunato, Michael—A C Weiber.... 169 40
25 Farrell, Henry—Mayor, Lane & Co.. 978 95
25 Filer, Adolph—E L Oppenheim...... 295 97
25 Foland, Peter—S J Lanahan.......... 454 26
27 Fletcher, John William—Harvey Lyman..........(D) 637 34
29 Fitzgerald, Henry—Benedict Fischer. 98 17
29 Frenger, Jacob—George Ehret....... 1,099 45
30 Foley, Joseph—John Post............ 118 08
30 Force, Freeman B—B F Martin, comm'r.......... 110 00
30 Fogg, John C—Thomas Monahan.... 3,689 53
30 the same——G W Robinson...... 1,741 83
31 French, George B—Solomon Barnett 647 79
31 Fogg, John C—Board of Water Commissioners of the Village of Sing Sing.......... 664 00
31 Frohne, William C—S J Herschman.. 37 10
31 Furst, Alexander—People State N Y 500 00
31 Flaviu, M J—J R Warner.......... 814 74
25 Gilmartin, James—Siegfried Rosenberg.......... 217 79
25 Green, George, exr — Scott Lord, guard..........costs 85 05
25 the same——R M Morgan, guard..........costs 170 12
27 Gerhart, Morris—L J Boniface....... 139 00
27 Gartner, Adam—Nathan Sapierstein. 76 48
27 Gibbs, Lulu—Elkan Stone........... 158 32
28 Geirke, Herman / Griesmeyer, Charles } W J Humphreys......... 99 05
28 Gilhooly, Patrick H—J F Arnold..... 1,720 22
28 Gies, Franz—A G Huptel............ 185 73
29 Goddard, Walter Z—C W Schwarting 246 70
29 Gunn, John G—R P Hoyt........... 192 93
29 Goerlitz, Philip—A S Nichols......... 1,040 70
30 Gearon, Michael—C W Ferris........ 105 70
30 Grinspan, Ephraim—Arnold Kohn.... 919 37
30 the same——Alois Kohn......... 1,360 64
31 Greeley, Peter—John Emmons....... 473 37
25 Hawley, Frank V—N S Spencer...... 86 93
25 Hartung, Lorenzo R—J H Heroy..... 173 47
27 Hackett, Thomas J—Martin Eckhardt 24 00
27†Heldman, John—G P Clements...... 29 50
27 Hirschfield, Samuel—Sigmund Kraus 176 81
27 Harstadt, Henry—G W Venable..... 91 50
28 Houghton, George L—L S Chase...... 42 37
28 Hirsch, Albert—W H De Camp...... 636 61
29 Hawkes, Henry—Karl Mathiasen..... 307 02
29 Harris, Edward P—Cady & Nelson Co (Lim).......... 344 07
29 Hong, Ju / Hong, Chow / How, Ju } J S Ngow.......... 47 00
29 Hauguy, Edward—Western Nat Bank 98 61
29 Haas, Joseph—J F Spaulding........ 118 10
30 Hagan, Thomas—Margaret Hagan... 1,105 32
30 Haviland, Henry—John Young...... 389 69
30 Horowitz, Salo A—J S Goldsman.... 223 38
30 Hartwell, Louise M—C H Willson ... 229 96
30 Hunter, Thomas / Hunter, James } C T G. Chace.... 621 73
30 Horton, Dudley R—E H Hinton...... 129 24
31 Hausner, Samuel—T B Hidden..... .. 156 02
31 Hamilton, William G—I M Muro.... 5,694 85
31 Harper, Tacie McD—Chatham Nat Bank.......... 903 69
31 Hart, Alexander R——the same...... 794 44
25 Indorsky, Isaac / *Indorsky, William } F E Rosen...... 427 40
30 Jaeger, Lionel—Benjamin, Hyams... 391 65
25 Kennedy, Emma / Kennedy, Henry } James Flynn..... 665 50
27 Khuner, Norbert C—Mount Morris Electric Light Co.......... 70 15
27 Kramer, Morris—S E Bloomberg.... 42 50
28 Kneeland, Stillman F—L A Williams 179 27
28†Kent, Edward H—L S Chase......... 38 97
28†Kelly, Robert T——the same... ..... 38 78
28 Kirwan, John P—People State N Y.. 2,000 00
29 Kruder, Adolph / Kruder, Frank F / Kline, Charles } Isaac Scheuer..... 311 72
29 Kopperel, Gabriel—Charles Schlesinger.......... 167 54
25 Levy, Julius / Levy, Augustus H / Levy, Moses S } Nathan May.... 20,482 09
25 Loeb, Max—David Garrison........ 71 19
27*Lehr, Andrew—Columbus Market Co 109 50
27†Landau, Frances—Hayward Cleveland.......... 176 80
28 Lamphere, George W—S P Flannery. 222 87
28 Lyon, John H—L S Chase........... 44 37
29 Lees, Samuel—R R Cornell 168 26
29 Le Roy, Otis S—Benedict Fischer.... 98 17
29 Lund, Peter W—L W Towt.......... 96 02
29 Lowenstein, Henry M—J C Starck... 72 34
29 Liscomb, Alfred A—A J Miller...... 70 72
29 Lehmann, William — India Wharf Brewing Co.......... 399 48
30 Leary, Mary E—W H Walling....... 269 36
30 the same——D G Ryer....... ... 340 33
30 Lendy, Richard—J T Shackleford ... 12 00
30 Lawrence, Mary J—Fourteenth St Bank.......... 119 05
30 the same——the same........... 219 33
31*Leary, Mary E—F F Lowenfels...... 153 95
31 Levy, Herman / *Levy, Aaron } Engelbert Hardt... 2,141 85
31 the same——William Wood...... 192 57
31 Ladd, Alfred W—J E Van Doren.... 140 73
31 Lamorte, Francesco—People State N Y.......... 3,000 00
25 Martin, Robert C—Rose Brick Co.... 4,054 14
25 Mitchell, Charles—N S Spencer....... 86 98
25 Miller, Oscar H—J E Linde.......... 135 90
27 Mullins, Patrick—Matt Taylor Paving Co.......... 24 87
28 Miller, Augustus F—L H Cramer..... 39 50
28 MacKinney, William H—W H Talbot.......... 214 04
28 Menzies, John, Jr—W T Mosel....... 93 01
29 Montgomery, Frank L—E R Jobnes. 161 27
29 Mann, Isaac—W P Raynor.......... 349 05
29 Mason, A J—Columbia Downing, Jr. 262 55
29*Morgan, Guendoline—Ludwig Renn.. 155 00
29 Muir, William—S R Ten Eyck....... 1,037 38
29 Morris, Frederick—Columbia Bank.. 2,615 02
29 Metzger, Charles F—Chatham Nat Bank.......... 331 88
30 Martin, Archibald M—B F Martin, comm'r.......... 110 00
30*Murphy, John—Meriden Britannia Co.......... 292 80
30 Meyer, Nathan—Samuel Roebuck.... 86 60
30 Martin, I Kinsley — Baltimore & Ohio R R Co.......... 21,997 96
30 Murphy, Emily J—Albert Russmann. 5,515 00
31 Meyer, Edwin O—Jennie E Thorley.. 112 79
31 MacMahon, Thomas J—Mary S Davis. 282 37
31 Morgan, George D—G A Le Blanc.... 93 69
31 Muller, Gus—William Harvey.... ... 86 47
31 Molner, Herman—R P Lyon......... 38 50
27 McMahon, Ellen, admrx Thomas McMahon—N Y Elevated R R Co.costs 56 65
27 the same——the same........costs 128 09
28 McEathron, James E—C M Hillman.. 130 05
28 MacKinney, William H—W H Talbot.......... 218 04
29 McDermott, John—J P Mones........ 96 14
30 McCarthy, Frank—R B Poucher 71 63
30 McCann, Patrick—Nathaniel Waterbury.......... 45 00
30 McQuade, Hugh—C T G Chace 621 72
30 McQuillen, James S—Real Estate Exchange and Auction Room (Lim)..........costs 74 13
31 MacMahon, Thomas J—Mary S Davis. 282 37
31 McCormick, George Troop—Alice E Schoenberger, extrx..........costs 47 10
31 McKenna, Margaret—D B Dunham.. 296 66
31 McGuire, John—J E Simmons, recvr 34,044 75
27 Noonan, Peter J—James Wallace..... 673 21
28 Nubb, John—Christian Kneip 80 30
28 Nicholson, J Elliott—W P Wentworth 217 54
30 Neuberger, Jacob / Neuberger, Silas W } German Exchange Bank. 2,262 25
31 Newton, Henry A—J P Tuttle. 119 89
31 Nightingale, James—Botany Worsted Mills.......... 104 17
28 Ogden, William F—L S Chase 50 50
29 O'Neill, Dennis—Samuel Crooks...... 1,821 79

20 Odell, John B—E A Landon.......... 45 19
30 O'Brien, Miles M—U S Trust Co, trustee.......... 535 36
31 O'Kane, James—N Y Architectural Terra Cotta Co.......... 297 84
24 Pirsson, William—Edward Holland.......... costs 18 24
25 Peck, Nathan—Rose Brick Co.......... 4,054 14
28 Peck, Edward M—Francis Dougherty. 601 69
28 the same——F C Boynton.......... 391 64
29 Pape, Charles—E G Barrett.......... 147 15
29 Prendergast, George F—B S Johnson 485 66
30 Proops, Isaac—B F Martin, comm'r.. 110 00
30 Pinckney, William J—Julia B Wilkins, extrx.......... 159 62
31 Poly, Adolph—W H Hoffman.......... 82 10
24 Reilly, John; Reilly, Edward } Nat Ice Co.......... 169 99
25 Razutis, Anthony—Matthias Yodyszus.......... 215 20
25 Ross, Mary E—Adolf Gans.......... 114 52
27 Renauld, John B—Morris Building Co.......... 134 48
27 Richards, Al E—J L Steinhardt.......... 27 50
27 Reiss, Bernhard—Solomon Siegel.......... 20 16
28 Riley, Maria—Anna Morales.......... 117 32
28 Rankin, William H—J F Arnold.......... 1,720 22
28 Riker, C Lawrence—William Kinscherf.......... 274 72
29 Risley, Joseph H—G W Curtis.......... 452 46
29 the same——the same.......... 498 40
29 Ross, William H—Jacob Yost.......... 5,195 29
29 Rubin, Charles—Solomon Bachrach.. 188 94
29 Reiper, Henry—G P Lies.......... 80 00
29†Ruben, Louis M—Charles Seale.......... 32 55
29 Risley, Joseph H—C H Meyer.......... 412 03
29 Ross, William H—S R Ten Eyck.......... 1,087 38
30 Robinson, Frank—F P Osborn.......... 493 20
30 Reves, Catharine—Samuel Lord.......... 632 09
30*Rosenstock, Benjamin—Sol Lindenborn.......... 440 63
30 Reilly, William B—Anna M Banks.......... 1,884 15
30 Rathbun, Jason P—F B Blauvelt.......... 264 47
31 Rapp, Francis B; Rapp, John W } William Delamater 18 73
31 Revell, William W—L N Hershfield.. 497 83
31 Reilly, William B—J P Mones.......... 1,259 35
31 the same——C E Maxfield.......... 250 42
31 the same——Jose Gomez.......... 1,243 09
31 the same——George Lester.......... 660 13
31 the same——S W Giles.......... 221 79
31 the same——Hipolito Dumois.......... 173 25
25 Schwack, John J—N J Benson.......... 150 49
25 Stout, Emily B—W Van Campen.......... 633 34
25 Spearing, William—John Delahunty. 129 87
25 Scriba, Augustus M—U S Nat Bank.. 2,715 78
25 Sinclair, James—S J Lanahan.......... 1,433 83
25*Staats, John H——the same.......... 454 26
27 Sigel, Samuel—Louis Levene.......... 29 50
27 Schneider, Louis H—N Y Press Co (Lim).......... 700 88
28 Schneider, Louis H—Isaac Fromme.. 694 62
28 Sjvberg, Carl—B K Stickle.......... 358 17
28 Schrage, Adam—W H Schmobl.......... 351 67
28 Simmons, James F—N Y Life Ins Co. 94 93
28 Schmidt, John M—A G Hupfel.......... 185 73
28 Stafford, William J—N A Merritt.......... 305 16
29 Sommer, Moritz—Washington Mills Co.......... 360 42
29 the same——R S Frost.......... 676 56
29 Schlamovitz, David—D P Morse.......... 163 03
29 the same——Edwin Wallace.......... 474 15
29 Streifler, Jacob—Frank Gass.......... 124 18
29†Seycora, Albert—Henrietta Rice.......... 65 89
29 Schwab, Gabriel; Schwab, Nathan; Schwab, Abraham; Schwab, Leo L } Siegfried Rosenberg.......... 308 03
30 Sotscheck, Charles—C A Aimone.......... 208 97
30 Scribner, G Hilton—Thomas Monahan 3,689 53
30 Schnaars, Diedrich—Conrad Stein.......... 2,022 94
30 Sribner, Gilbert H; Sribner, Howard } G W Robinson.. 1,741 53
30 Satterle, Livingston—Baltimore & Ohio R R Co.......... 21,997 96
31 Scribner, Gilbert H—Board of Water Comm'rs of Village of Sing Sing.......... 664 00
31 Straus, Louis—Western Nat Bank.......... 3,600 12
31 Sedransky, Morris—Alois Kohn.......... 144 44
31 Stewart, John—C D Rust.......... 119 88
31†Sause, Richard—Beadleston & Woerz 193 05
31 Sweeny, Stephen E—William Forster. 168 91
31 Schmidt, Hermann——the same.......... 108 48
28 Smith, Thomas R H—L S Chase.......... 69 18
31 Smith, Waitstill A; Smith, John Y } Andrew Dutcher 273 50
31 Smith, Ira; Smith, Charles I } A D Edson.......... 137 88
25 Acme Wood Fibre Co—Goodyear Rubber Co.......... 113 86
25 The Metropolitan Gas Light Co of Elizabeth, N J—J D Walsh.......... 796 56
25 The N Y Elevated R R Co; The Manhattan Railway Co } Lewis Seasongood.......... 2,561 93
27 Brooklyn Fastener Co—W E Dodge.. 157 79
27 The J J Nichols Mfg Co—Ansonia Brass and Copper Co.......... 140 28
27 The American Opera Co (Lim)—M W Whitney.......... 9,339 62
27 The Cartaret Club—L D Hosford.......... 537 30
28 The Lithographic Art Journal Publishing Co—Paul Berger.......... 79 72
28 Easton Electric Co—C A Murphy.......... 1,874 20
28 J H Bonnell & Co (Lim)—Western Nat Bank.......... 3,287 33
28 the same——the same.......... 1,424 31
28 the same——the same.......... 1,170 67
28 the same——the same.......... 1,105 95
28 The New York Underground Railway Co—John Newton, comm'r...costs 112 62
28 Facer Refrigerating and Ice Machine Co—T E Hogg.......... 13,647 21
29 The Walter Higgins Mfg Co—P A Welch.......... 1,339 80
29 Pneumatic Dynamite Gun Co—Richard Irvin.......... 42,386 73
29 The Fred Hower Brewing Co (Lim)—Scranton & Lehigh Coal Co.......... 1,207 73
29 Ducker Portable House Co—American Field Publishing Co.......... 235 60
29 The Pneumatic Dynamite Gun Co—O B Potter.......... 187 68
29 the same——the same.......... 1,396 19
29 Leo Austrian & Co—Adolf Van Praag 410 56
30 The Massachusetts Benefit Assoc—Emily Williams.......... 3,053 18
30 Hudson River Boot and Shoe Mfg Co—Poughkeepsie Transportation Co. 436 03
30 the same——James Mulvein.......... 1,886 68
30 J H Bonnell & Co (Lim)—Western Nat Bank.......... 432 06
30 The Ackerly & Gerard Co—D H Roberts.......... 575 62
30 The Hudson River Boot and Shoe Mfg Co—Bank of America.......... 1,469 09
31 The London Toilet Bazaar Co—William Albrecht.......... 183 98
31 Union Pavement Co—Osgood Welsh.. 922 33
31 The Stephany Perfume Co—George Lueders.......... 529 27
31 The Lawrence Curry Comb Co—Keller Printing Co.......... 125 38
31 The American Standard Electric Light Co—Laura L Preston.......... 119 99
31 United Zylonite Co; American Zylonite Co } Charter Oak Nat Bank.. 5,159 23
31 J H Bonnell & Co (Lim)—Western Nat Bank.......... 1,024 88
31 the same——the same.......... 1,344 58
31 The Ideal Sanitary Co—W C Wagner.......... 623 00
27 Thornton, Matthew—Barstow Stove Co.......... 89 40
27 Tyler, John B R—J H McGuire.......... 124 98
29 Thompson, James—James Boland.......... 161 65
29 the same——N Y Gas Fixture Co. 343 30
29 Taylor, Warren S; Taylor, Clarence M } J M Robb.......... 96 80
29 Taylor, Jacob—Equitable Life Assurance Society..........(D) 2,447 77
29 the same——the same..........(D) 1,365 49
29 the same——the same..........(D) 8,369 07
29 the same——the same..........(D) 5,754 69
29 the same——the same..........(D) 5,247 51
29 the same——the same..........(D) 4,692 12
31 Thomas, Edward E—T M Dougherty 107 00
27 Von Lehe, Catherine—Ernest Querino.......... 89 78
28 Vom Lehn, Richard—Simon Katzenstein.......... 273 41
28 Voss, Herman E—Nettie Tyson.......... 80 50
28 Vernon, Edward—W P Wentworth.. 99 53
31 Vincent, Belle—Elizabeth Stebbins.......... 86 91
30 Valentine, Robert H C—Chatham Nat Bank.......... 281 76
27 Van der Perren, Ferdinand—M M Hirsh.......... 837 01
25 Wheeler, De Witt C—Abraham Garside.......... 50 85
25 Wilson, William J—E S Jaffray.......... 2,819 15
28 Wodenscheck, Charles O—Sophia Wodenscheck.......... 317 75
28 Werner, Gottlieb—Wm Ottman & Co 294 92
28*Wick, Jacob—W H Schmobl.......... 351 67
29 Ward, John B—G O Cruttenden.......... 131 76
29 Wyman, John A—James White.......... 83 66
29 Welch, Deshler; Welsh, Deshler } Mrs Frank Leslie.......... 500 32
29 Wagner, Albert—A D Pape.......... 32 50
30 Walsh, Patrick—John Post.......... 118 08
30 Wilson, Moses R—J J Campbell.......... 140 15
30 Walker, Edward B—E H Hinton.......... 129 24
31*Weil, Isidor—Henry Abegg.......... 837 59
31 Welteck, Ernest—Emil Unger.......... 129 00
31 Williams, Clothilde B—Mary O'Connell.......... 516 82
31 Wattenberg, Ferdinand A—William Forster.......... 108 48
27 Young, Louis—C E Martin.......... 78 98

KINGS COUNTY.

July

28 Ames, Eliza J—E A Gillespie.......... $704 57
24 Baker, Henry C—G B Ellis.......... 44 67
24 Bower, Samuel—G Brandeis.......... 106 25
24 Beuson, Michael; Beaudet, Homer J } D Marx..........(D) 9,993 19
24 the same——the same..........(D) 9,714 16
24 Bills, James A—The Butler Hardware Co.......... 155 94
25 Bierschenk, Peter F—W Rankin..(D) 5,452 03
25 Best, H C sued as Henry C—O A Gordon.......... 121 16
28 Baruth, Henry—E Wallace.......... 616 03
28 the same——J Chambers (Lim).......... 259 57
24 Cox, Henry E—G L Wood.......... 356 09
28 Carter, Charles H—W E Rider.......... 70 89
30 Cheetham, Alfreda A—White, Potter & Paige Mfg Co.......... 155 90
30 Cleveland, Henry—S R Ten Eyck.......... 1,087 38
24 De Camp, Cornelius M—Butler Hardware Co.......... 155 94
27 Davenport, William B, Public admr Kings Co as admr, &c Devine, Mary, dec'd } Mary Clark 202 78
28 Driggs, W Lincoln—S D Bond.......... 143 86
29 Donovan, John, Jr—P A Welch.......... 1,170 87
30 Drew, Gershon H—Catharine Ward.. 40 00
25 Ellis, William H—H Henjes.......... 257 17
24 Fellows, Franklin J—B Moore & Co.. 136 42
24 Foss, Samuel—G A Kingsland.......... 61 85
25 Francis, Arthur—W Rohde.......... 23 85
27 Fellows, Franklin—T G Knight.......... 100 23
29 Finley, Henry T—J T Scott.......... 318 16
24 Gaffney, James—W J Lynam.......... 267 50
28 Grube, Frederick L—G Rehn.......... 58 44
24 Hennessy, John—G Brandeis.......... 106 25
24 the same——the same.......... 204 62
24 Heckman, James A—Wright & Co (Lim).......... 1,560 56
29 Harris, Edward P—Cady & Nelson Co (Lim).......... 344 07
29 Huber, August—W H Hamilton.......... 180 66
30 Hummel, Henry H—S L Tredwell.......... 92 18
27 Jones, W William H—G W Brown, exr.......... 102 68
28 Josiah, George—C Gans.......... 41 25
29 Jones, Joseph R—J B Huntting.......... 16 10
24 Kenney, Margaret—C Lane.......... 205 28
30 Kindleman, Frank—A C Bechstein.......... 124 71
30 Lansdell, Henry S—W Barri.......... 242 47
30 Lawrence, Edson—Wilson & Baille Mfg Co.......... 513 47
24 Miner, Mary L—J Mullins.......... 155 70
24 McConnell, Julia—R M Hickey.......... 32 77
25 Mersereau, Charles E—M H Murray.. 98 18
27 Meyer, Gesene—M J Gibbons.......... 219 60
27 Mott, John H—Otto Huber Brewery. 168 75
27 Moore, Frank S—W Vogel.......... 19 27
28 Meyer, George—A P Wilson.......... 24 85
28 McDermott, Thomas—P Weidmann.. 174 25
29 Meyer, Gesine; Meyer, Henry } O Huber Brewery.. 46 12
30 Mendenhall, Lorenzo—New York and Brooklyn Casket Co.......... 159 64
30 the same——the same.......... 158 94
30 McDermott, John—J P Mones.......... 96 14
30 McDermott, Thomas—S Streit.......... 135 32
30 Muir, William—S R Ten Eyck.......... 1,087 38
24 O'Hara, Thomas—T McCann.......... 666 11
29 O'Neill, Dennis—S Crooks.......... 1,821 79
29 Ochs, William—F W Koch.......... 123 20
24 Pearson, Eugene—S B Solomon.......... 826 27
24†Robertson, "Daniel" S—P A Johnson 35 20
24 Rogers, Joseph E—T McCann.......... 663 11
24 Reilly, Barbara—Catharine A Hurley..........(D) 4,016 33
27 Rothenback, John—L Bossert.......... 31 94
28 Renauld, John B—Morris Building Co 134 48
28 Raab, William—H Gehrksen.......... 90 55
28 Ryan, Mark E—H Miles.......... 34 63
28 Richards, Al E—J L Steinhardt.......... 27 50
29 Redfield, Frank W—R C Moffat.......... 93 75
30 Reid, Matilda; Reid, Hugh } G Brandies.......... 507 05
30 Ross, William H—S R Ten Eyck.......... 1,037 38
30 the same——J Yost.......... 5,195 29
24 Smith, Daniel A—P Barthel.......... 122 62
24 Scott, Charles B—S B Solomon.......... 826 27
24 Searing, Theodore W—C F Lawrence 104 33
24 Smith, John H—I Pierce.......... 78 36
24 Stockholm, Clara—P Moloney.......... 159 53
25 Smith, Frank L—W Rankin..........(D) 5,452 03
25 Svenlin, Alfred—W Rohde.......... 126 58
25 Seifert, Adolph C—G T Riley.......... 129 60
25 Strout, Emily B—O W Van Campen. 653 34
27 Seekamp, John H—J F Heinbockel.. 2,115 00
27 Schaefer, John—W S Williams.......... 78 69
28 Scott, David H—G F Chapman....(D) 1,055 83
28 Schneider, Louis H—N Y Press Co (Lim).......... 700 88
29 Sheldon, Cevedra B—S Winslow..(D) 3,709 31
29 Skelly, John—S Williamson.......... 46 10
30 Smith, Clarence H—White, Potter & Paige Mfg Co.......... 155 90
28 the same——Fromme Bros.......... 694 62
24 The Fred Hower Brewing Co—J Sibert.......... 179 80
24 Thompson, James—F C Knowles & Co.......... 136 08
27 The Brooklyn Fastener Co—W E Dodge.......... 157 79
27 The admr, &c, Mary Devine, dec'd—Mary Clark.......... 202 78
28 The Eastern Electric Co—Murphy & Metcalf.......... 1,874 20
28 the same——the same.......... 521 15
29 Thornton, Matthew—Barstow Stove Co.......... 89 40
29 The Fred Hower Brewing Co (Lim)—Scranton and Lehigh Coal Co.......... 1,207 78
24 Van Sloaten, Mary L—J Mullins.......... 155 70
24 Van Wynen, Sebastian—G B Ellis.......... 44 67
27 Vandewater, Frank P—G W Brown, exr, &c.......... 102 68
29 Vacoas, Michael P—G W Venable.......... 284 20
29 Vandenburg, Peter T—J T Scott.......... 318 16
29 Vom Lehn, Richard—S Katzenstein. 273 41
24 Williams, Benson J—C Voght.......... 218 00

SATISFIED JUDGMENTS.

NEW YORK.

July 25 to 31—Inclusive.

Andrews, Charles S—W E Stewart. (1891).......... $678 89
Byrne, John—People State N Y. (1889).......... 500 00
Brooklyn Fastener Co—N H Van Winkle. (1891).......... 171 75
Brennan, Thomas—Henry Loeb. (1891).......... 839 67
Same——A T Buckout. (1891).......... 115 79
‡Beaudet, Homer J—David Marx. (1891).......... 9,993 19
‡Same——same. (1891).......... 9,714 16
Bessell, John W—F L Froment. (1891).......... 625 06
Barry, John F and Samuel L—E S Greeley & Co. (1890).......... 2,886 90
Crowe, Thomas—A H Mayer. (1891).......... 73 24
Crow, Moses R—James Sawans. (1890).......... 353 29
Cartwright, Frederick G—E S Greeley & Co. (1890).......... 2,886 90
Central Trust Co—Michael Gernsheim. (1890).......... 601 00
Cates, Henry S—Mark Goodwin. (1891).......... 404 91
Same——A R Ackert. (1891).......... 377 65
Same——W H Mattison. (1891).......... 536 28
*Cassell & Co (Lim)—H W McNeal. (1888).. 109 62
*Same——same. (1887).......... 1,359 80
Demarest, H H—S B Higenbothem, trustee. (1889).......... 566 60
Same——C B Brinkerhoff. (1889).......... 108 86
Davenport, William B, admr Nauchen Tannenbaum—Albert Behrens. (1891).......... 310 59

Dearing, Benjamin—W H Mattison. (1891).... 536 28
Donahue, William—James Sawans. (1890).... 853 29
Downes, George E—Michael Gernsheim. ('90). 601 00
Eastern Lumber Co—C B Curtis. (1891). 97 75
England, William H—Evan Williams. (1886).. 2,023 19
Friend, Julius—Arnold Friedman. (1885)..... 377 09
Same—Meyer Rosenblatt. (1885).... ..... 1,508 13
Same—Nat Butchers' and Drovers' Bank. (1885).......... 267 36
Same—Isaac Hess. (1885).............. 317 09
Same—Arnold Friedman. (1885)..... ..... 678 75
Farmers' Loan and Trust Co, trustee—Michael Gernsheim. (1890).......... 801 00
Gillette, Daniel G—W J Crosby. (1891)........ 206 57
Gutmann, Nathan—James Barrett. (1891)... 75 11
Houston & Texas Central Railway Co No 1 / Huntington, Collis P } Michael Gernsheim. (1890).. 801 00
Hahn, Michael—John Guth. (1890).... .. .... 873 76
Irvine, Allan A—W H Mattison. (1891).. .... 536 28
Same—A R Ackert, (1891)... .... 377 66
Same—Mark Goodwin. (1891)............ 404 91
Koenig, Adolph—People State N Y. (1889)... 500 00
Krakauer, David—James Barrett. (1891)..... 75 11
Lawton, J Warren—Kate F Brown. (1889).... 89 73
Same—same. (1888)..................... 4,391 33
Lett, William F—Guardian Fire Ins Co. (1888) 282 17
Mutual District Messenger Co (Lim)—J W Harrison. (1891)................ 262 88
Mascher, John—Eastman Co. (1891) 146 41
Manhattan Railway Co—W P Abendroth. (1891)................... 8,017 41
Newcomb, Mary A—R W Hall. (1891) 438 91
New York Elevated R R Co—W P Abendroth. (1891)................... 8,017 41
Olcott, Frederic P—Michael Gernsheim. (1890) 801 00
O'Neil, Samuel M—E M Kielly. (1891).... .... 86 53
Ramsey, Peter N—Vanderbeck Iron Works Co. (1891)..................... 2,531 18
Schlief, Louis C—A J Horgan.. (1890)..... ... 46 53
U S Illuminating Co—John Doorley. (1891)... 2,770 01
Varley, Rosanna—Health Department. (1887). 59 50

*Vacated by order of Court. †Suspended on Appeal ‡Released. §Reversal. ‖Satisfied by Execution.

KINGS COUNTY.

July 17 to 23—Inclusive.

Hatten, Stephen—J O Sullivan* (1891)........ $381 06
The Coney Island & Brooklyn R R Co—C Catalanotto. (1889)..................... 1,149 04

MECHANICS' LIENS.

NEW YORK CITY.

July

25 Arthur av, w s, 200 s Pelham av, 25x118. Thomas Wilson agt William Murray, debtor, and Wehner & Schafer, owners... $275 00
25 Washington st, No. 457, n e cor Watts st, 70x20. Philip Schuyler agt E. M. Emberg, owner, and G. W. Lanphere, contractor.. 53 63
25 Sixty-third st, n s, 300 w 8th av, 75x100.5. J. L. Mott Iron Works agt Robert Carey, Richard Everett, Esther E. and Martin J. Barrow, owners, and Robert Carey, contractor........ 180 00
25 Waverley pl, No. 12, s s, 25 w Mercer st, 25x94. Altieri & Carretta agt John Doe, owner, and K. N. Smith & Co., contractors... 200 00
25 Eighty-third st, s s, 175 w 9th av, 25x100. J. R. Block agt John Chisholm, owner and contractor 400 00
27 Willett st, No. 132, e s, 83.6 s Houston st, 18.6x57.5. Farber & Schneider agt Louis Aaron, owner and contractor............ 1,100 00
27 Eighty-third st, s s, 175 w Columbus av, 25x100. Anton Larsen agt John Chisholm, owner and contractor 100 00
27 Arthur av, w s, 208 s Pelham av, 25x117.6. J. A. Woolf agt Ernest Wehner and Joseph Schafer, owners, and Wm. Murray, contractor........ 468 99
27 Fifty-second st, Nos. 513-517, n s, 175 w 10th av, 75x100.5. W. H. C. Hornum agt Joseph B. Husted, owner, and Hanschildt & Muller, contractors........ 500 00
28 One Hundred and Second st, Nos. 120-128, s s, 300 w 9th av, 100x100. Rufus Darrow agt Joseph R. Black, debtor, and Thomas J. McGuire, owner 124 75
28 Eighth av, No. 2782, e s, 50 s 148th st, 25x100. W. M. Waite agt Peter Hart, owner and contractor........ 23 72
28 Leroy st, Nos. 55 and 57, n s, 200 w Bedford st, 50x100. Schoeller & Winbladh agt Stevens, McElroy & Co., owners and contractors........ 235 00
28 Madison av, Nos. 1533-1537, e s, 75x100. John Dempsey agt Mrs. James Gault, owner, and Nicholas L. Demarest, contractor.... 150 00
28 One Hundred and Twentieth st, No. 14 E., s s, 25x100. Same agt same.... .... .. 150 00
29 One Hundred and Forty-first st, n s, 300 e Boulevard, 50x100. J. & W. C. Spears agt Carss & Hewlett, debtors and owners 3,048 00
29 Amsterdam av, w s, extends from 95th to 96th st, 201.5x175.4. Canda & Kane agt Andrew T. Doyle, owner and contractor. (Continued from July 31, 1890)........ 5,257 76
29 Ninety-eighth st, n s, 293 e Amsterdam av, 156.6x—. Louis Rosenbaum agt John W. Button, owner and contractor........ 1,300 00
29 Kingsbridge road, n w cor 181st st, 50x100. George Hubert, Jr., agt Catherine L. Beekman, owner, Rudolph Christ, lessee, and George F. Huskinson, contractor.... 40 00
29 Broadway, Nos. 715-727, n w cor Washington pl, runs north 200 to Waverley pl, x west 200 to Mercer st, x south 100 x east — x south — to Washington pl, x east 100 to beginning, known as New York Hotel. R. J. Anderson agt Henry Cranston, owner and contractor 46 19
29 Seventy-seventh st, n s, 100 w West End av, 209x100. O. D. Person agt Francis M. Jenks, owner, and Johann Grundlach, contractor 300 35
29 Ninety-fourth st, No. 47 n s, 375 e 9th av, 14.3x100.8. L. D. Hosford agt Davis & Fay, owners and contractors 150 00
30 Lexington av, No. 660, w s, 100 n 55th st, 25x100. John Sheeran agt Morris & Police Byk, debtors and owners........ 135 00
30 Madison av, s e cor 130th st, 100x70. Burrows & Smith agt Marie Gault, owner, and James Gault, contractor 337 62
30 One Hundred and Eighteenth st, s s, 65 e Madison av, 100x100. Same agt Samuel Harris, owner, and Herman and Marie Masche and Bernhard Ginsburg, contractors........ 250 00
30 One Hundred and Twentieth st, s s, 125 w 8th av, 75x100.11. Joseph Di Verniero agt James Thompson, owner and contractor. 629 00
30 Park av, s w cor 93d st, 100.8x105. Arthur Brown agt Downey & Curry, owner and contractor 175 00
30 Convent av, n w cor 143d st, 100x100. Abraham Steers agt Louise M. Hartwell, owner and H. E. Hartwell, contractor........ 185 22
30 One Hundred and Twentieth st, s s, 125 w 8th av, 75x100.11. Steindler & Hahn agt James Thompson, owner, and Erslew & Nilson, contractors........ 400 00
30 Eighty-ninth st, Nos. 438 and 440, s s, 157 w Av A, 50x100.8. Arthur Gorsch agt Mrs. Bertha Von Barber, owner and contractor........ 464 11
30 Seventy-eighth st, s s, 100 w Amsterdam av, 75x100. John Heerline agt Arthur Boehmer, owner, and McLoughlin, Clegg & Co., contractors........ 10 00
30 Same property. Patrick Simpson agt same. 10 12
30 Ninety-fourth st, n s, 150 w Columbus av, 100x100. Thomas Heaney agt James T. Brady, owner, and McLoughlin, Clegg & Co., contractors........ 11 87
30 Same property. John Heerline agt same.. 16 00
30 Same property. James Dempsey agt same. 14 62
30 Same property. Patrick Simpson agt same. 29 25
30 Same property. Edward Barry agt same.. 14 69
30 Ninth av, Nos. 309 and 311, e s, 50 s 75th st, 50x100. John Walsh and Michael Crowley agt Allen A. Irvine and John Smith, owners, and Allen A. Irvine, contractor. 445 00
30 Manhattan av, n e cor 121st st, 100x100. Same agt Henry Schneider and Allen A. Irvine, owners, and Allen A. Irvine, contractor........ 744 55
31 Spring st, Nos. 131-137, n s, 98.2x109. John Kehoe agt John and Philip Goerlitz, owners and contractors........ 4,000 00
31 Waverley pl, No. 175. Louis Jean agt William C. Bermiston, owner, and J Ehrig, contractor........ 12 50
31 Same property. John McCarty agt same.. 12 50
31 Same property. Frank Wiltz agt same. .. 10 50
31 Same property. John Wolf agt same .. 10 00
31 Ninety-fourth st, n s, 150 w Amsterdam av, 100x100. John Coleman agt James Brady, owner, and A. M. Clegg, contractor.. .. 11 25

KINGS COUNTY.

July

25 Macon st, s w cor Howard av, 93.6x100. W. H. and J. T. Bierds agt Clarence Lincoln, Emily Gilfoy, Thomas Purcell, Grove M. Harwood, Mary Leonhardt and Morris Isaacs, owners, and Clarence Lincoln, contractor........ $1,826 45
25 Same property. Graff & Co. agt Clarence Lincoln, owner and contractor........ 345 00
25 Second st, s s, 296 w 7th av, 101.10x95. Nilson & Svenson agt Julia A. Skidmore, owner and contractor........ 402 00
25 First st, s s, 305 w 5th av, 118x100. William Van Horne agt William S. Hale, owner and contractor 975 00
25 Bergen st, n s, 100 e Ralph av, 220x107.1. Stephen Delaney agt Mary E. Mason, Paul W. and Forosojean Ledoux, owners, and Mary E. Mason, contractor 130 00
25 Hinsdale st, w s, 225 n Livonia av, 25x100. Rudolph Reimer & Co. agt A. D. Hyde & Co., owners and contractors........ 74 92
25 Broadway, n e cor Jefferson av, 100x100. Samuel M. Weekes agt C. Henry and Annie J. Moller, owners, and Jacob Bisson, contractor 6,576 60
27 Broadway, n e cor Jefferson av, 100x100. Gfroehrer & McCarty agt C. Henry and Annie J. Moller, owners, and Jacob Bisson, contractor........ 2,670 00
27 Same property. Jacob A. Bissen agt C. Henry and Annie J. Moller, owner and contractor 16,005 00
27 Sixty-sixth st, n s, 375 e 6th av, 50x100. Hobby & Doody agt Peter Janson, owner and contractor........ 370 00
27 Twentieth st, s s, 300 e 4th av, 50x100. Hobby & Doody agt Carl Thorstenson, owner, and K. P. Kragelund, contractor........ 819 66
28 Prospect pl, s s, 250 e Rogers av, 34x100. James Keenan agt James E. Jenney, owner, and William H. Burhans, contractor 700 00
28*Fourth st, s s, 97.110 e 6th av, 440x100. William J. Fitzpatrick agt Moses & Fanton, owners and contractors........ 8,479 00
28 Broadway, n e cor Jefferson av, 100x100. Philip Dugro agt C. Henry and Annie J. Moller, owners, and Jacob Bisson, contractor........ 517 00
28 Howard av, s w cor Macon st, 100x93.6. Frederick W. Lawrence agt Clarence Lincoln, owner and contractor........ 901 14
28 Macon st, s s, 93.6 w Howard av, 108x100. Martin D. Walsh agt Clarence Lincoln, owner and contractor........ 450 00
28 Patchen av, s e cor Halsey st, 100x200. H. F. Burroughs & Co. agt Hiram Bedell and William E. Valentine, owners, and Hiram Bedell, contractor 718 35
28 Albany av, e s, extends from Park pl to Butler st, 14 houses. James Keenan agt Otto Schubkegel and James A. Loucks, owners and contractors........ 1,200 00
28 Garnet st, s s, 100 e Court st, 100x100. Joseph Logan agt Alfred E. Hartington, owner and contractor........ 1,220 00
28 Sixty-sixth st, n s, 375 e 6th av, 25x100. Thomas Robinson agt Peter Johnson, owner and contractor........ 146 10
29 Seventh av, w s, 50 s 57th st, 25x100. John E. Lindner agt Robert Carling, owner and contractor........ 150 00
29 Fifth av, e s, 50 s 50th st, 25x100. Same agt John Holt, owner and contractor........ 25 00
29 Pulaski st, Nos. 239-269, n s, 100 w Sumner av, 330x100. Reisert & Orth agt Frederick Hower Brewing Co., owners and contractors........ 12,432 05
29 Woodbine st, n s, 125 w Knickerbocker av, 100x100. B. Brinkman & Co. agt Albert Berkmeier, owner and contractor........ 110 00
29 Howard av, e s, 133 s Herkimer st, 34x89. Funk & Lehnert agt Eliza Reed, owner, and Ernst D. Yarber, contractor........ 718 00
29 Fulton st, s s, 22 e Hoyt st, runs east 30 x south 70 x east — x south 100 x west 90 to Hoyt st, x north 100 x east — x north 70. Charles S. Buell agt A. J. Namm, owner, and John Prosser & Son, contractor..... 1,308 92
29 Sunnyside av, n s, 150 e Barbey st, 50x100. Earl A. Gillespie agt William B. Howard, owner and contractor........ 636 67
30 Sutter av, s s, 50 w Watkins st, 50x100. Louis Parmer agt Isaac and Sarah Krupitzky, owners and contractors........ 191 00
30 Macon st, s s, 93.6 w Howard av, 108x100. Jeremiah Hackett agt Clarence Lincoln, owner and contractor........ 1,000 00
30 Bergen st, n s, 100 e Ralph av, 220x107.2. Wilhelm Kaubitzsch agt Isaac Mason, owner and contractor........ 22 95

Editor RECORD AND GUIDE:

The lien filed against us by W. J. Fitzpatrick is for plumbing materials and labor for twenty-three houses complete, six of which have not the foundations in yet. The entire lien covers materials and labor *not furnished.* We have paid promptly every payment when due under his contract, and estimates made show that the payments exceed the value of all materials and labor furnished by him.

MOSES & FANTON.

SATISFIED MECHANICS' LIENS.

NEW YORK CITY.

July

28 One Hundred and Eighteenth st, Nos. 54-62 E., 100x100. August Kissling agt Lipman Kingsberg and Marie Masche. (Lien filed (July 6, 1891)........ $647 00
29 One Hundred and Eighteenth st, s s, 60 e Madison av, 100x100. C. E. Gates & Co. agt Mary Masche. (May 15, 1891)........ 119 82
29 Same property. J. W. Binney agt Marie Masche. (June 17, 1891)........ 72 98
29 Tiebout av, w s, 50 s Clark st, 25x—. J. S. Lawlor agt Wm. H. Duncan and Perry & Schoonmaker. (April 15, 1891.) (Released)........
29 Same property. Joiner Planing & Moulding Co. agt same. (May 22, 1891.) (Released).
29 Same property. C. E. Gates & Co. agt same. (April 16, 1891.) (Released).......
30*One Hundred and Eighteenth st, s s, 60 e Madison av, 100x—. G. B. Robbins & Co. agt M. Masche. (June 3, 1891)........ 148 99
30*Same property. L. L. Ellsworth agt Margaret and Herman Masche. (June 12, 1891)........ 148 50
30 *Fourth st, No. 168, s s, 106 w Cornelia st, 20x—........ } Cornelia st, No. 5, n w s, 75 s 4th st, 25x—. Patrick Devine agt William Rankin and John Mallin. (Feb. 3, 1891)........ 60 00
31 Thirty-first st, No. 215, n s, 175 w 7th av, 25x100. James O'Shea agt Mary and John Wilson. (July 17, 1891)........ 248 00
31 Twenty-sixth st, Nos. 334-336 E., s s, 50x100. Canda & Kane agt Michael McCormick and Henry Madden. (July 27, 1891)...... 993 35
31 Houston st, Nos. 369 E. Nathan Hutkoff agt Siegmund and Ignatz Friedman and D. Slink (June 17, 1891)........ 54 00
31‡Twenty-fourth st, n s, 271.7 e 9th av, 78.4x—. J. J. Gorman and N. O. Sylvander agt James McFarland and Frederick Woods. (June 16, 1891)........ 3,937 00
31 One Hundred and Sixty-second st, s s, 145 e Prospect av, 35x85. Joiner Planing and Moulding Co. agt Timothy Flood. (July 29, 1891)........ 310 21
31 Ninety-fifth st, Nos. 106 and 108 W., 50x100. Albermarle Soapstone Co. agt Francis J. Hillenbrand. (July 23, 1891)........ 252 00
31 Madison av, No. 1200, s w cor 87th st, 100.8x62.2. See & Conover agt Frederick H. Correll and Charles Gueden. (April 18, 1891)........ 905 00
31 Twenty-sixth st, Nos. 334 and 336 E., 50x—. Canda & Kane agt Michael McCormick and Henry Madden and Martin Diskin. (July 27, 1891)........ 462 35

*Discharged by depositing amount of lien and interest with County Clerk.
‡Discharged by order of Court on filing bond.

KINGS COUNTY.

July

23 Howard av, s w cor Macon st, 100x200. Rudolph Reimer & Co. agt Clarence Lincoln, owner and contractor. (July 9, 1891)........ $1,965 00
23 Hicks st, n e cor West 9th st, 20x80. Spence Bros. agt George Balfe, owner and contractor. (May 2, 1891)........ 900 00
25 Bushwick av, east cor Aberdeen st, 40x90. Robert J. Walsh agt Louisa and John Reilly, owners and contractors. (March 25, 1890)........ 410 00
25 Kingston av, n e cor Pacific st, 80x96. Graff & Co. agt Franklin J. Fellowes, owner and contractor. (June 10, 1891)... 750 00
27 Central av, e s, extends from Putnam av to Cornelia st, 200x100 John Ernst & Son agt John T. Barnard, owner, and Joseph Hopkins, contractor. (July 24, 1891.) (Deposit)........ 325 00
28 Saratoga av, n w cor Decatur st, 100x120. Potts Bros agt Kate S. and Samuel R. Good, owners and contractors. (July 27, 1891)........ 230 00
28 Flushing av, Nos. 616 and 618, s s, 300 e Marcy av, 50x100. Simon and Louis Drezner agt Bluma Katz and Mayer Katz, owners and contractors. (June 2, 1891)........ 78 00
28 Same property. Rosenberg & Co. agt same owners and contractors. (May 15, 1891).. 270 00
28 Seigel st, No. 72, s s, 150 e Ewen st. Aloris Flohl agt Nathan Beshadsky, owner and contractor. (July 14, 1891) 113 00
28 Cooper st, s e s, 250 n e Evergreen av, 100x155.6. John C. Austin agt Hannah M. Rose, owner, and Thomas J. Allen, contractor. (July 27, 1891)........ 1,719 60
28 Utica av, w s, 79.9 n St. Marks av, 50x100. John Hennessy agt Catherine E. Ryerson, owner, and Charles H. Berrian, contractor. (May 19, 1891)........ 400 00

29 Noble st, n s, 365 e Franklin st, 25x100. Meserole & Walker agt William P. Morrissy, owner, and Smith & Duffy, contractors. (June 22, 1891)........................ 782 94
30 Sixth st, n s, 297 w 5th av, 95x100. Richard Cronin & Sons agt E. G. Gollner, owner and contractor. (July 25, 1891.) (Deposit) 262 80

BUILDINGS PROJECTED.

The first name is that of the owner; ar't stands for architect, m'n for mason, c'r for carpenter and b'r for builder.

NEW YORK CITY.

SOUTH OF 14TH STREET.

Bowery, No. 105, five-story brk building, 25x78 tin roof; cost, $20,000; agent, H. Trowbridge, 33 Howard st; ar't. L. F. Heinecke. Plan 1079.

Broad st, Nos. 64–68, ten-story stone, brk and terra cotta building, 98.7x69.1, iron, concrete and tile roof; cost, abt $400,000; Mrs. C. Morris, Throggs Neck, N. Y.; ar'ts, Youngs & Cable. Plan 1084.

Greenwich st, No. 368, six-story brk building, 25.5x90, tin roof; cost, $40,000; Amalie Coon, 317 West 176th st; ar't, G. A. Schellenger. Plan 1080.

Eldridge st, Nos. 196 and 198, two five-story brk and stone flats, 24x78.1, tin roofs; cost, $17,-500 each; Elizabeth Herdtfelder, on premises; ar't, C. Rentz. Plan 1087.

10th st; No. 209 E., five-story brk flat, 25x84, tin roof; cost, $18,000; A. Happel, 65 East 3d st; ar'ts, Boekell & Son. Plan 1085.

BETWEEN 14TH AND 59TH STREETS.

12th av, n w cor 37th st, bulkhead line, iron freight shed, 85x100, tin roof; cost, $14,000; lessees, Penn. R. R. Co., 2 Exchange pl, Jersey City. Plan 1076.

44th st, s s, 175 e 11th av, five-story brk and stone flat, 25x90, tin roof; cost, $18,000; J. Mulholland, 445 West 48th st; ar't, J. W. Cole. Plan 1092.

3d av, No. 923, rear, frame shed, 14x30, tin roof; cost, $150; G. Stewart, 221 West 42d st. Plan 1088.

BETWEEN 59TH AND 125TH STREETS, EAST OF 5TH AVENUE.

115th st, n s, 235 e Pleasant av, two-story brk building, 44x38.4, iron and slate roof; cost, abt $7,000; Standard Gas Co., 2 Cortlandt st; m'ns, J. & L. Weber. Plan 1091.

1st av, Nos. 1624 and 1626, two five-story brk flats, 20.4x84.10, tin roofs; cost, $16,000 each; agents and att'ys, T. M. & G. W. Fanning, 315 Madison av; ar't, W. Graul. Plan 1089.

BETWEEN 59TH AND 125TH STREETS, WEST OF CENTRAL PARK WEST AND 8TH AVENUE.

66th st, n s, 332 e 9th av, five-story brk and stone flat, 25x87, tin roof; cost, $20,000; ow'r and b'r, I. M. Grenell, 672 Columbus av; ar't, C. M. Youngs. Plan 1090.

NORTH OF 125TH STREET.

160th st, s s, 111 e St. Nicholas av, two three-story and basement brk and stone dwell'gs, 18x50, tin roofs; total cost, $27,000; E. Lewis, 8 West 135th st; ar't, R. R. Davis. Plan 1096.

169th st, n s, 150 e 11th av, one-story frame dwell'g, 21x37, tin roof; cost, $1,300; J. Rahill, Boulevard and 130th st; ar't, J. A. Stone. Plan 1094.

185th st, s s, 225 w 10th av, two-story brk and frame dwell'g, 25x35, tin roof; cost, $5,000; F. C. Smith, 639 East 143d st; ar't, W. H. Russell; c'r, G. W. Corson. Plan 1086.

St. Nicholas av, n w cor 158th st, frame shed, 25x38, gravel roof; cost, $125; lessee, F. Mierisch, 10th av, bet 155th and 156th sts; c'r, P. Costenbader. Plan 1078.

23D AND 24TH WARDS.

Bainbridge av, e s, 15.5 s Travers st, two three-story frame dwell'gs, 20x42, shingle roofs; cost, $4,500 each; ow'r and b'r, W. J. Lee, Fordham, N. Y.; ar't, L. A. Virtue. Plan 1083.

Brook av, w s, 125 n 143d st, two-story brk and stone stable, 30x52, tin roof; cost, $3,000; R. McLaughlin, 363 Brook av; ar'ts, French, Dixon & De Saldern. Plan 1077.

Clinton av, w s, 95 n 177th st, three two-story frame dwell'gs, 20x30, tin roofs; cost, $2,500 each; Mary Seiferd, 942 East 175th st; ar't, E. P. Murphy; c'r, T. J. Blair. Plan 1074.

Clinton av, e s, 95 n 177th st, two-story frame dwell'g, 20x30, tin roof; cost, $2,500; Lena Seiferd, 942 East 175th st; ar't and c'r, same as last. Plan 1075.

Stebbins av, e s, 313 n 167th st, rear, two-story frame stable, 24x48, gravel roof; cost, $200; S. R. Parker, Intervale av, near 167th st; ar't, C. C. Churchill. Plan 1081.

Washington av, w s, 342.6 s 175th st, two three-story brk and stone dwell'gs, 18.6x56.6, tin roof; cost, $5,000 each; Sarah I. Wyckoff, 1773 Washington av; ar't, T. E. Thomson. Plan 1082.

Aqueduct av, w s, 400 s Van Courtlandt av, frame shed, 85x20, tar paper roof; cost, $300; lessee, F. Pistone, Villa av; c'r, C. W. Vreeland. Plan 1093.

Ogden av, e s, 220 n Devoe st, two story frame dwell'g, 18.6x42.8, tin roof; cost, $1,500; J. Byrnes, Lind av; ar't, W. A. Gorman. Plan 1097.

3d av, 300 w of 134th st, 190 s of ——, brk chimney, 10.2x10.2x100; cost, $2,000; Mott Iron Works, 84 Beekman st. Plan 1095.

KINGS COUNTY.

Plan 1389—Greene av, No. 228, s s, 100 e Grand av, one three-story brk carpenter shop, 25x60, tin roof, iron cornice; cost, $4,000; ow'r and c'r, W. H. Tunison, 270 Franklin av; ar't, G. Ladue.

1390—Van Sielen av, e s, 100 s Livonia av, one two-story frame dwell'g, 20x30, tin roof; cost, $1,500; Sarah A. Brewster, Schenck av; ar't and c'r, W. A. Sloan; m'n, J. Tench.

1391—Wyckoff av, No. 30, one three-story frame (brk filled) store and dwell'g, 22x32, tin roof; cost, $3,800; Edmund Stein, 32 Wyckoff av; ar't, H. E. Funk.

1392—Warwick st, w s, 105 n Fulton av, one two-story frame dwell'g, 20x32, tin roof; cost, $2,600; ow'r and c'r, Peter J. Kerr, Essex st, near Arlington av; ar't, C. Infanger.

1393—Railroad av, s e cor Conduit av, one two-story frame office and dwell'g, 18x20, tin roof; cost, $300; Magdalena Spechts, near premises; ar't, C. Infanger.

1394—Montauk av, e s, abt 100 s Atlantic av; one two-story frame wood-working mill, 40x60, gravel roof; cost, abt $3,000; Charles Hancock, Snediker av.

1395—Eldert st, n s, 100 and 160 e Evergreen av, three two-story and basement frame (brk filled) dwell'gs, 20x45.8, tin roofs; total cost, $5,000; Chas. F. Gastmeyer, 53 Bleecker st.

1396—Livonia av, s e cor Osborn st, one one-story frame tailor shop, 20x12, tin roof; cost, $200; Sidenberg & Alomby, on premises; ar't, A. J. Warren.

1397—Mill st, s s, 60 e Columbia st, one one-story frame dwell'g, 21x30, gravel roof; cost, $200; F. Plennis, 18 Mill st.

1398—Livonia av, s s, 100 w Osborn st, one one-story frame blacksmith shop, 20x24, tin roof; cost, $100; G. Skienfeld, Thatford av.

1399—Van Pelt av, s e cor North Henry st, one three-story frame (brk filled) store and tenem't, 28x48.6 and 44, tin roof; cost, $3,500; Henry Bindrim, 133 Meeker av; ar't, F. J. Berlenbach, Jr.; b'r, not selected.

1400—Rutledge st, s s, 125 w Wythe av, one one-story brk boiler and engine room, gravel roof and brk cornice; cost, $2,000; T. G. Christmas, Wythe av, near Rutledge st; ar't, D. Hunt; b'r, W. & T. Lamb, Jr.

1401—3d av, n w cor Sackett st, one two-story frame carpenter shop, 50x70, gravel roof; cost, $800; ow'r, ar't and b'r, W. J. Conway, 414 Union st.

1402—Steuben st, e s, 225 s Myrtle av, one three-story brk carriage factory, 25x65, tin roof and brk cornice; cost, $6,000; George A. Knott, 206 West 53d st, New York; ar't, C. Huntington; m'n, M. Walsh.

1403—College pl, No. 16, w s, one four-story brk stable, 50x79.6, tin roof and brk cornice; cost, $20,000; ow'r and ar't, Chas. M. Burtenshaw; b'rs, J. J. Bentzen and J. Freeman.

1404—Madison st, s s, 225 e Howard av, one three-story brk dwell'g, 25x75, gravel roof and wooden cornice; cost, $5,000; Marquardt Bros., 693 Lexington av; ar't, J. H. Brock; m'n, T. D. Kelly; c'rs, Brock & Lindemann.

1405—St. Marks av, s s, 219 w New York av, one three-story brk and Belleville stone dwell'g, 35x56, tin roof, terra cotta cornice; cost, $18,000; Thomas Newcomb, New York and Atlantic avs; ar't, G. P. Chappell.

1406—St. Marks av, s s, 219 w New York av, one two-story brk stable, 56x32, tin roof, wooden cornice; cost, $8,000; ow'r and ar't, same as last.

1407—De Kalb av, s s, 300 e Irving av, one two-story frame (brk filled) dwell'g, 25x25, tin roof; cost, $1,500; ow'r and ar't, J. Betz, 184 Jefferson st; b'rs, J. Rueger and C. Wahler.

1408—Belmont av, n e cor Van Sielen av, one two-story frame store and dwell'g, 25x55, tin roof; cost, $3,900; Elias Helgans, Eastern Parkway and Van Sielen av; ar't, C. Infanger; b'rs, J. Pohlmann, Jr., and J. Fench.

1409—Seigel st, No. 46, one three-story frame (brk filled) tailor shop, 25x20, tin roof; cost, $1,500; ow'rs and b'rs, Rosenberg & Feinberg, 74 Seigel st; ar't, H. Vollweiler.

1410—Harman st, s s, 350 e Central av, two three-story frame (brk filled) tenem'ts, 25x50, tin roofs; cost, each, $4,500; ow'r and b'r, Wm. Berlinger, 169 Stanhope st; ar't, H. Vollweiler.

1411—Hart st, No. 715, 175 w Hamburg av, one one-and-a-half-story frame stable, 32 and 30x15, gravel roof; cost, $125; John Moore, on premises.

1412—4th st, s s, 389.6 e Smith st, one three-story frame tenem't, 22x42, tin roof; cost, $2,800; Edw. Donohue, 40 4th st; ar't, M. J. Murphy; m'n, J. J. Cody; c'r, M. H. Murphy.

1413—45th st, s s, 220 e 4th av, one two-story and basement frame dwell'g, 20x36, tin roof; cost, $2,800; Edward Zohn, 133 43d st; ar't, C. P. Robeder; b'rs, Smith & Robeder.

1414—Putnam av, n s, 200 e Reid av, five two-and-a-half-story and basement brk and Nova Scotia stone dwell'gs, 20x43, tin roofs, wooden cornices; cost, each, $5,000; ow'r, ar't and b'r, William O. Forrester, 1000 Herkimer st.

1415—Glenmore av, n s, 100 w Ashford st, one two-story frame dwell'g, 22x40, tin roof; cost, $2,000; John Hahn, Atlantic av, cor Cleveland st; ar't, C. Infanger.

1416—Cook st, No. 21, one four-story frame (brk filled) tenem't, 25x50, tin roof; cost, $5,000; Mary Kohl, on premises; ar't, H. Smith; b'r, not selected.

1417—Thatford av, s s, 100 e Glenmore av, two three-story frame (brk filled) tenem'ts, 25x50, tin roofs; cost, $3,500 each; owr and b'r, J. Stern, 172 Gwinnett st; ar't, H. Smith.

1418—Barbey st, e s, 225 n Blake av, three two-story frame tenem'ts, 16.8x32, tin roof; total cost, $4,500; Mary Heyser, 2734 Fulton st; ar't, J. H. Heyser; b'rs, H. Schwartz and M. Fitzmuller.

1419—Eastern Parkway, s s, 25 w Thatford av, one one-story frame tailor shop, 20x30, tin roof; cost, $300; Ch. Ratner, 245 Rockaway av.

1420—Elton st, w s, 275 n Arlington av, one two-story and attic frame dwell'g, 20x32, shingle roof; cost, $3,200; ow'r, ar't and b'r, Howard N. Acker, 258 Arlington av.

1421—52d st, s s, 100 w 4th av, four two-story and basement frame dwell'gs, 20x40, tin roofs; cost, each, $3,000; Foley & Eade, 3d av and 52d st; b'rs, Spence Bros.

1422—Shepherd av, w s, 200 s Blake av, one two-story frame dwell'g, 25x55.1, tin roof; cost, $3,000; Louis Thiele, Sheffield av, near Eastern Parkway; ar't, C. Infanger.

1423—Jamaica av, s s, 175 w Hemlock st, one one-story frame stable and shed, 18x65, gravel roof; cost, $175; Samuel Seaman, 503 Jamaica av; b'r, S. Van Sise.

1424—Throop av, w s, 39 n Gates av, one two-story brk supply depot, 26x25x70, tin and slate roof, iron cornice; cost, $10,000; Brooklyn Assoc. for Improving the Condition of the Poor, 104 Livingston st; ar't, J. Mumford; b'rs, C. Cameron and W. E. Booth.

ALTERATIONS NEW YORK CITY.

Plan 1418—Washington st, No. 489, side walls repaired and front rebuilt, with interior alterations and repairs; cost, $200; J. B. Ginocchio, 43 Prospect st, Jersey City.

1419—40th st, No. 16 East and 39th st, No. 13 E., one-story and basement extension, 9.8x8, and interior alterations; cost, $500; S. A. Warner; ow'r and ar't, on premises.

1420—14th st, Nos. 3 and 5 W., show windows repaired; cost, $800; lessee, J. H. Little, 64 East 86th st; ar't, J. O. Bunce; c'r, J. B. Franklyn.

1421—5th av, No. 426, new show window; cost, $300; att'y, J. M. Mitchell, 60 West 9th st; ar't, J. O. Bunce; c'r, F. Wingen.

1422—37th st, No. 10 W., one-story and basement extension, 8.4x28, and walls altered; cost, $2,000; W. Whitlock et al. on premises; ar't, W. W. Smith; b'r, E. D. Garnsey.

1423—West End av, No. 163, new fence wall in rear; cost, $800; Mrs. B. Norton, on premises; m'n, J. B. Woodruff.

1424—110th st, No. 175 E., windows altered; cost, $400; O. H. P. Archer, Jr., manager, 7 West 127th st; c'r, J. Halstead.

1425—3d av, No. 2082, windows altered; cost, $400; manager and c'r, same as last.

1426—Monroe st, No. 245, west wall rebuilt; cost, $250; J. Eberhardt, 247 Monroe st; m'n, M. Dugan.

1427—Lewis st, No. 111, new store front; cost, $500; P. Ganz, on premises; ar't, F. Ebeling; c'r, G. Galef.

1428—3d av, No. 1228, interior alterations; cost, $950; estate J. Kelly, 1202 Broadway; c'r, P. Roberts.

1429—22d st, No. 33 E., main building raised one story, extension raised three stories, interior alterations and new bath-rooms on three floors; cost, $4,000; Mrs. E. B. Grannis, on premises; ar't, H. Horenburger.

1430—114th st, No. 175 E., interior alterations; cost, $1,500; Mrs. E. Goldman, 210 East 118th st; ar't, A. I. Finkle.

1431—Madison av, No. 86, one-story extension, 17x16.5; cost, $700; F. O'Neill, on premises; ar'ts, Ogden & Son.

1432—45th st, No. 3 E., interior alterations, walls altered, &c.; cost, $2,700; Church of the Heavenly Rest, 551 5th av; ar'ts, Little & O'Connor; b'r, L. A. Burke.

1433—49th st, No. 47 W., two-story extension, 16x16; cost, $950; Lydia W. Gage, on premises; c'rs, Crockett & Weeks.

1434—88th st, No. 203 E., three-story extension, 26x21; cost, $1,400; J. H. Gray, 2 East 94th st; ar'ts, Ogden & Son.

1435—49th st, No. 340 W., driveway changed to store and living rooms, walls altered, &c.; cost, $800; H. Tongan, 525 West 49th st; ar't, J. W. Cole.

1436—25th st, Nos. 422–426 E., interior alterations; cost, $250; H. A. Reed, sec'y, on premises; m'n, J. Whyte.

1437—55th st, No. 104 W., interior alterations; cost, $2,400; N. Y. Athletic Club, on premises; ar't, C. W. Clinton; b'rs, Hoffman & Co.

1438—17th st, No. 311 W., interior alterations; cost, $2,000; Harriet F. Howe, on premises; ar't, J. H. McClelland; c'r, J. C. Lawrence.

1439—86th st, No. 130 E., repair damage by fire; cost, $40; estate R. Theall, 45 Wall st; c'r, A. Leitch.

1440—49th st, No. 13 W., walls altered and new bay; cost, $1,150; J. P. Marquand, on premises; ar't, F. H. Smith; b'r, P. H. Casey.

1441—West, Bethune and 12th sts and 13th av, interior alteration for elevators; cost, $6,000; agent, J. H. Johnston, 8 5th av; engineers, Copeland & Bacon.

1442—Boulevard, w s, 100 n 78th st, one-story extension, 20x12; cost, $600; D. Clarke, on premises; m'n, J. Batton; c'r, C. D. Hook.

1443—South st, East River, Piers 22 and 23, awning altered; cost, $1,500; Fulton Market Fishmongers' Assoc., Fulton Market; ar't, J. B. Rice.

1444—10th st, Nos. 457 and 459 W., interior alterations, walls altered and new fronts; cost, $1,-600; agent, L. Schultze, 49 3d av; ar't, H. Horenburger; c'rs, Schultze & Lambeck.

1445—10th av, No. 96, interior alterations and

new front; cost, $1,200; agent, ar't and c'rs, same as last.

1446—Pitt st, No. 66, interior alterations, walls altered and new front; cost, $700; H. Przeworsky, 59 Suffolk st; ar't, H. Horenburger.

1447—53d st, No. 225 E., five-story extension, 19.6x20, closets and dumb waiter removed to extension; cost, $4,000; Elizabeth Lewers, 136 East 43d st; ar't, G. F. Pelham.

1448—44th st, No. 107 W., new sills and lintels; cost, $200; Mary A. Dongan, on premises; m'n, J. F. Nelson.

1449—Irving pl, s e cor 18th st, interior alterations; cost, $500; J. S. Huyler, 281 Lenox av; ar'ts, Berg & Clark; m'n, C. T. Wills.

1450—6th av, No. 193, one-story extension, 14x25 2; cost, abt $800; lessee, Mary A. Linberr, 157 West 12th st; m'n, G. W. Lithgow.

1451—German pl, No 640, moved to new foundation; cost, $150; A. Neary, on premises.

1452—83d st, No. 33 W., walls altered; cost, $4,000; C. H. Lindsley, 195 Lenox av; ar't, C. W. Lindsley.

1453—125th st, Nos. 268 and 270 W., one story extension, 25x49 and walls altered; cost, $6,000; lessee, C. Weisbecker, 330 West 125th st; ar't, F. H. Hines; c'r, T. F. Hines.

1454—53d st, Nos. 431-435 W., walls altered; cost, $2,000; J. Heidenreich, on premises; ar't, M. V B. Ferdon; b'r, J. Held.

1455—Beach st Pier 26 (new) North River, one and two-story extension, 78x101.8; cost, $16,500; lessees, Old Dominion S. S. Co., 235 West st; ar't, R. P. Steats.

1456—6th av, bet 43d and 44th sts, repair damage by fire; cost, $14,000; Sixth Avenue R. R. Co., on premises; m'ns, R. L. Darragh & Co.; c'rs, Bogert & Bro.

1457—3d av, No. 1540, raised one story; cost, $1 000; L. Reiss, on premises; ar't, E. Wenz.

1458—27th st, Nos 554 and 556 W., rear, one-story extension, 18.6x30; cost, abt $300; ow'r and c'r, J. Williams, on premises.

KINGS COUNTY.

Plan 718—Jefferson av, No. 209, add one story to extension; cost, $800; F. W. Woolworth, on premises; b'rs, W. & T. Lamb and R. B. Ferguson.

719—Court st, No. 513, new store front; cost, $300; N. Seitz, on premises; b'r, D. Powell.

720—Dean st, No. 1714, one-story frame extension, 10x10, tin roof; cost, $100; George A. Hand, on premises; ar't, W. Campbell.

721—Moore st, No 23, one-story frame extension, 14x14, tin roof; cost, $300; L. Klimm, on premises; ar't, H. E Funk.

722—Broadway, No. 314, raised 5 ft. on brk wall, also one-story brk extension, 21 and 22x10 and 11, tin roof; cost, $800; Betsey Hamblin, 259 Division st; ar't, W. Jones; b'rs, B. Potter and J. L. Chapman.

723—Schenck av, e s, 200 n Arlington av, two-story frame extension 20x19.6, tin roof; cost, $600; ow'r, ar't and b'r, S. T. Hollister, 106 Barbey st.

724—Hendrix st, e s, 200 n Fulton st, building raised 30 inches on brick foundation; cost, $1,200; First Baptist Church, East New York; b'rs, Mr. Cook and Mr. Hughes.

725—4th av, No 124, three-story brick extension, 16.6x26; cost, $1,500; ow'r and b'r, Mrs. Cochrane, 124 4th av; ar't, T. McMahon.

726—Clymer st, No. 80, straighten and strengthen walls; cost, $75; Chas. Holtenroth, on premises; b'r, W. Stryker.

727—President st, No. 555, flat gravel roof; cost, $300; Frank Fosit, on premises.

728—Gates av, No. 897, two-story brick and iron extension, 29x7, tin roof, iron cornice; cost, $400; Chas. J. Warren, 1577 Atlantic av.

729—Boerum pl, n w cor State st, add one story, mansard tin roof; cost, $1,500; J. Curley, on premises; ar't, C. Werner; b'r, not selected.

730—Whipple st, No. 29, two-story brick extension, 15x24, tin roof; cost, $1,000; H. Seiler, on premises; ar'ts, D. Acker & Son; b'rs, M. Armendinger and C. Hestermann.

731—49th st, n s, 140 e 3d av, brk foundation; cost, $300; Henry Kellebberdt, 3d av, cor 28th st.

732—55th st, s s, 160 w 6th av, one-and-a-half-story frame extension, 11.6x26, tin roof; cost, $100; ow'r, ar't and b'r, Ed. B. Nimmo, 57th st, near 5th av.

733—Washington Park, No. 208, one-story brk extension, 9.6x16, tin roof; cost, abt $500; G. D. Mathews, on premises; ar't, J. Mumford; b'rs, S. W. Reeve and S. Booth.

734—21st st, n s, 140 e 3d av, flat gravel roof; cost, $200; ow'r, ar't and b'r, Jos. Nelmowski, 131 21st st.

735—Walcot st, No. 82, raised 4.6 on brk walls; cost, $1,000; Mrs. Mullady, on premises; ar't, D. J. Lynch.

736—India st, No. 43, three-story frame extension, 15x25, tin roof; cost, $1,600; Conrad Schmid, on premises; m'ns, McGarry & Moran; c'r, R. Gasser.

737—Ainslie st, No. 159, one-story frame extension, 16x18, tin roof; cost, $150; Mrs. Cowperthwait, on premises; b'rs, A. Huber and C. Flood.

738—Myrtle av, No. 39, flat gravel roof, also one-story brk extension, 22x45, gravel roof; cost, $2,000; Angeline E. Darling, 26 Court st; b'r, H. V. Terboss.

739—Columbia st, Nos. 217 and 219, new brk piers and iron columns, cellar and first story; cost, $4,000; Yauch & Biggers, 219 Columbia st; ar't, C. Werner; b'r, C. M. Detlefsen.

740—Freeman st, 217 w West st, one-story brk extension, 18.9x42.8, iron roof and cornice; cost, $2,000; New York Dye Wood Extract Co., 55 Beekman st, New York; b'rs, Barton & Nickel.

741—Ashford st, w s, 175 n Liberty av, flat tin roof; cost, $350; Michael Huber, on premises.

742—State st, No. 383, new piers under rear; cost, $150; Stephen Fallon, State st, cor Bond st; b'r, F. Connelly.

743—Atlantic av, s w cor Hinsdale st, four-story brk extension, 28x37, and one-story brk shop, 45x72, brk roof; cost, $5,000; J. Kellow, on premises; ar't, A. H. McGeehan; m'ns, Potts Bros.; c'r, T. Gronen.

MISCELLANEOUS.

BUSINESS FAILURES.

Schedule of assignments for the four weeks ending July 31, 1891:

	Liabilities.	Nominal Assets.	Real Assets.
Andrews, Proctor...	$1,888 42	$1,331 51	$750 00
Austin, Martin J. and Mary E......	4,427 58	3,587 21	1,482 26
Schmidt, Ellen... Booth, Samuel..... Snook, John A.....	29,737 00	146,942 89	5,879 26
Brencher, Conrad....	2,327 03	2,372 42	1,150 06
Collins, Catharine....	5,146 91	2,906 74	1,802 96
Engel, Leopold..... Stern, Rachel.......	6,097 75	1,909 40	1,050 00
Freeman, Alfred A. Roper, Henry...... Haight, Effingham C..................	225,807 56	471,834 00	43,996 31
Harmer, Mary.......	2,841 13	1,567 75	959 28
Hartung, Lorenzo R..	16,251 92	16,642 06	13,632 94
Hunter, Moritz......	5,430 23	1,673 78	1,250 00
Heiler, Raphael.....	6,662 06	4,293 99	2,284 08
Lexow, Rudolph G..	9,258 10	2,621 81	810 81
McQuillan, David....	4,599 68	7,181 43	3,697 67
Morris, Abraham.....	7,251 80	4,945 86	2,568 50
Pulver, Andrew P....	15,851 74	4,988 44	3,838 67
Rosenheim, Isidor.. Mack, Isaac S.......	229,561 59	196,845 97	101,845 99
Romain, Stephen M..	1,032 30	3,243 49	1,917 64
Schrimer, Edward...	6,308 62	3,825 32	1,261 18
Van Voorhis, William W............ Schuyler, Herman P	167,358 51	100,881 88	10,000 00
Wright, George W...	1,711 74	2,680 45	2,189 20
Woolman, George S.	10,784 74	11,356 08	6,711 88
Walter, John....... Crane, Joseph M...	3,424 25	2,673 60	1,325 00

N. Y. ASSIGNMENTS—BENEFIT CREDITORS.

April

27 Lawton, Nelson A. (dealer in hay, grain and feed, at No. 309 Washington st), to Alfred Ely; preferences, $250.

27 Collins, Catharine (dressmaker, at No. 52 West 18th st), to Alonzo C. Farnham; preference, $141.

29 Yasinki, Casmir W. (retail dealer in hardware, &c., at No. 2248 3d av), to George B. Curtiss; preferences, $1,085.

30 Avery, John C. (broker in investment securities, at No. 115 Broadway), to Louis C. Whiton; preference, $5,000.

30 Eustace, James A. (dealer in jewelry and antique goods, at No. 1216 Broadway), to George H. Ball; without preferences.

KINGS COUNTY.

GENERAL ASSIGNMENTS.

July

30 Hart, Alexander R. to Frank E. O'Reilly.

ADVERTISED LEGAL SALES.

REFEREES SALES TO BE HELD AT THE REAL ESTATE EXCHANGE AND AUCTION ROOM (LIMITED), 59 TO 65 LIBERTY STREET, EXCEPT WHERE OTHERWISE STATED.

August

Madison st, No. 281, n s, 47.8 e Jefferson st, 47.8x100, five-story brk tenem't, by R. V. Harnett & Co. (Amt due $23,058) 4

22d st, No. 44, s s, 257 e 6th av, 23x98.9, four-story stone front dwell'g, by William Kennelly. (Amt due $28.960) 4

116th st, No. 54, s s, 82.11 e Madison av, 27.1x101, five-story brk flat, by William Kennelly. (Amt due $3,074; prior mort. $25,000)........ 4

144th st, No. 454, s s, 214 e 10th av, 20x99.11, four-story brk dwell'g, by James C. Lalor. (Amt due $2,742)........ 4

144th st, No. 458, s s, 178 e 10th av, 17x99.11......
144th st, No. 452, s s, 234 e 10th av, 21x99.11......
Two three-story brk dwell'gs......
by James C. Lalor. (Amt due on No. 458 $2,819, and $3,746 on No. 452)........ 4

144th st, No. 466, s s, 100 e 10th av, 21x99.11, three-story brk dwell'g, by James C. Lalor. (Amt due $3,223)........ 4

101st st, No. 203, n s, 90 e 3d av, 20x100.11, four-story brk store and tenem't with two-story brk building on rear, by B. L. Kennelly........ 5

Av A, Nos. 28-30, e s, 88.6 s 3d st, 44x120, five and three-story brk assembly rooms, by J. F. B. Smyth. (Amt due $42,845)........ 5

Lexington av, No. 497, e s, 80 n 47th st, 20.5x100, five-story brk tenem't and store........
47th st, Nos. 119 and 121, n e cor Lexington av, 50x80, two five-story stone front flats........
by John T. Boyd. (Amt due $75,553)........ 6

Riverside Drive, No. 100 / 82d st, Nos. 318-326 { begins Riverside Drive, s e cor 82d st, runs east 161.1 x south 102.2 x west 16.8 x north 19.4 x west 32 x north 18.8 x west 14.4 x north 15.6 x west 8.4 x north 26.6 x west 79.9 to Riverside Drive, x north 24.2 to beginning, five four-story stone front dwell'gs, by Wm. R. Brown. (Amt due $4,244; prior morts. $—........ 7

7th av, No. 2812, s w cor 130th st, 25x100........
7th av, No. 2810, w s, 25 s 130th st, 37.5x100........
7th av, No. 2808, w s, 62.5 s 130th st, 37.5x100........
Three five-story brk flats with store in No. 2812........
by E. F. Raymond. (Amt due on No. 2812, $14,085; on No. 2810, $11,462, and $10,928 on No. 2808........ 7

50th st, No. 539, n s, 500 w 10th av, 25x100.5, five-story brk tenem't with stores, by R. V. Harnett & Co. (Amt due $3,548; prior morts. $7,000)........ 10

Amsterdam av, Nos. 641-649, n e cor 91st st, 136.5x100, five five-story brk flats with stores, by R. V. Harnett. (Amt due $29,132; prior morts. $120,000)........ 10

KINGS COUNTY.

Aug.

Cumberland st, No. 140, w s, 177.3 n Myrtle av, 25x100, three-story frame dwell'g; assessed value, $2,500; by G. F. Elliott, ref., at County Court House; partition........ 3

McDonough st, No. 333, n s, 280 w Stuyvesant av, 20x100........
McDonough st, No. 331, n s, 300 w Stuyvesant av, 20x100........
Two three-story brk dwell'gs; assessed value, $7,000 each........
by Michael Furst, ref., at County Court House.. 8

Prince st, No. 90, e s, 238.9 n Myrtle av, 21.3x85; partition; by T. A. Kerrigan, at 13 Willoughby st 3

Union st, n s, 200 w 8th av, 18.9x90........
Union st, n s, 312.6 w 8th av, 18.9x90........
Union st, n s, 331.3 w 8th av, 18 9x90........
Three three-story brown stone dwell'gs; assessed value, $11,000 each........
by Jere. Johnson, Jr., at the Real Estate Exchange, 189 and 191 Montague st........ 4

King st, s w cor Conover st, 100x100; assessed value, $4,000; partition........
Prospect av, No. 157, n s, 375 e 3d av, 25x52.6x25.1x50.7, three-story frame dwell'g; assessed value, $1,600; partition........
by J. Cole, at 389 Fulton st........ 4

Hendrix st, w s, 100 s Eastern Parkway, 100x100, two-story frame dwell'g on plot; assessed value, $3,100........
Greene av, Nos. 855 and 857, n w cor Stuyvesant av, 50x100, two four-story brk apartment houses, corner with store; assessed value, $20,000
Throop av, No. 549, e s, 61.7½ s Hancock st, 21.8½x81, four-story brown stone flat and store; assessed value, $9,500........
Stone av, w s, 42 n Pacific st, 58x80, three three-story frame dwell'gs; assessed value, $3,350 each........
by T. A. Kerrigan, at 13 Willoughby st........ 5

Palmetto st, n w s, 275 n e Knickerbocker av, 25x100, vacant; assessed value, $300........
Sedgwick st, s s, 225 w Columbia st, 18.9x100; all right, title and int........
Sedgwick st, s s, 100 w Columbia st, 125x100; all right, title and int., glass factory; assessed value, $10,000........
by T. A. Kerrigan, at 13 Willoughby st........ 6

62d st, s s, 480 w 14th av, 20x100, New Utrecht, frame dwell'g, by T. A. Kerrigan, at 13 Willoughby st........ 7

LIS PENDENS, KINGS COUNTY.

July

Bergen st, n s, 356.3 w Nevins st, 18.9x100. James Dunn agt Bertrand Clover; att'y, George B. Dunn........ 24

Rockaway av, s e cor Livonia av, 100x100. Lazarus Belfer agt Louis Ganz; action to recover deposit; att'ys, Judge & Durack........ 24

Herkimer st, n s, 145 e Hopkinson av, 15x100. Selena D. G. Gronlund agt Karl Viktor; att'y, James A. Hudson........ 24

Union st, s s, 92 w 5th av, 100x190 to President st.
5th av, n w s, 74.6 s w Union st, 20.6x92........
Union st, s w s, 92 n w 5th av, runs southwest 74.6 x southeast 92 to 5th av, x southwest 20.6 x northwest 92 x southwest 95 to President st, x northwest 100 x northeast 190 to Union st, x southeast 100. John Devlin agt Daniel Doody; att'y, Horace Graves........ 24

Same property. Same agt same; same att'y........ 24

21st st, n s, 125 e 6th av, 160x100. Stephen R. Sturges agt James R. Robb; att'ys, Sturges & Roby. 25

Ocean Parkway, w s, 100 s Av E, 60x250 to East 5th st, Flatbush. D. Lewis Grant agt John Erickson; foreclos. mech. lien; att'y, E. L. Heydecker........ 25

Atlantic av, s w cor Eldert av, 32.1x—x31x(11.1). William P. Roome agt Dennis O'Neill; notice of attachment; att'y, F. A. Thomson........ 25

Bushwick av, s e cor Williamsburgh turnpike, 25x100. Mary A. Werkmeister agt Andrew Holz; action to set aside deed; att'y, H. D. Birdsall.. 25

Duffield st, e s, 100 n Johnson st, 130x100. Isidore Cohen agt Angelo Mondolfo; att'y, Benjamin Wright........ 25

Lexington av, n s, 326 e Reid av, 34x100. Edwin S. Updike agt Victor P. P. Erslev; att'y, Russell Walden........ 25

2d av, s e s, extends from 43d st to 44th st, 200.4x350........
3d av, east cor 45th st, 100.2x200........
3d av, n w s, 25.2 s w 21st st, runs northwest 100 x northeast 25.2 to 21st st, x northwest 50 x southwest 100 x southeast 50 x southwest 24.10 x — to av, x northwest —........
Ernest H. Fischer agt Catharine B. Fischer; partition; att'y, Horace Graves........ 25

Kingsland av, w s, 298.3 n Nassau av, 19x100....
Kingsland av, w s, 279.3 n Nassau av, 19x100....
Kingsland av, w s, 317.3 n Nassau av, 19x100....
Louis St. Amant and Frank La Manna and ano. trustees agt Jonas Feldberg; 3 actions; att'ys, Wells & Waldo........ 27

Pellington pl, w s, lots 105 and 106 map Williams & Furman, runs south 48.3x west 100 x north 50 x east 99.2 x southeast —. Grace Rome agt Margaret Van Ostrand; att'y, J. R. Allaben........ 28

Van Voorhis st, n w s, 117 s w Evergreen av, 17x100. Moses P. Prout agt Mary N. McLaren; att'y, Wm. H. E. Jay........ 28

Van Voorhis st, n w s, 100 s w Evergreen av, 17x100. Same agt same; same att'y........ 28

Van Voorhis st, n w s, 134 s w Evergreen av, runs northwest 100 x southwest 18 x southeast 51.9 x southwest 1 x southeast 48.2 to st, x northeast 17. Same agt same; same att'y........ 28

Van Siclen av, e s, 100 s Blake av, 50x100. Rudolph Reimer agt Josephine Quinn; att'y's, Sackett, Lang, Reed & McKewan........ 28

Brooklyn and Jamaica plank road, s s, 106.2 e Sheffield av, 44.1x74x40x51.2. Joseph A. Kene agt Cornelius Donovan; att'y's, McGuire & Low. 28

Broadway, n e s, 96 s e Hull st, 29x100. Samuel Hancock agt Henry J. Hancock; action to set aside deed; att'ys, Jacobs & Butcher........ 28

4th av, n w cor 40th st, 25x100. Michael Gilligan agt Margaret A. Oakley; partition; att'y, William A. Crowe........ 29

Broadway, s s, 420 w Brooklyn av, 40x100, Flatbush. Edward Egolf agt Ann Carolin; att'y, John A. Lott, Jr........ 29

Lots 65 and 66 map Gilbert S. Thatford, 26th Ward. Jacob De Bevoise admr. Jacob De Bevoise agt William Neagle; same att'y.... 29
Broadway, Nos. 129-131, n s, 195.2 w Driggs st, 43.4x100. Harry M. Lynch agt Isabella Conly; partition; att'y, Arthur C. Butts.... 29
3d st, s w cor 7th av, 22x90. Sarah A. Bergen agt Mary A. Poole; att'y, B. Wright.... 29
3d st, s s, 44 w 7th av, 22x90. Same agt same; same att'y.... 29
Gates av, n s, 287.6 e Reid av, 20.10x100. Henry F. Balk agt George H. Box; att'y, Theo. Burgmyer.... 29
Fulton st, east cor Somers st, 127.4x27.11x124.3. Helen S. Rapelye agt Francis McMahon; att'y, Edward F. Brown.... 30
20th st, No. 156, s s, 260 w 4th av, 25x100. Henry W. Clear individ. and exr. Bridget Clear agt Bridget Seery; action to establish lien; att'y, John C. Kinkel.... 30

RECORDED LEASES.

NEW YORK. Per Year

Broadway, No. 826, n e cor 12th st. J. Waldron Gillespie to Samuel D. Folsom; 5 years, from May 1, 1896.... $8,000
Bowery, No. 27, front basement. Albin Wibom to Charles Hoffmann and John O. Regan; 9 10-12 years, from July 1, 1891.... 240
Christopher st, No. 154, s w cor Washington st. Margaret O'Neil to William Burns; 3 years, from May 1, 1891.... 1,300, 1,500
Delancey st, No. 215. Clinton Ogilvie to William Simpfendorfer; 3 years, from May 1, 1892.... 800
Fulton st, No. 140, store floor, basement and cellar. Margaret J. Spader, Amelia R. Moore, Maria L. Hegeman individ. and extrx, Mary G. Schwackhamer, Eveanna Rae, John G. Moore, Boltis Moore and Eloise M. Scheeper to Lazarus Spero; 3¾ years, from Aug. 1, 1891.... 4,500
Mulberry st, No. 58, front and rear buildings. Vito Cimino to Luigi Mega; 2 7-12 years, from Oct. 1, 1889.... 3,000
Mott st, No. 215, store and basement. Antonio and Michele Vilenzio to Franceso and Lorenzo Ciaffoni; 2 years, from May 1, 1891.... 260
Warren st, No. 118. Edgar L. Reynolds to Padecken & Raap, with Ludwig Mayer as guarantor; 5 years, from May 1, 1895.... 2,500
West Houston st., No. 55. Mary E. and Louis V. Appell to Charles Frey; 5 years, from May 1, 1891.... 1,500
28th st, No. 32 W. Edward P. Dickie to John J. McGrath; 10 1-6 years, from Dec. 1, 1891.... 3,600, 5,000
33d st, No. 29 W., store and rear apartments. Townsend Dickinson to Michael Sheridan; 2¾ years, from Aug. 1, 1891.... 420
32d st, n s, 300 e 1st av, boiler house. The New York Steam Co. to The Standard Gas Light Co., New York; 5 years, from July 24, 1891.... 250
39th st, No. 508 W., store floor on west side. Thomas Morrow to John Hughes; 4 10-12 years, from July 1, 1891.... 360, 420
45th st, No. 45 W. Marguerite Perrier to Christine Obenauer; 3 years, from May 1, 1891.... 2,600
73d st, No. 320 E., store floor and basement. Ignatz Schultz and Samuel Kopp to Martin Krikava; 3 years, from May 1, 1892.... 420
145th st, No. 321 W., store. Thomas F. Russell to Louis W. Kessel; 4½ years, from Aug. 1, 1891.... 540, 900
Av A, No. 1599, store and four rear rooms. Adam Stahl and Eva his wife to George Moeller; 5 years, from Aug. 1, 1891.... 1,104, 1,164
Av A, No. 1453, store, back room and part cellar. John H. Heckmann to Hermann Boymann; 5 years, from June 1, 1891.... 720, 900
Amsterdam av, No. 1065. Emil C. G. Von Pein to Adolph Pflughaupt; 10⅓ years, from Jan. 1, 1891.... 3,900, 4,000
Courtlandt av, No. 820, store floor and cellar. William Wolfrath to Hans Pohlmann; 4¾ years, from Aug. 1, 1891.... 552
Morris av, No. 692, store. A. Kuster to Conrad Lotiuk; 3 years, from May 1, 1891.... 264, 300
Park av, No. 1805, store and ground floor. Nora Dolan to Maggie McCarron; 3 years, from May 1, 1890.... 420
Tremont av, No. 760 } Gottfried Schultz to Bathgate av, No. 1901 } Joseph H. Rheinish; 3 11-12 years, from July 1, 1891.... 1,056
1st av, No. 82, store floor and basement. Margaret Scheig to Herman N. and August H. Postel; 3 years, from May 1, 1892.... 2,000
1st av, No. 2386, store floor. Amelia F. Berg to Henry J. McGivney; 3¾ years, from Aug. 1, 1891.... 540
2d av, No. 1945, corner store, floor and cellar. Emil Broggelwirth to Friedrich Huners and George Lebers; 5 years, from Aug. 1, 1891.... 1,380
3d av, No. 1785. Louise Ellis to Patrick Clark; 8 years, from May 1, 1891.... 1,950
5th av, s e cor 33d st, corner store, rear rooms and front cellar. John W. Haaren to Henry Ettinger; 5 years, from May 1, 1890.... 900, 1,200
7th av, No. 276, store floor. Morris Abrahams to Andreas Schmidt; 4¾ years, from Aug. 1, 1891.... 840
8th av, No. 870, n e cor 52d st. Albert J. Adams to Patrick Cashin; 10 years, from May 1, 1891.... 4,000, 4,500
9th av, No. 794, store floor and basement. Samuel A. Cutner to Charles S. Albers; 3 5-12 years, from Dec. 1, 1890.... 750, 780

CHATTELS.

NOTE.—The first name, alphabetically arranged, is that of the Mortgagor, or party who gives the Mortgage. The "R" means Renewal Mortgage.

NEW YORK CITY.

JULY 24 TO 30—INCLUSIVE.

SALOON AND RESTAURANT FIXTURES.

Brosen, Bernard. 1871 3d av....D Mayer. $530
Brown, E D. 278 Pearl....Thurber, Whyland Co. Restaurant Fixtures. 200
Belatta, Michael. Olie st, Williamsbridge....J Kuntz B Co. 200
Benson & Halford. 2097 2d av and 166 E 96th st . American Guar. Assoc. Restaurant and Furniture. 100
Bolger, Martin. Riverdale av....D Mayer. Saloon Pump. (R) 87
Breid, Michael. 125th st and Manhattan st....D G Yuengling, Jr. 2,70
Borman, Fritz. 64 Wooster.... G Ehret. (R) 1,000
Breunig, Frank. 134 E 7th....V Loewers. 2,989
Burns, Joseph. 340 Bowery....W C Scheuing. 443
Boyman, Herman. 1453 Av A....Bernheimer & S. 800
Carroll, Thomas. 1509 Av A.... J Eichler B Co. (R) 800
Carroll, Thomas. 1731 1st av....J Eichler B Co. (R) 700
Celer, John. 529 E 5th....J Kuntz B Co. (R) 595
Clampett, James. 332 Grand....R W Block. 4,000
Clancy & Hennessy. 791 8th av....I Roth. 2,000
Same....same. Bar Cabinet Work. 300
Clarke, Patrick. 854 6th av....J Ahles B Co. (R) 800
Considine, M S. 19 W 26th .. C and A Bereuter. Pool. 650
Crowe, Thomas. 509 W 59th ....L B Crowe. Hotel. 1,700
Calanne, August. 331 7th av....Beadleston & W. Pump. 90
Casidy, Michael. 325 West....M Hochstein. Restaurant Fixtures. 300
Coleman, Peter. 322 E 29th....M Seitz. (R) 225
Cusack, D F. 799 Washington....Burr B Co. 800
Dabritz & Co. 436 Broadway....Rubsam & H B Co. 800
Deufel, J and F. 413 E 38th....J Eichler B Co. (R) 400
Dixon, J J. 661 2d av....H Elias B Co. (R) 2,500
Doyle, Peter. 248 5th av... Langdon & G B Co. (R) 1,500
Dwyer, Michael. 453 E 138th....G Ehret. 1,000
Donahue, Julia M. 247 W 61st....M Van Rensselaer, Jr. 375
Dougherty, Joseph. 580 10th av....Beadleston & W. 980
Dykes, M M. 28 Canal....Welz & Zerweck. (R) 300
Dietrich, Herrmann. 88 1st av....J Hoffmann B Co. (R) 1,500
Dannecker, John. 989 1st av....F Oppermann, Jr. 700
Doernich, J and W. 167 E 105th....J Ruppert. 1,500
Ehler & Lind. 322 Greenwich ...H Meyer. (R) 4,559
Eibel, Henry. 327 E 43d....J Eichler B Co. (R) 400
Engel, Sam. 214 Broome....I Milgrann. Restaurant Fixtures. 250
Fay, W J. 164 Madison....Wagner & S. Pool. 150
Ferraro, Sebastiano. 2206 1st av....Feigenspan B Co. 400
Same....same. Pool. 165
Same....same. Pump. 90
Flannery, John P. 536 Hudson....C Stein. (R) 8,000
Fairchild, Frederick. 487 6th av ...J Kahn. Restaurant Fixtures. (R) 935
Fischer, Robert. 199 E 4th....G H A Meyer. (R) 500
Fitzgerald, Michael. Boston road and Southern Boulevard....J Kuntz B Co. 325
Fenton, Patrick. 228 Cherry....Bernheimer & S. Ice House. 120
Same....same. Pump. 91
Gregory, Minnie. 30 and 32 Oak....J Wallace & Son. 150
Gorman, T R. 445 E 13th ...J Kuntz B Co. 400
Grull, Barbara. 1407 Av A....J Ruppert. 2,000
Heinevetter, Ann. 78 Greene....J Hoffmann B Co. (R) 1,350
Hughes, John. 508 W 29th....H Vogel. Bar Fixtures. 350
Holian & Mani. 411 Broadway....J Kern. 1,628
Hughes, Edward. 308 West....M Van Rensselaer, Jr. (R) 710
Hughes, John. 508 W 89th....P Doelger. 750
Heim, B and E. Broadway, 74th and 75th sts....G C Engel. Restaurant Fixtures. (R) 3,400
Holzmann, Charles. 355 Broome....Rubsam & H B Co. 1,000
Jakob, J F. 1025 E 137th....P & W Ebling B Co. 400
Jakubovics, Leopold. 248 E 3d....Bernheimer & S. Pool Table. 143
Keilty, Henry. 2142 3d av....J Eichler B Co. (R) 1,325
Kivlehan, P T. 1341 1st av... Bernheimer & S. Saloon Box. 164
Kommel, B. 24 Allen....D Mayer. 500
Lenz, Katie. 494 Amsterdam av ...Bernheimer & S. Saloon Pump. 110
Same....same. Saloon Ice House. 130
Landwehr, Richard. 332 E 53d....Consumers B Co. 800
Lau, Joachim. 195 Av A....J & M Haffen. 1,954
Langness, Christian. 156 Duane....W Horrmann. (R) 350
Leary, Mary. 623 9th av... G Ehret. 1,844
Lester, Julius. 17 Clinton pl....Wagner & S. Pool. 130
Lipschitz, A & L. 152 Rivington....Feigenspan B Co. 250
Loonie, Maurice. 964 1st av....P & W Ebling B Co. 1,500
Lynch, Frank. 454 11th av....Mutual B Co. 500
Lebherz, John. 130 Spring... J Hensler. (R) 1,100
Lehmann, William. 101 Allen....Anchor B Co. 500
Leopold, Frances. 1112 Vanderbilt av....D Mayer. 400
McGirney, Owen. 721 11th av....Burr B Co. (R) 500
Mueller, George. 1599 Av A....Gottlieb & Fried. 365
Mankin & Haffen. 836 Washington ...J & M Haffen. 3,145
McCaull, Owen. 33 Downing....J Ahles B Co. 600
McCue, Patrick. 724 E 11th....Fitzgerald B Co. (R) 1,500
McFarland, Michael. 55th st and 11th av... P Doelger. 870
Mosser, Gregor. 1500 1st av....J Kuntz B Co. 725
Moskovits, Adolf. 244 Stanton ...Wagner & S. Pool Table. (R) 10
McGarry & McGuinness. 34 Marion....J Ahles B Co. (R) 700
Nixon, Claudius. 423 E 22d....J & M Haffen. 650
O'Brien, James. 1805 Park av.. H Koehler & Co. 850
O'Reilly, Hugh. 146 Monroe....V Loewers. (R) 225
Oakley, M J. E 14th st....Mutual B Co. 1,015
O'Connor, John. 319 Berry st, Brooklyn....F & M Schaefer B Co. 1,300
Phelan, Joseph. 230 W 18th....J Cunningham. (R) 1,500
Pohlmann, Hans. 820 Courtlandt av....A Hupfel's Sons. 1,000
Prendeville, Thomas. 877 2d av....H Clausen & Son B Co. (R) 1,200
Poellet, Louis. 96 Willett....V Loewers. 500
Prince, Henry. 27 West Houston .. B Heim. Restaurant Fixtures. (R) 600
Quinlan, C M. 69 Oliver . .J Wallace & Son. 1,000
Rheinish, J H. 760 Tremont av....Emma Rheinish. 2,500
Reiss, Wilhelmine. 53 Greenwich....W Horrmann. (R) 300
Rosenheim, Max. 235 E 107th....V Loewers. 863
Ryan, Thomas. 90 Chatham sq....Bernheimer & S. 850
Rappolt, F X. 705 E 12th....G Ringler & Co. 500
Russo, Domenico. 232 Elizabeth....H Elias B Co. 800
Same. 72½ Mulberry....same. 700
Roth & Silver. 130 Pitt ... M Seitz. 650
Seppenfeldt, William. 60½ 1st av....Bernheimer & S. 600
Schlotterbeck, Marie. 438 E 17th....P Doelger. 400
Sergi & Capellini. 128 Baxter....P Schaefer & Son. 800
Sheridan, Michael. 219 W 32d ...P Doelger. 600
Siegfried, Adam. 183 Duane....H M Cordts. 5,400
Stelzle, Leonard. 754 8th av....J Kuntz B Co. 1,200
Straub, Aquilin. 815 1st av....P Doelger. 350
Scherer, Heinrich. 18 Bond....L Epstein. Restaurant Fixtures. 200
Schiuder, Elise. 59 Forsyth....W Peter. (R) 50
Schmidt, Louis. 6 Centre....J Steingester. (R) 3,000
Schneider, Bessie. 60 Thomas....H Elias B Co. 1,000
Schutzel, Frederick. 121 1st av....A Hupfel's Sons. 1,000
Singer, Markus. 154 Attorney....Bernheimer & S. 900
Steiner, Simon. 427 E 59th ..D Mayer. (R) 350
Schuler, George. 96 Allen....J Eichler B Co. (R) 700
Siemers, F. 195 West....H Elias B Co. (R) 800
Stoll, Fr. 84 Cortlandt....Rubsam & H B Co. 2,000
Sullivan, Frank. 9 Bowery....A Wiborn. (R) 1,829
Sullivan, James. 656 Water....V Loewers. 225
Toebing, William. 216 E 120th....P & W Ebling B Co. 1,200
Thompson, Joseph. 420 W 42d....G Ringler & Co. 600
Trainor, F J. 65th st and 3d av... J Everard. 1,015
Wahlers, Frederick. 66 Vesey....Beadleston & W. Ice Box. 100
Weiss, David. 25 Lispenard....L Appel. Restaurant Fixtures. 800
Wieble, Reinhald. 518 10th av....V Loewers. 1,175
Winters, Theodore. 93 Oliver....D Mayer. 800

HOUSEHOLD FURNITURE.

Anderson, Charles. 221 E 97th....Dreisacker & Co. 130
Allen, Anna. 69 E 12th... O'Farrell & Co. 195
Adler, H B. 212 East Broadway....J Rubenstein. 183
Axtell, Mrs M. 58 Prospect pl....T Kelly. 382
Beggs, Louisa. 75 W 100th....T Kelly. 129
Bodden, Mrs Genie. 135 E 49th....T Kelly. 189
Bougnet, Louis. 253 E 10th....Krakauer Bros. Piano. 187
Buell, J F. 148 E 52d ...Krakauer Bros. Piano. 350
Bauerle, Gertrude. 126 E 12th....E Hermes. 260
Beury, Eugenie. 226 W 4th... J Gregg & Co. 129
Baldwin, Bella. 81 W 89th... H Mannes & Son. 116
Basler, George. 182 Chrystie....H S Eisler. 102
Behan, Peter. 119 9th av....Friel & Hand. 142
Bessey, Phoebe M. 859 9th av....Friel & Hand. 211
Block, E. 70 E 4th .. W H Butler. Safe. 230
Briggs, G E. 239 E 81st....Friel & Hand. 192
Bryan, J H. 875 Manhattan av....F O Benedict. 300
Buerger, Arthur. 314 E 119th....Blasius & Sons. Piano. 375
Carlisle, May. 138 E 48th....H Israel & Sons. 381
Carr, Mrs A L. 19 Watts .. D M Brown. (R) 170
Conklin, Mary. 9 Stanton....H Israel & Sons. 142
Collins, James. 83 Pike slip. .Jordan & M. 123
Coffey, Kate. 119 W 60th....L Baumann. 260
Cronin, Julia. 441 E 81st .. Dreisacker & Co. 175
Cockcroft, Eva. 987 Lexington av....C E Pierce. 130
Cronhardt, Louis. 138th st and Willis av....H Thoesen. 195
Cullen, Adelia M. 521 E 119th....Simpson & P. Piano. (R) 114
Cody, Annie. 48 Leroy. ..T Kelly. 126
Creamer, F D. 150 E 27th ...Fennell & Pye. (R) 232
de Wolfe, A R. 216 W 34th... E C Hinsdale. 100
Dexter, Adelia. 17 1st....W A Meyer. 200
Drinse, Charles. 425 E 79th .. H S Eisler. (R) 105
Dunn, Helen. 270 W 39th ...E S Webster. (R) 150
Drummond, Mrs K. 105 E 89th....T Kelly. 128
Drott, Christian. 103 E 27th....S I Herschmann. 912
Eife, A F. 175 E 10th....Simpson & P. Piano. (R) 246
Elsberg, Rebecca A. 114 E 58th....M Gearon. 800
Etchingham, John. Ogden av....W J Ruddell. 181
Fogarty, Mrs D J. 155 W 133d....T Kelly. 176
Fitzgerald, T W. 104 W 99th... J Gregg & Co. 228
Glass & Buckmaster. 557 5th av....J A Philbrick. (R) 640
Gleason, M J. 251 E 109th.... T Kelly. 320
Gottlieb, Herman. 1606 3d av ...Krakauer Bros. Piano. 325
Gibbs, C B. 210 Alexander av....H Mannes & Son. 194
Hawkins, Mary. 237 W 32d....J S Rice. 119
Henrich, Amelia. 748 Columbus av....S Baumann. 135
Hiscano, A R. 122 W 63d ...L Baumann. 159
Hassett, Kate. 501 W 59th... J Gregg & Co. 123
Hasson, Ellen. 213 Fulton. .T Kelly. 244
Hartog, Alphonse. 231 W 16th ...O'Farrell & Co. 113
Hardegg, Frederick. 137 W 104th....W Scott. 200
Johnson, Nellie. 160 Waverley pl....C H Lyon. 100
Jay, E Grace. 34 W 132d....T Kelly. 155
Johnston, Annie L. 209 Columbus av....T Kelly. 144
Jacobsen, C E & M E. 160 W 23d....M A Birtles. 500
Jones, J M. 138 W 16th....S J Evans. 100
Kayser, Gustav. 41 1st av....Krakauer Bros. Piano. 375
Kneip, John. Cor W 4th st and 10th st .. T Kelly. 265
Kiernan, Maggie. 225 W 10th....O'Farrell & Co. (R) 434
Klepper, Max F. 216 E 113th....A C Hinz. 315
Krauss, A F Mrs. 32 W 27th....C F Walters. 580
Kuilbock, E F. 313 W 42d....H C Lampe. 120
Lamb, Mary. 408 W 50th....O'Farrell & Co. 111
Lenon, Mamie A. 31 Bayard....J Rubenstein. 232
Livingston, Mary E. 218 E 82d....T Kelly. 181
Lichtenstein, David. 188 Henry....J Rubenstein. 500
Linzbach, Maxim. 222 E 6th....Friel & Hand. 116
McGraw, Michael. 302 W 69th....G Reubel. 110
Meriman, Mary. 2 Grove.... C E Pierce. 130
Miner, Ella. 151 E 46th....J Moriarty. 238
Mourey, Auguste. 122 Waverley pl....D Ficken. 1,000
McKinney, W L. 218 W 17th ..T Kelly. 110
McLean, J C. 35 Morton....T Kelly. 126
Meehan, Mrs Edward. 265 Mercer....T Kelly. 141
Madden, E and K A. 303 W 14th ...M F Cagney. 102
Mora, Antonio. 45 W 60th....N Good. 65
MacLellen, C F. 219 W 40th....O'Farrell & Co. 259
Norton, Anna. 211 W 53d ...R B De Casanova. 170
Nugent, Della. 245 E 45th ...Manges Bros. 124
Nathan, Abo Mrs. 74 Division....H Israel & Sons. 144
Owens, Mrs H E. 81st st and 9th av....Fennell & Pye. (R) 303

O'Donnell, Mrs. 439 10th av... J S Rice. 114
Pinkowsky, Morris. 347 E 81st....H S Eisler. 100
Paine, W E. 236 E 118th....Manges Bros. 203
Praeger, Samuel. 243 E 57th....H Thoesen. 132
Priess, Anna. 57 W 16th....J Moriarty. 790
Quinn, Ellen. 71 Clarkson....Jordan & M. 105
Raymond, Jas. 29 Broadway....Brooklyn Furn Co. 425
Riehl, Katherina. 623 E 152d....Simpson & P. Piano. 275
Roberts, G R. 329 to 333 Lenox av....J Bierhoff. Arthur Hall. 351
Rakentine, Charles. 236 E 85th....Friel & Hand. 138
Rascover, Hannah. 228 E 105th....Friel & Hand. 147
Reilly, Mary. 173 E 96th....Dreisacker & Co. 137
Rosenstock, Moritz. 156 W 138th....L Heidenheimer. 588
Schulze, C F. 124 2d....L Gort. 450
Silsby, Annie. 118 W 29th....L Baumann. 147
Smith, Mary D. 281 W 114th....L Baumann. 195
Struck & Schniefert. 938 8th av....G Beck. 188
Sussmann, Chas. 112 Hester ...E Wolf. 200
Scheider, Jacob. 40 Lexington av....Basch & Greenfield. 115
Same... Nellie Scheider. 800
Scholtz, Conrad. 781 E 63d....C E Pierce. 100
Smidt, Fannie. 420 E 79th....Manges Bros. 166
Smith, Almira G. 7 W 19th ...W H Appleton. 1,250
Steansbury, Mary A. 70 W 107th ...G W Mercer. 300
Schlater, W E....J Fyfe. 150
Simpson, May. 217 W 15th....T Kelly. 203
Same....same. 356
Stevens, Mary I. 155 E 123d....T Kelly. 126
Strefbel, Marie. 2069 Bathgate av....T Kelly. 265
Stahl, Leonard. 249 E 86th....J Moriarty. 129
Travis, Carrie. 136 W 37th....Rosa B De Casanova. 835
Taylor, Alice. 327 W 51st....S Baumann. (R) 304
Taylor, A D. 557 W 50th....L Baumann. 167
Tobin, J S. 681 E 134th....J Moriarty. 144
Viano, A and N. E 18th st, bet Broadway and 4th av....J & J Dobson. 700
Vibbard W H. 267 W 123d....T Kelly. 139
Walkowisky, Sam. 347 E 51st....J Rubenstein. 200
White, Mrs George. 132 W 15th....T Kelly. 125
Wight, Mrs M A. 106 W 52d... T Kelly. 310
Welsh, Mrs Michael. 406 E 18th ...D M Brown. 227
Williams, Vara E. 81 W 89th....H Mannes & Son. 409
Wheat, Sarah. 159 E 119th....O'Farrell & Co. 194

MISCELLANEOUS.

Altmann & Maykels. 65 Walker....A Aaronson. Machinery. 150
Arnstein, Finkelstein Co. 658 Broadway ...Hall's Safe Co. Safe. 175
Bean & Finnerty. 80 8th av....Lamson Consol S S Co. Register. 150
Barr, Rosalie S. 618 8th av....P F Turner. Store Fixtures, &c. 2,000
Bachert & Bach. 598 Broadway... A Schwaab. Barber Fixtures. 62
Behrmann, H J & Co. 69 Ludlow....E Burger. Wagon. 250
Berlin & Bertram. Lincoln av and 132d st....H Spies. Machinery. (R) 1,800
Blanchard, Clara. 82 Wooster....L Thompson & Co. Machinery. 101
Bloom, Moses. 22½ Catharine... B Meier. Store Fixtures. 50
Brandus, Edward. 30 Broad ...American Writing Machine Co. Typewriter. 99
Brownson, J M. 39 Harrison....G A Moss Presses. (R) 1,550
Same ...C J Moss. Presses. (R) 2,880
Bruno, P W. 118 Ludlow and 118 Orchard....L Kaufold. Confectionery Fixtures (R) 800
Beck, Fr, & Co....State Trust Co. Machinery, &c. (R) 194,000
Barns, C E. 37 Great Jones....Mosler Safe Co. Safe. 100
Block, Jacob. 45 Chrystie ...J Lester. Horse, Truck, &c. 100
Butow & Degenfeld. 201 Hester....G R Fischer. Butcher Fixtures. 400
Cajazzo & Caroselli. 55 Mott....R Rossi. Barber Fixtures. 265
Carter, R J ...M Armstrong & Co. Coach. (R) 925
Combes, John. 834 Broadway....S. D. Folsom. Office Fixtures. 800
Claus, Peter. 639 and 641 Kent av, Brooklyn....J S & G F Simpson. Electric Fixtures. 70
Cohnfeld, Rachel. 92-96 Bleecker....Marvin Safe Co. Safe. 500
Cooke, Thomas. 247 W 41st....J L Sheehen. Cab. 69
Cherouney Printing and Pub Co. 23 Vandewater ...C B Cottrell & Sons. Press. (R) 750
Coari, Louis. 359 W 59th and 361 and 363 W 59th ....L Losi. Confectionery Fixtures, &c. (R) 4,000
Diamond, Morris. 111 Delancey....B Meier. Store Fixtures. 100
Dow, C L A. 628 W 34th ...C L A Dow, Jr. Horse, Truck, &c. 500
Erff, Charles. 18 Waverley pl....E F Boehmann. Barber Fixtures. 255
Eustace, J A. 1216 Broadway....M Frank, Jr. Store Fixtures. 250
Egloff, August. 24 Prince....E Cole. Butcher Fixtures. 1,000
Eppinger, Leopold. 215 East Houston....C Seidenspinner. Butcher Fixtures. 300
Fibrone Mfg Co. 300 and 302 Monroe....T H Wheeler. Machinery. 14,748
Flieg, T. 10th av and 151st st....Lamson Consol S S Co. Register. (R) 210
Forrester, Kate. 80 Skillman av, Brooklyn... W V Mulford et al. Horse, Wagon, &c. 200
Frosch, Herman. 27 1st av....S Blaut. Bakery Fixtures. 300
Gardner, W C. 52 New Bowery....S J Weaver. Horses, Trucks, &c. 1,000
Grote & Frische. 1602 2d av and 223 E 83d st....J H Meyer. Grocery Fixtures. (R) 2,700
Gude, C H. 435 W 56th ...L Eibs. Grocery Fixtures. (R) 350
Gysbers, William C. 856 9th av....J W Gysbers. Office Fixtures, &c. 1,000
Goldberg, Samuel. 179 Stanton....C Haller. Machine 50
Guariglia, Patrick. 197 Division....G Santabicia. Barber Fixtures. 175
Geisler, Christian. 300 E 73d....F Behre & Bro. Grocery Fixtures. 810
Hagan, Thomas. 1362 3d av ... M Hagan. Gent's Furnishing Fixtures. 3,500
Hartung, G C. 775 9th av....Lamson Consol S S Co. Register. 300
Hoffmann, Philip. 182 East Houston....M Meyer. Machine. 98
Hartmann, William. 52 Lexington av....Lamson Consol S S Co. Register. (R) 210
Heyman, Mike....C Huller. Machine. 60
Hindle & Wright. 22 Beekman....E C Hinsdale. Machinery. 375
Hoehn, Christian. 118 Pitt....A Schaus. Horse and Milk Wagon. 400
Horn, Adam & Co. 24 Delancey....I Reith. Bakery Fixtures. 200
Jaffe, Abel. 9½ Essex....C Konigsberg. Grocery Fixtures, &c 100
Jacob & Grossman. 82 Forsyth ...Marvin Safe Co. Safe. 120
Joiner, Walter. 476-480 E 139th....S A Wood's Machine Co. Machinery. 72
Jordan, G F. 1036 10th av ...L C Kiefer. Horse, Wagon, &c. 50
Kaldenberg, F J. Nassau and Beekman sts.... Marvin Safe Co. Safe. 495
Kelly, T P and J A....M Armstrong & Co. Coaches, &c. (R) 1,400
King, Thomas. 66 University pl....D Smith. Stationery and Cigar Fixtures. 100
Klein, Herman. 306 E 3d....E Weil & Co. Machines. 298
Knauer, J H. 352 E 82d... A Knauer. Milk Wagon, Horse, &c. 800
Krause, J R. 501 Tinton av....L Rothschild. Horse and Fixtures, &c. 500
Kneppler, Rasquin and Porr. 165-171 Grand....R Hoe & Co. Press, &c. 1,837
Kraus, F R. 57 Ann....J Wenger. Machinery. 750
Krisch, Jacob. 108 Mercer....A Schwaab. Barber Fixtures. 87
Kuechenmeister, Frederick. 686 8th av....H Mandelbaum. Cigar Fixtures, &c. 271
Kennedy, James. 115 E 22d....D Daly. Cab. (R) 42
Kopf, Diederich. 513 6th....C H Tuthill. Horse, Milk Wagon, &c. 300
Leibe, Daniel. 2159 5th av.. H Ettinger. Drug Fixtures. 2,200
Lees, Samuel. 19 Barclay....Emma J Lees. Office Fixtures. 125
Lessner, Charles. 1661 3d av and 206 E 101st st ....S Hagedorn. Horse, Ice Wagon, &c. 250
Linquiti, Parquale. 205 7th av....M A Fitzgerald. Machines. (R) 175
Lawson, John. 504 W 35th ....W Lawson. Horses, Trucks, &c. (R) 2,000
Liquori, Antonio. 43 Washington....R Rossi. Barber Fixtures. 200
Licht, L. 155 E 44th....J P McHugh & Co. Machinery. 1,204
Locke, George. 991 1st av....Smith & Sills. Bakery Fixtures. 439
Meyer, John. 1483 2d av....L Link. Barber Fixtures. 100
Same....D Sauermann. Barber Fixtures. 100
Marti, Joaquin. 875 6th av....J Gonzalez. Store Fixtures. 160
Malnik, Nathan. 4 Norfolk... K Cohen. Machines. 80
Mankin, G B. Little 12th and Washington sts ..Mosler Safe Co. Safe. 190
Merritt, Cornelius. 204 E 123d....Chappell-Chase-Maxwell Co. Undertaker's Fixtures. 808
Miller, William....M Armstrong & Co. Coach. 900
Marlborough Hotel Co. Broadway and 36th st ....Knickerbocker Trust Co. Franchises, &c. (R) 250,000
Meyer, Frederick. 90th st and Western Boulevard....H Meyer. Horses, &c. 1,200
Nole, Anchea. 345 E 23d... M Pittaro. Barber Fixtures. 150
Niemann, Henry. 10th av and 151st st....Warren & Stratton. Bakery. (R) 660
N Y Smelting and Refining Co....J Hendricks and others. Franchises, &c. 17,000
Same....same. Franchises, &c. 20,000
Olivati, Ercole. 203 Bowery....A Petrone. Barber Fixtures. 174
Orth, John. 392 Bowery ...Lamson Consol S S Co. Register. (R) 210
Pearson & Fife. 27th st and Broadway and Coleman House....J H Rodgers. Hotel Fixtures. (R) 25,000
Phelps, G H. 169 W 126th... A W Selkirk. Dentist Fixtures. 250
Piening, Otto. 151 Forsyth....M Klemm. Bakery Fixtures, &c. 500
Platte, J and C. 571 Courtlandt av....J Chegwidden et al. Grocery Fixtures. 85
Posito, Filippo. 138 6th av....A Schwaab & Son. Barber Fixtures. 425
Pocello, Francesco. 407 6th av....D Lisanti. Barber Fixtures. 230
Rasmussen, Hans. 573 W 34th....J Souvay. Barber Fixtures. 87
Reilly & Donohue. 158 W 55th....J Leonard. Blacksmith Fixtures. 235
Reilly, John. 107 W 49th....J Leonard. Blacksmith Fixtures. 112
Reinert, August. 309 E 115th....F J Minck. Horse, Wagon, &c. 53
Rabinowitz, Isaac. 65 Chrystie....M Radilorosky. Machinery. 200
Riegelhaupt, Heinrich. 250 E 2d....G Pius. Horse, Wagon, &c. 508
Ruehe, A E. 148th st and Brook av....C H Krug. Machinery. 500
Rothenberg, Jacob....Goodkind & Jacobowetz. Machinery. 70
Recht, Rosenbaum & Co. 773 1st av....Tegetmeier & Riepe. Horses, Trucks. 175
Reiss, Henry. 59 Greenwich....Marvin Safe Co. Safe. 200
Roth, Herrmann. 200 E 2d....S C Marum. Cigar Fixtures. 201
Schlesinger, Julius. 86 Wooster....Leha Schlesinger. Horses, Trucks, &c. 900
Schnell, Abraham. 347 E 70th... C Dierking. Butcher Fixtures. 217
Schott & Griesel. 241 3d av....Columbia Wagon Co. Wagon. 115
Sazza, James. 247 E 113th ...A Schwaab & Son. Barber Fixtures. 90
Schaffmeier, M J. 408 E 121st....H Moll. Horses, Trucks, &c. (R) 1,500
Scher, B & Co. 16 Monroe....J Stewart. Machinery. 200
Schwendinger & Friedman. 448 E 72d....Burr B Co. Bottler Fixtures. 225
Searing, T W. 118 Lincoln av....H Spies. Machinery. (R) 160
Seligman, Abraham. 88 Delancey....S Proser. Bologne Fixtures. 25
Staub, David. 87 Columbia....Bettie Freiman. Butcher Fixtures. 125
See, J E. 230 E 125th....Jane Peters. Presses. 300
Spann, J H ...N Compton. Surgical Fixtures, &c, on Storage. 110
Smith, H P. 412 Lenox av....J Sirivay. Barber Fixtures. 28
Sundermann, John. 2738 8th av....H Thalmann. Grocery Fixtures. 850
Tereru, Michale...S A Cohen et al. Horse, Wagon. 161
Toner, Joseph. 301 Henry ....J H Lippe. Coach, &c. (R) 481
Tim, David. 280 Broadway....L and S Tim. Office Fixtures, &c. 1,500
Vail, Annie E. Foot East 86th st .. W E Conway. Launch "Elsie V." 246
Voges, F. 125 Crosby ...Mosler Safe Co. Safe. 140
Weidemann, Trangott. 97 Clinton pl....N Althaus. Cigar Fixtures. 500
Watson, Mary. 541 W 53d....R Hill. Grocery Fixtures. 100
Wolf, Ellen. 88 Greenwich ...E Marscheider. Butcher Fixtures. 143
Young, H and C. 211 E 2d....A Sternberg. Press, &c. 150
Young, Thomas. 122 W 29th....Wm McClelland. Horse, Cab, &c. 45

BILLS OF SALE.

Barcalow, G B. 147 W 35th....Anna V McWilliams. Furniture and Horse. 300
Boyd, L M. 22 E 47th....E C Hinsdale. Furniture. 727
Bertie, Annie. 30 and 32 Oak....Minnie Gregory. Saloon. 1
Butt, Charlotte. 40 West End av....J & A Ritter. Furniture. 1
Carbone, Alfonso. 283 Bowery....F Bisnien. Barber Fixtures. ½ int. 250
Duhne, John. 2733 8th av....H Thalmann. Grocery Fixtures. 1,500
Fenz, Frederick. 187th st and Southern Boulevard....A Orthlieb. Horse, Cows, &c..... 150
Giordano, Raffaele. 35 Crosby....Comparato & Colombo. Saloon. 900
Same... same. Saloon. 900
Hanahan, M J. 846 6th av....J R White. Gents Furnishing. 1
Heiter, J G. 136 W 52d... W H Schumacher. Butcher Fixtures. 800
Kutner, Jane. 36 Bond....M Manas. Machinery. 1
Kemp, Richard....M Mayer. Store Fixtures, &c 1
Lambeck & Betz Eagle B Co. 66 Vesey....F Wahler. Saloon. 515
Levy, Martin. 1653 2d av....J DeJong. Gents Furnishing Store. 400
Lepore, Ariello. 60 Flushing av, Brooklyn.....S Petti. Barber Fixtures. 600
Loveday, Edwin. 1337 Broadway....Louisa Loveday. Store Fixtures. 2,000
Meyer, Fred. 232 6th .. Doris Meyer ...Books, Clothing, Jewelry, &c. 50
McCullough, Mary T. 1834 Lexington av....H Vandyke. Furniture. 200
Meyer & Silberstein. 91 Delancey....M Isenberg. Saloon Fixtures. 150
Munger, Thomas & Co. 173 Broadway ...H L Cowles. Office Fixtures. 219
Newman, John. 228 and 230 Stanton....H Newman. Hat Store Fixtures. 150
Pancamo, Antonio. 776 9th av....V Persico. Barber Fixtures. 115
Phillips, E B. 1894 3d av....A Ward. Stock and Store Fixtures. 400
Prescott, H S. 4 and 6 Duane....P B La Roche. Machinery. 200
Romain, G B. 221 W 125th....L Ascher. Paints, &c. 100
Schumacher, W H. 136 W 52d ...Annie Heiter. Butcher Fixtures. 800
Soden, James. 219 W 32d....M Sheridan. Saloon. 1,200
Thomson, George. 46 Broad....D D Ryer. Restaurant Fixtures. 1,100
Thalmann, Herman. 2733 8th av....John Sundermann. Grocery Fixtures. 1,200
Weissenburg, Karl. 554 W 50th .. B Walsh. Saloon. 800

ASSIGNMENT OF CHATTEL MORTGAGES.

Carroll, J W to F W Dunton. (Mort given by S Zipras, Aug 6, 1890). 1
Gabler, Julius to Theo Gabler. (A Hoffman, Feb. 20, 1891.) 95
Lavery, John to Bernheimer & S. (J S Medick, May 1, 1891.) 1
Mariano, Girardo to Feigenspan B Co. (M Patrissio, March 6, 1891.) 1
Silverman, Isaac, 401 Broadway to P Adelson. Debts, Safe and Fixtures. .

KINGS COUNTY.

JULY 23 TO 29—INCLUSIVE.

SALOON AND RESTAURANT FIXTURES.

Bachmann, L. 584 Bushwick av .. M Keller. $800
Brehm, J. 528 Flushing av. .Feigenspan B Co. 650
Brunssen, H. 70 Kent av....Claus Lipsius B Co. 250
Campbell, J. 169 Sackett....P Ballantine & Son. 1,500
Chapman, J. 1426 Bergen... E Ochs. 750
Cumings, J J. 564 Court....H B Scharmann & Sons. 500
Desmond, J. 487 18th....Long Island Brewery. 100
Davidson, R. 151 Furman....G Feigenspan. 700
De Pamo, W. 1783 Fulton... E Ochs. (R) 475
Foley, P B. 704 5th av....A Immig. 1,625
Febinger, P. 1261 Flushing av....C Frese. 450
Fleischmann, J. 23 Jamaica av....Claus Lipsius B Co. 300
Gilligan, J. 500 Henry ..Welz & Zerwick. 2,000
Gannon, P J. 497 Court....P Ballantine & Sons 1,000
Hampson, W T. 407 De Kalb av....W Ulmer. (R) 500
Hart, T A. 823 Myrtle av ..W Ulmer. (R) 500
Hack, C. 184 McKibbin. ..Joseph Fallert B Co. 700
Healey, P. Bridge st, s e cor Tillary st....H C Draper. 859
Higgins, P. 612 Clason av....S Liebmann's Sons B Co. 800
Johnson, G and E. 406 7th av....M Seitz. 585
Jud, G. 193 Wallabout....W Ulmer. 756
King, J. 89 Prospect av....N Seitz. (R) 850
Klett, P. H. 113 Withers....Williamsburgh B Co. 300
Kramer, Anna F. 192 Washington....A Schierenbeck. (R) 2,700
Krancke, F. 526 Wythe av....G Ringler & Co. 599
Krey, P C. 5th av and 34th st....M Seitz. (R) 400
Kaffenberger, P. 244 Court....J Eichler B Co. (R) 600
Kessler, H. 192 Middleton....Burger & Hower B Co. 466
King, J J and J Ridge. 653 3d av....Long Island Brewery. 1,900

Kreusling, J. 228 Cook... Burger & Hower B Co. 750
Landrock, J G. 818 Flushing av....Fort Hamilton B Co. 1,000
Maley, J. 540 Graham av... Berger & Hower B Co. 400
Miller, C. 79 4th av....H B Scharmann & Sons. 700
Mohrmann, C. 619 Fulton... J Ruppert. 5,000
Malone, Annie M and William J Phelan. 144 Court ...Long Island Brewery. 1,500
Matsam, H. 1039 Flushing av... Williamsburgh B Co. 415
McEnerney, J. 141 Gold... M T Garvey. 268
Niederegger, J. Liberty av, s e cor Shepherd av ...W Ulmer. 350
Reilly, J. 479 Humboldt....E Ochs. 700
Ruppel, Jr, H. 88 Wirbers .. Burger & Hower B Co. 400
Senior, C W R. 713 Myrtle av....G Malcom. (R) 1,000
Stewart, W. Park av, s e cor Canton st....H Elias B Co. 1,000
Schippers, F G. 828 Court....P Ballantine & Sons. 400
Stroh, J and T. 229 Rivington st, New York.... F Ibert. (R) 500
Simonson, H J. 708 Wythe av....J Cunningham Son & Co. 250
Steers, M. 11 Bogart....F Ibert. (R) 250
Strecker, K. 1021 Myrtle av....W Ulmer. 400
Thompson, H. 784 Broadway....Claus Lipsius B Co. 1,000
Thompson, G. 673 6th av....M Seitz. (R) 1,500
Von Hassel, P N. 38 South 3d....Burger & Hower B Co. (R) 500
Wioezemer, W. Eastern Parkway, n w cor Thatford av. M Seitz. 660
Wardell, J. 15 Boerum pl....H B Scharmann & Sons. 400
Winter, G and Eliz M. 497 Atlantic av....H Elias B Co. 1,000

HOUSEHOLD FURNITURE.

Arnold, W A. 1476 Pacific....C E Pierce. 100
Biederbick, H. 899 Willoughby av ..Commercial Credit Co. 100
Berrie, Mrs Jennie. 178 Pearl....H Israel & Sons. 512
Buck, W R. 560 Lexington av. . Fennell & P. 108
Clarke, Eliz. 79 Palmetto....A Schulz. 112
Coubro, J. 383½ Union ...W Weed. 180
Cochen, F. 324 Bedford av....Weschler & Abraham. 500
Courtney, Mrs J. 407 Decatur....I Mason. 107
Fitzgerald, J. 151 Baltic....Fennell & P. 203
Freeman, C M 560½ Gates av....F M Freeman. 500
Healy, B and Emma A West. 29 Nevins....H L Morris. 400
Harrison, Jessamine G. 184 Schermerhorn.... J W Hatch. 100
Jones, T. 147 4th av....O'Connor & T. 215
Jordan, Mrs C. 761 De Kalb av....T Kelly. 186
Jewell, Mrs V D. 76 Tillary....T Kelly. 121
Kline, N S. 136 1st pl. ..C E Pierce. 100
Lena Bros. 134 Rochester av....J Kaehl. 200
McGuire, E A. 526 Vanderbilt av....I Mason. 209
Mueller, C A W. 417A 7th av....M M Webster. 107
Miller, Sarah. 11 Brooklyn av ...C S Lacey. 187
Morrison, J F. 149½ Lexington av... Mullins & Sons. 226
O'Hearn, J S. 137 34th....A Pearson. 148
O'Malley, F. 256 Carroll....Sarah A Casanova. 300
Rowan, J. 66 President. . I Mason. 113
Salzman, Mrs. 338 Oakland. I Mason. 252
Schloesser, L. 415 Grove....L Baumann. 206
Sheppard, W W. 426 9th....J A Webb. (R) 520
Sproule, May M. 98 Fulton....McEnery & Co. 154
Thwaite, Amanda A. 268 Gates av....C L Balch. 5,000
Wilson, Mrs E. 324 State ...I Mason. 115
Weidhorn, C A. 818 Evergreen av....J Ryan. 600

MISCELLANEOUS.

Brownson, J M. 39 Harrison....C J Moss. Machinery. (R) 2,880
Same....same. (R) 1,550
Block, A. 50 Moore.. Archer Mfg Co. Barber Fixtures. 167
Bonrke, Anna. 76 Congress....N Langler. Tools, &c. (R) 150
Bowles, J J. 186 Atlantic av....Babcock Printing Press and Mfg Co. Press. 360
Beattie, N....W F Palmer. Horse. 100
Clarin, M....W B Davis. Coach. 400
Clausen & Son. 825 Fulton....J Y Watkins & Son. Confectionery Store. 110
Danzer & Smith. 333 Nevins....J Ruppert. Milk Wagon. 150
De Cesare, Nicola and Luigi. 60 Atlantic av... A Petione. Barber Fixtures. 344
Delaporte, A. 390 5th av....W T Delaporte. Cigar Store Fixtures and Tools. 400
Denig, J. 143 Troutman....A Schulte. Blacksmith Fixtures. 250
Fischer, V. 91 Union....T N Bowles. Barber Fixtures. 150
Fleischhauer, H J. 191 Court .. F W Fleischhauer. Drug Store Fixtures. 100
Flohn, H. 106 5th av....Archer Mfg Co. Barber Fixtures. 158
Francesco, Paolo, Paoletta & Co. 310 Bedford av....G Lordi. Barber Fixtures. (R) 106
Guerin, M J. 114 Bridge....J S Geurin. Bakery Fixtures. 700
Giles, G P. Guernsey st, near Nassau av....W T Palmer. Horses and Trucks. (R) 460
Harms, W. 98 Berry....F Kaiser. Grocery. 2,400
Hill, J T. 404 Tompkins av....M De Meza. Store Fixtures. 66
Lizo, A. 243 Court....Archer Mfg Co. Barber Fixtures. 365
Kneppler, Rasquin & Poor Lithographing Co. 165 Grand....R Hoe & Co. Press. 1,887
Kane, J A. 179 5th av....A D Puffer & Sons. Soda Fountain. 360
Klee, H W. 444 Bedford av....A Levy. Butcher Fixtures. 1,398
Koschorreck, A. 394 Myrtle av....A Kropke. Store Fixtures. 100
Kraus, F R. 57 Ann st, New York....J Wenger. Tools, &c. 750
Kindfoss, I and P Burts. 192 Fulton....C Dierking. Fixtures. 150
Lamb, A. 2049 Fulton .... Archer Mfg Co. Barber Fixtures. 146
Lambert, W W. 63 St Felix....F A Fraser. Printing Fixtures. 500
Lawee, A J. 253 North 2d....Archer Mfg Co. Barber Fixtures. 80
Lees, S. 19 Barclay....Emma J Lees. Fixtures. 125
McDonald and Burns....P Barrett....Wagon. 188
McClean, Mrs Ann. 77 Hudson av....W B Davis. Coach. 650
Moore, W T. 995 Fulton....W Heaney. Hat Store. 1,800
Martin, H. 701 Fulton. ..Nat Cash Register Co. Register. 175
Marino, G. Flushing av....T N Bowles. Barber Fixtures. 178
McGrath, S. 314 Adams.. .Archer Mfg Co. Barber Fixtures. 345
McKinney, J. 374 9th....H Eggers & Co. Grocery Fixtures. 600
Moran, J C. 169 Halsey ...J W Tufts. Soda Apparatus. 250
Olpin, Tillie. 631 Myrtle av....Manges' Bros. Furniture 141
Poppelbaum, T 109-117 Sanford....W Poppelbaum. Horse, &c. 185
Rustmann, J and F. 284 Driggs....W S Travis. Bakery Fixtures. 875
Rimuto, G. 418 Underhill av....Archer Mfg Co. Barber Fixtures. 176
Sheffield & Co. 141 Kosciusko....J P Rathbun & Co. Paper Cutter. 350
Sautter, C F. 335 Grand... J W Tufts. Soda Fountain. 1,000
Smith & Quintoraile. 261 Smith....N. Crastrataro. Barber Fixtures. 75
Wetjen, H... Barrett & B. Wagon. 193
Wilkinson, H. 77 Middleton....L Zealander. Cigar Fixtures. 100
Woodcock, J....Barrett & B. Wagon. 105
Waldeck, C. 21 Alabama av....K Waldeck. Barber Fixtures. 300
White, J B. 365 Flushing av....Archer Mfg Co. Barber Fixtures. 474

BILL OF SALE.

Beer, L. 63 Linden....A Leckner. Furniture. 500
Bierschenk, P. 99 Freeman....C Bierschenk. ½ part of Woodworking Business. 500
Brown, E....Jane Brown. Horse and Cart. nom
Eisele, C. 124 Graham av....Kathie Eisele. Fixtures. 500
Fahrenkopf, J. 70 Central av....Josephine Bieland. Candy and Cigar Store. 335
Folsom, C H. 292 Lafayette av....Annie E Folsom. Furniture. nom
Goldfuss, J. 112 Central av... G Goldfuss. Saloon Fixtures. 2,000
Gulick, E S. Lincoln pl....J P Philip. Horse and Wagon. 500
Herrling, Anna. 148 Troutman....J Denig. Blacksmith Shop. 425
Hoehling, C and H Jantzen. 360 Smith....C Grantz. Grocery Fixtures. 600
Leyh, G F, Jr .... Mary Hauser. Horses, Wagons, &c. 450
Poppelbaum, W. 109-117 Sanford....T Poppelbaum. Horse, &c. 185
Winters, J H. 3d av, cor 45th st....E G Buchanan. Drug Fixtures. 800

ASSIGNMENTS OF CHATTEL MORTGAGE.

Langler & Sons to Maria Danzer. (Mort given by Danzer & Smith, March 7, 1891.) nom
Pierce, D H to J Carden. (J C Clark, Nov. 6, 1890). nom

NEW JERSEY.

NOTE.—*The arrangement of the Conveyances, Mortgages and Judgments in these lists is as follows: the first name in the Conveyances is the Grantor; in Mortgages, the Mortgagor; in Judgments, the Judgment debtor.*

ESSEX COUNTY.

CONVEYANCES.

Ackerman, W A—Miles Downey, Hunterdon st. $2,000
Allen, W L—J L Klink, Rose st.... 875
Aschenbach, S G—J P McFadden, Stanton st.... 1
Baldwin, B E—S C Briant, Baldwin st.......... 1
Ball, Charles—M C Ball, Bloomfield.............. 500
Beck, Charles—M Rachlin, Broome st 1,000
Same——same, Broome st.... 1,500
Same——same, Broome st.............. ... 2,000
Bensmann, Caroline—W Moll, Clinton........... 1
Blake, J L—B S Baker, Orange...... 1,000
Booth, George—C Schuetz, East Orange......... 8,400
Burkhart, J A—J Finan, Orange............... 1
Burnett, A A—T W Hedden, e s Mt Pleasant av 235 s Parker st 25x100.............. 3,000
Burns, Catharine—P Higgins, Ferry st 1,075
Carroll, Bridget—J A Gillick, Tichenor st.. 1
Carver, W S—S P Gilbert, Bloomfield........ ... 800
Cockefair, J A—S P Gilbert, Bloomfield........ 500
Coolbaugh, F W—L Y Dake, East Orange....... 1
Copcutt, J B—A F Eckert, East Orange......... 3,150
Devine, Arthur—G Butts, South Orange 150
Same——H Baumen, Clinton.................. 115
Same——J L Klink, Rose st........ 875
Dodd, J F—S H Dodd, Bloomfield................. 3,000
Dodd, S J—R U Dodd, Montclair................ 1
Doebner, C F—O W Thener, Bergen st.... 1,175
Duryee, W R—J F Fields, Morris av............. 550
Feick, C A——same, Hunterdon st............... 775
Finan, A B—J A Burkart, Orange 1
Frelinghuysen, Frederick—C Van Ness, Emmet st........................ 1,400
Freeman, W A—H Jerolaman, Salt Meadow .. 200
Freye, H H—A Meeker, Orange................. 9,500
Fulcher, A M—A Traphagen, s e s Richmond st 269 s Bank st 30x91.... 4,000
Fullerton, Mary—F W Boroe, South Orange. .. 800
Gilbert, S P—M E Carver, Bloomfield.... 300
Same —M E Carver, Bloomfield 800
Gillick, J A—T Crowell, Tichenor st.... 1
Grass, Lena—E Hartig, Baldwin st............. 2,500
Gsell, Barbara—C Garrod, South Orange av.... 1,500
Hall, C L R—F Schmitt, Walnut st 800
Hanlon, George—M A Harrison, West Orange.. 4,000
Harrison, Martha—M Fanning, East Orange. .. 300
Harvey, J B—J B Bennett, Bloomfield.......... 600
Haug, E M—A Stokesberry, w s Garside st, 25x100.............. 4,700
Hayes, H W—G Spottiswoode, Orange.... 1
Heller, E G—J Dorney, South 9th st 1,500
Heyden, Edward—J Bellamy, Clinton.......... 400
Hoagland, M E—M J Speer, Astor st............ 750
Hopkins, Catharine—E Hopkins, Walnut st..... 10
Kane, Bartholomew—M Smith, Bergen st........ 1,300
Kimball, E A—Wm A Grant, Bloomfield........ 600
Kubach, Catherine—R Kraenzler, South 6th st. 4,000
Kummer, Valentine—H Benz, e s Fairview av, 176 s Spruce st, 100x150.............. 3,000
Lindsley, O W—C A Buso, East Orange.......... 800
Lloyd, Aaron—A E Trusdell, Belleville.......... 43
Lowenstein, Cilli—F Schwarz, w s Belmont av, 455 s Sidney st, 50x100.................. 8,000
Lewy, Philip—K Betz, North 5th st...... 450
Lum, C M—J R Pitcher Milburn 1
McKay, W R—M Ryan, East Orange 250
Meeker, Alfred—H Freye, West Orange. 4,200
Moll, William—C Bensmann, Clinton. 1
Nesler, C L—C Hoerner, Hunterdon st 600
Nevins, Thomas—C Anness, East Orange......... 27,000
Same——R W Lyle, East Orange.............. 40,000
Oberndorf, Julius—L Huxtable, Belleville....... 425
Osborne, J H—F Walz, Clinton....... 650
Pettit, John—C F Harrison, East Orange....... 27,000
Pitcher, H K—C M Lum, Milburn 1
Ragen, Catherine—G Muller, 6th Ward 600
Randall, J M et al—S L Wyman, East Orange... 1
Riker, William—W C Ward, Clinton av......... 1,800
Schlopfur, Jacob—F Dobbins, Caldwell 150
Seaver, S A C—S Hartshorn, Milburn 1,295
Same——same, Milburn............... 1,924
Smith, A B—S A C Seaver, Milburn............ 25
Smith, Patrick—M Burns, Ferry st............. 250
Standard B and L Assoc—T Lander, Forrest st. 1,800
Teed, Phebe—S A C Seaver, Milburn......... .. 10
Theuer, Charles—B Joachim, w s Boyd st 175 n Kinney st 25x100 4,800
The Protestant Foster Home Society—E A M Cumming, e s Mt Prospect av 200 s 2d av 50 x252...................... 5,000
Tuttle, G F—G Spottiswoode, Orange........... 2,065
Wakeman, E P—R D Brower, Milburn.......... 1
Ward, S C—C B Petterson, East Orange......... 2,900
Ward, W C—H F W Willkehr, Chadwick av.... 1,350
Warman, T E—C H Collins, Milburn............ 1
Wesler, J H—E C Beebe, South 12th st.......... 1
Whelan, E M—H Hardy, Poinier............... —
Whitehead, I C—E Jerolaman, Meadows......... 25
Whitehead, W S—H Jerolaman, Newark Meadows.... 25
Wilson, W G—M F Hopkins, Montclair.......... —
Wittcop, Chas—C Feigenspan, Milburn.......... 900
Wood, D H—J Fox, Montclair... 450
Woodruff, J W—J Koester, 4th st............... 600

MORTGAGES.

Adler, Caroline—G Schmitt, Rankin st.... 4,000
Baker, B S—J L Blake, Orange.................. 1,000
Becker, Charles—A Hupfel, William st...... .. . 2,000
Bedell, H A—H C Fisher, East Orange 4,000
Bensmann, Henry—I Waterfield, Clinton 1,400
Benz, Herman—A Steudele, Fairview av........ 400
Same— C Kummer, Fairview av............ 3,000
Brady, Bridget—P Ballentine & Son, Cabinet st. 500
Collins, C H—J H Watson et al, Milburn........ 3,500
Corby, C C—F J Love, Montclair 1,000
Cotterill, R H—M J Richmond, East Orange ... 2,500
Crane, P C—American Ins Co, East Orange..... 1,000
Crevier, J C—P M Hall, Montclair.............. 2,2 0
Cullen, T H—W P Smith, Orange............... 2,200
Darwin, A G—The Home Savings Inst, Bloomfield....................... 5,000
Same——same, Bloomfield..... 5,000
Da Paolo, Vincenzo—P Marcantonio, Orange.... 300
Dodd, S H—J F Dodd, Bloomfield... 2,500
Dorney, John—E G Heller, South 9th st......... 400
Same——Reliable B and L Assoc, South 9th st. 1,400
Downey, Miles—Warren Ackerman, Hunterdon st............................... 1,900
Eckert, A F—F Kays et al, East Orange... 2,000
Edwards, S M—Irvington B and L Assoc, Clinton.. 1,500
Fitzsimmons, Edward—P Fitzsimmons, Lexington st............... 1,000
Flood, John—Lyon & Sons' Brewing Co, Johnson st... 250
Fordham, M E—J H Jackson, Miller st.......... 500
Francisco, L F—R Haddon, Montclair......... ..10,000
Francis, W H—F M Pelletreau, South 6th st..... 1,400
Freiday, Annie—T L Smith, Orange........... 2,000
Freye, Henry—S Martin, West Orange.......... 2,000
Fuchs, Jacob—Reliable B and L Assoc, West Parker st 1,700
Garrod, Charles—B Gsell, South Orange av.... 600
Gegenheimer, J P et al—The Mechanics' B and L Assoc, Prince st............................ 4,000
Haley, A A— . Dougherty, South Orange av.... 2,750
Hanley, Elizabeth—F E Hedden, Orange... 2,500
Harriett, D F—Montclair B and L Assoc, Montclair....................................... 2,000
Harris, Theophilia—E L Hobson, Boudinot st... 1,000
Same——M T Barrett, Boudinot st.... 800
Harrison, C F—The Newark Fire Ins Co, East Orange.... 12,500
Hedden, F W—A A Burnett, Mt Pleasant av.... 1,500
Higgins, Patrick—H A Richard, Ferry st........ 350
Jacobus, Lucy—The American Ins Co, Boyden st 400
Joachim, Benjamin—M A Roder, Boyden st..... 400
Same——Standard B and L Assoc, Boyd st . 3,600
Kling, Philip—C Kamlah, Belleville........ 20,000
Same——same, Belleville.. 8,000
Same——same, Belleville...................... 7,000
Klink, J L—A Devine, Rose st 600
Same——W L Allen, Rose st.................. 600
Klink, Minnie—Security Savings Bank, 5th av... 1,000
Knoebel, Peter—C A Feick, Ferry st............ 250
Lee, Rose—The North End B & L Assoc, Ridge st.... 2,900
Lender, Titus—Standard B & L Assoc, Forrest st.................. 1,800
Livingston, Bennett, Jr—P Gans, Orange 300
Lyon, C E—L K Conklin, 5th av................ 600
Martin, S A—The Bloomfield Savings Inst, Montclair.................. 8,600
Moll, William—C Bensmann, Clinton............ 2,000
Monaghan, T J A—T Harding, 59th st 200
Metcalf, R F—A Dodd exr, Bloomfield.......... 7,000
Nolan, John—A H Campfield, East Orange . 400
Rachlin, Morris—C Beck, Broome st............ 2,500
Reynal, L S—N C Van Reyper, Montclair.. 400
Ryan, D J—Mutual B & L Assoc—Chestnut st.. 3,000
Schaible, John—M Buehler, Boyd st..... 2,500
Schmidt, Heinrich—E Knoeller, Magnolia st.... 2,000
Smith, C D—R J Stillwell, Clinton. 240
Stainsby, William—F B Allen exr, Prince st.... 1,000
Stryker, A A—L Leverich, North 17th st........ 3,000
Studer, A C—P H Edmonston, Montclair.... 3,500
Trabert, Louis—E E Coe exrs, West Kinney st.. 1,000
Traphagen, Albert—A M Fulcher, Richmond st. 3,400
Usher, William—F H Wismer, Canfield st 100
Viscidi, Philip—D Wilson, Bank st.... 5,000
Wadsworth, E M—People's Bank, East Orange. 2,500
Waldron, C A—M A Waldron, South Orange ... 225
Williams, R G—The Protestant Foster Society, Orange 4,600
Woods, Patrick—F Bonykamper, Jackson st.... 100
Woodward, Joseph—W Musgrove, Plane st.... 3,000
Wurster, Christian—Passaic B and L Assoc, Camden st........... 1,200
Zehner, Magdalena—Fireside B and L Assoc, Livingston st...... 400
Zehff, M A—Howard Savings Inst, Belleville.... 2,300

JUDGMENTS.

Greenberg, K—L Mendel.... 437
Huelsenbach, Ernest—Racine Wagon and Carriage Co 189
Man, Frederick—J R Pitcher.... .... 2[illegible]

Morris, A P—C B Smith et al. 326
Smith, M E—G M Titus. 343
Ulrich, T G—J S Crane et al. 504
Zehmer, Gottlieb—The Home Brewing Co. 259

CHATTEL MORTGAGES.

Benzing, G F—F Lisiewski, saloon. 900
Bestle, Gottlieb—F J Kastner, saloon. 380
Bush, H M—G B Snyder, horse and buggy. 150
Dempsey, James—The Essex Brewing Co, saloon 400
Dougherty, Joseph—F J Kastner, saloon. 150
Dunnigan, Catherine—C Bierman, furniture. 48
Feeney, Ellen—F Lisiewski, saloon. 575
Hector, Louis—F J Kastner, saloon. 616
Herrmann, John—M J Oakes, stock, shoes, &c. 100
Karp, Jacob—D Blackwood et al, horse and wagon. 50
Lang, John—F Lisiewski, saloon. 800
Ludwig, Edward—E E Dieffenbach, saloon. 200
McConnell, John—G Feigenspan, saloon. 817
McMahon, James—Lyon & Sons Brewing Co, saloon. 282
Nutzel, P B—F J Kastner, saloon. 400
Peter, Richard—F Lisiewski, saloon. 1,200
Weber, Philip—M Meyer & Son, horses and trucks. 300

HUDSON COUNTY.

CONVEYANCES.

Ahlgreen, Gustav—A Stendahl, Kearney. $1,050
Allen, Robert and M M Forrest—L C Hopkins, Kearney. 900
Same——L C Niff, Kearney. 535
Same——J Cameron, Kearney. 2,900
Baile, Mary—Adelheid M Duhume, J City. 10,000
Barnes, Reon—The Jersey City Terminal Railroad Co, J City. nom
Benson, Jas—D R Atwell, Hoboken. 5,800
Bliss, Amelia F—J Nimino, J City. 400
Bloodgood, Clara—T B O'Neill, J City. 1,800
Bond, J M—Catharine Lally, Hoboken. 50
Boorsem, Cornelia V V, by exr—W Redlich, J City. 1,000
Bramhall, W E—A A Parker, J City. 900
Branagan, J B—H E Pepper, North Bergen. 2,500
Brenner, Arthur—G Brenner, J City. nom
Brenner, Geo—G Shearer, J City. 400
Brickwedel, Johanna—J Spielmann, J City. 5,000
Brophy, Alice—J Kirly, Bayonne. nom
Burke, Timothy—E F Emmons, J City. 9,300
Carwick, Jno—The West Side Connecting R Co, Bayonne. 2,000
Cazassa, Antonio—T Carmody, Hoboken. 1,220
Chamberlain, Alonzo—Caroline V Green, J City. 5,250
Christie, Anna by exr—S Kelly, J City. 2,400
Clos, Rosaline—H H Schultze, J City. 5,800
Cosgrove, Susan A—J Davison, J City. 2,500
Coudert, F R—Cath Schieferstein, Bayonne. 2,000
Same——Eliza Schieferstein, Bayonne. 2,000
Cox, Geo—Margaret Bryan, North Bergen. 3,125
Craig, C P—O Frommel, Hoboken. 800
Craney, Ed—Mary A Craney, Kearney. nom
Dieck, C C F—J Rottjer, Hoboken. 13,000
Drassel, Fred—Elizabeth B Bergeman, J City. 9,250
Earle, Maria C—C F Ruh, North Bergen. 1,225
Edelstein, John—J Roche, J City. 6,000
Evarts, D R—O Peterson, J City. 8,300
Eoff, H A—Mary J Regan, Bayonne. 1,400
Feury, N E—Maria Jensen, J City. 1,200
Fox, Chas—F Zergner, Union. 800
Frommel, Oscar and Annie—G Costanzo, Hoboken. 550
Same——M Piero, Hoboken. 550
Gardner, E D—J Gardner, Union. nom
Hatch, Anna K—Marg M Amon, J City. 5,500
Hedderick, Jacob by sheriff—J S Gerdes, Weehawken. 1,425
Hicht, Emile—Anna Nordenholtz, West Hoboken. 8,500
Hinrich, Elizabeth W—A T Bruegmann, Guttenberg. 1,200
Hoboken Land and Impt Co—O Menaber, Weehawken. 4,000
Same——T Kirchgesner, West Hoboken. 900
Same——J E Coane, Hoboken. 3,115
Same——J A Rosenbaum, Hoboken. 4,000
Same——W Utz, Hoboken. 1,068
Hudson City Savings Bank—E Dougherty, J City. 1,700
Jewell, C C—P Abstein, J City. 2,800
Jones, J M—J L Blaher, J City. 1,350
Kingsbury, J A—M Forster, J City. 1,250
Kneale, F S—E Kneale, J City. 1,600
Kuver, William—H Stockfisch, West Hoboken. 565
Lewis, David—J Edelstein, J City. 4,200
McLaughlin, G S by trustee—G S McLaughlin, J City. ——
Meyer, G W—J Ludwig, West Hoboken. 600
Mccrey, Pat—R Mooney, Hoboken. nom
Mount, S C—J Wennagel, Bayonne. 250
Ogden, W B by exrs—J Randall, J City. 1,000
Owen, B C—T B Luther et al, J City. 4,750
Perkins, Cath T—F Delaney, West Hoboken. nom
Pierson, Susan J—H Jurgensen, J City. 1,300
Poirett, Nora—L Bidley, J City. 2,500
Rapp, Louis—S Rapp, Union. nom
Rapp, Samuel—Henrietta Rapp, Union. nom
Reilan, M K—C Dunn, Kearney. nom
Rice, S M—C W Mueller, J City. 1,500
Roach, William—B P McClane, Kearney. 1,300
Rosenbaum, J A—J E Coane, Hoboken. 1,500
Schneider, C A—C A Schneider, West Hoboken. nom
Shannon, Rose A—Harriet J Francesco, J City. 3,300
Sipp, Maria L by guard—Cath E Sipp, J City. 600
Soulard, W M—W V Garrison, J City. 2,800
Steele, Annie H—J Carr, Harrison. 1,000
Tagart, Laura V—J McKendry, Bayonne. 400
The Delta Co—A Miller, J City. 300
The Indian Spring Land Co—Emile Hicht, West Hoboken. 2,000
Same——H Roberts, Hoboken. 5,700
The Standard B & L Assoc—Barbara Biegner, Harrison. 3,000
Tonnele, Cecile by trustee—G Liederthal, J City 7,000
Utz, Will—W J Irving, Hoboken. 2,250
Vandall, Cath—J Kirwan, J City. 1,500
Van Emburgh, R J—O Verilhac, Kearney. 1,400
Van Emburgh, Thos—R S Pierce, Kearney. 500
Van Winkle, Aletta A—W Bender, J City. 3,000
Wanters, Sarah G—P S Bonner, Bayonne. 500
Whiton, Caroline W—P M Griffith, J City. 11,000
Same——West Side Connecting R R Co, J City. 777
Whiton, L C——same, J City. 2,592
Wickham, Jno—L P Druck, West Hoboken. 650

MORTGAGES.

Atwell, D R—Hoboken B & L Assoc, Hoboken, installs. 6,800
Baker, J G—Emeline Davison, Kearney, 1 year. 1,500
Biede, Ellen—H L Timken, J City, 1 year. 378
Biegne, John—Standard B & L Assoc, Harrison, installs. 5,000
Blaber, J L—J M Jones, J City, 1 year. 1,300
Bond, F J—M Charavay, J City, 2 years. 200
Bryan, Margaret—G Cox, North Bergen, 3 years 2,000
Bergman, Eliza B—C Pflining, J City, 3 years. 5,500
Burke, Timothy—J E Andrus, J City, 3 morts, each $2,500, 3 years. 7,500
Cameron, John—Ann Palmer, exr, Kearney, 3 years. 1,500
Same——R Allen, Kearney, 1 year. 350
Carstens, Nicholas—A Rader, Hoboken, 3 years. 600
Coane, J E—Hoboken Bank for Savings, Hoboken, 5 years. 5,000
Same——same, Hoboken, 5 years. 5,000
Crawford, Rebecca A—People's B & L Assoc, Kearney, installs. 5,000
Dieck, C & F—H Bahrenburg, Hoboken, 3 years. 6,000
Disque, Katharine—Maria Leich, J City, 1 year. 1,000
Dorr, Henry—Hoboken Bank for Savings, J City, 3 years. 1,000
Dowd, Dennis—The Hudson Trust and Savings Inst, West Hoboken, 5 years. 4,000
Dougherty, Edward—Hudson City Savings Bank, J City, 1 year. 1,000
Duhme, Adelheid M—Mary Baile, J City, 3 yrs. 5,500
Edmonds, Nettie L—J A Edmonds, Kearney, 3 years. 2,000
Edwards, W W—Sarah T Van Cleaf, J City, 1 year. 2,000
Same——Amelia L Van Cleaf, J City, 1 year. 1,500
Finn, Mary—Highland M B and L Assoc, J City, installs. 5,000
Frommel, Oscar—C P Craig, Hoboken, 1 year. 400
Gennert, Gregor—T McNally, Union, 3 years. 1,000
Giblin, Jas—Jno C Crevier, Hoboken, 3 years. 300
Goodard, Alice S E—Merchants Bank of Newport, North Bergen, 3 years. 5,004
Gray, Mary—C G Adolph, Weehawken, 3 years. 1,100
Greene, Caroline A—E Greene, Jr, J City, 3 yrs. 3,900
Hanson, J G—D Van Buskirk, Bayonne, installs. 600
Haas, Jno—The Hudson Trust and Savings Inst, West Hoboken, 5 years. 4,500
Henderson, John—J H Rudiger, J City, 3 years. 550
Heskard, Mary C—C L Corbin, Bayonne, 1 year. 150
Hill, Chas—Mutual Life Ins Co, J City, 1 year. 10,000
Joest, Leonhard—The Hudson Trust and Savings Inst, West Hoboken, 1 year. 1,400
Keeley, Martin—A Semrad, Hoboken, 5 years. 3,500
Same——T Forster, Hoboken, 1 year. 600
Kinkelin, Rose—The Hudson Trust and Savings Inst, West Hoboken, 3 years. 1,500
Kirwan, John—Catharine Vandel, J City, 2 yrs. 750
Klein, Joan—Hudson Co Caledonian B and L Assoc, J City, installs. 1,792
Kneale, Edward—The Industrial M B and L Assoc, J City, installs. 1,000
Lau, James—D Reardon, J City, 2 years. 500
Lindenthal, Gustav—Trustee of Cecile Tonnele, J City, 5 years. 6,000
Luther, T H and T J Murphy—The New Jersey Title and Guarantee and Trust Co, J City, installs. 2,500
McDermott, Timothy—Charlotte Muller, J City, 3 years. 5,000
McEvoy, T F—J P J McEvoy, J City, 1 year. 2,203
McInness, Elizabeth—A Dunken, J City, 3 years 1,500
Muller, Barthasar—C Schmidt, West Hoboken, 3 years. 1,500
Muller, C W—S M Rice, J City, 1 year. 1,500
Muller, Elizab—Henrietta Cheseborough, West Hoboken, 2 years. 600
Nepwoda, Joseph—The Hudson Trust and Savings Inst, North Bergen, 1 year. 4,000
Nimmo, Sarah J—Sarah A Kingsland, Bayonne, 3 years. 1,700
Peppers, H E—C Schmidt, North Bergen, 3 yrs. 1,300
Pierce, C A—Exr W Veitch, Kearney, 3 years. 2,000
Piero, Michael—O Frommel, Hoboken, 1 year. 800
Peterson, Oscar—Elizabeth Evart, J City, installs. 2,700
Rentschler, Adam—Passaic B & L Assoc, Kearney, installs. 5,000
Schieferstein, Elizabeth—F R Condict, Bayonne, 2 years. 1,500
Same——same, Bayonne, 1 year. 1,000
Sheehey, Margaret—Hoboken Bank for Savings, Hoboken, 1 year. 1,100
Skillman, Jacob—J H Newkirk, J City, 1 year. 800
Stendahl, Anton—G Gauls, Kearney, 1 year. 300
Trustees of St Peter and Paul Greek Catholic Church—Mina Silkowsky, J City, 1 year. 3,500
Tyler, N P—Mary E Miller, Bergen, 1 year. 500
Verilhac, Oscar—P Murder, Kearney, 1 year. 1,600
Wilkinson, Anna M—Jennie E Preston, Harrison, 1 year. 1,000
Zeigler, Frank—C Fox, Union, 1 year. 500

CHATTEL MORTGAGES.

Rorig, Caspar, Hoboken—The William Peter Brewing Co, saloon fixtures. 1,471
Brehm, Jno, J City—Jordan & Moriarty, furniture. 77
Clark, Cornelia, J City—C Birdsall, furniture. 130
Condon, Pat, J City—Beadleston & Woerz, saloon lease. 300
Eakens, William, Bayonne—C Feigenspan, saloon. 400
Eckhardt, L A, J City—E M Traves & Co, horse, wagon and harness. 315
Edwards, Maria, J City—Jordan & Moriarty, furniture. 50
Garrison, W L, J City——same, furniture. 83
Grant, P F, J City—Bernheimer & Schmidt, saloon and lease. 350
Halbohm, H W, Jr, J City—O N Van Campen & Son, grocery business, horse, wagon and harness. 230
Kett, W F, J City—Lembeck & Betz Eagle Brewing Co, saloon and lease. 421
Kirchhoff, C B, Hoboken——same, saloon and lease. 625
Link, Frank, Hoboken—Bernheimer & Schmidt, saloon and fixtures. 300
Macnal, G R and Pauline T, J City—A F Archibald, furniture. 1,000
McEwen, A C, J City—Eliza J Eveland, 2 boilers and 1 Green steam engine, with fixtures. 4,000
Murphy, Thos, J City—J J Tighe, saloon. 800
Nolan, Ellen W, Hoboken—L Bauman, furniture. 103
Noonan, Jas, J City—The Indian Wharf Brewing Co, saloon and fixtures. 250
Peter, Williams, J City—The Bavarian Brewing Co, saloon. 400
Riplo, Eliza, J City—C Birdsall, furniture. 100
Schultze, Jacob, J City——same, furniture. 130
Scott, J J, J City—The William Peter Brewing Co, saloon and fixtures. 600
Smith, Maria, J City—L Bauman, furniture. 99
Wakefield, O M, J City——same, furniture. 92
Wilson, A R, J City——same, furniture. 105

BILLS OF SALE.

Hansen, F C, Union—J A Ross, office furniture and ½ office. 400
Meyer, Robt, J City—A Meyer, horse, wagon, harness. 500

JUDGMENTS.

Egan, Mary—L B Frank. 299
Frisch, Frederick—M Latz. 1,204
Haege, Adolph—The Hudson Trust and Savings Inst. 330
Maddigan, James—J Connelly. 177
Mulcahey, James—Z Mulcahey. 158
Steinhauer, Mary—Sonn Bros. 327
Wholey, Dennis—Consumers' Coal and Ice Co. 108
Yoe, S P—A Speer. 205

MECHANIC'S LIEN.

The Bradley & Currier Co (Lim), claimant; Christian Becker, builder; William Peter, Jr, owner, Weehawken. 294

BUILDING MATERIAL MARKET.

BRICKS.—Reports upon the condition of the market for Common Hards cover no new suggestions, and receivers and dealers frankly confess they have about exhausted their fund of information. The situation has one merit in sustaining about the same general range of values as for two or three weeks past, indicating probably that cost has settled to about as low a level as it is likely to go, and may, if it gets any kind of a grip, take a turn for the better. The current week's business has been somewhat smaller than the preceding one, owing to a great deal of unfavorable weather, not only preventing work on buildings but also interfering with the handling of stock by those who might feel willing to pile away a little, and as arrivals did not appear to get a check there has in natural course been a larger amount afloat. The storms may have an effect to make some washed brick from the present production, which will come in later on, but down to date the quality has continued uniformly and remarkably fine, and it would be a very captious buyer who was unable to make a satisfactory investment either as to quality or price from the offering now available. Indeed at the low cost of material the wonder is that no more of it passes into consumption, as the improvement of real estate upon present basis would make it a formidable competitor with structures erected a comparatively short time ago, when the value line of all component parts was much higher. For Pales there has been a direct demand of fair proportions and, if quality is fine, $2.50 per M paid without much question, but faulty stock buyers did not appear to want at any price.

GLASS.—No very great amount of animation can be found on the local market for either domestic or foreign stock, yet there is a little moving out all the while, and some of the trade think business is quite as full as the average for this time of year. Holders are prepared to meet any ordinary call, both in the matter of quantity and assortment, and are adhering to a steady line of valuation. From primary sources the accounts are generally in good shape, and a letter from Pittsburg this week suggests that when production is resumed prices may be advanced. There is, however, evidently a fear that some trouble may arise over the question of wages.

HARDWARE.—The distribution of supplies to dependent interior points commences to increase somewhat, and operators are correspondingly hopeful. Local demand, however, does not improve to any extent, and for many lines of even staple goods the outlet is very much below the average for the season. To a certain extent dealers have provided for the contingency by keeping stocks a little low, but they have quite enough to satisfy any ordinary call made upon them. Prices as a rule are irregular, with a weakish sort of tendency, though the only recent reduction of importance is on Wood Planes, for which the modified discount sheet stands at 40 and 10 per cent on Molding and Fancy Planes; 50 and 10 on first quality Bench Planes; 55 and 10 on second quality do., and 25 and 10 on Apple, Box, and Rosewood Planes.

LATH.—There did not appear to be anything new in the conditions as compared with those prevailing one week ago. A few more parcels came to hand; but where they were not already under engagement buyers stood ready to negotiate promptly, and the only complaint receivers make is their inability to promptly satisfy all the custom that applies to them for stock. No advance has as yet been made in price, the figure on latest quotation standing at $2.25 per M, but it is strong enough at that, and was it sure that Northern stock would not come forward an uppish turn would at once develop.

LIME.—The market has improved in tone, and for Common the line of valuation and "quotation" is advanced to $1.00 per bbl. without changing the figure on Finishing and there is at the moment one price all around. Some cargoes have been dropping in right along, but they were apparently not equal to demand for the ordinary grade and hence the advance, though some operators seem to think that after a temporary flurry the figure will drop back again. Advices from the primary points indicate partial and cautious production with an effort to keep shipments down to moderate proportions.

LUMBER.—Reports differ as to the amount of business doing again, but only a few yards particularly well located for catching the cream of the trade seem to substantiate a claim for much animation, and as a whole the market cannot be called better than fairly active. For building consumption the deliveries are mainly on contract, with unusually few additional calls making, and where there is new trade found it seems to come in the main from furniture and other manufacturers. The attitude of dealers toward bulk lots of stock also appears quite indifferent, and they are standing out better than anticipated. It appears to be simply a matter of seeing no reason for hurrying investment, and embodies nothing in the way of objection to cost or the assortment available. Indeed, aside from the temporary absence of the Eastern product, there has been a plentiful offering, at a plane of valuation that cannot be considered unreasonable, and succumbing to the importunities of the salesmen working the market for all it is worth, dealers picking an odd lot here and another there, where the goods appeared peculiarly adapted to their wants, are probably taking more stock than generally supposed. From pretty much all primary sources the evidences indicate a measurable display of steadiness, but dealers looking somewhat anxiously for custom.

Eastern Spruce does not appear to have done quite as well as anticipated. Receivers for two or three weeks have had a decided advantage in the comparatively light arrival and the stoppage of production at some of the principal mills, and buyers compelled to negotiate could make little progress except at fairly full bids. The enforced demand however has turned out smaller than calculated upon, the voluntary inquiry amounted to practically nothing, and hence the paucity of supplies failed materially in its force as a stimulating factor. Dealers either had greater accumulation on hand than was anticipated, or consuming wants have been over-estimated, but it is certain that a feature which, under most circumstances, would cause a boom, has failed to give the seller any unusual advantage. Some specials are being handed in, but negotiations thereon proceed slowly in view of the full rates mill men ask at the present juncture.

Within a few days there have been some comparatively numerous arrivals of cargoes from both St. John and Maine ports, but most of them were under contract, and have been a long while afloat owing to adverse winds. All available for open market use found ready sale.

Piling continues in fair request, as it goes into a great deal of work under contracts that permit of no delay or suspension, so long as supplies are available at least. With continued arrivals and a good accumulation of logs in chains, offerings continue to balance current wants fully, and values do not seem as yet to get a foothold for improvement, though they are held at about level with some steadiness.

Hemlock is getting more attention and the market brightens somewhat. One of our largest dealers in Pennsylvania product informs us that at his office, located near the mills, orders are at last commencing to come in with some little showing of freedom, and, while he cannot say as well for the trade in this vicinity, there is, nevertheless, some increase, and it is a cheering straw. Supplies are plenty enough to meet all calls promptly, but kept well in band, and former rates supported with little or no difficulty.

White Pine finds its average proportion of demand on the distributive outlet, and is getting some increase of trade in the way of bulk parcels. The latter is not particularly conspicuous, but from the numerous agents running about with more or less liberal tenders, both as to variety and cost, dealers are finding it possible to pick up considerable stuff well adapted to their regular natural wants, and they contract accordingly. Western sellers appear to have the most success in obtaining custom at the moment. The export deal runs along about as before, a fair call developing for cheap stuff, but trade with "the River" affording no encouragement.

Yellow Pine meets with a moderately active call and mainly in the way of specifications for good assortments to come in later, or specials against some particular job. All demands can be and are promptly met with rates ruling in a general way about as before, though desirable custom is probably able to secure moderate unquotable favors. Some operators are quite sanguine that there will be a much healthier market before the fall season has progressed very far.

Carolina Pine is another wood upon which operators pin a great deal of faith, and they expect to retain advantage without much difficulty. Indeed, the very spirit of caution, so universal, is expected to benefit Carolina Pine, but inducing many buyers to seek a moderate cost article, and the calculation is that while the amount immediately handled may not prove very large, new custom will be introduced to the wood and discover its merits so well as to remain constant buyers in the future.

Hardwood cannot be called active, but there is a little ripple of trade all the while, the demand mainly from furniture manufacturers and the makers of miscellaneous products. Manufacturers of house trim are poor customers under the dual influence of unusually light calls from actual consumers and pretty fair stocks remaining on hand. Prices are nominally steady, but on bulk lots the general chances are in favor of buyers who will make up any respectable sized bill. The action of the railway companies in charging $1 per car demurrage where cars are detained longer than two days is less severely criticised by regular operators than at first. They find that the companies want the cars more than they do the money, are disposed to be lenient with the regular customers, but rigid with the casuals who use the tracks and cars for holding their stuff until it is sold, and it becomes more and more apparent that the enforcement of the rule is almost sure to shut off a great amount of rag-tag and bob-tail stuff for which the market has no use.

A recent decision by Board of General Appraisers, possibly of interest to some of the trade, is reported as follows:

W. J. Sloan vs. Collector at New York.—The merchandise is kiaki timber, sawed in such a manner as to be too small for shipbuilding or fit only for rowboats or small bay craft. It was assessed at 15 per cent ad valorem as cabinet wood not further advanced than being sawed. The importers claim exemption as ship timber. The Collector's decision is affirmed.

The exports of lumber, exclusive of hardwood, from the port of New York during the month of July were as follows:

	1890. Feet.	1891. Feet.
To West Indies	2,948,000	1,486,000
To South America	1,979,000	1,177,000
To East Indies	847,000	1,452,000
To Europe	121,000	18,000
Total feet	[illegible]	4,133,000
Previously reported	44,058,000	45,4[illegible],000
Total since Jan. 1	49,913,000	49,559,000

GENERAL LUMBER NOTES.

STATE.

The Albany market is reported by the *Argus* as follows:

The market this week is exceedingly dull and likely to remain so for a month to come. There is always more or less of a stagnation in business during July and August, but this year beats them all; in fact, it is a complete paralysis. The demand for lumber of all kinds has fallen off so that there is hardly enough shipping to keep the hands busy, and the break in the canal, which will take some time to repair, has stopped the receipts of lumber from the West. This, however, has no injurious effect on the market, as the majority of the yards are overstocked, and the temporary delay in receipts will give the dealers an opportunity to work off a little of the stock on hand. Some of the firms in the district claim to be even with last year on their sales, while others profess to be behind, but all look forward hopefully to a good trade in the fall. The demand, such as it is, seems to be pretty evenly distributed among the different grades and dimensions. One and one-quarter inch lumber of all kinds is scarce, while the stock of boards and shippers is hardly in excess of the demand. Cull spruce and hemlock, as well as good, is enjoying a fair trade, but orders are not as heavy as they should be. Hardwoods are in moderate demand. Canal freights to Albany, from all points, are lower than ever before, but there is a rumor of an advance in freights on the lakes, owing to a movement in grain, which, if true, will have a tendency to advance freights on the canal. There is a large quantity of lumber at the shipping points to come forward, but the break in the canal will prevent the dealers from obtaining advantage of the present low rates, which cannot prevail long at the best. Quotations remain unchanged, as the condition of trade does not warrant any fluctuations.

THE WEST.

The Northwestern *Lumberman* as follows:

In western white pine there are reasons to expect some advance in prices as winter approaches. The streams are low and the logs on many of them are either hung up or are coming slowly. Some of the mills on the Green bay shore have about exhausted their supply of logs, and their operators are talking of shutting down at an early day. Since all the season there has, in this market, been no oversupply of framing dimension or good common and better lumber, and the outlook of fall trade is good, the tendency is rather to an advance of prices than otherwise. Local consumption in this city is taking care of a vast amount of lumber. Added to the ordinary building requirement, the world's fair enterprise is calling for extensive bills of timber, joists and scantling, as well as other forms of lumber. This demand will swell to an immense aggregate as the work progresses, and is bound to be a pronounced feature of the trade here, no matter what condition of depression may prevail in other portions of the country. It will also have considerable influence in Wisconsin, Michigan and even in the south, as mills in that section will be called on to furnish a large amount of the stuff required.

The manufacturers and dealers on the upper Mississippi and throughout northwest Wisconsin have for several weeks past reported a large volume of trade. Some say that in point of the amount of lumber being disposed of, no reasonable man could complain. But prices are unremuneratively low. This is considered beyond explanation. But the cause of it is doubtless in the fact that the supply at outside points, especially in the south, is pressing into a common field of distribution, and northern lumber must sell at prices that are successfully competitive with rival product. Recent advices from the Dakotas are to the effect that the crop prospect in those regions is exceedingly bright. If there shall be no failure in the outcome it will insure a heavy demand in the northwest throughout the fall and winter.

Surveying the entire country, and noting various conditions and prospects, we can conclude that, though the expected revival of demand is tediously slow in coming, there are good grounds for looking for somewhat better times in the early fall, with a probability that the demand will rise to a heavy volume early in the coming year.

At Chicago the commission dealers say that the yard docks are well filled up with unpiled stock, which may have some influence in preventing dealers from taking hold freely. This is likely to be a feature of trade during the fall. Dealers have got into the habit of leaving lumber unpiled as long as possible for the purpose of selling it off dock and thus avoiding the expense of piling.

The Mississippi Valley *Lumberman* as follows:

There is no doubt that the low prices which have prevailed are due in a large measure to the financial stringency from which the country has not yet recovered. There has been a desire upon the part of many lumbermen to realize. In the west the bankers have gradually been fortifying themselves against the prospective large call for money to move the crops. There has been a disposition shown everywhere to accumulate money against the usual fall stringency and the situation now is not likely to be very much changed until after the money begins to flow back from the farmers and until the European demand for wheat—sure to be enjoyed—shall bring back some of the gold which has been going steadily across the water.

NAILS.—Business shows the usual erratic tendencies and reports at times are widely variable. On the average, however, there is probably nothing more than a good routine trade doing, and buyers obtain such stock as they desire at about former rates. We quote Cut at $1.65@1.75 per keg for car lots and $1.75@1.85 per keg for parcels from store, for iron, and add 5@10c. per keg for steel; Wire, $2.10@2.15 at mills, and 2.30@2.40 from store.

PAINTS, OILS, COLORS, ETC.—Trade is moving slowly, and without features or elements calling for extended notice or explanation. Buyers seem to have caught the hand-to-mouth method all the way from the actual consumer back to the largest jobber, and in so pronounced form that it would be folly to attempt forcing a change. Many dealers, however, assert that they are really doing about all that can be expected at this juncture, and predict a good fall and winter trade as the outcome of the liberal harvests now apparently secured. There will not be any very extensive local consumption, however, before spring. Supplies continue to be kept under good control and valued about as before, the sustaining of the late advance on white lead acting as quite a stay to the whole market and offsetting the decline in oil. Association Corroders' rates stand as follows: Lead in oil in kegs and dry lead in kegs, in lots of less than 500 lbs., 7¼c. net; in lots of 500 lbs to 5 tons at one purchase, 7c.; 5 tons to 12 tons, one purchase, 6¾c.; 12 tons and over, one purchase, 6¾c.; dry white lead in bbls. ½c per lb. less than price in kegs. Lead in oil 12½ lb. in tin pails, add 1c.; in 25 and 50 lb. tin pails, add ½c.; and in 1 to 5 lb. tin cans, assorted (100 lbs. in case) add 2½c. per lb. to keg price. Terms on lots on 500 lbs. and over, note or acceptance at sixty days, or 2½ per cent. discount will be allowed for cash paid within fifteen days of invoice date. To make either of the above required quantities any assortment of packages of white lead, red lead and litharge may be counted. The above quotations are free on board cars or boat at corroding point. Linseed Oil has a feverish sort of market, as buyers are uncertain what the next move on prices may be and are unable to shape their operations at the moment. We quote at general range at 42@44c. for Western, and 44@56c. for City. Spirits Turpentine has continued in buyers' favor under a steadily accumulating stock, and a moderate indifferent demand from all sources. We quote at 35¼@36½c. per gallon, according to quality, delivery, etc.

TAR AND PITCH.—Demand retains a fair amount of force and volume for this season of the year, but there is not much in the market at the moment. Stocks are so controlled as to insure steady rates and sellers appear cheerful. We quote Pitch at $1.70@1.75 per bbl.; Tar at $2.15@2.50, according to quantity, quality and delivery.

MISCELLANEOUS.

MISCELLANEOUS.

MISCELLANEOUS

REAL ESTATE RECORD AND BUILDERS' GUIDE.
ESTABLISHED MARCH 21st 1868.
DEVOTED TO REAL ESTATE, BUILDING, ARCHITECTURE, HOUSEHOLD DECORATION, BUSINESS AND THEMES OF GENERAL INTEREST

PRICE, PER YEAR IN ADVANCE, SIX DOLLARS.

Published every Saturday.

TELEPHONE - - - - CORTLANDT 1370.

Communications should be addressed to

C. W. SWEET, 14 & 16 Vesey St

J. T. LINDSEY, Business Manager.

VOL. XLVIII AUGUST 8, 1891. NO. 1,221

The publication offices of THE RECORD AND GUIDE *have been removed to Nos. 14 and 16 Vesey street, over The Mechanics' and Traders' Exchange, a few feet west of Broadway.*

THE NEW ARCHITECTURAL MAGAZINE.

The first number of THE ARCHITECTURAL RECORD *is issued to-day, and may be purchased at the Elevated Road stands, or book-sellers, or it may be ordered at the offices of publication, Nos. 14 and 16 Vesey street. It is not too much to say that every one who takes an intelligent interest in the Architecture, the construction or the embellishment of the buildings he lives in or frequents should subscribe to this magazine, which treats of all of these matters from the highest point of view, yet in a popular and interesting way. The contributors are men of repute—experts in the matters of which they treat. The magazine is profusely illustrated, contains sixty-four large plates of interiors and exteriors of buildings, new designs in electrical fixtures, furniture, etc. The paper used is of the best quality, and the printing, which has been done by "The Record and Guide" press, is an excellent example of the highest modern typography. Annual subscription: one dollar.*

DURING the past week stocks have shown that they could go up as well as go down, and a comparison of the closing prices of last week with those of Friday evening show a slight strengthening of the most important stocks on the list, excepting Union Pacific. There has been so much bear talk of late that it is well to keep the more encouraging aspects of the situation in mind. The operators on the short side of the market relied almost exclusively on the quickening of apprehensions already excited and in the circulation of rumors. Meanwhile, the general conditions, apart from the money market, have distinctly been growing more encouraging. Large crops do not always produce large railway earnings, but in the present year there will be practically no increase of mileage to create competition, break rates and destroy the opportunity of a big income.

NOT only the London Stock Exchange, but the different branches of English trade is in a stagnant state just at present. A condition of apprehension prevails the business of the whole kingdom and takes the life out of the market. Similar statements are in the main true of France, Germany and Austro-Hungary, the first of these still continuing apparently the most prosperous. With the exception of the Northern, all the great French railway companies show an increase in their receipts in the first six months of the present year, compared with 1890, both in the gross amount and in the mileage. The Lyons company gains 3,733,535 francs; the Western, 1,005,329 francs; the Orleans, 1,792,709 francs; the Eastern, 1,488,103 francs; the Southern, 635,188 francs; and the State lines, 506,490 francs. Spanish and Italian railways are also doing better than any one would expect from the recently depressed condition of their country's finances. The enormous increase in the traffic of the Suez Canal still continues. The total receipts from January 1st have been 47,980,000 francs, an advance of 10,150,000 francs from the figures of last year. It is not surprising under the circumstances that the price of the company's securities is steadily augmenting in value. In Berlin the depression has been deepened by the insecurity created by the swindling of the Deutsche Bank. The public look with distrust on the course of events; and even if this were not so, declining trade and advancing money rates would suffice to stifle any attempt to animate business. The harvest prospects are most unsatisfactory, and it is now feared that the home production of rye, a most important article in Germany, may this year come to only about 80 per cent. of what is considered a good medium harvest. Then the position of the banks is anything but satisfactory. For about a year or so they have done their best to increase their stock of liquid reserves; yet, though they were successful in a measure, it is doubted whether they were so to the full extent of their requirements. They are supposed still to hold large amounts of stock resulting from loan and syndicate operations, and in any case they could not afford to go into the market as buyers, except with the object of maintaining prices.

WHEN Mayor Grant, a year ago last spring, appointed the Belmont Rapid Transit Commission THE RECORD AND GUIDE indicated the unwisdom of putting into the hands of business men the solution of a question that turned mainly on engineering difficulties. The advice of a good engineer is not sufficient; it would have been wiser to have selected the Commission from among the best members of the American Society of Civil Engineers. Nevertheless, when under the terms of the new rapid transit act, the Mayor appointed another Commission of the same kind, we did not care to press the criticism, and in the ensuing months the Commissioners have proved themselves to be so trustworthy that any objection to their *personnel* would be the merest cavilling. The only stricture that could reasonably be made is that if the Commissioners had been Civil Engineers employed by the city to devote their whole time to rapid transit, the work might have been expedited. As it is, the manifold private interests of every one of the Commissioners, and the time these interests demands, must of course delay the completion of the task. As yet, however, the engineering problems have not been fairly tackled—that is, not in the reports which the Commissioners have made to the public. We are informed, moreover, that before they are given to the public, all the details of construction will be submitted to competent experts in the several departments. This is certainly a very wise measure. It shows that the Commissioners are not foolish enough to think that they know everything; they are willing to supplement their own knowledge by calling in expert opinion. Furthermore, it is wise for another reason. No matter what the plan of construction upon which the Commission decides, it is very sure to provoke some opposition. A large number of pushing men are peculiarly interested in particular systems and ideas. It will not be difficult for them either to convince or to persuade the newspapers that there is only one proper and adequate system of construction, and hence any plan, as we have said, will meet with criticism. Under such circumstances it is well that the Commissioners should be backed by a consensus of competent opinion, for the public authorities are undeniably sensitive to newspaper clamoring, when such clamoring does not deny sacred political obligations. What the effect of such a howl may be we all know from the experience of the Manhattan Railway Company. If the modest request of that corporation to improve its terminal facilities had been acceded to by the press we do not think that Mayor Grant and the Legislature would have proved to be stubborn.

LATE in June the commercial world was somewhat startled on reading in the daily press that an inland-built steamer of a peculiar construction called "whalebacks" had left Duluth, Minn., en route for Liverpool with a cargo of 95,000 bushels of grain. On the 21st of July, a cablegram from London announced the safe arrival of the vessel. Accompanying this announcement came the further piece of news that her cargo was "the first grain cargo shipped from a lake port direct to Liverpool without being re-handled." The wires flashed, and inside of twenty-four hours every live daily paper in the land had repeated the news, and stick full upon stick full of editorials had appeared on "the 'whaleback' as a new agent in commerce." It was gravely maintained by many writers that the new steel vessel would revolutionize ocean traffic, for at last direct waterway communication had been opened between the great Northwest and Europe.

IN the light of the frigid facts all the commotion over the "whalebacks" becomes exceedingly ludicrous. In the first place the cargo of the steamer in question—by name the Charles W. Wetmore—was not carried "direct to Liverpool without being rehandled." To believe for a moment that such a feat could be accomplished by a loaded vessel built on the lines of the Charles W. Wetmore betrays ignorance of the nature of the route to be traversed. No large vessel drawing over seven feet of water can possibly descend the rapids of the St. Lawrence in safety. The Charles W. Wetmore with her cargo draws not less than fifteen. The facts are that in entering the rapids she was lightened to five feet and her cargo conveyed by smaller boats to Montreal and there reloaded. The success of this voyage is not as it has been circulated through the daily press, "evidence that the proposition to establish direct communication between European and other ports and the port of Chicago is feasible." It demonstrates merely that vessels suitable for ocean service may be so constructed as to pass unloaded down the rapids of the St. Lawrence River. That such empty vessels may make the voyage without risk is not even shown, as yet. One of the "whalebacks" which accompanied the Charles W. Wetmore down the rapids, was so badly damaged that it was obliged to go into dry-dock at Montreal for repairs. Even had it been demonstrated by the recent venture that "whalebacks," cargo and all, could pass with a reasonable degree of safety from the lakes to the sea, the means of communication thus provided could hardly be expected to affect commerce to any perceptible extent, for the reasons that large vessels which have once descended the St. Lawrence can not return by this route. No vessel has ever yet ascended the rapids of the St. Lawrence river. The only possible way vessels can return, which have once descended the St. Lawrence to Montreal, is through the canals along the river, and then, if the vessel is large, it must be "cut in two" and towed. No one acquainted with the facts supposes that the "whalebacks" which have descended the river will ever return to the lakes. The most that can be said of the successful voyage of the Charles W. Whetmore is that thereby the construction of ocean craft has been made possible on the Great Lakes. Commerce between the Northwest and Europe will continue, for a time at least, through the old channels.

Artistic Ensemble in America.

THE commotion raised a short time since in Brooklyn over the location of the Beecher statue was a most healthy indication of the status of art in general life that has been manifested for some time. The location of monuments, even when paid for by the public purse, has not always stirred up communities in this country to prolonged and earnest discussion on the merits and demerits of various places, and that a controversy over nothing less than this question should have occurred in our sister city in the year of grace 1891 is a most commendable indication of the progress art and art meanings are making in this vicinity. It almost compensates for the unfortunate position of the statue that so keen an interest was aroused concerning it, for in truth a new era in the popularity of art may be expected when artistic things become matters of discussion in the daily press.

There can scarcely be two opinions on the situation of the statue with its back to the world, and, doubtless, could the soul of the great preacher animate it, his first action would be to turn and face the vista now behind him. The whole thing is an excellent illustration of the inability of the American people to understand the value of artistic arrangements. In this particular instance, if the matter were put to popular vote, there would doubtless be an overwhelming voice for reversing the statue; but its position was deliberately chosen by a body of intelligent men, with every advantage of advice and knowledge, but who, apparently, did not realize how much stronger and better the statue would appear with the City Hall as a background, instead of the uncertain and shifting ground of irregular streets and houses against which it is now projected.

Few things add so much to the value of a statue or monument as well-arranged accessories. The most beautiful work of art the hands of man has yet produced needs to be seen in appropriate surroundings in order to appear to best advantage and to produce the best effect. No people understand this better than the French, who have a special genius for arrangements and exhibit it both in the interiors of their buildings and in public places. The arrangement of the statues in the Greek and Roman galleries of the Louvre are masterpieces of artistic feeling, the system adapted not only rendering the works of art thoroughly visible to the student, but ornaments to the galleries. The same artistic treatment is to be noted in the public gardens of Paris. Few vistas in the world are more magnificent than the sweep from the Louvre to the Arc de Triomphe. The foreigner is, perhaps, amazed that so much space would be given up to pleasure gardens in the very heart of a great city, yet the enormous area so used is put to the best possible advantage. It is the artistic vistas which help to make Paris so delightful and take Americans there by the thousands for weeks at a time, all the year around. The gardens of the Tuileries, the Place de la Concorde, the Champs Elysees, with their thorough appreciation of artistic arrangements, are object lessons in ensemble that every American may well study to advantage.

The palace of the Trocadero on the heights overlooking the Seine is another example of the thorough manner in which the French make use of every feature capable of artistic treatment when the occasion arises. The fountains and flower-beds, the vases and statues employed in the decoration of these grounds produce a result of wonderful beauty—marred only by the gigantic Tower Eiffel—which it would be difficult to find on so elaborate a scale outside of Paris. The gardens at Versailles are arranged with the same discriminating taste, and a careful study of the ensemble is a pronounced feature of all the public places of the French capital.

It is also illustrated in many public buildings, though here limitations of municipal growth frequently prevent the freedom of action which characterizes the parks. It was an inspiration of genius which enabled Baron Haussmann to sweep away the enormous number of houses that were required to be destroyed for his improvements; yet, notwithstanding the architectural sameness of much of the new Paris, the men of this generation must admit the wisdom and forethought which regenerated their city. Paris is a city of pleasure and of art; a fickleness and lightness of character has been attributed to her inhabitants, to which they are scarcely fairly entitled. Yet the bright nature of the Parisians and their inherent love for art has given them the most beautiful and most popular capital in Europe.

The artistic feeling shown in the public places of Paris should form the theme of fruitful study by every American who has an opportunity to inspect them. And in no respect is Paris more different from New York, and shows how valuable it may be to a city to develop its ornamental possibilities. In New York all such ideas are brushed aside in the wild rush of business and imaginary economy as something quite unnecessary and a thorough waste of money. Any location, any position is deemed good enough for a statue if room is found for its pedestal; its situation is quite independent of its relations to its surroundings, while it is almost equally unknown to make any changes in the site which would add to its merits or permit it to increase the beauty of the location. The American method of preparing a park is to lay out some walks, provide some trees, grass and, above all, some benches for the toughs who most do congregate in these places, and remain satisfied that everything needful to the making of an artistic pleasure ground has been accomplished. The French method is vastly different. It is base to put forward a claim for art on the ground of the money it might bring in; but the example of Paris is unmistakable evidence that the contrary of these most American practices is a valuable artistic investment and richly remunerative financially.

IT was natural at the dinner given to the officers of the "White Squadron" by the Chamber of Commerce that congratulations should be interchanged as to the great boon which the new navy will be to the country; and doubtless everything said had this much truth in it—that a very fair beginning has been made. Nevertheless, evidences are not wanting that some of the ships are very disappointing. The Baltimore and the Philadelphia made trial trips that gratified everyone who had anything to do with their construction, but their subsequent performances have not been such that it would be wise to send them after the Majestic or the City of Paris. Furthermore, the second of these two wonders has proved to be top-heavy and has had to have her steel masts removed and wooden ones substituted. These facts may mean much or little; but when we remember how easy it is for officials to get up a fictitious enthusiasm over some matter that appeals to patriotic feeling and to what a small extent such enthusiasm would be qualified by knowledge of its object, we may be uncertain whether all this clapping of hands and unlimited mutual admiration is not the precursor of disappointment and recrimination. At all events we should be glad, for the sake of the security for the vast propertied interests of this city, to see a little more time given to fortifications. It is very certain that even if our fleet was three times the size it will be, it could not effectively protect the enormous coast line. New York should be so fortified that no fleet could with impunity come within shelling distance of the city. Its location makes it possible by the expenditure of a large sum to give the city an impregnable line of forts, battle works, etc.; and it is expenditure which the country cannot afford to shrink from now. The property involved is too enormous. The fleet itself, according to ex-Mayor Hewitt, is no inexpensive thing to maintain; although his utterances were not very explicit. The statement that the cost of running one of those new cruisers is just as large as the operating expenses of a railroad between New York and Philadelphia sounds big and simple. In reality it is one of those vague and meaningless comparisons which depend on a thousand contingencies for any satisfactory interpretation.

Seven Months of Real Estate.

APPENDED will be found the totals representing the real estate transactions in this city for the months of July, and for the whole seven months of 1891. Any one who has followed the figures thus far this year will observe that the new totals do not warrant conclusions different from those which we were compelled to draw from the old. The decreases in the number of the conveyances, mortgages and buildings, and the amount involved in their record still continues in about the same proportion as hitherto, and the facts which we have repeatedly pointed out as explaining the decreases account for them satisfactorily. It is obvious that the present year will be an off-year in New York real estate.

SEVEN MONTHS OF REAL ESTATE.

NEW YORK CONVEYANCES.

1891.	No. Conveys.	Amount.	No. Nom.	No. 23d & 24th W.	Amount.	No. Nom.
Jan.-June, inc.	8,119	$142,002,130	2,293	1,355	$5,949,076	353
July	1,705	17,851,046	343	307	1,162,219	67
Total.......	9,824	$159,853,176	2,636	1,662	$7,111,295	420

1890.						
Jan.-June, inc.	9,085	$168,171,807	2,807	1,324	$6,555,698	350
July..........	1,485	25,232,995	306	360	1,503,302	72
Total........	10,570	$193,401,802	2,613	1,698	$8,059,000	422
1889.						
Jan.-June, inc.	8,700	$159,740,685	1,915	1,478	$7,069,202	356
July....	1,218	20,634,434	279	324	1,041,423	76
Total.......	9,918	$180,375,119	2,194	1,802	$8,110,625	432

MORTGAGES.

1891.	No. Morts.	Amount.	No. at 5 p. c.	Amount.	No. at less than 5 p. c.	Amount.	No. to B. T. & I. Cos.	Amount.
Jan.-June, inc.	7,982	$99,188,254	4,111	$51,745,264	756	$16,627,264	1,179	$29,614,461
July........ ..	1,295	13,947,980	644	7,124,996	98	1,996,825	156	4,157,650
Total........	9,277	$113,136,234	4,755	$58,870,260	854	$18,624,089	1,335	$33,772,111
1890.								
Jan.-June, inc.	8,346	$151,336,743	4,025	$61,487,693	971	$59,539,630	1,208	$73,166,566
July....	1,378	18,492,689	716	9,250,865	142	3,949,650	179	5,528,800
Total........	9,724	$169,829,432	4,741	$70,738,558	1,113	$63,489,280	1,381	$78,695,366
1889.								
Jan.-June, inc.	7,739	$99,345,462	3,618	$45,450,882	972	$20,478,668	1,078	$25,636,968
July...	1,333	16,461,213	619	7,540,148	172	3,908,826	180	4,300,750
Total,.....	9,072	$115,806,675	4,257	$52,991,030	1,144	$24,387,494	1,258	$29,937,718

Includes mortgage given in February, 1890, by the Manhattan and Metropolitan Elevated Railway Companies on real and personal property to The Central Trust Co. for $40,000,000; also mort. given in March, 1890, by the Edison Illuminating Co. to The Central Trust Co. for $5,000,000.

NEW YORK BUILDINGS PROJECTED DURING SEVEN MONTHS, GIVEN BY DISTRICTS.

	1889. Jan. to July, inc.	1890. Jan. to July, inc.	1891. Jan. to July, inc.
Total No. of plans filed....	1,361	1,355	1,097
Total No. of buildings projected....	2,525	2,371	1,834
Estimated cost	$47,610,292	$51,240,941	$38,533,116
No south of 14th st	329	320	284
Cost	$11,581,893	$14,101,500	$10,373,000
No. bet 14th and 59th sts	226	276	221
Cost	$5,687,075	$10,006,520	$7,270,945
No. bet 59th and 125th sts, east of 5th av	445	398	253
Cost	$6,915,540	$7,288,255	$4,861,168
No bet 59th and 125th sts, west of 8th av	600	547	438
Cost	$18,975,050	$12,662,800	$10,776,600
No. bet 110th and 125th sts, 5th and 8th avs	60	88	39
Cost	$1,683,550	$1,809,000	$798,000
No. north of 125th st	306	225	139
Cost	$4,652,195	$2,650,018	$1,938,265
No. 23d and 24th Wards	552	517	460
Cost	$3,104,887	$2,722,848	$2,520,118

NEW YORK BUILDINGS PROJECTED DURING JULY, GIVEN BY DISTRICTS.

	1889. July.	1890. July.	1891. July.
Total No. of buildings projected	355	346	245
Estimated cost	$6,526,220	$5,542,430	$4,032,300
No. south of 14th st	29	41	38
Cost	$1,335,850	$1,242,850	$1,303,800
No. bet 14th and 59th sts	35	30	25
Cost	$836,700	$434,130	$440,700
No. bet 59th and 125th sts, east of 5th av.	90	52	33
Cost	$1,387,100	$1,009,390	$582,475
No. bet 59th and 125th sts, west of 8th av.	80	83	64
Cost	$1,845,000	$1,583,000	$1,235,000
No. bet 110th and 125th sts, 5th and 8th avs	1	21	2
Cost	$20,000	$419,000	$38,000
No. north of 125th st	37	24	16
Cost	$906,240	$356,500	$168,925
No. 23d an 24th Wards	83	95	67
Cost..d	$245,330	$497,560	$263,400

	1889 No. b'ld'gs.	1889 Cost.	1890 No. b'ld'gs.	1890 Cost.	1891 No. b'ld'gs.	1891 Cost.
Jan.-June, inc.	2,170	$41,084,072	2,025	$45,698,511	1,589	$34,500,816
July	355	6,526,220	346	5,542,430	245	4,032,300
Total.	2,525	$47,610,292	2,371	$51,240,941	1,834	$38,533,116

FOR THE MONTH OF JULY, 1891, CLASSIFIED.

	Flats and Tenem'ts No.	Flats and Tenem'ts Cost.	Private Dwell'gs No.	Private Dwell'gs Cost.	Hotels, Stores, Churches, Office Build'gs, &c. No.	Hotels, Stores, Churches, Office Build'gs, &c. Cost.	Miscellaneous, Stables, Shops, &c. No.	Miscellaneous, Stables, Shops, &c. Cost.
South of 14th st. ...	14	$470,000	..	....	6	$795,000	18	$238,800
Bet 14th and 59th sts	5	106,000	1	$35,000	1	150,000	18	149,700
Bet 59th and 125th sts, east of 5th av.	21	387,000	1	100,000	1	25,000	10	70,475
Bet 59th and 125th sts, west of 8th av	14	330,000	46	751,000	1	50,000	3	74,000
Bet 110th and 125th sts, 5th & 8th avs..	..	....	2	38,000	.	....	..	....
North of 125th st..	7	95,000	6	66,200	..	....	3	7,625
23d & 24th Wards..	5	68,000	46	148,550	1	25,000	15	26,860
Total for July 1891.	66	$1,281,000	102	$1,138,850	10	$1,045,000	67	$567,450
Total for July, 1890.	137	$3,034,000	125	$1,355,600	20	$785,500	64	$367,330

THE COSTLIEST BUILDINGS FILED DURING JULY 1891.

Location and Character.	Owners.	Cost.
Bleecker st, s s, 72.5 w Mercer st, eight-story store	L. Schlesinger	$190,000
Broad st, Nos. 64-68, ten-story office building.	Mrs. C. Morris	400,000
Lafayette pl, No. 55, seven-story factory	O. B. Potter	120,000
25th st, Nos. 551-555 W., six-story shop.	J. M. Cornell	75,000
5th av, No. 114, seven-story store	W. Ziegler	150,000
5th av, s e cor 72d st, five-story dwell'g	J. A. Burden	100,000
Six buildings, to cost		$1,035,000

FLATS, TENEMENTS AND DWELLINGS IN ROWS.

Boulevard, s w cor 78th st, six five-story flats.	Forster & Livingston	$175,000
77th st, s s, 104 w West End av, thirteen three-and-a-half-story dwell'gs	Stewart & Pursell	260,000
87th st, n w cor Av B, five five-story flats	Feehan & Hammer	82,000
90th st, s s, 100 e 10th av, four five-story flats.	L. M. Muller	80,000
92d st, Nos. 54-62 W., five three-story dwellings	T. Kilpatrick	75,000
103d st, n s, 100 e Riverside Drive, five three-story dwell'gs	Egan & Hallecy	80,000
Madison av, s e cor 132d st, six five-story flats.	F. Rohrs	81,000
West End av, n w cor 102d st, five three-story dwell'gs	D. Christie	83,000
West End av, s w cor 104th st, five three-story dwell'gs	Jane A. Brown	80,000
Fifty-four buildings, to cost		$996,000

KINGS COUNTY CONVEYANCES.

	1890. Number.	1890. Am't involved.	1890. Nom.	1891. Number.	1891. Am't involved.	1891. Nom.
January	1,342	$5,816,826	341	1,429	*$7,878,196	412
February	1,298	5,137,587	344	1,219	4,704,985	390
March	1,685	7,608,870	423	1,602	6,245,195	475
April	2,176	11,587,703	490	1,998	9,042,227	490
May	1,883	9,317,276	437	1,802	7,280,963	482
June	1,515	5,920,270	357	1,731	6,233,014	405
July	1,738	7,729,816	351	1,680	6,030,359	402
Total	11,631	$53,118,348	2,743	11,461	$47,354,939	3,056

KINGS COUNTY MORTGAGES.

	1890. No.	1890. Am't involved.	1890. No. at 5 per cent. or less.	1890. Am't involved.	1891. No.	1891. Am't involved.	1891. No. at 5 per cent. or less.	1891. Am't involved.
Jan.....	1,264	$4,994,740	798	$3,455,940	1,182	†$14,007,743	620	$2,417,480
Feb......	960	4,117,787	558	2,659,475	1,082	4,123,056	615	2,602,984
March .	1,272	5,643,729	780	3,916,105	1,229	5,147,777	682	3,072,480
April....	1,679	6,575,719	1,067	4,536,146	1,581	6,871,880	917	4,165,699
May	1,516	6,042,149	927	4,233,752	1,272	5,059,644	680	2,941,829
June....	1,322	5,468,301	772	3,987,174	1,460	5,654,829	792	3,727,914
July.....	1,446	5,785,961	901	3,879,466	1,468	5,050,339	777	3,014,425
Total..	9,459	$38,643,376	5,793	$26,617,358	9,274	$45,915,068	5,083	$22,152,811

*Includes seven deeds at a total of $2,560,000 given by the various sugar companies in Brooklyn to The American Sugar Refining Co. of New Jersey.

†Includes mortgage given by The American Sugar Refining Co. of New Jersey to The Central Trust Co. of New York, for $10,000,000.

KINGS COUNTY PROJECTED BUILDINGS.

	1890 Total No. b'gs.	1890 No. of brick b'gs.	1890 No. of frame b'gs.	1891 Total No. b'gs.	1891 No. of brick b'gs.	1891 No. of frame b'gs.	1890. Cost.	1891. Cost.
Jan	344	108	236	268	61	207	$1,407,615	$1,108,235
Feb. ...	388	158	230	350	160	190	1,816 425	1,545,895
March..	484	215	269	427	185	242	2,829,661	2,170,100
April...	525	249	276	563	305	258	2,406,950	3,177,072
May....	426	198	238	427	205	222	2,469,935	2,455,360
June...	547	274	273	299	122	177	2,632,739	1,873,275
July..	369	133	236	270	94	176	2,653,540	1,185,530
Total..	3,083	1,330	1,753	2,604	1,132	1,472	$16,216,865	$13,516,367

Investments—Good and Bad.

RAILROADS AND CROPS.—There is at the present moment a great agreement, and at the same time a great divergence of opinion among business men. It is agreed on all sides that the grain crops which are blessing the farmers this year cannot fail to improve the value of railroad securities; but there is a very marked and active discussion as to the time when that improvement will be seen. On one side it is claimed that the stock and bond markets are on the eve of a big advance; on the other that there is still a considerable period of waiting to be gotten through, and meantime the probabilities markedly point to a further decline in values. The arguments pro and con. are many enough to make an outsider's head swim and leave him confused and hopeless of deciding which way to incline in employing his money.

It is claimed that there will be an immediate advance because the wheat crop is beyond any doubt the largest this country has ever seen and there is every prospect that the corn crop will be enormous; that railroads of the wheat regions are taxed to their capacity to carry the grain the farmers are already shipping; that the fears of tight money this fall are being rapidly dissolved under the expectations that the demands of the interior from this centre will be small and a speedy gold import movement will begin. This favorable view of the interior movement is based on the belief that the Western banks have a very large surplus which must be exhausted before there is any occasion to call upon Eastern funds, and that such demand when made will be comparatively small. The reliance on any early Westward movement of gold finds its support in the fact that Europe is already and must continue to be a large purchaser of American grain, and in the belief that those purchases must be paid for in gold for the reason that Europe, and notably London and Berlin, have been denuded of American speculative issues, and consequently purchases of American grain cannot be offset by sales of American stocks, no alternative will be left to the buyers but to pay in gold. Some of the largest foreign houses in New York say the London and Berlin markets, which carry the great bulk of foreign holdings of American railroad issues, are bare of the active stocks, having disposed of those they did hold in this market during the year of trouble and depression they have just passed through. This opinion does not tally with the statements recently published by several of our railroad companies to show that the foreign holdings of their several stocks have shown no falling off. The bull view of the situation is generally favored in commission houses. The wish, however, may be father to the view; commission houses have very little share in the business of a professional and declining market such as we have seen, their best time being when the public are buying under the stimulus of advancing prices. It is not for a moment intended here to hint that the commission houses which take the sunniest view of the situation are not sincere in their views, but one's interests will affect one's opinions. These commission houses are premature, that is all, and are saving the reputation of the street for discounting the situation, in default of the market doing it as it ought to do, maintain the truth of the flattering traditions that has for so long attached to it.

The opposite view that delay and decline are necessary to enable the crops to be gathered and carried to market, and the necessary means created to benefit railroad securities, was explained in this column last week. It receives additional support from answers made to the arguments stated in the preceding paragraph. The fears of tight money are well founded, it is claimed, and the time has not yet come to test the accuracy of the statement, though it finds support already in the movement of the rates in Boston. The greater the movement of grain, the greater will be the demands for money to move it with. The New York banks apparently think it wise to be prepared for sudden demands, as they are keeping a large reserve within their control. Time loans are very hard to get, though money has been fairly easy in New York on call. The market is affected by the condition of certain railroad properties, and until these have reached their true value there can be no sure basis on which to start a healthy advance. On the question of gold imports the contending views are very extreme. Those who do not look for any large return of gold for some time say that the resources of Europe, being so very materially lessened by crop failures, it will not be able to pay for grain purchases in gold, but will, instead, sell securities in this market. A threatened movement of gold westward would so affect the European money market, that more than a few American stocks now on the investment list and largely held abroad would be undesirable to hold in view of the small dividends they pay. The sale of these would limit the return of gold to this side to very moderate proportions, considering the immense sums drawn from this side, for the rest of this year at least. Then, finally, it is claimed, and this does not permit of a moment's dispute, that the bond market which usually leads in a wholesome advance shows no sign of improvement, but on the contrary issues of merit barely hold their own under very small pressure to sell and that any large realizing demands would make the bond market as weak as the stock market has been.

Looking back, it can be seen how a previous great crop, that of 1884, affected the railroads. The wheat harvested that year amounted to 512,000,000 bushels St. Paul that year carried 36?,000 tons of freight more than in the previous year, but rates declined as did also earnings per mile. The next, also a great crop year, the same road had a further increase of 46?,000 tons of freight. Rates declined. but earnings per mile increased. In 1886 the freight moved increased by 6?0,000 tons, yet, owing to declines in rates, earnings per mile were less than in the previous year and in 1884. Manitoba carried less freight in 1884, on an increased mileage, than in 1883, It increased in 1885 and fell off again in 1886. Earnings per mile fell off each year. Northern Pacific had a largely increased freight tonnage in 1884, the first year of operating the through line, and increased earnings per mile. In 1885 there was a large falling off in both, and a recovery and increase in the tons carried, but not in mileage earnings in 1886. Each year saw an addition to the mileage of the system. Northwest in 1884 increased its tonnage and reduced its earnings per mile. The next year saw a falling off in both, and the next an improvement in both over the year immediately preceding. The roads just named are all great wheat carriers. The corn crop was larger in 1885 than in 1884. That year gave Burlington & Quincy an increase of 900,000 tons of freight, and the magnificent increase in gross earnings of $23 per mile. In 1886 there was a further increase in tonnage and a decrease in earnings per mile of $384. Atchison, with a continued increase of mileage and tonnage in the years 1883, 1884, 1885 and 1886, had declining earnings per mile until the last-named year, when the increase was $74 per mile. Missouri Pacific, on about the same mileage, had a tonnage decreasing during the years 1884 and 1885, and with 44 more miles of road, less tonnage than in 1883, though more than in the two succeeding years. Gross earnings declined about $400 per mile in 1884, $950 in 1885, and in the next year increased $200. These figures go to show that the increase of crop is not all gain to the railroads, but is partly offset by other things. It stands to reason, if the railroads are taxed to their capacity to carry grain, the merchandise and other movements must suffer. The great trouble with the railroads at the time of the last great crop was differences on the subject of rates, and hence they did not benefit as much as they should have done by their increased tonnage. Rates have a tendency to fall with the increase of railroad facilities, though the cost of handling has not. The crops of 1884 and 1885 did a great deal for the railroads and helped the advance of the summer of the latter year, but what has happened since to the railroads we have mentioned? Northwest is the only one that maintains its reputation, though it pays a smaller dividend than it did then. St. Paul has given up paying dividends on its common stock, Atchison has gone through reorganization, Missouri Pacific, Burlington and Manitoba have reduced dividends, and Northern Pacific has been financed into a dividend payer. Perhaps, under the immense influence of this year's crop the conditions will be reversed; at any rate, the prospectively large earnings of the present year will not have a continued increased mileage, on the part of the western roads, to compete with.

Those Harlem Bridges.

There was another hearing on Wednesday before the Park Board, upon the petition of the New York Central & Hudson River Railroad Company, to have the Madison and Third avenue bridges across the Harlem closed between 7 and 10 o'clock A. M. and 4 and 7 o'clock P. M. Frank Loomis, the company's attorney, appeared in its behalf, and quoted figures to show how great delays were caused to the trains on its road by the opening of the bridges for the passage of vessels during those hours. Ex-Justice Angel, who said he appeared for the owners of property and residents of the North Side, presented a petition said to bear several thousand signatures, in favor of the closing. The petitioners were actually yearning for more permanent ties to bind them to Manhattan Island.

Against the petition appeared Ex-Secretary Wm. C. Whitney, Daniel S. Lamont and Elihu Root, for the New York & Northern Railroad Company; Franklin Bartlett, for the Astor Estate; Andrew H. Green, and the representatives of several workingmen's organizations. It was shown that the New York Central Company had been ordered by the United States authorities to remove its railroad bridge or to raise it to a grade of 24 feet above high water mark, and that the company was fighting to avoid the expense of doing this. Its desire is to have the bridges made permanent and the river closed to commercial navigation. The board, after some further discussion, adjourned the matter until next Wednesday, when Commissioner Strauss is expected back from Europe, and the matter will be further considered.

Rapid Transit Breakers Ahead.

Incomplete and unofficial though they have been, the reports of the plans of construction which the Rapid Transit Commission is considering for the Broadway-Boulevard line have been sufficient to draw fire from two or three poorly-masked batteries from which nothing but opposition was to be expected, unless the work of the commission had conformed to the wishes of the persons manipulating the batteries. The contest was inevitable, but it was precipitated rather sooner than the commissioners had any reason to expect. However, it is fortunate rather than otherwise that the people have been given a foretaste of what they may expect from certain sources when the plans of the commission shall have been completed and presented to the Common Council for approval, as they are likely to be some time within the present or coming month.

The commissioners have taken sound and commendable steps to discount this class of opposition to their work in advance. They have had the plans of Messrs. Worthen and Parsons perfected and completed to the utmost details and have submitted them for criticism and report to a large number of the leading engineers of the country, taking care to avoid as far as possible any complications with engineers of any of the plans which have heretofore been unsuccessfully exploited in this city. Among the engineers to whom the plans have been submitted, it is unofficially reported, are—John Bogart, State Engineer and Surveyor, an expert in sanitary engineering; Theodore Cooper, of 35 Broadway, a well-known expert in iron construction; John Wilson, of Philadelphia, a member of the celebrated firm of Wilson & Sons, engineers for the Pennsylvania Railroad Company, and Octave Chanut, President of the American Association of Civil Engineers, a recognized authority in tunnel construction. There are several others, it is stated, in various parts of the country, to whom special parts of the plans have been sent, with the "schemes" of the authors figured out, so that they will be burdened with but little of the original work of the plans, but can devote all the time at their disposal to the technical examination and criticism of the plans which they have been requested to make.

When the reports of this formidable body of experts shall have been received, which, the commissioners hope will be before the end of next week, the commissioners will meet and consider them, and if they sustain the work done by the regular engineers of the board, will formulate their final report upon them, in which the choice will be made of the two plans, the other being completely suppressed, and this final report will be presented to the Board of Aldermen, as required by the Rapid Transit act. It will be backed up by the reports of the large body of consulting engineers referred to—not merely by a generally expressed opinion, but by reports in detail upon every feature of the plans upon which they shall have been called upon respectively to report If then there shall be found any who desire to set themselves up in judgment upon the work of the commission, the latter will be fortified behind a formidable breastworks of supporting opinion from the best authorities on the subject in the country. Under these conditions it is believed the people, who must ultimately decide the important question, will not be led into any prejudiced or one-sided expressions on the subject.

The main difficulty of securing Rapid Transit for New York City, it is admitted, will be in securing the consent of the owners of property on Broadway to the plan of the commission. Growing out of the multiplied efforts of private promoters to secure control of that all-important thoroughfare for an everlasting system of intermural transit and transportation, some few of the owners along the line have conceived a violent prejudice against any invasion of the street for any railroad structure whatever. Notions of the most ridiculous character about the danger to foundations from the vibrations that would be caused by the trains have been instilled and encouraged by rival claimants for the monopoly of the street, and to such an extent that some of the owners who are most affected with the fright are prepared to resist the construction of any kind of road whatever. They seem to be blind to the fact that the foundations of the most massive structures in the city have at times been laid bare, and deep trenches have been dug along the entire sidewalls of some of the heaviest of them to make way for some still deeper and heavier walls. They, also apparently disregard the fact that on many of the business streets of this and other large cities some of the heaviest railroading in the world is done into massive warehouses and along the street in front of them, and the owners are not apparently disturbed by foolish fears that the foundations of their buildings are in any danger. On 4th avenue and Hudson and Canal streets hundreds of heavily-loaded freight and passenger trains pass to and fro every day, as they have for years, and the first case has yet to be reported where the foundations of any building have been injuriously affected by the vibration caused by the trains. And in these cases no effort was ever made to lessen the vibration nor to overcome the effect upon the buildings along the streets of the constant passage of trains. All these matters have been given proper consideration by the commissioners and the plans which they will report, it is declared, will provide against any serious vibration and against anything more than the minimum of noise. Especial care has been given to the deadening of the tracks, and an engineer, now connected with the work, assured the reporter that the noise in the tunnels would not be so disagreeable as that on an elevated railroad train.

The plans will first be reported to the Board of Aldermen, and that body will be required to set a day not less than one week nor more than ten days distant when it will begin the consideration of the plans. In this it may be "assisted" by all the objectors the report may bring forth, and from present indications there will be enough of them, no matter what the report may show. For if one promoter should chance to find his scheme substantially carried out, the rest of that industrious fraternity will be disappointed and dissatisfied, and will do all in their power to prejudice the report before the people. To do this they will not hesitate to coddle for the time being all the fears of all the property-owners on the line of the road. Notwithstanding that they are nearly all on record as scouters of the notion that any underground road can be other than a great benefit to Broadway, or can in any manner injuriously affect the foundations of buildings, they will for the purpose of defeating the construction of the road belie their former declaration and join hands with the reactionaries who are sure to be found to oppose the building of a rapid transit railroad in Broadway. It is not doubted but that upon an intelligent and thorough understanding of the matter by the Broadway property-owners a great majority of them will cheerfully consent to the construction of the proposed road. But there is not the least bit of doubt but that the plan when reported will encounter the fiercest opposition from interested parties that can be brought to bear upon it. The citizens must be prepared to encounter and combat this opposition if New York is to have any relief from the present hide-bound and depressing condition of transit matters. The commission having the matter in charge is as well able to handle the subject as any five men in the community, and of their high characters and disinterestedness there is not the slightest doubt or suspicion whatever. And when their report is presented the people of New York may rest assured that no better work could reasonably be expected of any other commission, should the city try for a century to improve upon it.

As a matter of information in anticipation of the report, it may be stated that the decision of the commission will turn upon the question whether anything shall be done to provide Broadway with a permanent road-bed or not. In one of the plans which the commissioners are considering provision is made for a pipe gallery between the underground tunnels, in which it is designed to take care of all the underground pipe systems, so that they shall be accessible, not from the surface of the street, as was reported in the papers generally last week, but from the stations along the road, whence they can be got at any time for purposes of alterations or repairs. The same plan provides for a permanent roadway constructed in the most substantial and enduring manner, and designed to remain undisturbed by the corporations that control the pipe systems. Because it was intimated in one of the daily papers last week that it would be necessary to open the surface of the street for the purposes of construction, though for ever so small a space and for only a short interval at any one point, two of the leading papers condemned the plan off-hand, and declared just as an interested person who had written to one of the papers a letter upon the subject wanted them to do in support of a scheme which, while satisfactory enough for London, will not in the judgment of the most competent persons to judge, be at all satisfactory for New York City. Such criticism assumes that, notwithstanding American engineers have been on the ground studying the great questions for years, and are entirely familiar with the lay of the ground, a brace of English engineers may come over with a little scheme that has satisfied the Londoners, and have it preferred as the best that engineering skill can devise for this great city. National, not to say civic, pride would seem to be at a discount in such quarters.

The alternative plan of the commissioners makes no provision for the permanent roadway, but leaves the pipe systems and the roadway to take care of themselves. It provides for a wide tunnel, taking up the whole width of the street down just beneath the pipes and mains, and in which all four tracks of the proposed rapid transit road shall be laid. In both plans the road is intended to lie as near to the surface of the street as possible—in the former instance nearer to the surface than in the latter. In both cases the stations are designed to occupy the space just under the sidewalks, and to be accessible from the street by short flights of stairs conveniently placed in the areaways or within buildings to be secured for that purpose. So far as the location of stations is concerned that matter, it is said, will nearly regulate itself. There must be stations, as one of the engineers suggests, at Wall and Rector, Cortlandt and Fulton, City Hall and Chambers, White or Walker, Grand, Houston or Bleecker, 8th, 14th, 18th, 23d, 28th, 33d or 34th, 42d, 47th, 53d and 59th streets, and possibly at one or two other cross streets. But that is a part of the plan which, although planned and arranged for, is still to be determined by the commissioners.

Of the inestimable advantage a rapid transit road, such as is contemplated by the commission, would be to Broadway there is no sort of question. The benefits would begin to accrue at once from a great increase in the tide of travel, the one thing which gives value to real estate. With a permanent roadway this tide of travel would never be interrupted as it is now and always has been, by laborers tearing up the pavements to get at the subsurface works. With the cable road for local and the underground electric road for through and rapid travel Broadway would be the best equipped street in the world, and would accommodate with comparative comfort a larger tide of travel than any other street in the world. The plans of construction, together with the routes as already laid out, will undoubtedly be reported to the Board of Aldermen within a few weeks, and the city will be given an opportunity to say decisively whether it is ready to do the best thing that can be done now to give itself the relief it needs for its future growth, or whether it will reject the opportunity and will be content to drift along another decade or two until another and more enterprising generation comes along to do the thing that has now already been too long delayed and is becoming more expensive every hour.

The Plans.

There has been much said of late, and great interest awakened in the public mind, as to the plan of railway which the Rapid Transit Commissioners were likely to adopt. There seems to be little doubt that the borings on Broadway, and the careful investigations made by both the engineers and commissioners have compelled the abandonment of not only the Greathead system, so called, but of all deep-down tunnel structures. The recent report of the Commissioners contain the following significant resolution:

"*Resolved*, That the general plan of construction to a point near 96th street shall be either by double-deck tunnel, with two tracks upon each deck, or four tracks upon the level, as may be found, upon further examination and survey, to be most expedient, *and as near the surface as shall be found practicable*. From 96th street north the route is to be via viaduct to the Harlem River."

Several weeks since we placed before our readers a diagram of the rock formations beneath Broadway, and in our last issue gave some important facts bearing on the Greathead system. This week we present some of the plans covered by the foregoing resolution.

These plans provide for four tracks, and being all drawn on the *same scale* the reader can readily make his own comparisons.

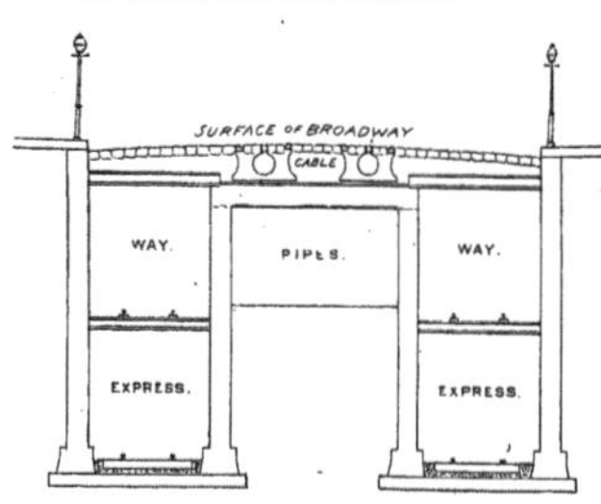

As to Plan 1 there is a criticism which THE RECORD AND GUIDE has always insisted upon, which we would again reiterate: The narrower and more confined a tunnel is the less pleasant and more dangerous it is, and a road thus constructed would make transfer of passengers, co-operation of trains, etc., difficult, though of course these disadvantages may be offset by important gains in the plan of which we speak. There is a general and well-founded aversion to a close, stuffy tunnel, which might lessen its patronage and income.

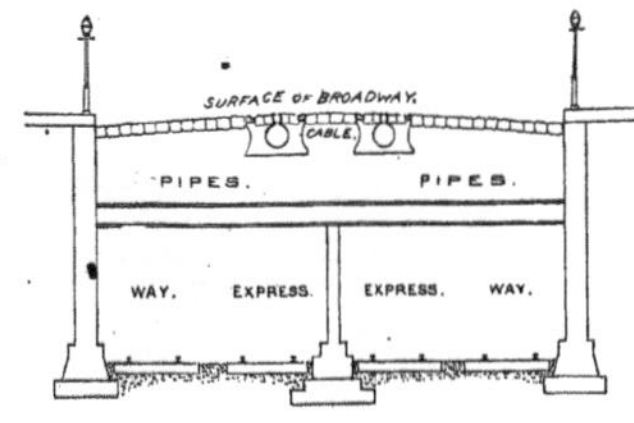

Plan 2 apparently can be constructed without tearing up the street; also, that the four tracks being on a level, ventilation from the sides and at the cross streets would in all respects be good.

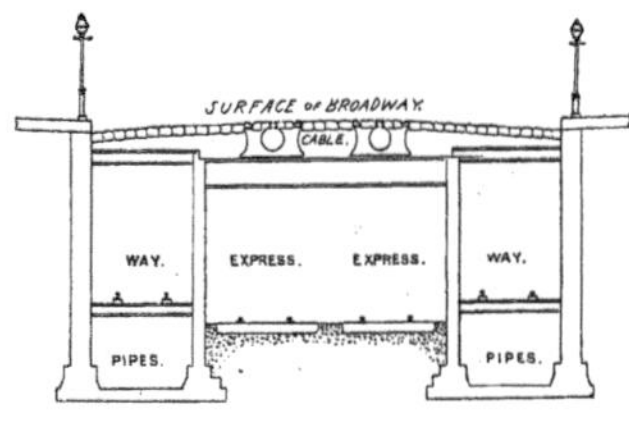

Plan 3, like plan 1, would require reconstructing the surface of the street and the consequent building of a pipe gallery, which in this plan is placed under the way trains, and adjacent to the buildings.

The question likely to cause the most discussion is whether a plan shall be selected similar to plan 2, leaving the pipes where they now are, and not disturbing the surface of Broadway; or, whether the surface of the street shall be reconstructed, a perfect road-bed made, and a suitable pipe-gallery constructed, substantially as in plans No. 1 and 3.

THE RECORD AND GUIDE presents an outline of the facts and plans for the consideration of our readers.

The Commissioners have thus far taken each step only after the fullest consideration and with rare good judgment; we feel confident that they will continue to do so to the end.

Chester Park.

[COMMUNICATED.]

THE UNUSUALLY HANDSOME SUBURBAN PROPERTY TO BE OFFERED AT AUCTION ON TUESDAY—PLOTS OF ONE-QUARTER TO ONE-THIRD OF AN ACRE AT PELHAMVILLE, WITH ELECTRIC LIGHTS, WELL-MADE STREETS AND SIDEWALKS, A PARK AND PLAYGROUND FOR TENNIS, ETC., STATUARY AND OTHER ATTRACTIVE FEATURES — INTELLIGENT PLANS AND RESTRICTIONS.

Rarely has a suburban property been offered which presents such an opportunity to buyers as that which is to be sold at auction on the Real Estate Exchange on Tuesday, the 11th inst., by John F. B. Smyth.

Chester Park is unquestionably one of the finest and most intelligently planned among the various suburban properties which have been offered for sale. In laying out and designing the park, the owner, Mr. Wm. T. Standen, actuary of a prominent life insurance company, and who resides at "The Homestead," Chester Park, had in view the establishment of a limited and select community of professional and business men and others of sufficient means or income to build a home where they could obtain the best enjoyment out of life without a large burden of expense. Mr. Standen recently had a good offer for nearly three-quarters of the park if he would consent to have it cut up into lots 20x100 or 25x100 instead of quarter-acre plots. This offer he declined, because it was abolutely antagonistic to the plan which he had in view from the time when he first started to improve the park.

Terrace, leading to the Green.

Main entrance to the Park.

THE RESTRICTIONS.

Chester Park is restricted. But the restrictions are made in a spirit of liberality, with a view to hamper the independent action of each resident as little as possible, aiming only at the control of such matters as would be likely to materially affect the well-being and comfort of the whole community. Each plot contains about one-quarter to about one-third of an acre, and on this only one house is allowed to be built, thus avoiding the sub-division of the plot and the marring of the beauty of the general surroundings. The only out-building allowed on each plot is a stable, which must be on the rear lot furthermost removed from the street.

THE WATER SUPPLY.

The park has an abundant supply of good, fresh water, pumped up out of rock by an artesian well from a depth of 147 feet below the surface, into a tank holding 30,000 gallons in reserve. There is sufficient force employed to carry it to the top stories of all the houses that may be erected there, and there is no restriction as to the quantity to be used, no charge being made by the owner. A very excellent idea was adopted in laying the water pipes on the rear line of the houses, instead of along the street in front. This will avoid the necessity of tearing up the roads whenever a leak or some trivial damage occurs to the pipes at any point. Over two miles of pipes have been laid. The water supply will be maintained and its cost met by the owner until two-thirds of the property shall have been disposed of.

LIGHTED BY ELECTRICITY.

Electric light is supplied to the park by the Eastchester Electric Light Company, at a cost, by contract, to each plot-owner, of $9 per annum, which is at the rate of less than 2½ cents per day. Arrangements have been made whereby the same plant can be run into the houses.

THE ROADWAYS.

The most costly improvement on the property was the laying out about one mile and a half of avenues, with roadways and sidewalks of an unusually fine character. The plan adopted was to dig out the roads three feet. They were then filled in with native stone to a depth of two feet, over which eight inches of gravel was placed. On top of this four inches of broken native stone was put, with small pieces of blue-stone of about one inch cube, and this, after the roller had made it level, formed the roadway. The consequence of this method of construction has been that a perfect drainage is formed, the water sinking at once into the earth. No mud forms, even after the severest rain storm. This character of roadway is probably one of the most substantial ever constructed and it has the additional merit of always having a clean appearance. The sidewalks are lined with trees and grass plots.

THE PUBLIC GREEN AND PLAYGROUND.

One of the most interesting features of Chester Park is the reservation, for all time, of two acres of ground in the midst of the property for use as a public green. This open space is to be ornamented with flower-beds

The Fountain.

and walks, as well as seats, and a contract has just been given out for the erection of three summer houses, two of which are to be circular and eighteen feet in diameter, the third being oblong in form and 16x40 feet in size. They will be constructed of rustic work, with shingled roofs, and they will form a pleasant and shady retreat in summer for ladies and children, for the latter of whom the green will form a healthy playground. Lawn tennis courts and an archery are also to be laid out on this little "park within a park," and numerous pieces of statuary have already been set in position on the green and on the terraces, consisting of deer, fawns, lions, etc.

RESERVING GROUND FOR A CLUB-HOUSE.

In addition to this, a plot of ground is to be reserved for the purpose of building a club-house and a place for indoor amusements, where the future residents of Chester Park may gather together in the evenings for music, dancing, lectures, readings and other entertainments.

A park laid out on such a basis as this is bound to be attractive. It is certain to bring together a settlement of cultured people, and it possesses all the attractions which are likely to give happiness and pleasure to those who may reside there. There are very few places within easy access of New York City that offer such advantages for the strictest privacy and home comfort in country life.

OTHER FEATURES.

The park has three entrances from the main public road, viz.: Pine avenue to the north and Willow avenue to the south, with Central avenue between. The entrance piers and receding walls are built of handsome granite and are imposing in size and of excellent workmanship, being surmounted by large bronze vases, in which flowers are to be kept in all seasons. In the largest piers terra cotta medallions are inserted, on which appear the words "Chester Park;" while on the smaller piers are similar medallions with the date of the construction of the park, viz.: "1890." There are also handsome ornamental piers on the green, surmounted by vases at each of its eight corners, the fountain in the centre being of bronze. At the eastern end, facing the main terrace, the whole width of this green forms a handsome terrace, with a flight of steps at the entrance from the Central avenue side.

The park is situated on high ground. Its westerly boundary is a strip of woods standing on a steep declivity leading to a ravine, through which runs the Hutchinson River. The drives in the vicinity of Chester Park are attractive, some of them passing through one or two of the oldest roads in the county.

In the course of a conversation Mr. Standen said: "I have built my home at Chester Park and intend to live there for many years to come. I am therefore naturally desirous of making it one of the most attractive places of residence in the county. The fact that we are only about half an hour's journey from the Grand Central depot will no doubt attract outsiders, and I have done everything human for the last eighteen months to make the park as perfect as possible. Every purchaser of a plot will receive $900 of actual value outside of the lot. In other words, $900 represents the capital and expenditure, pro rata, for each plot, outside of the actual cost of the ground. Visitors to Chester Park will at once observe what large expenditures have been made. We shall restrict our ground to houses costing not less than about $4,000. I shall run a stage to and from the depot directly the first house is built after Tuesday's auction sale, and I shall run this stage all the time, no matter how much I may lose; so that residents may either use their own carriages or the stage, as may be convenient. When two-thirds of the property has been sold, I will hand over the management of the park to the property-owners."

There is probably no property in Westchester County that can compare with Chester Park, except it be Rochelle Park, built by the Iselins, at New Rochelle. The intelligent policy of finishing everything at the beginning has been adopted, and thus, all that buyers, who wish to build, require to do is to "go and build"—water, electric light and other improvements being right at hand. There is no necessity to wait for these requisites. Herein lies the secret of the future success of Chester Park. OBSERVER.

The Blackman Suit.

Herbert B. Turner, the referee in the ejectment suit brought by one John E. Blackman, of evil repute, against Charles Riley, to recover a slice of Broadway property between 53d and 54th streets, on the east side, has just decided against Blackman. The decision removes the cloud of Blackman's claim from the entire Broadway front between 50th and 56th streets property valued at several millions of dollars. The property was, until 1762, part of a farm lying on both sides of the old Bloomingdale road, now Broadway, and extending from the common lands of the city to the Hudson River. It belonged to Cornelius Cosine and descended to his children.

Broadway was legally opened in 1847, and was straightened in 1869 by vacating along the east side, between 50th and 56th streets, the property to which Blackman laid claim, and by condemning and taking about an equal amount off the blocks on the west side of Broadway. In the act of 1869, providing for the straightening, it was provided that the vacated parts of the street might be acquired by the adjoining and abutting property-owners who should agree to pay the appraised price of it to the city. This all of them did and they became the nominal owners, at least of the property in question.

But Blackman claimed that the fee of the Bloomingdale road was never in the city, and that when part of it was vacated it reverted to the heirs of the last owner before the vacation—the heirs of Cornelius Cosine, who had never conveyed until he, Blackman, bought their title. Referee Turner found that the fee of the Bloomingdale road was vested in the city after the opening proceedings of 1847, if not before, and that the purchasers of the part vacated, under the straightening proceedings in 1869, took a good title from the city. Blackman was not present at the decision. He was in prison in Albany, on a charge of swindling not connected with his attempted grab of Broadway property.

Real Estate Notes.

Louis Stern, the dry-goods merchant, has taken title to five lots on the northeast corner of 5th avenue and 60th street, at an expressed consideration of $265,000.

John A. Rochford, on Tuesday last, turned over to The Bradley & Currier Company (Lim.), at a nominal consideration, No. 162 West 79th street, three-story dwelling, mort. $16,000; No. 340 East 93d street, five-story tenement, morts. $11,500; Nos. 111 to 117 West 96th street, four five-story flats, sub. to all liens; No 138 West 97th street, three-story dwelling, two-and-a-half lots on 99th street, north side, 275 east 10th avenue; No. 96 West 103d street, five-story flat, mort. $19,000; one lot on 118th street, north side, 460 east Lenox avenue, mort. $13,000; No. 255 West 120th street, three-story dwelling, mort. $10,000; No. 482 Lenox avenue, five-story flat, and Nos. 2193 to 2199 5th avenue and No. 4 East 134th street, being five five-story flats, on the southeast corner of 5th avenue and 134th street.

The Hebrew Free School Association and the Aguelar Free Library Society have obtained leave from Judge O'Brien, of the Supreme Court, to borrow $115,000 from "The Baron de Hirsch Fund" upon its property on the southeast corner of East Broadway and Jefferson street. There are mortgages of $56,500 on the property. These are to be retired, and the balance used in completing the Hebrew Institute, now being erected on the property.

The Congregation Chaari Zedek has obtained leave from Judge Barrett, of the Supreme Court, to execute to Franklin N. Billings a mortgage for $50,000 upon its property, Nos. 38 and 40 Henry street. It is proposed to erect a new house of worship on this site. The corporation has a cemetery at Bayside, L. I., and property in 88th street, between Park and Madison avenues, worth $30,000. Its Henry street place will be worth, when completed, $120,000. The total obligations of the corporation are about $60,000, and the cash assets $1,000.

Thomas F. Grady, John Connolly, and Samuel W. Milbank have been appointed by Judge Barrett as commissioners of Estimate and Assessment in proceedings to open Boston avenue between Sedgwick and Bailey avenues.

The New York Presbyterian Church has been given leave by Judge Barrett, of the Supreme Court, to mortgage its property at 7th avenue and 128th street for a loan of $100,000 from the Bowery Savings Bank. The money is to be used to cancel old mortgages.

Miss Gertrude Knelles wants the return of $177.95 paid for taxes in 1889 on premises belonging to the St. John the Baptist's Institution on the north side of 17th street, between 2d and 3d avenues.

Facts of General Interest.

The residents of Tremont are feeling happy over the completion of a long-promised improvement—the opening of a station at 177th street, on the Suburban road. Tremont can now be reached from the Harlem River on the Suburban road in seventeen minutes for a fare of only five cents, and the competition is having its effect in diminishing the revenue of the road, the New York & Harlem. The service on the Suburban may be generally commended, the cars being very comfortable and the trains frequent for that district of the city. There is one complaint, however, which is made against the road and that is that the trains about midnight are not long enough to carry all the passengers. Recently, it is said, the three-car train—the last for the night—was so crowded that half a-dozen or more persons who wished to embark could not do so and were forced to take the horse-cars instead. The train, too, was so crowded that it did not stop at the next station, and several people who were waiting for it there were left. The new station has only been open a few weeks and it is probable that everything is not yet working smoothly, so that criticism at this time would not be altogether just, but the Manhattan Company would do well to correct such errors as occurred on last Saturday night as soon as possible.

One of the oldest and best known auctioneers of suburban real estate showed a reporter of THE RECORD AND GUIDE his system for getting up circulars. It may seem strange to the uninitiated that a system is needed to get up circulars descriptive of suburban property, but such is the case, and the success of the auctioneer referred to is proof of the fact that the art of making circulars well is as important as making anything else well, and often of more consequence than having good property to sell. This auctioneer never gets out two circulars which are alike in any particular, if it is possible to avoid doing so, and as it is often necessary to say the same things in different circulars, the task is not an easy one. To facilitate matters he has a book of good phrases which deal with the points which it is desirable to touch on in a suburban circular such as means and kinds of transit, healthful location, scenery, terms, etc. Whenever he thinks of or hears a good phrase he puts it in his book and when he gets out another circular he has recourse to this valuable little compendium, which saves him from repeating himself. As a further help, he keeps a tabulated record of the various phrases he has used and when writing a new circular he keeps this before him and it acts as a sort of "don't" book.

Very small things will sometimes upset very large sales in the real estate world, as was well illustrated in a West Side broker's experience last week. The sale was of a large flat and store building on Columbus avenue, and it was not till the terms and everything else had been agreed upon that the technicality was discovered. Then it turned out that the wall of the house which was being sold was not quite plumb and overhung the neighboring property just 1 inch at the top of the house. The neighbor wanted a fabulous price to free the adjoining property, and this the owner would not pay, and as the would-be purchaser did not care to take any risk with the property he declined to complete the deal until there was a quit claim given by the adjoining owner. Consequently, the sale has not been completed and the broker will receive no commission, although he practically completed the sale.

A Quintet of West Side Houses.

[COMMUNICATED.]

It has been said, and with much truth, that the West Side of New York City can boast of handsomer private houses, taken as a whole, than any other section of the metropolis. This is particularly to be said of that section of the West Side between 70th and 95th streets. In the character of their exteriors and interiors, the private houses of the East Side, or of Harlem, or of the more southerly sections in the older quarters of the city, with a few exceptions, are of the older type, when electricity was not applied to dwellings, and when it was the rule to build row after row of plain brown stone front houses, which presented no particular architectural features worthy of mention.

But, *nous avons changé tout cela*, as the French would say. Not only have we changed in our style of exterior plan, but the finest woods from the forest, the best art of the woodworker and the cabinetmaker, the highest sanitary knowledge in plumbing, the best improvements in all those little conveniences that make a house what it ought to be—a perfect home—all these have tended to give the West Side a general superiority over other sections of the city where houses were built ten, twenty and thirty years or more since.

An excellent example of the West Side house is to be seen in the residences illustrated on this page. They have been built by James T. Hall, who recently disposed of several houses which he erected adjoining. The houses shown in the illustration contain Indiana limestone fronts. They give a cheerful appearance to the block, and the fine carving of the newel posts of the box stoop, and the general design of the latter, lend dignity to the exterior. The style adopted by the architect, Geo. H. Budlong, is of the Romanesque. The houses are four stories and basement in height, the top floor being ornamented with dormers and pediments. The most westerly house has three stories and basement in bay windows, while the other houses have one or two stories in bays. The stone work on the fronts is carved, rock-faced and tooled, and the whole, blended together, give a very rich appearance.

THE INTERIOR.

The interior of the houses do not belie their exterior. A glance at the centre house, which has recently been sold, and, which is a sample of the others, shows that the finest workmanship and best materials have been used. The storm doors, which are of oak, contain heavy plate-glass windows, running the entire length of the doors. The vestibule is entered through oak doors and contains high wainscoting in the same wood. Oak is also used in the entrance door to the hall, which is in panels, with carved borders. The hall is about 6 feet wide and from it the parlor is entered. This room is trimmed in maple and has a handsome mantel of special design, with fire-places faced in onyx, the hearths being tiled and the fenders and andirons being in brass. The window transoms are in stained cathedral glass.

THE MUSIC-ROOM.

The music room is entered directly from the parlor, and is separated from it by the simple arrangement of a screed of spindle-work. From this screed it is evidently intended that a portiere shall be suspended, and that this shall be the only division between the two rooms. This room, with the parlor and dining-room, can be thrown into one for receptions and other social entertainments.

James T. Hall, Owner. *Residences on Seventy-fifth street, between Columbus avenue and Central Park, West.* Geo. H. Budlong, Architect.

THE DINING-ROOM.

Passing from the music-room we enter the dining-room. This is unquestionably the handsomest room in the house. It is large and well-appointed. The floors are parqueted, the wainscotings are panelled in oak, and there is a handsome mantel and mirror, with tiled hearths and fire-places faced in onyx. The room is the full width of the house, and has a bay window. The butler's pantry beyond is unusually spacious, and is well-appointed in the matter of closets, etc. It has a parqueted floor, and contains a special rear flight of stairs leading down to the culinary department. This flight also runs to the top floor of the extension, which is two stories and basement in height.

THE UPPER FLOORS.

Ascending to the second floors we find a suite of bedrooms, with dressing-rooms communicating. This floor is trimmed in sycamore, and the front room is unusually large and contains an alcove to the south of the room which leads to the dressing-rooms. This feature is not often met with in modern houses. The dressing-rooms have parqueted floors and contain an abundance of wardrobe and closet room, the doors being inlaid with mirrors, which practically surround the rooms. The woodwork is in panels of white maple.

The bath-room on this floor is tiled and contains porcelain tub, nickel-plate plumbing exposed to view, a marble wash-stand and basin, etc. The floor is partly tiled and partly in inlaid oak. Close at hand, in the hallway from which the rear stairs are approached, is a large wardrobe closet intended as an adjunct to the bath-room.

The third floor contains four bedrooms and a bath-room, the latter with porcelain tubs and marble wash stand, nickel-plated plumbing, etc, similar to that on the second floor. The bedrooms are well appointed, and are in cabinet trim.

The fourth floor contains four rooms and a bath-room. The transoms in the front windows are of stained glass, and the main rooms have hard-wood mantels. The halls are surmounted by a dome light of stained glass, which sheds its rays over the lower halls and lights them up cheerfully.

The houses are not fully described without a mention of the front basement, which is in oak trim, and can be used as a billiard-room. It has mantel and mirror, closet, etc. The kitchen and laundry are appointed in the most approved manner.

Among the general features in these houses which strike the visitor are the excellent workmanship, whether in the stone-work, masonry or interior work, as well as the excellence of the materials used. The entire fronts and first-story rear are glazed with polished French plate-glass, the balance being of French glass of double-thickness. Each house has a separate sewer connection and the plumbing is of a high sanitary character. There is a complete system of speaking tubes, burglar-alarms and electric bells throughout, and each house is wired for electric lighting. The cabinet work, including the stairs and wainscoting, is in selected hardwoods of various kinds. All the floors are double and deafened. The mantels throughout have beveled plate mirrors and all the rooms are provided with open fire-places and tiled hearths and facings and are piped for gas logs. The cellars have a 4-inch flooring of high grade Portland cement and the sidewalks are of McKnight Flintic stone.

THE LOCATION.

The houses are within a few moments' walk of the 6th and 9th avenue elevated road stations at 72d street and Columbus avenue, and the 8th avenue, 10th avenue and Boulevard cars are easy of access. Central Park West can be seen from the front windows, while Riverside Park and Drive are within five minutes' walk. Communication with the East Side is made comparatively easy via the stages which run through from West to East 72d street, and the cross-town cars running through the Central Park at 86th street.

The houses are just being completed and will be placed upon the market next month.

OBSERVER.

The Opinions of Others.

President Geo. R. Read, of the Real Estate Exchange, said: "I think that down-town investment real estate is very much in favor now with the general capitalist. It supplies the place occupied fifteen years or so ago by Governments. It is firm, safe and returns a fair percentage, while Governments are so unprofitable that few people care to hold them. The investor, too, at the present time wants to be his own President, Secretary and Board of Directors, and have entire charge of his property, and this he can do only with real estate. Yes, I think that for investment real estate there is a bright prospect."

"What we need in the 23d Ward just now," said a local broker, "is one fare right through to the City Hall. Now that the Manhattan road has got control of the Suburban elevated they might make the price of the fare from Tremont 5 cents, and they would find it extremely profitable. Most of those who live or would like to live up here on the North Side are people in only moderate circumstances, and they do not feel that they can afford a double fare; so instead of residing in the 23d Ward they go to Brooklyn, Jersey City or Hoboken. I think I am right in saying that no one thing would help this ward so much as the reduction of the fare on the elevated road. The population would increase at a phenomenal rate, and I don't think the Manhattan people would find that they had lost anything by the change."

George Romaine said: "There is one weak point in real estate at the present time that I do not think is fully appreciated and that is the practice, quite general in many sections of the city, of selling houses on the smallest possible cash margins. Many men nowadays in receipt of fair incomes who rent houses are induced to buy a $15,000 or $16,000 dwelling, paying $1,000 or $2,000 cash and allowing the rest of the purchase money to remain on mortgage. They have been used to paying their $75 or $100 rent every month, but now they own the dwelling they reside in, so they increase their expenditures never thinking of the interest charges and the taxes that they will have to pay all in a lump. Suddenly the time for payment arrives and there is no money to discharge the debts; the man becomes involved and the house reverts to the original seller. This wouldn't happen if more money was required to purchase and fewer irresponsible parties were allowed to assume obligations that they couldn't discharge."

An Unimportant Strike.

The tin and sheet-iron workers who struck this week are still out.

At Messrs. Gillis & Geoghegan's about twenty men left work, demanding eight hours for the same pay as nine hours, which has hitherto been the length of a day's work. The firm offered to reduce the time of the outside men to eight hours, with the same pay as for nine hours, but the men declined this compromise, demanding that the inside men also have the time reduced to eight hours.

At Baker, Smith & Co. between thirty and forty men went out, and at E. Rutzler's about ten men went on strike. Until yesterday afternoon the men were still idle and both sides declare their determination to hold out. The wages of each man runs from $3 to $3.50 per diem.

Notes.

Judge Barrett, in the Supreme Court, this week, reduced the assessment levied on abutting property-owners for the regulating and grading of Clifton avenue (161st street) between St. Ann's and Union avenues, 31 9-10 per cent. In his opinion, the Judge says, "that it is a case of the advertisement of fictitious work, erroneous estimates and unbalanced bids. The assessment should be reduced on account of the fraud which is clearly established."

The testimony of the property-owners showed that the advertisement called for the removal of several thousand more cubic yards of earth and rock than were necessary to be or were removed, and that the commissioners approved the certificate of the work done notwithstanding these facts.

Personal.

John P. Kane, of the firm of Canda & Kane, building material dealers, is spending the summer with his family at Huntington, L. I., where he owns a very handsome place. Mr. Kane comes to business almost daily.

William P. Mangam and wife are spending the summer at Far Rockaway, L. I.

J. Jay Smith is rusticating at Pittsfield, Mass.

Charles E. Schuyler is staying at the Octagon House, Seabright, N. J.

J. Remsen Eckerson is spending a short time at Asbury Park, N. J.

Real Estate Exchange Matters.

The Real Estate Exchange balance sheet up to August 1st has been made out. It shows that on the 30th of June last there was a balance of $26,544.47, and that since then the receipts have amounted to $4,875.98, making a total of $31,420.45. Out of this amount a dividend of $12,500 has been paid, together with current office expenses of $2,102.81, making a total of $14,602.81. This leaves a balance of $16,817.64 on deposit to the credit of the Exchange.

Interesting to Architects and Builders.

HOT AIR ENGINE.

The Rider Hot Air Engine Company, of No. 37 Dey street, have, in connection with their hot air engine, a kerosene burner which dispenses with the necessity for using gas or coal, and is thus an important factor in the matter of economy.

* * *

PUMPS.

Henry R. Worthington has recently supplied a number of large compound pumps for the Imperial Fire Insurance Co., the Bank of the State of New York and the Bearsford Hotel. Among the other buildings of recent construction, supplied with the Worthington pumps, are the "Columbia," corner of Broadway and Morris street; the Jersey Central Railroad's headquarters, on Liberty and West streets; and Clinton Hall, on Astor place and 8th street. They have also been used in buildings all over the country, and as far west as San Francisco.

* * *

WATER-TIGHT CELLARS.

The fact that a considerable portion of the buildings erected in New York City have their cellars below tidewater, has made the cementing of cellars a special work. This is particularly so along the water front, where millions of dollars worth of valuable property now stands, over which, at the beginning of the century, the tide advanced and receded. Among those who have made a particular study of this kind of cementing is F. W. Lawrence, of No. 16 Exchange place, who has contracted for this class of work for the last twenty years, during which time he has effectively constructed many water-tight cellars along the river fronts and in the lower parts of the city. One of his recent contracts was for the cellar in the building owned by the Kunhardts, on the southeast corner of Broad and Beaver streets.

* * *

CERAMIC TUBS.

The Stewart Ceramic Company are the sole manufacturers, under Morahan's patents, of the only solid white crockery sinks and wash-tubs made. There are over two hundred of these tubs in one building alone—the "Dakota," on 72d street and Central Park West. The company have opened a branch office in Chicago, at Nos. 323 and 325 Dearborn street, under the management of W. N. Griffin. They have large offices and showrooms at No. 312 Pearl street, where a fine collection of their goods are to be seen.

Special Notices.

The Real Estate Loan and Trust Company, of No. 30 Nassau street, offers a good bargain to intending purchasers in a building on Broome street, near Greene, five stories high, rented to two tenants at $14,500 per annum. This parcel is offered at $182,000.

Contractors' Notes.

Bids will be received at the Department of Charities and Correction, 66 3d avenue, for materials and work for repairing rooms, plumbing, etc., at Bellevue Hospital, until 10 A. M., August 14th.

Strong, neat binders, especially made for THE RECORD AND GUIDE, can be obtained at this office. Those of our subscribers who wish to keep a file of the numbers in a compact form and in regular sequence, can have the binder delivered at their office on receipt of order by postal card. Price at office, $1.00, by mail, $1.19.

The Bedfordshire, Brooklyn. —Montrose W. Morris, Architect.

German Country House.

Real Estate Department.

There is nothing new to report in the Real Estate Market. The pronounced dullness experienced last week continues with unvarying conditions and about the same prospects of change. Little business is looked for or can be reasonably expected for at least a couple of weeks, and if matters brighten then it will be a surprise in many quarters. The market is neither weak nor unhealthy, but simply inactive, as it always is during the month of August, and there are no unusual circumstances to warrant the belief that this record will be broken. A hopeful sign is the preliminary inquiry for houses, both for sale and to rent, and these early indications are responsible for the bright views of the fall season advanced by the majority of the brokers.

THE AUCTION MARKET.

The Auction Market at the present time is almost featureless. Very little is being offered outside the sales necessitated by decrees of the courts, and these sales are almost entirely uninteresting. The property so offered is unimportant and of little moment to the general market, and the bidding is nearly always of the tamest character. That this state of affairs will immediately improve there is little hope, although there are signs which seem to indicate that the season will not be a late one. This coming week, for instance, Auctioneer John F. B. Smyth will offer on the Exchange nearly one hundred plots at Chester Park, a private park near Pelhamvillle, and if on the occasion of this sale the market develops any particular strength other suburban properties will be offered in rapid succession. Outside of this Chester Park sale, the auctioneers' announcements are devoid of anything interesting, consisting as they do of legal sales of a very ordinary character.

CONVEYANCES.

	1889. Aug. 2 to 8, inclus.	1890. Aug 1 to 7, inclus.	1891. July 31 to Aug. 6, inclus.
Number	192	263	268
Amount involved	$1,750,850	$5,581,360	$4,374,322
Number nominal	87	52	80
Number 23d and 24th Wards	38	40	60
Amount involved	$64,651	$251,070	$289,975
Number nominal	8	6	..

MORTGAGES.

	1889.	1890.	1891.
Number	175	271	243
Amount involved	$1,899,188	$3,596,664	$2,612,027
Number at 5 per cent	86	109	116
Amount involved	$1,126,012	$1,282,574	$1,340,175
Number at less than 5 per cent	16	89	12
Amount involved	$389,000	$411,900	$819,000
Number to Banks, Trust and Insurance Companies	27	34	24
Amount involved	$728,500	$367,250	$505,900

PROJECTED BUILDINGS.

	1889. Aug. 3 to 9, inclus.	1890. Aug. 2 to 8, inclus.	1891. Aug. 1 to 7, inclus.
Number of buildings	49	60	44
Estimated cost	$1,187,775	$1,078,810	$672,855

Gossip of the Week.

SOUTH OF 59TH STREET.

A rumor that the old Stevens House, on the southwest corner of Broadway and Morris street, had been sold to "Old Hutch," of Chicago Board of Trade repute, could not be verified. John F. Ames, the lessee, denied the rumor, and a call at the office of Horace S. Ely, agent for the property, did not elicit information of a definite character. It is said, however, on good authority, that negotiations for the sale are about to be or have already been concluded, but it has been directly through the owner, James Fielden, of San Francisco. The property was held at $700,000, and has a frontage of 139.11½ feet on Broadway, running back 117.8 feet in depth on the southerly line. It is 67 feet on Morris street and 132.6 wide on the westerly line, with an alley running through to Morris street at a point 183.5 feet west of Broadway. The hotel is five stories high in front and six stories in rear, and was one of the finest built in the early hotel days of this city.

Randolph Guggenheimer has sold to Wm. Ormiston Tait the block front on the west side of Park avenue, between 50th and 51st streets, for $150,000. The plot is 201.10x75, and Mr. Tait will improve the same by the erection of a six-story stable, from plans by Thomas Graham. The livery stable has already been leased for a period of twenty-one years, at an annual rental of $22,500.

Hiram Rinaldo & Bro. have sold to Fay & Stacom the lot, 25x100, No. 98 Henry street, on private terms, for improvement.

William R. Mason has sold for James Thompson the five-story improved tenement, 25x88x95.9, No. 324 West 37th street, for $29,000.

F. R. Houghton has sold to the Police Department for Schuster & Ruff Nos. 24 and 26 Macdougal street, size 50x100 feet, as a site for a new station house. The price paid was $40,000.

NORTH OF 59TH STREET.

F. A. Condit has sold for Elmore D. Alvord, of Bridgeport, Conn., to F. L. Wilmuith the five four-story dwellings, Nos. 312 to 320 West 89th street, for $137,500.

Charles Buek & Co. have sold No. 73 West 70th street, a four-story, high stoop, brick and brown stone front dwelling, 20x60x100.5, to Ernest Pfarrius for $35,000, and a similar dwelling, No. 75 West 70th street, to Haley Fiske for $36,000.

Charles E. Schuyler has sold No. 247 West 74th street, a three-story Queen Anne brick dwelling, 20x55x102.2, to H. D. Haven for $25,000.

J. W. & A. A. Teets have sold the three-story and basement brown stone house, No. 358 West 122d street, to Charles Weinmarth for $17,000, and a similar house, No. 360 West 122d street, to Jacob R. Wilkins for $16,750.

E. Sherman, as executor of the Day estate, has sold No. 141 West 122d street, a four-story brown stone dwelling, 16.8x60x102.2, for $17,500. This dwelling was purchased by the late Mr. Day, it is said, about three years ago for $19,500. This sale on one of Harlem's very best residence streets seems to corroborate the view advanced in THE RECORD AND GUIDE, a couple of weeks ago, in regard to the weakness of up-town real estate.

William P. Anderson has sold No. 170 West 93d street, a three-story, high stoop, brick and stone dwelling, 18x50x100, to Geo. Watson, of Newark, N. J., on private terms.

Ames & Co. have sold at private contract for Eagan & Halleey the three-story and basement brown stone private dwelling No. 243 West 103d street, size 17x50x100.11, to Samuel J. Clarke, Superintendent of the Providence & Stonington Steamship Company, on private terms.

LEASE.

Chas. E. Schuyler has leased for W. W. Conklin to J. Lehmaier for three years, at an annual rental of from $1,600 to $1,750, the three-story dwelling, No. 171 West 71st street.

Brooklyn

Corwith Bros. have sold for Mary A. Flynn the house and lot, No. 734 Leonard street, 25x25x100, to James A. and Wm. H. Post for $3,100.

C. H. Lock has sold the house on a lot, 25x100, No. 124 Pacific street, to Miss Leyden for $7,250.

CONVEYANCES

	1889. Aug. 1 to 7, inclus.	1890. July 31 to Aug. 6, inclus.	1891. July 30 to Aug. 5, inclus.
Number	317	426	419
Amount involved	$1,563,382	$1,257,597	$1,541,896
Number nominal	66	101	106

MORTGAGES.

	1889.	1890.	1891.
Number	244	241	348
Amount involved	$856,429	$1,626,629	$1,140,380
Number at 5 per cent. or less	139	173	184
Amount involved	$499,872	$871,461	$638,214

PROJECTED BUILDINGS.

	1889. Aug. 2 to 8, inclus.	1890. Aug. 1 to 7, inclus.	1891. July 31 to Aug. 6, inclus.
Number of buildings	93	92	79
Estimated cost	$435,307	$419,085	$373,095

Out of Town.

RICHMOND PARK, N. Y.—Ware & Odell have sold for the Ware estate one acre of ground at this place to a Mr. Kramer for $1,650, and three lots, 50x125 each, to a Mr. Barret for $1,050.

Out Among the Builders.

Thomas Graham is the architect for a six-story brick and stone livery stable which Wm. Ormiston Tait will erect on the plot, 201.10x75, west side of Park avenue, between 50th and 51st streets, at a cost of $130,000. The stable will accommodate 450 horses, and among other improvements it will be supplied with two steam elevators. It is the owner's intention to start work immediately and to make the stable as perfect as possible.

Frederick Ebeling is drawing plans for alterations which Barnett Levy, the owner, proposes to make in the building No. 97 Henry street. The alterations consist of interior improvements and a four-story and basement extension, 38 feet deep. The cost is estimated at $12,000.

Ferdinand J. Miller has drawn plans for the erection of a four-story house, 25x65, on the west side of Courtlandt avenue, 75 feet north of 156th street; Heinrich Hohmann, owner.

Two tenements, 50x70, are to be erected at Nos. 313 and 315 West 17th street for John McSweeney from plans by Charles H. Israels.

John Hauser is drawing plans for a two-story and attic frame dwelling, to be built by H. A. Strasse on the southwest corner of 161st street and Union avenue; cost not estimated.

Fay & Stacom will build a six-story apartment house on the lot, 25x100, No. 93 Henry street.

R. E. Rogers is drawing sketches for a three-story frame dwelling, 22x50, to be built by Wm. C. Jones, on the east side of Washington avenue, 210 feet south of 172d street, at a cost of $5,500.

The Police Department intend erecting a station house on the recently-acquired site, Nos. 24 and 26 Macdougal street. The size is 50x100. This station house will take the place of that now at Wooster and Prince streets.

J. O'Neill, the restaurateur, will build a seven-story hotel and restaurant, 26x98 in size, on the northeast corner of 6th avenue and 22d street, from plans by Danmar & Fischer, and will later add 28x69 on the street. The corner will cost $40,000, and will have an elevator, electric lights, etc.

The West Side Index

A few copies of the Ten Years' Index to Conveyances of West Side real estate can be had at the publication office of THE RECORD AND GUIDE, Nos. 14 and 16 Vesey street, at $5 per copy. The index is most valuable to brokers, lawyers and others who are desirous of keeping a list of the ownerships of property on the West Side. It is neatly bound, and is arrayed in the order of streets and avenues consecutively in such a simple manner that owners of property can easily be traced.

WANTS AND OFFERS.

(Advertisements strictly in accordance with this title will be inserted at the practically nominal rate of 10 CENTS *per line (agate). In figuring for themselves advertisers may count seven words for each line, the address to be taken as one line. The object of this department is to bring buyers and sellers into communication with customers. Advertisements must be marked "Wants and Offers Column," and sent to the office of publication, Nos. 14 and 16 Vesey Street, not later than 3 P. M. Friday.)*

SALES OF THE WEEK.

The following are the sales at the Real Estate Exchange and Auction Room for the week ending Aug. 7.

** Indicates that the property described has been bid in for plaintiff's account:*

R. V. HARNETT & CO.

Madison st, No. 231, n s, 47.8 e Jefferson st, 47.8x100, five-story brk tenem't. F. W. Foster. (Amt due $23,058) $70,625

WM. KENNELLY.

116th st, No. 54, s s, 82.11 e Madison av, 27.1x101, five-story brk flat. J. C. McDonald. (Amt due $3,074; prior mort. $25,000) 28,400

B. L. KANNELLY.

*101st st, No. 203, n s, 90 e 3d av, 20x100.11, four-story brk store and tenem't with two story brk building on rear. Wm. R. Rose ... 10,000

J. F. B. SMYTH.

Av A, Nos. 28 and 30, e s, 88.6 s 3d st, 44x100, five and three-story brk assembly rooms. D. M. Kellogg. (Amt due $42,845) 60,060

OTHER AUCTIONEERS.

*7th av, No. 2312, s w cor 136th st, 25x100, five-story brk flat with store. Moses Valentine and Jacob Rabinowitz. (Amt due $14,085) .. 48,075

*7th av, No. 2310, w s, 25 s 136th st, 37.5x100, five-story brk flat. Same. (Amt due $11,462) 40,650

*7th av, No. 2308, w s, 62.5 s 136th st, 37.5x100, five-story brk flat. Same. (Amt due $10,926) 40,650

Total $297,410
Corresponding week 1890 .... $415,322

BROOKLYN, N. Y.

For Week Ending August 6.

JERE JOHNSON, JR.

55th st s s, 90 e 16th av, 1 lot. Bollinger	$175
55th st, adj, 2 lots. Mastecello	320
55th st, adj, 2 lots. McDonald	320
55th st, adj, 4 lots. Hubbard	620
55th st, adj, 2 lots. B. Rapap t	8 0
55th st, adj, 3 lots. N. Miraldior	465
55th st, adj, 4 lots. H. F. McGail	600
56th st, n s, 90 e 16th av, 5 lots. Bolinger	975
56th st, adj, 3 lots. Douglass	480
56th st, adj, 3 lots. O'Brien	465
56th st, adj, 2 lots. Buhson	310
56th st, adj, 2 lots. Ewing	8.0
56th st, adj, 4 lots. A. Find	620
56th st, s s, 90 e 16th av, 5 lots. Thill	875
56th st, adj, 2 lots. Wm. Paine	360
56th st, adj, 2 lots. N. L. Brock	300
56th st, adj, 2 lots. Chas. Andrews	320
56th st, adj, 2 lots. A. Find	280
56th st, adj, 2 lots. G. W. McGowan	350
57th st, s s, 90 e 16th av, 2 lots. Thill	370
57th st, adj, 2 lots. Bollinger	360
58th st, s s, 200 w 16th av, 1 lot. G. Hendrick	185
58th st, adj, 1 lot. Buhson	185
58th st, adj, 4 lots. H. F. Cutting	840
58th st, adj, 4 lots. Thill	860
59th st, n s, 180 w 16th av, 1 lot. John Ewing	195
59th st, adj, 1 lot. M. Doyle	200
59th st, adj, 1 lot. J. Higgins	2?5
59th st, adj, 4 lots. M. E. Thill	800
59th st, s s, — w 16th av, 4 lots. P. Connolly	740
59th st, adj, 1 lot. Shelby	200
59th st, adj, 1 lot. Murphy	200
59th st, adj, 2 lots. John Doyle	400
60th st, n s, — w 16th av, 2 lots. J. Kelly	400
60th st, adj, 2 lots. M. Lyman	450
60th st, adj, 2 lots. M. Edwards	440
60th st, adj, 2 lots. F. Whittaker	450
16th av, s e cor 57th st, 5 lots. M. E. Thill	1,075
16th av, n w cor 59th st, 5 lots. J. Keller	1,175

OTHER AUCTIONEERS.

Cumberland st, No. 140, w s, 177.3 n Myrtle av, 25x100, three-story frame dwell'g. A. H. Williamson	3,600
Fenimore st, s s, 615.72 e Flatbush av, 100x125, Flatbush. Jacob V. Ackerman	6,050
King st, s w cor Conover st, 100x100. Carson Plake	11,125
*McDonough st, No. 333, n s, 280 w Stuyvesant av, 20x100 } McDonough st, No. 331, n s, 300 w Stuyvesant av, 20x100 } Two three-story brk dwell'gs. Elias J. Hendrickson	10,000
Prince st, No. 99, e s, 238.9 n Myrtle av, 21.3x85, three-story frame dwell'g. L. Arensberg	4,500
*Sedgwick st, s s. 225 w Columbia st, 18.9x100; all right, title and int } Sedgwick st, s s, 100 w Columbia st, 125x100; all right, title and int } H. S. Weaver	7,000
Prospect av, No. 157, n s, 375 e 3d av, 25x52.6x25.1x50.7, three-story frame dwell'g. Geo. Duncan	2,250
* Stone av, w s, 42 n Pacific st, 58x80, three three-story frame dwell'gs. John M. Stearns	8,500
Total	$71,100
Corresponding week, 1890	$48.925

CONVEYANCES.

Wherever the letters Q. C., C. a. G. and B. & S occur, preceded by the name of the grantee they mean as follows:

1st—Q. C. is an abbreviation for Quit Claim deed, i. e., a deed in which all the right, title and interest of the grantor is conveyed, omitting all covenants or warranty.

2d—C. a. G. means a deed containing Covenant against Grantor only, in which he covenants that he hath not done any act whereby the estate conveyed may be impeached, charged or encumbered.

3d—B. & S. is an abbreviation for Bargain and Sale deed, wherein, although the seller makes no express covenants, he really grants or conveys the property for a valuable consideration, and thus impliedly claims to be the owner of it.

NEW YORK CITY.

JULY 31, AUGUST 1, 3, 4, 5, 6.

Allen st, No. 103, w s, abt 125 s Delancey st, 25x87.6, five-story brk tenem't with stores. Morris Solomon and Henrietta his wife, Harry Harris and Dora his wife to Samuel Davis. July 31. $32,000

Bowery, No. 340, w s, 79 s Great Jones st, 26.6x106.4x25.4x98.10, four-story frame and brk store and tenem't. Ignazio Mercadante to Mary Mercadante his wife. Q. C. Aug. 4 nom

Central Park West (8th av), s w cor 94th st, 25.8x100, vacant. Partition. William N. Armstrong to Edward Hirsh. Aug. 4. 18,300

Central Park West (8th av), w s, 25.8 s 94th st, 50x100, vacant. Partition. William N. Armstrong to Bernard Cohen. Aug 4. 24,100

Delancey st, No. 100, n e cor Ludlow st, 19.3x75, five-story brk store and tenem't. Henry Sierichs and Augusta his wife to Marcus Jalien. *Mt.* $23,000. Aug. 1. 32,500

Dry Dock st, No. 2, w s, 75.4 s 11th st, 22.1x84x22.1x84, three-story brk tenem't. John Branigan to Joseph Branigan. *Mt.* $4,000. Aug. 3. 2,500

Duane st, No. 14, w s, 27.9 n William st, 19.11x51.1x20x51.4, four-story brk store and tenement with two-story brk building on rear. Simon Johnson, Cresskill, N. J., to Jacob Peiser. July 18. 18,000

East Broadway, No. 96, n s, abt 235 w Pike st, 25x76, three-story brk store and tenem't. Charles and Frederick Sylvester to Harry D. Haber. July 29. 20,250

East Broadway, No. 193, s s, 30 e Jefferson st, 17.4x65.6, new institute in course of erection. Myer S. Isaacs to The Hebrew Free School Assoc. *B. & S.* All liens. Dec. 31. nom

East Broadway, No. 191, s e cor Jefferson st, 30x65.6, new institute in course of erection. Same to Aguilar Free Library Soc. B. & S. All liens. Dec. 31. nom

Eldridge st, No. 196, e s, abt 80 n Rivington st, 24x87.6 three-story brk building. Frederick Finck and Antoinette his wife to Elizabeth Herdtfelder widow. Aug 1. 18,500

Eldridge st, No. 198, e s, 104.1 n Rivington st, 24x87.6, three-story brk tenem't. Lizzie wife of and George Herdtfelder and Natalie wife of and Louis B. Couch and Denton Fowler, Jr., to Elizabeth Herdtfelder widow. Q. C. and correction deed. July 21. nom

Essex st, No. 85, w s, 150.9 n Hester st, 25x87, six-story brk tenem't with stores. Wolf Cohen and Annie his wife to Annie Cohn. *Mt.* $30,500 July 30. nom

Greenwich st, No. 739, e s, 75.7 n Perry st, 18.8x77.10x20x84 10, three-story brk tenem't. Hamilton Walling and Elizabeth his wife to Edgar Logan. July 31. 8,080

Hamilton st, No. 39 } Monroe st, No. 34 } begins Hamilton st, n s, abt 175 w Market st, 16.10x82.9 to Monroe st, x19.7x77.4, each st contains a two-story frame and brk store and tenem't. Joseph D. Mayer and Fannie M. his wife to Randolph Guggenheimer and Salomon Marx. *Mt.* $10,000. July 31. See 134th st in 23d Ward. 14,000

Henry st, No 266, s s, 52.11 w Gouverneur st, 31x110.4x20.11x113, three-story brk tenem't. Harry Harris and Dora his wife to Morris Solomon. *Mt.* $16,000. Feb. 25. 27,000

Horatio st, No. 83, n s, 90.9 e Washington st, 23x84.3, three-story brk tenem't with two-story brk stable on rear. Jacob H. Conklin trustee Jacob Strout to Marx and Moses Ottinger. July 29. 9,850

Same property. Partition. Henry H. Anderson to same. July 29. 9,350

Houston st, No. 119, s s, 50 e Sullivan st, 25x95, five-story brk tenem't with stores. Lewis Myers and Eva his wife to Hugo Lederer. *Mt.* $25,000. Aug. 1. 38,250

Same property. Release mort. Hyman Schnitzer to Lewis Myers. July 27. nom

Hudson st, No. 242. }
Washington st, No. 255. }
Washington st, No. 253. }
Beach st, No. 7, and one lot in Park av and out of town property. }
Albert Lewis heir Albert Lewis dec'd and Harriet H. wife of and Albert Lewis, Jr., to Charles Schweinler, South Orange, N. J. Release all title. July 30. val. consid.

Kingsbridge road, n s, 150 w Hawthorne st, 100x250. Foreclos. Edgar Logan to Edward Kilpatrick. April 1. 8,000

Madison st, No. 136, s s, 188 e Market st, 25x100, five-story brk tenem't. Samuel Weil and Rachel his wife to Barnet Friedman and Samuel Harris. *Mt.* $29,000. July 30. See Oliver st. 44,500

Mott st, No. 183, w s, 147.2 n Broome st, 25.5x100, five story brk tenem't with stores Morris Willner and Rosanna his wife to Simon Selzer. *Mt.* $29,650. July 29. 34,500

Oak st, Nos. 41 and 41½, s s, abt 92 e James st, runs south 25 x east 7.8 x south 25.4 x east 1 x south 2.8 x east 12.9 x north — to Oak st, x —, three-story brk tenem't with stores. Margaret Harvey widow to John H. V. Arnold July 30. 500

Oliver st, No. 70, e s, 132.10 s Oak st, 26.4x100.8x25.6x100.2, five-story brk tenem't with stores. Barnett Friedman and Betsy his wife, Samuel Harris and Annie his wife to Samuel Weil. *Mt.* $23,500. July 28. See Madison st. 32,000

Oliver st, No. 65, w s, 46.2 s Oak st, runs west 50.2 x south 2.5 x west 20.7 x south 0.5 x west 29.8 x south 22.5 x east 99 6 to Oliver st, x north 25.3, four-story brk store and tenem't with five-story brk tenem't on rear. Rosanna wife of Michael Varley to Dora Harris. July 31. 19,000

Pearl st, No. 67 } Stone st, No. 32 } begins Pearl st, n s, 189.1 e Broad st, runs north 84.4 x west .06 x north — to Stone st, x east 19.10 x south 35.1 x east — x south 7.5 x west 3.4 x south 73.2 to Pearl st, x west 20.4, four-story brk store on Pearl st and three-story brk store on Stone st. Frank B. Treiber to Jefferson M. and L. Napoleon Levy. Sub. to mort. April 1, 1891. 50,000

Pitt st, No. 57, w s, 168.8 n Delancey st, 18.7x63, three-story brk store and tenem't Ignatz Kaufman to Samuel Stiller and Theresa his wife. *Mt.* $9,000. July 28. 11,100

Ridge st, No. 145, w s, 80 n Stanton st, runs west 25 x south 5 x west 50 x north 25 x east 75 to st, x south 20, four-story brk store and tenem't with four-story brk tenem't on rear. Katherine E. wife of Samuel Kopp to Gussie Luhr. July 29. nom

Same property. Gussie wife of Frederick Luhr to Samuel Kopp. July 29. nom

Sheriff st, No. 34, e s, abt 150 n Broome st, 21.10x100, five-story brk store and tenem't with two-story frame dwell'g on rear. Israel Lebowitz and Fanny his wife to Isaac Goldstein. *Mt.* $13,000. July 29. nom

Spring st, No. 55, n s, abt 75 e Marion st, 25.3x118x25x112 3, five-story brk tenem't with stores. Catharine A. Stevens to John Maggi. Aug. 3. 34,000

Spring st, No. 10, s s, 25.4 e Elizabeth st, 25.1x51.9x24 9x57.8, four-story brk store and tenem't. Bertha wife of Christopher H. Wiemann and John Muhlenbrink to Peter Massoth. July 6. 17,750

Stanton st, No. 176, n s, 75 e Clinton st, 25x100, four-story frame store and tenem't, with four-story brk building on rear. David K. Schuster and Sallie his wife to Bernard Galewski. *Mt.* $14,000. July 30. 20,750

Sullivan st, No. 77, e s, 200 s Spring st, 25x100, five-story brk store and tenem't. Florentina Isaacs to Harris Mandelbaum. July 28. 28,000

Sullivan st, No. 77, e s, 200 s Spring st, 25x100, five story brk store and tenem't. Harris Mandelbaum and Annie his wife to Marcus and Jacob S. Rosen. ⅙ part. *Mt.* $20,000. Aug. 3. nom

William st, No. 215 } North William st, No. 12 } begins William st, n w s, 70 n e from centre line of East River Bridge, runs northwest 70 to s e s of North William st, x northeast 3.3 x southeast 78 to William st, x southwest 17, four-story brk building. Louis Ceragioli and Augusta his wife and John and Frank Ceragioli and Eliza Yerance to Albert Tag. July 31. 16,000

Same property. Albert Tag to William and August Zinsser. B. & S. Aug. 1. 18,000

William st, Nos. 79 and 81, n w cor Liberty st, 36.7x34.8x38 8x44 2, five-story brk office building. Sarah M Garretson widow and Maria Jones to T. Gaillard Thomas. July 27. 80,000

3d st, No. 118, s s, 25 w Macdougal st, 25x100, five-story stone front tenem't with stores. Fanny Levy to Isidore Abrahams. *Mt.* $21,550. Aug. 6. 32,000

4th st, No. 166, w s, 76 n Cornelia st, 20x47.11x20x51.10, five-story brk tenem't. Bertha Striem to Hyman Garvar. *Mt.* $12,500. Aug. 1. 15,750

6th st, No. 543, n s, 70 w Av B, 20x90.10, five-story brk store and tenem't. Edward H. Hanigan and Annie M. his wife, Stamford, Conn., to George P. Herrmann. Q. C. June 10, 1880. nom

6th st, No. 726, s s, 238 e Av C, 30x97, five-story brk tenem't with stores. Marcus Lederer and Sofie his wife to Samuel Cohen. *Mt.* $19,500. July 28. 32,250

11th st, No. 150, s s, 169.9 e Greenwich av, runs south 43.4 x southeast 6.7 x southeast 13.9 x north 51.4 to 11th st, x west 18.9, three-story brk dwell'g. William C. Dick to Elizabeth Wood. *Mt.* $7,500. Aug. 5. nom

11th st, No. 148, s s, 207.3 e Greenwich av, runs south 57.3 x west 6.3 x northwest 13 9 x — to st, x east 18.9, omission, three-story brk dwell'g. William C. Dick to Elizabeth Wood. *Mt.* $7,500. Aug. 5. nom

12th st, No. 329 } Greenwich st, No. 799 } begins 12th st, n e cor Greenwich st, runs north 74.7 x east 77.10 x south 23 x west 53.3 x south 48.11 to 12th st, x west 21, six-story brk building on each st. Joseph D. Eldredge and Henrietta his wife to James C. Smith. *Mt.* $40,000. July 30. nom

13th st, No. 528, s s, 270 w Av B, 25x103.3, five-story brk tenem't with stores. Lewis Franklin and Amelia his wife to Adolph Steiner. *Mt.* $16,000. Aug. 3. 26,350

14th st, s s, 175 e 8th av, 25x103.3. Release morts. The Equitable Life Assurance Society of the U. S. to H. Henry Rader and Mathilde R. Griffeth. July 31. 10,000

17th st, Nos. 313 and 315, n s, 125 w 8th av, 50x92.2, two three-story brk tenem'ts with two two-story frame buildings on rear. Ascher Weinstein and Annie his wife to John McSweeney. *Mt.* $34,000. Aug. 3. nom

18th st, No 142, s s, 480 w 6th av, 23x92, two-story brk stable. H. Henry Rader and Mathilde R. Griffith widow to The Butterick Publishing Co. (Lim.) *Mt.* $5,000. July 24. 17,500

21st st, No. 311, n s, 599.10 e 9th av, 25.1x98.9, five-story stone front flat. James B. Gillie and Sarah E. his wife to Hugh Reilly. *Mt.* $20,000. July 29. nom

24th st, No. 18, s s, 396.7 w Broadway, 19x78.5x19x78.3, three-story brk building. William P. Lynch to Roean Spencer. *Mt.* $23,000. July 27. 30,000

25th st, No. 222, s s, 217.9 w 7th av, 15.6x98.9, four-story brk dwell'g. Annie V. and Emily C. Fox to Mary Griffiths. July 23. nom

25th st, No. 207, n s, 102 w 7th av, 21x98.9, three-story brk dwell'g. Esther Chuck to John H. McGinn. Aug. 3. 14,000

27th st, No. 138, s s, 120 e Lexington av, runs south 98.9 x west 20 x north 3.3 x west 5 x north 95.6 to 27th st, x east 25, three-story brk dwell'g. Joseph Kerr and Emma his wife to The Welsh Baptist Tabernacle. July 30. 25,500

27th st, Nos. 253 and 255, n s, 159.7 e 8th av, 49.9x98.9, two four-story brk stores and tenements with three-story brk building on rear. Margaret A. Post to Emilie S. Thackston. Q. C. June 20. 100

27th st, Nos. 103 and 105, n s, 60 e 4th av, 40x24.8, two three-story brk dwell'gs. Mary and Emma Turner, John W. Turner and Mary his wife, Richard W. Turner and Mary R his wife children and devises of Richard Turner, Maria E. wife of James H. Kent, Lillian wife of George W. Lippencott, Harriet and Emma Burton, children and heirs of Maria E. Burton, Ella G. and William A. Tooker, Jr., children and heirs of Sarah A. Tooker and William A. Tooker individ. and as exr of Sarah Tooker to Edward Cooper. July 29. 24,000

27th st, No. 446, s s, 175 e 10th av, 25x98.9, five-story brk flat. John V. Campbell and Elizabeth M. C. his wife to Ellen Ryan. *Mt.* $23,000. July 31. See 118th st. 34,000

29th st, Nos. 131 and 133, n s, 337 w 6th av, 38x28.7x—x38, two three-story brk dwell'gs. William L. Wilson to William P. Dixon. July 30. 15,250

Same property. James D. Sherwood and Mary

E. his wife, Peekskill, N. Y., to William L. Wilson. July 30. 20,000

29th st, s s, 380 w 6th av. Party wall agreement. Herbert M. Kinsley, Chicago, Ill., to Anna A. Boyle. July 31. nom

32d st, No. 42, s s, 168.10 e Broadway, 21x98.9, four-story brk dwell'g. Frank M. Blodgett and Isadora B. his wife to Mary E. Hanley. June 10. nom

33d st, No. 222, s s, 287.6 w 7th av, 20.10x68.3x 20.10x66 10, three-story brk dwell'g. Evangeline Stewart by William W. Fuller guard. to Lizzie W. Guy. 1-7 part. Aug. 4. 886

Same property. George G. Dunlop by Joseph Dunlop guard. to same. Infant's share. July 31. 885

Same property. Samuel J. Stewart, Chicago, to same. B. & S. July 20. nom

Same property. Isabella Noble formerly Guy, Margaret E. and Lizzie W. Guy and Joseph Dunlop to John O'Gara. July 31. 10,700

37th st, Nos. 550-554, s s, 100 e 11th av, 75x98.9, one, two and three-story frame buildings. Edward Joyce and ano. exrs. Felix Dougherty to Mary E. Joyce. Aug. 1. 18,100

Same property. Michael J. and John P. Dougherty to same. B. & S. July 30. nom

38th st, Nos. 330-334, s s, 175 w 1st av, 74x95.5x 75x104, three five-story brk tenem'ts. Maria N. Winne to August M. Weil. *Mt.* $65,000. July 31. other consid. and 100

41st st, No. 306, s s, 92 6 e 2d av, 16.3x67x17.10x 59.9, four-story brk dwell'g. Foreclos. Henry McCloskey to William P. Sheridan. Aug. 3. 7,500

43d st, No. 230, s s. 300 w 7th av, 16.8x100.5, four-story brk dwell'g. George R. Hamilton and Irene F. his wife to Albert H. Little. July 31. 16,000

44th st, No. 435, n s. 440 w 9th av, 20x100.4, four-story brk tenem't. Ann wife of James McCann to Patrick Kennedy. July 1. 11,500

45th st, No. 226, s s, 807 e 3d av, 26x100.4, five-story brk tenem't with stores. Jacob Arm and Frederika Arm his wife to Morris A. Eiseman and Abraham Sandberg. *Mt.* $8,000. July 30. 20,750

46th st, No. 152, s s, 205 w 3d av, 15x100.5, four-story stone front dwell'g. Anna E. Nebrbes to Emma A. Kassing. July 31. 18 000

48th st, No. 149, n s, 260 e 7th av, 20x100.5, four-story stone front dwell'g. George Kitching and Ella K his wife to Leopold Kahn. *Mt.* $12,000. July 31. See 124th st. 27,000

49th st, No. 109, n s, 150 w 6th av, 25x100.5, three-story brk store and tenem't with two-story frame building on rear. William G. Robinson and Augusta L. his wife to Park & Tilford. *Mt.* $12,000. Aug. 1. 20,000

50th st, Nos. 35 and 37, n s, 150 w 4th av, 50x 100.5, two five-story brk flats. Foreclos. Thomas F. Donnelly to The Equitable Life Assur. Soc. of United States. Aug. 3. 75,000

50th st, No. 123 E., conveys strip 5x7, forming part of premises given below. Emma A. Kassing to the trustees of St. Patrick's Cathedral. Aug. 1. nom

50th st, No. 123, n s, 80 w Lexington av, 20x 107.6, four-story stone front dwell'g. Same to same. Aug. 1. 22,000

51st st, No. 347, n s 150 w 1st av, 25x100.5, five-story brk store and tenem't. Louis M. Cohen to Morris H. Cohen. Aug. 5. nom

Same property. Morris H. Cohen to Sophie H. wife of Louis M. Cohen. B. & S. Aug. 6. nom

52d st, Nos. 539-543, n s, 300 e 11th av, 75x100.5, three five story brk tenem'ts, stores in Nos. 539 and 541. Gottfried J. Hauser and Annie his wife, Frank S. Price and Louise B. his wife to Edward B. Gethin. *Mt.* $45,000. Aug. 3. nom

52d st, n s, 200 e 11th av, 75x100.5. Release judgment. Michael Cain to G. Julius Huser and Frank S. Price. Aug. 3. nom

55th st, No. 428, s s, 340.7 w 9th av, 21.10x 100.5, two-story frame store and dwell'g with two-story frame dwell'g on rear. Adam Felferling to Barbara Loehr. Aug. 5. 6,000

57th st, No. 47, n s. 145 e 6th av, 25x100.5, four-story stone front dwell'g. Fannie R. and John R. Hazard by Harry Hubbard guard. to Ambrose K. Ely. Infants' shares. Aug. 6. 17,667

Same property. John C. Ross and Fanny R. wife of and Herbert Hazard to same. ⅔ part. Aug. 6. 35,333

64th st, No. 142, s s, 433 w 9th av, 17x100.5, four-story stone front dwell'g. Edward B. Gethin to Louise B. Price and Annie Hauser. C. a. G. *Mt.* $20,500. Aug. 1. nom

66th st, Nos. 243 and 245, n s, 150 e West End av, 50x100.5, two five-story brk and stone tenem'ts. E. Clifford Potter and Margaret S. his wife to James L. Cornell, Brooklyn, N. Y. *Mt.* $15,000. July 14. See 72d st. nom

68th st, No. 230, s s, 319.2 e 3d av, 18.2x100, three-story stone front dwell'g. Robert Froese and Henriette his wife to Esther S. Goldstein. *Mt.* $6,500. July 30. 14,000

69th st, No. 207, n s, 150 w West End av, 25x 100.5, five-story brk tenem't with stores. Percival S. Menken to Patrick Roache. Aug. 2. 25,000

72d st, No. 160, s s, 98 e Lexington av, 18x104.4, four-story stone front dwell'g. James L. Cornell, Brooklyn, N. Y., to Thomas R. Hughes, Weehawken, N. J. *Mt.* $15,000. July 30. See 66th st. nom

Same property. Thomas R. Hughes, Weehawken, N. J., to Eugene C. Potter. *Mt.* $19,500. July 30. See 66th st. nom

72d st, n s, 425 w 8th av, 50x102.2, vacant.
73d st, s s, 425 w 8th av, 50x102.2, vacant.
Al. Hayman and Minnie his wife to Richard M. Hooley. Q. C. ½ part. July 29. 20,000

73d st, No. 432, s s, 125 w Av A, 25x102.2, five-story brk tenem't. Max Cohen to Joseph Stang and David Hittner. *Mt.* $15,000. July 31. 23,250

74th st, No. 321, n s, 275 e 2d av, 25x102.2, five-story brk tenem't. Myer Hellman and Amelia his wife to Marianna Meyer. *Mt.* $11,000. Aug. 1. 17,250

75th st, Nos. 227-231, n s, 230 w 2d av, 75x102.2, three four-story brk tenem'ts. Ellen F. wife of Cornelius Leary to Fannie A. Lowenstein. *Mt.* $41,000. July 31. 47,000

75th st, No. 17, n s, 95 w Madison av, 20x102.2, four-story stone front dwell'g. Charles L. Tiffany and Harriet A. his wife to Albert Bellamy. Aug. 5. 36,000

76th st, No. 419, n s, 268 e 1st av, 20x102.2, five-story brk store and tenem't. Simon Abrahams and Lena his wife to Wolf Cohen. *Mt.* $9,000. July 31. 12,000

78th st, No. 217, n s, 241 w Amsterdam av, 20x 102.2, three-story stone front dwell'g. Adelaide L. and Mary E. Beekman to Blanche P. Flanagan. July 31. nom

78th st, No. 215, n s, 221 w Amsterdam av, 20x 102.2, three-story stone front dwell'g. Jacob M. Newman to Frank W. Larom. Aug. 1. 25,150

78th st, No. 307, n s, 83.2 w West End av, 16.4x 102.2, three-story brk dwell'g. Matthew C. Meyer and Julia M. his wife to Ella A. Monroe Hall. Aug. 4. 20,500

79th st, No. 328, s s, 287.6 w 1st av, 18.9x102.2, four-story stone front flat. Charles Rosenberg and Barbara his wife to Henry Gernshym. *Mt.* $9,000. Aug. 1. nom

Same property. Henry Gernshym, Brooklyn, to Charles Rosenberg. ½ part. *Mt.* $9,000. Aug. 1 nom

79th st, Nos. 433-437, n s, 460 e 1st av, 78x102.2, three four-story stone front tenem'ts. Jacob Schlosser and Margaret his wife to William Fritzel and Elizabetha his wife. *Mt.* $34,500. July 30. See 81st st. 52,500

79th st, No. 431, n s, 434 e 1st av, 26x102.2, four-story stone front tenem't. Same to same. *Mt.* $10,000. July 30. See 81st st. 17,000

79th st, No. 155, n s, 393 w 9th av, 19x102.2, three-story stone front dwell'g. Jean E. wife of Gilbert Tompkins to Jennie L. Denig. July 14. 24,000

79th st, No. 162, s s, 200 e 10th av, 17x102.2, three-story brk dwell'g. John A. Rochford to The Bradley & Currier Co. (Lim.) *Mt.* $16,000. Sept. 11, 1890. nom

80th st, No. 112, s s, 275.10 w Lexington av, 18.4x102.2, three-story stone front dwell'g. Bennett B. Schneider, South Orange, N. J., to Sarah wife of Louis Rubenstein. *Mt.* $8,000. Aug. 1. 15,800

81st st, No. 229, n s, abt 250 w 2d av, three-story brk tenem't with three-story frame dwell'g on rear.
32d st, No. 248, s s, 530 w 8th av, 20x98.9, three-story brk dwell'g.
James L. Lowry trustee of Henrietta E. Gibbins to Henrietta E. Guldenkirck formerly Gibbins. Aug. 4. nom

81st st, No. 413, n s, 231.6 e 1st av, 25x102.2, five-story brk tenem't. William Fritzel and Elizabetha his wife to Jacob Schlosser. *Mt.* $14,000. July 30. See 79th st. 21,500

81st st, No. 213, n s, 152.6 e 3d av, 25.6x102.2, five-story brk tenem't. Mary F., Thomasena V., Thomas N., Cora M., Owen L. and Oscar Smith by The Farmers' Loan and Trust Co. guard. to Margaret C. Smith. Infants' shares. *Mt.* $18,000. July 29. 16,075

Same property. Andrew A. Smith, Annie R. Pack and John J. Smith to same. ⅜ part. *Mt.* $18,000. July 24. 9,425

82d st, No. 608, s s, 148 e East End av, 25x83.8x 25.3x80.3, five-story brk tenem't. Louis Brandt, Henriette E. his wife and John Brandt to John Biezinger and Maria his wife. *Mt.* $12,000. Aug. 3. 19,400

84th st, s s, 275 e 10th av, 100x102.2, vacant.
84th st, Nos. 155-159, n s, 100 e 10th av, 75x 151.2x77x154.5, three five-story stone front flats.
Joel O. Stevens, late Under Sheriff, to Edna A. wife of William J. Gage. Deed on execution. Aug. 6. 2,981

85th st, Nos. 252-258, s s, 100 e West End av, 80x102.2, four five-story brk flats. Foreclos. Henry A. Robinson to Reuben W. Ross. *Mt.* $12,000. July 15. 5,000

Same property. Reuben W. Ross and Hattie N. his wife to Albert C. Henderson. *Mt.* $12,000. Aug. 6. 30,800

85th st, Nos. 330 and 332, s s, 350 e 2d av, 50x 102.2, two four-story stone front tenem'ts. Henry P. De Graaf and Amanda M. his wife to Karl M. Wallach. *Mt.* $21,000. July 31. 36,000

86th st, No. 64, s s, 203.7 w Park av, 31.11x102.2, five-story stone front flat. Edward Oppenheimer and Mathilde his wife to George Finck. July 27. nom

Same property. Edward Philips and Theodora his wife to same. Aug. 2. nom

Same property. George Finck to Rose Wilson. *Mt.* $35,000. July 22. 50,000

Same property. Rose Wilson to Robert W. Taller. *Mt.* $35,000. July 22. nom

86th st, No, 520, s s, 223 e Av A, 28x102.2, four-story brk tenem't. Hattie Frank to Anna Hauck. *Mt.* $13,500. Aug. 3. 21,000

89th st, s s, 113.4 w Madison av, 25x100, vacant. Clarissa L. Crane widow and devisee of Thomas Crane to William O. Tait. *Mt.* $9,500. July 27. 13,500

Same property. William O. Tait and Maggie J. his wife to Isaac Untermyer. *Mt.* $9,500. July 31. nom

89th st, No. 223, n s, 225 w 2d av, 25x100.8, five-story brk tenem't. Henriette wife of Jacob Harris to Leopold Barth. *Mt.* $12,500. Aug. 3. 20,100

93d st, No. 340, s s, 75 w 1st av, 25x75.8, five-story brk tenem't. John A. Rochford to The Bradley & Currier Co. (Lim.) *Mt.* $11,500. Oct. 27, 1890. nom

94th st, Nos. 16 and 18, s s, 143.9 w 8th av, 37.6x 100.8, two four-story stone front dwell'gs. Peter Herche and Louisa his wife to Moritz Pinner. *Mt.* $46,000. July 31. nom

96th st, Nos. 111-117, n s, 200 w 9th av, 125x 100.11, four five-story brk flats. John A. Rochford to The Bradley & Currier Co. (Lim.) All liens. Nov. 18, 1890. nom

97th st, No. 138, s s, 347 w 8th av, 18x100.11, three-story stone front dwell'g. John A. Rochford to The Bradley & Currier Co. (Lim.) All liens. Sept. 13, 1890. nom

97th st, No. 72, s s, 100 e 9th av, runs south 100.11 x east 21.1 x northeast 39.5 x north 61.8 to 97th st, x west 24.6, five-story brk flat. Adolph Franke and Christina his wife to Robert Franke. *Mt.* $17,500. July 22. nom

Same property. Robert Franke to Christina Franke. *Mt.* $17,500. July 22. nom

99th st, n s, 275 e 10th av, 60.2x101x64.1x100.11, vacant. John A. Rochford to The Bradley & Currier Co. (Lim.) Oct. 14, 1890. nom

101st st, n s, 320 e 1st av, 75x—, vacant. Augustus N. Denman, Des Moines, Iowa, and Mary A. his wife, William M. Denman, Mount Vernon, N. Y., and Jennie A. his wife, Annie M. and Mary F. Tompkins, Dallas, Texas, Ashael A. Denman, Denver, Col., Francis H. Denman, Aspen, Col., Caroline P. and Arthur R. Denman, Newark, N. J., to Esther A. Wheaton. *Mt.* $4,000. June 5. 8,250

101st st, s s, 75 e Amsterdam av, 25x100 11, five-story brk flat. Robert J. McGirr and Mary A. his wife to Edward Karsch. *Mt.* $18,500. July 30. 24,000

101st st, No. 229, n s, 175 w 2d av, 25x100.11, four-story brk tenem't. Simon Adler and Emma his wife, Henry S. Herrman and Jennie his wife to Henry Harder and Hildegard his wife. *Mt.* $10,000. July 23. 13,500

102d st, No. 74 and 76, s s, 100 e Columbus av, 60x100.11.
102d st, No. 68, s s, 220 e Columbus av, 30x 100.11.
Three five-story brk flats.
Henry C. Acker and Emma L. his wife to Annie L. Gardner. All liens. July 1. nom

102d st, Nos. 208-214, s s, 160 e 3d av, 100x100.11, four five-story brk tenem'ts with stores in Nos. 212 and 214. Jonas Weil and Theresa his wife and Bernhard Mayer and Sophia his wife to Benedict A. Klein. July 28. 97,200

Same property. Benedict A. Klein and Karoline his wife to Jonas Weil and Bernhard Mayer. *Mt.* $54,000. Aug. 4. nom

103d st, No. 96, s s, 80 e 9th av, 19 6x100.11, five-story stone front flat. John A. Rochford to The Bradley and Currier Co. (Lim.) *Mt.* $19,000. Oct. 14, 1890. nom

103d st, Nos. 247, n s, 133 e West End av, 17x 100.11, three story stone front dwell'g. John J. Egan and Mary his wife and Daniel Hallecy and Mary his wife to William C. Flanagan. *Mt.* $13,500. July 29 19,000

105th st, No. 59, n s, 175 e Columbus av, 25x 100.11, five-story brk flat. Release mort. Edward Shuttleworth to William L. Wilson. June 23. 544

Same property. Release mort. Isaac S. Steindler and Max Hahn to same. July 23. 157

Same property. Release mort. William Wilkening to same. July 23. 70

Same property. Release mort. Michael McGrath and George Burns to same. July 23. 773

Same property. Release mort. John Comisky and Frank Dobson to same. July 23. 50

Same property. Release mort. Charles Hartman to same. July 23. 300

Same property. Release mort. Luke Highton to same. July 23. 175

Same property. Release mort. Enoch C. Bell to same. July 23. 250

Same property. Release mort. Christopher Nally to same. July 23. 350

Same property. William L. Wilson to James D. Sherwood. *Mt.* $22,000. July 30. 38,000

105th st, n s, 175 e Columbus av, 25x100.11. Release mort. Rody McLaughlin to William L. Wilson. July 23. 150

Same property. Release mort. John and James Dobson to same. July 23. 130

106th st, No. 321, n s, 300 w 1st av, 25x100.11, four-story brk tenem't. Hubert Madden and Mary his wife to Bertolomeo Cassazza. *Mt.* $7,500. July 31. 17,350

106th st, No. 321, n s, 300 w 1st av, 25x100.11, four-story brk tenem't. Bertolomeo Cassazza to Giovanni Cassazza. ½ part. Q. C. Aug. 5. nom

Same property. Giovanni Cassazza to Julianna Cassazza. ½ part. Q. C. Aug. 5. nom

107th st, No. 161, n s, 133 e Lexington av, 17x 100.11, four-story stone front flat. Mary A. Bulkley to Hulda Goldstein. July 30. 12,500

107th st, No. 165, n s, 167 e Lexington av, 17x 100.11, four-story stone front flat. Justus L. Bulkley and ano. exrs. Joseph E. Bulkley to Wolff Morris. July 29. 12,400

107th st, No. 81, n s, 49 w 4th av, 16x100.11, three-story stone front dwell'g. George F. Goldstein to Hulda Goldstein. Aug. 6. 13 000

109th st, No, 123, n s, 211.3 e 4th av, 18.9x100.11,

four-story brk tenem't. John N. Michel and Elizabeth his wife to Joseph I. West. July 31. 8,500

111th st, No. 10, s s, 100 e 5th av, 19x100.11, five-story stone front flat. John Hickey and Ann his wife to Alice F. wife of William D. Lent. *Mt.* $15,000. Aug. 5. nom

112th st, n s, 378.4 w 3d av, —x—. Party wall agreement. William Lyman and Fannie his wife with Kate wife of Francis Rogers. May 8. nom

113th st, No. 152, s s, 320 w 3d av, 25x100.10, two-story frame dwell'g. Ellen Ryan to John V. Campbell. July 31 See 27th st. 10,000

115th st, No. 19, on map No. 15, n s, 135 w Madison av, 25x100.11, five-story brk flat. Louis Stern and Caroline his wife to Levi L. Kessler and Amanda his wife. *Mt.* $18,000. July 31. nom

116th st, No. 417, n s, 199 e 1st av, 20x100.11, three-story stone front dwell'g. Emil J. wife of George N. Manchester to Elizabeth Herdtfelder. *Mt.* $12,000. July 31. 15,000

118th st, n s, 460 e Lenox av, 25x100.11, vacant. John A. Rochford to The Bradley and Currier Co. (Lim.) *Mt.* $12,000. Oct. 14, 1890. nom

119th st, No. 30, s s, 630 e Lenox av, 15x100.11, three-story stone front dwell'g. John B. Smith and Bertha his wife to Samuel E. Ayres. *Mt.* $10,000. July 1. See Madison av in 23d Ward. July 1. 14,500

119th st, No. 305, n s, 75 e 2d av, 19.3x100.11, four-story stone front dwell'g. Partition. Samuel Cohn to Johanna Marco. *Mt.* $8,500. Aug. 3. 12,075

120th st, No. 255, n s, 57 e St. Nicholas av, 16.8x100.11, three-story stone front dwell'g. John A. Rochford to The Bradley and Currier Co. (Lim.) *Mt.* $10,000. Oct. 14, 1890. nom

120th st, n s, 225 e 4th av, 20x100.11
144th st, n s, 200 e Willis av, 50x100
Release judgment. Eugene Kelly, and Eugene and Edward Kelly, and William Farrell and Joseph A. Donohue, of Eugene Kelly & Co., to William T. Washburn and ano. exrs. Benjamin Richardson. July 11. nom

120th st, n s, 225 e 4th av, 20x100.11 Sub. to mort. $9,000.
144th st, n s, 200 e Willis av, 50x100. Sub. to mort.
William T. Washburn and Emma Richardson exrs. and trustees of Benjamin Richardson to Mary A. wife of George D. Scott. Aug. 3. 17,350

123d st, Nos. 228 and 230, s s, 425 e 8th av, 50x100.11, three-story frame dwell'g and vacant. Eliza D. Dye to Harrison T. Slosson. *Mt.* $13,500. July 24. 18,500

Same property. Harrison T. Slosson to Elizabeth K. Smith. *Mt.* $13,500. July 31. 24,000

123d st, Nos. 221 and 223, n s, 218 e 3d av, 33.8x100.11, two five-story stone front flats. Robert H. Mathews and Fannie C. his wife to John Morrisey. *Mt.* $32,000. July 30. 38,500

124th st, No. 100, s e cor 4th av, 30x100.11, five-story brk flat. William E. Diller and Elizabeth A. his wife to Robert Wallace. *Mt.* $40,000. Aug. 1. nom

125th st, n s, 100 e 7th av as widened, 50x99.11, vacant. Serafino Magliola and Victoria his wife to Emanuel Heilner, Moses J. Wolf and Adolph M. Bendheim. *Mt.* $46,000. July 31. 69,000

128th st, No. 67, n s, 140 w 4th av, 25x99.11, five-story stone front flat. Robert H. Mathews and Fannie C. his wife to James E. Sullivan. *Mt.* $21,000. July 30. 28,500

128th st, No. 67, n s, 140 w 4th av, 25x99.11, five-story stone front flat. James E. Sullivan and Alice M. his wife to Charles R. Sullivan. *Mt.* $21,000. Aug. 1. 14,250

129th st, No. 312, s e cor St. Nicholas av, 32.10x99.11x47.8x101, five-story brk flat. Frank P. Perkins and Lizzie his wife, Irvington, N. Y., to Augusta C. A. Sigfus, Tarrytown, N. Y. *Mt.* $50,000. July 29. nom

129th st, s s, 135 e Lenox av, 75x99.11. Release mort. Marx and Moses Ottinger to Patrick Hogan. July 14. 27,000

Same property. Release mort. Same to same. July 14 9,600

130th st, No. 224, s s, 282.6 w 7th av, 17.6x99.11, three-story stone front dwell'g. Robert H. McCutcheon and Julie E. his wife to Henrietta M. Montross. *Mt.* $10,000. Aug. 3. 17,000

134th st, Nos. 189 and 191, n s, 150 e 7th av, 50x99.11, two five-story stone front flats. Leopold Kahn to George Kitching. *Mt.* $36,000. Aug. 1. See 48th st. 56,000

135th st, No. 179, n s, 175 e 7th av, 25x99.11, four-story stone front dwell'g. Fernando C. Candee, Jr., and Mary L. his wife to Charles H. Southard. *Mt.* $20,600. July 27. 25,000

135th st, Nos. 5–15, n s, 110 w 5th av, 106.8x99.11, six four-story brk dwell'gs. Warren B. Smith, Yonkers, to William Verdon. July 25. 78,500

170th st, n s, 125 e 11th av, 25x100. James Rowan and Ann his wife to James Calhoun. *Mt.* $1,400. Aug. 6. nom

170th st, n s, 100 e 11th av, 25x100. James Calhoun and Mary his wife to James Rowan. *Mt.* $1,000. Aug. 6. nom

180th st, s s, 125 w Amsterdam av, 50x100. Pauline Simon to Oliver B. Bridgman. July 12. 4,900

183d st, s s, 423.4 w 10th av, 376.8x104.11. Mason Young and Louisa H. his wife to George Schindler. Aug. 2. 35,000

183d st, s s, 423.4 w 10th av, 376.8x104.11. George Schindler to Andrew J. Connick and Thomas J. Colton. *Mt.* $23,000. Aug. 3. 38,000

Av A, Nos. 1425 and 1427, s w cor 76th st, 51.1x100, two five-story brk tenem'ts with stores. Harriet B. Webster to Frederick Rohrs. Sub. to mort. June 24. nom

Av A } begins Av A, n w cor 101st st, runs
101st st } west 293 x north 100.11 x east 75
102d st } x north 100.11 to 102d st, x east 218 to Av A, x south 201.11, one-story frame buildings and vacant. Richard N. Denman trustee to Augustus N. and William M., Anna or Annie M. Denman, Mary F. Tompkins, Asahel A., Francis H., Carrie or Caroline P. and Arthur R. Denman. June 2. nom

Amsterdam (10th) av, No. 585, e s, 53.10 n 88th st, 28.4x100, five-story brk tenem't with stores. Foreclos. Herman W. Vanderpoel to The New York Life Ins. Co. July 29. 23,200

Amsterdam (10th) av, w s, 297.4 n Kingsbridge road, 39.11x221.4x44.1x202.7 Charlotte A. Lyon to Peter J. McCoy. *Mt.* $12,000. Aug. 1. See 7th av. 22,500

Audubon av, e s, 50 n 180th st, 25x100. Pauline Simon to Carl R. Eberth. June 8. 2,550

Columbus av, No. 953, e s, 25.11 s 107th st, 25x75, five-story brk flat with stores. William Buhler to Newell Martin. July 30. nom

Edgecombe av, No. 202, e s, 340.7 s 145th st, 21.5x64x21.5x88.5, two-story frame dwell'g. Catharine Connor widow to Catharine B. and Margaret L. Connor. Aug. 4. 8,000

Lenox av, No. 482, e s, 24.11 n 134th st, 25x85, five-story brk flat with stores. John A. Rochford to Edwin A Bradley, Montclair, N. J., and George C. Currier. All liens. Sept. 11, 1890. nom

Lexington av, No. 740, s w cor 59th st, 20.5x75, four-story brk (stone front) dwell'g. Normand Smith and Elena his wife, Kiene Valley, N. Y., to James W. Ketcham. *Mt.* $12,000. July 10. nom

Same property. James W. Ketcham and Appolonia his wife to Benjamin Sire. *Mt.* $32,000. July 31. 40,000

Lexington av, No. 1830, w s, 80.11 n 113th st, 20x73.10, four-story brk flat. William H. and Mary Henenstal to Mary C. Sweeney. *Mt.* $7,000 and int. from Feb., 1891. Aug. 4. 13,000

Lexington av, No. 1449, n e cor 94th st, 19.8x95, three-story brk stone front dwell'g. Mary E. wife of and George Fox, Stamford, Conn., to Mary Louise wife of Richard I. Fox. Aug. 6. 14,000

Manhattan av, No. 399, w s, 55.11 s 117th st, 18x50, three-story stone front dwell'g. Robert C. Winters and Annie A. his wife to Thomas J. Reilly trustee. *Mt.* $6,000. Aug. 1. 13,000

Madison av, w s, 50.11 s 107th st, 25x100. Release mort. James McCreery to Lizzie T. Brady widow. July 30. 19,532

1st av, No. 932, e s, 25.1 n 51st st, 25.1x74, four-story brk tenem't with stores. Margaretha Zeller widow to Frederick Frevert and Franziska his wife. Aug. 1. 18,500

1st av, No. 2209, w s, 50 n 113th st, 25x75, five-story brk tenem't with stores. Teresa wife of Matthew Coogan to Nicola Laino and Catharine his wife. *Mt.* $10,000. July 30. 17,500

1st av, w s, 50 n 119th st, 25x75. Release mort. Edwin A. Bradley and George C. Currier to Teresa Coogan. July 31. nom

Same property. Release mort. Murray Hill Bank to same. July 31. nom

2d av, No. 1598, w s, 127.8 n 82d st, 25.6x101.8, four-story brk tenem't with stores. George Bernhard and Elise his wife, San Francisco, Cal., to Olaf Wasboe. All title. *Mt.* $8,000. July 30. nom

2d av, No. 1889, w s, 75.11 s 98th st, 25x96, five-story brk tenem't with stores. Harris Levy and Jennie his wife to Christoph A. Schuber. *Mt.* $11,000. July 30. 17,900

2d av, No 452, e s, 59.2 s 26th st, 19.7x74, four-story brk store and tenem't. Israel Josefsohn and Theresa his wife to Barnett Greenstone. *Mt.* $11,000. July 31. 18,120

2d av, No. 2256, e s, 20.11 s 116th st, 20x80, four-story brk store and tenem't. Alice Brady to Samuel Fleck. *Mt.* $10,400. Aug. 1. 12,875

2d av, No. 2263, w s, 20.10 n 116th st, 20x70, four-story stone front store and tenem't. Partition. Walton Storm to Abram G. More. July 31. 11,200

3d av, Nos. 260–264 } begins 3d av, n w cor 21st
21st st, Nos. 153–157 } st, 50x75, four five-story brk tenem'ts, with stores on av. Sally wife of John E. Todd, Long Ridge, Conn., Daisy wife of Andros Weed, New Canaan, Conn., and Annie D. Gardner, New Canaan, Conn., heirs George Gardiner to Harriet A. Gardiner widow. Trust deed. July 30. nom

Same property. Release dower. Harriet A. Gardiner widow to Sallie wife of John E. Todd, Daisy wife of Andros Weed and Annie D. Gardiner. July 31. nom

Same property. William W. Gardiner and Sarah A. his wife to Seth C. Weed. ½ part. July 30. 29,500

5th av, No. 2147, e s, 25 n 131st st, 25x99, five-story brk flat. Henry H. Glass to Jacob and Joseph Levy. *Mt.* $16,000. Aug. 6. 24,500

5th av, No. 263, s e cor 29th st, 24.9x100, five-story brk store. Walter Rutherfurd to Philip L. Runkle. Q. C All title. July 30. nom

Same property. Partition. Charles N. Morgan to same. July 31. 178,200

Same property. Philip L. Runkle to Charles H. Besson, Hoboken, N. J. B. & S. Aug. 3. nom

Same property. Charles H. Besson to John C. Runkle. Aug. 3. nom

5th av, n e cor 80th st, 77.2x100, vacant.
80th st, n s, 100 e 5th av, 49.9x102.2, vacant.
George W. Vultee to Louis Stern. *Mt.* $200,000. Aug. 3. 265,000

Same property. Collis P. Huntington and Arabella D. his wife to George W. Vultee. Aug. 3. 275,000

5th av, Nos. 2193–2199 } begins 5th av, s e cor
134th st, No. 4 } 134th st, 99.11x100, four five-story brk flats with stores in Nos. 2197 and 2199 on av and five-story brk flat on st. John A. Rochford to Edwin A. Bradley, Montclair, N. J., and George C. Currier. All liens. Oct. 14, 1890. nom

7th av, No. 2003, e s, 17.11 n 120th st, 17x77, three-story stone front dwell'g. Peter J. McCoy and Anna R. his wife to Charlotte A. Lyon. *Mt.* $13,500. July 27. See Amsterdam av. 20,500

7th av, No. 587, e s, 39.1 n 41st st, 20x71.4x20.2x73.10, four-story brk store and tenem't. Daniel Underhill to James W. Ketcham. April 15. 30,000

8th av, No. 259 } begins 8th av, s w cor 23d st,
23d st, No. 310 } runs south 18.6 x west 73 x south 37.10 x west 27 x north 56.4 to 23d st, x east 100, five-story brk tenem't with stores on av and three-story brk dwell'g on st. John P. Windolph to Israel Lowenstein. *Mt.* $50,000. July 2. 55,000

9th av, Nos. 855–859 } begins 9th av, w s, 25.5
56th st, No. 404 } s 56th st, runs west 100 x north 25.5 to 56th st, x west 25 x south 100.8 x east 25.2 x north 3.5 x east 100 to 9th av, x north 75, three six-story brk flats with stores on av and one six-story brk flat on st.
9th av, No. 861, s w cor 56th st, 25.5x100, six-story brk flat with store.
Abraham H. Hummel and Benjamin Steinhardt to Maria N. Winne. *Mt.* $165,000. July 30. 250,000

11th av, n w cor 30th st, 31.6x100, vacant. Gertrude V. C. Hamilton to John Jordan. Sub. to mort. July 30. 14,000

11th av, e s, 150 n 187th st, 25x100. Henry T. Thompson to Henry W. Droge. July 6. 3,500

12th av, s e cor 30th st, 49.4x100, vacant.
29th st, s s, 600 w 11th av, 50x98.9, vacant.
Henry L. Sprague as assignee of Schuyler Hamilton, Jr., to Gertrude V. C. Hamilton. *Mt.* $25,000. June 17. 430

MISCELLANEOUS.

All property, &c. General assign. Abraham Backer to Benjamin F. Einstein. Aug. 3. nom

All rights, licenses, privileges and franchises. Herzog General Electric Co. to The Farmers' Loan and Trust Co. Trust deed. July 16. 300,000

23d and 24th WARDS.

Croton Aqueduct, e s, 132.10 n Highbridge st, 50x133 to Edenwood av, x50x—. Release mort. Mary Hill to Elizabeth E. T. wife of George A. Hill. July 17. nom

Same property. Elizabeth E. T. wife of George A. Hill to Julia A. Thorn. July 20. 3,500

Evelyn pl, s s, 175 w Jerome av, 50x100. Foreclos. Augustus C. Brown to Joseph F. Stier. *Mt.* $3,000. July 30. 500

Fort Independence st, w s, north ½ plot 71 map W. O. Giles property, 24th Ward, 25x106.10x23.9x111.1. Thomas O'Reilly and Norah his wife to Frederick Smith. Aug. 4. 800

Freeman st, n s, 60 e Chisholm st, 30x85. Mary wife of August Peklo to Emil Wejvoda. July 31. 1,000

John st, s w s, lot 50 map East Tremont, 33x150. Edward J. Cronin and Margaret his wife to Devinia Dorgan. July 31. 2,860

Opdyke st, n w cor Oneida av, 200x151.6x200x154.5. Charles R. Treat and Julia H. his wife to Carlos Warner and Charles D. Smith. July 16. nom

Orchard st, n e s, part of plot 101 map of Claremont, 25x100. Bridget wife of Daniel McCarty, Sr., to Richard O'Brien. July 1. 2,500

South pl, s w cor Bronx av, abt 583.8x631x449.6 to Bronx av, x 300, abt 5 acres and houses Mary L. Tiffany to Phil Moore Leakin, East Orange, N. J. Aug. 1. 22,500

Same property. Phil M. Leakin, East Orange, N. J., to The East Harbor New York Land Co. Aug. 3. nom

Tiffany st, w s, 296.3 n 165th st, 30x100. Elizabeth F. Parker to Frederick Krause and Albertina his wife. *Mt.* $1,600. July 28. 3,300

Tiffany st, e s, 129.8 s 167th st, 25x100. James J. Fitzpatrick and Margaret D. his wife to George Price. July 24. 425

Same property. Charles C. Churchill to same. July 23. 425

Same property. Release mort. Susan B. Hutchison widow, Brooklyn, to Hans Reinhardt and Charles C. Churchill. July 27. 300

Willard st, s s, 300 e Keppler av, 50x100. Jane Potter individ. and extrx. Wm. Hy. Potter to Christine Ehlers. July 29. 850

134th st, n s, 375 e Willis av, 50x100. Fredericke Mayer widow to Randolph Guggenheimer and Salomon Marx. *Mt.* $21,000. July 31. nom

Same property. Randolph Guggenheimer and Eliza his wife and Salomon Marx and Betche his wife to Joseph D. Mayer. *Mt.* $21,000. Aug. 3. See Hamilton st. 33,000

138th st, No. 631, n s, 130.3 w Willis av, 26.3x100. John Cotter and Sarah his wife and Nicholas Cotter and Eliza his wife to John M. Tracy. *Mt.* $14,500. Aug. 1. nom

148th st, s s, 94 w Courtlandt av, 37x100. Charles Schledorn and Johanne his wife to Adolph Hank. Sub. to assessm'ts. Aug. 1. 8,000

149th st, n s, 120.8 e Morris av, 50x100. William McKenna and Lizzie his wife to Dennis

W. Moran. ½ part. Taxes and sales for same. Aug. 4. 250

163d st, s s, 99 w 3d av, 50x100. Partition. William N. Armstrong to Magdalena Holland. March 5. 4,200

170th st, No. 842, s s, 197.7 e Fulton av as monumented, runs south 119.4 x west — x north 118 to st, x east 16.11. Fernando Wood and Delia C. his wife to William Reimer and Albert Schubert. July 31. 4,400

170th st, No. 838, s s, 33.4 w of centre line, bet Fulton and Franklin avs, 16.8x113x16.6x114. Fernando Wood and Delia C. his wife to Mary E. Schroeder. Aug. 5. 4,400

Bathgate av, e s, 150.9 s 179th st, 36x56.4x36x55. Robert S. and Cornelius E. Anderson trustees Cornelius V. Anderson to L. Napoleon Levy. July 30. 1,000

Same property. Robert S. Anderson and Mary A. his wife, Cornelius E. Anderson and Mary H. his wife, William S. Anderson and Lucy B. his wife, Mount Vernon, N. Y., and Mary E. wife of and James Montgomery, Brooklyn, N. Y., heirs of Cornelius V. Anderson to same. July 30. nom

Bathgate av, e s, 216 s 175th st, 27x114x27x112; also,
Bathgate av, adj above on n s, 54x—.
Bathgate av, adj above on s s, —x—.
Bathgate av, adj 2d parcel, —x—.
Plinny Ayres, Kate L. Watkins and Samuel E. Ayres to each other. Agreement as to location of property described in will of Albert Ayres. July 1. nom

Boston av, as widened, at intersection lands of The Suburban Land Improvement Co. and lands Marion Bathgate, runs northwest 160 x south 55.6 to Boston av, x east 150, contains 1 607 1,000 city lots. Marion Bathgate widow to The Suburban Land Improvement Co. July 18. 2,600

Briggs av, n w s, 227.4 n e Travers st, 50x100. William H. Birkmire and Louisa his wife to George W. Haigh. July 18. 1,400

Brook av, e s, 75 n 141st st, 25x100. Pauline Simon to Henry Morgenthau. *Mt.* $14,150. Aug. 3. nom

Cambreling av, w s, 200 n Bayard st, 50x89.5. Sarah C. wife of and Alfred E. Fountain, Jr., to Francis Trainor. July 27. 1,300

Cauldwell av, w s, 181 n Clifton st, 36x100. Release mort. R. Clarence Dorsett to John W. Decker. July 31. nom

Same property. Release mort. Annie Ormiston to same. July 31. nom

Same property Release mort. Francis S. Phraner exr. Caroline M. Hitchcock to Annie Ormiston July 31. 3,000

Same property. John W. Decker to George Silva. *Mt.* $10,000. June 29. See Westchester av. 17,000

Cauldwell av, w s, 349.9 n Westchester av, 50x115. Harvey F. Johnson and Ruth his wife, Haverstraw, N. Y., to Abraham Bennett. July 27. 2,000

Creston av, e s, 150 n 183d st, 50x105. Release mort. Amelia V. Wilson to William H. Walter. July 30. nom

Creston av, e s, 175 n 183d st, 25x105. William H. Walter and Sarah E. his wife to Frank N. Mesch and Elizabeth his wife. July 30. 900

Creston av, e s, 150 n 183d st, 25x1'5. Same to William C. Adams and Margaret A. A. his wife. July 30. 900

Crotona av, n s, 128.6 e Broad st, 25x90.11x25x89.11. Mary H. wife of Clark Wright to Otis W. Boyden. June 29. 1,050

Courtlandt av, e s, 156.4 s 152d st, 25x100. Angela Sauter widow to Mary wife of Joseph Wirsing. Aug. 1. 4,900

Eagle av, e s, 312 n Westchester av, 150x115. Harvey F. Johnson and Ruth his wife to Jacob Riehl and Anton Rinschler. July 25. 7,200

Forest av, e s, 145.2 s 165th st, 94.10x300, excepting part taken for Fulton av, also excepting as follows
Forest av, e s, 145.2 s 165th st, 25x120.
Foreclos. Frederick Smyth to Simon and Mayer Loeb. Feb. 24, 1890. 7,550

Franklin av, n w s, 179 n e 170th st, 25x127. Gotleib Fromer to Selma Fromer. *Mt.* $2,000. March 14. gift

Intervale av, n w s, 378.11 s w Home st, 50x125.2x50x127.11. Thomas O'Rorke and Margaret A. his wife to Lavina E. Patrick. *Mt.* $2,500. Aug. 3. 4,250

Keppler av, n w cor Willard st, 75x100. Carlos Warner, New York, and Charles D. Smith, Londonderry, Vt., to Ida L. Senior. B. & S. May 29. nom

Madison av, e s, 243 s Fitch st, 27x113.3x27x112.2. Samuel E. Ayres to John B. Smith. Aug. 1. See 119th st. 3,000

Mott av, e s, 179 s 165th st, 60x125x60x125. Janet wife of George W. McAdam to Walter Wilkens. August 5. 6,500

Opdyke av, n s, 200 w 4th st, 230x148.3x211x151.6. James C. Cloyd, Oyster Bay, N. Y., to W. R. Lamberton, Pelham Manor, N. Y. *Mt.* $3,000. July 20. 3,600

Prospect av, s e s, lot 85 map East Tremont, 66x150. Frederick Grote and Maria C. his wife to William Clinton. Dec. 1, 1866. 400

Prospect av, s e s, n ½ lot 85 map East Tremont, 33x150. John Leddy and Jane L. his wife to James McMahon. *Mt.* $375. Aug. 1. 750

Prospect av, s e s, all of lot 84 same map, 66x150. Catharine Clinton to John Leddy. Aug. 1. 1,500

Prospect av, w s, 80 s Lebanon st, 25x100. John Leddy and Jane L. his wife to Lawrence Duffy. Sub. ½ mort. $900. Aug. 1. 950

Robbins av, e s, 100 n 151st st, 25x105. George P. Amon and Rosina his wife to Ferdinand Christen. Aug. 1. 2,950

Taylor av, w s, 94.5 s Columbia av, 23.5x102.10. Ellen Donohue to Mary wife of Patrick Reid. July 29. 2,700

Villa av, e s, 510.3 n Southern Boulevard, 23x86.2x25x87.5. Edward W. Parsells and Leonora his wife, Jersey City, to James F. Geoghegan and Mary E. his wife, joint tenants. *Mt.* $115. July 30. 500

Villa av, e s, 271.6 s Van Cortlandt av, 25x124.6x25x124.1 Edward W. Parsells and Leonora his wife, Jersey City, to Adalbert Voss. July 16. 650

Washington av, s w cor 173d st, 50x105. Diedrich Muller and Lena his wife to Anton Rinschler and Jacob Riehl. *Mt.* $7,000. Aug. 1. 10,500

Webster av, e s, 75 n Mosholu Parkway, 25x108.8x28.7x122.5. Robert N. Quinn and Charlotte F. his wife to Mary A. Thompson. July 17. 1,075

Westchester av, s s, 281 e Bergen av, runs east along Westchester av and across Brook av 508.4 to w s Port Morris Branch R. R., x south to westerly side St. Anns av, x south 74 x west and crossing Brook av to former channel mill brook, x north along curves to line at right angles to point of beginning and south therefrom, x north 137, with all title in streets and mill brook excepting part taken for Brook av. Henry E. Janes and Amelia M. his wife to Edward R. Janes. 1-9 part. July 27. nom

Westchester av, north cor proposed 162d st, runs west 150.9 x north 123.7 x east 60.9 x east 53.9 x south 153 to av, x southeast 49. John W. Decker to R. Clarence Dorsett. *Mt.* $4,000. June 29. consid. omitted

Same property. George Silva and Mary his wife to John W. Decker. *Mt.* $4,000. July 31. See Cauldwell av. 10,000

Willard av s s, 275 e 2d st, 50x200 to Clinton av. William J. Riley and Catharine his wife and Margaret Riley children and devisees of James Riley to Elizabeth wife of Alexander Campbell. July 31. 2,000

2d or Bainbridge av, s s, 24 n e from line late of Twenty-fourth Ward Real Estate Assoc. and 175 e of old William st, 25x125, h & l. Walter J. Lee and Carrie his wife to Phœbe A. Cornell. July 31. 6,500

Macombs Dam road, lot begins at centre line Loring av as laid down on map at point 205 n 206th st, runs east 170 to w s Macombs Dam road, x north 75 x west 170 to centre Loring av, x south 75. Martha J. wife of and David McClenahan, Parkville, L. I., to James Morrison. July 12. 4,000

Old Post road from New York to Albany, adj land of Jonathan Odell, runs northwest — x northwest — x northwest — x nothwest — to Lispenard Stewarts land, x northeast — x southeast — x southeast — x southeast — to said road, x southwest — x southwest — to said lands of Odell at beginning, contains 17 acres. Christian F. Tietjen and Caroline E. his wife to Adolph G. Lackman and Gottfried Walbaum, Hoboken, N. J. *Mt.* $12,000. July 13. 55,000

Lot begins at division line bet lands of Suburban Land Improvement Co. and Margaret Bathgate, 159.11 w Boston av, 28.4x149.4x irreg., 2 736-1,000 city lots. Suburban Land Improvement Co. to Marion Bathgate. July 14. nom

Lot in 23d Ward, bounded north by land of Chesebrough, east by Long Island Sound or East River, south by land of Jacob Van Wagener and west by Harlem River & Portchester Railroad. Agreement of ratification and attornment. Louis J. Heintz to Charles M. Vandervoort. June 14. nom

LEASEHOLD CONVEYANCES.

Baxter st, No. 7. Assign. lease. Frank Ferretti to The J. Kress Brewing Co. 694

Bowery, No. 30, part of store in New England Hotel. Assign. lease. New York Breweries Co. (Lim.) to Ferdinand R. Minrath. Aug. 4. 5,000

Broad st, No. 91. Surrender lease. William Aufenanger and Charles Schwarm to Horatio Gomez trustee Hetty Gomez. March 31. nom

Same property. Assign. lease. Carl Weczerzeick to William Aufenanger and Charles Schwarm. nom

Broadway, Nos. 1195-1203, upper portions. Assign. lease. Adelaide Herrmann to Alfred C. Cheney trustee July 25. nom

Same property. Assign. lease. Alexander Herrmann to Adelaide Herrmann. March 18. nom

9th st, No. 41, n s, 222.7 e University pl, 25x92.3. Assign. lease. Charles B. Atkinson exr. William H. Atkinson to Sarah Ettlinger. Aug. 1. 7,000

19th st, s s, 190 e Av A, runs southwest 98.10 x southeast 69.8 x northeast 24 4 x northeast 26 x northeast 32.3 x southeast 19.2 x northeast 30 to st, x northwest 122.6. Agreement modifying terms of lease and fixing yearly rent at $1,125 in place of $1,000. The N. Y. Steam Co. to The Standard Gas Light Co., New York. July 30. nom

19th st, s s, 275 e 9th av, 25x92. Assign. lease. Henry W. Howell exr. Alice W. Babcock to Louisa Babcock. July 30. nom

22d st, n s, 79 w 8th av, 21x84.4. Consent to assign. lease. Mary E. wife of John P. R. Wells with consent of Katharine T. Moore to Thomas Ennis. nom

32d st, No. 219 W. Assign. lease. Michael Sheridan to Peter Doelger. July 28. nom

46th st, s s, 125 w 8th av, 18.9x100.5. Assign. lease. Jessie F. Clark to James Barber, Englewood, N. J. nom

57th st, s s, 115 w 1st av, 60x73.5x60.2x77.8. Rebecca S. and William H. Mills to Congregation Adas Israel. 21 years, from Jan. 1, 1892, per year, 1,000

1st av, No. 975. Assign. lease. Paul Rohl to The Henry Elias Brewing Co. Aug. 1. nom

1st av, No. 93. Assign. lease. Louis Celce to John Hempel. nom

1st av, e s, 38 s 19th st, 18x70. Henry Parish exr., &c., Mary Griffin to Henry Monheimer. 21 , from May 1, 1889, per year, taxes and years 300

Same property. Assign. lease. Henry and Hannah Monheimer to Cary Levenson. 4,500

3d av, w s, 165.11 n 10th st, 23.8x78. Assign. lease. George E. Annett to Arthur Blue. 13,625

7th av, No. 582. Assign. lease. James F. Kinney to John S. Reilly. Aug. 1. nom

8th av, s w cor 23d st, 18.6x73.
23d st, s s, 73 w 8th av, 27x56.4.
Assign. lease. John P. Windolph to Israel Lowenstein. nom

Pier No. 24, East River, ½ part, also ½ of slip and bulkhead lying west of same. Surrender lease. People's Steamboat Co. to Samuel L. Storer et al. trustees for the Fulton Market Fishmongers' Assoc. Aug. 1. nom

Assign. indeft. lease. Diedrich Otteman to Richard and John Harms. March 12. nom

---

KINGS COUNTY.

JULY 30, 31, AUGUST 1, 3, 4, 5.

Ashford st, e s, 125 n Arlington av, 37.6x100. Elizabeth Bennett to De Witt C. E. Baisley. $1,500

Ashford st, w s, 200 s Arlington av, 12.6x97.10. Thomas Everit to Alexander F. Zundt and James Stewart. *Mt.* $1,000. 2,600

Bainbridge st, s s, 250 w Lewis av, 40x100. Mary E. wife of and Alfred W. Welch to Henry Nieland, Jr. 4,400

Bainbridge st, n s, 137.6 w Ralph av, 18.9x100, h & l. Samuel R. Good to Arend Lutjen. All liens. 6,000

Bainbridge st, n s, 23 e Saratoga av, 18.6x100. Victor J. Dowling, of New York, to William H. Good. nom

Bainbridge st, n s, 78.6 e Saratoga av, 18.6x100, h & l. Victor J. Dowling to William H. Good. B. & S. nom

Same property. William H. Good to John R. Hughes. *Mt.* $4,000. 6,500

Barbey st, e s, 205 n Wortman av, 20x100. William A. Watson to Nicholio Vichelo. 250

Bergen st, s s, 150 e Paca av, 50x127.9. Abraham Livingston and John T. Coyle to Julius Miller and Samuel Cohen. 1,450

Bergen st, s s, 100 w Hopkinson av, 100x127.9. John D. and Catharine Ditmis and Georgiana J. Remsen heirs Martin G. Johnson to Charles M. Thompson. 1,400

Same property. Charles M. Thompson to Rose Rosenfield. 2,000

Bergen st, s s, 325 w Hopkinson av, 50x127.9.
Bergen st, s s, 225 w Hopkinson av, 25x127.9.
Mary wife of and Frederick Kuckuk to Elizabeth L. Schultz. *Mt.* $4,700. exch

Berriman st, e s, 235 n Stanley av, 20x100. William H. Jackson, of New York, to George J. Southgate. 150

Bleecker st, n s, 90 w St. Nicholas av, 40x100. Leonhard Emig to Jacob Manneschmidt and Margaretha his wife. exch

Boerum st, n s, 587.9 e Bushwick av, runs north 52.5 x east 15.1 x south 8 x east 10 x south 42.8 to Boerum st, x west 25. Eliesabetha wife of and Heinrich A. Mahla to John Klein and Lina his wife. B. & S. nom

Same property. John Klein and Lina his wife to Henry Roth. *Mt.* $1,200. See Floyd st. 2,400

Boerum st, s s, 175 e Lorimer st, 25x100. Ludwig Jordens to Isaac, Gustav and Samuel Dreyer. *Mt.* $1,800. 32,000

Broadway, n e s, 60 n w Madison st, 20x100, h & l. Sarah wife of Jacob Jacoby to Mary wife of John Nimmo. *Mt.* $4,500. 8,500

Broadway, s w s, 75 n w Conway st, 50x100. Release mort. Lottie A. wife of F. G. Soper to Susan M. Spencer. nom

Broadway, n e s, 145 n w Johnson av, 25x100. Margaretha widow and Henrietta Metzger and Mina S. wife of Solomon Bender to Leopold Metzger. nom

Broadway, n s, 101.2 e Troy av, 269.11x84.4x250.8x124.3, Flatbush John J. Drake to Albert Seele. *Mt.* $1,000. 1,820

Butler st, No 55, n s, 160 w Smith st, 20x100. Annie A. De Bowes to Charles E. Power. B. & S. 2,500

Butler st, n s, 330 w 5th av, 20x144.3x20x144.4. John P. Crawford to Robert Furey. nom

Carroll st, s s, 212.1 e 6th av, 39x136.5x35.9x136.8, h & l. Margaret E. Conlon to Henry Franke. Sub. to morts. nom

Cheever pl, s e s, 95 n e Degraw st, abt 20x½ block. Bridget Murphy to Catherine Doyle. Morts. and taxes. 5,400

Chester st, n w cor Eastern Parkway, 50x100, hs & ls. Matilda Weinberger and Lena Hershkovics to Louis Bella. *Mt.* $1,000. 2,000

Chestnut st, w s, 1,950 n 4th st, 25x150. Edward E. Comstock to Mathilda Benedict. *Mt.* $2,100. 2,400

Cleveland st, e s, 125 n Eastern Parkway, 25x98.4. George Schade to John Bessler. 3,000

Clifton pl, n s, 50 w Nostrand av, 25x100. Samuel Hopkins to Peter Haskell. *Mt.* $3,000. 3,450

Cooper st, n w s, 159.7 n e Broadway, 19.7x100, h & l. Bertha Uehlinger to Hermann Reiche. All liens. 6,800

Cooper st, s e s, 200 n e Evergreen av, 50x100. Andrew Miller to Robert Miller. n m

Same property. Robert Miller to Lillian Miller. nom

Cornelia st, n w s, 125 n e Bushwick av, 50x100. Mary H. wife of Elias J. Hendrickson to James W. Lamb. 4,500

Columbia st, e s, 20.3 s Woodhull st, 19.11x70, h & l. James Calvert to Matilda Jacobs. *Mt.* $6,000. 9,000

Cumberland st, w s, 91.10 n Atlantic av, runs west 40 x northwest 35.6 x north 17 x southeast 35.1 x east 40 x south 20. Maximillian Lang to Thomas C. Raine, Jr. *Mt.* $3,500. 6,000

Cumberland st, w s, 376.10 n Atlantic av, 20x100. Foreclos. John Courtney, sheriff, to Maximillian Lang. 4,225

Cumberland st, e s, 13 n Atlantic av, 20x91.3x21x82.4, h & l. Martha A. Knight to Robert Knight her husband. nom

Dean st, n s, 150 w Hopkinson av, 25x107.2. Cornelia J. Sarvin, of New York, to James McMahon. 300

Dean st, n s, 100 w Hopkinson av, 50x107.2. Alexander P. Bell, of New York, to same. 600

Dean st, n s, 50 w Hopkinson av, 50x107. Enoch C. Bell, of New York, to same. 600

Dean st, n s, 175 w Hopkinson av, 50x107.2. John J. Bell, of New York, to same. 600

Decatur st, n s, 210 w Reid av, 20x100. Daniel Lauer to Mary E. wife of William G. Miller, of Hempstead, N. Y. *Mt.* $5,000. exch

Decatur st, s s, 380 w Patchen av, 20x100. Elizabeth wife of Alvaro Garcia to Achille Fouquet and Margaret his wife. 5,000

Decatur st, s s, 154 e Ralph av, 54x100. William J. Northridge to Elizur Cable. *Mt.* $13,500. nom

Same property. Charles M. Marsh to William J. Northridge. 2,700

Degraw st, s s, 277.11 w 5th av, 19.2x100. Peter Kelly to Margaretha Schoen. *Mt.* $3,500. 6,700

Degraw st, s s, 297.1 w 5th av, 19.2x100. Peter Kelly to Margaretta and Julius Schmidt, of New York. *Mt.* $3,500. 6,700

Dresden st, e s, 150 n Arlington av, 50x100. Bridget Duffield widow to John Voell. 950

Dupont st, s s, 560 w Manhattan av, 25x100. Thomas Anderson to John E. Judge, of New York. 6,000

Eagle st, n s, 68 w Oakland st, 32x50. Release mort. Katharina Desch to Sophia Plath, Nikolas Droge and Christian Koch exrs. Claus Plath. nom

Eagle st, n s, 66.7 w Oakland st, 33.5x50. Nicholas Droge, Christian H. Koch and Sophia Plath exrs. Claus Plath to Matilda Weinberger and Lena Herskowics. 1,600

Same property. Release dower. Sophia Plath widow to same. nom

Earl st, n s, 360 w Brooklyn av, 20x100, Flatbush. Edward Egolf to Mary Mahon. 250

Eastern Parkway, n s, 60 w Milford st, 40x90. Effingham H. Nichols to William T. Goundie. 750

Eastern Parkway, n s, 25 w Osborn st, 21.5x100x21.3x100. Herbert C. Smith to John Power. 685

Eastern Parkway, n s, 125 e Thatford av, 28.7x100x28.9x100. Samuel Barnett to Jacob Soloweitzik, of New York. 2,800

Eastern Parkway, s s, 100 e Thatford av, 25x100. Andrew R. Culver to William Brown. 500

Eastern Parkway, s s, 100 e Thatford av, 53.4x100. William Brown to Barnet Levin and Max Gittlesohn. 1,750

Eldert st, n w s, 215 s w Evergreen av, 20x100. Release mort. Virginia A. Kleine to J. Christian Johnson and Mary his wife. nom

Eldert st, s s, 293 e Evergreen av, 18x100, h & l. Helen M. Buttle to George R. Hankinson. 4,500

Elton st, e s, 100 n Liberty av, 50x90. Charles E. Cummings to Markus and Edward Ehrlich, of New York. *Mt.* $5,500. 7,000

Essex st, w s, 380 n Ridgewood av, 20x100.
Essex st, w s, 340 n Ridgewood av, 20x100.
Edward F. Linton to Thomas Corker. 1,600

Fleet pl, e s, 275 n Myrtle av, 25x56x25x57. Sarah I. and James Watson heirs William W. Watson to Ann F. Watson. 2,660

Floyd st, s s, 275 w Throop av, 25x100. Wilhelmina Israel to Henry Roth. *Mt.* $2,500. exch

Same property. Henry Roth to John Klein and Lina his wife, joint tenants. *Mt.* $2,500. See Boerum st. 5,200

Floyd st, n s, 150 w Sumner av, 25x100. Emma Paul a devisee of Ernst Paul to Josephine Seider. All title. *Mt.* $3,500. 2,545

Folsom pl, n s, 85 w Essex st, 15x80, h & l. Laura Rooney to Rudolph Duncker. 1,900

Frost st, s s, 300 w Kingsland av, 25x100. James Roseman to James P. Clark. *Mt.* $400. 1,400

Fulton st, n e cor Pine st, 113x105x107x119.3. Marenus J. Goodenough to Frederick, Richard and Otto Kampfe. 5,500

Fulton st, n e cor Pine st, 93.9x87.5x87.10.
Fulton st, n w cor Pine st, runs west 46.11 x north 98.3 x west 153.6 to Market st, x north 50 x east 200 to Pine st, x south 140.7.
Release mort. Anna L. Short and ano. exrs. John J. Petet to Marenus J. Goodenough. 1,800

Fulton st, n e cor Van Siclen av, 100x100. James McGuigan to Gerd. H. Meyn. 8,000

Garfield pl, n e s, 281.3 n w 6th av, 17.6x107.8x17.6x106.10. George A. Annable to Ellen Hickey. 7,000

Grand st, n e s, 204.11 s e Driggs st, 20x92.1x20.1x98.9. Maria L. wife of John H. Matthews, Newark, N. J., Frances W. Blackwell, Emma L. wife of Samuel B. Tisdale, Gertrude B. Wiley widow and Thomas G. Evans to Henry Seeba. C. a. G. 10,000

Grand st, n s, 150.1 e Berry st, 21.8x60.10x20.10x62.6. George S. Raymer, Idaho Springs, Col., to Morris Isaacs. *Mt.* $5,000. 10,500

Gwinnett st, n s, 364 e Harrison av, 22x100. Joseph Neger to Heyman Margoies and Moses Goldberg, of New York. *Mt.* $3,000. 7,250

Halsey st, s e s, 120 n e Evergreen av, 20x100. Ernestine Gastmeyer to Helene Heuschober, New York. 4,500

Hancock st, n s, 358.4 e Reid av, 16.8x100. Wesley A. Law to Clara H. Law. nom

Hancock st, s s, 296 e Sumner av, 18x94.6x18.1x96.2. Samuel W. Hurley to John W. Douglass. *Mt.* $5,000. exch

Hancock st, s s, 300 e Reid av, 21.6x100. Frederick Ulrich to Franceska Hanson. 5,000

Hart st, s s, 158 w Marcy av, 19x100. Charles H. Berry, Norwalk, Conn., to Helen L. Blondel. Q. C. nom

Same property. Helen L. Blondel to Cornelia W. wife of Charles H. Berry, Norwalk, Conn. *Mt.* $5,000. nom

Hart st, n s, 100 w Tompkins av, 25x100. James C. Charlock to Frederick De Ath. 2,750

Hart st, s e s, 100 n e Central av, 22.6x75, h & l. William Lindermann to Bernhard Janzer. *Mt.* $4,000. 5,000

Havemeyer st. Party wall agreement. William C. H. Muller with Jane M. Howard. —

Hemlock st, w s, 316.8 s Jamaica turnpike, 25x85.1. Catherine Molloy to James McCadden. 500

Herkimer st, s e cor Howard av, 25x98. Clara wife of John H. Ernst to Charles Stehling. *Mt.* $5,800. 12,000

Herkimer st, s s, 200 w Nostrand av, 50x185.6 to Herkimer pl. Sarah L. Smith, New York, to Stephen P. Sturges. *Mt.* $5,950. exch

Heyward st, s s, 114.10 e Bedford av, 19x100. Asahel T. Mitchell to Vina A. Sumner, of Syracuse, N. Y. *Mt.* $3,000. nom

Hicks st, w s, 100 n Lorraine st, 60x86.6. Joseph Foley to Annie C. wife of Isedro W. Hultgren. 1,650

Same property. Release mort. Livingston Gifford exr. George Gifford to Joseph Foley. 400

High st, s s, 186.7 w Washington st, 25.2x98.5 to alley. Adolph Pfeiffer to Frederick Jansen. 25,000

Hinsdale st, e s, 150 n Sutter av, 25x100. Martha A. Wilkin to Mary E. Cook, of Newtown, N. Y. *Mt.* $2,550. 2,800

Hooper st, n w s, 225 n e Marcy av, 60x100.
South 5th st, n e cor Rodney st, 41x60.
Lizzie J. wife of Alfred Hodges, Caroline A. wife of Frank B. Smith and Ephraim Johnson heirs Cornelius L. Johnson to Grace M. Johnson. ¾ part. exch

Hooper st, n w s, 285 n e Marcy av, 20x100.
South 5th st, n w cor Rodney st, 23x80.
South 4th st, s s, 65.9 w Union av, 20x85. ¾ part.
South 5th st, s w cor Rodney st, 60x75. ⅝ part.
Caroline A. wife of Frank B. Smith, Ephraim Johnson and George M. Johnson heirs Cornelius L. Johnson to Lizzie J. wife of Alfred Hodges. exch

Hopkins st, No. 116, s s, 25x100.
Chester st, s w cor Sackett st, 100x100.
Contract to exchange property. John Hasselbach with David Klein. nom

Hopkins st, n s, 250 e Marcy av, 25x100. Eva Bottman to Frank Mahr. *Mt.* $2,800. 5,900

Hopkins st, s s, 450 e Marcy av, 25x100. David Israel Schiff to Max Manes. *Mt.* $4,300. 6,150

Hull st, n s, 375 e Rockaway av, 37.6x100. Michael J. Boylan to Margaret McLaughlin. nom

Hull st, n w s, 116.6 n e Bushwick av, 16.6x100. John C. Rogers to Kate Schnabe. *Mt.* $1,800. 2,800

India st, n s, 153.4 e Franklin st, 16.8x100. James E. Brown to Michael Toomey. *Mt.* $2,500. 5,000

Jackson st, n s, 125 w Lorimer st, 100x100. George Ledogar to Elizabeth Ledogar his wife. nom

Jackson st, s s, 125 w Graham av, 25x100. John H. Schafer to Jacob and Henry Nelson, of New York. *Mt.* $3,000. 6,300

Jerome st, e s, 100 s Dumont av, 10x100. August H. Dahl to James H. Brundage. 350

Jerome st, e s, 200 n Livonia av, 20x100, h & l. James H. Brundage to Charles Johnson. 2,450

Jerome st, e s, 225 s Vienna av, 20x100. William Brown to John F. Maguire. *Mt.* $2,000. 250

Johnson pl, n w cor Union st, 150x100, Flatbush. Foreclos. Gerard M. Stevens to John J. Duff. *Mt.* $1,200, taxes, &c. 1,775

Kosciusko st, n s, 100 w Stuyvesant av, 16.8x100, h & l. Bernhard Bauer to John Bauer. 2,500

Leonard st, e s, 80 n Powers st, 20x100. Foreclos. Robert Merchant ref. to Lizzie and Theresa Beheim. 3,300

Leonard st, e s, 450 n Calyer st, 25x100. Mary A. widow of Lawrence J. Flynn to James A. and William H. Port. 3,100

Linwood st, w s, 200 n Ridgewood av, 50x100. Samuel Albert to Frank E. Hart. *Mt.* $3,630. 5,100

Livingston st, n s, 25 e Nevins st, 16.8x75. Jacob S. Koechlein to James Johnston. 5,000

Luquer st, n e s, 154.6 s e Henry st, 25x100. James Shepherd to Felix Bozzo, John Moresco and John Canova. *Mt.* $5,000. 11,500

Lorimer st, e s, 60 s Ainslie st, 20x100, h & l. Eliza J. Rockwell, Harriet Bessey, Lydia A. Mohr and Charles A. Bessey to Mary E. Sandell, East Orange, N. J. Q. C. nom

Mackay pl, s s, 150 e River road, 50x90x50x95, New Utrecht. Release mort. Elizabeth P. Child, of Litchfield, Conn., to Catharine I. Mackay. nom

Same property. Release mort. Horace Bacon, of New York, to Catherine I. wife of John Mackay. 25

Same property. Catherine I. Mackay to Moe S. Lott. nom

Macon st, n s, 490 e Ralph av, 90x100. Richard Mullowney to Joseph A. Cross. *Mt.* $16,435. nom

Macon st, n s, 253.4 e Reid av, 16.8x100, h & l. Frank C. Swimm to Bell K. Scott. *Mt.* $3,800. 6,300

Macon st, s s, 375 e Reid av, 18x100, h & l. James G. Roberts to Mary Reardon. *Mt.* $4,500. 7,750

Madison st, s e s, 386 s w Knickerbocker av, 18x100. Release mechanic's lien. The Tilly & Van Hagen Co. to George A. Craig. nom

Madison st, s e s, 390 n e Central av, 20x100. Emil F. Wildner to Christopher Bargfrede. *Mt.* $2,250. nom

Madison st, s s, 218.9 e Franklin av, 18.9x100. George L. Marinor to Eleonora Rick. *Mt.* $2,500. 4,825

Madison st, n w s, 152 n e Hamburg av, 18x100. John Cooper to Edi Posner and Pincus Burger. nom

Madison st, s e s, 386 s w Knickerbocker av, 18x100, h & l. George A. Craig to David McKelvey. 4,200

Same property. Release mort. James C. Brower to George A. Craig. 1,944

Same property. Release mort. Mary J. Pillon to same. 84

Same property. Release mort. Annie C. Craig to same. 150

Malbone st, n w cor Nostrand av, runs west 90 x north 80 x west 10 x north 20 x west 25.2 to old Nostrand av, x north 124.6 to Sullivan st late old Bedford road, x northeast 25.6 x northeast 7.6 x northeast again 25.11 x again northeast 7.6 x east 85 to av, x southwest 44 x south 200. Daniel Doody to Jane H. Cowdrey, Edgewater, N. Y. Q. C. nom

Market st, w s, 1,442 s Brooklyn and Jamaica pike, 25x150. Lillian H. wife of Francis H. Miller to Alexander S. Cook. 650

McDonough st, s s, 306.3 e Ralph av, 18.9x100, h & l. Thomas H. Radcliffe to Martha V. Travers, New York. *Mt.* $4,500. 6,800

McDonough st, s s, 250 w Patchen av, 35.8x100. John Pierce to Henry B. Hill. 3,210

McDonough st, s s, 464.4 e Reid av, 35.8x100. Release mort. Joseph C. Hoagland to John Peirce. 2,475

McDougal st, s s, 150 e Hopkinson av, 56.3x100. William Andrews and August Nickel to Jane Lansing. *Mt.* $12,750. 16,500

McKibbin st, s s, 144.9 w Ewen st, 25x100. Moritz Scharfman and Joseph Littmann to Joseph Zirinsky. *Mt.* $9,700. 13,000

Melrose st, n w s, 100 s w Knickerbocker av, 25x100. Wilhelm Kempf to Michael Girkes. *Mt.* $3,000. 5,175

Melrose st, n w s, 175 s w Knickerbocker av, 25x100, h & l. Bernard Rokus to William Koehler. *Mt.* $3,000. 5,450

Milford st, w s, 550 n Liberty av, 25x100, h & l. Michael J. McCann to Edward Carmody. *Mt.* $1,500. 2,400

Moffat st, n w s, 153.4 s w Bushwick av, 19.2x100. Jabez R. Parsons and Thomas A. Watson to Albert M. Seaman. *Mt.* $3,650. 5,500

Monroe pl, w s, 225 s Clark st, 25x100. Annie L. widow Edward S. Howard to Annie Howard. *Mt.* $10,000. nom

Montgomery st, s s, 125 e 18th st, 25x100, Flatbush. John Reis and Henry B. Davenport to Robert Dorn. 1,800

Morrell st, w s, 25 n Moore st, 25x75, h & l. Theresa Goodkind widow to Simon H. Whiteman. *Mt.* $4,000. 5,575

Myrtle st, s s, 300 e Evergreen av, 50x95. Release judgment. Anne E. Schirzel to Margaretha Bossert. 140

Moore st, s s, 275 e Graham av, 25x100. Semche Simon to Abraham and Joseph Weltman. *Mt.* $7,000. 12,500

Moore st, s s, 100 w Graham av, 25x100. Abraham and Louis Roaschinsky to Morris Simiansky. *Mt.* $3,700. 7,150

Moore st, s s, 50 e Leonard st, runs south 57.7 x northeast 45.4 x southeast — x north 74.2 to st, x west 50. Henry Seiler to Henry Roth. 8,500

North Henry st, e s, 254.3 n Van Pelt av, 17x100. Charles Engert to Henry Garrick. 3,500

North Oxford st, e s, 499.11 s Park av, 19.5x100. Release dower. Anne F. Watson widow to Sarah I. and James Watson. nom

North Oxford st, w s, 262.3 s Park av, 25x100. Frederick J. and John J. Adler to Jeannette Adler. nom

Osborn st, s w cor Sutter av, 25x100. William H. Ellis to Benjamin Sachs. 3,500

Osborn st, w s, 175 s Blake av, 50x100. Israel M. Cohen and Marks Jacobs to Thomas Goldstein. 1,600

Palmetto st, s e s, 100 n e Central av, 25x100. Caroline Kloetmann to Anton and Anna E. Ullingeo. 6,000

Palmetto st, n w s, 380 n e Central av, 20x100. Margareth M. Boehm to George Closset. *Mt.* $2,000. 3,400

Pacific st, No. 124, s s, abt 192 e Henry st, 25x100, h & l. Charles H. Lock to Mary A. Leyden. *Mt.* $4,000. 7,250

Pacific st, n s, 55 e Franklin av, runs north 45.10 x northeast 5.5 x north 51.10 x east 20 x south 100 x west 25. Thomas D. Carpenter, Jr., to Wm. C. Boone, Jr. *Mt.* $8,000. 13,500

Pearl st, e s, 118 s Nassau st, 24x102.9. Stephen P. Sturges to Sarah L. Smith. *Mt.* $14,000. exch

Plymouth st, Nos. 321 and 323, n s, being 28.3x100. Eugene H. Vanderbilt to L. K. Reynolds, of Stockport, N. Y. *Mt.* $11,000. 21,000

Powell st, e s, 250 n Liberty av, 25x100. William Field admr. John S. E. Field to Charles E. and William Field, each ½ part. 2,300

Same property. Charles E. Field to Charles C. Hoffmann. ½ part. 1,150

Same property. William Field to same. ½ part. 1,150

President st, s s, 383.4 w Columbia st, 16.8x100. Foreclos. John Courtney to James Usher. 775

President st, n s, 217 e 6th av, 62.6x95. William L. Perkins to Alexander J. C. Skene. *Mt.* $5,000. 15,000

Pulaski st, s s, 194.10 w Sumner av, 50.11x100, h & l. Maria Roberts to Frederick W. Klein and Elise his wife. exch and 10,500

Same property. Release mort. The Bulmer Lumber Co. to Maria Roberts. nom

Same property. Release mort. C. B. Keogh Mfg Co. to same. consid. omitted

Pulaski st, s s, 479.3 e Throop av, 51.1x100. Release mort. Louis W. Schaefer to Maria and Essex Roberts. 200

Pulaski st, s s, 479.3 e Throop av, 51.1x100. Release mort. Edwin O. Phelps to Maria Roberts. 10,185

Quincy st, s s, 60 w Patchen av, 20x100, h & l. John P. McQuaid to Elizabeth Decker. *Mt.* $3,500. 7,750

Richardson st, n s, 95 w Herbert st, runs north 59 x west 15.11 x north 15 x again west 0.10 x south 62.5 to st, x east 22. Bertha Kaufmann to Anna T. Schiel. *Mt.* $1,350. nom

Rutledge st, s s, 153.1 w Bedford av, 18.5x100. Mary E. wife of William C. Dunn to Eli H. Bishop. *Mt.* $3,000. exch

Ryerson st, w s, 183.11 n Park av, 40x100. Robert Woodcock to Charles H. Bulkley. 7,500

Sackett st, s s, 57.9 e Hicks st, 19.3x100. Partition. Leicester Holme to Anna M. Roes. 4,050

Sackman st, w s, 200 n Belmont av, 25x100. Lewis Hurst to Tracy Coit. 650

Scholes st, n s, 100 e Lorimer st, 55x100. Robert Brass to John Kopf and Mina his wife, joint tenants. *Mt.* $4,500. 8,500

Scholes st, n s, 100 e Lorimer st, 55x100. Charles Bethon and William Gans to John Kopf. *Mt.* $5,000 nom

Same property. John Kopf to David Michel. *Mt.* $5,000. 6,700

Same property. David Michel to David Gluck. *Mt.* $5,000. 8,500

Seigel st, s s, 75 e Ewen st, 25x100. Gerson Levy to Wolf Plotel and Benjamin Rosenthal, of New York. *Mt.* $8,300. 9,800

Seigel st, No. 95, n s, 100 w Graham av, 25x100. Jonas Feldberg, Sarah Barasch and Henry Meyer to Tillie Frank and Anny Mintz. *Mt.* $11,000. 18,800

Sherman st, e s, 140 s Greenwood av, runs east 133 x south 10 x southwest 31.3 x west 127 to Sherman st, x north 40, Flatbush. Henry Rudloff to George J. and Daniel D. Waugh. *Mt.* $2,000. 3,650

Stagg st, s e cor Bogart st, 50x100. Peter Hillenbrand to John A. Eppig. 3,500

Stanhope st, n w s, 250 n e Hamburg av, 25x100. John Eich to William Ramsey and Catharine his wife. 6,100

Stanhope st, n w s, 225 n e Hamburg av, 25x100. Simon G. Meyer to Valentine Kohl, of New York. *Mt.* $3,000. 6,700

Stanhope st, n w s, 375 n e Hamburg av, 125x100. Theodore F. Jackson to Wilhelmina Schwenck, of New York. 6,625

Stanhope st, s e s, 140 n e Hamburg av, 20x100. James White to Joseph Ryan. *Mt.* $4,200. nom

Starr st, n w s, 125 s w Hamburg av, 25x100, h & l. Frank Eitel to William Schultz. *Mt.* $1,500. 3,000

Starr st, s s, 325 e Central av, 25x100. John Hermann to Theobald Kemer and Anna his wife. 2,600

Stockton st, n s, 150 w Throop av, 25x95. Anna G. Schiel to Bertha Kaufmann. 7,000

Steuben st, No. 243, e s, 175 s De Kalb av, 22.4x100. Moritz Pinner, Elizabeth, N. J., to Peter Herche. *Mt.* $11,000. nom

Steuben st, e s, 152.8 s De Kalb av, 22.4x100, h & l. Same to same. *Mt.* $10,000. nom

Strong pl, e s, 99.11 s Harrison st, 25.1x120x25x120, h & l. Mary L. Mather widow to Thomas Williams. 7,000

St. James pl, w s, 123 s Fulton st, 18.9x100, h & l. Anna M. wife of Toswill E. Harrison to Hugh Rose Hill trustee. nom

Suydam st, s e s, 200 n e Hamburg av, 25x100. John Clement to Charles P. Muller, of New York. *Mt.* $3,000. 6,400

Suydam st, n w s, 175 s w Knickerbocker av, 25x100, h & l. August Sedlmeir to Karl G. Lehmann and Katharina his wife, joint tenants. *Mt.* $3,000. 6,200

Suydam st, s e s, 235 s w Knickerbocker av, 75x100. Theodore F. Jackson to John Clement. 4,050

Suydam st, s e s, 125 n e Hamburg av, 50x100. Theodore F. Jackson to Peter J. Brahm. 2,725

Sydney pl, n w s, 506.8 n State st, 22x100. Annie C. Lindeman to Crowell Hadden, Jr. 10,200

Ten Eyck st, n s, 75 w Bushwick Boulevard, 25x50. Release mort. Abram Cooke to Mendel Levy. nom

Same property. Mendel Levy to Esther Harris 3,800

Van Buren st, s s, 314.3 w Reid av, 14.3x100.
Van Buren st, s s, 357 w Reid av, 14.3x100.
Irwin Heasty to Andrew Donnelly. *Mt.* $6,250. nom

Vanderbilt st, n s, 1,030.7 e 18th st, 29x80, Flatbush. Andrew Wilson to James F. Bergen. 1,800

Walworth st, e s, 306.8 s Willoughby av, 16.8x100. Catharine Brady to Elizabeth Brady. gift

Warwick st, w s, 200 n Eastern Parkway, 25x100. Eugene R. Tichenor to George Alexander. *Mt.* $2,891. 3,850

Washington st, w s, 80.10 s Concord st, 26.6x105.9x26.6x106.1. Elizabeth R. Levison widow to the trustees of the New York and Brooklyn Bridge. 30,000

Washington st, w s, bet Concord and Tillary sts, at the s e cor land now or late of Francis Howard, 29x125. Asa W. Parker to the trustees of the New York and Brooklyn Bridge. 30,000

Watkins st, e s, 100 s Livonia av, 50x100, h & l. Ann E. Sullivan to Isaac and Annie Harris. 3,100

Watkins st, e s, 75 n Dumont av, 25x100. Frank C. Lang trustee of J. G. Williamson dec'd to James O'Halloran. Confirmation deed. nom

Weirfield st, n w s, 321 s w Central av, 20x100. Contract. L. J. Lippmann to James M. Shay. 2,500

Whipple st, n w s, 180 n e Throop av, 25x100. Joseph Hyman to Saja Guttman, of New York. *Mt.* $4,100. 6,000

Windsor pl, s s, 79.10 w 8th av, 18x100. Thomas Brown to George A. Webster. *Mt.* $4,000. 6,000

York st, n s, 25 w Green lane, 25x100. Emanuel Weill to Aaron and Louis Davidson, of New York. 6,000

2d st, s s, 100 w 8th av, 27.9x95. John Adamson to Albert E. White. *Mt.* $2,125. nom

2d st, s s, 127.9 w 8th av, 80x95. Cornelius E. Donnellon to Albert E. White. *Mt.* $6,684. nom

2d pl, s w cor Clinton st, 16x118.5. John W. Peckett to James A. Townsend. 7,750

3d st, s s, 180 e Smith st, 88x100. Edward M. Townsend individ and as exr. Belinda R. Townsend to Vina A. Sumner, of Syracuse, N. Y. 8,875

South 3d st, s s, 50 e Keap st, 25x20. Fanny Wallach to Herman Bleck. 1,500

South 3d st, s s, 20 w Rodney st, 20x47.6; also,
South 3d st, s s, 50 e Marcy av, 25x95; also,
Hewes st, n w s, 116.6 s w Bedford av, 20x80;
14th st, n e s, 297.10 n w 7th av, 50x100.
Lizzie J. wife of Alfred Hodges, Ephraim Johnson and Grace M. Johnson heirs Cornelius L. Johnson to Caroline A. wife of Frank B. Smith. ¾ part. exch

3d pl, s s, 275 w Court st, 25x100. Rebecca M. wife of Daniel Ferry to Peter Mallon. 5,000

4th st, s w s, 455.6 s e Smith st, 22x100. James E. Raleigh to Michael Raleigh. 1-6 part. nom

Same property. James E. Raleigh to Michael, James and Annie Raleigh. 1-6 part. nom

North 4th st, n e s, 175 n w Driggs st, 25x100. Foreclos. Robert Merchant, ref., to Daniel E. Kain. 5,000

South 4th st, s w s, 225 s e Hooper st, 25x90.3x25x90.6. Frederick W. Klein to Maria Roberts. exch

Same property. Maria Roberts to Andrew R. Baird. *Mt.* $4,100. nom

South 4th st, n s, 153.6 e 4th st, 25x95. Theodore B. Case to Carl Hermann, of New York. *Mt.* $3,000. 7,000

South 5th st, n e s, 25.6 s e Hewes st, 24.6x89x24.6x89.6, h & l. Lewis P. Nostrand to Christopher Weber. *Mt.* $5,300. 6,500

5th st, s s, 137.10 e 5th av, 15x100. Francis Curran to Emma F. Callanan. *Mt.* $2,500. nom

5th st, s w s, 97.10 n w 5th av, runs southwest 100 x northwest 300 x southwest 100 to 6th st, x northwest 200 x northeast 200 to 5th st, x southeast 500. Frank A. Barnaby to Charles D. Burwell. All liens. nom

6th st, s s, 180 w 4th av, 115x100. Release judgment. George R. Brown to Emil Lindburg. 150

7th st, n s, 132.6 w 5th av, 17.6x100. Annie M. wife of John E. Molone to John E. Malone in trust for Ellen Malone. *Mt.* $3,000. 5,500

7th st, s s, 256.2 w 7th av, 16.8x100. Franklin J. Fellows to Daniel Doody. Q. C. nom

Same property. Daniel Doody to Annie A. Suydam. *Mt.* $5,000. nom

9th st, s s, 296.4 e 5th av, 53.7½x80. Pedro Riesgo, of New York, to William Wetterer, of New York. 10,000

Same property. William Wetterer, of New York, to Anna Riesgo. Sub. to all liens, &c. 10,000

9th st, n s, 22.10 e 7th av, 110x90.
Pacific st, s s, 150 w 6th av, 25x110.
7th av, s e cor Carroll st, 222x96x230.11x96.5.
Abbot L. Dow trustee to Franklin Trust Co. substituted trustee of Margaret H., Cornelia H. and Caroline Dow. nom

North 9th st, s w s, 240 n w Driggs st, 38.9x100. Rose Ireland widow, Mary, Rose W., Joseph and John Ireland children of Patrick Ireland to Thomas H. Ireland. All liens. 3,400

10th st, n e s, 398 n w 3d av, 25x100. William H. Kent to Sarah Tolson. nom

11th st, s w s, 213.5 n w 8th av, 75x100. James Jack to Henry E. Murphy. *Mt.* $4,000. 5,700

12th st, n e s, 296.5 s e 5th av, 16.8x100, h & l. Terence F. Ferguson to John Assip and Timothy J. Buckley. *Mt.* $3,750. 6,000

12th st, s s, 222.10 w 7th av, runs south 100.3 x west 15.1 x north 0.3½ x west 7.5 x north 100 x east 22.6. Henry T. Bauman, of Jersey City, to Daniel W. Talcott, of New York. *Mt.* $5,750. nom

13th st, s s, 166.7 w 5th av, 18.9x100. Harriet L. Thompson to Jane E. Foote. 4,400

Bay 13th st, s e s, 95 n e Bath av, 30x80, Bath Beach. Karl Bochmuller to John Henni. 560

Same property. Release mort. John Henni to Karl Bochmuller. nom

18th st, n s, 78 w 7th av, 18x ½ block. William C. Brooke to Catharine Trobue or Trobue. 2,800

Bay 22d st, n w s, 410 s w 86th st, 65x96.8, New Utrecht. George P. Gott to Robert L. Wood. nom

Bay 26th st, n w s, 160 s w Benson av, 60x96.8, New Utrecht. Annie K. Kaltenbach to Emma L. wife of William P. Palmer. *Mt.* $787. 1,800

Bay 29th st, s e s, 180 s w Benson av, runs southwest 160 x southeast 193.4 to 22d av, x northeast 180 x northwest 96.8 x southwest 20 x northwest 96.8, New Utrecht. Cornelius Furgueson, Jr., to George Eckstein. 6,000

Bay 32d st, n w s, 80 s w 86th st, 60x96.8, New Utrecht. James Gascoine to Charles Corey. ½ part. 550

Same property. Anna E. widow John G. Cozine individ. and with James Gascoine as exr. John G. Cozine to same. ½ part. 550

47th st, n s, 85 e 3d av, 20x100.2. Frederick Seifried and Frederick Gommel to Hermann Schroeder. 1,000

Same property. Release mort. Jacob Heim, New York, to Frederick Seifried and Frederick Gommel. 1,000

49th st, s s, 380 e 8th av, 10x100.2 New Utrecht. James V. S. Woolley to Sophie M. Olsen. 175

51st st, s e s, 100 n e 8th av, 80x100.2.
51st st, s e s, 180 n e 8th av, 20x100.2.
52d st, n e s, 80.3 n w 9th av, 20x102.2, New Utrecht.
Michael J. Bergen to Annie Gaffney. 785

54th st, n s, 380 w 3d av, 17.6x100.2. Levi V. Martin to Thomas R. H. Fitzgerald and Elizabeth his wife. *Mt.* $2,200. 3,600

56th st, s w s, 100 n w 12th av, runs northwest 26 x west 14.9 x southwest 95.7 x southeast 40 x northeast 100.2, New Utrecht. Release mort. Hope H. Colgate to The Blythebourne Improvement Co 200

57th st, s w s, 140 s e 7th av, 20x100.2. Charles W. Lundqvist to James Preston. 200

57th st, s s, 180 w 2d av, 20x100.2. Albert L. French to John and James Van Dyk. *Mt.* $2,500. 4,400

64th st, s s, 600 w 14th st, 20x100, New Utrecht. Effingham H. Nichols, of New York, to Louisa Heintz, of Parkville, N. Y. 215

64th st, s w s, 300 n w 7th av, 20x81.7; also,
65th st, n e s, 120 n w 8th av, 40x100, New Utrecht.
Claus Doscher to Nicholas Molinari. 405

67th st, s s, 140 e 11th av, 20x130, New Utrecht. Margaretha Reichenbach to Anna B. Sorenson. 350

67th st, s s, 450 e 4th av, 50x100, Bay Ridge. Georgianna wife of Frank Jacobus to Charles W. and William A. Van Ness. 900

75th st, n s, 426 w 18th av, 40x100, New Utrecht. John H. Hanley to George S. Francis. 585

76th st, westerly cor 11th av, 120x200 to 77th st, New Utrecht. Hoik D. Campbell to Thomas K. Schmerhorn. 2,900

Av B, s w cor East 4th st, 100x100, Flatbush. Foreclos. Wilmot T. Cox ref. to The Brooklyn and New York Arcanum Building and Loan Assoc. 2,000

Av Y, s w cor East 14th st, 100x50, Gravesend. Mary A. wife of and Duncan J. McKinlay to Charles T. Sumner. 700

Albany av, w s, 38.11 n Butler st, 16.8x85. Charles S. Taber and George C. Case to Irwin Heasly. *Mt.* $3,500. 5,500

Atlantic av, s s 144.4 e Henry st, runs south 80 x east 20.4 x south 100 to Pacific st, x east 64 x north 100 x west 32.11 x north 80 x west 51.6. Lyman S. Burnham and Hugh Boyd to Kate P. widow, Henry P. and Katharine children and heirs of Henry P. Journeay. Q. C. nom

Atlantic av, n e s, 201.2¾ s e East New York av, 32.7x83.6x81x south 77.6. Release mort. Frederick T. Hill to Catharine Molloy. nom

Same property. Catherine Molloy to John Meyn. *Mt.* $10,000. 16,500

Atlantic av, s w s, abt 61 s e Warren st, 50x145, New Utrecht. Peter Wilkinson to Philip Kralzer. 800

Bedford av, e s, 112 s Prospect pl, 20x90x20.4x86. James Gowdy to William Burrows. 2,500

Bedford av, e s, 65.9 n Grand st, 18x59.3x17.6x61.4, h & l. Foreclos. John Courtney to Bernard and Philip Katz, Paterson, N. J. 500

Bedford av, e s, 20 s Wallabout st, 20x67. John W. McCaffrey son and devisee of Letitia McCaffrey widow and devisee of Patrick McCaffrey to David M Koehler. nom

Blake av, s w cor Watkins st, runs west 200 to Osborn st, x south 100 x east 200 x north 100. George M. Walgrove, of New York, to Bernhard J. Pink. 5,000

Blake av, n e cor Sackman st, 100x100. Lewis Hurst to Leah Siegel, of New York. Sub. to mort. 2,200

Bushwick av, west cor Pilling st, 20x70.4. Henry Weil to Richard Morrisey. nom

Clason av, w s, 80 s Lexington av, 20x100. Ethelbert T. Swezey, of Colorado, to Maria I. Swezey, of Cornwall-on-the-Hudson, N. Y. gift

Clinton av, w s, abt 150 s Myrtle av, 75x200 to Vanderbilt av, hs & ls. Lavenia wife of William H. Beard to William H. Beard. B. & S. 1890. nom

De Kalb av, s w cor Reid av, 24.6x80. John Bauer to Bernhard Bauer. 7,500

De Kalb av, s e s, 275 s w Hamburg av, 25x100. A. H. August Arwo to Carl W. Bauermeister. 6,525

De Kalb av, s s, 250 w Lewis av, 25x100; also,
Interior lot on centre line block bet De Kalb av and Kosciusko st 450 w Lewis av, runs south 1.10 x northwest to centre line said block x east — to beginning.
Margaret, Peter P. and Edward C. Curtis heirs of Patrick Curtis to Joseph Short, Jr. 1,500

Evergreen av, s w s, 80 n w Harman st, 20x100. Elizabeth wife of and James Wilder to Henrietta Singer widow. 4,400

Flushing av, n s, 65 w Knickerbocker av, runs west 25 x north 84.1 x northeast 44.4 to av, x southeast 8.4 x southwest 21.8 x south —. Sigmund Bleyer to Hermann Katt and Annie his wife, joint tenants. 10,000

Flushing av, s s, 65 e Nostrand av, 35x100. Louise Erdman to Hemon Lottman. *Mt.* $5,000. 9,500

Franklin av, w s, 177.9 n Park av, 45x112.2x45 x111.5. Thomas H. Bullick to V. T. Lockwood. *Mt.* $`5,000. nom

Gates av, w s, 4. 6 o Downing st, 22.6x84. Mary L. wife of and John W. Douglass to Samuel W. Hurley, of New York. exch

Gates av, No. 291, n s, 146 e Franklin av, 16x 100, h & l. Mary E. Barnes to Emma J. wife of Frank H. Phillips. *Mt.* $4,250. nom

Glenmore av, s e cor Berriman st, 125x100. Release mort. Samuel Burhans, Jr., to Marenus J. Goodenough. 1,000

Glenmore av, s e cor Berriman st, 50x100. Marenus J. Goodenough to Mary wife of Thomas Smith. 1,600

Glenmore av, s o cor Christopher av, 100x100. Julia wife of and Philip Hyer to Morris Levy, of New York. 3,200

Glenmore av, n s, 25 w Christopher av, 26x100. Charles Stahner to Morris Levy, of New York. *Mt.* $200. 720

Graham av, e s, 25 n Varet st, 25x100. Louis Jung to Frederick Luhrsen. *Mt.* $4,300. 6,200

Graham av, e s, 75 s Ainslie st, 25x100.
Hooper st, n w s, 305 n e Marcy av, 20x100.
South 5th st, n s, 41 e Rodney st, 20 6x60.
Richardson st, s s, 60 e Ewen st, 40x50.
Taylor st, s e s, 300 s w Wythe av, 106x100. ⅝ part.
North 4th st, s e cor Berry st, 25x60.
Union av, w s, 53.3 s South 4th st, runs south 22 x west 68.4 x northwest — x east 80 7.
Rodney st, w s, 53 s South 4th st, runs west 25 x south 22 x west 19.9 x south 28 3 x west 19.9 x south 28.3 x west 34.2 x south 23.11 x east 78.11 to Rodney st, x north 78.6 to beginning.
Rodney st, e s, 41.6 s South 4th st, runs east 70 x south 60.1 x west 8.6 x south 39.10 x west 61.6 to Rodney st, x north 100 to beginning. ⅝ part.
Lizzie J. wife of Alfred Hodges and Caroline A. wife of Frank B. Smith and Grace M. Johnson heirs Cornelius L. Johnson to Ephraim Johnson. exch

Grand av, e s, 129.6 s Flushing av, 30x100. Eliza Sheridan to James Harrigan. B. & S. C. a. G. 1,400

Greene av, n w s, 25 s w Irving av, 25x83.7x25x 84.9. Joseph Weidner and John Haas to Lazarus Almuly. 6,100

Greene av, s e s, 218.10 s w Central av, 15x100, h & l. Lillie Cohen to Anna Ficker. *Mt.* $2,950. nom

Greene av, n s, 75 w Hamburg av, 25x200 to Harman st. George Covert to Heinrich Langlos. 13,000

Greene av, n s, 430 w Patchen av, 20x100. Frank H. White and Frank H. White, of Ridgewood, N. J., to William Herron. *Mt.* $8,750. 1,600

Hamburg av, w s, 60 n Troutman st, 20x60. John Wahl to Mary wife of Adam Nunner. *Mt.* $2,000. 5,000

Hamburg av, n e s, 100 s e Woodbine st, 18.9x 80. Release mort. James Gascoine to Jacob Manneschmidt. nom

Same property. Jacob Manneschmidt to Leonhard Emig and Carolina his wife. 4,000

Hamilton av, w s, 66.6 s Columbia st, runs south 75 x west 59.5 x northwest 59.5 to st, x north 75 x southeast 27.11 x east 27.11 to av. Moses Schwartz to Charles Schwartz. ½ part. *Mt.* $2,000. 3,000

Hopkinson av, n w cor Dean st, 107.2x50. Florence A. wife of and James A. Dunbar to James McMahon. 600

Howard av, e s, 200.10 s Herkimer st, 16 10x98. Foreclos. John Courtney, Sheriff, to Nathan Kaplan. 1,760

Howard av, w s, 117.3 n St. Marks av, runs southwest 100 x south 32.2 x northeast to Howard av, x north 32.2. Clarence Dickerson to Frederick W. Carruthers. ⅜ interest. 274

Hudson av, w s, 58.4 s John st, 16.8x90. Foreclos. John Courtney, Sheriff, to Emilie W. Dana. 3,000

Hudson av, e s, 104.2 s Myrtle av, 50x100.5, hs & ls. William H. Ferguson to Silas A. Condict. nom

Jefferson av, s s, 200 e Lewis av, 50x100. Mary wife of William N. Reardon to James G. Roberts. B. & S. *Mt.* $3,500. 6,000

Jefferson av, s e s, 311.6 n e Evergreen av, 18x 100. Timothy G. Sellew to Lucy Cornell. Sub. to mort. nom

Jefferson av, s e s, 174 n e Broadway, 18x100. Joseph A. Cross to Lowell V. Brown. *Mt.* $3,-000. nom

Johnson av, s s, 143 e Bushwick av, 50x100. Esther Sweet, New York, to Louis Berman, New York. *Mt.* $7,000. 10,250

Judson av, w s, 50 s Washington pl, 50x100, 26th Ward. Ferdinand Krooss to Louisa F. wife of Nicholas F. Brockmann. 6,000

Kingston av, n e cor Pacific st, 96x80. Daniel Doody to John F. Hart. 37,000

Lafayette av, n s, 575 e Reid av, runs east 54.6 x northeast 135.7 to s w s Broadway, x northwest 92.9 x southwest 80.7 x south 7.9 x west 25 x south 100. Elizabeth E. Hutchins widow to Samuel D. Hunter. *Mt.* $9,000. 25,000

Lee av, s w s, 91 n w Rutledge st, 15x81.8.
Park av, n s, 75 e North Portland av, 25x87.7 x25.6x92.8.
Jeannette and John J. Adler to Frederick J. Adler. nom

Lee av, w s, 20 s Lynch st, 20x80, h & l. Theodore Wulp to Charles Rayber and Catherina his wife. 9,500

Lee av, n e s, 66.8 s e Wallabout st, runs northeast 78.7 x south 15 x southeast 10.6 x southwest 76.2 to Lee av, x northwest 25. Henry Roth to Wilhelmine Israel. *Mt.* $4,000. exch

Lee av, n e s, 50 n w Middleton st, 25x75. Louis Beer and Michael Schaffner to Conrad Schaffner, of New York. 11,000

Lewis av, n w cor Pulaski st, 20x79.10. August Beneke to Mary C. Hale. 5,400

Lewis av, e s, 60 s Lexington av, 20x100. Hardy H. Dignam, New York, to Frank Hyde. *Mt.* $6,700. nom

Lexington av, s s, 259 w Nostrand av, 32x100, h & l. Rose Wilson to George Finck. 15,000

Lexington av, s s, 200 e Patchen av, 17x100. Carrie wife of William Tilly to Tinie M. Smith. B. & S. Taxes, &c. nom

Liberty av, s s, 50 e Osborn st, 100x100. Herbert C. Smith to Charles and Charles W. Tomlin. 4,000

Livonia av, s s, 50 e Thatford av, 25x100. Joshua Fletcher to Morris Ableson. *Mt.* $500. 1,100

Livonia av, s w cor Christopher av, runs south 229.6 x west 201 to Stone av, x north 232.8 x east 200. Charles F. Griffith to Bernhard J. Pink. 7,200

Livonia av, s e cor Stone av, runs south 232.8 x east 100 x north to Livonia av, x west 100. Bernhard J. Pink to Harris Fein and Simon and Louis Young. 4,250

Lott av, s s, extends from Watkins st to Osborn st 200 x — to New Lots road, 45 lots. Henry J. Putnam to Henry E. Woodward, Morristown, N. J. 20,250

Lott av, s s, extends from Stone av to Watkins st, 200x — to New Lots road, 39 lots. Henry W. Putnam to William Bryce, of Madison, N. J. 17,550

Marcy av, s w s, 100 s e Hewes st, 20x100. Eliza Ross to Elizabeth A. Green. nom

Miller av, w s, 80 s Arlington av, 20x75. George, John W. and Joseph T. Fletcher to Marie Hermann. *Mt.* $2,500. nom

Myrtle av, n s, intersection s e s Himrod st, runs east along av 92.10 x north 73.11 x northwest 14.3 to Himrod st, x southwest 117.10; also,
Himrod st, s e s, 117.10 n e Myrtle av, runs southeast 14 3 x south 73.11 to av, x east 25 x north 84.4¾ x northwest 24 8 to st, x southwest 25 to beginning.
John J. Brady to Thomas F. Magner. *Mt.* $2,000. 5,500

Myrtle av, s s, 80.3 e Willoughby av, runs south 84.11 x northeast 25.11 x north 78.1 to Myrtle av, x west 25. Henry W. T. Mali, of New York, to Edward Hendrickson. 1,200

Same property. Edward Hendrickson to Joseph G. Wischerth. nom

Nostrand av, w s, 25 n Butler st, 82.10x107.10x 83.2x100, Flatbush. Patrick J. Kenedy to Julia Kane. 1,000

Ovington av, n w cor Stuart av, 103.5x170x 113.8x170.3, New Utrecht. George Self to John J. Page. 2,000

Ovington av, n s, 200 w 12th av, 40x130.1x40x 129.7, New Utrecht. James V. S. Woolley, of New York, to Bernard J. Shanley. 400

Patchen av, s e cor Lexington av, 20x90. Robert Smith to Elizabeth Wilder. 5,350

Pennsylvania av, e s, 100 n Broadway or Eastern Parkway, 25x110. George Lederle to Emilie Kehle. *Mt.* $4,000. 6,200

Prospect av, n s, 85 w 5th av, 20x100x20.4x100. Annie A. Suydam to Daniel F. Doody. nom

Prospect av, s s, 199 e 5th av, 0.8½x80.2x0.11x 80.2. Daniel Doody to Jane H. Cowdrey. B. & S. nom

Prospect av, n s, 245 e 7th av, 25x100. Joseph P. Fuels to Mary E. Barnes. *Mt.* $4,000. exch

Prospect av, s e cor 8th av, runs east 20 x south 55 x east 0.6 x south 25.2 x west 20.6 to 8th av, x north 80.2, h & l. Henry E. Murphy to Jennie L. Brown. *Mt.* $12,000. 16,000

Same property. Release mort. William Post committee of John Rogers to Henry E. Murphy. 12,000

Same property. Release mort. James Jackson to same. nom

Putnam av, s e cor Lewis av, 25x100. Kate Acor to Hermann Lange. 6,000

Putnam av, n e cor Lewis av, 25x100. Eli H. Bishop to Fanny Bishop. *Mt.* $20,000. nom

Putnam av, n s, 185 e Stuyvesant av, 40x100. Release mort. John Marsh to John Mitchell and Charles Herr. 1,600

Putnam av, s s, 295 w Stuyvesant av, 20x100. Eli H. Bishop to Mary E. Dunn. *Mt.* $8,000. nom

Ralph av, s e cor McDonough st, runs south 90 x east 88 x south 10 x east 75 x north 100 to McDonough st, x west 113. Release mort. Asa W. Tenney to Thomas H. Radcliffe. 8,500

Ridgewood av, s w cor Essex st, 40x90. Christian W. C. Dreher to John Mehan. 2,000

Ridgewood av, s s, 80 e Essex st, 20x90. Wilmot D. Losee to Charles S. Cook. *Mt.* $1,600. 3,300

Riverdale av, n e cor Stone av, runs north 270 x east to Christopher av, x south to Riverdale av, x west — to beginning; also,
Stone av, e s, 230 s Livonia av, runs east to Christopher av at point 229.6 s Livonia av, x west to e s Stone av, x north 2.8.
Abram Simon, Haskel Silberman and Simon Alker to Max Cohen and Barnet Friend. *Mt.* $4,000. 10,250

Rockaway av, s e cor Dean st, 114.5x100. William M. Miller to Mary E. Cook, Newtown, L. I. *Mt.* $2,300, taxes, &c. 5,000

Saratoga av, s e cor Bergen st, runs east along st 77.5 x southwest — to av, x north 13.6. Clarence Dickerson to Frederick W. Carruthers. ⅜ part. 160

Saratoga av, s e cor Decatur st, 100x115.6. Samuel R. Good to William H. Good. Sub. to morts. nom

Saratoga av, n e cor Marion st, 22x78.
Saratoga av, e s, 41.4 n Marion st, 29x78.
Saratoga av, e s, 100.4 n Marion st, 60x78.
Thomas A. McWhinney to Jacob Aaronson. nom

Schenck av, w s, 300 n Blake av, 25x100. Albert H. W. Van Siclen to Sven Johanson. nom

Shepherd av, w s, 225 n Liberty av, 25x100. Louise M. and Charles E. Thomas to Emily C. Siemon. 550

Same property. William Townsend to same. Q. C. 30

Snediker av, e s, 225 s Riverdale av, 25x100. Charles S. Cook to Wilmot D. Losee. exch

St. Marks av, n s, 450 e Grand av, 150x126. John H. and William R. Doherty to Thomas W. Hynes. *Mt.* $5,000. 10,000

St. Marks av, s s, 250 e Howard av, runs east 50 x south 127.9 x west 75 x north 42.9 x east 25 x north 85. Aline wife of and George Oertel to Mary A. Dowdell. 1,500

Stone av, n e cor Riverdale av, 267.4x— to Christopher av, x270.6 to Riverdale av, x west 200. Thomas McGee to Abram Simon, Haskel Silberman and Simon Alkor. *Mt.* $4,000. 8,360

Stone av, e s, 230 s Livonia av, runs east to w s Christopher av at point 229.6 s Livonia av, x west back to Stone av, x north 2.8. Bernhard J. Pink, Harris Fein, Simon and Louis Young to Abram Simon, Haskell Silberman and Simon Alker. B. & S. 325

Same property. Release mort. Charles F. Griffith to Bernhard J. Pink et al. nom

Sunnyside av, n s, 270 w Miller av, 50x250 to Highland Boulevard. John N. Smith to Abby J. wife of James A. Bills, of Newtown, N. Y. *Mt.* $3,500. nom

Thatford av, e s, 100 n Belmont av, 25x100. Barnet Levin and Max Gittelsohn to Philip Sigle. *Mt.* $1,800. 3,100

Thatford av, e s, 125 s Sutter av, 25x100. Abraham Ruth to Louis Cohen, of New York. *Mt.* $1,700. 2,950

Throop av, w s, 50 n Stockton st, 25x100. Nannetta Weinstein widow to Louis Berman and Ferdinand Feldblum. *Mt.* $4,900. 5,950

Washington av, e s, 90 n Park av, 40x200 to Hall st. Julian Lucas to Isaac S. Long, William Martin and John A. Kunkel. *Mt.* $7,000. 25,000

Waverly av, e s, 625 n Myrtle av, 18 9x100, h & l. Augustus Busener to Frank McIntyre. 4,250

Willoughby av, n w cor Grand av, runs west 24 x north 94 x east 14.1 x south 7.1 x east 9.8 to Grand av, x south 87, h & l. Edward Judson to Isaac, Joseph D., and Henry Lewis. *Mt.* 13,000. 17,000

Willoughby av, s s, 219.4 e Nostrand av, 19.4 x100, h & l. Augustus Wulfing, Jr., to Alexander Rosengarden and Frederica his wife. B. & S. nom

Same property. Alexander Rosengarden and Frederica his wife to Louise Wulfing. B. & S. nom

Wyckoff av, e s, 75 n Ralph st, 25x100. John and Ludwig Kuntz to Frederick Leyer and Sopha his wife. *Mt.* $3,500. 6,050

Wythe av, e s, 87.10 n Division av, 23.5x100.2x 18.9x100.4. Peter Adrian to Patrick Hayes. 8,500

Same property. Patrick Hayes to John McLoughlin, New York. 8,500

2d av, n w s, 50.2 s w 41st st, 50x100. Francis Nully to Maurice Daly and Annie his wife. *Mt.* $2,500. 7,625

3d av, n w s, 75 n e 14th st, 25x98. Annie wife of Jacob Levy to Jacob Shepsky, New York. *Mt.* $3,000. 4,500

3d av, n e cor 47th st, 40.2x85, bs & ls. Frederick Seifried and Frederick Gommel to Herman Schroeder. *Mt.* $17,000. 23,500

3d av, s e s, 80.2 s w 31st st, 20x100. Franklin Koehler and ano. exrs. Margaret A. Tretjen otherwise Tietjen to Margaret Everard. *Mt.* $1,500. 3,350

Same property. Martena G. Peterson, Adelina E. Koehler and Anna M. Schanz devisees Margaretha Tretjen to same. *Mt.* $1,500. 3,350

3d av, e s, 55.2 s Prospect av, 25x100. Fanny wife of Louis F. Herold, Ida wife of Charles Friedrich and Emil Landgraf heirs Charles W. Landgraf to Gunther Vonnoh. *Mt.* $1,700. 4,250

8d av, e s, 50 n 10th st, 40x80, hs & ls. Helene Steneck widow Henry W. and Adeline S. G. Steneck heirs Henry C. Steneck to Herman Bolte. 12,000

4th av, e s, 50.2 n 52d st, 20x100. James C. Foley to John A. Kernan. 1,000

5th av, east cor 19th st, 25x100. Joseph Dempsey to Frederick, Christian and Henry Hutwelker, of Hutwelker Bros. 10,000

6th av, s w cor 20th st, 100x100. John O'Connor to John D. Murphy. 20,000

6th av, n w s, 44.4 n e Prospect av, 18x80. Foreclos. John Courtney to Adolph H. Henriques, New York. *Mt.* and int. $3,725. 600

6th av, s w cor 66th st, 50x100; also,
Herbert st, s e cor Monitor st, 25x100.
Patrick Clancy, of New York, to Mary Hart. nom

12th av, w s, 80 n 66th st, 20x100, Bath Junction. James V. S. Woolley to Emil H. J. Heyser. 200

20th av, easterly cor 82d st, 200 to 81st st, x 100 to 21st av; also,
83d st, n e s, 320 s e 20th av, runs southeast 380 to 21st av, x northeast 200 to 82d st, x northwest 380 x southwest 200 to beginning, New Utrecht.
Cornelius Furguson to Albert Franke. 27,000

20th av, south cor 82d st, 100x120. Same to George Eckstein. 1,500

20th av, east cor 83d st, 100x120. Same to Harry A. Gubner. 1,500

20th av, south cor De Bruyns lane, being near centre of 83d st, runs south to angle in lane, x southwest along lane to 20th av, x northeast —
20th av, s e s, at centre line bet 80th and 81st sts, runs southeast to n s Kings Highway, x west to 20th av, x northeast — .
80th st, s w s, 100 s e 20th av, runs southwest to Kings Highway, x east to 80th st, x northwest —, New Utrecht
John L. Nostrand to Cornelius Ferguson. exch

20th av, n w s, intersection e s De Bruyns lane, runs northeast to Kings Highway, x southeast to 20th av, x southwest to beginning, New Utrecht. Cornelius Furguson to John L. Nostrand. nom

20th av, s e s, 600 n e Benson av, 100x96.8, New Utrecht. John F. Berry to Margaret Berry. nom

Brooklyn and Jamaica turnpike, s s, 27 e Locust av, 81x186x81x153; also,
Brooklyn and Jamaica turnpike, s e cor Locust av, 27x154.
Anna C. Meyn to Catharine Molloy. 6,000

Canarsie Landing road, abt 1 acre, adjoins W. Matthews.
Canarsie Landing road, indeft., 79x91, Canarsie.
William W. Silliman to Ella H. W. Silliman. Q. C. 200

Interior part of lot 224 map of P. Calyer farm, 24.2x0.4 inclusive x 24. Release mort. Greenpoint Savings Bank to Mary Roach. nom

Interior lot on centre line bet 80th and 81st sts, at point 100 s e 20th av, runs northeast 10.6 x southwest to said centre line, x southeast 11.6, New Utrecht. Cornelius Ferguson to John L. Nostrand. nom

Lots 151-169, 172-183 and 188-202, block 4; also 203-210, 213-216, 219-237 and 245-249, block 5; also lots 403-413 block 10; also lots 484-502, 525, 526 and 527 block 11; also lots 547-551, 565-558, 561, 562 and 563, block 12, all inclusive on map No. 1 of 618 lots, Cowenhoven farm, New Utrecht. Release mort. Cornelius Cowenhoven to Effingham H. Michols, of New York. 13,500

Lots 513-524, 534, 535 and 536, 542-546, block 11; also lots 573-587 block 12; also lots 599 and 615-618, all inclusive, same map. Release mort. Magdalena Cowenhoven admrx. Garret Cowenhoven to same. 4,600

Lot at Canarsie, begins at point 200 s w road to Canarsie Landing, 50x100. Fanny A. wife of John C. Matthews to John H. Mills. 300

Lot 66 map property John Emmons, Gravesend. Charles T. Sumner to Mary A. McKinley. 1,000

Lot 182 map of W. Nichols, New Lots. James W. Wadsworth, Comptroller State New York, to John H. Millard, Poughkeepsie, N. Y. Tax deed. 1880. nom

Lot 178 same map. Same to same. Tax deed. 1880. nom

Lots 178 and 182 same map. John H. Millard to Leila E. Marsh, Lansingburgh, N. Y. Q. C. 50

Lot 200 S J. Stewart property, Belleplaine.
Lots 367 and 374 map First Mfg. District, East New York.
Lot 6 block 17 map 2 M. G. Johnson's survey.
Lot 186 map Williamson homestead.
Lot 28 map of R. Clancy property, Flatbush.
Same to same. Q C. 150

Lots 217 and 218 map Williamson homestead, Kings County. Same to same. Q. C. 50

Lots 2050, 2051 and 2071-2076 inclus. block 6, 2126 and 2131 block 7, and 2261, 2262, 2263, 2197, 2198 and 2199 block 8, map E. H. Nichols property, Lefferts Park. Release mort. Albert V. B. Voorhees to Effingham H. Nichols. 2,000

Lots 203-208 inclusive block 5 map 1 of Cowenhoven farm, New Utrecht. Effingham H. Nichols to Bernard Larzelere. 1,200

Lots 561, 562 and 563 block 12 same map. Same to Cathrine Morgan. 462

Lots 188 and 189 block 4 same map. Same to John Gewehr. 360

Lots 573 and 574 block 12 same map. Same to John Murphy. 270

Lots 174-178 block 4 same map. Same to Lawrence A. Weber. 950

Lots 231 and 232 block 5 same map. Same to Thomas G. Allen. 390

Lots 233 and 234 block 5 same map. Same to Lucy C. Palmer. 390

Lots 403-407 and 413 block 10 same map. Same to Sophie Hunter. 1,250

Lots 160 and 161 block 4 same map. Same to Louis Olsen. 390

Lots 235-237 block 5 same map. Same to Hugh M. Keenan. 570

Lots 213 and 214 block 5 same map. Same to Henry Armand. 410

Lot 191 block 4 same map. Same to Nels Swenson. 180

Lot 210 block 5 same map. Same to Emil Schmidt. 205

Lot 209 block 5 same map. Same to Max Schmidt. 205

Lots 224 and 225 block 5 map 1, map of Cowenhoven farm. Same to Louis Blankenfeld. 400

Lot 575 block 12 map 1 of Cowenhoven farm, New Utrecht. Same to John Maguire. 145

Lots 219, 220 block 5 same map. Same to Rudolph Schwenker. 330

Lot 599 block 14 same map. Same to Patrick J. McHenry. 65

Lots 484-488 and lots 494-496 block 11 same map. Same to Walter Harper. 1,520

Lots 615-618 block 16 same map. Same to Matthew Muthes. 540

Lots 534-536 and lots 542-546 block 11 same map. Same to Christian H. and Roelofina Joosten. 1,155

Lots 151 and 152 block 4 and 576-578 and 584-587 12 same map. Same to William Hurlflock 1,275

Lotsn522-524 block 11 same map. Same to James Dane or Dawe. 405

Lots 157-159 block 4 same map. Same to Edward H. Diehl. 570

Lots 193-197 block 4 same map. Same to Medart Singer. 925

Lots 579-583 block 12 same map. Same to John F. Hackett. 725

Lots 408-412 block 10 same map. Same to Thomas Hogan. 1,000

Lots 153-156 block 4 and 547-551 and 555 and 556 block 12 same map. Same to Annie Hogan. 2,110

All dower and estate of John H. Hicks. Jane M. Hicks to John H. Hicks her husband. val. consid

Receipt for legacy under will of Maurice Roche. John Reagan to exrs. of Maurice Roche. 500

Similar receipt. Margaret Daley general guard. John Daley to same. 500

Similar receipt. David T. Roche general guard. David Roche to same. 950

WESTCHESTER COUNTY.

JULY 29 TO AUGUST 4—INCLUSIVE.

BEDFORD.

Van Tassel, Chas. exrs. of, to Jos. O. Miller, s s Main st, adj Theresa Crist, 20x200. $2,775

CORTLANDT.

Depew, Martha M. exr. of, and ano. to John McGee, e s Depew st, 183 s Elm, 40x150. 400

Sage, Wm. H. to Emilie J. Eden, 55 acres adj Philip Van Cortlandt. 2,000

Simpkins, Benj. R. to Emma Valentine, s s Brown st, adj John R. Denike, 40x100. 2,000

EASTCHESTER.

Avery, Benj. B. to Mary E. Holmes, s s Elm pl, adj Sue West Newell, 85x106. 6,000

Bernstein, Eliz'h A. to Hattie B. Hunt, n s "The Bluff," 112 e Union pl, 55x150. 1,600

Same to Wm. B. Davis, s s same, 232 w Jno. P. Holler's land, 50x106. 1,650

Berrian, Mary E. to Jas. Wilson, w s N. Y. Post road, adj Floyd Stevenson, abt 2 acres. 4,000

Easton, Mary L. to Eliza Munro, part lot 40 s s Madison st, East Mt. Vernon, 29.6x92. 2,750

Gay, Margt. C. to Wm. Allen, w s 2d st, 162 n 20th av, Wakefield, 62x105. 1,000

Same to Jas. McKenzie, w s 2d st, 100 w 20th av, 62x105. 1,000

Same to Richard Van Anden, part lot 889 and 852 s s 18th av, 110x114. 1,800

Hine, Julia O. to Lewis R. Streeter, w s Summit av, 699 n Sidney, 100x156. 4,600

Henneberger, Herman to Mary C. McCourt, lots 10 and 11 w s South 9th av, 50x105. 1,050

Lomas, Cornelia A. to Josephine S. Finn, w s Cottage av, 300 n Sidney, 60x110. 2,500

Lawlor, Nellie A. to Wm. Shoebottom, s s Madison st, 270 e Franklin av, 27x94. 1,800

Lyon, Clarence M. to Wm. Bossert, lot 14 s e s Union st map Ferry property, 34x100. 500

Marks, Isaac to Robt. McKeand, part lot 245 s e s Greenwich st, West Mt. Vernon, 30x100. 1,600

Newman, Anna J. to John Boyle and ano., part lot 296, map Teutonia Homestead Assoc., 37x336. nom

Oakley, Abijah exr. of, to Chas. Henricks, s e cor 1st st and 5th av, 47x32,6x52x33. 10,000

Oakley, Marietta to Thos. Oakley, n s White Plains road, adj grantee, 108x348x142x299. 2,000

Slavin, Michael to Elizh. O'Brien, south ½ lot 59 e s White Plains road, Waverly, abt 106x200. 851

Trede, John, Jr., to Louisa M. Kuntzmann, lot 73 n w s Matilda st, Washingtonville, 50x100. 3,000

Underhill, Henry M. to The Home Building and Land Co., lots 100 and 125, map lots at Tuckahoe. 500

Williams, Thos. to John Rellstab, part lot 121 e s 9th av, Central Mt. Vernon, 25x100. 1,325

GREENBURGH.

Brayton, Fred. H. and ano. to Otto Vogel, lots 50 and 51, map Chester Park. 325

Briggs, Harriet to Alf. E. Miller, s s Tarrytown and White Plains road, adj Saw Mill River, abt 13 acres. 8,500

Miller, Alfr. E. to Aug. T. Gillender, same property. nom

Fairchild, Clara to Fannie E. Lawrence, s s Ashford road, 300 w Railroad, 20 acres. 14,187

Lawrence, Fannie E. to Madeline Pierce, same property. 16,214

Hatch, Theodosia to John Potts, n e cor Union and Sunnyside avs, 1½ acres. 3,000

Jones, Cyrus P. and ano. to Margt. Storms and ano., lots 164-169 map lots at Ardsley. 585

Mauterstock, Jos. W. to Julia Becker, s s old road from Beekmantown to Unionville, 65 x—. 2,400

Sigafus, Augusta C. to Frank P. Perkins, lot 15 map west part Steph. B. Tompkins farm, 4½ acres. nom

MAMARONECK.

Larchmont Manor Co. to Edw. F. Caldwell, s w cor Circle and Walnut avs, abt 101x175. 2,135

MOUNT PLEASANT.

Farrington, Cath. to Wm. E. Andrews, n s road from Pleasantville to depot, adj Pickle house, 5 acres. 1,100

Smadbeck, Louis to John Eagan, lots 714 and 715, Sherman Park. 250

Same to Emil Kossman, lot 375. 100

Same to Mary Morris, lots 117, 535, 536 and 537. 450

Same to Wm. McGrath, lot 207. 400

Same to Charlotte M. Hayden, lot 862. 100

Same to Henry S. Albright, lot 1065. 200

Same to Jos. S. Lesser and ano., lots 949-954, 941, 942, 943, 1188, 1189 and 1092. 1,875

Same and ano. to Mary D. Briggs, lots 205 and 206, Lakehurst Villa Park. 500

Wheeler, Ira to Geo. H. Wheeler, n s Railroad av, adj John I. Thorn, 62x—. 1,800

Wheeler, George H. to Millard F. Hammond, s s Jackson st, adj Chas. M. Lane, 27x90. 175

NEW ROCHELLE.

Lambden, John to Minnie Dankwerts, w s White Oak st, 191 n Summit av, abt 64x200. 425

Larkin, Carrie L. to John R. Philip, lot 112 e s Woodland av, Residence Park, 80x182. nom

Manhattan Life Ins. Co. to Letitia I. Jones, lot 8 block G. Rochelle Park. 2,000

Stern, Regina to Jas Wright, s s Morgan st, 200 w Weyman av, 100x75. 600

Wheeler, Fannie to Julia M. Secord, s e cor Union pl and Washington av, abt 35x100. 1,700

NEW CASTLE.

Adams, Emily B. to Morris Duklauer, N s Smith av, adj Emory Dingee, 90x330. 2,000

OSSINING.

Larkin, Francis to Harriet Raymond, n s Lincoln pl, adj S. O. Washburn, 50x180. 2,600

Mutual Life Ins. Co. to Aaron Herzberg, 24 acres, Post road, adj Jas. Edsall, 24 acres. 15,000

PELHAM.

Crewell, Baltis F. to Theo. L. Taylor, lot 256 e s 6th av, Pelhamville, 100x100. 100

RYE.

Drew, Geo. F. to Wm. R. Young, s s Olivia st, 171 e Regent, 50x106. 200

Same to Michael Jones, n s same, 375 e same, 50x95. 125

Finnegan, Ann to Patrick O'Malley, s e s Locust av, adj N. J. Sands, 51x125. 2,225

Mead, Benj. to Wm. Kelly, w s Railroad av, adj grantor, 1½ acres. 750

SCARSDALE.

North End Ld. Imp Co. to Oliver A. Hyatt, n w s White Plains road, 200x300. 3,500

WESTCHESTER.

Camp, Hugh N. to Thos. Clarkin, lots 253, 254, 255, 279, 280 and 307 to 310, McGraw estate. 2,065

Clocke, G. De Witt to Emma J. Carter, e s Barker av, 67 n Julianna st, 66x125. 1,360

Jacobson, Abram to Jacob Jacobson, lot 119 map part Givan Homestead. nom

Mace, Levi H. and ano to Fred C Dexter, lots 54-68 and 141-154, Laconia Park. 6,000

Same to Wolfe C. Cohen, lots 49, 50 and 51. 600

Mapes, John S. to Vincent C. Ferris, s s Maitland av, 200 w Mapes av, abt 50x100. 405

Same to Edw. S. Kennion, n s Maitland av, 275 w Mapes, 100x100. 840

Nerenberg, Henry to Mary L. Brown, w s Elm st, 175 n Maple, 25x100. 200

Same to And. B. Brown, w s Elm st, 100 n Maple st, 25x100. 200

Williams, Susan E. to Jas. C. Cooley, s s Zulette av, 200 w Mapes av, 25x100. 200

Shirmer, Chas. D. to Isaac S. Wood, lots 73 and 74 w s Hickory st, Bronxwood Park. 1,400

YONKERS.

Andersen, And. to Gramatan Park Co., lots 74, 75 and 76, Armour Villa Park. nom

Bangs, Francis S. et al. to Edwin K. Martin, s w cor Parkville av and Undercliff st; 6½ acres. 28,500

Druid Hill Park Co. to And. Andersen, lots 393-396, Mohegan Park. 740

Same to Katie Wirth, lots 397 and 398. 820

Dickson, John to David F. Cotton, w s South Waverly st, 275 e Herriott, 50x115. nom

Delahanty, Bridget to Frank Knapper, e s Bellevue av, 241.6 n Robert av, 6 acres. 5,000

East Side Land Co. to Jacob H. Simberlund, lots 28 and 29, Shearwood Hill. 1,050

Herriot, J. Groshon exr. of, to Patrick H. Murphy, lots 21 and 23 map estate grantor. 980

Jones, Cyrus P. and ano. to Jas. Coghlan, lot 5 block A grantor's map. 330

Same to Philip Ramsey, lots 7 and 28 block C. 650

Johnston, Richard to Aaron Machin, n s Chestnut st, 75 — Victor, 25x100. 2,800

Kilgour, Mary to John J. Sloan, s s Ash st, 420 e Oak st, 25x100. 3,500

Ludlow, Thos. W. to Chas. Scheeck, w s Livingston st, 277 s Morris st, 50x147. 1,100

McDonald, Patrick to John J. Murray, lot 725 Nepperhan av City map. nom

Murray, John J. to Patrick McDonald, lot 711 Nepperhan av City map. nom

Monrovia Park Co. to Henry S. Moore, lots 159-163, Monrovia Park. nom

Same to Edw. L. Harriott, lots 153 and 154. nom

Same to Mary J. Lounsbury, lots 92 and 93. 300

Same to Rob't W. Lounsbury, lots 94 and 95. 300

Same to Rob't M. F. Luyster, lots 131 and 132. 350

Same to Jane B. Duval, lots 84 and 85. nom

Same to Edw. S. Peck, lot 140. nom

North End Land Co. to Eleanor H. Almond, n s Dunwoodie st, 200 e Yonkers av, 25x100. 310

Same to Wm. P. Tompkins, s s Alida st, 175 e Yonkers av, 190x—. 1,715

Siers, Daniel to Jennie E. Roy, n s Poplar st, 175 e Beech st, 25x100. 3,000

Sherwood, Marg't J. to Bridget Nolan, e s Palisade av, 37.6 n Carlisle pl, 37.6x84. 6,000

Shonnard, Fred. to Munson S. Millspaugh, lot 292 Edward pl City map. 135

Wheeler, John to Geo. W. Cobb, s s Highland av, adj W. T. Van Zandt, 60x150. 4,500

YORKTOWN.

Covert, Cath. A. to Bertha Harrison, tract on road from Baptist Church to Crompond road, 23 acres. 2,000

MORTGAGES.

N TE.—*The arrangement of this list is as follows. The first name is that of the mortgagor, the next that of the mortgagee. The description of the property then follows, then the date of the mortgage, the time for which it was given, and the amount. The general dates used as headings are the dates when the mortgage was handed into the Register's office to be recorded.*

Whenever the letters "P. M." occur, preceded by the name of a street, in these lists of mortgages, they mean that it is a Purchase Money Mortgage, and for fuller particulars see the list of transfers under the corresponding date. Whenever the rate is not given, read as 6 per cent.

NEW YORK CITY.

JULY 31, AUGUST 1, 3, 4, 5, 6.

Abraham, Theresa wife of and Afred to Isaac Fromme. 126th st, s s, 150 w 4th av, 20x99.11. July 21, due Aug. 1, 1892. $2,500

Abrahams, Isidore to Fanny Levy. West 3d st. P. M. Aug. 6, installs. 3,450

Allen, Charles E. to Henry L Bogert guard. of Harriet L. Bogert. 51st st, n s, 200 e 3d av, 20x100.5. July 30, due July 30, 1894, 5½ %. 9,000

Aufenanger, William and Charles Schwarm to George Ehret. 91 Broad st. Lease. July 30, demand. 2,000

Bernstein, Max and Annie his wife mortgagors with George Marcus and Charles Loewenstein trustees Bernhard Mayer mortgagees. Extension of mortgage. July 31. nom

Blumberg, Moses I. and Ida Epstein mortgagors with Annie E. Underhill mortgagee. Extension of mortgage. July 24. nom

Brady, Lizzie F. to John K. Bangs. Madison av, w s, 50.11 s 107th st, 25x100. May 15, 3 years, 5 %. 20,000

Brown, James A. Superintendent of the Bond and Mortgage Department of the EQUITABLE LIFE ASSURANCE SOCIETY of the U. S. to Albert H. Little. Declaration that mortgage made by William S. Maddock Dec. 14, 1888, was never recorded. July 31. nom

Bauer, Frederick to Bernheimer & Schmid. 7th av, No 377. Saloon lease. Aug. 1, note, demand. 1,000

Bingham, Anna M. wife of and Leander K. to THE FRANKLIN SAVINGS BANK. 143d st. n s, 125 w College av, 49.8x100. July 31, 1 year, 5 %. 8,500

Brauns, Angelina to Mary A. Dale. 77th st, n s, 91.8 e 2d av, 16.8x102.2. Aug. 3, due Oct. 5, 1894, 5 %. 1,000

Brockner, Ambrose E. to John Boyd and ano. exrs. Jane Boyd. West st, No 421, e s, 86.9 s w 11th st, 23x88.11x23x81.9. July 22, 3 years, 5 %. 7,000

Breihof, Sebastian, Baltimore, Md., and Sophia Breihof widow to "The Redemptorists." 1st av, e s, 63 n 4th st, 21x87.11. Lease. July 1, 5 years, 5 %. 3,000

Byrne, James J. to Herman Fox and William A. Klingler exrs. Helena Smith. 26th st, s s, 7? w 10th av, 28x148.1. Aug. 1, 1 year. 1,20.

Bennett, Abraham to Harvey F. Johnson, Haverstraw, N. Y. Cauldwell av. P. M. July 27, 3 years or sooner, 5 %. 1,200

Bridgman, Oliver B. to Henry Morgenthau. 180th st. P. M. June 12, due June 15, 1892, 5 %. 3,400

Bellamy, Albert to Charles L. Tiffany. 75th st. P. M. Aug. 5, due Aug. 6, 1894. 4½ %. 20,000

Brady, Lizzie F. widow to William Mitchell trustee Clarissa E. Curtiss dec'd. Madison av, s w cor 107th st, 25.11x100. Aug. 6, due July 1, 1894, 5 %. 28,000

Campbell, John V. to TITLE GUARANTEE AND TRUST CO. 113th st. P. M. July 31, due Aug. 6, 1892, 5 %. 5,000

Same to Laemmlein Buttenwieiser. Same property. P. M. Sub. to last mort. July 31, due Oct. 1, 1891. 1,800

Cushing, Catherine wife of Thomas to TITLE GUARANTEE AND TRUST CO. 42d st, s s, 317.2 w 8th av, 16.8x98.9. July 6, 3 years, 5 %. 8,500

Christen, Ferdinand to Andreas Wrede. Robbins av. P. M. Aug. 1, 3 years. 1,200

Campbell, Elizabeth wife of Alexander to William J. and Margaret Riley. Willard av. P. M. July 31, due Aug. 1, 1894, 5 %. 1,000

Clarke, Sarah H. widow to Jessie C McBride. 26th st, No. 130, s s, 350 w 6th av, 25x98.9. July 31, 3 years. 800

Cohen, Samuel to Marcus Lederer. 6th st, s s, 288 e Av C. P. M. July 28, installs. 5,300

Cohen, George J. and Samuel Blumenthal to George E. Hyatt, Brooklyn. 84th st, s s, 350 w Columbus av, 50x102.2. Aug. 3, 1 year. 40,000

Cohen, Bernard to Frederic J. Middlebrook, Brooklyn. Central Park West, w s, 25.8 s 94th st P. M. Aug. 5, 1 year or sooner, 5 %. 8,000

Same to same. Central Park West, w s, 50.8 s 94th st. P. M. Aug. 5, 1 year or sooner, 5 %. 8,000

Conley, John to William Hall Columbus av, n e cor 74th st, 54.2x100. Aug. 1, 6 months 10,000

Conkling, John C. F. to THE NORTHERN BUILDING, SAVINGS AND LOAN ASSOC., New York. Villa av, e s, 583.3 n Southern Boulevard, 25 x82.4x25x83.7. June 30, installs. 1,750

Cooper, Howard to Henry Cooper. Bowery, No 281, n e cor Houston st, 23x70.1. July 31, due Aug. 1, 1896, 4 %. 30,000

Daly, Mary D. wife of Augustin to Charlotte M. Tytus. Riverside av, e s, 27 n 116th st, 53.8x75.6 to w s old Bloomingdale road, x60.4 x47.10, with all title in old road. June 30, 3 years. 11,000

Davis, Samuel to Jennie L. Kohn. Allen st P. M. July 31, due Aug. 1, 1896, 5 %. 21,000

Same to Morris Solomon and Harry Harris. Same property. P. M. July 31, 3 years 3,000

Dickie, Perry to THE IRVING SAVINGS INST., City New York. Washington st, No. 382, w s, 20x62. July 6, 1 year, 5 %. 6,000

Decker, Paul G. to Sarah K. Wright. 3d av, n e cor 161st st, 25.6x93.8x25.6x92.5. Aug. 1, due July 1, 1894, 5 %. 20,000

Decker, John W. to Charles A. Runk. 161st st, n s, 92 5 e 3d av, 54x100. July 30, due Aug. 1, 1892, 5 %. 1,500

Doyle, Andrew T. to John Sweeny. Amsterdam av, w s, 25.8 s 96th st, 25x89.3. Aug. 1, note. 1,000

Dempsey, William to William H. Simonson. 133d st, No. 54, s s, 175 w Park av, 20x99.11. July 17, demand. 1,838

Donohue, Patrick K. to Francis Bourne. Franklin av, s e s, lot 122 part subdivision 2 map of Morrisania, 42.6x185.5. July 16, 5 years, 5 %. 2,000

Eiseman, Morris A. and Abraham Sandberg to Jacob Arm. 45th st. P. M. Sub to mort. $8,000. July 30, installs, 5 %. 8,750

Ehlers, Christine to Jane Potter trustee William H. Potter dec'd. Willard st. P. M. July 29, due Aug. 4, 1894, or sooner, 5 %. 425

Ebbinghausen, George H., Mamaroneck, N. Y., to George R. Lansing. 7th av, s e cor 23d st, runs east 175 x south 98.9 x west 50 x south 9 6 x west 25 x south 39.10 x west 100 to av. x north 148.1. 1-10 part. July 13, 5 years 5,000

Endlich, Sophia to Paulina Breivogel. 83d st, No. 431, n s, 300 e 1st av, 25x102.2. July 31, due July 1, 1896, 5 %. 11,250

Flanagan, Blanche P. to Adelaide L. and Mary E. Beekman. 78th st. P. M. Sub. to mort. $10,000. July 31, installs. 10,000

Flannery, Simon P. to Louis B. Binsse and ano. trustees Delia Binsse. City Hall pl, s s, 202.2 w Pearl st, 20.3x99.5x20.5x—. Aug. 1, 3 years, 5 %. 10,000

Friedman, Barnet and Samuel Harris to Samuel Weil. Madison st. P. M. July 30, installs. 2,000

Fritzel, William and Elizabetha his wife to Jacob Schlosser. 79th st, Nos. 433-437 E. 3 P. M. morts., each $2,500. July 30, due Feb. 1, 1892. 7,500

Same to same. 79th st, No. 431 E. P. M. July 30, due Feb. 1, 1892. 3,500

Fish, John and Jacob Miller to Charles H. Spitzner. 28th st, n s, 125 w 2d av, 25x98.9. Aug. 1, due Aug. 3, 1896. gold, 23,000

Frevert, Frederick and Franziska his wife to Margaretha Zeller. 8th av, No. 96, e s, 38.8 s 15th st, 19.4x73.6. Aug. 1, installs, 4½ %. 10,000

Same to same. 1st av. P. M. Aug. 1, 5 years, 4½ %. 8,500

Frame, John to William Hall's Sons. 127th st, n s, 145 e Park av, 70x99.11. Sub. to morts. July 8, due Dec. 1, 1891, or sooner. 6,500

Fitzpatrick, Bridget D. widow to THE EMIGRANT INDUST. SAVINGS BANK. 3d av, w s, 50.5 n 112th st. Aug. 5, 1 year, 4½ %. 2,000

First German Baptist Church of Harlem to Southern New York Baptist Assoc. 118th st, s s, 250 e 3d av, 50x100.5. Aug. 5, payable when mortgagor ceases to be recognized by mortgagee. gold, 14,500

Gawtry, Mary L. widow to James W. Smith trustee for Helen A. Kent. 30th st, n s, 220 e Madison av, 20x98.9. July 27, due July 28, 1894, 5 %. 3,000

Goldberg, Jacob and Rosalie his wife to Adelaide Abraham. 10th av, s e cor 88th st, 25 8 x100. July 1, 5 years, 5 %. 8,000

Greenstone, Barnett to Israel Josefsohn. 2d av. P. M. July 31, installs. 4,000

Griffiths, Mary to THE NEW YORK SAVINGS BANK. 25th st, s s, 202 3 w 7th av, 31x98.9. July 22, due Dec. 1, 1892, 4½ %. 15,000

Same to Lambert Suydam. Same property. Sub. to last mort. Aug. 3, 2 years 2,500

Giblin, Michael and James W. Taylor to Edward Oppenheimer and Isaac Metzger. 75th st, s s, 400 w Columbus av, 125x102.2. Jan. 30, due Feb. 1, 1892, or sooner. 55,000

Galewski, Bernard to David K. Schuster. Stanton st. P. M. July 30, due Sept. 15, 1892, or sooner. 3,000

Graham, Amelia M. to THE TITLE GUARANTEE AND TRUST CO. Bridge st, No. 25, n s, 24x 64.7x26x65. July 28, due Feb. 1, 1892, 5 %. 12,000

Goodman, Louis to Hyman Schnitzer. Delancey st, No. 188, n s, 63.3 e Attorney st, 23.3x 86.5. Collateral for notes. Aug. 3, installs. 6,000

Goldstein, Esther S. to Robert Froese. 68th st. P. M. Aug. 3, due Jan. 30, 1895, 5 %. 3,500

Goldstein, Hulda to Mary A. Bulkley. 107th st. P. M. July 30, due Aug. 1, 1896, 5 %. 9,000

Guldenkirck, Henrietta E., Brooklyn, to James P. Campbell. 81st st, No. 229 E., n s, 25x100; 33d st, No 348, s s, 530 w 8th av, 20x98.9. Aug. 4, 1 year or sooner. See Conveys. 445

Same to Margaret Lowry. Same property. Aug. 4, 1 year or sooner. 413

Gutekunst, Johanna to August Hassey. Av B, e s, 102.3 n 82d st, 25.6x100. Aug. 6, 3 months. 1,000

Gilman, Henry K., Flushing, L. I., to Stephen H. Olin, committee &c., of Benjamin Page. 106th st, s s, 550 e 9th av, 37.6x100.11. July 22, due Aug. 1, 1892, 5 %. 7,500

Goodwin, Frank J. to George Ehret. 8th av, s w s cor 24th st. Lease. Aug. 5, demand. 4,500

Henderson, Albert C. to Reuben Ross. 85th st, s s, 100 e West End av, 80x102.2. Aug. 6, 3 months. 25,000

Same to same. Same property. P. M. Aug. 6, 3 months or sooner. 18,800

Helmken, Otto to George F. Martens. 126th st, s s, 185 e 8th av, 40x99.11. July 14, 1 year. 2,500

Hirschhorn, Joseph to Peter Doelger. Bleecker st. No. 124, s w cor Wooster st. Lease. July 5, demand. 1,800

Hannan, John W. to August Freutel. Myrtle av, w s, 44.1 n 176th st, 24.10x100x24.6x100. Aug. 3, due Feb. 14, 1894. 1,000

Harris, Marks to Jacob Nussbaum. Av C, No. 24, e s, 25x92.10. Lease. July 22, demand, 5 %. 1,650

Haigh, George W. to William H. Birkmire. Briggs av. P. M. Aug. 4, 3 years or sooner, 5 %. 900

Herter, Peter to Simon A. Asch. Pearl st, No. 484, n s, 274.11 w Park row, runs north 42.3 x northeast 80.6 x west 25 4 x southwest 77.2 x south 48 to Pearl st, x east 25.1. Sub. to mort. $37,500. Aug. 4, 2 years. 8,000

Haber, Harry D. to Stephen Merrihew and ano. trustees for Edwin T. Putnam. East Broadway. P. M. July 29, due Nov. 1, 1894. 5 %. 14,000

Same to Charles Sylvester. Same property. Sub. to last mort. July 29, due Aug. 1, 1892. 1,500

Hagan, Susanna V. to Paul Gantert & Son. Amsterdam av, s w cor 79th st, 102.2x100. May 19, installs. 2,500

Hirsh, Edward to Isaac Fry. Central Park West and 94th st. P. M. Aug. 4, 1 year, 5 %. 12,000

Higgins, James and James King to Frederic J. Middlebrook, Brooklyn. 90th st, s s, 299.6 e 2d av, 25x100.8. Aug. 1, due Aug. 3, 1894, 5 %. 13,500

Hayward, Belle D. wife of and William A. to Frederick D. Tappen and ano. trustees Ann E. Cairns dec'd. 20th st, s s, 133.4 e 9th av, 16.8x91.11. July 30, 3 years, 5 %. 9,000

Hauck, Anna widow to Hattie Frank. 86th st. P. M. Aug. 3, due Dec. 1, 1892. 4,000

Harder, Henry and Hildegard his wife to Henry Jacobowicz. 101st st. P. M. July 31, due July 1, 1893. 1,000

Howell, Helen E. and Byron C., Westfield, S. I., to The St. Luke's Home for Indigent Christian Females. 97th st, s s, 144 e Columbus av, 19x100.11. Aug. 5, 3 years, 5 %. 19,000

Hummel, Frederick P. and Katie his wife to George J. Horn. 86th st, s s, 75 9 w Av A, 22x102.2. Sub. to mort. $12,000. Aug. 1, due July 1, 1893. 2,000

Hogan, Patrick to Louis Roller. 129th st, s s, 162.6 e Lenox av, 27x99.11. Aug. 5, 1 year. gold, 1,500

Same to same. 129th st, s s, 189.6 e Lenox av, 20.6x99.11. Aug. 5, 1 year. gold, 1,000

Herdtfelder, Elizabeth to Frederick Finck. Eldridge st, No. 196, e s, 80 n Rivington st, 24x88.7. Aug. 1, due Feb. 1, 1892, 5 %. 16,000

Hogan, Patrick to Jacob K. Lockman. 129th st, s s, 135 e Lenox av, 27.6x99.11. July 31, 5 years, 5 %. gold, 23,000

Same to George G. De Witt and Jacob K. Lockman trustees Sarah Talman dec'd. 129th st, s s, 189.6 e Lenox av, 20.6x99.11. Error. July 31, 5 years, 5 %. gold, 16,500

Same to George G. Kip, Morristown, N. J. 129th st, s s, 162.6 e Lenox av, 27x99.11. July 31, 5 years, 5 %. gold, 22,500

Hughes, Thomas R., Weehawken, N. J., to James L. Cornell, Brooklyn. 72d st, No. 160. P. M. July 30, due July 31, 1892, 5 %. 4,500

Hugues, Henri to Amelia wife of Lee Wolff. 37th st, s s, 133.2 e 8th av, 16.7x98.9. July 31, 3 years, 5 %. gold, 6,000

Harris, Dora to Rosanna Varley. Oliver st, No. 65. P. M. July 31, 3 years, 5 %. 15,000

Jetter, Thomas to Mary G. Kugelman. Madison av, s e cor 134th st, 100x60. July 31, 6 months, 12,000

Joyce, Mary E. to Elizabeth Herb. 37th st, s s, 100 e 11th av, 75x98.9. P. M. Aug. 1, 3 years, 5 %. 12,000

Klein, Benedict A. to Caroline L. Macy. 102d st, s s, 160 e 3d av. P. M. July 28, due Aug. 4, 1894, 5 %. gold, 13,500

Same to same. 102d st, s s, 210 e 3d av. P. M. July 28, due Aug. 4, 1894, 5 %. gold, 13,500

Same to Mary J. Kingsland, Mt. Pleasant, N. Y. 102d st, s s, 185 e 3d av. P. M. July 28, due Aug. 4, 1894, 5 %. gold, 13,500

Same to same. 102d st, s s, 234.9 e 3d av. P. M. July 28, due Aug. 4, 1894, 5 %. gold, 13,500

Kaufman, Ignatz to Ignatz Gluck. Pitt st, No. 57. P. M. Sub. to mort. $7,000. July 25, installs. 2,000

Kervan, Matthew C. and Charles to Hyman and Henry Sonn. Amsterdam av, e s, 275 s 133d st, 75x100. July 31, due Jan, 1, 1892. 27,000

Same to same. Willis av, w s, 25.2 n 145th st, 49.9x107.6x50x107.1. July 31. Collateral to last mortgage to extent of 5,000

Ketcham, James W. to Meyer L. Sire. Lexington av, s w cor 59th st, 20.5x75. July 31, 2 years, installs, 5 %. 8,000

Same to Normand Smith. Same property. P. M. July 10, due Oct. 1, 1892, 5 % 12,000

Ketcham, James W. to Daniel Underhill. 7th av. P. M. April 15, 5 years, 5 %. 28,000

Kilpatrick, Edward to Sarah M. Shotts, Yonkers, N. Y. Kingsbridge road. P. M. April 1, 3 years, 5 %. 8,000

Kitching, George to Elizabeth A. wife of John G. Parr. 57th st, No. 428, s s, 273.4 e 1st av, 22.1x111x — x109. July 28, 5 years, 5 %. 8,000

Kerr, John to Peter Kelaher. 121st st, n s, 325 e 2d av, runs east 50 x north — x northwest 38.9 to 122d st, x west 5 x south 100.11 x west 20 x south 100.11 to beginning. Lease. July 31, notes. 3,500

Kennedy, Patrick to Ann wife of James McCann. 44th st. P. M. July 1, 3 years, 5 %. 5,500

Kaliske, Theresa wife of and Henry S. to The United States Trust Co. of New York. Madison av, No. 1281, e s, 68.8 n 91st st, 17x68. Aug. 6, due Aug. 1, 1894, 5 %. 12,000

Lane, Smith E. to Smith Ely. Lexington av, e s, 49.4 s 28th st, 12.4x60. Sept. 23, 1890, 1 year. 4,500

Larom, Frank W. to Jacob M. Newman. 78th st, n s, 221 w Amsterdam av. P. M. Sub. to mort. $14,000. July 1, installs, 5 %. 5,500

Same to same. Same property. P. M. Aug. 1, 3 years, 4½ %. 14,000

Levenson, Cary to Henry and Hannah Monheimer. 1st av, e s, 38 s 19th st, 18x70. Lease. July 30, 5 years, 5 %. 2,500

Lippe, Joseph F. to Charlotte Schweyer. West st, No. 195, 18.1x43.8x3.8x36 to Caroline st, x14.4x79.3 July 31, 2 years, 5 %. 10,000

Little, Albert H. to The Equitable Life Assur. Soc. of the United States. 43d st, s s, 300 w 7th av. P. M. July 31, due Jan. 1, 1893, or installs, 5 %. 11,000

Logan, Edgar to Frederick J. Middlebrook, Brooklyn. Greenwich st. P. M. July 31, 1 year or sooner, 5 %. 6,000

Same to same. Same property. P. M. July 31, 1 year or sooner. 1,500

Laino, Nicola and Catharine his wife to Teresa Coogan. 1st av. P. M. July 30, due July 1, 1893, or sooner. 3,000

Langrebe, William F. and Mortimer C. and Henry S. and Louis De Nobriga to Samuel G. Derrickson. Courtlandt av, n w cor Gouverneur st, 115.7x150x115.10x150. Secures counsel's lien on performance of services. July 1. 23,333

Lederer, Hugo to Lewis Myers. West Houston st. P. M. Aug. 1, 3 years or sooner. 4,000

Leakin, Phil Moore, East Orange, N. J., to Lyman Tiffany and ano. exrs. and trustees Charlotte L. Fox. Bronx av and South pl. P. M. Aug. 1, 1 year or sooner, 5 %. 15,000

Leddy, John to Catharine Clinton. Prospect av. P. M. Aug. 1, due Aug. 3, 1894, or sooner. 750

Leporin, Henry F. to George Ehret. Amsterdam av, w s, bet 158th and 159th sts, 33.4x114. Lease. Aug. 3, demand. 3,500

Lowenstein, Fannie A. to Ellen F. Leary. 75th st. P. M. Sub. to morts. July 31, installs., 5 %. 3,500

Lecour, Aimee R. wife of and Eugene H. to Catharine A. Taylor et al. trustees for Albertina S. Pyne, Kate W. Winthrop, Mary Lewis, George C. and Henry A. C. Taylor. Mercer st, Nos. 117 and 119, w s, 200 n Spring st, 50x100. Aug. 5, 3 years, 4½ %. 50,000

Lustig, Arnold to Mrs. Frank Leslie. 116th st, s s, 125 e Lenox av, 50x100.11. Aug. 3, due Aug. 5, 1892, 5 %. 5,000

Leahy, Gregory and Annie his wife to Abraham Steers. 98th st, n s, 375 e 9th av, 25x100.11. Sub. to mort. $21,000. Aug. 5, 3 months. 557

Levy, L. Napoleon to Robert S. Anderson and ano. trustees Cornelius V. Anderson dec'd. Bathgate av. P. M. July 30, 1 year or sooner. 600

Levy, Fanny mortgagor with Smith Ely, Jr., mortgagee. Extension of mort. Aug. 1. nom

McMasters, John D. to Marie B. Boss. Jackson av, w s, n ½ lot 77 map of Belmont, 50x100. Aug. 5, due June 11, 1896. 600

McCoy, Peter J. to Charlotte A. Lyon. 10th av. P. M. Aug. 1, 1 year. 2,500

Morris, James J. to The Emigrant Industrial Savings Bank. 71st st, No. 112, s s, 125 e Park av, 25x100.5. Aug. 3, 1 year, 4½ %. 7,000

McFarland, Joseph to Hardwood Decorative Co. 24th st, n s, 297.9 e 9th av, 26.1x98.9x26.3x98.9. Sub. to mort. $25,000. July 31, 1 year. 5,876

Moeller, George to Burr Brewing Co. Av A, No. 1599. Store lease. Secures chattel mort. July 25, note. 1,000

Morris, Wolff to Justus L. Bulkley and ano. exrs. of Joseph E. Bulkley. 107th st. P. M. July 29, due Aug. 1, 1896, 5 %. 9,000

Mandelbaum, Harris to The Farmers' Loan and Trust Co. Sullivan st, No. 77. P. M. July 28, due July 31, 1894, 5 %. 20,000

Messoth, Peter to Bertha A. wife of Chris. H., Jr., Wiemenn and Anna M. and John Muhlenbrink. Spring st. P. M. July 6, due July 1, 1894, 5 %. 10,000

McGuire, James F. to Ambrose K. Ely and Mary J. Walker and Emily A. Watson exrs. Madison st, s s, 64.4 w Catharine st, runs south 155.4 x west 139.9 to Oliver st, x north 34.10 x east 69.4 x north 99.11 x east 24.9 x north 21.7 x west 0.8 x north 7.3 to Madison st, x east 44.2. July 31, 3 years, 5 %. 50,000

Same to Smith Ely. Same property. Sub. to last mort. July 31, 3 years or installs. 15,000

McQuade, George E. to P. Ballantine & Sons. Chambers st, No. 15, cor City Hall pl. Lease. July 31, note. 2,000

McMillan, Samuel to The United States Trust Co. of New York. 42d st, n s, 350 w 8th av, 25x100.5. July 29, due Aug. 1, 1894, 5 %. 25,000

Maggi, John to Catharine A. Stevens. Spring st. P. M. Aug. 3, installs, 5 %. 27,000

Morrison, James to Julia Stanbery. Loring av, centre line, 205 n 206th st, 75x170 to Macomb's Dam road. July 31, due Aug. 1, 1896, 5 %. See Conveys. 6,000

McCormick, Michael and Henry Madden, of McCormick & Madden, to Canda & Kane. 26th st, Nos. 334 and 336, s s, 125 w 1st av, 50x98.9 Sub. to morts. $52,441. July 31, 6 months. 1,000

Mayer, Joseph D. to Randolph Guggenheimer and Salomon Marx. 134th st, n s, 375 e Willis av, 3 lots. 3 P. M. morts., each $2,667. Aug. 1, 1 year, 5½ %. 8,000

McSweeney, John and Mary his wife to Ascher Weinstein. 17th st. P. M. Aug. 3, due May 1, 1892, or sooner. 20,000

Same to same. Same property. P. M. Aug. 3, 1 year or sooner. 11,000

O'Brien, Richard to Adolph G. Hupfel. Orchard st. 23d Ward. P. M. Aug. 1, 1 year. 2,500

O'Gorman, Mary wife of Edward to J. & M. Haffen. 149th st, n s, 225 e Courtlandt av, 25x100. July 31, due Aug. 1, 1896, 5 % 2,500

Ogden, Samuel B. to Gideon Fountain. Brook av, s e cor 149th st, 75x100. Aug. 6, 2 years. 25,000

Price, Louise B. and Annie Hauser to Edward B. Gethin. 64th st. P. M. Aug. 1, 1 year, or sooner. 1,000

Phillips, Henry and Johannah his wife to Morris Jacobson. Madison st. P. M. Aug. 3, installs. 8,000

Pitt, Malcolm R. to The German Savings Bank, New York. 4th av, No. 405, e s, 23.5 n 28th st, 22.8x80. Aug. 4, due Aug. 5, 1894. 12,000

Patrick, Lavinia E. to Margaret A. O'Rorke. Intervale av. P. M. Aug. 3, due Aug. 1, 1893, or sooner, 5 %. 650

Pierce, Guly E. wife of and Lewis L. to The Mutual Life Ins. Co. of N. Y. 54th st, n s, 100 e 8th av, 18.9x100.5. July 30, due Aug. 3, 1892, 5 %. 6,000

Potter, E. Clifford and Margaret S. his wife to Jane Potter extrx. Joseph Potter. 66th st, Nos. 243 and 245, n s, 125 e West End av, 2 lots, each 25x100.5. 2 morts., each $2,000. July 14, due July 31, 1892, 5 %. 4,000

Radebold, William and Edward Wenz to Young, Gerard & Co. 5th av, s w cor 116th st, 51x100. Sub. to morts. $70,000. July 20, due May 18, 1893. 1,750

Romaine, Benjamin F. Jr., to The Germania Life Ins. Co. 97th st, n s, 135.6 e Columbus av, 16x100.11. Aug. 3, due Aug. 1, 1892, 5 %. gold, 14,500

Same to same. 97th st, n s, 151.6 e Columbus av, 16x100.11. Aug. 3, due Aug. 1, 1892, 5 %. gold, 15,000

Same to same. 97th st, n s, 167.6 e Columbus av, 16x100.11. Aug. 3, due Aug. 1, 1892, 5 %. gold, 15,000

Same to same. 97th st, n s, 183.6 e Columbus av, 16.6x100.11. Aug. 3, due Aug. 1, 1892, 5 %. gold, 14,500

Reilly, Hugh to James B. Gillie. 21st st. P. M. July 29, due Aug. 1, 1892, 5 %. 2,500

Reynolds, Catharine F. wife of and Jesse to Caroline Wandell. 98th st, n s, 75 w Columbus av, 25x75.11. July 31, 1 year. 3,500

Reid, Mary to Ellen Donohue. Taylor av. P. M. July 29, installs, 5 %. 2,100

Roggenkamp, August to Robert W. Cooper. 176th st, s s, 50 e Fleetwood av, 50x125. July 31, 3 years, 5 %. 4,000

Rabbe, Frederick to Charles Brodmann. West 12th st, n e cor Hudson st, 25.6x80x16.6x80.6. Aug. 1, due July 1, 1894, 5 %. 6,000

Reim, Maggie heir Barbara Koetzner to August Freutel. 151st st, n s, 300 w Courtlandt av, 25x116.4x25x116.3. Aug. 3, due July 1, 1894. 300

Rubenstein, Sarah wife of and Louis to Bennett B. Schneider, South Orange, N. J. 80th st. P. M. Aug. 1, installs, 5 %. 3,800

Riehl, Jacob and Anton Rinschler to Harry F. Johnson, Haverstraw, N. Y. Eagle av. P. M. July 27, 3 years or installs, 5 %. 4,000

Reimer, William and Albert Schubert to Fernando Wood. 170th st. P. M. July 31, 5 years or installs, 5 %. 3,000

Russak, Benjamin to Amelia B. Lazarus. Madison av, n e cor 114th st, 26x91. July 14, 3 years, 5 %. 27,000

Reilly, Hugh to Robert Freese. 117th st, s w cor Lexington av, 23.11x100.11x24x100.11, Sub. to morts. $30,000. Aug. 5, 3 months or sooner. 4,000

Reilly, Thomas J. as trustee to Robert C. Winters. Manhattan av. P. M. Aug. 1, 6 years. 2,000

Reilly, Adeline wife of and Hugh J. to The Title Guarantee and Trust Co. 19th st, n s, 455 e 7th av, 15x62. July 17, 1 year or sooner, 5 %. 4,000

Ryan, Ellen to John V. Campbell. 27th st. P. M. July 31, due Aug. 1, 1893. 3,000

Stevens, Sarah J. P. wife of Ogden to Jacob Hays. 32d st, s s, 155 e Lexington av, 15x62.6. Aug. 1, due June 24, 1892. 1,000

Smith, Thomas S. and Mary E. his wife to Maurice Roberts. 3d av, e s, 80.2 s 51st st, 20.1x76. July 28, note. 200

Stang, Joseph and David Hittner to Max Cohen. 73d st. P. M. Sub. to mort. $15,000. July 31, installs. 5,590

Steiner, Adolph to Lewis Franklin. 13th st. P. M. Sub. to mort. $16,000. Aug. 3, installs, 5 %. 2,350

Salmon, James H. to Almira J. Brown, Milburn, N. J. 105th st, No. 152, s s, 275 e Amsterdam av, 25x100.11. July 31, 3 years, 5 %. 18,000

Savage, John, Providence, R. I., to The Mutual Life Ins. Co., New York. John st, s s, 74.4 e Nassau st, 25.4x51.9. Already mortgaged to party of 2d part. July 31, 1 year. 1,400

Savage, Cornelius to Sophia C. Ridden, Brooklyn. 129th st, n s, 181.3 w 7th av, 18.9x99.11. ½ part. July 25, 3 years. 600

Schuber, Christoph A. to Harris Levy. 2d av, No. 1829. P. M. July 30, due Jan. 1, 1892, 5 %. 4,000

Smith, Elizabeth K. wife of and Albert E. to Harrison T. Slosson, Bedford, N. Y. 123d st, s s, 425 e 8th av. P. M. July 31, due Jan. 25, 1893. 10,000

Spencer, Rosan to William P. Lynch. 24th st. P. M. July 27, 2 years, 5 %. 4,500

Stanton, Jemima to Eliza Clark. 25th st, n s, 130 w 3d av, 165x197.5 to 26th st. 1-5 part. July 24, demand, 5 %. 4,000

Sheridan, William P. to Peter Sheridan. 41st st. P. M. Aug. 3, 4 years or sooner, 5 %. 4,000

Schwarz, Jacob to The Emigrant Indust. Savings Bank. 113th st, s s, 27 e 4th av, 27x100.10. Aug. 4, 1 year, 4½ %. 12,000

Shady, James H. to Mary A. O'Reilly. 6th av, e s, 48 n 53d st, 21.6x75. Aug. 3, due Aug. 1, 1893, 5 %. 5,000

Silva, George to John W. Decker. Caldwell av, w s, 181 n Clifton st. P. M. June 29, due June 1, 1896, 5 %. 500

Same to same. Caldwell av, w s, 199 n Clifton st. P. M. June 29, due June 1, 1896, 5 %. 500

Sullivan, James E. and Charles R. to James E. Sullivan guard. of Mary A., Clara M. and Georgina F. Sullivan. 128th st, No. 67, n s, 140 w 4th av, 25x99.11. Aug. 1, 1 year, 5 %. 4,500

Sweeney, Mary C. to Christopher Kelly. Lexington av. P. M. Aug. 4, 3 years, 5 %. 6,000

Schwartz, Philip to Henrietta Holzderber. 8th av, w s, 75.5 n 53d st, 25x100. Aug. 5, 5 years, 5 %. 4,000

Stein, Dora wife of and Simon to Adam Happel. Suffolk st, No. 84, e s, 84.6 s Delancey st, 23x100.2. Aug. 5, 1 year, 4 %. 1,500

Smith, Frederick to Thomas O'Reilly. Fort Independence st. P. M. Aug. 4, 1 year or sooner. 400

Schindler, George to Mason Young. 183d st. P. M. July 2, 1 year, 5 %. 23,000

Stanley, Arthur T., Harry Hall, Sheldon H. and Royal M. Bassett stockholders in Stanley & Hall to Royal M. Bassett. Consent to mortgage. Aug. 5. nom

Schroeder, Mary E. to Fernando Wood. 170th st, No. 838 E. P. M. Aug. 5, 3 years, 5 %. 2,500

Schmidt, Mary widow to John Jorritsma. 157th st, n s, 275 e Courtlandt av, runs east 25 x north 100 x west 22 x south 75 x west 3 x south 30. Aug. 4, due April 1, 1894. 250

Tiffany, Annie Du B. wife of and Charles, Dobbs Ferry, N. Y., to Albert B. Chandler exr. Oran S. Baldwin. 41st st, s s, 91.8 e Lexington av, 16.8x80. Aug. 5, due Oct. 1, 1894, 5 %. 8,500

The Congregation Chaari Zedek otherwise Congregation Shaari Zedek to Franklin N. Billings, Woodstock, Vt. Henry st, Nos. 38 and 40, s s, 270.9 e Catharine st, 53.6x100. Aug. 4, due Aug. 1, 1896, 5 %. gold, 50,000

Tait, William O. to Clarissa L. Crane. 89th st. P. M. July 27, due July 31, 1892, or sooner, 5 %. 4,500

Thorn, Julia A. wife of and Thomas H. to Robert A. B. Dayton trustee Anson Blake. Croton Aqueduct, e s, 132.10 n Fordham road. P. M. July 31, due Nov. 1, 1894, 5 %. 3,000

The Welsh Baptist Tabernacle to Peter A. H. Jackson. 27th st. P. M. Aug. 3, 3 years, 5 %. 16,000

The Catholic Club of the City of New York to THE BOWERY SAVINGS BANK. 59th st, s s, 225 w 6th av, 75x110.10. Aug. 3, 1 year, 4½ %. gold, 160,000

The New York Presbyterian Church to THE BOWERY SAVINGS BANK. 7th av, n e cor 128th st, 99.11x100. Aug. 5, 5 years, 5 %. gold, 100,000

Same to the trustees of the Presbytery of New York. Same property. Sub. to last mort. Aug. 5, payable when mortgagor severs connections with mortgagee. 12,500

The Hebrew Free School Assoc., of New York, and Aguilar Free Library Society to The Baron de Hirsch Fund. East Broadway, s s, 30 e Jefferson st, runs east 65.4 x south 87.6 x west 95.4 to Jefferson st, x north 22 x east 30 x north 65.6 to beginning; East Broadway, s e cor Jefferson st, 30x65.6. Aug. 5, due Jan. 1, 1893, or sooner, 5 %. 115,000

Thurber, Horace K. to Mrs. Frank Leslie. 12th st, s s, 337.6 e 7th av, 20.10x103.3. Aug. 4, due Aug. 5, 1896, 5 %. 15,000

The Metropolitan Telephone and Telegraph Co. to THE MERCANTILE TRUST CO. trustee. All real estate, rights, privileges and franchises acquired since May 24, 1888. Supplemental to prior mort. for $2,900,000. Aug. 1.

Umpreville, Charlotte to John Bussing, Jr. 3d av, Nos. 3471 and 3473, n w s, 172.9 n e 167th st, 49.3x100x5?x—. Aug. 6, 3 years. 7,700

Verdon, William to Warren B. Smith, Yonkers, N. Y. 135th st, n s, 110 w 5th av, 6 lots. 6 P. M. morts., each $12,500. July 25, 3 years. gold, 75,000

Same to same. 135th st, n s, 110 w 5th av. P. M. July 25, 3 years. gold, 3,500

Verdon, William to Peter Patry. 135th st, n s, 163.8 w 5th av. 17.8x99.11. Secures bond of mortgagor and Fred. R. Mens. July 30, due Nov. 10, 1891. 3,000

Vettel, Francis to THE EAST RIVER SAVINGS INST. Av A, No. 217, w s, 77.6 n 13th st, 25.11x100. Aug. 3, 1 year, 5 %. 20,000

Vultee, George W. to Nathaniel Niles. Broadway or Boulevard, s e cor 63d st, runs east 128.4 x south 84.11 x west 25 x north 62 x west 85 to Boulevard, x north 25; Boulevard, e s, 25 s 63d st, 24x73x20x85; Boulevard, e s, 49 s 63d st, 20x62x17x73. Sub. to mort. $71,433. July 1, due Jan. 1, 1893. 5,000

Vultee, George W. to Collis P. Huntington. 5th av and 80th st. P. M. Aug. 3, 2 years or sooner, 4¾ %. 200,000

Wall, John L., Harrison, N. Y., to Magdalene M. Craft. 50th st, No. 60, s s, 721 w 5th av, 20x100.5, Lease. July 27, due Sept. 21, 1892. 12,000

Whitlock, William and Bache McE. to Gilbert A. Robertson Home, a corporation. 37th st, No. 10, s s, 206 w 5th av, 19.5x98.9. July 31, due Aug. 1, 1894, or installs, 5 %. 15,000

Wheaton, Esther A. to William M. Denman, Mt. Vernon, N. Y., and Arthur R. Denman, Newark, N. J. 101st st. P. M. July 31, due Aug. 1, 1892, 5 %. 4,000

Warner, Carlos and Charles D. Smith, Londonderry, Vt., to Charles R. Treat. Opdyke st, n w cor Oneida av. P. M. July 16, due Aug. 1, 1894. 500

Walsh, William M. to William H. Scott. 101st st, n s, 150 e Columbus av, 25x100.11. Aug. 1, due Jan. 1, 1892. 2,100

Waters, Thomas to Alexander L. Bowie. 11th av, No. 660, e s, 25.1 s 48th st, 25.1x100. July 1, 3 years, 5 %. 1,000

Weed, Seth C. to William W. Gardiner. 3d av, n w cor 21st st. P. M. July 30, due Aug. 1, 1894, 5 %. 20,000

Wehrmann, Arthur to J. Sophia Eilers. Columbus (9th) av, No. 646, w s, 75.8 n 91st st, 25x80. July 13, due Oct. 1, 1892, 5 %. 5,000

Weinstein, Morris and Kity his wife and Morris Margovitz and Necony his wife to Ascher Weinstein, Fisher Lewine and Harris Mandelbaum. Division st, Nos 243, s s, 46 w. Montgomery st, 23x48.6x23x48.7. Aug. 3, 3 months. 3,000

KINGS COUNTY.

JULY 30, 31, AUGUST 1, 3, 4, 5.

Abt, Helena to John Greubel. Ingraham st, n s, 200 w Morgan av, 25x100. Aug. 4, 5 years, 5 %. $3,500

Ableson, Morris to Joshua Fletcher. Linnington av. P. M. April 11, 3 years. 300

Akermann, Josephine to Henry W. Meyer, Glendale, L. I. Broadway. P. M. Aug. 4, installs. 7,750

Alexander, George to Eugene R. Tichenor. Warwick st. P. M. Aug. 3, 4 years. 450

Alexander, Henry to Ann E. McCaddin. South 9th st, s s, 104 e 2d st, 25x100. July 31, 3 years, 5 %. 2,000

Almuly, Lazarus to The Bushwick Co-operative Building and Loan Assoc. Greene av. P. M. Aug. 1, installs. 6,000

Same to Joseph Weidner and John Hass. Same property. 2d mort. Aug. 1, due Feb. 1, 1897, 5 %. 700

Bragaw, John to William Kenney. Plot at Gravesend, adj lands of William Morris and Gravesend Bay at high water line, 55 acres. March 19, demand. 1,000

Bauer, Bernhard to John Robertson. De Kalb av, s w cor Reid av, 24.6x80. Aug. 4, 3 years, 5 %. See Conveys. 5,500

Balk, Henry F. to William Williamson, Flatbush, L. I. Skillman st, w s, 174.10 s Myrtle av, runs south 37 x west 100 x north 35 x east 5 x north 2 x east 95. July 30, due May 1, 1893. 1,000

Same to Rebecca C. wife of Henry F. Balk. Sam property. July 30, due Feb. 28, 1892, 5 %. 4,500

Bargfrede, Christopher to Emil F. Wildner. Madison st, s e s, 390 n e Central av, 20x100. Aug. 3, installs, 5 %. 750

Bauermeister, Carl W. to A. H. August Arwo, De Kalb av. P. M. Aug. 1, 5 years, 5 %. 5,000

Beasley, Alfred L. to Horace F. Burroughs. Putnam av, s s, 154.6 e Ralph av, 24.6x100. July 24, 1 year. 1,850

Same to same. Putnam av, s s, 130 e Ralph av, 24.6x100. July 24, 1 year. 1,850

Becker, Herman and Patrick to The Title Guarantee and Trust Co. 6th st, s s, 180 w 4th av, 115x100. Aug. 1, demand. 20,000

Bella, Louis to Matilda Weinberger and Lena Herskowics. Chester st, Sackett st. P. M. July 29, installs. 250

Bellamy, Mary A. wife and Robert J. to The Co-operative Building Bank. Bergen st, s s, 98.4 e Hopkinson av, 19.4x100. June 30, installs. 2,000

Bennett, John to Henry A. Latimer. Clifton pl, s s, 240 w Nostrand av, 20x100. Aug. 1, 1 year. 350

Bergin, James F. to Andrew Wilson. Vanderbilt st, Flatbush. P. M. July 14, installs. 1,475

Berman, Louis to Esther Surut. Johnson av. P. M. July 30, installs, 5 %. 750

Berman, Louis and Ferdinand Feldblum to Nannetta Weinstein. Throop av, w s, 50 n Stockton st, 25x100. July 31, 6 years. 1,900

Bessey, Charles A., Samuel A. and Charles Alonzo, Sarah J. wife of Charles W. Sheffield, Mary A. Reeves, Clara E. wife of Robert Keeler and Willie A. Bessey to Maria E., Cecelia J. and Josephine Cassidy. Lorimer st, e s, 40 s Ainslie st, 20x80. July 25, 5 years, 5 %. 1,200

Blazo, Augustus W. to Edwin C. Low. Lewis av, n w cor Jefferson av, 22x90. May 12, 1 year, 5 %. 5,000

Bolte, Herman to Diederich H. Wersebe. 3d av. P. M. July 29, 3 years, 5 %. 5,000

Bossert, Margaret wife of and Philip to The Dime Savings Bank of Williamsburgh. Cooper st, n w s, 160 s w Bushwick av, 25x100. July 31, 1 year, 5 %. 3,250

Brahm, Peter J. to Theodore F. Jackson. Suydam st. P. M. July 28, 1 year or sooner, 5 %. 1,325

Bills, Abby J. wife of James A., Newtown, L. I., to John N. Smith. Sunnyside av, n s, 200 w Miller av, 50x250 to Highland Boulevard. Aug. 4, 2 months. 650

Broach, John H. to Howard C. Conrady. McDonough st, n s, 225 w Tompkins av, 40x100, July 29, 2 years. 2,000

Brockmann, Louisa F. to Ferdinand Krooss. Judson av. P. M. Aug. 1, 3 years, 5 %. 5,000

Same to Casper Koster. Same property. Aug. 1, 3 years, 5 %. 1,000

Brown, Jennie L. to Henry E. Murphy. Prospect av. P. M. Sub. to mort. $10,000. July 28, due July 29, 1894. 2,000

Same to John Pullman. Same property. P. M. July 28, 5 years, 5 %. 10,000

Brown, Mary E wife of and George W. to Lucy R. Blanke. Lafayette av, s s, 452 e Bedford av, 23x100. July 28, 3 years. 600

Budion, Catherine wife of and John to Joseph Von Hatten. Sumpter st, n s, 275 w Howard av, 25x100. July 30, due July 1, 1896, 5 %. 1,500

Budlong, Morris M. to Julia M. Budlong guard. Josephine H. and Robert H. Haseltine. Madison st, n e cor Nostrand av, 20x80. July 13, due Aug. 1, 1893, 5 %. 5,500

Burns, Hugh to Patrick J. Carlin. 5th av, n w s, 75 n e 15th st, 25x100. July 31, 1 year. 1,500

Burr, Townsend, Jr., to The Bedford Bank. Monroe st, s s, 100 w Nostrand av, 25x100. Feb. 14. secures credits

Bursch, Frederick J. W. to Caroline and Charlotte Hewlett. 14th st, n s, 320 w 2d av, 86x100. Aug. 3, due May 1, 1894, 5 %. 2,500

Burwell, Charles D. to Frank A. Barnaby. 5th st, s w s, 97.10 s e 4th av, 300x100; 5th st, s w s, 97.10 n w 5th av, 100x100; 6th st, n e s, 397.10 n w 5th av, 200x100. July 30, demand. 4,000

Clement, John and Anna his wife to Theodore F. Jackson. Suydam st. P. M. July 29, 1 year, 5 %. 1,700

Closset, George to Margareth M. Boehm. Palmetto st. P. M. July 29, 3 years, 4½ %. 700

Cobb, Sylvester R. and Sarah A. his wife, Brooklyn, and Mary L. Nightingale, Paterson, N. J., to James A. Connell. Dean st, n s, 387.6 e New York av, 37.6x114.5. July 30, due Aug. 1, 1892, 5 %. 6,000

Cohen, Louis to Hyman Kaplan. Montauk av, e s, 140 n Blake av, 30x100. June 29, 3 years, 5 %. 200

Colegate, Edward to The Title Guarantee and Trust Co. Monroe st, s s, 279.7 e Lewis av, 19.11x100. July 29, 3 years, 5 %. 2,500

Cook, Mary E., Newtown, L. I., to J. C. and H. C. Smith & Koepke. Rockaway av, s e cor Dean st, 114.5x100. July 29, demand. 2,700

Cook, Charles S. to Wilmot D. Losee. Ridgewood av. P. M. Sub. to mort. $1,600. Aug. 1, installs. 1,150

Coit, Tracy to Lewis Hurst. Sackman st. P. M. July 15, due July 28, 1893. 400

Cornell, Lucy to Timothy G. Sellew. Jefferson av, s e s, 311.6 n e Evergreen av, 18x100. Aug. 1, installs. 4,000

Cosgrave, Ellen to Herman B. Scharmann. 4th av, south cor 52d st, 180.4x100. July 30, 5 years, 5 %. 7,000

Culhane, Daniel to John H. Ackerman. Driggs st, s e s, 156.3 n e Union av, runs northeast 102.4 to Van Pelt st, x east 28.7 x south 100 x southwest 77.9 x northwest 79.9 to beginning. Aug. 4, 5 years. 5,000

Cush, Adelia to Catherine M. Rickins. 37th st, s s, 125 e 3d av, 25x100.2. July 31, 3 years. 300

Daly, Maurice and Anne his wife to Francis Nulty. 2d av, w s, 50.2 s 41st st, 50x100. July 31, due Oct. 1, 1891, 5 %. 500

Same to Gertrude Prince, Flatbush, L. I. Same property. P. M. July 31, 3 years, 5 %. 3,000

Davidson, Aaron and Louis to Emanuel Weill. York st. P. M. Aug. 1, 5 years or sooner, 5 %. 5,000

De Ath, Frederick to John N. Eitel. Hart st, n s, 100 w Tompkins av, 50x100. July 30, 1 year, 5 %. 4,000

Donnelly, Andrew to Irwin Heasty. Van Buren st, s s, 357 w Reid av. P. M. July 27, 2 years. 1,725

Same to same. Van Buren st, s s, 314.3 w Reid av. P. M. July 27, 2 years. 1,725

Doody, Daniel F. to Title Guarantee and Trust Co. Prospect av. P. M. July 29, due July 31, 1894, 5 %. 2,500

Donahue, Edward to Equitable Co-operative Building and Loan Assoc. 4th st, s s, 389.6 e Smith st, 22x100. July 31, installs. 3,750

Dorn, Robert to John Joy, of Renslaerville, N. Y. Montgomery st. P. M. Aug. 3, 3 years. 800

Dornheim, John P. G. to The Title Guarantee and Trust Co. Eldert st. P. M. Aug. 5, 1 year, 5 %. 3,000

Doubleday, Frank N. to Benjamin P. Davis exr., &c., Benjamin W. Davis. 2d av, e s, 100 s 4th st, 108x215. Aug. 1, 2 years, 5½ %. 11,000

Dowdell, Mary A. to The Serial Building Loan and Savings Inst. St. Marks av, s s, 250 e Howard av, runs east 50 x south 127.9 x west 75 x north 42.9 x east 25 x north 85. July 21, installs. 2,000

Dreher, Christian W. C. to Julius Muller. Wyona st, e s, 175 n Fulton av, 25x100. July 28, 3 years. 500

Dreyer, Isaac, Gustav and Samuel to Ludwig Jordens. Boerum st. P. M. July 31, 3 years, 5 %. 1,000

Duncker, Rudolph to Laura Rooney. Folsom pl, n s, 85 w Eldert av, 15x80. Aug. 3, 3 years. 1,100

Dunn, James and Mary A. his wife to John W. Hayes. 4th st, s s, 320 w Bond st, 20x107.8x20.5x108.4. Aug. 1, 3 years. 1,700

Dunn, Mary E. to Eli H. Bishop. Putnam av, s s, 295 w Stuyvesant av, 20x100. July 31, notes. 2,000

Same to The Brooklyn Trust Co. Same property. July 31, 1 year, 5 %. 8,000

Ehrlich, Markus and Edward to Charles E. Cummings. Elton st, e s, 100 n Liberty av, 50x90. July 31, 5 years, 5 %. 5,500

Eich, John to Severin Linsenmeyer and Katharina his wife. Park av, n s, 275 w Tompkins av, 25x100. Aug. 1, 5 years, 5 %. 3,500

Erk, Maria to Michael Zimmer. Ingraham st, n s, 225 w Morgan av, 25x100. Aug. 4, 5 years, 5 %. 3,500

Everett, Susan M. to Isaac Steigerwald. Washington st, Nos. 323–327. Lease. Aug. 4, demand. 500

Eybel, Catharine wife of John to John F. Eybel. Conselyea st, n s, 125 w Ewen st, 25x100. July 27, due Aug. 1, 1896, 5 %. 900

Fein, Harris and Simon and Louis Young to Charles F. Griffith. Livonia and Stone avs. P. M. Aug. 1, 3 years, 5 % 2,200

Fenwick, Mary F. wife of and William H. to Jane Thompson. Lorimer st, w s, 250 n Nassau av, 25x100. Aug. 1, 5 years, 5 %. 3,800

Ferry, Rebecca M. to Eliza J. Smith. Sackett st, n e s, 835 n w Columbia st, 50x200 to Degraw st; Sackett st, n e s, 810 n w Columbia st, 25x100; Sackett st, n e s, 125 w Van Brunt st, 50x100. May 9, due May 1, 1896. 9,000

Same to same. Same property. July 7, 5 years. 6,000

Same to same. Same property. July 7, 5 years. 2,000

Findlay, Georgiana L. wife of William to Alexander Findlay, Ronkonkoma, L. I. Clermont av, w s, 228.4 s Greene av, 20x70.7; Adelphi st, e s, 234.7 s Greene av, 15x29.5x15x29.4. July 29, 1 year. 500

Fischer, Johann to William Ulmer. Scholes st, n s, 125 w Lorimer st, 25x100. July 29, 1 year, 5 %. 1,000

Fitzgerald, Thomas R. H. to Levi V. Martin. 54th st, n s, 380 w 3d av. P. M. July 28, installs. 600

Fitzsimmons, Michael to James S. Bearns. 2d av, s e cor 9th st, runs east 73.4 x south 71 x east 51.6 x south 29 x west 25 x south 24.6 x west 83.10 x south 75.6 to 10th st, x west 66.2 to av, x north 200. May 14, 1 year, 5 %. 5,000

Fowler, Bernard to Michael Lamm. Washington av, w s, 25 n Gates av, 25x100. July 30, 1 year. 2,500

Frank, Tillie and Anny Mintz to Henry Meyer. Seigel st. P. M. July 29, installs. 5,000

Garrick, Henry and Phebe his wife to The Kings County Savings Inst. North Henry st. P. M. July 1, 1 year, 5 %. 1,750

Same to Charles Henry. Same property. P. M. 2d mort. July 1, installs. 5 %. 1,250

Gans, Henry to Henry Gartelmann, Flushing. Liberty av, n s, 115.1 e Lincoln av, 30x111.4x30x111.10. July 29, 3 years, 5 %. 1,000

Geib, Adam and Theresia his wife to Nickolaus Ziegler. Hull st, n s, 25 e Saratoga av, 25x100. July 14, due July 1, 1896, 5 %. 2,000

Gillespie, William to George H. Pendleton. Bergen st, s s, 345 e Vanderbilt av, 25x131. Aug. 1, due Nov. 1, 1893. 500

Given, Robert to Anna W. Townsend, North Hempstead, L. I. Chauncey st, s s, 233.4 e Patchen av, 16.8x100. July 30, due Aug. 1, 1896, 5 %. 2,200

Gluck, David to David Michel. Scholes st. P. M. Aug. 4, 5 years or installs, 5 %. 2,500

Goldstein, Thomas to Marks Jacobs. Osborn st. P. M. July 31, 1 year or installs. 800

Good, William H. mortgagor and J. H. Puels mortgagee with Title Guarantee and Trust Co. Agreement that new loan of $19.500 by said Guarantee Company shall be a prior lien to a mortgage held by said Puels. nom

Good, William H. to Title Guarantee and Trust Co. Saratoga av, s e cor Decatur st. 100x115.6. July 29. 19,800

Good, William H. and Sarah his wife to Charles D. King. Bainbridge st, n s, 23 e Saratoga av, 18.6x100. July 30, 1 year, 5 %. 1,600

Granger, John J. to Jaques Van Brunt. Lots 136 and 137 map mortgagees property, New Utrecht. July 27, 3 years. 500

Griffiths, Charles A. to Catharine S. Griffiths. North 3d st, n e s, 85.5 n w Bedford av, 25x85. March 2, 5 years, 4 %. 2,000

Gubner, Harry A. to Albert Franke. 20th av, east cor 83d st, 100x120, New Utrecht. Aug. 1, 5 years, 5 %. 1,500

Guttman, Saja to Joseph Hyman. Whipple st P. M. July 31, installs, 5 %. 800

Hackett, John F. and Catharine Kiernan to Effingham H. Nichols. Lots 579-583 block 12 map No. 1, Cowenhoven farm, New Utrecht. July 22, 2 years, 5 %. See Conveys. 360

Hadden, Jr., Crowell to Crowell Hadden. Sydney pl. P. M. Aug. 1, 1 year, 5 %. 6,000

Hale, Mary C. to Florence B. and Alice M. Dike. Lewis av, Pulaski st. P. M. Aug. 4, 1 year. 1,000

Same to same. Same property. Aug. 4, 5 years. 3,500

Hallen, Catherine E. to Elizabeth Remsen. Lots 217 to 220 map A. W. Parker, Bath Beach. July 31, 1 year. 600

Harrigan, James to The Brooklyn Mutual Building and Loan Assoc. Grand av, e s, 129.6 s Flushing av, 30x100. July 29, installs. 1,400

Harris, Esther to Mendel Levy. Ten Eyck st. P. M. July 30, due Aug. 1, 1896, 5 %. 3,100

Hart, John F. to Daniel Doody. Kingston av, n e cor Pacific st. P. M. July 3, due Aug. 1, 1892. 5,000

Hanson, Franceska to Frederick Ulrich. Hancock st. P. M. Aug. 1, 5 years, 5 %. 3,400

Haynes, Gilbert to Catharine M. Trimble. Van Voorhis st, s s, 100 e Evergreen av, 200x100. Aug. 1, 3 months. 117

Hennemann, Caroline to Joseph Bolton. North Oxford st, w s, 168.1 s Flushing av, 25.3x100. Aug. 5, 3 years, 5 %. 600

Hermann, Carl to Theodore B. Case. South 4th st. P. M. Aug. 1, 5 years, 5 %. 2,500

Herrmann, Marie wife of Charles to George, John W. and Joseph T. Fletcher. Miller av. P. M. July 21, 2 years. 700

Hess, Frank to Emily Obernier. Johnson av, s w cor Lorimer st, 50x100. Aug. 1, 3 years. 400

Heuschober, Helene wife of and Henry to The Title Guarantee and Trust Co. Halsey st. P. M. Aug. 1, 1 year, 5 %. 2,000

Same to Ernestine Gastmeyer. Same property. 2d mort. Aug. 1, 3 years, 5 %. 1,000

Hickey, Ellen to The Title Guarantee and Trust Co. Garfield pl. P. M. Aug. 1, due Aug. 5, 1894, 3 %. 4,000

Hill, Henry B. to Charles G. Tousey, Clinton Corners, N. Y. McDonough st, s s, 267.8 w Patchen av. P. M. July 29, 3 years, 5 %. 3,500

Same to same. McDonough st, s s, 249.8 w Patchen av. P. M. July 29, 3 years, 5 %. 3,500

Hogan, Annie to Effingham H. Nichols. Lots 153-156 block 4 and 547-551 and 555 and 556 block 12 map 1, Cowenhoven farm. July 22, 2 years, 5 %. See Conveys. 1,055

Hogan, Thomas to Effingham H. Nichols. Lots 408-412 block 10 map 1 of Cowenhoven farm. July 22, 2 years, 5 %. See Conveys. 500

Hopkins, Samuel mortgagor with Junius A. Fuller mortgagee. Extension of mort. July 28. nom

Hultgren, Annie C. to Joseph Foley. Hicks st. P. M. July 31, due April 30, 1897, or installs. 1,150

Hunecke, Frederick to Theodore S. Lowndes, South Norwalk, Conn. Franklin st, n e cor Eagle st, 24.6x72. July 25, 5 years, 5 %. 10,000

Same to same. Franklin st, e s, 24.6 n Eagle st, 24x72. July 25, 5 years, 5 %. 6,500

Same to same. Franklin st, e s, 48.6 n Eagle st, 31.6x72. July 25, 5 years, 5 %. 6,500

Hunter, Samuel D. to Elizabeth E. Hutchins widow. Lafayette av. P. M. Aug. 3, 3 years, 5 %. 12,424

Hurley, Samuel W. to Thomas S. Strong trustee for Lewis B. Strong. Gates av. P. M. July 31, due Aug. 1, 1894, 5 %. 4,000

Hutwelker Bros. to Joseph Dempsey. 5th av and 19th st. P. M. July 30, 5 years or installs, 5 %. 8,000

Israel, Wilhelmine to Henry Roth. Lee av. P. M. July 31, installs. 3,600

Jacobs, Matilda to E. Sinnamon Calvert. Columbia st. P. M. July 30, 3 years, 5 %. 2,750

Jahn, Gustave A. to Eliza J. Smith. Road from Flatbush to Brooklyn, e s, property Alletta Hess, 1 acre, Flatbush. June 1, 5 years, 5 %. 5,000

James Methodist Episcopal Church, Brooklyn, to Williamsburgh Savings Bank. Reid av, w s, 100 s Monroe st, 47x100. July 31, 1 year, 5 %. 13,000

Jansen, Frederick, New York, to The Title Guarantee and Trust Co. High st, s s, 186.7 w Washington st, 25.2x98.5 to alley. Aug. 1, demand. 15,000

Janzer, Berhard and Mamie his wife to William Lindemann. Hart st. P. M. Aug. 3, due Aug. 1, 1896, or installs, 5 %. 4,000

Jervis, Mary L. wife of and Henry C. S. to Joseph W. Campbell. South Portland av, e s, 150 s Hanson pl, 20x85. Aug. 4, 2 years. 1,000

Johnson, Charles to Jacob Cozine. Jerome st, e s, 900 n Livonia av. P. M. Aug. 1, demand. 1,500

Same to James H. Brundage. Same property. P. M. Aug. 1, installs. 300

Johnson, J. Christian to Twiss Bermingham guard. Josephine M. Power. Eldert st, n w s, 215 s w Evergreen av, 20x100. July 31, 4 years, 5 %. 4,000

Johnson, Hannah M. to Helen M. Organ. Throop av, w s, 83.4 s Hart st, 16.8x100. Aug. 3, 3 years, 5 %. 500

Jones, Cadwallader M. to William M. Jones. Monroe st, s s, 166.8 e Tompkins av, 16.8x100. Aug. 1, 3 years, 5 %. 1,400

Judge, John E. to The Stuyvesant Co-operative Building and Loan Assoc. Dupont st, s s, 560 w Manhattan av, 25x100. Aug. 5, installs. 5,000

Kain, Daniel E. to Theodore F. Jackson subtrustee Wm. Taylor dec'd. North 4th st. P. M. July 15, due Aug. 1, 1894, 5 %. 3,000

Same to Joseph A. Burr, Jr. Same property. P. M. July 15, due Aug. 1, 1892. 2,000

Kaplan, Elias to Mary L. Douglass. Watkins st, w s, 275 s Bay av, 25x100. July 31, due Aug. 1, 1892. 3,000

Kaplan, Nathan to Sophia L. Schroder. Howard av. P. M. July 8, 1 year. 1,500

Kaufman, Bertha to Anna T. Shiel. Stockton st. P. M. July 24, 2 years. 1,150

Katt, Herman to Sigmund Bieyer. Flushing av. P. M. July 29, due Aug. 1, 1898, 5 % 7,000

Kerner, Theobald and Anna his wife to John and Catharine Herrmann. Starr st. P. M. Aug. 2, due July 1, 1894, 5 % 1,100

Kirsch, Louis and Martin, of Kirsch Bros., to The New York Sandy Hook Pilot's Charitable Fund. Keap st. P. M. July 27, due July 1, 1896, 5 %. 3,000

Klein, John to Henry Roth. Floyd st. P. M. July 31, installs. 1,500

Klein, Frederick W. and Elise his wife to The Williamsburgh Savings Bank. Pulaski st, s s, 194.10 w Sumner av, 25.5x100. Aug 1, 1 year, 5 %. 4,000

Koch, Wilhelmina to Frederick Bonawitz. Palmetto st, s s, 500 w Central av, 25x100. July 28, 3 years, 5 %. 300

Koehler, William to Bernard Rokus. Melrose st, n w s, 175 s w Knickerbocker av, 25x100. Aug. 1, 2 years, 5 %. 1,000

Kohl, Valentine to Simon G. Meyer. Stanhope st, n w s, 225 n e Hamburg av, 25x100. Aug. 1, 2 years, 5 %. 700

Koller, Marie widow to Amelia Jobum. Willoughby av, s s, 253.6 e Broadway, 21.6x77x21.6x76.7. Aug. 4, due July 1, 1894, 5 %. 1,000

Kraus, Frank R. to John P. Free. Folson pl and Linwood st. P. M. July 31, installs. 800

Kringstin, Solomon to Mary W. Smith. Eastern Parkway, s s, 100.1 e Rockaway av, 25x100. July 30, due Jan. 1, 1892. 1,500

Lamb, James W. to Mary H. Hendrickson. Cornelia st. P. M. July 31, 2 years, 5 %. 4,000

Lang, Maximilian to The Title Guarantee and Trust Co. Cumberland st. P. M. July 7, due July 31, 1892, 5 %. 3,000

Langlos, Heinrich to George Covert. Barman st. P. M. July 25, due July 1, 1896, 5 %. 5,000

Same to same. Greene av. P. M. July 25, due July 1, 1896, 5 %. 5,000

Ledogar, Elizabeth wife of and George to Robert Rhinow. Jackson st, n s, 125 w Lorimer st, 100x100. July 30, due July 1, 1894, 5 %. 3,500

Levy, Samuel and Sali Cohen to Stephen B. Sturges. Eastern Parkway, s s, 50.1 e Rockaway av, 25x100. July 29, demand. 3,500

Levy, Barnet and Max Gittlesohn to William Brown. Eastern Parkway. P. M. Aug. 1, 1 year. 1,350

Little, William M. to Teresa M. Devin. McDonough st, s s, 135 e Sumner av, 20x100. July 31, due Jan. 1, 1897, 5 %. 2,500

Lohmann, Karl G. and Katharina his wife to August Sedlmeir. Suydam st, n w s, 175 s w Knickerbocker av, 25x100. Aug. 1, 5 years, 5 %. 2,000

Lottman, Hymon to Louise Erdman. Flushing av. P. M. July 25, installs. 3,500

Lynch, Mary E. to Alfred Williams. Clinton st, w s, 40 s West 9th st, 30x90. May 8, 4 years, 5 %. 6,000

Lyon, Sarah A. wife of James to William E. Lyon, Banksville, Conn., exr. Newman C. Lyon. Pulaski st, n s, 280 w Tompkins av, 20x100. July 24, due July 1, 1893, 5 %. 2,085

Magnus, Charlotte mortgagor with The Title Guarantee and Trust Co. mortgagee. Extension of mort. July 31. nom

Mahon, Andrew to Edward Egolf. Earl st, Flatbush. P. M. June 1, 2 years, 5 %. 400

Margolis, Heyman and Moses Goldberg to Joseph Neger. Gwinnett st. P. M. July 30, due July 1, 1896, or installs., 5 %. 2,250

Manes, Max to David and Israel Schiff. Hopkins st. P. M. July 29, due Feb 1, 1893, 5 %. 350

Martin, William B. and Patrick J. Lee to The Methodist Episcopal Hospital. Garfield pl, s s, 269.10 e 7th av, 19.6x100. Aug. 3, due Dec. 1, 1894, 5 %. 9,500

Same to same. Garfield pl, s s, 250.4 e 7th av, 19.6x100. Aug. 3, due Dec. 1, 1894, 5 %. 9,500

Same to The Long Island Loan and Trust Co. trustee of John A. Cross dec'd. Garfield pl, s s, 289.4 e 7th av, 19.6x100. Aug. 3, due Dec. 1, 1894, 5 %. 9,000

Same to Wesleyan University. Garfield pl, s s, 328.4 e 7th av, 19.6x100. Aug. 3, due Dec. 1, 1894, 5 %. 9,500

Same to same. Garfield pl, s s, 308.10 e 7th av, 19.6x100. Aug. 3, due Dec. 1, 1894, 5 %. 9,500

Max, Harris to Mary W. Smith. Osborn st, e s, 75 s Sutter av, 25x100. July 31, 5 years 3,000

McBean, Archibald N. to James H. Watson and James H. Pittinger, of Watson & Pittinger. 2d st, s s, 177.10 w 6th av, 30x95. July 29, demand. 470

McCadden, James to Agata Carnet. Hemlock st, w s, 316.10 s Jamaica turnpike, 25x85.1x25x85.6. July 1, 3 years. 1,800

McCormack, Cornelius to Thomas Flood. Eagle st, s s, 200 e Oakland st, 25x100. Aug. 1, 3 years, 5 %. 1,000

McIntyre, Frank to Title Guarantee and Trust Co. Waverly av. P. M. July 20, due July 31, 1892, 5 %. 1,200

McKelvay, John to George B. Forrester. Underhill av, w s, 20 n Pacific st, runs west 80 x north 20 x east 30 x south 0.2 x east 50 to av, x south 19.10. Aug. 3, 1 year. 1,000

Medler, Joseph to Crescentia Saile, New York. Hale av, w s, 250 s Ridgewood av, 25x100. Aug. 3, due Aug. 1, 1892. 300

Meis, Mina wife of and Henry to The German Savings Bank, Brooklyn. Broadway, n e s, 34.4 s e Debevoise st, 34.4x101.7x25x125.2. July 31, due Dec. 1, 1892, 5 %. 11,000

Meyer, William and Mary L. his wife to P. Ballantine & Sons, a corporation. Fulton st, Nos. 12, 14 and 16. Lease. July 30, note. 3,000

Meyn, Gerd. H. to James McGuigan. Fulton st, n e cor Van Siclen av. P. M. July 31, 5 years, 5 %. 5,500

Michel, Leopold to John and Joseph Graetzer. Flushing av, s s, 275 e Nostrand av, 25x100. Aug. 1, 3 years, 5 %. 5,000

Miller, Jane to James D. Rankin and James Ross. Macon st, n s, 218 e Patchen av, 3 lots, each 18x100. 3 morts, each $1,072. Sub. to prior mort. $4,500. July 29, 1 year. 3,216

Miller, Henry to The Kings County Savings Inst. Jefferson av, No. 460, s s, 356.8 e Throop av, 16.8x100. Aug. 4, 1 year, 5 %. 1,500

Miller, Julius and Samuel Cohen to Bertha Cohen. Bergen st. P. M. July 30, due July 31, 1892, or sooner. 950

Mills, John H. to Fanny A. Mathews. Lot at Canarsie, 200 s w road to Canarsie Landing, 50x100, to right of way of Fanny A. Mathews, Canarsie. July 1, 2 years. 250

Minturn, Raymond to The East Brooklyn Savings Bank, Brooklyn. Sunnyside av, n s, 150 w Miller av, 50x250 to Highland Boulevard. Aug. 4, 1 year, 5 %. 5,000

Mitchell, John and Charles Herr to Williamsburgh Savings Bank. Putnam av, n s, 188.4 e Stuyvesant av, 18.7x100. July 28, 1 year, 5 %. 4,500

Same to same. Putnam av, n s, 206.9 e Stuyvesant av, 18.7x100. July 28, 1 year, 5 %. 4,500

Molloy, Catherine to Frederick T. Hill. Atlantic av, n e s, 201.3 s e East New York av, 32.7x83.6x31x77.6. July 30, due Aug. 22, 1893, 5 %. gold, 10,000

Same to Edward A. Ackerly. Logan st, e s, 94 s Jamaica av, 50x100. July 21, 3 years. 750

Same to Nannette Marks. Jamaica av or plank road, s s, 54 e Logan st, 54x136x50x115. July 21, 3 years. 1,000

Moran, Michael to Williamsburgh Savings Bank. Central av, east cor Eldert st, 25x80. July 31, 1 year, 5 %. 4,000

Morgan, Cathrine to Effingham H. Nichols. Lots 561-563 block 12 map 1 of Cowenhoven Farm, New Utrecht. July 21, 2 years, 5 %. See Conveys. 230

Morrissey, Richard to Henry Weil. Bushwick av. P. M. July 31, installs., 5 %. 5,700

Muller, William to Albert H. W. Van Sielen. Sutter av, s e cor Hendrix st, 50x100. Aug. 1, 3 years 1,200

Mulvihill, Michael to The Dime Savings Bank, Brooklyn. Putnam av, s e s, 180 n e Broadway, 4 lots, each 20x100. 4 morts, each $3,000. July 30, 1 year, 5 %. 12,000

Murphy, Henry E. to William Post committee John Rogers. 11th st, s w s, 213.5 n w 8th av, 75x½ block. July 29, due Dec. 1, 1891. 21,000

Muthes, Matthew to Effingham H. Nichols. Lots 615 618 block 16 map 1 of Cowenhoven farm. July 22, 2 years, 5 %. See Conveys. 270

Myers, William H. to The Williamsburgh Savings Bank. Bushwick av, s w s, 21 n w Moffat st, 40x75. July 30, 1 year, 5 %. 4,000

Neger, Joseph to Mathias Neger. Gwinnett st, 22x100. P. M. July 24, due July 1, 1896, 5 %. 3,000

Neumeyer, John P. to John Dunphy. Lots 119, 120 and 121 block 6, Gravesend, map filed by Mary E. C. Johnson. Aug. 3, 2 years, 5 %. 200

Nunner, Mary wife of and Adam to John Wahl and Babette his wife. Hamburg av. P. M. Aug. 4, 10 years, 5 %, 2,000

O'Neil, John M. to Hans S. Christian. 4th av, e s, 59.6 n Butler st, 56x98.4. July 22, 5 years. 7,125

O'Brien, Patrick to Joseph Liebman and Theodore Obermeyer. 45th st, s s, 140 e 4th av, 60x100.2; 3d av, e s, 75.2 n 47th st, 25x100. July 31, due Aug. 1, 1892, 5 %. 8,000

O'Connor, John to The F. & M. Schaefer Brewing Co. Berry st, No. 349. Lease. July 28, demand. 1,800

Olsen, Henry mortgagor with Henry R. Reid mortgagee. Extension of mort. July 23. non

Page, John J. to Bushwick Co-operative Building and Loan Assoc. Ovington and Stewart avs. P. M. Aug. 1, installs. 4,000

Parmer, Ada wife of Lewis to Mary W. Smith. Watkins st, w s, 100 s Eastern Parkway, 51.6 x100. July 31, due Sept. 1, 1891. 600

Peterson, Charles G. to The Title Guarantee and Trust Co. 7th st, s s, 147.6 w 7th av, 75.4 x100. Building loan. July 31, demand. 20,000

Pink, Bernhard J. to Charles F. Griffith. Livonia av and Christopher av. P. M. Aug. 1, 3 years, 5 %. 1,800

Same to George M. Walgrove. Watkins st, s w cor Blake av. P. M. July 29, due Aug. 1, 1894, 5 %. 3,500

Plotel, Wolf and Rosa his wife and Benjamin Rosenthal and Sarah B. his wife to Gerson Levy. Seigel st. P. M. July 30, installs., 5 %. 4,550

Power, John to Mary W. Smith. Eastern Parkway, n s, 25 w Osborn st, 21.3x100. July 31, 5 years. 1,850

Puels, Joseph P. to Clinton D. Burdick. Prospect av. n s, 245 e 7th av, 25x100. July 27, due July 24, 1893. 400

Radcliffe, Thomas H. to John C. Schenck. McDonough st, s s, 138 e Ralph av, 18.8x100. July 31, 3 years, 5 %. 4,500

Same to same. McDonough st, s s, 100 e Ralph av. 19x100. July 31, 3 years, 5 %. 5,000

Same to same. McDonough st, s s, 119 e Ralph av, 19x100. July 31, 3 years, 5 %. 5,000

Same to same. McDonough st, s s, 81 e Ralph av, 19x90. July 31, 3 years, 5 %. 5,500

Same to same. McDonough st, s s, 62 e Ralph av, 19x90. July 31, 3 years, 5 %. 5,500

Radcliffe, Thomas H. to George Cook. McDonough st, s s, 119 e Ralph av, 19x100. Sub. to mort. $5,000. July 31, 1 year. 1,000

Radley, Margaret A. to Alma Meeker. Lee av, e s, 20 n Rutledge st, 16x77. May 13, 5 years, 5 %. 800

Raine, Jr., Thomas C. to Maximilian Lang. Cumberland st. P. M. July 13, installs, 5 %. 1,500

Ramsey, William to John Eich. Stanhope st. P. M. Aug. 1, due Oct. 1, 1892, 5 %. 2,100

Ranken, John M. to John Griffin. Penn st, s s, 77 e Lee av, 23.8x100. July 14, due July 1, 1896, 5 %. 5,000

Raymond, Amelia wife of Joseph D. to Lottie N. Palmer. Stuyvesant av, e s, 47 n Halsey st, 19x83. July 31, 1 year or sooner. 500

Raymond, Benjamin C. to Patrick G. Hughes. Macon st, n s, 58 w Ralph av, 18x100. Sub. to mort. $4,500. Aug. 2, 1 year. 1,000

Raymond, John V. to The Title Guarantee and Trust Co Clason av, e s, 128.4 s Atlantic av, 2 lots, each 16.7x70. 2 morts., each $1,200. July 31, 3 years, 5 %. 2,400

Reardon, May to James G. Roberts. Macon st. P. M. Aug. 3, 5 years or sooner. 550

Reiche, Hermann to Bertha Ueblinger. Cooper st, n w s, 159.7 n e Broadway, 19.7x100. Aug. 1, 1 year or sooner, 5 %. 1,350

Reid, John and Henry B. Davenport to Johanna Scholz. Montgomery st, n s, 150 e 18th st, 25x100x25x—, Flatbush. July 31, 3 years. 1,000

Reilly, John to Cornelius Macardell, Middletown, N. Y. Bainbridge st, s s, 25 e Ralph av, 18x100. July 31, demand. 1,000

Reincke, William to Obermeyer & Liebmann. Flushing av, No. 913. Lease. Aug. 1, demand. 600

Rick, Eleonora to George L. Marinor. Madison st. P. M. July 31, 3 years. 1,800

Riley, Morris to Frederick Cobb. Bergen st, s s, 325 w Howard av, 25x127.9. July 24, due July 15, 1894. 50

Rissler, Charles to William and Abby Laytin and ano. trustees Wm. Laytin dec'd. Harrison av, s e cor Wallabout st, 25x84. July 31, 3 years, 5 % 7,500

Same to same. Harrison av, e s, 25 s Wallabout st, 25x84. July 31, 3 years, 5 %. 5,000

Roberts, Maria wife of Essex to Philippina Hoeffner. South 4th st. P. M. Aug. 1, 3 years, 5 %. 3,100

Same to C. B. Keogh Mfg. Co. Same property. Aug. 1, 1 year. 1,000

Roes, Anna M. to Leicester Holme. Sackett st. P. M. July 30, 5 years, 5 %. 2,835

Rollins, Elisha B. to The Mutual Life Ins. Co., New York. Poplar st, s e cor Columbia st, 20.6x75.3. July 31, 1 year, 5 %. 2,500

Rosenbaum, Augusta to Richard Long. Broadway, No. 477, n e s, abt 190 n w Johnson av, 23.6x ½ block. Sub. to mort. $7,500. Aug. 1, 1 year, 5 %. 1,500

Same to The Williamsburgh Savings Bank. Same property. Aug. 1, 1 year, 5 %. 7,500

Rosenfeld, Rose to Catherine Molloy. Bergen st. P. M. July 31, due Aug. 1, 1894. 1,700

Rosner, Eli and Bertha his wife and Pencus Burger to John Cooper. Madison st. P. M. 2d mort. July 28, installs. 1,000

Ross, Jennie L. to Thomas Brennan. Fulton st, s s, 260 w Stone av, 20x100. Aug. 5, installs. 3,450

Same to same. 2d st, s s, 197.10 w 7th av, 19.8 x100 Aug. 5, installs. 2,880

Ryan, Emma H. wife of Michael P. to Marshal Tucker and Charles Brewster, of Tucker & Brewster. Henry st, w s, adj land of Margaret E. Goldstone, 35x139.6, Coney Island. July 27, due Sept. 30, 1891. 350.

Roth, Henry to Henry Seiler. Moore st. P. M. July 30, due Aug. 1, 1893, 5 %. 4,000

Rowland, Sidney L. to James A. Inness trustee John W. Inness. Bedford av, e s, 200 n Willoughby av, 25x100. July 1, 3 years, 5 %. 1,500

Sachs, Benjamin to William H. Ellis. Osborn st, s w cor Sutter av, 25x100. Aug. 3, installs, 5 %. 2,700

Sandell. Mary, East Orange, N. J., to Maria E. Cassidy et al. exrs. Mary A. Cassidy. Lorimer st, e s, 60 s Ainslie st, 20x100. July 25, 5 years, 5 %. 1,000

Sands, Frederick to Lemmy A. Halstead. Ridgewood av, s w cor Linwood st. P. M. July 31, 1 year. 800

Schachne, Peril and David to Fredericka Knapp. Blake av. P. M. July 30, due July 1, 1896, or sooner, 5 %. 1,000

Schaffner, Conrad to Charlotte Bass. Lee av. P. M. Aug. 5, 3 years, 5 %. 6,000

Schildt, Henry to S. Liebmann's Sons Brewing Co. Myrtle av, n e cor Tompkins av, 25x100. June 12, 1 year, 5 %. 4,000

Schmidt, Margaretta wife of and Julius to Peter Kelly. Degraw st. P. M. Aug. 5, 1 year, 5 %. 2,500

Schroeder, John to Joseph Hake. Lot 37 block 100 on 22d Ward assessm't map. Aug. 1, due July 1, 1894. 700

Schwarz, Henry to Eliza Buttner. Spencer st, w s, 175 n Willoughby av, 25x100. July 1, 5 years, 5 %. 4,000

Schwenck, Wilhelmina to Theodore F. Jackson. Stanhope st P. M. Aug. 1, 1 year. 6,125

Schultz, William to Frank Ertbal. Starr st, n w s, 125 s w Hamburg av, 25x100. Aug. 1, 1 year, 5 % 700

Scott, Bell K. to Frank C. Swimm. Macon st, n s, 253.4 e Reid av, 16.8x100. Aug. 3, due May 1, 1895. 1,100

Scott, James to John Jones. Norman av, s s, 50 w Jewel st, 25x70. July 31, due Aug. 1, 1894, 5 %. 2,000

Same to same. Norman av, s s, 25 w Jewel st, 25x70. July 31, due Aug. 1, 1894, 5 %. 2,000

Same to same.. Norman av, s w cor Jewel st. 25x70. July 31, due Aug. 1, 1894. 3,000

Seebs, Henry to Lydia M. White, New York. Grand st. P. M. July 13, due Aug. 1, 1894, 5 %. 5,000

Seibert, Jacob to Henry Decker. 83d st, s w s, 280 s e 22d av, 60x100, New Utrecht. Aug. 1, 3 years, 5 %. 2,500

Seider, Josephine wife of Charles formerly Josephine Paul and Emma Paul devisees Ernst Paul to The Williamsburgh Savings Bank. Floyd st, n s, 150 w Sumner av, 25x100. Aug. 3, 1 year, 5 %. 3,500

Seele, Albert to John J. Drake. Broadway, n s, 101.2 e Troy av, runs east 270 x north 84.4 to s s Malbone st, x west 250.8 x south 124.3, Flatbush. July 31, due Aug. 1, 1891, 5 %. 365

Shanley, James to Amelia E. Louis. 25th st, s s, lot 43 block 30 on 8th Ward map. Lease. Aug. 1, 1 year. 775

Shepsky, Jacob to Annie Levy. 3d av. July 29, 5 years or installs. See Conveys. 3.000

Sherwood, Samuel T. to Elcy A. Martin. 47th st, n s, 140 e 4th av, 20x100.2. July 1, 1 year. 800

Sibley, Albert to Joseph P. Puels. Quincy st, s s, 100 w Throop av, 187.6x100. July 30, demand. 25,000

Same to Andrew D. Baird. Same property. Sub. to above. July 30, demand. 36.000

Siegel, Leah to Louis Hurst. Blake av, n e cor Sackman st. P. M. July 28, 2 years. 500

Simon, Abram, Haskel Silberman and Simon Alker to Jacob Strauss. Stone av, n e cor Riverdale av, 267.4x— to Christopher av, x 270.6 to Riverdale av, x west 200. July 7, 2 years. See Conveys. 4,000

Singer, Henriette to Elizabeth Wilder. Evergreen av. P. M. July 29, due Aug. 1, 1893, 5 %. 1,800

Singer, Medart to Effingham H. Nichols. Lots 193-197 block 4 map 1 Cowenhoven farm, New Utrecht. July 21, 2 years, 5 %. See Conveys. 460

Skelton, Christopher P. to Martha A. Adams. Buffalo av, w s, 37.10 n Atlantic av, 17x45, May 19, due May 1, 1895. 1,500

Same to same. Buffalo av, w s, 54.10 n Atlantic av, 17x45. May 19. due May 1, 1894, 5 % 1,500

Skidmore, Julia A. to The Brooklyn Door and Sash Co 2d st, s w s, 337.10 n w 7th av, 40x 95; 2d st, s w s, 397.10 n w 7th av, 20x95. Sub. to morts. $21,100. July 21, 3 months. 4,100

Smith, Sarah L. to S. Perry Sturges. Pearl st. P. M. July 29, due July 10, 1893. 2,500

Smith, William H. to Ernst G. Stache. Huron st, s s, 125 e West st, 50x100. July 1, 1891, due in July, 1891, 5 %. 1,500

Smith, Mary wife of Thomas to Marenus J. Goodenough. Glenmore av. P. M. Aug. 3, 1 year. 1.000

Snyder, Nicholas R. to Charles and Frederick Figge, of Figge Bros. Monroe st, n s, 282.3 w Sumner av. 17.9x100. Aug. 1, 1 year. 1,700

Stern, Lisette widow to Dan Lodge No. 9 Independent Order Free Sons of Israel. Garden st, n e s, 385.10 s e Flushing av, 20 x 86.11 x 39.1 to Bushwick av, x north 20 x west 45.2 x southwest 43.5. July 1, 4 years, 5 %. 1,500

Stehlin, Charles to Martin Ibert. Howard av, s e cor Herkimer st, 25x98. July 31, due Aug. 1, 1896, 5 %. 6,000

Southgate, George J. to William H. Jackson. Berriman st. P. M. June 1, 3 years. 75

Straub, George to The Williamsburgh Savings Bank. Myrtle av, n s, 200 e Throop av, 25x 100. Aug. 3, 1 year, 5 %. 7,500

Spencer, Susan M. widow to The German Savings Bank, Brooklyn. Broadway, s w s, 75 n w Conway st, 50x100. July 18, due Dec. 1, 1892, 5 %. 4,000

Strout, Emma L to James Seymour, Jr., Auburn, N. Y. Park pl, n s, 274 7 e 6th av, 20x 100. Feb 25, 2 years. 7,000

Stockford, Charles E. and Grace his wife to James Hunter. Nassau av, s w cor Newell st. 75x100. July 1, 2 years. 5,000

Sumner, Vina A., Syracuse, N. Y., to Edward M. Townsend exr. Belinda R. Townsend. 3d st, s s, 180 e Smith st. P. M. July 28, due Aug. 1, 1894, 5 %. 3,250

Same to same. 3d st, s s, 199 e Smith st. P. M. July 28, due Aug. 1, 1894, 5 %. 3,250

Tangerman, Thomas to Helena Fuchs. Bushwick av, east cor Stanhope st, 19.6x64.11x19.6 x65.3. May 8, due Aug. 1, 1892. 1,500

Taylor, Ella M. to John Andrews. Butler st. P. M. July 29, installs. 1,160

The House of the Good Shepherd to The Emigrant Industrial Savings Bank. Rockaway av, Hopkinson av, Pacific st and Dean st—the block and buildings. Aug. 1, 1 year. 4,000

The United Builders' Assoc. to The German Savings Bank, Brooklyn. Hart st, n w s, 350 n e Hamburg av, 25x100. Aug. 3, due Dec. 1, 1892, 5 %. 2,500

Thien, Henry G. to Caroline Rathje. 14th st, s w s, 320 n w 3d av, 16x88.8x16x88.9. Aug 3, due July 1, 1894, 5 %. 1,000

Thompson, William A. to Harriet L. Thompson. 20th st. P. M. Aug. 4, 5 years, 5 %. 3,400

Thompson, Charles M. to John D. and Catharine Ditmis and Georgienna J. Remsen. Bergen st. P. M. July 17, 6 months. 800

Tedebush, August to William Laytin et al. trustees Wm. Laytin dec'd. Cornelia st, n w s, 100 s w Evergreen av, 3 lots, each 25x100. 3 morts., each $4,000. Aug. 3, 3 years, 5 %. 12,000

Tomlinson, Charles and Charles W. to Herbert C. Smith. Liberty av. P. M. June 3, 3 months. 9,500

Toomey, Michael to James E. Brown. India st. P. M. July 31, 2 years 1,300

Townsend, James A. to John W. Prokett. 2d pl, s w cor Clinton st, 16x113.5. August 8, 3 years, 5 %. 3,000

Tregman, Henry M. W. to Mark B. Knight. Flatbush. East New York av, s s, 89 w Troy av, 16.5x100.1x12.3x100, Flatbush. July 31, demand. 208

Travers, Martha V. to Thomas H. Redcliffe. McDonough st. P. M. July 29, due July 30, 1893, 5 %. 1,200

Ullinger, Anton and Anna E. his wife to Caroline Kloetmann. Palmetto st, s e s, 100 n e Central av, 25x100. July 29, 5 years or installs. 4,000

Urso, Michael and Peter Cazza to Hugo J. Panzer, Lakewood, N. J. 14th av, e s, 20 s 66th st, 20x100. Aug. 1, due July 1, 1894. 1,000

Van Dyk, John and James to Albert L. French. 57th st, s s, 180 w 2d av, 20x100.2. Aug. 1, 3 years, 5 %. 1,000

Vennob, Gunther to Emil Landgraf. 3d av. P. M. July 31, due July 1, 1892, 5 %. 800

Voorheis, Georgie A. to John Lott Nostrand. North Van Sielen av, 204.3 w Av L, 50x309.10 x56.0½x272.3, Gravesend. Aug. 3, due May 1, 1892. 200

Vrooman, John F. to Angeline A. Davis, Huntington, L. I. Powell st, w s, 216 6 n Liberty av, 16.8x100. July 30, 3 years. 2,000

Walsh, Thomas A. to The Mutual Life Ins. Co. of New York. Court st, s e cor Lorraine st, 19.9x100. July 31, 1 year. 4,000

Wangle, George J. and Daniel D. to Henry Rudloff. Sherman st, Flatbush. P. M. July 21, due Aug. 1, 1894, 5 %. 500

Weber, Christopher to Lewis P. Nostrand. South 5th st. P. M. July 31, 5 years, 5 %. 5,300

Weber, Lawrence A. to Effingham H. Nichols. Lots 174-178 block 4 map No. 1, Cowenhoven farm. July 22, 2 years, 5 %. See Conveys. 475

Webster, George A. to Thomas Brown. Windsor pl, s s, 79.10 w 8th av, 18x100. Aug. 5, 2 years. 1,500

Weis, Phillipp and Christine his wife to The German Savings Bank. McKibbin st, s s, 100 w Graham av, 25x100. Aug. 1, due Dec. 1, 1892, 5 %. 4,000

Weltman, Abraham to Semche Simon. Moore st. P. M. Sub. to mort. $7,000. July 31, installs. 3,500

White, Albert E. to Cornelius E. Donnellon. 2d st, s s, 100 w 8th av. P. M. July 29, demand. 11,191

Same to same. Same property. Building loan. July 29. 28,809

Wiarda, John C. to Ernest G. Stache. Greene st, n w cor Provost st, 150x100. July 1, 5 years. 8,000

Wienholz, Maria formerly Wrede widow to Matilda and Mary E. Calder. Clermont av, w s, 84.5 s Park av, 20x100. Aug. 1, 3 years, 5 %. 2,000

Williams, Thomas to Gardiner Van Nostrand exr. and trustee of John J. Van Nostrand. Strong pl. P. M. Aug. 1, 5 years, 5 %. 6,000

Wilmer, Lydia W. wife of John R. to The Williamsburgh Savings Bank. Bushwick av, n e s, 18.9 s e Bleecker st, 18.9x79.8x18.9x 80.2. Aug. 4, 1 year, 5 %. 1,250

Whiteman, Simon H. to Theresa Goodkind. Morrell st. P. M. July 29, 1 year. 500

Wilson, Simon C., Baldwins, L. I., to Augustus E. Kissam. Osborn st, n e cor Dumont av, 25x100. Aug. 3, 3 years. 3,000

Wills, Emily R. to The German Savings Bank, Brooklyn. Bedford av, s w s, 100 s e Rutledge st, 19x80. July 28, due Dec 1, 1892, 5 %. 4,000

Wingerath, William to Mary Strybing. 16th st, n s, 135.9 w 8th av, 19x100. July 31, 3 years. gold, 4,000

Wischerth, Joseph G. to Edward Hendrickson. Myrtle av. P. M. Aug. 3, due Aug. 1, 1893, 5 %. 1,350

Wittenfeld, Christian to William M. Gibson. Macon st, s s, 200 e Patchen av, 25x100. July 31, 1 year, 5 %. 250

Woodward, Henry E. to Henry W. Putnam. Lott av, Watkins st and Osborn st. P. M. July 29, 3 years 14,175

MORTGAGES----ASSIGNMENTS.

NEW YORK CITY.

JULY 31 TO AUG. 6—INCLUSIVE.

Abraham, Adelaide to Isaac Fromme. $3,000

Adler, Frederick J. and Jeannette, Brooklyn, to John J. Adler, Brooklyn nom

Appel, Emanuel to George W. Galinger. 2,512

Barnard, Henry to William N. Coler, Jr., Newark, N. J nom

Bearns, Joseph H., Brooklyn, to Joseph H. Bearns trustee Alexander M. Fischer. 53,000

Black, Alexander G to Loftin Love. nom

Balfour, John, Balburne, Scotland, to Sophia R. C. Furniss et al. trustees of Clementina Furniss. 13,000

Campbell, John V. to Joseph L. Buttenwieser. nom

Cohen, Samuel to Marcus Lederer. 5,950

Coogan, Teresa to Pasquale Caponigri. 3,000

Decker, John W. to R. Clarence Dorsett. 2 assigns. nom

Furniss, Sophia R. C. et al. trustees of Clementina Furniss to The Title Guarantee and Trust Co. 13,153

Friedman, Barnett and Samuel Harris to Samuel Weil. 1,500

Forner, Henry C., Philadelphia, to John A. Bickel, Philadelphia. 2,500

Gluck, Ignatz to Joseph Larchan. 2,000

Goldberg, Nathan M. to Paulina Ryshpan. 600

Guyer, Louise M., otherwise Senouille, Hoboken, N. J., to Celestine Progler. 5,000

Gordon, Katie admrx. Stephen T. Gordon to Thomas K. Egbert. 8,000

Goble, Joseph F. and ano. exrs. and trustees George S. Goble to Joseph F. Goble guard. of Addison S Goble. 6,050

Gernshym, Henry and Charles Rosenberg to Barbara Rosenberg. 3,000

German-American Real Estate Title Guarantee Co. to Margaretha Hoffmann. 12,500

Gray, James F. to The Murray Hill Bank. nom

Goldstein, William H. et al. exrs. Sophie Goldstein to Jennie wife of William H. Goldstein. 5,000

Hodes, Morris and Gabriel S. Lavendol to Nellie C. Van Reypen. 1,000

Harison, Richard M., Astoria, L. I., to Irving Grinnell et al. trustees Gardiner G. Howland dec'd. 14,500

Hassett, Edmund J. to James F. Hassett. 1,200

Hay, George W. admr. George Hay to Charles E. Allen. 100

Hardwood Decorative Co. to John E. Coar. nom

Same to Charles S. Bardwell, Sumers E. and Charles N. Robinson, Minneapolis, Minn. 2,000

Same to same. 5,879

Hyatt, George E., Brooklyn, to Franklin Brush. nom

Hyatt, George E. to Henry W. Ford trustee Augustus H. Ward dec'd. 5 assigns. nom

Jencks, Francis M. to The St. Luke's Home for Indigent Christian Females. nom

Kittel, Joseph J. to William S. Hawkins. 2,000

Lippe, Joseph F. to Edward Schweyer. 3,000

Lazarus, Amelia B. et al. exrs. Jacob H. Lazarus to Amelia B. Lazarus. nom

Lazarus, Jacob H. to Sophia Tobias 17,500

Loew, Sarah L. to Charles R. Parfitt, Stamford, Conn. 2,000

Manning, William D. to William Hall's Sons. nom

Middlebrook, Frederic J., Brooklyn, to Thomas C. T. Crain as Chamberlain of the City of New York 8,040

Same to same. 9,081

Same to same. 14,126

McDowell, Hugh and John C. Heney to May G. Melius. 3,500

Marshall, Abby S. wife of Charles C. formerly Story to Ursula Story, Bayonne, N. J. 10,000

Myers, Lewis to Rebecca Zemansky. 4,000

New, Tobias, Brooklyn, to Horace G. Wood. nom

Nichols, Adelbert S. to Joseph M. De Veau. 800

Newman, Jacob M. to William Hall's Sons. nom

Newburgh Savings Bank to Francis M. Jencks. 10,000

Oliver, Alfred C. to John E. Coar. nom

Progler, Celestine, Hoboken, N. J., to Louise M. Guyer. consid. omitted

Phillips, Samuel to Babette Cohen. 5,000

Rusch, Cecile trustee of Cecile Genton to Caroline E. Hughes, Brooklyn. 9,000

Reynolds, G. Emily, Piermont, N. Y., to Augustus T. Gillender committee Alice F. M. Wood. 5,039

Ruff, August to Marx Reiss. 4,000

Russ, Edward admr. John Guyer to Celestine Progler, Hoboken, N. J. consid. omitted

Sheldon, George R. to Abraham Stern and Ascher Weinstein. 20,000

Sire, Meyer L. to Edward F. Browning. 8,000

Sullivan, John, Mt. Vernon, N. Y., to William B. Cook, Morris County, N. J. 2,400

Saberski, Rosa to Sarah Saberski and Aaron Green. 2,000

Steinhardt, Rosalie to Russell Murray. nom

Taylor, Henry A. C., Newport, R. I., to Wesley G. Lyon trustee Gilbert S. Lyon dec'd. 9,910

Thurston, William R. surviving trustee Lindley Murray dec'd to William R. Thurston et al. trustees Lindley Murray dec'd. nom

The Equitable Life Assurance Society of the U. S. to Albert H. Little. nom

The N. Y. Infirmary for Women and Children to the Orphan Asylum Society, City N. Y. 9,000

Same to same. 8,097

The Manhattan Life Ins. Co. to Title Guarantee and Trust Co. 6,000

Tobias, Sophia to Amelia B. Lazarus. 17,500

Title Guarantee and Trust Co. to John H. Linsly and Otis W. Booth exrs. and trustees of Jared Linsly. 15,000

Title Guarantee and Trust Co. to The Excelsior Savings Bank. 15,000

Same to Alexander Munn guard. of Helen L., Frederick L. and Roger H. Lutz. 12,000

Title Guarantee and Trust Co. to Sarah A. Taylor. 4,000

Same to Charles R. Henderson exr. John C. Henderson. 5,500

Title Guarantee and Trust Co. to Sara Welt. 5,500

White, William C. to Myer Hellman. 2 assigns., each $3,000. 6,000

Wright, Sarah K. to Mary Bedford, Brooklyn. 5,061

Wolff, Lee to William C. White. 2 assigns., each $3,000. 6,000

Wood, Horace G., Brooklyn, to Mary A. Scott. 2,200

Weil, Jonas and Bernhard Mayer to Gustave Jacobs. 2,652

Wrede, Andreas to John Ernst. 517

Zeller, Margaretha to Maria Fuehrer. nom

KINGS COUNTY.

JULY 30 TO AUGUST 5—INCLUSIVE.

Bowers, Mary L., South Evanston, Ill., to George W. Brush. nom

Burroughs, William H. to Hamilton Trust Co. $2,000

Brown, Frank F. to Jeremiah E. Tracy. 21,000

Budlong, Morris M. to Julia M. Budlong, guard. Robert H. Hazeltine. 1,000

Burke, Bridget to Theodore E. Green and ano. exrs. William Green. 2,900

Carpenter, James O. to William H. Lyon. 800

Cook, Mary E., Newtown, L. I., to J. C. & H. C Smith & Koepke. nom

Daley, Joseph B. to William L. Bond. 2,000

Devoe, Jasper, Greenburg, N. Y., to George H. Walker, Jr., New York. 200

Dixon, William H. to Charles H. Bedell, Newtown, L. I. 3,456

Dunn, Harriet E. to Julia A. Schenck. 2,000

Fuehrer, Maria widow to Hartmann F. Gundrum. 2,033

Gillespie, Earl A., Woodhaven, L. I., to The Bedford Bank. 1,000

Germania Savings Bank, Kings County, to Louise wife of John Leippert. nom

Hart, John F. to Asa W. Parker, Hempstead, L. I. 2,000

Hicks, Caroline to Allen H. Baxter. 2,000

Hurlburt, Lawrence to Ferdinand B. Hanck or Hauck. 900

Henni, John to Mary Vanderveer. 4,000

Harrison, Ann to William E. Philips. consid. omitted

Jackson, William H. to James Bolton. 275

Same to same. 100

Same to same. 345

Johnson, Ephraim admr. Cornelius L. Johnson to Ephraim Johnson. 15,167

Same to Caroline A. wife of Frank B. Smith. 4,017

Same to Lizzie J. wife of Alfred Hodges. 4,417

Same to Grace M. Johnson. 519

Same to same. 1,699

Kings County Trust Co. to Edwin O. Phelps. consid. omitted

Klots, John T. exr., &c., John Devoe to Willard S. Watson. nom

Klots, Walter J. to Alexander Underhill. 1,000

Langlos, Heinrich to Henry Loeffler. 2,300

Law, Edwin C. to Howard M. Smith. 5,000

Lamb, James W. and Albert J. to James W. Lamb. 1,900

Linton, Edward F. to John Beach. 1,070

Lovell, H. A. to Gage & Wallace. nom

La Roche, William J. to William F. Sheridan. 1,000

Michel, David to Leopold Michel. nom

Maguire, Charles E. to William J. Kay. 500

McColloch, John to Albert H. W. Van Sielen. 450

Murphy, Henry E. to James Jack. 2,000

Nassau Trust Co., Brooklyn, to John W. Phelps. 15,000

New York Infirmary for Women and Children to John T. Willets treas. of the Endowment Fund of the Schofield Normal and Industrial School of Aiken, S. C. 7,000

O'Connor, John to John Connor, Jr. 4,000

Otten, Luer and George to Germania Savings Bank, Kings County. 20,000

Perigord, Adele de T. Duchesse de Dino to Frederick Taiber. 1,029

Powell, Sarah H. to Joseph T. Willets trustee Maria M. Hobby dec'd. 5,500

Puels, Joseph P. to Kings Co. Trust Co. 25,000

Pullman, John to Hamilton Trust Co. 10,000

Rehout, Mary to Bertha Rodding. 2,000

Rodding, Bertha to H. Koehler & Co. 2,000

Roth, Henry to John L. Gaus. 1,500

Reynolds, Charles H. to Alexander Underhill, Jr. 1,000

Schimmel, Anton to The Orphan Home. 3,800

Title Guarantee and Trust Co. to Emma Savage. 1,200

Same to George S. Ingraham. 4,500

Same to Mary J. Brunsen. 1,000

Same to Dorothee Sander. 2,000

Same to William E. Selpho. 2,500

Same to Walter Thackray. 1,000

Same to Mary J. Brunsen. 3,500

Same to same. 2,500

Same to same. 3,500

Same to Florence M. Larcomb. 3,000

Same to The Riverhead Savings Bank. 2,000

Same to Lucy P. Le Brun. 4,[illegible]0

Same to same. 6,500

Same to Charles R. Harrington et al. trustees David Carll. 2,500

Same to same. 2,500

Same to Jeanette Henry. 3,000

Tunis, Stephen W. to Carrie H. McCormick, Hamilton, N. J. nom

Tracy, Jeremiah E., Plainfield, N. J., to John B. Hagenbuchle. 21,000

Watson, Ann F. admrx. of William W. Watson to James Watson. 3 assigns. nom

Same to Sarah I. Watson. nom

Same to Ann F. Watson. nom

Watson, Willard S. to John T. Klots exr. and trustee John Devoe. 9,000

Same to Phebe E. Leverich extrx. Augustus A. Leverich. 2,000

Wilder, Elizabeth to Robert Smith. 1,800

Zirnisky, Joseph to Moritz Scharfman and Abraham J. Littmann. 1,300

JUDGMENTS.

In these lists of judgments the names alphabetically arranged, and which are first on each line, are those of the judgment debtor. The letter (D) means judgment for deficiency (*) means not summoned. (†) signifies that the first name is fictitious, real name being unknown. Judgments entered during the week, and satisfied before day of publication, do not appear in this column, but in list of Satisfied Judgments

NEW YORK CITY.

August

4 Ahrens, Henry—Metropolitan Telephone and Telegraph Co. $17 62

4 Aronsen, Alexander—Moses Shlanowsky 531 05

4 Adam, James A / Adam, Angelo } Patrick Cassidy 512 44

5 Appleton, Samuel E—Allen Fitch 365 02

5 Ainslie, George H—C K Hammitt 33 29

6 Antonio, Jonnelli—Gottlieb Schnabel 110 00

3 Boylan, Michael J—A C Haynes 1,714 24

3 Bencke, John—James Dwyer 85 82

4 Benke, John—P H Siebern 837 86

4 Bensel, Rebecca—Richard Grant Co 194 99

4 Bonnell, John Harper—Chatham Nat Bank 2,284 10

4 Beers, John D—Henry Leute 427 15

4 Biggs, Edward M—G A Radtke 87 45

4 Burr, William H—Gustav Hoeltze 139 14

5 Bene, Lizzie—George Quimby, exr 535 28

5 Begley, Alexander—O'Reilly, Skelly & Fogarty Co 99 77

5†Bodine, Thomas C—G O Walbridge 100 93

5 Barclay, Annie—James Hawthorne 32 50

6 Berrian, William H—John Lees 207 90

6 Brennan, Thomas J—Empire State Brewing Co 81 17

7*Bailey, Harry B—Alice J Williams, trustee 1 083 50

7 Banks, Thomas W—J G Van Camp 83 79

7 Bonnell, John Harper—Chatham Nat Bank 1,075 62

7 Bloch, Morris—Michael Jackson 28 00

7 Bennett, Samuel T / Bennett, Celiant } William Berger. 238 95

7 Block, Hugo—Herman Rosenberg 1,856 07

7 Barratt, George—Patterson Bros 495 32

7 Bernard, Joseph—C W Dorn 31 90

7 Burns, Michael—Henry Campbell, assignee 88 97

1 Colvin, William P—Maurice Somborn 124 10

1 Conkling, John B—Thomas Vernon 5,170 58

1 Cohn, Bernard—W R Potts 276 16

4 Christie, William—Manhattan Brass Co 33 12

4 Carpenter, Robert B—G. W. McLean, recvr 136 83

4 Campbell, Barney J—Fitzgerald Brewing Co 212 65

4 Crosher, James—G W M Reed Bitter Co 95 03

5 Cohen, Bernhardt—Daniel Katz 191 26

5 Charlier, Elie S—Clarence McKim 420 86

5 the same—the same 1,003 83

5 Copp, Richard—L. S. Tenney 167 50

6 Church, Richard—Charles McBurney 181 59

6 Cox, Charles P—Abraham Philips 212 22

6 Curtiss, William H—W. H. H. Miller 1,538 07

6 Clearwater, Edward—J. L. Morgan 623 95

6 Carle, Severyn B—Campbell Printing Press and Mfg. Co. 70 53

6 Campbell, John—Nathaniel Waterbury 250 35

6 Costello, John C—Rose M. Hughes 412 84

6 Chapman, George D, as recvr—Railroad Equipment Co 361 00

the same——the same 285 00

the same——the same 266 00

the same——the same costs 706 70

6 the same——the same 1,650 00

7 Clark, Robert—James Biglen 256 92

7 Cooney, Frank J; Cooney, Michael J } Bernard Cahn 573 87

7 Crawford, Robert J—Abraham Steers 120 21

1 Decker, Adolphus M—A J Hood 181 05

3 Dollaway, Alvah J—Mt Morris Electric Light Co 656 30

4 Davis, John C—W J Eaton 230 55

4 De Man, William—Mary Samuels 125 00

4 †De Wint, Frederick A; †De Wint, Elizabeth C } Joseph Beck 246 91

4 Danziger, Edward—Central Stamping Co 300 00

4 Dodson, E Newton—Campbell Printing Press & Mfg Co 239 46

4*Doe, John—E S Jaffray 3,966 79

5 Deyfuss, Bernard—Leopold Ullman 2,617 86

5 the same——E C Philbrick 1,622 62

5 Day, Peter S—Mary L Day 279 85

6 Devlin, James; Dearing, Albert G } C N Lawson 185 88

6 Dick, George N—S T Birdsall 153 80

6 Delabarre, Elizabeth—Peter McChesney 52 20

6 Devlin, William P—W H Higgins 147 50

7 Dolan, Hugh—James Biglen 256 92

7 Dunn, James—W M Van Lier 71 59

7 Davis, Abraham—Philip Wagner 186 63

5 Everett, Charles E—Peter Lang 769 92

6 Erkes, Max—Jacob Ruppert 260 11

6*Engel, Leopold—Adolph Ziegler 211 17

3 Fischman, Joseph—Louis Rosen 75 50

3 Fiske, Edgar A—August Muller 144 62

4 Fay, Anna B—W J Eaton 230 55

4 Finelite, Abraham—George Munro 67 00

4 Fagan, James—Bethel Chair Co 141 09

4 Fontaine, Allen—G A Radtke 87 45

4†Friedland, Abraham S—Moses Shlanowsky 531 05

4 Fusco, Guiseppe—Patrick Cassidy 512 44

4 Farley, Thomas H—Riverside Bank 73 47

5 Flynn, Peter H—G W Venable 269 51

5 Foster, Henry C—Long Branch Banking Co 1,448 89

6 Fash, Mary C—P H Monaghan 259 50

6*Foder, Sigmund—Adolph Ziegler 211 17

7†Frank, Bernard A—David Hochner 94 50

7 *Freeman, Alfred A; Freeman, Marcus L } Garfield Nat Bank 2,136 02

1 Grinspan, Abraham—Bernhard Weinberger 1,418 87

3 Gray, Charles E—Lloyd Milnor 168 85

4 Gross, Anthony; Gross, James } Bethel Chair Co 141 09

4 Gross, Philip—L S Keller 180 30

5 Glover, John M—Zerlina Rosenfield 625 33

6 Goldsmith, Adolph—G S Van Hoesen, as late Sheriff of Cortland Co, N Y 1,433 85

7 Goerlitz, Philip—East River Lead Co 524 70

7 Grinspan, Abraham—Jacob Levy 27 50

7 Guastavino, Raphael—Ludwig Baumann 78 79

1†Heilpen, George—Harris Silberman 96 12

1 Haight, Ellen Jane Harper—Chatham Nat Bank 2,234 10

1 Hirsch, Albert—Bank of New Hanover, of Wilmington, N C 2,651 06

3 Hausmann, Frederick—E C Korner 497 97

3 Hauf, Anna—Philip Stein 250 08

4 Hart, Gustavus—W R Thomas 76 20

4 Horton, Charles G—T H McNamee 192 94

4 Henningsen, Jacob—William Schade 29 69

4 Hart, Alexander—Western Nat Bank 1,172 02

4 Haynes, Ella—George Mason 97 46

4 Harper, William D—Western Nat Bank 624 08

4 Horwitz, Philip—Michael Rosencranz 325 74

4*Humphries, John—W B Weir 111 87

5 Haring, Sarah B—Margaret R Quackenbos 271 74

6 Haaga, Joseph—Barbara Walther 914 94

6 Haas, Christian—M B Edinger 522 22

6 Heumann, John—Louis Goldsticker 156 00

6 Hodes, Simon—V Loewers Gambrinus Brewery Co 169 05

6†Hallett, George G—G H Felt 259 50

6 Hays, George F—D S Wells 2,505 42

6 Howell, Eugene N—E R Ladew 19,448 00

6 Herzog, Sigmund—Carl Klemm 7,420 50

6 Hass, Frank X—J F Wittemann 154 64

6 Hahn, Charles—G B Morrell 160 97

6 Haughey, Edward—Empire State Brewing Co 80 22

7 Hallet, Granville G—Western Nat Bank 221 71

7 Hamilton, Walter—Harriet B Fisk 89 63

7 Haas, Leonard J—Philip Wagner 185 12

7 Haut, John—Henry Seelig 260 75

7 Henman, John—Henry McShane Co (Lim) 106 68

7 Huber, John—J A Roth 111 61

7 Hays, Simon; Hays, Maurice S; Hays, Henry S } Abraham Rosenberg 739 97

7 the same——the same 731 94

7 Hofelfinger, John—J P Windolph 586 16

7*Haight, Effingham C—Garfield Nat Bank 2,136 02

7 Hewlett, Frederick—Hiram Snyder, assignee 360 72

7 Hutchison, Marcus——the same 274 38

5 Inness, Frederick A—J H Foote 17 63

7 Irons, James R—Thomas Clark 91 50

7 the same——Frederick Smart 90 75

7 the same——John Laubinger 91 45

3 Jacobowsky, Louis—Tradesmen's Nat Bank 1,007 78

4 Jackson, Walter M—W B Baldwin 5,190 64

7 Jonnelli, Antonio—Gotlieb Schnabel 110 00

3 Katzenberg, Julius—H H Salmon, exr. (D) 6,135 32

3 Kelly, James E, assignee William L Lowden, Jr, and Archibald Rutherford—Mutual Bank costs 367 72

3 Kiefer, Christian—David Greenfield 207 40

4 Kayser, Frederick K—Henry Leute 427 15

4 Kane, James—Isidor Hirsch 145 42

5 Kirschbaum, George; Kirschbaum, Max } Josephine F Lindenstein 117 64

5 Kelly, Frank—J H Luken 122 50

6 Kennell, Joseph A—Warren Scarborough 82 50

6 Kellogg, George A—T H Sheldon 145 92

6 Kissling, August—W M Van Lier 70 99

7 Kenyon, A C, Jr—New Home Sewing Machine Co 533 98

7 Koper, Henry—Garfield Nat Bank 2,136 02

1 Lawrence, Mary J—E D Griggs 266 10

3 Lind, James—Robert Main 230 03

3 Lett, William F, Jr; Lett, Frederick R } Serafin Sanchez 526 46

Lehmann, Charles—Herman Baetjer 851 03

3 the same——the same 641 78

4 Leshnovner, Abraham; Leshnovner, Elias } Nathan Sommer 172 50

4 Lynch, Michael—M F Phelan 228 02

4 Lippmann, Israel—Joseph Batt 302 08

4 Loughlin, George—William Wuerz 40 00

5 Lynch, James—Charles Perceval 132 80

Lancaster, James H—E C Stout 29 42

5 Lees, Samuel—C B Hewitt 207 19

5 Luce, Clarence S—G R Brown 174 01

6 Leeper, James—John Fyfe 62 50

6 Lustig, Arnold—G S Van Hoesen, as late Sheriff of Cortland County, N Y 1,433 85

6 Lake, James R S—H A Ehrmann 231 91

6 Lehmaier, Ludwig—Carl Klemm 7,420 50

7 Luce, Clarence S—H C Meyer 45 99

7 Lord, John G—J G Van Camp 83 79

7 Lees, Samuel—Enterprise Mfg Co of Pa 202 30

7 Lindheim, Minnie—Herman Rosenberg 1,856 07

7 Lowther, Sarah E; Lowther, John R } Chemical Nat Bank 679 77

1 Meuer, Frank—Hirsch Feldstein 150 62

1 Miller, Robert H—Chatham Nat Bank 641 43

3 Myers, Sinclair—N J Haines 395 68

3 Muller, Conrad, Jr—Philip Stein 250 08

3 Martin, Patrick—August Muller 71 62

3 Myers, Sinclair—Murray Hill Bank 247 04

3 Meyer, Siegmund T; Meyer, Arthur L } W H Brandt 436 81

4 Max, Margowski—George Munroe 67 00

4 Macnaughtan, Francis J—Samuel Cocking 214 97

4 Meyer, Arthur L; Meyer, Siegmund T } George Mackenzie 229 37

4 Murray, Thomas—J A Roebling's Sons Co 1,199 99

4 Moran, P—T L Arthur 101 50

5 Meyer, Siegmund T; Meyer, Arthur L } G W Tice 1,511 56

5 Moore, Charles V—F S Naylor 20,658 96

6 Milair, Gustave A J—Brett Lithographing Co 322 03

6 MacFarlan, Hamilton—G F Swift 179 30

7 Manson, Sinclair—Saugatuck Iron Works Co 161 43

7 Morrison, Daniel—John Boland 88 50

7 Maier, Elio—Alois Kohn 221 32

7 Miller, Isaac—T C Campbell 841 52

3 McGuire, John J—P & W Ebling Brewing Co 351 00

4 Macnaughtan, Francis J—Samuel Cocking 214 97

4 McDermott, Patrick J—M R Cook 344 00

4 McDonald, Theodore F—A H Allen 1,431 76

5 McGivney, Owen—Riverside Bank 73 47

6 McGilliwie, Alexander—W J Quinlan trustee 149 10

6 MacFarlan, Hamilton—G F Swift 179 30

7 McLean, Cornelius—John Gillies, exr. 137 16

7 McDougall, Allan S—F W Nostrand 85 97

4 Nebb, John—Henry Herrmann 237 00

1 O'Kane, James—R E Thibaut 98 00

4 O'Connor, John—Patrick Cassidy 555 28

5 Onderdonk, William M—F S Naylor 20,658 96

5 Osborn, Robert A—Albert Barnes 297 36

6 *O'Keefe, Jeremiah; O'Keefe, Michael } W. R. Waters 125 01

6 O'Conner, John J—Empire State Brewing Co 181 21

7 O'Connor, John—Philip Smith 147 47

1†Philips, Joseph—Joseph Kandel 84 69

5 Powers, Robert C—William Delamater 110 56

5 Parmer, Joseph—D. H. Roberts 590 41

6 Parke, Henry C; Parke, A. J } Second Nat. Bank 801 80

6 Phillips, Frederick—Charles Parrish 501 41

6 Phillips, Frederick; *Phillips, Walter C } R. H. Williams 1,039 04

6 Pincus, Sam—Samuel Isaacs costs 64 19

6 Pini, Carlos—Oscar Huttlinger 80 07

6 Phillips, Frederick; Phillips, Walter E } Charles Parrish 529 75

7 Pine, Charles H—James Whiteside 99 57

3 Reilly, Joseph B—N J Haines 395 68

4 Reinheimer, Edward—L S Keller 422 96

4 Richenstein, William—Campbell Printing Press and Mfg Co 239 46

4 Reid, David—W B Weir 111 87

5 *Roff, Bela B; Roff, Henry R } Manhattan Brass Co 129 07

6 Rosenbaum, Joseph—Henry Liepmann 153 61

6 Ruser, Henry—Union Distilling Co 312 69

6 Raduziner, Adolph—Adolph Zieger 211 17

7 Reynolds, Hayden P—August Marschall 405 65

7 Risley, Joseph H—Chemical Nat Bank 577 19

7 Rissinger, John—Rudolph Bendler 37 00

1†Steinmetz, William R—George Klingmann 18 75

1 Sutherland, William—C F Risley Co 35 37

1 Sheridan, Frank P—T S Atwater 28 50

1 Schilt, Ike F—Henry Liepmann 81 12

3 Stephens, Richard W—A C Haynes 1,714 24

3 the same——Thomas Vernon 5,231 47

3 Sterner, Winfield S—Michael Stachelberg 206 59

3 the same——T B Main 323 34

3†Swenson, Edward—Mt Morris Electric Light Co 80 64

3*Storey, Edwin A—W S Hill 221 38

3*Scott, George H—Murray Hill Bank 247 04

3 Saxe, Simon P—J S Pinchbeck 128 62

4 Schneider, Louis H—D P Morse 3,868 05

4 the same——Office Specialty Mfg Co 70 52

4 Schwab, Nathan—Gorham Mfg Co 135 00

4 Strauch, Christian—Knickerbocker Brewing Co 104 87

4 Sotscheck, Carl—Fr Beck & Co 288 70

4 Sturtevant, William Hatch—Equitable Life Assurance Society (D) 31,420 66

4 Straus, Louis—Frederick Muller 10,186 75

4 the same——William Kossler 7,201 62

4 Stiles, Kimball H—C M Barstow 237 90

4 Stollmack, Solomon—Michael Rosencranz 325 74

5 Summerhays, Charles K—Edison General Electric Co 1,195 73

5 Sommer, Moritz—Joseph Wild 228 38

5 Sreiber, Morris—Moses Mendelsohn 575 68

5 Schäfuss, George C—Robert Stahl 1,471 39

5 Stark, Joseph—G R Brown 114 32

5 Sagel, Conrad—A N Barker 399 94

5*Schmidt, Edmund P—Albert Barnes 297 36

5 Strauss, Julia—Alfred Salomon costs 63 88

5 Stapleton, Thomas; Stapleton, Joseph F } John Murray 1,345 33

6 Scott, James T—G S Van Hoesen 1,433 85

6 Sotscheck, Carl—J A Stock 246 56

6 Strait, Ebenzer S—T E Greacen 175 01

6 Stetson, Alexander M—Thomas Lidgerwood 97 95

6 Stevenson, James—Gustave Daniel 32 26

6 Stevens, Laura—W H Higgins 281 10

6 *Stern, Max; *Stern, Bachel } Adolph Zeiger 211 17

7 Sloman, Selim—Meyer Mamlock 2,587 20

7 Struthers, Robert S—G D Whitehead 41 50

7 Scanlon, Thomas E—T J Carroll 31 00

3 Smith, Richard W—August Kramer 29 50

4 Smith, Franklin H—G F Perkins 1,555 75

6 Smith, Matthew—Solomon Pritz 337 00

6 Smith, James M—Frederick Hillier 83 88

7 Smith, John—W E Stewart 1,496 00

1 Joseph B Tiffany & Co—Thomas Strahan & Co 241 50

1 The Jenness Miller Publishing Co—Eugene Higgins 337 59

1 The Lexington Improvement Co—W R Potts, exr 276 16

3 Loudon Toilet Bazaar Co—H A Dickie 680 47

3 Joseph B Tiffany & Co—W T Merserau 285 25

3 the same——E H Faulkner 173 00

3 the same——J H C Nevins 146 00

3 The European Importing & Grocery Co—C F Coffin 98 53

3 London Toilet Bazaar Co—W A Cole 529 85

4 Memphis, Little Rock & Indian Territory R R Co—Percival Roberts 10,110 87

4 the same——the same 10,124 20

4 Bank of North America—Herman Aaron, assignee 560 48

4 Joseph B Tiffany & Co—J M Constable 632 05

4 The Mayor, Aldermen, &c—Henry McDonough 25 84

4 J H Bonnell & Co (Lim)—Western Nat Bank 624 08

4 Rapid Printing Co—Carsten Offerman 121 43

4 London Toilet Bazar Co—J W Thompson 3,163 90

4 J Parker Read Co—Samuel Lees 2,036 23

4 The Mayor, Aldermen, &c—M L Carroll 85,234 89

4 the same——Walter Langdon 60,051 36

5 The Lexington Improvement Co—G W Tice 1,511 56

5 the same——the same 486 36

5 The Stephany Perfume Co—George Lueders 1,783 19

5 The Memphis, Little Rock & Indian Territory R R Co—Zug & Co (Lim) 7,591 19

5 The Metropolitan Elevated Railway Co; The N Y Elevated R R Co; The Manhattan Railway Co } Annie Steinhardt 771 74

5 The J J Nichols Mfg Co—Manhattan Brass Co 183 74

5 The Mirror Lake Hotel and Improvement Co—Theodore Schmalholz 1,215 43

5 Ackerly & Gerard Co—C E Pell 1,072 89

5 J Parker Read Co—Manhattan Watch Co 461 14

6 The N Y Cordage Co—Lindley Murray 11,627 63

6 The Excelsior Dynamite Co—Fred Longway 146 56

6 The Saugatuck Iron Works Co—G H Felt 259 50

6 Rapid Printing Co—E C Eustace..... 168 95
The Central Construction Co—Railroad Equipment Co............ 361 00
6 the same—the same.............. 285 00
6 the same—the same............ 266 00
6 the same—the same............1,650 00
6 the same—the same........costs 760 70
6 The Lackawanna & South Western R R Co—Railroad Equipment Co.costs 760 70
6 the same—the same............ 988 50
6 National Patent Co—Gustav Daniel... 66 75
6 J Parker Read Co—Bertha Laws...... 363 00
7 Belford Co—Adams & Bishop Co..... 558 30
7 The Brooklyn Cross Town R R Co—Rachel Pollock. ....costs 79 13
7 The Hudson River Boot and Shoe Mfg Co—E R Ladew..............17,928 21
7 The Mayor, Aldermen, &c—G L Green.............................. 103 84
7 The European-American Supply Co—Morton Decker..................... 146 79
3 Toucey, Donald, assignee Guy C Hotchkiss, Field & Co—Baltimore & Ohio R R Co..................costs 584 01
3 Tracy, Gurdon—Michael Stachelberg. 206 59
3 the same—T B Main.......... 323 34
3 Taylor, Thomas—L W Mack......... 87 07
4 Townsend, William A—C F Loutrel..21,845 93
5 Tiernan, Hugh P—Edgar Wright.... 328 69
7 Turner, William H—Joseph Josephson.................................. 73 36
5 Vagt, Charles F / Vagt, Charles J H } Burroughs & Mountford Co.. 189 35
6 Vernam, Remington—William Noe. 476 21
7 Van Riper, Romaine—Henry Heywood 465 62
1 Wheeler, Thomas M—Francis Gooldy 773 85
1†Woods, W D—Second Nat Bank... .. 773 68
3 Wyckoff, Jacob F—F A Palmer......1,263 01
3 Whiting, Holland S—B F Tracy.... 74 01
3 Wilson, Lucius E—W S Hill. 221 38
3 Wasbauer, Alexander—S J Weaver.. 228 50
4 Weinstock, Leo—Josephine F Lindenstein.................................. 165 97
4 Wilkes, George / Wilkes, Lizzie T } George Mackenzie 229 37
4 Walsh, James—Isidore Hirsch... .... 145 43
4 Wallis, William — Knickerbocker Brewing Co................ .... 159 87
4 the same—the same............ 156 21
4 Wilson, William J—E S Jaffray.....3,966 79
5 Walter, Alexander A—R T Wilson.. 67 50
5 Walsh, John F—William Delamater. 110 56
6 Wormser, Leo—G S Van Hoesen.....1,453 85
6 Wurz, Charles—C A Burgess........1,224 00
7 Weaver, William W—Robert Currie.. 454 29
7 Walford, Robert M G—Alice J Williams, trustee..........................1,083 59

KINGS COUNTY.

July and August

1 Bormann, Louis—F Hafke..........$465 00
1 Borowski, Max T—G Griffin......... 82 30
4 Beatty, Edmond—H Suden........... 43 60
4 Boettcher, Walter F—Edison Electric Illuminating Co....................... 71 52
4 Briody, Patrick N—M Cullen......... 100 45
5 Battermann, George E—J Engel.... 124 79
6 Brice, William—W Massey B Co..... 68 24
31 Connolly, Joseph—I Weissenhorn.... 56 60
1 Clark, Henry F—Agnes L Yenin..... 800 81
4 Colyer, Joseph H—W Kenny 95 17
6 Carroll, John J / Carroll, David F } J Gage........... 146 35
5 De Man, William—Mary Samuels.... 125 00
1 Feverty, E—Broadway Bank of Brooklyn.............................. 347 52
3 Frazer, Alexander—G Johnson.......1,514 87
5 Fagan, James—Bethel Chair Co....... 141 09
6 Fowler, Warren C—M Rofrano...... 214 60
1 Good, Samuel R—M Gallagher....... 110 35
1 Garcia, John J—R C Williams....... 94 50
1 the same—S J Berry.......... 40 81
5 Gross, Anthony / Gross, James } Bethel Chair Co.... 141 09
5 Garczynski, Caroline R—G F Gilman. err..................................8,284 78
5 Gross, Anthony / Gross, James } Bethel Chair Co.... 141 09
5 Garczynski, Catharine R—G F Gilman..................................8,284 78
1 Hart, Alexander R—Chatham Nat Bank.................................. 794 44
1 Hill, Charles E—E W Dunston....... 125 83
4 Hausmann, Frederick—E C Rorner... 497 97
5 Haak, Frederick—J B Bowden....... 722 65
6 Harvey, Mary J—R A Hastings...... 25 80
6 Hunger, Theodore / Hunger, Pauline } Gerrin, Payson & Co............ 46 06
4 Irwin, George—M Hood............... 77 60
31 Johnson, August—F Mittnight....... 33 08
3 Johnson, William—L Rasch.......... 58 39
3 the same—H Arnold........... 21 14
4 Jackson, Walter M—W B Baldwin..5,190 64
30 Kindleman, Frank—A C Bechstein.. 124 71
31 Krey, George / Krey, Adam } C Schussner 108 42
4 Kyle, Peter Y—M Rofrano....... ... 167 97
5 Keeling, Philip—C Froeb............ 98 59
6 Krumm, Charles—Leibinger & Oehm B Co.................................. 96 44
31 Lott, Albert—J Z Lott............. 223 47
1 Lett, William F—H W Haas... ..... 315 37
5 Landrock, John G—N Y Life Ins Co. 105 99
5 Leverich, Henry M—Eaton, Cole & Burnham.............................. 469 62
5 Lynch, James—C Percival........... 132 80
5 Linde, Amelia—C Froeb............. 98 59
5 Lynch, James—C Percival........... 132 80
5 Linde, Amelia—C Froeb............. 98 59
6†Lowenstein, "Benjamin"—Manhattan Shoe Co............................. 54 10
31 McMullen, Archibald C—M Davis... 107 93
31 Meyer, George and Gesene—J C Crevling.............................. 161 50
1 Meyer, Gesine—W B A Jurgens...... 391 01
4 Marquardt, Jacob—S Liebmann's Sons.............................. 307 88
5 Manning, James J—S Streit......... 142 23
5 Milair, Gustav A J—Brett Lithographing Co......................... 832 03
5 Maroney, Michael—J Andrews....... 50 25
5 McDermott, Patrick J—M B Cook.... 244 10
5 McNamara, Daniel—R J Galligan....1,056 44
6 Moll, William A—B Moore & Co.....1,623 05
6 Minnis, William H—O Goerke... .... 114 02
6 McGilluire, Alexander L—W J Quinlan.................................. 149 10
30 Nolan, Thomas—T Tracy........... 62 56
1 Newton, Henry A—J P Tuttle....... 119 85
31 O'Brien, Daniel—I Weissenborn..... 123 60
1 O'Connor, Margaret—P Heffernan.... 23 10
31 Pendergast, George F—B S Johnson.. 485 66
5 Pearce, John—Eaton, Cole & Burnham.................................. 469 62
5 Pearson, Eugene—S B Solomon 841 40
1 Roth, Martin—S R Ten Eyck........ 113 45
1 Roth, Martin—W Grandman......... 113 45
3 Rosse, Louis / Rosse, Auguste } W Ulmer........... 264 12
3 Rosse, Louis / Rosse, Augusta } W Ulmer 264 12
5 Rogers, Joseph C—T E Quion........ 171 69
5 the same—the same............ 47 32
30 Smith, Clarence A, Mfg Co—White, Potter & Paige 155 90
30 Stout, Charles S—G Covert.......... 241 76
31 Schlamovitz, David—E Wallace..... 474 15
31 Stilson, Samuel J—A Reimer......... 764 74
31 Schlamovitz, David—D P Morse..... 163 03
3 Schneider, Louis H—D P Morse......3,808 05
3 Smith, Richard W—A Kramer...... 29 50
4 Schuck, Philip, Jr—M D Stern....... 84 52
5 Simmons, James F—N Y Life Ins Co. 94 93
5 Scott, Charles B—S B Solomon....... 841 40
6 Sheldon, Cevedra B—C J Ryder..... 95 78
31 The admr, &c, Adam Krey—C Schlussner.............................. 108 42
4 Tragman, Deitrick—H Suden........ 48 60
4 Turner, William C—M Rofrano...... 107 97
5 The Fred Hower Brewing Co (Lim)—M O'Keffee.......................21,498 84
5 The Hazzard Gold Mining Co—W E Philips.............................43,946 92
30 Van Zandt, Charles E—F W Myers.. 173 48
30 Warren, Thomas E—M De Mello..... 243 75
31 Weiland, Andrew—I B Esberg....... 38 37
1 Wolf, John J—S Liebmann's Sons Brewing Co........................ 871 74

SATISFIED JUDGMENTS.

NEW YORK.

August 1 to 7—Inclusive.

Averill, William W—T E Turner. (1877)....$2,549 57
Booth, Samuel—Union Nat Bank of Frenchtown, N J. (1891).....................4,524 75
Burrows, W T—G H Norfolk. (1886) 185 13
Brandon, Edward—Eleazer Bowen. (1891)...14,118 93
Same—Horace Bowen. (1891) 528 69
Same—W H Speer. (1891)...................4,798 23
*Burke, Michael T N—People State N Y. (1886) 500 00
Bencke, John—James Dwyer. (1891)......... 85 82
Same—P H Siebern. (1891)... .... 827 86
Craig, George A and Annie C—Union Stone Works. (1891)............................ 341 15
Carpenter, Robert B—Durland's Riding Academy Co. (1891)....................... 140 42
Coogan, Matthew—Health Department. (1889) 55 87
Cornish, Charles E and Louis M, exrs Charles L Cornish—Aaron Butler. (1891)........... 404 80
Same—same. (1891).......................... 65 75
Donohue, James—Oscar Goerke. (1885)....... 138 77
Donnelly, Patrick—E R Gibson. (1890)........ 84 58
Same—same. (1890)...... .... 359 83
Same—same. (1891) 77 77
Ewing, Justus E—J S Mathews. (1891)....... 264 60
Ely, William F—G H Norfolk. (1886) 184 13
Frankel, Max—Patrick Kennedy. (1891)...... 108 42
Fouche, William W—J Le B Willard. (1891).. 208 71
Faulkner, Henry N—C H K Curtis. (1891)..... 123 71
Hill, James M—W J Morgan & Co. (1891)..... 415 18
Horton, Annie M—H M Hitchings. (1891)..... 583 81
Hauser, Gottfried J—W H Higgins. (1891).... 339 49
Same—H E Stevens, Jr. (1891)............. 345 78
Same—George Hagemeyer. (1891)........ 222 82
Same—August Banbahn. (1891).... .... 583 94
Same—Sims Lumber Co. (1891)........... 415 86
Same—Peter Patry. (1891)................. 134 60
Hawkes, Henry—Karl Mathiasen. (1891)... .. 257 04
Ingersoll, James H, as guard Wilhelmine L Van Cleft—W L Van Cleft. (1888)..........8,532 66
Ingersoll, Ida M—M E Ingersoll. (1887).......53,405 76
Same—Auguste Pottier. (1887)...........50,836 26
Jennings, Walter B—Maranda Lane. (1890)..1,645 48
Jackson, Homer B—Michael Mahony. (1887). 105 37
Same—Louis Waefelaer. (1882)............ 158 16
Lawton, J Warren—Kate F Brown. (1891)... 122 78
Loriot, Henry—J E Whitcomb. (1890)......... 304 73
Levenson, Samuel—J A Flack, as Sheriff. (1891).................................. 178 73
Lohrano, William—P H Sichern. (1891). 827 86
Same—James Dwyer. (1891)............... 85 82
McQuillen, James S—Real Estate Exchange and Auction Room (Lim.) (1891)......... 74 13
Same—same. (1890)..... .. .. 96 72
Maduro, Solomon—H M Hitchings. (1891)..... 588 81
McDermott, John—J P Noues. (1891)......... 96 14
McClelland, Louise—Emma Helmken, admrx. (1889).................................. 184 77
Marsden, Yates—Nineteenth Ward Bank. (1889)................................... 527 84
Moores, William—Patrick Kennedy. (1891)... 108 42
McCarthy, John H, as Marshall—Abraham Hahn. (1891).............................. 242 72
Palme, Julius—Hamburg Filiale der Deutschen Bank. (1891).............................1,354 00
Price, Frank S—Peter Patry. (1891).......... 134 60
Same—Sims Lumber Co. (1891)........... 415 86
Same—August Banbahn. (1891)............ 686 94
Parkhurst, Eliza W, extrx Sylvester C Parkhurst—C P Berdell. (1887)................. 93 81
Same—same (1886).............................1,252 54
Same, indivi'd and extrx Sylvester C Parkhurst—Lizzie A Miller. (1886)............. 579 54
Same—same. (1887)............................. 99 01
*Plath, Ernest—F E Kappenberg. (1891)...... 821 06
Rasines, Antonio—Patrick Kennedy. (1891).. 108 42
Snook, John A—Union Nat Bank of Frenchtown, N J. (1891)...............................4,524 75
§Schneider, Bennett H—M T McMahon, recvr. (1882).................................. 379 65
Smith, Annie W—John Kidlon. (1890) 250 64
Schirmer, Gustav—D D Russell. (1888).......2,209 07
Scoville, Mrs Jennie L M—Otis Corbett. (1891) 388 61
*Sting, David—People State N Y. (1886)..... 500 00
Strong, Samuel A—Austin Finegan, assignee. (1891).................................. 80 88
Stanfield, Hope G—C D Metz. (1889).... ..... 50 00
Stanfield, Frederick Otis—same. (1889).... 90 00
Standard Busching Machine Co. (1891).......1,717 12
Schwarz, Charles—Edwin Wallace. (1888).... 120 11
Transmitting Dynamometer Co, under Hamilton Ruddicks patent—Edward Bassett. (1889) 1,479 60
Tooker, William A, Jr, and Ella J—L M Hornthal. (1887).............................. 80 68
Tooker, Ella G—Gustave Lippman. (1887).... 154 55
Von Prochazka, Joseph O—R B Gray. (1888). 117 25
Welwood, Thomas—J P Puels. (1891)......... 490 72

*Vacated by order of Court. †Suspended on Appeal ‡Released. §Reversal. ||Satisfied by Execution.

KINGS COUNTY.

July 31 to August 6—Inclusive.

Becker, Herman—J Stabler. (1890) $349 47
Brady, Thomas—C Ropke. (1885) 90 13
Becker, Herman—L & J J Hickey. (1889)..... 46 50
Same—F J Firth. (1889)....................... 95 80
Bailey, William T—F Aldridge. (1891) 149 62
Croner, Benjamin—E M Townsend. (1889).... 61 47
Same—same. (1891)........................ 119 29
Same—same. (1889)........ .... 64 42
Foote, Warren—R D Stryker. (1889)........... 897 11
Flaherty, William J—D Strong. (1891)........ 73 10
Holland, Samuel G—W J Elliott. (1890)....... 3 6 87
Jones, William H—G W Brown. (1891)..... .. 102 68
Kelly, Edward T—D Strong. (1891) 73 10
Knorr, John—F Voelk. (1888).................. 201 74
McCaffrey, John W—G W Ferris. (1891)..... 449 98
Smith, Thomas—Hobby & Doody. (1888)..... 153 72
Vandewater, Frank P—G W Brown. (1891)... 104 68

MECHANICS' LIENS.

NEW YORK CITY.

Aug.

1 Ninety-eighth st, n s, 268.6 e 10th av, 156.5x113.6. Bernard Marrey agt John W. Lintton, owner and contractor $176 93
1 Sixty-third st, n s, 300 w 8th av, 87.6x100.5. J. L. Mott Iron Works agt Esther E. Barron, owner, and Robert Carey, contractor 180 00
1 One Hundred and Twentieth st, s s, 125 w 8th av, 75x100.11. Dempsey & Smith agt James Thompson, owner and contractor. 3,631 85
1 Lexington av, No. 666, w s, 75.5 s 56th st, 24.6x90. F. A. Wendel agt Morris M. Byk, owner, and — Walsh, contractor 179 00
1 One Hundred and Twenty-third st, Nos. 142-150, s s, 200 e 7th av, 100x100. Hollister Mfg. Co. agt Elizabeth K. Smith, owner, and Hardwood Decorative Co., contractor.............................. 270 81
3 Forty-second st, No. 559, n s, 100 e 11th av, 25x100. Albermarle Soapstone Co. agt Mary A. Barron, owner and contractor... 140 00
3 Arthur av, w s, 208 s Pelham av, 25x117.6. H. H. Meise agt Ernest Wehner and Joseph Schafer, owners, and William Murray, contractor.............................. 58 00
3 Ninety-eighth st, Nos. 220-224, s s, 225 w 2d av, 75x100. John O'Hare agt William Dempsey and John Smith, owners and contractors.............................. 200 00
3*One Hundred and Twenty-eighth st, n s, 135 e Lenox av, 75x99.11. Michael Zertina agt Patrick Hogan, owner and contractor ... 355 20
3 Eighth av, s w cor 102d st, 100x100. Richard Flanagan & Co. agt Joseph O'Connor and James Stevenson, owners, and Joseph O'Connor and Charles H. Bliss, att'y, contractors.............................. 1,750 00
3 Ninety-eighth st, n s, 268.6 e 10th av, 156x100. J. W. Binney agt John W. Hutton, owner and contractor.............................. 82 74
3 Amsterdam (10th) av, n e cor 91st st, 100x137. Same agt Edward Smith, owner, and John Reisinger, contractor.............................. 168 13
3 Twenty-fourth st, Nos. 341-345, n s, 272 e 9th av, 79x100. Breretan & McIntosh agt Joseph McFarland, owner, and Hardwood Decorative Co., contractor.............. 149 00
3 Madison st, n w cor 115th st, 81x100. Same agt William McEntee, owner, and Hardwood Decorative Co., contractor.... ..... 268 00
3 Central Park West, n w cor 104th st, 100.11x100. J. G. Wilson agt John J. Carey, owner and contractor.............................. 2,145 00
4 Forty-second st, No. 559, n s, 100 e 11th av, 25x100. Murray & Hill agt Mary A. Barron, owner, and same and William Spearing, contractor.............................. 59 00
4 Amsterdam av, n e cor 91st st, 125x100. Peter McIntyre agt Edward Smith, owner, and contractor.............................. 250 00
4 Fourteenth st, s s, 100 e Av C, 234x100. Wm. Eckert & Co. agt William H. Muldoon, owner and contractor.............. 973 10
4 Kingsbridge road, n w cor 181st st, 50x100. G. F. Huskinson agt Catharine L. Beekman, owner, and Rudolph Christ, contractor.............................. 326 27
5 West End av, e s, 62.2 s 84th st, 60x100. James Slattery agt Frederick P. Foster, owner and contractor.............................. 500 00
5 Madison st, No. 414, s s, 87 e Montgomery st, 26.11x115. J. J. Kierst agt Joseph Solomon, owner, and Charles W. Heine, contractor.............................. 165 00
5 One Hundred and Twenty-third st, Nos. 142-154 W., s s, 150x100. Vanhorne, Griffen & Co. agt Elizabeth K. Smith, owner, and Hardwood Decorative Co., contractor.... 572 38
5*Twenty-fourth st, Nos. 341-345, n s, 271.7 e 9th av, 78.4x98.9. Cassidy & Adler agt Joseph McFarland, owner, and Gorman & Sylvander, contractors..........................4,007 30
5 Arthur av, w s, 200 s Pelham av, 25x118. Dominico Schiavone agt Wehner & Scha-

fer, owners, and William Murray, contractor 11 25
5 Same property. Bart Schiavone agt same. 18 00
5 One Hundred and Thirty-fifth st, No. 17, n s, 208 w 5th av, 17x100. J. I. Brady agt Frederick W. Mears and John W. Fisher, owners and contractors 250 00
5 One Hundred and Fifty-seventh st, s s, 25 w Barry av, 25x100. S. B. Leary agt James Thompson, debtor and owner........ 56 00
5 One Hundred and Twentieth st, s s, 125 w 8th av, 75x100.11. Manchester & Philbrick agt James Thompson, owner and contractor 655 58
5 Manhattan av, n e cor 121st st, 100x100. J. H. Collins agt Henry Schneider, owner and contractor........ 343 00
6 Twenty-fourth st, n s, 271.7 e 9th av, 78.4x98.9. Hanlon & Ryan agt Thomas Snape, debtor, and Joseph McFarland, owner, and Frederick Wood, contractor 2,550 00
6 Ninety-eighth st, n s, 268.5 e 10th av, 156x100. J. P. Duffy & Co agt John W. Hutton, owner and contractor........ 170 50
6 Eighty-seventh st, Nos. 150 and 152, s e cor Lexington av. Francesco Ricci agt Fretelli Caviuato, owner, and same or Jose Cavinato, contractor........ 25 42
6 Ninety-eighth st, Nos. 22-224, s s, 225 w 2d av, 75.2x100. August Kaehler agt Wm. Dempsey and John Smith, owners, and P. Blumenthal, contractor........ 29 50
6 Madison st, s s, 6..4 w Gouverneur st, 26x—. Schnatz & Massoth agt Joseph Salomon, owner, and Charles W. Heine, contractor. 750 00
6 Riverside Drive, s e cor 82d st, 109.3x122.4x102.2x161.1. Cream City Furniture Co. agt Squire & Whipple, owner and contractor........ 2,080 00
6 Ninety-eighth st, Nos. 220-224, s s, 225 w 2d av, 75x100. T. G. Hoyer agt Wm. Dempsey and John Smith, owner, and P. Blumenthal, contractor........ 114 88
6 Pelham av, s s 58.2 e Hoffman st, 25x108. James Kern agt Ida M. Ayars, owner and contractor........ 52 71
6 Eighth av, s w cor 103d st, 100.11x100. Mohawk Valley Lumber Co. agt Joseph O'Connor, owner and contractor........ 5,500 00
6 One Hundred and Twenty-eighth st, n s, 135 e Lenox av, 75x—. Miacho Fortunato agt Patrick Hogan, owner, and same and Mary Hogan, contractor 346 24
6 One Hundred and Fourteenth st, n s, 495 w 5th av, 75x—. Same agt Peter Biringer and Emil Haensgen, owner and contractor 639 75
6 One Hundred and Thirty-fourth st, s e cor Madison av, 60x100. Michael Conforti agt Thos. Jette, owner, and Thomas McCormack 3,492 00
6 One Hundred and Thirty-fifth st, Nos. 5-17, n s, 110 w 5th av, 125x—. William Grier agt Warren B. Smith, owner, and John W. Fisher, John R. Meres and James Vernon and wife, contractors 450 00
6 Watts st, n e cor Washington st, 20x70. Philip Schuyler agt John Mulvihill, owner, and G. W. Lamphere, contractor 53 63
6 Eleventh st, Nos. 314 and 316, s s, 288.4 e 2d av, 88.8x—. James Dunn agt John O'Connor, owner and contractor........ 375 75
6 Same property. James Dunn and W. J. Moody agt same 700 00
‡7 Bowery, n w cor Great Jones st, 25x100. Canda & Kane agt Michael Noonan, owner, and John E. Darragh, contractor........ 135 18
7 Broadway, s e cor Leonard st, 75x150. Same agt same owner, and N. Y. Life Ins. Co., contractor........ 165 00
7 West End av, Nos. 441-459, w s. Thomas Osborne agt W. E. D. Stokes, John J. Brewster, Francis M. Jencks and Squire & Whipple, owners, and Squire & Whipple, contractors 8,000 00
7 Waverley pl, Nos. 175, n s, 30x—. Patrick Dawson agt William Bornstein, owner, and John Ehrig, contractor 9 50

‡*Editor* RECORD AND GUIDE:

The lien filed against me by Michael Zettina for $355.20 is entirely unjust, as he has not fulfilled his contract nor finished his work. I shall bond the lien and fight it in Court.

P. HOGAN.

¶*Editor* RECORD AND GUIDE:

This lien is filed upon the request of Gorman & Sylvander, the contractors.

CASSIDY & ADLER.

KINGS COUNTY.

July

31 Troy av, n e cor East New York av, 100x100. John R. Hughes agt D. Tragman, owner and contractor........ $400 08
31 Broadway, n e cor Jefferson av, 100x100. John J. O'Brien agt C. Henry and Annie J. Moller, owners, and Jacob Bisson, contractor........ 51 30

Aug.

1 Van Voorhis st, s s, 100 w Bushwick av, 100x100. C. H. Reynolds & Sons agt Fred. Amman, owner, and Amzi D. Vreeland, contractor 660 06
1 Navy st, n s, 75 w Myrtle av, 50x100. Thomas Sheffield agt Henrietta Fiske, owner, and William H. H. Glover, contractor........ 575 00
1 East Nineteenth st, w s, 200 s Av A, 50x100, Flatbush. Lemuel N. Martin agt Margaret E. Chatfield, owner, and William Crozier, contractor........ 356 00
1 Woodbine st, No. 45 (see Lien). Peter Egan agt Albert Berckmeier, owner and contractor........ 140 00
1 East Nineteenth st, w s, 200 s Av A, 50x100, Flatbush. William Crozier agt Margaret C. Chatfield, owner and contractor........ 825 00
1 Moore st, n s, 150 w Ewen st, 25x100. Peter Kunzweiler agt Meyer and Rachel Rich, owners and contractors 6,160 00
3 Seventeenth st, s s, 200 e 5th av, 25x100. Adaline A. Newman agt Mary E. Zeyhle, owner, and John Stabler, contractor........ 45 74
3 Troy av, s w cor East New York av, 100x100. Earl A. Gillespie agt D. Tragman, owner and contractor........ 275 83
3 Woodbine st, 20 feet from Knickerbocker av, 90x100 (see Lien). Peter Egan agt Albert Berckmeier, owner and contractor.. 140 00
3 Weirfield st, n s, 100 e Evergreen av, 159x100. John C. Austin and George Mehrman agt Annie Herzog, owner, and James A. Bills, contractor........ 1,000 00
3 Central av, n e s, extends from Cornelia st to Putnam av, 200x90. Joseph Hopkins agt John T. Barnard, owner and contractor 16,000 00
3 Same property. Guiseppe Cannella agt Joseph Hopkins, owner and contractor... 295 00
3 Howard av, s w cor Macon st, 100x116. Bulmer Lumber Co. (Lim.) agt Clarence Lincoln, owner and contractor........ 1,538 88
3 East Nineteenth st, w s, 200 s Av A, 50x100, Flatbush. Ross & Snyder agt Margaret E. Chatfield, owner, and William Crozier, contractor........ 400 00
3 Pulaski st, s s, 479.8 e Throop av, 159.7x100. George Iles agt Maria Roberts and Frederick W. and Elise Klein, owners, and Essex Roberts, contractor........ 150 00
4 East Nineteenth st, w s, 200 s Av A, 50x100, Flatbush. Charles A. Lundine agt Margaret E. Chatfield, owner, and William Crozier, contractor........ 218 00
4 First st, s s, 100 w 7th av, 100x100. Brereton & McIntosh agt Hardwood Decorative Co., owners and contractors........ 195 28
4 Central av, n e s, extends from Cornelia st to Putnam av, 200x100. Dugan Mfg Co. agt Joseph Hopkins and John T. Barnard, owners and contractors........ 735 86
4 Sixthteenth st, s s, 90 e 9th av, 29.9x200 to Windsor pl, 22 houses. William Stone agt John Aslip and Timothy Buckley, owners and contractors........ 1,428 92
5 Lewis av, w s, extends from Jefferson av to Putnam av, 200x90. A. S. Nichols & Co. agt Augustus W. Blazo, owner and contractor........ 1,062 91
5 East New York av, s w cor Troy av, 100x100. Earl A. Gillespie agt Henry M. W. Tragman, owner and contractor........ 291 61
5 Bainbridge st, n s, 115 e Saratoga av, 180x100. Kilian Bros. agt J. Mason Kirby, owner and contractor........ 1,190 00
5 Watkins st, w s, 100 n Sutter av, 25x100. Louis Bossert agt Elias Kaplan, owner and contractor 515 46
5 Eighty-second st, n e s, 80 s e 23d av, 4x100, Gravesend. John Lambert agt Mary E. Case, owner and contractor........ 75 00
5 Twentieth st, s s, 800 e 4th av, 20x100. Dennis Norton agt Carl Thorstenson, owner and contractor........ 100 00
5 Bergen st, s s, 290 e Brooklyn av, 60x100.. }
Bergen st, s s, 350 e Brooklyn av, 40x105.7. }
H. F. Burroughs & Co. agt Joseph M. Pilcher & Co., owner and contractor........ 918 87
6 Garnet st, Nos. 30-36, s s, 100 e Court st, 100x100. Edward H. Bailey agt Alfred E. Harrington, owner and contractor........ 355 44
6 Same property. Peter McCadden agt same owner and contractor........ 231 60
6 Poplar st, n e cor Hicks st, 25x100. The New York Gas Fixture Co. agt Ida N. Edwards 80 00
6 Twenty-first av, e s, 95 n Cropsey av, 30x40. Abraham H. Rosenblum agt Kate F. Monjo, owner and contractor........ 342 00
6 Central av, n s, 40 w Cornelia st, 160x100.1. Frank Luberto agt Joseph Hopkins, owner and contractor........ 62 00
6 Fiftieth st, n s, 100 w 4th av, 80x100. Bradley & Currier Co. (Lim) agt John Koski, owner and contractor........ 1,203 63
6 Sunnyside av, s s, 150 e Barbey st, 50x100. Frederick Schluchtner agt William B. Howard, owner and contractor........ 214 30

SATISFIED MECHANICS' LIENS.

NEW YORK CITY.

Aug.

3 One Hundred and Thirty-fifth st, Nos. 5-17 W., n s, 125x—. William Grier agt John W. Fisher, Fred R. Meres and Warren B. Smith. (Lien filed June 12, 1891)........ $450 00
3 Same property. John Fallon agt Warren B. Smith, John W. Fisher and Fred. R. Meres. (June 19, 1891)........ 795 00
3 Same property. C. H. Southard agt same. (Aug. 4, 1891)........ 135 87
3 Same property. Elsworth Miller agt same. (May 5, 1891)........ 125 00
3 Same property. Henry Strader agt same. (Mar. 5, 1891)........ 39 00
3 Same property. Abraham Steers agt same. (April 18, 1891)........ 100 18
3 Same property. Patrick Cassidy agt Warren B. Smith, John W. Fisher and Wm. Verdon. (April 9, 1891)........ 1,411 76
3 Same property. Dimock Fink & Co. agt John W. Fisher and William Verdon. (April 7, 1891)........ 279 94
3 Same property. Jacob Myer agt same and John Fallon and Fred. Speth. (April 13, 1891)........ 85 50
3 Same property. George Muller agt — Fisher and — Meres. (Mar. 30, 1891)... 49 12
3 Same property. Union Stove Co. agt Warren B. Smith, John W. Fisher and Fred. R. Meers. (April 24, 1891)........ 102 00
3 One Hundred and Thirty-fifth st, Nos. 13 and 15 W., 40x100. George McMullen agt John Smith, John W. Fisher and Fred'k R. Meres. (April 6, 1891)........ 65 00
3 One Hundred and Thirty-fifth st, No. 15 W., n s. Thomas Conwell agt John W. Fisher and Fred. R. Meres. (Feb. 21, 1891)........ 97 00
3 Ninth st, No. 11, n s, 200 e 5th av, 25x92.3. Morton & Chesley agt Charles Burrall Hoffman. (July 16, 1891)........ 4,308 30
3 Willett st, No. 184, e s, 18.6x—. Farber & Schneider agt Louis Aaron. (July 27, 1891)........ 1,100 00
4†Seventh av, s e cor 57th st, known as The Music Hall. Beers & Kuenstner agt Andrew Carnegie and Isaac A. Hopper & Co. (June 19, 1891)........ 5,512 00
4 Cedar st, No. 13, n s, 25x100. J. V. Schaefer & Co. agt Importers' and Traders' Club and Steiner & Hirschfeld. (Aug 1, 1891). 2,118 00
4 One Hundredth st, Nos. 207 and 209 E., 40x100. Levy & Twobig agt Phillip B. Smith. (June 20, 1891)........ 250 00
4 One Hundred and Twenty-fifth st, Nos. 145 and 147 W., 50x—. Percy Jacobs agt James S. Kelly and The Harlem Republican Club. (June 18, 1891)........ 256 85
4 One Hundred and Thirty-fifth st, Nos. 5-15 W., 106.8x99.11. F. R. Meres and Peter Patry agt Warren B. Smith. (April 11, 1891)........ 30,386 42
5 Same property. S. C. Johnson pres't, agt same and Fred. R. Meres. (May 4, 1891). 681 12
5 One Hundred and Thirty-fifth st, No 17 W., 18.4x100. Same agt John W. Fisher and Fred. R. Meres. (May 4, 1891)........ 118 52
5 Fifty-second st, Nos. 539-543 W., 75x—. August Jacob agt Gottfried J. Hauser and Frank S. Price. (Jan. 24, 1891)........ 275 00
5*Fifty-second st, Nos. 539-548, 75x—. William and Thomas Morton and David Brown agt Hauser & Price. (April 25, 1891)........ 190 00
5*Same property. Thomas Moore agt same and Wm. E. Graham. (Jan. 28, 1891)........ 30 85
5*Same property. John Mathews agt same. (Jan. 28, 1891)........ 18 25
6 One Hundred and Forty-first st, n s, extends from Convent av to Hamilton terrace, block x 70. W. G. Leeson agt St. Lukes Episcopal Church and Jones & Co. (July 22, 1891)........ 1,822 60
6 One Hundred and Thirty-fifth st, No. 17 W., 18.4x100. Adamant Mfg. Co. agt John W. Fisher. (April 18, 1891)........ 345 00
6 Madison av, s e cor 120th st. Thomas and J. F. Stapleton agt Mary Gault and S. M. Saunders. (Dec. 29, 1890)........ 88 00
6 Willett st, No 184, e s, 18.6x60. W. H. Schmohl agt Louis Aaron and L. Farber. (June 12, 1891)........ 159 48
6 Same property. Schnatz & Massoth agt Louis Aaron and Farber & Schneider. (June 16, 1891........ 560 00
7 Sedgwick av, w s, 50 n 184th st. William Clarke agt Elizabeth S. Roe and E. H. Smith. (May 25, 1891)........ 450 00
7 Same property. Same agt same. (April 4, 1891)........ 445 00
7 One Hundred and Fifty-fourth st, s s, 125 w Courtlandt av, 25x100. James W. Colwell's Sons agt Frantz Lotz and Catharine C. Twomey. (July 16, 1891)........ 221 85
7*Fifty seventh st, No. 154, s e cor 7th av, 150x175. Henry Schoenemann and 14 others agt Andrew Carnegie, Adolph Scherer, Charles Block and Charles Schneider; 15 liens. (June 6, 1891) 953 74
7 Leroy st, Nos. 61 and 63, n s, 200 w Bedford st, 50x100. J. W. Finney agt Stevens & McElroy and John Reisinger. (Aug. 4, 1891)........ 45 57
7 Eighty-sixth st, n s 200 w 8th av, 50x—. W. S. Burton agt. Mrs. G. Livingston Morse and J. C. Nobis. (May 29, 1891) ... 97 03
7 Catharine st. Nos 53 and 55, e s. W. H. Brandt agt Eliza L. Miller. (Dec. 31, 1890) 160 00

†Vacated and cancelled by order of Court.

*Discharged by depositing amount of lien and interest with County Clerk.

KINGS COUNTY.

July

29 Forrest st, n s, 180 e Bushwick av, 80x100. F. W. Davis & Bro. agt Claus Lipsius Brewing Co., owner, and Arci & Murray, contractors. (Lien filed May 13, 1891)... $1,000 00
30 Pacific st, n s, 200 e Stone av, abt 50x100, two flats. R. Cummings' Sons agt J. C. Truax, owner and contractor. (Feb. 19, 1891)........ 401 45
30 Eighth av, s e cor Prospect av, 90x150. Herman J. Hoff agt Henry E. Murphy, owner and contractor. (Dec. 15, 1890)........ 413 10
30 Same property. John Q. Maynard agt same owner and contractor. (Jan. 16, 1891) 350 00
31 Forty-fifth st, n s, 300 e 5th av, 40x100. Thomas and Robert Edgerton agt John L. Parish, owner, and A. D. Hyde & Co., contractors. (July 16, 1891)........ 200 00

Aug.

3 Sixth st, s s, 180 w 4th av, 100x115. Andrew Johnson agt Emil Lindberg, owner, and Lindberg & Olsen, contractors. (July 8, 1891)........ 100 00
3 Fulton st, s s, 22 e Hoyt st, 20x70........ }
Hoyt st, e s, 70 s Fulton st, 100x90........ }
Howell & Saxtan agt A. I. Namm, owner, and John Prosser & Son, contractors. (Aug. 1, 1891)........ 772 31
5 Fulton st, s s, 22 e Hoyt st, 20x70........ }
Hoyt st, e s, 70 s Fulton st, 100x90........ }
Kelty Bros. agt A. I. Namm, owner, and John Prosser & Son, contractors. (Aug. 1, 1891)........ 1,000 00
6 Same property. Charles S. Buell agt same owner and contractor........ 1,308 92
7 Fourth st, s s, 97.10½ e 6th av, 440x100. William J. Fitzpatrick agt Moses & Fanton, owners and contractors. (July 28, 1891).. 8,479 00

BUILDINGS PROJECTED.

The first name is that of the owner; ar't stands for architect, m'n for mason, c'r for carpenter and b'r for builder.

NEW YORK CITY.

SOUTH OF 14TH STREET.

Crosby st, No. 49, five-story brk and stone warehouse, 25x90 and 100, tin roof; cost, $15,000; o'w'r, ar't and b'r, Louis Korn, 261 Broadway. Plan 1109.

King st, n s, 84.2 w Congress st, three five-story brk and stone flats, 16 and 25x65, tin roofs; cost, $58,000; Michael McCormick and Henry Madden, 319 East 50th st; ar't, J. Hauser. Plan 1118.

10th st, Nos. 299-303 W., four-story brk storage warehouse, 76.3x97.11, cement and asphalt roof; cost, $90,000; Beadleston & Woerz, 291 West 10th st; ar't, O. C. Wolf; m'n, J. L. Weber; c'r, J. F. Moore. Plan 1124.

BETWEEN 14TH AND 59TH STREETS.

49th st, No. 617 W., one-story iron and frame shed, 15x17; cost, abt $75; Richard F. Harris, 541 9th av. Plan 1111.

BETWEEN 59TH AND 125TH STREETS, EAST OF 5TH AVENUE.

85th st, n s, 96 w Av B, eight five-story brk and stone tenem'ts, each 24.11x77, tin roofs; cost, $17,000 each; Jos. Schreiner, 110 West 131st st; ar't, John Hauser. Plan 1100.

112th st, n s, 150 e 5th av, five-story brk flat, 25x74, tin roof; cost, $20,000; John Shields, 1715 Madison av; ar't, J. C. Burne. Plan 1105.

121st st, No. 405 E., one-story frame shed, 15x35, tar and gravel roof; cost, $150; Wm. Austin, 2412 Forest av; ar't, J. P. Walther. Plan 1107.

121st st, No. 405 E., rear, one-story frame wagon shed, 50x15, tar and gravel roof; cost, $150; ow'r and ar't, same as last. Plan 1108.

Madison av, n e cor 59th st, four-story brk and stone business building, 100.5x90, tin and tile roof; cost, $125,000; Leo Schlesinger, 128 East 74th st; ar'ts, Buchman & Deisler; m'ns, List & Lennon. Plan 1116.

Park av, w s, 75 n 103d st, five-story brk and stone flat and stores, 25.11x64.6, tin roof; cost, $16,500; Mull & Fromer, 1588 Washington av; ar't, J. J. Vreeland. Plan 1117.

89th st, s s, 113.4 w Madison av, seven-story brk and stone hotel, 25.6x96.8, tin roof; cost, $45,000; ar't and b'r, Thomas Graham, 20 East 91st st; c'rs, Dawson & Archer. Plan 1120.

BETWEEN 59TH AND 125TH STREETS, WEST OF CENTRAL PARK WEST AND 8TH AVENUE.

65th st, s s, 395 w 10th av, three-story brk stable, 30x100, tar and gravel roof; cost, $15,000; Jas. Buhler, 41 Harrison st; ar't, J. P. Leo. Plan 1103.

West End av, n w cor 83d st, six three and four-story brk, stone and terra cotta dwell'gs, each abt 19x80; cost, $18,500 each; Gerald L. Schuyler, 8 Henderson pl; ar'ts, Lamb & Rich. Plan 1110.

23D AND 24TH WARDS.

Ernescliff pl, s s, abt 700 e Jerome av, two-story frame dwell'g, tin roof; cost, $1,500; David Cunningham, on premises; m'ns, Emery & Forsyth. Plan 1112.

Kingsbridge road, s s, 81 s Nindham pl, two-story frame stable, 15x29, shingle roof; cost, $500; Agnes S. Kirse, Newark, N. J.; ar't and b'r, N. M. Whipple. Plan 1101.

Ponus st, s s, 450 w Boston av, two-and-a-half-story frame dwell'g, 21x42, shingle roof; cost, $2,580; Jas E. Algeo, 537 East 84th st; ar't, Louis Koelle; b'r, F. Lessor. Plan 1098.

175th st, n s, 425 w Fleetwood av, two-story frame dwell'g, 18x26.6, shingle roof; cost, $1,500; Victor L. Veyrac, 251 West 16th st; ar't, W. Graul. Plan 1104

Riverdale av, w s, 450 n Sidney st, two-story frame dwell'g, 24x28, shingle roof; cost, $3,500; John A. Berrian, Jr., Kingsbridge; ar't and b'r, S. L. Berrian. Plan 1099.

Tinton av, e s, 80 s Home st, two-story and attic frame dwell'g, 22x48, shingle roof; cost, $5,000; Mary E. Day, 341 Willis av; ar't, H. S. Baker. Plan 1106.

Washington av, No. 1023, w s, 75 s 165th st, rear, one-story frame stable, 18x13, tin roof; cost, $200; Chas. Zimmerman, 714 East 165th st. Plan 1102.

Home st, s s, 87.9 e Intervale av, two-story frame stable, 18x24, shingle roof; cost, $500; Peter Stumpf; ar't, M. J. Garvin; b'rs, Wisswell & O'Brien. Plan 1114.

Lowmede st or Madison av, 12 n Scribner st, two-story frame workshop, 25x50, gravel roof; cost, $1,500; ow'r, ar't and b'r, John A. Knox, Marion av, Fordham. Plan 1121.

Powell pl (proposed), s w cor Commerce av (proposed), one-story frame shed, 65x16, gravel roof; cost, $500; N. Y. Gas Engine and Power Co., Morris Dock; ar't, Chas. McKinney. Plan 1119.

176th st, s s, 150 e Fleetwood av, two-story frame dwell'g, 22x57.8, one-story frame stable, 24.6x18, tin and shingle roof; total cost, $7,000; Wm. McNable, 1066 Park av; ar't, C. Stegmayer. Plan 1122.

Bathgate av, No. 1620, e s, 60 n 172d st, two-story frame dwell'g, 17x35, tin roof; cost, $2,400; George L. Hurd, 1638 Bathgate av; ar't, J. M. Fisher; b'r, J. M. Wilson. Plan 1115.

Taylor av, s e cor Kingsbridge road, two-story frame dwell'g, 19x40, tin roof; cost, $1,500; Mrs. Eliza Campbell, 897 Caldwell av; ar't, J. J. Vreeland. Plan 1118.

Webster av, e s, 435 n 170th st, three three-story frame dwell'gs, 16.8x50, tin roofs; cost, $4,500 each; Sarah C. Ottiwell, 75 Lexington av; ar't, Louis Kayer. Plan 1123.

KINGS COUNTY.

Plan 1425—Seigel st, No. 14, one one-story frame wheelwright shop, 22x60, tin roof; cost, $200; Michael Hesbergh, 670 Putnam av.

1426—Thatford av, w s, 100 n Dumont av, one three-story frame store and dwell'g, 18x36, tin roof; cost, $5,500; Jas. Morris, Osborn st.

1427—Livonia av, n e cor Osborn st, one three-story frame (brk filled) store and tenem't, 25x60, tin roof; cost, $6,500; A. Matthews; ar'ts, D. Acker & Son.

1428—Humboldt st, w s, 75 n Stagg st, one four-story frame (brk filled) tenem't, 25x57, tin roof; cost, $6,500; Geo. Dietrich; ar'ts, D. Acker & Son.

1429—Seigel st, No. 89, one four-story frame tenem't, 25x55, tin roof; cost, $6,500; G. Levy & Co.; ar'ts, D. Acker & Son.

1430—New York av, w s, 35 n Park pl, one two-story and attic brk dwell'g, 21x58, tin and slate mansard roof, wooden cornice; cost, $17,000; Nathan T. Beers, 97 Gates av; ar't, G. P. Chappell.

1431—Bedford av, s e cor North 12th st, two four-story brk dwell'gs, 30x68.9, tin roofs, iron cornices; cost, each, $15,000; Christian Friedmann, 174 South 9th st; ar't, C. Rentz.

1432—Walworth st, n s, abt 150 w Park av, one four-story brk factory for car fixtures, 100x40 and 35, gravel roof, brk cornice; cost, $14,750; Binns estate, Brooklyn; ar't, H. Gilvarry; b'rs, Buchanan & Riley.

1433—Knickerbocker av, No. 205, e s, 25 s De Kalb av, one one-and-a-half-story frame stable, 12x13, gravel roof; cost, $75; M. F. Munz, on premises; b'r, C. Bott.

1434—Hart st, n s, 100 e Wyckoff av, one two-story frame (brk filled) dwell'g, 20x45, tin roof; cost, $1,500; ow'r, ar't and b'r, Jos. Eirich, 988 Hart st.

1435—Seigel st, No. 44, one four-story frame (brk filled) tailor shop, 25x85, tin roof; cost, $2,000; M. J. Kaplan, on premises; ar't, H. Smith; b'r, not selected.

1436—Vermont st, w s, 50 n Belmont av, one two-story frame dwell'g, 20x40, tin roof; cost, $2,000; Catharine Ochs, 235 Delancey st, New York; ar't and b'r, C. S. Haviland.

1437—4th av, n w cor 44th st, one three-story frame (brk filled) store and tenem't, 28x60, tin roof; cost, $7,575; John B. Gorgers, 4th av, near 44th st; ar'ts, H. L. Spicer & Son; b'r, J. H. French.

1438—Knickerbocker av, s e cor De Kalb av, three three-story frame (brk filled) stores and tenem'ts, 25x56, tin roofs; cost, $4,200 each; George Koch, Greene av and Stuyvesant av; ar't, F. J. Lessing.

1439—Wyckoff av, e s, 50 s Stockholm st, one one story frame dwell'g, 25x25, tin roof; cost, abt $500; Martin Klett, 80 Av A, New York; ar't, T. J. Beir.

1440—Putnam av, w s, 117.6 s Central av, seven two-story frame (brk filled) dwell'gs, 17.6x42, tin roofs; cost, each, $2,000; owr's and c'rs, J. W. Lamb & Son, 1068 Putnam av; ar't, A. J. Lamb; m'n, C. Vincent.

1441—Putnam av, n s, 100 w Central av, one two-story and basement frame (brk filled) dwell'g, 17.6x42, tin roof; cost, $2,500; ow'rs, ar't and b'r, same as last.

1442—Evergreen av, w s, 75 s Van Voorhis st, one one-story frame wood-shed, 12x16, felt roof; cost, $15; John Hedderick, 724 Evergreen av.

1443—Suydam st, s s, 225 w Knickerbocker av, one three-story frame (brk filled) tenem't, 25x57, tin roof; cost, $4,500; John Clement, on premises; ar'ts, D. Acker & Son.

1444—Gates av, s s, 250 w Knickerbocker av, one three-story frame (brk filled) store and tenement, 25x57, tin roof; cost, $4,500; John Lyons, on premises; ar'ts, D. Acker & Son.

1445—Wyckoff av, s w cor Gates av, four three-story frame (brk filled) tenem'ts, 30 and 25x60, tin roofs; cost, total, $20,000; W. H. Barton, 10 Cooper av; ar't, B. Finkenseiper; b'r, not selected.

1446—Scholes st, s s, 100 w Leonard st, one four-story frame (brk filled) tenem't, 25x65, tin roof; cost, $8,000; H. Hoffmann, 135 Leonard st; ar't, F. Holmberg.

1447—Ewen st, w s, 100 s Jackson st, one four-story frame (brk filled) tenem't, 25x60, tin roof; cost, $5,000; Leopold Michel; ar'ts, D. Acker & Son.

1448—Atlantic av, s w cor Warwick st, one one-story frame stable, 14x20, felt roof; cost, $80; A. K. Thau, on premises.

1449—Suydam st, n s, 200 e Hamburg av, one three-story frame (brk filled) store and tenem't, 25x57, tin roof; cost, $7,000; Peter Prahm, 1054 Willoughby av; ar't, F. Holmberg.

1450—2d st, s s, 100 w 8th av, five three-story and basement brk and brown stone dwell'gs, 21x46.4, tin roof and iron cornice; cost, $6,500 each; ow'r and ar't, A. E. White, 445 1st st; b'r, not selected.

1451—Sumner av, w s, 125 s Decatur st, four one-story brk stores, 25 and 26x40, gravel roofs, wooden cornices; cost, each, $600; ow'r and c'r, Henry J. Brown, 389 Herkimer st; art, F. B. Smith.

1452—Clifton pl, n s, 400 w Nostrand av, two three-story brk flats, 25x60, gravel roof and iron cornices; cost, each, $10,000; ow'r and b'r, Chas. F. Hunt, 480 Putnam av; ar't, F. L. Hine.

1453—Gates av, s s, 100 w Hamburg av, one three-story frame (brk filled) store and tenem't, 25.1x60.2, tin roof; cost, abt $4,000; ow'r, ar't and b'r, Otto Singer or Linger, 1175 Greene av.

1454—6th av, w s, 20.2 n 49th st, one two-story frame dwell'g, 20x55, tin roof; cost, $2,000; ow'r, ar't and b'r, James Montgomery, 209 44th st.

1455—6th av, w s, 75 n 49th st, one one-story frame carpenter shop, 15x18, tin roof; cost, $75; ow'r, ar't and b'r, same as last.

1456—Dean st, n s, 83.4 e Utica av, sixteen two-story frame dwell'gs, 17x38, gravel roofs; cost, $1,800 each; Chas. A. Martin, 43 Pilling st; ar't, C. Terry.

1457—Boerum st, n s, 175 w Lorimer st, one six-story frame (brk filled) tenem't, 25x63, tin roof; cost, $6,800; Charles Naeber, Stuyvesant av, cor Pulaski st; ar't, Th. Engelhardt; b'r, not selected.

1458—Lorimer st, s e cor Conselyea st, three three-story frame (brk filled) stores and tenem'ts, 20x63, tin roofs; cost, each, $4,500; James J. McEntee, 501 Grand st; ar't, T. Engelhardt; b'r, not selected.

1459—Nassau av, n s, 75 w Newell st, one one-story frame store, 17x25; gravel roof; cost, $325; E. & C. Schwindt, 134 Manhattan av; ar't and b'r, A. Van Dien.

1460—Sullivan st, s s, 125 w Richards st, one three-story frame tenem't, 25x54, tin roof; cost, $5,500; Catharine Leonard, 59 Sullivan st; ar't and b'r, T. Brownell.

1461—Dumont av, n e cor Thatford av, one three-story frame store and tenem't, 25x55, tin roof; cost, $4,500; Jos. Morris, Osborn st.

1462—Lewis av, w s, 82 s Quincy st, one two-story and basement brk and brown stone dwell'g, 18x38, tin roof and iron cornice; cost, $4,200; Henry Peters, Stuyvesant av, cor Lafayette av; ar't, T. Engelhardt; b'r, not selected.

1463—22d st, s s, 250 e 6th av, one two-story and basement frame (brick filled) dwell'g, 22x42, tin roof; cost, $3,500; ow'r and b'r, Mrs. M. Donnelly, 324 22d st; ar't, C. B. Fish.

1464—Fulton st, s s, 100 w Hoyt st, one three and four-story brk store, 36 and 102.6x300; cost, $75,000; Mrs. Lucy E. Stoddard, 517 Fulton st; ar't, W. H. Beers; b'r, not selected.

1465—Irving st, n s, 250 e Van Brunt st, one one-story brk coal shed, 50.6x71.4, gravel roof; cost, $3,000; Marx & Rawolle, on premises; ar't, E. Claus; b'r, F. J. Ashfield.

1466—Irving st, n s, 250 e Van Brunt st, one one-story brk dwell'g, 50.6x29, gravel roof, brk cornice; cost, $5,400; ow'r, ar't and b'r, same as last.

1467—Washington st, Nos. 233 and 235, one two-story brk storehouse, 26.5x108, gravel roof, brk and stone cornice; cost, $10,500; B. McCaffrey, Tillary and Washington sts; ar't, J. G. Glover; b'r, not selected.

1468—Stone av, w s, 75 n Belmont av, one three-story frame store and tenem't, 25x25, tin roof; cost, $4,500; Morris Berman, 306 Cherry st, New York.

1469—Knickerbocker av, s e cor Flushing av, one one-story frame stable, 12x10, felt roof; cost, $50; Jos. Hemel, on premises.

ALTERATIONS NEW YORK CITY.

Plan 1459—28th st, No. 32 W., two-story brk extension, 22.6x27.6, concrete and asphalt roof; cost, $10,000; J. J. McGrath, Plaza Hotel; ar'ts, De Lemos & Cordes.

1460—56th st, No. 36 W., interior alterations; cost, $5,000; E. H. Johnson, on premises; ar't, F. Jacobson.

1461—9th st, Nos. 320 and 322 E., walls altered; cost, $1,000; Wm. Milleg, 77 East 3d st; ar't, F. A. Sieghardt.

1462—24th st, No. 18 W., two-story and basement brk extension, 19x20, tin roof; cost, $1,500; R. L. Spencer, 779 Lexington av, Brooklyn; ar't, S. Sass.

1463—Summit av, w s, 618 w Bainbridge av, two-story frame extension, 16x12, tin roof; cost, $500; A. Fournier, on premises; ar't, J. C. Kerby.

1464—Park st, Nos. 52-60, interior alterations; cost, abt $2,000; R. M. Donaldson, 54 Park st; ar't, W. Satterly.

1465—57th st, Nos. 239 and 241, walls altered; cost, 10,000; G. Lozelling, 239 East 57th st; ar't, C. W. Lozelling.

1466—Vanderbilt av, e s, 25 n 171st st, building to be moved; cost, $200; Daniel Sheahan, n e cor 171st st and Vanderbilt av.

1467—5th av, s e cor 35th st, repair damage by fire; cost, $20,000; Liberty Ins. Co., 130 Broadway; b'r, R. A. Farmer.

1468—Central st, No. 120, walls altered; cost, $2,000; Anthony Milles, 132 Worth st; ar't, B. W. Berger.

1469—River av, s e cor Palisade av, one-story frame extension, 7.6x18.8, shingle roof; cost, $350; Henry W. Sackett, Riverdale; ar't, L. A. Osborne.

1470—Washington st, No. 561, interior alterations and walls altered; cost, $100; Wm. B. Foreman, on premises.

1471—6th av, No. 14, repair damage by fire; cost, $1,000; David Silberstein, 10 6th av; ar't and b'r, J. D. Miner.

1472—Locust av, n e cor 13th st, building to be moved, &c.; cost, $1,300; Central Gas Light Co., cor Alexander av and 143d st; ar't, H. S. Baker.

1473—127th st, Nos. 50 and 52 W., s s, 310 e Lenox av, raise one story, also three-story brk extension, tin roof; cost, $4,500; M. A. McCormack, 50 West 127th st; ar't, J. H. Valentine.

1474—86th st, n s, 80 e Amsterdam av, new gallery and staircase in Sunday-school; cost, $——; Park Presbyterian Church, A. B. Price, trustee, 63 West 90th st; ar't, N. M. Whipple.

1475—34th st, No. 136 W., interior alterations; cost, $5,000; S. F. and W. C. Adams, 432 5th av; ar't, D. and J. Jardine.

1476—45th st, No. 6 E., interior alterations, walls altered; cost, $2,000; Margaret H. Trevor, 20 East 48th st; ar't, Murray & Howard.

1477—3d av, No. 965, e s, 40 s 58th st, walls altered; cost, $650; Julia A. Blake, 461 Gold st, Brooklyn; ar't, J. Wolf.

1478—Madison st, s s, 96 e Oliver st and Oliver st, e s, 122 s Madison st, walls altered, &c.; cost, $25,000; Alart & McGuire, 68 and 70 Madison st; ar't, J. M. Farnsworth.

1479—University pl, s e cor 11th st, one-story brk extension, tin roof, also interior alterations and walls altered; cost, $15,000; A. S. Rosenbaum, 5 East 73d st; ar't, A. Wagner; b'rs, P. Tostevin's Sons.

1480—37th st, No. 36 W., interior alterations; cost, $1,200; John F. Scott, 29 West 55th st; ar't, J. H. Taft.

1481—Attorney st, No. 128, walls altered; cost, $1,200; lessee, Casper V. Stumpf, 92 Av B; ar'ts, Schneider & Herter.

1482—28th st, No. 107 E., walls altered; cost, $4,500; Stohlmann, Pfarre & Co., on premises; ar't, R. L. Daus; c'r, H. I. Smith.

1483—Suffolk st, No. 23, repair damage by fire; cost, $500; Sarah Marks, on premises; ar't, H. Horenburger.

1484—18th st, No. 436 E., two-story brk extension, 17x58, tin roof; cost, $2,000; Frank Vattel, 328 East 18th st; ar't, B. W. Berger.

1485—10th av, No. 818, five-story brk extension, 25x22, tin roof, walls altered; cost, $10,000; John Budki, on premises; ar't, H. Davidson; m'n, G. A. Zimmerman's Sons.

1486—13th st, No. 13 W., walls altered; cost, $1,500; Harris Mandelbaum, 181 Henry st; ar't, M. Bernstein; c'r, H. Fischel.

1487—50th st, s e cor 10th av, one-story brk extension, 10x19, tin roof; cost, $1,000; Wm. Fendrich, 730 10th av; ar't, J. W. Cole.

1488—8th av, No. 2785, s w cor 148th st, repair damage by fire; cost, $1,500; Francis M. Wilmurt, New Rochelle, N. Y.; b'r, L. C. Webster.

1489—7th av, No. 279, walls altered; cost, $800; Mrs. Mary Stroh, on premises; b'r, W. McFarland.

KINGS COUNTY.

Plan 744—Gold st, No. 414, flat tin roof; cost, $600; H. W. Gourley, on premises; ar't and b'r, J. F. Richartz.

745—De Kalb av, No. 936, add two stories, gravel roof; also one-story brk extension, 25x45, gravel roof, new store front; cost, $2,500; ow'r, ar't and b'r, Wm. W. Dougherty, 936 De Kalb av.

746—Baltic st, n s, 108 w 5th av, three-story and basement brk extension, 20x10, tin roof; cost, $600; C. S. Woodhull, 5th av, bet Baltic and Warren sts.

747—Elton st, e s, 135 n Blake av, two frame extensions, one front and one rear, 20x15 and 20 x10, tin roof; cost, $700; Philip Lebrian, 276 Av B, New York.

748—19th st, No. 379¼, one-story frame extensions, 16x13, tin roof; cost, $75; Emile B. Thoret, on premises; b'r, J. B. Lenton.

749—Henry st, No. 82, flat tin roof; cost, $500; George Kinne; b'r, J. Wohlman.

750—Nassau st, n w cor Navy st, flat tin roof; cost, $700; Josephine Cassaday, 42 Navy st; b'rs, J. McKeefrey and B. H. Body.

751—Clinton av, No. 345, two-story and basement brk extension, 67x22 and 16, tin roof; cost, $9,000; A. J. Pouch, 315 Greene av; ar't, W. A. Mundell; b'rs, C. Cameron and Long & Barnes

752—Atlantic av, No. 1295, one-story brk extension, 30x20, tin roof; cost, $250; J. Dunn, 1295 Atlantic av.

753—Conover st, No. 218, new store front; cost, $450; H. Fenkelday, 220 Conover st; b'r, C. M. Detlefsen.

754—Bedford av, e s, 53 s Atlantic av, one-story brick extension, 14x42, gravel roof; cost, $300; Eugene G. Blackford, Bedford & Herkimer sts; b'rs, G. H. Stone & Son.

755—Myrtle av, No. 265, add two stories to extension; cost, $1,500; Mr. Biggert, on premises; ar't and m'n, J. Thatcher; c'r, E. S. Boyd.

756—Smith st, s e cor Livingston st, rebuild front wall, new store front; cost, $500; James McCormick, 131 North Oxford st; b'r, F. Connelly.

757—20th st, s s, 160 w 4th av, raised 10 feet on frame story; also three-story frame extension, 20x15, tin roof; cost, $800; John O'Neil, on premises; b'rs, J. Campbell and A. E. Smith.

758—Dean st, Nos. 1140 and 1142, add one-story to extension; cost, $750; Robert Proddow, 104 Montague st; ar't, W. H. Burhans; b'rs, Lynch & Dalton.

759—Smith st, No. 19, two-story brk extension, 25.2x37, tin roof; cost, $3,500; P. H. McNulty, 12 Gallatin pl; ar'ts, W. Field & Son; b'r, F. J. Ashfield.

760—Columbia st, No. 173, rebuild front wall and new store front; cost, $1,060; P. Noonan, 169 Columbia st; b'r, M. Gibbons.

761—Union av, w s, 55 s North 12th st, add one story, gravel roof; cost, $700; John Doyle, 333 Union av; b'r, N. Crahen.

762—North 11th st, n s, 72 e Bedford av, three-story brk extension, 12x65, tin roof, west wall taken out from first story to roof, iron girders, &c.; cost, $2,000; Christian Friedmann, 174 South 9th st; ar't, C. Rentz.

763—5th av, w s, 52 n 20th st, one four-story frame extension, 16.8x20, tin roof; cost, $400; Mrs. Fitzsimmons, on premises; b'rs, Spence Bros.

764—Broadway, e s, 40 s Flushing av, cut opening in centre wall, steel beams, girder, &c.; cost, $500; George, Henry and Louise Heerle, 212 South 9th st; b'r, J. P. Ryan.

765—Wallabout st, e s, 84 n Harrison av, new store front; cost, $150; Ch. Rissler, 324 Bleecker st; ar't, B. Finkensieper; b'r, C. Rissler.

766—Jerome st, No. 162, two-story frame extension, 13x6.6, tin roof; cost, $500; Nuns of St. Dominic; ar't, F. J. Berlenbach, Jr.; b'r, not selected.

767—Myrtle av, No. 1252, interior alterations; cost, $200; B. Simon, on premises; b'r, L. Loeser.

768—Skillman av, s e cor Ewen st, add one story, flat gravel roof; cost, $500; E. Golden & Son, on premises.

MISCELLANEOUS.

BUSINESS FAILURES.

N. Y. ASSIGNMENTS—BENEFIT CREDITORS.

July

31 Jordan, Louis (general brokerage, at No. 5 Beekman st), to George W. Bowman; without preferences.

Aug.

3 Backer, Abraham (dealer in commercial paper, at No. 285 Broadway), to Benjamin F. Einstein; without preferences.

6 Dillingham, Charles T. (bookseller and publisher, at Nos. 718 and 720 Broadway), to John H. Kitchen; preferences, $26,137.

ADVERTISED LEGAL SALES.

REFEREES SALES TO BE HELD AT THE REAL ESTATE EXCHANGE AND AUCTION ROOM (LIMITED), 59 to 65 LIBERTY STREET, EXCEPT WHERE OTHERWISE STATED.

August

Amsterdam av, Nos. 641-649, n e cor 91st st, 136.5 x100, five five-story brk flats with stores, by R. V. Harnett. (Amt due $29,132; prior morts. $120,000)........ 10

50th st, No. 539, n s, 500 w 10th av, 25x100.5, five-story brk tenem't with stores, by R. V. Harnett & Co. (Amt due $3,548; prior morts. $7,000).... 10

42d st, No. 25, n s, 354.2 w 5th av, 20.4x100.5, four-story stone front store and dwell'g, by R. V. Harnett. (Leasehold; action No. 1; amt due $5,420)........ 11

Same property, by R. V. Harnett, (Leasehold; action No. 2; amt due $10,650)........ 11

10th av, No. 319, w s, 74.1 n 28th st, 24.8x100, three-story brk tenem't with stores, ¾ part, by William Kennelly........ 11

133d st, Nos. 161-167, n s, 125 e 7th av, 100x99.11, four five-story brk flats, by B. L. Kennelly. (Amt due $18,878; prior mort. $——)........ 12

8th av, No. 2140, e s, 51.4 s 116th st, 25.5x100, one-story brk stores, by James L. Wells. (Amt due $3,830)........ 12

53d st, Nos. 208-214, s s, 68 w 7th av, 68x60.5, four four-story stone front dwell'gs, by Richard V. Harnett. (Amt due $16,008)........ 13

65th st, No. 138, s s, 458 e 10th av, 20x100.5, four-story stone front dwell'g, by Richard V. Harnett. (Amt due $21,242)........ 17

71st st, No. 114, s s, 138.1 w Columbus av, 19x100.5, four-story stone front dwell'g, by Smyth & Ryan. (Amt due $10,784)........ 17

Amsterdam (10th) av, No. 307, e s, 70.4 n 74th st, 17x81, four-story brk dwell'g, by J. F. B. Smyth. (Amt due $14,909)........ 17

KINGS COUNTY.

Aug

Walworth st, w s, 261.10 s Myrtle av, 18.9x100, two-story brk dwell'g; assessed value, $2,000; by T. A. Kerrigan, at 45 Broadway, E. D........ 11

Broadway, Nos. 151 and 153, n s, 195.2 w Driggs st, 43.4x100, two three-story brk flats and stores; assessed value, $19,000; all right, title and interest; by Taylor & Fox, at 45 Broadway, E. D.... 12

Franklin av, s w s, lot 37 map of 28 building sections at Bath, filed June 28, 1854, New Utrecht, 51x359.6 to New Utrecht Bay, x50.4x362.4....
Franklin av, s w s, lot 38 same map, 50x362.4 to New Utrecht Bay, x97.11x373.7........
Franklin av, s w s, abt 105 s e Bath, New Utrecht and Greenwood plank road, 50x373.7 to New Utrecht Bay, x10x370.5........
Franklin av, s s, 255 s e New Utrecht to Bay road, formerly plank road, 50x355.10 to New Utrecht Bay, x50.2x359.8........
by J. Cole, at 380 Fulton st........ 12

Glenada pl, w s, 100 s Decatur st, 49.9x100, two four-story stone apartment houses........
Glenada pl, w s, 149.9 s Decatur st, runs west 100 x south 38.2 x east 24.11½ x south 6.10 x east 77.2½ to Glenada pl. x north 50.8 to beginning, two four-story apartment houses; assessed value, together, $56,000........
by Edward G. Nelson, ref., at County Court House........ 12

Hendrix st, w s, 100 s Eastern Parkway, 100x100, two-story frame dwell'g on plot; assessed value, $3,100........
44th st, No. 189, n e s, 275 s e 3d av, 25x100.2, three-story frame dwell'g and store; assessed value, $1,800........
by T. A. Kerrigan, at 13 Willoughby st........ 12

Herkimer st, n w cor Rockaway av, 20x80, three-story brk dwell'g; assessed value, $4,200........
Herkimer st, n s, 20 w Rockaway av, 20x80........
Herkimer st, n s, 40 w Rockaway av, 20x80, two three-story brk dwell'gs; assessed value, $3,800 each........
Pacific st, s s, 497.4 e Rochester av, 16.8x107.2⅝, two-story frame dwell'g; assessed value, $1,400........
Palmetto st, n w s, 275 n e Knickerbocker av, 25 x100, vacant; assessed value, $300........
Vanderveer st, s e s, 80 s w Bushwick av, 16.10x 100; assessed value, $2,000........
Throop av, No. 549, e s, 61.7½ s Hancock st, 21.8½x81, four-story brown stone flat and store; assessed value, $9,500........
by T. A. Kerrigan, at 13 Willoughby st........ 13

Union st, n s, 200 w 8th av, 18.9x90........
Union st, n s, 312.6 w 8th av, 18.9x90........
Union st, n s, 331.3 w 8th av, 18.9x90........
Three three-story brown stone dwell'gs; assessed value, $11,000 each........
by Jere. Johnson, Jr., at the Real Estate Exchange, 189 and 191 Montague st........ 13

New Utrecht road, w s, adj land William Cole, 35.3 x143.7x63.8x143.7, New Utrecht, by William Hughes, ref., at County Court House........ 14

College pl, No. 16, e s, 127.11 n Love lane, 20x50, two-story brk stable; partition; assessed value, $2,000; by T. A. Kerrigan, at 13 Willoughby st.. 17

Flushing av, n w cor Franklin av, runs west 120.9 x north 196 x east 24.2½ to Wallabout st, x east 106 to Franklin av, x south 200.4 to beginning, also all right, title and int. which Alexander Dugan had to a triangular parcel on Wallabout st, adj above, being 23.10 on Wallabout st, x4x—, moulding mill; assessed value, $25,000; by Geo. L. Fox, ref., at County Court House........ 17

LIS PENDENS, KINGS COUNTY.

July

Decatur st, n s, 100 e Saratoga av, 100x100. Ellen Wilson agt Emma Davis et al.; att'y, A. C. Fransioli........ 31

Warren st, n s, 75 w Smith st, 25x75. Sarah Stetson, formerly McSorley, agt Elizabeth W. Van Duyne et al.; att'y, H. M. McKean........ 31

St. Marks av, n s, 175 w Grand av, 25x182.2x26.6x 173.8........
Dean st, s s, 140 w Kingston av, 20x100........
Artilissa V. Gearon agt Walter E. Switzer et al.; att'y, M. Gearon........ 31

East New York av, n w s, 190 s w Sackman st, 20x 81.4x20.10x75.3. John L. Culver agt Mary E. Dewey........ 31

Essex st, e s, 260 n Ridgewood av, 20x100. Phebe R. Kissam agt Harry W. Harding; att'y, W. R. Kissam........ 31

Bedford av, s w cor Rodney st, 133x100. Bradley & Currier Co. (Lim.) agt Charles W. Andress et al.; att'y, E. H. Moeran........ 31

Aug.

Vanderbilt av, e s, 49.4 n Dean st, 24.9x70........
Vanderbilt av, w s, 25 n Pacific st, 25x75........
Donovan & Heron agt Phillip and Hannah Sullivan; action for specific performance; att'y, J. J. Leary........ 1

7th av, w s, 40 n 4th st, 30x88. Metropolitan Life Ins. Co. agt Garwood W. Powell et al.; att'ys, Arnoux, Ritch & W........ 1

7th av, w s, 21 n 4th st, 19x88. Same agt same; same att'y........ 1

Prospect av, s w s, 254 n w 8th av, runs southwest 90.4 x northwest 46 x northeast 10.4 x northwest 50 x northeast 80 to av, x southeast 90. Newman H. and R. C. Raymond agt Robert W. Fielding et al.; foreclos. mechanic's lien; att'y, C. W. Wright........ 1

Chauncey st, s s, 78 e Saratoga av, 190x100. Adrianna Smith and C. Trimble agt Thos. A. McWhinney and Jacob Aronson; action for recession of contracts and accounting; att'y, S. Williams........ 1

Greene av, s e cor Lewis av, 200x100. George B. Spratt agt Moses Schlansky; action to compel re-conveyance; att'y, I. N. Miller........ 1

North 6th st, n e s, 45 s e 7th st, 20x100; ½ part. John McLaughlin agt Antonio Ferrazzo and Pietro Ghigliotti; action to set aside conveyance for alleged fraud; att'y, E. J. Dunphy........ 1

South 4th st, No. 253, n s, 100 e Havemeyer st, 25x 95. Nellie C. Van Keypen agt Marie Bruninghaus et al.; att'ys, Wells & Waldo........ 1

Bedford av, s w s, 50 s e Penn st, 25x70. Marie E. Jacobson agt Marie Bruninghaus et al.; same att'y as last........ 1

Gold st, w s, 479.4 s Willoughby st, 16.2x115. Stephen B. Sturges agt Henry de Zavala; att'ys, Sturges & Roby........ 3

Putnam av, n s, 380 e Broadway, 20x100. Earl A. Gillespie agt Eliza M. Winter; att'y, Geo. F. Alexander........ 4

Gates av, s e s, 125 s w Bushwick av, 20x100. Same agt Michael Tanner; same atty........ 4

Livonia av, s e cor Osborn st, 20x100. Hyman Simon agt Abraham Seidenbergh; action on attachment; att'ys, J. C. & H. C. Smith & Koepke 4

Tompkins av, s w cor Gates av, 20x100. The Riverhead Savings Bank agt Margaret A. A. Burns; att'y, Timothy M. Griffing........ 4

Dean st, n s, 419.5 e Rochester av, 16x107.2. William G. Boulton trustee John Boulton agt Joseph Hopkins, Jr.; att'ys, S. F., F. H. & H. Cowdrey. 4

Dean st, n s, 435.5 e Rochester av, 16x107.2. Same agt same; same att'ys........ 4

Dean st, n s, 467.5 e Rochester av, 16x107.2. Same agt same; same att'ys........ 4

Kosciusko st, s s, 100 w Stuyvesant av, 25x100. John Hehr agt Christina Roessle; action for specific performance; att'y, Fernando Solinger.... 5

Fulton st, s s, 200 e Stone av, 50x100. David H. Beyea agt James H. Watson; att'y, James Demorest........ 5

27th st, w s, 140 s Voorhees av, 132x80x132x140, Gravesend. Albert Philip and ano. admrs. Catharine A. Philip agt Leonard Knox; att'y, Wm. Sullivan........ 6

Broadway, Nos. 129 and 131, n s, 195.2 w Driggs st, 43.4x100. Harry M. Lynch agt Belle I. Couly; partition; att'y, Arthur C. Butts........ 6

Stone av, w s, 65.2 n Bergen st, 42x100. Leon Rollac agt John W. Davis; att'ys, Sackett, Lang, Reed & McKewan........ 6

RECORDED LEASES.

NEW YORK.	Per Year
Baxter st, No. 7, store floor. Solomon Friedman to Frank Ferretti; 4 10-12 years, from July 1, 1889........	$426
Bleecker st, No. 124, s w cor Bleecker st. Phillip Sammet to Joseph Hirschorn; 3¾ years, from Aug. 1, 1891........	2,400
Broad st, No. 24, part of. Ellen A. Adee widow, George A. Adee, Clara T. A. wife of M. Dwight Collier, Philip H., Frederic W., Edwin M. and Ernest R. Adee heirs George T. Adee to Samuel B. Clark and Charlotte L. Robins; 8 years, from May 1, 1891........	10,000
Broadway, cor Canal st, basement occupied by lessee. Eliza J. Smith extrx. Thomas Smith to Theodore Kruger; 5 years, from May 1, 1891........	2,500
Chambers st, No. 15, cor City Hall pl. Maria L. Groves to Arthur McQuade; 4 years 5½ months, from Nov. 15, 1890........	2,000
Same property. Agreement to extend lease for 8 years on original terms. Maria L. Groves to George E. McQuade. July 11........	nom
Greenwich st, No. 160, store and front and rear basements. Elias and Philip Sobel to Charles J. Reuter; 5 years, from May 1, 1891	1,260
Greenwich st, No. 273 / Greenwich st, No. 271 — stores and basements. John H. Welsh to Gustav and Ferdinand Buck; 5 years, from May 1, 1893........	1,800
Howard st, No. 12, all. Adelheid M. Duhme and ano. extrxs. Martin Duhme to John P. Friedhoff and Henry Meyer, of Friedhoff & Meyer; 10 years, from July 1, 1891........	1,600
Hudson st, No. 527, store and basement. Caroline W. Sommer to Samuel A. Suydam; 5 years, from May 1, 1890........	900, 1,000
Mulberry st, No. 52, basement. Federico Chieffo to Luigi Di Meo and Orario Discepolo; 3 years, from May 1, 1891........	240
Mulberry st, No. 111, w s, 106.1 n Canal st, 25x 100. Peter F. Gallagher to Pasquale Lovaglio; 5 years, from Aug. 1, 1891........	2,880
Prince st, No. 11, all. Elizabeth A. Corcoran to Salvato Di Matteo; 3 years, from May 1, 1891........	1,200
Southern Boulevard, n e cor 136th st, 28x75x25 x70. Ann Murtaugh to George Stuhl; 5 years, from March 1, 1892........	900
William st, No. 83. Charles Kramer to George Meister and William Messing; 4 years, from May 1, 1890........	390

Washington st, No. 892. Michael Lawless to Frederick Lemmermann; 3 years 9 months, from Aug. 1, 1891 ... 1,000
Willett st, No. 132, store floor. Louis Aron to Carl Schmieder; 7 years, from May 1, 1891 .. 420
13th st, No 535 E., store and bakery. Martin Derx to Kundiguna Durf; 5 years, from May 1, 1891 ... 300
33d st, Nos 518-532 W., all ... }
32d st, No 531 W., shop on rear ... } Henry Howard to Robert H. Howard and Childe H. Childs; 5 years, from Jan. 1, 1889. 13,000
41st st, No. 141 W., all. Eliza Railings to William H. Meade; 10 years, from June 1, 1891 .. 2,800
105th st, No. 305 E. Matthew Coogan to Sigmund Schulhof; 5 years, from July 1, 1891 .. 480
108th st, No. 167 E. Sebastian Sander to Julius and William Doemich; 3 years 9 months. 720
113th st, No. 125 E., all. Mary L. and Catharine E. Brady to Annie Kelly; 4 years, from Aug. 1, 1891 ... 300
161st st, No. 987 E. E. S. Berger to Julius Hagemeier; 2 11-12 years, from June 1, 1891 198, 240
Amsterdam av, w s, bet 158th and 159th sts. 37.4x114, three-story frame building and extension. Chauncey G. Stone to Henry F. Leporin; 3 years, from May 1, 1891 ... 1,500
Park (4th) av, s e cor 125th st. James Everard to James Williams; 6 years, from July 1, 1891 ... 2,900
1st av, No. 500, n e cor 29th st, store floor and front cellar. Christian H. Sonnenschmidt to H. Koehler & Co., a corporation; 5¾ years, from Aug. 1, 1891 ... 1,200
1st av, No. 177. Edward Kafter exr. Henry Cogan to John Kress Brewing Co.; 5 years, from June 10, 1891 ... 1,500
1st av, No. 975, store, basement and part first floor. Henry Knobloch to Frederick Schloesser; 3 years, from May 1, 1890 ... 1,000
Same property. Frederick Schloesser to Paul Kohl. Assign. lease. Aug. 1 ... consid. omitted
3d av, No. 1316, store, basement second and third floors. Jacob and Louis Vogel to Louisa Schenck; 5 years, from May 1, 1891 .. 1,500
3d av, No 92, w s, all. Libbie O. Rykert to Lauretz Jorgensen; 5 years, from May 1, 1891 ... 1,740
3d av, No. 1001, n w cor 60th st, store and basement. John H. D. Meyer and Maria C. his wife to Thomas McNamara; 6¼ years, from Aug. 1, 1891 ... 1,800, 2,000
3d av, n w cor 130th st, summer garden in rear of above, begins 71 w of 3d av, runs west 115 x 88 Mark Mayers to Michael Shine; 3 years, from May 1, 1890 ... 900, 1,200
6th av, No. 408, all. Martin Herman to David C. Long; 5 years, from May 1, 1891 ... 3,000
7th av, No. 377, s e cor 31st st, store, basement, second floor and room on third floor. Margaret Berg to Frederick Bauer; re-recorded; 5 years, from May 1, 1887 ... 1,500
8th av, No 521, n w cor 26th st, store and basement. John J. and Annie E. Bannan to Francis Rogers; 2 years, from May 1, 1891 ... 3,100, 3,400
8th av, No. 258, s e cor 24th st. Elizabeth Aymar extrx. John J. Aymar to Frank J. Goodwin; 3 years, from May 1, 1889 ... 2,500
Same property. Same to same; 5 years, from May 1, 1892 ... 2,500
9th av, No. 694, store. August Graefe to Christian F. Kappler; 5 years, from May 1, 1891 .. 440
10th av, No. 756, store, basement and half first floor. Wilhelm A. Dieterich to John Oehler; 3 1-6 years, from Aug. 1, 1891. 1,000
12th av, n w cor 129th st. 45x— to land of The New York Central & Hudson River R. R., x south to 129th st, x east 62.4. Mary G. Pinkney to Jonathan O. Armour; 10 years, from April 1, 1891 ... 1,000

CHATTELS.

Note.—The first name, alphabetically arranged, is that of the Mortgagor, or party who gives the Mortgage. The "R" means Renewal Mortgage.

NEW YORK CITY.

JULY 31 TO AUGUST 6—INCLUSIVE.

SALOON AND RESTAURANT FIXTURES.

Albrecht, Lorenz. 11 E 7th....G Ehret. (R) $1,000
Alport, J. Sedgwick av and 171st st....D Stevenson. 675
Arndt, Mulligan & Haas. 149 East Houston....P Weiss. 6?0
Aufenanger & Schwarm. 91 Broad ...G Ehret. 2,000
Bauer, F. 377 7th av....Bernheimer & S. 1,000
Becker, Henry. 549 9th av ...G Ehret. (R) 2,200
Bergin, Patrick. 481 10th av....I Roth. 2,200
Blank, Christopher. 641 E 9th....J Eichler B Co. (R) 400
Bloechlinger, Joseph. 201 South 5th av....J & M Haffen. (R) 700
Braun, Lisette B. 1866 Park av....India Wharf B Co. (R) 1,000
Breithuth, Leopold. 414 E 71st....G Ringler & Co. (R) 900
Baier, H. 25 Columbia....O Huber Brewery. 600
Bazart, J. 302 E 71st .. J Doelger's Sons. (R) 5?0
Bergen, J. 1075 3d av ...J B Bereuter. Billiard Table. 420
Breitenstein, J. 101 South 5th av....W Kollorz. 4,500
Brooks, E. 119 W 10th....J C G Hupfel B Co. 619
Baumann, M. 237 E 106th ...H Elias B Co. (R) 350
Bock, G. 234 E 102d....G Ehret. 1,030
Borst, J E. 135 Lawrence....D G Yuengling, Jr, B Co. (R) 200
Bischoff, G. 1067 1st av. . G Ehret. (R) 3?0
Bland, Minnie. 386 Rider av ...J & M Haffen. 3?0
Boody, A. 49 Bowery....G Ehret. 800
Bury, G M. 333 E 47th....J Ables B Co. 350
Callanan, W J and P K Mulligan. 342 West... S Liebmann's Sons B Co. 5,000
Callum, C. 1080 9th av... J Kress B Co. 2,500
Collin, M. 723 E 9th....M Seitz. 425
Conway, J G. 22 Columbia... D Stevenson. 768
Coleman, P. 285 Cherry....H Elias B Co. 400
Deguan, Kate. 102 E 10th ..Fitzgerald B Co. 1,000
Delarey, B. 1470 2d av....D Stevenson. (R) 1,500
Desmond, W J. 1204 8th av....J Hoffmann B Co. 3,000
Dorrhofer, Jacob. 428 E 62d....Burr B Co. 800
Dowling, P. 410 E 18th....D Mayer. 400
Drucker, M. 130 Delancey....D Mayer. 1,900
Fechter, A J. E 17th st....C E Birkenhauser (R) 1,500
Feuerbach, Jacob. 509 5th....G Ehret. (R) 1,500
Ferretti, F. 7 Baxter....J Kress B Co. 694
Fleig, Babbetta J. 10th av bet 167th and 168th sts ...G Ehret. (R) 1,800
Franz, William. 751 2d av....Jos Doelger's Sons. 641
Fitzgerald, J. 2190 8th av ...A B Marx. Billiards. 850
Frish, A. 259 East Houston ...S Liebmann's B Co. (R) 700
Goodwin, F J. 278 8th av....G Ehret. 4,500
Grassmuck, J. 155th st, near St Nicholas av....G Ehret. (R) 7,000
Grenz, C F. 228 E 74th... F Oppermann, Jr. 400
Gebhard & Clayborne. 251 Water....G Ehret. (R) 1,000
Groh, E. 86 Willett... S Liebmann's Sons B Co. 850
Gutman, N & H. 1561 2d av....Burr B Co. 1,100
Haakonsen, Martin. 347 Spring....Bernheimer & S. (R) 250
Hammer, Edward. 45 and 47 New Chambers .. Bernheimer & S. (R) 1,000
Healey, D. 2058 1st av... D Stevenson. (R) 300
Heim, B & E. Western Boulevard and 74th and 75th sts .. G C Engel. Restaurant Fixtures. 3,004
Hillebrandt, Henry. 515 Pearl....G Ehret. (R) 750
Hasting, K. 434 E 59th....J Doelger's Sons. 600
Hirschhorn, J. 124 Bleecker....P Doelger. 1,800
Hoefer, M and A. 192 Allen....S Liebmann's Sons B Co. (R) 450
Johnson, C. 1943 Lexington av....J Ruppert. (R) 1,000
Krikava, M. 320 E 73d....C Krikava. 500
Kaiser, T. 418 East Houston ...G Ehret. 1,500
Koblwey, D. 234 E 5th....India Wharf B Co. 300
Kammitter, F. 793 1st av....S Liebmann's Sons B Co. 800
Kennell, J A & W. 41 Ann....J Hoffman B Co. 500
Krejci, J. 304 E 71st... V Loewer's G B Co. 750
Law, Joachim. 193 Av A....I Boehm. (R) 1,300
Lehmann, William. 101 Allen....Anchor B Co. Beer Pump. 70
Levy & Edelman. 231 Rivington....Bernheimer & S. Cellar Box. 110
Same....same. Beer Pump. 71
Same....same. Ice House. 95
Lockley, P C. 329 4th av....L Bradt. Restaurant Fixtures. 100
Ladjing, J. 13 South William and 57 Stone ... I Steigerwald. Restaurant Fixtures and Furniture. 3,200
Leporin, H F. 1088 Amsterdam av ...G Ehret. 3,300
Lane Bros. 680 6th av....Beadleston & W. 300
Lynch, M. 615 Amsterdam av ...P Dunne Liquor Business. 2,300
Maurer, G H and P C. 2221 8th av....J Kress B Co. (R) 870
Michels, W. 654 8th av....G Ehret. (R) 2,000
Moeller, G. 1599 Av A....Annie Kubeck. 1,200
Mallon, J. 16 Gansevoort....T Mallon. 100
McCarthy, P. 241 E 28th .. J Ables B Co. 154
Michaelis, H. 2190 4th av....Beadleston & W. (R) 1,000
Moeller, G. 1599 Av C....Burr Brewing Co. 1,000
Massett, Lawrence. 608 Water....Danenberg & Coles. 300
McCormick, R T. 426 W 31st....S Munch, exr. (R) 500
McHugh, F. 177 1st av ...J Kress B Co. 500
McLean, J J. 8 and 10 South Pearl st, Albany, N Y ... M B Carpenter, exr of. 1,850
McQuade, G E and A. 15 Chambers....P Ballantine & Sons 2,000
Meyer, Henry. 85 2d av....J Eichler B Co. (R) 500
Meyer, William. 146 W 19th....H B Scharmann & Son. 350
Murphy, H C. 126 W 19th....Finck & Son. 500
Newhans, Moses. 98 Av C....G Ringler & Co. (R) 1,250
O'Neill, J. 79 Pike slip....P Wehlmann. 600
Osuato, A. 109 Mulberry....H Elias B Co. 1,500
Oschmann, P. 406 E 6th .. S. Liebmann's Sons B Co. (R) 500
Ott, T. 2384 Old Broadway....D G Yuengling B Co. 1,200
Pollitzer, E. 426 E 81st....Beadleston & W. Saloon Ice Box. 135
Quigley, H J. 545 W 30th....H Van Renselaer, Jr. 500
Rehm, Teresa 347 W 38th....Eva Bechtel, extrx G Bechtel. 500
Roberts, T. 348 West....G Ringler & Co. 3,000
Reilly, E. 419 W 48th....Bernheimer & S. (R) 1,000
Rosenhagen, H. 158 Orchard....Lena Fischer. 175
Reubert & Ruschmeyer. 191st st and 10th av .. G Ehret. (R) 5,000
Roetting & Beckmann. 447 6th av....Bernheimer & S. (R) 1,226
Rohl, P. 975 1st av....H Elias B Co. 1,000
Rosenwasser, Adolf. Division st....Burger & Hower 500
Sauer, J. 403 W 41st....V Loewer's G B Co. 1,078
Schroeck, M. 43 1st....V Loewer's G B Co. 300
Sergi & Capellini. 128 Baxter... Burr B Co. 800
Sexton, T. 426 W 42d....D Stevenson. (R) 500
Silberman & Badner. 62 Pitt ...H B Scharmann & Son. 1,0?0
Silva, Manuel. 1321 1st av... P T Kivlehan. 500
Spiwak, L. 89 Allen....D Stevenson. (R) 2,000
Steinbeck, W A. 3d av, s e cor 16th st....P Doelger. 2,000
Stimmel, August. 1248 2d av....G Ehret. (R) 650
Stroh, J and T. 229 Rivington....F Ibert. (R) 5?0
Stuercke, J G. 179 West Houston....J H & H Wellbrock. 594
Sullivan, M. 401 West....Burr B Co. (R) 550
Szkalla, A C. 165 Allen ...P Weidmann. 600
Schindler, P. 214 E 41st....J C G Hupfel B Co. 250
Sheehan, T. 25 Monroe....C Frese. (R) 1,100
Stadler, C. 548 W 43d....Schmitt & S. 300
Stark, C. 453 Washington....Bernheimer & S. (R) 350
Stefani, C. 165 Bleecker....Bernheimer & S. (R) 600
Stronczer, S. 249 2d....G Roesinsky. 500
Schaaf, W. Boulevard, near 111th st....G Ehret. (R) 350
Schmidt, A. 276 7th av.. R Braun. 650
Schnakenberg, C & D. 148 E 14th....P & W Ebling B Co. 1,500
Schopen, H. 76 2d av... Eliz Schopen. 1,000
Strauss, A. Western Boulevard, n w cor 80th st....D G Yuengling, Jr, B Co. (R) 1,500
Schauer, V G. 529-533 Broadway and 91 Spring st. ..G Thomson. Bar and Restaurant Fixtures. 138
Timmins, T F. 2349 8th av....D G Yuengling, Jr, B Co. (R) 1,500
Troiano, Agostino. 62 Baxter....H Elias B Co. 350
Van Slomski, S F. 130 Forsyth....Burr B Co. 856
Vonder Lieth, J D. 183 William....Consumers' B Co. 2,?0
Vollkommer, A. 74 Lewis ...J Eppig. (R) 250
Walsh, Bernard. 554 W 50th... P Doelger. 500
Walsh, P D. 116 Madison....Burr B Co. 1,?00
Wavra, Josef. 213 E 71st ...H Vogel. 7?0
Weinstock, M. 86 Henry....Sekosky Bros. 817
Wiel & Cable. 978 3d av....J Kress B Co. (R) 350
Wilson, Thomas. 304 W 10th ...M I Reynolds. 800
Winkelmeyer, Max. 62 Ann....J Eichler. (R) 2,000
Weik, W. 518 E 16th.... F Oppermann. 1,000
Zaeffel, O. 421 West... G Ringler & Co. 834
Zatulowsky & Linsky. 97 Chrystie....E D Farrell. Tables, &c. 199
Zirpoli & Luciano. 437 E 113th....Bernheimer & S. (R) 400

HOUSEHOLD FURNITURE.

Anderson, Hilda. 160 W 20th....J Moriarty. 309
Ash, Imogene. 1137 Washington av....W E Wheelock & Co. Piano. (R) 105
Adams, Hattie. 23 E 27th... Jordan & M. (R) 203
Allen, Mrs. 115 E 54th ...B Milach. 483
Addis, W H. 328 W 12th ...D O'Farrell & Co. 145
Allen, Alice S. 106 W 123d ...S Baumann. (R) 842
Arthurs, Annie. 330 W 49th....J Baumann. 102
Boniface, Louisa. 64 Rivington. ..G Schuster. (R) 250
Berara, M de la C....318 E 19th....J Baumann. (R) 883
Bell, A A. 222 9th av....J N Ramsdill. 150
Bithom, Hariette. 108 E 86th....J Moriarity. 347
Block, Emil. 39 E 132d ...Spies Bros. 331
Hoady, O Mrs. 78 3d av ... H S Eisler. (R) 156
Bowland, E S. 237 W 105th ...G Browne. 2,500
Brambrinck, George. 98 St. Marks pl....J Moriarty. 182
Burns, Bessy. 428 W 58th ...O'Farrell & Co. 116
Cabrera, Mary J. 610 6th av ...Jordan & M (R) 104
Cahill, Mary F. 88 Lewis....R M Walters. Piano. 200
Cambeis, Mary A. 353 W 29th. J C Hegeman. 209
Clement, Theresa. 21-24 Desbrosses....Lincoln I & G Co. 100
Crane, Julia M. 56 W 40th... F W Savin. Carpets. 400
Carroll, W T. 238 E 56th ...L Baumann. 148
Christal, Amelia. 439 W 23d.. .Rosa B De Casanova. 110
Clune, P W. 500 E 8th.. .Carey & Sides. 275
Culvosa, C. 484 Pearl....L Baumann. 183
Challet, Elise. 43 W 21st....J Grafton. 3,?0
Chase, C S. 308 W 22d. .H Thoesen. 131
Collert, J. 1182 3d av ..H Thoesen. 563
Crowell, O V. 148 E 84th....H Thoesen. 129
Davidson, I. 19 E 115th....D M Brown. 378
Dana, Kath A. 7 5th av ...M M Dana. 510
De Witt, M J. 467 W 57th....J W Aylward. 1,000
Downing, M H. 40 E 26th....J H Little. 188
De Ville, H L. 118 E 119th .. Krakauer Bros. Piano. (R) 123
Dion, Leopold. 241 W 32d .. L Baumann. 120
Douglass, Katie. 75 Christopher....J Baumann. (R) 112
Elkan, Mrs E J. 265 W 19th....O'Farrell & Co. 229
Emmrich, F. 29th st, near 6th av....Krakauer Bros. Piano. 140
English, Ida. 102 E 52d....Dreisacker & Co. 264
Edwards, Sarah J. 243 W 34th....S Green. 250
Eichelman, J C. 307 W 120th....Lincoln I & G Co. 100
Elton, Edith. 125 W 28th... D O'Farrell & Co. (R) 292
Fitzpatrick, T. 1038 3d av....L Baumann. 193
Frank, Rosa. 222 E 55th....J Baumann. 148
Ford, Marie L. 217 W 42d. Carrie Kingsbury. 765
Foley, Mary A. 366 W 45th....O'Farrell & H. 129
Foster, J W. 438 E 52d .. H S Eisler. 174
Foster, William. 315 E 70th....L Baumann. 123
Frank, M. 439 E 80th ...American Guarantee Assoc. 100
Fuerst, John. 210 E 25th....L Baumann. 159
Fullerton, Mamie. 154 E 108th .. E D Farrell. 121
Florence, T F. 147 W 123d....R L Epstein. Piano. 200
Ghetti, L G. 468 Lenox av....W E Wheelock & Co. Piano. (R) 145
Goeler, Richard. 34 8th av....Financial Credit Co. Piano. 100
Gates, Jessie M. 210 E 97th....D O'Farrell & Co. (R) 165
Gelhaar, E 987 6th av... J Gregg & Co. 333
Gunther, F. 30 E 4th ...L Baumann. 180
Gorman, Anna A. 156 St Anns av....Dreisacker & Co. 173
Heimelman, A. 774 Greenwich... D M Brown. 128
Hoe, J A. 2335 7th av....J H Little. 631
Hughes, W. 1818 Amsterdam av ...L Baumann. 205
Hallenbeck, Mary E. 263 W 63d....W E Wheelock & Co. Piano. (R) 258
Hamburger, J. 223 E 111th ...Alexander Bros. 151
Hartwell, T H. 256 W 21st....J C Collins. 448
Heffelshenner, J T. 208 W 103d ...L Baumann. 517
Hennessy, Lizzie. 230 E 70th .. J Moriarty. 198
Hennessy, Mamie....E D Farrell. 131
Hermon, J A. 1420 6th av....T Willis. 370
Hill, Harriet. 257 W 30th... J Moriarty. 232
Hoffmann, Joseph. 414 W 39th.. Alexander Bros. 234
Howard, Mary F. 104 W 52d....J F Manges. (R) 233
Hughes, L R. 113 W 62d....W E Wheelock & Co. Piano. (R) 140
Huxford, S H. 71 E 107th... Financial Credit Co. 150
Julian, L E. 335 W 41st .. R Silverman. (R) 107
Johnson, J. 3415 3d av....A Bernstein. 163
Jordan, A A. Boston av, near Perot st ...D O'Farrell & Co 146
Jordan, E. 432 W 53d....J Baumann. 136
Kain, T. 163 Varick....L Baumann. 2?6
Kuenkel, H. 1578 Broadway....Anna Lepcke. 250
Keeler, Louise. 143 E 29th....O'Farrell & Co. 126
Kellam, D L. 281 Greenwich...Lincoln I & G Co. 500
Keohane, J F. 179th st ... J J McGrorty. 158
Klepper, M F. 218 E 11th. ..A C Hinz. 84
Kusel, A H and W S. Storage....R J Knox. 82
King, Rose. 24 Bleecker....J Moriarty. (R) 513
Lev, Philipine. 101 E 65th....Jordan & M. (R) 224
Lebelle, Ida. 412 W 42d... M Strauss. 262
Laice, J H. 80 E 116th ...J H Little. 612
Leckie, W. 396 3d av....L Baumann. 148
Magnus, H H. 535 E 83d....Spies Bros. 391
May, A S. 361 W 118th....American Guarantee Assoc. 50?
McCann, Kate. 116 W 23d ...N Y F Co. (R) 100
McDonald, W F. 110 New York av, Jersey City ...Lincoln I and G Co. 200
McHenry, Josephine. 16 W 4th....Jordan & M. 104
McMahon, Nellie. 158 W 15th ...J Baumann. 259
Middlemiss, Anna R. 72 W 45th.... R Halsey.(R) 921
Mollenhauer, E and W F T. 100 E 6th. ..Amer Guar Assoc. 125
Mowton, G M. 187 W 135th ...J & J Dobson. 92
Muhl, G J. 104 E 76th....S Heyman & Co. 100
McGuire, W P. 510 E 84th....H Thoesen. (R) 465
MacLellan, C F. 210 W 40th....O'Farrell & H. 289
May, Nellie J. 208 W 48d ... F T Higgins. 603
Mandelkern, Joseph. 237 Broome....H Israel & Son. (R) 156
McEvoy, Mary. 419 W 53d....J Early. 135

Mansfield, Louise. 417 E 69th.…W E Wheelock & Co. Piano. 300
McInery, Maria. 232 E 32d… D Purcell. 1,500
Mendelsohn, P. 54 Pike.… E D Farrell. 205
Moore, Emma. 152 W 103d.…T Willis. 166
Morin, Mathilda. 505 W 52d… J Baumann. (R) 100
Morrell, C J. 602 E 144th.…J Moriarty. 158
Morton, Jennie. 108 W 123d.…L L Frost. 2,500
Moss, Joseph. 550 E 16th.…J Moriarty. 51
McKenna, Margaret. 261 W 123d.…R L Epstein. Piano. 200
Morton, Nettie. 179 E 108th.…C H Sleight. 100
Porchette, John. 157 Wooster.…C R Rugger. 750
Porter, M E. 59 E 8th …Fennell & Pye. 140
Porter, G. 276 7th av.…Brooklyn F Co. 170
Palmer, S R. 345 E 2?th.…J Baumann. 653
Pike, Mrs S. 101 E 80th… J H Little. 285
Randel, S. 77 Division.…H Israel & Son. 501
Regan, C. 248 W 33d …L Baumann. 112
Reute, W T. 418 W 48d.…L Baumann. 285
Rosenberg, E. 88 Greenwich …Jordan & M. 151
Robinson, Hattie P. 37 W 42d… S Russell. 300
Ryerson, Georgie A.…S I Herschmann. 134
Raferty, Julia. 6 Renwick.…R M Walters. Piano. 215
Rauh, Theodore. 301 W 47th.…W E Wheelock & Co. Piano. 450
Read, Harry. 210 E 10th.…J Moriarty. (R) 144
Richmond, J S.…Gately & Williams. 265
Riel, B, Mrs. 349 W 45th.…W E Wheelock & Co. Piano. 250
Rohrs, F. 511-517 E 70th.…J Rohrs. Oil Cloths, &c. 326
Salomon, Felix. 151 W 132d.…F J Brechtel. (R) 189
Schwenkel, W. 516 E 88d… Jordan & M. (R) 108
Sheeley, W H. 236 W 128d.…W E Wheelock & Co. Piano. (R) 110
Sichler, Richard. 1929 3d av.…H Israel & Sons. 180
Smith, S C & M M. 100 W 92d.…Lincoln I & G Co. 200
Stern, Joseph. 365 Pleasant av.…H Israel & Son. (R) 328
Stratford, Patrick. 420 W 56th.…O'Farrell Co. 119
Scheible, E and Sarah. 1232 3d av.…E C Hinsdale. 100
Spanner, Carolina. 125 Elizabeth.…W Schlaeppi. 100
Sullivan, Kate. 424 W 53d.…L Baumann. 167
Sontag, G J. Cauldwell av, s w cor 165th st.…S Heyman & Co. (R) 304
Stein, C. 1061 Myrtle av.…L Baumann. 111
Stilwell, Emma. 415 W 47th.…Manges Bros. 100
Steinmetz, P C. 258 E 83d.…Manges Bros. 209
Thompson, W H. 142 Willis av …Dreisacker & Co. 157
Tomassek, Eliza. 242 E 83d… S Heyman & Co. 355
Taussig, Chas. 147 E 48th.…F J Brechtel. (R) 189
Totten, J W. 215 W 104th.…J Sketchley. 200
Theinhardt, Clara. 258 W 55th.…Amelia Graeff. 700
Valentine, Isaac. 57 E 86th… L Baumann. 123
Von Doenhoff, Helen. 159 E 63d.…Alexander Bros. 737
Valentine, I. 57 E 86th.…L Baumann. 207
Vincent, Fanny. 258 W 39th… J H Little. 141
Wilson, G N. 317 W 58th.…J Gregg & Co. 255
Windsor, Helen. 14 E 24th.…S Baumann. 481
Woolston, A. 158 Delancey.…Jordan & M. 102
Washburn, C M. 71 E 108th.…M H C Foster. 100
Williams, F and H. 327 W 112th.…Commercial Credit Co. 200
Wiltsie, Rhoda. Spuyten Duyvil, N Y. …Margaret French. 250
Weber, Theo. 152 W 25th.…J Baumann. (R) 205
Weed, Mrs Fred K. 14 E 125th.…D Schwarzkopf. 750
Whitehurst, Mrs B D. 115 W 27th.…H Israel & Sons. (R) 150
Williams, Carrie P. 227 W 4th.…C E Pierce. 130
Wolf, E F. 167 E 90th …E D Farrell. 166
Wolf, Kittie. 60 1st.…E D Farrell. 186
Wood, Mary E. 125 W 61st.…C E Pierce. 180
Wright, G H. 159 W 84th.…L Baumann. 151
Weber, A. 252 W 43d.…American Guar. Assoc. 500
Wright, Mary E. 251 W 43d.…E C Hinsdale. 190
Yeager, Mary. 99 E 4th.…Jordan & M. (R) 105
Zander, Mary. 104 E 11th.…W E Wheelock & Co. Piano. (R) 196

MISCELLANEOUS.

Ahrens, Louis. 508 W 31st.…H Ahrens. Horse, Wagon, &c. (R) 350
Althans, C H. 340 W 126th.…J W Tufts. Soda Fixtures. (R) 150
Anastasi, Francesco. 590 3d av.…A Schwaab. Barber Fixtures. 61
Ahlgrim, O. 1631 2d av.… Y Heinemann. Candy Store. 900
Ametram, N. 405 W 38th.…A Fasano. Barber Fixtures. 100
Abrahams, H. 155 Suffolk.…P Leidersdorf. Machines, &c. 100
Baier, S. 637 E 13th.…Y Friedman. Grocery Fixtures. 100
Baroslowsky, M. 63 Elizabeth.…J Perlman. Sewing Machines. 150
Bell, W R. 1st av and 100th st.…M F Schwieman & Co. Machinery. 965
Bender, M F. 357 W 14th.…J W Tufts. Soda Apparatus. 582
Burgess, R. 322 Greenwich.…H F Ehler. Restaurant Fixtures. 125
Bree, D, Jr.…M Donovan. Horses, Trucks. 300
Benedict Popular P Co. 37 Bond.…Damon & Peets. Press. 125
Burrows, J H. 487 10th av.…M J La Place Martin. Horses, &c. 300
Bauer, J. 30 Washington Market.…Anna M Hemmer. Stand. 400
Bellucci, Maria. 7½ Mulberry.…Irene Campana. Grocery Fixtures. 110
Bieth, J. 430 8th av.…Mary A Heidelberger. Bakery Fixtures. 400
Branagan, John. 73 Roosevelt.… Joseph Branagan. Milk Business. 500
Bennette, Frank. 48 E 110th.…A Schwaab. Barber Fixtures. 108
Brown & Skinner.…Insurers Automatic Fire Ex Co. Fixtures. 4,250
Buck, G and F. 292 1st av. ..W F Trautwein. Bakery Fixtures. 1,000
Bursky, F H. 208 E 34th.…O W Van Campen & Son. Grocery Fixtures. 90
Buth, G and F. 292 1st av.…S Valentine & Son. Bakery Fixtures. 1,000
Capriola, Felice. 762 11th av… V Lombardi. Barber Fixtures. 25
Clark & Dolan. 62d st and East River.…New England Brown Stone Co. Machinery, &c. 2,283
Comerford, M. 327 W 26th.…Marvin Safe Co. Safe. 150
Conklin, R S. 40 W 60th.…N & L Henry. Horses. (R) 360
Conlan, H. 521 W 38th.…T H Benedict. Horse. 500
Cordes, Laura A. 434 W 46th.…P Eisenbauer. Grocery Fixtures. 115
Corlies, George. 34 and 36 North Moore.…H Griffin & Sons. Machinery. 1,200
Cummings, J B. 56 Madison.…H Lawton. Presses. 273
Carroll, W. 108 W 32d… A L Winne. Cigar Fixtures. 100
Cline, J W & Son. 44 Ahn.…Lincoln I & G Co. Machinery. 135
Dieckman, J E. 167 E 121st J Cunningham Son & Co. Undertaker's Wagon. 400
Duffy, James. 202 and 204 East 102d.…J H Lippe. Hearse, &c. 3,296
De Leo, C. 135 E 110th… J Blase. Barber Shop. 240
Devoe, W T.…Damon & Peets. Press. 105
Esposito, Camillo. 188 Canal.…A Schwaab. Barber Fixtures. 95
Farina, Raffaelo. 2342 Old Broadway.…V Zipuldi. Shoe Shop Fixtures. 50
Finch, F L. 170 East 106th.…H G Zaunie. Drug Fixtures. 525
Fisher, J O, manager of The Monitor Press. 106 Liberty.…A C Fisher. Printing Office. 700
Forman, Ralph. Reade and Elm.…American Mfg Co. Machinery, &c. 293
Gerson, Mrs E. 248 Divison.…Bennett & G. Soda Fixtures. 300
Grinspan, Abraham. 200 Rivington.…East Side Bank. Clocks, &c. 300
Grossman, M and J Weiser. 17 Division.…L Heinsfurter. Butcher Fixtures. 200
Ginsburg, B. 180 Orchard… Liberty Machine Works. Press 90
Gray, C, Jr. 909 6th av.…F H Hobbs. Presses, &c. 150
Hawes, H E… H C Zehner. Machinery. 400
Hilton, J. 89 Nassau.…Hall's Safe and Lock Co. Safe. 150
Holmes, J. 4 Pearl.…Liberty Machine Works. Press. 600
Hunt, W H. 301 W 123d …A E Woodman. Horses, Trucks, &c. 3,000
Haas, F X. 30 Suffolk.…J H Bates. Horse, Truck, &c. 250
Hart, H C, successor to Jos Anderson.…J W Tufts. Soda Fixtures. (R) 346
Haiman, W. 87 Ridge.…A Greenspan. Machinery. 25
Higgins, F A. 659 9th av .. J W Tufts. Soda Fixtures. (R) 100
Horr, F J. 330 Cortlandt.…J M Ruhl. Barber Fixtures. 400
Hall & Prodgers 79 Mercer.…W Prodgers. Machines, &c. 2,500
Hanover, H, and Joseph H D Rehberger. 35 South 5th st, Brooklyn … A Hanover. Printing Office. 975
Same.…L M Ernst Printing Office 400
Johnson & Eagan. 618 E 142d .. E Johnson. Horses and Wagons. 450
Jonik, Marie. 2449 2d av.…A Adler & Co. Bakery Fixtures. 200
Kasschan, Minna, doing business as Star Plating Works. 17 Bond.…H Spies. Machinery. 651
Kremrich, W, and J Kemmer, Jr, of Kremrich & Kemmer. 717-721 E 5th.…J Kemmer, Sr. Machinery, &c, Cabinet Factory. 1,000
Kelly, J. 536 W 43d.…J H Lippe. Coaches. 342
Kong, C C. 19 Bowery.…Coon & Kim. Theatrical Fixtures. 350
Kyle & Minnerly. 48 Horatio.…J H Van Houten. Horses, Trucks, &c. 400
Lohrand & Behnke. 563 2d av.…P H Siebern. Store Fixtures, &c. 800
Lussen, G L. 169 E 129th.…Dunham & Co. Coach. (R) 120
Levy, L. 54 Sheriff.…M Solomon. Sewing Machines. 200
Lauer, C C. 240 E 56th.…C Harris. Butcher Fixtures. 500
Mayers, M. 3d av, n w cor 130th st.…M Shine. Summer Garden Fixtures. secures rent
Metropolitan Telephone and Telegraph Co.… Mercantile Trust Co. Rights, Privileges and Franchises. 2,000,000
Marotine, Alice. 25 South 5th av.…G Papot. Fixtures and Furniture. 300
McGeorge, P A. 220 William.…W McGeorge, Jr. Presses, &c. (R) 17,220
McSwyny, Kate. 240 Broadway.…Mary Kearney. Shoe Store. 1,000
Same.…W E Blanchard. Shoe Store. 1,429
Monahan, J. 511-518 E 118th.…W Galvin. Horses, &c. 800
McDowell, W H. 33 E 133d.…W C McDowell. Horse, &c. (R) 650
Mount Morris Electric Light Co .. Central Trust Co. Franchises. (R) 950,000
Mull & Fromes. 1583 Washington av.…A A Mull. Horses, Trucks, &c. 500
Mullady, John. 79th st, bet Avs A and B.…H J Hanlon. Blacksmith Fixtures. 200
Nathan, Daniel. 87th st and Madison av .. T Cote. Barber Fixtures. 500
Neulist, G. 296 E 4th.…J Weiss. Ice Wagon, &c. 350
Parrish, B. 62 East Broadway.…Bennett & G. Soda Fixtures. 200
Post, W G. 284 Willis av.…J W Tufts. Soda Apparatus. 225
Pracees, I. 381 6th av.…B Weinberger. Barber Fixtures. 100
Rowe, J. 108 E 142d.…M Mack. Coaches. 175
Ruebe, A E. 148th st, s s, 270 w Brook av.…C H Krug. Machinery. 500
Reid, D. 305 W 30th.…R Beggs. Grocery Fixtures. 125
Rubin, Barnet. Chrystie and Canal sts.…J W Smith. Truck and Horse. 100
Roma, F. 208 E 14th.…A De Santis. Barber Fixtures. 400
Rosenberg, A. 153 West Broadway.…Manhattan Type Foundry. Type. 30
Rneth, J and E Bartolicius. 756 Greenwich.…H Dantel. Tools, &c. 300
Simone, M and F Fanizzi. 566 7th av.…R Ramforth. Barber Fixtures. 204
Stein, I. 113 Lewis.…Strause & Israelson. Butcher Fixtures. 125
Schwartung, Henrietta R. Ogden av, cor Wolf st.…C H Goess. Horse, Grocery Fixtures. 1,000
Scudder, R B. 163 W 15th.…Dunham & Co. Coach. 400
Silberman, Meyer. 98 Hester.…J A Raab. Butter Ice Box. 45
Starace, Michael. 397 3d av …N Cappiello. Barber Fixtures. 600
Strohmenger, C L, Jr. 493 6th av.…R L Dick. Store Fixtures, &c. 2,000
Schink & Steinbach. 68 East Broadway.…Liberty Machine Works. Press. 589
Schoenberger, L. 27 Centre …Liberty Machine Works. Printers Fixtures. 851
Schwarz, W. 2103 2d av.…H Hammond. Grocery Fixtures. 100
Stanley & Hall. 31 Frankfort.…R M Bassett. Machinery. 6,000
Stapleton, T and J F. E 104th st …J C Murray trustee. Horses, Trucks, &c. 135
Stern, L. 261 2d.…W Buermann. Livery Business, Horses, Wagons. 600
The South Publishing Co. 76 Park pl.…Babcock P P Mfg Co. Press. (R) 1,280
Tilden, Lilian E F. England… H Isaacs and ano. ½ share in estate real and personal of M Tilden dec'd. £8,000
Tafel, J. 1589 Av A.…J Nickolaus. Store Fixtures. (R) 175
Tannelli, Antonio. 686 11th av.…V Lombardi. Barber Fixtures. 25
Tancitelli & Capriola. 445 W 52d.…V Lombardi. Barber Fixtures. 185
Thompson, Walter. Liverpool.…C C Monroe. Yacht Clara. 4,000
Tessmer, A. 222 E 82d… P Heinrich. Printing Office. 514
Tietze, C …A Benk. Horse, &c. 250
Volkhardt, A. 33 Av A .. Liberty Machine Works. Press. 145
Walton, T. 245 8th av… Lamson Co. Cash Register. 165
Weinstock, L. 1766 Amsterdam av.…J McLean. Butcher Fixtures. 290
Woodworth, C & Co. 116 W 23d… J W Tufts. Soda Apparatus. 1,200
Weiss, A. 6 City Hall pl …Ely Weiss. Press, &c. 500
Woelfle, W. 156 E 87th.…G F & E C Swift. Baker Fixtures. 100
Wash Out Mfg Co. 17 Hubert.…E Montamer. Machinery, &c. 250
Weidman, G L. 1211 Broadway.…A Curtis. Confectionery Fixtures. 340
Wiedemann, H. 292 Bowery.…W Murray. Barber Fixtures. 250
Zeisler, L. 8 Av B …J Weiss. Barber Fixtures. 160

BILLS OF SALE.

Ainsworth, James. 120 Walker.…Catherine Ainsworth. Machinery. 4,000
Barbarita, Raphaele. 867 3d av.…G Fiscella. Shoe Shop Fixtures, &c. 100
Blumenthal, L. Ogden av, cor Wolf st.…H R Schwartung. Grocery. 475
Buonsignore, G & F. 77 Greenwich av… V Farengo et al. Barber Fixtures 260
Baker, F S. 212 W 103d W Baker. Furniture. nom
Barcalow, G B. 147 W 35th, Broadway and 36th st …Annie V. McWilliam. Furniture, also Horse, &c. 300
Crawford, R J. 246 W 125th.…Wright & Williams. Carpenter Shop. 100
Clifton, J G. 108 Spring.…D Kerbs. Cigar Fixtures. 1
Dorrance, Kate B 432 5th av.…R G Berry. Tailor Fixtures. 888
Epple, Rosa. 328 Broome.…G and C Oltmann. Saloon. 1,200
Elsing, E B. 88 Ridge.…M Roth. Saloon. nom
Feinsod, H and L. 27 Ludlow.…I Feinsod. Saloon Fixtures. 200
Friedman, Lena. 62 Baxter.…A Troiano. Saloon. 550
Graefer, N H. 956 10th av.…J Oehler. Drug Fixtures. nom
Gasser, A. 18 Greenwich.…W Redigahn. Saloon Fixtures. 2,600
Gauer, Charles. 2061 3d av.…Lisette Gauer. Bottling Business. nom
Heitlinger, A. 88 Ridge ..E B Elsing. Saloon. nom
Hepp, F. 161 Av B.…F Birkenmeir. Grocery. 305
Kingsbury, Carrie C. 247 W 42d.…Maria L Ford. Fixtures. 1,080
Loriot, H. 136 Fulton.…A Calvet. Tools, &c. 600
Losi, L. 82d st and Columbus av.…L Coari. Restaurant Fixtures. 5,000
Oehler, J. 756 10th av.…O P M Liebrenz & Co. Drug Fixtures. 1,700
Ortmann, F. 288 Canal… P Henig. Saloon and Restaurant. 6,000
Perlman, D.…Scheurer & Kalchheim. Horse and Wagon. 70
Pertsch, F and W. 1 and 3 Broome.…B Gunst. Engine, &c. nom
Reinert, Frederick.…Annie Reinert. Horse, Truck, &c. 700
Roth, Herman. 200 E 2d.…S Helfish. Cigar Fixtures. 100
Russell, H A. 298 West Houston.…H McNeilly. Grocery Fixtures. 500
Rockfeller, N B. 1007 2d av.…G F Kitchell. Milk Business. 1,050
Selig, M. 1541 1st av… Sophie Selig. Bakery Fixtures. 300
Segal, Rosa. 202 Rivington ..S Witner. Candy and Cigar Store. 140
Schoesser, F. 975 1st av.…P Rohl. Saloon. 1,900
Zauner, K H. 170 E 106th …H G Zauner, Jr. Drug Fixtures. 500

ASSIGNMENTS OF CHATTEL MORTGAGE.

Ehret, G to Bernheimer & S. (Mort given by J Bannon, Oct 8, 1889.) 1,500
Ruppert, J to Bernheimer & S. (C. Grube, Feb 7, 1889.) 1,800

KINGS COUNTY.

JULY 30 TO AUGUST 5—INCLUSIVE.

SALOON AND RESTAURANT FIXTURES.

Anderson, Chas. 25 Union.…India Wharf B Co. $300
Buekl, Philip. 40 Knickerbocker av… Burger & Hower Brewing Co. 800
Blase, Henry. 505 Marcy av.…George Ehret. 450
Bohanna, Michael. 358 Hamilton av.…D Stevenson. 600
Borrmann, Minna. 254 Marion.…Michael Seitz. 600
Bahrenburg, John H. 675 6th av.…Obermeyer & L. 425
Bonner, Michael. 211 and 213 Park av.…Wm Ulmer. 3,500
Catterson, B and T. 510 Manhattan av …S Liebmann's Sons B Co. 1,000
Corbett, Thomas. 1235 De Kalb av.…S Liebmann's Sons B Co. 800
Cosgrove, John J. 774 Grand.…S Liebmann's Sons Brewing Co. 1,000
Dierks, Otto. 244 Columbia.…J Hoffman Brewing Co. 1,650
Eschman, Wm. 68 Metropolitan av.…L Eppig. 500

Everett, Susan M. 323, 325 and 327 Washington ..I Steigerwald. Restaurant Fixtures. 500

Faltack, Paul. 134 Dupont....S Liebmann's Sons Brewing Co. 280

Farrell, Jas F. 413 Smith....Beadleston & Woerz. 100

Forster, Joseph. 47 Johnson av....Wm Ulmer. 300

Gerckens, Aug. Liberty av, cor Barbey st .. Frank Ibert. 250

Gemmel, Philip. 1057 Flushing av....C Frese. 568

Gieges, Theodore. 461 20th....S Liebmann's Sons B Co. 800

Grill, Fred. 275 and 277 Ellery....Anne Grill. 7,800

Haesloop, Chris P. 1560 Fulton....S Liebmann's Sons B Co. 1,800

Heik, August. 595 Kent av....S Liebmann's Sons B Co. 1,500

Howard, James. 3d av, cor 19th st... India Wharf B Co. 400

Hughes, Catharine. 721 Dean....Abbott B Co. 500

Hanisch, Julius. 168 Gwinnett....Otto Huber. (R) 550

Hanfield, Franz S. 487 Broadway....Wm Ulmer. 500

Hayden, F. 108 Manhattan av....Otto Huber. (R) 800

Healy, Patrick. 33 Hoyt....Long Island Brewery. 8,000

Hildebrandt, Albert. 194 Union av .. Otto Huber. (R) 650

Holsten, George. 1167 Bedford av....Beadleston & Woerz 4,000

Jacobson & Swanson. 116 Sackett ...J Hoffman Brewing Co. 1,232

Kelly, Andrew. 1068 De Kalb av....Williamsburgh Brewing Co. 300

Kenny, Chas E. 144 West...S Liebmann's Sons Brewing Co. 1,850

Koehnel, Elize. 193 Johnson av....Burger & Hower Brewing Co. 595

Kuhlken, Henry F. 1013 Fulton....Jacob Ruppert. 646

Kern, Louis. 46 Ten Eyck....G Feigenspan. 600

Kienzle, Michael. 181 Stockton....Wm Ulmer. 600

Kilgallen, Patrick. 263 Hamilton av....India Wharf B Co. 300

Kossmann, M. 133 Leonard....C Frese. 400

Lapp, Charles. Liberty av, cor Cypress av.... Charles Frese. 200

Letziesen, Vinzens. 1200 Meserole....Welz & Zerweck. 400

Larkin, Michael. 432 Hicks....Wm Ulmer. 1,000

Leimer, Fred. 281 Scholes....Otto Huber Brewery. 110

Malion, Robert. 228 Pearl ...Bachman Brewing Co. 500

Mangels, H. 14 Alabama av....H Schierloh. 100

Mass, Christian and A E Gundlach. 1096 Bedford av....H D Laue. 4,500

McCabe, Thos. 195 Franklin....S Liebmann's Sons Brewing Co. 1,000

McMahon, John F. 109 Flatbush av....M McDowell. 200

Marquardt, Gottfried. 1 Delmonico pl....George Ehret. 450

Meyer, Wm. 12, 14 and 16 Fulton....P Ballantine & Sons. 3,000

Mahnken, Henry. 171 Spencer....S Liebmann's Sons B Co. 2,400

McEvilly, James. 18 India Wharf ... India Wharf B Co. 1,800

Newsburger, E. 156 Leonard....Otto Huber Brewery. 800

O'Connor, John. 349 Berry....F & M Schaefer Brewing Co. 1,800

Pigot, Michael A. 14 Myrtle av....Wm Ulmer. 1,500

Rankel, George. 50 Lorimer....L Eppig. 496

Rath, Peter W. 648 Wythe av....Otto Huber B. 1,725

Reinig, J A. 120 Boerum....L Eppig. 300

Reneke, Wm. 913 Flushing av....Obermeyer & Liebmann. 600

Rohm, Wm. 470 Humboldt ...Joe Fallert Brewing Co. 550

Rothang, M J. 906 Herkimer....Eppig & Ibert. 450

Russo, M. 134 North 6th....John Kress Brewing Co. 350

Sauer Bros. 21 Grand....George Ehret. 5,000

Sintef, Henry. 939 De Kalb av ...Joseph Eppig. 600

Van Sickell, Wm M. 808 Fulton .. India Wharf B Co. 1,600

Weinrach, Jacob. 391 Liberty av....F Ibert. 350

Walsh, James J. 872 Broadway....John J Reilly. 200

Wichman, C 623 Atlantic av....Claus Lipsius Brewing Co. 600

Wills, H & J. 143 Kent av... P Weidman. 2,800

Wiebauer, Wm. 150 Union av....Ernest Ochs. 750

Woedebeck, O. 197 Humboldt ...Williamsburgh B Co. 100

Zaun, Henry. 315 Rockaway av....L Eppig. 440

HOUSEHOLD FURNITURE.

Abearnes, Ida E. 134 Amity....Financial Credit Co. 130

Best, Frederick. 721 Macon ...C T Kendrick & Co. 181

Boschen, Fred W. 623 Douglass ...Wm J Weidersum. 575

Bingham, Letitia. 266 Franklin av....Jas McEnerey & Co. 200

Brier, John 692 President....F W Whipple 475

Carmichael, Nellie. 450 Franklin av....Anderson & Co. Piano. 255

Checkley, E. 111 Rutledge....A Schulz. 193

Cowen, Mrs R. 474 Madison....C T Kendrick & Co. 142

Elliott, Jane D. 424 Greene av....P L Spence. 175

Faulkner, Mrs J J. Reid av....C T Kendrick & Co. 112

Ford, Joseph B. 370 Hancock ...The Commercial Credit Co. 255

Gill, Stephen. 133 Schermerhorn....Thos F Mulqueen. 245

Haskell, Peter. 383 Lexington av....Geo L Mariner. 250

Haines, H A. 810 Adam....E Driscoll & Bro. 479

Houstoun, A M. 644 Hancock....E C Hinsdale. 190

Klompus, H. 85 Bartlett....C T Kendrick & Co. 193

Langefeld, H E. 146 Stockton....C T Kendrick & Co. 342

Lincoln, Clarence. 968 Jefferson av... E C Hinsdale. 200

Maloney, M E. 26 Bushwick av . A Schulz. 106

Maun, Mary. 258 13th....A Pearson. 144

Marks, Mrs L. 8 Vernon av....C T Kendrick & Co. 237

McGann, Tessie. 265 Bergen....Anderson & Co. Piano. 285

Neily, John. 1116 Prospect pl....Anderson & Co. Piano. 300

Newman, I. 64 Gerry....C T Kendrick & Co. 350

Purrington, M A. 563 Quincy....C T Kendrick & Co. 133

Riley, Samuel J. 87 Skillman....C T Kendrick & Co. 129

Rodewald, Fred. 683 Van Buren....C T Kendrick & Co. 102

Rogers, J J. 166 Walworth....Mullins & Sons. 123

Ryan, Edward. 104 Rockaway av....A Schulz. 102

Scott, Lizzie. 44 Prospect....A Pearson. 147

Staples, Henry. 118 Somers ...Anderson & Co. Piano. 200

Thompson, Mrs F. 30 Broome....Mullins & Son. 177

Underhill, C A. 136 Madison....Commercial Credit Co. 260

Van Pelt, Frank. 427 Gold....E Driscoll & Bro. 195

Vengels, H. 805 Park av....J C Hegeman. 128

Von Bistramb, C F. 703 3d av .. E Schoppen. 600

Walker, Ansella 606 10th ...C E Pierce. 100

Ward, Mrs E. 739 Franklin av....C T Kendrick & Co. 190

Zimmer, Louis L. 53 Pineapple....Mary C Van Brunt. 375

MISCELLANEOUS.

Bader, Henry. 458 Grand....Louis Bader. Jewelry store. 250

Bartenhagen, Wm. 243 South 4th....G A Gardner. Milk Business. 200

Bettfreund, Adolph. 305 Floyd....Maria F Bettfreund. Grocery Fixtures. 1,100

Cohen, M. 57 and 59 Scholes...M Abrahams. Tailoring Business. 150

Connors & Gunyan. 63 Kent....J C Stead. Horses, Wagon, &c. 360

Cottrill, Jr, Wm A. Liberty av and Linwood st ....R S Schmidt. Butcher Shop. 150

Cully, John. 344 Hudson av....D B Dunham. Coach. 850

Demarest, A A. 156 Maiden lane, New York.... M W Thomson. Office Fixtures. 250

Frisbie, J W. 415 Bridge....John Kipp. Blacksmith Tools. 300

Fahlbusch, Wm. 118 5th av....Philipp Grimm. Barber Shop. 200

Gello, V and A Dablerl. 316 North 2d....Archer Mfg Co. Barber Shop. 895

Glinns Sons. 47 Herbert ...D B Dunham. Coaches. (R) 480

Holden, Henry ...J Downey. Buggy. 115

Hopkins, Thomas....D B Dunham. Coach. (R) 264

Hanover, Henry. 35 South 5th....L M Ernest. Presses. 400

Same... Aaron Hanover. Presses, &c. 975

Koehler, Fred. 253 Bushwick av....E D Leng. Barber Shop. 100

Lee, Linda M. 113 and 115 Sterling pl....George L Thompson. Livery Stable. 13,000

Lescewicz, Frank. 407 Nostrand av....A Johnston. Fixtures &c. 73

Lessels, Edgar A. 588 Fulton....Adolph Kleint. Bakery Fixtures. 1,000

Lewinske, Philip. 166 Dikeman....J Lewinske. Machinery. 1,000

Lange, Henry A. 121 Grand....Jas W Tufts. Soda Water Apparatus. 337

Mullady, Daniel. 6 and 8 Hunts alley....D B Dunham. Coaches. (R) 928

Nelson, Emil. 316 Columbia....Campbell Printing Press and Mfg Co. Press. 660

Neuberger, Jacob S. 936 Madison....A Adams. Fixtures, &c. 500

Ratjen & Co, J H. 13 Columbia Heights.... Wm H Ratjen. Grocery Fixtures. 650

Rhinehart, Charles F. 193 Spencer....Beers Frost. Horses, Trucks, &c. 1,450

Roeder, Annie B. 79 Meserole....G Grauer. Butcher Shop. 800

Schertl, Leonhard. 276 Kent av....L Friedl. Horses, Wagon, &c. 152

Scotto, Joseph....Robert B Maxwell. Horse and Harness. 125

Simonis, Charles....J Downey. Phaeton. 170

Simon, Hugo. 489 7th av....A D Puffer & Sons. Soda Water Apparatus. 500

Spadavecchia, Anne. 74 Flatbush av....Mary A Doodey. Confectionery Fixtures. 600

BILL OF SALE.

Ainsworth, James. 120 Walker st, New York ....C A Ainsworth. Machinery. 4,000

Frankel, Edward. 607 Bushwick av....Jacob Schutz and Charles Samuels. Pool Table. 125

Frost, Beers. 193 Spencer....C F Rhinehart. Horses, Trucks, &c. 3,150

Gardner, G A....William Bartenhagen. Milk Route. 400

McDermott, Thos. 90 Prince....Denis Duhig. Saloon Fixtures. 250

Meyer, George. Glenmore, cor Sheffield av.... G Mueller. Bakery Fixtures. 500

Patterson, Howard....Benj M Whitlock. Copyright mort $1,000. 500

Piper, Fred W and Edward De Brauwere, Coney Island ...Piper & Co. Hotel and Restaurant. nom

Rempel, John. 104 Flushing av....W Staiegele. Produce Business. 550

Stradley, Luke. 17 and 19 Park row, New York ...J Van Brunmer. Furniture. 1,500

NEW JERSEY.

NOTE.—*The arrangement of the Conveyances, Mortgages and Judgments in these lists is as follows: the first name in the Conveyances is the Grantor; in Mortgages, the Mortgagor; in Judgments, the Judgment debtor.*

ESSEX COUNTY.

CONVEYANCES.

Allen, F B—W Stainsby, Prince st $1,200

Allen, William—K Kelaher, Hudson st 2,000

Arnold, George—E H Snyder, South Orange .... nom

Beach, D H—C H Beach, South Orange 2,700

Blanchard, T C E—A S Allen, South 14th st 100

Breakenridge, J H—E A Grungler, Clinton 900

Buermann, August—A Ulrich, Badger av 600

Same——L E Webbe, Vanderpool st 2,160

Butts, A E—J R Taggart, Wright st .... nom

Cadmus, James—T J Regan, North 11th st 600

Cansbrook, John trustee—Phoenix Hose Co, Bloomfield .... nom

City of Newark—F Viscidi, Drift st 1,500

Corbally, T J—J Hensler, Jr, Patterson st 1,200

Coyne, James—P Munn, East Orange 1,100

Coyle, John—H Siff, s w cor Central av and Lock st 30x40 4,200

Devine, Arthur—Karl Stutz, South Orange 300

Dodd, G F—C A Taylor, Orange 605

Dodd, G F—D MacRorie, Orange 605

Doremus, E O—L Mansbach, Orange 5,000

Doremus, H M—H R Alberson, High st 2,150

Dreyer, Florian—M A Rudman, Bank st .... nom

Dwyer, J R—T Honig, Sussex av 1,200

Edwards, S M—F C Cummings, Augusta st 700

Eisele, J C—W Scarlett, Clinton .... nom

Field, J W—M S O'Connor, West Orange 625

Finnegan, John—A Weiber, Madison st 2,000

First Congregational Church—Essex Land Co., s s Clinton st 339 e Broad st 80x86 28,200

Fischer, F A—E L Eppinger, Springfield av 1,500

Gardner, C A—H L Pierson, South Orange 25

Geraldo, Nicholas—L Wolf, 16th av .... nom

Gould, Ezra—G W Betts, n s Fulton st 251 e Broad st 22x160 7,000

Same——M K Weis, Walnut st 3,500

Graeff, F A—W H Allen, South Orange 35,000

Grant, Patrick—J Coyle, Nuttman st 2,500

Gray, T J—J Clark, Broad st 2,000

Grummon, C A—H E Grummon, Bloomfield .... nom

Grummon, R S—C A Grummon, Bloomfield .... nom

Guenther, J U—G H A Seibt, South 14th st 525

Gyles, T A—B McCabe, Franklin .... nom

Gyles, T A—G R Hill, Franklin .... nom

Hall, Edward—O Akers, Bloomfield 2,000

Haines, C S—L S Pierson, e s Broad st 37 s Fair st 61x59x78x123x81 74,100

Harrison, C J—J Boehner, West Orange 250

Havemeyer, W F—J G Faron, South Orange 2,500

Hoeler, P J—M Horowitz, w s Bruce st 37x120 7,200

Hotz, Annie—W P Rommel, Hillside av .... nom

Jackson, William—C E Wheeler, Milford av 317

Jatkowsky, Max—L Mendel, s s Mercer st 100 w Broome st, 25x100 8,000

Jones, S W—J A Stivers, West Orange .... nom

Kastenhuber, A M—T H Wilcox, Bloomfield 7,500

Kirkpatrick, Alexander—G Molinari, Orange st. nom

Kubler, John—F Tegen, Jr, e s Jelliff av 108 ft n Avon av, 25x100 3,000

Kurfess, Risina—L C Herold, Magazine st 2,100

Lauer, William—O Milford, w s Barclay st 377 ft n Spruce st 25x69x43x68 3,000

Lichtenberger, Louise—L Aff, New York av 100

Lindsley, L L—J B Walker, East Orange 200

Lindsley, O W—M E Mackinson, East Orange 300

Linnett, Thomas—G Linnett, Penna av .... nom

Lloyd, A B—S B Ferris, Montclair 2,750

Love, F J—Bank of Montclair, Montclair 8,500

McCarter, T N—W Zilliff, Belleville av 1,000

Same——G Zelliff, Belleville av 1,000

McDougall, J M—J G Vermilye, e s Bruen st 130 n Green st 28x85 4,960

McPheeters, W S—M A Birtles, Wright st 1,500

Moeller, John—W Stainsby, Corey st 1,000

Navatier, E C—C H McIntire, Clinton 1,100

Orange M E Church—J H Lecher, Orange 5,500

Osborne, J H—E A Underwood, Clinton 900

Parkinson, William—R G Williams, Orange .... nom

Parsons, Jane—M L Cueman, Bloomfield 25

Phoenix Hose Company—E Ward et al, trustees, Bloomfield .... nom

Pyne, P R—F Dreyer, Bank st 1,200

Roff, O M—C M Roff, w s Halsey st where it intersects Morris Canal 26x150 10,500

Rommel, W P—H Hotz, Hillside av .... nom

Rowe, Michael—J F Fields, Warren st 2,500

Scarlett, William—J B Scarlett, Clinton .... nom

Scheerer, G O—C Fischer, Clinton 700

Schmidt, Casper—A Haun, Bergen st 2,600

Security B and L Assoc—C Finnegan, Clinton .... nom

Shipman, Daisy—W S Norris, Garside st 2,200

Smith, H H—N Schneider, Bloomfield 565

Smith, M J—S M Smith, East Orange 2,000

Smith, T J—C R Miller, East Orange 4,500

Snyder, E H—E C Sherman, South Orange 800

Same——G Arnold, South Orange .... nom

Same——K J Baldwin, South Orange 400

Stivers, J A—S E Jones, West Orange .... nom

Stockhammer, Solomon—I Bass, w s Carlton st 92 s Court st 25x100 4,600

Tag, Albert et al—F E Mackay, James st 2,600

Thompson, James—L M Gerbert, Orange 6,000

Townsend, A S—L E Creede, East Orange 3,750

Van Reyper, A E—R Hozack, Belleville 168

Van Riper, P H—A G Miller, Montclair 11,250

Viscidi, Filippo—A Napoliello, Drift st 825

Wilbur, Wilhelmina—M Bergen, South Orange 6,000

Woodruff, Obadiah—M A Wightman, s w cor High and Bank sts 55x100 12,000

MORTGAGES.

Allen, W H—F A Graeff, Orange 19,000

Same——same, Orange 19,000

Andrae, Huldreich—Enterprise B and L Assoc, North 11th st 5,000

Andrus, Cornelia—A Areson, Montclair 2,500

Same——C Bohn, Montclair 2,500

Baldwin, K I—Orange B and L Assoc, South Orange 300

Ball, Isaiah—F H Smith, Jr, East Orange 3,500

Beach, C H—D H Beach, South Orange 1,000

Bergen, Martin—W Wilbur, South Orange 3,000

Betts, G W—A Sickel, Fulton st 3,500

Blum, George—G Krueger, Clinton 600

Boehner, John—J O'Rourke, West Orange 150

Burgesser, Philip—H Burgesser, Sr, Orange st 4,000

Clegg, Kershow—E Mulford, Orange 250

Cogan, R E—Fidelity Title and Deposit Co, Montclair 4,500

Cooper, W E—M W Jacobus, Montclair 5,000

Corcoran, Patrick—C Meeley, Montclair 3,000

Crane, Henry A—Mutual B and L Assoc, 4th st 8,600

Creede, L E—A S Townsend, East Orange 2,500

Damiano, Francisco—J M Trimble, Commerce st 1,100

Darwin, K V—National Shoe and Leather Bank, Bloomfield 1,500

Doremus, C J—M Evans, Webster st 400

Embury, P A—J K Field, West Orange 7,000

Essex Land Co—First Congregational Church, Clinton st 1,400

Fields, J F—M Rowe, Warren st 1,300

Finnegan, Catharine—Security B and L Assoc, Clinton 900

Freeman, G C—Half-Dime Savings Bank, Orange 1,000

Froehlich, Gervasius—C Kuffner, Prince st 2,000

Frome, M E—J M Smith, North 9th st 1,000

Same——same, North 9th st 1,000

Same——Knights of Pythias B and L Assoc, North 9th st 600

Fuller, L C—Howard Savings Inst, 4th st 10,000

Gallagher, M A—E Adams, Clifton av 4,300

George, John—Hearth Stone B and L Assoc, 9th av 4,200

Gould, G W—H W Banta, Caldwell 4,000

Hann, Adam—H Geiger, Bergen st 1,000

Helmstetter, John—M E Smith, Hayes st 300

Herbold, Jacob—S R Ward, 14th av 200

Hill, William—Knights of Pythias B and L Assoc, Forrest st 1,300

Hog, Anton—A Younger, Aqueduct st 200

Honig, Theresa—J R Duryee, Sussex av 1,000

Horowitz, Moritz—P J Hoeler, Bruce st 600

Horowitz, Moritz—The Savings B and L Assoc, Bruce st 6,200
Hotz, Herman—The Washington B and L Assoc, Hillside av 400
Huger, William—J Huger, Monmouth st 1,000
Jaques, Irvington—H G Martin, South Orange 2,100
Joergens, Theodore—The Newark German B and L Assoc, Court st 1,400
Kelaher, Kate—The Savings B and L Assoc, Hudson st 1,600
Kincart, Sarah—The Mutual B and L Assoc, Shipman st 900
Klink, Minnie—J Klink, 5th av 2,600
Kobl, Charles—J H Breakenridge, Clinton 325
Kurzchenkel, Robert—J Parker, Broome st 2,500
Leber, Adolph—The Savings B and L Assoc, Morris av 600
Lee, Rose—E M Colie, Ridge st 680
Mansbach, Louis—E O Doremus, exr, Orange 2,000
Mansbach, Louis—E O Doremus exr, Orange 2,000
Matthews, C B—Prudential Ins Co, N J R R av 9,500
Maynard, M A—J Jenkins, Montclair 16,000
Mendel, Lena—Max Jatkowsky, Mercer st 1,000
Miller, T S—G B Turrell, South Orange 6,000
Mills, S D—C P Derrius, East Orange 800
Morfilt, Jennie A—W R Ward, East Orange 2,000
Morse, S E—T H Decker, Garside st 2,500
Niebling, Michael—J H Breakenridge, Clinton 2,000
Norris, W S—F S Flohn, Garside st 400
Same—G T Casebolt, Garside st 1,000
O'Connor, Arthur—E F Tichenor, Filmore st 400
O'Connor, M S—J W Field, West Orange 525
Pain, W J—J Wharton, 3d st 2,000
Parsil, S B—F T Johnson, Milburn 1,000
Peit, Sophia—Howard Savings Institution, East Orange 1,000
Pierson, L S—C S Haines, Broad st 2,500
Same—same, Broad st 2,500
Same—C S Haines exr, Broad st 10,000
Rautuscha, Michael—E H Affert, East Orange 600
Roemer, E S—N Feick, Washington st 500
Sayre, A E—P T Lewis, Bank st 2,000
Scarlett, Wm—John D Van Duyne, Clinton 1,000
Schwartz, Josephine—C A Feick, South 8th st 200
Siff, Harry—Home B & L, Central av 3,000
Sindle, R S—E A Rayner, Bloomfield 100
Smith, H T—Knights of Pythias B & L Assoc, Jelliff av 2,000
Smith, S M—E Mulford, East Orange 1,000
Sperber, John—Phoenix B & L Asso, South 17th st 1,500
Squier, Albert C—J L Brewster, West Orange 2,900
Squier, T E—F M Squier, East Orange 300
Same—S F Squier, East Orange 400
Ulrich, Anna—A Buerman, Badger st 500
Van Riper, P H—American Ins Co, Montclair 2,000
Van Winkle, F J—J Jaeger, Bloomfield 600
Verone, Luigi—Tenth Ward B and L Assoc, Bedford st 3,800
Vreeland, E S—Mutual Benefit Life Ins Co, Burnet 500
Weis, M K—Fourteenth Ward B and L Assoc, Walnut st 3,200
Weiss, Albert—Home B and L Assoc, Court st 1,400
Wilebir, Andreas—J Wharton, Madison st 700
Williams, I M—M S Williams, Orange 2,000
Zimmerman, T L—North End B and L Assoc, Belleville 2,000

CHATTEL MORTGAGES.

Barker, Mamie—C Treiz, saloon 305
Blauvelt, P M—F C Edwards, horses and trucks 60
Same—E A Blauvelt, horses and trucks 600
Benton, Thomas—J Ketcham, furniture 42
Blanchard, W L—E Alsdorf, piano 235
Carrington, J L—F L Huff, furniture 100
Clayton, C D—Hills Union Brewing Co, saloon 500
Davenport, I W—F L Huff, furniture 100
Dietrich, Frederick—M Sucker, saloon 600
Doyle, James—E C Doyle, horses, &c 500
Eckert, G M—M Eckert, furniture 250
Eisele, Gustav—J G Eisele, grain, groceries, &c 1,500
Farly, Thomas—C Gaffney, horse and wagon, &c 1,200
Fetzer, Matthias—F J Kastner, saloon 250
Flocke, E A—J S Holmes, Jr, furniture 60
Futzinger, Retter—C Buerman, furniture 130
Gonsior, John—A Glueckman and ano, furniture 50
Gonsior, John—J Zaburowsky, furniture 100
Haeberle, Albert—C Trefz, saloon 2,050
Haller, Emma—F Lisiewski, saloon 700
Hofer, John—J Ketcham, furniture 130
Kimkler, John—F Lisiewski, saloon 700
Klittish, Christoph—P Ballantine & Sons, saloon 200
Kurz, Wilhelm—F J Kastner, saloon 425
Larine, Henry—J M Hann, furniture 65
Leonard, E B—W V Egbert & Co, horses and wagons, &c 3,661
Mallet, Sophie—J Ketcham, furniture 100
National Cash Register Co—N Keller, register 175
Neale, Joseph—L C Vossmeyer, furniture 70
Oviatt, W T—E S Clymer, furniture 200
Reup, Peter—F J Kastner, saloon 500
Ruppel, W F—same, saloon 660
Seker, F J—F L Huff, furniture 100
Shupe, Gustina—M Raphael, horse and harness 75
Suchawerski, Julia—C Feigenspan, saloon 510
Szottack, Julius—M Raphael, horse and wagon 70
Terry, H T—J T Terry, pictures, crockery, &c 30
Virnoche, Maxime—T Burk, gun rack, guns, &c 363
Wagner, Albert—Gotfried Krueger Brewing Co, saloon 747
Same—L Murrill, furniture 773
Webb, R M—W C Heilman, furniture 100
Weiser, Emil—Hill's Union Brewing Co, horse and wagon, &c 150
Whyte, Thomas—C Tresz, saloon 800
Wirkle, Ludwig—J Carroll, bakery fixtures 100

JUDGMENTS.

Dwyer, John—E G Heller et al 685
Honeywood, E F et al—The H B Claflin Co 2,105
Mucklow, H L—H Hoch and ano 1,008
Nellis, Alvina—H Schuessler 388
Romine, J W and ano—J J G McShane 442
Ulrich, F G—J S Crane & Co 504

HUDSON COUNTY.

CONVEYANCES.

Allen, Robert—H V Vulte, Kearney $1,700
Anderson, H A—W Gardner, J City 250
Andes, John—J Selfridge, Union nom
Boethe, Maria—Catharine W Jud, J City 5,000
Bostwick, Frances M—Lizzie S Weed, J City 900
Brand, Leopold—Emma Bultz, Union 5,000
Browning, J H—Catharine Norton, J City 730
Same—Eugenia C Coleman, J City 730
Browning, J H—R J Allen, J City 1,200
Burnham, F G—T Welwood, Harrison 8,304
Bruns, J N—W Bruns, J City 28,000
Burton, Harriet G—J E Leete, Bayonne 1,500
Chancellor, Mary—R W Dewey, Hoboken 3,050
Close, Ellen M—N Kemann, Bayonne 700
Conway, Jno—O Haars, Union 600
Crevier, J C—Louise L McDougall, Hoboken 7,500
Cunningham, Ann—H Birtley, Hoboken 350
Donnell, Gertrude—The Central N J Land and Improvement Co, Bayonne 1,000
Dundon, Jane—Nellie Hurley, Bayonne nom
Egbert, T K—C H Reilley, J City 500
Eggers, H C E—T B Black, Hoboken 7,500
Eilshemius, H G—Sophia J Kerr, Kearney 1,560
Eoff, H A—P Mansfield, Bayonne 350
Eppens, Fred P—J A Eppens, Hoboken nom
Eppens, J A—Sophia E Eppens, Hoboken nom
Everett, Matilda by exr, by City Collector—H Harney, J City 431
Eilshemius, H G—R Davidson, Kearney 409
Same—W F Clemmons, Kearney 2,300
Fitch, Harriet—Sarah J Starin, J City 425
Garland, Hugh—A Cassidy, J City 700
Haege, Adolph—L Brand, Union 5,000
Hansen, F C—J A Ross, Union 350
Hemkein, Anna C—Theresa Gavazzi, Union 850
Hetherington, J W—Margaret Hetherington, J City 730
Hillock, Margaret—C Buchholtz, Hoboken 2,000
Hollister, Geo—E K Lane, Bayonne nom
Holton, Mary D—Mary V Craig, J City 4,250
Howell, Mary—Nellie Hurley, Bayonne nom
Hurley, Jeremiah—Nellie Hurley, Bayonne nom
Joeckel, Geo—T Schumann, Hoboken 6,000
Kelsall, Nora T—G Howarth, Kearney 6,400
Kingsland, E W—H J Trumble, J City 2,700
Kiolon, Ellen M—D F Reed, Hoboken nom
Krutina, Fred—Lovetta Liverding, Union 1,000
Kuldosher, Vincent, by sheriff—C L Demarest, Bayonne 500
Lawrence, G K—C H Julk, J City 900
Leete, Edgar L, by sheriff—Harriet G Burton, Bayonne 700
Lewis, Albert—C Schweinler, Hoboken 600
Long, James and Henry Milter, by sheriff—J Brady, Bayonne 1,725
Loury, Catharine—Nellie Hurley, Bayonne nom
McCoy, Mary J—C Keegan, Guttenberg 106
Meyer, Elise—H L Meyer, Bayonne nom
Meyers, Moses—S W Brown, Kearney nom
Monahan, James—Ellen Walsh, Harrison 75
Moody, N D—O E Sharrot, J City 3,000
Mulcahey, J H—J Mulcahey, Hoboken nom
Nichols, E H—E P Kennelly, J City 350
North Jersey Land Co—W N Jennings, Kearney 500
Ogden, W B, by exrs—W Bretz, J City 2,000
O'Sullivan, Cornelius, and Hanorah Condon, by sheriff—H Crongar, Harrison 7,000
Otten, Louis—H Harnes, Hoboken 12,250
Peltke, Albert—W Gardner, J City 1,100
Phillips, Alpha—A McConnack, Bayonne 400
Plenty, Josephus—The Plenty Horticultural and Skylight Works, J City 7,750
Rudiger, J M—J Henderson, J City 750
Schaefer, Anna—H Roeber, Union 200
Schleman, Robert—R Schlemon, Union 3,325
Schlick, Marie—Sophie Erdmann, J City 5,600
Schultz, Valentine—A Schmidt, Bayonne 250
Schultz, Otto—M Baader, West Hoboken 8,500
Same—O Poeschel, West Hoboken nom
Same—same, West Hoboken nom
Same—W Braunstein, West Hoboken 20,000
Selfridge, Jane—J Andes, Union nom
Siegfried, Adam—J V Shelly, West Hoboken 900
Seel, Chas—P Yost, West Hoboken 1,000
Smith, E S—A Smith, Weehawken 250
The Central Railroad Co of New Jersey—The Central New Jersey Land and Improvement Co, Bayonne nom
The Kearney Land Co—A Hantfinger, Kearney 225
The Kearney Land Co—J Ehmann, Kearney 450
Van Buskirk, Dewitt—The Central N J Land and Impt Co, Bayonne nom
Van Buskirk, J H—C F J Anderson, Bayonne 3,400
Van Emburgh, Benj—Annie M Van Emburgh, Kearney 150
Van Sann, Isaac—J Dickinson, J City 1,000
Wellinghoff, Lucie—H W Meyer, J City 1,275
Wittreich, Chas—Emma Sutz, Union 1,500
Worden, Carrie—E J Sparenberg, Hoboken nom
Same—same, Hoboken nom

MORTGAGES.

Abbott, Isabella F—J Van Horn, J City, 3 years 3,200
Adam, Thos—P Fuller trustee, Bayonne, 5 years 3,250
Same—Mary E Babbitt, Bayonne, 5 years 1,750
Allen, G D—M V Stringham, Bayonne, 1 year 125
Allen, R J—The Improved Land and L Assoc, J City, installs 1,400
Altfelix, Chris—Elsworth Post No 14, Dep of N J, Grand Army of Rep, Union, 3 years 700
Andres, Maggie—Hudson Trust and Savings Inst, Union, 3 years 1,200
Brown, Hannah C—Exrs J L Ogden, J City, 3 years 1,800
Brennan, G F—Katie Brennan, J City, 1 year 500
Butz, Emma—L Brand, Union, 3 years 5,000
Christie, Geo—J Van Horn, J City, 3 years 3,200
Clemmons, W F—Cecile E Eilshemius, Kearney, 3 years 3,000
Coleman, Abraham—J H Browning, J City, 5 years 500
Craige, Marie V—Mary D Holton, J City, 1 year 1,350
Dast, J A—Fifth Ward Savings Bank, J City, 1 year 1,200
Davidson, Rich—Cecile E Eilshemius, Kearney, 3 years 3,600
Dickinson, James—Lafayette M B and L Assoc, J City, installs 1,000
Dixon, Mary—Emil Leuly, Union, 1 year 500
Erdmann, Sophie—R Mathesheimer, J City, 5 years 2,000
Eschroy, Flora—Sophie Schick, 3 years 2,000
Fagin, James—Harrison and Kearney B and L Assoc, Kearney, installs 1,400
Farrant, W S—The Highland M B and L Assoc, J City, installs 600
Gardner, Will—A Pattkee, J City, 2 years 100
Same—Hudson City M B and L Assoc, J City, installs 1,000
Garland, Hugh—A Cassidy, J City, 3 years 304
Giberson, A P—W G Nelson, J City, 1 year 125
Glickman, Isaac—Caroline Schoenfeld, Bayonne, 1 year 600
Gross, Philip—R Simpson, J City, 1 year 1,500
Hartung, Julia—C Jambel, J City, 2 years 500
Hoffmann, J A—The Indian Spring Land Co, West Hoboken, 3 years 400
Howarth, Geo—The Howard Savings Inst, Kearney, installs 3,000
Jud, Catharine M—A Boethe, J City, 2 years 1,400
Kerr, Sophia J—Cecile E Eilshemius, Kearney, 3 years 1,060
Kermann, Nicholas—Ellen M Close, Bayonne, 3 years 250
Kestner, Chas—Francis Lebans, Guttenberg, 3 years 1,700
Kockendoerfer, Will—S Connors, Hoboken, 5 years 2,000
Kuhlen, Will—W Dietrich, J City, 3 years 400
Kyuast, Robert—The Town of Union B and L Assoc, Union, installs 800
Lofgerst, Karl—W W Jennings, Kearney, 1 year 200
Loughman, Lucy—The Greenville United B and L Assoc, J City, installs 8,845
Lyons, Thomas—The Lembeck & Betz Eagle Brewing Co, J City, 1 year 1,000
McCordts, Fred—Mary L Sleight, Kearney, 3 years 1,250
McDermott, Timothy—Charlotte Miller, J City, 3 years 5,000
McEvoy, J B—J P J McEvoy, J City, 10 years 1,785
McEvoy, J P—same, J City, 1 year 5,345
McGee, Lucy—A A Rich, West Hoboken, 1 year 200
Menzel, Gustav—W H Schmidt, North Bergen, 5 years 500
Moran, Thos—Adelaide Umbry, J City, 5 years 1,500
Muller, John—Guard Mary E Sisson, J City, 3 years 5,000
Mulcahey, John—Hudson Trust and Savings Inst, Hoboken, 3 years 1,300
Neale, C E—Exrs G T Neale, Bayonne, 5 years 1,400
Same—E J Hen, Bayonne, 5 years 500
Olesmann, Mary C—Eugene Richard, West Hoboken, 3 years 250
Otis, Emma—Rosaline Wappelsberg, Union, 5 years 1,000
Owens, Cornelius—F Frelinghuysen, Kearney, 1 year 700
Pelegrino, Gennaro—Hoboken B and L Assoc, Hoboken, installs 5,000
Pfeifer, Fritz—C Fabeck, Guttenberg, 5 years 600
Pilch, D B—H S White, J City, 1 year 1,000
Poeschel, Osman—D F Reed, West Hoboken, 3 years 3,000
Redlich, William—Exrs Cornelia V V Booraem, J City, 3 years 500
Ryan, Matthew—Howard Richards, Bayonne, 3 years 750
Scharf, Henry—Exr Chas G Sisson, J City, 3 years 3,000
Sharrot, G E—C A Stillman, J City, 5 years 2,000
Schlich, Marie—R Mathesheimer, J City, 1 year 750
Schnell, Christian—West Side Mutual B & L Assoc, Union, installs 2,000
Schumann, Theo—G Joeckel, Hoboken, 5 years 4,000
See, Rachel V W—People's B & L Assoc, Kearney, installs 7,800
Skelly, J V—Susan Luxton, West Hoboken, 3 years 2,400
Smith, J P—People's B & L Assoc, Kearney, installs 1,500
Soule, D E—New Jersey Title Guarantee and Trust Co, J City, installs 1,500
Sparenberg, E J—The Hudson Trust and Savings Inst, Hoboken, 3 years 8,000
The Crescent Hall School—Highland M B & L Assoc, J City, installs 5,600
Thoulowe, Geo—C Dort, J City, 5 years 900
Tumble, H J—E W Kingsland, J City, 5 years 1,700
Walsh, Ellen—Adeline Nicolas, Harrison, 1 year 1,000
Walsh, John—Maggie C Lutkins, J City, 5 years 3,000
Wamke, John—A C Foye, J City, 1 year 2,200
Wanner, Jacob—W W Kobb, Bayonne, 3 years 700
Welwood, Thos—F G Burnham, Harrison, 3 years 7,000
Winblad, J E—Hudson City M B & L Assoc, J City, installs 200
Wienaber, Otto—Hoboken Ld & Impt Co, Hoboken, 4 years 7,300
Zeliff, Jethu E—The Knights of Pythias B & L Assoc, Kearney, installs 400

CHATTEL MORTGAGES.

Bailey, John and John M Gillespie, Kearney—T D Bailey, butcher shop fixtures, horses, wagons and harness 2,000
Blacher, Mary A, Jersey City—G Dessecker, coffin wagon 150
Borges, Fred, Hoboken—P Ballantine & Son, saloon and grocery store, horse, wagon and harness 800
Bower, J D, J City—C Birdsall, furniture 310
Broas, Julia, J City—J Bauman, furniture 82
Brown, Elsworth, Jersey City—T F Dennin, horse, wagon, harness and milk business 175
Bujson, John, J City—C Birdsall, furniture 160
Conlin, Maggie, Hoboken—H Thoesen, furniture 82
Delo, J B, Jersey City—Beadleston & Woerz, saloon and lease 250
Dmoth, Helen, J City—L Bauman, furniture 148
Ebert, Maggie, J City—L Bauman, furniture 134
Ernest, Louis, J City—Beadleston & Woerz, saloon 700
Enstic Mfg. Co, Bayonne—Donegan & Swift, 25 horse power Metropolitan engine and boiler 590
Farrell, Richard, Jersey City—Beadleston & Woerz, saloon and lease 475
Franz, Catharine, J City—L Bauman, furniture 89
Frisch, Fred, J City—M Lotz, cigar store and fixtures and stock 1,204
Gansberg, Fritz, J City—The William Peter Brewing Co, saloon fixtures 120
Geist, O R, Secaucus—Marvin Safe Co, safe 90
Gordan, W J, J City—J J Herbert, horse, wagon, harness 125
Gormley, Frank, J City—C F Walters, piano 255
Harvey, C T, J City—Marvin Safe Co, safe 55
Hauf, F S, J City—J W Tufts, soda water fountain 2,565
Hoffman, W C, Union—The William Peter Brewing Co, saloon 900
Johnson, Isabella, Bayonne—C Birdsall, furniture 130
Kane, Samuel, J City—D Bauman, saloon and lease 1,000
Lowe, C M, J City—L Bauman, furniture 114
Magee, Chas, West Hoboken—L Bauman, furniture 20
Mahnken, A C, Bayonne—National Cash Register Co, 1 No 4 register 225
Martindale, Emma S, J City—J Bauman, furniture 204
Melchoir, Ludwig, Union—William Peter Brewing Co, saloon fixtures 500
Moeller, A G, J City—W Kerr, drug store 900
O D M Baker & Co, J City—Marvin Safe Co, safe 158
O'Donnell, Nellie, Bayonne—Marvin Safe Co, safe 45
Pallard & Co, J City—J W Tufts, soda water fountain, &c 735
Pinney, C A, Montclair—C Birdsall, furniture 130
Prime, J H, J City—C Birdsall, furniture 160
Sabelberg, John, Hoboken—J Eitzen, cigar store 75

Schultz, Bernard, J City—Matilda Alexander, stock and fixtures, store 500
Shields, John, J City—C F Walters, piano 115
Sohn, Fred and Emma, Bayonne—H A Yust, stock and fixtures 50
Traquair, W M, Bayonne—J Bauman, furniture 500
Von Atzinger, Louis, West Hoboken—L Ulrich, cows, horse, wagon and harness 400
Von Atzinger, Louis, West Hoboken—L Ulrich, 12 cows, horse, wagon and harness 400

BILLS OF SALE.

Davis, Theresa, J City—D Davis, tailoring business, horse, carriage, &c 2,500
Dueben, Gottlieb, Union—H Dueben, horses, harness and coaches .... nom
Fitzgerald, James and Eugene, partners as Fitzgerald Bros, J City—J Ramsay, stock and fixtures, store 421
Knoffler, George, J City—H Sturcke, grocery store, horse, wagon 2,000
Koller, Jacob, J City—B H Luiken, grocery, hay and feed business 1,200
Skrivanick, George, Hoboken—G Gondolfo, grocery store 201
Youmans, T J, J City—R Corriell, horses, wagons, &c 500

JUDGMENTS.

Crampien, W G; Cook, Jessie; McIoness, William; McIoness, John—Elizabeth Blauvelt 39
Duggan, J P—Lembeck & Betz 132
Same—N Whalen 778
Haege, Adolph—Dorothea Semaes 1,012
Kelleher, Nicholas—Callahan & Co 276
Singewald, Ewald—C Stein 671

BUILDING MATERIAL MARKET.

BRICKS.—Another week has passed without bringing to light any new features upon the general market, and conditions remain practically as they were all last month. Business is going on continually, but it is upon such an even keel that neither buyer or seller gains any advantage, and operator after operator, when applied to for information, has the one monotonous reply, an unsatisfactory trade at unchanged prices. Last Monday some forty loads came in, from which, through deliveries on standing contracts and fresh sales, twenty-seven were delivered, and subsequent arrivals have kept a fluctuating surplus of from ten to thirteen loads always available and of a general run of quality that could not fail to please the most captious. There were a few extras or fancies, to be sure, for which special customers were willing to pay a little premium, and we "hear" that $5.50 per M is sometimes touched, but it must be a very fine load to reach $5.25 per M, and any quantity of good useful stock can be had at $5 and under. Actual consumption has probably been fuller during the week because the weather was better, but neither consumption or piling as yet keep even with the supply, and until that balance is reached, with the scale turned somewhat in the opposite direction, it will probably be somewhat difficult to infuse a firmer tone into values. Pales still have a fairly steady custom, and all the really fine parcels seem to have found a place at $2.50 per M, but receivers talk as though the current average supply was quite as much as required, and evidently do not care to see an increase. There does not appear to be anything new from primary points. Manufacturers keep on making and sending brick, and no one pretends to guess when they will stop.

LATH.—At just about the time of publication of our last report prices took a sudden header, and on the perpendicular tumble as low as $2.10 per M was touched, though for bulk of business $2.15 was inside, and there has since been a tendency toward rather more strength. Receivers who were last week talking about the unassailable position of the market and their ability to put the price up if they desired, explain the contradictory result upon the basis of wind. That is, the ordinary wind provided by nature, which had been blowing from the Eastward for several days continuously, and picked up and brought along both the expected and "unexpected" cargoes, some of only three or four days' clearance overhauling others that had been out a week or more, and about everything afloat seemed to rush in together, and a not uneven result followed. Having found an outlet for bulk of their supply, sellers again commence to talk quite chipper about what they expect to do in matter of recovering ground, and it is quite likely that should buyers be compelled to invest just now they would have to pay more money; but it will probably require another week to test the true status of the market. The Eastern people still claim indifference toward stock from other localities, but are nevertheless making an anxious effort to keep posted on the movements of those likely to offer Northern stock.

LIME.—The quotation given out is $1 per bbl. all around, and as it comes to us from responsible operators the figure is accepted. Yet there are some suspicious indications carrying an impression that the entire body of the trade does not stand right up to the mark, and if there be any cutting at all it is in the usual quarters. Arrivals have been quite full this week, but most of them seem to have been wanted up to the present writing, and additions expected are said to be small.

LUMBER.—Dull, is the word employed by most operators in reporting upon conditions of trade, but it must needs be used with a great deal of emphasis to fully convey an impression of the manner of expression in majority of cases. Hopes of an expansion of the distributive business have failed to materialize; indeed, on the whole, the yard trade, if anything, is less animated than a couple of weeks ago, and although August has fairly opened the desire of dealers to invest in supplies does not appear to have taken any really fresh or decided impetus. It is possible that the standing-off policy may be running to an extreme, but nevertheless certain that buyers are unusually indifferent toward all classes of stock, and the bulk of the business transacted may be traced to the full attendance of salesmen and their persistent efforts to secure custom. Generally the claim is for fairly sustained values, and for most goods figures are certainly low enough in all reason, but under ruling conditions of trade it does not require much stretch of imagination to suggest that desirable customers obtain allowances of which no publication is given.

Eastern Spruce still stands as a mark of disappointment to receivers. The actual fact of a suspension of product and very light shipments stood without question; yet every attempt to impress upon local buyers the natural strengthening influence of such conditions proved utterly fruitless, and as soon as a few arrivals put in an appearance it was found that demand was just about as indifferent as at any time this season, and any attempt to realize would result in taking off the moderate gain made at the outset. Even the Up-River trade could not be depended upon to afford any relief, and had it not been for the pretty good demand obtained down through the Long Island towns and villages it might have been difficult to get rid of the stock, even as small as it was. However, we find receivers unwilling to abandon a feeling of hope in regard to fall trade. They report a somewhat greater number of special orders coming in, and appear to be strongly impressed with the assertions of manufacturers that production will be abandoned unless a better line of prices is obtainable, the plea, of course, being a want of margin on shipments. It does not appear, however, that manufacturers make any reference to recent reduction in price of logs or the number of vessels almost begging for freight at very low rates. It is generally admitted that the local dealers have stood well together in sustaining yard rates, but suggestions that they attempt forcing a further advance seems to be about as ill-advised as could be imagined at this juncture.

Piling is meeting with some demand, but not at all in proportion to the supply, and there is a growing accumulation in chains. Such conditions are naturally against any increase of value, and quotations remain as before.

Hemlock continues to meet with some little demand from local and near-by points and operators feel as hopeful over it as circumstances will admit, though the principal trade secured at the mills is for distribution to other localities. The association of Pennsylvania manufacturers is successful in preventing free offerings and in keeping a fairly steady line of values.

White Pine remains in very much the former general situation, and there is practically nothing new to suggest since our last. Very few dealers make an open call for stock, because there is no necessity to do so in the face of the generous offering tendered them, and of a competition among sellers that insures an easy range of values. Even with their indifferent feeling, however, buyers cannot in all cases resist the bargains now and then available, and are gradually getting quite a little amount under engagement. Export trade dull, but there is a hope that the reciprocity treaty with the West India Islands will open the door for quite a good business in coarser grades of stuff at least.

Yellow Pine is very dull and very uncertain in value as operators are quite reticent over the situation. It is quite unlikely that stock now here could be sold except at a loss were any further shading to be made on cost, and while possibly new engagements might be made at primary points on pretty easy terms the condition of trade offers little inducement for investment. The export trade continues moderate and unsatisfactory, and much complaint comes from primary sources.

Carolina Pine is reported as doing fairly well, even by the more conservative operators, and as a rule dealers manage to book quite a little business weekly. This is a cheering comparison with other woods, and it is to be hoped will become even more pronounced as the season progresses. Prices are well sustained on all standard qualities of stock.

Hardwoods continue to move slowly, and without new or important feature worthy of note. For consumption there is a little stock going out, but principally in a routine sort of way, and toward fresh yard supplies dealers retain very much the old indifferent mood. They do not object particularly to negotiating now and then, but wait until the tender is made, and it is a reasonable surmise that they obtain comparatively easy terms even on leading descriptions, though no admission to that effect can be heard. Some export demand prevails, but accompanied by the usual provision that only the best quality must be tendered to insure successful negotiation.

GENERAL LUMBER NOTES.

ENGLAND.

Of the Liverpool market the *Timber Trades Journal* says:

The supplies of pine timber from Canada continue to be upon a very moderate scale so far as the import of logs is concerned, but pine deals are still coming forward in a liberal manner, and there is at present no sign of the direful scarcity which some of the American and Canadian papers interested in the wood trade there are anxious to make us believe is at hand. If they will take our advice they will moderate their transport, and not rush into such wild and exaggerated statements that apparently give them so much delight. They overshoot the mark, and fail entirely to touch the mark they want to hit.

The pitch pine business for the season seems to be almost at an end, if it can be said that it has an end, for the introduction of steam tonnage into this trade during the past few years has altogether revolutionized it. Some few vessels, both sailing and steamships, are on the way here from various ports with pitch pine timber. With the exception of one or two steamers which may call at Pensacola or adjacent ports to complete their cargoes, all are sailing ships.

THE WEST.

The Northwestern *Lumberman* as follows:

A special feature of the present situation is the firmness with which white pine is held at initial points. This is the case in the face of the fact that the season's trade has not been brisk, the Eastern requirement having been particularly slow and meager. All season the movement at Lake Erie points and in Saginaw valley has been quiet. Yet manufacturers and holders of bulk stock have manifested little disposition to sacrifice values. In this city prices for everything in the shape of white and Norway pine, except for the coarser grades of inch lumber, have averaged higher than last year. It is a remarkable thing that prices have been so well maintained against the measure of apathy among buyers that has prevailed. The manufacturers have done wisely in refusing to force lumber on an unwilling market. It would have been unsafe to do so, in many instances, in the existing rather uncertain state of credits. Manufacturers of white pine are generally in such solid condition that they can better afford to hold their lumber than to urge it on buyers that are financially weak.

One would naturally think, however, that the men who are known to be financially sound would this season be able to buy lumber at their own price. But they have found that such a conclusion were vain. Manufacturers have all season had firm faith in the value of their product, and were bound to hold it until the reaction should come.

At the Chicago yards:

Piece stuff is still based on $10.25 for strictly short, though when the tally includes a considerable percentage of 18 and 20 foot stuff or 2x12 or small timbers, it easily commands $10.37½ to $10.50. The tendency is to stiffen on the more desirable tallies.

The Chicago *Timberman* says:

Some of our hardwood dealers are beginning to ask themselves, and others as well, how long it will be before trade begins to show some symptoms of renewed activity. There is certainly not a great deal doing at the present time, and it is just as certain that trade for the past four or five months has been disappointing, more, however, because it has not come up to the expectation than because the volume has been less than the average. From the way demand started in the first of the year, many were led to believe this would be an exceedingly good year for trade, and are disappointed because their expectations have not been realized.

Last fall the great trouble was in finding plenty of quartered oak to keep the trade supplied, but this fall it begins to look as though there would be difficulty in finding buyers for all the stock offered. Prices do not show much change as yet, but it should be remembered that early in the season anything went that was dry enough to go into the kiln, while at the present time buyers are very particular both as to grade and dryness.

As was stated last week there is as yet no surplus stock of plain sawed red oak, and prices paid by dealers are about the same as those current three months ago. Plain sawed white oak is in good supply, but is held reasonably firm at old prices.

Basswood and soft elm are still moving quite freely, considering the dull state of trade, but prices for these woods do not improve, nor are they likely so long as the supply is as abundant as at present.

Demand for maple is slow, unless it be for flooring strips, and these are only moved when offered at low prices.

Dealers in cypress in this market are not boasting of a booming trade, but nevertheless there is an increasing quantity of this stock being consumed from month to month. Architects and builders are beginning to realize that there is no longer any doubt about getting supplies as required, and for that reason cypress is more frequently specified for interior work than formerly. Tank manufacturers long since discovered that no other wood answers their purposes so well as this, and regarding its qualities as a roofing material there is no question.

The Mississippi Valley *Lumberman* says:

With the exception possibly of Minneapolis, the production of white pine lumber does not promise to be large. Low water has hung up many of the drives and in the Wisconsin Valley, on the Menominee and along the Green Bay shore points the mills have been compelled to shut down in many cases for want of logs. La Crosse, too, is not as freely supplied as her mill men might wish, while failure to get out the logs on the Rum has resulted in shutting down all the mills at Anoka. Low water on the Chippewa and St. Croix is limiting the supply of logs for the down river mills. The cut of white pine lumber does not promise therefore to be as large proportionally, as the sale that is found for it.

Within the past few days more activity has been noted among the lumber dealers at Bay City and Saginaw. Several large sales have been made. The lumber is to go in almost equal proportion eastward and into Ohio.

METALS.—COPPER — Ingot continues very dull on pretty much all outlets and the tone of the general market extremely weak. Indeed, since our last, offerings have been openly made at a considerable reduction in cost and it is believed a still further fractional shading would be allowed buyers who might consent to handle round lots of stock. On an average range of valuations we quote at 12¼@12½c. for Lake, and 11¾@12c. for casting brands. Manufactured Copper has also found a comparatively narrow and uncertain outlet, buyers generally refusing to handle anything beyond the natural wants of the moment, but the list rates are understood to be quite well adhered to. We quote as follows: Sheet, not above 30x72 in., 16 oz. and over, 25c.; do, 14 to 16 oz., 23c.; do, 12 to 14 oz., 24c.; do, 10 to 12 oz., 25c.; do, 8 to 10 oz., 28c.; do under 8 oz, 30c. Sheets longer than 72 inches add 1c. for 12@14 oz., 2c. for 10@12 oz, and 3c. for 8@10 oz. Sheets, not above 36x96 in., 16 oz and over, 22c.; do, 14 to 16 oz, 24c.; do, 12 to 14 oz, 26c.; do, 10 to 12 oz, 30c.; do, 8 to 10 oz, 33c. Sheets longer than 96 inches 22c. for over 32 oz, and add 1c. for 16 to 32 oz.; 3c. 14 to 16 oz.; 5c. 12 to 14 oz, and 13c. for 8 to 10 oz. Sheets, not above 48x96, 32 to 64 oz, 22c.; do, 16 to 32 oz, 25c.; do, 14 to 16 oz, [illegible]; do, 12 to 14 oz, 29c.; do, 10 to 12 oz, 33c. Sheets wider than 48x96 and longer, 22@25c. for 32 to 64 oz. and over, 27@28c. for 16 to 32 oz, 29c. for 14 to 16 oz and 34c. for 12 to 14 oz. All bath tub sheets, per lb., 16 oz, 27c.; 14 oz, 29c.; 12 oz, [illegible]; and 10 oz, 35c. Bolt copper ¼ inch diameter and over, 28c. Circles, 60 diameter and less, 3c. above price of sheets of same thickness; circles, 60 to 96 do do, 5c. do; circles, 96 do and over, 6c. do. Segment and pattern sheets, 3c. above price of sheets required to cut them from. Cold or hard rolled copper, 1@2c. per lb. above the foregoing prices. Copper bottoms, 26@32c. per lb. IRON—Scotch Pig is seldom referred to at the moment, and if it finds custom at all it is upon special orders. We quote more or less nominally at $22.00@24.50 per ton, according to brand. American Pig of best quality and used for the finest castings, remains quite steady on the support of comparatively moderate supplies. For bulk of supply, however, the tone is a trifle weak and on low grade there is undoubtedly a great deal of quiet cutting continually going on. We quote at $16.50@18.00 per ton for No. 1 X foundry; $15.50@16.50 for No. 2 X do. and $14.00@15.00 for Gray Forge. Old material practically has no demand of a regular character and the general market is in a nominal, stupid sort of condition. As a rule, however, holders manage to prevent any great quantity of stock from coming upon the market. We quote at about $20.50@21.50 for old rails; $20.00@21.00 for No. 1 wrought scrap; $17.00@18.00 for cast scrap and $17.00@17.50 for car wheels. Manufactured Iron does not appear to be moving in a very satisfactory manner, and there is more or less complaint to be heard among the trade generally. There is, however, no great pressure to secure custom and former rates are quite generally asked. We quote Common Merchant Bar ordinary size, at 2.00@2.10c. from store, and refined at 2.30@2.60c; Rods, round and square, 2.9@2.4c. Bands, 2.40@2.60c.; Norway Nail Rods, 4@4c. and domestic sheet on the basis of 3.00@3.%c. for common Nos. 10@16. Other descriptions at corresponding prices, with 1-10c. less on large lots from cars. Steel rails meet with some attention from time to time, but principally on small orders, and 1,000-ton lots seem to be the maximum purchase for the time being. There is said to be a little accumulation of stock making, but the combination rate is well adhered to in all cases. We quote standard sections $30 per ton at mill, with usual advance for delivery at tide water. Pig Lead, after easing off a fraction, has since remained about steady, but without much animation, and at the present writing the position is pretty dull. We quote at ... 4. 5c. per lb. The manufactures of lead are quo... at 7c. for Pipe, 7¾c. for Sheet, 15c. for Tin-lined Pipe, and 37½c. for Block Tin Pipe. Pig Tin for consumption moves quite slowly, the speculative element is indifferent, and values do not get any solid support. We quote at about 20@20.10c. for round lots, and 20⅛@20¼c. for jobbing parcels. Tin Plate is offered with some moderation and care and holders do not appear anxious to realize. The demand, however, has been moderate, with movement confined mainly to ordinary jobbing parcels. We quote prices as follows: I. C. Charcoal, ⅛ cross assortment Melyn grade, $6.50@6.55, each additional X add $1.50; I. C. Charcoal, ⅛ cross assortment, Allaway grade, $6.00@6.05, each additional X add $1; Charcoal terne, M. F. grade, 14x20, $7.50@7.55; M. F. grade, 20x28, $15.50@15.55; Worcester, 14x20, $5.75@5.80; Worcester 20x28, $11.40@11.45; Dean grade, 14x20, $5.25@5.30; Dean grade, 20x28, $10.50@10.55; D. R. D. grade, 14x20, $4.85@4.90; D. R. D. grade, 20x28, $10.00@10.05; I. C. Coke, Penlan grade, $5.20@5.25; J. B. grade, 14x20, $5.40@5.45; I. C. Bessemer steel, squares, $5.75@5.80 basis; I. C. Siemens steel, squares, $5.85@6.00 basis. Spelter secures moderate and unimportant attention, but the supply well located and prices firm. We quote $5.05@5.15 for Common Western, according to brand

NAILS.—On all regular outlets there is a little stock moving, but not enough to bring the market up into a condition of animation, and operators generally continue to find fault. Threats of reduced production continue without materializing, and prices are inclined to range easy if anything. We quote Cut at $1.50@1.60 per keg for car lots and $1.75@1.85 per keg for parcels from store, for iron, and add 5@10c. per keg for steel; Wire, $2.00@2.05 at mills, and 2.20@2.35 from store.

PAINTS, OILS, COLORS, ETC.—There is a great deal of uniformity, and indeed monotony, in reports over the various descriptions of stock. Operators try to be cheerful, naturally, but it is evident that it requires considerable stretch of imagination to present any very pronounced good points in relation to even some of the most thoroughly staple articles, and business as a whole is not panning out according to calculations. On the other hand, however, there is an evident determination to retain a fair measure of hope, and predictions of improvement to come soon are to be heard, as it is calculated that no matter how closely buyers may confine themselves to actual wants they must order with greater liberality to keep up an assortment. Supplies are plenty enough and prices generally rule about steady. There has been no evidence of any cut on the White Lead list. Association Corroders' rates stand as follows: Lead in oil in kegs and dry lead in kegs, in lots of less than 500 lbs., 7½c. net; in lots of 500 lbs to 5 tons at one purchase, 7c.; 5 tons to 12 tons, one purchase, 6⅞c.; 12 tons and over, one purchase, 6¾c.; dry white lead in bbls. ½c. per lb. less than price in kegs. Lead in oil 12½ lb. in tin pails, add 1c.; in 25 and 50 lb. tin pails, add ½c.; and in 1 to 5 lb. tin cans, assorted (100 lbs. in case) add 2½c. per lb. to keg price. Terms on lots on 500 lbs. and over, note of acceptance at sixty days, or 2½ per cent. discount will be allowed for cash paid within fifteen days of invoice date. To make either of the above required quantities any assortment of packages of white lead, red lead and litharge may be counted. The above quotations are free on board cars or boat at corroding point. Linseed Oil is fairly active and somewhat steadier as the most persistent cutter of rates on Western product seems to be getting a little tired and now asks a little more money. We quote at general range at 37@40c. for Western, and 44@56c. for City. Spirits Turpentine remains quiet and valued about as before, though at the close the market is somewhat firmer on the influence of improved advices from the South. We quote at 35½@36½c. per gallon, according to quality, delivery, etc.

TAR AND PITCH.—Business has been somewhat irregular, but not very liberal at any time, as buyers invest mainly for immediate wants. Moderate supplies well in hand, however, insure good support to values throughout. We quote Pitch at $1.70@1.75 per bbl.; Tar at $2.15@2.50, according to quantity, quality and delivery.

MISCELLANEOUS

BUILDING MATERIAL PRICES

LUMBER.

Appended quotations are based almost wholly upon prices obtained for goods from first hands. Yard rates necessarily range much higher owing to the expenses attending sorting out and grading cargo and even car lots, besides which must be added the cost of handling and carrying until consumers are ready to invest. Terms of sale also p o important factors and, altogether, it is impossible to give a line of retail quotations thoroughly reliable in character.

SPRUCE—Eastern—special cargoes delivered N. Y.	$16 00 @ 17 00
Random cargoes, narrow	13 50 @ 14 50
Random cargoes, wide	14 50 @ 16 00
PILING—Eastern—cargo rates:	
Ranging 30@40 per cent 12 inch butt, 35 to 40 ft average length	4 @ —
Ranging 45@50 per cent 12 inch butt, 35 to 40 ft average length	4¼@ 4½
Ranging 50@60 per cent One-half 12 inch butt, 38 to 40 ft average length	4¾@ 5
Two-thirds 12 inch butt, 38 to 42 ft average length	5½@ 6
Three-fourths 12 inch butt, 40 to 45 ft average length	5¾@ 6
All 12 inch butt and up, 40 to 45 ft average length	6 @ 6¼
Piece stick, 40 feet each	4 00 @ —
do. 45	6 00 @ —
do. 50	8 00 @ —
do. 55	12 00 @ —
Inch spars, per inch	20 @ 22
Scaffolding poles, each	60 @ 1 00
Clothes poles, 45 to 65 feet, each	3 00 @ 6 00
HEMLOCK:	
Penn. joist	12 00 @ 12 50
do. boards	13 00 @ 13 50
do. timber, 20 ft and under	12 50 @ 13 00
do. do. 22 to 24 ft	13 00 @ 13 50
do. do. 26 to 28 ft	13 50 @ 14 00
do. do. 30 to 32 ft	14 00 @ 15 50
do. do. 34 to 36 ft	15 50 @ 16 00
do. do. 38 to 40 ft	16 50 @ 17 50
WHITE PINE—Good uppers and select, 1 to 2 inch	40 00 @ 48 00
Upper and select, 2½ to 4 inch	50 00 @ 58 00
Shelving	26 00 @ 31 00
Pickings, 1 inch	33 00 @ 36 00
Cutting-up, 1 inch	25 00 @ 28 00
Bracket plank	30 00 @ 35 00
Dressing-boards	18 00 @ 29 00
Box, inch	13 50 @ 14 00
Box, thick	14 50 @ 15 50
West India shippers	16 00 @ 19 00
Rio Janeiro do.	20 00 @ 21 00
River Plate do.	29 00 @ 30 00
Australia do.	25 00 @ 30 00
YELLOW PINE—Random cargoes delivered N. Y.	18 00 @ 21 00
Ordered cargoes	22 00 @ 23 00
Flooring	21 00 @ 22 00
Step plank	26 00 @ 28 00
Common siding	13 00 @ 14 00
Heart face boards	20 00 @ 21 50
Car orders	21 00 @ 23 00
At Atlantic ports, f. o. b.	12 50 @ 15 00
At Gulf ports, f. o. b.	11 50 @ 13 00
North Caroline pine timber	13 50 @ 15 00
do. flooring 1 inch	16 00 @ 22 00
do. do. 1¼	16 50 @ 22 50
do. do. 1½@2 inch.	24 00 @ 25 00
do Shipping culls or box	12 00 @ 14 00
do Plain and mottled ½@1½ inch.	18 50 @ 25 50
Ash, white	36 00 @ 48 00
Elm	20 00 @ 22 50
Oak, plain	37 00 @ 41 00
Oak, quarter sawed	52 00 @ 55 00
Oak, quarter sawed, extra thick	56 00 @ 60 00
Redwood	45 00 @ 52 50
Maple, clear	28 00 @ 33 00
Chestnut, clear	33 00 @ 35 50
Cypress, clear	30 00 @ 32 50
Black Walnut, good to choice	130 00 @ 140 00
Black Walnut, ordinary to fair	100 00 @ 120 00
Black Walnut, ⅝	78 00 @ 83 00
Black Walnut, selected and seasoned	150 00 @ 155 00
Black Walnut counters	110 00 @ 150 00
Black Walnut, culls	35 00 @ 40 00
Black Walnut, rejects	50 00 @ 53 00
Cherry, wide	110 00 @ 115 00
Cherry, good	85 00 @ 100 00
Cherry, ordinary	65 00 @ 80 00
Whitewood, inch	30 50 @ 32 50
Whitewood, ⅝ inch	24 50 @ 26 00
Whitewood, 1¼ to 2½ inch	32 00 @ 34 00
Shingles, Pine, 16 inch, extra	2 75 @ 3 10
do 18 inch, extra	4 10 @ 4 30
do 16 inch, clear butt	2 90 @ 3 10
do 16 inch, stocks	4 50 @ 4 60
do 18 inch, stocks	5 30 @ 5 40
Shingles, Cypress, 6x20	8 00 @ 10 00
do larger sizes	11 00 @ 16 00
do sawed	6 00 @ 9 00
Cedar—Medium to large	6¼@ 7½
do. —Extra large	7¾@ 8
Mahogany—Small	6½@ 7½
do —Medium	8 @ 8½
do. —Large	9½@ 12
do. —Extra Large	12½@ 14

REAL ESTATE RECORD AND BUILDERS' GUIDE.
ESTABLISHED MARCH 21st 1868.
DEVOTED TO REAL ESTATE. BUILDING ARCHITECTURE, HOUSEHOLD DECORATION,
BUSINESS AND THEMES OF GENERAL INTEREST

PRICE, PER YEAR IN ADVANCE, SIX DOLLARS.

Published every Saturday.

TELEPHONE - - - - CORTLANDT 1370.

Communications should be addressed to

C. W. SWEET, 14 & 16 Vesey St.

J. T. LINDSEY, Business Manager.

VOL. XLVIII AUGUST 15, 1891. No. 1,222

The publication offices of THE RECORD AND GUIDE *have been removed to Nos.* 14 *and* 16 *Vesey street, over The Mechanics' and Traders' Exchange, a few feet west of Broadway.*

Readers of THE RECORD AND GUIDE *may subscribe to the new illustrated quarterly,* THE ARCHITECTURAL RECORD, *by sending their names and addresses to the offices of publication, Nos.* 14 *to* 16 *Vesey street. Annual subscription,* $1.00.

THE advance in, and subsequent stability of, the Grangers is affecting the whole stock list, and it seems as if the corner has been turned for a good long bull movement. Issues whose defects can not be offset by grain carriage or the prospect thereof, appear to have discounted their demerits for the time being, at least, and it would not be surprising if the advance became general. Northern Pacific, which surprised its friends by lagging when other grain carriers were moving up, took a jump, and Union Pacific began to recover its losses yesterday. Reports of earnings on the North and Southwestern roads are showing substantial increases, which will also swell the incomes of the Eastern trunk lines. There may be set-backs from causes too often alluded to here to need mention now, but it must be admitted that the outlook has the most satisfactory aspect for an increase in stock values. The recent advance in the Grangers has been too well maintained, and the solid benefits of the crops are too near at hand to allow of any other conclusion.

ONE of the most marked indications of the way in which many British investments have suffered since the Baring failure is afforded by the position of the finance and trust companies. Nothing exactly similar to these companies exists in this country. They have been founded ostensibly for the purpose of securing to small investors the advantages commanded by large capital and wide knowledge in the remunerative employment of money; that is, their bonds and stock would be sold into comparatively small holders, and the money thus received would be employed in the way that seemed most advantageous to the directors. For the first two or three years of their existence—during the speculation of 1889 and 1890—they were remarkably successful and distributed large profits to their shareholders; but their managers either could not or did not forsee the prospective collapse, and when it came they were loaded up with issues of dubious value, which could be sold only at a heavy loss. It was owing largely to the purchases of these trust companies that London Stock Exchange quotations were raised to such an extravagant level a few years ago. These facts are well known, and investors have consequently been selling their trust company shares with their usual haste and indiscrimination. A list has recently been published of the highest prices recorded for the shares of twenty-nine of these companies compared with the present quotations. The list shows declines amounting in some cases to 60 per cent and in many to more than 80 per cent. The general fall in the value of securities would account for some portion of this shrinkage, but there are other and more special influences at work. The trusts were mainly creatures of the recent speculation; they went largely into the underwriting and promoting business, and they still retain the mass of securities they thus accumulated. Their managers have naturally been subject to much severe criticism, which no doubt has been largely deserved. The chief cause for the present position of the trust companies is the vicious system of founders' shares, which made the managers of these concerns eager to distribute extravagant dividends, for they were thus given the opportunity of securing the return of capital originally invested in their founders' shares several times over in one year. It by no means follows from all this that these finance companies have not a perfectly legitimate place. As in all such enterprises the security of the investor rests ultimately on the honesty and ability of the directors or manager, for there is no doubt that a shrewd man with ample capital can invest money to better advantage than can ignorant people of small means. It should be remembered that if the inflation and consequently the collapse was caused largely by the trust companies, that other inflations, with far less substance to them, have the product of incautions lack of knowledge, united with a little spare money.

WE print in another column a review of the foreclosure sales held since the beginning of this year. It deserves the serious attention of everyone interested in real estate—of fiduciary institutions, capitalists, building material merchants and others. The review discloses a condition of affairs very far from satisfactory—a condition, moreover, which is of rather long standing, for our investigations last year showed that an exactly similar state of affairs existed. Why is it that this year more than 20 per cent of all the parcels offered under foreclosure failed to sell for an amount equal to the charges upon them? In answering this question there is of course a strong temptation to search for causes outside of the real estate field, and having found some, to magnify them and insist that they are completely explanatory. There can be, of course, no doubt that the strained and unsettled state of the money market during the past year has caused not a little of the unsatisfactory condition of the real estate market. It has not, however, been the real cause, but only—if the phrase may be used—the *disclosing* cause, the accidental circumstance which revealed what already existed. The foreclosure suits last year, when there was no special tightness of money, were unsuccessful, just as they have been this year, so that it is apparent that we must get beyond the monetary troubles of last Fall.

IN the first place, it seems to us that too large a part of the new building is done under such financial conditions that nothing but the best of luck and the most prosperous of times will enable all parties to pull through successfully. Very mildly adverse circumstances are sufficient to knock the fictitious element out of the operations. In many of the foreclosure sales we see what this fictitious element amounts to, for it does not follow that because a piece of property does not bring the charges against it that we are to conclude that the market is weak or values have tumbled. Quite apart, however, from the keying up of prices due to the speculative system of building, there is no doubt that in certain sections of the city real estate has been held at pretty high figures, not too high, perhaps, if the future be taken into consideration; but it is hard to realize on the future in dull times. Some of the property mortgaged has had a good deal of the "future" in it, and this the foreclosure suits have readily eliminated. Another fact has to be pointed out, of which we speak in our review, it is that property is not always sold under foreclosure proceedings in a manner that insures the best market price of the moment.

THE Rev. Mr. Stiggins, when asked what tap he preferred, replied that all tap was mere vanity. Mr. Weller, as we remember it, admitted the truth of this, but pressed the reverend gentleman for some statement as to which of these vanities was least vain. And Mr. Stiggins confessed that he thought some rum, with hot water, and sugar, partook less than any other drink of the nature of the devil. In a similar spirit, we may say that experience has proved the vanity of placing too much reliance on newspaper anticipations of the reports of the Rapid Transit Commission, but that under the present circumstances there appears to be a certain amount of information circulating which is less vain than much of the same kind. This information is to the effect that the Commissioners have abandoned any system of deep tunnels, and, whatever else they do, will run their cut as near the surface as possible. So much, indeed, they have already declared in their report; but nobody paid much attention to it, because of the varying conceptions which exist regarding the limits of the possible in this matter. According to our authority, the limit which the Rapid Transit Commissioners put upon their ability to approach the surface of the street with their tracks is scarcely any limit at all, and that the Commissioners are practically hesitating between two plans, both of which provide for tunnels very near the surface. This may or may not be the whole truth; but it is worth while to consider what the consequences will be in case it is the whole truth. Broadway has been the chosen land and the summum bonum of all rapid transit schemers since New York first began to grow along the line of that thoroughfare; and the danger to which the street has always been subjected has tended to make property-owners most suspicious of any attempt to gain possession of the street. They have fought to the bitter end every scheme which seemed but ever so little to threaten the security of their property, and have killed at least one plan which would have made that street unique and most efficient for its purpose. The question arises: Will they pursue the same policy in reference to some similar plan of construction, if this were proposed by the

Rapid Transit Commission? It must be remembered that there will be some considerable difference between the conditions under which former schemes were proposed and the circumstances of the present plan. The Commissioners are public officials—men of recognized conservatism and ability. They will have no pecuniary interest in favor of any one system of construction, but are evidently endeavoring to reach a solution with a single eye for the public interests. The worst that they can be reproached with is then an error of judgment, and the danger of this is minimized by their intention to have every detail of their arrangements carefully scrutinized by acknowledged experts. The presumption then in favor of any plan they may select is overwhelming; and we believe that many Broadway property-owners so far appreciate this as to give their consent to the plan. Whether enough of them hold off to make a recourse to the Supreme Court necessary it is impossible to predict. Certainly the owners of vaults extending beyond the house line are not likely to take kindly to a surface tunnel. If litigation does arise it will certainly be most unfortunate. Every few months lost is of great importance.

Paying too Dearly for the Whistle.

APPLICATION at the Dock Department offices fails to uncover any report from that department of a later date than 1888. It is not to be presumed that this was the last report made. We know for a certainty that several reports have been made since 1888; and were we to wade through the official records we could no doubt find an account of receipts and expenditures for the last two or three years. But the keeper of the archives for the department knows of nothing later than 1888, and so, in the form of fugitive reports, it will not be worth while to try to bring down knowledge on the wing.

The figures for 1888, however, will form a good enough basis for calculation. The total income of the Dock Department for that year was $1,320,684. But rents have increased since then, new piers have been built, and it is reasonable to presume that the current income is somewhat greater. Say that it is $1,500,000. This estimate cannot be very far out of the way, and we will use it as a basis for calculating the value of the improved water-front property of the city.

The principal at 6 per cent, represented by a net income of $1,500,000, would be a few thousand more than $25,000,000. But in estimating the value of the property we are not at liberty to estimate so liberally. There are expenditures as well as receipts to be considered. There are the salaries paid to the Commissioners and to the engineer corps. Then there is a very considerable body of dock laborers and helpers of one kind or another under pay, and there is an equipment of dredges, scows, tugs, pile drivers and such like machinery for making improvements and keeping the water front in good condition. The annual net income of the Dock Department under the most economical and honest management possible would have to be placed very much below $1,500,000, and the principal would have to be correspondingly reduced. We should not be justified from a business point of view in placing the value of the property at the half of $25,000,000. As a matter of fact it is worth next to nothing when considered as a means for reducing the tax levy and relieving the burdens of individual taxpayers. It is, however, as it is very well known, the source of a very considerable degree of corruption.

Now, let us look upon a reverse picture, imaginary if you will, but easily made objective. Let us suppose this property to be in the hands of individuals, and on this supposition we will be entirely justified in estimating it at the full valuation of $25,000,000. We would be justified in estimating it at twice or thrice $25,000,000, indeed, for we all know the resources of individuals and of individual enterprise for increasing the value of property, and our water front has always been a field that might have offered unlimited opportunities. But say that the value would be only $25,000,000 and then estimate what it would pay in taxes. It would certainly pay more than the city has ever received from the Dock Department.

But this is only a narrow view of the subject. If it could be shown that the possession of the water front by the city operated beneficially on the commerce of the port, it could be reasonably maintained that the municipal government should continue to hold it even though it contributed nothing to the public resources and was a source rather of increased than of diminished taxation. But this is precisely what no man in his senses will undertake to show; and it is just because possession of the water front by the city has operated mischievously on our arrangements for receiving, shipping, and storing merchandise, driving it to Brooklyn, Jersey City, Staten Island, and elsewhere, that the question of taxation becomes pertinent. We find that we are paying for a whistle that makes such wretchedly bad music that we are forced to inquire the cost; and when we learn that we are expected not only to play the piper but to pay the piper, it is time to call the music off.

The truth is, we have an anomalous water front system in New York unparalleled elsewhere in the United States and as foreign to all our political ideas and our constitutional theories as it is possible to imagine. Save a few men who have temporarily lost their heads there is no one in this country who looks upon a government as a fit operator in fields that should be left open to private enterprise, and least of all can the party that has ruled New York from time immemorial stand forward and defend municipal ownership of the water front on principle. The situation here has come down to us as an inheritance from pre-revolutionary times; and the Democratic party would simply stultify itself were it to engage in its defense. The most that it can say in its own defense is that it simply accepted a situation which it did not create and would not have created had it had the ordering of our municipal household at the start. But at the same time, it would be forced to confess that it has not been so active as it ought to have been in extricating itself from a false position.

Consistently with our theories of government, as interpreted by any intelligently led party in the United States, the city of New York has no more business with the water front than it has with the bakeries, and we think, upon the whole, that the public would find a greater advantage in giving the city a proprietary interest in the bakeries than it has ever gained from its ownership of the piers. Men inclined to hair splitting may say that there is a difference. They may talk learnedly of the principles of eminent domain that are involved in the lands under water, and say that the bakeries are covered by no such complication. But the most beneficent use that any government ever made of the right of eminent domain was to sell its real estate holdings to whoever would improve, reserving to itself merely its right of police regulation.

There is no use of dreaming dreams over these lands under water that are in the possession of the city. They will never be improved on any comprehensive plan so long as they remain in the possession of the city. Public sentiment is against municipal intrusion in productive work; and this sentiment is not cherished alone by the great body of the people. It is shared by the best men in public office, and it will always be strong enough to hold in check, cripple, and practically defeat any movement made in opposition to the general tread of opinion. Men are jealous of their rights. They want no colossus, even though it may be only a municipal colossus, blocking their way and holding them back from legitimate fields of enterprise.

The most profitable use that could be made of the piers would be to give them away to whoever will undertake a comprehensive work of improvement, and as for the unimproved lands under water, still remaining in the possession of the municipal government all around the island, the sooner they are sold to the riparian property-holders the sooner the city will have some money in bank that can be used for the payment of its debts. Our landed estate at present is a source rather of poverty than of riches.

We really think that our riparian property-holders are seeing too many lions in the way when casting about for the means of improving their situation. They seem to think that the city would hold on to this property with the tenacity of a bulldog, and that any movement on the part of individuals to obtain possession, acting either by themselves or through syndicates, would be met by a rebuff. This is the impression, and it seems to be very general. But the city is certainly not holding on with any great tenacity. For proof we have only to point to the fact that the municipal government has already alienated about half its holdings, and the reason probably why it has not sold out the remaining half is to be found in the fact that it has not been besieged with sufficient urgency.

There is no reason to think that the city will stand in the way of a comprehensive movement for giving to the riparian property-holders their rights to the lands under water. Why should it stand in the way? We have already called attention to the worthlessness of its holdings as a source of public revenue, and there is nothing in the little patronage controlled through the Dock Department to make anybody lose his head. When the riparian property-holders make an earnest effort to get possession of the lands under water they will not find the task so very difficult.

It should be very well understood nevertheless that concerted action is necessary, and that no other movement can be very fruitful. As we have seen in the past, individuals can do but very little while the city with its large holdings lies like a reef along shore and makes financial navigation almost impossible. At present, too, our wate front is involved in a fog, and men can only discover clear skies by looking beyond the rivers.

TO appreciate the unmeasured esteem in which Mr. Lowell was held by his fellow Americans, one has only to read the tributes to his memory, published by the New York papers. In the *Advertiser* we are told that his death "removes one of the shining lights of our literature," that in England he was "regarded not so much as a representative American as a thoroughly cultivated cosmopolitan, whom no country could especially claim and any country might be proud of," and "that it was by showing the cultivated man this country can produce that Mr. Lowell rendered his chief service to America abroad." The *Herald* says that "Lowell's death is an unspeakable loss to the great company of scholars," and that though "Fame may hesitate to rank Lowell among the proudest poets we have produced, she will readily concede that in all his work there was a remarkable degree of grace and graciousness." The *Tribune* differs a little from the *Advertiser*, but we judge that the difference is superficial rather than profound. It says "that what was best in Mr. Lowell's work was what was distinctively American in thought and purpose," and that "as his brilliant address on Democracy bore witness, his life abroad did not spoil his Americanism." The *Recorder* is most unlimited in its grief. It says that "the death of James Russell Lowell is a contribution to the eternities which no nation, however opulent in intellectual resources, can afford," that it "comes as the falling of one of the pillars of the State," that the "'Commemoration Ode' will divide with the 'Ode to Immortality' the poetical honors of the century," and "that the heart and soul of a nation are not insensible to whatever is highest and best in human endeavor which can give us so brilliant and worthy a son." The *Sun* alone of all the papers flavors its tribute with a bit of criticism and politics. It says that "that sacred gift of supreme imagination, that resistless lifting of the subject and the artist above the levels of ordinary feeling, is always wanting in him after all, and we are obliged to fall back towards the commonplace and respectable," and "that his political ideas became tinctured with an admixture of Pharisaic moral sentiments too strong to leave his judgment of public questions strong and comprehensive." How well was James Russell Lowell known to his journalistic countrymen!

The first number of *The Architectural Record* is now for sale at the elevated railroad stands, and all stands throughout the Union and at the leading booksellers. It is of the same size as the *Century*, printed on fine paper, and contains sixty-four superb illustrations.

Investments—Good and Bad.

THE BEAR RECORD.—We have had about thirty days in which the bears have held control of the market, and a glance at the results of their operations is timely, and may be advantageous in guiding future operations. The opportunity for the selling movement came from the fact that the market was a speculative one purely and simply, and that opportunity was increased by the difficulties which some important properties found themselves in, some from inherent defect and some from an inability to finance under the conditions prevailing, and some from both causes. The character of the market has seemingly undergone little change. The public is not thoroughly in it; yet there is a very steadfast holding to certain properties, which shows how strong has been the faith of their possessors in their merits. The damage done by the month's selling movement is almost wholly confined to properties whose antecedents, connections and conditions would not admit of similar faith on the part of their owners. It is not by any means a bad sign that this careful discrimination has been made. One of the most encouraging features after a long depression is the repression of what may be called the anomalies and what in the street is called liquidation, though that term is scarcely applicable to the decline in securities, which from their nature ought never to have gone up.

While merited punishment has been meted out to issues which owed their value to meretricious manipulation, there was a class of stocks which on the whole showed sturdy and successful resistance to depressive measures, and in the particular instances where declines were forced, recovered their losses wholly or in great part with admirable swiftness. This was the grain carrying class. A comparison of the quotations will show that their prices, at the times when the bear movement began and ended, differed very little. Atchison, Burlington & Quincy, St. Paul, Rock Island and Missouri Pacific are particular instances of this fact. Northern Pacific and Union Pacific may be quoted to the contrary. But they only serve to show the discrimination that has been used by buyers. Most notable for strength in the active list has been Atchison. On July 17th this stock was 32⅝ (the lowest figure for any particular day is chosen as best suited to the purposes of this article) and on August 11, when the selling movement culminated, 32¾, a difference of ⅛. Between the dates mentioned it had sold down to 30⅜, the fluctuations being limited within 2¼ points. Its recovery from depression was very quick, its lowest figure on August 3d being 32⅛, since when it has at no time sold down more than ⅝. In thirteen days Burlington & Quincy was sold down 6⅛ points, in the same time it recovered its losses and gained a point in addition. St. Paul, though the greatest anomaly on the whole list, shows no sign of the selling to which it has been subjected, the quotations at the end of the movement being about the same as they were at the beginning, although in the fight it had declined 5 points. St. Paul is unique. A strong circle of friends and a great partiality on the part of the room-trader, keeps the no-dividend payer higher than some dividend payers, at the price of some bonds which have favor in certain quarters and surprisingly near some bonds of real admitted merit. If there is one thing that should throw doubt upon the genuineness of the buying movement which set in a few days ago, it is the position of St. Paul which suggests the question, how is it possible to base a permanent advance on the quotations which such a stock makes? Next to Atchison, Rock Island has been held best. This stock on July 17 was 72¾; in two weeks it was sold down 3¾ points—in the same space of time that Burlingtoon & Quincy and St. Paul lost 6 and 5 points respectively—rallied in one week 2 points and developing a sudden buying spirit make another 3 points in twenty-four hours. Missouri Pacific being a Gould stock came in for some of the bearish attention lavished on Union Pacific; but it has shown fair powers of recuperation. During fourteen days the price was depressed only 2 per cent and in a like period recovered the whole of that loss. The exceptions in the grain carriers Union Pacific and Northern Pacific both show large losses for the thirty days and in both cases there is a suffering from financing. Northern Pacific lost 6 points in two weeks and in a like period recovered only 1¾. Union Pacific has but one record—continuous loss since July 17, the rallies being slight and the relapse severer as time went on until t had sold down 10 points, from which it has recovered 2. The decline in the last-mentioned stock is not in the least remarkable, it was foretold in the last annual report to those who studied its contents, and in the reports of its declining earnings. With its previous earnings it was unable to prevent the rolling up of an immense floating debt, and with earnings declining the outlook could not encourage an advance in price. It was at one time thought that Mr. Gould and his friends did as much harm as was possible to Union Pacific, but it does not appear to have fared any better in the hands of Mr. Adams. Mr. Adams had a theory that Union Pacific was handicapped by extensions being restricted under the contract with the Government. He saw rivals pushing across it and alongside of it, and, all its troubles arising therefrom. As far as he could he favored extensions. The Oregon Short Line was acquired, the Lincoln & Nebraska and the Union Pacific, Denver & Gulf built, and other connections made, but they did not help Union Pacific, which with its great floating debt, its growing indebtedness to the Government, apparently impossible of settlement, and the guarantee burdens it has taken on of late years, must offer sorry contemplation to the holders of its stock.

Where the bear movement has been really successful is among the list of Southwesterners. Louisville & Nashville and the Richmond Terminal and allied issue do not recover their losses. In the one case it is owing to the increase of capital, and in the others to an absence of value. There has been, too, considerable permanent damage among specialties, such as Cordage, Chicago Gas, Tennessee Coal and Iron, etc. The Coalers have been strong. Reading & Lackawanna are both selling about as high as they were a month ago. The moral of all this is that there has been careful and quiet buying in the stocks which are likely to benefit most by the favorable conditions in the situation, the great crop and the European demand for cereals. It is not so much a bull market as a favoring of the grain carriers, and as these are many their strength and advances give an appearance more favorable that the situation actually warrants. The drawbacks to a general advance have been before alluded to here and they still exist, but it is evident that their effect will be less on grain carriers than on other issues; it is even probable that the latter may suffer in being thrown over to acquire the former, and will have to await developments before their prices will improve materially. Before the movement can become general there must be a settlement of doubts as to money, and there must be more confidence among investors in issues of merit. There has been within a few days some signs of renewed activity in bonds, but a most distinguishing feature for a good while past, and still conspicuously apparent, is the neglect of good things. Manhattan has only touched par for a moment, while New York Central is oftener below it than at it. Atchison 4s, while speculation moves the incomes up, stick below the 5 per cent. selling basis as do also other good bonds, such as the Reading and Kansas & Texas 4s. Such things are not usually among the signs of an immediately active and healthy bull movement.

The Death of Mr. George Jones.

In the death of Mr. George Jones, proprietor of the New York *Times*, at Poland Springs, Me., on Wednesday, American journalism loses its most sterling and exemplary exponent. Of the principal facts in his career of eighty years the people have already been made acquainted by the daily press. But the contemporaries of the newspaper, of which he was the ruling spirit, would naturally not be expected to dwell at much length upon those predominating and creditable features of the man and his journal in which they are, for the most part, deplorably deficient. The biography of George Jones and the history of the New York *Times* are necessarily inseparable. The predominating traits of his character were well reflected in the great journal to which the ripened and perfected energies of his life were devoted.

In the earlier years, it is recorded, the editorial tone and position of the *Times* were inspired almost entirely by its brilliant first editor, Henry J. Raymond. But one incident of that period illustrates conspicuously the superior quality of the heart and mind of the man whose death has just left so large a vacancy in the ranks of American journalism. The *Times*, in common with other papers, had been printing a certain class of medical advertisements, when one day, feeling that they had grown too rank for the countenance of the *Times*, Raymond went into the business office and said: "Mr. Jones, about how much do we make out of these medical ads.?" Mr. Jones had the figures compiled and replied: "About $60,000 a year." "Now, suppose that we discontinue all of that?" said Raymond. "Agreed," was the prompt reply, and without any ostentatious parade of virtue the medical advertisements were quietly dropped out of the paper. Mr. Jones was unswerving in the determination that his paper should be clean and wholesome in the character of the matter it placed before its readers.

During the war of the rebellion the *Times* was a staunch and able supporter of the Union, and it was one of the first to declare in favor of the enfranchisement of the slave. Its only great mistake, which was afterwards admitted, was in the support of Andrew Johnson, after that statesman had launched upon his erratic career. The death of Mr. Raymond in 1869 threw the whole responsibility of the paper upon the shoulders of the only survivor of the original partnership, Mr. Jones. Many supposed t because he had never taken an active part in the editorial management of the paper that he was incapable of its direction, but after a short and disagreeable experience with an English editor, who was discharged after an unsuccessful effort to supplant Mr. Jones in the control of the paper, he assumed the editorial direction, as he had always had the business management of the paper. He presently began the memorable and successful crusade against the corrupt municipal government under which the city was being robbed of millions of dollars every year, and in the course of the next few months not only exposed and led to the destruction of the notorious Tweed ring, but established the standard of American journalism on a higher plane than it had ever before occupied.

In that great issue, in which Editor George Jones was tempted with a money bribe amounting to the enormous sum of $5,000,000 if he would only refrain from publishing the facts he had in hand about the doings and stealings of the thieves then in control of the city government, he stood manfully for the high principle which carried him and the *Times* safely through the trials of that contest for honesty and uprightness, and established the claim of the newspaper to the confidence and support of the people. From this high standard he never was known to recede. And when, a few years later, the masses seemed to demand from their newspapers a morbidly sensational style in the presentation of news, he stood against this new phrase of newspaper immorality quite as courageously and creditably as against corruption in office. The result is that the newspaper which he did more than any other man to establish on its present sound basis of honesty, respectability and independence survives in competent hands, one of the very few good and able examples we have of what an American newspaper should be. While in no sense an editorial writer, and in that respect nearly the opposite of his early great contemporary, Horace Greeley, Mr. Jones exhibited all the qualities of a wise and sagacious leader of public opinion, and in the selection of an able and respectable corps of editorial workers to carry out the policy of which he alone was the author, did all that is required of the proprietor of a great newspaper by the public welfare.

Foreclosure Sales.

The foreclosure sales of city property held since January 1st of this year have been far from satisfactory. The average weekly number of such sales for the first seven months of 1891 is from nine or ten to a dozen—a very material increase over the figures for last year. But the increase in number is not the only cause for complaint. Hardly a week has passed when one, two or three of the parcels offered under decrees of foreclosure have not sold for an amount below what was due for mortgages and costs. Doubtless the financial stringency of last fall accounts for many of the sales and perhaps for some of the failures to sell satisfactorily; but in face of the statement made so frequently by real estate men that the tightness in the money market last fall had no perceptible effect on real estate values, what explanation can be made of the fact that over 20 per cent of all the parcels offered under foreclosure failed to sell for an amount equal to the charges against them.

The location of the property, too, seems an indorsement of the view that real estate is weak and that the property was really not over-mortgaged, but rather that values took a slump in consequence of the strained money market. Last year about this time, when we analyzed the foreclosure sales, it was found that the greatest number of unsuccessful legal sales was on the west side, between 59th and 125th streets, west of 8th avenue, where building was most active. This year matters have been reversed, and although the west side is still the most active section in the number of buildings being erected, the east side, between 59th and 125th streets, east of 5th avenue, occupies first place in the table of unsuccessful foreclosure sales.

Another discouraging feature of these foreclosure sales is the fact that they are not confined to any one or two sections of the city, but are widespread, stretching from South street down town up into the 23d and 24th Wards on the north side. An analysis of the sales shows that of the fifty-eight cases where the parcels disposed of failed to bring the amounts due upon them, three were in the district south of 14th street; five were between 14th and 59th streets; ten were located between 59th and 125th streets, west of 8th avenue; twenty-two were in the section bounded by 59th and 125th streets, 5th avenue and the river; one was situated just north of Central Park and south of 125th street; nine were located north of 125th street and south of the Harlem River, and the remaining eight were located on the north side.

These figures taken from the records show that something is wrong either with real estate values or with the mortgagees, who have, in the past, advanced money too liberally on real estate where values were not fixed and certain. Of course there are exceptions to this statement. In some cases, doubtless, property is sold at auction under legal decrees for very much less than it is really worth, simply because the terms under which it is disposed of are so confusing and bewildering and require so much study to get at the truth in them, that the ordinary buyer does not care to take his chances in bidding for the property. This evil should be corrected. The legal notice should state exactly how much is due on the property, as simply as possible, and give an idea of how far work on the house (if, as is often the case, the building is in course of construction) has progressed. The practice of reading off a list of liens, claims and counter-claims against a piece of property which is offered to a miscellaneous crowd of bidders, who have no means of ascertaining the exact condition of affairs, is highly unsatisfactory. It generally has the effect of closing the competition to everyone but the plaintiff who, in most cases, takes advantage of the situation and bids astonishingly low.

We give below a few instances of where property sold under foreclosure has failed to bring the amount due upon it for mortgages and costs. The other cases mentioned above can be found by a search of THE RECORD AND GUIDE for the last seven months.

*Goerck st, Nos. 104–108 } begins Goerck st, e s, 246.7 n Rivington
Mangin st, Nos. 95–99 } st, runs east 100 x north 34.10 x east
100 to Mangin st, x north 65.9 x west 100 x south 36 x west 100 to Goerck st, x south 75 to beginning, three five-story brk tenements with stores on Goerck st, and vacant lots on Mangin st. (Amt due $11,741; prior morts. $86,800) $69,600

13th st, No. 5, n s, 150 e 5th av, 19.9x103.3, four-story brk dwell'g. (Amt due $11,006; leasehold 6,050

*50th st, Nos. 35 and 37, n s, 150 w Park av, 50x100.5, two five-story brk flats. (Amt due $95,175) 75,000

*50th st, Nos. 39 and 41, n s, 75 w 4th av, 74.11x100.5, two five-story brk flats. (Amt due $142,464) 100,000

*66th st, Nos. 42–48, s s, 375 w 8th av, 100x100.5, four five-story stone front flats. (Amt due $53,881) 40,000

*83d st, Nos. 122 and 124, s s, 225 w 9th av, 50x102.2, two five-story brk flats. (Amt due $14,595; prior mort. $25,450) 17,000

106th st, Nos. 63–69, n s, 200 e Madison av, 100x100.11, four five-story brk flats. (Amt due $76,956) 61,500

*Madison av, Nos. 1570–1576, w s, 24.11 s 106th st, four five-story brk flats, each 19x100. (Amt due $106,094) 80,000

*112th st, n s, 125 w Lenox av, 25x100.11, five-story brk flat. (Amt due $2,330; prior morts. $20,000) 21,275

*129th st, Nos. 306–310, s s, 125 w 8th av, 75x99.11, three five-story brk flats. (Amt due $35,436; prior morts. $56,000) 78,000

Park (4th) av, Nos. 1980–1986 } begins Park av, n w cor 133d st, 100
133d st, Nos. 63 and 65 } x140, four five-story brk flats
with stores on av and two five-story brk flats on st. (Amt due $89,899) 51,000

*135th st, n s, 104 e Southern Boulevard, 100.7x75. (Amt due $29,565) 24,000

*Railroad av, e s, 100 s w lot 47 on map of Village Morrisania, 25x150 .... }
Railroad av, e s, 250 s 11th st, 50x150 .... }
(Amt due $7,689) 3,500

* Indicates that the property described has been bid in for the plaintiff's account.

Readers of THE RECORD AND GUIDE *may subscribe to the new illustrated quarterly,* THE ARCHITECTURAL RECORD, *by sending their names and addresses to the offices of publication, Nos.* 14 *to* 16 *Vesey street. Annual subscription,* $1.00.

Sale of the Stevens Hotel.

THE RECORD AND GUIDE last week reported that the Stevens House was about to be or had been sold. This rumor is now substantiated by deeds which have just been placed on record, of which the following is a description, in brief:

Broadway, Nos. 21–27 } begins Broadway, s w cor Morris st, runs
Morris st, No. 1 } south 95.2 x west 119.6 x north 59.4 x east
45 x north 46.6 to Morris st, x east 90, five and six-story brk (Stevens House) hotel on Broadway and three-story brk store on Morris st. James Phelan and Alice his wife to Wm. H. Mairs, Brooklyn, N. Y. Aug. 17. exch

8th av, Nos. 2287 and 2289 } begins 8th av, s w cor 123d st, 50.11x
123d st, Nos. 302 and 304 } 71.3x50.11x71.2, two five-story brk stores and flats on av and two three-story brk dwell'gs on st.
123d st, Nos. 310 and 312, s e cor St. Nicholas av, 49.3x50.11x17.11 to av, x59.9, two three-story brk dwell'gs.
St. Nicholas av, e s, 59.9 s 123d st, 21x34.5x—x40.3, vacant.
Wm. H. Mairs to Jas. Phelan, of San Francisco. *Mt.* $44,000. Aug. 12. nom

The figures do not transpire, but it will be seen that Mr. Phelan takes Mr. Mairs' property, subject to a mortgage of $44,000, while a mortgage deed recorded shows that Mr. Mairs takes Mr. Phelan's property subject to a purchase money mortgage of $460,000, at 5½ per cent, due August 12, 1898, or sooner.

The sale is reported to have been made directly between the two principals. John F. Ames, the lessee, holds his tenancy from month to month only, a long lease which he held having expired a few months ago. It is not improbable that the new owner has a view to the improvement of the site by a handsome modern structure as he owns Nos. 17 and 19 Broadway, which adjoins the Stevens House. This property is about 44.9x119 in size, and was purchased by Mr. Mairs from Geo. F. Johnson in February last, the price not being named.

The Real Estate Auctioneers' Association.

The articles of association of the Real Estate Auctioneers' Association have been issued in pamphlet form and can be obtained of the secretary.

The article on membership reads: "Any real estate auctioneer, or partner of any real estate auctioneer, doing business in the city of New York, whose character and standing is vouched for by a member of the association, may be eligible for membership, must be proposed by a member at a regular meeting and seconded." A majority vote only is necessary to an election. The initiation fee is $10 and the annual dues a like amount.

The objects of the association as defined in the pamphlet are as follows: "The objects of this association shall be the general welfare of the real estate auction business; the promotion and facilitating the sale of real estate and other properties at auction and otherwise; the support and advocacy of every movement that tends to elevate the real estate business and to inspire that feeling of confidence and mutual reliance between owners of realty, auctioneers and brokers that should at all times exist."

The executive committee, consisting of nine members, has power to make contracts and purchases, to call meetings, to pass upon the eligibility of those proposed for membership, and to "suspend, fine, or by a four-fifths vote of all the members of the committee expel any member charged with conduct which endangers or may endanger the welfare, interests or character of the association."

The officers of the association at present are as follows: President, James L. Wells; Vice-President, J. Thos. Stearns; Secretary, Jas. S. McQuillen, and Treasurer, Wm. M. Ryan.

The lease of the room at Nos. 27 and 29 Pine street until recently held by the Association has been given up, and just now they have no auction room for the transaction of their business, as they will not take possession of 111 Broadway until May 1, 1892. A member of the association, who was questioned as to the reasons for giving up the room, said that they had no use for it during the summer anyway, that the building was in litigation, and the only lease possible in consequence was from month to month, that they would take possession of their new quarters at 111 Broadway on the first of May next, and altogether they considered the leasing of Nos. 27 and 29 Pine street as a needless expense, inasmuch as they could secure the room for sales if they should want it before May next. The same auctioneer said that the members of his association had given up any idea of reconciling their interests with those of the Real Estate Exchange, and that they would make no fight at the next election at the Exchange.

The Insurance on the Old Christ Church.

Everyone who has passed the ruined structure once occupied by the communicants of the erstwhile fashionable church on the southeast corner of 5th avenue and 35th street has wondered what the fate of the structure would be.

Last week the Liberty Insurance Co. filed plans for repairing damage by fire to the building, to cost $20,000. As the plans were filed by that company the impression got abroad that Lewis S. Samuel had sold the property to them. Inquiry at the offices of the company shows that this is not so, but that Mr. Samuel, who held a policy of $25,000 in the company, demanded the entire sum in settlement for damage done to the church by the fire which took place last fall. The company demurs at this, and have resolved to repair the church and place it in as good condition as it was before the fire occurred. This explains the filing of the plans. The affair may end in a lawsuit.

The property covers a plot 62.9x125. It was offered at auction about five years ago, and was knocked down at $207,500. It was transferred by Christ Church to Fredk. Billings for $315,000 in June, 1890, and was conveyed by that gentleman to Mr. Samuel, the present owner, in May, 1890, at a nominal consideration. The latter has offered it at private sale for some time, but has not found any one willing to give his figure.

The Sheet-Iron Workers Strike.

The strike of between sixty and seventy tin and sheet-iron workers at the shops of Baker, Smith & Co., Gillis & Geogbegan and Enoch Rutzler still continues, and has not changed in its aspect since our last issue. The men are still demanding from $3.00 to $3.50 per day for eight hours' work instead of nine, and the three employers are standing together in a determination not to yield. The men are not willing to accept a proportionate reduction in their pay that a decrease of one hour's work per day would mean. Their strike is for eight hours and the same pay as for nine hours.

It is not probable that the men will hold out very long, as their organization is not a strong one. The object seems to have been to obtain the desired concession from the three firms named above, and then to tackle other firms in the hope of meeting with similar success.

Newark News.

NEWARK, N. J.—The following plans have been filed at the Building Department: J. Duerr, 2-sty fr factory, 24x28, 22 Magazine st; S. F. Schnetz, 2½-sty fr dwg, 25x37, 55 Johnson av; G. Lapp, 3-sty fr dwg, 22x40, 310 South 6th st; J. Regan, 1-sty brk stable, 14x40, extension 16x30, rear, of 398 Plane st; F. Gehring, 2½-sty fr dwg, 21x32, 117 Johnson st; E. Remson, 2-sty fr dwg, 18x28, 308 Peshine av; Seb. Pfarr, 2-sty fr stable, 42x17, 735 South 17th st; W. Zahn, 1½-sty fr pigeon house, 20x14, 124 Littleton av; Isaac Champenois, 2-sty brk stable, 20x50, rear, 10 Spruce st; Newark Plank Road Co., 2-sty fr dwg, 18x28, West End Passaic Bridge; J. F. Barrett, 3-sty fr tenem't, 40x56, 93 and 95 Summit st; Wm. H. Taylor, 3-sty fr dwg, 23x30, 163 Elizabeth av; New York Roofing Co., two 2-sty brk office and stable, 32x36 and 30x28, 13–19 Division st; Mrs. Augusta Ebbinghousen, 3-sty brk flat, 23x41, cor Grant and Spring sts; C. H Guild, 2-sty fr dwg, 21x52, Chadwick av; Emele Roussell, 2½-sty fr tenem't, 20x82, 418 South 9th st; John M. Williams, 2-sty fr dwg, 20x40, 248 Aqueduct st; Thomas Hellrigle, 2-sty fr stable, 15x24, cor 14th av and Bergen st; R. E. Hunt, two 2½-sty fr dwgs, 17x42, 207 and 209 3d st; Louisa Spaeth, 1-sty brk, 16x16, 135 Academy st; Rich. Schwirten, 2-sty fr dwg, 22x45, 394 Hunterdon st; St. Aloysius Church, 2-sty fr church and school, 32x58, Esther st; Geo. Brown, 2-sty fr stable, 36x23, 219 Mt. Prospect av; Philip Viceidi, 3-sty fr tenem't, 28x56, 16 Drift st; Luigi Vorono, 3-sty fr dwg, 15x38, 4 Bedford st; Theresa Honig, 2-sty fr dwg, 22x30, cor Sussex av and Hecker st; Mrs. F. T. Ellithorpe, 1-sty fr stable, 20x16, 259 North 7th st; Mrs. Myron W. Morse, 2-sty fr dwg, 18x32, cor Garside st and 3d av; Home Brewing Co., 2½-sty brk brewery, 40x75, 15–17 Hudson st; Oscar Hudd, 2-sty fr dwg, 21x38, 152 Van Buren st; C. S. Osborne, two 2-sty fr dwgs, 16x32, 89 Ann st; Wheeler & Russell, 3-sty brk engine room, 16x13, extension 33x64, cor N. J. R. R. av and Miller st; Wheeler & Russell, 1-sty fr hat factory, 28x153, cor N. J. R. R. av and Vanderpool st; Albert Spaeth, 2-sty fr, extension 14x30, 23 Howard st; Charles Buerman, 2-sty fr stable, 15x14, rear, 412 Clinton av; Charles Buerman, 3-sty fr dwg and store, 22x50, 412 Clinton av; Frank Schreck, 2-sty fr dwg, 22x38, 43 Bremen st; Patrick Cox, 2-sty fr dwg, extension 12x25, 207 Warren st.

Real Estate Notes.

The Sixth Street Baptist Church has been given permission by Judge O'Brien to mortgage the church property for $20,000 to the pastor, Rev. Daniel C. Potter, in lieu of salary for ten years' services. The mortgage is to be paid in one year, with 5 per cent interest.

Francis P. Burke has taken title at $110,000 to four lots on the south side of 72d street, 350 east West End avenue.

The title to a portion of the old Twenty-second Regiment Armory on 14th street, north side, 300 west of 6th avenue, size 100x200, running through to 15th street, has passed this week to The Mayor, etc., at $203,405.

Notice is given that the Board of Street Opening and Improvement propose to alter the map or plan of the city of New York by laying out 188th and 189th streets, between Amsterdam and Wadsworth avenues, in the 12th Ward, said 188th and 189th streets to be 60 feet wide, between the lines of Amsterdam and Wadsworth avenues.

Robert and Ogden Goelet are gradually acquiring the block front on the east side of Broadway, between 31st and 32d streets, and their purchases are even extending down each of the side streets toward 5th avenue. It is only recently that they purchased the "San Carlo," on the corner of 31st street and Broadway, together with a couple of houses in the rear on 31st street; and this week they have taken title to No. 42 West 32d street, which is a four-story dwelling, the second house from the Hotel Imperial, on the corner of 32d street. The intervening lot, No. 44, is also owned by the Goelets and is being improved by them by the erection of a nine-story addition to the Hotel Imperial.

New Incorporations.

The Parkside Land and Improvement Co. on Saturday last filed a certificate of incorporation for the purpose of purchasing real estate, improving, selling and leasing the same in the County of Westchester, N. Y. The capital stock shall be $22,000, divided into 220 shares of $100 each. The directors' names are as follows: Geo. A. Peters, James M. Townsend, Jr., and Charles H. Young, of New York, W. W. Bissell, New Rochelle, N. Y., and Bradford Rhodes, Mamaroneck, N. Y.

The first number of *The Architectural Record* is now for sale at the elevated railroad stands, and all stands throughout the Union and at the leading booksellers. It is of the same size as the *Century*, printed on fine paper, and contains sixty-four superb illustrations.

The Opinions of Others.

James L. Wells said: "The outlook for suburban real estate this fall is, I think, very good. Very much depends, of course, on the location and general desirability of the property, and nearly as much more on the manner of laying it out. Even good property will not sell when buyers have any difficulty in understanding the restrictions and reservations on the part of owners. Maps and terms of sale should be as simple as possible, so that the buyer will run no chance of getting confused. An instance of the danger of such confusion was brought to my notice last year, when very acceptable suburban property was offered, on the map of which the streets showed only 30 feet wide. The sellers, however, reserved the right to lay gas and water mains under the 15 feet at the front of each lot. Those who attended the sale did not seem to understand what it all meant, so that the bidding was tame and dispirited from the start and the sale was not a success. Another thing that owners of suburban property should not do, and that is to offer any great number of lots at one time. My experience is that buyers are indifferent when a large number of lots are offered at one time, thinking that the property will be sold anyway, and if they hold off they will get the lots at their own figures. If owners would offer their holdings in smaller divisions I think they would do better than when they offer 500 or 1,000 lots at one time. Then, too, advertisements of suburban property should state simply and as plainly as possible the facts about the lots to be offered, adding nothing to the truth, and the sales will be attended by a greater measure of success than if glowing, meaningless words are used, whose only object readers think is to deceive. As I say, inquiries and requests for circulars of property which is to be offered in the fall reach my office every day, and altogether the outlook is very satisfactory."

Joseph D. Smyth said: "I do not think that vacant, restricted suburban property can ever meet with much of a success at public auction. The people who would buy suburban property are clerks and others of the same class who are frightened off when they find that they cannot build anything but a $4,000 or $5,000 house on a $1,500 lot, and the speculators do not like to take hold because of the risk there is in it. If owners improved their property with small desirable dwellings, I think there would be a better chance of their selling their lots than when the plots are offered with nothing but heavy restrictions upon them, which generally confuse and nearly always frighten the small investor".

"It is very hard to close sales of any kind just now," said James E. Leviness. "When the seller is in town the buyer is not to be found and by the time we have the buyer the seller has disappeared. And even when one has succeeded in getting both parties together some little matter comes up which upsets the sale. Only a short time ago I succeeded in signing a contract for a Broadway store and the sale fell through because there was a mortgage of $65,000 on the property which still had two years to run. The holder of the mortgage would not cancel it for less than six month's interest and this the buyer refused to pay. Taking it all in all I think this summer has been a pretty hard one for the brokers."

D. Y. Swainson, of the firm of L. J. Carpenter, said: "The Real Estate Exchange should have a complaint bureau where brokers and other real estate men could send complaints, incorrect bills, etc., for correction by any of the public departments. If an efficient man was in charge of such a bureau an immense deal of trouble could be saved the real estate community, and evils in the municipal departments against which an individual is powerless would I think be speedily remedied."

Fine Printing of All Kinds.

Personal.

S. M. Blakely is spending the summer with his family at East Moriches, L. I.

J. M. Flanagan is spending a vacation in Sullivan County, N. Y.

Benjamin Sturges has just negotiated a loan of $15,000 on the Emanuel Episcopal Church, corner of Smith and President streets, Brooklyn.

Interesting to Architects and Builders.

BRICK.

The Raritan Hollow and Porous Brick Co. have just begun the delivery of fire-proofing material at the Astor hotels, on 5th avenue and 33d street and 5th avenue and 59th street. These are said to be the largest fire-proofing contracts ever let out in this city. They are also furnishing the same character of material to the Van Ingen building on 5th avenue and 21st street, and the buildings of the Franklin Trust Company in Brooklyn and the Prudential Life Insurance Company in Newark, the latter of which is to be thirteen stories high.

***

CEMENT.

Messrs. Johnson & Wilson, of Aldrich Court, state that they have sold more cement this year than in any previous year. A. J. Swift, chief engineer of the Delaware & Hudson Canal Co., in writing to them, says: "The Saylor's American Portland Cement, which we have purchased from you during the last two years, has proved entirely satisfactory, and in my opinion is as desirable for railroad engineering as any imported Portland Cement we have used." In concluding his letter Engineer Swift says: "We propose to continue using it as our standard cement until something equally as good and less expensive shall appear upon the market."

***

IRON AND STEEL WORK.

Messrs H. Stutzer & Co. are doing the work for a six-story, iron front building on Broadway and South 8th street, Brooklyn. They are also putting up the Breezy Hill Bridge in Prospect Park. This is the first time that the electro-plating process has been applied to outside work, the difficulty being to treat the material so that it will not rust after being exposed to all the changes of the weather.

***

VENETIAN BLINDS.

The Venetian blind is evidently superseding the cumbersome and more expensive box-shutter. The Albany Venetian Blind Company, whose blinds are being used from Maine to the Pacific Coast, have had much to do with this change. They devote themselves exclusively to the manufacture of Venetian blinds of simple construction, with all the objectionable features of the old style of blind done away with. The simplicity, durability and cheapness of these blinds, combined with their superb finish, appear to have attracted builders in the principal towns and cities all over the country. The company have contracts in hand for apartment and dwelling houses, schools, hotels, etc. Among the buildings which they have recently supplied are the "Nevada" on the Boulevard and 69th street, and the "Monterey" on Morningside avenue and 114th street. They are represented in all the principal cities, their New York agent being W. G. Orr, of No. 150 Broadway.

***

GALVANIZED SHEET IRON.

J. T. Wagner, of No. 108 Chambers street, has about finished the ornamental work for the cornices and bay windows of the Dugro Hotel on 5th avenue and 59th street. There is a very elaborate frieze on the main cornice. It is a bas-relief, and is stamped out bold and clear. Mr. Wagner's work on the tower of the Madison Square Garden is progressing rapidly, the statue of Diana, 18 feet high, which is to be placed on the apex, being nearly completed.

***

STEAM HEATING.

Messrs. Gillis & Geogbegan have been awarded the contract for the steam-heating of the new Astor hotel on 5th avenue and 59th street, which, it is said, is a $100,000 contract. Among their many engagements ahead are the contracts for supplying the building of the Manhattan Storage and Warehouse Co. on 7th avenue, 52d and 53d streets, where they will put in four large boilers, 5½x16, for power. They are also supplying a Roman Catholic Institution in Wheeling, West Virginia, with three of their largest boilers, and they are said to have enough contracts on hand to keep them busy for a year. They will shortly remove to the six-story building erected for their occupancy at Nos. 33 and 35 South 5th avenue, near Bleecker street.

***

SALE OF MAHOGANY VENEERS.

Messrs. Daniels & Co., of No. 202 Centre street, have ceased to exist, and their property will be sold at auction toward the end of the month. Their stock consists of sawed and cut mahogany veneers.

***

TERRA COTTA.

The Perth Amboy Terra Cotta Company are engaged in making the terra cotta for the Equitable building in Baltimore, which, in general design, is similar to that of the Imperial Hotel, on Broadway and 32d street, though somewhat larger in proportion. Among other material now being manufactured by them is the terra cotta for the Havemeyer office building on Cortlandt, Church and Dey streets, which is said to be by far the largest contract given out on terra cotta work this season.

***

SKYLIGHTS.

J. C. French & Son, of No. 452 Canal street, have just finished the patent lights for the "Nevada" apartment house on the Boulevard, between 69th and 70th streets, and the large skylights for the Hotel Endicott on Columbus avenue, 81st and 82d streets. They are also working on the new Grammar School at 3d avenue and 157th street. They have recently placed in their factory an Edison Electric Motor to run their machinery, which has proved a source of convenience and economy.

***

HYDRAULIC PIPE WORK.

The contract for all the hydraulic pipe work for Judge Dugro's Hotel, on 5th avenue and 59th street, has been awarded to George Franklin, who has also secured a similar contract on the Hebrew Orphan Asylum on East Broadway and Jefferson street. The demand for hydraulic pipe work seems to be on the increase. Mr. Franklin states that his orders will keep him exceptionally busy for months to come.

***

GAS FITTINGS.

The jewelry store of C. W. Schuman & Sons, on Broadway and 22d street, has been very extensively and elaborately fitted up by J. F. Palmer's Son. They do considerable gas fitting in the upper wards, and some fine examples of their work are to be seen at No. 13 East 17th street.

***

TEARING DOWN OLD BUILDINGS.

Thos. E. Tripler & Son have just torn down the old New England Hotel on the Bowery, Elizabeth and Bayard streets, to make way for the building to be erected for the Third Avenue Cable Company. They are also tearing down the old Merchants' Hotel on Cortlandt street. This well-known building material firm have torn down the old buildings on sites on which some of the most prominent structures in New York City have since been erected.

***

IRON CONSTRUCTION.

The Atlas Iron Construction Co., whose incorporation we noticed some six months ago, have since erected large shops on Monmouth street, between 13th and 15th streets, Jersey City, and equipped them with the most modern and approved machine tools. The company is about to move from the eighth floor of the *Times* building to more spacious quarters on the tenth floor, having quite outgrown their present room-space. They are engaged on several buildings in New York, Brooklyn and elsewhere, and one of the contracts recently secured by them was that for the ten-story office building which is being erected on the corner of Broad and Beaver streets for Mrs. John A. Morris, from plans by Youngs & Cable. In this building all the walls are carried on columns and girders of iron and steel, the outside walls being intended only as a buttress against the inroads of the weather, their greatest thickness being but 16 inches. The saving in floor space through this character of construction is considerable, as the thickness of the walls under the old method would have been at least 4 feet.

Important to Property-Holders

Notice is given to the owner or owners of all houses and lots affected thereby, that the following assessments have been completed and are lodged in the office of the Board of Assessors for examination by all persons interested, viz.:

No. 1.—Receiving basins on the northeast and southeast corners of 96th st and Boulevard.

No. 2.—Receiving basins on the northwest and southwest corners of 108th st and Boulevard.

No. 3.—Receiving basin on the southeast corner of 98th st and 1st av.

No. 4.—Alteration and improvement to sewer in Ludlow st, bet Delancey and Broome sts.

[The limits embraced by such assessments include all the several houses and lots of ground, vacant lots, pieces and parcels of land situated on—

No. 1.—Blocks bounded by 95th and 97th sts, Amsterdam av and Boulevard.

No. 2.—West side of Boulevard, commencing half way bet 107th and 108th sts, northerly to half way bet 108th and 109th sts.

No. 3.—South side 98th st, from 1st av to the East River.

No. 4.—Both sides of Ludlow st, from Broome to Delancey st; east side of Orchard st, from Broome to Delancey st, and south side of Delancey st, from Ludlow to Orchard st.]

All persons whose interests are affected by the above-named assessments, and who are opposed to the same, are requested to present their objections in writing to the Chairman of the Board of Assessors, at their office, No. 27 Chambers street, within thirty days from Aug. 13th.

The above-described lists will be transmitted, as provided by law, to the Board of Revision and Correction of Assessments for confirmation on the 14th day of September, 1891.

Special Notices.

We are pleased to note the co-partnership lately announced between Benj. Prince and Y. J. Muir under the firm name of Prince & Muir, manufacturers of fine Parquet flooring, Wainscotings, etc., at 501-505 East 70th street. Mr. Prince has, in the few years he has devoted to this line of work, won for himself a good reputation among many leading architects and builders for turning out strictly first-class work. His partner, Mr. Muir, is a son of Mr. James Muir, who has borne an excellent reputation as a reliable plumber in this city for many years.

H. F. Clinton, of No. 220 William street, offers for sale a plot of 655 acres adjoining New Rochelle, about one mile from the depot. Larchmont Manor Station is only five minutes' walk from the property. This is an excellent opportunity to purchase for investment and improvement.

Joseph Marren gives notice that he has transferred to his sons, James P. and William E. Marren, the business known as the Grand Central Iron Works, at No. 157 East 44th street.

Schloss Valore, Erbaut von Architekt Tubeuf in Paris.

Notice.

We are in receipt of the July numbers of the *Westminster* and *Edinburgh Reviews*, from the Leonard Scott Publication Company, of No. 231 Broadway. Both of these issues contain interesting contributions. In the former Theodore Stanton has the second of a series of articles on Abraham Lincoln, and Mr. J. T. Cunningham enters into a vigorous and convincing polemic against the new Darwinists. Other articles of scarcely less interest follow. In the *Edinburgh* the papers on Talleyrand, Kipling, and London architecture, are admirable and instructive bits of writing.

Readers of THE RECORD AND GUIDE *may subscribe to the new illustrated quarterly,* THE ARCHITECTURAL RECORD, *by sending their names and addresses to the offices of publication, Nos.* 14 *to* 16 *Vesey street. Annual subscription,* $1.00.

Real Estate Department.

The real estate market at the present time is absolutely without movement. Nothing is being done, nothing can be done. The brokers are working hard enough on the various transactions which they have underway, but by the time, when after much labor they get the terms agreed upon, one of the parties to the negotiation goes out of town, where it is not easy to reach him, and perhaps the other negotiator leaves town also before contracts can be signed. When accidents do not prevent the closing of contracts quibbling or hesitancy does, and so it comes about that nothing is done. This state of affairs results, of course, from the indifference with which everyone is regarding real estate transactions at the present time. Both buyers and sellers seem to be of the opinion that it is wiser to wait for the fall market, and all efforts on the part of the brokers to hasten matters have proved and probably will continue to prove futile. Even large sales like that of the Stevens House, reported last week, where the negotiations have been going on for a long time, seem to be at an end for the present. And certainly if these hold-over transactions from the spring or winter's business cannot be closed the prospect for new deals at the present time is not bright. The fall market cannot be expected for nearly a month yet, but when it does come good judges say there will be an active business. In the meantime, important preliminary work is being done, and it is progressing in such a satisfactory way that great results are expected.

THE AUCTION MARKET.

The sales at auction during the week have been as few in number and as unimportant in character as they well can or will be. The only city property disposed of at auction was three different parcels which had to be sold to satisfy judgments of foreclosure. None of these three sales are possessed of features that would interest the general market, so that details of the sales are unnecessary. Besides the foreclosures sales, however, some suburban property was offered. Chester Park, near Pelhamville, had been so thoroughly and extensively advertised that success in some measure was looked for. These anticipations were disappointed. The heat of the auction room on the day of sale, Tuesday, was unendurable, and the fifty or sixty people who faced the auctioneer's stand were absolutely devoid of the enthusiasm and spirit so essential to the success of a suburban sale. The auctioneer knocked down about twenty-nine plots, each containing between four and five city lots, and really sold but nine or ten of them out of the eighty-six which the owner had offered. The prices for these were $625 to $725 and $1,500 and $1,800 for some of the better corners. It is doubtful if the most attractive property would have sold well on such an exceedingly warm day, and it is to the heat that the failure of the sale is partially attributed, but doubtless another cause had a larger share in the failure. The lots were sold with a restriction against the building of any house which should cost less than $4,000, and it is very likely that this clause frightened off those who would, under other circumstances, have been willing enough bidders.

The announcements for next week show no improvement over those to which the real estate world has been accustomed for some time past. In the way of city property there are only forced sales, and the out of town real estate is of a not very attractive kind. The dull season with the auctioneers shows no sign of drawing to a close just yet, and it will be more or less in the nature of a surprise if anything much is stirring for a month to come. The preliminary work, however, goes on without interruption, and the indications are that the resulting offerings will be of a fairly interesting kind.

CONVEYANCES.

	1890. August 8 to 14 inc.	1891. August 7 to 13 inc.
Number	193	127
Amount involved	$3,492,371	$2,241,310
Number nominal	70	53
Number 23d and 24th Wards	44	34
Amount involved	$121,447	$201,760
Number nominal	11	7

MORTGAGES.

	1890.	1891.
Number	192	199
Amount involved	$2,147,209	$2,763,114
Number at 5 % or less	76	106
Amount involved	$974,790	$1,047,600
Number at less than 5 per cent	24	9
Amount involved	$342,000	$740,000
Number to Banks, Trust and Ins. Cos	30	29
Amount involved	$392,500	$863,500

PROJECTED BUILDINGS.

	1890. August 9 to 15 inc.	1891. August 8 to 14 inc.
Number of buildings	55	18
Estimated cost	$1,139,950	$699,050

Gossip of the Week.

SOUTH OF 59TH STREET.

S. Harris & Co. have sold to Daniel Rothstein for J. Ochs, Nos. 244 and 246 Elizabeth street, two five-story double tenement houses, on plot 50x98, for $55,000.

S. M. Blakely has sold for Wm. J. Roome to Mrs. Rose Heyman the four-story brick tenement, No. 555 West 32d street, for $12,000.

NORTH OF 59TH STREET.

J. W. Stevens has sold for Increase M. Grenell to the Rev. Thomas Dixon, pastor of the 23d street Baptist Church, No. 61 West 94th street, a three-story brown stone dwelling, 19x55x100.8, on private terms; and for John McKean to J. F. Cordes, No. 70 West 93d street, a five-story brown stone dwelling, 27.6x87x100.8, for $32,000.

R. Peblemann has sold for Gordon Bros. to John Sasse, No. 422 Amsterdam avenue, a five-story buff brick double flat, 25x70x82, for $28,000.

Jacob M. Newman has sold to P. Gomprecht's Sons, No 334 Columbus avenue, a five-story brick and stone flat and store, on private terms.

Frank L. Fisher & Co., it is reported, have sold for Wm. Lanchantin to Mrs. J. L. Adams, of Morristown, N. J., No. 313 West 89th street, a three-story brick and brown stone dwelling, 20x55x104.2, for $24,000.

LEASE.

Jesse C. Bennett has leased for Richard Wightman to Dr. F. Spencer Halsey, No. 125 West 69th street, a three-story dwelling, 17x50x100, for five years, at an annual rental of $1,500.

Brooklyn

Corwith Bros. have sold for Emily H. W. Behnken the house and lot No. 93 Manhattan avenue, 20x36x75, to Carl A. F. Striepecke, for $5,000.

J. P. Sloane has sold for the estate of Maria E. Gay the two-story frame dwelling, 20x32, on lot 25x100, No. 82 Oakland street, to Andrew Valentine, for $2,600.

Boyd & Co. have sold for F. Yost to Mrs. Susie E. Boyd the three-story dwelling, on plot 40x137, No. 297 Park place, for $13,000.

CONVEYANCES.

	1890. August 7 to 13 inc	1891. August 6 to 12 inc
Number	259	240
Amount involved	$1,006,891	$957,647
Number nominal	74	83

MORTGAGES.

	1890.	1891.
Number	219	240
Amount involved	$828,184	$1,081,446
Number at 5 per cent. or less	117	130
Amount involved	$628,250	$696,415

PROJECTED BUILDINGS.

	1890. August 8 to 14 inc.	1891. August 7 to 13 inc.
Number of buildings	140	60
Estimated cost	$566,150	$371,500

Out of Town.

MT. VERNON, N. Y.—Boyd & Co. have sold for Mrs. Susie E. Boyd to F. Yost the corner of 2d and Cleveland streets for $6,000.

Builders—Out of Town.

GREENPOINT, L. I.—Constable Bros. have completed plans for an extension in brick and stone to be built for Poulson & Eger at their foundry at this place.

WANTS AND OFFERS.

(Advertisements strictly in accordance with this title will be inserted at the practically nominal rate of 10 CENTS *per line (agate). In figuring for themselves advertisers may count seven words for each line, the address to be taken as one line. The object of this department is to bring buyers and sellers into communication with customers. Advertisements must be marked "Wants and Offers Column," and sent to the office of publication, Nos. 14 and 16 Vesey Street, not later than 3 P. M. Friday.)*

WANTS.

TO MASONS AND BUILDERS.—A thoroughly reliable man wants a position as foreman (bricklayer); 25 years experience; best of references. Address, "FOREMAN," RECORD AND GUIDE.

WANTED.—A capitalist who will erect a warehouse, if same is leased for a term of years. NAYLER, office of RECORD AND GUIDE.

YOUNG MAN AS SALESMAN in West Side real estate office; salary and commission; state references and experience. WEST SIDE, RECORD AND GUIDE.

WANTED.—Property to let or for sale; registration free. E. A. TREDWELL, 41 Park row

WE HAVE several clients who desire first mortgage loans on improved and well-located property; executors and administrators are invited to communicate with us. SOLOMON BENEDICT & CO., 165 Broadway.

$200,000 TO INVEST in good paying flat or tenement property; send full particulars to 709 Columbus av. Aug. 8-15. HENRY H. DREYER.

Real Estate Wanted.

WANTED TO PURCHASE, for cash, a three-story and basement 18-foot front house in good neighborhood, between 23d and 50th sts., 6th and 9th avs. Address, BUYER, RECORD AND GUIDE office.

OFFERS.

Dwellings and Flats.

FOR SALE.—Five new first-class four-story and basement private dwellings, Nos. 109, 113 and 113 East 46th street, and Nos. 462 and 464 Lexington avenue; all leased to desirable tenants, or can arrange to give possession to some of them if desired. For further particulars, apply to The C. GRAHAM & SONS CO., 99 East 43d st.

BUYERS, ATTENTION!—145 to 165 West 95th st.; sizes 18 and 20x62.6x100; the most attractive three-story and basement houses, with two modern bath-rooms, open plumbing, tiled walls, mosaic floors, butler's pantry, laundry and wine vault in extensions; magnificent saloon floors; hardwood cabinet trim throughout. Special prices and convenient terms offered to prompt buyers; inspection solicited. For further particulars apply on premises or THE AMSTERDAM IMPROVEMENT CO., 15 Cortlandt st.

OFFERS.

SUMMER PRICES.—Safe investments; property paying 10 per cent net; corner dwellings and business property; good neighborhood; first-class order. KETCHAM, owner, 120 Broadway.

WASHINGTON HEIGHTS.—Only $15,000, $4,000 cash, balance on mortgage; new house, hardwood trim and floors; walls frescoed; porcelain bath; tiled bath-room. Apply to owner, W. G. ALGER, 45 Pine st.

FOR SALE.—A newly-built double flat in Essex st., now fully tenanted and returning 7 per cent. net on price asked, or 9½ per cent. on investment required. Full particulars and accounts. FULLER & FROTHINGHAM, 945 Broadway, cor 22d st

FOR SALE.—West 47th st., near Broadway. A very desirable four-story, high stoop, brown stone house, 20x52x100; price, $32,000. FULLER & FROTHINGHAM, 945 Broadway, cor 22d st.

FOR SALE OR TO RENT.—East 35th st., near Lexington av. A very desirable English basement house in perfect order; price, $19,000; rent, $1,600. FULLER & FROTHINGHAM, 945 Broadway, cor 22d st.

WANTED.—Unimproved property on Boulevard, 8th or 10th av, in exchange of single flats. WILLIAM H. ALLEN, 38 Park row.

BARGAINS.—Single tenement improved, or cold water flats and lots in exchange or cash. WILLIAM H. ALLEN, 38 Park row.

WEST 89TH ST., near Boulevard. Nos. 260, 262 and 264; new three-story brown stone. CHAS. L. RITZMAN, Owner. July4-e.o.w.4t. 941 Broadway.

FOR SALE.—At a sacrifice, new five-story double flats, near 125th st. L station. Address, Aug. 1—1aw-9w. BUILDER, 319 East 125th st.

BUY THE BEST.
72D ST., THE PARK DRIVEWAY.
SEVERAL 25-FOOT PALATIAL RESIDENCES.
ONE SUPERBLY DECORATED.
NONE MORE ELEGANT AND SPACIOUS.
The best judgment of long experience has been given to their construction. The most critical will be satisfied in the taste displayed and the excellent character of the workmanship and material; prices reasonable. F. CRAWFORD, 114 West 72d st. July 11-1aw8w.

FOR SALE—2443 8th av.; 26.3½x100; easy terms; commission allowed brokers; apply at Mar. 28-u-f. ROOM 19, 156 Broadway.

OFFERS.

FOR SALE—210 and 212 West 105th st.; five-story apartments; each, 25x89x100; decorated and carpeted; apply at ROOM 19, 156 Broadway. Mar.28-u-f.

Vacant Lots.

TWO FULL LOTS, south side 125th st., 150 feet west of 10th av., very cheap; will exchange. J. H. WELLWOOD, 247 West 125th st., room 17.

FOR SALE.—On easy terms, nine first-class lots, ready for immediate improvement, on south side 116th street, commencing about 130 feet east of 7th avenue. The C. GRAHAM & SONS CO., A 15—4t 309 East 43d street.

100TH ST., between 2d and 3d avs; ten lots, cheap; all mortgage if improved. July11-1aw8w. EDWIN A. ELY, 108 Gold st.

40 CHERRY ST., between Roosevelt and Franklin sq., 32x84, vacant; $12,000; accommodating terms. EDWIN A. ELY, 108 Gold st. July11-1aw8w.

Improved Property.

PLANING MILL, branch of my business, for sale.—Is located at 24th st. and 11th av., on four or five city lots, leased ground, and consists of two and three-story brick buildings and adjoining sheds; also 80 horse-power engine and boiler, planers, moulders, saws, etc., all in good running order and now in operation; will leave a portion of value on bond and mortgage three years; this offers splendid opportunity to enlarge wood-working industry or to secure good mill business to add thereto. For further particulars, etc., apply to EBEN PECK, 24th st. and 11th av. Advertiser intends to continue his lumber business now carried on at above address. Aug. 15-22-29

Brooklyn Real Estate for Sale.

DESIRABLE INVESTMENT.—Eight-story apartment house; best location in Brooklyn; might exchange equity over $125,000 at 4½ per cent. J. 20—uf. Apply 60 Broadway, Room 311.

LARGE FACTORY for sale; price, $28,000; the land itself supposed to be worth the money. Apr 4-uf FIRST NATIONAL BANK, Brooklyn, N. Y.

Miscellaneous.

A PARTY ABOUT TO BUILD A FIVE-STORY factory, 50x98, in Harlem, near water-front, will lease the three upper floors and build to suit tenant. Terms very moderate. Address May 16 u. f. OWNER, 409 E. 107th St.

SALES OF THE WEEK.

The following are the sales at the Real Estate Exchange and Auction Room for the week ending Aug. 14.

** Indicates that the property described has been bid in for plaintiff's account.*

R. V. HARNETT & CO.

53d st, Nos. 208-214, s s, 68 w 7th av, 68x50.5, four four-story stone front dwell'gs, A. W. Farmer. (Amt due $16,008) $52,500

Amsterdam av, Nos. 641-649, n e cor 91st st, 136.5x100, five five-story brk flats with stores. Simon Arendt. (Amt due $29,132; prior morts. $120,000) 156,200

R. L. KENNELLY.

133d st, Nos. 161-167, n s, 125 e 7th av, 100x99.11, four five-story brk flats. Chas. Schlesinger. (Amt due $18,878) 37,000

Total $245,700
Corresponding week 1890 .... $243,850

BROOKLYN, N. Y.

FOR WEEK ENDING AUGUST 13.

JERE. JOHNSON, JR.

*Herkimer st, n w cor Rockaway av, 20x80, three-story brk dwell'g. Brayton Burrill, exr $5,000

*Herkimer st, n s, 20 w Rockaway av, 20x80, three-story brk dwell'g. Charles A. Moran, trustee 4,000

*Herkimer st, n s, 40 w Rockaway av, 20x80, three-story brk dwell'g. Mary M. Burrill 4,000

*Pacific st, s s, 497.4 e Rochester av, 16.8x127.9½, two-story frame dwell'g. Sarah Chauncey Savage trustee 2,000

*Palmetto st, n w s, 275 n e Knickerbocker av, 25x100, vacant. Charles Johnston.......... 850

*Union st, n s, 200 w 8th av, 18.9x90..........
Union st, n s, 312.6 w 8th av, 18.9x90..........
Union st, n s, 331.3 w 8th av, 18.9x90..........
Three three-story brown stone dwell'gs.... Henry F. Ogden.......... 21,000

*Vanderveer st, s e s, 80 s w Bushwick av, 16 10x100. Sarah Chauncey Savage.......... 2,000

*Walworth st, w s, 261.10 s Myrtle av, 18.9x100, two-story brk dwell'g. Frederick Behrens, trustee.......... 2,000

*44th st, No. 159, n e s, 275 s e 3d av, 25x100.2, three-story frame dwell'g and store. The Daily News Building, Savings and Loan Asso.......... 3,500

Throop av, No. 549, e s, 61.7½ s Hancock st, 21.8⅝x81, four-story brown stone flat and store. William K. Gilchrist.......... 10,000

OTHER AUCTIONEERS.

North 3d st, No. 56, w s, abt 206 s Kent av, two-story frame dwell'g. John D. Wacker...... 2,850

*Franklin av, s w s, lot 37 map of 28 building sections at Bath, filed June 28, 1854, New Utrecht, 51x359.6 to New Utrecht Bay, x 50.4x364.4..........
Franklin av, s w s, lot 38 same map, 50x362.4 to New Utrecht Bay x97.11x378.7..........
Franklin av, s w s, abt 105 s e Bath, New Utrecht and Greenwood plank road, 50x 378.7 to New Utrecht Bay, x10x370.5..........
Franklin av, s s, 256 s e New Utrecht to Bay road, formerly plank road, 50x355.10 to New Utrecht Bay, x50.2x359.8..........
Resale. Herbert Vaughan.......... 20,000

Kingsland av, Nos. 295-299, w s, 279.3½ n Nassau av, three three-story brk tenem'ts. John J. Drake.......... 7,650

Total.......... $84,350
Corresponding week, 1890.......... $81,069

CONVEYANCES.

Wherever the letters Q. C., C. a. G. and B. & S occur, preceded by the name of the grantee they mean as follows:

1st—Q. C. is an abbreviation for Quit Claim deed, i. e., a deed in which all the right, title and interest of the grantor is conveyed, omitting all covenants or warranty.

2d—C. a. G. means a deed containing Covenant against Grantor only, in which he covenants that he hath not done any act whereby the estate conveyed may be impeached, charged or encumbered.

3d—B. & S. is an abbreviation for Bargain and Sale deed, wherein, although the seller makes no express covenants, he really grants or conveys the property for a valuable consideration, and thus impliedly claims to be the owner of it.

NEW YORK CITY.

AUGUST 7, 8, 10, 11, 12, 13.

Broadway, Nos. 21-27 } begins Broadway, s w Morris st, No. 1 } cor Morris st, runs south 95.2 x west 119.6 x north 59.4 x east 45 x north 46 6 to Morris st, x east 90, five and six-story brk Stevens house hotel on Broadway and three-story brk store on Morris st. James Phelan and Alice his wife, San Francisco, Cal, to William H. Mairs, Brooklyn, N. Y. Aug. 17. See 8th av. exch

Chestnut st, No. 26 } begins Chestnut st, e s, New Bowery, No. 24 } 23.3 s Madison st, 25.1 x44 10 to New Bowery, x 35.4x69.10½, three-story brk building. Susan M. Riorden, Michael W. Hughes and Mary C. Adams to Joseph Hughes. Q. C. June 25. nom

Same property. Michael J. Barrett an heir of Michael Barrett and Ellen his wife to same. Q C June 25. $333

Same property. Delia Dugan, Irene Florence, Marion and Theresa Barrett heirs Michael Barrett to same. Q. C. June 25. 500

Same property Release dower. Catharine Barrett to same. July 29. nom

Division st, No. 248, n s, abt 140 e Attorney st, 19.5x93x17.4x101, three story frame (brk front) store and tenem't with four-story brk building on rear. Release dower. Julie Raduziner wife of Adolph to John Ambacher. Aug. 10. nom

Same property. John Ambacher to Samuel Dorman and Edmund Kohn. *Mt.* $20,500. Aug. 10. nom

Essex st, No. 109, w s, abt 200 s Rivington st, 25x87.6, five-story brk tenem't with stores. Charles Dexheimer and Emma his wife to Ernestine wife of Joseph Kiwi. *Mt.* $12,000. Aug. 13. 33,000

Horatio st, No 76, s s, abt 144 5 w Greenwich st, 25x87.5, four-story brk tenem't. Jacob H. Conklin trustee Jacob Straut to Mitchell A. C. Levy. Aug. 12. 13,500

Same property. Partition. Henry H. Anderderson to same. July 30. 13,500

Hester st, No. 182, s w cor Mulberry st, 25x57.3, three-story frame (brk front) store and tenem't. John H. Hayes to Mary A. Neacy. Q. C. Aug. 6. nom

Same property. Mary A. Neacy to William Hartfield and Abraham Nelson. July 30. 22,000

Jersey st, No. 4 } begins Jersey st, s s, abt 97 Marion st, No. 89 } e Crosby st, 24x66.5 to Marion st, x25.3x65.7, four-story brk store and tenem't on Jersey st and three-story brk store and tenem't on Marion st. John Hayes to John S. Hawley and Herman W. Hoops Aug. 10. 18,000

Laight st, No. 57, s w cor Collister st, 25x87.6, two and three-story frame stores. James Pyle and Esther A. his wife to Du Bois Smith. July 29. nom

Lewis st, No. 53, w s, 150 n Delancey st, 25x100, four-story brk store and tenem't with three-story brk tenem't on rear. William Newman and Rosa his wife and Rebecca wife of Simon Danziger to Sarah wife of Sigmund Berkowitz and Hannah Meyer widow. *Mt.* $10,000. Aug. 5. 19,500

Mott st, Nos. 57 and 59. Agreement granting easement to construct door in dividing fence to use water closets, &c. S. Levy to Isaac Marx. Aug. 6. nom

Same property. Cancellation of agreement. S. Levy to Isaac Marx. Aug. 6. nom

New Croton Aqueduct, n e cor 147th st. Party wall agreement. Diantha A., Rowena M. and Elias B. Southworth to John G. Moore. Aug. 8. 250

Norfolk st, No. 31, w s, 150 s Grand st, 25x100, three-story frame (brk front) store and tenem't with five-story brk tenem't on rear. Rachel Solomon to Samuel Parnas. *Mt.* $22,250. Aug. 10. 14,100

Pearl st, Nos 284 and 286, s e cor Beekman st, runs southeast 53.10 x southwest 31 x south 11.6 x southwest 10.2 x northwest 69.6 to Pearl st, x northeast 40.2, seven-story brk store and office building. John Pettit, East Orange, N. J., and Alida R. his wife to Charles E. Tracy. *Mt.* $100,000 and easements. June 26. nom

Pitt st, No. 62, e s, 150 s Rivington st, 25x100, three-story brk store and tenem't with three-story brk tenem't on rear. Anne Kasner to Semche Simon. *Mt.* $18,000. July 30. 21,900

Rose st, No. 34, n w s, 63.10 s w Duane st, runs west 85.9 x south 15.10 x west 30.8 x south 4.5 x southeast 107.8 to Rose st, x northeast 20.10, two-story brk store Philip Ochsenreiter to David Peters, Bayside, L. I. *Mt.* $5,000. Aug. 11. 16,000

Spring st, No. 192, s s abt 75 e Sullivan st, 25 x100, five-story brk tenem't with stores. August Ruff and Mena his wife to Elizabeth wife of Nicholas Brooks. *Mt.* $38,000. Aug. 10. 48,000

Washington st, No. 327, e s, 66.6 n Jay st, 20x 80, two-story brk store. Partition. Walton Storm to John H. Newton. Aug. 7. 25,600

West st, No. 331 } being West st, s
King st, Nos. 132-138 } e cor King st,
Washington st, Nos 536-540 } runs east along
Charlton st, Nos. 133 and 135 } King st 168 3 x south 80 x again east 80 to Washington st, x south 70 x west 120 x south 50 to Charlton st, x west 38.8 x north 96.11 x west 14.4 x north 73 5 x west 70 to West st, x north 30.1, six-story brk building on West st, vacant lots on King st, three and four-story brk stores on Washington st and two three-story brk tenem'ts on Charlton st George S. Coe and John S. Kennedy trustees to James Pyle Aug. 8. 155,000

Same property. William A Booth and William T. Booth and Mary S. his wife, James H. Peters and Mary A. his wife to same. Q. C. Aug. 6. nom

1st st, No. 22, n s, 87 w 2d av, 16.3x75, three-story brk tenem't. Elise Lotze widow to Adam Happel. July 23. 19,700

1st st, No 24, n s, 70 w 2d av 17x75, three-story brk store and tenem't. Gotthardt Strich and Catharine his wife to Adam Happel. July 22. 10,700

3d st, No 235, n s, 367.3 e Av B, 20.3x96, three-story brk store and tenem't, with three-story brk tenem't on rear. Edward R. Schneider to Christina Schneider. *Mt.* $4,000. Aug. 1. 12,500

4th st, No. 101, s s, 200 e 2d av, 25x96.2, five-story brk tenem't. Francis Hillenbrand to Frederick Eisele. ½ part. *Mt.* $28,000. Aug. 6. 6,608

9th st, No. 212, s s, 64.6 e Stuyvesant st, 18.2x 75, three-story brk building. William Waller and Margaret his wife to William B. Waller. B. & S. ½ part. *Mt.* $15,000. Aug. 6. nom

12th st, No. 530, s s, 420.6 e Av A, 25x103.3, five-story brk store and tenem't with four-story brk tenem't on rear. Henry Stoehr and Helena his wife to Louis M. Rosenthal. *Mt.* $7,000. Aug. 13 20,000

12th st, No 337, n s, 64.10 w Greenwich st, runs north 41.6 x west 9.7 x north 35.4 x west 7 10 x south 79.10 to 12th st, x east 18, three-story brk dwell'g. Emanuel Salomon exr. Rebecca Salomon to Truman A. Brown. *Mt.* $3,650. Aug. 1. 7,400

Same property. Truman A. Brown to George V. N. Baldwin *Mt.* $3,650. Aug. 1. nom

13th st, No. 529, n s, 371 e Av A, 25x103.3, five story brk tenem't with stores. Philip Carpenter to Margaretta Klotz. Release lien. Aug. 6. nom

13th st, No. 161, n s, 100 e 7th av, 20x103.3, three-story brk dwell'g. George Finck to Minna Rost. *Mt.* $15,000. Aug. 13. 20,000

14th st, n s, 300 w 6th av, 100x103.3.
15th st, s s, 300 w 6th av, 100x103.3.
Portion two-story brk old 22d Regiment Armory.
Edward L., Edith L. and Maud L. Hall by Richard M. Harison guard. to The Mayor, &c, New York. 3-24 part Aug. 6. 22,701

Same property. John T. Hall and Catherine C. his wife, Catharine T. wife of Eugene Schieffelin, Margaret T. wife of Edward L. Ludlow, Anna R. wife of Elliott Roosevelt, Elizabeth R. wife of Stanley Mortimer, Valentine G. Hall to same. 21-24 part. May 29. 158,905

19th st, No. 319, n s, 200 w 8th av, 21.4x92, three-story brk dwell'g. Partition. Joseph O. Brown to Sarah J. wife of Charles Miller, Jr. Aug. 13. 17,000

23d st, No. 452, s s, 200 e 10th av, 24x98.9, five-story stone front dwell'g. George W. Van Siclen to Sarah J. Van Siclen. *Mt.* $19,000. Aug. 7. 31,000

24th st, Nos. 213-217, n s, 195.2 e 3d av, 68.4 x98.8; Nos. 213 and 215, two-story brk stable; No. 217, three-story brk dwell'g. Foreclos. Martin T. McMahon to John B. Doerr. Aug. 6 44,500

25th st, No. 332, s s, 200 w 1st av. 25x98.9, five-story brk tenem't. Philipina Brubacher to Philipina Keicher. Q. C. May 13. nom

25th st, No. 334, s s, 175 w 1st av, 25x98.9, five-story brk tenem't. Philipina Keicher to Philipina Brubacher. Q. C. May 13. nom

26th st, No. 262, s s, 80 e 8th av, 20x49.4, three-story brk dwell'g. William H. Bowden to Ellen Bowden his wife. *Mt.* $4,000. June 4. nom

26th st, No. 264, s s, 60 e 8th av, 20x49 4, three-story brk dwell'g. Same to same. *Mt.* $4,500. June 4. nom

29th st, Nos. 301 and 303, n s, 52.2 e 2d av, 50 8x 29.6 to old Maria st, x50x35.6, four-story brk building. Anthony J. Dittmar and ano. trustees P. Goerlitz to William G. Marchall. C. a. G. *Mt.* $14,000. Aug. 5. 18,000

29th st, No, 155, n s, 290 e 7th av, 25x116.3 to old Stewart st, x25x113.10, five and six-story brk factory with two-story frame dwell'g on rear. William H. Bowden to Ellen Bowden. *Mt.* $17,762. June 4. nom

32d st, No. 42, s s, 168.10 e Broadway, 21x98.9, four-story brk dwell'g. Mary E. Hanley to Robert and Ogden Goelet. Aug. 12 80,000

32d st, No. 555, n s, 175 e 11th av, 25x98.9, five-story brk tenem't with stores and three-story brk tenem't on rear. Minnie J. Rice to Rose Byman. *Mt.* $11,000. Aug. 5. 12,000

39th st, No. 309, n s, 125 w 8th av, 25x98.9, five-story brk tenem't with stores. Josephine wife of Herman Ury, Jennie wife of Louis Bloch, Henrietta wife of Gottlieb Glauber, Herman A. Brodek and Fannie his wife, Jacob, Gustave A. and Caroline widow and heir of Adolph Brodek to John N. Michel *Mt.* $9,000. Aug. 6. 25,000

43d st, Nos. 547-551, n s, 100 e 11th av, 75x100.11, one and two-story frame and brk factory. Henry Rice exr. and trustee Maria Jones to Henry P. Havens. ½ part. Jan. 2. 9,000

44th st, No. 134, s s, 100 e Lexington av, 20x 100.5, three-story stone front dwell'g Partition. Walton Storm to Abram G. More. Aug. 7. 15,000

46th st, No. 66, s s, 136.5 e 6th av, 16.8x100.5, four-story stone front dwell'g. Ella Neuberger, Frankfort-on-Main, Germany, to Jacob Neuberger. All liens. April 16. nom

47th st, No 330, s s, 200 w 1st av, 25x100, four-story brk tenem't with three-story brk tenem't on rear. Ottilie Heumann to Rosa Jung and Marie L. Dauenhauer. *Mt.* $6,000. July 30. See 86th st. exch

49th st, No. 10, s s, 191.2 e 5th av, 16.2x100.5, four-story stone front dwell'g. Albert Bellamy and Charlotte his wife to Katherine H. Gould. *Mt.* $20,000. Aug. 6. 87,500

52d st, No. 234, s s, 350 e 8th av, 20x100.5, four-story stone front dwell'g. Percival S. Menken to Ella F. Pell. *Mt.* $21,000. Aug. 7. 27,500

Same property. Rachel H. Menken to Percival S. Menken. B. & S. March 17. nom

52d st, No. 234, s s, 350 e 8th av, 20x100.5, four-story stone front dwell'g. Foreclos. Charles Strauss to Robert Ganz. Re-recorded. Jan. 16, 1891. 26,800

52d st, No. 326, s s, 313 e 2d av, 19x100.5, four-story stone front dwell'g. Albert Jaret and Dora his wife to Anne Kasner. *Mt.* $10,500. July 30. 13,750

53d st, No 409, n s, 150 w 9th av, 25x100.5, five-story brk tenem't with stores. Sherwood Aldrich, Colorado Springs, Col., and Florence M. his wife to William K. Thorn, Newport, R. I. C. a. G. *Mt.* $25,000. July 31. nom

54th st, No. 542, s s, 300 e 11th av, 25x156x25.3x 152.6, three-story brk store and tenem't. Foreclos. Edward Bassett to Andrew Doerrschuck. All title. *Mt.* $750. July 17. 1,650

57th st, No. 417, n s, 139.9 e 1st av, 16.8x100.4, three-story stone front dwell'g. Henrietta Wimpfheimer widow to Caroline Ehrle. Q. C. Aug. 2. nom

60th st, Nos. 41 and 43, n s, 100 e 9th av, 50x 100.5, two five-story stone front flats. Stephen Ballard and Abby his wife to Harvey Teny or Terry, Mount Harmon, N. C. Q C. June 30. nom

Same property. Silas B Brown and Elizabeth E. his wife to same. *Mt.* $75,000. June 30. exch

65th st, n s, 125 w Central Park West, 75x100.5, vacant. David F., Annie, Louisa and Mary Kimberly to Esther A. Wheaton. July 25. 30,000

69th st, No 307 on map No. 305, n s, 125 w West End av, 25x100.5.
69th st, Nos. 311 and 313 on map Nos. 309 and 311, n s 175 w West End av, 50x100.5.
Three five-story brk tenem'ts with stores.
Fredricke Mayer widow to Gordon Pier. *Mt.* $27,000 May 21. consid. omitted.

Same property. Gordon Pier to Fredricke Mayer. Aug. 8. consid. omitted

70th st, No. 73, n s, 160 e Columbus av, 20x 100.5, four-story brk dwell'g. Release mort. Harriet Overbiser to Charles Buek and Abbie B. his wife. Aug. 10. 3,000

Same property. Charles Buek and Abbie B. his wife, Westport, Conn., to Emma C. wife of Ernest Pfarrius. *Mt.* $23,000. Aug. 4. 35,000.

72d st, s s, 350 e West End av, 100x102.2, vacant. Hannah M. Halpin widow to Francis P. Burke. *Mt.* $40,000. Aug. 10. See 85th st. 110,000

72d st, n s, 30 w Lexington av, 125x102.2, vacant. Moses J. Wolf and Katie wife of and

Emanuel Heilner and Lewis Z. Bach to Lorenz Weiher. Q. C. Aug. 10. nom

72d st, No. 48, s s, 24 w Park av, 23x73, four-story stone front dwell'g. Richard W. Buckley and Josephine G. his wife to Ludwig Raecke. Mt. $34,000. Aug. 12. 61,000

74th st, No. 165-69, n s, 150 w 3d av, 60x102.2, three four-story stone front tenem'ts. Ida wife of Joseph Shultz to Blanche and Fanny H. Yams. Mt. $27,000. Aug. 13. 55,000

78th st, s s, 225 w 10th av, 50x100, vacant. John A. Rochford to Edwin A. Bradley and George C. Currier. ½ part. Oct. 17, 1890. nom

78th st, No. 307, n s, 83.2 w West End av, 16.4x102.2, three-story brk dwell'g. Ellen J. Pearson to Matthew C. Meyer. Aug. 4. 18,500

79th st, Nos. 415 and 417, n s, 225 e 1st av, 58x102.2, two four-story stone front tenem'ts. Jacob Schlosser and Margaret his wife to Moritz Weisskopf. Mt. $23,000. Aug. 1. See 1st av. 35,000

83d st, No. 508, s s, 148 e Av A, 25x102.2, five-story brk tenem't. Mt. $10,000.
83d st, No. 501, n s, 76.6 w Av A, 25x102.2, five-story brk tenem't with stores. Mt. $12,000.
Joseph Schneider and Maria his wife to George Herbener. Aug. 12. 39,000

85th st, No 134, s s, 318 w 9th av, 18x102.2, four-story brk dwell'g. Catharine wife of Francis P. Burke to Hannah M. Halpin. Mt. $14,500. Aug. 6. See 72d st. 30,000

86th st, No. 334, s s, 275 w 1st av, 30x102.2, four-story stone front flat. Rosa Jung to Michael Heumann. Mt. $14,000 and assessm't for park in 12th Ward. July 29. See 47th st. exch

86th st, No. 336, s s, 245 w 1st av, 30x102.2, four-story store front flat. Marie L. Dauenbauer to same. Subject as above. July 29. See 47th st. exch

88th st, n s, 175 w 9th av, 50x100.8, vacant. Charles Meyerhoff to John Adamson, Brook-. Mt. $11,500. Aug. 11. 17,500

88th st, n s, 96 w Av B, 150x100.8, vacant. Lambert Suydam to Joseph Schreiner. Assessed for East River Park extension. Aug. 7. 36,000

Same property. Esther A. Wheaton to Lambert Suydam. Mt. $14,000. May 12. 100

88th st, No. 179, n s, 116.8 e Amsterdam av, 16.8x100.8, three-story stone front dwell'g. Samuel R. Donnellon and Jennie M. his wife to William H. Morton. Mt. $14,000. July 29. nom

92d st, s s, 100 e 5th av, 75x100.8; also all title to strip, 3.10⅝x100.8, adj above. Release mort. Randolph Guggenheimer and Isaac and Samuel Untermyer to Thomas Graham. Aug. 8. nom

Same property. Release mort. Same to same. Aug. 8. nom

92d st, s s, 100 e 5th av, 53.4x100.8. Release mort. The Bowery Savings Bank to same. July 31. 20,000

92d st, s s, 153.4 e 5th av, 21.8x100.8. Release mort. The Manhattan Savings Inst to same. July 24. 20,000

92d st, s s, 158 e 5th av.
92d st, s s, 178.11 e 5th av.
Declaration of Thomas Graham that strip 3.10⅝x ½ block bet above lots shall be used as alley with gate on 92d st for use of owners and occupants of above. Aug. 11.

94th st, s s, 100 e 10th av, 68x94.7 to Apthorps lane, x68.1x91.2. Release mort. John A. Gwynne to Walden P. Anderson. Aug. 6. 14,000

96th st, s s, 96.9 e West End av, 0.8x26.4. Release mort. John A. Aspinwall trustee John W. Minturn to David Christie and Alice L. his wife. April 28. nom

97th st, No. 25, n s, 281 w 8th av, 19x100.3, three-story brk dwell'g. Edward H. Pirsson to Katharine C. wife of John A. Beall. Mt. $14,400. Aug. 8. nom

Same property. John A. Beall to Edward H. Pirsson. Mt. $14,400. Aug. 8. nom

98th st, No. 33, n s, 375 e 9th av, 25x100.11, five-story stone front flat. Gregory Leahy and Annie his wife to William T. and James Bingham, of Bingham Bros. Aug. 5. nom

104th st, No. 10, s s, 150 w Central Park West, 18.11x101x23x100.11, five-story brk flat. Alma L. Coddington et al. exrs. Homer Morgan to Emeline Johnston. July 11. nom

105th st, n s, 175 e Columbus av, 25x100.11. Release mort. Joseph P. Carney to William L. Wilson. July 23. 153

105th st, No. 70, s s 142.10 e 9th av, 21.6x100.11, five-story brk flat. Julia Renoud to John Duke, Brooklyn. Mt. $10,000 and taxes, and contract for loan of $12,000. April 24. nom

106th st, Nos. 63-67, n s, 199.6 e Madison av, 75.6x100.11, three five-story brk flats. Foreclos. Frederick G. Gedney to Samuel M. Cohen. Sub. to judgment of foreclos. and sale. Aug. 7. 1,500

106th st, Nos. 63-69, n s, 200 e Madison av, 100x100.11, four five-story brk flats. Foreclos. Same to same. Aug. 7. 60,000

108th st, n s, 175 e 5th av, 95x100.9, vacant. William G. Peck and Ida D. his wife to Edward M. Scudder. July 24. 100

108th st, n s, 175 e 5th av, 95x100.9, vacant. Edward M. Scudder to Frederick Rohrs. Mt. $8,000. ½ part. C. a. G. Aug. 11. 14,250

Same property. Hewlett and Edward M. Scudder and Lewis C. Ledyard trustees Henry J. Scudder to same. ½ part. July 24. 14,250

109th st, No. 234, s s, 200 w 2d av, 25x100.10, five-story brk tenem't with stores. Charles T. Harbeck, Islip, N. Y., to Sophia C. wife of Charles T. Harbeck. Mt. $14,000. July 15. nom

111th st, No. 99, n e cor 4th av, 16x100.11.
111th st, No. 111, n s, 95.8 e 4th av, 15.11x100.11.
111th st, No. 129, n s, 239 e 4th av, 15.11x100.11.
Three three-story stone front dwell'gs. John H. Bloodgood and Elizabeth his wife to George W. Bryant. Mt. $5,500. May 19. consid. omitted

116th st, s s, 100 w 8th av. Party wall agreement. Jarvis B. Smith to Charles H. Von Dehsen. Aug. 11. 125

118th st, n s, 460 e Lenox av, 75x100.11, vacant. John A. Rochford to The Bradley and Currier Co. (Lim.) Mt. $18,000. Oct. 14, 1890. (Corrects error in last issue.) nom

119th st / Claremont av { begins 119th st, s s, at intersection with w s of Old Bloomingdale road, at point 9.4 w Claremont av, runs south — x east to Claremont av, x north to 119th st, x west to beginning, being part of Bloomingdale road. Cornelius R. Duffie et al. trustee Jane A. Gibson to Charles C. and Henry M. Taber. May 19. 25

123d st, No. 238, s s, 39.2 w 8th av, 15.11x50.11, three-story stone front dwell'g. James Armstrong, Brooklyn, to William H. Mairs. Q. C. Aug. 7. nom

124th st, No. 227, n s, 287 w 2d av, 20x100.11, three-story stone front dwell'g. William Allan to The Harrisonville Co-operative Building Association of New York. Mt. $8,000. Aug. 3. 17,500

126th st, Nos. 285 and 287, n s, 275 w 7th av, 50x99.11, two four-story stone front flats. William Allan to The Harrisonville Co-operative Building Association of New York. Aug. 3. 50,000

132d st, No. 5 E. Charles C. Luhrs to John H. and Louis C. Luhrs, joint tenants. In trust for grantor's use until Feb. 10, 1893, to be then reconveyed to him. Aug. 10. nom

Amsterdam (10th) av, n e cor 68th st, 75.5x100.
Columbus (9th) av, s w cor 102d st, 100.11x100.
99th st, s s, 175 w 8th av, 25x100.11.
5th av, e s, 25 s 101st st, 25x100.
Julia, Alice and Michael and Ellen Barrett by Adolph Rosenthal guard. to William T. Graff. Sept. 1, 1888. 675

Av A, Nos. 1374 and 1376, e s, 52.2 n 73d st, 50x98, two five-story brk tenem'ts with stores. Lewis Krulewitch and Betsy his wife to Adam Moran. Mt. $40,000. Aug. 8. 50,000

Av A, No. 1372, e s, 27.2 n 73d st, 25x98, five-story brk tenem't with stores. Mendel W. Greenberg to Adam Moran. Mt. $20,000. Aug. 11. 29,000

Av A, No. 1394 / 74th st, Nos. 503 and 505 { begins Av A, n e cor 74th st, 22.2x98, one-story brk store on av and two two and three-story brk and frame stores and tenements on st. Samuel Kempner to Charles Meier. C. a. G. Aug. 11. 14,500

Av D, No. 133, w s, 26 n 9th st, 20.6x70, three-story brk store and tenem't. Osias Chroback to Mary Chroback. Mt. $8,000. Aug. 7. nom

Columbus (9th) av, Nos. 1289-1293 / Manhattan st / 124th st { begins Columbus av, s e cor 124th st, runs south 100.11 x east 200 x north 93.11 to Manhattan st, x northwest 15.1 to 124th st, x west 186.7, four five-story brk flats, store in No. 1293 on av, and four five-story brk flats on sts. Nathan Wise and Delphine his wife, Adolph M. Bendheim and Henrietta his wife to Henry M. Bendheim. Mt. $24,500, taxes, &c. C. a. G. Aug. 2. nom

Madison av / 5th av / 108th st / 109th st { the block. William G. Peck and Ida D. his wife to Edward M. Scudder. Q. C. All title. July 25. 100

Morningside av, s w cor 119th st. 100.11x100, vacant.
119th st, s s, 100 w Morningside av, 50x100.11, vacant.
Charles E. Tracy and Jennie B. his wife, Charles E. Tracy exr. &c., Charles Tracy, Charles E. Tracy, John P. Morgan, Frederick S. Hoppin and Francis G. Brown trustee to Joseph W. Spencer, East Orange, N. J. July 20. 28,000

Park av, No. 1687, e s, 101.8 s 119th st, 25x90, five-story brk tenem't with stores. George Schwegler and Eva his wife to Katharina Michel. Aug. 10. 19,500

West End av, e s, extends from 69th to 70th st, 200.10x100, vacant. John A. Rochford to The Bradley & Currier Co. (Lim.) Mt. $83,000. Sept. 11, 1890. nom

West End av, No. 519, s w cor 90th st, 24x90, four-story brk dwell'g. Foreclos. William Sulzer to Eugene Mehler. Aug. 10. 37,900

1st av, No. 1209, w s, 50.5 n 65th st, 25x92, five-story brk tenem't with stores. Moritz Weisskopf and Karolina his wife to Jacob Schlosser. Mt. $16,000. Aug. 1. See 79th st. 24,000

1st av, w s, 100.5 n 43d st. Party wall agreement. August I. Tegetmeier and Ignatz A. Riepe to Dennis Harrington. July 15. nom

1st av, w s, 46.1 s 12th st, 45.10x100. Release mort. Julius Weill, Titusville, Pa., to Sarah Feiner. Aug. 11. 3,000

2d av, No. 1917-1927 / 99th st, No. 233 { begins 2d av, n w cor 99th st, 151.3x105, six five-story brk tenem'ts with stores on av and one five-story brk tenem't on st. Charles G. Martin and Maria M. his wife to William C. Martin. B. & S. C. a. G. Aug. 7. nom

2d av, No. 1945, n w cor 100th st, 25.11x100, five-story brk tenem't with stores. Emil Brogelwirth and Pauline E. his wife to Louis Bossert. Mt. $25,000. Aug. 1. nom

2d av, Nos. 2028 and 2030, e s, 50.11 n 104th st, 50x75.
2d av, No. 2036, e s, 50.11 s 105th st, 25x75.
Three four-story stone front tenem'ts with stores.
Bernhard Bopp to Emma Bopp. All liens. Dec. 24, 1890. nom

2d av, No. 2130, e s, 75.8 s 110th st, 25.2x75, four-story brk store and tenem't. John W. and David G. Baird exrs. John Baird to Max Brummel. June 30. 15,000

Same property. John W. and David G. Baird, Carrie M. Crowe and Sophia A. O. Baird heirs John and Sarah Baird to same. Q. C. June 30. nom

5th av, No. 802, e s, 52.7 n 61st st, 22.9x98, five-story stone front dwell'g. Jabez A. Bostwick and Helen C. his wife to Frances E. Allen. July 22. 140,000

5th av, Nos. 2228 and 2230, w s, 49.11 s 136th st, 49.6x85, two five-story brk stores and flats. John A. Rochford and Minnie L. C. his wife to Francis M. Wilmurt. Aug. 5. nom

7th av, No. 587, e s, 39.1 n 41st st, 20x71.4x20.2x73.10, four-story brk store and tenem't. James W. Ketcham and Appolonia his wife to Henry B. Sire. Mt. $28,000. Aug. 7. 37,000

7th av, No. 2420, n w cor 141st st, 49.11x75, five-story brk flat. John A. Rochford and Minnie L. C. his wife to The Bradley & Currier Co. (Lim.) Mt. $40,000. Aug. 5. nom

8th av, Nos. 2287 and 2289 / 123d st, Nos. 302 and 304 { begins 8th av, s w cor 123d st, 50.11x71.3x50.11x71.2, two five-story brk stores and flats on av and two three-story brk dwell'gs on st.
123d st, Nos. 310 and 312, s e cor St. Nicholas av, 49.3x50.11x17.11 to av, x59.9, two three-story brk dwell'gs.
St. Nicholas av, e s, 59.9 s 123d st, 21x34.5x—x40.3, vacant.
William H. Mairs, Brooklyn, to James Phelan, San Francisco, Cal. Mt. $44,000. Aug. 12. See Broadway. nom

All one-half of Maria st, as shown on Kips Bay farm map immediately adjacent to and adj lot 40 on said map. Samuel Jones and Martha B. his wife, Sarah R. and Catharine S. Jones, Mary A. Seabury widow, Catharine C. Peck widow heirs Samuel Jones to Mary Quinn widow. Q. C. Re-recorded. April 8, 1887. nom

MISCELLANEOUS.

Release legacy and receipt. Samuel Goldstein heirs Sophie Goldstein to William H. Goldstein et al. exrs. Sophie Goldstein. Aug. 5. 2,000

23d and 24th WARDS.

Ann st, lots 44 and 45 map Mary S. Shipley property, West Farms, 24th Ward, 46.6x96.8x69.2x98. James Butler to James E. Algeo and Eliza J. his wife. July 29. 800

Beech terrace, n e cor Crimmins av, 111.1x100. The William R. Beal Land Improvement Co. to Alfred B. Hall. July 5. 9,500

Beech terrace, s s, 111.1 e Crimmins av, 75x100.
Oak terrace, n e cor Crimmins av, 86.1x100.
Oak terrace, s e cor Crimmins av, 86.1x100.
Oak terrace, s s, 136.1 e Crimmins av, 50x100.
Same to Andrew J. McCord. July 8. 20,675

Fox st, w s, 62.2 s 167th st, 41.9x29.3x47.2x46. Bessie Butler wife of and Edward to Frank McGarry. Mt. $1,200. Aug. 10. 2,000

Home st, Nos. 1070-1076, s w s, 134.9 n w Intervale av, 75x87.3x83x58.6. Treffle H. Allard to Marie L. Allard. Mt. $8,000. Aug. 13. nom

Mott Haven Canal, s w cor 138th st, 4 lots. Contract. John H. Cheever to James and Olin J. Stevens. Aug. 12. 30,000

Oak terrace, n s, 86.1 e Crimmins av, 50x100. The William R. Beal Land Improvement Co. to Wilbur L. Molyneaux. July 8. 4,000

Oak terrace, s s, 86.1 e Crimmins av, 50x100.
Beekman av, w s, 50 s Beech terrace, 25x100.
William R. Beal Land Improvement Co. to Franklin Lynch. Aug. 8. 6,000

Orchard st, n s, 100 e Madison av, 5x125. Release mort. Susan Jefferson, Jr., to Thomas Jefferson. Aug. 6. nom

Same property. Thomas Jefferson and Annie L. B. his wife to August Koelsch. Aug. 6. nom

Sidney st, e s, 75 w Westchester av, 15x250. Release mort. Amelia A. Thorn, Riverdale, N. Y., to Florence A. Bartlett. Aug. 6. nom

Same property. Florence A. Bartlett to Rachel B. Longacre. Aug. 6. 950

134th st, n s, 375 e Willis av, 50x100. Joseph D. Mayer and Fannie M. his wife to Adam Gebhardt. Mt. $29,000. July 31. 34,250

138th st, n s, 104 w Willis av, 26.3x100. John Cotter and Sarah his wife and Nicholas Cotter and Eliza his wife to Mary McGuire. Mt. $14,500. Aug. 10. nom

142d st, s s, 150 e Clifton av, 100x100. Mary McGuire to Frederick Folz. Aug. 10. nom

145th st, n s, 100 e Willis av, 25x100. John Cotter and Sarah his wife to Frederick Folz. Mt. $2,000. July 30. nom

145th st, n s, 100 e Willis av, 25x100. William Rumble and Henrietta his wife to John Cotter. Q. C. July 29. nom

146th st, n s, 289.6 w Brook av, 0.6x100. Nicholas J. O'Connell and Mary L. his wife to Elizabeth wife of Hugh Reilly. C. a. G. All liens. July 31. 500

146th st, n s, 290 w Brook av. Party wall agreement. Same to same. July 31. nom

147th st, n s, 225 e Brook av, 25x100. Frederick Folz and Susannah S. his wife to Julius Wanner. Aug. 6. 2,750

147th st, n s, 200 e Brook av, 25x100. Same to Peter F. Wanner. Aug. 6. 2,750

157th st, n s, 150 w Elton av, 50x100. Patrick Murphy and Kate his wife to Thomas Quigley. *Mt.* $2,600, assessm'ts $313. Aug. 10. 7,325

176th st, n s, 425 w Fleetwood av, 25x125. Lewis G. Morris to Victor L. Veyrac. Aug. 8. 800

183d st, n s, 100 w Creston av, 25x100. Charles Pitchie and Charlotte his wife to George Banger. June 24. 3,700

Bathgate av, e s, 283.4 n 173d st, 16.8x120. Cyrus Lawton and Sarah M. his wife to Newbury D. Lawton. *Mt.* $2,000. May 18. 3,750

Beekman av, n w cor Beech terrace, 125x125. The William R. Beal Land Improvement Company to William R. Beal. Aug. 8. 12,750

Beekman av, w s, 25 s Oak terrace, 100x100. William R. Beal Land Impt. Co. to Henry B. Hall. Aug. 8. 8,000

Beekman av, s w cor Beech terrace, 50x100. William R. Beal Land Improvement Co. to Francis B. Chedsey. July 8. 4,500

Beekman av, w s, 75 s Beech terrace, 50x100. Same to John A. Norman. Aug. 8. 4,000

Central av, s e s, lots 50 and 51 map Upper Morrisania, 100x115. Bridget Curry to John P. Kerrigan. *Mt.* $3,000. July 30. 10,750

Cambreling av, w s, lot 308 map S. Cambreling et al, 24th Ward, 25x87.6. David A. Merrick to The College of St. Francis Xavier, New York. July 30. nom

Fairmount av or East 175th st, No. 946, s s, abt 100 w Franklyn av, 25x150. Mary Seiferd to Roman Arnold. Aug. 3. 5,500

Intervale av, s e cor 167th st, runs south 30 x east 75 x south 60 x east 25 x north 90 to st, x west 100. Frank McGarry to Johann C. Merkle. Aug. 7. 1,200

Morris av, e s, 175 n 164th st, runs east 104.11 x north 25 x east 80.11 x north 35 x west 185.10 to av, x south 60. Arthur Parrett to Elizabeth Parrett. *Mt.* $3,600. Aug. 6. 5,000

Prospect av, s e s, 291.6 n e Westchester av, 25x122.6x31.10x102.9. Annie S. McCormack to Charles D. Ogden. Aug. 10. 1,750

Sheridan av, w s, 265 n Ella st, 100x163.
Sheridan av, w s, 365 n Ella st, 50x163.
Hiram R. and Henry Dater trustees Philip Dater to Thomas Byrnes. Aug. 4. 11,250

Union av, e s, 125 n Glen av proposed, 25x200 to another new road. Henry J. Sawyer and Sarah A. his wife, Joliet, Ill., to Jenny A. Carew, Norwich, Conn. Aug. 11. 1,310

Union av, e s, 100 n Glen av proposed, 25x200 to another new road. George Cameron and Maggie R. his wife to same. May 22. 1,450

Washington av, e s, 78 s 180th st, 25x100.4x22.4 x100.4. Theodore Stalp to Amanda A. Stalp. All liens. Re-recorded. Aug. 5. 500

Washington av, e s, 78 s 180th st, original line, 25x100.4x23.4x100.4, h & l. Theodore Stalp to Amanda A. Stalp. All liens. Aug. 5. 500

Kingsbridge and West Farms road, s w s, 75 n w Madison av, 50x145x42x119, except portion taken for opening 3d av. John A. Knox and H tt his wife to William Pfoh, Jr. July 28e ie 10,500

Lot No. 824 map of land at Riverdale belonging to Joseph Rosenthal showing parcel sold to Redmon, begins at a stone monument, runs northeast 125 to centre of way leading to Bettners' lane as opened, x— to centre of another lane, x south — x east — x south 131.5 x east to beginning, 2½ acres, with all title in said roadways. The New York Life Insurance and Trust Co. trustee Fannie Meiklebam and Robert E. Robinson exr. William A. Meiklebam to I. Lawrence Aspinwall. C. a. G. Aug. 8. 23,750

LEASEHOLD CONVEYANCES.

Attorney st, No. 60. Assign. lease. Hannah Lavendol to Sarah Hodes. nom

Same property. Assign. lease. Morris Hodes to Hannah Lavendol. nom

Attorney st, No. 62.
Ridge st, No. 55.
Assign. lease. Degel Maehne Rubin, a corporation, to Brisk Delito Lodge of American Star Order, an association. 2,900

Clinton pl, n e cor University pl, 35.6x98.11x 38.9x94.2. Trustees of the Sailors Snug Harbour to Trow City Directory Co. 21 years, from May 1, 1876, per year, taxes and 1,000

Same property. Consent to assign. lease. Same to same. nom

Same property. Assign. lease. The Trow City Directory Co. to Trow Directory Printing and Bookbinding Co. nom

Cherry st, No. 448, n s, 100 e Jackson st, 25x100. Assign. lease. Thomas Black to William M. Thatcher, receiver. nom

Forsyth st, No. 123, w s, 25x100. Assign. lease. Henry Muhlhauser to Bella Neugass. 5,500

Pike st, w s, 45 n Henry st, 22.6x85.9. Surrender lease and quit claim to buildings. Ellen Kenney to Joseph Huber. Aug. 10. 4,750

3d st, s s, 325 w Av A, 25x90. William Astor to Christian Jaeger individ. and Catharina Geyer and Christian Jaeger exrs. Jacob Geyer. 20 years, from May 1, 1880, per year, taxes and 350

4th st, s s, 225 w Av A, 25x96.2. Franklin H. Delano et al. trustees for John J. Astor to Daniel Franzreb. 20 years, from May 1, 1879, per year, taxes and 350

45th st, n s, 230 e 8th av, 20x100.5. Charles F. Southmayd and James F. Chamberlain trustees for Henry Astor to Sarah J. McMurtry admrx. John McMurtry. 20 years, from Feb. 1, 1891, per year, taxes and 480

Columbus av, No. 851. Assign. lease. Samuel Einstein and August Schneider to Jacob Frank. val. consid.

1st av, No. 2003, all title, under lease, free of encumbrances. August Niewohner and Doretta his wife to John Simon. Aug. 1. nom

3d av, No. 2374. Assign. lease. Solomon Buttner to H. Koehler & Co. 2,500

3d av, w s, 38 n 16th st, 18x60.
16th st, n s, 80 w 3d av, 20x92.
16th st, n s, 60 w 3d av, 20x92.
Assign. lease. Louis Lese to Pincus Lowenfeld, Morris Goldstein and Mark Blumenthal. 27,000

7th av, n w cor 47th st, 75.5x64 to Broadway, x 76 to st, x 45. John Murtha to John Appell. 20 years, from May 1, 1891, per year, 6,000

9th av, No. 56. Assign. lease. Anton Klause to Annie Hamann. nom

KINGS COUNTY.

AUGUST 6, 7, 8, 10, 11, 12.

Ashford st, e s, 85 s Stanley av, 40x100. Katharine D. Salmon to Henry C. Becker. $120

Ashford st, e s, 213.7 n Atlantic av, 50x100. Release mort. Thomas B. Smith to Louis Ilsemann. 1,000

Bancroft pl, w s, 90 n Atlantic av, 30x90x30.10 x90. Louisiana I. Gleason to Benjamin Armstrong. 1,300

Bartlett st, No. 55, n w s, 175 s w Throop av, 25 x100, h & l. Nicolaus Schoendorf to Frederick Noll. 5,000

Bergen st, s s, 250 w Hopkinson av, 25x127.9, h & l. Peter Yung to Mary J. Cook. 1887. 600

Same property. Mary J. Cook to Alexander Ray. 500

Bergen st, s s, 100 w 3d av, 25x100. Herman Sacks to Michael D. Quigley. *Mt.* $4,000. 8,000

Broadway, centre line, at intersection e s Canarsie av, runs east to point 120 e of Canarsie av, x north to centre block, bet Broadway and Milton st, x west 136.8 to av, x southeast —, excepting land taken for Leffert av, Flatbush. Horatio L. Olcott to Adam Scherff. 1,000

Broadway, s s, 40 w Macon st, 20x100. Henry W. Meyer, of Glendale, L. I., to Josephine wife of Alphons Hermann. 8,750

Broadway, n e s, 96 s e Hull st, 29x100. Henry J. Hancock to Matthew Dignan. *Mt.* $3,-500. 6,000

Same property. Samuel Hancock to same. Q. C. 250

Butler st, n s, 350 w 5th av, 120x144.2x120x 143.11. John P. Crawford to Kate C. Henderson et al., exrs, &c., Isaac Henderson. nom

Chauncey st, s s, 250 e Ralph av, 25x100, h & l. Lawrence Cahill to Mary Cahill. *Mt.* $2,500. nom

Chester st, w s, 175 s Sackett st, 25x100, h & l. Eva Schreiber to Levi Gross. *Mt.* $1,500. 2,400

Chestnut st, e s, 524 s Jamaica av, 50x150. John Delaney to Caroline Beck. 2,000

Cleveland st, e s, 110 s New Lots road. 40x100. Adolph Sussman to Sarah Lang. 600

Cook st, No. 187, 25x100. Contract for property. Jacob Untereiner with David Stern. 2,400

Covert st, n w s, 239 n e Evergreen av, 18x100. Hyde & Gload Mfg. Co. (Lim.) to The New York Building and Loan Banking Co. *Mt.* $2,750. 4,800

Dean st, s s, 280 w New York av, 20x100. Sarah E Fisher to Mary R. King. 13,500

Dean st, n s, 340 e 4th av, 20x80. Partition. Gerard M. Stevens to Jennie Dresdner. 3,350

Dean st, n s, 360 e 4th av, 20x80. Partition. Same to Jane McClenahan. 3,300

Decatur st, n s, 247 w Throop av, 18x100. Thomas Wood to Elizabeth M. Whelan, of Newark, N. J. *Mt.* $7,000 and foreclosure proceeding. exch

Decatur st, n s, 211 w Throop av, 18x100. Same to same. *Mt.* $8,200. exch

Decatur st, n s, 229 w Throop av, 18x100. Peter S. Servis, of Elizabeth, N. J., to Elizabeth M. Whelan, of Newark, N. J. *Mt.* $8,500, taxes 1890 and 1891. nom

Degraw st, s s, 316.3 w 5th av, 19.2x100. Peter S. Kelly to Emil Lachmann. *Mt.* $3,500. 6,700

Degraw st, s w s. 200 n w Van Brunt st, 50x 100. Rebecca M. Ferry to Marion S. Sheldon. 4,000

Degraw st, n s, 266.11 w Columbia st, 16.9x100. John Kennedy, Gravesend, to Regina Doppmann. 2,800

Devoe st, s s, 139 w Lorimer st, 60x100. Foreclos. Robert Merchant to Roswell Eldridge. 5,000

Devoe st, s s, 199 w Lorimer st, 3.2x103.3x10.5x 100. George W. Payntar to Roswell Eldridge. 1,250

Decatur st, n s, 220 e Sumner av, 20x100. George B. Stoutenburg to Louisiana J. Gleason. *Mt.* $5,000. 7,500

Devoe st, s s, 161.4 e Union av, 26.5x100.2x24.7 x100.3. Margaret Downs to John J. McConville. 4,500

Duffield st, Nos. 93-103, e s, 100 n Johnson st, 130x100. Jacob Finkelstone to Angelo Mondolfo. nom

Eastern Parkway, s s, 25 e Thatford av, 25x 100. Meyer Marcus to Baruch Seermann. ½ part. 350

Eastern Parkway, s s, 25 e Osborn st, 25x100. Barnet Frank and Simon Rose to Harris Schoenzeit and Susman Schwartz. *Mt.* $2,200 8,725

Eastern Parkway, s e cor Osborn st, 25x100. Harris Max to Jacob Weiss, of New York. *Mt.* $2,750. 4,500

Eldert st, s s, 275 e Evergreen av, 18x100. Juan B. C. Phillips to Helen M. Buttle. *Mt.* $3,250. nom

Ellery st, n s, 175 w Sumner av, 25x100. Joseph Weidner to Adolph Schlessinger. *Mt.* $3,000. 5,600

Fennimore st, n s, 360 e Rogers av, 60x100.
Fennimore st, n s, 465 e Rogers av, 60x100, Flatbush.
William Bowers to Maria L. Lyon, Fall River, Mass. nom

Floyd st, n s, 275 w Sumner av, 25x100. Mary Hertling to William Koster. Q. C. 1,700

Frost st, s s, 125 w Leonard st, 25x50x26.6x41.7. Mary wife of Martin Carroll to Martin Carroll. *Mt.* $650. nom

Frost st, s s, bet Lorimer and Leonard sts, interior, being lot 37 block 24 on assessm't map 15th Ward. Mary wife of Martin Carroll to Martin Carroll. B. & S. nom

Fulton st, n s, 85.7 w Spencer pl, runs northeast 75 x north 15.6 x west 2.4 x north 1 x west 12 x southwest 84.7 to st, x 20 to beginning; also,
Fulton st, n s, 65.7 w Spencer pl, runs north 66 x northwest 9.10 x west 16 x south 75 x east 20 to beginning.
Clara M. wife of John S. Nugent to John S. Nugent. *Mt.* $7,500. nom

Fulton st, n s, 305.8 w Nostrand av, 80x70. Charles A. Betts to Annie S. wife Charles W. Betts. *Mt.* $10,000. nom

Fulton st, s s, 280 e Franklin av, runs south 100 x east 27.2 x south 3.1¼ x east 56.4 x north 80 x west 80 to beginning. Release of easement. Eugene G. Blackford et al. to William H. Scott. nom

Halsey st, n s, 167.2 n Broadway, runs north 43.6 x northeast 3.4 x northwest 20 x southwest 15 x northeast 3.4 x south 47.2 to st, x east 20. John Bamberger to Helen M. Beetles. nom

Halsey st, n s, 127.6 w Throop av, 16.8x100. John de Vries, Jr., New York, to Howard T. Montgomery, New York. Sub. to mort. nom

Halsey st, n s, 167.2 w Broadway, runs north 43.6 x northeast 3.4 x northwest 20 x southwest 15 x southeast 3.4 x south 47.2 x east 20 to beginning. Helen M. Buttle to Frederick Zimmerman. 1,000

Hancock st, n s, 156 w Lewis av, 18x100. Robert W. Reid, of New York, to Edward P. Brennan. nom

Hancock st, n s, 156 w Lewis av, 18x100. Edward P. Brennan to George and Thomas J. Jenkins, of New York. *Mt.* $6,000 nom

Harman st, s e s, 75 s w Hamburg av, 25x100. Release mort. Theodore F. Jackson et al. trustees Loftis Wood to George Covert. 8,600

Harman st, s e s, 125 s w Hamburg av, 50x100. Darwin R. James to Louisa Cronenweth. 2,900

Harman st, s e s, 100 s w Hamburg av, 25x100. Same to George C. Klein. 1,450

Harman st, s e s, 100 n e Central av, 50x100. Release mort. Theodore F. Jackson et al. trustees Loftis Wood to Darwin R. James. 23,250

Hicks st, e s, 75 n Nelson st, 25x100. William Mulvey to Margaret Donohue. 1,800

Hemlock st, e s, 125 s Griffin pl, 25x100. Israel Y. Cochrane to Elouise wife of and Ulysses Brown. *Mt.* $1,500. 2,300

Humboldt st, e s, 100 n Scholes st, 25x100. Joseph Cohen to Theresa Goodkind, of New York. *Mt.* $2,840. exch

Humboldt st, w s, 75 n Stagg st, 25x100. Louis Dietz to John Dittrich and Mary his wife, joint tenants. 3,350

Jackson st, s s, 150 e Union av, 25x100. Barbara widow John Knab to David Knab. nom

Jefferson st, e s, 60 n Baltic av, 20x60, h & l. Charles O. Johnson to Peter O. Johnson. *Mt.* $300. 1,000

Jerome st, w s, 120 s Blake av, 40x100. Mary wife of John V. Sanborn to David P. Ellis, of Jackson, Miss. 700

Kosciusko st, s e s, 273.9 n e Broadway, 50x98.9. Joseph H. Colyer to Peter L. and Thomas W. Lucas. *Mt.* $2,000. 6,000

Kosciusko st, n s, 72 w Reid av, 16x100. Annie C. Van Winkle to Grace E. M. Rawlins. 3,300

Leonard st, e s, 34 n Norman av, 16x60, h & l. Martin Elbert to Mary H. Collard. 3,700

Linwood st, e s, 165.11 s Fulton av, 18x51.6x18 x54.4. Joseph Neideregger to Maggie wife of Charles G. Schliepes. *Mt.* $950. 1,700

Luquer st, n s, 120 e Henry st, 2.6x107. John L., Thomas B. and Louis P. heirs of Lucinda Gratacap to William Littmann. Q. C. 50

Macon st, n s, 350 s Reid av, 25x200 to Halsey st. Carrie Grove, of Amityville, N. Y., to Frank C. Swimm. 5,000

Madison st, s s, 319 e Lewis av, 19x100. James C. North to Mary wife of James C. North. nom

Magenta st, n s, 125 w Crescent st, 25x100. Patrick O'Connor to Cornelius Leary. 430

Malbone st, n s, 320 w New York av, runs north 127.9 x west 20 x south 107.4 to e s Clove road, x27.3 to Malbone st, x east 2. Timothy C. Conklin to Annie E. wife of Martin Zimmermann. 300

Market st, e s, 125 s Glen st, 25x100. Nicholas L. and Ida Rapelje to Arthur Grimes. 450

McDonough st, n s, 280 w Stuyvesant av, 20 x100; also,
McDonough st, n s, 300 w Stuyvesant av, 20x 100.
Foreclos. Michael Furst ref. to John J. De Revere. 10,000

McDonough st, n s, 400 e Tompkins av, runs

north 200 to Macon st, x east 13 x south 80 x east 15 x south 120 to st, x west 28 to beginning. Harlan P. Halsey to John Fraser. 7,925

Monroe st, n w cor Lewis av, 24x100, h & l. Daniel McDicken to John H. Ficken. *Mt.* $9,000. 17,050

Same property. Release mort. Thomas S. Strong to Daniel McDicken. 1,000

Monroe st, n s, 231.4 e Throop av, 19.4x100, h & l. Henry De Zavala to Gertrude C. De Zavala. B. & S. 2,000

Montague st, n s, bet Henry and Clinton sts. Josephine B. Thayer and Ida F. Taft, of Milford, Mass., Adla M. Andrews, Henry A. Claflin and John C. Thompson to Charles F. Claflin. Q. C. nom

Moore st, s s, 100 w Morrell st, 25x100. Louis Lurie to Isaac Horowitz. *Mt.* $2,500. 2,100

Moore st, n s, 75 w Morrell st, 25x50. Theresa Goodkind widow, of New York, to Joseph Cohen. *Mt.* $3,940. exch

Navy st, w s, 127.4 s De Kalb av, 25x100.5. Adolph Skrzyneki to Caroline Skrzyneki his wife nom

Nevius st, s e cor President st, 05x100, also in Flatbush.
Vanderbilt st, s s, 355 e Short st, 15x100, bad error.
William H. Bierds to Eliza A. Bierds. Liens $6,500. nom

North Henry st, e s, 271.3 n Van Pelt av, 17x100. Charles Iugert to Henry Rassiga 3,500

Ormond st or pl, e s, 74.9 s Jefferson st, 20.2x130, h & l. Mary H wife of David Anderson to Bridget wife of George P. Buckley. 6,500

Otsego and Greene sts, Monticello and Delavan sts—the block—48 lots, old 9th Ward. Frederick, Alfred and Eugene Devereux to Edward Lavin. 8,500

Osborn st, e s, 150 n Livonia av, 50x100. Lemuel Weil to Harris Fein and Nathan Nelson, of New York. 950

Osborn st, e s, 125 s Eastern Parkway, 25x100. Release mort. Herbert C. Smith to Abraham Ruth. 700

Pacific st, n s, 125 e 4th av, 25x90. Isaac Goldstein, of New York, to Israel Lebowitz, of New York. *Mt.* $8,500. nom

Pacific st, n s, 141 w Troy av, 17x100. James H. Watson and James H. Pittinger to Patrick J. Tracy. *Mt.* $3,000. 3,500

Plymouth st, s s, 83 w Bridge st, runs west 24.8 x south 100 x east 17.6 x north 25.6 x east 6 8 x north 74 6. Rodger Mullin to James L. Truslow. 4,900

Same property. Rodger Mullin to same. B. & S. nom

President st, s w s, 413 s e 8th av, 19x100. Patrick Sheridan to David W. Stein. *Mt.* $12,000 nom

Quincy st, s s, 217 w Tompkins av, 16.6x95. Lowell V. Brown to Albert Woodruff. *Mt.* $5,000. exch

Quincy st, s s, 300 e Patchen av, 25x100. A Stewart Walsh to Jennie Eastmont. 2,500

Radde pl, e s, 136 s Herkimer st, 15.6x97.6. Laura wife of and Dionie M. Hunger to John B. C. Woodcock. *Mt.* $2,500. 4,800

Rapelyea st, s s, 100 w Hicks st, 25x100, h & l. Ellen T. wife of John Collins to Martin Olsen and Gustaf Johanson. *Mt.* $2,000. 3,100

Richardson st, n s, 137.8 w Humboldt st, 24x5 2x20 6x65 James Meakim to Patrick Ronan and Ellen his wife, joint tenants. 1,000

Richmond st, w s, 850 n 3d st, 25x150. George L. Smith to Joseph Stamper. 725

Sackett st, n s, 125 w Van Brunt st, 125x100. Rebecca M. Ferry to Eliza J. Smith. *Mt.* $56,000. 62,000

Sackman st, e s, 150 n Eastern Parkway, 75x100. Emma Quinn to Abraham Dmerstein, of New York. 2,100

Sackman st, w s, 100 s Eastern Parkway, 50x100. James G. Roberts to Harris Max. *Mt.* $1,100. 2,800

Sackman st, e s, 100 s Livonia av, 100x100 Herman F. Koepke to Abraham Goldman and Harris Levy, of New York. 2,400

Schermerhorn st, s s, 275 w 3d av, 20x88, h & l. Peter Mallou to Sabine L. wife of Peter Mallon. *Mt.* $3,000. nom

Skillman st, w s, 407.9 w Myrtle av 50x100. Emanuel New, of New York, to Susan O'Brien *Mt.* $4,000. 10,000

South Oxford st, w s, 453 n Lafayette av, 27x100. William J. Brown, of New York, to John F. James. Sub. to morts., taxes, &c. 300

Stanhope st, n w s, 100 s w Evergreen av, 18 9x100. Abbie J. Dillworth to Carl Franck, of New York. 3,800

Starr st, n s, bet St. Nicholas and Wyckoff avs, being lot 32 block 1161 assessm't map, 18th Ward. John C. McGuire, Registrar of Arrears, to Bernard Mahon. 50

Starr st, n s, bet St. Nicholas and Wyckoff avs, being lot 33 block 1161 assessm't map, 18th Ward. Same to same. 50

St. Felix st, e s, 275 s De Kalb av, 16.8x85. John L. Young exr., &c., Isaac H. Young to Herman Posbergh. 6,500

Sumpter st, n s, 125 e Patchen av, 17x100. George Schreiber to Christina R. Schreiber. *Mt.* $600. nom

Sumpter st, n s, 175 w Howard av, 25x100. Elizabeth E. wife of Walter A. Howard to Emil Dietze. 2,000

Sumpter st, s s, 375 e Ralph av, 25x100. Bernard Remmert or Bernhard Remert to Louise E. wife of Philip Eller. nom

Same property. Louise wife of Philip Eller to Bernard Remmert and Eva his wife. nom

Suydam st, s e s, 175 n e Hamburg av, 25x100 Lena Weis to Peter J. Brahm. 1,350

Suydam st, n w s, 200 s w Knickerbocker av, 25x100. August Seabmeir to Margaretha Bienenstein, of New York. *Mt.* $3,000. 6,200

Tompkins pl, e s, 221 11 n Degraw st, 22x112.6. Ansel Jones, of Saybrook, Conn., to Mary B. wife of Theodore Fisher. *Mt* $4,500. 7,250

Troutman st, n w s, 86 2 s w Bushwick av, 25x100, h & l. Foreclos. John Courtney to Charlotte Wills extrx of John Wills. 7,550

Warwick st, w s, 175 s Eastern Parkway, 25x100 Thomas W. Porter and Annie C. Porter widow to George Schade. 525

Warwick st, w s, 251.7 s Fulton st, 16.8x95, h & l Emma wife of and James I. Newman to Frank L. Wallett. 8,500

Watkins st, s e cor Dumont av, 50x100. Contract. Max Mehlman with Harris Deminskey. 1,325

Same property. Assign. of contract. Harris Deminsky to Betsie Cohn. 1,450

Same property. Betsy Cohn, of New York, to Isidor Meyers and Augusta Davis. 525

Watkins st, e s, 50 n Riverdale av, 25x100. Mary E. Cook, Newtown, L. I., to Solomon Dubroff. *Mt.* $1,500. 2,300

Watkins st, e s, 75 n Riverdale av, 25x100. Same to Abraham Dubroff. *Mt.* $1,200. 2,200

Weirfield st, n w s, 335 n e Bushwick av, 20x100. Caroline Hughes to Conrad Meyer. *Mt.* $2,000. nom

Woodbine st, s e s, 100 n e Hamburg av, 20x100. Release mort. Anna E. Cozine individ. with James Gascoine exrs, &c., John G. Cozine to George W. and Charles H. Francisco. 2,338

Same property George W. and Charles H. Francisco to Edward Krueger. nom

3d st, s s, 47 e Smith st, 57x80. Edward M. Townsend individ. and as exr. Belinda R. Townsend to William O. Sumner. 13,212

5th st, s w s, 280 4 n w 7th av, 19.11x100. Lucinda Campbell, of New York, to Jennie C. Keough. nom

10th st, n s, 140.9 w 5th av, 20x100. Richard Nash to John McCormick. 6,500

10th st, n s, 273 4 e 8th av, 19.6x92.6. Thomas Brown to Richard Nash. *Mt.* $7,000. 11,000

12th st, n s, 70.4 e 5th av, 14.11x60. Foreclos. John Courtney, Sheriff, to James Warner. 1,300

12th st, s s, 2d and 3d avs, being lot 38 on assessment map 22d Ward block 100. The City of Brooklyn to James Ennis. Q C. 725

13th st, n s, bet 2d and 3d avs, being lot 28 on assessment map 22d Ward block 100. City of Brooklyn to James Ennis. Q. C. 525

18th st, s s, 173 2 w 4th av, 34.9x100. Catherine E. Duysters, of New York, to Frank W. Belmont. Q. C. *Mt.* $11,000. All int. 3,750

Same property. Robert L. Du Buisson, of Texas, heir Catherine Du Buisson to Frank W. Belmont. *Mt.* $11,000. All int. 3,750

Same property. Mary F. Du Buisson, of New York, and George H. Du Buisson, of Montclair, N. J., heirs of Catherine Du Buisson to same. All int. 7,500

16th st, n s, 135 9 w 8th av, 19.1x100. Release mort. Daniel Doody to William Wingerath nom

Same property. Release mort. James H. Watson and James H. Pittinger to William Wingerath. nom

Same property. Release mort. Ezra D. Bushnell to same. 3,000

Bay 26th st, s e s, 100 n e Cropsey av, 60x96.8, Bath Beach. William Keegan to Cornelius Ferguson 1,650

Bay 34th st, n w s, 380 s w 86th st, 60x96.8, Bensonhurst. Alfred B. Potterton, N. Y., to Elizabeth Ferry. 1,200

Bay 34th st, n w s, 440 s w 86th st, 60x96.8, Bensonhurst. John S. McClure to Elizabeth Ferry. 1,200

36th st, n s, 83 w 4th av, 43x100.2, h & l. Cathrina Svenlin to Jacob Morgenthaler. *Mt.* $8,250. nom

48th st, n s, 180 w 4th av, 20x100.2. Samuel T. Sherwood to Ralph Walsh. *Mt.* $2,500. 4,300

52d st, s s, 240 e 4th av, 20x100.2. Maren wife of and Henry H. Lee and Hans Hanson to Arndt H. Olsen. 2,800

55th st, n s, 125 w 2d av, 25x100.2. Thomas Markey to Louis H. Schenck. *Mt.* $1,200. 2,400

57th st, s s, 220 from 1st av, 55x100.2. Contract. Christian Gihman to John H. French. 1,300

64th st, n s, 520 w 14th av, 40x97.8x40x97.1. Effingham H. Nichols, of New York, to W. Rea Pattison, Washington, D. C. 400

70th s s, 210 w 15th av, 40x100, Lefferts Park. James V. S Woolley to Charles H. Rogers. 520

72d st, n s, 350 w 15th av, 40x100, New Utrecht. James V. S Woolley to Augusta Willendrup. 400

76th st, n s, 150 w 15th av, 20x100, Lefferts Park. James V. S. Woolley to Jane F. Murphy. 150

82d st, n s, 100 e 2d av, 80x109.4, New Utrecht. William W. and Robert M. Spence, Frank Forshew and Sylvester E. Coffin to Phoebe Howe. 2,000

82d st, n s, 100 e 2d av, 80x109 4, New Utrecht.
81st st, s s, 380 e 2d av, 20x109 4.
Release mort. Rulef J. Van Brunt to William W. and Robert M. Spence, Sylvester E. Coffin and Frank Forshew. 1,250

84th st, n e s, 300 n w 22d av, 60x100, Bensonhurst. James D. Lynch to Hilton R. Freeman. 1,050

84th st, s w s, 120 n w 23d av, 60x100, New Utrecht. James D. Lynch to Henry J. Westover. 1,050

Albany av w s 138.11 n Butler st, runs west 108 x north to point 155.7 n from Butler st, x east 114 to av, x south 16.8. Charles S. Taber and George C. Case to William Herod. *Mt.* $3,500. 5,500

Albany av, w s, 55.5 n Butler st, 16.8x85. Charles S. Taber and George C. Case, of Flatbush, to Ellen Sullivan. *Mt.* $3,500. 5,500

Atlantic av, s w s, 240.6 s e Flatbush av, runs southeast 20.2 x southwest 79.5 x northwest 1 x northwest 20.3 x northeast 72.11; also,
Atlantic av, s s, 220.6 s e Flatbush av, runs southeast 20 x southwest 72.11 x northwest 20.11 x northeast 66.9.
Partition. Gerard M. Stevens referee to Peter H McNulty. 12,700

Atlantic av, s s, 150 e Saratoga av, 16.8x100. Release mort. Thomas T. Barr to Alfred Ogden. nom

Atlantic av, s s, 150 e Saratoga av, 100x100. Alfred Ogden to George E. Schmoll. *Mt.* $5 000. nom

Av X, n s, extends from East 14th st to East 15th st, 200x200, Gravesend. William Sloan to John Lange and James Kaine. *Mt.* $3,900. exch

Bedford av, s e cor Madison st, 20x100. John D. Sticht to Annie G. Sticht. *Mt.* $5,000. 12,000

Berriman av, late Atkins av, w s, 120 s Eastern Parkway, 80x100. Charles Wildner to Betsey Berwin. 1,500

Buffalo av, w s, 54.10 n Atlantic av, 17x45, h & l Christopher P. Skelton to Anna M. Donahue. 2,400

Buffalo av, w s, 20 n Atlantic av, 17.10x45. Christopher P. Skelton to John G. Collins. *Mt.* $600. 2,600

Buffalo av, w s, 37.10 n Atlantic av, 17.10x45. Same to Margaret E. Clark. *Mt.* $600. 2,400

Buffalo av, e s, 77.9 s Park pl, 25x100. John Robinson to Catharine wife of Peter White. Taxes, assessm'ts, &c., from 1888. 950

Bushwick av, w s, 80 n Siegel st, 20x100, h & l. William H. Wiecke to Leon Botengoff, New York. 5,550

Same property. Release mort. The Williamsburgh Savings Bank to William H. Wiecke. nom

Bushwick av, s w s, 25.10 n w Cook st, 25.10x61x25x67.6 Sub. to mort. $4,200.
Graham av, e s, 25 n Seigel st, 25x100. ½ of this only. Sub. to mort. $6,300.
Louis Dimond to Leah Dimond. nom

Bushwick av, s w s, 25.10 n w Cook st, 25.10x61x25x67.6. ½ of this only. Sub. to mort. $4,200.
Graham av, e s, 25 n Seigel st, 25x100. ½ part of this only. Sub to mort. $6,300.
Leah Dimond to Harris Dimond. 5,000

Central av, s w s, 60 n w Harman st, 20x80. Katie wife of and Charles C. Kreppel to Frederick A. Spenn. exch

Clason av, e s, 196.11 s Fulton st, 21.6x80.6x22.3x2.11x95 8, h & l Charles A. Betts to Annie S. wife of Charles W. Betts. *Mt.* $5,000. nom

Coney Island av, s w cor Greenwood av, 60 8x116.1x30 4x120, Flatbush. Jennie V. Wilbur to Nathan Bidwell. 2,500

Flushing av, s s, 250 e Nostrand av, 25x100. David Stern to Barnet Bershatsky. *Mt.* $5,000 9,400

Flushing av, s s, 225 e Nostrand av, 25x100. David Stern to Joseph Resnick. *Mt.* $5,000. 9,750

Flushing av, s s, 225 e Nostrand av, 50x100. Leopold Michel to David Stern. *Mt.* $10,000. nom

Flushing av, s s, 100 e Marcy av, 25x100. Nathan Rosenthal to Frank Pelevger and Pincus Kessler, of New York. *Mt.* $3,400. 5,140

Franklin av, e s, 40 s Putnam av, 20x80. Emma C. Merryweather wife of Charles A. to John Muller. *Mt.* $4,500. 6,200

Fort Hamilton av, s w cor Denyses lane, 243 4x312.4x314 6. Daniel I. Lewis to The Bay Ridge Park Improvement Co. nom

Foster av, s s, 91.8 w Florence st, runs south 141 2 x west 13 10 x east 99.3 to East 3d st, x north 36.5 to Florence st, x north 142.2 to Foster av, x west 91.8, New Utrecht. Margaret Myles to Henry P. O'Farrell. *Mt.* $3,000. exch

Gates av, No. 286, s s, 238 w Bedford av, 17x110. Albert Woodruff to Lowell V. Brown. *Mt.* $3,250. exch

Gates av, n s, 139 w Stuyvesant av, 19.6x100. William H. Bierds to Eliza A. Bierds. nom

Glenmore av, n s, 75 w Miller av, 25x100. James Livingston to Albert G. Liebereuz. 2,587

Greenpoint av, n s, 100 e Provost st, 50x95. Jeremiah V. Meserole to Bridget wife of Patrick O'Brien. 2,000

Greenpoint av, n s, 150 e Provost st, 50x95. Same to Bernard Tierney. 2,000

Greene av, e s, 33.4 s Evergreen av, 16.8x50, h & l. Louis Folks to Mary J. wife of James H. McCormick. *Mt.* $2,000. 2,800

Greene av, n w s, 75 s w Irving av, 25x82.4x25x81.2. Joseph Weidner to John Haas. *Mt.* $3,000. nom

Greene av, n w s, 50 s w Irving av, 25x83.7x25x84.4. John Haas to Joseph Weidner. *Mt.* $3,000. nom

Greene av, n w s, 75 s w Hamburg av, 25x100. Release mort. Theodore F. Jackson et al. trustees of Loftis Wood to George Covert. 8,600

Greene av, s s, 250 w St. Nicholas av, 20x100. Conrad Nill to Margaretha Nill. *Mt.* $3,000. nom

Greene av, s e s, 203.10 s w Central av, 30x100. Release mort. Rosa Levy to Lillie Cohen. nom

Greene av, s s, 60 w Sumner av, 19.6x100. Thomas B. Bryant to J. Sophia Eilers, of New York. Mt. $5,000. 9,000

Hale av, e s, 124.10 s Ridgewood av, 24x101. John A. Seely to Peter E. Lawrence. 550

Hamburg av, s w s, 20 s e Ralph st, 30x100. Maria Heinstadt to Margaret Hynes. Mt. $600. 2,800

Hamburg av, e s, 50 s Suydam st, 25x100. Frank Nuss to Simon G. Meyer. 1,400

Hegeman av, s s, 40 e Cleveland st, 40x85. Adolph Sussman to Katherine F. Unkelbach. 490

Hegeman av, s s, 80 e Cleveland st, 20x85. Josef Pietschmann to Katherine F. Unkelbach. 310

Hopkinson av, e s, 195 s Herkimer st, 56x97.6, h & l. Albert G. Baker to Margaretha Hemmer. Mt. $17,600. 26,000

Jamaica av, s s, 92 w Schenck av, runs south 92.9 x west 8 x south 50 x west 75 x north 110 to Jamaica av, x northeast 89.1. Alexander F Zundt and James Stewart to Thomas Everit. Mt. $1,800 3,500

Same property Elizabeth V. wife of Alexander F. Zuudt to Thomas Everit. Q C. nom

Jefferson av, s s, 223.4 e Throop av, 16.8x100. Foreclos. John Courtney to Maximillian Lang. 5,135

Jefferson av, s s, 80 e Lewis av, 63x100. Release mort. Henry C. Needham exr. Henry M. Needham to Theodore W. Swimm. 5,500

Jefferson av, n s, 23 e Tompkins av, 19x80.3. h & l. Cornelia A. Bell to Mendel Levy. Mt. $4,500. 8,500

Kingsland av, n w cor Richardson st, 50x100. John M. Stearns to Michael Sullivan. 2,200

Kingsland av, w s, 273.9 n Van Cott av, runs west 70 x south 0.2 x west 30 x north 20.2 x east 100 to av, x south 20 to beginning. Benedict Brenner and Charles Hagmaier to Charles Hagmaier. Mt. $1,500. nom

Kingston av, n w cor Bergen st, 40x100x74.5x60x114.5x160. Silas A. Condict to John H and William R. Doherty. Mt. $8,000. exch

Lafayette av, No. 615, n s, 383.4 w Marcy av, 16.8x100.
Lafayette av, No. 771, n s, 75 e Throop av, 16.8x100.
Lafayette av, No 740, s s, 278.4 w Throop av, 21 8x100.
George B. Forrester to Edgar Y. Hubles. 12,000

Lexington av, s s, 215 e Clason av, 15x100. William H Caswell, of New York, to John H. Caswell, of New York. nom

Liberty av, s s, 60 w Milford st, 20x90. Effingham H. Nichols, of New York, to Mary E. Laing. 475

Liberty av. s e cor Bradford st, 100x175 John Adamson to George W. Chauncey. Mt. $6-500. nom

Linnington av, s s, extends from Thatford av to Rockaway av, 200x100. Louis Hirsch and Papy Cohn to Jacob Goldblatt and Marks Rapps. Mt. $1,700 2,200

Linnington av, s w cor Williamson av, 100x100. George L and David F. Wilber heirs of David Wilber and M. B. Wilber widow to Mary E Cook, Newtown, L. I. 2,000

Manhatten av, w s, 60 s Nassau av, 20x75, h & l. Emilie H. W. wife of Henry Behnken to Carl A. Striepecke. 5,000

Marcy av, w s, 180 s Macon st, 37x110. Charles A. Betts to Charles W. Betts. nom

Montauk av, e s, 130 s Belmont av, 60x100. Joseph Vernon, of Hoboken, N. J., to Charles H. Machin. 945

Myrtle av, s s, 245 e Lewis av, 5x200 to Vernon av. Aaron Raymond, of New York to Clara wife of Richard L. Leggett. nom

Myrtle av, n s, 350 w Lewis av, 25x100. Release mort. James W. Watson and James H. Pittinger to Max Hallbeimer. nom

Nassau av, s s, 75 w Russell st, 75x100. Jeremiah V. Meserole to Andrew E. Walker. 4,250

Ovington av, n e cor 14th av, 100x97.2x100x99.11, Lefferts Park. Effingham H. Nichols to John S. Brooks. 1,725

Prospect av, n s, 273 w 3d av, 44.1x43x44x47.10. Elizabeth L. Chinnock to Frederick W. Rowe. B. & S. and C. a. G. nom

Same property. Frederick W. Rowe to Joseph P. Puels. Mt. $3,000. exch

Putnam av, s s, 179 e Ralph av, 24.6x100. Charles Lewis to Paul E. Walters. Mt $7,200. 13,500

Putnam av, s s, 189 w Howard av, 17x100, h & l S. Burrage Reed to Mary E. Callahan. Mt. $4,500. 5,400

Putnam av, n s, 200 e Broadway, 40x100. Robert L. Moores and Charles A. Le Quesne to George Burns and Michael McGrath. Mt. $13,000 and taxes 1890. nom

Putnam av, n s, 298 w Sumner av, 17x100. Robert W. Reid, of New York, to Edward P. Brennan. Mt. $5,250. nom

Putnam av, n s, 298 w Sumner av, 17x100 Edward P. Brennan to George and Thomas J. Jenkins, of New York. Mt. $5,150. nom

Railroad av, e s, abt 245 s Brooklyn and Jamaica turnpike, 25x100. Margaretha Reich to Theophile Henky. 2,000

Ralph av, n e cor Decatur st, 22.6x100. Release mort. Asa W. Tenny to Charles B. Reynolds. 3,000

Reid av, w s, 50 n Macon st, 50x100. Bernard Levino to William M. Wilson. Mt. $4,500. 5,000

Reid av, e s, 22 n Hancock st, 38x100. Benjamin F. Constable to Lipman Arensberg. Mt. $12,000. exch

Ridgewood av, s s, 60 w Linwood st, 20x100. Caroline L. Everit to Harriet Harden. Mt. $1,500. 2,950

Riverdale av, s e cor Wyckoff lane, runs north to s s Eastern Parkway, x east to point near centre Van Siclen av, x south along line bet Wyckoff and Van Siclen's properties to land conveyed to C. B. Vanderveer, x west—x south to s s Riverdale av, x west —, excepting part taken for streets. Joanna S. Bogert to Edward F. Linton. 1-16 part. Sub. to life estate Sarah Wyckoff. 10,812

Same property. William F. Wyckoff exr. and trustee of Jacob S. Wyckoff to same. 5-16 part. Sub. to life estate Sarah Wyckoff. 54,062

Rockaway av, w s, 50 n of line bet D. B. Ames and W. Kouwenhoven, 25x100, Flatlands. Sarah Morris widow, Jersey City, to James Ford. Sub. to taxes and sales therefor. nom

Same property. James Ford to Thomas McGee. 175

Rockaway av, w s, 200 s Eastern Parkway, 25x100. Harriet A. wife of Charles R. Miller to Sabra E. Gregg. Q. C. 100

Sackman av, w s, 105 6 s Livonia av, 59x100. Paul W. Ledoux to Louis and Joseph Eisenberg and Marsey Rosenblum. 1,200

Schenck av, n w cor Van Brunt av, 45x100. Frederick A. H. Rackerbrandt, of New York, to John H. Greten. 400

Schenck av, e s, 175 s Blake av, 25x100. Albert H. W. Van Siclen to Tito and Domenico Constantine. Sub. to mort. 450

Schenectady av, n s, 84.2 n Dean st, 18x113.7x20x119.3 Levin Robbins to John Donerson Sub. to sewer assessments. 1,000

Sheffield av, e s, 100 s Eastern Parkway, 50x100. George Sattler to Rosa Haller. Assignment of title derived through an adverse possession for 31 years 300

Sheffield av, e s, 75 s Glenmore av, 25x100. Wm. Haug to Clara Lehmann. 1,000

Shepherd av, e s, 286.9 s Ridgewood av, 16 7x101.10. Zipporah L. Hollister to Matilda Kurz, of New York. Mt. $1,774. 2,900

Shepherd av, w s, 100 n Gay st, 25x100. Jane L. Smith to Emily C. Siemon. Q. C. 20

Stone av, w s, 100 s Livonia av, 25x100. Ann E. Sullivan to John T. Sullivan. nom

Same property. John T. Sullivan to Isaac Greenman. 525

Stone av, w s, 75 s Livonia av, 25x100. Patrick Mulligan to Isaac Greenman, of New York. 525

Stone av, w s, 125 s Livonia av, 25x100. Ann E Sullivan to Isaac Greenman, of New York. 525

St Marks av, s s, 275 e Rockaway av, runs south 46 8 x southeast 41.4 to East New York av, x east 25 x northwest 33.9 x north 39 to St. Marks av, x west 25 to beginning. Eleonora J. Decker to Charles A Bormann. 1,000

Same property. Charles A. Bormann to Christine Bormann his wife. Mt. $800. nom

St. Marks av, n s, 320 e Franklin av, 20x128.6. Release mort. John L. Voorhees commissioner, &c., to Mary E. wife of Levi Fowler. nom

St. Marks av, n s, 125 w Underhill av, 25x131. Foreclos. John Courtney, Sheriff, to Wm J. Hart. 8,000

St. Marks av, n s, 150 w Underhill av. 25x131. Foreclos. John Courtney, Sheriff, to Wm. J. Hart. 7,800

Thatford av, w s, 75 n Belmont av, 25x100. Louis Ratner to Meyer Sosnovitch, of New York. Mt. $3,000. 5,750

Thatford av, e s, 200 s Glenmore av, 25x100. Nathan Hyman, of New York, to Jacob Malz Mt. $1,500. 3,500

Thatford av, e s, 150 n Livonia av, 25x100. Release mort. Gilbert S. Thatford to Pauline Hartmann. nom

Underhill av, w s, 38 10 n Pacific st, 0.2x50. Mary E. Murtha to John McKelvey. Q. C. nom

Underhill av. w s, 39.10 n Pacific st, 0.2x50. John McKelvey to Anna Greve. Q. C. nom

Van Cott av, n e cor Manhattan av, 50x100. John S O'Connor, of White Mills, Pa., to Julius Manheim. 8,475

Washington av, s s, 250 w 3d st, 50x100, Flatbush. John Cole to Andrew Wilson. 2,500

Williamson av, w s, 175 s Sutter av, 25x100. Bartholomew Baumann to Hannah Bennett nom

Willoughby av, n w cor Skillman st, 35x83. John H. Rowland to D. Von Deylen, of New York. 11,550

Wythe av, w s, 19.8 s South 10th st, 36.1x50. Partition. Walton Storm ref. to Mary M. More. 6,450

3d av, e s, at n e s of 96th st, 104x167.2x100x138.8, New Utrecht. John H. Schroder to Ulrich Maurer, Adolf J. Jacobson and Christ H. Meller. 4,000

4th av, w s, 25.2 n 52d st, 50x100, Henry Kettelhodt to Annie E. Lavelle, of New York City. 2,575

4th av, w s, 50.2 n 52d st, 25x100. Annie E. Lavelle to Bridget Dineen. 1,287

4th av, w s, 100 s 6th st, runs west 160 x south 100 to 7th st, x east 100 x north 50 x east 60 to av, x north 50. Frank J. Schwab to Henry Putzel, of New York. Mt. $3,500. nom

4th av, w s, 20.2 n 33d st, 60x80. James J. Edwards, of New York, to Isabella Stirling. Mt. $3,800. 2,700

4th av, e s, 87.6 n Butler st, 28x98.4. Release mort. Hans S. Christian to John M. O'Neil. 2,375

Same property. John M. O'Neil to Susanne L. Ehmer. Mt. $9,000. 13,000

5th av, e s, 52 n President st, 28x102. Henry P. O'Farrell to Margaret Myles. Mt. $15,500. exch

5th av, n w s, 62 s w 2d st, 28x81.10, h & l. John W. Moran to Louise Egelhoff. Mt. $9,500. 16,000

6th av, n w cor Union st, 19x92. William H. H. Childs to Louis Schelling. 16,000

6th av, e s, 158.6 n Middle st, 18x99. Foreclos. Clark D. Rhinehart, Sheriff, to Schuyler E. Brumley as admr. of Sanford S. Brumley. 2,025

7th av, w s, 43 n 12th st, 19x44.10. John H. and William R. Doherty to Silas A. Condict. Mt. $6,000. nom

All of lots 488 and 489 sectional map No. 4 of part of Fort Hamilton not heretofore conveyed by one Schaeffer to anyone or taken from him for opening 86th st, with all title in New Utrecht and Lafayette avs and said 86th st. Charles E. Hill to Bay Ridge Park Improvement Co. B. & S. 100

Gore plot at s s of F. Allens and n w s of party of 2d part, New Utrecht, runs southwest 1,087.1 x northeast 1,044.6 x east 107.4. Holk D. Campbell to Bay Ridge Park Improvement Co. nom

Interior plot, 38.7 n of Prospect av and 232.9 e of 3d av, runs north 30 x east 42.4 x south 30 x west 42.4. Annie D. wife of Aaron D. Osborn to Henry Bohlen. nom

Kings highway, e s, adj Carolina L. Tams, New Utrecht, runs northeast 959.4 to point 440 s w 12th av, x southwest 827.5 to centre 81st st, x southeast 80 x southwest 130 x northwest 142.
Parcel begins on centre line bet 81st and 82d sts, 12th and 13th avs, at its intersection with Kings highway, runs northwest 113.10 x northeast 57.5 to centre Kings highway, x southeast 127.3.
Release mort. The Long Island Loan and Trust Co. to The Bay Ridge Park Improvement Co. nom

Lot No. 140 block 3 map 221 lots Michael J. Bergen, New Utrecht. James V. S. Woolley to George E. West. 200

Lot 139 block 3 same map. Same to same. 200

Lots 142 and 143 block 3 same map. Same to Dennis Hickey. 400

Lot 190 block 4 map No. 1 618 lots Couwenhoven farm, New Utrecht. Effingham H. Nichols to John More. 180

Lots 497-502 block 11 same map. Same to Arend N. Teenga. 990

Lots 215 and 216 block 5 same map. Same to Margaret Spear. 400

Lots 98, 99, 100 and 103 block 2 map 221 lots Michael J. Bergen, New Utrecht. James V. S. Woolley to Patrick Campbell. 600

Lot 148 block 3 same map. Same to Thomas J. West, Jersey City. 200

Lots 215 and 216 map Asa W. Parker, New Utrecht. George Duncan to Frederick O. Miller. 650

Lots 192 and 198-202 block 4 map 1 of Cowenhoven farm. Effingham H. Nichols to Albert Cohn. 1,190

Lots 162 to 165 block 4 map 618 lots, Cowenhoven farm, New Utrecht. Effingham H. Nichols, of New York, to James Woodhead. 720

Lots 489 to 493, 525 to 527 block 11 same map. Same to Frank H. Holland. 1,470

Lots 179 and 180 block 4 same map. Same to Mary J. and Margaret McDevitt. 380

Lots 245 to 249 and lot 228 block 5 same map. Same to John Nicholson. 1,200

Lots 181, 182 and 183 block 4 map 618 lots Cowenhoven farm, New Utrecht. Effingham H. Nichols, of New York, to Henry Klee. 570

Lots 278-282 and 298-302 and 297, 310, 311 and 337-340 and 395-398 and 404-411 and 423-426 and 366 and 367 map of 430 lots of J Worth and V. A. Strawson, Flatbush. Jacob Worth and Vincent A. Strawson to Jacob Worth. Mt. $5,400. nom

Lots 283-287 and 296 and 303-309 and 341, 342, 347-349 and 373, 374 and 383-[illegible] and 359-394 and 413, 429, 430 and 416 and 417 same map. Same to Vincent A. Strawson. Mt. $6,500. nom

New lots road n w cor Wyckoff lane, runs north to point 56 s Belmont av, x west to e s Pennsylvania av, at point 87 s Belmont av, x south to New Lots road, x east —, excepting portion taken for sts. Abraham L. Hopkins to Edward F. Linton. ⅛ part. 70,000

Parcel of salt and fresh meadow in 26th Ward, bounded by bay and property of Scholl, Lefferts & Wyckoff. 9 14-100 acres. Gilliam Schenck to Williamson Rapalje and John H. Ireland. 571

Plot of land bounded north by Livonia av, east by Powell st, south by land late Thomas B. Lott and west by Sackman st. Kunigunda Buhn extrx. John Buhn to Herman F. Koepke. 7,800

Plot of land, bounded north by Degraw st, west by New York av, south by the middle line of Remsen av and east by land John T. Martin. William H. Murr to James D. Rankin and James Ross. 1,200

Plot begins 440 s e 12th av at south line of Fallens property, runs southwest 1,044 6 x northeast in five courses 1,087.1 to Fallen land, x northwest 107.4, New Utrecht. Bay Ridge Park Improvement Co. to Graham K. Anderson. nom

Plot of land New Utrecht, bounded northeast by land of De Russey, southeast by land Reotgert Stillwell, &c., 280x85. James A. Sargent to Jane E. Johnson. Q. C. 100

Same property. Comptroller New York State to James A. Sargent. 17

Salt meadows, in 26th Ward, bounded west by fresh meadow formerly Jacob Cozine east by salt meadow formerly Michael Duryea south by the bay and west by salt

meadow formerly Michael Duryea, contains 8 acres; also,
Salt meadows, bounded east by meadow of John Cozine west by meadow John Blake north by meadow Garret Cozine and south by the bay, contains 6 acres, ½ part; also,
Salt meadows, 5 acres on bay adj John Blake and Christ. Lott, ½ of one-half long lot.
Sabra L. Duryea widow to Williamson Rapelye and John H. Ireland. 906
Yellow Hook to New Utrecht road, n s, adj J. J. Voorhies, J. A. Emmons et al., 14 acres 2 roods, New Utrecht, excepting portion conveyed by Anna Hinckley to Amelia Gubner. Charles E. Hill to The Bay Ridge Park Improvement Co. *Mt.* $16,400. nom
Agreement as to the conduct of dissolved copartnership. William H. Bierds with John T. Bierds. nom
All title in property conveyed by grantees to grantor, excepting part conveyed herewith to said grantor by Annie D. and De C. Osborn. Henry Bohlen to Annie D. and A. De Camp Osborn. nom
General release. Harriet Stock to Alexander Semelis. 1,000

WESTCHESTER COUNTY.

AUGUST 5 TO 11—INCLUSIVE.

EASTCHESTER.

Bernstein, Eliz'h A. to Emily J. Dearborn, e s Union pl, 560 s Prospect av, 50x124. $1,750
Berry, Mary S. to Victoria Ridgway, lot 7 w s White Plains road, map Townsend estate, 9¼ acres. 7,500
Behrman, Mary S. to Metha Von Heyn, n e s Mt. Vernon av, 35 s e Bond st, 40x100. 12,000
Doremus, Lizzie B. to Townsend Wandell, part lot 625 w s 7th av, Mt. Vernon, 50x105. nom
Forster, Fred. P. to Chas. T. Lovall, lot 162 grantors map Chester Hill, 50x100. 800
Hall, Mary J. to Bertha Hookey, lot 990 e s 14th av, Mt. Vernon, 100x105. nom
Houlihan, Patrick to Nellie A. Lawlor, lot 416 w s 5th av, Mt. Vernon, 100x105. 3,000
Jeannerett, Sarah S. to Armenia Carpenter, part lot 1049 n s Stevens av, Mt. Vernon, 50x100. 4,000
Johnson, Fred. to Jacob Schuermann, lot 60 e s 10th av, Central Mt. Vernon, 50x100. 1,300
Lasker, Moses to Cornelius Donovan, part lot 459 w s 4th av, Central Mount Vernon, 50x100. 2,100
Lachenauer, Geo. to Henry Siegfried and ano., w s 11th av, 300 s 3d st, 112x115x80x110. 5,000
Lomas, Robt. I. to Wm. J. Lynsky and ano., lots 246, 247 and O, n w s Catherine st, Washingtonville, 116.8x—. 1,450
Merritt, Eliz'h M. to Nicolaus Wilhelm, lot 278 s e s Marion st, Washingtonville, 50x100. 600
Muller, Kath. to Louise Miller, part lot 408 n w s Greenwich st, West Mount Vernon, 40x125. other consid, and 350
Penfield, Geo. J. to Samuel Thomas and ano., lots 233 and 234 n w s Pell Place, South Mount Vernon, 66.8x100. 1,300

GREENBURGH.

Bliss, Albert E. to Wm. J. Preston, lot 4 e s Washington st, map Bliss Bros. property, 35x100. 1,200
Le Roy, Jacob trustee of to Julia D'A Jones, w s Oak st, adj grantee, abt 595x300, and gore bet Oak and Coles avs. 2,500

MAMARONECK.

Burns, Patrick to Cornelius Sheehan, lot adj Rushmore and Nevils, 100x150. 800
Daymon, Wm. D. and ano. to Rueben R. Richards and ano., lots 26–31 Mamaroneck av, Homestead Park, 200x150. 3,600
Mutual Life Ins. Co. to Wm. D. Daymon and ano., lots 3–12 w s Mamaroneck av, Barnard property, abt 328x1,000. 10,000
Whipple, Dorris to Mary J. Vincent, s s Union av, 1,100 w White Plains av, 50x—. 1,140

MOUNT PLEASANT.

Barnhart, J. W. to Mary Carpenter, e s Barnhart av, 100 n Francis st, 25x86. 350
Conlon, Francis A. to Rev. Wm. H. Tole, tract road from Fair Grounds to Kensico Station, abt 50 acres. 15,000
Same to The Church of St. John, 24 acres w s same road. nom
Foster, Caroline et al., W. M. Skinner ref., to Stephen Washburn, 21 acres on road from Pleasantville to Unionville. 4,450
Huler, Johanna to Magdalen Schreyer, lots 10 and 11 Cortlandt st, North Tarrytown, 100x125. 6,000
Smadbeck, Louis to Wm. Fredericks, lots 1144 and 1145 Sherman Park. 400
Same and ano. to Pattie E. Jenks, lots 97–100 Lakehurst Villa Park. 500
Same to Malachy Byrne, lots 25 and 26. 325
Smith, Wm. R. to Anthony Fisch, lot 3 block 9 map Lake Kensico. 100
Same to S. A. Swart, lots 61–64 block 6. 400
Same to W. Soenneker, lots 67 and 68 block 5. 190
Same to Wm. Stagg, lots 24, 25 and 26 block 9. 195
Same to Chas. Schneider, lots 40 and 41 block 10. 200
Same to Isabella Lessard, lot 16 block 6. 100
Same to Thos. Dunn, lot 15 block 6. 100
Same to Jas. Y. Cochran, lots 39 and 40 block 6 and 49 block 3. 370
Same to Elmwood Carpenter, lots 18–21 block 9. 310

NEW ROCHELLE.

Bachmann, Herman to John Wackerbarth, e s Av A, 115.7 n Grove av, 25x100. 500
Bliss, Alicia M. to John New, lot 50 and part 49 and 51 e s Lawton st, map Benj. Seacord property, 55x137. 5,890

OSSINING.

Storms, Sarah A. to Geo. W. Storms, w s Scarborough road, 75x200. 500

RYE.

Damon, Carrie M. et al., M. Dillon ref., to John Ryan, lot 85 w s Centre st, Mt. Jefferson, 50x100. 825
Merritt, Jas. and ano. to Bridget McEvoy, lot 21 n s Ellendale av, Washington Park, 50x150. 240
Same to Louis Praeger, lots 121 and 122 s s West William st, 100x110. 372
Same to Louisa Merritt, lot 117 s s West William st, 50x109. 167

SCARSDALE.

North End Land Improvement Co. to Chas. W. Montgomery, n w s White Plains road adj Barry, 200x300. 1,500
Montgomery, Chas. W. to Chas. D. Immen, part same lot, 100x300. 750

WESTCHESTER.

Camp, Hugh N. to Leah Rosenfield, lots 293 and 294, map McGraw estate. 600
Duncan, Wm. F. to Robt. C. Phair, lots 111 and 112, map property grantor. 1,150
Same to Christopher Carlisle, lots 109 and 110. 859
Estwick, Chas. Hy. to Geo. W. Eccles, part lot 279 s s 10th av, Wakefield, 50x114. 2,800
Fairchild, Clara to Fred. M. Farwell, s w cor Van Cortlandt st and Guion pl. 1,600
Hyland, Wm. J. to Mary McGurl, s s Halperine st, 98 e Main, 25x115. 700
Jones, Theo. De G. to Margt. T. Hackett, n s Briggs av, 250 e 4th st, 50x209. 1,500
McGann, Jane to Harry Overington and ano., east ½ 201 s s 9th st, Unionport, 50x216. 600
Same to Hannah M. Hurlbut, west ½ same, 50x216. 600
Mace, Levi H. and ano. to Ambrose S. Wildey, lots 15 and 16 n s Ash av, Lacoma Park, 50x100. 500
Muller, Aug. to Louisa Richter, s s Green av, 200 w Mapes av, 25x100. nom
Merrill, Maria L. to Patrick J. Crough, lot 91 s s 1st av, New Jerome, 90x125. 550
Sims, John to Stephen T. Moen, lot 1137 w s 2d st, Wakefield, 109.6x105. 1,700
Sinclair, Margt. to Laura M. Powers, n e cor Duncomb av and Juliana st, 125x164x157x70. 1,500
Same to same, e s Barker av, 233 n Elizabeth st, 66.8x100. 8,200

WHITE PLAINS.

Purdy, Liv. R. to John H. M. Luhrs, tract cor North st and Rosedale road, 8¼ acres. 4,000
Sutton, Chas. D. to Margt. D. Banks, w s Stewart pl, adj grantor, 40x145. 675

YONKERS

Armour Villa Park Assoc. to Mary M. Hinman, lot 262. nom
Barnes, Ella L. to Patrick Formey, lot 71 w s 1st st, map Hyatt farm, 50x100. 450
Edwards, Adah et al. to Jane McLain, lots 16, 17 and 21, e s Cornell av, Lowerre Station. 1,800
Same to Jas. A. Witcher, lot 15, e s Cornell av. 600
Same to Jas. J. Edwards, lots 15–18, n s Cornell av. 800
Same to Annie Gillespie, lots 18, 19 and 20, e s Cornell av. 1,800
Gramatan Park Co. to Jas. Romano, lots 99 and 100. 270
Hartung, Dorothea to Dorothea Werner, part lot 254 map Hyatt farm, 50x117. 275
Herriot, J. Groshon exr. of to Mary E. Sickley et al, lots 87, 88 and 89, e s Beech st, 75x98. 1,080
Same to Edward Mee, lot 84, e s Beech st, 25x98. 230
Mee, Edw. to Ann Siers, same lot. 310
Haney, Mary A. and ano. J. H. Ferguson, ref., to Thos. Haney, s s St. Marys st, 75 e Riverdale av, 25x98. 1,590
Jones, Cyrus P. et al. to Thos. Lee, lots 1 and 2 block A grantors map. 750
Same to John Gasspard, lots 7 and 8 block A. 750
Kingsbury, Jas. A. and ano. to Henry J. Fegan, No. 149 w s Orchard st, 25x125. nom
Lowerre, Seaman to Albert G. W. Starke, lots 18, 19 and 20 e s Van Cortlandt Park av, Lowerre Station. 890
Maguire, Mary E. to Wm. E. Thorne, e s Bronx River road, adj New York city line, 175x100. 1,459
Same to John H. Thorne, e s same, 215 n New York city line, 125x100. 1,049
Monrovia Park Co. to Albert E. Cowdrey, s s Euclid av, 225 w Ridge st, 50x100. nom
Smith, Cornelius to Soren R. Sorenson, lot s s Swain st, 75x150. nom
Springer, Regina to Walter Fox, 37 acres road from Hunts Bridge to Bronxville, adj John R. Hoole, ½ interest. 18,500
Wangenstein, Fred. to Ludwig Kuenstler, n w cor Riverdale av and Washington st, 100x90. 13,750

YORKTOWN.

Travis, Annie C. to E. Munson Frost, The Jas. L. Travis farm, 206 acres. 9,000

MORTGAGES.

Note.—The arrangement of this list is as follows. The first name is that of the mortgagor, the next that of the mortgagee. The description of the property then follows, then the date of the mortgage, the time for which it was given, and the amount. The general dates used as headings are the dates when the mortgage was handed into the Register's office to be recorded.

NEW YORK CITY.

AUGUST 7, 8, 10, 11, 12, 13.

Allen, Frances E. widow to Jabez A. Bostwick. 5th av. P. M. July 22, due Aug. 1, 1894, or installs, 5 %. $100,000
Amidon, Georgiana M. wife of James R. to The Citizens' Savings Bank. West End av, n e cor 83d st, runs north 81.10 x southeast 175.11 x north 6.1 x east 86.1 to Boulevard, x south 70.2 to 83d st, x west 260.4. Aug. 7, 1 year or sooner. gold, 140,000
Aspinwall, J. Lawrence to Henry Parish. Lot 84 map of land at Riverdale, 24th Ward, of Joseph Rosenthal. P. M. Aug. 8, due Aug. 10, 1894, 5 %. 16,000
Adamson, John, Brooklyn, to Charles Meyerhoff. 88th st. P. M. Aug. 11, due Dec. 22, 1892, or sooner, 5 %. 4,500
Ahrens, John E. to Henry Middendorf. 2d av, e s, 60.5 n 42d st, 20x80.6. Sub. to mort. $5,000. Aug. 11, due July 20, 1894, 5 %. 3,000
Arnold, Anna mortgagor with Zoe D. Underhill guard. of Walter D. and Ruth Underhill mortgagee. Extension of mort. April 24. nom
Allard, Treffle H. to The Harlem Savings Bank. Home st, s s, 178 e Stebbins av, 16.4x80.9x17.6x87.2. Aug. 12, 1 year, 5 %. 2,000
Same to same. Home st, s s, 194.4 e Stebbins av, 16.9x74.2x17.11x80.9. Aug. 12, 1 year, 5 %. 2,000
Same to same. Home st, s s, 211.1 e Stebbins av, 17.1x68.1x18x74.2. Aug. 12, 1 year, 5 %. 2,000
Same to same. Home st, s s, 228.2 e Stebbins av, 24.10x58.6x26 7x68.1. Aug. 12, 1 year, 5 %. 2,000
Aldrich, Sherwood, Brooklyn, to William K. Thorn, Newport, R. I. 53d st, n s, 150 w 9th av, 25x100.5. P. M. March 1, 1890, demand. 4,000
Biersack, Christian to Conrad Muller. 121st st, No. 434, s s, 225 w Pleasant av, 25x100.11. Aug. 12, due Jan. 1, 1895, 5 %. 14,000
Burd, Charles W. to Mary E. Moulton. Hull av, n s, 51 w Suburban st, 45x110. Aug. 11, due Aug. 15, 1892, 5 %. 1,500
Byrne, Michael J. to Byrne & Tucker. 84th st, s s, 275 w 9th av, 30.8x102.2. July 31, 3 years, 5 %. 5,000
Byrnes, Thomas to Hiram R and Henry Dater trustees Philip Dater dec'd. Sheridan av. P. M. Aug. 10, 3 years or sooner, 5 %. 6,250
Brummel, Max to John W. Baird and ano. exrs. John Baird. 2d av. P. M. June 30, 5 years or installs., 5 %. 10,000
Brummel, Max mortgagor with John W. Baird and ano. exrs. John Baird. Extension of mort. Aug. 12. nom
Banger, George to The Railroad Co-operative Building and Loan Assoc. 188d st, n s, 100 w Creston av, 25x100. P. M. June 24, installs., 5 % 3,750
Bauer, Friedrich to Ernest C. Bliss et al. exrs. William Bliss. 31st st, s s, 125 w 1st av, 50x98.9. Aug. 13, due Aug., 1896, 5 % gold, 15,000
Brownell, Asa C., Brooklyn, to Leonard D. Hills, Amherst, Mass. Brown pl, w s, 85 s 138th st, 40x82.6. Aug. 8, 1 year. 5,000
Brothers, Mary wife of and Charles and Minnie wife of and Abram Brothers to Melancthon W. Borland and ano. trustees of Sarah L. Coit. Allen st, e s, 180 s Grand st, 20x87.6. Aug. 13, 5 years, 5 %. 14,000
Bendheim, Henry M. to Nathan Wise and Adolph M. Bendheim. Columbus or 9th av and 124th st. P. M. June 2, due Jan. 1, 1892. 44,000
Same to Adolf Kerbs. Same property. P. M. Sub. to last mort. June 2, due Jan. 1, 1892. 16,050
Brisk Delito Lodge of the American Star Order to Lewis Goldberg. Attorney st, No. 62; Ridge st, No. 55. Lease. May 1, demand. 200
Bruckmann, Fredericke widow to Jacob Rieser. 10th st, No. 424, s s, 321.4 w Av D, 25x92.3. Aug. 12, due Aug. 1, 1893. 1,000
Baker, Ella to Barbara Stahl. Edenwood av, w s, 237.8 n St. James st, 75x106 to Croton Aqueduct. Aug. 11, 3 years, 5 %. 1,000
Bormann, Conrad to Ella Breslauer. 65th st, No. 302, s s, 64 e 2d av, 18x76.2x18.2x73.5. Aug. 10, 3 years. 100
Brooks, Elizabeth to August Ruff. Spring st. P. M. Aug. 10, 2 years or sooner. 6,600
Balheimer, George L. mortgagee. Certificate as to subordination of morts. and extension thereof. Aug. 8. nom
Bendinger, August to August L. Martin. 76th st, n s, 230 e 3d av, 25x102.2. Sub. to morts. $12,000. Aug. 10, demand. 3,625
Brunjes, Martin to John D. A. Stoeckel. Robbins av, n w cor of st leading from said av to e s of Terrace pl, 50x100, part lot 325 map of East Morrisania. Aug. 7, 5 years, 5 %. 4,500
Bryant, George W. to John H. Bloodgood. 111th st, No. 111, n s, 95.8 e 4th av, 15.11x100.11. P. M. May 29, due June 30, 1894, 5 %. 3,000
Same to same. 111th st, No. 99, n e cor 4th av, 15x100.11. P. M. May 29, due June 30, 1894, 5 %. 8,500

Same to same. 111th st, No. 129, n s, 239 e 4th av, 15.11x100.11. P. M. May 29, due June 30, 1894, 5 %. 8,500

Brown, Truman A. to Edith N. Wharton. West 12th st. P. M. Aug. 1, 3 years, 5 %. 2,350

Brown, Joseph and Mary his wife to Daniel J. Brown. 105th st, s s, 193.9 w 1st av, 18.9x100.9. July 28, 5 years, 600

Buttner, Simon to H. Koehler & Co., a corporation. Bowery, No. 304. Saloon lease. Aug. 8, demand. 1,500

Same to same. 3d av, No. 2374. Saloon lease. Aug. 8, demand. 1,000

Buzzini, S., W. P. Molo, B. Malizia, Mannini E. Dimoni, V. Zucca, V. Camovito, John, John B. and Francis Cavagnaro, A. Albertini, Camisa Domanico, Guiseppe Rezziti, A. Jagmetti, J. Baltramini, Henry Giering, Rud Bullo, Angelia Sartori, Clemente Demaron, Andrea Dellera, Enrico Chevola, Guiacomo Cavasco, A. Ragaglia, Charles Devy, Leonard Quanchi and H. T. Salari to Cosmopolitan Range Co. Consent of stockholders to execution of mort. July 30. ——

Berkowitz, Sarah wife of and Sigmund, Brooklyn, and Hannah Meyer widow to Henry A. Bogert guard of Mary E. Bogert. Lewis st. P. M. Aug. 5, due Aug. 1, 1894, 5 %. 12,000

Same to William Newman and Rebecca wife of Simon Danziger. Same property. 2d mort. Aug. 5, installs. 5,000

Boehm, Caroline wife of Samuel C. to Justus L. Bulkley et al. exrs. and trustees Daniel B. Fayerweather. 80th st, n s, 149.9 e 5th av, 25.1x102.2. July 22, due Aug. 7, 1896, 4½ %. 55,000

Campbell, John V. to Joseph L. Buttenwieser. Monroe st, No. 244, s s, 269.3 e Scammel st, 24.9x97.8; 113th st, No. 152, s s, 320 w 3d av, 25x100.10. Aug. 7, demand. 4,000

Clark, Cyrus to THE MUTUAL LIFE INS. CO. of New York. 7th av, w s, 25.2 n 49th st, 75.3 x— to Broadway, x—x—. Aug. 5, due Aug. 11, 1894, 5 %. 110,000

Civill, Acton T., Caroline B. widow, Sarah A. B. and Emma B., Coeymans, N. Y., to THE EAST RIVER SAVINGS INSTITUTION. James slip, Nos. 3 and 5, w s, 24 s Cherry st, 31.10 x36.2x31.6x36.2. Aug. 3, 1 year, 5 %. 6,000

Cleyton otherwise Clayton, Michael to Thomas Neilson. Jackson av, w s, lot 79 map of Belmont Village, 50x100. Aug. 6, 4 years. 500

Crasto, Rebecca L. to Robert A. Sands guard. of Henry H. Sands. 126th st, n s, 231.5 e Lenox av, 17.10x99.11. Aug. 5, 4 years, 5 %. 10,000

Same to Mary J. and Horace P. Averill, Brooklyn. Same property. Aug. 5, 2 years or sooner. 2,500

Caballero, Ramona A. A. to Henry E. Jones. 26th st, n s, 100 w Lexington av, 14.3x98.9. Sub. to mort. $9,000. Aug. 13, 1 year. 2,000

Cameron, Alexander to Eliza L. Macy. 96th st, s s, 300 w Columbus av, 25x100.8. Aug. 12, 3 years, 5 %. 20,000

Same to Sarah H. Powell. Same property. Aug. 12, 3 years, 5 %. 2,000

Same to same. 96th st, s s, 325 w Columbus av, 25x100.8. Aug. 12, 3 years, 5 %. 2,000

Same to Caroline L. Macy. Same property. Aug. 12, 3 years, 5 %. 20,000

Same to John A. James, London, Eng. 96th st, s s, 350 w Columbus av, 25x100.8. Aug. 12, 3 years, 5 %. 22,000

Same to Charles W. and Henrietta S. Haskins trustees Henrietta W. Havemeyer. 96th st, s s, 375 w Columbus av, 25x100.8. Aug. 12, 3 years, 5 %. 21,000

Camp Memorial Church to The American Congregational Union. Chrystie st, No. 141, w s, 23.4x105.2. July 3, due —— 13,000

Chalfin, Jane V. wife of and Samuel F. to George L. Ingraham and ano. trustees Daniel P. Ingraham dec'd. 214th st, centre line, 182.3 w from exterior bulkhead line, runs west 300 x south 129.11 x west 150 to 9th av, x south 129.11 x east 375 x north 129.11 x east 75 x north 129.11 to beginning. Aug. 5, due Aug. 6, 1894, 5 %. gold, 3,250

Chedsey, Francis B. to William R. Beal Land Impt. Co. Beekman av. P. M. July 8, 3 years, 5 %. 600

Delaney, John to Nellie D. Traphagen, Brooklyn. Webster av, e s, 122.1 n 171st st, 50x105.8 to Mill Brook, x50x102. Aug. 6, 3 years, 5 %. 700

Donnellon, Samuel R., Brooklyn, to James W. Green trustee for the Mohawk Valley Lumber Co., Fultonville, N. Y. 88th st, n s, 199.6 e Amsterdam av, 3 lots, each 17x100.8. 3 morts., each $1,000. Sub. to prior mort. $44,000. Aug. 6, 1 year. 3,000

Doerr, John B. to THE FARMERS' LOAN AND TRUST CO. 24th st. P. M. Aug. 6, 3 years, 5 %. 25,000

Same to MURRAY HILL BANK. Same property. P. M. Aug. 6, 1 year. 19,000

Downey, Charles and George W. Curry to Manchester & Philbrick. Park av, s w cor 93d st, 100.8x105. Sub. to mort. $50,000. Aug. 10, 6 months or sooner. 2,250

Daniels, Ellen T. widow to George L. and Arthur Ingraham trustees Daniel P. Ingraham. 166th st, n s, 95 e Audubon av, 50x95. Aug. 12, 3 years, 5 %. gold, 3,750

Dempsey, Mary E. V. and Winifred A. to George P. Herrmann. 74th st, n s, 34.6 w Lexington av, 17x72.2. Aug. 13, 2 years, 5 %. 1,500

Durand, Albert W. to THE AMERICAN SURETY CO. of New York. 50th st, No. 357 n s, 597.6 w 8th av, 19.2x100.5 Secures guardian's bonds of mortgagor and Rufus L. Scott. July 24.

De Long, Emma J. mortgagor with THE TITLE GUARANTEE AND TRUST CO. mortgagee. Extension of reduced mortgage at 4½ %. Aug. 13. nom

Embree, John C. to Richard H. Casey. Fairmount pl, s s, 372 w Marmion av, 25x60.1x25 x67.7. Aug. 4, 4 years, 5 %. 1,500

Edwards, Rebecca A. S. wife of William L. formerly Kerr to Rose wife of Robert O'Byrne. Perry av, n e cor Ozark st, 25x100. Aug. 11, 1 year. 175

Entwistle, John to THE HARLEM SAVINGS BANK. 135th st, n s, 125 e St. Anns av, 6 lots, each 16.8x100. 6 morts., each $3,500. Aug. 6, 1 year, 5 %. 21,000

Folz, Frederick to Rosa E. Rainsford. 142d st, s s, 150 e Brook av, 4 lots. 4 P. M. morts., each $1,250. Aug. 10, 3 years, 5 %. gold, 5,000

Gault, Mary wife of James to Julius Lipman, and William Cohen. Madison av, s e cor 120th st, 40x75. Sub. to mort. $42,000. Aug. 7, due Feb. 1, 1892. 15,418

Same to same. Madison av, e s, 80 s 120th st, 20.11x75. Sub. to mort. $17,500. Aug. 7, due Feb. 1, 1892. 2,500

Same to Light & Louther. Madison av, s e cor 120th st, 100.11x75. Sub. to morts. $117,143. Aug. 7, due Feb. 1, 1892. 1,437

Same to Cassidy & Adler. Madison av, s e cor 120th st, 100.11x75. Sub. to morts. $99,210. Aug. 7, due Nov. 6, 1891. 2,515

Same to The New York Lumber and Wood Working Co. Madison av, s e cor 120th st, 40x75, sub. to morts. $67,418; Madison av, e s, 40 s 120th st, 40x75, sub. to morts. $30,-000. Aug. 7, demand. 7,310

Gault, Mary wife of James to Rosalie Wittner. Madison av, s e cor 120th st, 40x75. Aug. 7, 1 year, 5 %. 42,000

Gault, Mary wife of and James to James W. Smith trustee for Maria L. Debon and remaindermen. Madison av, e s, 40 s 120th st, 40x75. Aug. 6, due Aug. 7, 1894, 5 %. gold, 30,000

Same to Francis J. Gasquet and John Duer trustees for Marie Marshall and remaindermen. Madison av, e s, 80 s 120th st, 20.11x75. Aug. 6, due Aug. 7, 1894, 5 %. gold, 17,500

Graham, James M. to Henrietta Gaus. 51st st, n s, 376.8 e 3d av, 33.4x100.5. Sub. to morts. $37,751. Aug. 3, due Dec. 1, 1891, or sooner. 2,700

Graham, Thomas to THE GERMANIA LIFE INS. CO. 92d st, s s, 100 e 5th av, 75x100.8, all; 92d st, s s, 175 e 5th av, 1.11x100.8, all title; 92d st, s s, 175 e 5th av, 3.11x100.8, all title. Aug. 11, due Aug. 1, 1893, 5½ %. gold, 93,000

Same to Randolph Guggenheimer and Isaac and Samuel Untermyer. 92d st, s s, 100 e 5th av, 75x100.8. Aug. 10, 6 months. 15,000

Goff, Sophie wife of and Charles A. to THE WASHINGTON LIFE INS. CO. Cannon st, Nos. 92–100, e s, 75 s Stanton st, 102.6x100. Aug. 12, due June 1, 1896, or sooner, 5 %. 55,000

Goff, Sophie to George I. Bassermann. Same property. Aug. 12, 5 years or sooner, 5 %. 7,000

Gunn, William and Andrew Grant to THE CITIZENS SAVINGS BANK. Amsterdam av, n w cor 78th st, 102.2x100. Aug. 11, 1 year. 110,000

Same to same. Same property. Sub. to last mort. Aug. 11, due Feb. 1, 1892. 47,000

Same to Julius Lipman and William Cohen. Same property. Sub. to mort. $110,000. Aug. 11, due Feb. 1, 1892. 35,375

Garlan, Joseph to Bernheimer & Schmid. 58th st, No. 203 W. Saloon lease. Aug. 12, note, demand. 500

Gray, Christopher to THE HARLEM SAVINGS BANK. Park av, n w cor 126th st, 48x90. Aug. 12, 1 year, 5 %. 25,000

Same to same. Same property. Aug. 12, 1 year, 5 %. 1,000

Same to William H. Colwell. Park or 4th av, n w cor 126th st, 74.11x90. Aug. 13, 1 year. 524

Geery, Anna S. wife of and Isaac J., Stamford, Conn., to Burrall Hoffman. Canal st, n w cor Mulberry st, 26.7x72.5x25.8x80.10. Aug. 7, due Feb. 10, 1892, or sooner. 5,000

Hyams, Blanche and Fanny to Ida Shultz. 74th st, Nos. 165–169, n s, 150 w 3d av, 3 lots. 3 P. M. morts., each $3,000. Sub. to mort. on each of $9,000. Aug. 13, 3 years, 5 %. 9,000

Hall, Henry B. to William R. Beal Land Improvement Co. Beekman av. P. M. July 8, 3 years, 5 %. 2,100

Hall, Alfred B. to William R. Beal Land Impt. Co. Beech terrace. P. M. July 8, 3 years, 5 %. 450

Healy, Aaron, Brooklyn, to Justus L. Bulkley et al. exrs. and trustees Daniel B. Fayerweather. Ferry st, n e cor Gold st, 75.2x111.7 x92.3x92.4. Aug. 12, 3 years, 4½ %. 150,000

Hinton, George H., Clifton, N. J., to Eugene H. Hinton. 8th av, s e cor 20th st, 25x100. Sub. to mort. $11,500. Aug. 12, 1 year. 1,000

Haefelin, Joseph to Horace F. Hutchinson. 11th av, e s, 110.11 s 165th st, 25x100. Aug. 4, demand. 3,000

Hangen, Leonard mortgagor with Thomas J. Falls agent and att'y of Thomas J. Falls and Thomas F. Stevenson mortgagee. Extension of reduced mortgage. Aug. 7. nom

Hanover, Hannah wife of and Henry to Frederick D. Tappen and ano. trustees Ann E. Cairns. 10th av, e s, 24.8 s 31st st, 19.5x100. Aug. 7, 3 years, 5 %. 10,000

Heermance Co., a corporation, to Robert Hewitt trustee. Greenwich st, Nos. 309–313; Reade st, Nos. 145–151. Leases and franchises, &c. Secures bonds. July 1, installs. 35,000

Hamman, Annie to Bernheimer & Schmid. 9th av, No. 56. Saloon lease. Aug. 10, note, demand. 1,000

Hawkes, Henry, Greenwich, Conn., to Timothy Flood and Edward Fredrich. 131st st, Nos. 23 and 25, n s, 285 w 5th av, 50x99.11. Sub. to morts. Aug. 1, due Sept. 1, 1891, or sooner. 9,543

Hartfield, William and Abraham Nelson to Mary A. Neacy. Hester and Mulberry sts. P. M. July 31, due Aug. 1, 1892, or sooner, 5 %. 15,000

Hawley, Rinaldo W., Sylcauga, Ala., to Rinaldo W. Hawley trustees for Fred M. and Frank L. Hawley. 12th av, w s, 75.11 n 102d st, 25x100 to exterior line. June 20, 1 year. 5 %. 1,000

Hawley, John S., Brick Church, N. J., and Herman W. Hoops to THE IRVING SAVINGS INSTITUTION. Mulberry st, s w cor Jersey st, 72x225.4x64.10x214.11; Mulberry st, w s, bet Prince and Houston sts, 26.9x35.7x41.8x 84.6, adj land of trustees Lying-in Hospital; Marion st, e s, 140 n Prince st, 65x84.6x53x 88. Aug. 8, 1 year, 4½ %. 100,000

Henry, John A. to THE UNION SAVINGS BANK of Westchester County, Mamaroneck, N. Y. 5th st, s s, 100 w Washington av, 50x100. Aug. 8, 1 year. 3,000

Johnston, Emeline wife of and William H. to John M. Scribner guard. of Mary and Elizabeth Scribner. 104th st. P. M. July 15, 3 years, 5 %. 14,000

Kelly, John to Mount Sinai Lodge No. 135 of the Independent Order Odd Fellows. 76th st, s s, 100 w Av A, 25x102.2. Aug. 11, 1 year, 5 %. 3,000

Kouba, Emil to T[illegible] GREENWICH SAVINGS BANK. 7th av, [illegible] 22 s 15th st, 22x100. Aug. 10, due Aug. 1, 1[illegible], 5 %. 3,000

Kerrigan, John P. [illegible] Bridget Curry. Central av. P. M. July [illegible], due Aug. 12, 1894, or sooner, 5 %. 1,000

Kiwi, Ernestine wife of and Joseph to Jacob A. Geissenhainer and ano. trustees Henry Elsworth dec'd. Essex st. P. M. Aug. 13, 5 years, 5 %. 20,000

Levy, Mitchell A. C. to Frederic J. Middlebrook, Brooklyn. Horatio st. P. M. Aug. 12, 1 year. 10,000

Levett, Alexander to Jennie wife of and Robert H. Spriggs. Grand st, n s, 129.8 e Varick st, 66x83 to alley, x66x72. July 8, 2 years, 5 %. 5,000

Levison, Elizabeth R., Brooklyn, to THE NEW YORK LIFE INS. AND TRUST CO. Madison av, e s, 74.1 n 27th st, 24.8x100. Aug. 8, 3 years, 4½ %. 20,000

Lange, Frederick to The Tremont Building and Loan Assoc. Marion av, e s, 75.3 s Rockfield st, 25.1x108.2x25x110. Aug. 8, installs. 2,000

Lazarus, Sarah, Josephine, Frank and Annie, and Agnes wife of Montague Marks, and Mary wife of Leopold Lindau to Franklin N. Billings, Woodstock, Vt. Broadway, n w cor Exchange alley, x28.6x203.7 to Trinity pl, x28.5x202.4; Liberty st, Nos. 95 and 97, n s, 237.9 w Broadway, runs north 48.4 x north 53.7 x north 16.8 x west 30 x south 119 to Liberty st, x east 30; 14th st, n s, 100 e 10th av, runs north 103.3 x east 50 x north — to 15th st, x east 100 x south — to 14th st, x west 150 to beginning; Harrison st, Nos. 34, 36 and 38, n e cor Washington st, 60.5x50x60.9x50. July 1, 6 years, 4 %. gold, 290,000

Leahy, Gregory to Bingham Bros. 98th st, n s, 375 e 9th av, 25x100.11. Aug. 5, 3 months. 677

Lowinstamm, Julius to Jacob Smalls. 3d av, No. 1674, w s, 25.5 s 94th st, 26x100. June 3, 1 year, 5 %. 1,000

Lynch, Franklin to The William R. Beal Land Improvement Co. Beekman av. P. M. July 8, 3 years, 5 %. 1,400

Lee, William W., Wilkesbarre, Pa., heir and devisee of Andrew Lee to William C. Price committee of Minnie Lee. 58th st, No. 132, s s, 316.8 w 6th av, 16.8x100.5. ⅜ part. July 30, 3 years. 2,500

Martin, William C. to Charles G. Martin. 2d av, w s, 26 n 99th st, 3 lots. 3 P. M. morts., each $2,000. Aug. 7, 6 months. 6,000

McGuiness, Edward to George E. Hyatt, Brooklyn. 85th st, s s, 225 e 3d av, 49.10x102.2. Aug. 4, due Jan. 1, 1892, or sooner. 2,000

Metzler, John H. and Annie M. his wife to Magdalena Schulze. Fairmount pl, n s, 450 w Marmion av, 20x100. Aug. 7, due July 25, 1894. 1,500

Metzler, John H. to John J. Brady. Elsmere pl, s s, 202.4 e Prospect av, 20x100. Aug. 6, due July 1, 1894, 5 %. 2,000

Muller, Michael to Bernheimer & Schmid. 1st av, No. 1549. Saloon lease. Aug. 8, note, demand. 4,000

Mars, Henrietta A., Brooklyn, to Lewis S. Marx. Willow st, n s, lots 2, 3 and 4 map of East Morrisania, lying east of the branch R. R., part of farm of Gouverneur Morris, contains 6 72-100 acres. Aug. 7, note. 500

McGirr, Robert J. to William Hall's Sons. 84th st, s s, 91 e Amsterdam av, 84x102.2. July 8, due Dec. 1, 1891, or sooner. 10,000

Michel, Katharina to George Schwegler. Park av. P. M. Aug. 10, 5 years, 5 %. 12,000

Myles, Andrew, Brooklyn, to Henry P. O'Farrell, Brooklyn. 17th st, n s, 100 e 9th av, 25x92. Sub. to mort. $5,500. July 31, due Feb. 1, 1893, without interest. 1,000

Mairs, William H., Brooklyn, to James Phelan, San Francisco, Cal. Broadway and Morris st. P. M. July 17, due Aug. 12, 1893, or sooner, 5½ %. 460,000

Mansfield, William to A. Hupfel's Sons. 3d av, No. 2995, n w cor 154th st. Lease. Aug. 4, note, demand. 2,800

Meier, Charles to Bertha Cohn. Av A and 74th st. P. M. Aug. 11, 5 years, 5 %. 8,000

McCormick, Michael and Henry Madden, of McCormick & Madden, to Margaret T. Nally. 26th st, Nos. 334 and 336, s s, 125 w 1st av, 50x98.9. Sub. to mort. $53,441. Aug. 8, 6 months. 1,000.

Michel, John N. to Anthony W. Miller. 39th st. P. M. Aug. 11, due Feb. 12, 1893, 5½ %. 4,000

Molyneeux, Wilbur L. to William R. Beal Land Improvement Co. Oak terrace. P. M. July 8, 3 years, 5 %. 1,200

Mulvihill, Cornelius J. to Steffen Dieckmann, Hoboken, N. J. 75th st, n s, 223 e Av A, 5 lots, together in size 125x95.7x126.8x116.5. 5 morts., each $12,000. Aug. 11, 3 years, 5 %. 60,000

Same to same. Same property. 5 morts., each $2,000. Each sub. to prior mort. $12,000. Aug. 11, 1 year. 10,000

Miller, Sarah J. wife of Charles, Jr., to Vassar College, Poughkeepsie, N. Y. 19th st, No. 319, n s, 200 w 8th av, 21.4x92. Aug. 13, 3 years, 5 %. 11,000

Miller, Robert to The Franklin Savings Bank. 11th av, e s, 53.4 s 173d st, 21.8x100. Aug. 13, 1 year, 5 %. 7,000

Nolan, John J. to Frank D. Carley, Tuxedo, N. Y., and Daniel G. Brown, Newburg, N.Y. Intervale av, w s, 293.10 n Westchester av, 50x100. June 16, 5 years or sooner, 5 %. 1,000

Newton, John H. to Jeremiah G. Tracy, Plainfield, N. J. Washington st. P. M. Aug. 7, 6 months, 5 %. 7,500

Norman, John A. to William R. Beal Land Improvement Co. Beekman av. P. M. July 8, 3 years, 5 %. 800

Nagel, Frederick, Sing Sing, N. Y., to Reginald P. B. Johnson. Morris av, n w cor 183d st, 150x106.9x150x108.8. Aug. 1, 1 year, 5 %. 5,000

O'Donelau, James to W. F. Fisher & Co, Sayreville, N. J., a corporation. 53d st, s s, 275 e 11th av, 125x100.5. Sub. to morts. $87,500. Aug. 11. 5,750

O'Donohue, Joseph J., Jr., to Alfred C. Clark guard. of Robert S. Clark. 73d st, s s, 188 e West End av, runs south 100 x east 12 x south 2.2 x east 7 x north 102.2 to st, x west 19. Aug. 10, due July 10, 1896, 4 %. 20,000

Ogden, Charles D. to Annie S. McCormick Prospect av. P. M. Aug. 10, 1 year, 5 % 1,450

O'Brien, Timothy to The Emigrant Indust. Savings Bank. Cherry st, n s, 243.4 e Market st, 19x72x19x72.5. Aug. 11, 1 year, 4½ %. 2,000

Pfob, William, Jr., to George Hewlett, Great Neck, L. I. Kingsbridge and West Farms road, w s, 75 n Madison av, 50x145x42x119, except part taken for widening 3d av. July 28, 5 years 5,500

Same to John A. Knox. Same property. Sub. to last mort. July 28, 5 years, 5 %. 4,500

Pier, Gordon to Fredericke Mayer. 69th st, n s, 125 w West End av. P. M. Aug. 4, due Sept. 1, 1892. 3,365

Same to same. 69th st, n s, 175 w West End av. P. M. Aug. 4, due Sept. 1, 1892. 4,805

Same to same. 69th st, n s, 200 w West End av. P. M. Aug. 4, due Sept. 1, 1892. 4,805

Post, Andrew J., Jersey City, N. J., and William H. McCord to William R. Beal Land Improvement Co. Beech terrace, Oak terrace and Crimmins av. P. M. July 8, 3 years, 5 %. 10,900

Pandolfi, Gaetano to Bernheimer & Schmid. 107th st, No. 301 E. Saloon lease. June 4, demand 600

Prehn, John to Peter Doelger. Broome st, No. 278. Saloon lease. Aug. 13, demand 5,000

Quinn, William to John Quinn. 132d st, s s, 385 w 5th av, 60x99.11. All title. July 1, 6 months, 5 % 500

Queripel, Adaline to The Title Guarantee and Trust Co. 156th st, s s, 150 w Courtlandt av, 50x100. Aug. 10, 3 years. 2,500

Regan, Annie wife and James to Daniel Regan. 124th st, No. 60, n s, 178 w 4th av, 17x100.11. Aug. 10, 3 years. 5 %. 5,000

Rosenbaum, Louis to Marks Cohn. Av B, w s, 40.2 s 6th st, 47.1x69.6x abt 18x60.1. P. M. May 1, installs. 3,000

Roe, Elizabeth L. wife of and Andrew J. to Alfred J. Taylor trustee for Kathleen K. Taylor. Sedgwick av, w s, 150 n from n s of a proposed st, 20 ft. wide, extending westward from said av and monumented, 50.3x79.7x50.7x76.8. July 24, due Aug. 1, 1894. 2,000

Raecke, Ludwig to Richard W. Buckley. 72d st. P. M. Aug. 12, installs, 5 %. 14,000

Reilly, Elizabeth to Henrietta Cohn. 146th st, No. 719, n s, 265 w Brook av, 25x100. Aug. 7, 3 years, 5 % 5,000

Rohrs, Frederick to Edward M. Scudder. 108th st, n s, 175 e 5th av, 95x100.9. Sub. to mort $21,000. Aug. 11, 1 year. 5,000

Same to Hewlett Scudder et al. trustees Henry J. Scudder dec'd. Same property. ½ part. P. M. July 24, 1 year, 5 %. 13,000

Same to Edward M. Scudder. 134th st, n s, 175 w Alexander av, 25x200 to 135th st. Aug. 11, 1 year. 2,500

Rosenthal, Louis M. to Henry Stoehr. 12th st. P. M. Aug. 13, 5 years or installs., 5 %. 7,000

Roessert, Emil to Frederick P. Hummel. 90th n s, 325 e 2d av. P. M. June 8, due Sept. 1, 1892, 5 % 2,500

Same to same. 90th st, n s, 300 e 2d av. P. M. June 8, due Sept. 1, 1892, 5 %. 2,500

Stadecker, Leopold and Jacob Emsheimer to Justus L. Bulkley et al. exrs. Daniel B. Fayerweather. Thompson st, Nos. 34-38, e s, 164.8 n Grand st, 61.10x94x61.10x94; South 5th av; Nos. 190-194, w s, 125.3 s Broome st, 59.5x68.7x59.5x68.3. July 27, due Nov. 1, 1894, 4½ %. 80,000

Skidmore, William to Martin J. Bickey and Ellen his wife. 52d st, s s, 555 w 11th av, 20 x100.5. All title. April 20, due May 1, 1896, 5 %. 1,100

Shaepering, Frederick to Sarah A. Hardy. Marion av, e s, 50.2 s Rockfield st, 25.1x110x25x112.3. Aug. 6, due Mar. 26, 1896. 350

Southworth, Diantha A., Rowena M. and Ellis B. to George R. Williams trustee John Southworth dec'd. 147th st, n e cor New Croton Aqueduct, 50x99.11. Aug. 7, 10 years or sooner, 5 %. 16,000

Sasse, John and Diedericke G. his wife to Louis Borstelmann. Spring st, No. 195, n s, 25 e Sullivan st, 21.3x75. Aug. 10, due July 1, 1896, 5 %. 4,000

Schreiner, Joseph to Lambert Suydam. 88th st. P. M. Aug. 7, due Sept. 1, 1892, or sooner. 36,000

Same to same. Same property. Aug. 7, due Sept. 1, 1892, or sooner. 39,000

Schneider, Joseph mortgagor with Eliza Wiener trustee of Pauline Sill mortgagee. Extension of mort. at reduced interest. Aug. 4. nom.

Scudder, Edward M. to William G. Peck, Greenwich, Conn. 108th st. P. M. July 24, 1 year, 5 %. 8,000

Smith, Du Bois to James Pyle. Laight st, s w cor Collister st. P. M. July 29, due Aug. 1, 1892, 5 %. 15,000

Tetedoux, Eliza J. mortgagor to Emmett J. Howell individ. and guard. of George W. Howell proposed assignee. Acknowledgment of notice of assignment and certificate as to amount due thereon. Aug. 7. nom

The Music Hall Co. of New York (Lim.) to The Bowery Savings Bank. 7th av, s e cor 57th st, runs south 175 x east 100 x south 25.10 to 56th st, x east 25 x north 100.10 x east 25 x north 100 to 57th st, x west 150 to beginning. June 26, 1 year. gold, 50,000

Thorn, William K., Newport, R. I., mortgagor with Edith N. Wharton mortgagee. Extension of reduced mortgage. Aug. 5. nom

Ueckermann, Marie to Lambert Suydam. 87th st, s s, abt 125 w 4th av, 50x98.4. Aug. 12, due Jan. 1, 1892. 9,000

Wallace, James to The Greenwich Savings Bank. 7th av, n w cor 49th st, 25x96. Aug. 12, due Aug. 1, 1894, 5 %. 35,000

Wyatt, Ida S. wife of and Harry to Carsten H. Meyer, Brooklyn. 93d st, n s, 268.9 w 9th av, 18.9x74.1 to Apthorps lane, x18.9x73.8, with all title in said lane, being a strip 18.9x18.4 Aug. 11, 6 months, 5 %. 3,000

Weisskopf, Moritz to Jacob Schlosser. 79th st. P. M. Aug. 1, installs. 2,700

Wheaton, Esther A. to David F., Annie and Louisa Kimberly. 65th st, n s. P. M. Aug. 25, 3 years or sooner, 4½ %. 23,000

Wanner, Julius to Frederick Folz. 147th st, n s, 225 e Brook av. P. M. Aug. 6, 3 years, 5 %. gold, 1,000

Same to same. 147th st, n s, 200 e Brook av. P. M. Aug. 6, 3 years, 5 %. gold, 1,000

Widmayer, William F. to George R. Lansing. 7th av, s e cor 23d st, runs east 175 x south 98.9 x west 50 x south 9.8 x west 25 x south 39.10 x west 100 to av, x north 148.1. Aug. 10, 3 years. 20,000

Zurleiden, Jacob and Fanny his wife to Lucas Glockner. 114th st, No. 237, n s, 175 w 2d av, 25x100.11. Aug. 8, due July 1, 1896, 5 %. 3,000

KINGS COUNTY.

August 6, 7, 8, 10, 11, 12.

Allen, John T and Nathaniel Proskey to Theresa A. Cannon. 4th st, n e s, 256.10 n w 5th av, 21x95 July 31, due Feb. 1, 1892. $800

Same to same. 4th st, n e s, 277.10 n w 8th av, 20x95 July 31, due Feb. 1, 1892. 2,200

Allan, John T. and Nathaniel Proskey to Watson & Pittinger. 6th st, n e s, 217.10 n w 5th av, 40x100. Aug. 6, notes. 1,800

Acor, Kate wife of and Lewis to Hannah K. wife of Garret D. Van Vranken, Hempstead, L. I. Jefferson av, n s, 235 e Stuyvesant av, 20x100. Aug. 12, due May 1, 1894, 5 %. 6,000

Allison, James to Clarence W. Birdsall. Conselyea st, s s, 125 w Ewen st, 25x100. Aug. 10, due July 1, 1894. 300

Anderson, Graham K. to Long Island Loan and Trust Co. Plot beginning at intersection s s land Franklin Allen and n w s land Bay Ridge Park Impt. Co., New Utrecht, runs southwest 1,087.1 x northeast 1,044.6 x east 107.4 to beginning, New Utrecht. May 13, due Feb. 6, 1894, 5 %. 130,000

Andrews, Archibald to Lucy P. Le Brun. Broadway, n s, 50 e Hooper st, 25x100. Aug. 10, 3 years, 5 %. 6,000

Baird, Henrietta wife of and John to Richard M. Wyckoff et al. exrs. John S. Andrews. Baltic av, n s, 75 e Henry av, 25x100. Aug. 10, 2 years. 500

Barker, Samuel to Henry C. Soap, Kingston, N. Y., and Frank M. Andrus, Roxburg, N. Y. Stone av, w s, 158 n Blake av, 25x100. Aug. 6, installs. 650

Battalora, Matilda wife of and Felix to Title Guarantee and Trust Co. Tompkins av, e s, 84 s Vernon av, 20.8x100. Aug. 6, 1 year, 5 %. 7,000

Bershatsky, Barnet to David Stern. Flushing av. P. M. Sub. to mort. $5,000. Aug. 5, 5 years or installs, 5 %. 3,000

Betts, Charles A. to Charles W. Betts. Fulton st, n s, 85.2 w Nostrand av, runs east 39.6 x north — x west to point 80 n Fulton st, x south 80, except strip 0.6 wide along w s of above. Feb. 13, due Sept. 1, 1891. 12,000

Birdsall, Anna E. wife of Henry D. to Millard F. Smith. Taylor st, No. 150, s e s, 184 n e Bedford av, 21x100. Aug. 4, 1 year. 600

Blaisdell, Julia A. to Lizzie Eckstein. New Utrecht av, n w cor 59th st, runs north 148 x west 110 x south 46.3 x southwest 43 to st, x east 143.6. Aug. 12, due July 1, 1892. 200

Bliss, Eliphalet W. to The Brooklyn Savings Bank. 1st av, w s, 82.6 n 66th st, runs west 200 x west 200 x south 112.6 to centre 66th st, x west 275.6 x west — x south — x east 1,337.6 to 1st av, x north 1,249.9. Aug. 5, due Aug. 6, 1892, 5 %. 50,000

Bliss, Clara J. to Morris H. Dillenbeck. 5th av, n s, 60 e 3d st, 20x75. Aug. 6, 2 years. 300

Bienenstein, Margaretha to August Sedlineir. Suydam st, n w s, 200 s w Knickerbocker av, 25x100. Aug. 8, due Aug. 1, 1896, 5 %. 2,200

Bormann, Charles A. to Eleonora I. Decker. St. Marks av. P. M. July 16, 2 years. 800

Botengoff, Leon, New York, to William H. Wiecke. Bushwick av, w s, 80 n Seigel st, 20x100. P. M. Aug 6, 3 years, 5 %. 4,550

Bongartz, Elizabeth wife of and Adam. 3d av, n e cor 38th st, 40.2x100. Aug. 6, 1 year, 5 %. 1,300

Broach, John H. to Charles Small. McDonough st, n s, 205 w Tompkins av, 20x100. Aug. 11, 1 year. 1,600

Same to same. Same property. Aug. 11, due Aug. 1, 1896. 5,000

Brown, William to Frederick T. Hill trustee. 7th st, s s, 147.10 w 6th av, 225x100. Sub. to mort. $15,000. Aug. 5, 1 year. 3,500

Brown, Isabella wife of William to Frederick T. Hill trustee. 3d st, s s, 228.10 e 5th av, 22x190 to 4th st. Sub. to mort. $5,000. Aug. 11, 3 months. gold, 1,224

Buckley, Bridget wife of and George to Mary H. wife of David Anderson, Rockville Centre, L. I. Ormond st or pl. P. M. Aug. 10, 5 years, 5 %. 5,000

Burckett, Sarah W. wife of Charles F. Burckett to Frederick E. Pitkin exr. President st, s s, 132 w 8th av, 30x100. Aug. 10, 5 years. 6,000

Bullocke, Mary to Catharine E. L. Duryee. 2d av, w s, adj land of Mary Bullocke, 627.9 x342.8 to a lane, x661.6x344.11, New Utrecht. Aug. 5, 2 years. 8,000

Bush, Wesley C. to Henry Weil. St. Marks av, n s, 225 e Kingston av, 100x135.7. Aug. 8, 3 years. 10,000

Calder, Alexander G. to The Williamsburgh Savings Bank. 12th st, n e s, 137.10 s e 4th av. 8 lots, each 20x100. 8 morts., each $3,000. Aug. 4, 1 year, 5 %. 24,000

Campbell, Patrick to The Brooklyn Trust Co. Bergen st, n s, 100 w Grand av, 25x100. Aug. 8, 1 year, 5 %. 1,000

Campbell, Paul to Magdalena Ubres widow, Hart st, s s, 149.2 e Wyckoff av, 20x100. Aug 5, due July 1, 1896, 5 %. 1,800

Cohen, Joseph to Theresa Goodkind. Moore st. P. M. Aug. 1, installs. 940

Chauncey, George W. to The Title Guarantee and Trust Co. Liberty av, s e cor Bradford st, 100x100. Aug. 1, due Aug. 11, 1892, 5 %. 4,000

Cheeks, Orlando L. and William H. to The South Brooklyn Savings Inst. Hancock st, s s, 40 w Marcy av, 20x90. Aug. 6, 1 year, 5 %. 2,000

Cooper, Nicholas mortgagor with Silas Ludlam. Extension of mort. Aug. 6. nom

Cropsey, James to Jane E. Cropsey, Hillsborough, N. J. Bath av, west cor Bay 35th st, 165.4x201.3x165.3x250.4, New Utrecht. Aug. 6, 1 year. 1,500

De Revere, John J. to Elias J. Hendrickson. McDonough st, 300 w Stuyvesant av. P. M. Aug 3, due Nov. 1, 1894, 5 %. 6,000

Same to same McDonough st, 280 w Stuyvesant av. P. M. Aug. 3, due Nov. 1, 1894, 5 %. 6,000

Same to Phebe Ryan. McDonough st, 300 w Stuyvesant av. P. M. Sub. to mort. $6,000. Aug. 3, due Aug. 1, 1893. 1,500

Same to same. McDonough st, 280 w Stuyvesant av. P. M. Sub. to mort. $6,000. Aug. 3, due Aug. 5, 1893. 1,500

Dervan, Peter to Jennie V. Wilbur. Schenectady av, w s, 207 s Montgomery st, 50x100. July 15, due July 1, 1893, 5 %. 200

De Zavala, Gertrude C. to Francis E. Dana. Monroe st, n s, 231.4 e Throop av, 19.4x100. Aug. 1, demand. 1,000

Diehl, Jr., William to Thomas Marchant. Bradford st, s e cor Arlington av, 25x100. Aug. 8, 3 years, 5 %. 3,000

Dietze, Emil to Elizabeth E. Howard. Sumpter st. P. M. July 30, 5 years. 1,000

Dinerstein, Abraham to Emma Quinn. Sackman st. P. M. Aug. 6, 2 years. 1,100

Donaldson, Marie I. to Rachel M. Gilsey and ano. exrs. John C. C. Gilsey. Park av, s s, 81.6 e Prince st, 25.2x127.8. Aug. 4, 5 years. 1,600

Donelson, John to Lydia Brooke. Schenectady av. P. M. July 27, due Jan. 1, 1893. 500

Dowley, Mary H. to A. S. Nichols & Co. Macon st, n s, 185 w Howard av, 18x100. Aug. 7, due Feb. 7, 1892, 5 %. 550

Dreyer, Richard to Eburn F. Haight. Cornelia st, s e s, 35 s w Evergreen av, 140x100. Sub. to mort. $22,400. Aug. 10, 1 year, 5 %. 10,500

Same to The Williamsburgh Savings Bank. Same property. 7 morts., each $3,200. Aug. 10, 1 year, 5 % 22,400

Same to same. Cornelia av, south cor Evergreen av, 35x100. Aug. 10, 1 year, 5 %. 7,000

Dubroff, Abraham to Mary E. Cook, Newtown, L. I. Watkins st. P. M. Aug. 5, installs. 700

Dubroff, Solomon to same. Watkins st. P. M. Aug. 5, installs. 400

Driggs, Emily L. M. wife of and Edmund to The Orphan Asylum Society, Brooklyn. Ocean av, w s, 275 s Av A, 60.3x160.9x113.9x 151.7, Flatbush. Aug. 1, 3 years, 5 %. 4,500

Eastment, Jennie to A. Stewart Walsh. Quincy st, s s, 300 e Patchen av. P. M. June 10, 5 years, 5 %. 2,000

Same to same. Same property. Aug. 10, due Nov. 1, 1891. 500

Elizabeth, Grace and Maria Rawlins to Broadway Dry Goods Co-operative Building and Loan Assoc. Kosciusko st. P. M. Aug. 11, installs. 3,000

Egelhoff, Louise to John W. Moran. 5th av, n w s, 62 s w 2d st, 28x81.10. Aug. 6, 3 years or installs, 5 %. 3,500

Eisenberg, Louis and Joseph and Marsey Rosenblum to Paul W. Lecoux. Sackman av. P. M. July 29, due Aug. 1, 1894. 600

Ennis, Eliza to Stephen C. Halstead. Baltic st, s s, 166 4 w Clinton st, 24.6x100. Aug. 8, 2 years. 500

Fagan, Mary A. to Louisa A. Crane. 11th av, s e cor 61st st, 75x100. June 16, due Dec. 12, 1891, 5 %. 400

Farrell, James to Ann McGuigan. Dean st, n s, 435 w Franklin av, 20x110. Aug. 10, 2 years, 4 %. 1,000

Fassnacht, William to Michael Seitz. Bushwick av, n e cor McKibbin st, 28x98.9x26.7x 100. Aug. 8, 3 years, 5 %. 1,100

Ficken, John H. to Hermann Ficken. Lewis av, n w cor Monroe st. P. M. Aug. 3, due Aug. 6, 1894, 5 %. 3,000

Ficker, Anna to Lillie Cohen. Greene av. P. M. Aug. 1, installs, 5 %. 1,500

Fitzsimmons, Owen to The Greenpoint Savings Bank. Van Cott av, n e cor Leonard st, 24 10 x 80.3x45.2x70.11. Aug. 8, 1 year, 5½ %. 1,000

Fleck, Joseph to Peter Doelger. Leonard st, w s, 75 s Calyer st, 21.3x80. Aug. 8, 5 years, 5 %. 3,000

Same to same. Leonard st, w s, 103 s Calyer st, 22x100. Aug. 8, 5 years, 5 %. 2,000

Flint, John to A. E. Sumner. Cleveland st, e s, 246.10 n Atlantic av, 50x100. Aug. 7, 1 month. 3,000

Fowler, Mary E. wife of and Levi to A. M. Sweet & Son. St. Marks av, n s, 320 e Franklin av, 20x128 6. July 31, 1 year or sooner, 5 %. 7,500

Francis, George S. to John Hanley. 75th st, n s, 426 w 18th av, 40x100, New Utrecht. Aug. 3, installs. 285

Franck, Carl to Abbie J. and Sarah A. Dillworth. Stanhope st, n w s, 100 s w Evergreen av, 18.9x100. Aug. 10, 1 year. 5 %. 600

Same to Anna C. Fleischmann. Same property. Aug. 10. 5 years, 5 %. 2,500

Fraser, John to Harlan P. Halsey. McDonough st, n s, 400 e Tompkins av, 28x120; Macon st, s s, 200 e Tompkins av, 13x80. July 10, due July 25, 1893, 5 %. 7,000

Freeman, Hilton R. to James D. Lynch. 84th st, New Utrecht. P. M. 3d mort. July 28, due Nov. 1, 1891. 750

Same to Frank D. Carley and Daniel G. Brown. Same property. Aug. 7, due April 7, 1893, installs, 5 %. 1,000

Same to same. Same property. Aug. 7, 3 years, 5 %. 2,000

Friel, Bridget to Henry Krudener. Partition st, w s, 200 s Conover st, 25x100. May 4, 3 years, 5 %. 1,400

Gallagher, John to Cornelius Gallagher. 36th st, s w s, 310 s e 3d av, 75x100. July 22, 3 years, 5 %. 2,400

Gleason, Lousiana I. to George B. Stoutenburg. Decatur st. P. M. Aug. 10, due Aug. 31, 1894. 1,125

Golman, Abraham and Harris Levy to Herman F. Koepke. Sackman st. P. M. Aug. 11, 3 years. 888

Gore, Calvin and Rachel A. wife of and Nicholas B. Hooper, of Hooper & Gore, to Seaman L. Pettit, Hempstead. Ellery st, s s 225 w Marcy av, 150x100. Aug. 22, 1 year. 4,000

Greene, Julia S. wife of and J. Warren to Samuel T. Valentine et al. trustees Stephen Valentine dec'd. Willow st, w s, 25 s Orange st, 25x100.6. Aug. 1, 3 years, 5 %. 5,000

Greenman, Isaac to Ann E. Sullivan. Stone av, w s, 125 s Livonia av. P. M. Aug. 1, 5 years or installs. 415

Same to Patrick Mulligan. Stone av, w s, 75 s Livonia av. P. M. Aug. 1, 5 years or installs. 358

Same to John F. Sullivan. Stone av, w s, 100 s Livonia av. P. M. Aug. 1, 5 years or installs. 358

Haag, Fredericke widow, Anna M. and Anton F. to Peter Kaufmann, Dobbs Ferry, N. Y. Elm st, n s, 400.4 e Evergreen av, runs north 87 x west 0.4 x north 58 x east 25 x south 95 x west 24.8 to beginning. Security for bond. Aug. 6 2,000

Hagen, Winston H. to Elihu Thomson, Lynn, Mass. Hancock st, n s, 245 e Sumner av, 20x 100. July 15, due July 31, 1896, 5 %. 6,500

Same to same. Hancock st, 265 e Sumner av, 20x100. July 15, due July 31, 1896, 5 %. 6,500

Hahn, Andrew and Christian to David Springsteen, Newtown, L. I. Harman st, s e s, 250 n e Central av, 25x100. Aug. 8, 3 years, 5 %. 3,500

Same to Zariah W. Monfort. Harman st, s e s, 275 n e Central av, 25x100. Aug. 8, 3 years, 5 %. 3,500

Same to same. Harman st, s e s, 200 n e Central av, 2 lots, each 25x100. 2 morts., each $3,500. Aug. 8, 3 years, 5 %. 7,000

Same to Cornelia M. Covert trustee Helena Covert dec'd. Harman st, s e s, 100 n e Central av, 4 lots, each 25x100. 4 morts., each $3,500. Aug. 8, 3 years, 5 %. 14,000

Halstead, Stephen C. to Lemmy A. Halstead et al. exrs. Stephen Halstead. 2d av, s w cor 41st st, 25.2x100. Aug. 5, 3 years, 5 %. 1,500

Hanes, Nathan to Stephen C. Halstead. 2d av, n s, 178.6 e Shore road, 60x100, New Utrecht. Aug. 7, 1 year. 300

Harden, Harriet to Caroline Eeverit. Ridgewood av, s s, 60 w Linwood st, 20x100. July 25, due Aug. 1, 1891, 5½ %. 1,150

Hay, George T. to Charles S. Whitney and ano. exrs. James F. Whitney. 1st pl, n s, 265 e Clinton st, 25x100. Aug. 1, 1 year. 1,000

Harrington, John J. to The Bushwick Co-operative Building and Loan Assoc. Powers st, n s, 150 w Ewen st, 25x100. Aug. 4, installs. 1,000

Harris, George to Edward S. McVey. North 6th st, n s, 275 e Havemeyer st, 25x100. Aug. 1, 1 year. 175

Harris, Isaac to Ann E. Sullivan. Watkins st. P. M. Aug. 3, 5 years or installs. 2,100

Hemmer, Margaretha to Albert G. Baker. Hopkinson av. P. M. Aug. 7, 2 years. 718

Hendrickson, Hannah M. to Hendrica B. Ryder exr. Jason B. Hendrickson. Jefferson av, n s, 101 w Franklin av, 21x100. May 1, 1 year, 5 %. 500

Holland, Frank H. to Effingham H. Nichols, New York. Lots 489–493 and 525–527 block 11 map No. 1. &c., Cowenhoven farm, New Utrecht. July 22, 2 years, 5 %. 1,070

Hood, Sarah L and Joseph to Ordon K. Powell. Gold st, w s, 75 n Prospect st, 22x75. July 24, 1 year. 1,000

Same to same. Smith st, s e s, 94.5 s w Livingston st, 19.4x100. July 24, 1 year. 1,000

How, Phoebe to Rulef J. Van Brunt. 21 av, n e cor 82d st, New Utrecht. P. M. Aug. 4, due Aug. 1, 1894, 5 %. 1,000

Hughes, Catharine to the Abbott Brewing Co. Underhill av, n w cor Dean st. Saloon lease. July 30, demand. 500

Hullgren, Annie E. to Harriet E. Dunn. 54th st, s w s, 350 n w 3d av, 20x100.2. Aug. 7, 2 years. 600

Hymes, Margaret to Maria Heinstadt. Hamburg av. P. M. Aug. 10, 5 years, 5 %. 1,900

Ilsemann, Louis to Elizabeth J. King. Ashford st, e s, 213.7 n Atlantic av, 3 lots, together in size 50x100. 3 morts., each $1,700. Aug. 7, due Aug. 1, 1894. 5,100

Jeandheur, Frederic C. to Mary E. Corley, Newburg, N. Y. Stagg st, s s, 100 e Union av, 25 x100. Aug. 1, 5 years, 5 %. 6,000

Jahr, Josephine to Edward J. D. Barnett. Johnson st, s s, 340.9 e Gardner av. runs east 132.2 x southeast 84.1 to Flushing av, x southwest 125.9 x northwest 89.11 x north 30.2 to beginning. July 28, 5 years, 5 %. 5,500

Johnson, J. Christian and Mary his wife to Avery T. Brown and William W. Starr, Jr. trustees Abraham Lockwood. Eldert st, n w s, 195 s w Evergreen av, 20x100. Aug. 1, 3 years, 5 %. 3,000

Same to same. Eldert st, n w s, 155 s w Evergreen av, 20x100. Aug. 1, 3 years, 5 %. 4,000

Johnson, J. Christian to Phebe E. Valentine, Queens, L. I. Eldert st, n s, 175 w Evergreen av, 20x100. Error. Aug. 10, 5 %. 4,000

Same to Virginia A. Kleine. Eldert st, n w s, 95 s w Evergreen av, 100x140. Aug. 10, demand. 20,000

Kearney, James to Mary R. Bennett. 3d st, s e cor Hoyt st, 84x190.9 to 4th st. Aug. 6, 3 years. 28,500

Same to Robert P. Jacoby, Newport News, Va. Same property. Aug. 6, 2 years. 14,845

Same to William H. Nafis. Same property. Aug. 6, 2 years. 1,688

King, Mary R. wife of Albert B. to Sarah E. Fisher, Dean st. P. M. Aug. 1, due Aug. 7, 1894, 5 %. 8,000

King, Mary R. to Parke Godwin, N. Y. Willoughby av, n s, 165 w Tompkins av, 20 x 100. Aug. 1, 5 years, 5 %. 3,500

Krueger, Edward to Marie Wallach. Woodbine st. P. M. Aug. 11, 5 years, 5 %. 3,000

Lachmann, Emil to Peter Kelly. Degraw st. P. M. Aug. 8, 1 year, 5 %. 1,000

Laing, Donald to William A. Cook. Glenmore av, s s, 60 w Milford st, 20x90. July 10, 3 years. 2,000

Lang, Sarah to Adolph Sussman. Cleveland st. P. M. July 23, 3 years, 5 %. 150

Lavin, Edward to William T. Welp. Otsego and Greene sts, Monticello and Delavan sts. P. M. Aug. 11, 3 years. 2,500

Lawrence, Peter E to Jacob T. Van Siclen. Hale av, e s, 124.10 s Ridgewood av, 24x101. Aug. 7, 3 years. 800

Lieberenz, Albert G. to James Livingston. Glenmore av. P. M. Aug. 8, 5 years, 5½ %. 1,500

Lieder, William J. A. to Barbara Schuch. Myrtle av, s s, 150 w Sumner av, 150x100. Aug. 4, 1 year. 1,000

Lott, Moe S. to Mary E. Bennett, Mackay pl, s s, 150 e River road, 50x90x50x95, New Utrecht. Aug. 1, 5 years. 3,000

Lowe, Robert to Edward Sutcliff. Montauk av, e s, 150 n Eastern Parkway, 40x100. July 1, 1 year. 500

Lyons, Henry B. to Margaret wife of John F. Berry. Berkeley pl, s w s, 123.4 s e 5th av, 18.1x95. Aug. 6, 3 years, 5 %. 5,500

Same to same. Berkeley pl, s w s, 105.3 s e 5th av, 18.1x95. Aug. 6, 3 years, 5 %. 5,500

Same to Lawrence V. Cortelyou and Caroline A. Rushmore. Berkeley pl, s w s, 87.2 s e 5th av, 18.1x95. Aug. 6, 3 years, 5 %. 5,500

MacDonald, Ranald H. to Archibald G. King trustee, Weehawken, N. J. 2d pl, n s, 120 w Clinton st, 23.4x133.5. Aug. 5, due Aug. 1, 1896, 5 %. 6,000

Madn, Louis to Julia W. Latimer. Vernon av, s s, 168 w Throop av, 32x100. Aug. 6, 3 years, 5 %. 9,500

Same to Mary E. Peck. Same property. Aug. 6, 1 year. 3,200

Malton, Peter to Anna J. Lockwood. Willoughby st, n s, 72.9 w Prince st, runs west 24.6 x north 78.4 x northeast 25 x east 10.7 x south 100 to beginning. Aug. 5, 2 years, 5 %. 3,500

Manheim, Julius to John S. O'Connor, White Mills, Pa. Van Cott av, n e cor Manhattan av. P. M. Aug. 10, 3 years, 5 %. 4,250

Same to Seventeenth Ward Bank. Manhattan av, n e cor Van Cott av, 115.10x203.6x87 11x 203.6. Aug. 10, note. 3,500

Marcus, Meyer and Baruch Seerman to Mary W. Smith. Eastern Parkway, s s, 25 e Thatford av, 25x100. Aug. 5, 3 months. 1,000

Maguire, Catherine F. wife of and John to Earl A. Gillespie, Woodhaven, L. I. Pennsylvania av, w s, 150 s Glenmore av. Aug. 4, due Nov. 1, 1891. 325

Matthews, Susan wife of and Owen to Theodore L. Lutkins, Jr. Pacific st, s s, 140 e New York av, 20x100. Aug. 10, due Aug. 11, 1893, 5 %. 4,000

Max, Harris to James G. Roberts. Sackman st, w s, 100 s Eastern Parkway. Aug. 5, 2 years. 700

McCall, Mary M. to Jennie V. Wilbur. 48th st, n e s, 250 n w 12th av, 50x100.2. Aug. 6, 3 years. 2,000

McClenahan Jane to The Title Guarantee and Trust Co. Dean st, n s, 340 e 4th av, 2 lots, each 40x80, 2 morts., each $2,000. Aug. 6, 3 years, 5 %. 4,000

McCormick, Mary J. wife of James H. to Louis Folkes. Greene av. P. M. Aug. 5, 1 year, or on execution of release of dower by Johanne wife of said Louis Folkes. 500

McConville, John J. to Margaret L. Deraismes, New York. Devoe st. P. M. Aug. 10, 3 years, 5 %. 2,500

McKenna, Margaret wife of and Matthew to The Title Guarantee and Trust Co. South 8th st, s s, 69 w Driggs st, 23x100. Aug. 7, 1 year, 5 %. 4,000

McNulty, Peter H. to William J. Gaynor trustees Andrew McClennan. Atlantic av, s w s, 220.6 s e Flatbush av, 2 lots. 2 morts., each $5,750. P. M. Aug. 10, due Sept. 1, 1894, 5 %. 11,500

Mercle, Henry and Sarah J. Pirsson mortgagors with William Banta mortgagee. Extension of mort. July 17. nom

Meserole, George H. to Louisa C. Spencer. Fennimore st, n s, 245 e Rogers av, 20x100. April 8, 3 years. 450

Metz, Adam to Caroline Broistedt. Bleecker st, n s, 300 w Central av, 25x100. Aug. 5, 5 years, 5 %. 3,500

Miller, Mary E. to Carsten H. Meyer. 7th st, n s, 297.6 e 4th av, 3 lots, together 50.4x100. 3 morts., each $4,000. Aug. 6, 3 years. 12,000

Monsees, John to Clark T. Hamilton. Bergen st, n s, 170 11 w Rockaway av, 14.5x107.2. Aug. 11, 1 year. 300

Moses, Charles H. and Henry B. Fanton, Jr., to William L. Dowling. 4th st, s s, 97.10 e 6th av, 74x100; 4th st, s s, 157.10 w 7th av, 4x 100. Aug. 7, demand. 36,000

Mueller, William C. H. to The German Savings Bank, Brooklyn. Havemeyer st, e s, 51 n South 4th st, runs east 47 x north 15 x east 33 x north 5 x west 80 to st, x south 20. Aug. 6, due Dec. 1, 1892, 5 %. 5,000

Mullowney, Richard to Edwin Booth, Boston. Halsey st, s w cor Ralph av, 22x100. Aug. 5, due July 1, 1894, 5 %. 18,000

Same to same. Halsey st, s s, 22 w Ralph av, 6 lots, each 18x100. 6 morts., each $4,000. Aug. 5, due July 1, 1894, 5 %. 24,000

Same to trustee of the Sustentation Fund of the Reformed Episcopal Church, &c. Halsey st, s s, 130 w Ralph av, 18x100. Aug. 5, due July 1, 1894, 5 %. 4,000

Same to same. Halsey st, s s, 148 w Ralph av, 18x100. Aug. 5, due July 1, 1894, 5 %. 4,000

Same to The Metropolitan Life Ins. Co. New York. Halsey st, s s, 166 w Ralph av, 17x100. Aug. 5, due Oct. 1, 1894, 5 %. 4,000

Same to same. Halsey st, s s, 183 w Ralph av, 17x100. Aug. 5, due Oct. 1, 1894, 5 %. 4,000

Same to James L. Ross. Halsey st, s s, 58 w Ralph av, 18x100. Sub. to mort. $4,000. Aug. 7, 1 year. 1,000

Same to same. Halsey st, s s, 76 w Ralph av, 18x100. Sub. to mort. $4,000. Aug. 7, 1 year. 4,000

Mullowney, Richard to James D. Rankin and James Ross. Halsey st, s s, 112 w Ralph av, 3 lots, each 18x100. 3 morts., each $1,000. Sub. to mort. of $4,000 on each. Aug. 7, 1 year. 3,000

Mullowney, Richard to James D. Rankin and James Ross. Halsey st, s s, 166 w Ralph av, 17x100. Sub. to mort. $4,000. Aug. 7, 1 year. 1,000

Munson, Emily M. wife of and Walter D. to Amelia Smith, Yaphank, L. I. Throop av, e s, 56 n Lexington av, 18x100. Aug. 8, due Aug. 10, 1894, 5 %. 3,000

Nash, Richard to George J. Weybrecht. 10th st, n s, 273.4 e 8th av, 19.6x92.6. Aug. 6, due July 1, 1901, 5 %. 4,000

New York Building Loan Banking Co., of New York, to Hyde & Gload Mfg. Co. Covert st, n w s, 239 n e Evergreen av, 18x100. July 31, due Aug. 1, 1896, or sooner, 5 %. 750

Nicholson, John to Effingham H. Nichols, N. Y. Lots 243 and 245–249 block 5 map No.

1, &c., Cowenhoven farm, New Utrecht. July 22, 2 years, 5 %. 600

Noll, Frederick to Nicolaus Schoendorf. Bartlett st, No. 55. P. M. Aug. 7, 9 years, 5 %. 4,500

Obenauer, Carrie B. wife of and Robert H. to Katie Nicklaus. Linwood st, w s, 150 s Blake av, 25x90. Aug. 4, 5 years or sooner, 5 %. 1,350

O'Connell, John J. to William T. Trim. 50th st, s s, 250 w 6th av, 25x100.2. July 25, 2 years. 900

Olsen, Arndt H. to Harriet E. Dunn. 52d st. P. M. Aug. 3, 3 years. 1,500

Same to Maren Lee and Hans Hanson. Same property. Aug. 3, installs, 5 %. 1,300

Parmer, Ada wife of Lewis to Mary W. Smith. Watkins st, w s, 100 s Eastern Parkway, 51.6 x100. Aug. 11, demand. 225

Phillips, Ellen T. to Julia A. Smith. Hawthorne st, s s, on line which at n s of Winthrop st is 2,905.7 e of Flatbush av, 50x106, Flatbush. Aug. 10, 5 years. 1,600

Prentiss, Jennie to William W. Walsh and ano. exrs. and trustees of Edward Clarke dec'd. Carroll st, n s, 99 w Court st, 22x100. June 1, 1 year, 5 %. 4,500

Pritchard, James to William E. Rabell, Emily A. Stanley and Angelina M. Horton. Throop av, n e cor Van Buren st, 50x100. Aug. 5, due Aug. 1, 1894, 5 %. 7,500

Rassinge, Henry to The Kings County Savings Inst. North Henry st. P. M. July 1, 1 year, 5 %. 1,750

Same to Charles Engert. North Henry st. P. M. Sub. to mort. $1,750. Aug. 1, installs, 5 %. 1,250

Ray, Alexander to Serial Building Loan and Savings Inst. Bergen st, s s, 250 w Hopkinson av, 25x127.9. Aug. 7, installs. 600

Reichart, Sarah to The Williamsburgh Savings Bank. Tompkins av, e s, 40 n Floyd st, 20x100. Aug. 7, 1 year, 5 %. 3,000

Resnick, Joseph to David Stern. Flushing av. P. M. Sub. to mort. $5,000. Aug. 5, 5 years or installs. 5 %. 3,250

Reynolds, William W. to Charles Siedler, Morristown, N. J. Decatur st, s w cor Glenada pl, 85x100. Sub. to morts. Aug. 6, 3 months or sooner. 7,500

Reynolds, Charles G. to Marion S. wife of Henry A. Alderton. Ralph av. n e cor Decatur st, 22.6x100. Aug. 1, 3 years, 5 %. 10,000

Rhodes, George H. to Clark T. Hamilton. Bergen st, n s, 185.5 w Rockaway av, 14.7x 107.2. Aug. 11, 1 year. 800

Robbins, Thomas H. to Asa W. Frisbie, Willsborough, N. Y. St. Marks av, s s, 184 e Vanderbilt av, 16x131. May 21, installs. 800

Rowe, Frederick W. to George W. Douglas. Prospect av, n s, 273 w 3d av, 44.1x43x44x 47.10. Aug. 1, due Jan. 1, 1893. 1,000

Saddington, John F. mortgagor with Cornelius N. Hoagland. Extension of mort. Jan. 4. 1886. —

Scheling, Louis to James H. Rich. 6th av, Union st. P. M. June 8, due Aug. 6, 1894, 5 %. 8,000

Scherf, Adam to Freeman Clarkson and ano. trustees Eibe A. Steers Broadway centre line, at intersection with e s of Canarsie av, runs east to point 120 e Canarsie av, x north — x west 136.8 to av, x southeast —, Flatbush. Aug. 11, due Aug 1, 1894, 5 %. 500

Schlieper, Maggie wife of Charles G. to Joseph Neideregger. Linwood st. P. M. Aug. 5, installs, 5 % 450

Schlesinger, Adolph to Joseph Weidner. Ellery st. P. M. Aug. 4, 5 years, 5 %. 1,100

Schmall, George E. to Thomas H. Leggett trustee for W. L. Franklin. Atlantic av, s s, 150 e Saratoga av, 16.8x100. Aug. 11, 3 years, 5 %. 2,500

Schmitz, Henry E. to Philip Umstadter. Cleveland st, w s, 150 s Arlington av, 25x100. Aug. 8, due July 1, 1894, 5 %. 600

Schoenzeit, Harris to Barnet Frank and Simon Rose. Eastern Parkway. P. M. Aug. 3, installs. 525

Schreiber, Henry to Joseph Von Hatten. Bergen st, s s, 350 w Buffalo av, 25x100. Aug. 5, due July 1, 1894, 5 %. 1,200

Seidenbergh, Abraham and Rochmiel Abramovitz to Mary W. Smith. Livonia av, s e cor Osborn st, 20x100. Aug. 10, 3 months. 1,000

Solomon, Joseph and Hyman Goldberg to William H. Baker. Eastern Parkway, n s, 100 e Christopher av, 25x100. Aug. 1, 3 years. 3,000

Sosnovitch, Meyer to Louis Ratner. Thatford av. P. M. Sub. to mort. $3,000. Aug. 10, installs. 1,750

Spann, Frederick A. to Katie Kreppel. Central av. P. M. Aug. 8, 5 years or installs. 1,500

Same to Title Guarantee and Trust Co. Same property. Aug. 8, 5 years. 1,500

Spencer, Theodore to Martin Alletzhausser, Woodhaven, L. I. Market st, w s, 975 n Record pl, 25x150. Aug. 1, 5 years, 5 %. 1,600

Stearns, William G. to John A. L. Aimer and ano. trustees for Anne M. Vought. Elton st, w s, 263.5 n Atlantic av, 25x100. Aug. 7, 3 years. gold, 3,000

Stevens, Caroline to Hermann F. Krvoss. St. Marks av, n s, 208.9 e Carlton av, 16.3x131. Aug. 6, due Aug. 1, 1894, 5 %. 1,000

Stirling, Isabella to James J. Edwards. 4th av. P. M. Aug. 7, due Aug. 10, 1894, 5 %. 750

Striepecke, Carl A. F. to Emilie H. W. Behnken. Manhattan av. P. M. Aug. 10, 5 years, 5 %. 4,000

Studer, Mary to The Williamsburgh Savings Bank. Putnam av, s s, 182.6 w Tompkins av, 17.6x100. Aug. 7, 1 year, 5 %. 1,400

Sullivan, Cornelius A. to Cornelius Sullivan. Buffalo av, w s, 82.8 n Bergen st, 16.4x55. July 29, 10 years, 4 %. 1,800

Sullivan, Michael to John M. Stearns. Kingsland av, w s, 18 n Richardon st. P. M. Aug. 5, 3 years. 1,400

Same to same. Kingsland av, w s, 34 n Richardson st. P. M. Aug. 5, 3 years. 1,400

Same to same. Richardson st, n s, 80 w Kingsland av. P. M. Aug. 5, 3 years. 1,400

Same to same. Kingsland av, n w cor Richardson st. P. M. Aug. 5, 3 years. 2,000

Suydam, Annie A. to The South Brooklyn Savings Inst. 7th st, s s, 256.2 w 7th av, 16.8x 100. Aug. 11, 1 year, 5 %. 3,000

Sumner, William O. to Edward M. Townsend exr. Belinda R. Townsend. 3d st, s s, 47 e Smith st, 3 lots. 3 P. M. morts., each $3,250. Aug. 5, 3 years, 5 %. 9,750

Sutterlin, Ernst F. to The Williamsburgh Savings Bank. Cooper st, s e s, 168.2 s w Bushwick av, 34x100. Aug. 12, 1 year, 5 %. 8,300

Same to same. Cooper st, s e s, 202.2 s w Bushwick av, 34.2x100. Aug. 12, 1 year, 5 %. 8,500

Swimm, Frank C. to Carrie Grove. Macon st; Halsey st. P. M. Aug. 1, 3 years, 5 %. 4,000

Swimm, Theodore W. to The Title Guarantee and Trust Co. Jefferson av, s s, 80 e Lewis av, 53x100. Aug. 7, demand. 22,500

Syreen, Charles to William Entwistle. 5th av, n w s, 18 n e 13th st, 15x60. Aug. 1, 3 years, 5 %. 2,500

Taylor, Henry S. to William McMonegal. 48th st. P. M. Aug. 6, due Jan. 2, 1892, 5 %. 500

The Kings Co. Improvement Co. to The Seventeenth Ward Bank. Kingsland av, e s, 48.9 n Van Cott av, 75x100. July 18, demand. 3,000

The Solidarity Watch Case Co. to Thomas and Augustin Walsh. Chestnut st, w s, 125 n of new unnamed st, 75x150. Aug. 10, 3 years. 8,000

Same company. Consent of stockholders to mortgage.

Thompson, Lillian wife of Richard to Daniel B. Halstead. Rodney st, s s, 100 w Bedford av, 22.4x100. *Mt.* $7,000. July 27, 2 years. 4,000

Tracy, Patrick J. to James H. Watson and James H. Pittinger. Pacific st, n s, 141 w Troy av. P. M. June 6, due Oct. 1, 1895. 1,300

Treu, Marie wife of Richard to Thomas W. Harries. Lee av, w s, 121 n Rutledge st, 15x 81.8. Aug. 6, 3 years, 5 %. 2,500

Vaccas, M., Coney Island, to Vaccas & Co. The Bowery Walk, s s, adj T. Reis, 55x100. West End Casino. Lease. July 9. 2,000

Vollweiler, Henry to Clemens Muller and ano. trustees. Hart st, n s, 100 e Broadway, 40x 75. Aug. 6, due May 1, 1895. 2,600

Von Graff, Roderick to Robert Morgan. 4th st, n e s, 297.10 n w 8th av, 20x95. Sub. to mort. $20,000. July 29, due May 1. 1892. 650

Vreeland, George to Stephen C. Halstead. 4th st. n s, 114.11 w 6th av, 17.4x95. Aug. 5, 2 years. 400

Walker, Andrew E. to Jeremiah V. Meserole. Nassau av. P. M. Aug. 4, 1 year. 3,250

Wallett, Frank L. to The Mount Morris Co-operative Building and Loan Assoc. Warwick st. P. M. Aug. 10, installs. 3,500

Walter, Paul E. to Charles Lewis. Putnam av. P. M. Aug. 1, 1 year. 1,800

Wheeler, Louise F. wife of James B. to Margaret Stevenson. Underhill av, s w cor Dean st, 25x100. Aug. 7, 1 year. 1,000

White, Catharine wife of and Peter to John Robinson. Buffalo av. P. M. Aug. 11, due July 1, 1892. 175

Wichert, Joseph to John Backer. Boerum st. P. M. Aug. 8, 5 years, 5 %. 4,000

Wilson, Andrew to John Cole. Washington av, Flatbush. P. M. July 27, installs. 2,807

Wilson, William M. to The East New York Savings Bank. Reid av, w s, 50 n Macon st, 50x100. Aug. 10, 1 year, 5 %. 12,000

Woodcock, John B. C. to Laura wife of Divine M. Munger. Radde pl, No. 18, e s, 136 s Herkimer st. 15.6x97.6. Aug. 10, demand. 500

Woodhead, James to Effingham H. Nichols, New York. Lots 162-165 block 4 map No. 1, &c., Cowenhoven farm, New Utrecht. July 22, 2 years, 5 %. 360

Zimmermann, Annie E. wife of Martin to Timothy C Conklin. Malbouc st, Flatbush. P. M. Aug. 11, installs. 2,500

MORTGAGES----ASSIGNMENTS.

NEW YORK CITY.

AUGUST 7 TO 13—INCLUSIVE.

Bijur, Nathan to Adolph Prochownick, trustee. nom

Crawford, George to The Hudson River Bank. nom

Clark, Robert P. and Hugh Dolan, of Clark & Dolan, to The New England Brown Stone Co. nom

Clark, Alfred C. guard. of Frederick A. Clark to Alfred C. Clark guard. of Robert S. Clark. $20,000

Dingee, Caroline M. to Samuel Woolverton. nom

Fisher, Harris M. to Jennie Simons. 4,000

Gordon, Katie admrx. Stephen T. Gordon to Kittie Gordon. 7,000

Same to same. 500

Hildebrand, Catherine M. E. et al. exrs. and trustees John H. G. Hildebrand to John H. Tietjen. nom

Happel, Adam to Elise Lotze. 2,000

Same to Gotthardt Strich. 2,000

Same to Elise Lotze and Gotthardt Strich. 5,000

Same to Gotthardt Strich and Elise Lotze. 2,675

Haaren, John W. to Bessie Glass. 1,000

Same to same. 2,793

Same to Betsey Glass. 5,000

Same to Henry H. Glass. 4,009

Same to same. 3,015

Same to same. 5,119

Jencks, Francis M. to Emmett J. Howell individ. and guard. of George W. Howell. 2,500

Johnston, Emeline to John W. Haaren. 1,000

Kelly, Angus and ano. exrs. Jane A. Kelly to Angus Kelly. 1,800

Levy, Fanny to L. Napoleon Levy. other consid. and 337

Lipman, Julius to Charles A. Troup trustee. 2,000

Mayer, David to Carrie Mayer. 4,500

More, Abram G. admr. John O. More to Mary E. More, Marlborough, N. Y. 13,139

Martin, Charles G. to Catharine A. F. Casanova. 2,000

Same to Edward F. Browning. 2,000

Same to same. 2,000

Murray, Mary G. L. wife of Francis W. to Lyman Tiffany and ano. exrs. and trustees Charlotte L. Fox. 6,000

Moran, Adam to Lewis Krulewitch. 6,000

Meikleham, William exr. Anne C. Cannon to Henry Parish. 2,500

Oppenheimer, Bertha wife of Jacob to Henry Hartmann. 700

Perry, Oliver H. exr. Mary A. Perry to Charles E. Strong. 10,000

Prochaska, Josefa to Frank Sovak. 250

Roe, Joseph B. exr. Frances A. Howell to Francis M. Jencks. nom

Staudinger, Mary A. extrx. Rudolph Staudinger to Morris Feigel. 500

The Mutual Life Ins. Co. of New York to Edith N. Wharton. 3,745

The Mutual Life Ins. Co. of New York to The Title Guarantee and Trust Co. 19,000

Title Guarantee and Trust Co. to The State Trust Co. guard. for Edna C. Harwood. 8,000

Title Guarantee and Trust Co. to Mabel D. L. Sandford. 8,500

Troup, Charles A. trustee to Albert H. Leszynski trustee. 2,000

Tietjen, John H. to Catharine M. E. Hildebrand. nom

Whittemore, William L. and ano. exrs. William T. Whittemore to Alice G. T. wife of Charles T. Whittemore. 2 assigns. nom

William R. Beal Land Improvement Co. to Julia Huerstel. 1,382

William R. Beal Land Impt. Co. to William R. Beal. 1,400

Wise, Nathaniel to Richard H. L. Townsend. 3,500

KINGS COUNTY.

AUGUST 6 TO 12—INCLUSIVE.

Bailey, Frank to Elmer E. Fingarr. $600

Benjamin, Joseph to Charles Wildner. 1,300

Burroughs, William H. to Ellen L. Kitchen. 3,000

Backer, John to Charlotte Backer. nom

Baumann, Bartholomew and Anna E. to Jennie Friedman. 600

Bergen, Cornelius J. admr. Anna M. Bergen to Frank H. Steers. 1,100

Cock, Augustus G. exrs. Mary Titus to Henrietta Titus. 1,500

Collins, Stephen W. to Richard Collins. 1,000

Cook, Mary E. to John C. and Herbert C. Smith and Herman F. Koepke, of J. C. and H. C. Smith & Koepke. nom

Cranford, George C. to William Sullivan. 1,000

Culver, Andrew R. to Tina D. Delehanty. consid. omitted

Carpenter, Elnathan to Richard Collins. 1,000

Denton, Charles C. and Oscar exrs. Charles Denton to Garret J. Garretson trustee for Elias P. Hicks. 3,000

De Beixedon, Daniel K. to David Murray. 100

Fleich, Michael to Flora C. Fleich. nom

Frank, Barnet and Simon Rose to Rebecca Katz. 485

Garrahan, John and Gorge and John Burke to Patrick G. Hughes. 1,150

Gillespie, Earl A. to The Bedford Bank. 1,030

Grunig, Louis to Peter Kaufmann. 2,000

Harris, Julia D. to Susan Strong. 10,000

Haydock, William H. to Jeannette A. Haydock. 2,000

Huttenbocker, Rosina to Christina A. Scholl. 1,500

Jackson, Theodore F. exr. Maryott Hodgetts to Sarah L. Hodgetts. 2,040

Same to same. 408

Kleine, Virginia A. to Sarah M. Striker. 1,500

Same to Catharine Spurr and Sarah M. Striker. 1,500

Kneuth, Christian to Alexander Underhill, Jr. 1,025

King, Charles D. to Robert Main. 1,500

Leverich, John T. admr. Sarah Leverich to William M. Ingraham. 1,700

Lang, Teresa to Theodore Kiendl. 200

Mackenzie, Anna C. S. trustee Cath. C. Stevens to Henry H. Stevens. 14,200

Mott, Thomas exr. Hannah C. Mott to Katharine A. Mott. nom

Maguire, Caroline F. to Sallie R. Wemmel. 150

O'Berry, Loftis W. to Theodore F. Jackson et al. trustees Loftis Wood. 3,000

Proctor, Albert W. S. to Sarah J. wife of Henry S. Vanderveer, Newtown, L. I. 912

Phelan, Gussie L. to Henry Weil. 740

Rust, Charles D. to Almon W. Griswold. 1,875
Ryan, Joseph to John G. Price. 1,000
Rome, Grace to John Hahn. 704
Roth, Henry to Jacob Ernst. 500
Schwabeland, Henry to E. Christian Korner. 250
Steers, Frank H. to John B. Meyenborg, Jr. 1,528
Same to Freeman Clarkson and ano. trustees Eibe H. Steers. 1,100
Shelly, Abram C. to Hans C. Pfalzgraf. 2 assigns. nom
Sisto, Joseph to The Budweiser Brewing Co. (Lim.) 500
Smith, Mary W. to Peter B. Koechlein, Bound Brook, N. J. 3,000
Skelton, Christopher P. to Martha A. Adams. 1,500
Suydam, John to William M. Ingraham. 1,300
Swift, Gustavus F. and Edwin C. to Williamsburgh Savings Bank. 13,000
Schuyler, Lulu D. wife of Richards K. to Duncan E. McKenzie. 1,500
Taiber, Frederick to Edgar J. Taylor. 1,030
Thorne, Mary A. W. and as extrx. George A. Thorne to Walter S. Tuttle. 2,000
Taaffe, John P. to Alice L. Pearsall admrx. of Oliver D. Pearsall. 1,000
Trustees of the Jones Fund for Support of the Poor to Henry S. Gilbert. 1,500
Title Guarantee and Trust Co. to College Point Savings Bank. 20,000
Same to The Riverhead Savings Bank. 1,200
Same to same. 1,200
Same to Erastus W. Hawkins. 4,000
Same to Hamilton Trust Co. 15,000
Same to Susan M. Pooley. 3,000
Title Guarantee and Trust Co. to The Kings County Trust Co. 5,000
Underhill, Edward C. exr. Abraham Underhill to Mary T. Tatum. 2,500
Vollweiler, Henry to Clemens Muller and ano. trustees, &c. 2,600
Weiber, Lorenz F. J. to Katherine F. Van Wyck. 3,000
West Brooklyn Land and Improvement Co. to Eugenia McCauley. 2,500
Woodhull, Ann M. wife of Jesse C. to Caroline A. Remsen. 1,500
Worth, Jacob and Vincent A. Strawson to Charles T. Stewart. 2,492
Westfall, George F. and ano. exrs. Diedrich Westfall to James H. McCormick. 7,000
Whitney, Scudder V. to Henry S. Gilbert. 1,000

JUDGMENTS.

In these lists of judgments the names alphabetically arranged, and which are first on each line, are those of the judgment debtor. The letter (D) means judgment for deficiency (*) means not summoned. (†) signifies that the first name is fictitious, real name being unknown. Judgments entered during the week, and satisfied before day of publication, do not appear in this column, but in list of Satisfied Judgments.

NEW YORK CITY.

August

11 Adams, Henry C—Chas Schaeffer....$238 19
11 Andress, Charles W—A D Baird.....1,548 16
11 the same——the same............3,057 29
12 *Altman, Bernhard / Altman, Samuel } Max Bowsky..1,798 36
12 Archer, John J—Raymond Lead Co.. 219 13
13 Andress, Charles W—Glens Falls Terra Cotta and Brick Co...............1,089 40
14 Adler, Phillip—Max Lehmann........ 140 00
8 Birmingham, Ernest F—H L Bridgman........................... 637 43
8 Bittner, John—D B Britton..... .... 168 00
10 Berger, Joseph A—Charles White....1,035 75
10 Bensel, Frank O—Metropolitan Telephone and Telegraph Co............ 66 80
11 Benjamin, Sender—Meyer Wolff..... 195 99
11 Bonnell, John H—Nat State Bank of Camden............................4,050 63
11 the same——the same.............3,040 61
11 Blake, Patrick J—Herman Krenzler.. 27 42
11 Bonnell, John Harper—Bank of New York...............................5,050 31
11 Bernstein, Morris—Theodore Litbauer. 174 62
11 Banks, Peter G—C H Reed........... 177 56
11 the same——the same............ 124 63
11 Bonnell, J Harper—John Munroe....12,032 91
11 the same——the same............3,967 05
12* the same —— Washington Nat Bank............................. 939 26
12 Bonnell, John Harper—Nat Bank of Republic............................ 722 99
12 the same——the same............ 922 77
12 the same——Chatham Nat Bank.10,085 68
12 Burlingham, Albert S / Bonnell, John Harper } the same..... 174 90
12 Bedell, Hiram—Sims Lumber Co..... 183 33
12 Bertrand, Henry C—Joseph Beck..... 86 12
12 Burgess, Levi G—H W O Edye.......1,076 21
13 Benke, John——J H Mohlman Co.... 371 88
13 Bacigalupo, Charles—Domenico Stabile............................. 110 70
13 Brown, Charles H—J W Mason...... 128 82
14 Bonnell, J Harper—W D Barnes.....2,031 33
14 Benson, James A—E F Amsler....... 72 49
14 Bonnell, J Harper—Nat Shoe and Leather Bank......................1,016 82
14 Burrows, John P / *Burrows, James C } D G Ryer...... 159 30
14 Brosman, Jeremiah M—Oscar Taussig 528 44
8 Cohn, Casper L—G W McLean, recvr 85 41
8 Callanan, Bridget T—Chas Wood..... 98 02
8 Crosber, James—R A MacAndrews... 120 22
10 Carley, Michael E—H W Haas...... 27 49
10 Cook, Martin—J F Wilson.......... 218 49
11 Cohen, Solomon—Henry Meyer...... 35 82
11 Cohen, Jacob—Abraham Teplitzky... 38 51
13 Crawford, John—Cleveland Rolling Mill Co..............................4,260 83
12 Cohen, Israel—Julius Kamber........ 163 21
13 Canavan, Michael—G W Venable.... 336 75
13 Cassidy, Asa R—Chatham Nat Bank..2,031 03
14 Coffey, Thomas—J W McKnight..... 74 07
14 Chenoweth, Henry—W G Schuyler...2,360 07
14 Carling, James H—Michael Martin... 106 73
8 Dondero, Charles—J G Touisseu... .. 60 23
11 Dunn, Lawrence J—Andrew Meurer.. 325 84
11 Dreyfus, Bernard—W S Bate........ 120 54
11 Davidson, Ephraim—Jas M C Martin. 159 87
11 Dougherty, James—Theodore Westing 213 55
11 Dejongh, Abraham D—L L Lathrop.. 422 56
11 Dwyer, Charles J—C H Lohr....costs 25 40
12 Doran, Myles—S C Boehm......... .. 461 31
12 Day, Martin H / Day, Mary T } J W Bissell........ 102 07
12 Davidson, Ephraim—Philip Rudolph. 262 15
12 Doggrell, William—G W Venable.... 632 02
13 Delaney, William J—G B Robinson... 307 21
14 Dieter, Elias—F E Heath........... 524 69
14 Dolan, Hugh—N J O'Connell......... 727 12
14 Dunbar, Whitman Nickerson—H A Kearney..........................1,147 32
14 Deaves, Ada / *Deaves, Rillie A } Thomas & Wylie Lithographing Co 1,224 35
14 Dietz, Carl—Anton Feser........... 558 24
8 Edelmuth, Louis—Bernard Feifer.... 831 00
8 Elliss, Edward S—Manufacturers' Nat. Bank of Newark.............. 794 30
10 Elias, William—C L Amvander...... 209 50
10 English, Michael—Peter Barry....... 196 45
11*Estes, Maria L—Louis Klein.........1,171 81
11 the same——Charles Barrez...... 268 77
11 Evans, William—W J Ruddell....... 37 60
12 Ely, Goddard Alice S—Albert Baer..1,802 16
14 Ehrlich, Abraham—Peter Lang...... 102 50
7 Flynn, Peter H—The Western Nat. Bank.......................... 179 31
8 Fine, Christopher—Henry White..... 171 68
8 Freedman, Louis—S J Weaver....... 171 76
8 Farrington, John A / Farrington, Jonas S } Esther Frank... 188 29
10 Franke, Frederick A—John McCormick............................ 179 62
10 Fallon, Thomas L—Chas Simon, assignee........................ 144 29
11 Farley, John—Chas F Rohmann.... 567 17
12 Frisbie, Eaton N—M H Arnot........7,058 99
12 Flynn, John J—Henry Campbell..... 500 86
12 Flavin, Martin J—Elkan Naumburg.. 748 65
12*Flynn, James—S C Boehm.......... 461 61
12 Fowler, George—Mark Schmuckler... 85 53
13 Farley, John—Henry Emrich......... 643 13
13 the same——F P Williams.... ... 229 31
13 Furber, Jesse H—E A Bradley.........1,794 57
13 Farley, John—Louis Ettinger........1,086 26
13 Fisher, John H—David Jones Co..... 404 29
13 Finelite, Abraham—George Munro... 67 00
14 Fellerman, Abraham—Z S Finn...... 42 50
14 Ficker, Herman—Edward Siegman... 201 98
14 Farley, John—N Y Furniture Supply Co.................................. 80 39
14 Fursman, William L—Thomas & Wylie Lithographing Co.............1,224 35
8 Gilmour, John—The Saugerties Bank. 507 31
8 Graham, James H—J H Sotereadis... 68 50
8 Goold, Michael—Coleman Brewing Co 167 11
11 Grossman, Francis B—J K Krieg.... 570 27
11 Goldstein, David—William Demuth.. 130 66
12 Gavigan, John—S C Boehm...... .. 448 84
12 Goddard, Alice S Ely—Albert Baer..1,802 16
14 Godfrey, August—Henry Eggers..... 87 41
14 Griswold, Margaret D—J R Churchill, trustee................................ 427 80
14 Grossman, Ada—Thomas & Wylie Lithographing Co.....................1,224 35
7 Hallett, Granville G—Western Nat Bank................................ 221 71
7 Hamilton, Walter—Harriet B Fisk... 89 63
7 Hass, Leonard J—Philip Wagner.... 186 62
8 Holcomb, Irving—W E Tefft..... .... 438 12
8 Harper, William D—The Mfr's Nat Bank of Newark.................. 794 30
11 the same——Nat State Bank of Camden...........................4,050 63
11 the same——the same............3,040 61
11 Heiser, Charles W—Geo Gennerich... 175 87
11 Herman, Abraham—Julius Schwabach............................. 628 73
11 Herrmann, Henry, Jr—Consolidated Fire Works Co of America........ 73 41
11 Harper, William Durbin—Bank of N Y Nat Banking Assoc..............5,050 31
11 Harper, William D—Chatham Nat Bank.............................1,076 84
11 the same——John Munroe.......12,032 91
11 the same——the same............3,967 05
12 Hard, Henry D / Hard, Charles M } Cleveland Rolling Mill Co..........4,260 88
12 Hagan, Thomas—Louis Auerbach.... 258 77
12 Hurley, Joseph C—N Y & Sea Beach Railway Co....................... 821 03
12 Harper, William D—Washington Nat Bank............................ 939 26
12 Hart, Alexander R—Nat Bank of Republic........................ 722 99
12 Heimerdinger, Berthold M—Richard Davidson........................ 130 61
13 Healy, Charles — Frederick Oppermann, Jr...................... 801 34
13 Hildebrand, John—Louis Davis...... 102 50
13 Harper, William D / Harper, Tacie McD } Chatham Nat Bank.........7,557 51
13 Herrmann, Alexander — Josephine Henley.......................... 285 67
14 Harper, William D—W D Barnes.....2,031 33
14 the same——Nat Shoe and Leather Bank.............................1,016 82
14 Haines, Napoleon J. Jr—A S Bacon.. 303 04
14 Howell, Eugene N—Clinton Bank....1,510 70
14 the same——the same.............1,613 73
14 the same——the same.............1,614 51
14 the same——the same.............1,776 11
14 Hunter, Rillie A—Thomas & Wylie Lithographing Co...............1,224 35
13 Invinizzi, Baptiste—Guiseppe De Carlini............................. 61 18
11 John, Louis—Mary C Hopper........ 2,007 50
11 Jester, Peter—Ellen M Pike........... 109 50
11 Jacobson, George / Jacks, Thomas F } Ezekiel Hunu, Jr, assignee........ 535 87
11 Jordan, Mary—W J Ruddell......... 114 06
12 Jackson, John L—J S Gans 1,173 79
10 *Kreuder, Adolph / Kline, Charles / *Kreuder, Frank } Henry Woods.....1,775 13
10 Kelly, John—Morris Feigel........... 46 92
11 Koneman, Frederick—W D Godley... 82 22
13 Kreuder, Adolph / Kreuder, Frank L / Klein, Charles } T J Little........ 98 48
13 Knox, J Armoy—First Nat Bank of Houston........................ 277 61
7 Lissberger, Lazarus—S H Salome.... 38,287 51
8 Lawrence, John D / Lawrence, Mary J } T H Watson..... 190 95
10 Lenz, Albert—Wm Walsmann....... 71 43
11*Lublin, Joseph—Louis Klein...........1,171 81
11 the same——Chas Barrez......... 268 77
11 Lester, Sidney / Lester, Josephine } Simon Heinbach.. 151 84
11 Lasher, Louis—E U Steiner, assignee.. 178 46
12 Levinthal, Morris / Levinthal, John } Philip Epstein.... 29 07
12 Lydecker, Garrett P—Mount Morris Bank............................ 124 51
13 Lohrand, William—J H Mohlman Co. 371 88
13 Lynch, Michael—C H Childs......... 100 11
13 Lurie, Morris—Bernhard Levison.... 265 37
14 Luckemeyer, Edward—Michael Coleman, comm'r.................costs 89 60
14 Levy, Julius / Levy, Augustus H / Levy, Moses D } Julius Ballin 2,489 95
8 Molloy, Anthony—J Corbett.......... 116 98
8 Mulholland, Bernard J—S S Toombs. 136 92
8 Meyer, Gustav H A—H A Brunke.... 391 55
11 Maguire, John J—David Jones Co.... 393 61
11 Masche, Maria—Abner Armstrong.... 52 50
11 Miller, Robert H—Western Nat Bank.1,060 60
11 Mitchell, Charles R—A D Baird......1,548 16
11 the same——the same.............3,057 29
12 Masche, Herman—Ezekiel Fixman... 387 99
13 Menton, Joseph A—J A Bernholz..... 832 55
13 Mitchell, Charles R—Glens Falls Terra Cotta and Brick Co.................1,089 40
13 Moore, Elric L—S M Rook........... 175 43
13 Murphy, John W—J W Mason....... 128 82
13 Moen, Edward A—Silas Nourse...... 465 00
13*Margowski, Max—George Munro.... 67 00
13 Myers, Sinclair T—Hiram Snyder.... 393 21
14 Miller, Walter R—C H Richter...... 28 00
14 Morgan, Henry—A D Knapp.... ... 107 37
14 Meier, William G—F & M Schaefer Brewing Co.......................... 228 23
14†Mars, Hannah A—T B Kniffin...... 99 09
14 MacLaughlin, George C—W M Van Lier................................ 72 31
14 Mulligan, John—John McCormick... 90 42
14 MacLaughlin, George C—W M Van Lier................................ 72 31
10 McCabe, Agnes A—Second Nat Bank. 453 96
11 McGlynn, Patrick—John Glackner... 537 67
10 Nehb, John—J R Naham, Jr......... 77 27
11 Nollman, Charles H—Thos Wright...1,040 95
11 Newman, William M—Hattie Fernbacher.......................... 691 78
11 Norris, Maggie F—Hyman Sonn..... 130 67
13 Nichols, Jacob J—Nat Pahquioque Bank..............................1,536 86
13 the same——the same............1,535 59
11 Ott, George—The Delamater Iron Works............................ 40 15
8 Pulver, Andrew—Art Publishing Co. 789 99
8 the same——T W Morris......... 802 51
11 Petrus, Ella—Max Salmon........... 82 66
12 Prendergast, George F—H R Brown..1,093 06
12 Peck, Edward M—Sims Lumber Co.. 222 74
12 the same——the same............ 510 83
12 the same——the same............ 452 37
12 Pulver, Andrew P—A A Fishel...... 520 51
12 the same——Pierce & Bushnell Mfg Co............................ 130 38
12 the same——King Mfg Co........ 189 73
12 the same——H C Bainbridge..... 89 18
12 the same——C M Taber.......... 212 01
13 Page, Alfred R—G E Faile.......... 245 74
13 Pettit, James H—Robert Beatty...... 84 53
7 Raduziner, Adolph—Alois Kohn.... 231 32
7 the same——Lenox Hill Bank.... 121 92
7 the same——the same........ ... 102 76
7 Reavis, James A Peralto—Peters & Calhoun Co........................ 294 48
8 Roberts, Austin J / Roberts, Walter J } S S Olcott......3,619 39
10†Romaine, William R—Gustave Grossman............................ 104 00
10 Reamer, Job B—J S H Clark 1,330 89
11 Robinson, Charles—Homer Ladd..... 28 82
11 Russell, Philip A J—F C Travers 86 37
11*Reisner, Ignatz—William Demuth.... 130 66
11 Rosenfeld, Moses L—Abraham Teplitzky............................ 38 51
12 Root, James H—Washington Nat Bank............................ 939 26
12 Ruck, John—W G Schuyler.........22,757 37
12 Ray, William H—Nat Bank of Republic.............................. 922 77
13 Raub, Andrew—Charles Fink........ 385 89
14 Root, James H—Nat Shoe and Leather Bank..............................1,016 82
14 Ross, Ruth—Charles Wehle.......... 38 57
14 *Reinheimer, Emanuel / Reinheimer, Leopold } M L Read.... 31 93
14 the same——W N Flint.......... 33 76

14 Rothenbach, John—Anton Feser..... 553 24
7 Schutz, Bernhard—S H Salomo. 38,287 51
8 Shotwell, Townsend W—P S Ross.... 253 98
8 *Strauss, Moses / Strauss, Julius } John G Smith........ 2,814 49
8 Schwarting, Charles W—E C Korner 1,721 65
8 Scully, John J—L G Morris.......... 276 17
8 *Sife, Jacob F / Sigler, Isaac, sued as / Sigler, Jacob } D R Corbin... 30 49
10 Sonand, Abraham—Lewis Sylvester.. 126 77
10 the same——the same............ 81 75
11 Sturtevant, Edgar F—J R Jarvis 91 81
11 Stroeblein, Mary—Solomon Zadek.... 77 45
11 Schanning, Frederick—Louis Klein.. 1,171 81
11 the same——Charles Barrez...... 268 77
11 Sinclair, Margaret—Kate Murphy... 770 09
11 Switzer, Walter E—Peters & Calhoun Co.............................. 781 46
12 Schagrin, Adolph—Joseph Goldfuss.. 93 64
12 Spring, John H—Nat Bank of Republic............................ 87 87
12 Sullivan, Maurice J—Mount Morris Bank. 73 49
12 St John, Cortlandt—H W O Edye.... 1,076 21
13 Simpson, Samuel W—Charles Rosenberg......... .... 134 87
13 Scott, George H—Byram Snyder..... 398 21
14 Stone, Howard C—G W Atwood 70 75
14 Steele, Edward J—Charles Web 38 67
14 Shires, William C—A S Bacon....... 303 04
14 Schlotterbeck, Christian—R C Johnson................................ 395 61
12 Smith, Alfred—Christian Jourgensen. 168 00
13 Smith, James H—G R Brown........ 31 50
13 Smith, Herbert R—C C Camerden.... 181 77
7 J H Bonnell & Co (Lim)—The Western Nat Bank............................ 4,037 39
7 The N Y Elevated Railroad Co / The Manhattan Railway Co } Charles Nette... 8,708 75
7 The Casa Grande Improvement Co—Peters & Calhoun & Co............ 294 48
8 Gilds Company—G W McLean, as recvr 85 93
8 The China Mutual Ins Co—M B Heilner............................... 792 80
8 J H Bonnell & Co (Lim)—Manfrs' Nat Bank of Newark............... 794 30
10 the same——The Western Nat Bank 329 02
10 the same——the same........... . 223 23
10 West Florida & Alabama Railway Co—W O Wyckoff................ 143 88
10 E B Benjamin Mfg Co—Sarah Benjamin.......... .... 3,864 87
10 the same——Seth S Terry 2,563 69
10 The Mayor, Aldermen, &c—R A Wathaus...................................... 519 37
10 North River Lumber Co—The Tunis Lumber Co............................ 8,189 06
10 The Mayor, &c—Allan McLane Hamilton................................ 519 37
11 The Alden Book Co—J M Walcut.... 429 12
11 the same——Orren Sherwin....... 1,949 47
11 the same——E T Sawyer.......... 1,888 48
11 the same——W S Phillips..... ... 1,120 84
11 J H Bonnell & Co (Lim)—Bank of New York............................ 5,050 31
11 the same —— The Western Nat Bank.................................... 1,060 60
11 the same——the same.............. 4,035 38
11 the same——John Munroe 12,032 97
11 the same——the same............. 3,967 05
12 J H Bonnell & Co (Lim)—W D Barnes 1,174 26
12 The Alden Book Co—George Langdon 821 00
12 J H Bonnell & Co (Lim)—Nat Bank of Republic..... .... 722 99
12 the same——the same........ ... 942 77
12 the same——the same............ 964 80
12 The United Purchasers' Discount Co—G A Laridon.................... ..... 135 10
13 The Fibrone Mfg Co—T H Wheeler.. 2,090 32
13 the same——Thomas Wheeler.... 2,107 32
13 the same——T H Wheeler......... 2,113 32
13 the same——the same............. 2,119 84
13 the same——the same............. 2,193 62
13 the same——the same...... ..... 2,100 82
13 the same——the same 1,830 12
13 the same——the same............ 1,070 32
13 the same——F H Allen........... 1,298 32
13 the same——E H Allen............ 1,298 32
13 American Scotch Iron Co—Phoenix Foundry and Machine Co.......... 493 07
13 The London Toilet Bazaar Co—Morris Heimerdinger........ .... 4,214 16
13 The Fibrone Mfg Co—Edward Kasebier.... .... 1,583 54
13 Saranac Improvement Co (Lim)—Mary Herter..... .... 13,435 42
14 J H Bonnell & Co (Lim)—W D Barnes. 2,031 33
14 The Fibrone Mfg Co—Meinhard Alsberg.................................. 207 38
14 The Alden Book Co—Lovejoy Co..... 612 76
7 Tegethoff, Charles—Hiram Snyder, assignee................................ 129 66
10 T[illegible]er, William E—G W Campbell.... 172 95
11 T[illegible] William H—Bridget Conklin.... 3,657 50
11 the same——the same............ 110 52
11 the same——the same.... .... 67 62
14 Thom, David R, Jr—Joacquin Rodriquez 109 54
10 Varian, I L—Eastmans Co of N Y... 937 21
12 Vette, John / Vette, Diederich } E C Korner 314 59
12 the same——H C Webb,.......... 787 18
12 Valentine, Robert H C—Nat Bank of Republic 964 80
12 Vernam, Florence G—Daniel Wadsworth........................ .... 967 08
14 Voight, Albert G—T B Munroe,...... 345 86
14 Vreeland, Jacob C—F W Meeker..... 47 30
12 Van Cleve, Garret—F W Meeker..... 209 51
8 Willman, John—Juan Casas..... .... 107 22
8 Wood, Alexander G—Isaac P Martin. 184 49
8 Walsh, Roger—Illinois Type Founding Co........................... 1,008 14
8 Wemple, Henry Y—Ellen W Cutts... 349 75
11 Weinstein, Jacob—C F Hodsdon..... 37 01
11 Ward, Catherine—Lucy M Copeland.. 106 10
12 Wadsworth, Edwin—Adaline M Wadsworth. 4,587 86
12†Wetterau, Charles—Edward Noettling.... .... 61 50
12 Wagner, George—Amelia Berg....... 72 50
12 Wilding, Walter—Thomas Miller..... 171 47
12 Williams, William R—William Birss. 240 72
12 Weisenberg, Barnet—Leopold Wise.. 213 52
13 Wyatt, Irving—A J Hood............ 182 18
13†Walsh, Mary J—D M Koehler........ 98 80
14 Ward, John B—H W Voorhees........ 192 18
14 Wah, Yee Pon—Louie Wing......... 350 20
14 Weyrauch, Charles—D G Gautier.... 147 55
14 Wilson, James—E N Dickerson...... 3,210 25
13 Zugner, Peter J—Metropolitan Telephone and Telegraph Co........... 42 51
13 Zimmermann, Mrs Albias—Richard Vom Hofe...... .... 361 17

KINGS COUNTY.

August

7 Ainslie, George H—C K Hammitt.... $33 29
11 Andress, Charles W—A D Baird..... 3,057 29
11 the same——the same............ 1,548 16
11 the same——C Dehler.... .... 605 39
13 Andress, Charles W—Glens Falls Terra Cotta and Brick Co... .... 1,084 40
8 Bedell, Edwin J / Bedell, Hiram } P W Ledoux....... 93 85
8 Burke, Richard J—The Long Island Brewery.... .... 607 08
10 Benedict, Edwin H—T Stratton...... 156 72
10 Baldwin, Frank—F G Smith.......... 93 71
10 Blossfield, Charles H—W Mackey.... 371 30
13 Bedell, Hiram—Sims Lumber Co..... 188 33
8 Collins, Charles H—Central Gas & Electric Fixture Co 769 91
10 Curran, Patrick—J Rappold & Bro... 45 30
11†Conklin, "Mary"—W Rohde......... 111 64
11 Cohen, Jacob—A Teplitzky........... 38 51
6 Dunn, Lawrence J—A Meurer........ 345 84
7 Dlanhey, Vincent—F Rosenthal...... 36 50
11 Dudley, Henry J—E F Patten........ 189 49
13 Duclos, Joseph M—J Hodgson........ 84 26
11†Elford, "Mary"—W Rohde.......... 120 72
8 Farley, Thomas H—Riverside Bank.. 73 47
8 Fingleton, Henry W—M Brock....... 88 25
8 Fischman, Joseph—L Rosen.......... 75 50
11 Fullerton, William—A Watson....... 488 12
12 Fingleton, Henry W—Otto Huber Brewery...... .... 68 25
13 Ferrall, John—B Weill............... 70 25
7 Good, Samuel R—L Bossert.......... 94 59
8 Gasser, August—E Heller........... 358 46
10 Giebl, Peter—Thurber, Whyland & Co.................................. 48 45
13 Gibson, John F—G N Percey 94 50
13 Geine, George—H S Christiansen 96 57
13 Gunn, Thomas—B Weill.... .... 70 26
8 Hawley, Lucius P—A J Nutting...... 154 77
8 Hebeler, Nicholas—Long Island Brewery..................................... 500 78
12 Hennesy, John—J Urell.............. 148 57
7 Inness, Frederick A—J H Foote...... 17 63
10 Ingraham, Alexander K—Lumber Exchange Bank.................... ... 419 58
10 Jacobson, Abram—W P Ellison...... 70 14
10 Jenny, James E—G T Tucker........ 705 35
7 Knox, John—C A Franc.......... .... 120 81
11 Kneeland, Stillman F—L A Williams. 179 27
7 Lacy, Eliza C—G R Brown.......... 70 37
7 Lowther, Sarah E / Lowther, John R } Chemical Nat Bank of N Y. . 679 77
13 Lober, Albert—D Wolff............. 127 45
7 Moore, John F—L M Holton......... 85 97
7 Meyer, George / Meyer, Gesine } Caroline Traum.... 110 50
8 McGivney, Owen—Riverside Bank... 73 47
8 Meierdiecks, George—E Heller....... 358 48
10 Mulholland, Bernard J—S S Toombs. 136 92
10†McDermott, Patrick J — Thurber, Whyland & Co........ .... 89 80
11 Meyer, Bertrandt / Meyer, Thresa } H G Somborn.... 168 06
11 Mitchell, Charles R—A D Baird...... 1,548 16
11 the same——the same.... .... 3,057 29
12 McCabe, Agnes A—Second Nat Bank City of New York.................. 453 96
12 Mitchell, Charles R—C Dehler........ 605 39
13 Mitchell, Charles R — Glens Falls Terra Cotta and Brick Co.......... 1,089 40
7 O'Connor, Emeline / O'Connor, Frances B } M E Cobb. (D) 628 41
8 O'Hea, Michael—Long Island Brewery......................... .... 120 20
11 O'Keefe, Jeremiah / O'Keefe, Michael } G Beck........ 77 30
13 O'Neill, Anne—Mason Au & Magenheimer Confectionery Mfg Co..... 34 60
10 Parkes, John F / Parkes, Frederick W } Lumber Exchange Bank 419 58
7 Renchen, Martin—G Gennerich...... 72 31
7 Radner, Louis—E Kuhnla 73 85
10†Roth, John P—Thurber, Whyland Co. 91 92
11 Rosenfeld, Moses L—A Teplitsky.... 88 51
13 Robbins, Thomas H—J Howell....... 1,070 16
7 Schorling, Herman H—O Mather..... 108 13
8 Smith, Thomas H—J May........... 89 97
10 Sieling, Diedrich—W P Ellison... ... 70 14
10 Shannon, Thomas—Nat Cash Register Co................................ 117 70
10 the same——the same........... 53 60
11 Simonson, Isaac C—C Dietrick...... 8,523 92
12 Switzer, Walter E—Peters & Calhoun Co.................................. 781 46
13 Shelly, Michael—W J Osborne....... 98 77
13 Sterry, T Hunt—W E Stratton....... 178 16
13 Sullivan, James E—G N Percey.. .. 94 50
13 Schlim, William H—D Wolff. 127 45
7 The County of Kings—K G Sutherland 197 95
11 Thompson, Frank M / Thompson, Albert W } G L Wood.... 23 22
10 Von Dreele, Philip H / Von Dreele, Annie M } H Von Dreele. 5,049 61
11 Voege, Henry—J Behrens............ 84 60
11 Van Tuyl, William T—W Davison... 146 01
11 Weaver, William W—R Currie....... 484 29
11 Wadsworth, Edwin — Adaline M Wadsworth................ .... 4,587 86
12 Wilding, Walter—T Miller..... ..... 171 47
13 Warner, Gilbert L—G R Avery...... 101 13
13 Waller, Frederick—F D Secor....... 43 46

SATISFIED JUDGMENTS.

NEW YORK.

August 8 to 14—Inclusive.

Barnes, Oliver W—Wm W Carner, trustee. (1891) $343 76
Brockman, Lenore / Butler, Edward } People State N Y. (1891). 500 00
Byrne, Andrew—John Bell. (1891)............ 402 70
*Byrne, James E—E C Fronk. (1890)........ 1,068 32
Same——same. (1888)........................ 984 17
Campbell, Timothy J—Richard Sharp. (1880). 77 60
Coogan, Matthew—Loudon & Manchester Plate Glass Co (Lim). (1884)..................... 235 51
†Doyle, Andrew T—A Hall Terra Cotta Co. (1891)... 77 18
†Same——same. (1891)......... .... 959 18
Fletcher, Walter K—Thomas Cook. (1891).... 2,046 37
Hauser, Gottfried J—J L Toch. (1891)........ 36 24
Hauser, Gottfried J—Annie Carr, extrx. (1891) 238 90
Hauser, G Julius—Wm Breen. (1891) 192 81
Same——The United States Supply Co. (1891) 17 51
Herter Bros—Charles Volckhauser. (1891).... 321 15
†Jenks, Francis M—Edward Kearney. (1891). 127 45
Kohn, Arnold—Richard Sharp. (1880)...... .... 77 60
Same——G H Farley. (1883)... .... 28 40
Levy, Annie—Henry Solomon. (1885).... ... 868 68
*Lippmann, Israel—Jacob Barnett. (1891).... 923 71
Levy, Annie—Raphael Lewisohn. (1886).... 4,135 12
Same——Henry Solomon. (1886)..... ...... 1,094 95
Same——Adolph Sternfeld. (1886) 3,447 46
Same——Benjamin Stearns. (1885)......... 717 09
Same——Nathan Sekulsky. (1885).......... 349 09
Same——Abraham Levinson. (1885)........ 1,217 09
Same——Isaac Frey. (1885).................. 317 09
Levy, Samuel—George Wiemers. (1880)... ... 75 17
Madden, William J—J S Seymour. (1891)..... 379 89
Mahoney, Michael—Utley Hare. (1891)....... 75 24
Same——same. (1890)......................... 1,103 23
*McNiece, James—John Bell. (1891) 626 55
Same——same. (1891).... .... 402 70
Masten, Frederick—Richard Kempe. (1891)... 117 12
Price, Frank S—J L Toch. (1891)............. 36 24
Price, Frank S—Annie Carr, extrx. (1891) ... 238 90
Raduziner, Adolph—Arnold Kohn. (1891).. . 1,269 62
Same——Frederick Kafferman. (1891)...... 819 91
Same——Alois Kohn. (1891)................ 952 67
Rendel, Henry—Delamater Iron Works. (1890). 88 47
†Schirmer, Gustave—F S Myers. (1891)....... 242 44
Stout, Sarah L—J W Mudgett. (1891)........ 298 94
Scholes, Mary J—J W Mudgett. (1890)........ 77 50
Washington Cold Storage Co—Beberdick Anton. (1891) 73 88
Wannemacher, John—Thomas Cook. (1891). 2,046 37

*Vacated by order of Court. †Suspended on Appeal ‡Released. §Reversal. ||Satisfied by Execution.

KINGS COUNTY.

August 7 to 13—Inclusive.

Burns, Patrick G—R Johnson. (1890).......... $429 90
Brooks, Julius—S F Rothschild. (1891).... ... 67 44
Briody, Patrick N—M Cullen. (1891).......... 100 45
Burns, Hugh—P J Carlin. (1891).............. 1,047 58
Colligan, Peter—E Kirmss. (1891) 186 89
Craig, George A / Craig, Anne C } The Union Stove Works. (1891) 341 15
Craighead, John P—Brooklyn City R R Co. (1887)... 394 32
Froeligh, William B / Froeligh, Mary L } S H Millard. (1891)..... 159 14
Folkes, Louis / Folkes, Johanna } R D Birdsell. (1891)....... 114 75
Folkes, Louis—W Battermann. (1891)....... 578 27
Jackson, Homer B—J Derundem, Jr. (1882). 352 92
Loeser, Frederick—Liebmann's & Owings. (1890)..... .... 310 75
Same——same. (1891).... . ... 81 16
Same——same. (1890).................... ... 107 75
Same——same. (1891). 89 81
Monzani, Eliza J and Julia T—Richard P Monzani. (1891)....... .... 158 27
Smith, Eliza—G H Roberts. (1882).. .... 497 39

MECHANICS' LIENS.

NEW YORK CITY.

Aug.
8 Garden av, No. 82, n s, 150 w Prospect av, 10 x abt 130. James A. Wolf agt Michael Roos, owner, and E. Keller, contractor.................. .... $244 38
8 Sixty-third st, No. 31, n s, 337.6 w Central Park West, 37.6x100.5. Robert Carey agt Richard Everett and Margaret his wife, owners and contractors 5,150 00
8 Twenty-fourth st, No. 138 W., n s, 24x125. George Washington agt Mary Headleston, owner and contractor..................... 45 00
8 Twenty-fourth st, No. 329, n s, 250 e 9th av, 25x98.9. Thos. H. Snape agt John McKee, owner and contractor...................... 210 00
10 Hamilton pl, e s, 38 s 142d st, 72x85. Ingbrigt Mikkelson agt Mary A. Stevens, owner, and Mark A. Stevens her husband, contractor. 250 00
10 One Hundred and Second st, s s, 100 e Boulevard, 50x87. Joseph Belello agt Lewis M. Muller, owner, and G. MacLaughlin, contractor.. 500 00
10 One Hundred and Fifteenth st, s s, 275 e 5th av, 175x100. Pasquale Streppone agt

Conrad Muller, Jr., owner and contractor.... 389 00

10 Sixty-third st, n s, 300 w 8th av, 37.6x100. Benedict, McIlroy & Fowler agt Martin J. Barron and John J. Carey, owners and contractors.... 520 53

10 Twenty-fourth st, No. 517 W., n s, bet 10th and 11th avs, 25x100. Wm. H. Cornet agt Charles and George Rapp and Chas. Stevens, owners, and Charles Stevens, contractor.... 175 00

11 One Hundred and Second st, s s, abt 100 e Boulevard, 50x119.7. Candee & Smith agt Lewis M. Muller, owner and contractor.. 283 80

11 Forty-second st, No. 559, n s, bet 10th and 11th avs, 25x100. A. S. Nichols agt Mary A. Barron, owner, and Wm. Spearing, contractor.... 121 06

11 Thirty-fifth st, No. 41, n s, 381.3 e 6th av, 21x100. Philip Smith agt Janette Pirrson, owner and contractor.... 508 50

11 Ninety-eighth st, Nos. 220-224, s s, 225 w 2d av, 75x100. Samuel Veliagori agt Wm. Dempsey and John Smith, owners, and P. Blumenthal.... 22 75

11 Eighty-fifth st, Nos. 73-77, n s, 150 w Park av, 65x100. John Iselhard agt Martin J. Harkert, owner, and Tom Dunn, contractor.... 10 00

11 Same property. Frank Koehler agt same 86 00

11 Same property. Henry Sommermeyer agt same.... 64 00

12 Norfolk st, No. 178, e s, 172.4 s Houston st, 22.1x100. Fischer & Deutsch agt The Congregation Ohaw Zedack, owner, and Isaac Unger, contractor.... 171 69

12*Seventh av, n w cor 56th st, 50.5x78. W. H. Cornet agt N. B. Mortimer, owner and contractor.... 1,645 75

12 Fifty-third st, s s, 350 w 10th av, 125x100. Frank Graziadio agt ——, owner, and James C. O'Donelan, contractor.... 268 62

12 One Hundred and Eighteenth st, s s, 240 w Park av, 100x100.11. Vermont Marble Co. agt Bernhard Ginsburg, Maria and Herman Mascha, owners and contractors.... 21 40

12 Ninety-eighth st, Nos. 220-224, s s, 225 w 2d av, 75x100. Joseph Cobolewsky agt Dempsey & Smith, owners, and P. Blumenthal, contractor.... 20 85

12 Sixteenth st, No. 345, n s, 250 e 9th av, 25x100. C. J. Everett agt Henry W. Deane, owner and contractor.... 68 34

13*Seventh av, n w cor 56th st, 50x100. Canda & Kane agt Nellie B. Mortimer, owner and contractor.... 2,086 59

13 Twenty-fourth st, No. 517 W., n s, 25x100. Charles Zanini agt George Rapp and Charles Stevens, owners, and Charles Stevens, contractor.... 190 00

13 One Hundred and Tenth st, s s, 100 w Madison av, 50x100. G. B. Robbins & Co. agt J. O'Connor, owner and contractor.... 81 85

13 Norfolk st, No. 175, w s, 223.4 s Houston st, 25x100. Davis Wolf and Louis Kidansky agt Samuel Frank, owner and contractor.... 200 00

13 Park av, s w cor 93d st, 81x85. William Heney agt Downey & Curry, owners, and John Driscoll, contractor.... 42 00

13 Same property. Patrick Grady agt same.. 84 50

13 Same property. Hugh McCourt agt same. 19 00

13 One Hundred and Thirty-third st, Nos. 32-36, s s, 410 w 5th av, 75x99.11. L. F. Manes agt Jacob Wick, owner, and Charles Deickmann, contractor.... 95 00

13 Fox st, w s, abt 200 n 165th st, 3 lots. H. G. McClelland agt Leopold R. True, owner and contractor.... 285 00

13 Seventy-second st, Nos. 422-428, s s, 313 e 1st av, 100x100. J. B. McCoy & Co. agt John McLean and John J. Molloy, owners and contractors. (Continued from Aug. 14, 1891).... 475 00

13 One Hundred and Fourth st, s s, 175 w 8th av, 25x100. Philip and Charles Bierschank agt Robertson & Gammie, owners and contractors.... 225 00

14 One Hundred and Sixty-third st, No. 676, s s, 440 e Courtlandt av, 25x100. Henry Sproessig agt Mary Ann Holohen, owner and contractor.... 127 07

14 Hampden st, s s, 50 w Andrews av, 50.10x100. Charles Cavagnaro agt Mary Adriance, owner, and Thomas Wilson, contractor.... 95 00

14 Park av, w s, 30.8 s 93d st, 70x100. John Driscoll agt George W. Curry and Charles Downey, contractors.... 275 00

14 Eightieth st, Nos. 170-182, s s, abt 110 e 10th av, 135x100. Mathias Gerst agt August and Morris Schneider, owners and contractors.... 1,000 00

14 Ninety-sixth st, n s, 70 e Lexington av, 125x100.11. Clark & Dolan agt Owen F. McElroy, Jr., and William McElroy, owners and contractors.... 3,590 00

14 Catharine st, Nos. 53 and 55, e s, 47.3 n Moore st, 27.6x—. Frederick Jenth agt Eliza Louisa Miller, owner and contractor.... 483 45

14 Twenty-first st, n s, 300 w 8th av, 25x—. Canda & Kane agt William H. Cornet, owner and contractor.... 1,791 18

14 Park av, Nos. 1807-1809, e s. Henry Taylor agt William H. McCarthy, owner, and John Sheehy & Son, contractors.... 8,400 00

14 Madison av, e s, 50 s 136th st, 25x—. Same agt C. T. Leonard, lessee, and John Sheehy & Son, contractors.... 150 00

14 One Hundred and Tenth st, Nos. 223 and 225, n s, 300 e 3d av, 50x—. W. Z. Wenzel agt E. D. Farrell, owner, and Thomas McCarthy, contractor.... 98 95

14 Home st, Nos. 1070-1076, s s, 154 e Stebbins av, 70x—. Richard Zobelt agt Treffle H. Allard, owner and contractor.... 707 50

14 Fox st, w s, 151 n 165th st, 50x—. P. G. Decker agt Leopold R. Trew, owner and contractor.... 563 60

**Editor* Record and Guide:

These liens are unjust. In the case of Cornet there was nothing due for ninety days from this date, as per contract signed by Wm. H. Cornet. In the case of Canda & Kane a check was held by the parties advancing the money as the building progressed, but by an oversight was not indorsed; payment was offered yesterday to have lien satisfied, but principal was out of town and lien could not be released; payment is now ready. Mrs. N. B. Mortimer.

KINGS COUNTY.

Aug.

7 Howard av, s w cor Macon st, 100x93.6. T. B. Willis and Bro. agt Mary Leonhardt, Emily Gilroy, Thomas Purcell, George M. Harwood, Morris Isaacs and Clarence Lincoln, owners and contractors.... $650 57

7 Eleventh av, s w cor 62d st, 66.9x64x88.10x60, New Utrecht. Bay Ridge Mfg. Co. agt Andrew Johnson, owner and contractor.. 264 15

7 Sunnyside av, n s, 150 e Barbey st, 50x100. Fred Schluchtner agt William B. Howard, owner and contractor.... 214 00

8 Rockaway av, w s, 300 n Eastern Parkway, 50x100. James O'Connor agt Samuel Levy, owner, and L. Rattner and Charles F. Harles, contractors.... 50 00

8 Gates av, n s, 275 w Hamburg av, 25x100.. } Gates av, s s, 125 w Hamburg av, 25x100.. } Francis Cramer agt John F. Tilman, owner and contractor.... 14 00

8 Gates av, n s, 275 w Hamburg av, 25x100. } Gates av, s s, 125 w Hamburg av, 25x100. } Patrick Curley agt John F. Tilman, owner and contractor.... 81 00

8 East 19th st, w s, 200 s Av A, 50x100, Flatbush. William T. Cowenhoven agt Margaret E. Chatfield, owner, and William Crozier, contractor.... 65 00

8 East New York av, n e cor Troy av, 100x100. Rudolph Reimer & Co. agt D. and Henry M. Tragman, owners and contractors.... 178 00

8 Pulaski st, Nos. 239-269, n s, 100 w Sumner av, 330.6x100. John Auer agt The Frederick Hower Brewing Co., owner and contractor.... 10,000 00

8 Driggs av, s s, 25 w North Henry st, 2 houses. William Meade agt Frank Lehnard and Mr. Blazer, owners and contractors.... 33 00

10 East 19th st, w s, 200 s Av A, 50x100, Flatbush. William J. Spence agt Margaret E. Chatfield, owner and contractor.... 574 00

10 Van Voorhis st, s s, 100 w Bushwick av, 75x100. R. G. Phelps agt Frederick Amman, owner, and Amzi D. Vreeland, contractor. 609 19

10 Union st, n s, 115 e Henry st, 140x100. Norman R. Neiley agt Charles W Andress and Charles R. Mitchell, owners and contractors.... 5,000 00

10 Henry st, e s, bet Van Siclen av and Coney Island Creek, 40x150, Coney Island. Conrad Lebhardt agt —— Slavin, owner, and —— Rubens, contractor.... 75 00

11 Pulaski st, n s, 100 w Sumner av, 330.6x100. Frederick Wunder agt The Frederick Hower Brewing Co. (Lim.) owner and contractor.... 10,402 15

11 Saratoga av, s w cor Fulton st, 80x100. New York Architectural Terra Cotta Co. agt George H. Gibby, owner and contractor.... 600 00

11 Schenck av, w s, 100 n Arlington av, 100x100. Charles F. Moeck agt Eugene R. Tichenor, owner and contractor.... 20 00

12 Bergen st, s s, 200 w Troy av, 25x119 John Irish agt William H. Cornell, owner and contractor.... 24 38

12 Same property. Robert McKee agt same owner and contractor.... 19 94

12 Market st, e s, 100 n Fulton st, 45x150. F. W. Koch & Co agt John Reiss, owner, and Stephen B., George W. and Westley Rose, owners and contractors.... 800 00

13 Livonia av, s e cor Osborn st, 20x100. Earl A. Gillespie agt Abraham Seidenbergh and Rochmiel Abramovitz, owners, and G. Schnefeld.... 700 00

SATISFIED MECHANICS' LIENS.

NEW YORK CITY.

Aug.

8 Ninety-eighth st, n s, 375 e Columbus av, 25x102.2. Andrew Geoghegan agt Gregory Leahy, Agnes and Frank Reynolds. (Lien filed June 24, 1891).... $200 00

8‡Fifty-seventh st, No. 154, s e cor 7th av, 150x175. Adolphe Scherrer agt Andrew Carnegie and the Music Hall. (May 9, 1891)..4,799 50

8‡Fifty-seventh st, s e cor 7th av, 125x— to 56th st, x25x—x— to 7th av x, 175. John D. Beers and Edward Kuenstner agt The Music Hall Co. of New York, and Isaac A. Hopper & Co. (July 23, 1891).... 6,980 00

8‡Same property. Same agt The Music Hall Co. of New York (Lim.) (July 28, 1891)..2,012 00

10 Thirty-fourth st, No. 157 W. James Ross agt Mrs. V. M. Hallett and Annie C. Hallett. (July 8, 1891).... 108 75

10†Seventy-sixth st, No. 350, s s, 375 w 1st av. John M. Pitts agt Georgiana F. Webster. (March 19, 1891).... 174 00

10†Same property. Christian Bambach agt same. (Feb. 10, 1891).... 94 00

10 Madison av, s e cor 130th st, 100x70. Burrows & Smith agt Marie and James Gault. (July 30, 1891).... 337 12

11 One Hundred and Twenty-third st, Nos. 142-150 W. Hollister Mfg. Co. agt Elizabeth K Smith and Hardwood Decorative Co. (Aug. 1, 1891).... 270 81

11 Same property. Same agt same. (Aug. 1, 1891).... 127 50

11 One Hundredth st, Nos. 207 and 209 E. Hooper & Shipman agt Philip H. Smith and George Breitenback. (June 27, 1891). 90 00

12 One Hundred and Third st, n e cor Madison av, 75x100.11. John Pelose agt Charles E. Bonwell and John S. Scott. (April 22, 1891).... 50 00

12 Same property. Vermont Marble Co. agt Charles E. Bonwell. (April 9, 1891).... 251 50

12 Same property. Perth Amboy Terra Cotta Co. agt same. (April 7, 1891).... 3,150 00

12 Same property. Benedict, McIlroy & Fowler agt same. (April 11, 1891).... 570 11

12 Same property. Adam Mitchler agt same. (April 15, 1891).... 297 85

12 Same property. August Boruholz agt same and John Scott (April 6, 1891).... 600 00

12 Same property. A. G. Pucci agt same. (April 14, 1891).... 350 00

12 Broadway, s e cor Leonard st, 75x150. Canda & Kane agt N. Y. Life Ins. Co. and John E. Darragh. (Aug. 7, 1891).... 165 00

12 Bowery, n e cor Great Jones st, 25x100. Same agt Michael Noonan and John E. Darragh. (Aug. 7, 1891).... 135 18

12‡Henry st, Nos. 251-255, n s, 19 e Montgomery st, 56x86. T. J. Hardenbergh agt Maurice Levy and Peter J. Conner. (March 24, 1891).... 230 00

12 Seventy-sixth st, s s, 350 e 2d av. J. S. Haft agt G o gi a F. Webster. (April 3, 1891) e r. an.... 126 40

13 Seventy-second st, s s, 100 e West End av. Fenn & Braxmar agt William Miller. (Feb. 7, 1891).... 214 00

13 Homes st, s s, 176 e Stebbins av, 75x100. Weber & Strom agt Triffle H. Allard, Fred'k Rouseau and Albert McCone. (July 16, 1891).... 78 39

13 Broadway, n e cor Bleecker st, 58.6x149.11. Elgar & Sheehan agt Manhattan Savings Inst. and Cheney & Hewlett. (Apr. 13, 1891).... 990 00

13 Same property. Hopkins & Co. agt same. (Jan. 29, 1891).... 675 00

13 Same property. Achille Bataille agt same. (Jan. 29, 1891).... 1,000 00

13 Same property. C. S. Harris assignee agt Manhattan Savings Inst. (April 25, 1891) 3,082 53

13 Manhattan av, n e cor 121st st. Philip and Charles Bierschank agt Henry Schneider and Allen A. Irvine. (May 12, 1891).... 375 00

13 One Hundred and First st, n s, 350 w Columbus av, 50x100.11. Bowes & Coombes agt Irvine & Co. (May 8, 1891).... 368 40

13 Eighty-fifth st, Nos. 73-77 E., n s. Albert Oellig agt Martin J. Hackett. (April 27, 1891).... 135 00

14 One Hundred and Nineteenth st, n s, 125 w 8th av, 75x100. N. Y. Gas Fixture Co. agt James Thompson (June 17, 1891).... 325 00

14 Same property. Natl. Barrow and Truck Co agt same. (June 11, 1891.... 121 50

14 Same property. J. L. Stothers agt same and Emma T. Coleman and James Merchant. (June 15, 1891).... 510 00

14 Same property. Hoopes & Shipman agt James Thompson and J. August Kissling. (June 20, 1891).... 130 00

14 One Hundred and Nineteenth st, No. 305, n s, 125 w 8th av, 25x—. Charles Just agt James H. Merchant and J. Halstead Dunn. (Aug. 10, 1891).... 60 00

14 Fifty-second st, Nos. 513-517, n s, 175 w 10th av, 75x100.5. W. H. C. Hornum agt Joseph B. Husted and Hauschildt & Muller. (July 27, 1891).... 500 00

14 Anthony av, e s. C. E. Gates & Co. agt Frederick Schappering. (May 19, 1891).. 254 74

14 One Hundred and First st, n s, 275 w 9th av, 25x100. A. R. Ackert and August Schroeder agt Henry S. Cates and Allen Irvine. (May 14, 1891).... 350 00

14 Waverley pl, No. 12, s s, 25 w Mercer st, 25x—. Altieri & Caretta agt K. N. Smith & Co. and John Doe. (July 25, 1891).... 200 00

‡Discharged by order of Court on filing bond.
†Discharged by order of Court.

KINGS COUNTY.

Aug.

7 Madison st, s e s, 386 s w Knickerbocker av, 18x100. New York Gas Fixture Co. agt George A. Craig, owner and contractor. (Release mechanic's lien, filed June 4, 1891, for $78).... nom

8 Leonard st, n e cor Frost st, 25x100. Louis Bossert agt Mary E. Hower, owner, and Louis Mehrmann, contractor. (Aug. 7, 1891).... $1,960 00

8 Sixteenth st, Nos. 385-391, n s, 134.5 w 8th av. William Donnelly agt William Wingerath, owner and contractor. (June 8, 1891).... 23 00

8 Hicks st, No. 25, n e cor Poplar st, 25.3x75. Washington Bulkley agt Ida Edwards, owner, and John Edwards, contractor. (July 30, 1891).... 507 50

8 McDonough st, s s, 175.5 e Sumner av, 100x100. John Garrahan and George Burke agt Michael Rofrano, owner and contractor. (July 3, 1891).... 275 00

10 Chestnut st, w s, 198 s Fulton av, 75x100. Hodgkiss & Co. agt Solidarity Watch Case Co., owner, and J. Le Clair & Son, contractors. (July 1, 1891).... 85 14

11 Same property. Ernst Kuhnla agt same owner and contractor. (July 7, 1891).... 92 00

11 Bergen st, s s, 150 w Schenectady av. Michael Lynch agt A. & M. McGarvey, owners, and Peter Modeste, contractor. (July 6, 1891).... 225 00

11 Bergen st, s s, 290 w Brooklyn av, 60x100. } Bergen st, s s, 350 w Brooklyn av, 40x105.7. } H. F. Burroughs & Co. agt Joseph M. Pilcher, owner, and J. M. Pilcher & Co., contractors. (Aug. 6, 1891).... 913 87

12 McDonough st, s s, 175.5 e Sumner av, 99.7x100. Charles R. Weeks & Co. agt Michael Rofrano, owner and contractor. (June 18, 1891.) (Order of Court.... 124 10

12 Fennimore st, s s, abt 125 w Clove road, 50x80. John Williams agt Gaetano Pranzo, owner, and Alexander Woods, contractor. (June 12, 1891.) (Deposit).... 22 75

13 Driggs av, s s, 25 w North Henry st, 50x100. Thomas Broderick agt —— Fleckhower, owner, and Funk & Lehnert and Peter Anker, contractors. (Aug. 11, 1891.) (Deposit).... 16 00

13 Same property. William Kellegher agt same owner and contractor. (Aug. 11, 1891.) (Deposit).... 16 00

13 Bainbridge st, n s, 115 e Saratoga av, 180x100. Kulan Bros. agt J. Mason Kirby, owner and contractor. (Aug. 5, 1891).... 1,190 00

BUILDINGS PROJECTED.

The first name is that of the owner; ar't stands for architect, m'n for mason, c'r for carpenter and b'r for builder.

NEW YORK CITY.

SOUTH OF 14TH STREET.

Greenwich st, w s, 75.3 n Clarkson st, seven-story brk warehouse, 50.2x165.5 and 168.4, tin roof; cost, $35,000; James McClenahan, 461 8 av; ar'ts, Thom & Wilson. Plan 1127.

11th av, w s, bet 12th and 13th sts, bulkhead line, one-story galvanized iron ferry house, 110x90, tin roof; cost, $8,000; Pennsylvania R. R. Co., 233 South 4th st, Philadelphia. Plan 1135.

BETWEEN 14TH AND 59TH STREETS.

17th st, Nos. 313 and 315 W., two five-story brk and stone flats, 25x70, tin roofs; cost, $17,000 each; ow'r and b'r, J. McSweeney. 188 West 102d st; ar't, C. H. Israels. Plan 1134.

BETWEEN 59TH AND 125TH STREETS, EAST OF 5TH AVENUE.

72d st, n s, 30 w Lexington av, seven-story brk and stone flat, 125x93, tin roof; cost, $375,000; Lorenz Weiher, 14 East 76th st; ar't, L. F. J. Weiher, Jr. Plan 1132, substituted for plan No. 93.

BETWEEN 59TH AND 125TH STREETS, WEST OF CENTRAL PARK WEST AND 8TH AVENUE.

69th st, n s, 225 e Columbus av, five four-story and basement stone dwell'gs, 20x60, tin roofs; cost, $21,000 each; ow'rs and ar'ts, Thom & Wilson, 1267 Broadway. Plan 1128.

110TH TO 125TH STREET, BETWEEN 5TH AND 8TH AVENUES.

123d st, s s, 40 e Lenox av, four-story and basement brk library and apartment building, 34x90.4 and 70.4, tin and tile roof; cost, $50,000; Harlem Library, 2238 3d av; ar't, E. K. Bourne; m'ns, White & Anderson; c'r, B. Walther. Plan 1130.

23D AND 24TH WARDS.

Mt. Hope pl, s s, 225 w Fleetwood av, frame shed, 25x18, tin roof; cost, abt $250; J. Dewhurst, on premises; ar't, C. S. Clark. Plan 1125.

Southern Boulevard, n w cor Webster av, three (?) two-story frame dwell'gs and stores, 50x60, tin roofs; cost, $8,000; F. Grimley and ano., 157 East 51st st; ar't, J. S. O'Meara. Plan 1129.

Mott av, e s, 179.6 s 165th st, two-and-one-half-story frame dwell'g, 33x54, slate roof; cost, $7,000; Florence Wilkens, 630 Walton av; ar't, W. F. Stickles. Plan 1126.

Commerce av, n e cor Powell pl proposed, frame stable, 34x24, gravel roof; cost, $800; Gas Engine and Power Co., Morris Heights; ar't, C. McKinney. Plan 1133.

Vanderbilt av, e s, 160 s 178th st, three-story frame dwell'g, 20x55.6, tin roof; cost, $6,000; D. Flynn, on premises; ar't, J. J. Vreeland. Plan 1131.

KINGS COUNTY.

Plan 1470—Van Sielen av, e s, 175 n Blake av, one two-story frame dwell'g, 20x30, tin roof; cost, $1,800; o'r and c'r, Henry T. Smith, 300 Elton st; m'n, A. Hensinger.

1471—Buffalo av, e s, 60 s Butler st, one one-story frame dwell'g, 17x24, tin roof; cost, $700; John Kemper, on premises.

1472—North 12th st, No. 146, s s, 100 e Berry st, one one-story frame shed, 20x50, gravel roof; cost, $450; Hermann Schmidt, 51 North 3d st; ar't, H. E. Funk.

1473—Broadway, s w cor Halsey st, one four story brk store and tenem't, 18x46.2 and 31.9x38.9 and 40, tin roof; cost, $13,500; James Conway, 1578 Broadway; ar't, Th. Engelhardt; m'n, M. Smith; c'r, not selected.

1474—Lafayette av, n s, 258 w Reid av, four two-story and basement brk dwell'gs, 18x40, tin roofs, wooden cornices; cost, $4,500 each; ow'rs, ar'ts and b'rs, George Fletcher & Bros., 38 Grove st.

1475—Fulton st, n w cor Clinton st, one two-story and basement brk and Lake Superior stone Bank and offices, 50.9 and 49.11x122.6, tin roof, stone and brk cornices; cost, $48,000; The Brooklyn Bank, Fulton st; ar't, W. B. Tubby; b'rs, P. J. Carlin and Long & Barnes.

1476—Lexington av, s s, 275 w Grand av, one one-story brk shop for electric light, 28x76, iron roof, iron cornice; cost, $3,500; Edison Illuminating Co.; b'rs, J. McKeefey and B. H. Body.

1477—De Kalb av, s s, 200 w Reid av, one two and three-story brk stables and dwell'g, 50x96, gravel and slate roof, terra cotta cornice; cost, $15,000; Henry Batterman, Broadway and Flushing avs; ar'ts, P. J. Lauritzen and W. & T. Lamb.

1478—Hamburg av, e s, 50 s Stockholm st, one three-story frame (brk filled) store and tenem't, 25x50, tin roof; cost, $4,000; Jacob Klett, 190 Flushing av; ar't, E. Schrempf.

1479—Columbia st, e s, 800 s Halleck st, one two-story frame store and dwell'g, 25x50, gravel roof; cost, $2,000; trustees Wm. Beard dec'd, Erie Basin; b'r, H. Turner.

1480—Hamburg av, e s, 50 n Suydam st, two two-story frame (brk filled) stores and tenem'ts, 25x65, tin roofs; total cost, $7,000; ow'rs and b'rs, J Eich and S. G. Meyer, 175 Stanhope st; ar't, F. Holmberg.

1481—Flushing av, n s, 228.5 e Morrell st, one three-story frame (brk filled) store and tenem't, 25.6 and 25x55 and 50, tin roof; cost, $4,500; ow'r and b'r, Christopher Schneider, 867 Flushing av; ar't, T. Engelhardt.

1482—Ashford st, e s, 100 s Ridgewood av, three two-story and attic dwell'gs, 13 and 25x36 and 27, shingle roofs; cost, $3,500 each; F. E. and W. F. Scofield, 145A Kent st; ar't and c'r, E. G. Vail, Jr.; m'n, D. H, Hulse.

1483—Grand av, No. 307, being 50 s Greene av, one three-story brk carpenter shop, 25x50, gravel, roof, wooden cornices; cost, $3,500; ow'r and c'r, W. H. Tunison, 270 Franklin av; ar't, G. Ladue.

1484—President st, s s, being west of Clinton st, one four-story brk tenem't, 20x62, tin roof, iron cornice; cost, $7,500; Daniel Buckley, 30 Sterling pl; ar't, W. M. Coots; m'n, J. Donahue; c'r, day's work.

1485—Schermerhorn st, n s, 194 w 3d av, two five-story brk and brown stone tenem'ts, 36x70, tin roofs, iron cornices; cost, total, $40,000; R. von Graff, 164 7th av.

1486—Schermerhorn st, n s, 150 w 3d av, two five-story brk and brown stone tenem'ts, 22x72, tin roofs, iron cornices; cost, total, $20,000; same as last.

1487—Schermerhorn st, n s, 238 w 3d av, two five-story brk and brown stone tenem'ts, 22x72, tin roofs, iron cornices; cost, total, $20,000; same as last.

1488—Varet st, s s, 175 e Graham av, one four-story frame (brk filled) tenem't, 25x60, tin roof; cost, $6,500; Mrs. Kleinlein, on premises; ar'ts, D. Acker & Son.

1489—47th st, s s, 160 e 4th av, five two-story basement, cellar and attic brk dwell'gs, 20x40, tin roofs, wooden cornices; cost, $3,200 each; Alexander Waldron, 48th st and 4th av; ar'ts, H. L. Spicer & Son.

1490—52d st, n s, 100 e 4th av, five two-story basement and cellar frame (brk filled) dwell'gs, 20x38, tin roofs; cost, each, $2,500; —— Hamilton; ar'ts, H. L. Spicer & Son.

1491—Covert st, s w cor Hamburg av, one three-story frame (brk filled) store and tenem't, 24x65, tin roof; cost, $3,000; I. B. Booth, 716 Hancock st; ar't, F. W. Ames; b'r, J. N. Booth.

1492—Cook st, n w cor While st, one three-story brk enamel factory, 125x69, gravel roof, brk cornice; cost, $18,500; Iron Clad Mfg. Co., 22 Cliff st, New York; ar't, F. Weber; b'rs, I. & J. Van Riper & Co. and T. Davies.

1493—Varet st, s s, 155 e Ewen st, two four-story frame (brk filled) stores and tenem'ts, 22.6x50, tin roofs; cost, each, $6,500; Isaac Horowitz, Ellery st; ar'ts, D. Acker & Son.

1494—Miller av, e s, 275 s Fulton av, one two-story frame dwell'g, 21x38, tin roof; cost, $2,800; Frances L. Lewis, Atlantic av, near Miller av; ar't, C. Infanger.

1495—Bergen st, s s, 325 e Rochester av, one one-story frame wagon shed, 25x24, tin roof; cost, $75; Henry Schreider, Rochester av and Dean st.

1496—Thatford av, w s, 125 s Eastern Parkway, one three-story frame store and tenem't, 25x55, tin roof; cost, $4,800; Salmonsen & Ringinsky, Belmont av.

1497—State st, n s, 100 e Smith st, one five-story brk store, 30x90, tin roof, iron cornice; cost, $29,000; Vosburgh Mfg. Co., Fulton and Smith sts; ar't, G. P. Chappell.

1498—Canton st, n s, 67.6 w Myrtle av, one one-story iron front movable photographic gallery, 17x25, glass and iron roof; cost, $185; G. W. Heatley, 117 Waverly av.

1499—St. Marks av, s s, 427.6 e Utica av, one three-story frame tenem't, 20x40, tin roof; cost, $2,800; James McCormick, 1029 Bergen st; ar't, C. Infanger.

1500—New Jersey av, w s, 250 n Fulton av, one three-story frame tenem't, 25x57, tin roof; cost, $4,300; August Klaus, Jamaica av, cor New Jersey av; b'rs, H. Ries and D. Cook.

1501—Stockholm st, n s, 225 e Hamburg av, one two-story frame tailor shop and dwell'g, 25x26, tin roof; cost, $2,000; Frank Winteraht, 189 Hamburg av.

1502—Wyckoff av, No. 32, one three-story frame (brk filled) store and tenem't, 25x55, tin roof; cost, $5,300; Edmund Stein, 34 Wyckoff av; ar't, H. E. Funk.

1503—Flushing av, s w cor Beaver st, one two-story frame (brk filled) wagon factory, 51.3 and 72.3 and 19.9x50.6, tin roof; cost, $4,800; Wm. Wallmann, 33 Fayette st; ar't, H. E. Funk.

1504—Myrtle av, s s, 60 e Bleecker st, five three-story frame (brk filled) dwell'gs, 20x45, tin roofs; cost, $3,200 each; ow'r and c'r, Edward Thompson, 18 Garden st; ar't, J. Thompson; m'n, R. Murphy.

1505—Belmont av, s s, 150 e Hendrix st, one two-story frame tenem't, 25x36, tin roof; cost, $3,000; Patrick Collins, Shepherd av, near Blake av; ar't, J. McMurda; b'r, P. Keenan.

ALTERATIONS NEW YORK CITY.

Plan 1490—31st st, No. 11 E., one-story extension, 10x7; cost, $1,000; agent, W. H. Smith, 945 Broadway; ar't, Bruce Price; c'rs, G. & C. Brown.

1491—131st st, n s, 50 w Amsterdam av, three-story and basement extension, 40x51, interior alterations, rear wall altered, doors and windows changed; cost, $35,000; Manhattan Dispensary, on premises; ar'ts, Buchman & Deisler; m'n, C. A. Cowen.

1492—7th st, No. 11, new show window; cost, abt $500; Susan Semler, on premises; ar'ts, Kurtzer & Rohl; c'rs, Thies & Folz.

1493—157th st, No. 609 E., raised 2 feet, two-story extension, 19x12; cost, $500; O. Judge, on premises; ar't, F. L. Blom.

1494—161st st, No. 521 W., two-story and basement extension, 30.4x29, interior alterations, &c.; cost, abt $2,900; H. Pomeroy, 24 West 135th st; ar't, P. H. J. Kruider.

1495—Mott st, No. 5, walls altered; cost, $1,200; L. Silverstone, 188 Park row; ar't, F. Wandelt.

1496—Madison av, n e cor 126th st, interior alterations; cost, $150; St. James M. E. Church, 37 West 127th st; c'r, C. W. H. Elting.

1497—24th st, No. 517 W., dig out cellar 3 ft; cost, $300; H. Rapp, on premises.

1498—13th st, No. 122 E., repair damage by fire; cost, $3,000; lessee, A. Dulge, 243 East 14th st; b'rs, Clark & Co.

1499—Broadway, No. 1424, new elevator; cost, $——; D. S. McElroy, 246 Lexington av; ar't, J. M. Dunn.

1500—5th av, No. 319, doors and windows altered; cost, $5,000; Knickerbocker Club, on premises; ar'ts, McKim, Mead & White.

1501—Exchange pl, Nos. 45 and 47, raised one story; cost, $10,000; W. K. Aston, 603 5th av.

1502—4th av, e s, bet 67th and 68th sts, one-story extension, 4x6.9, and walls altered; cost, $300; H. Calkin, prest., 147 West 49th st; ar't, J. E. Terhune.

1503—53d st, No. 343 E., interior alterations and new skylights; cost, $900; J. N. A. Griswold, 355 5th av; ar'ts, Ogden & Son.

1504—21st st, No. 315 W., windows altered; cost, $100; J. Reilly, on premises; m'n, M. Gillespie; c'r, O. Henderson.

1505—Elizabeth st, Nos. 208 and 210, north wall altered; cost, $235; Brush Electric Ill. Co., Times Building; ar't, H. O. Ockershausen; m'ns, Burton & Nickel.

1506—112th st, No. 413 E., foundation altered; cost, $100; M. Ganly, 2188 1st av.

1507—Locust av, s w cor 139th st, raised one story, new slate roof; cost, $8,500; Central Gas Light Co., 142d st and Alexander av; ar't, H. S. Baker.

1508—3d av, 280 west of and 210 south of 134th st, wall rebuilt and altered, new wood and iron roof; cost, $3,000; Mott Iron Works, 84 Beekman st; ar't, A. G. Thomson.

1509—113th st, No. 408 E., interior alterations; cost, $15; H. McNally, 161 East 118th st; ar't, J. J. Vreeland.

1510—2d av, No. 113, extension altered; cost, $1,500; lessee, O. A. Kopetzki, on premises; ar't, E. W. Greis.

1511—79th st, No. 153 W., two-story extension, 8.1x13; cost, $600; att'y, G. A. Denig, Hotel Beresford; m'n, J. Batton; c'r, C. D. Hook.

1512—Grand st, No. 330½, one story extension, 12.6x20; cost, $900; agent, M. J. Adrian, 308 East Broadway; art's, Boekell & Son; b'r, S. Niewenhous.

1513—34th st, Nos. 349 and 351 E., interior alterations; cost, $15; Haiss Bros. lessees, on premises.

1514—Fulton st, Nos. 191 and 193, interior alterations, walls altered; cost, $10,000; Fire Dept., 157 East 67th st.

1515—55th st, No. 52 E., four-story extension, 4.8x4.8, new bay, windows altered; cost, $2,000; Celia F. Howell, on premises; b'rs, Morton & Chesley.

1516—Bleecker st, Nos. 414-416, tank on roof; cost, $300; P. M. Wilson, 144 West 22d st; b'rs, Harkness Fire Extg. Co.

1517—9th st, No. 41 E., roof raised, interior alterations and windows altered; cost, $2,500.

1518—Westchester av and Bronx River, interior alterations, walls altered; cost, $3,500; T. Bolton, West Farms, N. Y.; ar't, J. Stroud.

1519—Varick st, No. 204, new front and doors, cost, $300; S. D. Wilson, 153 West 73d st; c'r, L. Sibley.

1520—Allen st, No. 165, interior alterations; cost, $50; S. Sigel, on premises; c'r, M. Levy.

1521—Broadway, No. 652, tank on roof; cost, $250; W. S. Defendorf, 1251 Lexington av; c'r, P. H. Murphy.

1522—45th st, N. Y. C. Railway yard, roof repaired; cost, $2,000; N. Y. C. & H. R. Railway Co., 42d st station.

1523—Pearl st, No. 323 and Cliff st, No. 80, walls altered, court changed and roofed in, new elevator, new windows and general repairs; cost, $12,000; N. L. Munro, Plaza Hotel; ar't, F. T. Camp; m'ns, Bunn & Co.; c'r, T. Henley.

1524—Grand st, No. 365, repair damage by fire; cost, $600; agent, W. H. Griffin, 86 Stockholm st, Brooklyn; ar't, H. Horenburger.

1525—17th st, Nos. 425 and 427 W., new store fronts; cost, $500; Catharine S. Herrman, 340 West 14th st; c'r, P. Herrman's Son.

1526—Blackwell's Island, opposite 53d st, four-story extension, 20.8x27; cost, $7,000; City of New York, 66 3d av; ar'ts, Withers & Dickson.

KINGS COUNTY.

Plan 769—Leonard st, No. 56, three-story frame extension, 25x28, tin roof; cost $3,000; —— Greenblat, 119 Boerum st; ar't, H. E. Funk.

770—Central av, n w cor Gates av, one-story frame extension, 25x25, tin roof; cost, $500; M. Pepper, on premises; b'r, C. Welsher.

771—Broadway, No. 1403, one-story brk extension, 40x22, tin roof; cost, $1,200; Russell W. McKee, 750 Willoughby; ar't, J. Harbison; b'rs, K. Reilly and Brock & Lindemann.

772—Jefferson av, s w cor Marcy av, one-story brk extension, 12x9.8, slate roof; cost, $3,000; Trinity Presbyterian Church, on premises; ar't, M. W. Morris; b'r, T. B. Rutan.

773—Lafayette av, Nos. 73 and 75, three-story brk extension, 20.10x44, front wall and interior alterations; cost, $5,000; B. Roessler, 65 Lafayette av; ar't, A. F. Norris; b'r, not selected.

774—Van Brunt St, No. 517, front and interior alterations; cost, $500; Mrs. Kinney, on premises; ar't, O. Neilson.

775—Noll st, No. 137, add one story; cost, $500; August Krieg, on premises; ar't, E. Schrempf; b'r, not selected.

776—Rockaway av, Nos. 254 and 256, raised 2 feet on brick wall; cost, $325; C. Chambers, 2084 Dean st.

777—Johnson av, n w cor Scott av, 18th Ward, raised 7 feet on stone and brk foundation; cost, $850; Mrs. Mayer, on premises.

778—South 9th st, Nos. 39-47, six-story brk extension, 47.2x100, tin roof; cost, $15,000; Wm. Vogel, on premises; ar't, W. H. Gaylor; b'r, W. & T. Lamb.

779—Boerum st, No. 5, one-story frame extension, 22x50, tin roof; cost, $1,200; Wm. Emich, on premises; ar't, H. E. Funk.

780—Cleveland st, e s, 300 n Liberty av, raised 8 feet, also extension at rear of basement, 9x15; cost, $600; J. Meister, 216 Cleveland st.

781—Walcott st, No. 78, building straightened up, new brk foundation; cost, $500; N. McManus, 380 Van Brunt st; b'r, M. Riele.

782—Barbey st, w s, 150 s Liberty av, raised 10 feet on frame story; cost, $500; Ludwig Kappes, on premises; ar't, C. Infanger.

MISCELLANEOUS.

BUSINESS FAILURES.

N. Y. ASSIGNMENTS—BENEFIT CREDITORS.

August

10 Farley, John (furniture dealer, at Nos. 2794, 2796, 2798 and 2863 3d av), to George Beck; preferences, $1,990.19.

10 Teschner, Wolfgang (Manufacturer of ladies' and children,s underwear, at Nos. 265 and 267 Canal st), to Louis Werner; without preferences.

KINGS COUNTY.

GENERAL ASSIGNMENTS.

Aug.

12 Bullwinkel, Martin H. to H. F. Stegmann.

11 Dorgeval, Polydore to George J. Yestner.

ADVERTISED LEGAL SALES.

REFEREES SALES TO BE HELD AT THE REAL ESTATE EXCHANGE AND AUCTION ROOM (LIMITED), 59 TO 65 LIBERTY STREET, EXCEPT WHERE OTHERWISE STATED.

August

65th st, No. 138, s s, 458 e 10th av, 20x100.5, four-story stone front dwell'g, by Richard V. Harnett. (Amt due $21,242)........ 17

71st st, No. 114, s s, 130.1 w Columbus av, 19x100.5, four-story stone front dwell'g, by Smyth & Ryan. (Amt due $10,784)........ 17

Amsterdam (10th) av, No. 307, e s, 70.4 n 74th st, 17x81, four-story brk dwell'g, by J. F. B. Smyth. (Amt due $14,909)........ 17

10th st, No. 213 E., n s, abt 200 e 2d av, three-story brk dwell'g, by William Kennelly. (Partition sale)........ 18

34th st, No. 211, n s, 137.6 e 3d av, 12.6x98.9, three-story stone front dwell'g, by William Kennelly. (Amt due $1,203; prior morts. $8,000)........ 18

144th st, n e cor Bradhurst av, 32.4x99.11x21.4x100.6, by Smith & Ryan. (All right, title and int. which Jacob Strider had on March 5, 1890)........ 18

82d st, No. 348, s s, 101.5 w 2d av, 19.3x102.2, three-story stone front dwell'g, by D. P. Ingraham & Co. Amt due $7,604)........ 20

Av A, Nos. 1314-1320, n e cor 70th st, 100.4x98, four and five-story brk planing mill, &c., by R. V. Harnett & Co. (Amt due $34,234)........ 20

Riverside Drive, No. 100 } begins Riverside Drive,
82d st, Nos. 318-326 } s e cor 82d st, runs east 161.1 x south 102.2 x west 16.8 x north 10.4 x west 82 x north 18.8 x west 14.4 x north 15.6 x west 6.4 x north 26.6 x west 79.9 to Riverside Drive, x north 24.2 to beginning, five four-story stone front dwell'gs, by Wm. R. Brown. (Amt due $2,244; prior morts. $—........ 21

52d st, No. 521, n s, 275 w 10th av, 25x100.5........ }
52d st, No. 523, n s, 300 w 10th av, 25x100.5........ }
Two five-story brk tenem'ts........ }
by Wm. Kennelly........ 21

61st st, No. 347, n s, 132.4 w 1st av, 25x100.5, five-story brk tenem't, by Richard V. Harnett. (Amt due $16,858)........ 21

69th st, Nos. 322-331, n s, 350 w West End av, 125x100.5, five five-story brk tenem'ts, by W. R. Brown. (Amt due $7,656; prior morts. $—)........ 24

74th st, Nos. 435 and 437, n s, 150 w Av A, 50x102.2, two five-story brk tenem'ts, by James C. Lalor. (Amt due $19,268)........ 24

79th st, Nos. 171-175, n s, 205 e Amsterdam av, 45x102.2, three three-story stone front dwell'gs, by William Kennelly. (Amt due $26,302)........ 24

KINGS COUNTY.

Aug.

College pl, No. 16, e s, 127.11 n Love lane, 20x50, two-story brk stable; partition; assessed value, $2,000; by T. A Kerrigan, at 13 Willoughby st........ 17

Flushing av, n w cor Franklin av, runs west 120.9 x north 196 x east 24.2½ to Wallabout st, x east 106 to Franklin av, x south 200.4 to beginning, also all right, title and int. which Alexander Dugan had to a triangular parcel on Wallabout st, adj above, being 23.10 on Wallabout st, x4x—, moulding mill; assessed value, $25,000; by Geo. L. Fox, ref., at County Court House........ 1

Hancock st, Nos. 942-949, n w cor Saratoga av, 67.4x95x67, gore, three-story brk stable; assessed value, $8,400........ }
Bay 32d st, n w s, 200 n e Benson av, 60x96.8, Bensonhurst........ }
by T. A. Kerrigan, at 13 Willoughby st........ 18

Greene av, Nos. 796-812, s e cor Lewis av, 200x100, ten two-and-a-half-story brk dwell'gs; assessed value, $3,000 each; and one four-story brk flat with store on corner; assessed value, $6,000....

Greene av, Nos. 855 and 857, n w cor Stuyvesant av, 50x100, two four-story brk apartment houses, corner with store; assessed value, $20,000

Washington av, s s, 150 e 3d st, 50x100, Flatbush.

Lot at Gravesend, begins at Atlantic Ocean at division line bet old lots 22 and 23 on one side and old lots 20 and 21 on the other side, as shown on Kowolski's map of common lands of Gravesend, Coney Island, runs north — x west — x south to ocean, x east to beginning, except strip 40 ft. wide condemned for use of New York & Coney Island R. R. Co., and part lying south of centre of Surf av; partition........ }
by T. A. Kerrigan, at 13 Willoughby st........ 19

Atlantic av, n s, 50 w Gunther pl, 15x98.7, vacant; assessed value, $700; by J. Cole, at 389 Fulton st. 20

Marcy av, Nos. 578 and 580, w s, 100 s Myrtle av, 50x100, two-story frame (brk lined) dwell'g; assessed value, $4,000; by Edward Moran, ref., at County Court House........ 21

Atlantic av, No. 423, n s, 230 e Bond st, 25x100, three-story brk tenem't with frame rear; assessed value, $4,500; by T. A. Kerrigan, at 13 Willoughby st........ 24

LIS PENDENS, KINGS COUNTY.

Aug.

Newtown road, at n w cor of land of William M. Betts, runs south 92 x northwest 109 to Newtown road, x east 67.8........ }
Diamond st, s s, 175 e Schenectady av, 25x190........ }
Grand st, s w s, 125 n w 9th st, 25x77........ }
Grand st, s s, 25 e 8th st, runs west 0.3x77........ }
Fulton st, n s, adj land of John Doughty, 24x110, ndeft........ }
Roma M. Meade agt Daniel E. Sickles et al.; partition; att'y, Frank B. Colton........ 6

Butler st, s s, 458 e Nostrand av, 16.8x100. Mutual Life Ins. Co. agt Brewster Conklin; att'y, Robert Sewell........ 7

Cedar st, s s, 255 w Evergreen av, 20x91. The Lafayette Fire Ins. Co., Brooklyn, N. Y., agt Annie T. Mariga; att'y, David F. Manning........ 7

60th st, n s, 60 e 12th av, 20x102.2. The Brooklyn City Co-operative Building and Loan Assoc. agt Michael Morgan; att'ys, McGuire & Low........ 7

Carroll st, n s, 95 w Hicks st, 20x100. William H. Beard exr. Archibald Johnson agt Bridget Nallin; att'y, Willard S. Pladwell........ 7

Dean st, n s, 280.7 w Buffalo av, 111.9x107.2. James H. and Franklin Lee agt James W. Lane. Action for conveyance; att'y, Tallmadge W. Foster........ 8

Sidney pl, No. 52, w s, 125.6 n State st, 21.1x101.9x28.9x100. The Commercial Alliance Life Ins. Co. agt Mary L. Van Slooten; atty's, Patterson, Buel, Toucey & Whiting........ 8

Dupont st, s s, 275 e Manhattan av, 25x100........ }
India st, s s, 225 w Manhattan av, 25x100........ }
India st, n s, 325 w Manhattan av, 25x100........ }
George W. Wheeler agt Timothy S. Wheeler; partition; att'y, James F. Quigley........ 10

Park pl, n s, 154.7 e 5th av, 20x100. George W. Armstrong agt Margaret T. Griffiths; att'y, H. B. Blauvelt........ 11

President st, s s, 382.6 w 5th av, 17x100. George R. Brown agt Henry Dundas; att'y, Robert T. Rhodes........ 11

President st, s s, 365.6 w 5th av, 17x100. Same agt same; same att'y........ 11

Winthrop st, s s, 2,911.6 e Flatbush av, runs east 40 x south 122.6 x east 20 x south 122.6 to Robinson st, x west 60 x north 245, Flatbush. Francis E. Dana exr. Fannie M. S. Jenkins agt Annie M. Tait; att'y, Theo. Bergmyer........ 11

South 2d st, s w s, 75 n w 11th st, 25x120. Edgar J. Taylor agt Emma Taiber; att'y, T. J. Taylor. 11

2d st, n s, 90.9 w 7th av, 20x100........ }
2d st, n s, 110.9 w 7th av, 20x100........ }
2d st, n s, 130.9 w 7th av, 20x100........ }
William L. Dowling agt Roderick Von Graff; 3 foreclos. suits; att'y, Cornelius Doremus........ 11

Myrtle av, s s, 480.7 e Lewis av, 19.9x100. Henry Waterman agt Fritz Schreyer; att'ys, Jackson & Burr........ 13

Norman av, n e cor Guernsey st, 25x95........ }
Eckford st, e s, 200 n Nassau av, 25x100........ }
Annie L. McCabe agt Catharine McCabe; partition; att'y, J. Tracey Langan........ 13

Degraw st, s s, 431.5 w 5th av, 19.2x100. Lyman D. Calkins agt Albert M. Crouter; att'y, Cornelius Doremus........ 13

2d st, n s, 150.9 w 7th av, 20x100. Same agt William L. Dowling; same att'y........ 15

RECORDED LEASES.

NEW YORK. — Per Year

Broadway, No. 813, second, third and fourth floors. Peter J. Kahler to Frank P. Macnabb; 5 years, from May 1, 1892........ $2,450

Broome st, No. 275. The estate of Maria C. Cadwalader to John H. Prehn; 4 years, from May 1, 1890........ 1,200

Bowery, No. 27, upper part with ¼ part of cellar. Albin Wiborn to John O'Regan; 10 years, from May 1, 1891........ 1,800

Eldridge st, No. 218, basement store floor. Lewis Adelson to Joseph Sawicki; 10 years, from Aug. 1, 1891........ 840

Grand st, No. 280. Richard G. Barcalow to George H. Lubis; 5 years, from May 1, 1889. 1,550

Greenwich st, No. 273 } store and basement of
Greenwich st, No. 271 } No. 273 and second story of Nos. 271 and 273. John H. Welsh to Gustav and Ferdinand Buck; 5 years, from May 1, 1893. (Corrects error in last issue)... 1,800

Houston st, No. 216 E., store floor, cellar and second and third floors. Harriet Gale to John W. Aldag; 3 years, from May 1, 1891... 600

Hester st, Nos. 73 and 75. Barney Isaacs to Hyman Jalowsky; 5⅚ years, from Aug. 1, 1891........ 515

Hudson st, No. 463, except top floor. D. Edwin O'Neil to Henry M. O'Neil; 5 years, from May 1, 1891........ 1,560

Hamilton st, No. 16, front and rear. William H. McKinney to Charles Scalichting; 5 years, from May 1, 1892........ 800

James st, No. 74. William Hart to Andrew Barbieri and John Mangini; 5 years, from Aug. 15, 1891........ 1,100

Liberty st, Nos. 92 and 94, store on ground floor. Charles Schlesinger to Max Nathan; 7 years, from May 1, 1890........ 6,000

Liberty st, Nos. 92-94, fourth loft. Max Nathan to Charles Schlesinger; 6 years, from May 1, 1891........ 1,500

Pell st, No. 15. John H. Voss to Harry Leeking; 4⅝ years, from Sept. 1, 1891........ 1,680

White st, No. 98, n w cor Elm st. Mary E. Brennan to William Schierenbeck, Elizabeth, N. J.; 5 years, from May 1, 1893........ 1,600

13th st, No. 158 W. Timothy J. Kiely to Sadie M. Eaton; 3 years, from Sept. 1, 1891........ 1,550

14th st, No. 5 W. Julius J. Lyons to John H. Little; 5 years, from May 1, 1891........ 5,500

41st st, No. 42 E. Frank T. Warburton exr. Adolphus F. Warburton to Katharine wife of H. Hobert Porter, Jr.; 3 years, from Oct. 1, 1891........ 1,700

58th st, No. 203 W. James C. Miller to Joseph Garlan; 3 years, from May 1, 1892........ 1,200

77th st, No. 330 E., west part of store. Springmeyer Brothers to Samuel Veit; 8 months, from Sept. 1, 1890........ 240

81st st, No. 358 E. Henry Oellig to Michael Muller; 5 years, from July 15, 1891........ 1,500

104th st, No. 307 E. Henry Lochmueller to Antonio Florio; 5 years, from June 1, 1891........ 1,080

107th st, No. 301 E. Michael and Anna Scheringer to Gaetano Pand ifi; 5 years, from June 1, 1891........ 1,200

141st st, s s, 40 e 1st av, one-story store. Thomas Foy to Charles P. Bell; 5 years, from July 1, 1891........ 200, 240

Park av, n w cor 113th st, corner store. John S. Scott to William D. Hinck; 5 years, from May 1, 1892........ 1,200

Park av, No. 1052, store. Abraham Steers to Robert T. Dorion; 5 years, from May 1, 1890. 720, 900

1st av, n e cor 43d st, 70.5x150. John Harrington to John J. Harrington; 5 years, 8 months and 21 days, from Aug. 10, 1891........ 5,000

1st av, No. 1448, store, first floor and front part of cellar. Mary Vondrash to Sophie Strauch; 3 years, from May 1, 1890........ 720

Same property. Assign. lease. Sophie Strauch to The Fred Hower Brewing Co. (Lim)........ nom

Same property. Assign. lease. William J. McCarthy, Jr., to Adolph Schwerkolt........ 1,075

Same property. Assign. lease. Adolph Schwerkolt to Antonie Klauser........ nom

2d av, No. 2064, store and apartments on third floor. Frederick Wolters to Christian Ziegler; 5 years, from Jan. 19, 1891........ 900

3d av, No. 965, store and part cellar. Julia A. Blake to Adolph Stoessel; 5⅚ years, from Sept. 1, 1891........ 1,000

3d av, No. 2374, ground floor. Henry Hunneke to Simon Buttner; 9¾ years, from Aug. 1, 1891........ 2,000, 3,000

3d av, No. 2445. William H. Buxton to Frederick Holland; 8¾ years, from Aug. 1, 1891.. 780, 840

9th av, No. 56. John B. Scott to Annie Hamann; 2 years, from May 1, 1893........ 1,100

10th av, No. 740, basement and store. George Zehnder to John J. Zehnder; 4 11-12 years, from June 1, 1891........ 900

10th av, No. 517, store and bakery. John Kohler to Valentine Saelzer; 5 years, from July 1, 1891........ 770

CHATTELS.

NOTE.—*The first name, alphabetically arranged, is that of the Mortgagor, or party who gives the Mortgage. The "R" means Renewal Mortgage.*

NEW YORK CITY.

AUGUST 7 TO 13—INCLUSIVE.

SALOON AND RESTAURANT FIXTURES.

Albrecht, Lorenz. 117th .. G Ehret. (R) $1,000

Albrecht, Joseph. 107 Av C... Bernheimer & S. (R) 800

Alten, Meta H. 115 West Broadway....G Ehret. (R) 1,000

Adamko, Andrew. 725 E 6th....Bernheimer & S. 450

Albert & Tabak. 192 Broome....C Shapiro. Restaurant Fixtures. 100

Brown & Brower. 72 East Broadway....J Everard. (R) 1,532

Rayer, Etienne. 33 Bowery....J Kress B Co. (R) 750

Biondi, Sbarra & Riccio. 75 Mulberry....Budweiser B Co. 650

Boley, Benjamin. 951 1st av....J C G Hupfel B Co. 500

Burghard, Geo. 110 3d av....M Eckstein B Co. (R) 1,200

Buttner, Simon. 2374 3d av ...H Koehler & Co. 1,000

Bergin, Patrick. 484 10th av....W L Flanagan. 3,500

Berthold, C A. 251 Bowery....G Ehret. (R) 2,000

Bondy, Arthur. 49 Bowery ...I Lindemann. Restaurant Fixtures. 4,000

Buttner, Simon. 304 Bowery....H Koehler & Co. 1,500

Berge, Christ. 544 W 29th....V Loewers (R) 700

Bernstein, Morris. 226 Broome....D Mayer. (R) 1,000

Blake, P J. 2739 8th av....Bernheimer & S. (R) 2,000

Blint, Gus. 5 Norfolk....S Liebmann's Sons B Co. 600

Christ, Sebastian. 535 W 110th....Bernheimer & S. (R) 1,300

Cagiano, Venanzo. 430 E 112th....Bernheimer & S. (R) 300

Clark, J C and J J. 176 Madison ...C Frese. 725

Coakley, Frank. 911 6th av....J Ruppert. (R) 600

Converse, J L. 116 Wall....White, Hentz & Co. 6,232

Cooper, John. 553 Hudson....Bernheimer & S. (R) 600

Clancy & Hennessy. 791 8th av....Beadleston & W. 1,400

De Boer, J H. 130 E 85th....Wagner & S. Pool Table. 150

Devery, Patrick. 124th st and 1st av....D Stevenson. 900

Drahos, Joseph. 426 E 73d....Budweiser B Co. 368

Duffy, P H. 442 Washington....Lawrence Myers Co. 800

Doehle, Daniel. 777 3d av ...G Ehret. (R) 1,800

Duhrkoop, C H. 83 3d av....G Ehret. (R) 1,068

Davoren & Kerwick. 858 3d av....Beadleston & W. (R) 4,000

Edmonds, John. 327 W 25th....J J Buckley. 500

Eisler, L. C. 378 7th av....F Melzer. Pool Table. (R) 20

Esberg, I B. 215 7th....L Ehrman. 300

Esberg, I B. 215 7th....M Esberg. 550

Engelsberg, Ernst. 224 1st av....G Ringler & Co. 600

Engster, Albert. 125 Elizabeth....Budweiser B Co. 400

Fayman, Salomon. 48 Allen....Leibinger & Oehm B Co. (R) 700

Frank & McKesson. 130 W 23d....Mary E McKesson. 2,000

Fuchs, Michael. 614 E 9th....Budweiser B Co. (R) 1,500

Fackhamm, John. 77 Lexington av....P & W Ebling. 4,800

Falk, Dominick. 406 and 408 7th av....G Ehret. (R) 2,000

Farrell, M J. 189 Worth....F & M Schaefer B Co. (R) 2,000

Same. 21 Chatham sq....same. (R) 2,000

Flynn, Edward. 20 Bowery....S Liebmann's Sons B Co. 1,500

Fay, J J. 180 Amsterdam av....J Everard. 3,000
Garlan, Joseph. 203 W 58th....Bernheimer & S. 500
Geromanos, Lizzie. 30 Carmine....Burr, Son & Co. (R) 525
Gombossy & Eisenman. 294 Bowery....Rubsam & H B Co. (R) 3,200
Gorman, John. 542 W 29th....Fitzgerald Bros. Ale Pump. (R) 100
Grimm, Thomas. 436 East Houston....S Liebmann's Sons B Co. 790
Gundlach, John. 162 2d av....Bernheimer & S. (R) 500
Goossen, Herman. 73 E 88th....J Everard. 507
Gardella, Louis. 161 Worth....India Wharf B Co. 200
Gas, E and K. 46 Av A....J Ruppert. (R) 5,400
Gough, Edward. 508 10th av....G Ehret. (R) 900
Grassmuck, Joseph. 120 Nassau....G Ehret. (R) 5,500
Grote, George. 349 Hudson ...J G Grote. Restaurant Fixtures. 400
Gruetter, Arnold. 555 9th av....V Loewers. 550
Gaiser, Louis. 182 Ludlow. ..Budweiser B Co. (R) 1,650
Glaser, Bertha. 342 E 49th ...D M Koehler. (R) 300
Hamann, Annie. 56 9th av.. .Bernheimer & S. 1,000
Hayes, Edward. 685 2d av....Budweiser B Co. (R) 851
Hustedt, Hermann. 1740 Lexington av....G Ehret. 1,000
Hauser, Jacob. 419 E 82d....Bernheimer & S. (R) 850
Hein, Albert. 209 E 40th....G Ehret. (R) 800
Hoffman, Jacob. 169 Av C....Burr B Co. 400
Horling & meller. 174 E 106th....Bernheimer & S. (R) 2,300
Koedding, Balthasar. 885 2d av....F Oppermann, Jr. 600
Kolm, Fritz. 1448 1st av....F Hower B Co. 500
Kraatz, Albert. 1794 3d av....F Oppermann, Jr. 500
Ketchum, H S. 794 8th av....A H Gardner &c. Restaurent. 350
Kief, John. 436 E 58th....J Kress B Co. 600
Kaiser, Charles. 263 7th av.. .Burr B Co. (R) 1,600
Lanigan & Barry. 1433 Av A....C O'Neill. 600
Lochhead, J R. 100 Broome....D Stevenson. 800
Malchow, Charles. 740 11th av....Budweiser B Co. 950
Manning, Joseph. 2231 2d av....J Ruppert. 600
Maglio, Antonio. 252 Elizabeth ...T R Lane. 60
McAuliffe, C & M. 183d st and Ryer av....A Westphal. 500
McDonald, P T. 526 W 27th....V Loewers. (R) 350
McQuillan, Edward. 1210 1st av....P Doelger. (R) 1,000
Meehan, Patrick. 253 10th av....Bernheimer & S. (R) 300
Merz, John. 1544 2d av....F Hower B Co. 100
Mulhern, J T. 1349 2d av....P Doelger. (R) 2,000
Muller, Michael. 1549 1st av....Bernheimer & S. 4,000
Mansfield, William. 2995 3d av....A Hupfel's Son. 2,800
Maurel, Louise. 25 South 5th av....A Cohendet. Restaurant Fixtures, &c. 605
Same....C R Ruegger. Furniture. 120
McKallen, Felix. 218 E 89th ...P Doelger. (R) 281
Masona, Dominic. 60 Baxter....V Loewers. 250
Medau, P G. 2756 8th av....F & M Schaefer B Co. 500
Morris, John. 991 10th av ...Bernheimer & S. (R) 1,000
Nichels, Joseph. 1803 9th....Bernheimer & S. (R) 1,500
O'Reilly, Myles. 69 Gansevoort....M Van Rensselaer, Jr. 200
O'Connor, L & H. 1959 2d av....H Vogel. (R) 355
Same....F & M Schaefer B Co. (R) 500
O'Connor, T E. 51 Beach....Fitzgerald Bros. Ale Pump. (R) 150
Peschke, Otto. 149 Essex....J C G Huppel B Co. 1,000
Prehn, J H. 275 Broome....P Doelger. 5,000
Pick, Henry. 80 Nassau....A Bondy. Restaurant. 1,040
Pfriemer, Joseph. 128 Columbia....J Doelger's Son. 500
Pye, John. 109 West Houston....Budweiser B Co. (R) 2,350
Pohl, George. 76 7th av....J C G Hupfel. 6,000
Quirk, J M. 443 W 16th... M Van Rensselaer, Jr. (R) 1,000
Quick, William. 401 E 34th....F Baar. 8,317
Rosenberg, Louis. 105 Cannon....F Rosenberg. Pool. 100
Rugen, Catharine. 40 South st and 34 Old slip ....Haaren & Meinken. 6,500
Rocco, Verrilli & Co. 193 Hester....P Schaefer & Co. 3,300
Rottler, Bernhard. 121 Broome....Budweiser B Co. (R) 800
Schaffer, G. W. 859 3d av....J Kress B Co. (R) 1,500
Schnoper, Martin. 169 2d....Budweiser B Co. (R) 300
Schoenberger, Pinctos. 61 Cannon....D Stevenson. 200
Soobda, Joseph. 231 E 3d....Budweiser B Co. 1,600
Spiegel, H. 502 8th av....Brunswick-Balke-C Co. Pool Table, &c. 225
Sutter & Idler. 95 and 97 Pearl and 80 Stone.... J Kress B Co. (R) 3,000
Safran, Max. 1875 3d av....Wagner & S. Pool. 150
Schmadeke, F W. 371 Washington....G Ehret and others. (R) 500
Schoemann, Theresa. 1380 3d av....Beadleston & W. (R) 1,500
Siegfried, Adam. 183 Duane....Beadleston & W. 2,000
Schneider, Gottlieb. 1583 1st av....H Elias B Co. 700
Tranquillini, Hannes. 7 St Marks pl .... E Loenthal. Restaurant Fixtures. 300
Tighe, J C. 10th av and 102d st....H Koehler & Co. (R) 3,699
Taaffe, Ellen. 635 W 46th....D Stevenson. 600
Tivers, Thomas. 76th st and 10th av....Budweiser B Co. (R) 450
Ulrich, George. 1502 Av B....G. Ehret (R) 2,000
Van Clief, Jacob. 212 E 127th....C Iba 475
Von Gerichten, William. 126 E 120th... F & M Schaefer B Co. (R) 900
Walfish & Pariman. 98 Clinton... Restaurant Furniture Co. Restaurant Fixtures. 20
Wakely, James. 42d st and 6th av....J Everard. 10,150
Wieben, John. 58 Thomas....Bernheimer & S. (R) 1,500
West, S F. 20 Bowery....S Liebmann's Sons B Co. 10,000

HOUSEHOLD FURNITURE.

Ahern, K and N. 188 E 100th....A Romer. 147
Allen, Anna. 68 E 12th....O'Farrell & Co. 258
Anderson, F M. 345 W 21st ...F G Smith. Piano. (R) 175
Anderson, A B. 116 E 123d....J Moriarty. (R) 165
Ap l, Elizabeth. 808 1st av... Simpson & P. Piano. 190
Alvarez, Joseph. 171 E 107th....J Moriarty. 117
Angle, Isabella. 112 W 32d....W E Wheelock & Co. Piano. 350
Bayne, Mary E. 296 W 142d....W E Wheelock & Co. Piano. 160
Bessoe, C L. 984 6th av....E C Hinsdale. 190
Beggini, Mary F. 988 10th av....R M Walters. Piano. (R) 174
Blunt, C and E S. 1 W 83d....E C Hinsdale. 255
Buday, Bertha. 307 E 74th....W E Wheelock & Co. Piano. 250
Bertault, Edward. 102 W 94th... L Baumann. (R) 223
Bach, Nina. 59 2d av....Fennell & Pye. (R) 158
Beatty, Mary F. 332 E 35th....Jordan & M. 119
Bernstein, Jacob. 155 E 104th....H S Eisler. 100
Bennett, Tillie....J Moriarty. 152
Blackburn, J N. 319 W 134th....J Baumann. 211
Brennan, Kate. 714 3d av....Krakauer Bros. Piano. (R) 154
Brennan, Louisa A. 195 Prince ...J Gregg. Piano. 298
Borot, H E. 105 Madison av....S Knapp Co. (R) 171
Calcagui, Lena F. 315 W 144th....J Baumann. 540
Carroll, Mary A. 260 W 16th....H Thoesen. 167
Carlisle, May. 188 E 48th....H Israel & Sons. 417
Carsebohm, Lillie. 1766 9th av....S Hyman & Co. (R) 126
Church, Alice. 212 E 97th....O'Farrell & Co. 142
Same....same. 150
Casey, E J. 120 E 120th....W E Wheelock & Co. Piano. 200
Cronin, Laura. 450 W 50th....W E Wheelock & Co. Piano. 375
Daly, Nellie J. 592 E 137th....W E Wheelock & Co. Piano. 300
Drummond, C L. 221 W 133d....L Baumann. 128
Dinkelberg, F P. 83 W 86th....J Baumann. (R) 121
Disney, Joseph. 441 W 39th....Simpson & P. Piano. (R) 150
Duke, Georgia. 220 E 18th... J Gregg. (R) 120
Durlacher, J F. 73 E 121st....Manges Bros. 435
Eaton, Sadie M. 158 W 13th....T J Kieley. secures rent
Finckbohm, Leno. 430 E 17th....H S Eisler. 108
Fischer, Mary. 2251 7th av....Bollermann & Son. Piano. 325
Flynn, P J. 138 W 60th... L Baumann. 191
Frueh, August. 9 Spruce....E C Hinsdale. 190
Grass, A W. 135 W 101st....Alexander Bro. 187
Gurvitch, Isidor. 18 Market....Alexander Bro. 477
Gracie, George. 209 E 95th....J Moriarty. 268
Gardner, Patience M. 146-150 W 53d....M A Birtles. 1,460
Guttmann, Malvine. 332 E 123d....Krakauer Bros. Piano. 270
Galt, Mary I. 37 and 38 Gramercy Park....S Knapp & Co. (R) 2,850
Gillette, Mrs R. 212 W 46th ...S Knapp & Co. (R) 430
Hanley, Sarah F. 441 Canal ...Simpson & P. Piano. (R) 103
Hart, Mrs G W. 14 E 29th....S Knapp & Co. (R) 479
Hull, Ella E. 341 W 55th....J Moriarty. 310
Same. 101 Lexington av....same. 392
Hilman, G E. 138 W 43d....T E Thompson. 250
Johnson, G H. 167th st and 10th av....Dreisacker & Co. 128
Judge, Margaret. 430 W 46th....J Baumann. 118
Khuen, Frank. 155 Amsterdam av....J Baumann. 483
Klemm, Leopoldine. 234 E 21st .. L Baumann. 214
King, Thomas. 298 Henry....Jordan & M. 153
Lindsey, Jennie. 145 W 16th....Jordan & M. 359
Lochhead, J R & A. 100 Broome....P H Cavanagh. 100
Lowenberg, Rose. 77 W 47th....Amer Guar Assoc. 150
Lusk, O L. 322 W 23d... C E Pierce. 130
Lembach, Theodore. 409 E 52d....W E Wheelock & Co. Piano. 300
Lawrence, Ruby. 1028 6th av. ..J Baumann. 583
Leima, Lorenze. 536 W 48th....J Baumann. 171
Marcus, Abram. 11 E 1st S Green. 1,000
McCarthy, J W. 501 W 59th....Manges Bros. 140
McGowan, Elizabeth. 288 E 48th....J Baumann. 149
Mendoza, Bella. 57 Bond....Manges Bros. (R) 110
Monge, Abel. 345 E 20th....J Baumann 776
Mayo, Peter. 335 E 23d....W E Wheelock & Co. Piano. 250
Meeks, Annie. 167 W 22d... L Baumann. 702
Marr, Geo. 121 Allen . J Moriarty. 137
Martin, Mary. 244 E 21st ... J Moriarty. 180
Martin, Maria. 56 Stanton. ..Voss & Law. 1,500
McInerney, R and M. 234 E 32d....B Feeney. 251
Meallet, Louisa. 151 W 62d....Jordan & M. 117
Minzesheimer, Clara. 646 Lexington av.... Krakauer Bros. Piano. 250
Maloney, Dean Mrs C. Amsterdam av... S Hyman & Co. 114
Neumark, A. 324 E 52d ....Krakauer Bros. Piano. 325
Nelson, Laura. 239 W 126th....J Baumann. 129
Newman, Jennie. 2205 5th av....J Baumann. 246
O'Brien, Mattie. 231 E 21st....J Moriarty. 198
Same. 234 E 21st....same. 198
O'Connell, J P. 221 W 67th....O'Farrell & Co. 121
Ostrowsky, W. 159 2d ...H S Eisler. (R) 206
Perez, Ensebio. 369 W 40th....L Baumann. 175
Price, Lettie. 224 W 62d....L Baumann. 198
Pearson, Elizabeth. 1514 10th av....J Moriarty. (R) 110
Petersen, Anna. 264 W 22d... J Gregg. 166
Phillips, S. 83 Delancey....Simpson & P. Piano. (R) 180
Quigley, M J. 52 Spring....Fennell & Pye. (R) 120
Quinn, M E. 253 W 15th....L Baumann. 184
Reed, Emily. 439 W 57th....J Baumann. (R) 165
Reilly, Louise. 22 Barrow....J S Rice. 125
Rein, M J. 312 Spring....Fennell & Pye. (R) 129
Reuton, Louis. 413 E 82d....J S Rice. 118
Rixa, Alex. 1268 Lexington av....S Hyman & Co. 191
Rosenberg, George. 346 E 85th .. S Hyman & Co. 127
Sharp, Mary E. 12 and 14 E 28th....L Baumann. 172
Simons, J W....M Bender. 277
Smiller, Sarah. 119 W 56th....C E Pierce. 130
Somerville, John. 39 King....O'Farrell & Co. 204
Sudeck, Gustav. 204 E 65th....W H Knox. 100
Sartoris, Minnie. 25 W 31st....S Baumann. 351
Smith, Maggie. 140 W 27th... L Baumann. 102
Smith, Bridget. 509 W 49th....M Wichelhaus. (R) 140
Strauss, Max. 491 2d av....J Moriarty. 128
Schloming, Harry. 362 W 116th....L Baumann. 341
Stepan, Johanna. 159 E 95th....L Baumann. 297
Schacht, Mary. 423 E 14th....G Leist. 200
Starkey, Lizzie....Gately & W. 229
Stewart, W H. 454 W 58th....J Baumann. 136
Trauebman, Josephine. 10 Rivington....Alexander Bros. (R) 260
Turner, Julia. 214 W 33d....O'Farrell & Co. 166
Tray, J J. 226 W 4th....Krakauer Bros. Piano. 160
Toohill, A F. 164 E 100th....Manges Bro. (R) 107
Vedder, A F....M Vedder. (R) 100
Weisiger, P. 58 and 60 W 19th....S Knapp & Co. (R) 1,230
Westropp, Maggie. 533 W 46th....H Thoesen. 112
Wilson, Hattie. 314 W 59th....J Baumann. 350
Wheelock, J A. 326 W 36th....C E Pierce. 100
Williamson, Ada. 105 W 40th....J F Manges. (R) 254
Wilson, G E. 744 Broadway....L Baumann. 231
Woods, Margaret. 70 W 106th....J C Hegemann. 134
Washington, Elizabeth. 453 6th av....L Baumann. 114
Waters, R E and C. 798 6th....R B De Casanova. 135
Wengel, K C. 227 W 67th....L Baumann. 127
Wild, William. 337 2d av....Amer Guar Assoc. 100
Zeien, H. 248 W 124th....J J Coogan. 119

MISCELLANEOUS.

Alsdorf, John. 98 Columbus av....C L Rickerson. Drug Fixtures. 750
American Preserves Co. 754 Washington.... Hall's Safe and Lock Co. Safe. 170
A W Lindsay Type Foundry. 76 Park pl....D W Bruce. Machines, &c. (R) 5,000
Arnowitz, L. 418 10th av and 442 W 33d st....C F Pierce. Machinery. 130
Bertram, Ferdinand. Morris Dock....G Eicke. Bottler Fixtures. 650
Bobb, William. 802 10th av....P Westphal Barber Fixtures. (R) 190
Brettler, Marx. 537 E 18th....S Baer. Grocery Fixtures. 100
Burhenne & Demuth. 42 W 67th....P Pryibil. Machinery. 81
Burnett, Charles. 40 W 18th....D Daly. Horse and Cab. 60
Bassemir, John. 247 Centre....Dora Bassemir. Machinery. 1,000
Bottger, Annie. 254 W 47th....C H Tuthill. Horses, Wagon, &c. 1,834
Bottjer, C A. 254 W 47th .. Bischoff & Meyerhoff. Horses, Truck, &c. (R) 603
Buggie, Henry. 321 1st av....M L Merrill. Drug Fixtures. (R) 750
Bihler & Duffy. 305 Pearl....T E Gaskill et al. Machinery, &c. 1,000
Bleibler, Martin. 48 Av D....C Jaeger. Horses, &c. 350
Blitzer, H. 69 Clinton....P Reidenbach. Wagon. 150
Bolger, Edward. 335 E 59th....J Cunningham Son & Co. Coach. 200
Boyd & Co. 2269 7th av....Marvin Safe Co. Safe. 135
Brown, Ezra. 542 Hudson....R S Brown. Wagons, &c. 1,600
Brown, William. 529 W 45th....W Garms. Horses, Trucks, &c. 457
Buckley & Wood. 220 William....H L Bridgman....Machines. (R) 781
Brinke, C H. 296 Hudson....Lamson Consol S S Co. Register. 140
Campbell, James. 136 Liberty... Marvin Safe Co. Safe. 168
Caplin, H and H. 46 Grand .. R Caplin. Press, &c 800
Citro, Ginseppe. 43 Mulberry....V De Vita. Bakery Fixtures. 140
Cohen & Einbinder. 97 Allen....M Silbermann. Butcher. 50
Cosmopolitan Range Co. 245-249 Centre....F Cavagnaro. Franchises, &c. 5,000
Cohen, Daniel. 1 Ridge and 261 Division.... Lincoln Ind G Co. Butcher Fixtures. 100
Call, G & Co....Young & Farrell Diamond Stone Sawing Co. Machinery. (R) 13,277
Cooney, P J. 501 E 144th....P Pryibil. Machinery. 130
De Intinis & Marotti. 162 Greenwich....L Cucci. Barber Fixtures. 176
Delany Bros....G Dessecker. Coffin Wagon. 275
Dentel, Paul. 307 E 115th. ..J Heck. Wagon. 80
Ellis, Margaret. 1788 Broadway....H Heups. Store Fixtures. 267
Eggler, F, Jr. 62d st and 11th av... A C Manning & Co. Machinery. 1,250
Elliott, W B ...N Y City Ice Co. Horse, Wagon, &c. (R) 800
Fitzpatrick, C B. 47 Great Jones... J Matthews. Soda Fixtures. 960
Fina, Carmine. 597 3d av....G Lordi. Barber Fixtures. 38
Finan, James. 202 E 77th....J Cunningham Son & Co. Harness. 100
Frohwein, Otto. 1260 3d av....A D Puffer & Co. Soda Fixtures. 800
Finnegaro, Andrew....T Quinn. Horse. 75
Flesch & Slomin. 118 Ridge....A Barenfeld. Drug Fixtures. 100
Gillie, G B and J B. 161st st and Jerome av.... Shaler & Hall Quarry Co. Machinery, &c. 7,000
Gerson, Mrs E. 248 Division ...Bennett & G. Bottler Fixtures. 300
Gibson Electric Co....F Storrs trustee. Franchises, &c. (R) 20,000
Grossman, Geo. 622 W 131st and 421 E 120th.... A M Stein & Co. Horses, Carts, &c. (R) 1,500
Gibb, Bros & Moran... Campbell P P Co. Press. (R) 900
Gibb Bros....Campbell P P Co. Press. (R) 3,050
Same....same. Press. (R) 2,400
Same....same. Press. (R) 110
Heenni, Charles G Dessecker. Coach. (R) 125
Hickson, Mary. 540 W 56th....Lamson Consol S S Co. Register. 140
Huneke, D. 207 7th av....Lamson Consol S S Co. Register. 150
Hay, Peter. 58 Clinton . .W Scott & Co. Press, &c. 2,900
Henne, William. 3d st and Av D ...A C Manning & Co. Machinery. 1,250
Heernance Company. 309-313 Greenwich and 145-151 Reade....R Hewitt trustee. Machinery, &c. 35,000
Horwitz & Shrieber. 59 Forsyth....Sekowsky Bros. Store Fixtures. 623
Hubel & Plechinger. 345 E 81st....E Marscheider. Butcher Fixtures. 234
Hurst & Co. 134 and 136 Grand....Mosler Safe Co. Safe. 235
Hay, Peter. 58 Centre....R Schinzel. Press, &c. 3,200
Hertz & Green. 2154 2d av....J Stewart. Machines. 65
Hickok, W P. 317 Broadway....N Herder. Type. 70

Horowitz, Harris. 120 Hester....R Ginsburg. Machines. 67
Hull, Lewis R. 218 W 16th....L Thayer. Horses and Ice Wagons. (R) 848
Joiner, Walter. 476-480 E 139th ...S A Woods Machine Co. Machinery. 265
Krebs, Friedrich. 1411 Lexington av....C Eisenfelder. Barber Fixtures. 90
Kessel, Margaret....India Wharf B Co. Horse. 150
Kaufmann, Herman. 242 E 80th....Abels & Co. Horses, Trucks, &c. 200
Kenny, T A, Jr. 15 Attorney....P A Cassidy. Wagon. 140
Krenrich & Kemmer. 228 E 44th....Berlin Machine Works. Machi ery. 750
Lopes & Caliva. 855 1st av ..P Saprenza. Barber Fixtures. 120
Lemcke, Chris. 218 St Nicholas av....Lamson Consol S S Co. Register. 140
Lingemann, George....F Glamann. Truck. 50
Lally, Ellen S. 617 2d av....J J O'Connell. Butcher Fixtures. 300
Lumley, A T. 8 Park pl....F Willets. Press, &c., of N. Y. Illustrated News. (R) 5,000
Lyman, Jacob. 98 Sheriff....P Ronder. Machines. 110
Lynch, M J. 207 E 110th....A A Stein. Type, Presses, &c. 2,500
Levensohn & Spector. 44 Canal....J Stewart. Machines. 412
Martelli, Santo. 280 Mott....A Doino. Bakery Fixtures. 70
Megna, S. 773 2d av....A Beesley. Grocery Fixtures. 180
Meise, H H. 151 and 158 E 128th....D Wakeman. Machinery. (R) 1,200
Merkel, August. 2562 8th av....A Merkel. Butcher Fixtures. 700
Mohlmeyer, William. 246 W 17th....F Gokenholz. Grocery Fixtures. (R) 1,200
Moody, W J. 150 W 4th ...R Donnelly. Horses, Carts, &c. 600
Mack, Edward....G Meyer. Coach. 100
Manecke, Philip. 50 Centre....E Lunitz. Drug Fixtures. (R) 1,750
Manhattan Tea and Portrait Co. 38 Great Jones....Mosler Safe Co. Safe. 110
Mason, J A. 203 E 124th....W Scott & Co. Press. 875
Meyer, H M. 710 Washington.....G Meier. Horses, Trucks, &c. 400
Mucciacciaro, N & Co. 54 Spring ...W H Butler. Safe. 175
Murphy, Patrick. 403 E 47th....A Canning. Machinery. (R) 105
Meier, F and M. 601 Water... A Fischer. Bakery. (R) 1,600
Meier, Gustav. 2031 2d av....E Marscheider. Butcher Fixtures. 85
Macomber, R W....J H & C J Malone. Horses, Milk Wagons, &c. 850
McGowan, P & P. 204 E 81st....T Hagan. Machinery. 500
Michel, Valentine. 462 E 144th....H Eggers & Co. Grocery Fixtures. 112
Newman, H. 88 Pitt....J Stewart. Machine. 14
Parrett, Arthur. 191 and 193 Worth....J McPartland. Machinery. 10,000
Peyser, Nat....P Barrett. Truck. 100
Quinn, J E. 2220 3d av....Bramhall, Deane & Co. Range, &c. (R) 90
Ringersen, Jacob. 690 E 154th. ..E Sturzenegger. Machines. 150
Rose, W A....P Barrett. Truck. 285
Richardson & Gibb....Campbell P P Co. Press. (R) 1,500
Richardson, M T... Campbell P P Co. Press. (R) 1,600
Ruttenberg & Rosenberg. 139 and 139½ Madison....J Stewart. Machines. 375
Schuss, Marie ..J Heiling. Horse, Wagon, &c. 100
Schwarze & Cohn. 131 South 5th av....E Siegman. Machines. 1,530
Seabold, R S....Blake & Sullivan. Grocery Fixtures. 250
Studley, F J. 309 E 11th....A A Clute. Horse, Wagon, &c. 100
Sweet, W N & Co. 28 Reade ...Hall's Safe & Lock Co. Safe. 150
Sainberg, L. 107 William....J L Morrison & Co. Machine. 80
Schiro, Vittorio. 185 Av C....F Arra. Barber Fixtures. 125
Schreiner, John. 60 White....L A Dischinger. Barber Fixtures. 1,500
Sherlock, Mary....G Meyer. Coach. 100
Shields, Edward....G Meyer. Coach. 350
Sostmann, William. 60 Varick....H Harms. Grocery Fixtures. 800
Stafford, E B and A G. 508 3d av... A D Puffer & Son. Soda Fixtures. 775
Stollmack, Solomon. 47 Canal....J Rubenstein. Photo Fixtures. 100
Schmolze & Weifenbach. 88 Fulton....R. Hoe & Co. Press. 3,250
Schlitz, John. 869 9th av....P Schlitz. Barber Fixtures. 250
Stockfisch, Emma M. 35 Amsterdam av.... Koenig & S. Grocery Fixtures. 1,168
Thie, Otto. 17 John....H Jaeger. Jewelry Fixtures. 750
Same....L Schottmiller. Jewelry Fixtures. 400
Tassi, Raphael. 6 Gouverneur slip....L Palermo. Machinery. 900
Thomson & Co. 55 Dey....C Craske. Presses, &c. (R) 2,175
Thompson, R G. 149 E 130th....E Decker. Horses, Tools, &c. 2,800
Utjer, Henry. 2631 8th av....M Peters. Truck. 600
Vette Bros....P Barrett. Truck. (R) 75
Warren & Fowler. 76-78 Varick....L B Huse. Presses, &c. (R) 2,525
Welling, Joseph. 1491 Sullivan....J B Thorpe. Wagon, &c. 200
Young & Cook. 256 W 30th....A Busby. Horses, &c. 145

BILLS OF SALE.

Appel, Louis. 25 Lispenard....D Weiss. Restaurant Fixtures 1,500
Beck, David. 181 South ...M Klinkowstein. Saloon Fixtures. 1,000
Chieffo, Onofrio. 52 Mulberry... A Sarro. Grocery Fixtures. 1,500
Condon, Michael....P Cadley. News Stand, &c. 20
Cordts, H M. 183 Duane....A Siegfried. Saloon Fixtures. 6,000
Dondero, Charles. 192 Wooster .. Catarina Rossi. Grocery Fixtures. 200
De Benedetto, Antonio. 200 Park row....G Marrone. Tailor Fixtures. 150
Eilenberg, Berthold. 42 Division....H Bergman ....Machines. 200
Harrison, Mary R. 104 W 58th....W H Harrison, Paintings, &c. 1,000

Kleeblatt, Max. 305 E 83d....S Kleeblatt. Saloon Fixtures. 350
Koenig, Josephine. 149 E 89th....Elizabeth Weiss. Furniture, &c. 2,000
Konig & Schuster. 35 Amsterdam av....Emma M Stockfisch. Grocery Fixtures. 1,168
Miller & Woodbridge....McCreery Bros. Patent "Columbus Egg." 1,000
Muller, Anna. 2302 2d av....Louisa Sprague. Confectionery Fixtures. 400
Penta, Emanuel. 656 Broadway....N Giuliano. Barber Fixtures. 50
Rottner, Samuel. 85 Stanton....S Aaronowitch. Grocery Fixtures. 446
Rosenberg, M L. 2180 8th av....M Condon. News Stand, &c. 20
Schulz, Valentine. 929 2d av....P Buckel. Saloon Fixtures. 1,450
Scheibe, Marie and L. 2182 8th av. ..B Fischer & Co. Grocery Fixtures. 388
Schuler, Eugen. 1583 1st av....G Schneider. Saloon. 1,300
Taylor, James. 327 W 25th....J Edmonds. Saloon Fixtures. 1,000
Zehnder, George. 740 10th av ...J J Zehnder. Bakery Fixtures. 1

ASSIGNMENT OF CHATTEL MORTGAGES.

Kaufman, Isaiah to L Arnstein. (Mort given by I Ledermann, July 31, 1890). 1

KINGS COUNTY.

AUGUST 6 TO 12—INCLUSIVE.

SALOON AND RESTAURANT FIXTURES.

Abraham & Weill. 512 Flushing av... J Weill. Restaurant Fixtures. $200
Ahlers & Paulsen. 164 Johnson....P Weidmann. 500
Albini, V. 71 Adams....H B Scharmann. (R) 250
Beatty, W. 707 3d av....M Seitz. 600
Boser, G. 178 Ewen....J Kress B Co. (R) 700
Bouquet & Loeffler. 34-36 Maujer and 26 Maujer... J Kress B Co. (R) 734
Blohm, A. 223 Kent av....Burger & Hower B Co (Lim). 1,000
Boyan, Julia. 225 Broadway....J Ruppert. 3,000
Burggraf, J and Emma. 545 Grand....M Seitz. 700
Bertsh, A. 25 Ten Eyck....J Fallert B Co. (R) 600
Cassidy, P. 346 Franklin av....Catherine Byrne. 655
Churchill, A E. 320 Van Brunt ...M Eckhoff. 600
Clark, F H. 316 Bedford av....Claus Lipsius B Co. 1,000
Collins, J F. 474 Bergen....D Yuill. 500
Clahane, H. 351 Grand... Rubsam & Herrmann B Co. (R) 400
Downs, P. 1596 Broadway....M Seitz. (R) 1,645
Doyle, E and J Matthews. 777 Washington av ....Budweiser B Co. 310
Dietz, C C and G F McArdle....96 Hudson av.... P Weidmann. 68
Dockendorf, Emma. 141 Montrose av....Fort Hamilton B Co. 500
Dunn, J L. 40 Willoughby... Long Island Brewery. 1,500
Darraugh, A. 490 Manhattan av....J Fallert B Co. 1,500
Erzinger, J. 155 Harrison av....J Doelger's Sons. 400
Feldmann, H. 222 Hamburg av....Leibinger & O B Co. 550
Farrell, M J. 182 Worth, N Y....F & M Schaefer B Co. (R) 2,000
Same. 21 Chatham sq, New York....same. (R) 200
Fischer, A. 30 Sumner av ...Leibinger & O B Co. (R) 550
Graf, Elise and J. 61 Cook....Leibinger & O B Co. (R) 450
Hannon, T. 3d av, n e cor 19th st ...J Ruppert. (R) 500
Hartmann, P. 208 Moore....J Kress B Co. (R) 1,430
Hornung, J F. 28 Boerum pl....Leibinger & O B Co. (R) 1,500
Heck, L. 1497 Gates av....Leibinger & O B Co. (R) 519
Hoppe, H. Fulton av and Williams pl....Eliz Meltzer. (R) 300
Hons, H. 61 South 8th....Claus Lipsius B Co. 1,000
Hayden, F T and H W Stevens. 580 and 582 Fulton....G H Huber. 3,500
Kaffenberger, P. 244 Court st....J N Grunewald. 1,200
Keller, R. 60 Graham av....L Epig. 100
Kennedy, J. 1854 Fulton....Welz & Zerwick. 352
Koner, J. 84 Seigel... Burger & Hower B Co. 500
Kretschmer, Mary. 1069 Flushing av....Fort Hamilton Brewing Co. 666
Kenna, J. 245 Hoyt.....Budweiser B Co. (R) 1,325
Lellig, J. 217 Johnson av....Leibinger & O B Co. (R) 529
Luca, H. 99 Nostrand av....Leibinger & O B Co. (R) 300
McAulay, W. 3 Somers....Anna Bunger. 1,128
Same....W Ulmer. 775
Metzger, F. 218 Graham av....Welz & Zerwick 2,000
Mount, C A. 273 Nassau....Budwieser B Co. 1,500
Mueller, J. 170 McKibbin.... M Seitz. 570
McNamara, T. 688 Bedford av ...E Ochs. 500
Meyer, R. 826 Myrtle av....Otto Huber Brewery. 3,000
McEnery, J. 141 Gold....Claus Lipsius B Co. 300
O'Brien, J....C Hart. Scow. (R) 1,000
O'Donnell, T M. 548 Vanderbilt av....Abbott B Co. 500
O'Brien, D. Atlantic av, cor Sackman st.... Budweiser B Co. (R) 135
Ott, G. 983 Flushing av....Leibinger & O B Co. (R) 300
Peterson, J. 1663 Broadway....Leibinger & O B Co. (R) 500
Porcio, P. 36 Main....H B Scharmann. (R) 250
Peters, Clement. 592 De Kalb av....Christopher Peters. 2,000
Phillips, G C. 1606 Bushwick av... F Roos. 300
Peterson, M and J. 503-507 Hamilton av.... Williamsburgh B Co. 400
Pollak, L. 441 Broadway ...Burr B Co. 1,000
Rogers, T. 324 19th....J Fallert B Co. 500
Ryan, E. 1058 3d av....Abbott B Co. 500
Ryan, E. 936 4th av. ..Abbott B Co. 500
Rath, Bertha. 548 Wythe av....O Huber Brewery. 1,725
Reese, L. 217 Court....Olena & Craig. (R) 2,000
Ropke, F. 951 Herkimer....W Ulmer. 1,050
Rapp, A. 72 Diamond....J Kress B Co. (R) 1,220
Rapporte, A. 30 Osborn....Budweiser B Co. 400
Sander, H. 869 Bedford....Leibinger & O B Co. (R) 800
Schanz, J. 165 Fort Greene pl....M Seitz. 612
Skelly, G W. 125 Bushwick av.....Budweiser B Co. (R) 1,000

Schaffel & Flack. 56 Moore....Wagner & S. Pool Table. 160
Schaffel, B & H Flack. 56 Moore....Burger & Hower B Co (Lim). 500
Schumacher, L. 722 4th av... H E Kane. 500
Saltzmann, D. 349 Leonard....J Kress B Co. 800
Schmidt, C. 16 Havemeyer....J. Everard. 822
Schneider, W. 15 Old Coney Island road....Abbott B Co. 300
Treiber, J. 182 Stagg....E Ochs. 300
Thornton, J E. 129 24th....M Seitz. 656
Wagner, M. 93 Clay....H Greenfeld. 800
Wild, J. 378 Leonard....W H Griffith & Co. Billiards. 100
Wisbauer, W. 150 Union av....E Ochs. 750
Wright, R S. 280 Kent av....P Doelger. 741
Zehe, C M. 341 Nevins....C Steffens. (R) 962

HOUSEHOLD FURNITURE.

Albrecht, Mrs H. 71 Lorimer....J Mason. 167
Alm, C G. 775 Atlantic av....J Michaels. 121
Barnum, C H. 70 Decatur....I Mason. 111
Brown, Jennie S. 506 Grand av....J Michaels. 127
Barg, W T. Myrtle av, cor Marcy av ...C T Kendrick & Co. 228
Berry, J T. 464 Belmont av....J McEnery & Co. 155
Bicknell, J. 180 Jay....Sarah J Casanova. 117
Brown, A M. 2069 Dean....S I Shimberg. 100
Brown, Mrs S E. 1087 Atlantic av....I Mason. 132
Burns, Lillian. 272 Berry ..L Baumann. 243
Cregan, S A. 174 Hall ...L Baumann. 179
Califas, Mrs J. 1103 3d av....I Mason. 110
Conklin, W H. 508 Herkimer....R G Lockwood's Sons. 76
Dorge, E....Krakauer Bros. Piano. 165
Duane, May. 104 Summit....Simpson & P. Piano. 125
Deming, E. 335 St Marks av....W D Crowell. 110
Fleming, J S. 417 Waverly av... J R Wood. 250
Fonseca, F E. 161 State....J McEnery & Co. 559
Gerson, H. 540 Marcy av....C T Kendrick & Co. Carpets. 118
Howell, G S. 91 Spencer st...C T Kendrick & Co. 256
Kennedy, Melinda. 658 Bedford av....Mary A. Birtles. 280
Jones, Maria. 2106 Dean....R Silverman. 105
Lazarus, J S. 215 Lorimer . .Jacob Bros. Piano. 255
Le Paige, C E. Coney Island ...Mathushek & Son Piano Co. Piano. 100
Lord, A. 177½ Floyd st....C T Kendrick & Co. 146
Ludwig, W. 1223 Gates av...C T Kendrick & Co. 185
McMahon, Mary. 798 Myrtle av....C T Kendrick & Co. 114
Mathews, Mrs J. 172 Elizabeth ...I Mason. 158
McInerney, Mrs J H. 295A McDougal....I Mason. 288
McLaughlin, Ellen. 35 Little Nassau....H S Eisler. 101
Mitchell, W H. 11 Ainslee....J Baumann. 230
Monds, Elizabeth. 1631 De Kalb av....W Weed 250
Mulrenan, W. 151 23d....I Mason. 263
Orderbing, A A. 61 Tompkins pl ...L Baumann. 236
Omy, F. 1845 Broadway... H S Eisler. 135
Phelps, I. Fulton st....W R Woodward. Office. 500
Pritchard, J. Bedford av . .. Jacob Bros. Piano. 145
Pfaff, Lena. 93 Eldert....L Baumann. 220
Post, C. Gravesend, L I....F W Heinrich. Piano. 125
Richmond, Fannie. 137 34th.....I Mason. 100
Renaud, E Anna. 166 De Kalb av....W D Crowell. 210
Smith, Adelie E. Ridgewood av.. .A Schulz. 155
Solon, Mary E. 247 Frost .... Jacob Bros. Piano. 235
Sattler, G. 740 Myrtle av....C T Kendrick & Co. 265
Schaible, Katie. — Elton....C T Kendrick & Co. 120
Schneider, J W. 15 Coney Island road ...E Driscoll & Bro. 144
Thornburg, Annie S and E D. 303 Putnam av.... Haviland & Sons. 105
Thompson, W. Blythebourne....C H Ten Eyck. 100
Timmins, E F. 270 St Marks pl.. .L Baumann. 125
Walton, Annie. 190 Pacific ...Kate Gehrig. Piano. (R) 100
Waugh, G J. Sherman av.. I Mason. 271
Walker, Celestina S. 131 Garfield pl....H V Monahan. 251
Ward, Harriet. 420A Halsey .. J Baumann. 833
Whelan, Mrs E. 237 and 239 Quincy. 120

MISCELLANEOUS.

Adriance, B. Plymouth st, cor Jay st....N Johannsen. Machinery. (R) 609
Bohm, C. 266 Stagg....J Nicklaus. Grocery Fixtures. 150
Broedel, F & Co. 133 Reid av....M Ruppert. Barber Fixtures. 100
Brinkmann, M. 333 South 3d....A Streelmann. Cigar Store Fixtures. 500
Carver, W Capes. Knickerbocker av, cor Madison st....W Carver. Machinery. 1,000
Cartmell, J. Enfield st, cor South road....T J Walters. Cows. 1,500
Cook, David and C A Wilson. 181 4th av....Liberty Machine Works. 350
Cornehlsen, C. 556 Marcy av....H Butt. Milk Route. 500
Davids, C H. Madison st....J Drew. Horse, Wagon, &c. 300
Doe, W S. 619 3d av....J Strathan. Fixtures. (R) 753
Esposito, N and V. 7 Union....S Littman. Barber Fixtures. 712
Ferrante, G A. 47 Atlantic av....R Rossi. Barber Chairs. 70
Feldman, W. 159 Division av ...C Hous. Candy and Ice Cream Store Fixtures. 2,500
Hopkins, J. Monroe st, near Howard av.. .G E Parmelee. Horses. 1,000
Huckans, Bogardus & Dodge, 354 7th av. .. Charlotte S. Dodge. Machinery. 1,000
Hatch, J A....J H Buck. Canal Boat (R) 900
Hoy, P. 58 Centre....Walter Scott & Co. Presses. 2,960
Hayes, W E. 586 Gates av... J W McInnes. Butcher Fixtures. 250
Klein, W. 55 Throop av....Knickerbocker Ice Co. Wagon and Horse. 781
Leidner, J B. 766 Park av....A A Schmidt. Barber Fixtures. 800
Loftus, E. Flatbush....A Pearson. Wagon, &c. 100
Leifels, J J....P Barrett. Truck. 280
Meyer, W. 12-16 Fulton....A C & C Fisher. Hotel Fixtures. 1,850
Mierisch, B. 1203 Myrtle av....Puffer & Sons Mfg Co. Soda Fountain. 175
Muehlhausen, L. 341 Central av....E Seemar. Cigar Store and Pool Room. 200
Neidhart, O. 451 Graham av .... H Maier. Drugs. 1,300
Neumann, C. 789 Broadway....G Frank. Store Fixtures. 175

Oleson, Charles. Hamilton av and Henry st.... J Caulfield. Horse. 100
Roach, Anna M. 140½ Fulton ...O Persanvosky. Fixtures. 115
Schneider, G. 109 Varick....L Schneider. Grocery Fixtures. (R) 500
Spadavecchia, Anne. 570 Atlantic av....Matilda Cacace. Ice Cream Saloon and Factory. 355
Steffens, H W & E A. 44 Myrtle av....W B A Jurgens. Store Fixtures. 2,482
Schlitz, J. 58 Moore....J Cunningham Son & Co. Coach. (R) 123
Schmand, C. Linwood st, near Liberty av....H Fleck. Horses. 850
Walters, T J. 1443 Fulton....J Cartmell. Safe. 150
Wilhelm, S & Co. 118 Union ...Mosler Safe Co. Safe. 105
Wilson, W M.....D B Dunham. Coach. 325
Zeydel, H. 184 and 186 Floyd....Emilie Zeydel. Bottling Business. 600

BILLS OF SALE.

Bedell, H. ..F Shaw, Office Furniture. 105
Bencke, A. 102 Lewis av....Mary C Hale. Carpets, &c. 100
Bongartz, Ferd 90 Graham av... Frank Bongartz. Drug Fixtures. 800
Bullwinkel, M H. 652 Gates av....D Menken. Grocery Fixtures. 1,700
Butt, H. 536 Marcy av....C Cornehlsen. Milk Route. 800
Lynch, J. 896 Myrtle av .. R Meyers. Saloon Fixtures. 5,500
Pritchard, J. 304 Bedford av ...Wolff Sons. Saloon Fixtures. 1,500
Pelcyger, F and P Kessler. 82 Graham av....N Rosenthal. Store Fixtures. 1,672
Wiebusch, L. Clason av, n w cor Flushing av ....Lynch & Roe, Saloon Fixtures. 600

ASSIGNMENTS OF CHATTEL MORTGAGES.

Hotchkiss & Co to W M Richards, Jr. (Mort given by C B Townsend, Sept 18, 1888). 400
Shimberg, S to J Irving. (A M Brown, Oct 25, 1890). nom

NEW JERSEY.

NOTE.—*The arrangement of the Conveyances, Mortgages and Judgments in these lists is as follows: the first name in the Conveyances is the Grantor; in Mortgages, the Mortgagor; in Judgments, the Judgment debtor.*

ESSEX COUNTY.

CONVEYANCES.

Bailey, C M—E Brandt, n w cor South Orange av and 6th st 72x100....$15,000
Bayles, C I—P Wilcox, Montclair....12,750
Bell, James—E B Aymar, East Orange.... nom
Bigelow, A G—T C Ennever, Montclair....12,000
Blaicher, F E—H Oelke, South 11th st.... 600
Same——R Ledig, South 14th st.... 500
Bonykamper, William—S A Bonykamper, Bonykamper av.... nom
Breakenridge, J H et al—C Kohl, Clinton.... 700
Same——M Niebling, Clinton.... 4,000
Breintnall, J H H et al—O Monheimer, 13th av. 2,200
Brison, David—M A Park, Milburn.... 900
Brokaw, L T—S A C Seaver, Milburn.... 500
Brower, R D—R Porter, Milburn.... 1,600
Cadmus, A A—P Gerbert, Bloomfield.... nom
Carter, K B—T Thieme, Belmont av.... 625
Colyer, Joseph—N Hutin, Chestnut st.... 2,400
Condit, E M—J A Egner, West Orange.... 608
Condit W P—T N Gray, Orange.... 900
Conover, W H—J Breen, North 4th st.... 600
Coolbaugh, F W—F Drinkwater, East Orange.. 3,600
Cort R M—W L Glorieux, Irvington.... nom
Crowell, L F—J Huebner, South 9th st.... 1,875
Dobbinson, Hannah—T Fay, East Orange.... 205
Dodd, R N—S J Dodd, Montclair.... nom
Dod, Robert—A J Fletcher, Littleton av.... nom
Duffy, Ellen—J D Duffy, Orange.... nom
Fields, J F—W McGuire, Warren st.... 800
Fish, C J et al exrs—E Plant et al, first tract s s Cedar st n w cor James F Fowler's land 30x104, 2d tract rear line of lots fronting on Cedar st 183 w Broad st 92x41x72x6x24x24, 3d tract n s Morris Canal adj e s 2d tract, 6x22x4x22. (Corrects error as to amt in issue of July 25)....35,000
Fish, Della J——same. Same property.... nom
Fish, Clara J widow——same. Same property. 35,000
Freeman, J M—J Stevens, East Orange.... 1,800
Same——J Bell, East Orange.... 1,314
Fuller, L C—O Picard, Central av.... 1,000
Gerbert, A M—F E Gerbert, Bloomfield.... nom
Same——same, Bloomfield.... nom
Same——same, Orange.... nom
Gerbert, Peter—L Richards, Bloomfield.... 1,100
Same——same, Bloomfield.... ——
Gerbert, F E et al—P Gerbert, Bloomfield.... nom
Gerbert, F E——same, Bloomfield.... nom
Glorieux, W L—R M Coit, Irvington.... nom
Hadley, M C—C V Lewis, Clinton.... 1,200
Haines, L J—J W Vreeland et al, e s Badger av 50 s A Buerman 25x80.... 4,000
Hauser, Simon—W Doremus, e s Adams st 340 s Ferry st 50x09.... 3,900
Hann, Adam—C Schmidt, South 15th st.... 1,400
Harrison, Martha—R Bibbins, East Orange.... 250
Harrison, Ira—J Harrison, Livingston.... 408
Hartshorn, Stewart—J R Pitcher et al, Milburn. 15,000
Hawkins, D L—E T Lindsley, East Orange.... 22,500
Hebard, A A et al—F M Olds, Belleville.... 4,250
Helwig, Seibert—W M Power, Montclair.... 170
Henderson, William—J L Millar, Orange.... 660
Houston, Gavin—R D Brower, South Orange.... 480
Hunter, H I et al—J Kubler, South 19th st.... 2,000
Keasbey, A Q—A H M Beyer, South 9th st.... 625
Lamont, A M exr—F Mackin, Parkhurst st.... nom
Lindsley, E T—D L Hawkins, East Orange.... 20,000
Lister, J C—Lister's Agricultural Chemical Works, Esther st.... 1,180
Same——A P McLoughlin, Joseph st.... 805
Same——St Aloysius Church, Esther st.... 1,910
Same——W M A Fleming, Albert av.... 575
Lockwood, L G—J M Mead, Caldwell.... 714
Lyon, D M—E White, East Orange.... 1,000
Mackin, Francis—A R Fordyce, s e cor Broad and Parkhurst sts, 75x100....11,875
Maier, Jacob—M D Van Winkle, Bloomfield.... 325
McCormick, H D—W M Whitlock, North 11th st.... 1,000
McGrath, C A—I A Person, North 5th st.... 1,700
Messler, I H—A E Ryerson, Bloomfield.... 100
Muller, Otto—E Ball, Franklin.... nom
Palmer, T L—C H Palmer, Amsterdam st.... 275
Parkinson, Wm—N A Mullen, West Orange.... 4,500
Poinier, J D—C A Schanze, Milford av.... 500
Priest, J A—A McPharlan, Caldwell.... 25
Richmond, Eleanor—J Crowell, trustee, East Orange.... nom
Riker, Adrian—The Rapid Transit Street Railway Co, Hunterdon st.... 1,200
Reeves, H M—W E Gray, s s Emmett st 125 w Penna av 25x100.... 4,750
Rochford, J A—The Bradley & Currier Co (Lim), North 5th st.... 425
Russell, C M—J M Sayre, w s Broome st 150 s Waverly pl 100x100.... 6,750
Ryerson A E—M Ryerson, w s Broad st adj s line T H Stephens 25x105.... 5,000
Ryerson, A M—F B Ryerson, Nassau st.... 1,000
Ryerson, F B—A Wood, Nassau st.... 2,200
Same——A E Ryerson, w s Broad st and s line T H Stephens 25x105.... 5,000
Sayre, J M—C M Russell, undivided ½ n s Crawford st 100 w Washington st 53x100.... 5,720
Schneider, Edward, Jr—E Schneider, Morris av. nom
Schneider, Edward—E Schneider, Jr, Morris av. nom
Serbe, A F—L Serbe, Bergen st.... 800
Shannon, William—J Elliott, East Orange.... 3,000
Slater, G W—M D Van Winkle, Bloomfield.... 325
Smith, John—J Heffel et al, n w cor Bleeker and Colden sts 30x105.... 3,150
Smith, Patrick—J Heffel, n w cor Bleeker and Colden sts 30x105.... 3,150
Snyder, E H—M Reinhardt, South Orange.... 325
Snyder, E H et al—M Reinhardt, South Orange. 875
Snyder, E H—W Parkinson, South Orange.... 2,000
Sohnle, John—C Trinter, Kipp st.... 1,200
Stager, Thomas—The East Jersey Water Co, Franklin.... 8,000
Stapff, Julius—J F Egner, w s Plane st s e cor land Mrs Whitney 30x94.... 7,000
Stiles, Mary—W Hill, Sr, Bloomfield.... 300
Sunfield, E C et al—M W Gould, Newark Meadows.... 50
Suburban Home Assoc—I A Person, Montclair.. 500
Tichenor, A H—Lewis Rockwell, Fairmount av 850
Tichenor, H T et al—M Schmidt, Hunterdon st.. 500
Tichenor, William—M Corcoran, Montclair.... 250
Tomkins, Ambrose—H Ehrlich, Franklin.... 250
Tieppe, H M—J Kelly, Orange.... 500
Van Horce, D A—W Doremus, e s Mulberry st 126 s Thomas st 75x148.... 3,500
Ward, A L—E G Ward, Bloomfield.... 2,500
Ward, J M—I Harrison, Livingston.... 1
Werman, T E—A G Kramer, West Orange.... 5,000
Weidenfeld, Camille—R Weidenfeld, West Orange....30,000
Same——J Byrne, West Orange.... 3,000
Welsh, S A—A Devine, Central av.... 1,800
Wilde, Joseph—J H Bradshaw, Orange.... 4,000
Williams, E H—I H Patrey, East Orange.... 700
Wright, E H—St Augustine Roman Catholic Church, Norfolk st.... nom

MORTGAGES.

Agens, W A—F Frelinghuyser, Broad st.... 5,000
Allen, W L—A S Ralmer, Avon av.... 550
Same——E B Reeves, Hunterdon st.... 450
Andlauer, Frederick—F J Kastner, Somerset st. 6,000
Aymar, E B—S S Sands, East Orange.... 800
Batten, George—The Mutual Benefit Life Ins Co, Montclair.... 6,000
Baumgartner, John—M Wedel, South 7th st.... 3,500
Beyer, A H M—A Q Keasbey, South 9th st.... 325
Blanck, Gertrude—E Condit, Orange.... 100
Brandt, Emma—C M Bailey, South Orange av.. 8,000
Brown, A N—M Stoutenburgh, Bellville av.... 2,400
Church of the Sacred Heart, Bloomfield—The Mutual Benefit B and L Assoc, Bloomfield... 21,000
Cinnamon, Julius—The Freeman's Ins Co, Court st.... 5,000
Cook, A T—The Fidelity Title and Deposit Co, Halsey st.... 950
Conklin, W T—The Orange National Bank, Montclair.... 465
Corwin, A D H—J H Cuthill, Mt Prospect av.... 2,800
Crowell, John trustee—Orange Savings Bank, East Orange.... 2,250
Curtis, W F—Montclair B and L, Montclair.... 3,000
Denner, Henry—B Gsell, New st.... 2,050
De Witt, W H—American Ins Co, Montclair.... 3,000
Dickerson, Adrian—Fidelity Title and Deposit Co, Bloomfield.... 5,000
Duffy, Charles—Mutual B and L Assoc, Academy st.... 600
Ebbinghausen, Augusta—C Schleuer, Spring st. 5,000
Ebner, Ferdinand—E Storklie, Morris av.... 2,000
Egbert, W S and as exr—E C Latesinger, Lafayette st.... 474
Egner, Josephine—A H B Howe, West Orange.. 700
Egner, J F—J Stapff, Plane st.... 1,500
Same——German Savings Bank of Newark, Plane st.... 3,500
Elliott, John—W Shannon, East Orange.... 2,750
Ennever, T C—A G Bigelow, Montclair.... 4,500
Same——same, Montclair.... 5,500
Fee, J F—L Headley, Broad st.... 2,000
Fowler, Martha—J H Stewart, 1st st.... 1,300
Franz, R J—A J Sigler, Summer av.... 3,500
Fuhr, J H—E Geppert, Lafayette st.... 1,600
Gallagher, S C—M C Tichenor, Bloomfield.... 1,000
Geppner, Emilie—F J Kastner, South 18th st.... 200
Glennon, M A—A W Lintott, Belleville.... 600
Gless, A S—M A Hay, Niagara st.... 1,700
Gregory, Bridget—G T Casebolt, Murray st.... 500
Heffel, Jacob—T J Lintott, Bleecker st.... 1,500
Hahn, Nora—J Collyer, Chestnut st.... 500
Hammer, Neals—S Martin, Orange.... 3,000
Heyl, A H W—E M Burnett, Somerset st.... 200
Hildebrandt, August—W Una, Prince st.... 200
Hills, H B—Woodside B and L Assoc, Lincoln av.... 3,000
Huebner, John—L F Crowell, South 9th st.... 944
Jatkowski, Aaron—J Hirschberg, Prince st.... 1,000
Kennedy, R A—W H Hussey, East Orange.... 1,000
King, C M—J H H Breintnall, Belleville av.... 2,000
King, R W—J H Baldwin, Montclair.... 1,100
Kingston, M L—Fireman's Ins Co, Crawford st. 2,750
Klein, Frederick—H B Schureman, Clinton.... 2,000
Knapp, Andrew—E N Peck, Orange.... 2,400
Kramer, A G—H M Ward, West Orange.... 1,000
Kroll, Peter—E Butz, River road.... 2,000
Kubler, John—H J Huster, South 19th st.... 100
Lambert, G R—Fireside B and L Assoc, Fairmount av.... 4,000
Le Cato, Lillian—S A Dickinson, West Orange.. 3,000
Lee, P W—Aaron Ward et al exrs, South 12th st. 100
Ledig, Richard—M E Smith, South 14th st.... 1,000
Lindsley, E T—D L Hawkins, East Orange.... 2,500
Logan, William—P H Edmonston, Montclair.... 5,000
Mackay, F E—A Tag, James st.... 2,100
Mechuer, J P—P J King, Belleville.... 500
Mersfelder, Louisa—Wilkinson, Gaddis & Co, No 403 Washington st.... 1,491
Millar, J L—T Weir, Orange.... 2,070
Mullen, N A—W Parkinson, Orange.... 3,900
Oelke, Herman—F E Blaicher, South 11th st.... 300
Palmer, A C—M Green, East Orange.... 1,000
Patrey, I H—E H Williams, East Orange.... 650
Picard, Otto—L C Fuller, Central av.... 900
Pitcher, J R—S Hartshorne Milburn.... 12,500
Porter, John—R A Gopsill, Montclair.... 6,000
Post, Henry—S S Dobbins, Caldwell.... 700
Raphael, Maurice—J Dreyfuss, South 15th st.... 6,000
Reinhardt, Mary—E H Snyder, South Orange.. 600
Rizzolo, Alfonso—J M Trimble, 8th av.... 4,000
Robinson, Jophia—West End B and L Assoc, South 7th st.... 3,000
Sheldon, Sarah—C M Borrie, Parker st.... 2,500
Sherman, E C—E H Snyder, South Orange.... 525
Sikorra, Andreas—C Schiener, Fairview av.... 3,000
Schneider, Edward—E Wirtz, Morris av.... 1,500
Simpson, A J—A J Heller, Spruce st.... 4,000
Smith, Grace—A B Clark Academy st.... 5,125
Stoutenburgh, A E—M A Bay, R R av.... 1,500
Theime, George—E Theime, Somerset st.... 6,000
Tobin, Elizabeth—Montclair B and L Assoc, Montclair.... 200
Trinter, George—Passaic B and L Assoc, Kipp st. 1,000
Trustees of First Baptist Church, Bloomfield—Mutual Benefit Life Ins Co, Bloomfield.... 10,000
Tubbs, C B—A B De Camp, Montclair.... 1,230
Van Wagenen, Herbert—P H Edmonston, Montclair.... 5,000
Varley, Thomas—H Holden, 2d st.... 1,600
Walsh, Mary—M A Smith, Chambers st.... 50
Wadsworth, E M—Mutual Life Ins Co of New York, East Orange....20,000
White, Edward—D M Lyon, East Orange.... 500
Williams, C A—Corporation for the Relief of Widows and Children of Clergymen, Orange. 2,400
Wood, K B—F J Love, Montclair.... 5,000

CHATTEL MORTGAGES.

Barker, O W—J Ketcham, furniture.... 100
Campbell, J M—F L Huff, furniture.... 100
Douney, Timothy—German American Brewing Co, saloon.... 250
Elphinstone, A C—C E Young, oil cans &c.... 500
Gruschov, Morris—M Harris, butcher fixtures.. 45
Harrison, Joseph et al—M A Brewster, horses and wagons.... 475
Jennings, Halsey—C Bierman, furniture.... 130
Kaelber, Fritz—F Lisiewski, saloon.... 625
Klein, Frederick—H B Schureman, machinery.. 1,000
Leonard, J H—Lyon & Sons Brewery Co, saloon. 192
Lisiewski, Frederick A—S K Nesler, brewery... 5,000
McNaughton, J. M—J Ruckelshaus, furniture... 69
McNaughton, Josephine—L Bloomer, furniture. 36
Meterie, Julia—J W Smith, furniture.... 140
Oswald, Herman—F Lisiewski, saloon.... 800
Platt, F G—G P Johnson, furniture.... 300
Raphael, Maurice—S Oury, stock, horses, carriages and harness.... 4,800
Schweickert, Peter—C Bierman, furniture.... 130
Same——E H Putnam, furniture.... 130
Serbe, A F et al—W T Serbe, stock groceries.... 3,729
Smith, Spencer et al—C M Wintermute, saloon. 115
Thompson, S M—German-American Ins Co, saloon.... 450
Wedel, N H—M Wedel, barber fixtures.... 100

JUDGMENTS.

Herbst, A R—G Krueger Brewing Co.... 807
Hyman, Regina—A Stein et al.... 1,358

HUDSON COUNTY.

CONVEYANCES.

Layerl, S R—J Hüdne, Hoboken.... nom
Bouton, Rebecca M by trustee—W G Bumsted, J City....$2,700
Brady, Julia M—A Corby, J City.... 1,850
Bulkley, Mary J—Rose A Shannon, J City.... 2,710
Claflin, C F—A Voelker, J City.... 3,500
Coles, F W—Rosina Purcell, J City.... 4,200
Colwell, Michael—Bridget Trainor, Kearney.... 1,700
Combes, Mary E—J J Duffey, Bayonne.... 2,610
Connolly, T J—Mary Kane, J City.... 750
Cunliffe, Michael—The Mayor and Aldermen, J City.... 230
Darling, W H—W G Bumsted, J City.... nom
Davis, J P N—Mary A Lively, Kearney.... 2,1 0
Doherty, P H—J J Herbert, J City....13,000
Drescher, Chas by exrs—J Zink, West Hoboken. 400
Same——R Brupbacher, West Hoboken.... 800
Edsall, Ellen Y—Sophia Walz, J City.... 3,000
Eilshemius, H G—Louisa Walters, Kearney.... 850
Gacquin, Mary and Martin Ward by master—D E Cleary, J City.... 2,400
Galbraith, C S—F M Fise, North Bergen.... nom
Garretson, G R—G H Jones, J City.... nom
Gassmann, Andrew—J Gassmann, J City.... 900
Grass, John—Caroline Wagner, Guttenberg.... 1,375
Gravier, A J—W Kelly, Bayonne.... 1,700
Grevillot, Madeline—C Allen, North Bergen.... 2,400
Grimes, Ann—Mary A Grimes, J City.... nom
Gugel, Caroline—Mary A Zimber, West Hoboken 1,000
Hansen, F C—H Behrens, Union.... 40
Herbert, J J—P H Doherty, J City....13,000
Hartman, Emily—J Orr, J City.... 650
Hess, Katharine—P C Scharwaechter, Union... 2,000
Hoboken Ld and Impt Co—J G Hibdner, Hoboken.... 3,800
Same—J Keresey, Hoboken.... 3,700
Inwight, J C—The Keystone National Savings Loan and Ins Co, J City.... 1,500
Jennings, W N—K Lofquist, Kearney.... 1,000
Kissam, Sarah J—D M Birdsall, J City.... nom
Lawrence, W A—R V W Sell, Kearney.... nom
McGinniss, Chas—J A Moore, J City.... 5,050
Minnix, Jace—L Wilenton, North Bergen.... 500
Miller, Johanna—H Walker, Guttenberg.... 800
Monahan, Patrick by assignee—P Monahan, Bayonne.... nom
Mueller, John—J Bodeman, West Hoboken.... 2,000
Same——J Keller, West Hoboken.... 700
Newman, John—Lena D Newmann, Bayonne... nom
Nichols, E H—A Walters, J City.... 200
Ogden, W B by exrs—W Eckers, J City.... 1,000
Page, Emma F—A Corby, J City.... 075
Page, Will by guard——same, J City.... 100
Paxton, E T—A B Dayton, J City.... 2,500
Platt, Catharine M exrs of Frederick L Platt—T K Halstead, J City.... 4,500
Pullman, C G—Lizzie Schieferstein, Bayonne... 220
Sandford, J H—Marie A Rhode, Bayonne.... 3,400
Schroll, Mary—Lena Schroll, J City.... 900
Schultz, Otto—W Braenstein, West Hoboken....20,000
Schwind, J P—H Hoffman, J City.... 3,300
Simonson, Michael—A Von Fell, J City.... 1,575
Smith, H C by trustee—The Mattison Methodist Episcopal Church, Bayonne.... nom
The Central N J L and Impt Co—Anna F Plumb, Bayonne.... nom

The New Jersey Warehouse & Guaranty Co—The Jersey City, Newark & Western R R Co, J City	181,376
Thompson, Margaret F—J Thiersten, J City	200
Tierney, Myles—R Kelly, Hoboken	11,500
Tierney, Myles—Gaetanno Centanni, Harrison	550
Van Rensselaer, Emile—J O'Ahern, J City	600
Vreeland, Jane by exr—W Vreeland, J City	3,000
Vreeland, Peter—Exr Jane Vreeland, J City	nom
Same——G Heckmann, J City	nom
Vreeland, Washington——same, J City	600
Walker, Herman—G H Mager, Guttenberg	400
Same——C W Blackmore, Guttenberg	900
Same——H Hersler, Guttenberg	1,200
Walters, Alex—D Landrine, J City	250
Wescott, W P—C D Farand, Bayonne	350
Weston, H D—Eliza T Palmer, J City	2,450
Wetmore, F G—Exr Margaret A Graham, J City	4,100
Whitney, Aletta M—J J Melich, J City	1,500
Whyard, Sarah J—A McGimpsey, J City	450

MORTGAGES.

Allen, Cornelius—C Pratt, North Bergen, 5 years	1,500
Blackmore, C W—H Walker, Guttenberg, 5 years	300
Brady, James—Jennie E Kennedy, Bayonne, 3 years	1,100
Brupbacher, Rob—Salena Egolf, West Hoboken, 5 years	700
Burton, Jos—W Gulken, Union, 1 year	300
Cunliffe, Michael—K K Stearns, J City, 1 year	150
Daumann, J F—H F A Michels, J City, 3 years	5,000
Desmann, R A—F A Von Bemuth, West Hoboken, 1 year	8,200
Dowitsch, Andrew—F C Hausen, North Bergen, 1 year	400
Faulkner, Kate—H Puster, J City, 1 year	500
Frank, W F—C Soffcke, North Bergen, 3 years	425
Frericks, Henry—Metha Humken, J City, 1 year	1,000
Furey, Anna C—Sarah Post, J City, 5 years	2,000
Furey, Catharine E——same, J City, 5 years	4,800
Graham, Margaret—Provident Inst for Savings, J City, 1 year	2,000
Gravatt, Chas—North Hudson Co B and L Assoc, West Hoboken, installs	400
Grimes, Mary A—Maggie C Lutkins, J City, 5 years	5,000
Hackett, Will—A J C Foye, J City, 1 year	1,500
Halstead, T W—The Paulus Hook B and L Assoc, J City, installs	4,400
Hamilton, Barbara—P Kupper, J City, 3 years	2,000
Hersler, Henry—H Walker, Guttenberg, 2 years	800
Hildner, Jos—The Hudson Trust and Savings Inst, Hoboken, 3 years	8,000
Kaiser, Aug—Rosa Baumgarten, Hoboken, 3 years	300
Kelly, Bryan—M Tierney, Hoboken, 3 years	2,500
Same——same, Hoboken, 3 years	2,500
Kelly, Will—A J Gravier, Bayonne, 5 years	1,600
Kelsey, M H—The Excelsior M B and L Assoc, Issue 3, J City, 1 year	800
Kren, C G—P Rittberg, West Hoboken, 3 years	1,700
Lavaggi, J C—A De Barbieri, West Hoboken, 3 years	1,000
Lively, Mary A—J P N Davis, Kearney, 3 years	1,100
Monahan, Pat—Greenville B and L Assoc, J City, installs	3,650
Murphy J J—Greenville United B and L Assoc, J City, installs	2,211
Newkirk, J H—Gussie Langendorf, J City, 3 years	1,000
Nugent, B H—Exr J L Ogden, J City, 5 years	4,000
O'Ahern, John—Emile Van Rensselaer, J City, 1 year	250
Philips, Mary—H Von Glahn, J City, 5 years	1,800
Plumb, Ann E—Sarah A Kingsland, Bayonne, 3 years	2,500
Ridgeway, Daniel—Josephus Hughes, West Hoboken, 1 year	640
Shannon, Rose A—The Union B and L Assoc, J City, installs	5,000
Smith, W V V—J G Willard, Union, 5 years	2,200
Seery, John—Anna M Lord, Bayonne, 3 years	2,000
Smith, Ann—Sarah A Kingsland, J City, 3 years	500
Steel, Annie—H H Stuhr, J City, 1 year	200
Thierstein, John—Excelsior M B, Series No 2, Issue 3, J City, installs	3,000
Viehrolg, F G—The William Peter Brewing Co, Union, 1 year	350
Walker, Herman—J Meller, Guttenberg, 1 year	400
Wholey, Dennis—C P Vreeland, Bayonne, 2 years	500
Wileslon, Louis—Jane Munna, North Bergen, 3 years	1,200

CHATTEL MORTGAGES.

Austar, Hattie, Hoboken—H Thoesen, furniture	125
Bainbridge, John, J City—C Birdsall, furniture	100
Buchi, Arnold, West Hoboken—Lembeck & Betz Eagle Brewing Co, saloon	2,500
Connelly, Mary T, J City—C Birdsall, furniture	100
Cosgrove, Jno or Joseph, J City—D Stevenson, saloon	200
Creveling, William, J City—John Mullins & Co, furniture	148
Fritsche, Richard, Hoboken—The Bachman Brewing Co, saloon	1,100
Same, Hoboken——Emil Beekmann, furniture	600
Griffin, Joseph and Ernest Struck, partners Griffin & Struck, J City—The Manhattan Type Foundry, 1 30-inch paper cutter with extra knife	155
Grimmler, Martin, J City—G Schmidt et al, saloon	225
Haege, Adolph and Theophilus Butz, partners as Haege & Butz, Union—A Schwartz, factory and machinery	13,300
Henkel, W J, J City—The Lembeck & Betz Eagle Brewing Co, saloon	390
Jacquemot, Hyppolyte, Seacaucus—Christian Schwarz, horses, wagon, harness, 225 greenhouse sashes, 4 greenhouses	300
Jones, A H and Ann, J City—A Kurston, furniture	490
Martone, Antonio, Hoboken—Francesco Marinelli, barber shop	60
Meissner, Tillie, J City—John Mullins & Co, furniture	180
Messmer, Fritz, West Hoboken—P Birdsall, furniture	220
Murrer, James, J City—The James Cunningham Son & Co, Berlin coach	308
Nevins, W D and E J Nooman, partners as Nevins & Nooman, J City—W J Lenrerich, horse, wagon, harness, lumber and moulding machinery	250
Same——Janet Nevins, horse, wagon, harness, lumber and moulding machinery	227
Same——Maud Dingwall, horse, wagon, harness, machinery	380
Same——I O Bruner, horse, wagon, harness, machinery	927
Rapp, Adolph, J City—The Jacob Hoffman Brewing Co, saloon	2,500
Steinhman, Matthias, Hoboken—H Heyman, dry, fancy and millinery goods, stock and fixtures	630
Same——The H B Claflin Co, dry, fancy and millinery goods, stock and fixtures	1,994
Same——J Smith, dry, fancy and millinery goods, stock and fixtures	500
Tewkburg, Annie, J City—H Manners, furniture	284
Viehwig, F E, Union—The William Peter Brewing Co, saloon and fixtures	600
Winans, G H, Kearney—Eliz A Winans, machinery and hat factory	500

BILLS OF SALE.

Fahrendorff, Herman by exrs, Hoboken—Sarah E Guinan, frame house	2,000
Mueller, Jno, West Hoboken—J Bodemann, two embroidery machines	1,000
Todd, C W, J City—D Reardon, horse, wagon, harness and milk business	100
Wallace, Louise, J City—T Gallagher, horse, wagon, harness, ice box and milk wagon	75

JUDGMENTS.

Corbery, Mary—R S Hudspeth	62
Downs, C L—First National Bank	617
Garrett, W H and Joseph partners, as Garrett Bros—P A Nech	542
Haege, Adolph and G T Butz—Gloneux & Woolsey	12,404
Same——The Newark Watch Case and Material Co	8,004
Killeen, Martin—Delia Conklin	47
McKee, James and Rosanna and C A Edwards—D B Dunham	301
McKenna, Pat—The F & M Schaefer Brewing Co	357
Ormsby, C A—F M Foye	25
Reddy, Joseph—C Feigenspan	311
Reisch, Max—M A Lesser	304
Schwartz, Solomon—The William Peter Brewing Co	976

MECHANICS' LIENS.

Blachowski, Stanislaus, owner; Talfelski & Collin, contractors; Ray & McIntyre, claimant, Bayonne	92
Cohn, Morris, John Morrisy and Sarah R Nathan, owner; J Phillip, et al, contractors; Frank A Lawson, claimant, Hoboken	78
Long, Thos, owner; J J Rhodes, contractor; Thos A Murphy & Co, claimant, Harrison	72
Peters, William, owner; Christian Becher, contractor; The Bradley & Currier Co (Lim), claimant, Weehawken	204
Rothstein, Rebecca, builder and owner; W S Emery, claimant, Bayonne	2,235

BUILDING MATERIAL MARKET.

BRICKS.—"Nothing new" appeared to be the refrain again regarding the general condition of the market, and the greater the number of operators conversed with the more convincing became proof of the reliability of the statement. A great many brick have been handled, more probably than might have been expected, considering the intensely warm weather of the forepart of the week; but every time a call was made, the stock was there to meet it, with quite a bunch to spare, and sellers could not obtain any advance on price. Indeed it is doubtful if they made the effort with the evidences of almost certain failure before them, and it has become almost a foregone conclusion that no hardening on value can be secured until the flow of supplies and the daily consumption reach a closer balance. We still notice an absence of complaint over quality. Now and then there is a load a little "off," but generally the makes of the various localities are right up to their best standard, and it requires something of unusual attraction to command a premium over the average best cargo rate, which cannot be placed at better than $5.25 per M, and some of the trade think even that a little full. Pales remain about steady, with some little demand, but the supply is large enough to go around. We again learn that some of the gentlemen in the trade with whom we converse in canvassing the market have been taken to task for telling us the truth. Who and what the complainants are we did not inquire, nor do we care; their status is shown from the position they assume. We desire to say to them, however, that the reports in this journal are intended to be as nearly absolutely correct as it is possible to make them from information obtainable; that they are dictated by no individual or clique, but compiled after careful comparison of views with reliable members of the trade representing all shades of opinion, and by a gentleman who probably understands his business quite as well as any of the fault-finders imagine they can instruct him. Furthermore, there is no law compelling the reading of these reports, and people who do not like honest, straightforward statements may possibly find consolation elsewhere.

HARDWARE.—A deal much behind the average for the season is taking place, and the market shows far from really satisfactory features. Still, of late buyers have appeared to show a trifle more interest, and that creates a somewhat hopeful feeling that first symptoms of fall trade are developing. Local consumption promises least, and especially in way of builders' hardware, mechanics' tools, etc. Prices are irregular and not over strong, but no important changes of late announced, except on Wrought Iron Pipe, which shows a decline of 10 per cent., while Boiler Tubes 3@6 inches are up. The discount sheet is on Butt, 52½ per cent on black and 42½ on galvanized; on Lap, 62½ for black and 50 for galvanized; Boiler Tubes up to 2¾ inches, inclusive, 55 per cent.; do, 3 to 6 inches, inclusive, 60 per cent.; do, 7 inches and larger, 55 per cent.; and casing 55 per cent.

LATH.—That sharp reaction on values predicted has not come yet, and up to the present writing the market is really not much better than last week, though the turn of advantage is in sellers' favor. Receipts have been smaller as anticipated, but so has the demand, and previous large amounts handled making many dealers temporarily independent, and even out of the market, custom was a trifle slack. Under the circumstances it is not unnatural to find some discrepancies in expressed views of values, but it looks just about this way. If anyone had much to sell at the market it might be difficult to exceed $2.10@2.15 per M, while on the other hand a direct demand would be very apt to add at least 10c., and possibly more to those figures.

LIME.—Up to the present writing the market appears to be unchanged and $1.00 is quoted for Rockland, with a renewal of the claims that no cutting is known to have taken place on standard stock, except, possibly, on tail end of cargoes. Outside Eastern makes, it is admitted, may sell a little off. The arrivals have been small, but dealers are pretty well filled up and receivers do not care for many additional cargoes at the moment. There is, also, considerable stock coming in from outside sources; State, Jersey and Ohio available, it is understood, at 80c.@85c. per bbl. and that satisfies a great many wants.

LUMBER.—Reports over the condition of business differ in no essential particular from last week, except possibly that the added annoyance of hot weather contributed to the feeling of lassitude among operators. The presentations of attractive parcels at comparatively low figures has led to some deals in both coarse and hard woods, and dealers who require special cuts for assortment have also negotiated and closed to some extent, but demand does not wake up into energetic, stimulating action, and grumbling on the selling side comes in natural order of things. What makes matters more disagreeable is that buyers have no particular cause for complaint as regards either the quantity, variety or cost of stock offering, but simply adhere to the policy of refusing to negotiate because they think there is no occasion for hurry. We find, however, that in addition to the now almost unquestioned poor prospect for extensive building operations, a great many operators are revolving and pondering upon the financial situation, with a tendency to entertain a fear that legislation upon silver and other matters may act as a serious disturbing factor to trade of all kinds. It is, however, getting along toward the time when lumber dealers will have to decide between continued theorizing and apathy, and commencing the work of accumulating winter supplies.

Eastern Spruce remains practically the same in most leading particulars. The arrivals have been smaller, as might have been expected after the recent large fleet, and with a fair outlet it has not been particularly difficult to maintain a reasonably steady line of value, but demand was scattered and lacking the concentration of force necessary to act as a stimulating factor and apparently not prepared to provide for any great quantity of stock. In the matter of specials some receivers claimed to have booked an encouraging additional quantity, others grumble as much as ever, and it shows that in this division of negotiations also there is the same tone of irregularity. The fact is buyers feel no real anxiety about the balance of the season whatever and still confine their investments as closely to actual wants as possible. No other locality is looking up the supply and some recent Boston quotations are much below this market, and all talk to the contrary notwithstanding it is not imagined that the curtailment of production will be as great as claimed. Northern Spruce is reported scarce at primary points, and the mills on the upper Hudson are said to have obtained very few logs through any of the recent rains, but Albany dealers have bought with some freedom in Canada.

Piling does not find a satisfactory market, and conditions remain dull and unsettled. Some increase of demand has been shown since our last, but against it was an ample offering, including some fresh arrivals, and sellers generally appeared willing to accept former figures and seek additional custom on the same basis.

Hemlock has fair demand, but cannot be put upon the active list so far as this locality is concerned. Agents for the Pennsylvania product report most of the calls as coming from a sort of regular custom for ordinary assortment, with buyers making no objection to cost, but still disinclined to anticipate the future to any extent. The mills, however, are getting more orders from various sources, and manufacturers feel correspondingly encouraged. Albany dealers are reported to have bought fairly in Canada, owing to the scanty supply of logs at the State mills.

White Pine develops no really new features. There is no feeling of doubt that supplies will be plenty enough, and therefore buyers feel justified in moving slowly and resisting the blandishments of the drummers who tender them assortment and quantity to suit all needs. There is, however, almost as a matter of course, something doing all the while, mainly to come forward, and including all standard grades, from ordinary box up, and at about the same rates for some time ruling, giving position a nominally steady tone. A considerable quantity of stuff has been coming to hand of late from Canada, all, or nearly all, on old contracts.

Yellow Pine, according to some reports, would seem to have no friends at all and is undoubtedly still pretty dull, affording little opportunity for business on a direct open offering. Some trading, however, occasionally takes place over special orders presented and supposed to be at about former rates. What these rates are, however, is something of a problem, as operators generally manifest a very reticent spirit and seem to strive to give as little information as possible, which is not a reassuring feature.

Carolina Pine meeting with about as good a demand as last week, some of the trade think a little better, and is evidently filling a great many nooks and crevices in the general volume of trade that competing products cannot reach. The supply is ample, but seems to be under control and held for steady rates.

Hardwoods has probably a steady market for all leading kinds of stock, and it would be difficult to secure any concessions of a noticeable character. That is due in a measure to the careful manner in which offerings have for some time been made, for while there are a great many representatives of manufacturers and interior dealers evidently ready, and even a little anxious to place larger quantities, they recognize the conditions to be such as to warrant only a very careful tender. There is nothing particularly new as to the different descriptions, except an occasional reference to walnut, as likely to have some revival, not as a leader, however, but simply in somewhat fuller proportion than in the past few years. At primary points the markets continue to be reported dull.

GENERAL LUMBER NOTES.

STATE.

The Albany *Argus* as follows:

Business has improved a little in the market in the past ten days. The demand for better grades of pine has been stronger and considerable lumber has been shipped from the district, in all about ten or twelve million feet of lumber. Inch and a quarter lumber is in good demand, but the stock is light, and the same might be said of certain grades of inch lumber.

Culled spruce is in excellent demand, and orders are being placed on fall trade to take advantage of present quotations. The stock of spruce lumber for the present is light. The mills on the upper Hudson have practically shut down for the present.

From present indications the outlook for the fall trade is favorable and the dealers are in hopes of keeping up the average of sales with those of last year. The receipts of lumber last week were heavy and the yards are overstocked.

Hard woods have had a good steady trade all season and the stock on hand is in splendid condition. Shingles and lath are in good demand with a good stock on hand.

Canal freights to Albany have advanced of late to their old standard of $1.50 from Buffalo and Tonawanda to Albany. There is considerable lumber at the shipping points to come forward; dealers are holding it back on account of the crowded condition of the yards here.

ENGLAND.

The London *Timber Trades Journal* says:

In the pitch pine trade things are again beginning to move; it is reported that there are five steamers now on their way to London. Two we know of with some 1,000 loads of sawn timber to add to the stocks here. We hear that there are very few vessels at Pensacola. The question is whether the shipowners will hold out for better rates later on or take what offers now. This the next few weeks will decide. The belief is that pitch pine freights will come down, as owners will be hardly likely to keep their ships doing nothing if cargoes are to be had.

THE WEST.

The Northwestern *Lumberman* as follows:

In the producing regions around the lakes there is some apprehension felt as to whether the log supply will be sufficient to keep the mills running till the usual time to shut down. Some of the mills at Cheboygan are now running on half time, and others have logs enough on hand to run but about three weeks longer. Like conditions prevail at other points in northern Michigan. There is no doubt but that a large aggregate of logs are hung up on the smaller streams. Late September rains may bring them in o mill boom, but the situation at present is considered uncertain.

There is an urgent call for bill timber at Manistee and Ludington, as well as on the Huron shore. A good many long logs have been got out this summer, but their owners are holding them firmly for what they consider a sure thing in the fall and winter demand. There has lately been a livening up in the requirement for car sills, which strengthens the hands of holders of long logs and their product.

Trade is still reported quiet in the Saginaw valley, though there has recently been some increase of inquiry and sales.

The only drawback on prospects for a heavy movement of lumber during the coming three months is the scarcity of cars. At this early period in the season the railroads begin to tighten up on the reins, delivering no more cars than possible. The grain movement is absorbing cars rapidly, and the stringency will become worse as the fall approaches. The trouble will probably be less in this city than at northern points for the reason that so many cars will arrive with grain which can be loaded out with lumber. But there will be some difficulty here. Dealers who have a shipping business from Wisconsin points are deeply apprehensive of the approaching blockade, and advise their customers to get their lumber forward as soon as possible. It would be well for country dealers to heed this advice.

The *Timberman* says of the Chicago yard trade:

The relative condition of stocks on hand is practically unchanged. As a general thing assortments are in very good shape, but there is still the customary shortage of clear inch boards, etc. Firsts and seconds clear inch is selling at $47 to $50, thicker bringing $44 to $47. A selects, 2 in., bring $38 to $40; 1¼ and 1½ in., $37 to $39. B selects, 2 in., $34 to $35; 1¼ and 1½ in., $31 to $32. Prices for C selects range from $21.50 to $26 for 1¼, 1½ and 2 in. On good lumber considerable apparent difference in prices is found in the different yards, but it is all due to different methods of grading.

Twelve inch common boards are selling between yards at $14.50 to $15.50 for 12, 14 and 16 feet, $17 for 18 ft. and $16 for 10 ft.

Rough fencing and fencing flooring are not quite so stiff in price as earlier in the season. Demand is still good but there is a more ample supply, although there is not any too much of No. 1. For No. 1 fencing rough, prices range from $14.50 to $16, according to length. No. 2 is worth $1 to $1.50 per thousand less.

Piece stuff continues to sell at the old prices, based on $12 for the short lengths. There is a good supply of everything except long, wide joist, but prices are proportionately higher on all long lengths. Hemlock piece stuff is selling well at $2 to $2.50 per thousand less than pine, and there is an excellent demand for hemlock plank for paving purposes.

The first week of August does not show any material improvement in the demand for hardwoods, but the fact that prices remain unchanged in the face of light inquiry may be taken as an indication that dealers expect to see orders coming in more freely before the month is ended. At present it would appear that neither the furniture nor interior finish factories are greatly rushed. At least they are not calling upon hardwood dealers for any great amount of stock. But as neither of these lines has done much so far this season, there will likely be plenty doing in both during the fall months.

So far prices on all classes and grades of hardwoods have held up remarkably well, but unless demand becomes more active soon there is bound to be a break, for lumber is coming in more rapidly than it is being consumed and the piling space in yards is already pretty well utilized.

The Mississippi Valley *Lumberman* as follows:

Not all the mills are getting logs as freely as was anticipated would be the case. The boom on the St. Croix has been shut down for a week or more, very few logs are being got out of the Chippewa and the La Crosse mill men see the end of their supply. Over in the Wisconsin valley and at Green Bay shore points low water has limited the log supply. Some interruption will occur with the mills at Minneapolis but the production at this point for the season will be very large. Elsewhere it is now evident that the cut will not be proportionately as large as the consumption now promises to be.

Despite complaint which has been heard all the season, the shipments of lumber from Bay City for the month of July show a most gratifying increase over the same month during the past two years, exceeding the output of 1889 by nearly 10,000,000 feet, and that of 1890 by over 16,000,000 feet. This increase is taken by vesselmen as an indication of better times and as a result they are very sanguine of a good business during the remainder of this season.

PAINTS, OILS, COLORS, ETC.—A moderately active business is about all that can be found for any article on the list, though in some instances there has been a slight increase since our last. Buyers are acting very much as they have done all the season, confining orders to well determined wants, and the hope for an extension of trade is in the increase of those wants. In making up invoices customers are found to be taking standard qualities of stock in about the usual relative proportion, and keeping away from anything in the way of fancies, except as the latter may be required to maintain a store assortment. The impression prevails that we shall not have much of local competition this fall, but the prospects outside are more encouraging and are thought to indicate, at least, average takings. Offerings plentiful enough, and, while easy in their views, holders can hardly be called weak or inclined to shade on values. Outside makes of White Lead are the only ones upon which "cut" rates are named. Association Corroders' rates stand as follows: Lead in oil in kegs and dry lead in kegs, in lots of less than 500 lbs., 7⅛c. net; in lots of 500 lbs to 5 tons at one purchase, 7c.; 5 tons to 12 tons, one purchase, 6⅞c.; 12 tons and over, one purchase, 6¾c.; dry white lead in bbls. ⅛c per lb. less than price in kegs. Lead in oil 12½ lb. in tin pails, add 1c.; in 25 and 50 lb. tin pails, add ½c.; and in 1 to 5 lb. tin cans, assorted (100 lbs. in case) add 2½c. per lb. to keg price. Terms on lots on 500 lbs. and over, note or acceptance at sixty days, or 2½ per cent. discount will be allowed for cash paid within fifteen days of invoice date. To make either of the above required quantities any assortment of packages of white lead, red lead and litharge may be counted. The above quotations are free on board cars or boat at corroding point. Linseed Oil does not readily settle down to a uniform market. The cutting on price is not so severe or general, but irregularities now and then develop, especially on the commoner makes. Supplies seem to be ample. We quote at general range at 37@40c. for Western, and 44@56c. for City. Spirits Turpentine has not been particularly active, and the business was confined in the main to small odd parcels desired for immediate positive requirements. Supplies here, however, are under good control, and with supporting advices from the South values are quite firm. We quote at 36@37c. per gallon, according to quality, delivery, etc.

NAILS.—A moderate unsatisfactory demand is still recorded, and it is a disagreeable market apparently throughout. Prices do not change, because they are already low beyond reason as a peg against further decline, and demand lacks sufficient competition to act as a stimulus. We quote Cut at $1.50@1.60 per keg for car lots and $1.75@1.85 per keg for parcels from store, for iron, and add 5@10c. per keg for steel; Wire, $2.00@2.05 at mills, and 2.20@2.35 from store.

TAR AND PITCH.—Consumers want very little on fresh orders, having provided for most present requirements by contract. The demand in consequence is slowish and unimportant, and the market does not amount to much. With small stocks holders are firm on valuation. We quote Pitch at $1.70@1.75 per bbl.; Tar at $2.15@2.50, according to quantity, quality and delivery.

BUILDING MATERIAL PRICES

LUMBER.

Appended quotations are based almost wholly upon prices obtained for goods from first hands. Yard rates necessarily range much higher owing to the expenses attending sorting out and grading cargo and even car lots, besides which must be added the cost of handling and carrying until consumers are ready to invest. Terms of sale also prove important factors and, altogether, it is impossible to give a line of retail quotations thoroughly reliable in character.

SPRUCE—Eastern—special cargoes delivered N. Y.	$15 50	@	16 50
Random cargoes, narrow	13 00	@	14 00
Random cargoes, wide	14 50	@	15 50
PILING—Eastern—cargo rates:			
Ranging 30@40 per cent 12 inch butt, 35 to 40 ft average length	4	@	—
Ranging 45@50 per cent 12 inch butt, 35 to 40 ft average length	4¼	@	4½
Ranging 50@60 per cent One-half 12 inch butt, 38 to 40 ft average length	4¾	@	5
Two-thirds 12 inch butt, 38 to 42 ft average length	5½	@	6
Three-fourths 12 inch butt, 40 to 45 ft average length	5¾	@	6
All 12 inch butt and up, 40 to 45 ft average length	6	@	6¼
Piece stick, 40 feet each	4 00	@	—
do. 45	6 00	@	—
do. 50	8 00	@	—
do. 55	12 00	@	—
Inch spars, per inch	20	@	22
Scaffolding poles, each	60	@	1 00
Clothes poles, 45 to 65 feet, each	3 00	@	6 00
HEMLOCK:			
Penn. joist	12 00	@	12 50
do. boards	13 00	@	13 50
do. timber, 20 ft and under	12 50	@	13 00
do. do. 22 to 24 ft	13 00	@	13 50
do. do. 26 to 28 ft	13 50	@	14 00
do. do. 30 to 32 ft	14 00	@	15 50
do. do. 34 to 36 ft	15 50	@	16 00
do. do. 38 to 40 ft	16 50	@	17 50
WHITE PINE—Good uppers and select, 1 to 2 inch	40 00	@	48 00
Upper and select, 2½ to 4 inch	50 00	@	58 00
Shelving	26 00	@	31 00
Pickings, 1 inch	31 00	@	35 00
Cutting-up, 1 inch	25 00	@	28 00
Bracket plank	30 00	@	35 00
Dressing-boards	18 00	@	22 00
Box, inch	13 50	@	14 00
Box, thick	14 50	@	15 50
West India shippers	16 00	@	19 00
Rio Janeiro do.	20 00	@	21 00
River Plate do.	29 00	@	30 00
Australia do.	25 00	@	30 00
YELLOW PINE—Random cargoes delivered N. Y.	18 00	@	21 00
Ordered cargoes	22 00	@	23 00
Flooring	21 00	@	22 00
Step plank	26 00	@	28 00
Common siding	13 00	@	14 00
Heart face boards	20 00	@	21 50
Car orders	21 00	@	23 00
At Atlantic ports, f. o. b.	12 50	@	15 00
At Gulf ports, f. o. b.	11 50	@	13 00
North Caroline pine timber	13 50	@	15 00
do. flooring 1 inch	16 00	@	22 00
do. do. 1¼	16 50	@	22 50
do. do. 1½@2 inch	24 00	@	25 00
do Shipping culls or box	12 00	@	14 00
do Plain and mottled ½@1½ inch	18 50	@	25 50
Ash, white	38 00	@	43 00
Elm	20 00	@	22 50
Oak, plain	37 00	@	41 00
Oak, quarter sawed	52 00	@	55 00
Oak, quarter sawed, extra thick	56 00	@	60 00
Redwood	45 00	@	52 50
Maple, clear	28 00	@	33 00
Chestnut, clear	33 00	@	35 50
Cypress, clear	30 00	@	39 50
Black Walnut, good to choice	130 00	@	140 00
Black Walnut, ordinary to fair	100 00	@	120 00
Black Walnut, ⅝	78 00	@	88 00
Black Walnut, selected and seasoned	150 00	@	155 00
Black Walnut counters	110 00	@	150 00
Black Walnut, culls	35 00	@	40 00
Black Walnut, rejects	50 00	@	58 00
Cherry, wide	110 00	@	115 00
Cherry, good	85 00	@	100 00
Cherry, ordinary	65 00	@	80 00
Whitewood, inch	30 50	@	32 50
Whitewood, ⅝ inch	24 50	@	26 00
Whitewood, 1¼ to 2½ inch	32 00	@	34 00
Shingles, Pine, 16 inch, extra	2 75	@	3 10
do 18 inch, extra	4 10	@	4 30
do 18 inch, clear butt	2 90	@	3 10
do 16 inch, stocks	4 50	@	4 60
do 18 inch, stocks	5 30	@	5 40
Shingles, Cypress, 6x20	8 00	@	10 00
do larger sizes	11 00	@	16 00
do sawed	5 00	@	9 00
Cedar—Medium to large	6¼	@	7½
do. —Extra large	7¾	@	8
Mahogany—small	6½	@	7½
do —Medium	8	@	8½
do. —Large	9¼	@	13
do. —Extra Large	12½	@	14

PRICE, PER YEAR IN ADVANCE, SIX DOLLARS.

Published every Saturday.

TELEPHONE - - - - CORTLANDT 1370.

Communications should be addressed to

C. W. SWEET, 14 & 16 Vesey St.

J. T. LINDSEY, Business Manager.

VOL. XLVIII AUGUST 22, 1891. NO. 1,223

The publication offices of THE RECORD AND GUIDE *have been removed to Nos. 14 and 16 Vesey street, over The Mechanics' and Traders' Exchange, a few feet west of Broadway.*

IN spite of some very active work on the part of the reactionists it will hardly be thought possible that there is now, in the face of the realization of hopes for the crops an uncompromising bear in existence. The stock market has yielded but little and some stocks which were not particularly active on the advance have made gains in the interval of waiting. It is rest rather than reaction. If the volume of buying is not quite equal to that of the selling, it is so great as to be very promising for the next move. Under the bright prospect of a good foreign market for cereals, the return of gold this way and consequently plenty of money in the hands of the people with the consequent enormous expansion of business, whatever doubts clouded the mind only a few weeks ago are being rapidly dispelled. It is becoming even a dangerous matter to hint that free silver legislation by the ensuing Congress may undo what the agricultural and industrial prosperity may have done. President Harrison recently and Secretary Forster previously have given such emphatic expression to the opposition of the administration to unlimited coinage of the white metal that all who share their views, on this point at least (and they are the best elements of most business circles), begin to hope that Congress will not be a disturbing influence only to find itself checkmated by the President. To come back from general to particular influences on the market, Union Pacific with its load of floating obligations has been responsible for most of the deterring influence, and this it will continue to be probably until those obligations are safely provided for. All things considered, the stock has acted well for the past few days, indicating a near end of its troubles with its creditors. Northern Pacific securities, which have not advanced like some others, have shown indications of moving up on the first favorable opportunity. A reaction of two or three points would be a very healthy thing, as it would at once decide intending buyers who are now hesitating. It is not an altogether unknown thing, one should remember, however, for the market to make a much larger advance than seen in this latest movement without reacting at all, and the strength of the week suggests that this is one of those occasions.

IT is interesting to note that the Manchester Ship Canal Company, which has been spending millions of pounds in the task, certain to be ultimately successful, of making Manchester a seaport, is now in financial straits. Either the credit of the corporation has fallen so low, or the English market is at present so inhospitable to speculative undertakings, that the company has been unable to raise fresh capital for the prosecution and completion of the work. Consequently the Manchester corporation has stepped into the breach and tided the company over its difficulties. Municipal stock to the amount of £1,500,000 has been issued, and the corporation has sanctioned the payment to the Canal Company for five weeks of money sufficient to meet running expenses not exceeding £40,000 a week. This, however, would not exhaust one-seventh of the total issue of stock, and the opinion is prevalent that still more assistance will have to be rendered. The company will shortly issue a report showing exactly where it stands; and upon such a report will be based any future action. It is significant, however, of the present difficulty of obtaining funds in London that an enterprise already so far advanced and so certain of ultimate success should be reduced to such straits. The probabilities are that the city corporation itself will have to undertake the completion of the work. All the European markets are, however, in a decidedly apprehensive and sensitive condition. The prices of the securities principally dealt in on the Paris and Berlin Bourses have undergone an enormous shrinkage, from which there is no prospect of immediate recovery. There is very certain to be a severe drain of gold to this country; and manufacturers have to face an increased price of labor, owing to an increased cost of food. In Germany the depression in trade is creating a great deal of complaint. Two such important industries as the iron and steel and the textile trades are described as "languishing." It is becoming evident that however good crop may restore to this country most of the commercial activity of the years of 1889 and 1890, that Europe will suffer from a protracted and severe season of dullness and depreciation.

THE Rapid Transit Commissioners have given out a description of the West Side route above 121st street. As every one familiar with that part of the city knows, the ground is very irregular all the way to the Yonkers line, and any road on which the grades are not to be steep must alternately run well below and well above ground. Consequently a succession of tunnels and viaducts will have to be built, the latter of which will be very expensive to construct. A detailed description of this will be found in another column. Here it is sufficient to say that the first of these viaducts will be 3,500 feet long, and at highest point 64 feet above the surface. This, however, does not compare with the viaduct that begins at Fort George and continues to 213th street, a distance of 4,300 feet. At the crossing of Sherman's Creek it will be 110 feet above high water mark. The rest are small compared with this difficult piece of construction; but some of them run through private property, which will, of course, have to be condemned. At the present, as we scarcely need say, there is no traffic along the line of the route sufficient to pay for the large cost of such a road. For some years any corporation operating the route will run trains north, say of the line of Washington Bridge, at a heavy loss; and it will be necessary to do this in order to build up the district. The bidders for the franchise will fully understand the full bearing of this fact, and it is likely to make them touch that part of the route most gingerly—at all events until they can see more clearly what their traffic returns will be on the southern portion of the route. If they are forced to bid on the franchise all at once, the portion of earnings, if any, which they would be willing to make over to the city will be largely diminished by the knowledge that several miles of expensive road will have to be operated for future rather than for present returns. Now that the financial situation is clearing up, however, and it looks as if the year 1892 was going to be most prosperous, the prospects of selling the franchise advantageously are far better than they were.

WHILE thoroughly sympathizing with residents roundabout the Boulevard and 132d street, who are trying to prevent the Standard Gas-light Company from erecting a gas tank in their vicinity, we very much fear that their efforts will be ineffectual. President Wilson of the Health Board doubts whether the Health Board has power to interfere; and his doubt is justified by common sense. It would be very difficult to show that a gas tank is unhealthy. It is not, of course, a pleasant object to have next door, and it will undoubtedly injure the value of real estate in the neighborhood; but we cannot understand in what way any injury which it may inflict will come within the jurisdiction of the Health Board. It is a case where the property-owners ought to have protected themselves. Experience has repeatedly shown that the only safe method of preserving a neighborhood from the nuisances of undesirable improvements is by an adequate restriction of the property against them. Otherwise it is dangerous for anyone to build a good row of houses or to try to create a neighborhood of a uniformly pleasing and unobjectionable character. The buyers of the houses are always subject to be blackmailed by some rascal who files plans for a stable in order to be enabled to sell his lot at an extortionate figure; and this project of the Standard Gas-light Company is but an exaggerated instance of what may happen to any locality not thus properly protected. The most desirable parts of the West Side have all been built up under restrictions that excluded not only nuisances in the ordinary sense, but any building that would tend to lower a certain high standard of improvement. We have frequently pointed out that the property-owners of Washington Heights must needs follow this example. That part of the city is next in line of improvement, and it possesses every natural advantage fitting it to become a delightful residential section. In certain parts of the Heights these restrictions have been made; but if the section is to have even such a small measure of uniformity as has been accorded to the West Side, the restricted area must be largely increased.

A NOVEL suggestion is made by the *Times* for incorporation into the next bill amending the building laws—a suggestion which we very much fear was dictated rather by the natural refinement of the writer than by any very careful consideration of what should or should not be included within the ample limits of such a statute. The opening by the Association for Improving the

Condition of the Poor of a new bath-house in a section of the city where flesh is normally dirty has so stirred the imagination of that journal that it pictures to itself a bath-room on every floor of a tenement house, and the picture is so fascinating that it demands that such a feature be made a "requirement" of tenement houses. No doubt, if such a provision did exist, and the builders of tenements were obliged to furnish a bath-tub with every floor, there would be more baths taken in New York City then than there are now; but whether the increased cleanliness would be sufficient to pay for the expense which would attend the innovation is a matter which is far more doubtful. We do not believe that any improvement or convenience introduced into a building by the law, the use or neglect of which was optional on the part of the tenants, would be of any great value. The statute rightly provides for such essentials to life and safety as fire escapes and air shafts. The occupant needs no urging either to breathe the purer air thus obtained, or to hurry down the iron scaffolding if he needs must. But a bath-room would be a very different matter. The demand for such facilities is not strong at the present time in Cherry street; we do not believe that the owner of a building would find the new feature a very tempting one to would-be tenants. In all probability the bath-room would be let with one of the tenements, and the lessee would place a board on the top of the sink and a grimy lodger on top of the board. This could be even partially prevented only by a system of incessant inspection on the part of the Health Department, the expense of which would be enormous and the utility but very meagre. No, such are not the kind of provisions that should be included in building laws. Health and safety must at the present time be forced down the throats of the tenement-house population. In many of the "model" buildings of London all the various conveniences provided by the thoughtful philanthropists have been used simply as a common ground for the vicious and degraded to follow their inclinations. It would be an excellent plan for the city to establish bath-houses after the manner of the Association for Improving the Condition of the Poor, but any further than that it would be futile to go.

Cities Made to Order.

IT was formerly urged that an all-wise providence must have created the earth, because there was no great city but had been supplied with some large body of water, river, lake or sea, to float its commerce and to enable it to communicate with neighboring peoples. Were there no such over-watching wisdom, it was thought, how unfortunate for those cities that had been omitted in the distribution of natural favors!

The time has now come when natural advantages are relatively of ever-diminishing importance in the competition of city with city. Even the ascendancy of New York was secured, or assured, in the first instance by an artificial means of transportation, the Erie Canal. Most of the leading Western cities owe their prominence more to "enterprise" than to the possession of greater natural advantages than the rivals they have distanced. In the early days of Nebraska's development Omaha was not as well located as Florence to the north of her, or Bellevue to the south of her, but she secured the territorial capital, the terminus of the Union Pacific road, and so her own future. The mills at Minneapolis and the State capital at St. Paul would hardly have made the twin cities what they are had they not also had a rate of about three mills per ton per mile on flour and wheat to Chicago. Statistics show that the entire net increase of population from 1870 to 1890, twenty years, in Illinois, Wisconsin, Iowa and Minnesota (except the new section, which has not yet felt the effects of discrimination), was in cities and towns possessing competitive rates; and further, that nearly all the non-competitive towns and villages decreased in population.

It is this decisive influence of artificial highways upon the future of towns that makes it possible for a group of railway officials, operating as a land company, to speculate in real estate with absolute certainty of success. The old-fashioned speculator in the lots of new towns trusted to his ability to select the spot having the greatest natural advantages, and then proceed to advertise his discovery. If he boomed a place without natural advantages it collapsed either before or after he was ready for it to do so. Now the question as to which is to be the leading town of a given section is not a question of physiography, but largely of finance. It will be decided mainly by the men that control the construction and administration of the railways. This is so evident that in many instances in the West the best route from the standpoint of the engineer for a new road is ignored and some unexpected and relatively impracticable route is selected in order to give the officials an opportunity to buy real estate low and sell it high. The most important question about a new town is, therefore, who is interested in it?

It is reported that a group of Eastern capitalists have agreed to construct a great city on the shores of Puget Sound, and, of course, to build the railroads that will make it a success, and to start there industries that will insure a population of 10,000 within ninety days. It illustrates what we have already said that men are investing in this new city before it is named or located. Three strong rivals stand ready to dispute the supremacy of the unborn and nameless infant. Seattle presumed upon her natural advantages and the prestige of age and expected to be the San Francisco of the northern Pacific coast without a struggle. But the Northern Pacific Railroad appreciated the modern conditions of city building better, reached the Sound south of Seattle, cleared away the forest and founded the city of Tacoma. Now the Great Northern Railroad, which is well on its way toward the Sound, is reported to have selected Fair Haven as the proper location of the metropolis of that region, and will bend every energy to secure the concentration of business there. These three cities stand ready to resist the encroachments of a new rival, but it is doubtful if they will be able to prevent its existence and prosperity. Every one seems to feel that it is a question not of natural advantages but of enterprise and capital.

Competition of some kinds is the life of business, as so often asserted; but there are varieties of competition that are emphatically the death of business and of all prosperity. The wasteful paralleling of railroads is brought about partly by the wasteful over-multiplication and over-development of cities. The strong drift to the great centers of population shown by the census returns is partly inevitable, but it is also in part factitious and mischievous. It is in some sort the result of the manipulation of railroad construction and administration by officials who are interested in urban real estate. The only consolation is that where the thing is so overdone, as it appears to be in Washington at the present time, those who engage in it are likely to defeat their own purposes, and to lose rather than gain by their gigantic operations. Yet this is an unworthy consolation after all, for whether the great operators gain or lose the community as a whole will probably lose, in the first place by direct waste of capital and effort, and in the second place by a distorted and unsatisfactory development of its industries.

Investments—Good and Bad.

Bond Buying.—One, and it may almost be said the most favorable, feature in the situation is the good bond buying seen for a week past. Of course, back of this buying is a more healthy condition of the business situation, but the buying itself is the best symptom of the genuineness of the recovery. We have more than once pointed out that an advance, unaccompanied by a sign of returning confidence among investors, was likely to be of limited duration. Any one who will compare the list of bond sales for some time past cannot fail to be struck with the increase in the volume of purchases, and the way they are distributed among all attractive issues. Consequently, if our position is the correct one, and it is the one that experience suggests, there can be no doubt whatever that the present movement is genuinely bull, and that such will be the character of the speculative and investment markets for some time to come. No such advances as we have yet seen can possibly have discounted all the good there is in the situation or any very large part of it, and, while admitting that reactions will come or that the development of adverse influences may from time to time create set-backs, there is yet ample time to participate in the benefits of the advance. Houses, whose business is largely in the investment lines, are reporting the receipt of large buying orders each day, and a very much larger inquiry regarding bonds than they have known for a year. From that it would seem as if, though the market may take wholesome rests, that the hesitation to advance will be of short duration, and that the time for anything like a reaction has not yet come.

It was natural that the new buying should be first seen in the speculative issues, because they suffered most during the periods of depression and offered the largest promise of profit as soon as the advance began. Large amounts of this class of bonds have been bought for investment, and still larger amounts, probably, taken into margin accounts. These facts will account for the heavy buying from day to day of Atchison 4s and incomes, Kansas & Texas 4s and seconds, the Texas, Pacific and Wabash issues, St. Louis & Southern Terminal, Northern Pacific 5s, and even the much-abused and despised Richmond Terminal bonds. But there has also been inquiry for high-priced bonds and some business, limited because business in such securities always is more or less limited in comparison with the other classes, they being held on the excellent theory that it is well to keep a good thing when one has it. Notwithstanding the advances that have been made, the present prices of bonds do not come up to the figures of last year, and if such a substantial advance as was then seen could be effected in 1890, when the only arguments for a bull movement were the cheapness of money and previous depressions it is perfectly within the bounds of reason to anticipate that a market rising upon the largest grain crop in the history of the country, with a simultaneous falling off in the returns to the European farmer, will at least carry prices up to the figures of last year and probably a good way beyond it. This is provided, of course, that the evils in the situation will not be greater than can now be seen. There is one fact that should be borne carefully in mind by the investor, and that is that under any and every circumstance that can now be imagined there are many bonds on the list which, during the present movement, will change from speculative to investment issues. These are more particularly the bonds of recently reorganized roads which the time have not yet permitted to settle into their proper places. They are very large issues, and the fact of their size will always maintain a certain activity in them, but the influences of the movement just begun will not cease to be felt until these bonds have not only substantially advanced, but also not until they have proved the permanence of their value. In seeking such a bond the investor is advised to turn his attention to the Atchison, Kansas & Texas, St. Louis, Arkansas & Texas, Atlantic & Pacific and other 4 per cent new issues which will bear investigation. The cases are not in all respects alike. In some particulars a comparison may be made with the West Shore 4s. These bonds have back of them the guarantee of one of the first railroads in the country and have so long to run that any discount or premium changes the rate of interest which they pay only infinitessimally. They are a large issue, $50,000,000, and while issued at a good discount, have been on the market six years yet always showing some activity, even in the dullest times they rarely sell below par and then only fractionally. The West Shore 4s, however, are currency bonds, and in this respect later issues of the same denomination have an advantage over them. As with the West Shore 4s, so it is with other 4 per cent bonds we have named, and also with some bonds paying higher rates of interest, while their value will secure for them higher quotations, the extent of the issue will always keep open a market for those who wish to dispose of them. For evidence that good bonds have not discounted the excellent prospect, the quotations can be referred to with the utmost confidence. Some months ago we indicated some bonds it was then good to buy, and notwithstanding the great depression and almost utter stagnation in the bond market seen since, those bonds are higher to-day than they were then. This may be thought to qualify the expectation of a further advance, were it not for the fact that to-day's prices are so much below those of a year ago. For instance, the Atchison 4s were two days ago 80¾, but sold in 1890 as high as 88, the Atlantic & Pacific 4s are nearly 10 points below the highest of last year, the Kansas & Texas 4s 6 points, Reading 4s 4 points, and even the West Shore 4s 6 points below the highest of 1890. It is not alone in the 4 per cent issues that these discrepancies of prices in the two years are seen. In the 5 per cent. issues as a rule it is even more marked. Brooklyn Elevated Seconds reached 90⅛ in 1890, and recently sold at 84⅛; Hocking Valley 5s touched 88⅛ last year, five or six points higher than recent quotations; Wisconsin Central first quoted on Wednesday last at 87, sold last year at 104⅛. This last-named bond has been the subject of a good deal of diligent inquiry lately, but current quotations do not encourage transactions. There is a good margin for the expectation of profit in the prices at which Wabash 1sts, Iowa Central 1sts, Milwaukee, Lake Shore and Western Extensions and Improvements, New York, Ontario & Western Consols, St. Louis & San Francisco 1st Trusts, Wabash 1st, and the other 5 per cent bonds are selling compared with the prices at which they sold last year. It must not be taken that there is any intention here to convey the idea that because a bond sold high last year it must necessarily sell high this year. That is not the intention at all. The idea intended to be conveyed is that the situation warrants an advance in the price of any particular bond more than did the events which brought about the advance of last year, provided the merits of that bond remain unimpaired. For instance, while we say Atchison 4s should sell as high as they did last year, we would not say the same of Richmond Terminal 5s. There is no question that Kansas and Texas 4s are worth as much as they were last year; but there is some doubt whether Northern Pacific Consol 5s will reach last year's figures. If any road should benefit by the great wheat crop, it should be Northern Pacific, which runs through and has as its tributaries many wheat-growing states and territories, but its securities have not shown the same vim in advancing as have other grain roads, and that fact makes the expression of an opinion on the prospective value of its issues more of a matter for hesitation than in other cases, though it is probable that the selling and consequent lagging comes from foreign holders who are necessitous, and is not occasioned by any defects in the property which the good business on hand should not offset. It will be seen from all this merely that it is now as always, an act of wisdom for the investor to temper his confidence with discretion.

The Rapid Transit Outlook.

The Rapid Transit Commission has been broken up with sickness and vacations this week and nothing of an active character has been done by it. But the consulting engineers, on the other hand, have had so much to do that they could not finish their assigned tasks, and the commission is forced to wait for them.

The engineers of the commission have, however, completed the surveys of the West Side route from Fort George to the Yonkers line. As completed, this line will extend straight out 11th avenue, by a viaduct 4,300 feet long, to the high ground on the Isham property at 213th street, just west of the Kingsbridge road; thence it diverges to eastward to 217th street, at what would be the intersection of Audubon avenue, if the latter were extended thus far.

From this point the road follows the line of Audubon avenue produced, across the new Government Canal, which is crossed by a viaduct 60 feet above high water, and across the Spuyten Duyvil Creek at the same elevation, and by alternate viaducts and tunnels, as a hill or a hollow is encountered, to a point just north of Delafield lane. Thence the road is to diverge a little to the westward, continuing to the intersection of Rock and Forest streets, and thence along Forest street to the northern city limit.

Along this West Side route there will be eight or nine viaducts of from 500 to 4,300 feet in length, and from 15 to 110 feet above the surface of the ground. The country traversed, from 121st street to the northern terminus, is some of the prettiest in the city, and is capable of containing a large population and of supplying a large patronage to the road when completed. Now it is out of the market for improvement, for want of proper and adequate transit facilities. But with a rapid transit railroad in operation along the line designated by the engineers of the commission, there is not the slightest doubt but that it would be rapidly improved and inhabited.

"The Architectural Record"—What Is Thought of It.

Office of T. Buckler Ghequier, architect, No. 227 St. Paul street, Baltimore.

August 10, 1891.

To the Editors of the Architectural Record:

I write to assure you of my hearty commendation of your first number. I have read every article through word by word and have examined most carefully the illustrations and find no fault. If the present standard is kept up it deserves every success.

Can you not get from some one who can write interestingly an article or so on the "Proper Relations of Architect and Client?"

Very truly yours, T. Buckler Ghequier.

Hazlehurst & Huckel, architects, 410 Walnut street, Philadelphia.

August 11, 1891.

The Architectural Record:

Gentlemen—The first number of your *Record* reached us to-day, and let us say in reply that we are more than pleased with the magazine, both as regards its text and illustrations, and we consider you are filling a want long felt in a fresh, scholarly, architectural review, aside from the building journals and building trade journals, and giving a much better field for such articles on architecture as have appeared from time to time in the *Century* and *Harper's* magazines, also reaching more directly those especially interested. Hazlehurst & Huckel, per S. Huckel.

J. H. Scharn, architect, Room 43, Thorpe Block, Indianapolis, Ind.

August 12, 1891.

The Architectural Record:

I have received the first number of the *Architectural Record*, but in driving home I have lost it out of my buggy, and am not able to trace it so as to get it back. Will you send me another in place of it? Whatever the cost may be I certainly will pay, and you may send it C. O. D. to my address. J. H. Scharn.

Edward P. Doan, architect, No. 500 Main street, Orange, N. J.

Aug. 17, 1891.

Editor Architectural Record, 14 to 16 Vesey street:

Dear Sir—Inclosed please find check for year's subscription from July 1, 1891. If the following numbers are as good as the first it will become a very successful magazine. Edward P. Doan.

Greg Vigeant, architect, 59 Dearborn street, Room 610, Real Estate Board Building, Chicago, telephone 2888.

Aug. 10, 1891.

The Architectural Record:

Vol. I., No. 1., received and appreciated. G. Vigeant.

Office of Albert H. Humes, architect, Nos. 163 and 165 Dexter street, Central Falls, R. I.

Aug. 18, 1891.

To *The Architectural Record*, New York, N. Y.:

I am very much satisfied with your first number, and if that standard is followed I think your circulation will increase rapidly. I value this first number very much.

You will please find inclosed money order for one year's subscription and $1. Albert H. Humes.

Mead & Taft, contractors and manufacturers, Established 1843, Cornwall Landing, N. Y.

Aug. 18, 1891.

The Architectural Record, 14-16 Vesey street, N. Y. City.:

Gentlemen—Inclosed please find postal note in payment of subscription to *The Architectural Record*. Am pleased with first copy received.

Wm. E. Jackson.

The Tax Rate for 1891.

The tax rate for 1891 has been fixed at $1.90 per cent, as anticipated in The Record and Guide six weeks ago. This rate will be on all property, both real and personal, except the personal estates of certain corporations, joint stock companies and associations which are exempt by law from local taxation for State purposes, on which the tax will be $1.686 per cent. Of the former the amount to be assessed is $1,707,868,828, and of the latter $77,988,510, a total of $1,785,857,338.

While the tax rate is thus reduced .07 per cent as compared with the tax rate of 1890, the total assessed valuation is increased by $88,878,948 over last year. The full figures of assessed valuations, by wards and in totals, of both real and personal estate, were published in The Record and Guide of July 11th last.

Important Suburban Sales.

Two important sales of suburban real estate have taken place this week.

The estate of Stephen H. Thayer have sold thirty-two acres near Woodlawn station, on the New York and Harlem Road, for about $70,000.

Dr. A. W. Lozier, whose building operations on the West Side have been quite extensive during the last few years, has purchased about eighty-two and one-third acres of high ground on the Hartsdale road, near Elmsford depot, on the New York and Northern Railway. The seller was Elverton R. Chapman, of the firm of Moore & Schley, bankers and brokers, Union Trust Company building, and the price is said to be about $24,000. It is at Elmsford that Charles T. Barney and Augustus T. Gillender and their respective syndicates are making extensive improvements.

Street Improvements on the North Side.

Up on the North Side the work of preparing the district for the occupancy of the millions who are coming from all parts of the world to make New York their permanent home goes bravely on. Where the streets have been legally opened and the city is in possession of the property, adjoining property-owners are pressing with impatience for the new Department of Street Improvements to hasten the work of improvement. Owners know that every dollar spent in sewering, grading, curbing, flagging and paving, where the work is properly done, adds ten to the market value of their property; and they have not been so discouraged by the dull times and stagnation in the real estate market yet to lose hope in a speedy turning of the tide in their favor. While they remain thus hopefu they will continue to make their preparations to welcome the buyer and settler, when he shall choose to put in his appearance.

Commissioner Heintz is doing everything in the line of his official duty to help the district along. Every delegation of property-owners, and they come every day, is given the most interested attention, and its request is attended to as fast as it can be managed in the order in which it comes before him. The Commissioner is himself a resident and property-owner in the district, and is just as desirous to see the district developed as anybody else. Within the last month seventeen contracts have been awarded, of which eleven are now under way and six are awaiting the action of the Comptroller upon the sureties of the contractor. They are given herewith, together with the estimated amounts of cost of the work:

REGULATING AND GRADING.—139th street, from Willis to St. Ann's avenue, $6,438.50; 155th street, from Courtlandt to Railroad avenue, $3,182.25; Bristow street, from Stebbins avenue to the Boston road, $6,139.93; Devoe street, from Ogden to Bremer avenue, $4,895.40; 138th street, from Rider to Railroad avenue, $3,758.25; Chisholm street, from Jennings street to Stebbins avenue, $11,102.73; Hampden street, from Sedgwick to Jerome avenue, $19,909.75; 147th street, from Brook to St. Ann's avenue, $1,656.70; 169th street, from Franklin avenue to 167th street, $34,819; 154th street, from Courtlandt to Morris avenue, $2,845.80; and 167th street, from Vanderbilt to 3d avenue, $2,750.40.

REGULATING, GRADING AND PAVING.—145th street, from 3d avenue to 146th street, $5,270.25; 138th street, from Railroad Avenue to Madison Avenue Bridge, $9,442.75; Brook avenue, from 132d to 156th street, $86,719.

SEWERING.—Locust avenue, from 139th to 141st street, $1,748; German place, from Westchester avenue to 156th street, $4,221.85.

CURBING AND FLAGGING.—Boston avenue, from Jefferson to Tremont avenue, $9,026.75.

Of work already cut out for the future there are four contracts advertised to be let next Thursday, as follows: Flagging Brook avenue, from 165th street to 3d avenue; regulating and grading 170th street, from 3d to Franklin avenue; and regulating and paving Morris avenue, from 148th to 152d street, and from 139th to 140th street.

Specifications have also been prepared and proposals will soon be invited for other improvements to be made this fall, among them the following, which have been decided upon:

REGULATING AND GRADING.—College avenue, from Morris avenue to 146th street; 173d street, from Vanderbilt avenue to 3d avenue, and from the Harlem Railroad to Weeks street; 38th street, from the Southern Boulevard to Locust avenue; 184th street, from Jerome to Vanderbilt avenue; and Burnside street, from Westchester avenue to Sedgwick.

REGULATING, GRADING AND PAVING.—134th street, from Brook avenue to the Southern Boulevard; 135th street, from Brook to Cypress avenue; 143d street, from 3d avenue to 144th street; 149th street, from the Harlem Railroad to Mott avenue.

PAVING.—153d street, from 3d to Courtlandt avenue; 167th street, from Vanderbilt to 3d avenue.

SEWERING.—132d street, from Brook to Trinity avenue; Wales avenue, from 149th to Kelly street; 161st street, from Sheridan to Mott avenue; Southern Boulevard, from summit west of to summit east of Willis avenue, and from Brook avenue to 137th street; John street, from Brook to Eagle avenue; and Brook avenue, from tidewater to 165th street.

The work of maintenance and repairs is also receiving the attention of Commissioner Heintz, some 200 men, in gangs of from three to twenty, being busy upon this branch of the department work nearly all the time. Over 25,000 cubic yards of broken stone have been placed upon the roads most in need of repair this year and 11,000 more will be asked for in the next batch of proposals.

The New Appraiser's Stores Site.

Judge Wallace, of the United States Circuit Court, on Monday last, handed down a decision in the condemnation proceedings begun by the United States Government against Patrick J. Roon and Ida L. Pryor. Frederick D. Tappan, Henry L. Burnet and Alexander P. Ketchum have been appointed commissioners to appraise the value of the three lots owned by the defendants and to make the proper awards, subject, of course, to confirmation by the court. The commissioners are directed to hold their first meeting in the Post-office Building on August 27th, at 3 o'clock P. M. The details of this suit are probably well known to readers of THE RECORD AND GUIDE, having been referred to more than once in these columns.

It seems from the evidence in the case that when the government decided to locate the appraiser's stores on the West Side they made a contract with John Lindley, a lawyer, for the purchase of the block bounded by Barrow, Washington, Christopher and Greenwich streets, at $500,000, although at the time Mr. Lindley owned none of the property. Mr. Lindley succeeded, however, in having Trinity Church corporation convey to the Government the sixteen lots which they owned for $321,000, and he also purchased on his own account last February, No. 635 Washington street, 25x105.5x25x104.8, for $22,500, and No. 639 Washington street, 26x106.10, for a similar sum, making a total of $45,000. These two lots Mr. Lindley immediately reconveyed to the government for $99,000, or $44,000 more than he had paid for them. This sale left only $80,000 for the three remaining lots on the block, and the owners refused to accept this amount as compensation, claiming that the proportion of payment was lower than what had been paid to Lindley for his lots. After ascertaining that he could not purchase the remaining three lots on the block, and previous to January 1st, as per contract, Mr. Lindley notified the government of the fact and the present condemnation proceedings are the result.

The lots in dispute are No. 637 Washington street, 26x105 4x26x106.1, owned by Ida L. Pryor and located between the two lots which Lindley personally conveyed to the government. Mrs. Pryor purchased this lot in 1875 for $6,000, and since then there has been no conveyance. The two lots owned by Patrick J. Roon are Nos. 662 to 666 Greenwich street, 57x100.8x49.9x71.2, and he purchased them April 21, 1888, at a foreclosure sale for $9,900 above the mortgage of $22,500. A search of the records fails to reveal any transfers that will help the commissioners in deciding upon their awards. The only recent sales upon which it would be proper to base an appraisal are those of the other owners on the block to the government, and if these are used the contention of Mr. Roon and Mrs. Pryor that their property is worth more than the $80,000 offered them must be sustained.

New Incorporations.

The Trevino Land Company have filed a certificate of incorporation in the County Clerk's office for the purpose of dealing in real estate. The capital stock is $5,000, divided into 500 shares at $10 each. The names of the directors are Mariner A. and Victor A. Wilder, Thomas S. Bullock, Samuel Bingaman, Frank Rudd, George E. Walters and Teofilo H. Gimbernat.

Personal.

Morgan D. McMonegal, of McMonegal & Eckerson, has just returned from a successful fishing trip at Lackawaxen, Pa.

T. L. Reynolds will spend a short time at Middletown Springs, Vt.

William Waldorf Astor, who is now abroad, has no present intention of returning to this country. In social circles it is not expected that Mr. Astor will visit New York until after the close of the coming winter season at least, and it is whispered that he may make his permanent residence abroad.

William Astor, up to a short time ago, was staying at the Pacific Hotel, Chicago. He has now left that city and gone on to Denver and other Western cities, but whether with a view to making real estate investments or not we are unable to say.

Karl M. Wallach left for Europe on Thursday last, to be gone six months.

Fifty cents apiece will be paid for indices to Volume XLIII. of THE RECORD AND GUIDE, at the office, 14 to 16 Vesey street.

Interesting to Architects and Builders.

CEMENT.

The demand for the Stettin Grislow Portland cement continues unabated. Emil Kanter, of No. 126 Liberty street, who is the sole agent for the United States, has taken orders this season for about 45,000 barrels in New York City alone, exclusive of large orders from all parts of the country.

* * *

BRICK.

The Lorillard Brick Works Company, of Lorillard, N. J., are turning out a fine quality of repressed brick and special designs in terra cotta ornaments. They are running up to their fullest capacity on hand burned and porous terra cotta fire-proof building material, and have made several additions to their plant, enabling them to turn out a greater quantity of work than before.

* * *

PAVING.

The Matt. Taylor Paving Company have secured the contract for all cement work to be laid at the Manhattan Storage and Warehouse Company's fire-proof building on 7th avenue, 52d and 53d streets, on which they will commence their work on September 1st. They are also completing their contract on the new Holland House, which is to be ready for occupancy about September 15th. The company has other contracts for fire-proof buildings.

* * *

VENETIAN BLINDS.

The Venetian Blind Company, of Burlington, Vt., whose New York offices are in the *World* building, have extended their factory three times in three years, and are now adding a three-story building, 36x100 in size, to their present structure. Their blinds have a very extensive reputation, and are sold in every state and territory in the Union, in Canada, South America and Europe. The company are shipping millions of feet to Europe every year. They sold in New York city and Brooklyn alone over 33,000 sets of blinds in 1890, and will more than double this, they say, in 1891. They have in Geo. D. Wright, who is the head and front of the firm, a most able manager.

* * *

STEAM HEATING.

Messrs. Blake & Williams, of No. 197 Wooster street, are doing all the steam work for the Brooklyn Post-office, which will be completed about November 1. They are also doing the steam-heating work on the new Fifth Avenue Theatre. Among their other contracts is that on the handsome Leiter residence in Washington, D. C.

* * *

CORNICE WORK.

Louis Dreyer, of No. 339 West 18th street, is doing all the cornice work and roofing on the Dugro Hotel, on 5th avenue and 59th street, which is a ten thousand dollar contract. He is also doing similar work on the six flats being built by P. & J. Schaeffer on 13th street, between 1st and 2d avenues, and has many other orders on hand.

Notice to Property-Owners.

CITY OF NEW YORK, FINANCE DEPARTMENT,
COMPTROLLER'S OFFICE, August 17, 1891.

In pursuance of Section 916 of the "New York City Consolidation Act of 1882," the Comptroller of the City of New York gives notice to all persons, owners of property affected by the following assessment lists, viz.:

SEWERS.

Bridge st, bet Broad and Whitehall sts.

Boulevard, e s, at 129th st, alteration and improvement.

Madison av, bet 107th and 109th sts.

Madison av, bet 116th and 117th sts.

Madison av, bet 125th and 127th sts.

Madison av, bet 128th and 129th sts.

Madison av, bet 134th and 135th sts.

1st av, bet 45th and 46th sts.

4th (Park) av, w s, bet 71st and 73d sts, and in 72d st, bet Park and Madison avs, alteration and improvement.

13th av, e s, bet Little West 12th and 13th sts. and in 13th st, bet 10th and 13th avs.

63d st, bet Amsterdam and Columbus avs, extension of sewer.

77th st, bet Boulevard and Amsterdam av.

89th st, bet Boulevard and 10th av, with curve into 10th av (west side), extension of sewer.

99th st, bet Madison and 5th avs.

99th st, bet Boulevard and West End av.

102d st, bet Boulevard and West End av.

104th st, bet Harlem River and 1st av.

126th st, bet 10th av and Boulevard.

East 142d st, bet Rider and 3d avs, with a branch in Morris av., bet 142d and 143d sts.

East 147th st, bet Willis and Brook avs.

153d st, bet 8th and Bradhurst avs.

RECEIVING BASIN.

On northwest corner of 131st st and Amsterdam av.

REGULATING, GRADING, CURBING AND FLAGGING.

5th av, from 138th st to the Harlem River.

139th st, from Rider to Morris av.

139th st, from 8th av to the first new av west of 8th av.

139th st, from 10th av to 425 feet west of Boulevard.

140th st, from North 3d to Morris av.

140th st, from 7th to 8th av.

142d st, from 8th to Bradhurst av.

146th st, from 8th av to the Harlem River.

147th st, from 8th av to Harlem River.

147th st, from 10th av to Boulevard.

148th st, from St. Nicholas av to the Boulevard.

149th st, from St. Nicholas to Amsterdam av.

East 166th st, from Vanderbilt to 3d av, and laying crosswalks.

PAVING.

Sylvan pl, from 120th to 121st st, with granite blocks.

Boston av, from 3d av to 167th st, with trap blocks and laying crosswalks.

Madison av, from 94th to 105d st, with granite blocks and laying crosswalks.

Madison av, from 108th to 110th st, with granite blocks and laying crosswalks.

Rider av, from 135th to 144th st, with trap blocks.

The Southern Boulevard, from the easterly crosswalk of 3d av to the easterly crosswalk of Willis av, with trap blocks.

Westchester av, from the westerly crosswalk of Brook av to the westerly crosswalk of Trinity av, with granite blocks.

1st av, from 125th to 126th st, with granite blocks and laying crosswalks.

10th av, from 110th to Manhattan st, with granite blocks and laying crosswalks.

69th st, from West End av to the line of the Hudson River Railroad, with granite blocks.

75th st, from 8th to 9th av, with asphalt.

78th st, from Boulevard to Riverside Drive, with granite blocks.

84th st, from 10th av to the Boulevard, with granite blocks and laying crosswalks.

85th st, from Boulevard to Riverside Drive, with asphalt.

87th st, from West End av to Riverside Drive, with asphalt.

87th st, from 8th to 9th av, and from 10th av to the Boulevard, with asphalt block pavement and laying crosswalks.

88th st, from Boulevard to West End av, with asphalt.

88th st, from West End av to Riverside Drive, with granite blocks.

89th st, from Boulevard to Riverside Drive, with granite blocks and laying crosswalks.

96th st, bet 8th and 9th avs, with asphalt.

96th st, from 9th to 10th av, with asphalt.

96th st, from 10th av to the Boulevard, with granite blocks and laying crosswalks.

101st st, from 8th av to the Boulevard, with granite blocks and laying crosswalks.

102d st, from 1st av to the Harlem River, with granite blocks.

103d st, from Amsterdam av to the Boulevard, with asphalt and laying crosswalks.

104th st, from Boulevard to Riverside Drive, with granite blocks and laying crosswalks.

105th st, bet Park and 5th avs, with granite blocks and laying crosswalks.

114th st, from Madison to 5th av, with granite blocks.

125th st, from Manhattan st to the Boulevard, with granite blocks and laying crosswalks.

128th st, from Av St. Nicholas to 8th av, with asphalt and laying crosswalks.

130th st, from 10th av to the Boulevard, with granite blocks and laying crosswalks.

133d st, from 8th av to Av St. Nicholas, with asphalt and laying crosswalks.

134th st, bet St. Nicholas and 8th avs, with asphalt and laying crosswalks.

138th st, from the westerly crosswalk of 3d av to the westerly crosswalk of Rider av, with granite blocks and laying crosswalks.

138th st, from 3d to St. Ann's av, with granite blocks.

139th st, from 3d to Willis av, with trap blocks.

149th st, from 3d to Robbins av, with granite blocks.

REPAVING.

Bethune st, from West st to 13th av, with granite blocks.

Houston st, from Washington to West st, granite blocks and laying crosswalks.

Lewis st, from Delancey to Houston st, with granite blocks and laying crosswalks.

Little West 12th st, from Washington st to 10th av, with granite blocks.

Mangin st, from Grand to Houston st, excepting block bet Stanton and Rivington sts, with granite blocks and laying crosswalks.

Washington st, from Clarkson to Spring st, with granite blocks and laying crosswalks.

FLAGGING, CURBING, ETC.

E s Boston av, from Jefferson to Bristow st, and laying crosswalks at intersection of Prospect and Boston avs.

E s Park av, from 115th to 116th st, and s s of 116th st, from Lexington to Park av.

N e cor Park av and 120th st, extdg abt 50 ft. on Park av and 100 ft. on 120th st.

In front of Nos. 805, 807, 809 and 811 1st av.

E s 3d av, from 92d to 93d st, and on the n s of 92d and s s of 93d sts, extdg abt 150 ft. easterly from 3d av.

S s of 59th st, from 7th av to Broadway.

S s 69th st, bet 2d and 3d avs.

Both sides of 69th st, from Boulevard to West End av.

Both sides of 78th st, from 10th av to the Boulevard.

Both sides of 86th st, from 8th to Riverside av.

Both sides of 87th and 88th sts, bet Madison and 5th avs.

S s of 90th st, from Park to Madison av.

S s of 95th st, extending westerly from Columbus av about 225 ft.

Both sides of 96th st, from 8th av to the Boulevard.

Both sides of 96th st, from 8th av to the Boulevard.

N s of 116th st, bet Park and Madison avs.

Both sides of 120th st, from 7th to St. Nicholas av.

N s of 132d st, from 7th to 8th av.

FENCING VACANT LOTS.

On the n e and n w cors of Madison av and 108th st.

On the n w cor of 8th av (Central Park West) and 74th st.

On the n s of 69th st, commencing abt 175 feet east of the Boulevard and extdg easterly about 75 feet.

On the s e cor of 72d st and Madison av.

On the n s of 76th st, bet Columbus av and Central Park West.

On the s e cor of 88th st and Columbus av, extdg abt 120 feet on Columbus av and 101 feet on 88th st.

On the s s of 95th st, extdg a distance of abt 200 feet westerly from Columbus avenue.

On the s s of 99th st, bet 8th and 9th avs.

On the block bounded by 105th and 106th sts and Madison and Park avs.

On the s s of 111th st, bet 5th and Madison avs.

On the n s of 117th st, from Park to Madison av.

On the block bounded by 119th and 120th sts, Madison and Park avs.

On the s s of 135th st, bet Park and Lenox avs.

—which were confirmed by the Board of Revision and Correction of Assessments, August 7, 1891, and entered on the same date in the Record of Titles of Assessments, kept in the "Bureau for the Collection of Assessments and Arrears of Taxes and Assessments and of Water Rents," that unless the amount assessed for benefit on any person or property shall be paid within sixty days after the date of said entry of the assessments, interest will be collected thereon as provided in section 917 of said "New York City Consolidation Act of 1882."

The above assessments are payable to the Collector of Assessments and Clerk of Arrears, at the "Bureau for the Collection of Assessments and Arrears of Taxes and Assessments and of Water Rents," between the hours of 9 A. M. and 2 P. M., and all payments made thereon on or before October 7, 1891, will be exempt from interest as above provided, and after that date will be subject to a charge of interest at the rate of 7 per cent per annum from the date of entry in the Record of Titles of Assessments in said Bureau to the date of payment.

In the matter of the application of the Board of Street Opening and Improvement at the City of New York, relative to acquiring title (wherever the same has not been heretofore acquired) to Cammann street (although not yet named by proper authority), extending from Fordham road to the Harlem River Terrace, in the 24th Ward; also to Harlem River Terrace (although not yet named by proper authority), extending from Cedar avenue to Fordham road, in the 24th Ward; also to East 137th street (although not yet named by proper authority), extending from the westerly line of Locust avenue to the easterly line of the Southern Boulevard, in the 23d Ward.

The Commissioners of Estimate and Assessment in the above-entitled matters, give notice to all persons interested in these proceedings, and to the owner or owners, occupant or occupants, of all houses and lots and improved and unimproved lands affected thereby, and to all others whom it may concern, to wit: that they have completed their estimates and assessments, and that all persons interested in this proceeding, or in any of the lands affected thereby, and having objections thereto, do present their said objections in writing, at No. 51 Chambers street (Room 4), on or before the twenty-sixth day of September, 1891, and said Commissioners will hear objections thereto within ten week days next after the said twenty-sixth day of September, 1891; that their report will be presented to the Supreme Court, at a Special Term thereof, to be held on the ninth day of October, 1891, at the opening of the Court on that day, and that then and there, or as soon thereafter as counsel can be heard thereon, a motion will be made that the said report be confirmed.

Contractors' Notes.

Sealed bids or estimates for furnishing the materials and work required for repairing rooms, plumbing, etc., Bellevue Hospital, will be received at the office of the Department of Public Charities and Correction, No. 66 3d avenue, in the City of New York, until 10 o'clock A. M., Friday, August 28, 1891.

Sealed bids or estimates will be received at the Department of Public Parks, at its offices, Nos. 49 and 51 Chambers street, until 11 o'clock A. M., on Wednesday, August 26, 1891, for repairing and resurfacing the macadamized roadway of a certain portion of "The Plaza," at 59th street and 5th avenue, and "The Circle," at 59th street and 8th avenue; for the construction of mason and granite work for seven parks in Park avenue, between 60th and 67th streets. Blank forms for proposals and forms of the contracts which the successful bidder will be required to execute can be had at the office of the Secretary, and the plans can be seen and information relative to them can be had at the office of the Department.

Bids or estimates, inclosed in a sealed envelope, will be received at the Department of Public Works, until 12 o'clock M., on Tuesday, September 1, 1891: For flagging 8 feet wide and reflagging, curbing and recurbing the sidewalks on Delancey street, from Mangin to East street; flagging 8 feet wide and reflagging, curbing and recurbing the sidewalks on west side of Tompkins street, from Broome to Delancey street; flagging full width and reflagging, curbing and recurbing the sidewalks on north side of Hester street, from Suffolk to Clinton street; flagging full width and reflagging, curbing and recurbing the sidewalks on north side of 86th street, from Madison to 5th avenue; flagging full width and reflagging, curbing and recurbing the sidewalks on east side of 5th avenue, from 86th to 91st street; regulating and grading F street, from northerly line of Dyckman street to Bolton road, and setting curbstones and flagging sidewalks therein; regulating and grading Dyckman street, from Hudson River to exterior street, and setting curbstones and flagging sidewalks therein. Blank forms of bid or estimate, the proper envelopes in which to inclose the same, the specifications and agreements, and any further information desired, can be obtained at Room 5, No. 31 Chambers street.

Estimates for preparing for and laying pavement and plank roadways on new-made land on and in rear of the cribwork bulkhead, from East 138th street to north of East 140th street, on the Harlem River, will be received by the Board of Commissioners at the head of the Department of Docks, on Pier "A," North River, until 1 o'clock P. M. of Thursday, September 3, 1891. Bidders are requested, in making their bids or estimates, to use the blank prepared for that purpose by the Department, a copy of which, together with the form of the agreement, including specifications, and showing the manner of payment for the work, can be obtained upon application therefor at the office of the Department.

Real Estate Department.

There is some improvement to be noted in the real estate market this week, though the degree is not great enough to encourage the hope that the season of fall business has opened up in earnest. The most sanguine among real estate men do not look for a real revival of activity for at least two weeks yet, and meantime they expect the most pronounced dullness, for during these last weeks in August nearly every one who can so arrange it is away, or is trying to get away for a last visit to the country. The purchase of lots on 5th avenue, therefore, by Mr. William Astor, and the several interesting private house sales reported in our "Gossip" column are more in the nature of surprises than expected results. There is, however, a strong inquiry in nearly all classes of real estate that bodes well for the coming season if the demands made by owners for their property are not unreasonable. The strongest interest is manifested in sterling investment property and in the better classes of private dwellings, and brokers whose main business is in that line of holdings say that anything which is at all desirable will be quickly taken up if the prices asked are not prohibitive. In other classes of real estate, while the demand is not quite so active, it is still good, and those who ought to know say that it will be even better if the general business throughout the country is all that is anticipated. Altogether the prevailing opinion among the most reliable and best-informed real estate men seems to be that while the fall will bring forth no boom it will be an active season at satisfactory prices.

THE DOINGS IN THE AUCTION MARKET.

The past week in the auction room has been the dullest of the season thus far, and it is not likely that it will be equalled in this respect for some time to come. On no day during the week has the attendance at the Exchange exceeded fifty persons, and during the larger part of the week it has not reached that number. Those, too, who in the main make up the auctioneers' audiences are not of the important market-making character. In consequence of this, absolutely nothing is being sold that has a general interest for the real estate world. The few foreclosure sales are of the most unimportant character, and it is seldom that they engage the attention of any but the parties interested. During the week, in addition to the few legal sales, an attempt was made to dispose of three parcels of New Jersey real estate. In every instance the attempt was met with a failure so pronounced and decided that other owners will probably hesitate before offering any country holdings for some time to come. One of the parcels offered was the Elberon Hotel and the celebrated "Garfield" cottage, with a considerable tract of land. This sale had been fairly well advertised, and the historical interest which attached to the property it was thought would surely draw a crowd. And yet the property was offered to an audience of about twenty-five men, none of whom showed any anxiety to buy, and after one bid by an outsider and two bids by representatives of the owners the property was bought in at $62,000, a figure admittedly below its value.

Next week there will be but few sales outside an uninteresting list of legal offerings, and the outside announcements are not of the kind to attract real estate people in general. The auction market it will be seen is very dull, and the auctioneers' announcements are not numerous or important enough to warrant any statement as to the time of improvement. In the meantime there is a great deal of talk about the prospects of the fall season, and although the news about city offerings is rather scarce the suburban property and that in the outlying wards promise very well. Already large lot sales in the 23d and 24th Wards are the talk of the market, not to mention large holdings outside the city limits which will be offered to the small buyer in the form of building lots. If these sales attain only a measure of the success that is expected of them the season will be a very satisfactory one.

CONVEYANCES.

	1890. August 15 to 21 inc.	1891. August 14 to 20 inc.
Number	194	168
Amount involved	$3,527,056	$2,561,542
Number nominal	58	42
Number 23d and 24th Wards	52	30
Amount involved	$244,357	$93,340
Number nominal	18	6

MORTGAGES.

	1890.	1891.
Number	214	187
Amount involved	$2,441,003	$1,887,451
Number at 5 % or less	106	92
Amount involved	$1,371,891	$1,017,580
Number at less than 5 per cent	20	6
Amount involved	$481,000	$50,000
Number to Banks, Trust and Ins. Cos	52	26
Amount involved	$1,083,700	$406,250

PROJECTED BUILDINGS.

	1890. August 16 to 22 inc.	1891. August 15 to 21 inc.
Number of buildings	72	32
Estimated cost	$2,084,950	$536,850

Gossip of the Week.

SOUTH OF 59TH STREET.

Douglas Robinson, Jr., & Co., we hear, have sold for Mrs. Caroline W. Whiton to E. Clinton Potts, No. 7 East 53d street, a four-story brown stone front dwelling, on lot 21x100.5, for $43,500.

Plunkitt & McKenna have sold for Kate Gallagher, Nos. 322 and 324 West 49th street, to Thomas Smith on private terms.

Ames & Co. have sold for Emanuel Regnier the three-story, high stoop, brick dwelling, No. 111 West 28th street, 21.5x55x98.9, to Mrs. W. Dunn for $18,000.

Andrew Kopple and Henry Wise have sold to John Maggi and Rocco Marasco the five-story brick tenement, 25x118, No. 55 Spring street, for $32,000.

NORTH OF 59TH STREET.

Geo. R. Read has sold for Jas. Stillman, the merchant, to William Astor, the three lots on the northeast corner of 5th avenue and 65th street, 75.5x100, for $215,000.

street, a four-story brown stone, uncompleted dwelling, 20x55 and extension x102.2, to C. A. Whiting for $37,000, and for the same owner to Robert F. Little, No. 116 West 76th street, a similar house, also for $37,000.

John G. Prague has sold No. 81 West 86th street, a four-story Lake Superior red stone front dwelling, 20x56, with 19-foot extension x102.2, to the President of the West Side Bank, John W. B. Dobler, for $50,000. Brokers, Fairchild & Yoran.

Samuel Colcord has sold to Ex-Alderman O'Dwyer, No. 43 West 76th street, a four-story stone front dwelling, 20x56x102.2, on private terms.

T. E. D. Power has sold for D. Willis James to S. F. Jenkins No. 138 West 86th street, a four-story brown stone dwelling, 21.6x60 with a 19-foot extension x half the block, on private terms.

R. C. Vilas has purchased from John G. Prague through T. E. D. Power No. 73 West 86th street, a four-story brown stone front dwelling, 20.6x60 and a three-story extension x102.2, on private terms.

Beverley Ward has sold for Thomas Butler et al. to Wm. Patchell one lot on the north side of 120th street, 100 feet west of Amsterdam avenue, for $3,350.

Stabler & Smith have sold for James Cunningham to a Mrs. Herring No. 318 West 117th street, a five-story brick and stone flat, for about $24,000.

L. J. Phillips & Co. have sold for Patrick Farley No. 114 West 76th

Jesse C. Bennett, it is reported, has sold for Foster & Livingston, one of their two remaining houses, on the south side of 82d street, between Central Park West and Columbus avenue. The house is a four-story brown stone, 18x56x102.2, and it was disposed of on private terms. It was impossible to ascertain the name of the buyer.

The 23d Ward branch office of L. J. Phillips & Co. have sold for John McMillen to Jacob Westheimer the two lots, on the southwest corner of 150th street and Morris avenue, for $7,000, and the southwest corner of 149th street and Bergen avenue, for Mrs. Keller for $5,000.

Karl M. Wallach has sold the two five-story double tenements, 25x85x102, Nos. 433 and 435 East 73d street, for $43,000. Mr. Wallach has purchased from S. O'Connor the five-story double tenement, No. 326 East 74th street on private terms.

LEASES.

Chas. E. Schuyler has leased for R. P. Martin to a Miss Putnam, No. 196 West End avenue, a three-story Queen Anne dwelling, for three years, at $1,800 per annum.

Ascher Weistein has leased No. 50 West 28th street to Edward May for ten years at $3,750 to $4,000 per annum.

Frederick Winant has leased for J. Woodbridge Davis to V. Henry Rothschild the four-story dwelling, No. 645 Madison avenue, for three years at $3,000 per annum.

Brooklyn

Corwith Bros. have sold for George and Annie Hassenfratz the house and lot No. 110 Oak street, 22x34, lot 25x84x100, to Louis and Marie Rebele for $3,700.

J. P. Sloane has sold for Gen. J. V. Meserole the plot of ground, 100x 100, on the west side of Diamond street, 25 feet north of Calyer street, to Albert and Jennie Rolfing for $1,000.

George F. Edwards has sold for W. H. Burroughs the plot, 16.8x100, with two-story and basement brown stone dwelling thereon, at No. 160 Huntingtou street, on private terms.

Judge Bartlett, of the Supreme Court, has granted the trustees of the First Baptist Church permission to sell their property at the corner of Pierrepont and Clinton streets to the Brooklyn Savings Bank for $200,000. The Bank will erect a handsome office building on the site.

CONVEYANCES.

	1890. August 14 to 20 inc	1891. August 13 to 19 inc.
Number	242	250
Amount involved	$832,729	$894,518
Number nominal	57	66

MORTGAGES.

Number	246	232
Amount involved	$810,304	$657,860
Number at 5 per cent. or less	153	120
Amount involved	$560,354	$356,927

PROJECTED BUILDINGS.

	1890. August 15 to 21 inc.	1891. August 14 to 20 inc.
Number of buildings	58	88
Estimated cost	$302,910	$508,670

Out of Town.

EAST NEW YORK.—George F. Edwards has sold for W. H. Burroughs to Geo. Baecker the plot, 20x100, with three-story and basement frame dwelling thereon, at No. 12 Snediker avenue, on private terms.

Out Among the Builders.

J. C. Burne has plans on the boards for a five-story brick and stone flat, 20x75, which Andrew Judge will build on the north side of 128th street, 244.6 west of 5th avenue, at a cost of $16,000.

F. Ebling will draw plans for extending and altering the building at No. 248 East 55th street, owned by Charles Harnischfeger. A four-story and cellar extension, 26x15.6 and 11.6 will be added, and a new vault, 15x30x8, built under the sidewalk. The estimated cost is about $10,000

Out of Town.

GREENPOINT, L. I.—Constable Bros. have plans under way for a large semi-fire-proof factory to be built here for the Hecla Iron Works.

JACKSONVILLE, FLA.—Edgar K. Bourne will draw plans for a four-story brick and stone building, 107x120, to be built for S. B. Hubbard on the corner of Main and Forsyth streets. The interior will be finished in cypress and Georgia pine and arranged for business purposes. The cost will be about $50,000.

WANTS AND OFFERS.

(Advertisements strictly in accordance with this title will be inserted at the practically nominal rate of 10 CENTS *per line (agate). In figuring for themselves advertisers may count seven words for each line, the address to be taken as one line. The object of this department is to bring buyers and sellers into communication with customers. Advertisements must be marked "Wants and Offers Column," and sent to the office of publication, Nos. 14 and 16 Vesey Street, not later than 3 P. M. Friday.)*

WANTS.

THE advertiser, who has handsome offices and large connection among builders, desires agencies for merchandise in their line on commission. Address, P. O. Box 791, New York City.

Real Estate Wanted.

WANTED—A property in Southern California, value $60,000 to $100,000; vicinity of San Diego, Los Angeles or San Francisco preferred; brokers noticed. W. J. COLE, 32 Liberty st., New York.

OFFERS.

Dwellings and Flats.

A SEVEN-ROOM HOUSE, full lot, $2,500; terms to suit. POWERS, Grand av., near 4th st., Woodlawn.

FOR SALE.—At a sacrifice, new five-story double flats, near 125th st. L station. Address, BUILDER, 319 East 125th st. Aug. 1—1aw-9w.

FOR SALE.—Five new first-class four-story and basement private dwellings, Nos. 109, 113 and 119 East 45th street, and Nos. 462 and 464 Lexington avenue; all leased to desirable tenants, or can arrange to give possession to some of them if desired. For further particulars, apply to The C. GRAHAM & SONS CO., 309 East 43d st.

BUY THE BEST.
72D ST., THE PARK DRIVEWAY.
SEVERAL 25-FOOT PALATIAL RESIDENCES.
ONE SUPERBLY DECORATED.
NONE MORE ELEGANT AND SPACIOUS.
The best judgment of long experience has been given to their construction. The most critical will be satisfied in the taste displayed and the excellent character of the workmanship and material; prices reasonable. F. CRAWFORD, 114 West 72d st.
July 11-1aw8w.

FOR SALE—2443 8th av.; 26.8½x100; easy terms; commission allowed brokers; apply at ROOM 19, 156 Broadway. Mar. 28-u-f.

FOR SALE—210 and 212 West 105th st.; five-story apartments; each, 25x89x100; decorated and carpeted; apply at ROOM 19, 156 Broadway. Mar. 28-u-f.

OFFERS.

Vacant Lots.

FOR SALE.—Two lots on West 58th st., between 10th and 11th avs.; a fine site for a factory; a reasonable offer will be considered; no rock. OWNER, RECORD AND GUIDE.

EASTERLY FRONT BOULEVARD, with 200 ft. on 86th st. and 264 ft. on 85th st.; one or more plots. OTTO ERNST, South Amboy, N. J. Aug. 22-1aw-8w.

A GOOD FACTORY SITE for sale cheap, consisting of five lots, 125x100 ft. (corner), near Newtown Creek. Address: OWNER, 564 Manhattan av, Greenpoint.

TWO LOTS, southeast corner 10th av. and 209th st.; cheap. POWERS, Grand av, near 4th st, Woodlawn.

PLOT of five (5) choice lots, ripe for improvement, 92d st. Madison and 5th avs. B. A. & G. N. WILLIAMS, JR., 68th st and Av A. Aug 22-1aw4w.

FOR SALE.—On easy terms, nine first-class lots, ready for immediate improvement, on south side 116th street, commencing about 130 feet east of 7th avenue. The C. GRAHAM & SONS CO., 309 East 43d street. A 15—4t

100TH ST., between 2d and 3d avs; ten lots, cheap; all mortgage if improved. EDWIN A. ELY, 108 Gold st. July11-1aw8w.

40 CHERRY ST., between Roosevelt and Franklin sq., 32x64, vacant; $12,000; accommodating terms. EDWIN A. ELY, 108 Gold st. July11-1aw8w.

Improved Property.

FOR SALE OR TO LEASE.—One of the best lighted and strongest factory buildings on the west side, just below 59th st; main building five stories and cellar having a frontage of 150 feet on st. by 68 ft. in depth; boiler house and stable detached; main building can be extended to a 200 ft. frontage; lots 100 ft. deep. FACTORY OWNER, RECORD AND GUIDE.

TO LET OR TO LEASE.—Two floors of a factory, 25x98 light on all sides, 1st av and 107th st; terms moderate. J. REEBERS' SONS, 409 East 107th. Aug. 22-uf.

OFFERS.

A BUSINESS PROPERTY, located in the centre of a wholesale trade in the City of New York, to exchange on the basis of a 5 per cent net income, with an equity of about $200,000; suburban and out-of-town property will be considered. OWNER, 174 REAL ESTATE RECORD.

PLANING MILL, branch of my business, for sale.—Is located at 24th st. and 11th av., on four or five city lots, leased ground, and consists of two and three-story brick buildings and adjoining sheds; also 80 horse-power engine and boiler, planers, moulders, saws, etc., all in good running order and now in operation; will leave a portion of value on bond and mortgage three years; this offers splendid opportunity to enlarge wood-working industry or to secure good mill business to add thereto. For further particulars, etc., apply to EBEN PEEK, 24th st. and 11th av.
Advertiser intends to continue his lumber business now carried on at above address. Aug. 15-22-29

Brooklyn Real Estate for Sale.

FLATS, 93 Concord st., Brooklyn, near the Bridge; five-story double flat property, in perfect order and always rented for $2,300 per year, paying easily 15 per cent. per annum on investment; terms easy. Apply to owner. R. J. KELLEY, 377 Broadway, New York. Aug. 22-1aw4w.

DESIRABLE INVESTMENT.—Eight-story apartment house; best location in Brooklyn; might exchange equity over $125,000 at 4½ per cent. Apply 60 Broadway, Room 311. J. 20—uf.

Country Property.

A GREAT BARGAIN will be given for cash or exchange for flats or tenements; a fine place at Nyack, 20 miles; river view; fine house, all improvements; stable, carriage house; fruit. Also place at Irvington; all free and clear; brokers noticed. W. J. COLE, 32 Liberty st.

Miscellaneous.

A PARTY ABOUT TO BUILD A FIVE-STORY factory, 50x98, in Harlem, near water-front, will lease the three upper floors and build to suit tenant. Terms very moderate. Address OWNER, 409 E. 107th St. May 16 u. f.

SALES OF THE WEEK.

The following are the sales at the Real Estate Exchange and Auction Room for the week ending Aug. 21.

** Indicates that the property described has been bid in for plaintiff's account:*

SMYTH & RYAN.

*71st st, No. 114, s s, 186.1 w Columbus av, 19x 100.5, four-story stone front dwell'g. F. W. Lockwood. (Amt due $10,784)	$32,000

J. F. B. SMYTH.

Amsterdam av, No. 307, e s, 70.4 n 74th st, 17x 61, four-story brk dwell'g. Wm. Bryan. (Amt due $14,909)	15,350

WM. KENNELLY.

10th st, No. 213 E., n s, abt 200 e 2d av, three-story brk dwell'g. Thos. D. Day, Jr.	16,650
84th st, No. 211, n s, 137.6 e 3d av, 12.6x98.9, three-story stone front dwell'g. L. N. Levy. (Amt due $1,203; prior morts. $8,000)	9,420

B. L. KENNELLY.

*Ryer av, e s, 308 n 184th st, 25x164.3x25.6x 162.6, vacant. Industrial Co-operative Building and Loan Assoc	2,500

R. V. HARNETT.

*61st st, No. 347, n s, 182.4 w 1st av, 23x100.5, five-story brk tenem't. (Amt due $16,858). Henrietta Cohn	10,000
Total	$85,950
Corresponding week 1890	$194,980

BROOKLYN, N. Y.

FOR WEEK ENDING AUGUST 20.

College pl, No. 16, e s, 197.11 n Love lane, 20x 50, two-story brk stable. Carrie Shay	$2,900
Hancock st, Nos. 943-949, n w cor Saratoga av, 67.4x95x67, gore, three-story brk stable. W. T. Klots & Bro's. Sons	10,200
Bay 32d st, n w s, 200 n e Benson av, 60x96.8, Bensonhurst. Ronald K. Brown	5,110
Atlantic av, n s, 80 w Gunther pl, 15x96.7, vacant. John R. Anderson	850
*Flushing av, n w cor Franklin av, runs west 120.9 x north 196 x east 24.2½ to Wallabout st, x east 106 to Franklin av, x south 200.4 to beginning, also all right, title and int. which Alexander Dugan had to a triangular parcel on Wallabout st, adj above, being 23.10 on Wallabout st, x4x—, moulding mill. Loftis W. O'Berry	13,500
*Greene av, Nos. 796-812, s e cor Lewis av, 200x 100, ten two-and-a-half-story brk dwell'gs, and one four-story brk flat with store on corner. Spencer Aldrich	58,000
Washington av, s s, 150 e 3d st, 50x100, Flatbush. Richard L. Wyckoff	1,550
Total	$87,110
Corresponding week, 1890	$38,180

CONVEYANCES.

Wherever the letters Q. C., C. a. G. and B. & S occur, preceded by the name of the grantee they mean as follows;

1st—Q. C. is an abbreviation for Quit Claim deed, i. e., a deed in which all the right, title and interest of the grantor is conveyed, omitting all covenants or warranty.

2d—C. a. G. means a deed containing Covenant against Grantor only, in which he covenants that he hath not done any act whereby the estate conveyed may be impeached, charged or encumbered.

NEW YORK CITY.

AUGUST 14, 15, 17, 18, 19, 20.

Boulevard or Broadway } begins Boulevard, 63d st } s e cor 63d st, runs east 123.4 x south 84.11 x west 25 x north 69 x west 85 to Boulevard, x north 25.
Boulevard, e s, 25 s 63d st, 24x73x20x85.
Boulevard, e s, 49 s 63d st, 20x62x17x73.
All vacant.
George W. Vultee to Jacob B. Tallman. *Mt.* $76,433. July 20. other consid. and $20,000

Bowery, No. 393, or 3d av, e s, 24.4 s 6th st, 24.2x60.1, five-story stone front tenem't with stores. Partition. Martin T. McMahon to Mary Sander, Atlantic City, N. J. Aug. 17. 38,000

Catharine st, No. 55, e s, abt 48 n Monroe st, 13.6x104.6x13.6x103.4, portion of five-story brk store and tenem't. John Miller trustee Eliza Peck to Eliza L. Miller. Aug. 18. 7,000

Central Park West, No. 468, w s, 20 s 107th st, 30.11x100, with all title to strip adj on n s, 3x100, five story brk flat. William Noble and Elizabeth his wife to Charles Noble. *Mt.* $35,000. Aug. 15. nom

Central Park West, w s, 20 s 107th st, 30.11x100, with all title to slip adj on n s, 3x100. Charles Noble and Esther his wife to William Noble. *Mt.* $49,132. Aug. 15. nom

Cherry st, No. 228 } being Cherry st, n w cor Pelham st, No. 7 } Pelham st, runs north 135 x west 39.3 x south 38.6 x east 10 x south 100 to Cherry st, x east 29, one six-story brk building on each st. Peter C. Wodzicki and Theodora C. his wife to Karl M. Wallach. *Mt.* $55,000. Aug. 14. See 75th st. 70,000

Cherry st, No. 272, n s, 130.8 w Jefferson st, 26.1 x113.7x26.1x113.1, five-story brk tenem't with stores. Alden S. Swan and Mary A. his wife to Benedict A. Klein. *Mt.* $16,750. Aug. 20. 26,000

Cherry st, No. 270, n s, 156.9 w Jefferson st, 26.1x114x26.1x113.7, five-story brk tenem't with stores. Same to same. *Mt.* $16,750. Aug. 20. 26,000

Same property; also,
Cherry st, No. 272, n s, 26.1x113.7x26.1x113.1. }
Benedict A. Klein and Karoline his wife to Jonas Weil and Bernhard Mayer. *Mt.* $40,-000. Aug. 20. 52,000

Chrystie st, No. 214, e s, 274.3 s Houston st, runs east 75 x south 24.9 x west 22.11½ x south 0.2 x west 24 x north 0.8½ x 28 to st, x north 24.10, six-story brk tenem't with stores. Peter C. Wodzicki and Theodora C. his wife to Karl M. Wallach. *Mt.* $19,300. Aug. 14. See 75th st. 30,000

Cornelia st, Nos. 1 and 3, n w cor West 4th st, 40.11x75x26.10x76, five-story brk tenem't with stores. William Rankin and Elizabeth his wife to John Rankin. Aug. 14. 75,000

Cornelia st, n w cor West 4th st, 40.11x75x 26.10x76. John Rankin and Mary his wife to William Rankin. *Mt.* $33,000. Aug. 17. nom

Eldridge st, No. 85, w s, 125 s Grand st, 25x100, five-story brk store and tenem't. Isidor V. Wittenberg and Blanche his wife to Oscar E. A. Wiessner. *Mt.* $27,000. Aug. 18. 36,000

Elm st, No. 207 } begins Elm st, e s, abt 315 Marion st, No. 26 } n Broome st, 20x41 to Marion st, x 21x35.2, two story frame and brk tenem't. Peter Leesoine and Susan his wife to Albert Etgel and Emanuel Kronaeher. Q. C. Aug. 17. nom

Emerson st, s w cor Cooper st, 25x100. Fannie E. Lawrence to Mathew McQuade. *Mt.* $720. Aug. 14. 1,340

Goerck st, No. 90, e s, 81.3 n Rivington st, 15.4 x99.11, five-story brk tenem't. Foreclos. Rollin H. Lynde to Henry Frohwitter. Aug. 18. 10,000

Harrison st, No. 52, n s, 115 e West st, 20x75. }
Harrison st, Nos. 54 and 56, n s, 75 e West st, 40x75.
Three four-story brk stores. }
William C. Renwick et al. trustees William R. Renwick to Gustav L. Lawrence. ½ part. Taxes, &c. Aug. 6. 32,500

Same property. Thomas Patten and Annie S. his wife to same. ½ part. Aug. 6. 32,500

Henry st, No 211, n s, 24 e Clinton st, 22.6x85, five-story brk tenem't. Charles L. Cohn to Tobias Krakower and Abraham Kraner. *Mt.* $13,000. June 3. nom

Houston st, No. 326, n e s, abt 200 e Av B, 23 x83.5x23x81.11, five-story brk store and tenement. }
Houston st, No 316, n s, abt 190 e Av B, 24.11x88.1x24.10x89.9, four-story brk tenement with stores. }
Aaron H. Schutz and Rachel his wife, Julius Schutz, Clara Bloom, Fanny Biath and Eliza Strauss to Hartwig I. Phillips. Aug. 6. nom

Houston st, No. 369, s s, 104.4 e Pitt st, 20.6x 100, three-story brk store and tenem't with three-story brk building on rear. Ignatz Friedman and Fanny his wife to Adolph and Samuel Ullman. *Mt.* $18,000. Aug. 18. 23,100

Houston st, Nos. 370-374 E. Party wall agreement. Jacob Asch and Herman Rushin to Ignatz Meirowitz and Samuel Altman. July 29. 425

Jefferson st, No. 25, e s, 75 s Henry st, 25x23.10, three-story brk tenem't. Abraham Rosenthal and Sarah R. his wife to Abraham Goldberg. *Mt.* $6,000. Aug. 11. 7,050

Jersey st, No. 2 } begins Jersey st, s s, 74 e Marion st, No. 88 } Crosby st, 22.2x65 to Marion st, x22.2x65a three-story brk tenem't on each st. William Cohen and Fannie his wife and Henry Lipman to John S. Hawley, Brick Church, N. J., and Herman W. Hoops. *Mt.* $7,500. Aug. 11. 12,500

Jersey st, No. 6 } begins Jersey st, s s, 144.3 w Marion st, No. 87 } Mulberry st, 24.6x66.4 to Marion st, x26x67.4, three-story brk tenement on Jersey st and two-story brk tenem't with stores on Marion st. Leo Schlesinger and Rachel his wife to John S. Hawley and Herman W. Hoops. *Mt.* $4,959. Aug. 17. 11,500

Madison st, Nos. 203 and 205, n s, 60.1 e Rutgers st, 34.7x46.2x34 5x46.2, five-story brk tenem't. Morris Jacobson and Eva his wife to Henry and Johannah Phillips. *Mt.* $20,000. Aug. 3. 33,000

Madison st, No. 261, n s, 47.2 e Clinton st, 21.6x 68.2, five-story brk tenem't. Patrick Gallagher and Mary his wife to Abraham Levinson and Alexander Rittmaster. *Mt.* $16,000. Aug. 17. 22,000

Madison st, n s, 68.8 e Clinton st, runs north 68.2 x east 1.5 x north 32.1 x east 23.6 x south 100.3 to st, x west 25. Same to same. *Mt.* $26,000. Aug. 17. 40,000

Perry st, No. 41, n s, 125 e 4th st, 25x95, two-story brk dwell'g with two-story brk stable on rear. Hannah H. Purdy to Joseph C. Divine. *Mt.* $17,000. July 10. other consid. and 5,280

Ridge st, No. 31, w s, 61.6 s Broome st, 20x75, three-story brk store and tenem't. Johanna, William J. and Constantine J. McCarthy and Ellen his wife and John McCarthy to John Finley. *Mt.* $5,000. Aug. 17. 14,000

Stanton st, No. 302, n w cor Lewis st, 25x58, three and four-story brk and frame store and tenem't. William J. Gallagher to The First Nat. Bank of Texarkana, Texas. ¼ part. Sub. to mechanic's lien $553. Aug. 3. 1,500

Washington st, Nos. 481-487, e s, 51.6 n Canal st, 84.3x80x83.5x80, one-story frame sheds, coal and wood yard. J. Fred Pierson and Susan A. his wife to Morris S. Herrman. July 20. 47,000

Water st, No. 351, s s, abt 105 w James slip, 16.4x75, four-story brk store and tenem't. David B. Hart and Priscilla his wife to Siegmund T. Meyer. *Mt.* $4,500. June 30. 10,000

West Broadway, Nos. 28, 30 and 32 } being Duane st, Nos. 154 and 156 } West Broadway, s w cor Duane st, 54.3x49.7x54.8x 49.10, three and four-story brk stores. James Gibson, White Plains, N. Y., to Horace K. Thurber. Aug. 17. 60,000

Same property. Horace K. Thurber and Nancy his wife to William G. Weld, Newport, R. I. Aug. 17. 61,750

Willett st, No. 133, w s, 50 s Houston st, 25x50, two-story frame store and tenem't. Margaretha Hebbel widow to Morris Jacobson. *Mt.* $3,000. Aug. 17. 8,250

3d st, No. 69, n s, 305 e 2d av, 20x96.2, four-story brk tenem't. Carrie Bock widow to Henry Delhougne. *Mt.* $12,000. Aug. 17. 25,800

3d st, No. 58, s s, 98 e Av A, 22x88.6, five-story brk tenem't with five-story brk tenem't on rear. Partition. Martin T. McMahon to John Becker. Aug. 19. 23,550

3d st, No. 160, s s, 120 e Av A, 24.9x105.11x24.4 x105.11, five-story brk store and tenem't with four-story brk tenem't on rear. Partition. Same to same. Aug. 19. 27,800

6th st, No. 204, s s, 82.8 e 3d av, runs south 44.3 x southwest 4.6 x west 0.9 x south 49 x east 25 x north 97 to st, x west 22.6, four-story brk tenem't with stores and five-story brk tenem't on rear. Partition. Martin T. McMahon to Mary Sander, Atlantic City, N. J. Aug. 7. 25,100

6th st, No. 202, s s, 60.1 e 3d av, runs south 48.6 x east 20.8 x northeast 4.6 x north 44.3 to st, x west 22.6, four-story brk tenem't with store. Partition. Same to same. Aug. 7. 15,400

8th st, No. 318, s s, 308.4 e Av B, 19.10x97.6, four-story brk tenem't with three-story brk building on rear. Sarah wife of and Philip Wertheimer to Ignatz Bleier. *Mt.* $9,000. Aug. 17. 15,300

10th st, No. 271, n s, 219 w Av A, 25x94.8, five-story stone front tenem't with stores. Simon Hoffmann and Bertha his wife to John Tierney. *Mt.* $22,800. Aug. 14. 34,500

14th st, No. 40 } begins 14th st, s w s, University pl, No. 79 } 53 1 s e University pl, runs southwest 130.4 x northwest 62.3 to University pl, x northeast 26 x southeast 33.6 x northeast 102.3 to 14th st, x southeast 26.10, five-story brk store. Charles Lamson and Elizabeth R. his wife to Charles H. Marshall. July 31, 1855. nom

18th st, No. 417, n s, 365 w Av A, 25x92, four-story brk store and tenem't. Mary A. Madden to John Mathews. *Mt.* $4,000. April 20, 1883. 5,250

27th st, Nos. 253 and 255, n s, 159.7 e 8th av, 49.9 x98.9, two four-story brk stores and tenem'ts with three-story brk building on rear. William Schnell formerly husband of Susan A. Schnell to Emilie S. Thackston. Q. C. May 20. 1,000

Same property. Thomas A. Storm, Stormville, N. Y., and Emilie S. wife of Charles A. Thackston to Ascher Weinstein. July 16. 28,000

29th st, No. 233, n s, 175 w 2d av, runs west 25 x north 98.9 x east 8.5 x southeast — x south 67.4, four-story brk store and tenem't with three-story brk tenem't on rear. Luke McDermott and Frances D. his wife to Simon T. Levy. Aug. 13. 13,500

32d st, No. 105, n s, 68 w 6th av, three-story brk dwell'g. Option to purchase to lessee and agreements. Caroline E. Hiffert to Garret D. Rhinehart. Aug. 12. 18,000

32d st, No. 557, n s, 150 e 11th av, 25x98.9, five-story brk tenem't with stores and four-story brk tenem't on rear. }
32d st, No. 553, n s, 200 e 11th av. 25x98.9, five-story brk tenem't with stores. }
Carl G. A. Hoble and Sophie his wife to Arnold J. D. Wedemeyer, of Liberty, N. Y. *Mt.* $13,000. Aug. 20. See St. Nicholas av. nom

36th st, No. 241, n s, 360 e 8th av, 18.6x98.9, four-story brk dwell'g. Annie T. Harris widow to John Ravensburg. *Mt.* $8,000. Aug. 17. 12,500

36th st, No. 358, s s, 125 e 9th av, 25x98.9, five-story stone front flat. William Drought and Julia his wife and Charles J. Carew and Jenny A. his wife, Norwich, Conn., to Herman Weissmann and Frank J. Britt. *Mt.* $35,000. Aug. 13. 34,500

37th st, No. 206, s s, 100 w 7th av, 20.10x60, four-story brk store and tenem't. Jacob Krause and Sarah his wife to Louis Friedenberg. *Mt.* $5,500. April 1. 12,650

39th st, No. 243, n s, 350 e 8th av, 16.8x98.9, five-story stone front dwell'g. Antonia Bachiller, Ponce de Leon, to John H. McGinn. Aug. 17. 14,500

40th st, No. 311, n s, 175 w 8th av, 25x98.9, six-story brk building. Archibald Culbert and Rachel I. his wife, John Culbert and Carrie his wife to Julius Stern and Jacob Saalberg. *Mt.* $17,000. Aug. 17. 30,000

40th st, No. 218, s s, 214.3 w 7th av, 14.3x98.9, four-story brk dwell'g. Bertha wife of J. W. Brinkmann to Marguerite wife of Celestine Gautier. Aug. 14. 10,000

Same property. Owen E. Abraham to Bertha wife of J. W. Brinkmann. Aug. 14. 10,000

41st st, No. 238, s s, 127 w 2d av, 26x98.9, five-story brk tenem't. John Herrick trustee to Mary wife of John F. Melia. *Mt.* $8,000. Aug. 17. 15,700

43d st, Nos. 547-551, n s, 100 e 11th av, 75x100.5, two-story frame and brk factory, &c. Henry P. Havens and Marion H. his wife to Sarah J. Rice. ½ part. Q. C. March 10. 9,000

48th st, No. 555, n s, 125 e 11th av, 25x100.4, five-story brk tenem't. Theodore Palmer to Eleanor Dougan. *Mt.* $15,000, taxes, &c. July 29. 25,000

50th st, No. 419 (Dunscomb pl), n s, 175 e 1st av, 20x100.5, five-story stone front dwell'g. Charles Reinwarth and Louisa his wife to William N. Sternkopf. Aug. 19. 16,500

51st st, No. 147, n s, 175 e 7th av, 25x100.5, four-story brk tenem't. William H. Doty and Elizabeth MacC. his wife to John O. Hoyt. *Mt.* $18,000. Aug. 15. nom

52d st, Nos. 510 and 512, s s, 131.8 w 10th av, 45 x100.5x51.10x—, two and three-story brk and frame buildings. Joseph J. Curran and Mary A. his wife, Francis Goodman and Emma his wife, John Marx and Eliza his wife, Owen Melaney and Sophie his wife, Josephine and Margaret Curran to John J. and William A. Curran. All title. Aug. 17. 15,000

53d st, No. 30, s s, 439.6 e 6th av, 18x100.5, four-story stone front dwell'g. Edward Engel to James A. McCormick. *Mt.* $2,000. July 30. 13,500

54th st, Nos. 427 and 429, n s, 394 e 1st av, 50x 100.5, two-story brk stable with one-story frame shed on rear. Partition. J. Warren Greene to Daniel Herbert. Aug. 13. 17,200

56th st, Nos. 422 and 424, s s, 325 w 9th av, 50x 69.2x50.5x75.5, two five-story brk tenem'ts. Edward J. Bannon and Catherine his wife to Joseph M. Ledwith. *Mt.* $24,000. Aug. 14. 32,000

59th st, No. 547, n s, 200 e 11th av, 25x100. }
59th st, Nos. 535 and 537, n s, 325 e 11th av, 50x100.
Three four-story brk tenem'ts with stores. }
Foreclos. Somerville P. Tuck to Edith H. Simmons. *Mt.* $35,000. Aug. 18. 1,600

62d st, s s, 100 e 11th av, 200x100.5, vacant. Emma A. Stockinger to Bertha Smith. *Mt.* $32,000. Aug. 19. nom

70th st, n s, 273 e Av A, 25x100.5. Release mort. Henry W. Ford trustee Augustus H. Ward to Frederick Rohrs. Aug. 19. 12,350

Same property. Release mort. The Bradley & Currier Co. (Lim.) to Frederick Rohrs and Louisa his wife. Aug. 20. nom

71st st, No. 114, s s, 136.1 w Columbus av, 19x 100.5, four-story stone front dwell'g. Foreclos. John S. Cram to Amelia B. wife of Frederick W. Lockwood, New Caanan, Conn. *Mt.* $21,750. Aug. 17. 32,000

73d st, No. 262, s s, 188 e West End av, runs south 100 x east 12 x south 2.2 x east 7 x north 102.2 to st, x west 19, four-story brk dwell'g. Henry McCloskey to Marie L. wife of Joseph J. O'Donohue, Jr. B. & S. Aug. 18. nom

Same property. Joseph J. O'Donohue, Jr., and Marie his wife to Henry McCloskey. B. & S. Aug. 18. nom

73d st, No. 179, n s, 46 e 10th av, 18x76.8, four-story stone front dwell'g. Foreclos. Richard B. Kelly to The First National Bank of Sing Sing. *Mt.* $15,500. July 31. 10,000

73d st, No. 177, e s, 64 e 10th av, 18x76.8, four-story brk dwell'g. Foreclos. Same to same. *Mt.* $15,500. July 31. 14,000

73d st, No. 181, n s, 28 e 10th av, 18x76.8, four-story brk dwell'g. Same to same. *Mt.* $15,-500. July 31. 9,000

75th st, Nos. 233-239, n s, 125 w 2d av, 105x102.2, four four-story brk and stone front tenem'ts. Karl M. Wallach to Peter C. and Theodora C. Wodzicki. *Mt.* $49,000. Aug. 14. See Cherry and Chrystie sts. 85,000

76th st, n s, 300 w 8th av, 50x102.2, vacant. Mary E. Yost to Mary E. Yeakle. All liens. Aug. 15. nom

84th st, No. 521, n s, 253.5 e Av A, 19.5x102.2, three-story stone front dwell'g. Ferdinand Landmann, Hempstead, L. I., to Clara wife of Ferdinand Landmann. Aug. 17. nom

84th st, No. 36, s s, 435 w 8th av, 20x102.2, three-story brk dwell'g. Partition. Thomas H. Barowsky to Elizabeth F. Hand. Aug. 18. 15,000

85th st, No. 26, s s, 289 w 8th av, 20x102.2, four-story brk dwl'g.
85th st, No. 30, s s, 279 w 8th av, 21x102.2, four-story stone front dwell'g.
John A. Rockford to Francis M. Wilmurt. Sub. to mort. Oct. 14, 1890. nom

88th st, No. 145, n s, 408 e Amsterdam av, 17x100.8, three-story stone front dwell'g. John C. Heney and Sarah his wife to Hugh McDowell. ½ part. *Mt.* $20,000. Aug. 14. nom

88th st, n s, 115.8 e Amsterdam av, 16.8x100.8. Release mort. D. Newton Barney to Samuel R. Donnellon. July 30 nom

95th st, No. 207, n s, 140 6 w Amsterdam av, 27.6x100.9x31.8x100.8, five-story brk flat. Andrew T. Doyle and Annie C. his wife to John J. Lynes, Brooklyn. *Mt.* $25,900. Aug. 18. 34,500

100th st, No. 48, s s, 427.10 w 8th av, 19.4x100.11, four-story brk dwell'g. James G. Gardiner to David H. McAlpin. C. a. G. *Mt.* $13,800. Aug. 20. nom

101st st, No. 223, n s, 335 e 3d av, 25x100.11. four-story brk tenem't. Benjamin Oestreicher and Henrietta his wife to Solomon Wallenstein. *Mt.* $8,000. Aug. 15. 13,600

104th st, No. 211, n s, 125 w 10th av, 25x100.11, five-story stone front flat.
104th st, No. 215, n s, 175 w 10th av, 25x100.11, five-story stone front flat.
106th st, No. 121, n s, 245 w 9th av, 20x100.11, four-story brk dwell'g.
107th st, s s, 245 w 9th av, 20x100.11, one-story frame stable.
Margaret J. Lange to Norman S. Dike. Aug. 14. See 116th st. nom

105th st, No. 220, s s, 230 e 3d av, 15x100.9, two-story stone front dwell'g. John F. Hinners and Rose his wife to Annie Cochrane. *Mt.* $3,450. Aug. 1. 8,250

111th st, No. 10, s s, 100 e 5th av, 19x100.11, five-story stone front flat. John Hickey and Ann his wife to Alice F. Lent. *Mt.* $15,000. Aug. 5. nom

113th st, No. 125, n s, 196.8 e 4th av, 16.8x100.11, three story frame dwell'g. William B. Brady to Mary L. Brady. Q. C. All title. *Mt.* $2,500. Aug. 30, 1888. 500

Same property. Edward J. Brady to same. Q. C. All title. *Mt.* $2,500. Dec. 10, 1889. 500

116th st, s s, 260 w 9th av, 60x100.11, vacant
116th st, Nos. 169 and 171, n s, 173.6 w 3d av, runs west 34.6 x north 100.11 x southeast 1.0½ x south 5 x northeast 5 x southeast 26.6 x south 100.11, two three story stone front dwell'gs.
Edward Lange and Margaret J. his wife to Norman S. Dike. Aug. 14. See 104th st. nom

117th st, No. 441, n s, 394 e 1st av, 16,8x100.10, two-story brk dwell'g. Sarah A. Fagan to Edward W. Hoegberg. *Mt.* $3,000. Aug. 12. nom

Same property. Edward W. Hoegberg to Edward B. Fagan. *Mt.* $3,000 Aug. 13. nom

119th st, No. 307, n s, 94.3 e 2d av, 18.9x100.11, four-story stone front tenem't. Partition. Samuel Cohn to Fanny Froehlich. *Mt.* $8,500. Aug. 13. 11,950

120th st, No. 540, s s, 437.6 e Av A, 18.9x100.11, two-story brk dwell'g. Partition. William H. Willis to James T. Moynagh. Aug. 20. 4,400

121st st, Nos. 61 and 63, n s, 188.6 e Madison av, 46x100.11, two four-story stone front flats. *Mt.* $30,000.
132d st, No. 165, n s, 115 e 7th av, 20x99.11, three-story brk dwell'g. *Mt.* $12,000.
75th st, Nos. 56 and 58, s s, 100 e Columbus av, 40x102.2, two four-story stone front dwell'gs.
75th st, Nos. 48-52, s s, 162 e Columbus av, 58x102.2, three four-story stone front dwell'gs.
75th st, Nos. 42 and 44, s s, 240 e Columbus av, 40x102.2, two four-story stone front dwell'gs. *Mt.* $228,000 on last 3 parcels.
James T. Hall and Helen M. his wife to The James T. Hall Building and Decorative Co. Aug. 11. nom

122d st, s s, 66.1 w St. Nicholas av, 50x100.11, vacant. Frederick Hulberg and Marie L. his wife to Adele Hutton widow. Aug. 13. See St. Nicholas av. 17,000

122d st, No. 358, s s, 218 w Manhattan av, 16x100.11, three-story stone front dwell'g. A. Alonzo Teets to Charles Reinwarth. Aug. 1. 17,000

123d st, No. 210, s s, 144 w 7th av, 15x100.11, three-story stone front dwell'g. Annetta Currie to Lydia M. Sullivan. *Mt.* $9,000. Aug. 11. 16,500

125th st, No. 133 W.
95th st, No. 48 W.
Assign rents. W. Le Roy Washburn to Chester W. Palmer. Collateral. July 29. ——

128th st, n s, 244.8 w 5th av, runs north 85 x west 15.6 x north 14.11 x west 5 x south 99.11 to st, x east 20.6, vacant. John W. Hagren to Andrew T. Judge. Aug. 6. 8,000

129th st, Nos. 158 and 160, s s, 185 w 3d av, 50x99.11, two three-story frame dwell'gs. William T. Washburn and Emma Richardson exrs., &c., Benjamin Richardson, to William H. Payne. *Mt.* $5,000. July 21. 17,300

129th st, s s, 185 w 3d av, 50x99.11. Release mort. Eugene Kelly to William T. Washburn and Emma Richardson exrs. Benjamin Richardson. July 11. nom

Same property. Release judgment. Eugene Kelly individ., Eugene Kelly, William Farrell, Edward Kelly and Joseph A. Donahue, of Eugene Kelly & Co., to same. July 11. nom

134th st, Nos. 6 and 8, s s, 135 w 5th av, 50x99.11, two five-story stone front flats. John A. Rochford to Francis M. Wilmurt. All liens. Sept. 11, 1890. nom

134th st, No. 223, n s, 233.4 w 7th av, 16.8x99.11, three-story stone front dwell'g. Charlotte M. wife of Horace W. Chipman to Rougier Thorne, Flushing, L. I. B. & S. *Mt.* $8,000. Aug. 13. nom

Same property. Rougier Thorne, Flushing, L. I., to Horace W. Chipman. B. & S. *Mt.* $8,000. Aug. 13. nom

142d st, No. 210, s s, 141.6 w 7th av, 16 6x99.11, three-story stone front dwell'g. Louis Weber and Mary C. his wife to John Kelly. *Mt.* $7,000. Aug. 15. 15,000

169th st, s s, 145 e Audubon av, 25x85. Charles Scheidecker and Madelina his wife to P. Johann Ebbecke. *Mt.* $1,500. Aug. 17. 3,500

178th st, n s, 100 w Wadsworth av, 50x100. Pauline Simon to Rachel wife of William Mulgrew. Aug. 9. 5,050

179th st, n s, 150 w Audubon av, 50x100.
178th st, n s, 175 w Audubon av, 50x100.
Audubon av, e s, 21.11 s 178th st, 60x95.2x66.1x95.
182d st, s s, 120 e Audubon av, 100x70.
Pauline Simon to Joseph H. Cain. June 15. 22,725

179th st, n s, 100 w Audubon av, 50x100. Pauline Simon to Henry Armbrust, Union Hill, N. J. June 15. 4,750

180th st, s s, 120 e Audubon av, runs south 100 x west 25 x south 100 to 179th st, x east 125 x north 100 x west 25 x north 100 to 180th st, x west 75. Pauline Simon to Joseph H. Cain. June 15. 18,075

Audubon av, n w cor 180th st, 25x100.
Audubon av, s w cor 182d st, 70x150.
Kingsbridge road, s e cor 182d st, 25.3x95.11x25x99.5.
Pauline Simon to Jacob Blumauer. July 12. 21,050

Same property. Jacob Blumauer to Leo Schlesinger. *Mt.* $14,735. June 12. 21,050

Av A, No. 141 } being Av A, s w cor 9th st,
9th st, No. 440 } 27x85.6, five-story brk tenement with store on av and five-story brk tenem't on st. Partition. Martin T. McMahon to Elias Jacobs. Aug. 19. 48,750

Av A, No. 1394 } begins Av A, n e cor
74th st, Nos. 503 and 505 } 74th st, 22.2x98, one-story brk store on av and two two and three-story brk and frame stores and tenem'ts on st. Charles Meier and Auguste C. J. his wife to Charles Meier. *Mt.* $8,000. Aug. 11. nom

Av A, n e cor 74th st, 22 2x98. Charles Meier and Auguste C. his wife to Samuel Kempner. Sub. to mort. Aug. 19. nom

Columbus av, No. 941, n e cor 106th st, 25.11x75, five-story brk flat with stores. Caroline A. Buhler to William Buhler. Sub. to mort. Aug. 19. nom

Edgecombe av, No. 88, e s, 108.11 n 138th st, 18x85, three-story brk dwell'g. Martin L. Rickerson and Sarah J. his wife to George De Forest Smith. *Mt.* $13,000. Aug. 17. exch

Edgecombe av or road, n e cor of former 172d st, 764.6 to centre of former 170th st, x108.9 to High Bridge Park, x631.3x60.1, vacant. James McCloud and Sarah A. his wife and John J. Mahony to Hugh Stevenson. Aug. 15. See Riverside av. 150,000

Lexington av, No. 1354, w s, 60.6 s 90th st, 20.1x81, four-story brk flat. Henry W. York and Lillie F. his wife to John Canavan. *Mt.* $10,000. Aug. 12. 16,000

Lexington av, No. 1074, w s, 34.2 s 76th st, 17x80.
Lexington av, No. 1070, w s, 68.2 s 76th st, 17x80, two three-story stone front dwell'gs.
John A. Rochford to Francis M. Wilmurt. All liens. Sept. 1, 1890. nom

Lexington av, No. 190, w s, 67.8 s 32d st, 22x80, three-story brk dwell'g. John B. Haskin and Jane his wife to Lewis A. Mitchell. Aug. 14. nom

Madison av, Nos. 1590 and 1592, w s, 25.11 s 107th st, 50x100, two five-story stone front flats. Lizzie F. Brady to Gottlieb Jetter. *Mt.* $40,-000. Aug. 15. 54,000

Madison av, No. 1699, e s, 50.5 n 112th st, 25x75, five-story brk flat. Millard F. Dakin to Meyer Jonasson. *Mt.* $16,000. Aug. 14. 22,000

Morningside av, s w cor 119th st, 100.11x100, vacant.
119th st, s s, 100 w Morningside av, 50x100.11, vacant.
Maria N. wife of Dwight H. Olmstead to Joseph W. Spencer, East Orange, N. J. July 3. nom

Riverside av, n e cor 83d st, 57.4x107.6x52.2x83.9, vacant. Hugh Stevenson to James McCloud and John J. Mahony. Aug. 18. See Edgecombe av. 37,500

South 5th av, e s, 125 n Grand st, 25x100. Release mort. Augustus T. Gillender committee Alice F. M. Wood to Thomas Eagleton. July 28. nom

St. Nicholas av, w s, 100.11 n 121st st, 59.3x96.11x50.5x128, vacant. Adele Hutton widow to Frederick Hulberg. Aug. 13. See 122d st. 20,750

St. Nicholas av, e s, 126.7 n 141st st, 75.11x93x74.11x83.7, vacant. John Kelly and Johanna his wife to Louis Weber. *Mt.* $10,000. Aug. 15. 20,000

St. Nicholas av, Nos. 366 and 368, e s, 60.7 n 128th st, 40.5x77.8x40x83.7, two five-story brk flats. Arnold J. D. Wedemeyer and Anna his wife to Carl G. A. Hohle. *Mt.* $37,000. Aug. 11. See 32d st. nom

1st av, No. 607, w s, 50.9 s 35th st, 24.1x75x23.4x75, four-story brk tenem't with stores. Solomon Miller and Minnie his wife to Samuel Kempner. Sub. to mort. Aug. 19. nom

2d av, No. 1548, e s, 127.2 n 80th st, runs east 100 x south 25 x east 94 x north 20 x west to av at point 144.2 n 80th st, x south 17, two-story brk store and tenem't. Margaret E. Adriance to Patrick Reynolds. Q. C. Aug. 11. 250

2d av, No. 681, s w cor 37th st, 24.9x65x24x55, four-story brk store and tenem't with two-story brk stable on rear. Mary A. Humes extrx. Hugh Humes to Hannah C. Hartzell. Nov. 12, 1890. nom

2d av, No. 1465, w s, 25 n 76th st, 26.6x100, four-story brk tenem't with stores. Moses Lehmann and Mina his wife to Anthony, Charles J. and Joseph Miller. *Mt.* $13,500. July 31. 22'500

2d av, Nos. 894 and 896, e s, 50.3 s 48th st, 50.2x100, two five-story brk stores and tenem'ts. Partition. Martin T. McMahon to Marx Ottinger and Max S. Korn. Aug. 19. 45,400

3d av, No. 1831, e s, 25.11 n 101st st, 25x90, five-story brk tenem't with stores. Jonas Weil and Theresa his wife and Bernhard Mayer and Sophia his wife to Julius Dreyfus. *Mt.* $22,000. Aug. 13. 29,500

3d av, No. 1070, w s, 50.5 n 63d st, 25x100, five-story stone front store and flat. Partition. S. L. H. Ward to Eliza Millhauser. Aug. 13. 41,000

7th av, Nos. 882-886, n w cor 56th st, 50.5x78, one-story brick and frame buildings, new buildings projected. Nellie B. Mortimer to William Noble. *Mt.* $58,000. Aug. 15. 72,132

8th av, No. 2459, w s, 282.11 s 133d st, 26.4x100, five-story brk tenem't with stores. Peter Bauer and Louisa F. his wife to Mary C. wife of James H. Laird. Aug. 13. 27,500

8th av, s e cor 153d st, 97x8.8x94.4x34.2, vacant. Nathaniel Jarvis, Jr., and M. Louise his wife to George A. Greene. Aug. 15. 4,000

9th av, No. 707, w s, 75.4 n 48th st, 25x100, five-story brk store and tenem't. Paul Worms to Albert Bruijlants. Aug. 14. 41,500

11th av, Nos. 653-657, w s, 25 5 s 48th st, 75x70, three five-story brk tenem'ts with stores. Simon Haberman and Rosie his wife to Pauline Heilbrunn. *Mt.* $40,500. July 30. 57,000

MISCELLANEOUS.

All dower in estate of Daniel Becker, Sr., deceased, in City of New York. Elizabeth wife of and John Becker to Mary Sander, Elias Jacobs, Marx Ottinger, Max S. Korn, Carl Henn and Katharina his wife and other purchasers. (See deeds from Martin T. McMahon, referee, in this week's issue.) Aug. 19. nom

Appointment of new trustees of Buffalo Branch of Erie Railway Co. and The Erie Railway Co. J. C. Bancroft Davis to J. C. Bancroft Davis and Charles Steele. April 1. nom

Appointment of new trustee of The New York & Erie R. R. Co. in place of James Brown. Same to same. April 1. nom

Appointment of new trustee of The New York & Erie R. R. Co. in place of John Davis. Same to same. April 1. nom

Rejection of provisions in lieu of dower contained in will of George Graham. Elizabeth Graham widow to estate of George Graham. Sept. 18, 1890.

23d and 24th WARDS.

Fort Independence st, e s, part lot 56 map W. O. Giles property. 30x70x28.10x70. Diary Younkheere to William Stark. Aug. 19. 690

Marcy pl, n e cor Mott av, 164.4x102.9x158.7x103.3. Lydia A. wife of and Francis F. Reynolds to Thomas L. Reynolds. *Mt.* $2,000. Aug. 17. nom

Pyne st, n e cor Bayard st, 100x100. Edward Reilly and Mary A. his wife to Hugh Doon. *Mt.* $1,600. Aug. 15. 3,100

Rogers pl, w s, 203.10 n Westchester av, 50x72.4x60x72.4, error. John J. Daly and Bella his wife to Thomas L. Reynolds. Sub. to mort. Aug. 12. nom

Rogers pl, w s, 203.10 n Westchester av, 50x72.4x60x72.4.
Sheridan av, e s, lots 221 and 222 map Inwood, 50x110.2x51.1x120.9.
Release judgment. John J. Daly to Thomas L. Reynolds. Aug. 13. nom

138th st, s e cor lands Harlem River & Portchester R. R. Co., 75x208.10 to 137th st, x75x208.10. The De La Vergne Refrigerating Machine Co. to The New York, New Haven & Hartford Railroad Co. and The Harlem

River & Portchester Railroad Co. April 1. nom

146th st, n s, 325 e Willis av, 75x100. David Tetslaff and Martha his wife to John H. and Peter F. Meyer. Aug. 12. 9,600

147th st, s s, 325 e Southern Boulevard, 25x100. Robert A. Cheesebrough to John Heuffing. Aug. 6. 900

148th st, n s, 325 w Morris av, 25x106.6. Mary F. wife of Patrick McGrath to James P. Cells. Aug. 7. 2,500

152d st, n s, 95.5 e Morris av, 24.10x100. William A. Hustace and Amy B. his wife. Mount Vernon, N. Y., to Lawrence Ryan. Aug. 14. 1,750

154th st, n s, 275 e Courtlandt av, 25x—. Agreement to remove encroachments on notice. Rose Rice with Adolph Attmann. June 3. nom

158th st, n e s, 150 n w Courtlandt av, 25x100. Hugh Thompson to Charles Schreiber and Barbara his wife, joint tenants. Aug. 10. 2,200

Av C or Trinity av, w s, 100 n Cedar pl, 25x100. Catharine Kansky to Frederick E. Kunst. Aug. 18. 1,175

Brook av, s e cor 149th st, 75x100. Samuel B. Ogden to Gerard Fountain. Mt. $25,000. Aug. 17. 4,300

Eagle av, w s, 526.10 s Westchester av, runs west 120 x south 50 x east 30 x north 25 x east 90 to av, x north 25. Release mort. Elizabeth Seiler to Margaret Brown. Aug. 15. 200

Eagle av, w s, 551.10 s Westchester av, 25x90. Margaret wife of and James Brown to Michael J. Donohue, Charles W. Callaghan and Katie his wife and William Kenyon and Ettie his wife. Sub. to mort. Aug. 15. 2,300

Edenwood av, centre line, at intersection n s Highbridge st, runs east 145.10 x north 115.5 x west 125 x south 190.6. John H. Eden and Mary D. his wife to Daniel Buckley. July 30. 7,500

Forest av, e s, 47.6 n 161st st, 29x135. Hermann Hering and Anna his wife to Alphonse Rinschler. Aug. 6. 8,000

Central av, s e s, lots 50 and 51 map Upper Morrisania, 100x115. Bridget Curry to John P. Kerrigan. Mt. $3,000. July 30. (Corrects error in last issue.) 6,750

Franklin av, e s, 73 n 169th st, 23.9x125x23.6x125. Sarah A. Appleton to Z. S. Sampson. Aug. 17. 4,250

Franklin av, e s, 96.9 n 169th st, 23.9x125x22.9x125. William G. Appleton and Catharine his wife to same. Aug. 17. 4,250

Jefferson av, s e s, lot 197 map Samuel Ryer Homestead, 25x100. Jacob Ramsteck and Louise A. his wife to Edward J. Deegan. Aug. 17. 1,000

Marion av, w s, 577 n Kingsbridge road, 61.6x160.2x61.7x157.6. August Frank and Johanna his wife to Frederick Jacobs. ½ part. July 2. 2,000

Marion av, e s, 151.10 s Travers st, 75.11x82x75.6x85. George W. Robins to Sarah Jackson. Mt. $1,125, taxes, &c. Aug. 18. 2,600

Sheridan av, e s, lots 221 and 222 map Inwood, 50x110.2x51.1x120.9. Kate O'Hara, Schraalenburgh, N. J., to Thomas L. Reynolds. Sub. to mort. Aug. 3. nom

Stebbins , e s, 513.2 n 165th st, 25x170.10x25.4x166.8, avMary E. Stillwell widow to Elizabeth F. Parker. Aug. 14. 1,400

Washington av, n w cor 161st st, 34x40.4x67.3x25.6. Henrietta wife of and Morris Franklin to Newbury D. Lawton. Aug. 10. 1,300

Washington av, e s, 75.2 s 171st st, 25x98.6x25x100.3. Israel C. Jones and Phebe M. his wife to Martha Neumann. July 29. 8,750

Washington av, w s, 50.2 s 184th st, 50.2x115x50x119.6. Joseph Wodicka and Julia his wife to William Walsh. Mt. $800. Aug. 19. 3,025

Washington av, e s, 75.2 s 171st st, 25.1x94.6x25x100.3. Israel C. Jones to Martha Neumann. July 29. 8,750

Webster av, e s, 435.5 n 170th st, 50x121 to Mill Brook, x50.10x129.8. Anna M. Z. wife of Charles F. de Montsaulmin to Sarah C. Ottiwell. July 2. 2,700

2d av or Fordham to Williamsbridge road, s e s, 150 n e Williams st, 25x125. Walter J. Lee and Carrie his wife to Marcus W. Hall. Mt. $4,500. Aug. 18. 16,750

3d av, s e s, 362.11 n e Grove st, 36x180 to Mill Brook, x36x164. Leopold to Joseph Loewy. All title. Aug. 1Loewy nom

Main Post road leading from New York to Boston, adj land late of John Carroll, runs southeast 61.1 x southeast again 6.1 x southwest 3.1 x northwest 64 x again northwest 9.6 to road, x northeast 25. Patrick McManus and Mary his wife, Peoria, Ill., to Richard D. Williams. July 10. 1,300

LEASEHOLD CONVEYANCES.

Broadway, No. 641. Assign. lease. S. H. Stone & Co. to Isidor C. Istel. nom

45th st, n s, 210 e 8th av, 20x100.5. Charles F. Southmayd and James F. Chamberlain trustees for Henry Astor to Levi H. Marsteller. 20 years, from Aug. 1, 1891, per year, taxes and 480

7th av, No. 781. Assign. lease. Gustav T. Von Glehn to Charles Kollmann. nom

Same property. Assign. lease. Charles Kollmann to Adolph Von Oehsen. nom

11th av, s w cor 30th st, 49.4x100. The New York Life Ins. and Trust Co. exrs., &c., Richard Ray to John A., James B., Arthur J., Thomas L., Julia A., Clara C., Eugenia M. and Elizabeth J. Moore. 21 years, from May 1, 1891, per year, taxes and 1,300

Assign. lease made by Herman Meyer July 23, 1888. George Heilshorn to Consumers' Brewing Co., N. J. (Lim.) nom

KINGS COUNTY.

AUGUST 13, 14, 15, 17, 18, 19.

Adams st, s s, 426.1 w Coney Island plank road, 25x101.11x25x101.8, Flatbush. Charles H. Fitzgerald to Joseph Fitzgerald. $2,600

Ashford st, w s, 200 s Arlington av, 12.6x97.6, h & l. Alexander T. Zundt and James Stewart to Hiram S. and Charlotte Lyon. Mt. $1,000. 2,800

Bainbridge st, n s, 156.3 w Ralph av, 18.9x100, h & l. Orville D. Lankford to Victor J. Dowling, New York. 500

Bergen st, n s, 200 w Vanderbilt av, 24.8x110, h & l. Foreclos. John Courtney to The Kings Co. Co-operative Building and Loan Ass c. 4,000

Bergen st, s s, 250 w Hopkinson av, 25x127.9. Alexander Ray to William and Mary McCord. Mt. $600. 650

Boerum st, s s, 100 w Lorimer st, 25x100, h & l. John Backer to Joseph Wiebert. 6,000

Bradford st, e s, 100 s Liberty av, 75x100. George W. Chauncey to Patrick Brophy. 2,500

Carroll st, s s, 270 w Clinton st, 20x90. New York Life Ins. Co. to Sarah A. Dowling. 6,500

Cheever pl, e s, 133.7 n Degraw st, 20x88.6, h & l. Lewis Josephs to Katie wife of Thomas Thorgerson. 6,000

Columbia st, e s, 60 s Centre st, 19x100. Joseph Bosch to Valentine Bosch, New York. nom

Clarkson st, s s, 180 w Schenectady av, 20x100, h & l, Flatbush. Solomon Kohn to John Goetz. Q. C. nom

Same property. Partition. Samuel G. Adams to John Goetz. 850

Dean st, s s, 100 e Rockaway av, 25x107.2. Contract. Laura P. Gibbs to George Grossing. 3,000

Dean st, s s, 225 w Rockaway av, 25x107.2, h & l. Charles Killeen to Mary Ascher. Mt. $2,275. 2,625

Degraw st, s s, 300 w Smith st, 25x100. Joseph M. Williams individ. and exr. of Martha S. Williams to Bernard Callaghan. 4,500

Decatur st, s s, 76 e Patchen av, 20x82x17.3x82, h & l. Isabelle B. wife of John N. Booth to Charles H. Reynolds. B. & S. nom

Same property. Release mort. Paul W. Ledoux to Isabelle B. Booth. nom

Same property. Charles H. Reynolds to Louis Ellinghausen. Mt. $2,800 5,175

Duffield st, e s, 100 s Concord st, 25x100. Thomas Stratton to Timothy Doris. 3,000

Eldert st, n w s, 195 s w Evergreen av, 20x100. J. Christian Johnson to Frederick C. Wiederhold. Mt. $3,000. nom

Same property. Release mort. Virginia A. Kleme to J. Christian Johnson. nom

Essex st, w s, 90 s Ridgewood av, 20x100, h & l. James Miller to Elizabeth Gegenheimer. Mt. $2,500. 3,800

Essex st, w s, 988 n New Lots road, 25x95. Emma wife of Frank Winkenbach to Solomon B. Kraus. 400

Ewen st, n e cor Jackson st, 33.4x75. John P. Cowley to James Kelly. 3,550

Ewen st, n w cor Moore st, 25x75, h & l. Mary A. Zimmer to Jonas Feldberg and Sarah Barusch. Mt. $3,000. 12,500

Fernald st, s s, 194.6 w Hudson av, 40x100, Flatbush. Edward C. Ellis to Mary J. Coo er. 600

Floydpst, n s, 315 e Nostrand av, 25x100, h & l. Louis Beer and Michael Schaffner to Conrad Schaffner, New York, 10,250

Same property. Release mort. Charles Diemer to Louis Beer and Michael Schaffner. nom

Floyd st, n s, 215 e Nostrand av, 25x100. Louis Beer and Michael Schaffner to Jacob Schilb. Mt. $4,000. 10,000

Fort Greene pl, e s, 191 s Hanson pl, 20.6x100, h & l. Helena M. L. wife of and Frederick Schneider to James, Michael and Patrick Scanlan, of J. M. & P. Scanlan. Mt. $4,000. 200

Fulton st, s s, 164.5 s w Franklin av, 56x117, h & l.
Fulton st, s s, 169.9 e Bedford av, 40x100, hs & ls.
William H. Mairs to James Phelan, San Francisco. Mt. $56,000. exch

Garfield pl, s s, 275 w 6th av, 150x100. Brooklyn Life Ins. Co. of the City of New York to Sarah A. wife of George W. Hunt 18,750

Garnet st, s s, 100 w Court st, 100x100. Elijah L. Robbins and ano. exrs. and trustees Daniel A. Robbins to Alfred E. Hartington. 5,000

Garnet st, s s, 100 e Court st, 25x100. Albert E. Hartington to John A. Schad. 8,500

Same property. Release mort. Peoples Trust Co. to Alfred E. Hartington. 5,000

Gerry st, n s, 100 e Harrison av, 25x100, h & l. Margaretha Schaefer to William Meth. 2,880

Greene st, n s, 200 e Provost st, 583.5x125. Lewis Walker to William H. Meserole. ½ part. Sub. to mort. $24,000. 17,000

Gwinnett st, n w s, 100 n e Harrison av, 22x100. Jacob, Frank, Henry, Bennie and Lizzie Heiser, Susie wife of Jacob Hafner, Margaretha Harzberger, Anna Heizer widow, Hannah wife of Charles Publie and Martin Heiser heirs Christian Heiser to Mary Heiser widow. Q. C. nom

Halsey st, n s, 425 e Lewis av, 100x100, hs & ls. John H. Knapp to Charles A. Knapp, Norwalk, Conn. Mt. $27,000. 1887. nom

Halsey st, s s, 81.3 w Patchen av, 18.9x75, h & l. Charles G. Reynolds to Frederick Cowdrey. Mt. $3,750. 5,500

Halsey st, s, 375 e Reid av, 25x100. Joseph C. Hoagland to Frank C. Swimm. 2,000

Halsey st, n s, 300.4 e Reid av, 17.8x100. Elizabeth Tuthill to Helena M. L. wife of Frederick Schneider. 5,500

Henry st, w s, 84 n Woodhull st, 21x100, h & l. Charles A. Kaufman to August Henpel. Mt. $6,000. 2,250

Heyward st, No. 150, s s, 278 w Marcy av, 18.6x100, h & l. Walter H. z to George W. Richards. Mt. $3,20Fit gerald 6,000

Harman st, n w s, 408 n e Evergreen av, 18.6x100. George D. M y to Elizabetha Blessmann. Mt. $1,500a ran 3,800

Hart st late Elm st, n s, 310 w St. Nicholas av, 20x81.3x20x80.10. Benjamin Thompson to Joseph Eirich. 650

Hart st, s s, 100 w Hamburg av, 25x100, h & l. Albert Tremmel to Caspar Rauch and Margaretha his wife, joint tenants. ½ part. 3,475

Henry st, w s, 76.3 n Pineapple st, 25x69.3. Francis E. Gordon to Ellen Kenney, New York. Mt. $5,000. 7,000

Herkimer st, n s, 183.4 w Saratoga av, 16.8x100, h & l. Charles J. Hoernlein to Herbert Albertson. Mt. $2,300. 3,300

Herkimer st, s s, 64 w Nostrand av, 20x92.9, h & l. Charles W. Moller to Dorothea P. Moller. B. & S. Mt. $1,500. nom

Himrod st, s e s, 570 s w Central av, 79x100. William Ruthmann to Katie Kreppel. exch

Hinsdale st, e s, 150 n Sutter av, 25x100. Mary E. Cook to Hugh Corduan. Mt. $2,550. 2,800

Irving pl, w s, 425 s Gates av, 25x100. Helen M. Simpson to Clinton W. and Edward M. Barlow. 2,500

Irving pl, w s, 400 s Gates av, 25x100. Helen M. Simpson et al. trustees Alexander Simpson to same. 2,500

Jackson st, n s, 75 e Ewen st, 25x50. John P. Crowley to Toney Russo and Frank Masino. 3,000

Jefferson st, s e s, 100 s w Central av, 25x100, h & l, Flushing. Peter Kraemer to Conrad Abmeier. 7,000

Jerome st, w s, 40 n Blake av, 20x100. Bernard Smyth to James Smyth. 250

Kosciusko st, s s, 300 e Reid av, 25x100. Margaret Emrich to Gustav A. H. Bauer. 3,500

Kosciusko st, n s, 223.6 w Reid av, 19.2x100. Alfred J. L. Brucks to Henrietta Cronacher. Mt. $1,500. 3,000

Leonard st, w s, 83.4 n Jackson st, 16.8x abt 75, h & l. George W. Richards to Henry Reineke. 2,600

Linwood st, w s, 500 n Arlington av, 25x100. Barbara Munz to Ernst Munz. Sub. to morts. 3,000

Lorimer st, n w cor Jackson st, 25x100, h & l.
Jackson st, n s, 100 w Lorimer st, 25x100.
Alfred Martin, Jr., to Harriet Martin. All liens. nom

Macon st, No. 713, n s, 22.6 e Ralph av, 17.6x100. F. Augustus Conkling to Greenleaf W. Crossman, New York. Mt. $4,000. nom

Macon st, s s, 302.4 e Reid av, 18x100, h & l. James G. Roberts to Sarah E. Lusk. Mt. $4,500. 7,250

Madison st, n s, 80.8 w Franklin av, 19.4x60, h & l. Jennie F. B. Cowles widow to Benjamin L. Cowles. Q. C. nom

Madison st, n w s, 260 n e Hamburg av, 100x100. James Gascoine to Adolphus Gload. ½ part. nom

Same property. Ann E. Cozine widow and Jas. Gascoine exrs. John G. Cozine to same. ½ part. 2,562

Madison st, s e s, 410 n e Central av, 20x100. Emil F. Wildner to Franz Kahle. Mt. $2,300. nom

Malbone st, s s, 300 e Brooklyn av, 107x148.6x140.10x107.11, 24th Ward. Mary McCarthy to Daniel McCarthy. 1,200

McDonough st, s s, 249.8 w Patchen av, 0.4x100. Henry S. Lampher to Henry B. Hill. 30

Same property. Release mort The Brooklyn Trust Co. to Henry S. Lamphear. nom

North Henry st, e s, 203.3 n Van Pelt av, 17x100. Charles Engert to Samuel Harper. 3,500

Osborn st, e s, 50 n Glenmore av, 50x100. Herbert C. Smith to David Stern. 1,400

Osborn st, n e cor Glenmore av, 50x100. Same to Johannes Feldberg. 1,775

Osborn st, e s, 150 n Blake av, 25x100. Pauline Hartmann to Simon Gunsberg and Reuben Epstein. Mt. $1,200. 1,850

Osborn st, e s, 125 s Eastern Parkway, 25x100. Abraham Ruth to Morris Goldberger. 925

Pacific st, n w cor Clinton st, 90x75. The Pacific Street Methodist Episcopal Church to John Adamson. B. & S. Mt. $12,000. 21,000

Pearl st, w s, 177 n Tillary st, 20.3x102.11x20.8x102.11. E. Sinnamon Calvert to Herman Sacks. Mt. $3,000. 6,500

Poplar st, w s, lot 5 map of R. Totler property, Flatbush, 25x100. Mary J. Owen to Mary Jordan. 1,500

President st, s s, 150 e Franklin av, 25x131. John McCabe, New York, to James Conley. 550

Prospect pl, s s, 84 w Buffalo av, 16x52.9. William L. Beers to Greenleaf W. Crossman. Mt. $1,250. nom

Prospect pl, s s, 52 w Buffalo av, 16x52.9. Same to same. Mt. $1,250. nom

Quincy st, n s, 186 w Patchen av, 18x100, h & l. Henry Battermann to Sarah M. Warren widow. 5,750

Sackett st, No. 103, n s, 192 w Columbia st, 19x100, h & l. Benjamin C. Thayer to Louis and Emilie Berg. 6,000

Sackman st, e s, 125 n Liberty av, 25x100. Charles Harlin to Cornelius N. Muessig. Correction deed. nom

Sands st, n s, 60 w Hudson av, runs north 80 x west 9.2 x north 20 x west 10.10 x south 100 to st, x east 20. James Entwistle to Emanuel Weill. 4,250

Seigel st, n s, 175 w Humboldt st, 25x100, h & l. Salomon Friedland to Samuel and Annie S. Abelow. *Mt.* $900. 4,375

Seigel st, s s, 50 w Leonard st, 25x100. Lena Fischer to Bernard Buchenholz. 7,000

Seigel st, s s, 50 w Leonard st, 25x100. Bernard Buchenholz to Gerson Levy. *Mt.* $5,000. 3,500

Smith st, e s, 102 n Livingston st, runs east 44.2 x north 3 10 x east 59.10 x north 25.2 x west 104 to Smith st, x south 29. Mercy L. widow and Isaac H. Cary to Margaret V. McNulty. 17,500

Same property and other property. Release of legacy. Sanford C. Hardy, Providence, R. I., to Isaac H. Cary individ. and as exr. and Mercy L. Cary widow. nom

Stanhope st, s e s, 100 s w Irving av, 150x100. Otto Muhlbauer to Darwin R. James. *Mt.* $4,000. exch

Starr st, n w s, 195 s w St. Nicholas av, 25x100. George Deutsch to John L. Rossteuscher. nom

Starr st, n w s, 97.3 n e Wyckoff av, 25x100. Leonhardt Martin to Paul Westfall. 800

Starr st, n w s, 97.3 n e Troutman st, 25x100. Leonhardt Martin to Paul Westphal. Correction deed. 800

Strong pl, w s, 225 s Harrison st, 25x100.9. William Post exr of Abraham P. Skinner to Abram S. Post, Great Neck, L. I. 10,000

Strong pl, w s, 225 s Harrison st, 25x109 9, h & l. William Post, Great Neck, L. I., to John Assip and Timothy J. Buckley. 14,000

Stockton st, n s, 150 w Throop av, 25x90. Bertha Kaufmann, Newtown, L. I., to Simon Hartmann and Frieda his wife, Babylon, L. I. *Mt.* $5,350. nom

Suydam st, s e s, 275 n e Hamburg av, 25x100. Lena Weis to Philipp Kemp and Jacob Jaeger. 1,400

Taylor st, n s, 140 w Wythe av, 20x100. George Libricht or Lebrecht to William Lebrecht. *Mt.* $2,000. nom

Same property. William Lebrecht to Catherine Libricht. *Mt.* $2,000. nom

Troutman st, n e s, 92 n e Wyckoff av, 25x200 to Starr st. Rachel Wilder widow to Leonhardt Martin. 1887. 570

Troutman st, s e s, 92.1 n e Wyckoff av, 25x100. Leonhardt Martin to Paul Westfall. 700

Troutman st, s e s, 92.1 n e Wyckoff av, 25x100. Leonhardt Martin to Paul Westphal. Correction deed. 700

Van Voorhis st, n w s, 287 s w Evergreen av, 16.10x100. John W. McLaren to William J. Higginson. 4,200

Van Voorhis st, n s, 151 w Evergreen av, runs west 51 x north 100 x east 2 x north 100 to Schaeffer st, x east 50 x south 100 x west 1 x south 100. Virginia A. Kleine to Mary E. wife of Moses H. Gentleman. *Mt.* $4,000. nom

Wallabout st, s s, 84 e Harrison av, 16x50, h & l. Charles Rissler to Samuel and Davis Eisler. 2,200

Walworth st, e s, 390 s Willoughby av, 65x100. Frank R. Moore to Marcie Dunn. nom

Same property. Marcie Dunn to Frank R. Moore. *Mt.* $13,000. nom

Walworth st, w s, 290 s Willoughby av, 20x100, h & l. Frank H. Tyler to Abbie C. Smith. *Mt.* $2,600. exch

Warwick st, w s, 368.3 s Fulton st, 25x95. Sarah A. Haviland widow to John Downes and Annie his wife. *Mt.* $1,500. 3,030

Weirfield st, n w s, 80 n e Evergreen av, 20.2x100, h & l. Annie Herzog to John C. Austin and George Mohrmann. *Mt.* $4,700. nom

Windsor pl, n e s, 97.10 s e 7th av, 17x100, h & l. William E. Kay to Margaret Seibel, Patterson, N. J. *Mt.* $400. 4,000

North 2d st, No. 135, n s, 25x69.5x25x70. Michael Becker to William R. Beeston. 1,200

North 2d st, s s, 50 w Havemeyer st, 37x91x33.3x94.6. Joseph Schmeling to Ciro and Antonio Gaimari and Paolo Langone. Assessm't. 5,000

South 2d st, s s, 50 w 6th st, 24.3x96x24.5x95. Andrew Weigel to Frank Mace. nom

North 3d st, s s, 51.9 e Berry st, 27.4x71.3x26.2x72. Eliza A. M. wife of James Quinn to William E. Stokum. C. a. G. nom

Same property. William E. Stokum to James Quinn. C. a. G. nom

3d pl, s s, 41.8 w Court st, 20.10x133.5. Charles Quenzer to Charles A. Muller. 6,400

3d pl, s s, 41.8 w Court st, 20.10x½ block. Margaret B. wife of Marmont B. Edson to Charles Quenzer. nom

North 5th st, n s, 125 e Roebling st, 25x100. Margaret E. wife of John B. McCaffrey and Catharine M. Gleason heirs Patrick Gleason to Francesco Calicchio. 3,800

North 5th st, s s, abt 125 e 6th st, begins at point 23.6 s said North 5th st, runs north 23.6 to st, x east 25 x south 17.2 x again south 95.2 x west 25 x north —. Rosanna Fagen widow, Annie T. Byrnes, Rose E., Thomas J. and Cornelius Fagen heirs Garrett or Gerald Fagen to Anthony Laveglia. 5,500

South 5th st, s s, 42.10 w 6th st, 21.5x80, h & l. Peter J. Eckes to Jacob Urwitz. *Mt.* $3,000. 5,800

6th st, s s, 228.10 e 6th av, 17x100. Adolph Schroeder to Nelson L. Tuck, Philadelphia, Pa. *Mt.* $7,500. nom

6th st, s s, 217.8 e 5th av, 20.1x100, h & l. Fannie M. wife of Josie Pando to John Banker. 4,500

North 6th st, s s, 150 w Berry st, 25x100. Catharine Rogers to John W. Frey. 6,000

7th st, n e s, 233.4 n w 9th av, 19x100. Mary A. Kieff to Albert B. Schofield. 9,000

North 7th st, No. 255. Contract. John B. Ferrall to Jules & Edward Wolff, of Wolff Bros. 4,000

North 8th st, s w s, 200 n e Wythe av, 25x100. Lizatta wife of Albert Schnibbe to Albert Schnibbe. nom

9th st, n s, 172.10 e 7th av, 19.6x100, h & l. Anna, William and Joseph S. Whiteside to Thomas A. Bond. 5,360

Same property. Robert and Mary Whiteside by Anna Whiteside guard. to same. 2,142

13th st, s s, 175 w 8th av, 122.10x100. David Atkin to David J. Atkin nom

14th st, s w s, 147.10 s e 6th av, 25x100. Jane Royce widow to Eliza J. Cochran. nom

16th st, n s, 154.9 w 8th av, 38.2x100. Release mort. Ezra D. Bushnell to William Wingrath. 6,000

21st st, n e s, 285 n w 4th av, 25x100. Frank A. Belling to John Szeikowski. 2,500

41st st, n s, 350 e 5th av. 50x100.2. Patrick Whelan trustee to Mary A. Whelan. nom

Same property. Mary A. Whelan to Henry McCready, New York. 2,400

45th st, s s 220 e 3d av, 20x100.2 James G. Carroll to James Galloway. *Mt.* $2,300. 4,600

47th st, s s, 180 w 3d av, 40x100. Samuel J. King to Gottfried Fischer. 1,400

48th st, s s, 380 e 3d av, 16x100.2. William Bibl to John R. Schoonover. *Mt.* $2,534, taxes, &c. nom

52d st, n s, 100 e 4th av, 240x100.2. Stephen Martin to Charles and Alfred Hamilton. *Mt.* $2,537. 9,000

53d st, n s, 160 w 8th av. 40x100.2, New Utrecht. Henry Kettelhodt to Florence I. Driscoll. 600

55th st, n e s, 200 s e 4th av, 80x100.2, 8th Ward. Michael Smith to Patrick Smith. 2,500

55th st, w s, 100 n w 14th av, 50x100.2, New Utrecht. West Brooklyn Land and Improvement Co. to Sherwood Aldrich. 700

57th st, n s, 360 e 3d av, 20x100.2. George H. Parshall to Thomas Ostrick. 825

57th st, n s, 280 e 3d av, 20x100.2. Same to Hannah Bennett. 800

66th st, s s, 180 e 13th av, 40x100, Lefferts Park. Effingham H. Nichols to Eugene J. Spear, New York. 460

72d st, s s, 570 w 15th av, 40x100, New Utrecht. James V. S. Woolley to Jennie L. Bennie. 400

73d st, s s, 490 w 15th av, 20x100, New Utrecht. Bengt. Carlson to Olaf M. Olsen. Q. C. 178

74th st, s s, 590 w 15th av, 20x100, New Utrecht. James V. Woolley to Gregory I. Leahy. 160

76th st, s s, 463.7 e 4th av, 160x100, New Utrecht. Thomas B. Miniter to Andrew Halley. ½ part. Sub. to morts. See 3d av. nom

80th st, s s, 120 e Narrows av, 40x109.4, New Utrecht. Rulef J. Van Brunt to William J. Ward. 600

81st st, n s, 280 e Narrows av, 40x109.4, New Utrecht. Rulef J. Van Brunt to Louis Blankenfeld. 600

Atlantic av, s s, 212.3 w Clason av, 100x120. Release mort. Stephen B. Sturges to John F. Hart. nom

Atlantic av, No. 2266. Contract. James Nevins to James H. Hart. 2,600

Av B, n s, 551.7 w Ocean av, runs north 401.1 x southwest 291 6 x south 91.3 x east 140 x south 200 to Av B, x east 130, Flatbush. Emeline Gallup widow to John McElvery. 6,000

Av D, centre line, s s, extends from e s Ocean Parkway to centre East 7th st, 250x140, Flatbush. Release mort. Mary B. Ward, Walter R. Gilbert, Jr., Thomas C. and John B. H. Oakley to Peter H. McNulty. 3,059

Av D, s s, extends from Ocean Parkway to East 7th st, 250x100, Flatbush. Peter H. McNulty to De Witt D. Cook. 7,000

Bay Ridge av, s s, 330 w 15th av, 20x100, Lefferts Park. James V. S. Woolley to Daisey E. F. Culin. 280

Bedford av, n e cor Heyward st, 22x100. Margaret wife of Nicholas Mulvihill to Frederick Borghard. *Mt.* $13,000. 26,000

Central av, s w s, 80 n w Harman st, 20x80. Henry A. Beiler to Katie Kreppel. Q. C. nom

Same property. Katie Kreppel to William Ruhmann. exch

Christopher av, e s, 200 n Belmont av, 25x100. Annie Levy to Joseph Berger and Samuel Mishel. *Mt.* $900. 900

Christopher av, e s, 200 n Belmont av, 25x100. Lewis Hurst to Annie Levy, New York. 800

Christopher av, w s, 150 s Belmont av, 50x100. Pauline Hartmann to Joseph Singer. *Mt.* $900. 1,500

Clason av, e s, 87.9 n Myrtle av, 25x90.10x25x90.8. Lipman Arensberg to Benjamin F. Constable. *Mt.* $8,000. exch

Clinton av, No. 97. Release judgment. John F. Brown to Ariette Baird. 300

De Kalb av, s e s, 175 n e Hamburg av, 25x100. George Ochs to Peter Scheimeister. *Mt.* $3,000. 6,200

De Kalb av, s e s, 200 n e Hamburg av, 25x100. George Ochs to Ferdinand Lenz. *Mt.* $3,000. 6,200

Evergreen av, north cor Eldert st, 20x100. James Gascoine to John Christen. ½ part. nom

Same property. Anna E. Cozine widow individ. and with James Gascoine exrs. John G. Cozine to same. ½ part. 5,000

Flatbush av, No. 95, e s, 269.10 n Hanson pl, 20x66.7x20x64.7.
Flatbush av, No. 91, e s, 309.10 n Hanson pl, 20x70.9x20.1x68.8.
Mary A. McGivern to Ira Perego. 20,000

Franklin av, s s, 692 w 3d st, 69x115.6x69x—, Flatbush. John W. Maloney to Mary F. and Margaret A. Maloney. Reserves life estate. gift

Same property. William Dredger to John Maloney. Q. C. nom

Gates av, s s, 255.7 w Lewis av, 19.5x100, h & l. William R. Young to Edward L. Britt, Jr. *Mt.* $5,000 and taxes 1890. 6,750

Gates av, n s, 375 w Reid av, 25x100. James Kelly to John P. Cowley. 3,000

Gates av, n s, 175 e Stuyvesant av, 25x100. Herman E. Wagner to Maria A. Baxter. 6,000

Georgia av, e s, 150 s South Carolina av, 25x100. Elizabeth wife of George W. Bassett to Henry Kurz and Sophia his wife. 1,750

Greene av, n w s, 60 s w Evergreen av, 20x80. Annie L. wife of S. G. Bedell to Josef A. Haven. *Mt.* $2,900. 3,950

Greene av, n s, 20 e Stuyvesant av, 30x100, hs & ls. George Koch to Henry Roemer. *Mt.* $10,500. 17,675

Greene av, n w s, 456 s w Central av, 18.6x100, h & l. Otto Singer to Gustav Doerle and Christina his wife. *Mt.* $2,000. 4,500

Greene av, s s, 100 e Grand av, 25x100. George H. Stover to William H. Tunnison. 3,500

Greene av, n w cor Irving av, 25x84.4x25x85.5, h & l. Gustav Feigenspan to Thomas C. Higgins. *Mt.* $4,000. exch

Greene av, n w s, 474.6 s w Central av, 18.6x100, h & l. Otto Singer to John Bittorf and Caroline his wife. *Mt.* $2,000. 4,500

Greene av, s s, 206 e Patchen av, 20x100.2. William D. Day to Lucinda B. Winter. *Mt.* $4,000. nom

Johnson av, No. 87, n s, 100 w Leonard st, 25x100 Jacob Manheim to Hyman Friedman. *Mt.* 4,990. 7,800

Knickerbocker av, n e s, intersection s s Thames st, runs east 100.3 x south 22.8 x southwest 60.6 x northwest 83. Ernst Augustin to Minna Feigenspan, of Newtown, N. Y. *Mt.* $2,000. nom

Knickerbocker av, n w s, intersection n s Thames st, runs east 61.4 x north 53.2 x southwest 77.3 x southeast 25. Peter Blank to same. *Mt.* $2,500. nom

Knickerbocker av, south cor De Kalb av, 75x100. Louis Beer to George Koch and Frederick Koerner *Mt.* $3,246. 6,500

Lafayette av, No. 12, s s, 100.7 e Navy st, 20.1x91.9x20x89.2. William N. Crane and ano. trustees Walter F. Brush dec'd to Ira Perego. 8,500

Lafayette av, n s, 331.3 e Sumner av, 18.9x100. Alexander McKnight to Annie L. Gabriel. *Mt.* $6,000. nom

Lexington av, s s, 343.9 w Throop av, 18.9x100. Mary J. Rougan widow to Catharine Zimmer. *Mt.* $2,800. 4,800

Livonia av, s e cor Sackman st, 50x100.
Powell st, w s, 100 s Livonia av, runs south 121 x west 200 to Sackman st, x north 21 x east 100 x north 100 x east 100.
Herman F. Koepke to Abraham Ruth. 4,250

Livonia av, s s, 50 e Sackman st, 100x100. Herman F. Koepke to Benjamin Marder. 2,200

Livonia av, n s, 25 w Thatford av, 25x100. Pauline Hartmann to Gussie Simon. *Mt.* $1,300. 1,850

Livonia av, s w cor Powell st, 50x100. Herman F. Koepke to Sam. Ruginsky and Hyman Tallie, New York. 1,225

Manhattan av, w s, 81.5 n Van Cott av, 150x100, h & ls. Joseph Loewy to Leopold Loewy. All title. *Mt.* $9,000. nom

Mermaid av, s e cor West 15th st, runs south 50 x east 112.6 x north 40.2 x northwest 21.1 x west 92.1, Gravesend. Albert D. Buschman to Catharine Jones. 1,000

Montauk av, e s, 130 s Belmont av, 20x100. Charles H. Machin to John Fulton. 350

Morgan av, e s, 50 s Thames st, 25x100. George Eckert to Magdalena wife of Peter Borst. *Mt.* $3,650. 6,125

Montrose av, s s, 50 w Bushwick av Boulevard. 25x100. Charles Werner to Anton Schimmel and Elizabeth his wife, joint tenants. 5,300

Myrtle av, n s, 300 w Tompkins av, 20x100. Annie L. Gabriel to Alexander McKnight. *Mt.* $2,000. nom

Myrtle av, n s, 38 w Harman st, 25xx91.2x27.1x101.7, h & l. Darwin R. James to Otto Muhlbauer. *Mt.* $3,500. exch

Nostrand av, w s, 56.7 n East Broadway, 289 to Linden Boulevard, x12x289.4.
East Broadway, n s, 100 w Nostrand av, runs north 293.10 to Linden Boulevard Sections, x east 12 6 x south 294.6 to East Broadway, x west 25.5, Flatbush.
Trustees of the Reformed Protestant Dutch Church to George C. Sexton. 500

Nostrand av, e s, 110 n Hart st, 18x100. John H. Woolley to Agnes Roever. *Mt.* $4,000. 4,400

Patchen av, e s, 80 s Monroe st, 20x80, h & l. John H. Gustin to Caroline Ellinger. *Mt.* $2 000. 3,600

Prospect av, w s, 486 n Greenwood av, 12.6x150, Flatbush. Christopher J. Prehn to Charles Prehn. *Mt.* $1,550. 1,750

Prospect av, n s, 273 w 3d av, 44.1x43x44x47.10. Joseph O. Fuels to Philip Spitzenberg. *Mt.* $3,000. nom

Putnam av, s s, 423 w Ralph av, 27x100. Charles G. Wharry to Uriah B. Swan. nom

Same property. Uriah B. Swan to Virginia R. wife of Charles G. Wharry. nom

Putnam av, s s, 90 w Lewis av, 180x200 to Jefferson av.
Lewis av, s w cor Putnam av, 22x90.
Augustus W. Blazo to Andrew D. Baird. *Mt.* $34,500. 7,000

Putnam av, n s, 175 e Ralph av, 50x100, h & l. Peter E. Peters to John H. Jessen. 5,000

Putnam av, n s, 80 w Howard av, 20x100, h & l. James Sweet to Annie wife of and George Fickeissen. *Mt.* $1,900. 3,450

Putnam av, n s, 320 e Broadway, 20x100. Robert L. Moores and Charles A. Le Quesne to Charles B. Wheeler. *Mt.* $6,500, taxes, &c. 9,000

Ridgewood av, s e cor Ashford st, 100x100. Edward F. Linton to Theodore M. Le Beau. 4,300

Same property. Release mort. Williamsburgh Savings Bank to Edward F. Linton. 1,400

Rockaway av, e s, at n e cor D. Vanderveer's farm, runs east abt 700 to centre of Fresh Creek, x north — along same 150 x west 200 x north 120 x west 215 to av, x south abt 425, Flatlands. Frederick Balz to George Underhill. 6,500

Shepherd av, e s, 140 n Ridgewood av, 20x 102.4.
Shepherd av, e s, 240 n Ridgewood av, 20x 102.5.
Release mort. Williamsburgh Savings Bank to Edward F. Linton. 700

Same property. Edward F. Linton to James Graham. 1,600

Stanley av, n e cor Elton st, 100x85. Johanna wife of William Dieckman to Andrew Steven. 1,000

Stewart av, south cor 73d st, 80.1x102.1x80x 106.3, New Utrecht. Prospect Land and Improvement Co. to Adolf Scharsich. 1,110

St Marks av, s s, 168 e Vanderbilt av, 32x131. Lillian F. Naylor wife of Joseph F. to Thomas H. Robbins. All liens. nom

Stone av, w s, 181 n Blake av, 44x100. Hyman Arkave to Meyer Shakofsky. ½ part. *Mt.* $2,890. nom

Same property, all. Meyer Shakofsky to Rosa Shakofsky *Mt.* $2,890. nom

Stone av, w s, 150 n Blake av, 23x100, h & l. Henry C. Soop and Frank M. Andrews to Samuel Barkin, New York. *Mt.* $1,700. 2,550

Stone av, e s, 200 n Blake av, 50x100. Herbert C. Smith to Louis Regenbogen, Samuel Davis, William Schechtel and Louis Cohen. 1,200

Stone av, w s, 150 n Belmont av, 25x100. Laura wife of and Divine M. Munger to Marcus Berman and Jacob Lipsky. 825

Stone av, e s, 50 n Glenmore av, 25x100. S. Ferris Owen to Louis Goldsohn and Harris Schurtz. 755

Stuyvesant av, s w cor Quincy st, runs south 25 x west 80 x south 18.9 x west 20 x north 43.9 to Quincy st, x east 100, h & l. George M. Rothstein to Henry Meis and Mina his wife. *Mt.* $10,000. 22,000

Sunnyside av, n s, adj A. W. Monfort on west, 477 3x423.1x339.5x413.5, 26th Ward.
Sunnyside av, n s, at east line of land of City of Brooklyn, 140.11x671.3x235.11x433 6 x786.6x292.4. The two pieces taken together contain 7 394 1000 acres.
Marietta wife of C. Washington Colyer to the City of Brooklyn. 30,596

Sunnyside av, n s, 14 3-1000 acres party in Newtown. John C. Schenck to The City of Brooklyn. 59,402

Sunnyside av, n s, adj. J. C. Schenck on east, 6 203-1000 acres, 26th Ward. Azariah W. Monfort to same. 31,015

Thatford av. w s, 125 s Sutter av, 50x100. Charles Ruskin to Frank Rosenberg. *Mt.* $2,-350. nom

Thatford av, w s, 100 n Dumont av, 25x100. Lewis Hurst to Joseph Morris. 900

Union av, n e cor Johnson av, 50x75. Rosa, Henry, Leopold, Bertha and Emma Newman heirs Phillip Newman to Solomon Blumenstock. 14,300

Vernon av, s s, 82.4 e Lewis av, 18x80. Thomas J. De Gray to Aaron Kodziesen. *Mt.* $3,200. 7,000

Washington av. Party wall agreement. George R. Brown to Francis S. Fitch. nom

Willoughby av, n s, 152.8 e Kent av, 17.6x100. Annie Gabriel to Hester A. McKnight. *Mt.* $2,000. nom

Wyckoff av, n e cor Ralph st, 25x98.1x25x97 3, h & l Gustav Feigenspan to Jacob Blank. $4,500 exch

Wyckoff av, north cor Madison st, 25x94.11x 25x95.7.
St. Nicholas av, s w s, 25 s e Jefferson st, 25x 90.
James M. McNamara to Ignatz Martin. nom

3d av, w s, 120 s 6th st, 20x100. Andrew Halley to Thomas B. Miniter. B. & S. *Mt.* $700. See 76th st. nom

4th av, w s, 58 n 14th st, 56x86.10, h & l. Release mort. Lester A. Lewis to William H. Norris and William Bowers. 3,300

Same property. William H. Norris and William Bowers to D. Brainerd Ray, New York. *Mt.* $20,000. nom

7th av, w s, 20 s 14th st, 40x100. William H. Bierds to William Forkel. *Mt.* $12,500. exch

8th av, s e cor 11th st, 30x82, h & l. *Mt.* $14,-000.
8th av, e s, bet 11th and 12th sts, 18x100, h & l. *Mt.* $5,000.
Allison V. B. Norris and William C. Turner contracts to exchange above property with George Potts for farm 151¾ acres in Blooming Grove, Pa., with appurtenances. —

9th av, e s, extends from 16th to Windsor pl, 200x90.
9th av, n e cor 16th st, 50x97.10.
John Assip and Timothy J. Buckley to William Post. 26,000

9th av, e s, 20.2 n 18th st, 20x100. Michael Smith to Patrick Smith. 2,750

10th av, s e cor 71st st, 100x100, h & l, Bay Ridge Park. Bay Ridge Park Improvement Co. to Fred. C. Cocheu 6,000

24th av, n w s, 200 s w 86th st. 60x96.8, Bensonhurst. James D. Lynch to Joseph Assenheim. 1,050

24th av, n w s, 140 s w 86th st, 60x96.8, Bensonhurst. Same to Louis J. Assenheim. 1,050

25th av, s s, 499.1 w Harway av, 82.4x83.1x6 6, Gravesend. Patrick Keady recvr to Michael Murphy. B. & S. 810

25th av, n s, 471.2 w Harway, 193.4 to Gravesend Bay, x30.7 to The Brooklyn City R. R. Co.'s land, x194.8, Gravesend. Same to The Brooklyn City R. R. Co. B. & S. 3,525

Lots 123 and 141 map Henry Lehmann, Canarsie, Flatlands. Release mort. John Z. Lott to Henry Lehmann. 250

Lots 41, 42, 47 and 48 map heirs of Samuel G. Stryker, Gravesend. Michael Dowling to William H. McMahon. 900

Lot 141 map 151 lots town of Gravesend, surveyed by Charles Crook, 1889. William H. McMahon to Michael Dowling. 200

Lots 166-169 block 4 map No. 1 Cowenhoven farm, New Utrecht. Effingham H. Nichols to Charles J. Kinsey. 720

Lots 183-187 and 226-230 map of H. C. Pfalzgraf property, New Utrecht. Contract, Hanz C. Pfalzgraf to Adolph Ketchum. 2,600

Lots 119, 200, 234, 235, 299, 300 and 310 map 405 of J. Wechsler, Flatbush. William Matthews et al. exrs and trustees Henry Johnson to Joseph Wechsler. 825

Lots 414 and 415, New Utrecht, h & ls. William P. Rae to Albert E. Chamberlin. 3,750

Lot bet Major R. De Russey and N. Court and Esther Stillwell, 85x280, Gravesend. William H. Stillwell to Jane E. Johnson. nom

Parcel on Jamaica Bay, Flatlands, 75x200, with right of way to Rockaway av. Henry Lohman to The Canarsie Yacht Club. *Mt.* $600. 1,000

Section 86 on commissioners' map for opening and grading 18th av, New Utrecht. John H. Maloney to Mary F. and Margaret A. Maloney. gift

Road leading from the Brooklyn and Jamaica plank road Van Wicklen Mill at Plunders Neck at intersection of the new road leading from said road to New Lots, 6 72-100 acres, h & ls. James D. Davies to John C. Blackwell. 6,500

General release, especially from a pending action at law. Clara Hausten to George A. Reynolds. 1,000

WESTCHESTER COUNTY.

AUGUST 12 TO 18—INCLUSIVE.

CORTLANDT.

Catlin, Austin H. and ano. to Nathan L. Ely, lot 12 n s Bay st, map property grantors, 40 x150. $400

EASTCHESTER.

Archer, Gilbert F. to Henrietta J. De Graw, s e cor 8th av and Bridge st, 50x100. 6,500

Gescheidt, Albert F. to Max Bonaventura, lots 66 and 84 South Washingtonville. 1,400

Miller, Louise to Karoline Gundlach, part lot 408 n w s Greenwich st, West Mt. Vernon, 40x125. 1,600

Murray, Jas. to Thos. Leonard, lots 5 and 6 s s Highland av, East Waverly, 200x210x200x 200. 1,300

Martens, Edw. to Edmund H. Sheaff, w s Cottage pl, 100 s Sidney av, 50x125. 3,500

Sheaff, Edmund H. to Edw. Martens, e s Park av, 150 s Sidney, 50x125. 3,500

Treuer, Wm. H. to Geo. W. Bard, n s Monroe st, 234 e Franklin av, 25x91. 350

GREENBURGH.

Bassford, Abrm. to Anna M Korman, n s road from Central av to Harts Corners, adj M. E. Church, 150x—. 1,500

Buchanan, Jane to Eugene Jones, w s Broadway, adj Caruthers, 2 acres. 21,000

Jones, Cyrus P. and ano. to Edwin C. Johnson, lots 33 and 34 map lot at Ardsley. 270

Same to Henry H. Schop, lots 6, 7 and 8. 650

Same to Paul Lindberg, lots 193 and 194. 190

Same to Wm. A. Walton, lots 170-173. 400

Same to Annie M. Simms, lots 104 and 105. 360

Same to Chas. Schneider, lots 160 and 161. 200

Same to Chas F. Kranz, lots 175 and 176. 310

Same to Margt. Hilley, lots 23 and 24. 300

Same to Johanna Hilley, lots 20, 21 and 22. 495

Same to William Devereux, lot 86. 255

Same to Sarah Devereux, lot 87. 255

Same to Jas. Coalter, lots 110-113. 520

Same to Robt. C. Phair, lots 45, 46, 61 and 62. 800

Same to Cath. Rogers, lots 146 and 147. 215

MOUNT PLEASANT.

Smadbeck, Louis to Lena E. Schofield, lots 1016 and 1017, Sherman Park. 350

Same to Julias A. Weigand, lots 200 and 201. 300

Same to Jas. H. Gannon, lots 1106 and 1107. 400

Same to Henrietta Delalie, lot 1158. 250

Same to Eichold & Miller, lots 244-247. 500

Same to Margt. E. McDonald, lot 1066. 200

Same to Johanna Weis, lot 37. 150

Same to Martin Weis, lot 602. 150

NEW ROCHELLE.

Ferguson, Geo. to Edw. B. Tefft, w s Centre av, adj grantee, 75x141. 300

Gregg, Jas. A. S. to Edw. A. Seymour, s e cor Pelhamville road and Mayflower av, abt 80x 125. 900

Manhattan Life Ins. Co. to Harriet H. Thompson, lot 14 block F, Rochelle Park. 1,700

OSSINING.

Kipp, Martha H. to Fanny M. Spencer, n s Croton turnpike, adj S. R. Stone, 11 acres. 9,000

PELHAM.

Horton, Geo. W. to Elizb. H. McLure, e s Main st, 50 s Pilot av, 50x110. 500

Sparks, Wm. H. to Eastchester Investment Co., lot 347 s s 6th st, Pelhamville, 100x100. 600

RYE.

Belmont, Frank W. to Geo. H. Du Euisson, s w cor Regent and West sts, 400x100. 13,000

Kelemen, Jane E. exr. of to Abner B. Mills, lots 3, 7, 8, 20, 22, 36, 38, 49, 50 and 51 map West Rye. 2,300

Merritt, Jas. S. et al. to Hannah Flood, s e cor West William and Ridge sts, abt 500x123. 1,375

Whittemore, John H. to Frank Gralla, lot 40 n s Irenbyl av, grantors map, 50x153. 400

WESTCHESTER.

Camp, Hugh N. to Jos. Harth, lot 330 map McGraw estate. 175

Same to Morris Dworetzky, lots 331 and 332. 350

Same to Jas. T. McGovern, lots 15, 16 and 17. 1,350

Cipolla, Carmine to Dora A. Williams, lot 359 n s 5th av, Wakefield, 100x114. 5,200

Dexter, Fred. C. to Bertha K. Wirman, part lot 1135 w s 2d st, Wakefield, 27.4x105. 2,000

Mace, Levi H. to Constant J. Sperco, lots 173-176 and 254-257, Laconia Park. 1,700

Place, R. Nelson to Geo. Herold, lot 86 n s 4th st, Unionport, 100x108. nom

Suby, Martin to Wm. V. Ruppert, lots 250 and 251 n s 12th av, Wakefield, 205x114. 3,000

WHITE PLAINS.

Butler, Chas. to Wm. A. Rowley, the Wright farm e s Broadway, 51½ acres. 34,000

Rowley, Wm. A. to Mt. Morris Real Estate Assoc., same property. 34,000

YONKERS

Barnes, Ella L. to Frank McElroy, lot 72 w s 1st st, map Hyatt Farm. 650

Frey, Rev. Bonaventure to Christian Kolosius, lots 29 and 31 w s Constant av, map property grantor and ano., 50x100. 600

Same to Henry Spruck, lots 33 and 35, adj above. 600

Same to John C. M. Jacob, lots 37 and 39, adj above. 600

Same to Aug. Zeininger, lots 41 and 43, adj above. 600

Same to Eleanor Kunz, lots 45, 47 and 49, adj above. 1,200

Same to Anthony Kunz, lots 51, 53 and 55, adj above. 1,200

Same to Clemens Henger, lots 49, 51, 53 and 55 Shounard pl, same map. 2,000

Herriott, J. Groshon exr. of G. Le Cate Myers, lot 92 e s Beech st. 300

Same to Minnie Sutherland, lot 93, adj above. 485

Lawrence, Fannie E. to John H. McCabe, part lot 253 Hyatt Farm. 250

Shounard, Fred to Cath. Rafferty, lot 719 Nepperhan av, City map. 200

Wales, Jane H. to Anna Wallace, lot 5 n s Odell av, map Gray Oak, 88.9x211. nom

Wallwork, Sarah to Edw. L. Peene, n s Maple st, 126.3 e Lincoln st, 25x134. 3,000

MORTGAGES.

NOTE.—*The arrangement of this list is as follows. The first name is that of the mortgagor, the next that of the mortgagee. The description of the property then follows, then the date of the mortgage, the time for which it was given, and the amount. The general dates used as headings are the dates when the mortgage was handed into the Register's office to be recorded.*

Whenever the letters "P. M." occur, preceded by the name of a street, in these lists of mortgages, they mean that it is a Purchase Money Mortgage, and for fuller particulars see the list of transfers under the corresponding date. Whenever the rate is not given, read as 6 per cent.

NEW YORK CITY.

AUGUST 14, 15, 17, 18, 19, 20.

Arnold, Eliza wife of and Edmund S. F. to THE TITLE GUARANTEE AND TRUST CO. 1st av, No. 502, e s, 24.8 n 29th st, 24.8x75. Aug. 14, 3 years, 5 %. $7,000

Aust, Harriet to The Home Mutual Building and Loan Assoc. 165th st, n s, 33.6 w Jackson av, 16.8x71. Aug. 15, installs. 1,600

Aymar, Benjamin, Orange, N. J., to Frederic J. Middlebrook, Brooklyn. 8th av, n e cor 34th st, 59x60. Aug. 15, 1 year or sooner, 5 %. 5,000

Aymar, Benjamin, East Orange, N. J., to THE CONNECTICUT MUTUAL LIFE INS. CO., of Hartford, Conn. 8th av, n e cor 34th st, 59x60. Aug. 18, 1 year, 5 %. 5,000

Armbrust, Henry, Union Hill, N. J., to Henry Morgenthau. 179th st. P. M. June 15, 3 years, 5 %. 3,325

Same to Frank Yoran. Same property. Aug. 20, 6 months, 5 %. 175

Blumauer, Jacob to Henry Morgenthau. Audubon av, n w cor 180th st. P. M. June 12, due June 15, 1894, 5 %. 2,800

Same to same. Audubon av, s w cor 182d st. P. M. June 12, due June 15, 1894, 5 %. 8,575

Same to same. Kingsbridge road, s e cor 182d st. P. M. June 12, due June 15, 1894, 5 %. 3,360

Bornhagen, Dorothea wife of and Frederick to THE EMIGRANT INDUSTRIAL SAVINGS BANK. Bond st, n s, 106.6 w Bowery, runs west 25 x north 75 x east 19.6 x south 50 x east 5.6 x south 25. Aug. 18, 1 year, 4½ %. 8,000

Brushaber, Louis to THE BOWERY SAVINGS BANK. Macombs Dam road, e s, lot 4 map of Thomas W. Ludlow, 24th Ward, except part taken for Burnside av. Aug. 18, 1 year, 4½ %. 5,000

Balzer, Nicholas to Thomas Rothmann. Willett st, w s, 79.2 n Stanton st, runs west 50.1 x north 4.11 x west 25.1 x north 25.1 x east 75 to Willett st, x south 30.1. Lease. Aug. 1, 1 year, 5 %. 2,000

Beaudet, Homer J. to The Bradley & Currier Co. (Lim.) Boulevard or Public Drive, s w cor 85th st. 102.5x98.7x102.2x100.10. Aug. 13, 3 months. 8,000

Same to The East River Mill and Lumber Co. Same property. Sub. to last mort. Aug. 13, 1 month. 16,000

Same to The Bradley & Currier Co. (Lim.) 27th st, n s, 368 w 9th av, 82.11x98.9. Aug. 13, 3 months. 6,000

Same to Manchester & Philbrick. Same property. Sub. to last mort. Aug. 13, 3 months. 17,000

Beaudet, John and Ernest P. to Manchester & Philbrick. Mount Morris av, s w cor 121st st, 100.11x100. Sub. to morts. Aug. 18, 3 months. 4,000

Buckley, Daniel to John H. Eden. Highbridge st. P. M. July 30, due Aug. 15, 1893. 6,500

Bleier, Ignatz to Sarah Wertheimer. 8th st, s s, 308.4 e Av B, 19.10x97.6. Aug. 17, installs, 5 %. 2,300

Bliss, Eliza S. wife of Charles F. mortgagor with Dwight H. Olmstead exr. Noah T. Pike mortgagee. Extension of mort. at 5 %. June 4. nom

Burne, William C to William Stone trustee. 78th st, Nos. 164–170, s s, 150 w 3d av, 100x102.2. Sub. to morts. July 30, due Sept. 1, 1891. 8,785

Barrett, John to Charles H. Meserau. Cedar st or pl, n s, 75 e Forest av, 25x100. Aug. 17, 3 years, 5½ %. 2,200

Becker, John to THE DRY DOCK SAVINGS INST. 3d st, s s, 98 e Av A, 22x88.6; 3d st, s s, 120 e Av A, 24.9x105.11x24.4x105.11. Aug. 19, due Aug. 20, 1892, 5 %. See Conveys. 26,000

Bensel, Rebecca widow to Alice S. Constant. Morton st, s s, 205 e Hudson st, 25x100. Aug. 7, due May 31, 1892, 5 %. gold, 1,000

Cain, Joseph H. to Henry Morgenthau. Audubon av, e s, 21.11 s 178th st. P. M. June 15, 3 years, 5 %. 3,409

Same to same. 179th st, n s, 95 e Audubon av. P. M. June 15, 3 years, 5 %. 4,560

Same to same. 179th st, n s, 170 e Audubon av. P. M. June 15, 3 years, 5 %. 3,040

Same to same. 180th st, s s, 120 e Audubon av. P. M. June 15, 3 years, 5 %. 5,009

Same to same. 179th st, n s. 150 w Audubon av. P. M. June 15, 3 years, 5 %. 3,325

Same to same. 178th st, n s, 175 w Audubon av. P. M. June 15, 3 years, 5 %. 2,870

Same to same. 182d st, s s, 120 e Audubon av. P. M. June 15, 3 years, 5 %. 3,150

Same to same. 182d st, s s, 170 e Audubon av. P. M. June 15, 3 years, 5 %. 3,150

Cavinato, Luigi, Steffano, Natale and Guiseppe to Harriet A. Phelps trustee George D. Phelps dec'd. 53d st, No. 419, n s, 275 w 9th av, 25x100.5. Aug. 14, 3 years, 5 %. gold, 20,000

Same to Marx and Moses Ottinger. Same property. Sub. to last mort. Aug. 14, 1 month. 2,101

Same to The Bradley & Currier Co. (Lim.). Same property. Sub. to morts. $22,101. Aug. 14, 1 month. 8,403

Crawford, George mortgagor with Louis Dannhauser mortgagee. Extension of mortgage at increased interest. Aug. 7. nom

Conover, Daniel D. to THE QUEENS COUNTY BANK. Av A, s w cor 24th st, 49.5x81.5. Sub. to mort. $25,000. Aug. 17, note, 3 months. 25,000

Curran, John J. and William A. to Merced D. M. and Emilia J. B. Greene. 52d st, s s, 131.8 w 10th av, 45x100.5x51.10x—. Aug. 17, 3 years, 5 %. gold, 10,000

Same to Margaret Curran. Same property. Aug. 18, 3 years, 5 %. gold, 2,500

Same to Josephine Curran. Same property. Aug. 18, 3 years, 5 %. gold, 2,500

Conner, William M. to Milton Robbins individ. and as trustee. Broadway, s w cor 26th st, St. James Hotel. Lease. Aug. 18, demand. 75,000

Donnellon, John to Sarah H. Powell. 145th st, s s, 260 e Amsterdam av, 40x99.11. Aug. 13, 3 months. 20,000

Deegan, Edward J. to Jacob Ramsteck. Jefferson av. P. M. Aug. 17, 3 years, 5 %. 500

Dreyfus, Julius to Jonas Weil and Bernhard Mayer. 3d av. P. M. Aug. 13, demand. 6,000

Dale, Anna T. wife of James S. to Orison B. Smith trustee Anne Seguin. 139th st, s s, 250 e Willis av, 25x100. July 10, 3 years, 5 %. gold, 15,000

Dautel, John G. to Margaretha Widman. 163d st, n s, 200 e Washington av, 100x217.10. Aug. 15, due July 1, 1894, 5 %. 6,000

Delhougne, Henry to Carrie Bock. 3d st. P. M. Aug. 17, due Aug. 1, 1892, 5 %. 1,800

Donohue, Michael J., Charles W. Callahan and Katie his wife, William Kenyon and Ettie his wife to Margaret Brown. Eagle av. P. M. Aug. 15, due March 28, 1893, 5 %. 200

Dresber, Bernard to Isaac Schlachter. Sheriff st, No. 81, w s, 125 n Rivington st, 25x100. Aug. 17, installs. 4,000

Epstein, Samuel to John H. Burt. 62d st, n s, 279 w 1st av, 17x100.5. Sub. to mort. $3,900. Aug. 10, due Aug. 13, 1892. 2,000

Eveleth, Walter, Joseph J. Kelly and George W. Comstack stockholders of Eveleth Printing Co. Consent to mortgage of company's properties and franchises for $5,000. Aug. 14.

Eagleton, Thomas to Augustus T. Gillender committee of Alice F. M. Wood. South 5th av, Nos. 196, 198 and 200, w s, 120.11 n Grand st, 59.5x70; South 5th av, e s, 125 n Grand st, 25x100. July 28, 3 years, 5 %. 21,000

Ely, Goddard, Alice S. wife of and Ely to Mary L. March extrx. John P. March. 15th st, No. 27, n s, 520 e 6th av, 25x103.3. Aug. 18, 3 years, 5 %. gold, 25,000

Ersley, Bertha M. with Buffalo Door and Sash Co. both mortgagees. Agreement as to priority of mortgages made by Conrad Muller, Jr. July 22. nom

Eggers, George W. to Julia S. Bryant, Cummington, Mass. 100th st, No. 19, n s. 224 6 w 8th av, 25x100.11. Aug. 19, 3 years, 5 %. gold, 15,000

Same to same. 100th st, No. 21, n s, 249 6 w 8th av, 25.6x100.11. Aug. 19, 3 years, 5 %. gold, 15,000

Same to Joseph Fox. 100th st, n s, 100 w Central Park West, 175x100.11. Sub. to morts. $92,000. Aug. 19, due Oct. 9, 1891. 8,000

Eltz, Jacob to Charles Lehritter. 54th st, n s, 175 w 10th av, 100x100.5. Aug. 18, due Sept. 1, 1893, 5 %. 4,000

Flannery, Thomas E. to Conrad Stein. Greenwich st, No. 802. Saloon lease. Aug 12. 3,564

Finley, John to THE EMIGRANT INDUST. SAVINGS BANK. Ridge st, w s, 81.6 s Broome st, 20x75. Aug. 14, 1 year, 4½ %. 5,000

First Hungarian Congregation Ohab Zedek to THE MUTUAL LIFE INS. CO. of New York. Norfolk st, e s, 175 s Houston st, 100x100. Already mortgaged to mortgagee. Aug. 5, due Aug. 12, 1892, 5 %. 10,000

Fish, John, New York, and Jacob Miller, Long Island City, to Henri Strasbourger. 28th st, n s, 125 w 2d av, 25x98.9. Sub. to mort. $23,000. Aug. 14, 2 years or sooner. 5,000

Frohwitter, Henry to Sophie and John Bohnet exrs. and trustees Mary Braun. Goerck st. P. M. Aug. 13, 3 years, 5 %. 7,000

Same to Katharine Meusch. Same property. P. M. Sub. to last mort. Aug. 13, due Nov. 1, 1892. 1,500

Fritz, Egbert P. to Alice A. Hallock and ano. exrs. George G. Hallock. 26th st, No. 250, s s, 215.6 e 8th av, 21.4x98.9. Aug. 14, 1 year, 5 %. 10,000

Gautier, Marguerite wife of Celestin to The Empire State Widows and Orphans Society. 40th st. P. M. Aug. 14, due Sept. 15, 1891, 5 %. 6,000

Gallup, Albert to Samuel N. Hoyt. 12th st, No. 5 E., n s, 25x114x26x107. Aug. 19, 1 year. gold, 2,000

Herbert, Daniel to Deborah A. Haviland, Brooklyn. 54th st, n s, 394 e 1st av, 50x100.5. Aug. 13, due July 1, 1894, or sooner, 5 %. 5,000

Hoyt, Ellen M. wife of and Russell P. with James H. Smith and Abel Crook. Trust agreement affecting property on n s of 74th st and out-of-town property. Jan. 17, 1888. nom

Herdtfelder, Elizabeth to George L. Pease trustee Augustus Brown. Eldridge st, e s, 125 n Stanton st, 25x87.6. Aug. 14, 3 years, 5 %. 12,500

Hopkins, Thomas and Margaret his wife to Franklin Seymour. Weeks st, n w cor 174th st, 50x100. July 1, 5 years. 600

Heilbrunn, Pauline to Simon Haberman. 11th av, w s, 25.5 s 48th st, 75x70. Aug. 15, 3 months. 5,000

Henry, David to Mary J. Henry. 121st st, s s, 325.4 e 2d av, 24 8x100.11. Aug. 10, 5 years, 5 %. 3,000

Herrman, Morris S. to J Fred. Pierson. Washington st, Nos. 481–487. P. M. July 20, due May 1, 1895, 5 %. 30,000

Huerstel, Julia wife of Gustav to Sarah L. Myers. Boston road, s e s, 236 n e 165th st, runs east 101.1 to Cauldwell av, x south 97.9 x west 163.10 to road, x northeast 117.1. Aug. 15, due Aug. 17, 1894, 5 %. 8,000

Hulberg, Frederick to Adele Hutton. St. Nicholas av. P. M. Aug. 13, due Sept. 1, 1892, 5 %. 15,750

Hartzell, Hannah C. wife of and Elmer E. to Edward Smith. 2d av, No. 681, s w cor 37th st, 24.9x65x24x65. Aug. 10, 2 years, 5 %. See Conveys. 5,000

Heydecker, Isaac and Abraham Harris mortgagors with John Vincent exr., &c. Extension of mort. Aug. 8. nom

Hagen, Susanna V. to Ernest F. Amsler. Amsterdam av, s w cor 79th st, 102.2x100 Aug. 17, due Nov. 18, 1891. 1,000

Holmes, Benjamin, Brooklyn, to THE MUTUAL LIFE INS. CO. of New York. 39th st, s s, 125 w 1st av, 25x98.9. July 31, due Aug. 18, 1892. 11,000

Same to same. 39th st, s s, 150 w 1st av, 25x98.9. July 31, due Aug. 18, 1892. 11,000

Same to same. 39th st, s s, 175 w 1st av, 25x98.9. July 31, due Aug. 18, 1892. 12,000

Holmes, Benjamin, Brooklyn, to Thomas L. Concklin. 115th st, n s, 245 e 1st av, 25x58.1 x36x85.4. Aug. 30, 3 years, 5 %. 12,000

Hoyt, Ellen M. wife of and Russell P. to Howard and Maria H. Beck. 74th st, n s, 310 e West End av, 20x102.2. July 8, 3 years, 5 %. 18,000

Same to Harmon W. Hendricks. Same property. Sub. to last mort. Aug. 14, due Aug. 19, 1894. 2,250

Same to William C. Spelman, Brooklyn. Same property. Sub. to mort. $20,250. Aug. 13, due Sept. 1, 1892. 6,000

Jacobs, Elias to The Baron de Hirsch Fund. Av A, No. 141. P. M. Aug. 19, 3 years, 5 %. 25,000

Same to same. 9th st, No. 440 E. P. M. Aug. 19, 3 years, 5 %. 6,000

Jordan, James F. to The J. Chr. G. Hüpfel Brewing Co. 9th av, No. 861, s w cor 36th st. Store lease. Aug. 17, demand. 5,000

Jenkins, George and Thomas J. to The Bradley & Currier Co. (Lim.) 118th st, s s, 100 e 8th av, 200x100.11. Sub. to morts. $105,000. July 10, 4 months. 17,200

Judge, Andrew T. to John W. Haaren. 128th st. P. M. Aug. 6, 8 months. 8,000

Jacobson, Morris to Mary Hitchcock, Morristown, N. J. Willett st. P. M. Aug. 17, due Sept. 1, 1892, 5 %. 6,000

Kanenbley, Herman F. exr. August Kanenbley mortgagee to Archibald and John Culbert. Certificate that amount due on mortgage is $12,000. Aug. 14. nom

Kenny, John to Thomas W. Harries, Brooklyn. Gambril st, n s, 346.8 e Marion av, 25x100. Aug. 12, due Aug. 14, 1894. 3,000

Klein, Benedict A. to Alden S. Swan, Brooklyn. Cherry st, No. 270, n s, 156.9 w Jefferson st. Sub. to mort. $16,750. Aug. 20, 3 years. See Conveys. 3,250

Same to same. Cherry st, No. 272. Sub. to mort. $16,750. Aug. 20, 3 years. See Conveys. 3,250

Larkin, William R. to THE HARLEM SAVINGS BANK. St. Nicholas av, e s, 108.8 n 126th st, runs east abt 55.10 x east 41 9 x north 17.2 x west 95.1 to av, x south 17.7. Aug. 13, 1 year, 5 %. 7,000

Laird, Mary C. wife of and James H. to Peter Bauer and Louisa F. his wife. 8th av. P. M. Aug. 13, installs., 5 %. 22,000

Lee, Walter J. to THE METROPOLITAN TRUST CO. trustees Catharine L. Gould. 2d av or road, from Fordham to Williamsbridge, s e s, 150 n e William st, 25x125. Aug. 17, 3 years, 5 %. 4,500

Lewis, Edward to Seth M. Milliken. 160th st, s s, 147.4 e St. Nicholas av, runs south 100 x west 35 x north 50 x west 1 x north 50 to st, x east 36. Building loan. Aug. 14, due July 1, 1892. 10,000

Levinson, Abraham and Alexander Rittmaster to Patrick Gallagher. Madison st, n s, 47.2 e Clinton st. P. M. Aug. 17, installs, 5 %. 5,000

Levy, Simon J. to Joshua W. Bowron, Sing Sing, N. Y. 29th st. P. M. Aug. 15, 5 years, 5 %. 10,000

Little, Joseph J. to THE GREENWICH SAVINGS BANK. 45th st, No. 23, n s, 300 w 5th av, 25 x100.5. Aug. 12, due Aug. 15, 1892, 5 %. 30,000

Lawrence, Gustavus L., Brooklyn, to William C. Renwick et al. trustees William R. Renwick dec'd. Harrison st. P. M. Aug. 6, due Aug. 19, 1894, 5 %. gold, 32,500

Same to Thomas Patten. Same property. P. M. Sub. to last mort. Aug. 6, due Aug. 19, 1892. gold, 10,000

Lynch, Robert V. to David Webster exr. Caroline Webster. St. Nicholas av, e s, 101.8 s 159th st, 25.5x255.7 to Edgecombe av, x 25x 261.11. Sub. to morts. Aug. 19, 2 years. 3,500

Lamb, Tessie A. and Mamie C., Katie C. and John P. Phelan heirs Catherine and Walter Phelan to Sophie Kanenbley. Columbia st, No. 12, e s, 100.2 s Broome st, 21.11x65. 4-5 part. Aug. 20, 2 years, 5 %. 2,000

McKenna, Richard M. to Peter Doelger. 3d av, n w cor 137th st. Lease. Aug. 19, demand. 2,500

Miller, Jacob, L. I. City, and John Fish to Alexander B. Coxe, Philadelphia, Pa. 29th st, No. 237, n s, 125 w 2d av, 25x98.9. Aug. 20, 1 year, 5 %. gold, 22,500

Same to Alexander Brown, Philadelphia. 29th st, No. 239, n s, 100 w 2d av, 25x98.9. Aug. 20, 3 years, 5 %. gold, 22,500

Mitchell, Lewis A. to Addison Thomas et al. trustees of Catherine d'Anglemont, Paris, France. Lexington av, w s, 67.8 s 32d st, 22 x79.11x22x79.10. P. M. Aug. 19, 3 years, 5 %. gold, 11,000

Moore, Hiram M. to THE UNION DIME SAVINGS INST. 114th st, n s, extends from Manhattan av to Morningside av, 68.3x100.11x135x118.9. Aug. 20, due Nov. 1, 1892, 5 %. 110,000

Same to Frederick P. Forster. Same property. Aug. 20, demand. gold, 50,000

Same to M. Dasher Wylly. Same property. Aug. 20, 1 year. 20,000

Moynagh, James T. to Frank Taylor. 120th st. P. M. Aug. 20, due July 1, 1894. 1,000

Mattmuller, Annie to John Bussing, Jr. Prospect av, e s, 69.6 s of proposed new st, 15x100. Aug. 19, installs. 3,000

Same to same. Prospect av, e s, 84.6 s of proposed new st, 15x100. Aug. 19, installs. 3,000

McCormack, Mary A. wife of and Michael to THE BOWERY SAVINGS BANK. 127th st, s s, 310 e Lenox av, 50x99.11. Aug. 19, 1 year, 4½ %. 12,000

Mulch, Theodore H. to Ferdinand Schindele. Amsterdam av, No. 1055, w s, 50.5 n 66th st, 25x90. Aug. 18, due Aug. 1, 1892. 5,000

Marx, David to Edward Oppenheimer and Henry and Edward Hirsh. 8th av. s w cor 114th st. 100.11x225. Aug 19, 1 year or sooner. 85,000

McGinn, John H. to Frederic J. Middlebrook, Brooklyn. 39th st. P. M. Sub. to mort. $9,000. Aug. 15, due Aug. 17, 1892. 1,000

Same to same. Same property. Aug. 15, due Aug. 17, 1894, 5 %. 9,000

Melia, Mary wife of and John F. to THE BOWERY SAVINGS BANK. 41st st. P. M. Aug. 17, 2 years, 4½ %. 12,000

Mulgrew, Rachel wife of William to Henry Morgenthau. 178th st. P. M. June 9, due June 15, 1894, 5 %. 3,000

McCarthy, Julia to Edward Stein. 20th st, No. 204, s s, 520 w 2d av, 20x78. Lease. May 29, 1890, demand. 300

McGerrity, Michael otherwise Garrity to John Ochse. Centre Market pl, No. 1, e s, 72 3 n Grand st, 17.5x58.10x17.5x59.6. Aug. 15, 1 year. 1,000

Merchant, James H. to James Stokes, West Orange, N. J. 119th st. n s, 125 w 5th av, 25x100.10. Aug. 6, 1 year. 18,000

Meyer, Siegmund T. to David B. Hart. Water st. P. M. June 30, 2 years or sooner, 5 %. 3,000

Meyer, Siegmund T. to Robert C. Rudd. Water st, No. 351, s s, 16.4x75. Sub. to morts. $75,000. June 30, 2 years. 2,000

Milhauser, Eliza wife of and Napthali A. to Adelaide Abraham. 3d av. P. M. Aug. 13, demand. 5,000

Miller, Sarah J. wife of Charles, Jr., to Isaac and Abraham L. Fromme. 19th st. P. M. Aug. 13, demand. 1,361

Miller, Eliza L. to Frederick A. Snow. Catharine st, Nos. 53 and 55, e s, 54x106.5x54x103.4. Aug. 18, due Aug. 1, 1892. gold 27,000

Moore, Edward to Isaac N. Hebberd. 127th st, s s, 151 w 3d av. 53.5x99.11. Aug. 10, 1 year. 1,000

Noble, Charles to Nellie B. Mortimer. Central Park West, w s, 90 s 107th st, 30.11x100. Aug. 15, due Aug. 17, 1892, or sooner. 14,132

Neumann, Martha to Israel C. Jones. Washington av, e s, 75.2 s 171st st, 25.1x94.6x25x100.3. July 29, installs. See Conveys. 7,750

Ottiwell, Sarah C. to Anna M. Z. wife of Count Charles F. de Montsaulmin, Paris, France. Webster av. P. M. July 2, 3 years or installs, 5 %. 2,000

Ottinger, Marx and Max S. Korn to The Baron de Hirsch Fund. 2d av, No. 894. P. M. Aug. 19, 3 years, 5 %. 14,000

Same to same. 2d av, No. 896. P. M. Aug. 19, 3 years, 5 %. 14,000

Pfaff, George C. to Samuel L. Laderer. 85th st, n s, 373 e Av A, 25x102.2. Aug. 19, 1 year. 3,500

Pearson, Sorelle to Conrad Stein. 9th av, No. 269. Saloon lease. Aug. 17, demand. 4,396

Parker, Elizabeth F. to Mary E. Stillwell. Stebbins av. P. M. Aug. 14, 3 years, 5 %. 600

Phillips, Hartwig I. to THE GERMAN-AMERICAN REAL ESTATE TITLE GUARANTEE CO. East Houston st. P. M. Aug. 6, due Aug. 13, 1893, 5 %. 12,000

Poissonnier, Henri to John F. Edwards, Brooklyn. 45th st, n s, 250 w 2d av, 25x100.5. Aug. 18, 1 year. 1,500

Pucci, Annunciata wife of and Antonio G. to William Scott. 113th st, n s, 215 w Pleasant av. 25x100.11. Aug. 19, due Sept. 1, 1892. 3,500

Rohrs, Frederick to Theodore M. Barnes exr. and trustee Edwin R. Barnes. 70th st, n s, 273 e Av A, 25x100.5. Aug. 20, 3 years, 5 %. gold, 12,350

Same to Charles S. Longhurst. Same property. Aug. 20, 1 year. gold, 1,000

Ramsey, William H. to George Crawford. 35th st, Nos. 241, 243, 245 n s, 331 e 8th av, 69x98.9. Sub. to morts $62,000. Aug. 14, due Sept. 15, 1891. 500

Rankin, John to THE GERMAN SAVINGS BANK, New York. Cornelia st. n w cor West 4th st, 40.11x75x26.10x76. Aug. 12, due Aug. 14, 1892. See Conveys. 33,000

Rinschler, Alphonse to Hermann Hering. Forest av. P. M. Aug. 6, due Aug. 15, 1896, or installs, 5 %. 5,000

Rabadan, Adeline E. wife of Charles to James J. Phelan trustee Walter Stevenson dec'd. Ernescliff pl, n s, lot 514 map G. F. & H. S. Opdyke, 24th Ward, 25x97.5x25x96 8. July 1, 3 years, 5 %. 2,000

Same to same. St. Georges crescent, s s, 175.9 w Grenada pl, runs west 50 x south 94 x east 25 x south 96.8 to Ernescliff pl, x east 25.4 x north 187.7. July 1, 3 years, 5 %. 2,000

Ruff, Charles to THE UNITED STATES TRUST CO. of New York. 7th st, No. 97½, n s, 142.5 e 1st av, 19x97.6. Aug. 18, due Sept. 1, 1896, 5 %. 19,000

Same to same. 7th st, No. 99, n s, 161.5 e 1st av, 26.4x97.6. Aug. 18, due Sept. 1, 1896, 5 %. 26,000

Rosenbaum, Louis to August Hassey. Av B, w s, 40.2 s 6th st, 47.1x99.6x abt 13x60.1. Aug. 12, due July 1, 1894, or sooner. 3,000

Schreiber, Charles and Barbara his wife to Hugh Thompson. 158th st P. M. Aug. 10, due Aug. 17, 1893, 5 %. 1,200

Schuler, Frederick mortgagor with Francis H. Macy exr. mortgagee. Extension of mort. Aug. 13. nom

Scott, John, Jr., to The F. & M. Schaefer Brewing Co. 3d av, No. 2180; 119th st, No. 186 E. Saloon lease. Aug. 17, demand. 3,000

Sauter, John G. mortgagor with Jemima Thallon mortgagee. Extension of reduced mortgage. July 1. nom

Same with Hewlett Scudder et al. exrs. and trustees Henry J. Scudder. Extension of mortgage and waiver of gold coin payment. Aug. 6. nom

Stevenson, Hugh to James McCloud and John J. Mahony. Edgecombe av or road and 172d st. P. M. Aug. 15, due Aug. 18, 1896, 5 %. 100,000

Siegfried, Adam to Beadleston & Woerz. Duane st, No. 183. Saloon lease. Aug. 10, demand. 2,000

Schirmer, Gustav to THE GERMAN SAVINGS BANK. 16th st, s s, 171 e 4th av, 33x103.3. July 9, 1 year. 50,000

Schloss, Isabella R. wife of Henry W. to William and Louis Ottmann trustees Jacob Ottmann dec'd. 79th st, s s, 85 e 3d av, 20x102.2. Aug. 8, 3 years, 4½ %. 8,000

Stock, Bernhard and Mary his wife to THE HARLEM SAVINGS BANK. Morris av, w s, 100 s 155th st, 25x99.7 to Railroad av, x 28.8x85.7. Already mortgaged to mortgagee Aug. 12, 1 year, 5 %. 750

Sempson, Z. S. to Sarah A. Appleton. Franklin av, e s, 73 n 169th st. P. M. Aug. 17, 3 years, 5 %. 4,950

Same to William G. Appleton. Franklin av, e s, 96.9 n 169th st. P. M. Aug. 17, 3 years or installs. 5 %. 2,550

Sander, Mary, Atlantic City, N. J., to Waldron P. Brown and ano. trustees for Julia E. Brown. 6th st, No. 202, s s, 60.1 e 3d av. P. M. Aug. 7, due Aug. 19, 1894, 5 %. gold, 10,000

Same to Julia E. Soutter trustee James T. Soutter, Jr., dec'd. 6th st, No. 204, s s. 82.8 e 3d av. P. M. Aug. 7, due Aug. 19, 1894, 5 %. gold, 15,000

Sander, Mary, Atlantic City, N. J., to George H. Byrd. Bowery. P. M. Secures bond of mortgagor and Christian Sander. Aug. 17, due Aug. 19, 1894, 5 %. gold, 24,000

Seagrist, Francis W., Jr., to Nicholas Seagrist. Boulevard (11th) av, w s, extends from 140th to 141st st, 199.10x125. Aug. 18, due Jan. 1, 1892. 4,000

Sedgwick, Henry D. mortgagor with Caroline L. Nones mortgagee. Extension of mort. Principal to be paid in gold coin. Aug. 9. nom

Sergeant, Alice P. wife of and Joseph R. to THE MUTUAL LIFE INS. CO. of New York. Troy st, e s, 115.4 s Sidney st, 187.1x238 to w s Berrian st proposed, x249.3x271. Aug. 15, 1 year. 8,000

Spiess, Caspar, Brooklyn, to Mary A. Rabbage. 14th st, n s, 216 e Av A, 25x103.3. Aug. 15, 1 year. 1,000

Sackett, Sarah E. to THE TITLE GUARANTEE AND TRUST CO. 126th st, No. 19, n s, 212.6 e 5th av, 17.5x99.11. Aug. 18, 3 years, 5 %. gold, 10,000

Schmitt, Florian and Anna his wife to Joseph Henning. Willis av, e s, 50 n 146th st, 25x100. Aug. 1, 5 years or sooner. 5½ %. 10,000

Stark, William to Samuel L. Berrian. Fort Independence st. P. M. Aug. 19, 3 years, 5 %. 400

Taylor, Mary H. wife of and Thomas B., Rye, N. Y., to Josephine Wandell. 54th st, No. 115, n s, 124.10 e 4th av, 16.10x100.5. Aug. 20, due Jan. 20, 1893, 5 %. 1,000

Tipping, Edward to William Halls Sons. 69th st, n s, 275 w Columbus av, 75x100.5. Aug. 14, due Feb. 1, 1892, or sooner. 20,000

Thompson, Olivia wife of George W. to THE TWELFTH WARD SAVINGS BANK. 3d av, w s, 68.7 s 128th st, 16.8x100. Aug. 15, 1 year, 5 %. 7,000

The Church of the Archangel to The Corporation of Trinity Church. St. Nicholas av, s w s, 58.11 s e 118th st, 57.5x117.5x50x87.9. Sub. to mort. $17,000. July 7, 2 years, 5 %. 8,000

The House of the Holy Comforter Free Church Home for Incurables to Adele Kneeland and Alice K. Munroe. 2d av, No. 149, w s, 72.10 n 9th st, 32.5x125. Aug. 10, 1 year, 5 %. 4,000

Treu, Leopold R. to Hollister Mfg. Co. Fox st, w s, 161 n 165th st, 50x100. Aug. 17, demand. 779

Ullman, Adolph and Samuel to Ignatz and Sigmund Friedman. Houston st. P. M. Aug. 18, installs. 2,000

Von Oehsen, Adolph to Peter Doelger. 7th av, No. 781, n e cor 51st st, 22.5x75. Lease. Aug. 13, demand. 7,000

Weissmann, Herman and Frank J. Britt to William Drought, New York, and Charles J. Carew, Norwich, Conn. 36th st. P. M. Aug. 13, installs. 4,500

Wodzicki, Peter C. and Theodora C. his wife, Brooklyn, to Karl M. Wallach. 75th st. P. M. July 17, installs. 10,000

Wallenstein, Solomon to Benjamin Oestreicher. 101st st. P. M. Sub. to mort. $8,000. Aug. 15, 2 years, 5 %. 1,000

Walters, Louisa M. formerly Cregier to John A. Weekes, Jr. 116th st, n s, 159 e 1st av, 18x100.10. Aug. 17, due Nov. 1, 1892. 2,000

Wiessner, Oscar E. A., Brooklyn, N. Y., to Isidor V. Wittenberg. Eldridge st. P. M. Aug. 13, due Dec. 15, 1891. 2,000

Wendel, Katie, Jr., formerly Neber to Edward Karsch. Amsterdam av, w s, 99.11 n 181st st. 70.1x100x72.4x100. Aug. 17, 1 year. 2,000

Williams, Richard and Edward Jones to Judson S. Todd. Lexington av, n e cor 54th st, 25.5x100. Aug. 17, due Jan. 1, 1892. 36,500

Weinstein, Ascher to Frederic J. Middlebrook, Brooklyn. 27th st, n s, 159.7 e 8th av. P. M. Aug. 19, 1 year or sooner, 5 %. 11,000

Same to same. 27th st, n s, 184.5 e 8th av. P. M. Aug. 19, 1 year or sooner, 5 %. 11,000

Wedemeyer, Arnold J. D. Liberty, N. Y., to Claus Haaren. 32d st, n s, 150 e 11th av. P. M. Sub. to morts. $7,000. Aug. 20, 3 years or sooner. 4,000

Same to same. 32d st, n s, 200 e 11th av. P. M. Sub. to mort. $6,000. Aug. 20, 3 years or sooner. 4,000

Williams, Richard D. to Benjamin Nors. Main Post road from New York to Boston. P. M. July 30, 2 years. 700

Zahn, Franz and Ida his wife to Sarah H. Hewlett, Brooklyn. Dutch st, e s, 102.11 s Fulton st, 22.8x72.11x23.11x72. Lease. Aug. 17, 5 years. gold, 3,000

KINGS COUNTY.

AUGUST 13, 14, 15, 17, 18, 19.

Adams, Matilda E. to Earl A. Gillespie, Woodhaven, L. I. Thatford av. P. M. July 2, due Oct. 1, 1891. $550

Adler, Herman to Ernst Goetz. Warwick st, w s, 200 s Liberty av, 25x100. Aug. 8, 3 years. 300

Ahmeier, Conrad, Flushing, L. I., to Margarethe A. E. Douglas. Jefferson st, s e s, 100 s w Central av, 25x100. Aug. 14, 5 years, 4 %. 6,000

Ahrens, Caspar to Henry F. Rosenbrock. Hamilton av, n e s, 111.4 s e Centre st, runs northeast 38.2 x north 51.2 to Centre st. x west 14.2 x south 37.4 x southwest 37.6 to av, x southeast 19.7. Aug. 14, due July 1, 1894, 5 %. 2,000

Albertson, Herbert to Charles J. Hoernlein. Herkimer st. P. M. Aug. 15, installs., 5 %. 700

Alrich, Sherwood to The West Brooklyn Land and Improvement Co. 55th st. P. M. July 25, due Aug. 1, 1894, 5 %. 350

Ascher, Mary to Kate A. wife of Charles Killeen. Dean st. P. M. Aug. 17, due Aug. 18, 1894, 3½ %. 300

Assenheim, Louis J. to James D. Lynch. 24th av, n w s, 140 s w 86th st. Aug. 6, due Aug. 14, 1893, 5 %. See Conveys. 735

Same to same. 24th av, n w s, 200 s w 86th st. Aug. 6, due Aug. 14, 1893, 5 %. See Conveys. 735

Aston, Frederick, Alfred A. and Walter F. to Elizabeth and William G. Walter. Java st, s s, 175 e Oakland st, 25x100. Sub. to mort. $700. Aug. 1, 1 year, 5 %. 400

Atkins, David J. to The Title Guarantee and Trust Co. 13th st, s s, 175 w 8th av, 122.10x100. Aug. 13, demand. 23,500

Banker, John to Caroline E. Morton. 6th st. P. M. Aug. 4, 3 years, 5 %. 3,000

Baldinger, Louis to Morris Handler, Newark, N. J. Hopkins st, s s, 125 e Marcy av, 18.9x100. Aug. 10, due Feb. 10, 1894, 5 %. 525

Balling, August E. H. to The East Brooklyn Savings Bank, Brooklyn. Park av, n e cor Franklin av, 40x77.9. Aug. 13, 1 year, 5 %. 6,500

Barnett, Rosa wife of and Morris and Hulda wife of Benjamin Hill to Michael Minden. Pennsylvania av, w s, 175 n Glenmore av, 25x100. Aug. 18, 1 year, 4 %. 1,000

Bassett, Elizabeth. Woodhaven, L. I., to Dora Krauss. Liberty av, s s, 25 w Georgia av, 25x100. Aug. 15, due July 1, 1893, 5 %. 500

Bauer, Gustav A. H. to Louis Bauer. Kosciusko st, s s, 300 e Reid av, 25x100. Aug. 17, 5 years, 5 %. 400

Same to Margaret Emrich. Same property. P. M. Aug. 17, 2 years, 5 %. 2,700

Beer, Louis and Michael Schaffner to Kings Co. Savings Inst. Floyd st, n s, 215 e Nostrand av, 25x100. Aug. 15, 1 year, 5 %. 4,000

Bennett, Hannah to Caroline E. Morton. 57th st, n s, 380 e 3d av, 20x100.2. Aug. 17, 3 years, 5 %. 3,000

Bessler, John to George Schade. Cleveland st, e s, 125 n Eastern Parkway, 25x98. P. M. July 30, 5 years. 1,800

Same to same. Cleveland st, e s. 125 n Eastern Parkway. 2d P. M. July 30, installs. 600

Best, Louis and Barbara to Lena Weis. De Kalb av, s w s, 300 n e Irving av, 25x100. Aug. 15, 3 years, 5 %. 1,400

Betts, Elmira to Lizzie Gray. Bushwick av, south cor Kossuth pl, 23.5x72x23.5x71.6. Aug. 17, 3 years. 500

Bevington, Charles E. to Hannah Hitchings extrx. Charles F. Hitchings. Arlington av, s s, 50 e Cleveland st, 25x100. Aug. 13, due Aug. 1, 1894. 3,000

Bigelow, Anna E. to Caroline A. Rushmore. 53d st, s w s, 90 n w 4th av, 20x100.2. Aug. 18, 3 years, 5 %. 2,500

Bittorf, John and Caroline his wife to Otto Singer. Greene av, n w s, 474.6 s w Central av, 18.6x100. Aug 13, 3 years, 5 %. 1,500

Blackwell, John C. to James D. Davies. Road leading from Brooklyn and Jamaica plank road and Van Wicklen's mill, &c. P. M. Aug. 14, 5 years or installs. 5,300

Blankenfeld, Louis to Ella M. Van Brunt. 81st st. P. M. Aug. 15, 3 years, 5 %. 300

Blazo, Augustus W. to Edwin C. Low. Lewis av, s w cor Putnam av, 22x90. May 12, 1 year, 5 %. 5,000

Blinn, Ernest H. to Title Guarantee and Trust Co. Broadway, north cor Stewart st, 20x75. Aug. 19, 3 years, 5 %. 5,000

Blumenstock, Solomon to Rosa, Henry, Leopold, Jennie, Bertha and Emma Newman. Union av, n e cor Johnson av. P. M. Aug. 15, 5 years, 5 %. 4,000

Bond, Thomas A. to Ellen wife of Michael F. Lyons. 9th st, n s, 172.10 e 7th av, 19.6x100. Aug. 14, due in Aug., 1894, 5 %. 5,000

Bonert, Louis to The Title Guarantee and Trust Co. 10th st, s w s, 399.8 s e 7th av, 80.4x100. Aug. 14, demand. 20,000

Bopp, Adolph to Anna M. Bopp his wife. Sands st. n s. 125 w Hudson av, 25x100. Aug. 15, due July 1, 1892. 1,000

Bormann, Sophia J. to William L Middendorf. East New York av, s s, 200 e Albany av, 30x100. Aug. 1, 1 year, 5 %. 1,400

Boyan, Julia to Jacob Ruppert, New York. Broadway, n e cor Roebling st. Store lease. Aug. 6, demand. 3,000

Brophy, Patrick to George W. Chauncey. Bradford st. P. M. Aug. 15, 3 years, 5 %. 2,000

Buchenholz, Bernard to Lena Fischer. Seigel st. P. M. Aug. 14, installs., 5 %. 1,200

Calicchio, Francesco to Margaret C. McCaffrey. North 5th st. P. M. Aug. 17, 5 years, 5 %. 2,400

Callaghan, Bernard to Atlantic Co-operative Savings and Loan Assoc. Degraw st, s s, 300 w Smith st, 25x100. Aug. 19, installs. 5,400

Cassidy, John T. to Elizabeth A. Walters. Skillman st, e s, 132.9 n Myrtle av, 25x100. Aug. 10, 3 years. 1,500

Chamberlin, Albert E. to William P. Rae. Lots 414 and 415 block 13 map 1,197 lots, Flatbush and New Utrecht, of W. Ziegler. P. M. Aug. 11, installs. 1,800

Christen, John to Title Guarantee and Trust Co. Evergreen av and Eldert st. P. M. Aug. 18, 1 year, 5 %. 5,000

Same to James Gascoine individ. and with ano. exrs. John G. Cozine. Same property. 2d mort. Aug. 18, installs. 3,500

Cochen, Fred. C. to Cornelius Cowenhoven. 10th av and 71st st. P. M. Aug. 17, due Nov. 1, 1894. 3,500

Cook, De Witt D. to Mary B. Ward, Walter R. Gilbert, Jr., Thomas C and John B. H Oakley. Av D and Ocean Parkway, Flatbush. P. M. Aug. 15, due Mar. 24, 1893, 5 %. 3,000

Conradi, Marie widow to Edward Krueger guard. Alexander Conradi. Stockton st, s s, 190 e Nostrand av, 25x92.3. Aug. 1, demand, 5 %. 1,200

Corey, Charles to James Gascoine individ. and with Anna E. Cozine exrs. John G. Cozine. Bay 32d st, New Utrecht. July 17, 2 years, 5 %. 500

Crossman, Greenleaf W., New York, to F. Augustus Conkling. Macon st. P. M. Aug. 12, installs, 5 %. 2,400

Crossman, Greenleaf W. to William L. Beers. Prospect pl, s s, 84 w Buffalo av. P. M. Aug. 15, 4 years. 750

Same to same. Prospect pl, s s, 52 w Buffalo av. P. M. Aug. 15, 4 years. 750

Daly, Mary P. to Margaret Reynolds. Poplar st, s s, 85.7 w Henry st, 42.4x100.7. Already mortgaged to party of 2d part. Aug. 14, 2 years. 500

Day, William D. to Lavilla Day. Greene av. s s, 206 e Patchen av, 20x100.2. Aug. 1, 3 years, 5 %. 4,000

Dlauhy, Vincenz and Victoria his wife to Williamsburgh Brewing Co. Bushwick av, n e s, 79.8 s e Vanderveer st, 20x79.6. Aug. 11, 1 year. 300

Doris, Timothy and Sarah his wife to The Title Guarantee and Trust Co. Duffield st. P. M. Aug. 14, 3 years, 5 %. 2,000

Dower, Andrew J. to Mary Townshend. 10th st, n s, 308.3 w 3d av, 21.11x100. Aug. 13, 3 years, 5 %. 2,000

Dower, Christiana wife of Andrew J. to Ettie Townshend. Union st, s s, 100 w Hoyt st, 16.8x98. Aug. 13, 1 year. 2,000

Dowley, Michael and Mary H. to Lawrence Hurlburt. Macon st, n s, 239 w Howard av, 18x100. Aug. 12, 1 year. 1,000

Driscoll, Florence to Henry Kettelhodt. 53d st, n s, 160 w 8th av, New Utrecht. P. M. Aug. 15, 3 years, 5 %. 500

Driscoll, Catherine to Matthew Hooker. 3d av, w s, 40.2 s 52d st, 20x80. Aug. 3, 4 years, 5 %. 1,500

Dunleavy, James to South Brooklyn Co-operative Building and Loan Assoc. 49th st, n s, 100 e 6th av, 20x100.2. Building loan. Aug. 18, installs. 2,250

Dunn, Marcie to Thomas C. Balderson et al. trustees of the Order of Tonti. Walworth st, e s, 390 s Willoughby av, 32.6x100. Aug. 17, 3 years, 5 %. 6,500

Same to same. Walworth st, e s, 422.7 n Willoughby av, 32.5x100. Aug. 17, 3 years, 5 %. 6,500

Eckes, Peter J. to Nathaniel L Nathan. South 5th st, s s, 42.10 w 6th st, 21.5x80. Aug. 17, due Aug. 15, 1894, 5 %. 3,000

Eisler, Samuel and Davis to Charles Rissler. Wallabout st. P. M. Aug. 15, installs. 1,600

Ellingbausen, Louis to Charles H. Reynolds Decatur st. P. M. Aug. 10, 1 year. 325

Feldberg, Johannes to Herbert C. Smith. Osborn st and Glenmore av. P. M. Aug. 8, 3 months. 1,725

Feldberg, Jonas and Sarah Barusch to Jacob P. Zimmer. Ewen st, Moore st. P. M. Aug. 18, 6 months, 5 %. 5,500

Same to Michael Seitz. Ewen st, n w cor Moore st, 25x75. Aug. 17, 5 years, 5 %. 4,000

Finley, John to The Emigrant Industrial Savings Bank. Nelson st, n s, 150 w Court st, 21.2x100. Aug. 14, 1 year, 4½ %. 4,000

Fitzgerald, Joseph to Charles H. Fitzgerald, New York. Adams st. P. M. Aug. 11, installs. 1,300

Frederick, Eleanor to Michael Seitz. Wythe av, w s, 60 s Clymer st, 40x60. June 19, due June 20, 1893. 2,500

Frey, John W. to Catharine Rogers. North 6th st. P. M. Aug. 18, 2 years, 5 %. 3,000

Same to Paul Weidmann. Same property. Aug. 18, installs, 5 %. 3,000

Friedman, Hyman to Jacob Manheim. Johnson av. P. M. Aug. 12, installs. 1,800

Fulton, John to Eliza J. Brown. Montauk av, e s, 130 s Belmont av, 20x100. Aug. 12, 3 years. 2,000

Gaimari, Ciro, Antonio and Paolo Langone to Josepha Schmaeling. North 2d st. P. M. Aug 10, due July 1, 1896, 5 %. 3 000

Galloway, James to James G. Carroll. 45th st. P. M. July 30, due Nov. 1, 1894, 5 %. 1,300

Gegenheimer, Elizabeth wife of Anthony to James Miller. Essex st, w s, 90 s Ridgewood av, 20x100. Aug. 14, installs. 700

Gentleman, Mary E. wife of and Moses H. to Virginia A. Kleine. Van Voorhis st. P. M. July 31, demand. 16,000

Ginzburg, Simon and Reuben Epstein to Pauline Hartmann. Osborn st. P. M. Aug. 5, installs. 350

Gload, Adolphus to James Gascoine individ. and with Ann Eliza Cozine exrs. John G. Cozine. Madison st, n w s, 260 n e Hamburg av. P. M. July 15, 6 months. 5,125

Graham, James to The Williamsburgh Savings Bank. Shepherd av, e s, 140 n Ridgewood av, 20x102.4. Aug. 13, 1 year, 5 %. 1,800

Same to same. Shepherd av, e s, 240 n Ridgewood av, 20x102.5. Aug. 13, 1 year, 5 %. 1,800

Green, Alsop V. to Ann E. wife of Joseph Boyes. Eastern Parkway, s s, 60 e Berriman st, 20x100. Aug. 15, due Nov. 1, 1894. 1,800

Hallaren, John D. to The Title Guarantee and Trust Co. 6th av, s e cor 1st st, 100x90. Builders loan. Aug. 18, demand. 10,000

Same to W. F. Fisher & Co. 6th av, e s, 60 s 1st st, 20x90. Sub. to mort. $10,000. Aug. 18, 6 months. 700

Hall, William F., Pompton, N. J., to Andrew J. Dower. Clinton av, w s, 241.9 s Park av, 100x100. Aug. 6, 1 year. 6,000

Harper, Samuel to Charles A. Engert. North Henry st. P. M. Sub. to mort. $1,750. July 1, installs, 5 %. 1,250

Same to The Kings County Savings Inst. Same property. July 1, 1 year, 5 %. 1,750

Hart, John F. to Oliver B. Van Beuren, Hoboken, N. J. Atlantic av, s s, 212.3 w Clason av, 4 lots, each 25x120. 4 morts., each $7,000. Aug. 13, 3 years. 28,000

Same to Stephen B. Sturges. Same property. Aug. 13, demand. 4,000

Hartington, Alfred E. to The German-American Real Estate Title Guarantee Co. Garnet st, s s, 100 e Court st, 25x100. Aug. 14, due Aug. 15, 1894, 5 %. 4,000

Haven, Joseph A. and Mary A. his wife to Annie S. Bedell. Greene av. P. M. Aug. 15, due Feb. 15, 1894, or installs. 500

Hedenkamp, Diedrich to William Ulmer. South 9th st, n s, 37.6 w 6th st, 18.9x80. Aug. 14, 1 year, 5 %. 500

Henderson, Mary A. to Elizabeth Taber et al. exrs. Franklin W. Taber. Albany av. P. M. July 27, due Aug. 14. 1892. 500

Higginson, William J. to John W. McLaren. Van Voorhis st. P, M. July 27, due Feb. 27, 1896. 1,100

Hill, Henry B. to Charles G. Tousey. McDonough st, s s, 249.8 w Patchen av, 15x—. Confirmation mort. Aug. 11. 4,500

Hopkins, Harry F. C. to George Covert. Bleecker st, s e cor Knickerbocker av, 20x80. Aug. 12, 1 year. 1,320

Huber, August to Katharina Grubel. Stockholm st, n w s, 108.2 s w Wyckoff av, 25x100. Aug. 1, due July 1, 1894, 5 %. 500

Hunt, Sarah A. wife of and George W. to The Brooklyn Life Ins. Co. Garfield pl, s s, 275 w 6th av, 150x100. P. M. 6 months. 18,750

Same to same. Garfield pl, s s, 275 w 6th av, 150x100. Aug. 12, demand. 12,000

Jacobs, Fanny wife of and Lewis to The Title Guarantee and Trust Co. 13th st, n e s, 60 n w 5th av, 2 lots, each 18.11x50. 2 morts., each $2,000. Aug. 18, 3 years, 5 %. 4,000

Jessen, John H to Peter E. and Caroline Peters. Putnam av. P. M. Aug. 11, 2 years, 5 %. 2,000

Jonas, Catharine to Albert D. Buschman. Mermaid av and West 15th st. P. M. Aug. 12, 3 years. 500

Jones, E. Willard to The Title Guarantee and Trust Co. McDonough st, n s, 250 e Lewis av, 20.6x100. Aug. 17, 3 years, 5 %. 8,000

Jordon, Sarah to Sarah Holman. Centre st, w s, 400 s Eastern Parkway, 50x100. April 6, 5 %. 3,250

Kaufmann, Charles A. to August Heupel. Henry st, w s, 84 n Woodhull st, 21x100. Agreement to reconvey on payment of $2,000. Aug. 17. nom

Kinsay, Charles J. to Effingham H. Nichols. Lots 166–169 block 5 map No. 1 Cowenhoven farm. July 22, 2 years, 5 %. See Conveys. 300

Kirby, J. Mason to Theodore and William Kilian, of Kilian Bros. Bainbridge st, n s, 205.6 e Saratoga av, 90x100. 2d mort. Aug. 8. 1½ years. 1,190

Kirk, Sarah E. mortgagor with Thomas Berry. Extension of mort. Aug. 12. nom

Kiso, August to The Title Guarantee and Trust Co. North Henry st, w s, 105 n Nassau av, 20x100. Aug. 15, 1 year, 5 %. 1,100

Koch, George and Frederick Koerner to Louis Beer. Knickerbocker av and De Kalb av. P. M. July 28, 4 months. 3,128

Kronheim, Moses to Dore Kronheim. Withers st, s s, 125 e Ewen st, 25x100. July 23, due Jan. 1, 1893, 5 %. 600

Kurz, Henry and Sophia his wife to Elizabeth wife of George W. Bassett, Woodhaven, L. I. Georgia av, e s, 150 s South Carolina av, 25x100. Aug. 15, due Sept. 1, 1896, 5 %. 1,000

Lacey, Herbert D. to William H. Crocker, San Francisco, Cal. Remsen st, No. 120, s s, 200 e Henry st, 25x143.4x25x145. 1-12 part. Aug. 14, note. 2,000

Lachmann, Emil to William Bedford. Meeker av, s s, 160.8 w North Henry st, 25x107.6x28.10x93. July 1, 3 years, 5 %. 1,500

Lamb, James W. and Albert J. to The Williamsburgh Savings Bank. Garden st, n e s, 305.10 s e Flushing av, 20x63.1x25.3x78.7. Aug. 13, 1 year, 5 %. 1,600

Lampe, Edward to John Y McKane. Voorhies pl, e s, 131.2 n Coney Island road, 50x100, Coney Island. Aug. 4, note 500

Laveglliar, Anthony to Rosanna Fagen. North 5th st. P. M. Aug. 17, installs, 5 %. 3,000

Le Beau, Theodore M. to Benjamin P. Davis exr. Benjamin W. Davis. Ridgewood av, s e cor Ashford st, 84x100. Aug. 18, 3 years. 8,800

Lenz, Ferdinand and Leopoldine his wife to George Ochs. De Kalb av, s e s, 200 n e Hamburg av, 25x100. Aug. 18, 5 years, 5 %. 2,200

Levin, Barnet and Max Gittelsohn to The East New York Savings Bank. Thatford av, s w cor Blake av, 25x90. Aug. 13, 1 year. 1,600

Same to same. Thatford av, w s, 25 n Blake av, 3 lots, each 25x90. 3 morts., each $1,600. Aug. 13. 4,800

Lieberman, Chaie to Alice wife of Thomas McGee, Flatlands, L. I. Rockaway av. P. M. Aug. 15, 5 years. 1,150

Lusch, Charles F. to John F. Nelson. St. Marks av, n s, 436 w Carlton av, 21x131. Aug. 15, 6 months 1,000

Lyon, Hiram S. and Charlotte to Alexander F. Zundt and James Stewart. Ashford st, w s, 200 s Arlington av, 12.6x97.6. July 30, installs. See Conveys. 1,650

Maier, Frank to Peter B. Koechlein. Vermont av, e s, 300 n Fulton av, 125x81. Aug. 7, due Sept. 1, 1892. 1,500

Marder, Benjamin to Herman F. Koepke. Livonia av. P. M. Aug. 11, installs. 312

Same to same. Same property. P. M. Aug. 11, 3 years. 888

Marsh, Ellen B. to William Matthews et al. exrs., &c., Henry Johnson. Macon st, n s, 255 w Lewis av, 20x100. Aug. 19, 3 years. 5 %. 5,500

McBean, Archibald N. to William H. Bierds. 2d st, s s, 177.10 w 6th av, 60x95. Aug. 1, 1 year. 775

McCabe, Christopher and Christina his wife to John Dobbin. 44th st, s s, 433 e 3d av, 20x100.2. June 9, 1 year, 5 %. 92

McBride, Sarah M. wife of and John A. to Anna wife of James Stafford. 10th st, s w s, 228 n w 9th av, 18x100. Aug. 13, 2 years. 5 %. 5,000

McCormick, Mary A. to Robert Shaw. Prospect av, s w s, 150 s e 4th av, 25x75. Aug. 19, 3 years, 5 %. 4,000

McElvery, John and Robert Getty to Emeline Gallup. Av B. P. M. Aug. 12, 3 years. 4 000

McGann, Richard to The Kings Co. Trust Co. Franklin av, n e cor Butler st, 20x75. Aug. 13, due Aug. 17, 1892, 5 %. 4,500

McMahon, William H. to Michael Dowling. Lots 48–47, 41 and 42 map of S. G. Strykers heirs. Gravesend. Aug. 12, 3 years. 425

McNulty, Margaret V. to Isaac H. Cary. Smith st. P. M. Aug. 12, 5 years, 4½ %. 15,000

Meagher, Michael to The Emigrant Industrial Savings Bank. Flatbush av. n e s, 69.10 n w Hanson pl, 20x46.1 x east 4.4 to Raymond st. x south 19.10 x southwest 42.5. Aug. 18, 3 years, 4½ %. 4,000

Meis, Henry and Mina his wife to George M. Rothstein and Balbina his wife. Stuyvesant av, s w cor Quincy st. P. M. 2d mort. Aug. 17, 1 year or installs. 7,000

Metzer, William to Michael Seitz. Barbey st, w s, 145 s Hegeman av, 20x100. July 10, 1 year, 5 %. 125

Miller, Henry and Mary his wife to Theresia Bill. Johnson av, n s, 80 e Bushwick av, 25x100. Aug. 8, due July 1, 1896, 5 %. 4,000

Same to same. Graham av, e s, 25 n Boerum st, 50x100. Aug. 8, due July 1, 1896, 5 %. 5,000

Miller, Jane to The Brooklyn Door and Sash Co. Macon st, n s, 273 e Patchen av, 18x100. Sub. to mort. $4,500. Aug. 4, 1 year. 1,875

Miller, George A. and Robert with The Title Guarantee and Trust Co. mortgagees. Agreement as to priority of morts. made by John D. Hallaren. Aug. 17. nom

Moller, Dorothea P. to Edward F. De Beixedon, Tarrytown, N. Y. Herkimer st, s s, 640 w Nostrand av, 20x92.9. Aug. 14, 3 years. 500

Morris, Joseph to Agnes Macauley. Thatford av, w s, 100 n Dumont av, 25x100. July 28, 2 years 2,000

Mueller, Amalia to William Laytin et al. trustees William Laytin. Starr st, n w s, 100 s w Hamburg av, 25x100; Starr st, n w s, 150 s w Hamburg av. 50x100. Aug. 14, 3 years, 5 %. 5,000

Muessig, Cornelius N. to Henry Miller. Sackman st, e s, 125 n Liberty av, 25x100. Aug. 1, 3 years. 1,800

Muhlbauer, Otto to Mary E. wife of Darwin R. James. Myrtle av. P. M. Aug. 3, 3 years, 5 %. 1,000

Mullowney, Richard to Horatio S. Stewart. Halsey st, s w cor Ralph av, 22x100. Sub. to mort. $13,000. Aug. 7, 1 year. 5,000

Same to same. Halsey st, s s, 22 w Ralph av, 18x100. Sub. to mort. $4,000. Aug. 7, 1 year. 1,000

Murphy, Daniel to Lawson Sproulle. North 8th st, n w cor Roebling st, 25x100. Aug. 10, 4 years, 5 %. 2,000

Muller, Charles A. to Charles Quenzer. 3d pl. P. M. Aug. 18, 5 years, 5 %. 4,400

Murphy, James to Kings Co. Savings Inst. Grand st, n e s, abt 210 s e 4th st, 25x100.10 to North 1st st, x25x99.9. Aug. 15, 1 year, 5 %. 1,000

Nicholson, John to Constantia A. P. Duppen widow. 35th st, s w s, 160 s e 3d av, 20x100.2. Aug. 13, due Aug. 15, 1896, 5 %. 1,200

O'Donnell, Timothy M. to The Abbott Brewing Co. Vanderbilt av, No. 548. Store lease. Aug. 6, demand. 500

O'Dougherty, Patrick to Margaret Stevenson. Lafayette av, s s, 40 w Portland av, 20x80. Aug. 13, due Aug. 1, 1894, 5 %. 2,500

O'Raw, Patrick to William F. Corwith. Newell st, w s, 350 s Meserole av, 25x100. Aug. 14, 1 year. 300

O'Raw, Patrick to William F. Corwith. Newell st late 7th st, w s, 350 s Meserole av, 25x100. Aug. 14, 1 year. 500

Ostick, Thomas to Ella E. Morton. 57th st, n s, 360 e 3d av, 20x100.2. Aug. 17, 3 years, 5 %. 3,000

Pelcyger, Frank and Pincus Kessler to Susan wife of Alexander Rosenthal. Boerum st, n s, 150 e Graham av, 25x100; Flushing av, s s, 100 e Marcy av, 25x100. Aug. 14, due Dec. 15, 1891. 340

Perego, Ira to Church Charity Fund of Long Island. Flatbush av. P. M. Aug. 15, 1 year, 5 %. 10,000

Perego, Ira to William N. Crane and ano. trustees Walter F. Bush, Jr., dec'd. Lafayette av. P. M. Aug. 19, 3 years, 5 %. 6,500

Pitt, John R. to The Title Guarantee and Trust Co. Macon st, s s, 98 e Ralph av, 5 lots, each 18x100. 5 morts., each $4,000. July 31, 3 years, 5 %. 20,000

Prosser, John to Samuel G. Stanley. Lots 105 and 106 and part 104 map on amended map of Linden Terrace Beautiful Villa Sites, Flatbush. Aug. 13, 2 years, 5 %. 1,000

Quigley, Michael D. to Herman Sacks. Bergen st. P. M. July 30, due July 24, 1896, installs. 3,000

Radcliffe, Thomas H. to Emilie K. Eeks. McDonough st, s s, 138 e Ralph av, 18.8x100. Sub. to mort. $4,500. Aug. 11, 1 year. 800

Radcliffe, Thomas H. to Emelie K. Eeks. McDonough st, s s, 100 e Ralph av, 19x100. Sub. to mort. $5,000. Aug. 17, 1 year. 1,000

Rahmann, George to Mary Stothard. Stanhope st, n w s, 137.6 s w Evergreen av, 18.9x100. Aug. 1, 5 years, 5 %. 2,300

Rauch, Casper to Charles J. Hobe. Elm st, s s, 100 w Hamburg av, 25x100. Aug. 14, 3 years, 5 %. 3,500

Rauch, Casper and Margarethe to Albert Tremmel. Elm st, s s, 100 w Hamburg av, 25x100. Aug. 14, 2 years, 5 %. 900

Raymond, Benjamin C. to George C. Cranford. Macon st, n s, 22 w Ralph av, 18x100. Sub. to mort. $4,500. Aug. 11, 1 year. 1,000

Raymond, Benjamin C. to Horatio S. Stewart. Macon st, n w cor Ralph av, 22x100. Aug. 17, due Sept. 15, 1891. 1,625

Regenbogen, Louis, Samuel Davis, William Schechtel and Louis Cohen to Herbert C. Smith. Stone av. P. M. July 28, 3 months. 1,000

Reineke, Henry to George W. Richards. Leonard st, w s, 33.4 n Jackson st, 16.8x75. Aug. 12, 5 years, 5 %. 800

Rhodes, Mary A. S. to Andrew D. Baird. Fulton st, s s, 325 e Rochester av, 20x100. Aug. 11, 1 year, 5 %. 250

Ruginsky, Sam. and Hyman Tallie, New York, to Herman F. Koepke. Livonia av and Powell st. P. M. Aug. 11, 3 years. 450

Same to same. Same property. Aug. 11, installs. 325

Russo, Toney and Frank Wasino to John P. Cowley. Jackson st. P. M. Aug. 6, 4 years, 5 %. 2,400

Ruth, Abraham to Herman F. Koepke. Livonia av, s e cor Sackman st, 50x100. Aug. 11, 3 years 409

Same to same. Powell st. P. M. Aug. 11, 3 years. 3,273

Sacks, Herrman to E. Sinnamon Calvert. Pearl st. P. M. Aug. 14, installs. 5 %. 3,000

Sangnier, Sarah wife of and Prosper to Jane H. wife of Joseph S. Wright, Valley Stream, L. I. Howard av, w s, 27.8 n Bergen st, 79.6x100. Aug. 11, 3 years. 1,000

Schade, Emilie to Elizabeth Meltzer. Stanhope st, n w s, 175 n e Hamburg av, 25x100. Sub. to mort. $3,500. August 11, 3 years, 5 %. 250

Schafer, John to Juliet L. Pinckney, both of Gravesend, L. I. Lake st, e s, 178.2 n Av U, 20x75, Gravesend. Aug. 17, 3 years. 300

Schaffuer, Conrad to Jean H. Tompkins. Floyd st, n s, 315 e Nostrand av, 25x100. Aug. 17, 3 years, 5 %. 6,000

Scharsich, Adolph to Harry W. Denzler and Louise his wife. 66th st, w s, 100 s 5th av, 25x100.2; Stewart av, south cor 73d st, 80.1x102.1x80x101.3, New Utrecht. Aug. 18, due July 1, 1894. 1,000

Simon, Gussie to Pauline Hartmann. Livonia av. P. M. June 19, due Sept. 19, 1894. 325

Singer, Joseph to Pauline Hartmann. Christopher av. P. M. Aug. 1, due May 1, 1892. 150

Slevin, Emma J. to The Millinery Building and Loan Assoc. Henry st, s e s, adj W. Thompson, Coney Island, 4,822 sq feet. Aug. 14, installs. 500

Schneider, Jacob F. and Magdalena his wife to The German Savings Bank, Brooklyn. Hart st, s s, 225 e Hamburg av, 4 lots, each 25x100. 4 morts., each $2,500. Aug. 12, due Dec. 1, 1892, 5 %. 10,000

Schneider, Helena M. L. to The Friends Academy, Locust Valley, L. I. Halsey st, n s, 300.4 e Reid av, 17.8x100. Aug. 18, 3 years. 4,000

Smith, Walter E. to Frederick D. Hart. Milford st, w s, 175 n Liberty av, 50x100. Aug. 13, 6 months. 120

Speer, Emma wife of and Richard C. to The Kings Co. Trust Co. 17th st, s w s, 481.3 n w 5th av, 18.9x100.2. Aug. 18, 1 year, 5 %. 1,900

Stein, David to Herbert C. Smith. Osborn st. P. M. Aug. 8, 3 months. 1,400

Steven, Andrew to Johanna Dieckman. Stanley av and Elton st. P. M. Aug. 10, due Aug. 1, 1896, 5 %. 800

Straub, George to Williamsburgh Savings Bank. Myrtle av, n s, 75 e Throop av, 25x100. Aug. 3, 1 year, 5 %. 7,500

Szeikowski, John to Frank A. Belling. 21st st. P. M. Aug. 17, installs. 1,000

Taylor, Sarah to Emeline E. Brower. Harrison av, e s, 25 n Wallabout st, 25x100. Aug. 14, 1 year. 6,000

Taylor, Arthur to Henry Albert. Macon st, s s, 235.10 e Stuyvesant av, 19.2x100. Aug. 14, 3 years, 5 %. 4,000

Thorgerson, Katie wife of Thomas to Lewis Josephs. Cheever pl. P. M. Aug. 13, due July 1, 1894, or installs. 3,000

Throckmorton, Job to Christian W. Yutte, Hoboken, N. J. Taylor st, s e s, 142 n e Bedford av, 21x100. Aug. 14, 3 years. 2,500

Urwitz, Jacob to Peter J. Ecker. South 5th st. P. M. Aug. 18, 2 years or installs, 5 %. 1,300

Vanderveer, Harriet J. wife of John R. to David A. Fithian. Carlton av, e s, 330 n Lafayette av, 22.6x100. July 3, 2 years. 700

Victory, Jane wife of and Charles to The Title Guarantee and Trust Co. Glenmore av, n e cor Sheffield av, 100x100. Aug. 18, 3 years, 5 %. 4,000

Von Dreele, Philip H. and Annie M. his wife to Henry Von Dreele. Road leading from New Lots road to Forbells Landing on Plunders Neck, e s, adj J. H. Torborg, abt 12 acres, 26th Ward. July 1, 5 years, 5 %. 5,000

Vrooman, John F. to Anna L. Owen, New York. Powell st, w s, 200 n Liberty av, 16.6x100. Aug. 10, 3 years. 2,000

Wall, Mary J. to Jennie V. Wilbur. Fernald st, s s, 140 e Albany av, 20x100, Flatbush. Aug. 12, due Nov. 1, 1894, 5 %. 340

Ward, William J. to Ella M. Van Brunt. 80th st. P. M. Aug. 15, 3 years, 5 %. 300

Warnock, Owen to David A. Fithian. Hamilton av, s w s, 88 s e Hicks st, runs southwest 37.6 x south 20 x east 2.3 x northeast 45.11 to av, x northwest 25. Aug. 13, 1 year. 500

Warren, Sarah M. widow to Henry Battermann. Quincy st. P. M. May 1, 1 year, 5 %. 4,800

Weild, David to John Feeney. Hancock st, n s, 180 w Throop av, 18x100. Aug. 14, 3 years, 5 %. 5,000

Weill, Emanuel to Bernard Vogel. Sands st. P. M. Aug. 18, due Sept. 1, 1893, 5 %. 2,000

Weinberger, Matilda and Lena Herskowics to Nicholas Droge et al. exrs. Claus Plath. Eagle st. P. M. July 31, 3 years. 1,000

Weingerath, William to John W. Freckelton et al. exrs. and trustees John W. Freckelton. 16th st, n s, 154.9 w 8th av, 19.1x100. Aug. 13, 3 years. 4,000

Same to Oliver Davidson, East Rockaway, L. I. 16th st, n s, 173.10 w 8th av, 19.1x100. Aug. 13, due May 1, 1894. 4,000

Willcox, Edwin C. to Charles Griffen et al. trustees Frederick Willets, residuary trustee. Secures debt of Edwin C. Willcox and Edward R. Johnes. Herkimer st, n e cor Hopkinson av, 30x100. Aug. 14, due Dec. 31, 1892, 5 %. 17,000

Young, Celia to Albert Brous. Lots 99 and 100 Conklin et al. property, Canarsie. P. M. July 1, 5 years. 1,000

MORTGAGES----ASSIGNMENTS.

NEW YORK CITY.

August 14 to 20—Inclusive.

Bussing, John, Jr., to David Stevenson. $2,000

Cornell, James L., Brooklyn, to Leopold Gusthal. 4,000

Dempsey, William and John Smith, of Dempsey & Smith, to Maria N. Winne. nom

Eden, John H. to The Mutual Life Ins. Co. of New York. 4,000

Fay, Michael and William Stacom to John Braun. 5,062

Gifford, Silas D., Eastchester, N. Y., to Ellen McKenna. 1,000

German-American Real Estate Title Guarantee Co. to Armand Levy and ano. trustees Theodore Levy dec'd. 15,000

Same to The Peoples Trust Co. 18,000

Hagan, Matthew to Thomas Hagan. nom

Haar, H. M. et al. exrs. Susanna Kress to Wilhelmina Miller. 8,500

Hummel, Frederick P. to Theodore Sattler. 5,000

Jacobson, Morris to Charles H. Reed. 8,000

James, John A. exr. Frank L. James to Joseph Van Vleck, Montclair, N. J. 15,500

Same to same. 15,500

Kiwi, Ernestine to Charles Dexheimer. 8,000

Lipman, Julius to Charles A. Troup trustee. Re-recorded. 2,000

Mayer, Fredericke to Randolph Guggenheimer and Salomon Marx. 3 assigns. nom

More, Abram G. admr. John O. More to Mary M. More. 10,000

March, Mary L. exr. John P. March to Frederick H. and Frederica W. Trow and Augusta C. Korber. 14,000

Morris, Elizabeth wife of John to Robert W. Cooper. 1,000

Paskusz, Jacob to Moses Goodman. nom

Parmly, Erick and ano. trustees for Ehrick K. Rossiter and Anna R. Adams to Gertrude Dreyfous. nom

Purdy, Samuel G. exr. Stephen Secor to Thomas H. Purdy, Harrison, N. Y. 2,200

Purdy, Thomas H. admr. Ann Purdy to Thomas Purdy, Harrison, N. Y. 449

Rankin, William to Anthony W. Miller. consid. omitted

Roller, Louis to Simon Adler and Henry S. Herrman. 1,200

Same to same. 1,000

Rolston, Rosewell G. trustee Roswell S. ague dec'd to The Farmers' Loan and Trust Co. 15,000

Tredwell, John H. et al. exrs Peggy Smith to Ann Augusta Carpenter. nom

The Peoples Trust Co., Brooklyn, to The German-American Real Estate Title Guarantee Co. 15,000

The Mutual Life Ins. Co. of New York to The Title Guarantee and Trust Co. 95,000

Title Guarantee and Trust Co. to Luther Kountze and ano. exrs. Mantegnie Ward. 2,500

Title Guarantee and Trust Co. to George J. Schermerhorn. 27,500

Same to Emily, Laura, Frederick and Percy Sandford. 4,500

Title Guarantee and Trust Co. to The German Society of the City of New York. 10,000

Troup, Charles A. trustee to Albert H. Leszynsky trustee. Re-recorded. 2,000

Van Riper, Charles to Laura F. Van Riper. 4,800

Vogler, Charles E. to Dwight H. Olmstead 2,500

Weekes, Henry de F. to Christ Church, Oyster Bay, L. I. 3,027

KINGS COUNTY.

August 13 to 19—Inclusive.

Adams, Matilda E. to Earl A. Gillespie. $200

Anderson, John C. trustee for George G. and John C. Barnard to John Weber and ano. trustees of George G. and John C. Barnard. Assigns 9 morts. nom

Bushnell, Ezra D. to Elizabeth Buch. 2,375

Bossert, Jacob to Hugo Weil, New York. 1,200

Bay Ridge Mfg. Co. to Henry G. Hoblin. 150

Candee, Evelina wife of Julius A. to Julia A. Candee. 1,500

Cummings, Samuel, Philadelphia, Pa., to Margaret McReynolds. 2,000

Davis, Cordelia, Boston, Mass., to Sarah M. Caton. 2,100

De Mund, Phebe E. to Albert V. B. Voorhies. 2,135

Downing, George S. and ano. admrs. Simonson M. Suydam to Catharine A. Suydam. 1,500

Same to same. 1,900

Same to same. 1,750

Downing, George S. and ano. admrs. of Simonson M. Suydam to Catharine Ann Suydam. 2,000

Dresdner, Isidore to Louisa Schuck. 800

German-American Real Estate Title Guarantee Co. to The Peoples Trust Co. 4,000

Hendrickson, Edward to Cross, Austin & Co. 1,000

Hart, Frederick D. to Hannah Hitchings extrx. Charles F. Hitchings. 1,600

Hassell, Jane to Charlotte L. Mundy. nom

Hill, Henry B. to The Bradley & Currier Co. (Lim.). 800

Kings Co. Trust Co. to The Peoples Co-operative Building and Loan Assoc. nom

Ledoux, Paul W. to Geneva C. Stopenhagen. 227

Ledoux, Paul W. to Geneva C. Stopenhagen. 600

Lincoln, Clarence with Morris Isaacs. Agreement to make two conditional assigns. of morts. perpetual. nom

Levy, Julius to Mathilde Isaac. 1,500

Martin, Levi V. to Lawrence Hurlburt. 600

Martin, Ignatz to Charles C. Kreppel. 2,400

Moss, Frank exr. Maltby G. Lane to Charles D. Smith, Huntington, L. I. 2,600

McElhinny, Michael to Louis Froehlich. 1,500

Mueller, Amalia to William Laytin et al. trustees William Laytin. 3,000

Mundy, Charlotte L. formerly Kelly to James Millar. 2,000

Nassau Trust Co., Brooklyn, to Charlotte L. Mundy. nom

Powell, Sarah H. to Sarah J. Moore. 5,000

Rollac, Leon to Henry W. Lee. 2,387

Ratner, Louis to Louis Bossert. 1,575

Ruth, Abraham to Herbert C. Smith. nom

Roth, Henry to The New York Gas Fixtures Co. 750

Sedlmeier, August to William Bayer. 2,000

Steinebrei, Henry and Elise to Louis J. and Katharina Hoffmann. 2,570

Stryker, Anna J. to Nellie S. Van Kleek. 1,500

Samelson, Samuel and Pincus Ronginsky to Jacob W. Erregger. 900

Schneider, Rosa to Julius Dewald. 1,500

The Williamsburgh Savings Bank to Joanna K. Jewell. 2,000

Thompson, Clarence admr. of Albert J. Reynolds to Anna L. Strong admrx. James Kenyon. val. consid

Thomas, Samuel W. et al. exrs. William H. Thomas to Melvin Stephens et al. exrs. Nathan Stephens. 4,077

Title Guarantee and Trust Co. to Elizabeth Hawthorne. 4,500
Same to John Lee. 5,000
Same to Mary A. Littlewood. 3,750
Same to The Church Charity Foundation, L. I. 3,000
Same to same. 8,000
Same to Robert Hunter. 4,000
Same to The Riverhead Savings Bank. 2,000
Townsend, James A., Elmira, N. Y., to Clarence A. Thompson admr., &c. of Owego, N. Y. 300
Union Trust Co., New York, guard. George B., Clara I. and Franklin H. Youngs to Thomas Berry. 6,000
Wunnenberg, John A. to Esther Wunnenberg. 1,000
Wildner, Emil F. to Joseph Elsbeck and Magdalena his wife. 750

JUDGMENTS.

In these lists of judgments the names alphabetically arranged, and which are first on each line, are those of the judgment debtor. The letter (D) means judgment for deficiency (*) means not summoned. (†) signifies that the first name is fictitious, real name being unknown. Judgments entered during the week, and satisfied before day of publication, do not appear in this column, but in list of Satisfied Judgments.

NEW YORK CITY.

August

15 Altman, Cecilia / Altman, Charles } R E Wood........ $32 50
15 the same —— Henry Schwanewede........................ 32 50
15 Andrews. Proctor H—Cyrus Clark... 70 15
17 Appel, Emanuel — Caroline Schoenberg................................2,017 60
17 Ainsworth, James—Metropolitan Telephone and Telegraph Co........... 42 80
17 Angell, Harold G — Southern Nat Bank.....................................7,181 27
18 Ashmore, Herbert E—C O Reilly.... 48 34
19 Ainsworth, James—Katie Macooll.... 290 23
15 Behlmer, John F—Highlands Chemical Co.............................. 29 73
15 Bonnell, John Harper—Bank of N Y Nat Banking Assoc....................1,278 69
15 the same——the same............1,002 59
15 Brigham, Daniel W—Manhattan Oil Co.................................... 92 70
17 Bliss, Charles H—T J Dunn, exr.......1,188 95
17 Belvin, Mary—James Talcott......... 300 12
18 Brady, James H—T G Dunn.......... 289 93
18 Bonnell, J Harper—Webster Paper Co.......................................2,266 07
18 Brower, Lena—Richard Vom Hofe.... 244 00
18 Bonnell, Tammisin H—Chatham Nat Bank.......................................9,471 17
19 Brada, John E—Louis Youngling.... 665 02
19 Byrnes, Jeremiah J—Johanna Gilmartin.............................. 238 18
19 Bates, Oliver G—Mayor, Lane & Co.. 1,539 47
19 Blath, William—Raphael Elias...... 148 95
19 Bissell, Rush W—Washington Nat Bank....................................1,041 42
19 Bechter, Conrad—Jacob Schwarz.... 182 20
19 Behlmer, John F—Peter McDowell.... 478 06
19*Bohrmann, Julius H—C J Horstmann 159 88
20 Brown, Henry C—D D Mangam...... 341 48
20 Beekman, John C—G B Brown...... 508 42
20 Brooks, James Wilton—Henry Blendermann.............................. 154 80
20 Bell, Jessie—Hyman Schnitzer......... 41 85
20 Brennan, Thomas—Excelsior Elevator Guard and Hatch Cover Co......... 225 78
20 Boocard, Pauline—Lucy E Smith..... 459 01
20 Bruno, Gus—Reinhold Busse.......... 246 94
20 Bonnell, John Harper—Bank of N Y Nat Banking Assoc.... .... 570 10
20 Bernstein, Samuel G—Edward Siegman.................................... 355 05
21 Bini, Lawrence F—Henry Cohen..... 118 97
21 Bliss, Charles H—James Slattery..... 575 88
21 Barnum, Stephen C—Henry Bauendahl....................................1,026 15
21*Behnke, John—Henry Eggers......... 222 29
15 Carlin, John / Carlin, Mary E } William Fiss......... 558 01
17 Coyle, John—John Keresey......... 173 56
17 Cree, Eugene H—Charles Wiesbecker. 222 49
18 *Cooney, Frank / Cooney, Michael J } Hyman Sonn.... 219 08
18 Calvert, Wilber F—J G Smith....... 177 55
19 Collins, Joseph Edmund—Gertrude A Collins.... .... costs 200 77
19 Carr, Benjamin J—G S Hamlin, assignee.................................. 132 87
19 Crosber, James—A C Barnes......... 86 42
20 Coulson, William—Samuel Druiff ... 129 84
20 Clark, Robert P—James Fitzpatrick. 337 22
21 Considine, Michael S—David Jones Co.. 74 96
21 Crosby, George—Henry Bauendahl...1,026 15
15†Doe, John—R E Wood.... .... 32 50
15 the same——Henry Schwanewede 32 50
17 Davidson, Max—Alexander Frank... 32 50
17 Deirerlein, John—A H Leathern...... 27 50
18 Devine, Patrick / Devine, John } Abraham Steers.... 397 15
18 Dattlebaum, Charles—J W Block.... 986 45
18 Dougherty, James—H W Benedict...1,563 01
18 the same——the same.............1,622 65
18 Donovan, James T—Adolph Alexander.. 171 11
19†De Mott, Charles M—J C Gazley 82 00
19†Day, Edward M—Standard Gas Light Co.. 51 51
19 Dreyfuss, Bernard—W E Dodge..... 280 41
20 Dolan, Hugh—James Fitzpatrick.... 337 22
20†de Sotolongo, Thomas E—Mary Lyness.. 85 08
20 De Mott, Clifford M—Herbert Reeves 156 06
20 the same——the same... .... 384 81
20*De Carlins, John—Herrmann Weiller 109 38
21 Dreyfuss, Bernard—Otto Gerdau..... 653 00
21 Dwyer, William—Orlando Marine.... 288 49
19 Evatt, John G—Peck Bros & Co...... 328 47
19 Eldridge, Samuel—Mayor, Lane & Co.. 90 52
21 Ehlers, Henry—N Y Veal and Mutton Co 95 62
21 Earley, Terence J—Orlando Marine.. 288 49
19 Fuller, Edward J—Samuel Lord...... 133 80
19 Fleisch, Benjamin—Ludwig Renn.... 145 00
19 Fleming, Thomas J—Charles Schlesinger.................................... 104 05
20*Flanagan, John F—Union County Bank.. 306 38
21 Fielbig, George J—Richard Tangeman 38 55
21 Fromm, Sarah—Marc Eidlitz, exr.... 342 91
21 French, George B—Solomon Barnett. 640 85
15 Graham, James H—Fray Zahn....... 72 84
17 Grant, George—T E Greacen......... 89 25
17 the same——J W Mason.......... 140 98
18 Gay, William — Lithographic Art Journal Publishing Co............. 27 64
18 Griffith, Charles E—John McCormick. 277 16
18†Goldstein, Nathan—Isaak Goldstein.. 39 78
18 Glackemeyer, Auguste—S E Smith... 44 64
19 Green, Douglass—W F Owens........ 552 97
19 Gordon, Isaac—Jacob Shapiro........ 86 50
19 Garrison, James M / Garrison, John M } Myer Gans...... 300 00
19 Gaunder, Joseph E—Ludwig Renn... 145 00
19 Grunberg, Caroline, admrx — Mary Dietz 77 12
19 Gebhardt, Adolph—C J Horstmann.. 159 58
15 Hauser, Julius G—John Barnutz... .. 628 82
15 Harper, William Durbin—Bank of N Y Nat Banking Assoc.............1,278 69
15 the same——the same 1,002 59
17 Herman, Abraham—W A M Stenz... 147 66
17 Hilliker, Albert H—H S Deshon.. ... 38 27
17 Horling, Frederick—Anthony Fischer 30 28
17 Henjes, Henry—W H Ellis.......costs 32 72
18 Holmes, Edward—C S Kiggins........ 79 52
18 the same——W P Raynor........ 75 83
18 Harper, William D—Webster Paper Co..2,266 07
18 Harding, H L—J A Bornstein 107 90
18 Howell, Eugene N—Importers and Traders Nat Bank.......................4,840 64
18 Hill, Harry—H C Browning.........1,599 09
18 Haines, Andrew G—H W Gray..costs 105 00
19 Hochstadter, Oscar J / Hyatt, Belden F } Robert McCord 93 20
19 Hanson, Andrew—Abraham Berliner 137 00
19 Hirsch, Rozelio—Charles Scarth. 97 85
19 Horstmann, Richard—Mayor, Lane & Co..1,817 84
19 Harris, Hiram W—B M Whitlock.... 134 52
19 Harris, Herman L—Standard Gaslight Co.................................... 31 06
20 Harding, Joseph M—J W Fiske..costs 88 75
20 the same——J M Harding Mfg Co ....costs 66 55
20 Hart, Alexander R—Chatham Nat Bank..1,491 09
20 Hamlin, John—Bradley & Co......... 161 94
20 Hug, Joseph—U S Illuminating Co... 24 83
20 Holcomb, William F—L F Genet Lumber Co............................ 322 49
20 Heumann, John—Thurber, Whyland Co.. 437 99
20 Harper, William Durbin—Bank of N Y Nat Banking Assoc............. 570 10
21 Hartung, Lorenzo R—C H Willson. . 192 35
21 Hogg, Julia D—W & J Sloane....... 714 86
21 Healey, Thomas—T F Breen.......... 206 05
21 Harrington, Jeremiah F—Edgewood Poultry Co.... .... 274 83
15 Ihrcke, Rudolph—C W Bachmann.... 36 17
19 Iseneke, Joseph J—Charles Sobiesinger... .... 63 57
20 Invernizzi, Battista—Herrmann Weiller.. 109 38
17 Jenne, Louis—I C Ogden, Jr 1,246 25
17 the same——the same............5,653 37
17 James, Edward F—Horace, Waters & Co.. 158 50
19 Jones, William C—The Sidney....... 186 35
21†Jackson, Andrew W—First Nat Bank of Ashbury Park..................... 284 00
21 Joyce, John H—D G Yuengling, Jr, Brewing Co.............................. 259 00
15 Krueger, Daniel—C W Bachmann.... 36 17
15 Kinne, George P—Edward Philips... 86 57
18 Klein, Henry—Louis Leviseur....... 120 00
19 Kelly, Lawrence / Kelly, John } G S Hamlin, assignee. 1,638 97
19†Koester, Laurence—George Ringler & Co.. 172 00
19 Kloeck, Carl A / Kloeck, Carl A, Jr } D A Vanhorne. 396 52
19 *Kreuder, Adolph / Kreuder, Frank F / Kline, Charles } John Shepard... 722 87
19*Kurschbaum, Jacob—H B Claflin.... 208 03
20 Kaufmann, Max—Gustave Goldman. 332 27
20 Keogh, Christopher B—A R Brown. 794 67
21 Katz, Sara—Louis Schoenberg......1,457 38
21 Ketzlich, Joseph—Claus Lipsius Brewing Co.................................. 103 63
15 Lenz, Ellen—H S Mott............... 183 04
15 L'Hommedieu, Sylvester Y—Maurice O'Meara....................................2,254 07
15 Leyrer, Louis G—Israel Block........ 183 28
15 Levy, Reuben—Bernhard Ginsberg... 41 48
15 Luetzeler, George—M A C Levy.. ... 268 62
17 Langan, Patrick T / Langan, Joseph P } H K Miller..... 324 63
17 L'Hommedieu, Sylvester Y—Southern Nat Bank... .... 7,181 27
18 Levy, Herman L / *Levy, Aaron } J W Goddard.... 493 53
18 the same——M R Wendell........1,623 11
18 Lawrence, John D / Lawrence, William C } E D Griggs. 226 81
18 Lees, Samuel—L N Lovell............ 170 79
18 the same——R J Waddell......... 137 18
19 Leyrer, Louis G—T F Hoctor........ 103 31
19 Lowther, Sarah E—C F Osley....... 77 10
19 Leonard, William H—Johanna Gilmartin.......................... . 238 18
19 Lohman, David V—Premier Cycle Co.1,177 05
20 Lovey, Morris—J S Gans.............. 63 00
20 Lewis, Parke—Hyman Schnitzer..... 41 85
20 Lake, Louis N—T C Oakley........... 459 49
20 Leonard, Robert W—C E Chinnock. 1,484 59
21 *Ludwig, Bernhard J / Ludwig, Isidor / *Ludwig, Morris J } Manhattan Electric Light Co (Lim)..... 105 73
21 Leake, Edward C—H W Day.... ... 296 91
21 Levy, James C—J S Simpson......... 39 21
21 Lohrand, William—Henry Eggers.... 222 29
21 Lawson, Louise—Thomas Graham.... 321 28
21 Liard, Frank—Marc Eidlitz, exr..... 342 91
21 Lamb, Julia D—W & J Sloane....... 714 86
21 Lees, Samuel—Marie Brown........ . 170 19
21 Langenstein, Conrad—William Hatfield.......................... ...... 7 55
17 Meuer, Pauline—Israel April.......... 164 19
17 Muller, George A—Leopold Herzberg 162 39
18 Marion, David M—Lewis Sylvester... 95 47
18 Murphy, Matthew—D M Koehler.... 140 89
19 Menzel, Otto—Robert McCord........ 93 20
19†Meyer, Gazina—R G Thomas......... 301 00
19 Meyer, George—Townsend Cushman. 90 00
19†Meyer, Mary—Michael Edesheimer... 96 60
19 Moran, John C—George Hollister.... 203 00
19 Murphy, Matthew—J L Hasbrouck... 152 94
19 Martin, Crowell H—Shelton Co...... 77 61
19†Murray, John, Jr—Standard Gas Light Co.................................. 35 09
19 Minuse, John P / Minuse, Carrie D } D P Vanhorne... 73 38
19 Morris, Ellis—William Reitlinger.... 690 52
19 Meyer, Jacob J—H B Claflin Co..... 208 03
20 Miller, Wilbur J—J M Thorburn..... 125 75
20 Maxfield, Mrs T R / Maxfield, T R } S M Hoye..... 110 69
20 Myers, Sinclair—Union County Bank 166 31
20 Maguire, John F—Edward Barr Co (Lim)... .... 144 95
20 Murphy, John / Murphy, Mary Ann } Fifth Nat Bank. 2,042 30
21 Moeller, Carl—Kent & Stanley Co... 266 65
17 McCormack, Francis—David Neighbour.................................. 143 86
19 McEvoy, Henry—Mayor, Lane & Co. 1,493 30
21 McGlynn, Joseph L—Abraham Shoemann............. ...... 42 50
21 McNiece, James—E E Ensley 185 43
15 Nathan, Victor—M A C Levy........ 208 62
17 Noble, William L—John Dunn....... 45 50
18 Nelson, Peter D—John McKesson..... 93 98
20 Nolan, James—P J Bresnan.... ..... 150 58
15 Ott, George, Jr—John Gordon........ 378 47
17 O'Connor, Eleanor—John Keresey... 266 95
17 O'Shaughnessy, John F—Nat Commercial Bank of Albany............ 528 37
19 Osborne, Thomas—W H P Bogart... 107 83
19 Ostheim, Abraham—Barnett Sturman 98 21
15 Platt, John E—Erwin Fery 74 75
17 Peruein, Max—Alexander Frank..... 32 50
17 Parrett, Arthur—Max Bernstein......2,543 68
17 Phelan, John—J A Frazee........... 564 37
18 Pullis, William—W H Rogers........ 145 72
18 Pullar, Joseph H—R G Pullar....... 100 54
18 Phillips, John Y—Reinbold Von der Emde.. 36 50
18 Perrine, Howland D—H C Hardy ... 173 63
19 Pulver, Andrew P—John Muller.... 447 00
19 Petersen, Herman—Burger & Hower Brewing Co (Lim).... .... 124 20
20 Pinkel, Katharine—Charles Townsend 27 20
20 Price, Walter S—J C Overbirer..(D)1,349 44
15 Reichenberg, Jacob—Bernhard Ginsberg.. 41 48
15 R , Henry—Union Distilling Co... 356 34
17 Rusler, Henry / Resler, Christopher } Charles Gulden. 98 27
17 Regensburger, Melville H—Aaron de Cordova.................................. 65 90
17 Rattray, Robert J—Gorham Mfg Co. 171 00
17*Regenhard, Frederick — Dominick Adams.. 48 20
18 Ruck, John—Margaret H Kilpatrick.. 534 90
18 the same——the same........... 528 90
19 Ross, J Stewart—Benedict Fischer.... 556 03
21 Roberts, Austin J / Roberts, Walter J } Peter Walrath. 215 43
21 Rosenstein, Henry—M F Topken..... 118 10
21 Roche, Frank J—Edgewood Poultry Co.. 274 83
15 Schwenk, Samuel K—William Turnbridge 197 69
17 Schilling, John F—David Neighbour. 143 86
17 Steinmetz, Christian—George MacKenzie.. 175 69
17 Sale, Winfield B—William Turnbridge.. 133 01
18 Steinherz, Leon / Sternberz, Otto } Claus Lipsius Brewing Co.... 117 78
18 Scribner, Isaac T—O C Wilson....... 177 27
19 Sheehan, Patrick J—G S Hamlin, assignee....................................1,289 43
19 Simpson, John E—Mayor, Lane & Co.. 195 63
19 Striefler, Jacob—Jacob Schwartz ... 182 20
19 Semansky, Harris N—P R Mitchell... 377 85
20 Susswein, Haiman—Abraham Unger. 517 38
20 Scott, George H—Union County Bank.. 306 38
20 the same——the same............. 166 31
20 Shevlin, Frank H—Frank Moss....... 117 50

21 Symonds, William H—N F Martin... 139 71
21 Stegner, Christian — Claus Lipsius Brewing Co... 138 34
21 Sterner, Winfield S—S G Patterson.. 389 00
18 Smith, George C—Manhattan Electric Light Co (Lim)... 112 84
19 Smith, Addison, Jr / Smith, Jessie Ives } Twelfth Ward Bank... 306 88
19 Smith, Ira / *Smith, Charles I } J C Quick... 133 00
20*Smith, Theoplis G—Union County Bank... 166 81
20 Smith, Henry C—A R Brown... 794 67
21 Smith, Edgar M / Smith, Scudder } Holyoke Card and Paper Co... 850 89
15 Banker & Campbell Co (Lim)—Henry Durk...27,909 45
15 J H Bonnell & Co (Lim)—Bank of New York Nat Banking Assoc... 1,278 69
15 the same—the same... 1,002 59
15 Banker & Campbell Co (Lim)—William Neumann... 821 89
15 the same—F P Prial... 172 90
17 The American Fibre Assoc / The Tompkins Paper Stock Co } Nat Commercial Bank of Albany 528 37
18 The Mankey Decorative Co—S J Albright... 105 18
18 The Fibrone Mfg Co—William Zinsser... 1,246 75
18 Banker & Campbell Co (Lim)—John Wilkinson Co... 909 00
18 The Kentucky Consolidated Oil and Natural Gas Co (Lim)—J H Warner 59 50
18 United Cloak and Suit Cutters' Benevolent Assoc—J H Myers... 104 50
18 J H Bonnell & Co (Lim)—Western Nat Bank... 921 52
18 the same—the same... 139 04
18 the same—the same... 494 54
18 E B Benjamin Mfg Co—Nat Park Bank... 597 29
18 the same—the same... 3,547 20
18 Belfords Magazine Co—Peter Adams Co... 194 61
19 The London Assurance Corporation—Giles Everson... 1,281 62
19 The Fire Ins Assoc of London, England—the same... 1,281 62
19 The Phœnix Ins Co of Hartford, Conn—the same... 2,793 26
19 The Westchester Fire Ins Co—the same... 1,606 11
19 The N Y Bowery Fire Ins Co—the same... 1,606 11
19 The Liberty Ins Co—the same... 1,281 62
19 The Fire Assoc of Philadelphia, Pa—the same... 1,281 62
19 The Williamsburgh City Fire Ins Co—the same... 1,606 11
19 Belfords Magazine Co—Peter Adams Co... 268 42
19 The Mayor, Aldermen, &c—John Sullivan... 510 31
19 the same—John Boyle... 240 00
19 the same—Louis Zimmerman... 660 00
19 Eastern Electric Co—Samuel Rowland...15,364 99
19 E G Blakslee's Sons Iron Works—Columbus and Hocking Coal and Iron Co... 781 73
20 The Persian Rug and Carpet Co—John Morgan... 262 00
20 The Alden Publishing Co—Orren Sherwin... 2,082 05
20 J H Bonnell Co (Lim)—Bank of N Y Nat Banking Assoc... 507 10
20 Cary & Moen Co—McNab & Harlan Mfg Co... 521 67
20 the same—J C Cook... 225 89
21 Banker & Campbell Co (Lim)—J N Goldbacher... 1,660 71
21 the same—Percival Tattersfield. 232 37
21 The Hudson River Boot and Shoe Mfg Co—E W Dean... 860 12
21 The Fibrone Mfg Co—G F Blake Mfg Co... 361 58
21 The Arizona Cattle Co—Emile Hubner... 1,073 87
17 Timmer, Ernest—Dominick Adams.. 48 20
17 Thompson, Joseph R H—Metropolitan Telephone and Telegraph Co... 38 65
18 Townsend, Dwight—C O Reilly... 48 34
19 Tisch, Moses—Standard Gas Light Co 20 54
21*Tracy, George—S G Patterson... 389 00
21 Timony, Mary A—Thurber, Whyland Co... 132 21
21 Tremper, William—the same... 120 66
15 Vette, Di d ich / Vette, Johner } Abram French Co 103 13
18 the same—Philip McManus... 525 99
18 Veimeister, George A / Veimeister, Edmund C } J M Weil.. 133 96
19*Vogel, Robert G—George Ringler & Co... 172 00
19 Vogeler, Waldemar—Louis Wahl... 238 97
18 Van Sicklen, William—W H Rogers. 145 12
21 Van Steenburgh, Burhaus / Van Steenburgh, Bernhard } Peter Henderson & Co... 166 70
15 Williams, George E—M L Williams.. 1,583 79
15 Woolverton, William H, as president N Y Transfer Co—Ann McManus.. 5,493 21
17 Webster, Jacob—J M Valentine... 243 48
17 Wischnewetzky, Florence K—Eliza M Jermyn... 329 83
17 Walch, Charles—Edward Vogel... 168 37
17*Weil, Isador—James Talcott... 369 12
18 Wolff, Louis—M B Edinger... 162 00
18 Welch, George Swift—J L Cavanagh. 142 05
19 Wade, Richard A—Standard Gas Light Co... 80 73
19 Weinstein, David—Morris Demby... 658 42
19 Wisbauer, George / *Wisbauer, Lena } Emil Calman... 105 00
20 White, Charles J—Julius Somborn... 345 78
21 Webster, Jacob—Tradesmen's Nat Bank... 863 40
21 White, Whitman V—G R Brown... 591 34
21 Weaverson, Frederick—Samuel Harrington... 122 05
21 Westermeyer, Edward, Jr—William Hatfield... 14 35
21 Wood, Samuel S—J M McMahon... 245 69
18 Young, Annie V—Occidental Oil Co.. 282 79
18 Yost, Abraham—Saugatuck Iron Works Co... 154 16
21 Zimmerman, Ernest—J T Long... 109 50

KINGS COUNTY.

August
15 Adams, Frank E—W G White... $418 15
18 the same—the same... 123 73
14 Bonnell, John H—Nat Bank of the Republic, N Y... 722 99
15 Blyn, Louis—L Z White... 136 80
19 Baily, William T—W Jessen... 104 74
17 Carroll, John J / Carroll, David F } M F McGoldrick. 219 26
18 Clark, Hayden—W J Grov... 171 80
18 Crotty, Richard D / Crotty, Holton M } Commercial Bank 447 76
19 Cozine, William—J M Graff... 41 45
19 Cronin, David—C Heidelberger... 204 36
20 Campbell, Frank R—Rebecca E Corbett... 27 85
17 Dick, George N—S T Birdsall... 153 80
18 Delauhey, William J—G B Robinson... 307 21
19 Devantry, Joseph—C P Kalkenbreuner... 44 48
20 Dattlebaum, Charles—J & W S Block 986 45
14 Fellerman, Abraham—L S Finn... 42 50
20 Fuller, Edward J—Lord & Hatch... 133 80
15 Glassey, Samuel—M & D Levy... 122 57
19†Gleason, "James"—W Rohde... 75 25
14 Hart, Alexander R—Nat Bank of the Republic... 722 99
14 Hans, Jacob—H Roeber... 200 35
14 Hubbard, Harlan P—H Christian... 87 06
15 Henry, T A sued as Thomas A—L Z White, Jr... 69 41
17 Hochstadter, Oscar J / Hyatt, Belden F } R McCord... 93 20
18 Hosch, Morris—A & M Jacobs... 276 27
18 Homburger, Rudolph—H F Luce... 230 22
19 Hackett, William—J M Graff... 41 45
19 Henjes, Henry—W H Ellis... 32 72
20 Jonsen, Peter R—Michael J McDonough... 184 94
14 Kinkel, Konrad—H Loeffler... 46 04
14 Koneman, Frederick—W D Godley... 82 22
15 Kirkland, William—D L White... 418 15
15 the same—the same... 125 73
15 Klee, Henry W—M & D Levy... 122 57
15 Kirkland, William—D L White... 123 73
19 Kirby, Mary A—Mason, Au & Magenheimer Confectionery Mfg Co... 180 99
14 Lester, Jr, Joseph H—J Feiber... 311 15
17 Levy, Julius / Levy, Augustus H / Levy, Moses S } Joseph Ballin... 2,489 95
20 Lawson, Benjamin S—J F Rogers... 405 30
14 Marshall, William H—Christiana Marshall... 422 59
14 Metz, Adam / Metz, Margaretha } E A Konter... 61 75
17 Menzel, Otto—R McCord... 93 20
17 Meyer, Gesene—Wechsler & Abraham... 220 01
19 Morford, Frederick, otherwise Fred—W H Rogers... 33 27
19 Mulvielle, William / †Mulvielle, "Mary" } W Dowling... 166 56
19 Markowitz, Herman—A D Ginsberg.. 85 75
19 Major, Kenneth S—R A Hastings... 77 81
14 Nichols, Jacob J—Nat Pahquioque Bank... 1,535 59
14 the same—the same... 1,536 86
17 Nobbe, William L—J Dunn... 45 50
20 Nollman, Charles H—Wright & Winsor... 1,040 95
14 Ogilvie, Kate B and George L—Brooklyn and N Y Arcaunum Building Loan and Savings Assoc... 2,272 50
13 Pendergast, George F—H R Brown.. 1,093 06
14 Palmer, Benjamin W—J Freiber... 311 15
15 Philion, Achille—E B Haines... 297 75
19 Pullis, William—W H Rogers... 145 12
14 Rhodes, Andrew—J Kerwin... 58 75
15 Robbins, Thomas H—B F Hobby... 529 01
18 Reilly, Thomas D—R S Neely... 962 80
20 Robbins, Frank—John Feeney... 179 79
20 Reynolds, James I—Ed McGarvey... 26 25
15 Schwenk, Samuel K—W Tumbridge.. 197 69
17 Stroehlein, Mary—S Zadek... 77 45
17 Stovenel, Kate A—N B Cohn... 160 30
19 Smith, Levi—A G Fisher... 42 75
14 The J H Bonnell & Co (Lim)—Nat Bank Republic N Y... 722 99
14 Terry, Julia A and Wm H Marshall, of Marshall & Terry—Christiana Marshall... 422 59
15 Twichell, G H, sued as George H, first name unknown—E H Muncie... 127 41
15 The Banker & Campbell Co (Lim)—H Denk...27,909 45
18 the same—The J Wilkinson Co. 909 00
18 Tonjes, Charles F—Louise Neumann.. 1,251 37
18 the same—P Weidmann... 645 06
19 The Fred Hower Brewing Co (Lim)—Kings Co Bank, Brooklyn... 1,032 63
19 the same—the same... 1,528 13
20 The Eastern Electric Co—Samuel Rowland...15,364 99
19 Van Sicklen, William, otherwise Pullis—W H Rogers... 145 12
15 Williams, George E—M L Williams.. 1,583 79
19 Wolff, Louis—M B Edinger... 162 00
19 Weinstein, David—M Demby... 658 42

SATISFIED JUDGMENTS.

NEW YORK.

August 15 to 21—Inclusive.

Aluminum Process Co—R D Sawyer. (1891) $17,772 10
Brown, Warren C—Campbell Printing Press and Mfg Co. (1887)... 130 82
Bode, Charles—T R A Hall. (1886)... 41 36
Boswell, Eugene S—Pedro Riesgo. (1890)... 157 32
Busse, William—Fire Dep't. (1885)... 59 50
Same—same. (1886)... 59 50
Craig, George A—Brooklyn Gas Fixture Co. (1891)... 225 43
Denninger, Frank—L E Ransom. (1891)... 98 85
†Doyle, Andrew T—James Numan. (1891)... 1,237 34
Fitz, Charles R—George Smith, Jr. (1891)... 1,031 01
Goddard, Alice S Ely—Albert Baer. (1891)... 1,802 15
*Gould, Frederick H—Lucius Moses. (1891).. 3,942 55
*Same—H S White et al. (1891)... 5,351 42
*Same—J S Crouse, assignee. (1891)... 1,701 09
Gillies, John S—Patrick Barker. (1891)... 55 50
Gerst, Henry—H A Butterfield. (1879)... 330 06
Goldsmith, Adolph—G S Van Hoesen, as late Sheriff of Cortlandt Co. (1891)... 1,483 85
*Hodges, Amory G—Lucius Moses. (1891)... 3,942 55
*Same—H S White et al. (1891)... 5,351 42
*Same—J S Crouse, assignee. (1891)... 1,701 09
Jackson, Homer B—J H Cort. (1891)... 97 97
Kauffmann, Franklin—H A Butterfield. (1879) 330 06
Kasnowitz, Max—J E Mergott Co. (1891)... 197 15
Losee, Albert—S T Birdsall. (1887)... 1,109 01
Lester, Joseph H, Jr—Joseph Ferber. (1891). 311 15
Same—same. (1890)... 312 49
Lustig, Arnold—G S Van Hoesen, as late Sheriff of Cortlandt Co. (1891)... 1,483 85
New York, New Haven & Hartford R R Co—Owen Sweeney. (1891)...28,582 17
Same—G T Shambow. (1891)... 100 70
Same—same. (1890)... 5,314 01
*Neilson, Mathilda—Sarah E Taylor. (1891).. 415 52
Palmer, Benjamin W—Joseph Ferber. (1891). 311 15
Same—same. (1890)... 312 49
Purdy, Herschel—Campbell Printing Press and Mfg Co. (1887)... 130 82
Rowe, David A—Campbell Printing Press and Mfg Co. (1887)... 130 82
*Read, William G—Lucius Moses. (1891)... 3,942 55
*Same—H S White et al. (1891)... 5,351 42
*Same—J S Crouse, assignee. (1891)... 1,701 09
Soltan, Robert—J G Curtis. (1891)... 3,309 06
Scott, James T—G S Van Hoesen, as late Sheriff of Cortlandt Co. (1891)... 1,483 85
State Nat Bank—St Nicholas Bank. (1890)... 813 29
Same—same. (1891)... 247 07
Sullivan, John J—W H Hussy. (1885)... 4,376 62
Wormser, Leo—G S Van Hoesen, as late Sheriff of Cortlandt Co. (1891)... 1,483 85
*Willard, Edward K—Lucius Moses. (1891)... 3,942 55
*Same—H S White et al (1891)... 5,351 42
*Same—J S Crouse, assignee. (1891)... 1,701 09
Ward, Martin J—Pedro Riesgo. (1890)... 157 32

*Vacated by order of Court. †Suspended on Appeal ‡Released. §Reversal. ‖Satisfied by Execution.

KINGS COUNTY.

August 14 to 20—Inclusive.

Baker, Henry C—Evans & Corwins. (1891)... $120 35
Same—G B Ellis. (1891.) (Execution)... 54 67
Craig, George A—Brooklyn Gas Fixture Co. (1891)... 225 43
Cosby, James—Catharine Cosby. (1891)... 786 82
Miller, James—A Swanson. (1889)... 68 04
Niewoehner, Frederick—J H Siems. (1891.) (Execution)... 96 10
Noll, William A—B Moore & Co. (1891)... realized 76.00 on 1,623 05
Roth, Martin—W Grandeman. (1891.) (Execution)... 94 68
Sanford, James A—H H Frost. (1891)... 100 00
Scholes, Mary J—J W Mudgett. (1890)... 77 50
Stockholm, Clara—P J Mahoney. (1891)... 159 28
Van Wynen, Sebastian—G B Ellis (1891.) (Execution)... 54 67

MECHANICS' LIENS.

NEW YORK CITY.

Aug.
15 One Hundred and Second st, s s, 100 e Boulevard, 50x100. William Brooks & Son agt Louis M. Miller, owner, and George C. MacLaughlin, contractor... $128 25
15 Eighty-fifth st, n s, 70 w 4th av, 65x102.2. L. P. Beck agt Martin J. Hackett, owner and contractor... 500 00
15 Home st, Nos. 1070-1076, s s, 154 e Stebbins av. Brady & Anderson agt Treffle H. Allard, owner, and same and A. C. McCone, contractor... 150 00
15 Same property. J. J. Coyne agt Treffle H. Allard, owner and contractor... 490 00
15 One Hundred and Twenty-third st, Nos. 140-150 W., s s. Richardson & Boynton Co. agt Elizabeth K. Smith, owner and contractor... 890 00
17 Fox st, w s, 75 n 165th st, 50x100. C. E. Gates & Co. agt L. R. Treu, owner and contractor... 63 18
17 Inwood av, e s, 175 s Wolf pl, 50x130. Klemens Mueller agt John F. Eichler, owner and contractor... 40 00
17 Manhattan av, No. 12, n e cor 121st st, 100x100. Philip and Charles Bierschank agt Henry Schneider, owner, and Allan A. Irvine, contractor... 550 00
17 Twenty-seventh st, Nos. 431-435, n s, 368 w 9th av, 83x100. Dimock, Fink & Co. agt Homer J. Beaudet, owner and contractor... 4,266 55
17 One Hundred and Fifth st, Nos. 221-225, n s, 100 w Amsterdam av, 75x100.10. Matthesius & Vollosio agt Christian H. Schultheiss, owner and contractor... 2,181 14
17 Seventy-sixth st, n s, 200 e 10th av, 75x102.2. C. B. Keogh Mfg. Co, agt Duncan C,

McKinley and James B. Gunn, owners and contractors 342 00
17 Broadway, n w cor 36th st, 77.11x90.4x75x118.8. The Smith & Adler Co. agt C. A. Blanchard & Co. and C. A. Blanchard & Co., owners and contractors 5,375 00
17 Rivington st, No. 313, s s, 75 e Lewis st, 25x100. Gabriel Galef agt Adolph Gross and —— Solomon, owners and contractors 165 00
18 Washington av, No. 875, s w cor 161st st, 25.8x114 1 to William st, x25x124.8x7.7. Henry Sproessig agt Julius and Clara Keutel, owners and contractors 250 00
18 Fox st, w s, 161.1 n 165th st, 50x100. C. H. Kirke agt Leopold Treu, owner and contractor 146 00
18 Fox st, w s, 150 n 165th st, 50x100. E. T. Hawkins agt Leopold R. Treu, owner and contractor 105 30
18 West End av, s e cor 72d st, 100x100. Thomas Osborne agt Squier & Whipple and W. E. D. Stokes, owners and contractors 8,000 00
18 Seventy-second st, n s, 100 e West End av, 100x100. Same agt same 6,000 00
18 Eighty-sixth st, s s, 160 e Riverside Drive, 100x100.11. Same agt Squier & Whipple and Francis M. Jencks, owners and contractors 5,000 00
18 Lewis st, No. 27, w s, 100 n Broome st, 25x100. W. P. Youngs & Bros. agt Harriet B. Webster, owner and contractor 244 43
18 Eighteenth st, n s, 401.3 w 8th av, 23.4x—. Peter Wagner agt David Mackay, owner and contractor 1,932 84
18 Walton av, w s, 300 s 161st st, 75x100. John Bodemann agt John F. Rourke, owner, and John Fricker, contractor 14 00
18 Same property. J. M. Gehring agt same 85 75
18 Same property. Edward Brander agt same property 25 75
19 One Hundred and Sixty-first st, s w cor Walton av, 25x80. R. J. & W. H. McCracken agt same 325 00
19 Walton av, w s, 200 s 161st st, 50x60. Same agt same 325 00
19 One Hundred and Fifty-sixth st, No. 563, n s, 300 w Courtlandt av, 50x150. Same agt John Hetzel, owner, and John Fricker, contractor 225 00
19 One Hundred and Fifty-sixth st, n s, 300 w Courtlandt av, 100x163. William Huck assignee agt same 102 36
19 Fifty-third st, s s, 275 e 11th av, 125x100.5. Morton Bros. & Co. agt James O'Donelan, owner and contractor 1,750 00
19 One Hundred and Twenty-eighth st, No. 5, s s, 110 e 5th av, 22x100. F. E. Stair agt Mary J. Newgeon, owner, and Edward D. Stair, contractor 67 00
19 Manhattan av, n w cor 114th st, runs north 100.1 x west — to Morningside av, x southeast 118.9 to 114th st, x east 68.3 to beginning. Canda & Matthews Mfg Co. (Lim.) agt Hiram Morton Moore, owner and contractor 6,760 00
19 Prince st, n e cor South 5th av, 20x71.3. Samuel Nichols & Son agt Frank Reeber, owner and contractor 168 00
19 One Hundred and Twentieth st, s s, 125 w 8th av, 75x100.11. Patterson Bros. agt James Thompson, owner and contractor 304 77
19 Av C, No. 285, w s, 88 s 17th st, 23x58. John Glasbrenner agt Mary Reilly, owner and contractor 18 00
20 One Hundred and Fifty-sixth st, n s, 300 w Courtlandt av, 100x100. Max Schneckenburger & Son agt Joseph Hetzel, owner, John Friger, contractor 135 00
20 Manhattan av, n w cor 114th st, runs north 100.11 x west — to Columbus av, x southeast 118 to 114th st, x east 68.3 to beginning. Bartholemew Donovan agt H. Morton Moore, owner and contractor 622 00
20 Riverside Drive, s e cor 82d st, 109.3x122.4x102.2x161.1. Dunn Bros. agt Squier & Whipple, owners and contractors 4,950 00
20 Fox st, w s, 151 n 165th st, 50x100. Willson, Adams & Co. agt Leopold R. Treu, owner and contractor 309 88
20 Third av, No. 2313, e s, 99.11 n 125th st, 25x80. R. J. McDonald agt Louis J. Kahn, owner, and Percy Jacobs, contractor 1,120 30
20 Hamilton pl, e s, 38 s 142d st, 72x85. Richard Birmingham agt Mary E. Stevens, owner, and Mark Stevens, contractor 60 00
20 Walton av, w s, 200 s 161st st, 50x100. Wm. Huck assignee Louis Falk agt John O'Rourke, owner, and John Fricker, contractor 25 78
20 Twelfth st, No. 625 E., n s. Isaac Hoffman agt ———, owner, and A. Gottlieb, contractor 87 50
20 One Hundred and Fifty-sixth st, n s, 300 w Courtlandt av, 150x—. Max Hoetzel agt Joseph Hoetzel, owner, and John Fricker, contractor 39 00
20 Same property. Karl Stahl agt same 44 00
20 Same property. Heinrich Wieder Kehr agt same 18 00
20 Amsterdam av, s w cor 99th st, 40x100. T. F. Hoctor agt L. Rogers, owner and contractor 253 16
20 Eightieth st, Nos. 170-182, s s, 105 e Amsterdam av, 145x102.2. E. B. Holborow agt Morris & Abraham Schneider, owner and contractor 2,245 15
20 Ninety-fourth st, No. 39, n s, 300 w 8th av, 18x100. Alfred Boote agt Edward Van Orden, owner and contractor 155 50
21 Macdougal st, s w cor 4th st, 34.5x86, known as No. 39½ Washington sq. James Fay agt Martin Disken, owner and contractor. (Continued from Aug. 25, 1890) 2,208 77
21 Ninety-second st, s s, 100 e 5th av, 150x—. John Dawson and William Archer agt Thomas Graham, Randolph Guggenheimer, Isaac and Samuel Untermeyer, owners, and Thomas Graham, contractor. 9,000 00
21 Madison av, s w cor 59th st, 25x113. Same agt same 25,500 00
21 Honeywell st, e s, 95 s Samuel st, 25x—. Owen Toher agt Mr. Bowman, owner, —— Soule, contractor, and D. Kent, subcontractor 26 00
21 One Hundred and Eighty-fourth st, s s, 500 w Andrews av, 50x—. Thomas Wilson agt Mary L. Adriance, owner, and Thomas J. Clarke, contractor 252 90
21 Twenty-fourth st, Nos 335-339 W., 77x100. W. H. Cornet agt Joseph McFarland, Frederick Woods, Thomas H. Snape, owners, and Frederick Woods and Thomas Snape, contractors 900 00

KINGS COUNTY.

Aug.
14 Woodbine st, n w s, 25 s w Knickerbocker av, 200x100. Michael Mayer agt Albert Berckmier, owner and contractor $1,946 45
14 Cleveland st, w s, 350 s New Lots road. 50x100. Rudolph Reimer & Co. agt Philips & Smith, owners and contractors 339 42
14 Twelfth av, n w cor 58th st, 100x100, New Utrecht. C. A. Windt agt Martha Jul, owner, and Emil Kibler, contractor 178 00
14 Twelfth av, n w s, 75 n e 58th st, 20x100, New Utrecht. Same agt Ida Hofler, owner, and Emil Kihler, contractor 173 00
14 Watkins st, w s, 250 s Sutter av, 25x100. Lynch & Gormley agt Solomon Morris, owner, and Abraham Stone, contractor 675 00
14 Twelfth av, s w cor 57th st, 60x100, New Utrecht. C. A. Windt agt Emil Kihler, owner and contractor 173 00
15 Cooper st, e s, 200 n Knickerbocker av, 75x115. Bulmer Lumber Co. (Lim.) agt Stephen B. and George Rose, of Rose Bros., owners and contractors 878 00
15 Leonard st, n e cor Frost st, 25x100. Louis Bossert agt Mary E. Hower, owner, and Louis Mehrmann, contractor 1,960 00
15 Watkins st, w s, 100 s Eastern Parkway, 26.6x100. Annie Levy agt Ada Parmer, owner and contractor 350 00
15 Columbia Heights, No. 208, w s, 200 n Pierrepont st, 33x98. Schratwieser & Hilton agt Mary S. Hewsey, owner and contractor 347 00
15 Covert st, n w s, 175 s w Evergreen av, 25x100. Thomas Hanlon agt Wenzel Korb, owner, and P. F. Fitzgerald, contractor 627 00
17 East New York av, s s, 150 e Albany av, 40x100. Edward Ferguson agt James Bowen, owner, and John Galloway, contractor 46 00
17 Greene av, n e cor Lewis av, 200x100. Fenberg & Co. agt Moses Schlansky, owner and contractor 500 00
17 Cooper st, e s, 200 n Knickerbocker av, 75x115. Bulmer Lumber Co. (Lim.) agt Stephen B., George and William Rose, owners and contractors 837 00
17 Seventh st, n s, 200 w 5th av, 60x100. George Gough agt Mary Miller, owner, and George Miller, contractor 51 97
17 Broadway, n e cor Jefferson av, —x—. Andrew D. Baird & Co. agt Jacob Besson, owner, and A. J. & C. H. Moller, contractors 2,600 00
17 Pulaski st, n s, 100 w Sumner av, 330.6x100. John Rueger agt The Frederick Gower Brewing Co. (Lim.), owner and contractor. 9,588 92
18 Macon st, s w cor Howard av, 93x100. Rudolph Reimer & Co. agt Clarence Lincoln, owner and contractor 1,223 00
18 Pacific st, s s, 100 e Rockaway av, 102x107.2. Samuel Glazer agt Robert S. Neely, owner and contractor 250 00
18 Seventh st, n s, 297.6 e 4th av, 50.4x100. Watson & Pittinger agt Mary E. Miller, owner, and George Miller, contractor 385 86
18 Eighth av, s e cor 11th st, 100x120. L. E. Mansfield agt Albert F. Norris and Wm. Turner, owners and contractors 175 00
18 Second st, s s, 87.9 e Smith st, 20x100. Thomas B. Stevenson agt James Thompson, owner and contractor 26 00
19 Market st, e s, 650 n 6th st, 25x150. Earl A. Gillespie agt John Reiss, owner, and Rose Bros., contractors 568 06
19 Market st, e s, 300 n Fulton st, 21x100. Patrick Cain agt same owner and contractor. 40 00
19 Hancock st, s s, 81 e Throop av, 69.6x100. Henry H. Thorpe agt Robert S. Neely, owner and contractor 1,185 00
19 North 7th st, No. 255, n s, 145 w Havemeyer st, 25x100. Edward Burke agt John B. Ferrall, owner and contractor 150 00
19 Union st, n s, 130 e Henry st, 140x100. Charles E. Ring agt Charles W. Andress and Charles R. Mitchell, owners and contractors 1,200 00
19 Commerce st, No. 59, s s, 350 e Van Brunt st, 25x65. Davis & Fay agt A. & M. McKinzie, owners, and The Facer Refrigerating and Ice Machine Co., contractors 138 30
19 Third av, Schermerhorn st and Flatbush av, gore. John F. Richartz agt George H. Rice, owner and contractor 1,750 00
20 Seventh st, n s, 50.4 e 4th av, 50.4x100. Johnson & Phelan agt Mary E. and George Miller, owners and contractors 244 83
20 Halsey st, s s, 118.3 e Patchen av, 100x100. Richardson & Boynton Co. agt Hiram Bedell and William E. Valentine, owners, and Thomas Pedell, contractor 174 63
20 Fifteenth st, s s, 107.8 e 8th av, 72x100. Same agt Edwin J. Bedell, Thomas McCann, William Martin and Thomas Fitzpatrick, owners, and Edwin J. Bedell, contractors 79 96
20 Forty-second st, n s, from 1st av to New York Bay, 800x100 ....
Forty-second st, s s, from 1st av to New York Bay, 600x100 ....
Hewitt Boice agt The Bush Co. (Lim.), owner, and William Kenney, contractor 789 00
20 Ocean Parkway, w s, 100 s Av E, 60x250 to East 5th st, Flatbush. Jacob Morgenthaler agt Ellen Graham, owner, and J. F. Richartz & Brother, contractors 374 50
20 Ocean Parkway, w s, 160 s Av E, 60x250 to East 5th st, Flatbush. Same agt Fannie Leslie, owner, and same contractors 275 50
20 Kent av, n w cor Rutledge st, 40x80. George W. Evans agt H. M. Warren, Jr., owner, and F. W. Baldwin, contractor 75 00
20 Madison st, s s, 100 e Hamburg av, 100x100. Jacob Willman agt George A. Craig, owner and contractor 561 19
20 Henry st, n s, 70 e Coney Island Creek, 40x129, Coney Island. Theodore McKane agt John and Jane Slaven, owners, and William Ruben, contractor 625 00
20 Third av, No. 528, s s, 78 e 12th st, 20x100. James F. Frazer agt Jacob Klein and Beadleston & Woerz, owners, and John J. O'Brien and Jacob Klein, contractors 49 00

SATISFIED MECHANICS' LIENS.

NEW YORK CITY.

Aug.
15‡Madison st, Nos. 261 and 263, n s, 48.8x100.3. D. P. McCarthy agt Patrick Gallagher. (Lien filed Aug. 18, 1890) $400 00
17 One Hundred and Twenty-third st, Nos. 142-152 W., s s. Vanhorne, Griffen & Co. agt Elizabeth K. Smith and The Hardwood Decorative Co. (Aug. 5, 1891) 572 38
18 Thirty-fifth st, No. 125 E., n s. M. J. Harris agt Sidney S. Harris and John T. Moore. (Nov. 21, 1890) 70 00
18 Norfolk st, No. 175. Davis Wolf and Louis Kidansky agt Samuel Frank. (Aug. 13, 1891) 200 00
18 Ninety-sixth st, n s, 70 e Lexington av, 125x100.11. Clark & Dolan agt Owen F., Jr., and William McElroy. (Aug. 14, 1891) 3,500 00
19 Seventh av, n w cor 56th st, 50x75. Phoenix Iron Co. agt Nellie B. Mortimer. (Aug. 17, 1891) 2,116 00
20 Ferry st, n e cor Gold st, 76x96. Phoenix Iron Co. agt A. Healy & Sons and Cheney & Hewlett. (Jan. 28, 1891) 6,231 37
20 Broadway, Nos. 1365-1369, s w cor 37th st. G. I. Roberts & Bros. agt Charles A. Blanchard, Charles H. Ayers, The Marlborough Hotel Co., The C. A. Blanchard Co. and Louis L. Todd. (May 21, 1891) 1,682 71
20 Southern Boulevard, s w cor Decatur av, 50x200. William Clarke agt —— Katz and H. Rosenbaum. (July 20, 1891) 379 70
20 Twenty-fourth st, Nos. 341-345 W., 79x100. Brereton & McIntosh agt Joseph McFarland and Hardwood Decorative Co. (Aug. 5, 1891) 149 00
20 Madison av, n w cor 115th st, 81x100. Same agt William McEntee and Hardwood Decorative Co. (Aug. 3, 1891) 268 00
20 Seventh av, n w cor 56th st, 50x100. W. H. Cornet agt Nellie B. Mortimer. (Aug. 12, 1891) 1,645 75
20 Same property. Canda & Kane agt same. (Aug. 13, 1891) 2,086 52
20*Broadway, n w cor Dey st, 75x150. W. G. Fordham agt The Western Union Telegraph Co. and James B. Smith. (Aug. 15, 1891) 1,400 00
21 One Hundred and Twentieth st, s e cor Madison av, 70.6x100. J. Krause & Co agt James and Marie Gault. (June 8, 1891) 591 00
21 One Hundredth st, n s, 80 w 4th av, 20x100. Catherine Irvin agt Edward J. Kelly. (Jan. 19, 1891) 256 44
21 One Hundred and Thirty-fifth st, Nos. 5-17 W., 125x—. William Grier agt John R. Vernon and wife, Warren B. Smith, John W. Fisher and John R Meyers. (Aug. 6, 1891) 450 00
21 One Hundred and Forty-third st, s s, 419 e Boulevard, 56x100. P. J. Ryan agt Mrs. Hannah M. Halpin. (July 2, 1891) 800 00

*Discharged by depositing amount of lien and interest with County Clerk.

‡Discharged by order of Court on filing bond.

KINGS COUNTY.

Aug.
14 Driggs st, s s, 25 w North Henry st. William Meade agt —— Blazer and Funk & Lehnard, contractors. (Lien filed Aug. 8, 1891). (Deposit) $23 00
15 Sixth av, s e cor 1st st, 100x90. W. F. Fisher & Co. agt Roderick Von Graff. (July 15, 1891) 1,040 63
15 Somers st, No. 117, n s, 90 e Stone av, 20x100. Robert W. Starr agt M. Chorinski, owner, and Washington L. Baker, contractor. (July 16, 1891) 6 25
17 Dresden st, w s, 95.7 n Atlantic av, 30x150. James B. Wood & Co. agt Mr. P. Mullin, owner and contractor. (July 22, 1891) 52 25
17 Christopher st or av, w s, 250 s Sutter av, 150x100. Ole Harrison agt George A. Remsen, owner, and John Barrett, contractor. (June 20, 1891) 196 00
18 Ocean av, w s, 100 s Av E, 25x100, Parkville. John Williams agt Mrs. Graham, owner, and John Erickson and Richartz Bros, contractors. (July 18, 1891) 675 00
18 Av E, s w cor Ocean Parkway, 200.1x300, Flatbush. George Schmidt agt Helen and James F. Graham, owners, and Reichartz Bros., contractors. (July 23, 1891) 20 00
18 Rockaway av, w s, 300 n Eastern Parkway, 50x100. James O'Connor and Samuel Levy, owners, and L. Rattner and Charles F. Harles, contractors. (Aug. 8, 1891.) (Deposit) 50 00
18 Henry st, e s, bet Van Siclen av and Coney Island Creek, abt 40x150, Coney Island. Conrad Lebhart agt —— Slavin, owner, and —— Rubens, contractor. (Aug. 10, 1891.) (Deposit) 75 00
18 De Kalb av, s s, 150 w Marcy av, 100x100. Johnson & Phelan agt Elizabeth S. Maitland, owner, and Charles H. Collins, contractor. (July 9, 1891) 167 57

BUILDINGS PROJECTED.

The first name is that of the owner; ar't stands for architect, m'n for mason, c'r for carpenter and b'r for builder.

NEW YORK CITY.

SOUTH OF 14TH STREET.

Washington st, No. 693, frame shed, 21x17, tin roof; cost $25; J. P. McGovern, on premises; ar't, M. V. B. Ferdon. Plan 1146.

6th av, s w cor 11th st, six-story brk and stone warehouse, irreg., tin and slate roof; cost, $95,000; J. Glass, 426 West 23d st; ar't, G. A. Schellenger. Plan 1148.

BETWEEN 14TH AND 59TH STREETS.

37th st, No. 28 W., five-story cellar and basement brk and stone dwell'g, 23 11x61.6, with extension, 22.6x9.6, tin roof; cost, $25,000; Dr. C. McBurney, 40 West 36th st; ar't, W. W. Smith; m'n, J. J. Tucker; c'rs, Hoe's Sons. Plan 1150.

45th st, s s, 300 e 1st av, one and three-story brk building, 50 and 28x100 and 50, fire-proof felt roof; cost, $25,000; Schwartzchild & Sulzberger, on premises; ar'ts, Ogden & Son. Plan 1153.

BETWEEN 59TH AND 125TH STREETS, EAST OF 5TH AVENUE.

116th st, s s, 25 e Lexington av, five-story brk and stone flat, 25 89.6, tin roof; cost, $22,000; ow'r and m'n, J. Fish, 355 West 122d st; ar't, F. Baylies. Plan 1137

103d st, n s, 27 w Park av, two five-story brk and stone flats, 26 and 27x60, tin roofs; cost, $15,000 each; ow'rs and b'rs, Mull & Fromer, 1583 Washington av; ar't, J. J. Vreeland. Plan 1138.

Lexington av, s w cor 103d st, two and three-story brk and stone church and dwell'g, 47 and 22x78 and 40, tin and slate roof; cost $30,000; F. Willenbrook and ano., 165 East 95th st; ar't, F. Weonemer. Plan 1147.

Park av, n w cor 103d st, five-story brk and stone flat, 27x70, tin roof; cost, $20,000; ow'rs and b'rs, Mull & Fromer, 1583 Washington av; ar't, J. J. Vreeland. Plan 1160.

BETWEEN 59TH AND 125TH STREETS, WEST OF CENTRAL PARK WEST AND 8TH AVENUE.

71st st, s s, 125 w Central Park West, five four-story and basement stone dwell'gs, 20x58 with extension, tin roof; cost, each, $20,000; att'y, D. T. Kennedy, 19 West 74th st; ar't, G. A. Schellenger. Plan 1157.

Riverside av or drive, n e cor 102d st, iron and glass conservatory, 27x84; cost, abt $7,000; W. F Foster, on premises; ar't, J. Wooley. Plan 1156.

St. Nicholas av, w s, 100.11 n 121st st, four-story brk and stone stable, 59 3x193.10 and 96.11, cement or tin roof; cost, $36,000; F. Hulberg, 265 West 125th st; ar't, R. R. Davis. Plan 1154.

NORTH OF 125TH STREET.

Kingsbridge road, e s, 100 n 178th st, two-story brk dwell'g, 20x45, tin roof; cost, $5,000; R. McGarity and ano., 203 East 63d st; ar't, G. A. Schellenger. Plan 1149.
Schlesinger. Plan 1143.

136th st, n s, 475 w Lenox av, stone church, 50x120, slate roof; cost, $40,000; C. D. Baker, St. James av; ar't, C. C. Haight. Plan 1141.

159th st, s s, 125 e Boulevard, three-story frame dwell'g, 22x34, tin roof; cost, $6,50 ; J. McAllister, on premises; ar't, J. Barry; b'r, W. McFarland. Plan 1139.

2d av, n w cor 129th st, iron elevator tower and gallery, no size given, iron roof; cost, $25,000; Manhattan Railway Co., 71 Broadway. Plan 1155.

23D AND 24TH WARDS.

Bolton road, w s, bet 212th and 214th sts, brk and cement store house, 32x35, tin roof; cost, $1,50 ; Sisters of Mercy on premises; ar't, F. S.

Southern Boulevard, n s, 35 e Briggs av, two-story and attic frame dwell'g, 27.6x41.6, slate roof; cost, $7,000; C. Uihlein, 11th st and Western Boulevard; b'rs, McElroy & Son. Plan 1145.

143d st, No. 740 E., five-story brk and stone flat, 25x73, tin roof; cost, $22,000; G. Connor, 117 Forsyth st; ar't, C. Rentz Plan 1136.

179th st, n s, 88.4 w Vanderbilt av, two-story frame dwell'g, 16 8x36.6, tin roof; cost, $2,500; T. Oakes, 775 2d av, ar't, R. Lomax. Plan 1142.

Mapes av, e s, 165 n Samuel st, two story frame stable, 20x20, tin roof; cost, $250; T. J. Dolan, on premises; b'r, W. Murran. Plan 1140.

3d av, e s, 212.6 s 169th st, three-story brk stable, 30x149.4, tin roof; cost, $15,000; D. Mayer, 1043 5th av; ar't, W. Guggolz. Plan 1144.

Potter pl, s s, 400 w Bainbridge av, frame shop, 14x18, gravel roof; cost, $75; E. C. Weymann, on premises. Plan 1158.

157th st, n s, 1 6.6 e Alexander av, one-story brk building, 7.8x27, tin roof, cost, $800; St. James R. C. Church, on premises; ar't, C. A. Millner, Jr.; b'r, J. Cotter. Plan 1152.

Anthony av, e s, 80 n 175th st, two two-story and attic frame dwell'g, 18x40, shingle roof s; cost, $4,000 each; ow'r and b'r, H. Masche, n e cor Fulton av and 177th st; ar't, A. Boehmer. Plan 1151.

Stebbins av, e s, 413 n 165th st, two-story frame dwell'g, 21x37, tin roof; cost, $2,700; C. Rennhauser, 1040 Hall pl; ar't, J. J. Vreeland; b'r, J. H. Metzler. Plan 1159.

KINGS COUNTY.

Plan 1506—57th st, s s, 200 w 2d av, one two-story and basement frame (brk filled) dwell'g, 20x38, tin roof; cost, $2,500; John H. French 4th av, cor 47th st.

1507—Richardson st, n s, 80 w Kingsland av, one two-story frame dwell'g, 20x30, gravel roof; cost, $1,200; Michael Sullivan, Hancock st, near Lewis av; ar't, O. E Hoffses.

1508—Kingsland av, w s, 18 n Richardson st, two two-story frame dwell'gs, 16x30, gravel roofs; cost, $1,200 each; ow'r and ar't, same as last.

1509—Kingsland av, n w cor Richardson st, one two-story frame store and dwell'g, 18x40, gravel roof; cost, $1,500; ow'r and ar't, same as last.

1510—Seigel st, No. 87, one four-story frame (brk filled) shoe shop, 25x28, tin roof; cost, $2,500; P. Rosenzweig, 239 Van Buren st; ar't, H. Smith.

1511—De Kalb av, s s, 43 e Graham st, one three-story brk store and tenem't, 23x45, tin roof, wooden cornice; cost, $5,000; Wm. Vauthen, 444 De Kalb av.

1512—Moore st, No. 138, one four-story frame (brk filled) tenem't, 25x52, tin roof; cost, $6,000; I. Horowitz, 185 Ellery st; ar'ts, D. Acker & Son.

1513—Boerum st, s s, 175 e Ewen st, one four-story frame (brk filled) tenem't, 25x52, tin roof; cost, $6,500; A. Greenstone, 981 Myrtle av; b'r, not selected.

1514—Sheffield av, s e cor Glenmore av, one three-story frame store and tenem't, 25x57, tin roof; cost, $5,600; Lucas Glockner, 152 Henry st; ar't, C. Infanger.

1515—McKibbin st, Nos. 102-106, three four-story frame (brk filled) tenem'ts, 25x85, tin roofs; cost, each, $7,000; J. Meyer, on premises; ar'ts, D. Acker & Son.

1516—Boerum st, No 54, rear, one two-story frame (brk filled) stable, 25x25, tin roof; cost, $1,800; J. Dreirer, on premises; ar'ts, D. Acker & Son.

1517—Hancock st, n s, 91 w Ralph av, one two-story and basement brk dwell'g, 19.4x30, tin roof, iron cornice; cost, $4,000; S. G. Holland, on premises; ar'ts, D Acker & Son.

1518—Kent av, w s, 40 n Cross st, one one-story brk gas factory, 35.8 and 34.4x18.10, tin roof, iron cornice; cost, $3,000; Nassau Gas Co., Kent av and Cross st; b'rs, J. H. Dewes & Bro. and T. Davies.

1519—Kent av, w s, 464.3 n Cross st, one one-story brk purifying house, 42x190, slate roof, brk cornice; cost, $25,000; ow'r and b'rs, same as last.

1520—Kent av, w s, 405.9 from Cross st, two one-story and basement brk engine-house, &c., 47x61 and 31, slate roofs, brk cornices; cost, each, $10,000; ow'r and b'rs, same as last.

1521—Kent av, w s, 405.9 n Cross st, two one-story brk generator and retort house, 38x96x79, slate roof and brk cornice; cost, $30,000; ow'r and b'rs, same as last.

1522—Van Pelt av, n e cor Humboldt st, one two-story frame (brk filled) office, 17x20, tin roof; cost, $200; ow'r and b'r, Charles Engert, 152 Montrose av; ar't, F. J. Berlenbach, Jr.

1523—6th av, s e cor Prospect av, four four-story brk tenem'ts, 23 and 25.8x56 and 80.2, tin roofs, iron cornices; total cost, $25,000; ow'r and b'r, James Jack, 454 9th st; ar't, W. M. Coots.

1524—Bristol st, w s, 100 n Eastern Parkway, one three-story frame store and dwell'g, 20x60, tin roof; cost, $300; Emil Reinking, Liberty av and Alabama av; ar't, A. J. Warren.

1525—Schermerhorn st, s s, 50 e 3d av, one six-story and basement brk and terra cotta public hall and meeting rooms, &c., 75x95x95, Sparham cement roof, copper cornices; cost, $125,000; Young Women's Christian Assoc., Johnston Building; ar'ts, J. C. Cady & Co.; b'rs, B. Robinson & Co.

1526—Broadway, n e cor Hart st, eight two story frame (brk filled) stores, 26x60, tin roofs; cost, each, $2,000; Phillip Levy, Broadway, n w cor Thornton st; ar't, H. Vollweiler; b'r, not selected.

1527—Lorimer st, w s, 250 n Nassau av, one three-story frame (brk filled) tenem't, 25x50, gravel roof; cost, $5,000; Mary F. Fenwick, 534 Leonard st; ar't and c'r, W. H. Fenwick; m'n, C. C. Gately.

1528—Central av, w s, 81 s Cooper st, one two-story frame zinc factory, 19x35, tin roof; cost, $200; F. Bremer, on premises.

1529—De Kalb av, s w cor Fort Greene pl, one four-story brk and Lake Superior stone tenement, 20 and 30x58.8, tin or gravel roof, iron cornice; cost, $10,000; Ella E. Seaman, 10 Fort Greene pl; ar'ts and b'rs, L. W. Seaman & Son.

1530—Monroe st, n s, 110 e Stuyvesant av, two two-story and basement brown stone dwellings, 20x45, tin roofs, wooden cornices; cost, each, $4,500; ow'r, ar't and b'r, H. Grassman, 840 Hancock st.

1531—Hart st, n s, 100 w Tompkins av, two two-story and basement brown stone dwell'g, 15.8x40, tin roof, iron cornice; cost, $4,000 each; ow'r and m'n, Fred. De Ath, 127 Hart st; ar't, M. J. Morrill; c'r, not selected.

1532—Elton st, w s, 510 s New Lots road, one two-story frame dwell'g, 18x30, tin roof; cost, $2,000; Elliot D. Martin, Elton st, near Sutter av; ar't, L. F. Schellinger; b'r, R. Obermauer.

1533—Cornelia st, w s, 84 e Central av, five two-story and basement frame (brk filled) dwell'gs, 18x42, tin roofs; cost, $2,500 each; ow'rs and c'rs, Raymond & Donly, 759 Macon st; ar't, C. W. Raymond.

1534—Harman st, s s, 95 w Wyckoff av, two three-story frame (brk filled) stores and tenements, 25x56, tin roof; cost, $4,000 each; Daniel Fink, 376 Bimrod st.

1535—Barbey st, e s, 140 s Duryea av, one two-story frame dwell'g, 18x27, tin roof; cost, $1,400; Joseph C. Howard, 1070½ De Kalb av; ar't, L. F. Schillinger; b'r, F. Gunderman, Jr.

1536—Grand st, s s, 58 e La Grange st, one one-story frame blacksmith shop, 29x33, gravel roof; cost, $200; James Cook, Jr., 215 Powers st; c'r, C. F. Caufield.

1537—Bleecker st, No. 60, rear, one one-story frame cigar shop, 19.9x11, tin roof; cost, $150; John Heitmann, on premises.

1538—Broadway, s e cor Palmetto st, rear, one one-and-a-half-story frame carpenter shop, 16x10, tin roof; cost, $200; Gesina E C. Ahrens, 77 Butler st; ar't and c'r, G. A. Schanz.

1539—Milton st, s s, 125 e Franklin st, one three-story brk flat, 25x65, tin roof, iron cornice; cost, $8,500; P. F. O'Hare, Manhattan av, near Milton st; ar't, F Weber; b'r, J. Rooney.

1540—Sutton st, w s, 83.9 n Van Cott av, one one-story frame stable, 20x26, tar paper roof; cost, $100; ow'r and cr, O. W. Humphries, 194 Kingsland av.

1541—Diamond st, e s, 200 s Nassau av, one three-story frame (brk filled) tenem't, 25x65, gravel roof; cost, $5,000; Winnefred McGloin; ar't, F. Weber; b'r, J. Fallon.

1542—Liberty av, n s, 25 w Van Siclen av, one two-story frame stable, 50x27, tin roof; cost, $970; M. F Deininger, 1774 Fulton st; ar't, C. Meins; b'r, A. Henslager.

1543—Cook st, No. 126, one four-story frame (brk filled) shop, 25x35, tin roof; cost, $3,000; David Stern, 86 Seigel st; ar't, W. Schmallheiser; b'r, not selected.

1544—Cook st, No. 137, n s, 150 w Bushwick av, one four-story frame (brk filled) tailor shop, 25x35, tin roof; cost, $3,000; ow'r and ar't, same as last.

1545—Montauk av, e s, 130 s Belmont av, one two-story frame dwell'g, 20x30, tin roof; cost, $2,300; John Fulton, Essex st and Blake av; b'r, D. Laing.

1546—Lombardy st, s s, 200 w Morgan av, two one-story frame sheds and stables, 18x20, gravel roofs; cost, $75; Charles E. Lund, 81 Devoe st.

1547—Barbey st, w s, 175 s Sutter av, one two-story frame dwell'g, 20x30, tin roof; cost, $1,500; ow'r, ar't and b'r, Geo. Olsen, on premises.

1548—North 10th st, s s, 125 w Kent av, one one-story frame (brk filled) dwell'g, 22x41, gravel roof; cost, $1,000; Margaret Curry, 63 Kent av; ar't, F. Weber.

1549—Williams av, w s, 175 s Belmont av, one two-story frame dwell'g, 20x30, and extension, 11x14, tin roof; cost, $2 000; John Miller; b'rs, J. P. W. N. Free and D L. Nash.

1550—Hancock st, n w s, 90 s w Central av, eighteen two-story and basement frame (brk filled) dwell'gs, 20x45, tin roofs; cost, each, $3,000; ow'rs, ar'ts and b'rs, L. J. Lippmann & Co., 142 Eldert st.

1551—Schaeffer st, s s, 150 w Evergreen av, two three-story frame (brk filled) tenem'ts, 20 and 30x60, tin roofs; cost, $3,000 and $5,000; Mary C. Gentleman, 1658 Jefferson av; ar't and b'r, J. W. Wilton.

1552—Van Voorhis st, n s, 150 w Evergreen av, two three-story frame tenem'ts, 20 and 30x60; cost, $3,000 and $5,000; ow'r, ar't and b'r, same as last.

ALTERATIONS NEW YORK CITY.

Plan 1527—50th st, No 237 W., extension raised one story, walls altered; cost, $3,000; ow'r and b'r, O T. Mackey, 165 West 81st st.

1528—48th st, No 452 W., interior alterations, front altered; cost, $300; I. Boehm, 104 East 71st st; ar't, G. F. Pelham.

1529—Av A, No. 269, walls altered; cost, $3,000; Catherina Hermann, on premises; ar't, J. Weibter.

1530—40th st, No. 44 W., extension raised one story; cost, $700; Lillie T. Martin, on premises; m'ns, Rose & Co.; c'r, G. McKenzie.

1531—119th st, No. 102 E., roof altered, interior alterations; cost, $1,932; Mrs H. Eisenprice, admrx, 2021 Lexington av; c'r, J. Cain.

1532—41st st, No. 3 6 W., interior alterations, walls altered; cost, $200; C Wagner, 190 Amsterdam av; ar't, J. W. Cole; c'r, C. Becker.

1533—33d st, No. 12 E., interior alterations, walls altered; cost, $2,000; lessee, Helen E. Chadwick, 467 5th av; ar'ts, Hubert, Pirsson & Hoddick.

1534—23d st, No. 215 E., walls altered for new show window; cost, $500; J. D. Powell, 122 East 24th st; m'ns, Powell & Bro.; c'r, A. Steel.

1535—3d av, No. 532, interior alterations and walls altered; cost, $500; lessee, E. L. Reynolds, Holbrook, New York; c'r, J. McLoughlin.

1536—154th st, n s, 100 e Courtlandt av, extension raised one story; cost, $100; Sophia Mochus, 609 East 154th st; ar't, E. Stichler.

1537—33d st, No. 407 W., rear walls altered; cost, $150; J. Downey, on premises; ar'ts and b'rs, Eidlitz & Son.

1538—Crosby st, Nos. 79-83, tank on roof; cost, abt $ 50; G. G. Williams, 34 West 58th st; b'rs, Insurers' Automatic Fire Extinguishing Co.

1539—18th st, Nos. 59 and 61 W., one-story extension, 49.4x40 6, interior alterations and walls altered; cost, $5,000; J. L. Tonnele, 48 East 68th st; ar't, M. V. B. Ferdon; b'r, R. Macbeth.

1540—11th av, No. 764, raised one story, one-story extension, 25.5x20; cost, $2,000; Mrs. A Murphy, on premises; ar't, J. W. Cole; b'r, C. Murphy.

1541—Walker st, No. 107, interior alterations and walls altered; cost, $1,000; agent, W. H. Carpenter, Mamaroneck, N. Y.; m'n, A. Schrage.

1542—50th st, No. 8 W., chimney altered; cost, $250; F. Cromwell, on premises; ar't, P. W. Roos; b'r, G. Mulligan.

1543—Oliver st, No. 26, four-story extension, 14.2x18; cost, $2,800; Christina K. Brown, on premises; m'ns, Blevin & Sheeran; c'r, J. Power.

1544—8th av, Nos. 432 and 434, walls altered; cost, $317; J. B. Scott, 258 West 24th st; b'r, T. A. Davis.

1545—6th av, Nos. 210 and 212, interior alterations and walls altered; cost, $3,500; lessee, J. F. De Lury, 335 West 15th st; a'rt, J. B. Franklin; b'r, N. Connor.

1546—117th st, No. 448 E., two-story extension, 8 8x15; cost $500; A. J. Fisher, on premises; ar't, A Spence; c'rs, Gardner & Sons.

1547—118th st, No 337 E., walls altered; cost, $300; Lena Baritali, 101 East 9th st; ar't, J. C. Burne.

1548—Dyckman st, s s, bet Kingsbridge road and Hudson River, one-story extension, 9.6x12 6, building moved; cost, abt $400; B L. Ackermann, on premises; m'ns, Emery & Forsyth; c'r, M. McQuade.

1549—26th st, No. 402 E., new steel and brk roof, walls altered, tank house on roof; cost, abt $2,500; C. H. Schultz, 440 1st av; ar't, L. Thouvard.

1550—3d av, No. 1394, repair damage by fire; cost, $250; O. Marshall, on premises; b'r, J. D. Miner.

1551—129th st, Nos. 158-160 E., foundation and walls altered, one-story extension, 50x100; cost, $4,500; W. H. Payre, 98 Park av; ar't, C. A. Millner, Jr.; b'r, A. Arctander.

1552—49th st, No. 17 W., new light shaft and tank on roof; cost, $3,000; H. D Auchincloss, 11 West 57th st; ar't, R. H. Robertson.

1553—135th st, Nos. 144 and 146 W., interior alterations; cost $275; lessees, Corn, Kaliske & Co., on premises; c'r, T. F. Hines.

1554—Christopher st, No 115, interior alterations; cost, abt $350; J. W Dimmick, 31 Madison av; c'rs, Ryan & Bro.

1555—42d st, No. 23 W., one-story extension, 21 x48; cost, $1,300; T. M. Barnes, 755 Madison av; ar't, G. G. Bradley; c'r, W. L. Goetchius.

1556—Tremont av, No. 761, interior alterations and new front; cost. $400; Carolina Weiner, on premises; b'r, C. F. Kunz.

1557—1st av, No. 298, new front; cost, $700; W. S. Haight, 24 1st av; ar't. F. Ebeling.

1558—Av D, No. 42, new front; cost, $300; M. Frenkenthal, 363 East Houston st; ar't, H. Horenburger.

1559—2d av, No 8, front wall altered and new steps; cost, $375; att'y, F. W. Sommer, on premises; ar't, B. W. Berger.

1560—Beach st, No. 74, brk wall in rear; cost, $1,000; W. Rhinelander, 18 West 48th st; ar'ts, Hubert, Pirsson & Hoddick.

KINGS COUNTY.

Plan 783—Sumpter st, No. 135, two-story frame extension, 12x12, tin roof, new wall under new extension; cost, $850; Albert A. Otto; ar't, C. Infanger; b'r, J. J. Pirrung, Jr.

784—Flushing av, n s, 100 e Graham av, five-story brk extension, 74 8 and 136x96, tin and slate roof, iron cornice, east and rear walls removed and replaced with columns and girders, interior alterations, new freight elevator; cost, $75,000; H. Batterman, Broadway and Flushing av; ar't, P. J. Lauritzen.

785—Johnson av, No. 346, one-story frame extension, 13x44, gravel roof; cost, $100; Lemuel Weil, 184 Humboldt st.

786—5th av, s e cor Union st, two-story brk extension, 21,6x20, tin roof and front alterations; cost, $1,500; H. Rohrs, on premises; ar't and b'r, W. J Conway.

787—De Kalb av, No. 689, alterations for store and flats; cost, $5,500; Joseph Innis, 145 Lefferts pl; b'r, J. Hodgson.

788—Sumpter st, No. 58, add one-story, flat tin roof; also three-story brk extension, 29.9x18, walls rebuilt, interior alterations; cost, $4,500; Henry Wend, 60 Sumpter st; ar't. C. Infanger.

789—Tiffany pl, Nos. 14 and 16, new freight elevator; cost, $300; day's work; R. S. Hobbs, on premises; m'n, J. Alled.

790—Carroll st, n w cor Nevins st, raised 3 ft on brk foundation; cost, $100; John S. Loomis, Baltic st, cor Nevins st; b'r. J. J. O'Brien.

791—Henry st, from Pacific to Amity st, three-story brk extension, 25.6x11.6; tin roof, iron cornice; cost. $22,000; Long Island College Hospital, on premises; ar't, W. B. Tubby; b'rs, J. Thatcher and L. W. Seaman, Jr.

792—Jefferson av, No. 51, two-story and basement brk extension, 14.6x14.6, tin roof; cost, $1,100; Gayton Ballard, 51 Jefferson av; ar't and b'r. G. Halbert.

793—Cock st, No. 5, one-story frame extension, 11x19 6, tin roof, front and interior alterations; cost, $400; J. & C. Frass, 9 Cook st; ar'ts, Danman & Fischer.

794—Marion st, No. 192, one-story brk extension, 16x30, tin roof; cost, $500; Martin Carl, on premises; b'rs, P. Husemann and H. G. Amter.

795—Columbia st, No 175, rebuild front wall and new store front; cost, $1,000; P. May, on premises; b'rs, M. Gibbons & Son.

796—22d st, No. 315, raised 1 foot, also two-story frame extension, 16x25, tin roof; cost $8 0; Mrs. A. Walsh, on premises; ar't and c'r, L. H. Raymond.

797—Columbia st, Nos. 178 and 180, rebuild foundation and first story walls; cost, $450; Mrs. Pratt, 71 Hamilton av; b'r. J. F Nelson.

798—Atlantic av, Nos. 1389-1393, one-story brk extension, 46 and 60x66, glass roof; cost, $750; H. W. Whippermann, on premises; ar'ts and b'rs, Lord & Burnham.

799—Greene av, No. 271, front alterations, &c.; cost, $150; Dennison Mfg. Co., 198 Broadway, New York; b'r, W. H. Tunison.

800—Greenpoint av, No. 315, raised 8 ft on brk wall; cost, $100; Alex. Holmes, on premises.

801—Devoe st, No 141, one-story frame extension, 9x12, tin roof; also brk piers instead of posts; cost, $150; ow'r and c'r, C. Taft, on premises; m'n, J. Weaver.

MISCELLANEOUS.

BUSINESS FAILURES.

N. Y. ASSIGNMENTS—BENEFIT CREDITORS.

August

17 Casse, Alfred J. and William J. Lackey (composing firm of Casse, Lackey & Co., manufacturers of window shades, at No. 275 Canal st), to Edward McCue; preferences, $7,000.

18 Johnston, George R., Stephen S. and George D. Tallman, general partners, and Edward Spaeth and Edward D. Thurston, special partners (Johnston, Tallman & Co., importers, dealers and manufacturers in fireworks, notions, toys, &c., at No. 41 Barclay st and No. 387 West 12th st), to John M. Young; without preferences.

20 Perreins, Charles A. (cigar manufacturer, at No. 25 Old slip), to Willit P. Gaylor; preferences, $2,177.26.

21 Dane, William P. (paper dealer, at No. 61 Beekman st), to Samuel P. Prentiss; preferences, $16,199 58.

21 Hyde, Eugene M. (dealer in machinery and supplies, at No. 85 John st), to Alton H. Kimball; without preferences.

PROCEEDINGS OF THE BOARD OF ALDERMEN AFFECTING REAL ESTATE.

* Under the different headings indicates that a resolution has been introduced and referred to the appropriate committee. † Indicates that the resolution has passed and has been sent to the Mayor for approval ‡ Passed over the Mayor's veto.

NEW YORK, Aug 18, 1891.

CURBSTONES SET AND SIDEWALKS FLAGGED.

Boulevard, e s, from 63d to 65th st.
Dock st, s s, from the railroad to Riverview terrace.
Riverview terrace, w s, from junction of Sedgwick av to Dock st.
Riverview terrace, e s, from junction of Sedgwick av to a point 558 feet therefrom.
George st, from Boston av to w s of Prospect av.
64th st, both sides, from Central Park West to Boulevard.
Columbus av, from 93d to 94th sts, full width.
Railroad av West, from Morris av to 165th st.
} where not already done.†

FENCING VACANT LOTS.

90th st, n s, from Park to Madison av.†

CROSSWALKS.

Dock st, at intersection of Riverview terrace.
George st, from Boston av to Prospect av.
119th st, from Lexington to 7th avs.
124th st, from Mount Morris av to Lenox av.
Riverview terrace, at on a line with n and s s of Dock st.
Railroad av West, from Morris av to 165th st.
} where not already done.†

MAINS.

Broadway (24th Ward), from Kingsbridge road to Garden st and through Garden st to Southern Boulevard; water.†
Kappock st, from Spuyten Duyvil Parkway to Johnson av; water.†

REGULATING, GRADING, PAVING, ETC.

George st, from Boston av to w s of Prospect av.†
Railroad av West, from Morris av to 165th st.†

PAVING.

119th st, from Lexington to 7th av; granite block.†
124th st, from Mount Morris av to Lenox av; granite block.†

GAS LAMPS.

Two lights in front of Madison Square Garden; at owner's expense.†
Four lamps in front of St. Michael's Church, Nos. 377 and 379 9th av.†

APPROVED PAPERS.

Resolutions passed by the Board of Aldermen calling for the following improvements have been signed by the Mayor for the week ending August 15, 1891. *Indicates that the Mayor neither appoved nor objected thereto, therefore the same became adopted.

PAVING.

114th st, from Manhattan to Columbus av; asphalt.*
117th st, from 8th to Columbus av, asphalt.*
122d st, from Manhattan to Columbus av.*

FLAGGING, ETC.

Riverview terrace, e s, from Sedgwick av to point 55 ft, therefrom.
Riverview terrace, w s, from Sedgwick av to Dock st

ADVERTISED LEGAL SALES.

REFEREES SALES TO BE HELD AT THE REAL ESTATE EXCHANGE AND AUCTION ROOM (LIMITED), 59 to 65 LIBERTY STREET, EXCEPT WHERE OTHERWISE STATED.

August

69th st, Nos. 323-331, n s, 350 w West End av, 125x100.5, five five-story brk tenem'ts, by W. R. Brown. (Amt due $7,656; prior morts. $ —)... 24
74th st, Nos. 435 and 437, n s, 150 w Av A, 50x102.2, two five-story brk tenem'ts, by James C. Lalor. (Amt due $19,298)........ 24
79th st, Nos. 171-175, n s, 205 e Amsterdam av, 45x102.2, three three-story stone front dwell'gs, by William Kennelly. (Amt due $26,302)........ 24
65th st, No. 138, s s, 458 e 10th av, 20x100.5, four-story stone front dwell'g, by Richard V. Harnett. (Amt due $21,242)........ 24
144th st, No. 466, s s, 100 e 10th av, 21x99.11, three-story brk dwell'g, by James C. Lalor. (Amt due $3,223)........ 25
144th st, No. 454, s s, 214 e 10th av, 20x99.11, four-story brk dwell'g, by James C. Lalor. (Amt due $3 742)........ 25
42d st, No. 25, n s, 354.2 w 5th av, 20.4x100.5, four-story stone front store and dwell'g, by R. V. Harnett. (Leasehold; action No. 1; amt due $5,420)........ 25
Same property, by R. V. Harnett, (Leasehold; action No. 2; amt due $10,650)........ 25
144th st, No. 458, s s, 178 e 10th av, 17x99.11.....
144th st, No. 452, s s, 254 e 10th av, 21x99.11.....
} Two three-story brk dwell'gs........
by James C. Lalor. (Amt due on No. 458 $2,819, and $3,746 on No. 452)........ 25
10th av, No. 319, w s, 74.1 n 28th st, 24.8x100, three-story brk tenem't with stores, ¾ part, by William Kennelly........ 25
168th st, s s, 31.10 e Concord or Forest av, 20x125, by J. T. Stearns. (Amt due $4,402)........ 26
76th st, s s, 300 w West End av, 44x102.2, vacant, by J. F. B. Smith. (Amt due $7,754; prior morts. $9,000)........ 31
116th st, No. 54, s s, 82.11 e Madison av, 27.1x101, five-story brk flat, by William Kennelly. (Amt due $4,892; prior morts. $25,000)........ 31
Park av, Nos. 565-569, e s, 75 3 s 63d st, 66.5x100.1x 6 x100, five-story brk flats "Lonsdale," by William Kennelly. (Amt due $10,967; prior morts. $90,000)........ 31

KINGS COUNTY.

Aug.

Atlantic av, No. 423, n s, 250 e Bond st, 25x100, three-story brk tenem't with frame rear; assessed value, $4,500; by T. A. Kerrigan, at 13 Willoughby st........ 24
Roebling st, No. 248, w s, 71.8 s South 3d st, 23 9x 105, three-story brk dwell'g and two story frame dwell'g in rear; assessed value, $4,000..
North 1st st, No 54, s w s, 141.6 s e Kent av, 25x 140.8x25.6x142.11, three-story frame dwell'g and two-story frame dwell'g in rear; assessed value, $2,600........
} by T. A. Kerrigan, at 13 Willoughby st........ 25
Furman av, No. 73, n s, 187 e Bushwick av, 34.7x 100x187x100, two-story frame dwell'g and two-story frame carpenter shop in rear of plot; assessed value, $2,400; by T. A. Kerrigan, at 13 Willoughby st........ 26
Prospect av, No. 171, n e s, 515 s e 3d av, 20x82.10¾ x 20.9¾x61.3¼, two-story brk dwell'g; assessed value, $2,100; by Van Nater Stilwell, referee, at County Court House........ 26
St. Marks av, Nos. 671 and 673, n s, 150 w Nostrand av, 50x125.3¼, two-and-a-half-story brk detached dwell'g on plot; assessed value, $11,500; by Jere. Johnson, Jr., at the Real Estate Exchange, 189 and 191 Montague st........ 26

LIS PENDENS, KINGS COUNTY.

Aug.

High st, s s, 175 8 e Jay st, runs south 45.5 x west 0.8 x south 32.3 x east 25.8 x north 72.8 to High st, x west 24.9. Patrick Walsh agt John Walsh; amended partition; att'ys, Judge & Durack..... 14
Rockaway av, s e cor Glenmore av, 25x100 1. Andrew Lemon agt Rosa Johns; att'y, Andrew Lemon........ 14
9th st, centre line, s w s, 490 n w 3d av, 25x100. Thomas A. Fitzsimons agt Rose Fitzsimons; partition; att'y, Thomas J. Molloy........ 14
Jefferson av, s s, 410 e Howard av, 20x100. Josephine D. Powers agt George B. Bleydenburgh; att'y, Charles E Taber........ 14
Jefferson av, s s, 420 e Howard av, 20x100. Irwin Heasty agt same; same att'y........ 14
Plymouth st, n s, 200.1 e Hudson av, 28.2x100. John A. Latimer agt Mary A. Donlon; att'ys, Rolle & Snedeker........ 14
Gates av, n w s, 1 0 s w Knickerbocker av, 17.6x 97.6. The Dime Savings Bank, Brooklyn, agt Elizabeth A. Williams; att'y, J. Lawrence Marcellus........ 14
Mumbys alley, w s, 139.6 n Nassau st, 16.11x20.4 Trustees of New York and Brooklyn Bridge agt Charles W Stenzel; action to acquire title to real estate; att'ys, Bergen & Dykman........ 14
Mumbys alley, w s, 96.7 n Nassau st, 14.9x20.4. Same agt Amelia V. Brecht; similar action; same att'ys........ 14
Mumbys alley, w s, 104.10 n Nassau st, 17.2x20.4. Same agt Michael White; similar action; same att'ys........ 14
Liberty st, n w cor Concord st, 25x40. Same agt Alfred J. Cammeyer; similar action; same att'ys........ 14
Liberty st, w s, 25 n Concord st, 41.6x40. Same agt Isaac H. Cary; similar action; same att'ys.. 14
Nassau st, No. 13, n e cor Mumbys alley, 25x98.8 to another alley. Same agt Samuel W. Day; same att'ys........ 14
Fulton st, Nos. 241 and 243, w s, 27.6x41.8x27.5 x42. Same agt Edward Rorke; similar action; same att'ys........ 14
Liberty st, w s, 25 n Sprague's alley, 25x40. Same agt John Wood; similar action; same att'ys.... 14
Liberty st, No. 229, w s, 25 s Spragues alley, 25 2x 40.7x25.2x40.8. Same agt Charlotte A. Mathez; similar action; same att'ys........ 14
Fulton st, No. 239, w s, 27.6 n St. Anns Church, 20.6x41.5x20.6x41.8. Same agt William Wise; similar action; same att'ys........ 14
Fulton st, e s, 301.3 n Tillary st, runs north 16.1 x east 9 x east 18.1 x south 17.1 x west 114. Trustees of New York and Brooklyn Bridge agt Thomas J. Leary; action to acquire real estate; atty's, Bergen & Dykman........ 14
Fulton st, Nos. 251 and 253, e s, 231.1 n Tillary st, 35.2x128x35.6x115.6. Same agt Charles N. Peed; similar action; same att'ys........ 14
Fulton st, No. 237, part of, begins Liberty st, w s, 48 n St. Anns Church, 23.6x41.8x23.6x41.5. Same agt Sarshette W. Cochrane; similar action; same att'ys........ 14
High st, No. 14, s s, 25 e Mumby's alley, 25x70. Same agt Ann Nicholl; similar action; same att'ys........ 14
Fulton st, No. 257, e s, 192.7 n Tillary st, 39.6x115.6 x40x107. Same agt Jennie C. Reynolds; similar action; same att'ys........ 14
Fulton st, No. 171, part of, begins Mumby's alley, w s, 122.7 n Nassau st, 16 11x20.4. Same agt Thomas J. Leary; similar action; same att'ys.. 14
Nassau st, No. 11, n w cor Mumby's alley, 20.4x53. Same agt Thomas R. Schemerhorn; similar action; same att'ys........ 14
Fulton st, Nos. 283 and 285, part of, begins Liberty st, w s, 50.1 s Sprague's alley, 50.6x41.2x50.6x 40.7. Same agt Charles Urban; similar action; same att'ys........ 14
Fulton st, Nos. 259 and 261, e s, 192.7 n Tillary st, 28x95.6x28x107. Same agt Aaron S. Robbins; similar action; same att'ys........ 14
Fulton st, No. 249, e s, 267.4 n Tillary st, 17x127x 17 6x123. Same agt Millicent North; similar action; same att'ys........ 14
Liberty st, w s, 66.6 n Concord st, 102.8x40. Same agt Eliza C. Farnham; similar action; same att'ys........ 14
Fulton st, Nos. 273 and 275, e s, 47.4 n Tillary st, 37.5x61.6x irreg. Same agt Eliza Clark; similar action; same att'ys........ 14
Fulton st, No. 265, e s, 167.6 n Tillary st, 2 .2x87x 28x95.6. Same agt Robert L. Cutting; similar action; same att'ys........ 14
Nassau st, No. 15, n s, 25 e Mumby's alley, 25x50. Same agt Nehemiah Denton; similar action; same att'ys........ 14
High st, No. 10, s w cor Mumbys alley, 20.4x51. Same agt Valentine Schmitt; similar action; same att'ys........ 14

Fulton st, No. 277, s s, 22.4 n Tillary st, 25x irreg. Same agt Eliza J. Smith et al. trustees Thomas Smith; similar action; same att'ys.............. 14

Fulton st, No. 107, w s, 67.9 s Nassau st, runs west 40 x north 24 x southeast 10.9 x south 13.8 x west 38.5 to st, x south 4.3. Same agt Isaac H. Cary; similar action; same att'ys................ 14

Fulton st, Nos. 177-181, parts of, begins Mumbys alley, w s, 53 n Nassau st, 37.7x20.4. Same agt Daniel Lord, Jr.; similar action; same att'ys.. 14

Fulton st, n w cor Spragues alley, runs north 75 x west 40 x south 25 to alley, x east 40. Same agt Mary D. Milne; similar action; same att'ys. 14

Nassau st, Nos. 12 and 14, s w cor Liberty st, runs south 63.6 x west 38.5 x north 13.3 x northwest — x north 39 to Nassau st, x east 40. Same agt Nelson G. Carman, Jr., trustee George S. Cary; similar action; same att'ys.................. 14

Furman st, w s, 213.8 n Pierrepont st, 274.11x301.2 to East River bulkhead line, x277x320.4. Samuel H. Seaman agt Samuel McLean; notice of attachment; att'ys, Parsons, Shepard & Ogden... 15

Schermerhorn st, n s, 150 w 3d av, 160x100.9. Cornelius E. Donnellon agt Roderic Von Graff; att'ys, Bergen & Dykman.... 15

13th st, s s, 190.4 w 4th av, 17.6x100. Christina M. McKenna agt Clara M. Parkhurst admrx. George A. Parkhurst; att'y, J. C. McCachen............ 15

Columbia st, w s, 58 s Degraw st, 21x100. Henry Doell agt Barbara Doell; partition; att'y, James C. Church.............. 17

Jefferson av, s s, 180 w Nostrand av, 20x100.....
Jefferson av, s s, 200 w Nostrand av, 20x100.....
Jefferson av, s s, 220 w Nostrand av, 20x100.....
Jefferson av, s s, 240 w Nostrand av, 20x100. ..
Jefferson av, s s, 260 w Nostrand av, 20x100.....
Jefferson av, s s, 320 w Nostrand av, 20x100.....
Thomas H. Elliott exr. Stephen Pettus agt Samuel J. Jones; 6 foreclos. suits; att'ys, Hoadly, Lauterbach & Johnson.......................... 17

Butler st, e s, 100 s Hoyt st, 25x100. Fanny M. Kelly agt John F. Kelly; partition; att'y, A. C. Fransioli... 18

Pulaski st, n s, 294.5 e Throop av, 330.6x100. Antony Reisert agt The Fred. Hower Brewing Co. (Lim.); foreclos. lien; att'y, Oliver W. Beals 18

Schenck st, w s, 111.4 s Flushing av, 25x100. Margaret Anderson agt Thomas Anderson; partition; att'ys, Osborn & Beatty.................. 18

Union st, n s, 100 w 4th av, 50x95. George K. Brown agt Samuel McBride; att'y, Robert F. Rhodes.. 18

Willoughby av, s s, 20 w Steuben st, 20x80. Rebecca Mitchell agt Edward J. Barber; att'y, George L. Carlisle.................. 19

Bainbridge st, n s, 180 e Howard av, 18x100. James H. Watson and James H. Pittinger agt Elizabeth Higginson; att'y, J. Herbert Watson...... 19

Prospect pl, s s, 250 e Rogers av, 33.4x100. Same agt James E. Jenny; same att'y................. 19

Foster av, s s, adj land Maria Duryee, runs south 118 x west 25 x north 118 to av, x east 25......
Foster av, n s, 600 w 3d st, 200x100, New Utrecht.
John B. Meyenberg, Jr., agt Michael Feeney; att'ys, Dana & Clarkson........................ 19

Palmetto st, n w s, 320 n e Central av, 20x100. Thomas Berkeley agt Julius A. Mosby; att'y, Bolton Hall............ 19

Somers st, s s, 100 w Stone av, 100x100...........
Truxton st, n s, 100 w Stone av, 100x100... .....
Fulton st, s s, 100 e Hopkinson av, 100x100..... .
William H. Scott agt Marion O. Crumpler; att'y, Bolton Hall 19

Ocean pl, w s, 147.8 s Herkimer st, 19.4x97.6. William M. Evans agt Henry C. Baker; att'y, Noah Tebbetts.. 20

Fulton st, No. 227, part of, begins Liberty st, s w cor Spragues alley, 25x40. Trustees of N. Y. and Brooklyn Bridge agt John F. Coots; action to acquire real estate; att'ys, Bergen & Dykma . 20

Fulton st, No. 247, e s, 284.4 n Tillary st, 16.11 to Liberty st, x130x17x127. Same agt John Blake; similar action; same att'ys 20

Fulton st, No. 279, n e cor Tillary st, runs east 25 x northeast — x west 7 x southwest 29 to Fulton st, x south 22.4. Same agt Martha M. Huyler; similar action; same att'ys.................. 20

North 10th st, n s, 125 w Bedford av, 50x100. St. Georges Roman Catholic Church, Brooklyn, agt Mathias Yodyszus; action to compel reconveyance; att'ys, Klein & Rendich................ 20

RECORDED LEASES.

NEW YORK. Per Year

Broadway, No. 299, store or room B on ground floor. Isaac H. Hunter, agent for Stillman & Hubbard, to Frederick A. Cauchois; 4 10-12 years, from July 1, 1891........................ $12,000

Duane st, No. 153, store and part cellar. Anthony Fischer to Henry W. Cordts; 5 years, from May 1, 1890............................ . 1,200

Same property. Assign. lease. Henry M. Cordts to Adam Siegfried......... .. .... nom

Jay st, Nos. 48 and 50. Patrick Skelly to William H. Amerman and Arthur W. Paterson; 8⅔ years, from Feb. 1, 1891 ....4,100, 4,200

Mercer st, Nos. 127-131. Lazarus Rosenfeld to Jos. Schultz & Co.; 6 years, from Feb. 1, 1891......... 6,000

Varick st, No. 26, n e cor Beach st, store and part basement. Henry McArdle to Denis O'Neill; 2 years 8 months and 11 days, from Aug. 19, 1891.................................... 1,000

Wooster st, Nos. 108 and 110, north part of second loft. Louis Kahn and Morris Burganer to Ramon Velez; 2½ years, from Aug. 1, 1891............ 800

28th st, No. 215 E., store. Henry Schumacher & Sons agents for Naretta Weber to Samuel Miller; 3⅔ years, from Sept. 1, 1891 360

34th st, No. 46 E. Anna Moore to Charles T. Parker; 5 years, from Oct. 1, 1891......... . 2,560

49th st, No. 340 W., store and three rooms. Henry Touyan to John Warnock; 5 years, from Nov. 1, 1891......................... ... 600

59th st, No. 241, store and rear rooms. Caroline Dillenberg to Mary O'Connor; 5 years, from July 21, 1891.... 360

Same property. Assign. lease. Mary O'Connor to The Burr Brewing Co...... .... nom

104th st, No. 339 E., store and rear rooms. Dominico Farende to Michael Gestaro; 4 years, 8 months and 13 days, from Aug. 13, 1891.... 192

Same property. Assign. lease. Michael Gestaro to Burr Brewing Co..................... nom

107th st, No. 151 E. Gustav Basch to Lewis Morris and Henry Steinhardt; 7 years, from May 1, 1891................ 1,950

Willis av, No. 223, store and rear rooms and part cellar. John A. Foote to Ferdinand Hildebrandt; 3 years, from May 1, 1891...... 540,000

1st av, No. 1129, store and extension. Henrietta Katz to Bernard Quinn; 5 years, from May 1, 1891...................................... 900

3d av, No. 222. Thomas K. Foster to Patrick J. O'Keeffe; 9 years, from May 1, 1891. ....2,500, 2,700, 2,800

Same property. Assign. lease. Patrick J. O'Keeffe to James Everard................... nom

3d av, No. 2180,
119th st, No. 186 E.
John Muller to John Scott, Jr; 4⅜ years, from Aug. 15, 1891.................................... 2,700

3d av, No. 2327, store and part cellar. John C. Fry, Brooklyn, to Asa Lemlein and Benjamin Jacobs, of A. Lemlein & Co.; 2¾ years, from Aug. 1, 1891........ 880

3d av, n w cor 137th st. Margaret Kratch to Felix McKenna; 18 years, from Sept. 1, 1891. 900

Same property. Assign. lease. Felix McKenna to Richard McKenna.... .... nom

9th av, No. 861, store on ground floor. Maria N. Winne to James F. Jordan; 10 years, from Aug. 13, 1891.......... 3,000

9th av, No. 92, store floor, &c. Caroline wife of and Frederick Kellar to Robert B. Rouband; 4 10-12 years, from July 1, 1891........ 720

10th av, No. 96, store floor. Henry H. Diercks to John and Henry Neus; 4⅔ years, from Sept. 1, 1891.............................. 1,500

CHATTELS.

NOTE.—The first name, alphabetically arranged, is that of the Mortgagor, or party who gives the Mortgage. The "R" means Renewal Mortgage.

NEW YORK CITY.

AUGUST 14 TO 20—INCLUSIVE.

SALOON AND RESTAURANT FIXTURES

Arberg, Diedrich. 817 2d av....G Ehret. $600
Bayer, Etienne. 33 Bowery....J Kress B Co. 800
Bissikummer, A E. 2187 2d av....J Ruppert. 650
Burns, Michael. 230 Mulberry....India Wharf B Co. 500
Bean, John. 80 8th av....Henry Elias B Co. 2,035
Bergami, Giacomo. 122 South 5th av....Bachmann B Co. 600
Callum, Charles. 780 Columbus av... H Held. 1,500
Cassel, J & S. 1600 Railroad av....India Wharf B Co. 745
Craig, Patrick. 228 3d av....Bernheimer & S. (R) 4,000
Cunneen, Carroll. 188 Bleecker....H Elias B Co. (R) 1,500
Cangro, Antonio. 333 E 113th....D Mayer. 277
Dunn, Terence. 216 E 56th....J Wallace & Son. 330
Donnelly, P C. 435 11th av....Beadleston & W. Pool Table, &c. 100
Dunn, Patrick. 10th av and 196th st....A Hupfel's Sons. 300
Deyerberg, H H. 27 10th av....G Bechtel exr of. 2,500
Edsall, Clara L. 41 and 43 W 125th....P Bartlett. Restaurant Fixtures. (R) 950
Egan, F J. 837 8th av....H Vogel. 850
Eiser, Paul. 245 E 77th....Wagner & S. Pool Table. 145
Engel, Leopold. 75½ Columbia....D Mayer. (R) 588
Frankewitch, George. 525 E 5th....M T Garvey. 100
Fried, Philip. 118 and 120 Columbia....J Hoffman B Co. (R) 1,000
Felt, Henry. 10th av and 186th st....A Hupfel's Sons. 300
Flannery, T E. 802 Greenwich....C Stein. 3,563
Fatula, John. 249 2d . S Liebmann's Son B Co. 600
Furlong, John. 386 Canal....Beadleston & W. (R) 2,000
Faller, Charles. 95 E 4th....Bachmann B Co. 1,000
Fino, James. 168 Thompson....Burr B Co. 500
Gestaro, Michael. 339 E 104th....Burr B Co. 400
Garbade, Louis. 91 Walker....S Liebmann's Sons B Co. 300
Griesbaber, John. 505 W 50th ...Bachmann B Co. (R) 900
Hall, Samuel. 534 W 34th and 608 W 43d.... Amer Guar Assoc. Saloon and Furniture. 100
Heins & Stahlhut. 96 Gold....G Seeburg. 232
Same....same. 200
Huber, August. 196 E 3d .. F Ibert. 300
Hedenkamp, D. 155 and 157 Washington....W Ulmer. (R) 2,000
Hure, Mathilda. 2609 8th av....Bernheimer & S. (R) 3,000
Hellshorn, George. 121 11th av....Consumers B Co. 6,000
Joyce, Thomas. 161 W 53th.. .H Vogel. 350
Jacob, Aron. 71 Suffolk. ..H B Scharmann & Son. 1,500
Jordan, J F. 861 9th av....J C G Hupfel B Co. 5,000
Kaufmann, C A. 73 New. ..J Hoffmann B Co. 3,000
Khuen, Frank. 155 Amsterdam av....Bachmann B Co. 1,450
Kaufman, Elise. 1438 1st av....J Kuntz B Co. 500
Kessel, Eleanor A. 321 W 145th....C Iba. 400
Kaplan, Morris. 134 and 136 Canal....W Peter. (R) 3,000
Kaufmann, C A. 73 New....M D Stern. 400
Krikava, Martin. 320 E 73d... J Kuntz B Co. 500
Laserovitz, Abraham. 50 Delancey .... H B Scharmann & Son. 1,000
Langhorst, F W. 158 E 23d....J C Boettner. 3,500
Mueller, R C. 36 Catharine....J Cusick. (R) 1,500
Murphy, W F. 258 Madison....S Wurzburg. (R) 600
Muhs, H F. 186 Monroe....Danenberg & Coles. (R) 447
Mack, A. 216 E 80th ...Bernheimer & S. (R) 500
Manahan, Patrick. 532 11th av....V Loewers. (R) 360
Mappes, Philip. 520 9th av....V Loewers. (R) 966
McCann, P C. 340 W 16th....M Seitz. 350
McGrath, James. 46 Spring....Beadleston & W. (R) 1,800
McKeen, T J. 178 Av C....S Liebmann's Sons B Co. 4,000
McKenna, R M. 2521 3d av ...P Doelger. 2,500
Nehring, Charles. 344 W 38th....F Hower B Co. 705
Nemec, Frank. 1283 1st av....F Hower B Co. 650
Neville, J J. 545 3d av....Wagner & S. Pool Table. 300
Organ, J J. 167th st and 10th av....J Beck. 1,500
Ohl, Herman. 300 Broome....Bernheimer & S. 400
O'Connor, Mary. 241 E 59th....Burr B Co. 500
Pearson, Sorelle. 269 9th av....C Stein. 4,306
Pfleiderer, Christian. 84 Delancey....H B Scharmann & Sons. 200
Pfriemer, Joseph. 128 Columbia....J Ruppert. 900
Rosenhagen, Henry. 158 Orchard....J Wallace & Son. 450
Schmidt, Andreas. 276 7th av....C Stein. 650
Singer, Markus. 154 Attorney....Bernheimer & S. Pool Table. 140
Sullivan, M. 319 Bowery....Rubsam & H B Co. 2,000
Schmitt, George. 627 E 16th....H B Scharmann & Sons. 500
Schuster, G H. 49 Franklin....J H Meieldierck. Saloon Pump. 75
Semis, L. 225 Delancey....C Dierking. Pool Table. 95
Sinnot, A J. 201½ Whitehall....G Ehret. 2,200
Schrader, Anna M. 412 Brook av....A Hupfel's Sons. 900
Schultze, Marie. 2670 8th av....Bernheimer & S. (R) 1,000
Scott, John, Jr. 2180 3d av and 186 E 119th st .. F & M Schaefer B Co. 3,000
Siemon, W T. 76 Spring ....J Kuntz B Co. 375
Smith, M J & D T. 438 Greenwich....Bernheimer & S. (R) 1,000
Stewart, W F. 42 Carmine....W Peter B Co. 2,700
Schinek, Herman. 137 West Broadway... J & A Doelger. 880
Summerfield, H & F. 17 Clinton pl....Burr B Co. 800
Vincent, Patrick. 88 Essex ...H B Scharmann & Sons. 600
Von Oehsen, Adolph. 781 7th av ..P Doelger. 7,000
Wavra, Joseph. 313 E 71st...J H Bereuter. Pool Table. 145
Weil, Hermann. 312 E 4th....J Eichler B Co. 1,500
Weiss, J & Son. 102 1st....I Rosenfeld. Restaurant Fixtures. 100
Wewer, Richard. 940 Washington av....P & W Ebling B Co. 800
Weiben, John. 58 Thomas....J Plangemann. (R) 1,000
Wiegand, John. 110th st and Southern Boulevard....D G Yuengling, Jr. B Co. (R) 1,000
Wilzig, Paul. 85 E 4th....G Bechtel. (R) 4,210
Wintermeyer, Bernhard. 15 Bowery....H Elias B Co. (R) 2,700
Wollman, S & J. 505 Canal....B & P Katz. 800
Wunschmann, Joseph. 232 W 28th....M Groh's Sons. (R) 400
Walch, Charles. 149 Greenwich....Bachmann B Co. (R) 3,000
Ward, Michael. 461 4th av....G Ehret. 3,500
Wolf, Joseph. 104 E 1st....J Ruppert. 950
Wolff, V G. 242 E 126th ...P Schoenhofen B Co. 1,500
Zimmermann, Charles. 192 Ludlow....W Horrmann. (R) 1,100

HOUSEHOLD FURNITURE.

Aarons, Annie A. 1767 Park av....Fennell & Pye. 149
Allen & Rowland. 229 W 16th....J Baumann. 430
Allport, J G. Sedgwick av....Fennell & Pye. 218
Ange, George. 255 W 40th....O'Farrell & Co. 499
Aron, Max. 2224 5th av....Manges Bros. 417
Alexander, W Y. 1797 Lexington av....J Baumann. (R) 225
Barlow, Ellen. 8 W 22d....Brooklyn F Co. 532
Bermingham, Miss. 206 E 45th....J Moran. 158
Boger, Celia M. 507 E 118th....Dreisacker & Co. 164
Berge, Belle. 1473 Lexington av....H Mannes & Son. 213
Beynroth, Mrs W H. 164 W 83d....J Early. 155
Bortle, W E. 625 E 137th....H Mannes & Son 193
Brown, Frank. 254 W 45th .. S Baumann. 209
Byrnes, K. 313 E 56th....H Thoesen. 122
Baron, Richard. 171 E 4th....L Baumann. 174
Barton, J W. 334 W 42d....L Baumann. 201
Bauer, Louis. 2106 2d av....J Kabatchnick. 134
Beaid, L W. 164 Bainbridge av....Krakauer Bros. Piano. 165
Berge, Ludevicko. 336 E 20th....H S Kisler. 252
Bishop, Mary. 208 E 122d....Fennell & Pye. 111
Burrows, Mrs C. 12 Cannon....D M Brown. 108
Cronin, Mrs M. 252 E 62d ...D M Brown. (R) 100
Cunningham, J B. 107 W 62d....W E Wheelock & Co. Piano. (R) 159
Clark, E A. 216 W 53d....T Bamber. 224
Connell, Mary A. 735 E 137th....Jordan & M. (R) 190
Cummings, William. 40 E 28th....Lord & T. 212
DeBedts, Alice. 263 W 25th....J Baumann. (R) 185
Dunn, John. 304 E 33d....B M Cowperthwait & Co. 122
De Seve, Werner. 1748 1st av....A Bernstein. 225
Doran, Mrs J. 218 E 80th....A Bernstein. 135
Dorsey, R C. 206 W 41st....L Baumann. 175
Donnelly, Bridget. 204 E 32d....Manges Bros. 188
Easton, Helen. 308 W 43d....H Mannes & Son. 207
Ehrlich, David. 160 E 68th....American G Assoc. 100
Finkelstein, J L. 361 6th av....J P Delehanty. 161
Foster, Albert. 49 E 129th....G Reubel. 107
Friedrich, Dora. 103 E 14th....A Feusch. 225
Fun, Franzisco. 1135 1st av....Geo Fennell & Co. 168
Fox, R A. 8th av, bet 93d and 94th sts....J Baumann. 177
Gates, Jessie M. 226 W 17th....O'Farrell & Co. 417
Gedalge, Julius. 651 E 6th... G Reubel. 131
Giriaid, Mrs E. 261 W 39th....J Moran. 246
Glassburg, M. 77 Columbia....J A Schwarz. 124
Greene, James. 27 Jackson pl, Brooklyn ...J Kabatchnick. 164
Grundman, Ada M. 41 Hopkinson av, Brooklyn ....Fennell & Pye. 105
Greene, E C and L E. 319 W 16th....J C Hegemann 125
Gilbert, F R. 233 W 49th....J Early. 1,195
Haldimand, Annie. 45 W 66th....W E Wheelock & Co. Piano. (R) 119
Harrison, Nellie. 570 7th av....E O'Brien. 400
Hart, Mabel. 107 W 40th....Kate Williams. 500
Hennelly, Mrs Patrick. 240 Av A ...G Reubel. 102
Herbert, Lizzie....J Moriarty. 150
Horwitz & Speiriber. 69 Forsyth....N Altschuler. 140
Houghton, Eva. 273 W 38th....O'Connor & Treacy. 130
Hester, E M. Storage....C E Pierce. 180
Ingram, Maggie. 519 W 52d....F T Higgins. 115
Ironside, Elizabeth. 17 W 99th ...O'Farrell & Co. 259
Joiner, Sophie. 666 E 144th....Fennell & Pye. 963
Jones, Mathew. 30 W 9th.. H Thoesen. 1,907
Jovine, Antonio. 47 E 7th....S I Herschmann. 125
Kraus, G. — E 78th....S I Herschmann. 146
Kelly, John. 115 W 60th....O'Farrell & Co. 119
Kerpen, Alfred. 160 E 4th....E Wolf. 144
Krouse, Rose. 54 Sheriff....H S Eisler. 102
Kube, Mrs Bruno. 333 E 81st....D M Brown. (R) 132
Laubliner, Rosa. 328 52d....J R Keane & Co. 457

Lassalle, S G. 229 Waverley pl....Lord & Taylor. 608
Lesser, Ettie. 10 E 66th....J Moriarty. (R) 115
Lima, Lorenzo. 556 W 48th....J Baumann. 130
Lewis, Annie 116 W 29th....B M Cowperthwait & Co. 537
Lindau, V H and L. 127 E 71st....J & J Dobson. 217
Lindsay, J A. 10 Bayard....Jordan & M. (R) 213
Lippencott, R H. 1133 Madison av...W E Wheelock & Co. Piano. 275
Middleton, E. 321 W 50th....Brooklyn F Co. 880
Missel, Ida. 302 E 26th Geo Fennell & Co. 129
Mann, W D and M E. 9 and 11 W 30th....A M Bigelow. 1,100
Melillo, Gaetano. 7 Elizabeth....J Nabatchnick 198
Monaghan, J H. 695 E 135th....Fennell & Pye. 156
Moran, Michael. 302 E 49th....J Moran. 154
Moses, A. 173 E 74th....J R Keane & Co. 281
Murray, Michael. 886 2d av... G Reubel. 162
Musch, Francis. 523 E 85th ...Krakauer Bros. Piano. 175
Myers, C W. 562 1st av....H S Eisler. 200
Meaney, Mary. 342 E 8th....R M Walters. Piano. 200
Mathews, J J. 154 3d av....Manges Bros. 175
McWilliams, Magdalene. 188 8th av....O'Farrell & Co. 177
Meeks, Annie. 167 W 22d...L Baumann. 114
Nielsen, Emma. 850 Tinton av....Fennell & Pye. 101
Nichols, C L. 486 St Nicholas av....Amer Guar Assoc. 100
O'Callaghan, Lizzie. 2070 3d av....Fennell & Pye. 134
Owen, W B. 273 W 117th....J Moran. 202
Olinsky, Barney. 429 E 72d....Carey & Sides. 104
Pinckney, H F A &c. 102 W 84th....Meyer & Lange. 1,000
Porter, Kate. 124 W 31st....S Woods. 1,500
Peters, Robert. 146 W 61st....J Baumann. 194
Putter & Cohen. 36 Forsyth....B M Cowperthwait & Co. 205
Quinn, J J. 167 E 99th....Dreisacker & Co. 167
Reeve, F A. 191 W 134th ...J Baumann. 325
Rodding, Bertha. 365 E 123d....B A Trowbridge. 300
Rosell, Laura. 4 W 136th ...F T Higgins. 156
Rosenthal, Anna. 238 E 104th....Fennell & Pye 107
Rooney, Mrs J. 307 E 97th . D M Brown. 135
Rhodes, Kittie. 312 W 47th....H Mannes & Son. 194
Rosenberg, Chas. 333 E 30th....L Baumann. (R) 138
Rosenstein, E & H. 210 E 48th....E Basch. (R) 1,200
Sweeney, Daniel. 427 W 36th....L Baumann. 149
Silberstein, A J. 845 Columbus av....J Baumann. 162
Smith, F E. 2162 7th av....H Thoesen. 239
Smith, Stella. 2451 2d av ...Fennell & Pye. 133
Sprague, H B. 1383 Lexington av....Fennell & Pye. 357
Sangster, M V. 411 W 51st....H Mannes & Son. 264
Sharkey, Libbie. 13 W 56th. ..J Baumann. (R) 222
Silk, Mary A. 248 W 14th....J & J Dobson. 109
Sparrow, Ida. 66½ W 10th....J Baumann. (R) 149
Stockmar, C B. 215 E 25th....Geo Fennell & Co. 197
Storms, Christian S. 248 W 16th....W F Severance. 124
Turk, Hattie. 109 E 85th....J Baumann. 257
Tobey, Mary T. 20 Montgomery....R M Walters. Piano. 148
Weneck, Annie. 1558 3d av....J R Keane & Co. 232
Weston, Margaret. 420 E 66th....L Baumann. 148
Wolfarth, Laura J. 208 W 60th....J Rubenstein. 107
Walsh, Martin. 221 E 69th....J Early. 135
Watson, Gertrude. 988 6th av....L Baumann. 155
Wilbur, Marie. 256 W 43d....L Baumann. 207
Wurtz, Regina. 315 E 6th....Geo Fennell & Co. 127
Zagot, Meldel. 858 2d av . Brooklyn F Co. 427

MISCELLANEOUS.

Ackerle, H G. 180 Columbus av....P A Cassidy. Wagon. 75
Angel, Isaac. 96 Broadway....H Stern. Office Fixtures. 657
Atkinson, M B. 19 Platt....J E Durgin. Press. 471
Atlanta Boat Club. Harlem River and 7th av....W Tuttle. Boat House, &c. 1,500
Austin, S W. Highbridge....A Lamarte. Horses and Milk Wagon. 102
Avignone, Frank. 1874 3d av....A Schwaab & Son. Barber Fixtures. (R) 154
Antel, Louis. 101½ W 63d....P Westphal. Barber Fixtures 300
Badgley & Schultz. 268 Henry....Archer Mfg Co. Barber Fixtures. (R) 58
Balzer, Amelia. 119 Willett ... C Krauch. Horse, Wagon, &c. 750
Beck, Reuben... J Gottsleben. Coach. 500
Bergin, Patrick. 10th av and 37th st....National Cash Reg Co. Register. 200
Bolton, Henry. 150 E 50th .... Wolff Bros. Horse. 90
Borgwardt, Frederick. 135 W 27th....F O Richter. Machines. 600
Bruchle, C J. 1029 Boston road....P Pryibil. Machinery. 415
Buttre, J C. 32 Courtlandt....F E Francisco. Press. (R) 1,000
Barrett Electric Co. 10 Cedar .. Prentiss Tool Co. Machinery. 456
Biggane, M J. Vesey and West sts, Washington Market . D McLaughlin. Stands, &c. 1,650
Brannigan & Kilgannon....J O'Leary. Horses, Trucks, &c. 400
Buelow, L C. 321-323 E 122d....P Mueller. Horse, Wagon, &c. 90
Copeland, Ewance. 455 7th av, 148 and 150 W 35th st ...W Hall. Undertaker Fixtures and Horses. 5,000
Cavalle & Digirolamo. 118 9th av ...S Littman. Barber Fixtures. (R) 61
Conner, W M. St James Hotel... M Robbins. Leasehold. 75,000
Coughlin, John. 379 and 381 Madison....Wolff Bros. Horse. 300
Cummings, William. 1193 Broadway....Marvin Safe Co. Safe. 120
Cabricci, T. 110th st and 2d av....Archer Mfg Co. Barber Fixtures 810
Canary, Timothy. 513 E 19th....T Canary. Horses, Coaches, &c. (R) 2,000
Cramer, C & H. 149th st and Walton av....C C Cramer. Grocery Fixtures. 800
Davids, C H. 126 Liberty....E C Hinsdale. Office Fixtures. 190
Dayboch, N. 44 Essex....Archer Mfg Co. Barber Fixtures. 87
Delia, Leonardo. 441 1st av....A Schwaab & Son. Barber Fixtures. 264
Same....same. Barber Fixtures. 264
Dean, E. 1 Broadway....Marvin Safe Co. Safe. 140
Dragna, Simone. 345 E 121st ...A Schwaab & Son. Barber Fixtures. 460
Dragna & Lorello. 200 W 67th....A Schwaab & Son. Barber Fixtures. (R) 164
Dicenta, Frank....Roger Wheel Co. Horses and Truck. 150
Davidson, M. 813 Av A....Hall's Safe and Lock Co. Safe. 35
De Leo & Brogna. 16 Franklin....G Loveli. Barber Fixtures. 132
Donaghey, David. 37th st and 7th av....M McPatton. Horses, &c. (R) 100
Drucker, M. 130 Delancey . Lamson Consol S S Co. Register. 210
Eberle, Philip. 416 E 23d ...J Weiss....Barber Fixtures. (R) 28
Esposito, Vincenzo. 459 W 33d....S Littman. Barber Fixtures. 277
Eugenhofer, Henry. 2750 8th av....National Cash Reg Co. Register. 175
Farengo, Vincenzo. 77 Greenwich av....A Schwaab & Son. Barber Fixtures. 306
Feigensohn, David. 189 East Broadway....L Bresloff. Drug Fixtures. 1,000
Frankel, Solomom. 58 Av D....M Krieger. Store Fixtures. 300
Freese, Anna. 514 E 137th....Koster & Son. Piano. 185
Fanning, E L. 277 6th av. ..J Metz. Press. 40
Frank, August. 1549 Av A... Lamson Consol S S Co. Register. 210
Friedrich, Heinrich. 108 E 14th....A Fensch. Drug Fixtures. 225
Feldman, Joseph. 1st av, bet 92d and 93d sts....Archer Mfg Co. Barber Fixtures. 515
Fruchtenicht & Ullrich. 370 Greenwich ...A Cossin. Horses, Trucks, &c. 2,075
Glickman, Abraham. 29 Suffolk....M Silberman. Store Fixtures, &c 200
Greenberg, C. 84 Hester....M Greenberg Machinery. 180
Gallo, Nasale. 384 Water ...G Scalese. Barber Fixtures. 75
Gardner, E B. 287 and 289 Western Boulevard ....D Thomas. Butcher Fixtures. 400
Gallagher, J E. 1680 2d av. National Cash Reg Co. Register. 175
Geduldig, Carl. 501 9th av....H Welsh. Laundry Fixtures. 250
Hosuedel, Frank....G Dessecker. Coffin Wagon. 375
Hirschel, Joseph. 186 Orchard. ..C Marscheider. Butcher Fixtures. 150
Hoffmann, G B. 8th av and 127th st....Donigan & Neilson. Wagon. 250
Horwath, Emerich. 251 E 35th....P Westphal. Barber Fixtures. 55
Jackman, Michael. 119th st and 10th av, 77th st and West End av....E Lee. Horses, Carts, Machinery, &c. 2,000
Jenkins, Margaret. 222 W 67th... D Finerty. Grocery Fixtures. 100
Kregan & Cully. 735 11th av....National Cash Reg Co. Register. 175
Kallma , A F & Co. 49 E 2d....O Lehmann. Office Fixtures. 40
Koch, Henry. 612 E 83d....G A Devermann. Horse and Milk Wagon. 150
Koehler, A F. 391 7th av....W Huber. Bakery Fixtures. 100
Kopelman, S T. 236 Broome....Lamson C S S Co. Register. 140
Korngut, Adolf. 53 Av B....S Korngut. Butter and Egg Fixtures. 100
Krieger, Marx. 58 Av D....R Krieger. Butcher Fixtures. 350
Krieger, Marx. 102 Columbia....S Zinsler. Store Fixtures. 400
Kearney, Luke. 217 E 23d ...F Thistleton. Cab. 200
Kurtz & Metz. 782 1st av....M Metz. Horse, Wagons, &c. 500
Kennel, P F. 610 E 12th ...W Meles. Horses, Trucks. 500
Kerby, J A. Bathgate av and 174th st....D Seligman. Horses, &c. 815
Lawria & Cachione, 48 Sullivan....J Souvay. Barber Fixtures. 118
Luckert, W J. 33 Norfolk .... J Burkhard. Horse. (R) 25
Lipiansky, Barnett. 35 Jefferson....C Dierking. Butcher Fixtures. 231
Lisiecke, F F. 124 Chambers....W Scott & Co. Machinery. 850
Lagroute, Frank 130 East Houston....A Schwaab & Son. Barber Fixtures. 87
Lally, P J....Wolff Bros. Horse, Cab, &c. 102
Levy, Edward. 86 East Broadway ...Wolff Bros. Horse. 165
Lisanti, Antonio. 808 2d av....A Schwaab & Son. Barber Fixtures. 260
Mahon, J F. 1431 2d av....M Mahon Cigar Fixtures. (R) 500
Marzuelo, Ginsippi. 164 W 4th....A Petrone. Barber Fixtures. 30
Miller, William....M Armstrong & Co. Coach. 2,050
Mischke, Charles. 164 W 27th....Prentiss Tool Co. Machinery. 280
Monahan, Edward ...W B Davis. Coupe. (R) 400
Martinellie, Antonio. 82 W 90th....S Littman. Barber Fixtures. (R) 80
Modeman, G H. 502 3d av and 125th st and 5th av....Amer Guar Assoc. Dental Fixtures. 450
Muller, Louis. 61 Av C....F Muller. Confectionery. 1,000
Marcus, P and H. 2659 3d av....W C Bates. Store Fixtures. 150
McMurray, William....Th McMurray. Tools, &c. 1,000
McNiff, Joseph....S Jolly Horse. 105
Metz, A & C.. 60 John...Campbell P P Co. Press, &c. (R) 2,744
Moore, Herman.. 122 Willett....A J Wolff. Horse, &c. 150
Mott, Anthony. 2088 7th av....J N Blasi. Barber Fixtures. 600
Muller, August. Westchester....L Richter. Horse, Wagon, &c. 150
Macgowan, R W. 28 and 30 Beekman....J A Slipper exr. Press, &c. (R) 1,400
Marion, Thomas. 431 E 47th st....J Marion. Horses and Ice Wagon. (R) 700
McDonald & Wiggin. 82d st and Amsterdam av ... E T Eddy, Jr. Bottling Fixtures. 300
Mueller, William. 358½ W 44th....F Wendel. Barber Fixtures. 200
Murphy, J. — W 4th .. D W Cochran. Horses, Ice Wagon, &c. 1,000
Nichols, R W. 2384 8th av....Day & Beers. Store Fixtures. 500
Napoli, Guiseppe. E 129th....A Schwaab & Son. Barber Fixtures. 475
North Side Pub Co. 175th st and 3d av....Babcock P P Co. Press. 2,450
Nussbickel, Jacob. Jerome av....C W Schwarting. Greenhouse Fixtures. 88
Otto, Theodore. 149 Baxter... Prentiss Tool Co. Machinery 270
Pfister, V and V. 254 Bowery ..G Bulle. Machinery, Tools, &c. 100
Phillips, W H. 38 Park row ...J S Fogotston. Office Fixtures. 400
Pravate, Antonio. 2317 3d av.. I Daino. Barber Fixtures. 108
Pancomo, Antonio. 776 9th av....A Schwaab & Son. Barber Fixtures. 70
Platt, C J & Co....J Gottsleben. Coach. 750
Price, Jesse....Campbell P P Co. Press, &c. (R) 3,294
Palumbo, Peter. 252 E 125th....Archer Mfg Co. Barber Fixtures. 200
Palumbo, Pietro. 122 Lincoln av ..Archer Mfg Co. Barber Fixtures. (R) 451
Pellen, Max. 218 Delancey....Archer Mfg Co. Barber Fixtures. (R) 195
Pepino, Raffaele. 49 Bleecker....Archer Mfg Co. Barber Fixtures. 536
Rosenbaum, W E. 593 Columbus av.... National Cash Reg Co. Register. 175
Rapid Printing Co....E Lyman. Press, &c. (R) 10,000
Reder, Welhelem. 127 Rivington....J L Gottlieb. Barber Fixtures. 63
Regan, J T....G Dessecker. Coffin Wagon. 350
Rosenberg, Abraham. 153 East Broadway....F Wesel Mfg Co. Press, &c. 80
Schramek, Luft & Co. 146 Centre....J B Beatty. Press, &c. 1,200
Schwarz, Auguste. 39 and 41 Delancey....A Hildebrandt. Bakery Fixtures. 300
Scott & Co. Athens, N Y....W H Brown. Hotel Fixtures. 8,687
Seekamp, Henry. 159 Alexander av....G A Ehlers. Grocery Fixtures. 139
Stable, T L. 356 W 125th....J Mathews. Soda Fixtures. (R) 730
Snyder, Frederick....J Gottsleben. Coach. 140
Coscano, Savior. 243 E 24th ...A Schwaab & Son. Barber Fixtures. 176
Stenger, Peter. 1475 1st av....G Geiss. Butcher Fixtures. (R) 150
Sticca, Nicola. 70 Oliver....A Schwaab & Son. Barber Fixtures. 259
Savage, Alexander. 39 South 5th av....Hutchinson & Co. Horses, Coaches, &c. 2,000
Schwartz, Wm. 343 E 80th....Archer Mfg Co. Barber Fixtures. (R) 246
Tiedemann, Henry. 851 1st av....C F Gennerich. Grocery Fixtures. 1,000
Towle, F S. 54 and 56 Fulton....C Towle. Machinery. 2,062
Tucker, Thomas. 156th st and 10th av .. A Worms. Barber Fixtures. (R) 220
Uhlerch & Seyler. 191 Broome and 397 Grand ... Lincoln I and G Co. Furniture and Store Fixtures. 300
Valiquet, L P. 228 Centre.... Prentiss Tool Co. Machinery. 213
Walker, John....M Armstrong & Co. Coach. (R) 560
Weinman & Co. 43 Park ...G Kempf. Machinery. 200
Wilmot & Traub. 26 New....G Discoard. Fixtures, &c. 075
Winters, J C. Fulton Market....E G Blackford. Stand, &c 400
Wood, Susan A. 140 W 39th....J Rudd. Horses. (R) 400
Woodworth, C & Co .. J W Tufts. Soda Fixtures. 1,200
Wyatt & Bristoll. 17 Ann... Duparquet, Huot & M Co. Range, &c. 111
Welker, J. 218 E 34th....A J Bilhoefer. Surgical Fixtures. 500
Wainslock, Morris. 86 and 88 Henry....Bishop & Babcock Co. Machinery. 154
Westermann, T R. 1062 2d av....National Cash Reg Co. Register. 200
Wilson, J W. 13th st and 8th av....National Cash Reg Co. Register. 200
Yung, Ferdinand. 57 Av B...A Welzel. Butcher Fixtures 100
Yetter, J. L. 107 and 109 E 130th .... W H Stuckey. Horses, Trucks, &c. 400
Zimmerman & Steiber. 9 and 11 Baxter....C Stevens. Machinery. 500
Zimmermann, Hyman. 720 E 11th ...P Paskall. Machines. 50
Zarrelli & Pizzuti. 51 Spring ...Marvin Safe Co. Safe. 150
Ziniti, Frank. 1547 2d av....A Schwaab & Son. Barber Fixtures. 33

BILLS OF SALE.

Bultmann, Diederich. 149th st and Walton av. ..C & H Cramer. Grocery Fixtures. 1,000
Carey, Jane. 2369 2d av...J Rielly. Stock and Fixtures. 200
Clark, J J. 228 E 125th....W R Clark. Tools, &c. 300
Dondero, Charles. 192 Wooster....Catrina Rossi. Grocery Fixtures. 200
Dinkelmann, Aloys. 23 Centre.. Safran & Bloch. Saloon Fixtures. 10,500
Erhart, L. J. 444 E 14th....Emily Erhart. Saloon Fixtures. 500
Fallon, T L. 385 3d av... Theresa J Fallon. Hat Store Fixtures. 300
Geismar, B P. 226 W 67th....Sophie Geismar. Butcher Fixtures. 250
Graff & Newman....J Boyle & Co. Machinery. 1
Hausmann, August. 152 South....H Von Glahn. Saloon. 3,500
Hart, Walter. 114 Liberty....Catharine Hart. Machinery. 1
Henriques, A F....E B st J Henriques. Estate of R Henriques. 100
Kollmann, Chas. 781 7th av....A Von Ohsen. Saloon Fixtures. 12,000
Moeller, Henry. 2267 7th av ...A Wagner. Grocery Fixtures. 505
Munch, George. 963 Kingsbridge road....A Wiesler. Butcher Fixtures. 100
Meyer & Gerken. 410 W 38th....Anna E Otto. Grocery Fixtures. 848
Patterson, H A. 82 Broadway .. Mrs A O Smith. Office Furniture, &c. 250
Studley, F J....Agnes A Clute. Horse, Wagon, &c. 100
Toland, Hugh. 159 E 32d....Jane Toland. Horse, Harness, &c. 1
Ubrisco, Camillo. 2186 1st av. C Ubrisco. Saloon Fixtures. 1,000
Weisman, H and M. Jerome av and 165th st....J A Striker. Hotel Furniture, &c. 3,912
Wallace, John. 174th st and 3d av....Ann Wallace. Horses, Trucks, &c. 500
West, Bella....F Rode. Piano. 90
Wagner, Adolph. 2267 7th av....J H Mohlman. Grocery Fixtures.

ASSIGNMENTS OF CHATTEL MORTGAGES.

Elsworth, Joseph to J C Divine. (Mort. given by Henry Divine, April 22, 1891.) 2,500
Fakas, Lazer to J Alexander. (A Goetzel, Jan. 28, 1891.) 300

KINGS COUNTY.

AUGUST 13 TO 19—INCLUSIVE.

SALOON AND RESTAURANT FIXTURES.

Agster, J. 284 Devoe....E Ochs. $550
Borchers, W. 559 Kent av....W Ulmer. 4,000
Burke, J J. 406 Ralph av....E Ochs. 450
Clark, P T. 684 Evergreen av....F Munch. Brewery. 400
Doherty, J. Hudson av and Prospect st....T C Lyman & Co. (R) 500
Dowling, T. 311 17th....Bachmann B Co. 1,700
Eichhorn, Jr, C. 166 Central av....F Ibert. (R) 685
Elheran, A. 161 Eagle....S Liebmann's Sons B Co. 600
Fitzgerald, J. 552 3d av....Obermeyer & L. 975
Fleischmann, G. 230 Cook....J Eppig. 6.0
Flynn & Dowling. 459 Fulton ...J H Albohn. Restaurant Fixtures. 300
Frank, Mary. 159 Boerum ...Berger & H B Co. (R) 900
Gehrig, G. 134 Maujer ...J Eppig. 600
Gnad, W. 362 Carroll....Sophia Munch and ano exrs F Munch (R) 900
Hart, M C. 88 42d....Berger & H B Co. (R) 500
Heise, H. 181 Kent av ...W Ulmer. 750
Hemmerich, A. 11 Hamburg av....J Eppig. (R) 350
Herzog, G. 414 E 5th....J Eppig. (R) 800
Hoffmann, Henry W. 65 Park av....F & M Schaefer B Co. 1,000
Hoffmann, H W. 65 Park av....F & M Schaefer B Co. Ice Box. 140
Johnson, C H. 97 Canton....Feigenspan B Co. 600
Joyce, J and M. Sullivan. 2079 Fulton....M Seitz. 1,162
Kennedy, T. 340 Myrtle av ...W A Miles & Co. (R) 1,200
Kinowski, J. 496 Liberty av... F Munch Brewery. 150
Kneuer, G. 350 Johnson av....Williamsburgh B Co. 200
Kreuscher, Jr, P. 501 Broadway....Dannenberg & Coles. (R) 1,692
Klebesch, G. 1196 3d av....M Worn & Sons. 1,200
Miller, G W. 67 Manhattan av ...L Eppig. 455
Maloney, F. 291 3d av....Danenberg & Coles. Ice Box. (R) 105
Maloney & Plunkett. 271 3d av... Danenberg & Coles (R) 600
Martin, L 789 Grand ... E Zimmer. Restaurant Fixtures. 200
McMonagle, J. 735 Myrtle av....Danenberg & C. 735
McGuinness, M. 52 5th av....J Fallert B Co. 1,000
Meyer, C L. 161 Columbia....M Seitz. 250
Morris, L. 187 Pennsylvania av....Burger & H B Co. 700
Nelson, J. 47 Carroll....Danenberg & C. 400
Numberg, R. 228 Ewen....Louise Schrammar. 500
O'Brien, W D. 461 5th av ...J Ruppert. 1,000
O'Donnell, J. 541 Clinton....J Hoffmann B Co. (R) 2,000
Ott, J. 246 Jefferson....L Eppig. 300
Pohndorf, J H. Nassau av, n w cor Lorimer st ....D G Yuengling, Jr, B Co. 1,000
Peters, L. 281 Ainslie ... Rubsam & H B Co 700
Reymers, E H. 641 Park av....S Liebmann's Sons B Co. 875
Roseman, J. 400 Graham av....S Liebmann's Sons B Co. 400
Reinhard, Emil. 26 Maujer st....J Kress B Co. 1,000
Riordan, E. 762 4th av... Lyman & Co. (R) 450
Ruckdeschel, G. 276 Atlantic av... M Ackermann. (R) 325
Richter, C. 1465 Broadway ...J S Sharpe. Restaurant Fixtures. 150
Schrammar, Louise. 228 Ewen ...R Numberg. 600
Sommer, J. 496 Liberty av....Leibinger & O B Co. 200
Schaardt, W. 2972 Atlantic av ...Long Island B. 500
Schaefer, E. 1268 3d av....E Ochs. 602
Schmidt, A. 161 Saratoga av....F Ibert. 600
Schreiner, J. 17 Van Cott av....W Ulmer. 850
Strauss, H W. 52 Underhill av....Williamsburgh B Co. 400
Simonson, C W. 25 Broadway....W Ulmer. 1,500
Stahl, J. 344 Graham av....Williamsburgh B Co (Lim.) (R) 700
Tonjes, Anna. 707 Bedford av....Obermeyer & L. 2,000
Taylor, Samuel T. 349 Manhattan av... Wagner & S. Billiard Table. 190
Wild, J. 378 Leonard....M Worn & Sons. 3,000
Wachtel, F. 1021 Myrtle av ... W Ulmer. 500
Wendt, A. 349 7th av... J Hoffmann B Co. (R) 1,300
Wursthorn, C. 247 Central av....J Eppig. 700

HOUSEHOLD FURNITURE.

Baluka, A and E. 49 Middagh....J C Hegemann. 236
Barry, Mary. 328 29th....L Baumann. 105
Borden, C E. 177 St James pl... Waterbury & Marshall. 400
Breen, W. 130 56th ...E A Kisselberg. 100
Buckhardt, L. 33 Starr st... C T Kendrick & Co. 119
Coote, H G. 471 and 473 Hudson av ... Lydia Day. 517
Danley or Danby, J B....G C Sexton. 100
Davison, H. 46th st....T F Ryan. 233
Egger, J L. Vesta av, near Sutter av....I Mason. 191
Geer, T R. 348 Lafayette av....Cowperthwait & Co. 249
Gilliland, R. 147 Manhattan av....Mullins & Sons. 115
Heyman, Christina. 710 4th av....L Baumann. 137
Heymans, C. 710 4th av... L Baumann. 154
Hollock, J H. 257 Humboldt....C T Kendrick & Co. 150
Holton, W 256 Palmetto....C T Kendrick & Co. 297
Hegre, Annie E. 143 Lawrence ... T Cassin. 158
Jackson, T. 1244 St. Marks av....J A Schwarz. 120
Kennedy, J. 73 88th....Mullins & Sons. 147
Ketcham, V C. 273 Skillman .... Josephine Black. 400
Lord, Mrs Augusta. 425 Atlantic av....O'Connor & T. 105
Lowther, J R and S E. 716 Nostrand av....Financial Credit Co. 300
Mars, Henrietta A. 288 President....Amer Guar Assoc. 400
McGuire, Elizabeth. Railroad av, near Danforth st....H Thoesen. 365
Martin, P C and Anna. Flatbush av....E C Hinsdale. 100
McGrath, Kate B. 1 North 1st....E D Farrell. 138
Machumnsohn, L. 37 Lorimer....C T Kendrick & Co 204
McDonough, Mrs M J. 87 Sands....I Mason. 176
Quick, E H. 300 Livingston....D Moriarty 169
Rosenfeld, D. 616 Lexington av ...Simpson & P. Piano. 425
Rooney, Annie. 706 East 5th....R M Walters. Piano. 175
Shaw, R. 62 North Oxford ... I Mason. 114
The Michael J Divine Assoc. 118 Wythe av. Jacob Bros. Piano. 215
White, F. 82 Stuyvesant av....F J Brechtel. 182
Willard, I. W. 70 South 4th....J H Little. 370
Zipp, O A. Fort Hamilton ...T Kelly. 149

MISCELLANEOUS.

Ash, C E. South road and Enfield st....Gertrude Cartmell. Wagon. 150
Althuser, N. 149 Columbia... J Rohmer. Store Fixtures, Horse and Wagon. (R) 210
Behnken, H. 255 Sumner av....National Cash Register Co. Register. 200
Bodenstab, H. 90 Graham av....F Boogartz. Drug Fixtures. 400
Boyle, Bridget. 163 Dupont....B Weill. Horses, Wagons, &c. 100
Bistramb, C H. 708 3d av ...E Schopen. Fixtures. 350
Cornell, E F and J McCloskey. 21 and 23 Hoyt ...W B Davis. Coach. 450
Costello, J E. 515 Kent av....Prentiss Tool and Supply Co. Planing Machine. 150
Donahue, B S. 76 St Marks av....J Donahue. Store Fixtures. 2,247
Dunham, W L. 289 9th....C H Collins. Drug Fixtures. 1,000
Devine P. 230 York....H Jacobs. Tools, &c. 280
Doyle, P. 183 Hudson av....National Cash Register Co. Register. 175
Eggers, W. 79 Washington....Prentiss Tool and Supply Co. Tools. 230
Friel, J H. 344 Hudson av... W B Davis. Horses. (R) 150
Gallagher, M....W B Davis. Landau. (R) 150
Gallagher, M. 172 Pacific....W B Davis Coach. (R) 625
Gerrity, J. 274 Grand....Wolff Bros. Horses. 250
Green, W H. 80 Fulton....Sophia J Cruger. Machinery, &c. 460
Gallo, T. 554 Graham av....M Borchetta. Barber Fixtures. 120
Henry, W. 490 Throop av .... W B Davis. Horses, &c. (R) 500
Henry, W. 461 Madison....W B Davis. Victoria. (R) 600
Hiller, P. 941 Grand....Anna M Hiller. Cigar Stores. 150
Huppert, M. 163 and 165 North 7th....Alma Huppert. Blacksmith Fixtures. 150
Laffel, F T. 468 Court....R A Holcke. Barber Fixtures. 226
Lange, Louisa. 558 Driggs....L Winterbauer. Bakery Fixtures. 800
Lange, W. 634 7th av....J H Luppens. Bakery Fixtures. 150
Lang, L W. 496 8th av....D Lohmann. Produce Business. 300
Same——Lamson Store Service Co. Register. 235
Madadcy, W. 200 Tillary....W B Davis. Coach. (R) 400
Mallady, J J.....W B Davis. Coach. (R) 875
McCaul, J F. 283 Raymond....W B Davis. Coach. (R) 300
Mullady, D. 15 Grace Court alley....D B Dunham Coaches. 1,540
Mercurio, S & O. 172 Hoyt....A Schwaab & Son. Barber Fixtures. 285
Musso, P. 232 Hamilton av....A Schwaab & Son. Barber Fixtures. 145
Ohlmann & Bockelmann. Folsom pl and Linwood st....R Dierking. Grocery. 400
Polhemus, Josephine and C W. 3d av and 2d st ....J M Horton Ice Cream Co. Ice Cream Saloon. 2,000
Reilly, O. 264 Jay... W B Davis. Coach. (R) 125
Richmond, M O. 41 and 67 West av, Wallabout Market ... G B Gerow. Market Fixtures. 150
Schnepf, E. 243 Fulton ...Sarah L Hunter admrx W F Hunter. Photographic Gallery. 150
Tims, R....W B Davis. Coach. (R) 150
Treber, C. 138 Franklin....G Hagemeyer. Undertaker Fixtures, Horses, &c. (R) 3,000
Torborg, J G & L G. 1041 Liberty av... National Cash Register Co. Register. 175
Winters, J C. Fulton Market, New York....E G Blackford. Fish Business. 400
Winters, J H. 1098 3d av....Tarrant & Co. Drug Fixtures. 866
Witty, W N ... G C Sexton. Coupe. 100
Wyatt & Bristoll. 17 Ann st, New York....Duparquet, Huot & Co. Ranges. 111

BILLS OF SALE.

Berkson, H. 645 5th av....M Bodker. House Furnishing Good Store Fixtures 900
Bongartz, F. 90 Graham av....H Bodenstab. Drug Fixtures. 600
Campbell, J D. 141 Claremont av....Jennie E Campbell. Horse and Wagon. nom
Draper, J. 191 Gold....L Weill. Butcher Fixtures. 425
Dierking, R. Folsom pl and Linwood st....L Ohlmann and R Bockelmann. Grocery Fixtures. 800
Edelblum, M, and J Kaminetz. 149 Harrison av ....H Burwitz. Store Fixtures. 250
Finken, Meta. 128 North 10th....A Schnibbe. Saloon Fixtures. nom
Goodman, P. 228 Ewen... Louisa Schrammar. Weiss Beer Business. 200
Menken, D. 652 Gates av....J H D Fangemann. Grocery Fixtures. 1,800
Morrissey, J. 735 Myrtle av....J McGonigle. Saloon Fixtures. val consid and 500
Paton, J. 560 State....J B Crawford. Store Fixtures. 2,000
Quantin, E H. Court st, also Washington st.... Estella M Quantin. Personal Property and Furniture. 700
Suydam, C....J P Rathbun & Co. Presses. 109

ASSIGNMENT OF CHATTEL MORTGAGES.

Ciancimino, Eliz R to Shepard, Terry et al. (Mort given by P Ciancimino, May 7, 1891). nom
Ennis, J J to The Long Island Brewery. (T Keenan, May 7, 1891. nom
Ibert, F to The Williamsburg B Co. (A Mittelstaedt, May 18, 1891.) 400

NEW JERSEY.

NOTE.—*The arrangement of the Conveyances, Mortgages and Judgments in these lists is as follows: the first name in the Conveyances is the Grantor; in Mortgages, the Mortgagor; in Judgments, the Judgment debtor.*

ESSEX COUNTY.

CONVEYANCES.

Ackerman, T W—P Coons, Franklin.......... $200
Alberson, C G—H R Alberson, Marshall st...... nom
Baldwin, J G—F R Baldwin, East Orange..... nom
Baldwin, J M—T E Walmsley, West Orange... 8,000
Ball, Isaiah—E M Wadsworth, East Orange..... 6,000
Bauerlein, Nicholas—B Sohm, East Orange.... nom
Bergen, H A—M Bergen, North 7th st .... nom
Same—S Bergen, Bloomfield av.............. nom
Breintnall, J H H et al.—W Schaub, Bank st.. 1,800
Buermann, August—Henry Buerman, Clinton.. 9,500
Same—J H Cummings, Avon av............. 1,500
Burling, John—J A Williamson, South Orange. 100
Butterworth, Elizabeth—M E Hammond, East Orange.......................... 1,800
Campfield, A H—J H S Willey, East Orange.... 562
Casale, John—F Casale, s w cor Drift and Factory sts, 106x29x107x25 (conveys his one-third share in same)........................ 4,166
Same—M Casale, s w cor Drift and Factory sts, 106x29x107x25 (conveys his one-third share in same)........................ 4,166
Coeyman, Minard—The Peabody Land and Loan Co. of America, Coeyman st............. 600
Coeyman, Samuel——same, Mt Prospect av..... 900
Condit, M A—P Scherrer, South Orange......... nom
Culver, J C—J S Bryant, s w cor N J R R av and King st 97x115x16x125......................... 10,000
Daniel, S C—Bloomfield Savings Inst, Bloomfield 1,000
Dassing, Valentine—G Bornemann, Clinton and South Orange.............................. 11,000
De Forest, F M—G MacAndrew, e s Morris Canal adj land W A Lighter 210x143x699x295x614.. 4,250
Devine, Arthur—E S Flohn, 2d av............. nom
Same——F Hellstrom, South Orange.......... 100
Dodd, Robert—W E McDougall, w s South 6th st 339 s 13th av 50x100 5,000
Dodd, S E—D T Clark, South Orange............ nom
Eisele, J C—C Steigler, w s Hunterdon st 81 s 14th av 100x40x50x50.................... 8,200
Ely, Edwards—W B Ely, s s Elm st 300 e Mulberry st 25x99.......................... 4,500
Ely, W B—E Ely, Market st 2,000
Everitt, R A—T Fox, Orange................... 450
Firth, John—A A Stryker, East Orange......... nom
Flohn, E C—L Bech, 2d av.................... nom
Garrabrant, Eugene—J O Mara, Montclair...... 2,900
Gerth, Julius—A Smith, South Orange......... 2,500
Gibbons, Edward—M F Zahn, Littleton av 1,200
Gray, Thomas N—Orange Wheelmen, Orange... 1,050
Hartshorn, Stewart—R Humphrey, Milburn.... 2,250
Hotz, Annie—E Oppel, Johnson av 2,800
Hughes, W P—T Mickill, Montclair............. 675
Keasbey, A Q—M Schoenheit, South 9th st...... 625
Kemp, Samuel—Edith Glover, South 18th st..... nom
Kent, J N—C W Monroe, East Orange.......... 6,500
Lindsley, O W—K Egan, East Orange........... 370
Lister, J C—E Planer, Esther st. 250
Same——P Hunt, Esther st.................. 258
Same——W H Rowe, Esther st 655
Mallia, John—J Conroy, Orange................ 500
Martin, C W—J R Conlan, Bloomfield.......... 615
McMurtry, William—G M Keasbey, Clinton av... nom
McWilliams, A C—C H Schrack, East Orange... 1,100
Miller, Ernestine—C Schmidt, Littleton av..... 1,750
Mohl, John—J Hensler, Jr, southeasterly cor Patterson st and Hamburg pl 44x50x48x31x 99....................................... 11,000
Moore, F W—G MacAndrew, Morris Canal..... 400
Newark Savings Inst—P Fitssimmons, South 9th st...................................... 870
Parkinson, William—B Mulhern, Orange........ 1,400
Same—E M Lawrence, West Orange.......... 770
Reinehart, C F—M E Roof, Montclair............ 225
Riker, W H—C R Smith East Orange 1,000
Rolf, Fannie E—W A Woodbury, South Orange 1,050
Ross, A S—A S Ross, Jr, Milburn............... nom
Scerrer, Peter et al—O S Thompson, South Orange.................................. nom
Schmidt, J A—C C Hilfer, Littleton av.......... 1,200
Shanley, B M—N J Bay R R Co, n w cor Peddie and Ridgewood avs 50x50, n e cor Peddie and Ridgewood avs 50x250, n e cor Peddie and Belmont avs 50x260, n e cor Peddie and Hillside avs 50x260, n e cor Peddie and Johnson avs 50x209x50x203............................ 10,500
Silvey, Joseph et al—M J Dnegan, Bloomfield... 600
Smith, C R—W B Riker, East Orange........... 3,500
Smith, Edwin—I Young, vq st.................. 500
Smith, J M—C S Cooper, Clifton av............ 1,050
Smith, M B—F N De Forest Newark Meadows.. nom
Stemmle, Charles—T E Stemmle, East Orange.. nom
Stern, Henrietta et al—M Schweikart, South 14th st.................................... 750
Sullivan, M F—F C Doonald, West Orange...... 350
Same — P J McCormick, West Orange........ 300
Tichenor, William—J H Kent, Montclair. .. 125
The Peabody Land and Loan Co of America—J F McLagan, e s Mt Prospect av 400 n Grafton av 25x132.......................... 3,200
Todd, R F—M Treichler, n s Chestnut st 172 w Orchard st 25x100.......................... 5,000
Van Buskirk, L A—C Pienovi, Wilsey st 2,000
Ward, Joseph, Jr—L Lehman, e s Essex st 214 n James st 25x100............................ 3,200
Williams, B S—M E Plummer, Orange.......... 500
Williams, J R—J M Smith, Orange 50
Winans, S K—P A Baldwin, East Orange....... 5,000
Zilliox, Phillip—M A Zilliox, w s Prince st 425 s Montgomery st, 25x100.......................... 4,300

MORTGAGES.

Baldwin, P A—S K Winans, East Orange........ 4,000
Benedict, E F—J Moller, South Orange......... 1,085
Blaney, Thomas—The Firemans Insurance Co, Piersons alley 800
Bornemann, George—V Dassing, Clinton........ 8,700
Brislin, Michael—L Gillespie, Franklin......... 550
Brown, M J—J H Condit, Orange 2,300
Buermann, Henry—A Buermann, Clinton........ 6,000
Burke, Patrick—M Colgate, Orange............ 1,200
Cadmus, James—The Fidelity Title and Deposit Co, Jelliff av 2,500
Same——same, Jelliff av..................... 2,500
Caffrey, Thomas—F Becameyer, Chatham st ... 200
Same——The Chancellor of the State of New Jersey, Chatham st......................... 1,900
Cochran, R M—The American Ins Co, land formerly of J H Stephens........................ 700
Collins, B F—S B Winans, Livingston.......... 147
Conlan, J R—C W Martin, Bloomfield............ 375

Connett, Rose—Montclair B & L Assoc, Montclair 4,600
Connolly, M E—R S Gould, Camden st 300
Cussack, John—N J Zinc and Iron Co, Chappel st 600
Drescher, August—S A Bonykamper, Bowery st 500
Dreyer, Florian—C Fischer, Banks 1,800
Duggan, M J—Essex Co B & L Assoc, Bloomfield 1,100
Dunn, James—P Hauck, Belleville 150
Ely, Edwards—W B Ely, Market st 7,000
Evans, W H—A Rodel, Frelinghuysen av 2,500
Finter, W F—C A Feich, Congress st 10,000
Fitzsimmons, Patrick—A E Trusdell, 12th av 450
Fox, Thomas—C Blanchard, Orange 500
Fredericks, L L—Howard Savings Inst, Montclair 4,000
Gilbert, Harris—C Skelly, Rutgers st 1,800
Guerin, Daniel—J Guerin, Orange 1,875
Hammond, M E—E Butterworth, East Orange 600
Hansen, H C—Passaic B and L Assoc, Ferry st 5,600
Hansen, Hans—J S Schwarz, Ferry st 700
Harzord, Barbara—F Bonykamper, Delancy st 210
Same——F Bonykamper, Jr, Delancy st 1,000
Havell, Christina—F L Flohn, Webster st 250
Huxtable, Lewis—Belleville B & L Assoc, Belleville 500
Jacobus, H V N—M E Stuart, Caldwell 1,100
Kearny, Mary—F J Kearny, Milburn 250
Keegan, C E—W G Butterly, N Y av 3,000
Lehman, Leser—J Ward, Jr, Essex st 2,000
Lisiewski, F A—J Stapff, Hayes st 40,000
McDougall, W E—R Dodd, South 6th st 2,379
McLaughlin, A P—J C Lister, Joseph st 402
Miskell, Thomas—F J Love, Montclair 400
Moffit, M A—The Howard Savings Inst, Sheffield st 200
Munn, R D—J H Stewart et al exrs, Avon av 1,500
O'Connor, Arthur—G W Wredenmayer, Fillmore st 631
Plummer, M E—R S Williams, Orange 200
Pierson, S A—L Leverich, Green st 3,000
Same——same, Green st 3,000
Raphael, Maurice—F Grub, South Orange 1,500
Rehmann, C F—M Porsch, Norfolk st 2,000
Remsen, A E—Fourteenth Ward B and L Assoc, Peshine av 1,400
Riker, W H—C R Lamb, East Orange 475
Rogers, A D—P Beck, Congress st 2,100
Rowe, W H—J C Lister, Esther st 327
Schoenheit, Mary—A Q Kessbey, South 9th st 225
Schreck, Franz—V Fray, Bremen st 2,000
Schweikhardt, Martin—H Stern, South 14th st 650
Seward, K S—S Cornelia, East Orange 8,000
Sohm, Barbara—N Bauerlein, East Orange 1,500
Spatola, Gerardo—S De Nicola, Bovden st 300
Steigler, Charles—J C Eisle, Hunterdon st 1,210
Same——Washington B and L Assoc, Orange 6,000
Streeter, C C—East Orange B and L, Chester av 1,400
The Orange Wheelman—The Orange B and L Assoc, Orange 3,000
Vreeland, E S—Mutual Benefit Life Ins Co, Plane st 4,000
Vreeland, J W—H P Cook, Bergen av 500
Weber, J, Jr—W Book, Ferry st 1,000
White, E S—Eighth Ward B and L Assoc, 3d av 500
Williams, James—F H Goble, N Y av 1,000
Woodbury, W A—F E Rolf, South Orange 650
Yeomans, G H—J S Duffy, Orange 300

CHATTEL MORTGAGES.

Allen, E H—W S French, furniture 400
Bird, W A—Henry Thoesen, furniture 113
Baboudreick, Gustav—M Robinson, horses and wagons 800
Bourne, C R—J Ketcham, furniture 130
Colandra, Jos—Hirschfield & Co, safe 90
Fuente, Ralph, Jr—R Fuente, store fixtures 1,991
Gelb, Max—J Serlen, horse 44
Greiner, Robert—G Krueger, saloon 1,050
Howarth, A C—J M Ham, furniture 100
Johnson, G E—M Raphael, horse 120
Jones, I F—T R Williams, wagons, &c 500
Limeberg, George—W Grohmann, horses 100
Macrae, Daniel—D Schoenstein, butcher shop 200
Mouarque, M C—P H Hanley, furniture 78
Murtaugh, Grace—C Bierman, furniture 400
National Cash Register Co—C Schutte, cash register 173
Oelkers, J B—The Celluloid Co, celluloid goods 2,001
Paddock, George—P H Hanley, furniture 68
Pitt, Theresa—C Biermann, piano 42
Primrose, E H—H Y Campfield, furniture 4,056
Servos, Samuel—E Berla, horses, &c 190
Tracy, Winnifred—W K Rankin, store fixtures 238
Whelan, J J—I L Haff, piano, pictures, &c 78
Winkler, Conrad—The Prentiss Tool Supply Co, machinery 185
Ziruth, Belle—C Bierman, piano 100

JUDGMENTS.

Bugg, O T—W R Hinsdale 895
Evan, W H—A Zabriskie 528
Kitchell, F P—R N Brundage 1,008
Moll, L M—W G Hainski 671
Raphael, Morris—O P Wakeman 682
Sumner, H R—M Christopher 259

HUDSON COUNTY.

CONVEYANCES.

Allen, Robert and M M Forrest—J T Easton, Kearney $200
Same——C H Beaver, Kearney 200
Archibald, S A and R F et al—A B Archibold, J City ..... nom
Archibold, S A and R F—Annie G Reed, J City ..... nom
Archibold, R F and A B et al—S A Archibold, J City ..... nom
Archibold, S A and A B et al—R F Archibold, J City ..... nom
Same——Annie E Reed, J City ..... nom
Behr, Frederick—C Koster, J City 2,800
Barry, Edward—A Archibald, J City ..... nom
Brett, P W—H Niederlitz, West Hoboken 450
Brigham, L F—E P Buffett, J City ..... nom
Same——A B Dayton, J City 850
Brohn, Mary A—R W Bacot, J City 1,000
Burns, John—P Kandler, Union 2,050
Carson, Ann J—R Fishbourne, J City 2,000
Condit, Fillmore—J R Carlson, Kearney 200
Conway, John—J Burton, Union 600
Cubberly, J H—T Burke, J City ..... nom
Dayton, A B—D W Lawrence, J City 600
Doermer, Emile—H J Bonn, Union 3,500
Donnell, Gertrude A—P E Dimler, Bayonne 400
Edelstein, John—J Roche, J City 268
Frommel, Oscar—G Luciano, Hoboken 550
Same——M Riccio, Hoboken 350
Fuller, Dwight B—F Wilson, Kearney 7,000
Garbs, D H—T J Cronin, Bayonne 380
Gifford, Livingston—Mary P Dunham, J City 60
Good, W E—T A Davis, J City 735
Hansen, F G—H J Bonn, Union 5,000
Hoboken Land and Impt Co—M Obry, Weehawken 190
Jennings, W N—C Van Benschoten, Kearney 2,500
Jones, Mary—J T Gibbons, J City 2,900
Kaiser, Carl—Charlotte Kline, Bayonne 3,000
Kerrin, Patrick—B Naughton, Harrison 2,100
Latour, Elleuor—C Kaiser, Bayonne 3,000
Lawless, Anne—J J McCormick, J City 2,200
Ludwig, John—G Ludwig, West Hoboken ..... nom
Lutz, Caroline—John Lutz, J City 4,000
Mansell, Robert—C H Weller, Bayonne 1,500
May, Adam—A Meyer, J City 2,213
McCarthy, John—D Dempsey, Bayonne 650
McDonald, E F—B Naughton, Harrison 450
Same—same, Harrison 1,500
Meller, Charles and E J Lemon by Sheriff—C Jaeger, J City 400
Mitchell, F W—H B Stone, J City 550
Mooney, Richard—Elizabeth Mooney, Hoboken ..... nom
Murphy, J J—M J Donovan, J City 150
Nuge, W F—F C Hansen, Union 500
O'Connor, Edward—M O'Connor, J City 100
Parker, A A—G L Betcher, J City 1,000
Parker, C W—N Sanborn, Bayonne ..... nom
Pfeifer, G C—B M Shanley, J City 17,500
Phillips, A J—Maggie L Gleason, Kearney 475
Pratt, Elizabeth A—Martha A Greenfield, Harrison 1,600
Reed, Annie E and R F Archibald—S A Archibald, J City ..... nom
Same——same, J City ..... nom
Roche, James—J Edelstein, J City 6,000
Rockford, J A—The Bradley & Currier Co (Lim), J City ..... nom
Rose, G C—A Vom Fell, J City ..... nom
Rutherford, Charlotte L—Isabella Crookall, Kearney 1,700
Schmidt, W H—J Diedrich, Union 800
Schultz, Otto—P D Laugel, West Hoboken 14,400
Same——E Steffan, West Hoboken 9,000
Smith, A L—Eleanor B G Kirkman, Kearney 200
Steinson, Annie—A Greener, Guttenberg 3,600
Steel, Ann—C Helwig, J City 2,500
Stringham, M V—Anna Booth, Bayonne 500
The Central N J Land and Imp't Co—R Mansell, Bayonne 1,500
The Kearney Land Co—J Kestner, Kearney 200
Thomas, Trustie—A Meise, J City 2,700
Uffert, E B—J G Maier, Harrison 5,000
Van Buskirk, James H—A J Gablen, Bayonne 3,500
Van Wagenen, H N—Harriet Robert, J City 700
Vreeland, Hartman—J H Van Buskirk, Bayonne 900
Weller, C H—R Mansell, Bayonne 1,500
Wiesset, Sophie—A Frey, J City 2,400
Young, Henry by exrs—M Quinn, Harrison 2,400

MORTGAGES.

Ahrens, Emond F—Martha L Deraismes, Union, 3 years 600
Alexander, W J—North Hudson Co B and L Assoc, West Hoboken, installs 200
Aussell, R H—The Greenville B and L Assoc No 2, Bayonne, installs 5,295
Bechle, Mary D—The Palisade B and L Assoc, West Hoboken, installs 2,000
Benatar, Louis—Guard Lucio Anes, Kearney, 3 years 1,700
Berenbroick, Frederick—L Berenbroick, Union, 1 year 500
Biggane, M J—D McLaughlin, J City, 2 years 1,000
Bolan, Timothy—Mary Stumpf, Harrison, 1 year 1,800
Bonn, H J—Emily Doermer, Union, 2 years 2,500
Breslin, James—Exr C G Nisson, Harrison, 3 yrs 1,000
Brooke, Margaret L—Admr J Boye, Bayonne, 1 year 1,800
Butler, Bridget—Greenville B and L Assoc, Bayonne, installs 6,165
Dakin, J A—J Doscher, J City, 3 years 1,000
Dietz, Caspar—Margaretha Huber, J City, 3 years 2,000
Dunler, P E—H Richards, Bayonne, 3 years 1,200
Emmons, E F—T F Blodgett, J City, 2 years 700
Farrand, C D—The Security B and L Assoc, Bayonne installs 3,200
Finck, Peter—A Stenken, J City, 3 years 500
Fisher, R F—P G Walter, J City, 3 years 500
Flynn, John—Ann Behenery, Harrison, 4 years 1,000
Gallien, A J—The Harrington B and L Assoc, Bayonne, installs 2,400
Same——J H Van Buskirk, Bayonne, 5 years 938
Garrison, W V—The Cartaret M B and L Assoc, J City, installs 1,000
Same——same, J City, installs 1,000
Gleason, Maggie L—A J Phillips, Kearney, 3 yrs 225
Gould, G H—Margaret A Ryman, Bayonne, 3 years 1,300
Gray, Charlotte S—The Provident Inst for Savings, J City, 1 year 1,000
Greenfield, George—Exrs Katharine E Hahn, Kearney, 2 years 750
Grieder, Adolph—L Becker, Guttenberg, 3 years 2,000
Hansen, F C—W F Kurze, Union, 2 years 2,500
Harney, Margaretha C—Provident Inst for Savings, J City, 1 year 2,500
Helwig, Carl—Pavonia B and L Assoc, J City, installs 2,400
Kandler, Paul—J Burns, Union, 5 years 1,000
Kenny, Ellen—Ann E Trusdell, Harrison, 1 year 750
Kestner, Joseph—J Swackhammer, Kearney, 2 years 1,000
Koster, Christian—W Drecktrade, J City, 4 years 1,500
Kieby, August—C T Jones, West Hoboken, 6 years 650
Luciano, Guiseppe—O Frommel, Hoboken, 3 years 850
Lutz, Barbara—Elizabeth Muller, Hoboken, 3 years 1,500
Maier, J G—W Bissell, Harrison, 1 year 1,800
Same——P Hauck, Harrison, 1 year 2,900
McGimpsey, Alex—A Pfhigh, J City, 3 years 400
McKaig, Archibald—Phoenix L and B Assoc, J City, installs 500
McKelvy, J W—A Campbell, J City, 3 years 3,700
McKnight, H B—S B Vreeland, J City, 3 years 6,000
Meyer, August—The Excelsior Mutual B and L Assoc, series 2 issue 4, J City, installs 2,200
Mueller, C W—Spencer M Rice, J City, 1 year 1,000
Mullally, Mary A—Hudson Trust and Savings Inst, West Hoboken, 7 years 2,500
Newkirk, Eliz—J H Newkirk, J City, 1 year 1,000
O'Connor, J S—Excelsior M B & L Assoc, J City, installs 3,800
Purcell, Rosanna—F W Coles, J City, 1 year 450
Rath, James—L E Huyler, Bayonne, 5 years 850
Reed, Annie E—A B Archibald, J City, 7 years 1,800
Sanborn, Noah—The Bayonne B Assoc No 2, Bayonne, installs 3,000
Somers, Helen—J P Northrop, J City, 3 years 9,000
Stone, H B—F W Mitchell, J City, 3 years 400
Taylor, Katharine—Exrs R Paterson, Kearney, 6 years 3,500
Tivy, Peter—Hoboken Bank for Savings, Hoboken, 3 years 4,000
Trustees of the Zion's Church of Evangelical Assoc—F Werffenbach, J City, 3 years 2,000
Van Benschoten, Chas—W N Jennings, Kearney, installs 400
Wade, M E—Lizzie Schoppinger, J City, 1 year 500
Weisbecker, Henry—G Vreeland, J City, 3 years 3,000
Wilson, Fred—The Sun and Evening Sun Building M L and Accom Fund Assoc, Kearney, installs 625
Witte, Louisa—The Gottfried Krueger Brewing Co, J City, 1 year 380

CHATTEL MORTGAGES.

Bosenberg, C H, Hoboken—A Schleuss, store and fixtures 500
Buchbinder, William, J City—John Matthews Apparatus Co, soda water fountain 325
Corvin, Gaetano, J City—V Cartolano, grocery store 400
Crambelli, Arnold, West Hoboken—P Aquadro, horse wagon, harness 200
Davis, D D, North Bergen—W B Hausen, horse 150
Eckhardt, L A, J City—H Frericks, butcher fixtures 600
Evans, G S, J City—J P Rathbum, shafting 60
Same——same, 2 printing presses 300
Same——same, 30-inch paper cutter 100
Fredrichs, B J, Kearney—J Ketcham, furniture 130
Graham, A L and Peter, J City—J P Rathbum, 2 printing presses 300
Hennesy, T W, J City—Johanna Weber, hat and cap store 1,000
Hill, Geo, J City—C Flod, horse, wagon 80
Howald, Albert, J City—The F & M Schaefer B Co, saloon and lease 728
Kemp, C H, J City—H D Trearck, horse and wagon 70
Kessler, Fred, J City—C Stein, saloon 275
Lyons, T F, Bayonne—Christian Feigenspan, saloon fixtures 600
McCartney, Annie, Hoboken—The Duparquet, Knot & Monense Co, 1 No 4 hard coal broiler and base, 4 gallons, Manhattan urn 72
Meyer, Adam, J City—Lewis & Tremble, horse, 1 Matthews generator, 3 fountains, 2 bottling benches, &c, and 300 boxes 700
Mortone, Antonio, Hoboken—M Pierro, barber shop 81
Moury, Samuel, Bayonne—Marvin Safe Co, safe 55
Ormsly, C A, J City——same, safe 75
Schipman, Henry, J City—Lembeck & Betz B Co, saloon and lease 430
Schubert, Louis, Union—The William Peter Brewing Co, saloon 400
Sinaewald, E C, Hoboken—Leith & Co, saloon fixtures 75
Steinmann, Wilhelmine, Hoboken—H Heymann, furniture 650
Zeiger, Frank, J City—Bernheimer & Schmidt, saloon 1,000
Same——E A Rohlfs, saloon 600

BILLS OF SALE.

Helvig, H A J and C A Waite, J City—Iron Clad Mfg Co, stock, tools, fixtures, machinery, &c 9,550
Taylor, Robert, North Bergen—Eliza Taylor, horse, wagon, harness, coaches ..... nom

JUDGMENTS.

Driscoll, Michael—The F & M Schaefer Brewing Co 436
Giroux, Arthur, Rudolph Vesman and Theodore Oesman—F Hall 33

MECHANICS' LIENS.

Cohen, Morris, John Morring and Sarah B Nathan, owners; J Phillip and M Nathan, builders; F A Lamson, claimant, Hoboken 78 03
The German Pioneer Verein of J City, owners; C A Crowley, contractor; The A A Griffing Iron Co, claimant 109 20

ASSIGNMENT FOR BENEFIT OF CREDITORS.

Winans, G H, Newark, to The Fidelity Title and Deposit Co; assets, $12,300; liabilities, $23,137.

BUILDING MATERIAL MARKET.

BRICKS.—One of the peculiarities of the market for some time past has been the absence of speculative suggestions. Ordinarily when a business falls into unfavorable and disagreeable conditions, operators with a commendable and natural spirit are inclined to put forth various ideas and theories intended as a forecast of early improvement and as an aid to its development. Earlier in the season something of that kind was noticeable on the brick market, but as week after week passed with monotonously unchanged conditions and scarcely a fluctuation in value, leading and authoritative operators have abandoned all attempts to report beyond the mere fact that, whatever the demand might happen to be, there was always plenty of stock for it, in both quantity and quality, with a surplus to spare, and no foundation apparent upon which there seemed the least probability of obtaining an immediate improvement in values. This week history repeats itself in all general particulars. Demand has been fair right along from day to day, the weather not interfering with work or the handling of stock; but buyers found a supply of good quality awaiting them and something left over in first hands. Prices, too, seem to be just the same as we have advised for a long while, some of the specials or extra fine lots commanding $5.50, but $5.25 per M more generally representing the average top figure on open market, and thence along down according to quality, etc. The demand for Pales seems to have fallen off again, and $2.25 per M is now about all that can be depended upon. While, as already noted, the market shows no quotable change, there are two or three little straws which appear to be of a promising character, and anything in that line certainly deserves notice. First, we find that the surplus supply has not run quite so full, and probably in partial explanation of that it is said that several manufacturers on the latest shipments made requested that after boats had discharged here that they seek freight at other yards. This plainly indicates a tendency to reduce shipments, and is the more significant from the fact that there is evidently no concert of action in the movement.

LATH.—Although this is a market that probably fluctuates with greater frequency than any other in the line of material, it does not, as a matter of fact, develop other than comparatively staple influences. On a small run of arrivals for a time values gradually harden until they get up to about $2.25 per M, when buyers commence to object and receivers of Eastern keep a sharp eye on those who might be likely to bring in something from the North. Then comes a little bunch of cargoes, generally said to be unexpected, prices take a tumble down toward $2.00 and then commence the recuperative process once more. At the moment there is not much buoyancy, the recent arrivals having proven quite full, and with previous amounts in hand, dealers naturally feel more or less indifferent. Still receivers are managing to keep the market upon a fairly steady basis, and while sales have been made at $2.05 per M the latest business was at $2.10 for Eastern, and that is now generally admitted to be about inside. From advices at hand, too, it looks as though there was very little stock now afloat. An interesting feature in connection with this market is the sale of a cargo of Michigan White Pine Lath. The stock is coming here by one of the new steel steam barges built at the West, and known as the S. O. No. 55. She sailed from West Superior, Mich., via the lake, canal and St. Lawrence River and thence via ocean to this harbor, and is due from 22d to 25th. The lath are supposed to have been taken as a make-shift cargo rather than make the voyage light, and consist of 1,081,600 pieces 1½ inch wide, ⅜ inch thick, 4 feet long and 50 to bundle, showing nice clean bright stock, as per sample received. The vessel and cargo are consigned to Scammell Bros., of this city, who will order them to Elizabethport to unload the lath, having been sold at $2.20 per M to estate of D. J. Boice, of Plainfield, N. J. It is not likely that Michigan Lath will become a commodity on this market, but the deal is a unique one in its way and the details are worthy of record and preservation.

LIME.—There is as usual considerable uncertainty permeating the market, and more or less contradiction in some of the statements made. It looks, however, as though there was no real dearth of supplies, and while for certain purposes, or to satisfy the demands of sentiment, special makes are insisted upon, the ordinary run of consumption has found a considerable offering of la e that it could get along with very well, and some of it comparatively cheap. Since our last the market has remained pretty steady, the arrivals of Rockland proving moderate, with demand enough to take care of the cargoes at old rates, while of other productions the tenders are said to have been less liberal, and it is thought some shippers are getting a little tired of the prices they were compelled to accept.

LUMBER.—So far as the general market is concerned it retains the former features, and a moderate unsatisfactory trade is reported in pretty much all cases. For some goods there has undoubtedly been an increase of the movement during week, but operators do not consider the volume or form of business at all up to standard for the season, and complaint is common on all sides. Upon investigation it is not difficult to locate responsibility for conditions as they prevail, and we find the same old spirit of caution permeating the entire market through which about all demands are confined to immediate requirements and the major portion of the labor of negotiation must be undertaken by the seller. Of course such influences do not help values, yet, fortunately, the position is under very fair control, and a further shrinkage on the line of cost is for the present prevented.

Eastern Spruce gained nothing in tone, and some of the expressions of receivers very emphatically convey an idea of the feeling of dissatisfaction they entertain toward the market. Buyers have shown much greater ability to stand off than was expected, not only in the matter of randoms, but with specials, and it is very evident that there is a disinclination to see any very heavy supply offering, and a constant dread that it will come. Reports from some of the mills are quite independent in character, but there seems to be enough of them at work to produce all the stocks required, and no one is much alarmed over the present outlook for supplies. Cargo rates are somewhat variable, but so far as known dealers do not swerve from the uniform line of valuation agreed upon at commencement of the season.

Piling has found a little more demand this week in part engagements of parcels for delivery later on in the season, but the offering proved quite equal to the necessities of the case, with a little to spare, and it is still a difficult matter to do better with values than keep them about steady at the previous low range.

Hemlock undergoes little or no variation, though if anything there is a growing tendency to business. That terrible worm about which so much has been written certainly has not destroyed this year's supply and does not appear to be creating any great amount of alarm about the future among buyers, but against natural wants the inquiry increases somewhat, and the natural possibilities favor a further growth. Prices remain much the same as for some time past, with a hardening tone claimed.

White Pine has been arriving to some extent in the way of contract deliveries, and the local accumulation grows in consequence. Dealers in most cases claim to be making no really new engagements, but this is denied by agents of both Western and Canadian product, who assert that where they can make a tender of desirable goods at about former cost there is less difficulty in attracting attention than heretofore, and now and then some fair orders can be booked. Business, however, is not what it should be, and fall trade is slower than usual in developing. There have been some fair export clearances of late, but principally of low grade stuff.

Yellow Pine may be called nominally unchanged, as there is very little lucid information to be obtained on the general market. Some operators intimate a better character to the demand, others grumble and growl over the indifferent character of the trading, but everything goes to show that buyers retain about all the advantage in matter of price. Southern advices are not of a character to convey an impression that manufacturers are in a position to refuse any reasonable offer.

Carolina Pine for certain classes of work of cheap and medium character retains much favor, and is sufficiently staple to meet with very fair demand even amid the dull time hanging over other kinds of stock. Receivers admit they might do more business without feeling much inconvenience, but claim ability to support values at about the old range all around.

Hardwoods are meeting with some demand for manufacturing purposes, and probably actual consumption is, if anything, on the increase. This, however, does not influence the wholesale market greatly if at all, as not only are manufacturers very well stocked themselves, but jobbers generally are prepared to meet any ordinary call without difficulty and feel no pressing necessity for additional stocks. It is, therefore, necessary for sellers to keep up the skirmishing in order to maintain trade and they find no grip with which to stiffen values. Rumors of cut rates on p p a lack confirmation, but there is no buoyancy, and oak is a little slack.

Shingles have for some time past been meeting with only a limited sort of call and there is complaint generally. Especially do operators in cypress shingles express disappointment over the waning demand for their goods and the difficulty experienced in keeping values in good shape. They console themselves, however, with the apparent evidence that the goods really lose nothing in popularity, and with recovery in general trade must secure full proportionate benefit.

GENERAL LUMBER NOTES.

STATE.

The Albany *Argus* reports as follows:

There has been a very good tone to the market the past week. While nobody has been rushed, there has been a good steady trade in which all hands participated. There have been a larger number of buyers in town than for some time, but the orders placed were for odds and ends in small quantities. Dealers anticipate an excellent fall trade. Judging from present indications some are inclined to believe that prices will be higher next fall and considerable higher next spring. The receipts of lumber during the past ten days have been moderate. Spruce and Hemlock remain unchanged. The demand is exceeding the supply of culled spruce. Hard woods are in good demand.

GREAT BRITAIN.

The *Timber Trades Journal*, reporting a public sale at Dundee, says it was fairly well attended, and the proceedings were fairly brisk, a large amount of business being done in the various classes of goods. The leading feature was the Quebec cargo just landed. The waney pine was an excellent shipment. The large wood brought from 2s. 11d. to 3s. 1d., the medium sizes from 2s. 8d. to 2s. 9d. and the smaller wood 2s. 6d. to 2s. 7d. The square pine was cleared out at 2s. 10½d. 1st pine deals 12 in. broad and short lengths from 8 ft. brought 2s. 8d. to 2s. 1¼d.; narrow widths of short lengths, 2s. 2d. to 2s. 6d.; common white battens, 6½x2½, fetched 1 1-16d. to 1⅛d.; and white, 9x3, 2d.

THE WEST.

The Northwestern *Lumberman* as follows:

Low water in northwestern streams continues to annoy lumber producers, and in different localities, including the Saginaw and Chippewa valleys, apprehensions are felt regarding a continuous log supply. So far retarded drives have done little to reduce white pine production, but should the dry spell continue any length of time many mills will be affected.

A money stringency is becoming more apparent in the west, which seems to have been caused by the closer scrutiny of paper by banks whose caution has been increased by the Howell and other lumber failures. The assignment on Thursday of the St. John & Marsh Company, of Chicago and elsewhere, having a chain of yards in Kansas and Colorado, emphasizes this condition. It was forced to the step by slow collections and inability to obtain banking accommodations that would enable it to tide over without sacrificing assets. A conservative tendency is also noted in the cargo market, where the recent carefulness of buyers has been remarked upon.

At Chicago there has been a slight decline in activity, which is not regarded significant.

In the Saginaw valley there appears to be only a fair hot weather business, visiting buyers having been scarce. Stocks are being worked down, however.

In Chicago:

It has been a moderately active week at the docks, little changes in the situation being noted. No big fleet has come in, cargoes having been scattered along in a manner to cause little inconvenience and to keep up an average movement of business. Prices appear to have hugged previous quotations closely. While cargoes have not hung fire long an apathy has been apparent in trade, which seems to have been the outcome of recent financial disturbances. Caution is manifest on the part of both buyer and seller. The latter is extra careful of credits, and the former is slow about taking on any obligations that he can not see a thoroughly clear way of meeting. Perhaps it is the conservative among the buyers who are thus influenced, but it is evident that the complications of the Howell failure are upon the minds of many and have produced an impression.

At the yards, the intense heat that characterized the after half of last week doubtless took away some of the little energy that had recently pertained to trade. At any rate, early this week the movement seemed to have slackened off from that of the week previous. Yet such rising and falling, ebbing and flowing, has been a peculiar feature of this season's business. Perhaps by the time this report reaches the reader, there will again a strong current of demand set in. The planing mills do not appear to be more than fairly busy and there is no rush in the yards. Yet some dealers report a gain in average volume of distribution since August came in, and it is believed that there will continue to be a steady rise until the full volume of the fall trade begins, which should not be far off.

The Chicago *Timberman* says:

There is no particular change to note in the condition of the local hardwood market. Some dealers report a better business since the first of August, but there is as yet small indication that trade is recovering from its usual midsummer dullness. With plenty of stock being offered, the scalper has been securing a good share of the factory trade, and the yard dealers have had to suffer accordingly.

Quarter-sawed oak is very dull as compared with a year ago at this time. The production this season has been immense, and at the same time, for one reason or another, demand has fallen away, leaving a big surplus on the market at the present time. Prices have been gradually growing weaker all summer, and are now from $4 to $6 per thousand lower than they were in the spring, with a very limited inquiry.

Plain-sawed red oak has weakened lately, but more because of a weak market than because of over-production. Prices on this wood will undoubtedly recover as soon as the fall trade opens.

There is a better demand for lower grades of oak than for good. Close competition among manufacturers has forced them to cut corners wherever they can and for many purposes they have found it safe to use the poorer grades, in place of the better, while the completed work is practically just as good.

Cherry is not as active as it was earlier in the season, but there is still sufficient demand to take all the high grade stock that arrives at about old prices. Cull cherry is very dull and common only fairly active.

The Mississippi Valley *Lumberman* as follows:

The usual Western car famine is inevitable, and this fall it promises to be even more than usually deleterious to traffic. This is especially true in the Northwest, where immense crops of grain will tax the equipment of all the roads to the utmost. It is noteworthy that retail stocks all through this section are not in condition for the fall trade, and that there must in consequence be a vast movement of lumber to meet the consumptive fall demand. In the South the situation is even more unpromising. But this is a difficulty for which retailers are largely responsible and which can best be remedied by the early placement of orders for the fall trade. No matter what efforts the railroads may make, so long as three months' trade is concentrated into thirty days there is bound to be trouble about cars.

METALS.—COPPER—Ingot, following our last report, continued to recede in value until an additional ¼@½c. per lb. was taken off, with fair selling on the downward turn. At 12c., however, while buyers were willing to go on, holders became a little stubborn and have since offered with reduced freedom, leading to a somewhat narrower market throughout. On an average range of valuations we quote at 12⅛@12¼c. for Lake, and 11½@12c. for casting brands. Manufactured Copper meets with no unusual demand, and some of the trade think the movement unusually slow. It is understood, however, that values are well sustained and the market free from a surplus product. We quote as follows: Sheet, not above 30x72 in., 16 oz. and over, 25c.; do, 14 to 16 oz., 23c.; do, 12 to 14 oz., 24c.; do, 10 to 12 oz., 25c.; do, 8 to 10 oz., 28c.; do under 8 oz. 30c. Sheets longer than 72 inches add 1c. for 12@14 oz., 2c. for 10@12 oz. and 3c. for 8@10 oz. Sheets, not above 36x96 in., 16 oz and over, 22c.; do, 14 to 16 oz., 24c.; do, 12 to 14 oz., 26c.; do, 10 to 12 oz., 30c.; do, 8 to 10 oz., 33c. Sheets longer than 96 inches 22c. for over 32 oz. and add 1c. for 16 to 32 oz.; 3c. 14 to 16 oz.; 5c. 12 to 14 oz., and 13c. for 8 to 10 oz. Sheets, not above 48x96 32 to 64 oz., 23c.; do, 16 to 32 oz., 25c.; do, 14 to 16 oz., [illegible]; do, 12 to 14 oz., 29c.; do, 10 to 12 oz. 33c. Sheets wider than 48x96 and longer, 22@25c. for 32 to 64 oz. and over, 27@[illegible]c. for 16 to 32 oz., 29c. for 14 to 16 oz and 34c. for 12 to 14 oz. All bath tub sheets, per lb., 16 oz., [illegible]; 14 oz., 29c.; 12 oz. [illegible]; and 10 oz. 35c. Bolt copper ¾ inch diameter and over, 24c. Circles, 60 diameter and less, 3c. above price of sheets of same thickness; circles, 60 to 96 do do, 5c. do; circles, 96 do and over, 6c. do. Segment and pattern sheets, 3c. above price of sheets required to cut them from. Cold or hard rolled copper, 1@2c. per lb. above the foregoing prices. Copper bottoms, 26@32c. per lb. [illegible] Pig has become such an entirely nominal article that, aside from maintaining a line of approximating valuations in our regular table of quotations, it is no longer worthy of notice. American Pig has a very slow and generally unsatisfactory demand. There is possibly more doing than a month ago, yet not enough to give the market an animated tone, and it is pretty well conceded that a much broader outlet is required to round up matters in thoroughly healthy form. About old valuations made, though on some of the common lots shading is not uncommon. We quote at $16.25@18.00 per ton for No. 1 X foundry; [illegible]@16.50 for No. 2 X do. and $14.00@15.00 for Gray forge. Old material remains in a very quiet condition, and the market presents no really new features worthy of remark. Supplies are not extensive enough to be urged into notice, but holders willing to sell and likely to accept at least former rate. We quote at about $20.00@21.50 for old rails; $20.00@21.0[illegible] for No. 1 wrought scrap; $17.00@18.00 for cast scrap and $17.00@17.50 for car wheels. Manufactured Iron meets with some demand, but it is of an irregular sort of character, and the market not altogether satisfactory in form. About old rates, however, are current for standard shapes and sizes. We quote common merchant Bar ordinary size, at 2.00@2.10c. from store, and refined at 2.30@2.50c; Rods, round and square, [illegible]c. Bands, 2.40@2.50c.; Norway Nail Rods, [illegible], and domestic sheet on the basis of 3.00@[illegible]c. for common Nos. 10@16. Other descriptions at [illegible] prices, with 1-10c. less on large lots from [illegible]. Steel rails undergo little or no change. The demand is moderate and uncertain from all quarters, and few contracts are being placed; but manufacturers remain steady and quite generally insist upon full former rates. The amount booked by the associated mills for 1891 delivery was a trifle under 851,000 tons, and deliveries are within 175,000 tons of that amount. We quote standard sections $30 per ton at mill, with usual [illegible] delivery at tide water. Pig Lead has been quite irregular at times, with rather an uppish tendency, but at the moment the turn is somewhat in buyers' favor. We quote at 4.45@4½c. per lb. The manufactures of lead are quoted at 7c. for Pipe, 7½c. for sheet, 15c. for Tin-lined Pipe, and 27½c. for block Tin Pipe. Pig Tin receives more or less attention from the speculative element, but consumers still stand off and have to be urged by positive necessity before they will invest. We quote at about 20.15@20.30c. for round lots, and 20.30@20½c. for jobbing parcels. Tin Plate does not get much attention from large buyers, most of whom are well supplied, but there is a fair general movement of small lots at steady rates. We quote prices as follows: I. C. Charcoal, ½ cross assortment Melyn grade, $6.40@6.45, each additional X add $1.50; I. C. Charcoal, ½ cross assortment, Allaway grade, $5.90@6.00, each additional X add $1; Charcoal terne, M. F. grade, 14x20, $7.50@7.55; M. F. grade, 20x28, $15.50@15.55; Worcester, 14x20, $5.75@5.80; Worcester, 20x28, $11.25@11.30; Dean grade, 14x20, $5.25@5.30; Dean grade, 20x28, $10.50@10.55; D. R. D. grade, 14x20, $4.85@4.90; D. R. D. grade, 20x28, $10.00@10.05; I. C. Coke, Penlan grade, $5.40@5.45; J. B. grade, 14x20, $5.45@5.50; I. C. Bessemer steel, squares, $5.75@5.80 cash; I. C. Siemens steel, squares, $5.85@6.00 basis. Spelter has been offered with a little more freedom, and rates were easier, though sellers exhibit no special anxiety to realize. We quote $5.00@5.10c. for Common Western, according to brand.

NAILS.—There is a good enough demand up to the natural and positive wants of the hour, and there it stops. Buyers have no speculative spirit whatever, and contend against all arguments intended to convey a suggestion that investment against the future is judicious. About the former general line of valuation is retained, but irregularity occasionally develops, mainly in buyers' favor. We quote Cut at $1.50@1.60 per keg for car lots and $1.75@1.85 per keg for parcels from store, for iron, and add 5@10c. per keg for steel; Wire, $2.00@2.05 at mills, and 2.20@2.35 from store.

PAINTS, OILS, COLORS, ETC.—Trade seems to be improving somewhat, though very slowly, and there is still a great deal of complaint among operators over the general conditions of the market. As previously intimated, not much is expected of the local run of custom for some time, at least, but there is a great deal of interior trade that should have been heard from and the delay is not fully understood, even allowing for the cautious tendencies of buyers. Manufacturers and dealers, however, feel fair assurance that the country generally will, sooner or later, want larger amounts, in view of the large crops and other evidences of prosperity. The accumulations of supplies in first hands embody all in the way of assortment that would naturally be required under ordinary conditions and are easily available, but offered without pressure and values pretty steadily adhered to. On White Lead there seems to be no irregularity on the combination production. Association Corroders' rates stand as follows: Lead in oil in kegs and dry lead in kegs, in lots of less than 500 lbs., 7½c. net; in lots of 500 lbs to 5 tons at one purchase, 7c.; 5 tons to 12 tons, one purchase, 5¾c.; 12 tons and over, one purchase, 6¾c.; dry white lead in bbls. ½c per lb. less than price in kegs. Lead in oil 12½ lb. in tin pails, add 1c.; in 25 and 50 lb. tin pails, add ¼c.; and in 1 to 5 lb. tin cans, assorted (100 lbs. in case) add 2½c. per lb. to keg price. Terms on lots on 500 lbs. and over, note or acceptance at sixty days, or 2½ per cent. discount will be allowed for cash paid within fifteen days of invoice date. To make either of the above required quantities any assortment of packages of white lead, red lead and litharge may be counted. The above quotations are free on board cars or boat at corroding point. Linseed Oil has some minor irregularities still, but on the whole the inclination of the market is to steady up and maintain a healthier measure of uniformity on really desirable makes. We quote at general range at 37@40c. for Western, and 44@58c. for City. Spirits Turpentine does not change in value to any noticeable extent, and the market as a whole is free from unusual feature. Supplies appear to be ample and advices from the South are as a rule supporting. We quote at 36@37c. per gallon, according to quality, delivery, etc.

TAR AND PITCH.—The market has about former general features. Not much force can be found in the demand from any quarter, and buyers invest only when compelled to, but as accumulated supplies are moderate, holders have a fair advantage and calculate upon full rates. We quote Pitch at $1.70@1.75 per bbl.; Tar at $2.15@2.50, according to quantity, quality and delivery.

MISCELLANEOUS.

ATLANTIC WHITE LEAD AND LINSEED OIL COMPANY,

Manufacturers of

ATLANTIC" PURE WHITE LEAD.

The best and most reliable White Lead made and unequaled for uniform

Whiteness, Fineness and Body.

RED LEAD AND LITHARGE,

PURE LINSEED OIL,

Raw, Refined and Boiled.

Atlantic White Lead & Linseed Oil Co.,

287 PEARL STREET, New York.

A. KLABER,

Importer of and Worker in

MARBLE, ONYX & GRANITE

Steam Works,

236 to 244 EAST 57th STREET,

4th 2d Av Elevated R. R. Station NEW YORK

National Chimney Tops.

(Patented.)

The most efficient Chimney Cowl in use. Down drafts and smoky flues cured; a wonderful increase of draft obtained.

WARRANTED "SURE."

The spiral part enlarging as it goes upward, admits the air on all sides, and the wind striking it in any direction is given an upward tendency, thus helping to produce the desired effect.

IRA G. LANE, Patentee.

207 East 64th Street.

WATER-TIGHT CELLARS.

F. W. LAWRENCE, 16 & 18 Exchange Place.

MISCELLANEOUS.

TOWN OF UNION, HUDSON COUNTY, N. J.

NOTICE TO BUILDERS.

Proposals for the Construction of a Town Hall.

SEALED proposals will be received by the Board of Council of the Town of Union, at the Town Hall, corner of Lewis Street and Palisade Avenue, on

Monday, August 31st, 1891,

at 8 P. M., for the construction of a Town Hall, according to plans and specifications now on file in the Clerk's office of said Town and at the office of the Architects, Messrs. French, Dixon, & De Saldern, Broadway and 57th Street, New York City, where they can be examined by any person interested therein. Bids will be received for the entire work, or for separate parts thereof, according to the specifications, and the successful bidder or bidders will be required to furnish bonds equal to the amount of the bid. All information necessary in relation to said contract can be had from the Town Clerk, and from the above-named Architects, and the Board reserves the right to reject any or all bids, if deemed for the interest of the Town so to do.

Town of Union, August 15th, 1891.

By order of the Board of Council.

LOUIS FORMON,
Town Clerk.

J. P. EKSTROM'S

Ventilator

— AND —

Stove Pipe RING and HOLDER

COMBINED.

A sure means of removing excessive heat, smoke, cooking odors, etc.

Equally adaptable to old or new houses.

Send for circulars.

GEORGE E. READ,

MANUFACTURER,

90 Nassau St., N. Y.

FIDELITY RANGE.

Pat. April 29, 1890.

ELEVATED BOILER,

Plain or Hot Air, Right or Left Hand, with or without Hot Closets.

Just the thing for Flats and Small Houses.

Send for circulars.

Isaac A. Sheppard & Co.,

PHILADELPHIA OR BALTIMORE.

GEORGE W. LITHGOW,

GENERAL REPAIRS TO BUILDINGS

41 King Street, New York.

MISCELLANEOUS

HUGH M. CAMP & SONS VALLEY IMPROVED CEMENT ABSOLUTELY HYDRAULIC

SOLD BY ALL DEALERS IN BUILDERS' SUPPLIES.

UNIFORM, RELIABLE, CHEAP

55 Liberty St., N. Y.

J. C. French & Son,

VAULT AND SIDEWALK

LIGHTS

Of every Description.

No. 452 Canal Street New York.

OPERATORS FOR TRAP DOORS

TICE & JACOBS

MANUFACTURERS OF

Jacobs' patent Concrete Lights

AND ALL KINDS OF PATENT LIGHTS FOR

Sidewalks, Roofs, Floors Etc.

Telephone 211 Cortlandt. 510 PEARL St N.Y.

JAMES MATHEWS & SON,

Sole agents and Manufacturers of

MAX KELLING'S Patent

FIRE-PROOF IRON

Dumb Waiter Doors and Casings, Sashes, Windows, Shutters and Wall Closets.

The most durable and cheapest articles in the market.

PRICES:

$3, $4, $6, $7, $8 and upward, according to size and style.

Illustrated catalogue, price list and references sent on application.

Over 5,000 in use in this city.

Main Office & Salesroom,

172 E. 110th St.

Branch & Factory,

510 & 512 E. 20th St.

Excelsior, Pat. Dec. 3, 1889.

RAPP SHEET METAL WORKS.

Man'f'rs of

RAPP'S PAT. IRON

Dumb Waiter DOORS AND FRAMES.

Send for illustrated catalogue and price list.

Indorsed by the leading architects and builders as being the best and cheapest Fire-Proof Door made.

Pat. May 6th, 1890.

J. W. RAPP, Sole Agent,

315-319 E. 94th St., N. Y. City.

Stewart Ceramic Company,

SOLID WHITE CROCKERY BUTLER'S PANTRY, KITCHEN, STATIONARY WASH TUBS, SLOP AND CORNER SINKS.

312 Pearl St. Cor. Peck Slip.

HENRY McSHANE CO.,

(LIMITED.)

Plumbers', Steam & Gasfitters' Supplies

Telephone, 215 39th. 625 AND 627 SIXTH AVENUE.

Sanitary Specialties.

BUILDING MATERIAL PRICES

LUMBER.

Appended quotations are based almost wholly upon prices obtained for goods from first hands. Yard rates necessarily range much higher owing to the expenses attending sorting out and grading cargo and even car lots, besides which must be added the cost of handling and carrying until consumers are ready to invest. Terms of sale also prove important factors and, altogether, it is impossible to give a line of retail quotations thoroughly reliable in character.

SPRUCE—Eastern—special cargoes delivered N. Y.	$16 00	@	17 50
Random cargoes, narrow	13 00	@	14 00
Random cargoes, wide	14 50	@	15 50
PILING—Eastern—cargo rates:			
Ranging 30@40 per cent 12 inch butt, 35 to 40 ft average length	4	@	—
Ranging 45@50 per cent 12 inch butt, 35 to 40 ft average length	4¼	@	4½
Ranging 50@60 per cent One-half 12 inch butt, 38 to 40 ft average length	4¾	@	5
Two-thirds 12 inch butt, 38 to 42 ft average length	5½	@	6
Three-fourths 12 inch butt, 40 to 45 ft average length	5¾	@	6
All 12 inch butt and up, 40 to 45 ft average length	6	@	6¼
Piece stick, 40 feet each	4 00	@	—
do. 45	6 00	@	—
do. 50	8 00	@	—
do. 55	12 00	@	—
Inch spars, per inch	20	@	22
Scaffolding poles, each	80	@	1 00
Clothes poles, 45 to 65 feet, each	3 00	@	6 00
HEMLOCK:			
Penn. joist	12 00	@	12 50
do. boards	13 00	@	13 50
do. timber, 20 ft and under	12 50	@	13 00
do. do. 22 to 24 ft	13 00	@	13 50
do. do. 26 to 28 ft	13 50	@	14 00
do. do. 30 to 32 ft	14 00	@	15 50
do. do. 34 to 36 ft	15 50	@	16 00
do. do. 38 to 40 ft	16 50	@	17 50
WHITE PINE—Good uppers and select, 1 to 2 inch	40 00	@	48 00
Upper and select, 2½ to 4 inch	50 00	@	58 00
Shelving	26 00	@	31 00
Pickings, 1 inch	33 00	@	36 00
Cutting-up, 1 inch	25 00	@	28 00
Bracket plank	30 00	@	35 00
Dressing-boards	18 00	@	22 00
Box, inch	13 50	@	14 00
Box, thick	14 50	@	15 50
West India shippers	16 00	@	19 00
Rio Janeiro do.	20 00	@	21 00
River Plate do.	29 00	@	30 00
Australia do.	25 00	@	30 00
YELLOW PINE—Random cargoes delivered N. Y.	18 00	@	21 00
Ordered cargoes	22 00	@	23 00
Flooring	21 00	@	22 00
Step plank	26 00	@	28 00
Common siding	13 00	@	14 00
Heart face boards	20 00	@	21 50
Car orders	21 00	@	23 00
At Atlantic ports, f. o. b.	12 50	@	15 00
At Gulf ports, f. o. b.	11 50	@	13 00
North Caroline pine timber	13 50	@	15 00
do. flooring 1 inch	16 00	@	22 00
do. do. 1¼	16 50	@	22 50
do. do. 1½@2 inch.	24 00	@	25 00
do Shipping culls or box	12 00	@	14 00
do Plain and mottled ½@1½ inch.	18 50	@	25 50
Ash, white	36 00	@	43 00
Elm	20 00	@	22 50
Oak, plain	37 00	@	41 00
Oak, quarter sawed	52 00	@	55 00
Oak, quarter sawed, extra thick	56 00	@	60 00
Redwood	45 00	@	52 50
Maple, clear	28 00	@	33 00
Chestnut, clear	33 00	@	35 50
Cypress, clear	30 00	@	32 50
Black Walnut, good to choice	130 00	@	140 00
Black Walnut, ordinary to fair	100 00	@	120 00
Black Walnut, ⅝	78 00	@	83 00
Black Walnut, selected and seasoned	150 00	@	155 00
Black Walnut counters	110 00	@	150 00
Black Walnut, culls	35 00	@	40 00
Black Walnut, rejects	50 00	@	53 00
Cherry, wide	110 00	@	115 00
Cherry, good	85 00	@	100 00
Cherry, ordinary	65 00	@	80 00
Whitewood, inch	30 50	@	32 50
Whitewood, ⅝ inch	24 50	@	26 00
Whitewood, 1¼ to 2½ inch	32 00	@	34 00
Shingles, Pine, 16 inch, extra	2 75	@	3 10
do 18 inch, extra	4 10	@	4 30
do 18 inch, clear butt	2 90	@	3 10
do 16 inch, stocks	4 50	@	4 60
do 18 inch, stocks	5 30	@	5 40
Shingles, Cypress, 6x20	8 00	@	10 00
do larger sizes	11 00	@	16 00
do sawed	6 00	@	9 00
Cedar—Medium to large	6¼	@	7½
do. —Extra large	7¾	@	8
Mahogany—Small	6½	@	7½
do —Medium	8	@	8½
do. —Large	9¼	@	12
do. —Extra Large	12½	@	14

ESTABLISHED MARCH 21st 1868.

DEVOTED TO REAL ESTATE. BUILDING ARCHITECTURE, HOUSEHOLD DECORATION, BUSINESS AND THEMES OF GENERAL INTEREST

PRICE, PER YEAR IN ADVANCE, SIX DOLLARS.

Published every Saturday.

TELEPHONE - - - - CORTLANDT 1370.

Communications should be addressed to

C. W. SWEET, 14 & 16 Vesey St.

J. T. LINDSEY, Business Manager.

VOL. XLVIII AUGUST 29, 1891. NO. 1,224

The publication offices of THE RECORD AND GUIDE *have been removed to Nos. 14 and 16 Vesey street, over The Mechanics' and Traders' Exchange, a few feet west of Broadway.*

THERE are times when even reason appears to be unreasonable, and it is only on looking backward that one sees that what appeared to be unreason was simply the doubt naturally attaching to all things earthly. Thus reason points to a continuance of the advance in prices on the stock market, while the fact that the advance has continued for a month with no setback to speak about creates a doubt of the justness of its conclusion. It is easy to determine whether an opinion is correct or how far correct when all the circumstances that can possibly go toward making it are presented for consideration. In the stock market this is never the case; there are always influences creating themselves which are most likely to come to the front at the most unexpected moment and change the conditions sometimes trivially and sometimes wholly. At one time it appeared that the reaction which the traders had so long worked for would come near the end of this week, but the faith of the buying public in the future of the railroads prevented it and even carried prices beyond any point previously seen this year, if we leave one or two cases out of account. With a continuance of such faith, no reaction of importance need be looked for. The reports of frost in the Northern wheat line failed of great influence, for the good reason that frost cannot now prevent the wheat crop from being a large one and, in even the threatened districts, larger than last year. With this fact in view and a probability of good prices for wheat, the farmer's position is not one to excite discouragement. Should the frost reach the corn, there might be more room for alarm, but not until it does. With the farmer prosperous general business will be good and values increase in all markets, and especially in the markets which employ the savings of the community. It is under such anticipations as these that stock and bond quotations continue to advance, and that realizations are more than offset by new buyings—and it is under them that prices will continue to rise. Foreign exchange is now an active bull feature, the quotations are gradually falling, and as the times are as exceptional as they were in the spring when the movement was Eastward, we may expect to see gold come this way before the rates for bills touch the importing point, as we saw it go out when rates were below the exporting point. The return of gold should naturally be a further inducement for prices to go up; but it will not be surprising if on the movement so caused a great deal of stock is thrown on the market, bringing reaction and ultimately forcing a new basis for a new advance.

THE state of trade in Great Britain is very clearly shown by the foreign trade figures for July. They were smaller, both as regards imports and exports, than in July, 1890. In the case of the imports the decrease was very slight—less than 1 per cent; but the decline in exports amounted very nearly to 10 per cent. The falling off in the imports is, however, peculiarly noticeable, when it is borne in mind that the movement during the first half of the year resulted in a considerable increase. In a similar way, the decline in exports during July has been much greater than the figures for previous months would lead one to expect. These lower totals for foreign trade, especially when taken in conjunction with other evidence, such as the decrease in railway freight traffic and in the amount of bankers' clearings, undoubtedly bear conclusive testimony as to the dullness which exists in trade. So far as the foreign trade statistics are concerned, however, it should be remembered that the July of 1890 was a month of exceptional activity, due to the desire on the part of foreign manufacturers and American importers to accumulate as large stocks as was possible before the prospective increase of duties went into effect. If anything, however, a somewhat better feeling is beginning to prevail not only in Great Britain but on the Continent. Stocks are somewhat more active; and confidence seems to be slowly returning. The American department of the London Exchange has, of course, moved with the New York market; and there can be no doubt but that English financiers are taking an increasing interest in the American securities. The negotiations between the Austro-Hungarian, German and Swiss delegates as to the proposed treaty of commerce are dragging along very tardily. The difficulty of coming to an agreement seems to be the fault mainly of the Swiss representatives. Switzerland is an exemplification of the truth so often forced upon the minds of our own countrymen that a nation which takes the protective road must travel far. Up to a few years ago Switzerland was regarded like Great Britain, as a free trade country—not free trade, however, in the British acceptation of the term, for low revenue duties were placed on very many articles. But the Swiss Treasury, becoming depleted through the country's increasing military expenses, these duties were raised, and the raises proving acceptable to manufacturers, protectionist notions spread until last winter the Federal Assembly voted an autonomous customs tariff, by which the duties on a great many articles were raised to so high a rate that they are now the chief hindrance to an agreement between the three negotiating countries. It seems probable that for the present the disagreements will prove to be insurmountable, and that another meeting will take place between the delegates from Germany, Austria-Hungary and Italy for the conclusion of the treaty of commerce between these three countries, leaving Switzerland to join later.

DESPITE his apparently small chances of election every friend of good government should be glad to see Andrew D. White the Republican gubernatorial candidate this fall. It would distinctly be a case in which the high character and commanding abilities of a nominee would redeem the political methods which were the efficient cause of his nomination. When Abram S. Hewitt was put up by Tammany as its candidate for Mayor, everyone knew that Mr. Hewitt would represent, not his temporary backers, but an intelligent and invincible desire to secure good government for the city. In the same way and for the same reason we should feel confident that Andrew D. White would not use his office for the purposes of Platt, but in what he considered to be the best interests of his constituents; and representing as he would a distinctly higher plane of political morality than the leadership of Hill admits of in the New York State democracy, he could conduct his campaign on the salutary if not very successful issue of opposition to the methods of our Senator-Governor. That he would make a good running candidate is, however, a matter which is more than doubtful. It is plain that his nomination is not by any means decided upon, and that the possibilities thereof has been thrown prominently forward only for the purpose of testing public, or, more correctly, newspaper feeling. Neither will this test, we fear, be entirely satisfactory to Mr. White's friends. His name has drawn forth respectful tributes even from the Democrats; but in case he was nominated it seems probable that the latter would concentrate their batteries on what is considered to be an indefensibly weak spot in Mr. White's record—his opposition to universal suffrage in large cities. He would be accused of being a radical and implacable demophobist; the coarse prejudices of the mob would be opened on behalf of his opponent and we should have a campaign which would be far from comforting to believers and nourishers of what is best in the American democracy.

APART from any considerations as to Mr. White's affiliation to either of the political parties, it would be grossly unjust to make his opinions as to universal suffrage a bar to his election as Governor; and if his opponents are successful in stirring up an effective mass of public prejudice against him, they would fittingly emplify an evil in democracy which provides a reasonable basis and perhaps a partial justification for his opinion. Mr. White has never questioned the expediency of universal suffrage in the election of President, Governor or Mayor; but, like all observers of the politics and economics of the country, he has found our cities "the rotten spots in our body politic," and he has sought for some efficient means to eradicate the sore which, in his opinion, is threatening the vitality of the whole political system. The expedient which he would adopt to this end is the creation of boards, to be elected by the property-owners alone, with sole authority to spend the public money. How far this expedient would remove the evils from which our municipalities are suffering, we have no intention of discussing. It may be said that the question raised is outside the area of practical discussion; for the suffrage when once granted can be taken away again only under the most exceptional conditions. But in what way, we should like to know, does the holding of such an opinion disqualify a man from attending satisfactorily to the duties of Chief Executive of this commonwealth?

Obviously to any right-minded man it would be no disqualification at all. If universal suffrage was to be an inevitable issue in the campaign, or if Mr. White by any official action could give actuality to his opinions, the believers in manhood suffrage would, of course, be justified in opposing him strenuously; but as we all know the question is no more germane to any possible official action on the part of Mr. White than is the question of original sin. The introduction of the issue would be simply a detestable piece of demagoguery. Yet, if Mr. White is nominated, who can doubt but that the opposing candidate and his support will amplify at great length on his own great love for the people and his great confidence in them, and will cast many a hypocritical slur on one who is honest and courageous enough to assume an unpopular position. One would expect to hear such degrading and windy-mouthing from a ward politician; but the appointed representatives of State organization ought to be above such pot-house politics.

FROM all accounts the philo-Russian demonstrations in France have been childish in their extravagance. A crowd of school-boys engaged in parading noisily through the streets of a city in celebration of some victory in athletics could not be more antic and unrestrained in their rejoicings or more silly in the exhibition of gratified vanity than the French have been lately. Much of the talk is really dangerous in its inflammability. At Gap an entertainment given by the officers of the Fifty-second Regiment was the occasion for a great display of enthusiasm, and M. Saint Romaine, Deputy for the Department of the Isere, while lecturing in the presence of the Prefect of that district, said that two days before, when he was at the fete of the Seventy-fifth Regiment of Romans, he heard the officers exclaim, "We have never been so prepared." This was quite true, and when they cried in France "Aux arimes, citoyens!" from the banks of the Volga to the shores of the Baltic the Russian people would reply, "Formez vos batailions!" A continual diet of this sort of stuff acting on the excitable French nature might easily lead to some outbreak were it not that the governments of both France and Russia are very well aware that they are in no condition to go to war at the present time. Russia, particularly, with an unusually short crop and her peasantry suffering from destitution, and in many districts from actual or prospective starvation, is for the time being practically bound over by nature to keep the peace. People are not wanting in France who appreciate the ludicrous extremities of feeling to which the country has been carried by its hatred of Germany. One writer in a Paris journal has invented a few amusing telegrams designed to betray the silly side of the gushing accounts forwarded from all parts of the provinces. He relates how in a restaurant a waiter who was serving the sweets to a patron, placed the dish on the table with a loud "Charlotte Russe"—whereupon everyone present arose and sung the Russian national anthem, followed by the "Marseillaise." In another place a man who was walking quietly down a street pulled out a cigar-case. Immediately thirty of the passers-by wrenched it from his grasp, and hugged him with cries of "Vive le Tzar." The explanation of this peculiar demonstration is to be found in the fact that the cigar-case was of Russia leather. The whole town was illuminated that evening. It may be doubted if the spirit of Russia worship can long stand a little common-sense satire of this kind.

WITH a palpable discrimination against the numbers ninety-nine and one hundred and one a committee of one hundred "champions of the people" has recently been formed for the purpose of freeing Battery Park from the grasp of Gould. It is evident that the organizers of the recent "popular uprising" against the nefarious grab have had the greatest difficulty collecting one hundred "citizens" who were willing to serve on this many-headed committee. The number of good names that have expressed a hearty sympathy with the movement in the abstract, but declined to accept the proffered place among the "champions of the people" is astonishingly large. Within a few days the "Rev. Dr." (*sic*) Morgan Dix, Theodore Roosevelt, the "Rev. Dr." (*sic*) Thomas Gallaudet, Everett P. Wheeler and George W. Curtis have all pleaded lack of time or some other disability as a reason for declining to become "champions." Evidently this "popular uprising" differs from others of the same kind. Ordinarily we might expect public-spirited citizens to take on gladly the *Times*-honored burden of championship; but the conclusion is forced upon us that this "popular uprising" has been misnamed. The faithful ones must take refuge in the comforting assurance that they are following their own best lights; but they should not disguise from themselves the esoteric character of the illumination. The committee of champions have not yet organized; but they have made up their minds that they will do so on next "Wednesday, Thursday or Friday." According to the oracle of the "popular uprising," they intend to go about the work with an unexpected amount of discretion and caution. They "will not assume at the beginning that the fight is won," which certainly shows an admirable amount of self-denial. We can well imagine how keenly they must desire to make such an assumption. We are assured, "on the contrary, that operations for the future will be discussed as if the campaign were entirely new and as if the committee had the greatest possible obstacles to overcome." This is right. If obstacles of that superlative character known as the "greatest possible" were not to be overcome, it is obvious that the committeemen would be misnamed "champions." Undoubtedly the campaign is "entirely new." Seldom has a "popular uprising" in our experience grown old so slowly. All the work is still to be done. That a resolution containing the Board of Aldermen's "pious opinion," that Battery Park ought to be vacated has been passed was doubtless something; but it was something entirely useless. As we pointed out at the time the Board of Aldermen is not at present a representative body; its resolutions do not arouse interest and command respect, particularly when the expression of opinion is simply of a dialectical order. Nothing has as yet been accomplished, and, as the oracle says, "the members of the committee will have every opportunity to exercise the utmost zeal and the strongest endeavor toward ousting the squatter from the people's pleasure ground." Right again, you trumpet of champions. The "popular uprising" will will undoubtedly offer a truly moral occasion for those who uprise. Their motto should be: "Effort without expectation."

Was the Taylor Building Unsafe?

THE dreadful accident which occurred on Saturday last in Park place, by which sixty-one lives were lost, has been the chief topic of conversation during the past week. Just what caused the collapse of the building and the fire which ensued immediately thereafter, will never be accurately known. A careful examination shows that the walls were constructed of good brick and of thicknesses quite up to the requirements of the building law at the time when, in 1872, the building was erected. The mortar was excellent, being in part cement mixed with the lime and sand. The wooden girders, 12x14, and the floor timbers, 3x14, and placed 16 inches from centres, were of good quality, and reasonably well anchored and strapped. The interior cast iron columns were much smaller than would be allowed at the present time, being only 9 inches diameter in the first story and lessening 1 inch in each story until in the fifth story their diameters were only 5 inches. On the floor of the upper story stood six steam printing presses, and on the next floor below stood four similar presses. The paper, lithograph stones and other materials, together with machinery of various kinds, made up a load on the several upper floors greatly in excess of the safe carrying capacity of the structure which was intended only for light manufacturing or office purposes, although similar overloading quite general in the older down-town buildings. But in this case there was an element of danger quite common to corner buildings. The fallen building was but the rear portion of the building known as Nos. 245 and 247 Greenwich street, on the southeast corner of Park place, having a frontage of about 38 feet on Greenwich street and a depth of 135 feet on Park place. The structure as a whole was divided by two cross-walls about midway of the length, forming a hallway, with staircases for entrance to the westerly and easterly portions. It was the easterly portion where the disaster occurred. Considering this latter portion as a separate building, and it was known as Nos. 68 to 74 Park place, the building had a frontage of about 65 feet, by a depth of about 35 feet, with a height of five stories, or about 67 feet above the sidewalk, and a basement below. The basement and first story were divided by brick cross-walls into four separate small stores, one being occupied as a restaurant, the next adjoining as a drug store, the third as a paint store and the fourth was vacant. The walls that divided the stores did not extend above the floor of the second story. The upper floor beams and the roof beams were carried on one line of wooden girders, supported by iron columns, running across the width of the lofts, parallel with Park place, and the floor beams ran in the direction of the lesser distance, the depth of the lofts, so that on each upper story the ends of the beams rested respectively on the front wall and on the rear wall and on the girder centrally placed between these two walls. The rear wall was solid, as it abutted against the wall of an adjoining building, which latter was three stories in height. The front wall was full of window openings, for the entire light came in from the street side. Usually when a building more than 25 feet in width occupies an inside lot, the girder runs from a pier of the front wall to the rear, and floor beams run in an opposite direction, with their ends resting on the side walls. Had this plan been adopted in the case of the fallen building, probably it would be standing to-day. The presses on the two upper stories stood in a line facing the front or street wall, in the same direction as the floor beams, and the vibration and shock of the running presses had a tendency to sway the heavily-weighted floors backwards and forwards from the rear wall to the front wall. The ends of floor beams only rest 4 inches on a wall. The rear wall could not be swayed to the extent that the front wall could, for another building stood against it for about half its height. Did the swaying finally release the beams from their bearings on that rear wall, or from their bearings on the front wall, thus allowing the floor to drop, carrying death and destruction in its downward flight and throwing the front wall out into the street? No column of support gave way, for in that event the collapse would have been toward the centre and the street wall would have been dragged inwardly instead of being pushed outwardly. Or did an explosion of naphtha or benzine in the basement of the paint store or the drug store, in this structurally weak and overloaded building, throw out the front wall and bring down the upper floors? It is said that the flames shot through the fallen mass with rapidity and burned intensely, and apparently showed the presence of some gaseous explosive. An intricate network of broken gas pipes were contributing, however, to that very same appearance. There was no boiler on the premises, steam being supplied from an outside source. At the time of the accident only three, or at most four, of the printing presses were in motion. Were these running at an accelerated rate of speed for the very reason that the others were not consuming power? Or did a belt catch and cause an unusual or sudden jar? And was one of the floors in some one place unusually overweighted? Generally when a building gives from overloading, some premonition is given by the creaking of timbers and noise of materials tearing asunder. If there was no explosion, what caused the ignition—was it the friction of the falling material that started the flames or the range in the basement? What happened inside the building at the moment of collapse will never be accurately known, as death has sealed the lips of those who could have told.

It is a singular omission in the present building law, as in all the previous ones, that while the thicknesses for bearing walls are minutely specified for given heights, yet there is no restriction as to the number or size of openings for windows or doors that may be placed in such walls, and thereby more or less weakening them. In the last revision of the law which unfortunately failed to get through the Legislature, this defect was to be remedied by the following requirement: "If any horizontal section through any part of any bearing wall in any building shows more than 25 per cent area of flues and openings, the said wall shall be increased 4 inches in thickness for every 10 per cent, or fraction thereof, of flue or opening area in excess of 25 per cent." The thickness of walls in the fallen building were 16 inches above the level of the second story floor beams, up to the roof beams, except that the front wall was 20 inches in thickness on account of being faced with pressed brick, laid in running bond, but this 4 inches of the thickness is not counted in under the law as the face brick has next to no bonding in with the brick-work back of it. The front wall was a bearing wall, with the usual number of window openings, and it would have had to be the thickness that it was even if it was not a bearing wall, which unfortunately it was as it carried the ends of the floor beams of the several upper stories.

The humane work of recovering the bodies from the ruins of the fallen building has been done at the expense of the city under a section of the building law which says:

"In case of the falling of any building or part of any building in the city of New York, if persons are known or believed to be buried under the ruins thereof, it shall be the duty of the fire department to cause an examination of the premises to be made for the recovery of the bodies of the killed and injured, and for that purpose said department shall employ laborers and materials, as may be necessary, to perform said work as speedily as possible, and the comptroller of the city of New York is authorized and directed to provide the funds to prosecute said work until completed. And for the purpose of providing the money for said work the board of estimate and apportionment are hereby authorized to transfer to the order of the comptroller such sums as may be necessary, from any unexpended or excessive appropriation of the then current, or of any previous year, or to issue revenue bonds payable out of the taxes of the next ensuing year."

Prior to the passage of the 1885 law, or what was known as the Esterbrook law, as prepared by a Committee from the several building trade organizations, no provision existed in any law for the rescue of injured persons or the recovery of bodies from the ruins of a building. It required five years to get the Esterbrook law through the Legislature. That law made it incumbent on the owner of the building, when required so to do by a notice from the Chief of the Fire Department, to immediately have the debris removed and an examination made; and in case of the owner's failure to commence the work within five hours after the notice had been served, the Chief could then employ laborers, and the expense should be a valid claim on the owner of the land. When the next revision was made, in the 1887 law, which is the one at present in force, the Committee took into consideration the possible difficulty in finding an owner, and of the delay that would ensue anyway, and the leisurely way in which an owner might possibly prosecute the search. To secure prompt action and because it is a matter of public concern far beyond the interests of an owner, the Committee decided to put the duty and the expense on the city, and the section which we have quoted above was drafted. Certain persons whom it would be useless now to recall by name, holding official positions and speaking for the city, opposed the change and the saddling of such possible expense on the city. It looked as though the proposed alteration had to be abandoned when an appeal was made to Richard Croker, who was at that time one of the fire commissioners. Promptly and decisively Mr. Croker said "Certainly, the committee are right; let the section stand as they have prepared it." It is to the credit of Mr. Croker's head and heart at that time that the search of the Park place ruins could now be made with the vigor and effectiveness that it finally was. The search was first commenced by the Chief of Police, in ignorance of the fact that the law made it incumbent on the Fire Department to take the work in hand. It was nearly two days after the accident occurred before the officials of the Fire Department woke up to what was their duty. The scandal of a similar delay should never occur again.

Investments—Good and Bad.

CATS AND DOGS.—If to buy, then what to buy? With this question repeated over and over again in his mind, his finger on his lips, his eye upon the tape which is reeling out quotations as fast as he can read them, the would-be buyer stands the picture of steadfast contemplation and in fact lost in the possibilities of his query. It is a position of considerable danger, not to his person but to his purse. There are times when a prick of a pin, as children tell their fortunes, will with certainty indicate a profitable purchase; or to be more correct there are times when a backward look will tell that had a pin been stuck on a particular day at any part of the list it would have indicated a profitable purchase, because everything moved up. But, notwithstanding a rare precedent or two, sensible people do not decide upon their purchases in this way, luckily for them. It is a good rule to look for merit whatever the times. There are people, however, who in a manner allow the list to be pricked for them. They are the people who are deceived into purchasing worthless stocks or bonds by artful manipulation of quotations, and it is to them that a few words of advice are offered. With the means and a desire to purchase, it is very hard to resist the wiles of the manipulator. A man goes into the Street when the market is well advanced with the hope of buying something which has been still, but which will show him a profit. He cannot see any attraction in a stock that has gone up 10 or 12 points, and ordinarily he is right, but in this exceptional case he is wrong, consequently he looks around for a stock that has not moved, or has risen slightly if at all. He soon finds what he is seeking in, say, X Y Z, which has been held nominally at 20 for a long time and now moves up by a quarter, and sometimes a half per cent at a time, 2 or 3 points. If he buys it is ten chances to less than one that some years later he tells a friend confidentially that he has carried X Y Z for so many years, and has never had a chance to get his money back.

In times of activity the temptation to the insider to secure a market for the rattletrap he has had no option, but to carry is too great to be resisted. A few wash sales may help to dispose of some of his superfluous stock, and generally the proceeds of every hundred shares sold is so much profit. It is, it must be admitted, one of the indispensable features of the situation that things which have been for so long a time unsalable are now being brought into trading. If the situation was not a very good one, their owners would not pay commissions for the washes, knowing that it would be only so much money thrown away. But with all things looking rosy and the prospects of a great speculation in the near future what are known as cats and dogs are exposed for sale in the market place. Nothing can be done without the public, so it is the fault of the public that these wares are brought out. It is the public who take the venture. The promoter who has paid little or nothing for the goods is always ready to take the cash, so that he can create some more cats and dogs for the next great rise, whenever it may be. The buying is conducted on the principle that the times are so good and the prospects for a large supply and rapid circulation of money so certain, that anything and everything must go up. It is in the expectations of, or with the view of inducing such a principle into being, that the stock market has recently seen a shower of, if it has not rained, cats and dogs. Rapid quotations have sent out and up South Carolina, with its enormous floating debt, and Laclede Gas Common in the face of growing obligations to the preferred stock under the cumulative dividend clause. Atlantic and Pacific, with its enormous bonded debt ahead, Des Moines and Fort Dodge, with nothing to warrant it at all, the East Tennessee and kindred issues, to say nothing of coal and other mining issues. Any one interested in learning how people are induced to buy rubbish can do so by following the sales from day to day. It will be seen that they commence with a few hundred shares, all wash, that they grow to a thousand or two, partly wash and partly genuine, and if they grow further, it can generally be taken that the public is in it and then prayers for the safety of buyers are in order. It has been some years since the cats and dogs have had any show, not since the fall of 1886 certainly. A comparison of prices then and now, or of a few weeks back, will be an instructive lesson as to what will happen to the man who deals too long in them and has them just before they begin to go down under the influence of a change in the times. That is a good way off, though. A mariner commences his voyage provided with all the information he can get of the rocks and shoals he may encounter; he does not refuse the voyage but provides against its dangers. Low as well as high-priced stocks will in the speculative movement just entered bring profit to the buyer, if he is not too rash in buying and gets out in time.

In the long list of cheap stocks there are, of course, some which have merit and are not merely tokens to be cast this way or that according to the wave of speculation. Among such Southern Pacific, Chesapeake & Ohio and Hocking Valley, for example, deserve attention. Southern Pacific has an immense capital, $116,000,000 outstanding out of $150,000,000 authorized, but it is practically sole owner of the largest and best parts of the properties it operates. Last year it earned a surplus on stock of about 2 per cent, though this was offset two-thirds by advances to leased lines. For the first half of this year net earnings increased nearly a million dollars, the greatest gain being made on the roads owned. With other Southwestern roads making large increases in earnings, it is natural to expect that Southern Pacific will show corresponding gains. With less promise, the stock has sold higher than it does now. In 1886 it moved between 30¾ and 41⅛, the next year between 29⅝ and 36⅝, in 1888 between 19 and 27½, in 1889 between 21½ and 37⅛; last year its lowest price was 22½ and its highest 37⅛, and this year it has risen from 23 in January to 37⅛. Chesapeake & Ohio earned, in the fiscal year ended June 30th last, nearly a million dollars gross and half a million dollars net more than in the previous fiscal year, and earnings since the close of the fiscal year maintain their increase. Hocking Valley, in the first half of the current year, earned something more gross and about the same net as in the like period of 1890. The July report showed substantial gain in gross earnings. All these roads have, in the dull days of recent years, met their engagements promptly; the bad points in Chesapeake & Ohio and Hocking Valley especially have been very thoroughly exposed, in the first case by reorganization and in the second by litigation, and it is not unreasonable to suppose that they, as well as other stocks of as good record, will now benefit by the good times come and coming.

Notice to Property-Owners.

BOARD OF ASSESSORS.

OFFICE OF THE BOARD OF ASSESSORS,
No. 27 CHAMBERS STREET.
NEW YORK, August 21, 1891.

Notice is given to the owner or owners of all houses and lots affected thereby, that the following assessments have been completed and are lodged in the office of the Board of Assessors for examination by all persons interested, viz.:

No. 1.—Sewer and appurtenances in 139th st, from Brook to St. Ann's av and in St. Ann's av, bet 138th and 142d sts. with a branch in 141st st.

No. 2.—Sewer and appurtenances in East 151st st, bet Railroad av East and Courtlandt avs, with a branch in Morris av, bet 151st and 152d sts.

No. 3.—Sewer in 82d st, bet Boulevard and Amsterdam av.

No. 4.—Sewer in Park av, w s, bet 92d and 93d sts. with alteration and improvement to present sewer in 92d st bet Park and Madison avs.

[The limits embraced by such assessments include all the several houses and lots of ground, vacant lots, pieces and parcels of land situated on—

No. 1.—Both sides of 141st st, from Trinity to St. Ann's av; both sides of 139th st, from St. Ann's to Brook av; east side of Brook av, from 138th to 139th st; both sides of St. Ann's av, from 138th to 142d st, and both sides of Crimmins and Beekman avs, commencing abt 360 ft. s of 141st st northerly to a point distant abt 350 ft. n of 141st st on Crimmins av and abt 525 ft. n of 141st st on Beekman av.

No. 2.—Both sides of 151st st, from Railroad av East, to Courtlandt av, and both sides of Morris av, from 151st to 152d st.

No. 3.—Both sides of 82d st, from Boulevard to Amsterdam av.

No. 4.—West side of Park av, from 92d to 93d st, and both sides of 92d st, beginning at Park av and running westerly abt 150 ft.]

All persons whose interests are affected by the above-named assessments, and who are opposed to the same, or either of them, are requested to present their objections in writing to the Chairman of the Board of Assessors, at their office, within thirty days from the date of this notice.

The above-described lists will be transmitted, as provided by law, to the Board of Revision and Correction of Assessments for confirmation on the 22d day of September, 1891.

In the matter of the application of the Board of Street Opening and Improvement of the City of New York, relative to acquiring title, wherever the same has not been heretofore acquired, to Cedar avenue (although not yet named by proper authority), extending from the westerly line of Sedgwick avenue, opposite to the junction of Burnside and Sedgwick avenues, to Fordham road, in the 24th Ward, as the same has been heretofore laid out and designated as a first-class street or road by the Department of Public Parks. The Commissioners of Estimate and Assessment in the above-entitled matter, give notice to all persons interested in this proceeding, and to the owner or owners of all houses and lots and improved and unimproved lands affected thereby and to all others whom it may concern, to wit: that they have completed their estimate and assessment, and that all persons interested in this proceeding, or in any of the lands affected thereby, and having objections thereto, do present their said objections in writing at their office, No. 51 Chambers street, on or before the 8th day of October, 1891, and that the said Commissioners will hear parties so objecting within ten week days next after the said 8th day of October, 1891, and for that purpose will be in attendance at said office on each of said ten day [illegible] o'clock P. M.

FINANCE DEPARTMENT,
COMPTROLLER'S OFFICE, August 25, 1891.

The Comptroller of the City of New York gives notice to all persons, owners of property, affected by the assessment list in the matter of acquiring title to certain lands in the 12th Ward of the City of New York, bounded on the west by Avenue B, on the north and east by the Harlem and East Rivers, and on the south by East 86th street, for a public park, as laid out under and in pursuance of the provisions of chapter 320 of the Laws of 1587, was confirmed by an order of the Supreme Court, dated May 27, 1891, and entered in the County Clerk's Office, June 12, 1891, and that, unless the amount assessed for benefit on any person or property shall be paid on or before the expiration of sixty days from the date of this notice, that is to say, on or before the 26th day of October, 1891, interest will be charged thereon at the rate of 6 per cent per annum, from the date of confirmation of said assessment, to wit: the 27th day of May, 1891, as provided by section 4 of said chapter 320 of the Laws of 1887.

The above assessment is payable to the Collector of Assessments and Clerk of Arrears, at the "Bureau for the Collection of Assessments and Arrears of Taxes and Assessments and of Water Rents," Room 31, Stewart Building, between the hours of 9 A. M. and 2 P. M., and all payments made thereon on or before October 26, 1891, will be exempt from interest as above stated, and after that date will be subject to a charge of interest on the amount of the assessment at the rate of 6 per cent per annum from the said date of confirmation thereof to the date of payment.

Contractors' Notes.

Sealed bids or estimates will be received at the office of the Department of Public Charities and Correction, No 66 3d avenue, until 10 o'clock A. M., of Friday, September 4, 1891, for furnishing the materials and work required for building a pavilion for alcoholic patients at Bellevue Hospital, New York City; also for steamheating a pavilion for the incurables, Almshouse, Blackwell's Island, New York; also for a water-closet tower at Charity Hospital, Blackwell's Island; also materials and work required in the erection of addition to Harlem Hospital, and repairing pavilion D, Randall's Island, New York City. Further information, etc., may be had upon application at the department.

Estimates for repairing the crib-bulkhead between Piers 47 and 48, East River; also for preparing for and extending Piers, old 57 and 58, with appurtenances, near the foot of Bloomfield street, North River, and for preparing for and repairing the crib-bulkhead at Pier, old 58, will be received by the Board of Commissioners at the head of the Department of Docks on Pier "A," foot of Battery place, North River, in the City of New York, until 1 o'clock P. M. of Thursday, September 10, 1891.

Sealed bids or estimates will be received by the Commissioner of Street Improvements of the 23d and 24th Wards, at his office, No. 2632 3d avenue, corner of 141st street, until 3 o'clock P. M., on Thursday, September 10, 1891, at which place and hour they will be publicly opened, for furnishing and delivering, where required, broken-trap rock stone and trap-rock screenings and Tomkins Cove blue stone, along certain roads, avenues and streets in the 23d and 24th Wards, in the City of New York; also for constructing sewer and appurtenances in 132d street, from Brook avenue to summit west of Trinity avenue, and branch in St. Ann's avenue, between 132d street and Southern Boulevard, and for regulating, grading, setting curb stones, flagging the sidewalks and laying crosswalks in College avenue, between Morris avenue and 146th street.

The Market.

E. A. Crûiksbank: "Our renting has commenced and we are now quite busy with it. From present indications, and if the general business of the country is as good as it promises to be, I think we will have a satisfactory market in the fall."

H. H. Cammann: "There is promise of a fair general business in the fall. There will be no boom, and it is better that there should be none; but for investment property and private houses there will, I think, be a very good market."

Hall J. How: "The outlook promises very well for the fall. Already there is an active inquiry, and although business is very dull just now, as it generally is at this season of the year, I think that it will very shortly improve. We are not in for a boom, but rather for a steady and generally satisfactory market."

Geo. R. Read: "The prospect for the fall is very good. I think we will have a tip-top market."

New Members.

The following names have been posted for membership in the Real Estate Exchange: A. F. Schwannecke, by J. F. B. Smyth, and Frederick Winant, by James L. Wells.

Personal.

C. E. Harrell has just returned from a two months' trip to Puget Sound, Washington.

Real Estate Notes.

The Equitable Life Assurance Society has begun a suit in the Supreme Court to foreclose mortgages aggregating $200,000 upon the property of the New York Steam Company, including Nos. 174 and 176 Washington street and Nos. 13, 15 and 17 Front street.

The House of Rest for Consumptives have conveyed to The St. Luke's Hospital about fifty lots lying on Gray street, Anthony avenue, Crane place, Popham street, Morris street, and Prospect and Lexington avenues (24th Ward), at an expressed consideration of $100,000.

Title has passed from Samuel Weeks to The Children's Aid Society at $40,000 for premises known as Nos. 219 and 221 Sullivan street, with six two-story frame front and rear buildings thereon.

Patrick J. Roon, Ida L. Pryor and others, the owners of t[illegible]ing lots on the block bounded by Washington, Christopher, Greenwich and Barrow streets, which the United States Government require for the site for their new appraisers' stores, this week filed an appeal from Judge

Wallace's decision appointing commissioners to appraise and condemn the land. The matter, it is said, will be carried to the Supreme Court.

The Opinions of Others.

J. J. Plummer said: "There is scarcely a lot on the West Side, between 70th and 93d streets, at the present time available for improvement. This section is essentially one of private houses, but of not very expensive private houses. It is out of the question for a builder on the West Side to take hold of lots at $14,000, $15,000 or $16,000 and improve them without loss, and yet where prices have not already reached those figures they are rapidly advancing towards them. This is all or nearly all traceable to the building loan operators who buy lots at fair prices and re-sell with a loan at a considerably enlarged figure, which, of course, does not represent the true value of the lot, but the value of the lot with the building loan. Adjoining property-owners do not understand this, and so they put their prices on a level with the high figures of the building loan operator, and of course, they cannot dispose of them, not having the operator's advantages and facilities for doing so. The result is, that while there are plenty of unimproved lots and a very lively demand for three-story, 20-foot reasonable houses on the West Side, nothing is doing because owners of lots will not sell at figures which would enable builders to improve at a profit, and builders when they do buy these expensive lots put up houses whose cost is above the demand of the market."

Cyrille Carreau said: "The coming fall market reminds me of the fall market of 1887. In that year business had been very dull for some time, and when the fall came the only business the brokers had to do was of the hold-over kind which had lain over from the spring. This business was taken up and pushed to a successful conclusion, and other transactions that had not been anticipated were also closed, and altogether the brokers had a very good season of it. I only hope my experience of 1887 may be repeated and I shall rest satisfied."

Frank G. Swartwout said: "There has been a good deal of talk lately about Harlem foreclosure sales, but do you know for the last month or so at least there have been less foreclosure sales in Harlem than in any other part of the city. Last week there was only one such sale, and it was so far uptown that it should not properly be called Harlem. Then, too, the foreclosure proceedings were brought about not by any weakness in real estate itself, but by the absconding of the builder, who left town as soon as he received the payment on his first tier of beams. In this way many of the foreclosure sales in this section of the city can be traced to special outside causes, and I think it would be hard to say the same thing about other parts of the city."

J. Averit Webster said: "The builders are having rather a hard time of it just now. With the prevailing price of lots and the addition of the loan operators' profit it is almost impossible for a builder to get out of an operation and make anything. The loan operators are not satisfied with the old profit of $1,000 a lot, they want $2,000 or $2,500, and with the high values which owners set on their vacant property it is hard to get hold of any lots where there is a margin for the builder. Another trouble that they have is the practice now so common of giving one, two or three months' free rent. There are a lot of 'rounders' now who go around from one flat to another and get free rent. These people have given flat property such a bad name that buyers will not believe that flat or tenement property produces a good income no matter what proof you give them that your tenants are bona fide rent payers. The remedy for this is for the builders to stop giving more than the broken part of a month's rent free, and for the builders to black list non-rent-paying tenants."

"I think it is a perfect outrage the way Jay Gould and the Manhattan Elevated road is talked about," said George A. Denig to a reporter. "The Manhattan system has done more to develop and benefit New York than all the other means of transit within the city limits combined. Its service is cheap, good, very safe and generally satisfactory, and it would be more so if the road was only allowed to extend and improve its present lines. Jay Gould is not a philanthropist, we all know that. He is running the elevated roads, as any other man would run them, to make money; but, at the same time, he is giving a longer and better ride for five cents than can be had anywhere else in the world. The talk about preserving Battery Park for the people is absurd. No greater service can ever be got out of the park than by allowing the elevated roads to make the extensions and improvements that they wish. The people of the whole city would be benefited by such a step and no one would be harmed, for, even after the improvements had been made, there would be lots of room for the few hundred more or less questionable characters who now use the park, and whom the daily newspapers call the "people," to move around in. And I would allow the elevated roads not only to improve their present system, but to build new lines. New Yorkers don't want and won't have an underground system after using the elevated roads."

"I lay all the stagnation in Harlem real estate to the World's Fair boom," said C. Henry Mead. "When that boom was at its height owners of Harlem real estate of every kind raised their prices, and although we did not get the Fair they have never lowered their figures. The consequence is that although every one wants to sell bad enough, nothing is doing, and investors who would be very glad to put their money into up-town real estate are deterred from doing so by the unreasonable prices which owners demand. The indications are, however, that matters will change this fall. Prices will come down and money which is now lying idle in the banks and trust companies will be put into real estate. Everything, however, depends on prices becoming more reasonable. If they remain at their present high notch I do not think there will be much business done."

"No one wants to touch flats nowadays," said Thomas L. Reynolds. "They have been boomed up so high on a fictitious basis that it does not matter what percentage you show they are very hard to sell. All over town free rent varying in length of time from one to four and sometimes five months is being given, and even after that period of time it is hard to get any money out of your tenants. Some owners not satisfied with giving free rent advertise that they will pay your moving expenses! Is it any wonder that investors are suspicious of flat property?"

"It seems to me," said an old-time owner, "that the Rapid Transit Commission is courting opposition by laying out routes that they know are opposed by some of New York's largest real estate owners. Take the underground route under Broadway as an instance. The owners along that thoroughfare, numbering some of the richest and most influential men in the city, have more than once evidenced their dislike to any underground system in Broadway because they say it endangers the great structures along the street. The assurances of the engineers that it will not do so seemingly count for nothing. The prejudice has taken deep root and is not to be disturbed. With the knowledge that this commission had of how Broadway owners had opposed the arcade system, which is certainly as good and probably better than the one proposed, I cannot understand how they came to designate Broadway as the route. The road would have been for all practical purposes just as central either one block east or one block west of Broadway, and instead of the owners along the latter street using their large influence against the road they would have been in favor of it."

Edward Cabot Wilde said: "There is a practice very common among brokers and at the same time troublesome to them, which I wish could be done away with. It is that of giving around to other brokers the houses on your own books. It is not at all an unusual thing for brokers to bring me houses which are for sale, asking me to enter them on my books against their names, and if I sell them I am, of course, expected to divide the commission. Many of these houses come to me in the natural course of events direct from the owners, but if the broker comes and rattles off a description of the house before I have time to say a word, and I then tell him that I have or will get the house, he thinks I am playing a sharp trick with him. For my part I wish brokers would not offer me houses until they have found out in some indirect way whether I want them or not. When I get orders for a house that is not on my books I go around to other brokers and ask if they have a 25-foot house between such and such streets at such and such a price, and I think that if other brokers would do likewise they would find it a very much more satisfactory plan than the present one, where houses are thrust on you whether you will or no."

Important to Architects and Builders.

YELLOW PINE.

The well-known firm of A. T. Decker & Co. has recently been incorporated under the laws of New Jersey, with the title of "A. T. Decker Company," the capital stock being $100,000, in 1,000 shares of $100 each, all of which has been subscribed for. This firm has been established since 1874, and they are the largest dealers in yellow pine in this city. They have a regular line of sailing vessels from Jacksonville, Fla., and also receive large shipments weekly by steamer from points in Georgia and Florida direct. Their stock at their yards, foot of Bethune street, comprises an assortment of all sizes and lengths, and is one of the largest in town. A. T. Decker is president of the new company, and Chas. Hersey, treasurer.

* * *

DISPOSING OF BUILDING MATERIAL.

F. M. Hausling, of No. 614 E. 14th street, has recently torn down St. Paul's Methodist Episcopal Church on 4th avenue and 22d street. The marble which composed all the interior of the church was sold by him to the Rev. Thos. McLaughlin for the new Catholic church at New Rochelle. The pews were purchased by the Church of the Ascension in Mount Vernon.

* * *

ELECTRICAL WORK.

The New York Electrical Engineering Company, of which Eugene M. Smith is manager, are doing considerable wiring and electric light work about the city. Among the recent contracts completed by them is that on Messrs. Jones & Co.'s building at No. 361 6th avenue (wiring for the Edison system) and No. 130 West 23d street, near 6th avenue, where they wired for fifty lights. They have also put in a complete plant at Rockaway Beach for the Grand Ocean Hotel, including an engine, boiler and dynamos. They have in addition a number of contracts under way for architects, who pronounce their work to be very reliable.

* * *

MOSAIC WORK.

The Wood Mosaic Company, of No. 315 5th avenue, are doing the flooring for David H. King's hotel on 43d street, near 5th avenue. They are also contractors for the wood mosaic in the forty-three houses of which John G. Prague is architect and part owner, on West 86th and 87th streets. They are said to be the only firm manufacturing end wood mosaic, which is of great durability and strength of construction.

* * *

MAHOGANY.

J. R. Graham, Jr. has just received a fine stock of mahogany and mahogany veneers, the latter of which are used extensively among decorators, and are to be seen at his yards on 11th avenue and 30th street.

* * *

CARPETS, SHADES, ZINC PLATES, ETC.

Henry Rauch & Son, of No. 24 Avenue B, have just received the contract for furnishing the flat at the southwest corner of 134th street and Lenox avenue, for Mr. Thompson, the owner. He has also the contract for supplying the carpets and shades to the three flats on East 85th street, being built for Louis Wirth. He has just completed the work on four flats in 104th street, between 1st and 2d avenues.

***

BRICKS.

The Baltimore brick is still in great demand. It has been furnished in very large quantities for years by J. C. Hendrickson, sole agent, No. 267 Broadway, New York. It is supplied in the quantities required, and is said to be unsurpassed among the brick brought to this market. Mr. Hendrickson has supplied this brick for the pumping station of the Brooklyn Water Works, East New York, just about completed, and for the large building at Baldwins, L. I. Among other contracts in which the Baltimore brick was used is the Presbyterian Hospital on Madison avenue and 70th street.

***

CEMENT.

Erskine W. Fisher, of No. 18 Broadway, who is thoroughly identified with the Stettin "Anchor" brand of Portland Cement, states that during his visit to Germany, early in the year, he made arrangements for much heavier supplies of this brand, for which he has been turning away orders for the last three years. He is now receiving regular shipments by steam and states that he is in a position to quote on any contract where the quality is taken into consideration.

***

HOW TO ECONOMIZE ON STEAM PLANT.

It has been remarked that over 96 per cent of the steam users in New York City are unfamiliar with the appliances for producing steam. The result is that owners who are obliged to operate steam plants for supplying the heat, light and power necessary in carrying on their regular business are more or less at the mercy of their engineers. With the knowledge that the proprietor is ignorant of the workings of the engine and boiler-room, the engineer may make demands and incur expenses under a plea of necessity that he would not suggest if those in authority over him understood engine-room practice as well as himself. Besides, if he felt himself responsible to those having experience and knowledge equal to his own he would not feel safe in either neglecting his plant or shirking his duties.

It is here where the usefulness of the steam contractor comes in. Assuming, as he does, the entire responsibility of the plant, the owner or lessee feels assured of proper service, without any of the care and vexation incident to securing it. It is not generally known that such contractors exist, and those who may be unaware of the fact are referred to the Hall Steam Power Company, the oldest contractors in this line in New York. They make yearly contracts for the entire care of steam plants, furnishing the engineer, fireman and all coal supplies. They can be addressed at No. 211 Centre street, where estimates can be obtained.

***

STEAM HEATING.

Messrs. Hitchings & Co., of No. 233 Mercer street, are doing the heating work for the new stations of the Suburban Elevated Railway. They also heat in winter the water-pipes connecting the stations with the street, a distance of about 17 feet. It is considered an easy matter to send heat upward, but it is said that this is the first time heat has been forced down to heat water-pipes in winter to keep them from freezing.

***

IRON-WORK.

John Riehl & Bro., of the Metropolitan Iron Works, No. 304 East 95th street, are putting in a much larger boiler and engine in their shops. Owing to the increased demand for their work they have not hitherto been able to turn out as much as desired. With their new facilities this will be remedied, and they expect to be in full running order the first week in September.

New Incorporations.

The Daily News Building, Savings and Loan Association filed a certificate of incorporation in the County Clerk's office on August 26th. The object of this company is the purchase and improvement of real estate, etc. The names of the trustees are W. H. Leffingwell and thirteen others.

A similar certificate was filed by the Fernwood Park Land and Improvement Co. for the purpose of purchasing and improving real estate in the town of Greenburg, Westchester County, N. Y. The capital stock is $50,000, divided into 500 shares of $100 each. The directors of this company are Benjamin G. Glover and eight others.

Real Estate Department.

The real estate market is in about the same condition as it was last week. Not very much business has been done, and while there was considerable inquiry in many of the brokers' offices there are very few new transactions under way. Many of the largest dealers and capitalists and brokers also are still out of town, and the best informed among real estate men do not think they will return until after Labor Day. It will then be several days before they get settled down to serious business, so that a revival of activity cannot be looked for much before the 15th of next month. The talk among the brokers continues of the brightest kind, and most of them are looking for an active season with good prices. The renting season is well started now, and the reports from all quarters are encouraging. In the case of small three-story houses the supply does not equal the demand, but so far as can be seen it is only in these three-story houses that there is as yet any scarcity.

THE SALES OF THE WEEK.

As anticipated in this column last week, little has been done at auction since last Saturday. An insignificant lot of foreclosure sales of a very unimportant character and one suburban sale complete the list of the week's business. The foreclosure sales possess no features of interest to the general market unless the slowness which attended the sale of a house and lot on East 168th street can be taken as such. In this instance it was evident that the plaintiff did not wish to buy in the property, and there was a long and awkward pause before he made a bid. For a few moments it looked as though even this forced sale would not go through, and the men in the crowd kept suggesting bids of $100 to $200 to each other. The auctioneer, however, finally succeeded in getting a bid, and he quickly knocked the property down to the plaintiff at $3,000.

The suburban sale was of a number of villa sites at Central Valley, New York, about an hour and a-half's ride from this city. The country roundabout, it is said, is an exceedingly pleasant one for residence, and in the vicinity are the dwellings of several well-known people, included in the number being Thomas C. Platt. The improvement company that owned the property cut it up most wisely. In the centre of these villa plots is a large open circle and radiating from it are the various drives, giving to each plot a desirable location and making the open of the settlement in the middle of the dwellings instead of off to one side, as is so often the case. Auctioneer Morris Wilkins, who had charge of the sale, disposed of eleven plots, varying in size from a little over one-half to not quite one and three-quarters acres in size. The price was so much per acre, the lowest figure being $360, while the highest price obtained was $555. Among the buyers were Richard Ficken, Henrietta Ficken, Jas. C. Ryder, David Connell and James M. Barnes.

THE ANNOUNCEMENTS.

Next week promises to be very dull on 'Change. The auctioneers have practically nothing to offer, and, indeed, several of the most prominent among them have not yet returned to town, which is an indication that they do not expect very much just yet themselves. The foreclosures sales are of the tamest character, and it is only here and there that a bill announcing property at public auction has made its appearance, and these sales, it must be remembered, do not take place for a week or two yet. The auction market for city property, it will be observed, is very dull, with no very great prospects of immediate improvement. In the suburbs and the outlying wards of the city a more satisfactory state of affairs is to be observed. One or two large sales are announced for next month already, and the bills of others which are booked for the early fall will doubtless make their appearance very soon. Among those settled on or talked of are Richard V. Harnett's sale of 536 lots at South Bensonhurst, Jere. Johnson's sale of 400 lots at New Utrecht, Jas. L. Wells sales in Bedford Park and the vicinity, and a reported sale of seven hundred lots on the North Side by an auctioneer who has just applied for membership in the Exchange, A. P. Schwannecke. All these sales, however, are some way ahead, the first of them not taking place until Labor Day, so that until then we cannot expect any auction activity, even in the suburbs.

CONVEYANCES.

	1890. August 22 to 28 inc.	1891. August 21 to 27 inc.
Number	165	106
Amount involved	$2,613,646	$1,412,948
Number nominal	48	38
Number 23d and 24th Wards	89	40
Amount involved	$656,115	$197,170
Number nominal	13	11

MORTGAGES.

	1890.	1891.
Number	185	161
Amount involved	*$3,898,958	$1,503,678
Number at 5 % or less	66	72
Amount involved	$869,014	$840,780
Number at less than 5 per cent	18	6
Amount involved	$218,000	$82,000
Number to Banks, Trust and Ins. Cos	34	41
Amount involved	*$2,824,700	$930,535

PROJECTED BUILDINGS.

	1890. August 23 to 29 inc.	1891. August 22 to 28 inc.
Number of buildings	68	20
Estimated cost	$1 390,350	$322,734

*Includes mortgage given by the Mount Morris Electric Light Co. to the Central Trust Co. for $2,000,000.

Gossip of the Week.

SOUTH OF 59TH STREET.

Geo. R. Read has sold for Jas. G. Wallace to W. M. Martin No. 136 Prince street, a five-story brick warehouse, on lot 25x101, on private terms.

E. H. Ludlow & Co. have sold for James C. Fargo, president of the American Express Co., to Frank B. Martin the four-story, high stoop, brown stone dwelling, about 19 6x49.6, No. 124 East 37th street, on private terms.

Chas. H. Yarnall has sold to Augustus Spagbaro, No. 207 Elm street, a three-story brick house, 20x41, for $9,000.

H. S. Hewson, it is reported, has sold for Kelly & Ramsgate, No. 55 South 5th avenue, 25x100, for $27,750.

G. W. Dunham has sold No. 29 West 37th street, a four-story brown stone dwelling. The lot has a frontage of 18 feet by a rear width of 12 feet and a depth of about 60 feet.

NORTH OF 59TH STREET.

C. K. Bill has sold for Bernard S. Levy the three five-story and Tiffany brick front flats and stores covering the plot, 100x102.2, on the southwest corner of Amsterdam avenue and 78th street. Two of the houses are 35 feet front and the third 30 feet. The purchaser, W. H. Vredenburgh, of Monmouth Beach, New Jersey, paid more than $200,000 for the property, but the exact figure it is impossible to ascertain.

Francis Crawford has sold to a Mr. O'Day, of Buffalo, No. 128 West 72d street, a four-story Indiana limestone front dwelling, 25x60, and extension, 20x102.2, for about $80,000.

W. E. D. Stokes has sold to Dr. Albert F. Sawyer the four-story brick and stone dwelling, 22.8x85x98, on the northwest corner of 86th street and West End avenue, for $75,000.

The Manhattan Elevated Railroad Company are said to be making extensive purchases along the line of their Suburban Road, in the 23d and 24th Wards. It is said that the company is buying property along its present line and in the neighborhood of its proposed extension, and that as soon as they have secured as much property as possible at low prices they will proceed with improvements to their line, which it is said they already contemplate. Vice-President Gallaway, of the Manhattan Company, could not be seen in relation to the above rumor so that as the story stands now it is unverified. We give it for what it is worth.

Fairchild & Yoran inform us that the buyer of the house No. 81 West 86th street, reported last week, was C. F. Tietjen, of the West Side Bank, not John W. B. Dobler as reported.

Garrett D. Clark has sold for Joseph Donald to W. K. Richardson the three-story dwelling No. 232 West 132d street, for $14,500; and for R. V. Davis to W. E. Parsons the three-story dwelling No. 233 West 132d street, for $12,500.

Jesse C. Bennett has sold for Foster & Livingston to John H. Staats, of R. P. & J. H. Staats, the dock and bridge builders, No. 26 West 82d street, a four-story brown stone house, 18x56, and extension, x102.2, for $35,000. This sale was mentioned last week.

LEASE.

C. E. Harrell has leased for Jas. H. Havens and Robert C. Winters to the Hall Steam Power Co. the six-story building now in course of erection, about 100x100 in size, Nos. 167-173 Wooster street, for ten years, from May 1st, 1892, at $17,000 per annum.

Brooklyn.

J. P. Sloane has sold for the Carroll estate the two-story store, 22x30, lot 25x100, No. 152 India street, to James McGuckin for $2,350.

Corwith Bros. have sold the lot, 25x100, on the east side of Diamond street, 125 feet south of Calyer street, for J. V. Meserole to George Sweeting for $400; and the lot, 25x100, on the north side of Green street, 150 feet west of Provost street, for Michael Toomey to John C. Wiarda for $900.

CONVEYANCES.

	1890. August 21 to 27 inc	1891. August 20 to 26 inc
Number	279	202
Amount involved	$1,099,314	$816,735
Number nominal	76	75

MORTGAGES.

Number	208	205
Amount involved	$975,398	$642,534
Number at 5 per cent. or less	124	125
Amount involved	$738,343	$444,834

PROJECTED BUILDINGS.

	1890. August 22 to 28 inc.	1891. August 21 to 27 inc.
Number of buildings	70	88
Estimated cost	$58[illegible],650	$532,660

White Plains.

M. McCormick has sold for the Mutual Life Insurance Company to Jno. Schappert, the builder, the 100 acres at White Plains, with mansion, outhouses, etc., known as Kennedy Farm, on the east side of Broadway, running to Harrison road. Mr. Schappert will lay out this farm in villa plots and improve the same.

Out Among the Builders.

J. C. Burne has plans on the boards for five five-story brick and brown stone flats to be built by Wm. J. Mathews on the north side of 88th street, 36.8 east of Madison avenue, at a cost of $125,000. One flat, 27.6x90, will accommodate three families on a floor; three others, 25x90, are to be built for two families on a floor, and the remaining house will be a single flat, 25x90 in size.

Boring, Tilton & Mellen have begun the consideration of plans for a handsome residence to be built at Mt. Morris avenue and 121st street for A. G. Hupfel. The house will be a four-story and basement stone structure finished in the most thorough manner with every convenience. The scheme for the interior arrangement, if carried out as at present developed, will give a frontage on the avenue of 90 feet and a depth of 35 feet. The cost will be in the neighborhood of $100,000.

Geo. F. Johnson, who recently purchased the three five-story flats, on plot 100x100, on the northeast corner of 7th avenue and 127th street, contemplates altering them into a seven-story apartment hotel. Mr. Johnson proposes to remove the stoops, put in a line of stores on the avenue, add two stories to the present buildings, put in elevators and make other interior alterations and improvements, which will cost him, he thinks, upwards of $20,000.

R. E. Rogers will furnish plans for the addition which the trustees of the Home for Incurables, at Fordham, will make to the boiler and laundry building of that institution. The cost of the alterations will be $4,000.

Ernest Molwitz will build a five-story tenement, 25x65, on the south side of West 144th street, 100 feet west of 8th avenue, from plans by Hugo Kafka.

Charles Rentz has plans on the board for a five-story flat house at No. 266 Henry street, for Moritz Solomon.

Out of Town.

MADISON, N. J.—C. Powell Karr has completed plans for a two-story and attic frame cottage, 36x40, to be built for Henry Steadrath. The house will be finished with all modern improvements and is to be cabinet-trimmed in part, including mantels of original design.

MT. LORRETTO, S. I.—Benjamin E. Lowe is the architect for the new stone and brick church to be built here for the congregation of the Mission of the Immaculate Virgin, Rev. Father James J. Dougherty, rector. The edifice will be 85x190 in size, with a central spire of iron and slate 235 feet high. The church proper will rest upon a basement 18 feet high, which is to be finished as a chapel for ordinary uses. The walls will be finished in plaster relief, while the ceiling will be groined in ash. The seating capacity will be about 3,500, and the cost something over $275,000, which is the amount of estimates now in, not including the twenty-eight stained glass windows, which will be 9x22 in size and which are to be imported from Munich. The corner stone will be laid Sept. 13 by Archbishop Corrigan and many church dignitaries, and it is expected that some 20,000 spectators will witness the ceremonies. Mr. Lowe is also the architect for the four-story brick and stone laundry building, 65x135, with extension, 40x40, now building for the Mission. This building will be fitted with every first-class appliance in the way of machinery, and is to cost $60,000.

WANTS AND OFFERS.

(Advertisements strictly in accordance with this title will be inserted at the practically nominal rate of 10 CENTS *per line (agate). In figuring for themselves advertisers may count seven words for each line, the address to be taken as one line. The object of this department is to bring buyers and sellers into communication with customers. Advertisements must be marked "Wants and Offers Column," and sent to the office of publication, Nos. 14 and 16 Vesey Street, not later than 3 P. M. Friday.)*

OFFERS.

100TH ST., between 2d and 3d avs; ten lots, cheap; all mortgage if improved.
July11-1aw5w. EDWIN A. ELY, 103 Gold st.

40 CHERRY ST., between Roosevelt and Franklin sq., 32x64, vacant; $12,000; accommodating terms. EDWIN A. ELY, 103 Gold st.
July11-1aw8w.

Brooklyn Real Estate for Sale.

FLATS, 93 Concord st., Brooklyn, near the Bridge; five-story double flat property, in perfect order and always rented for $2,300 per year, paying easily 15 per cent. per annum on investment; terms easy. Apply to owner.
R. J. KELLEY, 377 Broadway, New York.
Aug. 22-1aw4w.

OFFERS.

PLATE-GLASS CORNER on avenue thoroughfare, 17th Ward, Brooklyn, half block from big shipyard; suitable for saloon; price, $3,800; easy terms.
J. P. SLOANE,
Aug. 29-1aw5w. 343 Manhattan av., Brooklyn, E. D.

$16,000—BARGAIN—Four-story double house on Broadway, near Myrtle av.
JACOB MARKS, 250½ Stockton st., Brooklyn.

DESIRABLE INVESTMENT.—Eight-story apartment house; best location in Brooklyn; might exchange equity over $125,000 at 4½ per cent.
J. 20—uf, Apply 60 Broadway. Room 311.

Improved Property.

TO LET OR TO LEASE.—Two floors of a factory, 25x98 light on all sides, 1st av and 107th st; terms moderate. J. REEBERS' SONS,
Aug. 22-uf. 409 East 107th.

OFFERS.

PLANING MILL, branch of my business, for sale.—Is located at 24th st. and 11th av., on four or five city lots, leased ground, and consists of two and three-story brick buildings and adjoining sheds; also 80 horse-power engine and boiler, planers, moulders, saws, etc., all in good running order and now in operation; will leave a portion of value on bond and mortgage three years; this offers splendid opportunity to enlarge wood-working industry or to secure good mill business to add thereto. For further particulars, etc., apply to
EBEN PEEK, 24th st. and 11th av.
Advertiser intends to continue his lumber business now carried on at above address. Aug. 15-22-29

Miscellaneous.

A PARTY ABOUT TO BUILD A FIVE-STORY factory, 50x98, in Harlem, near water-front, will lease the three upper floors and build to suit tenant. Terms very moderate. Address
May 16 u. f. OWNER, 409 E. 107th St.

SALES OF THE WEEK.

The following are the sales at the Real Estate Exchange and Auction Room for the week ending Aug. 28.

• Indicates that the property described has been bid in for plaintiff's account:

WM. KENNELLY.

79th st, Nos. 171-175, n s, 205 e Amsterdam av, 45x102.2, three three-story stone front dwellings. J. O. Baker. (Amt due $26,302)...... $27,000

J. C. LALOR.

•74th st, Nos. 435 and 437, n s, 150 w Av A, 50x102.2, two five-story brk tenem'ts. N. Cowen. (Amt due $19,288)........................ 24,000

OTHER AUCTIONEERS.

•69th st, Nos. 323-331, n s, 350 w West End av, 125x100.5, five five-story brk tenem'ts. Hubert Van Wagenen. (Amt due $7,656; prior morts, $——)........................ 34,020

•168th st, s s, 81.10 e Concord or Forest av, 50x125. Thomas McCrane. (Amt due $4,402).. 3,000

Total........................ $88,020
Corresponding week, 1890, no sales took place on the Exchange.

BROOKLYN, N. Y.

FOR WEEK ENDING AUGUST 27.

•Roebling st, No. 248, w s, 71.3 s South 3d st, 23.9x105, three-story brk dwell'g and two-story frame dwell'g in rear. Louis Rohdenberg........................ $8,000

North 1st st, No. 54, s w s, 141.6 s e Kent av, 25x140.8x25.6x142.11, three-story frame dwell'g and two-story frame dwell'g in rear. Huntington Page........................ 2,700

•Furman av, No. 73, n s, 187 e Bushwick av, 34.7x100x187x100, two-story frame dwell'g and two-story frame carpenter shop in rear of plot. Henry Weil........................ 1,200

•Marcy av, Nos. 578 and 580, w s, 100 s Myrtle av, 50x100, two-story frame (brk lined) dwell'g. William S. Oakley........................ 10,000

New Utrecht road, w s, adj land William Cole, 85.8x143.7x83.8x143.7, New Utrecht. Catharine Tidd........................ 406

Total........................ $22,906
Corresponding week 1890........................ $3,325

CONVEYANCES.

Wherever the letters Q. C., C. a. G. and B. & S occur, preceded by the name of the grantee they mean as follows:

1st—Q. C. is an abbreviation for Quit Claim deed, i. e., a deed in which all the right, title and interest of the grantor is conveyed, omitting all covenants or warranty.

2d—C. a. G. means a deed containing Covenant against Grantor only, in which he covenants that he hath not done any act whereby the estate conveyed may be impeached, charged or encumbered.

3d—B. & S. is an abbreviation for Bargain and Sale deed, wherein, although the seller makes no express covenants, he really grants or conveys the property for a valuable consideration, and thus impliedly claims to be the owner of it.

NEW YORK CITY.

AUGUST 21, 22, 24, 25, 26, 27.

Allen st, No. 9, w s, abt 75 s Canal st, 25x87.6
Allen st, No. 11, w s, abt 50 s Canal st, 25x87.6.
Two five-story brk tenem'ts with stores.
Sarah wife of Israel Wolff to Manassah L. Goldman. *Mt.* $30,000. ½ part. August 22. nom

Bleecker st, No. 125, on map No. 127, n s, 50 w Wooster st, 25x100, four-story brk store and tenem't. Mitchell A. C. Levy to William S. Kane. Sub. to mort. Aug. 21. nom

Same property. William S. Kane and Gertrude his wife to Mitchell A. C. Levy. Sub. to mort. Aug. 21. nom

Broadway, n w cor 28th st, 77.11x57.6x72.9x85.4. Release mort. John Gilsey to Pauline and Daniel E. Starr. Aug. 18. nom

Broome st, No. 423, s s, abt 50 e Crosby st, 25x100x25x108; also strip on rear extdg to alleyway 12 feet wide with use of same, seven-story brk store. Ernest F. Tucker to Anna Schell widow. 1-32 part. May 20. $2,000

Cannon st, No. 52, e s, 100 n Delancey st, 25x100, four-story brk store and tenem't. Alter Gottlieb and Celia his wife to Abraham J. Bleistift. *Mt.* $16,750. Aug. 25. 17,250

Chrystie st, No. 214, e s, 274.3 s Houston st, runs east 75 x south 24.9 x west 22.11 x south 0.2 x west 24 x north 0.8½ x 28.0½ to st, x 24.10, six-story brk tenem't with stores. Karl M. Wallach to Emma Engel. *Mt.* $19,300. Aug. 18. nom

Cherry st, No. 50, n s, 37.5 e Roosevelt st, 19.3x80x21.4x80, three-story brk tenem't with stores. Michael T. N. Burke to Charles Friedman. Aug. 1. 7,250

Cornelia st, Nos. 1 and 3, n w cor 4th st, 40.11x75x26.10x76, five-story brk flat with stores. William Rankin and Elizabeth his wife to Charles Euler. *Mt.* $33,000. Aug 17. 75,000

Coenties slip, No. 31, w s, abt 40 n South st, four-story brk store and tenem't. William M. Rice, Lewiston, Id., and Sarah M. his wife to Austin C. Chandler. Q. C. June 8. nom

Goerck st, No. 102, e s, 22.7 n Rivington st, 25x98.10, five-story brk tenem't. Henry Strauss and Fanny his wife to Jacob Larchan and Rebecca his wife. *Mt.* $16,000, and taxes 1891. Aug. 27. 22,500

Hester st, No. 65 } begins Hester st,
Ludlow st, Nos. 35 and 35½ } n w cor Ludlow st, 21.10x100, lot 1150 map James Delancey, three-story frame (brk front) store and tenem't on Hester st and two-story brk tenem't with stores on Ludlow st. Louis Minsky and Esther his wife to Joseph Kassel. *Mt.* $21,000. Aug. 25. nom

Leroy st, Nos. 55 and 57, n s, abt 200 w Bedford st, 66.3x60.4x53.4x61.6, two five-story brk flats. Owen McElroy, Jr., to John W. Stevens and Owen McElroy, Sr. B. & S. All title. All liens. Aug. 1. nom

Ludlow st, No. 52, e s, abt 137 s Grand st, 20x87.6, four-story brk store and tenem't with two-story frame building on rear. Louis Minsky and Esther his wife to Joseph Kassel. *Mt.* $26,250. Aug. 25. nom

Sullivan st, Nos. 219 and 221, e s, 250 n Bleecker st, 50x100, two two-story frame (brk front) dwell'gs with four two-story frame dwell'gs on rear. Samuel Weeks and Anglesea his wife to The Childrens Aid Society. Aug. 27. 40,000

Water st, No. 674, n s, 125 w Jackson st, 25x100, five-story brk tenem't with stores. Elias G. Brown and Julia S. D. his wife to Benjamin Lichter. *Mt.* $7,500. Aug. 26. 15,000

2d st, Nos. 47, 49 and 51, s s, 100 e 2d av, runs south 29 x east to point 121.6 from 2d av, x south 15 x east 40 x north 9.11 x north 10 x north 27 to st, x west 63.4.
2d st, Nos. 53-57, s s, 163.4 e 2d av, runs east 62.8 x south 45 x west — to point 161.6 e 2d av, x north 10 x north 27 to st.
Allotted in partition to Samuel A. Goldschmidt.

3d st, No. 34, s s, 90 e Wooster st, 22x75.
127th st, No. 20 E.
2d av, No. 2180, e s, 18.10 n 112th st, 19x80.
Allotted in partition to George B. Goldschmidt.

3d st, No. 36, s s, 68 e Wooster st, 22x75.
123d st, No. 341 E.
2d av, No. 2182, e s, 37.10 n 112th st, 19x80.
Spring st, No. 186, s s, 50 w Thompson st, 16.8x75.
Allotted in partition to Edward Goldschmidt.

7th st, No. 38, n s, 225 w 2d av, 25x74.10, three-story brk tenem't. John E. Kaughran to Charles Guntzer. *Mt.* $9,000. Aug. 15. 17,500

18th st, No. 416, s s, 244 e 1st av, 25x92, five-story brk tenem't. Partition. Martin T. McMahon to Mary Sander. Atlantic City, N. J. Aug. 7. 13,900

27th st, No. 502, s s, 60 w 10th av, 15x24.8, three-story brk store and tenem't. Contract. Peter O'Neill to Louis Becker. Aug. 5. 1,400

Same property. Assign. contract. Louis Becker to Adolph Schaefer. Aug. 18. 250

27th st, No. 448, s s, 150 e 10th av, 25x98.9, five-story brk tenem't. Thomas Stone to Mary C. wife of said Thomas Stone. *Mt.* $20,400. July 30. nom

32d st, No. 42, s s, 168.10 e Broadway, 21x98.9, four-story brk dwell'g. Mary E. Hanley to Robert and Ogden Goelet. Aug. 5. 80,000

33d st, Nos. 518-532, s s, 225 w 10th av, 200x98.9, one, two, five and seven-story ale brewery, malt house, stables, &c.
32d st, No. 531, n s, 375 w 10th av, 25x98.9, six-story brk storage house.
Elizabeth J. Childs, Henrietta S. and Robert H. Howard and Angelina Pawley exrs. and trustees Henry Howard with consent of Robert H. Howard and Childe H. Childs to Robert H. Howard and Elizabeth J. Childs. June 8. nom

37th st, No. 530, s s, 400 w 10th av, 12.6x98.9, four-story brk dwell'g. James S. Hopkins to Herman Wronkow. *Mt.* $5,000. Aug. 21. 5,250

43d st, No. 333, n s, 350 e 9th av, 25x90, five-story brk tenem't with stores. Dorinda E. Hyatt widow, Catskill, N. Y., to Walden Pell. 1-16 part. Sub. to 1-16 of morts. Jan. 15. 1,000

47th st, Nos. 119 and 121 } begins 47th st, n e cor
Lexington av, No. 497 } Lexington av, runs east 50 x north 80 x east 50 x north 20.5 x west 100 to av, x south 100.5, two five-story brk (stone front) flats on 47th st and five-story brk store and flat on av. Bridget wife of Martin Disken to Charles Wise and Sali Simonson. Q. C. Aug. 20. nom

Same property. Henry W. Benedict trustee creditors of Martin Disken to Charles Wise and Sali Simonson. C. a. G. *Mt.* $82,000. Aug. 20. 102,500

48th st, No. 311, n s, 150 e 2d av, 25x100.5, five-story brk tenem't with stores. Partition. Martin T. McMahon to Mary wife of Christian Sander. Aug. 18. 16,000

48th st, No. 309, n s, 125 e 2d av, 25x100.5, five-story brk tenem't with stores. Partition. Same to Carl Heim and Katharina his wife. ½ to each. Aug. 27. 16,500

57th st, No. 433, n s, 301.5 w Av A, 20x100.5, three-story stone front dwell'g. Isidor Stark and America his wife to Sali Stark. *Mt.* $8,000. Aug. 27. 4,500

57th st, No. 8, s s, 175 e 5th av, 25x100.5, four-story stone front dwell'g. Siegmund T. Meyer to Edmund Dodge. All liens. June 23. other consid. and 3,000

63d st, No. 413, n s, 206 e 1st av, 25x100.5, five-story brk tenem't. Floyd M. Horton and Dollie S. his wife to Franz C. Doscher and Wilhelmina his wife. *Mt.* $9,000 and taxes 1891. Aug. 25. 15,500

73d st, n s, 250 w 1st av, 75x102.2, vacant. Release dower. Caroline M. Lockwood widow to Mary A. Lyddy widow. July 15. nom

Same property. Mary A. Lyddy now Mary A. wife of Thomas E. Fitz Gerald to The Bohemian Benevolent and Literary Assoc. *Mt.* $16,000. July 1. 21,000

74th st, Nos. 435 and 437, n s, 150 w Av A, 50x102.2, two five-story brk tenem'ts. Foreclos. David P. Ingraham, Jr., to Newman Cowen. *Mt.* $15,000. Aug. 26. 9,000

76th st, n e cor Madison av, 45x102.2, vacant. Foreclos. Augustus C. Brown to Alfred P. Dix and John J. Phyfe. Aug. 24. 39,150

83d st, Nos. 445 and 447, n s, 119 w Av A, 69.1x29x69.4x19.6, one-story frame and two-story brk buildings. William A. Smith exr. George Jones to Michael Conlan and Terence Gannon. *Mt.* $5,000. July 30. 9,000

82d st, No. 118, s s, 175 w 9th av, 25x102.2, five story stone front flat. John Chisholm and Annie his wife to James Thomson. Sub. to mort. Aug. 21. nom

84th st, s s, 275 e Amsterdam av, 100x102.2, vacant. Edna A. wife of William J. Gage to Frank A. and Adolphus E. Stevens. *Mt.* $13,000. Aug. 19. 46,000

85th st, No. 108, s s, 126.5 e 4th av, 18.1x102.2, three-story stone front dwell'g. Charles Rosenberg and Barbara his wife and Henry Gernshym to Sarah Katz, New York. *Mt.* $9,000. March 28, 1891. 13,000

89th st, No. 264, s s, 52 e West End av, runs east 30 x south 67.8 x west 18 x north 43 x west 12 x north 24.8, four-story brk dwell'g. Release mort. Charles T. Barney, Francis M. Jencks and William E. D. Stokes to Jacob Brandt. Aug. 26. nom

Same property. Release mort. Armintha Merritt to same. Aug. 22. nom

Same property. Release mort. Alfred M. and Samuel N. Hoyt and James W. Jackson trustees Mary I. Hoyt to Frank L. Smith. May 5. nom

Same property. Jacob Brandt to Armintha Merritt, Springfield, Mass. Aug. 26. 30,000

93d st, No. 70, s s, 126 w Park av, 21x100.8, five-story stone front flat. Francis J. Schnugg and Carrie H. his wife to Henry Meyer. *Mt.* $19,000. Aug. 18. 28,000

93d st, No. 72, s s, 105 w Park av, 21x100.8, five-story stone front flat. Francis J. Schnugg and Carrie H. his wife to Henry Waters. *Mt.* $19,000. Aug. 18. 28,000

95th st, Nos. 145-165, n s, 150 e Amsterdam av, 200x100, eleven three-story stone front dwellings. Amsterdam Impt. Co. to Bernard Cohn. *Mt.* $188,000. Aug. 19. nom

98th st, No. 202, s s, 92.6 w Amsterdam av, 26x100.11, five-story brk flat. Sebastian Kerner and Mary his wife to John Freienstein. *Mt.* $10,000. Aug. 25. 25,300

103d st, Nos. 158-166, s s, 177.5 e 10th av, 150x 104.10x150x105.6, five five-story brk flats. James McNiece and Mary A. his wife to Peter McParland. *Mt.* $168,920. Aug. 21. 173,020

106th st, No. 209, n s, 150 e 3d av, 20x100.11, four-story brk tenem't. Mitchell Hershfield and Henrietta his wife to Henry Goldstone. *Mt.* $9,000. Aug. 3. 12,000

107th st, No. 73, n s, 113 w 4th av, 16x100.11.
107th st, Nos. 67 and 69, n s, 145 w 4th av, 33 x100.11.
Three three-story brk dwell'gs.
The New York Life Ins. Co., New York, to William S. Cooper. B. & S. C. a. G. July 1. 32,250

112th st, No. 206, s s, 115 e 3d av, 20x100.10, three-story frame dwell'g. Caroline A. Kelly to Catharine Meighan. Sub. to lien $4,000. Aug. 25. nom

114th st, No. 153, n s, 376.3 w 3d av, 18.9x100.11, three-story brk dwell'g. Bridget McGuire widow to Marie L. Depierre. *Mt.* $5,000. Aug. 25. 10,500

122d st, No. 360, s s, 234 w Manhattan av, 16x 100.11, three-story stone front dwell'g. A. Alonzo Teets to Jacob R. Wilkins. *Mt.* $6,-000. Aug. 1. 16,750

127th st, Nos. 310 and 312, s s, 175 w 8th av, 50x 99.11, two four-story brk flats. John Bottomley and Susan A. his wife to Anna M. Steers. B. & S. *Mt.* $22,500. Aug. 20. nom

128th st, Nos. 257-261, n s, 150 e 8th av, 108x 100.11, three four-story stone front flats. David Greenfield, Albany, Ga., and Julia his wife to Herman Wronkow. *Mt.* $50,000. July 27. nom

130th st, n s, 550 w 11th av, old line, 50x99.11, one-story frame building. James Saxton to Alexander Lockwood. *Mt.* $7,500. July 1. 8,250

130th st, No. 43, n s, 375 e 6th av, 20x99.11, four-story stone front dwell'g. The L. F. Genet Lumber Co. to Mary wife of William R. Lowe and Gertrude G. McVay. *Mt.* $16,-500. July 27. 21,000

144th st, s s, 100 w 8th av, 25x100. Agreement as to easement for light and air. Ernest Molwitz individ. and trustee with Board of Health, New York. Aug. 24. nom

Amsterdam (10th) av, Nos. 701-715 } begins Amsterdam av,
94th st, Nos. 123-175
95th st, Nos. 122-174
n e cor 94th st, 201.5 to 95th st, x555x201.6 to 94th st, x545. Frances J. wife of Henry J. MacLean and daughter of Augustus L. Clarkson to the grantors of Levinus Clarkson the younger. Confirmation deed. Aug. 8. nom

Amsterdam (10th) av. No. 709, e s, 100.8 n 94th st. 25x82, five-story brk flat with stores. John Bushmann and Fredericke his wife to William S., Jessie H. and Ellen MacLean. *Mt.* $15,000. June 30. 25,250

Audubon av, e s, 24.11 n 185th st, 29.4x95x29x 95. Mary Flaherty widow to John Dempsey. *Mt.* $2,695. Aug 25. 4,000

Greenwich av. No. 35, w s, 45 s Charles st, 21x 84.10x20.6x80.5, excepting strip 5x9.6 from n w cor of said lot, three-story brk tenem't with stores. Jacob Klinger and Sophie his wife to Anthony Burdorf. Aug. 22. nom

Same property. Anthony Burdorf to Sophie Klinger. Aug. 24. nom

Lenox av, s w cor 137th st, 149.11x75, vacant. Charles E. Runk and Aurelia E his wife to William Rankin, *Mt.* $36,000. Aug. 18. exch

Lexington av, No. 1055, s e cor 75th st, 17.2x55, three-story brk (stone front) dwell'g. Ascher Weinstein and Annie his wife to Mordecai S. Kauffman and Manuel Goldberg. *Mt.* $10,000. Aug. 3. nom

Sherman av, n s, 100 w Emerson st, 150x150. Richard C. Voth to E. Clifford Potter. *Mt.* $6,000. May 18. nom

1st av, Nos. 1689 and 1691, w s, 70.6 s 88th st, 40.2x100.
29th st, No. 51 E.
Allotted in partition to Philippine E. Von Stade.

2d av, No. 1427, w s, 60.2 n 74th st, 20x77, four-story stone front store and tenem't. Joseph Cohen and Lena his wife to Wilhelmina V. Grimm. *Mt.* $10,000. Aug. 22. 18,125

2d av, Nos. 1849-1855, s w cor 96th st, 100.11x 76.5, four five-story brk flats with stores.
96th st, Nos. 230-236, s s, 76.5 w 2d av, 100x 100.11, four five-story brk flats, store in No. 236.
William A. Middleton, Brooklyn, to Emeline wife of J. Worden Gedney. Sub. to morts. Aug. 24. nom

3d av, Nos. 1828-1844, n w cor 101st st, 130.11 x100.
Madison av, Nos. 51-55, n e cor 125th st, 99.11 x72.8.
56th st, No. 24, s s, 51 w Madison av, 26x73.
34th st, n s, 360 e 2d av, 20x97.6.
Lowell Lincoln assignee John F. Plummer individ, and of John F. and Albert T. Plummer and William S. Darling, of John F. Plummer & Co., to William L. Strong. Sub. to morts. Aug. 19. 118,000

Same property. John F. Plummer and Emily M. his wife to same. B. & S. June 25. nom

Same property. William L. Strong to Hookanum Co. et al. Declaration of trust. Aug. 27. nom

6th av, Nos. 70 and 72, e s, 30.3 s Waverley pl, runs east 59 x north 4.5 x east 0.8 x north 21.6 to Waverley pl, x east 5.6 x south 60.1 x west 68 to av, x north 34.4.
Waverley pl, No. 126, ss, 66.11 e 6th av, runs south 60.1 x east 7.7 x south 22 x west 2.2 x south 22 x east 18 x north 102.5 to pl, x west 26.5
Allotted in partition to May Goldschmidt.

6th av, No. 74, s e cor Waverley pl, runs south 30.3 x east 59 x north 4.5 x east 0.8 x north 21.6 to pl, x west 61.5.
123d st, No. 335 E.
119th st, No. 508 E.
Allotted in partition to lawful issue of John Goldschmidt dec'd.

9th av, No. 498, e s, 24 9 s 38th st, 24.8x100, three-story frame tenem't with stores. Edward Antes to Clara H. Antes. B. & S. Aug. 1. other consid. and 35,000

All right, title and int. in and to Pier (old), No. 23, North River, commonly known as Vesey st Pier, and Pier (old), No. 24, North River, including 109.4 of bulkhead or wharf property incident thereto or connected there with on w s West st, next southerly of Barclay st ferry, with land under water and riparian rights. William J. Cruger and May his wife, Griffin, Ga., to The Mayor, &c. B. & S. All title. Aug. 18. 33,333

MISCELLANEOUS.

All title being one undivided int. in estate of Eliza Pooler dec'd. Mary A. Green to Melissa G. Ballentine. Oct. 30, 1890. nom

All title in real and personal estate of Thomas C. Chalmers dec'd. Thomas C. Chalmers and Inez L. his wife to Joseph F. Stier. Deed of defeasance. Aug. 21. 6,500

23d and 24th WARDS.

Ackerman st, s e cor Varian st, 27x90, h & l. Maximilian Polsenski to Greenleaf W. Crossman. Aug. 27. 2,800

Anthony st, e s, opposite the centre line of the block bet Summit av and Jefferson st, runs east 108.2 x south 50 x west 104.1 to st, x north 50.2, being lots 135 and 136 map of New York City private park, 24th Ward. Charles H. Rogers and Carrie L. his wife to James H. Marvin. *Mt.* $500. Aug. 21. 1,150

Drive, s s, 339.1 w from corner formed by intersection of s e s of Drive with s s of Holl pl, runs south 79.4 to lane, x west 54.4 x north 57.6 to Drive, x east 25. Thomas McHugh and Rose his wife to Kate Lynch. Aug. 26. 400

Gray st, s s, extends from Anthony av to Crane pl, 200x230 to 175th st.
Anthony av, s w cor Popham st, runs west 307.7 x south 135.6 to Morris st, x southeast 250 x northeast 85 to Anthony av, x north 159.6.
Morris st, s s, extends from Prospect av to Lexington av, 223x243 to Gray st, x200x217.
The House of Rest for Consumptives to St. Luke's Hospital, City of New York. *Mt.* $36,-500. June 1. 100,000

Orchard terrace, south cor Fordham to West Farms road, 56 to Garden av, x100x79.5 to road, x102.7. Eliza Van Schaick to Giuseppe Botta and Vingenza his wife. Aug. 27. 1,800

Penfold st, s s, lot 122 map George Faile property 24th Ward, 25x100. Joseph Murphy, Jr., to Joseph Murphy. Aug. 22. 800

Samuel st, n e s, lot 38 map East Tremont, 66x 150. Henry J. Dalton and Augusta M. his wife to Mary E. Welsh. Aug. 25. 1,400

Warren st, n w cor Lexington av, 104x76x100x 104. Edward Stichler to Julia F. Stichler. *Mt.* $1,060. Dec. 8, 1890. nom

Weeks st, w s, part lot 16 map of Mt. Hope, 25 x98 4. William E. Hackett and Margaret Hackett widow to Catherine M. Williams. *Mt.* $300. Aug. 25. 1,300

134th st, No. 970, s s, 250 e Cypress av, 16.8x 103 8. Charles Hohl and Anna his wife, Arnold Anderhalden and Theresia his wife to William Werner. *Mt.* $2,500. Aug. 24. nom

134th st, No. 972, s s, 266.8 e Cypress av, 16.8x 103.8. William Werner and Lina his wife, Arnold Anderhalden and Theresia his wife to Charles Hohl. *Mt.* $2,500. August 24. nom

134th st, No. 974, s s, 283.4 e Cypress av, 16.8x 103.7x16.8x103.8. Charles Hohl and Anna his wife and William Werner and Lina his wife to Arnold Anderhalden. *Mt.* $2,500. Aug. 24. nom

138th st, s s, 500 e Willis av, 16.8x100. John F. Dowd to John H. Whittle. B. & S. C. a. G *Mt.* $8,000. Aug. 4. nom

Same property. John H. Whittle and Harriet L his wife to Jonathan Whittle and John W. Wood. *Mt.* $8,000. Aug. 12. 11,000

138th st, s s, 245 e Southern Boulevard, 17.6x 100. Jacob D. Romer and Eliza his wife to Elizabeth G. Madden. *Mt.* $4,000. July 28. 4,500

144th st, n s, 425 e Willis av, runs north 41.6x west 0.8 x south to 144th st, at point 0.4¾ west from point of beginning, x east 0.4¾. Fannie M. E. Lancaster to Gustav and Sophie Stepbach. Q. C. Aug. 21. 20

144th st, n s, 400 e Willis av, 25x100. Annie J. wife of and Francis E. Walkley to same. Aug. 22. 6,000

144th st, n s, 450 e Willis av, runs north 41.6x east 0.8 x southwest to 144th st, at point 0.4¾ from beginning, x west 0.4¾. Annie J. Walkley to Fannie M. E. Lancaster. Q. C. Aug. 21. nom

146th st, s s, 100 e Willis av, 25x100. Agnes Walsh to John N. Schramm. *Mt.* $3,000. Aug. 20. 5,500

158th st, s w s, 100 s e Washington av, 23.4x100 x20.1x100. John Green and Lizzie Normoyle, formerly Green, to William C. Trull and Anthony McOwen. Feb. 17. (See Wales av. nom

Clinton av, n s, 275 w 2d st, 25x200 to Willard av. Emma A. Willard to Abraham G. More. July 14. 650

Cauldwell av, w s, 397 n Clifton st, 18x100. Release mort. Sumner R. Stone exr. Caroline M. Hitchcock to Annie Ormiston. Aug. 21. 4,000

Same property. Release mort. Annie Ormiston to John W. Decker. Aug. 21. 1,600

Same property. Release mort. R. Clarence Dorsett to same. Aug. 21. nom

Same property. John W. Decker to Margaret F. Walsh. *Mt.* $4,000. Aug. 21. 8,500

Cauldwell av, s w cor 156th st, 52.6x52 6x20x 52.6. Charles D. Ogden to Kate T. Bowen. *Mt.* $3,000. Aug. 27. 5,550

Fulton av, e s, 118.6 n 169th st, 7.11x175. James L. Haight and Julia his wife, Brooklyn, to Henrietta Hartung. Q. C. Aug. 25. nom

Lind av, east cor Devoe st, 64x90x—x107.2. Release mort. The Home Ins. Co., New York, to Abraham L. Casey and Maria E. his wife. Aug. 26. nom

Morris av, w s, 50 n Buckhout st, 25x126 6x25x 126 9. Luke S. Van Zandt and Emma V. his wife to Joseph T. Bedford. June 27. 1,800

Morris av, e s, 93.5 n Denman st. 26x100.3. Harry Overington exr. Margaret Heyburn to John Heyburn and Eliza E. Golden. Aug. 20. nom

Same property. Eliza E. Golden to John Heyburn. Q. C. Aug. 20. nom

Morris av, e s, 231 s Highbridge road, 24x131. Sarah A. Lisk to Augusta R. Corris. *Mt.* $3,000. Aug. 17. 5,000

Perry av, e s, 250 s Scott av, 50x110. Robert N. Quinn and Charlotte F. his wife to Adelaide M. Sheak. *Mt.* $470. July 29. 1,600

Strong av, n s, 162.11 e Tinton av, 21x82.11. Max Goldnick and Ida his wife to Anna C. Thiel. *Mt.* $1,750. Aug. 22. 3,450

Tinton av, s e cor Denman pl, 17x95. John C. Fahl and Clara his wife to Frank Benassai and Malvina his wife. *Mt.* $8,000. August 25. 5,500

Union av, e s, 175 s 165th st, 50x165.7x50x165.4. August and Frank Fechteler and Mary Haehnel devisees Julius Fechteler to Charles Schledorn. Aug. 21. 3,700

Wales av, e s, 17 n 147th st, 16.6x100. William C. Trull and Jeanne B. his wife, Anthony McOwen and Ellen his wife to John Green and Lizzie Normoyle. *Mt.* $2,000. Aug. 17.. See 158th st. 4,000

Webster av, e s, 105.8 n Anna pl, 15.4x90. Sarah C. Ottiwell to Herbert A. Shipman. *Mt.* $10,-000. Aug. 20. 5,750

Webster av, e s, 90.4 n Anna pl, 15.4x90. Same to Walter E. M. Zborowsky. *Mt.* $10,000. Aug. 20. 5,750

Webster av, e s, 75 n Anna pl, 15.4x90. Same to same. *Mt.* $10,000. Aug. 20. 5,750

3d av, e s, south ½ of lot 230 map Mt. Eden, &c., 25x100. Elizabeth M. Sandford formerly Ferguson to John Baron. Aug. 22. 500

Lot 48 map of property of The Metropolitan Real Estate Assoc., Fordham Ridge. Isidor Stark to Sali Stark. Aug. 27. 500

Lot 416 map part of Charles Berrian farm, Fordham. Killian Drabold and Emma his wife to The West End Co-operative Building and Loan Assoc. May 26, 1890. nom

Lot 412 same map. Foreclos. John A. Foley to The Industrial Co-operative Building and Loan Assoc. Aug. 21. 2,500

LEASEHOLD CONVEYANCES.

West st, No. 128. Assign. lease. Frederick H. Mueller to The Burr Brewing Co. nom

Same property. Assign. lease. Adolph Koch to Frederick H. Mueller. nom

13th st, n s, 225 w 10th av, 50x103. Assign. lease. Bridget Cuff admrx. John Cuff to Henry M. Livor. 4,000

13th st, Nos. 614 and 616 E. Assign. lease. Franz C. and Wilhelmina Doscher to Floyd M. Horton. 2,500

46th st, n s, 220 e 5th av, 20x100.5. Hannah G. Gerry to Charles R Leaycraft admr. Agnes J. Leaycraft. 20 years, from May 1, 1891, per year, 1,260

83d st, n s, 119 w Av A, 72.7x29.4x69.4x19.6. Assign. lease. William A. Smith exr. George Jones to Michael Conlan and Terence Gannon. nom

7th av, No. 76, s w cor 15th st. Assign. lease. Henry Bening to The J. Chr. G. Hupfel Brewing Co. nom

8th av, e s, 50 s 20th st, 25x100. Mary E. Moore to William D. Southard trustee and admr. Thomas Southard. 21 years, from May 1, 1890, per year, taxes and 1,000

9th av, No. 861. Cancellation of lease. Frederick Picker to Maria N. Winne. nom

Assign. indeft. lease made by John J. Astor to Michael Lawless in 1880. Michael Lawless to Robert V. Lawless. May 2, 1891. 15,000

KINGS COUNTY.

AUGUST 20, 21, 22, 24, 25, 26.

Bainbridge st, n s, 164 w Patchen av, 16x100, h & l. Jacob H. Roberts to Concepcion Castellanos. $5,000

Bainbridge st, n s, 291.8 e Saratoga av, 4x100. Release mort. John G. Dettmer to J. Mason Kirby. nom

Bancroft pl, w s, 90 n Atlantic av, 30x90x30.10 x90. Benjamin Armstrong to James D. Rankin and James Ross. 1,300

Barbey st, e s, 60 s Dumont av, 40x100. Norah A. Cashen to Ellen T. Regan. nom

Bergen st, n e s, 150 n w Underhill av, runs

northeast 157.10 x north 3.8 x west 26.8 x southwest 147.6 to Bergen st, x southeast 25. Henry Newman to Bertha Kaufmann. *Mt.* $3,000. exch

Bergen st, s s, 275 w Rockaway av, 25x127.9. Jacob Pirrung to Anna M. Bodmann. 600

Berriman st, e s, 95 n Stanley av, 20x100. William H. Jackson to Jessie Ferguson. 150

Bleecker st, w s, 290 s Hamburg av, 100x100. Joseph Levy and Henry S. Naul to Meinrad Keck, Simon Kitt and Jacob Miller. *Mt.* $2,500. 5,200

Boerum st, n s, 125 e Graham av, 25x100. Marx Krackow to Lena Fischer. *Mt.* $6,500. exch

Bushwick pl, w s, 80.5 s Montrose av, 23.7x77x 25x84.3. Charles Ernst to Herman Witt. 2,400

Butler st, n s, 180 w Kingston av, 50x100. Alla Otis to Ella S. Benton, Boston, Mass. nom

Carroll st, s s, 327 w 7th av, 17.3x184.7.
Dean st, n s, 25 w 6th av, 20x77.6.
Release mort. Catharine M. Gomez admrx. Domingo M. Gomez to Catharine J. wife of Louis Monjo, Jr. 10,000

Central pl, n e s, 219.10 s e Greene av, runs southeast 17.3 x northeast 120 x northwest 22.2 x southwest 69.1 x north 1.8 x southwest 51. Margaretha Kutschbach to Phillip Bremer. *Mt.* $1,500. 4,500

Cheever pl, n w s, 166.8 s w Harrison st, 16.8x 88.6, h & l. William Moylan to Matthew T. Brennan. *Mt.* $2,000. 5,560

Cleveland st, e s, 246.10 n Atlantic av, 50x100. Arthur E. Sumner to John Flint. 3,500

Clinton st, e s, 125 n Nelson st, runs east 90 x south 25 x west 20 x south 75 x west 70. John Caulfield to Francis Speir, Jr. *Mt.* $24,000. 39,500

Clinton st, e s, 113.4 n Warren st, 22.8x92.3x 22.8x91.10, h & l. Elizabeth F. and Gerard Lester, Alice B. Lawrence, Florence L. Burchard and Helen C. Whitney heirs Joseph H. Lester to Joseph H. Lester. Q. C. nom

Conover st, s w cor King st, 100x100. Partition. Jacob Brenner to Carsten Plate. 11,125

Cooper st, n w s, 100 s w Bushwick av, 25x100, h & l. Edward E. Kelly to Henry Diehm. 8,400

Court st, w s, 18.3 n Union st, 18.2x80. Carrie L. Decker to Carrie M. Vreeland. 1887. 6,000

Court st, w s, 300 n Degraw st, 25x112.6. Same to same. 1887. 10,000

Court st, n w cor 1st pl, runs north 21 x west 55 x north 59 x west 20 x south 80 x east along 1st pl 75. Walter D. Hoag to Carrie M. Vreeland. 1887. 20,000

Crown st, n s, bet New York and Nostrand avs, being lot 50 block 36 assessm't map 24th Ward. John C. McGuire, Registrar of Arrears, to City of Brooklyn. 31

Dean st, No. 1514, s s. 100 w Schenectady av, 16 x107. Frank B. Wakeman to William Linson, New York. *Mt.* $1,600. 3,000

Debevoise st, cor Fleet st, being lot 1 block 139 assessm't map 11th Ward. Jas. C. McGuire, Registrar of Arrears, to City of Brooklyn. 4,077

Decatur st, n s, 75 w Throop av, 80x100. Edward K. Wilder to John Gordon. *Mt.* $6,000. exch

Decatur st, s s, 250 e Stuyvesant av, 25x100. John A. Treusch to Emma Treusch. 125

Degraw st, s s, 335.5 n 5th av, 19.2x100. Peter Kelly to Emil Lachmann. *Mt.* $3,500. 6,790

Eastern Parkway, n s, extends from Osborn st to Watkins st, 200x100. Jacob Miller to Abraham Levine. ½ part. *Mt.* $4,000. nom

Eastern Parkway, n w cor Osborn st, runs west 25 x north 100 x west 21.3 x north — x east 45.10 to st, x south 250. Release mort. Claus Luehrs, Mineola, L. I., to Herbert C. Smith. 2,000

Eastern Parkway, s w cor Chester st, 100x100. David Klein to Henry Vollweiler. 3,600

Eldert st, s e s, 95 s w Evergreen av, 140x— to line of W. Covert farm, x—x—. Mary E. Koster to Virginia A. Kleine. nom

Same property. Abram S. Cassidy to Mary E. Koster. 4,500

Elton st, w s, 325 s Stanley av, 20x100. John T. Toner to Joseph Carroon. 200

Essex st, w s, 100 n Arlington av, 20x100. Edward F. Linton to Harmon A. Whitlock. 750

Essex st, w s, 100 n Ridgewood av, 20x100. Release mort. Thomas Monahan to Edward F. Linton. 510

Ewen st, Nos. 114 and 112. Agreement as to encroachment. Phillip Feldmann with Edward Karutz. 100

Ewen st, e s, 25 s Devoe st, 18.4x75, h & l. Martha J. wife of Charles B. Paul to Charles B. Paul. nom

Frost st, s s, bet Lorimer and Leonard sts, being lot 37 block 24 on assessm't map of 15th Ward. Martin Carroll to Denis Carroll. B. & S. C. a. G. nom

Frost st, s s, 125 w Leonard st, 25x50x26.6x41.7. Martin Carroll to Denis Carroll. *Mt.* $650. nom

Fulton st, s s, 25.6 w Linwood st, 25.6x96.1x25x 101.3. Salvator and Elizabeth Rizzo to John P. Kane. nom

George st, s s, 250 w Knickerbocker av, 25x100, h & l. Goswin Schmitt to George Hagenmueller. *Mt.* $3,000. 5,600

Grand st, s w cor Leonard st, 20x100. Hugh Smith to Bernard Smith. *Mt.* $10,000. 17,000

Grand st, Nos. 247 and 249, n e s, 264.11 s e Driggs st, 40x85.5x40.1x88.9. Maria L. wife of John H. Matthews, Newark, N. J., Frances W. Blackwell, Emma L. wife of Samuel B. Tisdale, Gertrude B. Wiley widow, Long Island City, and Thomas G. Evans, New York, to Louis Laumann. C. a. G. 18,500

Grattan st, s s, 125 e Bogart st, 25x100. George Fitz to George Durst. *Mt.* $500. 2,300

Graham st, e s, 337.4 s Willoughby av, 24.4x 91.5, h & l. Herbert Reynolds to Margaret wife of Herbert Reynolds. *Mt.* $1,600. nom

Halsey st, s s, 248.4 e Sumner av, 16.8x100. Dewitt, Eugene and Eliza C. Tappan to John B. C. Tappan. 5,000

Halsey st, n s, 150 w Howard av, 16.8x100, h & l. Lucy W. Ralphs to George Burns and Michael McGrath. *Mt.* $2,137. exch

Halsey st, n s, 325 e Sumner av, 25x108.10x25.2x 105.4. Louisa Cavanagh widow to John Foley. *Mt.* $400. nom

Same property. John Foley to The City of Brooklyn. 3,250

Hancock st, n w s, 90 s w Central av, 360x100. Timothy G. Sellew to Leopold J. Lippmann. nom

Hancock st, n s, 412.6 e Reid av, 18.9x100, h & l. Asa W. Parker to Mary E. wife of Daniel H. Renton. *Mt.* $3,000. 6,000

Hancock st, n s, 270 e Bedford av, 20x100. John H. Wallace to Leonard M. Allen. nom

Harman st, s e s, 400 n e Central av, 100x100. Release mort. Theodore F. Jackson et al. trustees of Loftis Wood to Darwin R. James. 3,000

Harrison st, s s, 55.9 w Court st, 20x91.5. Carrie L. Decker to Carrie M. Vreeland. 1887. 5,000

Hart st, s e s, 120 n e Broadway, 20x73.3. Bertha Kaufmann, Newtown, L. I., to Henry Newman. *Mt.* $5,800. exch

Henry st, e s, 76.5 s 4th pl, runs east 104.6 x south 50 x west 27.6 x south 9 x west 77 to Henry st, x north 59. M. Howell Topping and ano. exrs. Robert E. Topping and Mary H. F. Topping his widow to George R. Riley. 100

Same property. George R. Riley to M. Howell Topping and ano. exrs. Robert E. Topping. 100

Herkimer st, n s, 82 w Kingston av, 18x100. Julia B. F. wife of John D. Fish to Theodore Wulp. *Mt.* $3,000. exch

Hewes st, No. 212, s s, 63 w Marcy av, 20.5x98, h & l. Horris Adler to Rosa Newman. 8,450

Hopkins st, s s, 425 e Marcy av, 25x100. John Hasselbach to David Klein, New York. *Mt.* $4,500. nom

Hopkins st, s s. 150 s Tompkins av, 25x100. Julius Zeuner to Gustave Kuhn and Rosina his wife. *Mt.* $2,500. 4,000

Jackson st, n s, 250 e Lorimer st, 25x100, h & l. Mary Shevlin to Frank F. Seebolzer. 2,950

Jackson st, n s, 175 e Leonard st, 25x100. Mary M. Atwater, Callicoon, N. Y., to Catharine M. Carroll. 1,800

Jefferson st. Party wall agreement. John Doyle with Gayton Ballard. nom

Jerome st, w s, 60 s Dumont av, 40x100. Catherine Cummings to Norah A. Cashen. 650

Leonard st, s e cor Scholes st, 75x100. Elizabeth Baumgaertner widow, Barbara Woerner, George and August Baumgaertner heirs John Baumgaertner to John Baumgaertner. All title. 30,000

Linwood st, w s, 100 s Blake av, 50x90.
Linwood st, w s, 200 s Blake av, 150x90.
William Rosenbush to Frederick E. Kalkbrenner. ½ part. 110

Livingston st, No. 313, n s, 41.8 e Nevins st, 16.8 x80. William Irvine to James Johnston. *Mt.* $2,600. nom

Livingston st, n e cor Nevins st, 25x100. Charlotte wife of Rotch Kerr and daughter of Carman Stringham to James Johnston. 9-20 parts. Sub. to life estate of Charlotte Stringham and mort. 3,825

Same property. Cecelia Langdon, daughter of L. Stringham and heir of C. Stringham, Jr., Rockville Centre, L. I., to same. 1-20 part. Sub. as above. 637

Same property. Lucinda wife of Skidmore Pettit and daughter of Carman Stringham to same. 6-20 parts. Sub. as above. 3,825

Same property. Edward Rutledge to same. ½ part. Sub. as above. 319

Same property. Parmedia M. Stubbs heir C. Stringham, Jr., to same. 1-40 part. Sub. as above. 319

Same property. Charlotte Stringham widow to same. All title, also life estate. Sub. to mort. 3,250

Same property. Cecila wife of Henry Wood daughter of C. Stringham to same. 6-20 parts. Sub. to life estate and mort. 3,825

Logan st, w s, 150 s Belmont av, 20x100. George H. Sprink to Joseph Stamper. 250

Logan st, w s, 1,550 n 2d st, 25x150. Eliza and William N. Strong to Frederick Grob. 800

Logan st, w s, 1,625 n 2d st, 25x150. Frederick Grob to Eliza and William N. Strong. 800

Lombardy st, s s, 250 w Morgan av, 25x100. Jeremiah V. Meserole to William Reinstagen. 400

Lombardy st, s s, 275 w Morgan av, 25x100. Same to same. 1,500

Macon st, s s, 98 e Ralph av, 90x100. Release mort. Ransom F. and Walter F. Clayton and Bernard Levino to John R. Pitt. 2,000

Macon st, n s, 270 e Reid av, 80x100. David S. Beasley to Frank C. Swimm. 6,900

Madison st, s s, 176 w Lewis av, 20x100. Ellen J. Moore to Alfred Sims. *Mt.* $3,500. 7,500

Madison st, s e s, 376 s w Knickerbocker av, 18x100. David McKelvey to George A. Craig. 4,200

Madison st, s e s, 385.8 s w Knickerbocker av, 18x100, h & l. Georg A. Craig to David McKelvey. 4,200

Madison st, s e s, 295.8 s w Knickerbocker av, 18x100, h & l. Same to Edward Fisher. 4,200

Madison st, s e s, 120.5 n e Hamburg av, 20x100, h & l. George A. Craig to Ellen H. Costello. *Mt.* $?,300. 4,400

Madison st, s e s, 100 n e Hamburg av, 20.5x100, h & l. George A. Craig to Louis Ceiner. *Mt.* $2,400. 4,500

Madison st, s e s, 331.8 s w Knickerbocker av, 18x100, h & l. Same to Elizabeth F. Driscoll widow. *Mt.* $2,300. 4,200

Madison st, s e s, 403.8 s w Knickerbocker av, 18x100, h & l. Same to Elizabeth F. wife of Henry Wade. 4,200

Madison st, s e s, 350 s w Knickerbocker av, 18x100.
Madison st, s e s, 314 s w Knickerbocker av, 18x100, h & l.
Sophie wife of Louis Gelb to George A. Craig. nom

Madison st, s e s, 404 s w Knickerbocker av, 18 x100. Elizabeth E. wife of Henry Wade to George A. Craig. nom

Madison st, s e s, 349.8 s w Knickerbocker av, 36x100, h & l. George A. Craig to Sophie wife of Louis Gelb. 9,000

Madison st, s e s, 313.8 s w Knickerbocker av, 18x100, h & l. Same to George A. List. *Mt.* $2,300. 4,500

Madison st, s e s, 278 s w Knickerbocker av, 17.8x100, h & l. Same to William Grosser. *Mt.* $2,300. 4,200

Madison st, s e s, 140.5 n e Hamburg av, 20x100, h & l. Same to Felix Ceder. *Mt.* $2,400. 4,400

Madison st, s e s, 421.8 s w Knickerbocker av, 17.11x100, h & l. Same to John D. Jager. *Mt.* $2,300. 4,200

Market st, e s, 50 s Glen st, 25x100. Nicholas L. Rapelje to Helen Burke. 450

McDougal st, s s, 206.3 e Hopkinson av, 18.4x 100, h & l. Margaret Weir to John E. Callinan, New York. *Mt.* $4,500. 6,500

McDougal st, s s, 275 e Howard av, 25x100. Theodore Staff to Ansslom S. Bryant. 2,000

Moore st, n e cor Leonard st, 25x75. Henry C. McBrair, Livingston, N. J., to David Bloom, Isaac Ginsburg and Israel Feldman. 6,500

Moore st, s s, 25 w Humboldt st, 25x80. John Lannig to Abraham and Louis Rodschlinsky. *Mt.* $5,000. 8,000

Moore st, s s, 264 e Bushwick av, 25x100. Kaufman Fischer and Ferdinand Feldblum to Marx Krackow. *Mt.* $2,900. exch

Osborn st, w s, 175 n Blake av, 50x90, h & l. Julia Levin to Louis Glattstine. *Mt.* $1,500. 3,400

Osborn st, w s, 200 n Blake av, 25x100, h & l. Same to same. ½ part. *Mt.* $1,700. 1,400

Same property. Louis Glattstine to Esther Levin. ½ part. *Mt.* $1,700. 1,475

Osborn st, w s, 175 n Blake av, 50x90. Louis Glattstine to Esther Levin. *Mt.* $1,500. 3,500

Osborn st, w s, 200 n Blake av, 25x100. Abraham Goldstein to Israel Rosenthal. ½ part. *Mt.* $1,700. 1,600

Osborn st, w s, 175 s Temporary st, 25x100. Same to same. *Mt.* $1,250. 3,500

Osborn st, w s, 200 n Blake av, 25x100. Israel Rosenthal to Mary G. Goldstein. ½ part. *Mt.* $1,700. 1,650

Osborn st, w s, 175 s Temporary st shown on map Gilbert S. Thatford property, 25x100. Same to same. *Mt.* $1,250. 3,600

Palmetto st, s e s, 150 s w Knickerbocker av, 17x100. Release mort. Virginia A. Kleine to James S. Leonard. nom

Same property. Mary E. Koster to Karoline and Robert Schutter. *Mt.* $2,500. nom

Palmetto st, s e s, 125 n e Central av, 50x100. Caroline Kloetmann widow to John Knoebel. 2,100

Parkway, n e cor. Utica av, being lot 67 block 169 assessm't map 24th Ward. John C. McGuire, Registrar of Arrears, to City of Brooklyn. nom

Pearl st, w s, 105.3 s Johnson st, 20x60. Edwin H. Burnett and ano. exrs. and trustees of Charlotte Burnett to Theodore C., Lottie B. and Gertrude L. and Ida B. Burnett. nom

Pierrepont st, n s, 206.8 e Hicks st, 27.6x— to centre Love lane, h & l. Charles D. Burwell to Maria L. Gallup, Springfield, Mass. ½ part. B. & S. *Mt.* $20,000. nom

Powers st, s s, 75 w Leonard st, runs west 24.9 x south 100 x west 0.3 x south 100 to Grand st, x east 25 x north 100. Albert Karutz to Anton Heiberger and Franziska his wife. *Mt.* $5,500. 21,250

Powell st, w s, 200 n Liberty av, 16.6x100. John F. Vrooman to August Steitz. *Mt.* $2,000. 3,100

Powell st, w s, 216.6 n Liberty av, 16.8x100. Same to James E. Seaman. *Mt.* $2,000. 3,100

President st, n s, 327 e 7th av, 20x100. Frank L. Corwin to Charles E. Rogers. *Mt.* $13,500. nom

Prospect pl, s s, 250 e Rochester av, runs south 127.9 x east 85 x south 127.9 to Park pl, x east 40 x north 127.9 x west 25 x north 127.9 to Prospect pl, x west 100. Isaac Halstead to George F. Van Doorn. 2,900

Prospect pl, s s, 160 w Albany av, 16x100. Catharine Sullivan to Irwin Heasty. *Mt.* $2,000. 4,500

Quincy st, s s, 24 w Throop av, 76x80. Release mort. Title Guarantee and Trust Co. to William M. Gibson. nom

Quincy st, s s, 81 w Throop av, 19x80, h & l. William M. Gibson to Emilie M. Askew. *Mt.* $4,500. 8,000

Rush st, No. 58½, s s, 231.8 e Wythe av, 16.8x 100. Franz Krieger to Elizabeth wife of Edward Metz and Matilda wife of Frederick Rolf. nom

Rutledge st, n e cor Marcy av, 21.4x60, h & l. John Brentano to Thomas J. De Gray. *Mt.* $2,000. 6,000

Sackett st, n s, 128.6 w Court st, 21.6x100. Bernard J. McCann to John Mooney. *Mt.* $4,000. 6,112

Sackman st, e s, 258.4 n Liberty av, 16.8x100, h & l. Frederick Heinemann to Wilhelm Vogt. *Mt.* $1,000. 2,200

Schaeffer st, n w s, 137.6 s w Knickerbocker av, 12.6x100, h & l. Sidney M. Williams, Jersey City, to Ellen F. wife of Joshua J. Pim. *Mt.* $800. 1,500

Seigel st, n s, 175 e Graham av, 25x100, h & l. Salomon Konig to Samuel Parshelsky. Q. C. Correction deed. nom

Skillman st, e s, bet De Kalb and Willoughby av, being lot 60 block 46 assessm't map 7th Ward. John C. McGuire, Registrar of Arrears, to City of Brooklyn. 1,341

South Elliott pl, e s, 212.6 s Hanson pl, 20.10x100. George P. Rowell to Herman Posbergb. 6,400

South Elliott pl, w s, 72.2 s De Kalb av, 19.10x86x20.3x81.11. Partition. Gerard M. Stevens to Josephine L. Ross. 6,200

Stagg st, n s, 25.6 w Bogart st, 18.1x87.4x94.10 Joseph Maurer to Adam Fischer and Minna his wife, joint tenants. 2,300

Stagg st, s s, 25 w Lorimer st, 25x75, h & l. William Staats to George Staats. ½ part. Sub. to mort. $2,000. 1,500

St. Johns pl, s s, 185.5 w 7th av, 8.6x100. Emily C. Thallon to William L. Dowling. 1,000

Same property. Release mort. Jemima Thallon to Emily C. Thallon. nom

Van Buren st, s e s, 244 n e Broadway, 18.9x100, h & l. Hugo Schoening to Eugene Verdin and Mary his wife, joint tenants. *Mt.* $3,000. 5,000

Vanderveer st, s e s, 260 n e Broadway, 16.6x100. Contract. James H. Hart to Nellie Hearon. 2,900

Walton st, n s, 350 e Marcy av, 25x100, h & l. Alois Barth to Jacob Kappeler. All liens. nom

Walton st, n w s, 100 s w Harrison av, 25x100, h & l. Same to same. All liens. nom

Warren st, s s, bet Court and Smith sts, being lot 34 block 203 assessm't map 10th Ward. John C. McGuire, Registrar of Arrears, to City of Brooklyn. 609

Watkins st, w s, 175 s Sutter av, 25x100. Hannah Bennett to Abraham Goldstein. Taxes, &c. 565

Same property. Release mort. Elizabeth C. Halcott, New York, to Hannah Bennett. 500

Watkins st, w s, 175 s Sutter av, 25x100. Abraham Goldstein to Israel Rosenthal. 750

Same property. Israel Rosenthal to Mary Goldstein. 775

Wolcott st, n e s, 265 s e Richards st, 20x100. Benjamin Schelinsky to John J. Wheeler. 2,400

Woodbine st, s e s, 246 n e Hamburg av, 18x100. Release mort. Anna E. Cozine and James Gascoine exrs. John G. Cozine and James Gascoine individ. to George W. and Charles H. Francisco. 2,344

Same property. George W. and Charles H. Francisco to Harry Otterbein and Mary his wife. nom

South 2d st, s s, 55.10 w Rodney st, 19.2x60. Esther Isaacs to Thomas W. Power. 3,300

4th st, s s, 197.10 w 7th av, 18x100, h & l. Charles H Moses and Henry B. Fanton, Jr., to Louis H. Myers, Jr. *Mt.* $6,250. nom

4th st, s s, 271.10 w 7th av, 20x100, h & l. Same to M. L. Moses. *Mt.* $6,950. nom

4th st, s s, 252.10 w 7th av, 19x100, h & l. Same to F. M. Moses. *Mt.* $6,600. nom

4th st, s s, 215.10 w 7th av, 18x100, h & l. Same to S. F. Morse. *Mt.* $6,250. nom

4th st, s s, 291.10 w 7th av, 20x100, h & l. Same to A. J. Dynes. *Mt.* $6,950. nom

4th st, s s, 233.10 w 7th av, 19x100, h & l. Same to Eliza A. Fanton. *Mt.* $6,600. nom

4th pl, s s, 100 w Smith st, 25x100, h & l. Michael Daly to George F. Elliott. *Mt.* $3,500. nom

6th st, s s, 228.10 e 6th av, 17x100. Nelson L. Tuck to Thomas H. Robbins. *Mt.* $7,500. nom

7th st, s s, 147.5 w 7th av, 0.4x100. Nellie M. wife of Frederick O. Ernesty to Charles G. Peterson. 175

Same property. Release mort. Isaac J. Cahen to Nellie M. wife of Frederick O. Ernesty. nom

10th st, n e s, 117.10 n w 8th av, 20x100. James F. Ransom to N. Charles Mogren. *Mt.* $6,500. 8,900

North 10th st, s w s, 175 n w Bedford av, 25x100. Jacob Boelger to John Fischer. 2,200

13th st, s s, bet Gowanus Canal and 2d av, being lot 39 block 96 assessm't map 22d Ward. John C. McGuire, Registrar of Arrears, to City of Brooklyn. 154

13th st, s s, bet Gowanus Canal and 2d av, being lot 35 block 96 assessm't map 22d Ward. Same to same. 154

13th st, s s, bet Gowanus Canal and 2d av, being lot 36 block 96 assessm't map 22d Ward. Same to same. 154

13th st, s s, bet Gowanus Canal and 2d av, being lot 44 block 96 assessm't map 22d Ward. Same to same. 154

13th st, s s, bet Gowanus Canal and 2d av, being lot 42 block 96 assessm't map 22d Ward. Same to same. 154

13th st, s s, bet Gowanus Canal and 2d av, being lot 43 block 96 assessm't map 22d Ward. Same to same. 154

13th st, s s, bet Gowanus Canal and 2d av, being lot 53 block 96 assessm't map 22d Ward. Same to same. nom

13th st, s s, bet Gowanus Canal and 2d av, being lot 45 block 95 assessm't map 22d Ward. Same to same. 154

13th st, s s, bet Gowanus Canal and 2d av, being lot 54 block 96 assessm't map 22d Ward. Same to same. 554

13th st, s s, bet Gowanus Canal and 2d av, being lot 50 block 96 assessm't map 22d Ward. Same to same. 54

13th st, s s, bet Gowanus Canal and 2d av, being lot 41 block 96 assessm't map 22d Ward. Same to same. 154

13th st, s s, bet Gowanus Canal and 2d av, being lot 40 block 96 assessm't map 22d Ward. Same to same. 154

13th st, s s, bet Gowanus Canal and 2d av, being lot 27 block 96 assessm't map 22d Ward. Same to same. 154

15th st, s s, bet 2d and 3d avs, being lot 60 block 94 assessm't map 22d Ward. John C. McGuire, Registrar of Arrears, to City of Brooklyn. 193

15th st, s s, bet 2d and 3d avs, being lot 66 block 94 assessm't map 22d Ward. Same to same. 100

15th st, s s, bet 2d and 3d avs, being lot 62 block 94 assessm't map 22d Ward. Same to same. 193

15th st, s s, bet 2d and 3d avs, being lot 48 block 94 assessm't map 22d Ward. Same to same. 308

15th st, s s, bet 2d and 3d avs, being lot 52 block 94 assessm't map 22d Ward. Same to same. 193

15th st, s s, bet 2d and 3d avs, being lot 54 block 94 assessm't map 22d Ward. Same to same. 308

15th st, s s, bet 2d and 3d avs, being lot 56 block 94 assessm't map 22d Ward. Same to same. 379

15th st, s s, bet 2d and 3d avs, lot 36 block 94 assessm't map 22d Ward. Same to same. 154

15th st, s s, bet 2d and 3d avs, lot 37 block 94 assessm't map 22d Ward. Same to same. 154

15th st, s s, bet 2d and 3d avs, being lot 42 block 94 assessm't map 22d Ward. Same to same. 231

15th st, s s, bet 2d and 3d avs, being lot 38 block 94 assessm't map 22d Ward. Same to same. 231

15th st, s s, bet 2d and 3d avs, being lot 38 block 94 assessm't map 22d Ward. Same to same. 269

15th st, s s, bet 2d and 3d avs, being lot 46 block 94 assessm't map 22d Ward. Same to same. 302

16th st, n s, 124 e 8th av, 18x100. Agnes Morgan to William J. Fitzpatrick, Thomas McCann and William Martin. All liens. nom

17th st, n s, 275 e 6th av, 25x90. Simon J. Harding to Jacob Blumberg, New York. 6,000

17th st, s s, 124 w 6th av, 19x100. Phillip R. F. Sparling to Joseph Rieder. 2,650

Bay 20th st, s e s, 500 s w 86th st, 50x96.8, New Utrecht. Gilbert Hoffman to Adoniram J. White. 4,500

Bay 20th st, s e s, 200 s w 86th st, 60x96.8, New Utrecht. Adoniram J. White to Adaline Hoffman. 1,200

East 21st st, e s, 155.10 n Caton av, 125x110, Flatbush. Partition. William H. Greene to Charles Crooke. 8,000

26th st, s w s, 100 n w 3d av, runs northwest 100 x southwest 100.2 x southeast 119.10 x northeast 75 x northwest 19.11 x northeast 25.2. Frank L. Corwin to Arnold A. Lewis. All liens. nom

Bay 28th st, s e s, 100 n e Cropsey av, 160x96.8.
Bay 25th st, s e s, 100 n e Cropsey av, 120x96.8, Bath Beach.
Frank G. Hennings to Ferdinand W. Keller. 9,000

36th st, n s, 82 w 4th av, 43x100.2. Jacob Morgenthaler to George C. Jeffery. *Mt.* $6,500. 10,500

41st st, n e s, 150 s e 12th av, 25x100, New Utrecht. Julia wife of Ado Glaeser to Frank Rudolph. Deed delivered as collateral security. 800

53d st, n e s, 240 n w 5th av, 40x102.2. George A. Traver to John J. Tracy. Q. C. nom

Same property. John J. Tracy to Kitty L. Traver. Q. C. nom

56th st, n s, 320 e 3d av, 80x100.2. Release mort. Edward T. Hunt exr. and trustee Thomas Hunt to George H. Parshall. 1,358

64th st, s s, 170 w 13th av, 30x100, Bath Junction. James V. Woolley to Luanna A. Davison. 262

67th st, n s, 580 e 14th av, 26.11x100x23.3x100, Lefferts Park. Effingham H. Nichols to Gustaf Wilson. 800

73d st, s w s, 86.6 n w 7th av, 360x100.
Stewart av, south cor 73d st, 160.2x98x160x106.3.
7th av, east cor 72d st, 32.11x43.5x39.3x30.8, New Utrecht.
Release mort. Anna C. Hegeman et al. to George Edgett. 2,025

77th st, n s, 106.6 e 4th av, 440x100, New Utrecht. Charles E. Rogers to Frank L. Corwin. B. & S. All liens. nom

80th st, s w s, 220 s e 11th av, 80x100, New Utrecht. Hoik D. Campbell to Julius Hertz. 1,000

83d st, n e s, 64 n w 24th av, 60x100, Gravesend. James D. Lynch to Henry Currier. 900

East 94th st, s w s, 50 s e of H. L. Schmeelk, 50x100, Flatlands. Hermann Lohmann to Gustaf Nystrom. 400

Alabama av, w s, 125 n Sutter av, 25x100, h & l. Lena wife of Frederick W. Durchholz to Barbara Durchholz. *Mt.* $2,100. 3,500

Atkins av, e s, 310 n Hegeman av, 20x100. Ella Hoffman to Amanda M. Whelan. 180

Av G, n s, 89.6 e 92d st, 61.10x136.8x61.10x137, Canarsie. John H. Ireland to Charles H. Sargood, Flatlands. 2,500

Bedford av, s e cor Hancock st, 36.3x50x1.6x14.4x38x59.7. Christian Friedman to John A. Dilliard. nom

Belmont av, n s, 125 w Watkins st, 25x100. John Bechthold to Elizabeth Stephens. B. & S. *Mt.* $1,000. nom

Same property. Charles H. Stephens to John Bechthold. *Mt.* $1,000. nom

Belmont av, n s, 109 e Linwood st, 16x100, h & l. Sven Johanson to Andrew Weeking. 1,800

Belmont av, n s, 87.1 w Essex st, 16x100. Andrew Gulbrandsen to Robert K. Anderson. 1,800

Bushwick av, n w cor Schaefer st, 20x75, h & l. Charles A. Wehr to John Prehn, New York. *Mt.* $5,500. nom

Bushwick av, s w s, 94.6 s e Vanderveer st, 37x73.2. Kate T. wife of Alfred Ogden to Charles Schneidt and Katharina his wife. *Mt.* $6,000. 8,000

Carlton av, w s, 170 s Flushing av, 24x100. Charles M. Rex to James Dunn. 4,250

Central av, s w s, 50 s e Jacob st, runs southwest to boundary bet lands of parties hereto, x northeast to Central av, x southeast 1.11. Manly A. Ruland to Philip Steingotter. Q. C. nom

Central av, n e s, 80.3 n w Grove st, 20x80, h & l. Anna Martin to Theodore Beusher. nom

De Kalb av, s s, 415 w Nostrand av, 20x100, h & l. John Assip and Timothy J. Buckley to Kate T. Lynch. *Mt.* $2,500. 3,962

East New York av, s s, 114.6 w Kingston av, 60x100, Flatbush. Jane Brague, New York, to John E. Callinan. 1,200

Same property. John E. Callinan to Margaret Weir. 1,500

East New York av, east cor Rockaway av, runs south 103.5 x east 57.10 x north 40 x northwest 78.7 to East New York av, x southwest 34.5. Theodore Wulp to Irving Fish. *Mt.* $5,000. exch

Evergreen av, n e s, 25 n w Hancock st, 75x100. Lucy G. wife of Edwin Miner to Charles and William Lehmann. 4,500

Evergreen av, s s, 81.9 w Ralph st, 18.3x100. William H. Hunter to Adam Schliesman. *Mt.* $1,500. 3,525

Gates av, s e s, 375 n e Central av, 25x100. Daniel Mayers to Annie B. wife of Henry Smith. *Mt.* $2,500 and tax 1890. 4,250

Gates av, n e s, 183.4 s w Knickerbocker av, 16.8x84.8x17.2x88.11, h & l. George J. Koch to Agatha Dietzel. *Mt.* $1,000. 3,000

Gates av, s s, 48.9 e Lewis av, 18.9x80, h & l. George W. Godward to Martin L. Rickersen. 7,800

Gates av, n s, 44.6 w Clason av, 43.6x82x44.6x79. George H. Chinnock to Elizabeth L. Chinnock his wife. Sub. to morts. nom

Gates av, n w s, 250 n e Central av, 25x105.3x25.1x103.6. Horace Graves guard. of Jennie A., Ella C. and Cassie Knapp to Alice G. Bradley, Long Branch. 180

Same property. Release dower. Agnes Knapp to same. 50

Gelston av, n w s, 300 n e Atlantic av, 50x116.3, New Utrecht. Martin J. O'Rourke to William A. Westaway. Sub. to mort. 1,500

Glenmore av, s s, 58 e Snediker av, 25x100, h & l. Barbara Durchholz to Lena Durchholz. *Mt.* $1,800, taxes, &c. 3,000

Gravesend av, w s, bet Van Siclen and Floyds, 80.10x—x98x—, Gravesend, excepting portions thereout. Lawrence Van Sicklen to Jane wife of William K. Voorhees. ⅙ part. nom

Greene av, s e s, 340 n e Irving av, —x100x90x—. Oscar Case to Susan E. Fingarr. All liens. nom

Jefferson av, s s, 23 w Patchen av, 72x75. Charles Burkhardt to Jacob Nehrbass. *Mt.* $4,500. 6,500

Jefferson av, s s, 162.6 w Stuyvesant av, 15.10x100. Thomas G. Bunker to Annie M. Bunker. *Mt.* $3,500. nom

Jefferson av, s s, 150 e Patchen av, 43x100. John H. Heidgerd to Mary T. wife of Samuel J. Williams. 5,500

Johnson av, s s, 75 w Gardner av, 80x200 to Ingraham st.
Johnson av, n s, at centre line Gardner av, runs west 228 to centre of creek, x northerly along same to branch of same at point 49 n Randolph st, and 141.6 of Gardner av, x east along said branch 101.6 to centre of ditch at point 40 w of Gardner av, and 48.9 n Randolph st, x southeast along ditch 57.6 to Randolph st, x southeast 93.1 to centre Gardner av, x253.
Montrose av, s e cor Stewart av, runs east 200 x south to n s Randolph st, at point 230 e Stewart av, x west 80 x north 100 x west 150 to Stewart av, x north 100.
Arthur Settle to Edward and Alfred Settle. All title. nom

Johnson av, s s, 243 e Bushwick av, 25x100. Juliana Schneider to Stanislaus R. Blumke. Confirmation deed. B. & S. nom

Johnson av, s s, 39.6 e Bushwick av, 19.9x75. Jennie Levin to Henry Berbert. *Mt.* $4,000. 4,900

Kent av, w s, 50 s of John Bierbrowers land, 25x100. William B. Dunley and Jane Armstrong heirs Sarah E. Dunley to George W. Armstong. 1-9 part. nom

Kent av, n w cor Little Nassau st, being lot 10 block 14 assessm't map 7th Ward. John C. McGuire, Register of Arrears, to City of Brooklyn. 1,253

Kingsland av, w s, 125 s Herbert st, 25x100, h & l. Foreclos. John Courtney to George W. Sammis. 1,500

Knickerbocker av, s w s, 25 s e Stanhope st, 25x80. Charles H. Wagner and George Gutting to Ludwig Jordens and Dorothea his wife. *Mt.* $4,000. 6,400

Knickerbocker av, s w s, 75 s e De Kalb av, 25x100. James J. Murray to Ellen Murray. *Mt.* $840. 1,400

Knickerbocker av, s w s, 40 n w Linden st, 40x100. Daniel E. McEwen to Ignatz Martin. 1,400

Lafayette av, n s, 312.6 e Sumner av, 18.9x100. Alexander McKnight to Simon Batt, New York. *Mt.* $6,000. 9,750

Lafayette av, n s, 275 e Sumner av, 37.6x100. Release mort. Sarah A. Abbott to Alexander McKnight. nom

Lafayette av, s s, 258.4 e Lewis av, 16.8x100, h & l. Giddings H. Pinney to Carrie Bartow. 6,500

Lewis av, Van Buren st, —x100x26x100. Deed location worthless. George C. Jeffery to Jacob Morgenthaler. *Mt.* $5,000. 9,000

Lexington av, s s, 78 e Nostrand av, 22x100, h & l. Andrew L Winton, Bridgeport, Conn., to Francesca wife of Julius W. Buttner. *Mt.* $5,000. 9,100

Livonia av, s s, 100 w Watkins st, 80x100. Jacob Strauss to Amelia Pachinsky, New York. *Mt.* $1,200. 1,600

Marcy av, w s, 100 s Park av, 25x100. Joseph Schmitt to Florian Kammer. *Mt.* $3,000. 7,000

Marcy av, w s, 100 s Myrtle av, 50x100, h & l. Forcelos. Edward Moran to William S. Okie. 5,000

Morgan av, e s, 50 s Thames st, 25x100. Dorothea Zerr to George Eckert and Kunnigunda his wife. *Mt.* $4,000. 4,250

Patchen av, s w cor Jefferson av, 75x95. Release mort. Anna Reynolds and Samuel Teather exrs. Thomas Reynolds to Charles Burkhardt. nom

Patchen av, w s, 20 n Putnam av, 80x80. Eliza Reed to Frances G. Underhill. nom

Patchen av, e s, 43 s Hancock st, 19x80. Richard R. Lane to Martha wife of Richard Van Riper. *Mt.* $2,500. 5,250

Prospect av, n e s, 270 s e 7th av, 25x100, h & l. William C. Behrens to Jens Kamman. *Mt.* $1,800. 2,725

Prospect av, n e s, 387.11 n w 8th av, 16.8x100, h & l. Agnes wife of Thomas S. Gilbert to Samuel Ukrainsky. *Mt.* $1,600. 3,600

Putnam av, s s, 158.6 e Reid av, 19.6x100. Francis D. Jackson to Morris Adler. *Mt.* $4,000. 6,800

Putnam av, n s, 220 e Broadway, 20x100, h & l. George Burns and Michael McGrath to Samuel E. Gatechair and Lucy W. Ralphs. *Mt.* $6,500. exch and 137

Putnam av, n s, 140 e Reid av, 20x100, h & l. William O. Forrester to Arthur Herring. *Mt.* $5,000. 9,250

Same property. Release mort. John Cassidy to William O. Forrester. 1,000

Putnam av, n s, 250 w Patchen av, 20x100. Sadie E. Rice to Marcus Sayre, Newark, N. J. All liens. nom

Railroad av, w s, 75 n Griffin pl, 25x100. Frank C. Lang to Stephen Mafera. 500

Railroad av, w s, 100 n Griffin pl, 25x100. Same to Christiana E. Lohrentz. 500

Reid av, e s, 25 s McDonough st, 25x75, h & l. Jacob Nehrbass to Charles Burkhardt. *Mt.* $4,500. 9,575

Rochester av, w s, 87.9 n St. Marks av, 40x91.3. David Burkert to William Emken. 1,700

Rockaway av, w s, 225 s Broadway, 25x100. Alice McGee to Chaie Liebeman. *Mt.* $1,150. 1,750

Saratoga av, s e cor Decatur st, 100x115.6. Release mort. Jacob G. Dettmer to William H. Good. 7,000

Schenck av, e s, 25 s Van Brunt av, 20x100. Ellen Gibbs to Charles Woollam. 125

Schenectady av, e s, 130 s Herkimer st, 18.6x100. Irving Fish to Theodore Wulp. *Mt.* $2,400. exch

Snediker av, e s, 415 n Liberty av, 20x100. William H. Burroughs trustee Charles F. Burroughs to George Baecker. 2,100

St. Marks av, n s, 360 e Franklin av, 20x128.6. James D. Rankin and James Ross to Ella M. Robbins. *Mt.* $6,500. 9,600

St. Nicholas av, e s, 80 s Greene av, 20x90. James J. Murray to Ellen Murray. 2,600

Stone av, e s, 225 s Rapelje av, 25x100. John Negron to Elizabeth wife of Edwin Myring. 1,150

Stuyvesant av, n e cor Chauncey st, 20x100. John Gordon to Edward K. Wilder. *Mt.* $7,000. exch

Sutter av, n w cor Hendrix st, 25x100. George Crawford to Eliza wife of and Thomas McMillan, joint tenants. 2,250

Thatford av, w s, 75 s Belmont av, 25x100. Jacob Axelrod and Isaac Levingson to Wolf Feier and Samuel Hirsch, New York. *Mt.* $1,950. 4,400

Throop av, n e s, 75 s e Bartlett st, 25x95, h & l. Jacob Hirsch and Lena Fischer to Marx Krackow. *Mt.* $5,000. 6,650

Utica av, w s, 87.9 s Bergen st, 40x100. Rosina Russell to Ella M. Cole. 8,000

Willoughby av, n s, 275 w Stuyvesant av, 18.9x100, h & l. Anna wife of Julius Kuttner to Geza C. Liszka. *Mt.* $5,000. 8,250

Wyckoff av, south cor Myrtle st, 25x100.8. Aegidius Schuler to Martin Schuler. nom

Same property. Martin Schuler to Carolina Schuler. nom

2d av, s w cor 13th st, being lot 1 block 96 assessm't map 22d Ward. John C. McGuire, Registrar of Arrears, to City of Brooklyn. 385

2d av, w s, bet 13th and 14th sts, being lot 3 block 96 assessm't map 22d Ward. Same to same. 308

2d av, w s, bet 13th and 14th sts, being lot 4 block 96 assessm't map 22d Ward. Same to same. 308

3d av, e s, 50 s 39th st, 25x100. Johanna M. and Francis J. Pierret and Annie Rappel to Maria Vaccarezza. 4,225

3d av, west cor 87th st, 25x100.
3d av, north cor 88th st, 100x100, New Utrecht.
David D. Field to Anthony McNeely. 4,140

3d av, w s, 50.2 n 48th st, 25x80, h & l. Solomon Sonin to Marcus Solomon, Port Elizabeth, N. J. *Mt.* $8,000. 9,000

4th av, e s, 41.10 n 57th st, 33.4x100. William Magnor to William Simpson. 1,600

4th av, s w cor 35th st, 20.2x82. Richard Chidwick to Addie wife of George Plate. *Mt.* $3,500. exch

5th av, s e s, 25 s w 22d st, 33.4x100. George Plate to Richard Chidwick. *Mt.* $3,500. exch

5th av, e s, 40 n 38th st, 20x85, h & l. Cornelius Duffy to Anastatia Feehan, New York. *Mt.* $2,500. 4,627

7th av, w s, 21 n 1st st, 29x80. John A. Rochford to Francis M. Wilmurt. *Mt.* $13,000. nom

10th av, n e cor 71st st, 80x100.
10th av, n e cor 70th st, 60x100.
70th st, n s, 100 e 10th av, 20x100.
70th st, s s, 100 e 10th av, 80x100, New Utrecht.
Release mort. Eloy Ann Martin extrx. Isaac Martin to Fred C. Cocheu. nom

10th av, n e cor 70th st, 60x100.
70th st, n s, 100 e 10th av, 20x100, New Utrecht.
Bay Ridge Park Improvement Co. to Fred C. Cocheu. 5,000

13th av, w s, 80 n 67th st, 40x100, *Lefferts Park.* Effingham H. Nichols to Edward Mueller. 500

13th av, n e cor 54th st, runs north 125.2 x east 100 x south 25 x east 23 x south 102.2 to 54th st, x west 125, New Utrecht. The West Brooklyn Land and Improvement Co. to Robert B. Snowden. *Mt.* $40,000. 3,500

14th av, e s, 40 s 64th st, 60x100, New Utrecht. Effingham H. Nichols to Henry C. Sibbert. 900

18th av, n w s, 250 s w 86th st, 96.8x100, New Utrecht. Catherine J. wife of James W. Johnson formerly Fettretch, Denver, Col., to James L. D. O'Reilly, New York. *Mt.* $1,600. 2,800

Interior lot, 100 w Evergreen av and 40.2 s Eldert st, runs south 34.10 x east 5 x north 34.10 x west 5. Annie Herzog to Virginia A. Kleine. nom

Same property. Release mort. James M. McNamara to Annie Herzog. 100

Same property. Release mort. Henry H. Adams, County Treasurer, to same. nom

Lots 2244-2246 and 2264-2266 and 2253-2256 block 8, and 2359-2361 block 12, and 2398-2402 and 2441, 2442 block 13 map of 630 lots of E. H. Nichols, Lefferts Park. Release mort. Albert V. B. Voorhees to Effingham H. Nichols. 2,000

Lot in town of New Lots, 26th Ward, begins on w s of road leading to the mill, at intersection with land of Jacob L. Van Wicklen, 14 59-100 acres. Patrick Keady, recvr., to Henry W. Rozell. 9,475

Same property. John Bragaw to Henry W. Rozell. Q. C. nom

Same property. Henry W. Rozell to Joseph H. Colyer. 10,475

Lots 393 and 394 map Dudley Field property, New Utrecht, begins at centre of block 400 from s e s of 3d av, runs northeast 23.11 to land of May and others, x southeast 69.11 to centre line of block, x northwest 107.4. David D. Field to Robert C. McIntyre. 110

Lot at Canarsie, Flatlands, adj lands of Abrams & Snare, 33x114. Sub. to right of way on s e s. Henry W. Schmeelk to Harriet J. Prosser. 150

Part lot 108 Wyckoff tract, Coney Island, 60.1 x154.3x62.2. Release mort. Terence Jacobson to Barbara Groll widow and heirs of Joseph Groll. 224

All of mortgaged premises, being 259.7 e of 6th av. Release mort. Mary J. Sproule trustee James Sproule to William Flanegan. nom

Brooklyn city line, at point 260 e Knickerbocker av, runs north to point 100 from Cooper st, x east — to said city line, x south —. Eliza Reed to Alexander Underhill, Jr. nom

Gaufel Creek, n w s, meadow lot, 25x100, Flatlands. James Savage to Margaret S. Smith. 125

Gaufel Creek, n w s, meadow lots, 50x100, Flatlands. Same to Edwin Hoogland. 200

Assignment judgment. William Deterling to Lena Durchholz. 729

WESTCHESTER COUNTY.

AUGUST 19 TO 25—INCLUSIVE.

BEDFORD.

Palmer, Bryant S. to Maggie A. Gallagher, e s Palmer av, adj grantee, 50x150. $200

CORTLANDT.

Catlin, Austin H. and ano. to Thos. Brennan, w s Smith st, adj C. A. Thorne, 45x146. nom

Hart, Jas. to same, w s Nelson av, adj J. S. Hart, 56x150. 1,680

EASTCHESTER.

Andrews, Walter E. to Leopold L. Barzaghi, s s new road, 102 w Pondfield road, abt 101x100. 1,400

Bullard, John E. and ano. to Walter N. Wier, lot 72 w s Johnson st, grantor's map, 30x86. 275

Same to Irena L. Albister, lot 81 e s same st, 25x100. 275

Darling, Alf. B. et al. to Annie A. Smith, w s Rich av, 637 n Sidney, 75x125. 3,157

Fischel, Henry and ano. to Richard J. Seder, lot 70 n w s Greenwich st, West Mt. Vernon, 78.9x125. 1,000

Fischer, Wolf to Michael Biedermann, lot 99 n w s Bond st, West Mt. Vernon, 28x100. 2,800

Hoysradt, Edwin to Mary Berghorn, lot 312 n e s Becker av, Washingtonville, 50x100. 1,175

Lichtenhein, Chas. E. to Mary A. Baker, n w cor 10th av and 7th st, 90x106x93x128.5. 3,000

Miller, Nicholas to Chas. Wilkens, lot 200 e s Catharine st, Washingtonville, 25x100. 1,900

Mager, Fred. to Susie E. Hulsizer, part lot 902 w s 11th av, Mt. Vernon, 33.4x105. 4,900

Same to Mary J. Stuckey, part lot 901 w s 11th av, Mt. Vernon, 25x105. 4,100

Owen, Susannah to Annie A. Campbell, w s Garden av, 150 s Park av, 50x200. 1,600

Plath, Chas. to Wensel Kucera, lot 217 s e s Catharine st, Washingtonville, 50x100. 650

Reynolds, John J. to Agnes L. Rowland, part lot 897 w s 11th av, Mt. Vernon, 25x105. 3,150

Treuer, Pauline to Martha Wilson, part lot 71 w s Franklin av, East Mt. Vernon, ⅛ acre. exch and 500

Treuer, William H. and ano. to Geo. H. Dedler, n s Monroe st, 209 e Franklin av, 25x91. 300

Same to Thos. Thorn, n s same, 159 e Franklin av, 50x91. 705

Van Anden, Rich. to E. Leonard Gay, part lot 889 and 852 e s 18th av, Wakefield, 110x114. 1,900

Wilson, Martha to Pauline Treuer, lot 35 e s 1st av, Mt. Vernon, 50x210. exch. and nom

Westcott, Ezbon S. to Chas. H. Hallock, w s White Plains road, 300 s Westchester av, abt 31x170. 550

GREENBURGH.

Bradley, David O. to Sidney Martin, s s Ashford av, 150 w Ogden pl, 25x100. 400

Brant, Grace P. to Jas H. Moran and ano., e s Maple av, 146 s Chatterton Hill road, abt 150x115. 1,100

Cunningham, Mary H. and ano. to Gilbert A. Buck, w s Livingston av, 175 n North Chauncey Drive, 150x100. 2,100

Same to J. Henry Carpenter, e s same, adj above, abt 150x140. 835

Freund, John to John Schlachter, lot adj grantee, 20x50. 300

Jones, Cyrus P. and ano. to Chris. Carlisle, lots 25, 26, 27 and 40 map lots at Ardsley. 615

Same to Jennie C. Wright, lots 37 and 38. 218

Same to Eugene C. Pichards, lot 47. 180

Lester, Sarah E. to Francis A. Conlon, n e cor Washington av and Chatterton Hill road, 300x—. 3,800

McCollough, Mich. to Mary A. Cronan, lot 30 n s Main st, Dobbs Ferry, 50x150. 1,000

Mutual Life Ins. Co. to Mich. McCullough, s s Av A, 550 e Storms st, 40x144. 2,500

Schlachter, John to John Freund, n e cor Warren st and Old Broadway, 94x76x105x65. 1,650

MAMARONECK.

Carroll, John to Thos. Kane, part lot 67 w s Mamaroneck av, Spencer map, 25x100. 1,000

MOUNT PLEASANT.

Canning, John C. to Ansen Husted, n s Beekman av, adj grantor, 50x135. 1,300

Clark, Isaac to Chas. W. Yerks, n s Railroad av, adj public school, 61x200. 250

Nauds, Fred. to Gustav Wenzler, lot 1090, Sherman Park. 450

Smadbeck, Louis to Annie Ziegler, lot 985, Sherman Park. 225

Same to Victoria Feerst and ano., lots 707-711. 750

Same to Sophie Bayer, lot 558. 100

Same to Leonce Fraissinet, lot 1109. 200

Same to Rosa Fraissinet, lot 1108. 200

Same to Anna Durr, lot 540. 100

Same to Mary Goede, lot 630. 150

Same and ano. to Wm. F. Connor, lots 63 and 64, Lakehurst, Villa Park. 300

NEW ROCHELLE.

Burns, Wm. to Julia Burns and ano., lots 50, 51 and part 30 and 31 s e s Bayard st, map property John I. V. Westervelt, 100x150. 600

Gregg, Jas. A. S. to Anna N. Lynn, e s Gloucester pl, 277 s Mayflower av, 23x124. 175

Lambden, Jos. to John McEwen and ano., w s Hillside av, 100 n Mayflower av, 50x140. 450

Mulligan, Hugh to John H. Humes, n e s Webster av, 502 n w Old Boston road, 60x173. 4,500

Renner, John to John C. Jaeger, s e cor Av A and Union av, 75x112. 6,000

Sheahan, Jeremiah F. to Frazer Coulter, lot 189 n s Chestnut lane, Residence Park, 75x140. 2,000

Strang, Fred. A. to Mott Emigh, lot 10 block B, Rochelle Park. 1,900

OSSINING.

Larkin, Francis to And. I. Ferguson, lot 5 n s Agate av grantor's map, 50x164. 500

PELHAM.

Leviness, Joshua to John Nuffer, s s West Prospect, 504 w Main st, 200x100. 3,100

RYE.

Damon, Carrie M. et al. M. Dillon, ref., to Eloise Burns, e s Centre st, 301 s Westchester av, 50x199. 600

Drew, Geo. F. to Emilie O'Sullivan and ano., n s Olivia st, 425 e Regent st, abt 150x90. 175

Merritt, Jas. S. and ano. to Carrie A. Brundage, n s Merritt st, 50 s Ellendale av, 50x100. 260

Same to John Guernsey, n s West William st, 150 e Merritt st, 100x150. 200

Ward, Wm. L. and ano. to The Portchester Athletic Assoc., n s Irving av, 258 w Smith av, 100x100. 2,400

WESTCHESTER.

Buckel, Mary J. to Susan A. Snedeker, w s Glebe av, 255 Westchester turnpike, 75x247. 8,600

Clocke, G. De Witt to Emma J. Carter, n s Julianna st, 100 e Barker av, 25x100. 500

Same to same, s s Barker av, 34 n Julianna st, 33x100. 680

Cooper, Margt. et al., J. B. Lockwood ref. to Carl Diem, lot 1 n s Main st, map estate Wm. Cooper, 25x100. 1,050

Mace, Levi H. and ano. to Martin Suchey, lots 11-14, Laconia Park. 800

Same to Alfred Haines and ano., lots 166-169. 1,200

Mensch, Matthias to Leo L. Buchmann, e s Av D, 83 n 12th st, Unionport, 25x105. 250

Ovens, John to Matthies B. Tipper, n w s Boston road, 25 s w Thwaites pl, 25x107. 400

Snedeker, Susan A. to Mary J. Buckel, s s Pelham Bridge road, 76 e Baxters Corners, 50x140. 3,000

Shelton, Rosalie T. to Emanuel Burlando, n s 2d av, 197 e White Plains road, 100x114. 1,500

Saxe, John M. to Wm. Briggs et al., s s Guerlain pl, 103 w Theriot av, abt 50x120. 4,000

WHITE PLAINS.

Albro, Wm. H. to Jas. W. Webster, n e cor Court st and Post road, 100x100x59x105. 1,800

Close, Odle et al. to Henry S. Moore, lots 8 and 11 s s Railroad av map estate Elisha Horton. 3,500

YONKERS

Bruno, Rich. to Wm. Bailey, lot 104 map property Caroline E. Lowerre. 550

Butler, Wm. A. to John B. Sullivan, e s South Broadway, 206 s Lawrence st, abt 77x125. 2,700

Doerner, Peter to Henry Wallwork, n s Main st, 72.6 w Warburton av, 25x50. 7,000

Dusenberry, Chas. to Francis Wise, n s Swain st, adj W. H. Underhill, 74.6x— 1,500

Dwyer, Anthony to Winifred Dwyer, w s Clinton st, 125 n St. Mary's st, 25x100. nom

Edwards, Adah and ano. to Henry George. Lots 23 and 24 block 2, map property Lowerre Station. 1,200

Same to Lewin Pennington, lot 9 block 3. 550

Same to Sadie H. Fulton, lots 22 and 23 block 3. 1,100

Same to Oscar P. Wittiger, lots 2 and 3 block 3. 1,050

Same to Edw. Linden, lot 21 block 3. 550

Same to Fred. D. Gibb, lots 23 and 24 block 4. 700

Same to Herbert R. Miller, lots 28 and 29 block 4. 700

Same to Henry L. Springsteen, lots 24 and 25 block 4. 700

Same to William D. Springsteen, lots 26 and 27 block 4. 700

Herriot, J. Groshon exr. of, to Wm. McKellar, Lot 73 w s Beech st, 25x100. 360

Same to Duncan Buchanan, lot 72 w s Beech st, 25x100. 360

Jones, Cyrus P. and ano. to Mary A. Judge, lot 17 block A and 27 block C grantors map. 500

Same to Clarence J. Ramsey, lot 8 block C. 375

Same to Michael Mallen, lots 1 and 2 block E. 750

Same to Jas. Meara, lot 13 block D. 255

Same to Jas. Hackett, lots 4 and 5 block G. 495

Same to Wm. Brown, lots 6 and 12 block H. 540

Same to Chas. Sullivan, lots 3 and 4 block B and 24 block C. 855

Lowerre, Seaman to Frank Schuch, e s South Broadway, 100 n Randolph st, 75x103. 4,500

Monrovia Park Co. to Joshua W. Lounsbury, n s Euclid av, 350 w Ridge st, 100x100. nom

Nugent, And. P. to Arthur Littlefield, south ½ lot 143 Hyatt farm. nom

Rice, Wm. B. to Edw. L. Wells et al., 42 acres e s Saw Mill River road, adj Chas. Runyon. 100,000

Stewart, Margt. to Mary C. Ryan, e s Woodworth av, 50 s Lamartine, 25x80. 1,215

Wangenstein, Fred. to Geo. P. Amon, n s Downing st, 156 w Riverdale av, 50x102. 2,175

Ware, Enoch R. trustee of, to Edw. N. Barrett, s w s Richmond av, 220 n w Kimball av, 150x125. 1,050

MORTGAGES.

NOTE.—*The arrangement of this list is as follows. The first name is that of the mortgagor, the next that of the mortgagee. The description of the property then follows, then the date of the mortgage, the time for which it was given, and the amount. The general dates used as headings are the dates when the mortgage was handed into the Register's office to be recorded.*

Whenever the letters "P. M." occur, preceded by the name of a street, in these lists of mortgages, they mean that it is a Purchase Money Mortgage, and for fuller particulars see the list of transfers under the corresponding date. Whenever the rate is not given, read as 6 per cent.

NEW YORK CITY.

AUGUST 21, 22, 24, 25, 26, 27.

Amsler, Ernest F. with Julius Lipman and William Cohen both mortgagees. Agreement as to priority of morts. made by Susanna V. Hagen. Aug. 24. nom

Bedford, Joseph T. to Luke S. Van Zandt. Morris av. P. M. June 27, due Aug. 27, 1894, or installs., 5 %. $1,000

Bowen, Kate T. to James W. Ogden. Cauldwell av and 156th st. P. M. Aug. 27, installs., 5 %. 1,250

Boyd, Elizabeth widow, Brooklyn, to THE TITLE GUARANTEE AND TRUST CO. South 5th av, Nos. 186 and 188, w s, 80.2 s Broome st, runs south 45.3 x west 68.2 x north 25.3 x east 6.2 x north 19.11 x east 62 to beginning. Aug. 27, 2 years, 5 %. 18,000

Baron, John to Elizabeth M. Sandford. 3d av. w s, south ½ lot 230 map of Mount Eden, 25x100. Aug. 22. 200

Braender, Frederick and Emily his wife to John H. Borgstede. 83d st, s s, 82 e Av A, runs south 120 x east 16 x north 17.10 x east 25 x north 102.2 to st, x west 41. Sub. to mort. $13,000. Aug. 1, 1 year or sooner. 2,064

Baubahn, Heinrich D. A. to John Muth, Jr. 2d av, No. 2154, e s, 75.11 s 111th st, 25x100. Aug. 22, due Jan. 1, 1893. 2,500

Bohemian Benevolent and Literary Assoc. to Frederic R. and Charles Coudert trustees. 73d st. P. M. July 1, due Aug. 20, 1896, or installs, 5 %. 10,000

Burne, William C. to Joseph W. Babcock. 113th st, s s, 152.3 w 5th av, 17.9x100.11. Sub. to morts. Aug. 15, 6 months. 3,700

Barnes, Jacob J., Jersey City, N. J., to Henry M. Bendheim. 106th st, n s, 265.6 w 9th av, 59.6x100.11. June 24, due Nov. 1, 1891. 6,000

Benassai, Frank and Malvina his wife to John C. Fahl. Tinton av and Denman pl. P. M. Aug. 25, installs, 5 %. 1,700

Bleistift, Abraham J. to Alter Gottlieb. Cannon st, e s, abt 100 n Delancey st, 25x100. Aug. 25, due Jan. 1, 1892. 2,750

Bohmer, Ferdinand, Jr., to William G. McCrea. Morris pl, n w cor 161st st, 140.6x180. Aug. 21, 3 months, notes. 15,000

Bradley & Currier Co. (Lim.) with M. Dasher Wylly and W. Wilton Wood mortgagees and Frederick Rohrs and Louisa his wife mortgagors. Agreement to release mortgaged premises. Aug. 21. nom

Same with Mary M. Post. Agreement as to priority of morts. made by Frederick Rohrs and as to application of mortgage moneys. Aug. 22. nom

Conlan, Michael and Terence Gannon to William A. Smith exr. George Jones. 83d st. P. M. July 30, due Aug. 21, 1892, 5 %. 5,000

Cooper, William S. to THE NEW YORK LIFE INS. CO. 107th st, n s, 113 w 4th av, 3 lots. 3 P. M. morts., each $9,675. July 1, installs, 5 %. 29,025

Same to Meyer L. Sire. 107th st, n s, 113 w 4th av, 16x100.11. Aug. 21, installs, 5 %. 1,500

Same to same. 107th st, n s, 145 w 4th av, 16x100.11. Aug. 21, installs, 5 %. 1,400

Same to same. 107th st, n s, 161 w 4th av, 17x100.11. Aug. 21, installs, 5 %. 1,300

Cohn, Bernard to NEW YORK LIFE INS. CO. 95th st, n s, 150 e Amsterdam av, 11 lots, each 18x100. 11 morts, each $14,000. Aug. 19, 3 years, 1st 6 months 6 % and after 5 %. See Conveys. 154,000

Condon, Patrick W. to Peter Doelger. 1st av, No. 295, s w cor 17th st. Store lease. Aug. 25, demand. 2,500

Christopher, Charles R. and William H. to THE BROADWAY SAVINGS INST. Spruce st, s s, 47.2 w William st, runs west 20 x south 49.6 x east 78.1 to William st, x north 25.4 x west 52.1 x north 24.8 to beginning, being No. 22 Spruce st and No. 181 William st. Aug. 14, due Sept. 1, 1892, 4½ %. 30,000

Casey, Maria E. wife of and Abraham L. to Thomas Johnston. Lind av, s e s, 58.6 n e Devoe st, 25x100x—x—. Aug. 17, due Aug. 15, 1896, or installs., 5 %. 7,000

Crossman, Greenleaf W. to Maximilian Polsenski. Ackerman and Varian sts. P. M. Aug. 27, 5 years, 5 %. 2,300

Dederer, Ida E. wife of Abijah M. to Anna wife of John Hesdorfer. 17th st, n s, 120.6 w Av B, 25x92. Aug. 27, 3 years. 3,000

Duke, John, Brooklyn, to George E. Hyatt, Brooklyn. 105th st, s s, 142.10 e Columbus av, 21.6x100.11. Aug. 25, due Feb. 1, 1892, or sooner. 5,000

Same to Thomas Hagan. Same property. Sub. to last mort. Aug. 25, 5 months. 3,000

Same to Henry H. Lloyd. Same property Sub. to morts. $8,000. Aug. 25, due Jan. 21, 1892, or sooner. 7,000

Doscher, Franz C. and Wilhelmina his wife to Floyd M. Horton. 63d st. P. M. Aug. 25, installs. 2,500

Depierre, Marie L. to Bridget McGuire. 114th st. P. M. Aug. 25, 2 years, 5½ %. 2,500

Dessau, Simon to Schnatz & Massoth. Broadway, w s, 83 s Clinton pl, 26x100. Lease. Aug. 25, due Sept. 1, 1891. 6,000

De Latasa, Fidelma V. widow to Mary L. Hays. 93d st, No. 123, n s, 283.1 w Columbus av, 16.11x72.5 to old line, x16.11x71.5, with all title to strip in rear 16.11x18.4. Aug. 24, due Aug. 1, 1893. 2,000

Deyerberg, Henry H. to Eva Bechtel extrx. George Bechtel. 10th av, No. 27. Store lease. Aug. 19, demand. 2,500

Engel, Emma to Karl M. Wallach. Chrystie st. P. M. Aug. 18, demand. 11,000

Ericson, Lars G. to Edward H. Van Ingen and David T. Leahy. Walton av, w s, 166.8 n 150th st, 16.8x100. Aug. 20, 3 years, 5 %. 2,000

Eitze, Edward to Henry Beste trustee for Pauline G. Onativia. 36th st, No. 216, s s, 605 e 8th av, 21x98.9. Aug. 24, due Nov. 1, 1892, 5 %. 9,000

Edmunds, Isaac A. to Beadleston & Woerz, a corporation. Rutgers slip, No. 69. Store lease. Aug. 24, demand. 2,500

Same to same. Same property. Store lease. Aug. 24, demand. 2,500

Euler, Charles to William Rankin. West 4th and Cornelia sts. P. M. Sub. to mort. $33,000. Aug. 17, 3 years or installs. 22,000

Friedman, Charles to Michael T. N. Burke. Cherry st. P. M. Aug. 1, 6 years or installs, 5 %. 6,000

Freienstein, John to Sebastian Kerner and Mary his wife. 98th st. P. M. Aug. 25, 5 years, 5 %. 5,000

Gallagher, Kate and Joseph F. to Matilda Rothschild. 114th st, s s, 300 w 1st av, 30x100.11. Sub. to morts. $18,900. Aug. 22, 3 months or sooner. 1,000

Grimm, Wilhelmina V. wife of and Louis to Joseph Cohen. 2d av. P. M. Aug. 22, due Jan. 1, 1892. 3,000

Goldstein, Mary L. to Franz Bilz. 1st av, e s, 50.11 s 110th st, 25x95. April 8, 5 years. 1,500

Gaylor, Clarence W. to Elliott C. Davidson, Hull, Ia. 114th st, n s, 245 e 5th av. P. M. July 24, installs. 1,717

Same to same. 114th st, n s, 270 e 5th av. P. M. July 24, installs. 1,717

Gilsey, Andrew et al. exrs. Peter Gilsey and Andrew, Charles, Peter, Henry and John Gilsey and Mary wife of Peter Gardner and Pauline wife of Daniel E. Starr to THE UNITED STATES TRUST CO. of New York. Broadway, n w cor 28th st, 21.2x77.10x19.9x85.4. Aug. 20, due Aug. 1, 1892, or installs., 5 %. 40,000

Same to same. Broadway, w s, 21.2 n 28th st, 28.9x67.6x26.11x77.10. Aug. 20, due Aug. 1, 1892, or installs., 5 %. 30,000

Same to same. Broadway, w s, 49.11 n 28th st, 27.11x57.6x26.1x67.6. Aug. 20, due Aug. 1, 1892, or installs., 5 %. 30,000

Gantert, Paul and Edward A. of Paul Gantert & Son, with Julius Lipman and William Cohen both mortgagees. Agreement as to priority of mortgages made by Susanna V. Hagan. Aug. 24. nom

Haggerty, William F. to Mary Totten. Prince st, No. 22, s s, 23.9x123.6x23.9x129. Aug. 20, 3 years. 2,500

Hartwell, Louise M. to Howard A. Stevens. Convent av, w s, 59.11 n 143d st, 20x100. Sub. to mort. $18,000. Aug. 25, 1 year. 2,500

Howe, Bridget wife of Michael to James M. Gifford. Hoffman st, w s, lot 106 and north ½ lot 105 and south ½ lot 107 map of Rev. W. Powell, Fordham, 24th Ward, 100x100. Aug. 21, demand. 170

Hagan, Susanna V. to Burrows & Smith. 79th st, s s, 40 e 10th av, 40x102. Sub. to mort. Aug. 21, demand. 7,445

Hartwell, Louise M. to THE NEW YORK LIFE INS. CO. Convent av, n w cor 143d st, 19.11x100. June 29, 1 year. 26,000

Same to same. Convent av, w s, 19.11 n 143d st, 20x100. June 29, 1 year. 20,000

Same to same. Convent av, w s, 39.11 n 143d st, 3 lots, each 20x100. 3 morts., each $18,000. June 29, 1 year. 54,000

Same to Stephen B. Sturges. Convent av, n w cor 143d st, 99.11x100. Sub. to morts. $62,500. Aug. 20, demand. gold, 6,412

Same to Thomas A. McIntyre. Same property. Sub. to morts. $68,912. Aug. 20, due Oct. 10, 1891. 17,710

Same to Canda & Kane. Convent av, w s, 19.11 n 143d st, 20x100. Sub. to morts. Aug. 25, due Aug. 20, 1892. 3,000

Same to William J. Bailey. Same property. Sub. to morts. Aug. 25, 1 year. 3,875

Same to Charles De Hart Brower. Convent av, n w cor 143d st, 19.11x100. Sub. to mort. $26,000. Aug. 21, 3 months. 8,220

Same to Thomas Hagan. Convent av, w s, 79.11 n 143d st, 20x100. Sub. to mort. $18,000. Aug. 25, 6 months. 3,282

Honig, Moses to John R. Bleecker, Brooklyn. Av C, No. 123, w s, 20 s 8th st, 19.4x83. Aug. 25, 5 years, 5 %. 4,000

Same to William S. Bleecker. Same property Equal lien with last mort. Aug. 25, 5 years, 5 %. 3,000

Same to Jacob Schlosser exr. and trustee Christian L. Nunnenkamp. Same property. Aug. 25, due Jan. 1, 1892, 5 %. 1,000

Hummel, Frederick P. to Louis Brandt. Kingsbridge av, s e s, 192 n e Terrace View av, 52.5x146.11x44.3x134.10. Aug. 24, demand. 1,000

Hatton, Elizabeth wife of Jonathan to Sarah U. Perkins, Brooklyn. Forest av, w s, 121.4 n Wall st and 123.9 n 165th st, 75x200. Sub. to mort. $6,000. Aug. 27, 1 year. 500

Heim, Carl and Katharina his wife to Merritt Trimble. 48th st. P. M. Aug. 19, 3 years, 5 %. gold, 10,000

Same to William Glaeser and Mary his wife. Same property. P. M. Sub. to last mort. Aug. 27, 3 years, 5 %. 4,000

Howard, Robert H. and Elizabeth J. wife of Childe H. Childs to THE UNION DIME SAVINGS INST. 33d st, s s, 225 w 10th av, runs west 200 x south 98.9 x east 25 x south 98.9 to 32d st, x east 25 x north 98.9 x east 150 x north 98.9 to beginning. Aug. 22, due May 1, 1896, or installs, 5 %. 75,000

Jordan, James F. to H. Koehler & Co., a corporation. 9th av, No. 861. Saloon lease. Aug. 18, demand. 500

Jacob, August to Frank E. Wise. 80th st, s s, 225 w 3d av, 25x102.2. Aug. 25, demand. 5,000

Kane, William S. to Henry A. Barling et al. trustees Edward M. Robinson dec'd. Bleecker st. P. M. Aug. 21, 3 years, 5 %. 35,000

Kauffman, Mordecai S. and Manuel Goldberg to Ascher Weinstein. Lexington av and 75th st. P. M. Aug. 3, installs. 3,000

Kornahrens, George C. to Oliver B. Tweedy, Plainfield, N. J. 126th st, No. 308, s s, 175 e 2d av, 25x99.11. Aug. 26, due Dec. 1, 1894, 5 %. gold, 10,000

Kennedy, Thomas F. to John M. Lyon, Portchester, N. Y. Ogden av, n e cor Union st, 59x100. Aug. 15, 1 year. 500

Lyman, Jennie mortgagee to Edward H. Horner mortgagor. Certificate of payment of $3,000 on account of mortgage and of amount due thereon. Aug. 11. nom

Lay, Jacob and Catharine E. his wife to Emil Gabler et al. trustees Ernst Gabler. Jackson av, w s, 450 n Columbia av, 25.8x100. Aug. 20, due Aug. 21, 1896, 4½ %. 1,000

Levy, Louis to THE BOWERY SAVINGS BANK. Baxter st, No. 64, s w cor Franklin st, 25x54.9 x25x56.10. Aug. 21, 1 year, 4½ %. 16,000

Levy, Lewis mortgagor with George E. Blanke mortgagee. Extension of mort. July 31. nom

Lichter, Benjamin to Elias G. Brown. Water st. P. M. Aug. 26, installs, 5 %. 5,000

Same to Fanny Cohen. Same property. Sub. to morts. $12,500. Aug. 26, demand. 7,500

Lockwood, Alexander to James Saxton. 130th st. P. M. July 1, 12 years or sooner, 5 %. 7,500

Lowe, Mary and Gertrude G. McVay to Horace Anderson. 130th st, n s, 375 e Lenox av, 20x 99.11. Sub. to morts. Collateral. Aug. 20, due Feb. 1, 1893. 3,000

Lynch, Kate to Thomas McHugh and Rose his wife. "Drive," 24th Ward. P. M. Aug. 26, 2 years or sooner, 5 %. 225

Livor, Henry M. to Bridget Cuff admrx. John Cuff. 13th st, n s, 225 w 10th av, 50x103. Lease. Aug. 18, installs. 3,000

Lynd, Robert B. to THE WASHINGTON LIFE INS CO. 84th st, n s, 70 w Madison av, 75x 102.2. Aug. 27, due Dec 1, 1891. 210,000

Merritt, Armintha wife of and William J. to Ehrick Parmly and ano. trustees for Ehrick K. Rossiter and Anna R. Adams. 89th st, s s, 52 e West End av, runs east 30 x south 67.8 x west 18 x north 43 x west 12 x north 24.8 to beginning. Aug 27, 5 years, 5 %. gold, 20,000

Meyer, Henry to Isaac and Julius Meyer, Kingston, N. Y. 93d st, s s, 126 w Park av, 21x100.8. Aug. 27, due Dec. 30, 1894, 4½ %. 17,000

Madden, Elizabeth G. to Delia Gibson. 138th st, s s, 175 e Southern Boulevard, 17.6x100. Aug. 26, 1 year or sooner. 765

McNiece, James to THE METROPOLITAN LIFE INS. CO., New York. 103d st, s s, 209.5 e Amsterdam av, 27x105.3x27x105.4. Aug. 14, due Oct, 1, 1896, installs, 5½ % 1st year, 5 % after. 24,000

Same to same. 103d st, s s, 177.5 e Amsterdam av. 32x105.4x32x105.6. Aug. 14, due Oct. 1, 1896, installs, 5½ % 1st year, 5 % after. 27,000

Same to same. 103d st, s s, 263.5 e Amsterdam av, 27x105x27x105.1. Aug. 14, due Oct. 1, 1896, installs, 5½ % 1st year, 5 % after. 24,000

Same to same. 103d st, st, s s, 236.5 e Amsterdam av, 32x105.1x32x105.3. Aug. 14, due Oct. 1, 1896, installs, 5½ % 1st year, 5 % after. 27,000

Same to same. 103d st, s s, 205.5 e Amsterdam av, 32x104.10x32x105. Aug. 14, due Oct. 1, 1896, installs, 5½ % 1st year, 5 % after. 27,000

Same to Bradley & Currier Co. (Lim.) 103d st, s s, 177.5 e Amsterdam av, 150x104.10x150x 105.6. *Mt.* $140,200. Aug. 14, 3 months or installs. 20,053

Same to same. Same property. Sub. to morts. $130,200. Aug. 14, 1 year or installs. 10,000

Same to Daniel J. Carroll. Same property. Sub. to morts. $157,831. Aug. 14, 1 year. 900

Same to Morris Steinhardt. Same property. Sub. to morts. $129,000. Aug. 21, 30 days. 1,219

Same to Thomas Roberts Stevenson Co. Same property. Sub. to morts. $167,153. Aug. 14, 1 year. 878

Same to William Gould. Same property. Sub. to morts. $154,053. Aug. 14, 1 year. 3,100

Same to Thomas Hagan. Same property. Sub to morts. $161,253. Aug. 14, 1 year. 2,000

Same to James Curran. Same property. Sub. to same mort Aug. 14, 1 year. 1,800

McNiece, James to Joseph Marren. 103d st, s s, 177.5 e Amsterdam av, 150x104.10x150x 105.6. Aug. 21, note, due Nov. 24, 1891. 1,071

Murray, Michael to Regine A Hafferberg. Morris av new, e s, part lot 254 map of Melrose South, 25x70.3. Aug. 10, 5 years, 5 %. gold, 2,600

McGough, Henry to Susan A. Tier, Eastchester, N. Y. Union st, n s, lot 39 map of North Melrose, 23d Ward, 50x100. Aug. 21, due April 19, 1894, 5 %. 2,500

Meares, Richard to Schwarzschild and Sulzberger. 6th av, s e cor 40th st, 59.6x100. Lease. Aug. 24, demand. 9,000

Murphy, Annie to Bessie A. Foley. 136th st. No. 242, s s, 319.2 e 8th av, 17.6x99.11. July 15, demand after 60 days' notice, 4 %. 6,000

Ottiwell, Sarah C. to William E. M. Zborowski, Melton Mowbray, England. Webster av, e s, 435.5 n 170th st, 50x121 to Mill Brook, x 50.10x129.8. Sub. to mort. $3,000. Aug. 1, 3 years or sooner, 5 %. 12,500

Phelps, Louis N. to Julius Lipman. 8th av, s e cor Bleecker st, runs northeast 44.11 x southeast 40 x east 17.2 x south 22.5 x west 76.9 to st. x north 27.7 to beginning. Aug. 10, 2 months or sooner. 3,000

Pettit, Frank, Brooklyn, to J. Henry Work and ano. exrs. and trustees John C. Work. 20th st, s s, 239.6 e 4th av, 26.8x92; interior lot in rear of above, 26.8x22, being No. 13 Gramercy Park or 114 East 20th st. July 28, 1 year. 20,000

Pearsall, Margaret A., Lawrence, L. I., to THE MANHATTAN SAVINGS INST. 2d av, w s, 49.8 n 25th st, 24.6x100. Aug. 25, 1 year, 5 %. 5,000

Same to same. 45th st, s e cor Lexington av, 18.9x70. Aug. 25, 1 year, 5 %. 5,000

Pope, William B. and Mary B. his wife to Henry Offerman, Brooklyn. Park av, s e cor 81st st, 51x100. Aug. 25, 1 year. 7,000

Phillips, Hartwig I. to THE GERMAN-AMERICAN REAL ESTATE TITLE GUARANTEE CO. Houston st, No. 316 E. Aug. 27, 2 years, 5 %. 12,000

Reinwarth, Charles to Louisa Reinwarth. 122d st. P. M. Aug. 20, 3 years, 4½ %. 6,000

Rohrs, Frederick to The Bradley and Currier Co. (Lim.) 70th st, n s, 273 e Av A, 25x100.5. Sub. to morts. $13,350. Aug. 20, 3 months. 2,500

Same to Edward M. Scudder. 133th st, s s, 100 w Alexander av, 50x100. Aug. 21, due Nov. 1, 1891. 5,000

Same to Mary M. Post, Hoboken, N. J. 102d st, n s, 27 e Park av, 3 lots, each 25x100.11. 3 morts., each $1,000. Aug. 21, due Oct. 1, 1891. 3,000

Ringen, John to Hewlett Scudder et al. exrs. and trustees Henry J. Scudder. Willis av, No. 372, e s, 25 s 143d st, 24.11x98.8. Aug. 26, due Dec. 1, 1894, 5 %. gold, 12,000

Sander, Mary wife of Christian to Leon Oliver. 48th st. P. M. Aug. 18, 3 years, 5 %. 10,000

Sheak, Adelaide M. to Robert N. Quinn. Perry av, e s, 250 s Scott av, 50x110. July 29, due Nov. 13, 1893, 5 %. 330

Schramm, John N. to Agnes Walsh. 146th st. P. M. Aug. 20, due Nov. 19, 1891. 1,700

Smith, Elizabeth K. to James Rogers. 123d st, s s, 174.6 e 7th av, 16x100.11. Aug. 4, demand. 1,400

Stephach, Gustav and Sophie his wife to Annie J. Walkley. 144th st, n s, 400 e Willis av, 25 x100. Aug. 22, 5 years, 5 %. 4,000

Same to same. Same property. Sub. to last mort. Aug. 22, 2 years or sooner, 5 %. 600

Schweebius, George to Susan A. Tier, Eastchester, N. Y. 153d st, s s, 150 w Courtlandt av, 25x100. Aug. 22, due July 22, 1894. 500

Stevens, Mary J. wife of and Henry E. to THE FRANKLIN SAVINGS BANK. 55th st, s s, 145.10 w Broadway, 20x100.5. Aug. 25, 1 year, 5 %. 10,000

Sauter, George and Charles E. Deppermann to THE CITIZEN'S SAVINGS BANK. 157th st, s s, 125 w Amsterdam av, 25x99.11. Aug. 25, 1 year, 5 %. gold, 12,000

Same to same. 157th st, s s, 150 w Amsterdam av, 3 lots, each 16.8x99.11, 3 morts., each $7,000. Aug. 25, 1 year, 5 %. gold, 21,000

Tompkins, Sophia H., East Orange, N. J., Mary A. Wright, Bogata, N. J., and Johnston Knight, Bogata, N. J., to THE TITLE GUARANTEE AND TRUST CO. 30th st, No. 349, n s, 213 e 9th av, 13.6x98.9. Re-recorded. July 14, 2 years 2,000

Tripler, Thomas E. to Anna wife of John Hesdorfer. 17th st, n s, 145.6 w Av B, 25x92. Aug. 27, 3 years. 3,000

Same to same. 17th st, n s, 170.6 w Av B, 25x 92. Aug. 27, 3 years. 3,000

Thatcher, James to THE TWELFTH WARD SAVINGS BANK. Jefferson av, n w s, 537 n e Tremont av, 25x200. Aug. 19, due Aug. 25, 1892. 2,500

Thiel, Anna C. to Max Goldnick and Ida his wife. Strong av. P. M. Aug. 22, 6 years or installs, 5½ %. 1,200

The Catholic University of America to Mary Feeney. Riverside av or Drive, e s, 450 n 122d st, 25x100. Aug. 19, 3 years, 5 %. 6,000

Thomas, Anna wife of Daniel to Elizabeth Wegford. 65th st, s s, 300 e West End av, 25x100.5. Aug. 15, 5 years, 5 %. 4,000

Ullmann, Max to The John Kress Brewing Co. West st, No. 404. Saloon lease. Aug 20, demand. 1,000

Uihlein, Frank A. and Anna Elizabeth wife of Conrad Kerner, Catharine wife of Valentine Maickol and Mary wife of Henry Peters to Amelia A. wife of John B. Passite. 89th st, n s, 250 w 1st av, 25x100.8. Aug. 18, due Aug. 24, 1894, 5 %. 10,000

Same to same. 89th st, n s, 275 w 1st av, 25x 100.8. Aug. 18, due Aug. 24, 1894, 5 %. 10,000

Vermilye, Thomas E., Jr., and Celeste B. Vedder widow to The General Synod of the Reformed Church in America. 12th av, s w cor 132d st, 52x83 to low water mark of Hudson River, x15x74, with land under water, &c. Aug. 18, 1 year. 12,000

Van Vechten, Jessie L. wife of Cuyler, New Brighton, S. I., to Jane L. Swift, Elizabeth, N. J. Elizabeth st, Nos. 49 and 51, w s, 175.1 n Canal st, 50x94.6. Nov. 30, 1889, demand, 5 %. 10,000

Verdon, William to The Yale Shaft and Iron Co. 135th st, n s, 110 w 5th av, 18.4x99.11. Aug. 10, notes. 2,500

Wall, Elizabeth M. wife of and Matthew J. to Martha L. Andrews. 122d st, n s, 115.6 w from e s 2d av, 14x100.11. Error. Aug. 18, 1 year. 500

Walsh, Margaret F. to John W. Decker. Cauldwell av. P. M. Aug. 21, installs. 3,000

Werner, William, Charles Hohl and Arnold Anderhalden to Louis Engel. 127th st, s s, 250 e Cypress av, 3 lots, each 16.8x103.8. 3 morts., each $2,500. Aug. 24, 1 year. 7,500

Wickham, Christopher to Herbert B. Turner, Englewood, N. J., trustee. Railroad av, s e s, 191 n e 167th st, 50x150. Sub. to mort. $2,-000. Aug. 25, 1 year, 5 %. 500

KINGS COUNTY.

AUGUST 20, 21, 22, 24, 25, 26.

Adams, Calvin T. to Title Guarantee and Trust Co. St. Johns pl, s s, 220.2 w 6th av, 20x123.9 x20x122.7. Aug. 21, 1 year, 5 %. $5,000

Anderson, Anders J. to Eugene M. Berard committee. 28th st, s s, 475 e 3d av, 25x100.2. Aug. 19, due Aug. 20, 1894, 5 % 2,000

Anderson, Robert K. to Maria E. Schneider. Belmont av. P. M. Aug. 20, 3 years. 800

Same to Andrew Gulbrandsen. Same property. Aug. 20, installs, 5 %. 500

Anhalt, Margaretha to Ferdinand Heuer. South 2d st, s s, 157.10 e 1st st, 22x95. Aug. 24, 3 years, 5 %. 2,000

Atwell, Joseph B. to Mary E. Miller, New Rochelle, N. Y. Dean st, s s, 386 e Franklin av, 20x100. Sub. to mort. $2,000. Aug. 22, 6 months. 550

Baumgaertner, John to August Baumgaertner. Leonard st, s e cor Scholes st, 100x100. Sub. to morts. $17,000. Aug. 20, 5 years, 5 %. 5,000

Same to Elizabeth Baumgaertner. Same property. Sub. to morts. $5,000. Aug. 20, 5 years, 5 %. 12,000

Same to Barbara Woerner. Same property. Sub. to morts. $17,000. Aug. 20, 5 years, 5 %. 6,000

Same to George Baumgaertner. Same property. Sub. to morts. $17,000. Aug. 20, 5 years, 5 %. 4,600

Beatty, Catherine wife of and George F. to Martha McCormick. 14th st, n s, 218.2 e 8th av, 19.8x100. Aug. 17, 3 years, 5 %. 4,000

Bloch, Henry to South Brooklyn Savings Inst. Bridge st, w s, 125 s Johnson st, 25x107.6. Aug. 22, 1 year, 5 %. 3,000

Bloom, David, Isaac Ginsberg and Israel Feldman to Sarah H. Powell, New York. Moore and Leonard sts. P. M. Aug. 17, 1 year, 5 %. 3,000

Blumberg, Jacob to Simon J. Harding. 17th st, n s, 275 e 6th av. P. M. Aug. 14, installs. 1,000

Same to The German-American Real Estate Title Guarantee Co. Same property. P. M. Aug. 14, due Aug. 19, 1894, 5 %. 3,000

Brahm, Peter T. and Caezilia his wife to Susan P. Du Bois trustee for Frances E. Du Bois. Suydam st, s e s, 175 n e Hamburg av, 25x 100. Aug. 22, 3 years, 5 %. 3,000

Burgtorf, Theodore R. to Louise Staudenbaur. Gates av, n s, 165 e Sumner av, 20x100. Aug. 18, 1 year. 500

Burkhardt, Charles to Anna Reynolds and ano. exrs. Thomas Reynolds. Jefferson av, s s, 23 w Patchen av, 72x75. Aug. 13, due June 15, 1893, 5 %. 4,500

Burtonshaw, Charles J. to Edwin F. Knowlton. College pl, w s, 109.2 n Love lane, 50x82. Aug. 19, due Aug. 25, 1892. 15,000

Busher, Theodore to Charles Feuring. Central av, n e s, 80.3 n w Grove st, 20.2x80. Aug. 20, due Sept. 1, 1896, 5 %. 2,400

Begly, Hugh J. to Title Guarantee and Trust Co. Navy st, w s, 75 s Bolivar st, 25x100. Aug. 25, 1 year, 5 %. 5,000

Beunie, Jennie L. to Sarah M. Bergen. 72d st, s s, 570 w 15th av, 40x100. Aug. 19, 1 year. 200

Cochran, Israel Y. to Rope & Co. Hemlock st, e s, 150 s Griffin pl, 50x100. Aug. 8, demand. 1,500

Carroll, Catherine M. to William Beaford. Jackson st. P. M, Aug. 11, due Aug. 31, 1896, 5 %. 1,000

Castellanos, Conception to The Title Guarantee and Trust Co. Bainbridge st, n s, 164 w Patchen av, 16x100. Aug. 18, 1 year, 5 %. 950

Ceder, Felix to George A. Craig. Madison st, s e s, 140.5 n e Hamburg av, 20x100. Sub. to mort. $2,400. Aug. 19, installs. 1,300

Ceiner, Louis to George A. Craig. Madison st, s e s, 100 n e Hamburg av, 25.5x100. Sub. to mort. $3,300. Aug. 19, installs. 650

Same to same. Same property. Aug. 19, installs. 800

Ceiner, Louis to George A. Craig. Madison st, s e s, 100 n e Hamburg av, 20.5x100. Sub. to morts. $3,000. Aug. 19, installs. 300

Cochen, Fred. C. to Sarah E. Weller and ano. exrs. Alfred T. Weller. 10th av, n e cor 70th st, New Utrecht. P. M. Aug. 20, 1 year. 3,500

Cole, Ella M. to Rosina Russell. Utica av. P. M. Aug 3, due Aug. 20, 1901, 5 %. 2,550

Corwin, Frank L. to Charles E. Rogers. 77th st, n s, 106.6 e 4th av, 440x100, New Utrecht. Aug. 14, due Sept. 1, 1892. 5,500

Couts, Albert to The Brooklyn Mutual Building and Loan Assoc. Liberty av, n s, 27.6 e Jefferson st, 25x100. Aug. 20, installs. 1,200

Craig, Adam to The Title Guarantee and Trust Co. South 1st st, n s, 75.10 w Marcy av, 49.2 x77x50x72. Aug. 22, 1 year, 5 %. 6,000

Craig, George A. to William Laytin et al. exrs. William Laytin. Madison st, s e s, 439.7 s w Knickerbocker av, 3 lots, together 60.5x100. 3 morts., each $2,400. Aug. 14, 3 years, 5 %. 7,200

Same to same. Madison st, s e s, 313.8 s w Knickerbocker av, 3 lots, each 18x100. 3 morts., each $2,300. Aug. 14, 3 years, 5 %. 6,900

Same to same. Madison st, s e s 421.8 s w Knickerbocker av. 17.11x100. Aug. 14, 3 years, 5 %. 2,300

Same to same. Madison st, s e s, 278 s w Knickerbocker av, 2 lots, each 18x100. 2 morts., each $2,300. Aug. 14, 3 years, 5 %. 4,600

Costello, Ellen H. to George A. Craig. Madison st, s e s, 120.5 n e Hamburg av, 20x100. Sub. to mort. $2,400. Aug. 19, installs. 1,500

Costelloe, Nellie wife of and Thomas to Phebe A. Underhill, New York. Monroe st, n s, 272.6 w Lewis av, 19.2x100. Aug. 19. 3 years, 5 %. 4,000

Crocker, James to Jacques Sandmeyer, trustee Rebecca Grove. 5th av, e s, 50 s 14th st, 12.8x97.10. Aug. 18, 3 years, 5 %. 1,000

Currier, Henry to James D. Lynch. 83d st, n e s, 60 n w 24th av, 60x100. Aug. 8, due Aug. 11, 1895, 6 %. 630

Cummings, Robert J. to Alfred Wagstaff guard. Snediker av, e s, 50 n Belmont av, 50x100. Aug. 17, 3 years. 2,450

De Gray, Thomas J. to John Brentano. Rutledge st, n e cor Marcy av P. M. Aug. 20, 5 years, 5 %. 2,000

Diehlmann, Katharina wife of Charles F. to Michael Jacobs. Stockton st, s s, 150 w Lewis av, 25x100. Aug. 20, 5 years, 5 %. 3,500

Diehm, Henry to The Williamsburgh Savings Bank. Cooper st, n w s, 100 s w Bushwick av, 25x100. Aug. 20, 1 year. 5 %. 4,000

Dillard, John A. to Christian Friedman. Bedford av and Hancock st. P. M. Aug. 20, 5 years. 10,000

Doody, Daniel F. to Julia E. Brick. 44th st, s w s, 133.9 n w 4th av, 54.3x100.2. Aug. 12, 1 year. 7,700

Same to William M. Ingraham. 44th st, s w s, 80 n w 4th av, 53.9x100.2. Builders loan. Aug. 12, demand. 2,750

Dowd, Jerome A. to Peter Blank. Harman st, n s, 270 w St. Nicholas av, 20x100. Aug. 15, 3 years, 5 %. 1,000

Dowling, William L. to Emily C. Thallon. St. Johns pl. P. M. Aug. 15, due Nov. 1, 1891, 5 %. 1,000

Same to Rulef J. Van Brunt. 3d av, n w cor 85th st, runs west 310 x north 100 x east 75 x north 100 to 84th st, x west to 2d av, x north — x east to point 110 w 3d av, x south — x southeast — to av, x south —, New Utrecht. Aug. 13, 1 year. 5,500

Duffy, James J. to The Germania Savings Bank, Kings County. Gold st, e s, 100 n Johnson st, 25x85. Aug. 18, 1 year, %. gold, 51,500

Dunn, James to Charles M. Rex. Carlton av. P. M. Aug. 21, 1 year. 800

Durchholz, Barbara to Lena Durchholz. Alabama av, w s, 125 n Sutter av, 25x100. June 20, 1 year. 600

Durchholz, Lena mortgagor with Lucy A. Huntington and Herbert C. Smith. Extension of mort. June 2. ——

Edwards, Ida W. wife of and John to Clarence W. Hillyer. Hicks st, n e cor Poplar st, 25x100. Aug. 20, 3 years, 5 %. 20,000

Emken, William to Anna Sohmor. Rochester av. P. M. Aug. 21, due Sept. 1, 1893, 5 %. 1,000

Feier, Abraham and Samuel Hirsch to Jacob Axelrod and Isaac Levingson. Thatford av. P. M. Aug. 21, installs. 1,050

Finn, Maurice to John D. Prince, Jr., and ano. exrs. George R. Cutler. Bay 13th st, e s, 225 n Bath av, 100x108.4. Aug. 18, 5 years. 2,200

Fischer, Adam to Regina Heilmann. Stagg st, n s, 25.6 w Bogart st, 18.1x87.4x94.10 (?). Aug. 13, due July 1, 1894, 5 %. 500

Fisher, Edward to George A. Craig. Madison st, s e s, 295.8 s w Knickerbocker av, 18x100. Aug. 14, 1 year, 5 %. 200

Gelb, Sophie wife of Louis to George A. Craig. Madison st, s e s, 367.8 s w Knickerbocker av, 18x100. Aug. 19, installs. 480

Same to same. Same property. Aug. 19, installs. 720

Same to same. Same property. Sub. to mort. $2,780. Aug. 19, installs. 500

Same to same. Madison st, s e s, 349.8 s w Knickerbocker av, 18x100. Sub. to mort. $2,300. Aug. 19, 1 year. 1,900

Same to William Laytin et al. trustees William Laytin. Madison st, s e s, 367.8 s w Knickerbocker av, 18x100. Aug. 14, 3 years, 5 %. 2,300

Gilligan, Jeremiah J. to The Title Guarantee and Trust Co. Garfield pl, s s, 272.10 w 8th av, 4 lots, each 18.9x100. 4 morts., each $8,000. Aug. 21, 3 years, 5 %. 32,000

Gomez, Catharine M. admrx. of Domingo M. Gomez mortgagee with Catharine J. wife of and Louis Monjo mortgagors. Agreement to release portions of mortgaged premises upon payment of sums due on same. Feb. 24, 1891.

Gresser, William to George A. Craig. Madison st, s e s, 178 s w Knickerbocker av, 17.8x100. Aug. 19, installs. 725

Grosser, William to George A. Craig. Madison st, s e s, 278 s w Knickerbocker av, 17.8x100. Sub. to mort. $2,200. Aug. 19, installs. 475

Gauen, Franz to Martha Blanke. McDougal st, Nos. 55 and 57, 41.6x103. Contract recorded as mortgage. Aug. 24. 3,300

Groesbeeck, Sylvester to Thomas Read. Vanderbilt av, w s, 175 n Gates av, 20x100. Aug. 24, due August 25, 1894. 1,000

Gunn, Annie wife of and Albert W. to Title Guarantee and Trust Co. Jefferson av, s s, 208.4 w Ralph av, 16.8x100. Aug. 20, due Aug. 26, 1894, 5 %. 2,000

Heiberger, Anton to Albert Karutz. Grand st. P. M. Aug. 25, 5 years, 5 %. 3,500

Hertz, Julius to Frank Bailey. 80th st. P. M. Aug. 20, 1 year. 300

Horton, Katharina to Nelson T. Samson trustee for Catharine A. Samson. 56th st, n e s, 200 s e 14th av, 50x100.2. June 16, 1 year. 400

Hyde, Florence E. to Henry Weil. Greene av, n s, 125 w Stuyvesant av, 16.4x100, Aug. 22, 1 year, 5 %. 874

Jager, Johann D. to George A. Craig. Madison st, s e s, 421.8 s w Knickerbocker av, 17.11x100. Sub. to mort. $2,800. Aug. 19, 3 years, 5 %. 200

Same to same. Same property. Sub. to mort. $2,300. Aug. 19, 5 years. 500

Jennings, Joseph G. to David Banks. Madison st, n s, 176 e Bedford av, 20x100. Aug. 22, due Aug. 1, 1896, 5 %. 5,500

Johnson, Charles G. to Abraham C. Shelley. Ovington av, n s, 140 e 12th av, 40x136.4x40x135.10, New Utrecht. Aug. 15, due Jan. 2, 1893. 300

Johnson, James to Brooklyn Trust Co. Nevins st, n e cor Livingston st, runs east 58.4 x north 80 x west 16.8 x south 5 x west 16.8 x north 25 x west 25 to Nevins st, x south 100. Aug. 25, 1 year, 5 %. 15,000

Jordens, Ludwig and Dorothea his wife to Charles H. Wagner and George Gutting. Knickerbocker av. P. M. Aug. 25, 5 years, 5 %. 1,400

Kammer, Florian and Elizabeth his wife to Joseph Schmitt and Mary his wife. Marcy av. P. M. Aug. 18, 3 years, 5 %. 1,000

Karl, Martin to The Germania Building, Savings and Loan Inst. Marion st, s s, 81.8 w Ralph av, 19.4x100. Aug. 20, due Oct. 1, 1893. 550

Kaufmann, Bertha to Henry Newman. Bergen st. P. M. Aug. 24, 3 years, 5 %. 2,200

Keiser, Henry and Otilia his wife to Jacob Keiser. 3d st, No. 164, s s, 169.6 e Av A, 24.9x105.11. Aug. 19, due Jan. 1, 1895, 5 %. 4,000

Keller, Ferdinand W. to Frank G. Hennings, Hoboken, N. J. Bay 25th st, s e s, 100 n e Cropsey av, New Utrecht. P. M. Aug. 18, 2 years, 5 %. 1,500

Kempf, Charles to The Title Guarantee and Trust Co. Duffield st, e s, 213 n Willoughby st, 21x100.3. Aug. 15, due Aug. 20, 1892, 5 %. 1,000

Klein, David to Henry Vollweiler. Hopkins st. P. M. Aug. 17, installs. 240

Koster, Mary E. to Abram S. Cassedy, Newburgh, N. Y. Eldert st. P. M. Aug. 24, due Sept. 1, 1892, 5 %. 3,500

Krackow, Marx to Jacob Hirsch and Lena Fischer. Throop av. P. M. Aug. 24, 2 years, 5 %. 800

Kamman, Jens to William C. Behrens, Mt. Vernon, N. Y. Prospect av. P. M. Aug. 25, 1 year. 200

Lippmann, Leopold J. to Timothy G. Sellew, New York. Hancock st, n w s, 90 s w Central av, 360x100. Aug. 25, demand. 44,100

Lachmann, Emil to Peter Kelly. Degraw st. P. M. Aug. 20, 2 years, 5 %. 1,000

Lamert, Henry C. C. to Frederick Weil. 12th av, e s, 40.2 n 59th st, 20x100, New Utrecht. Aug. 20, 1 year. 100

Laubenberger, Philip to Ebenezer Kellum. Columbia st, w s, 37 s Sackett st, 42x80. Aug. 19, due May 1, 1894, 5 %. 6,000

Laumann, Louis and Ida his wife to Kings Co. Trust Co. Grand st. P. M. Aug. 5, 1 year, 5 %. 9,000

List, George A. to Henry Vollbracht. Madison st, s e s, 313.8 s w Knickerbocker av, 19x100. Sub. to mort. $2,300. Aug. 19, 2 years, 5 %. 400

Lubben, Lisette to Henry Kettelhodt. 53d st. P. M. Aug. 19, 5 years. 1,200

Lewis, Arnold A. to John J. Hardy. 26th st, s w s, 80.1 n w 3d av, 219.11x200.4 to 27th st, x219.10x200.4. Aug. 1, 5 years. 12,306

Mafera, Stephen and Christiana E. Lobrentz to Guernsey Sackett. Railroad av. P. M. and building loan. Aug. 1, demand. 1,500

Maynard, Edwin P. to Helen Martense. East 18th st, e s, 150 n Av A. 50x100, Flatbush. Aug. 19, 5 years, 5 %. 5,300

Martin, Ignatz to Daniel C. McEwen. Knickerbocker av. P. M. Aug. 25, 1 year. 700

McMillan, Eliza wife of Thomas formerly O'Connell to William O. Moore et al. exrs. Abraham Underhill, Warwick st. P. M. Aug. 24, 5 years. 2,250

McBride, Thomas B. to Charles W. Lundqvist. 57th st, s w s, 100 s e 7th av, 40x100. Aug. 22, 3 years. 600

McCann, Thomas, William J. Fitzpatrick and William Martin to Bernard Levino. 8th av, e s, extends from 15th to 16th st, 200x160. Building loan. Aug. 1. 8,100

Meister, John to Albert Brons. Jefferson st, e s, 300 n Liberty av, 25x90. July 1, 5 years, 5 %. 600

Menzel, Christian to Bernard Cruse, Jr. Roebling st, w s, 96 n Grand st, 22x71x22.2x73.6. Aug. 20, 3 years. 700

Mertens, Elizabeth to Peter Blank. Myrtle st, s s, 250 e Evergreen av, 25x95. Aug. 12, 3 years, 5 %. 3,500

Miller, Mary E. wife of and George M. to James H. Watson and James H. Pittinger, of Watson & Pittinger. 7th st, n s, 297.10 e 4th av, 50x100. Sub. to mort. $1,360. Aug. 21, demand. 487

Same to Peter A. Johnson and John J. Phelan, of Johnson & Phelan. Same property. Sub. to morts. for $1,360 and $356. Aug. 21, demand. 255

Same to The Title Guarantee and Trust Co. Same property. Aug. 21, 3 months. 1,360

Monahan, Bernard to Anne Allen. 16th st, s w s, 97.10 s e 11th av, 25x100. Aug. 15, 7 years or installs. 1,000

Moore, Alice wife of and John W. to John E. Mason. 13th av, n e cor 65th st, 80x50.3x80.2x45.3, New Utrecht. Aug. 6, 3 years. 400

Moore, William R. to David A. Fithian. Jerome st, w s, 200 n Duryea av, 40x100, Aug. 22, 2 years. 100

Morrissy, Henry mortgagor with John T. Willets admr. Extension of mort. Aug. 19. nom

Nebrhass, Jacob and Peter to Cornelia M. Covert trustee Helena Covert. Lewis av, e s, 100 n Stockton st, runs east 41.5 x northeast 30.10 x northwest 50 x southwest 16.2 x west 20.9 to av, x south 50. Aug. 21, 3 years, 5 %. 2,500

Newman, Rosa to Caroline Broistedt. Hewes st, s s, 63 w Marcy av, 20.5x98. Aug. 21, 5 years, 5 %. 2,000

Nystrom, Gustaf to Anna A. Schmeelk. East 94th st. Aug. 1, 5 years. See Conveys. 1,000

Otterbein, Henry to The Title Guarantee and Trust Co. Woodbine st. P. M. Aug. 25, 3 years, 5 %. 2,000

Prehn, John to Charles A. Wehr. Bushwick av, Schaeffer st. P. M. Aug. 25, 2 years, 5 %. 3,000

Pachinsky, Amelia, New York, to Jacob Strauss. Livonia av late Linnington av, s s, 100 w Watkins st, 80x100. Aug. 20, 1 year, 5 %. 1,200

Pfeffer, Otto to George Ruettinger. Ewen st, w s, 25 s Siegel st, 25x75. Aug. 22, due Jan. 1, 1894, 5 %. 1,500

Pim, Ellen F. wife of Joshua J. to Sidney M. Williams, Jersey City, N. J. Schaefer st, n w s, 137.6 s w Knickerbocker av, 12.6x100. July 31, 3 years. 400

Power, Thomas W. to Esther Isaacs. South 2d st. P. M. Aug. 20, due Sept. 1, 1894, 5 %. 2,000

Raphael, Louis to William W. Stoll. Moore st, No. 29, n s, 175 w Ewen st, 25x100. Aug. 14, 5 years, 5 %. 4,000

Reinshagen, Henry to Jeremiah V. Meserole. Lombardy st. P. M. Aug. 20, 5 years. 500

Renton, Mary E. wife of Daniel H. to Asa W. Parker, New Hamburg, N. Y. Hancock st. P. M. Aug. 20, installs. 2,550

Rice, George H. to William D. and George W. Anderson. Schermerhorn st, n e cor 3d av, 46.6 to Flatbush av, x southeast 83.2 to Schermerhorn st, x69. Aug. 19, 3 months. 2,357

Rieder, Joseph to The South Brooklyn Co-operative Building and Loan Assoc. 17th st. P. M. Aug. 18, installs. 2,500

Riley, Edward to The Williamsburgh Savings Bank. Bedford av, e s, 43.11 s Bergen st, runs east 40.6 to Rogers av, x south 30.11 x west 45.9 to Bedford av, x north 21. Aug. 21, 1 year, 5 %. 6,250

Same to same. Bedford av, s e cor Bergen st, 43.11x406 to Rogers av, x 43.1 to st, x 81. Aug. 21, 1 year, 5 %. 6,250

Riley, George R. to James M. and Harriet M. Halsey guards. of Lydia M. Halsey. Henry st, e s, 76.5 s 4th pl, 16.6x60. July 1, 5 years, 5 %. 2,000

Same to same guards. of Edward B. Halsey. Henry st, e s, 92.11 s 4th pl, 16.6x60. July 1, 5 years, 5 %. 2,000

Same to James M. Halsey guard. of Mortimer H., Juliette and Mary A. Gray. Interior lot, 76.5 s 4th pl and 60 e Henry st, runs south 50 x east 44.6 x 50 x 44.6, with alley, &c. July 1, 5 years, 5 %. 1,800

Same to Esther M. Hedges, Easthampton, L. I. Henry st, e s, 76.5 s 4th pl, 33x60. July 1, 1 year, 5 %. 1,000

Same to Warren A. James trustee of George L., Minnie H. and Gertrude M. Bliven. Henry st, e s, 109.5 s 4th pl, 20x60, reserves passageway. July 1, 5 years, 5 %. 3,000

Rodschinky, Abraham and Louis to John and Margaretha Lannig. Moore st. P. M. Aug. 15, 5 years, 5 %. 5,000

Ross, Josephine L. to The Brooklyn Savings Bank. South Elliott pl, w s, 74.2 s De Kalb av, 19.10x86x20.2x81.11. Aug. 20, 1 year, 5 %. 4,000

Ross, Jennie L. to Frank L. Tapscott. 2d st, s s, 80 w 7th av, 40x100. Aug. 17, demand. 1,000

Ross & Snyder with The Title Guarantee and Trust Co. mortgagees. Extension of mort. made by John D. Hallaren. Aug. 21. nom

Reilly, John H., Jersey City, to William J. Courtney. Shepherd av, e s, 125 n Duryea av, 25x100. Aug. 25, 1 year. 200

Reiner, Wilhelmine to Hermann A. E. Muller. Strong pl, e s, 260 n Degraw st, 16.6x106.2. July 1, 5 years, 4 %. 4,000

Riggs, Walter B. to The F. & M. Schaeffer Brewing Co. Atlantic av, No. 2541, n e cor Williams av. Lease. Aug. 25, 1 year. 1,500

Schaeffler, Alfred to Timothy Perry. Kingsland av, e s, 220 s Nassau av, 20x100. Aug. 21, 5 years. 3,000

Scheimeister, Peter to George Ochs. De Kalb av, s e s, 175 n e Hamburg av, 25x100. Aug. 18, 5 years, 5 %. 2,200

Schnitzer, August to Beadleston & Woerz. Oakland st, n e cor Greene st, 25x75. Lease. Aug. 21, demand. 970

Schmoll, George E. to Alberto Verastegin. Atlantic av, s s, 166.8 e Saratoga av, 6 lots, each 16.8x100. 6 morts., each $2,400. Aug. 21, due Aug. 15, 1894, 5 %. gold, 14,400

Schubert, Anna E. to Ferdinand Munch Brewery. Harrison av, east cor Heyward st, 23x80. May 21, 3 years. 700

Seaman, James E. to John F. Vrooman. Powell st. P. M. Aug. 19, installs, 5 %. 500

Seaton, Charles to Frederick Middendorf. Schenck av, w s, 127 s Jamaica av, 25x100. Aug. 22, demand. 200

Shay, John and Catharine Dowd widow heirs of Ann Shay to Lawrence Fitzpatrick. Bergen st, n s, 475 w Vanderbilt av, 25x73.8x68.1x102.5. Aug. 22, 3 years, 5 %. 850

Sheen, Isaac to George Scheinfeld. Dumont av, s s, 25 e Thatford av, 25x100, Aug. 19, due Sept. 1, 1898. 525

Shults, Christopher to Simon E. Bernheimer and Josephine Schmid, of Bernheimer & Schmid. Louis pl, e s, 78 s Herkimer st, 20x 49. Aug. 18, 1 year. 600

Smith, Annie B. wife of Henry to Robert S. Neely. Gates av. P. M. Aug. 22, installs. 750

Snowden, Robert B. to The West Brooklyn Land and Impt. Co. 13th av, n e cor 54th st. New Utrecht. P. M. Aug. 12, 10 years. 3,500

Solomon, Joseph and Hyman Goldberg to Kunigunde Buhn. Eastern Parkway, n s, 125 e Christopher av, 25x100. Aug. 19, 3 years. 3,000

Speir, Jr., Francis to John Caufield. Clinton st, e s, 125 n Nelson st. P. M. Aug. 21, 5 years, 5 %. 5,500

Same to Moses T. Pyne. Same property. P. M. Aug. 21. 8,000

Sprague, William E. to Janet Pirnie and ano. exrs. John M. Pirnie. Adelphi st, w s, 109 s Myrtle av, 25x100. Aug. 19, due April 21, 1894, 5 %. 500

Staats, George to Michael Mehling. Stagg st, s s, 25 w Lorimer st, 25x75. Aug. 20, 3 years, 5 %. 1,500

Steinfeld, Minna to Mary W. Smith. Rockaway av, e s, 225 n Belmont av, 25x100.1. Aug. 24, 3 months. 1,800

Steitz, August to John F. Vrooman. Powell st. P. M. Aug. 19, installs, 5 %. 500

Stevens, Fannie to Phebe A. wife of John H. Akley, Hempstead, L. I. 3d av, e s, 25 s Pacific st, 25x100. Aug. 24, due Nov. 1, 1894, 5 %. 2,000

Surgood, Charles H. to John H. Ireland. Av G. P. M. Aug. 20, 5 years, 5 %. 2,000

Seebolzer, Frank F. and Mina E. his wife to Anna M. Jager. Jackson st. P. M. Aug. 22, due Dec. 29, 1893. 700

Swimm, Frank C. to Elizabeth U. Hitchcock, Poughkeepsie, N. Y. Macon st, n s, 270 e Reid av, 4 lots, each 17.6x100. 4 morts., each $5,500. Aug. 26, 3 years or installs, 5 %. gold, 22,000

The Welcome Primitive Methodist Church to Martha Humphries. Clason av, w s, 475 n Myrtle av, 50x126.2. Lease. Aug. 17, note. 500

Tumbridge, William appoints Charles A. Seymour new trustee under trust mortgage. Aug. 19. nom

Ukraiusky, Samuel to Agnes Gilbert. Prospect av. P. M. Aug. 20, installs, 5 %. 1,200

Vaccarezza, Maria to Daily News Building Savings and Loan Assoc. 3d av. P. M. Aug. 15, installs. 3,700

Van Doorn, George F. to Isaac Halstead. Prospect pl. P. M. Aug. 13, 1 year, 5 %. 1,500

Van Ostrand, Margaret wife of and John W. to Williamsburgh Savings Bank. Pellington pl, w s, 272.8 n Brooklyn and Jamaica plank road, runs west 100 x north 100 x east 99.2 x southeast to pl, x south 98.3. Aug. 24, 1 year. 5 %. 3,000

Wade, Elizabeth E. to William Laytin et al. trustees William Laytin. Madison st, s e s, 403.8 s w Knickerbocker av, 18x100. Aug. 14, 3 years, 5 %. 2,300

Waldron, Alexander to Hans S. Christian. 3d av, s w cor 45th st, 40.2x100. Aug. 3, 1 year, 5 %. 1,180

Wallau, Marie L. to The Title Guarantee and Trust Co. State st, n s, 141.8 e Hoyt st, 16.8 x100. Aug. 20, 1 year, 5 %. 4,500

Wasmer, Herman J. to Title Guarantee and Trust Co. Buffalo av, e s, 138.7 n Atlantic av, 19.3x100. Aug. 24, 3 years, 5 %. 2,000

Same to same. Buffalo av, e s, 157.10 n Atlantic av, 19.3x100. Aug. 24, 3 years, 5 %. 2,000

Weeking, Andrew to Sven Johanson. Belmont av. P. M. Aug. 20, installs, 3½ %. 450

Same to Maria E. Schneider. Same property. Aug. 20, 3 years. 800

Werner, Theodor H. to Maria Fink. De Kalb av, n w s, 200 n e Hamburg av, 25x100. Aug. 24, 3 years, 5 %. 3,500

Same to Louis Fink. De Kalb av, n w s, 175 n e Hamburg av, 25x100. Aug. 24, 3 years, 5 %. 3,500

Westphal, Paul to William Ulmer. Troutman st, s e s, 92.1 n e Wyckoff av, 25x100; Wyckoff av, n e s, 25 s e Troutman st, 25x93.5x25x 93.9; Wyckoff av, n e s, 50 s e Troutman st, 25x94.6x25x93.5 Aug. 19, 1 year, 5 %. 4,000

Whigam, Bertha E. wife of and Cornelius J. to George A. Jarvis. Van Buren st, s w cor Throop av, 20.9x80. Aug. 20, 3 years, 5 %. 5,000

Whitlock, Harmon A. to Magdalena Brommer widow. Essex st, w s, 100 n Arlington av, 20 x100. Aug. 22, 3 years. 2,000

Wichmann, Sophie wife of and Peter to The Dime Savings Bank of Brooklyn. Jay st, e s, 46.6 n Tillary st, 43.6x57.6x43.7x57.6. Aug. 24, 1 year, 5 %. 500

Wieler, John to Rosalie Heilmann. 46th st, n s, 300 e 4th av, 20x100.2. Aug. 24, 3 years, 5 %. 1,800

Wilder, Edward K. to Edward H. Wilson. Stuyvesant av, Chauncey st. P. M. Aug. 20, 1 year, 5 %. 3,000

Same to John Gordon. Same property. 2d mort. Aug. 20, 1 year, 5 %. 1,000

Wildner, Emil F. to Elizabeth Lautenkloz. Madison st, s s, 150 w Hamburg av, 20x100. Aug. 20, due Jan. 1, 1894. 1,200

Wilhelm, Elizabeth widow to Joseph Liebmann and Theodore Obermyer. Union av, south cor Scholes st, 30x75. Aug. 20, 5 years, 5 %. 1,500

Wingerath, William to Read Gordon and ano. exrs., &c., William H. Dilworth. 16th st, n s, 192.11 w 8th av, 18.9x100. Aug. 21, 3 years. 4,000

Witt, Herman and Theresa his wife to Charles Ernst. Bushwick pl, w s, 80.5 s Montrose av, 23.2x77x25x84.3. Aug. 12, 5 years, 5 %. 1,800

Woods, Rebecca A. wife of and Alexander to The Union Co-operative Building and Loan Assoc. Bergen st, n s, 200.9 e Troy av, 56.3x 138.7x—x119.1. Aug. 21, installs, 5 %. 4,400

Wheeler, John J. to John Gerity. Wolcott st. P. M. Aug. 26, 5 years, 4 %. 2,000

MORTGAGES----ASSIGNMENTS.

NEW YORK CITY.

August 21 to 27—Inclusive.

Adler, Simon and Henry S. Herrman to Rosa B. de Casanova. $1,000

Bowers, John M. trustee Franklin Osgood to Louise L. Williams. consid. omitted

Boettner, John C., Christian Hachemeister, Frederick A. Ringler exrs. George Ringler and John C. Boettner exrs. William Orth to George Ringler & Co., a corporation. nom

Boettner, John C. and Christian Hachemeister, of George Ringler & Co., to same. nom

Behre, John H., Brooklyn, to Frederick A. Behre. 3,000

Butts, Augustus E. to Walter E. Ward. 1,000

Cummins, Patrick, Bernard Lenehan and Richard W. Kane, of R. W. Kane & Co., to Hugh Young, Chicago, Ill. 2,784

Cheesebro, Denison P. to William S. Whitman. 1,300

Decker, John W. to R. Clarence Dorsett. nom

Dunn, Alfred B. to Mitchell A. C. Levy. 3,000

Eddy, Sarah J. extrx. James Eddy to Caroline F. Hoelzle. 5,055

Ford, Henry W. trustee Augustus H. Ward dec'd to The Lawyers Title Ins. Co. of New York. 16,475

Same to same. 16,475

Fayen, John F. to William L. Strong. 4,047

Gillender, Augustus T. to G. Emily Reynolds, Piermont, N. Y. 15,000

Goodman, Sarah to Frederick P. Forster 3,500

Garrison, David, George C. Reukauff and Edward B. Staggers, of Hall & Garrison, to Henry A. Renkauff. nom

Greenwood, Mary A. to Robert S. Rudd exr. Joseph Rudd. 2 assigns. nom

Gebhard, William H. exr. Frederick C. Gebhard to August Limbert trustee Frederick C. Gebhard dec'd. nom

Gordon, Katie to Erastus Crawford. 4,500

Hays, Jacob to Hubert Van Wagenen and ano. guards. of children of David Louderback. 1,000

Hellman, Myer to Gustav Lange. 3,000

Hornberger, George and Louisa his wife to Elias Jacobs. 6,000

Hyatt, George E, to John B. Whiting trustee. nom

Haggerty, George A. to Thomas Hagan. 4,000

Herrman, Jennie to Frederick P. Forster. 4,000

Howe, Robie S. to The Title Guarantee and Trust Co. 1,000

Harsett, James F. to The Title Guarantee and Trust Co. 1,200

Kraus, Charles T. and August C. Hassey to Louisa C. Miller. 6,450

Leland, Francis L. to William Fletcher. Re-recorded. 10,000

Middlebrook, Frederic J., Brooklyn, to Alexander S. Webb trustee of Catharine S. Coles dec'd. 11,000

Mertens, William to Catharina F. Krug. Freiburg, Germany. 18,149

Montag, Michael to Herman Hering. 2,000

Marks, Cecil A. to Hugo S. Mack. nom

Ormiston, Annie to Sumner R. Stone and ano. exrs. Caroline M. Hitchcock. 4,000

Potts, Arthur to Charles J. Gillis. 6,000

Rothschild, Matilda to Peter Doelger. 1,100

Richards, Nancy L. wife of Joseph to Susan E. Ferris. 3,000

Sire, Meyer L. to Catharine A. F. Casanova. 1,500

Same to same. 1,300

Same to same. 1,400

The Canda-Mathews Mfg. Co. (Lim.) to Simon Adler and Henry S. Herrman. 1,790

Title Guarantee and Trust Co. to The Mercantile Trust Co. as agent of E. D. M. Waterman. 5,000

Title Guarantee and Trust Co. to Eleanor S. Keys. 7,500

Uihlien, Frank A. to Charles F. and Dora Hally. 6,000

Webb, Alexander S. trustee for Catherine S. Coles dec'd to Louise L. Williams. consid. omitted

Winslow, Edward to Henry W. Ford trustee Augustus H. Ward. 25,000

Waters, Rosa to Francis J. Schnugg. 9,075

Whiting, John B. trustee to Henry W. Ford trustee of Augustus H. Ward dec'd. 16,000

Whiting, John B. trustee to Henry W. Ford trustee Augustus H. Ward dec'd. Re-recorded. 16,000

Wilmot, De Borden to Susan O. Hoffman, Flushing, L. I. 5,000

KINGS COUNTY.

August 20 to 26—Inclusive.

Antonides, Ida and ano. exrs., &c., John Antonides to Margaret wife of John F. Berry. $7,000

Armstrong, Jane individ. and as admrx. of Sarah E. Dunley to William B. Dunley, Jane and George W. Armstrong. 4,000

Bentley, John to The John St. M. E. Church Trust Fund Soc., New York. 2,500

Berckmeier, Albert to Walter J. Klots. 1,400

Bruggner, John to Mary J. Pillon. other consid. and 200

Brown, Thomas to William C. O'Keeffe and James H. McKenna. 1,500

Benham, John C. exr. Sarah Benham to Charles A. Murphy. 6,056

Same to same. 2,910

Brockmann, Henry to Henry Nieland, Jr. 1,375

Cochran, Israel Y. to Rope & Co. nom

Cooke, Nathaniel B. and ano. exrs Leander Sarles to Leander H. Sarles guard. Susan A. Sarles. 3,000

Cohn, Amalie to Nathan Levy. 750

Craig, George A. to The Tilly & Van Hagen Co. 1,209

Same to The New York Gas Fixture Co. 300

Same to The Bulmer Lumber Co. (Lim). 1,900

Same to George C. Hollister. 600

Same to John C. Austin and George Mohrmann. 1,300

Same to Raeburn Latourette & Co. 500

Same to Mary J. Pillon. 1,000

Same to Charles S. Lynan. nom

Same to same. 500

Same to The Dugan Mfg. Co., Brooklyn. 480

Same to William Goetschins. 200

Same to The Hyde & Gload Mfg. Co. (Lim.) 475

Dexheimer, Charles to Anna M. Bopp. nom

Same to same. nom

Driscoll, Elizabeth F. to James C. Brower. 2,000

French, Albert L. to William C. O'Keefe and James H. McKenna. nom

Fletcher, George, John W. and Joseph T. to Phebe R. Kissam. 700

Franklin Trust Co. to The Brooklyn Savings Bank. 175,000

Godwin, Parke to Kate C. Henderson et al. trustees Isaac Henderson dec'd. 2,450

Heiberger, Anton and Franziska his wife to Albert Karutz. 10,500

Knight, Mark B. to Hans S. Christian. 100

Kingsley, Isabe to William H. Sage. 2,000

Looff, John H. to Caroline Broistedt. 5,000

McLaughlin, Edmund M., Jr., and ano. exrs. Edmund McLaughlin to Peter Kramer. 6,000

Moss, Frank exrs. Maltby G. Lane to Durias Seacordof, of New Rochelle, N. Y. 2,256

Murphy, Charles A. to John C. Benham, of Hudson, N. Y. 6,056

Same to same. 2,910

Osborn, Charles W. and ano. exrs. Peter B. Schoonmaker to Martin V. Schoonmaker. 3 assigns. nom

Ostick, Thomas and Margaret his wife to William Hunt. nom

Packard, Ralph G. to Charles Dexheimer. 500

Packard, Josiah S. to Charles Dexheimer. 500

Pope, Hannah to George Self and Harriet M. his wife. 2,600

Rudolph, Henry to Mina Roswall. 1,000

Robbins, Aaron S. to Olin G. Wallridge. 15,000

Rushmore, Anna M. to David A. Fithian. 200

Sage, William H. to Charles E. Rogers. 2,000

Simon, Semche to Marks Kirshbaum. nom

Stuckey, Alfred to William H. Stuckey. nom

Tappen, John B. C., Glen Cove, admr. Mary Tappen to John B. C. Tappen. 4,000

Same to same. 3,000

Same to Eugene Tappen. 1,000

The German-American Real Estate Title Guarantee Co. to Edwin Sherman guard. for Albertine. Frederic and Clara Dav. 3,000

Title Guarantee and Trust Co. to Giddings H. Pinney. 6,000

Same to Elizabeth Briggs. 2,500

Same to Brooklyn Trust Co. 10,000

Same to Robert A. Lindsay. 4,500

Same to same. 4,000

Same to Franklin Trust Co. 17,115

Same to same. 31,037

Same to same. 20,000

Same to same. 33,051

Same to George B. Forrester. 1,900

Underhill, Edward C. exr. Abraham Underhill to Sophia Loffler. 3,000

Willets, John T. and ano. exrs. Hannah W. Underhill to John T. Willets admr. of Lydia T. Post. 3,600

JUDGMENTS.

In these lists of judgments the names alphabetically arranged, and which are first on each line, are those of the judgment debtor. The letter (D) means judgment for deficiency (*) means not summoned. (†) signifies that the first name is fictitious, real name being unknown. Judgments entered during the week, and satisfied before day of publication, do not appear in this column, but in list of Satisfied Judgments.

NEW YORK CITY.

August

25 Arden, Henry—Title Guarantee and Trust Co. $41 80

25 Angell, Harold G—Danbury Nat Bank 3,671 85

25 Arnold, John F—Jacob Hoffmann Brewing Co. 392 64

25 the same——the same 563 61

26 Asmus, Charles—F W Devoe & Co. 81 34

26 Aaronson, Alex I—State Bank 526 53

27 Ames, John F—James Phelan 6,343 64

26 Allen, William S—Edward Kirkpatrick 158 14
27 the same—Hempstead Bank 427 43
27 Anderson, John—A P Dienst 158 75
27*Altman, Bernard; Altman, Samuel } S P Hyman 3,000 96
28 Allen, Melville E—G W Brower 418 19
22 Bernard, Joseph—Joseph Schrage 116 42
22 Benedix, Gustave—Ignatz Weissenborn 159 45
22 Bailey, William—Joel Swope 41 22
24 Bernstein, Philip—B B Zippert 818 49
24 Banzett, William E—G R Hill 346 24
24 Brockhuyzen, John H—Elizabeth M Barry 24 50
24 Borrmann, Ludwig—C H Krug 1,303 05
24 Beresford, Walter S—J R Platt 273 14
25 Brockway, Frank S—Emilio Arecco 139 37
25 Burke, Michael L—J M Griggs 267 50
25 Baker, William—N Y Glass Co..costs 23 47
25 Butler, Jacob D—John Birkenstock 222 81
25 Barnum, Stephen C—Ernest Fouquet 358 99
25 Bordell, Ann—Herrman Weiller 85 67
25†Bailey, William D—Rufus Waterhouse 367 19
25 Butler, Frank—F A Bartram 150 37
25*Brown, Thomas J—Jacob Hoffman Brewing Co 568 61
26 Burke, Michael L—J M Griggs 267 50
26 Branagan, John—Richard Vom Hofe 344 24
26 Beh, Mary A—J G Johnson 495 81
26 Bertin, Paul—Paul Guerin 6,604 54
27 Bonnell, John H—Carl Goepel 5,281 59
27 Bonnell, John Harper—Bank of Harlem 1,017 34
27 Barry, T—C P Chapman 87 42
28*Bradley, Alfred B—First Nat Bank 2,257 37
28 Bonnell, John Harper—Dobbs Ferry Bank 1,004 62
28 Braendle, Edmund—Victoria Natural Water Spring Co 101 49
28 Benson, Andrew E—D W King 238 18
28 Bonnell, John Harper—Chatham Nat Bank 585 65
22*Cotes, Henry S—J W MacKnight 334 31
22 Carpenter, Robert B; Cornell, Joseph; Cornell, Samuel } Rudolph Rannow 1,124 62
24 Cambreling, Stephen C—John Mason 198 20
25 Cameron, Allen J; Cameron, Letitia } C A Spalding 137 44
25 Crosby, George—Ernest Pouquet 358 99
25 Cohen, Casper; Cohen, Charles } Max Bernstein 77 31
25 Cady, Edward W—L C Josephs 270 09
25 Cummings, William—L H Viemeister 122 81
25 Christie, William—J G Batterson 961 46
25*Chatfield, Oscar—Frederick Roeth 97 87
25 the same—the same 97 90
26 Cooper, Louis; Cooper, Anna } William Faust 98 41
27 Cohen, Barnett—Samuel Zirinsky 95 85
28*Connor, John R—Clara Delafield 131 75
24 Dolan, James F—Millstone Granite Co 5,894 07
26 Deeves, John R—Robert Wilson costs 86 09
26 Dreyfuss, Bernhard—E D St George 301 72
28 Delabarre, Arthur P—T H Beeckman 328 76
24 Fischman, Joseph—Louis Rosen 131 72
24 Finkle, Alexander I—Metropolitan Telephone and Telegraph Co 125 87
25*Falk, Isaac; Falk, Zachariah; Falk, Joseph J; Falk, George W } Albert Tower 1,859 09
25 Fitzgerald, Matthew J—Katie E Fitzgerald 180 50
26 Friedland, Abraham S—State Bank 526 52
27 Fruchtenicht, John—H C Schrader 170 06
27 Fuller, Eugene F—C M Berrian 88 78
27 Feist, Henry—J B Goodman 39 88
27 Feld, Anne—Franz Eberlein 118 70
27 Flannigan, Mary—J F Heinbockel 335 00
27*Fleming, Michael J—Edge Hill Wine Co 134 30
27 Finberg, Jacob—Catherine Bagot 97 15
25 Gardner, George; Gardner, Charles E } Henry Wehle 105 78
25 Griswold, Margaret D—H M Brigham 445 00
26*Greene, Edward C—Paul Guerin 6,604 54
27 Gleason, John—Edge Hill Wine Co 134 30
27 Graham, James H—Franz Zahn 72 58
22 Hamert, Frank—Moses Guggenheim 244 60
24 Hankins, Samuel M—S A Johnson 402 34
24 Hay, James, Sr; Hay, James, Jr; Hay, John; Hay, Archibald } Sylvester Sawyer 194 72
24 Howell, Eugene N—Clinton Bank 5,041 57
25 Hecksher, Meyer N—Tradesmen's Nat Bank 4,026 18
25 Hartung, Lorenzo R—George Hagemeyer 1,361 40
25 the same—G W Lumb 187 52
25 Howes, Elbert D—Henry Wehle 105 78
25 Halsey, Charles B—O O Clark 96 90
25 Bunold, Joseph—Jacob Hoffmann Brewing Co 641 36
25 Horsfall, John B—Frederick Roeth 97 87
25 the same—the same 97 90
26 Howell, Eugene N—Bank of America 4,554 21
27 Hoyt, Russell P—C H Harman 580 26
27 Harper, William D—Carl Goepel 5,281 59
27 Harper, William Durbin—Bank of Harlem 1,017 34
27 Hofele, F W—C P Chapman 75 11
27 Heller, Emil—[illegible] Westheimer 34 78
27 Hirschfield, David—John Baehr 127 60
27†Hallheimer, Martin—C F Oxley 90 72
27 Hart, Alexander R—Western Nat Bank 816 33
27 Harper, William D—the same 494 08
28 Harper, William D—Dobbs Ferry Bank 1,004 62
28 Hemmens, John—William Ganseberg 144 75
28 Hunt, George S; Hunt, William H; Hunt, Caroline O } Germania Bank 3,795 56
28 Harper, William D—Chatham Nat Bank 585 65
22 Irvine, Allan A—J W MacKnight 334 31
27 Isaacs, Nathan—C L Cohn 87 91
22 Johnson, Charles E—Joseph Yesky 162 06
26 Jackson, Henry—Abraham Seligsberg, admr 3,498 20
24 Kearns, Thomas—S J Lanahan 970 46
25 Koch, George—Henrietta Rice 133 42
25 Kallman, Moritz—Hulda Fuss 67 50
26 Knox, J Amory—South Texas Nat Bank 328 46
26*Kalmus, Philip—Dwight Ashley 275 70
27 Knauth, Percival—Philip Van Volkenburgh, Jr, admr costs 254 00
22 Longworth, Thomas F—H W Hass 131 74
24 Leibold, Charles—John McCormick 189 60
24 Leopold, Henry—Anna Leopold costs 195 17
25 L'Hommedieu, Sylvester Y—Danbury Nat Bank 3,671 85
25 Lynch, William—Jacob Hoffmann Brewing Co 458 11
26 Levy, Samuel—Alexander Goldberg 777 20
26 Leon, Charles—Tobias Lesser 850 88
26 Leigh, Louis—Henry Pohts 157 72
26 Lamberton, Alfred S—Cady & Nelson Co (Lim) 300 32
27 Lyon, Charles J—C H Evans 138 12
28 La Badie, Joseph E—J A McElhinny 259 50
24 Moore, John—Alfred Hopcroft 110 73
24 Metzger, Charles F—G L Kelty 493 90
24*Marxson, Oscar—C H Krug 1,303 05
25 Muller, Mary R; Muller, Lewis M } J L Kearney 452 86
25 Mayhew, Edward C—G A Radtke 348 22
25 Miller, William H—J R Berbling 229 85
25 Murphy, Daniel—J J Froelich 167 00
26 Myers, Charles S—Dwight Ashley 275 70
27 Martin, Robert C—Highland Nat Bank 20,227 98
27 Montgomery, James—C C Dodge 566 53
27 Mulrain, Frances—George Wood, assignee 77 91
27 Miller, Robert H—Western Nat Bank 542 70
28 Magill, Harry N W—Edward Siegman 631 43
28 Meyer, Samuel—Benjamin Fitch 200 93
28 the same—D C Cowan 181 52
28 Mahnken, Maria—J C Fraser 46 50
26 McManus, Patrick H—C H Willson 241 46
26 McCullagh, Matilda—James Culgin 149 08
27 McGowan, Patrick; McGowan, Peter } Boynton Furnace Co 414 85
22 Nigey, Lena—Edward Siegman 190 25
25 Nesbit, William H—Rand Drill Co 181 57
25 Nash, Isidore—Jacob Delmonte 261 40
26 Newburg, Jacob A—Henry Heywood 85 50
26 Nostrand, Warner H—E T Throop 1,055 73
27 Nielson, Max—O W Van Campen 128 00
28 Nightingale, James—H T Gaddum 1,158 54
25 O'Hea, Michael—Long Island Brewery 120 22
27 Ollendorf, George—C J Billwiller 155 00
24†Pohlmann, Mary—J E Bernard 172 68
25 Price, William J—Gilbert & Barker Mfg Co 104 00
26 Parker, Orrin C—J H Hentz 241 17
26 Perbacs, Gaysa—Robert Jones 46 91
27 Peck, Nathan—Highlands Nat Bank of Newburgh 20,227 98
27 Piper, William—Joseph Beck 202 00
27 Pfaeffle, Frederick—J J Froelich 102 00
27 Patterson, Charles H—M C Kellogg 325 52
28 Pitts, James—First Nat Bank 2,257 37
24¶Quinn, Michael J—P C Grening 531 60
26 Quick, Woodward F—C H Willson 538 80
26 the same—the same 241 46
22 Rodermond, Richard B—Edward Smith & Co 93 42
22 Roberts, William H H—Robert Rae 149 92
24 Rogers, Myron W—F W Devoe & Co 713 43
24 Ross, William H—August Muller 274 02
25 Rogers, Myron W—D C Belknap 208 11
25 Reilly, Lawrence—Jacob Hoffmann Brewing Co 442 61
25*Rossi, Louis—J G Batterson 961 46
27 Radice, Pasquino S—Eagle Brewery 224 00
28 Root, James H—Chatham Nat Bank 585 65
22 Spiewack, Louis—Louis Rosen 113 12
22 Silverstein, Morris; Silverstein, Samuel } Edward Siegman 424 77
24 Steinmetz, M V B—August Muller 70 93
24 Stiller, Julius—W E Callender 26 50
25 Sause, Richard E—William Walsmann 139 52
25 Sause, Richard C—R J Chapman Co 100 97
25 Strom, Nathan—Sigismund Haubenstock 31 50
25 Schaefer, Edmund; Schaefer, Carl; Schaefer, Edward } J T Lamm 102 24
26 Schultz, Henry—Metropolitan Telephone and Telegraph Co 86 37
27 Sternberger, Morris S—Joseph Simpson 534 98
27†Schwert, Mary—Rosa Herschman 63 07
27 Sutter, Alexander—Amelia Westheimer 45 50
27 Schilt, Isaac F—L S Schilt 318 87
27*Samuels, Isaac; Samuels, Leo } Danenberg & Coles 147 00
27 Stark, Isidor; Stark, Edward J; Stark, Gustav } Sali Stark 3,017 50

¶ *Editor* RECORD AND GUIDE:

The judgment entered against M. J. Quinn is a misunderstanding. THORNTON, EARLE & KIENDL.

27 Schreiber, John H—G W Venable 71 04
27 Schonberger, Louis—G B Erdelyi 34 50
28 Schilt, Isaac F—Herman Levy 119 73
28 Shirley, Charles—William Ganseberg 144 75
28 Simmons, Patrick J—William Ottmann & Co 77 78
28 Sutherland, William—Clara Delafield 131 75
22 Smith, John M, as trees of Brooklyn Lodge No 38, Order of Tonti—John Coar 54 00
22 The Fibrone Mfg Co—Charles Kunzo 345 72
23 Flour City Life Assoc—Life Union 1,228 72
22 Banker & Campbell Co (Lim)—John Wilkinson Co 331 05
22 Mankey Decorative Co—Patrick Moore 90 36
22 the same—I T Williams 467 51
22 the same—the same 697 23
24 The Mayor, Aldermen, &c—F S Beard 684 14
24 Cape Breton Construction Co—Klim, Linder & Bauer Lithographing Co 131 74
24 American Standard Electric Light Co—the same 224 34
25 Banker & Campbell Co (Lim)—James Huggins 205 07
25 The Home Ins Co—J J Gorman, Sheriff 1,026 14
25 the same—the same costs 27 50
25 The Flour City Life Assoc—Charles Schwarzwaelder 5,094 79
25 The McWilliams' Printing Co—James Mitchell 140 24
25 The Taconic Marble Co—J S Newberry 286 47
26 The Mayor, Aldermen, &c—Louisa D Kane 17,799 99
26 the same—W G Langdon 58,514 31
26 the same—the same 57,461 44
26 the same—Matthew Wilks 19,767 18
26 the same—the same 59,416 89
26 the same—Cecilia L Nottbeck 58,348 10
26 The American Loan and Trust Co—Louis Bauer 2,047 08
26 the same—the same 2,046 75
26 the same—the same 1,029 55
26 the same—the same 2,054 79
26 Banker & Campbell Co (Lim)—John Wilkinson Co 908 51
26 the same—the same 846 69
27 Ursuline Convent of St Teresas, N Y—J P Koch, Jr 654 93
27 the same—Patrick Dougherty 1,492 20
27 J H Bonnell & Co (Lim)—Carl Goepel 5,281 59
27 The American-Scotch Iron Co—T G Strong 1,028 91
27 J H Bonnell & Co (Lim)—Western Nat Bank 429 97
27 the same—the same 1,597 15
27 the same—the same 816 33
27 the same—the same 494 08
27 the same—the same 542 70
27 E B Benjamin Mfg Co—Nat Park Bank 1,009 47
28 The Hillis Plantation Coffee Co—Martha G Seggermann 148 87
28 Banker & Campbell Co (Lim)—L B Hamilton 212 17
28 the same—the same 87 37
28 The McElwee Mfg Co—First Nat Bank of Wellsville 2,257 37
28 Banker & Campbell Co (Lim)—J P McGovern 190 70
28 J H Bonnell & Co (Lim)—Dobbs Ferry Bank 1,004 62
28 Taconic Marble Co—W & J Sloane 545 26
22 Thorne, Arthur—F W Devoe & Co 713 43
22 Toher, Owen—William Coogan 30 00
24 Troper, Louis—P Libeman 80 23
25 Thorne, Arthur—D C Belknap 208 11
25 Trautwein, William—Adolphe Halbran 494 15
26 Thode, William F—J M Alsgood 248 38
27 Tiernan, Hugh P—Robert Currie 120 39
27†Tiernan, H P—Nathaniel Waterbury 92 98
27 Thompson, Walter R—J H Ernst 134 00
28 Thompson, Joseph R H—Sims Lumber Co 472 08
28 Tandlich, Henry—Lewis Sylvester 117 04
27*Ullrich, Carl—H C Schrader 170 06
26 Van Voorhis, Cornelius W—W M Woods, exr 785 11
28 Van Volkenburg, Philip, Jr, admr Antonio J Moderno—Percival Knauth 184 62
22 Woerner, Albert M—Valentin Kolb 397 96
24 Weill, Leopold; Weill, John } M F Schenkeisen 71 30
24 Wolff, Edward L—L J Pooler 22 50
25 Walker, Frank R—Wm Cabble Excelsior Wire Mfg Co 171 33
25 White, Robert J—Park & Tilford 128 50
25 Welch, H H—F P Gordon 5,198 83
26 Weinberg, Jacob—Jacob Delmonte 261 40
27 Wynne, Henry G—Harriet Eads 1,023 00
27 Willis, Henry M—J A Frazee 87 20
27 Webster, Thomas—Third Nat Bank 2,014 99
28 Ward, James—Stephen Ward 228 68
28 Walsh, Mary J—Jacob Engel 111 83
22 Yost, Fernando—J L Mott Iron Works 767 37

KINGS COUNTY.

August

22 Adams, Frank E—D L White $328 44
25 Anderson, Franz V—W F Hooney 72 88
25 Anderson, Mary—W F Hooney 72 88
26 Adams, Frank—Third National Bank of Buffalo 354 93
21 Behrens, Henry—D Weirich 137 67
22 Bedell, Edwin J—D L White 328 44
25 Baumgras, Clarence M—G F Chapman 233 73

26 Bisinkoff, Morris—B Blank 61 67

21 Craigen, George J—J J Snyder........ 515 30

24 Carpenter, Charles H — Brooklyn Union Pub Co.......................... 201 81

24 Chase, Henry A—J D Mallonee...... 97 19

25 Crofoot, John B—M F Brown......... 283 36

25 Commerce, Fanny / Cohn, Joseph } C Goldstein...... 147 17

25 Cook, Frank—J A Webster........... 95 38

22 Doggrell, William—Venable & Heyman.......................... 632 02

27 Duffy, Michael J—Lang, Bernheimer & Co.......................... 325 47

27 Darcy, William, sued as John—John H E Sand.......................... 70 33

22 Ehlers, Henry—N Y Veal and Mutton Co.......................... 95 62

20 Franke, Frederick A—J McCormick.. 179 62

22 Flanagan, William L—W A Abbott.. 261 96

25 Fischman, Joseph—L Rosen.......... 121 73

25 Friedlein, Anna—John H Hoeft...... 215 09

25 Fitzpatrick, Lawrence—H J Braker.. 49 30

27 Fleming, Thomas J—C Schlesinger... 104 05

20 Griffith, Charles E—J McCormick.... 277 16

21 Godley, Jonathan L / Godley, Voorhees I } Fidelity and Casualty Co, N Y 98 53

21 Gordon, Isaac—J Shapiro............ 86 50

20 Heilsborn, Henry—G Merritt......... 47 53

21 Hanson, Andrew—A & M Berliner... 137 00

22 Hamlin, John—Bradley & Co......... 161 94

24 Hornborg, Axel G—M Louise Jeauson.......................... 201 74

27 Hutchins, Edgar A—J Woods......... 32 60

21 Kloeck, Carl A / Kloeck, Jr, Carl A } D A Vanhorne.. 396 52

21 Kerrigan, Mary—Henry Strauss..... 79 44

22 Kirkland, William—D L White...... 323 44

26 the same——Third Nat Bank of Buffalo.......................... 354 93

21 Lowther, Sarah E—Oxley, Giddings & Enos.......................... 77 00

26 Lake, Louis N—T C Oakley.......... 459 49

21 Maxfeld, Mrs T R / Maxfield, T R } S M Hoye...... 110 09

21† Meyer, "Mary"—M Edesheimer..... 96 60

21† Meyer, "Gazina"—R G Thomas...... 301 00

21 Meyer, George—T Cushman 90 00

21 Moran, John C—G Hollister......... 203 00

22 Martin, Henry—Venable & Heyman. 34 43

24 Marshall, William H—H M Birkett.. 409 59

25 McKennee, Joseph H—Walter T Klots & Bros Sons.......................... 228 08

25 Muller, Mary R / Muller, Lewis M } J L Kearney..... 452 86

26 Murphy, Daniel—Joseph J Froelich .. 107 00

26 Metzger, Charles F—G L Kelty...... 493 90

25 O'Neil, John M—National Cash Register Co.......................... 27 60

20 Pearson, Eugene—S B Solomon...... 176 25

21 Perrine, Howland D—H C Hardy..... 173 03

22 Perbacs, Gavsa—R Jones........... 46 91

24 Parmer, Joseph—D H Roberts....... 390 41

26 Potter, Samuel P—F H Smith........ 82 28

26 Richardson, Charles A—J Brugger... 140 25

26 Ross, J Stewart—R Fischer.......... 556 03

20 Scott, Charles B—S B Solomon....... 176 25

21 Schliep, Louis C—H Miles........... 32 75

22 Smith, John M treasurer—J Coar.... 54 00

24 Simons, Emanuel—G W Evans....... 38 10

21 The Baker & Campbell Co (Lim)—J N Goldbacher.......................... 1,860 71

22 The New York Breweries Co (Lim)—W A Abbott.......................... 758 19

22 Treasurer of Brooklyn Lodge No 58 of The Order of Tonti—John Coar.... 54 00

25 Timony, Mary A—Thurber, Whyland & Co.......................... 132 21

25 The Fred Hower Brewing Co—A S Minner.......................... 32 25

25 Trooper, Louis—Libeman & Mayer... 80 23

26 Tayntor, Albert I—S Perry Smith... 28 90

26 Tilman, John F—R O Ernst.......... 133 55

26 Thode, William F—J M Alsgood..... 248 38

26 The Fred Hower Brewing Co—M Levy 227 19

21 Wisbauer, Jorge / ‡Wisbauer, "Lena" } E Calman...... 105 00

24 Wardrobe, Thomas—Coleman Carriage and Wagon Co 279 67

22 Yost, Fernando — J L Mott Iron Works.......................... 767 37

SATISFIED JUDGMENTS.

NEW YORK.

August 22 to 28—Inclusive.

Baker, Samuel H—James McMurray. (1889).. $42 50

Blake, Matthew / Baldwin, Delia } William De Lamater. (1891).......... 113 22

Crandall, William E—John Morrow. (1887) .. 553 21

Same——same. (1887).......... 284 37

Same——J W McKnight. (1887).......... 1,050 24

Same——R E Wilcox. (1887).......... 369 35

*Curiel, Herman K—W W Watkins. (1891)... 993 33

Dalzen, Allan C—Adolph Luthy. (1879)....... 3,315 89

Darling, William S—J H Van Blarcom. (1891) 1,275 17

*Flanagan, William L—W A Abbott. (1891)... 261 96

Grumberg, Caroline, admrx—Mary Dietz. ('91) 77 12

Hiller, George—Max Lehmann. (1891)........ 160 30

Hillery, James M—E A Decker. (1891)........ 461 31

Hamel, Francis—F A Van Dyke. (1877)....... 1,100 38

*Hauser, Julius G—John Barnum. (1891)..... 628 82

Hartwell, Louise M—C H Willson. (1891) 229 96

*Hopkins, Franklin W—Albert Hurwitz. (1890) 253 19

Kilpatrick, Walter F—First Nat Bank of Chattanooga. (1891).......... 2,001 20

Lincoln, Lowell as assignee John T Plummer & Co—F C Linde. (1891) 176 57

Lyon, Frederick W—Isaac Gottscho. (1887)... 181 50

Lyons, William M—August Goertz. (1890).... 354 90

Little, E Knox—J W McKnight. (1887)....... 1,050 24

Same——R E Wilcox. (1887).......... 369 35

Mayor, &c—Hannah Cohen. (1890).......... 8,378 88

Same——same. (1891).......... 77 97

Same——R A Witthaus. (1891).......... 519 37

Same——J H Strahan. (1891).......... 5,000 00

Same——Timothy Donovan. (1891).......... 420 05

Same——M H Moore. (1891).......... 143 19

Same——A McL Hamilton. (1891).......... 519 37

Same——Oliver Von Courtlandt. (1891)..... 139 28

Same——Jerome Brady. (1891) 272 59

Same——Hannah Cohen. (1891).......... 436 75

Same——Peter Larkin, admr. (1891)........ 2,000 00

Same——G L Green. (1891).......... 103 84

Mayor, &c—Thomas Ferris. (1891).......... 86 70

Same——W F Thompson. (1891).......... 295 42

Same——C W Ackerman. (1891).......... 59 67

Same——W P Mitchell. (1890).......... 8,969 24

§Morse, G Livingston—Holmes & Griggs Mfg Co. (1888).......... 3,257 76

McGovern, James S—People State N Y. (1890) 100 00

*McNiece, James—E E Ensley. (1891).......... 185 43

Mann, Charles—Jacob Ruppert. (1884).......... 227 68

Minden, Michael—H S Christiansen. (1885)... 58 89

Newman, Hugh—People State N Y. (1890).... 100 00

*N Y Breweries Co (Lim)—W A Abbott. (1891) 758 19

Pyke, Robert S—F A Van Dyke. (1877)....... 1,100 38

Plummer, John F and Albert T—J H Van Blarcom. (1891).......... 1,273 17

Roylance, Edgar W—First Nat Bank of Chattanooga. (1891).......... 2,001 20

Ryan, Michael—Mark Goodwin. (1891)........ 335 60

Ross, George—Joseph Bierhoff. (1891)....... 168 78

Smith, Albert E and Elizabeth K—Joseph Bierhoff. (1891).......... 168 78

Sharkey, William—H S Christiansen. (1885).. 58 89

Stevens, Henry E, Jr—First Nat Bank of Chattanooga. (1891).......... 2,001 20

Schlachter, John—Willson, Adams & Co.(1888) 249 38

Stiebeling, George C — Henry Feldman. (1889).......... 413 03

Tuttle, Ezra A—J W McKnight. (1887)....... 1,050 24

Same——R E Wilcox. (1887) 369 35

Von Raven, Leo—William Kramer. (1891) ... 607 65

*Woolner, Adolph, Jr—W W Watkins. (1891). 993 33

*White, Stephen V—Albert Hurwitz. (1890)... 252 19

*Vacated by order of Court. †Suspended on Appeal ‡Released. §Reversal. ‖Satisfied by Execution.

KINGS COUNTY.

August 21 to 27—Inclusive.

Hawley, Lucius P—A J Nutting. (1891)........ $154 77

Haack, Wilhelmina—W Hope. (1886).......... 157 26

Jackson, Homer B—Benham & Stoutenborough. (1881).......... 256 00

Losee, Albert—S S Birdsall. (1881).......... 1,109 01

Maurer, Jacobine—Kraussmann & Fredericks. (1887).......... 88 39

Reinhart, James M—Ida Peil. (1888) 632 39

Robinson, Mary A—Sarah Wortman. (1890) (Vacated).......... 86 25

Same——same. (1887) (Vacated).......... 708 49

Same——same. (1889) (Vacated).......... 101 41

Stockholm, Clara—P J Mahoney. (1891) 159 28

Sanford, James A—H H Frost. (1891).......... 100 00

The Brooklyn City and Newtown R R Co—Emily J Pike. (1891).......... 1,714 79

MECHANICS' LIENS.

NEW YORK CITY.

Aug.

22 Thirty-ninth st, n s, 125 w 11th av, 100x100. Rufus Darrow agt K. N. Smith & Co., debtors, and J. N. Koster, owner.......... $574 80

22 Madison av, s w cor 89th st, runs west 139.4 x south 100 x east 64.4 x north — x east 75 to Madison av, x north 25.8 to beginning. W. E. Lyon agt Thomas Graham, owner and contractor.......... 2,332 21

22 Ninety-second st, s s, 100 e 5th av, 151.8x100.8. Same agt same.......... 1,188 93

22 Eighty-ninth st, n s, 113.4 w Madison av, 51.1x100.8. Same agt same.......... 1,475 00

22 Twenty-seventh st, n s, 368 w 9th av, 81.11x100. Anton Larsen agt Homer J. Beaudet, owner and contractor.......... 180 00

22 Forty-ninth st, No. 122 W., s s, 25x—. Frank Schaeffler agt Prescott & McLoughlin, owners, and Prieble & Co., contractors.......... 120 00

22 Fifty-third st, s s, 350 w 10th av, 125x100. Vermont Marble Co. agt James O'Donelan, owner and contractor.......... 686 80

22 Fox st, Nos. 56-58, w s, 135 n 156th st, 50x100. A. S. Nichols agt Leopold R. True, owner and contractor.......... 90 00

22 Madison av, s w cor 89th st, 25x113. Josephine Collins agt Randolph Guggenheimer, Isaac and Samuel Untermeyer and Thomas Graham, owners, and Thomas Graham, contractor.......... 6,000 00

22 Eighty-ninth st, n s, 113 w Madison av, 51.1x—. Same agt same.......... 1,500 00

24 Ninety-second st, n s, 100 e 5th av, 151.8x100. Francis Keil & Son agt Thomas Graham, debtor, and Isaac and Samuel Untermyer, Randolph Guggenheimer and Thomas Graham, owners.......... 1,881 61

24 Same property. Freeman & O'Neil Co. agt same.......... 37,000 00

24 Same property. John Renehan agt Isaac and Samuel Untermeyer and Randolph Guggenheimer, owners, and Thomas Graham, contractor.......... 5,216 77

24 Eighty-ninth st, n s, 113.4 w Madison av, 51.1x100.8. Willson, Adams & Co. agt Thomas Graham, owner and contractor.......... 1,059 04

24 Madison av, s w cor 89th st, runs west 139.4 x south 100 x east 64.4 x north — x east 75 to Madison av, x north 25.8 to beginning. Same agt same.......... 4,943 48

24 Ninety-second st, s s, 100 e 5th av, 151.8x100.8. Same agt same 1,429 94

Ninety-second st, s s, 100 e 5th av, 151.8x—. Eighty-ninth st, n s, 113.4 w Madison av, 51.1x—.......... 24 Madison av, s w cor 89th st, runs west 138.10 x south 100 x east 63.10 x north 74.3 x east 75 to Madison av, x north 25.8 to beginning.......... } Frederick Haas agt Thomas Graham, Randolph Guggenheimer and Isaac and Samuel Untermeyer, owner, and Thomas Graham, contractor.......... 4,336 15

24 Ninety-sixth st, n s, 70 e Lexington av, 125x100. Allen & Campbell agt Owen F. McElroy, Jr., and William McElroy, debtors and owners.......... 1,200 00

24 Boulevard, s w cor 85th st, 102.2x98.7x102.2x105.10. Carr & Ball agt Homer J. Beaudet, owner and contractor.......... 5,000 00

24 Third av, e s, 100 s 126th st, 25x100. Sextus Bradenstein agt Louis Kahn, owner, and R. J. McDonald, contractor.......... 210 00

24 One Hundred and Fifth st, Nos. 305-311, n s, 100 e 1st av, 100x100. Henry Schluter agt Matthew Coogan, owner and contractor.......... 418 00

24 One Hundred and Forty-first st, No. 592, s s, 250 w 3d av, 25x100. John Hartmayer agt Terrence McGuire, owner, and Thomas Moorcroft, contractor.......... 200 00

24 One Hundred and Twenty-third st, Nos. 140-150 W., s s. Richardson & Boynton Co. agt Elizabeth K. Smith, owner and contractor.......... 890 00

25 Twenty-first st, Nos. 222 and 224 W., s s, 50x100. Thomas Cutler agt John McClutchey and Thomas Kenney, debtors, and Michael Gillespie, owner.......... 12 00

25 Eighty-ninth st, n s, 113.4 w Madison av, 51.1x100. See & Conover agt Thomas Graham, owner and contractor.......... 6,113 04

25 Chambers st, No. 129, n e cor West Broadway, 76.1x—x75.8x100.1. P. G. Lough agt Charles F. Wilday, owner, and Central Complete Combustion Mfg. Co., contractors.......... 464 62

25 One Hundred and Fifteenth st, n s, 500 e Pleasant av, 44x44. Vigna & Orrigoni agt Standard Gas Co., owners, and W. V. and John Weber, contractors.......... 110 00

25 One Hundred and Eighteenth st, s s, 240 w 4th av, 100x100.11. Burrows & Smith agt Samuel Harris & Bernhard Ginsburg, owners, and Herman and Mary Masche and Bernhard Ginsburg, contractors...... 250 00

25 One Hundredth st, n s, 130 e 3d av, 50x80. Herman Anderson agt Phillip H. Smith, owner, and William Jayne, contractor... 26 25

25 Forty-third st, No. 321, n s, 275 w 8th av, 25x100.5. N. Y. Architectural Terra Cotta Co., agt Richard J. Keeffe, owner, and Thomas Farrell, contractor.......... 1,340 00

25 Lexington av, w s, 75.11 s 56th st, 25x70. Patrick Leddy agt Poline Byk, owner, and Morris Byk, contractor 170 00

25 Ninety-second st, s s, 100 e 5th av, 155.7x100.8. P. J. Cooney agt Thomas Graham, owner and contractor.......... 2,050 00

25 Same property. L. R. Hartung Co. agt Randolph Guggenheimer and Isaac and Samuel Untermeyer and Thomas Graham, owners, and Thomas Graham, contractor. 1,082 25

25 Madison av, s w cor 89th st, 25x113. W. E. D. Vincent agt same.......... 2,050 00

25 Amsterdam (10th) av, s w cor 99th st, 40x100. Bowes & Son agt L. Rogers, owner and contractor.......... 50 00

25 One Hundred and Second st, s s, 100 e Boulevard, 50x100. Bowes & Combs agt Lewis M. Muller, owner, and George C. MacLoughlin, contractor.......... 315 00

26 Ninety-second st, s s, 100 e 5th av, 150x100. J. L. Mott Iron Works agt Thomas Graham, Samuel and Isaac Untermeyer, owners, and Thomas Graham, contractor 575 00

26 Same property. George Call & Co. agt same and Randolph Guggenheimer, owners, and Thomas Graham, contractor.... 4,600 00

26 Eighty-ninth st, s s, 113 w Madison av, 25x100. W. E. D. Vincent agt same.......... 330 00

26 Eighty-ninth st, n s, 113.4 w Madison av, 51x100. Same agt same.......... 450 00

26 Ninety-second st, s s, 100 e 5th av, 150x100. Same agt same.......... 600 00

26 Same property. J. S. Conover & Co. agt same 1,800 00

26 Leroy st, Nos. 57-63, n s, 64x100. John Madden agt Stevens, McElroy & Co., owners, and Clark & Dolan, contractors.. 100 00

26 Ninety-sixth st, n s, 70 e Lexington st, 103x100.11. John Madden agt Owen F. McElroy, Jr., and William McElroy, owners, and Clark & Dolan, contractors.......... 150 00

26 One Hundred and Fifteenth st, s s, 275 e 8th av, 175x100. Maxwell & Dempsey agt Muller & Hauff, owners and contractors. 276 00

26 Bainbridge av, w s, 452.10 n Travers st, 70x185. Douglas, Dolan & McMaster agt Eunice C. Lawrence, owner and contractor. 103 00

26 Warren st, No. 67, s s, 25.6 w College pl, 25.6x50. W. G. Robinson agt John Duesing, owner, and George W. Willerhausen & Co., contractors.......... 53 39

26 Ninety-second st, n s, 70 e Lexington av, 125x100.11. Pelham Hod Elevating Co. agt Owen F. McElroy, Jr., and Wm McElroy, debtors and owners.......... 192 50

27 One Hundred and Eighteenth st, n s, 90 e Madison av, 150x100.11. Hickey & Greene agt The Amsterdam Improvement Co., owner and contractor.......... 1,056 13

27 Washington st, No. 698. T. G. Patterson agt John P. McGovern, owner and contractor.......... 5,778 68

27 Madison av, s w cor 89th st, runs west 138 x south 100 x east — x north 75 x east — to Madison av, x north 25 to beginning. Patrick Fogarty agt Thomas Graham, debtor, and same and Randolph Guggenheimer and Isaac and Samuel Untermeyer, owners.......... 2,101 70

27 Manhattan av, n e cor 121st st, 100.11x25. John Murray agt Henry Schneider, owner, and Allen A. Irvine, contractor.... ... 261 00

27 Fifty-eighth st, Nos. 108 and 110, s s, 100 w 6th av, 40x100. Edward Tipping agt Charles T. Barney, owner, and Mankey Decorative Co, contractor.......... 1,100 00

27 Thirty-fourth st, Nos. 126 and 128, s w cor Lexington av, 95x117.6. James D. Powell & Bro. agt The Lexington Improvement Co., owner and contractor.......... 706 71

28 Third av, e s, 99.11 n 125th st, 25x80. A. B. Johnson & Co. agt Louis J. Kahn or The N. Y. Beef Co., owner, and R. J. McDonald and Percy Jacobs, contractors... 477 55

28 Fifty-eighth st, Nos. 106-110 W., s s. P. and F. Corbin agt Charles T. Barney, owner, and Mankey Decorative Co., contractors. 406 79

28 Norfolk st, e s, 200 s Houston st, 25x—. J. M. Leonhardt agt First Hungarian Opal Zedeck Verein, Leopold Herman pres't, owner, and Patrick Gallagher, contractor 1,333 00

KINGS COUNTY.

Aug.

21 Leonard st, n e cor Frost st, 25x100. Palmer M'f'g. Co. agt Mary E. Howe, owner, and Louis Mehrmann.......... $664 32

21 Van Voorhis st, s e s, 260 n e Central av, 40x100. Adam Wagner agt Clemens Dehler, owner and contractor 648 25
21 Throop av, w s, 40 s Stockton st, 60x100. Val. Bruchhauser & Bro. agt The German Evangelical Protestant Church.......... 8,500 00
21 Ewen st, No. 378, e s, 25 s Withers st, 25x100. Joseph Hunt agt Catherine Coleman, owner, and McGarry & Moran.......... 889 20
21 Navy st, s w cor Nassau st. Sylvester Ross agt John Ryan, owner, and Matthias Zang.......... 700 08
21 Second st, s s, 177.10 w 6th av, 80x95. Central Gas and Electric Fixture Co. agt Archibald N. McBean.......... 301 70
21 Fulton st, s s, 76.7 w Linwood st, 25x90. Earl Gillespie agt William Reuss, owner, and K. F. Schmidt.......... 1,000 00
21 Monroe st, s s, 141.8 w Tompkins av, 16.8x100. Stillman Soule agt Sarah J. Thistle, owner and contractor.......... 677 01
21 Stone av, w s, 125 s Belmont av, 25x100. Annie Sherry agt Elias Rudermann and Abraham Orzpersky, owners and contractors.......... 25 00
21 Harrison pl, n s, 100 w Morgan av, 100x100. Tony De Luka agt Orphans Home of the Sorrowful Mother, owner, and Jacob Besson 154 15
21 Cooper st, s s, 315 w Knickerbocker av, 60x100 Bulmer Lumber Co. agt Stephen B., George, Joseph W. B. and Kate Rose and Ole Harrison, owners and contractors... 887 00
21 East 95th st, n e s, 100 n w Av M, Canarsie, 50x—. William F. Grunhard agt Mary A. Cook, owner, and August Wonsousky, contractor.......... 58 54
22 Seventh st, n s, 297.6 e 4th av, 50.4x100. William H. Bierds agt Mary E. Miller, owner, and George N. Miller, contractor.......... 202 15
22 Arlington av, s e cor, 60x100 (see Lien). Hyde & Gload Mfg Co. agt Isidore Warren, owner and contractor.......... 145 25
22 Johnson av, No. 35, 25x100. Jarashow & Kaplan agt —— Rosenthal, owner and contractor.......... 60 00
22 St. Marks av, Nos. 242-250. American Stoneware Co agt Thomas H. Robbins, owner and contractor.......... 27 00
22 Patchen av, w s, extends from Macon to McDonough st, —x100. Same agt same.. 117 00
22 Marion st, s s, 50 w Rockaway av, 20x100. Same agt same.......... 72 00
22 Eastern Parkway, s s, 25 e Thatford av, 25x100. Louis Bossert agt B. Seerman, owner and contractor.......... 657 97
22 Madison st, s s, 100 e Hamburg av, 220x100. Joseph Cannello agt George A. Craig, owner and contractor.......... 285 00
24 Broadway, n e cor Jefferson st, 100x100. Greenthaler & Halpin agt A. J. & C. H. Moller, owners and contractors.......... 283 00
24 Fourth st, n s, 297.10 e 7th av, 100x100. Charles G. Rice agt Roderick Von Groff, owner and contractor.......... 137 50
24 Sixth st, s s, 180 w 4th av, 100x115. Same agt H. Beckerowner, and contractor 87 50
24 Watkins st, w s, 250 s Sutter av, 25x100. Earl A. Gillespie agt Solomon Morris, owner, and A. Stone, contractor.......... 805 16
24 Saratoga av, n e cor Bainbridge st, 100x116. Reilly & Timony agt Kate and Samuel R. Good and Victor J. Dowling, owners and contractors.......... 125 00
24 Pulaski st, s s, 479.3 e Throop av, 152 9x100. Terrence Ferguson agt Maria Roberts, Frederick W. Klein and Elise Klein, owners, and Essex Roberts, contractor.......... 67 50
24 Same property. David Sheppard agt same owners and contractor.......... 143 36
25 Bedford av, s e cor Rodney st, 138x100. King & Adams agt Charles W. Andress and Charles R. Mitchell owners and contractors.......... 257 00
25 Cooper st, s s, 315 w Knickerbocker av, 60x100. Walter T. Klots & Bros. Sons agt Stephen B., George and William Rose, owners and contractors 300 87
25 Cooper st, s s, 300 w Knickerbocker av, 22x50. Same agt T. J. Scharffenberg, owner, and Rose Bros., contractors 190 88
25 Leonard st, n e cor Frost st, 25x100. Louis Mehrmann agt Mary E. Hower, owner, and Frederick Hower, contractor.......... 2,877 00
25 Same property. Keupp & Poetsch agt Mary E. Hower, owner, and Louis Mehrmann and Frederick Hower, contractor.. 1,060 00
25 Navy st, s w cor Nassau st, 25x78. J. Schindele's Sons agt John Ryan, owner, and Matthias Zang, contractor.......... 398 00
25 Cleveland st, e s, 350 s New Lots road, 50x100. Rudolph Reimer & Co. agt Philips & Smith, owners and contractors.......... 339 42
25 First st, n s, 306 w 5th av, 90x100. Law & Gale agt W. S. Hale, owner and contractor.......... 144 00
25 Seventh av, w s, 50 s Lincoln pl, 100x100. Same agt same owner and contractor... 100 00
25 Willoughby st, n w cor Hudson av, 20x75. William V. Williamson agt John Braun, owner, and Joseph Harter, contractor... 360 00
25 Fourth st, s s, 97.10 e 6th av, 440x100. Thomas McCann agt Moses & Fanton, owners and contractors.......... 1,000 00
25 Third st, n s, 431.9 e 6th av, 44x100. Same agt same owner and contractor.......... 465 00
25 Market st, e s, 300 n Fulton st, 21x100. Walter T. Klots & Bros. Sons agt John Reiss, owner, and Rose Bros., contractors.......... 191 26
25 Flushing av, s e cor Grand av, 25x100. Same agt John Von Glahn and J. H. Von Glahn, owners, and Rose Bros., contractors.......... 96 61
25 Pulaski st, n s, 100 w Sumner av, 380.6x100. Isidor Meck agt Fred. Hower Brewing Co., owners and contractors.......... 9,185 96
25 Fourth st, s s, 138 w 7th av, 114x100. William J. Fitzpatrick agt Charles H. Moses and Henry B. Fanton, S. T. and M. L. Moses, A. J. Daynes, Eliza A. and Emma G. Fanton and Louis H. Myers, owners, and Moses & Fanton, contractors.......... 1,621 44
26 Fourth st, s s, 157.10 w 7th av, 40x100. William J. Fitzpatrick agt Charles H. Moses and Henry B. Fanton, owners and contractors.......... 200 00
26 Fourth st, s s, 197.10 w 7th av, 18x100. Same agt Louis H. Myers, owner, and Moses & Fanton, contractors.......... 270 24
26 Fourth st, s s, 215.10 w 7th av, 18x100. Same agt S. F. Moses, owner, and Moses & Fanton, contractors.......... 270 24
26 Fourth st, s s, 233.10 w 7th av, 19x100. Same agt Elizabeth A. Fanton, owner, and Moses & Fanton, contractors.......... 270 24
26 Fourth st, s s, 253 w 7th av, 19x100. Same agt Emma G. Fanton, owner, and Moses & Fanton, contractors.......... 270 24
26 Fourth st, s s, 271.10 w 7th av, 20x100. Same agt M. L. Moses, owner, and Moses & Fanton, contractors.......... 270 24
26 Fourth st, s s, 291.10 w 7th av, 20x100. Same agt A. J. Dynes, owner, and Moses & Fanton, contractors.......... 270 24
26 Fourth st, s s, 97.10 e 6th av, 286x100. Same agt Charles H. Moses and Henry B. Fanton, owners and contractors.......... 6,657 76
26 Ralph av, n e cor Macon st, 100x400. William C. Fisher agt F. Augustus Conkling, owner, and S. G. Holland and F. A. Conkling, contractors.......... 251 32
26 Second st, s s, 457.11 e 5th av, 75x100. Traitel Bros. agt A. N. McBean, owner and contractor.......... 205 42
26 Fourth st, s s, 97.10 e 6th av, 440x100. Thomas McCann agt Moses & Fanton, S. F. Moses, H. J. Dynes, Eliza A. Fanton, F. M. Moses, M. L. Moses and Louis H. Meyers, Jr., owners, and Moses & Fanton, contractors.......... 1,000 00
26 Pulaski st, n s, 100 w Sumner av, 380.6x100. Brennan & Colligan agt The Fred Hower B. Co. owners and contractors.......... 1,003 38
26 Eighth av, s e cor 11th st, 120x100. Fox & McCarty agt Allison V. B. Norris and William Turner, owners and contractors. 136 00
26 Arlington av, s e cor Hendrix st, 60x100. Hyde & Gload Mfg. Co. agt Isidore Warren, owner and contractor.......... 145 25
26 Livonia av, s e cor Osborn st, 20x100. George Scheinfeld agt Abraham Seidenberg and Rachmiel Abramowitz, owners and contractors.......... 1,295 00
27 Fourth st, s s, 97.10 e 6th av, 440x100. Thomas O'Hara agt C. H. Moses and H. B. Fanton, Jr., owners and contractors.. 481 00
27 Halsey st, s s, 100 e Patchen av, 100x100. William Donnelly agt Hiram Bedell, owner and contractor.......... 50 00
27 Fourth st, n s, 197.10 w 8th av, 100x95. W. F. Fisher & Co. agt Roderick Von Graff. 1,251 21
27 Seventh st, n s, 214.1 e 4th av, 68.9x100. Berg & Bjorkman agt George and Mary Miller, owners, and George Miller, contractor.... 105 00
27 Greene av, n s, 100 w Bushwick av, 56x100. Jacob May agt Thomas Goodwin, owner and contractor.......... 102 82

SATISFIED MECHANICS' LIENS.

NEW YORK CITY.

Aug.
22 One Hundred and Third st, Nos. 158-166 W., s s. Culbert Bros. agt James McNiece. (Lien filed June 16, 1891) $370 73
22 Same property. Joseph Marren agt same. (July 1, 1891).......... 1,558 43
22 Same property. John Kingston agt same and Andrew Byrne. (June 18, 1891)...... 489 00
24 One Hundredth st, n s, 80 w 4th av, 20x80. Ernest Hall agt Edward J. Kelly. (July 7, 1890).......... 475 38
24 Third st, No. 70, s s, 80 w South 5th av, 25x—. Samuel Nichols & Son agt B. Barretti and Charles A. Cowen. (Aug. 12, 1890)... 310 60
24*Third av, No. 2813, e s, 99.11 n 125th st, 25x—. R. J. McDonald agt Louis J. Kahn and Percy Jacobs. (Aug. 20, 1891).......... 1,190 30
25 Fifty-third st, s s, 100 e 11th av, 150x—. Jackson Architectural Iron Works agt Eva Stafford. (Feb. 16, 1891) 279 90
25 One Hundred and Eighteenth st, s s, 65 e Madison av, 100x100. Burrows & Smith ag Samuel Harris, Herman and Mary Matsche and Bernhard Ginsburg. (July 30, 1891).......... 250 00
26*Third av, No. 2813.. Fritz Eisner and nine others agt same and Sextus Bridenstein and Roderick J. McDonald. (Aug. 25, 1891).......... 89 30
26 Convent av, n w cor 143d st, 100x100. J. M. McArdle agt Louise M. Hartwell. (July 9, 1891).......... 2,400 00
26 Same property. Rody McLoughlin agt same. (June 18, 1891).......... 300 00
26 Same property. Abraham Steers agt same and H. E. Hartwell. (July 30, 1891..)..... 185 22
26‡One Hundred and Twenty-eighth st, n s, 135 e Lenox av, 75x99.11. Michael Zettina agt Patrick Hogan. (Aug. 3, 1891).......... 355 20
27‡Same property. Maicho Fortunato agt same and Bridget Hogan. (Aug. 6, 1891). 346 24
27 Arthur av, w s, seventh building south of Pelham av. C. E. Gates & Co. agt Ernest Wehner and D. Kent. (July 24, 1891) 150 00
27 Arthur av, w s, 200 s Pelham av, 25x—. Domenico Schiavone agt Weimer & Schaeffer and William Murray. (Aug. 5, 1891).......... 11 25
27 Same property. Bart Schiavone agt same. (Aug 5, 1891).......... 18 00
27 Same property. J. A. Woolf agt same. (July 27, 1891).......... 468 99
27 Same property. Thomas Wilson agt same. (July 25, 1891).......... 275 00
27 One Hundred and Fifth st, No. 62 W., 22x100.11. Michael Spinelli and Bro. agt Mary O. Nesbit. (April 29, 1891).......... 344 50
28 Madison av, s e cor 134th st, 100x60. Michael Conforti agt Thomas Jette and Thomas McCormack. (Aug. 6, 1891).......... 3,492 00
28 Twenty-first st, No. 325 W., 25x100. Canda & Cane agt William H. Cornet. (Aug. 14, 1891).......... 1,791 08

‡Discharged by order of Court on filing bond.
*Discharged by depositing amount of lien and interest with County Clerk.

KINGS COUNTY.

Aug.
19 Garnet st, s s, 100 e Court st, 100x100. Joseph Logan agt Alfred E. Hartington, owner and contractor. (Lien filed July 28, 1891).......... $1,220 00
19 Same property. Peter McCaden agt same owner and contractor. (Aug. 6, 1891).... 281 80
19 Same property. The Hyatt Co., New York, agt same owner and contractor. (Aug. 8, 1891).......... 365 44
20 Madison st, s e s, 109 n e Hamburg av, 220x100. New York Gas Fixture Co. agt George A. Craig, owner and contractor. (June 4, 1891) 634 06
20 Same property. The Tilly & Van Hagen Co. agt same owner and contractor. (June 5, 1891).......... 1,209 50
21 First st, s s, 100 w 7th av, 100x100. Brereton & McIntosh agt John Kolle, owner, and Hardwood Decorative Co., contractor. (Aug. 4, 1891).......... 193 23
22 Hicks st, n e cor Poplar st. 25.3x99.9. Sheehey & McGarry agt Ida M. Edwards, owner, and John Edwards, contractor. (July 6, 1891) 120 00
22 Same property. New York Gas Fixture Co. agt same owner and contractor. (Aug. 6, 1891).......... 80 00
22 Same property. John S. Loomis agt same owner and contractor. (June 26, 1891)... 456 13
22 Same property. Henry McShane & Co. agt same owner and contractor. (June 20, 1891).......... 695 70
22 East 31st st, w s, lots 50 and 51 on block 3 Reformed Dutch Church property, Flatbush. Peter J. Heffron agt Richard Peyton, owner, and George J. Craigen, contractor. (July 22, 1891.) (Deposit)...... 49 49
22 Eighth st, n s, 100 e 4th av, 100x100. Matt Taylor Paving Co. agt Paul Gantert, owner and contractor. (June 9, 1891).......... 300 00
25 Pacific st, s s, extends from Rochester av to Buffalo av, 31 houses; also.......... } Dean st, n s, 100 w Buffalo av, 500x100... } Thomas B. Jackson, Jr., agt Joseph Hopkins, Jr., owner and contractor. (Sept. 8, 1890) 165 78
25 Same property. George W. Evans & Co. agt Joseph Hopkins, Jr., owner and contractor. (Aug. 15, 1890).......... 859 00
25 Same property. Same agt same. (Nov. 25, 1890) 33 25
25 Pacific st, s s, 80 e Rochester av, 520x100. The Union Stove Works agt same owner and contractor. (Aug. 27, 1890).......... 465 00
25 Schenck av, e s, 162 n Arlington av, 75x100. Gustaf Widen agt Thomas F. Parker, owner and contractor. (April 30, 1891)... 90 00
25 Same property. Louis Bossert agt same. (April 29, 1891).......... 323 87
25 Same property. Rudolph Reimer agt same owner and contractor. (April 27, 1891)... 256 15
25 Marion st, n s, 130 w Hopkinson av, 50x100. Augustus C. Becker agt Charles Hunt, owner, and A. M. Sagar & Bro., contractors. (Feb. 28, 1891) 169 62
26 Navy st, e s, 61.7 n Myrtle av, 50x100. George W. Wright agt Henrietta Fisk, owner and contractor. (April 14, 1891)... 45 00
26 Same property. Same agt William H. H. Glover, owner and contractor. (April 10, 1891).......... 45 00
25 Dean st, n s, 280.7 w Buffalo av, 137.10x—. William H. Cable agt James A. Lane, owner and contractor. (May 16, 1891).... 637 33
26 Same property. Joseph D. Clayton agt same owner and contractor. (May 16, 1891).......... 395 00
26 Central av, e s, extends from Putnam av to Cornelia st, 200x100. John Ernst & Son agt John T. Barnard, owner, and Joseph Hopkins, contractor. (July 24, 1891).... 325 00
25 Schenck av, e s, 162 n Arlington av, 213x100. Otto Gebelien agt Thomas F. Parker and Elizabeth M. Rapelje, owners, and Thomas F. Parker, contractor. (June 12, 1891).......... 59 30
24 Wallabout st, No. 396. Joseph Wagner agt Peter Wehle, owner and contractor. (June 16, 1891).......... 1,520 00
26 Seventh st, n s, 297.6 e 4th av, 50.4x100. Watson & Pittinger agt Mary E. and George Miller, owners and contractors. (Aug. 19, 1891).......... 385 85
26 Same property. Johnson & Phelan agt same owners and contractors. (Aug. 20, 1891).......... 244 88
26 Broadway, n e cor Jefferson st, 100x100. Greenthaler & Halpin agt C. Henry and Annie J. Moller, owners, and Jacob Bisson. (Aug. 24, 1891) 285 00
26 Same property. A. D. Baird & Co. agt same. (Aug. 17, 1891).......... 2,600 00
26 Same property. Louis Gfroerer agt same owner and contractor. (July 27, 1891)... 2,670 00
26 Same property. Samuel M. Weeks agt same owner and contractor. (July 25, 1891).......... 6,576 60
26 Same property. Philip Dugro agt same owner and contractor.......... 517 00
26 Fulton st, n s, 25.6 w Elton st, 25.6x106 2x25x101. Henry McShane & Co. agt Rebecca Koop, owner, and Ernst Loerch and Rose Bros., contractors. (June 8, 1891). ..... 256 0[illegible]

BUILDINGS PROJECTED.

The first name is that of the owner; ar't stands for architect, m'n for mason, c'r for carpenter and b'r for builder.

NEW YORK CITY.

SOUTH OF 14TH STREET.

Henry st, No. 98, five-story brk and stone flat, 25x88 6, tin roof; cost, $20,000; Fay & Stacom, 337 Pleasant av; ar't, C. Rentz Plan 1161.

Pearl st, s w cor William st. eight-story and basement brk factory, 100.6x89.9, tin roof; cost, $220,000; J. Whalen, 155th st and St. Nicholas av; ar't, W. H. Hume. Plan 1166.

Franklin st, Nos. 54 and 56, six-story brk, iron, stone and terra cotta building, 50.1x100, tin roof; cost, $80,000; J. T. Williams, 871 Madison av; ar't, C. R Behrens. Plan 1180.

Willett st, No. 133, four-story brk flat, 25x40, tin roof; cost, $16,000; Jacobson & Margovitz, 152 Clinton st; ar't, F. Ebeling. Plan 1173.

BETWEEN 59TH AND 125TH STREETS, EAST OF 5TH AVENUE.

73d st, n s, 323 e Av A, two-story and basement brk stable, 25x97.8, tin roof; cost, $7,500; J. McGee and ano., 513 East 75th st; ar't, J. J. F. Gavigan. Plan 1169. as

83d st, n s, 71.3 w 2d av, five-story brk and stone flat, 28x94, tin roof; cost, $26,000; Sheehy Bros., 338 East 84th st; ar't, J. C. Burne. Plan 1162.

1st av, s w cor 64th st, four-story brk factory, 50.5x100, tin roof; cost, $10,000; lessee, D. P. Chesebro, on premises; ar't, M. Hensel. Plan 1172.

91st st, s s, 225 e 5th av, five-story brk and stone flat, 25.6x88, tin roof; cost, $22,000; R. W. Thain, 231 East 87th st; ar't, J. Hauser. Plan 1178.

Blackwell's Island, opposite 78th st, two-story brk building, 195x44, slate roof; cost, $25,000; Mayor, &c., 66 3d av; ar'ts, Withers & Dickson. Plan 1175.

NORTH OF 125TH STREET.

Wadsworth av, w s, 25 n 179th st, two-story and basement frame dwell'g, 22x30, shingle roof; cost, $2,800; F. T. McKee, 171st st, near West Boulevard; b'r, E. Palmer. Plan 1164.

Academy st, s s, 475 w Kingsbridge road, frame structure, 5x13, wooden roof; cost, $8; ow'r and b'r, W. Duncans, on premises. Plan 1176.

23D AND 24TH WARDS.

Garfield pl, n s, 100 w Valentine av, two-story and attic frame dwell'g, 26.6x47.2, shingle roof; cost, $5,000; Marie A. Klein, 17 West 100th st; ar't, S. B. Reed; c'r, F. Robinson. Plan 1165.

Rockfield st, n s, 100 w Bainbridge av, one-and-a-half-story frame dwell'g, 16x25, shingle roof; cost, $900; Emily Burnham, 220 West 110th st; ar't and c'r, C. W. Vreeland; m'n, T. Johnston. Plan 1167.

150th st, s s, 3,451 e Harlem River, frame shed, 40x100, tarred roof; cost, $550; ow'r and b'r, E. T. Smith, 317 East 150th st. Plan 1170.

Anthony av, e s, 5.7 n 175th st, two-story frame dwell'g, 18x39, shingle and tin roof; cost, $3,500; H. Humphreys, 577 Ash st; ar't, S. P. Barry. Plan 1171.

Brook av, w s, 125 n 170th st, two-story frame stable, 25x25, tin roof; cost, $400; L. Kayser, n e cor Webster av and Anna pl. Plan 1168.

Courtlandt av, w s, 75 s 158th st, one-story frame shop, 25x35, gravel roof; cost, $400; lessee, H. Reymers, 607 East 158th st; ar't, C. F. Lohse. Plan 1163.

Rockfield st, s s, 291 e Marion av, two-story frame building, 25x40, tin roof; cost, $2,500; Ellen Eichele, 486 9th av; ar't, A. Pfeiffer. Plan 1174.

Valentine av, e s, 231 n Clark st, frame shed, 32x19, wooden roof; cost, $25; W. W. Edwards, High Bridge road and Tiebout av; c'r, T. C. Lisk. Plan 1170.

Webster av, n s, 100 s 180th st, one-story frame stable, 13x20, gravel roof; cost $150; lessee, R. E. Osborne, on premises. Plan 1177.

KINGS COUNTY.

Plan 1553—Atlantic av, s s, 260 e New York av, one three-story brk stable, 40x70, tin roof, brk cornice; cost, $8,000; W. J. Skelley, 572 Fulton st; ar't, T. F. Houghton; b'rs, J. C. Carlin and J. C. Sawkins.

1554—Hicks st, w s, 40 s Bush st, one-and-a-half story frame shop, 20x30, tin roof; cost, $250; Annie Holtgen, 132 54th st; ar'ts, H. L. Spicer & Son.

1555—Nassau st, Nos. 49, 51 and 53, one four-story brk stable, 43.11 and 42.7x98.4, gravel roof, iron and brk cornice; cost, $15,000; Jas. Constable, 202 Fulton st; ar't, J. G. Glover; b'r, not decided.

1556—St. Marks av, n s, 350 e Rockaway av, one three-story frame (brk filled) tailor shop, 22x45, tin roof; cost, $300; Joseph Kreinik, 2921 Atlantic av; ar'ts, Danmar & Fischer.

1557—Sumner av, s w cor Jefferson av, one four-story brk flat, 24x65, tin roof, iron cornice; cost, $10,000; Henry C. Evers, 447 Manhattan av; ar't, C. Dunkhase; b'r, not selected.

1558—Atlantic av, s s, 150 e Schenectady av, one one-story frame smoke house, 30x50, tin roof; cost, $400; ow'r and ar't, John Fischer, 813 Herkimer st.

1559—Oakland st, No. 125, w s, 100 n Norman av, one three-story frame tenem't, 25x50, gravel roof; cost, $3,000; ow'r and c'r, John H. Murphy, 324 Oakland st.

1560—4th av, s w cor 23d st, one two-story frame store and dwell'g, 25x50, tin roof; cost, $3,000; Elizabeth Stabler, 140 21st st; b'r, J. Stabler.

1561—Broadway, e s, 80 s Cooper st, one one-story frame store, 20x70, tin roof; cost, $1,150; Joseph Lawson, 1197 Broadway.

1562—Wyona st, w s, 150 n Fulton av, one two-story frame church, 43 and 40x74, tin roof; cost, $8,000; trustee, German Evangelical Church; president, Christian Schwicker, Jamaica av; ar't, A. McLean; b'r, M. R. Thompson & Co.

1563—Kent av, North 6th and North 7th sts and East River, one four-story brk barrel factory, 200x540, gravel roof, brk cornice; cost, $75,000; Brooklyn Cooperage Co., 181 Front st, New York; ar't, A. Krause; m'ns, Carpenter & Woodruff and Libby & Keese.

1564—Fulton st, n s, 45.8 w Nostrand av, one five-story brk and brown stone flats, 39.6x65, tin roof, iron cornice; cost, $25,000; Betts Bros., Fulton st and Nostrand av; ar'ts, Thayer & Wallace.

1565—Decatur st, n s, 75 w Throop av, four two-and-a-half-story and basement brown stone dwell'gs, 20x45, tin roofs, iron cornices; cost, each, $5,000; ow'r and b'r, John Gordon, 374 Clermont av; ar't, R. Dixon.

1566—Suydam st, s s, 300 e Hamburg av, one one-story frame paint shop, 25x13, tin roof; cost, $60; Nathan Jaeger, 1112 Willoughby av; ar't, H. Vollweiler; b'r, not selected.

1567—Osborn st, n e cor Livonia av, one three-story frame store and tenem't, 25x55, tin roof; cost, $3,500; S. C. Velson, 2499 Atlantic av.

1568—Moore st, No. 34, rear, one two-story frame stable, 25x13.6, tin roof; cost, $350; S. Rath, on premises; ar't, R. Von Lehn.

1569—Vernon av, n s, 339 e Nostrand av, six two-and-a-half-story and basement brown stone dwell'gs, 18.6x43, tin roofs, wooden cornices; cost, each, $5,500; ow'r and m'n, John Parkin, 40 Vernon av; ar't and c'r, J. W. Parkin.

1570—St. Johns pl, s s, 160 w 7th av, three three-story brown stone dwell'gs, 19.6x47, tin roofs, iron cornices; cost, each, $7,500; Wm. L. Dowling, 683 President st; ar't, R. W. Firth; b'r, not selected.

1571—Melrose st, n s, 100 e Knickerbocker av, two three-story frame (brk filled) tenem'ts, 25x57, tin roofs; cost, each, $5,000; ow'r and b'r, Jos. Weidner, on premises; ar'ts, D. Acker & Son.

1572—54th st, n s, 400 e 6th av, one two-story frame dwell'g, 20x36, tin roof; cost, $1,000; ow'r and ar't, Michael Miller, 1127 3d av; c'r, I. Munson.

1573—Seigel st, n s, 100 e Leonard st, one four-story frame tenem't, 25x85, tin roof, brk cornice; cost, $7,500; Mrs. B. Keller, on premises; ar'ts, D. Acker & Son.

1574—Jackson st, n e cor Ewen st, one four-story frame (brk filled) store and tenem't, 18x55; gravel roof; cost, $4,200; James Kelly, 86 Berry st; ar't, F. Weber; b'r, J. Fallon.

1575—Ewen st, e s, 18 n Jackson st, one four-story frame (brk filled) store and tenem't, 15.4x55, gravel roof; cost, $4,000; ow'r, ar't and b'r, same as last.

1576—Partition st, No. 133, one four-story frame store and tenem't, 20x50, tin roof; cost, $7,000; John Wolf, 133 Partition st; b'r, D. J. Lynch.

1577—Buffalo av, e s, 25 n St. Marks av, one one-story frame milk shed, 10x23, tin roof; cost, $25; B. I. Shaffer; ar't and b'r, W. D. Bogart.

1578—Norwood av, w s, abt 490 n Fulton st, one two-story frame dwell'g, 20x35.6, tin roof; cost, $2,400; Mary L. Bennett, Logan st, near Jamaica av; b'rs, A. V. Green and C. Baur.

1579—Navy st, w s, 102.5 s De Kalb av, one two-story brk, electric station, 27x42.9, gravel roof; cost, $7,000; Citizens Illuminating Co., on premises; ar't, T. F. Houghton; b'r, Mr. Guilfoyle.

1580—Glenmore av, n s, 25 w Christopher av, one three story frame store and tenem't, 26x80, tin roof; cost, $5,000; Morris Levy, 49 Pike st, N. Y.

1581—4th av, s w cor 34th st, five four-story brk stores and tenem'ts, 20x50, tin roofs, wooden cornices; cost, each, $10,000; Nicholas McCool, Jr., on premises; ar't, E. D. Morris.

1582—Apollo st, s s, 200 s Nassau st, one one-story frame dwell'g, 20x24, felt roof; cost, $150; ow'r and b'r, James Berger, 526 East 14th st, N. Y.

1583—Kingston av, n w cor Bergen st, two three-story brown stone apartment houses, 21 and 19x55, tin roofs, wooden cornices; cost, $17,000; Jno. H. Doherty & Bro., 286 Flatbush av; ar't, W. M. Coots; b'r, day's work.

1584—3d st, s s, 220 w 7th av, one seven-story brown stone double flat, tin roof, 44x67, iron cornice; cost, $55,000; ow'r and b'r, Moses Fanton, 7th av and 4th st; ar't, G. M. Miller.

1585—Harrison st, s w cor Van Brunt st, river front, two seven-story brk warehouses, 60x170, gravel and cement roofs, brk cornices; cost, $102,000; Brooklyn Pier and Storage Co., 31 State st, N. Y.; ar't and b'r, T. Stone.

1586—Troutman st, No. 65, one one-story frame (brk filled) tailor shop, 22x15, tin roof; cost, $400; Geo. Lebonar, on premises; ar't and b'r, E. Schneider.

1587—Orient av, n s, 160 w Guilford st, one three-story frame (brk filled) dwell'g, 32x30, gravel roof; cost, $3,000; N. A. Conklin, 16 Orient av; ar't, F. J. Berlenbach, Jr.; b'r, not selected.

1588—Jerome st, e s, 100 and 164 s Dumont av, two two-story frame dwell'gs, 18x30, tin roofs; cost, $1,900 each; J. H. Brundage, Jerome st.

1589—Huron st, No. 207, n s, 150 w Oakland st, one three-story frame coach house and dwell'g, 25x52, gravel roof; cost, $3,000; ow'r and b'r, John H. Murphy, 324 Oakland st.

1590—Richardson st, No. 38, one one-story frame blacksmith shop, 20x24; cost, $50; Simon Simonwitz, on premises.

1591—Logan st, w s, 75 s Etna st, one one-story frame shed for stable, 14x18, shingle roof; cost, $125; George Merrick, on premises; b'r, S. Van Sise.

1592—Chestnut st, w s, 100 n Ridgewood av, one two-story and attic frame dwell'g, 16 and 20x28, and one-story extension, 18x14, shingle roof; cost, $2,000; George Beach, Logan st.

1593—McDougal st, n s, 230 w Stone av, four three-story frame (brk filled) flats, 20x45, tin roofs; cost, total, $16,000; William M. Brown, 114 Cumberland Heights; ar't, E. Dennis; b'r, C. Trimble.

1594—Carroll st, No. 529, 100 w 4th av, one three-story brk flat, 25x43, tin roof, wooden cornice; cost, $3,500; ow'r and b'r, Tony Lupe, on premises; ar't, G. M. Miller.

ALTERATIONS NEW YORK CITY.

Plan 1561—Arthur av, w s, 194 n Kingsbridge road, one-story extension, 20x14; cost, $160; J. Reilly, on premises.

1562—177th st, s s, 150 w Fleetwood av, one-story extension, 16x9; cost, $500; Emma A. Halsey, 370 East 177th st; c'r, J. N. Emlirt.

1563—9th st, No. 440 E., roof raised and internal alterations; cost, $450; E. Jacobs, 57 East 80th st; ar'ts, Kurtzer & Rohl.

1564—3d st, No. 191 E., new show window; cost, $250; W. Klein, on premises; ar'ts, Kurtzer & Rohl.

1565—84th st, No. 247 E., two-story extension 18.10x6; cost, $2,500; C. Rosenberg, 121 East 80th st; ar't, C. Baxter.

1566—Vanderbilt av, s w cor 176th st, moved from 177th st, roof raised, one-story extension, 13.6x30, interior alterations, new tower, bay, &c.; cost, $5,000; J. Thos. Stearns, pres't, 1757 Bathgate av; ar't, A. E. Davis.

1567—Vandewater st, No. 29, roof raised and walls altered; cost, $2,500; G. Munro, 15 West 57th st; ar't, S. B. Reed.

1568—78th st, No. 145 W., two-story extension, 14x8.4; cost, $1,150; Mrs. G. F. Rinke, on premises; m'n, J. G. Lord; c'r, G. G. Newbery.

1569—86th st, No. 167 E., one-story extension, 20x29; cost, $700; J. J. Carroll, 148 East 86th st; ar't, J. H. White; m'ns, Reilly & Bickerstaff.

1570—Kingsbridge road, n s, 142.2 e Marion av, two-story extension, 12x60; cost, $500; W. W. Edwards, Tiebout av and Highbridge road; ar't, T. C. Lisk; m'n, T. Johnston.

1571—23d st, Nos. 560–568 W., repair damage by fire; cost, $1,500; J. C. Fincken, 79 4th st, Hoboken, N. J.; m'n, —— Tyson; c'r, J. B. Purdy.

1572—Washington av, No. 1364, building raised above foundation 12 feet, new story built and extension raised one story, interior alterations and walls altered; cost, $5,000; W. W. Gardiner, on premises; b'rs, Wiswell & O'Brien.

1573—125th st, No. 207 W., interior alterations, new front; cost, $200; M. Baumann, agent, 163 East 113th st.

1574—3d av, No. 2194, one-story extension, 25.9x47.3, interior alterations, walls altered; cost, $2,000; J. B. Guttenberg, 113 East 116th st; ar't, J. P. Walther.

1575—Tremont av, No. 539, two-and-a-half-story extension, 14x28.3, interior alterations and walls altered; cost, $500; W. Schultz, on premises; ar't, A. E. Davis.

1576—Morris av, w s, 50 s 153d st, interior alterations and walls altered; cost, $1,150; D. Fitzpatrick, 152d st and Morris av; ar't, A. Pfeiffer.

1577—East Broadway, No. 186, roof raised 8 ft.; cost, $2,500; lessee, Basehkopf, on premises; ar't, H. Horenburger.

1578—West Washington Market, repair damage by fire; cost, $9,000; City New York, 31 Chambers st.

1579—3d av, w s, 125 s 156th st, one-story extension, 22x24, interior alterations and walls altered; cost, $500; lessee, W. Hafner, 3027 3d av; ar't, C. C. Churchill; c'rs, Wiswell & O'Brien.

1580—9th av, s e cor 54th st, one-story extension, 16x300; cost, $1,000; L. P. Foulk, Superintendent, 185 West 79th st; ar't, J. W. Cole; b'r, G. L. Haag.

1581—River av, n s, 950 w Riverdale av, two-story and basement extension, 10x18, interior alterations, new fire-place, two new bay windows and walls altered; cost, $20,000; G. P. Morosini, 71 Broadway; ar'ts, D. & J. Jardine.

1582—Delancey st, No. 301, interior alterations and repairs and new fronts; cost, $5,000; J. Horowitz, 204 East Broadway; ar't, F. Ebeling.

1583—Broadway, s e cor 32d st, nine-story extension, 42x94.9; cost, abt $150,000; Robert Goelet, 9 West 17th st; ar'ts, McKim, Mead & White; m'ns, Reid & Co.; c'rs, Norcross Bros.

1584—34th st, No. 146 W., four-story and basement extension, 25x44, interior alterations, portion front wall rebuilt; cost, $18,000; ow'r and ar't, Geo. Keister, 55 West 33d st.

KINGS COUNTY.

Plan 802—Atlantic av, No. 256, one story brk extension, 20x30, tin roof; cost, $2,100; Ernest Weidling, 16 Webster pl, New York; b'rs, G. McCoskey and H. Tormey.

803—Ewen st, n w cor Moore st, add one story of frame, tin roof; also four-story frame extension, 25x25, tin roof; cost, $3,000; A. Barosch, 95 Seigel st; ar't, H. Smith; b'r, not selected.

804—Columbia st, No. 177, new front wall; cost, $1,000; P. Halley, 44 Carroll st; b'rs, M. Gibbons & Sons.

805—Middleton st, No. 75, one-story brk extension, 12x22, tin roof; cost, $400; H. Frederick, on premises.

806—Dean st, No. 1126, add one story to extension and rebuild east wall of same; also two-story brk extension, 13x10.9, tin roofs; cost, $500; Albert J. Delatour, on premises; b'rs, H. Read and M. H. Berry.

807—Ewen st, No. 142, add one story to extension; also two-story frame extension, 25x15, tin roof; cost, $300; H. Schoenhour, on premises; c'rs, Becker & Rueger.

808—Park pl, No. 1170, raised 6 ft. on frame story; cost, $275; M. Jackson, 1170 Park pl.

809—Montauk av, e s, 137 n Liberty av, one-story frame extension, 18.9x6, felt roof; cost, $50; Walter E. Smith, on premises.

810—Seigel st, No. 46, front and interior alterations; cost, $200; ow'rs and b'rs, Rosenberg & Feinberg, 74 Seigel st; ar't, H. Vollweiler.

811—East New York av, n s, 150 w Stone av, one-story frame extension, 12x36, tar roof; cost, $175; ow'r and ar't, Jacob Lehman, on premises; b'r, A. Gauthie.

812—Partition st, No. 82, new chimneys and interior alterations; cost, $450; Joseph Foley, 82 Partition st; ar't and c'r, G. Hausen; m'n, J. Spratt.

813—State st, No. 118, three-story brk extension, 25x16.6, gravel roof; cost, $2,100; John F. Robertson, 118 State st; ar't, C. Werner; b'r, C. H. Collins.

814—Belmont av, s e cor Osborn st, one-story frame extension, 25x20, tin roof; cost, $150; L. Ratner, Rockaway av.

815—Carroll st, n s, 192 e 6th av, two-story and basement brk extension, 36.6x28, tin roof; cost,

$5,000; Sisters of St. Joseph, Flushing, L. I.; ar't, C. Werner; b'rs, O. Nolan and P. F. O'Brien & Son.

816—Columbia st, No. 517, raised 10 feet on frame story; cost, $200; Jere Moriarty, on premises.

817—Bergen st, Nos. 504 and 506, one-story brk extension, 50x25, tin roof, interior alterations, &c.; cost, $2,300; Olivet Chapel, on premises; ar't, F. S. Benedict; b'rs, C. G. Lloyd & Co.

818—Sackett st, No. 460, one-story and basement brk extension, 9x14, tin roof; cost, $450; William Orr, on premises; b'rs, E. Keenan and M. Cullen.

819—19th st, No. 411, one-story frame extension, 25x5, tin roof; cost, $100; ow'r, ar't and c'r, Wm. H. Washburne, 426 18th st; m'n, —— McCoffin.

820—Barbey st, No. 234, extend foundation under entire building; cost, $65; Ernest Gabreller on premises.

821—Cleveland st, No. 222, raised 3 ft. on brk foundation; cost, $200; Jacob Benziger, on premises.

822—Broadway, No. 738, interior alterations, elevator, &c.; cost, $500; Frederick Bauer, 738 Broadway; ar't, T. Engelhardt; b'r, C. Schneider.

823—43d st, at foot of, one-story frame extension, 30x80, gravel roof; cost, $300; The Cowles Engine Co., on premises.

824—Herkimer st, No. 640, two-story and basement frame extension, 7x31, tin roof; cost, $325; —— Allen, on premises; ar't, A. Hill; b'r, S. I. Jarvis.

825—Smith st, No. 120, one-story brk extension, 21x19, tin roof; cost, $1,200; Theo. Rehn, on premises; ar't and b'r, C. Dietrick.

826—Waterbury st, n e cor Maujer st, one-story frame extension, 20x25, tin roof; cost, $200; L. D. Scanlan, 293 Menjer st; ar't and b'r, J. Hopel or Hapel.

MISCELLANEOUS.

BUSINESS FAILURES.

N. Y. ASSIGNMENTS—BENEFIT CREDITORS.

August

24 Elbe, Isidor (manufacturer of diamond jewelry, at No. 42 Maiden lane), to Gustave Gomprecht; preferences, $23,963.98.

28 Carr, Walter and Delwin B. and William H. Sneckner (composing firm of Walter Carr & Co., commission merchants and produce dealers, at No. 15 Harrison st), to Robert J. Dean; without preferences.

28 Ernst, J. Eugene (importer of East India merchandise, at Nos. 91 and 93 Wall st), to Charles G. Nichols; without preferences.

KINGS COUNTY.

GENERAL ASSIGNMENTS.

Aug

27 Thomas, Samuel E. to Isaac Lublin.

PROCEEDINGS OF THE BOARD OF ALDERMEN AFFECTING REAL ESTATE.

APPROVED PAPERS.

Resolutions passed by the Board of Aldermen calling for the following improvements have been signed by the Mayor for the week ending August 22, 1891. *Indicates that the Mayor neither appoved nor objected thereto, therefore the same became adopted.

PAVING.

141st st, from e s Alexander av to w s of Willis av; paved with trap block and crosswalks laid at intersecting and terminating avs.

ADVERTISED LEGAL SALES.

REFEREES SALES TO BE HELD AT THE REAL ESTATE EXCHANGE AND AUCTION ROOM (LIMITED), 59 to 65 LIBERTY STREET, EXCEPT WHERE OTHERWISE STATED.

August

76th st, s s, 300 w West End av, 44x102.2, vacant, by J. F. B. Smith. (Amt due $7,754; prior morts. $9,000) 31

116th st, No. 54, s s, 82.11 e Madison av, 27.1x101, five-story brk flat, by William Kennelly. (Amt due $2,822; prior morts. $25,000) 31

Park av, Nos. 565-569, e s, 75.3 s 63d st, 66.5x100.1x60x100, five-story brk flats "Lonsdale," by William Kennelly. (Amt due $10,967; prior morts. $90,000) 31

Sept.

28th st, Nos. 516-528, s s, 225 w 10th av, 150x98.9, seven two, three and four-story brk tenem'ts, stores in Nos. 520 and 524, and seven two-story brk and frame buildings on rear, by William Kennelly. (Partition sale) 1

Park (4th) av, No. 668, w s, 86.5 s 69th st, 16x61, four-story brk dwell'g, by J. T. Stearns. (Amt due $30,764) 1

114th st, No. 322, s s, 262.6 e 2d av, 18.9x100.11, four-story brk tenem't, by B. L. Kennelly. (Amt due $9,852) 2

Madison av, No. 1678, n e cor 111th st, 15x70, three-story brk (stone front) dwell'g, by R. V. Harnett & Co. (Amt due $1,492; prior morts. $7,000; sold May 24, 1890, for $11,500) 2

1st av, No. 2406, n e cor 123d st, 26x75, four-story brk store and tenem't, by R. V. Harnett. (Amt due $11,018; leasehold) 2

98th st, s s, 150 e 10th av, 200x100.11, vacant, by Wm. Kennelly. (Amt due $38,511) 2

Waverley pl, No. 152, s w s, 243 n w 6th av, 22.3x97, four-story brk dwell'g, by Charles S. Brown. (Amt due $10,817) 3

22d st, No. 44, s s, 257 e 6th av, 28x98.9, four-story stone front dwell'g, by William Kennelly. (Amt due $38,960) 3

65th st, No. 22, s s, 200 w 8th av, 25x100.5 ....
65th st, No. 24, s s, 225 w 8th av, 25x100.5 ....
Two five-story stone front flats ....
by William Kennelly. (Amt due on each $9,321; prior morts., $——, and sold Jan. 11, 1890, for $48,300) 3

82d st, No. 348, s s, 161.5 w 2d av, 19.8x102.2, three-story stone front dwell'g, by D. P. Ingraham & Co. (Amt due $7,604) 3

8th av, No. 2550, n e cor 136th st, 24.11x80 ....
8th av, No. 2552, e s, 24.11 n 136th st, 25x80 ....
8th av, No. 2554, e s, 49.11 n 136th st, 25x80 ....
8th av, No. 2556, e s, 74.11 n 136th st, 25x80 ....
8th av, No. 2558, e s, 74.11 s 137th st, 25x80 ....
8th av, No. 2560, e s, 49.11 s 137th st, 25x80 ....
8th av, No. 2562, e s, 24.11 s 137th st, 25x80 ....
8th av, No. 2564, s e cor 137th st, 24.11x80 ....
Eight five-story brk flats with stores ....
by Peter F. Meyer. (Amt due on No. 2550 $14,154 and $13,096 on No. 2564 and abt $9,914 each on Nos. 2552 to 2562) 4

42d st, No. 25, n s, 354.2 w 5th av, 20.4x100.5, four-story stone front store and dwell'g, by R. V. Harnett. (Leasehold; action No. 1; amt due $5,420) 5

Same property, by R. V. Harnett. (Leasehold; action No. 2; amt due $10,650) 5

KINGS COUNTY.

Aug.

Prospect av, No. 171, n e s, 515 s e 3d av, 20x62.10¾ x 20.9¾x61.3¼, two-story brk dwell'g; assessed value, $2,100; by Van Mater Stilwell, referee, at County Court House 31

Sept.

Lot at Gravesend, begins at Atlantic Ocean at division line bet old lots 22 and 23 on one side and old lots 20 and 21 on the other side, as shown on Kowolski's map of common lands of Gravesend, Coney Island, runs north — x west — x south to ocean, x east to beginning, except strip 40 ft. wide condemned for use of New York & Coney Island R. R. Co., and part lying south of centre of Surf av; partition; by T. A. Kerrigan, at 13 Willoughby st 1

Macon st, No. 446, s s, 272.6 w Stuyvesant av, 17.6 x100, two-and-a-half-story brk dwell'g; assessed value, $5,000; by T. A. Kerrigan, at 13 Willoughby st 2

Glenada pl, Nos. 12-16 (late Albany av), w s, 100 s Decatur st, 49.9x100, two four-story stone apartment houses ....
Glenada pl, Nos. 18-22 (late Albany av), w s, 149.9 s Decatur st, runs west 100 x south 38.2 x east 24.11½ x south 6.10 x east 77.2¼ to Albany av, x north 50.3 to beginning, two four-story apartment houses; assessed value, together, $56,000 ....
by Edward G. Nelson, ref., at County Court House 4

Vanderbilt av, e s, 167.4¾ s Park av, 28x85, by John H. Wilson, referee, at County Court House 4

LIS PENDENS, KINGS COUNTY.

Aug.

North 6th st, s s, 150 w 2d st, 50x100. John Schreyer agt Jane McInroy individ. and admrx. of Donal McInroy; att'y, A. O. Salter 20

Kosciusko st, s s, 20 e Lewis av, 20x80. George O. Ditmis agt Patrick Concannon et al.; att'y, R. H. Coll 21

Prospect st, No. 123, n s, 175 w Bridge st, 25x75 ....
Prospect st, No. 105, n s, 100 e Jay st, 25x61; also, New York property ....
William L. Whiting agt Adelaide B. Stillwell et al.; action for partition; att'y, J. A. Balestier 21

Decatur st, n s, 229 w Throop av, 18x100. Moses Sahlein agt John C. Bushfield et al.; att'ys, Boardman & Boardman 21

4th st, n e s, 297.10 n w 8th av, 100x95. Henry Ginnel agt Roderick Von Graff et al.; att'ys, Johnson & Lamb 22

Carroll st, s w s, bet 4th and 5th avs, 200 from 4th av, 20x61.9x20x62.8. Patrick Cunningham agt James Cunningham; action to bar claim to inheritance, &c.; att'y, J. P. Philip 22

Graham av, e s, 25 n Scholes st, 25x100. Ferdinand M. Theriot exr. Marie T. March agt Jacob J. and Huldah K. Seebach; att'y, E. L. Lowe 22

18th st, n e s, 75 s e 6th av, 30x100.2. Katharine H. Taber agt William Kennedy et al.; att'ys, Garretson & Eastman 22

14th st, s s, 176 w 3d av, 16x90. Sarah H. Dodge agt William Kennedy et al.; att'ys, Garretson & Eastman 22

Market st, e s, 100 n Fulton st, 25x150. William H. Nolte and F. W. Koch agt John Reiss et al.; att'ys, Hurd & Grim 22

South 4th st, n s, 100 e Havemeyer st, 25x95. William Coit agt Arthur B. Gritman et al.; att'y, Alex. McKinny 24

13th st, s s, 173.2 w 4th av, 17.2x100. Ernest Adler agt Clara M. Parkhurst admrx., &c.; att'y, J. C. McEachan 24

Summit st, s s, 89.6 e Hicks st, 18x100. Ellen F. Lane agt Ann Hogan widow et al.; att'y, N. D. Pelty 24

Halsey st, s e cor Patchen av, 200x100. Horatio S. Stewart agt Hiram Bedell et al.; att'y, G. S. Ingraham 25

Madison st, s s, 20 e Howard av, 40x100. Twenty-sixth Ward Bank agt Robert L. Moores et al.; att'ys, Thornton, Earl & K. 25

Temple Court, centre line, e s, 160.8 n Seeley st, 14 x100, Flatbush. Richard Collins agt Thomas B. Robbins et al.; att'y, S. W. Collins 25

Temple Court, centre line, e s, 146.8 n Seeley st, 14 x100. Same agt same; same att'y 25

Temple Court, centre line, e s, 132.8 n Seeley st, 14 x100. Same agt same; same att'y 25

Lot at Sheepshead Bay, adj land of A. A. Emmens, runs south 176 x east 300 x north 186 x west —. John J. Cummins agt Mary A. Cummins; partition; att'y, John J. Cummins 25

York st, both sides, from Main st to Hudson av. Brooklyn Elevated R. R. Co. agt Joseph B. Markey et al.; action to acquire easement; att'ys, Hoadly, Lauterbach & Johnson 25

Hudson av, both sides, from York st to Park av. Same agt Anna Taylor; similar action; same att'ys 25

1st pl, s s, 225 e Court st, 25x133.5. Herman Wronkow agt James Finlay; att'y, D. Solis Ritterband 26

Jefferson av, s s, 260 w Nostrand av, 20x100. Thomas H. Elliott exr. Stephen Pettus agt Samuel J. Jones et al.; att'ys, Hoadley, Lauterbach & J. 26

21st st, s s, 225 e 3d av, 75x100. Peter A. Johnson agt John and Eliz. Stabler; action to set aside alleged fraudulent deed; att'y, W. J. Gaynor 26

Union st, n s, 100 w 8th av, 100x90. Alice and G. A. Crocker agt Erwin G. Gollner et al.; att'ys, Evarts, Choate & Beeman 26

Columbia st, e s, 50 n Church st, 20x83.6. Maurice Fitzgerald agt Ellen Sullivan et al.; att'y, G. W. Pearsall 26

RECORDED LEASES.

NEW YORK.

Per Year

Bleecker st, No. 311. William and David Huyler representing the Huyler estate to Asher M. Sachs; 3 years, from May 1, 1891 .... $900

Bowery, No. 25, second to fifth floors. Melancthon Burr, Jr., and Harris Lyons agents of William Cooper estate to Henry Peymann and Martin J. Kirby; 5¼ years, from Feb. 1, 1891 3,200

Bowery, No. 57½, store floor and cellar. John J. D. Meyer to Martin J. Kirby; 5 years, from May 1, 1891 1,280

Broad st, Nos. 105 and 107 ....
Water st, Nos. 24 and 26 ....
John F. E. Meissner to Hermann Schutte; 4 years, from May 1, 1892 3,800

Delancey st, No. 84, n w cor of Orchard st, No. 117, saloon. William Stern to Christian Pfleiderer; 5 years, from May 1, 1891 804

Greenwich st, Nos. 552 and 564 ....
Washington st, No. 541 ....
Patrick H. Nealis to Daniel Barry; 3¾ years, from Aug. 1, 1891 2,100

Leonard st, No. 15, store floor and cellar. Julius Schinkowsky to Peter Tidemann; 2 8-12 years, from Aug. 26, 1891 660

Ridge st, No. 145, front and rear. Samuel Kopp and Frederick Luhr to Abraham Michael; 2 10-12 years, from July 1, 1891 1,300

Same property. Assign. lease. Abraham and Rachel Michael to David Beck .... nom

Rutgers slip, No. 69, first floor. William Lane to William Rohlfs; 5 years, from Sept. 1, 1889 1,200

Same property. Assign. lease. William Rohlfs to Isaac A. Edmunds .... nom

Same property. William Lane to same; 2 years, from Sept. 1, 1894 1,200

West st, No 167, Louise Nuzzarini to Robert Ernst; 5 years, from Sept. 1, 1892 3,800

Same property. Assign. lease. Robert Ernst to William J. Williamson .... nom

Same property. Assign. lease. William J. Williamson and Frederick W. Hayward, of Williamson & Hayward, to James S. Kelly .... nom

23d st, No. 525 W. Frederick Wood to Edwin Outwater; 5¾ years, from Aug. 1, 1891 1,800

41st st, No. 248 W. James Gray to Roger V. Bonnell; 5 years, from Feb. 1, 1890 1,260

Same property. Assign. lease. Roger V. Bonnell to Helen Bonnell .... nom

41st st, No. 254 W. Assign. lease. Same to same .... nom

41st st, No. 129 W. John W. Timpson to Joseph B. Cross; 5 years, from May 1, 1891 1,500

81st st, No. 435 E. East store floor, three rooms on second floor, and front basement. John Fischer to John Pospisil; 3 years, from May 1, 1891 420

94th st, No. 161 W. Caroline Ross to Mathilde A. Ferdon; 3 years, from Sept. 1, 1891 1,200

Av B, No. 275, store and basement. Bartholomew Green to David Stevenson; 5¾ years, from Aug. 1, 1891 1,400

Av D, No. 112, store floor and cellar. John Brodbeck to Leopold Walter; 5 9-12 years, from Aug. 1, 1891 720

Amsterdam av, No. 1417, store. Thomas Moloney to Joseph Graef; 3 years, from Aug. 1, 1891 720

2d av, No. 88, three upper floors. Adolph Seelig and John H. Taylor to Robert Hobenstein; 3 years, from May 1, 1891 1,400

3d av, No. 1338, store and living apartment. Lewis E. Ransom to Charles Apt; 4⅔ years, from Sept. 1, 1891 1,400

7th av, n e cor 124th st, 100x125, second floor. The Columbus Market Co. to George Kraemer; 5 7-12 years, from Oct. 1, 1891 4,000

8th av, No. 890. Richard Mock to Patrick Sullivan; 4 years, from May 1, 1892 2,400

Same property. Assign. lease. Patrick H. Sullivan to Burr Brewing Co. .... nom

10th av, No 27, store and cellar. William J. Ryan to Frank Reeber; 4 years, from May 1, 1891 1,900

Same property. Assign. lease. Frank Reeber to Henry H. Deyerberg .... nom

CHATTELS.

NOTE.—The first name, alphabetically arranged, is that of the Mortgagor, or party who gives the Mortgage. The "R" means Renewal Mortgage.

NEW YORK CITY.

AUGUST 21 TO 27—INCLUSIVE.

SALOON AND RESTAURANT FIXTURES.

Arnstein, Alois. 419 E 70th....Burr B Co. $735
Abrams, William. 21 Clinton....M Seitz. 600
Aull, John. 900 3d av....J Ahles B Co. (R) 1,200
Baruch, Julius. 420 W 42d G Ringler & Co. 600
Borst, G W and W A. 396 Pleasant av....G Ehret. (R) 800
Brachmann, F W. 252 Fulton....J Doelger's Sons. (R) 375
Broche, Albert. 1883 Park av....J H Bereuter. Pool Table. (R) 150
Barmbold, Frederick. 108 8th... J Feldman. 152
Bertolotti, Angelo. 75 Thompson....Bernheimer & S. 140
Broderick, M J. 559 Morris av....D Stevenson. 460
Behrens, D H. 1651 Madison av....G Ringler & Co. 2,000
Bolefka, John. 585 E 118th....G Ehret. (R) 600
Brannigan, Richard. 789 11th av....J Ruppert. (R) 4,000
Barry & Lanigan. 1433 Av A....G Ehret. 1,600
Celentano, Pietro. 324 E 11th....Feigenspan B Co. 505
Carley, Maria C. 861 10th av ..Long Island Brewery. (R) 3,098
Cohn, A J. 239 E 73d... J Eichler B Co. (R) 500

Carney, Patrick. 2176 Park av ...J Hagerty & Co. 1,750
Cogan, E C. 12 Centre....J Foulke, Jr. 650
Colombara, Giovanni. 183 Bleecker....J Kress B Co. 500
Capparelli & Vaccaro. 65 Elizabeth....Abbott B Co. (R) 225
Dankers, Herman. 2639 8th av....G Ehret. 1,000
Dwyer, Michael. 29 Jones....Burr B Co. 500
Doran, Michael. 205 E 121st....D Stevenson. 500
Duerr, Frederick. 123 Stanton....C Stein. (R) 300
Duff, Patrick. 697 3d av....E T Moran. 1,000
Drummond, Angus. 355 West....M L Brophy. Restaurant. 669
Doran, James. 165 E 126th....G Ringler & Co. (R) 1,494
Edmunds, I A. 69 Rutgers slip....Beadleston & W. 2,500
Eckhardt, Franz. 104 and 106 E 48th....V Steiniger. 1,525
Engelhardt, Joseph. 231 Av A....G Ringler & Co. (R) 400
Erk, Rudolph. 388 E 10th....P Weidmann. 700
Freund, Edward. 490 E 59th....L I Brewery. 2,000
Falling, C E. 419 E 82d....C Stein. 550
Flynn, P H. 54th st and 9th av....C P Hawkins' Sons. (R) 785
Fox, Elizabeth. 1070 3d av....V Loewers. 900
Gerlach, A W. 460 Bedford....W Ulmer. (R) 4,000
Gondon, P W. 296 1st av....P Doelger. 2,500
Gans, Gertrude. 414 Washington....Abbott B Co. 1,000
Goldman, Nathan. 126 Hester....J Ferber. Restaurant Fixtures. 55
Goodrich, F W. 664 5th av....J Ahles B Co. (R) 400
Gossweyler, Fred. 323 W 39th....J Gossweyler. Liquors, &c. 2,000
Grassing, Charles. 628 E 13th....P Weidmann. 300
Harkin, J J. Broadway and Bleecker st....W Peter B Co. Pump. 158
Same——same. Ice Box. 75
Hayward & Williamson. 38 West Houston....J S Kelly. 1,000
Hinck, John. 456 Pearl....B Robitscher et al. 487
Hart, Peter. 19th st and 10th av....T Burke. 1,500
Hess, Julius. 10 1st av....J Ruppert. 1,000
Hildenbrand, Nicholas. 405 E 81st....G Ehret. 1,075
Hughes, James. Broadway and Van Courtland av....D Stevenson. (R) 100
Huynes, Henry. 677 5th av ...J Everard. 1,687
Husala, Philip. 393 2d av ..J C G Hupfel. (R) 700
Hylan & Meehan. 102 Centre ...W Peter. (R) 5,311
Hirtz, C H. 5 Norfolk....S Liebmann's Sons B Co. 600
Hubert, J H. Southern Boulevard and 3d av....J Eichler B Co. (R) 5,000
Holtgrewe, Henry. 823 E 43d....G Ehret. (R) 600
Jung, John. 235 E 107th...V Loewers. 863
Jordan, J F. 861 9th av....H Koehler & Co. 500
Same....M N Winne. 1,500
Joyce, Thomas. 161 W 55th... G Ehret. 1,500
Knupfer, M W. 72 Rivington...J Eichler B Co. 500
Kaupmann, Frederick. 147 E 4th....W Ulmer. (R) 800
Kraatz, Johanna. 1794 3d av....F Oppermann, Jr. 500
Koch, Theresia. 1275 1st av....Schmitt & S. 600
Lindstrom, Frederick. 6 Battery pl ... B Geiger. 190
Langhorst, Anton. 1586 1st av....G Ringler & Co. (R) 473
Lemmermann, Fred. 832 Washington... J Ruppert. 450
Levins, Patrick. 336 Av A....D Stevenson (R) 300
Leer, Henry. 106 Av B... A B Marx. Pool Table. 165
Link, Julius. 534 2d av....H Koehler & Co. 440
Lowenwicth, Joseph. 86 Eldridge....A B Marx. Pool Table. 150
Madden, M I. 1159 2d av....D Mayer. (R) 1,000
Mahon, John. 42 and 44 Washington....C Mahon. 1,900
Meier, George. 826 E 40th....Lembeck & Betz. 700
Mueller, F H. 128 West....Burr B Co. 2,000
Mattheslus, J C. 148 8th....G Ehret. (R) 1,500
Marello & De Minno. 62 Mulberry....P Neutarieri. 200
McEvoy & Dunn. 219 Canal....W L Flanagan. (R) 600
Nolan, Michael. 532 W 43d....D Stevenson. (R) 269
Nugent, J B. 700 3d av...J C G Hupfel B Co. (R) 4,000
O'Brien, J J. 74 New Chambers....J Fallert B Co. 650
O'Connor, Elinor. 1373 3d av....D Stevenson. (R) 1,500
O'Connor, T A. 928 E 33d....H Koehler & Co. 600
O'Gorman, Mary. 861 1st av....G Ehret. 2,000
O'Gorman, Mary. 861 1st av....E Poen. 200
O'Halloran, Edward. 36 Market....Hirsch & S. 1,267
O'Leary, Denis. 212 Monroe....W Ulmer. (R) 800
Ohry & Henig. 84 Av A....W Ulmer. 1,877
Peterson, B D. 455 8th av....A Peterson. (R) 490
Pitilli, Luigi. 268 E 108th....J Fallert B Co. 735
Pusch, Elizabeth A. 731 3d av....J Eichler B Co. (R) 2,000
Pospisil, Jan. 435 E 81st ...W Cohn. 800
Richards, Jean. 668 8th av....J Kress B Co. 300
Rottmann, Jacob. 608 W 52d....G Ehret. (R) 1,900
Rittershausen, Louis. 113 Clinton....W Horrmann. (R) 650
Schachel, William. 761 1st av ...G Ehret. 1,629
Schimpff, Clement. 56 Av C....J Doelger's Sons. 900
Sheridan, T P. 56th st and 6th av....H Held 600
Siemers & Rathyen. 272 Bleecker....J Dewender. 765
Sullivan, P H. 390 8th av....Burr B Co. 1,000
Saueriand, Anthony. 231 West....H Eibsen. 3,200
Strong, Patrick. 302 E 107th....Burr B Co. 700
Schraedler, Jakob. 130 Chrystie....J Hoffmann B Co. (R) 600
Seeber, Fred'k. 127 E 110th....F Oppermann, Jr. 400
Totten & Gregory. 197 3d av ...S Liebmann's Sons B Co. 300
Traver, G A. 54 Church... C G Carlsten. Restaurant Fixtures. 400
Tremer, Andrew. 452 W 38th....V Loewers. 245
Tripp, Henry. 404 Lenox av... Beadleston & W. saloon Ice Box. 80
Tierney, John. 12 Christopher....V Loewers. 600
Ullmann, Max. 404 West... J Kress B Co. 1,000
Vail, B F. 327 8th av....L Bradt. Restaurant Fixtures. 1,000
Van Clief, Jacob. 212 E 127th....India Wharf B Co. 750
Van Clief, Jacob. 212 E 127th....C Iba. 175
Verschleiser, Max. 101 Hester....Feigenspan B Co. 500
Walther, Louis. 286 Bowery . H Vogel. 800
Weiman, Gustav. 452 W 37th....A Kremer B Co. 500
Weyrauch, Wm. 115 Rivington....F Oppermann, Jr. 2,200
Wind, Geo. 808 E 49th....F Oppermann, Jr. 500
Woitke, Gustav. 88 Rivington....Anchor B Co. 233
Winkelmeyer, Max. 150 Eldridge....J Eichler B Co. (R) 600
Werniger, Oscar. 85 Cherry....P Weidmann. 250
Williams, Frank. 627 E 9th....J Doelger's Sons. (R) 500
Wallace, T J and J P. 36 6th av....G Ringler & Co. (R) 2,093
Werther, Gustav. 2346 2d av....G Ringler & Co. 1,082
Zimmer, Henry. 163 Mott....G Ringler & Co. 500
Zweig, Rebecca. 86 Suffolk....I Gluck. 25

HOUSEHOLD FURNITURE.

Allen, Alice S. 157 W 44th....B M Cowperthwait & Co. 179
Allen, Annie. 68 E 12th....O'Farrell & Co. 498
Allen, George. 1732 Madison av . J H Little. 387
Allen, Dollie and Ella Rowland. 229 West 16th ....J Baumann. 507
Axtell, Mimi. 347 E 113th....S Heyman & Co. (R) 118
Allison, Theo. 729 Amsterdam av .. J H Little. 154
Aveson, W D. 332 Lenox av....B M Cowperthwait & Co. 149
Baker, Francis. 327 E 30th... S Heyman & Co. 219
Barron, Mary A. 559 W 42d....B M Cowperthwait & Co. 156
Baum, Virginia. 2148 Lexington av....Amer Guar Assoc. 100
Beck, M. 134 Rivington....S I Herschmann. 242
Bender, Geo. 234 E 6th....Fennell & P. (R) 150
Bloch, Tilly. 200 Chrystie....S I Herschmann. 170
Brazendale, Edward. 801 10th av....L Baumann. 141
Burk, Mary. 195 West Houston....B M Cowperthwait & Co. 133
Burke, Maggie. 342 Madison....Jordan & M. 109
Burt, C A, Jr. 315 W 36th....A Ballin. 157
Boelsen, Marie. 1705 3d av....Simpson & P. Piano. 150
Buck, Susan E. 136 W 46th....J Baumann. 278
Bird, D W. 107 W 104th....J Gregg. 110
Blewett, M E. 221 W 14th ...S Knapp & Co. 338
Boock, Annie. 353 W 42d....H Thoesen. 118
Buckley, Bridget. 239 W 80th....S Heyman & Co (R) 122
Barry, Patrick. 412 E 81st....J Rubenstein. 135
Braun, Margaret. 339 E 21st....Manges Bros. 185
Culberth, E B. 313 W 22d ...J Baumann. 695
Castor, E A. 47 Perry....L Z Murray. 349
Chase, Laura. 19 Pell....B M Cowperthwait & Co. 125
Clabaugh, William. 177 Waverley pl....J H Little. 151
Clark, R. 1576 Park av....B M Cowperthwait & Co. 115
Clinton, D E. 177 E 60th ...S Heyman & Co. 144
Coffey, Ellen E. 308 E 20th ...Lincoln Ind & G Co. 125
Cogan, Patrick. 143 W 30th A Ballin. 148
Corliss, W E. 1689 9th av....B M Cowperthwait & Co. 145
Corridan, Mary. 1862 Lexington av....B M Cowperthwait & Co. 146
Crosby, Catherine. 550 E 143d....B M Cowperthwait & Co. 195
Cunningham, Margaret. 422 W 29th....A Ballin. 137
Chandler, Jennie G H. 38 E 10th S I Knight. (R) 2,922
Clarke, Maude K. 111 E 28th ...L Baumann. 194
Clayton, Mamie. 251 W 32d....L Baumann. 160
Daly, Margaret. 131 E 84th....J R Keane & Co. 594
Davenport, Mamie. 56 Oak . Jordan & M. 139
D E Finn Assoc. 157 Hudson ...B M Cowperthwait & Co. 276
del'Espee, L H. 222 E 15th....E C Hinsdale. 162
Depken, Fred. 202 E 114th....Jordan & M. 138
Dietrich, William. 430 E 15th....G Reubel. 129
Duffy, F A. 384 St Nicholas av .American Guar Assoc. 100
Durkin, Jane. 417 Pearl....B M Cowperthwait & Co. 129
Darragh, E A and A F. 219 W 15th....M Furman. 600
Dearman, Johanna. 143 E 15th....E Carl. 1,100
De Waters, Viola. 345 W 21st....O'Farrell & Co. (R) 207
Evans, Annie. 141 W 46th....S Knapp & Co. 939
Enders, Hermine. 160 Av B....S Heyman & Co. 138
Erber, Regina. 228 E 4th....Krakauer Bros. Piano. 340
Feldmann, Benny. 150 E 50th ...S Heyman & Co. 204
Flaherty, J F. 402 E 15th....J Moriarty. 162
Fleming, C P. 316 W 36th....Manges Bros. 136
Fleming, Elizabeth. 30 E 18th....L Baumann. 116
Field, Annie. 515 W 121st....J Coyne & Co. 139
Fox, Morris. 255 E 72d....S I Herschmann. 215
Farnham, Bessie D. 335 4th av....J Baumann. 270
Friedlander, Theresa. 14 E 73d....J Baumann. 176
Fahrenholz, Amelia. 135 W 45th ...J Baumann. 140
Freeman, Oakley. 56 E 105th ...S J Evans. 100
Gannon, James. 169th st and Walton av....Manges Bros. 166
Gardiner, Frank. 308 E 20th....T E Thompson. 250
Gathard, Mary. 310 W 53d....D Schwarzkopf. 1,292
Gorman, Anna. 156 St Anns av ...S Baumann. 168
Guthrie, S J. 5 E 115th... C E Pierce 130
Glover, C N. Webster av, 169th and 170th sts....Fennell & Pye. 152
Gott, Margaret A. Sheepshead Bay, L I....D Brown. 2,500
Green, Mary. 114 Rivington....S I Herschmann. 132
Grimes, G B. 228 W 41st....O'Farrell & Co. 167
Galligan, J J. 204 E 32d ...J Moriarty. 259
Gallenbiek, Charles. 449 W 39th....H Thoesen. 117
Gippert, Annie. 347 E 17th....H S Eisler. 156
Guntting, Frank. 55 W 98th ...S Heyman & Co. (R) 100
Homer, Charles. 128 East Houston....H S Eisler. 230
Hughes, Francis. Inwood....H Thoesen. 125
Hadley, C P. 2283 7th av....J H Little. 317
Hartog, Alphonse. 231 W 16th....O'Farrell & Co. 168
Hershhef, Hermann. 179 Madison....A Ballin. 152
Hickey, J J. 472 Pearl... B M Cowperthwait & Co. 197
Hill, Harriet. 257 W 30th....J Moriarty. 243
Hommedieu, Mrs M L. 48 Greenwich av....J Moriarty. 192
Houston, Bebie L. 166 E 78th....J Baumann. 497
Hetzel, E L. 22 E 125th....C E Pierce. 130
Jaupol, Moris. 647 E 13th....H S Eisler. 160
Jennings, Hattie. 119 W 26th....O'Farrell & Co. 335
Johnson, Jennie W. 219 W 46th....O'Farrell & Co. 289
Johnston, Mrs F R. 267 W 40th....J H Little. 242
Kay, Emil. 164 E 28th....S I Herschmann. 149
Keegan, Mary. 78 Mangin....B M Cowperthwait & Co. 139
Keely, Ella. 86 E 3d....J Moriarty. 123
Kiernan, Rosie. 426 W 45th....Alexander Bros. 144
Kilburn, Catherine. 188 W 4th....O'Farrell & Co. 201
Kohnstamm, E H. 533 W 125th....S Heyman & Co. 175
Kortum, Bertha. 301 E 87th....S Heyman & Co. 244
Keppler, Lena. 133 W 15th....L A McGinley.(R) 3,000
Kuhsel, Mary. 300 E 5th....S I Herschmann. 229
Libreton, Pauline. 38 Clinton pl....C E Pierce. 130
Livingston, May. 154 W 32d....S I Herschmann. 964
Lampart, Josephine B. 321 W 17th....Dreisacker & Co. 137
Levien, J J. 152 E 86th....S Heyman & Co. 281
Lester, Helen V. 342 Lenox av....L Baumann. 113
May, Tillie. 91 Catharine....Jordan & M. 117
Millner, C A, Jr. 454 College av....J Baumann. 166
Maganu, Mary J. 146 Madison....Jordan & M. 100
Marcus, Benaro. 3 Jackson....S I Herschmann. 221
Matthews, Annie. 200 E 81st....L Baumann. 114
Matthews, Mamie. 133 W 60th....L Baumann. 208
McArthur, William. 3 W 103d....H Thoesen. (R) 213
McCarthy, Lizzie. 44 Rivington....A Hahn. 140
McCutchen, Frank. 509 W 23d....J H Little. 387
Meinhard, Adam. 335 W 59th....E Waldect. 200
Meyer, A and J. 1047 Prospect av....R F Stevens. 157
Middleton, Sedgwick. 139 W 83d....J H Little. 116
Moore, Bessie. — W 16th....S I Herschmann. 137
Morache, Mrs. H. 100 W 73d ..J H Little. 206
Morgenstern, M. 1629 Lexington av....J Kabatchnick. 203
Morse, May A. 120 W 61st....B M Cowperthwait & Co. 220
Mount, Mary L. 110 E 26th....L Baumann. 216
Marcus, Fannie. 151 E 112th....Krakauer Bros. Piano. 340
Maschek, Theodore. 217 W 33d....O'Farrell & Co. 217
Meagher, M E. 228 E 78th....S Heyman & Co. 254
Meehan, Margaret. 114 E 114th....J Baumann. 227
Meyers, Louis. 1838 3d av....Krakauer Bros. Piano. 225
Mark, Rudolph. 150 Henry....J Rubenstein. 623
McVicar, A H. 229 E 70th....J Moriarty. (R) 159
Norcross, I W, Jr. 200 and 202 W 38th....I W Norcross, Sr. 1,800
Naumann, Lottie. 128 W 67th....A Ballin. 286
Nolan, Celia. 161 E 113th....Dreisacker & Co. 174
Neidelhamp, John. 354 W 12th....L Baumann. 185
O'Connor, Bridget. 763 10th av....O'Farrell & Co. 111
Pelton, L C. 8 Broome....J Lewin. 139
Petigney, F T. 1670 Madison av ..L Baumann. 112
Priess, Anna. 57 W 16th....J Moriarty. 150
Perry, E H. 38 W 21st....L Baumann. 115
Ramer, Mary. 127 Forsyth....Fennell & P e. (R) 198
Riley, Ellen C. 169 W 34th....A Ballin. 272
Rosenblatt, H R. 976 3d av....S Heyman & Co. 289
Rueffer, Annie. 39 Cooper....J H Little. 294
Rallins, Alice. 418 W 52d....J Baumann. 177
Rade, J and S. 321 E 33d....W A Buckley. Piano. 350
Schneider, Anna. 229 E 14th....J Moriarty. (R) 247
Storms, Jennie. 241 E 75th....J Baumann. 155
Stuusehr, Israel. 254 Henry....J Rubenstein. 119
Schneider, Elise. 1361 Lexington av....J Gregg. 156
Steinthal, H. 523 E 12th....H Thoesen. 111
Sanger, Fanny. 415 E 118th .. L Baumann. 516
Schwarz, I, Mrs. 2121 8th av....J H Little. 312
Seymour, Emma. 1988 Lexington av .... W Weed. 100
Sherwood, F M. 344 Lenox av....J Lewin. 138
Smith, Lillie. 243 W 34th....J Baumann. 123
Smith, Lillian. 252 W 43d....C W Matthews. 105
Solan, Julius. 20 Pike....Alexander Bros. 206
Spanger, L. 1582 Madison av....S Heyman & Co. 174
Stanton, Jas. 65 E 105th ...J H Little. 212
Salmonson, Frederick. 26 W 135th....L Baumann. 135
Singhi, H U. 169 E 111th....L Baumann. 298
Smith, J S. 332 W 11th....L Baumann. 280
Thompson, Catherine. [illegible] W 33d....J Baumann. 171
Thornton, Ida. 151 W 22d....S Knapp & Co. 795
Tunison, Mattie L. 48 W 97th....E Marks. 225
Thomashefsty, Bores. 120 Forsyth ...J Rubenstein. 167
Van Campen, Mary R. 137 and 139 E 21st ...J T Rathbun. (R) 3,610
Van O'Linda, Josie. 100 W 61st....J Baumann. 197
Van Campen, Mary R. 137 and 139 E 21st....Havana National Bank, of Havana, N Y. (R) 17,732
Vasseliades, Constantine. 357 W 23d....J Baumann. (R) 174
Vogel, Mary F. 805 Washington ...Manges Bros. 235
Vollmer, G. 405 E 82d... S Heyman & Co. (R) 136
Walroud, Howell. 181 E 120th....Krakauer Bros. Piano. 160
Williamson, Albert. 1435 Broadway....O'Farrell & Co. 456
Williams, Ellen. 202 E 114th....W Daly. (R) 500
Winslow, Charlotte. 121 W 97th.... J Baumann. 162
Watson, Carl. 158 E 112th....B M Cowperthwait & Co. 184
Webb, Harry. 140 W 63d....B M Cowperthwait & Co. 120
Weinberg, Bernard. 1981 2d av....B M Cowperthwait & Co. 205
Williamson, Albert. 1435 Broadway....O'Farrell & Co. 391
Wilson, Mrs W B. 2208 7th av....B M Cowperthwait & Co. 214
Wilson, W R. 540 W 47th....A Ballin. 177
Wiswell, Nellie B. 42 W 132d....Dreisacker & Co. 226
Wilkins, Gertrude. 27 7th av....L Baumann. 130
Wilson, Lizzie. 986 6th av....J Baumann. 695
Weld, G W. 18 W 26th....B Croner. 500
Williams, W F. 8th av, bet 92d and 93d sts....J Baumann. 130
Young, Malora. 225 W 74th....J Baumann. 139
Zerbe, J S. Pulitzer Building....B M Cowperthwait & Co. 170
Zerrenthin, Fritz. 404 E 117th....B M Cowperthwait & Co. 158

MISCELLANEOUS.

Albers, John. 995 6th av....S Green. Grocery Fixtures. 300
Altiere, P & Bro. Lenox av, 111 and 112th sts....H Frank. Horses, Trucks, &c. 3,000
Anderson, W H & S. 452 6th av, 204 W 23d....S Brown. Type, Press, &c. 800

Aron & Kleinkopf. 73 Willett....F & G Haag & Co. Barber Fixtures. 345
Anderson, Alexander. 23-27 Vandewater....G Mathers' Sons. Presses, &c. 9,000
Aaronson, Andrew. 66 Suffolk....J P Rathbun & Co. Cutter. (R) 121
Ader, Adolph. 243 Delancey....G Pins. Barber Fixtures. 72
Arteaga, Serapio. 52 Broadway....M Lopez. Cigar Fixtures. 675
Belmont, Antonjio. 188 Canal....A Schwaab & Son. Barber Fixtures. (R) 21
Bockee, J J....E Sherman. Yacht. 1,151
Burger, Jacob. 6?8 9th av....National Cash Register Co. Register. 200
Beneditti, Raeffaele. 42 Madison....C E Pierce. Drug Fixtures. 130
Barry, Michael. 137th st, bet 5th and 6th avs...P Brinckmann. Horses, Trucks, &c. 800
Baum, Lippmann. 93 Ridge....P Reidenbach. Truck. (R) 220
Bleibler, Martin. 48 Av D....B Fischer & Co. Grocery Fixtures. 150
Brown, David. 110 W 53d....Sonn Bros. Horses and Trucks. (R) 275
Cassidy, John. 147 Fulton .. H C Neer. Machinery. (R) 1,080
Copeland, Ewance. 148 W 35th....J Cunningham Son & Co. Coach. 587
Cuney, Patrick ...D P Nichols & Co. Cab. 500
Cohen, Meyer. 425 9th av....L Cohen. Gents' Furnishing Goods. 48
Corriglio, Zucchine. 2082 2d av....Marvin Safe Co. Safe. 255
Cuddy, William. 108 Hester....M Hanan. Store Fixtures. 100
Culver, C H. 8 E 125th....J W Tufts. Soda Fixtures. (R) 700
Callelli, Dominico. 356 1st av....A Schwaab & Son. Barber Fixtures. (R) 31
Cappello, C A. 1126-1130 Lexington av....S Littmann. Barber Fixtures. 784
Colohan, Wm....G Dessecker. Coach. 600
Dreyer, August. 125 Pearl....National Cash Reg. Co. Register. 225
Dithridge Flint Glass Co....Atlantic Trust Co. Fixtures, &c, &c. (R) 100,000
Davis, L E. 1 and 3 Union sq....Rosa B De Casanova. Office Fixtures. 135
Delaney, Dennis. 585 Greenwich....National Cash Register Co. Register. 175
Eiser, Anton....P Strobel & Sons. Tables, Chairs, &c. (R) 73
Eiselt, Henry. 249 Eldridge....H Corell. Horse Wagon, &c. 150
Equinian & Tashjian. 12 Frankfort .. Campbell P P Co. Press 400
Freireich, Joseph. 265 Rivington....P Feinberg. Wagon. 115
Feinberg, Peter. 103 Stanton....E Newfeld. Tools, &c. 100
Finklesten, J L. 361 6th av....Canton S and Dental Chair Co. Dental Fixtures. 90
Fischer, R W. 407 4th av....G Fischer. Butcher Fixtures. 1,246
Finan, James. 1507 1st av....J Cunningham Son & Co. Coach. (R) 131
Glueck, Adolf. 58 Sheriff....J Weitzer. Grocery Fixtures. 100
Green, Williame 324-328 Pearl....Van Allens & B. Press. (R) 2,050
Glanckopf, Rosalia. 68 Av B... D Eichner. Safe. 40
Gorga, Raffaele. 574 Grand....A Trondera. Barber Fixtures. ½ int. 165
Gruber, K C. 323 East Houston... F G Haag & Co. Barber Fixtures. 196
Glickman, A and R. 29 Suffolk....S Benjamin, Grocery Fixtures. 135
Haessig, F A. 784 Washington....O A Leister. Drug Fixtures. (R) 600
Holland Bros. 588 Highbridge road....E Baker. Horses and Store Fixtures. 1,000
Horwitz & Schreiber....Sekosky Bros. Store Fixtures. 85
Howes & Williams. 64 Fulton....T W & C B Sheridan. Cutter. (R) 133
Herzog, Henry. 406 W 41st....H Diggelmann. Horses, Wagon, &c. 1,200
Harrje, F and H. 86th st and Park av. . H Sturcker. Grocery Fixtures. 1,600
Horowitz, Moses. 69 Forsyth....Lamson Consol S S Co. Register. 140
Hubner, Louis. 145 E 90th....D Fernschild. Grocery Fixtures. 2,000
Hardenbergh, George. 113 Nassau....G H Sandborn & Sons. Machinery. 220
Heumann, John. 2140 8th av....Standard Pump Co. Machinery. 141
Howe, Bridget. Fordham....J M Gifford. Horses, Trucks, &c. 170
Hoyt, Bros. 712 E 145th....H Weil. Horses, Trucks, &c. 1,450
Iron Car Equipment Co ...Central Trust Co. Franchises, &c. (R) 600,000
Intermann, C H. 330 Bleecker....National Cash Register Co. Register. 225
Jacobson, Jacob. 165 Attorney....L Heinsfurter. Butcher Fixtures. 200
Jones, Frederick ...D B Dunham. Coach. 825
Jaschke, Herman. 1168 2d av....Roberts & Collin. Bakery Fixtures. 150
Joiner, Planing and Moulding Co. 476-480 E 139th....E Stichler. Machinery. agreement
Kieferdorf, F F. 75th st and Columbus av....Fischer Bros. Drug Fixtures. 808
Kohn, Edward. 510 Hudson....E Kohn. Horse, Wagon, &c. 125
Kalisky, John. 1395 2d av ...Korner & S. Grocery Fixtures. 187
Katzmeier, F A. 2027 7th av....Canton Surgical and Dental Co. Dental Fixtures. 100
Kiene, William. 227 Sullivan....Weeks, Parr & Co. Bakery Fixtures. (R) 300
Kleinschmidt, Louis. 648 Broadway... P Westphal. Barber Fixtures. 148
Kuko, Louis. 275 Delancey....J Brille. Machines. 100
Lopez, Rosasio. 310 E 8th.. .G Pins. Barber Fixtures. 302
Laux, J G. 96 Varick....G H Hachenberg. Butcher Fixtures. 500
Same....C F Becker. Horse, Cart, &c. 500
Lawson, G B. Delhi, N Y....American Writing Machine Co. Typewriter. 110
Lenahan, J M. 102d st and East River....Union Blue Stone Co. Horses, Trucks, &c. 1,430
Levy & Weinstein. 12 Ludlow....F W Hahn. Machines. 128
Lewson, George. 2318 2d av....S Bilden. Drug Fixtures. 3,500
Lieboff, Sam. 49 Canal....J Uzlaner. Barber Fixtures. 60
Macy, C E. 17 8th av ...I H Macy. Laundry Fixtures. 295
McClary, J A. 112 Front ..American Writing Machine Co. Typewriter. 60
Same....same. Typewriter. 60
McEathron & Waite. Railroad av, bet 176th and 177th sts....J C Watson & Co. Horses, Trucks, &c. 800
Michel, Jennett. 1517 1st av....B Fischer & Co. Grocery Fixtures. 200
Michel, Fred. 193 1st av....J C Klatze. Bakery Fixtures. 383
Minuilie, Michiele. 332 1st av....A Busby. Barber Fixtures. 250
Same....G Bernava. Barber Fixtures. 175
Mueller, E E. 1560 Madison av....National Cash Register Co. Register. 175
McAdams & Duane. 164 Division....J Cunningham Son & Co. Coach, &c. (R) 467
Meares, Richard. 40th st and 6th av....Schwarzschild & Sulzberger. Hotel Fixtures. 9,000
Merinsky, S. 438 Pearl....A Wirsching. Lithographing Stones. 628
Maclean, F E. 779 2d av....T J Thomburg. Drug Fixtures. 1,070
Magee, Worrall & Richards. 223 Grand .Marvin Safe Co. Safe. 120
Manhattan Turn Verein. 314-316 E 63d....W F Behrens. Fixtures, &c. 150
McHugh, Frank. Av A and 11th st....National C Reg Co. Register. 175
National Stove Co., Peekskill, N Y....N Y Stove Works. Fixtures, &c. 2,500
Oppenheimer, Simon. 47th st and East River....I Reuss. Horse, Wagon, &c. 275
Otto, Henry. 10 Av A....S Blant. Bakery Fixtures. (R) 800
Oxly, J A. 124 Liberty....National C Reg Co. Register. 175
Ohmann, Herman. 70th st and 9th av....L Heilbrum. Horses, &c. 402
Pecoraro, Enrico. 2330 2d av....A Schwaab & Son. Barber Fixtures. (R) 397
Perrino, Rosario. 1083 3d av....A Schwaab & Son. Barber Fixtures. 493
Pisarra, Angelo. 574 Grand....R Gorga. Barber Fixtures. ½ int. 165
Patton, Isabella. 696 9th av... E B Banks. Butcher Fixtures. 300
Penrose & Co. 27 Rose. ..Van Allens & B. Press, &c. (R) 9,455
Quinn, D F. 338 W 25th....J Cunningham Son & Co. Coach. 400
Richards, Alice R. 75 Fulton....J S Huyler. Machinery, &c. (R) 1,836
Roberts, J S. 168 E 112th....R Gill. Carpenter Fixtures. 300
Risk, William. 855 E 137th....Smith & Sills. Horse, Wagon, &c. 100
Reardon, D and B. 97th st, bet Lexington and 4th avs....D Murray. Horses, &c. 300
Reynolds, E W. Horatio st and North River and 115 Withers, Brooklyn....I W Reynolds. Horses and Trucks. 871
Schaffner, L P 26 W 3d... Lamson Consol S S Co. Register. 210
Slomin, Mary. 90 Stanton....J Flesch. Drug Fixtures. 682
Smith, J B....D F Morgan Boiler Co. Boilers, &c. 565
Stolba, John. 1108 1st av....J Cunningham Son & Co. Coach. (R) 525
Sussels, J & D. 82 Ridge....R Spahn. Machines. 125
Schwarze, Julius. 79 and 81 Crosby.. .E E Levi. Machinery, &c. Secures Rent. 1,000
Same....same. Machinery, &c. 3,800
Simon, Leon. 146 South 5th av....D E Adams. Machines. (R) 300
Solomon, Philipp. 27 Allen....L Lesser. Bakery Fixtures. 50
Span & Mandelbaum. 112 Canal....M Schustak, Store Fixtures. 1,000
Spring Weld Tube Co 43 John....Hall's Safe and Lock Co. Safe. 145
Strohsahl, August. 1731 Av A....J Arfmann. Horses, Truck, &c. 600
Sunderman, J H Gouverneur and Front sts....H P Havens. Machinery. (R) 3,500
Schmid, Chas. 2d av and 116th st....Jackson & Co. Butcher Fixtures. 165
Scinrca, Ginseppe. 624 8th av....P Ventuzieri. Barber Fixtures. 208
Seitz, Peter. 26 8th av....P Westphal. Barber Fixtures. 104
Sheehan, J L. 247 W 41st....D B Dunham. Coach. 1,350
Sganga, Salvatore. 943 8th av....A Schwaab & Son. Barber Fixtures. (R) 151
Siebenborn, H A. 470 W 23d....A Mohl. Drug Fixtures. 250
Teppewein, Ernst. 260 1st av....A B Stratton. Bakery Fixtures. (R) 1,145
Tobin, Michael....C Keegan. Horses, Trucks. 700
Same....same. Horses, Trucks, &c. 700
Same....same. Horses, Trucks, &c. 1,200
Taylor, Mary A. 160 E 125th....A D Puffer & Co. Soda Fixtures. 1,600
Vogel & Herman. 15 2d....L Weinfeld. Cigar Fixtures. 40
Vopelak, Joseph. 74th st and Av A....National C Reg Co. Register. 800
Wobbekind, A. 24 Market....National C Reg Co. Register. 200
Wanke & Co. 8 Lafayette pl....J Stewart. Machinery. 95
Same....J Stewart. Machines. 121
Weinberg, Israel. 10 Suffolk....F W Hahn. Machines. 85
White, Johanna. 31 and 33 10th av... P McManus. Machinery. (R) 1,000
Washburn, H L. Storage....D T Warren. Office Fixtures. 150
Ziegelmeier, Joseph 536 6th.. .J Ziegelmeier. Grocery Fixtures. 50

BILLS OF SALE.

Atkinson, M B. 19 Platt....W F Farrington Co. Press, &c. 1
Birkenstamm, Fritz. 207 E 76th....E Malter. Saloon. 1,100
Dukek, Charles 307 E 115th....M L Christopher. Horses, Milk Wagons, &c. 2,500
Eitner, Otto. 36 E 4th....J R Albrecht. Cigar Fixtures. 400
Engel, Joseph. 168½ Attorney....Samath & Weiss. Liquors, &c. 1,900
Eckhoff, Henr . 370 9th av....Anna W Meyer. Grocery Fixtures. 3,200
Fraenkel, Samuel. 102 Columbia....Rosa Krieger. Milk Fixtures, Horse, &c. 425
Gendel, Jacob. 94 Bayard .... Anna Gross. Clothing Fixtures and Furniture. 1,500
Krieger, Marx. 102 Columbia....S Fraenkel. Milk Fixtures, Horse, &c. 400
Knob, Jacob. 32 Av A....J Kammer. Butcher Fixtures. 275
Koch, F E. 48 Av D... M Bleibler. Grocery Fixtures. 250
Little, L M. 324 W 47th....J E Little. Piano. 50
Same....same. Furniture. 100
Lehmann, Max. 1?60 1st av....S Eichengren. Horse and Harness. 60
Myer, Babatta. 1087 Park av....Clara Myer. Grocery Fixtures. 225
Marri & Patolo. 126 Mott....Gregorio & De Vito. Saloon. 1,225
Miraglia, Raffaele. 35 Mulberry... Teresa Petito. Grocery Fixtures. 600
Norton, J T. Washington Market....S Underhill. Stand. 100
Stetler, Carrie S. 252 W 38th....L Kendel. Furniture. 325
Sullivan, Mortimer. 319 Bowery....Ellen Sullivan. Saloon. 2,000
Scotchoff, M....Louis Bradell. Tobacco Fixtures, &c. 1
Whitney, Amanda. 320 E 42d....W Balding. Furniture. 350
Wolf, Rosa. 592 3d av....A Wolf. Store Fixtures, &c. 100
Washburn, Abbie S. 383 and 385 W 52d....A L Washburn. Machinery, &c. 200

ASSIGNMENTS OF CHATTEL MORTGAGES.

Butler, Elizabeth to J Butler. (Mort given by Jas Hunter, Oct 16, 1890.) 1
Krieger, Marx to Rosa Krieger. (S Fraenkel, Aug 17, 1891.) 300
Rosenfeld, Leo to Emil Rosenfeld. (F Freedman, May 15, 1891). 1,200

KINGS COUNTY.

AUGUST 20 TO 26—INCLUSIVE.

SALOON AND RESTAURANT FIXTURES.

Bode, F. 142 George....J Doelger's Sons. $600
Beecher, H. 232 Suydam....J Eppig. 524
Broglie, L. 95 Morgan av....J Eppig. 650
Connelly, J. 195 Wythe av....F Hower B Co. 600
Connelly, J. 138 Patchen av....I Roth. 665
Dorn, A and F Edzard. 204 Ewen....E Ochs. 1,000
Duffy, M L. Myrtle av, n w cor Navy st....F Munch. (R) 700
Dougherty, J. 227 Hudson av....M Seitz. 800
Eckert, J. Blake av and Linwood st....India Wharf B Co. 635
Enrich, W. 5 Boerum pl....Elizabeth Meltzer. 600
Eagan, Cath E. 605 5th av....H Koehler & Co. 1,800
Furnald, H W. 1307 Broadway ...F Fedderke. Pool Table. 175
Gleichmann, A. 47 Jamaica av....Danenberg & Coles. 600
Gaiser, A. 99 Morrell....J Eppig. 350
Gerlach, Albert W. 460 Bedford av....W Ulmer. (R) 4,000
Hiller, G. 357 Kent av....India Wharf B Co. 800
Healy, P. 33 and 33½ Hoyt....L I Brewery. 1,888
Jacoby, F. 72 Goerck, New York....F Ibert. 200
Knoblach, J. 487 Liberty av....Leibinger & O B Co. 225
Kaspar, G. 246 Jefferson....L Eppig. 300
Meigel, J. 190 Harrison av....M Seitz. 500
Mahon, J. 42 Washington....C Mahon. 1,800
McGrath, M and P. 1408 Bergen....J Murtaugh. 700
McKeown, C V. 359 5th av....Long Island Brewery. 1,250
Meyer, H. Ashford st, cor Liberty av....Wiggins & Co. Pool Table. 200
Madden, Luke. 466 Manhattan av....S Liebmann's Sons B Co. 600
May, B. 244 Wyckoff av....F Ibert. 700
Offermann, D. 55 Ralph av....W Ulmer. 100
Parisette, Christine. 215 Ewen....P Weidmann. 500
Pink, F and P Lehnert. 318 Melrose....F Eller. 350
Quigley, J F. 193 Driggs....E Ochs. 900
Satter, J N. 25 Graham av....J Kissinger. Oyster Saloon. (R) 300
Scheib, P. 403 Bushwick av....J Kress B Co. 1,500
Schiffmann, W. 97 Scholes....J Kress B Co. 560
Schneider, Morris & Max. 23 Seigel....J Doelger's Sons. 425
Schnitzer, A. Greene st, n e cor Oakland st....Beadleston & W. 270
Shanley, J. 70 Van Brunt....P Weidmann. 215
Siemsen, W. 216 North 2d....W Ulmer. (R) 250
Sheridan, Mary E. 1074 Broadway....E Miller. (R) 3,500
Scholler, J. 907 Grand....J Wallace & Son. 600
Shea, T J. 179 Franklin....F Hower B Co. 600
Temme, C. 130 Hamburg av... Abbott B Co. 460
Vansize, G A. 257 South 2d....S Liebmann's Sons B Co. 1,000
Wolpe, B. 52 Underhill av....Williamsburgh B Co. 400
Weissler, F. 165 Graham av....E Ochs. 420
Williams, M. 267 Humboldt....Burger & H B Co. 700
Wisely, P G. 197 Saratoga av....Welz & Zerwick. 450
Wadsworth, A W. 1346 Gates av....F Hower B Co. 686
Wrieden, J C. 536 7th av....W Ulmer. (R) 600

HOUSEHOLD FURNITURE.

Antonillo, C. 23 Central av....D Lauriano. 400
Arthur, Ellen. 398 Henry ...Eleanor Kisselburg. 200
Bremer, F. 1402 Bushwick av....Brooklyn F Co. 203
Brown, G T. 1 Alice court....Brooklyn F Co. 267
Burns, Edith E. 395 Bridge....A Pearson. 614
Bernard, D E. 248 14th....I Mason. 126
Borgendahl, A F. 362 Atlantic av....A Pearson. 1[illegible]
Brown, J. 137 Nassau ..I Mason. 205
Curry, Mary. 15 Patchen av....Mullins & Sons. 153
Clark, Katie. 989 St Marks av....C T Kendrick & Co. 173
Cummings, Lillian. 70 Ellery....L Z Murray. 121
Dean, W M. 585 Willoughby av... M Botteberg. 140
Dewees, W H. 598 Bergen....L Baumann. 134
Douglass, F. 185 Adams....L Baumann. 131
De Julio, Mrs J. 139 34th....Brooklyn F Co. 174
Donato, F. 88th st....Brooklyn F Co. 140
Galvin, J. 805 Park av....C T Kendrick & Co. 122
Goud, J T. 448 Gates av....J McEnery & Co. 117
Harvey, W F. Lee av and Middleton st....A C Flatley. 121
Hausen, Mary L. 250A Livingston....L Z Murray. 244
Hilton, Jessie. 256 Palmetto....A White. Piano. 100
Hall, Mary E. 52 2d pl....Lincoln Indorsement and Guarantee Assoc. 150
Hanan, J D. 842 1st....Annie Hanan. 1,000
Hardman, Bessie. 345 Clason av....Mullins & Sons. 287

Hayes, Louisa. Hammels Station... Cowperthwait & Co. 379
Kingsley, E A. 211 Halsey....Financial Credit Co. 900
Lincoln, Minnie D. 425 6th....L Z Murray. 154
Lockwood, S. 881 Halsey....Kendrick & Co. 320
Meissner, C. Parkville, L I....R M Walters. Piano. 135
Martin, L A. 163 Wilson....Brooklyn F Co. 247
McAuley, A B. 109 Huron....Brooklyn F Co. 255
Mooney, Marie E. 132 Calyer... J Moriarty. 185
Morse, Kittie C. 1003 Putnam av....L Baumann. 540
Mullins, R. 909 Stuyvesant av....W R Willis. 148
McConnell, R E. 147 Hooper....I Mason. 717
Nistad, P. 186 Middleton....Brooklyn F Co. 249
O'Grady, E. Staten Island....R M Walters. Piano. 200
Pfeister, Christina. 29 Stockton....L Baumann. 158
Pickave, Clara. 274 52d....J Browne. 116
Rose, A F. 69 Clermont av....D Moriarty. 193
Saunders, F. A. and K W. 93 Johnson....H S Eisler. 223
Silverberg, J. 593 Van Buren....Brooklyn F Co. 248
Smith, Annie. 26 Skillman av....A Schulz. 175
Salg, C. 54 Throop av....C T Kendrick & Co. 108
Scheper, Annie. 103 Luquer....L Z Murray. 114
Silberstein, S. 228 Stockton....C T Kendrick & Co. 294
Stafford, Emma. 182 5th av....O'Connor & Treacy. 112
Warren, Nancy P. 241 Washington....P White. 650
Wilkenning, L H. 1389 Fulton....Brooklyn F Co. 154
Wolf, Ida. 60 High... Manges Bros. 206

MISCELLANEOUS.

Bahr, H P. 679 Grand....A D Puffer & Sons Mfg Co. Soda Fountain. (R) 100
Bandolin, H. 230 Graham av....Archer Mfg Co. Barber Fixtures. (R) 148
Bennett, Annie M....Heath & Co. Canal Boats and Mules. 250
Bowers & Bros. 387 Wythe av....Empire State Type Founding Co. Type. 151
Bernson, N. 679 4th av....J M Markert. Coal and Ice Business. 1,350
Cook, F. Coney Island... R Schermerhorn. Drug Fixtures. 1,000
Doyle, P. 133 Hudson av....Nat Cash Register Co. Register. 175
Finkle, E. 371 Fulton....Marvin Safe Co. Safe. 120
Frank, A. 135 Central av....M Pfiester. Horse, &c. 275
Goldstein, A. 141 Osborn....Betsy Goldstein. Sewing Machines. 250
Green, Mrs R E 1064 Bedford av ...J W Tufts. Soda Apparatus. (R) 105
Gabriel, S. 242 9th av ...Archer Mfg Co. Barber Fixtures. (R) 315
Gray, B E. 892 Bergen....F Plunkett. Horses. 500
Grenzig, J A. 35 South 5th....A Hanover. Presses. 775
Same....L M Ernst. Presses. 200
Herring, C. 167 Central av... Archer Mfg Co. Barber Fixturos. 375
Herman, H. 573 Franklin av....Archer Mfg Co. Barber Fixtures. 100
Kelly, D....Smith & Co. Truck. 300
Kleock, E T....P Barrett. Truck. (R) 460
Kopf, D W. South 3d and Hooper sts....Nat Cash Register Co. Register. 175
Kuster, A C. 2641 Atlantic av....Phebe E Leverich. Milliner and Fancy Goods. 900
Levin, J. Osborn st, near Blake av....L Glattstine. Sewing Machines. 1,000
Madden, L. 707 Bedford av....Nat Cash Register Co. Register. 175
Maragier, P. 169 Court....Archer Mfg Co. Barber Fixtures. (R) 512
Martin, C J. 964 Lafayette av....C Pfeiff. Bakery Fixtures. 200
McAtamny, P. 46 Greenpoint av....National Cash Register Co. Register. 175
Moussette, O J. 174 North 4th .. A Vogeley. Machine. 800
Mucia, A. 316 Broadway....F & G Haag & Co. Barber Fixtures. 192
Oldham, J. White st, cor Elm st....W W Goodrich. Machinery. (R) 1,915
Petrino, J. 827 Flushing av....Archer Mfg Co. Barber Fixtures. (R) 145
Reitz, J. 367 Hooper....Nat Cash Register Co. Register. 175
River and Rail Electric Light Co....Central Trust Co. Rights, Patents and Franchises. 250,000
Rache, D F and E D Hawkins, Jr....F Capps. Printing Office. 640
Schutt, J H. 51 Lincoln pl.... Koke Bros. Horse, &c. 115
Searles, H C... J W Tufts. Soda Apparatus. 200
Taylor, R. 57 Liberty....Catharine Taylor. Horses, Cabs, &c. 1,000
Van Beuren, R A. 254 State....Singer Mfg Co. Sewing Machines. 169
Welcome Primitive Methodist Church. Clason av....Martha Humphries. Frame Church. 500
Woodcock, J....P Barrett. Wagon. 170

BILLS OF SALE.

Berge, J. 1499 Fulton... G Hahn. Bakery Fixtures. 300
Berge, J. 2013 Fulton ...J & H Trieschmann. Bakery Fixtures. 1,325
Berner, P. 93 East av, Wallabout Market....B Bloch. Market Stands. 750
Ferry, D. ..W A Ferry. Real Estate Office. 150
Hanover & Cobbeng. 35 South 5th....John A Grenzig Jr. Machinery. 1,500
Macullar, Parks & Co 1188 Bedford av....Charlotte Bergman Machinery, &c. 879
Markert, G. 679 4th av....Johanna M Markert. Coal Business. 200
Markert, J M. 679 4th av....N Bernson. Coal and Ice Business. 1,350
O'Conner, D. 17 Red Hook lane....N Green. Horse. 134
Seigel, Sophie. 162 Tompkins av....A H O Schroter. Furniture. nom
Sangsler, J M & G. 589 Park av....Sporck & Kuhn. Horses and Trucks. 450
Tunison, Caroline. 46 Clifton pl....Lilian M Tunison. Furniture. 300

ASSIGNMENT OF CHATTEL MORTGAGES.

Boltstein, M to C A Muller. (Mort given by Mary A McCarthy, Dec 5, 1890.) nom
Cross, Joseph A to Welcome Primitive Methodist Church. (Robert Brocklehurst, Jan 20, 1891.) 150
Glanz, R to M Moore. (Emma P Cooper, April 10, 1891.) nom
Hausmann, Bertha A to B Fischer & Co. (Eveline Sheldon, Aug. 13, 1890.) val consid
Koehler, D M to Myer L Myers. (M McNally, Dec 5, 1889.) nom
Welcome Primitive Methodist Church to Martha Humphries. (Robert Brocklehurst, Jan 20, 1891.) nom

NEW JERSEY.

NOTE.—The arrangement of the Conveyances, Mortgages and Judgments in these lists is as follows: the first name in the Conveyances is the Grantor; in Mortgages, the Mortgagor; in Judgments, the Judgment debtor.

ESSEX COUNTY.

CONVEYANCES.

Akers, Charles—M A Hall, Bloomfield....$2,000
Arbuthnot, M A—E A McCurdy, Belleville av... 1,500
Baldwin, J V—F H Baldwin, Caldwell.... 1
Beach, J C—I S Anderson, Montclair.... 7,500
Bell, James—A J Levi, East Orange.... 720
Brown, Ogden—P D Brown, South Orange.... 2,000
Butler, H C—H McChesney, Livingston.... 1
Same——same, Milburn.... 7,500
Butler, O D—H McChesney, Livingston.... 100
Campbell, C S—H Bogert, Bloomfield.... 1,000
Coe, Theodore et al exrs—W Perkins, 14th av.. 2,867
Connelly, J E—J Redden, Wakeman av.... 1
Crawford, C G—F Quant, South Orange.... 280
Davenport, Archibald—J Neavy, Caldwell.... 55
Dale, J A—W C Hutchins, South 10th st.... 1
Ennis, Ellen—E B Ennis, Webster st.... 1
Essex and Hudson Land Improvement Co—J C Wilson, Locust st.... 1,200
Edwards, T P—J M Gwinnell, South Orange av. 850
Fitzpatrick, Richard—Caldwell R R Co—Caldwell.... 272
Gwinnell, J M—I M Edwards, e s South 7th st 288 s 13th av 75x100.... 5,300
Hartmann, Emile—M E Worthen, Belleville.... 70,000
Heller, P J—Caldwell R R Co—Caldwell.... 100
Higgins, Michael—G W Courter, Montclair.... 325
Hitchcock, C R—E T Lindsley, Orange.... 3,500
Holmes, L N—O E English, Milburn.... 2,500
Holzhauer, H J—E Marsh, Wimans av.... 2,000
Howard Savings Inst—O Milford, Barclay st... 1,825
Hubbell, G W et al—J McG Demorest, Orchard st.... 1,200
Jackson, S B—W Eberhardt, Elm st.... 1
Same——same, Walnut st.... 1
Same——same, Elm st.... 1
Kane, Mary—M Roe, Chatham st.... 125
Kitchell, J F—W B Dod, w s Summer av 85 from Bloomfield av 35x94.... 4,000
Kolb, J F—M V Kern, Charlton st.... 1,600
Lamb, Peter—C Schmidt, Littleton av.... 1,650
Lehlbach, Gustav—H Ill, Lafayette st.... 1,100
Liebstein, Joseph—J Woodward, South Orange av.... 1
Lindsley, E T—C R Hitchcock, East Orange.... 1,500
Lister, J C—B Dunn, Catherine st.... 245
Same——B Smith, Albert av.... 400
Same——J Whealon, Esther st.... 530
Lydig, P H et al—G L Wilmerding, West Orange....18,333
Matthews, P A—Caldwell R R Co, Caldwell.... 100
McChesney, Hubert—H C Butler, Orange.... 6,000
Milford, Oscar—F Lezgus, 18th av.... 1,400
Morris, J R—W S Hare, East Orange.... 550
Mt Pleasant Cemetery Co—J J L Adams, e s Fairmount av 50 n Godet st 100x100.... 4,500
Neary, John—P Russ, Caldwell.... 50
Ost, Catharine—A Isler, Livingston st.... 1,400
Parkinson, William—M J Brown, Orange.... 780
Pfister, Antionette—D Trimbel, Prince st.... 1
Poinier, John—G Crawford, South Orange.... 200
Richards, M S—J Sheridan, Vincent st.... 340
Roth, Lazar—H Levy, Prince st.... 1
Roth, Phillip—R Notte, Adams st.... 2,400
Same——same, s s South Market st 58 e Adams st 12x54.... 4,000
Scheider, Bernard—L R Scheider, Lentz av.... 1
Scheider, G E—B Scheider, Lentz av.... 1
Scheerer, George O—Susan Cook, Clinton.... 350
Schroeder, F O—A Naegele, w s Belmont av 150 s Kinney st, 100x25x100.... 4,000
Sherman, L I—M S Sherman, High st.... 1
Sherman, Moritz S—R Sherman, High st.... 1
Simonson, John—J C Crane, Bloomfield.... 150
Sloat, Emma—Caldwell R R Co, Caldwell.... 1,000
Sullivan, M F—J McCormick, West Orange.... 300
Sweet, N D—J D Pierson, East Orange.... 1
Taylor, J C—W H Bowen, South Orange.... 650
Terhune, J E—J Stapff, West Washington st 153 s Spruce st 37x200x48x200.... 20,000
Thompson, J B—Caldwell R R Co, Caldwell.... 1
Tolmen, James—A Munser, Clinton.... 508
Torrey, John, Jr—C J Bayles, Montclair.... 5
Triebel, Ludwig—P Laig, Prince st.... 2,250
Vertryck, S A—W J Donnelly, n s Baldwin st 123 w Washington st 17x87x50x30x20.... 4,750
Ward, C W—L Scheiner, 5th av.... 1,500
Wendel, Frederick—Mt Pleasant Cemetery Co, Fairmount av.... 50
Williams, Augusta et al—E W Hine, Orange.... 4,500
Woodward, Joseph—P Lowy, South Orange.... 625
Wribke, Frederick—J Merz, Spruce st.... 1,200

MORTGAGES.

Adams, J J L—Mt Pleasant Cemetery Co, Fairmount av.... 3,000
Bach, Ralph—M B Lindsley, Caldwell.... 1,400
Baldwin, F H—H F Harrison, Caldwell.... 300
Bogert, Harry—C S Campbell, Bloomfield.... 800
Brower, J C—E Ball, Roseville av.... 500
Same——same, Roseville av.... 2,000
Buck, Christian—T Oakes, Bloomfield.... 1,700
Burns, Michael—H Stetson, Orange.... 180
Campbell, P H—Sarah E Dodd, South Orange... 1,250
Casth, William—J Wharton, 6th av.... 1,500
Coras, Richard—H A Harvey, East Orange.... 2,000
Courter, J L—Daniel Lawrence, cor Littleton av and Bank st.... 500
Craig, T H—C U Heath et al exrs, East Orange.. 3,000
Donnelly, W J—C A Feick, Baldwin st.... 2,100
Dunn, Bernard—J C Lister, Catherine st.... 121
Duncan, C B—Herman Knoderer, Elm st.... 1,500
Fanning, Mary—Washington B and L Assoc, East Orange.... 2,000
Farley, J J—C R Crane, Montclair.... 4,000
Ford, H S—F H Earle, 7th av.... 500
Galbraith, A H—A A S Wiss, 4th av.... 150
Garg, Peter—A Davis, Prince st.... 500
Garton, E M—A Z Genung, East Orange.... 1,800
Goeller, Frederick—J A Clark, Winans av.... 700
Same——same, Winans av.... 900
Haines, L J—A Buermann, Badger av.... 600
Same——J H Jackson, Badger av.... 2,000
Hannegan, E C—J C Culberson, East Orange.... 1,000
Hemming, Frank—F Frelinghuysen, Norfolk st. 5,060
Hitchcock, C R—E T Lindsley, East Orange.... 300
Hitchcock, J M—M H Tichenor, Irvington.... 3,000
Holey, J A—H M Childs, East Orange.... 800
Isler, Abraham—A Ost, Livingston st.... 1,100
Jacobus, A M—M E Pierson, Caldwell.... 300
Jacobus, P E—J H Hush, Caldwell.... 750
Jardine, Christina—S L M Ward, Clifton av.... 4,000
Kelly, Daniel—Roseville B and L Assoc, cor Warren and Bergen sts.... 4,500
Kothe, Christian—Knights of Pythias B and L Assoc, Howard.... 2,400
Levy, Hannah—Firemens Ins Co, cor Prince and Kinney sts.... 6,000
Liebstein, Samuel—Mechanics' B and L Assoc, Bedford st.... 300
Manser, Alice—J Tolman, Clinton.... 383
Marsh, M F—N Fredericks, Franklin.... 1,200
McChesney, Hubert—Hettie C Butler, Milburn and Livingston.... 3,000
McCurdy, E A—Howard Savings Inst, Belleville av.... 500
Miller, Samuel—J M Cornell, South Orange.... 2,500
Milford, Oscar—Washington B and L Assoc, Barclay st.... 1,950
Notte, Rocco—Philip Roth, South Market st.... 5,400
Olds, F M—E N Campfield et al, trustees, Belleville.... 2,700
Osborn, G H—J S Howkins, Clinton.... 500
Perkins, William—T Coe et al exrs, cor South 6th st and 14th av.... 3,200
Pierson, J D—W Pierson, East Orange.... 500
Robrecht, F P—A Rorbecht, Fairview av.... 2,000
Russomanno, Lorenzo—Hearthstone B and L Assoc, 8th av.... 900
Solomon, R G—J H Breintnall, Montgomery st.. 5,000
Scannell, Lawrence—Montclair B and L Assoc, Montclair.... 200
Schoenfeld, Flora—F Bornstein, Belmont av.... 112
Snyder, W F—Security B and L Assoc, South Orange.... 500
Stryker, A A—L Leverich, East Orange.... 3,000
Studer, A C—E A Fuller, Montclair.... 500
Sturgis, Ophelia—H F Bailey, Clinton.... 1,000
Utter, J S—Lafayette Mutual B and L Assoc, Ridgewood av.... 4,000
Van Iderstine, W H—Woodside B and L Assoc, Elwood av.... 3,000
Van Ness, E A—State B and L Assoc, Summer av.... 400
Varian, S T—Fidelity Title and Deposit Co, East Orange.... 5,500
Ward, W C—Protection B and L Assoc, Clinton. 4,000
Wheeler, John—W Pierson, Orange.... 2,000
Yetter, Wilhelmina—Catharina Barkhorn, Montgomery st.... 3,000
Zarra, Nicola—Hearthstone B and L Assoc, 8th av.... 1,300

CHATTEL MORTGAGES.

Bowman, W T—E S Thorn, horse, &c.... 500
Brown, Margaret—J Moriarty, furniture.... 130
Bugg, O T—A E Eisele, furniture.... 340
Creveling, W S—L Bloomer, furniture.... 500
De Mont, J W—J Ketcham, furniture.... 86
Dunham, W D—L Bloomer, furniture.... 65
Ellis, D C—H A Bambridge, store fixtures.... 150
Fleisner, Christopher—A Hahn, press.... 450
Freder, Louis—A Schwaab & Son, barber shop furniture.... 20
Gasser, Mary—M Kane, furniture.... 26
Goff, William—M Raphael, horse, &c.... 125
Halligan, Peter—B J Quinn, horses and wagons. 1,000
Heath, Frank—J Ketcham, furniture.... 54
Hewitt, Daniel—A Lloyd, furniture.... 75
Huber, George—M Kane, horses, wagons, &c.... 54
Jung, George—F J Kastner, saloon.... 175
Kriedel, J L & Son—C W Clayton, machinery... 1,000
Lambrecht, John—K Jubert, factory fixtures... 200
Markert, Charles—H Hemendinger, furniture... 1,000
Masker, William—E M Lawrence, horses, &c.... 150
Moffet, F N—F C Edwards, furniture.... 200
Moschkowitz, Aaron—Eideser Lodge N 2, O B J of N J, machinery.... 15
National Cash Reg Co—F Azoy, cash register... 175
Preedee, J G—C W Clayton, horses, &c.... 350
Raimo, A—A Schwaab & Son, barber shop furniture.... 25
Rizzolo, Felix—Home Brewing Co, saloon.... 350
Roberts, William et al—R M Stiles, machinery.. 200
Rosenkrans, W R—German-American Brewing Co, horses.... 400
Swan, Alfred—W S Richardson, furniture.... 570
Thompson, E M—Peterson Consolidated Brewing Co, saloon.... 1,000
Ulrich, F J—F Beckmever, pictures, &c.... 100
Weston, Thomas—T Charlesworth, machinery.. 200

HUDSON COUNTY.

CONVEYANCES.

Ahrens, Mary E—Maria A. Nichol, Hoboken.... $2,000
Alexander, Jane A and Margaret Kilpatrick by sheriff—R J Alexander, Union.... 1,000
Auld, Charlotte A—G Roth, Union.... 3,000
Baier, William—P Donohue, North Bergen.... 350
Barnes, F C—M H Kelsey, J City.... 775
Bastan, Chas—F Wild, J City.... 1,000
Bastan, Chas by city collector—W Seechal, J City.... 928
Becker, Louis—L T Fruttchey, Union.... 800
Bedler, Fanny E—R English, J City.... 5,000
Bell, Henry—N S Woolley, North Bergen.... 400
Bennett, Margaret and James Bennett—Elizabeth Scanlon, J City.... 400
Booraem, Cornelia V V by exrs—G B Cole, J City.... 800
Boyle, Louis—E Russ, Hoboken.... nom
Brooks, W J—W Peterkeir, J City.... 53,075
Bruns, Annie—W Bruns, J City.... 40,000
Buddington, W S—W D Salter, J City.... nom
Byrn, M L—J Honiss, Kearney.... 200
Byrnes, Matthew—R E Naylor, Bayonne.... nom
Close, Eva B—S L Lewin, Bayonne.... 375
Collins, Gilbert—C Bastan, J City.... nom
Collins, Gilbert and W G E See——same, J City. nom
Combes, Mary E—Kate A Knapp, Bayonne.... 800
Condit, Fillmore—J Eckert, Kearney.... 125
Same——H Astley, Kearney.... 125
Same——same, Kearney.... 125
Currey, Richard and Jennie—Hilric J Bonn, Union.... 8,250
Currey, Richard—Dorothea Bermes, Union.... nom
Currey, Richard, Jennie S and Lella F—Dorothea Bermes, Union.... 5,500
Duff, Eliza and William by sheriff—J J Devill, Hoboken.... 2,300
Forman, J G—L Boye, Hoboken.... 4,625
Fruttchey, Jere—Cecilie Becker, Union.... nom

Fuller, D B—R Buchana, Kearney	1,300
Garrett, Robert—Julia Garret, J City	nom
Hansen, F C—The William Peter Brewing Co, Union	2,000
Hencken, H M—Emma W A Hencken, J City	nom
Heppenheimer, W C—W Kennedy, Hoboken	450
Hermann, Adam—G M Zurk, Union	850
Hodge, Mary—Susan A Hann, Bayonne	3,000
Ligoot, A J by exrs—J Jaekle, J City	1,200
Mappal, Ferdinand—C J Bott, Union	780
McCroskey, J B—G Kessler, North Bergen	750
McKensey, Bernard—Elizabeth Smith, Union	1,550
Mitchell, G K—E T Battley, J City	2,300
Moran, Susan, J C Crevier and A R Meyer, by sheriff—J C Crevier, Hoboken	1,050
Naylor, R E—Mary A E Byrnes, Bayonne	nom
Nichols, E H—W J Hulford, J City	150
North Jersey Land Co—J Anderson, J City	1,350
O'Neill, W M—W Bruns, J City	nom
Rodefeldt, J F, by sheriff—H Walker, Guttenberg	50
Roehrer, George—A Schaefer, Union	2,950
Russ, Edward—Bertha Boye, Hoboken	nom
St Michaels Passionist Monastery—P M Weldon, West Hoboken	nom
Same——P Quirk, West Hoboken	nom
Salter, W D—Mary E Budington, J City	nom
Saulter, Christopher and George—A H Pitchford, Union	nom
Scanlon, Elizabeth—Mary A Haley, J City	1,400
Schluck, Julius—H Brown, J City	2,675
Schmidt, Philip—F Behnker, Union	2,250
Schoone, C I—Mary Bindernagel, Union	750
Siegfried, Adam—Emil Junger, J City	750
Same——F W L Wenninger, J City	750
Smythe, Owen—J McDonald, Union	300
Steil, C F—Mimma Steil, Guttenberg	nom
Steil, Mina—C F Steil, Guttenberg	nom
St Martin, Eliza—H W Harper, Hoboken	3,000
Stolt, Chas—J Schumm, Union	3,000
Symes, J H—W Koch, Union	300
The Bergen Point Methodist Episcopal Church—J A Kirkendall, Bayonne	—
The Hoboken Land and Improvement Co—D P Westervelt, Hoboken	10
Tierney, Myles—Jane E O'Brien, Hoboken	6,600
Toffey, Adeline S—G Wilson, J City	1,200
Tonnele, Cecile by trustee—P Vander Boire, J City	400
Van Buskirk, Emma—J H Browning, Bayonne	100
Van Winkle, Elizabeth, Margaret L and A A—Mary F Van Winkle, J City	nom
Van Winkle, Eliz and A A—Margaret L Van Winkle, J City	nom
Van Winkle, Margaret L and A A—Elizabeth Van Winkle, J City	nom
Vietor, G F and Thomas Achelis et al by sheriff—M Hammerschlag, Hoboken	50,000
Vile, T T—T R Hornblower, J City	625
Walker, Herman—J Burkhardt, Guttenberg	1,550
Weissensee, Andrew—J J Froehlich, North Bergen	—
Wescott, W P—E W Rover, Bayonne	325
Westervelt, D P—P E Hall, Hoboken	2,770
Wickham, John—Emil C R Hecnrich, West Hoboken	700

MORTGAGES.

Bahr, Annie H—J G Christ, Bayonne, 1 year	135
Battey, E T—Lincoln B and L Assoc, J City, installs	2,400
Same——G K Mitchell, J City, installs	290
Bonn, H J—R Curry, Union, 1 year	6,000
Browne, Henry—E Cordean, J City, 3 years	1,650
Buchanna, Robert—The Kearney B and L Assoc, Kearney, installs	800
Brickwedel, Johanna—C Witte, Hoboken, 3 years	1,500
Budington, Mary E—Highland M B and L Assoc, J City, installs	1,000
Burch, Maria T—The Hudson City Mutual B and L Assoc, J City, installs	2,200
Callaghan, John—M Clausen & Son Brewing Co, Bayonne, 1 year	1,900
Casper, Jacob—Henry Mayer, Hoboken, 3 years	1,500
Deinroth, John—Emma Schmidt, Union, 2 yrs	500
Dewey, C M—Cartaret M B and L Assoc, J City, installs	5,000
Duffy, J J—G Cadmus, Bayonne, 2 years	1,300
English, Richard—H E Bedler, J City, 5 years	4,000
Finlay, Jeannette M—J Fleming, Bayonne, 3 years	1,500
Frank, J E—G G Vreeland, J City, 10 years	10,000
Fruttchey, Livera T—L Becker, Union, 3 years	1,300
Gehrs, Dietrich—The Hudson City Savings Bank, J City, 1 year	900
Gleitsmann, G L—G Gerisch, Union, 5 years	1,000
Goeger, Anna—V Ruthart, Union, 3 years	2,000
Hahn, George—C Witte, Hoboken, 3 years	4,400
Hammerschlag, Moritz—A L McDermott, J City, 3 years	25,000
Heinrick, E C—J Wickhane, West Hoboken, installs	450
Junger, Emil—A Siegfried, J City, 4 years	350
Klein, Herman—F U Hermann, Guttenberg, 3 years	400
Knapp, Kate A—Mary E. Combes, Bayonne 5 years	800
Same——D B Salter, Bayonne, 5 years	2,000
Lewin, S L—The Industrial Co-op B and L Assoc, Bayonne, installs	2,000
McCauslin, Thomas—W V Mulford, J City, 2 years	500
Newmann, Gustav—Adeline Emboff, J City, 3 years	2,000
O'Brien, J E—M Tierney, Hoboken, 5 years	3,950
Peterkin, William—W J Brooks, J City, 3 years	2,500
Puckridge, A P—The New Jersey Title Guarantee and Trust Co, J City, 2 years	2,075
Raven, E W—The Security B and L Assoc, Bayonne, installs	2,800
Roedel, Adam—G Schumann, J City, 2 years	550
Rottman, William—C F Rub, Union, 6 years	1,900
Schumm, Jacob—C Stoll, Union, 5 years	1,500
Schwersquth, Henry—Town of Union B and L Assoc, Union, installs	5,000
Smith, W F—Victoria Shipman, Kearney, 1 year	600
Smith, Elizabeth—Martha L Deraismes, Union, 1 year	500
Staats, Richard—The Greenville B and L Assoc, Bayonne, installs	2,945
Stilson, Lyula H—Bayonne B Assoc No 2, Bayonne, installs	3,000
Van den Boire, Pierre—W D Edwards trustee, J City, 2 years	1,600
Van Winkle, Mary F—The Star Mutual B and L Assoc, J City, installs	5,000
Warren, John—P Van Emburgh, Kearney, 1 year	2,000
Wenninger, F W L—A Siegfried, J City, 3 years	300
Wild, Frank—C Bastan, J City, 1 year	300
Wildey, W L—The Kearney B and L Assoc, Kearney, installs	1,400

CHATTEL MORTGAGES.

Bolinsky, William, J City—F Melger, pool table	110
Caspar, Frank, J City—Adam Schwarb & Son, barber shop fixtures	313
Cummnui, Guseppe, J City—same, barber shop fixtures	300
Dillon, Patrick, Bayonne—Lembeck & Betz Eagle Brewing Co, saloon	650
Di Marsi, Michaele, J City—Adam Schwarb & Son, barber shop fixtures	105
Dohrmann, Henry and Fred, partners as Dohrmann & Bro, Hoboken—W Gudehus, milk wagon	130
Duggan, J P, J City—The Burr Brewing Co, saloon and lease	300
Ellis, Leawens, Hoboken—D Bermes, saloon	142
Same, Hoboken—H Fischer, saloon	175
Feudtner, Jacob, J City—Emma Von Rdonitz, machinery, tools, &c, used in ornamental iron works	325
Frost, Thomas, J City—The Burr Brewing Co, saloon	100
Gerrity, James, J City—Wolff Bros, 2 horses	350
Grimm, Herman, Hoboken—Frances McDonough, coach	300
Hasselbrock, Dederick, Hoboken—B Fischer & Co, grocery store, horse, wagon	1,500
Jackson, Charles, J City—O Taussig, saloon fixtures	200
Keating, M F, J City—The National Cash Register Co, one No. 3 Register	175
Krisgen, Charles, J City—G Luhrman, clothing and gents furnishing store	300
Lohmann, Adolph, Union—The William Peter Brewing Co, saloon fixtures	450
Maturo, Filippo, Hoboken—The F & M Schaefer Brewing Co, saloon fixtures	650
Mockridge, A W, J City—W F Day Bro, furniture	75
Murphy, John, J City—Lembeck & Betz Eagle Brewing Co, saloon fixtures	375
Nash, Joseph, West Hoboken—Fannie Mucudei, horse, wagon, harness	500
Nicasto, Louis, Hoboken—Adam Schwarb & Son, barber shop fixtures	201
Oldenburg, Diederich, J City—The James Cunningham Son & Co, undertaker's wagon	400
Reger, L O, J City—B Weill, horses, trucks and wagon	500
Rogers, C J, J City—H Rohlfs, saloon	400
Ross, Michael, Hoboken—Bernheimer & Schmid, pool table	140
Rubaishy, George, J City—The Burr Brewing Co, saloon	550
Schierenbech, F H, Hoboken—H Bahrenburg, horse, wagon, harness	500
Scheider, John, Hoboken—A Kiesewetter, horse, wagon, harness	160
Schroeder, August, Hoboken—The Burr Brewing Co, saloon	500
Shaber, Frank, Hoboken—T H Muirdierk, saloon fixtures	350
Solimine, Domenico, J City—Adam Schwarb & Son, barber shop fixtures	180
Steinman, Wilhelmina, Hoboken—The H B Claflin Co, store and fixtures, dry goods	1,613
Unger, John, Union—The William Peter Brewing Co, pool table	125
Wagner, Albert, Hoboken—Lembeck & Betz Eagle Brewing Co, saloon and lease	400

JUDGMENTS.

Crossley, C A—The A A Griffin Iron Co	984
Hasselbrock, Dederick—B Fischer & Co	1,504
Hedden, A L—D B Duncan	294
Murphy, M V—S Lord	408
The Rectors, Wardens and Vestrymen of Grace Church in Greenville, J City—J Dodds..costs and	523

BUILDING MATERIAL MARKET.

BRICKS.—Last week we noted just a faint hope entertained among some of the trade that manufacturers were about curtailing shipments and possibly making ground upon which to build an improvement in the condition of the market. Nothing has come of it as yet, however, the conditions of affairs if anything proving somewhat less satisfactory inasmuch as the overrun of supplies was constantly liberal and buyers seemed to move with a greater degree of lassitude. The dog-day weather may have had something to do with the indifferent character of the demand, but the more direct influencing features are probably to be found in the completion of considerable work; indifference about starting in on new jobs, and stock enough piled away to take up pretty much all the immediately available storage room. Beyond the natural calculation for interest and carrying expenses it seems to be generally admitted there is little to figure upon regarding propriety of investing in brick at current cost; indeed, buyers rarely complain of price, yet there is no special speculative attraction, and purchases can be and are made without hurry. The quality retains old excellent average, and we allow former quotations to stand, our figures only being exceeded by exceptional goods under special conditions. Nothing definite can be learned from the points of production as to manufacturers' intentions and some of the trade commence to think they will keep on making brick until frost stops them.

CEMENT.—In common with all kinds of structural material, cement has been passing through a decidedly unpropitious season. So discouraging indeed have been the conditions, that we felt fully warranted in abstaining from any special reference to the market beyond such as might be necessary to preserve the proper line of valuation. Briefly, it is the one story of shrunken outlet, too poor a prospect ahead to suggest speculative investment and a surplus supply. For domestic grades a few very good contracts were made early in the year, and there was for a while some good open market trading during spring months; then came the development of inertia, hastened somewhat by the lumbermen's labor troubles and the effect upon building, with slow dragging trade ever since. Naturally all buoyancy was taken out of values, but considering the influences at work the depression was decidedly less than might have been expected, and there was really no general giving way on values at all. Some business in Rosendale product was done at 85c. per bbl., but under special conditions and not really acceptable as a basis for quotation, as the lowest rate to be depended upon was 90c. per bbl. Manufacturers of domestic cement have had an advantage in ability to shut down production and ease up on shipments whenever disposed, and this has been used so judiciously as to go a long way in neutralizing the disagreeable condition of demand.

Imported cement has never been so plenty, and in its relation to the supply available never was demand so slow and indifferent. Last year, up to September 1st, the total receipts of foreign cement at the port were 590,227 bbls., and this year, down to the present writing, some three or four days short of corresponding period, the receipts are 884,220 bbls., of which 242,825 came from Great Britain, and 641,395 from the Continent. This difference is due to the fact that manufacturers on the other side and importers here were not as a rule bound by any freight engagements from the U. K., and were therefore in a position to curtail supplies whenever the condition of trade suggested, while on the contrary from the Continent extensive and binding contracts had been made with transportation companies, and operators had to decide between paying for the empty freight room or bringing out cement, and they choose the latter. Some new brands have come forward; but the offering was mainly of established goods and quality therefore has proven all right. Of course, there has been miscalculation upon the extent of the consumption. In this locality private enterprises have run slowish and upon a decreasing scale, and public work though quietly absorbing a great deal of stuff is now up to volume calculated upon. On interior calls, between here and Chicago, the business was really quite fair at times, but the far west trade has fallen off about 50 per cent, owing to partial subsidence of some of the building booms and to financial stringency. The effect upon importers must at once be obvious and they have generally felt discouraged and perplexed, especially as some trials at reducing price to absolute cost or less failed as an attraction for demand. Surplus supplies have been handled as well as they could under the circumstances, some sending to interior and some storing here, with a probability that the quantity in this port unsold is greater than ever before. Prices for months have been quite irregular, running on a sort of sliding scale to suit the deal in hand, but at the moment may be placed at about $2.20@2.25 per bbl. for Belgian, $2.30@2.50 for English, and $2.30@2.50 for German; the outside figures somewhat full for cargo lots.

LATH.—There has not been much of a market during the week. Unsold arrivals were comparatively moderate, which was fortunate, as the demand also run small, many of the best customers not having been heard from at all, owing to the accumulations they now have in yard. The few buyers coming upon market, however, had no special advantage, but on the con rary, were compelled to pay a little more money, and the latest sale we learn of was at $2.15 per M. At the close it is claimed that most of the Provincial stock afloat has reached this port, and only a few cargoes from Maine known to be due, which excites the usual predictions from receivers, but draws no orders.

LIME.—The market is reported steady for first-class Eastern stock, and quoted at $1 all around, but some brands from "outside" points are understood to have sold at a fractional shading. State and Western goods are available, but offered with less freedom than a short time ago, as the market momentarily seems to have a sufficient supply.

LUMBER.—In the matter of distribution there has not been much improvement, so far as really new orders are concerned, and except with the very favorably located yards business remains on the dull list somewhat longer than was anticipated. Dealers are feeling a little more hopeful in regard to the incoming month, but many of them evidently entertain grave doubts about any revival of demand for building purposes this fall of sufficient volume to create stimulating animation. As a natural sequence, attention turns toward bulk lots with continued doubt and hesitation and the principal effort on the part of buyers is to make a calculation upon quantity that will closely limit their investment to natural requirements. On the whole, however, there has been a little more inquiry of late, picking up odd lots available, making contracts for tenders by travelers, etc., and in placing special bills required to maintain a regular yard assortment. In very few instances has cost varied materially and the major portion of advantage remains upon side of buyers.

Eastern Spruce has found pretty much the same general market for some time advised. Up to present writing the arrivals are comparatively light, and a customer who might happen to call for stock would be placed at some disadvantage, but in a general way receivers are well aware that the outlet could not provide for any considerable quantity of any description, and there is nothing of a really promising character in the situation, while valuations stand much the same as for some little time past or, say, about $13@14 for narrow, $14@15 for 9 to 12 inch and $15@16 for 10 to 12 inch, with specials at ordinary difference. For the latter there has been more inquiry of late, especially bills calling for 24 to 25-foot stuff, and as high as $18 has been made in exceptional cases. Advices from the East are generally found to be framed in firm sort of tone, and it is now reported that so many vessels are seeking freight in other directions that manufacturers will be unable to send forward a liberal supply this fall even if they want to.

Piling continues in comparatively moderate demand, the basins are full of stock, with further additions likely from any arrivals that may take place, and value gets no buoyancy. Dealers say there is no cutting from old rates because they were already too low for further shading, and some of them are discouraged enough to predict no advance until after the close of the season at least.

Hemlock remains steady and on its natural merit some operators think would gain a trifle in value. Demand here does not amount to much as yet, but has shown some increase of interest, and there is a gain in the run of orders from outside sources quite satisfactory to manufacturers, who still appear able to control the supply and prevent a surplus offering. The cheapness of competing woods, however, acts as a drawback to any raise in cost at the moment, and lightness of the Northern production could not have developed at a better time for the general good of the market.

White Pine is increasing in supply as stock continues to come forward on contract, the arrivals said to include ordinary grades in the main, but in good fair proportion of the better qualities showing up. A great deal of the stuff was bought last winter under the rush of Canadian supplies but some lots of this season's investment, and include parcels picked up from time to time from bargains tendered as we have recorded in our reports. At the moment, however, there is a little more in the way of natural demand as dealers commence to appreciate the lapse of time and think it about as well to stir themselves gradually toward looking up such stuff as they know must be purchased.

Yellow Pine is the worst on the list and the market simply dull and nominally unchanged. Outside of some natural special orders there appears to be scarcely anything doing at all, and upon whatever may be consummated the reticence of operators is of that intense description that renders it impossible to obtain any information in matter of prices. They are undoubtedly quite low.

Carolina Pine presents much the same general features previously advised. The market on local account is not an active one by any means, but quite on a par with business doing in other kinds of stock, and there is said to be a steady increase of orders from outside custom.

Hardwoods retain old features, the furniture men calling for fair quantity of stock, other manufacturers comparatively little, and dealers negotiating for fresh supplies in a moderate and indifferent manner. Rates rule about as for some time past with tone easy, but not weak, and the offering fair with ability to increase if necessary. Quartered Oak is popular but plenty of it prevents buoyancy, and the chances are that plain Red Oak will do much better in price owing to its scarcity. Poplar has fair average demand, and is supposed to be selling at old rates. Other woods moving mainly in job lots and without special feature worthy of detail.

GENERAL LUMBER NOTES.

GREAT BRITAIN.

The *Timber Trades Journal* as follows:

LONDON.

It seems as if there was something of truth in the report of a big import to London of pitch pine. One or two cargoes have been diverted to this port, amongst which have just arrived the Asloun, a big steamer from Pascagoula, now discharging in Canada Dock 1,700 loads of sawn timber; and another large sailing ship, the Campbell, sailed from Queenstown last week for London, with about 1,300 loads of sawn and hewn, shipped at Pensacola. These additions to the dock stocks will probably bring them up level with last year. The Capulet steamer, mentioned last week, is now discharging her cargo, which was one of Baars' shipments.

LIVERPOOL.

Though we have had several large steamers here during the week with sawn pitch pine we have not had any further auction sales. Some few cargoes . . . steamers are either landing or on the way here with market cargoes of sawn pitch pine timber, but how they will be dealt with on arrival cannot be determined at present. It may be fairly taken as an indication of the view held by shippers that the large cargo of sawn timber per ss. Ramon de Larrinaga is being stored by Messrs. Robert Coltart & Co., as well as a portion of the cargo per ss. Architect. The shippers, as well as their brokers, seem to be of the opinion that prices cannot be worse, and that there is but little risk in holding these goods for a future market.

GLASGOW.

The complaints this year by importers of pitch pine have been more than usually numerous and serious in respect of quality, average size and short measure; compensation may, with some little difficulty, be obtained, but compensation will not substitute good wood for inferior or increase the size contracted for. It is very difficult for firms to deal with difficulties and breaches of contract individually, and never before did there exist a greater necessity for a trade combination to enforce fulfilment of contracts.

A cessation for some time in the imports of walnut (small sized) would benefit the market, as stocks would soon become reduced from present large bulk by the steady consumption that goes on and better prices then be obtainable.

THE WEST.

The Northwestern *Lumberman* after reviewing the generally dull condition of trade says:

How long will this state of things continue? lumbermen are anxiously inquiring. Probably until midwinter or next spring. Though a large small grain and early fruit crop has been harvested, prices for which are yielding the farmer a good profit, there must be a certain amount of liquidation accomplished before money will begin to go into improvements on a scale sufficiently large to be felt as a special impetus to the lumber trade. when the financial condition among farmers and country merchants shall become easy, and surpluses of profit begin to flow into the banks, real estate matters will begin again to boom, and a revival of the lumber trade always follows that. Simultaneously with this will come a renewal of activity on the part of the railroads and among manufacturers, both influences in favor of the lumber trade.

Dealers in all the large centres have apparently about made up their minds that there will be no phenomenal demand for lumber this fall. They only anticipate a fair trade, but look for a good demand next winter and spring. This is in consonance with the opinion more recently expressed in these columns.

The amount of stock on hand in the principal markets is not so burdensome as to be a menace to prices, even though the fall trade should be only fair. There has been little over-production in the northern pine belt, and very little anywhere. The southern manufacturers have felt the need of orders all summer, and there has been considerable piling in the southwest. But a more recent demand is demonstrating that it will not take long for the surplus to disappear. Prices all over the country have been surprisingly maintained in view of the slowness of demand. Even in the south, where weakness has been the most pronounced, there has lately been a tendency to a firmer feeling, especially in respect to yellow pine. * * *

Reports from shipping points in Wisconsin are to the effect that a lively movement is prevailing at such sources of supply. This may, in a measure, account for the slack shipping demand here. The mill points are getting the lion's share of the full car load trade, as they have done in recent years. Chicago dealers will have to look lively for their portion of the trade. In doing so they must make competitive prices, and that is what prevents an advance. This year cargo values have been steady and firm. Stocks have been put in at a slight advance on prices that prevailed last year. Now the Wisconsin men come into a common territory, and undersell the Chicago dealer. Verily the latter has a hard time between the two horns of the dilemma. However, should there be an extraordinary demand during the fall and winter, as; is anticipated,; Wisconsin will be unable to furnish all the lumber that will be wanted.

The following extracts are from the *Timberman* ;

It would seem as if the price of lumber could not be much lower than at present and the producers survive, although the retailers are not taking advantage of the situation with their usual spirit. It is doubtless owing to the fact that prices have receded on yellow pine and other commodities continu usly during the past year and the conviction becoming general that they have not reached the bottom. Trade is always dullest when prices are low, but the reaction which has already been felt to some extent in the white pine trade and in the hemlock markets is almost sure to prove a stimulus to traffic in yellow pine.

It almost seems that manufacturers of yellow pine, many of them at least, are working for the public's good, although they are not entitled to any great amount of credit for b nevolence on that account, for their labors are involuntary. The frugality of the people and the keenness of competition have compelled them to put up with a very meagre compensation in ome instances and, in others, to endure actual losses. Th y are supported, as a manufacturer told me at St. Louis last week, a good deal as the towns' poor in New Hampshire was said to be, "half the year on the recollections of the past, and the other half year on anticipations of the future." * * *

There is a great deal of speculation with regard to the future of quart r-sawed oak. From present indications it would seem that demand is turning more to plain-sawed, and many dealers doubt if they will ever be able to get the quartered stock back to old prices. Last winter they were paying all the way from $42 to $50 for stock not particularly dry, and were only too glad to take all that was offered. Just now prices range from $34 to $40, and buyer are very particular as to quality and state of dryness. It is true that these low prices are in a great measure occasioned by the fact that nearly every manufacturer has been quartering his logs this season, but it is also true that the demand for quartered oak, as compared with that of plain-sawed, has been much less this year than last.

There is considerable stock arriving right along, but most of it is on contract. There are dealers, however, who are still buying more than they can sell, in the firm belief that there will be demand for it all before the season is over. Quotations remained practically unchanged; but are somewhat weaker on most items than they were during July.

A slightly improved demand is reported for cherry and good walnut, but there is not much of either to be found. The better demand noted is caused by a more active inquiry from the exporters, and good prices are realized on all stock suitable for this trade.

The Mississippi Valley *Lumberman* says:

The feeling among Northwestern lumbermen is undoubtedly more bullish than it has been at any time in many months. There is reason to believe that trade from this out will be measured only by the capacity of the railroads to carry the lumber which may be ordered to its destination.

Southern manufacturers who have been under a cloud for several months past are already beginning to enjoy considerable trade in the prairie States west of the Missouri River, where the harvest is completed and much of the grain is already marketed.

The recent failures in the lumber trade have caused lumbermen's paper to be scrutinized with considerable care lately and the money stringency is undoubtedly contributing something to t e low prices which prevail, and which is the only present cause for complaint in the trade. The manufacturers have set on foot, however, a movement for better prices which promises to be successful. Collections are already reported much better than they have been and while the demand for money to move the crops will make the money market close, many old scores will be paid off and accounts of long standing erased from the books of both wholesalers and retailers.

NAILS.—The market makes no general or positive improvement. There is again some talking about cutting down production in order to put up prices, but it does not appear to frighten buyers in any way or add to the demand against future wants. The latter is probably the main objective point in order to secure a dumping-ground for surplus stock. We quote Cut at $1.50@1.60 per keg for car lots and $1.75@1.85 per keg for parcels from store, for iron, and add 5@10c. per keg for steel; Wire, $2.00@2.05 at mills, and 2.20@2.35 from store.

PAINTS, OILS, COLORS, ETC.—It is difficult to discover many, if any, really new points or suggestions in the current run of reports. Even the proverbially bullish element in the trade is compelled to admit disappointment with the movement thus far and are compelled to fall back upon their hopes for support. Not much is expected locally as conditions are hardly in form for good consumption, but interior dependent points are calculated upon to make a much better business. The portions of country thus far heard from has neither the desire or the credit to invest freely, but territory now about opening up with new orders is in much better condition and has given preliminary evidence of a willingness to handle fair quantities of stock. Available supplies are plenty enough for the use of the present market and an increase can be made without difficulty, if necessary. All along the line prices are about steady. There is the usual talk about irregularitie on White Lead but nothing proven. Association Corroders' rates stand as follows: Lead in oil in kegs and dry lead in kegs, in lots of less than 500 lbs., 7½c. net; in lots of 500 lbs to 5 tons at one purchase, 7c.; 5 tons to 12 tons, one purchase, 5⅞c.; 12 tons and over, one purchase, 6¾c.; dry white lead in bbls. ¼c per lb. less than price in kegs. Lead in oil 12½ lb. in tin pails, add 1c.; in 25 and 50 lb. tin pails, add ½c.; and in 1 to 5 lb. tin cans, assorted (100 lbs. in case) add 2½c. per lb. to keg price. Terms on lots on 500 lbs. and over, note or acceptance at sixty days, or 2½ per cent. discount will be allowed for cash paid within fifteen days of invoice date. To make either of the above required quantities any assortment of packages of white lead, red lead and litharge may be counted. The above quotations are free on board cars or boat at corroding point. Linseed Oil meets with about an ordinary proportion of trade call, but the tone is irregular. Valuation retains some steadiness on the better makes, but evidences of irregularity on under grades continue and Western manufacturers are still working the local market. We quote at general range at 37@40c. for Western, and 44@56c. for City. Spirits Turpentine has been somewhat irregular, with tendency rather in buyers' favor at times, but the supply appears to be kept very well in hand and at the close a somewhat stronger and more uniform tone is infused into the market. We quote at 36@37c. per gallon, according to quality, delivery, etc.

TAR AND PITCH.—Operations are of moderate calibre and confined in the main to such parcels as can be turned over into consuming channels quickly. Supplies, however, are well controlled and owners have the confidence to induce them to insist upon previous rates. We quote Pitch at $1.70@1.75 per bbl.; Tar at $2.15@2.50, according to quantity, quality and delivery.

MISCELLANEOUS.

MISCELLANEOUS

MISCELLANEOUS.

TOWN OF UNION, HUDSON COUNTY, N. J.

NOTICE TO BUILDERS.

Proposals for the Construction of a Town Hall.

SEALED proposals will be received by the Board of Council of the Town of Union, at the Town Hall, corner of Lewis Street and Palisade Avenue, on

Monday August 31st, 1891,

at 8 P. M., for the construction of a Town Hall, according to plans and specifications now on file in the Clerk's office of said Town and at the office of the Architects, Messrs. French, Dixon, & De Salderp, Broadway and 57th Street, New York City, where they can be examined by any person interested therein. Bids will be received for the entire work, or for separate parts thereof, according to the specifications, and the successful bidder or bidders will be required to furnish bonds equal to the amount of the bid. All information necessary in relation to said contract can be had from the Town Clerk, and from the above-named Architects, and the Board reserves the right to reject any or all bids, if deemed for the interest of the Town so to do.

Town of Union, August 15th, 1891.

By order of the Board of Council.

LOUIS FORMON,
Town Clerk.

ARCHITECTURAL WOOD WORKERS.

MISCELLANEOUS.

MISCELLANEOUS

BUILDING MATERIAL PRICES

LUMBER.

Appended quotations are based almost wholly upon prices obtained for goods from first hands. Yard rates necessarily range much higher owing to the expenses attending sorting out and grading cargo and even car lots, besides which must be added the cost of handling and carrying until consumers are ready to invest. Terms of sale also prove important factors and, altogether, it is impossible to give a line of retail quotations thoroughly reliable in character.

SPRUCE—Eastern—special cargoes delivered N. Y.	$16 00	@	17 50
Random cargoes, narrow	13 00	@	14 00
Random cargoes, wide	14 50	@	15 50
PILING—Eastern—cargo rates:			
Ranging 30@40 per cent 12 inch butt, 35 to 40 ft average length	4	@	—
Ranging 45@50 per cent 12 inch butt, 35 to 40 ft average length	4¼	@	4½
Ranging 50@60 per cent One-half 12 inch butt, 38 to 40 ft average length	4¾	@	5
Two-thirds 12 inch butt, 38 to 42 ft average length	5½	@	6
Three-fourths 12 inch butt, 40 to 45 ft average length	5¾	@	6
All 12 inch butt and up, 40 to 45 ft average length	6	@	6¼
Piece stick, 40 feet each	4 00	@	—
do. 45	6 00	@	—
do. 50	8 00	@	—
do. 55	12 00	@	—
Inch spars, per inch	20	@	22
Scaffolding poles, each	60	@	1 00
Clothes poles, 45 to 65 feet, each	3 00	@	6 00
HEMLOCK:			
Penn. joist	12 00	@	12 50
do. boards	13 00	@	13 50
do. timber, 20 ft and under	12 50	@	13 00
do. do. 22 to 24 ft.	13 00	@	13 50
do. do. 26 to 28 ft.	13 50	@	14 00
do. do. 30 to 32 ft.	14 00	@	15 50
do. do. 34 to 36 ft.	15 50	@	16 00
do. do. 38 to 40 ft.	16 50	@	17 50
WHITE PINE—Good uppers and select, 1 to 2 inch	40 00	@	48 00
Upper and select, 2½ to 4 inch	50 00	@	58 00
Shelving	26 00	@	31 00
Pickings, 1 inch	33 00	@	35 00
Cutting-up, 1 inch	25 00	@	28 00
Bracket plank	30 00	@	35 00
Dressing-boards	18 00	@	22 00
Box, inch	13 50	@	14 00
Box, thick	14 50	@	15 50
West India shippers	16 00	@	19 00
Rio Janeiro do.	20 00	@	21 00
River Plate do.	29 00	@	30 00
Australia do.	25 00	@	30 00
YELLOW PINE—Random cargoes delivered N. Y.	18	@	21 00
Ordered cargoes	22	@	23 00
Flooring	21	@	22 00
Step plank	26	@	28 00
Common siding	13	@	14 00
Heart face boards	20	@	21 50
Car orders	21	@	23 00
At Atlantic ports, f. o. b.	12	@	15 00
At Gulf ports, f. o. b.	11	@	13 00
North Caroline pine timber	13	@	15 00
do. flooring 1 inch	16	@	22 00
do. do. 1¼	16	@	22 50
do. do. 1½@2 inch	24	@	25 00
do Shipping culls or box	12	@	14 00
do Plain and mottled ½@1½ inch	18	@	25 50
Ash, white	36 00	@	48 00
Elm	20 00	@	22 50
Oak, plain	37 00	@	41 00
Oak, quarter sawed	52	@	58 00
Oak, quarter sawed, extra thick	56	@	60 00
Redwood	45	@	52 50
Maple, clear	28	@	33 00
Chestnut, clear	33	@	35 50
Cypress, clear	30	@	32 50
Black Walnut, good to choice	130	@	140 00
Black Walnut, ordinary to fair	100	@	120 00
Black Walnut, ⅝	78	@	83 00
Black Walnut, selected and seasoned	150	@	155 00
Black Walnut counters	110	@	150 00
Black Walnut, culls	35	@	40 00
Black Walnut, rejects	50	@	58 00
Cherry, wide	110	@	115 00
Cherry, good	85	@	100 00
Cherry, ordinary	65	@	80 00
Whitewood, inch	30 00	@	32 50
Whitewood, ⅝ inch	24 00	@	26 00
Whitewood, 1¼ to 2½ inch	32 00	@	34 00
Shingles, Pine, 16 inch, extra	2 75	@	3 10
do 18 inch, extra	4 10	@	4 30
do 18 inch, clear butt	2 90	@	3 10
do 16 inch, stocks	4 50	@	4 80
do 18 inch, stocks	5 30	@	5 40
Shingles, Cypress, 6x20	8 00	@	10 00
do larger sizes	11 00	@	1[illegible] 00
do sawed	6 00	@	9 00
Cedar—Medium to large	6¼	@	7½
do. —Extra large	7¾	@	8
Mahogany—Small	[illegible]	@	[illegible]
do —Medium	8	@	8½
do. —Large	9½	@	12
do. —Extra Large	1½	@	14

DEVOTED TO REAL ESTATE, BUILDING ARCHITECTURE, HOUSEHOLD DECORATION, BUSINESS AND THEMES OF GENERAL INTEREST

PRICE, PER YEAR IN ADVANCE, SIX DOLLARS.

Published every Saturday.

TELEPHONE - - - - CORTLANDT 1370.

Communications should be addressed to

C. W. SWEET, 14 & 16 Vesey St.

J. T. LINDSEY, Business Manager.

VOL. XLVIII SEPTEMBER 5, 1891. No. 1,225.

UNDER pretense of imminence and removal of danger from frost, but really on some heavy realizing and correspondingly heavy new buying, the stock market has maintained its advance and in some cases has made net gains in the past week. Such a movement as this has not been seen for so long that it puzzles everyone not familiar with the history of this market. It is a case where experience rather deters than helps to success. The traders, the men who are in it all the time, who assiduously watch the movements of prices and have eyes active to discover domestic or foreign complications or extrications likely to move quotations one way or the other, have long since taken their profits and, with the exception of the few who see the unusualness of the movement and have bought again, have been working industriously for a reaction. That stocks should have made the advances they have, some as much as 17 or 18 points from the lowest on the last decline, with only a reactive movement now and then of a point or two is certainly unusual; but that, instead of giving ground for belief in a certain heavy decline, ought to prove that the situation is one not to be judged by ordinary conditions. The trader who applies the rules good in times when the market fluctuates five or six points one way or the other will lose his money. The present movement resembles a political crisis, when neither party will take hold of some question vital to the public but only important to the politician as a means of gaining or holding power, which the public takes up and compels its representatives to carry. In the stock market both bull and bear were quite content to send the ball back and forth within a 5 per cent limit, but suddenly it was snatched from them and sent out of sight. We have passed so many feared dangers without mishap that confidence grows apace. This month has opened without disclosing that the government has any difficulty in dealing with the matured 4½s. Money in spite of the increase in the volume of stock business is easy, and some passing of interest which was feared has not happened. There is a strong hope, too, that present fears of trouble in particular cases may prove as lightly founded. In reviewing the whole situation, and for the moment the most just conclusion arrived at, would be that there is a grip upon the market which can put prices much higher, but as the movement so far can only be characterised as a speculative one there is always a danger of scare and a consequent break. If the demand for investment bonds had been maintained in the good proportions of three weeks ago, there could only be one view of the situation, but when, as now, good bonds are selling below, and in cases very much below stocks, paying little if anything more and sometimes not so much, there is always room to apprehend a readjustment of the quotations. Viewed for the future, there is no doubt whatever that a bull movement is only now in its initial stage.

THE foreign markets are at the present time quite devoid of new features. It is not too much to say that almost the sole condition affecting prices is the condition of the cereal market. Any speculation in which English operators are at present indulging is carried on in American securities. Other issues are dull and weak. In a similar way Berlin is occupied with the grain situation, and its effects on Russian securities, which are of course weak and feverish. Neither is there likely to be any change in this respect throughout the fall. For a month past the political situation has been far from assuring; but now it is apparent that the winter will be passed without any disturbance. With that much certainty the foreigners must rest content.

ON Thursday evening last, the committee of one hundred "champions of the people," as the *Times* calls them, minus "quite a number," assembled in one of the parlors of the Hotel Brunswick. The meeting was called only for the purpose of constituting an executive committee, which is to bear the brunt and heat of the battle. This committee numbers nine of the champions. The meeting was so very free from incidents of importance, that we should not deem it necessary to grant it any attention, was it not that the future plans of the committee were revealed. They are going to make an onslaught on the Park Commissioners, and if defeated there, carry the case to the Legislature. Alderman Morris thought that the executive committee ought to address to each candidate for the Senate, the Assembly and the Board of Aldermen a list of questions prepared to define the attitude of every candidate in regard to this movement. We do not think that if Alderman Morris' advice is adopted they will chose the path of wisdom. There is no objection that we can see in committing the candidates for aldermen to the displacement of the elevated tracks in Battery Park, because the aldermen cannot do anything but pass resolutions which nobody cares anything about. But in the Legislature there is every reason to believe that the champions of the people will be on the defensive, and that is something that champions should never be. People who have been following the course of public sentiment, particularly in the upper wards, are very well aware that the Manhattan Company has been gaining rather than losing ground this summer, for there can be no doubt that Mr. Gould's agents have secured in their favor (by corrupt means, no doubt,) the logic of events; while opposed to this there is nothing but a mass of sentiment, partly due to misunderstanding, partly peurile, partly contemptible. The logic of events has been saying more and more clearly all summer that during the necessarily long interval before the Rapid Transit Commissioners can get any part of any route in operation, that the traveling public will need somewhat better accommodations, and as the pressure grows more unendurable the logic of events will speak still louder. We by no means predict the triumph of the Battery Park "grabbers," but without doubt next winter their voices will be heard high throughout the city. The champion's mouthpiece stated last week that the obstacles in the way of the movement were the "greatest possible." Now it is obvious that even according to the words of the mouthpiece the conflict will be nothing better than the old one between an irresistible force and an immovable body. But what if this "greatest possible" obstacle should itself get under way. Manifestly its momentum would be tremendous. Could the champions withstand it? We cannot say; but think of the possible spectacle—champions put to rout. It would be a sorry sight.

THE Socialistic programme, or rather programmes, so far as drawn up, receive a good deal of vague sympathy and support from people who are not so well off as they fancy they deserve to be, because it is thought that a closer division of production by polls instead of by merit, or what passes for merit, would give everyone a very sufficient competency. The Massachusetts Bureau of Statistics has published some figures which run counter to these anticipations. Investigations made by the Bureau show that the average yearly wages of work-people of both sexes employed by individuals and firms engaged in manufactures, amount to $362.23, while the employers receive $517 each, which represents both salary and profit. The average is lower in the case of corporations, for it appears that the workmen engaged by them receive average wages of $333.22, but then the stockholders realize only $379 on their investment. These figures certainly afford no glimpses of the Socialistic millennium. Indeed, if these figures be correct, it is hard to see by what process of equal division the average earnings of work-people is to be much increased. We do not believe that very many people would give up their chances of getting "what they can" for an assurance of their "average," even with their share of the employer's and stockholder's net profit added thereto. These figures possess no scientific accuracy and are little better than a guess based upon a mass of data, for which the taxpayers in Massachusetts had to pay pretty heavily. They are not, however, so far from the truth as to be without a lesson for visionaries.

THE English builder, so far as we know, has never been a person of very much interest to his New York prototype. Building is not an international affair, being on the contrary the most local of the large industries of a country. Nevertheless, since there are some men in London and elsewhere throughout England who make money by speculative and contract building, their New York brethren in trade may be interested to learn a little something about their ways, particularly as that something is nothing to their good. According to the report of the English Inspector-General of Bankruptcy, the English speculative builders are men of a "bad system." Taking the country through, the Inspector-General states that while bankruptcy in those trades which are based on credit is decreasing, that of the non-trading class is increasing or remaining steady. In other words, business proper in England is becoming more secure all the time. There is, however, one trade to which this does not apply—the building trade, itself one of the four largest classes of failures.

The reason for this is, according to our Inspector-General, that the speculative builder seems to consider it his business to erect buildings without due regard to the laws of demand and supply. The only limit on his operations is that imposed on his power of mortgaging. Frequently starting with little or no capital, he has no difficulty in obtaining sites of land on lease; the lessor, knowing that the moment the requisite materials are brought on the ground that the value of his land is certain to be improved in any case, is perfectly indifferent to the lessee's means. Having thus obtained the lease, the builder proceeds to order the materials. Timber, brick, cement, etc., are obtained on long credit, the usual period being about six months. As the buildings progress there is no difficulty of obtaining advances on mortgage to the extent of about two-thirds or three-fourths of their actual cost. These advances are obtained long before the bills for materials become due, so that the builder is no longer hampered by want of ready money. As his operations increase, his credit increases correspondingly. His trade bills are met with more or less regularity for a time, but the discharge of one obligation is generally simultaneous with the contracting of other and larger ones. Sometimes a building may be disposed of for cash, but as a rule it is by a mortgage and not by sale that the requisite funds are supplied. Of couise, he can only borrow a portion of the value, but for some years his trade credit easily supplies the margin; and he may even be regarded and regard himself as a man of capital. But the day of reckoning inevitably comes. To meet the increasing pressure every resource available for borrowing is resorted to, and second and third charges are given to bankers and other pressing creditors over properties already mortgaged. The debtor has as a rule no debts due to him over which he can give a charge, but furniture and similar property is too often pledged to his relatives and even to his wife or his marriage trustees in consideration of alleged advancer, and when at last the bubble bursts and bankruptcy supervenes, his estate is found to have entirely disappeared. Readers may, perhaps, recollect cases in New York similar to this typical case in England. After making full allowance for the difference in the laws between the two countries and the customs of the trade, there can be no doubt of the similarity in this—that too many builders build for no other reason on earth than that they can.

Chicago and the Fair.

TWO years ago last August, when the agitation in favor of holding the World's Fair in New York was begun, it was claimed by those who were most zealous in furthering the project that, if New York secured the Fair, it would constitute an enormous stimulus to business of all kinds. Not only would the influx of visitors crowd the city, fill the hotels and bring customers to the stores and theatres, but the familiarity which thousands of strangers would thus obtain with the various attractions and advantages of New York life would be of enduring benefit. Trade connections of a permanent character might be formed, and many who could afford it would be tempted to repeat their visit to the metropolis. On the other hand, it was alleged that the confusion and bother produced by a hot crowd of scurrying strangers, the interruption thus caused to regular business, and the diversion of energy required to entertain them and to meet their requirements would very nearly, if not quite, offset whatever spasmodic stimulation trade might receive. As for any possibility of permanent benefit—that was scouted as a fanciful assumption. The controversy is long since dead, and we have no wish to revive it. At the writing, we can recall no reasonable pretext for any such celebration being held in this city until the three hundredth anniversary of the landing of Henry Hudson; and we shall not have to begin to prepare for that until a good quarter of a century or more is passed. But there can be no doubt that even if some industries would have been hampered by the holding of the Fair in New York, and a great deal of bother incurred and money wasted, that real estate, particularly in the upper wards, would have been supplied with a cause for activity; which during the present year, at least, it has sorely needed. Here, also, there would have been a great deal of forced adaptation to the various requirements of an enormously enlarged transient population. Hotels, theatres, lodging houses and various places of entertainment would have been built, which not only would have become useless for their peculiar purposes after the ending of the Fair, but which would for some years have been quite valueless—until, that is, the city grew up to them. Nevertheless, a very important permanent advantage would have been secured in the necessarily rapid construction of a rapid transit line to accommodate the crowds from all over the city which would wish to visit the Fair grounds. As it is, rapid transit is still in the far distant future.

Whatever permanent assistance the Exposition may render to Chicago, it is very certain that the temporary effects are everything that was anticipated. The coming Fair has proved to be a tremendous stimulus to activity in the building trades and in real estate circles. The year 1890 was a good year for building and for real estate all over the country. It was the biggest year New York, Brooklyn, Boston and many other cities have ever seen; but it was particularly big for Chicago. In that year permits were issued for 11,544 new buildings, to be erected at an estimated cost of $47,373,-200, a sum nearly twice as great as that spent by Philadelphia and Brooklyn, although their population is not very much smaller. During the same year the exchanges of real estate in Cook County aggregated in value $237,831,586, of which $194,303,532 represented city property, and $43,528,054 suburban property. What this enormous total means can best be shown through a comparison with the similar figures for New York. In 1890 the aggregate of value involved in such of the transfers in this city, for which a consideration was expressed, was $282,047,609. Between Cook County and New York there is a difference in our favor amounting to about $45,000,000, while between the city proper and New York the difference in favor of the latter verges on twice that sum. In view of the fact that the area of Chicago is 175 square miles while that of New York is only forty-one square miles, this difference may not seem to make the comparison very much worse for New York; but there are a number of other conditions to be considered. The population of New York is 700,000 or 800,000 larger than that of Chicago, but the more important factor is the much higher level of real estate values in this city. The population of Brooklyn is just about half that of New York, and within 200,000 of that of Chicago; but the aggregate value represented in the transfers in Kings County during 1890 was only $81,618,104, and Brooklyn real estate was very active during that year. We might illustrate our point still further, but we think that it is already sufficiently established. Real estate in Chicago is certainly more active than real estate in New York, and this activity has been continued into the present year. There are at present in the course of erection in that city five buildings, the estimated cost of which is more than one million dollars. One of these buildings is twenty-two stories high, and will cost $3,000,000; another is eighteen stories high, and will cost $2,000,000. Furthermore, it cannot be doubted that this quickening and enlargement of operations is largely the result of the prospective World's Fair. We fully expect that the coming two or three years will be years of great and substantial prosperity for Chicago. A large part of the region which will be most benefited by the enormous crops of this summer and the excellent prices at which they will be sold is more or less completely tributary to that city. In consequence its trade will undoubtedly undergo a great expansion, and money will be made hand over fist. The danger is that stimulated by this enlargement of business and by the money brought there through the World's Fair that a boom will set in on the top of the already slight inflation of values—a boom which will be succeeded by an inevitable and disastrous collapse.

It is becoming increasingly certain that Chicago will make the World's Fair a credit to the country. When that city obtained the sanction of Congress to the location of the International Exhibition within its boundaries many of the New York newspapers turned up their metropolitan noses and talked superciliously about an inter-state fair, the impossibility of giving an Exposition held in such a place an international character, and so on. Scarcely any of them had a large enough spirit and sufficient patriotism to sink their chagrin at being beaten in the fight and to direct their energies towards assisting Chicago in the great and difficult work of rousing the people of the country to support the undertaking. It is needless to say that Chicago has got along very well without them. Unfortunately, the responses by the Legislatures of the different States to appeals for money have not by any means been all that they should have been. Very frequently, owing to jealousy or some equally petty political reason, the appropriations embodied in the original bills were cut down; and in not a few States the bills failed to pass. We regret to say that among these latter New York must be numbered; and for this our patriotic, disinterested and broad-minded Governor is responsible. Indications are not wanting, however, that in all the States people are becoming more and more zealous in furthering the interests of the Fair. There has never been any doubt but that the best business men of the country, those whose products represented our finest craftsmanship and most improved methods would do their best to give to the Exposition a truly and comprehensively expressive character; and with their co-operation Chicago can spare the half-hearted assistance and defy the ill-concealed enmity of political foes and commercial rivals. The commissioners from this country have been enthuiastically received abroad; and the two greatest nations of Europe—the nations whose arts and industries are most highly developed—are committed to a hearty support of the Fair. A good deal of the best organizing and artistic talent that the United States possesses has been enlisted in its service; and Americans can rest confident that the energy and ability which has made Chicago the great city which it is at present, will make the Exposition of 1892-93 as completely representative of the content and scope of this country as the Paris Exposition of 1889 was representative of the content and scope of France.

Investments—Good and Bad.

UNION PACIFIC BONDS.—The tendency to overdo things, for which security-holders are remarkable, is becoming apparent in the quotations for Union Pacific bond issues. There was a time when both stock and bonds of this property were sought for at figures unwarranted by its merits. Going to the other extreme, there seems now to be a tendency to throw over the bonds, at least without regard to merit at all. There is ground for hesitation in buying the stock at current figures and perhaps some justification for selling it to place the proceeds where they will give less anxiety. With the floating debt all provided for by the three-year notes the creditors are asked to take, the stock would merely have the control value and such other value as speculation might give it; the prospects of both together would not make it very attractive around current figures. There may be some combination under consideration which, if carried out, would send the stock up for the time being, and there may be difficulties to face not yet made known to the public which, when known, will have a tendency to send the price down very materially. The rapid fluctuations it has lately undergone and the improbable stories accompanying the advances, both advance and story only lasting until the latter could be contradicted, show that the stock could be manipulated wholly for purposes of speculation. For these reasons the conservative will fight shy of it until something more definite is known. It may be said that in the decline of this year Union Pacific has discounted the bad in its situation; certainly in the rally of ten points it has discounted the substantial good in a property so beset with trouble.

With the bonds it is different. Current quotations are made in part by forced sale of collateral in the liquidation of some of the company's loans. But they also show an over anxiety on the part of holders and the buyers of its securities. The basis on which some of the bonds are selling is pretty nearly what might be expected if a receivership was declared to be inevitable and a disintegration of the system probable. Naturally, this is most apparent in the securities that would be most affected in the event of danger to the integrity of the system as it now stands, such as guaranteed bonds of leased lines. But some of its best issues which, should the improbable worst occur run only a danger of delay in payment of interest, have sold to yield more than 5 per cent on the investment. The last-mentioned issues are undesirable, it is true, in having only a few years to run, but this fact ought to help the underlying and collateral issues. Whatever fortune for good or evil Union Pacific is likely to meet, a breaking up of the system is most highly improbable; amalgamation and not disintegration is found to be the wisest policy in dealing with distressed properties nowadays; witness Atchison and other recently reorganized railroad companies. What has been found good in those cases would also be found good in others. Therefore, if the necessities or distrust of the present holders of Union Pacific bonds continues, stronger and more confident investors will be able to make some very advantageous purchases.

While there may be no need for haste in making purchases, and in fact good need for careful study and discrimination in the employment of money in Union Pacific bonds, some of the recent figures prove that sales have been made without regard to anything but realizing the principal of loans, for which the bonds so sold were deposited as security. Not only do the best Union Pacific issues sell below a 5 per cent basis, but some of its minor issues have made quotations to pay from about 6 to 8¾ per cent. With no question of Union Pacific's ability to keep up payment of interest and guarantees such figures would be impossible, or at most possible only for a very short space of time indeed. Even with the financial troubles which now perplex the management some of the Union Pacific bonds are cheap at recent figures. For instance, Utah Southern generals and extension firsts have sold, the former to pay 7.40 per cent on the investment and the latter 7.25 per cent. Such figures can only be the result of forced sales. Utah Southern was long ago taken into the Union Pacific system by an exchange of 11 Union Pacific, selling at the time above par, for 10 Utah Central, with which Utah Southern had previously been amalgamated on equal terms. It now forms an integral part of the system, and is only distinguished from the general system by its outstanding bonds. Union Pacific, Denver & Gulf first consolidated gold 5s have sold on a 7 per cent basis, yet the property on which it is based earns its interest, and has besides the Union Pacific backing. With doubt for the security of the system, there would be reason for the low prices brought by Atchison, Colorado & Pacific 6s, Union Pacific, Lincoln & Colorado first guaranteed and others, but as has before been stated there is very little apparent ground for such doubts. Even the Union Pacific collateral trust 4½s ought to find better prices than they do. The collateral of the bond is only bonds of a road dependent on Union Pacific for means to pay its interest; but so long as Union Pacific can maintain its guarantee, so long is the collateral good, but the bond is also a direct obligation of Union Pacific. While there are many who do not think well of its financial position at the present moment, there are few or none whose word is worth anything who will affirm that the company is facing bankruptcy. It would be strange, indeed, if a great property like Union Pacific could not in these times of commercial cheerfulness manage to find a way out of its difficulties, great though they be. When those difficulties are removed, while the stock may not and perhaps should not advance, there is no doubt whatever that a change will be seen in the quotation for its bonds.

BROOKLYN ELEVATED.—"A Subscriber" writes us: "Several years ago I bought some shares of the Brooklyn Elevated Railroad. I would like to know something about it and what the prospects are. It is seldom quoted, and I have not been able to find out anything about it. If you can throw any light on it I should appreciate it very much." "A Subscriber" should keep his shares. The Brooklyn Elevated is developing new territory which must be given time to grow, but its future is very promising. The company has paid all its fixed obligations, and in two years created a surplus of $157,873, after writing off the deficiencies of previous years, and reports a satisfactory cash balance on hand. The steady growth of earnings is very satisfactory. Some months ago some Brooklyn Elevated sold for 35, a price which indicates considerable faith on the part of the buyer. Present quotations merely nominal and not representing transactions are 22 and 26.

A Builder in Trouble.

Thomas Graham, the architect and builder, who has just finished eight private dwellings on 92d street, near Madison avenue, and who is now engaged on the "Graham" apartment hotel, is embarrassed in a business way. Within ten days, liens have been filed against him amounting to more than $100,000, and all work on the buildings he is erecting has come to a standstill. Mr. Graham is now trying so to arrange matters with his creditors that the loss of time and money in the completion and disposal of his buildings will be reduced to a minimum.

With this end in view, three meetings of his creditors have been held. The first was on Monday, the second on Wednesday, and the last on yesterday afternoon. In a general way, it is proposed to appoint three trustees from among the creditors to look after the interests of those concerned and to as rapidly as possible complete and dispose of the property. There are a number of details, however, upon which the creditors are not agreed and, until these are finally settled upon, matters will be at a standstill.

Mr. Graham is out of town resting from the strain that has been put upon him lately, and as his address could not be learned, it was impossible to get a statement from him. A creditor, who is also a friend of Mr. Graham's, furnished the following figures and explanation: The indebtedness amounts, roughly speaking, to $140,000, and the assets are, as near as they can be estimated, a little under $100,000 in excess of the liabilities. This estimate is not, of course, based on the value of the holdings in their present unfinished state, but rather what they will be worth when they are put on the market, provided real estate values remain on their present level.

The trouble was precipitated, it is said, by Mr. Graham's inability to pay a note of $3,000 which came due on Saturday last, owing to the fact that he had not received his loan on his 92d street houses. He had secured the loan from an insurance company, but the lawyer who was to search the title was out of town and the work was delayed. From this loan Mr. Graham would have received about $25,000 after paying off his building loan. One of his houses had been sold and title was to be given on September 1st, and from this sale there would have been an additional $13,000 in cash. With this money he could have tided over his affairs, but the loan was delayed and the liens which have been placed on the 92d street houses prevent the owner from giving title.

The first lien was placed on the property by the holders of the unpaid $3,000 note. They filed a lien for $9,000 against the 92d street houses, and of $24,500 against the hotel property, and, of course, everyone else who was engaged on the buildings took fright and liens were filed as rapidly as possible, with the result that all work is stopped, and the creditors are now trying to find out how they can go on again.

At the meeting of creditors in Guggenheimer & Untermyer's office yesterday afternoon three trustees were appointed to complete the 92d street houses and offer them on the market. They are Frederick Haas, a creditor, who represents Thomas Graham, John Casey, who represents Freeman & O'Neill, and John Renahan, representing the other creditors. As soon as the loan is obtained, and the houses spoken of above conveyed, the title to the other seven houses will be put in the names of these trustees, who will pay off the creditors pro rata as the money is received. After the just liens against this property are paid off the surplus money will be used to complete the 89th street job, and when all claims against the hotel are settled Mr. Graham will receive the residue. The creditors were unable to reach any conclusion in the 89th street matter, and it will be necessary to hold at least one more meeting to arrange the details of that. Mr. Graham is to be employed as the agent of the trustees, but he has no power to make any contracts or to bind the trustees in any way.

Real Estate Notes.

The plans have been filed in Brooklyn during the past week for two large and costly buildings. One is to be built on Wythe avenue, west side, 25 south of South 11th street, being a six-story factory, to cost $350,000, while the other will be a one and three-story armory to be erected by the State of New York on Bedford avenue, west side, extending from Atlantic avenue to Pacific street, at an estimated cost of $283,459.

The five-story brick store, known as No. 40 East 14th street and No. 79 University place, has been transferred to John Downey, the builder, for $245,000.

Edward L. Keyes has conveyed to John L. B. Mott the three-story brick dwelling, size 25x80, No. 1 Park avenue, on the northeast corner of 34th street, for $110,000.

Plans were filed last week for a nine-story extension, size 42x94.9, to the Hotel Imperial, on Broadway, southeast corner 32d street, for Robert and Ogden Goelet. The improvement will cost $150,000.

New Incorporations.

The United States Home Providing Association filed a certificate of incorporation in the County Clerk's office, on August 29th, for the purpose of purchasing and improving real estate. The capital stock is $12,000, divided into 240 shares of $50 each. The directors are Leon M. Kramer, Elias J. Friedland, Simon Landres, Jacob Ash and Barnet Bletstein.

The Railroad Brotherhood Savings and Building Association filed articles of association on September 4th, for the purpose of purchasing and improving real estate. The capital stock is to be divided into shares of $250 each. The names of the directors are M. N. Clapp and twenty-nine others.

Personal.

Thomas Lyons, of Lyons & Bath, arrived on the Arizona on Monday last, from Europe, where he made a stay of considerable length.

Frank R. Houghton says: "The demand for houses on the West Side to rent is greater than the supply, and there has been recently a marked improvement in the rents obtained for them."

Real Estate Department.

THE SALES OF THE WEEK.

There is some improvement to be noted in the real estate market this week, although the number of transactions does not greatly exceed those reported in our last issue and nothing of any particular importance has been closed. But if the tangible results of the week's work do not show great improvement the general feeling does. The summer torpor is gradually giving way before the very general prophecies of fall prosperity and the reports upon which those prophecies are based. In the first place the renting in nearly all sections of the city is better than it was at this time last year. The rents, except in rare cases, remain the same, but they are paid more willingly and readily and there is a steadiness of demand in nearly all parts of the city that is a very good sign. Added to this is a very general sentiment that no booming methods will avail this fall, and if the effort to keep business on a legitimate and sound basis is successful the indications are that a large, steady business will be done. The inquiry for nearly all kinds of property is quite active, considering the fact that we are only in the first week in September, and if prices will only be kept down to reasonable figures there is little doubt that many sales will be closed in the near future. There is talk of several large transactions already current, but as yet they are only in the first stages which lead to consummation, and even when completed there will doubtless be an effort made to keep the facts from the public.

The sales at auction during the past week present little that is of general interest. They have been mainly foreclosure sales, with here and there a partition sale; but all of them have been of a legal character, with the exception of a small parcel in Mt. Vernon, sold at public auction. These legal sales have all been of parcels where the selling price has been below $50,000. In the case of the foreclosure sales the selling price has exceeded the charges against the property, so far as those are known, and that fact is, at least, a very satisfactory one. The active bidders, often the only bidders at the sales during the past week, have been the parties in interest, although the daily attendance on the Exchange floor shows a very considerable increase over that of the past summer months.

THE ANNOUNCEMENTS.

The auctioneers' bills show nothing more in the way of new sales than what was spoken of in this column last week. The auction branch of the real estate business is probably duller than any other just now and the auctioneers themselves show no particular desire to hurry matters along. In fact in several instances owners who wished to offer their property early this month have been advised by their auctioneers to defer it for a little while until the market becomes more active. A general feeling of confidence in the coming fall auction market is preventing any undue haste on the part of the auctioneers, and the result will probably be all that they desire. Property offered at this time under existing circumstances stands very little chance of meeting with a successful sale. Everything is in an unsettled state, as is to be expected between seasons, and no one seems to have any very decided notion of what they want to do. In a few weeks this feeling will have given place to one of a more certain direction and determination, and then with attractive offerings a very good business should be done.

On Thursday, September 10th, Richard V. Harnett & Co. will sell the frame dwellings at Nos. 173 and 175 East 123d street.

CONVEYANCES.

	1889. Aug. 30 to Sept. 5, inclus.	1890. Aug. 29 to Sept. 4, inclus.	1891. Aug. 28 to Sept. 3, inclus.
Number	182	209	167
Amount involved	$3,366,655	$1,582,379	$2,467,639
Number nominal	37	57	48
Number 23d and 24th Wards	35	36	37
Amount involved	$178,367	$172,400	$150,091
Number nominal	11	12	9

MORTGAGES.

	1889.	1890.	1891.
Number	127	101	170
Amount involved	$1,066,285	*†$9,128,244	$1,608,674
Number at 5 per cent	57	72	61
Amount involved	$520,674	*$6,194,500	$642,755
Number at less than 5 per cent.	14	23	7
Amount involved	$276,500	$604,000	$156,750
Number to Banks, Trust and Insurance Companies	11	31	18
Amount involved	$248,100	*†$7,287,900	$505,250

PROJECTED BUILDINGS.

	1889. Aug. 31 to Sept. 6, inclus.	1890. Aug. 30 to Sept. 5, inclus.	1891. Aug. 29 to Sept. 4, inclus.
Number of buildings	56	36	31
Estimated cost	$725,140	$1,429,080	$345,090

*Includes mortgage given by the United States Electric Light and Power Co. to the Union Trust Co. for $5,000,000.

†Includes mortgage given by the Standard Gas Light Co. to The Mercantile Trust Co. for $1,500,000.

Gossip of the Week.

SOUTH OF 59TH STREET.

Charles S. Brown has sold for Daniel S. McElroy to Anson W. Hard No. 51 Park avenue, a four-story dwelling adjoining 37th street, on private terms. Mr. McElroy purchased this dwelling less than a month ago from Charles Steinway.

John N. Golding has sold for D. B. Van Emburgh to John W. Stirling No. 3 West 47th street, Columbia College leasehold, a four-story brick dwelling, 29x55x100. The price is said to have been $47,500.

B. Flanagan & Son have sold for Henry Stewart No. 156 West 53d street, a four-story brown stone dwelling, 18.8x65x100, for $15,000.

Ward Belknap has sold for Chas. W. Rose to Mrs. Mary J. Mitchell the three-story brick dwelling, 14x60x100, No. 305 East 31st street, on private terms.

Fairchild & Yoran have sold for M. Simpson the three-story frame building, on lot 22.6x100.5, No. 410 West 47th street, to a builder for improvement, on private terms.

NORTH OF 59TH STREET.

Wm. J. Mathews has sold the uncompleted five-story and basement brick and stone flat, 36.8x96, on the northeast corner of Madison avenue and 88th street, for $110,000. The purchaser is R. H. Mathews, a brother of the builder, and it is said he has resold the building to Isaac Hoagland.

Cyrille Carreau has sold for Dr. James J. Phelan to Wm. J. Mathews, the builder, the five lots on the north side of 88th street, 36.8 feet east of Madison avenue, for $50,000 for improvement.

Chas. F. White has sold for J. Hassell to J. H. Weinberg No. 233 West 100th street, a four-story, brown stone, high stoop dwelling, 25x60x100, for $30,000, and for A. Robison to J. Hassell Nos. 103 and 105 West 105th street, two five-story brick flats, each 25x70x100, for $46,500.

Arthur Gorsch has sold for Judge Langbein to a Mrs. Bernstein No. 203 East 82d street, a three-story and basement brown stone dwelling, 18x55x82, for $13,350.

Hunt & Wendell have sold for Foster & Livingston to James F. Ryan No. 28 West 82d street, a four-story brown stone dwelling, 18x56x100, for $35,000.

F. Zittel has sold for Breen & Nason to C. H. Wilcox No. 115 West 75th street, a four-story brown stone dwelling, 20x55x102.2, for $35,000.

Mark P. Brennan, it is reported, has sold the two five-story brick and stone flats Nos. 133 and 135 West 83d street, on private terms.

Stabler & Smith have sold for James Cunningham the two five-story brown stone flats, each 25x80x100, Nos. 111 and 113 West 117th street, on private terms.

Frederick Aldhous, it is reported, has sold No. 21 West 74th street, a four-story brown stone dwelling, 25x60x104, with a dining-room extension 28 feet deep. The price, it is said, was something less than $65,000.

The firm of L. J. Carpenter have sold for A. M. Mitchell to Charles Smith, a builder, the northwest corner of 101st street and 2d avenue, 100.8x100, for $33,500, for improvement.

LEASES.

Richard D. Kehoe has leased for J. B. Morrow the private dwelling, No. 85 West 134th street, for eighteen months, at the yearly rental of $900, to Henry Mendelson.

W. E. Jackson has leased for Mrs. Addractte Goodwin to David D. Newill, No. 32 West 70th street, a four-story brown stone dwelling, 20x56x102.2, for three years, at $2,000 per annum; and for George G. Rockwood, the photographer, to C. P. Armstrong, Jr., the three-story 18-foot dwelling, No. 256 West 88th street, for three years, at $1,350 per annum.

T. A. Burnett reports that he has leased the four-story brown stone dwelling, No. 36 East 64th street, for Joseph I. West, at $2,500 per annum; and for A. M. Palmer a similar house, No. 763 Madison avenue, also at $2,500 per year.

Frank R. Houghton has leased No. 62 West 72d street, a four-story dwelling, furnished, for A. Sober to Theo. Marburg, recently of Baltimore, for one year, for $4,500. This is said to be the highest rent yet obtained for any private house west of Central Park. The same broker has leased the dwelling No. 152 West 72d street for three years, at $3,000 per annum, for Dr. W. H. Tutt to E. G. Hime, of Brazil.

Brooklyn.

Corwith Bros. have sold the two three-story brick stores and dwellings, 25x50x95 each, Nos. 149 and 151 Franklin street, for Geo. T. Benton and Josiah H. Benton, to Peter Merkens for $12,000; and the one-story frame building, on lot 25x50, No. 18 Herbert street, for Margaret Small, to Henry Rehder for $550.

Ward Belknap has sold for the Backley estate to Peter J. Jacobus No. 62 Warren street, a three-story and basement brick dwelling, 25x55x100, on private terms.

J. P. Sloane has sold for William W. Campbell the vacant lot on the north side of Eagle street, 275 feet west of Provost street, to John Griffin for $1,000.

CONVEYANCES.

	1889. Aug. 29 to Sept. 4, inclus.	1890. Aug. 27 to Sept. 3, inclus.	1891. Aug. 26 to Sept. 2, inclus.
Number	257	266	298
Amount involved	$1,076,963	$1,279,569	$1,133,703
Number nominal	58	61	73

MORTGAGES.

	1889.	1890.	1891.
Number	210	225	269
Amount involved	$889,530	$851,556	$846,194
Number at 5 per cent. or less	131	140	123
Amount involved	$613,100	$635,067	$306,395

PROJECTED BUILDINGS.

	1889. Aug. 30 to Sept. 5, inclus.	1890. Aug. 28 to Sept. 4, inclus.	1891. Aug. 27 to Sept. 3, inclus.
Number of buildings	80	66	56
Estimated cost	$434,325	$280,400	$385,499

Out Among the Builders.

John C. Burne, architect, is preparing plans, etc., for a large apartment house to be built by John Keirns on Sylvan place, west side, between 120th and 121st streets, facing the new Court House. It will have a frontage of 126 feet, by a depth on the corner of 93 feet. It will be six stories high and have an exterior of brown stone, terra cotta and buff brick. The interior will be finished in cherry. All recent improvements, such as steam heat, passenger and freight elevators, electric light, etc., are to be placed in the building.

Richard R. Davis has plans on the board for two five-story flats, 25x87.6, to be erected at Nos. 228 and 230 West 123d street, by E. K. Smith.

The northwest corner of 101st street and 2d avenue, 100.8x100, is to be improved by the erection of four five-story tenements and stores. The owner is Charles Smith, a builder, who has just purchased the lots.

The report, which found circulation last week, that Charles W. Dayton would improve the ground which he owns on Broadway, adjoining the Washington building, by the erection of a twenty-six-story office building does not seem to have much foundation in fact. In several quarters it was asserted that the report was started to boom the land and enable the holder to sell out at a handsome profit to some man or syndicate attracted by the magnitude of the undertaking. In order to ascertain what truth there was in the story, a reporter of THE RECORD AND GUIDE called on Mr. Dayton at his office. Mr. Dayton said that there was nothing definite in the matter as yet. Several architects, he said, who knew that he owned the ground, had drawn designs for office buildings and submitted them to him voluntarily. He said that these designs were for large buildings of various heights, but that he was not ready, just yet, to adopt any of them. When the cable road is finished on Broadway, the Custom House site on Bowling Green finally acquired and other contemplated improvements in the vicinity are well under way, he will set about organizing a company for the construction of some large building; but until then nothing definite will be done. At present, Mr. Dayton says, investors have not been educated up to the point where they will readily take part in an enterprise of the kind projected by him; but he hopes before long that they will see the advantages of it, and when the bonds are put upon the market he expects that they will be eagerly taken up. Mr. Dayton says he has held the property at too great a sacrifice up to the present time to part with it now.

Out of Town.

HERKIMER, N. Y.—King & Symonds have drawn plans for a brick and stone round-house, with seven stalls, and asphalt roof, to be built for the Adirondack & St. Lawrence Railway Company.

WANTS AND OFFERS.

(Advertisements strictly in accordance with this title will be inserted at the practically nominal rate of 10 CENTS *per line (agate). In figuring for themselves advertisers may count seven words for each line, the address to be taken as one line. The object of this department is to bring buyers and sellers into communication with customers. Advertisements must be marked "Wants and Offers Column," and sent to the office of publication, Nos. 14 and 16 Vesey Street, not later than 3 P. M. Friday.)*

WANTS.

WANTED, in exchange for excellent plot of ground on the West Side, splendid neighborhood, established character, near 8th av, equity $75,000; a good investment property, preferably down town, must be well rented and bring good returns.
X Y Z, RECORD AND GUIDE.

A YOUNG MAN, 26, who has had seven years' practical experience in the real estate business, desires employment; references unexceptionable.
INDUSTRY, RECORD Office.

AN AUCTIONEER requiring the services of a man, 25, who understands the business, and who can furnish unquestionable references, will please address.
ACTIVE, RECORD Office.

SITUATION WANTED.—As superintendent or foreman for an architect, builder or speculator. Address,
C. J. D., RECORD AND GUIDE.

AN ENERGETIC YOUNG MAN, with considerable knowledge and experience in the real estate business, desires to connect himself with an established office. Will furnish capital for part interest.
L. B., RECORD AND GUIDE.

WANTED.—A position in a real estate office by a young man of twenty years, who has had some experience, and can furnish references. Address,
RELIABLE, RECORD Office.

BUILDER desires position as foreman. Address,
D., 122 7th av.

WANTED—West side, avenues or streets, flats from 60th to 96th sts. to buy, four or six together; direct from builders. Send full particulars to
MAX SIMON,
791 Columbus av., near 99th st.
Aug. 29—Sept. 5.

Real Estate Wanted.

WANTED FOR PHYSICIAN.—House, good width, between 35th and 57th sts., Madison and 5th avs.; limit, $125,000. Owners and brokers address.
H. T. SCHELLHASS, 171 Broadway.

OFFERS.

Dwellings and Flats.

GREAT SACRIFICE! For sale—2101 5th av; four-story decorated brown stone residence; street asphalted.

HOTEL TO EXCHANGE for residence in New Jersey, within 30 miles north; satisfactory reasons. Address,
OWNER, 1175 Fulton av.

SEVERAL remunerative business establishments for flats or tenements; $70,000 ranch for income producing city property; city properties for country, and vise versa; large list now ready for prompt exchanges.
WHITING, 45 Broadway.

WASHINGTON HEIGHTS, 170th st., just east of Amsterdam av., full lot; large rooms; frescoed ceilings; hardwood trim and floors; porcelain bath; $15,000; $4,000 cash, balance mortgage.
Owner, W. G. ALGER, 45 Pine st.

OFFERS.

43D ST., NEAR BROADWAY.—Private house, very central location; one block of "L" station; five horse cars near the door; price, $20,000; terms to suit.
GEO. SEGEE, 59 Liberty st., room 33.

$34,000—New five-story steam-heated flat; rent, $3,840; choice investment property.
TREACY, 101 Western Boulevard, near 64th.

NEAR 5TH AV., between 28th and 32d sts.; a very rare investment; 25x100; well rented; must be sold.
GEO. SEGEE, 59 Liberty.

EXCHANGE.—A 30-foot front flat four-story, 2d av., Harlem; equity about $10,000; for a private house in good neighborhood or flat on street. Call Sunday all day.
BRUDI, 214 East 87th st.

EXCHANGE.—Several three-story private houses on Prospect Hill, Yorkville, for lots or flats, separate or together; will give bargain. Call Sunday.
BRUDI, 214 East 87th st.

FOR SALE.—Five-story double flat, 27x85x100, close to Mount Morris Park; all rented to colored tenant for $3,048 per year; price $28,000, mortgage $19,000; chance in a life time; owner going to Europe to live. Call Sunday all day.
BRUDI, 214 East 87th st.

FOR SALE.—At a sacrifice, new five-story double flats, near 125th st. L station. Address,
Aug. 1—1aw-9w. BUILDER, 319 East 125th st.

FOR SALE.—Six new cabinet-trimmed three-story and basement brown stone private dwellings, Nos. 142-112 West 123d st.; prices reasonable and brokers commissions allowed. For further particulars apply at office of
FRED'K. M. LITTLEFIELD, 156 Broadway.
Aug. 29-uf.

FOR SALE.—2443 8th av and 210 and 212 West 105th st.; commission allowed brokers. Apply at
Aug. 29-uf. Room 19, 153 Broadway.

FOR SALE—2443 8th av.; 26.3½x100; easy terms; commission allowed brokers; apply at
Mar. 28-u-f. ROOM 19, 156 Broadway.

FOR SALE—210 and 212 West 105th st.; five-story apartments; each, 25x89x100; decorated and carpeted; apply at ROOM 19, 156 Broadway.
Mar. 28-u-f.

Improved Property.

PLANING MILL, branch of my business, for sale.—Is located at 24th st. and 11th av., on four or five city lots, leased ground, and consists of two and three-story brick buildings and adjoining sheds; also 80 horse-power engine and boiler, planers, moulders, saws, etc., all in good running order and now in operation; will leave a portion of value on bond and mortgage three years; this offers splendid opportunity to enlarge wood-working industry or to secure good mill business to add thereto. For further particulars, etc., apply to
EBEN PEEK, 24th st. and 11th av.

Advertiser intends to continue his lumber business now carried on at above address. Sept. 5-1aw4w

TO LET OR TO LEASE.—Two floors of a factory, 25x98 light on all sides, 1st av and 107th st; terms moderate. J. REEBERS' SONS,
Aug. 22-uf. 400 East 107th.

OFFERS.

Vacant Lots.

FOR SALE.—Agents take notice, at great sacrifice, two corner lots in Armour Villa Park. Address,
F. BOYD, Tremont, N. Y.

A CHANCE! for builders, wood-workers, etc.; two full lots, with machinery, shop, office, stable; very cheap; below 60th st.
PETER A. LALOR, 1035 3d av., near 61st st.

FOR SALE.—Five lots, northeast corner Willis av. and 137th st, 100x125; easy terms; all ready for improvement; splendid location. Apply to
Sept. 5—1aw4w. JAMES CARNEY, 137 East 52d st.

PLOT of five (5) choice lots, ripe for improvement, 92d st, Madison and 5th avs.
B. A. & G. N. WILLIAMS, JR.,
Aug 22-1aw4w. 68th st and Av A.

FOR SALE.—On easy terms, nine first-class lots, ready for immediate improvement, on south side 116th street, commencing about 130 feet east of 7th avenue. The C. GRAHAM & SONS CO.,
A 15—4t 309 East 43d street.

EASTERLY FRONT BOULEVARD, with 200 ft. on 86th st. and 261 ft. on 85th st.; one or more plots.
OTTO ERNST,
Aug. 22-1aw-8w. South Amboy, N. J.

Brooklyn Real Estate for Sale.

FLATS, 93 Concord st., Brooklyn, near the Bridge; five-story double flat property, in perfect order and always rented for $2,300 per year, paying easily 15 per cent. per annum on investment; terms easy. Apply to owner.
R. J. KELLEY, 377 Broadway, New York.
Aug. 22-1aw4w.

DESIRABLE INVESTMENT.—Eight-story apartment house; best location in Brooklyn; might exchange equity over $125,000 at 4½ per cent.
J. 20—uf. Apply 60 Broadway, Room 311.

PLATE-GLASS CORNER on avenue thoroughfare, 17th Ward, Brooklyn, half block from big ship-yard; suitable for saloon; price, $3,800; easy terms.
J. P. SLOANE,
Aug. 29-1aw5w. 343 Manhattan av., Brooklyn, E. D.

Country Property.

A BEAUTIFUL HOME NEAR MARIETTA, GA., 20 miles from Atlanta; perfectly healthy, climate highly recommended for throat and lung troubles; 762 acres, partly cleared; house 11 rooms, excellent order; extensive outbuildings; five acres of ornamental grounds about house; railway station on premises; west side city; property considered in exchange. (Folio 5,778).
PHILLIPS & WELLS, Tribune Building.

Miscellaneous.

BASEMENT TO LET—On the s w cor of 73d st and Columbus av, at a very moderate rental; good for a plumber, carpenter or electrician; rent, $22.50; lease dated Oct. 1st. Apply on premises.

A PARTY ABOUT TO BUILD A FIVE-STORY factory, 50x98, in Harlem, near water-front, will lease the three upper floors and build to suit tenant. Terms very moderate. Address
May 16 u. f. OWNER, 400 E. 107th St.

SALES OF THE WEEK.

The following are the sales at the Real Estate Exchange and Auction Room for the week ending Sept 4.

** Indicates that the property described has been bid in for plaintiff's account:*

R. V. HARNETT & CO.

*Madison av, No. 1673, n e cor 111th st, 15x70, three-story brk (stone front) dwell'g. (Amt due $1,492; prior morts. $7,000; sold May 24, 1890, for $11,500). J. George Flammer.......	$13,450
*1st av, No. 2406, n e cor 123d st, 26x75, four-story brk store and tenem't. (Amt due $11,018; leasehold). Wm. H. Beadleston....	7,000

WM. KENNELLY.

28th st, Nos. 510-528, s s, 225 w 10th av, 150x98.9, seven two, three and four story brk tenem'ts with stores in Nos. 520 and 524, and seven two-story brk and frame buildings on rear. John S. Stokes..................	42,000
*65th st, Nos. 22 and 24, s s, 200 w 8th av, 50x100.5, two five-story stone front flats. Katherine M. Mabley. (Amt due on each $9,321; sold Jan. 11, 1890, for $48,300)	$36,450
116th st, No. 54, s s, 81.11 e Madison av, 27.1x101, five-story brk flat. (Amt due $2,822; prior morts. $25,000). J. J. MacDonald............	31,015

A. H. MULLER & SON.

*8th av, Nos, 2550-2564, e s, bet 136th and 137th sts, 199.10x80, eight five-story brk flats and stores. Equitable Life Assur. Soc. (Amt due $86,784)............................	170,750

J. F. B. SMYTH.

76th st, s s, 330 w West End av, 44x102.2, vacant. (Amt due $7,754; prior morts. $9,000). Jos. Slevinbach..................................	21,400

OTHER AUCTIONEERS.

Waverley pl. No. 152, s w s, 243 n w 6th av, 22.3x97, four-story brk dwell'g. G. B. Howard. (Amt due $10,817)	14,500
83d st, No. 348, s s, 101.5 w 2d av, 19.8x102.2, three-story stone front dwell'g. Oscar Baum. (Amt due $7,604)	8,230
Park (4th) av, No. 658, w s, 80.5 s 69th st, 16x81, four-story brk dwell'g. (Amt due $30,754). Ellen E. Ward..................................	31,150
Total..	$380,963
Corresponding week, 1890........................	$1,801,950

BROOKLYN, N. Y.

For the week ending Sept. 3, no sales took place.
Corresponding week 1890.. .... $124,190

CONVEYANCES.

Wherever the letters Q. C., C. a. G. and B. & S occur, preceded by the name of the grantee they mean as follows:

1s—Q. C. is an abbreviation for Quit Claim deed, i. e. a deed in which all the right, title and interest of the grantor is conveyed, omitting all covenants or warranty.

2d—C. a. G. means a deed containing Covenant against Grantor only, in which he covenants that he hath not done any act whereby the estate conveyed may be impeached, charged or encumbered.

3d—B. & S. is an abbreviation for Bargain and Sale deed, wherein, although the seller makes no express covenants, he really grants or conveys the property for a valuable consideration, and thus impliedly claims to be the owner of it.

NEW YORK CITY.

AUGUST 28, 29, 31, SEPTEMBER 1, 2, 3.

Allen st, No. 195, w s, 175 n Stanton st, 25x88.3 x25x83.2, five and six-story brk tenem't with store. Ernst Rejall and Katharina his wife to Marks Levin. *Mt.* $28,000 and easements. Aug. 25. $26,000

Baxter st, No. 52, w s, 49.5 n Leonard st, 18.3x 33.8x16.6x43, five-story brk store and tenement. Hyman Claman and Ida his wife to Charles I. Williams. *Mt.* $7,000. Aug 6. 15,250

Baxter st, Nos. 44 and 46, south cor Leonard st, runs northwest 11.6 x west 90.9 x south 50 x east 100 to Baxter st, x north 43.5; No. 44, five-story brk tenem't with stores and three-story brk tenem't on rear; No. 46, four-story brk tenem't with stores and three-story brk tenem't on rear. Lewis Levy and Rachel his wife to Alexander Simonetti. *Mt.* $27,500. Sept. 1. 66,500

Beach st, No. 5, n s, abt 40 w West Broadway, 18.9x80, three-story brk tenem't. Maria wife of William H. Way to Irene Way. Aug. 27. nom

Bowery, No. 30, n w cor Bayard st, 30x151. Release judgment. Caleb D. Gildersleeve to Ferdinand R. Minrath. Aug. 5. 414

Broome st, No. 508, n s, 41.2 w South 5th av, 21.9x80, three-story brk store. Pete J. Brady to Joseph Wallach. Aug. 26. nom

Cannon st, No. 81, w s, 90 n Rivington st, 20x 82, three-story brk tenem't. Adolph Roth and Rosa his wife, Adolph Ullman and Mary his wife to William Hausman. *Mt.* $7,000. Aug. 31. nom

Cannon st, No. 83, w s, 110 n Rivington st, 20x 82, three-story brk tenem't. Adolph Ullman and Mary his wife, William Hausman and Riki his wife to Adolph Roth. *Mt* $7,500. Aug. 31. nom

Cannon st, No. 85, w s, 130 n Rivington st, 20x 82, three-story brk tenem't Adolph Roth and Rosa his wife, William Hausman and Riki his wife to Adolph Ullman. *Mt.* $7,500. Aug. 31. nom

Columbia st, Nos. 82 and 84, e s, 100 n Rivington st, 50x118, two five-story brk tenem'ts with stores. Huldah wife of and Joseph Wittner, New York, and Emanuel Glauber, Brooklyn, to Morris and Isaac Cohen. *Mt.* $65,000. Sept. 3. See Henry st. 95,000

Delancey st, No. 186, n s, 43.6 e Attorney st, 19.9x86-5½x19.9x86.6, three-story brk tenem't. Mary Craft widow to Louis Goodman. B. & S. Aug. 12. 11,000

Division st, No. 88, n e cor Eldridge st, 24.7x 75.4 to alley, x21.10x86.6, three-story brk tenem't with stores. Ellen H. Wilcox widow trustee Benjamin Albro to Kate R. Wilcox. Aug. 31. 30,000

Essex st, No. 118, e s, 125 s Rivington st, 16x80, three-story brk store and tenem't. Simon Rehmer and Regina his wife to Bernhard Zeller. *Mt.* $8,500. Aug. 31. 12,750

Goerck st, No. 33, w s, 150 n Broome st, 24.11x 100, five-story brk tenem't. Isaac Amdursky to Herman Oppenheim. *Mt.* $19,000. Sept. 1. 30,000

Henry st, No. 46, s s, 290 w Market st, 25x100, four-story brk tenem't. Morris Goldstein and Sarah his wife to Henry Pasiosky. *Mt.* $17,000. Aug. 31. nom

Henry st, No. 166, s s, abt 104.1 w Jefferson st, 26.1x100, five-story brk tenem't.
Henry st, No 164, s s, abt 130.2 w Jefferson st, 26.1x100, four-story brk tenem't.
Henry st, No. 168, s s, abt 78 w Jefferson st, 26.1x100, two-story brk tenem't.
Morris Cohen and Betsey his wife and Isaac Cohen and Rachel his wife to Hulda Wittner, New York, and Emanuel Glauber, Brooklyn. *Mt.* $84,500. Sept. 3. See Columbia st. 109,000

Houston st, No. 326, n e s, abt 290 e Av B, 23x 81.11x23x88.5, five-story brk store and tenement. Hartwig I. Phillips to Clara Bloom, Fanny Blath, Eliza Strauss, Julius and Aaron H. Schutz. *Mt.* $12,000. Aug. 14. nom

Houston st, No. 316, n s, abt 190 e Av B, 24.11x 88.1½x24.10x89.9, four-story brk tenem't with stores. Same to same. Aug. 27. nom

Madison st, No. 148, s s, abt 157 w Pike st, 25x 100, three-story brk tenem't with five-story brk building on rear. Aaron Rosenberg and Jetta his wife to Nathan and Marks Rosenberg. Q. C. and correction deed. Aug. 28. nom

Same property. Nathan Rosenberg and Sarah his wife and Marks Rosenberg to Mary Schlomberg, Washington, D. C. *Mt.* $21,500. Aug. 28. See Suffolk st. 30,000

Madison st, No. 355, n s, 216 e Scammel st, 23.10 x96, five-story brk tenem't with stores. Louis Minsky and Esther J. his wife to Abraham Kassel. *Mt.* $17,250. Aug. 31. See 75th st. 24,000

Madison st, No. 414, s s, 400 e Jackson st, 25.2 to junction of Grand st, x99.7x25.2x100, three-story brk tenem't with stores. Elizabeth Hauschild widow to Thomas F. and James E. Burke. Aug. 13 18,000

Market st, No. 16, e s, 75 n Henry st, 25x86, two-story brk dwell'g. Rebecca Isear to Isaac Gelles. *Mt.* $10,500. July 31. 19,500

Mulberry st, No. 169, w s, abt 175 n Grand st, 25x 100, four-story brk tenem't with four-story brk tenem't on rear. Simon M. Roeder and Jennie his wife to Carmella P. Labbate. *Mt.* $15,000. Sept. 2. 25,000

Mulberry st, No. 110, e s, abt 125 n Canal st, 25x100.
Mulberry st, No. 112, e s, abt 150 n Canal st, 25x100.
Two five-story stone front stores and tenements
Abraham Kassel and Ida his wife to Vito Cimino. *Mt.* $50,500. Aug. 28. 74,000

Mulberry st, No. 53, e s, abt 200 s Bayard st, 26.11x88.3x28x—, three-story frame (brk front) store and tenem't with four-story brk tenem't on rear.
85th st, s e cor Madison av, 63x100.8x—x—, one-story frame buildings and vacant.
Joseph O'Connor, Newark, N. J., to Fannie G Reeve, Brooklyn, N. Y. *Mt.* $2,500. May 19. nom

Norfolk st, No. 125, w s, 19.9 s Rivington st, 20.3x50, four-story brk store and tenem't. Matyas Kukoly and Susanna his wife to Herman Stern. *Mt.* $10,000. Aug. 27. 13,725

Perry st, No. 74, s s, 184.8 e Bleecker st. 20x 94.11, three story stone front dwell'g. Martha Kemp to Emily Jacobus. *Mt.* $10,000. Sept. 2. 19,000

Rivington st, No. 178, n w cor Attorney st, 25x 100, five-story brk tenem't with stores. Harris Rosenthal and Sarah his wife to Samuel Davis. *Mt.* $35,000. Aug. 31. See 18th st. 56,500

Rivington st, No. 313, s s, 75 e Lewis st, 25x100, five-story brk tenem't with stores. Adolph Gross and Mallie his wife and Louis Solomon and Ida his wife to Ludwig Zodikow and Louis Lewinthan. *Mt.* $18,750. Aug. 31. 24,750

Sheriff st, No. 107, w s, 100 n Stanton st, 25x 100, five story brk tenem't. Charles Weisberger and Mary his wife to Rachel Gross. *Mt.* $23,500. Aug. 31. 37,000

Sheriff st. No. 113 w s, 175.1 n Stanton st, 24.11 x100, three-story brk building with five-story brk factory on rear. David Lese to Marks Levin. *Mt.* $10,500. Sept. 1. See Suffolk st. 18,500

Spring st, No. 55, n s, abt 75 e Marion st, 25x 118x25.3x112.3, five-story brk tenem't with stores. John Maggi and Louisa his wife to Rocco M. Marosco. *Mt.* $27,000. August 29. 33,500

Suffolk st, No. 12, e s, abt 75 n Hester st, 25x50, five-story brk tenem't with stores. Mary Shlomberg, Washington, D. C., to Nathan and Marks Rosenberg. *Mt.* $21,500. Aug. 31. See Madison st. 26,750

Suffolk st, No. 125, w s, 100 n Rivington st, 25x 100, five-story brk tenem't with stores and five-story brk tenem't on rear. Marks Levin and Betsie his wife to David Lese. *Mt.* $21,000. Sept. 1. See Sheriff st. 35,000

Suffolk st, No. 186, e s, 60.8 s Houston st, 19.4x 74.10x19.5x75, three-story brk store and tenement with three-story frame tenem't on rear. Moses Finklestone and Johanna his wife to Hattie Cohen. Aug. 31. nom

Same property. Hattie wife of Barney Cohen to Morris Rosenbloom. *Mt.* $10,600. Aug. 31. See Willett st. 15,000

Willett st, No. 49, w s, 44.8 n Delancey st, 25.1x 88, with use of alley adj on west side, four-story brk tenem't with three-story brk tenem't on rear. Morris Rosenbloom and Malka his wife to Hattie Cohen. *Mt.* $15,625. Aug. 31. See Suffolk st. 20,000

William st, No. 214, all that portion of same not taken for Brooklyn Bridge and being a gore, bounded southeast by No. 18 Rose st, northeast by No. 216 William st and west by land of N. Y. & Brooklyn Bridge, vacant. Victoria and Julia Mann and Margaretha Alexander, Hoboken, N. J., Theresa Salomon, White Plains, and Franz Mann and Wilhelmina his wife to The Metropolitan Realty Co. 5-6 part. Sept. 2. 2,917

Same property. Mechtides Mann by Wm. Zinsser guard. to same. 1-6 part. Sept. 3. 583

3d st, No. 23, n s, 150 w 2d av, 25x96.2.
4th st. No. 74, s s, 150 w 2d av, 25x96.2.
Four-story brk verein building and vacant.
The Aschenbradel Verein to Ascher Weinstein. Sept. 1. 55,000

9th st, No. 635, n s, 223 w Av C, 20x92.3, four-story brk store and tenem't. Frank Steinberger and Bertha his wife to Rosa Ehrlich. *Mt.* $10,000. Sept. 1. 12,250

10th st, No. 254, s s, 100 e 1st av, 28x92.3, four-story brk tenem't with four-story brk tenement on rear.
Interior lot, 46.2 s 10th st and 90 e 1st av, 10x 23.1, vacant.
Catharine Kraemer widow to Charles Kraemer, Brooklyn. B. & S. C. a. G. June 24. 1890. nom

14th st, No 40 } begins 14th st, s s, 53.1
University pl, No. 79 } e University pl, runs southwest 130.4 x northwest 63.8 to University pl. x northeast 26 x southeast 33.6 x northeast 102.8 to 14th st, x southeast 26.10, five-story brk store. William A. Butler, Jr., and John L. Lamson exrs. Elizabeth R. Lamson to John Downey. 1-5 part. Aug. 31. nom

Same property. Daniel S. Appleton and Jessica C. his wife and Malvina Appleton heirs Malvina W. Appleton ,to same. All title. Q. C. Aug. 27. nom

Same property. Charles H Marshall and William A. Butler exrs. Charles H. Marshall to same. Aug. 5. 245,000

Same property. William A. Butler trustee Helen M. Haseltine to same. 1-5 part. Aug. 31. nom

Same property. Mary R. wife of and William A. Butler, Yonkers, N. Y., to same. Q. C. All title. Aug. 5. nom

18th st, No. 342, s s, 300 e 9th av, 25x92, five-story stone front flat. Samuel Davis and Dora his wife to Harris Rosenthal. *Mt.* $23,000. Sept. 2. See Rivington st 40,000

21st st, No 23, n s, 388.1 w 5th av, 25x98 9, four-story stone front dwell'g. John C. Barnard to Mary A. B. wife of Alfred Wagstaff. 1-5 part. C. a. G. Nov. 1, 1890. 4,000

24th st, Nos. 125 and 127, n s, 80 w Lexington av, 45x98.9, six-story brk flat. Samuel G. Revans and Mary his wife to Hattie B. wife of Henry G. Allen. *Mt.* $105,000. Aug. 18. nom

26th st, Nos 328 and 330, s s, 200 w 1st av, 50.2 x98.9x50.4x98.9, five-story brk glass factory. The Matthews Decorative Glass Co. to George and John H. Matthews. Sub. to mort. July 1. 45,000

26th st, No. 310, s s, 136 w 8th av, 18 10x98.9, three-story stone front dwell'g. Virginia Hall to Benjamin F. Cohen. Sept. 1. 11,900

26th st, No. 312, s s, 155 w 8th av, 18.6x98.9, three-story brk dwell'g. John H. Armstrong and Mary H. his wife to same. Sept. 1. 12,000

26th st, No. 332, s s, 175 w 1st av, 25x98.9, four-story brk store and tenem't with four-story brk tenem't on rear. Joseph Steinert and Agnes his wife, Oyster Bay, L. I., to Minnie L. Simon. *Mt.* $5,500. Sept. 1. 15,500

27th st, Nos 103 and 105, n s, 80 e 4th av, 40x 24.8, two three-story brk dwell'gs. Edward Cooper and Cornelia R his wife to Edward Cooper et al. trustees Peter Cooper dec'd. C. a. G. Sept 2. 24,000

32d st, No. 45, n s, 606 w 5th av, 18x98.9, four-story stone front dwell'g. Mary A. R. wife of and John O'Brien to David D. Davis. Aug. 29. 39,500

33d st, No. 210, s s. 151.8 e 3d av, 16.8x98.9, three-story stone front dwell'g. Henry Kominsky and Rachel wife of and Benjamin Kominsky and Jennie wife of and Samuel Kominsky to Samuel Kominsky and Betsy S. his wife. All title. Aug. 31. 7,000

33d st, No. 207, n s, 84.10 w 7th av, 15x98.9, three-story stone front dwell'g. Abraham Stern to Mordecai S Kaufmann and Manuel Goldberg. *Mt.* $9,500. Sept. 1. nom

41st st, No. 412, old No. 188, s s, 183 w 9th av, 20.6x98.9, four-story brk store and tenem't. John L. Held heir John L. Held to Charles A. Held. 1-6 part. Aug. 11. 1,155

41st st, No. 311, n s, 133.4 e 2d av, 16.8x98.9, four-story brk tenem't. Margaret I. Fox to Honora Fox. *Mt.* $6,000. Aug. 26. 10,000

46th st, No. 117, n s, 225 w 6th av, 25x100.5, four-story brk tenem't with stores. Richard Stackpoole and Laura his wife to Flora I. wife of Charles Bradbury. *Mt.* $9,000. Aug. 29. nom

47th st, No. 410, s s, 127.6 w 9th av, 22.6x100.5, three-story frame dwell'g. Mary A. Gore and Alice A. and John J. Ward to Maria S. Simpson. *Mt.* $3,000. Sept. 1. 9,500

47th st, No. 410, s s. 127.6 w 9th av, 22.6x100.5, three-story frame dwell'g. Maria S. Simpson to James J. Buckley. *Mt.* $6,000. Sept. 1. 10,300

48th st, No. 153, n s, 290 e 7th av, 20x89.9x20.2x 90.5, four-story stone front dwell'g. Eliza wife of and David Klauber to John Lelong and Mary his wife. *Mt.* $16,000. Aug. 17. 22,000

48th st, Nos. 322 and 324, s s, 250 w 8th av, 50x 100.5, two five-story stone front dwell'gs. Mary Gallagher to Thomas Smith. *Mt.* $38,000. Sept. 1. nom

48th st, No. 544, s s, 550.4 w 10th av, 19.8x100.5, five-story stone front tenem't. William Stolzenberg and Sophie his wife to D. Frederick Ebbers. *Mt.* $1,000. Sept. 1. 10,150

49th st, No. 209, n s, 135.8 e 3d av, runs east 20.11 x north 14 x northwest 37.3 x west 14 x south 50.4, three-story brk dwell'g. Fannie S. Beebe to George A. Haggerty. Aug. 31. 8,250

49th st, No. 412, s s, 156.3 w 9th av, 18.9x100.5, five-story brk tenem't. John McKelvey and Rose his wife, Robert Dick and Katie his wife to Albert Derlick. Sept. 1. 26,000

51st st, Nos. 408 and 410, s s, 150 w 9th av, 50x 100.5, two five-story brk tenem'ts. James Lee and Emeline his wife to Mary A. Timken. B. & S. July 15. gift

57th st, No. 415, n s, 153.10 w 9th av, 21.2x100.5, four-story stone front dwell'g. Matilde McKee, Bensonhurst, L. I., to Amalia Stepper. *Mt.* $19,500. Aug. 10 See 61st st. nom

59th st, n s, 90 e Madison av, 0.6x100.5. Release mort. The Manhattan Life Ins. Co to Catherine B. Chenoweth. Sept. 2. nom

Same property. Release mort. William H.

Newschafer exr. Catharine Newschafer to Catharine R. wife of Alexander C. Chenoweth. Aug. 29. nom

Same property. Catharine R. wife of Alexander C. Chenoweth to Leo Schlesinger and Joseph Hecht. Sept. 2. 1,250

59th st, n s, 90 e Madison av. Party wall agreement. Same to same. Sept. 2. nom

61st st, No. 415, n s, 220 e 1st av, 20x90.1x20.3x93.3, three-story brk dwell'g. Louis N. Schnepp to Annie N. Schnepp. Aug. 27. 100

61st st, No. 227, n s, 350 e 11th av, 25x100.5.
61st st, No. 229, n s, 375 e 11th av, 25x100.5.
Two five-story brk tenem'ts.
James E. Hoctor to Amalia Stepper. *Mt.* $30,000. May 22. nom

Same property. Amalia Stepper to Mathilde McKee, Bensonhurst, L. I. *Mt.* $30,000 Aug. 25. See 57th st. nom

62d st, No. 316, s s, 174.6 e 2d av, 25x100.5, five-story brk tenem't. Adolph Pawel and Emma his wife to Joseph Rosenberg. Sub. to morts. Aug. 31. 25,000

62d st, No. 314, s s, 149.6 e 2d av, 25x100.5, five-story brk tenem't. Same to Sigmund Tynberg. Sub. to morts. Aug. 31. 25,000

63d st, No. 112, s s, 200 w 9th av, 25x100.5, five-story stone front flat. James B. Murray to Charles C. Cranmer. B. & S. *Mt.* $18,000. Aug. 10. 29,675

Same property. Charles C. Cranmer and Mary A. his wife to Thurlow W. Coulter. B. & S. *Mt.* $18,000. Aug. 31. 30,000

70th st, No. 75, n s, 140 e Columbus av, 20x100.5, four-story brk dwell'g. Charles Buek and Abbie B. his wife to Haley Fiske. *Mt.* $23,000. Sept. 2. 36,000

72d st, No. 428, on map No. 426, s s, 380 e 1st av, 25x102.2, five-story brk tenem't. Robert Garcewich to Annie Nelkin. ½ part. Sub. to mort. Aug. 28. nom

73d st, No. 29, n s, 18 w Madison av, 15x80, four-story stone front dwell'g. Esther D. wife of Pincus Pohalski to Rosa Gavin. *Mt.* $15,000. Sept. 1. 23,000

74th st, No. 326, s s, 250 e 2d av, 25x102.2, four-story brk dwell'g. George Connor to Samson Wallach. *Mt.* $8,000. Sept. 1. 13,000

74th st, No. 323, n s, 300 e 2d av, 25x102.2, five-story brk tenem't with stores. Nathan Federgreen and Sarah his wife to Pauline wife of Henry Holck. *Mt.* $14,000. Sept. 1. 16,500

74th st, No. 247, n s, 170 e West End av, 20x102.2, three-story brk dwell'g. Mary De W. wife of Charles E. Wallack to Emma L. wife of Henry D. Haven. *Mt.* $21,000. September 1. 25,000

75th st, No. 182, s s, 225 w 3d av, 18x102.2, four-story stone front flat. Joseph Schneider and Maria his wife to Benjamin Korminsky. *Mt.* $8,000. Sept. 1. 15,000

75th st, No. 109, n s, 169.8 e Park av, 26.8x102.2, five-story stone front flat. Abraham Kassel and Ida his wife to Louis Minsky. *Mt.* $25,000. Sept. 1. See Madison st. 34,000

75th st, No. 22, s s, 25.7 w Madison av, 25x102.2, four-story stone front dwell'g. Siegmund T. Meyer to Peter J. Brady. Q. C. Aug. 27. nom

75th st, No. 107, n s, 143 e Park av, 26.8x102.2, five-story stone front flat. Joseph Kassel and Jeanetta his wife to Louis Minsky. *Mt.* $24,300. Aug. 24. nom

76th st, s s, 300 w West End av, 44x102.2, vacant. Elizabeth W. Aldrich to Spencer Aldrich. All liens. Aug. 26. nom

76th st, n s, 249.11 e Columbus av, 0.0¾x102.2. Release mort. James McMahon to Alfred S. Lascelles. June 8. nom

Same property. Alfred S. Lascelles and Helen his wife to Samuel Colcord. B. & S. June 11. other consid. and 100

76th st, n s, 151 w West End av, 28x102.2, vacant. James R. Smith and Mary F. his wife to Leonard Jacob, Jr. C. a. G. July 25. nom

78th st, Nos. 200-204 } begins 78th st,
Amsterdam av, Nos. 368-376 } s w cor Amsterdam av, 100x102.2, three five-story brk flats, stores in corner building. Bernard S. Levy and Henriette his wife to William H. Vredenburgh. *Mt.* $115,000. Sept. 1. See 134th st. nom

79th st, No. 339, n s, 100 w 1st av, 27.10x102.2, four-story stone front tenem't. Ellen Summers to Jacob Froman. *Mt.* $19,500. Aug. 29. 25,555

80th st, No. 422, s s, 251 w Av A, 26x102.2, five-story brk tenem't. Michael Gebhard and Katharina his wife to Joseph Riehl and Agnes his wife. *Mt.* $10,000, and street opening assessm't. Aug. 31. 23,200

80th st, No. 329, n s, 225 w 1st av, 25x102.2, four-story stone front tenem't. Julia Elsbach to Samuel First. *Mt.* $10,000. Sept. 1. 14,500

80th st, No. 207, n s, 100 e 3d av, 25x102.2, five-story stone front flat. Amalie Schellenberger widow to Elise Hauser. *Mt.* $13,500. Aug. 27. 24,500

82d st, No. 26, s s, 319 w Central Park West, 18x102.2, four-story stone front dwell'g. William Forster and Maggie E. his wife and James Livingston and Margery his wife to John H. Staats. *Mt.* $22,000. Aug. 26. 35,000

82d st, No. 174, s s, 102.3 w 3d av, runs south 120.5 x west 11.3 x northwest 18.8 x north 109.5 to st, x east 25.7, four-story brk dwell'g. Edward Rafter and Cecilia M. his wife to Elizabeth C. Lewis. *Mt.* $16,000. Aug. 24. 26,000

82d st, No. 343, n s, 150 w 1st av, 25x102.2, five-story stone front tenem't, Thomas Moore and Annie his wife and John McLaughlin and Margaret his wife to George C. Pfaff. *Mt.* $14,000. Sept. 1. 24,500

83d st, No. 406, s s, 131 e 1st av, 25x102.2, five-story stone front tenem't. George Mundorff and Mary his wife to George Riebl. *Mt.* $13,000, assessm'ts, &c. Aug. 1. 24,000

85th st, No. 216, s s, 205 e 3d av, 25x102.2, five-story brk tenem't. Louis Wirth and Barbara his wife to Philip F. Donohue. *Mt.* $18,000. Aug. 28. See 134th st, 23d Ward. 30,000

87th st, No. 130, s s, 66.1 w Lexington av, 17.6x100.8, four-story stone front store and flat with one-story frame building on rear. Matilda and Charles Struppmann, Jr., Jersey City, to Sarah Myers. Q. C. December 16, 1889. nom

87th st, No. 128, s s, 304.4 e 4th av, 17x100.8, four-story stone front flat. Matilda and Charles Struppmann, Jr., Jersey City, to Henry W. Meyer. Q. C. Re-recorded. July 13, 1889. nom

90th st, Nos. 75 and 77, s s, 100 e 9th av, 37.6x100.8, two three-story stone front dwell'gs. Thomas D. Valentine, New Rochelle, N. Y., to Matthias B. Valentine, New Rochelle, N. Y. *Mt.* $36,000. June 1. 64,000

90th st, s s, 150 w 9th av, 25x100.8, vacant. Frederick W. Sauer and Magdalena his wife and Conrad Gross and Lena his wife to Gottlieb F. Weber. *Mt.* $12,500. Aug. 31. nom

90th st, No. 137, n s, 375 e 4th av, 25x100.8, three-story frame dwell'g with two-story frame building on rear. Michael McCabe, Woonsocket, R. I., to Emma G. Conboy. Q. C. Re-recorded. July 11. nom

Same property. Emma G. Conboy to John Weber. Sept. 1. 16,700

93d st, No. 170, s s, 135 e Amsterdam av, 18x100.8, three-story stone front dwell'g. Walden P. Anderson to George Watson. *Mt.* $18,250. Aug. 31. nom

93d st, No. 70, s s, 25 10 e Columbus av, 27.6x100.8, five-story stone front flat. John McKean, Orange, N. J., and Hattie L. his wife to John F. Cordes. *Mt.* $18,000. Aug. 28. 31,600

94th st, No. 45, n s, 375 e 9th av, 14.3x100.8, three-story brk dwell'g. John C. Davis and Harriet his wife and Anna B. wife of W. Lewis Fay to Thomas Hilson. Re-recorded. May 5. nom

Same property. Thomas Hilson to Henry M. Livor. C. a. G. Sept. 1. 200

95th st, s s, 200 e 2d av, 100x100.8, vacant. Susan Kilpatrick to James Kilpatrick. *Mt.* $12,500. May 1. 22,500

95th st, Nos. 145-165, n s, 150 e Amsterdam av, 200x100, eleven three-story stone front dwellings. Bernard Cohn and Amy E. his wife to The Amsterdam Improvement Co., N. J. *Mt.* $210,000. Aug. 26. nom

98th st, Nos. 150-154, s s, 150 w 3d av, 75x100.11, three four-story stone front tenem'ts. Smith Ely to Adam Moran. B. & S. Sept. 1. 46,500

100th st, No. 226, s s, 180 w 2d av, 25x100.7, five-story brk tenem't. Elkin Farmer and Wilhelmina his wife to Emma C. Barnes. *Mt.* $15,000. Aug. 28. 21,000

103d st, n s, 166 e West End av, 17x100.11, three-story stone front dwell'g. John J. Egan and Mary his wife and Daniel Hallecy and Mary his wife to Samuel J. Clark. *Mt.* $13,500. Aug. 29. 19,000

103d st, Nos. 159 and 161, n s, 180 w 3d av, 60x100.11, two four-story brk flats. Julia A. wife of Frederick Frank and John H. Frank to Theodore Gunsel. *Mt.* $20,000. Sept. 1. 37,250

105th st, No. 305, n s, 100 e 2d av, 25x100.11, five-story brk store and tenem't. Release mort. William N. Crane trustee to Matthew Coogan. Aug. 28. 12,124

Same property. Release mort. The Bradley & Currier Co. (Lim.) to same and Theresa his wife. Aug. 28. om

Same property. Release mort. The Murray Hill Bank to same. Aug. 27. nom

105th st, Nos. 319 and 321, n s, 240 e 2d av, 40x100.11, one and two-story frame buildings. Peter Steinmann and May M. his wife to Nicholas Dullmeyer. *Mt.* $3,700. Aug. 27. nom

106th st, No. 209, n s, 150 e 3d av, 20x100.11, four-story brk tenem't. Henry Goldstone to Henrietta Hershfield. *Mt.* $7,000. September 2. 12,500

108th st, No. 160, s s, 133 e Lexington av, 17x100.11, four-story stone front flat. Samuel, Moses and Esther Stern, Tillie wife of Louis Schwaab and Michael Stern to Anna Streep. *Mt.* $6,000. Sept. 1. 12,000

110th st, No. 228, s s, 310 e 3d av, 25x100.11, four-story brk tenem't. Samuel Altheimer and Rosa his wife to Katharine and Adolph Harz. *Mt.* $8,300. Sept. 1. 13,500

110th st, No. 152, s s, 25 e Lexington av, 25x100.11, four-story stone front tenem't. Minnie L. wife of Marcus Simon to Joseph Steinert, Oyster Bay, L. I. *Mt.* $13,000. September 1. 17,000

112th st, n s, 150 e 5th av, 25x100.11, vacant. Bernard Cohen and Rosalie his wife to John Shields. Sub. to taxes, &c. July 24. 7,000

113th st, No. 405, s s, 95 e 1st av, 25x100.10, three-story brk tenem't with two-story frame building on rear. Saverio Gallo and Caterina his wife and Joseph Gallo and Jennie his wife to Michele Paolantonio and Felix Mainella. *Mt.* $5,500. Aug. 20. 14,500

114th st, Nos. 21 and 23, n s, 245 e 5th av, 50x100.11, two five-story brk flats. Elliott C. Davidson, Hull, Ia., and Mary C. his wife to Clarence W. Gaylor. *Mt.* $34,000. Aug. 24. 39,000

120th st, No. 124, s s, 90 w Lexington av, 25x100.10, five-story brk flat. Daniel W. McWilliams and Helen F. his wife to William E. Crandall. *Mt.* $17,000. Sept. 3. 30,000

123d st, Nos. 221 and 223, n s, 218 e 3d av, 33.8x100.11, two five-story stone front flats. John Morrisey to Morris Cohen. ½ part. ½ morts. $32,000. Aug. 28. nom

123d st, No. 73, n w cor Park av, 20x100.11, four-story brk flat. John M. Robinson and Carrie E. his wife to Henry Gieschen. Aug. 24. 19,000

124th st, No. 108, s s, 102.6 w Lenox av, 27x100.11, five-story stone front flat. Timothy Flood and Rosa his wife, Joseph J. Van Note and Emma E. his wife to William Hallisy. *Mt.* $24,000. Aug. 31. 36,000

128th st, No. 58, s s, 235 e Lenox av, 25x99.11, five-story brk flat. Leo Dinkelspiel to Edward L. Rieser. *Mt.* $25,500. Aug. 31. 28,000

133d st, No. 54, s s, 175 w Park av, 20x99.11, three-story stone front dwell'g. William Dempsey and Mary his wife to Mary Cahill. *Mt.* $9,838. Aug. 26. nom

133d st, No. 19, n s, 217.6 e 5th av, 17.6x99.11, two-story brk dwell'g. John Smith to James Everard. Sept. 1. 6,500

134th st, Nos. 71-79, n s, 197.6 e 6th av, 87.6x99.11, five three-story brk dwell'gs.
135th st, s s, 197.6 e 6th av, 87.6x99.11, five three-story brk dwell'gs.
William H. Vredenburgh and Bessie H. his wife, Freehold, N. J., to Bernard S. Levy. Sept. 1. See 78th st. nom

181st st, n s, 25 e Wadsworth av, 100x100. Pauline Simon to Charles Weinberg. *Mt.* $10,400. June 15. 17,600

Amsterdam av, w s, 50 s 121st st, 25x100, vacant. Partition. Leicester Holme to William R. Larkin. Sept. 1. 3,800

Amsterdam av, w s, 75 s 121st st, 25x100, vacant. Partition. Same to same. Sept. 1. 3,700

Av B, No. 261, e s, 88.3 s 16th st, 26.6x88, five-story brk tenem't with stores.
Highbridge road, n w s, 87.9 s w Kingsbridge road, runs southwest 44.11 x southwest 5 x northwest 106.6 x northeast 1.9 x northeast 42.6 x southeast 106.6.
Charles F. McCabe to Rose wife of said Charles F. McCabe. Aug. 12. nom

Edgecombe av, No. 36, e s, 89.10 s 137th st, 17.6x90, three-story brk dwell'g. Samuel J. Beacom to John Demarest, Rowayton, Conn. *Mt.* $14,200. Sept. 1. nom

Lenox av, No. 470, e s, 79 11 n 133d st, 20x84, five-story brk store and flat. Foreclos. William Sulzer to William McIlroy. Sept. 1. 18,900

Lexington av, No. 965, e s, 20.5 n 70th st, 20x75.6, four-story brk dwell'g. Jacob Schmitt and Elisabetha his wife and Henry Weiler and Anna his wife to Franz Rebhan. Aug. 31. 27,500

Lexington av, No. 965, e s, 20.5 n 70th st, 20x75.6, four-story brk dwell'g. Franz Rebhan to Henriette Popper. *Mt.* $15,000. Aug. 31. nom

Madison av, s e cor 134th st, 100x60, four five-story brk flats with stores projected. Foreclos. Isaac Fromme to Thomas Jetter. *Mt.* $8,000. July 18, 1890. 20,000

Park av, No. 1, n e cor 34th st, 25x80, three-story brk dwell'g. Edward L. Keyes and Sarah L. his wife to John L. B. Mott. Aug. 27. 110,000

Park (4th) av, No. 1052, w s, 50.8 s 87th st, 25x80.11, five-story brk store and flat. Release mort. Henry F. Wells to Abraham Steers. Aug. 31. nom

Same property. Abraham Steers and Susan C. his wife to Clementine Metzger. *Mt.* $20,000. Aug. 31. 30,000

Park av, No. 1754, s w cor 122d st, 25.11x80, five-story brk flat with stores. Henry D. Van Seggern and Catharine his wife, George W. H. Menkens and Annie his wife to John H. Rose. Sept. 1. 36,000

Park av, No. 51, e s, 25 n 37th st, 21x80, four-story stone front dwell'g. Marie A. wife of Charles H. Steinway to Daniel S. McElroy. *Mt.* $25,000. Aug. 31. 55,000

Park (4th) av, No. 688, w s, 86.5 s 69th st, 18x81, four-story brk dwell'g. Foreclos. Thomas D. Husted to Ellen E. Ward, Roslyn, L. I. Sept. 2. 31,150

Pleasant av, No. 335, w s, 50 s 118th st, 18.6x75, three-story stone front dwell'g. John R. Smith to Ella L. Gault. Aug. 24. nom

South 5th av, No. 136, n w s, 125 n e Spring st, 25x69.6x25x69.4, four-story brk store and tenem't with three-story frame building on rear. Denison P. Chesebro and Harriet P. his wife to George Noakes. *Mt.* $14,000. Aug. 28. 20,500

West End av, No. 40, n e cor 66th st, 25.5x100, five-story stone front store and flat. George Roll to Samuel H. Denton. *Mt.* $22,000. Sept. 1. 35,000

1st av, No. 397, w s, 49.4 n 23d st, 24.8x75, four-story brk tenem't with stores. Rachel A. Cartwright widow, Newark, N. J., to Rachel A. wife of Jasper Lynch. June 22, 1888. nom

2d av, No. 1633, s w cor 85th st, 27.2x80, four-story brk stone front tenem't. Max Borger to Israel Schneittacher and Betty his wife. *Mt.* $23,000. Aug. 31. 36,500

3d av, No. 1953, e s, 106.2 s 108th st, 17.8x100, four-story brk store and tenem't. Philip Bernhardt and Florence D. his wife to John G. Lindenberger and Christiana his wife. *Mt.* $8,000. Sept. 2. 21,500

5th av, No. 1042, e s, 46.10 n 85th st, 22x100, four-story stone front dwell'g. William E. Crandall and Mary F. his wife to Arthur J. Noonan, Assistant Treasurer. *Mt.* $36,080. Sept. 3. 75,000

7th av, No. 2185, e s, 49.11 n 129th st, 25x96, five-story brk store and flat. Rachel Hurwich wife of and Max to Josephine Heyer, Wilkesbarre, Pa. *Mt.* $16,000. Aug. 31. 36,000

9th av, No. 477, w s, 100 n 36th st, 25x75, five-story stone front tenem't with stores. Peter Albert and Margaretha his wife to Christian Dohm. Sept. 5, 1889. 25,000

Interior lot, centre line, bet 75th and 76th sts, 344 w West End av, runs west 31 x north — x southeast to a point 344 w West End av, x south — to beginning. Mary R. wife of Albert W. Harris to Spencer Aldrich. B. & S. Aug. 29. nom

Interior lot, 200 w West End av and 54.5 s 76th st, runs south 47.9 x west 100 x north 51.3 x southeast —. Elizabeth P. Skinner, Kate V. L. Howell, Mary W. Currie, Mary Tiedemann and Andrew Shiland, Jr., and Ada L. his wife to same. B. & S. *Mt.* on this and other property $92,000. April 21. nom

23d and 24th WARDS.

Anthony st, e s, lots 135 and 136 map New York City Private Park, 50.2 x 104.1 x 50 x 108.2. James H. Marvin and Emily C. his wife to Carrie L. Rogers. Aug. 26. 1,250

Bettners lane, centre line, adj south boundary line Mary J. Jones, 4 52-100 acres, with land under water, &c. Mary J. Coxe to Robert A. Johnston. Sept. 1. 22,500

Bettners lane, centre line, adj south boundary line Mary J. Jones, 4 73-100 acres, with land under water, &c. Ida F. wife of James H. Fraser to same. Aug. 12. 22,500

Cordova pl, w s, 213.7 s Courtlandt av, 25x100x25.1x100. Bernhard Freeman, Samuel Freehof and Rosa his wife, Brooklyn, N. Y., to Cornelius Gleason and Bessie his wife. Aug. 19. 500

Elsmere pl, n s, 150 w Marmion av, 25x100. Elisha P. Murphy to Agnes K. Murphy. July 16. nom

Fox st, w s, 311 s 165th st, 25x100. Eugene F. W. Braunsdorf and Catherine P. his wife to Martin McInerny and Pat'k J. Kelly. Q. C. Aug. 27. nom

Fox st, w s, 504.6 s 165th st, 25x100. Catherine Braunsdorf to Patrick J. Kelly. *Mt.* $2,000. Aug. 28. 3,700

Gourverneur st, s s, west ½ lot 264 map of Melrose South, 25x118.6. Carl Hulster and Julia his wife to Caroline Rumpf. Sept. 1. 2,725

Hoffman st, n w s, south ½ lot 110 map Powell farm, Fordham, 25x100. Release encroachment. Patrick Donnelly to Michael Carlos and Annie his wife. Sept. 1. nom

Jacob st, n s, lots 288 and 289 on unnamed map, 50x100, indeft. James J. Finn, Mount Vernon, N. Y., to Kate E. Finn. March 18, 1890. 1,200

Rockfield st, n s, 725 e Marion av, 25x126.5 to Jerome Park Railway Co., x25x126.6. William S. and Charles W. Opdyke to Josephine M. Mallahan. Taxes, &c., since June 1, 1883. Oct. 22, 1889. 287

Tiffany st, w s, 326.3 n 165th st, 30x100. George A. Minasian, Brooklyn, to Albertina Krause. Sept. 1. 850

134th st, s s, 183.4 e Willis av, 16.8x100. Philip F. Donohue to Louis Wirth. *Mt.* $7,000. Aug. 28. See 85th st. 12,000

135th st, s s, 100 w Alexander av, 50x100. Release mort. W. Wilton Wood, Huntington, L. I., to Frederick Rohrs. Aug. 29. nom

137th st, n s, 256.6 e Alexander av, 75x100. Dominick Weiss to The Ursuline Convent. B. & S. *Mt.* $12,000. June 9. nom

137th st, s s, 98 e Willis av, 27x100. William Seitz and Emma his wife to Babetta Groll. *Mt.* $21,500. Aug. 29. 31,500

138th st, s s, 75 e Southern Boulevard, —x100x25x100. Patrick Whelan trustee for Mary A. Whelan to Julius M. Cayson. *Mt.* $6,300. July 22. exch

146th st, s s, 275 w Brook av, 25x100. James Sullivan and Susan his wife to William Roach. Aug. 31. 3,375

152d st, n s, 500 w Courtlandt av, 100x100. Charles L. Konollman, Philadelphia, Pa., and Lizzette his wife, Charles L., Jr., and William H. Konollman and Amelia E. Eckel devisees Amelia Dennel to Sophia wife of John Lerch. Aug. 29. 7,475

154th st, n s, 220.3 e Morris av, 25x100. W. Y. Mortimer and A. E. his wife to Nicholas Schaefer. Aug. 3. 2,000

154th st, n s, 195.3 e Morris av, 25x100. Same to Peter Schaefer and Kunigunda his wife. Aug. 3. 2,000

169th st, s s, 73 w Intervale av, 30x44.3x32.2x32.7. Mary E. Cox to John N. Emra. Aug. 24. nom

Same property. John N. Emra and Marie R. his wife to William H. Gray. Aug. 24. nom

Beach av, s w cor 147th st, 200x200 to Tinton av. Clara F. Ruszits individ. and with Welcome G. Hitchcock and Emil J. Stake exrs. John Ruszits to John Y. Hallock. All liens. July 1. 2,000

Same property. John Y. Hallock to Walter D. Burke, Anthony McOwen, Henry G. Autenrieth and Edward R. Merrill. *Mt.* $8,000 and assessm'ts. Sept. 2. nom

Fleetwood av, w s, lot 80 map Charles Berrian farm, 25x100. Emma L. wife of Samuel N. Hyde to Thomas O'Reilly. Aug. 15. 600

Intervale av, e s, 340 s 167th st, 25x100. William N. Armstrong and Mary F. his wife to John W. Jackson. B. & S. July 30. 400

Inwood av, e s, 225 s Wolf pl, 25x130. Wiltshire Payne to John F. Eichler and Mary M. his

Same property. John F. Eichler and Maria M. his wife to Felix Krupp. Aug. 28. 1,000

Nathalie av, w s, lot 32 map 16 villa sites and 80 lots Anthony estate on Kingsbridge Heights, 37.9x133x1.10x127.9. Augustus S. Frazee to Alfred L. Larkin. Sept. 2. 900

Prospect av, w s, 105 s 165th st, 65x187.6. Mary wife of William Haehnel, August F. Frank Fechteler to Oscar Rudolph. Sept. 3. 5,500

Retreat av, n w s, part of lot 27 map East Ward of Melrose, runs northwest 100 x east 50 x southeast 100 to av, x southwest 50, excepting part taken for 149th st. Barbara Keller otherwise Magdalena B. Keller widow to Henry R. A. Carey, Portsmouth, N. H. Taxes, &c. Aug. 31. 5,000

Rider av, w s, 768 s w 144th st, 75x125 to Mott Haven Canal. John J. Moore and Mary A. his wife to Thomson-Houston Electric Co. Sub. to mort. Sept. 30, 1889. 10,000

Same property. Thomson-Houston Electric Co. to The North New York Lighting Co. Aug. 3. nom

Trinity av, e s, 380 n 161st st, 20x100. Robert C. Tucker to Robert C. Tucker, Jr. Q. C. Sept. 1. 1,800

Tinton av, No. 822, e s, 200 n Cedar st, 35.9x148.3x35.6x148. Frank W. Carmon and Mary J. his wife to Henry Mallebre. All liens. Aug. 29. 5,400

Worth av, n e cor Warren st, runs north 413 to Spring st, x west 50 to Worth av, x south 413 to Warren st, x east 50.
Worth av, s e cor Warren st, runs south 190 x southwest — x north 218 to st, x east 50.
Milicent C. Weeks widow and Jennie Hall, Farmingdale, L. I., to Kate Lurch. Q. C. May 18, 1891. nom

West Farms to Hunts Point road, w s, adj Nathan Hulet's land, 27x90x25x100. Edna M. Pawson to George Pawson. *Mt.* $125. Sept. 1. gift

Parcels 10 and 11 on damage map for opening George st from Boston road to Prospect av in 23d Ward. Charles P. Diefendorf to Mayor, &c., New York. July 7. 3,004

Parcel 6 on damage map for opening Railroad av West from Morris av to East 165th st, 23d Ward. Release mort. Bowery Savings Bank to Mayor, &c., New York. July 14. nom

LEASEHOLD CONVEYANCES.

Cherry st, No. 448, n s, 100 e Jackson st, 25x100. Assign. lease. Thomas Black to Bernard J. York. nom

Division st, No. 88. Assign. lease. John Wilken to Kate R. Wilcox, Middletown, N. Y. 1,741

Dutch st, No. 12. Assign. lease. Reformed Dutch Church to James A. Gilbert. nom

Same property. Consent to assign. lease. Same to same. nom

Houston st, No. 17 W.
Mercer st, No. 174.
Assign. lease. Adelheid Roes extrx. John Roes to Henry Bening. nom

Park row, No. 103, all. Rebecca C. Wayne to Michael Solomon. 16 years, from May 1, 1895, per year, 1,900

Park row, No. 103, all. Same to same. 5 years, from May 1, 1890, per year, 1,806

4th st, s s, 225 w Av A, 25x96.2. Assign. lease. Daniel Franzreb to Joseph Eck and Maria his wife 8,000

9th st, No. 30 W. Assign. lease. Rosalie Schoenberg to Max Scheuer. 950

32d st, No. 105 W. Agreement varying terms of lease and option to purchase. Caroline E. Hiffert to Garret D. Rhinehart. August 28. nom

34th st, No. 264 W. | Assign. leases and rents.
9th st, No. 30 W. | Rosalie Schoenberg extrx. Joseph Rosenfield to Henry Fera. 2,100

34th st, Nos. 160-164 E. | Assign. leases. John
3d av, No. 498 | A. Sause to Conrad Stein. nom

Willis av, n e cor 134th st. Assign. lease. Charles Jones to Eugene F. Degnan. nom

1st av, w s, 124.9 n 21st st, 24x100. Assign. lease. Henry Diefenthaler to Michael Horrner. 11,500

1st av, No. 2386. Assign. lease. Henry J. McGivney to D. G. Yuengling Brewing Co. nom

3d av, w s, 38 n 16th st, 18x60.
3d av, w s, 20 n 16th st, 18x60.
16th st, n s, 80 w 3d av, 20x92.
16th st, n s, 60 w 3d av, 20x92.
Assign. leases. Pincus Lowenfeld, Morris Goldstein and Mark Blumenthal to Daniel Ohl. 21,250

8th av, n e cor 125th st. Assign. lease. Abraham Lyons to Joel B. Kaufman. nom

KINGS COUNTY.

August 27, 28, 29, 31, September 1, 2.

Adelphi st, w s, 58 n Greene av, 19x67, h & l. Elizabeth L. wife of George H. Chinnock to Frederick J. Greve. *Mt.* $5,600. exch. and $1,100

Bainbridge st, n s, 277.2 e Saratoga av, 18x100. Sub. to mort. $5,000. J. Mason Kirby to Isaac Taylor. Contract to exchange for property at Lindenhurst, Babylon, on s s of Hoffman av, 100 w Wellwood av, 25x99. Sub. to mort. $1,200.

Bainbridge st, n s, 137.6 w Ralph av, 18.9x100. Release mort. Howard M. Smith trustee for The Bedford Bank to Samuel R. Good. nom

Same property. Aren Lutjen to Joseph E. R. Boudreau. *Mt.* $3,500. 5,500

Bartlett st, s s, 250 w Throop av, 25x100. Will-

Bergen st, s s, 100 e Buffalo av, 120x100, hs & ls. Edward Parkes to George C. Hollister, Rochester, N. Y. nom

Bergen st, s s, 143.7 e Clason av, 72x131, hs & ls. George R. Brown to Joseph L. Burton. All liens. nom

Bergen st, s s, 460 w 5th av, 60x100. Mary De Languillette, Ida L. Cahill and Louis C. Koch heirs of Leo E. Koch to Gertrude Koch widow, of Woodhaven, N. Y. nom

Bergen st, n s, 341.8 w Rockaway av, 16.8x107.2, h & l. John P. Shea to Mary Hurley, New York. *Mt.* $1,725. 80

Bond st, w s, 20 n Livingston st, 20x63. John Gibb to Aa S. Robbins, of New York. *Mt.* $3,500. ron 10,000

Bond st, e s, 80.9 n Schermerhorn st, 20x75. Margaretha wife of Henry Mugge to Philipp Ochsenreiter. 7,750

Broadway, n e s, 20 s e Woodbine st, 20x100, h & l. Bernard T. Biffar to Samuel Tobias. *Mt.* $3,500. 8,500

Broadway, s w s, 41.1 n w Whipple st, 20.6x80.5 to alley, x 20x85.1, h & l. Henry Sauerbrunn to Albert Wiener. *Mt.* $7,600. See George st. 15,000

Butler st, s s, 341.4 e Nostrand av, 16.8x100, h & l. John Andrews to Ella M. Taylor. *Mt.* $4,187. 5,750

Cleveland st, e s, 280 n Hegeman av, 20x100. Adolph Sussman to Mary V. Donnelly. 235

Cleveland st, e s, 260 n Hegeman av, 20x100. Same to John J. Coogan. 235

Cleveland st, e s, 246.10 n Atlantic av, 50x100. Emma A. wife of Perrin H. Sumner to Arthur E. Sumner. Q. C. nom

Clinton st, e s, 65.6 n 2d pl, 17.8x76.6, h & l. James J. Ferry to Catherine G. Ferry his wife. *Mt.* $5,000. nom

Clifton pl. Party wall agreement. Charles F. Hunt with Michael J. Campbell. val. consid.

Chester st, e s, 750 s Sackett st, 25x100. Joseph Holtzer to Isaac Fox and Marcus Ciment. 1,450

Clarkson st, s w cor Albany av, 40x92.1, Flatbush. Frank C. Lang to Patrick Crown. 700

Cook st, n s, 150 e White st, 25x100. Elward Karutz to Sebastian Schaffer. *Mt.* $3,000. 6,375

Cornelia st, n e s, extends from Central av to Hamburg av, 600x100. Virginia A. Kleine to Michael Dowley. *Mt.* $24,000. See Macon st. nom

Covert st, s e s, 381 n e Evergreen av, 25.6x101.2. City of Brooklyn to Charlotte A. Sutherland. Q. C. nom

Covert st, n w s, 347 n e Evergreen av, 18x100, h & l. Mathew Montgomery to Lizzie wife of Peter W. Sylvester. *Mt.* $3,000. 4,250

Cooper st, s e s, 347.6 n e Evergreen av, 19.6x100. Release mort. Augustus S. Bedell to Thomas J. Allen. nom

Same property. Hannah M. Rose to Robert Smith. *Mt.* $2,200. exch

Degraw st, n s, 55.4 e Van Brunt st, 20x59.6. John Hennessy to Amelia J. wife of Robert W. Ray, of New York. 2,500

Dean st, s w s, 180 n w 3d av, 20x100, h & l. Charlotte E. Miller to Mary M. Crawford. 5,500

Dean st, No. 181, n s, 190 w Bond st, 20x100. Margaret A. wife of James E. Young to John Goetz. *Mt.* $3,500. 6,900

Dean st, s s, 275 w Vanderbilt av, 25x110, h & l. Oliver, Amelia, Joseph and Catharine Marshall heirs Oliver Marshall to Michael Bracken. 2,000

Earl st, n s, 400 w Brooklyn av, 40x100, Flatbush. Edward Egolf to Andrew Mahon. 500

Eldert st, n w s, 411 n e Evergreen av, 19x100. Leopold J. Lippmann to Frank X. Heim. nom

Same property. Release mort. Ann E. Cozine extrx. and James Gascoine individ. and exr. John G. Cozine to Leopold J. Lippmann. 2,408

Ellery st, s s, 375 w Marcy av, 25x100. Maria Kunzweiler to W m Schwartz, of New York. *Mt.* $3,200. illia 6,450

Essex st, e s, 450.7 n Atlantic av, 25x100. Mary J. Higgins to Alfred Beinhauer, of New York. *Mt.* $3,100. nom

Ewen st, w s, 50 s McKibbin st, 25x98.6. Eva Bach to Joseph Levi and Morris Blum. *Mt.* $3,500. 7,800

Ewen st, s w cor Stagg st, 25x72. Marcus or Markus Bach to Eleck Sundel and Gerson Krackauer, New York. 13,500

Fillmore pl, No. 24, being North 1st st, s s, 128 w Roebling st, 20x60. John Keresey to Harris and Abraham Blum. 5,000

Fort Greene pl, w s, 250 s Hanson pl, runs west 60.3 x southwest 26.8 x south 14.3 x northeast 35.1 x east 54.4 to pl, x north 20. Long Island R. R. Co. to Frank W. Crocker, Chelsea, Mass. *Mt.* $6,000. 8,038

Same property. Release mort. Central Trust Co., New York, to same. nom

Floyd st, n s, 240 e Nostrand av, 25x100. Louis Beer and Michael Schaffner to Emilie Rhinow. *Mt.* $4,000. See Park av. 10,250

Ford st, e s, 298.10 n East New York av, 25x99.10, Flatbush. Margaret Curtin to Matthew Dolan. 600

Fulton st, s s, 75 w Miller av, 25x100, h & l. John A. Davies to Jane L. Smith. *Mt.* $1,500. 2,000

Fulton st, s s, 100 w Miller av, 25x100. Partition. Robert Merchant to David Rosenberg. 1,750

Fulton st, s s, 75 w Miller av, 25x100. Partition. Same to John A. Davies. 1,700

Fulton st, n w cor Bradford st, 25x100, h & l. Herman Wichert to Maria Degnan. 4,000

Fulton st, n s, 70 e Georgia av, 30x147.3 to Jamaica av, x31.10x136.7. Louis Liedtke to

Fulton st, s s, 50 w Miller av, 25x100, h & l. Partition. Robert Merchant to Quinton R. Parker. 1,550

George st, n s, 129 e Evergreen av, runs north 67.5 x north 28.9 x southerly 89.9 to st, x west 25.6, h & l. Albert Wiener to Henry Sauerbrunn. *Mt.* $2,200. See Broadway. 4,000

Halsey st, No. 782, s s, 83.6 e Ralph av, 19.5x100. John T. Barnard to Frederick Bauer. *Mt.* $5,000. 6,500

Halsey st, n s, 145 w Sumner av, 20x100, h & l. Ernst Rost to Clara Rost. nom

Halsey st, n s, 105 w Sumner av, 20x100. Louis F. Schmidt to Rosa Schmidt. nom

Hancock st, s s, 280 w Lewis av, 20x100. William Warmbrum to Matthew Robb. See McDonough st. 2,000

Hancock st, n s, 245 e Sumner av, 40x100. Leonard D. Hills to Winston H. Hogner. *Mt.* $13,000. (Correction.) nom

Harman st, s e s, 275 n e Central av, 25x100, h & l. Andrew and Christian Hahn to Magdalena Stahl. *Mt.* $3,500. nom

Harman st, s e s, 250 n e Central av, 25x100. Andrew and Christian Hahn to Valentine Reiss. *Mt.* $3,500. 7,500

Harman st, s e s, 195.9 s w Wyckoff av, runs southeast 89.8 x southwest 425 to Irving av, x northwest 110.2 to Harman st, x northeast 425. Ann E. Crouse widow to John F. Gantz. Correction deed. 1853. nom

Hawthorne st, s s, 360.6 w Nostrand av, 60x106, Flatbush. Release mort. Asa W. Parker to John F. Hart. nom

Hayward st, s s, 240 w Lee av, 16x100, h & l. Mary wife of and John McCartney to Pauline Morgenroth. 3,550

Hendrix st, w s, 150 s Delmont av, 25x100. Michael Devitt to Patrick Collins. 800

Herkimer st, s s, 200 w Utica av, 25x185.6 to Old Brooklyn & Jamaica R. R. Bernard Hefferan to Anne Hefferan. All morts, taxes, &c. 1,300

Herkimer st, s s, 325 w Utica av, 25x185.6 to Brooklyn & Jamaica R. R. George H. Gould exr. David H. Gould to William H. Reynolds. 1,000

Herkimer st, n s, 20 w Rockaway av, 20x80. Foreclos. John Courtney, Sheriff, to Charles A. Moran as trustee Anne A. Moran. 4,000

Herkimer st, n s, 40 w Rockaway av, 20x80. Foreclos. Same to Mary N. Burrill, of New York. 4,000

Herkimer st, n w cor Rockaway av, 20x100. Foreclos. Same to Drayton Burrill exr. Anna Morris. 5,000

Hicks st, w s, 35 n Sackett st, 20x93. James G. Gallagher to Joseph F. Kennelly, South Orange, N. J. *Mt.* $1,900. 3,600

High st, n s, 115 w Bridge st, 25x100 to alley. Helen K. and Wm. G. Leask exrs. Margaret I. Hurdes formerly Leask to John Brown and Margaret his wife. 5,500

High st, e s, 46.3 w Gold st, 23.3x97.6x22.11x97.5, h & l. Honora Farrell to Owen D. McGovern, New York. 7,750

Himrod st, s s, 170 w St. Nicholas av, 40x100. Sarah A. C. Moore to Joseph Fritz. 800

Himrod st, s e s, 375 n e Central av, 25x100. Darwin R. James to Dorothea Bies. 1,500

Himrod st, s e s, 200 s w Hamburg av, 25x100. Release mort. Theodore F. Jackson et al, trustees of Loftis Wood dec'd to Darwin R. James. nom

Hopkins st, s s, 600 w Marcy av, 26x100, h & l. Isaac A. Edmunds to Johanna Rohlfs. *Mt.* $2,900. nom

Hopkins st, n s, 234.5 e Throop av, 23.4x100. Carl A. Katt to Henry Roth and Joseph E. Middle. *Mt.* $5,000. 8,400

Hull st, s s, 419.5 e Stone av, 60x100. Release mort. Mary M. Fagan to David B. Brower. nom

Same property. Mary M. Fagan to same. 3,060

Huron st, n s, 345 e Franklin st, 25x100, h & l. Max Berliner to Peter Russell. Sub. to morts. 4,350

Jerome st, e s, 140 s Blake av, 20x100. Charles F. Duryea to Josephine A. Thibaut, of New York. 350

Kosciusko st, No. 325, n s, 175 e Throop av, 25x100, h & l. Louisa Schoppa to Annie C. Itzen. *Mt.* $2,500. 3,500

Leonard st, s e cor Johnson av, 25x100. Isaac, Gustav and Samuel Dreyer to Jacob Zirinsky. *Mt.* $5,600. 7,600

Lincoln pl, s s, 359 e 7th av, 25.6x100, h & l. Henry Gaullier to George H. Fletcher. 17,000

Linden st, s s, 76.2 w Wyckoff av, 25x92.6x25x93, h & l. Peter Riebling to Mary Sedlemayer, New York. *Mt.* $3,500. 6,500

Livingston st, n w cor Bond st, 20x63. John Gibb to Aaron S. Robbins, of New York. 15,000

Logan st, e s, 175 n Liberty av, 50x100. Liona Ryan to Benjamin J. Guerra. *Mt.* $1,300. 2,900

Macon st, n s, 400 e Ralph av, 180x100, hs & ls. Eliza J. Ames to Benjamin C. Raymond. Sub. to liens. nom

Macon st, s s, 338.8 e Reid av, 18.4x100, h & l. James G. Roberts to Agatha Kelsch, New York. *Mt.* $4,500. 7,250

Macon st, n s, 436 e Ralph av, 18x100. Michael Dowley to Virginia A. Kleine. *Mt.* $5,300. See Cornelia st. nom

Macon st, s s, 84 w Ralph av, 18x100. Walter F. Clayton to George F. Turner and Annie his wife, joint tenants. *Mt.* $4,000. 7,250

Macon st, s s, 95 e Ralph av, 90x100. Release mort. Frank Bailey to John R. Pitt. nom

Macon st, s s, 320.4 e Reid av, 18.4x100, h & l. James D. Roberts to Mary A. Valentine. *Mt.* [illegible]

Madison st, n w s, 188 n e Hamburg av, 18x100. Pauline J. La Burt, of New York, to Adolph I. Fritsch. *Mt.* $3,250. 3,700

Madison st, s s, 125 e Ralph av, 25x100. Amy J. wife of Isaac Reynolds to Abram Rutan. *Mt.* $1,000. 1,600

Madison st, n w s, 170.7 n e Wyckoff av, 25x100. Mariana wife of and Joseph Scheuermann to Lorenz Schnell. 1,430

Marion st, s s, 350.2 e Howard av, 74.10x100. William H. Reynolds to Elizabeth P. McNab. 4,000

McDonough st, n s, 175 e Sumner av, 20x100. Matthew Robb to Susan Warmbrum. 8,000

McDonough st, n s, 91 w Reid av, 16.6x100, h & l. Mary F. Malcolm to Thomas W. Henderson. *Mt.* $3,000. See Hancock st. 5,600

McDonough st, n s, 300 w Stuyvesant av, 20x100, h & l. John J. DeRevere to William W. Share. *Mt.* $7,500. nom

McDonough st, s s, 90.4 w Ralph av, 18x100. John G. Craig to Sara J. Craig. *Mt.* $5,800. 6,800

McDonough st, s s, 108.4 w Ralph av, 18.4x100, h & l. Carrie Sarles to Mary E. wife of George W. Brown. *Mt.* $5,200. exch

McDougal st, s s, 275 e Stone av, 25x100, h & l. George H. Smith to Margaretha Lewis. B. & S. and C. a. G. *Mt.* $3,000. 3,500

Same property. Margaretha Lewis to William D. and Elizabeth Stolz, New York. *Mt.* $4,500. 2,000

McDougal st, n s, 25 w Saratoga av, 25x100, h & l. Katerina wife of Luis Pollack to George Knauer, New York. *Mt.* $2,500. 4,100

McDougal st, s s, 150 e Hopkinson av, 18.9x100, h & l. Jane Lansing to James T. or F. Curry. *Mt.* $4,250. 5,500

McDougal st, s s, 168.9 e Hopkinson av, 18.9x100, h & l. Same to Andrew L. Dalton. *Mt.* $4,250. 5,500

McDougal st, s s, 187.6 e Hopkinson av, 18.9x100, h & l. Same to same. *Mt.* $4,250. 5,500

McDougal st, n s, 230 w Stone av, 80x100. Charles A. Silver to William M Brown. 7,000

McKibbin st, s s, 200 w Morrell st, 25x100. Magdalena Klockert to Abraham Kemp. nom

McKibbin st, n s, 250 w Ewen st, 25x100. Max A. Dassau to Isaac Greenblatt and Simon Loeb. *Mt.* $2,700. 6,500

McKibbin st, s s, 200 w Morrell st, 25x100. George P. Knockert to Abraham Kemp. *Mt.* $2,900. 3,400

Melrose st, n s, 75 e Bushwick av, 25x100, also strip adj on west side of above lot, .01x50, party wall. Elisabeth Schano widow to Leonard Hefter. 9,400

Middleton st, s e s, 200 n e Marcy av, 25x100. Marie Lang to Michael and Anna Spatz, joint tenants. *Mt.* $1,900. 6,200

Monroe st, s s, 486.6 w Throop av, 19.3x100. Charles E. Griffin to Martha J. Vogel. *Mt.* $3,000. 7,800

Montague pl, n s, 78 e Hicks st, 51x100. Frederick J. Stone, of New York, to Delmar W. Heath. *Mt.* $125,000. nom

Navy st, w s, abt 126.9 n De Kalb av, 25x100, h & l. Ann Killam to John De Mott. 4,600

Newton st, n s, 180 s w Graham av, 25x62.7x32.5x82.3. William C. Traphagan, of New York, to James A. Davies. 500

Oakland st, e s, 225 n e Nassau av, 25x100. Jessie E. Gay, of Carthage, N. Y., and Edward G. Gay to Andrew Valentine. 2,600

Oakland st, w s, 175 n Nassau av, 25x100. Mary E. V. wife of Joseph E. R. Boudreau to Silas W. Quick. 3,150

Oliver st, s s, 297.11 e Shore road, 200x51.9x200.4x64, New Utracht. Elizabeth A. Thorn to Robert M. A. Coming. *Mt.* $1,122. nom

Orange st, n s, 74.5 w Henry st, 50.4x100.9x50.8x100.9. Lucetta B. Phelps to Edwin D. Phelps. nom

Osborn st, w s, 325 s Dumont st, 25x100. Wolf Yonack, of New York, to Samuel Rosenbaum and Charles Faber. 500

Osborn st, w s, 300 s Dumont st, 25x100. Morris Weinstein, of New York, to same. 500

Osborn st, w s, 150 n Glenmore av, 25x100. Herbert C. Smith to Louis Lebewohl. 600

Osborn st, n w cor Rapelje st, 100x150. Rosa N. Geis to Joseph Newborg. *Mt.* $800. 2,500

Park pl, n s, 100 e Clason av, 40x131. Mary E. Yost to Susie E. Boyd, of Tea Neck, N. J. 12,000

Pacific st, s s, 148.6 w Nevins st, 21.6x100. Release bond, &c. Christopher Heinrich to Philip Heinrich. nom

Pacific st, s s, 497.4 e Rockaway av, 16.8x107.3. Foreclos. John Courtney, Sheriff, to George G. Hill. 2,000

Pacific st, n s, 101 w Utica av, 203.5x108.7x245.10x100. William Herod to Thomas S. Denike. 10,000

Pacific st, s s, 497.4 e Rochester av, 16.8x107.3.
Vanderveer st, s e s, 80 s w Bushwick av, 16.10x100.
George A. Hill to Francis H. Cowdrey. nom

Pacific st, n s, 504 e Rochester av, 16x100, h & l. Frederick Dhuy, Jr., to Kate A. Hughes. *Mt.* $1,600. 3,600

Pacific st, n s, 266.8 e Hoyt st, 16.8x100. Rachel Elliot to Thomas Walsh. 6,000

Powers st, s s, 132.7 e Olive st, 25x65.11x25.5x70.5. William R. Meinell to Franz Franz. 2,700

Powers st, s s, 132.7 e Olive st, runs south 70.5 x northeast 25.5 x north 65.11 x west 25. Franz Franz to Johann W. Eufinger. *Mt.* $1,500. 2,400

President st, s s, 216.6 e Henry st, 25.6x100. George B. Dearing to Joel W. Sherwood. *Mt.* $12,000. exch

Richardson st, s s, 150 w Lorimer st, 25x100. Herman Rhein to Mali Rice, Newark, N. J. *Mt.* $300, and paving assessm't. 1,550

Rock st, n s, 100 e Bogart st, 25x100, h & l. George Herold to Herman Kuck. 2,000

Rutledge st, s e s, 384 s w Harrison av, 28x100, h & l. John H. Dewes to Edward Keesy and Phebe his wife. *Mt.* $6,000. 10,700

Sackman st, Powell st, Dumont and Livonia avs—the block, 500x200. A. Judson Palmer to Hirsch Wilkenfeld. *Mt.* $9,500. 20,000

Schaeffer st, n w s, 425 n e Division av now Broadway, 25x100. August C. Scharmann to Henry Scherf. 9,050

Scholes st, w s, 100 e Graham av, 25x100.
Scholes st, n s, 200 e Graham av, 25x100.
Lina Wisbauer widow and George Wisbauer t Edward, L i H., George, John A., Francklin, Celius, Alfred T. and Joseph J. Wisbauer. nom

Seigel st, s s, 25 w Leonard st, 25x75, h & l. Valentin Reiss to Smith Ely, New York. 4,200

Seigel st, n s, 181.6 e Leonard st, 24x100. Morris Levin to Israel Habar. *Mt.* $6,200. 8,800

Seigel st, s s, 100 w Graham av, 25x100, h & l. Israel Jarashon to Jacob and Michael Lewis. *Mt.* $9,100. 14,000

Seigel st, n s, 122.6 w Ewen st, 24x100. Henry Meyer and Jonas Feldberg to Harris Wolf and Jacob Piser. *Mt.* $25,000. 15,000

Seigel st, s s, 125 w Graham av, 25x100, h & l. Louis Rosenthal to Leo Katz. nom

Seigel st, n s, 225 e Graham av, 25x100. Elizabeth Timmes to George Gutting and Charles Wagner. *Mt.* $3,000. 6,500

Same property. George Gutting and Charles Wagner to Lasar Lurie. *Mt.* $5,500. 6,200

Seigel st, n s, 122.6 w Ewen st, 24x100. Release mort. Henry Meyer to Harris Wolf and Jacob Piser 1,000

Stagg st, n s, 175 w Ewen st, 25x102.4x—x94.7. Helena Lungershausen to Joseph Neger. *Mt.* $3,000. 7,500

South Elliott pl, w s, 254.2 s Hanson pl, 20.6x100. Jose Gestal to Marie A. Loewenstein, of New York. *Mt.* $1,750. 6,800

Stanhope st, n w s, 100 s w Irving av, 50x100. Darwin R. James to Pincus Seifters. 2,300

Stanhope st, s e s, 80 s w Knickerbocker av, 20x75. George Gutting and Charles A. Wagner to Josephine Ganter. *Mt.* $3,500. 4,925

St. Johns pl, s s, 373 w 6th av, 19x127.6, h & l. George W. Hanley to Concepcion T. de Venecia. 9,500

Steuben st, No. 139. Party wall agreement. Mary A. McCloskey and George A. Knott. 500

Stockton st, s s, 325 e Throop av, 25x100, h & l. Andrew Mahr to Henry Sowisky and Katharine his wife. *Mt.* $3,200. 7,600

Stockton st, n s, 150 w Sumner av, 25x100, h & l. George Covert to Philipp Chlebowski, New York. 4,400

Suydam st, s s, 225 w Evergreen av, 25x95. Elise Knieriem to Mine Wehler. 4,250

Union pl, s w cor Lott st, runs south 115 to Butler st, x west 20 x north 90 x west 80 x north 25 to Union pl, x east 100, Flatbush. George J. Craigen to Eliza Craigen. *Mt.* $6,660. 1,200

Vanderveer st, s e s, 80 s w Bushwick av, 16.10x100. Foreclos. John Courtney, Sheriff, to George G. Hill. 2,000

Van Voorhis st, n w s, 100 w Evergreen av, 51x100; also,
Van Voorhis st, n w s, 203 w Evergreen av, 85x100.
Robert H. Irish to Alice B. Bedell. Sub. to all liens, &c. nom

Van Voorhis st, n w s, 219 w Evergreen av. 34x100. Alice B. Bedell to The Dugan Manufacturing Co. Sub. to all liens, &c. nom

Wallabout st, n s, 103 w Marcy av, 25x70.10x29.5x86.4, h & l. Jacob Bossert to Charles F. Stadler. *Mt.* $2,700. 6,400

Warwick st, e s, 125 n Eastern Parkway, 25x90, h & l. Abraham L. Hopkins to John W. Gottlock. 2,950

Warwick st, w s, 20 n Blake av, 40x100. Theodore Kiendl to Charles E. Maguire. 800

Watkins st, e s, 100 n Riverside av, 50x100, h & l. Michael Sullivan to Joseph Levin and Sara Borenstein. *Mt.* $3,000. 4,200

Winthrop st, n e cor East 45th st, runs north 421.4 x east 200 to East 46th st, x south 423.2 to Winthrop st, x west 200 to beginning.
East 46th st, e s, 100 n Winthrop st, runs north 324.1 x east 200 to Schenectady av, x south 328.6 x west 200 to beginning; also,
Schenectady av, n e cor Winthrop st, runs north 100 x east 100 x north 20 x west 100 to av, x north 140 x east 100 x north 80 x west 100 to av, x north 90.4 x east 200 to East 48th st, x south 434.9 to Winthrop st, x west 200 to beginning, Flatbush.
Theodore E. Fogg, of Philadelphia, Pa., to Lizzie A. Shaw, of Finderne, N. J. 22,000

Woodbine st, s e s, 264 n e Hamburg av, 18x100, h & l. George W. and Charles H. Francisco to Richard Kurth. nom

Same property. Release mort. Anna E. Cozine extrx. and James Gascoine individ. and as exr. of John G. Cozine to George W. and Charles H. Francisco. 2,344

Willow st, e s, 50 n Cranberry st, 50x25. Foreclos. Judah B. Voorhees to William Roberts. Confirmation deed. 2,000

Woodbine st, s e s, 210 n e Hamburg av, 18x100. Ann E. Cozine extrx. and James Gascoine individ. and exr. of John G. Cozine to George W. and Charles H. Francisco. 2,346

Same property. George W. and Charles H. Francisco to Clementine wife of Louis Gruner. nom

Windsor pl, n e s, 218.8 s e 7th av, 18.10x100, h & l. William E. Kay to Charles A. Enggren. Mt. $1,150. 4,450

Wolcott st, s w s, 76 s e Richards st, 19.4x100. John Terrett to Thomas Henry. Mt. $1,200. 2,850

1st st, s s, 188.7 w Bond st, 20x84.7x20x85.1. Edward Lavin to Thomas and Mary Enright. 4,000

South 1st st, n e cor Roebling st, 25x77. Martha C. Jennings widow and sole devisee of Ebenezer Jennings to Adam Schulz. 5,100

2d st, s s, 225.2 e 6th av, 36.4x95. Release mort. James McLaren to William H. Norris and William Bowers. 2,380

Same property. Release mort. Lester A. Lewis to William H. Norris and William Bowers. 3,300

Same property. William H. Norris and William Bowers to Amanda M. Drummond. Mt. $12,000. nom

North 2d st, n s, 175 e 2d st, 25x100. Frederick Moschette to William H. Schliffer. 4,800

5th st, s w s, 97.10 n w 5th av, runs southwest 100 x northwest 300 x southwest 100 to 6th st, x northwest 200 x northeast 200 to 5th st, x southeast 500 to beginning. Charles D. Burwell to Frank A. Barnaby. Mt. $4,000. nom

6th st, n s, 397.10 w 5th av, 100x100. Charles D. Burwell, Frank A. Barnaby and Susan E. Fingarr to Ervin G. Gollner. Mt. $4,100. 9,000

6th st, n e s, 277.10 n w 5th av, 20x100. Release mort. The Title Guarantee and Trust Co. to Henry H. Cochran. nom

Same property. Charles D. Burwell and Frank A. Barnaby to Charles H. Denison. nom

7th st, s s, 339.10 w 8th av, 20.9x100, h & l. Mary Rich to Benjamin C. Anderson. 7,000

North 7th st, n s, 225 e Roebling st, 25x100. John B. Ferrall to Jules and Edmund Wolff. Mt. $3,500. 4,000

East 8th st, w s, 320 n Av B, 40x120.5, Flatbush. Thomas W. Kavanagh, Chicago, to Mary J. Owen. 500

9th st, s s, 245.9 w 4th av, 20x90, h & l. Ann S. Ives widow, Alice R. wife of George K. Goodwin and Henry B. Ives to Cornelius Drew. 4,000

9th st, s w s, 125 n w 2d av, 25x200 to 10th st. Timothy J., Patrick A., Dennis I. and Thomas A. Nolan to John T. Nolan. Q. C. nom

10th st, n s, 125 w 2d av, 25x100. John F. Nolan to Patrick McGonigle. 675

North 10th st, s w s, 75 s e Roebling st, 100x100. Caroline D., Alice W. and Howard W. Hayes and Mary H. wife of Louis Pennington, Newark, N. J., to Thomas P. Graham. 2,600

11th st, s s, 281.2 e 4th av, 16.8x100, h & l. Ann Cosgrove to Charles B. Barker. 4,700

15th st, s w s, 225 n w 6th av, 14.3x100. Signor A. Buckley to Rynier S. Rutan. Mt. $1,000. 2,100

15th st, s w s, 97.10 s e 7th av, 25x100. James J. Ferry to Catharine G. Ferry his wife. Mt. $6,000. nom

17th st, No. 327A, n e s, 187.6 s e 6th av, 17.6x80. Katharina wife of John P. Munch to Caroline wife of Lazarus Brilliant and Sallie wife of Henry Brilliant. Mt. $1,500. 3,000

17th st, s w s, 220 n w 10th av, 20x100.2. Robert Walsh to Michael W. Conway. 1,600

20th st, s w s, 64.9 n w 5th av, 17.5x75. Horace W. Couillard to Brooklyn City Co-operative Building and Loan Assoc. nom

39th st, s s, 175 e 6th av, 25x100.2; also,
39th st, s s, 200 e 6th av, 25x100.2.
J. Augustus Randel to John Randel. nom

39th st, s s, 316.8 w 3d av, 16.8x100.2.
39th st, s s, 333.4 w 3d av, 16.8x100.2.
William A. Helwig to Johanna Helwig. Sub. to morts. 100

40th st, n e s, 1,044 n w 2d av, 150x200.4 to 39th st, with use of roadway to 2d av. The Phenix Chemical Works to Henry W. Johns, of New York. 20,000

40th st, s s, 125 w 3d av, 125x100.2. Robert W. Drummond to William H. Norris and William Bowers. nom

45th st, s s, 280 e 3d av, 20x100.2, h & l. James G. Carroll to Patrick R. F. Sparling and Margaret his wife. Mt. $2,300. 4,600

46th st, n s, 280 e 7th av, 80x100.2. Kate Hurst to Virginia Lowey. nom

51st st, n s, 100 w 7th av, 25x100.2. Catherine Battermann widow to Alexander McGregor. 1,300

52d st, s s, 286.8 w 3d av, 16.8x100.2, h & l. John A. Lindsey or Lindsay to Annie L. wife of William W. Greene, Uniontown, Pa. Mt. $2,000. nom

Same property. Annie L. wife of William W. Greene to Anna M. C. wife of William O'Donoghue. Mt. $2,000. 3,200

53d st, n e s, 160 s e 7th av, 40x140.5x42.1x153.8.
54th st, n e s, 500 n w 8th av, 20x100.2.
Jerome F. Callahan to James Costello. 600

55th st, s w s, 260 s e 8th av, 80x100.2. Frank D. Creamer to Joseph F. De Castro. 1,600

55th st, s w s, 350 s e 14th av, 25x100.2, New Utrecht. West Brooklyn Land and Improvement Co. to Minnie Frothingham. 500

57th st, s s, 200 e 3d av, 20x100.2. Jarvis Masters to Thomas Dunn. Mt. $266. 760

57th st, s s, 120 w 3d av, 20x100.2, h & l, 8th Ward. William S. Hassan to Esther wife of Thomas Pitt, Nyack, N. Y. Mt. $2,700. 4,600

61st st, n s, 360 w 11th av, 20x100, New Utrecht. Edward Kavanagh, of New York, to George G. Hallock. 150

61st st, s w s, 320 s e 7th av, 40x— to N. Y. & Sea Beach R. R., x—x—, New Utrecht. Carrie M. Hatten to Jennie Roberts. nom

Same property. Jennie Roberts to Adolph Weissbein. 500

67th st, s s, 100 e 11th av, 40x130, New Utrecht. Gustav Reichenbach to The Brooklyn City Co-operative Building and Loan Assoc. Sub. to mort. nom

70th st, n s, 570 w 15th av, 40x100, Lefferts Park. James V. S. Woolley to James Kelly, New York. 520

72d st, s s, 235.10 w 18th av, 40x100, New Utrecht. James McClelland to John T. McClelland. 400

75th st, s s, 110 w 15th av, 40x100, Lefferts Park. James V. S. Woolley to Maggie A. Farrell. 350

82d st, n e s, 220 s e 22d av, 120x100, New Utrecht. James D. Lynch to John R. Conway. 2,400

Albany av, s e cor Lefferts av, 100x100, Flatbush. Sterling E. Edmunds to David C. Reid. Mt. $1,000. 50

Atkins av, e s, 175 s Liberty av, 40x100. Marenus J. Goodenough to George Grolimund. 900

Atkins av, e s, 100 s Liberty av, 175x100. Release mort. Samuel Burhans, Jr., to Marenus J. Goodenough. 1,575

Atkins av, e s, 90 n Hegeman av, 20x100.
Hegeman av, n s, 40 e Atkins av, 20x90.
William H. Jackson to Constantine Bernauer. 465

Atlantic av, s s, 25 w Bond st, 01¼x90. Henry Kohler to Ernest A. Hoffmann exr. of August T. Schweitzer. Q. C. 30

Atlantic av, s s, 25 w Bond st, 20x90. Ernest A. Hoffmann exr. August T. Schweitzer to Patrick Drew. 7,000

Belmont av, s s, 25 e Watkins st, 25x100, h & l. Moritz Goldberg to Joseph and Philip Krinko. Mt. $1,900. 2,900

Belmont av, s w cor Powell st, 100x300. James G. Roberts to Morris Kaplan, Jacob Epstein and Fannie Levy, of New York, and Jacob Liebmann. Mt. $4,500. 8,400

Bushwick av or Woodpoint road, e s, bet lots of W. J. Conselyea and A. Hultz, 25x100 to land of Reformed Protestant Dutch Church, Bushwick, h & l. Angilo Masone sometimes called John Rose to Jelice Dicco and Andrea Angeloso. ⅝ part. Sub. to mort. $3,700. 5,000

Carlton av, w s, 137.3 s Park av, h & l. William R. Lowe and George P. H. McVay to The L. F. Genet Lumber Co. Mt. $15,500. 21,000

Carlton av, e s, 252 s Park av, 25x100, h & l. Mary A. Hanlon to James Quinn. 4,250

Central av, s w s, 100 s e Linden st, 25x100. Anna wife of Anton Herbst late Bauer to Bertha Kaufmann, of Newtown, N. Y. Mt. $4,300. exch

Central av, south cor Van Voorhis st, 100x100. Edward P. Loomis to Anna Martin. nom

Central av, s w s, 40 n w Ivy st, 20x100. Albert E. Schalkenbach to Adam Baum. Mt. $2,200. 2,900

Christopher av, n e cor Lott av, centre lines, runs north to centre Newport st, x east to centre Sackman st, x north to Lotts land, x east to Van Sinderens, x south to centre Lott av, x west —, being 142 lots. Maria L. Linington widow and sole devisee of John Linington to James G. Roberts and Charles G. Reynolds. Mt. $39,700. 56,800

De Kalb av, n s, 154.4 e Wyckoff av, 20x100. Margaretha Pfeiffer to Katharina Diehlmann. Mt. $1,150. exch

Evergreen av, w s, 75 n De Kalb av, 50x100. Franz Franz to William R. Meinell. Mt. $7,000. exch. and 3,300

Flushing av, n e cor Bushwick av, runs north 124.3 x east 74.9 x south 118.4 x west 71.1. George W. Conselyea and Anna M. Irwin to Jacob Manneschmidt. 16,000

Flushing av, n e cor Nostrand av, 25x63.10x51.8x82.1. Joseph Mentz, of New York, to Israel Josefsohn, of New York. nom

Same property. Israel Josefsohn to Joseph Mentz. nom

Flushing av, s s, 350 w Tompkins av, 25x100. Simon Rudolph to Esther Surut. Mt. $7,000. 11,000

Franklin av, w s, 240 s Willoughby st, 25x101.11x25x101.2. Hannah E. Pearsall to Georgiana wife of Henry Burton. 2,900

Gates av, n s, 80 w Vanderbilt av, 20x75. William Schoefer to Louise Ruhle. ½ part. 1,500

Gates av, Nos. 1182 and 1184, s e s, 55.1 s w Evergreen av, 40x100. Herman Vehstedt and Henry Roth to Joseph Kunz. Q. C. Correction deed. nom

Same property. Joseph Kunz to William J. Kaiser. Mt. $9,000. exch

Greene av, n w cor Carlton av, 20.10x75. John W. Newbery to Jenny Vyncker. Mt. $6,000. nom

Greenpoint av, s s, 71.10 w Manhattan av, 80x95. George H. Gerard to Conrad Heidelberger. 22,857

Greenpoint av, s s, 151.10 w Manhattan av, 60x95. Willis H. Young, of Hempstead, N. Y., to same. 17,143

Greenwood av, s w cor East 4th st, 45x105.7x11x100, Flatbush. James V. Wilbur to Anna M. Ferris. 475

Greenwood av, s w cor East 4th st, 45x105.7x11x100.
Greenwood av, s w cor East 3d st, 60x105.7x25.10x100, Flatbush. Anna M. Ferris to George W. McGarl. 1,125

Hamburg av, n e s, 75 s e Suydam st, 25x100. John Raber to John Wischerth. Q. C. nom

Jefferson av, s s, 325 n e Bushwick av, 18.9x100. Anna wife of George Koch to Joseph Peck. Mt. $2,350. nom

Same property. Joseph Peck to George Koch. Mt. $2,350. nom

Kingsland av, e s, 102.2 n Division pl, 25x114x25x108. Smith E. Hendrickson to Joseph Kreppin. 1,350

Knickerbocker av, n e s, 600 n w Putnam av, 20x67. Louis H. Dewery to William Luchan. 480

Knickerbocker av, n e s, 580 n w Putnam av, 20x68. Same to Dennis Cosgrove. 480

Knickerbocker av, s w s, 125 n w Himrod st, 25x80. George Gutting and Charles A. Wagner to Elizabeth Timmes. Mt. $3,500. 6,500

Lafayette av, s s, 452 e Bedford av, 28x100. Mary E. wife of George W. Brown to Carrie Sarles. Mt. $2,400. exch

Lafayette av, n s, 148 e Reid av, 16x100, h & l. William S. Gahagan to Emery J. Hampton. 2,650

Lee av, e s, 93.8 s Wallabout st, 25x76.2x35x81.3. Henry Roth to Isaac Simon. Mt. $4,000. 8,500

Lewis av, w s, 100 s Monroe st, 19x81. Frederick B. Norris to Annie B. wife of George H. Stevens. nom

Lewis av, e s, 82 n Madison st, 18x100. William J. Pearson to Robert B. Stokes. Mt. $4,000. 5,800

Liberty av, n e cor Milford st, 50x100. John J. Messer to Bessie Naughton. 1,500

Manhattan av, w s, 125 s Calyer st, 25x100, h & l. Amos W. and A. Silkworth exrs. Rebecca Silkworth to Amos W. Silkworth. Mt. $1,500. provision in will and 5,000

Marcy av, n w cor Wallabout st, being on assessment map 19th Ward lot 1 block 97. John C. McGuire, Registrar of Arrears, to Walter Duggan. 61

Marcy av, e s, 80.6 s Quincy st, runs east 57 x north 0.6 x east 34 x south 20 x west 91 to Marcy av, x north 19.6. Phillips Abbott to George H. Chinnock. Mt. $6,000. nom

Marcy av, n w cor Wallabout st, runs north 17.10 x west 13.9 x south 15.10 to st, x east 23.2 to beginning. Walter Duggan to Henry Reges. nom

Same property. Henry Reges to Charlotte Dugan. nom

Montrose av, n s, 125 w Leonard st, 25x100, Isaac Goodman and Max Karol to Abraham Friedman. Mt. $6,800. 9,000

Myrtle av, n s, 64.1 w North Oxford st, 20x87.2x20.5x91.3. Frank C. Joslin to Edward Jantzer and Christian Xeller. Mt. $4,000. 10,000

New York av, e s, 80 s Fulton st, 20x80. John F. C. Elfers to Samuel J. Hughes. Mt. $2,000. 6,300

Nostrand av, e s, 19.6 s Herkimer st, 19.4x100, h & l. C. Henry Edwards to Elizabeth wife of Hugh Lawton. Mt. $3,000. 5,250

Park av, s s, 280 w Marcy av, 25x100. Emilie wife of Julius Rhinow to Louis Reer and Michael Schaffner. Mt. $2,700. See Floyd st. 6,500

Patchen av, e s, 80 n Decatur st, 20x100, h & l. George Evans to Catharine Schmidt. Mt. $3,500. nom

Prospect av, n e s, 515 s e 3d av, 20x62.11x20.10x61.3. Foreclos. Van Mater Stillwell to Catharine A. wife of William J. Golden. 9,900

Putnam av, n s, 100 e Howard av, 40x100. Robert L. Moores and Charles A. Le Quesne to William H. Waters. Mt. $17,000. exch

Putnam av, s s, 324 e Stuyvesant av, 19x100. Charles Isbill to Marion H. Tibballs. Mt. $4,500. 8,700

Putnam av, s s, 216 e Lewis av, 19x100. Kate Acor to Eleanor C. Winham. Mt. $6,500. 11,300

Putnam av, s s, 228.6 e Ralph av, 121.6x100. Alfred L. Beasley to Charles Lewis. Mt. $7,500. nom

Putnam av, s s, 275.6 e Reid av, 19.6x100. Charles H. Lohr to Charles Lewis. Mt. $4,500. 7,500

Putnam av, s s, 203.6 e Ralph av, 25x100. Charles Lewis to Charles H. Lohr. Mt. $7,200. 13,500

Railroad av, w s, 325 s Liberty av, 25x100. Jane L. Smith to Morris C. Seifert. 325

Rapalje av, n w cor Ocean av, 150x100. Pinkas Ganz to Rosa N. Geis. Mt. $800. See Throop av. exch

Same property. Morris Feldman to Pinkas Ganz. Mt. $800. 2,400

Ralph av, n w cor Park pl, 20.7x100; also,
Ralph av, w s, 60.7 n Park pl, 40x100.
Elizabeth Brand to John W. Eckelkamp. 2,050

Rockaway av, e s, 100 n Sutter av, 75x100. Marks Jacobs and Israel M. Cohen to Anna Leinfelder, of Flatlands, N. Y. 3,450

Reid av, w s, 50 n Macon st, 50x100. William M. Wilson to Bernard Levino and Walter F. Clayton. Mt. $12,000. nom

Ridgewood av, n s, 75 e Seigel av, 25x100. William J. Hamilton trustee to Sarah Gilmartin. by order of Court

Saratoga av, e s, 126.8 s McDonough st, 17.9x80, h & l. Andrew D. Baird to Isabella H. Kipp. Mt. $3,500. 6,300

Schenectady av, e s, 55.7 s Bergen st, 50x100. Mary Kunath widow to David Stern. Mt. $3,100. 7,000

Shepherd av, w s, 125 s Eastern Parkway, 25x100. Clara E. Cobb to Thomas Davies. 1,209

Snediker av, e s, 415 n Liberty av, 20x100. George Baecker to John Pertsch, New York. 2,350

St. Nicholas av, n e cor Hart st, 74x90x72.4x90. Charles Reuschenberg and Otto F. Struse to Herman Apeler and George Geyer. 2,200

Sutter av, s w cor Essex st, 48x100. John Flood to William A. Northridge. ½ part. Mt. $4,800. 3,000

Sutter av, n e cor Elton st, 90x100. Louisa D. Pratt to John Denninger and Louisa his wife. 1,800

Thatford av, w s, 100 n Belmont av, 25x100.1. Louis Ratner to Bernhart Kershkowitz, of New York. *Mt.* $3.000. 5,800
Throop av, n e cor Van Buren st, 50x100, hs & ls. James Pritchard to Mary wife of John Grogan. *Mt.* $7,500. 20,500
Throop av, w s, 75 s Quincy st, 5x100. Joseph P. Fuels to William M. Gibson. Q. C. Correction deed. nom
Throop av, e s, 25 n Wallabout st, 25x59.2x26.9x68.8. Rosa N. Geis, of New York, to Pinkas Ganz. See Conveys. exch
Throop av, w s, 75 n Ellery st, 25x100. Henry Wassmuth to William Ruoff and Emelia his wife and Louis Lavigne and Katie his wife, joint tenants. *Mt.* $2,500. 6,500
Vanderbilt av, s e cor Atlantic av, 25x70, h & l. Maria wife of William Fehleisen to Thomas Kelty. 8,500
Same property. Thomas Kelty to Thomas Kane. nom
Van Pelt av, n w cor Russell st, runs west 25 x north 100 x west 75 x north 75 x east 100 to Russell st, x south 175.
Russell st, w s, 150 s Van Pelt av, 25x100.
Phebe A. Watson wife of Beriah A. Watson, Jersey City, to Charles Engert. 4,900
Same property. Release mort. Theodore F. Wolfe to Phebe A. Watson. nom
Wyckoff av, e s, 75 n Greene av, 25x86.2x25x85.6. Kaspar Wahler and Jacob Beslet to John Frank. *Mt.* $3.000. 6,025
5th av, w s, 25.2 s 23d st, 75x100. Alexander M. White to Joseph Braun. 8,400
6th av, w s, 36 n 7th st, 16x78.10. Joel W. Sherwood to James W. Dearing. exch
22d av, n w s, 200 n e Cropsey av, 50x96.8, New Utrecht. Release mort. Amelia A. and George A. Gunther exrs. C. Godfrey Gunther to J. Bentley Squier. 312
Lot No. 157 map building lots, Canarsie, Conkling, Hendrickson & Remsen, Mary H. Conklin extrx. Henry Conkling to Hannah Cousins. 150
Lot 81 sectional map No. 5, Fort Hamilton. Benjamin B. Baptiste to Emma P. Zipf. 250
Lot 394 map of J. Worth and V. A. Strawson, Flatbush. Vincent A. Strawson to Jacob Worth. nom
Lot 336 and ½ of 313 same map. Jacob Worth to Vincent A. Strawson. nom
Lots 309 and 310 plot 2 map of G. Stryker dec'd, Gravesend. Whitfield Terriberry to William W. Sarles. 400
Lots 311 and 312 plot 2 same map. Mary T. wife of and William Stone to William W. Sarles. 400
Interior lot, 33 4 e Roebling st and 100 s South 1st st, runs east 66.8 x north 44.9 x west 66.8 x south 44.9. Henry L. Goodwin, East Hartford, Conn., to Ida Gunstone. B. & S. 2,000
Interior lot, 165 s Herkimer st and 405 e Utica av, runs east to centre Hunterfly road, x south to land Brooklyn & Jamaica R. R. Co., x west to point 405 e Utica av, x north — to beginning. Peter A. Blake to Anson H. Naylor, of New York. *Mt.* $1,700. exch
Unionville to Gravesend road, w s, at right of way, bet Schmidt and Stryker, Gravesend, 6 acres. Edward Tobin to Thomas J. Cummin. Option to purchase for $9,000. 500

WESTCHESTER COUNTY.

AUGUST 26 TO SEPTEMBER 1—INCLUSIVE.

BEDFORD.

Gorham, David F. to Mary J. Milmore, w s Middle Patent road, adj Cath. Church, 2 acres. $600
Mathews, Tertulus G. to Henry J. Fisher, w s road from Mt. Kisco to Jas. Wood's, 60x—. 200

CORTLANDT.

Butler, Adelaide L. to Blanche Frost, s e cor Nelson av and Decatur st, 50x100. 750
Green, Chas. P. to Wm. E. Flockton, n s Cortlandt st, adj Jas. O'Brien, 38x90. 450
Same to Emma G. Flockton, n s same st, adj above, 39x90. 850
Chaskel, Jas. et al., D. H. Hunt referee, to Fred. Jacobi, n s Main st, adj Geo. Dayton, 30 acres. 18,500
Simpkins, Benj. R. to Addie F. Hancock, lot 95 s s Maple st map Depew lots. nom

EASTCHESTER.

Allerton, Rachel W. and ano. to Fred. W. Chivvis et al., s e cor White Plains and New Rochelle roads, 51 acres. 57,000
Berry, John to Margt. L. Nesbitt, part lot 432 w s 5th av, Mt. Vernon, 50x105. 6,650
Bernstein, Elizh. A. and ano. to Jas. A. Young, s s "new" road, adj Wm. B. Davis, 50x106. 1,650
Same to Wm. H. McCloy, s s same, adj above, 50x106. 1,600
Same to Ida C. Shotwell, n e cor Union pl and "new" road, 100x112. 4,400
Boyd, Susie E. to Mary E. Yost, lots 106 and 107 n e s Cleveland av map Penfield property, 100x—. 6,000
Burtis, Alb. S. to Seaman Burtis, part lot 331 s s Cortlandt av, West Mt. Vernon, 26x125. 650
Bussing, John, Jr., to John J. Reynolds, part lot 72 n w s North Terrace av, West Mt. Vernon, 55x125. 1,500
Cranford, Kenneth to Melville S. Page, lots 31-34 s s St. Owen pl. 1,200
Chivvis, Ferd. et al. to Thos. Thorne, s e cor White Plains and New Rochelle roads, abt 5 acres. 8,000
Donohue, Annie to Emma Kairies, lot 117 w s Railroad av, West Mt. Vernon, 35x—. 1,250
De Groot, Alice E. et al. to Wm. H. Bard, lot 120 Fulton st, Washingtonville, 50x100. 425
Hallock, Sanford to same, lot 326 n w s Matilda st, 50x100. nom
Stearns, Sarah A. to Jos. K. Stearns, lot 938 s s 16th av, Wakefield, 100x114. 1,000
Underhill, Henry M. to Peter G. Kramer, e s Wallace st, 131 n Underhill st, 25x50. 175
White, Wm. to Chas. Stabl, lot 107 w s 9th av, Central Mount Vernon, 49x100. 1,800
Wright, Katie L. to Geo. J. Beitel, s s Lincoln st, 190 w Fairview av, 25x101. 400
Walreth, Allie N. to Wm. H. Bard, s ½ lot 71 South Washingtonville. nom

GREENBURGH.

Cunningham, Mary H. and ano. to Patrick Osborn, s s Ashford av, 75 w Railroad, 25x100. 500
Decker, Harriet S. to Geo. W. Vultee, w s Saw Mill River road, adj Jos. Coles. 20,000
Vultee, Geo. W. to The Fernwood Park Land Co., same property. 45,500
Dobbs Ferry Landy Co. to Jas. Busher, lot 31 map property grantors. 700
Same to Alice E. Butler, lots 55 and 56. 1,500
Same to Cath. R. Calkins, lots 41 and 42. 1,500
Same to Mort. T. Cowperthwaite, lot 64. 560
Same to Moses J. Freund, lot 22. 500
Same to Lee E. Foise, lots 20 and 21. 1,000
Same to Asher Foise, lot 14. 1,000
Same to Thos. Grant, lot 29. 850
Samo to Cath. Mulcahy and ano., lots 36 and 37. 1,400
Same to Cath. Murphy, lots 15 and 16. 1,700
Same to David N. Prime, lot 46. 475
Same to Cath. Rogers, lots 28, 60 and 61. 1,915
Same to Anton Treuling and ano., lots 38 aud 39. 1,600
Same to David L. Woodall, lot 12. 1,175
Jones, Cyrus P. and ano. to Abr. Le F. Elting, lots 17, 18 and 19 map lots at Ardsley. 388
Pierce, Madeline to Wilson H. Blackwell, s s Ashford road, w Railroad, 20¼ acres. nom
Blackwell, Wilson H. to D. W. Beswick, lots 604-607, 610 and 611 grantors map, Ardsley. 700
Same to Marie L. Dolson, lots 566 and 567. 275
Same to Maria L. Dolson, lot 564. 150
Same to Fred. A. Herz, lot 676. 175
Same to Frank P. Hoffman, lots 568, 571, 572 and 581. 520
Same to Emma Hoffman, lot 569 and 570. 250
Same to Jos. Israel, lot 642. 135
Same to Moses Israel, lot 643. 135
Same to Sarah A. Jones, lots 658 aud 659. 250
Same to J. Edw. Mangels, lot 677. 160
Same to Geo. E. Morey and ano., lots 708 to 711. 720
Same to John J. Murdock, lots 540, 541, 608 and 609. 720
Same to Alb. A. Salt, lots 535, 536 and 715. 695
Same to Jas. Tamagin, lot 732, 733 and 734. 570
Same to Chas. H. Van Aken, lots 538 and 539. 450
Same to Wm. H. Zahn, lot 675. 175
Same to Geo. E. Burr, lots 577 and 578. 350
Same to Matilda Hoag, lot 713. 130
Same to Edw. Ransom, lots 693, 694, 561 and 562. 870
Same to Lizzie Sampher and ano., lots A and 527 to 530. 500
Same to Mary T. Waters, lots B and 505. 450
Same to Wm. A. Walter, lots 549 and 550. 360

HARRISON.

Bull, Clara R. to Wm. R. Bull, e s Harrison av, 579 s Halstead av, abt 275x375. 3,000

MOUNT PLEASANT.

Smadbeck, Louis to Margt. A. Bormann, lots 489 and 499, Sherman Park. 200
Same to Margt. Schoenherr, lots 1310 and 1311. 350
Same to Willett Pary, lots 546, 547, 548, 651 to 655 and 657. 1,000
Same to Fred. Nauds, lot 74. 150
Same to Minna Nands, lot 97. 125
Same and ano. to Gustav Surdez and ano. lots 43, 44 and 45, Lakehurst Villa Park. 300
Same and ano. to Sarah A. Schorah, lots 381 and 382. 250

NEW ROCHELLE.

Downey, Henry B. to Albert Smalley, w s North st, 202 n Burling lane, 25x102. 750
Same to Josephine Smalley, adj above, 40x102. 1,200
Graff, Elizh. A. to Mary A. McGuirk, s s, Washington av, 65 e Webster, abt 30x70. 400
Iselin, Adrian, Jr., to Jeremiah F. Sheahan, lot 6 n s Elm st, Neptune Park, 70x133. 1,800
Miller, Mary E. to Jerome B. Latour, Jr., s w s Centre av, 50 s e Banker pl, 50x150. 2,250

OSSINING.

Herzberg, Aaron to The Westchester Town Site Co., 24 acres on Albany Post road, adj Jas. Edsall. 25,000
Williams, Ginerva to Harriet Parsons, n s Broad av, adj Marie L. Olivet, 60x126. 3,200

PELHAM.

Godfrey, Aug. to Ezra Daggett, lot 178 s s 4th st, Pelhamville, 100x100. 3,800
King, Eliz'h R. R. exr. of, to Philip Flynn, lot 341 e s Main st, bet Beach and Cross sts. 450

RYE.

Merritt, Jas. S. and ano. to Chas. Hanson, s e cor Ellendale av and Ridge st, 100x100. 325
Same to Mark A. Bradley, n s West William st, 150 w Merritt st, 50x150. 258

WESTCHESTER.

Brown, Zeno B. to Henry Nerenberg, e s Cottage Grove av, 246 s Guerlain pl, 25x110. 350
Brown, And. B. to Robt. J. McCracken, w s Elm st, 150 n Maple st, 25x100. nom
Buchanan, Annie D. to Thomas C. Cameron, e s 2d av, 140 n 1st st, Olinville, 40x100. 3,000
Camp, Hugh N. to John J. Schwing, lot 243 map McGraw estate. 300
Same to John H. Chase, lots 361 and 362. 310
Clocke, G. DeWitt to Emma J. Carter, e s Barker av, 133 n Julianna st, 33x125. 680
Same to same, n e cor Barker av and Julianna st, 34x100. 725
Cooper, Marg't et al. Jas. B. Lockwood, ref., to Wm. Torpey, lots 7 and 8 n s Main st map property Wm. Cooper, abt 48x100. 1,700
Crust, Emily to Mary Scharder, lot 1151 e s Railroad terrace, Wakefield, 109.6x105. 1,200
Graham, Wm. H. to Kath. M. Wilhelm, lot 162 s s 5th av, Wakefield, 100x114. 600
Gertz, Jos. to Herman Meyer, s e cor 2d st and 12th av, Wakefield, 64x105. 1,300
Mace, Levi H. to Marcus Henneberry and ano. lot 283 s s 7th av, Wakefield, 100x114. 1,550
Mapes, John S. to Henry Miller, s s Maitland av, 250 w Mapes av, abt 50x125. 470
Walker, Robert E. to Jas. C. Cooley, s s Eastchester road, 200 e Main st, abt 57x110. 1,500

WHITE PLAINS.

Barnes, Samuel J. et al, to Wm. T. McNeilly, s w s Lafayette st, 433 s e Fisher av, 50x105. 400
Same to Otto W. Guldemeister, n e s same, 172.7 s e Fisher av. 100x110. 800
Dusenberry, Chas. C. to Ida D. Hope, lot 10 Highland av, Highland Park, abt 3 acres. 5,000

YONKERS.

Columbia Land aud Improvement Co. to Chas. J. Rodd, lots 6 and 7 e s River av, 50x—. 1,000
Same to Ella C. Fowle, lot 8 adj above, 25x—. 500
Dickson, John to Ann Siers, lot 85 e s Beach st Herriot map, 25x98. 335
Edie, Richard, Jr., to Daniel Siers, lot 86 adj above, 25x98. 375
Ford, Cath. to John Hanifin, lots 413 and 414 map Shonnard lots. 300
Herrict, J. Groshon exr. of to Richard Edie, Jr., lot 86 e s Beach st, 25x98. 280
Kiely, Wm. P. to John Crawford, west ½ lot 61, Clinton st, 50x25. 562
Monrovia Park Co. to Geo. P. Phyfe, s s Euclid av, 100 w Ridge st, 75x100. nom
North End Land Co. to Marg. E. Thurber, e s Yonkers av, 50 n Wilbur st, 25x100. 500
Roys, Jennie E. to John Myers, n s Poplar st, 175 e Beech st, 25x100. 3,000
Siers, Ann to Jennie M. Hyatt, lot 84 e s Beech st, Herriot map, 25x98. 400
Same to And. Gowen, lot 85, adj, 25x98. 400
Shonnard, Fred. to John Hanihu, lot 667, Nepperhan av, City map. 230
Same to Ellen Cody, lot 290, Edward pl. 140
Sullivan, John B. to Marcia F. Butler, lots 37, 39, 45 and 47 n s Yonkers av, Nodine Hill. 9,800
Turner, Cornelia J. to Emilie B. Turner, e s Warburton av, adj grantee. 1,500
Yonkers North End Land Co. to John J. Melin, n w cor Tompkins and Marion avs, 51x100. 1,000

MORTGAGES.

NOTE.—The arrangement of this list is as follows. The first name is that of the mortgagor, the next that of the mortgagee. The description of the property then follows, then the date of the mortgage, the time for which it was given, and the amount. The general dates used as headings are the dates when the mortgage was handed into the Register's office to be recorded.

Whenever the letters "P. M." occur, preceded by the name of a street, in these lists of mortgages, they mean that it is a Purchase Money Mortgage, and for fuller particulars see the list of transfers under the corresponding date. Whenever the rate is not given, read as 6 per cent.

NEW YORK CITY.

AUGUST 28, 29, 31, SEPTEMBER 1, 2, 3.

Allen, Hattie B. to Samuel G. Revans. 24th st. P. M. Sub. to mort. Aug. 18, installs. $13,000
Appleby, Arthur B., Spottswood, N. J., to THE MUTUAL LIFE INS. CO. of New York. 7th av, No. 913, es, 50 s 58th st, 25x91. Sept. 3, 1 year, 5 %. 11,000
Arberg, Diedrich to George Ehret. 2d av, No. 817. Store lease. Aug. 25, demand. 600
Born, Philip to Alfred De Witt, Hyde Park, N. Y. Av A, No. 1016, e s, 25.5 n 55th st, 25x79.8. Sept. 3, 5 years, 5 %. 12,000
Boyd, Elizabeth to Pittsburgh Plate Glass Co., Pa. South 5th av, w s, 80.2 s Broome st, runs south 45.3 x west 68.2 x north 25.3 x east 6.2 x north 19.11 x east 62. Aug. 27, 3 months. 1,200
Bryant, James S. to Alexander M. Lane, Eastchester, N Y. 144th st, n s, 525 e Willis av, 25x100. Aug. 8, 3 years. 2,000
Bonfils, Belle B. wife of Frederick G., Peekskill, N. Y., to Ada A. wife of Herbert A. Shipman. Webster av, n e cor 171st st, 22.1x96.6 to Mill Brook, x27.9x95.1. Sub. to mort. $595. Aug. 28, 1 year. 500

Bridenburg otherwise Bridenburgh, Daniel to THE GERMAN SAVINGS BANK, New York. 39th st, s s, 375 w 10th av, 25x98.9. Re-recorded. April 2, due April 8, 1893. 3,000

Bannen, John to William Hall's Sons. 126th st, n s, 110 w 2d av, 75x100.11. Aug. 27, due Dec. 31, 1891. 6,000

Bernes, Emma C. to Elkin Farmer. 100th st. P. M. Aug. 28, installs. 4,000

Bauhahn, Henry D. A. to Thomas D. Mason and ano. trustees Sidney Mason dec'd. 121st st, n s, 300 e 3d av, 25x100.10. Sept. 1 3 years, 5 %. gold, 18,000

Beekman, Livingston and Etta and Emma Louderbach to Henrietta Beekman. 29th st, No. 48 W. Secures interest and taxes Jan. 25, 1887. 8,500

Burke, Thomas F. and James E. to Jeannette wife of Henry E. Nicond, Newark, N. J. Madison st. P. M. Sept. 2, 5 years, 5 %. 11,000

Same to Augustus F. Holly. Same property. P. M. 2d mort. Sept. 2, 6 months. 3,000

Canaan, Simon to Karl M. Wallach. Ludlow st, No. 16, e s, 19x87.6. Sept. 1, demand. 1,000

Cassin, James to Marie Obry. Amsterdam av, s e cor 24th st, 149.11x100. Sept. 1, 8 years, 5 %. 3,000

Cohen, Benjamin F. to Frederic J. Middlebrook, Brooklyn. 26th st, s s, 136 w 8th av. P. M. Sept. 1, 1 year, 5 %. 7,500

Same to John H. Armstrong. 26th st, No. 312, s s, 155 w 8th av. P. M. Sept. 1, 1 year or sooner, 5 %. 9,000

Cohen, Morris and Isaac to Hulda Wittner, New York, and Emanuel Glauber, Brooklyn. Columbia st. P. M. Sub. to mort. $43,000. Sept. 3, installs. 6,000

Connell, Hugh G. and Ellie E his wife to Patrick F. Ferrigan. 124th st, n s, 227 w 2d av, 20x100.11. Sept. 1, 5 years or sooner. 2,500

Coogan, Matthew to THE FARMERS' LOAN AND TRUST CO. 105th st, No 305, n s, 100 e 2d av, 25x100.11. Aug. 28, 3 years, 5 %. 15,000

Same to The Bradley & Currier Co. (Lim.). Same property. Sub. to last mort. Aug. 28, 1 month. 2,000

Cryan, Harriet N. wife of and James A to THE MUTUAL LIFE INS CO of New York. 123d st, s s, 333.4 w 6th av, 16.8x100.11. Already mortgaged to mortgagee. Aug. 31, 1 year, 5 %. 250

Cimino, Vito to Abraham Kassel. Mulberry st, No. 110; Mulberry st, No. 112. P. M. Aug. 28, due Sept. 1, 1893. 10,000

Cohn, Bernard to Eugene H. Davis, Montreal, Can. 95th st, Nos. 147-165, n s, 150 e Amsterdam av, 10 lots, each 18x100. 10 morts., each $5,000. Aug. 26, 1 year or sooner. 50,000

Same to same. 95th st, No. 145, n s, 330 e Amsterdam av, 20x100. Aug. 26, 1 year sooner. 6,500

Cokelet, Edward to George G. Reynolds, Brooklyn. Barrow st, Bedford st, Commerce st, all real estate in above block of which Stephen Cokelet died seized, being No. 71 Barrow st and lot adj on west and premises in rear of both on Commerce st. ¼ part. Aug. 27, 2 years. 2,000

Coppola, Giacomo to Julius B. Denicke. Elsmere pl, n s, 450 w Marmion av, 25x100. Aug. 28, 5 years or installs. 2,000

Conover, Lawrence V. to Daniel E. Seybel. 161st st, n s, 222.3 w Elton av, 100x89.8x100x87.11. Aug. 20, due Sept. 15, 1894, 5 %. 12,000

Dankers, Herman to George Ehret. 8th av, No. 2619, w s. Lease Aug. 25, demand. 1,000

Davis, David D., Wilton, N. H., to Mary A. R. wife of John O'Brien. 32d st. P. M. Sept. 1, 2 years or sooner, 4½ %. 26,000

Davis, Samuel to Harris Rosenthal. Rivington and Attorney sts. P. M. Aug. 31, due Jan. 10, 1892. 2,000

Decker, John W. to Paul G. Decker. Clifton st, n s, 92.5 e St. Anns av, 54x100. Sept. 2, due Sept. 1, 1892, or sooner. 5,600

Degnan, Eugene F. to A. Hupfel's Sons. Willis av, n e cor 134th st. Store lease. Aug. 28, note. 4,477

Delabarre, Elizabeth M. wife of Walter E. to Edward Delabarre, Conway, Mass. 22d st, s s, 257 e 6th av, 23x98.9. Sub. to mort. $25,000. Aug. 31, due Sept. 1, 1892. 1,000

Derlick, Albert to Emma D. Van Vleck and ano. trustees Patrick Dickie dec'd. 49th st. P. M. Sept. 1, 5 years, 5 %. 15,000

Same to Augustus F. Holly. Same property. P. M. Sub. to last mort. Sept. 1, 1 year. 1,500

Dodge, Mary S. to Amanda Wolf. 76th st, No. 10, s s, 198 w Madison av, 21.11x102.2. Aug. 29, due March 1, 1893. 5,000

Day, Eliza H. wife of and Warren H., Bridgeport, Conn., to THE MUTUAL LIFE INS. CO. of New York. 132d st, n s, 500 e Trinity or Cypress av, 100x210 to 133d st. Aug. 27, due Aug. 31, 1892. 7,000

Dalton, Thomas to THE MUTUAL LIFE INS. CO. of New York. Av A, No. 291 and 18th st, No. 441, begins Av A, n w cor 18th st, 22x90; 74th st, s s, 175 e 2d av, 25x102.2. Sept. 3, 1 year, 5 %. 11,000

Dressel, Charles and Mary his wife mortgagors with Helene Fuld mortgagee. Extension of mort. Sept. 3. nom

Ebling, Jacob to Henry Weiler. 90th st, n s, 325 e 4th av, 50x100.5. Aug. 29, 1 year or sooner. 6,000

Eck, Joseph and Maria his wife to Daniel Franzreb. 4th st. P. M. Aug. 31, installs., 5 %. 4,000

Ely-Goddard, Alice S. to Park & Tilford, a corporation. 15th st, No. 27, n s, 375 w 5th

Ebbers, D. Frederick to THE FRANKLIN SAVINGS BANK. 48th st. P. M. Sept. 1, 1 year, 5 %. 5,000

Frey, John A. to Louisa Watson. 56th st, s s, 250 w 1st av, 61x100.5. Sept. 1, 1 year, 5 %. 7,000

Fiske, Haley to Charles Buek. 70th st. P. M. Sept. 2, installs. 6,250

Gelles, Isaac to Frederic J. Middlebrook, Brooklyn. Market st. P. M. Sept. 2, installs. 14,000

Gelles, Isaac and Sarah his wife to Rebecca Isear. Madison st, No. 87, s s, 29x100. Aug. 1, 2 years. 6,000

Gieschen, Henry to John M. Robinson. 123d st and Park av. P. M. Aug. 24, due Sept. 1, 1893, 5 %. 14,000

Goodman, Louis to Mary Craft. Delancey st. P. M. Aug. 12, 1 year or sooner, 5 %. 7,500

Gunsel, Theodore to Julia A. wife of Frederick Frank and John H. Frank. 103d st. P. M. Sept. 1, 4 months or sooner, 5 %. 7,250

Grotrian, Christian to Mina Fischer. Eldridge st, No. 122, e s, 25x87.6. Aug. 25, 3 years, 5 %. 6,000

Goldman, Manasseh L. to THE UNION TRUST CO., New York. Canal st, No. 74, s s, 47.7 w Allen st, 20.4x49.7x20.5x49.7; Canal st, No. 76, s s, 68 w Allen st, 20.2x49.7; Canal st, s s, 62.7 e Eldridge st, 25x75; Allen st, No. 9, w s, 25x87.6; Allen st, No. 11, w s, 25x87.6. Aug. 28, 3 years, 5 %. 90,000

Galway, Harry to John and John J. Bell, of John Bell & Son. Columbus av, w s, 75.9 n 97th st, 25.1x100. Sub. to mort. $26,000. Sept. 3, 6 months or sooner. 2,000

Gunning, Ellen McK. to THE MUTUAL LIFE INS. CO., New York. Columbus av, e s, 50.5 n 70th st, 75x100. Aug. 27, 1 year. 60,000

Hickey, Elizabeth F. wife of John J. to Harriet H. Van Alst, Brooklyn. Union av, s w cor Home st, 70x100. Sept. 3, 1 year. gold, 2,000

Huber, Louisa wife of and Jacob mortgagors with William Weismann, Frankfurt-on-Main, mortgagee. Extension of mort. Sept. 3. nom

Hartwell, Louise M. to James Thomson. Convent av, w s, 59.11 n 143d st, 20x100. Sub. to morts. Aug. 25, 1 year. 3,000

Healy, Aaron to Alfred Gilman admr. Winthrop W. Gilman. Ferry st, n e cor Gold st, 24.10x99.9x40.5x92.4; Ferry st, n s, 24.10 e Gold st, 50.4x111.7x51.10x99.9. Aug. 22, payable on certain contingencies, 4½ %. 15,000

Heyer, Josephine wife of Oscar, Wilkesbarre, Pa., to Rachel Hurvich. 7th av. P. M. Aug. 31, 10 years or installs. 7,500

Halliday, Joseph and Mary J. to THE EMIGRANT INDUST. SAVINGS BANK. Park av, e s, 53.8 n 90th st, 28x88. Aug. 31, 1 year, 4½ %. 16,000

Same to Jeremiah J. Campion, Jr. Same property. Sub. to last mort. Aug. 31, 1 year. 2,000

Hafelin, Arnold mortgagor with Ludwig Falk mortgagee. Extension of mort. July 13. nom

Harz, Katharine and Adolph to Samuel Altheimer. 110th st. P. M. Sept. 1, 1 year or installs, 5 %. 700

Hawkins, Annie wife of Charles legatee of Thomas Dunphy to Frederick Brommer guard. of Henry D. Bultmann. Market st, No. 49, w s, 27x88. Sept. 1, 3 years, 5 %. 3,000

Haven, Emma L. wife of and Henry D. to Mary DeW. wife of Charles E. Wallack. 74th st. P. M. Sub. to morts. $17,000. Sept. 1, 3 years, 5 %. 4,000

Holck, Pauline to Nathan Federgreen, Monticello, N. Y. 74th st. P. M. Aug. 1, installs, 5½ %. 5,000

Same to same. Same property. P. M. Sept. 2, due Dec. 1, 1891, 5½ %. 500

Isidor, Franziska mortgagor with Samuel B. Sexton mortgagee. Extension of mort at 5 %. Mar. 27. nom

Isear, Rebecca wife of Sacherize to Frederick Schuchardt. Henry st, No. 184, s s, 71.6 e Jefferson st, 23.10x100.2. Sub. to mort. $14,000. July 29, due Aug. 1, 1893. 3,000

Same to same. East Broadway, No. 194, n s, 26.1x70. Lease. Collateral to last mort. July 29, due Aug. 1, 1893. 3,000

Jetter, Thomas to John Tigges. Madison av, s e cor 134th st, 100x60. Aug. 28, 6 months. See Conveys. 4,000

Same to John W. and David G. Baird exr. John Baurd. Same property. Aug. 27, 3 years. 16,000

Same to Michele Conforti. Same property. Sub. to mort. $16,000. Aug. 28, 6 months. 3,492

Same to George W. Richards. Same property. Aug. 31, due Dec. 1, 1891, or sooner. 8,000

Jacob, Leonard, Jr., to James R. Smith. 76th st. P. M. July 25, due Aug. 20, 1892, or sooner. 44,800

Same to same. Same property. Building loan. July 25, due Aug. 20, 1892, or sooner. 40,000

Johnston, Robert A. to Mary J. Coxe. Betters lane, middle line, adj land late of Mary J. Jones now of heirs of James E. Bettner, at Riverdale, 24th Ward, contains 4 52-100 acres. P. M. Sept. 1, 3 years or sooner, 5 %. 17,000

Same to Ida F. wife of James H. Fraser. Betters lane, middle line, adj land formerly of Mary J. Jones, Riverdale, 24th Ward, contains 4 73-100 acres. P. M. Aug. 12, due Sept. 1, 1894, or sooner, 5 %. 17,000

Justiniani, Jennie C. to Henry D. Winans. Lexington av, No. 458, w s, 19 n 45th st, 16.6x68. Sub. to mort. $14,000. Aug. 25, due Sept. 15, 1892, or sooner. 5,000

Judge, Hugh and Michael McFarland to Beadleston & Woerz. 3d av, No. 1799. Saloon

Jefferds, Edwin I. to George Ehret. 8th av. No. 382. Store lease. Aug. 20, demand. 4,000

Korminsky, Benjamin to Mary Harris. 165th st, n w cor Lafayette st, 50x89.8x56.2x66; Lafayette st, w s, 86 n 165th st, 25x100. Sept. 1, 2 years. 1,200

Same to Anna Baron. 75th st, No. 182, s s, 225 w 3d av, 18x102.2. Sept. 1, 2 years. 1,500

Lese, David to Marks Levin. Suffolk st. P. M. Sept. 1, 2 years or sooner. 1,000

Laforge, Isabella to Carson G. Archibald. 25th st, s s, 200 e 9th av, 50x98.9. Aug. 26, 2 years, 5 %. 2,000

Larkin, William R. to Leicester Holme ref. Amsterdam av, w s, 50 s 121st st. P. M. Sept. 1, 5 years, 5 %. 2,470

Same to same. Amsterdam av, w s, 75 s 121st st. P. M. Sept. 1, 5 years, 5 %. 2,405

Lewis, Samuel to Solomon Feinberg. Eldridge st, e s, 75.3 s Stanton st. 31.2x88.6. Sept. 2, due March 2, 1893. 5,000

Labbate, Carmella P. to Henry de F. Weekes. Mulberry st. P. M. Sept. 2, due Sept. 1, 1892, or sooner. 6,000

Marx, Davis and Rebecca his wife to Sender Jarmulowsky. Monroe st, No. 56, s s, 25.1x92.8x25.1x92.6. Aug. 28, notes. 5,000

McElroy, Daniel S. to Marie A. wife of Charles H. Steinway. Park av. P. M. Aug. 31, due Sept. 2, 1896, 5 %. 10,000

McKee, Osbourne H. and Mathilde his wife, Bensonhurst, L. I., to Celine Rheinhold. 61st st, n s, 350 e 11th av, 50x100.5. Aug. 31, due May 1, 1892, or installs. See Conveys. 6,000

McGuire, Joseph to Thomas McGuire and ano. trustees John Dowling dec'd. 60th st, s s, 195.8 w 3d av, 20x100.5. Aug. 27, 5 years, 4½ %. 18,000

McGuiness, Lizzie wife of and Edward to Judson S. Todd. 85th st, n s, 250.10 e 3d av, 25.7x101.6x25.1x102.1. Aug. 27, due Feb. 1, 1892. 20,000

Moris, Martha to David Webster exr. Caroline Webster. Robbins av, s w cor passage connecting Robbins av with Terrace pl, 25x100. Aug. 28, 3 years. 2,000

Mahoney, Daniel to Sarah A. Wright, White Plains, N. Y. Cottage st, east ½ lot 189 map of Mott Haven, 25x110. Sept. 1, 3 years. 200

Marshall, Hannah B. wife of and David W. to Richard S. Emmet trustee of Emma S. Bowman. 165th st, s s, 117.2 e Delmonico pl or Grove av, 17.2x94.2. Sept. 1, 3 years, 5 %. 3,500

McIlroy, William to THE NEW YORK LIFE INS. CO. Lenox av. P. M. Aug. 10, installs, 5 %. 16,000

Minsky, Louis to Abraham Kassel. 75th st. P. M. Sept. 1, installs. 2,000

Montanus, John J. and Emil to Henrietta E. and Minna S. Montanus. 85th st, n s, 244 e 1st av, 25x102.2. 2d mort. Sept. 1, 3 years, 5 %. 3,000

Moran, Adam to Ambrose K. Ely. 98th st, s s, 150 w 3d av, 3 lots. 3 P. M. morts., each $11,000. Sept. 1, 5 years, 5 %. 33,000

Mott, John L. B., Bellport, L. I., to Edward L. Keyes. Park av and 34th st. P. M. Aug. 27, due Sept. 1, 1892, 4½ %. 55,000

Mutzig, Charles E. to George Ehret. Grand st, Nos. 137 and 139. Lease. Aug. 31, demand. 2,000

Mars, Henrietta A., Brooklyn, to Charles Johnson. 152d st, n s, lots 1-4 map of East Morrisania, 753x428.5x254.5x374x391, contains 6 72-100 acres, except parts taken for Prospect, Union, Tinton and Wales avs. July 20, note. 500

Martin, Patrick to H. Koehler & Co., a corporation. 18th st, No. 410 E. Saloon lease. Sept. 2, demand. 550

Matter, John to THE FRANKLIN SAVINGS BANK. 44th st, n s, 300 e 11th av, 25x100.5. Aug. 4, 1 year, 5 %. 6,000

Nevers, Henry K. to William Ray. 129th st, No. 220, s s. 217 w 7th av, 17x99.11. April 29, 3 years, 5 %. 3,500

Ohl, Daniel to Pincus Lowenfeld, Morris Goldstein and Mark Blumenthal. 3d av, Nos 168 and 170, w s, 20 n 16th st, 36x60; 16th st, Nos. 145 and 147, n s, 100 w 3d av, 40x90. Lease. P. M. Sept. 1, installs, 5 %. 12,500

Oppenheim, Herman to Isaac Amdursky. Goerck st. P. M. Sub. to mort. $19,000. Sept. 1, 5 years or installs, 5 %. 4,250

Pfaff, George C. to Thomas Moore and John McLaughlin. 83d st. P. M. Sept. 2, 1 year or installs, 5 %. 2,000

Prague, John G. to John C. Tomlinson. 86th st, n s, 72.6 e 9th av, 20x100.8. Sub. to mort. $30,000. Aug. 31, 1 year, 5 %. 10,000

Putzel, Rose D. to Jacob Scholle et al. exrs. and trustees Abraham Scholle. 80th st, No. 58, s s, 199 e Madison av, 18x102.2. Aug. 31, due Sept. 1, 1894, 4½ %. 18,750

Paolantonio, Michele and Felix Mainella to Saverio and Joseph Gallo. 113th st. P. M. Aug. 20, due Sept. 1, 1893, or sooner, 5 %. 2,500

Regnier, Emile to Delilah L. Shorb. 50th st, Nos. 106 and 108 W. Lease. Sept. 1, notes. 4,000

Roach, William to James and Susan Sullivan. 146th st. P. M. Aug. 31, due Feb. 31, 1892, 5 %. 1,800

Riehl, Joseph and Agnes his wife to Michael Gebhard. 80th st. P. M. Aug. 31, installs. 5,700

Roschlau or Roschlan, George to Conrad Stein. 10th av, w s, 25.5 s 51st st, 25x100. Sept. 1, 5 years or installs, 5 %. 12,000

Ross, John H. to Henry D. Van Seggern and George W. H. Menkens. Park av and 122d st. P. M. Sept. 1, 5 years, 5 %. 28,000

Rosenbloom, Morris to Barney Cohen. Suffolk

Roth, Adolph to Sigmund Cohn. Cannon st, No. 83, w s, 110 n Rivington st, 20x82. Sept. 1, installs. 1,000

Ruff, Anthony to THE NEW YORK SAVINGS BANK. 108d st, s s, 325 w 9th av, 25x100.11. Sept. 1, due Dec. 1, 1892, 4½ %. 10,000

Ruck, John M. to Joseph P. Sauer, Jersey City, N. J. 3d av, e s, 27.2 n 75th st, 55.3x105. Aug. 31, 1 year or sooner. 20,000

Rebhau, Franz to Jacob Schmitt and Henry Weiler. Lexington av. P. M. Sub. to mort. $15,000. Aug. 31, installs, 5 %. 4,000

Same to THE DRY DOCK SAVINGS INST. Same property. Aug. 31, due Sept. 1, 1892, 5 %. 15,000

Rohrs, Frederick to Hattie Kottek. Av A, s w cor 76th st, 51.1x100. Building loan. Aug. 21, 6 months. 15,000

Same to Mary M. Post. 102d st, n e cor Park av, 27x100.11. Aug. 21, due Oct. 1, 1891. 2,000

Shields, John to Bernard Cohen. 112th st, n s, 150 e 5th av, 25x100.11. July 24, due Aug. 24, 1892. 7,500

Same to same. Same property P. M. July 24, due Aug. 24, 1892. 7,000

Stein, Viktor and Wilhelmine his wife to Jacob Siegel. Fordham (3d) av, e s, 119.5 n 167th st, 30x120. Aug. 27, 5 years, 5 %. 3,000

Sullivan, Norah wife of and Thomas J. to Eleanor K. O'Connor. 109th st, s s, 139 w Lexington av, 19x100.11. Aug. 27, 3 years, 5 %. gold, 5,500

Stolpe, Paul to Bernheimer & Schmid. Beaver st, Nos. 82 and 84 and No. 131 Pearl st. Saloon lease. Aug. 31, note, demand. 1,500

Sherman, Helen R., New Preston, Conn., to Adolph Prowchownick trustee. 55th st, s s, 146.8 e 4th av, 18.9x100.5. Aug. 31, due Sept. 1, 1894. 4,000

Schlomberg, Mary, Washington, D. C., to Nathan and Marks Rosenberg. Madison st. P. M. Aug. 31, installs. 2,750

Schnelle, William to Charles Dexheimer. Essex st, w s, 100 s Stanton st, 25x89.4. Lease. Sept. 1, installs. 2,000

Simonetti, Alexander to Lewis Levy. Baxter st. P. M. Sept. 1, 5 years or installs. 27,500

Simpson, Maria S. to Frederic J. Middlebrook. 47th st. P. M. Sept. 1, 1 year or sooner, 5 %. 6,000

Sackman, Peter mortgagor with THE TITLE GUARANTEE AND TRUST Co. mortgagee. Extension of mort. at 5 %. Sept. 1. nom

Seiferd, Lena to Helen A. Reagles widow. Fairmount av or 175th st. P. M. Aug. 31, 3 years, 5 %. 2,500

Simon, Minnie L. wife of Marcus to Joseph Steinert, Oyster Bay, L. I. 26th st. P. M. Sept. 1, installs, 5 %. 6,750

Stoddard, Emmet R. to Jennie C. Johnston. Cooper st, n s, 250 w Hawthorne st, 50x200 to Seaman av. Sept. 2, 3 years. 2,000

Sause, John A. to Conrad Stein. 34th st, Nos. 160, 162 and 164 E., and 498 3d av. Saloon lease. Sept. 2, demand. 6,000

The Church of St. James to William P. O'Connor. Henry st, n s, 240 w Market st, 25x80. Aug. 31, due Sept. 1, 1892, 5 %. 7,500

The Ursuline Convent to THE MUTUAL LIFE INS. CO. Southern Boulevard, Marion av, Travers st and Bainbridge av—block, except so much as lies north of s s of Old Williamsbridge road, and also excepting a triangular gore in s e cor of said plot. July 30, due Aug. 17, 1892. 80,000

Tabele, Maria M. to Henry C. Meyer. 127th st, No. 130, s s, 524.9 w 3d av, 16.11x99.11x16.10x99.11. Aug. 13, 5 years, 5 %. 3,000

Tiggs, John mortgagee with Michele Conforti proposed owner. Agreement as to priority of mortgages made by Thomas Jetter and said Conforti. Aug. 28. nom

Ullman, Adolph to Sigmund Cohn. Cannon st, No. 85, w s, 130 n Rivington st, 20x82. Sept. 1, due Jan. 1, 1893. 1,000

Vredenburgh, William H., Freehold, N. J., to Bernard S. Levy. Amsterdam av and 78th st. P. M. Sept. 1, 4 months. 30,000

Walker, Fernando R. to THE MANHATTAN SAVINGS INST. 3d av, n w cor 32d st, runs west 100 x north 49.5 x east 25 x south 24.8 x east 75 to av, x south 24.9 to beginning. Sept. 3, 1 year, 5 %. 10,000

Williams, Charles J. to Hyman Claman. Baxter st, No. 52. P. M. Sept. 1, installs. 5,000

Witt, August, Lackawaxen, Pa., to Newbury D. Lawton, New Rochelle, N. Y. 164th st, s s, 48.7 e Brook av, 16.9x87.10x28.1x65.4. July 24, 1 year. 1,800

Same to Eliza J. Bradley. 164th st, s s, 32 e Brook av, 16.0x65.4x27.8x43.1. July 24, 1 year. 1,400

Weber, John to Emma G. Conboy, Woonsocket, R. I. 90th st. P. M. Sept. 1, 3 years or sooner, 5 %. 15,000

Weinstein, Ascher to Frederic J. Middlebrook. 3d st. P. M. Sept. 1, 1 year or sooner, 5 %. 15,000

Same to Eliza M. Gillespy. 4th st. P. M. Sept. 1, 3 years, 5 %. 23,000

Weinstock, Morris to Bernheimer & Schmid. Henry st, Nos. 86 and 88. Saloon lease. Sept. 1, note, demand. 2,000

Wagstaff, Alfred to THE MUTUAL LIFE INS. Co., New York. Liberty st, s s, 112.6 e Greenwich st, runs east 47.4 x south 52 x west — x south 59 to Cedar st, x west 45 x north 59 x east — x north 52, being Nos. 114 and 116 Liberty st and 119 and 121 Cedar st. Aug. 27, 1 year. 110,000

Washburn, Arthur S. to Carolyn C. Vermeule. 95th st, s s, 245 e 9th av, 17x100.8. Collateral.

Work, James H. to THE MERCANTILE TRUST Co. admr. Jules B. Gimbernat. Clinton pl, n s, 100 w 5th av, 56.6x93.11. Sept. 2, due Sept. 4, 1896, 5 %. 40,000

Wells, Jennie T. to Valentine Schussler. 41st st, s s, 125 w 8th av, 25x98.9. Aug. 31, due Jan. 1, 1897, 5 %. 11,500

Weymann, Ernst C. to Henry Von Bergen. Potter pl, s s, 766.4 e Anthony or Marion av, 50x43.8x50x43.8. July 1, 2 years. 800

Wilcox, Kate B., Middletown, N. Y., to N. Taylor Phillips and Sophia P. Hendricks. Division st, No. 88, n e cor Eldridge st, 24.7x75.4 to alleyway, x21.10x86.6. Sept. 2, 3 years, 5 %. See Conveys. gold, 10,000

Werner, William, Charles Hohl and Arnold Anderholden to Gustavus, Emil and Edward Robitzek. 134th st, s s, 266.8 e Cypress av, 16.8x103.8. Aug. 24, 1 year, 5 %. 2,500

Same to same. 134th st, s s, 283.4 e Cypress av, 16.8x103.8. Aug. 24, 1 year, 5 %. 2,500

Zeller, Bernhard to Simon Rehmer. Essex st. P. M. Aug. 31, installs. 2,250

KINGS COUNTY.

AUGUST 27, 28, 29, 31, SEPTEMBER 1, 2.

Abelow, Samuel and Annie S. to Salomon Friedland. Seigel st. P. M. Aug. 19, due Aug. 17, 1892. $400

Ajello, Michele L. to Luigi Scotto di Quacquaro. President st, No. 32, s s, 23 e Van Brunt st, 22x80. Aug. 28, 5 years, 5 %. 700

Als, Jacob to Henry Scholl. 17th st, n s, 183.4 w 7th av, 17.10x90.2. Aug. 27, due Sept. 1, 1896, 5 %. 1,200

Andersen, Anton to Frederick Klebbe. 59th st, s s, 260 e 11th av, 20x100.2. July 1, 3 years. 1,000

Bacon, Jeremiah J. to Margaret Fryer. Jay st, e s, 78 n Sands st, 34x25.6. Aug. 19, 7 months. 250

Beasley, David S. to The Title Guarantee and Trust Co. Greene av, s s, 340 e Throop av, 160x100. Aug. 27, demand. 42,000

Bernauer, Constantine to William H. Jackson. Atkins av. P. M. July 28, 3 years. 195

Beer, Louis and Michael Scheffner to The Kings Co. Savings Inst. Floyd st, n s, 240 e Nostrand av, 25x100. Aug. 28, 1 year, 5 %. 4,000

Bracken, Michael to Robert Murphy. Dean st. P. M. Aug. 27, 3 years, 5 %. 1,500

Benziger, Xavier to Michael Nuber. Cleveland st, e s, 150 n Liberty av, 25x90. Aug. 31, due Sept. 1, 1894. 150

Bliss, John A. to The Title Guarantee and Trust Co. Dean st, n s, 380 w New York av, 20x100. Aug. 31, 3 years, 5 %. 7,500

Bloch, Philipp and Julia his wife to Philip Bloch guard. Frederick and Karl H. Vollmer. Berry st, s e s, 50 n e North 9th st, 25x100. Aug. 18, 1 year, 4½ %. 800

Blum, Harris and Abraham to John Keresey. North 1st st. P. M. Aug. 26, 3 years, 5 %. 2,000

Blumke, Stanislaus K. to The Bushwick Savings Bank. Johnson av, s s, 243 e Old Bushwick av, 25x100. Aug. 31, due Sept. 1, 1892, 5 %. 3,000

Bray, Bridget wife of and Patrick J. to Marcella Daly. Degraw st, n s, 310 e Smith st, 20x100. Aug. 31, 3 years, 5 %. 2,800

Brown, John to The Title Guarantee and Trust Co. High st, n s, 115 w Bridge st, 25x100. Aug. 25, due Aug. 27, 1894, 5 %. 2,500

Brown, William M. to Emerson W. Perry. McDougal st, n s, 230 w Stone av, 80x100. Aug. 13, demand. 8,000

Same to Charles A. Silver. McDougal st. P. M. Aug. 13, demand. 7,000

Brundage, James H. to John Hahn. Jerome st, e s, 80 s Dumont av, 20x100. Aug. 29, 3 years. 1,800

Braun, Joseph to Alexander M. White. 5th av. P. M. Aug. 25, due Sept. 1, 1894, 5 %. 3,400

Brenner, John F. to Charles Engert. Skillman av, s s, 250 e Union av, 25x100. Sept. 1, 30 days, 5 %. 3,425

Benedict, Jennie to Christopher Prince and ano. exrs. Sarah B. Prince. 5th st, s s, 223.4 e 6th av, 17.9x100. Sept. 1, due June 17, 1896, 5 %. 1,000

Callahan, Mary E. to James Callahan. Putnam av, s s, 189 w Howard av, 17x100. Sept. 1, demand. 1,000

Chandler, William G. and Elizabeth his wife to Anna L Schwarzenbach. 59th st, s s, 220 w 12th av, 40x100.2. Sept. 1, due Oct. 7, 1894, 5 %. 1,700

Clement, John C. to Edward C. Reinhardt. Suydam st, s s, 225 w Knickerbocker av, 25x100. Sept. 1, 3 years, 5 %. 3,000

Conzen, Lawrence to Henry Gutkes. 10th st, n e s, 75 n w 2d av, 25x100. April 15, 1 year, 5 %. 1,000

Cowley, John P. to Caroline Kloetmann. Skillman av, n w cor Ewen st, 25x75. Aug. 31, due Sept. 1, 1892, 5 %. 2,000

Carpenter, James O. to William H. Lyon. Pacific st, n s, 40 e Brooklyn av, 40x100. Sept. 1, due March 1, 1892. 5,000

Colyer, John to John F. Nelson. 9th av, s e s, 80 n e 64th st, runs southeast 80 x northeast 20 x southeast 295.6 to Fort Hamilton av, x northeast 79.3 x northwest 397.11 to 9th av, x southwest 16.10, New Utrecht. Aug. 29, demand. 500

Chlebowski, Philipp, New York, to George Covert. Stockton st. P. M. Aug. 25, 5 years, 5 %. 1,200

Chinnock, George H. to Phillips Abbott. Marcy

Christensen, Margaretha, Newark, N. J., to The South Brooklyn Co-operative Building and Loan Assoc. 22d st, s s, 325 e 3d av, 25x100. Aug. 25, installs. 1,250

Cogan, John J. to Adolph Sussman. Cleveland st. June 9, due June 15, 1894. See Conveys. 141

Collins, Adelaide L. wife of James to Rose M. wife of William A. Watson. Ashford st, w s, 125 s Vienna av, 40x100; Ashford st, e s, 125 s Vienna av, 60x100; Wortman av, n w cor Barbey st, 40x85; Wortman av, n s, 40 w Barbey st, — to M. S. Duryeas lane, x85; Stanley av, s s, 40 w Warwick st, 60x85; Wortman av, n s, 40 e Barbey st, 60x85; Barbey st, e s, 225 n Wortman av, 80x100. Aug. 21, due Jan. 21, 1892, 5 %. 2,250

Collins, Charles H. and Frank Bailey with The Title Guarantee and Trust Co. all mortgagees. Agreement as to priority of morts. made by Herman Becker and Patrick Maloney. Aug. 29. nom

Conway, John R., New York, to James D. Lynch. 82d st, n e s, 220 s e 22d av, 120x100. Aug. 22, due Aug. 29, 1894, 5 %. 1,900

Cornelius, Mary F. to Lucy W. Peck. Greene av, n s, 337.6 e Tompkins av, 18.9x100. Sept. 1, 3 years, 5 %. 2,000

Craigen, George J. to Peter Lawson, Jersey City, N. J. Union pl, s w cor Lott st, runs south 115 to Butler st, x west 20 x north 90 x west 80 x north 25 to Union pl, x east 100, Flatbush. Aug. 28, demand. 1,060

Craigen, George J. to J. T. E. Litchfield & Co. Butler st, n w cor Lott st, 20x90x80x25x100x115, Flatbush. Aug. 31, due Oct. 1, 1891. 2,719

Crooke, Charles to Alois Lazansky. Lots 31-36 map Crooke estate, Flatbush. Aug. 25, due Sept. 1, 1892. 3,000

Davies, John A. to Emilio del Pino. Fulton st. P. M. Aug. 28, due in Aug. 1892. 1,500

Day, William D. to Richard P. McCully. Ralph av, south cor Broadway, 68.7x48.3x48.10, gore. Aug. 26, due Sept. 1, 1893. 1,000

Degnan, Maria to Hannah D. White. Fulton av and Bradford st. P. M. Aug. 26, 2 years. 1,000

Denison, Charles H. to Minerva A. Ketcham. 6th st. P. M. June 24, due Sept. 1, 1894, 5 %. 4,500

De Venecia, Concepcion T. to Philip Neidlinger. St. Johns pl, s s, 373 w 6th av, 19x128x19x127.6. Aug. 27, 3 years, 5 %. 4,500

Dillon, Catherine, Mary L., Anastasia and Eliza by George Corey guard. and James Dillon to Margaret G. McGrain. Navy st, e s, 113 s Tillary st, 25x100. Aug. 26, 3 years, 5 %. 700

Dolan, Matthew and Catharine his wife to Margaret Curtin. Ford st. Aug. 27, installs. See Conveys. 450

Donnelly, Mary V. to Adolph Sussman. Cleveland st, e s, 280 n Hegeman av, 20x100. June 9, due June 15, 1894. 141

Denike, Thomas S. to Susan E. Blodgett, Stockbridge, Mass. Pacific st, n s, 231.8 w Utica av, 4 lots. 4 morts., each $1,800. P. M. July 31, due Nov. 1, 1894. 7,200

Same to Helen Embury. Pacific st, n s, 199 w Utica av, 2 lots. 2 morts., each $1,800. July 31, due Nov. 1, 1894. 3,600

Same to Samuel T. and George W. Skidmore exrs. James H. Skidmore. Pacific st, n s, 182.8 w Utica av. P. M. July 31, due Nov. 1, 1894. 1,800

Same to same. Pacific st, n s, 166.4 w Utica av. P. M. July 31, due Nov. 1, 1894. 1,800

Same to Mary A. Skidmore, Great Neck, L. I. Pacific st, n s, 150 w Utica av. P. M. July 31, due Nov. 1, 1894. 1,800

Same to Aymar Embury. Pacific st, n s, 133.8 w Utica av. P. M. July 31, due Nov. 1, 1894. 1,800

Same to Frank J. Blodgett. Pacific st, n s, 101 w Utica av, 2 lots. 2 morts., each $1,800. P. M. July 31, due Nov. 1, 1894. 3,600

Dowley, Michael to Virginia A. Kleine. Cornelia st, s e s, 84 s w Hamburg av, 432x100. Building loan. Aug. 18. 33,600

Same to same. Central av, east cor Cornelia st. P. M. Aug. 18, demand. 13,700

Dunn, Robert J. to Elizabeth Kolb. Lot 288 map 430 lots of Jacob Worth and Vincent A. Strawson, Flatbush. Aug. 21, 3 years. 500

Drew, Cornelius to Phebe Stilwell. 9th st. P. M. July 30, 3 years. 2,600

Egan, Mary E., Jamaica, L. I., to Augustin and Thomas Walsh. 7th st, n s, 100 w 3d av, 140x100; 6th st, s s, 200 w 3d av, 40x100. Aug. 31, 3 years. 5,000

Eiermann, Frederick to Emeline Gallup. Jerome st, w s, 240 s Blake av, 20x100. Aug. 15, 3 years. 1,000

Enfinger, Johann W. to Franz Franz. Powers st. P. M. Aug. 31, installs, 5 %. 300

Enright, Thomas and Mary to Edward Lavin. 1st st. P. M. July 8, installs. 3,500

Evans, Sarah C. wife of and George A. to The Mutual Life Ins. Co., New York. Washington av, e s, 180 s Willoughby av, 40x200 to Hall st. Aug. 28, 1 year. 18,000

Eckelkamp, John W. to Elizabeth Brand. Ralph av, n w cor Park pl, 20x100; Ralph av, w s, 60.7 n Park pl, 40x100. Sept. 1, 3 years, 5 %. 800

Enggren, Charles A. to William E. Kay. Windsor pl. P. M. Sept. 1, installs. 1,150

Feldman, Israel to Jacob Paskus. Seigel st, n s, 225 w Leonard st, 25x100; Seigel st, n s, 100 w Leonard st, 25x100. Sept. 1, 1 year. 1,000

Frank, John and Rosa his wife to Kaspar Wahler and Jacob Boslet. Wyckoff av.

Fowler, Mary E. wife of and Levi to John L. Voorhies, Comm'r of Investment, Gravesend. St. Marks av, n , 340 e Franklin av, 20x128.6. Aug. 24, 3 years. 7,500

Frishe, Friedrich and Gertrude to The German Savings Bank, Brooklyn. Lorimer st, w s, 100 s Ten Eyck st, 24x89.7. Aug. 10, due Dec. 1, 1892, 5 %. 3,000

Fritz, Joseph to Sarah A. C Moore. Himrod st. P. M. Sept. 1, 1 year, 5 %. 800

Fuhr, Jacob to Charles Engert. Skillman av, s s, 225 e Union av, 25x100. Sept. 1, 30 days, 5 %. 3,585

Fagan, Dora J. to Agnes H. Davies. Somers st, s s, 620 e Stone av, runs west 20 x south 45.5 to Brooklyn and Jamaica plank road, x southeast 24.2 x north 58.10. Aug. 26, 1 year. 890

Fischer, Emma to Janet and James Pirnie exrs. and trustees John M. Pirnie. Lafayette st, s s, 150 e Grand av, 18.9x100. Sept. 1, due Dec. 5, 1894, 5 %. 3,000

Fisk, Henrietta to The Title Guarantee and Trust Co. Navy st, e s, 61.7 n Myrtle av, 50x100. Aug. 26, demand. 3,500

Fisk, Henrietta to Edward T. Nicoll. Navy st, e s, 61.7 n Myrtle av, 50x100. Sub. to mort. $23,500. Aug. 28, due Dec. 1, 1891. 1,550

Flanagan, William to William Gibbens. St. Johns pl, s s, 279.7 e 6th av, 20x93.6x—x94.4. Aug. 27, 3 years, 5 %. 7,000

Same to same. St. Johns pl, s s, 259.7 e 6th av, 20x94.4x—x95.2. Aug. 27, 3 years, 5 %. 7,000

Fletcher, George H. to Charles E. O'Hara trustee for Warren B. Sage. Lincoln pl. P. M. Aug. 6, due Aug. 27, 1894, 4½ %. 12,000

Fowler, Bernard to Davis Barnett. Clinton av, e s, 155.4 s Gates av, 27x120. Aug. 26, demand. 2,000

Franz, Franz to Charles E. Dillon, Jamaica, L. I. Powers st, s s, 132.7 e Olive st, 25x65.11x25.5x70.5. Aug. 27, 3 years, 5 %. 1,500

Friederici, Frank to Franz Kannengieser and Louise his wife. Hamburg av, north cor Madison st, 25x80. Aug. 10, due July 1, 1896. 4 %. 900

Frothingham, Minnie to West Brooklyn Land and Improvement Co. 55th st. P. M. Aug. 16, 4 years, 5 %. 300

Graham, Thomas P. to Alice W. Hayes, Newark, N. J. North 10th st, s w s, 75 s e Roebling st, 100x100. April 20, 3 years or installs, 5 %. 1,500

Ganter, Josephine to George Gutting and Charles A. Wagner. Stanhope st. P. M. Aug. 27, 5 years, 5 %. 900

Ganz, Pinkas to Rose N. Geis. Throop av. P. M. Aug. 27, due Aug. 24, 1894. 3,550

Gillman, Boaz to Jacob C. Bergen, Jamaica, L. I. Suydam pl, w s, 94 s Herkimer st, 21x97. Aug. 28, 2 years. 500

Gilmartin, Sarah to Julia Carroll widow. Ridgewood av, n s, 75 e Seigel av, 25x100. Aug. 31, 2 years. 250

Goetz, John to Margaret A. wife of James E. Young. Dean st. P. M. Aug. 26, 5 years, 5 %. 3,500

Gollner, Ervin G. to Charles D. Burwell, Frank A. Barnaby and Susan E. Fingarr. 6th st, n s, 397.10 w 5th av. P. M. Sub. to mort. $17,500. Aug. 1, demand. 3,900

Same to The Title Guarantee and Trust Co. Same property. Aug. 1, demand. 18,900

Gottlock, John W. to The East Brooklyn Co-operative Building Assoc. Warwick st. P. M. Aug. 26, installs. 3,500

Greenblatt, Isaac to Regina Loeb. McKibbin st. P. M. Aug. 31, due Sept. 1, 1892, 5 %. 900

Grogan, Mary wife of and John to James Pritchard. Throop av, Van Buren st. P. M. Aug. 25, due Sept. 1, 1896. 10,000

Gruner, Clementine wife of and Louis to The Title Guarantee and Trust Co. Woodbine st. P. M. Aug. 31, 3 years, 5 %. 2,000

Same to George W. and Charles H. Francisco. Same property. 2d mort. Aug. 31, installs. 1,300

Gutting, George to The Williamsburgh Savings Bank. Putnam av, s e s, 175 n e Bushwick av, 50x100. Aug. 26, 1 year, 5 %. 5,000

Gutting, George and Charles Wagner to Elizabeth Timmes. Seigel st. P. M. Aug. 31, 1 year, 5 %. 500

Golden, Catharine A. to The Hamilton Trust Co. Prospect av. P. M. Sept. 1, 1 year, 5 %. 1,000

Guerra, Benjamin J. to Liona Ryan. Logan st. P. M. Aug. 26, installs. 1,400

Heath, Delmar W. to Reuben Ross. Montague pl, n s, 78 e Hicks st, 51x100. Sub. to morts. Sept. 1, due March 1, 1892. 10,000

Heidelberger, Conrad to Willis H. Young, Hempstead, L. I., Greenpoint av, s s, 151.10 w Manhattan av. P. M. Sub. to mort. on this and other property $25,000. Sept. 1, 1 year. 9,857

Same to George H. Gerard. Greenpoint av, s s, 71.10 w Manhattan av. P. M. Sub. to mort. on this and other property $25,000. Sept. 1, 1 year. 5,143

Same to Charles H. Reynolds. Greenpoint av, s s, 71.10 w Manhattan av. P. M. Sept. 1, 5 years, 5 %. 25,000

Heim, Frank X. to William O. Moore et al. exrs. Abraham Underhill. Eldert st, P. M. July 20, 3 years, 5 %. 2,500

Same to Leopold J. Lippmann. Same property. 2d mort. July 20, installs, 5 %. 500

Hemmer, Anna M. wife of and Peter to Margaretha Hemmer. Hopkinson av, e s, 167 s Herkimer st, 28x97.6. Aug. 1, 1 year. 1,000

Habar, Israel, New York, to Morris and Nancy Levin. Seigel st. P. M. Aug. 29, 4 years. 1,250

Hampton, Emery J. to The East Brooklyn Co-operative Building Assoc. Lafayette av. P. M. May 25, 1891, installs.; this mort. was recorded Aug. 27, 1891, and re-recorded Aug. 29, 1891. 2,750

Hampton, Harriet L. wife of and Louis G. mortgagors with Henriette S. Corradi, New York. Extension of mort. April 9. nom

Hart, John F. to John Lahey, Gravesend, L. I. Hawthorne st, s s, 360.6 w Nostrand av, 60x106, Flatbush. Aug. 1, due Aug. 24, 1894, 5 %. 5,000

Hefter, Leonard to Elisabeth Schano widow. Adams st. P. M. Aug. 31, 5 years, 5 %. 6,400

Heisman, Hyman to Catharine Z. Bogert. Grand st. s s, 98.3 w Bedford av, 25x100. Aug. 27, 3 years, 5 %. 4,500

Hill, George G. to Sarah C. Savage trustee Elihu Chauncey. Pacific st, s s, 497.4 e Rochester av. P. M. Aug. 26, 1 year, 5 %. 2,100

Same to Sarah C. Savage individ. Vanderveer st. P. M. Aug. 26, 1 year. 1,900

Hirshkowitz, Bernhart to Louis Ratner. Thatford av. P. M. Aug. 26, installs. 1,800

Hoffmann, Henry W. to Sophia H. Howard, London, Eng. Park av, n e cor North Elliott pl, 20.6x44.7x26x44.11. Aug. 28, 1 year, 5 %. 6,000

Hughes, James to Joseph Liebmann and Theodore Obermeyer. Greenpoint av, s s, 75 e Moultrie st, 25x130. Aug. 28, 1 year, 5 %. 500

Humphrey, Owen W. to Peter Doelger. Van Cott av, n w cor Sutton st, 100x103.9. Aug. 27, 3 years, 5½ %. 15,000

Itson, Annie C. wife of and Henry to Charles A. and Louisa Schoppa, Park Ridge, N. J. Ellery st, s s, 300 w Tompkins av, 12.6x100. Aug. 26, 1 year. 300

Jenkins, Theodore S. to Samuel Hubbard. Van Siclen st, w s, 428.3 s Av "T," 126x143.5. Aug. 31, 3 years. 1,500

Johns, Henry W. to The Phenix Chemical Works. 40th st. P. M. Aug. 1, 5 years. 20,000

Kaplan, Morris, Jacob Epstein, Fannie Levy and Jacob Lieberman to James G. Roberts. Belmont av, s w cor Powell st, 100x300. Aug. 25, due Feb. 25, 1893, or sooner. 1,350

Kemp, Abraham to George P. Klockert. McKibbin st. P. M. Aug. 24, installs, 5 %. 2,900

Kempton, Edwin to The Title Guarantee and Trust Co. Adelphi st, w s, 199.6 s Greene av, 18.6x100. Aug. 27, due Sept. 1, 1894, 5 %. 2,500

Kipp, Isabella H. to Andrew D. Baird. Saratoga av, e s, 126.8 s McDonough st, 17.9x80. Aug. 26, 3 years or installs. 2,300

Kouwenhoven, Caroline wife of and Johannes to Joseph Brennan. Neck road, n s, 412.8 e of Jane E. Stillwell, 4 11,167-43,500 acres, except part conveyed to Mary C. Hatton. Aug. 25, due Feb. 19, 1894. 500

Kriete, Johann, Astoria, L. I., to Richard F. Carpenter. South 8th st, s w cor Berry st, 50x75; Berry st, w s, 75 s South 8th st, 25x72. Aug. 28, 3 years, 5 %. 8,000

Krimko, Joseph and Philip to Moritz Goldberger. Belmont av. P. M. July 30, 5 months. 300

Kuck, Hermann to The John H. Shults Co-operative Building and Loan Assoc., Brooklyn. Rock st. P. M. Aug. 31, installs. 2,200

Kunath, Mary to David Stern. Flushing av. P. M. Aug. 31, due Sept. 1, 1894, 5 %. 1,600

Kunz, Joseph to William J. Kaiser. Bartlett st. P. M. Aug. 31, 5 years, 5 %. 5,500

Kurth, Richard and Jane F. his wife to George W. and Charles H. Francisco. Woodbine st. P. M. Sub. to mort. $2,000. Aug. 25, installs. 2,000

Same to The Title Guarantee and Trust Co, Same property. P. M. Aug. 25, 3 years, 5 %. 2,000

Knapp, John L., Andrew and Henry, of Knapp Bros., to The South Brooklyn Savings Inst. Harrison st, n s, 21.6 w Hicks st, 42.8x94.10. Sept. 2, 1 year, 5 %. 2,000

Kopf, Claus to Anna M. Winterberg. Av L, east cor East 94th st, 100x175, Canarsie. May 10, due July 1, 1893, 5 %. 2,000

Kreppein, Joseph and Marie his wife to Smith E. Hendrickson. Kingsland av. P. M. Aug. 1, 5 years. 800

Levi, Joseph and Morris Blum to Eva Bach. Ewen st. P. M. Aug. 31, 5 years, 5 %. 3,300

Lurie, Lasar to George Gutting and Charles Wagner. Seigel st. P. M. Sept. 1, installs. 1,700

Leahey, John C. to Harvey W. Pearce, Whitestone, L. I. North 7th st, n e s, 125 n w Berry st, 25x100. Aug. 29, due Sept. 1, 1893. 1,000

Lebewohl, Louis to Herbert C. Smith. Osborn st. P. M. Aug. 20, due Sept. 1, 1891. 600

Levin, Joseph and Sara Borenstein to Michael and Ellen Sullivan. Watkins st. P. M. Aug. 1, installs. 900

Lewis, Jacob and Michael to Israel Jarashow. Seigel st. P. M. Aug. 29, due Sept. 1, 1896. 2,900

Lewis, Margaretha to George H. Smith. McDougal st. P. M. Aug. 29, installs, 5 %. 1,500

Loewenstein, Marie A. to Jose Gestal. South Elliott pl. P. M. Aug. 29, due April 1, 1893, 5 %. 1,500

Mailhouse, Emma to Isabella Mullen. Baltic st, n e s, 198 s e Henry st, runs northeast 99.10 x southeast 23.7 x southwest 41.4 x southwest 58.7 to Baltic st, x northwest 25. Aug. 31, 3 years. 500

McDermott, Peter to Charles H. Reynolds. Greenpoint av, n s, 550 e Manhattan av, 25x100. Aug. 31, 5 years. 250

McNab, Elizabeth P. to William H. Reynolds. Marion st. P. M. July 23, due Aug. 1, 1892. 3,500

McGonigle, Patrick Samuel O'Connor. 10th st. P. M. Sept. 2, no int. 600

Merrick, George W. to Crescentia Saile. Locust st, w s, 1,687.6 n 2d st, 37.6x100. Aug. 31, due Sept. 1, 1892. 750

Mould, Edward to Crescentia Saile. Chestnut st, w s, 78.2 s Jamaica av, 25x100. Aug. 24, 2 years or sooner. 500

Maguire, Charles E to Theodore Kiendl. Warwick st. P. M. Aug. 26, 1 year. 500

Malcolm, Mary F. wife of and Charles E. to Ida F., Harriet E. and Oliver T. Hewlett. McDonough st, n s, 92 w Reid av, 16.6x100. Aug. 31, due May 1, 1894, 5 %. 3,000

Manneschmidt, Jacob to George W. Conselyea and Anna M. Irwin. Flushing av and Bushwick av. P. M. Sept. 1, 1 year, 5 %. 12,800

Martin, Anna to Edward P. Loomis. Van Voorhis st. P. M. Aug. 27, 3 years, 5 %. 3,000

Martin, Edward to Freeman Clarkson and ano. trustees Elizabeth Steers dec'd. Grant st, s s, 25 e New York av, 25x93.11, Flatbush. Aug. 15, demand. 150

Marvin, William H. to Tunis G. Bergen. 28th st, s s, 300 w 5th av, 25x100.2. Aug. 27, due Sept. 1, 1894, 5 %. 3,800

McBean, Archibald N. to James D. Rankin and James Ross. 2d st, s s, 227.9 w 8th av, 20x95. Aug. 26, 1 year. 774

McGarl, George W., New York, to Anna M. Ferris. Greenwood av, East 3d st. P. M. Aug. 19, 5 years, 5 %. 450

Mehrmann, Louis to Louis Bossert. Jefferson st, w s, 248.6 s Fulton av, 25x100; Jefferson st, w s, 280.8 n Atlantic av, 25x100. Aug. 22, 4 months. 1,794

Miller, John to Gustave Meiners. Williams av, w s, 175 s Belmont av, 25x100. Aug. 28, 5 years. 1,800

Morgenroth, Pauline wife of and Henry to Mary wife of John McCarney, Sea Cliff, L. I. Heyward st. P. M. Aug. 15, 5 years, 5 %. 2,500

Moores, Robert L, and Charles A. Le Quesne to Benjamin Moore & Co., a corporation. Putnam av, n w s, 260 n e Broadway, 20x100. Aug. 20, notes. 1,324

Mowbray, Andrew to Charles J. Patterson. Schermerhorn st, n e s, 142.6 n w Bond st, 50x100.9; 17th av, w s, 325 n Bath av, 75x108.4, New Utrecht. Aug. 26, 1 year. 1,200

Nathan, Isaac and Israel Lippmann to Goodman Shapiro, Abraham Dinnerstein and Mayer Max. Thatford av, w s, 100 n Riverdale av, 50x200 to Rockaway av. June 22, installs. 125

Norris, William H. and William Bowers to James McLaren. 40th st, s s, 170 w 3d av, 80x100. Aug. 31, due May 6, 1891. 2,380

Same to Albro J. Newton. 40th st, s s, 125 w 3d av, 125x100.2. Aug. 31, due July 16, 1892. 2,600

Neger, Joseph to Helena Lungershausen. Stagg st. P. M. Aug. 31, 3 years, 5 %. 1,000

O'Donoghue, Anna M. C. to Teresa Lang. 52d st. P. M. Aug. 17, 3 years, 4 %. 600

Peer, Lucretia S. widow and William H. Peer to The Greenpoint Savings Bank. Meserole av, s w cor Lorimer st, 25x100. Sept. 1, 1 year. 1,000

Park, Alfred to Phebe E. Rork, Lansing Co., Mich. Hamilton av, n w s, 574.11 n e Concord st, 25x100x24.9x100. Aug. 28, due Aug. 27, 1894, 4½ %. 912

Parmer, Ada wife of and Lewis to Mary W. Smith. Watkins st, w s, 100 s Eastern Parkway, 51.6x100. Aug. 26, demand. 200

Peiffer, Margaretha to Katharina Diehlmann. Stockton st, s s, 150 w Lewis av. P. M. Aug. 31, due Sept. 1, 1894, 5 %. 1,500

Pertsch, John to Michael Kamp. Snediker av. P. M. Aug. 26, 3 years, 5 %. 1,450

Pitlage, Ellen G. to John Conselyea. Leonard st, w s, 25 s Jackson st, 25x69.11x25x71.2. Aug. 28, 3 years. 600

Phythian, Thomas to Albert Berry. Warren st, n w s, 50 n e Lexington av, 50x125. Aug. 10, due July 1, 1896. 1,200

Quick, Silas W. to Adolphus F. Quick. Oakland st. P. M. Aug. 31, 3 years. 2,500

Quinn, James to The Equitable Co-operative Building and Loan Assoc. Carlton av. P. M. Aug. 26, installs. 4,750

Radcliffe, Thomas H. to Emilie K. Ecks. McDonough st, s s, 62 e Ralph av, 19x90. Sub. to morts. $5,500. Aug. 29, 1 year. 1,000

Redding, Mary to Mary L. Myers, New York. Navy st, n e cor Johnson st, 16.11x100.5x7.4x25x98.10. Aug. 26, installs. 135

Regan, Thomas F. to Thomas P. Mulligan. Atlantic av, s s, 25 w Clinton st, 21.8x80. Mar. 19, 2 years, 5 %. 1,000

Reynolds, William H. to The Title Guarantee and Trust Co. Hancock st, s s, 255 w Tompkins av, 20x100. Aug. 29, 1 year, 5 %. 8,000

Same to same. Hancock st, s s, 215 w Tompkins av, 20x100. Aug. 29, 1 year, 5 %. 8,000

Same to same. Macon st, n s, 237.6 w Marcy av, 5 lots, each 19.6x100. 5 morts., each $7,500. Aug. 28, 3 years, 5 %. 37,500

Reynolds, William and William H. to same. Hancock st, s s, 195 w Tompkins av, 20x100. Aug. 29, 1 year, 5 %. 9,000

Same to same. Hancock st, s s, 175 w Tompkins av, 20x100. Aug. 29, 1 year, 5 %. 8,000

Rice, Mali, Newark, N. J., to Hermann Rhein. Richardson st. P. M. Aug. 28, due Sept. 1, 1897. 650

Roberts, James G. and Charles G. Reynolds to Maria L. Linnington. Riverdale av, Sackman st. P. M. Aug. 14, due May 1, 1896. 5,600

Same to same. Sackman st, Newport st. P. M. Aug. 14, due May 1, 1896. 5,000

Same to same. Sackman st, Newport st. P. M. Aug. 14, due May 1, 1896. 5,000

Same to same. Sackman st and Lott av. P. M. Aug. 14, due May 1, 1896. 5,000

Same to same. Christopher av, Newport st. P. M. Aug. 14, due May 1, 1896. 5,000

Same to same. Christopher av and Lott av. P. M. Aug. 14, due May 1, 1896. 5,000

Same to same. Christopher av and Lott av. P. M. Aug. 14, 1½ years. 3,000

Same to same. Sackman st and Riverside av. P. M. Aug. 14, due May 1, 1896. 6,160

Robinson, Mary wife of and Henry to John B. Myenborg, Jr. Flatbush av, south cor Malbone st, —x—, Flatbush. All title. Aug. 24, due Aug. 1, 1892. 200

Rodrigues, Mansel to Henrietta D. Dexter, Nallego Co. Temple Court, Flatbush. P. M. Aug. 13, due Sept. 1, 1896. 600

Rohlfs, Johanna wife of William to William Laue. Hopkins st, s s, 600 w Marcy av, 25x100. Aug. 24, 2 years. 339

Same to David Mayer. Same property. Aug. 24, 1 year. 1,391

Royar, Frederick, Jr., and Carolina his wife to Frederick Royar, Sr. Harrison av, e s, 50 n Gerry st, 25x100. Sept. 1, 5 years, 5 %. 2,700

Ruoff, William and Emelia his wife and Louis Lavigne and Katie his wife to Henry Wassmuth. Throop av. P. M. Aug. 31, due Sept. 1, 1894, 5 %. 1,000

Russell, Peter to Max Berliner. Huron st. P. M. Aug. 27, installs. 1,350

Rutan, Rynier S. to Signor A. Buckley. 15th st. P. M. Aug. 31, due Sept. 1, 1894, 5 % 900

Radcliffe, Thomas H. to Jacob C. Bergen. McDonough st, s s, 156.8 e Ralph av, 18.8x100. Sub. to mort. $4,500. Aug. 31, 1 year. 800

Read, Amelia J. to Thomas Carroll. Degraw st. P. M. Sept. 2, 2 years. 750

Reiche, Carl to Andrew Ginter. Troutman st, n s, 100 w Hamburg av, 40x100. Aug. 31, due Sept. 1, 1893, 5 %. 300

Rook, Nora A., Newport, R. I., to The Germania Savings Bank, Kings Co. Schermerhorn st, s s, 168 w Hoyt st, 22x100. Sept. 2, 1 year, 5 %. gold, 3,000

Ross, Josephine L. to John H. Vanderveer. South Elliott pl, w s, 72 2 s De Kalb av, 19.10 x86x20.3x81.11. Sept. 2, 1 year. 300

Ruth, Abraham to Warren B. Sammis, Edgewater, N. J. Osborn st, e s, 175 s Eastern Parkway, 25x100. Sept. 1, 2 years. 2,000

Sarles, Carrie to Lawrence Hurlburt. McDonough st, s s, 108.4 w Ralph av, 18.4x100. Aug. 28, installs. 1,200

Schenkel, Christina to The Bushwick Savings Bank. Hart st, n s, 59.4 w Central av, 44x71. Aug. 31, due Sept. 1, 1892, 5 %. 2,000

Scherf, Henry to August C. Scharmann. Schaeffer st, n w s, 425 n e Division av. P. M. Aug. 25, 3 years, 5 %. 6,000

Same to same. Same property. Aug. 25, 3 years, 5 %. 1,500

Schmidt, Catharine to George Evans. Patchen av. P. M. Aug. 25, due Sept. 1, 1894, 5 %. 600

Schmitt, Magdalena widow and Joseph G. Schmitt heir Andrew Schmitt to Charlotte Barnett. Central av, e s, 25 s Starr st, 25x100. Aug. 27, 3 years, 5 %. 2,100

Schwab, William to Catharina Lipsius. Melrose st, n w s, 250 n e Knickerbocker av, 25x85. Aug. 25, due Sept. 1, 1892, 5 %. 3,500

Same to same. Melrose st, n w s, 225 n e Knickerbocker av, 25x85. Aug. 25, due Sept. 1, 1892, 5 %. 3,500

Sedlmayer, Mary to Peter Riebling. Linden st. P. M. Aug. 27, 2 years. 1,900

Seifters, Pincus to Mary E. wife of Darwin R. James. Stanhope st. P. M. Aug. 28, 3 years, 5 %. 1,300

Simon, Isaac to Henry Roth. Lee av. P. M. Sept. 1, 1 year. 2,500

Simpson, William to Ellen Byrne. Hoyt st, n e cor Carroll st, 20x90. May 30, 2 years. 300

Smith, Wilmer C. to Charlotte Leavens. Van Sielen av, w s, 100 s Arlington av, 25x100; Miller av, e s, 125 s Arlington av, 40x100; Aug. 28, 3 years, 5 %. 2,000

Sparling, Philip R. F. and Margaret his wife to James G. Carroll. 45th st. P. M. Aug. 29, 2 years. 300

Spatz, Michael and Anna to Marie Lang. Middleton st. P. M. Aug. 27, due Sept. 1, 1894, 5 %. 1,100

Squier, J. Bentley to Cornelius Cowenhoven. 22d av, n w s, 200 n e Cropsey av, 50x96.10. Aug. 27, 3 years. 4,000

Stader, Charles F. and Elizabeth his wife to Jacob Bossert. Wallabout st. P. M. Aug. 25, installs, 5 %. 2,000

Starrett, George to The Title Guarantee and Trust Co. Hancock st, s s, 133.4 w Marcy av, 16.8x100. Aug. 27, 3 years, 5 %. 5,000

Same to same. Hancock st, s s, 100 w Marcy av, 16.8x100. Aug. 27, 3 years, 5 %. 5,000

Stewart, Martha W. to Laura E. Mills. Clermont av, w s, 95.1 n Greene av, runs west 71.10 x north 6.11 x west 13.3 x south 30 x east 13.3 x north 2.7 x east 71.7 to av, x north 20.6. Sept. 1, 3 years, 5 %. 3,000

Stevens, Annie B. wife of George H. to Elizabeth A. Whiting. Lewis av. P. M. Sept. 1, 3 years, 5 %. 5,000

Same to Frederick B. Norris. Same property. P. M. Sept. 1, 1 year, 5 %. 1,000

Strubel, John and Barbara his wife to Thomas W. Kiley. Wyckoff av, s w s, 25 s e De Kalb av, 29.10x90.11. Aug. 31, due Nov. 30, 1892. 1,015

Sucker, Frank, Bertha and Emma Sucker to Lizzie Sucker. Newell st, w s, 416.5 n Van Cott av, 28x100. June 30, due July 1, 1894, 5 %. 2,000

Strawson, Vincent A. to Richard Thall. Lots 283-287, 296, 303-309, 313, 341, 342, 347, 348, 349, 373, 374, 383-386, 389-393, 412, 416, 417, 429 and 430 map Worth & Strawson, Flatbush. Sept. 1, 3 years. 2,800

Sullivan, Michael and Ellen his wife to The Hall Sash and Door Company. Rockaway av, e s, 43.4 n Glenmore av, 36.8x100. Aug. 28, due Sept. 1, 1891. 1,000

Schliffer, William H. to Ann M. and Emma C. Barkley. South 2d st. P. M. Sept. 1, 2 years, 5 %. 800

Schnell, Lorenz to Francis E. Clark. Troutman st, n w s, 170.7 n e Wyckoff av; 25x100. Sept. 1, 1 year. 200

Schwartz, William to Maria Kunzweiler. Ellery st. P. M. Sept. 1, installs, 5 %. 2,250

Stoll, Margaretha wife of Frederick to Caroline Boistedt. Ellery st, s s, 300 e Throop av, 25x100. Sept. 1, 5 years, 5 %. 2,000

Sundel, Eleck and Gerson Krakauer, New York, to Emily Obernier. Ewen st, s w cor Stagg st, 25x72. Sept. 1, 5 years, 5 %. See Conveys. 8,000

Same to Markus Bach. Same property. Sept. 1, 3 years. See Conveys. 2,500

Tangeman, George P. to Benjamin A. Sands. Union st, n s, 207 w 7th av, 23x90. Sept. 1, 1 year. 8,500

Thorne, Annie L. to The South Brooklyn Savings Inst. 10th st, s w s, 246 n w 9th av, 18x100. Sept. 2, 1 year, 5 %. 3,400

Tibbals, Marion H. to Charles Isbill. Putnam av. P. M. Aug. 31, 2 years, installs. 2,400

Turner, George F. to Walter F. Clayton. Macon st, s s, 84 w Ralph av. P. M. Aug. 28, installs. 2,300

Valentine, Mary A. to James G. Roberts. Macon st. P. M. Aug. 28, 2 years. 1,000

Van Riper, Martha wife of and Richard to Lawrence Hurlburt. Patchen av. P. M. Aug. 25, installs. 1,000

Vichelo, Nichelio and Antonia to William A. Watson. Barbey st, e s, 205 n Wortman av, 20x100. Aug. 4, 3 years. 5 %. 225

Valentine, Andrew to The Long Island Building and Loan Assoc. Oakland st. P. M. Aug. 6, installs. 3,000

Walther, Caroline to Anthony Straub. Central av, n e s, 25 n w Suydam st, 25x100. Sept. 1, 5 years. 800

Warmbrunn, Susan to Matthew Robb. McDonough st. P. M. Sept. 1, installs, 5 %. 2,200

Welcher, Charles to The Williamsburgh Savings Bank. Gates av, s e s, 184 1 n e Evergreen av, 25x100. Sept. 1, 1 year. 5 %. 4,000

Wichmann, Sophia wife of and Peter to The Dime Savings Bank, Brooklyn. Jay st, e s, 46.6 n Tillary st, 43.6x57.6. Sept. 1, 1 year, 5 %. 1,000

Walling, Thomas, Somerville, N. J., to Joseph H. Pratt. Patchen av, n e cor Putnam av, 20x100. Aug. 31, 1 year. 800

Walsh, Thomas to The South Brooklyn Savings Inst. Pacific st. P. M. Aug. 1, 1 year, 5 %. 3,000

Wagner, Frank W. to Sophie Iverson. 22d st. P. M. July 23, 6 years. 600

Wiener, Albert to Henry Sauerbrunn. Broadway. P. M. Aug. 26, 2 years, installs. 2,600

Wilkenfeld, Hirsch to A. Judson Palmer. Sackman st, Powell st, &c. P. M. July 1, 3 years. 6,500

Wingerath, William to Samuel Dean. 16th st, n s, 135.9 w 5th av, 76x100. Aug. 26, 1 year. 1,475

Wisbauer, Lina widow, Edward, Louis H., George, John A., Franklin, Celia L., Alfred T. and Joseph A. heirs Charles Wisbauer to Benjamin Moore & Co. Scholes st, n s, 100 e Graham av, 25x100; Scholes st, n s, 200 e Graham av, 25x100. Aug. 24, due Feb. 18, 1892, 5 %. 4,997

Withers, Sarah E. to Emma C. Barnes, New York. Hancock st, n s, 121 w Reid av, 18x100. Re-recorded. April 1, 1891, due May 1, 1895, 5 %. 1,700

Zirinsky, Jacob to Isaac, Gustav and Samuel Dreyer. Leonard st, s e cor Johnson av. P. M. Sept. 1, 5 years, 5 %. 1,600

MORTGAGES----ASSIGNMENTS.

NEW YORK CITY.

AUGUST 28 TO SEPTEMBER 3—INCLUSIVE.

Broadbelt, William to Theodore Connoly. $2,518

Bendheim, Henry M. to Benjamin L. Wertheimer. 2 assigns. nom

Blauvelt, James C., Brooklyn, to Eugene Stephens, Closter, N. J. 550

Benner, Mary S. and ano. exrs. Hiram Benner to Frank Yoran substituted trustee Hiram Benner dec'd. order of Court

Chesebro, Denison P. to William S. Whitman. Re-recorded. 1,300

Cohn, Sigmund to Rosa Schoeffel. 1,000

Same to same. 1,000

Chamberlain, Jacob A. and Albert S. Roe, of Chamberlain, Roe & Co., to Jacob A. Chamberlain. 10,000

Deering, James A. to Henry D. Winans. 5,000

Same to same. 3,000

de Forest, Henry W. trustee of Harriet C. Cheney to Maude L. Norton guard. of Augustus Norton. 4,500

Decker, Paul G. to Frederick C. McCormack. nom

Drought, William and Charles J. Carew to Jenny A. Carew, Norwich, Conn. 4,500

Duffy, Philip exr. Ellen Kane to James J. Phelan. 1,200

Delaney, John P. to Vincent J. Delaney. nom

Ellison, Eliza to Elizabeth D. Chaloner. 15,000

Faas, Carrie to John W. and Ernst A. Haaren and Ernst A. Meinken, of Haaren & Meinken. 1,019

German-American Real Estate Title Guarantee Co. to The Mercantile Trust Co. as agent for E. D. M. Waterman. 8,000

Same to James M. Wentz trustee Joseph H. Weller dec'd. 7,000

Geib, Agnes now wife of Joseph Riehl to Michael Gebhard. 6,000

Greenblatt, Louis to Hyman Schnitzer. 2,060

Ghiglione, Angelo, Staten Island, to John Boyd. 3,000

Hurvich, Rachel to Jacob and Mary Rosenbaum exrs. Philip Rosenbaum. 7,500

Hall, Charles A. trustee of James A. Hall, Gloversville, N. Y., to Oliver Getman, Johnstown, N. Y. 1,500

Immen, Luer to The F. & M. Schaefer Brewing Co. 5,000

Knox, Louise W. and ano. trustees for Jeanie de F. K. Barbour to Henry W. de Forest trustee of Harriet C. Cheney. 4,500

Kings County Trust Co. to The German-American Real Estate Title Guarantee Co. nom

Kunhardt, Henry R. and Henry Rocholl trustees to New York Dispensary. 8,066

Lennon, William F. to Rosalie Epstein. 2,000

Lennon, William F. to Isaac Schlachter. 1,500

Same to Henri Strasbourger. 1,500

Levy, Harris to Marks Levy. 4,000

Luyster, Peter, Jr., exr. Peter Luyster to Catharine L. Fairweather and Cornelia L. Luyster. val. consid.

Morgenthau, Henry to Moses Goldsmith. nom

Morgenthau, Henry to Simon Adler and Henry S. Herrman. nom

Same to Emanuel Heilner, Moses J. Wolf and Morris Mayer. nom

McCabe, James J. to William M. Thornton. 2,250

Middlebrook, Frederic J., Brooklyn, to Christopher D. Robert, Parkville, L. I. 10,026

Same to John M. Bowers trustee Franklin Osgood dec'd. 14,136

Middlebrook, Frederic J., Brooklyn, to B. A. R. Seymour. 1,002

Same to same. 1,007

Ohl, Daniel to Pincus Lowenfeld, Morris Goldstein and Mark Blumenthal. 4,050

Parsons, Margaret B. trustee Margaret W. Pirnie dec'd to Sarah F. Pirnie widow. 2 assigns. order of Court

Same to Mary E. Pirnie and William G. DeWitt trustees Henry Pirnie dec'd. 3 assigns. order of Court

Roe, Albert S. trustee Jacob Aims dec'd to J. Aims Chamberlain. 20,192

Revans, Samuel G. to Joseph F. Stier. 13,000

Redmond, William F. exr. Ann A. Carpenter to Phebe Carpenter, Brooklyn. 2 assigns. nom

Schneittacher, Israel and Betty to Max Borger. 6,045

Schnitzer, Hyman to Hannah Schnitzer. nom

Stephens, Eugene, Closter, N. J., to James Taveniere and Darius S. Johnson. 550

Taber, Elizabeth, Brooklyn, to Jane Romaine. 1,050

The Bank for Savings in the City of New York to Jacob A. Chamberlain and Albert S. Roe, of Chamberlain, Roe & Co. 10,000

Title Guarantee and Trust Co. to Peter Arens, New Durham, N. J. 18,000

Ursuline Convent to Catharine A. Mower, Buffalo, N. Y. 1,355

Weber, Gottlieb F. to Frederick W. Sauer and Conrad Gross. 2,544

Weil, Samuel to Samuel Schweitzer. nom

Wood, Anna J., Huntington, L. I., to Heyward Scudder. 2,500

KINGS COUNTY.

AUG. 27 TO SEPT. 2—INCLUSIVE.

Andrews, Felix exr. Eliza Andrews to William Andrews. $6,000

Andrews, William to The Title Guarantee and Trust Co. 6,007

Ayers, Samuel to The Title Guarantee and Trust Co. 3,500

Abbott, Philip to Annie B. Ritterband. 1,000

Barnes, Emma C. to Elkin Farmer. 1,700

Brown, John T. trustee for John J. Miller to John J. Miller. nom

Chase, Adele R. St. F. extrx. Franklin Chase to Elizabeth W. Aldrich. 3,110

Cozine, John H., of Manor, L. I., to William H. McKee. 590

Currier, George C. to William W. Hebberd. nom

Clark, Belle to Ida Barnes. 1,045

Clark, Frances E. to John B. Binns. 1,000

Davison, Emeline, Rockville Centre, L. I., to Susan M. Abrahams, Pearsalls, L. I. 2,000

Same to Woodhull Skidmore, East Moriches, L. I. 3,500

Dare, Edward H. to A. Maria Brown. 3,000

Dugan Mfg. Co. to William W. and Charles R. Rope and George W. McChesney. nom

Doody, Daniel to Asa W. Parker. 5,000

Everit, Thomas exr. Valentine Everit to David A. Fithian. 800

Eich, Henry to Henry Liebmann. 3,000

Gordon, Frances E. to W. R. Spooner. 605

Geis, Rosa N. to Joseph Newborg. 3,550

Gibson, Henry C., Philadelphia, Pa., to C. Brown McCullough. 1881. nom

Howard, Elizabeth E. to Philip L. Balz, Jr. 1,000

Hurlburt, Lawrence to Alfred Fitzroy. 1,000

Same to Edward W. Vanderbilt. 325
Hawkins, William to Alanson W. Adams. 1,200
James, Mary E. wife of Darwin R. to Anna L. Short and ano. exrs. John J. Petit. 15,500
Kunzweiler, Maria to George Straub. 1,377
Krause, Elizabeth to John Gramm. 875
Maguire, Charles E. to Theodore Kiendl. 700
Moores, Robert L. and Charles A. Le Quesne to Watson & Pittinger. nom
Miller, John J. to John T. Brown. nom
Nolte, William H. and Frank W. Koch to Hugo Weil. 800
Parker, Asa W. to Daniel Doody. nom
Rankin, James D. and James Ross to Lawrence Hurlburt. consid. omitted
Raymond, Blanch E. to Raeburn, Lataurette & Co. nom
Ryan, Patrick J. and Kate Smith admrs. Margaret Gallagher to Josephine McQuade. 400
Rose, Nettie M. to Anna C. Hegeman, Elizabeth Bennett, Rebecca B. Lott and Jennie Cropsey. 2,878
Roth, Henry to Jacob Manneschmidt. 2,100
Rudderman, Rosa to Jacob W. Erreger. 300
Smith, Mary W. to Emily F. Dingley. 2,150
Smith, Robert to Joshua M. Whitcomb. 1,800
Scheidt, John H. to Lorenz Leopold. 800
Steers, Alfred E. and William C. to Frank H. Steers. 1,019
Stoutenburg, George B. to Rankin & Ross. 1,125
Sussman, Adolph to The Kings Co. Trust Co. Assign. of 41 morts. 5,000
Thayer, Joseph S. et al. exrs. Maria Brown to Edward H. Dare. 5,000
Thorn, Lillie C. to George B. Forrester. 1,500
The American Casualty Insurance and Security Co., Baltimore, Md., to Alexander Munn guard. Helen L., Frederick L. and Roger H. Lutz. 6,134
The American Steam Boiler Ins. Co. to The American Casualty Ins. and Security Co., Baltimore, Md. 6,233
Title Guarantee and Trust Co. to The Brooklyn Trust Co. 7,500
Same to Edward E. Sprague trustee for Elizabeth K. Lathrop. 2,000
Same to William H. Chapman exr. Samuel Wanser. 1,100
Same to College Point Savings Bank. 9,500
Same to same. 7,000
Same to Lizzie F. Kretzschmar extrx. Francis A. Moran. 4,500
Same to same. 2,000
Same to same. 8,000
Same to Stephen D. Horton trustee for William J. Horton. 7,000
Same to same. 5,000
Same to Edward D. White and ano. exrs. John S. Thorne. 8,000
Same to same. 9,000
Same to same. 8,000
Treviranus, Johanna S. to Bernard Rourke. 774
Tyler, Frank H. to Elizabeth L. Chinnock. nom
Vorbach, Margaretta to Paulina A. Summers. 1,700
Volke, Fredericke to John Hornl. 3,500

JUDGMENTS.

In these lists of judgments the names alphabetically arranged, and which are first on each line, are those of the judgment debtor. The letter (D) means judgment for deficiency. (*) means not summoned. (†) signifies that the first name is fictitious, real name being unknown. Judgments entered during the week, and satisfied before day of publication, do not appear in this column, but in list of Satisfied Judgments.

NEW YORK CITY.

Aug. and Sept.

31 Ainsworth, James—J W Sisson...... $74 14
2†Anton, Antonio—David Biskinty.... 51 80
2 Angel, Isaac—Garfield Nat Bank.... 426 67
2 Ahlers, Frederick—J Chr G Hupfel Brewing Co.......... 75 60
3*Aquilar, Ancelmo—Jacob Delmonte.. 187 91
4 Adams, Frank—Tunis Lumber Co.... 158 28
29 Brennan, Thomas—J A Wilson...... 1,075 16
29 Bonnell, J Harper—Nat Bank of North America.......... 1,435 22
31 Brown, A F Allen, as pres't Holland Purchase Co—J Y Johnston........ 579 36
31 Bechstadt, Charles F—Morris Steinheimer.......... 2,167 50
31 Bosch, Joseph—Eleazer Jackson...... 147 42
31 Bertram, Joseph—H F Burchard..... 185 84
31 Brownell, Robert B—G W Venable.. 158 72
1 Bonnell, John Harper / Bonnell, Tammisin H } Chatham Nat Bank...... 2,533 54
1 Bishop, William M—J H Johnston... 731 70
1 Bernstein, Philip—G A Le Blanc..... 310 08
1 Berksin, H—John Boyd.......... 565 58
1 Bencke, John—William Lang........ 107 62
2 Brady, Lucy A—Samuel Earnest.... 105 75
2 Bezmonawich, Aaron—Aaron Walder 615 00
2 Blackman, John E—Charles Riley... 1,945 67
2 Bonnell, Tammisin H / Bonnell, John Harper } Chatham Nat Bank...... 3,230 85
2 Bonnell, John Harper——the same... 587 62
2 Belford, Robert J—Garfield Nat Bank 426 67
2 Bonnell, John Harper / Bonnell, Tammisin H } Nat Bank of Republic... 3,055 89
2 the same——the same.......... 8,101 39
3 Bender, John—D B Toucey, assignee.. 244 78
3 Bartels, Carl—M P Daly.......... 141 46
3 Barretoni, Caesar A—W C Boone, recvr.......... 3,174 05
3 Barcolow, George—E A Behringer.... 199 11
3 Barcolow, George B—E W Youmans. 236 21
3 Balcom, Clark—Metropolitan Telephone and Telegraph Co.......... 31 60
3 Borchardt, Joseph—Julius Knopf.... 94 50
3 Braun, John—Jacob Doelger........ 236 00
4 Barrow, David—Julia R Rawls...... 120 82
4 Bonnell, John Harper—Bank of N Y Nat Banking Assoc.......... 840 59
4 the same——the same.......... 854 39
4 the same——the same.......... 1,592 86
4 Bonnell, J Harper—Globe Paper Co.. 104 18
4 Bowen, Jason M—Louis Weddigen... 8,469 92
29 Corbett, Lawrence—J L Hasbrouck.. 159 24
29 Clark, Herman—Citizen's Saving and Loan Assoc.......... 831 19
29 the same——State Nat Bank of Ohio.......... 882 84
31 Cummins, Henry—C De H Brower... 308 14
31 Clune, Margaret—G W Venable...... 175 65
31 Crosher, James—Joseph Sigel....... 113 30
31 Coar, John—A R Ackert.......... 122 05
1 Conkling, John B—Florence W Beers. 30 46
1 Chapman, Charles—Gertrude Rockwell.......... 17 77
1 Collins, Frank S—T J Shea.......... 418 00
1 Crowford, William G—J L Hasbrouck 101 47
2 Collins, Dennis B—P G Fleming...... 157 02
2 Clark, Herman—Julius Anderson.... 95 45
2 Crump, Helen—W & J Sloane........ 133 76
2 Cumisky, Thomas—David Mayer.... 147 90
2 Clark, Herman—Second Nat Bank of Warren.......... 3,573 71
2 the same——Exchange Bank of Madison, Ohio.......... 2,050 31
2 Clift, Thomas—William Schlemmer.. 119 00
2 Clarke, William D—J W Nicholson.. 1,192 59
2 Casey, William C—Edward Joyce... 113 35
2 Carifi, Nicola / Carifi, Luciano } Antonio Galella.... 302 75
3 Carroll, Robert F—A T Carroll...... 223 21
3 Cadzow, William—James Williamson 360 09
4 Coulter, Mary—David Jones Co...... 396 64
4 Comstock, Alexander—B S Wise.... 75 77
4 Cubberly, Jesse—William Campbell.. 89 77
4 Creed, Sarah C—Anna B Hutcheson.. 240 52
4 Conklin, William—J T Lee.......... 459 50
4 the same——the same.......... 563 65
4 the same——the same.......... 563 66
4 Cogswell, William L / Cogswell, John D R / admrs. Elizabeth R Cogswell } Edith H Simmons 2,006 54
4 Carr, William H—Thomas Cloke.... 98 80
29 Demarest, Henry H—Andrew Thomson.......... 83 69
29 the same——the same.......... 501 75
29 Dolen, James E—Abraham Steers.... 1,050 49
29 Dunlap, Benjamin F—Acme Staple and Machine Co.......... 81 70
31 Delany, John P—Elizabeth M Delany. 1,245 54
31 Dyett, Charles H—Abraham Siegel... 87 26
1 Devlin, Michael—James Stewart..... 317 17
1 Delany, John P—W I Rosenfeld...... 132 00
1 Dorr, Thomas—William Fiss........ 194 69
2 Davis, George P—R W Weir........ 231 00
2 de Murguiando, Carter—W E Dodge. 300 90
3 Douherty, James—John Bowes....... 187 09
3 Dunn, John—Lawson Valentine Co... 101 96
3 Doyle, Patrick J—Robert Peyton.... 456 48
3 Daly, Patrick J—Samuel Wilson..... 194 99
3 Donat, Rudolph—H T J Kline....... 248 45
4 Dubsky, Adolph—Philip Rudolph.... 124 26
31 Ekstrom, Alfredo—Catharine H Ranney.......... 215 11
31 Emanuel, Solomon A—Jacob Nathan. 10 62
1†Ehrenspeck, Herman—Louis Wolfsky 126 81
2 Eibsen, Hermann—August Lutz..... 170 62
3 Eichler, Fried—Jacob Raichle........ 364 01
31 Foote, Herbert W—Tradesmens Nat Bank.......... 798 31
31 Friebe, Henry F—Bishop & Babcock Co.......... 580 99
31 Falk, Benjamin—Austin Hall....... 373 65
31 Fry, David—Isaac Wyman.......... 826 70
1 Flaherty, Simon—Metropolitan Brewing Co.......... 232 83
2 Fry, David—Samuel Eichberg....... 610 55
2 Flieg, John—David Mayer.......... 174 50
2 Fox, Michael—L S Friedberger..... 200 18
2 Fleisch, Benjamin—Ludwig Renn... 142 00
2 Farrington, Jonas S / Farrington, John A } Hugo Josephy 761 49
3 Fitzgibbon, Maurice—E A Behringer 199 11
3 the same——E W Youmans...... 236 21
3 Finney, Thomas J—Metropolitan Telephone and Telegraph Co....... 76 14
4 Fisher, John H—C H Childs......... 141 21
4*Fairclough, Edward—Thomas Cloke.. 98 80
29 Graham, James H—M D Stern....... 175 21
31 Ginsberg, Wolf—David Eisenberg.... 265 00
1 Grovesteen, William F—William Koch.......... 13 00
2 Graf, Julius—T C Lyman.......... 87 57
2 Gaunder, Joseph E—Ludwig Renn.. 142 00
2 Gormley, John, admr Michael Gormley—John Masterson.......... 465 80
2 Gould, Frederick H—Lucius Moses... 3,691 09
2 the same——the same....... costs 251 46
2 the same——Giles Everson et al.. 1,295 99
2 the same——the same.......... 3,755 47
2 the same——the same.......costs 300 05
2 the same——E C Wright.......... 1,747 96
3 Gilmartin, James—Robert Peyton.... 456 48
3 Gombossy, Max—Charles Weisflog... 267 50
4 Gearon, Michael—David Jones Co.... 319 69
4 Gaeta, Angelo—Antonia Carretta.... 186 41
4 Goldgrabe, Dederick H—Edgewood Distilling Co.......... 191 16
4 Griffin, William H—F X Ganter..... 74 87
29*Hubbell, Julius C—First Nat Bank of Plattsburgh.......... 499 74
29 Harper, William D—Nat Bank of North America.......... 1,435 99
31 Hermann, Alexander—Julius Bien.... 741 70
31 Harris, Jacob—B L Price.......... 18 12
31 Higgins, Paul J—H Clausen & Son Brewing Co.......... 438 88
31 Heinzer, John—H W Rosenbaum.... 44 50
31 Henderson, Frederick D—W F Severance.......... 134 69
1 Holmes, Joseph—S J Luckings....... 327 54
1 Hoelder, Ferdinand—G A Blessing... 163 35
1 Harper, William D / Harper, Tacie McD } Chatham Nat Bank.......... 2,533 54
1 Howser, Horace—W E Sperling...... 158 22
1 Hagan, Thomas—V H Rothschild.... 178 68
1 Hartwell, Louise M—Henry McShane Co (Lim).......... 688 28
1†Henriques, David—Henry Grub...... 85 89
1 Hart, Peter—Metropolitan Brewing Co 253 65
2 Herman, Abraham—Emil Oelbermann.......... 90 67
2 Hughes, Henry—Benno Loewy....... 168 12
2 Holmquist, Frederick L—A H Schoff. 81,706 42
2 Harper, William D—Chatham Nat Bank.......... 587 62
2 Hathaway, Frederick A—Thurber, Whyland Co.......... 307 65
2 Harper, William D / Harper, Tacie McD } Nat Bank of Republic........ 3,055 89
2 Hodges, Amory G—Lucius Moses..... 3,691 60
2 the same——the same.......costs 251 46
2 the same——Giles Everson et al.. 1,295 90
2 the same——the same.......... 3,755 47
2 the same——the same.......costs 300 05
2 the same——E C Wright.......... 1,747 96
3 Hart, Alexander R—Western Nat Bank.......... 1,006 46
3†Handler, J—B F Tuthill.......... 131 87
4 Harper, William Durbin—Bank of N Y Nat Banking Assoc.......... 840 59
4 the same——the same.......... 1,593 86
4 the same——the same.......... 854 39
4 Hauser, Gottfried—J M Canda...... 1,164 11
4 Huck, Reinhard—German-American Ins Co.......... 292 86
4 Herrmann, Alexander—Francis Higgins, recvr.......... 1,683 69
4 Hertzfield, Joseph—Joseph Sawyer... 739 13
4 Howell, Henry C—Clarence Clayton. 500 18
4 Hodes, Regina—Emanuel Pisko...... 74 87
4 Harper, William D—Globe Paper Co. 104 18
2 Irving, James—T R McNell.......... 249 84
29 Jones, Clarence H—First Nat Bank of Plattsburgh.......... 499 74
1 Jackman, Michael—Andrew Henderson.......... 112 67
1 Johnston, Robert A—A A Gardner.. 27 50
2 Johnson, Charles F—Maria N Johnson.......... 2,830 10
3 Jenkins, Maross—C S Carter........ 123 96
31 Kaiser, John—H W Rosenbaum...... 44 50
1 Kegel, Joseph—Leopold Brand....... 189 71
1 Kneppler, Charles M—James Phelan. 370 84
1 Kattenhorn, Frederick—Cordt Gerken.......... 963 63
1*Krugler, John F—Herman Dorn..... 38 71
1 Kempner, Bernard M—Joseph Moss.. 416 10
1 *Kreuder, Adolph / Kline, Charles / *Kreuder, Frank F } Samuel Fuld.... 182 25
2 Krafft, John C—Samuel Cupples Wooden Ware Co.......... 280 94
3 Kissling, August—Louis Hoopes..... 259 34
4 Kaletsky, Samuel—Samuel Hirsh.... 98 16
4*Kirkland, William—Tunis Lumber Co 158 28
4 Kelly, John P—Bazilius Busch...... 126 46
4 the same——the same.......... 111 80
4 Kilpatrick, T Judson—C V Sidell.... 146 00
4 Kenyon, Norman S—Real Estate Record Assoc.......... 71 81
29 Lederer, James L—Acme Staple and Machine Co.......... 81 70
31†Levy, Henry—I D Einstein.......... 728 62
31 Lennon, Edward—Marie Brown..... 112 72
31 Loewenstein, Jacob E—H W Rosenbaum.......... 44 50
1 Lawrence, Thomas J—George Smith, Jr, admr.......... 810 44
1 Leigh, Louis—Herman Dorn......... 38 71
1 Love, Samuel—Adolph Weber....... 252 95
1 Lohrand, William—William Lang.... 107 62
2 Lissner, Salem / Levenson, Michael } Benno Loewy.... 649 49
2 Lamoreaux, James M—Thurber, Whyland Co.......... 137 49
2 Lindenborn, David—John Baehr...... 400 00
2 Levy, Julius / Levy, Augustus H / Levy, Moses S } William Lauterbach.......... 3,746 25
2 Leonard, Robert M—George Haseltine 331 83
3 Leahey, Thomas—Jacob New......... 221 25
3 Lowrey, James P—J M Constable.... 149 87
3 Lippmann, Otto—George Ehret...... 256 41
3†Lyons, Bernard—G D Royston....... 87 30
4 Lees, Samuel—Beadleston & Woerz.. 151 66
4 Laviada, Antonio—J A Medina...... 2,210 44
4 Linnington, Timothy B—R S Bourne. 592 80
4 Levy, Israel—Joseph Sawyer........ 475 36
29 Martin, Crowell H—First Nat Bank of Plattsburgh.......... 499 74
29 Morris, Ellis—S S Long.......... 269 59
29 Meyer, Siegmund T / Meyer, Arthur L } D W Moran.... 199 89
31 May, Albert S—Elizabeth Jahnel..... 761 50
31 the same——J T McPaul.......... 270 54
31 May, Albert S / *May, Frida } Elizabeth Jahnel... 632 87
31†Mason, Mary—Harry Newman....... 34 14
1 Milair, Gustave A J—D T Warron.... 1,225 44
1 Milair, Gustave A J / Milair, Luise B } the same........ 4,839 44
1 Madlin, Charles—Levi Dexter........ 103 23
1 Muller, Lewis M—W F Carroll....... 449 05
2 Mass, Henry—Max Deckinger....... 65 13
2 Macmichael, Samuel—J W Hatch, assignee.......... 139 68
2 Meyer, George—H H Muller.......... 152 34

2 Mcss, Joseph F—W & J Sloane....... 126 57
2 Moneseh, Fannie—Morris Eschwege.. ....costs 49 29
2 Mandeville, Henry; Mandeville, Heury C—Schillinger Fire Proof Cement and Asphalt Co.. 295 77
2 Masten, Robert—Thurber, Whyland Co.... 307 65
3 Meyer, Frederick—J C Huser........ 76 58
3 Mitchell, John J—J G Jansen........ 21 91
3 Morton, William O—James Wright... 136 35
3 Meyer, Henry—G F Weeden 460 88
3 Morsch, Andrew—Edward Siegman.. 107 78
4 Morgan, George P—M B Beelman.... 76 92
4 Meyer, Siegmund T; Meyer, Arthur L—Mechanics' Nat Bank of Trenton 428 13
4 Muldoon, William H—John McGrath. 500 58
4 Mullen, John J—Campbell Printing Press and Mfg Co.......... 73 13
4 Melick, Jacob A—J T Lee....... .... 563 65
4 the same——the same............ 459 50
4 the same——the same............ 563 66
4 Meyer, Siegmund T; Meyer, Philip L—John Webb.... 5,934 63
4 Machette, Edwin V—Real Estate Record Assoc.............. 71 81
4 Moen, Edward A—P W Moen, admr. 48,885 23
29 McSwyny, Bryan G—James O'Day... 642 12
31*McPaul, John F—Elizabeth Jabnel... 632 87
31 McMahon, Michael J—Alsensche Portland Cement Fabriken............ 606 02
1 McKeon, Thomas—German Exchange Bank.............. 207 23
1 McManus, Mary—Christopher Nally.. 2,084 25
1 McIndoe, Walter J—Sarah J Raynor 153 14
1 McGrath, William — Metropolitan Brewing Co 304 00
2 McCann, Patrick—E C Korner....... 630 28
2 Macmichael, Samuel—J W Hatch, assignee.............. 129 08
2 McCullough, Willis J—United Electric Light and Power Co............ 76 93
3 McBride, Patrick F—J G Jansen..... 21 91
3 McCarthy, James — Catharine V Feury.............. 1,582 60
4 McKenna, Patrick—Timothy Callahan.............. 182 14
4 McNab, George R—Isaac Stern.. .... 289 51
31 Nightengale, James—Joseph Meyer.. 136 29
1 Newman, Isaac—L J Maguire....... 277 07
3 New, Moses—E G Chatain............ 104 98
29*O'Brien, John—State Nat Bank of Ohio.............. 882 84
29 the same——Citizen's Savings and Loan Assoc.............. 881 19
2 O'Brien, John—Julius Anderson...... 95 45
2 Ochs, Moses—Hugo Josephy.......... 136 69
2*O'Brien, John—Second Nat Bank of Warren.............. 3,573 71
2 the same——Exchange Bank of Madison, Ohio.............. 2,050 31
4 O'Hagan, Frank——David Jones Co.. 228 21
4 O'Meara, Patrick B—P J Fleming.... 141 50
31 Piser, Abraham—B L Price.......... 18 12
4*Pakelinsky, Susan—Samuel Hirsh.... 93 16
4 Price, Frank S—J M Canda.......... 1,164 11
31 Roberts, William H H—George Engert.............. 95 10
31*Reed, Charles P—F V Burton........ 120 63
1 Rosenfeld, Leo—Lucien Wolf... .... 241 23
1 Root, James H—Western Nat Bank.. 1,431 99
1 Rhodes, Alexander R—Metropolitan Brewing Co.............. 294 81
2 Roper, Osmer W—C C Luckey....... 826 10
2*Reynolds, Milton H—Thurber, Whyland Co.............. 307 65
2 Read, Charles P—H E Brown 441 58
2 Read, William G, Jr—Lucius Moses.. 3,691 09
2 the same——the same.......costs 251 46
2 the same——Giles Everson et al.. 1,295 90
2 the same——the same............ 3,755 47
2 the same——the same......costs 300 05
2 the same——E C Wright......... 1,747 96
3 Ravel, Augustin—Jacob Delmonte.... 187 91
3 Roch, Ernest—J H Norwood......... 232 69
4 Roach, William—David Jones Co.... 151 54
29 Schneider, George—Frederick Robitscher.............. 100 41
29 Saehr, Gottlieb—J M Thorburn...... 107 80
31 Schlotterbeck, John—Morris Greenwald.............. 160 11
31 Sterner, Winfield S—C F Biele....... 117 50
31 Schlosser, Henry—H W Rosenbaum.. 44 50
31 Surbeck, Eibe F—G W Venable...... 98 47
31 Sprague, Watson N—Gustav Rau.... 469 13
31 Schieber, Leopold—Isaac Wyman ... 820 70
1 Spielberg, John—Charles Herr....... 452 98
1 Slug, Ju—Ming Low............... 342 20
1 Schlegel, Frederick — Metropolitan Brewing Co.............. 222 93
2 Schieber, Leopold—Samuel Eichberg. 610 55
2 Schlotterbeck, Christian — Esther Dreyfous.............. 1,337 87
2 Schade, Herman—J J Froelich...... 191 00
2*Smalley, Mahlon C—T F Johnson.... 80 55
2 Springer, William P—Garfield Nat Bank.............. 426 67
2 Strauss, Samuel — Harlem Lighting Co.............. 85 61
3 Schey, Joseph—Emma Schey........ 155 57
3 Stephens, James G—Wilhelmina Fuhr 30 50
3*Sollinger, Emil—J G Jansen......... 21 91
4 Scharmann, Frederick—H B Scharmann.............. 8,742 87
4 Schnaars, Elizabeth—August Koenig. 693 85
4 Schwarting, Charles W—R D Uffelman.............. 669 88
4 Scholes, Mary J—Joseph Seeman 187 01
4 Still, Allan—B S Wise............... 72 72
4 Schroeder, Charles—J S Foster....... 1,153 00
4 Satterlee, John; Simmons, James A—John Webb.... 5,934 63
4 Streiffer, Jacob—A J Stewart........ 575 82

31 Smith, R Earle—J J Mead.......... 194 44
2 Smith, Joel B—W H Barlow........ 418 15
3 Smith, Thomas S—X T Bates...... 391 54
4 Smith, Edgar M; Smith, Scudder—Megargee Paper Mills.......... 209 70
29 The Knickerbocker Storage Co (Lim)—James Savage, Jr.............. 470 31
29 J H Bonnell & Co (Lim)—Nat Bank of North America.............. 1,435 22
31 The Mayor, Aldermen, &c — G L Green.............. 103 73
1 Belford Magazine Co — Alexander Belford.............. 7,041 51
1 J J Nichols Mfg Co—A L Doremus ....costs 27 55
1 The Firm Printing Press Co—G A Ohl.............. 4,439 49
2 Hudson River Boot and Shoe Mfg Co—C A Vinal.............. 367 96
2 Banker & Campbell Co (Lim)—Gendron Iron Wheel Co.............. 500 00
2 South Brooklyn Steam Engine Works—Third Nat Bank.............. 2,240 65
2 Casa, Grande Improvement Co—Co-operative Building Bank.......... 270 59
2 J H Bonnell & Co (Lim)—Nat Bank of Republic.............. 3,055 89
2 the same——the same............ 8,101 39
3 Cohnfeld Company—Lewis Seasongood.............. 1,775 02
3 J H Bonnell & Co (Lim)—Western Nat Bank.............. 1,527 52
3 the same——the same............ 1,212 75
3 the same——the same............ 1,006 46
3 The Manhattan Railway Co; The Metropolitan Elevated Railway Co—Eliza L Hinschberger 1,031 84
3 Flour City Life Assoc—W H Law.... 1,720 85
3 Joseph B Tiffany Co—E P Treadwell. 530 18
3 N Y Refrigerating Construction Co—J T Noye Mfg Co..... 375 78
4 J H Bonnell & Co (Lim)—Bank of N Y Nat Banking Assoc.............. 840 59
4 the same——the same............ 854 39
4 the same——the same............ 1,592 86
4 N Y & Berkshire Marble Co—N Y Newspaper Union.............. 530 18
31 Tracy, Gurdon—C F Biele.......... 117 50
1 Templeman, Charles B—W H Oliver. 58 43
1 Teator, Harvey L—B F Tuttle....... 235 45
1 Townsend, Maurice; Townsend, Edward N; Townsend, Solomon S—Pottstown Iron Co.... 92 51
2 Thorpe, William H—J W Hatch, assignee.............. 3,812 20
3 Townsend, Edward N — Benjamin Altman.............. 137 30
4 Tregaskis, John—D B Van Wagenen. 95 81
4 Tallman, Jacob B—John Webb...... 5,934 63
4 Tenney, Herman J—J C Cochran Co. 108 05
4 Thomas, George H—Catharine Feitner.............. 434 22
2 Urban, Henry A—Mary A Fitzpatrick, admrx.............. 74 73
1 Vondy, Thomas D—Sarah J Raynor. 153 14
2 Vlasto, Solon J; *Vlasto, Demetrius J—J I Mediano. 1,164 84
2 Vroome, Philip A—T F Johnson..... 80 55
3 Von Graff, Roderick—St Nicholas Bank.............. 250 60
3 Vieu, Henry A, exr Andrew Leonard—Elizabeth C Leonard.............. 1,721 96
31 Van Gelder, John S—F V Burton..... 120 63
2 Van Gelder, John—H E Brown...... 441 58
3 Van Engers, Abraham J—Sheldon Leavitt.............. 89 66
31 Weider, John A—Alsensche Portland Cement Fabriken.............. 696 02
31 Willard, Albert B—Mayor, Lane & Co.............. 160 53
1 Woolston, George F—T C Power..... 32 15
1 the same——the same........... 32 15
2 Wendel, Louis—J W Hatch.......... 158 71
2 Williams, William C—T C Lyman.... 321 80
2 Whipple, Benjamin A — Thurber, Whyland & Co.............. 307 65
2 Willard, Edward K—Lucius Moses... 3,691 09
2 the same——the same........costs 251 46
2 the same——Giles Everson et al.. 1,295 90
2 the same——the same............ 3,755 47
2 the same——the same........costs 300 05
2 the same——E C Wright.......... 1,747 96
3 Wilson, Mary—West Side Bank...... 83 09
3 Williams, William R—Hewitt Boice.. 173 89
3 the same——Ephraim Mower.... 94 69
3 Westcote, William J—W W Astor... 954 40
3 Wellington, Samuel B—Bankers' Safe Deposit Co.............. 225 12
4 White, Robert J—David Jones Co.... 76 61
4 Wierster, Stephen C—Bessie Loucheim.............. 96 89
4 Whitson, Arlington R—F C Thomas. 122 50
2 Young, Joseph—J W Hatch, assignee 372 90

KINGS COUNTY.

Aug. and Sept..

1 Allen, William S—E Kirkpatrick.... $158 14
28 Borrmann, Ludwig—C H Krug...... 1,303 05
28 Bullock, Arthur W—S G Condit..... 5,130 75
1 Bosch, Joseph—E Jackson............ 147 42
2 Bogert, O Gordon, exr Cuthbert O Gordon—H R Gordon, admr........ 82 31
2 Baker, Henry C—Fannie E Metcalfe. 472 15
3 Berksin, H—J Boyd................ 565 53
28 Cameron, James; +Cameron, Eliza—D M Somers...... 193 34
1 Casey, William C—J Bohnet, Jr..... 1,028 10
2 Carpenter, Charles H—J R Townsend. 173 79
1 Dietz, Carl—A Feser................ 553 24
1 Doran, Myles—Leibinger & Oehm Brewing Co.............. 66 00
31 Flannigan, Mary—J F Heinbockel.... 355 00
31 Finken, John—H Fleer.............. 68 09
3 Felty, Albert J—F Emmerick........ 111 10
3 Fielder, D P—Hyde & Gload Mfg Co. 111 74
2 Gordon, Cuthbert O, exr of—H R Gordon, admr.............. 82 31
2 Gregory, John—W T Klots & Bro's Sons.............. 522 45
28 Hennessey, John R—H Sengstaken.... 78 84
28 Huebans, John—T F Dinnegan....... 101 70
29 Higgins, Patrick—M E Deyo 40 25
29 Hoffman, Julius—G A Koruder...... 19 65
31+Hallheimer, Martin—C F Oxley...... 90 72
1 Herse, Ernest M—J Goetz, Jr........ 57 30
1 Higgins, Paul J—H Clausen & Son Brewing Co.............. 438 88
3 Jones, Walter; *Jones, B H—George A Hawkins... 124 21
31 Koster, Caspar—H Fleer............ 68 09
1+Kirchner, Luke—Leibinger & Oehm Brewing Co.............. 72 60
2 Kampfmuller, William—E Huber et al exrs O Huber.............. 532 46
28 Lang, Louis—M Heim............... 117 86
28 Lang, Jr, Louis——same............ 229 95
28 Lawrence, Edson—F Meyer.......... 52 75
31 Lenk, Margaretha—J Schnetter..(D) 15,890 22
1 Loew, Herman G—J Bohnet, Jr...... 1,023 10
2 Lynes, Lillian M; Lynes, Isabella, as admrx, &c, of Lynes, William B dec'd—W C Dornin....(D) 1,710 49
28*Marxson, Oscar—C H Krug.......... 1,303 05
28 Moseman, George H—W B Lindsay.. 381 17
28 McBean, Archibald—T Sheffield ..... 2'3 31
29 Martin, Harry—M E Deyo........... 51 35
29 Miller, Sarah—G L Spaulding........ 7 25
29 Mulrain, Frances—G Wood.......... 77 91
1 Milair, Gustave A J; Milair, Gustave A J; Milair, Luise B—D T Warren.(D) 4,839 44
2 Muller, Lewis M—W F Carroll....... 440 05
31 Nielson, Max—O W Van Campen.... 128 00
29 Osman, Peter—M Hirsch............ 36 04
29 Palmer, W W—B Russell............ 561 63
31 Piper, William—J Beck 202 00
31 Pfaeffle, Frederick—J J Froehlich... 162 00
3 Queckenbush, Hester — Margaret A Morris.............. 119 20
29 Reid, Jessie V—G L Spaulding....... 7 25
1 Rothenbach, John—A Feser.......... 553 24
31 Samuels, Isaac; Samuels, Leo—Danenberg & Cole... 147 00
31 Stabler, John—O O'Keeffe........... 64 40
2 Sullivan, James E—L Otten, exr..... 637 29
3 Scharmann, Frederick—H B Scharmann.............. 8,742 87
3 +Sager, "Albert M"; +Sager, "John"—G Henricke...... 43 74
28 The Perfecto Mfg Co—W H Atkinson 193 34
28 Thomsen, Inga—A T Nielsen......... 88 64
29 The Muller Bronze Co—L Ruble 522 49
31 Thompson, Walter R—J H Ernst..... 134 00
31 The admr, &c, Irene Yung—H Fleer.. 68 09
31 The Easton Electric Co—J S Simpson. 273 49
1 The Muller Bronze Co—E A Hanson.. 1,070 53
1 the same——the same........... 533 49
1 the same——the same........... 2,100 24
2 The exr, &c, Cuthbert O Gordan dec'd—H R Gordon, admr.............. 82 31
2 The admrx, &c, of William B Lynes dec'd—W C Dornin.........(D) 1,710 49
2 Urban, Henry A—Mary A Fitzpatrick, admrx.............. 74 73
3 Von Graff, Roderick — St Nicholas Bank.............. 259 60
28 Wildermuth, John G—M Heim....... 117 86
28 Wildermuth, John D——the same.... 229 95
29 Wingert, Charles W—H B Lyons..... 27 80
2 Williams, Reginald R—H S Stewart.. 140 35
3 Wintermeyer, Louis—G Cudlipp..... 164 77
31 Yung, Ireno—H Fleer............... 68 09

SATISFIED JUDGMENTS.

NEW YORK.

August 29 to September 4—Inclusive.

Broadway & Seventh Av R R Co—Nellie Fowler. (1890).............. $1,693 50
Same——same. (1891).............. 69 15
Bourquin, Henry—August Marschall. (1891). 191 00
Same——Achille Starace. (1891).......... 106 36
Barnes, Oliver W—Edward Vaughan. (1891).. 167 27
Crandall, William E—M B Mayhar. (1887).... 604 65
‡Cole, William L—Seventh Nat Bank. (1889). 918 16
Cassidy, Peter A—James Fay. (1886)........ 79 40
Clark, Cyrus—Elizabeth A L Hyatt. (1885)... 203 27
Same——same. (1885).............. 222 85
Claflin, John—H N Bailey. (1891).......... 98 25
Coogan, Matthew—Thomas Farrell. (1891).... 155 43
Citizens Ins Co—P P Baldwin. (1891).......... 1,533 81
Daniel, August—Salomon Reiss. (1891)........ 411 31
Epstein, Simon and Isaac L; Eames, Edward E—H N Bailey. (1891).......... 98 25
Fairchild, Horace J; Force, Dexter N—H N Bailey. (1891)..... 98 25
Goldberg, Leo, Benjamin and Louis J—S I Mayer. (1891).............. 1,062 79
Harris, Hiram W—B M Whitlock. (1891)...... 184 52
Jennings, James—F W Dietz. (1888).......... 218 27
Same——Martin Jennings. (1881).......... 259 14
Same——same. (1881).............. 1,628 27
Same——W H Stacy. (1881).............. 197 85
Same——Ezra Benedict. (1881).............. 111 80
‡Kilpatrick, Walter F—Nat Bank of Newburgh. (1889).............. 1,632 02
‡Same——same. (1889).............. 2,085 26
Same——same. (1889).............. 900 88
Same——same. (1829).............. 942 26
Same——same. (1889).............. 902 02
Same——same. (1889).............. 554 41
Same——same. (1889).............. 2,148 52
Same——same. (1889).............. 1,845 72
Same——same. (1889).............. 1,854 91
Same——same. (1890).............. 1,758 93
Same——same. (1889).............. 888 99
Same and Frank—I T Williams. (1889)...... 970 69
‡Same——Seventh Nat Bank. (1889).. .... 918 16
Kemp, Peter G—Cornell Vosburgh. (1890).... 8,264 76

Little, E Knox—M B Mayhar. (1887) 604 65
Lscombe, William H—Health Dept. (1891)... 59 87
Lebec, Charles—Salomon Reiss. (1891)........ 411 81
Moreau, Gustave—Salomon Reiss. (1891).. .. 411 81
N Y Protective Assoc—J H O'Connell, as president. (1889)................ 1,537 97
Same—H W Unger. (1888)................ 623 58
O'Shaughnessy, James F—Charles Reilly, comm'r. (1891)................ 110 00
Peloubet, Seymour S—Edward Thompson. (1882)................ 126 44
Riley, James—Thomas Farrell. (1891)........ 155 49
Robinson, Daniel—H N Bailey. (1891)........ 98 25
Sakolsky, Harris—Moses Leontesco. (1891)... 215 00
*Schoenberg, Rosalie—Morris Eschwege. ('91). 434 49
Schmadeke, Frederick—W Mertens. (1891)... 350 08
Sofia, Deodora—Pasqualo Carfagino. (1890).. 249 25
Tertrais, Charles—Salomon Reiss (1891).. ... 411 81
Tuttle, Ezra A—M B Mayhar. (1887)........ 604 65
True, Benjamin K—William Ottmann. (1890). 180 34
Weller, Henry S—R H Pollock. (1884)........ 42 35
Winne, Willis A—Cornell Vosburgh. (1890)... 3,264 75
Walworth, George S—G R Reardon. (1891).... 347 29

*Vacated by order of Court. †Suspended on Appeal. ‡Released. §Reversal. ‖Satisfied by Execution.

KINGS COUNTY.

August 28 to September 3—Inclusive.

Altenbrand, Albert—Geneva Nat Bank. (1891) $1,147 75
Burcher, Walter V—W Berri. (1891) 319 26
Craig, Adam—Emma Moore. (1890) 646 49
Good, Samuel R—Michael Gallagher. (1891)... 110 55
Hoffmann, George—Minna Hoffmann. (1891). 92 27
Leask, William G—Patrick H. McElroy. (1890) 475 75
Mann, Charles } Broadway Bank, Brooklyn
Mann, Babette } (1891)................ 497 95
Minden, Michael—H S Christiansen. (1881)... 58 89
Reynolds, William W—W Berri. (1891) 319 26
Sharkey, William—H S Christiansen. (1881).. 58 89
Schwarze, Charles—Broadway Bank, Brooklyn. (1891)................ 427 25
Wood, Celia—Theo Mentzinger. (1889)...... 44 20
Wallace, John W—A Tomb. (1891)........ 78 00

MECHANICS' LIENS.

NEW YORK CITY.

Aug.

29 Ninety-second st, s s, 100 e 5th av, 150x100.8. T. J. Dunn agt Thomas Graham, Randolph Guggenheimer and Isaac and Samuel Untermeyer, owners, and Thomas Graham, contractor $835 00

29 Eighty-ninth st, n s, 113.4 w Madison av, 51x100. Same agt same........ 732 00

29 Madison av, s w cor 89th st, runs west 138 x south 100 x east — x north — x east — to Madison av, x north 25 to beginning. Same agt same 1,050 00

29 One Hundred and Twenty-fifth st, No. 332, s s, 375 e 2d av, 25x122. Abraham Steers agt Henrietta Spiegel wife of Morris Spiegel, owner, and Patsy Zoccola, contractor. 500 00

29 South st, No. 8, n e cor Moore st, 15x19. William Martin agt Edward J. Landers, owner, and Edward G. Vail, contractor... 47 00

29 South st, n e cor Moore st, 12x100.7x11.9x100.7. P. M. Weldon agt same........ 60 00

29 One Hundred and Fifteenth st, n s, 200 w 5th av, 45.2x80. Coons & Bradbury agt Adam Gebhardt, owner, and Peter Halpin, contractor........ 110 00

29 Ninety-sixth st, n s, 70 e Lexington av, 100x100.11. John Madden agt Owen F. McElroy, Jr., and William McElroy, owners, and Clark & Dolan, contractors........ 150 00

29 Courtlandt av, n e cor 150th st, 50x150. Pelham Hod Elevating Co agt Fred. Koopman, debtor and J. M. and Henry Muller, owners........ 88 25

31 Lexington av, No. 666, w s, 100 s 56th st, 25x100. Samuel Adler agt Poline and Morris Byk, debtors and owners........ 80 00

31 Twenty-ninth st, Nos. 215 and 217 E., n s, 50x100. C. B. Keogh Mfg. Co. agt M. Sheehy, owner, and Edward M. Hackett, contractor........ 725 00

31 Ninety-eighth st, n s, 300 e 10th av, 175x110. Eric Anderson and 8 others agt John W. Hutton, debtor and owner........ 228 10

31 Bainbridge av, known as Nos. 24, 25 and 26 on map of Bedford Park, w s, — s Southern Boulevard. 82.6x188.7x75.6x210.11. C. W. Vreeland agt Eunice C. Lawrence, owner and contractor........ 1,020 64

31 Sixty-fifth st, Nos. 29 and 31, n s, 175 w 8th av, 75x100. Preston Lutterloh agt J. O'Brien, owner, and Rondel & Hunter, contractors........ 12 25

31 One Hundred and Fourteenth st, s s, 300 w 1st av, 30x90. Hoopes & Shipman agt Joseph F. Gallagher, owner, and George Brietenbach, contractor........ 200 00

31 One Hundred and Ninth st, n s, 150 w 1st av, 25x100. K. N. Smith & Co. agt Frank Ruggiero, owner and contractor........ 5,000 00

31 Berry st, n s, 225 w Anthony av, 25x90. C. W. Lard agt Michael Reid, owner, and Theodore Rhein, contractor........ 376 71

Sept.

1 Barrow st, Nos. 52 and 54, n s, 100 e Bedford st, 50x100........ } Grove st, Nos. 19 and 21, n s, 50 e Bedford st, 50x51........ } C. E. Dornbusch agt Alphonse Hogenauer, owner, and Joseph Gallick, contractor........ 85 00

1 Amsterdam av, n e cor 194th st, 100x—, Harlem River. J. O. Clement agt Charles C. Wendel, owner, and Henry Taylor, contractor........ 439 00

1 Park av, s w cor 93d st, 110x119. Olsen & Co. agt John Doe, owner, and Downey & Curry, contractors 224 00

1 Eleventh st, Nos. 314 and 316, s s, 250 e 2d av, 50x100. F. M. Hausling agt John O'Conner, owner and contractor........ 125 00

1 Fourteenth st, s s, 88 w Av. C, 244x100. Hughes & Scanlon agt William H. Muldoon, owner and contractor........ 7,050 00

1 Fifty-third st, s s, 350 w 10th av, 125x100. Albert Taubert agt James Volkening and James O'Donelan, owners, and James O'Donelan and David Davies, contractors 550 00

1 Amsterdam av, n e cor 194th st, 100x— to Harlem River. Miller & Robinson agt Charles C. Wendel, owner, and Henry Taylor and L. & J. Kelly, contractors.... 100 05

1 Park av, Nos. 1807 and 1809, e s, 69.4 s 125th st, 62.8x90. Henry Taylor agt William H. McCarthy, owner, and John Sheehy & Son, contractors........ 1,789 05

1 One Hundred and Fifth st, n s, 70 e Madison av, 50x100.11. Manchester & Philbrick agt John O'Connor, owner and contractor.. . 1,500 00

1 One Hundred and Sixth st, Nos. 123-127, n s, 265 w Columbus av, 60x100. Thomas Lawler agt Jacob Barnes, owner and contractor........ 42 25

2 Park av, n e cor 78th st, 75x100. F. W. Sossel agt Augustus F. Swartzler, owner, and Chas. Suckintick, contractor...... 30 00

2 South st, No. 8, n e cor Moore st, 12x100.7. R. S. Seckerson agt Edward J. Landers, owner, and E. G. Vail, contractor........ 200 00

2 One Hundred and Twenty-fifth st, Nos. 233 and 235 W., n s, 50x100. I. E. Marsh agt Lippman Toplitz owner, and John Ryan, contractor........ 97 50

2 Sixty-sixth st, Nos. 132-136, s s, 125 w Boulevard, 75x100. G. J. Schnatz and Charles Massoth agt Thomas and Margaret Shannon, owners and contractors. (Continued from Sept. 9, 1891)........ 630 00

2 One Hundred and Twentieth st, s s, 125 w 8th av, 75x100. McDougall & Potter agt James Thompson, owner and contractor........ 175 52

2 One Hundred and Nineteenth st, n s, 125.6 w 8th av, 75x100. Same agt same owner, and August Kissling, contractor 319 13

2 Warren st, No. 67, s s, 25.6 w College pl, 25.6x50.1. Charles Burger agt Louis W. Duesing, owner, and George W. Willershausen & Co., contractors........ 115 00

2 Eighteenth st, s s, 100 w 5th av, 75x92. P. G. Hubert and A. O. Hoddick agt Blanche H. de Logerot, owner, and Richard de Logerot, contractor........ 5,000 00

3 Park av, n e cor 78th st, 75x100, H. D. Jahnsen agt Joseph Schwarzler, owner, and Charles Siekendick, contractor....— 14 80

3 Same property. Bruno Eberhardt agt same........ 10 00

3 Fourteenth st, No. 103, n s, 48 e 4th av, 18x75. James Hodge agt Frederich & Co., owners and contractors 122 21

3 Bathgate av, Nos. 1753 and 1755, w s, bet 174th and 175th sts. Mara Engelberg agt — Cox, owner, and — Reinhard, contractor 17 00

3 Bainbridge av, w s, 452.1 n Travers st, 82.6x—. Frank Shepperd agt Eunice C. Lawrence, owner and contractor........ 70 00

3 Eighty-ninth st, n s, 113.4 w Madison av, 51.1x—. G. B. Robbins and H. W. Bell agt Thomas Graham, owner and contractor........ 72 52

3 Forty-ninth st, No. 122, s s, bet 6th and 7th avs. H. F. Siebold agt Prescott & McLaughlin and — Bach, owners, and Priebe & Co., contractors........ 259 23

3 Fifty-third st, s s, 350 w 10th av, 125x—. Bernard Marrey agt James O'Donelan, owner and contractor........ 41 21

3 Washington av, w s, 25 s 184th st, 25x100. Owen Toher agt Mrs. C. T. Lapinne, owner, and Whittle & Dowd, contractors. 620 66

3 One Hundred and Twentieth st, s s, 125 w 8th av, 75x—. August Kissling agt John Thompson, owner and contractor 430 00

3 One Hundred and Nineteenth st, Nos. 307-311, n s, 125 w 8th av, 75x—. Same agt James Thompson, owner and contractor. 427 13

4 Fort Independence st, w s, known as southerly half of lot, No. 68, map of the Giles estate, 25x148.7x27.3x142.5. W. J. Holmes agt John H. Klein, owner, and William J. Connell, contractor........ 225 00

4 Simpson st, w s, 171.7 n 169th st, 25x—. Abraham Steers agt John Walsh, owner, and Thomas A. Lynch, contractor 120 74

4 One Hundred and Sixth st, Nos. 123-127, n s, 265 w Columbus av, 60x—. Moses Lubelsky agt Jacob John Barnes, owner and contractor 212 78

4 Ninety-eighth st, n s, 478 w 5th av, 25x—. Thomas Roberts Stevenson Co. agt A. Reynolds, owner and contractor........ 152 50

4 One Hundred and Fifty-third st, n s, 194 e 10th av, 26x—. J. E. Darragh agt Mary Francis Disbrow, owner, and William Baker, contractor........ 227 00

4 Amsterdam av, e s, the only building bet 194th and 195th sts, 50x—. Rapp & Johnson Lumber Co. agt C. C. Wendell, owner, and Henry Taylor, contractor.... ... 790 65

4 One Hundred and Tenth st, s s, 100 w Madison av, 50x100. George Mackenzie agt John O'Connor, owner and contractor.... 200 20

KINGS COUNTY.

Aug.

28 Lot 787 map Linden Terrace Beautiful Villa Plots, Flatbush. Ross & Snyder agt Anna Dudley, owner, and Edgar S. Homans, contractor........ $812 00

28 Eighth av, s e cor 11th st, 100x190. Albert Goble agt Allison V. B. Norris and William C. Turner, owners and contractors... 192 68

28 Watkins st, w s, 250 s Sutter av, 25x100. Schmidt & Espersredt agt Solomon Morris, owner, and Abraham Stone, contractor........ 53 00

28 Watkins st, e s, 25 n Dumont av, 50x100. Same agt H. Wilkenfeld and N. Ritterman, owners and contractors........ 290 00

28 Willoughby st, s s, 22 w Prince st, 20x66. James W. Thompson agt Marie and Jacob Rathgabeer, owners and contractors. 36 73

28 Walworth st, e s, 390 s Willoughby av, 65x100. Hobby & Doody agt Frank R. Moore, owner, and William P. Rae and John Daly, contractors........ 619 21

28 Clinton st, e s, 65.6 n 2d pl, 17.4x76.6. Thomas Silk agt James J. Ferry and John McGahie, owners, and James J. Ferry, contractor........ 258 84

28 Sackett st, n s, 125 w Van Brunt st, runs west 125 x north 200 to Degraw st, x east 50 x south 100 x east 75 x south 100. Thomas Silk agt Rebecca M. Ferry and Eliza J. Smith, owner, and Daniel Ferry, contractor........ 757 15

28 Leonard st, n e cor Frost st, 25x100. Schratwieser & Hilton agt Mary E. Hower, owner, and John Wild, contractor........ 223 00

29 Clinton st, e s, 65.6 n 2d pl, 17.3x76.6. Thomas Silk agt James J. and Catherine G. Ferry, owners, and James J. Ferry, contractor........ 258 84

29 First st, s s, 305 w 5th av, 108x100. Michael M. Fox agt William S. Hale, owner and contractor........ 58 00

29 Nassau st, s w cor Navy st, 25x73. The Palmer Mfg. Co. agt John Ryan, owner and contractor........ 220 00

29 Sixteenth st, n s, 134.5 w 8th av, Nos. 385-391. Brooklyn Door and Sash Co. agt William Wingerath........ 846 88

29 Seventh st, n s, 297.6 e 4th av, 50.4x100. Same agt Mary E. Miller, owner and contractor........ 234 00

29 Nassau st, s w cor Navy st, 25x73. William Martin agt John Ryan, owner, and Matthias Zang, contractor........ 365 00

29 Douglass st, n s, 233 e Albany av, 127.9x48. William H. Stokes agt William C. Turner, owner and contractor........ 325 00

29 Third st, n s, 431.9 e 6th av, 44x100. Hobby & Doody agt Charles H. Moses and Henry Fanton, of Moses & Fanton, owners and contractors 488 84

31 Fourth st, s s, 97.10 e 6th av, 440x100. Charles E. Rogers & Co. agt Moses & Fanton, owners, and S. F. Moses, H. J. Dynes, Eliza A. Fanton, F. M. and M. L. Moses and Lewis H. Meyers, contractors. 1,100 39

31 Broadway, n e cor Jefferson av, 100x100. Isidor Mock agt C. Henry Moller and Arnid J. Moller, owners, and Jacob Bisson, contractor 155 00

31 Sixteenth st, n s, 192.11 w 8th av, 75x100. John Weisenborn agt William Wingerath, owner and contractor........ 639 39

31 Eastern Parkway, s s, 25 e Thatford st, 25x100. Norman & O'Brien agt B. Seerman, owner, and John Hogan, contractor...... 74 50

31 Rockaway av, e s, 100 s Eastern Parkway, 25x100. Same agt same owner and contractor........ 74 50

31 Fourth st, s s, 100 e 6th av, 440x100. Paul Rofrano agt Moses & Fanton, owners and contractors........ 215 00

31 Third st, n s, 431.9 e 6th av, 44x90. Same agt same owner and contractor........ 751 56

31 First st, s s, 305 w 5th av, 90x100. Miller & Anderson agt W. S. Hale, owner and contractor........ 178 00

Sept.

1 Sixty-sixth st, s e cor 11th av, 22x100, Bath Beach. John Gall agt Magi Reichenback, owner and contractor........ 222 00

2 Greene av, No. 456, s s, 888.4 w Nostrand av, 16.8x100. Benjamin H. Neuman agt Nellie C. Riley, owner, and Edward E. and Nellie C. Riley, contractors........ 120 00

2 Sixty-third st, n s, 240 w 14th av, 20x100, New Utrecht. Louis Willumsen agt John Healy, owner and contractor 32 50

2 Auburn pl, No. 3 } Canton st, No. 97 } Brooklyn Door and Sash Co. agt Lipman Arensberg, owner, and Frederick M. Fogg, contractor........ 625 03

2 Wyckoff av, No. 33........ } Troutman st, e s, 147.2 n Wyckoff av, 25x100........ } Boerum st, No. 99, n s, 25x106........ } Jacob Nasel agt — Edmundstein, owner, and Herman E. Funk, contractor. ... 1,215 00

3 Christopher st, e s, 200 n Belmont av, 25x100. Rope & Co. agt Joseph Berger and Samuel Machel, owners and contractors.. 375 00

3 Same property. David Levy agt Annie Levy, owner, and Joseph Berger, contractor........ 90 00

SATISFIED MECHANICS' LIENS.

NEW YORK CITY.

Aug.

31 Seventh av, No. 2185, e s, 50 n 129th st, 25x100. Henry Taylor agt Max Hervich and Lizzie McComb. (Lien filed June 30, 1891) $47 50

Sept.

2 Rivington st, No. 313, 25x100. Gabriel Galef agt Adolph Gross and — Solomon. (Aug. 17, 1891) 165 00

2 One Hundred and Fifth st, Nos. 221-225 W., 75x100.10. Matthesius & Vollosio agt Christian H. Schultheiss. (Aug. 17, 1891). 2,131 14

2*Ninety-fifth st, No. 68, s e cor Columbus av, 80x25. James Murray agt Mrs. Platho and Frank Leimeister. (July 11, 1891)... 60 00

2*Seventh st, Nos. 97 and 97½ E., 48.5x—. Balthaser Lautenschlager agt George Hornberger. (June 12, 1891)........ 200 00

3 9th av, s w cor 124th st, 100x75. J D Hicks agt Max Scharf and Welsh Bros. (Feb. 7, 1890)........ 185 00

3 Ninety-sixth st, n s, 70 e Lexington av, 125x—. Pelham Hod Elevating Co. agt Owen F. and William McElroy. (Aug. 25, 1891)........ 192 50

3 Same property. Allen & Campbell agt Owen F. McElroy, Jr., and William McElroy. (Aug. 24, 1891)........ 1,200 00

4 One Hundred and Fifth st, Nos. 305-311 E., n s, 100x—. Henry Schluter agt Matthew Coogan. (Sept. 2, 1891)........ 413 00

4 Same property. Same agt same. (Aug. 24, 1891)........ 413 00

4 One Hundred and Fifteenth st, n e s, 300 n e Pleasant av. Vigna & Orrigoni agt Standard Gas Co, and W. V. and J. Weber. (Aug. 25, 1891)........ 110 00

4 Third av (middle), bet 170th and 177th sts. Harris & Co. agt The N. Y., Suburban Rapid Transit Co., Stephen McGowan and John Doe. (Feb. 10, 1891)........ 683 38

4 Ninety-fourth st, n s, 100 w Columbus av, 50x—. Morton Bros. & Co. agt Francis J. Hillenbrand. (July 11, 1891)........ 1,900 00

4 One Hundred and Twenty-fifth st, Nos. 116 and 118, s s, 200 w Lenox av, 50x100. C. S. Harris assignee agt Edward D. Farrell. (April 28, 1891)........ 4,820 00

4 Hampden st, s s, 50 w Andrews av, 50.10x100. Charles Carognaro agt Mary Adriance and Thomas Wilson. (Aug. 14, 1891) 96 00

4 One Hundred and Eighty-fourth st, s s, 500 w Andrews av, 50x100. Thomas Wilson agt Mary L. Adriance and Thomas J. Clarke. (Aug. 21, 1891)........ 252 90

4 Ninety-second st, n s, 70 e Lexington av, 100x100.11. John Madden agt Owen F.

and William McElroy and Clark & Dolan. (Aug. 26, 1891)........ 150 00

4 Ninety-sixth st, n s, 70 e Lexington av, 100 x100.11. Same agt Owen F. McElroy, Jr., and William McElroy and Clark & Dolan. (Aug. 29, 1891)........ 150 00

4 Leroy st, Nos. 57-63, 64x100. Same agt Stevens & McElroy & Co. and Clark & Dolan. (Aug. 26, 1891)........ 100 00

*Discharged by depositing amount of lien and interest with County Clerk.

KINGS COUNTY.

Aug.

28 Sixth st, n s, 100 w 5th av, 100x100. H. S. Christian agt Sylvester Searing, owner and contractor. (Lien filed Sept. 26, 1890)........ $468 45

28 Henry st, e s, bet Coney Island plank road and Coney Island Creek, Coney Island. Conrad Labbardt agt Mrs. Emma Slevin, owner, and William Rubien, contractor. (Aug. 10, 1891)........ 75 00

28 Throop av, w s, 40 s Stockton st, 60x100. Valentine Bruckhauser & Brother agt German Evangelical P. Church, owner and contractor. (Aug. 21, 1891)........25,945 00

28 Forty-fifth st, n s, 300 e 5th av, 40x100.2. Hobby & Doody agt John L. Parish, owner, and A. D. Hyde, contractor. (July 13, 1891)........ 1:7 74

29 Sixth st, n s, 297.6 w 5th av, 96x100. Richard Cronin & Sons agt E. G. Gollner, owner and contractor. (July 25, 1891)........ 264 80

31 Sixth st, 180 w 5th av, 100x115. Charles G. Rice agt H. Becker, owner and contractor. (Aug. 24, 1891)........ 37 50

Sept.

1 Eighth av, e s, extends from 15th st to 16th st, 200x160. John Monahan agt Edwin J. Bedell, owner and contractor. (June 27, 1891)........ 102 83

1 Same property. The Long Island Brick Co. agt same owner and contractor. (June 23, 1891)........4,498 00

1 Same property. H. S. Christian agt same owner and contractor. (June 19, 1891)... 308 20

1 Same property. Taber & Case agt same owner and contractor. (June 17, 1891)... 213 00

1 Same property. William Martin agt same owner and contractor. (June 16, 1891)... 2,200 00

1 Woodbine st, n w s, 125 s w Knickerbocker av, 100x100. B. Brinkmann & Co. agt Albert Berkmeier. (July 29, 1891.) (Order of Court)........ 110 00

1 Woodbine st, w s, 20 w Hamburg av, 90x45. Peter Egan agt some owner and contractor. (Aug 1, 1891.) (Order of Court).... 140 00

1 Woodbine st, 20 from Knickerbocker av, 90 x100. Same agt same owner and contractor. (Aug 3, 1891.) (Order of Court).... 140 00

1 Woodbine st, n w s, 25 s w Knickerbocker av, 200x100. Michael Mayer agt same owner and contractor. (Aug. 14, 1891.) (Order of Court)........1,246 45

2 Greene av, e s, 100 n Bushwick av, 50x100. Jacob May agt Thos. Goodwin, owner and contractor. (Aug. 27, 1891)........ 102 82

3 Bath av, s s, 50 w Bay 19th st, 25x100, New Utrecht. Charles Stauche agt Mr. Simonson, owner, and Joseph Trautman and Mr. Larsen, contractors. (July 16, 1891)...... 18 00

BUILDINGS PROJECTED.

The first name is that of the owner; ar't stands for architect, m'n for mason, c'r for carpenter and b'r for builder.

NEW YORK CITY.

SOUTH OF 14TH STREET.

Jersey st, Nos. 2, 4 and 6, six-story brk factory, 70.7x61.6, copper roof; cost, $45,000; Hoops & Hawley, 324 West 20th st; ar't, J. R. Thomas. Plan 1198.

Walker st, No. 109, three-story brk building, 20x75, tin roof; cost, $6,000; agent, W. H. Carpenter, Mamaroneck, N. Y.; ar't, H. Horenburger; m'n, A. Schrage. Plan 1200.

BETWEEN 14TH AND 59TH STREETS.

18th st, Nos. 424 and 426 E, five-story brk stable, 50x89, tin roof; cost, $35,000; J. Bickmann, 327 East 18th st; ar't, B. W. Berger. Plan 1181.

BETWEEN 59TH AND 125TH STREETS, EAST OF 5TH AVENUE.

103d st, No. 315 E, frame shed, 25x14, gravel roof; cost, $100; T. Kiernan, 317 East 103d st. Plan 1184.

5th av, No. 852, four and five-story brk and stone dwell'g, 25x75.2 with 24.10 extension, tile and copper roof; cost, $60,000; H. O. Havemeyer, 1 East 66th st; ar't, C. C. Haight. Plan 1188.

BETWEEN 59TH AND 125TH STREETS, WEST OF CENTRAL PARK WEST AND 8TH AVENUE.

70th st, n s, 325 e 9th av, five four-story and basement stone dwell'gs, 20x60 with extension, tin roofs; cost, $20,000 each; J. Ruddell, 103 West 121st st; ar't, G. A. Schellenger. Plan 1192.

76th st, n s, 151 w West End av, four five-story brk and stone dwell'gs, three 20x55.4 and one 18x 55.4, all with extensions, tin roofs; cost, $18,000 each; Reuben Skinner, 314 West 76th st; ar't, M. Hensel. Plan 1191.

Columbus av, No. 691, rear, frame shed, 12x22, tarred roof; cost, $30; J. R. Eakins, 124 East 23d st; m'n, I. Gardiner; c'r, C. Bailey. Plan 1185.

NORTH OF 125TH STREET.

128th st, n s, 244.6 w 5th av, five-story stone flat, 20x75, tin roof; cost, $16,000; A. Judge, 164 St. Nicholas av; ar't, J. C. Burne. Plan 1194.

181st st, n s, 300 w Amsterdam av, five-story brk and stone flat, 25x89, tin roof; cost, $18,000; Clara A. Ruck and ano., 420 West 58th st; ar't, J. W. Cole; b'r, M. J. Barron. Plan 1183.

144th st, s s, 100 w 8th av, five-story brk and stone flat, 25x65, tin roof; cost, $12,000; E. Molwitz, 2707 8th av; ar't, H. Kafka; m'n, C. Andersen; c'r, C. T. Bruchle. Plan 1196.

23D AND 24TH WARDS.

170th st, s s, 86 e Vanderbilt av, four two-story frame dwell'gs, 16x48, tin roofs; cost, $2,000 each; Van Riper & La Coste, 378 Mott av; ar't, H. S. Baker. Plan 1190.

Crotona av, n s, 128 e Broad st, two-story frame dwell'g, 21x39, shingle roof; cost, $2,360; O. W. Boyden, 1791 Bathgate av; ar'ts, Hoar & Day; b'r, C. Pitchie. Plan 1193.

Eagle av, w s, 175 s 163d st, two-story and basement brk and frame dwell'g, 19x52, tin roof; cost, $3,000; Sarah Greenbaum, 1502 2d av; ar't, E. T. Richards. Plan 1189.

Grand av, n s, 150 w 1st st, frame and glass greenhouse, 33x100; cost, $500; P. Roemer, Woodlawn, N. Y.; ar't, G. P. Roemer, Jr.; m'n, J. New; c'r, W. A. Roemer. Plan 1187.

Johnson av, s s, 360 e Spuyten Duyvil Parkway, two-story frame dwell'g, 16x26, tin roof; cost, $1,200; J. W. Du Bois, Spuyten Duyvil, N. Y.; c'r, M. McQuade. Plan 1181.

Washington av, e s, 210 s 172d st, three-story frame dwell'g, 22x50, tin roof; cost, $4,500; C. W. M. Jones, House of Refuge, Randall's Island, N. Y.; ar't, R. E. Rogers. Plan 1182.

Elsmere pl, s s, 475 w Marmion av, two two-story frame dwell'gs, 20x30, with extensions, tin roofs; cost, abt $2,800 each; J. A. Gray, 131 West 35th st; ar'r, C. S. Clark. Plan 1197.

Hampden st, n s, 200 e Sedgwick av, two-story frame stable, 30x26, shingle roof; cost, $1,800; Sarah Y. Jackson, Fordham Heights, N. Y.; b'r, Tolin & Son. Plan 1199.

Southern Boulevard, s w cor Valentine av, two-story and attic frame dwell'g, 26x48, shingle roof; cost, $8,000; Hattie L. Hayward, 88 West st, South Norwalk, Conn.; ar't, E. K. Bourne; m'ns, Gillings & Co. Plan 1195.

KINGS COUNTY.

Plan 1595—Wythe av, w s, 25 s South 11th st, one six-story brk and brown stone factory, 44.6 and 26x175.6, tin roof, iron and brk cornice; cost, $350,000; McLoughlin Bros.; ar't, W. H. Gaylor; b'rs, W. & T. Lamb and G. A. Kingsland.

1596—21st st, s s, 80 w 7th av, one one-story frame dwell'g, 20x36, tin roof; cost, $700; ow'r and b'r, Henry Petersen, 325A 21st st; ar't, N. A. Taylor.

1597—Bergen st, s s, 100 w Hopkinson av, one three-story frame dwell'g, 20x44, tin roof; cost, $2,000; Rosa Rosenfeldt; ar't, C. M. Thompson; b'r, G. Schoenfeld.

1598—Shepherd av, w s, 100 n Ridgewood av, one two-story frame dwell'g, 19.6x32, tin roof; cost, $2,200; ow'rs and b'rs, Swift & Baker, 2921 Atlantic av; ar'ts, Danmar & Fischer.

1599—Essex st, e s, 100 n Ridgewood av, one two-story frame dwell'g, 19.6x32, tin roof; cost, $2,200; ow'rs, ar'ts and b'rs, same as last.

1600—Washington av, Nos. 77 and 79, abt 70 from Park av, one six-story brk and granite with iron columns wholesale egg store, 40x90, tin roof, iron cornice; cost, $2,900; S. S. Long & Bros., 82 Dey st, New York; ar't, T. E. Thomson; b'r, H. Getty.

1601—Stagg st, n s, 100 e Bogert st, one one-story frame stable, &c., 14x75, felt roof; cost, $265; Henry Berau, 621 Van Buren st.

1602—Ridgewood av, n w cor Dresden st, one one-story frame stable, 13x18, tin roof; cost, $75; Mr. Wickert.

1603—Keap st, No. 352, one two-story brk organ shop, 24x22, tin roof, brk cornice; cost, $1,-000; M. Schwarze, on premises; ar'ts, D. Acker & Son; b'r, J. Kleinklauss.

1604—47th st, n s, 280 w 3d av, one two-story frame stable, 20x50, gravel roof; cost, $1,000; C. B. Templeman, 1133 3d av; ar'ts, H. L. Spicer & Son.

1605—8th av, n w cor 16th st, one one-story brk church, 59 9 and 57.9x80, slate roof, wooden cornice; cost, $21,000; Brooklyn Baptist Church Extension Soc.; ar't, C. G. Jones; b'rs, F. Mapes and R. B. Ferguson.

1606—Chestnut st, w s, 782 s Jamaica av, one two-story and attic frame dwell'g, 20x30, tin roof; cost, $2,500; ow'r and c'r, Edward B. Mould, Logan st, cor Etna st.

1607—Van Voorhis st, n s, 150 w Evergreen av, and Schaeffer st, s s, 150 w Evergreen av, four three-story frame (brk filled) tenem'ts, 25x60, tin roofs; cost, $5,000; Mary E. Gentleman, 1058 Jefferson av; ar't and b'r, I. W. Welton.

1608—Bergen st, n s, 100 w Kingston av, three two-story basement and attic brk dwell'gs, 20x45, tin roofs, wooden cornices; cost, $6,000 each; J. H. Dorherty & Bro., 286 Flatbush av; ar't, W. M. Coots; b'r, day's work.

1609—6th st, n s, 397.10 w 5th av, six two-story and basement brk dwell'gs, 16.8x45, tin roofs, wooden cornices; cost, $24,000; ow'r and ar't, E. G. Goldner, 308 6th st.

1610—Bedford av, w s, bet Atlantic av and Pacific st, one three and one-story brk and Potsdam red stone armory, 198 2 and 210.4x485 and 408, corrugated iron or slate and tin roofs, iron cornices; cost, $283,459; State New York, Albany, N. Y.; ar't, J. G. Perry; b'rs, A. Pasquinni & Co.

1611—51st st, n s, east of 7th av, one one-story frame dwell'g, 20x40, tin roof; cost, $600; Ellen Parsons, 6th av and 51st st; ar't and b'r, E. Parsons.

1612—McDougal st, n s, 325 e Saratoga av, one one story frame tailor shop, 20x30, tin or gravel roof; cost, $1,200; ow'r and ar't, D. Davison, 134 Eldert st.

1613—Lombardy st, No. 32, s s, 225 w Morgan av, one one-story frame dwell'g, 25x26, gravel roof; cost, $500; Jas. Kelly, 148 Meeker av.

1614—Bushwick av, n e cor Myrtle av, two one-story frame stores, one 48 and 11x38 and one 24.6 x38, cement roof; cost, total, $3,500; J. T. Story; ar't, W. H. Gaylor; b'rs, S. L. Hough and S. Parks.

1615—28th st, s s, 300 w 5th av, one three-story frame tenem't, 25x52, tin roof; cost, $3,800; Wm. H. Marvin, 200 28th st; ar't, W. H. Wirth; c'r, J. R. Greene; m'n, not selected.

1616—Thatford av, w s, 125 s Eastern Parkway, one two-story frame tailor shop, 20x30, tin roof; cost, $400; Samelson & Rogensky, Belmont av.

1617—Putnam av, n s, 100 e Patchen av, four two-story and basement brk dwell'gs, 18.9x44, tin roofs; cost, $3,000 each; F. J. Mugford, 971A Putnam av; ar't, W. V. Young; b'r, not selected.

1618—McDonough st, n s, 360 e Tompkins av, two four-story and basement brown stone dwell'gs, 22x48, tin roofs, iron cornices; cost, $17,000; John Fraser, 44 Rochester av; ar'ts, A. Hill & Son.

1619—Monroe st, s s, 250 e Stuyvesant av, five two-story and basement sandstone dwell'gs, 17 and 18x45, tin roofs, wooden cornices; cost, each, $4,500; A. S. Walsh, 643 Madison st; ar'ts, A. Hill & Son.

1620—Willoughby av, s w cor Nostrand av, rear, one two-story brk stable, 40x18, tin and gravel roof, iron cornice; cost, $4,000; A. H. Topping, 489 Willoughby av; ar't, G. Makay; b'r, H. P. Smith.

1621—McDonough st, s s, 350 e Reid av, six two-story brown stone dwell'gs, 18 and 17.8x48, tin roofs, wooden cornices; cost, $4,700 each; C. G. Reynolds, 243 Reid av; ar'ts, A. Hill & Son.

1622—Ryerson st, e s, 73 n Myrtle av, one four-story brk store and flat, 27x50, tin roof, wooden cornice; cost, $9,000; Seth L. Keeney, 221 Clermont av. ar't, E. Van Voorhies; b'rs, R. E. Page & Co.

1623—Snediker av, e s, 150 s Hegemann av or st, one one-and-a-half-story frame dwell'g, 16x24, shingle roof; cost, $600; Elizabeth Morris, Christopher and Blake avs; b'r, J. W. Morris.

1624—22d st, n s, 150 w 6th av, one three-story frame (brk filled) tenem't, 22x45, tin roof; cost, $4,300; Ellen Malone, 285 22d st; ar't, W. H. Wirth; b'rs, N. Nelson and F. McCoppin.

1625—Bergen st, s s, 96 w Rochester av, one two-story frame dwell'g, 20x40, tin roof; cost, $1,500; Geo. Mahler, 204 Utica av; b'r, not selected.

1626—North 11th st, s e cor Berry st, one five-story brk blank book factory, 85x99, gravel roof, brk cornice; cost, $30,000; S. M. Vernon, 69 Duane st, New York; ar't, G. M. Walgrove.

ALTERATIONS NEW YORK CITY.

Plan 1585—26th st and East River (Bellevue Hospital grounds), interior alterations and new connecting bridge; cost, $6,500; Mayor, &c., City Hall; ar't, L. Eidlitz.

1586—3d av, e s, bet 181st and 183d sts, rear, raised one story and interior alterations; cost, $3,500; Home for Incurables, on premises; ar't, R. E. Rogers.

1587—Madison av, s w cor 133d st, interior alterations and walls altered; cost, $900; S. A. Thompson, on premises; ar't, M. L. Ungrich.

1588—135th st, No 568 E., interior alterations and front altered; cost, $1,000; W. H. Payne, 98 Park av; ar't, C. A. Millner, Jr.

1589—2d av, No. 556, new store front; cost, $280; C. S. Davis, Rochester, N. Y.; c'r, R. McGregor.

1590—Madison av, s w cor 111th st, new chimney; cost, $500; C. Carreau, 654 Madison av; m'ns, P. Tostevins Sons.

1591—Willis av, n e cor 134th st, one-story extension, 15x25, and new windows cut; cost, $800; J. D. Ohlssen, 663 East 134th st; ar't, A. Fowler.

1592—Cortlandt st, No. 33, interior alterations; cost, $2,500; W. H. Naething, on premises; c'r, C. Wendt.

1593—3d av, No. 4197, raised to grade; cost, $300; M. Eymer, on premises; ar't, C. F. Lohse.

1594—153d st, No. 511 E., raised one story and extended one story, 22x6; cost, $800; J. Siemering, on premises; ar't, C. F. Lohse.

1595—Courtlandt av, w s, 75 s 158th st, moved, new foundation; cost, $600; H. Reymers, 607 East 158th st; ar't, C. F. Lohse.

1596—Alexander av, n e cor 135th st, one-story extension, 20x36.6, interior alterations, walls altered; cost, $4,200; F. A. Schilling, on premises; ar't, A. Pfeiffer.

1597—2d av, No. 638, two-story extension, 28x 20.3; cost, $3,000; P J. Maloney, 339 East 58th st; ar'ts, Kurtzer & Rohl; c'r, E. Schulz.

1598—Amsterdam av, s w cor 94th st, one-story extension, 29.6x18.6; cost, $1,800; G. W. Eggers, 103 West 93d st; ar't, E. Wenz.

1599—45th st, No. 62 W., raised one story; cost, $3,000; Harriet M. Spraker, on premises; ar't, H. P. Seyfert.

1600—Aqueduct av, e s, 175 n 184th st, two-story extension, 12x8; cost, $100; att'y, S. H. Mapes, on premises.

1601—148th st, n s, 330 w Grand Boulevard, moved, new foundation; cost, $35; lessee, J. Farrell, on premises.

1602—55th st, No. 248 E., cellar extension, 26x 155; cost, $10,000; C. Harnischfeger, on premises; ar't, F. Ebeling.

1603—7th av, w s, bet 124th and 125th sts, interior alterations, walls altered; cost, $300; A. S.

Walker, Hotel Beresford; ar't, W. S. Jennings; m'ns, White & Anderson.

1604—Kingsbridge road, s s, 75 e Webster av, raised to grade and new foundation; cost, $500; F. Shepperd, Bainbridge av, Fordham, N. Y.

1605—Henry st, No. 97, cellar, basement and four-story extension, 16.1x37.2, new partitions, stairs and light shaft, walls altered; cost, $16,000; B. Levy, on premises; ar't, F. Ebeling.

1606—28th st, No. 50 W., one-story and basement extension, 14x7, interior alterations and walls altered; cost, $2,000; A. Weinstein, 808 Lexington av; ar't, C. H. Israels.

1607—Grand st, No. 364, one-story extension, 17.6x30, interior alterations, walls altered and new front; cost, $1,600; S. Conger, Summit, N. J.; ar't, H. Horenburger; c'r, F. Sackett.

1608—123d st, No. 73 E., one-story extension, 27x20, interior alterations and walls altered; cost, $4,000; H. Gieschen, 46 East 124th st; ar't, H. Horenburger; b'r, F. Sackett.

1609—Hudson st, n w cor Charles st, new store front; cost, $400; J. Schmitt, 971 Lexington av; ar't, C. Rentz.

1610—Washington av, w s, 88 n 177th st, moved and new foundation; cost, $100; W. Clarke, n w cor Washington av and 177th st; ar't, J. J. Vreeland.

1611—177th st, No. 711 E., one-story extension, 10x16; cost, $150; C. Heylman, on premises; ar't, J. J. Vreeland; b'rs, Heylman & Lally.

KINGS COUNTY.

Plan 827—Johnson av, No. 617, raised building 5 ft.; cost, $150; ow'r and b'r, Mr. Kruse, 199 McKibbinst.

828—South 1st st, No. 354, substitute flat for peak roof; cost, $550; Mrs. Bernard, 117 West 132d st, New York; c'rs, C. L. Johnsons Sons.

829—Navy st, w s, 77 s De Kalb av, add one story brk; cost, $1,000; Citizens Illuminating Co., Navy st, cor De Kalb av; ar't, T. F. Houghton; m'n, M. Guilfoyle.

830—Schenck av, No. 204, raised 3 ft.; cost, $250; ow'r and b'r, Mrs. Young, on premises.

831—Schermerhorn st, s s, 50 e 3d av proposed, to underpin about 25 ft. deep of e s wall; cost, $150; Board of Education; m'ns, Hugh & Robinson, 403 East 61st st, New York.

832—Eastern Parkway, n w cor Thatford av, one one-story frame extension, 22x46, tin roof, cost, $1,100; W. Wenezemer, on premises; cr's, Harrison & Gallagher.

833—Leonard st, n w cor Boerum st, interior alterations; cost, $700; Beller & Lieber, 36 Seigel st; ar't, H. Vollweiler; m'n, not selected.

834—Belmont av, No. 468, one two-story frame extension, 18x12, tin roof; cost, $450; John J. Keifer, on premises; m'n, August Henisinger.

835—Ewen st, No. 160, new store front; cost, $500; Mrs. Heinrich, on premises.

836—Nostrand av, No. 309, front and interior alterations; cost, $800; J. B. Ireland, 170 Broadway, New York; b'rs, J. J. Bentzen and H. J. Smith.

837—Broadway, s e cor Myrtle av, new show window and interior alterations; cost, $400; Julius Block, 246 Vernon av.

838—Seigel st, No. 42, add one-story, flat tin roof; cost, $800; Lewis Schackner, on premises; c'rs, Harrison & Gallagher.

839—Columbia st, No. 271, add one story to extension, front and interior alterations; cost, $1,500; H. Pepper, 281 Columbia st; ar't and m'ns; J. McGowan & Son; c'r, E. Perkis.

840—Lafayette av, n w cor South Oxford st, one-story brk extension, 24.6x14, tin roof; cost, $400; Oxford Club, on premises; ar't, J. L. Young; b'r, J. P. Fuels.

841—Vanderbilt av, No. 411, one one-story brk extension, 45x14, tin roof, internal alterations; cost, $1,850; ow'r, Dr. C. N. Hoagland, 410 Clinton av; ar'ts, Lamb & Rich; m'n, E. Jones; c'r, Geo. Lowden.

842—Eagle st, No. 229, add one story; cost, $1,100; ow'r, James A. Kenny, on premises; ar't, C. Dunkbase; b'r, not selected.

843—Harts alley, rear of No. 186 High st, one one-story brk extension, 24x10, tin roof; cost, $550; ow'r, O. D. McGovern, 21 Morton st, New York; b'r, &c., not selected.

844—Washington av, w s, 91.3 s Lafayette av, one story brk extension, 14 and 16x25, tin roof, wooden cornice; cost, $1,600; Clarence Creighton, on premises; ar't, C. B. Cutler, b'rs, J. M. Brown and Martin & Lee.

845—Henry st, No. 367, three-story brk extension, 6x17, tin roof; cost, $1,000; C. F. A. Hinrichs, 367 Henry st; ar't, A. Pauli; b'r, A. Goodsell.

846—Diamond st, No. 93, raised 9 feet on frame story; cost, $1,000; Mrs. Frank McCann, on premises.

847—Boerum st, No 26, one-story brk extension, 25x19.6, tin roof; cost, $250; J. Wickert & Co., 24 and 26 Boerum st; ar't, F. Wunder.

848—Fulton st, n e cor Pearl st, front altered, &c.; cost, $1,200; Wm. H. Douglass, on premises; ar't and b'r, O. K. Buckley, Jr.

849—Fulton st, Nos. 293-297, divide buildings by brk wall, new stairs, &c.; cost, $2,000; S. Wechsler & Bros., Fulton st; b'r, T. Donlon.

850—Gold st, No. 412, one-story and basement brk extension, 8x7, tin roof; cost, $150; J. Hennessy, on premises; ar't, H. Konig.

851—Oakland st, Nos. 401 and 403, one-story frame extension, 25x28, gravel roof; cost, $150; Thomas G. Pringle, on premises; b'r, J. C. Williams.

852—Eastern Parkway, near Alabama av, one-story frame extension, 40x108; gravel roof; cost, $1,500; ar't, O. F. Balston; b'r, Kings County L Road's men.

853—York st, No. 189, raised 8.6 on brk wall, also two-story brk extension, 22x12.6, tin roof; cost, $1,800; Wm. S. Catherwood, 94 Bridge st; ar't, J. G. Glover.

854—13th st, s s, 150 e 6th av, one and two-story brk extension, 50x79, tin roof; cost, $1,500; George Wessel, on premises; b'r, not selected.

MISCELLANEOUS.

BUSINESS FAILURES.

Schedule of assignments for the five weeks ending Sept. 4, 1891:

	Liabilities.	Nominal Assets.	Real Assets.
Arnold, Brainerd T...	$5,882.85	$5,960.99	$1,500.00
Avery, John C........	48,918.49	437,221.02	76,172.02
Byrne, William J.... Hartigan, Daniel J.	5,340.39	2,190.81	1,521.98
Bessey, Frederick A..	9,690.07	3,459.20	1,703.64
Farley, John.........	16,604.83	8,250.00	6,400.00
Jordan, Louis........	12,782.38	173,800.00	....
Johnston, George R. Tallman, Stephen S. and George D.... Thurston, Edward B. Spaeth, Edward....	92,691.30	96,808.12	41,411.29
Lawton, Nelson A....	8,371.02	4,061.42	3,132.92
Riker, Carroll L......	57,269.65	104,742.50	3,770.41
Satterlee, Livingston.... Bostwick, Charles B. Martin, Ira Kingsley........	150,177.14	193,224.93	116.60
Yasinski, Casmir W..	3,153.27	2,926.20	2,115.55

N. Y. ASSIGNMENTS—BENEFIT CREDITORS.

Aug. and Sept.

31 Cohen, Lipman (manufacturer of ladies' and children's cloaks, at No. 104 Division st), to Isaac Cohen; preferences $1,400.

1 James, Henry L., of Williamsburg, Mass., to Frank L. Learned; without preferences.

4 Capel, Henry A. and William B. McNulty (composing firm of Capel & McNulty, manufacturers of ostrich and fancy feathers, at No. 191 Mercer st), to Edward B. Goodman; without preferences.

4 Smith, Morris H. (sole surviving partner of F. D. Wallace & Co., stock brokers, at No. 56 Broad st), to John P. Crawford; preferences, $13,421.00.

KINGS COUNTY.

GENERAL ASSIGNMENTS.

Aug and Sept.

27 Thomas, Samuel E. to Isaac Lublin.

3 Vanderhoef, John V. E. to Edward C. Reiss.

ADVERTISED LEGAL SALES.

REFEREES SALES TO BE HELD AT THE REAL ESTATE EXCHANGE AND AUCTION ROOM (LIMITED), 59 to 65 LIBERTY STREET, EXCEPT WHERE OTHERWISE STATED.

Sept.

42d st, No. 25, n s, 354.2 w 5th av, 20.4x100.5, four-story stone front store and dwell'g, by R. V. Harnett. (Leasehold; action No. 1; amt due $5,420)........ 5

Same property, by R. V. Harnett. (Leasehold; action No. 2; amt due $16,650)........ 5

76th st, No. 311, n s, 200 e 2d av, 25x102.2, five-story brk tenem't with stores, by Smyth & Ryan. (Amt due $3,659)........ 8

144th st, n e cor Bradhurst av, 32.4x99.11x21.4x100.6, by Smyth & Ryan. (All right, title and int. which Jacob Striffler had on March 5, 1890)........ 8

184th st, s e s, 113.8 s Bainbridge av, 28.7x83.7x25x96.7, by R. V. Harnett & Co. (Amt due $2,263).. 8

184th st, s e s, 141.10 s Bainbridge av, 26.2x77.2x25x83.7, by R. V. Harnett & Co. (Amt due $2,263).. 8

Convent av, No. 61, e s, 599.6 n 141st st, 20x100, three-story brk dwell'g, by William Kennelly. (Amt due $16,269)........ 8

Jerome av, e s, at intersection with a line formerly known as the northerly line of village of Mount Eden and extending easterly along said line to lands formerly owned by Townsend Poole, x north and northwest to centre of a brook, x west along brook to Jerome av, x southwest along av to beginning, containing 5 39-100 acres, excepting and reserving a certain triangular parcel consisting of 1 acre of land and the av opposite, situate at s w extremity of said premises, beginning at intersection centre line of Jerome av with northerly line of village of Mount Eden and extending northeast along centre line 350 x southeast 300 to northerly line village of Mount Eden, x west 465 to beginning, by Smyth & Ryan. (Partition sale)........ 8

10th av, No. 319, w s, 74.1 n 28th st, 24.8x100, three-story brk tenem't with stores, ¾ part, by William Kennelly........ 8

123d st, No. 268, s s, 100 e 8th av, 25x100.11x25x100.8, five-story stone front flat, by A. H. Muller & Son. (Amt due $16,056)........ 9

114th st, No. 322, s s, 262.6 e 2d av, 18.9x100.11, four-story brk tenem't, by B. L. Kennelly. (Amt due $9,852)........ 9

55th st, No. 406, s s, 100 w 9th av, 23x100.5, four-story stone front dwell'g, by B. L. Kennelly. (Amt due $5,340)........ 10

87th st, No. 136, s s, 350 w 9th av, 20x100.8, four-story stone front dwell'g, by D. P. Ingraham & Co. (Amt due $24,156)........ 10

87th st, No. 142, s s, 410 w 9th av, 20x100.8, four-story stone front dwell'g, by D. P. Ingraham & Co. (Amt due $26,340)........ 10

Alexander av, s w cor 141st st, runs west 100 x south 100 x east 25 x north 25 x east 75 to Alexander av, x north 75 to beginning, by William Kennelly. (Amt due $6,588)........ 10

71st st, No. 407, n s, 94 e 1st av, 19x102.2, four-story brk store and tenem't........
111th st, No. 315, n s, 225 e 2d av, 25x100.10x24x100.10, four-story brk store and tenem't........
All the right, title and int. of Charles F. Rost had on Feb. 21, 1890, to the above, by Sheriff, at City Hall. (Sale under execution)........ 11

38th st, No 444, s s, 220.5 s e 10th av, 25x98.9, three-story frame tenem't with two-story brk building on rear, by R. V. Harnett. (Amt due $1,136)... 14

7th av, Nos. 2170-2178, s w cor 129th st, 99.11x75, five five-story brk stores and flats, by R. V. Harnett & Co. (Amt due $27,678; prior morts. $——)... 14

KINGS COUNTY.

Sept.

Hancock st, Nos. 702½ and 704, s s, 150 w Patchen av, 50x100, two story and basement brk dwelling and one-story frame dwell'g; assessed value, $4,700........
Sumpter st, No. 306, s s, 120 w Rockaway av, runs west 20.6 x south — x east .02 x south — x east 20.4 x north 100 to beginning, two-story frame dwell'g; assessed value, $1,000........
Atlantic av, No. 493, n s, 250 e Bond st, 25x100, three-story brk tenem't with frame rear; assessed value, $4,500........
by T. A. Kerrigan, at 13 Willoughby st........ 8

Duffield st, Nos. 91-103, e s, 100 n Johnson st, 130x100, Duffield terrace; assessed value, $42,000..
Macon st, No. 446, s s, 272.6 w Stuyvesant av, 17.6x100, two-and-a-half-story brk dwell'g; assessed value, $5,000........
62d st, s s, 480 w 14th av, 20x100, New Utrecht, frame dwell'g........
by T. A. Kerrigan, at 13 Willoughby st........ 9

Hull st, s s, 101.1 w Stone av, 16.8x100, two-story and basement brk dwell'g; assessed value, $2,500; at County Court House........

St. Marks av, Nos. 671 and 673, n s, 150 w Nostrand av, 50x125.3½, two-and-a-half-story brk detached dwell'g on plot; assessed value, $11,500; by Jere. Johnson, Jr., at the Real Estate Exchange, 189 and 191 Montague st........ 9

Herkimer st, n w cor Saratoga av, 100x120; assessed value, $22,000; by Charles H. Winslow, ref., at County Court House........ 10

Van Vourhis st, n w s, 269.11 s w Evergreen av, 17.0¼x100x16.11x100, two-story frame (brk lined) dwell'g; assessed value, $3,000; by T. A. Kerrigan, at 13 Willoughby st........ 10

Bedford av, No. 257, e s, 40.3 n South 1st st, 20.3x81x18.6x81, three story frame dwell'g and store; assessed value, $3,200; by T. A. Kerrigan, at 45 road way, E. D........ 10

Fulton st, s w cor Saratoga av, 100x80; assessed value, $11,000........
Pacific st, s s, 297.3 e Rochester av, 16.8x107.2⅝..
Pacific st, s s, 313.11 e Rochester av, 16.8x107.2⅝
Pacific st, s s, 330.7 e Rochester av, 16.8x107.2⅝..
Pacific st, s s, 347.3 e Rochester av, 16.7x107.2⅝..
Four two-story and basement frame dwell'gs; assessed value, $1,400 each........
by T. A. Kerrigan, at 13 Willoughby st........ 11

Jackson st, No. 170, s s, 100 e Graham av, 25x100, two-story frame dwell'g on rear; assessed value, $1,400; by Jacob Neu, ref., at County Court House........ 12

LIS PENDENS, KINGS COUNTY.

Aug.

Dean st, s s, 120 e Utica av, 20x107.5. Horace F. Burroughs agt Ann Donlon; att'ys, Fisher & Voltz........ 28

Dean st, s s, 100 e Utica av, 20x107.5. Same agt same; same att'ys........ 28

Jefferson av, s s, 180 w Nostrand av, 20x100......
Jefferson av, s s, 200 w Nostrand av, 20x100......
Jefferson av, s s, 220 w Nostrand av, 20x100......
Jefferson av, s s, 240 w Nostrand av, 20x100......
Jefferson av, s s, 260 w Nostrand av, 20x100......
Jefferson av, s s, 320 w Nostrand av, 20x100......
Thomas H. Elliott exr. Stephen Pettus agt Samuel J. Jones; 6 amended notices; att'ys, Hoadly, Lauterbach & Johnson........ 28

19th st, s w s, 475 s e 8th av, 50x100........
16th st, n s, 214.7 w 7th av, 25x100........
Annie Shields agt Michael Gorman; att'y, Alfred R. Page........ 28

Degraw st, n s, 363.2 e Schenectady av, runs east 6.10 x north 127.9 x west 32.1 x south 130.3........
Degraw st, n s, 390 e Schenectady av, 20x127.9...
Samuel B. Decker agt Amos S. Lampeear; action to have premises declared partnership assets; att'y, James P. Philip........ 28

Quincy st, n s, 775 e Bedford av, 100x100. William H. Aldrich agt Hannah C. Somers; action to determine title; att'y, C. D. Rust........ 29

Kingston av, n e cor Pacific st, 96x80. George E. Fahys agt Franklin J. Fellows; att'y, J. T. Marean........ 29

Adams st, No. 149, e s, 21.9x50........
Adams st, No. 234, w s, 20x100........
Adams st, No. 307, e s, 24x100........
Myrtle av, Nos. 176 and 178, s s, 37x71.10........
Myrtle av, No. 190, s s, 22x46........
Brooklyn Elevated R. R. Co. agt Rose Krafy; action to acquire real estate; att'ys, Hoadly, Lauterbach & Johnson........ 31

Lots 504 and 505 map Gilbert S. Thatford, East New York. Samuel Samuelson agt Isaac Glaser; action for specific performance; att'y, H. J. Morris........ 31

Columbia Heights, No. 204, w s, 248.1 n Pierrepont st, 37.3x150 to Furman st, x27.9x150. Charles H. Collins agt Mary S. Hewsey; foreclos. mechanic's lien; att'ys, Rochford & Stayton........ 31

Sept.

Ocean pl, e s, 98.7 n Atlantic av, 69x190 to Gunther pl. Leopold Michel agt Oscar H. Doolittle; att'y, Ira L. Bamberger........ 1

2d st, s s, 437.11 e 5th av, runs south 100 x east 3.1 x north 5 x east 76.11 x north 95 to st, x west 80. James Jack agt Archibald McBean; att'y, Marion A. Vinton........ 1

3d pl, n s, 40 e Henry st, 20x60, with all title to courtyard in front. The Title Guarantee and Trust Co. agt James J. Hagerty; same att'y.... 1

Steuben st, e s, 240 s Willoughby av, 16.8x100, George E. Elliott et al. trustees Morgan School Fund agt Francis G. Turner; att'ys, S. F., F. H. & H. Cowdrey........ 1

Steuben st, e s, 250.8 s Willoughby av, 16.8x100. Same agt same; same att'ys........ 1

Steuben st, e s, 273.4 s Willoughby av, 16.10x100. Annie B. Bedell agt same; same att'ys........ 1

Livingston st, n e s, 100 s e Hanover pl, 20x125. United States Trust Co., New York, agt William H. Noe; amended notice; att'ys, Stewart & Sheldon........ 1

Hudson av, e s, 175 s Water or Evans st, 25x127 to Navy Yard wall, x29.9x143.6. William B. Davenport, Public Adm'r, as adm'r of Charles P. Keely agt John McCarty exr. Peter McClean; att'y, Charles H. Otis........ 2

Seigel st, No. 83, s s, 125 w Graham av, 25x100. Jacob Koner agt Louis Rosenthal; action for specific performance; att'ys, Fisher & Volz........ 2

Howard av, n w cor Macon st, 100x185. Bernard Levino agt Eliza James; att'y, Wm. Ingraham. 2

Flatbush av, south cor Prospect pl, runs southeast 123.5 x south 2.6 x southwest 90 x 3.6 to av, x north 125, also gore adj on south, 50.8x40.8x90. J. Herbert Watson agt James Finlay; att'y, J. H. Watson, in person........ 2

Throop av, e s, 42.1 s Hancock st, 19.6x81. American Baptist Home Mission Society agt Ervin G. Gollner; att'y, S. Clinch.... 2

Warren st. n s, 140 e Columbia st, 25x99.10. John Martin agt Ann Ward; att'ys, McGuire & Low.. 2

Vandeveer st. n w s, 119.5 n e Broadway, 56.8x100. Adolph Vanrein exr. Lucy A. Vanrein agt William H. H. Glover; att'y. Otto F. Struse 2

Franklin st, e s, 50 n Huron st, 50x95. Sarah A. Foster agt Frederick K. Clark; action to restrain foreclos.; att'y, C. H. Williams 3

3d av, w s, 83.4 n Wyckoff st, 16.8x78. Emanuel New agt Julius Hansel; att'y, Herman Frank... 3

Henry st, e s, 75 n Carroll st, 25x117. Gwendoline Burgass agt Eleanor Rogers; att'y, Josiah T. Lovejoy.... 3

Lexington av, n s, 120 e Lewis av, 20x100. Sarah W. Collins agt Amelia W. Schelling; att'y, Stephen W. Collins.... 3

RECORDED LEASES.

NEW YORK. Per Year

Centre st, No. 116, front and rear. John P. Hauschild to Louis Dittenheimer and Peter Seaman; 10 years, from May 1, 1891.....$2,000, 4,000

Delancey st, No. 10, all. Ernst Plath to Emil Hagen; 5 years, from Sept. 1, 1891.........1,200, 1,500

Delancey st, No. 157. Louis Hyman to George Zwernemann; 3 years, from May 1, 1891.... 660

Grand Boulevard, e s, 75 s 78th st, all. Lena Colman to Peter J. Doolan and William O'Brien; 5 years, from May 1, 1891.......... 1,020

Grand st, Nos. 137 and 139, except part of No. 139. John T. McGuire to Charles E. Mutzig; 5 years, from Sept. 8, 1891.... 3,500

Grand st, No. 620, store. Maurice McCormick and George H. Mundorf to Emil Engelmann; 4⅔ years, from Sept. 1, 1891........ 480, 600

Henry st, No. 86, store and basement. Adolph Cohen and Harry Fischel to Morris Weinstock; 4⅔ years, from Sept. 1, 1891 900

Pearl st, No. 131, basement.....

Beaver st, No. 82, one-half basement........

James W. Murphy and Michael McCormack to Paul Stolpe; 2¾ years and 3 days, from July 28, 1891.... 1,500

West st, No. 176 ....

Warren st, Nos. 123 and 125....

Mary and Caroline T. Drake to John Glinsman; 7 years, from May 1, 1890.... 6,000

Worth st, No. 140. Alexander Patton agent for Margaret Creeden to Henry Kreiters; 4⅔ years, from Sept. 1, 1891.... 1,215

11th st, No. 434 E., store and cellar. Emanuel Kneisel to Michael Maher; 5 years, from May 1, 1891.... 216

40th st, No. 439 W., store and part basement. Babette Regel to Emma Blath; 5 years, from Aug. 1, 1889.... 456

Same property. Assign. lease. Emma Blath to Adolph Picker.... nom

Same property. Assign. lease. Adolph Picker to H. Koehler & Co.... 1,500

50th st, Nos. 106 and 108 W. Lucy A. Browne, Ronkonkoma, L. I., to Emile Regnier; 3 years, from Sept. 1, 1891.... 3,600

113th st, No. 85 E., east store and rear rooms. John S. Scott to John Degnan; 4⅔ years, from Aug. 1, 1891.... 600

Same property. Assign. lease. John Degnan to The Burr Brewing Co.... nom

113th st, n s, 204.5 e 3d av, runs east 155 x north 85.7 x southwest 5 x north 69.10 x west 150 x south 100.11. Francis Murphy to Moritz Samisch and Rudolph Hertz; 7 years, from Sept. 1, 1891.... 1,200

120th st, Nos. 207 and 209 E. Minnie W. Carson and John J. Carroll to Lewis Morris, Henry and David J. Steinhardt and Adolph and Edward Strasser; 2⅔ years, from Sept. 1, 1891.... 5,000

Amsterdam av, No. 691, all. George W. Eggers to S. Cushman & Sons; 5⅙ years, from Nov. 1, 1891.... 600, 900

Columbus av, No. 462, store. F. H. Walker to H. & S. Bloch; 5 years, from Nov. 1, 1891 ....2,000, 2,100

1st av, No. 537, store floor. John Shea to Henry Landwehr; 6 years, from May 1, 1891....960, 1,200

1st av, No. 1746, store, basement and rear rooms. Pauline Keller to Peter Geib; 3 years, from Sept. 1, 1891.... 300, 420

2d av, No. 817, store and cellar. Nicholas A. and Michael Hagerty to Diedrich Arberg; 5 years, from May 1, 1891....600, 650

3d av, No. 660, store and basement. George Rothmann to Jacob Heinrich; 5 years, from May 1, 1891.... 1,800

3d av, No. 1925, south store and part cellar. Patrick Norton to John D. and Theodore Strahmann; 6⅔ years, from Sept. 1, 1891. ....2,000, 2,500

9th av, No. 485, store and basement. Mary A. McGlynn trustee for Hugh A. McGrane to Charles M. Wendt; 3 years, from May 1, 1891.... 1,440

Same property. Assign. lease. Charles M. Wendt to William Hoberg and Dick Fitschen. nom

CHATTELS.

NOTE.—The first name, alphabetically arranged, is that of the Mortgagor, or party who gives the Mortgage. The "R" means Renewal Mortgage.

NEW YORK CITY.

AUGUST 28 TO SEPTEMBER 3.—INCLUSIVE.

SALOON AND RESTAURANT FIXTURES.

Bartels, Frederick. 165 Allen....P Weidmann. $600
Becker, P A. 2237 2d av....V Loewers. 400
Bernius & Huger. 600 10th av....Bernheimer & S. Saloon Beer Pump. 97
Same. 600 11th av....same. Saloon Ice House. 192
Braun, John. 227 E 51st....J Ruppert. 1,000
Burke, Michael. 130th st and North River....D G Yuengling B Co. (R) 1,700
Black, J H. 53 Frankfort....J Ruppert. (R) 1,000
Blath, Emma. 384 E 34th....Stiner & Munch. 1,500
Same. 232 W 30th....same. 1,500
Baaden, Anna. 259 3d av....J Haffen. (R) 300
Bachmann, Fred. 404 1st av....Schmitt & S. 900
Baresal, Paul. 94 and 96 Gansevoort....M K R Thumann. Restaurant Fixtures. 2,500
Bassen, Joseph. 1734 Amsterdam av....G Klein. 450
Bellotte, H A. 828 and 830 6th av....C A Ughettas. Restaurant Fixtures. 3,000
Bruckner, Hermann. 38 Stanton ...S Bruckner. Restaurant Fixtures. 400
Celia, Vincenzo. 319 E 115th....Budweiser B Co. 190
Cohen & Budwitzky. 88 Essex....H B Scharman & Sons. 400
Cotter, Sylvester. 1317 Av A....Bernheimer & S. (R) 500
Cuzze, Joseph. 332 E 115th ...Bernheimer & S. Pool Table. (R) 140
Degnan, E F. 138 Willis av....A Hupfel's Sons. 4,477
Deyerberg, H H. 27 10th av....C Iba. 2,000
Difnolo, Rigginaldo. 2089 2d av....C & A Bereuter. Pool Table. 140
Degnan, John. 85 E 113th....Burr B Co. 1,300
Dammer, Herman. 890 and 892 9th av...J Everard. 2,547
Doyle, J J. 154 W 10th....J Kress B Co. 1,000
Fino, Guiseppe. 175 Thompson...Bernheimer & S. (R) 385
Fleming, Thomas. 1111 1st av....H Koehler & Co. 1,500
Forster, Patrick. 23 Cherry....Budweiser B Co. 1,200
Frederick, G A. 157 Fulton....J C G Hupfel. (R) 1,700
Fuchs, Leonard. 636 E 12th....G Ringler & Co. 500
Glaser, Abraham. 731 St Anns av....J Eckert. Restaurant Fixtures (R) 400
Griffin & Dowling. 411 6th av ...F & M Schaefer B Co. (R) 3,000
Guterding, Jacob. 48 and 50 Orchard .... G Ehret. (R) 4,000
Same. 169th st and 10th av ...same. (R) 30,000
Grabendunkel, E F. 20 11th av ...Consumers B Co. 700
Griffin & Dowling. 411 6th av....P O'Neill. (R) 3,900
Geiger, J & B. 16 Greenwich ...M Eckstein B Co. 500
Gould, S A. 1805 Park av....J C G Hupfel B Co. 850
Gabriel, Barbara. 35 W 43d....Bernheimer & S. (R) 200
Gallagher, C D. 800 Westchester av....J Eichler B Co. 400
Hiller, John. 154 Allen....A Hupfel's Sons. (R) 350
Hannon, J M. 295 Av A....A Alsheimer. 775
Herzog, George. 414 E 5th....J Eppig. (R) 800
Hartung, G C. 775 9th av....Bernheimer & S. (R) 2,000
Hawranek, Vaclav. 1395 2d av....A Kraemer B Co. 660
Hulhausel, Wenzel. 410 E 59th....A Kraemer B Co. 850
Hamann, C J. 2711 8th av .. Bernheimer & S. (R) 500
Heinrich, William. 164 E 106th....P Buckel. (R) 850
Hertel, John. 228 5th....G Ehret. (R) 1,000
Holt, J W. 982 2d av....P Doelger. 1,282
Johnson, Andrew. 168 Cherry....E Meltzer. (R) 50
Judge & McFarland. 1738 3d av.. Beadleston & W. 3,000
Jefferds, E I. 382 8th av... G Ehret. 4,000
Jorg, Anton. 702 E 161st....A Hupfel's Sons. 500
Karcher, William. 103 Sheriff ...P & W Ebling B Co. (R) 300
Kruger, August. 976 E 163d....A Hupfel's Sons. (R) 100
Keller, Rudolph. 81 Division... J Ahles B Co. (R) 400
King, C W. 89 Bleecker....Bernheimer & S. 2,000
Klorum, Barnet. 17 Orchard....V Loewers. 1,400
Keegan & Cully. 735 11th av....Budweiser B Co. 1,000
La Vaglio, Pasquale. 113 Mulberry....Budweiser B Co. 800
Loretz, Honore. 326 Henry....Rubsam & H B Co. 550
Lynch, Bartley. 428 1st av....H Koehler & Co. 2,300
Lungershausen & Ebel. 114 E 3d....G Bechtel, exr of. 475
McMahon, J F. 724 2d av....J Kress B Co. 732
Martin, Patrick. 410 E 18th....D Mayer. 400
Meissner, Joseph. 1116 1st av....G Ehret. 1,080
Murphy, Denis. 517 W 42d. ..F & M Schaefer B Co. (R) 400
Macht, Victor. 369 Broadway....J Link. 1,000
Merkel, Julius. 325 Broome ...J Ruppert. (R) 1,200
Mueller, Rudolph. 36 Catharine....G W Schieck. Restaurant Fixtures. (R) 1,800
Mooney, Joseph. 241 E 59th....E Maher. Restaurant Fixtures. 250
Maher, Patrick. 10th st and Waverley pl....H Vogel. 685
Maher, F. 512 Pearl....H Koehler & Co. (R) 2,500
Maher, Thomas. 512 Pearl....H Koehler & Co. (R) 2,500
Martin, Patrick. 410 E 18th... H Koehler & Co. 550
Materlewicz ——. 185 Chrystie ...W Peters B Co. Pool Table. 150
McGivney, H J. 2386 1st av....D G Yuengling, Jr, B Co. 475
Moltzen, Christ. 1955 2d av....P Doelger. 590
Murphy, W F. 258 Madison....Bernheimer & S. (R) 2,300
Niclas, J F. 454 Washington....P Doelger. (R) 300
Neinert, August. 3 Goerck....E Meltzer. (R) 300
Neumeyer, Andreas. 158 Orchard... Welz & Zerweck. 450
O'Connor, John. 771 8th av....G Ehret. 1,500
O'Connor, William. 196 8th av....T C Lyman & Co. (R) 3,000
O'Hea, Michael. 146 Cherry....Budweiser B Co. 575
Ortmann, Fritz. Canal and Centre sts....Bernheimer & S. Saloon Ice House. 140
Same....same. Beer Pump 134
Picker, Adolph. 439 W 40th....H Koehler & Co. 1,500
Polizer, E. 426 E 81st....J H Bereuter. Pool. 150
Parke, C H. 18 6th av... T C Lyman & Co. (R) 250
Pakenham, Catharine. 308 Westchester av....P & W Ebling B Co. (R) 600
Pohlmann, Carl. 1422 2d av....Schmitt & S. (R) 808
Palmer, J D and C. 57 W 18th....H C Palmer. Restaurant Fixtures. 500
Placek, William. 556 1st av....J & A Doelger. (R) 1,800
Ruzzo, Antonio. 69 Mulberry....I Hirsch. 275
Rossini, Peter. 290 7th av....D Rossini. Restaurant Fixtures. 600
Radtke, Elise. 506 E 17th....P Doelger. 300
Richten & Rohrs. 26 Trinity pl....Wagner & S. Pool Table. 290
Roemer, Hermann. 197 Lewis....P Weidmann. 631
Ruckert, August. 786 10th av....Bachmann B Co. (R) 300
Rosenthal, I & Co. 88 West Houston....Budweiser B Co. 1,900
Sassmann, August. 104 E 110th....J C G Hupfel B Co. (R) 748
Sause, J A. 160 and 164 E 34th st and 498 3d av....C Stein. 6,000
Schelle, Wm....H Koehler & Co. Pool. ——
Scholly, Julius. 52 Stanton....P Doelger. (R) 1,300
Sheedy, M A. 421 West....G Ringler & Co. 500
Stenz, W H. 10th av, bet 99th and 100th sts....G Ehret. (R) 800
Sugrue, Michael. 41 Oliver....H Koebler & Co. (R) 156
Seidenwand, Joseph. 184 E 3d....J Hoffmann B Co. (R) 350
Stolpe, Paul. 82 and 84 Beaver and 131 Pearl....Bernheimer & S. 1,500
Sullivan, P H. 390 8th av....Burr B Co. 500
Sameth & Weiss. 108½ Attorney....D Mayer. 1,600
Schailes, Johannes. 566 Courtlandt av... J Eichler B Co. 400
Schelle, W....H Koebler & Co. Pool. ——
Schmitt, H L. 876 1st av....P I Schmitt. 8,000
Schnabel, Charles. 793 1st av....J Ahles B Co. 800
Stronezu, Stephan. 249 2d....H Freimuth. 800
Schiff, Adolf. 284 East Houston....J Toch. Restaurant Fixtures. 900
Schmidt, J P. 14 Av D....J Eichler B Co. 750
Siemon, W F. 76 Spring....J Kuntz B Co. 475
Treuge, J O. 58 Greenwich....J Kress B Co. 800
Tuck, W H. 207 1st av....M Moore. Restaurant. 500
Voisin, Joseph. 107 W 26th....Bernheimer & S. (R) 100
Von der Lieth, J D. 183 William....Consumers B Co. 280
Van Dahl, Henry. 59 Av B .. P Doelger. (R) 1,087
Same. 66 Broome....same. (R) 1,150
Same. 236 E 10th ...same. (R) 1,506
Wagner, Fred. 271 Av A... Budweiser B Co. 400
Weeks, G E. 56 Pike....D Mayer. (R) 1,885
Wainstock, Morris. 86 and 88 Henry....Bernheimer & S. 2,000
Wohlrab, Emil. 1240 Broadway....G Reaske. (R) 1,236
White, John. 137 Mott....Burr B Co. (R) 300
Warnke, J F. 242 Fulton... H Lemmermann. (R) 4,000

HOUSEHOLD FURNITURE.

Adams, Adolph. 229 Gold, Brooklyn....H Thoesen. 108
Anderson, W A & M E A. 187 W 80th....E C Hinsdale. 100
Auspitz, Antonette. 158 E 70th....L Baumann. 172
Ackerman, Mamie. 318 W 36th....L Baumann. 267
Beak, G g. 500 E 11th... B M Cowperthwait & Ceor e 224
Beresford, L. 102 W 44th T Kelly. 491
Berisford, Lizzie. 102 W 44th....T Kelly. 179
Bernheim, Rebecca. 27 Rutgers....L Baumann. 170
Blomgren, Gust. 218 W 128th....E C Hinsdale. 180
Borttgen, George. 34 Division.. B M Cowperthwait & Co. 195
Browning, Lilla M. 226 W 25th....J Baumann. 692
Ball, P J. 330 E 25th....F J Brechtel. (R) 135
Beals, Florence. 239 W 43d...L Baumann. (R) 101
Bennett, Mabel. 141 W 27th....J S Rice. 123
Brennan, William. 336 W 11th....O'Farrell & Co. 114
Brinson, Abby E. 106 W 47th.. M Gillig. 150
Brinson, Mrs A E. 106 W 47th... S Ballin. 198
Brodhead, G W. 49th st and 2d av....J Moriarty. 116
Brombacker, Ellen. 81 E 108th....J Moriarty. 180
Beekman, L and M O. 308 W 14th....M F Cagney. 102
Baros, S. 388 Grand....J Wolf & Son. 230
Bennett, W H. 144 W 28th....W Guinevan, exr of. 197
Chase, Sara B. 226 W 39th....O'Farrell & Co. (R) 176
Cody, Lizzie. 337 W 17th....O'Farrell & Co. 131
Conklin, J C. 1 Sheriff....Jordan & M. 200
Chadsey, N B and M T. 390 4th av....T Mooney. 150
Citron, Abraham. 142 Suffolk....M Neuman. 102
Clifton, Helen. 49 W 29th....L Baumann. 110
Camp, J T. 140 W 130th....J P Leo. (R) 1,215
Carhart, Fanny. 578 Mott av....L Baumann. 150
Charles, Mrs H E. 236 W 121st....T Kelly. 462
Curtis, Josephine. 108 W 47th....G Schuckman. (R) 800
Chipman, M G. 788 6th av....L Baumann. (R) 300
Colton, Mrs S K. 227 W 74th....W E Wheelock & Co. Piano. 325
Cullen, David. 510 W 28th....L Baumann. 199
Cunneen, Mamie. 434 Pearl....Jordan & M. 112
Dailey, Stella A. 205 W 31st....S Ballin. (R) 201
Dengler, Minnie. 148 Essex....Krakauer Bros. Piano. 209
Denning, W B. 260 W 122d. .T Kelly. (R) 180
Dayton, E R. 906 6th av....H Israel & Son. (R) 336
De Faletaus, Estelle. 111 E 75th....J Moriarty. (R) 219
Diossy, Mrs J. 126 W 47th....J Moriarty. (R) 400
Dannenfelser, Elise. 90 Macdougal....G A Kaltwasser. 300
Day, J H. 422 Willis av....J Gregg. (R) 108
Earlie, Emma. 388 3d av....H S Eisler. 204
Essing, Charles....Gately & W. 179
Farber, Jennie. 152 Ridge....H S Eisler. 110
Fay, Sadie. 342 W 18th. ..T Kelly. (R) 222
Feslger, John, Jr. 52 West End av....S Heyman. 147
Fitz, Mrs Patrick. 356 W 43d....H Thoesen. 205
Fox, G J. 210 E 43d....O'Farrell & Co. 195
Fraad, David. 55 Av D ...D M Brown. 297
Francis, J E. 520 W 35th....T Kelly. (R) 100
Friedman, Sadie. 31 W 24th....T Kelly. (R) 129
Friedlander, Siegfried. 140 E 97th....F J Brechtel. (R) 135
Frey, R G. 332 E 77th....Jordan & M. 162
Fairland, Marion. 701 6th av....J Baumann. 158
Fichler, Richard. 1929 3d av....H Israel & Son. 965
Friedman, Minnie. 153 E 97th....Fennell & Pye. (R) 110
Franklin, Jennie. 215 W 33th....L Baumann. 128
Gahan, James. 61 W 11th....T Kelly. 152
Gardner, Patience M. 148 W 53d....B M Cowperthwait & Co. 532
Gibb, Mrs M. 224 W 4th....T Kelly. 309
Gilbert, Helen. 110 E 41st....L Baumann. 128
Glover, C H. 742 Columbus av....T Kelly. 217
Gorman, Anna A. 156 St Anns av....Dreisacker & Co. 126
Gotthold, Ida. 664 Lexington av....J & J Dobson. 848
Gross, H. 23 E 114th....Fennell & P. (R) 416
Garr, Andrew. 436 W 58th....F J Brechtel. (R) 158
Garjen, Dietrich. Storage....J J Murphy. 220
Gotthold, Ida. 1064 Lexington av....J & J Dobson. 322
Green, Laura. 156 9th av ...O'Farrell & Co. 194
Greiger, Antoine. 158 E 46th....L Baumann. (R) 159
Gallagher, H P. 1654 2d av....J Baumann. 181
Gleason, Elizabeth L. 307 W 20th ...R M Walters. Piano. (R) 189
Ginsberg, Alex. 214 Madison....H S Eisler. 114
Haroth, Annie. 340 E 11th....H S Eisler. 179
Harrison, Addie. 356 W 116th....L Baumann. 225

Hill, M C. 397 7th av....F T Higgins. 193
Hogan, L A. 13 Market... R M Walters. Piano. (R) 190
Hall, Ella H. 70 Western Boulevard....T Kelly. 160
Haepern, Charlotte. 1695 2d av....H S Eisler. 131
Harrington, Ella H. 64 E 128th....Rosa B De Casemova. 270
Hart, L N. 3 Perry....W E Wheelock & Co. Piano. (R) 202
Hartley, Ray. 158 W 53d ...M Manges. (R) 436
Hesse, Eliza S. 1 W 83d....S Baumann. 147
Hewitt, Minnie. 26 Perry....J Moriarty. (R) 144
Hoffman, Isabella. 455 W 44th....L Baumann. (R) 123
Hagendorf, John. 137 Perry....O'Farrell & Co. 199
Hashagen, Jules. 73 E 82d....A Wix. 1,000
Hescote, H. 130 W 22d....T Kelly. 378
Holley, Libbie. 1014 3d av....Manges Bros. 114
Holmes, Mrs C E. 440 Lexington av....T Kelly. 185
Hoyt, Alice L. 902 E 138th ....Manges Bros. 373
Hull, Mary C. 349 W 37th....L Baumann. 180
Hull, T L. 147 E 21st....E C Binsdale. 635
Johnson, Carrie. 1968 7th av....L Baumann. 152
Jewell, J M. 596 E 134th....Dreisacker & Co. 176
Jaffe, Joseph. 341 E 82d....J Moriarty. 132
Jacobs, Bertha. 313 E 119th....R M Walters. Piano. (R) 150
Kern, I J. 235 and 237 W 14th....J Baumann. 2,930
Kranel, William. 70 9th av....L Baumann. 120
King, Adele. 240 W 14th ..L Baumann. (R) 179
Kosminski, Louis. 545 W 125th....L Steinbugler. 123
Kraus, Martin. 217 E 53d .. S Heyman & Co. 528
King, Mrs F M. 136 E 48th....H Thoesen. 175
Knight, Stephen. Stebbins av....P Gorman. (R) 500
Kane, Mary. 315 W 134th ....R M Walters. Piano. 175
King, Annie M. 157 W 49th.... T Kelly. 140
Livingston, May. 154 W 83d....S I Herschmann. 1,215
Loewenthal, A. 118 E 13th....J Bennett. 110
Lamm, J E. 216 E 89th....H Marsch. 450
Lampert, e S. 321 W 17th....Dreisacker & Glos phine 171
Levy, Isaac. 48 Eldridge....H S Eisler. 159
Leach, Julia E. 16 W 135th....L Baumann. (R) 122
Levy, Samuel. 206 E 86th....J Moriarty. (R) 387
Lyon, B A. 138 W 129th....American Guar Assoc. 100
Lange, Jean. 330 E 76th....J Baumann. 121
Masters, A, Mrs. 116 E 110th... H Israel & Son. (R) 118
McKenny, G W. 117 E 84th....F T Higgins. (R) 100
McNamara, George. Washington av and 189th st....W Reubel. 149
Merritt, Nellie. 108 E 120th....H Israel & Son. 313
Mettler, Augustus 28 W 143d....L Baumann. 150
Meyer, Lucien. 11 Jones....L Baumann. 113
Moran, Annie. 413 4th av. H Israel & Son. 190
Marsh, F C. 105 W 60th....L Baumann. 123
Marotine, Alice. 52 E 12th....P Lebreton. 150
McCloskey, Ed, Mrs. 380 W 49th....A Ballin. 161
McDermott, Annie. 214 W 46th....T Kelly. (R) 584
McDonald, Mary J. 170th st and Jerome av....T Kelly. (R) 100
McLoughlin, W J. 158 E 96th....J Gregg & Co. 101
Mullins, Eugene. 336 Robbins av....L Steinbugler. 255
Miller, B H. 378 8th av....H Thoesen. 112
Miller, Mary F. 125 W 3d....O'Farrell & Co. (R) 137
Magneson, John. 12 W 135th....T Kelly. 168
Masterson, Arabella C. 111 W 47th ...Kate Wiseman. 272
McDonald, H, Mrs. 157 W 49th....T Kelly. 189
McGhee, Bertha. 227 W 40th....L Baumann. 247
Meinell, G G. 222 W 128th....B M Cowperthwait & Co. 650
Melville, J H. 111 W 60th ...B M Cowperthwait & Co. 217
Miltion, Mary. 305 E 11th....S I Herschmann. 106
Muney, Susan. 1102 3d av....T Kelly. 138
Ney, Matilda. 226 W 144th....J Baumann. 262
Nathaway, Elizabeth. 148 W 62d....E D Farrell. 309
Odell, J D. 709 E 141st . G V House, Jr. (R) 149
Oliver, Lizzie. 1646 Madison av....B M Cowperthwait & Co. 618
Oppenheim, Jennie. 264 W 116th....T Kelly. 414
Palmer, W J. 200 W 108th... T Kelly. 344
Paul, Harry. 144th st and St Nicholas av....L Baumann. 265
Phillips, H and I. 194 Orchard....S I Herschmann. 285
Palmer, Eva. 341 W 81st....J S Rice. 115
Parker, Rosa. 140 W 27th....L Baumann. (R) 180
Paton, Jr, G S. 313 W 121st....L Baumann. 334
Patterson, H A and A S. 123 E 70th....E C Rinsdale. 440
Petrone, Raffaele. 1192 Charles....O'Farrell & Co. 189
Phibbs, James. 106 Canal. ..Jordan & M. 107
Pierce, Mrs W. 315 E 69th....E D Farrell & Co. 130
Parker, Agnes. 404 8th av....J Baumann. (R) 166
Phillips, Dororthy. 128 E 125th....J C de La Mare. 1,750
Quincy, J D. 287 Broadway....C Klebisch. 512
Quinn, J J. 869 10th av ... L Baumann. 157
Rodenburg, Maria. 224 W 37th....L Baumann. 323
Root, Mary. 1004 Av A....L Baumann. 114
Raschke, Gustav. 331 Broome....F J Brechtel. (R) 146
Reilly, S and M. 1131 3d av....Amer Guar Assoc. 100
Ries, H and S. 631 E 15th....N Wallach. 140
Riordan, Nellie. 814 3d av....L Baumann. 183
Rodenburgh Marie. 224 W 37th....L Baumann. 114
Rouget, Henrietta. 1 8 W 87th....N Y F Co. 184
Ruleberg, Gussie. 764 Columbus av....Fennell & Pye. 105
Requier, Emile. 106 and 108 W 50th ...D L Shorb. 4,000
Ross, Battie. 104 W 46th, 110 W 52d, 82 W 3d, 210 Wooster and 207 W 33d....H Israel. 3,000
Ruch, Fritz. 447 W 37th....W Guinevan, exr of. 117
Sacco, Joseph. 110 W 106th... E O'Callahan. (R) 231
Schweifert, Fred. 936 8th av....Dreisacker & Co. 121
Sweeney, Gus. Tinton av and 149th st....Dreisacker & Co. 126
Schmitt, Minnie. 2007 1st av....Krakauer Bro. Piano. 190
Schriber, Marie L. 411 and 413 W 57th ...P Duff 641
Schoez, Carrie. 1077 Columbus av....H S Eisler. (R) 110
Simmons, A H. 82 W 90th....E Marks. 210
Smith, Mattie. 87 W 3d .. F J Brechtel. (R) 106
Stephens, A B. 119 W 24th....Jordan & M. 113
Stetson, W L and C. 384 W 17th....J P Delehanty. 240
Simmons, Mary. 2009 Lexington av....L Baumann. 128
Schaefer, Theresa R. 112 E 81st....J E Kaltenbach. 100
Schroeder, H F. 264 W 35th....L Baumann. 308
Schultz, W H. 42 Beach....Manges Bros. 140
Sauch, J W. 65 2d ...H S Eisler. 105
Seawell, Annie. 339 W 23d....Financial Credit Co. 150
Seymour, Ida L. 21 W 18th....J C Oscar. 217
Shea, Jennie. 321 W 17th....T Kelly. 157
Simmons, Mary. 2009 Lexington av....L Baumann. 220
Starnes, W S. 243 E 33d....Lincoln I & G Co. 100
Teevan, John. 1859 2d av....J J McGrorty. 164
Taapp, Carl. 301 E 8th....L Baumann. (R) 158
Thomas, M A. 234 W 41th....T Kelly. (R) 155
Thomes, Mary E. 159 W 61st....L Baumann. 178
Thompson, F R. 146 W 68th... L Baumann. (R) 126
Tinkham, F A. 41 W 61st....H Thoesen. 428
Twiggs, Mrs M M. 224 E 27th....W E Wheelock & Co. Piano. 325
Toscey, Jennie. 214 W 48th ...W Guinevan, exr of. 258
Vanderberg, F M. 326 W 59th....J Moriarty. 312
Van Hevnigan, Jennie. 136 W 47th .. L Baumann. 471
Van Voorhis, W A. 99 E 7th....J Baumann. 211
Wallace, Mary A. 107 E 78th....J Gregg & Co. 140
Wallace, W H H. 164 E 92d....T Kelly. 216
Walters, Chas. 1712 1st av....Jordan & M. 233
Washburn, H L. 136 Liberty....B M Cowperthwait & Co. 171
Williams, Charles. 796 9th av....L Baumann. 197
Wheeler, Edmund. 1506 2d av....J Moriarty. 313
White, Mrs M A. 101 E 25th....N Y F Co. 104
Willett, W L, Jr. 152 E 27th....L Baumann. 215
Wilson, George. 230 West Houston....L Baumann. (R) 207
Woods, William. 302 E 102d....E D Farrell. 180
Wren, Nellie J. 236 W 121st....Brooklyn F Co. 106
Watts, D C. 66 and 68 W 38th....J & J Dobson. 279
Wiswell, Nellie B. 42 W 132d....Dreisacker & Co. 331
Williams, F D. 162 E 46th.... H Thoesen. 147
Yung, Fred. 419 E 5th....H Thoesen. 181
Zutte, Leon. 69 Chrystie....H S Eisler. 104

MISCELLANEOUS.

Abrams & Co. 6 Pell... Marvin Safe Co. Safe. 195
Aufeuangler & Schwarm. 89 Broad... Nat Cash Reg Co. Register. 176
Same. 58 Fulton....same. Register. 200
Austin, J R. 352 W 18th....A E Horton. Horses and Ice Wagon. 700
Auerbach, Rubin. 100 Essex. ..Liberty Machine Works. Press. 75
Abbes, Christopher. 118th st, 2d and 3d avs ...C Turk. Horse, Wag , &c. 200
Almy, E R. 307-311 E 127th....J J Carter, recvr. Horses, Coal Carts, &c. 847
Same....M Wells. Same. 991
Same... A Sulzer. Same. 3,200
Arienzo, Antonio. 178 Park row....T Stramiello. Barber Fixtures. 100
Beeck & Klute. 347 7th av....F Beeck. Tools, &c. 235
Bent, B C. Tremont... Lamson Consol S S Co. Register. (R) 210
Bloomer & Palmer. 78th st and West End av and 76th st and Columbus av....T F Otten. Horses and Milk Fixtures. 300
Bishop, J A. 207 Centre....Liberty Machine Works. Press. 348
Brash, Thos. 38 Bethune....Prentiss Tool Co. Machinery. 790
Baust, Jacob. 228 Eldridge....G Baust. Cigar Fixtures. (R) 250
Behrens, H L. 220 and 222 Columbus av....G W Holmes. Drug Fixtures. 1,000
Ballall, Fred. 167th and 169th....J Sohl. Horses and Garden Fixtures. 1,825
Same....R Buongiono. Horses and Garden Fixtures. 1,100
Banks, Michael F. 148 E 43d....Hincks & J. Coach. (R) 60
Beekman, Henry. 1885 3d av....O Fischer. Store Fixtures, Horses, &c. 500
Berger, Samuel. 430 East Houston....I Goldstein. Machinery. 400
Brennan, Thos. 84 West....Nat Cash Reg Co. Register. 115
Brown & Cohn. 21 Catharine....Mosler Safe Co. Safe. 150
Brown, J G. 51 W 10th....E S Chapin & Co. Paintings, &c. 17,831
Buchholz, Diedrich. 506 E 56th . H Diedrichs. Horse, Wagon, &c. 400
Burnham, G H & Co. 186 West Houston....Van Allens B Co. Press. 2,000
Behrmann, Adolph. 926 6th av ...Bavarian B Co. Bottling Fixtures. 200
Carolan, Nicholas. 182 Thompson....Hincks & J. Coach. (R) 225
Cassel, Charles. 350 E 76th....B Danner. Store Fixtures. 200
Corodin, J B. 66 Broadway, Brooklyn....Manhattan Type Co. Cutter. 121
Cotter, J C. 316 E 39th....J Mullane. Grocery Fixtures. 175
Coughlin, John. 379 and 381 Madison....Seligman & H. Horses, &c. 400
Corning, Emma I. 2279 and 2281 8th av....S M Seymour. Press, &c. 750
Conrade, Fred. 17 E 114th....H Hincks. Wagon. 105
Curtis, C L. 139-143 Centre ...Patterson G & H. Machinery. 100
Caplin, H & Co. 416 Grand ....Liberty Machine Works. Press. 800
Curtis, C L. 139-143 Centre....J Keller. Machinery. (R) 1,200
Callahan, P J....M Armstrong & Co. Coach. 325
Cooker, J B. 1557 Columbus av....E Walker. Cigar Fixtures. 200
Davidson, V. 51 and 53 Maiden lane....W H Butler. Safe. 235
Doering, O A. 304 E 95th....Prentiss Tool Co. Machinery. 300
de Preissig, E. 1031 1st av....E Winterbottom. Machinery. 128
Davis, J A, S M and J H. Foot W 39th st....D Hunter. Docks, Machinery, &c. (R) 3,000
Durando, Stephen. 230 W 47th....I S Clark. Horse, &c. 75
Deknatel, H A. 196 Elm....Mosler Safe Co. Safe. 104
Deppisch, Sabina. 228 E 102d....H Rice. Bakery Fixtures. 96
Eisenberg, P and H. 208 Stanton. ..P Marx & Sons. Peddler Carts. 165
Ellithorke, F T. 52 Rivington. . S Brodie. Horse. 250
Ellech, O. 139 Pitt....M Kaplan. Bakery Fixtures. 100
Freeman, R & Bro. 145-51 Rose....Babcock P P Co. Press. 2,500
Farrell, J J. 258 Av B....National Cash Register Co. Register. 200
Fenner, W J. 304 E 60th....H Diedrichs. Horse, Wagon, &c 300
Fornander, Alfred. 90 Fulton....G Fowler. Machines. 150
Fortgang, E. 164 Clinton.....P Reidenbach. Truck. 150
Foster, A W and A C. 21st st and Broadway....W Ottmann. Hotel Fixtures. (R) 2,700
Freutel, Charles. 147 Elm....A Freutel. Machinery. (R) 3,000
Fay, J J. 5 W 19th....M Donegan. Horses, &c. 600
Fleischhauer, Robert. 1472 1st av....J Rabiner. Cigar Fixtures. 33
Foley, J C. 17th st and 1st av....National Cash Reg Co. Register. 170
Gottschalk, Siegfried. 46 Stanton....Liberty Machine Works. Press. 140
Gunthert, William. 190 Amsterdam av....C Wagner. Butcher Fixtures. 100
Garry, Marco. 230 Mulberry....W H Butler. Safe. 220
Giles, F R. 8 Union sq....C H Unvergogt. Scenery, &c. 1,000
Girvin, J H. 549 W 18th....B G Mitchell. Horses, Trucks, &c. 300
Goebel & Schroeder. 645 2d av....Lamson Consol S S Co. Register. 250
Gouscher, Solomon. 108 Ridge....P Marx & Son. Peddler Carts. 96
Grassmock, Phil. 580 Amsterdam av....National C Reg Co. Register. 225
Gross, G B. 305 10th av....R Hill. Grocery Fixtures. 150
Gottlieb, Monas. 173 Clinton....A Paziner. Butcher Fixtures. 100
Hoff, F P. 44 E 14th....Liberty Machine Works. Press. 216
Hildebrand, Paul. 1042 Tiffany....P & W Ebling B Co. Bottling Fixtures. (R) 87
Hurd, Mary E. 43 W 89th....I C Winner. Horse, Cart and Furniture. 500
Hayward, H C. 167 E 84th....J Cunningham Son & Co. Coach. 550
Helck, H P. 726 Amsterdam av....Mosler Safe Co. Safe. 150
Hunt, W H. 301 and 303 W 125th....T Wright. Vans. 700
Hurley, Joseph. 116 1st, Hoboken, N J....National C Reg Co. Register. 200
Jewelers' Mercantile Agency....C E Carson et al. Franchises, &c. (R) 10,000
Jacobson, Adolph. 312 E 71st st and 1330 2d av....J Levinson. Cigar Fixtures, &c. 480
Kraemer, F and J, Jr ...G Dessecker. Coach. (R) 250
Kennedy, P J. 2591 8th av ...Lamson Consol S S Co. Register. 165
Keile, H W. 49 Forsyth....Y C Frost. Barber Fixtures. 1,096
Krikava, Chas....K Novotny. Horses, Trucks. 100
Kelly, Edward. 410 W 26th....Brown & Fleming. Horses, Carts, &c. (R) 1,000
Lake, Cortlandt. 186 E 44th....A A Lake. Machinery. (R) 2,000
Loan Star Boat Club....O Elsars. Boats, &c. 2,500
Lehman, Max. 1840 3d av....J A Willett & Co. Grocery Fixtures. 450
Lennox, John. 233 E 80th....Hincks & Johnson. Coach. (R) 625
Liesmann, Herman. 145 Alexander av....P Doelger. Bottler Fixtures. 500
Lindewurth, Catherine. 1582 9th av....R Hill. Grocery Fixtures. 150
Luzzi, Francesco. 222 East Broadway...M Meringolo. Barber Fixtures. 192
Lange, Frederick. 29 Macdougal and 624 Greenwich....J H Meinken. Horse and Furniture. (R) 600
Lennon, J J. Jerome av and 174th st....Korner & S. Horses, Carts, &c. 887
Miller, William....J Gottsleben. Coach. (R) 200
Miller, Charles. 10 W 63d....W H Sofield. Horse, Wagon, &c. 85
Mahler, W P. 266 Elizabeth....F Herbst. Horse, Wagon, &c. 400
Mahnken, Friedrich. 981 Columbus av....Koenig & Schuster. Grocery Fixtures. 210
Marvin Mfg Co. 48 Marion ..Mosler Safe Co. Safe. 200
McCaddin, H. 66 Madison....J Cunningham Son & Co. Coach. 175
Metcalf, W L. 154 W 55th....C T Barney. Paintings, &c. 329
Meumann, Emily H A. 97th st and Amsterdam av....T Koertge. Drug Fixtures. 1,500
Meyer, A W and F. 370 9th av....Smith & Sills. Store Fixtures. 500
Meyer, J E. 694 Elton av....H Gerken. Grocery Fixtures. (R) 595
Morris & Jorns. 89 South 5th av.. Hincks & J. Coach. (R) 300
Muller, Johann. 80th st and Riverside Drive....L Heilbrunn. Garden Fixtures. 300
Moore, Andrew....M Armstrong & Co. Coach. (R) 225
Nevin & Son, M W. 66 Prince....R H Pemter. Machinery. 500
Orlewitz, Herman. 2140 7th av....National C Reg Co. Register. 225
Pantiel, Theodore. 42 Pitt....H Brand. Butcher Fixtures. 25
Pecoraro, Leone. 858 Columbus av....S Nicastro. Barber Fixtures. 80
Rosenthal, Yetta. 188 and 190 Division....N Weisbaum. Livery Stable Fixtures. 500
Rothenbach & Dietz. 441 W 40th....A Arms, Jr. Butcher Fixtures. 70
Roth, Jacob. 1162 3d av....C B Gumb. Butcher Fixtures. 800
Riecke, Rebecca. 484 E 121st....Bischoff & Meyenhoff. Grocery Fixtures. 748
Riefel, H and G. 496 Hudson....J H Barrett. Store Fixtures. 330
Rigby, Burnham. 31 Union sq ...A G Fox. Furniture, Paintings, &c. (R) 1,100
Roth, Wilhelm. 814 E 75th....P Pryibil. Machinery. 130
Rendies, H J....Rouse, Hazard & Co. Bicycle. 80
Schlayer, Chas. 100 Centre....C Schlayer. Machinery. 1,058
Stelmann, Charles. 523-529 W 14th....D J Carroll. Horses, Trucks, &c. (R) 15,000
Straut, J J. 343 E 55th....N L Niver. Horses, Ice Wagon, &c. 700
Segalovitch, Samuel. 85 Ludlow....A Simon. Grocery Fixtures. 55
Scott & May. 15 Spruce....W Hogencamp. Press, &c. 1,687
Salamon, Dora. 219 Broome....J Levy. Bakery Fixtures. 1,000
Sauliac & Son. 26 Union sq....Mosler Safe Co. Safe. 160
Schmidt, Louis. 1992 2d av....R Hill. Grocery Fixtures. 75

Scholder, Maurice. 58 Broadway....F & G Haag & Co. Barber Fixtures. 70
Schreyer, Julius. 558 1st av....S Reitman. Cigar Fixtures. 100
Skeely & Larney. 325 E 38th....J Cunningham Son & Co. Coach. 150
Smith, C V....B M Shanley. Vessels, &c. (R) 13,000
Spinella & Sanicola. 248 Elizabeth....S Dejugelo. Grocery Fixtures. 100
Stein, Meyer. 86 Chrystie... S Weinstein. Machinery. 63
Stoecker, Paul 358 W 26th....Engilage & Liss. Grocery Fixtures. 100
Stockhoff, Herman. 106th st and Western Boulevard....W Stockhoff. Horse, Garden Fixtures, &c. 1,075
Turkheimer, Adolph. 1089 1st av....M L Bernard. Butcher Fixtures, &c. 75
Termini, Joseph. 38 Mulberry... W H Butler. Safe. 175
Thaler, Louis. 118 Ridge....M Kaplan. Bakery Fixtures. 40
Unverzagt, William. 117 W 46th....P Westphal. Barber Fixtures. 163
Valiquet, L P. 295 Centre....Prentiss Tool Co. Machinery. 205
Wood, F E. 146 W 39th ...J Rudd. Horse. (R) 100
Same... same. Horse. (R) 100
Waenstock, Morris. 86 Henry....National Cash Register Co. Register. 200
Walton, A & J. 15th st, near 8th av....J Goldstein, Horse, Wagon, &c. 80
Winter, L F. 418 and 420 W 27th....J H Havens. Machinery. (R) 250
Winterroth, J M. 719 and 755 1st av....E J Winterroth. Tools, Machinery. 2,000
Woop, Frederick. 74th st and East River ...F Woop. Tools, &c. (R) 875
Wolcott, E C. 282 8th av....W D Little. Horse and Fixtures, &c. 250
Same. 40½ 4th av....same. Store Fixtures. 200
Zimmermann Bros. 31 Norfolk... I Lipschitz. Machinery, &c. 100

BILLS OF SALE.

Abels, H J. 349 W 38th....Lena Roth. Leather Finding Fixtures, &c. 1,154
Blumenthal, L, auctioneer....S H Goldsmith. Fixtures. 275
Clark & Dolan. Foot E 62d....J Fitzgerald. Machinery, &c. 1
Drahos, Joseph. 426 E 73d ...Katie Drahos. Saloon Fixtures. 100
Ernst, J E....O H Ernst. Furniture, &c. 1
Fractional Share Co. 6 Wall....H J Brigham et al. Office Fixtures, &c. 400
Farley, E E. 78 3d av....P F Mathews. Stock, Fixtures, &c. 1,500
Franke & Co....S E Gee. Store Fixtures, &c. 1
Goldstein, Abram. 7 Norfolk....M Goldstein. Machines. 30
Same....same. Machines. 35
Graham, J H. 1925 3d av....J D & T Strahmann. Saloon Fixtures. 5,750
Irons, James. 103 E 130th and 61 E 130th....Ramsey Irons. Machinery and Furniture. 600
Irons, Ramsey. 103 E 130th and 61 E 130th....Margaret C Irons. Machinery and Furniture. 300
Jones, J H....R J Tripp. Furniture. (R) 1
Klaus, W J. 734 11th av....Magdelina Klaus. Butcher Fixtures. 800
Lange, George. 35 Ludlow....C H Burmeister. Horses, &c. 700
Little, L M... A P Clark. Yacht. 250
Lyons, Abraham. 125th st and 8th av. J B Kaufman. Fixtures, Stock, &c. 4,284
Master, S C....Gertrude E Master. Jewelry Fixtures, &c. 300
Murphy, Francis. 113th st, bet 2d and 3d avs....R Hertz. Coal Yard. 3,500
Mathes, C & H. 132 Pitt....P A Decker. Butcher Fixtures. 150
McDonough, Elizabeth. 230 E 29th....Mary McGuire. Butcher Fixtures. 125
Michels, Joseph. 107 Av C....J A Semon. Saloon Fixtures. 2,000
Monyea, E F. 14th st, bet 10th and 13th avs....Ann Gormley. Horses, &c. 1,500
Normann, Frederick. 41 Franklin....F Meyer. Saloon. 751
Napoletan, Michele. 97 Bayard....D Serry. Restaurant Fixtures. ½ int. 60
O'Brien, J and J. 1805 Park av....S A Gould. Saloon Fixtures. 1,600
Reilly, James. 2389 2d av....P Hipp. Stock, Fixtures, &c. 177
Reiser, Perl. 113 Ridge....I Teppich. Grocery Fixtures. 300
Rohlfs, William. 69 Rutgers slip....I A Edmonds. Saloon Fixtures. 1
Rotunno, John. 128 E 120th....P Benncasa. Barber Fixtures. 275
Salomon, Becie. 98 Orchard....J Salomon. Grocery Fixtures. 300
Stinner, F A. 3419 3d av....Barbara Stinner. Store Fixtures, &c. 1
Watson, I F. 385 9th av....C Sullivan. Confectionery Fixtures. 600

ASSIGNMENT OF CHATTEL MORTGAGES.

Jacob Hoffmann B Co to Bernheimer & S. (Mort given by G Baumgarth, Nov 12, 1890.) 1,500
McGuire, J T to G Ehret. (H Morsch, May 15, 1891.) 700
Wurzburg, Siegfried to T Euphrat. (W F Murphy, Sept 12, 1890.) 500
Same to same. (M Steitz, June 5, 1890.) 500

KINGS COUNTY.

AUGUST 27 TO SEPTEMBER 2—INCLUSIVE.

SALOON AND RESTAURANT FIXTURES.

Allan, F B. 90 Prince....Burr B Co. (R) $750
Atkins, R. 478 5th av....S Liebmann's Sons B Co. 200
Barnewold, W. 1664 Bergen....W Craft. 220
Barry, G. 494 5th av....Rubsam & H B Co. 1,200
Bermann, L. 951 Grand... Rubsam & Hormann B Co. 250
Bouquet, F. 117 Seigel....J Kress B Co. (R) 300
Brix, C. 100 Raymond....Williamsburgh B Co. 700
Cahill, L M. 728 5th av....O'Reilly & Co. Restaurant Fixtures. 2,500
Christianson, C. 819 Atlantic av....Bachmann B Co. 1,000
Daetsch, J. 21 Tompkins av....J Kress B Co. 1,010
Dalatkowski, A. Wyona av, s e cor Arlington av....F Ibert. 350
Dermody, W F. 74 Kent av. ..M Seitz. (R) 368
Desch, F. 45 Debevoise....M Seitz. 1,025
Dreyer, J H. 243 Bushwick av....H Both. 5,000
Evers, J. Gold st, s e cor Concord st....Leavy & Britton B Co. 500
Farren, W. 156 Fulton.. H B Scharmann & Sons. 600
Gorman, M. 441 Keap... W Ulmer. 900
Grassle, F. 659 Flushing av....H B Scharmann & Sons. (R) 750
Giacommo, R. 30 Maspeth av....Budweiser B Co. 130
Harrison, Ann. 1798 and 1800 Atlantic av....Budweiser B Co. 850
Same. 8 Utica av....same. 850
Hanser, J. 633 Broadway....J Doelger's Sons. 300
Kieffer, F. 47 Meserole....Welz & Z. 2,000
Klein, E. 282 Central av....J & A Doelger. (R) 1,200
Koerber, W. 32 Morgan av....Claus Lipsius B Co. 800
Loeffler, R. 100 Throop av....J Kress B Co. 1,800
Markert, H. 85 Leonard....Welz & Zerweck. 1,100
Miller, J. Driggs st, n w cor Eckford st....J Schoens. 800
Miller, J. 17 Van Cott av....W Ulmer. 350
Owens, P. 163 5th av... Obermeyer & L. (R) 1,500
Paddon, G. 760 Grand....J Jennings. 600
Schwarzel, C. 122 Throop av....Claus Lipsius B Co. 500
Seifreid, J and M. 813 Flushing av....Fort Hamilton B Co (Lim.) 1,000
Shaw, W F. 568 4th av....L I Brewery. 550
Shaw, W T. 568 4th av....W Hennessey. 1,250
Shea, T J. 73 Bedford av....Claus Lipsius B Co. 150
Simonson, C W. 25 Broadway....W Ulmer. 1,500
Straetz, G. 42 Varet....C Frese. 400
Scheland, C & A Langhorst. 10 Lee av....Obermeyer & L. (R) 1,500
Schnelle, W. 1298 Bushwick av....W Ulmer. 2,000
Shoenhaus, H 142 Ewen....Budweiser B Co. 1,460
Webb, J. 673 Hicks....Budweiser B Co. 450
Wolf, W V and G J. 304 Bedford av....Obermeyer & L. 600
Wertheimer, J. 104 Osborn....F Metzer. Billiard Table. 135
Westerhopf, B. 257 Greenpoint av....Claus Lipsius B Co. 400

HOUSEHOLD FURNITURE.

Anspitz, J and A. 100 Pineapple....A Freedman. 280
Austin, Pauline A. 65A Somers....L Z Murray. 217
Beckerman, J. 20 Stanhope....I Mason. 269
Browner, Annie T. 213 Butler....Caroline Barry. 130
Baker, M E. 66 Vanderbilt....F T Lyon. 227
Barker, J B. 205 Madison....S W Woolsey & Son. 131
Brown, Jennie S. 506 Grand av....M Schulz & Bro. 151
Calhoun, Annie. 289 Ewen....A Schulz. 108
Campbell, Mary A. 351 St Marks av....M Schulz & Bro. 131
Coffrey, J J. 81 India....A Schulz. 205
Dreagen, H G. 456 Van Buren....I Mason. 107
Darken, E D. 48 Cooper....Cowperthwait & Co. 308
Deacon, Mrs. 660 Herkimer....T F Mulqueen. 427
Deveau, Ella. 294 Ewen....A Schulz. 207
Donovan, M J. 226 46th....Cowperthwait & Co. 194
Elli, G A. 159 Cumberland....L Z Murray. 141
Gardner, M D. 155 Fulton... J Bunce. 1,800
Garnet, Sarah S J, and Susan McKinney....Commercial Credit Co. 150
George, W A. 87 Hicks ....Brooklyn F Co. 205
Hancock, J. Pacific st, near Sackman st....I Mason. 117
Harrold, R. 332 Stuyvesant av....J Baumann. 136
Holmes, G H. 320 Clifton pl....V A Russell. Piano. 115
Hosey, E. 674 Warren . L Z Murray. 251
Hale, J. 85 Gold....E Driscoll & Bro. 112
Jansen, Mary. Graham av, near Scholes st....L Chevallier. Piano. 175
Jones, Mary. 84 Ashland pl....Mullins & Sons. 197
Keys, J J. 663 Bergen st... Mullins & Sons. 155
Lane, M J. 736A Union ..M M Webster. 150
Lahey, R. 20 Hull... E Driscoll & Bro. 128
Lenhard, P. 884 37th .I Mason. 100
Marrin, M T. 559 Dean....I Mason. 120
Morgan, M. 641 Pacific... I Mason. 406
McCutcheon, F. 3 Willoughby....I Mason. 166
O'Neil, Kate. 200 23d....Mullins & Sons. 187
Paphebaum, H W. 63 Joralemon ...L Z Murray. 281
Peloubet, S S. 305 Madison....O D Rust. Piano. 1,400
Plunkett, H. 22 Walworth....I Mason. 104
Reilley, Mrs. 248 Pearl....I Mason. 112
Renhert, B. Eastern Parkway and Eldert st....B L Dinger. 107
Roles, Emma R. 2 Cornelia....D M Brown. 136
Stepenhausen, H. 278 Tillary....J C Hegeman. 133
Stevens, Mary C. 363 Driggs. ..M M Webster. 150
Steele, C. 85 Sterling pl....Mullins & Son. 151
Szag, G. 82 Court. . I Mason. 150
Worthington, F. 355 Dean....I Mason. 135
Wyman, R. 107 Stockton....I Mason. 224
White, R T. 309 W 41st ...C H Ten Eyck. 100
Whyte, Susan. 152 Kent av....J Baumann. 271
Wittman, J H. 277 Reid av....L Z Murray. 187
Woodbridge, Margaret S. 31 Ormond pl....L Z Murray. 202

MISCELLANEOUS.

Biaggi & Meccia. 695 Hicks....G Vento. Barber Fixtures. 100
Butt Bros. 12 Steuben....Marvin Safe Co. Safe. 120
Cohen, B. Brownsville....Hecht & Hamberger. Cows. 275
Curtis, C L. 189 Centre st, New York....J Keller Printing Office Fixtures. (R) 1,200
Davis, B. 152 Manhattan av....H T Lewis. Candy Store. 175
Edebohls, Mary. 178 Frost....Minna W Edebohls. Horses. 300
Fogarty, J J. Hamilton av and Columbia st....National Cash Register Co. Register. 175
Fortmann, B. 625 Vanderbilt av ...Nat Cash Register Co. Register. 200
Frohlich, J. 2992 Atlantic av....Mary Keeger. Butcher Fixtures. 400
Goldman, B. 7 Boerum....W H Butler. Safe. 130
Heffern, B A and J A. 664 Herkimer....A Randel. Horses, &c. 192
Hoberg, Rebecka ...H Lins & Sons. Horse and Wagon. 300
Hoenighausen, J. 250 Floyd....C Hoenighausen. Butcher Fixtures. 50
Hohmane & Maurer Mfg Co. 167 Plymouth....Prentiss Tool and Supply Co. Tools. 238
Jaeger, J. 181 Patchen av....Nat Cash Register Co. Register. 200
Lehman, Rebecca. 525 11th....Manges Bros. Fixtures. 140
Lewis, L F. 30 Clifton pl....Sarah A Casanova. Books and Paintings. 147
Lindau, F. New Lots road, near Wyckoff lane....Weil Bros. Cows. 583
Malone & Phelan. 144 Court....Nat Cash Register Co. Register. 175
Martin, A F... G Bungarz. Wagon. 122
Mann, E G. 315 Leonard....A F Zahn. Drug Fixtures. 2,000
Mann, E J. 315 Leonard... J C Hacker. Drug Fixtures. 2,000
McLoughlin, Ann and R J McConnell. 69 Warren....Arthur & Randel. Horses. 690
Meyer, W. 12 Fulton....Lamson C S S Co. Register. 500
Miller, E F. 1938 Fulton....J S Bernheimer & Bro. Tailor Fixtures. 175
Muller, H. 192 7th av....National Cash Register Co. Register. 200
Munger, L A & A S....A H Walker. Machinery 1,500
Navarra, M. 356 Myrtle av....S Legattolla. Barber Fixtures. 359
O'Connor, D. 17 Red Hook lane....J F Goodrich & Co. Coupe. 740
Palma, J S. 69 Court....Y C Frost. Barber Fixtures. 200
Price, J....Campbell P and Mfg Co. Press. (R) 3,294
Penrose & Co. 27 Rose st, New York ...Van Allens & B. Printing Office. (R) 9,455
Rathje & Hennessy. 578 4th av... W Hennesey. Trucks. 800
Reynolds, E W. 116 Withers....Isabelle W Reynolds. Horses, Trucks, &c. 872
Rehling, D. 167 Bedford av....H Schroeder. Wagons. (R) 1,000
Schmidt, H. 393 5th av....Liberty Machine Works. Paper Cutter, &c. 350
Seuling, W....A Goetz. Horse. 200
Schwartz, H. 569 Broadway....M Herskowitz. Shoe Store. 154
Semler, A. 197 Franklin....L Gardon. Store Fixtures. 600
Self, S. 31 Bedford av....W H Fenwick. Machinery. 700
Short, G D. 2529 Atlantic av....Lamson C S S Co. Register. 235
Sibbern, A. 147 Hudson av....Mary B Ryan. Store Fixtures. 2,000
Simonds, A C. 134 Carlton av....J F Clarke. Cart. 135
Smith, Carll V....B M Shanley. Horses, Carts, &c., Schooner George S. Page and Sloop Joseph C Knapp. 15,000
Stevenson, T. 83 Hudson av....D R Walker. Drug Store. 505
Tucker, A L. 38 Willoughby, 114 Bridge....J J Guerin. Store Fixtures. 1,300
Van Court, J H. 58 Fulton st, N Y....A W Schmitt. Machinery. 512
Same....same trustee for creditors. Machinery. 3,786
Wedermann, W. 313 Central av....M D Levy & Co. Store Fixtures. 165

BILLS OF SALE.

Bennett, W J. 26th Ward, Bennett's Casino ...L J Wing Co. Machinery. 400
Dowd, M J. 512 De Kalb av....Nannie T Dowd. Furniture. 700
Gross, Magdalena. 71 North 6th....J Curto. Barber Fixtures. 100
Gothar, L. 58 Lorimer....Emelia Handelmann. Piano. 250
Huefelein, F J. 13 McDougal....H Lapp. Saloon Fixtures. 746
Kaiser, J. 122 Throop av....C Schwerzel. Saloon Fixtures. 874
Kurz, A. 149 Stagg... J Heft. Butcher Fixtures. 125
Luck, H. 107 Sandford....C B Hurdt. Milk Route. 1,200
Lemmermann, H L. 254 Sumner av... F Lemmermann & Co. Indeft Business. 3,600
Moran, J J. Atlantic av, cor Carlton av....M McCarthy. Saloon Fixtures. 1,000
Racioppo, L. 442 Atlantic av....C Racioppo. Barber Fixtures. 600
Williamsburg B Co (Lim). 1692 Fulton....T L Hogan. Saloon Fixtures. 800
Wolf, M. 1856 De Kalb av....L Garment. Furniture. 30

ASSIGNMENTS OF CHATTEL MORTGAGES.

George Ringler & Co to J Murtaugh. (Mort given by Sarah Morgan, July 14, 1890). 1,000

NEW JERSEY.

NOTE.—*The arrangement of the Conveyances, Mortgages and Judgments in these lists is as follows: the first name in the Conveyances is the Grantor; in Mortgages, the Mortgagor; in Judgments, the Judgment debtor.*

ESSEX COUNTY.

CONVEYANCES.

Anderson, I S—C W English, Montclair......... $1,875
Same—J McNaughten, Montclair......... 1
Same—C A Goman, Montclair 1
Same—T E Baker, Montclair......... 1,040
Arnold, Jacob—A P Wolters, n s Bank st 30x101. 4,200
Atwater, Samuel trustee—E C Ward, South 10th st......... 1,000
Ayres, I H—W H Frothingham, Montclair...... 1,000
Baldwin, H R—M T Reeves, Livingston......... 150
Baldwin, J H—M C King, Montclair 1,640
Baldwin, P A—M Knolhoff, East Orange......... 5,500
Blakeslee, H K—M K Grant, Orange......... 1
Blamey, F R—W Wylie, Belleville......... 1,800
Booth, William—M A Tynan, South 9th st. ... 455
Breintnall, J H H et al—P J Hoeler, 13th av.... 2,200
Campbell, R C—E Hogg, Caldwell......... 450
Carragher, Peter—M Derbyshire, Belleville. ... 800
Chace, E I—E Bertolini, Montclair.........
Coe, Theodore et al—C Zeh, South 7th st......... 300
Conover, W H—T J Corbally, North 4th st...... 600
Cutti, Casare—E Bertolino, Montclair......... 1
Same—same, Montclair 1
Corby, Jane—P Degenhardt, Montclair......... 1
Same—same, Montclair......... 4,500
Crowell, L F—C Zeh, South 7th st......... 400
Dane, W P—S F Prentiss, East Orange .... —
Dangler, M A—A Bloemeke, Bruce st......... 2,600
Dawkins, Lewis—J A Peloubet, Bloomfield...... 1
Dean, E S—C Basile, n s Orange st 550 w Nesbit st 25x84......... 3,000

Dodd, Amzi et al exrs—P J Hoeler, 13th av 2,900
Drew, A T—G M Drew, East Orange 800
Earl, W H—F W Ward, Elizabeth av 1
English, M J—I S Anderson, Montclair 2,000
Fairchild, Emily—Morris & Essex R R Co, Orange 1
Faitoute, E C——same, e s Broad st adj land Wm H Harris 80x121 25,000
Fenner, Henry—E A Fenner, Newark Meadows. 1
Finlay, H P—Peoples Bank of Wilkesbarre, Pa., South Orange 24,500
Frothingham, W H—C W Ayres, Montclair 1,000
Gargan, Edward—A Stedenfeld, s s Inness st 490 s Lock st 60x138x130x60 4,000
Gould, Ezra—E J Schwarz, e s Columbia st 144 n Elm st 30x100 5,000
Goris, John—L Kull, South 10th st 700
Hankins, H F—C Colyer, s s Cottage st 261 e Mulberry st 25x111 and e s N J R R av 45 s Chestnut st 30x100 7,400
Hare, W S—M A Pring, East Orange 650
Hart, J H—E C Powler, East Orange 3,500
Hasse, Frederick—F Reheis, Jr, e s Newark st 351 n Elm 25x170 8,500
Hine, E W—A Williams, East Orange 2,500
Hilbig, F W—J Hart, e s Roseville av 125 n Orange st 35x91 4,000
Hill, William—O P Schaller, Hunterdon st 2,000
Hoffman, William—L Strucks, w s Mulberry st 19 s Beach st 25x90 4,300
Hunt, R E—E Mills, 7th av 1,000
Irvin, Charles—T P Murphy, Livingston 690
Jackson, John—F W Ward, Elizabeth av 1
Jacobus, C C—C E Bowen, East Orange 10,000
Jimmerson, N S—G Jacobus, North 2d st 1,750
Kenngott, Louis—T McLelland, South 18th st 1,500
Kelly, Mary—M Donnelly, West Orange 100
Lachenauer, Gustave—E Ziehr, e s Richmond st 147 n South Orange av 90x147x50x90x50 12,400
Lawless, Nicholas—W P Jaliaferro, East Orange 625
Lister, J C—A Camberbeach, Albert av 395
Same——E Toner, Albert av 380
Same——G Pope, Joseph st 1,030
Same——L Maybaum, s s Bowery st, 75 w Mott st 85x76x34x25x43x19x29x40x100 14,000
Same——R Stichlinger, Esther st 320
Same——J Fitzsimmons, Albert st 800
Same——W C Pope, Joseph st 240
Same——W Bauch, Jr, Esther st 510
Marsh, Josephine—A E Fryer, East Orange 3,390
Martin, C W—J A Peloubet, Bloomfield 1,200
Maurer, Otto—A K Nieder, Emmet st 1
McCauley, B T—E H Uffert, n s James st and e High st 25x85x36x84 7,480
McGovern, Owen—M Touery, Bloomfield 300
McGuire, M J et al—St Joseph's Catholic Church, Newark, Newton st 1,200
McLelland, Thomas—L Kenngott, s s South Orange av 29 e South 17th st 25x100 8,900
Monahan, S A—N Verzellino, Kinney st 1,950
Mutual Life Ins Co of N Y—T F Keer, Milford av 325
Nieder, John—O Maurer, Emmet st 1
Ohr, Christina—J Steiner, Garden st 1
Osborne, J H—N W Lawrence, Clinton 300
Pearce, James—C Pearce, West Orange 2,000
Pearce, Charles—J Pearce, West Orange 2,500
Peloubet, J A—J A Jamison, Bloomfield 4,000
Same——G Cantell, Bloomfield 1,200
Pinta, Michael—M Bilancia, Bleecker st 1,000
Post, W H—C M Post, Hill st 1
Preble, A M—E P Geach et al, Orange 4,222
Preble, G R—E P Geach, Orange 4,222
Ray, Adam—F J S Whitty, Wallace st 1,500
Roessner, Charles—C L Weeks, Hunterdon st 2,700
Rommel, August—A Kirschner, Napoleon st 1,200
Rowe, Francis—J C Wade, East Orange 500
Rowe, Michael—J Owens, 2d st 1,200
Seuffert, Michael—A Weiser, Littleton av 1,300
Strucks, Louis—M Hoffman, w s Mulberry st 19 s Beach st 25x90 4,500
Taylor, W H—W A Taylor, n s Tichenor st 235 e Orchard st 25x102 3,500
Tichenor, William—J Buehler, Montclair 250
Same——J H Kent, Montclair 125
Touery, P J—O McGovern, Bloomfield 300
The State Banking Co—C Reckner, Clinton 2,500
The Woodside B and L Assoc—B McDermott, Erie Place 100
Tynan, D F—D F Tynan, Sr, South 9th st 1
Tynan, M A—D F Tynan, South 9th st 1
Van Keyper, A E—J Pfaum, Belleville 400
Ward, F W—J P McFadden, Elizabeth av 1,900
Wightman, R C—J Combs, South 11th st 250
Williams, I M—A V Canniff, West Orange 750
Williamson, J A—J W Dow, Wyoming 1
Wolter, A P—J Arnold, Kossuth st 500
Zeh, Charles—M Strack, e s South 7th st 575 s 16th av 25x99 3,150

MORTGAGES.

Adams, A F—Roseville B and L Assoc, Mulberry pl 800
Adelma n, Seffer—C C Allen, Gotthart st 1,000
Anderson, I S—J C Beach et al exrs, Montclair. 400
Same——The Montclair B and L Assoc, Montclair 3,300
Balancia, Michael—Excelsior B and L Assoc, Bleecker st 3,500
Ball, M C—J W Baldwin, Bloomfield 2,000
Basile, Clementi—E S Dean, Orange st 2,750
Balz, Albert F—A Schmidt, South 6th st 1,500
Blashke, Anton—I Cockifair, Bloomfield 1,150
Bennett, C A—The Peabody Land and Loan Co of America, Mt Prospect av 500
Berla, Moritz—E H Green, Bank st 1,009
Bertolino, Eliza—Mutual Life Insurance Co of New York, Montclair 7,000
Blunt, Catherine—S Van Wyck, Montclair 5,440
Bodenweiser, Amelia—S E Richards, Orange 400
Brackin, Caroline—Reliable B and L Assoc, Mt Prospect av 2,000
Bradley, James—W C Headley, Bank st 139
Bundzleher, Maria—Washington B and L Assoc, Chestnut st 350
Canfield, E R—J Muir, Monmouth st 1,000
Carica, Vito—Enterprise B and L Assoc, O'Connel st 1,500
Conrad, Henry—C Geissele, Gotthart st 1,000
Cook, Frederick—J Wilde, Orange 3,000
Coully, John—Essex Co B and L Assoc, Lake st. 1,400
Decker, A V—J W Dawson, Ferry st 1,000
Donnelly, W J—M M Schneiber, Baldwin st 2,000
Eyrich, Emil—The American Ins Co, Camden st. 5,500
Fear, Henry—I S Anderson, Montclair 300
Fischman, Aaron—The Newark B and L Assoc, Prince st 500
Glover, W M—I S Anderson, Montclair 300
Harris, Marx—Passaic B and L Assoc, Boyd st 500
Herder, Ferdinand—E Butz, 18th av 1,500
Hillstrom, Frank—A Steadman, South Orange 500
Hogg, W E—H F Backus, Caldwell 1,500
Jacobus, S F—P L Mayer, Montclair 600
Jamison, J A—J A Peloubet, Bloomfield 1,800

Same—The Essex County Mutual Ins Co, Bloomfield 2,200
Jones, J E—F H Tiplin, Washington st 6,000
Same——H E Richards, Washington st 750
Kauch, William, Jr—J C Lister, Esther st 255
Kilcomin, M J—P Ballentine & Sons, Orange 680
Kiolehan, James—D J Creeden, Orange 500
Korn, E L—United States Credit System Co, Springfield av 2,800
Krueger, Nathan et al—Standard B and L Assoc, Montgomery st 7,000
Lefort, Katie—G Merritt et al exrs, Warren st 2,000
Lezgus, Frederick—F J Kastner, Mercer st 1,000
Lockwood, J H—C Akers trustee, Bloomfield 450
Logue, Mary—S Doughty et al exrs, Ferguson st 500
Matthews, C B—J S Page, Oliver st 5,500
Mayer, Anton—J Searing, Court st 1,350
McDermott, Bartle—The Woodside B and L Assoc, Erie pl 900
McLagan, J F—Howard B and L Assoc, Mt Prospect av 2,800
McNeill, Harriet—P Waldheim, South st 1,500
Memminger, Matthias—Orange Valley B and L Assoc, Orange 2,000
Mills, Hassey—S Doughty et al exrs, Wallace st 200
Nigg, Otto—Teutonic B & L Assoc, Rose st 800
Ormant, Edward—E Stanley 4,500
Owens, John—B Baldwin, 2d st 300
Polaner, Max—G Schoennamsgruber, Charlton st 3,000
Quinn, M F—J P Dusenberry, trustee, part of "Old Burrying Ground" 1,400
Rechner, Charles—The Mut B and L Assoc, Clinton 2,600
Reynolds, Michael—Enterprise B and L Assoc, Brill st 1,500
Robertson, Andrew—Roseville B and L Assoc, 4th st 600
Rogers, M A—C A Weick, Summer av 100
Ringland, R B—I S Anderson, Montclair 350
Rutan, J R—W W Jacobus, Somerset st 3,000
Schaller, O P—Wm Hill, Hunterdon st 1,800
Schill, Frederick—W Seidel, Charlton st 600
Schuetz, Ferdinand—C V Stoutenburgh, Camden st 800
Schwarz, E J—E Gould, Columbia st 4,000
Scudder, Emeline—The Howard Savings Inst, Springfield av 200
Seaman, G E—P J Cumerford, Orange 2,000
Sieger, F H—Fidelity Title and Deposit Co, South 8th st ..... ,000
Stedenfeld, August—J G Aschenbach, Inness st. 2,500
Strachan, David—M N Maxwell, East Orange 6,000
Thompson, L M—The Eighth Ward B and L Assoc, Badger av 1,800
Toner, Elizabeth—J C Lister, Albert av 190
Toth, Joseph—Passaic B and L Assoc, Prince st. 200
Tynan, Daniel—Norfolk B and L Assoc, South 9th st 500
Van Orden, J J—W Little, Jr, Caldwell 800
Verzellino, Nicola—S A Monahen, Adams st 310
Same——same, Kinney st 150
Wade, J C—F Rowe, East Orange 200
Weisse, Albert—C Weisse, Littleton av 300
Wild, Chas—H Ahrend, Kinney st 2,500
Williams, F E—A M Rollinson, East Orange 2,300
Wylie, William—S Forgie, Belleville 200
Yaufmann, John—J M Ward, Summer av 3,500
Zelliff, Winslow—J M Freeman, Belleville av 2,000

CHATTEL MORTGAGES.

Cramer, K H—C Bierman, furniture 130
Dowling, Edward—P Hauck, saloon 700
Edelhausser, Charles—E D Dennis, horse, &c 100
Gobel, Lena—M Kane, furniture 26
Hill, J A—P Ballantine & Sons, saloon 850
Hoffman, E H—Hamilton & Co, furniture 1,358
Kilcomin, M J—P Ballantine & Sons, saloon 630
Leibe, Henry—P H Hanley, machinery 145
Ludwig, Edward—C Feigenspan, saloon 325
Lyons, John—E Baer, horse 125
Marsh, C D—C Bierman, piano 100
Morton, Elizabeth—Hamilton & Co, furniture 275
National Cash Register Co—H H Gerrist, register 135
Olliner, Joseph—A Bleiweip, horse 95
Paddock, George—J H Mayell, furniture 243
Perkins, J E—G W Perkins, horses, &c 125
Reynolds, Peter—P Hauck, saloon 400
Riemer, G F L—P H Hanley, billiard table 58
Ross, Nettie—M Kane, furniture 40
Serbe, A F—W T Serbe, store fixtures 3,729
Stager, Julius—Essex Co Brewing Co, saloon 162
Thelen, C J—P Ballantine & Son, saloon 500
Travie, Michael—J Ettenberger, saloon 500
Van Riper, Eugene—D Blackwood, horses, &c 176
Winans, G H—E A Winans, machinery 500
Zeeb, J F—A Finger, furniture 150

HUDSON COUNTY.

CONVEYANCES.

Battin, S H—J J Degnan, J City $10
Bebus, J G—E Schindler, North Bergen 550
Benstead, Henrietta—C W Peroty, Kearney 2,000
Board, J M—R Kierseweller, Hoboken 45
Bowes, Richard—M Bowes, Hoboken ..... nom
Bowes, Thos—R Bowes, Hoboken ..... nom
Breitenbach, Otto—A Berisse, West Hoboken 6,300
Buchannan, L F—G Heitman, J City ..... nom
Same——same, J City 3,040
Cadmus, Geo—Clara Douglass, Bayonne 850
Cadmus, George—Emma Hartpener, Bayonne 425
Same——J J Duffy, Bayonne 2,610
Same——H R Hutchinson, Bayonne 274
Carroll, Roger—A Cuneo, Hoboken 2,650
Cherollier, Josephine—J Murphy, J City 2,900
Combes, Mary E—D Harnett, Bayonne 850
Condit, Fillmore—W Folen, Kearney 200
Culla, T F—R J Mahoney, J City 1,600
Currie, William—A Billings, Bayonne ..... nom
Drescher, Chas by exr—H Ruegg, West Hoboken 800
Drew, Patrick—U Schellein, J City 600
Eckert, Anna—J Ribe, Guttenberg ..... 25[illegible]
Edward, W H—Victoria H Ray, J City 1,250
Eilshemus, H G—A H Bell, Kearney 225
Same——W C Marion, Kearney 750
Eleveleth, Susan S—F Woodruff, J City ..... 3,6[illegible]
Epstein, Hannah—J Wetzler, West Hoboken ..... nom
Ewen, E D—W Thompson, Harrison 225
Ewen, Norman by exr—J Thompson, Harrison. nom
Fielder, J F—J W Ray, J City ..... nom
Fraleigh, E N—Jane A C Platt, Kearney ..... nom
Frances, R P by assignee—G Pase, Hoboken 8,200
Frances, R P—M Bowes, Hoboken ..... nom
Fridlieb, T R—Sarah Rophe, J City 600
Frey, Albert—P Pentland, J City 1,650
Goldberg, Lena—A Kohn, J City 5,000
Grieder, Adolf—J Grieder, Guttenberg ..... nom
Grieder, Jacob—Lydia Grieder, Guttenberg ..... nom
Guce, William—K Wahnung, West Hoboken 6,000
Harmer, Horace—A Billings, Bayonne ..... nom
Hart, Pauline T—C A Lewis, J City 2,600
Hoboken Land and Improvement Co—P Weigele, Hoboken 2,000
Same——R P Francis, Hoboken ..... nom
Same——same, Hoboken 1,800
Same——R P Francis, Hoboken 825
Same——The New York Thistle Curling Assoc, Hoboken 4,900
Hubbert, Wilhelmina—W J Hulford, J City 2,800
Johnston, Caroline—J Mulligan, Kearney 050
Johnson, Robert—Gesina Koster, J City 2,200
Kerrigan, Sarah C—W Niederlitz, West Hoboken 55
Knapp, Isaac—V Endres, West Hoboken 2,500
Knight, Patrick—G Lang, Union 1,175
Kirk, Franklin P—W W Hallock, West Hoboken 1,000
Kruse, Chas—E Russ, Kearney ..... nom
Leuthner, Maria—G C Rose, J City 1,200
Lewis, Mary P—J D Stover, Hoboken 5,220
Same——D Martens, Hoboken 5,130
Same——C Fall, Hoboken 5,220
Siegfried, Adam—C A Pierson, J City 750
Matthews, Peter—C Gimbel, Union 2,700
McCarren, Mary and Nellie, Edwin Bepet and C A Dubois by sheriff—J Warren, J City 5,868
McMann, Thos B—Mary J Wilson, J City ..... nom
Mead, Cathalina—Clara Douglass, Bayonne 425
Same——J G Koch, Bayonne 650
Same——J Wanner, Bayonne 600
Miller, C A F—J G Wolf, Union 1,500
Miller, W S—P Kerrin, Harrison ..... nom
Moersdorf, Johanna—Elizabeth De Marko, J City 600
Newkirk, Edgar—Jane D Newkirk, J City 1,050
Niehaus, G D—H Alber, J City 2,000
Noyes, Elizabeth S—Belle Metzler, J City 4,800
Ogden, W B by exrs—F Posser, J City 2,100
O'Hare, John, Jr—J O'Hare, Sr, North Bergen 2,000
Pape, Gotthold—Eva E Selvage, Hoboken 1,330
Pitman, W E by exrs—P H Hollwegs, J City ..... nom
Platt, D A—M Salinger, J City 1,000
Randall, F E—Emily Clarke, J City 1,150
Ray, Victoria H—J F Fielder, J City ..... nom
Ritchford, A H—J Emmel, Union 3,550
Ruh, C F—M Murray, North Bergen 1,600
Russ, Edward—Adele M Kruse, Kearney ..... nom
Schinzel, G H—O Frommel, Hoboken 2,200
Schultz, C S, assignee R P Francis—M Bowe, Hoboken 6,425
Siegfried, Adam—W Lutthias, J City 1,500
Smith, A F—F Raimon, J City 2,260
Skinner, J A—Adolph Rayson, Kearney 250
Speer, W H—W W Stuart, J City 4,500
Spillner, Mary L—H Spillner, J City 2,500
Stevens, Martha B—M Bowe, Hoboken 200
Same——same, Hoboken ..... nom
Stumpf, Jacob—A Hornkohl, Harrison 70
Symes, James H—C Loy, Union 350
The Board of Trustees of the Knox Presbyterian Church—F Condit, Kearney 800
The Provident Inst for Savings—Ida G DeLamater, Bayonne 600
The Ministers, Elders, Deacon of the Reformed Protestant Dutch Church—Mary D Knack, North Bergen 2,181
Thomas, J C—C W Thomas, J City ..... nom
Timannus, Charlotte—A Becker, J City 2,800
Vreeland, Peter—P J Wust, J City ..... nom
Wetzler, Joseph—V Maier, West Hoboken 850
Wilkinson, George—W Wilkinson, J City ..... nom
Wilkinson, Walter—Juliet B Wilkinson, J City nom

MORTGAGES.

Anderson, F E—J L Mathey, Weehawken, 3 years 1,500
Becker, Adam—New York Wakefield Co-operative B and L Assoc, J City, installs 2,500
Bell, A H—Cecile E Eilshemius, Kearney, 1 year 125
Beringer, Geo—F Posser, J City, 3 years 1,000
Billings, Albert—The Greenville B and L Assoc, Bayonne, installs 7,300
Bowes, Michael—Hoboken Bank for Savings, Hoboken, 1 year 6,500
Brackett, T W—The Pamrapo B and L Assoc, Bayonne, installs 840
Brooke, Lucy A—Margaret Cower, J City, 3 years 2,000
Butler, T A and Gabriel Balas—G R McKenzie, Hoboken, 5 years 20,000
Cadmus, J J—Hannah L Cadmus, Kearney, 1 year 2,000
Cash, Meyer—O Schultz, West Hoboken, 5 years 3,000
Cleary, M J—The Greenville B and L Assoc, J City, installs 4,280
Crevier, J C—Hoboken Bank for Savings, Hoboken, 3 years 6,000
Daly, Dennis—The Lafayette M B and L Assoc, J City, installs 1,200
De Lamater, Ida G—The Provident Inst for Savings, Bayonne, 1 year 500
Emmel, John—Anna M Dengler, Union, 5 years, 1,500
Endres, Valentine—I Knapp, West Hoboken, 6 years 1,900
Fickle, C J—Maria C Crowley, J City, 5 years 600
Foll, Chas—Hoboken Bank for Savings, Hoboken, 3 years 1,500
Fox, James—Pavonia B and L Assoc, J City, installs 2,200
Fraser, J S—Fairmount M B and L Assoc, J City, installs 800
Friese, Margaret—J Meibury, J City, 6 years 1,800
Frommel, Oscar—G H Schinzel, Hoboken, 1 yr. 1,000
Gimbel, Chas—Johanna C Barnstorf, Union, 5 years 2,000
Heitman, Gottlieb—L F Buchanan, J City, 3 years 1,500
Hollwegs, P H—J Kehrwald, J City, 3 years 8,000
Humbert, Louis—P G Walter, J City, 1 year 4,000
Hutchinson, Henry—G Cadmus, Bayonne, 1 yr 215
Hutchinson, Robert——same, Bayonne, 1 year 100
Kirchgesner, Theo—Palisade B and L Assoc, West Hoboken, installs 2,400
Kostner, Gesena—J Rugge, J City, 5 years 1,000
James, Julia—Jane Michell, West Hoboken, 3 years 500
Lewis, C A—Pauline T Hart, J City, 3 years 2,100
Lobey, Richard—The Star M B and L Assoc, J City, installs 4,000
Lutz, John—Juliet Lord, J City, 3 years 2,000
Lutz, K V—J Engerer, Guttenberg, 3 years 3,000
Machintosh, Jas—Jane Krowl, J City, 3 years 1,500
Mahoney, R J—Jersey City B and L Assoc, J City, installs 1,400
Maier, Victor—J Wurzler, West Hoboken, 2 years 200
Martens, Diederick—Hoboken Bank for Savings, Hoboken, 2 years 6,000
Marion, W C—H G Eilshemius, Kearney, 5 years 650
McArthur, John—People's B and L Assoc, Kearney, installs 3,200

McDonough, Pat—J Moylan, J City, 3 years 700
McNab, G A—T Belgin, J City, 1 year 976
Murray, Malachi—C F Ruh, North Bergen, 5 years 1,000
Nichol, Maria A—Mary E Ahrens, Hoboken, 5 years 1,700
Nugent, Annie E—D Campbell, Kearney, 3 years 600
Nierstedt, C H—The John Kress Brewing Co, J City, 1 year 1,000
Pape, Gotthold—S Fisher, Hoboken, 3 years 1,600
Perry, Geo—C Perry, Hoboken, demand 5,000
Polaher, Max—The Excelsior M B and L Assoc, Kearney, installs 800
Raimond, Felix—Agnes Van Horn, J City, 6 years 2,600
Ray, J W—The Provident Inst for Savings, J City, 1 year 2,400
Reid, J W—J Stumpf, Kearney, 3 years 5,000
Reilly, William—The Greenville B and L Assoc, Bayonne, installs 1,450
Renler, J J—Town of Union B and L Assoc, Union, installs 3,000
Rocci, Pasquale—Antonio Schiaffino, Hoboken, 1 year 200
Rose, G C—H Rollfs, J City, 3 years 1,500
Schweisguth, Henry—A Schlapfer, Union, 3 years 1,000
Selvage, Eva E—G Pape, Hoboken, 1 year 675
Sixon, Conrad—The Provident Inst for Savings, J City, 1 year 6,000
Smith, Charlotte W—The Hudson City Savings Bank, J City, 1 year 2,400
Stover, J D—Hoboken Bank for Savings, Hoboken, 1 year 3,000
Stuart, Walter—Monticello M B and L Assoc, J City, installs 3,600
Stuart, W W—W H Speer, J City, 5 years 1,341
Thompson, John—C H Nicoll, Harrison, 1 year .. 2,400
Van Buskirk, Dewitt—R W Parker, Bayonne, 3 years 2,000
Van Winkle, Elizabeth—The Columbia B and L Assoc, J City, installs 1,600
Wahnung, Karl—Theresa Reenoch, West Hoboken, 3 years 850
Ward, G E—F M Stone, Union, 1 year 800
Wanner, Jacob—The Pamrapo B and L Assoc, Bayonne, installs 2,520
Weber, Amelia—E Emiltheuen, J City, 1 year ... 5,000
Weigele, Philip—Trustee Cornelia L Fowler, Hoboken, 3 years 7,500
Wilson, Mary J—The Teachers' B and L Assoc, J City, installs 1,440
Wolf, J G—C A F Muller, Union, 5 years 1,500

CHATTEL MORTGAGES.

Adams, Bruce, J City—John Mullins & Co, furniture 174
Bellotte, Henry A and George Bauer, Weehawken—George Ringler & Co, the Eldorado restaurant and beer tunnel building at Weehawken 2,858
Borig, Caspar, Hoboken—National Cash Register Co, one No 3 register 200
Brengel, Adam, J City—C Birdsall, furniture ... 130
Burns, Richard, J City—L Bauman, furniture ... 180
Bushmonn, Bernard, Hoboken—J H Meierdierck, saloon and lease 1,300
Byrnes, Barnard, Bayonne—Hincks & Johnson, coach 850
Chamberlain, H T, J City—C Birdsall, furniture. 130
Conniff, John, J City—D Stevenson, saloon 355
Connors, M J, Hoboken—Bernheimer & Schmidt, saloon and lease 600
Cook, S E, J City—C Birdsall, furniture 100
Crosbey, Eleanor, J City—same, furniture 100
Crowley, Bernard, J City—Lembeck & Betz Eagle Brewing Co, saloon and lease 700
Delaney, William, J City—Marvin Safe Co, safe. 80
Dougherty, Mary, Bayonne—John Mullins & Co, furniture 189
Fields, Geo, J City—L Baumann, furniture 148
Funger, William, J City—H Schumacher, saloon 600
Fjarks, John, J City—F Wild, horse, wagon ... 165
Hunt, Mary, Hoboken—L Baumann, furniture .. 384
Jennings, James, J City—Lembeck & Betz Eagle Brewing Co, saloon 700
Kearney, Daniel, J City—J T Muller, saloon 800
Kinney, Thos, J City—C Birdsall, furniture 100
Mahon, Katie, J City—John Mullins & Co, furniture 216
Meyer, Anna, Hoboken—F Cordts, furniture .. 155
Mooney, T J, J City—L Bauman, furniture 145
Muller, C A, Hoboken—F Cordts, furniture 351
Norton, Michael, J City—Wilkinson, Gaddis & Co, grocery store 800
O'Connor, Thomas, J City—C Hertler & Son, butcher shop 1,548
Oldenburg, Dedrich, J City—Hincks & Johnson, Berlin coach 625
Rodgers, P E, J City—D Bermes, saloon 427
Siefried, Jacob, Harrison—A H Van Horn, furniture 248
The Asphalter-Slag Paving and Roof Co, Kearney—The Akron Iron Co, machinery 2,048
Theurrer, Rose, Hoboken—L Baumann, furniture 106
Wahnung, Karl, J City—Beadleston & Woerz, saloon 500
Wall, E C, Hoboken—C Birdsall, furniture 130
Wild, Frank, J City—A Heckt, blacksmith shop. 275

BILLS OF SALE.

Kirschenmann, Fred, J City—Frida Steber, bakery and lease 1,100
Kirschmann, Fred, J City—Frida Steber, bakery and lease 1,100
Rich, Sarah C, J City—Ellen G Vass, hotel furniture and fixtures ..... nom
Schumacher, Henry, J City—W Finger, saloon. 600
Schumacher, Henry, J City—W Funger, saloon. 600
Stewart, John, J City—J Jacobson, machine 67
Stewart, John, J City—J Jacobson, machine 67
Wild, Frank, J City—A Hecht, blacksmith shop and tools 275

JUDGMENTS.

Bemhannure, Chas—Gardner & Meeks 2,286
Brouse, C D—P C Vreeland 174
Corkery, Daniel—Consumers Coal and Ice Co ... 385
Du Bois, Jacob—Herkner & Steine 198
Fitzgerald, Eugene and James, as Fitzgerald Bros—Bernheimer & Schimdt 951
McDonald, Matthias—Gardner & Meeks 332
McKenna, Thomas and Frank Klein, as McKenna & Klein—Katz Bros 336
Newmann, Henry—The Jacob Hoffman Brewing Co 30
Rizzo, Michael—The Backmann Brewing Co ... 477
Rowe, Anna D or Anna D Gilman—T C Lyman & Co ..... costs and 6 cents
Strocker, J G—Exrs Johanna Kaiser .... costs and 460
Zimmerly, Jacob, Jr—Joseph Beck & Co 567

BUILDING MATERIAL MARKET.

BRICKS.—Market reports, when confined to their proper and legitimate sphere, are at the best plain matter of fact affairs, but when running along week after week and month after month in monotonously unchanged condition, they become disagreeable alike to writer and readers. Such has been the case for Common Hard brick for so long a period that we find it impossible to extract from the situation a single general idea, that has not been repeated until it is worn threadbare, and the only change developed since our last is a somewhat weaker tone. It seems to be the result of an increasing excess of supply over outlet and a consequent necessity for offering buyers greater favors as an attraction to secure their orders. Even that move, however, is successful in only a moderate degree, as, admitting the comparative cheapness of the stock, there is no place to put it if taken. We imagine from the statements made that the actual arrivals this week have been no greater, on the contrary somewhat smaller if anything, but actual consumption is decreasing through the completion of some jobs and the slow starting in of others, and as before advised most storage room is so fully occupied that little space remains for additions. On prices some stock coming to hand on contract may bring old figures, but none of the principal operators claim ability to obtain above $5.25 on open market, and from $5 down is the more general line of trading, while on Pales $2.25 is named for an extreme, with considerable less money accepted on some faulty goods. It is said that manufacturers are talking about shutting down for good on the 20th inst., but the report is made with a tone of skepticism that shows it has no solid foundation.

LATH.—It has been a light market again, with nothing of a particularly eventful character brought out. The offering was small, both on spot and to arrive, but that was particularly well suited to the nature of the more or less indifferent demand and receivers seemed to be very well satisfied that they had no larger quantity to take care of. Consumption is said to be fair, especially outside the city limits, and it is expected dealers will be heard from again before long. The run of sales as reported was at $2.10@$2.15 per M.

LIME.—Not unexpectedly, the market has settled back again to natural conditions and the valuation as now given is at 90c. for common, and $1 for finishing, Rockland brands, with the usual possibilities on outside makes. Supplies were not particularly full, but the demand seems to have become very well satisfied, and as a great many buyers still resort to the cheaper makes of State and Western stock, a few cargoes coastwise go a great ways.

LUMBER.—There is still a lack of positive animation in any section of the market, and a great many operators find occasion to repeat old complaints regarding dull condition of trade; yet, on the whole, there is certainly a gain over last week. City consumption is probably quite in the old slow form, but the suburban demand is picking up, and some dealers speak quite encouragingly of that outlet toward bulk lots; attention is also commencing to turn in a manner that promises a place for somewhat broader negotiation, and altogether the indications this week have a measure of cheerfulness not noticeable for a long while past. Sellers, so far as can be discovered, are disposed to meet the situation on a conservative basis, as it is evident enough buyers occupy the independent position, and are likely to find considerable advantage in the competition to secure their orders, as developed during balance of the season.

Eastern Spruce finds sale to a fair extent, yet hardly through any direct open demand anxiously awaiting an offering, but principally as the result of a sort of still hunt on the part of receivers. There are a great many yards carrying light stocks and others running down, with some of them located where evidence of increasing consumption may be noted, yet it seems impossible to stir up dealers into any thoroughly satisfactory manifestation of interest, and the market as a whole is ragged. There does not appear to be any special objection to cost, but simply the old flat refusal to negotiate at all, and that receivers find the most discouraging. From primary sources the complaints are coming in much the usual form, and manufacturers are still talking about shutting down for want of margin. Many of the mills are said to be working on specials only. Vessels as yet continue plenty and cheap.

Piling seems to be in quite as bad a way as ever and, with the exception of probably a little more business doing at the moment, operators have nothing of an improved character to report. Arrivals continue to drop in from time to time and with the liberal accumulation in chains it will take a pretty full deal to reduce supplies to a basis upon which a higher line of value may with safety be asked. Some two or three good sized jobs are said to be contemplated on the other side of the Hudson River, but no positive move as yet made.

Hemlock, in addition to the fair out of town demand before referred to, is getting a little more attention from local sources; enough to create encouragement without reaching a point of actual stimulus. With the Pennsylvania production well controlled and the State cut short, sellers have a very considerable advantage and seem to feel confidence in their ability to hold matters without much difficulty.

White Pine remains about steady, probably because it is already too low for a further cut on price; certainly the demand is not full enough to afford any real leaven, and the promises are a little uncertain. Some dealers who are large carriers generally, already have yards well stocked, in one instance the accumulation already piled is immense and that looks as though a great deal of fall trade would be missing, but smaller operators, it is claimed, all want stock, and predictions are making of an early improvement of demand, especially for the better qualities, as most of the free arrivals thus far have been of coarse stuff. Somewhat stronger talk comes from primary points, but it is not believed that any special attempt will be made to raise the line of value. From the cheaper grades of shippers, exporters have been sending out considerable stock to Brazil and to West Indies, and appear to hope for more demand.

Yellow Pine is at least no worse than at the date of our last and some of the reports appear rather more promising. One or two of the big concerns have been doing quite a distributive trade and think the chances now favorable for a further gain, and there is also a somewhat fuller run of orders for specials or occasionally good standard random. We also find a better word spoken for the f. o. b. trade, including orders filled, for England, the West Indies, and some sections of South America, with a hope expressed that the latter source of demand will be expanded through a speedy settlement of some of the political and financial difficulties. Prices generally remain low and unsatisfactory, but there is a whisper of movements on foot to perfect a combination among the trade through which the whole system of the market will be brought under control and many present difficulties remedied.

Carolina Pine has found a somewhat fuller demand, flooring in particular, stimulated by an increasing consumption in the suburban districts as well as at points outside this immediate locality. The offering was fair, however, and it has not cost desirable custom any more money to obtain stock.

Hardwoods are quiet all around. Some distribution into consumption takes place and there is a little buying on the part of receivers who now and then have some fair bargains tendered them, but nothing like real animation or any immediate tendency in that direction. The situation is well enough under control to insure a steady showing, yet the strength is not pronounced, and except on the very scarce and choice qualities any extra effort to realize would almost surely result in lowering the line of value. Export trade is taking a little, but wants it fine, and shows some inclination to contend against cost.

The exports of lumber, exclusive of hardwood, from the port of New York during the month of August were as follows:

	1890. Feet.	1891. Feet.
To West Indies	3,246,000	2,754,000
To South America	2,481,000	3,681,000
To East Indies	803,000	1,013,000
To Europe	551,000	195,000
Total feet	6,881,000	7,653,000
Previously reported	49,913,000	49,559,000
Total since Jan. 1	56,794,000	57,212,000

GENERAL LUMBER NOTES.

STATE.

The Albany market is reported by *Argus* as follows:

The past week brought no especial change in any line in the local market, and trade continues to move along in about the channel last reported. Pine seems to be about as quiet a feature as exists in the trade today, for outside of a few of the very large houses, there is but little doing. The demand, as a rule, is slow and shipping is very moderate. Still, in spite of the dullness, a stronger feeling prevails and the prediction of higher prices is freely made. Receipts from the west are fair, while of Canada pine the amount coming forward is quite large, and the district is amply stocked for all demands which the fall trade may make, except perhaps for 1¼-inch boards. Spruce culls are still the scarce article and there are practically no 1¼-inch in the market. In fact it is doubtful if a decent cargo could be gotten out of this market. Good spruce is also in very moderate supply, and with the shutting down of the northern mills for want of logs, the situation has become such that the principal dealers have been compelled to fall back on Canada spruce to help them out. This lumber which goes to England and France in large quantities in the shape of deals, is now being cut in sizes to suit this market. Some of the spruce men are very much gratified that they have at last received directions to ship some of the very large bills they have been holding for the convenience of their customers in New York. About the only trade of importance in hemlock is a p tt fair demand for 18-foot boards, other sizes and grades being largely neglected. The trade in the principal hardwoods is fairly active, and the market is ruling firm as quoted below. Shingles are also doing very well and the market is well stocked.

ENGLAND.

The *Timber Trades Journal* as follows:

The market is overdone with shipments of American whitewood (canary), and it is now difficult to sell even at prices which cannot remunerate shippers for their outlay. We notice a very large parcel just landed from one of the regular liners from Baltimore, which is unsold when we write. * * *

Referring to Canadian Pine, we are quite willing to believe all the shippers on the other side say as to probable shortage of supply and the increased cost of the goods there, but so long as consumers in the country are pressed to buy so long will their disbelief in the accuracy of these statements be maintained.

This is pretty much the same with the shippers of pitch pine timber. The recent sales must have resulted in heavy losses to the shippers. They may naturally say, when sales have to be made under such circumstances, and buyers are getting goods much under cost, that a reaction must shortly set in; but if, as is the case, we have cargo after cargo, steamer after steamer load thrust upon an already overloaded market, where is there a chance of prices coming back to a point profitable to the shippers? This is a condition of affairs lamentable from a shipper's point of view, but no one is responsible for it but the shippers themselves, backed up by their financial agents.

THE WEST.

The Northwestern *Lumberman* as follows upon the cargo market at Chicago:

After wobbling along under difficulties for a month the market is admitted to be offish. There is no longer any attempt to disguise the fact that short piece stuff is weak at $10 a thousand, and that boards have settled down about a dollar below the early season's quotations. The settling process has been going on for some time, but prices fluctuated according to the amount of stock offered, the terms demanded by the buyer, while all the time the commission men were holding hard to maintain prices. Recently a good deal of lumber has come in from Lakes Huron and Superior, and it has generally arrived in big tows or great single cargoes. Much of the time the docks of the larger yards have been crowded with unpiled lumber, bought in blocks at mill points and coming steadily all summer. This has been a drawback on market sales.

Coarse inch has gone off about $1 a thousand, and common 50 cents. Strips are still in good demand, though it is not very hard to overload the market with coarse stuff.

In respect to piece stuff slim jims have suffered less than short lengths, but a decline is shown by a willingness on the part of the seller to put in a sprinkling of 15 to 20 per cent of long lengths at the price of short lengths. In a measure this also applies to 2x12 and 2x14. When a tally shows lengths or sizes, long or short, that are not particulary demanded in the yard it gives the cargo a black eye. This is not the case when the market is strong and prices firm.

Advices from the mills on Lake Huron, Superior, and to some extent on Michigan, are to the effect that the mill docks are pretty well loaded up with lumber. On this account the outlook for an advancing cargo market in the immediate future is not bright.

At the yards:

Stocks are in a peculiar condition. Dealers have bought cautiously this year, though several have taken on large blocks. Heavy buying was mostly done early in the season. Since June dealers have been somewhat hampered by the conservatism of the banks and have not loaded up with their usual freedom. This had a somewhat depressing effect on the cargo market, which is seen in the recent sag in the price of piece stuff. But this careful going may have saved the dealers trouble. Should trade revive, and the market stiffen in the fall, dealers would regain confidence, the banks would relax, and purchase would be on a larger scale.

The *Timberman* as follows:

Demand for hardwoods has been somewhat more active during the past week, but dealers still report trade dull and prices hardly as satisfactory as they could wish. As a rule they look for a steadily increasing demand as the season advances, but with respect to prices, there are several who express the opinion that it will be some months, at least, before the market again shows that degree of firmness which is ultimately expected of it, because of improved financial conditions throughout the country.

There can be no doubt but that less oak is being consumed now than at this time a year ago, whatever the reason therefor may be. There is a great deal of oak being sold, however, and as the house-finish trade develops the demand is likely to improve. With plenty of stock still being offered prices, of course, continue somewhat weak, although it is claimed that high grade, quarter-sawed white oak is bringing as much money as ever. One dealer reports a couple of sales recently, amounting to three or four car loads, at full former prices, except that a small per cent of 1½-inch and 2-inch went in at the same price as the inch. For the ordinary run of stock, however, prices are from $5.00@3.00 per thousand lower than they were in the early spring, dealers paying about $36.00 @38.00 for inch.

Plain-sawed oak is quiet, with ample receipts. Prices have changed very little of late, $26 being about the average price paid by dealers for inch first and seconds, f. o. b. this city.

The Mississippi Valley *Lumberman* as follows:

The feeling in the lumber market in all the region west of Lake Michigan is one of exceptional strength and firmness. The demand is large for this season of the year, and even the most chronic bears in the trade are forced to admit that trade is likely to be limited only by the ability of the railroads to supply the cars.

Meantime a good many of the mills are shutting down. Low water has cut off the log supply. Comparatively few logs are coming out of either the St. Croix or the Chippewa, and many of the Mississippi River mills are without stock and have shut down. On the Wisconsin River the drouth has been felt and the majority of the mills have been shut down, some of them for the remainder of the season. All this is calculated to very materially reduce the output and leave the stocks, now by no means excessive, very badly depleted before spring. These conditions are all contributing to the stiffening of the market and new price lists are being sent out which show an advance of from fifty cents to a dollar. Orders have been so free with some of the Minneapolis firms that they have called in their traveling men.

METALS.—COPPER—Ingot has been in somewhat better demand with several very good deals made in lots on spot and to arrive and at hardening rates. At the close buyers and sellers seem fractionally apart in their views, but supplies are under control and quite unlikely to be urged upon the market. On an average range of valuations we quote at 12¼@12½c. for Lake, and 11½@12c. for casting brands. Manufactured Copper does not change much in value, the official quotations being quite generally adhered to, and all in all the tone is steady. Demand fair, with an inclination to increase if anything. We quote as follows: Sheet, not above 30x72 in., 16 oz. and over, 25c.; do. 14 to 16 oz., 23c.; do. 12 to 14 oz., 24c.; do. 10 to 12 oz., 25c.; do. 8 to 10 oz., 28c.; do under 8 oz, 30c. Sheets longer than 72 inches add 1c. for 12@14 oz., 2c. for 10@12 oz, and 3c. for 8@10 oz. Sheets, not above 36x96 in., 16 oz and over, 22c.; do, 14 to 16 oz, 24c.; do, 12 to 14 oz, 26c.; do, 10 to 12 oz. 30c.; do, 8 to 10 oz, 33c. Sheets longer than 96 inches 22c. for over 32 oz, and add 1c. for 16 to 32 oz.; 3c. 14 to 16 oz.; 5c. 12 to 14 oz. and 18c. for 8 to 10 oz. Sheets, not above 48x96 .32 to 64 oz, 22c.; do, 16 to 32 oz, 25c.; do, 14 to 16 oz, 27c. do 12 to 14 oz, 29c.; do, 10 to 12 oz. 33c. Sheets wider than 48x96 and longer, 22@25c. for 32 to 64 oz. and over. 27@ c. for 16 to 32 oz, 29c. for 14 to 16 oz and 34c. for 12 to 14 oz. All bath tub sheets, per lb., 16 oz. 7 c.; 14 oz. 29c.; 12 oz 3 c.; and 10 oz. 35c. Bolt copper, ¾ inch diameter and over, 22c. Circles, 60 diameter and less, 3c. above price of sheets of same thickness; circles, 60 to 96 do do, 5c. do; circles, 96 do and over, 6c. do. Segment and pattern sheets, 3c. above price of sheets required to cut them from. Cold or hard rolled copper, 1@2c. per lb. above the foregoing prices. Copper bottoms, 26@32c. per lb. IRON—American Pig continues to meet with only about a routine demand and there is nothing of a very pronounced character in the market at the moment. Evidence of an increasing interest among buyers is not wanting, however, and there is apparently faith in a comparatively early movement of somewhat fuller proportions. The leading and popular brands continue well together and steadily held, but inferior grades are unsettled, with tendency to weakness on price. We quote at $16.25@18.00 per ton for No. 1 X foundry; 15.50@16.50 for No. 2 X do. and $14.00@15.00 for Gray Forge. Old material has found only a slow uncertain sort of demand, and the market ruled quiet for all kinds of stock, though for general valuation about former figures are commonly named. We quote at about $20.50@21.50 for old rails; $20.00@21.00 for No. 1 wrought scrap; $17.00@18.00 for cast scrap and $17.00@17.50 for car wheels. Manufactured iron not very active, especially for this time of the year, and more or less complaint to be heard. There have, however, been some contracts made for shapes and specials, with about old rates generally obtained. We quote Common Merchant Bar ordinary size, at 2.00@2.10c. from store, and refined at 2.30@2.60c; Rods, round and square, 2.20@2.40c. Bands, 2.40@2.60c.; Norway Nail Rods 4@5c., and domestic sheet on the basis of 3.00@3.05c. for common Nos. 10@16. Other descriptions at corresponding prices, with 1-10c. less on large lots from cars. Steel Rails are meeting with a little more quiet attention, one or two of the larger railway companies manifesting an increased measure of interest, and the tone of the market has improved. It is, however, quite unlikely that an attempt to advance value will be made, any more than there was a tendency to weakness under dull conditions. We quote standard sections $30 per ton at mill, with usual advance for delivery at tide water. Pig Lead has shown some irregularity, but of late consumers seem to be satisfied with the amount of stock in hand, and the market is quieter. Moderate offerings serve to keep rates steady. We quote at 4.47½@4.52½c. per lb. The manufactures of lead are quoted at 7c. for Pipe, 7¾c. for sheet, 15c. for Tin-lined Pipe, and 37½c. for Block Tin Pipe. Pig Tin has undergone several fluctuations since our last, but the business continues principally speculative, consumers taking only enough for immediate wants. We quote at about 20@20.10c. for round lots, and 20¼@20½c. for jobbing parcels. Tin Plate is moving out fairly well, spot delivery, but buyers are non-speculative and will not anticipate future wants. Offerings under control and prices firm. We quote prices as follows: I. C. Charcoal, ½ cross assortment Melyn grade, $6.40@6.45, each additional X add $1.50; I. C. Charcoal, ½ cross assortment, Allaway grade, $5.90@6.00, each additional X add $1; Charcoal terne, M. F. grade, 14x20, $7.50@7.55; M. F. grade, 20x28, $15.50@15.55; Worcester, 14x20, $5.70@5.75; Worcester 20x28, $11.25@11.30; Dean grade, 14x20, $5.20@5.25; Dean grade, 20x28, $10.4 @10.50; D. R. D. grade, 14x20, $5.15@5.20; D. R. D. grade, 20x28, $10.00@10.05; I. C. Coke, Penlan grade, $5.45@5.50; J. B. grade, 14x20, $5.55@5.60; I. C. Bessemer steel, squares, $5.75@5.80 basis; I. C. Siemens steel, squares, $5.85@6.00 basis. Spelter has a slow sort of market, but well controlled supplies keep prices about steady all around. We quote $4.95 @5.10c. for Common Western, according to brand.

NAILS.—Business has been irregular in character. For cut, demand now light and buyers give no evidence of increasing their orders up to the close; but wire are selling freely and the movement is of a character to give the position a generally good firm tone. Production is as slow as conditions of market seem to warrant. We quote Cut at $1.50@1.60 per keg for car lots and $1.75@1.85 per keg for parcels from store, for iron, and add 5@10c. per keg for steel; Wire, $2.00@2.05 at mills, and 2.20@2.35 from store.

PAINTS, OILS, COLORS, ETC.—Demand continues in much the former general condition, about the only change being found in some increase of orders for future delivery. These are mainly against staple articles of production and simply booked as a precaution against slow delivery when demand shall become more general and active. Jobbers have advices to impress them with the belief that many vacancies exist in stocks and assortments at primary points, and as soon as the distribution commences the entire market must be benefited. Colors and mixed paints have been temporarily pretty dull, but of late attracted more demand, and are expected to sell freely this month. Block Chalk, at the recent decline, has become pretty steady in tone. Zincs are reported as making a fair seasonable demand, and operators appear to be very well satisfied with the market and all grades are held steadily. White Lead is somewhat irregular in price on sales from jobbers' hands, but producers remain steady and refuse to shade the regular rates. Association Corroders' rates stand as follows: Lead in oil in kegs and dry lead in kegs, in lots of less than 500 lbs., 7½c. net; in lots of 500 lbs to 5 tons at one purchase, 7c.; 5 tons to 12 tons, one purchase, 5¾c.; 12 tons and over, one purchase, 6¾c.; dry white lead in bbls. ½c per lb. less than price in kegs. Lead in oil 12½ lb. in tin pails, add 1c.; in 25 and 50 lb. tin pails, add ½c.; and in 1 to 5 lb. tin cans, assorted (100 lbs. in case) add 2½c. per lb. to keg price. Terms on lots on 500 lbs. and over, note or acceptance at sixty days, or 2½ per cent. discount will be allowed for cash paid within fifteen days of invoice date. To make either of the above required quantities any assortment of packages of white lead, red lead and litharge may be counted. The above quotations are free on board cars or boat at corroding point. Linseed Oil has ruled firmer owing to the reduced pressure of supplies. The Western competing stock seems to have disappeared, and that proves of material benefit to the general position. We quote at general range at 37@40c. for Western, and 44@56c. for City. Spirits Turpentine has not been very active, but with supplies here under better concentration and supporting advices from the South values are higher, closing strong. We quote at 37@38c. per gallon, according to quality, delivery, etc.

TAR AND PITCH.—Somewhat increased business has been done on regular outlets and the effect upon the market was stiffening, though without changing the general range of value. Supplies fairly balanced the inquiry in quantity and assortment. We quote Pitch at $1.70@1.75 per bbl.; Tar at $2.15@2.50, according to quantity, quality and delivery.

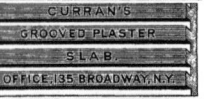

MISCELLANEOUS.

MISCELLANEOUS

REAL ESTATE RECORD AND BUILDERS GUIDE.
ESTABLISHED MARCH 21st 1868.
DEVOTED TO REAL ESTATE, BUILDING ARCHITECTURE, HOUSEHOLD DECORATION, BUSINESS AND THEMES OF GENERAL INTEREST

PRICE, PER YEAR IN ADVANCE, SIX DOLLARS.

Published every Saturday.

TELEPHONE - - - - CORTLANDT 1370.

Communications should be addressed to

C. W. SWEET, 14 & 16 Vesey St.

J. T. LINDSEY, Business Manager.

VOL. XLVIII. SEPTEMBER 12, 1891. No. 1,226

Next week there will be issued with the regular edition of THE RECORD AND GUIDE *a handsome supplement, illustrating and describing the growing suburban section traversed by the New York & Northern Railroad. Newsdealers and others desiring extra copies should send in their orders at once.*

THE EXHIBITION OF ARCHITECTURAL DRAWINGS.

One of the handsomest and most complete displays of architectural drawings will be opened next week in the exhibition halls of THE RECORD AND GUIDE, *at Nos. 14-16 Vesey street, to which all who are interested in architecture are cordially invited. The exhibition is free. There are on view over two hundred perspectives of the latest work done by all the leading architects of New York City. So excellent an opportunity for any one to familiarize himself with the best work of the day has not before been offered.*

ATTEMPTS to put up the stock market are for the moment no more successful than those to put it down. For almost a whole week it has maintained a waiting attitude with a movement here and there of a stock to equalize the advance and some slight concessions in those that advanced most; but in spite of heavy professional selling no general downward movement could be forced. Yesterday's attempt to rush prices up on the Government crop report was equally ineffective, for as soon as the first buying movement was over prices dropped to the figures of the previous day or two. There seems to be, as far as there can be an organized effort in a large market like the present, a general determination to await results in the grain regions and on trunk line issues. Southwestern securities are least in favor, the condition of cotton telling against them, and it may come that with the corn crop as assured as wheat now is, there will be a decided discrimination against them to favor the grangers and Eastern trunk lines. Gold imports promised to immediately become a larger bull factor.

THE English stock market is somewhat livelier and stronger; but all the activity and strength is concentrated in the American department. The other classes of securities do not find favor, and with reason. It is true that the financial position is now more satisfactory, and indications may be found of increasing confidence on the part of the public; but these facts alone are not considered sufficient. So far as English railway stocks are concerned there do not seem to be many inducements for purchasing. Harvest products are unsatisfactory, trade is stagnant, and money is bound to become dearer. Furthermore the traffic returns are disappointing; and although the companies are paying less for their coal than they were a year ago, their wages bill is heavier. Neither are foreign issues in favor. The Continent will also suffer from a deficient harvest, and this cannot fail detrimentally to affect the financial position. In addition, prices in many cases stand at a high level, and large quantities of stock are being financed which the holders would take advantage of any buying to turn into cash. About the only kind of properties which it is expected will be in a position to compete with the American securities for the favor of the British public are certain outlying industrial investments of good character which have suffered from the general fall in values. European economists are beginning gravely to consider the effects of the cereal shortage on the laboring population. The increased price of such a prime necessity as bread will, it is feared, cause a widespread and active discontent—particularly in those Continental countries where the struggle for existence is already severe and trying. The first of next May will not pass with as little disturbance as the first of last May. In Russia, of course, the effects of the bad harvests will be most disastrous; but apparently that country will escape, owing to the submissive nature of its population, any open revolt. What will be equally bad, however, large numbers of the peasantry will have nothing to sow with when seeding time comes around.

THE verdict rendered by the Coroner's jury in the case of the Taylor building disaster verifies the correctness of our opinion given before the jury entered upon their investigation, when we said that the cause for the accident would never be accurately known, as death has sealed the lips of those who could have told just what happened inside the building at the moment of collapse. The jury say they are unable to determine the cause of the shock which, after the death of the principal eye-witnesses, is not obtainable. The jury definitely find that the timbers and walls of the building were of fairly good material and construction, but that the iron columns were not as strong and as well constructed as they should have been, and that the fall of the building was due to "the breaking of one or more of the columns in or near the middle of the ground floor," by reason of some sudden shock applied to the exterior of the columns. Nothing is said in the verdict of the overloading of the floors, nor is any reference made to the destructive vibratory motion of the heavy steam presses that were located on the two upper stories.

THE verdict does not explicitly state whether the columns that the jurors believed to have been broken by shock were interior or exterior columns. On the ground floor (that is, the first story) there were three interior columns of cast iron, 9 inches in diameter and over an inch in thickness. Each column had to support a floor area of 16 by 16 feet for each of the four floors above and the roof in addition. By allowing a safe weight of 200 pounds per square foot on each floor, which is what the testimony showed was all that the floor timbers and girders could safely carry, each first story interior column had to support say 160 tons. This is about what such a column can safely carry, being only one-fifth of its ultimate crushing strength. Right here comes up an amazing oversight in presenting all the facts to the jury. Each of these columns rested on a brick pier only 24 by 20 inches square, or a sectional area of three and one-third superficial feet. The proper load to apply to a brick pier laid up in cement mortar is twelve tons per superficial foot. Thus, such a pier ought not to have had placed upon it more than 40 tons, which is only one-fourth of the safe load that the iron column immediately above it could carry. What the column could safely support would be the crushing load for the pier. The westerly brick pier was entirely destroyed by the collapse; and it so happens that this pier was at the very place where an explosion of some sort is alleged to have taken place. With the great weight resting upon that column to hold it rigidly in its upright position it would have required a terrific concussion of air to have overthrown it. If the verdict has reference to one of the exterior cast-iron box columns, the same reasoning applies for the application of a terrific force to overthrow any one of them, for upon them rested the brick wall of the front together with one-fourth of all the floors and contents of the building. Between each of the box columns were the ordinary wooden entrance doors with glass panels in same and fan-lights overhead. Most of the doors probably stood open, as the day was very warm. An explosion with force enough to break or even throw out of place one of those iron columns would have driven the entrance doors across the street. In the crush iron columns and all other kinds of materials were broken. The verdict leaves the question of what caused the collapse as open to opinions as before the jury undertook to solve the cause. The jury recommends that the Governor of the State call attention in his next annual message to the Legislature to the need of amendments to the building law. The jury also expressed their appreciation of the management and action of the Fire Department and its bureaus, both before and after this most lamentable disaster. In a future issue we shall refer more at length to the matters recommended by the Coroner's jury.

THE Board of Park Commissioners have acted rightly in denying the application of the New York Central & Hudson River Railroad Company for the closing of the drawbridges during certain hours of the morning and afternoon. The corporations, with their terminus at the Grand Central Depot, have never until lately been very solicitous of the comfort and convenience of their local traffic above the Harlem. If, despite their indifference, a considerable daily movement in and out of New York has been built up it will do them no harm to be placed in the position of being forced to make proper provision for it. The concession which they have asked for would encourage them in the procrastinating policy which they have pursued in the past. As the Park Commissioners point out, it would not be wise to take any step towards obstructing the navigation of a river which the national government is spending large sums of money on to improve. It is the Central that must raise its bridge, and so assume the burden of its own traffic instead of endeavoring to make the river trade interests pay part of the expenses. The Legislature can be pursuaded to grant the necessary authority to change the grade of the approaches, and with this consent obtained the reconstruction of the bridge ought not to take so very much time. Meanwhile the patrons of the road will suffer, and the improvement of the towns along its lines delayed; but this is better than the establishment of such a bad precedent as that of closing the draws. If there is to be a loss of time and money to be suffered by anybody, let those bear it to whom it belongs.

PRIVATE ownership of railways has received a wound in the house of a friend. That the blow dealt was unintentional makes it none the less effective. In advocating the consolidation of competing lines as the one means of reducing the cost of railway transportation to the minimum, and as a remedy for rate-wars, Mr. C. P. Huntington, in the current number of the *North American Review*, unwittingly condemns the system under which these rival lines were developed, and, in fact, the whole past of railroad operation in this country. For if, as the President of the Southern Pacific maintains, consolidation is better than the continuance of competition, surely it would have been better still if railroad traffic between any two commercial centres had been limited, in the first place, to one well-equipped line. As it is, the consolidation of competing lines between given centres would mean much higher freight and passenger rates than would be required to yield fair profits to a single line or system adequately equipped to conduct all the business between these points.

BUT much as the people may regret that they ever listened to the plea that the establishment of competing lines would serve to regulate railroad rates, they are not yet ready to place themselves completely at the mercy of private railroad corporations, as President Huntington, in urging consolidation, would have them do. The consolidation of all railroads of the country into one grand private system is not to be seriously considered as a solution to the railway question. The choice lies between the present competitive system and government ownership. Mr. Huntington does not advance a single argument in favor of consolidation, which cannot be urged with equal force for the nationalization of railroads.

Eight Months of Real Estate.

THE decreases which have been the marked feature of the records for the present year still continue during August, but the proportion of decrease has been increased in such way that the dose begins to become extremely unpalatable. During the first eight months of the present year 9,987 conveyances have been recorded, involving a total value of $169,831,027; during the same period of 1890, 11,473 conveyances were recorded, involving $210,-338,754. The decrease has been 1,486 or 13 per cent in number, and $40,507,727 or 19 per cent in amount. This is a heavy enough decline, but the shrinkage for the last month is double that of the whole period. During August, 1891, 668 conveyances have been recorded, involving $9,977,851; during August, 1890, 903 conveyances were recorded, involving $16,933,952, a decrease of 240 or 26 per cent in number, and $6,956,101 or 41 per cent in amount. The large disproportion between the percentage of decrease in the number of parcels transferred and the aggregate value involved shows that the falling off has taken place principally in expensive properties, and this is a conclusion which is sufficiently well explained by the obvious cause of the decline. The cause has been not so much the actual tightness of money as the lack of disposition of money-lenders to lock it up in mortgages, or of wealthy purchasers to lock it up in a form of property hard to dispose of. This explanation is partially borne out by the peculiar character of the mortgage filings. It is true that in the aggregate they do not decrease in anything like the same proportion as the conveyances decrease, which shows that more borrowing has been carried in proportion to the transferring than is either usual or healthy. But the important point is that far more than the usual proportion of this borrowing is being done at a high rate of interest. The decrease in the number of mortgages given at less than 5 per cent is large, that in the number of mortgages given at 5 per cent smaller, but still large; while those given at more than 5 per cent have had an ample and significant increase. Thus we see that a great many owners have wanted to borrow money on their holdings so badly that they were willing to pay high rates of interest, and that those who were not willing to pay such big prices for money found it difficult to obtain any. All this indicates rather weakness than strength.

Neither is a survey of the building tables reassuring. During the first eight months of the present year plans were filed for 1,954 buildings to be erected at an estimated cost of $40,843,931 and during the same period in 1890 for 2,644 buildings to be erected at an estimated cost of $57,312,401, a decrease of 690 or 22 per cent in the number, and $16,468,467 or 28 per cent in the estimated cost. Now turn to last month. During August 1891 plans were filed for 120 buildings to cost $2,310,818; during the same month in 1890 plans were filed for 273 buildings to cost $6,071,460, a decrease of 153 or 55 per cent in number, and $3,761,642 or 61 per cent in estimated cost. Of course this does not mean as much as it appears to mean, because a monthly table of building figures is very much subject to accidental variations, but even after making deductions on that score it shows very conclusively that buildings are not being disposed of in speculative districts with a rapidity that justifies the undertaking of new operations. It should, however, be remembered that the filings for one month represent the transactions of the month before. Lately the market has had a better feeling and a stronger tone; and this is but natural, for the apprehension which existed so long among money-lenders has been largely removed, and capital will again begin to return to real estate for investment. The year 1891 will nevertheless rank like 1888, as an off-year in New York realty, and those interested in the market should not disguise from themselves the fact that the dullness and the weakness, while due to a certain extent to general causes, are also to a certain extent due to a reaction from an activity that was somewhat feverish and prices that were a little too high. Nothing is to be gained by trying, as some of the morning papers are trying, to blow a boom on a turgid market; wind of a different kind is needed, and this, as we think, will be forthcoming in due time.

EIGHT MONTHS OF REAL ESTATE.

NEW YORK CONVEYANCES.

	No. Conveys.	Amount.	No. Nom.	No. 23d & 24th W.	Amount.	No. Nom.
1891.						
Jan.-July, inc..	9,321	$159,853,176	2,636	1,662	$7,111,295	420
August	663	9,977,851	218	164	751,499	36
Total.......	9,987	$169,831,027	2,854	1,826	$7,862,794	456
1890.						
Jan.-July, inc.	10,570	$193,401,802	2,613	1,693	$8,059,000	422
August.......	903	16,933,952	256	195	1,327,589	56
Total........	11,473	$210,338,754	2,869	1,888	$9,386,589	478
1889.						
Jan.-July, inc..	9,918	$180,375,119	2,194	1,802	$8,110,625	432
August........	740	12,883,002	167	150	516,128	47
Total.......	10,658	$193,258,121	2,361	1,952	$8,626,753	479

MORTGAGES.

	No Morts.	Amount.	No. at 5 p. c.	Amount.	No. at less than 5 p. c.	Amount.	No. to B. T. & I. Cos.	Amount.
1891.								
Jan.-July, inc.	9,277	$113,136,234	4,755	$58,870,260	854	$18,624,089	1,335	$33,772,111
August........	793	8,896,379	364	4,055,785	34	1,396,000	122	2,968,775
Total........	10,070	$122,032,613	5,119	$62,926,045	888	$20,020,089	1,457	$36,740,886
1890.								
Jan.-July, inc.	9,724	$164,829,432	4,741	$70,738,558	1,113	$63,489,280	1,382	$78,695,360
August.......	916	13,467,876	383	5,143,099	107	1,772,400	159	5,320,050
Total........	10,640	$188,297,308*	5,124	$75,881,657	1,220	$65,261,680	1,541	$84,015,416
1889.								
Jan.-July, inc.	9,072	$115,806,675	4,257	$52,991,030	1,144	$24,367,494	1,258	$29,937,718
August.......	802	9,168,945	360	4,026,444	87	1,740,220	111	2,631,250
Total.......	9,874	$124,975,620	4,617	$57,017,474	1,231	$26,107,714	1,369	$32,568,968

*Includes mortgage given in February, 1890, by the Manhattan and Metropolitan Elevated Railway Companies on real and personal property to The Central Trust Co. for $40,000,000; mort. given in March, 1890, by the Edison Illuminating Co. to The Central Trust Co. for $5,000,000; and mort. given in August, 1890, by the Mount Morris Electric Light Co. to the Central Trust Co. for $2,000,000.

NEW YORK BUILDINGS PROJECTED DURING EIGHT MONTHS, GIVEN BY DISTRICTS.

	1889. Jan. to Aug., inc.	1890. Jan. to Aug., inc.	1891. Jan. to Aug., inc.
Total No. of plans filed..................	1,505	1,515	1,187
Total No. of buildings projected........	2,777	2,644	1,954
Estimated cost..........................	$51,817,672	$57,312,401	$40,843,934
No south of 14th st.......................	367	342	297
Cost....................................	$12,375,895	$14,071,200	$10,960,025
No. bet 14th and 59th sts..............	244	311	247
Cost....................................	$5,981,375	$12,239,470	$7,390,030
No. bet 59th and 125th sts, east of 5th av	473	445	279
Cost....................................	$7,312,080	$8,163,055	$5,201,568
No bet 59th and 125th sts, west of 8th av	663	619	458
Cost....................................	$15,553,550	$13,594,800	$11,150,630
No. bet 110th and 125th sts, 5th and 8th avs	71	97	40
Cost....................................	$1,743,850	$1,060,625	$843,000
No. north of 125th st..................	314	262	146
Cost....................................	$5,313,895	$8,204,008	$2,035,594
No. 23d and 24th Wards................	610	568	507
Cost....................................	$3,539,927	$3,179,243	$2,663,098

NEW YORK BUILDINGS PROJECTED DURING AUGUST, GIVEN BY DISTRICTS.

	1889. August.	1890. August.	1891. August.
Total No. of buildings projected........	252	273	120
Estimated cost..........................	$4,207,380	$6,071,460	$2,310,818
No. south of 14th st....................	38	22	13
Cost....................................	$794,000	$569,700	$587,025
No. bet 14th and 59th sts...............	18	35	6
Cost....................................	$294,800	$2,232,950	$119,075
No. bet 59th and 125th sts, east of 5th av.	28	47	26
Cost....................................	$396,440	$674,800	$940,400
No. bet 59th and 125th sts, west of 8th av.	63	79	20
Cost....................................	$1,578,500	$1,282,000	$374,080
No. bet 110th and 125th sts, 5th and 8th avs	11	9	1
Cost....................................	$110,300	$151,625	$50,000
No. north of 125th st..................	36	37	7
Cost....................................	$661,700	$553,990	$97,308
No. 23d and 24th Wards................	67	51	47
Cost....................................	$435,040	$456,395	$142,980

	1889 No. b'ld'gs.	1889 Cost.	1890 No. b'ld'gs.	1890 Cost.	1891 No. b'ld'gs.	1891 Cost.
Jan.-July, inc..	2,525	$47,610,292	2,371	$51,240,941	1,834	$38,533,116
August	252	4,207,380	273	6,071,460	120	2,310,818
Total......	2,777	$51,817,672	2,644	$57,312,401	1,954	$40,843,934

FOR THE MONTH OF AUGUST, 1891, CLASSIFIED.

	Flats and Tenem'ts No.	Flats and Tenem'ts Cost.	Private Dwell'gs No.	Private Dwell'gs Cost.	Hotels, Stores, Churches, Office Build'gs, &c. No.	Hotels, Stores, Churches, Office Build'gs, &c. Cost.	Miscellaneous, Stables, Shops, &c. No.	Miscellaneous, Stables, Shops, &c. Cost.
South of 14th st	5	$94,000	..	....	6	$485,000	2	$8,025
Bet 14th and 59th sts	2	34,000	1	$25,000	..	....	8	60,075
Bet 59th and 125th sts, east of 5th av.	17	067,500	..	....	4	255,000	5	17,900
Bet 59th and 125th sts, west of 8th av	..	....	16	316,000	.	....	4	58,030
Bet 110th and 125th sts, 5th & 8th avs	..	....	..	....	1	50,000	..	....
North of 125th st	1	18,000	8	14,200	1	40,000	2	25,008
23d & 24th Wards	1	22,000	27	95,280	1	15,000	18	10,700
Total for Aug. 1891	26	$885,500	47	$450,580	13	$845,000	34	$179,738
Total for Aug. 1890	105	$2,577,000	98	$1,216,550	21	$2,023,125	49	$254,785

THE COSTLIEST BUILDINGS FILED DURING AUGUST, 1891.

Location and Character.	Owners.	Cost.
Pearl st, s w cor William st, eight-story factory	J. Whalen	$220,000
10th st, Nos. 299-303 W., four-story storehouse	Beadleston & Woerz	90,000
72d st, n s, 80 w Lexington av, seven-story flat	Lorenz Weiher	375,000
123d st, s s, 40 e Lenox av, four-story Library	Harlem Library	50,000
Madison av, n e cor 59th st, four-story business building	Leo Schlesinger	125,000
6th av, s w cor 11th st, six-story warehouse	J. Glass	95,000
Six buildings, to cost		$955,000

FLATS, TENEMENTS AND DWELLINGS IN ROWS.

Location and Character.	Owners.	Cost.
69th st, n s, 225 e Columbus av, five four-story dwell'gs	Thom & Wilson	$105,000
71st st, s s, 125 w Central Park West, five four-story dwell'gs	Att'y, D. T. Kennedy	100,000
88th st, n s, 96 w Av B, eight five-story tenements	Joseph Schreiner	136,000
West End av, n w cor 83d st, six three and four-story dwell'gs	Gerald L. Schuyler	111,000
Twenty-four buildings, to cost		$452,000

KINGS COUNTY CONVEYANCES.

	1890. Number.	1890. Am't involved.	1890. Nom.	1891. Number.	1891. Am't involved.	1891. Nom.
January	1,342	$5,216,826	341	1,429	*$7,878,196	412
February	1,298	6,137,587	344	1,219	4,704,985	390
March	1,685	7,608,870	423	1,602	6,245,195	475
April	2,176	11,587,703	490	1,998	9,042,227	490
May	1,882	9,317,276	437	1,802	7,230,963	482
June	1,515	5,920,970	357	1,731	6,233,014	405
July	1,738	7,729,816	351	1,680	6,020,339	402
August	1,274	4,696,970	322	1,238	4,251,552	327
Total	12,905	$57,815,318	3,065	12,699	$51,606,491	3,383

KINGS COUNTY MORTGAGES.

	1890. No.	1890. Am't involved.	1890. No. at 5 per cent. or less.	1890. Am't involved.	1891. No.	1891. Am't involved.	1891. No. at 5 per cent. or less.	1891. Am't involved.
Jan	1,264	$4,994,740	798	$3,455,240	1,182	†$14,007,748	620	$2,417,480
Feb	900	4,117,787	558	2,659,475	1,082	4,123,056	615	2,802,984
March	1,272	5,643,729	780	3,916,105	1,229	5,147,777	682	3,072,480
April	1,679	6,575,719	1,067	4,536,146	1,581	6,671,680	917	4,165,699
May	1,516	6,042,149	927	4,233,752	1,272	5,059,644	680	2,941,829
June	1,822	5,488,801	772	3,987,174	1,460	5,654,829	791	3,727,914
July	1,446	5,785,961	901	3,879,466	1,468	5,060,339	777	3,014,425
August	1,091	4,576,404	622	3,076,165	1,057	3,433,058	563	2,160,599
Total	10,550	$43,234,720	6,415	$29,693,523	10,331	$49,343,126	5,646	$24,316,410

*Includes seven deeds at a total of $2,560,000 given by the various sugar companies in Brooklyn to The American Sugar Refining Co. of New Jersey.

†Includes mortgage given by The American Sugar Refining Co. of New Jersey to The Central Trust Co. of New York, for $10,000,000.

KINGS COUNTY PROJECTED BUILDINGS.

	1890. Total No. b'gs.	1890. No. of brk, stone and iron b'gs.	1890. No. of frame b'gs.	1891. Total No. b'gs.	1891. No. of brk, stone and iron b'gs.	1891. No. of frame b'gs.	1890. Cost.	1891. Cost.
Jan	344	108	236	268	61	207	$1,407,615	$1,108,285
Feb	388	158	230	350	160	190	1,816,425	1,543,895
March	484	215	269	427	185	242	2,829,661	2,170,100
April	525	249	276	563	305	258	2,408,930	3,177,979
May	496	198	298	427	205	222	2,469,935	2,455,360
June	547	274	273	299	122	177	2,632,789	1,873,275
July	369	133	236	270	94	176	2,653,640	1,185,580
August	347	136	211	308	102	206	1,747,245	1,844,700
Total	3,480	1,466	1,964	2,912	1,234	1,678	$17,964,110	$15,361,067

AT the recent meeting of the British Association at Cardiff, an economist entered into an elaborate disquisition on the matter of the labor of women, and showed what was previously well known that their earnings are less by a large degree than those of men. In the manufacturing industries their pay varies between one-third and two-thirds less; and even when employed as teachers, clerks, telegraphers or compositors, they cannot command anything like an equal return. It is only in literature and art in which the distinctive personal flavor of the work renders it superior to competition that women receive a compensation that is equal to the compensation obtained by men. The explanation offered by the lecturer does not seem to be adequate. According to the reports, women received less, because they earned less. Ten hours' work from men produced a larger output than ten hours' work from women, and the former are paid proportionally. Now, doubtless, this is true in all industries in which power, endurance and persistence are the main requirements; but, as everyone knows, there are many industries in which these elements are subordinated to quickness of perception, neatness of workmanship and deftness of manipulation. All psychologists are agreed that women are far more nicely adapted to tasks demanding such qualities than are men; yet in these as little as in other lines of work, do they receive a return for their labor equal to the return received by the other sex. The explanation seems to be that women are practically subsidized laborers. Their fathers, brothers, or some members of their families as a rule help them by giving them rent or something else free. Consequently they can afford to accept less, whereas men who have families to support must hold out for a larger compensation. Whenever men are placed in a similar position—that is, when they are helped by other members of their families—their wages immediately begin to diminish. In the early factory days in England the operatives used to try to increase their earnings by getting employment for their whole families; but it was soon found the remuneration afforded to them all, in the long run, only equalled that which the man alone previously received. Women are in the same position, and so far as we can see will always remain so.

THE EXHIBITION OF ARCHITECTURAL DRAWINGS.

One of the handsomest and most complete displays of architectural drawings will be opened next week in the exhibition halls of THE RECORD AND GUIDE, *at Nos.* 14–16 *Vesey street, to which all who are interested in architecture are cordially invited. The exhibition is free. There are on view over two hundred perspectives of the latest work done by all the leading architects of New York City. So excellent an opportunity for any one to familiarize himself with the best work of the day has not before been offered.*

Investments—Good and Bad.

COMPARISONS AND CAUSES.—Of the many ways by which the character of the advance in the stock market may be tested, the best, perhaps, is the comparison of current quotations with those of previous years, and the causes which effected those quotations. When one considers that only a few weeks since prices were weak and men and things generally gloomy and depressed, and that now the outlook is rosy and prices very much higher, one is apt to overestimate the advance. It is with a more cheerful glance that one looks for instance at Burlington at 96 than at 79, but the thought will insist on rising, has not the advance gone as far as is safe and consistent with the merits of the property. If it were a question of investment alone Burlington would be plenty dear enough as a 4 per cent stock at 96, especially as it is no secret that as soon as the market will permit it, the C. B. & Q. Company will come forward as a large borrower in order to make some needed additions to its property and equipment, and in order to make use of the quarter of a million of dollars it has tied up in real estate in St. Louis for a couple of years or more. The investor must not overlook the fact in noting the prospects of our railroads all over the country to-day, that much of their increased earnings will be spent during the next year in enlarging equipment and putting the roads into condition to meet the demands for the Exposition of 1893, and consequently it is not improbable that some hopes of increased dividends may be disappointed. These expenditures will effect permanent good to the railroads, but they may require the stocks to wait their result before they benefit them in the way of dividends. These considerations effect the conservative and investment view of railroad securities.

There is an element, however, that is too pronounced to be lost sight of, or as it has been more graphically and quite as correctly put, the hurrah, and that is the speculative element, which comes in at intervals and upsets the best calculations on values. Every year it exerts its influence three or four times in a degree more or less marked, and leaves its impress in the recorded quotations. It is very pronounced now, and consequently this is a good time to see how far its influence has developed, compared with the powers it has shown in previous years. To do this is easy by comparing prices for a few years back. In such an examination of forty-nine stocks of every degree of activity, it has been found that few are selling at prices as high as the highest of 1889 and 1890, and not a few below the highest of the present year. The stocks of the forty-nine selected, whose current quotations are higher than the best of 1889 are: Canada Southern, Hocking Valley, Lake Shore, Reading & Wheeling and Lake Erie preferred; New York Central's and Southern Pacific's quotations are now at about the same as the best of 1889. Of the same forty-nine only three are selling higher than they did at any time last year, namely, Lake Shore and Erie Common and preferred. Current quotations of New York Central, Southern Pacific and Wheeling & Lake Erie preferred are about the same as when at their best last year. Twenty-three are selling at prices lower than at their best of even this year. These latter consist of stocks which are suffering some reaction after leading or being prominent in the advance, such as Burlington, Rock Island and others, some whose advance has not yet carried them up to the best of the year but will doubtless do so soon, as Lackawanna, Delaware & Hudson, Louisville & Nashville, Manhattan Elevated, Illinois Central, Manitoba and Pullman, and lastly stocks which have and still are suffering for the defects of the several systems they represent and containing among them Union Pacific, Oregon Improvement, Oregon Railroad and Navigation, Chicago Gas and the issues of the Wiman properties. It is remarkable that of so large a number as any forty-nine, to say nothing of their being the most active stocks, while some few come to or near it, Lake Shore should be the only one that is selling now higher than it has done at any time since January 1, 1889, a period of two years and three-quarters, in which, though, it must be admitted most of the time has been dull and of small business, there have been quite a number of periods of activity, that of the summer of last year being conspicuously good. Now the facts already given are not the only remarkable ones that claim attention in considering this question. One other is very important, and that is the extent of the difference between the highest prices of this and the two previous years. It would not be convenient, and would be, perhaps, unnecessary to give the figures of all, but taking the most important it will be found that Atchison is selling 7 points, Canada Southern 3, Jersey Central 8, Burlington & Quincy 14, St. Paul 8, Northwest 4, Rock Island 15, Three Cs 8, Lackawanna 5, Louisville & Nashville 13, Northern Pacific 13, Missouri Pacific 5, Pullman 8 to 10 and Western Union 3 points lower than the highest of last year. Compared with 1889 the differences are in many instances greater.

Of course the important question is, what does all this signify? That question is best answered by pointing to the circumstances under which the advances of recent years have been brought about. To what can any one point to as a general cause of advance in the market in the years 1889 and 1890 except that it was found at intervals that money was cheap and plentiful, and that the value of railroad securities have been very much depressed during times of inactivity and currency want. This year there is in addition to those features a certainty of great wealth coming into the hands of the community through the crops and the European demand for cereals, through the uprising to bustle of almost every, if not every industry in the country, all of which must benefit the railroads most of all. Therefore if the causes at work in the years 1889 and 1890 were able to effect a greater advance in the general market than we have yet seen, what should the causes now at work be able to effect?

INVESTOR wishes to know how to employ about $1,600 to earn 5 per cent per annum with safety. In this case Atchison or Missouri, Kansas & Texas 4s can be recommended with confidence.

"W B" is advised to consult our general articles on the stock market. We cannot undertake to more explicitly name stocks for speculative purchases.

WISCONSIN CENTRAL INCOMES.—To satisfy the inquiry of "Market" we would say the advance in Wisconsin Central Incomes is due in part to the general movement of the market and in part to improved earnings reported this year.

"A BROOKLYN READER" is justified in believing the situation favors the granger roads most. The best property in the West is undoubtedly Chicago & Northwestern, and if it is not dealt in so largely as some others it is because it is held in greater esteem for investment. At current figures and on their several records Lake Shore is not so attractive for investment buying as Northwest.

Rapid Transit on the East Side.

The Rapid Transit Commissioners expected to have been able to make public the reports of the consulting engineers upon the plans of construction of the Broadway line, yesterday, but at the last moment found that the reports were incomplete, that of State Engineer John Bogart not having been received. Engineers Octave Chaunte, Joseph Wilson and Cooper had filed their reports, and four of the commissioners, Messrs. Steinway, Starin, Spencer and Bushe spent the afternoon in reading them over. But they resolved to guard safely their contents until next Thursday, by which time they will be made ready for communication to the public.

A delegation was present at the meeting from the Twelfth and Nineteenth Wards' House and Real Estate Owners' Association, said to represent some 500 property-owners on and near Avenue A and 1st avenue, who were anxious that the board should do something for the East Side of the city. Conrad Harris, president; G. G. Lawrence, vice-president; Geo. G. Banzer, and Jacob Heil, secretary, presented the wishes of the association.

They said that most of their members lived over two blocks away from the nearest elevated railroad, and some of them as much as half-a-mile away. In the district between Grand and 92d streets and east of 1st avenue there was great need of rapid transit to give an impetus to improvements and to bring their property within easy communicating distance with the business sections of the city. There were 2,600 vacant lots in the district mentioned that would be improved as soon as a satisfactory transit system was provided.

A canvass of the district had satisfied the speakers that a two-track elevated road, constructed in the middle of the streets indicated and as far from the sidewalks as possible, would receive the consent of all the property-owners along the proposed lines. No third track and no storage of cars on the tracks would be tolerated. The committee suggested three routes, either of which would be satisfactory to the association. The first was an extension of the present 2d avenue road, from 23d street up 1st avenue to 57th street, to Avenue A, to 92d street at the Astoria ferry.

The second was also an extension of the Second Avenue road, but from Chatham square, through East Broadway, Rutgers street, Essex street, Avenue A, 23d street, 1st avenue, 57th street and Avenue A to 92d street at the Astoria ferry. The third route suggested was for an independent line beginning at the Battery, running through South street, Rutgers slip, Rutgers street, Essex street, Avenue A, 23d street, 1st avenue, 57th street and Avenue A to 92d street at the Astoria ferry. The first two routes were suggested in view of the assumed probability that the elevated railroad company would be the purchaser of the franchise and would construct the road. But if that company was not willing to construct either line the petitioners would undertake to find a purchaser of and the money to construct and operate the third line suggested. It was intimated to them that they would do well to make their proposition first to the elevated railroad company and see what it thought about the propositions. In the meantime the commission promised to take the suggestions under advisement.

The Value of "The Record and Guide."

NEW YORK, September 8, 1891.

Editor RECORD AND GUIDE:

Inclosed find check. * * * I must say this, that through THE REAL ESTATE RECORD AND GUIDE I recovered a commission for a piece of property this year in the Supreme Court, which property I sold in 1889, and carefully looking up the transfer of property in Brooklyn I saw the transfer which my customer bought without notifying me; even the builder did not notify me. Price of property was $21,000. So I must say THE GUIDE has paid me well. CHARLES BUERMANN.

Real Estate Exchange Matters.

The Board of Directors held a regular meeting on Tuesday afternoon. After the transaction of some routine business a letter was read from the New York Board of Trade and Transportation looking to the establishment of a State Board of Trade. The letter contained a request that two delegates be appointed by the Exchange as representatives at a convention to be held in October where the advisability of organizing a State Board of Trade is to be discussed.

A letter from the New York Tax Reform Association was read, asking the Exchange to indorse the views contained in their platform in order that the Association may go to the Legislature with a strong influence behind them. The matter was referred to the Legislative Committee. The platform is as follows:

1. The most direct taxation is the best, because it gives to the real payers of taxes a conscious and direct pecuniary interest in honest and economical government.

2. Mortgages and capital engaged in production or trade should be exempt from taxation: because taxes on such capital tend to drive it away, to put a premium on dishonesty and to discourage industry.

3. Real estate should bear the main burden of taxation: because such taxes can be most easily cheaply and certainly collected, and because they bear least heavily on the farmer and the worker.

4. Our present system of levying and collecting State municipal taxes is extremely bad, and spasmodic and unreflecting tinkering with it is unlikely to result in substantial improvement.

5. No Legislature will venture to enact a good system of local taxation until the people, especially the farmers, perceive the correct principles of taxation and see the folly of taxing personal property.

Therefore, we desire to unite our efforts in such ways as may seem advisable to keep up intelligent discussion and agitation of the subject of taxation, with a view to improvement in the system and enlightenment as to the correct principles.

An important letter from the attorneys for the Exchange was also read. It advises the Directors that the cumulative system of voting is prohibited under the new corporation law of the State, and hereafter the elections must be conducted on the non-cumulative system. The letter is as follows:

AUGUST 4th, 1891.

JAMES E. LEVINESS, Esq., Secretary Real Estate Exchange and Auction Room (Lim.), 59 Liberty street, City:

DEAR SIR—We find that the entire act Chapter 611 of the laws of 1875 has been repealed by the general corporation laws, Chapters 563, 564 and 567 of the laws of 1890. Sections Number 2, 4 and 27 by Chapter 563, which is known as a general corporation law. Sections, 5, 10, 11, 12, 13 to 28 inclusive and 28 and 29 by Chapter 564, known as the stock corporation law, and Section 1, 3, 6, 7, 8, 9, 30 to 39 inclusive by Chapter 567, which is known as the business corporation law. If you desire us to extract out of these three laws all that applies to the Real Estate Exchange and Auction Room, Limited, it will be quite laborious, and take much time. Perhaps it is sufficient to say now that they all govern you so far as their various provisions apply.

At all future meetings for stockholders for the election of directors or other purposes each stockholder, who is not in default in payment of subscriptions, shall be entitled to one vote for every share of stock held by him for thirty days immediately preceding the election or meeting. Such vote may be cast by proxy, except that no one can vote in person or by proxy upon any stock not in his possession, or under his control, or where he has ceased to retain the title thereto, notwithstanding it may stand in his name on the books. No stockholder shall sell his vote, or issue a proxy to vote, to any person for any sum of money or anything of value, and the inspectors can require an oath in the forms which are given in the stock corporation act from the stockholder, his agent, attorney or proxy. The act does not give us the right to cumulative voting and Section Number 54 of Chapter 564 governs your future elections and the way the votes should be cast. Your company can reorganize if it seems best to the directors to do so under Chapter 567, Section 5.

During the session of the last Legislature an attempt was made to suspend the going into effect of the corporation acts of 1890 until time was afforded to revise and amend them, which failed to pass.

It is the opinion of those engaged in this attempt that at the next session of the Legislature new acts founded upon those of 1890, with extensive alterations, will be substituted for them, and it might be well not to reorganize your corporation, but to live under the various provisions of these acts until this has been attempted, for they may be radically changed.

We have examined your present form of proxy and do not see any reason for changing it. Truly yours,

(Signed) STRONG & CADWALADER.

The directors have asked the attorneys for a further opinion on the new law.

Francis A. Curry has been elected a stock member of the Exchange, and E. Stanton Riker, Julius Friend, Albert F. Schwannecke, and Frederick Winant annual members.

Echoes of the Convention.

The Mechanics' and Traders' Exchange of this city has just received the following resolutions, elegantly engrossed and framed:

At a stated meeting of the Board of Directors of the Master Builders' Exchange of Philadelphia, held April 7, 1891, the following resolutions were unanimously adopted:

"*Resolved*, That the sincere thanks of this Exchange are herewith tendered to the members of the Mechanics' and Traders' Exchange of the City of New York, for the many fraternal courtesies extended our delegates and members during the session of the Fifth Annual Convention of the National Association of Builders, held in the City of New York, February 9 to 14, 1891.

"*Resolved*, That the cordial reception, generous hospitalities and liberal provisions made for the comfort, convenience and enjoyment of our members by the various officers and committees will ever be remembered."

They have been hung in a prominent position in the room of the Board of Managers, and are greatly admired, both artistically and as an expression of the fraternal intercourse existing between the various exchanges constituting the National Association of Builders.

Real Estate Notes.

The Metropolitan Realty Co. have taken title at $106,000 to the old buildings known as Nos. 18 and 20 Rose street and No. 216 William street.

James Stillman has conveyed to William Astor for $215,000 the three lots on 5th avenue, northeast corner 65th street.

Title has passed from James McCreery, the dry-goods merchant, to Sarah L. Keyes at $150,000 for the four-story brick and stone dwelling, known as No. 930 5th avenue, being on the northeast corner of 74th street, size of lot 27.2x100.

The Board of Aldermen on Tuesday last confirmed the taxes for the year 1891. The rate is fixed at $1.90 on $100.

Judge Pratt, in Supreme Court Chambers, in Brooklyn, confirmed the award of $74,000 made to the trustees of the Brooklyn Institute for their old building at Washington and Concord streets, that is to be torn down to make way for the bridge extension. The award will be accepted.

The Union Trust Co. of this city, which is the trustee of the first mortgage bondholders of the Brooklyn Water Front Warehouse and Dry Dock Co., secured from Judge Pratt in the Supreme Court, Brooklyn, a judgment of foreclosure and sale against the company for $314,850. This is the first important step toward the reorganization of the embarrassed concern.

Contractors' Notes.

Proposals for estimates for removing the existing earth, etc., between the westerly line of West street and a line 50 feet westerly therefrom, and from the northerly side of Franklin street, extended, to about the southerly side of Vestry street, extended, and preparing for and paving the same with granite or Staten Island syenite blocks, laying crosswalks and building the necessary drains or sewers, will be received by the Board of Commissioners at the head of the Department of Docks, at the office of said Department, on Pier A, foot of Battery place, North River, in the city of New York, until 1 o'clock P. M. of Thursday, Sept. 17, 1891.

Sealed bids or estimates will be received by the Department of Public Parks at its offices, Nos. 49 and 51 Chambers street, until 11 oclock A. M. on Wednesday, September 16, 1891: For alteration of the roads, walks and other improvements required in connection with the erection of the Washington Memorial Arch in Washington square; also for paving with rock asphalt or compressed asphalt tiles certain walks in the Riverside Park, between 72d and 79th streets.

Bids or proposals for grading, improving and fencing the grounds at several of the shafts of the New Croton Aqueduct; also for grading, improving and fencing the grounds of 135th street gate-house of the New Croton Aqueduct will be received at the Aqueduct Commissioners' office, No. 280 Broadway, until 3 o'clock P. M. on Wednesday, September 23, 1891.

Sealed bids or estimates will be received at the office of the Department of Public Charities and Correction, No. 66 3d avenue, in the city of New York, until 10 o'clock A. M. of Friday, September 18, 1891, for furnishing materials and work required for a water-closet tower at Charity Hospital, Blackwell's Island; also for materials and work required for repairing pavilion D, Randall's Island, New York City, and materials and work required in the erection of addition to Harlem Hospital.

Bids or estimates will be received at the Department of Public Works, No 31 Chambers street, until 12 o'clock M., on Thursday, September 17, 1891: For sewer in 122d street, between Boulevard and Claremont avenue, and in Claremont avenue, between 119th and 122d streets; also for repairing, painting and restoring the building damaged by fire in West Washington Market, between Gansevoort street, Grace, Lawton and 13th avenues, and for laying water-mains in 76th, 95th, 102d, 113th, 143d, 140th, 167th, Suburban and Jennings streets; in Webster, Scott, Decatur, Perry, Andrews and Aqueduct avenues, and in Signal, Coles and Poe places.

Sealed bids or estimates will be received by the Commissioner of Street Improvements of the 23d and 24th Wards, at his office, No. 2622 3d avenue, corner of 141st street, until 3 o'clock P. M., on Thursday, September 17, 1891: For readjusting curb-stone and laying crosswalks in and paving with trap-block pavement the roadway of 153d street, between 3d and Courtlandt avenues; for constructing sewer and appurtenances in Wales avenue, from summit south of 149th to Kelly street, and in Kelly street easterly to existing sewer; for regulating, grading, setting curb-stones, flagging the sidewalks and laying crosswalks in 173d street, between 3d and Vanderbilt avenue East; for regulating, grading, setting curb-stones, flagging the sidewalks and laying crosswalks in 163d street, between Brook and 3d avenues; for regulating, paving with trap-block pavement and laying crosswalks on 134th street, from the easterly crosswalk of Brook avenue to the westerly crosswalk of the Southern Boulevard; for regulating and paving with trap-block pavement the roadway of 135th street, and laying crosswalks, between the easterly crosswalk of Brook avenue and the westerly crosswalk of Cypress avenue; for regulating, grading, setting curb-stones, flagging the sidewalks and laying crosswalks in and paving with granite-block pavement the roadway of 143d street, between 3d avenue and 144th street.

Estimates for furnishing granite stones for bulkhead or river-wall, also estimates for removing all of the existing earth, etc., from the newly-made land for a width of 50 feet, extending from Dey to Vesey street, North River, and for paving the same with granite or Staten Island syenite blocks, laying crosswalks and building the necessary drains or sewers, will be received by the Board of Commissioners at the head of the Department of Docks, at the office of said department, on Pier "A," foot of Battery place, North River, in the City of New York, until 1 o'clock P. M., of Thursday, September 24, 1891.

Sealed bids or estimates will be received by the Department of Public Parks at its offices, Nos. 49 and 51 Chambers street, until 11 o'clock A. M., on Wednesday, October 7, 1891, for the construction of a bridge over the Harlem River at 155th street, to take the place of existing McComb's Dam or Central Bridge and in connection with viaduct now building on said street.

Notice to Property-Owners.

BOARD OF ASSESSORS.

OFFICE OF THE BOARD OF ASSESSORS,
No. 27 CHAMBERS STREET.
NEW YORK, Sept. 9, 1891.

Notice is given to the owner or owners of all houses and lots, improved or unimproved lands affected thereby, that the following assessments have been completed and are lodged in the office of the Board of Assessors for examination by all persons interested, viz:

No. 1.—Repaving 34th st, from 1st av to the East River (as far as the same is within the limits of grants of land under water), with trap blocks.

No. 2.—Paving 138th st, from 8th to Edgecombe av, with asphalt, and laying crosswalks.

No. 3.—Paving 120th st, from 7th to 8th av, with asphalt, and laying crosswalks.

No. 4.—Flagging and reflagging, curbing and recurbing s s of 113th st, from 5th to Madison av.

No. 5.—Curbing and flagging both sides of 142d st, from Amsterdam av to Hamilton pl.

No. 6.—Curbing and flagging 122d st, bet Manhattan and Columbus avs.

No. 7.—Flagging and reflagging, curbing and recurbing both sides of 32d st, from Lexington to 4th av.

No. 8.—Curbing and flagging s s of 60th st, bet 10th and 11th avs.

No. 9.—Paving 89th st, from 10th av to the Boulevard, with granite blocks, and laying crosswalks.

[The limits embraced by such assessments include all the several houses and lots of ground, vacant lots, pieces and parcels of land situated on—

No. 1.—Both sides of 34th st, from 1st av to the East River, and to the extent of half the block at the intersection of 1st av.

No. 2.—Both sides of 138th st, from 8th to Edgecombe av, and to the extent of half the block at the intersecting avs.

No. 3.—Both sides of 120th st, from 7th to 8th av, and to the extent of half the block at the intersecting avs.

No. 4.—South side of 113th st, from 5th to Madison av.

No. 5.—Both sides of 142d st, from Hamilton pl to Amsterdam av.

No. 6.—Northeast cor of 122d st and Columbus av.

No. 7.—Both sides of 32d st, from Lexington to 4th av.

No. 8.—South side of 60th st, from 10th to 11th av

No 9.—Both sides of 89th st, from 10th av to the Boulevard, and to the extent of half the block at the intersecting avs.]

All persons whose interests are affected by the above-named assessments, and who are opposed to the same, or either of them, are requested to present their objections in writing to the Chairman of the Board of Assessors, at their office, No. 27 Chambers street, within thirty days from the date of this notice.

The above-described lists will be transmitted, as provided by law, to the Board of Revision and Correction of Assessments for confirmation on the 10th day of October, 1891.

Errors in Recording Deeds.

Various daily papers, most prominent of which the New York *Herald*, have been complaining against the working of the Block System, as now operated in the New York Register's office. It is charged that over 800 mistakes have been made in recording deeds and mortgages in the New Block Index since January 1, 1891, and the article in question tries to atone for such mistakes in a half manner by showing that the papers had not been rightly located. This does not, however, remove the stigma from the officials of the Register's office, who are considered to be the parties answerable for the errors.

Deputy-Register Hanly asserts that under the present system it is almost an impossibility to make an error in either recording or indexing, owing to the system of checking in vogue. All papers recorded in the Register's office must be marked with the section and block numbers, as shown on the city map or under the head of miscellaneous. If correct the attorney or real estate conveyancer has done his duty, and all is right. So long, however, as people engaged in real estate transactions, lawyers and others, rely upon boys and incapable people to locate properties on the city map, and allow them to register deeds and mortgages thereunder, so long will there be a big list of errors for which the Register of the City and County of New York and his assistants are in no way responsible. To readers of THE RECORD AND GUIDE a perusal of a few back numbers relating to conveyances and mortgages (repeated) will show this.

Personal.

John R. Foley, Jr., the real estate broker, has returned to the city after an absence of two months in the Catskills.

Perez M. Stewart, the West Side builder, has returned to town ready for fall business. He says that real estate on the West Side is in splendid condition.

Special Notices.

HUNT & WENDELL

J. H. Hunt, who recently removed from the southwest corner of 72d street and Columbus avenue, has now associated with him Mr. H. M. Wendell, son of the late Nathan D. Wendell, ex-State Treasurer, of Albany, N. Y. Mr. Hunt has carried through many important transactions in real estate and mortgage loans, and is well known among West Side builders, residents and property-owners. His partner is one of the ablest among the junior real estate brokers on the West Side. They have charge of a large number of properties and give personal attention to the sale, rental and general management of realty in all parts of the city. The firm will hereafter be known as "Hunt & Wendell," with offices at

No. 249 Columbus avenue, southeast corner of 72d street. They are members of the Real Estate Exchange.

Have you ever given the subject of shelving careful thought? If so, are you not convinced that the kind you have been using comes far short of filling your needs! Sometimes you think you would like to alter the arrangement of your stock, but upon scanning the outlines of your shelving you conclude you cannot do so without first tearing it all to pieces and patching it together again at considerable expense. Then, as your business grows, you find some day that there isn't room enough on your shelves to hold the last big shipment that you are unpacking. True, there are gaps here and there, which, if they could only be united by some simple twist of the wrist, would give you all the additional space required; but then you cannot knock out your shelf partitions, nor stow away the new goods in the numerous small waste spaces appearing on all sides. Now, if you only had shiftable shelving you would be in no such dilemma, for you could then raise a shelf here or drop one there, move along this lot of stuff to unite more closely with the next and thus soon have ample room for the new stock, and that without wasting time waiting for a carpenter or having a big bill to pay for store improvements. If you are not already familiar with this kind of shelving write to the Koch C. B. Co., No. 380 Main street, Peoria, Ill., who will give you information about their shiftable shelf brackets, which are calculated to relieve not a little of the care of store-keeping.

Henry H. Dreyer, the West Side real estate broker, who this week closed two very important sales, has removed his offices to No. 435 Amsterdam avenue, southeast corner of 81st street.

On Friday, September 18th, at 3 P. M., the annual meeting of the C. Graham & Sons Co. will be held at its office.

The attention of readers is directed to the "Wants and Offers" at the end of the Real Estate Department.

Real Estate Department.

The week just past has been a busy one of preparation in real estate circles. Not very much has been accomplished in the way of consummated sales; that was not to be expected. Labor Day, of course, decreased the volume of business to some extent, but the real reason that there are not more transactions reported is attributable to the fact that there were few if any negotiations under way. The autumn season has only just opened, and the results of the work that is being done now may not be known for some few weeks yet. But that a satisfactory business will be done seems likely from all present indications. The inquiries for all classes of property are very numerous, and their tone implies that the inquirers are in earnest. Everyone is looking around just now to see where they will place their money, and while there may be some doubt as to which class of real estate will be most extensively dealt in there should be none as to ultimate purchases, for the attitude of the buyer is confident and owners show an inclination to be more reasonable than they have been.

Renting has not been so good as it is now for a long time past. South of 59th street it is already hard to find good houses for rent, and while up town there is not yet a scarcity except in a particular class of houses it seems likely that nearly of those now to rent will have been leased before the season closes. Flats, too, are renting more easily and at less sacrifice than they were, and if owners will only refuse to fill their houses with free-rent tenants there should be some activity in this particular line of investment. As a result of this improvement in rents several private houses have already been sold for investment, and we hear of other sales which will go through as soon as houses now on the market are rented. This is a healthy sign, and speaks well for the way New York real estate is regarded by the capitalist and investor.

THE AUCTION MARKET.

Practically no business has been transacted in the auction room during the past week. Of the few sales bulletined a number of the legal sales were adjourned, the only offering at public auction was bid in and the remaining sales of three or four parcels under foreclosure were of so insignificant a character that they are not worth examining in detail. The reception accorded the parcel which was voluntarily offered is a confirmation of the view advanced in this column lately, that as yet it is too early in the season to do a successful auction business. That this view is very generally shared by owners and others is evidenced by the very few new bills that have made their appearance this week. With the exception of A. H. Muller & Son's announcement of a sale of 233 lots on Washington Heights, these few new bills, too, are very uninteresting, embracing as they do only the most ordinary class of holdings. The Washington Heights sale does not occur until October 6th; but it is sure to be watched with the closest attention. The success of the Morgenthau syndicate sale of lots on the Heights last May was so phenomenal that its genuineness was called in question by many conservative real estate men. That their doubts were ill-founded seems proven by the fact that nearly all the deeds to the property have since then been recorded. Doubtless the entire success of last May has induced others who hold property in the neighborhood to put it upon the market, but the private sales of it have been so scattered and infrequent that it has been impossible to learn anything from them. This public auction sale next month, therefore, of a large number of lots at one time will be watched with all the more interest and attention, and especially so since it seems likely that the next great building movement on Manhattan Island will be located on the Heights. The lots to be sold are situated between 188th and 190th streets, Kingsbridge road and 10th avenue.

On Tuesday, Sept. 15th, Richard V. Harnett & Co. will sell the frame buildings on lot No. 157 Elizabeth street.

On Wednesday, September 23d, John F. B. Smyth will sell on the premises 168 choice city lots within 600 yards of the depot at Rahway, N. J. These lots front on Milton avenue, Lawrence, Totten and Hancock streets. Milton avenue, on which the plot faces, is the finest residence street of Rahway. Rahway is a city already. It has a population of 10,000, one of the finest public libraries in the State, seventeen churches, four good schools, banks, building and loan association, stores, hotels, gas, electric lights, good water and a good fire department. The streets are paved and sewered, and all the modern conveniences are available.

CONVEYANCES.

	1890. Sept. 5 to 11 inc.	1891. Sept. 4 to 10 inc.
Number	141	128
Amount involved	$3,193,676	$2,011,550
Number nominal	34	42
Number 23d and 24th Wards	80	30
Amount involved	$176,542	$43,325
Number nominal	7	8

MORTGAGES.

	1890.	1891.
Number	169	159
Amount involved	$2,690,542	$1,312,495
Number at 5 % or less	94	89
Amount involved	$1,197,318	$868,840
Number at less than 5 per cent	12	6
Amount involved	$444,000	$144,000
Number to Banks, Trust and Ins. Cos	31	20
Amount involved	$1,411,500	$308,000

PROJECTED BUILDINGS.

	1890. Sept. 6 to 12 inc.	1891. Sept. 5 to 11 inc.
Number of buildings	26	33
Estimated cost	$458,425	$364,025

Gossip of the Week.

SOUTH OF 59TH STREET.

Krakower & Co. have sold for I. Cohen to Hulda Wettner Nos. 164 to 168 Henry street, for $109,000. Mr. Cohen takes in part exchange the premises Nos. 82 and 84 Columbia street, at $95,000. Krakower & Co. have also sold No. 28 Columbia street, a five-story double tenement, to Max Cohen for $32,000.

H. R. Drew & Co. have sold for Theodore M. Burton the four-story brown stone dwelling, 21.6x60x98.9, No. 42 West 33th street, on private terms.

Wm. A. Wheelock has sold No 34 West 48th street, a four-story dwelling, on lot 20.6x98.9 (Columbia College leasehold), on private terms.

Fairchild & Yoran have sold for S. R. Johnson the three-story, high stoop, brick dwelling, No. 412 West 18th street, on private terms.

Ames & Co. have sold for Thomas Currie the three-story, high stoop, brick dwelling, No. 346 West 31st street, 20x50x98.9, to C. Fox for $15,250; and the three-story, high stoop, brick dwelling, No. 337 West 12th street, 18x50x84.6, for Emanuel Salomon to a Mr. Loos on private terms.

NORTH OF 59TH STREET.

Henry H. Dreyer has sold for John Casey to George Daiker the five-story buff brick and Indiana limestone front flat and stores, on the southeast corner of 81st street and Amsterdam avenue, for $140,000. The flat is not yet completed. It is 42x98x102.2 in size, is cabinet trimmed and contains all the modern improvements. Mr. Dreyer also sold for George Daiker a plot of five lots on Edgecombe avenue, 100 feet north of 145th street, for $53,000.

John Casey has sold the two five-story brown stone single flats, 21x85x102.2, Nos. 168 and 170 West 81st street, for $80,000. Broker, L. Froehlich.

Frank L. Fisher & Co. have sold for George J. Cohen to Fredk. Woodward the three four-story brown stone dwellings, 20x55, and extension x 102.2, Nos. 164 to 168 West 80th street, on private terms. Mr. Woodward has purchased the houses as an investment.

Frederick Aldhous has sold to V. Kirby, No. 18 West 75th street, a four-story brown stone dwelling, for $48,000. Mr. Kirby gives in part exchange a lot on the south side of 76th street, 100 feet west of Columbus avenue, valued at $16,000. It is said that Slawson & Hobbs negotiated the trade.

John Armstrong has sold for John J. Sheehan to Michael Stern No. 1414 5th avenue, a five-story brown stone and brick flat, on lot 29.11x100, for $35,500.

Dunn Bros. have sold to H. L. Pense, No. 338 West 87th street, a three-story dwelling, 20x55x100, for $23,500. The sale is claimed by Hunt & Wendell and McMonegal & Eckerson.

Chas. E. Schuyler has sold for Mrs. W. J. Merritt, No. 494 West End, avenue, a three-story brick and brown stone dwelling, 19x54x64, on private terms.

Goodman & Stern have sold for Francis Mitchell to Amalchen Schoenthal No. 104 East 108th street, a four-story double brick tenement, for $12,500.

J. W. Stevens has sold for W. P. Anderson No. 174 West 93d street, a three-story, high stoop dwelling, 18x50x100, to Theodore C. Gross, of Mexico, on private terms.

Hunt & Wendell have sold for Gunn & Grant the four-story dwelling, No. 311 West 88th street, on private terms.

Fairchild & Yoran have sold for B. Havanagh, No. 455 West 147th street, a three-story dwelling, 18.9x45x99.11, for $14,500.

LEASES.

Ames & Co. have leased for the Agate Estate the four-story, high stoop, brown stone dwelling, No. 612 5th avenue, for five years to Mrs. Helen E. Chadwick for $3,600 per year; for the same estate, No. 247 West 54th street, a three-story brown stone dwelling, to a Mr. Van Auken for two years at $1,500 per annum; for Mrs. Webster the three-story, high stoop, brown stone dwelling, No. 129 East 56th street, for three years to K. Woodman at $1,200 per annum; for the Phillips estate the four-story English basement dwelling, No. 238 West 25th street, for four years to a Mr. Voegtlin for $1,100 per annum; and for Mrs. Hallett the four-story English basement dwelling, No. 157 West 34th street, to a Mrs. Cole for three years at $2,100 per year.

James L. Libby & Son have leased for Hopper S. Mott No. 190 West End avenue to Benj. Leillard for $3,000 per annum.

Slawson & Hobbs have leased for Mrs. Annie Good to Mrs. H. Hitching, of Tarrytown, N. Y., No. 108 West 74th street, a four-story stone front dwelling, 20x60x102.2, for three years at $2,300 per annum.

Chas. E. Schuyler has leased for Mrs. Tripp to a Mr. Masten No. 128 West 71st street, a four-story dwelling, for three years at $2,100 per annum, and for John S. Ellis to ex-Mayor Francis M. Burdick, of Utica, the four-story dwelling, 18x50x100, No. 169 West 79th street, for three years at $1,800 per year.

Hunt & Wendell have leased for H. H. Salmon to A. Zabriskie No. 71 West 71st street, a four-story brown stone dwelling, for three years at $1,700 per annum.

Adams Bros. have leased to Mrs. Josephine R. Read for Chas. T. Barney the private residence No. 178 West 75th street, for three years, on private terms.

Brooklyn.

Corwith Bros. have sold the two-story frame dwelling, 25x40x100, No. 154 Calyer street, for Mary Welch to Mary B. Finn for $5,850.

H. S. Schellhass has sold for G. E. Hyatt to A. Caman the plot 80x80, on the east side of Patchen avenue, 20 feet south of Putnam avenue, on private terms.

J. P. Sloane has sold for the Goldberg estate the three-story frame double tenement, 25x52, with two-story rear dwelling, on lot 25x100, No. 132 Dupont street, to Lawrence Kaminskey for $6,450.

CONVEYANCES.

	1890. Sept. 4 to 10 inc	1891. Sept. 3 to 9 inc.
Number	272	260
Amount involved	$808,708	$782,649
Number nominal	73	59

MORTGAGES.

	1890.	1891.
Number	228	226
Amount involved	$934,720	$780,976
Number at 5 per cent. or less	135	105
Amount involved	$640,692	$399,024

PROJECTED BUILDINGS.

	1890. Sept. 5 to 11 inc.	1891. Sept. 4 to 10 inc.
Number of buildings	90	68
Estimated cost	$516,360	$226,360

Out Among the Builders.

A. Spence is drawing plans for four five-story brick and stone flats, 25x68, to be built by James T. Barry on the south side of 142d street, 100 feet west of 3d avenue, at a cost of $72,000; and for a five-story brick and stone flat, 37x90, to be erected at Nos. 310 and 312 West 20th street by James Meagher.

The Metropolitan Realty Co. will tear down the old buildings at Nos. 214 to 218 William street, running through to Nos. 18 and 20 Rose street, and erect on the site a large building the exact character of which has not yet been determined.

Brooklyn.

It is said that a new hotel, to cost $300,000, is to be erected on a plot 50x233, on the east side of Clinton avenue, near Greene. Frank A. Barnaby, of the firm of Charles A. Seymour & Co., is interested in the project.

Out of Town.

CHARLESTON, S. C.—F. P. Dinkelberg goes to Charleston to-day for the purpose of closing matters with C. Simonds, for whom he is to draw plans for a private dwelling. The house will be a two-story brick and stone residence, 76x80 in size, with rear ell extensions opening on an inner court. The interior will be cabinet trimmed throughout, and is to be completed in a first-class manner. The cost will be about $25,000.

UNIONPORT, N. Y.—F. A. Minuth has won the first prize in the competition for the extension of the Odd Fellows' Orphan Asylum. The plans embrace one three-story basement and attic brick and stone building, 50x75, and one two-story basement and attic, 30x50, with extension 20x30 The cost is estimated at $35,000.

WANTS AND OFFERS.

(Advertisements strictly in accordance with this title will be inserted at the practically nominal rate of 10 CENTS *per line (agate). In figuring for themselves advertisers may count seven words for each line, the address to be taken as one line. The object of this department is to bring buyers and sellers into communication with customers. Advertisements must be marked "Wants and Offers Column," and sent to the office of publication, Nos. 14 and 16 Vesey Street, not later than 3 P. M. Friday.)*

WANTS.

OWNERS, ATTENTION!—Experienced agent having charge of seven flat houses at present, desires to make a change for the better. Wants charge of several nice houses in good location, east side, up town; would occupy one flat for services; security given. OWNER'S ADVANTAGE, RECORD AND GUIDE. Sept. 12-19.

WANTED.—$54,000 mortgage on store property worth $90,000; bond A1.
JOHN PETTIT, 159 East 118th st.

OWNER OR BUILDER WANTING COMPETENT Superintendent address at once.
BUSINESS, RECORD AND GUIDE office.

WANTED.—COMSTOCK BLOCK MAPS—Complete or any part; state price and condition.
M., RECORD AND GUIDE Office.

WANTED.—A position in a real estate office, by a young man of 20 who has had experience and can furnish references. Address,
RESPONSIBLE, RECORD office.

GENTLEMAN of experience and ability having moderate income but unemployed seeks office work. Employment rather than salary important. Highest references. Address,
A. B. E., RECORD AND GUIDE.

Real Estate Wanted.

FIFTH AV.—A scientific club desires to rent for a term of years a large residence on the av, between 59th and 42d sts. Send terms and particulars to BOX 101, RECORD AND GUIDE office.

WANTED.—A dwelling between 6th and 8th avs. and 42d and 59th sts., at moderate price. Address, WILDER, RECORD AND GUIDE Office.

OFFERS.

Dwellings and Flats.

FIVE-STORY DOUBLE TENEMENT with stores; one vacancy; shows 16 per cent clean on investment, allowing vacancies, &c.
JOHN PETTIT, 159 East 118th st.

THREE-STORY AND BASEMENT, 13 rooms, 25x45x100, near Lexington av; $9,500; no mortgage.
JOHN PETTIT, 159 East 118th st.

FOR SALE.—Tenement on 56th st.; rents for $2,400, $21,000; tenement on West 18th st., rents for $3,480, $31,000; fall catalogues now ready and mailed on application. HIRAM MERRITT, 53 3d av.

SIX-STORIED BUILDING to sell or lease, 25x72; well-ventilated rooms; in good condition; 76th st., East, New York. Apply to ENGINEER, 17 John st. Sept. 11-1aw3w

FOR SALE.—At a sacrifice, new five-story double flats, near 125th st. L station. Address,
Aug. 1—1aw-9w. BUILDER, 319 East 125th st.

OFFERS.

FOR SALE.—Six new cabinet-trimmed three-story and basement brown stone private dwellings, Nos. 142-152 West 123d st.; prices reasonable and brokers commissions allowed. For further particulars apply at office of
FRED'K. M. LITTLEFIELD, 156 Broadway.
Aug. 29-uf.

FOR SALE.—2443 8th av and 210 and 212 West 105th st.; commission allowed brokers. Apply at
Aug. 29-uf. Room 19, 155 Broadway.

FOR SALE—2443 8th av.; 26.8½x100; easy terms; commission allowed brokers; apply at
Mar. 28-u-f. ROOM 19, 156 Broadway.

FOR SALE—210 and 212 West 105th st.; five-story apartments; each, 25x89x100; decorated and carpeted; apply at ROOM 19, 156 Broadway.
Mar. 28

FOR SALE.
BARGAIN TO QUICK BUYER.
Southeast corner Madison av. and 110th st., five-story steam-heated store and apartment, fronting 101 feet on Madison av. and 20 feet on 110th st.
Surface railroad on both av. and st.; mortgage, $25,000; 4½ %.
Will make terms easier if necessary; pays 12 % on $20,000 equity.
OWNER, 60 Liberty st., Room 2.

Improved Property.

PLANING MILL, branch of my business, for sale.—Is located at 24th st. and 11th av., on four or five city lots, leased ground, and consists of two and three-story brick buildings and adjoining sheds; also 60 horse-power engine and boiler, planers, moulders, saws, etc., all in good running order and now in operation; will leave a portion of value on bond and mortgage three years; this offers splendid opportunity to enlarge wood-working industry or to secure good mill business to add thereto. For further particulars, etc., apply to
EBEN PEEK, 24th st. and 11th av.
Advertiser intends to continue his lumber business now carried on at above address. Sept. 5-1aw4w

TO LET OR TO LEASE.—Two floors of a factory, 25x98 light on all sides, 1st av and 107th st; terms moderate. J. REEBERS' SONS,
Aug. 22-uf. 409 East 107th.

Vacant Lots.

ONE OR TWO LOTS in finest location in city, 102d st, and Riverside Drive, 50x101; several fine flats and private houses in same location. Address,
SCHUSSLER & CO., 14 East 111th st.

ATTENTION TO BUILDERS.—Full lot in Mott st.; leasehold; A1 lease for forty years; may be exchanged. Apply, C. FOSTER, 93 Delancey st.

FOR SALE.—100 feet in the 11th Ward, near Tompkins sq. For information address,
FOPPERT, office of RECORD AND GUIDE.

FOR SALE.—68th st., near West End av.; two lots, 50x100; not restricted.
E. SCHOONMAKER, 128 West 49th st.

OFFERS.

KINGSBRIDGE, 24TH WARD.—Two lots, ready for improvements; cash or part mortgage.
BUSICK BROS., 864 8th av.

FOR SALE.—Five lots, northeast corner Willis av. and 137th st, 100x125; easy terms; all ready for improvement; splendid location. Apply to
Sept. 5—1aw4w. JAMES CARNEY, 137 East 52d st.

PLOT of five (5) choice lots, ripe for improvement, 92d st, Madison and 5th avs.
B. A. & G. N. WILLIAMS, JR.,
Aug 22-1aw4w. 68th st and Av A.

EASTERLY FRONT BOULEVARD, with 200 ft. on 86th st. and 264 ft. on 85th st.; one or more plots.
OTTO ERNST,
Aug. 22-1aw-6w. South Amboy, N. J.

Brooklyn Real Estate for Sale.

FOR SALE.—A desirable corner property within a block and a half of City Hall; lot 44x60; frontage on two streets. Apply to
CHARLES CLARK, 371 Fulton st., Brooklyn.

TWO-THREE-STORY FRAME HOUSES to be removed at once. Apply at
386 Jay st., Brooklyn.

ATTENTION!—Is there anyone who has $5,000 to $15,000 cash? I will sell property that is paying 14 per cent net on this amount, the balance can remain on mortgage; it is Brooklyn property, in growing neighborhood; it must be sold, and no offer will be refused. A. N. McBEAN, 414 2d st, Brooklyn.

FLATS, 93 Concord st., Brooklyn, near the Bridge; five-story double flat property, in perfect order and always rented for $2,300 per year, paying easily 15 per cent. per annum on investment; terms easy. Apply to owner.
R. J. KELLEY, 377 Broadway, New York.
Aug. 22-1aw4w.

PLATE-GLASS CORNER on avenue thoroughfare, 17th Ward, Brooklyn, half block from big ship-yard; suitable for saloon; price, $3,300; easy terms.
J. P. SLOANE,
Aug. 29-1aw5w. 343 Manhattan av., Brooklyn, E. D.

Country Property.

FOR SALE.—In plots to suit; eligible building sites (commanding view of Sound for miles), on North st., Greenwich, Connecticut; price reasonable; terms easy; neighborhood aristocratic and fashionable. Apply to
FRED. J. STONE, owner, 60 Broadway, N. Y.
Sept. 12-uf.

FOR SALE OR EXCHANGE.—5,000 acres land heavily timbered with white and yellow pine; 3 large lakes on tract; suitable for park; will exchange for Brooklyn or city free and clear income property; no postals. Address,
R. MORISON, White Lake, Sullivan County, N. Y.

Miscellaneous.

A PARTY ABOUT TO BUILD A FIVE-STORY factory, 50x98, in Harlem, near water-front, will lease the three upper floors and build to suit tenant. Terms very moderate. Address
May 16 u. f. OWNER, 409 E. 107th St.

SALES OF THE WEEK.

The following are the sales at the Real Estate Exchange and Auction Room for the week ending Sept. 11.

** Indicates that the property described has been bid in for plaintiff's account:*

A. V. HARNETT & CO.

123d st, Nos. 173 and 175, n s, 156.8 w 3d av, 34.1x100.11x41.7x101.2, two-story and basement frame dwell'g. (Bid in) ...... —

SMYTH & RYAN.

76th st, No. 311, n s, 200 e 2d av, 25x102.?, five-story brk tenem't with stores. John Sheehan. (Amt due $8,689) $11,600

*Jerome av, e s, at intersection with a line formerly known as the northerly line of village of Mount Eden and extending easterly along said line to lands formerly owned by Townsend Poole, x north and northwest to centre of a brook, x west along brook to Jerome av, x southwest along av to beginning, containing 5 89-100 acres, excepting and reserving a certain triangular parcel consisting of 1 acre of land and the av opposite, situate at s w extremity of said premises, beginning at intersection centre line of Jerome av with northerly line of village of Mount Eden and extending northeast along centre line 350 x southeast 300 to northerly line village of Mount Eden, x west 465 to beginning. Wm. Kennelly 21,000

Alexander av, s w cor 141st st, runs west 100 x south 100 x east 25 x north 25 x east 75 to Alexander av, x north 75 to beginning. Muller & Oetjen 23,300

10th av, No. 319, w s, 74.1 n 28th st, 24.8x100, three-story brk tenem't with stores. ½ part. Edwin Farmhand 8,550

Total $64,450
Corresponding week, 1890 ...... $415,335

BROOKLYN, N. Y.

FOR WEEK ENDING SEPTEMBER 10.

Duffield st, Nos. 93-103, e s, 100 n Johnson st, 100x130. Duffield terrace. Maurice V. Freund .. $49,869

Hancock st, Nos. 702½ and 704, s s, 150 w Patchen av, 50x100, two-story and basement brk dwell'g and one-story frame dwell'g. Dennis Hayes 6,300

*Herkimer st, n w cor Saratoga av, 2?x80, two-story brk dwell'g and store unfinished. Thos. Brennan ...... 5,8?0

*Herkimer st, n s, 20 w Saratoga av, 80x80, four two-story brk flats unfinished. Noah Tebbetts 11,600

Saratoga av, w s, 80 n Herkimer st, 40x100, two two-story brk flats unfinished. Same 5,600

*Macon st, No. 446, s s, 272.6 w Stuyvesant av, 17.6x100, two-and-a-half-story brk dwell'g. Arthur Taylor 7,500

Sumpter st, No. 806, s s, 120 w Rockaway av, runs west 20.6 x south — x east .02 x south — x east 20.4 x north 100 to beginning, two-story frame dwell'g. Joseph Liebmann 2,000

Van Vourhis st, n w s, 269.11 s w Evergreen av, 17.0¾x100x16.11x100, two-story frame (brk lined) dwell'g. Julian Lucas 3,500

*Atlantic av, No. 423, n s, 250 e Bond st, 25x100, three-story brk tenem't with frame rear. Charles Emmons 4,800

Bedford av, No. 2?7, e s, 40.3 n South 1st st, 20.8x81x18.6x81, three story frame dwell'g and store. John F. Werner 4,900

Total $101,869
Corresponding week 1890 ...... $20,005

CONVEYANCES.

NEW YORK CITY.

SEPTEMBER 4, 5, 7, 8, 9, 10.

Barclay st, No. 52, s s, abt 215 e Greenwich st, 25x100, five-story stone front store.
Fulton st, No 207, n s, abt 200 w Church st, 24.11x82.4x25.6x—, five-story stone front store.
Louisa Lewis, Brooklyn, to Thomas H. Morrell, Elizabeth Sbegogue, Emma Hubbard and Fannie L Sill. June 8. nom

Bleecker st, No. 150, s s, 50 e Thompson st, 25x125, three-story brk store and tenem't with one-story frame building on rear. Alexander Fries to Mary Friedlander. All liens. Aug. 26. nom

Central Park West (8th) av, No. 285, w s, 80.4 s 84th st, 20x98, four-story brk dwell'g. Foreclos. John J. Adams to Charles H. Lindsley. June 16. $38,100

Same property. Charles H. Lindsley and Silvia A. his wife to William W. Green. Sept. 4. 46,000

Chrystie st, Nos. 23 and 25, w s, abt 150 n Bayard st, 37.8x70, two five-story brk stores and tenem'ts. Pauline Jacobs to Isaac Marx. *Mt.* $22,000. Sept. 1. See Mott st. 37,000

Cornelia st, Nos. 1 and 3, n w cor West 4th st, 40.11x75x26.10x76, five-story brk flat with stores. Charles Euler to Charles E. Runk. *Mt.* $55,000. Aug. 27. 75,000

Frankfort st, No. 9, s s, abt 115 e Nassau st, 28.8x103.9x32x104.3, four-story brk store and factory with two-story frame and three-story brk buildings on rear. Option to purchase fee. Joseph B. O'Connor, Mary E. Brennan, Mary O'Connor individ. and extrx. Joseph O'Connor, Annie W. O'Connor individ. and extrx. Charles O'Connor and as guard. of Margaret A. and Charles M. O'Connor and Charles T. Polhamus and Charles M. Brennan exrs. Charles O'Connor, Frances E. O'Connor, Margaret E. Shorthill and Agnes A. McCabe heirs, &c., Joseph O'Connor to Garret D. Rhinehart. Nov. 3, 1890. 48,000

Same property. Assign. contract. Garret D. Rhinehardt to Johanna H. Schmutz. Sept. 9. nom

Same property. Assign. contract. Johanna H. Schmutz to Louis W. Duesing. Sept. 9. nom

Same property. Assign. contract. Louis W. Duesing to Michael Foley. Sept. 9. nom

Same property. Option to purchase 1-12 int. in fee. Same to same. Sept. 9. 4,750

Hudson st, No. 571, w s, 24.10 n West 11th st, 24.10x76.9x25.2x77.8, three-story brk store and tenem't. Joseph Schader to James D. Smith and Sidney S. Darling. *Mt.* $5,000. Sept. 1. 20,000

Maiden lane, No. 139 / Fletcher st, No. 19 } begins Maiden lane, n e s, abt 52 s e Water st, 17x— to Fletcher st, five-story brk store. Rosenda Campbell widow, Rosenda I. and John F. Campbell to William H. Field. *Mt.* $11,000. Aug. 25. nom

Mott st, No. 57, n w s, abt 50 n e Bayard st, 25x100, five-story brk tenem't with stores and five-story brk tenem't on rear. Isaac Marx and Sarah his wife to Pauline Jacobs. *Mt.* $20,000. Sept. 9. See Chrystie st. 46,750

Park st, Nos. 31 and 33, 48x90. Agreement to exchange above, valued at $73,000, for
Broome st, No. 219, 25x100, valued at $40,000.
Morris Franklin, Henry B. Weselman and Fannie M. Updike with Henry and Clara Mass. Aug. 28. nom

Stanton st, No. 352, n s, 37.6 w Sheriff st, 18.9x60, three-story brk store and tenem't. Abraham Levy and Matilda his wife to Moses Davis and Hilda his wife. *Mt.* $5,000. Sept. 8. 10,500

Willett st, No. 55, w s, 125 n Delancey st, 25x100, three-story frame and brk store and tenem't with three-story brk tenem't on rear. Maria Koerber to Mary Knowles, Brooklyn. Sept. 9. 17,000

William st, No. 216, s e s, abt 220 n e Frankfort st, 25x100.
Rose st, No. 20, n w s, adj above on rear, 25x100.
Harriet Coles extrx. and trustee Harriet G. Johnson to Frederick A. Ringler. Confirmation deed. Sept. 1. nom

William st, No. 216, s e s, 25x100, five-story brk store with three-story brk building on rear.
Rose st, No. 20, n w s, 25x100, two-story brk store and four-story brk building on rear.
Rose st, No. 18, n w s, 187 n e Frankfort st, 30.5x112 x west 11.5 to land of New York and Brooklyn Bridge, x southeast 106, five-story brick store.
Frederick A Ringler and Mary his wife to The Metropolitan Realty Co. Aug. 31. 106,000

2d st, No. 248, s s, 197.2 w Av C, 25.2x74.1x25.2x72.2, five-story brk tenem't with stores. Elias Jacobs and Bertha his wife to Simon Hoffmann. *Mt.* $14,000. Sept. 2. 23,000

9th st, No. 626, s s, 315.6 w Av C, 27.6x93.11, five-story brk tenem't. Minnie wife of George Grau to Au[illegible] C. Renbel B. & S. All title. July 23. na nom

14th st, No. 40 / University pl, No 79 } begins 14th st, s w s, 53.1 s e University pl, runs southwest 130.4 x northwest 62.3 to University pl, x northeast 26 x southeast 33.6 x northeast 102.3 to 14th st, x southeast 26.10, five-story brk store. Charles H. Marshall and Josephine B. his wife to John Downey. Q. C. Sept 5. nom

17th st, Nos. 349 and 351, n s, 80 w 1st av, 42x92, two four-story brk tenem'ts with stores. Catherine E. Berkenbauer to Philip Sammet. *Mt.* $15,900. Sept. 8. 32,000

34th st, No. 146, s s, 275 e 7th av, 25x98.9, five-story stone front dwell'g. Partition. Robert E. Deyo to Emma P. Yergens, William W. and Edward M. Bliven, Yonkers, N. Y., and Ella M. Balderston, Philadelphia, Pa. Sept. 4. 39,250

Same property. Emma P. Yergens, William W. Bliven and Charlotte his wife, Edward M. Bliven and Cora E. his wife, Yonkers, N. Y., and Ella M. Balderston, Philadelphia, Pa., to George Keister. Sub. to mort. $6,000. Sept. 4. nom

37th st, No. 36, s s, 495 w 5th av, 25x98.9, four-story stone front dwell'g. George C. Flint Co., a corporation, to Amanda W. wife of John Abendroth. Q. C. Sept. 1. nom

Same property. Amanda W. Abendroth to Emily A. Scott. *Mt.* $20,000. Aug. 1. 50,000

40th st, No. 218, s s, 214.3 w 7th av, 14.3x98.9, four-story brk dwell'g. Daniel E. Bandmann, Missoula, Montana, to Owen E. Abraham. May 21. 10,000

Same property. Release dower. Millicent wife of Daniel E. Bandmann to same. June 12. 1,500

41st st, No. 24, s s, 96.7 w Madison av, 12.6x99.2x12.1x98.6, four-story stone front dwell'g. John M. Pinckney and Emma L. his wife, Samuel H. Kissam and Sarah J. his wife to Emma A. Streeter. B. & S. May 2, 1890. nom

41st st, No. 204, s s, 85 e 3d av, 20x74.1, four-story brk tenem't. David M. Koehler and Theresa his wife to A. Lester Heyer. *Mt.* $7,000. Aug. 29. 11,000

44th st, No. 526, s s, 375 w 10th av, 25x100.5, five-story brk tenem't. August Herzog to Frank Niesel. ½ part. ½ of morts. $15,500. Sept. 10. nom

45th st, Nos. 617-621, n s, 225 w 11th av, 56.3x100.5, three three-story brk dwell'gs. Eugene Higgins to Consolidated Gas Co. B. & S. April 28. 18,000

50th st, No. 140, s s, 260 w 3d av, 20x100.5, three-story brk dwell'g. Johanna Richard to Bernard Metzger. Taxes 1891. Aug. 13. 13,100

50th st, No. 138, s s, 280 w 3d av, 20x100.5, three-story brk dwell'g. Alexander McIntyre exr. Sarah Turner to Bernard Metzger. *Mt.* $6,000. Sept. 3. 12,500

Same property. John Turner, Rachel Young and Rebecca T. Lowery to same. Q. C. Sept. 3. nom

50th st, No. 158, s s, 140 e 7th av, 50x100.5, three-story stone front dwell'g. Elizabeth A. wife of and James D. Freeman to Ellen Summers. *Mt.* $2,000. Aug. 29. 18,500

50th st, No. 425, n s, 325 w 9th av, 25x100.5, four-story brk store and tenem't. John Schreyer to Martha M. Moore B. & S. C. a. G. *Mt.* $14,000 and all liens. Sept. 4. 1,800

52d st, No 240, s s, 175 w 2d av, 25x100.5, three-story brk dwell'g with two-story brk stable on rear. Monmouth H. Underhill and Clara B. Moore, White Plains, N. Y., Julia A. Tucker heirs M. H. Underhill, Sr., and Emily C. Underhill as assignee of said Monmouth H. Underhill to Hartman Linghbach. Q. C. and all title. Sept. 8. nom

Same property. Henry S. and Clara B. Moore and George H. Tucker exrs. of Monmouth H. Underhill, Sr., to same. Sept. 8. 12,100

53d st, No. 7, n s, 167 e 5th av, 21x100.5, four-story stone front dwell'g. Caroline W. wife of Augustus S. Whiton, to Leila R. wife of Edward R Merritt. Sept. 10. 43,500

53d st, No. 156, s s, 137.8 e 7th av, 18.8x100.5, four-story stone front dwell'g. Emily Stewart to Kate Amoss. Sept. 10. 15,000

55th st, No. 29, n s, 385 w 5th av, 17.6x100.5, four-story stone front dwell'g. Emily A. wife of John F. Scott to Walter J. Damrosch. Aug. 31. 27,000

55th st, No. 341, n s, 197.1 w 1st av, 17.10x100.5, three-story stone front dwell'g. Lois M. Fisher widow and extrx. William H. Fisher, Sarah A. Hawkes, Minnie E. Kennedy heirs William H. Fisher to Charles R. Price, Woodsburgh, L. I. *Mt.* $4,500. Sept. 8. 8,850

70th st, Nos. 309 and 311, n s, 150 e 2d av, 62.6x100.5, two five-story brk flats. Arthur Kenny and Catherine his wife to Henry Hirsch. *Mt.* $42,000. Sept. 3. nom

72d st, No. 44, s s, 385 w Central Park West, 20x102.2, four-story brk dwell'g. Dwight H. Olmstead to Maria N. Olmstead. *Mt.* $30,000. May 1. See 118th st. 80,000

72d st, No. 128, s s, 275 w 9th av, 25x102.2, four-story stone front dwell'g. Francis Crawford and Margaret his wife to Daniel O'Day, Buffalo, N. Y. *Mt.* $45,000. Sept. 1. 75,000

76th st, n s, 367.4 e 9th av, 18x102.2x18.4x102.2.
77th st, s s, 367.4 e 9th av, 18x102.2x18.4x102.2.
Vacant.
Rachel Clench widow and devisee and legatee of Holcroft L. Clench, Aledo, Ill., to William Britton. Q. C. Sept. 1. 100

78th st, No 166, s s, 120 e Amsterdam av, 20x102.2, four-story stone front dwell'g. Sarah J. Lozier to Elverton R Chapman. *Mt.* $22,000. Sept. 1. nom

79th st, Nos. 171-175, n s, 205 e Amsterdam av, 45x102.2, three three-story stone front dwellings. Foreclos. Wilbur Larremore to John O. Baker. Aug. 27. 27,000

81st st, No. 204, s s, 67.4 e 3d av, 17.1x80.10, three-story frame dwell'g. Adolph Cohen and Elise his wife to Norman L. Niver. *Mt.* $4,000. Aug. 31. nom

82d st, No. 28, s s, 337 w Central Park West, 18x102.2, four-story stone front dwell'g. William Forster and Maggie E. his wife and James Livingston and Margery his wife to Nora wife of James K. Ryan. *Mt.* $22,000. Sept. 3. 35,000

83d st, No. 534, s s, 148 w Av B, 25x102.2, five-story brk tenem't. Nathan Mayer to Agnes Drescher. *Mt.* $10,000. Aug. 21. nom

Same property. Frederick H. Drescher and Agnes his wife to Nathan Mayer. *Mt.* $11,000. Aug. 21. nom

86th st, No. 81, n s, 30 e 9th av, 20.6x100.8, four-story brk dwell'g. John G. Prague to Christian F. Tietjen. *Mt.* $30,000. Sept. 1. 50,000

87th st, No. 151, n s, abt 20 e Lexington av, 16.6x100.8, two-story brk dwell'g. Contract. Katharine Bollarth to Samuel Blum. Sept. 8. 7,500

93d st, n s, 325 w West End av, 50x100.8, vacant. Frank L. Smith and Magdalene his wife to William H. Myer. *Mt.* $10,000. April 20. nom

96th st, No. 66, s s, 120 e Columbus av, 20x100.8, four-story brk dwell'g. Sylvia A. Swinnerton to George H. Morris. *Mt.* $22,000. Feb. 16. nom

96th st, No. 132, s s, 330 w Columbus av, 25x100.8, five-story stone front flat. Alexander Cameron and Margaret his wife to Joseph A. Hoffmann and Emma his wife. *Mt.* $25,000. Aug. 14. 35,000

100th st, No. 283, n s, 200 e West End av, 25x101.10, three-story brk dwell'g. Joseph Hassell and Catharine S. his wife to Jacob B. Weinberg. Aug. 25. nom

100th st, n s, 200 e 11th av, 25x101.10. Jacob B. Weinberg and Frieda his wife to Amelia Robinson. *Mt.* $17,500. Sept. 9. nom

105th st, Nos. 103 and 105, n s, 75 w Columbus av, 50x100.11, two five-story brk flats. Amelia Robinson to Joseph Hassell. *Mt.* $25,500. Sept. 1. nom

105th st, n s, 125 e 2d av, 50x100.11. Release

mort. The Bradley & Currier Co. (Lim.) to Matthew Coogan and Teresa his wife. Sept. 4. nom

105th st, n s, 150 e 2d av, 25x100.11. Release mort. William H. Crane trustee to same. Sept. 4. 13,000

105th st, No. 307, n s, 125 e 2d av, 25x100.11, five-story brk flat. Matthew Coogan and Teresa his wife to Elise Lotze. *Mt.* $15,000. Sept. 4. 22,000

105th st, No 309, n s, 150 e 2d av, 25x100 11, five-story brk flat. Same to Adolph Henning. *Mt.* $15,000. Sept. 4. 22,000

117th st, No. 318, s s, 247.6 w 8th av, 26.3x100.11, five-story stone front flat. Release mort. Joseph B. Kaiser to Edward Cunningham. Sept. 3. 1,050

Same property. Edward Cunningham and Jane his wife to Mary A. Shea.. *Mt.* $17,500. Sept. 3. 25,000

117th st, No. 417, n s, 194 e 1st av, 18.9x100.11, four-story brk tenem't. Francis L. Vogelsberger and Friedericke his wife to John Rehhauser. Sept. 10. 10,800

117th st, No. 311, n s, 200 w 8th av, 25x100 11, five-story stone front flat. Release mort. Reuben Ross to Edward Cunningham. Sept. 9. nom

Same property. Edward Cunningham and Jane his wife to Mary H. Winans. *Mt.* $18,000. Sept. 9. 25,000

118th st { begins 118th st, n s, 300 e Amsterdam av, 150 to Morningside av, x100.11, vacant. Maria N. wife of Dwight H. Olmstead to Dwight H. Olmstead. *Mt.* $20,000. May 1. See 72d st. 75,000
Morningside av {

121st st, No. 209, n s, 143 w 7th av, 16x100.11, three-story brk dwell'g. Evelyn Randall to Edwin T. Greenfield. *Mt.* $13,500. August 13. 20,000

131st st, No. 6, s s, 120 w Mt. Morris av, 20x100 11, four-story stone front dwell'g. Samuel O. Wright and Maria T. his wife, Rockville Centre, N. Y., to Edgar Lockwood. *Mt.* $25,000. Aug. 20. 39,000

123d st, Nos. 332 and 334, s s, 308.2 w 1st av, 38.8x100.11, two four-story stone front tenements. Thomas Dougherty and Charlotte M. his wife to Catharine E. Rennert. *Mt.* $10,000. Sept. 3. 24,000

128th st, s s, 391.3 w 3d av, 18.9x99.11. Arthur E. Brown trustee to Maria E. Perris widow. Sub. to mort. $2,000, taxes, &c., and dower rights. See 2d av.

129th st, No. 220, s s, 217 w 7th av, 17x99 11, three-story stone front dwell'g. Henry K. Nevers to Lucy Nevers. April 29. nom

130th st, No. 18, s s, 160.2 w Madison av, 16.9x99.11, three-story brk dwell'g. Augustus Mayers to Mathilda Mayers. *Mt* $14,500. Sept. 9. nom

131st st, No. 235, n s, 390 e 8th av, 15x99.11, three-story stone front dwell'g. Manly A. Ruland and Jennie L. his wife to Mary S. wife of George B. Collier. *Mt.* $7,000. Sept. 1. 12,500

179th st, n s, 100 w Audubon av, 25x100. Henry Armbrust and Christina his wife, Union Hill, N. J., to George Metzger. *Mt.* $3,500. Aug. 31. nom

181st st, s s, 100 w Audubon av, 100x116.9. Pauline Simon to Isabella McCormack. *Mt.* $9,800. June 15. 22,800

181st st, n s, 125 w 11th av, 50x100. Same to same. *Mt.* $4,900. June 15. 8,800

187th st, centre line, at intersection centre line Audubon av, runs southeast 1,120 to Hudson River, x northeast to point 60 n e 188th st, x northwest 1,046 to av, x southeast 304.
187th st, centre line, at intersection centre line Audubon av, runs southeast 1,120 to Hudson River, x southwest to point 138 s w 186th st, x northwest 1,305 x northeast 303.
David Dudley Field to Cyrus W. Field, Robert E. Deyo and William Molloy. Trust deed. Sept. 3. nom

187th st proposed, s s, 125 e 11th av, 25x100. Catherine McIntyre to Jane McCloskey. Sept. 8. 2,400

215th st } plot contains 3 144-1,000 acres bounded by above, with land under water and rights of way, and sub. to rights of way.
214th st }
14th av }
Hudson River }

Lot begins at fence dividing lands of Joseph De Revira and Yetta Childs, at point 75 w 14th av, runs south 259.11 x west 359.5 to original high-water mark on east shore of Hudson River, x north 259.11 x east 382.3, 2 301-1,000 acres, with land under water and rights of way, and sub. to rights of way.

215th st, centre line, at n w cor of lot formerly occupied by Chas. L. Schneider as a garden, runs east 45 x south 280 to 214th st, x west 46 x north 280.8.
Francis Hathaway, New Bedford, Mass., to The National Bank of Commerce, of New Bedford. B. & S. June 15, 1887. nom

Amsterdam av, s w cor 180th st, 25x100. Pauline Simon to Abraham Goldsmith. *Mt.* $5,200. June 15. 10,100

Amsterdam av, No. 422, w s, 27.2 n 80th st, 25x82, five-story brk flat with stores. Robert and Joseph Gordon to John Sasse and Diedericke G. his wife. *Mt.* $19,000. Sept. 10. 28,000

Lexington av, No. 1641, e s, 25.11 s 104th st. 25x95, four-story brk (stone front) store and flat. Julia Muller by Hermann J. Muller att'y to Henry C. Meyer and Hannah his wife. All title. Q. C. *Mt.* $1,000. Sept. 4. nom

Same property. George Healy exr. Mary F. Hoyt to Henry C. Meyer. *Mt.* $11,000. Sept. 3. 15,000

Madison av, No. 1293, s e cor 92d st, 20.8x62.3, four-story brk dwell'g. Elizabeth C. Lewis to Edward Rafter. *Mt.* $17,000. August 18. 29,000

Park av, w s, 75 n 103d st, 0.11x27. Release mort. Richard H. L. Townsend to De Witt Mull and Gotlieb Fromer. Sept. 8. nom

Park av, No. 1056, s w cor 87th st, 25.8x80.11, five-story brk store and flat. Abraham Steers and Susan C. his wife to Matthew B. Brennan. *Mt.* $29,000. Sept. 8. 45,000

Same property. Release mort. Henry F. Wells to same. Sept. 8. nom

Wadsworth av, e s, 50 n 178th st, 25x100. Pauline Simon to J. Gerald Irwin, Jr. *Mt.* $1,000. June 15, 1891. 2,300

West End av, No. 343, w s, 22 n 81st st, 20x66, three-story brk dwell'g. Foreclos. Horace K. Doherty to Virgilio Del Genovese. June 10. 19,950

West End av { begins West End av, s e cor 102d st, 50.11x100, three three-story brk (stone front) dwell'gs on av and two three-story brk dwell'gs on st. Pauline Simon to Abraham Goldsmith. All liens. Sept. 3 1,000
102d st {

1st av, No. 2274 { begins 1st av, s e cor 117th st, 25.2x94, four-story brk tenem't with stores on av and three-story brk dwell'g on st. William T. Washburn and Emma Richardson exrs. and trustees Benjamin Richardson to Max S. Korn. *Mt.* $7,000. Sept. 8. 18,250
117th st, No. 402 {

Same property. Release judgment. Eugene Kelly individ. and Eugene and Edward Kelly, William Farrell and Joseph A. Donahue, of Eugene Kelly & Co., to William T. Washburn and Emma Richardson exrs. of Benjamin Richardson. April 13. nom

1st av, No. 1375, s w cor 74th st, 23x60, four-story brk tenem't with stores. Hermann Hinners and Louise his wife to Sarah Harris. *Mt.* $7,500. Sept. 9. 23,000

1st av } begins 1st av, n e cor 45th st, runs northeast 206.3 to brown monumental stone marked 15 on s s 46th st, x southeast 107.4 x — to Turtle Bay or East River, x south to 45th st, x west to beginning, land under water and right of way to bay. Vincent Boisaubin and Emma V. his wife, St. Louis, Mo., to Nathan Gabenheimer. 1-30 part. Aug. 19. 5,000
45th st }
46th st }

2d av, No. 2321 { begins 2d av, n w cor 119th st, runs west 100 x north 100.11 x east 20 x south 80.1 x east 80 to 2d av, x south 20.10, three-story frame store and tenem't on av and one-story frame building on st. Isaac H. Neuhaus and Charles H. Neuhaus and Theresa his wife to Henrietta Neuhaus. All liens. July 2. 20,000
119th st, No. 249 {

2d av, e s, 60.11 n 124th st, 20x80. Maria E. Perris widow to Arthur E. Brown trustee. Sept. 2. Deed in duplicate and release, Maria E. Perris pays in cash $3,900. See 128th st.

3d av, Nos. 1527-1533 } begins 3d av, n e cor 86th st, runs north 78 x east 100 x north 22 x east 25 x south 100 to 86th st, x west 125, three and five-story brk Parepa Hall with stores. Augustus C. Bechstein and Amelia his wife to Amzi L. Camp. All liens. Sept. 1. nom
86th st, Nos. 201 and 203 }

5th av, n e cor 104th st, 100.11x100.
104th st, n s, 100 e 5th av, 25x100.11.
One-story frame building and vacant.
Darius G. Crosby to James M. Constable. C. a. G. All liens. Sept. 4. nom

5th av, n e cor 65th st, 75.5x100, vacant. James Stillman and Sarah E. his wife to William Astor. Aug. 27. 215,000

5th av, No. 930, n e cor 74th st, 27.2x100, four-story brk and stone dwell'g. James McCreery and Fanny M. his wife to Sarah L. Keyes. Sept. 10. 150,000

8th av, No. 2383, w s, 25 n 126th st, 25x100, five-story brk store and flat.
Fleetwood av, n s, 33.7 w Popham st, 30x100.
Anastasia Power to Mary Power. Q. C. June 6. nom

Same property. Helena Power to same. Q. C. June 6. nom

Same property. Edward J. Power to same. Q C June 6. nom

8th av, w s, 25 n 126th st, 25x100.
Fleetwood av, n s, 33.7 w Popham st, 30x100.
James W. Power to Mary Power. Q. C. June 6. nom

8th av, No. 2783. Agreement to act as agent and janitor in consideration of use of store. Jane Leaycraft to William Hart. September 1. nom

11th av, e s, 25 s 180th st, 75x100. Pauline Simon to J. Gerald Irwin, Jr. *Mt.* $4,500. June 15. 10,800

Interior lot, begins at point 27 w Park av and 75 n 103d st, runs north 0.11 x west 26x0.11x26. Release mort. Richard H. L. Townsend to De Witt Mull and Gotlieb Fromer. Sept. 8. nom

Interior lot, begins at point 53 w Park av and 75 n 103d st, runs north 0.11 x west 27x0.11x27. Release mort. Same to same. September 8. nom

Interior lot, begins at point 93.8 s 19th st and 170 e 8th av, runs south 27.6 x east 8.4 x north 27.4 to beginning. Anna Shakespear guard. of and William A. and Irene A. Leggat to Joseph Farrell and Rebecca his wife. B. & S. Aug. 1. 125

23d and 24th WARDS.

Buckhout st, s s, 350 w Prospect av, 27 10x100x27.4x100. Charles Heylman and Harriet A. his wife, Henry Budelman and Virginia his wife to Elihu G. Hinckley. Sept. 4. 7,500

Pine st, w s, extends from Central av to Lafayette pl, 200x50. Henry Hirsch and Ella his wife Morris Victorius and Rachel his wife to John F. Crotty. Sept. 8. 2,000

Rockfield st, n s, 725 e Marion av, 25x126.5x25x126.6. Josephine M. wife of and Lawrence P. Mallahan to Susan M. Mallahan. Sept. 1. nom

Tiffany st, w s, 152.11 n 167th st, 60x125. Augusta wife of Joseph Peiser to John De Hart. *Mt.* $1,025. Sept. 2. 1,625

138th st, s s, 75 e Southern Boulevard, —x100x20x100. Julius M Cayson to Thomas Wood, Brooklyn. *Mt.* $6,300. Sept. 5. exch

154th st, n s, 288.4 w Courtlandt av, 16.8x100. Edward H. Moeran exr. Emma V. Kidder to Joseph Henning. Sept. 3. 3,750

154th st, n s, 170 w Elton av, 25x100. Charles Wurz to Lizzie Wurz. ½ part. *Mt.* $500. Aug. 31. 200

157th st, n e s, 175 s e Courtlandt av, 25x100. Fredericka wife of Edward Starke to Ottile Siedler. All title, Q. C. Sept. 4. 1,200

181st st, s s, part lot 208 map of Prospect Hill estate, Fordham, 50x100. Eliza Prescott widow to Charles Pitchie. Aug. 24. 1,100

Alexander av, No. 214, s e cor 137th st, 15x60. Jacob T. Nostrand and Sarah M. his wife, Huntington, L. I., to Carsten H. Bohlen. *Mt.* $8,000. Aug. 29. nom

Andrews av East to McCombs Dam road and Osborn pl. Release right of way by mutual agreement bet Catherine E. Schwab widow, Fanny C. wife of and Franklin Edson and Hugh N. Camp and Elizabeth D. his wife. Aug. 12. nom

Berrian av, e s, — n Southern Boulevard, runs southeast to point 100 s e Webster av and 24.11 n Southern Boulevard, x north 150 x west — to Berrian av, x south — to beginning. John J. Brady and Jennie M. his wife to Eliza Van Schaick. July 14. nom

Bathgate av, No. 2050, e s, 234 n 179th st, 18x70. Julia wife of Gustav Huerstel to Charles Pierrot. *Mt.* $2,000. Sept. 9. 4,000

Boston av, s e s, 250 s w Perot st, 25x93.9x25x93.8. Arthur Berry and Mary S. his wife to William N. Polhemus and Susan J. his wife. Aug. 24. 1,200

Boston av, s e s, 25 s w Perot st, 25x98.2x25x98.3. Same to Walter J. Hannan. Aug. 24. 1,200

Brook av, s e cor 164th st, —x32, gore. August Witt and Katharine his wife to Margaret Doyle. *Mt.* $1,800. Aug. 18. 2,500

Central av, s s, lot 71 map Upper Morrisania, 50x101x50x100.6. Henry Hirsch and Ella his wife, Morris Victorius and Rachel his wife to Matthew Smith. Sept. 8. 1,000

Kingsbridge av or Church st, w s, adj Church of the Mediator, 100x319. William C. and Ralph E. Prime exrs. Edward D. G. Prime to Alfred P. Clark and Michael J. Hart. Aug. 28. 1,800

Marion av, s e cor Campbell st, 65x84.11x40x78.1. William S. and Charles W. Opdyke to Isabell Merritt. Sept. 5. 1,250

Stebbins av, north cor Chisholm st, runs north 141.11 to Freeman st, x east 55.6 x south 28 x southeast 31.5 to Stebbins av, x southwest 122.9. Joseph Peiser and Augusta his wife to Denison P. Chesebro, Sub. to morts. Sept. 10. 2,600

Vanderbilt or Railroad av, e s, 100 n Fletcher st, 48x190. L. Napoleon Levy to George W. Hill. Sub. to mort. Sept. 1. 2,550

Villa av, e s, 225 n Potter pl, 50x100. James B. Powers and Mary A. his wife to Annie M. Healy. July 8. 1,200

Webster av, s e s, 75 n e Scott av, 50x183.2x50x184 9. Emile Pidoux and Celina his wife to John B. Armanino. Sept. 1. 2,300

Willard av, s w cor 1st st, 136.11x100x90.9x110.2. Laura T. wife of Herman K. Keller, South Mount Vernon, N. Y., to Benjamin H. Irving. Sept. 3. nom

Worth av, e s, lot 141 map Mount Hope, 18.5x101.1x24.3x100. Emily I. Wright, West Bergen, N. J., to Peter Leckler. Feb. 14 1885. 300

2d av, s s, lot 76 map No. 1 Hyatt farm. Thomas Curran and Martha T. his wife to Owen T. Martin. Sept. 8. 350

Kingsbridge to West Farms road, e s, bet Arthur av and Hoffman st, adj plot of John Murphy and wife, runs north — x west 1 4 x south — to road, x southeast 1.4. John Murphy and Mary his wife to Margaret Stonebridge. Sept. 5. 100

Lots 207 and 208 map Prospect Hill estate, Fordham.
181st st, s s, part lot 33 map heirs Rebecca Bassford, 124x150 to Valentine av, x123.6x149.1.
Peter Ryan to Eliza Prescott. Aug. 24. 4,000

Lot 209 map of Fisher farm, West Farms, 24th Ward. Assign. certificate of tax sale. Peter Ryan to Eliza Prescott. Aug. 24. nom

Lot 210 same map. Assign. certificate of tax sale. Same to same. Aug. 24. nom

LEASEHOLD CONVEYANCES.

Chatham sq, No. 23. Assign. lease. James Everard to Otto Huber Brewery. Aug. 29. nom

William st, No. 183, s e cor Spruce st. Assign. lease. John D. Von der Lieth to The Consumers' Brewing Co. (Lim.), New York. 2,480

13th st, n s, 150 e 5th av, 19.9x103.3. Mary S. Van Beuren heir Eliza M. Fonerden to W. Jennings Demorest. 21 years, from Nov. 1, 1892, per year, taxes and 1,000

32d st, No. 439 W., n s. Assign. lease. James McElroy to The Burr otherwise Bavarian Brewing Co. Sept. 4. nom

41st st, No. 143 E. Bill of sale and assign. lease. Abram R. Briggs to John P. Lein. 3,000

47th st, s s, 220 e 5th av, 20x100.5. Hannah G. Gerry to William W. Green. 20 years, from May 1, 1891, per year, taxes, &c., and 1,500

51st st, No. 2, s s, 123 w 5th av, 32.6x100.5x24.6 x92.5. Assign. lease. Henry W. Calhoun to Florence De W. wife of Elijah P. Sampson. Aug. 31. nom

Same property. Assign. lease. Elijah P. Sampson to Henry W. Calhoun. Aug. 31. nom

Same property. The trustees of Columbia College to Elijah P. Sampson. 21 years, from Oct. 1, 1886, per year, taxes, &c., and 1,198

Washington av, Nos. 1857 and 1859. Assign. lease. Frederick W. Burkhardt to George Scharrenbeck and A. F. Heiser. nom

1st av, No. 2406, n e cor 123d st, 26x75, four-story brk store and tenem't. Foreclos. Leasehold. Michael J. McKenna to William H. Beadleston. Sept. 3. 7,000

KINGS COUNTY.

SEPTEMBER 3, 4, 5, 7, 8, 9.

Ainslie st, n s, 175.6 e Union av, 17.6x100.3x20.8 x100.1. Frederick J. Greve to John and Ernest Lippert, of New York. *Mt.* $1,200. $3,400

Barbey st, w s, 150 s Liberty av, 25x100. Ludwig Kappes to George Dietrich. ½ part. 2,500

Same property. George Dietrich to Victoria Kappes. ½ part. 2,500

Bartlett st, n w s, 80 n e Throop av, 25x100, h & l. Jacob Schnautz to Valentine Voelker. 5,500

Beadel st, n s, 300 w Morgan av, 91x100.4x99.6 x100. Jeremiah V. Meserole to Benvanneda Wille. 1,400

Beaver st, s w s, 80 n w Park pl or st, 20x91.6. Amalia Gesele widow to Louis Beer and Michael Schaffuer. 4,000

Bergen st, s s, 153.8 e Carleton av, 17.10x131. Sarah E. wife of John E. Cleghorn to Rudolph Damm. 5,500

Bergen st, n s, 325 w Rockaway av, 16.8x107.2. Isaac V. Pratt, of Webster Grove, Md., to Israel Tuchsmann, New York. *Mt.* $1,725 and int., also taxes 1889, assessm'ts, &c. 2,275

Bergen st, n s, 257 e Troy av, 37.6x151.7x—x 128.7. Rebecca A. wife of Alexander Wood to Alexander Wood. nom

Bergen st, s s, 350 w Vanderbilt av, 50x100.3. Theodore Hunger to Pauline Hunger. *Mt.* $4,000. 7,000

Berriman st, e s, 175 s Wortman av, 60x167x 60.9x176.4. William H. Jackson to Bernard Bardon. 450

Bogart st, e s, 75 n Rock st, 25x100. Louis Windstein to George Herald. *Mt.* $1,750. 2,875

Broadway, n s, 60 w Furman av, 40x100. City of Brooklyn to Lucas Breitenstein. Q. C. nom

Butler st, s, 94 11 e Franklin av, 19.11x82.8x —x91.5, h & l. Foreclos. Gerard M. Stevens to Mary A. Simony. 3,050

Butler st, s s, 129.10 e Bedford av, 20x127.9. Party wall agreement. Fred'k A. Horsey with Catherine Beatty. nom

Butler st, s w s, 300 s e Smith st, 25x100. Frank Hyde to William B. Hurd, Jr. 4,400

Carroll st, n s, 125 w 4th av, 25x100. George S. Wheeler exr. Nancy B. Wheeler to Dominico Feurey. 1,500

Carroll st, n s, 125.4 w 4th av, runs north 32 x west 0.6 x north 68 x east 0.10 x south 100 to Carroll st, x 0.4. Donenico Feurey to Antonio Lupo. nom

Chestnut st, w s, 1,350 n 4th st, 25x150. George Beach to George C. Gillies. 2,690

Coney Island road, n e cor Brighton pl, 50x 135.7, Gravesend. Margaret E. Goldstone, of Shandaken, N. Y., to Margaret wife of John J. Snedeker. *Mt.* $4,000. 7,000

Chester st, e s, 300 n Eastern Parkway, 25x100. William Schwarz to Emma wife of Emil Reineking. 600

Cowenhovens lane, s w s, 720 s e Stewart av extension, 292.4 x 684 x 269.5 x 680.9, New Utrecht. Catharine H. Tallman by Mortimer C. Ogden committee to George W. Tubbs. 6,500

Cooper pl, w s, 190 s Herkimer st, 23x97. Morris Juskovits, New York, to William Reuter. *Mt.* $600. 1,250

Crescent st, e s, 31 n Glen st, 21x77. Charles S. Taber and George C. Case to Elizabeth Taber. *Mt.* $1,500. 900

Dean st, s s, 200 w New York av, 20x100. Sarah E. Fisher to Ella F. V. Proddow. 14,000

Dumont st, n s, extends from Christopher av to Sackman st, 200x100. Maria D. Palmer to Morris Rosenberg. 5,000

Eastern Parkway, n s, 25 w Osborn st, 21.3x 100.
Osborn st, w s, 100 n Glenmore av, 150x45x 150x45.4.
Release mort. Claus Luehrs to Herbert C. Smith. 2,000

Elton st, e s, 215.2 s Fulton av, 25x100, h & l. Howard M. Acker to George J. Collins. *Mt.* $2,800. 4,300

Eldert st, s s, 275 e Evergreen av, 18x100, h & l. Helen M. Buttle to Cynthia M. Powell. *Mt.* $2,750. 4,500

Essex st, e s, 160 n Ridgewood av, 20x100. Edward F. Linton to Minnie Josiah. 800

Same property. Release mort. Williamsburgh Savings Bank to Edward F. Linton. 350

Floyd st, n s, 137 e Nostrand av, 26x100. Jacob Stein to Josephina Richert. *Mt.* $5,000. 7,000

Floyd st, n s, 265 e Nostrand av, 25x100, h & l. Louis Beer and Michael Schaffner to Amalie Gesele. *Mt.* $3,600. 10,100

Fulton st, s w cor Nostrand av, 100x70. Charles A. Betts to Annie S. wife of Charles W. Betts. *Mt.* $14,000. nom

Fulton st, n e s, 60 s e Clason av, 20x91. Release dower. Babette Gnad widow to William F. Gnad. 1,737

Same property. Same to same. nom

Gerry st, n s, 125 e Harrison av, 25x100, h & l. John B. Mennier to William Meth. 9,800

Glenada pl, w s, 100 s Decatur st, 49.9x100, h & l. Foreclos. Edward G. Nelson to Charles D. Rust. Sub. to morts. $30,000 and action to foreclos. 50

Glenada pl, w s, 149.9 s Decatur st, runs west 100 x south 38.2 x east 24.11 x south 6.10 x east 77.2 to pl, x north 50.3. Foreclos. Same to same. Sub. to morts., &c. 50

Glenada pl, s w cor Decatur st, 100x85, hs & ls. Charles Siedler to William W. Reynolds. B. & S. 27,000

Same property. William W. Reynolds to Celvin C. Church. Sub. to morts. $59,000 and alley rights. nom

Greene st, n s, 150 w Provost st, 25x100. Michael Toomey to John C. Wianda. 900

Halsey st, s e s, 100 s w Central av, 20x100, h & l. James Gascoine to Harvey H. Mosier. nom

Hancock st, s s, 187.6 e Tompkins av, 17.6x100. Theodore J. Sederling to Matilda D. Meineke. 3,900

Hancock st, s s, 300 w Lewis av, 25x100. Foreclos. John Courtney, Sheriff, to Joanna B. Cook. 3,000

Hancock st, n s, 91.8 w Ralph av, 36.7x85, hs & ls. Martha K. wife of Thomas Chaffee to George Holland. 4,750

Hart st, s s, 125 e Throop av, 20x100. Mary E. Conklin, Emma F. Beverly, Sarah A., Ida E., Edward C. and Emily C. Ellis to Mary Ellis. nom

Harman st, s e s, 175 s w Hamburg av, 25x100. Darwin R. James to Gottfried Santer. 1,450

Henry st, e s, 80 s Union st, 20x99.6. Winant V. Pearce, of Wall, N. J., to Pauline Rimoldi, of New York. *Mt.* $4,000. 6,500

Hendrix st, e s, 225 s Belmont av, 25x100. John A. Davies to Michael Kane. *Mt.* $1,400. 2,600

Herbert st, s s, 170.6 w Humboldt st, 20x52. Margaret Small to William Rehder, Jr. 550

Herkimer st, s s, 120 w Rochester av, runs south 83.11 x west 16.9 x north 40.6 x north 43.6 to st, x east 18.8, h & l. Irving Fish to Ida E. Bailey. *Mt.* $2,006. exch

Hicks st, s e s, 80 s w President st, 20x100. John G. Heid to John Numer as trustee under will Sarah Heid. nom

Himrod st, n w s, 300 s w Knickerbocker av, 25 x100. George Gutting and Charles A. Wagner to Albert C. Gardner. *Mt.* $3,500. nom

Hopkins st, s s, 45 e Marcy av, 20x100x19.5x 99.5. August Luedicke to Jacob Amsterdam. *Mt.* $2,500. 3,000

Leonard st, w s, 46 s McKibbin st, 27x57. Nathan Lieber to Israel Mantel. Sub. to mort. 650

Leonard st, w s, 40 n Powers st, 20x50, h & l. William Kelly exr. Ann Daily to John B. Vogelbach. 2,600

Logan st, w s, 210 s Glenmore av, 20x100. Richard Tristram to James J. Tristram. 300

Logan st, e s, 744 s Brooklyn and Jamaica turnpike, 75x150. Waldemar Jansen, of Washington, D. C., to Rosanna Fulton. 3,000

Luquer st, n s, 229.6 e Henry st, 25x100. James Spaulding to Peter J. Higgins. 5,000

Luquer st, n s, 25 w Court st, 44.2x100. Patrick McAuliffe to Ellen McAuliffe his wife. nom

Macon st, n s, 400 e Ralph av, 18x100, h & l. Michael Dowley to Elizabeth wife of Thomas M. Valleau. *Mt.* $5,200. 6,400

Madison st, s s, 180 e Howard av, 40x100. Release mort. The Henry McShane Mfg. Co, of Baltimore City, to Robert L. Moores and Charles A. Le Quesne. nom

Madison st, s s, 220 e Howard av, runs south 100 x east 14 x northeast 53.8 x north 48.2 x west 28; also,
Madison st, s s, 180 e Howard av, 40x100.
Robert L. Moores and Charles A. Le Quesne to The Long Island Brick Co. *Mt.* $33,000. nom

Madison st, s s, 360 w Tompkins av, 20x100, h & l. Mary L. Barnard to Emma C. Merryweather. *Mt.* $3,300. 6,200

McDonough st, s s, 175 e Ralph av, 0.4x100. Release mort. The Methodist Episcopal Hospital to Thomas H. Radcliffe. nom

Milton st, n s, 631.8 e Franklin st, 75x95. Thomas C. Smith to The German Evangelical Lutheran St. Johns Church. 13,500

Monroe st, n s, 214.4 e Throop av, 17x100. Anna M. wife of Israel Bedwin to Esther C. Chapman. *Mt.* $5,750 and taxes 1889 and 1890. nom

North Henry st, w s, 80 n Van Pelt av, runs west 100 x north 20.6 x east 20.6 x north 26 x east 79.6 to st, x south 46 6. Henry Bindrim to Ernest A. Kroenke, John P. Friedhoff and Henry Sturke. *Mt.* $600. nom

Same property. Henry Kroenke to Henry Bindrim. *Mt.* $600. 2,200

Oak st, s s, 170 e Franklin st, 25x88x30x103. George Hassenfratz to Louis Rebele. 3,700

Oakland st, w s, 25 n Huron st, 25x100. Mary wife of Frederick Rummel to Patrick Kelly. Q. C. nom

Same property. Foreclos. Robert Merchant ref. to same. 3,400

Ocean pl, w s, 147.8 s Herkimer st, 19.4x97.6. Albert G. Baker to William M. Evans. *Mt.* $3,750. nom

Ocean pl, e s, 50.10 n Atlantic av, 16x80, h & l. James A. Hamblin to Jose Tineo. *Mt.* $2,200. 1,300

Osborn st, e s, 175 s Eastern Parkway, 25x100. Abraham Ruth to Morris Friedman, of New York. *Mt.* $2,000. 3,750

Osborn st, w s, 300 s Dumont av, 50x100. Samuel Rosenbaum to Moses Cohen. 1,375

Same property. Moses Cohen to Samuel P. Tostevinrope 1,200

Pacific st, s s, 350 e Albany av, 25x107.2. Catharine Price, of New York, to William L. Beers. nom

Pacific st, s s, 100 e Rockaway av, 50x107.2. Robert S. Neely to William A. Hancock. Sub. to mort. nom

Same property. William A. Hancock to Robert S. Neely. consid. omitted

Pacific st, s s, 450 e Vanderbilt av, 25x110. James H. P. Dawson to Michael Fenerty. 3,250

Prospect pl, s s, 105.5 w 6th av, 16.8x100.
Prospect pl, s s, 188.9 w 6th av, 33.4x100.
Prospect pl, s s, 188.9 w 6th av, 16.8x100.
Merritt H. Day, of Rapid City, South Dakota, to E. Eliza Knight, of Sparkhill, N. Y. *Mt.* $7,000. nom

Palmetto st, n w s, 320 n e Central av, 20x100, h & l. Charles B. Wheeler to Thomas Berkeley. B. & S. C. a. G. nom

Powell st, w s, 233.2 n Liberty av, 16.10x100. John F. Vrooman to Sarah E. Birmingham. *Mt.* $2,000. 3,000

President st, n s, 184.6 w 7th av, 16.6x95. Edwin Packard to Alfred H. Olena. *Mt.* $5,500. 9,500

President st, n e s, 272 s e 7th av, 20x100. Romeyn A. Salisbury to Louis B. Jones. *Mt.* $10,000. 15,500

Raymond st, e s, abt 50 n of Myrtle av and being on old map 255 n of Old Division st, 25 x56 as per deed and 66 as per map, x25.4x51. William Corcoran and Elizabeth G. his wife to Daniel Mahon and Margaret his wife. 3,200

Roebling st, w s, 71.3 s South 3d st, 23.9x105. Foreclos. John Courtney, Sheriff, to Louis Rohdenburg, of New York. 8,000

Sackett st, n s, 160.5 e Nevins st, 20.3x75, h & l. Catharine wife of and Patrick Whalen to The Fulton Municipal Gas Co. 3,500

Schaeffer st, s e s, 290 s w Hamburg av, 40x100. Cornelius J. Shute to William H. Friday, Jr. nom

Same property. Wm. H. Friday, Jr., to Cornelius J. Shute and Henrietta his wife. nom

Seigel st, s s, 125 w Graham av, 25x100, h & l. Leo Katz, New York, to Morris Berger. nom

Sherman st, e s, 100 s Greenwood av, 40x135x 40.1x132.4. Flatbush. Anna M. Ferris and Jennie V. Wilbur to Henry Rudloff. 1,050

Sherman st, w s, 105.7 s Greenwood av, 102.11x 100x68 9x105.7, Flatbush. Jennie V. Wilbur to John R. Benedict. 1,900

Sherman st, w s, 205.6 s Greenwood av, 40x100, Flatbush. Jennie V. Wilbur to Coleridge H. Benedict. 950

Sherman st, w s, 245.6 s Greenwood av, 40x100, Flatbush. Same to Theodore McFarland. 950

Stanhope st, s e s, 653 n e Evergreen av, 22x100. Release mort. Samuel Wells to Frederick Butt. nom

Same property. Frederick Butt to Henrietta Hager widow. 1,450

Stockton st, s s, 150 w Lewis av, 25x100. Katharine Diehlmann to Margaretha Pfeiffer. *Mt.* $3,500. exch

Stockton st, n s, bet Tompkins and Throop avs, being lot 14 block 41 assessm't map 21st Ward. The City of Brooklyn to Francis E. Clark. Q. C. 1,529

Varet st, s s, 175 e Graham av, 25x100. Anna D. Kleinlein widow, Maria T. Kleinlein individ. and as trustee of Balthasar and Maria T. Blass to George Dittrich. 3,400

Same property. George Dittrich to Maria T. Kleinlein. 3,400

Varet st, No. 74. John Blass et al. with Maria T. Kleinlein. Agreement of trust. nom

Varet st, s s, 147.10 w Bogart st, 25x100. Catherine Mengel widow to John B. Meunier. 2,950

Vermont st, e s, 300 n Fulton av, 125x81. Frank Maier to Stanhope C. Renwick, Amityville, L. I. *Mt.* $1,500. 4,250

Warren st, s s, 120.10 w 4th av, 20x100. George W. Anderson to Frances Muller. *Mt.* $2,-700. 3,300

Weirfield st, n w s, 321 s w Central av, 20x100. Leopold Lippmann to James M. Shay. Sub. to morts. nom

Willow st, No. 33, e s, 50 n Cranberry st, 50x25, h & l. Lena G. Roney to Rachael A. Van Kirk. 6,500

Willow st, e s, 50 n Cranberry st, 50x25. Fannie E. Spooner individ. and as extrx. Edward B. Spooner, of North Plainfield, N. J., to Lena G. Roney. 4,500

Yates pl, s e s, 150 n e Broadway, 50x100. Joseph T. Schmidt to George Biri and August his wife, joint tenants. 7,200

South 2d st, n s, 50 e Roebling st, 25x100. Dennis Wheeler, Ella wife of John Brainard, Lucy Peduzzi widow and Annie Sillen heirs James Wheeler to Peter Adrian. 4,250

South 4th st, n e s, 25 n w Hooper st, 25x95, h & l. Mattheus B to Wilhelmina Rothweiler. *Mt.* $6,000 and ck 14,800

South 5th st, s s, 100 w Rodney st, 20x112.2x20.2 x109 4. Annie S. Potts, Linden, N. J., to Patrick and William H. Olvany. 9,100

13th st, s w s, 194.1 n w 7th av, 19.2x100. Frank Hague and Mary A. wife of Joseph Glucksman to Mary A. Hague. *Mt.* $4,000. 6,500

East 18th st, w s, 350 n Av B, gore lot, bounded

northwest by line bet lands of parties hereto, Flatbush. John McElvery and Robert Getty to Gertrude B. Lott and Maria B. Story. nom

19th st, n e s, 175 n w 5th av, 25x100. John Gosling to Andrew E. Rudolph. 2,000

21st st, s s, 225 e 3d av, 75x100. Elizabeth Stabler to Elizabeth Schneider. 10,800

21st st, n s, 381 e 10th av, 25x125x95x100. Elizabeth Corrigan to Mary Corrigan. nom

26th st, s s, 80 1 w 3d av, 219.11x200.4 to 27th st, with all buildings, docks, land under water, &c. Arnold A. Lewis to William L. Proctor, Ogdensburgh, N. Y., 9-16 part, and John C. Hughson, Albany, 7-16 part. Sub. to morts. $32,829, and taxes 1889 and 1890. 38,474

Bay 26th st, n w s, 340 n e Benson av, 60x96.8, Bensonhurst. Sarah Petersen, of New York, to Charles W. Anderson, of Montclair, N. J. nom

Bay 38th st, s e s, 200 s w 86th st, 100x96.8, Bensonhurst. James D. Lynch, New York, to Alexander Stewart. 1,500

48th st, s s, 380 e 3d av, 16x100.2, 8th Ward. John R. Schoonover to Edward L. Callahan. Mt. $2,267. 3,100

51st st, s s, 220 w 3d av, 20x100.2, h & l. Thomas Dunn to Maria Dunn. 3,850

55th st, s s, 483.4 w 2d av, 16.8x100. George E. Wicks to Charles A. Erickson. Mt. $2,000. 3,200

55th st, s s, 175 e 2d av, 5x100. William S. Hassen to Ohne A. M. wife of Lars Larson. 300

59th st, n e s, 220 n w 17th av, 20x100.2, New Utrecht. Release mort. William A. Copp exr. Mary M. Warner to Hans C. Pfalzgraf. consid. omitted

70th st, s s, 160 e 10th av, 80x100, Bay Ridge Park. Bay Ridge Park Improvement Co. to Fred. C. Cocheu. 4,000

73d st, s w s, 370 s e 3d av, 40x100, h & l, New Utrecht. Charles A. Erickson to George E. Wicks. Mt. $4,000. 6,300

85th st, w s, 85.3 s lands Jacob P. Moore, 40x100, New Utrecht. Henry Schmidt to George Hagele. 600

95th st, n e s, 260 n w 3d av, 25x100, New Utrecht. William H. Sloan to Mary D. Neil. 425

Albany av, w s, 88.11 n Butler st, 16.8x85x16x85. Charles S. Taber to George C. Case. Mt. $3,500. nom

Arlington av, s s, 50 e Miller av, 50x100, hs & ls. Mary A. Lloyd to David Rosenberg. 3,400

Arlington av, s s, 30 e Warwick st, 34x100. Elizabeth V. Zundt to Augusta wife of Joseph Forbes. Mt. $1,000 and paving assessm't. 1,600

Atlantic av, s s, 445.2 e Carlton av, runs south 80.10 x northeast 99.4 to av, x west 57.6. Sarah Ramsey extrx. John Ramsey to Allen Ramsey. gift

Atlantic av, s s, 502.8 e Carlton av, runs south 123 x east 36.10 x north 117 x northwest 5.2 to Atlantic av, x west 31.6. Same to same. gift

Atlantic av, s s, 295.2 e Carlton av, runs south 80.6 x southwest 25.6 x south 13 x east 68.6 x northwest 36.2 x northeast 7.8 x south 89.1 to Atlantic av, x west 25. R. W. Townsend to George Marshall. 1877. 3,000

Bedford av, e s, 25 s Wallabout st, 20x67. David M. Koehler to Annie M. Tonyes. Mt. $2,500. 4,590

Benson av, n e s, 260.2 n w De Bruyns lane, 50x100, New Utrecht. Garret Wyckoff to Peter J. Carey. 3,500

Blake av, s s, 50 e Shepherd av, 25x100, h & l. George H. King to Frank Johnson. Mt. $1,400. 1,750

Carlton av, w s, 369 n De Kalb av, 16.11x100. Mattie S. wife of James G. De Witt to Julius B. Davenport. Mt. $5,500. 8,500

Central av, s w s, 25 s e Ralph st, 25x100. Adam Kaiser, Charles Rissler and August Todebusch to Sebastian Hoh and Peter Brun. Mt. $3,000. nom

Christopher av, e s, 200 n Belmont av, 25x200 to Sackman st. Release mort. John D. Ditmas, Georgianna J. Remsen and Catherine Ditmas to Lewis Hurst. 600

Clason av, w s, 79 n Degraw st, 52x100. Zacheus Bergen, Samuel W. Hollister and Robertson Trowbridge exrs. Robt A. Robertson to William H. Curtin. 2,300

Clinton av, e s, 146 s Fulton st, 33.4x120. Thomas T. and George E. Hogg to William Hurry. Q. C. nom

De Kalb av, n s, 306.3 w Stuyvesant av, 18.9x100. Louis Beer to Mary V. Lake. Mt. $2,600. 5,900

Flatbush av, south cor Prospect pl, runs southeast 123.5 x south 2.6 x southwest 90 x 3.6 to av, x north 120.5.
Interior lot, 3.6 e of Flatbush av, on line which is 120 s from south cor of Flatbush av and Prospect pl, runs northerly 90 x southerly 40.8 x southwest 50.8.
Merritt H. Day to E. Eliza Knight, of Sparkhill, N. Y. Sub. to mort. $103,000, and int. and taxes for 1890 and 1891. nom

Flatbush av, n e s, 88.4 n w Lafayette av, 20.7x65.4 to Navy st, x 20.2x57.4. John Ross and Fanny wife of Lewis Jacobs. 9,000

Flushing av, s s, 275 e Nostrand av, 25x100. Leopold Michel to Mary Kunath. Mt. $5,000. 12,000

Flushing av, n s, 75 e Vandervoort pl, 25x80.11, h & l. Albert Ruffle to George Gutting and Charles A. Wagner. Mt. $3,500. nom

Franklin av, e s, 170.3 n Butler st, 19.3x100, h & l. Howard T. Walden to Jane Timony. Mt. $2,250. 3,500

Franklin av, s e s, 100.4 s w Bergen st, runs southeast 24.7 x west 27 to av, x northeast 11.2 to beginning; also,
Interior lot, 100.4 s w Bergen st and 80 ft. southeast Franklin av, runs southwest 22.11 x north 25.2 x southeast 10.5.
Thomas McCann to Henry K. Fox. exch

Furman av, n s, 187 e Bushwick av, 34.7x100x—x100, h & l. Foreclos. John Courtney to Henry Weil. 1,200

Glenmore av, s s, 40 w Milford st, 20x90. Effingham H. Nichols to Annie C. Williams, New York. 350

Graham av, e s, 21.4 n Bayard st, 40x73, h & l. Ernest J. Eisemann to Adam Knoth. Sub. to mort. 9,000

Greenwood av, s e cor East 4th st, 31.4x100x12 and 50.6x88.4, Flatbush. Anna M. Ferris to George W. McGarl, New York. 725

Greenwood av, s s, 120 w Coney Island av, runs west 5 x southeast to point 116.1 w from Coney Island av, x north 30.4 to beginning, Flatbush. Jennie V. Wilbur to Theodore Magnus. 100

Hamburg av, n e s, 100 n w Madison st, 18.9x100, h & l. Jacob Manneschmidt to John Wahl. nom

Same property. Release mort. James Gascoine to Jacob Manneschmidt. 2,062

Hamburg av, w s, 25 s Suydam st, 25x100. Aurelia Fleischmann to Frederick Sterneckert, of New York. 6,700

Hamburg av, n e s, 75 s e Suydam st, 25x100. John Wischerth to John Eich. 1,500

Hopkinson av, e s, 167 s Herkimer st, 28x97.6. Anna M. wife of and Peter Hemmer, Jr., to Emma King. Mt. $10,500. nom

Jefferson av, n s, 190 w Ralph av, 200x100. Samuel M., Jane E. and Anna L. Meeker exrs. Samuel M. Meeker to Samuel Ayers. 11,500

Same property. Release dower. Jane E. Meeker widow to same. nom

Johnson av, n s, 100 e Lorimer st, 25x100. Ludwig Fink to Charles Schoenstein. Mt. $1,800. 5,800

Johnson av, s s, 125 w Graham av, 25x100. Elizabetha wife of and George Franz to Arnold Hoven. 7,000

Knickerbocker av, s w s, 75 s e Jefferson av, 25x100. John J. Hennemann to Gottlieb Markle. Mt. $2,500. 6,400

Lafayette av, n s, 575 e Reid av, runs east 54.6 x northeast 135.7 to Broadway, x northwest 92.9 x southwest 80.7 x south 7.9 x west 25 x south 100. Samuel D. Hunter to Emily A. Hunter and Adriana E. Simonson. Mt. $21,425. 25,000

Lee av, n e s, 50 n w Middleton st, 25x75. Conrad Schaffner to Joseph Kugler. Mt. $6,000. 10,000

Liberty av, n s, 250 e Crescent st, 25x100. William G. Osborn to Joseph D. Mallonee. Mt. $1,200, and taxes. 3,000

Livonia av, n s, 50 w Watkins st, 25x100. Arthur H. Wilson to Wolf and Nathan Loewenthal. Mt. $2,400. 2,700

Marcy av, w s, 226 s Macon st, runs west 110 x south to point 80 n Fulton st, x east to McDonough st or Marcy av, x north in two courses 64.10. Charles A. Betts to Annie S. wife of Charles W. Betts. Mt. $4,500. nom

Marcy av, n e cor Park av, 24.1x80; also,
Park av, n s, 80 e Marcy av, 20x80.
Peter J. Schneider to Martin Bullwinkel. Mt. $7,500. 17,000

Meeker av, s s, 160.8 w North Henry st, 25x93x28.10x107.5. Emil Lachmann to Clara A. Avery, of New York. Mt. $1,500. 3,000

Montauk av, w s, 90 s Hegeman av, 40x100. Christian Heber to Emma J. Stewart. Mt. $1,200. nom

Montauk av, w s, 280 s New Lots road, 20x100. William H. Jackson, of New York, to Benjamin L. Willen. 200

Myrtle av, s s, 56 w Hart st, 47x52.6x34.8x—. Robert Given to Elizabeth Munnich, New York. Mt. $4,500. 5,000

Norman av, e s, 900 n 2d st, 125x100. Wm. M. Lyddy, of New York, to George Strassner, of New York. nom

Norman av, s s, 125 e Jewel st, 25x95. Margaret wife of Joseph Beaver to Henry Stobbe. 1,000

Park av, s s, 50 e Spencer st, 25x100, h & l. Annie Tonyas to Margaretta wife of Luke Madden. 4,500

Putnam av, n s, 320 e Broadway, 20x100. Charles B. Wheeler to Robert L. Moore and Charles A. Le Quesne. nom

Putnam av, n s, 132.5 e Stuyvesant av, 18.7x100, h & l. John Mitchell and Charles Herr to John D. Rippe. 8,500

Ridgewood av, s s, 20 w Linwood st, 40x100. Frederick Sands to Philip M. Knight. Mt. $1,800. 7,400

Riverdale av, n e cor Thatford av, 50x100. Simon Levy to Michael Petrillo, New York. 865

Rockaway av, n w cor Sackett st, 50x100. Alexander S. Rosenthal, of New York, to John W. Brown. Sub. to all liens. 110

Rogers av, n e cor Grant st, runs east along st 30.4 x north 90.10 x west 31.6 x south 90.11, Flatbush. George Kerswill to Madelen Stroh. 3,100

Saratoga av, e s, 20 n Decatur st, 17.10x80. John W. Hussey to Andrew D. Baird. Mt. $3,500. nom

Schenck av, w s, 200 n Glenmore av, 25x100. Johanna Plambeck to J. Henry Kurtz. 1,250

Schenck av, w s, 125 s Vienna av late Van Brunt av, 40x100. James A. Henry to Joseph Spousta or Sponsta, New York. 225

Schenck av, w s, 275 s Glenmore av, 25x100. Jacob Fischer to Conrad Billing. Mt. $1,800. 3,400

Snediker av, e s, 137.6 s Sutter av, 15x100, h & l. John P. and Whitman M. Free to Hermann Stuber. 2,700

St. Marks av or pl, No. 673, n s, 150 w Nostrand av, 50x125.3, h & l. William Waring to Frak D. Creamer. Mt. $10,000. exch and 2,500

St. Marks av, s s, 300 w Rockaway av, 50x127.9. Release mort. Mechanics' Bank, Brooklyn, to Washington Sackmann. nom

St. Marks av, n s, 150 w Nostrand av, 50x125.3. Samuel E. Howard exr. George S. Cary to William Waring. 4,500

Stone av, w s, 200 s Blake av, 50x100. Sarah A. M. Kent to Mary E. Cook, Newtown, L. I. 1,100

Stone av, w s, 225 s Blake av, 25x100. Release mort. Same to same. 450

Stone av, w s, 24 n Bergen st, 41.2x100. Henry T. Gregory to Robert Smith. Mt. $3,500. 3,800

Stone av, w s, 210 s Riverdale av, 20x200 to Watkins st. Gustave Olson to Koppal Lubbal. 1,050

Stuyvesant av, e s, 60 n Quincy st, 20x88, h & l. Margaret A. and Timothy J. Cagney to M. W. Conway. Mt. $5,000 and int., and taxes 1889 and 1890. nom

Sutter av, n s, 16 w Osborn st, 16x100. Gilbert S. Thatford to Joseph Levy, of New York. 200

Thatford av, e s, 175 s Blake av, 25x100. Annie Solomon, of New York, to David and Jacob Zuckerman. 475

Thatford av, w s, 200 n Livonia av, 25x100. Pauline Hartmann to Jennie Green. Mt. $2,000. 2,300

Thatford av, e s, 225 s Eastern Parkway, 25x100. Samuel Samelson and Pinens or Pinkas or Pinkus Ronginsky to John Bergman. Mt. $3,000. 6,200

Throop av, e s, 61.7 s Hancock st, 21.8x81, h & l. Foreclos. John Courtney to William K. Gilchrist. 10,000

Tompkins av, e s, 41 n Van Buren st. Party wall agreement. Rachel A. Phillips to Richard C. Addy. 400

Troy av, w s, 200 s Herkimer st, 35.7x100, hs & ls. Walter Dickinson, New York, to Charles J. Warren. 4,650

Same property. Charles J. Warren to Emily M. Couch. 5,000

Van Siclen av, w s, 275 s Division av, 25x100. Louisa B. wife of Philip H. Reid to Frank Maier. 4,000

Vernon av, s s, 195 w Tompkins av, 20x100. Ann Robinson to Mary L. wife of Fernando C. Candee, Jr. Mt. $4,000. 7,400

Vienna av, s s, 75 e Milford st, 25x100. Charles A. Canavello, Englewood, N. J., to Henry F. A. Kurre, New York. Taxes and assessments. 150

Washingtoon av, s s, 150 e 3d st, 50x100, Flatbush. Foreclos. John Courtney to Richard L. Wyckoff. 1,550

Willoughby av, s s, 25 e Evergreen av, 25x95. Harlow N. Higinbotham to Hermann C. Huelle. 1,500

Wyckoff av, No. 275. Contract for property. Peter Riebling to Joseph Brautigam. 3,150

2d av, w s, 25.2 s 41st st, 25x100. Margaret Hagan, of New York, to Charles E. Gleason. 2,000

2d av, s w cor 57th st, 50.2x100. Release mort. Edward T. Hunt to James Cassin. 1,417

Same property. James Cassin to Letitia Barer. 4,000

3d av, southerly cor 11th st, 20x65. Katie wife of Peter McCarty to Eliza Plunkett widow. B. & S. All liens. nom

3d av, original line, w s, 50 s 94th st, 50x120, New Utrecht. Frank Moss exr. Maltby G. Lane to Andrew Lemon. 1,170

3d av, n w cor Schermerhorn st, runs west 75 x north 75 x west 57 x east 57.5 to Flatbush av, x south 52.11 to 3d av, x south 93.4. William H., Joseph B., Jr., and David F. Allee exrs. Joseph B. Allee to Percy G. Williams and Thomas Adams, Jr. Mt. $7,000. 40,000

4th av, w s, 50.2 s 55th st, 25x85. Joseph Foley to Johanna wife of Abraham Arens. nom

4th av, w s, 30 n 14th st, 28x86.10; also,
4th av, w s, 58 s 13th st, 28x86.10.
Release mort. Lester A. Lewis to William H. Norris and William Bowers. 3,300

Same property. William H. Norris and William Bowers to Frederick W. Payne, of Jersey City, N. J. Mt. $19,000. nom

4th av, s w cor 34th st, 100.2x100. E. Sinnamon Calvert to Nicholas McCool, Jr., of New York. 10,000

4th av, w s, 160.2 s 35th st, 20x82.
4th av, w s, 140.2 s 35th st, 20x82.
Frank D. Creamer to William Waring. Mt. $6,000. exch

5th av, e s, 25 s 13th st, 23x80. Release mort. Louisa Augustin, of Oyster Bay, N. Y., to Julius Augustin. nom

7th av, w s, extends from 52d to 53d st, 200.4x100. James Cassin to Stephen Martin. Mt. $882. 2,500

7th av, w s, 30.7 s Carroll st, 108.10x100. Foreclos. Gerard M. Stevens to Stephen B. Sturges. 10,000

10th av, s e cor 71st st, 100x100, New Utrecht. Fred. C. Cocheu to The Bay Ridge Park Improvement Co. Mt. $3,500. 6,000

Same property. Relase mort. Elsie A. Martin extrx. Isaac Martin to Fred. C. Cocheu. nom

10th av, n e cor 71st st, 80x100, Bay Ridge Park. Bay Ridge Park Improvement Co. to Fred. C. Cochen. 5,000

12th av, n w s, 40.2 s w 57th st, 60x100, New Utrecht. Richard B. Fithian to The Blythebourne Improvement Co. nom

13th av, westerly cor 59th st, 60.2x100. Release mort. James S. Suydam to Heloise M. L. Allin. nom

Same property. Heloise M. L. Allin to Josephine W. Faber, of New York. 1,625

14th av. south cor 55th st, 100.2x100, New Utrecht. West Brooklyn Land and Improvement Co. to William Duttmar, Jr. 2,125

20th av, east cor 76th st, centre lines, runs northeast to land of Cath. Jackson, x southeast along same to 22d av, x southwest to land of John J. Morrissey, x west along lands of Morrissey, Pfalzgraf and Nostrand to centre 76th st, point of beginning. William L. Dowling to Daniel W. Whitmore, Mt. Vernon, N. Y. ½ part. Sub. to mort. $23,392. nom

Interior lot, 100.4 s w Bergen st and 24.7 s e Franklin av, runs southeast 45 x north 18.9 x west 41. James H. Campbell exr. Barnabas Hammett to Thomas McCann. exch

Interior lot, 100 w Bushwick av and 57 6 n Devoe st, .06x20x.04x20. George C. Bedell, Jr., to Mary T. wife of Bernard F. Shevlin. nom

Lots Nos. 123 and 141 map Henry Lehmann, Flatlands. Henry Lehmann to Richard Gueller. 700

Lot No. 445 block 10 map No. 1 of 618 lots, Cowenhoven farm, New Utrecht. Effingham H. Nichols to Edward Mastaglio. 160

Lots Nos. 428, 429, 436 and 437 block 10 same map. Same to Christina Ewing. 620

Lot 430 block 10 same map. Same to Kate Brady. 155

Lots 333 and 334 block 8 same map. Same to Charles F. Blake. 230

Lots 1 and 2 block 1 same map. Same to Patrick Callen. 396

Lots 466 and 467 block 10 same map. Same to Thomas J. Ivans. 290

Lots 438, 439 and 468–471 block 10 same map. Same to George G. Hallock, Jr. 890

Lots 340 and 341 block 8, also lots 414–417, and lot 444 block 10 same map. Same to John Bollinger. 1,310

Lots 3 and 4 block 1 same map. Same to Frederick Witdich. 450

Lots 29–32 block 1 same map. Same to Patrick Connelly. 740

Plot in Flatbush, begins at line of land of Kings County at point 2,920.5 e Poor House road, runs south 702.6 to land of J. Neefus, x east 123.8 x north 706.2 x west 123.8, with right of way, &c., h & l Andrew Harth to Henry Hession, New York. 12,000

Part of lot 1-B of Wyckoff tract, Coney Island, 62.2x154.3 to Coney Island Elevated R. R., x60 1x171.10. Babetta Groll extrx. Joseph Groll to Louise Labro. 10,000

Same property. Release dower. Babetta Groll individ and as widow to same. nom

Coney Island road, n e cor Van Sielen pl, 49x 108, h & l, Gravesend. Foreclos. John Courtney to John Y. McKane. 3,500

Shore road, s e cor Oliver st, 25x140.5x25x147.11, New Utrecht. Edward I. Wilbur, Tuxedo Park, N. Y., to James P. Farrell. 2,775

WESTCHESTER COUNTY.

SEPTEMBER 2 TO 8—INCLUSIVE.

BEDFORD.

Adams, Henry B. to Geo W. Gardner, s e s road to Pines Bridge at Station, 89x126. $2,300

EASTCHESTER.

Armstrong, Cordelia to Jacob Lutz, w s Garden av, 100 s Park av, 50x200. 12,000

Same to Jessie E. Armstrong, e s Prospect av, 100 s Park av, 50x100. 1,000

Bard, Wm. H. to Margt. Blouk, lot 90 w s Fulton st, Jacksonville, 50x100. nom

Brick, Alex. et al. to John M. Dearborn, s w cor Prospect and Glen avs, 100x150. 8,500

Blouk, Margt. to Wm. H. Bard, part lot 168, n w s Fulton st, Washingtonville, 25x100. nom

Doremus, Morton R. et al. F. M. Buck, ref., to Isabella M. Burton, part lot 75, s e s Railroad av, West Mt. Vernon, 30x125. 1,895

Same to same, part same lot, 30x125. 1,895

Same to same, part lot 74 n e s Bridge st. 31.3x 100. 1,887

Same J S. Wood ref. to same, part same lot, 31.3x100 1,887

Same to same, part same lot, 31.3x100. 1,887

Same to same, part same lot, 31.3x100. 1,887

Foley, Edmund R. to Mary E Farrington, part lots, rear, 28, 29 and 30 South Washingtonville, 18x37. 725

Moore, Alice to Henry C. Wilken, w s Archer av, 125 s Sidney, 50x125. 1,950

Wilken, Henry C. to Henry P. Hyde, same property. 2,200

Richards, Annie et al. G. W. Hunt ref. to Henry Nolte, n e cor old White Plains road and a new st. 1,500

Nolte, Henry to Ann Kilduff, same property. 1,800

Rich, Peter exrs of, to Amalie Utz, e s Archer av, 116 old White Plains road, 50x135. 1,700

Ritterband, Jacob S. to Juliana Sponheimer, e s 3d st, 100 s 16th av, 28x100. 900

Roedel, Lillian C. et al. John H. Clapp ref. to John S. Hanson, lots 13 and 15, Dunham Park. 5,879

Thorn, Thos. to John J. O'Connor and ano., lots 1 and 2, Boulevard, map property grantor. 2,000

Same to Warren H. Barton, lots 10 and 11, e. Boulevard. 2,000

GREENBURGH.

Blackwell, Wilson H. to Louis Fuhs and ano., lot 640 map property grantor, Ardsley. 135

Same to Frank Warnier, lots 511, 512, 525 and 526 same map. 830

Chapman, Elverton R. to Sarah J. Lozier, w s road from Tarrytown road to Rock Scylla, 82 acres nom

Jones, Cyrus P. and ano. to Fannie E. Lawrence, lots 54, 57–60, 108, 109 and 118–125 map property grantor, Ardsley. 1,982

Roberts, Lewis to Lily C. Roberts, e s Belford road, 100 n Dayton av, 30x120 nom

MAMARONECK.

Fisher, John exrs. of, to Jas. L. Reynolds, 15 acres e s Old White Plains road. 7,000

MOUNT PLEASANT.

Briggs, Amos S. to Alb. E. Bliss and ano., lots 1, 2, 3, 8, 9, 16, 17, 18, 19, 23, 24, 25, 31, 32, 37, 38, 39, 40, 46, 47, 52, 53, 54 and 55, A B C D and E map property grantor. 4,525

Smadbeck, Louis to Jas J. McMahon, lots 1150 and 1151, Sherman Park. 300

Same to Alf. H. Koeller, lots 197, 198 and 199 400

Same to Martin Moran, lot 70 250

Same and ano to Charlotte M Baird, lots 325 and 326, Lakehurst Villa Park. 400

Same to Aug. Simonet and ano., lots 46, 47 and 48. 300

NEW ROCHELLE.

Ayres, Henrietta to Mary E. Pike, lot 9 block B, Rochelle Park. 1,200

Croft, Frances A., exr. of, to Rebecca McIntosh, lots 18, 26 and 27 map property grantor. 1,650

Disbrow, Susan W., exr. of, to Geo. Watson, lot 26 map plot 1, Huguenot Park. 350

Downey, Henry B. to Irene Strang, s s Lockwood's lane, 40 w May st, 40x10?. 800

Same to Ida E. Stewart, w s North st, 267 n Burling lane 25x105. 750

Rindge, Fred. H. to Louise Jacod, n e s Bancker pl, 215.6 s e Davis av, 50x150. 2,500

OSSINING.

Collingwood Wm H to Mary A. McCaffrey, e s Belleview av, 440 s Clinton av, 100x250. 1,000

Foshay, J. Burton to John P. Hermance, s w cor Post road and Everett av, 4 x130. 5,250

Larkin, Francis to Jas. T. Crane, n s Central av, adj grantee, 64x—. 1,800

Maplesden, Reuben H. to Patrick Lyons, lot 126 e s Prospect av, map Clark estate, 50x 125. 300

Same to Antonia M. Campion, s w cor State and William sts, 30x125. 3,000

Reynolds, Wm. to Bridget Nelson, w s Post road, adj Edw. McCann, 40.6x—. 750

PELHAM.

Bissell, Wm. W. and ano. to Parkside Land Co., part lot 67, s s Washington av, map Prospect Hill, 50x200. 500

Lamberton, W. R. to same, lot 57 s s same av. 600

Parkside Land Co. to Charles H. Young and ano., part lot 67 s s same av, 50x200. 500

POUNDRIDGE.

Kelt, Paulina to John W. Stevens, 21 acres adj Jane Reynolds. 700

Waterbury, John O. to Julia A. Peck, 8 acres, Stamford road, adj Cyrus Sarles. 650

RYE.

Merritt, Jas. S. and ano to Wilbur F. Moger, lot 115, s s West William st, Washington Park, 50x108. 167

Same to Lincoln G. Acker, lot 9 n s Ellendale av, 50x150. 202

Same to Thos. S. Townsend, lot 109 n s West William st, 50x150. 175

WESTCHESTER.

Camp, Hugh N. to Wm. Herrian, lots 317, 318 and 319 map McGraw estate. 570

Same to David Dunne, lots 250 and 251. 500

Carter, Emma J. to Jas. G. Robertson, e s Barker av, 100 n Julianna st, 3?x125. 4,?00

Clinton, Elizh. to Mary Lurig, s e cor Union and Railroad avs. 25x100. 415

Herold, Geo. to John C. Bowman, part lot 86 n s 4th st, Unionport, 100x108. 315

Heilman, Elizb. to Caspar Starke, s w cor Elliott av and King st, abt 55x270. 1,800

Johnson, Jos. Y. to Rebecca T. Creel, part lot 830 s s 6th av, Wakefield, 25x114 2,800

Rumsey, Cath. A. to Leroy Williams, part lot 995 s s 10th av, Wakefield, 50x114. 3,400

WHITE PLAINS.

Barnes, Samuel J. et al. to Anna E. Terry, s w s Lafayette st, 333 s e Fisher av, 50x105 400

Cleary, John to Daniel Cleary, lot 10 e s Brookfield st, map Fisher estate, 50x150. 500

Ferris, Kath. to Caroline Smith, part lots 5B and 5C w s Winchester st, map Fisher estate, 30x125. 183

Terry, Anna E to Samuel J. Barnes et al, part lot 2 n s Post road, map Fisher estate. abt 42x141. 400

YONKERS.

Barnes, Ella L. to Dorothea Hartung, lot 23 s s Scott av, Hyatt farm. 350

Belknap, Lydia E. to Mary E. Johnson and ano., e s Van Cortlandt Park av, 25 n Lawrence st, 25x100. 900

Dusenberry, Chas., Jr., to John C. Haynes, w s New st, 90 s Swain st, 25x100. 200

Druid Hill Park Co. to Henry E. Murgatroyd, lot 380 Mohegan Park. 185

Same to John E. Murgatroyd, lot 381. 185

Same to John B. Thatcher, lots 374, 375 and 403. 525

Duke, Eliza W. to Isabella T. Scotland, w s Warburton av, 350 — Gold st, 25x100. 2,000

Geul, Henry to Jeremiah Simmonds, s w s Oliver av, 214 s e Walnut st, 32 6x112. 2,800

Hobbs, Bailey to Thos. E. Hampson, s s Union pl, 100 w Woodworth av, 30.6x65. 1,750

James, Henry to Henry R. Parrott, n w cor Columbia av and Reade st, 100x100. 1,500

Jones, Cyrus P. and ano. to Eliza Port, lot 10 block A, map property grantor. 300

Lehman, Edmond to Edw. McConville, s e cor East Main and Kellinger sts, 25x75. 10,000

Same to Anna Schauer, lot 10 block E. 150

Same to Jos. Schauer, lot 11 block E. 150

Mutual Life Ins. Co. to Fred. Wangenstein, lots 45 and 51 w s Buena Vista av, city map, 50x 129.6 5,000

North, Lila V. to Frank D. O'Sullivan, lot 67 w s 1st st, Hyatt farm. 50x100. 500

Reynolds, Martha E. to John H. Byron, lot 34 w s Bronx River road, map Sherwood Park Land Co, 55x100. 1,050

Ryan, Timothy et al. J. F. Daly ref. to James C. Bell, w s Park av, 135 s Lake av, 100x218. 3,100

Sutphen, Melville to Jos. C. Wheaton, lot 14 w s Buena Vista av, Geo. Herriott map, 33x 100. 1,900

Twitchen, Elizh. to Wm. Quigley, lot 14 Hyatt farm. 900

Valentine, Clara M. to Thos. Costello, e s Cook av, 125 s Summerfield st, 25x100. 250

MORTGAGES.

NOTE.—The arrangement of this list is as follows. The first name is that of the mortgagor, the next that of the mortgagee. The description of the property then follows, then the date of the mortgage, the time for which it was given, and the amount. The general dates used as headings are the dates when the mortgage was handed into the Register's office to be recorded.

Whenever the letters "P. M." occur, preceded by the name of a street, in these lists of mortgages, they mean that it is a Purchase Money Mortgage, and for fuller particulars see the list of transfers under the corresponding date. Whenever the rate is not given, read as 6 per cent.

NEW YORK CITY.

SEPTEMBER 4, 5, 7, 8, 9, 10.

Anderson, Walden P. to Martha G. Farish. 93d st, No. 152, s s, 291 e Amsterdam av, 17x 100.8. Sept. 4, due Sept. 1, 1896, 5 %. gold, $14,000

Same to George de F. Lord. Same property. Sub. to last mort. Sept. 4, due Sept. 1, 1892. 2,500

Same to William McShane. 93d st, s s, 325 e Amsterdam av, 100x100.8. Sub. to morts. $128,000. Aug. 28, due Dec. 17, 1891. 4,000

Amoss, Kate to Hannah A. Davis. 49th st, s s, 143 w 6th av, 21.4x100.5. Sept. 10, 3 years, 5 %. 5,000

Same to Frederic J. Middlebrook, Brooklyn. 53d st, s s, 137.8 e 7th av, 18.8x100.5. P. M. Sept. 10, 1 year. 1,000

Same to same. Same property. Sept. 10, 5 %. 9,000

Aymar, William H., East Orange, N. J., to THE CONNECTICUT MUTUAL LIFE INS CO., Hartford, Conn. 8th av, No. 817, w s. 35.9 s 26th st, 17.6x62.6. Sept. 9, 2 years or sooner, 5 %. 11,000

Blauth, Adam to George Wilkinson et al. exrs. and trustees of Eliza May. Prince st, No. 171, n w cor Thompson st, 25x62x24.9x62. Sept. 4, 3 years, 5 %. 15,000

Same to Mary Meissel extrx. and trustee William Meissel. Same property. Sub. to last mort. Sept. 4, demand. 4,000

Brady, Patrick M. and Michael Farrel to Bernheimer & Schmid. 9th av, No. 642, n e cor 43d st. Saloon lease. Sept. 8, note, demand. 2,500

Buchsbaum, Justina mortgagor with POUGHKEEPSIE SAVINGS BANK mortgagee. Extension of mort. at 4½ %. Sept. 1. nom

Brennan, Matthew B. to Abraham Steers. 87th st. P. M. Sept. 9, 5 years or installs, 5½ %. 11,000

Brown, Samuel to Norman F. Nelson, Long Island City. Cottage st, lot 245 map Mott Haven, 50x100. Sept. 9, 1 year 250

Bull, Charles H. to Ephraim C. Gates, Calais, Me. Madison av, s e cor Marble st. P. M. July 29, due Sept. 10, 1896, 5 %. 3,000

Same to same. Same property. P. M. July 29, 1 year. 500

Brown, Robert I. to Ann C. Brown. 145th st. P. M. Aug. 15, 3 years. 9,600

Cammann, Oswald N., New Brighton, S. I., to Anna C. Wildey. Front st, No. 110, w s, 63.3 s Wall st, 21.1x83.8x21x83.7. Sept. 5, 5 years or sooner. gold, 2,500

Clark, Alfred P. and Michael J. Hart to William C. and Ralph E. Prime exrs. Edward D. G. Prime. Kingsbridge av. P. M. Aug. 28, due Sept. 1, 1894. 600

Colver, Mary L. wife of George B. to Manly A. Ruland, Brooklyn. 131st st. P. M. Sept. 1, 3 years. 3,500

Corrodi, John W. to Jacob Ruppert. Pearl st, No. 551. Store lease. Sept. 3, demand. 1,500

Cavinato, Luigi, Guiseppe, Natale and Steffano, of Cavinato Bros., to The New York Gas Fixture Co. Willis av, w s, 50 n 134th st, 25x81.6. Aug. 28, 1 year or sooner. 1,265

Coogan, Matthew to David McClure. 105th st, No. 307 and 309, n s, 125 e 2d av, 2 lots, each 25x100.11. 2 morts., each $14,000. Sept. 4, 3 years, 5 %. 28,000

Same to The Bradley & Currier Co. (Lim.). Same property. 2 morts., each $1,000. Sub. to last morts. Sept. 4, 3 years or sooner, 5 %. 2,000

Cropper, Rosina M. to William G. De Witt. Nassau st, No. 84, e s, 16.6x50. ½ part. Aug. 18, 2 years, 5 %. 2,500

Crotty, John F. to Henry Hirsch and Morris Victorius. Pine st, 24th Ward. P. M. Sept. 8, 2 years, 5 %. 1,667

Cahill, Mary to William Dempsey. 133d st. P. M. Aug. 26, 1 year. 1,000

Chesebro, Denison P. to Joseph Peiser. Chisholm st. e s, 113.9 n Stebbins av, 28x55.6. Sept. 10, 3 years, 5 %. 300

Same to same. Chisholm st, e s, 91.11 n Stebbins av, runs north 22 x east 55.6 x southeast 31.5 x southeast 25 x northwest 26.10 x east 37. Sept. 10, 3 years, 5 %. 300

Same to same. Chisholm st, e s, 69.11 n Stebbins av, runs north 22 x east 37 x southeast 26.10 x southwest 25 x northwest 22.3 x west 30.2. Sept. 10, 3 years, 5 %. 300

Same to same. Chisholm st, n e cor Stebbins av, 72.9x22.3x30.2x69.11. Sept. 10, 5 %. 400

Carbrey, Annie T., Mount Vernon, N. Y., to The Mutual Life Ins Co. of New York. 5th st, s s, 280 e 2d av, 20x96.2. Sept. 9, 1 year. 3,000

Casten, Henry and Amalia his wife mortgagors with Adolph Scheftel guard. of Edwin K., Florence R., Agnes K., Walter M., Herbert A. and Irene Scheftel mortgagee. Extension of mort. at 5 %. Aug. 1. nom

Dauphinais, Victoria F. to Wallis Iron Works, Jersey City, N. J. Morton st, Nos. 47 and 49, n s, 284.4 e Hudson st, 59x79.5x21.8x57. Sept. 8, due March 8, 1892. 6,000

Same to Julius Lipman and Moses Kind. Same property. Sept. 8, due Dec. 8, 1891. 3,500

Donovan, Timothy and Mary T. his wife to E. Augusta Tweed. Anthony av, e s, 130.9 n 175th st, 9.x170x98.11x142.6. Sept. 3, due Sept. 4, 1894, 5 %. 5,000

Dursie, Frank P. and Teresina his wife to Robert Courtright. Van Courtlandt av, s w cor Villa av, 29.7x122.6x25x128.4. Sept. 10, 5 years. 1,500

Davis, Moses and Hilda his wife to Abraham Levy and Matilda his wife. Stanton st. P. M. Sub. to mort. $5,000. Sept. 8, 6 years or installs. 3,500

Del Genovese, Virgilio to Mary M. Hartshorne, Highlands, N. J. West End av. P. M. June 10, due Sept. 4, 1894, 5 %. gold, 15,000

Damrosch, Walter J. to Ann E. Mitchell et al. exrs. Samuel L. Mitchell. 55th st. P. M. Aug. 31, due Sept. 4, 1894, 4½ %. 15,000

Same to Emily A. Scott. Same property. P. M. 2d mort. Aug. 31, due Sept. 1, 1893, 5 %. 6,000

De Hart, John to Augusta Peiser. Tiffany st, w s, 152.11 n 167th st, 60x125. Sept. 2, 3 years, 5 %. 1,025

Ebling, Philip and William to The Germania Life Ins. Co. 1st av, s w cor 101st st, 100.11 x325. Sept. 4, due Nov. 30, 1894, 5 % 25,000

Same to same. 1st av, n w cor 101st st, 100.11x325. Sept. 4, due Nov. 30, 1894, 5 %. 25,000

Same to same. 2d av, s e cor 101st st, 100.11x325. Sept. 4, due Nov. 30, 1894, 5 %. 25,000

Same to same. 2d av, n e cor 100th st, 100.11x325. Sept. 4, due Nov. 30, 1894, 5 %. 25,000

Eichler, John F. and Maria M. to Peter Graber. Inwood av, e s, 175 s Wolf pl, 50x130. Aug. 26, 1 year or installs, 5 % 1,100

Edelson, Louis and Abraham to Solomon Jacobs. Thompson st, No. 66; Oliver st, Nos. 74, 77 and 79. Sept. 8. notes

Egler, Frederick, Jr., to New York Produce Exchange. 11th av, n e cor 62d st, 100.5x100. Sept. 9, 1 year, 5 %. 35,000

Engel, William and Nanette Weber to The Emigrant Indust. Savings Bank. 35th st, No. 240, s s, 375 e 8th av, 25x98.9. Sept. 10, 1 year, 4½ %. 14,000

Same to Samuel J. Colgate. Same property. Sub. to above mort. Sept. 10, 1 year. 5,000

Evans, Isaac to Andrew H. Green. 160th st, s s, 219.4 e St. Nicholas av, 18x100. Sept. 10, due March 10, 1892. 1,000

Franke, Henry to The Title Guarantee and Trust Co. 112th st, n s, 120 w 5th av, 16x100.11. Sept. 10, demand, 5 %. 5,000

Fitzpatrick, Joseph to Matilda Eberhardt indivi. and as trustee for John H., Jr., August and Edward Eberhardt. Bathgate av, s e s, lot 4 map of Adamsville, 40x120. Sept. 4, due Sept. 15, 1896, 5 %. 5,000

Friedlander, Mary wife of and Albert to R. Augustine Smith et al. trustees Richard L. Campbell dec'd. Bleecker st. P. M. Aug. 26, due Sept. 2, 1896, 5 %. gold, 25,000

Frees, Valentine to The Bank Clerks' Co-operative Building and Loan Assoc. 155th st, s s, 275 e Courtlandt av, 25x100. Sept. 1, installs, 5 %. 1,000

Godfrey, Michael and Dennis Howard to Peter Doelger. 3d av, No. 639, n e cor 41st st. Store lease. Sept. 1, demand. 1,000

Green, William W. to The Washington Life Ins. Co. Beekman st, No. 74, n s, 114 e Gold st, 32.4x99.10x32.3x99.5. Sept. 4, due Dec. 1, 1892, 5 %. 15,000

Same to same. Central Park West. P. M. Sept. 4, due Dec. 1, 1893, 5 %. 25,000

Greenfield, Edwin T. to Evelyn Randall. 121st st. P. M. Sub. to mort. $13,500. Aug. 15, due Aug. 15, 1892, or sooner. 3,500

Gewirz, Louis to Haymann Wallach. Certificate that $1,750 is due on mort. Aug. 18. nom

Hannan, Walter J. to Hugh N. Camp. Boston av. P. M. Aug. 24, 3 years, 5 %. 500

Hutton, John W. to New York Anderson Pressed Brick Co. 98th st, n s, 268.6 e Amsterdam av, runs north 83 x northwest 15 x north 75.7 x east 164.2 x south 113 x west 156.6. Sub. to mort. $115,000. Sept. 5, due Oct. 1, 1891. 7,737

Heckman, John H. to George G. DeWitt and ano. trustees Sarah Talman dec'd. Av A, w s, 25.2 n 77th st, 27x74. Sept. 4, 5 years, 5 %. 10,000

Henning, Joseph to Edward H. Moeran. 154th st. P. M. Sept. 3, 1 year. 2,000

Herter, Rosamond wife of and Frank W. to The New York Savings Bank. 22d st, n s, 250 w 9th av, 25x98.9. Sept. 4, due Dec. 1, 1896, 4½ %. 14,000

Herter, Rosamond wife of Frank W. to Anthony Reiff. Same property. Sept. 5, due March 11, 1892, or sooner. 2,000

Hills, Charles to Isabella M. Hayes et al. extrxs. Stephen Hayes. 10th av, w s, 24.8 n 28th st, 24.8x100. Sept. 3, 5 years, 5 %. 7,000

Hill, George W. to L. Napoleon Levy. Vanderbilt or Railroad av. P. M. Sept. 1, 1 year, 5 %. 350

Hoffmann, Joseph A. and Emma his wife to Alexander Cameron. 96th st. P. M. Aug. 20, installs. 3,000

Hornberger, George to John A. Weekes. 7th st, n s, 94 e 1st av, 24.2x97.6. Sept. 3, due Nov. 1, 1896, 5 %. gold, 20,000

Same to Lorenza C. de Francia. 7th st, n s, 118.2 e 1st av, 24.2x97.6. Sept. 3, due Nov. 1, 1896, 5 %. gold, 20,000

Hemmer, Anna M. to George Ehret. 3d av, No. 1251, n e cor 72d st. Lease. Sept. 3, demand. 4,000

Higgins, James and James King to Frederic J. Middlebrook, Brooklyn. 90th st, s s, 324.6 e 2d av, 25.6x100.8. Sept. 8, 3 years, 5 %. 12,500

Irving, Benjamin H. to Laura T. Keller, South Mt. Vernon, N. Y. Willard av and 1st st. P. M. Sept. 3, 3 years or sooner, 5 %. 2,500

Jacobs, Pauline to Isaac Marx. Mott st, No. 57. P. M. Sept. 9, due Sept. 1, 1897. 7,750

Keyes, Sarah L. to William A. Brewer, Jr., and Edward B. Crowell exrs. Thomas Hope. 5th av, n e cor 74th st. P. M. Sept. 10, 1 year, 4½ %. 75,000

Kavanagh, Bernard J. to George Ehret. Park av, No. 1681. Store lease. Sept. 4, demand. 2,000

Keister, George to Emma P. Yergens, New York, William W. and Edward M. Bliven, Yonkers, N. Y., and Ella M. Balderston, Philadelphia. 34th st, s s, 275 e 7th av, 25x98.9. Sept. 4, 6 months, 5 %. 31,500

Kempner, Samuel to The German-American Real Estate Title Guarantee Co. Elizabeth st, Nos. 257-263, w s, 159 s Houston st, 4 lots, together in size 76.8x89.2x76.3x86.10. 4 morts., each $6,000. Sept. 3, 1 year, 5 %. 24,000

Krumwiede, Charles mortgagor with The Poughkeepsie Savings Bank mortgagee. Extension of mort. at 4½ %. Sept. 1. nom

Lerck, Sophia wife of John to August Freutel 152d st. P. M. Sept. 1, due Sept 1, 1894. 3,000

Lawton, Newbury D., New Rochelle, N. Y., to Jacob Poulin. 166th st, s s, 22 w Jackson av, 25x100. Re-recorded. April 1, 3 years, 5 %. 3,000

Same to same. 166th st, s s, 47 w Jackson av, 25x100. Re-recorded. April 1, 3 years, 5 %. 3,000

Lawton, Newbury D. and Hannah B. his wife, New Rochelle, N. Y., mortgagors with Jacob Poulin mortgagee. Agreement correcting errors in description of mortgages. Aug. 31. nom

Lingelbach, Hartman to Albert G. Morganstern exr. Charles L. Morganstern. 52d st. P. M. Aug. 1, 5 years, 5 %. 8,500

Levy, Lehman and Emil Meyer to Marie C. A. Richardson, Brooklyn, N. Y. 100th st, s s, 213 e 1st av, 50x100.11. Sept. 8, due Sept. 8, 1896, 5 %. 4,000

McGuinness, Edward and Daniel E. Reilly, of E. McGuinness & Co., mortgagors with The Poughkeepsie Savings Bank mortgagee. Extension of mort. at 4½ %. Sept. 1. nom

McKee, Thomas J. and Fernando Baltes exrs. and trustees Matthew Byrnes to Bernhard Beinecke. 5th av, s e cor 45th st, runs east 150 x south 100.5 x west 50 x north 25 x west 100 to av, x north 75.5 to beginning. Sept. 10, 1 year or sooner. 40,000

McLean, James to Schwarzschild & Sulzberger. River av, e s, 300 n James st, 100x250 to Gerard av; Arcularius pl, s s, 393.7 e Gerard av, 100x139x101.10x158.6. Secures bond of mortgagor and Charles F. and Frank Bond for building materials. Sept. 3. 7,500

Merritt, Isabell wife of and Charles to William S. and Charles W. Opdyke. Marion av and Campbell st. P. M. Sept. 5, 1 year. 800

Metzger, Bernard to Johanna Richard. 50th st, s s, 260 w 3d av. P. M. Aug. 13, due May 10, 1892, 5 %. 10,600

Same to Alexander McIntyre, exr. Sarah Turner. 50th st. s s, 280 w 3d av. P. M. Sept. 10, 8 months, 5 %. 4,000

Michael, Louis to Edward S. Clark, Cooperstown, N. Y. Bowery, Nos. 182 and 182½, w s, 75.1 s Spring st, 25.1x99.11x25x100. July 9, due Sept. 10, 1894, 4 %. 20,000

Martin, John and Emma J. his wife to Alexander List and Thomas Lennon. Samuel st, n e s, n w ½ lot 173 map of East Tremont, 37.6x133. Aug. 18. 800

Morrell, Thomas H., Port Richmond, S. I., to John H. V. Arnold. Barclay st, No. 52, s s, 25x100; Fulton st, No. 207, n s, 24.11x82.4x25.6x—. All title. Sept. 8, due Sept. 1, 1804. See Conveys. 400

Morris, George H. to William H. Lane. 96th st. P. M. Sept. 5, 6 months. 3,000

Same to Sylvia A. Swinnerton. Same property. P. M. 2d mort. Sept. 5, due March 5, 1893. 1,500

Muhlfeld, George A. and Mary his wife to John H. Powell, Newport, R. I. 17th st, s s, 338 e Av B, 25x92. Sept. 3, 5 years or sooner, 4½ %. gold, 6,000

Mull, De Witt and Gotlieb Fromer to Richard H. L. Townsend. Park av. P. M. July 6, demand. 12,000

McElroy, Owen F. and William to Allen & Campbell. 96th st, n s, 145 e Lexington av, 25x100.11. Sub to morts. $107,500. Sept. 3, 6 months or sooner, 5 %. 1,500

Same to Charles Forbes. 96th st, n s, 170 e Lexington av, 25x100.11. Sub. to morts. $107,500. Aug. 29, 6 months or sooner. 2,000

McKenna, Margaret to William M. Stilwell. 123d st, n s, 125 e 8th av, 50x100.11. Aug. 25, due Sept. 1, 1892, 5 %. 300

Mesick, Frank B. and Maria A. his wife to Maria Scaich. Travers st, proposed, s s, 100.11 w Marion av, 25x98.10x25x99.1; Marion av, w s, 50 s Travers st, 50x100x50x100.5; Travers st, s s, 100 w Valentine av, proposed, runs south 120.10 x west 175 x north 22.7 x west 50 x north 98 to Travers st, x east 225. June 10, 5 years or sooner, 5 %. 4,845

Moore, Martha M. to John Schreyer. 105th st, s s, 200 w Amsterdam av, 18.9x100.11. June 4, 1 year. 1,000

Same to same. 50th st, n s, 325 w 9th av, 25x100.5. P. M. June 4, 1 year. 1,500

Moser, Caroline wife of Martin to Louisa Hillsbrecht. Robbins av, s e s, 75 s w Fox st, 25x105. Sept. 4, due July 1, 1844, 5 %. 1,200

MacGuire, Dennis J. to H. Koehler & Co., a corporation. Watts st, No. 88. Saloon lease. Sept. 8, demand. 600

McCloskey, Jane to Thomas and Thomas, Jr., Courtney. 187th st, proposed. P. M. Sept. 8, 1 year. 1,200

McGrath, Mary J. to Abraham Steers. Crotona pl, w s, 134.9 s 171st st, 25x100. Sept. 9, 1 year, 5½ %. 2,515

Miller, Margaretha to The German Savings Bank. 18th st, n s, 160 w 1st av, 20x92. Sept. 9, 1 year. 1,500

Niver, Norman L. to Susan H. Geissenhainer extrx. Charles Burkhalter. 51st st, No. 204, s s, 67.4 e 3d av, 17.1x80.10 Sept. 5, 3 years, 5 %. gold, 5,000

O'Connor, Dennis to Peter Doelger. 59th st, No. 329 E. Lease. Sept. 3, demand. 600

O'Brien, James to Ambrose Snow et al. exrs. and trustees John S. Young. 65th st, n s, 200 w Central Park West, 20x100.5. Sept. 10, 1 year, 5 %. 14,000

Same to Charles P. Latting. Same property. Sub. to last mort. Sept. 10, 1 year, 5 %. 4,000

Owen, Sophia L. to The Harlem Savings Bank. 114th st, No. 165, n s, 241 w 3d av, 26.4x100.11. Aug. 12, 1 year, 5 %. 12,500

Orange, Elizabeth to Alfred Roe. 45th st, n s, 200 w 2d av, 25x100.5. Sept. 8, 1 year, 5 %. 500

Pfannenschmidt, Frederick to The German Savings Bank, New York. 10th av, No. 317, w s, 49.4 n 28th st, 24.8x100. Sept. 8, 1 year. 7,000

Pollock, Gustav to The Cook & Bernheimer Co., a corporation. Southern Boulevard, n w s, 125 s w 145th st, 25x100. Sept. 4, demand. 1,748

Phillips, Rebecca J. to Rachel Phillips and Samuel L. Hyman. Lexington av, w s, 79.5 s 64th st, 21x90. Sept. 3, due Sept 23, 1893, 5 %. 5,000

Prescott, Eliza to Peter Ryan. Valentine av and 181st st. P. M. Aug. 24, 2 years, 5 %. 1,000

Platt, Frederick E. to Abram T. and James Buckhout. Anthony and Burnside avs. P. M. Sept. 3, 10 years, 5 %. 6,500

Porr, Josephine N. to Lena Kuntz. 10th av, e s, 80.4 n 49th st, 25x100; 10th av, e s, 105.4 n 49th st, 15.2x100; 7th av, w s, 49.5 n 40th st, 24.8x60.11. Leasehold. Sept. 10, 1 year. 12,000

Palmenberg, Raymond P. and William F. and Emil T. to The Mutual Life Ins. Co. of New York. West 3d st, Nos. 89 and 91, n s, 125 w Thompson st, 50x100. Aug. 21, due Aug. 21, 1893. 45,000

Polhemus, William N. and Susan J. to Hugh N. Camp. Boston av. P. M. Aug. 24, due Aug. 24, 1894, 5 %. 720

Prowtin, William mortgagor with Julia E. Cameron. Extension of mort. at 5 %. Dec. 28, 1889. nom

Robinson, Thomas J. to Augustus Taber and ano. trustees Abraham S. Underhill. 8th av, e s, 24.7 s 112th st, 25.7x100. Sept. 9, 5 years, 5 %. gold, 18,000

Same to James Rogers. Same property. Sub. to last mort. Sept. 9, 6 months or sooner. 4,000

Same to Richard Cummings. 8th av, e s, 50.2 s 112th st, 25.2x100. Sub. to mort. $18,000. Sept. 9, 6 months. 2,000

Same to John Burke, Llewellyn Park, N. J. Same property. Sept. 9, 5 years, 5 %. gold, 18,000

Same to same. 8th av, e s, 75.4 s 112th st, 25.7x100. Sept. 9, 5 years, 5 %. gold, 18,000

Same to Abraham Steers. Same property. Sub. to last mort. Sept. 9, 1 year or sooner. 3,000

Rehbauser, John to Francis L. Vogelsberger. 117th st. P. M. Sept. 10, due Sept. 1, 1896, 5 %. 7,500

Reilly, Mary F. to Caroline Cornell, Brooklyn. Water st, No. 672, n s, 150 w Jackson st, 25x100. Sept. 3, 5 years, 5 %. gold, 5,000
Rohrs, Frederick to Hewlett Scudder, Northport, L. I. 134th st, n s, 150 w Alexander av, runs north 100 x east 50 x north 100 to 135th st, x west 75 x south 200 to 134th st, x east 25. Sept 2, 1 month. gold, 12,500
Rennert, Catharine E. to Frances C. wife of Thomas Beaty. 123d st, s s, 303.2 w 1st av. P. M. Sept. 3, due Sept. 8, 1894, 5 %. 6,500
Same to The Gilbert A. Robertson Home, a corporation. 123d st, s s, 322.6 w 1st av. P. M. Sept. 3, due Oct. 1, 1894, 5 %. 6,500
Roach, William and Catherine his wife to Charles H. Mersereau. 146th st, s s, 240 w Brook av, 50x100. Sept. 5, 3 years, 5 %. 1,800
Sachs, Julius to The Baron de Hirsch Fund. 59th st, s s, 200 w 6th av, 25x100.5. Sept. 3, due June 1, 1896, 5 %. 60,000
Sammet, Philip to Catharine E. Bukenhauer. 17th st. P. M. Sept. 8, installs, 5 %. 6,000
Smith, Elizabeth K. wife of Albert E. to William McShane admr. 123d st, s s, 190.6 e 7th av, 33x100.11. Sept. 8, 1 year. 1,640
Smith, Mathew to Henry Hirsch and Morris Victorius. Central av. P. M. Sept. 8, 2 years or sooner, 5 %. 833
Smith, James D. and Sidney S. Darling to Joseph Schader. Hudson st. P. M. Sept. 1, 5 years or sooner, 5 %. 8,000
Spencer, Joseph W. to Frederic J. Middlebrook. Morningside av, s w cor 119th st, 100.11x150. Sept. 8, 3 months. 15,000
Schreiner, George to Mary L. March extrx. of John P. March. 114th st, n e cor Lexington av, 25x100.11. Sept. 4, 3 years, 5 %. gold, 28,000
Same to same. 115th st, s e cor Lexington av, 25x100.11. Sept. 4, 3 years, 5 %. gold, 28,000
Seib, Anna M. to Leonard Seib. 82d st, n s, 156.6 w Av A, 25x102.2. Sept. 1, 2 years, 5 %. 1,000
Stubenbord, William to Augusta Meyer. 38th st, n s, 187 w 7th av, 20x98.9. Sept. 3, due Sept. 4, 1896, 5 %. 10,000
Summers, Ellen to Elizabeth A. wife of James D. Freeman. 50th st. P. M. Aug. 29, 5 years, 5 %. 9,000
Scharrenbeck, George and A. F. Heiser to A. Hupfel's Sons. Washington av, Nos. 1857 and 1859. Lease. Sept. 5, note, demand. 2,500
Smith, Jane to Caroline M. Cook. 22d st, No. 264, s s, 100 e 8th av, 25x98.9. Sub. to mort. $27,000. Sept. 9, 1 year or sooner. 6,000
Shea, Mary A. to Edward Cunningham. 117th st. P. M. Sept. 3, 1 year or sooner. 1,000
Smith, Elizabeth K. wife of Albert E. to Walter Scott. 123d st, s s, 190.6 e 7th av, 16x100.11. Sept. 4, 6 months. 600
Stearns, Jessie F. wife of Charles M. to Frederick A. Bacon. Cauldwell av, w s, 60 s 156th st, 20x52.6. Sept. 8, 3 years, 5 %. 800
Tolfree, James E. and Carrie his wife to Andrew Harman. Sniffen Court, No. 4. Aug. 20, 1 year, 5 %. 2,000
THE GERMANIA LIFE INS. Co. to Philip and William Ebling. 1st av, s w cor 101st st; 2d av, s e cor 101st st; 1st av, n w cor 100th st; 2d av, n e cor 100th st. Agreement to execute satisfaction piece. Sept. 4. nom
The Sixth Street Baptist Church to Daniel C. Potter. 6th st, s s, 110 w Av C, 67x94. Aug. 13, due Aug. 11, 1892, 5 %. 20,000
Van Schaick, Eliza to William B. Cook. Webster av, e s, 24.11 n Southern Boulevard, 150x100. Sept. 4, 3 years, 5 %. 4,600
Van Rensselaer, Killaen, Cornelia Van R. Erving, Catharine Van R. Atterbury formerly Van Rensselaer and Eleanor Van R. Fairfax with Edward S. Clark, Cooperstown, N. Y., both mortgagees. Agreement as to priority of mortgages made by Louis Michael. July 10. nom
Weinberg, Jacob B. to Richard H. Williams exr. William H. Macy (2d). 100th st. P. M. Aug. 25, due Sept. 3, 1896, 5 %. gold, 17,500
Wittnebert, Eliza wife of Caspar to Mary Gottsmann. 7th st, No. 212, s s, 233 w Av C, 25x90.4. Sept. 8, 1 year, 5 %. 800
Watson, Frances to Pasquale Caponigri. Rockfield st, n e cor Marion av, 25x147.9x35.5x128.4. Sept. 4, 1 year. 250
Wagner, Frederick and Caeser Artigo to George Ehret. 28th st, No. 137 W. Lease. Sept. 4, demand. 4,000
Wolff, Isaac to Samuel Valentine. Norfolk st, e s, 175 w Rivington st, 25x100. Aug. 20, 4 years or sooner, 5 %. 4,600
Yergens, Emma P., New York, William W. and Edward M. Bliven, Yonkers, N. Y., and Ella M. Balderston, Philadelphia, to THE LAWYERS' TITLE INS. CO. of New York. 34th st, s s, 275 e 7th av, 25x98.9. Sept. 4, 3 months. See Conveys. 6,000
Consent of stockholders to mortgage. G. B. Hodgman, J. M. Cornell, C. V. V. Powers, Wm. V. V. Powers, Sydney A. Smith, E. A. Matthiessen and A. R. Ledoux to The Deer Hill Co. (Lim.) July 31.

KINGS COUNTY.

SEPTEMBER 3, 4, 5, 7, 8, 9.

Amsterdam, Jacob to August Luedicke. Hopkins st, s s, 45 e Marcy av, runs east 20 x south 100 x west 19.5 x northwest — x north 99.6. Aug. 22, due Sept. 1, 1896, 5 %. $1,500
Same to same. Same property. Aug. 14, due Sept. 1, 1896, 5 %. 1,000
Adiekes, Magdelena M. and Emma C. his wife, Henry Ruppel mortgagors with Warren C. Hubbard mortgagee. Extension of mort. July 2. nom
Avery, Clara A., New York, to Emil Lachmann, New York. Meeker av. P. M. Sept. 1, 2 years, 5 %. 700
Ayers, Samuel to Samuel M. Meeker et al. exrs. Samuel M. Meeker. Jefferson av. P. M. Sept. 1, 3 years, 5 %. 10,500
Arens, Johanna wife of Abraham to Joseph Foley. 4th av. P. M. Sept. 3, 2 years, 5 %. 350
Bahrenburg, John H. to John Hollweg. Fulton st, n s, 20 w Verona pl, 20x80. Sept. 1, 5 years, 5 %. 4,000
Baright, Sophia W. wife of Edward P. to The Hamilton Trust Co. Dean st, n s, 324 w Nostrand av, 44x100. Sept. 4, 3 years, 5 %. 4,000
Benedict, John R. to Jennie V. Wilbur. Sherman st. P. M. Aug. 20, 3 years, 5 %. 1,500
Beer, Louis and Michael Schaffner to The Kings County Savings Inst. Floyd st, n s, 265 e Nostrand av, 25x100. Sept. 5, 1 year, 5 %. 3,600
Beers, William L. to Catharine Price. Pacific st. P. M. Sept. 1, 1 year. 575
Berger, Joseph and Samuel Misbel to Annie Levy. Christopher av. P. M. July 17, 4 months. 900
Betts, Charles A. to The Hamilton Trust Co. McDonough st, w s, 80 n Fulton st, runs north 46.6 to Marcy av, x northwest 18.4 x southwest 110 x south 46.6 x east 100. Sept. 3, 1 year, 5 %. 4,500
Birmingham, Sarah A. to John F. Vrooman. Powell st, w s, 233.2 n Liberty av, 16.10x100. Sept. 4, installs, 5 %. 900
Brownell, Asa C. to The Title Guarantee and Trust Co. State st, n s, 250 e Hoyt st, 100x100. Sept. 2, demand. 10,000
Bryans, A. K. mortgagor with Ella S. Robinson and Katharine M. Blanke. Extension of morts. July 27. nom
Barber, Letitia to James Cassin. 2d av, s w cor 57th st. P. M. Sept. 7, 3 years, 5 %. 2,500
Billing, Conrad to Jacob Fischer. Schenck av, w s, 275 s Glenmore av, 25x100. Sept. 8, 2 years or installs. 900
Bird, James R. to James M. Jackson. Putnam av, No. 122, s s, 81 w Franklin av, 20x100. Aug. 27, 1 year, 5 %. 500
Biri, George to Joseph T. Schmitt. Yates pl. P. M. Sept. 8, 5 years or installs, 5 %. 5,000
Brown, Mary E. to Lawrence Hurlburt. McDonough st, s s, 108.4 w Ralph av, 18.4x100. Sept. 5, 3 years, installs. 1,200
Caro, Blanch to Edward E. Stewarts. Osborn st. P. M. Sept. 1, installs, 5 %. 350
Collins, George J. to Howard N. Acker. Elton st. P. M. Sub. to mort. $2,800. Sept. 8, installs. 1,000
Creamer, Frank D. to Mary Knowlton. St. Marks pl. P. M. Aug. 25, 3 years, 5 %. 10,000
Callahan, Edward L. to John R. Schoonover. 48th st, s s, 380 e 8th av, 16x100.2. Sept. 1, installs. 532
Candee, Mary L. wife of Fernando C., Jr., to Ann Robinson. Vernon av. P. M. Aug. 27, due Sept. 1, 1893, 5 %. 2,200
Carey, Peter J. to Mount Morris Co-operative Building and Loan Assoc. Benson av, New Utrecht. P. M. Sept. 4, installs. 3,500
Carlile, Susan A. wife of and James to Samuel Carlile, Paterson, N. J. 5th av, n w s, 50 n e 14th st, 25x97.10. Aug. 1, 1 year. 2,600
Case, George C. to Elizabeth Taber et al. exrs. Franklin W. Taber. Albany av, w s, 88 11 n Butler st, 16.8x85. Aug. 21, due Dec. 1, 1891. 300
Cocheu, Fred. C. to The Peoples Trust Co. guard. of John A. Wilson. 70th st, s w s, 160 s e 10th av. P. M. Aug. 20, 1 year. 3,000
Same to same as guard. of William J. Shanley. 10th av and 71st st. P. M. Aug. 20, 1 year. 3,500
Colby, Rachel to Jeremiah Colby. 3d av, e s, 60.2 s 53d st, 20x80. Sept. 1, 1 year, 5 %. 1,435
Cook, Mary E., Newtown, L. I., to Sarah A. M. Kent. Stone av, w s, 200 w Blake av. P. M. July 23, demand. 900
Same to Lewis Hurst. Stone av, w. s, 225 s Blake av, 25x100. Aug. 22, 3 years. 800
Cosgrove, Mary to John Cleary. Summit st, n s, 220 w Hicks st. P. M. May 1, 1888, demand. 800
Couch, Emily M. to Ada Remsen, Flushing. Troy av. P. M. Sept. 2, 3 years, 5 %. 2,500
Curtin, William H. to Zacheus Bergen et al. exrs. Robert A. Robertson. Clason av. P. M. Sept. 3, 1 year. 1,300
Damm, Rudolph to Sarah E. Cleghorn. Bergen st. P. M. Sept. 3, due Sept. 1, 1896, or installs. 2,500
Dinnen, Francis P. to J. Wyckoff Van Sielen. Hendrix st, w s, 125 n Sutter av, 25x100. Sept. 5, 1 year. 900
Dittmar, William, Jr., to The West Brooklyn Land and Improvement Co. 14th av and 55th st, New Utrecht. P. M. July 1, due Sept. 1, 1895, 5 %. 1,275
Edmonston, S. S. mortgagee with Frank Johnston mortgagor. Extension of mort. Sept. 2. nom
Feurey, Domenico to George S. Wheeler exr. Nancy S. Wheeler. Carroll st. P. M. Sept. 1, 3 years. 1,500
Flint, John to Arthur E. Sumner. Cleveland st, e s, 246.10 n Atlantic av, 50x100. Sept. 4, 6 months. 500
Same to Charles N., Horace A. and Frederick B. P tt. Same property. Sept. 4, installs.ra 2,650
Frank, Barnet and Simon Rose to Mary W. Smith. Eastern Parkway, s s, 50 e Osborn st, 25x100. Sept. 4, demand. 400
Farrell, James P. to Edward I. Wilbur, Tuxedo Park, N. Y. Shore road and Oliver st, New Utrecht. P. M. Sept. 3, 5 years, 5 %. 1,665
Friedman, Morris, New York, to Abraham Ruth. Osborn st. P. M. Sept. 2, installs. 950
Faber, Josephine W. to Heloise M. L. Allin, New Utrecht. 13th av, west cor 56th st, New Utrecht. P. M. Sept. 8, 3 years, 5 %. 800
Fenerty, Michael to James H. P. Dawson. Pacific st. P. M. Sept. 1, 3 years, 5 %. 2,000
Free, John P. and Whitman M. to The City Savings Bank of Brooklyn. Sutter av, s s, 40 e Snediker av, 20x92.6. Aug. 17, due Nov. 1, 1892. 2,000
Same to same. Sutter av, s s, 60 e Snediker av, 20x92.6. Aug. 17, due Nov. 1, 1892. 2,000
Same to same. Snediker av, e s, 92.6 s Sutter av, 15x100. Aug. 17, due Nov. 1, 1892. 1,500
Same to same. Snediker av, e s, 107.6 s Sutter av, 15x100. Aug. 17, due Nov. 1, 1892. 1,500
Same to same. Snediker av, e s, 122.6 s Sutter av, 15x100. Aug. 17, due Nov. 1, 1892. 1,500
Same to William C. Wallace and ano. admrs. Joseph W. Douglass. Snediker av, e s, 137.6 s Sutter av, 15x100. Aug. 1, due Nov. 1, 1892. 1,500
Same to Julia W. Douglas. Sutter av, s s, 80 e Snediker av, 20x92.6. Aug. 17, due Nov. 1, 1892. 2,000
Same to same. Snediker av, e s, 152 s Sutter av, 15x100. Aug. 17, due Nov. 1, 1892. 1,500
Gibson, William M. to The Title Guarantee and Trust Co. Quincy st, s w cor Throop av, 24x80. Sept. 5, due Sept. 8, 1894, 5 %. 10,000
Green, George W. mortgagor with Frederick J. Greve mortgagee. Extension of mort. Sept. 1. nom
Gardner, Albert C. and Annie his wife to George Gutting and Charles A. Wagner. Himrod st. P. M. Sept. 1, 5 years, installs. 1,600
Gillies, George C. and Josephine C. to The First Reformed Prot. Dutch Church, Jamaica, L. I. Chestnut st. P. M. Sept. 1, 3 years. 1,300
Gillies, George C. and Josephine C. his wife to George Beach. Chestnut st, w s, 1,350 n 4th st, 25x150. 2d mort. Sept. 1, installs. 1,100
Gnad, William F. to Julius Lehrenkrauss. Fulton st, n e s, 60 s e Clason av, 20x91. Sept. 1, 1 year. 3,250
Green, Jennie to Pauline Hartmann. Thatford av. P. M. 2d mort. Sept. 1, installs. 500
Hancock, William A. to Robert S. Neely. Pacific st, s s, 100 e Rockaway av, 16.8x107.2. Sub. to mort. $1,834. Aug. 31, due Sept. 1, 1892. 300
Same to same. Pacific st, s s, 133.4 e Rockaway av, 16.8x107.2. Sub. to mort. $1,833. Aug. 31, due Sept. 1, 1891. 325
Same to same. Pacific st, s s, 116 8 e Rockaway av, 16.8x107.2. Sub. to mort. $1,833. Aug. 31, due Sept. 1, 1892. 325
Hennemann, John J. to Theodore F. Jackson et al. trustees of Loftis Wood. Knickerbocker av, s w s, 75 s e Jefferson st, 25x100. Sept. 2, due Sept. 1, 1894, 5 %. 2,500
Higgins, Henry J. to The Equitable Co-operative Building and Loan Assoc. Luquer st. P. M. Aug. 31, installs. 5,500
Hob, Sebastian and Peter Braun to Adam Kaiser, Charles Rissler and August Todebusch. Central av. P. M. Sept. 1, 2 years, 5 %. 900
Holt, Frank G. to The Serial Building Loan and Savings Inst. St. Marks av, s s, 300 w Rockaway av, 25x127.9 April 21, installs. 300
Hunger, Theodore to Marie E. Badeau et al. exrs. Nathaniel Niles. Bergen st, s s, 350 w Vanderbilt av, 50x94.9x—x100.3. Aug. 29, 1 year. 2,525
Hession, Henry to Andrew Harth] or Haeth Flatbush. Lot in Flatbush, 2,920.5 e Poor House road. P. M. Sept. 8, installs. 10,500
Holland, George to Martha K. Chaffee. Hancock st. P. M. September 8, 3 years, 5 %. gold, 4,750
Hoven, Arnold to Elizabetha Franz. Johnson av, s s, 125 w Graham av, 25x100. Sept. 8, due Oct. 1, 1896, or installs, 5 %. 6,000
Jackson, Amelia M. J. widow to Louis G. Engel. Dean st, s s, 216.8 e Nostrand av, 16.8x114.5. Sept. 8, due Sept. 1, 1892, 5 %. 500
Jacobs, Fanny wife of and Lewis to John Ross. Flatbush av. P. M. Aug. 31, 3 years, 5 %. 6,000
Johnson, Frank to George H. King. Blake av, s s, 50 e Shepherd av, 25x100. Sept. 8, due May 8, 1892, or installs. 200
Jones, John to The New York and Wakefield Co-operative Building and Loan Assoc. East Broadway or Church av, n s, at line bet Allgeo and Lahey, 28x219.5x33.7x219.2, Flatbush. Sept. 1, installs, 5 %. 2,500
Josiah, Minnie wife of and George to Rosalie T. Slade, Riverhead, L. I. Essex st, e s, 160 n Ridgewood av, 20x100. Sept 3, 3 years. 1,500
Kaiser, Marie L. wife of Christian formerly Stuermer to Lewis Hurst. Wyckoff st, No. 172, s s, 215 w Bond st, 20x100. Sept. 2, 6 months. 600
Knapp, John L., Andrew and Henry, of Knapp Bros., to The South Brooklyn Savings Inst. Harrison st, n s, 21 e Hicks st, 21x69.10. Sept. 5, 1 year, 5 %. 2,000
Knight, Mark B. to Henry H. Adams, County Treasurer. Webster st, n s, 260 e Albany av, 20x100, Flatbush. Sept. 3, 3 years, 5 %. 800
Krug, Emma wife of Louis to Henry S. Strauss. Hopkinson av, Nos. 217 and 219, e s, 167 s Herkimer st, 28x97.6. Sub. to morts. $10,500. Sept. 1, 1 year. 1,800

Karger, Samuel to Morris Minden and Simon Spandau. McKibbin st. P. M. Sept. 3, installs, 5 %. 700

Kelly, Patrick to Michael Danzlock. Oakland st. P. M. Aug. 11, 2 years, 5 %. 1,900

Kurtz, J. Henry to Johanna Plambeck. Schenck av. P. M. Aug. 22, due Sept. 1, 1896. 1,200

Knight, Philip M. to Frederick Sands. Ridgewood av, s s, 40 w Linwood st. P. M. Sub. to mort. $1,800. Sept. 9, 6 months. 700

Same to same. Ridgewood av, s s, 20 w Linwood st. P. M. Sub. to mort. $1,800. Sept. 9, 6 months. 700

Same to same. Ridgewood av, s s, 40 w Linwood st. P. M. Sept. 9, 6 months. 500

Same to same. Ridgewood av, s s, 20 w Linwood st. P. M. Sept. 9, 6 months. 500

Lippert, John and Ernest to Wilhelmina Ramge. Ainslie st. P. M. Sept. 3, due Jan. 1, 1894, 5 %. 700

Lubbal, Koppal to Gustav Olson. Stone av. P. M. Aug. 29, 3 years or installs 500

Lake, Mary V. to Louis Beer. De Kalb av. P. M. Sept. 2, 2 years. 500

Le Beau, Theodore M. to Julia W. Latimer. Ashford st, e s, 34 s Ridgewood av, 33x100. Sept. 3. gold, 6,000

Same to same. Ashford st, e s, 67 s Ridgewood av. Sept. 3. gold, 6,000

Levy, Davis, Jacob Jackson and Frank Glasser to Mary Bergan. Rockaway av, e s, 100 s Eastern Parkway, 25x100.1. Sept. 1, 3 years. 3,000

Levy, Joseph to Gilbert S. Thatford. Sutter av. P. M. Sept. 5, 10 years. 850

Liebmann, Louis and Herman to Henry Weil. Adams st, s w cor Tillary st, runs south 153.2 x west 114 x north 22 x west to Washington st, x north to Tillary st, x east —. Aug. 10, due March 1, 1892. 75,000

Lippmann, Leopold J. to Newbury H. Frost. Central av, Weirfield st, Old Bushwick road and Halsey st. P. M. Secures bond of mortgagor and Alexander Taylor. Sept. 3, due Dec. 1, 1891. 25,000

Same to same. Weirfield st, n w s, 81 s w Central av, 20x100. Secures bond of same persons. Sept. 3, due Dec. 1, 1891. 25,000

Loerenthal, Wolf and Nathan to Arthur H. Wilson. Livonia av. P. M. Sub. to mort. $1,300. July 28, installs. 1,100

Lund, Charles E. to Demas Strong. Devoe st, n s, 25 w Leonard st, 25x100. Sept. 2, 1 year, 5 %. 1,000

Lyons, John to The Long Island Loan and Trust Co guard. of Magdalena E. Schmadeke. Gates av, s e s, 250 s w Knickerbocker av, 25x100. Sept. 4, due Dec. 1, 1894, 5 %. 3,500

Madden, Margaretta wife of and Luke to Azariah W. Monfort. Park av, s s, 50 e Spencer st, 25x100. Sept. 1, 3 years, 5 %. 2,000

Magilligan, John to The Title Guarantee and Trust Co. 1st st, s s, 412.10 e 7th av, 3 lots, each 20x100. 3 morts., each $8,000. Sept. 5, 3 years, 5 %. 24,000

Magrath, Jemima to Albert W. S. Proctor guard. William J., Evaline F., Herbert and Arthur Magrath. Bergen st, s s, 180 w Clason av, 20x100. July 9, due May 1, 1893. 1,500

Mahon, Daniel to William Corcoran. Raymond st. P. M. Sept. 3, 2 years, 5 %. 1,600

Mangan, Sarah F. to Maria E. Krulder. Receipt for $500 on account of bond and mortgage. Oct. 18, 1883. 500

Martin, Ellen to Oscar Abrams and Charles A. Blohm. Sheepshead Bay road, n e cor West 3d st, 116.4x71x100 to st, x130.6, Coney Island. Sept. 4, due Sept. 3, 1896. 1,800

McAuliffe, Ellen wife of and Patrick to Jane C. Brown. Luquer st, n s, 25 w Court st, 44.2x100. Sept. 1, 5 years, 5 %. 5,500

McCann, Bernard J. mortgagor with George C. Blanke mortgagee. Extension of morts. Feb. 12. nom

McCready, Henry, New York, to Adelaide Van Dyk. 41st st, n s, 350 e 5th av, 50x100.2. Aug. 10, 1 year. 1,000

McGarl, George W. to Anna M. Ferris. Greenwood av, s e cor East 4th st, Flatbush. P. M. Sept. 3, 3 years, 5 %. 525

McGregor, Alexander to Catherine Battermann. 51st st. P. M. Sept. 1, 4 years. 900

Meyers, Israel to The Title Guarantee and Trust Co. Jay st, n s, 53 e Tillary st, runs east 22 x north 57.6 x west 7.6 x south 25 x west 14.1 x south 32.6. Sept. 3, 1 year, 5 %. 1,500

Meunier, John B. and Kunigunde his wife to Catherine Mengel. Varet st, s s, 147.10 w Bogart st, 25x100. Sept. 2, 5 years, 5 %. 800

Moores, Robert L. and Charles A. Le Quesne to Henry McShane Mfg. Co., of Baltimore City. Madison st, s s, 100 e Howard av, 40 x100. Sept. 3, note. 2,210

Moore, Ella E. to John C. Schenck. Schenck av, w s, 152 n Jamaica av, 25x100. Sept. 4, due Sept. 1, 1894. 4,000

Mosier, Harvey H. to The Title Guarantee and Trust Co. Halsey st. P. M. Aug. 31, 1 year, 5 %. 2,500

Mosier, Harvey H. and Carrie L. his wife to James Gascoine. Same property. 2d mort. Aug. 31, installs. 1,400

Mullowney, Richard to James D. Rankin and James Ross. Halsey st, s s, 158 w Ralph av, 17x100. Sub. to mort. $4,000. September 5, 1 year. 1,000

Manheim, Julius and Louis Helmken to The Greenpoint Savings Bank. Van Cott av, s s, 25 w Russell st, 25x92. Sept. 3, 1 year. 4,000

Same to same. Van Cott av, s w cor Russell st, 25x92. Sept. 3, 1 year. 6,000

Molloy, Catharine to Marianne Stelle. Brooklyn and Jamaica pike, s e cor Logan st, 54.2x 115.4x50x94. Aug. 31, 5 years 2,400

McCrodden, Charles to William H. Wartz. East 89th st, centre line at woodland of Johannes Lot, 132.4x southeast 309 to centre Flatlands av, x southwest 130 to centre East 89th st, x northwest 300.8, Flatlands. Sept. 1, 3 years. 400

McCool, Nicholas, Jr., to E. Simonson Calvert. 4th av, s w cor 34th st. P. M. July 20, demand. 10,000

Same to same. Same property. July 20, demand. 15,000

Merryweather, Emma C. to Mary L. Barnard. Madison st. P. M. Sept. 1, 1 year. 700

Meyer, Herman W. to Paul W. Ledoux. Schaeffer st, n s, 188 w Hamburg av, 16x98x16x98.2. Sept. 1, 2 years. 500

Miller, Jane wife of Abel to George C. Cranford. Macon st, n s, 200 e Patchen av, 54x 100. Sept. 8, due Dec. 1, 1891. 1,600

Muller, Frances to Phillip Butterfass and Barbara his wife. Warren st, s s, 120.10 w 4th av, 20x100. Sept. 8, 1 year, 5 %. 200

Naumer, John trustee Sarah Heid to Richard F. Carpenter. Hicks st, e s, 80 s President st, 20x100. Sept. 1, 3 years, 5 %. 5,000

Nissen, Helene wife of and George to Nicholas L. Cort. Rodney st, n w s, 251.11 s w Bedford av, 18.5x100. Sept. 9, 2 years. 4,000

Ochsenreiter, Philipp to Henry Stellwagen. Bond st. P. M. Sept. 1, 6 years, 5 %. 4,000

Pages, Paul H. to Mount Morris Co-operative Building and Loan Assoc. 15th av, north cor 67th st, 60x95.3x60x93.1, New Utrecht Sept. 4, installs, 5 %. 250

Parmer, Rebecca to Josephine D. Powers. Sackman st or av, w s, 164.6 s Livonia av, 60 x100. Sept. 3, 3 years. 500

Payne, Frederick W. to William H. Norris and William Bowers. 4th av, w s, 30 n 14th st. P. M. Sept. 1, 2 years. 1,000

Same to same. 4th av, w s, 48 s 13th st. P. M. Sept. 1, 2 years. 2,000

Petrillo, Michael to Simon Levy. Thatford av and Riverdale av. P. M. June 10, installs. 385

Phelps, Edwin O. and Robert S. Neely with William A. Bancock mortgagor. Agreement as to priority of mortgage. Aug. 26, 1890. nom

Powell, Cynthia M. to Helen M. Buttle. Eldert st. P. M. Sept. 3, installs, 5 %. 750

Prescott, Shubeal C. to Margaret N. Harteau. McDougal st, n s, 517 e Saratoga av, 24.5x 100x23.1x100. Sept. 2, 1 year. 200

Proddow, Ella F. V. to Sarah E. Fisher. Dean st. P. M. Sept. 1, 3 years, installs, 5 %. 9,000

Quinn, John to James Corrigan. Belmont av, n s, 50 e Schenck av, 50x100. Sept. 8, 3 years. 1,500

Radcliffe, Thomas H. to John C. Schenck. McDonough st, s s, 156.8 e Ralph av, 18.8x 100. July 31, 3 years, 5 %. 4,500

Reh, John J. and Andrew Smith to Michael Reh. Metropolitan av, n s, 502 e Olive st, 25 x100. Sept. 4, due Sept. 1, 1896, 5 %. 3,000

Same to same. Metropolitan av, n s, 527 e Olive st, 25x100. Sept. 4, due Sept. 1, 1896, 5 %. 3,000

Reigman, John to Samuel Samuelson and Pinkus Ronginsky. Thatford av, e s, 225 s Eastern Parkway, 25x100. Sept. 2, installs. 1,600

Rosenberg, David to Mary A. Lloyd. Arlington av. P. M. Sept. 8, 5 years, 5 %. 2,000

Rothweiler, Wilhelmina to Matthaus Beck. South 4th st. P. M. Sept. 1, 1 year, 5 %. 1,000

Rudloff, Henry to Jennie V. Wilbur, both of Flatbush. Sherman st, e s, 100 s Greenwood av, 40x134.10x40x132.4. Sept. 1, 3 years, 5 %. 2,500

Russell, George to The Peoples Trust Co. Jay st, w s, 125 s Myrtle av, 22x102.9. Sept. 4, 1 year, 5 %. 3,000

Radcliffe, Thomas H. to Jacob C. Bergen. McDonough st, s s, 156.8 e Ralph av, 18.8x100. Sub. to mort. $4,500. Aug. 21, 1 year. 800

Rebele, Louis and Marie his wife and George Hassenfratz to Annie his wife. Oak st. P. M. Sept. 1, 3 years, 5 %. 2,200

Reynolds, William W. to The Metropolitan Life Ins. Co. Glenada pl, n w cor Decatur st, 100x85. Agreement for loan of $54,000. June 23. nom

Same to Charles Frazier. Glenada pl, s w cor Decatur st, 50x85. Sept. 8, 2 months. 5,000

Same to The Metropolitan Life Ins. Co. Same property. Sept. 4, due Oct. 1, 1894, installs, 6 % first year, after 5 %. 30,000

Same to same. Glenada pl, w s, 50 s Decatur st, 50x85. Sept. 4, due Oct. 1, 1894, installs, 6 % first year, after 5 %. 24,000

Rockwell, Gertrude P. to Sarah M. Mygatt and ano. trustees Jacob A. Robertson. Myrtle av, n s, 60.3 w Gold st, 20x100. Aug. 26, due Nov. 1, 1894, 5 %. 14,000

Roesler, Bernard to The Peoples' Trust Co. Lafayette av, n s, 20 e Elliott pl, 20x80. Sept. 8, 1 year, 5 %. 5,000

Rosenberg, Morris to Maria D. Palmer. Christopher av. P. M. July 21, due June 25, 1894. 4,000

Rudolph, Andrew E. to The South Brooklyn Savings Inst. 19th st. P. M. Sept. 8, 1 year, 5 %. 1,000

Ruhl, Henry to Charles Kunz. Hart st, n w s, 275 n e Hamburg av, 25x100. Sept. 8, due July 1, 1893, 5 %. 2,000

Sandell, Mary E. to Maria E. Cassidy et al. exrs. Mary A. Cassidy. Lorimer st, e s, 60 s Ainslie st, 20x100. Sept. 5, 5 years. 300

Semelis, Alexander to Charles Vallender. Madison st, n s, 320 w Lewis av, 20x100. July 29, 5 years. 1,000

Sibley, Albert to The Title Guarantee and Trust Co. Quincy st, s s, 287.6 w Throop av, 10 lots, together 187.2x100. 10 morts., each $4,000. Sept. 9, 3 years, 5 %. 40,000

Same to William E. Bidwell trustee Robert Thompson, Jr. Quincy st, s s, 493.9 w Throop av, 18.9x100. Sept. 8, 3 years, 5 %. 4,500

Same to same. Quincy st, s s, 474.8 w Throop av, 19.1x100. Sept. 8, 3 years, 5 %. 4,500

Stuber, Hermann and Fredericke his wife to John P. and Whitman M. Free. Suediker av, e s, 137.6 s Sutter av, 15x100. Sept. 4, installs. 500

Schacbner, Louis to David Stern. Seigel st, s s, 150 e Leonard st, 25x100. Sept. 1, 1 year, 5 %. 1,000

Schade, George to Mary Morgan. Warwick st, w s, 175 s Eastern Parkway, 25x100. Sept. 3, 3 years. 1,800

Schenkel, Joseph to Margaret E. and Martha A. Farrell. Ewen st, e s, 20 s Ainslie st, 25x 100. Sept. 1, 3 years, 5 %. 1,500

Schneider, Elizabeth wife of and Napoleon to The Title Guarantee and Trust Co. 21st st. P. M. Sept. 3, 1 year, 5 %. 4,500

Schroff, Max to Kings County Trust Co. 67th st, s s, 340 w 2d av, 40x100. Sept. 3, 1 year. 1,000

Schlutter, Jr., Robert and Karoline wife of Robert Schlutter, Sr., to Mary E. Gentleman. Palmetto st. P. M. Aug. 25, installs. 975

Schoenstein, Charles to Ludwig Fink. Johnson av, n s, 100 e Lorimer st, 25x100. Sept. 1, 1 year, 5 %. 1,800

Seidel, Henry F. to Valentine Hammann. Ralph av, s w cor St. Marks av, runs south 20 x west 100 x north 50 x east — to St. Marks av, x58.11. Aug. 31, 3 years, 5 %. 2,000

Sharkey, Terrence to James Flanagan. Richard st, n e cor Partition st, 25x95. Sept. 4, 3 years. 8,000

Sherman, John T. to The Farmers' Loan and Trust Co. Remsen st, No. 35, n s, 250 w Hicks st, 25x100. ½ part. Sept. 3, 3 years, 5 %. 7,500

Sherwood, Samuel T. to Elcy A. Martin. 47th st, n s, 140 e 4th av, 20x100.2. Sept. 1, 1 year. 800

Sherwood, Samuel T. to Mary E. Seaman. 47th st, n s, 140 e 4th av, 20x100.2. Sept. 1, 3 years, 5 %. 2,500

Smith, Louisa to Peter Creifelds. Downing st, w s, 234.6 n Putnam av, 18.9x100. Sept. 3, 3 years, 5 %. 3,000

Sterneckert, Frederick to Aurelia Fleischmann. Hamburg av. P. M. Sept. 2, due Sept. 1, 1892, 5 %. 2,700

Stewart, Alexander to James D. Lynch. Bay 38th st, New Utrecht. P. M. Sub. to mort. $2,000. Aug. 12, 1 year, 5 %. 414

Same to Bernard Larzelere. Same property. Building loan. Aug. 12, 1 year. 2,000

Stewart, Eliza wife of and David S. to The Brooklyn Trust Co. Flushing av, n s, 400 e Bedford av, runs north 100 x west 50 x south 62.1 x northwest 1 x southwest 40.4 to Flushing av, x east 3.10. Aug. 17, 1 year, 5 %. 8,500

Stillwell, Edmund H. to The Brooklyn City Co-operative Building and Loan Assoc. 13th av, e s, 20 n 67th st, 20x100, New Utrecht. Sept. 3, installs. 1,600

Straub, George to The Williamsburgh Savings Bank. Myrtle av, n s, 150 e Throop av, 25x 100. Sept. 3, 1 year, 5 %. 7,500

Stroh, Madelen wife of and John to George Kerswill. Grant st, Flatbush. P. M. Sept. 4, 3 years, 5½ %. 2,000

Swimm, Frank C. to Elizabeth U. Hitchcock, Poughkeepsie. Macon st, n s, 40 e Reid av, 17.6x100. Aug. 26, 3 years, 5 %. gold, 5,500

Taylor, Sarah to Newbury H. Frost. Harrison av, e s, 25 n Wallabout st, 25x100. Sept. 3, due Dec. 1, 1891. 25,000

Tonyes, Annie M. to David M. Koehler. Bedford av. P. M. Sept. 8, 1 year. 500

Tubbs, George W. to M. C. Ogden committee Catharine H. Tallman. Cowenhovens lane or road, from Bay Ridge to New Utrecht lane, New Utrecht. P. M. Sept. 1, installs. 5,000

Taaffe, John P. to The Peoples Trust Co. Concord st, n s, 97.10 e Gold st, 25x100. Sept. 4, 1 year, 5 %. 6,000

Timony, Jane to Howard T. Walden. Franklin av. P. M. Sept. 1, 4 years. 750

Tineo, Jose to James A. Hamblin. Ocean pl, No. 29. P. M. Sub. to mort. $2,200. Sept. 1, due Dec. 1, 1894, or installs. 1,150

The German Evangelic Lutheran St. Johns Church to The Greenpoint Savings Bank. Leonard st, e s, 275 n Calyer st, 50x100. Sept. 4, 1 year, 5 %. 4,500

Tumelty, Patrick to Mary A. Leatz. Road from Flatlands to the Neck and Canarsie, adj land of Rem Hegeman, 61.6x128x61.6x143, Flatlands. April 28, 3 years, 5 %. 800

Vankirk, Rachel A. to Cornelius Van Blankenstein. Willow st, No. 33. P. M. Sept. 3, due April 1, 1893, 5½ %. 3,000

Voelker, Valentine to Jacob Schnautz. Bartlett st. P. M. Sept. 3, due Sept. 1, 1896, 5 %. 2,500

Same to Conrad Voelker. Same property. Sept. 3, due Sept. 1, 1898, 4 %. 1,000

Vogelbach, John B. to Azariah W. Monfort. Leonard st, w s, 40 n Powers st, 20x50. Sept. 2, 3 years, 5 %. 1,000

Walker, Andrew to The Williamsburgh Savings Bank. Essex st, e s, 90 s Ridgewood av, 4 lots, each 18.9x100. 4 morts., each $1,550. Sept. 2, 1 year, 5 %. 6,200

Wille, Benranned to Jeremiah V. Meserole. Beadel st. P. M. Aug. 20, 3 years. 800

Walker, Andrew E. to The Greenpoint Savings Bank. Oakland st, w s, 190.6 n Van Cott av. 25x100. Sept. 4, 1 year, 5½ %. 3,500

Warren, Isidora to Emma wife of James I. Newman. Arlington av, s e cor Hendrix st, 30x99.6. Sept 2, 2 years. 1,500

Wicks, George E. to Thomas Stratton. 55th st, s s, 483.4 w 2d av, 16.8x100.2. Sept. 3, 3 years. 2,000

Wallis, Charles E. to Caroline Hesse. Gravesend av, w s, 340 s highway passing village cemetery, runs west 110 x north 25 x west 113 to Lake st, x south 50 x east 123 to av, x north 25, Gravesend. July 13, due July 1, 1894. 1,400

Williams, Percy G. and Thomas Adams, Jr., to William H. Allee et al. exrs. Joseph B. Allee. 3d av, Schermerhorn st. P. M. Aug. 5 due on last day of February, 1892, or sooner, 5 %. 23,000

Wilson, Hilda E. to The Serial Building Loan and Savings Inst. St. Marks av, s s, 325 w Rockaway av, 25x127.9. April 21, installs. 300

Wilson, Samuel and Ada G. G. his wife to Edwin D. Wellin, Waterbury, Conn. Maple st, s s, 105 e Rogers av, 60x100. July 4, demand. 500

Wing, Laura L. to Helen Deland, Salem, Mass Fulton st, n s, 183.9 w Somers st, 20x78.8x20.1x80.11. Nov. 24, 1890, 1 year, 5½ %. 1,000

Wolf, Harris and Jacob Piser, New York, to Henry Meyer. Seigel st. P. M. Sept. 1, installs. 6,250

Yard, Julia S. wife of and Frederick A. to Thomas A. Watson. Putnam av, n s, 139 e Lewis av, 19x100. Sept. 1, due Jan. 1, 1892. 1,500

Zuckerman, David and Jacob to Erastus D. Benedict. Thatford av, e s, 175 s Blake av, 25x100. Sept. 1, 2 years. 300

MORTGAGES----ASSIGNMENTS.

NEW YORK CITY.

SEPTEMBER 4 TO 10—INCLUSIVE.

Astor, William W. and ano. exrs. John J. Astor to William W. Astor. nom

Atlantic Trust Co. to Elizabeth Wightman. $3,000

Blumenthal, August to Henry Stemme and John H. Huchting, of H. Stemme & Co. 1,000

Brady, John J. to John Halliday. 2,000

Brown, Edward J. and ano. exrs. Margaret Cleland to Susan Alvord extrx. Alonzo A. Alvord. 7,124

Conforti, Michele to Robinson Gill trustee. nom

Dodd, Gertrude W. wife of Bethuel L. and Annie C. Ward, Orange, N. J. to Joseph S. Carreau. 10,846

Ely, Smith to Edwin A. Ely. 15,000

Feinberg, Solomon to Sender Jarmulowsky. 5,000

Green, Kathrine to Ambrose S. Murray. 4,900

German-American Real Estate Title Guarantee Co. to Jacques E. Karelsen et al. exrs. Ephraim and Rozetta Karelsen. 6,000

German-American Real Estate Title Guarantee Co to Edwin Sherman trustee of Clifford W. and John H. Day. 7,000

Same to same. 2,000

Higbie, Richard, Babylon, L. I., to Atlantic Trust Co. nom

Heerbrandt, Carolina to Leopold Gusthal. 3,800

Kirke, Agnes S. to James P. Hoffman, Jr., Elizabeth, N. J. nom

Kernochan, James P. trustee of George L. Lorillard to John J. Wysong trustee for Marie Marshall. 4,500

Knowles, Helen A. widow to Elizabeth Wightman. 5,000

Levy, Abraham to Matilda Levy. nom

La Coste, James M. to Cornelius L. La Coste, Paterson, N. J. 500

Lambert, Patrick and James H. Mason, Brooklyn, to Margaret Miller widow, London, Eng. 3,058

Lake, Eleanor I. to Hannah W. Fardou. 1,750

Same to same. 2,500

Lowenfeld, Pincus, Morris Geldstein and Mark Blumenthal to Aaron Stone. 4,056

Merritt, Isabell to William S. and Charles W. Opdyke. 500

McCreery, J. Crawford to James McCreery. nom

Morgenthau, Henry to Abraham L. Newberger. nom

Same to Alfred T. Leward. nom

Same to Charles Weinberg. nom

Morgenthau, Henry to John Whalen. nom

Same to same. nom

Mayne, Charles to Brigitta Neustaedter. 12,000

O'Connor, John C., Jr., to Susan D. Bowers. 12,000

O'Reilly, Maria A. to Sarah Fitzpatrick. 2,910

Patterson, Albert M. exr. Mary M. Patterson to Mary H. Lockett. 4,500

Same to same. 4,500

Poth, John to Mitchel Valentine. nom

Phileman, Frederick to Frederick Gore. 5,000

Ross, Francis H. to Peter Wynen and John C. Heesters. 500

Steers, Abraham to Jennie Simons. 3,000

Schell, Edward trustee of Mary P. Cargill to Frederic A. Brown, trustee of Mary P. Cargill. 4 assigns. nom

Smith, Kate A. to Alfred C. Cheney trustee. nom

Sheldon, Francis D., Jersey City, N. J., to American Surety Co. of New York. 507

Schneider, Louis exr. Anna Schwarz to Frederick T. Hoffmann. 1,000

Schreyer, John to The West Side Bank. nom

Solomon, Morris to Harry Harris. 1,500

Stern, Abraham to Rebecca Zermansky. 4,000

Title Guarantee and Trust Co. to Mary T. Coles. 20,000

Same to The Atlantic Trust Co. 8,000

Title Guarantee and Trust Co. to Joseph F. Fradley. 12,500

Same to same. 18,000

Tigges, John to Mary G. Kugelman. nom

Tuck, Somerville P., New Brighton, S. I., to Edward B. Amend. 1,000

The House of Rest for Consumptives to St. Luke's Hospital in the City of New York. 19,000

Van Brunt, Thomas C. to Alfred C. Cheney trustee. nom

Valentine, Samuel to Minna Weller, Brooklyn. 4,000

Welch, Ellis G., Bergen Co., N. J., to J. Bleecker Miller. nom

Weiss, Samuel to Frederick Robitscher. 5,000

KINGS COUNTY.

SEPT. 3 TO 9—INCLUSIVE.

Augustin, Louisa to Jacob Steinert. $500

Beer, Louis and Michael Schaffner to Babette Freusberg. nom

Brown, William to Herbert C. Smith. nom

Burrell, John to Mary E. Fox. 1,800

Berckmeier, Albert to The Bulmer Lumber Co. 1,000

Betts, Charles W. to Charles A. Betts. 1,323

Same to same. 1,271

Same to same. 4,042

Same to same. 3,025

Same to same. 2,698

Same to same. 1,550

Same to same. 2,607

Same to same. 809

Constable, Benjamin F. to Caroline M. Conner. 1,000

Cronkhite, Elisha P. to Strouse, Loeb & Co., Philadelphia, Pa. 1,587

Crump, Anna E., Montclair, N. J., to Mary E. James. nom

Crump, Anna E., Montclair, N. J., to Mary E. James, Brooklyn. nom

Cohen, Isidore and Simon to Sigismund B. Wortmann. 9,032

Cole, Randolph H. to Michael J. Lynch. 4,500

Dennington, Frederick C. to Agnes H. Davies. 3,500

Donnellon, Cornelius E. to Ezra D. Bushnell. 3,000

Donohue, Florence J. to Alanson W. Adams. 1,210

Doody, Daniel to Stephen B. Sturges. nom

Douglas, George W. to John O. Hoyt, Jr. nom

Fitzpatrick, William J. to Thomas McCann. 4,000

Gillespie, Earl A. to Henry Taylor. nom

Grening, Paul C. to Daniel S. Arnold. 6,500

Hoagland, Cornelius to William E. Valentine. 4,000

Huber, Otto exr. Otto Huber to Herman and Catherine R. Reiners and Henry Bischoff. 4,592

Hyde, Frank to Adolphus Gload. nom

Hyde & Gload Mfg. Co. (Lim.) to Adolphus Gload. nom

Same to Frank Forshew. nom

Same to same. nom

Hartmann, Pauline to Earl A. Gillespie. 325

Same to same. 350

Same to same. 300

Kay, William E. to Hans S. Christian. 550

Kershner, Sophie nee Klinge to The Long Island Brewery. 3,684

Leggett, Thomas B. and ano. trustees William H. Leggett to Margaret L. Foote. 1,700

Levino, Bernard to Walter F. Clayton. 1,600

Levy, Simon to Morris Levy. 385

Leggett, Francis W. and Thos. B. trustees of William H. Leggett to Sarah R. Belden. 8,000

Luyster, Peter exr. Peter Luyster and Catharine L. Fairweather, Cornelia L., Sarah F., Margaret C. and Robert M. F. Luyster to Peter Luyster.
consid. paid to exr. $253 and to others nom

Radde, Marie to Agnes H. Davies. 1,000

Rissler, Charles and Adam Kaiser to August Todebush. 600

Redmond, William F. exr. Ann A. Carpenter to Mary S. wife of Calvin S. Carpenter. nom

Robbins, Richard D. and Eugenia B to George F. Rogers. nom

Schwickardi, Wilhelm to Julia A. Schwickardi. 1,000

Schneider, Elizabeth to The Title Guarantee and Trust Co. 1,500

Smith, Mary W. to Agnes H Davies. 500

Samelson, Samuel and Pinkus Ronginsky to Louis Bossert. 1,440

Title Guarantee and Trust Co. to Matilda S. Taylor. 2,500

Same to John S. Law. 5,000

Title Guarantee and Trust Co. to Robert Reiners and Gesche his wife. 12,000

Same to same. 7,000

Same to Garetta P. Hagemeyer. 6,000

Same to Gertrude A. Barr. 2,000

Title Guarantee and Trust Co. to The Brooklyn Trust Co. 3,000

Same to same. 2,000

Same to same. 2,500

Wood, Edward exr. Edward Tatum to Joseph M. Schilling. 500

Wilson, Emma A. to Jerry A. Wernberg. 381

JUDGMENTS.

In these lists of judgments the names alphabetically arranged, and which are first on each line, are those of the judgment debtor. The letter (D) means judgment for deficiency (*) means not summoned. (†) signifies that the first name is fictitious, real name being unknown. Judgments entered during the week, and satisfied before day of publication, do not appear in this column, but in list of Satisfied Judgments.

NEW YORK CITY.

Sept.

10 Alcock, Maskalyne—John Baehr..... $97 00

11*Adams, Fannie H—Sims Lumber Co.. 561 37

11 Andrews, Proctor H—Joseph Goldstein.......... 60 45

11†Althof, George F—O B Libbey....... 245 63

5 Backer, Abraham—Frank Rothschild 10,410 22

5 the same — Solomon Waxelbaum.......... 30,527 72

5 Belvin, Mary—John Menke.......... 519 40

5 the same—O J Boessneck..... 1,260 19

5 Bullinger, Eugene D—Augustine Smith.......... 238 96

8 Bugbee, Alfred S—Metropolitan Telephone and Telegraph Co.......... 20 97

8*Barcalow, George B — the same..... 30 14

8 Brooks, John—S B Dick ....costs 46 95

8 Bocock, John Paul—Ellen S Anchmuty.......... 252 50

8 Bartlett, Abner, Jr—Edward Fox.... 78 71

9 Bates, Charles F, Jr—Thomas McKay 256 95

9 Boyle, Andrew—Samuel Wilson...... 276 60

9 Bostwick, Charles R—J W Thompson 3,589 62

9 Barnum, Stephen C—E H Van Ingen. 86 17

10 Bechstedt, Charles F—John Bohnet.. 120 79

10 Butcher, Edward—Bernhard Finkle.. 232 86

10 Britton, Morton—J A Britton... .... 520 74

10 Bonnell, John Harper / Bonnell, Tammisin H } Chatham Nat Bank....... 602 50

10 Bagott, Richard H—H W Skerry.... 500 65

10 Bonnell, John Harper—Bank of N Y Nat Banking Assoc.......... 976 38

10 the same—the same.......... 1,642 40

10 Bennett, William J—Joseph Beck.... 393 00

10 Brooke, Charles W—Brunswick-Balke-Collender Co.......... 45 25

11 Backer, Abraham—Samuel Hyman. 14,826 87

11 the same—Henry Rico........ 89,736 88

11 the same—Henry Rice........ 45,929 98

11 the same—Samuel Hyman.... 12,605 39

11 Brown, Andrew B—Hudson River Beef Co (Lim).......... 98 19

11 Bleffert, Mathias—Charles Kunze.... 71 47

11 Beman, Charles H, admr Warren Beman—L L Todd.......... 1,527 21

11 Barrett, George H—A C Littell...... 42 02

11 Blascow, David H—Theresa Schoemann 60 30

11 Barns, Charles Edward—H J Weber.. 365 04

11 Brown, William—A B Smith......... 184 20

5 Coatsworth, Caleb J—L N Lukens .. 221 72

8 Cassidy, George H—J W Thompson.. 331 85

8 Curran, James W—B A Trowbridge. 137 55

8 Crolius, Walter S—Edward Zimmer. 84 03

8 Cohen, Meyer G—Metropolitan Telephone and Telegraph Co.......... 17 18

8 Collings, Albert T—Edward Eustace. 71 95

8 Cairns, John M—T H McArdle....... 76 67

8 Cairns, John M / Cairns, Agnes R } the same......... 494 92

8 Cristalli, Joseph M—W C Wunnenberg.......... 96 56

8 Cronson, Leon—Max Levy.......... 220 50

9 Coen, Edward P—Isidor Hirsch...... 149 03

9 Cushman, Daniel J—Joseph Sawyer. 1,928 49

9 Chapin, Ezra W—E A Wheelock.... 5,109 85

9*Clark, Robert—W C Reeber........ 124 91

9 Clar, Bernhard — Frederick Robitscher.......... 108 08

9 Crosby, George—E H Van Ingen..... 86 17

9*Caunold, Samuel—Marks Rinaldo.... 273 40

10 Cullen, Catherine—People State N Y. 1,000 00

10 Connoro, Michael—Abram Berliner.. 377 41

11 Crennan, Timothy S / Crennan, William } W C Ilsley.... 82 92

11 Caul, James—G W Venable..... .... 143 90

11 Carroll, Frank J—Charles Schlesinger. 727 22

11 Cullen, Philip—D M Koehler.... .... 94 23

11 Clarke, Robert P—Jacob Grein....... 134 95

5 Degirdo, Francesco—Nicola Zegga... 448 37

5 Dixey, Henry E—B J Ludwig....... 763 02

5 Dudley, Russell G—John Fyfe....... 111 26

8 Donohue, John—John Leonard....... 255 61

9 Dolan, Hugh—W C Reeber......... 124 91

9 de Barril, Robert—L H Viemeister... 96 63

9 Dvorak, Joseph—Emanuel Cadilek... 71 72

9 Deppisch, Henry—Jacob Peth........ 67 50

10 Davis, Amelia—J B Ryer.......... 89 84

10 Deutschberger, Friedrich—L S Friedberger.......... 82 50

10 Dwyer, Thomas H—Isabella Rummons.......... 244 00

10 Dew, Edwin—S J Lanahan.......... 1,069 06

10†Dunning, John—H H Thompson 61 13

11 Donnelly, Bernard E—Joseph Rothschild.......... 692 68

11 Dilks, Mary D—W J Ruddell......... 166 02

11 Dolan, Hugh—Jacob Grein...... .... 134 95

5 Eddy, Robert T—L N Lukens........ 221 72

9 Erdtmann, Henry / Erdtmann, William } P M Berger.... 11,948 09

10 Eakins, William R—I R Bruce... ... 1,287 88

10†Ewald, Edward J—Sarah E Ostrander, extrx.......... 78 00

8 Fitzgibbon, Maurice — Metropolitan Telephone and Telegraph Co....... 39 14
8 Frink, Edwin S——the same......... 437 05
9 Fazioli, Christoforo—James Saitta... 107 87
9 Fries, Louie K—Joanna Swayze..... 1,014 18
11 Field, Charles A—Oscar Unz........ 102 95
11 Faulhaber, Michael — Kate Faulhaber........................ 1,665 79
11 the same——the same............ 952 49
8 Galisky, Louis—Charles Falkenberg.. 335 40
9 Gilkinson, James—W K Murray.... 141 66
9 Gessner, William J — Isidore Rosenblath........................ 70 98
10 Gerety, John B—Patrick Gillea. 2,123 74
10 Griswold, Margaret D—J R Churchill, trustee........................ 431 38
11 Gaggin, Joseph J—W B Bunting, exr. 137 27
11 Goldgrabe, Dietrich H — Metta Schutte........................ 443 29
11 Gray, James Stuart—Minnie Rose.... 95 46
11 the same——the same............ 125 04
5 Haldane, Charles—Clinton Liberal Institute........................ 484 66
8 Hartung, Lorenzo R—William Booth, recvr........................ 290 65
8 Hubbell, Charles E—J M Guiteau.... 4,559 07
8 Hissette, Felix—E L Louis........... 308 99
8 Hutton, John W—The Salamander Works........................ 30 37
9*Hirsch, Rosalie—Valerie L Martin.... 2,490 04
9 Huwer, John W—Hower Brooke.... 10 00
9 Harper, William D—Western Nat Bank........................ 543 33
9 Hutton, John W—Joon Bowes........ 326 14
9 Hess, Ludwig—Moses Tanenbaum.... 63 40
10 Henderson, Russell H—J R Butterworth........................ 143 85
10 Hartkorn, Frank—L T Powell........ 168 40
10 Harper, William D / Harper, Tacie McD } Chatham Nat Bank.......... 602 59
10 Herrmann, Alexander—Francis Higgins, recvr........................ 9,516 08
10 Heimerdinger, Berthold M—U S Illuminating Co........................ 435 25
10 Harper, William Durbin—Bank of N Y Nat Banking Assoc........... 976 32
10 the same——the same............ 1,642 40
10 Herrmann, Alexander—Francis Higgins, recvr........................ 5,410 14
10 Hatch, Elias T—J G Van Camp..... 81 52
10 Havemayer, William M—C C Cammerden........................ 29 50
10 Hirsch, Rosalie—H J Libby........... 674 98
10 Haughey, Mrs Eliza—A E Messman.. 100 19
10 Henry, Helen M—Joseph Slevin.costs 1,149 52
11 Hubbard, Edson M—Board of Chosen Freeholders of Union County....... 412 88
11 Hosnedel, Frank—Charles Machovsky 104 56
5 Jerkowski, Marcus—Esther Jerkowski........................ 13,521 91
5 the same——C S Baum........... 5,093 99
5 Jordan, Joseph V—A L Heyer....... 348 25
5 Jewett, James C—Western Nat Bank 775 90
9 Jerkowski, Marcus—H J Hink....... 1,402 85
9 the same——Albert Robertson.... 2,186 14
9 the same——Simon Dessau..... 1,662 09
9 the same——F D Allen.......... 195 84
10*Jessup, John C—I R Bruce........... 1,287 88
5 Kahnweiler, Alfred B—F S Pinkus... 446 00
8 Kellogg, James B—Metropolitan Telephone and Telegraph Co.......... 74 68
9 Keenan, Hugh J—Thomas Roberts Stevenson Co........................ 541 82
9 Kruft, Frederick—Peter Koelble..... 146 24
9 Kanna, John—Henry Eggers........ 124 65
9 Kreutzberg, Henry—Henry Eggers.. 113 05
9 Kruft, Fred—Rudolph Laubenheimer 95 40
9 Kunzenman, Jacob — Daniel Brubacher........................ 156 84
9 Kelly, John—John Bowes........... 605 38
9 Kutner, Jane—Marks Rinaldo. 273 40
10 Kehoe, James R—J M Young........ 94 91
10 Klock, Levi R—E M Knox.......... 220 23
10 Kay, James—Robert Oliver.......... 67 50
10 Kaiser, William—David Mayer...... 813 00
11 Kirkland, William—Sims Lumber Co. 381 37
11 Kinkel, John—Hudson River Beef Co. (Lim)........................ 98 19
11 Kerr, Howard D—William Fischer... 408 34
11 Kiralfy, Elise M—Wolf Dazian....... 474 70
8 Lawrence, William P / Lawrence, Thomas J } J T McDowell... 471 85
9 Lane, Charles H—W H Williams.... 1,086 58
9 Lennon, Edward—Aiken, Lambert & Co........................ 144 34
9 Lemmel, Jacob—Joseph Sawyer...... 440 39
9 Loescher, Louis—August Horrmann, exr........................ 3,911 63
9 Lippincott, Jesse H—J W Thompson. 3,589 62
10 Lancaster, James H—Army and Navy Publishing Co........................ 121 69
10 Lemmel, Jacob—E S Clark.......... 673 60
10 the same——J B Case 1,323 17
11 Leaman, William S—William Fischer 408 34
11 Lowenthal, Charles, exr Fanny Lowenthal—Halsey Fitch........... 297 34
11 Levy, Louis—B M Cohen. 2,452 05
11 Lillis, Patrick—Peter Butterly........ 1,444 98
11 L'Hommedieu, Sylvester Y — Lawrence Johnson........................ 5,044 48
5 May, Albert S / *May, Frida } Ellen McPaul........ 685 47
5 Morsch, Henry—Duparquet, Huot & Moneuse Co........................ 72 65
8 Mills, James N—A C Haynes......... 100 03
8 Meyer, Siegmund T / Meyer, Arthur L } North American Iron Works.. 1,090 35
8 Maloney, D Quinlan—Charles Stern.. 171 66
8 Mandeville, Henry V—L B Lynch.... 3,423 94
9 Morrow, James—G H Stege.......... 227 52
9 Martin, Charles S—Valerie L Martin. 2,490 04
9 Miller, Robert H—Western Nat Bank. 705 80
9 Martin, Ira Kingsley—J W Thompson........................ 3,589 62
9 More, Mary J—E C Cockey.......... 429 90
9 Murray, Walter—Fourteenth St Bank. 118 48
9 Murray, Walter / Murray, Rose Mary } the same...... 576 00
10 Miller, Robert H—Chatham Nat Bank. 391 58
10 Moran, George R—R G Finlay....... 281 71
10 Moylan, William—M F Phelan....... 146 00
10 Martin, Charles E—H J Libby....... 674 98
11 Moeller, Henry—D F Ellis............ 275 76
5*McPaul, John F—Ellen McPaul .. 685 47
10 McIntire, John—Annie C Capowilliz. 77 50
10 McGuire, Cornelius F—Thomas McGovern........................ 91 31
10 McGowan, Thomas F—People State N Y........................ 1,000 00
10*McEvoy, James—Abram Berliner.... 377 41
11 McCarty, Thomas—Charles Bornkamp 13,465 83
8 Norton, Eliot—C A Hewins......... 87 57
9 Nolan, John J—Georgine von Januschowsky........................ 192 98
11 Nerenberg, Henry — Hudson River Beef Co (Lim)........................ 98 19
11 Newkirk, Edgar—William Fischer... 408 34
11 Nightingale, James—Edward His.... 1,074 87
10 Oppenheim, Louis — Morris Shidloosky........................ 108 00
10 O'Sullivan, John M — William McShane........................ 159 00
10 O'Connor, Mary—Robert Hill........ 513 61
11 Oetting, Frederick—Henry Eggers... 76 18
11 O'Donelan, James—Albert Taubert... 259 50
11 the same——the same........... 109 50
11 O'Brien, James—Consumers Brewing Co (Lim)........................ 161 73
8 Pollard, Stoddard W—Metropolitan Telephone and Telegraph Co....... 17 80
8 Porr, Josephine N—A E Crevier ... 518 22
10 Pullen, Edith—F G Smith........... 212 66
11 Peet, Alexander J—R J Horner...... 528 66
11*Paterson, Hugh Graham — Minnie Rose........................ 125 04
11 Queen, Montgomery—State Homeopathic Asylum for the Insane at Middletown........................ 131 53
5 Rudges, Charles—Valentine & Co.... 84 48
8 Reynolds, Michael—E C Heerwagen.. 419 39
9 Rogers, George W—Theresa Henry... 79 65
9 Rasquin, Kneppler—J M Fuchs. 397 75
9 Rice, James—John Bowes........... 605 38
9 Rebers, Henry—Henry Bischoff...... 1,568 89
10 Rendle, Arthur E—J W Beebe....... 254 80
10 Reed, Cassius H—Milton Robbins.... 530 94
10 Reynolds, Jessie—William Crawford. 1,701 00
10 Rasquin, Kneppler—Edmond Stack.. 1,964 47
10 the same——the same........... 1,585 61
10 the same——the same........... 239 14
11 Rosendahl, Albert—F A Schroeder... 880 09
11 Root, James H—Western Nat Bank.. 535 66
11 Richardson, George H, recvr Hawkins & Pearson—Charles Himmesbach.. 978 91
11 Rheinstrom, Joseph—G W Venable.. 339 14
11 Rosenstock, Besse—Julius Somborn.. 568 07
5 Schiff, John—Esther Jerkowski..... 13,521 91
5 the same——C S Baum........... 5,093 99
5 Stenzig, Elizabeth—Anna Barent..... 47 50
5 Seeley, James—J G Powers........... 328 22
5 Stark, Isidor / Stark, Edward J / Stark, Gustave } Joseph Hirsch..... 329 80
5 Stout, Thomas H—J S Decker......... 2,621 00
5*Struthers, Joseph—Augustine Smith. 235 96
8 Schueler, Abraham—Herman Dolinger........................ 244 81
8 Smyth, John M—Edward Eustace.... 71 95
8 Schoenberg, Herman—T P Galligan.. 272 83
9 *Stark, Isidor / Stark, Edward J / *Stark, Gustave } W E Iselin........ 1,285 58
9 Schiff, John—Albert Robertson....... 2,186 14
9 the same——H J Hink............ 1,402 85
9 Sanderson, Thomas—Thomas Roberts Stevenson Co. 541 82
9 Starin, Myndert W—C J Kaskel...... 36 21
9 Spratt, James—Michael Murphy...... 38 96
9 Schmidt, Edmund P—W H Williams. 1,086 58
9 Schneider, Louis H—Press Publishing Co........................ 819 75
9 Steward, John—Thomas Thedford... 86 85
9 Streifler, Jacob—Andrew Zerbau...... 189 43
9 Schwenk, Samuel K—F A Palmer... 1,270 16
9 Staab, William—August Horrmann, exr........................ 3,911 63
9 Schiff, John—Simon Dessau... ..... 1,662 09
9 Satterlee, Livingston—J W Thompson 3,589 62
9 Schiff, John—F D Allen.............. 195 84
9 Sprague, Watson N—J H Lyon...... 221 64
9 Sherman, Evan G—Marietta Ludington........................ 430 30
10 Saul, Charles / Saul, Isidore / Saul, Julius } F C Bill.............. 250 54
10 Shannon, John—C L Volkhausen..... 56 14
10 Sherwood, Frank M—H H Thompson. 61 12
10 Steinwedel, Eliza—L T Lazell........ 332 00
11 Schneider, Fritz—Kate Faulhaber.... 952 49
11 the same—— the same.... ...... 1,665 79
11 Schwerd, Louise—Julius Roubitsheck. 83 85
11 Silberstein, George—C E Feinberg.... 74 43
8 Smith, Frank — The Salamander Works........................ 30 37
9+Smith, Robert—Jacob Rubin.... .... 35 81
10 Smith, Archibald — Philipp Bierschenk........................ 144 94
5 The New and New Haven Automatic Sprinkler Co—W H Cummings 1,949 99
5 Saranac Improvement Co (Lim)—May Herter........................ 2,996 78
5 The Husted Investment Co—W O Wyckoff........................ 131 88
5 The Mayor, Aldermen, &c—Maicho Fortunato........................ 2,500 00
8 Porr Lithographing Co—A E Crevier. 518 22
8 Fonda Lake Paper Co—M M Belding. 1,606 87
9 Fred Hower Brewing Co (Lim)—Carl Ullmann........................ 1,318 85
9 J H Bonnell & Co (Lim) — Western Nat Bank........................ 220 51
9 the same——the same.. .... 497 02
9 the same——the same... .... 543 33
9 the same——the same....... .... 7,548 21
9 the same——the same............. 705 80
9 the same——Bank of Harlem..... 870 00
9 Porr Lithographing Co—J M Fuchs.. 397 75
9 North River Lumber Co—G H Knapp, exr........................ 545 66
9 Electro-Pneumatic Time Co — A M Baker........................ 583 67
9 the same——the same......... ... 525 92
9 Battenkill Paper Co—J H Lyon...... 221 64
9 Marks Adjustable Folding Chair—Marietta Ludington........ .... 430 30
9 Rapid Printing Co — Carsten Offerman........................ 122 05
10 The Willard Metal Co — American Wringer Co........................ 383 00
10 The American Loan and Trust Co—Louis Bauer 3,207 24
10 J H Bonnell & Co (Lim)—Bank of N Y Nat Banking Assoc............... 976 32
10 the same——the same............ 1,642 40
10 Lawrence Curry Comb Co—J M Jaegel........................ 95 69
10 Porr Lithographing Co — Edmond Stack........................ 1,964 47
10 the same——the same............ 1,585 61
10 the same——the same......... ... 239 14
10 John Boutes Sons Co—M D Ross..... 100 00
10 The Standard Chemical Co—Slar Co. 432 94
11 The Harlem Reporter Co—Sheffield Mfg Co........ .... 281 57
11 J H Bonnell & Co (Lim)—Western Nat Bank........................ 535 66
11 the same——the same............ 1,324 58
11 The Mayor, Aldermen, &c—P P McLoughlin........................ 1,565 75
11 N Y & New Haven Automatic Sprinkler Co—John Baehr........ ... . 537 00
11 The Barr Electric Mfg Co—John Dunbar........................ 30 09
11 The Masaniello Society and Laborers Union of Mutual Benefit—Giovanni Libretti........................ 133 83
11 Consolidated Printing and Publishing Co—H J Weber........................ 265 04
11 Benwood Loom Co—Anton Guendel.. 95 70
5 Thompson, James—John Harrison.... 71 21
5 Tobler, Walter Eugene—J D Lynch.. 79 60
5 Teator, Harvey L—Nathaniel Waterbury........................ 106 44
8 Thorne, Charles T—G W Herbert..... 29 50
10 Tiernan, Hugh P—J E Nichols....... 216 11
10 the same——the same........... 175 87
10 Tiernan, Hugh P / Tiernan, Hugh, Sr } the same....... 375 83
10 Tuohey, Michael W—Thomas McGovern........................ 91 31
10 Trevisone, Nicolo—Vincenzo Ruzzi... 54 50
8 Uher, Frank—K M Wallach....... . 47 50
9 Varrelmann, Gustave—P M Berger. 11,948 09
8*Van Emburgh, John A—Metropolitan Telephone and Telegraph Co....... 17 80
8 Van Syckel, Harry L—Edward Eustace........................ 71 95
10 Van Vorst, George W—E C Carpenter........................ 92 59
8 Wogan, John J—Barnston Tea Co (Lim)........................ 95 00
9 Whitfield, George—Adolph Newman. 709 39
9 Wolff, William—Henry Eggers...... 173 21
9 Wallace, William—J M Guiteau...... 317 02
9 White, Robert J—Langdon & Granger Brewing Co (Lim)........ .... 727 75
9 Williams, Joseph M—John Boyle..... 457 23
10 Wemple, Phebe J—Pryce Lewis..... 243 28
10 Wallace, Margaret C, individ and trustee Francis H Wallace—Joseph Slevin........................ 65,490 40
10 Wallace, Mary C / Wallace, Margaret T J / Wallace, Helen M / Wallace, Henry } the same ... .costs 1,149 52
11 Ward, John B—J H Berdan.. ...... 262 03
11 Webster, Harriet B—Newman Cowen 10,581 35
11 Young, Ammi V—Occidental Oil Co.. 283 16
11*Young, Thomas H—Oscar Unz....... 102 95

KINGS COUNTY.

Sept.
4 Aquilar, Ancelmo—J Delmonte...... $187 91
5 Arden, Henry—Title Guarantee and Trust Co........................ 41 80
8 Burke, Joseph F—F A Quintana..... 293 30
9 Burns, Gerald—Howard & Fuller B Co........................ 226 07
9 Breglia, Michele—V Gifuni.......... 39 50
10 Brown, Emily M—B Downer......... 130 10
10 Hoyle, John—M Cohn............... 43 45
10 Barps, Charles E—H J Weber........ 365 04
4 Clift, Thomas—W Schlemmer....... 119 00
8 Cooper, Louis and Anna—W Faust.. 98 41
9 Carroll, John J and David—T Silk... 378 55
9 Conselyea, Wallace A—J E Baker.... 285 11
9 Collings, Albert T—E Eustace... ... 71 95
4 Donaldson, Theodore P—J Machell.. 138 85
4 Dudley, Russell R—J Fyfe.... ...... 111 26
9 Di Giacomino, Rocco—V Gifuni 39 50
10 Eastman, Richard B—Howell & Saxton........................ 727 66
10 Erdtmann, Henry / Erdtmann, William } Berger & Wirth 11,948 09
3 Felty, Albert J—F Emmerich........ 111 10
3 Fielder, D P—Hyde & Gload Mfg Co. 111 74

5 Foulks, Thomas—F Leu.... 94 61
4 Gibby, George A—S A Kelly.... 163 07
9 Gibby, George H—T Silk.... 890 40
9 Gilbert, John—Hyde & Gload Mfg Co.... 439 98
10 Gould, Edwin—C F Hommel.... 494 00
4 Hogan, Cornelius J—G Ihnken.... 112 86
8 Harrington, Frederick—J M Conklin. 330 94
9 Harris, Edward P—Venable & Heyman.... 206 75
10 Harris, Henry H—M E Deyo.... 160 44
10 the same——the same.... 81 05
10 Harris, George S—C F Hommel.... 494 00
9 Johnson, Andrew—C Furgueson, Jr.. 150 63
9 Keenan, Hugh J—Thomas Roberts Stevenson Co.... 541 82
4 Lawrence, Edson—A M Suydam.... 121 47
4†Lyons, "Bernard"—G D Royston.... 87 30
5 Lewry, William J—Kingsland & Comstock.... 37 49
8 Levy, Julius; Levy, Augustus H; Levy, Moses S }—W Lauterbach.. 3,746 25
4 Morton, William A—J Wright.... 136 35
4 Muldoon, William H—J McGrath.... 500 38
4 Meyer, Henry—G F Weeson.... 450 88
4 McCarthy, James — Catharine V. Feurey.... 1,582 60
5 Morsch, Andrew—E Siegman.... 107 78
5 Mulligan, John J—J D Carroll.... 68 05
8 Marshall, William H—G H Smith.... 524 35
8 the same——Christiana Marshall. 419 35
8 McClane, Ezekiel—S Birwin.... 94 25
9 Meyer, Gesene—L Isenburger.... 209 52
9 Mugeno, Guiseppe—V Gifuni.... 39 50
10 McGovern, Charles H—Edison Electric Illuminating Co.... 39 27
10 Meyers, Gesene—I Nickels.... 146 20
10 Marquet, Frederick—C J Warren.... 134 67
8 Nommesson, Carlston—C P Skelton.. 188 50
8 Poole, Albert H—W H Ray.... 29 25
10 Pilcher, Joseph M—C F Hommel.... 494 00
10 Pigot, Michael A—L Schwager.... 77 85
4*Ravel, Augusta—J Delmonte.... 187 91
5*Renton, Fergus A—F Leu.... 94 61
8 Reitz, John—P R Farrell.... 63 25
9 Ryan, Matthew—T Silk.... 138 38
10 Rasch, William E—Boyle & Macy.... 177 89
4 Stroebel, Berth and Frederick—T Mc Gee.... 137 80
4 Schade, Herman—J J Froehlich.... 191 00
8 Scholes, Mary J—J Seeman.... 187 01
9 Seeley, James—J G Powers.... 328 22
9 Sanderson, Thomas — Thomas, Roberts, Stevenson Co.... 541 82
9 Smyth, John M—E Eustace.... 71 95
10 Strauss, Samuel—S Bell.... 167 75
4 Tilmau, John F—C H Tucker, Jr.... 417 72
5 Thomas, George H—Cath Feitner.... 434 22
8 The Greenpoint Turn Verein—C Heidelberger.... 101 25
8 Terry, Julia A—G H Smith.... 524 35
8 Tebo, William M—R Cronin.... 580 86
8 Terry, Julia A—Christina Marshall.. 419 35
8 The Muller Bronze Co—E A Hanson. 288 14
10 The Fred Hower Brewing Co (Lim)—C Ullmann.... 1,318 85
10 The Consolidated Printing and Publishing Co—Henry J Weber.... 365 04
4 Veimeister, George A and Edmund C—J M Weil.... 133 96
5 Vaccas, Michael—J W Hilliard.... 95 75
8 Von Graff, Roderick—G B Adams.... 110 00
9 Van Sycel, Harry L—E Eustace.... 71 95
9 Valenti, Raffelo—V Gifuni.... 39 50
10 Verrelmann, Gustave — Berger & Wirth.... 11,945 09
10 Waterson, George—M E Deyo.... 81 05

SATISFIED JUDGMENTS.

NEW YORK.

September 5 to 11—Inclusive.

American Zylonite Co—Nat Broadway Bank. (1891).... $10,091 80
*Arctender, Arthur—Twelfth Ward Bank. (1891).... 1,042 14
Brown, Michael—Joseph Stein. (1891).... 123 02
Black, Emma M—Mary A Anderson. (1887).. 19 30
Barber, William—United Nickel Co. (1888).... 519 57
Butler, S B—G T Homan. (1891).... 130 00
Blauth, Adam—John Elsey. (1886).... 78 70
Engstrom, Victor—Olivia Nelson. (1890).... 231 95
Foley, Thomas P — Nathaniel Waterbury. (1891).... 202 57
Haas, Bourchard—H B Claflin. (1883).... 863 34
‡Levenson, Michael—Benno Loewy. (1891).... 619 49
*Mandeville, Henry and Henry C—Schillinger Fire Proof and Cement Asphalt Co. (1891). 295 77
McCann, James—J A Weichman. (1890).... 38 54
*O'Connor, John J—Empire State Brewing Co. (1891).... 181 21
Reilly, Bryan—Edward Connaughton. (1891). 80 50
*Seabold, Jacob—Twelfth Ward Bank. (1891).1,042 14
Thompson Co (Lim), Richard—M H Taggart. (1891).... 359 00
United Zylonite Co—Nat Broadway Bank. (1891).... 10,091 80
Woehr, Henry—Charles Reilly, comm'r. ('90). 60 00
Wemple, Henry Y—E W Cutts. (1891).... 224 94
Waring, William—E G W Dietrich. (1891).... 703 02

*Vacated by order of Court. †Suspended on Appeal. ‡Released. §Reversal. ¶Satisfied by Execution.

KINGS COUNTY.

September 4 to 10—Inclusive.

Bailey, Wm Trist—W Jessen. (1891).... $104 74
Same—J McGroarty. (1891).... 300 00
Same—H Albert. (1891).... 235 53
†Cronin, "David"—C Heidelberg. (1891).... 204 33
Linde, Charles F; Smith, Wilmer C }—New York Nat Exch Bank. (1889).... 457 36
Suffern, George—Harriet Y Westlake. (1884). 9,583 83
Sheffield, Thomas B; Sheffield, Thomas }—First Nat Bank of Brooklyn. (1890).... 300 08

Tonjes, Annie M; Tonjes, Louis; Tonjes, Henry }—Morris Heyman. (1890).... 158 01
The Citizens' Ins Co, N Y—P P Baldwin. (1891). 1,583 81
Same——same. (1891).... 89 11

MECHANICS' LIENS.

NEW YORK CITY.

Sept.
5 Amsterdam av, n e cor 19th st, 100x100. C. E. Gates & Co. agt Charles C. Wendel, owner, and Henry Taylor, contractor.... $1,559 88
5 Pelham av, s s, 58.2 e Hoffman st, 25x108. J. M. Reid agt Ida M. Ayars, owner and contractor.... 133 86
8 One Hundred and Second st, No. 302, s s, 100 e 2d av, 25x88. George Gossweyler agt Mrs. Mary Diederich, debtor and owner.. 122 00
8 West End av, No. 501, n w cor 89th st, 24x90. Jacob Wimmer agt George W. and Henry M. Lawrence, owners, and Brinkman Skylight Works, contractor.... 100 00
8 Thirty-first st, No. 48, s s, 150 w 4th av, 25x100. M. C. Foertsch agt —— Daly, owner, and Bruno Ullrich, sub-contractor, and John Vance, contractor.... 76 16
8 Ninety-eighth st, n s, 275 e Columbus av, 25x100.11. Fred. Shoneweg agt Gregory Leahey and Frank Reinolds, owners, and Frank Reynolds, contractor.... 55 00
8 Twenty-fourth st, Nos. 341–345, n s, 271.7 e 9th av, 78.4x98.9. James Gough agt Joseph McFarland, owner, and Frederick Wood, contractor, and Thomas H. Snape, sub-contractor.... 300 00
8 Davidson av, n w cor Highbridge road, 75x75. I. J. Stapleton agt Thomas Thorn, owner, and William Huff, contractor.... 8 10
9 Third av, No. 2313, e s, 99.11 n 125th st, 25x100. W. H. Simonson agt Louis J. Kahn, owners, and Percy Jacobs, contractor, and Roderick J. McDonald, sub-contractor.... 169 93
9 Tenth av, s w cor 71st st, 100x100. Charles Pearson agt Reilly & Co., owners, and Paul Peterson, contractor.... 76 50
9 First av, Nos. 2207 and 2209; One Hundred and Thirteenth st, No. 355 } begins 1st av, n w cor 113th st. Louis Roller agt Theresa Coogan, owner, and Salvatore Marino, lessee and contractor. 278 00
9 Ninety-eighth st, Nos. 220–224, s s, 225 w 2d av, 75x—. Canda & Mathews Mfg. Co. (Lim.) agt William Dempsey and John Smith, owners and contractors.... 5,418 00
9 One Hundred and Sixth st, No. 338, s s, 225 w 1st av, 25x—. Same agt same.... 214 00
9 One Hundred and Twenty-fifth st, No. 332, s s, 249.6 w 1st av, 25.6x—. Patsy Zoccolo agt Morris Spiegel, owner, and same and Henrietta Spiegel, contractors.... 1,140 00
9 One Hundred and Thirty-fifth st, Nos. 5–17, n s, 110 w 5th av, 40x—. Fred. Speth agt Warren B. Smith, owner, and E. V. Fisher and Fred. Meres, contractors.... 147 00
9 Columbus av, No. 766, w s, 75 n 97th st, 25x100. Michael Tobin agt Harry Galway and Elias T. Hatch, owners, and Elias T. Hatch, contractor.... 100 00
9 Fifty-third st, s s, 275 e 11th av, 125x100. Same agt Henry Volkening, James O'Donelan and David Davis, owners, and James O'Donelan, contractor.... 161 65
9 West End av, No. 453, w s, bet 86th and 87th sts. Herman Boqumil agt Homer Lee, owner, and Clarence True, contractor.... 40 00
9 Sixty-first st, No. 303, n s, 75 e 2d av, 25x—. Morris Wolf agt Daniel A. Clarke, owner and contractor.... 50 00
9 One Hundred and Fifth st, n s, 70 e Madison st, 50x100.11. J. F. Pease Furnace Co. agt John O'Connor, owner and contractor.... 150 00
10 One Hundred and Seventeenth st, Nos. 363–365, s s, 100 e Morningside av, 100x100.11. J. L. Stothers agt Moses Samelson, debtor and owner.... 1,500 00
10 Ninety-eighth st, Nos. 220–224, s s, 225 w 2d av, 75x100. Doretta Niewohuer agt Dempsey & Smith, owners and contractors 306 25
10 One Hundred and Sixth st, s s, 200 w 1st av, 25x100. Same agt same.... 275 00
10*Ninety-eighth st, n s, 300 e 10th av, 175x100. August Swenson agt J. W. Hutton, owner and contractor.... 25 62
10 Same property. John Carlson agt same.... 28 15
10 Ninety-sixth st, s s, 70 e Lexington av, 100x100.11. John Madden agt Owen F. McElroy, Jr., and William McElroy, owners, and Clark & Dolan, contractors.... 150 00
10†Leroy st, Nos 57–63, n s, 64x100. John Madden agt Stevens & McElroy, owners, and Clark & Dolan, contractors.... 110 00
10 One Hundred and Seventeenth st, s s, 185 w 2d av, 50x—. J. E. Poole agt pastor and trustees of Little Zion Church, owners and contractors.... 75 00
10‡Amsterdam av, s w cor 79th st, 102.2x100. J. W. Russell agt Susanna Victoria Hagan, owner, and Thomas Osborne, contractor.... 963 60
10 Amsterdam (10th) av, n e cor 91st st, 136.4x100. J. & J. J. Bell agt Edward Smith, owner, and John Carew, contractor.... 167 39
11 Thirty-fourth st, s s, 125 e 8th av, 25x100. Richard Deeves agt Rosalia Schoenberg, owner and contractor.... 190 00
11 Av C, Nos. 78–82, e s, 48.6 s 6th st, 72.9x97.8. Louis Farber agt Congregation Menachim Zion, owner, and same and H. Silbermann, president, contractors.... 2,000 00
11 One Hundred and Second st, s s, 100 e 3d av, 35x100. Architectural Sheet Metal Works agt James Duffy, owner, and same and Michael Duffy, contractors.... 263 00
11 Ninety-sixth st, n s, 70 e Lexington av, 125x100. Clark & Dolan agt Owen McElroy, Jr., and William McElroy, owners and contractors.... 2,100 00
11 Ninety-first st, s s, 225 e 5th av, 76.6x100.5. Richard Hoar agt Bertha Volkening, owner, and R. W. Thain, contractor.... 340 00
11 Seventy-ninth st, Nos. 200–206, s e cor Amsterdam av. L. L. Ellsworth agt Susanna V. Hagan, owner, and Thomas Osborne, contractor.... 943 50

**Editor* RECORD AND GUIDE:

Referring to the lien filed by John Madden against our property on Leroy street we would say that the contractors, Clark & Dolan, have been paid in full for the job. STEVENS & MCELROY.

†*Editor* RECORD AND GUIDE:

In reference to the lien filed against our 96th street houses the contractors, Clark & Dolan, failed to comply with their contract, and have abandoned the same, compelling us to complete the work ourselves. MCELROY BROS.

‡*Editor* RECORD AND GUIDE:

The lien against myself and Thomas Osborne, who has no interest in the premises, filed by John W. Russell for $963.60, is unjust and will be contested. It will be discharged of record by deposit of the money or bonded immediately. My superintendent and the Inspector of Buildings have condemned more than one-half of the lumber for which the lien is filed. This lien will not affect the erection of the buildings in any way, as all my material men and contractors are secured, except as to the brown stone which is to be paid for out of the permanent loan. No person has any interest in the building except myself.

SUSANNA VICTORIA HAGAN.

KINGS COUNTY.

Sept.
4 Van Voorhis st, s s, 100 w Bushwick av, 75x100. G. F. Every agt Frederick Amman, owner, and Amzi D. Vreeland, contractor.... $70 00
4 Same property. The Bradley & Currier Co. (Lim.) agt same owner and contractor.... 869 00
4 Clinton st, e s, 65.6 n 2d pl, 34.6x76.6. William F. and Thomas A. Donovan, of Donovan Bros. agt James J. and Catharine G. Ferry, owner and contractor.... 748 06
4 Sackett st, n s, 125 w Van Brunt st, runs north 100 x west 75 x north 100 to Degraw st, x west 50 x south 200 to Sackett st, x east 125. Same agt Rebecca M. Ferry, Eliza J. Smith and Marion S. Sheldon, owners, and Rebecca M. and Daniel Ferry, contractors.... 3,867 75
5 Christopher av, e s, 200 n Belmont av, 25x100. The Wyandance Brick and Terra Cotta Co. agt Annie Levy Joseph Bergen and Samuel Meschell, owners, and Joseph Berger and Samuel Meschell and Reichert Bros., contractors.... 177 00
5 Warren st, s s, 150 e Smith st, 125x100. James Harley agt Board of Education, Brooklyn, owner, and John C. Carlin, contractor.... 630 50
5 Eastern Parkway, n w cor Osborn st, 45x100. George Covert agt John Power, owner and contractor.... 398 00
5 Herbert st, n e cor Monitor st, 100x200. John J. Kierst agt The Roman Catholic Church of St. Cecelia, owner, The Blue Ridge Marble Co., contractor.... 800 00
5 Columbia st, s e cor Amity st, 100x100. James Harley agt The Board of Education, Brooklyn, owner, and John C. Carlin, contractor.... 435 50
8 Van Voorhis st, s s, 100 w Bushwick av, 25x100. Lewis Finch agt Frederick Amman, owner, and Amzi D. Vreeland, contractor.... 215 00
8 Van Voorhis st, s s, 100 w Bushwick av, 25x100. J. M. Pilcher & Co. agt same owner and contractor.... 460 00
8 Nassau st, s e cor Navy st, 25x75. James Gaynor and William Walters, of Gaynor & Walters, agt John Ryan, owner, and Mattheis Zang, contractor.... 391 60
8 Eighth av, s e cor 11th st, runs east 120 x south 100 x west 20 x south 18 x west 100 to av, x north 118. E. J. Hayes & Bro. agt Wm. Turner and A. V. B. Norris, owners and contractors.... 84 00
8 Third av, w s, 50.2 n 48th st, 50x80. Jacobson & Margovitz agt Solomon Sorein, owner and contractor.... 1,575 00
8 Warren st, s e cor Columbia st, school. Patrick F. O'Brien & Son agt The Board of Education, Brooklyn, owners, and John C. Carlin, contractor.... 1,375 00
9 Caton av, n e cor East 21st st, 125x150, Flatbush. J. T. E. Litchfield & Co. agt Joseph Wurzler, owner, and George J. Craigen, contractor.... 903 62
9 Rockaway av, e s, 100 s Eastern Parkway, 25x100. Louis Bossert agt B Levy, owner, and B. Seermann, contractor.... 857 97
9 Seventh st, n s, 214.1 e 4th av, 68.9x100. Fox & McCarthy agt Mary E. Miller, owner, and George N. Miller, contractor.... 100 00
9 Sackett st, s s, 125 w Van Brunt st, runs west 125 x north 200 to Degraw st, x east 50 x south 100 x east 70 x south 100. Michael Dalton agt Daniel and Rebecca M. Ferry, Eliza J. Smith and Marion S. Sheldon, owners, and Daniel and Rebecca M. Ferry, contractors.... 1,115 00
10 Flatbush av, 3d av and Schermerhorn st, gore block. Charles S. Buell agt George H. Rice, owner, and J. F. Richartz & Bro., contractors.... 130 35
10 Clinton st, e s, 65.6 n 2d pl, 34.6x70.6. Henry McShane Mfg. Co., Baltimore, agt James J. and Catherine G. Ferry and John McGabie, owners, and Donovan Bros., contractors.... 381 56
10 Sackett st, n e s, 125 n w Van Brunt st, 125x100....; Degraw st, s w s, 200 n w Van Brunt st, 50x100.... } Henry McShane Mfg. Co., Baltimore, agt Rebecca M. Ferry, Marion S. Sheldon and Eliza J. Smith, owners, and Donovan Bros., contractors.... 2,190 45
10 Thatford av, e s, 100 s Glenmore av, 50x100. Patrick Creegan and Thos. Lyons agt Morris Handler and Samuel Balson, owners and contractors.... 1,410 00
10 Rockaway av, e s, 100 s Eastern Parkway, 25x100. Louis Bossert agt D. Levy, owner, and B. Seermann, contractor.... 381 34

10 Van Voorhis av, e s, 100 s Bushwick av, 75x100. Edmund Felgenhauer & Son agt Frederick Ammon, owner, and Amzi C. Vreeland, contractor.................... 129 00

10 Dean st, s s, 316.8 w Buffalo av, 66.8x107.2. Charles Blue agt Joseph D. Clayton, owner, and Joseph Hopkins, Jr., contractor.................... 325 00

10 Eighth av, Nos. 361-369 and Nos. 572-582 11th st, being 8th av, s e cor 11th st, 100 on av, 120 on st. Venetian Blind Co. agt Allison V. B. Norris and William C. Turner, owners and contractors 172 00

10 Sixteenth st, Nos. 385-391, n e s, 192.11 n w 6th av, 75x100. Venetian Blind Co. agt William Wingerath, owner and contractor 74 50

10 Seventh st, n s, 297.6 e 4th av, 50.4x100. T. F. Ferguson & Co. agt Mary E. Miller, owner, and Geo. M. Miller, contractor ... 650 00

10 Fourth st, n s, 297.10 w 8th av, 100x100. T. F. Ferguson & Co. agt Roderick Von Graff, owner and contractor.............. 26 10

10 Second st, Nos. 412-416, s s, 177.10 w 6th av, 80x100. T. F. Ferguson & Co. agt Archibald N. McBean, owner and contractor. (Vague lien).................... 64 34

10 Watkins st, e s, 175 n Blake av, 25x100. Emil Reineking agt Mrs. Danancher, owner, and Louis Ratner, contractor.... 100 00

10 Dumont av, n w cor Thatford av, 25x100. Same agt Abram Wolf and —— Goldstein, owners, and Louis Ratner, contractor.................... 225 00

10 Eighty-second st, n e s, 80 s e 23d av, 40x100, Bensonhurst-by-the-Sea. Cropsey & Mitchell agt Mary E. Case, owner, and Henry Case, contractor.................... 794 45

10 Lot at Coney Island, being part of old lot 19A on map common lands of Gravesend, 103.6x285x105.4x265.4. Same agt Agnes C. Durand, owner and contractor.......... 772 93

SATISFIED MECHANICS' LIENS.

NEW YORK CITY.

Sept.

5 Stanton st, No. 226, n s, 50 e Pitt st, 25x—. Adam Haffel agt Adolph Newman and George Whitfield. (Lien filed May 27, '89) $219 05

5 Same property. J. J. Mulry and George Nolan agt same. (May 29, 1889).......... 30 00

5 Same property. W. H. Schmohl agt same. (June 3, 1889).................... 113 46

5 Same property. Thomas Corcoran and William Fuller agt same. (May 21, 1889). 150 00

5 Same property. George Whitfield agt Adolph Newman. (May 31, 1891).......... 1,116 35

8 Washington av, s w cor 161st st. Henry Spoessig agt Clara Kreutel. (May 29, '91) 250 00

8‡Mott st, No. 57, w s. O'Brien & Lavelle agt Isaac Marx. (Feb. 17, 1891).............. 1,009 61

8 Park av, Nos. 1807 and 1809, e s. Henry Taylor agt William H. McCarthy and John Sheehy & Son. (Aug. 14, 1891)..... 8,400 00

8*Sixty-fifth st, Nos. 29 and 31, n s, 175 w 8th av, 75x—. C. P. Lutterloh agt J. O'Brien and Rondel & Hunter. (Aug. 31, 1891).. 12 25

9 Third av, centre line, bet 176th and 177th sts. United Building Material Co. agt Stephen McGowan, New York Suburban Rapid Transit Co. and John Doe. (Feb. 6, 1891).................... 683 38

10 Twenty-ninth st, Nos. 215 and 217 E., 50x100. C. B. Keogh Mfg. Co. agt M. Sheehy and Edward M. Hackett. (Aug. 31, 1891).. 725 00

10 Seventy-third st, n s, 323 e Av A, 25x—. Patrick Holohan agt Maurice Lawton and James McGee. (Jan. 8, 1891).............. 450 00

10*Seventy-sixth st, n s, 200 e 10th av, 75x—. C. B. Keogh Mfg. Co. agt Duncan C. McKinley and James B. Gunn. (Aug. 17, 1891).................... 842 00

11¶*Bleecker st, Nos. 358-366, s w cor Charles st, 100x50. Middleport Mfg. Co. agt William N. Sternkopf and John Kehoe or Keogh. (Sept. 9, 1891).................... 635 40

11¶*Prince st, No. 171 } begins Prince st, n w Thompson st, No. 125 } cor Thompson st, 25x75. Same agt John Doe and William N. Sternkopf. (Sept. 9, 1891).......... 161 64

11 One Hundred and Sixteenth st, s s, 160 w Madison av, 150x100.11. Malcolm & Taylor agt Dore Lyon. (May 26, 1891)...... 5,401 00

11‡Twenty-fourth st, No. 407 E., 25x100. Martin Smith agt John P. Banta. (July 8, 1891).................... 525 00

‡Discharged by order of Court on filing bond.
*Discharged by depositing amount of lien and interest with County Clerk.

¶*Editor* RECORD AND GUIDE:

The lien filed by Middleport Manufacturing Co. against me, on premises corner Prince and Thompson streets, corner Charles and Bleecker streets, and 129th street and 12th avenue, is unjust, as they have not completed their contract. I will contest the lien and fight it in Court.

WM. N. STERNKOPF.

KINGS COUNTY.

Sept.

4 Ocean Parkway, s w cor Av E, 200x300, Flatbush. D. Lewis Grant agt Helen and James F. Graham, owners, and John Erickson, contractor. (July 10, 1891)..... $138 80

8 Central av, n e s, from Putnam av to Cornelia st, 200x100. The Dugan Mfg. Co. agt John T. Barnard, owner, and Joseph Hopkins, contractor. (Aug. 1, 1891)..... 735 86

10 Greenpoint av, No. 198. The Ackerly & Gerard Co. agt Thomas Swain and Fanny Hamilton, owners, and James Stevenson and Louis F. Fischer, contractors. (Dec. 6, 1888).................... 140 00

10 First av, s w cor Wakeman pl, 300x300, New Utrecht. Joseph Marren agt E. W. Bliss, owner, and Rendle Co. (Lim.), contractors. (Feb. 11, 1891).............. 552 13

10 Clinton av, e s, 65.1 n Fulton st, 27x100. James Harley agt Bernard Fowler, owner, and David H. Fowler, contractor. (Sept. 5, 1891).................... 343 22

10 Washington av, w s, 28.3 n Gates av, 25x100. Same agt same owner and contractor. (Sept. 5, 1891).................... 1,001 79

8 Schaeffer st, 300 feet from Central av, 32x91.6x32x88.6. Henry H. Thorpe agt Robert S. Neely, owner and contractor. (July 17, 1891) (Order of Court).............. 151 00

10 Pacific st, s s, 100 e Rockaway av, 102x107.2. Samuel Glazer agt same owner and contractor. (Aug. 18, 1891.) (Deposit).... 250 00

9 Monroe st, s s, 141.8 w Tompkins av, 16.8x100. Stillman Soule agt Sarah J. Thistle, owner and contractor. (Aug. 21, 1891.) (Deposit).................... 677 01

BUILDINGS PROJECTED.

The first name is that of the owner; ar't stands for architect, m'n for mason, c'r for carpenter and b'r for builder.

NEW YORK CITY.

SOUTH OF 14TH STREET.

Elm st, No. 166, seven-story brk and stone building, 25x95.2, tin roof; cost, $35,000; F. Woehr, 224 East 18th st; ar'ts, Buchman & Deisler. Plan 1212.

BETWEEN 14TH AND 59TH STREETS.

2d av, No. 810, five-story brk flat, 25x88.6, tin roof; cost, $23,000; Weil & Mayer, 327 East 51st st; ar'ts, Schneider & Herter. Plan 1209.

11th av, n w cor 44th st, rear, one-story brk building, 25x30, tin roof; cost, $1,000; Margaret Cusack, 601 West 44th st; ar't, B. E. Lowe. Plan 1202.

BETWEEN 59TH AND 125TH STREETS, WEST OF CENTRAL PARK WEST AND 8TH AVENUE.

83d st, Nos. 31 and 33 W., two five-story and basement brk and stone dwell'gs, 20x55 with extension, tin and slate roofs; cost, $22,000 each; F. P. Hauck, East End Hotel, Rockaway Beach, L. I.; ar't, C. W. Lindsley. Plan 1211.

121st st, s s, 80 w Manhattan av, eleven three-story and basement stone dwell'gs, one 16x66.6, four 16x60 and six 15x60, tin roofs; cost, $12,500 each; A. A. Teets, 505 Manhattan av; ar't, J. A. Webster. Plan 1218.

23D AND 24TH WARDS.

Bush st, n s, 200 w Anthony av, two-story frame dwell'g, 22x32, wood roof; cost, $3,750; A. Jesser, 2295 Bathgate av; m'n, L. Williamsen; c'r, W. Haugaard. Plan 1210.

College st, s s, 100 e Hoffman st, one-and-a-half-story frame stable, 21x26, wood roof; cost, $300; W. J. Mitchell, on premises; ar't and c'r, C. W. Vreeland; m'n, P. Levetch. Plan 1203.

163d st, n s, 240 e Courtlandt av, two-story frame stable, 21x36, tin roof; cost, $800; Louisa Widder, 649 East 163d st; ar't, W. H. Berrian. Plan 1205.

181st st, s s, 94 w Valentine av, two-story frame dwell'g, 21x39, shingle roof; cost, $2,600; ow'r and b'r, C. Pitchie, 2987 3d av; ar't, A. Pfeiffer. Plan 1204.

Daly av, e s, 300 n Samuel st, two one-story frame and glass greenhouses, 50 and 70x17; cost, $300 each; Christina Schnaufer, on premises. Plan 1207.

Fulton av, w s, 200 n 169th st, two-story frame shop, 16x20, tin roof; cost, $200; F. Ludford, on premises. Plan 1208.

Intervale av, n s, 258.5 n 169th st, two-story and basement frame dwell'g, 22x40, tin roof; cost, $3,000; J. Corcoran, 978 2d av; ar't, J. J. F. Gavigan. Plan 1201.

Prospect av, e s, 269 n Westchester av, two-story and attic frame dwell'g, 22x33.6, with extension, shingle roof; cost, $6,500; C. D. Ogden, 731 Cauldwell av; ar't, M. J. Garvin. Plan 1206.

Boston Post road, w s, 370 s and 710 n 164th st, four three-story and basement brk, stone and terra cotta dwell'gs, 18x50, slate and tin roofs; cost, $10,000 each; Equitable Life Assur. Soc., 120 Broadway; ar'ts, Boring, Tilton & Mellen. Plan 1214.

St. Georges Crescent, s s, 100 e Cordova pl, one-story frame stable, 20x16, wooden roof; cost, $75; C. Rabadan, Ernescliffe pl, e Jerome av. Plan 1213.

152d st, n s, 100 e Morris av, two-story frame dwell'g, 22x40, tin roof; cost, $3,200; L. Ryan, 530 West 43d st; c'r, W. McEntyre. Plan 1216.

Fairmount av, s s, 447 w Marmion av, two-and-a-half-story frame dwell'g, 20x27, shingle roof; cost, $2,500; Ann Harvey, 249 Arthur av; ar't, R. Roberts. Plan 1215.

River av, n w cor 150th st, three-story brk factory, 200x150, tar and gravel roof; cost, $60,000; L. H. Mace, Williamsbridge, N. Y.; ar't, C. T. Mott. Plan 1217.

KINGS COUNTY.

Plan 1627—Humboldt st, No. 241, one four-story frame (brk filled) tenem't, 25x57, tin roof; cost, $5,500; John Schlenker, on premises; ar'ts, D. Acker & Son.

1628—Humboldt st, w s, 100 s Grand st, one four-story frame (brk filled) tenem't, 25x60, tin roof; cost, $6,500; Leopold Michel, Graham av, near Meserole st; ar'ts, D. Acker & Son.

1629—Hancock st, No. 992, one two-story and basement frame (brk filled) dwell'g, 20x38, tin roof; cost, $2,500; Joseph Collins, 66 Woodbine st.

1630—Bush st, s s, 60 w Hicks st, one two-story stable, 20x30, tin roof; cost, $800; Thos. C. Malon, 174 Sackett st; ar't, H. L. Spicer.

1631—Cook st, s s, 150 e Morrell st, one four-story frame (brk filled) tailor shop, 25x30, tin roof; cost, $3,000; D. Stern, 34 Seigel st; ar't, W. Schmalheiser.

1632—Bushwick pl, No. 274, rear, one two-story frame (brk filled) tailor shop, 25x30, tin roof; cost, $1,800; K. Meyer, on premises; ar't, H. Smith.

1633—Cook st, s s, 150 e Morrell st, one four-story frame (brk filled) tenem't, 25x48, tin roof; cost, $5,000; David Stern, 34 Seigel st; ar't, W. Schmalheiser.

1634—Cook st, n s, 150 w Bushwick av, one four-story frame (brk filled) tenem't and stores, 25x48, tin roof; cost, $5,000; ow'r and ar't, same as last.

1635—Cook st, n s, 150 w Bushwick av, one four-story frame (brk filled) tailor shop, 25x50, tin roof; cost, $3,000; ow'r and ar't, same as last.

1636—Moore st, No. 90, one three-story frame upholstering shop, 25x35, tin roof; cost, $2,000; A. Brand, on premises; ar't, H. Smith.

1637—Seigel st, No. 44, one four-story frame (brk filled) tenem't, 25x50, tin roof; cost, $4,000; L. Kaplan, on premises; ar't, H. Smith.

1638—4th av, w s, 100 s 36th st, one three-story frame store and dwell'g, 20x40, zinc roof; cost, $2,500; Michael Fitzgerald, 221 26th st.

1639—Montauk av, w s, 300 s Vienna av, one two-story frame dwell'g, 20x30, tin roof; cost, $1,400; William Herold, Montauk, near Vienna av; b'rs, J. Pohlmann, Jr., and J. Fensch.

1640—Hicks st, w s, 40 s Bush st, one frame open shed and horse stable, 26 and 60x66, board roof; cost, $200; ow'r and ar't, A. C. Holtgren, 132 54th st.

1641—Vesta av, w s, 63.11 n New Lots road, two two-story frame dwell'gs, 20x30, tin roof; cost, $1,200 each; Fritz Breitenstein, New Lots road, cor Vesta av; ar't, C. Infanger.

1642—Marcy av, n w cor Walton st, one three-story brk storage building, 38x75, gravel and felt roof or tiles, iron cornice; cost, $14,000; North American Iron Works, 88 and 90 Beekman st, New York; ar't, A. G. Thomson; b'r, not selected.

1643—Bainbridge st, n s, 150 e Reid av, one two-story brk stable and dwell'g, 20x44, tin roof and wooden cornice; cost, $3,000; W. Gorman; b'r, C. Collins.

1644—Flushing av, s s, 59.6 w Clinton av, one three-story brk kindling wood factory, 31.9 and 31x49 and 55, gravel roof and brk cornice; cost, $2,800; J. C. Kuneth & Co., on premises; ar't, D. E. Harris; b'r, not selected.

1645—McDonough st, n s, 384 e Tompkins av, one four-story brown stone dwell'g, 22x46, tin roof, iron cornice; cost, $16,000; John Fraser, 44 Rochester av; ar'ts, A. Hill & Son.

1646—Bergen st, No. 267, rear, one one-story brk boiler house, 25x20, gravel roof; cost, abt $150; William Roberts, on premises.

1647—Schaeffer st, s s, 75 e Bushwick av, one three-story frame (brk filled) store and dwell'g, 25x49.7, tin roof; cost, $6,000; Charlie Kappelmann, Gates av; ar't, F. Holmberg.

1648—Schaeffer st, s s, 75 e Bushwick av, rear, one two-story frame stable, 25x20, tin roof; cost, $500; ow'r and ar't, same as last.

1649—Hart st, s s, 180 e Wyckoff av, one two-story frame (brk filled) dwell'g, 20x45, tin roof; cost, $1,500; ow'r, ar't and b'r, C. Bechtel, 190 Evergreen av.

1650—8th av, s w cor St Johns pl, two four-story and basement brk and brown stone dwell'gs, 25x60, mansard slate and tin roofs, stone and iron cornices; cost, $31,000; Phil. J. Dwyer, 628 Carlton av; ar't, J. Mumford; b'rs, Martin & Lee.

1651—Dumont st, n s, 25 w Thatford av, one three-story frame store and dwell'g, 20x40, tin roof; cost, $2,500; ow'r and b'r, Joseph Morris, Osborn st; ar't, A. J. Warren.

1652—Dumont st, n s, 50 w Thatford av, one three-story frame store and dwell'g, 20x40, tin roof; cost, $2,500; Joseph Morris, Osborn st; ar't, A. J. Warren.

1653—Thatford av, w s, 125 n Dumont av, one three-story frame store and dwell'g, 20x45, tin roof; cost, $2,500; ow'r and ar't, same as last.

1654—Thatford av, w s, 250 n Dumont av, one five-story frame store and dwell'g, 20x40, tin roof; cost, $2,500; ow'r and ar't, same as last.

1655—Barbey st, w s, 100 n Sunnyside av, one two-story and attic frame dwell'g, 22 and 15x32, shingle roof; cost, $3,200; F. G. Hoyt, Cleveland st; ar't, C. E. Corby.

1656—1st av, w s, 40 n 57th st, one one-story frame dwell'g, 70x30, felt roof; cost, abt $600; Thomas Manning, 45 Beaver st, New York; c'r, Samuel Ayres; ar'ts, H. L. Spicer & Son.

1657—Garfield pl, s s, 275 w 6th av, eight two-and-a-half-story and basement brk and brown stone dwell'g, 18.9x45, tin and slate roofs, iron cornices; cost, $5,000; S. A. Hunt; ar'ts, Langston & Dahlander; b'r, G. W. Hunt.

1658—Bergen st, n s, 240 w Ralph av, six two-story frame (brk filled) dwell'gs, 17x42, gravel roofs; cost, each, $1,500; John White, 282 Marion st.

1659—East New York av, n s, 95 from St. Marks av, one one-story frame shop, 16x23, gravel roof; cost, $100; Cristina Bormann, St. Marks av, s s, near East New York av; b'r, C. A. Bormann.

1660—Morgan av, n w cor Metropolitan av, one one-story frame stable and shed, 33x25, gravel roof; cost, $180; Jacob Bahr, on premises.

1661—Evergreen av, No. 209, bet Hart and Cedar sts, one one-story frame wheelwright shop, 18.9x25, felt roof; cost, $55; William Coar, 33 Cedar st; b'rs, T. Tucker and E. Clark.

1662—Gerry st, n s, 100 e Harrison av, two four-story brk tenem'ts, 25x65, tin roofs, iron cornices; cost, total, $20,000; W. Meth & Son, 71 Gerry st; ar't, F. Holmberg.

1663—Orient av, No. 8, one two-story attic and basement frame (brk filled) dwell'g, 25x36, gravel roof; cost, $8,000; Geo. H. Remsen, 84 Maspeth av; ar't, F. J. Berlenbach, Jr.; b'r, not selected.

1664—Varet st, s s, 100 e Ewen st, three three-story frame (brk filled) tailor shops, 25x25, tin roofs; cost, each, $2,500; ow'r and b'r, Isaac Horowitz, 185 Ellery st; ar'ts, D. Acker & Son.

1665—Jefferson st, s s, 200 e Knickerbocker av, two three-story frame (brk filled) tenem'ts, 20x57, tin roofs; cost, each, $4,800; ow'rs and b'rs, A. Amann & Son, 1135 Willoughby av; ar'ts, D. Acker & Son.

1666—Seigel st, No. 89, one four-story frame (brk filled) tailor shop, 25x30, tin roof; cost, $8,000; ow'rs and b'rs, G. Levy & Co., Stockton st; ar'ts, D. Acker & Son.

1667—Linden st, s e s, 325 s w Central av, one three-story frame (brk filled) tenem't, 25x57, tin roof; cost, $3,500; ow'r and ar't, R. B. Muller, 37 Cornelia st; c'r, J. G. Hammel; m'n, not selected.

1668—Hendrix st, e s, 150 s Glenmore av, one two-story frame dwell'g, 19x26, tin roof; cost, $1,400; Theodore Stoff, Glenmore av; b'rs, F. C. Jaeger and J. Fench.

1669—Richardson st, n w cor Lorimer st, one one-story frame stable, 14x15, gravel roof; cost, $75; Fritz Westphal, 371 Lorimer st.

1670—Halsey st, n s, 80 w Central av, ten two-story and basement frame (brk filled) dwell'gs, 20x50, tin roofs; cost, $3,000 each; ow'rs, ar'ts, and c'rs, L. J. Lippmann & Co., 142 Eldert st; m'n, H. Allen.

ALTERATIONS NEW YORK CITY.

Plan 1612—Fulton st, No. 157, repair damage by fire; cost, $500; agent, J. M. Jackson, 8 Mercer st; c'r, M. H. Berry.

1613—29th st, No. 422 E., walls altered, new iron roof; cost, abt $5,000; U. S. Illuminating Co., Times Building.

1614—6th av, No. 258, interior alterations and foundation altered; cost, $1,000; agent, P. Kissam, 23 West 26th st; b'r, T. Bailey.

1615—155th st, No. 679 E., extension raised one story; cost, $120; Maria Moritz, on premises; ar't, F. J. Miller.

1616—6th av, w s, bet 50th and 51st sts, strengthened and repaired; cost, $6,000; H. Thompson, pres't, 40 West 59th st; ar't, H. O. Chapman; m'n, Darragh & Co.

1617—141st st, No. 73 W., two-story extension, 18x14, and general repairs; cost, $1,000; D. A. Fitzpatrick, on premises; ar't, M. L. Ungrich.

1618—Broome st, No 297, interior alterations and repairs and new front; cost, $1,300; A. Flisser, 327 East 119th st; ar't, M. L. Ungrich; b'rs, Holleath & Son.

1619—53d st, No. 7 E., two-story extension, 5 and 10x20, interior alterations and entrance changed; cost, $5,000; agents, Rosevelt & Son, 33 Wall st; ar't, W. H. Russell.

1620—70th st, n s, 80.3 e 3d av, one-story and basement extension, 28x41; cost, $6,000; Little Sisters of the Poor, 207 East 70th st; ar'ts, D. & J. Jardine.

1621—Forest av, e s, 47 n 161st st, raised to grade and moved, one-story extension, 22x15.6, interior alterations, walls altered and new foundation; cost, $3,500; A. Rinschler, on premises; ar't, A. Pfeiffer.

1622—Madison st, No. 141, interior alterations, walls altered and new front; cost, $3,000; L. Goodmann, 217 Henry st; ar't, F. Ebeling.

1623—27th st, Nos. 552-558 W., one-story extension, 16.4x30.6; cost, $500; ow'r and b'r, J. William, Greenville, N. J.; ar't, H. E. Ficken.

1624—Av A, n w cor 4th st, interior alterations; cost, $400; lessee, L. Kaufman, 61 St. Marks pl; ar't, Boekell & Son.

1625—Houston st, No. 209 E., interior alterations; cost, $50; C. Boettger, on premises; ar't, C. Lochman.

1626—178th st, No. 669 E., raised 18 inches, one-story extension, 20x14, chimneys rebuilt and new bay; cost, $700; H. C. Meyer, 705 Tremont av; m'n, B. Wilson; c'r, A. K. Royal.

1627—Park row, No. 105, one-story extension, 16.6x18, new front, walls altered, interior alterations; cost, $10,000; M. J. Callahan, 12 Chatham sq; ar't, F. Ebeling.

1628—42d st, No. 244 W., one-story extension, 17.2x11; cost, $1,200; W. H. McLaney, on premises; ar't, J. H. McDonald.

1629—Park pl, No. 25 and Murray st, No. 22, interior alterations, walls and chimneys repaired; cost, $1,000; H. A. Mott and ano., 48 West 59th st; ar'ts, D. & J. Jardine.

1630—Madison av, No. 178, two-story extension, 9.4x13; cost, $1,500; Eliza C. Oakman, on premises; ar't, T. D. Bush; b'r, G. Mulligan.

1631—7th av, n e cor 124th st, walls altered; cost, $1,400; Columbus Market Co., 100 East 60th st; b'r, W. S Jennings.

1632—54th st, No. 351½ E., interior alterations; cost, $700; W. Just, 152 4th av; c'r, A. Sturm.

1633—Broadway, No. 341, repair damage by fire; cost, $11,758; exr. B. L. Swan, Jr., 5 West 20th st; ar't, W. W. Smith; b'r, E. Smith.

1634—3d av, No. 1797, repair damage by fire; cost, $2,000; L. Sinsheimer, 13 East 80th st; b'r, L. C. Webster.

1635—West st, No. 331, raised two stories, walls altered; cost, $3,000; J. T. Pyle, Morristown, N. J.; b'r, H. Getty.

1636—Charlton st, No. 32, new bay window; cost, $250; agent, J. Cuddeback, 194 Varick st; c'r, L. Sibley.

1637—Stanton st, No. 52, one-story extension, 13x10, walls altered; cost, $750; lessee, D. D. Frereks, on premises; ar'ts, Boekell & Son.

1638—106th st, n s, 325 w Columbus av, wall along 107th st front, 250x4½ ft. high; cost, $2,500; Little Sisters of the Poor, on premises; ar'ts, D. & J. Jardine.

1639—11th av, No. 430, extension raised three stories and walls altered; cost, $3,000; ow'r and b'r, C. Shortmeier, 262 West 31st st; ar't, M. V. B Ferdon.

1640—57th st, No. 30 W., walls altered; cost, $150; Laura B. Marsh, on premises; ar'ts, Schastey & Co.; b'rs, Eidlitz & Son.

1641—25th st, No. 418 W., walls altered; cost, $150; F. W. Heucker, 423 West 24th st; ar't, B. McGurk; b'r, J. McKinney.

1642—German pl, No. 640, 23d Ward, one-story extension, 20x12; cost, abt $300; A. Neary, on premises.

1643—9th st, No. 438 E., interior alterations and walls altered for new front; cost, $1,000; E. Jacobs, 57 East 80th st; ar'ts, Kurtzer & Rohl.

KINGS COUNTY.

Plan 854—13th st, s s, 150 e 6th av, one and two-story brk extensions, 50x79, tin roofs; cost, $1,500; Geo. Wessel, on premises; b'r, not selected.

855—Floyd st, No. 238, flat tin roof; cost, $762; Wm. Riebling, on premises; b'r, L. Loeser.

856—Johnson av, No. 604, raised 4 ft. on brk wall; cost, $200; ow'r and b'r, Jacob Schuen, on premises; ar't, Th. Engelhardt.

857—Marcy av, No. 297, two-story brk extension, 22x25, tin roof; cost, $4,000; John P. Heins, on premises; ar't, J. W. Moulton; m'n, M. Smith; c'rs, Jenkins & Gillies.

858—South 5th st, No. 377, rear, rebuild end piers; cost, $25; Mr. Corterem, on premises; b'r, G. C. Quinn.

859—Seigel st, No. 87, add one story of frame, flat tin roof; cost, $1,000; A. Rosenzweig, 347 Van Buren st; ar't, H. Smith.

860—Remsen st, No. 155, two-story brk extension, 23x10, tin roof; cost, $1,200; F. H. Wunderlich, on premises; ar't, G. P. Crohen; b'r, H. H. Vought.

861—Prospect pl, n s, 200 w Troy av, add one brk story at one end, flat tin roof; cost, $1,500; St. Johns Home for Boys, St. Marks and Albany avs; ar't, T. F. Houghton; b'r, P. J. Carlin.

862—Hanover pl, No. 10, one-story and basement brk extension, 20x9.2, tin roof; cost, $300; Louis Bradt, on premises; ar't, J. Fenton; b'rs, W. Kane and J. Fenton.

863—Dean st, No. 1222, two story brk extension, 10x16, tin roof; cost, $775; Stephen H. Mills, on premises; ar't and b'r, J. B. Twaits.

864—Partition st, No. 166, raised 8 feet on frame story; cost, $70; Jane Sharp, on premises.

865—Bleecker st, No. 64, dig out cellar, brk foundation; cost, $200; James Kane, on premises.

866—Washington st, e s, 68 s Johnson st, new smoke stack for boiler; cost, $6,000; Abraham & Dunne, 428 Fulton st; ar't, G. L. Morse.

867—Greenpoint av, No. 287, raised 2 feet on posts; cost, $100; James Liddy, on premises; ar't and b'r, C. Merritt.

868—North Elliott pl, No. 108, new store front; cost, $300; ow'r and b'r, John Gallagher, on premises; ar't, A. Herbert.

869—Troutman st, No. 143, raised 12 feet on frame story; new foundation wall; cost, $500; Mrs. A. G. Heerlin, on premises; ar't, E. Schrempf; b'r, not selected.

870—Herkimer st, No. 1497, one-story frame extension, 10x13, shingle roof; cost, $75; ow'r and b'r, Jeremiah Fulkerson, on premises; ar't, C. M. Thompson.

871—Schenck st, No. 93, flat gravel roof; cost, $100; Margaret Shanley, on premises.

872—Schenck av, No. 204, one-story frame extension, 11x24, tin roof; cost, $150; Martha Yung, on premises; b'r, W. Max.

873—Nelson st, s s, 175 e Columbia st, new brk foundation; cost, $300; Mary Collins, 14 Nelson st

MISCELLANEOUS.

BUSINESS FAILURES.

N. Y. ASSIGNMENTS—BENEFIT CREDITORS.

Sept.

9 Leaman, William S. and Howard D. Kerr and Edgar Newkirk (composing firm of H. D. Kerr & Co., produce commission dealers, at No. 266 Washington st), to Arthur Lent; without preferences.

KINGS COUNTY.

GENERAL ASSIGNMENTS.

Sept.

4 Beaton, Peter to John P. Donnelly.
5 Linn, Edward to John P. Cranford.
5 Smith, Morris H. to John P. Cranford.
8 Boddy, Edward to Arthur Smith.
10 Teale, Robert E. J. C. to Charles R. Braine.
10 Morro, August T. to Charles R. Braine.

PROCEEDINGS OF THE BOARD OF ALDERMEN AFFECTING REAL ESTATE.

* Under the different headings indicates that a resolution has been introduced and referred to the appropriate committee. † Indicates that the resolution has passed and has been sent to the Mayor for approval. ‡ Passed over the Mayor's veto.

New York, September 8, 1891.

CURBSTONES SET AND SIDEWALKS FLAGGED.

Birch st, from Wolf st to Marcher av.†
157th st, from 3d to Railroad av.†

MAINS.

Boulevard, bet 96th and 145th sts; water.†
42d st, bet 2d and 3d avs; water.†
101st st, bet East River and 2d av; water.†
103d st, bet 2d and 5th avs; water.†
117th st, bet Madison and 5th avs; water.†
Park (4th) av, bet 94th and 100th sts; water.†
2d av, from 42d to 105th st; water.†

REGULATING, GRADING, ETC.

Birch st, from Wolf st to Marcher av.†
157th st, from 3d to Railroad av.†
170th st, from 3d to Fulton av; at expense of Henry Zeltner.†

FENCING VACANT LOTS.

107th st, from Park to Madison av.†
Madison av, bet 106th and 107th sts.†
Park av, bet 106th and 107th sts.†

PAVING.

118th st, bet Madison and Park avs; granite block.†
170th st, from 3d to Fulton av; at expense of Henry Zeltner; granite block.†

LAMP-POSTS ERECTED AND LAMPS LIGHTED.

20th st, in front of Nos. 29 and 31 E. } at owners' expense.†
125th st, s e cor Madison av. }
9th av, in front of No. 468. }
9th av, Nos. 371 and 381, in front of St. Michaels Church; four lamps.†

CROSSWALKS LAID.

Birch st, from Wolf st to Marcher av.†
118th st, bet Park and Madison avs.†
157th st, from 3d to Railroad av.†
170th st, from 3d to Fulton av, at expense of Henry Zeltner.†

APPROVED PAPERS.

Resolutions passed by the Board of Aldermen calling for the following improvements have been signed by the Mayor for the week ending September 5, 1891. *Indicates that the Mayor neither appoved nor objected thereto, therefore the same became adopted.

FENCING VACANT LOTS.

90th st, n s, bet Park and Madison avs.

PAVING.

124th st, from Mount Morris to Lenox av; granite block, with curbstones set and crosswalks laid at intersecting avs.

CURBSTONES SET AND SIDEWALKS LAID.

Boulevard, e s, from 63d to 65th st. }
64th st, both sides, from Central Park West to Boulevard. }
Columbus av, e s, from 93d to 94th st. }

ADVERTISED LEGAL SALES.

REFEREES SALES TO BE HELD AT THE REAL ESTATE EXCHANGE AND AUCTION ROOM (LIMITED), 59 to 65 LIBERTY STREET, EXCEPT WHERE OTHERWISE STATED.

Sept.

38th st, No 444, s s, 230.6 s e 10th av, 25x98.9, three-story frame tenem't with two-story brk building on rear, by R. V. Harnett. (Amt due $1,130)... 14

7th av, Nos. 2170-2178, s w cor 129th st, 99.11x75, five five-story brk stores and flats, by R. V. Harnett & Co. (Amt due $27,678; prior morts. $——)... 14

42d st, No. 26, n s, 354.2 w 5th av, 20.4x100.5, four-story stone front store and dwell'g, by R. V. Harnett. (Leasehold; action No. 1; amt due $5,425)........ 15

Same property, by R. V. Harnett. (Leasehold; action No. 2; amt due $10,650)........ 15

85th st, No. 44, s s, 375 e 9th av, 25x102.2, four-story stone front dwell'g, by A. H. Muller & Son. (Amt due $34,026)........ 15

134th st, No. 242, s s, 375 e 8th av, 25x99.11, five-story brk flat, by R. V. Harnett. (Amt due $28,647)........ 15

West End (11th) av, No. 42, e s, 25.5 n 66th st, 25x100........ }
West End (11th) av, No. 44, e s, 50.5 n 66th st, 25x100........ }
West End (11th) av, No. 46, e s, 75.5 n 66th st, 25x100........ }
West End (11th) av, No. 48, e s, 75.5 s 67th st, 25x100........ }
West End (11th) av, No. 50, e s, 50.5 s 67th st, 25x100........ }
West End (11th) av, No. 52, e s, 25.5 s 67th st, 25x100........ }
Six five-story stone front tenem'ts with stores. }
by J. N. Golding. (Amt due on each $10,890)... 15

West End av, No. 347, w s 62 n 81st st, 20x66, three-story brk dwell'g, by William Kennelly. (Amt due $4,217; prior morts. $18,000)........ 15

184th st, s e s, 113.3 s Bainbridge av, 28.7x83.7x25x96.7, by R. V. Harnett & Co. (Amt due $2,263)... 15

184th st, s e s, 141.10 s Bainbridge av, 26.2x77.2x25x83.7, by R. V. Harnett & Co. (Amt due $2,263)... 15

66th st, No. 217, n s, 275 w 10th av, 25x100.5, five-story stone front tenem't........ }
66th st, No. 219, n s, 300 w 10th av, 25x100.5, five-story stone front tenem't........ }
66th st, No. 221, n s, 325 w 10th av, 25x100.5, five-story brk tenem't........ }
by J. N. Golding........ 15

Houston st, No. 351, s s, 18.6 w Washington st, 18.9x50, three-story brk tenem't. 1-5 part........ }
Hester st, No. 211, n s, bet Baxter and Centre sts, runs west along st 24.11 x northeast 35.6 x northeast 66.6 x east 21.8 x southwest to beginning, five-story brk tenem't with stores. 1-5 part........ }
by R. V. Harnett & Co. (Amt due $4,359)........ 16

7th av { begins 7th av, n e cor 124th st, 100.11x125,
124th st { two-story brk market, &c., by A. H. Muller & Son. (Leasehold; foreclos. mech. lien) 16

Cherry st, No. 448, n s, 100 e Jackson st, 25x100, three-story brk stable, by Smyth & Ryan........ 17

27th st, No. 330, s s, 428 e 9th av, 22x98.9, three-story brk dwell'g, by P. F. Meyer. (Amt due $6,479)........ 17

52d st, No. 521, n s, 275 w 10th av, 25x100.5
52d st, No. 523, n s, 300 w 10th av, 25x100.5
Two five-story brk tenem'ts by Wm. Kennelly.... 21
65th st, No. 138, s s, 458 e 10th av, 20x100.5, four-story stone front dwell'g, by Richard V. Harnett. (Amt due $21,242).... 21
Av A, Nos. 393 and 395, s w cor 24th st, 49.5x81.5, vacant, all right, title and interest which Daniel D. Conover had on June 10, 1891, by Sheriff at City Hall. (Sale under execution).... 21

KINGS COUNTY.

Sept.

Jackson st, s s, 100 e Graham av, 25x100, by Jacob Neu, at County Court House.... 12
Hendrix st, w s, 100 s Eastern Parkway, 100x100, two-story frame dwell'g on plot; assessed value, $3,100
Spencer st, No. 166, w s, 78 n Willoughby av, 22x80, three-story frame dwell'g; assessed value, $2,100; partition
by T. A. Kerrigan, at 13 Willoughby st.... 15
Bedford av, Nos. 574-584, s w cor Rodney st, 133x100, three five-story stone apartment houses unfinished; assessed value, $85,000
Lot at Gravesend, begins at Atlantic Ocean at division line bet old lots 22 and 28 on one side and old lots 20 and 21 on the other side, as shown on Kowolski's map of common lands of Gravesend, Coney Island, runs north — x west — x south to ocean, x east to beginning, except strip 40 ft. wide condemned for use of New York & Coney Island R. R. Co., and part lying south of centre of Surf av; partition
by T. A. Kerrigan, at 13 Willoughby st.... 16
Degraw st, s s, 430 w Franklin av, 20x131, vacant; assessed value, $120; all right, title and interest; by T. A. Kerrigan, at 13 Willoughby st.... 17
Gwinnett st, No. 79, n w s, 85 n e Marcy av, 20x100, one-story frame brass foundry; assessed value, $1,900
Pacific st, s s, 480.8 e Rochester av, 16.8x107.2½, two-story and basement frame dwell'g; assessed value, $1,400
Somers st, No. 40, s s, 26 e Rockaway av, 18.6x99.3¼, three-story brk flat; assessed value, $5,000
by T. A. Kerrigan, at 13 Willoughby st.... 18
Georgia av, w s, 175 s Fulton av, 50x100, two two-story frame tenem'ts; assessed value, $6,000; partition; by T. A. Kerrigan, at 13 Willoughby st.... 21
Kosciusko st, No. 404, s s, 291.8 w Lewis av, 16.8x100, two-story frame dwell'g; assessed value, $1,800
Spencer st, No. 87, e s, 275 s Park av, 25x100, two-story frame dwell'g; assessed value, $1,000
Road from Village of Flatlands to the Neck and to Canarsie, n w s, 182.9 n e Hubbard st, 86.3x534.2x87x513.2, contains 1 acre, 5 36-100 perches, Flatlands, two-story frame dwell'g
New Utrecht road, e s, adj land of Protestant Dutch Church and Jos. H. Story, except portion taken for Prospect Park & Coney Island R. R. Co., Flatbush, two-story frame dwell'g; partition
by J. Cole, at 389 Fulton st.... 21

LIS PENDENS, KINGS COUNTY.

Sept.

St. Marks av, n s, 100 w Underhill av, 25x131. William L. Culbert exr. Nathaniel Culbert agt Thomas H. Robbins; att'y, J. Culbert Palmer.... 4
Palmetto st, n w s, 360 n e Central av, 20x100. Mary D. Clowes agt George Walker; amended notice; att'y, Joseph Aspinall.... 4
Roebling st, e s, 75 n North 5th st, 25x100. William Journeay agt Edward McDonnell; att'ys, Jackson & Burr.... 4
Stanhope st, s e s, 360 n e Hamburg av, 20x100. Theodore F. Jackson agt Clara K. Decker; att'ys, Jackson & Burr.... 4
Sands st, s w cor Gold st, 25x100
Sands st, s s, 25 w Gold st, 25x100
Gold st, n e cor Nassau st, 24.1x79.9
Mary A. Brady agt Katie Brady; action to recover dower; att'y, Thomas E. Pearsall.... 4
2d st, s s, 108.3 e 5th av, 60x100. Charles S. Kendall agt John L. Lansdell; att'y, Tallmadge W. Forster.... 5
Sheepshead Bay road, s s, 86.8 e West 5th st, 177x243.11 x west 171 x north 126.11 x east 14.10 x northwest 75 to beginning, Gravesend. August Michel agt Christian Michel; action to set aside deed; att'y, Sidney H. Stuart.... 5
Prospect pl, s s, 150 w Buffalo av, 50x127.9. Sarah Childrey agt John Robinson; action to set aside deed; att'y, J. Stewart Ross.... 5
4th pl, s s, 100 w Smith st, 25x100. David W. Binns agt Michael Daly; att'y, Frank A. Whelan.... 5
Jamaica av, s w cor Chestnut st, runs southwest 147 x west 150 x north 50 x east — x north 106 to av, x east 101.6. William Lardner agt Elihu J. Granger; partition; att'y, Wm. North.... 5
Eastern Parkway, s w cor Vesta av, runs south 360 to Sutter av, x west 450 to Powell st, x north 860 to Parkway, x east 450. Earl A. Gillespie agt The Brooklyn's Limited; att'y, George F. Alexander.... 5
Macon st, st, s s, 355 e Nostrand av, 20x100. Jemima Thallon agt Ellen M. Barlow; att'y, Ira O. Miller.... 8
Putnam av, s s, 218 e Reid av, 114x90. John Heinlein and William Rexer agt John Hennessy; forclos. mechanic's lien; att'y, H. C. Conrady.... 8
Parkway, s s, 350 e New York av, runs south 220.7 to Union st, x east 180.6 x north 228 to Parkway, x west 119.3. John Heyzer agt Mary E. Elkins; att'y, John H. Betts.... 8
Rockaway av, w s, 17 s Hull st, 16.8x75. Sarah L. Hodgetts agt Maria Roberts; att'ys, Jackson & Burr.... 8
Same property. Same agt John Raymond individ. and exr. Jeannette Raymond; same att'ys.... 8
Schenectady av, e s, 92.9 s Herkimer st, 37.5x100. John Andrews agt Irving Fish; att'y, John Andrews.... 9
Montague st, n s, 175 w Court st, 50x200 to Pierrepont st. Watson & Pittinger agt The Brooklyn Real Estate Exchange (Lim.); att'y, J. Herbert Watson.... 9
Gold st, w s, 100 n Myrtle av, 25x100.5. Minna Rufe agt Elizabeth Leiser; att'ys, Rabe & Keller.... 9
8th st, n s, 95.9 e 4th av, 110x100. Hugh J. Keenan agt Paul Geutert; action to establish and foreclos. vendor's lien; att'y, J. Herbert Watson.... 9
Prospect av, n e s, 400 s e 3d av, 25x54.4x25x52.5. Margaret B. Waldron and ano. admrs. John Waldron agt Terence McCormack; att'y, David Barnett.... 9
Macon st, s s, 93.6 w Howard av, 107.6x100. Walter F. Clayton agt Clarence Lincoln; att'y, James P. Philip.... 10
Atlantic av, s w cor Eldert av, 32.1x—x31x111.11. Lazarus Straus agt Dennis O'Neill; action on attachment; att'ys, Nathan, Sondheim & Rothschild.... 10
2d st, s s, 251.9 e 5th av, 17.6x100. Susan C. Strain and Mary R. Murphy agt John M. O'Neil; att'y, John A. Lott, Jr.... 10

RECORDED LEASES.

NEW YORK. Per Year

Delancey st, No. 180. Acceptance of new tenant by landlord. Bertha Levy to David Mayer.... nom
Pearl st, No. 551, basement and one-half cellar. Jane A. F. Frink, Ida F. Willcox and Lillie F. Ward widow and heirs of Isaac P. Frink, Newark, N. J., to John W. Carrodi; 3⅔ years, from Sept. 1, 1891.... $780
Sullivan st, No. 235. John H. Dorn to August Guidou; 5 years, from May 1, 1891.... 1,500
Wall st, No. 56, large basement office on east side. George P. Wetmore to Walter A. Phelan; 3 years, from May 1, 1891.... 1,650
Watts st, No. 66. Thomas C. and Gilbert Oakley, Jr., to Michael Walsh; 4 years, from May 1, 1891.... 870
Same property. Michael Walsh to Denis J. MacGuire; 3⅔ years, from Sept. 1, 1891.... 510
Same property. Assign. lease. Denis J. MacGuire to H. Koehler & Co., a corporation.... nom
West st, No. 371, n e cor Morton st. Marx and Moses Ottinger to Franccis Antoine; 1 year, from Sept. 15, 1891.... 3,500
3d st, No. 100 W., all. Arnold Vogt to Frederick A. Vogt; 5 years, from May 1, 1891.... 1,600
17th st, No. 9 E., parlor floor store. Margaret D. Griswold to Sebastian Sommer; 8¾ years, from Sept. 1, 1890.... 1,200, 1,500
34th st, No. 346 E., store. Thomas Murtha agent to C. F. Reibetanz; 3 years, from Sept. 1, 1891.... 180
36th st, No. 28 W., all. Almon W. Griswold to Robert C. Myles; 4 11-12 years, from Nov. 1, 1890.... 3,500
37th st, Nos. 343 and 345 W., first floor front and rear
37th st, Nos. 341, 343 and 345 W., basement and second and third floors
George F. Kek to John H. Ruhle and William H. Schleicher; 2 years, from Sept. 1, 1891.... 1,800
42d st, Nos. 53, 55, 57 and 59 W., all. The New York Real Estate and Building Improvement Co. to John P. Hayward, Mt. Vernon, New York; 3¼ years, from June 1, 1891, taxes, &c, and.... 7,500
50th st, No. 429 W., store, two rear rooms and part basement. Barbara Kay to Herman H. Rodewald; 5 years, from May 1, 1890.... 504
58th st, No. 356 W., all. George B. Frisbee to Gustavus A. Cohen; 3 years, from Oct. 1, 1891.... 1,900
59th st, No. 329 E., store floor. Thomas Golden, Patchogue, L. I., to Michael O'Connell; 3 years, from May 1, 1891.... 180
Same prop t . Assign. lease. Michael O'Connellto Denis O'Connor.... nom
120th st, No. 143 E., all. John Keirns to Edward F. Michaels; 4⅔ years, from Sept. 1, 1891.... 1,500
Amsterdam av, No 148, store and basement. W. Ruck to Margaret Sullivan; 2 years, from May 1, 1891.... 540
Park av, No. 1681, store and front basement. Gustave S. Boehm to Bernard J. Kavanagh; 10 years, from Sept. 1, 1891.... 1,000, 1,100, 1,200
Washington av, No. 1011, first floor and bake shop. Charles Zimmermann to Frederick Paschke; 5 years, from Sept. 1, 1890.... 300, 360
2d av, No. 877, store and basement. William Brandes to Thomas Prendeville; 5 years, from May 1, 1889.... 1,400, 1,500
Same property. Assign. lease. Thomas Prendeville to George Zimmerman.... nom
2d av, s w cor 40th st, store floor and front cellar. Thomas J. McCahill, Larchmont, N. Y., to John W. and James P. Foley; 5 years, from May 1, 1891.... 1,500
2d av, No. 689, and Nos. 201 and 203 East 41st st, all. Louise Immen to Henry C. Granneman; 4 11-12 years, from June 1, 1891.... 2,400, 2,500
Same property. Assign. lease. Henry C. Grannemann to M Godfrey and Dennis Howard; Sept. 1. ichael.... 2,800
3d av, No. 712, store and basement. David Moss and Morris Goldstein to Bernard D. Coyle; 5 years, from May 1, 1891.... 1,200
3d av, No. 1251, n e cor 72d st. Henry S. Strauss to Anna M. wife of Peter Hemmer, Jr.; 5⅔ years, from Sept. 1, 1891.... 4,000, 3,000
3d av, No. 2082. Oliver H. P. Archer to Bertha Solomon; 5⅔ years, from Sept. 1, 1891.... 2,000
6th av, No. 413, store and basement. Heyman Harris to Frederick W. Smith; 4⅔ years, from Sept 1, 1890.... 2,800
9th av, No. 602, n e cor 43d st. John Nugent to Patrick M. Brady and Michael Farrell; 7 years, from Nov. 1, 1891.... 2,800

CHATTELS.

Note.—The first name, alphabetically arranged, is that of the Mortgagor, or party who gives the Mortgage. The "R" means Renewal Mortgage.

NEW YORK CITY.

SEPTEMBER 4 TO 10.—INCLUSIVE.

SALOON AND RESTAURANT FIXTURES.

Arfmann, John, 464 E 144th....A Hupfel's Sons. (R) $800
Aufenanger & Schwarne. 91 Broad....J Aufenanger. 1,000
Barnes, J J. 1372 3d av....Bernheimer & S. (R) 2,000
Berger, Louis. 554 W 47th....Bachmann B Co. (R) 600
Berger & Wolken. 143 Broome....Steinhardt Bro & Co. (R) 1,518
Byrne, P J. 48 Peck slip....I Roth. 900
Brady & Farrell. 602 9th av....J Nugent. 3,450
Same....Bernheimer & S. 2,500
Same....J Nugent. 3,450
Barkhausen, August. 225 Bowery....W Peter B Co. 1,500
Binder, Rudolph. 610 Grand....Claus Lipsius B Co. (R) 3,000
Brandenburg, T. 192 East Houston....Claus Lipsius B Co. (R) 300
Brengel, Jacob. 7 1st av....J Eppig. (R) 605
Cashin, Patrick. 870 8th av....H Elias B Co. 5,000
Cashman, Thomas. 441 W 53d....Ph Schaefer & Son. (R) 408
Cashman & O'Keefe. 207 W 64th....D Stevenson. (R) 700
Christie, George. 318 11th av....V Loewers. (R) 239
Coen & Fonnan. 329 Bleecker....Rubsam & H B Co. (R) 1,000
Corrodi, J W. 551 Pearl....J Ruppert. 1,500
Cuzze & Florio. 322 E 104th....Bernheimer & S. Pool Table. (R) 135
Daubermann, Gottfried. 207 Av C....G Ringler & Co. 1,100
Daucher, Jacob. 73 Broome....J Ruppert. 5:0
Deile, Herman. 336 E 5th....Anchor B Co. (R) 300
Dorsch, H G. 127 W 67th....C Stein. (R) 3,000
Decker, Mary J. 4 Macdougal....S D Barnes. Restaurant Fixtures. 400
Deyerberg, H H. 27 10th av....C Iba. Pool Fixtures. 200
Same....F Melzer. Pool Fixtures. 175
Dwyer, T H. 105 Clinton pl....W Mason. 1,500
Ehrhardt, John. 1885 1st av....G Ehret. 2,000
Fierz, Jacob. 22 1st av....G Pfitzmayer. (R) 479
Flynn, Edward. 9 Bowery....S Liebmanns Sons B Co. (R) 1,500
Fricke, William. 71 Pearl and 38 Stone....G Ehret. (R) 2,000
Fuchs, J G. 1110 2d av....G Ringler & Co. 600
Franz, Charles. 191 East Houston....E Ochs. 875
Flueck, John. 227 E 42d....Claus Lipsius B Co. (R) 1,000
Same. 18 Crosby....same. (R) 1,500
Gelb, Morris. 219 Delancey....Burger & H B Co. (R) 600
Garbade, Louis. 91 Walker....S Liebmanns Sons B Co. 700
Gelb, Samuel. 711 E 5th....J & M Haffen. 600
Giles, P J. 880 8th av....W L Flanagan. 1,028
Gluck, Gustav. 319 W 17th....J C G Hupfel B Co. 620
Godfrey & Howard. 689 3d av....P Doelger. 1,000
Goebel, Julia. 315 Canal....Lembeck & Betz. 500
Gorman, William. 344 Madison....Fitzgerald B Co. (R) 300
Gross, Amalia. 34 2d av....J H Betts. Restaurant Fixtures. 250
Guterding, Jacob. 48-52 Orchard....A T Cornell. (R) 900
Hagemeyer, J A. 259 8th av....Windolph & Co. 19,500
Halohan, James. 852 11th av....H Wagner & Co. Pool Table. (R) 16
Hangen, Charles. 145 8th....S Liebmanns Sons B Co. (R) 1,000
Heiser, Michael. 310 E 80th....Bernheimer & S. 800
Hemmer, Anna M. 1251 3d av....G Ehret. 4,000
Herman & Schulz. 136 Beekman....S Liebmanns Sons B Co. 500
Hess, Peter. 143 Sullivan....J Altenburger, exr of. 1,500
Same....Bernheimer & S. 1,000
Holian & Maul. 411 Broadway....G Ehret. 1,500
Healy, Denis. 2058 1st av....A Hupfels Sons. 300
Jansen, J G. 742 7th av....G Ehret. (R) 3,000
Jansen, Theodore. 33 Stanton....G Ringler & Co. (R) 800
Jung, Gottlieb. 1144 1st av....Bernheimer & S. 2,000
Kelly, John. 334 E 61st....Mutual B Co. 531
Kasche, William. 17 Dutch....J Ruppert. (R) 350
Kavanagh, B J. 1681 Park av....G Ehret. 2,000
Same....S C Boehm Co. 1,000
Kempler, Harman. 31 Willett....Feigenspan B Co. 700
Kentner, U C. 212 Centre....J Ruppert. (R) 355
Kettner, J and J R. 272 E 3d....S Liebmanns Sons B Co. (R) 1,200
Klein, J and J. 33 Dey....India Wharf B Co. 450
Koch & Ruge. 2 Burling slip....J Hoffman B C. 650
Karp, Daves. 9 Essex....Feigenspan B Co. 500
Luhring, J H. 253 Centre....Beadleston & W. (R) 800
Lieb, Thos. 512 E 6th....G Ehret. (R) 400
Lilienthal, G F. 166 Maiden lane....Rubsam & H B Co. (R) 1,225
Lebkirchner, Jacob. 234-238 E 39th....J C G Hupfel B Co. 7,000
MacGuire, D J. 68 Watts....H Koehler & Co. 600
Manisof, Simon. 152 Stanton....Rubsam & H B Co. (R) 1,000
Michaels, Abram. 145 Ridge....H Steinhardt. (R) 400
Moisset, F A. 279 and 281 Greenwich....A Scharf. Hotel Fixtures. 800
Maguire, W E and M G. 653 Hudson....G Ehret. (R) 3,000
Maher, John. 374 10th av....Knickerbocker B Co. 575
Mass, H A. 9 Thames....American Guarantee Assoc. Restaurant Fixtures. 250
McAleer, John. 49 Broome....W Ulmer. (R) 400
McBridge, John. 108 Av D....S Liebmann's Son B Co. (R) 1,150
McCaffery, William. 1029 2d av....D Stevenson. 1,450
McElroy, James. 439 W 32d....Bavarian B Co. 600
McGorry, Felix. 418 3d av....F & M Schaefer B Co. (R) 1,500
McLaughlin, Cormack. 549 W 59th....W G Abbott. (R) 300
Miller, John. 1983 7th av....Bernheimer & S. (R) 2,000
Morrison, Michael. 1290 3d av....J Ruppert. (R) 1,700
Murphy, Arthur. 187th st and Jerome av....Bishop & B Co. 85
Maier, John. 1779 1st av....G Ehret. (R) 1,100
McCormick, M T. 425 W 31st....F Munch Brewery. 500
McKeon & Buckley. 1329 3d av....E Higgins. (R) 4,500
Muller, Henry. 431 7th av....G Ehret. (R) 500
Nixon, Claudius. 423 E 22d....Eagle Brewery. Saloon Pump. 87
O'Connor, Dennis. 329 E 59th....P Doelger. 600
Passchovitz, Moses....G Gerzog. Restaurant Fixtures. 100
Paterno, Domenico. 163 Hester....Feigenspan B Co. 150
Quinn, John. 352 Madison....Burr B Co. (R) 225
Redington, J F. 1469 Broadway and 153 W 42d....G Ehret. (R) 10,500
Richard & Albert. 668 8th av....Bishop & B Co. 150
Roth, Adam. 657 10th av....V Loewers. (R) 1,500
Ruppel, G g . 1548 Broadway....E McKee, exr ofeor e 366
Reeb, William. 155 Alexander av....J Ruppert. 1,800

Ryan, Edmund. 23 Chatham sq....O Huber Brewery. 6,500
Rettstadt, Henry. 212 South....Bavarian B Co. 600
Robertson, Alex. 407 3d av .. J H Bereuter. Pool Table. 140
Schacht, Mary. 421 E. 14th....Claus Lipsius B Co. (R) 900
Scharrenbeck & Heiser. 1859 Washington av ....A Hupfel's Son. 2,500
Schmidt, August. 214 E 4th....V Loewers. 418
Sambach, G J. 95 1st ...S Liebmann's Sons B Co. (R) 250
Schmid, Louis. 504 E 14th....Ph Schaefer & Son. (R) 500
Schmidt, E J. 444 Willis av....H Zeltner. (R) 1,000
Schmieder, Karl. 130 Willett....D Stevenson. 200
Senn, Otto. 526 10th av....V Loewers. (R) 408
Sexton, William. 1292 Broadway....Brunswick-B-C Co. Billiard Table, &c. (R) 6,306
Storch, August. 100 E 107th....H Fulling. (R) 1,989
Weil, David. 390 Madison....M T Garvey. 70
Wagner, Fred. 137 W 28th....J R Berbling. 2,000
Wagner & Artigo. 137 W 28th....G Ehret. 4,000
Same....same. A Ruehl. 2,000
Weiser, Anna. 482 E 76th.... J Ruppert. 400
Weber, F D. 128 Manhattan ...G Ehret. (R) 1,000
Wolff, V H. 15 Washington....Peter Schoenhafen B Co. 1,500
Zalisch, Joseph. 77 Eldridge....E Ochs. 650
Zorn, Augusta. 546 9th av....J Ruppert. 1,300
Zimmermann, George. 877 2d av.... W L Flanagan. 2,000

HOUSEHOLD FURNITURE.

Ackermann, Carrie B. 369 Lenox av ...Dreisacker & Co. 192
Albert, Emily. 123 W 15th.... J Moriarty. 318
Allen, G W and A S. 157 W 44th....E C Hinsdale. 130
Anderson, Emma. 224 Lexington av....J Moriarty. 208
Archibald, C H. 150 E 27th.... J Foulke, Jr. 174
Arnold, Dora. 266 W 39th....J Baumann. 326
Arnold, Dora. 266 W 39th....J Baumann. 382
Annis, Annie. 145 Essex....H Thoesen. 213
Arlington, J E, Mrs. 145 W 53d....J J Coogan. (R) 459
Beairds, John, Mrs. 237 E 29th....J J Coogan. 184
Bischoff, W, Mrs. 31 1st....J J Coogan. 240
Briggs, R M. 1675 Lexington av....W E Wheelock & Co. Piano. 190
Burns, Mary. 204 E 45th....L Baumann. 112
Begemann, Ella. 10 Beach....F Hoppe. 500
Belmont, Minnie. 227 W 15th....L Baumann. 160
Bennett, Edith L. 1607 Lexington av....R M Walters. Piano. (R) 137
Beringer, Carl. 45 E 112th....L Baumann. 254
Bettoni, Giovanni. 136 Eldridge....J Gregg & Co. 155
Bick, F H. 347 E 41st.... L Baumann. 193
Bolstridge, Caroline. 1634 East End av.... Amer Guar Assoc. 100
Boynton, Florence. 1556 Broadway....L Baumann. 276
Bartley, Sarah J. 59 W 98th....F G Smith. Piano. (R) 230
Bayer, Catherine. 622 E 141st....Jordan & M. (R) 120
Blake, Mabel. 145 W 53d....Alexander Bros. 1,340
Cabbell, Mrs C. 302 W 40th....McClain, S & Co. 168
Caceres, H D and M. 165 E 107th....E C Hinsdale. 180
Cadwell, C H. 109 W 62d....L Baumann. 179
Carroll, Bridget. 150th st and 7th av....P McCabe. 398
Carroll, T W. 388 E 86th....L Baumann. 137
Chalett, C de R. 48 W 21st....H Thoesen. 114
Churchill, Lillie. 207 E 14th....J Baumann. 333
Clifton, Viola. 228 W 26th....J Baumann. 431
Close, M J. 145 E 16th....Jordan & M. 709
Corrigan & Gillway. 205 E 14th....Jordan & M. 161
Cronk, M B. 1798 3d av....J Hoey. 350
Christ, Sebastian. 535 W 110th.... H Thoesen. 977
Clark, Nina. 250 W 43d .. L Baumann. 1,333
Covington, T H. 145 W 41st....O'Farrell & Co. 501
Clark, Stanley, Mrs. 403 W 42d....H Thoesen. 289
Clausman, Emile. 206 W 41st....W E Wheelock & Co. Piano. 300
Cobb, Hannah. 432 E 120th....L Baumann. 118
Cook, Eliza J. 141 E 12th....Jordan & M. 127
Darby, Thos. 69 E 114th....J J Coogan. 213
Darcey, Ellin. 215 W 66th.... H Thoesen. 152
Donnelly, H W. 226 E 21st....J J Coogan. 203
de Rancourt, Cora. 110 W 39th.... L Baumann. 621
Downing, M E. 594 E 134th....F G Smith. Piano. (R) 265
De Prato, Antonio. 226 Lexington av....L Baumann. 135
Deutschberger, F & L. 108 W 42d....American Guarantee Assoc. 300
Dickson, Annie. 250 W 41st....L Baumann. 154
Edwards, Marie. 108 E 8th....J Moriarty. 108
Farnham, F W. 300 W 120th .. J Baumann. 163
Fee, D J. 1117 10th av....J Baumann. (R) 140
Foley, Mamie. 487 10th av.... L Baumann. 117
Foster, Kate. 200 W 41st....L Baumann. 173
Foster, Victorine A. 63 W 92d....F G Smith. Piano. (R) 315
Friend, Lena. 314 E 56th....Alexander Bros. (R) 332
Friedman, S V. 234 W 51st....J Baumann. 470
Fairbanks, F. 140 E 48th....L Baumann. 159
Fowler, Clara A. 196 3d av....H Thoesen. 182
Gray, Hattie. 252 W 43d....I M Finkelstein. 370
Gibson, Edward. 159 W 41st....J F Doherty & Co. 125
Garside, Lizzie W. 250 W 123d....F G Smith. Piano. (R) 130
Geldern, Joseph. 84 E 3d....H Thoesen. 107
Gordon, G E. 350 E 74th....Alexander Bros. 134
Grinnon, Mrs J. 355 W 53d....Alexander Bros. 192
Horacek, Anna. Mt Hope, N Y City and 1685 Weeks st .. F G Smith. Piano. (R) 225
Howard, Mary F. 143 W 53d and 104 W 52d.... H Schnitzer. 300
Hendricks, S E. 424 E 116th .. W Weed. 250
Hendrickson, May. 309 3d av....Jordan & M. (R) 136
Hickey, D D. 226 E 28th....J Baumann. 382
Hunt, E H. 408 W 17th....L Baumann. 124
Huntley, J W. 149th st and Prospect av....A Moebus. (R) 500
Hackshall, Walter. 10th st and Hudson River ....L Baumann. 300
Hart, John. 344 1st av....J J Coogan. 126
Hausis, Dora. 265 W 19th....L Baumann. 125
Hope, John. 655 2d av ...L Baumann. 126
Jackson, J L and I. 82 E 81st ...Commercial Credit Co. 1,260
Jones, C H. 119 W 104th....J Baumann. 179
Kaiser, Pauline. 23 2d....P Kaiser. 276
Kiernan, Mary. 487 E 13th....J J Coogan. 208
Lewis, Annie. 84 W 3d....H Israel & Sons. 536
Livingston, Lizzie. 927 Broadway....L Baumann. 126
Lonrey, Annie. 357 E 10th....W E Wheelock & Co. Piano. 225
Lynch, J E. 77 E 108th.... H Thoesen. 110
Lenihan, W H. 20 Bedford....W J Ruddell. 179
Levy, Henrietta. 216 E 75th....J Baumann. 166
Madden, Margaret. 789 2d av ...H Thoesen. 137
McCarty, Julia L. 378 2d av ...H Mannes & Son. 140
McMahon, Kate. 318 E 57th .. L Baumann. 227
Meeks, Margaretta A. 224 E 49th....S Green. 215
Menne, Mary. 22 Van Dam.... Krakauer Bros. Piano. 260
Middleton, Mollie. 242 W 41st....J F Doherty. 145
Miller, Lena. 422 W 47th....J F Doherty & Co. 238
Milliken, Mary J. 211 W 53d....C M Mathews. 100
Murphy, James. 466 W 150th....J Gregg. 128
McKenna, P J. 53 Leroy....N Y F Co. 125
Murphy, Mary. 222 E 103d....Jordan & M. 134
Meeks, Annie. 167 W 22d....L Baumann. 984
Miller, B A. 33 Grove....J H Walker. Piano. 150
Mulholland, Katie. 106 W 17th....J Baumann. 165
Nelson, Nellie. 118 W 56th....O'Farrell & Co. 379
Nienstadt, Lena. 136 W 15th....Jordan & M. (R) 171
Nitcher, Alfred. 41 Attorney....H Mannes & Son. 150
O'Brien, J J. 74 New Chambers....Dreisacker & Co. 150
O'Brien, Mary. 39 Carmine....W J Ruddell. 155
Oegele, Fred. 1262 2d av....J Baumann. 346
Pepper, D and L K. 205 W 95th.. E C Hinsdale. 250
Pappenheimer, Lizzie. 113 W 56th....F G Smith. Piano. (R) 340
Rogers, Agnes. 406 W 25th.... O'Farrell & Co. 170
Reiss, Max. 16 E 8th ...Krakauer Bros. Piano. (R) 180
Rushmore, A E and J F. Storage....J J Trapp. 200
Sanderson, Bessie. 152 W 32d....W J Ruddell. 345
Bauer, E M and L. 123 E 58th....American Guarantee Assoc. 1,000
Seaton, Julia S. 224 E 10th....F S House. 1,000
Sharkey, Libbie. 113 W 56th....J Baumann. (R) 222
Same. 112 W 10th.... J Baumann. (R) 222
Sharpe, E E. 319 W 54th....J Baumann. (R) 203
Sinclair, Rose. 790 6th av....H Mannes & Son. 808
Snyder, J I and T....G W Vultee. (R) 100
Starace, Clelia. 231 E 13th....C E Pierce. 130
Storms, Jennie. 214 E 75th....J Baumann. 162
Summer, Hattie. 18 1st....E Weiss. 800
Swann, Louise. 38 W 67th....O'Farrell & Co. 133
Samuels, Cecelia. 10 E 85th ..Jordan & M. (R) 216
Schneider, Anna. 229 E 14th ...J Moriarty. (R) 242
Schnurer, Henry. 159 E 118th .. N Y F Co. (R) 144
Scott, J R. 319 W 116th....F G Smith. Piano. (R) 350
Slattery, John. 26 Henry....J Shilansky. 168
Schley, Geo. 174 W 96th....L Baumann. 116
Sheridan, W B. 312 E 25th.. .Manges Bros. 265
Smith, Mary. 21 Montgomery....W E Wheelock & Co. Piano. (R) 140
Slattery, M J. 172 E 88th....J J Coogan. (R) 149
Strycker, Mary F. 346 W 32d....L Baumann. 110
Taylor, Mary. 221 E 59th....Jordan & M. 327
Travis, H J. 2310 Monroe av....L Baumann. 171
Treanor, Patrick. 676 E 11th ...L Baumann. 225
Tucker, Elizabeth. 117 W 45th....T Willis. 505
Taub, Emma L. 133 E 118th....Alexander Bros. 100
Talcott, Frances L. 29 E 22d....G Colgate exr of. (R) 6,500
Theiss, Lizzie. 229 W 15th....J Moriarty. 267
Thompson, Frances. 142 W 103d....L Baumann. 173
Thorpe, Annie. 1588 1st av....J Moriarty. 211
Tobin, D H. 438 W 23d....H Mannes & Son. 672
Toy, Laura A. 325 W 57th....Bloomingdale Bros. 802
Tuttle, Madeline. 2292 2d av.... Bollermann & Son. Piano. 180
Vangelder, Katie. 29 East Broadway....Jordan & M. 192
Van Pelt, Emma. 222 E 84th.... B Fischer & Co. Piano. 400
Van Sanford, Reuben. 1488 Amsterdam av....L Baumann. 214
V Odress, Ella. 23 Forsyth....H Thoesen. 217
Willard, S H. 14 E 125th....E E Barkelew. 550
Walden, Grace. 151 16th ...J Gregg & Co. 110
Ward, Nettie. 1439 Lexington av....J Baumann. 136
Watts, Marion. 266 W 89th ...L Baumann. 113
Webb, H R and Z B. 347 W 22d....L Fitzgerald. 170
Werdenschlag, Abe. 497 Lexington av....J Baumann. (R) 175
Whitmarsh, F E. 211 E 14th....F H Babcock. (R) 200
Williams, Rosa. 250 W 41st....L Baumann. 186
Wilson, J H. 244 W 47th....L Baumann. 197
Woods, William. 98 E 4th....J Moriarty. 115
Walker, Carrie C. 350 W 58th....L Baumann. 171
Ward, Belle E. 307 W 43d L Baumann. 127
Waterman, C S. 1110 Washington av....L Baumann. 283
Weatherby, Geo. 410 W 46th....J Baumann. 113
West, Alice. 312 W 59th....W E Wheelock & Co. Piano. (R) 210
Yound, Ida B. 57 W 17th.... W E Wheelock & Co. Piano. 475
Young, F M. 29 W 31st....R Hurry. (R) 632
Zeener, Carrie. 116 E 117th....F G Smith. Piano. (R) 200

MISCELLANEOUS.

Alpert, Barnet. 115 Delancey....M Cohen. Butcher Fixtures. 50
Accles, J W... M Doran. Canal Boat. 3,000
Appleman, Anton. 931 10th av....Nat Cash Register Co. Register. 225
Basile, Giocinto. 204 E 59th....P Westphal. Barber Fixtures. (R) 30
Bernigiem, L L. 1093 3d av....C F Reibetawz. Cigar Fixtures. 175
Baumann, C. 125th st and 7th av... National Cash Register Co. Register. 175
Bassermann, Henry. 153 Chrystie....M Voss. Butcher Fixtures. 150
Bedner, Sam. 118 Chrystie....L Lesser. Bakery Fixtures. 100
Bennervitz, Peter. 1580 1st av....J Kuecks. Confectionery Fixtures. 270
Biber, Otto. 145 Reade....G S Montgomery. Machinery. 45
Buchhop, L F. 612 10th av....G H Spencer. Drug Fixtures. 1,750
Buchschats & Brendle. 159 Ludlow....C Wenzel. Machinery. 850
Busch, Charles. 7 Bowery....M Myer. Lodging House Fixtures. 2,500
Byrnes, Margaret M .... Averill & Gregory. Horses. 985
Capozzoli, L. 148 South 5th av....L Zula. Barber Fixtures. 100
Carr, Sadie. 365 Lenox av....M E Smith. Confectionery. 400
Casiraghi, August. 738 1st av....P Pryibil. Machinery. 175
Cohen, Abraham. 173 East Broadway....K Johalem. Tailor Fixtures. 200
Copeland, E. 148 W 35th....J M Quimby & Co. Hearses. 2,135
Cullen, P J. 88 Leonard....J G Wright. Woollen Goods. 4,800
Cuppers, Emil. 84 Amsterdam av....B Cuppers. Confectionery Fixtures. 600
Cauchois, F A. Broadway and Park pl....Lamson Consol S S Co. Register. 200
Coghlan, J D. 16 Washington....J M and I Griggs. Horses, Trucks, &c. 410
Crowley, Timothy. 124th st and 7th av....J Cunningham Son & Co. Coach. (R) 129
De Voe, W T. 2293 3d av....Damon & P. Printing Fixtures. 125
Daupel, William. 40 Stanton ...Warren & Stratton. Bakery Fixtures. (R) 600
De Revere, G B. 15th st and Union sq.... Beinecke & Co. Hotel Fixtures. (R) 13,000
Ditch, Harris. 27 Essex....L Lesser. Bakery Fixtures. 100
Dolcimascolo, Vincenzo. 683 3d av....A Lepore. Barber Fixtures. 375
Dryer, Leon. 247 W 41st....A Busby. Horse, Hansom, &c. 160
Esselborn, George. 9th av and 98th st....Jackson & Co. Butcher Fixtures. 400
Effler, Osmar. 998 1st av....M L Bernard. Jewelry Fixtures. 35
Enderlein, G W. 531 W 42d....J A Rudolf. Horse and Milk Wagon. 312
Feldman & Kaplan. 1783 1st av....Archer Mfg Co. Barber Fixtures. 587
Ferris, Jesse E ....J F McGuire. Horses, Trucks, &c. 2,000
Fisk & Foster. 291 W 11th....C Monk. Machinery. 500
Freiling, Peter. 136 Greenwich av....G W Gee. Barber Fixtures. 162
Fischer, H A and E C. 55 Madison....C Barthmann. Grocery Fixtures. 800
Foster Pub Co. Pulitzer Building....Mosler Safe Co. Safe. 150
Fanning, J P. 1991 2d av....Manhattan Type Co. Press. 340
Freebily, Lawrence .... M Armstrong & Co. Coach. 75
Frugone, Balletto and Gardella. 178 Park row ....Manhattan Type Co. Press. 440
Goodman, Isaac. 310 East Houston....Nat Cash Register Co. Register. 175
Garten, B. 38 Great Jones....Mosler Safe Co. Safe. 167
Gervasi, Paolino. 1032 10th av....A Schwaab. Barber Fixtures. 122
Granzio, Antonio. 254 E 110th....R Rainforth. Barber Fixtures. 33
Gautschy, Henry. 259 and 261 W 67th....M Zinderstein. Dyeing Fixtures. 1,000
Gerold, John. 637 E 13th....J McLean. Butcher Fixtures. 134
Gevardo, C. 1949 2d av....W Meyer. Barber Fixtures. 100
Greenwald & Anciss. 294 Rivington....R Brown. Butcher Fixtures. 100
Hahn, R J. 235 E 34th....W Williamson. Horses, Ice Wagon, &c. 300
Hamilton, F L. 18 Spruce....C B Cottrell & Sons. Press. (R) 200
Handwerker, Louis. 190 Columbus av .... G Bauer. Tailor Fixtures. 80
Hardy, S A. 574 2d av....F B Wadleigh. Fixtures, &c. 1,100
Heinrich, Philip. 61 Frankfort ...Manhattan Type Co. Fixtures, Machinery, &c. 2,250
Henery, Jeremiah ... M Armstrong & Co. Coach. (R) 104
Herriger, Reiner....M Armstrong & Co. Coach. (R) 410
Hiles, Charles, Jr. 224 E 6th .... Lena Hiles. Horses and Ice Wagons. 2,000
Hiller & Goldstein. 264 Broome....S Oshinsky. Machines. 100
Humbert, Nicholas. 237 Bowery....L A Humbert. Hat store Fixtures. 200
Handel & Levy. 627 2d av ...E Cole. Butcher Fixtures. 500
Howie, G W. Kingsbridge road....J Cunningham Son & Co. Coach. (R) 189
Jordan & Morrison....J W Tufts. Soda Fixtures. 450
Kasschaw, H F & M. 275 Bowery....H Spies. Horses, Office Fixtures, &c. (R) 1,000
Kling, Charles. 39 Attorney....C Bopp. Bakery Fixtures. 1,000
Knickerbocker Steamboat Co....People's Trust Co. Steamboats, &c. 140,000
Knoll, Mrs J L P. Asbury Park, N J....J Dumphy. Horses, &c. 2,395
Koenig, Charles. 588 Broome .... C Braun. Butcher Fixtures. 300
Kaiser, Morris. 259 Henry .. P Reidenbach. Wagon. 45
Leeds, W J. 12 W 14th....J Heyman. Dental Fixtures. 75
Lennon, J J. Jerome av and 174th st....S J Curtis. Horses, Trucks. 1,500
Ling, Adam. 204 E 54th....J Aull. Barber Fixtures. (R) 200
Lessner, Joseph. 67 Carmine....P Reidenbach. Wagon. 125
Martusciello, Michele. 67 Laight....V Zotta. Barber Fixtures. 100
Meyer, Frederick. 607 Water....C H Otten. Horses and Milk Wagon. 400
Macdonald, Alexander. 2345 3d av ... F J Schoff. Cigar Fixtures. 130
Mackey, Joseph. 106 and 108 Liberty....Fisher & Wesnage. Press, &c. 850
Mau & Bathmann. 35 Laidlow av, Jersey City ....C H Burmeister. Horses, &c. 1,500
Margaerta, L. 122 W 42d....Archer Mfg Co. Barber Fixtures. 921
Mass, Henry. 175 Eldridge....Archer Mfg Co. Barber Fixtures. 198
McGinn, J F. 64th st, 1st and 2d avs....H Mueller. Horse, Wagon, &c. 225
McNally, J F. 153 Clinton....J Gunst. Barber Fixtures. 100
McNulty, John. 308 Stanton....H Donohue. Horses, Carts, &c. (R) 1,000
Meyer, Michael. 1601 2d av....S Littman. Barber Fixtures. 70
Miller, William....M Armstrong & Co. Coach. (R) 260
Moskievitz, M. 147 Clinton....Canton Surg and Dental Co. Dental Fixtures. 80

Moore, Roger....M Armstrong & Co. Coach. (R) 150
Moors & Waidner... 187 Elm....C Waldner. Machinery. 500
Manen, P and M. 248 Elizabeth....S Sauniscole. Grocery Fixtures. 100
McGowan, P. 322 2d av....Nat Cash Register Co. Register. 175
Navo, Stefano. 175 Bleecker....F Bufano. Barber Fixtures. 175
Norz, Martin, Jr. 2467 3d av....A E Otto. Grocery Fixtures. (Satisfied Sept 8, 1891). 178
Oddo, Giovanni. 954 1st av....T Diliberti. Barber Fixtures. 250
Palumerie, V. 25 Ann....Archer Mfg Co. Barber Fixtures. (R) 361
Parish, Mrs. B. 62 East Broadway....Bennett & G. Soda Fixtures. 380
Perino, Chas. Lenox av and 131st st... Archer Mfg Co. Barber Fixtures. (R) 133
Perisi, A. 111 Chariton ..Archer Mfg Co. Barber Fixtures. 45
Pfister Book Binding Co....Chambers Bros Co. Machinery. 2,400
Patton, Joseph. 612 W 48th....J Cunningham Son & Co. Coach. (R) 427
Quinn, Arthur ...M Armstrong & Co. Coach. (R) 240
Reis & Lorenze. 203 E 30th....C W Dayton. Machinery. 3,500
Rogers, Joseph. 428 W 52d....P Bannon. Confectionery Fixtures. 50
Rosen, Joe. 56 Bleecker....J Munsky. Fixtures, &c. 150
Rosenstock, Abraham. 110 Essex....G Pius. Barber Fixtures. 140
Schlosser, Geo. 155th st and 8th av....National Cash Register Co. Register. 200
Schmidt, J M. 207 W 125th....Duparquet, H & M Co. Range, &c. (R) 375
Schroeder, Frederick. 438 E 77th....T Kruse. Horse, Ice Wagon, &c. 125
Searing, T W. 118 Lincoln av....Fay & Bardwell. Machinery. (R) 750
Sass, Max. 4 Forsyth .... J Stewart. Machinery. 120
Schoonmaker, John. 620 6th av....J Dalton. Fish Market Fixtures. 350
Skarvan, W. 1376 Av A....J Suchanek. Grocery Fixtures. 100
Schluter, John. 143 Greenwich....Lamson Consolidated S S Co. Register. 285
Sedgwick, Robert. 45 William....Mosler Safe Co. Safe. 110
Smith, W F. 203 E 124th ...M Plummer & Co. Press, &c. 225
Sternberg, Saul. 112 Goerck....W Koster, Jr. Wagon. 72
There, Maria. 584 W 40th....Warren & Stratton. Bakery Fixtures. (R) 200
Ullmann, Solomon. 415 E 113th....S Levy. Horse, Wagon, &c. 450
Vanderkar & McHaffie. 21 Ann....Manhattan Type Co. Type, &c. 97
Vandeskar & Hennion. 58 and 62 Broadway....C V A Blauvelt. Office Fixtures. 200
Ventrice, Jos. 39 W 125th....Archer Mfg Co. Barber Fixtures. 1,600
Viemeister, H W. South and Market sts....C H Meyer. Fixtures, &c. 10,000
Wilson, J E. 433 and 435 W 42d....J C De La Vergne. Machinery. 2,500
Winthrop Press. 255 Greene....M E Brister. Press, &c. 3,000
Wirz, Emil. 54 West End av....National C R Co. Register. 200
Wood, S A ...M Armstrong & Co. Coach. (R) 1,781
Wright & Pleasant. 159 W 41st....S Littman. Barber Fixtures. 165
Wagner & Lewis. 86 Greene....Mosler Safe Co. Safe 125
Washburn, Ida....M R Kunkely. Circus Tent. 394
Zangar, Emma. 116 Broome ...H Loffman. Drug Fixtures. 300
Zepser, C A. 248 Rivington....M J Koch. Barber Fixtures. 115
Zangen, Emma. 116 Broome ...L Leeser, Store Fixtures. 1,800

BILLS OF SALE.

Burmeister, C H. 35 Laidlow av, Jersey City ....Man & Bathmann. Horses, &c. 2,000
Briggs, A R. 143 E 41st....J P Lein. Horses, Trucks, Building, &c. 3,000
Carbone, Alfonso. 288 Bowery....N Vetromila. Barber Fixtures. ½ interest. 230
Chroback, O. 76 Orchard....Mary Chroback. Bakery Fixtures. 1
David, A A. 785 4th av . Theresa L David. Clothing Store, &c. 1
Dwyer, James. 22 Little West 12th....E Dwyer. Grocery Fixtures, &c. 219
Davidson & Perwein. 1983 3d av....A Hekseh. Hair Dressing Fixtures. 250
Ellis, D F. 1848 10th av....C T Seaman. Grocery Fixtures. 631
Ehrlich, Osias. 189 Pitt....D Jaffe. Bakery Fixtures. 240
Fay, Ellen. 792 9th av ...A P Smith. Butter and Egg Fixtures. 190
Gorey, T F. 2370 1st av....Elizabeth Hendricks. Grocery Fixtures. 550
Grannemann, H C. 41st st and 3d av....Godfrey & Howard. Saloon Fixtures. 2,300
Havens, Kate. 203 W 38th... Blanche Greene. Furniture. 1
Hoose, S E. 173 E 120th....E Greenslade. Horses, Trucks, &c. 350
Immen, Louise. 689 3d av....H C Granneman. Saloon Fixtures. 1,850
McCullough, J. 410 Madison....H & F Zanino. Horses, Trucks, &c. 2,500
McLaughlin, Winifred....Jesse E Ferris. Horses, Trucks, &c. 1,400
Meyer, Frederick. 607 Water....Annie Meyer. Horses and Grocery Fixtures. 215
Morison, S L. 3 North Washington sq....E C Hinsdale. Furniture. 250
Scheufele, John. 724 E 11th....Mary McCue. Saloon Fixtures. 1
Seaman, Adelaide G. 1823 10th av....D F Ellis. Grocery Fixtures. 631
Seixas, Rosalie S. 485 W 22d....E C Bramson. Furniture. 102
Trevisanello, Chas. 40 Grand .. C Herzenberg. Drug Fixtures. 1,000
Young, Frank. 144 Wooster....Martha Young. Fixtures, &c. 800

ASSIGNMENTS OF CHATTEL MORTGAGES.

Fisher & Wesnage to A C & M A Fisher. (Mort given by J Mackey, Sept 2, 1891). 850
Gennerich, C F to B Beirmeister. (Beirmeister & Wacker, Jan 14, 1891.) 1
Sulzer, Alfred to K A Sulzer. (E R Almy, Sept 2, 1891). 3,200

KINGS COUNTY.

SEPTEMBER 3 TO 9.—INCLUSIVE.

SALOON AND RESTAURANT FIXTURES.

Biba, F. 365 South 4th....Wagner & S. Billiard Table. $390
Baumann, J. 11 Newell....H Greenfeld. 500
Breit, M. 309 Johnson av....Ferdinand Munch Brewery. 597
Buck, C H. 67 4th av....S Liebmann's Sons B Co. 600
Burns, E. J. 77 Furman.. .O'Reilly, Skelly & Fogarty Co. 150
Berlin, W. 428 Graham av....O Huber. (R) 288
Bicker, F. 250 Ellery....Claus Lipsius B Co. (R) 900
Callahan, J. 591 Manhattan av .. P Doelger. 700
Campbell, J. 169 Sackett....P Ballantine & Sons. 2,000
Duffy, M. 336 Van Brunt....J W Metcalf. 1,000
Ellaus, J. 130 Forest....J Kress B Co. (R) 700
Esperti, E. 2048 Broadway....Feigenspan B Co. 700
Etter, A. 87 North Henry....Eva Bechtel, extrx. (R) 225
Emanuel, J. 32 Broadway....O Huber. (R) 1,200
Frankel, H. 66 Gerry....Feigenspan B Co. 550
Gallagher, Rose A. 228 5th av....G Ringler & Co. 2,590
Hassler, W. 686 5th av....J Fallert B Co. (R) 800
Janicke, R. 459 Keap....J Fallert B Co. (R) 670
Kapke, J. 959 Gates av....W Ulmer. 700
Keck, G. 254 Graham av....J Fallert B Co. (R) 500
Kilcoyne, P. 204 Reid av....J Eppig. 800
Kilduff, M. 181 South 6th....Abbott B Co. 800
Klein, A. 146 Gwinnett....L Eppig. 500
Kniest, M. 205 Driggs....Feigenspan B Co. consid omitted
Keely, M. 428 Carroll....Claus Lipsius B Co. (R) 225
Lesser, J. 192 Middleton....Burger & H B Co. 450
Lynes, J. 609 De Kalb av....Otto Huber Brewery. (R) 1,000
Mandler, L. 682 5th av....Claus Lipsius B Co. (R) 700
Madsen, P C. 371 Lorimer....P Westphal. 250
Maher, E. 335 Lorimer....J Ruppert. (R) 1,000
Maher, T F and L. 186 Grand .... Williamsburgh B Co. Pool Table. 125
McKenna, J. 37 Prince....Burr B Co. (R) 500
Mitchell & Bodkin. 214 Grand....P Weidmann. 200
Nelson, J. 47 Carroll....Danenberg & Coles. (R) 525
Niemann, A. 154 Maujer....Eliz Meltzer. 900
Ohlenschlager, H. 1134 Willoughby av....F Ibert. 300
Payne, C J. 419 Kent av....T J Bushell. 600
Purnhagen, Barbara. 665 Franklin av....Williamsburgh B Co. 500
Rickard, M. Gravesend....J S Slocum. 500
Schultz, F. 536 Driggs av....Burger & H B Co. 850
Stoehr, J. 141 Montrose av. ..Fort Hamilton B Co. 500
Salit, H. 41 Main....Claus Lipsius B Co. (R) 100
Schaeffner, C. 22 Melrose....Obermeyer & L. (R) 700
Schneider, J. Railroad av, s w cor Weldon st....Claus Lipsius B Co. (R) 150
Shannon, M. 169 Bedford av....Obermeyer & L. (R) 700
Shields, M. 100 Bridge....Claus Lipsius B Co. (R) 1,000
Scanlan, J P. 86 Norman av....P Doelger. 4,000
Schondorf, M. 139 Union av....H B Scharmann & Sons. 500
Seifried, J. 329 Kent av....S Liebmann's Sons B Co. 500
Shields, J W. 318 Grand....Williamsburgh B Co. 1,000
Sommers, H. 564 Wythe av....G Ringler & Co. (R) 2,100
Walsh, T F. 1117 Broadway....S Liebmann's Sons B Co. (R) 1,000
Walther, H O. 133 Leonard....C Freese. 400
Wilson, F W. 158 Division av....Wagner & Sanford. Billiard Table. 180
Weinberg, T. 81 North 6th ...O Huber Brewery. 1,000
Wharton, H F. 142 North 5th ..Claus Lipsius B Co. (R) 1,000
Woodside, W. 20 Elm pl....O Huber Brewery. 500
Yunge, J F. 314 North 2d....Claus Lipsius B Co. (R) 400
Zachmann, H. 119 Harrison av....F Melzer. Pool Table. 110
Zapp, J. 74 North 5th....Williamsburgh B Co. 350

HOUSEHOLD FURNITURE.

Alexander, G. 394 Warwick....Fennell & P. 236
Bjornquest, W. 458 Madison ...Mullins & Sons. 150
Bulger, T J. 179 Ainslie....Jacobs Bros. Piano. 207
Behn, C. 36 Alabama av....C T Kendrick & Co. 233
Butler, J W. 43 Floyd....C T Kendrick & Co. 204
Carey, Cath. 570 Vanderbilt av....Rosalie Langlette. 250
Cleary, Mary C. 5th av and 72d st ...M Bottstein. 110
Connolly, G C. 341 Marion....L Z Murray. 132
Deremody, Anne. 114 North 8th....Jacob Bros. Piano. 200
Duffie, J W. 92 Decatur....Dodd, Mead & Co. (R) indebtedness
Ellingham, Ellen. 11 Rochester av....C T Kendrick & Co. 119
Emans, J C. 2142 Fulton....C T Kendrick & Co. 155
Febo, Emily. 855 Sackett....T Kelly. 182
Freyland, J. 236 Wyckoff....C T Kendrick & Co. 199
Foster, E W. 152 28th....O'Farrell & H. 118
Fransioli, A. 582 Henry....R Day. 800
Finan, Mary. 95 Luquer....J McEnery & Co. 155
Fruh, G. 846 Flushing av....Jacob Bros. Piano. 285
Gillis, W L. 1286 Herkimer....Mullins & Sons. 248
Gegg, R E. 84 Grove....O'Connor & T. 199
Gorren, Selma. 41 South Oxford....J Baumann. 548
Graham, Mrs P. 1882 Pacific....J Rubenstein. 478
Griffen, R H. 620 McDonough....L Baumann. 521
Haggerty, Hannah. 128 Division av....L Baumann. 337
Hurst, E Clara. 258 Ryerson....Maria A Warner. 1,500
Jacobs, W S. 169 6th....J Coyne & Co. 166
Jaeger, Louisa. 708 Bushwick av....J Rubenstein. 188
Kane, J A. 222 5th av....T F Ryan. 342
Kohlman, Maggie. 406 Graham av....Jacob Bros. Piano. 895
Lane, E C. 748 Hancock....A Frey. 125
Liscomb, H C. 190 South 2d....Jacob Bros. Piano. 102
Le Clair, C. 151 Lawrence....L Z Murray. 101
Lobdell, W A. 18 Newell....R M Walters. Piano. 145
Ludwig, Louisa. 50 Central av....L Baumann. 102
Levy, C. 64 Gerry....C T Kendrick & Co. 311
Marinlso, W. 180 Central av....C T Kendrick & Co. 268
Marley, J H. 590 Willoughby av....C T Kendrick & Co. 284
McCuen, Isabel. 474 Carlton av....S Baumann. 178
McGuinness, J J. 155 Nassau....J Coyne & Co. 265
Miles, H. 1874 Bushwick av....C T Kendrick & Co. 223
Moorhouse, A. 289 7th....T Kelly. 158
Moorhouse, J K. 1067 Myrtle av....C T Kendrick & Co. 271
Munro, E A. 313½ State....L Z Murray. 375
MacIver, A S. 183 State ...T F Ryan. 118
McLaughlin, Mary. 474 Prospect av .... J Michaels. 323
Norton, J. Flatbush....J Baumann. 353
Nygren, W G. 89 4th av....J Michaels. 181
O'Mara, Katie. 314 State....T Lyons. 147
Phillips, T R. 261 Bainbridge....J & J Dobson. 153
Richardson, Delia. 52 Hicks....L Z Murray. 117
Rivoree, J E. 553 Gates av....T Kelly. 190
Shadley, Ida L. 97 Pierrepont....J Vanbrimmer. 1,200
Saulnier, H A. C T Kendrick & Co. 182
Scott, G. 966 Kent av....C T Kendrick & Co. 149
Shandley, T E. 424 Gold....C T Kendrick & Co. 174
Stall, C. 181 South 4th....C T Kendrick & Co. 114
Smith, O. 622 Grand....W Ulmer. 1,500
Thwaites, W. 248 Roebling.... Sarah A Bingham. Piano. 100
Teets, A S. 58 Fort Greene pl ...C T Kendrick & Co. 321
Thiel, A. 15th av and 74th st.. .Jacob Bros. Piano. 200
Turner, W J. 910 Driggs av....Jacob Bros. Piano. 180
Wellborg. 169 Wyckoff....T F Ryan. 163
Watson, P L. 85 St Marks av ...Mullins & Sons. 173
Wilson, Margt. 55 Morton....L Baumann. 136

MISCELLANEOUS.

Allen, L E. 975 Fulton....C Swezey. Bakery Fixtures. 1,000
Bistramb, C H. 703 3d av ... A C Fischer. Drug Fixtures. 200
Cobb, F W. 15 Elm....Martha Lalor. Machinery. 3,500
Cook, Hy, Jr, and John. 18th av and 86th st, Bath Beach....Levy & Dahlman. Meat Market, Horses, &c. (R) 600
Curtis, C. L. 139 Centre....Emily V. Curtis. Machinery. (R) 1,500
Culby, Minnie. 542 Atlantic av ...O'Connor & Treacy. Furniture. 136
Dlanhy, V A K. 1591 Bushwick av....A Kelly. Bottling Business. 175
Dunn & Murcott, of American Anvil Co....McDougall & P. Steam Hammer. 1,300
Emilians, M. St Marys Hospital....Mosler Safe Co. Safe. 225
Freeman, R & Bro. 45-51 Rose....Babcock Printing Press and Mfg Co. Press. 2,500
Hoerning, C K. 62 Graham av....Mosler Safe Co. Safe. 110
Haug, J. 132 Boerum....A Martin. Machinery. 500
Heinrich, P. 61 Frankfort....Manhattan Type Foundry. Printer's Fixtures. contingent liability, 6,750
Hirsch, Lena. 184 Johnson av....C Vogt & Son. Cigar Fixtures. 439
Jenkins, J D....Barrett & Brush. Wagon. 197
King, H C. 375 Fulton ...Mosler Safe Co. Safe. 100
Knudsen, P. 120 Clay....B H Tienken. Trucks. 700
Lippmann, W. Thatford st....S & B Strauss. Cows. 100
Lipinski & Babiak....J Downey. Wagon. 150
McCutcheon, F. 3 Willoughby....Mosler Safe Co. Safe. 120
McCue, M....M Armstrong & Co. Hansom. 550
McEnaney, J T and T L Duryea. 1063 De Kalb av... A Kelly. Bottling Business. 565
Miller, S J. 332 Keap ...J G Miller. Horses, Trucks, &c. 1,100
Nelson, C J. 571 4th av....Bath & Hayward. Horses, Ice Wagon, &c. 300
O'Brien, W D. 10th st and 5th av....Mosler Safe Co. Safe. 100
Ortlieb, M. 280 Nevins....G Wagner. Machinery. 300
Olufs, J. 452 Union....Archer Mfg Co. Barber Fixtures. (R) 405
Potts Bros. Cor East New York and Vesta avs ....Marvin Safe Co. Safe. 150
Panarello, S. Fenimore st....R Ramforth. Barber Fixtures. 185
Schwencke, C. 216 Flatbush av....M M Ramsay. Bakery Fixtures. 198
Sannenstrahl, H. 23 Wallabout Market ...J F Clarke. Wagon. 300
Stiles & Nichols. 259 Fulton....Marvin Safe Co. Safe. 105
Tucker, A L. 114 Bridge and 38 Willoughby....C Swezey. Bakery Fixtures and Furniture. 400
Same....same. Bakery Fixtures and Furniture. 400
Tietjen, H. Gates av, cor Marcy av .... H Borchers. Grocery Store Fixtures. 650
Winter, G. 497 Atlantic av....Mosler Safe Co. Safe. 105
Wentz, Annie ...M Armstrong & Co. Coach. 950

BILLS OF SALE.

Bowers, W H. 16 Fulton....J Engel. Saloon Fixtures. 2,300
Byrnes, M. 74 North 5th....J Zapp. Saloon Fixtures. 400
Ebert, Agatha. 97 Sanford....G Hein. Grocery Fixtures. 400
Gnad, Babette. 1087 Fulton....W F Gnad. Int in Saloon. 450
Haug, J. 132 Boerum....C Meyer. Machinery. 650
Kuhn, J. 77 Stagg....Mary Kuhn. Machinery. 600
O'Brien, Virginia E. Coney Island....J Lundy. Windsor Restaurant Fixtures. 1,400
Phillips, Annie M. 1067 3d av....C F Phillips. Candy store Fixtures. 150
Quabach, Anna J. 492 Grand... J Theurer. Saloon Fixtures. 550
Staudt, G. 2038 Fulton ..Eliz Staudt. Confectionery Fixtures. 300
Schneider, F and A E .. R Smith. Fixtures. 175
Scholl, M. 84 Broadway.. .J Scholl. Cigar Store Fixtures. 500
Shields, John W. 318 Grand....Jas W Shields. Saloon Fixtures. 5,500

Stilting, C H, 259 Myrtle av....H W Hardekopf, Store Fixtures. 1,800
Wolpe, B. 52 Underhill av....W Wolpe. Saloon Fixtures. nom

ASSIGNMENT OF CHATTEL MORTGAGES.

Dodd, Mead & Co to J F De Klyn. (Morts given by J W Duffie, Sept 16, 1890.) nom
Quabach, J T to Anna J Quabach. (B J Mulholland, Jan 22, 1891.) nom
Quabach, Anna J to J Theurer. (Assign of above.) 5)

NEW JERSEY.

NOTE.—*The arrangement of the Conveyances, Mortgages and Judgments in these lists is as follows: the first name in the Conveyances is the Grantor; in Mortgages, the Mortgagor; in Judgments, the Judgment debtor.*

ESSEX COUNTY.

CONVEYANCES.

Adams, William R—C J Sippell, Clinton.........$350
Anderson, I S—K Salmon, Montclair........612
Same——M Trainor, Montclair........650
Same——S S Edmonston, Montclair........2,105
Same——R B Ringland, Montclair........700
Same——S L Reeves, Montclair........1
Andrus, Cornelia—M Hayden, Montclair........3,000
Baldwin, E M—C L J Power, East Orange........10,000
Benedict, G L—L C Benedict, Montclair........1
Benedict, L C—F D Benedict, Montclair........1
Benkert, Sophia—L Gopfert, Bruce st........800
Bewkes, Henry—G Goetschins, Montclair........200
Bogie, A C—A P Law, Montclair........7,900
Breakenridge, J H—S O Runyon, Clinton........175
Bundschub, W C—J Bundschub, Norfolk st........1
Captain, Lewis—M Supenor, Caldwell........1,700
Chambers, M J et al, exrs A C Howard, Springfield av........1
Chandler, H L—Orange Heights Land Co, West Orange........249,000
Clapp, A B—F Seymour, South Orange........3,000
Clark, J A—E Tunison, w s Boyd st 177 s 18th av 24x108........3,000
Collins, Fred'k—O S Dodds, Cabinet st........2,000
Crane, Oliver—C H C Lyon, Montclair........1
Damiano, Francisco—J M Trimble, Commerce st........1
Dawkins, Louis—G Freeman, Bloomfield........1
Devine, Arthur—A Smith, South Orange........1,075
Dodd, Jane—J Gartland, Court st........1
Dodd, Michael—H Hardy, Howard st........1
Dodd, Michael guard——same, Howard st........1,894
Dodd, R N—J M Kinck, Montclair........2,750
Eckert, E V—C J Sippell, Clinton........350
Ehlers, J F—H Buppe, Bloomfield........1,600
Farrington, C E—F L Vanderhoof, Caldwell........300
Ford, W W—W Titus, Atlantic st........1,250
Froehlich, Samuel—J G Bray, Montclair........5,500
Gartland, Hugh—H Hardy, Howard st........1,1'0
Gartland, John —same, Court st........1,900
Geoffrey, N E—M Dunlop, Parker st........800
Geppert, M M—M Waldmann, Niagara st........1,500
Goetschius, George—W H Power, Montclair........700
Grand, d'Hauteville, S W—G C Brown, Broad st 2,500
Grimm, Rosina—R Grimm, 3) ft from cor Elm and Prospect 30x100x42x100........8,000
Gutbrod, A C—L F Huger, Monmouth st........1
Howard Savings Inst—James Dolan, Condit st. 2,300
Howell, J E—C G Hine et al, Washington av........1
Huger, William—A C Gutbrod, Monmouth st........1
Jaqui, Rosa—Orange Savings Bank, Orange........1
Jenkinson, G B—E Freund, Avon av........1,600
Kelly, George—E E Calder, e s Elizabeth av 50 s Hunter st, 25x109........3,300
Kernaghan, M E—F Mackin, Merchant st........1
Same——same, Napoleon st........6:0
Leary, Annie—J Dodd, Howard st........1
Lindsley, E T—S J Condit, East Orange........2,500
Same——same, East Orange........1,400
Same——same, East Orange........2,500
Lister, J C—E Kane, Joseph st........750
Same——J H Fitzgerald, Albert av........1,770
Same——M Mulcahey, Joseph st........275
Lyon, D H—C I Beck, South Orange........1,875
Martin, S M—M C Lynch, w s Mulberry st 50 n Emmett st 25x100........5,000
Mayor and Common Council of Newark—L R Trimble, Drift st........1,000
McGrane, M E—G James, Searing st........1,450
Mix, F H—T Groedel, n s Clinton av, 380 e Stratford pl 25x95x56x25x50x89........6,600
Moller, John—W Walton, East Orange........1
Morton, L P et al trustees—G C Brown, Broad st 1,250
N J Zinc and Iron Co—J Cuseck, Chapel st........1
Osborne, W D et al—W H Curtis et al, Scotland st........1
Pease, William—J C Crevier, Caldwell........1
Pfeiffer, Gottfried—A M Ortlieb, Ferry st........1
Potter, W S—G P Lydecker, South 12th st........2,200
Rau, Magnus—F Murray, Bergen st........1,400
Rindam, Patrick—F P Tully, Thomas st........1
Rothwell, John—M Hopkins, 8th av........2,400
Runge, Toni—W Riker, s s Hill st adj Jno Piersons land 25x76........4,000
Runyon, O E—D M Runyon, Clinton........600
Russell, Nathan—W W Collyer Co, East Orange. 400
Satterthwaite, K B—A H Larkin, Franklin........1,800
Schaible, John—J Isaac, e s Boyd st 175 s ——, 25x100........6,675
Scarlett, William—G R Walters, Clinton........500
Shay, C C—E Weeks, Newark st........1,500
Spottiswoode, George—H L Chandler, West Orange........32 000
Stern, Henrietta—C F Pfeiffer, South 14th st........950
Steigler, Herman—S Karlinsky, w s Morris av 100 s Court st 25x100........4,200
Sturgeon, Margaret—M Webb, Jr, East Orange. 7,500
Suydam, J P—B McDermott, Erie pl........200
The Mutual Life Ins Co—A B Clapp, South Orange........5,000
The Protestant Foster Home Soc—E W Clute, Summer av........1,000
Same——D Shipman, Summer av........2,000
Teed, A W—M E Halsey, Abington av........1
Tunison, Edward—J A Clark, Washington av........2,000
Same——M S Clark, Washington av........2,000
Waixel, David—C Wilhelm, Livingston st........1,000
Walton, William—W C Moller, East Orange........1
Webb, W C—E H Chandler, East Orange........7,500
Wilcox, Harriet—M E Loehnberg, Clinton........1,800

MORTGAGES.

Abeniste, Julie—J A Schmidt, Pennington st........850
Arnold, Michael—R A Firm guard, Lillie st........1,200
Arms, Roger N—W G Smith, Bloomfield........2,000
Bechlin, J C—G Miller, Johnson av........1,800
Bedell, H A—T Scott, East Orange........721
Brady, J G—S Froehlich, Montclair........4,500
Chandler, H L—G Spottiswoode, West Orange........12,000
Clapp, A B—Mutual Life Ins Co, South Orange........4,000
Clark, J A—A N Diltz, Washington av........1,800
Compton, C W—C Meyer, South 7th st........5,000
Conroy, James—W R Howe, Orange........700
Cooper, C S et al—J S Higbie extrx, Clifton av........2,000
Coit, R M—S M Aldridge, Orange st........3,000
Cusack, John—C Unckelbach, Chapel st........1,000
Degenhardt, Paul—W B Corby, Montclair........2,200
Dolan, James—The Howard Savings Inst, Condit st........2,000
Dumont, J W—A F Weaver, Pacific st........1,000
Dunlop, Maggie—E Bissland, Parker st........400
Faitoute, William—The Newark Fire Ins Co, Broad st........600
Ferguson, Charles—C Smith, Bloomfield........200
Fischmann, Lessor—The Washington B and L Assoc, Broome st........1,000
Fitzgerald, J H—J C Lister, Albert av........785
Garrabrant, Caroline—The Newark B and L Assoc, Nichols st........400
Garrabrant, M A—A A Sigler, Franklin........550
Garrison, F C—S W Pereston, Franklin........1,000
George, James L—The State B and L Assoc, Searing st........3,000
Grant, Bryan et al—The Essex Co B and L Assoc, Bloomfield........2,200
Grebe, Fred'k—D Wilson, Nelson pl........4,000
Groel, Adam—L Carpentier, Bergen st........800
Hans, Gertrude—C A Frick, South st........1,200
Hans, Gertrude—F Keuerauf, South st........1,000
Harrison, P H—S Atwater trustee, cor 9th av and South 9th st........2,000
Heitele, Max—J A Hay exr, South 11th av........1,500
Heery, Philip—T J Lintott, Academy st........1,600
Hild, Joseph—L Seitel, Jones st........1,000
Hopkins, Mary—J Rothwell, 8th av........1,900
Huber, Christian—V Dassing, South 18th st........850
Isaac, Joseph—J Schaible, Boyd st........5,675
Karlinsky, Sisli—Home B and L Assoc, Morris av........3,400
Same——H Steigler, Morris av........400
Kelly, John—C A Trippe, Orange........150
Kent, J H—Montclair B and L Assoc, Montclair. 1,400
Lamb, A W et al—Orange Savings Bank, East Orange........900
Law, Annie P—A C Bogle, Montclair........2,000
Lyon, D M—C Trefz, Bloomfield........5,000
Lyons, Patrick—P Bonykamper, Jr, Ferguson st 250
Matthews, Thomas—Assoc to provide, &c., a Home for the Friendless, Lemon st........1,100
McGrath, Patrick—Fidelity Title and Deposit Co, Dickerson st........2,000
Moore, C H—Trustees of Episcopal Fund, Fulton st........1,000
Murray, Frank—F T Johnson, guard, Bergen st. 700
Nisch, Margaret—S Neiss, Hunterdon st........800
O'Connor, Jno—M O'Connor, South Orange........100
O'Donnell, James—Chas Gallagher, Academy st 850
Oldham, W H—Tenth Ward B and L Assoc, cor Academy and Henry sts........500
Orange Mountain Cable Co—Fidelity Title and Deposit Co, West Orange........350,000
Parkhurst, M H—H A Allen, East Orange........1,000
Pieper, Theodore—S Doughty et al, exrs, Clinton av........3,000
Pittman, Philip—Union B and L Assoc, Gotthardt st........1,000
Potter, F M—J Donnelly, Howard st........1,500
Power, C L J—J G Baldwin, East Orange........5,700
Rhoades, C K—M H Pennington, South 10th st........800
Riggoloet, Donato—Security B and L Assoc, Lock st........800
Ritchie, T F et al—R F Ballantine, Orange........7,000
Schuckhaus, Peter et al—P Vollert, Van Buren st........1,500
Same——A Buermann, Ferry st........4,000
Schwitten, Richard—A Beck, Hunterdon st........2,500
Toler, Anastacia et al—F Bonykamper, Jr, Brill st........150
Van Nostrand, Harold—J S Higbie, Orange........3,000
Walters, Louisa—Security B and L Assoc, Clinton........1,200
Webbe, L E—W Doremus, Vanderpool st........5,000
Westervelt, C A—L Leverich, East Orange........3,000
Wilhelm, Christian—Mercer B and L Assoc, Livingston st........1,200
Wilmerding, J C et al—J G Heckscher et al, West Orange........13,750
Wilson, David—Newark Fire Ins Co, East Orange........500
Wood, W H—C Clark, Montclair........2,000
Worthington, L P—A Areson, Caldwell........4,800

CHATTEL MORTGAGES.

Allen, E B—W S French, furniture........400
Arndt, George—A H Winters, store fixtures........300
Barmettler, Josephine—J Vanflue, furniture........200
Blum, George—G Kaber, wagons, &c........125
Cody, David—J Lever, horses, &c........1,000
Damiano, Francesco—J M Trimble, saloon........1,500
Edwards, E O—J M Ham, furniture........65
Evans, W H—W D Perrine, horse, &c........1,800
Foerst, Joseph—G Krueger, saloon........312
Fruhinsfeld, Louis—G Krueger Brewing Co, saloon........1,150
Gadfield, Henry—M Kane, furniture........32
Gardner, W H—Marvin Safe Co, safe........70
Gaufman, Caroline—F J Kastner, saloon........485
Hayward, Charles—G Krueger Brewing Co, saloon........120
Hesse, Henry—Hills Union Brewery Co, saloon. 400
Howard, G W—C H Stewart, wagons, &c........182
Kenny, Horace— —— Kirschfield, safe........100
Kettler, Theodore—M Andlauer, wagons, &c........200
Knight, Richard—C Irving Cannon, furniture........259
Koehler, August—G Krueger Brewing Co, saloon........380
Kraemer, Charles—H G Nadler, store fixtures........1,750
Krufess, Edward—P Ballantine & Sons, saloon........700
Mackin, C F—C W Clayton, furniture........460
McFadden, John—F J Kastner, saloon........555
Moses, Merian—F C Willcox, furniture........300
Neill, James—J A Woods, machinery........550
Quick, W E—F J Kastner, saloon........1,000
Serien, Jacob—P Toldt, wagons, &c........75
Turnstead, G S—G B Swain, horses, &c........918
Weis, Joseph—I M Ramsey, machinery, &c........200
Wiener, S H—C Bierman, furniture........65
Yale Bros—Marvin Safe Co, safe........98

HUDSON COUNTY.

CONVEYANCES.

Baker, S S—Eliza A Johnston, J City........$2,100
Begiebing, H F—Emil F Begiebing, Union........nom
Brown, Michael—Winnie Heitshusen, J City........nom
Same——F Hetshusen, J City........nom
Cadmus, George—J W Randall, Bayonne........630
Carragan, Geo—Emmeth Smith, Bayonne........1,500
Carr, James—A H Pitchford, Union........1,600
Claflin, C F—J S O'Connor, J City........5,000
Clark, John—W Stewart, J City........700
Coster, Mary L—H Shanley, J City........5,500
Daly, John—J Hayden, J City........1,100
De Wint, Margaret S—J A De Wint, J City........nom
Dickinson, James—W J Moran, J City........5,200
Dillon, Ellen—D F Harms, J City........6,500
Doersching, Sophie S—O Schultz, West Hoboken........3,800
Eilshemius, H G—Sophia J Kerr, Kearney........650
Elsworth, Joe—Mary E Elsworth, Bayonne........nom
Feldman, Temma—S Friedman, Bayonne........800
Ferens, J R—J Hanestern, Union........400
Findlay, Alex—B Jacobowitz J City........4,250
Forman, G H—J Greener, J City........2,700
Forquer, Chas—Mary E Wood, Bayonne........nom
Frericks, Henry—Elizabeth E Bissell, J City........2,200
Gardner, John—Louisa Mecker, Union........1,750
Garthe, Elizabeth—Catharine Rose, Guttenberg. 100
Hanna, Rachel—Ida E Peterson, Kearney........3,700
Harper, W H—J J Hatfield, Hoboken........5,500
Hetshusen, Fred—M Brown, J City........nom
Horn, August—A Warmuth, Union........2,850
Keim, Louise—P Koster, Union........75
Lee, John—Wilhelm Koch, J City........150
Little, Julia W—The West Side Connecting R R Co, J City........1,037
Little, Mary—M T Barrett, Harrison........400
Lohmeyer, Herman—H McDougall, Hoboken........1,100
Matthews, F J—A M Klonowski, J City........3,250
McGovern, J F—Sophie S Doersching, West Hoboken........1,600
Mead, Cathalina—Mary E Barrows, Bayonne........450
Same——J W Randall, Bayonne........630
Mecker, Christopher—J Gardner, Union........400
Morehouse, J K—Fannie Nelson, J City........1,500
Morpeth, Anthony—C T Van Deren, Harrison........2,200
Same——Rhoda H Armitage, Kearney........500
Morpeth, R S—C T Van Deren, Harrison........2,500
Nelson, Fannie G—Georgianna Morehouse, J City........3,000
Nugent, J E—Annie E Nugent, Harrison........3,000
O'Brien, J—P O'Brien, J City........1,500
Oesmann, Marg't C—Caroline Gugel, West Hoboken........650
O'Hare, P J—M F Burns, J City........300
Pearsall, Annie E—Margaret A Wheelihan, J City........1,600
Percival, John—A McLaren, J City........425
Rochester, A W—T McEwan, Jr, J City........1,200
Schultz, Otto—A Quensel, West Hoboken........3,000
Schwietering, John—Josephine Deppenbrock, J City........nom
Shanley, Henry—J Depew, Jr, J City........2,300
Shepherd, Mary E—J M Van Nyckel, J City........1,500
Siegfried, Adam—G Lindenthal, North Bergen. 27,250
Stantford, W H by exrs—T Hepe, J City........1,250
Snyder, C N by sheriff—Mary Snyder, West Hoboken........500
Soft, L E—Dorothea Termes, Union........3,600
Thomas, J C—F Van Tassel, J City........2,200
Van Wagenen, Jacob—J J Birmingham, J City 6[illegible]
Wallace, Hiram—Annie Stiller, J City........800
Walker, Herman—Mary Wandrak, Union........5,000
Warrick, Woodward—Hattie W Travers, J City nom
Westervelt, D P—M Wright, Hoboken........1,500
Wigger, W M—The Sisters of Peace, J City........6,[illegible]
Willadsen, Jens—Mary P Lewis, Hoboken........14,000
Winfield, Abraham—Temma Feldman, Bayonne 600
Wolf, Philip—J Wolf, Union........275

MORTGAGES.

Anestern, J H—F Stahl, Union, 1 year........100
Furlong, Michael—The Hudson Trust and Savings Inst, Union, 3 years........1,500
Barrows, Mary E—Cathalina Mead, Bayonne, 3 years........225
Bissell, Elizabeth E—H Frericks, J City, 3 years. 1,700
Brutlon, Catharine—J A Reed, J City, 3 years........1,000
Brown, Jane A—J C Besson, Hoboken, 3 years........2,000
Ceburre, Marguret—Effie Van Buskirk, Bayonne, 3 years........2,500
Cole, G B—Hudson City M B and L Assoc, J City, installs........2,000
Conway, John—L Abbett, Union, 5 years........17,000
Dekamper, Minnie—J Ehmer, Union, 5 years........5,000
Depew, James, Jr—The Lincoln B and L Assoc, J City, installs........1,400
Fay, Michael—P Abstein, J City, 3 years........900
Feldman, Fenna—C C Steesman, Bayonne, 3 years........350
Finck, Henry—J E Andrus, J City, 1 year........500
Francisco, Harriet J—G Cleland, J City, 4 years 900
Gillespie, James—New Jersey Title Guarantee and Trust Co, J City, installs........1,200
Harper, H W—N H Cheseburgh, Hoboken, 1 yr. 2,000
Higson, Robert—Hudson City Mutual B and L Assoc, J City, installs........7,600
Hopkins, L C—W D Gilman, Kearney, 1 year........500
Howser, J C—Excelsior M B and L Assoc, Series 2 Issue 4, J City, installs........2,600
Hudson River Ice Co—S McBurney trustee, J City and elsewhere, 10 years........31,500
Hatfield, J J—W Harper, Hoboken, 1 year........1,500
Johnston, Eliza A—S S Baker, J City, 1 year........510
Klonowski, A M—The Security B and L Assoc, J City, installs........3,000
Koch, Wilhelmina—J Lee, J City, 3 years........100
Leistmann, Carl—H Greier, J City, 1 year........300
Lob, Christian—B Schultz, West Hoboken, 3 yrs. 2,200
May, Edward—Eliza T Camp, J City, 3 years........1,015
McComb, Joseph—The Fairmount M B and L Assoc, J City, installs........3,600
McEwan, G J—J Kemp, West Hoboken, 3 years. 2,400
McGuinness, Michael—The Provident Inst for Savings, J City, 1 year........12,000
Moran, Michael——same, J City, 1 year........1,000
Morehouse, Georgianna—Fannie G Nelson, J City, 3 years........1,500
Muller, Marie—H J Lutzen, J City, 3 years........3,000
Neitzemius, Matilda—The Pamrapo B and L Assoc, Bayonne, installs........2,520
Neever, Louisa—F Schumpen, Union, 5 years........6,000
O'Brien, Michael—F O Johnson, Bayonne, 5 years........600
O'Connor, J S—Jane Claflin, J City, 3 years........5,000
Peters, J A—M E La Croix, J City, 5 years........2,800
Paterson, John—J Stevens, Harrison, 1 year........2,400
Post, Frank—F Howe, J City, 1 year........1,800
Randall, J W—Cathalina Mead, Bayonne, 2 years........285
Same——G Cadmus, Bayonne, 3 years........2,065
Repetto, John—G Badaraco, Hoboken, 3 years. 600
Rochow, Chas—T J Preston, Harrison, 1 year........3,400
Schulz, Joe—G Weil, Guttenberg, 3 years........500
Schultz, Otto—J W Homer, West Hoboken, 1 year........3,000
Seibert, John—West End Co-operative B and L Assoc, West Hoboken, installs........5,000

Shanley, Henry—Mary L Coster, Hoboken, 5 years 4,500

Shea, Ellen J B—The Provident Inst for Savings, J City, 1 year 700

Stiller, Annie—H Wallace, J City, 3 years 500

Sweeney, Daniel—W H Beadleston, Bayonne, 2 years 500

The trustees of the First Baptist Church of Hoboken—Hoboken Bank for Savings, Hoboken, 1 year 14,000

Tolen, William—The Harrison and Kearney B & L Assoc, Kearney, installs 1,400

Van Deren, C T and P J Goodman—A Morpeth, Harrison, 1 year 1,100

Van Suckel, J M—E Denning, J City, 5 years 1,000

Van Winkle, Mary F—The Star M B and L Assoc, J City, installs 5.000

Von Tish, Hannah E—The Peoples B and L Assoc, Harrison, installs 400

Walter, Catharine—The Hudson City M B and L Assoc, J City, installs 1,000

W ndrak, Mary—F C Hausen, Union, 1 year 1,500

Wurster, John—T Schmidt, J City, 3 years 2,500

Wust, P J—The Hudson City M B and L Assoc, J City, installs 1,800

CHATTEL MORTGAGES.

Bade, William, Hoboken—The Rubsam & Horrmann Brewing Co, hotel and bar and fixtures 1,482

Barrkamp, F E, J City—Marvin Safe Co, safe 130

Bliem, Frank, J City—The Burton Brewing Co, saloon 457

Carver, W C, Hoboken—J Gregg & Co, furniture 128

Devlin, M E, J City—The Bachman Brewing Co, saloon 1,500

Dudrop, Felix, West Hoboken—Beadleston & Woerz, saloon and lease 800

Eberle, Joseph, J City—Christiana Grole, piano 109

Foley, Michael, Bayonne—H Manus & Son, furniture 339

Gereten, Joseph, West Hoboken—The William Peter Brewing Co, saloon 900

Hauser, Gustav, Hoboken—same, saloon and fixtures 4,000

Holland, Winnie, J City—L Bauman, furniture 182

Joralemon, Abram, Harrison—S C Joralemon, horse, wagon, harness 257

Kluess, Henry, Hoboken—G Ehret, saloon fixtures 300

Lamarda, Cono, J City—Gaetano D Eliza, barber shop 100

Liftschild, H T, Jr, J City—T Wright, horse, wagon, harness 175

Moeller, A G, J City—A D Puffer & Son, soda water fountain 347

O'Reilly, John, Hoboken—Lembeck & Betz Eagle Brewing Co, saloon 400

Rubatsky, Joseph, J City—The Bavarian Brewing Co, saloon 350

Schuessler, Chas, J City—Bernheimer & Schmidt, saloon and lease 750

Singewald, Minnie, Hoboken—Christian Feigenspan, saloon 650

Stevens, Henry, J City—T Kelly & Co, furniture 128

Same—same, furniture 208

Wehrenberg, Geo, J City—The William Peter Brewing Co, saloon and fixtures 1,572

Yahausen, K Y, J City—The India Wharf Brewing Co, saloon 250

BILL OF SALE.

Dean, S M, J City, by constable—P C Vreeland, horses, wagons, harness 700

JUDGMENTS.

Bauer, George—L Kirchner 38

Cordock, James—Annie Cordts 49

Driscoll, J J—N A Merritt 249

Farrier, G H—Paulus Hook Building and Loan Assoc 834

Grace, Catharine and Thomas—C Moore 32

Mahler, Mary and Richard—L Kirchner 132

Meyers, Albert—The William Peter Brewing Co 944

Newkirk, George—W Schranmann 2,230

O'Brien, W J—P McQuade 360

Schwartz, Solomon and August Myers as Schwartz & Meyers—H Kortlang 307

The North American Phonograph Co—A Darling 13,902

MECHANICS' LIENS.

Bruns, N, Jr, builder; Jno N and Werner Bruns, owners; The Union Stone Co, claimant, J City 128

Metzel, Francis, builder and owner; F Muller, claimant, Hoboken 815

Skurr, S A, owner and contractor; E W Keeney, claimant, J City 200

BUILDING MATERIAL MARKET.

BRICKS.—So far as general features are concerned almost any report given during the past five or six weeks might be repeated in portraying conditions prevailing since our last on the market for Common Hards. If there is any change at all it may be found in a lessened volume of trade and a still easier tone on values. The laborers who took a full holiday on Monday in many cases required two or three days extra to fully recover from the effects of their pleasure and work has been curtailed accordingly, though in any event the consuming wants were not particularly full, and storing as before advised is confined to occasional parcels, as most of the room is now fully occupied. In the meanwhile stock has continued to come forward in disagreeably large quantity, and while receivers were scarcely in a mood to push sales at all hazards the constant effort to find custom carries its natural effect and there was shading on cost in many cases. We do not alter the general range of quotations, because in exceptional instances it is claimed that $5.25 can still be obtained, but on bulk of stock business is reported at a shading of 12½@25c. per M from last week. Pales are also on the drag and it is said that even the Brooklyn inspectors are commencing to object to them, with prices toned down accordingly. A fine schooner load that has been held some time and finally put to forced sale commanded only $2.00, and custom was not easily found at that, while more ordinary quality sold at $1.75, possibly less. There is a gradual stoppage of work along the Hudson and an idea is entertained that the dull condition of trade may after all prove instrumental in leading to a pretty general shut down by the 20th of his month.

GLASS.—On the market for window glass business has for some time been in a dull and unsettled condition, and present chances for improvement are not particularly promising. The natural slow summer trade was intensified by the caution prevailing in regard to building operations generally, and finally the impatience of holders led to forced efforts in search of trade, with natural results to be found in more or less demoralization of values. This first developed on foreign stock, and it is intimated that importers cut and slashed rates well down to level of domestic product, but the latter weakened also, and was occasionally sold at unusually low rates. Of late, however, there has been a tendency to talk with greater confidence, and strong hopes entertained of getting rates upon a fuller level again, not through any indication of much, if any, increase of demand, as though the great uncertainty prevailing in regard to time when production at the American factories can be resumed. A short time ago a meeting of committees representing employers and employes failed to agree upon a scale of wages and, owing to certain formalities necessary, another conference cannot be held for several weeks; and even if an understanding is then arrived at, considerable additional time will be necessary to get the factories in working order. On old supplies, therefore, there is a chance for stiffening value somewhat. Plate is selling moderately, with only barely steady rates. Recently at a meeting of manufacturers and jobbers the former were requested to modify cost somewhat, and they complied to the extent of 5 per cent, though it is understood that one large manufacturer had previously been shading 10@12 per cent and selling exclusively to a combination of some half-dozen jobbers.

LATH.—Some few lots have come to hand and found custom, without the necessity of making a very extended search; yet it would appear there must have been sufficient, as values are not stimulated. One deal at least is reported as low as $2.05, but $2.10 appears to have been the more general rate, and $2 15 is claimed on a few transactions. In common with other material, lath find rather slow actual consumption at the moment, and dealers have a fair stock on hand; but there is said to be a somewhat more promising out-of-town call gradually developing.

LIME.—The market remains in about the same position as last week. Standard makes of Rockland have ruled steady in price throughout, and met a fair call, enough to exhaust the comparatively moderate arrivals without inconvenience to receivers. Other descriptions were somewhat irregular, but the offering seems to have been held in check to guard against effect of too much pressure upon an unwilling market.

LUMBER.—This has been a somewhat broken week, not confined so much to the loss of Monday, celebrated as a labor holiday, as to the subsequent influence, many workmen requiring an unusually long time to recuperate. Aside from that, however, which is of course only a temporary matter, the better undertone of late referred to seems to be progressive and we notice a more general inclination to speak hopefully regarding the prospects. There is a great deal of building definitely postponed until spring, but on the other hand evidences of a considerable coming on are noticeable and there is reason to believe that the apparent revival of confidence in commercial and financial circles is having beneficial influences upon lumber as well as other branches of trade. Dealers are not taking hold with avidity and many of them have already piled away considerable amounts of stock received during the summer months and up to date, but there are plenty who require a supply and they are commencing to take necessary steps for securing it. So far as can be learned they find fair quantities and assortment awaiting their negotiations, and while sellers are pretty steady for really desirable goods of all kinds there are few attempts to positively advance the line of cost, although some advices from primary sources indicate that manufacturers and dealers are quite determined to obtain more money on standard grades of stock. The export trade is fair, though outside of f. o. b orders at Southern ports, and the deals in hardwoods for Europe, business still runs mainly on cheap stuff.

Eastern Spruce is somewhat irregularly spoken of, and it seems evident all receivers are not having the same experience in placing cargoes. Complaints, however, are less frequent, and cheerful reports in some instances become rather pronounced, tending to show improvement in tone. It is, however, natural that dealers should commence to stir themselves a little, as the season is getting along gradually, and whenever a desirable parcel can be found within reach there seems little risk about taking it in, especially as the range of yard rates understood to be strictly adhered to affords a fair margin. There is continued talk at points of production about unprofitable markets and stoppage of saws, but the chances are that if a place is shown for it the lumber will be forthcoming.

Piling meets with more or less demand, but not enough to eat into the supply to any serious extent or afford sellers other advantage than checking further decline in value. There is, too, a belief that with improved feeling extant in the business world, many suggested improvements will take substantial form and lead to considerable winter work, especially should the season prove an open one.

Hemlock from up river is not bothering the market much this season, indeed it is said that some deliveries on contract are still rather short owing to scant supplies. The Pennsylvania manufacturers, however, supply a little more trade in this locality and at the eastward, and with a really good distribution to other interior points, some of them to the westward, the market as a whole has very fair shape. There is supply enough, but it is kept well under control and only allowed to come out about as required.

White Pine is now in very good supply so far as the low grades are concerned, and there commences to show up arrivals of the better qualities, the result of purchases made along from time to time during the season. Some new demand also prevails, for while dealers do not express anxiety regarding the general outlook either as to quantity or price, they tacitly admit that no further advantages are likely to come to them, and it is about as well to secure stock as it may come within reach as to wait longer. The scaling up of prices at the Minneapolis meeting seems to be viewed with indifference, except that some operators think it justified by conditions in that section, where trade is better than here. The reduced supply of dry stock in the Ottawa district, however, is spoken of with some respect.

Yellow Pine is commented upon somewhat favorably, and many operators are inclined to believe the market has passed its worst stage for this season. Between the sales of parcels for export before referred to, the placing of special bills on Northern account, and certain signs to indicate a probable consummation of the effort to curtail the output and regulate prices a greater degree of hopefulness is stimulated. There is very little car lot trade doing for random offering, deals for such delivery being mainly on specific orders.

A despatch from New Orleans on Thursday says: "A mammoth lumber contract was entered into here to-day between Mr. George S. Lacey, agent of the Keystone Lumber Company, and Messrs. Poitevant & Favre on the one hand, and a representative of the German Government as the other contracting party. The contract calls for the delivery at points in Germany, within eighteen months, of fifty million feet of pine lumber, and it is understood that the consignment will be used for the most part in the construction of railroads in the German Empire. The mills of Poitevant & Favre and those of the Keystone Lumber Company have each contracted for ten million feet and the remaining thirty million feet will be turned out by mills in this state and in Mississippi. Fully three-fourths of the lumber called for in the contract will be sent to Germany through this port, the rest going by way of Pascagoula, and the entire shipment will call for the utmost carrying capacity of one hundred ships.

Carolina Pine, according to report of a dealer, is not making any great "splurge" at the moment, but operators are getting in a considerable amount of fine work in quietly placing stock both with local and out-of-town custom, and maintaining steady rates on all first-class production. Some poor stuff is occasionally received, but as manufacturers have to pay for their carelessness by a reduction of price it is an evil likely to cure itself.

Hardwoods meet with only a moderate general demand and the market as a whole has practically no new features. In the matter of selection a great many small sales of poplar, and now and then a pretty full bunch, give it a prominent place, and oak, both plain and quartered, retains its favor. Other woods are handled irregularly, first one kind, then another appearing to get favor just as a class of custom may happen to be struck, but the regulars, such as ash, chestnut, hickory and maple, with a sprinkling of walnut, are probably most saleable. Prices are quoted about as before and are nominally steady, but buyers are thought to secure occasional moderate advantages.

GENERAL LUMBER NOTES.

CANADA.

The *Monetary Times* of Sept. 4th has the following, and it seems to confirm some of the reports of a prospective scarcity of Canadian lumber:

The latest mail advices from Great Britain seem to indicate that the careful reduction of import for some months at various ports there has brought the stocks on hand down to a point which renders an active demand more likely soon.

Some information of a significant character, bearing upon the lumber trade of Canada, was afforded in an interview held at Ottawa the other day with Mr. Todd, an English merchant in lumber and timber.

That gentleman, in speaking on the lumbering business in general, said that in England dealers in wood consider the statements made on this side of the Atlantic respecting the shortness of lumber here to be greatly exaggerated. Many of them, he said, will continue to be incredulous till they realize the truth by actual experiences. Quite recently, however, a few of the buyers who are better informed than others as to the condition of the Canadian markets have awakened up and have commenced buying.

The actual condition of stocks at Ottawa, for example, compared with their condition as the English people think them to be, is thus described by the Ottawa *Journal*: "Everybody here has been painfully aware for a year past that the stocks of dry lumber on the immense piling grounds of this city were being heavily drawn on, and that comparatively little new stuff was being made; and we all know that this summer large areas of the piling grounds have been almost bare, acres upon acres showing nothing but the growing grass, and the permanent rollers being the only visible evidence of the enormous stock of lumber once there. The dry stuff has been shipped away and there is very little left in the yards but green stuff just taken out of the water and sawn into lumber." The logical result of low stocks in the piling grounds and low stocks in the yards, of the wholesale reductions in numbers employed in the woods in the winter, the decreased output of all the going mills and shutting up altogether of other mills in the summer is, says the *Journal*, a brisk demand and hardening of prices. "The prospects, looked at all around, are good for solid improvement and increased prosperity for the lumber trade and all who depend upon it in Ottawa and the surrounding country."

GREAT BRITAIN.

The *Timber Trades Journal* gives following items:

Referring to auction sale at London it says:

American lumber of all sorts and sizes was next offered, without reserve, and cleared at low prices, as the broker said, "almost giving it away."

At Liverpool "the market is swamped with American whitewood logs, and, under the pressure of large arrivals, prices have gone down to a point about as low as ever known. This will, of course, have the effect of checking further supplies as soon as the results of present sales reach the shippers; but nothing excepting an entire cessation of supplies for some time will enable the market to recover itself."

At Glasgow:

It was referred to last week that the stock of Quebec deals in quarterly statement at 30th June last was very much less than at corresponding period in 1890; and, it may be said, next quarterly statement is likely to exhibit a still greater decrease under this year, because the Quebec deals landed here since 30th June last have been only about two-thirds of the quantity during like period in 1890, and deliveries recently have been fully maintained.

In particular, stocks of first, second and third pine deals are very light, and some considerable transactions recently in Quebec fourth pine deals have reduced them to very moderate compass, but there is a fairly ample supply on hand of Lower Port pine deals. Of Lower Port spruce deals the imports of late have been moderate, and present stock may be estimated as considerably less than at corresponding date last year.

THE WEST.

The Northwestern *Lumberman* as follows:

The commission men say that the past week has been the dullest one of the season on the cargo market. The yard men have been apathetic about buying any sort of lumber. Arrivals have been considerable, but it has been hard to work them off on any satisfactory basis. The yard men will not take hold in any case unless they can buy on sixty or ninety days' time. It appears as if either they had lumber enough or had resolved on a concert of action in insisting that time shall be given when lumber is sold. It will be remembered that a movement was made by the Yard Dealers' Association a year or more ago to change the order of things from cash to time payments. This the commission men objected to, and the association failed to secure full adherence to the plan. But the custom appears to have become about established without any definite action on the part of the association. The exigencies of trade has brought it into vogue as a kind of necessity.

The price of short-length piece stuff still hangs around $10 a thousand. Probably some indifferent stuff has been sold for a fraction less, but such deals are kept quiet. Since there is no urgent demand for piece stuff at the present time it is doubtless hard work to keep the price firm at $10.

Evidences of activity among the pine yards are numerous. Improved volume in shipments was noted in last week's report, and all signs now seem to point to a steady increase in business. It is not yet felt that the fall demand has set in, but it has cast its shadow before, and too many favorable reports of trade are received to make it reasonable to assume that there is not now a good average movement of lumber. Alongside dealers that report dullness or only a fair trade are arrayed others who assert that business is really good and has been for some time; that recent improvement has not been so notable as that concerns having large and well assorted stocks have been busy for weeks, while the call between yards for items to fill out bills is indicative of a generally good demand at this time. The number of cars everyday loaded and switched in the "Q" district is in itself evidence of briskness, and planing mills are reported uniformly busy. Some concerns report that they are having all they can do to advantage; in some instances business for August was ahead of that for July, and in various cases trade since spring is reported to have shown an increase of from 10 to 30 per cent as compared with the corresponding period of last year. Trade is not humping itself just now, but it is good enough.

The Chicago *Timberman* says:

Some of the local hardwood dealers report a good trade the past week, with increasing demand, but others say that this is because those dealers are slaughtering prices and that trade as a whole is not active. Certainly there is not as great activity in the yard trade as there was a year ago, but still it is probable that nearly as much lumber is being handled in Chicago as at that time. The large surplus stocks in all portions of the country give the car-load dealer a decided advantage over the yard dealer, and he is making the most of his opportunities. Several large mills have representatives in this city and are selling direct to the consumer at bout the same price they will sell to the yards, and are therefore capturing a good share of the trade.

Oak is as plentiful now as it was scarce last winter and yard prices are off from $2 to $3 to the thousand. Offerings are fair but the local trade is not disposed to buy heavily under present conditions. There is no doubt, however, but that oak will begin to move more freely during the present month, and while prices are not likely to reach the high water mark again this year, there are strong indications that they will do so before next spring.

The maple trade is steadily growing in volume, but prices are unchanged. Maple is being used much more extensively for manufacturing purposes than formerly and has come to be the leading flooring stock in this country.

High grade cherry is as ready sale as formerly at unchanged prices. Good walnut for export is wanted in excess of supply, but outside of this the trade in walnut is dull.

Selected red birch continues to improve in demand, but the call for this class of wood is not yet very extensive and dealers do not care to handle much of it at present prices.

Basswood and soft elm are selling freely, but there are excessive stocks of both and prices continue at the same low figure.

The Mississippi Valley *Lumberman* says that in the Saginaw valley the shipments during August were considerably less than for the same time last year. Vessels began arriving and loading very rapidly during the first of the month, and for a few days their owners were hopeful that the dull season had about ended, but the last half of the month was very dull. There is a large amount of lumber sold on the docks but its shipment will depend on the condition of the eastern markets. There is some talk of raising freight rates on the lakes.

NAILS.—Pretty much the former general story is repeated. Wire nails receive much favor and are filling many if not most of the immediate calls, but for cut the outlet is unsatisfactory, and manufacturers do not as yet find means to bring about a solid reform. We quote Cut at $1.50@1.60 per keg for car lots and $1.75@1.85 per keg for parcels from store, for iron, and add 5@10c. per keg for steel; Wire, $1.60@2.05 at mills, and 2.20@2.35 from store.

PAINTS, OILS, COLORS, ETC.—Business is picking up somewhat on the jobbing distribution, and there are said to be evidences of continued growth. The progress of the season helps matters somewhat, and while there is not much speculation in any of the deals, even to the extent of anticipating trade requirements in standard goods, it is calculated that custom on the "present necessity" basis must move quite a goodly portion of the supply. Some difficulty has been experienced in making collections, but on the whole the trade has not suffered materially, and the fine crops are calculated upon to improve the financial conditions in a large portion of dependent territory. Supplies and assortments now available are in good form to meet any ordinary call made upon them, and there are few complaints to be heard about difficulty in selection. Prices as a rule are kept in fairly steady position, and about the only shading is on second-hand parcels of White Lead. Association Corroders' rates stand as follows: Lead in oil in kegs and dry lead in kegs, in lots of less than 500 lbs., 7¼c. net; in lots of 500 lbs to 5 tons at one purchase, 7c.; 5 tons to 12 tons, one purchase,

9¾c.; 12 tons and over, one purchase, 6¾c.; dry white lead in bbls. ½c. per lb. less than price in kegs. Lead in oil 12½ lb. in tin pails, add 1c.; in 25 and 50 lb. tin pails, add ½c.; and in 1 to 5 lb. tin cans, assorted (100 lbs. in case) add 2½c. per lb. to keg price. Terms on lots on 500 lbs. and over, note or acceptance at sixty days, or 2½ per cent. discount will be allowed for cash paid within fifteen days of invoice date. To make either of the above required quantities any assortment of packages of white lead, red lead and litharge may be counted. The above quotations are free on board cars or boat at corroding point. Linseed Oil shows a somewhat irregular market, but as a rule price cutting is less severe and supplies seem to be well controlled especially the better qualities. We quote at general range at 37@40c. for Western, and 44@56c. for City. Spirits Turpentine continues in fair average jobbing demand and as the local stock is under control, with good accounts from primary points, prices are well sustained throughout. We quote at 37½@39c. per gallon, according to quality, delivery, etc.

TAR AND PITCH.—Business fluctuates somewhat, but operators act as though they were determined to make no complaint, and reports, as a rule, have steady tone in matter of valuation. Offerings are not of a liberal character, and made without pressure to realize. We quote Pitch at $1.70@1.75 per bbl.; Tar at $2.15@2.50, according to quantity, quality and delivery.

MISCELLANEOUS.

ATLANTIC WHITE LEAD AND LINSEED OIL COMPANY,

Manufacturers of

ATLANTIC" PURE WHITE LEAD.

The best and most reliable White Lead made and unequaled for uniform

Whiteness, Fineness and Body.

RED LEAD AND LITHARGE,

PURE LINSEED OIL,

Raw, Refined and Boiled.

Atlantic White Lead & Linseed Oil Co.,

287 PEARL STREET, New York.

A. KLABER,

Importer of and Worker in

MARBLE, ONYX & GRANITE

Steam Works,

238 to 244 EAST 57th STREET,

At 3d Av. Elevated R. R. Station NEW YORK

SHEA THE CLOTHIER

Cor. Broome and Crosby Sts., New York, is the only genuine dealer in leading American and European Tailors' Misfits at half price. Dress Suits for sale and hire. Established in 1869. **Also Ready-Made Clothing for Men and Boys.**

J. C. French & Son,

VAULT AND SIDEWALK

LIGHTS

Of every Description.

No. 452 Canal Street, New York.

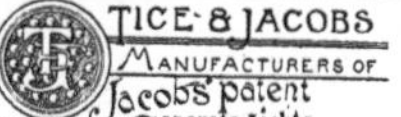

Material Men's Mercantile Association,

LIMITED

Reports and Ratings on BUILDERS & CONTRACTORS.

Daily Information as to Liens affecting Subscriber's Customers.

A Bureau of Quick and Reliable Information for

MATERIAL MEN.

[illegible] NASSAU ST., Tribune Bldg., NEW YORK.

MISCELLANEOUS

THE ANNUAL MEETING of the stockholders of THE C. GRAHAM & SONS COMPANY will be held at the office of the company, No. 309 East 43d Street, on FRIDAY, SEPTEMBER 18th, at 3 P. M.

GEO. G. BROOKS, Sec'y.

FIDELITY RANGE.

Pat. April 29, 1890.

ELEVATED

BOILER,

Plain or Hot Air, Right or Left Hand, with or without Hot Closets.

Just the thing for Flats and Small Houses.

Send for circulars.

Isaac A. Sheppard & Co.,

PHILADELPHIA

OR

BALTIMORE.

Furnaces and Ranges.

NOW IS THE TIME TO HAVE YOURS PUT IN REPAIR.

Send in your orders to one who has been in the business the past 25 years, and have your work properly done.

IRA G. LANE,

207 East 64th St.

GEO. E. READ, Agent, 132 Park Ave., N. Y.

G. W. BROMLEY & CO.'S

ATLASES of NEW YORK

just issued (1890).

Subscription price $15, for sale at $5 each.

J. H. MITCHELL,

ROOM 36 82 NASSAU STREET

O. A. PRICE,

—(STEAM)—

STAIR BUILDER,

415-417 E. 91st St., New York.

Estimates given. All work promptly attended to.

WM. H. OLIVER,

(Late Hobbs & Oliver.)

PLAIN and DECORATIVE PAINTING

Paper Hangings and Interior Decorations.

62 and 64 UNIVERSITY PLACE, . . . New York.

Telephone 833—21st St. ESTABLISHED 1846.

GEORGE W. LITHGOW,

GENERAL REPAIRS TO BUILDINGS

41 King Street, New York.

MISCELLANEOUS.

Our Position

ON AMERICAN TIN PLATE.

The numerous inquiries made of us as to how soon we would manufacture or distribute American plates that would be of the same class or high grade of excellence as those which we are now guaranteeing, render it necessary that we should publicly answer and define our position, which is as follows:

Up to this writing we are not aware of any American maker who can give us the quantity we daily require, and the all important guarantee required by this house; nor is it reasonable for us to expect it at this early period.

It must be known that months of time, thought and considerable money were expended by us before the best plates known to the American trade were put upon the market, and we assure the trade—**NOW** as we did **THEN**—that reputation with us is paramount. We shun misrepresentations just as we avoid their results, viz: unenviable notoriety.

As soon as we can secure American plates **equal to those we now guarantee, our patrons shall have them;** but we wish it understood that **OUR** idea of manufacturing tin plates is not that of **DIPPING** a plate made elsewhere and the use and **ABUSE** of a stamping machine. Any one familiar with the tin plate business knows full well such a plant (?) can be erected and in operation in a few days.

MERCHANT & CO.,

PHILADELPHIA, NEW YORK,

CHICAGO,

KANSAS CITY, LONDON.

JAMES MATHEWS & SON,

Excelsior, Pat. Dec. 3, 1889.

Sole agents and Manufacturers of

MAX KELLING'S

Patent

FIRE-PROOF

IRON

Dumb Waiter Doors and Casings, Sashes, Windows, Shutters and Wall Closets.

The most durable and cheapest articles in the market.

PRICES:

$3, $4, $6, $7, $8

and upward, according to size and style.

Illustrated catalogue, price list and references sent on application.

Over 5,000 in use in this city.

Main Office & Salesroom,

172 E. 110th St.

Branch & Factory,

510 & 512 E. 20th St.

RAPP SHEET METAL WORKS.

Man'f'rs of

RAPP'S PAT.

IRON

Dumb Waiter

DOORS

AND

FRAMES.

Send for illustrated catalogue and price list.

Indorsed by the leading architects and builders as being the best and cheapest Fire-Proof Door made.

Pat. May 6th, 1890.

J. W. RAPP, Sole Agent,

315-319 E. 94th St., N. Y. City.

A. T. DECKER CO.,

Wholesale and Retail Dealers in

GEORGIA AND FLORIDA

Yellow Pine

YARDS AND OFFICE:

FOOT OF BETHUNE ST., North River,

Telephone Call, 189 Spring. NEW YORK.

BUILDING MATERIAL PRICES

LUMBER.

Appended quotations are based almost wholly upon prices obtained for goods from first hands. Yard rates necessarily range much higher owing to the expenses attending sorting out and grading cargo and even car lots, besides which must be added the cost of handling and carrying until consumers are ready to invest. Terms of sale also prove important factors and, altogether, it is impossible to give a line of retail quotations thoroughly reliable n character.

SPRUCE—Eastern—special cargoes delivered N. Y.	$16 50	@	18 00
Random cargoes, narrow	13 50	@	14 00
Random cargoes, wide	14 50	@	16 00
PILING—Eastern—cargo rates:			
Ranging 30@40 per cent 12 inch butt, 35 to 40 ft average length	1	@	—
Ranging 45@50 per cent 12 inch butt, 35 to 40 ft average length	4¼	@	4½
Ranging 50@60 per cent One-half 12 inch butt, 38 to 40 ft average length	4¾	@	5
Two-thirds 12 inch butt, 38 to 42 ft average length	5½	@	6
Three-fourths 12 inch butt, 40 to 45 ft average length	5¾	@	6
All 12 inch butt and up, 40 to 45 ft average length	6	@	6¼
Piece stick, 40 feet each	4 00	@	—
do. 45	6 00	@	—
do. 50	8 00	@	—
do. 55	12 00	@	—
Inch spars, per inch	20	@	22
Scaffolding poles, each	60	@	1 00
Clothes poles, 45 to 65 feet, each	3 00	@	6 00
HEMLOCK:			
Penn. joist	12 00	@	12 50
do. boards	13 00	@	13 50
do. timber, 20 ft and under	12 50	@	13 00
do. do. 22 to 24 ft	13 00	@	13 50
do. do. 26 to 28 ft	13 50	@	14 00
do. do. 30 to 32 ft	14 00	@	15 50
do. do. 34 to 36 ft	15 50	@	16 00
do. do. 38 to 40 ft	16 50	@	17 50
WHITE PINE—Good uppers and select, 1 to 2 inch	40 00	@	48 00
Upper and select, 2½ to 4 inch	50 00	@	58 00
Shelving	26 00	@	31 00
Pickings, 1 inch	33 00	@	35 00
Cutting-up, 1 inch	25 00	@	28 00
Bracket plank	30 00	@	35 00
Dressing-boards	18 00	@	22 00
Box, inch	13 50	@	14 00
Box, thick	14 50	@	15 50
West India shippers	16 00	@	19 00
Rio Janeiro do.	20 00	@	21 00
River Plate do.	29 00	@	30 00
Australia do.	25 00	@	30 00
YELLOW PINE—Random cargoes delivered N. Y.	18 00	@	19 00
Ordered cargoes	19 50	@	21 00
Flooring	24 00	@	24 00
Step plank	26 00	@	28 00
Common siding	15 00	@	16 00
Heart face boards	22 00	@	23 00
Car orders	21 00	@	23 00
At Atlantic ports, f. o. b.	12 00	@	12 50
At Gulf ports, f. o. b.	11 50	@	12 50
North Caroline pine timber	13 50	@	15 00
do. flooring 1 inch	16 00	@	22 00
do. do. 1¼	16 50	@	22 50
do. do. 1½@2 inch.	24 00	@	25 00
do Shipping culls or box	12 00	@	14 00
do Plain and mottled ½@1¼ inch.	18 50	@	25 50
Ash, white	36 00	@	43 00
Elm	20 00	@	22 50
Oak, plain	37 00	@	41 00
Oak, quarter sawed	52 00	@	55 00
Oak, quarter sawed, extra thick	56 00	@	60 00
Redwood	45 00	@	52 50
Maple, clear	28 00	@	33 00
Chestnut, clear	33 00	@	35 50
Cypress, clear	30 00	@	32 50
Black Walnut, good to choice	130 00	@	140 00
Black Walnut, ordinary to fair	100 00	@	120 00
Black Walnut, ⅝	78 00	@	83 00
Black Walnut, selected and seasoned	150 00	@	155 00
Black Walnut counters	110 00	@	150 00
Black Walnut, culls	35 00	@	40 00
Black Walnut, rejects	50 00	@	53 00
Cherry, wide	110 00	@	115 00
Cherry, good	85 00	@	100 00
Cherry, ordinary	65 00	@	80 00
Whitewood, inch	30 50	@	32 50
Whitewood, ⅝ inch	24 50	@	26 00
Whitewood, 1¼ to 2½ inch	32 00	@	34 00
Shingles, Pine, 16 inch, extra	2 75	@	3 10
do 18 inch, extra	4 10	@	4 30
do 18 inch, clear butt	2 90	@	3 10
do 16 inch, stocks	4 50	@	4 60
do 18 inch, stocks	5 30	@	5 40
Shingles, Cypress, 6x20	8 00	@	10 00
do larger sizes	11 00	@	16 00
do sawed	6 00	@	9 00
Cedar—Medium to large	6¼	@	7¼
do. —Extra large	7¾	@	8
Mahogany—Small	6½	@	½
do —Medium	8	@	6½
do. —Large	9½	@	12
do. —Extra Large	12½	@	14

REAL ESTATE RECORD AND BUILDERS' GUIDE.
ESTABLISHED MARCH 21st 1868.

DEVOTED TO REAL ESTATE, BUILDING ARCHITECTURE, HOUSEHOLD DECORATION, BUSINESS AND THEMES OF GENERAL INTEREST

PRICE, PER YEAR IN ADVANCE, SIX DOLLARS.

Published every Saturday.

TELEPHONE - - - - CORTLANDT 1370.

Communications should be addressed to

C. W. SWEET, 14 & 16 Vesey St.

J. T. LINDSEY, Business Manager.

VOL. XLVIII SEPTEMBER 19, 1891. No. 1,227

Subscribers should see that they are supplied in this number with a copy of the "Northern Railroad of New York Supplement."

THE EXHIBITION OF ARCHITECTURAL DRAWINGS.

One of the handsomest and most complete displays of architectural drawings will be opened next week in the exhibition halls of THE RECORD AND GUIDE, *at Nos. 14-16 Vesey street, to which all who are interested in architecture are cordially invited. The exhibition is free. There are on view over two hundred perspectives of the latest work done by all the leading architects of New York City. So excellent an opportunity for any one to familiarize himself with the best work of the day has not before been offered.*

AT about the time when the gloomy-minded had confidently predicted injury to the corn crop by frost we are favored with specially good weather for that cereal almost to the extent of a supplemental summer. It may now be expected that the gloomy-minded will in a few days be predicting injury to the corn crop from want of frost. Meantime stocks are advancing so rapidly that favorable opinions are hardly expressed before they are verified. There has been a brisk movement all along the line now, and the Grangers have entered on the second stage of the advance; this is not quite so extensive as the first for the very good reason that the first rise included a recovery from over-depression as well as some discounting of the situation. Still it promises to be substantial. Everyone knows, or should by this time know, the immense influence a great crop has on the business of the country, and, combined with an unusual demand for cereals from abroad, that influence is correspondingly increased. Everyone knows, too, that stocks have not yet discounted all the good there is in the situation, nor will they for some time to come. We must, of course, have reactions at some time or another, and the greater the pace the more speedily we will come to the point where a decline will be in order; but a reaction of any moment is not, as a rule, heralded by such jumps in prices as we have seen for two or three days, but rather by hesitatory and indecisive fluctuations, Hence no important decline need be expected necessarily because of any increase in values yet seen. The tide is so strong in one direction that it would seem that should any one attempt to stem it, let him be ever so powerful individually, he would deserve only a pair of long ears for his pains. The crowd for the time being is pushing one way and the individual does not count at all. Still the movement is rapid and cannot go on for ever and a week, hence we may see a change, though there is now no waiting for time, tide or the opinions of newspapers.

NO small part of the strength of the present buying movement in the stock market apparently comes from London, and operators on this side are depending more or less on that centre for support and assistance in the work of putting up prices. It has been believed, and with reason, that since financial conditions are insecure the world over, with the almost single exception of this country, English investors would turn their eyes in this direction for the next few years, particularly since their holdings of American securities are less now than they were a couple of years ago. In view of this expectation, it is interesting to note what the English financial authorities have to say upon the prospects and standing of American issues. The *Economist* certainly cannot be charged with any prepossessions in favor of our railroads. Some of its recent criticisms have been not only severe, but unjustly severe. Yet the *Economist* recently, in an article on the wide fluctuations of our railroad stocks, said: "The future, however, is of more interest than the past, and what investors now seek to know is whether American railway shares are becoming more worthy to be regarded as investments, or, in other words, whether they are likely now to enjoy greater stability and prosperity. We are inclined to think they are, for several reasons." These reasons are that the most virulent competition is exhausted, that the State Legislatures are beginning to be more fair to the transportation interests, and that the local traffic is being more consistently and successfully developed, and in closing it recommends particularly the purchase of bonds. This is an interesting indication of the trend of English opinion; and we shall doubtless see in the future substantial effects from the increased confidence.

THE exasperating delays to which the local passengers of the Vanderbilt lines have been subject throughout this summer has, at all events, had the good effect of directing public attention to the matter; and so fast and free have been the criticisms showered on the management, that it is doubtless getting ready to mend matters so far as it can. Indeed, Vice-President Webb has said to a reporter "that elaborate and carefully prepared plans were under consideration for the relief of the congested suburban traffic," including a four-track bridge over the Harlem with entirely new approaches. Such an improvement would doubtless help to prevent much of the delay which now takes place in the uncomfortable tunnel and elsewhere; but quite obviously it would by no means meet adequately the needs of the present traffic, much less that of the future. The fact is, to use the emphatic but by no means exaggerated words of the *Evening Post*, "that everybody who lives above the Harlem River and has occasion to travel by the New York Central, the Harlem or the New York & New Haven Railroads is aware that the 'terminal facility,' known as the 'Grand Central Station,' has completely broken down and that the epithet 'Grand' applied to it has become more or less ridiculous. Not only is it inferior to the great stations of the leading capitals of the world but it is equalled by those of many second-rate provincial lines." And it follows from this inadequacy that these corporations must do something more than build a bridge over the Harlem if they wish to make their service at all adequate to their traffic. What this crying insufficiency is may be gathered from the fact that after each has discharged its passengers it has to go back six miles on the main line, to be broken up and made up over again, and has to be brought back six miles to resume its place in the time table. No wonder the New Haven Road is trying to find a southern outlet by means of the 2d avenue elevated tracks. It has been evident for some time that the Central officials do not intend any further enlargement of their present station. With any such intention in view they would never have permitted the erection of the large storage warehouse lately put up between Park and Lexington avenues, 43d and 44th streets, on land formerly occupied by the company. It would be too expensive. Everything points to a shifting of the principal terminus north of the Harlem. After this is done, however, the difficulty of distributing the passengers throughout the lower half of the city punctually and effectually will remain; and in order to compass this end, we do not see what better means the corporations could adopt than the controlling of the second route laid out by the Rapid Transit Commissioners. Such a connection would seem to be essential to the proper working of their system. There are several minor ways, however, in which the service can be improved immediately. One is the uniform utilization of clean and neat cars; another is to follow the example of the New York & Northern and to burn only hard coal. It is peculiarly unfortunate for Westchester County and the 23d and 24th Wards that they are served by corporations that are very liable to neglect their manifest duties to their patrons.

THERE have been some rejoicings in the Mugwump camp over what is known as the downfall of Hill. According to Saratoga dispatches during the past week, the Democratic convention passed completely beyond the Senator-Governor's control. He was opposed to the nomination of Flower, but could not prevent it; he was opposed to the nomination of Sheehan, but Chairman Murphy forced it on him; he was in favor of straddling the silver question, but the Croker and others insisted on the adoption of a flat-footed declaration in favor of "honest" money, so-called. In all the matters, other interests dictated the action of the convention; and as the New York machine is his only support, it has been loudly stated that the end of Hill as a political power has come. It may be so; but every presumption, every argument from the man's past career, every circumstance of the ostensible defeat argues a very different conclusion. It will be admitted, we suppose, that very possibly the correspondents may have been deceived by a lot of carefully-prepared lies and incidents, that a little comedy may have been staged for the purpose of turning the campaign in another direction from that which it was taking and of eliminating Hillism as an issue. Obviously it is to the Governor's interest that the virulent attacks to which he has been subjected should be discontinued; his candidacy at the Democratic National Convention would be materially strengthened thereby, and the only way in which this could be done is the temporary suppression of Hill as leader. Hence he would have a direct motive in creating the impression that has been created; and it would be perfectly possible for him to do so. On the other hand, notice the difficulty of the theory that his power has been completely superseded. For seven years the Democratic machine has been his personal property, and all his energies have been concentrated solely on the object of the Democratic Presidential nomination in 1892. Would such a shrewd man (he has repeatedly shown his shrewdness) be likely to relinquish his grip just on the eve of the final struggle? And if he saw the control of his machine snatched from his hands at the last moment, would he be likely to sit still and see it pass away without a contest? That he is a good fighter his opponents have reason to know. Furthermore, in the past, has he not worked in the most friendly way with Tammany? Has he not helped them and they helped him on every possible occasion? As to Flower, would he be likely to alienate a rich man of that stamp—a man who is liberal in his contributions to the strong box of his party? Would not the assistance of such a man be invaluable to him? And what better way of buying that assistance than the Democratic nomination for Governor of New York? Then take the silver plank. The organization in this State has done a popular thing in coming out against silver coinage, while by giving out that he is not responsible for the plank he has increased his acceptability to the southern and western Democrats. How much truth there is in this opposite view, we will not attempt to state; but it certainly possesses a large share of plausibility. Mr. Hill has always been devious, intricate and tricky in his political methods; and there would be nothing out of keeping with his political character in the hypothesis that his ostensible defeat is a huge hoax.

The Errors in Block Indexing.

A NUMBER of the daily newspapers have been printing accounts lately of the many errors in indexing arising from the working of the Block bill that went into operation on January 1st last; and in consequence some general and totally unjustifiable criticisms have been passed on the statute. That some errors have crept in, everybody familiar with the Register's office well knows; and furthermore these errors might, if uncorrected, have a disastrous effect on the security of titles. The law, as we have frequently pointed out, reduces the area of search from the county to the block. In making a search, no one is obliged to look further for instruments affecting the title to a given parcel than under the index of the block or blocks wherein the parcel is situated. Any paper not found after such a search is void against a bona fide purchaser. It is in this respect that the New York law differs from the New Jersey law, and from similar systems that obtain in some of the minor cities of the country. There it is only a convenience; here it is a material and indispensable part of the record. Hence it is absolutely necessary that the indexing should be accurate; and that every possible device should be adopted, and care taken to prevent errors and to correct them.

The mistakes which have crept in have been traced to well-known and to easily remediable causes. Since the indexing began more than 20,000 papers have been placed on record at the Register's office, and according to Deputy-Register Hanley only one error in indexing has been found traceable to the error of a clerk. In all the other cases, and according to the same authority, their number has been greatly exaggerated, the mistakes were those of lawyers or others who prepared the papers for record. Some of them were very natural, having arisen from the fact that a different set of maps were used in the Tax Department from those used in the Register's office; and the remedy lies obviously in the passage of a bill making the tax maps conform to the block maps. A bill to accomplish this object was introduced last session, but failed of passage owing to the Senate dead-lock. As the Tax Commissioners favor the legislation, it will certainly be again introduced next session, and in all probability passed. With this source of error eliminated, a proper system of checking will accomplish the rest. Under the present law the Register is obliged to notify the lawyers and have the correction made when the error is discovered, but he is not made responsible for the seeking of the error. He can, and, as a matter of fact, does accept the indorsement on the paper as indubitable. Now this divided or half responsibility is manifestly ridiculous. In the bill, as originally drawn, the Register was made responsible for indexing the instruments under the proper blocks, regardless of the indorsement, and the statute should be amended to that effect. No paper should be indexed until rectified, and the system of checking should make the appearance of any error quite impossible. In two minor ways, also, can the system be improved, and without any additional legislation. The Board of Estimate and Apportionment should appropriate sufficient money to pay the salaries of a couple of clerks, whose duty it should be to give all necessary information to people recording papers. Another improvement would be the keeping of all the index and record books belonging to one section in an alcove used exclusively for that section. At present, owing to some blunder in the making of the alcoves, they are too small.

On the whole the bill has undoubtedly worked very well. The system itself has been found to be fully adequate to the needs of the public in the matter of recording. All that has to be done is the making of certain corrections in the methods of carrying out the system, to the originator of which it is due to say that he fully anticipated all the sources of error, and would, if permitted, have provided for them. A method of simplifying the records and searches, which the title companies have adopted and used successfully for years, would surely seem to have been sufficiently tested. It is very necessary that any impression of failure should be removed, for at the next meeting of the Legislature a bill for re-indexing the records will be presented and will require strong public backing. This is the next step in land transfer reform in this State, and a much needed one. Indeed, it is the logical completion of the work begun by the present law, which is meaningless unless the principles underlying its provisions are made retroactive. The block-indexing statute has the advantage of giving to property-owners an assurance that searching will never become more difficult than it is now, at all events so far as the Register's office is concerned; but it is obvious that a system which works well in preventing the chaotic accumulation of real estate instruments, would also work well in arranging and simplifying those already in existence. Hence the work just begun should be vigorously pushed. New York started the movement in favor of land transfer reform and should be the first to have a working scheme in order. Some four or five States, including Massachusetts, Illinois, and one of the Dakotas, have Legislative Commissions at work inquiring into the feasibility of the Torren's Act and the general subject of land transfer reform. They should not be allowed to anticipate the action of the authorities of this State.

NO one, of course, supposes that the removal of Commissioner Beattie means clean streets or even cleaner streets. The deposition of that individual is nothing more than a piece of dictatorial humbug. The fact of the matter is, Tammany has discovered that it is much easier to give the public an occasional scapegoat than to clean the streets, so, whenever complaints become numerous and the newspapers more than ordinarily persistent in their criticisms, there is a "removal" or something else of the kind, which is supposed to meet the case, and afterwards everything goes on as before. Mr. Beattie's administration has not been of the character that we would like to see permanently established; but on the whole we do not think it has been worse than those of his predecessors. We even believe that this political person has done as well as he could, considering the fact that he was, like most politicians, totally unfit for the position he held, and besides was hampered by a system that had to be political in the first place, and then as efficient as it could be afterwards. The people of New York had better settle down at once to the knowledge that so long as this city is governed for "politics" mainly, the administration of the Street Cleaning Department will not be a whit more satisfactory than it is to-day. Until politics are put aside and government becomes a matter of business New York will remain one of the dirtiest and noisomest cities in Christendom. Why fool ourselves: our position is so obvious.

The Rapid Transit Plans.

The Rapid Transit Commission has received the reports of Octave Chanut, Theodore Cooper, Joseph Wilson and John Bogart, the consulting engineers to whom the Worthen and Parsons plans of construction of the Broadway-Boulevard line were referred for criticism and report, and has found in them so much more material for study and so many important points upon which it will have to decide that it could not come to an immediate conclusion upon them, but has set aside all of next week, from Tuesday on, for their consideration and decision.

President Steinway, with reference to the work of the consulting engineers, said: "It was an exceedingly fortunate idea, that of submitting the plans to this corps of engineering experts. The suggestions and criticisms made by them are full of importance. This report of Mr. John Bogart, which we have just read, is masterly and convincing. He has gone thoroughly and exhaustively into the subject, and has given us a good deal to think about. The other reports, which were opened last week, are equally valuable, showing that, notwithstanding all the study we had given to the matter, there were ideas and suggestions of great value that we had thus far overlooked.

"It will be necessary now to have abstracts of each report made and then for the commission to meet and consider the reports in detail and all together, and from the various suggestions and ideas received to make our decision. We have heard from Commissioner Spencer that he can be with us probably on Tuesday, certainly on Wednesday, and we will hold daily sessions thereafter until the matter is decided. We can form no conclusion as yet as to which plan will be selected, though it seems as if one of them, with some important amendments, will be the choice of the commission. The question of interference with traffic in Broadway will enter very largely into the consideration of the question, because it is a serious matter with Broadway property-owners. And while we feel that it would be a measure of superior economy in the long run to endure the disturbance of the street's surface a few months longer for the sake of the permanent roadbed that would be secured, we will have to pay serious attention to the wishes of property-owners in the matter. Besides, there are other important facts to be considered, which are embraced in the reports of the consulting engineers."

No official information regarding the contents of the reports of Messrs. Chanut, Cooper, Wilson and Bogart was given out, but THE RECORD AND GUIDE is reliably informed that the general tendency of the reports is favorable to the Worthen plan, of four tracks on one level, which would be 17 feet below the surface of the street. But for this plan, like the other, some important changes have been recommended. Mr. Chanut, for instance, has recommended that instead of running all four tracks down to the South Ferry, the road below City Hall Park shall be only a two-track road, with a loop running down through State street and back by way of Whitehall; and two of the tracks shall diverge at or near Mail street and form a loop under City Hall Park back to Broadway at Chambers street, forming a connection with Brooklyn Bridge, with a station just opposite the bridge entrance.

Others of the reports express, it is said, a clear preference for the Worthen plan of construction, for several reasons which are elaborately set forth. Some of them, stated briefly, are that in the Worthen plan the railroad question is kept entirely distinct and separate from the sub-surface pipe-conduit matter, which is considered a matter for the city authorities to deal with entirely separate from the rapid transit question. In the other plan it would be difficult to apportion the relative cost of the pipe-conduit and the rapid transit road, and this would be a serious objection to the scheme with investors. Then, it is believed, that, independent of the pipe-galleries, the double-decked road would cost 20 per cent. more to build than the other. It would require a much greater excavation, deeper foundations for the walls and more material of all kinds. Again, if there should ever happen to be a break down, or collision in the double-decked tunnel, it would be more difficult to get the passengers out and the obstruction cleared away than in the other and wider tunnel, where all four tracks would rest on *terra firma*.

Another superiority for the Worthen plan which is said to be mentioned in the reports is that the tunnel or arcade, which it would more closely resemble, would be better and more cheaply capable of lighting and ventilating. With its nearer approach to the surface of the street, and extending in one wide open stretch from side to side of the street, there would be opportunity of side lighting and ventilating at stations which would be inconvenient in the other plan. Furthermore, there would be fewer steps to climb in coming out of the stations in the Worthen plan, by an average of twelve at each station—an important consideration with aged and heavy persons, and one which would affect seriously the popularity of the proposed road. The Worthen plan provides for station platforms at a depth of but 17 feet below the surface of the street, while the Parsons plan would require a descent of twenty-four steps to the lower, or express tracks. In the Worthen plan the two middle tracks would be used for express purposes, the two side tracks for local traffic. At express stations the side tracks would make a detour around the stations under the sidewalks, and passengers would enter the express and local trains from opposite sides of the stations.

In the Worthen plan the pipe-gallery is not altogether lost sight of, for in the space of 7 feet 8 inches between the roof of the arcade and the surface of the street there would be ample space for the construction of the pipe-gallery whenever the city should determine to build it, and the roof of the arcade, with its supporting walls and columns would afford a solid and substantial foundation for the support of the upper roadway. Finally, it is said to be the opinion that the Worthen arcade can, if necessary, be constructed without disturbing the surface of the street, while the Parsons tunnel would cause an interruption of traffic over a third of the street in width at a time for two or three years. In either plan, electricity is held to be the only satisfactory motive power. All these considerations, and others which have not yet been made known, are to be considered and determined by the commission in detail, together with the designation of the points at which stations are to be provided, during the coming week. The commissioners hope to reach their conclusion upon them and to be able to report to the Board of Aldermen by the 1st of October.

The Municipal Building Project.

A site for the proposed new municipal building is again under discussion in the inner official circles. This time it is said that the majority of the commission appointed to select and acquire a site have fixed upon the *Staats Zeitung* block and the two irregular blocks across Chambers street from it as the property on which to erect the desired building. According to the informant of THE RECORD AND GUIDE, Mayor Grant has requested the Comptroller to call an early meeting of the commission for the purpose of considering and acting upon the matter.

The property referred to is embraced within the lines drawn from Tryon row, along Park row to Duane street, along Duane to Reade, along Reade to Centre, and along Centre to Tryon row, to Park row. It is intersected by Chambers street and by City Hall place. The plans, which have been elaborately worked out, provide for the condemnation of the entire tract, except the lot on the south side of Chambers street, 92 feet front, which is owned by the city, and therefore would not have to be condemned; to close City Hall place entirely and to construct an arcade through the proposed building covering Chambers street, but leaving it open for traffic as at present.

The site described would front 275 feet on Centre street, exclusive of Chambers street, which is 64.6 feet wide, and would make the entire Centre street front 339.6 feet; 96 feet 10 inches on Tryon row; 286 feet 9 inches on Park row, exclusive of Chambers street, or about 351¼ feet, that included; 119 feet 5 inches on Duane street, and, including City Hall place, which is 46 feet wide, 165 feet on Reade street. The assessed valuation of the property, including the city's lot, which is assessed at $40,000, is $895,000. Of this the *Staats Zeitung* represents $325,000. Upon inquiry at the *Staats Zeitung* office the story as above told was confirmed. But it was said that the taking of the *Staats Zeitung* property for this or any other purpose would be strenuously opposed by Mr. Oswald Ottendorfer. Mr. Ottendorfer would not accept $2,000,000 for the property in a voluntary transaction; and there was no public necessity which would justify the city authorities in paying any such price for it.

Important to Broadway Property-Owners.

We gladly print the following important letter:

"SEPTEMBER 15, 1891.

"*Editor* RECORD AND GUIDE:

"You will do a great service to the owners of property on Broadway and other streets which are being repaved by notifying them through your valuable paper that in almost every case where the new pavement is laid, it is done in such a way as to make the vaults of the buildings leak very badly. They can be made tight at a trifling expense before the new pavement is put down. After it is laid there is not only a delay in getting a permit to take it up again, but it is extremely expensive. I suppose the city's object in making it so was to prevent its being torn up again. However, if the vaults are not attended to before the paving is done they will have to be afterwards at a large expense to the owners and the discomfort of the general public.

F. SOUTHACK."

Special Notices.

In a few days there will be the usual scramble to get tax bills, and the usual tedious waiting in line to pay taxes. Few people enjoy the task of getting and paying a tax bill, or feel very certain when they are through that they have made correct payment. The Title Guarantee and Trust Company, of 55 Liberty street, has established a bureau to relieve owners of this unpleasant task. It registers the owner's lot, gives him, throughout the year, immediate notice when any tax, assessment, or water rate becomes payable, and procures and sends him the correct bill. If desired, it attends to the actual payment of the lien, saving the owner the necessity of going to any of the Departments at all. The company will guarantee that all such payments are correctly made, and will issue an annual certificate as to all tax liens on the lot. The charge is $2 per lot per annum, and the convenience and security to the owner are worth five times the amount. Owners of mortgages can use the bureau with like advantage. The company will, for the same charge, make and certify to them an annual search for taxes against each one of the mortgaged premises.

S. F. Jayne & Co., of No. 254 West 23d street and No. 59 Liberty street, offer a very desirable opportunity to manufacturers. They have for lease for a term of years the premises at No. 6 Gansevoort street, near Hudson. The buildings are substantial, the front one being four-story and basement, 25x41, and the rear one three-story and basement, 25x43. It contains a 12 horse-power steam engine and full machinery for wood-working. It is in first-rate order, and would be rented for the purpose of any business. Additional property running through the block can be obtained if wanted.

Thomas Curran, of New York City, manufacturer of Curran's Grooved Plaster Slab, has been quite successful, during the past six months, in introducing his grooved plaster slab. Its successful introduction is due not only to his strenuous and untiring exertions in putting it upon the market, but also to the obvious advantages which the slab itself possesses, and which are readily recognized and appreciated by the leading architects and builders. Among the many large contracts that he has had is one in which 60,000 square feet of this slab were used as a foundation for Portland cement finish on the exteriors and interiors of the new Eldorado buildings on Weehawken Heights, opposite 42d street, erected by the American Amusement and Exhibition Company. This is one of the largest contracts for exterior cement work on frame buildings ever done in this country. Messrs. McElfatrick & Son, architects of these immense buildings, consider this grooved plaster slab the cheapest and most practical foundation for exterior cement work and interior plastering ever brought to their notice, and think it is destined to prove an important factor in all future work of this kind.

John N. Golding, formerly with the firm of Adrian H. Muller & Son, and later a partner in the well-known firm of Brown & Golding, some time ago opened an office at No. 11 Pine street for the conduct of a general real estate business. Recently Mr. Golding has taken up a new branch of the business, auctioneering, and he bids fair to make as great a success in that as he has already done in selling and leasing property and managing estates. On Tuesday last, when several of the old-time auctioneers had sales at the Real Estate Exchange, there was in front of Mr. Golding's stand a larger crowd of interested bidders and spectators than at any of the other stands, and it seemed to be the general opinion of those present that the new auctioneer would make a success in the Auction Room. That such a corporation as the Equitable Life Assurance Society should have confidence enough in the new auctioneer as to intrust to him several important sales is certainly a flattering indication of the esteem in which Mr. Golding as an auctioneer is already held by the real estate community. To recommend him in his new line of activity Mr. Golding has an engaging manner, a clear and powerful voice and a courtesy in his treatment of bidders that cannot fail to attract the favorable attention of all those connected with the real estate business.

Henry H. Dreyer, the active West Side real estate broker, of No. 435 Amsterdam avenue, has closed several large sales of real estate within the past two weeks that have set people talking. Within that time Mr. Dreyer has sold property to the amount of nearly $450,000, and he is now engaged on a number of other transactions of greater or less magnitude, which it seems from present indications will be consummated. Mr. Dreyer was for a long time established at Columbus avenue and 93d street, where he did a large renting and collection business as well as a sales business. In his new offices at the southeast corner of 81st street and Amsterdam avenue, he has even better facilities for the transaction of a general real estate business. Mr. Dreyer has commended himself to all those with whom he has had any dealings by a strict attention to business, and by jealously guarding and serving the best interests of his patrons. It is safe to say that the record of this broker in the past for straightforward dealing and zealous service will be surpassed only by his record of the future.

A circular letter, issued by the directors of the Real Estate Loan and Trust Company to the stockholders of that institution, shows not only that the business of the company is in a very satisfactory condition, but that it has increased and is increasing rapidly. For instance, in the banking department in November, 1890, the number of depositors was 74, and August, 1891, 260, while between those dates the average balance of deposits had risen from $278,646 to $1,342,590, despite the recent tight money market. There was, no doubt, a vacant place in the commercial economy of this city which this institution has filled; for, although its real estate department was not fully organized until May the first of this year, it has been very successful. The real estate committee of the Board of Trustees consists of Messrs. Horace S. Ely, Herman H. Cammann and Douglas Robinson, Jr., and the company has already under its management over 100 pieces of property. A number of appraisals of an important character have been made, and the sales and leases of real estate effected have been large. The management of the company is in excellent hands, Henry C. Swords being President; Herman H. Cammann, Vice-President; Henry W. Reighley, Secretary; James M. Varnum, Counsel; Thomas H. Terry, Real Estate Officer. The endeavor of the officers of the company has been to make its investments and loans of the most current, conservative and secure character. The offices of the company are at 30 Nassau street.

The Union Iron Works have recently completed the contract for the iron work of the Columbia Building, 29 Broadway, and have moved their offices to that building. It is constructed on the principle of what is termed concealed iron work, a system of construction which effects a great saving in the thickness of walls, and consequent saving in valuable floor space. At present they are putting the finishing touches to a number of important contracts, among which may be mentioned the Hertel building, 71st street and Boulevard, R. S. Townsend, architect; the Sherry addition, on 5th avenue, McKim, Mead & White, architects, and Everard's Brewery, M. V. B. Ferdon, architect, and are now beginning work on the Young Women's Christian Association building in Brooklyn, J. C. Cady & Co., architects. We understand that the company have recently increased their capital for the purpose of providing for the extension of this work, and increased facilities for the conduct of their constantly enlarging business. The president of the company, P. Minturn Smith, has been identified with the iron business for the past twenty-five years, and is supported by an efficient corps of workers. We are assured that any contracts intrusted to them will be executed in a manner that will contrast favorably with that of the foremost concerns in the business. The company have recently issued a handsome illustrated catalogue, somewhat explanatory of the methods of construction adopted in the "Columbia," which they will be pleased to furnish, upon application, to those interested in this class of building.

Notable Purchasers of Real Estate.

Walter J. Damrosch has purchased No. 29 West 55th street from Emily A. Scott for $27,000.

Daniel O'Day, of Buffalo, the manager of the pipe line system of the Standard Oil Co., has purchased No. 128 West 72d street, one of Francis Crawford's houses, for $75,000.

The Opinions of Others.

V. K. Stevenson says: "I anticipate a speedy rise in city property necessitated by good prices for large crops and continued advances in stocks, and while real estate is always the last to feel these natural causes for a rise, still when the rise comes it will all come with a rush, and astonishment at quick advances will supplant present and past temporary dullness."

"The present market," said Frank E. Smith, "seems to be on a solid foundation. Prices are nearer their true level and altogether things are in pretty satisfactory shape. Renting of all kinds, but especially flat renting, has improved very much and if things continue as they are there is no reason why we should not have an active business. But don't let us have any boom. That will bring us back to the dullness which we seem to be getting over now."

Fifty cents apiece will be paid for indices to Vol. XLIII. (January to June, 1889,) of THE RECORD AND GUIDE at the office, 14 and 16 Vesey street.

Real Estate Department.

There is little new to report as to the condition of the real estate market this week. Generally speaking the complexion of things has not changed to any great extent, although business has taken on a more decided fall character. Renting, the main feature of the market, continues very good throughout the city, up town as well as down town, on the east as well as the west side. In some sections of the city this branch of their business, brokers say, has been better than it has been for several years past, and upon the unusual activity they base their hopes of a satisfactory selling market. The rents, it must be understood, have not, as a rule, increased, but applicants for flats and houses are more willing to pay the figures asked quickly and cheerfully, and they show an unusual anxiety to have leases signed. This state of affairs will unquestionably encourage investors and capitalists, and the result, the best judges of the market say, will be all that can be desired. Inquiry in the private house sections of the city continues very active and keeps the brokers busy. That their efforts are not unattended by success is evidenced by our reports of sales in the "Gossip" column. Many of the houses sold, it will be seen, are of the high-priced class, and this is a decidedly satisfactory sign, showing, as it does, that the rich men have confidence enough in New York real estate to buy dwelling houses for investment. As yet practically nothing has been done in lots or business property, but activity in these classes of holdings is hardly to be expected until next month. There is, however, as for private houses, an active inquiry, and it will be strange indeed if sales of vacant and improved business property of greater or less importance are not consummated before long. The general feeling in the market is very good. An active but healthy market is looked for, with prices good and sales fairly numerous.

THE SALES OF THE WEEK.

The auction market during the past week has been almost entirely uneventful. As we announced would be the case, little has been offered except parcels under foreclosure and, with the exception of the sale by the Equitable Life Assurance Society as plaintiff, even these sales have been small and unimportant. The two parcels voluntarily offered present very little of general interest. The northeast corner of 1st avenue and 69th street, a five-story flat said to rent for $4,500 per annum, sold for $38,200, and at no time during the sale was the bidding either enthusiastic or spirited, notwithstanding the efforts of the auctioneer to make it so. The other public auction sale of a lot on 118th street, near 5th avenue, was entirely unsuccessful and the owner was forced to bid it in in order to protect himself. The foreclosure sale by the Equitable Life was of nine tenements on the block bounded by 66th and 67th streets, 10th and West End avenues. This block, it may be remembered, was built by John M. Ruck with capital furnished mainly by the Equitable Society. A number of rumors have found circulation at different times to the effect that one syndicate or another had purchased the block, but all of them, including the interesting English syndicate story that attracted so much attention at the time, have proved to be without foundation. In consequence of this failure to dispose of all the houses satisfactorily the plaintiff was forced to foreclose on the remainder, and the first installment was offered on Tuesday last by Auctioneer John N. Golding, who will also have charge of the sale next Tuesday, when about twelve more of the houses are to be offered. The Equitable Company evidently did not wish to buy the houses in for they advertised them more or less extensively, and when the sale took place their agents showed no special anxiety to bid. The houses, too, were sold separately so as to give the small buyers a chance, but no one showed any special inclination to bid, so that the plaintiff corporation had to purchase them all at prices ranging from $16,250 to about $21,000 for each house. The other sales of the week do not call for special comment.

FUTURE SALES.

Next week the auctioneers will attempt to do a larger business than they have done for some time past. The announcements of city property to be offered show no great improvement over those for the past few weeks; but in the suburbs there is an activity that will be very satisfactory, if it is successful. Numerous new bills are out for sales in the near future, and others are talked of as settled, besides the other sales which will take place and which have already been mentioned in this column. Yet, notwithstanding the fact that so many lots are to be put upon the market, some of the best auctioneers do not regard the outlook as entirely favorable. They say that there is a diminished inquiry, and that so far as they can see the market for suburban property will be better next spring than it is this fall. However this is, owners are going ahead preparing and advertising their property, so that there will be numerous, if not altogether successful, sales within the next month or so. Owners, too, are spending a great deal more on their suburban properties than they used to do. Many of those that are to be offered shortly are not only graded and paved, but also contain gas, water and sewer-pipes, and all the city conveniences, so that the lots cannot be sold cheaply except at a great loss. It is to be hoped that the sales when they do occur will be attended with more success than is anticipated. To-day Jere. Johnson, Jr., will offer 500 lots near Rahway, N.J. and on Wednesday next John F. B. Smyth will offer 168 lots in the same town. On Tuesday next Auctioneer Johnson will offer 633 lots at Flatbush, and on the following day Richard V. Harnett & Co. will endeavor to dispose of 526 lots at South Bensonhurst. In addition to these sales next week there are announced for the near future 150 lots at Tuckahoe by A. F. Schwannecke, 100 plots of eight and ten lots each at Ardsley by Richard V. Harnett, 214 lots belonging to the Ryer Homestead, Tremont, by Jas. L. Wells, and by the same auctioneer 196 lots at Jerome Terrace, in addition to the sale on Washington Heights of 238 lots by A. H. Muller & Son.

On Tuesday, Sept. 22d, Richard V. Harnett & Co. will sell the two three-story brick dwellings Nos. 448 and 450 De Kalb avenue, and the three-story and basement dwellings Nos. 151, 153, 155, 157, 159 and 161 Butler street, between Hoyt and Bond streets, both parcels of Brooklyn property.

On Wednesday, Sept. 23d, Richard V. Harnett & Co. will sell 526 desirable lots, situated at South Bensonhurst, immediately adjoining Bensonhurst-by-the-Sea. The property belongs to Thomas J. Cummins and has on it a handsome private dwelling. It can be reached by the 39th street ferry and the electric road and by the Unionville station of the Brooklyn, Bath & West End Railroad. The titles are insured by the Title Guarantee and Trust Company.

On Thursday, Sept. 24th, Jere. Johnson, Jr., will sell on the premises, at 2 P. M., 200 desirable lots, now offered for the first time, on the celebrated Cowenhoven farm, in New Utrecht. The lots are situated between 60th and 63d streets and 15th and 18th avenues, and can be paid for in monthly installments. The grade is level and every lot is ready for immediate improvement. The property, surrounded by fine dwellings, is worthy the attention of people seeking small investments or suburban homes. The time from the Brooklyn Bridge is thirty minutes, or from the foot of Whitehall street, forty minutes. The title is insured.

CONVEYANCES.

	1890. Sept. 12 to 18 inc.	1891. Sept. 11 to 17 inc
Number	171	166
Amount involved	$2,427,455	$2,099,525
Number nominal	42	68
Number 23d and 24th Wards	35	31
Amount involved	$122,643	$147,475
Number nominal	8	10

MORTGAGES.

	1890.	1891.
Number	187	184
Amount involved	$2,585,494	$2,009,220
Number at 5 % or less	97	75
Amount involved	$1,646,914	$951,237
Number at less than 5 per cent	14	6
Amount involved	$363,106	$53,700
Number to Banks, Trust and Ins. Cos	37	30
Amount involved	$790,000	$613,250

PROJECTED BUILDINGS.

	1890. Sept. 13 to 19 inc.	1891. Sept. 12 to 18 inc.
Number of buildings	42	40
Estimated cost	$970,000	$1,356,400

Some Important Sales and Leases.

Bellamy & Winans have sold for James H. Goring the four-story dwelling, No. 42 West 54th street, for $55,000; for the estate of Judge Van Vorst to a Dr. Miller, No 811 Madison avenue, a four-story dwelling, on private terms; for Geo. W. Montgomery, who this week purchased a house on the West Side, to C. H. Childs. No. 8 East 54th street, for $53,500; and for Mrs. E. P. Beach the four-story dwelling, No. 56 East 57th street, for $63,750.

Bellamy & Winans, V. K. Stevenson and W. P. Seymour have leased for Mrs. Sanford to Col. W. H. Thompson, No. 812 5th avenue, between 62d and 63d streets, at $9,000 per annum.

Bellamy & Winans report that they have rented the following houses: No. 22 West 57th street to Jos. S. Decker; No. 39 East 57th street to E. H. Holbrook; No. 46 East 53d street to J. W. Clark; No. 39 West 49th street for A. S. Gorham; No. 1 East 74th street for F. Bianchi to A. Trowbridge, and No. 11 East 56th street to Colgate Hoyt.

Gossip of the Week.

SOUTH OF 59TH STREET.

William Rankin has sold to Ascher Weinstein, No. 237 West 18th street, a five-story brown stone double tenement, 25x82x92, on private terms. Mr. Weinstein gives in exchange Nos. 278 to 282 Madison street, a plot 70x100, with the old buildings thereon.

Ascher Weinstein has sold to Marks Kirchbourne, No. 235 West 18th street, a five-story brown stone double tenement, 25x82x92, on private terms; and to Edward C. Herrwagen, Nos. 194 and 196 West Houston street, a four-story factory, 25x60x125, also on private terms.

Max Simon has sold for a Mr. Manheim to a Mr. Brooker, No. 329 West 41st street, a four story double flat with rear house for $18,500. The size is 25x70x100. Mr. Brooker gives in exchange No. 71 West 99th street.

Louis Lese has sold to Ascher Weinstein, Nos. 337 to 341 West 18th street, and Nos. 338 to 342 West 19th street, a plot 75x200, with the old buildings thereon, on private terms.

E. H. Ludlow & Co. have sold to Martin & Bro., No. 129 East 36th street, a four-story dwelling, on private terms.

Wm. Kennelly has sold for Charles Weiland to C. C. Carvalho No. 108 East 45th street, a four-story, high stoop dwelling on private terms.

S. M. Blakely has sold for Mrs. M. C. Protheroe No. 208 West 46th street, a four-story brown stone dwelling, 20x50x100.5, to Mrs. B. H. Phillips, on private terms.

Wm. A. Wheelock has sold to C. W. Cass the four-story dwelling (leasehold), No. 34 West 48th street, for $25,000.

NORTH OF 59TH STREET.

Henry H. Dreyer has sold for John Casey to Geo. Daiker Nos. 176 and 178 West 81st street, two five-story brick and stone flats with all improvements, 37x91x102.2, for $148,500. It will be remembered that last week Mr. Dreyer sold the corner flat, adjoining, to Mr. Daiker for $140,000, and this, notwithstanding the fact that the flats are not entirely completed.

Frank L. Fisher & Co. have sold for F. Woodward to M. W. Cooke, No. 1987 7th avenue, a five-story double flat and store, 27x85x100, for $42,500; and for the same owner, No. 1985 7th avenue, a similar building, on private terms.

David T. Kennedy has sold to George W. Montgomery No. 5 West 74th street, a four-story brick dwelling, 20x60x104, for about $50,000.

Crevier & Woolley have sold for John D. Taylor the five-story flat and store on the southwest corner of 7th avenue and 121st street, on private terms The size is 40x85.

John Armstrong has sold for Radebold & Wenz to W. L. Brown, of Philadelphia, Nos. 6 and 8 West 116th street, two five-story flats, on plot 50x51, for $36,500.

Henry H. Dreyer has sold for George Daiker the northeast corner of 146th street and St. Nicholas avenue, a four-storp Indiana limestone front dwelling, 20.6x50, on lot 32.6x67, for $45,000; and for the same owner a similar residence, 20.6x50, on lot 30.6x69, on the southeast corner of 147th street and St. Nicholas avenue, for $45,000.

Giblin & Taylor have sold to Robert G. Irving No. 145 West 80th street, a four-story brick and stone dwelling, 21x55x102.2, for $33,000. Brokers, Walter Lawrence & Co.

J. W. Stevens has sold for Increase M. Grenell to J. W. Mapes No. 53 West 94th street, a four-story brown stone dwelling, 20x55x100, on private terms.

Jacob N. Weil has purchased from William Hayes the three-story and basement brick and stone dwelling on the southeast corner of Lexington avenue and 117th street, on private terms. Mr. Weil will take up his residence in the house next spring. Broker, S. V. Hervey.

F. Zittel has sold for the Rev. Dr. Edmund Guilbert, No. 56 West 76th street, a four-story brown stone dwelling, on private terms. The size is 18x56x102.2.

C. G. Dobbs has sold 250 West 104th street for Ellen M. Harlow to J. H. Stallman for $21,000.

Walker & Co. have sold to John M. Hogencamp, Nos. 259 and 261 West 124th street, two four-story brown stone front double flats, for $54,000. This property was purchased about five months ago by W. R. Martin from Robert T. Roosvelt, when the price is said to have been $50,000.

Max Simon has sold for a Mr. Walsh to a Mr. Oppenheimer, No. 73 West 101st street, a five-story double flat, 25x85x100, for $30.000.

Max Simon has sold for a Mr. Brooker to a Mr. Manheimer No. 71 West 99th street, a five-story double flat, 24.6x75x100.11, for $21,500. Mr. Manheimer gives in exchange No. 329 West 41st street.

V. K. Stevenson & Co. have sold to General Bassett, for the D. M. Chauncey Real Estate Co. of Brooklyn, the four story, high stoop, brown stone dwelling, 25x55x100, on the northwest corner of Convent avenue and 144th street.

John R. Foley & Son have sold for a Mr. Schneider to D. Kennedy, No. 261 West 121st street, a three-story brown stone dwelling, 16.8x50x100, on private terms.

Dr. Woolley, it is said, has sold the four-story dwelling, No. 1 West 121st street.

Squier & Whipple, it is reported, have sold three of their dwelling houses on West 96th street.

We hear that Wm. Lanchantin has sold one of his remaining houses on 89th street, near West End avenue.

LEASES.

Ames & Co. have leased for L. Morris the four-story brown stone dwelling No. 357 West 55th street, for three years, at $1,500 per year; No. 256 West 34th street, for H. Hammond, to C. Perry for two years, at $1,400 per year; for Mrs. Weed, the three-story brown stone dwelling No. 114 East 58th street, to Mrs. Elsberg for $1,400 per year; for J. B. Radley, the four-story high stoop, brown stone dwelling, No. 318 West 28th street, for three years, at $1,200 per year; for J. M. Ferber, the brown stone, English basement dwelling, No. 138 West 37th street, for $1,500 per year, to a Mr. McCue; for John Mack, the whole building, No. 365 5th avenue, opposite the Manhattan Club, to H. Carroll, for ten years, on private terms.

Richard D. Kehoe has leased for J. B. Morrow the private dwelling No. 83 West 134th street, for two years and seven months, at yearly rental of $900, to Mrs. Anna Stern.

Brooklyn.

J. P. Sloane has sold for Alfred T. Frost the two-story frame dwelling 25x30x100, No. 234 Eckford street, to Joseph Dougherty for $2,800.

Corwith Bros. have sold the three-story frame dwelling, 25x40x75, No. 50 Oakland street, for Conrad Meyer to Maurice G. Quinlan for $5,050.

CONVEYANCES.

	1890. Sept. 11 to 17 inc	1891. Sept. 10 to 16 inc
Number	285	285
Amount involved	$837,086	$873,434
Number nominal	72	85

MORTGAGES.

	1890.	1891.
Number	253	229
Amount involved	$994,832	$785,753
Number at 5 per cent. or less	138	123
Amount involved	$671,721	$498,891

PROJECTED BUILDINGS.

	1890. Sept. 12 to 18 inc.	1891. Sept. 11 to 17 inc.
Number of buildings	96	126
Estimated cost	$349,540	$528,473

Out of Town.

YONKERS, N. Y.—Ware & Odell and Jos. W. Archer have sold for Wm. B. Sewall, of Boston, about ten acres of ground on Kimball avenue, in the 2d Ward, opposite Richmond Park. The property is to be laid out in building plots.

MT. VERNON, N. Y.—Jefferson M. Levy and ex-Mayor Smith Ely have sold the McAvoy farm of about seventy acres for $70,000 to a syndicate, of which Dr. Eden is the president. The farm will be laid out in building lots.

Out Among the Builders.

Andrew Spence has plans on the boards for two five-story brick and brown stone flats, 25x74, to be built by James Meagher, on the north side of 111th street, 50 feet west of Madison avenue, at a cost of $36,000; and for a two-story frame dwelling, 20x35, which Wm. Weckwerth will build on the east side of East Vanderbilt avenue, 50 feet south of 187th street, at a cost of $1,800.

J. C. Burne is the architect for two five-story brick and brown stone dwellings, which Andrew Judge will erect on the south side of 132d street, 400 feet west of 5th avenue, at a cost of $40,000. They will be 25x69 feet in size, with an extension 13x7.

Wm. Rankin will improve the plot, 70x100, Nos. 278-282 Madison street, probably by the erection of tenement houses.

G. F. Pelham is preparing plans for six private dwellings to be built by Jas. Brown, on the north side of 91st street, 100 feet east of Amsterdam avenue. The houses will have brown stone fronts and hardwood interior finish. They will be 17x50, with two-story extensions, and are to cost about $17,000 each.

Brooklyn.

Thayer & Wallace are the architects for a one-story frame brick house, 200x275, to be built at Lorimer, Bayard and Newton streets, for the Brooklyn Transportation Company, at an estimated cost of $40,000.

Out of Town.

CHATHAM, N. J.—Swinnerton & Poole, of Newark, have plans on the boards for a three-story frame club-house, 50x117, to be built here by the Chatham Gun Club, at a cost of $8,000.

WANTS AND OFFERS.

(Advertisements strictly in accordance with this title will be inserted at the practically nominal rate of 10 CENTS per line agate). In figuring for themselves advertisers may count seven words for each line, the address to be taken as one line. The object of this department is to bring buyers and sellers into communication with customers. Advertisements must be marked "Wants and Offers Column," and sent to the office of publication, Nos. 14 and 16 Vesey Street, not later than 3 P. M. Friday.)

WANTS.

ADVERTISER would like to purchase the good-will of a fire insurance business. An excellent chance for a real estate man who finds it impracticable to give the insurance his proper attention.
INSURANCE, care of RECORD AND GUIDE.
Sept. 19—1aw4w.

OWNERS, ATTENTION!—Experienced agent having charge of seven flat houses at present, desires to make a change for the better. Wants charge of several nice houses in good location, east side, up town; would occupy one flat for services; security given. OWNER'S ADVANTAGE, RECORD AND GUIDE.
Sept. 12-19.

AN ACTIVE BROKER desires to enter in partnership with one having an established office.
OPPORTUNITY, RECORD AND GUIDE.

Real Estate Wanted.

WANTED.—West side private flat and tenement property to rent, collect, for sale or exchange.
J. HOLZ,
905 Amsterdam av, near 69th st., New York.

TO EXCHANGE.—Two cold water flats, well rented and built, 1st av, near 92d st.
A. TRUBE, Jr., corner 106th st. and 3d av.

OFFERS.

Dwellings and Flats

BARGAIN.—A two-story and basement all-brick house with brown stone trimmings, nine rooms and bath, all light; console mirror in front parlor; vestibule door; concreted cellar; coalbin in cellar, capacity 12 tons; sanitary plumbing; all improvements; two stoves, besides kitchen stove; heat whole house; burglar alarm all over house, cost $100; iron gate in basement; mosquito screens for all windows; house papered throughout one year ago; parlor ceiling and hall tinted; garden 100 feet deep, elegantly laid out with flowers and gravel walk; house 18x42; lot 18x185; five minutes' walk from Utica av station, Kings County L; price, $5,100; cash, $1,200; balance $600 yearly, with interest. Address,
K. A. E., 348 World.

THREE-STORY AND BASEMENT PRIVATE houses, 145-165 West 95th st.—Sizes 18x62x100 and 20x62x100, with second and third floor extension bathrooms; open plumbing; hardwood cabinet trim throughout and every modern improvement. Apply on premises or Amsterdam Improvement Co.'s office, 15 Cortlandt.

FOR SALE.—Five new first-class four-story and basement private dwellings, Nos. 109 113 and 119 East 45th st., and Nos. 462 and 464 Lexington av.; all leased to desirable tenants or can arrange to give possession to some of them if desired. For further particulars apply to
THE C. GRAHAM & SONS CO., 309 East 43d st.
Sept. 19-1aw8w.

SEDGWICK AV., MORRIS DOCK.—Elegant residence; ample grounds; 3½-story house; stable, chicken house; in first-class order. Particulars,
JOHN G. BORGSTEDE, 207 East 54th st.

THREE AND FOUR-STORY DWELLINGS, ALL sizes, all prices, all locations.
JOHN G. BORGSTEDE, 207 East 54th st.

TWO FOUR-STORY TENEMENTS, sixteen families each; rent, $3,456; price, $15,000 each.
JOHN G. BORGSTEDE, 207 East 54th st.

THREE-STORY DWELLING, RENTED IN FLOORS, $85 monthly; mortgage, $7,000, 4½ per cent; near 34th st. "L" station.
JOHN G. BORGSTEDE, 207 East 54th st.

FIVE-STORY tenement; 124th st.; full lot; price $15,250. Apply to
JOHN G. BORGSTEDE, 207 East 54th st.

86TH ST. CORNER; rents for $2,400; all improvements; want offer
JOHN G. BORGSTEDE, 207 East 54th st.

HARLEM.—Five-story tenement; twenty families; rents for $2,280; 16 per cent on investment. Particulars of JOHN G. BORGSTEDE, 207 East 54th st.

WASHINGTON HEIGHTS.—Amsterdam av; five-story flat and stores; near 145th st.; $6,000, $8,000 cash; balance mortgage. Particulars of
JOHN G. BORGSTEDE, 207 East 54th st.

CASH $6,000.—For sale, a cosy 16-foot brown stone, high stoop basement house, 111th st., near Madison av.; price $10,500, mortgage $4,500; more can remain if desired. Address,
H. D. HARRIS, owner, 71 Broadway.

FOR SALE.—A grand 25-foot four-story brown stone house, 80 feet deep, house, West 57th st., near 5th av.; asking only $93,000. Can be seen only by permits of HUNT & WENDELL,
249 Columbus av, southeast corner 72d st.

OFFERS.

FOR SALE.—On West End av., handsome, swell front brown stone and brick residence, 20 feet by 55; butler's pantry extension; hardwood and polished floors; beautifully decorated mirrors and elegant gas fixtures and gas logs; open fire places; price, inclusive fixtures and carpets, $40,000. Permits and particulars from HUNT & WENDELL, 249 Columbus av., near southeast corner of 72d st.

A FINE FIVE-STORY DOUBLE TENEMENT, renting for nearly $2,000 per annum; can be purchased for $19,000; mortgage $13,000; this is a good investment; lot 25x100. Apply to JAMES KENNY & SON, 80 East Houston st., near Bowery.

FIVE-STORY DOUBLE TENEMENT in 14th Ward, near this office; lot 25x100. Apply to JAMES KENNY & SON, 80 East Houston st., near Bowery.

$50,000.—Two five-story brick and stone flats, each 25x85x100, West 67th st.; mortgage, $28,000; rents, $4,800 per year.
GEO. F. EDWARDS, 106 Broadway.

$34,000.—Two four-story brick and stone flats, each 25 x 85 x 100; mortgage, $20,000; rent, $2,640, can be increased; Lexington av. GEO. F. EDWARDS, 106 Broadway.

$35,000.—Four-story, high stoop, brown stone dwelling, 19.6x55x100; mortgage, $14,000; West 71st st.
GEO. F. EDWARDS, 106 Broadway.

FINE SUBURBAN RESIDENCE; fourteen rooms; every improvement; sewer connection; fruit, vines; grounds, 54x120; near 174th st. L station; price $12,000; half cash. Address
E. F. HOLLISTER, 1584 Vanderbilt av.

SIX-STORIED BUILDING to sell or lease, 25x72; well-ventilated rooms; in good condition; 75th st., East, New York. Apply to ENGINEER, 17 John st.
Sept. 12-1aw3w

FOR SALE.—At a sacrifice, new five-story double flats, near 125th st. L station. Address,
Aug. 1—1aw-9w. BUILDER, 319 East 125th st.

FOR SALE.—Six new cabinet-trimmed three-story and basement brown stone private dwellings, Nos. 142-152 West 123d st.; prices reasonable and brokers commissions allowed. For further particulars apply at office of
FRED'K. M. LITTLEFIELD, 156 Broadway.
Aug. 29-uf.

FOR SALE.—2443 8th av and 210 and 212 West 105th st.; commission allowed brokers. Apply at
Aug. 29-uf. Room 19, 156 Broadway.

FOR SALE—2443 8th av.; 26.3½x100; easy terms; commission allowed brokers; apply at
Mar. 28-u-f. ROOM 19, 156 Broadway.

FOR SALE—210 and 212 West 105th st.; five-story apartments; each, 25x89x100; decorated and carpeted; apply at ROOM 19, 156 Broadway.
Mar. 28-u-f

Improved Property.

FACTORY BUILDING TO LET.—223 West 28th st., near 7th av., 25x85x100, five-story and basement; light three sides; a very fine factory building; rent, $2,500; without power. If tenant puts in power landlord will hire steam and power of him for adjoining building to extent of $1,200. Inquire
JACOB W. SMITH, 220 West 29th st.

FOUR-STORY and cellar factory building, very light; abundance of help; lots 125x100. Particulars of JOHN G. BORGSTEDE, 207 East 54th st.

PLANING MILL, branch of my business, for sale.—Is located at 24th st. and 11th av., on four or five city lots, leased ground, and consists of two and three-story brick buildings and adjoining sheds; also 80 horse power engine and boiler, planers, moulders, saws, etc., all in good running order and now in operation; will leave a portion of value on bond and mortgage three years; this offers splendid opportunity to enlarge wood-working industry or to secure good mill business to add thereto. For further particulars, etc., apply to
EBEN PEEK, 24th st. and 11th av.
Advertiser intends to continue his lumber business now carried on at above address. Sept. 5-1aw4w

OFFERS.

TO LET OR TO LEASE.—Two floors of a factory, 25x98 light on all sides, 1st av and 107th st; terms moderate. J. REEBERS' SONS,
Aug. 29-uf. 409 East 107th.

Vacant Lots.

FOR SALE.—On easy terms, nine first-class lots, ready for immediate improvement, on south side 116th st., commencing about 150 feet east of 7th av. THE C. GRAHAM & SONS CO, 309 East 43d st.
Sept. 19-1aw4w.

TREMONT AV., MORRIS HEIGHTS.—Three choice lots for sale; convenient to Jerome av., Berkeley Oval, Washington Bridge and Northern R. R. Depot; also lots at Tremont, near Elevated stations.
OWNER, 1014 East 175th st.

$20,000.—Two lots, Madison av, 49.11x75; easy terms.
GEO. F. EDWARDS, 106 Broadway.

EXCAVATED LOTS, with liberal building loan.
J. M. STRONG, JR., 60 Liberty st.

FOR SALE.—Five lots, northeast corner Willis av. and 137th st, 100x125; easy terms; all ready for improvement; splendid location. Apply to
Sept. 5—1aw4w. JAMES CARNEY, 137 East 52d st.

EASTERLY FRONT BOULEVARD, with 200 ft. on 86th st. and 264 ft. on 85th st.; one or more plots.
OTTO ERNST,
Aug. 22-1aw-8w. South Amboy, N. J.

FOR SALE.—Lots, with or without loans; private and tenement houses; single and double flats.
A. TRUBE, Jr., corner 106th st. and 3d av.

Brooklyn Real Estate for Sale.

FOR SALE.—88th st. and Fort Hamilton av., Brooklyn, 11 room house; all improvements; lot 100x116; will accept low figure if purchased before November 1st, or will rent furnished from November to May. FORT HAMILTON, RECORD AND GUIDE.

FOR SALE, or will let, that elegant new two-story and basement frame house, 147 Eldert st., Brooklyn; for two families; 12 rooms and two bath-rooms; all improvements; convenient to Halsey st. L station. Apply on premises, or 1281 Putnam av., near Central av., Brooklyn.

FOR SALE.—House worth $13,000, subject to a mortgage of $7,500, three-story and basement free-stone front; very elegant; hardwood; on Hancock st. Can be bought for $9,520. Call or address,
BENJ. STURGES, 671 Gates av., Brooklyn, N. Y.

BARGAIN.—Store property, 1507 Fulton st.; four-story brown stone; promising business block; must be sold; $2,500 cash required.
Sept. 19-26. EDWIN SPARKS, 102 Vesey st.

SPECIAL OFFERS in 26th Ward, Brooklyn (Brownsville), lots and plots.
ALFRED H. TOMPKINS, 2.6 Broadway, New York.

PLATE-GLASS CORNER on avenue thoroughfare, 17th Ward, Brooklyn, half block from big shipyard; suitable for saloon; price, $3,800; easy terms.
J. P. SLOANE,
Aug. 29-1aw5w. 343 Manhattan av, Brooklyn, E. D.

Country Property.

FOR SALE OR EXCHANGE.—Beautiful residence, high ground, on St. John's River, near Jacksonville, Fla.; 1,100 feet water front; 40 acres oranges, &c.; price $13,000; (photographs).
HENRY R. KING, 47 Cedar st.

$805 CASH, $1,195 mortgage.—Plot containing over 10 lots in Givan Homestead; fronts three streets. F. M. FARWELL, 208 Broadway.

FOR SALE.—In plots to suit; eligible building sites (commanding view of sound for miles), on North st., Greenwich, Connecticut; price reasonable; terms easy; neighborhood aristocratic and fashionable. Apply to
FRED. J. STONE, owner, 60 Broadway, N. Y.
Sept. 12-uf.

Miscellaneous.

BUILDING MATERIAL EXCHANGE.—Salesman who is a member of above would obtain liberal commission from Y. A., RECORD AND GUIDE.

A PARTY ABOUT TO BUILD A FIVE-STORY factory, 50x98, in Harlem, near water-front, will lease the three upper floors and build to suit tenant. Terms very moderate. Address
May 16 u. f. OWNER, 409 E. 107th St.

PRINTING.—Book, News and Job.
RECORD AND GUIDE PRESS,
14 Barclay, and 14, 16 Vesey sts

SALES OF THE WEEK.

The following are the sales at the Real Estate Exchange and Auction Room for the week ending Sept. 18.

** Indicates that the property described has been bid in for plaintiff's account.*

R. V. HARNETT & CO.

Elizabeth st, No. 157, 25.2x93.11x24.11x93.9, two-story frame and three-story brk building. S. Magliola.............. $15,500

49d st, No. 25, n s, 354.9 w 5th av, 20.4x100.5, four-story stone front dwell'g and store. H. C. Demarest. (Leasehold; amt due on two actions $16,070).............. 20,000

*184th st, s e s, 118.8 s Bainbridge av, 28.7x83.7 x25x96.7. Thomas J. Walls. (Amt due $2,263) 2,500

*18?th st, s e s, 147.10 s Bainbridge av, 26.2x77.2 x25x83.7. Same. (Amt due $2,263)........ 2,500

7th av, Nos. 2170-2178, s w cor 129th st, 99.11x75, five five-story brk flats and stores (uncompleted). L. S. Baker. (Amt due $26,678)... 125,850

13?th st, No. 232, s s, 375 e 8th av, 25x99.11, five-story flat. Louis C. Elterich.............. 24,500

A. H. MULLER & SON.

85th st, No. 44, s s, 375 e 9th av, 25x102.2, four-story stone front dwell'g. T. R. Hughes. (Amt due $34,016).............. 35,100

WM. KENNELLY.

West End av, No. 347, w s, 62 n 81st st, 20x66, three-story brk dwell'g. Wm. C. Hanna, Jr. (Amt due $4,217; prior morts. $16,000)....... 20,00

B. L. KENNELLY.

1st av, No. 1286, n e cor 69th st, 25.1x110x25.1x113, five-story tenem't and stores. Louis N. Philips 38,200

SMYTH & RYAN.

*Cherry st, No. 448, n s, 100 e Jackson st, 25x100, three-story brk stable.......... 3,000
118th st, s s, 219 w 5th av, 22x100.11. (Bid in).. ——

OTHER AUCTIONEERS.

*West End av, Nos. 42-52, e s, 25.5 n 66th st, 150x100, six five-story stone front tenem'ts and stores. Equitable Life Assurance Society. (Amt due $55,340).......... 121,500
*66th st, No. 217, n s, 275 w 10th av, 25x100.5, five-story stone front tenem't. Equitable Life Assurance Society.......... 17,000
*66th st, No. 219, adj, 25x100.5, five-story stone front tenem't. Same.......... 16,250
*66th st, No. 221, adj, 25x100.5, five-story stone front tenem't. Same.......... 17,200

Total.......... $469,100
Corresponding week, 1890.......... $330,925

BROOKLYN, N. Y.

For Week Ending September 17.

JERE. JOHNSON, JR.

57th st, n s, 80 e 21st av, 1 lot, New Utrecht. C. Gillman.......... $125
57th st, n s, adj, 4 lots. J. Q. Thompson.......... 520
57th st, s s, 80 e 21st av, 1 lot. C. Gillman.......... 125
57th st, adj, 2 lots. F. L. Brown.......... 260
57th st, adj, 2 lots. C. Boyhart.......... 250
58th st, s s, — e 21st av, 9 lots.......... 1,125
59th st, s s, — e 21st av, 5 lots.......... 775
59th st, s s, adj, 8 lots.......... 1,280
18th av, e s, 58th to 59th st, 10 lots. D. Puyman.......... 3,950
21st av, s w cor 59th st, 5 lots. C. Gillman.......... 960

OTHER AUCTIONEERS.

Degraw st, s s, 430 w Franklin av, 20x131, vacant; all right, title and interest. Agnes L. Yenni.......... 50
Fulton st, s w cor Saratoga av, 100x80. Noah Tebbetts.......... 25,500
*Pacific st, s s, 297.3 e Rochester av, 16.8x107.2⅝..........
Pacific st, s s, 313.11 e Rochester av, 16.8x107.2⅝..........
Two two-story frame dwell'gs..........
William Jervis.......... 4,000
*Pacific st, s s, 330.7 e Rochester av, 16.8x107.2⅝
Pacific st, s s, 347.3 e Rochester av, 16.8x107.2⅝.
Two two-story and basement frame dwellings..........
Sarah J. Chauncey.......... 4,000
Prospect pl, n s, 105.5 w 6th av, 20x81. Harriet E. Burke.......... 5,525
Bedford av, Nos. 574-584, s w cor Rodney st, 133x100, three five-story stone apartment houses unfinished. John Hennessy.......... 136,437

Total.......... $184,482
Corresponding week 1890.......... $214,015

CONVEYANCES

Wherever the letters Q. C., C. a. G. and B. & S occur, preceded by the name of the grantee they mean as follows:

1st—Q. C. is an abbreviation for Quit Claim deed, i. e., a deed in which all the right, title and interest of the grantor is conveyed, omitting all covenants or warranty.

2d—C. a. G. means a deed containing Covenant against Grantor only, in which he covenants that he hath not done any act whereby the estate conveyed may be impeached, charged or encumbered.

3d—B. & S. is an abbreviation for Bargain and Sale deed, wherein, although the seller makes no express covenants, he really grants or conveys the property for a valuable consideration, and thus impliedly claims to be the owner of it.

NEW YORK CITY.

September 11, 12, 14, 15, 16, 17.

Allen st, No. 83, w s, 99.10 s Hester st, 25.1x87.6, five-story brk tenem't with stores. Saul Federman and Annie his wife to Louis Sackin. *Mt.* $18,750. Sept. 15. $27,000

Bedford st, No. 53, w s, 75 n Leroy st, runs west 100 x north 15 x east 25 x north 10 x east 75 to st, x south 25, two-story brk dwelling with one and two-story brk and frame buildings on rear. Julius Dreyfus to Joseph L. Buttenwieser. *Mt.* $10,500. May 26. nom

Bleecker st, No. 143, n w cor South 5th av, 32.3x100, six-story brk store. James B. Morrow to Patrick H. McManus. C. a. G. Sept. 7. nom

Same property. Release judgment. John J. Daly to same. Sept. 11. nom

Same property. Patrick H. McManus and Mary his wife to James B. Morrow. All liens. Sept. 16. nom

Bleecker st, n w cor South 5th av, 32.3x100.
Wooster st, e s, 120 s Houston st, 75x100.
Release mort. Willson, Adams & Co. to Patrick H. McManus. Sept. 15. nom

Boulevard or Broadway | begins Boulevard,
65th st | n w cor 65th st,
runs west 114.11 x north 80.4 x west 25 x north 20.1 x east 81.6 to Broadway, x south 116.3.
65th st, n s, 525 e 10th av, runs east 50 x north 80.3 x west 25 x north 20.1 x west 25 x south 100.4.
One and two-story brk and frame buildings.
Martha E. wife of Thomas K. Egbert, New Jersey, and Catharine L. wife of George Lowther, Clara wife of Charles Greer, Rye, N. Y., to Hartwig I. Phillips. Sept. 8. 95,000

Boulevard | begins Boulevard, n w cor 65th st,
65th st | 116.3x106.6x100.5 to st, x164.11,
one and two-story brk and frame buildings. Hartwig I. Phillips to William Strauss. *Mt.* $75,000, taxes, &c. Sept. 14. 105,000

Broome st, No. 580, n s, 152.6 e Hudson st, 22.6x84.3, two-story brk tenem't.
Broome st, No. 578, n s, 175 e Hudson st, 22.6x84, two-story brk tenem't.
George W. Travers, Hoboken, N. J., and Francis A. his wife to Maurice Ahern. *Mt.* $16,500. Sept 14. 25,150

Cherry st, No. 35, s s, 96 w Roosevelt st, 15.8x75.4x15.6x76, four-story brk tenem't with stores. Daniel Rothstein and Lillie his wife to Levy Rothstein. *Mt.* $6,000. Sept. 14. nom

Clinton st, No. 47, w s, 150 s Stanton st, 25x100, five-story stone front tenem't with stores. Daniel Rothstein and Lillie his wife to Levy Rothstein. ½ part. *Mt.* $25,000. Sept. 14. nom

Clinton st, No. 250, e s, abt 20 n Cherry st, 20x71.11x19.11x71.11, three-story brk tenem't. Abraham Edelson and Annie his wife to Aaron Kaplan. *Mt.* $11,000. Sept. 15. 13,000

Delancey st, No. 256, n s, 78.8 e Sheriff st, 21x100, four-story brk store and tenem't with three-story brk factory on rear. Abraham Brown and Jeannette his wife, Isaac Haft and Dora his wife to Lena Abraham and Morris Smoley. *Mt.* $13,500. Sept. 15. 21,000

Same property. Lena Abraham to Simon Abraham. Sub. to mort. Sept. 15. nom

Delancey st, No. 301 | being Delancey st, s w
Lewis st, No. 41 | cor Lewis st, 25x75,
five-story brk tenem't with stores. Raphael Freedman and Fanny his wife to Jacob Horowitz. *Mt.* $23,000. Aug. 28. See East Broadway. 33,500

Delancey st, No. 276, n s, 75 w Cannon st, 25x75, five-story brk tenem't with stores. Henry Metz and Amelia his wife to Lob Reiss. Sept. 15. 24,500

East Broadway, No. 204, n s, 157.6 e Jefferson st, 26.4x65, five-story brk tenem't. Jacob Horowitz and Hannah his wife to Raphael Freedman. *Mt.* $15,000. Sept. 1. See Delancey st. 27,000

Elizabeth st, No. 246, e s, 282.11 s Houston st, 24.3x81.8, five-story brk tenem't with stores.
Elizabeth st, No. 244, e s, 307.2 s Houston st, 24.5x91.4x20.3x92, five-story brk tenem't with stores.
John Ochse and Maria his wife to Daniel Rothstein. *Mt.* $26,000. Sept. 14. 45,750

Elm st, No. 207 | begins Elm st, e s, abt 140 s
Marion st, No. 16 | Spring st, 20x41 to Marion
st, x 21x35.2, two-story frame and brk tenement. Albert Etzel and Catharine his wife, Emanuel Kronacher and Rachel his wife to Augustus Sbarbora. *Mt.* $5,000. Sept. 15. 9,000

Essex st, No. 12, e s, 144.6 s Hester st, 18.9x100x19x100, five-story brk store and tenem't with five-story brk tenem't on rear. Charlotte Hastorf to Bertha Finkelstein. *Mt.* $12,000. Aug. 15. 28,000

Grove st, No. 63, on map No 65 | begins Grove
Christopher st, No. 74 | st, n s, 110
w 4th st, 27x91.6x26x86.10, five-story brk tenem't with stores. John Goerlitz and Emma his wife to Adam Happel. *Mt.* $30,000. Sept. 14. 40,000

Leonard st, Nos 162, 164 and 166, s s, 79.2 w Baxter st, runs west 59.4 x south 40.1 x southeast 21.10 x south 7.11 x northeast 13 x south 8 x east 30 x south 9 x east 3.6 x northeast 52.9, three three-story brk stores and tenements. John Simmons and Mary M. his wife to Minnie Harder. *Mt.* $23,000. Sept. 5. 40,000

Lewis st, No. 30, e s, 125 n Broome st, 24.9x100, three-story brk tenem't with three-story brk tenem't on rear. Julius Rosenberg and Jette his wife to Adolf Duckler. *Mt.* $8,000. Sept. 15. 14,800

Macdougal st, No. 23, w s, 112.11 s Carlton st, runs south 25 x west 59.5 x again west 14.7 x north 14 x east 47 x again east 38.8, three-story frame (brk front) store and tenem't. Mary E. wife of Henry B. Weller to Joseph Rivara and Catharine his wife and Louis Laneri and Rosa his wife. Q. C. Sept. 15. nom

Maiden lane, No. 127 | begins Maiden lane, n e
Fletcher st, No. 11 | s, abt 60 n w Water
st, 19.9x82.4 to Fletcher st, six-story brk store. Isaac Bijur and Leopold Nachenbeim exrs. and trustees of Asher Bijur to Nathan Bijur. ½ part. Sept. 14. nom

Same property. Nathan Bijur to Lilly Bijur. Sept. 14. nom

Market st, No. 46, e s, abt 50 s Madison st, 25x87.8, three-story brk store and tenem't. Mathilde wife of Johanes M. Smith to Charles R Scruton. *Mt.* $11,000. Sept. 12. 17,500

Morton st, No. 56, s s, 205 e Hudson st, 25x100, three-story brk dwell'g. Rebecca Bensel to Carrie Bensel. *Mt.* $12,000. Aug. 24. gift

Oliver st, No. 76, e s, abt 100 n Cherry st, 26.2x100x25.8x100, five-story brk tenem't with stores.
Av A, s e s, lot 153 map Prospect Hill, Fordham, 50x130.6.
Catharine, Hannah M., Julia and Mary Daly heirs Daniel Daly to Catharine Daly widow. Q. C. All liens. Sept. 11. gift

Park st, No. 37, s s, abt 100 w Duane st, 25x98.6.
Park st, No. 39, s s, abt 75 w Duane st, 25x95.6.
Two six-story brk tenem'ts, store in No. 37, and a six-story brk tenem't on rear of each.
Olivia Christal and Mabel his wife to Henry R. and Kate Christal. *Mt.* $30,000. Sept. 15. 14,400

Same property. Catharine wife of Millard M. Moss, Brooklyn, Josephine and Eliza J. Christal to Samuel Aronson and Louis Gordon. *Mt.* $30,000. Sept. 15. 39,600

Prince st, No. 136, s s, 75 e South 5th av, 25x101, six-story brk store. John C. Wallace and Annie his wife to William M. Martin. *Mt.* $40,000. Sept. 15. nom

Pike st, No. 23, s e cor Henry st, 25x77.10, five-story brk tenem't with stores.
Henry st, No. 110, s s, 77.10 e Pike st, 33.6x25.1x33.6x25, five-story brk tenem't.
Pike st, No. 25, e s, 25 s Henry st, 25x111.4, five-story brk tenem't.
Louis Goodman and Rachel his wife to Jacob Rieser. *Mt.* $84,000. Sept. 16. 135,000

Pitt st, No. 29, w s, 175 s Delancey st, 25x100, five-story brk tenem't with stores. William Friedman to Hanie Friedman. *Mt.* $23,000. June 17. nom

Spruce st, No. 48, n w cor Gold st, 24.5x27.5x23.11x27.1, five-story brk store. Harrison P. Bowne, Brooklyn, N. Y., to Kate P. Knight, Orange, N. J. All title. C. a. G. Sept. 14. nom

Same property. Charles A. Wheeler, Brooklyn, N. Y., to same. All title. C. a. G. Sept. 14. nom

Stanton st, No. 178, n s, 80 w Attorney st, 20x99.6, three-story frame store and tenem't with six-story brk factory on rear. Annie wife of Leopold Hyman to Michael C. Miller. *Mt.* $15,000. July 20. 10,000

Wall st, No. 114, n s, 81.7 w South st, 21.11x72.7x22.2x72.7. ½ part.
Vesey st, No. 110 | begins Vesey st, n e cor
West st, No. 139 | West st, runs east 23.9 x
north 35 x east 9 x north 10.5 x west 8 x west 41.7 x south 43.9.
Front st, No. 261, s e cor Dover st, 22.2x76.11x21x76.10.
Jones lane, Nos. 4 and 6, 39.5x61.6x40.8x61.10.
James E. McAleer to Amy N. wife of James P. Cruger, Newburgh, N. Y. *Mt.* $65,000. Sept. 14. nom

Same property. James P. Cruger, Newburgh, N. Y., to James E. McAleer. *Mt.* $65,000. Sept. 14. nom

Willett st, No. 71, w s, 63 s Rivington st, 18.6x50, five-story brk store and tenem't. Max Landesman and Annie his wife to Meta Salberg. *Mt.* $10,250. Sept. 10. 13,750

Same property. Meta Salburg to Yotte Eichhorn. *Mt.* $10,250. Sept. 10. 14,500

William st, No. 218, s s, abt 245 e Frankfort st, 30.5x103x24.10x116.9, five-story brk store and tenem't. Elsner C. and Bernard G. Gunther to The Metropolitan Realty Co. Sept. 3. 35,000

3d st, No. 23, n s, 150 w 2d av, 25x99.4, vacant. Ascher Weinstein and Annie his wife to Michael Eay and William Stacom. *Mt.* $15,000. Sept. 1. 21,500

6th st, No. 429, n s, 250 w Av A, 25x90.10, five-story brk tenem't with stores. Henry Heller exr. John A. Klenert, otherwise called August Klenert to Max Rosenbaum. *Mt.* $15,000. Sept. 15. 28,500

6th st, No. 710, s s, 126 e Av C, 19.9x97, four-story brk store and tenem't. Contract. Henry Berkowitz to Isaac Kirschner. June 4. 16,550

9th st, No. 438, s s, 86.6 w Av A, 26.6x27, five-story brk tenem't. Ignatz Bauer, Jr., and Wilhelmina his wife to Elias Jacobs. *Mt.* $4,150. Sept. 15. 11,000

10th st, No. 193, n s, 109.4 w 4th st, 21.4x95, three-story brk dwell'g. Mathias Banta to Eloise J. Messer. Sept. 11. 1,500

12th st, No. 224, s s, 261.6 w 2d av, 23.4x106.6, five-story stone front tenem't. Thomas A. Ryan to Mary Ryan. Q. C. All title. Sept. 17. nom

13th st, No. 640, s s, 158 w Av C, 25x103.3, five-story brk store and tenem't. Abraham Katz and Mary his wife and Louis Maier and Ida his wife to George Meister, Sr., and Fanny his wife and Louis and Clara Meister. *Mt.* $10,000. Sept. 14. 16,900

18th st, No. 134, s s, 383 w 6th av, 23x92, two-story brk stable. Mary A. Chisolm, College Point, L. I., to William Crawford and James Simpson. C. a. G. Aug. 17. 18,000

Same property. William Crawford and James Simpson and Lulu D. his wife to Nicholas Sheldon, Providence, R. I. Aug. 17. 8,000

21st st, No. 235 W., n s, abt 735 e 8th av, 16.8x98.9, three-story brk dwell'g. Release dower. Elizabeth K. Hoyt, Binghampton, N. Y., to Bernard Travis, Katonah, N. Y. Aug. 17. nom

Same property. Bernard Travis and Margaret J. his wife, Katonah, N. Y., to Pauline M. Kauffman. Sept. 17. 12,000

22d st, No. 307, n s, 114.8 w 8th av, 14.8x98.9, four-story brk dwell'g. Caroline M. Conner to Jane M. Gano. Sept. 15. 7,000

22d st, No. 164, s s, 87.6 e 7th av, 18.6x85.6, four-story stone front dwell'g. William Morgan and Adelaide his wife to Mary and Kate Riordan. *Mt.* $9,000. Aug. 31. 21,750

24th st, No. 213, n s, 185.8 w 7th av, 21.5x98.9, three-story brk dwell'g. Thomas R. Hughes, Weehawken, N. J., to John S. Robinson. *Mt.* $15,000. May 20, 1891. nom

28th st, No. 230, s s, 345.7 w 7th av, 24.10x98.9, five-story brk store and tenem't with four-story brk tenem't on rear.
26th st, No. 143, s s, 475 w 6th av, 25x98.9, four-story brk store and tenem't with four-story brk tenem't on rear.
Nicholas McCool to Henry and Hyman Sonn. Sept. 16. nom

28th st, No. 111, n s, 164.3 w 6th av, 21.5x98.9,

three-story brk dwell'g. Emile Regnier and Elise his wife to William S. Dunn and Ellen his wife. *Mt.* $11,000. Sept. 1. 17,200

33d st, No. 36, s s, 166.8 e Madison av, 17.3x98.9, four-story stone front dwell'g. Logan C. Murray and Hattie G. his wife to Alfred S. Malcomson. *Mt.* $18,500. Sept. 16. 26,500

37th st, No. 29, n s, 467.6 w 5th av, runs north 98.9 x west 12.6 x south 39.9 x west 5.6 x south 59 x east 18, four-story stone front dwell'g. George H. Dunham and Eliza his wife to Isaac L. Kip trustee for Adelaide B. Harris. Sept. 10. 33,000

46th st, No. 525, n s, 400 e 11th av, 25x100.5, two-story frame dwell'g with two-story frame dwell'g on rear. Lizzie Wagner widow, Monica Scheffler and Cecilia wife of Augustus N. Mathieu to John Stich. Aug. 8. nom

51st st, No. 404, s s, 37 e 1st av, 18x100.5, three-story brk dwell'g. Herman G. Gordan and Emma E. his wife to Louis Kramer. *Mt.* $4,000. Sept. 1. 7,600

52d st, No. 430, s s, 250 w 9th av, 25x100.5, five-story stone front tenem't. James Lee to Emeline Lee. B. & S. July 15. nom

53d st, No. 41, n s, 243 e 6th av, 20x100.5, four-story stone front dwell'g. Isaac Bijur and Leopold Wachenheim exrs. and trustees Asher Bijur to Nathan Bijur. ⅙ part. Sept. 14. nom

Same property. Nathan Bijur to Lilly Bijur. ⅙ part. Sept. 14. nom

72d st, n s, 425 w Central Park West, 50x102.2, vacant.
73d st, s s, 425 w Central Park West, 50x102.2, vacant.
Richard M. Hooley, Chicago, Ill., to Rosina Hooley. B. & S. *Mt.* $60,000. Sept. 16. nom

75th st, No. 403, n s, 68 e 1st av, 20x51, three-story brk dwell'g. Rachel Gross to Max Peters. *Mt.* $3,500. Sept. 10. nom

76th st, No. 43, n s, 249.11 e 9th av, 20.1x100, four-story stone front dwell'g. Samuel Colcord and Alice B. his wife to Mabel Witherbee. *Mt.* $25,500. Sept. 11. 38,000

76th st, Nos. 116 and 118, s s, 165.1 w Columbus av, 40x102.2, two four-story stone front dwellings. Patrick Farley to Caroline W. Whiton. *Mt.* $50,000. Sept. 17. nom

79th st, No. 117, n s, 165 e Park av, 20x102.2, three-story stone front dwell'g. Joseph H. Lowenstein to Anna Lowenstein. All liens. Oct. 7. 24,000

83d st, No. 335, n s, 225 w 1st av, 25x102.2, five-story stone front flat. Thomas Moore and Annie his wife, John McLaughlin and Margaret his wife to Claus Wilkens. *Mt.* $15,000. Sept. 15. 26,500

86th st Boulevard } begins 86th st, n s, 225 e West End av, runs north 150.8 x east 92.2 to Boulevard, x south 50.1 x west 18.8 x south 100.8 to 86th st, x west 75, one-story frame building and vacant. Mary A. Jordon widow and Eleanor P. wife of Wellesley W. Gage to The United States Life Ins. Co. Dec. 20, 1890. nom

87th st, s s, 35.3 e Lexington av, 27x100.8. Release mort. The Bradley & Currier Co. (Lim.) to Luigi, Guiseppe, Steffano and Natale Cavinato. Sept. 5. nom

Same property. Release mort. Same to same. Sept. 5. nom

Same property. Release mort. Edward C. and Patrick Sheehy to same. Sept. 9. nom

Same property. Release mort. Same to same. Sept. 9. nom

Same property. Release judgment. Thomas C. Ennever to same. Sept. 2. 125

Same property. Release mechanic's lien. Giacinto Russiano to Luigi Cavinato. Sept. 10. 200

87th st, No. 139, n s, 317.6 w 9th av, 15x100.8, three-story brk dwell'g. Metropolitan Life Ins. Co., New York, to Peter Herche. C. a. G. Sept. 11. 20,000

87th st, No. 147, n s, 375 w 9th av, 16.8x100.8, three-story stone front dwell'g. Alfred P. W. Seaman to Samuel A. Seaman. *Mt.* $12,000. April 1, 1887. nom

88th st, No. 307, n s, 100 w West End av, 19x100.8, four-story brk dwell'g. Edwin H. Peck to Julia E. wife of Edwin H. Peck. Sept. 11. nom

88th st, No. 149, n s, 374 e Amsterdam av, 17x100.8, three-story stone front dwell'g. Hugh McDowell and Julia F. his wife to John C. Heney. *Mt.* $20,000. Sept. 14. nom

90th st, s s, 80 e Madison av, 33.4x100.8, vacant. William Lalor and Elizabeth A. his wife to Louis Wirth. *Mt.* $11,000. Sept. 15. 15,000

91st st, No. 332, s s, 150 w 1st av, 25x100.8, five-story stone front tenem't. Frederick W. Sauer and Magdalena his wife and Conrad Gross and Lena his wife to Gottlieb F. Weber. *Mt.* $12,500. Aug. 31. (Corrects error in issue of Sept. 5, 1891). 100

92d st, No. 12, s s, 196.11 e 5th av, 21x100.8, four-story stone front dwell'g. Contract. Thomas Graham to Max Richter. May 11, 1891. 30,000

92d st, n s, abt 50.0 e 5th av, 51.1x100.8.
92d st, n e cor Madison av, 11.1x100.8.
Nos. 41 and 43, one and two-story frame buildings.
Louis A. Gent and Maria L. his wife to Henry Schiffer. *Mt.* $30,000. Sept. 14. 52,000

93d st, No. 172, s s, 100 e Amsterdam av, 18x100.8, three-story stone front dwell'g. Walden P. Anderson to Alice wife of Theodore C. Gross. *Mt.* $18,750. Sept. 14. nom

97th st, No. 140, s s, 183 e Lexington av, 25x100.11, five-story stone front flat. Wilbur F. Washburn and Emma H. his wife, Yonkers, N. Y., to Caroline Uhlig. *Mt.* $17,000. Sept. 15. 23,500

Same property. John E. Andrus and Julia M. his wife, Yonkers, N. Y., to Wilbur F. Washburn. C. a. G. Sept. 15. nom

98th st, Nos. 205-209, n s, 110 e 3d av, 75x100.11, three five-story brk tenem'ts. Solomon Z. Lord et al. exrs. Russell F. Lord, Elizabeth S. Lord widow and devisee Walter S. Lord, Frederick E. Tracy and Anna L. his wife, Russell F. Lord and Mary F. his wife, James H. Lord, Mary S. Dimmick widow and John F. Parker and Lizzie his wife heirs Russell F. Lord to Henry M. Seely. Re-recorded. July 28, 1885. 1,000

Same property. Anna A. Tracy widow, Miles L. Tracy and Mary H. his wife, Henry L. Seely and Kate T. his wife, Charles W. Tracy and Mary M. his wife, George F. Bentley and Lucy T. his wife and Thomas H. R. Tracy and Lucy S. his wife heirs H. R. Tracy, Lucretia S. Dimmick extrx. and devisee Samuel E. Dimmick to Solomon Z Lord et al. exrs. Russell F. Lord. All title. Re-recorded. April 15, 1879. nom

98th st, s s, 385 e 3d av, runs south 100.8 x east 128.4 x north 74.9 x east 14.8 x north 26 to st, x west 143, vacant. Elizabeth C. McKibbin to Harriet P. Brown. Sept. 8. nom

102d st, No. 124, s s, 75 w Lexington av, 25x100.11, five-story brk flat. William J. Hendricks and Mattie H. his wife, Fleming Co., Ky., to Louis Michaelis. C. a. G. July 2. nom

103d st, No. 304, s s, 99.3 w West End av, 20x100.11, three-story brk dwell'g. Welcome R. Steinmetz to Wilbur F. Washburn. Sub. to mort. Sept. 15. 25,000

103d st, No. 302, s s, 79.3 w West End av, 20x100.11, three-story brk dwell'g. Same to same. Sub. to mort. Sept. 15. 25,000

103d st, No. 306, s s, 119.3 w West End av, 20x100.11, three-story brk dwell'g. Same to Thomas Hagan. *Mt.* $16,000. Sept. 15. nom

103d st, s s, 119.10 w West End av, 20x100. Thomas Hagan and Margaret his wife to Welcome R. Steinmetz. July 31. nom

103d st, No. 308, s s, 139.3 w West End av, 20.2x100.11, three-story brk dwell'g. Welcome R. Steinmetz to Wilbur F. Washburn, Yonkers, N. Y. Sub. to mort. Sept. 15. nom

108th st, No. 222, s s, 311 e 3d av, 24.6x100.11, four-story brk tenem't. Richard Cummings and Elizabeth his wife to John Hammer. Sept. 12. 12,500

114th st, No. 211, n s, 185 e 3d av, 25x100.11, five-story stone front flat. Regina Prosnitz to Charles E. Dettelbach. *Mt.* $17,000. Sept. 16. 23,000

117th st, No. 318, n s, 225 w 8th av, 25x100.11, five-story stone front flat. Release mort. Reuben Ross to Edward Cunningham. Sept 9. nom

Same property. Edward Cunningham and Jane his wife to Morris Wolf. *Mt.* $18,000. Sept. 12. 25,000

117th st, No 316, s s, 221 w 8th av, 26.3x100.11, five-story stone front flat. Thomas P. Dunne and Maria D. his wife to John D. Mennie. *Mt.* $18,000. Sept. 8. 22,500

117th st, s s, 100 e Columbus av, 100x100.11, four five-story brk flats. Moses Samelson and Dora his wife to William H. Green. Trust deed to secure creditors. Sept. 14. nom

118th st, No. 420, s s, 228.4 e 1st av, 15.7x100.11, two-story stone front dwell'g. Henrietta Studinski to Isidor Michelson. *Mt.* $3,600. Sept. 8. 7,000

119th st, s w cor Claremont av, —x—, being part of Old Bloomingdale road. Jane A. wife of Edward H. Cahill to Charles C. and Henry M. Taber. Q. C. July 19. nom

Same property. Cornelius R. Duffie, Jr., and Edith N. his wife to same. Aug. 18. nom

122d st, No. 249, n s, 318.4 e 8th av, 17.8x100.11, three-story stone front dwell'g. Nathan Kaplan, Brooklyn, and Sarah E. his wife to Adeline E. F. Praeger. *Mt.* $15,500. Sept. 8. 30,000

128th st, No. 239, n s, 425 e 8th av, 25x99.11, four-story stone front flat. Ida W. Phillips to Charles Cudlipp. *Mt.* $16,000. Sept. 15. 25,000

132d st, No 232, s s, 470 e 8th av, 15x99.11, three-story stone front dwell'g. Release mort. John Bell to Joseph Donaldson. Sept. 11. 1,250

Same property. Joseph Donaldson and Mary M. his wife to Mabel wife of William K. Richardson. *Mt.* $9,000. Sept. 11. 14,500

133d st, Nos. 161-167, n s, 125 e 7th av, 100x99.11, four five story brk flats. Foreclos. Leicester Holme to Charles Schlesinger. Sub. to mort. Sept. 14. 37,000

143d st, n s, 150 w 8th av, 25x99.11, vacant. George E. Sibley exr. Charles A. Clapp to Mary E. wife of George E. Sibley, Elizabeth, N. J. Aug. 25. nom

Same property. Mary E. wife of George E. Sibley, Elizabeth, N. J., to Henry C. Stetson. *Mt.* $2,000. Aug. 26. nom

143d st, n s, 175 w 8th av, 25x99.11, vacant. George E. Sibley exr. Charles A. Clapp to Samuel D. Clapp, Saratoga Springs, N. Y. Aug. 25. nom

Same property. Samuel D. Clapp and Helen C. his wife, Saratoga Springs, N. Y., to Henry C. Stetson. *Mt.* $1,000, taxes, &c. Aug. 26. nom

143d st, n s, 150 w 8th av, 50x99.11. Henry C. Stetson to Edward J. Kelly. Sept. 8. 8,000

144th st, No. 453, n s, 94.5 w Convent av, 21.5x99.11, three-story brk dwell'g. Harry J. Meyer and Jennie E. his wife to Sophia C. Hoffman. Sub. to mort. Sept. 10. 21,000

157th st, No. 506, s s, 150 w Amsterdam av, 16.8x99.11, three-story brk dwell'g. Charles E. Deppermann and Elizabeth his wife, George Santer and Lena his wife to John Becker and Elizabeth his wife. *Mt.* $7,000. Sept. 10. 14,500

157th st, No. 508, s s, 166.8 w Amsterdam av, 16.5x99.11, three-story brk dwell'g. Same to Robert E. De Forest, Bridgeport, Conn. *Mt.* $7,000. Sept. 10. 14,000

Amsterdam av, No. 148, w s, 75.5 s 67th st, 25x100, five-story stone front tenem't with stores. Wilhelmina Ruck to Louis E. Oxee. *Mt.* $22,250. Sept. 14. 28,500

Av A, s e cor 74th st, 25x77. Agreement as to easement for light and air. Francis J. Schnugg and Lambert S. Quackenbush trustees with The Board of Health, New York. Sept. 11. nom

Av C, Nos 255 and 257 } begins Av C, n w cor 15th st, No. 645 } 15th st, 45.9x88, two four-story brk tenem'ts with stores on av and two-story brk stable on st. Mary Reilly to Joseph F. Johnson. C. a. G. Sept. 16. nom

Av D, No. 123, w s, 95.6 n 8th st, 23.6x93, four-story brk store and tenem't. Isaac Schencker and Bella his wife to Dora R. Bernart. *Mt.* $8,500. Sept. 15. 13,000

Columbus av, n w cor 63d st, 25x100.5, all.
Columbus av, n w cor 70th st, 25x100.5, 1-5 part.
Columbus av, s w cor 73d st, 25x102.2, 1-5 part.
Columbus av, w s, extends from 86th st to 87th st, 201.5x30, 1-10 part.
95th st, n s, 100 w 3d av, 100x100.8, 1-5 part.
5th av, e s, 32 s 73d st, 22.7x130, with all int. in lane or passageway adj, 22.7x130, 1-5 part.
Greenwich st, e s, 39.8 s Dey st, 25.7x43.5x25x52.8, 1-5 part.
Babette Reckendorfer widow to Louis J. Reckendorfer her son. All liens. March 16, 1891. nom

Same property. Same proportionate parts. Same to Samuel J. Reckendorfer her son. All liens. March 16, 1891. nom

Columbus (9th) av, Nos. 881-891, n e cor 103d st, 166.11x100x160.11x100, five five-story brk flats with stores. Thomas Campbell and Sarah his wife to Welcome R. Steinmetz. Sub. to mort. Sept. 12. other consid and 100

Fort Washington av, centre line, 173.4 n e from a point in south line of L. Chittendens land which is 619.11 w Kingsbridge road, runs northeast 150 x southeast 445.7 x southwest 151.6 x northwest 465.11. Charles Euler to Charles E. Runk. *Mt.* $12,600. June 30. nom

Lexington av, Nos. 150 and 152, s e cor 87th st, 62.3x100.8, two five-story brk flats with stores in No. 150. Edward C. Sheehy and Maggie E. his wife and Patrick Sheehy and Bridget his wife to Luigi, Guiseppe, Steffano and Natale Cavinato. Q. C. and C. a. G. Correction deed. Sept. 1. nom

Mount Morris av, Nos. 35-38, s w cor 124th st, 100.11x100, six-story brk flat. Henry Franke and Eunice R. his wife, Brooklyn, to William B. Franke. 3-10 part. Sub. to mort. Sept. 5. nom

Park av, No. 51, e s, 25 n 37th st, 21x80, four-story stone front dwell'g. Hugh Cheyne et al. exrs. Alexander F. Sterling to Marie A. wife of Charles H. Steinway. Re-recorded. April 30, 1887. 41,000

Park av, e s, 25 n 37th st, 21x80. Daniel S. McElroy and Linda L. his wife to Sarah E. wife of Anson W. Hard. *Mt.* $25,000. Sept. 8. nom

Park av, No. 1143, e s, 20.5 n 91st st, 16x70, three-story stone front dwell'g. Nathan Kaplan and Sarah E. his wife to Adeline E. F. Praeger. *Mt.* $12,000. Sept. 8. 25,000

Pleasant av, No. 333, w s, 38.6 s 118th st, 18.6x75, three-story stone front dwell'g. Sender Jarmulowsky and Rebecca his wife to Amelia Levin. *Mt.* $6,000. Sept. 11. nom

St. Nicholas av, No. 336, s e cor 127th st, 18.11x77x18.9x74.2, four-story brk flat. William H. Moore and Mamie E. his wife to Annie B. wife of James Rogers. B. & S. *Mt.* $12,000. Sept. 2. nom

1st av, No. 1491, w s, 25 s 78th st, 25x100, five-story brk store and flat. Louis Wechsler to Isaac Bitterman. Sub. to mort. July 22. 33,500

1st av, Nos. 1295 and 1297, w s, 25.4 s 70th st, 50x77, two four-story stone front tenem'ts with stores. Theresa M. Hill widow, Jersey City, to Christina wife of Jacob Keller, Jersey City. B. & S. Sept. 2. nom

Same property. Jacob Keller, Jersey City, to Theresa M. Hill, Jersey City. B. & S. Sept. 2. nom

3d av, No. 777, n e cor 48th st, 25.5x93, four-story brk tenem't with stores. Frederick Moeller and Rachel his wife to Patrick J. Kennedy. *Mt.* $30,000. Sept. 15. 44,750

7th av, Nos. 2170-2178, s w cor 129th st, 99.11x75, four five-story brk flats with stores. Foreclos. James R. Cuming to La Force S. Baker, Chicago. Sept. 15. 11,000

8th av, No. 2550, n e cor 136th st, 24.11x80, five-story brk store and flat. Foreclos. David McClure to The Equitable Life Assur. Soc., United States. *Mt.* $16,500. Sept. 9. 27,000

8th av, No. 2564, s e cor 137th st, 24.11x80, five-story brk store and flat. Foreclos. Same to same. *Mt.* $16,000. Sept. 9. 29,000

8th av, No. 2560, e s, 49.11 s 137th st, 25x80, five-story brk store and flat. Foreclos. Same to same. *Mt.* $12,500. Sept. 9. 21,000

8th av, No. 2562, e s, 24.11 s 137th st, 25x80, five-story brk store and flat. Foreclos. Same to same. *Mt.* $12,500. Sept. 9. 19,000

8th av, No. 2558, e s, 74.11 s 137th st, 25x80, five-story brk store and flat. Foreclos. Same to same. *Mt.* $12,500. Sept. 9. 21,250

8th av, No. 2556, e s, 74.11 n 136th st, 25x80, five-story brk store and flat. Foreclos. Same to same. *Mt.* $12,500. Sept. 9. 18,000

8th av, No. 2552, e s, 24.11 n 136th st, 25x80, five-story brk store and flat. Foreclos. Same to same. *Mt.* $12,500. Sept. 9. 21,000

8th av, No. 2554, e s, 49.11 n 136th st, 25x80, five-story brk store and flat. Foreclos. Same to same. *Mt.* $12,500. Sept. 9. 20,500

MISCELLANEOUS.

All title of grantors in real and personal estate of John, Tammisin and Fletcher Harper. William D. Harper and Tacie McD. wife of and John H. Bonnell and Margaret C. his wife to Robert L. Harrison. All liens. April 18. nom

All title of grantor in residuary estate of Paul Spofford dec'd. Edward C. Spofford to Thomas W. Pearsall and Jacob Halstead. Trust deed. May 12. nom

23d and 24th WARDS.

Buckhout st, s s, 350 w Anthony av, 27.10x100x 27.4x100. Elihu G. Hinckley to Virginia Budelman. Sept. 8. 7,500

Ernescliffe pl, s s, 471.6 w Lisbon pl, 35.2x101.9 x25x103. Susan wife of Edward Rodier to John J. Kane. Aug. 27. 600

Potter pl, n s, 175 w unnamed st, lot 433 map No. 3 New York City Private Park, 25x100. Peter Ross and Mary his wife to Hannah M. Hynes. Sept. 14. 600

Potter pl, n s, 200 w unnamed st, lot 434 same map, 25x100. David Kay and Mary his wife to same. Sept. 14. 600

Rogers pl, e s, 642.4 n Westchester av, 30x81.8x 23.1x78.11. Contract. James McCarthy to Mary E. Burrell. June 15. 1,200

Samuel st. n e s, 132 n w Franklin av, 66x150. John F. Crotty and Mary F. his wife to James Y. Allen. Sept. 10. 1,400

Southern Boulevard, n s, 96 w proposed Webster av, 25x100. James Hynes and Hannah M. his wife to Fred. M. Edwards. Sept. 10. 2,200

135th st, s s, 220 w 3d av, 30x100. James Byrne and Mary his wife and Bridget Byrne to John H. Byrne. ⅓ part. Sept. 14. nom

135th st, n s, 104 e Southern Boulevard, 100.5x 75. Frederick C. McCormack to Phebe C. Rapelye. B. & S. Sept. 17. 33,000

136th st, n s, 231.6 e Alexander av, 50x100. James Brown and Mary his wife to Hannah Brooks. April 29. 12,000

137th st, s s, 1,000 w Home av. 50x110. Julia A. Sadlier and ano. exrs. Dennis Sadlier to Frederick Vollmar. July 17. 3,950

Same property. Release mort. The Metropolitan Savings Bank to same. July 17. nom

Same property. Release mort. John W. O'Shaughnessy to same. July 17. nom

147th st, n s, 241.5 e 3d av, 105.6x125.9x91.10x 128.2. Edward Willis and Margaretta C. his wife to Christian Schaefer. June 28, 1866. 1,500

165th st, s s, 250 w Trinity av, runs south 120.6 x west 100 x north 120.6 to 165th st, x east 39.11 x south 85 x east 20 to Cauldwell av, x north 85 to 165th st, x east 40.1. Release mort. John Bussing, Jr., to George P. Arbogast. Jan. 7. nom

166th st, s s, 275 w Forest av, 25x100. Newbury D. Lawton and Hannah B. his wife to Josephine T. Greene. *Mt.* $3,000. Aug. 25. 5,500

169th st, n s, part lot 40 map property Mrs. Henrietta Henwood, 23d Ward, contains 900 square feet. Henrietta Barnum to Henrietta V. Wheeler. C. a. G. Feb. 26, 1890. 250

187th st, s w cor St. Johns av, 25x100. Ella M. McClatchey to Edward Reilly. Sept. 4. nom

Anthony av, e s, at intersection with w s Burnside av, runs south 256.4 x west 102.7 x north 89.2 x west 100 to Anthony av, x north 144. Abram T. Buckhout and Martha his wife, James Buckhout and Sarah E. his wife to Frederick E. Platt. Sept. 8. 7,500

Arthur av, e s, lot 18 map known as Oak Tree plot, part farm Gouverneur Morris, 25x100. Robert Roberts to Robert Roberts and Jane his wife, joint tenants. *Mt.* $2,000. Sept. 16. nom

Bathgate av, w s, 178.3 s 180th st, 21.1x94.8. Justin Wohlfarth and Catherine his wife to Kate L. Osborn. *Mt* $2,500. Aug. 31. 4,800

Boston av, s e s, 250 s w Perot st, 25x98.8 to Armand pl, x25x95.2.
Boston av, s e s, 25 s w Perot st, 25x98.2 to Armand pl, x25x98.4.
Release mort. James M. Wentz, Newburgh, N. Y., to Arthur Berry. Aug. 24. nom

Brook av, w s, 125 n 170th st, 25x90. Louis Kaysser and Ottilie his wife to Margaretha Pape. *Mt.* $500. Sept. 11. 900

Cambreling av, w s, 200 n Bayard st, 25x87.6. Francis Trainor to Daniel McLean. Sept. 12. 600

Forrest av, n e cor George st, 75x100. Sadie A. Marvin widow to Frederick A. and Frank W. Marvin. C. a. G. Sept. 9. nom

Franklin av, n e s, lot 131 map Morrisania, 68x —x—x99. Theodora Ernst to Frank L. Schaller. Aug. 26. 6,500

Madison av, s e cor Marble st, 58x98.2x58x96. Ephraim C. Gates and Vashte R. his wife, Calais, Me., to Charles H. Bull. July 31. nom

Madison av, e s, 58 s Marble st, 50x100. Same to Henry F. Taylor. July 31. nom

Morris av, s w cor 150th st, 50x100. John McMillan and Mary his wife to Jacob H. Westheimer. Sept. 14. 6,750

Washington av, n w s, 50 s w 186th st, 50x100. Henry J. Masson and Sadie P. his wife to Fanny J. Masson. Sept. 14. nom

Willis av, s w cor 135th st, 25x81.6. Luigi, Guiseppe, Steffano and Natale Cavinato to Charles P. Faber. *Mt.* $21,500. Sept. 15. 34,500

Willis av, No. 403, w s, 50 s 144th st, 25x84. Harry C. Browning and Ida C. his wife to Arnold Adler and Adolf Sommer. *Mt.* $15,500 Sept. 15. nom

Lots 136-141 map Woodlawn Heights, belonging to Edward K. Willard. 24th Ward. Ephraim B. Levy to Mary E Monaghan. Sept. 10. 2,275

Lots 10 and 11 block 24 sections A and B map North New York, Morrisania. Jacob Cohen and Fanny his wife to Jacob Rose. Q. C. ½ part. Feb. 2, 1891. nom

Same property. Martin Schwayer exr. Christian Schaeffer to same. Feb. 25. 1,500

Lots 10 and 11 map Section A and B, North New York Jacob Rose and Ida his wife to Fanny wife of Jacob Cohen. B. & S. ½ part. Sept. 10. nom

LEASEHOLD CONVEYANCES.

Grand st, No. 40. Assign. lease. Charles Trevesanello to Charles Herzenberg. nom

West st, No. 127. Assign. lease. James S. Kelly to Ferdinand Neis. nom

6th st, No. 217 E. Assign. lease. Friedrich Suder to Paul Sheel. nom

19th st, s s, 70 e 1st av, 20x56. Assign. lease. Torpetus L. Herberger admr. John P. Herberger to Philip Jaeger. nom

Same property. Assign. lease. Philip Jaeger to Torpetus L. Herberger. nom

23d st, Nos. 70 and 72 W. Surrender lease. Hosea Higgins and Judson G. Wells to James McCreery. Sept. 15. 12,899

Same property. Assign. lease. Same to same. nom

23d st, No. 68 W., second floor. Surrender lease. Same to same. Sept. 15. 100

48th st, No. 209 E. Robert A. Chesebrough to Pearl Eytinge. 50 years, from May 1, 1891. gift

48th st, No. 34, s s, 452.6 w 5th av, 20.6x100.5. Trustees of Columbia College to Harriet E. W. wife of George D. Strong. 21 years, from Nov. 1, 1886, per year, taxes and 835

49th st, n s, 264 w 5th av, 25x100.5. Assign. lease. Mary B. Child to Emma B. Jennings. 36,500

3d av, No. 358. Assign. lease. Hermann Keris to The F. & M. Schaefer Brewing Co. nom

8th av, n e cor 15th st, 25x93.6. William Astor to Jonas and Samuel Weil and Bernhard Mayer. 20 years, from May 1, 1891, per year, taxes, &c. 1,750

8th av, e s, 77.2 s 16th st, 26.1x93.6. Same to same. 20 years, from May 1, 1891, per year, taxes, &c. 1,250

8th av, e s, 51.1 s 16th st, 26.1x93.6. Same to same. 20 years, from May 1, 1891, per year, taxes, &c. 1,250

8th av, s e cor 16th st, 25x93.6 Same to same. 20 years, from May 1, 1891, per year, taxes, &c. 1,750

8th av, e s, 25 s 16th st, 26.1x93.6. Same to same. 20 years, from May 1, 1891, per year, taxes, &c. 1,250

8th av, e s, 77.2 n 15th st, 26.1x93.6. Same to same. 20 years, from May 1, 1891, per year, taxes, &c. 1,250

8th av, e s, 51.1 n 15th st, 26.1x93.6. Same to same. 20 years, from May 1, 1891, per year, taxes, &c. 1,250

8th av, e s, 25 n 15th st, 26.1x93.6. Same to same. 20 years, from May 1, 1891, per year, taxes, &c. 1,250

10th av, No 812. Assign. lease. Thomas H. Farley to Peter McIntyre. nom

Agreement as to waiver of covenant in lease made between parties on Sept. 8, 1890. John A. Hagemeyer to John F. Windolph and Israel Loewenstein. nom

KINGS COUNTY.

SEPTEMBER 10, 11, 12, 14, 15, 16.

Aberdeen st, s e s, 210 s w Bushwick av, 20x 100. Thekla Merschoff to Adam Merschoff. *Mt.* $2,775. $4,200

Ashford st, w s, 290 s New Lots road, 40x100. Adolph Sussman to James Monks. Correction deed. 820

Barbey st, w s, 300 n Blake av, 25x100. Albert H. W. Van Sielen to George Olsen. Taxes, &c., from 1889. 350

Bedford st, e s, 345 s Fulton av, 20x100. Christine wife of and Ernest Schnopp to Peter Wagener. *Mt.* $2,000. 3,775

Bergen st, s s, 560 w 5th av, 20x100.
Wyckoff st, n s, 320 w 5th av, 20x100.
Release dower. Gertrude Koch, Woodhaven, to Louis Koch. nom

Bergen st, s s, 520 w 5th av, 40x100. Release dower. Gertrude Koch to Mary De Languilette. nom

Bergen st, n s, 291.8 e Rockaway av, 16.8x 107.2. James D. and Jennie E. Firth to William Davison. *Mt.* $1,800. 2,800

Bergen st, n s, 250 w Buffalo av, 65x107.2. Frank P. Martin to Gussie L. Phelan. All morts. nom

Bergen st. n s. 175 e Hopkinson av, 75x125.8x— x112.8. Augusta M. Hobe to Marion C. wife of J. Wheeler Smith. Sub. to assessm't. 1,800

Bergen st, n e s, 150 n w Underhill av, runs northeast 157.10 x north 3.8 x west 26.8 x southwest 147.6 to Bergen st, x southeast 25. Bertha Kaufmann to Elizabetha Weber, Breslau, L. I. *Mt.* $5,200. exch

Bergen st, n s, 80 e Boerum pl, 20x75. Sarah Chatterley to Otto Szyszka. 3,550

Boerum st, No. 155, n s, 25x100. Contract. Elisabetha Fruh formerly Zink to Samuel Pilzer. 8,400

Berkeley pl, n s, 270.6 w 8th av, 20x100, h & l. Mary E. wife of Joseph D. Higgins formerly Bowne to Abram S. Townsend. nom

Bond st, s w cor Degraw st, 25x85. Helena wife of and John E. Wulp to Thomas P. Kenna. *Mt.* $6,000. exch

Butler st, n s, abt 234.4 e Schenectady av, 175.4 x111.6x174.2x61, h s & l s. Gustavus M. Carroll to Ella T. Caffery. B. & S. 800

Butler st, s s, 358 e Nostrand av, 16.8x100, h & l. John Andrews to Frank L. Corwin. *Mt.* $3,750. 6,000

Calyer st, s s, 25 w Lorimer st, 25x100, h & l. Mary Welsh widow to Amelia W. Finn. 5,350

Carroll st, s s, 20.1 e Polhemus pl, 21x101.9x21.1 x103.9. John Magilligan agt Henrietta Obermeyer. *Mt.* $10,000. 17,000

Chester st, lots 179 and 180 map 262 lots Sarah A. Suydam, New Lots, 50x100 Harriet C. wife of Charles S. Brown to Daniel McEnerny. May 9, 1864. 250

Chestnut st, w s, 782 s Jamaica av, 25x100. Edward R. Vollmer to Edward F. Mould. 600

Court st, w s, 82 n 2d pl, 18x50, h & l. Mary A. A. Mayhew to Meline F. Beachoff. Sub. to encroachment. 8,300

Covert st, s s, 394 w Evergreen av, 18x100, h & l. Richard Geary to Miriam E. Cunningham. *Mt.* $2,400. 1889. 4,750

Same property. Miriam E. wife of Ira Lester formerly Cunningham, Tannersville, N. Y., to Roman Holzenthaler. *Mt.* $3,600. 4,800

Decatur st, s w cor Glenada pl, 85x100. Calvin C. Church to Mary E. Reynolds. *Mt.* $70,-247. nom

Dumont st, e s, s e cor Sackman st, runs east 200 to Powell st, x south 500 to Livonia av, x west 200 to Sackman st, x north 500 to beginning. Hirsch Wilkenfeld to Rosanna Rosenfeld. ½ share. *Mt.* $8,000. 10,000

Eastern Parkway, s w cor Amboy st, runs south 215.5 x west 100 x north 125 x west 25 x north 90.5 to Parkway, x east 125. John H. Vanderveer to Berthold J. Pink. *Mt.* $3,150. 4,500

East Broadway, s e cor Rogers av, 38x100x 36.10x100; also,
Erasmus st, n w cor Rogers av, 37x100x35x 100, Flatbush.
Gideon Mowlen to Joseph F. Bower. Sub. to mort. nom

Eldert st, n w s, 100 n e Evergreen av, 20x100. Lucinda Moadinger individ. and extrx. of John Moadinger to Ernestine Gastmeyer. 1,075

Eldert st, n w s, 160 n e Evergreen av, 40x100. Charles E. Silkworth to Ernestine Gastmeyer. 2,100

Fulton st, n w cor Pine st. runs west 47 x north 98.3 x west 53.6 x north 25 x east 100 to Pine st, x south 115.6. Marenus J. Goodenough to Frank Ehlers. 2,350

Fulton st, s s, 164.5 w Franklin av, 56x117.
Fulton st, s s, 169.9 e Bedford av, 40x100.
James Phelan, of San Francisco, Cal., to Thomas G. Splint. *Mt.* $56,000. nom

Fulton st, s s, 169.9 e Bedford av, 40x100. Thomas G. Splint to Latimer W. Crosby, of Trenton, N. J. *Mt.* $20,000. nom

Furnald st, n s, 94.6 w Hudson av, 20x100, Flatbush. Luke Mahon to Maria wife of Emides Furfino. 210

George st, s e s, 250 n e Central av, 25x94x27.10 x106.3. Nicholas Seagrist to Gottwald Jacob and Gertrude his wife, joint tenants. 1,600

Glenada pl, w s, 100 s Decatur st. Release of agreement as to encroachment, &c. Charles D. Rust to William W. Reynolds. nom

Graham st, e s, 429.10 s Flushing av, 25x75.10x 25x75.11. Vincenzo Ciardi or Ciarda and Angeline Ciardi or Ciarda to Francisco Ciardi or Ciarda. ½ part. *Mt.* $1,700. 600

Grove st, n w s, 91.3 s w Evergreen av, 23x87.6 x20x87.6, h & l. Henry Ruthmann to Jacob Schnautz. 5,050

Guernsey st, e s, 375 s Nassau av, 75x100.
Lorimer st, w s, 375 s Nassau av, 25x100.
Fredericke wife of Frederick Sauter to Franz A. Baier. 4,200

Hall st, w s, 227.10 s Park av, 20x100. Annie M. Curry to John J. Curry. nom

Halsey st, s e s, 240 n e Bushwick av, 20x100. Charles Woodruff to Sadie L. Woodruff. *Mt.* $8,000. nom

Same property. Sadie L. Woodruff to Helen Woodruff. *Mt.* $8,000. nom

Halsey st. No. 226, s s, 245 w Tompkins av, 20x 100. Absalom W. Dieter to Charles H. Tyson. *Mt.* $3,800. nom

Hancock st, s s, 80 w Howard av, 20x75, h & l. Gustavus M. Carroll to Tully F. Fanshaw trustee for Francis Borroto. 1,000

Hancock st, n s, 67.4 e Saratoga av, runs northwest 95 to av, x south 67 to st, x east 67.4. Foreclos. John Courtney, Sheriff, to Walter J. Klotz 3,700

Harman st, n w s, 375 n e Knickerbocker av, 25 x100. Release mort. Mary E. James to Joseph N. Sgier. 700

Same property. Joseph N. Sgier to Pauline Renoldi. *Mt.* $700. 1,237

Harman st. s e s, 300 n e Central av, 25x100. William Berlinger to Katie Katzmann. *Mt.* $3,500. 6,550

Harman st, s s, 325 e Central av, 25x100. William Berlinger to John Beiler. *Mt.* $3,500. 6,650

Harman st, s e s, 225 n e Central av, 25x100, h & l. Andrew and Christian Hahn to Albert Beck and Paulina his wife, joint tenants. *Mt.* $3,500. nom

Hemlock st, w s, 125 s Liberty av, 50x100. John H. Ives to John H. Kerrigan. 600

Hemlock st, w s, 125 s Liberty av, runs south 184.11 x west — x north 121.5 x east 100. Jane L. Smith to John H. Ives. nom

Hendrix st, e s, 150 s Glenmore av, 25x100. Thomas F. Lonney or Louney to Theodore Staff and Catherine his wife. Sub. to assessment. 1,000

Herkimer st, s e cor Howard av, 16x98. Caspar Lucke to Hermann Thielemann and Joseph G. Weisbaupt. *Mt.* $2,300. 4,350

Herkimer st, s s, 66 e Howard av, 16x98. Caspar Lucke to Thomas E. Haverty. *Mt.* $2,350. 4,350

Himrod st, s e s, 380 s w Central av, 20x100, h & l. John Sherman to Max Pannwitz. *Mt.* $2,000. 4,500

Hopkins st, s s, 100 w Marcy av, 25x100, h & l. Lawrence Woodworth to Rosanna Woodworth. B. & S. nom

Hoyt st, e s, 40 s Douglass st, 20x60.
Atlantic av, s s, 215.4 w Utica av, 16.8x100.
Teresa B. wife of August H. Brabe to Jennie A. Ives. *Mt.* $4,350. exch

Hull st, s s, 75 e Hopkinson av, 18.9x80, h & l. Alonzo E. De Baun to Fayette S. Barnum, New York. *Mt.* $3,500. exch

Humboldt st, e s, 125 n Scholes st, 25x100. Eliza Wolf to Gustav Hangarter. *Mt.* $3,000. 5,100

Humboldt st, w s, 75 n Maujer st, 25x100. Theresa wife of Lazar Braun to Leopold Michel. *Mt.* $500. 3,200

Huron st, s s, 225 w Oakland st, 25x100. Jeremiah Desmond and Catharine his wife who releases dower to Timothy Dermond. 2,000

India st, s s, 375 e Manhattan av, 25x100. Patrick McMahon, of New York, to Bridget wife of Patrick O'Brien. 2,100

Jay st, e s, 30 s Willoughby st, 20x87.6, h & l. Eliza Munro widow to Julius Colberg, Sr. *Mt.* $5,420. 12,000

Jay st, w s, 70 s Prospect st, 30x50, hs & ls. James Bothersall to Pauline Rimoldi. 6,500

Jefferson st, s s, 175 e Knickerbocker av, runs south 100 x east 23.6 x — x north 96.1 to st, x west 25. Jacob Boslet to Frank Spaeth. 1,250

Jerome st, w s, 100 n Eastern Parkway, 100x 100.
Eastern Parkway, s e cor Barbey st, 25x100.
Alois Lazansky to Theodore M. Le Beau. 4,000

Jerome st, s w s, 120 n w Repose pl, 60x49 4x60x 52.3. Foreclos. John Courtney, Sheriff, to Nathan Kaplan. 290

Johnson pl, n e s, bet E. Johnson's and R. Wanser, indeft. plot, Canarsie. Eve Patterson to Sarah Van Pelt. nom

Johnson pl, n e s, bounded southeast by land of Dianah Ferguson, southwest by land Richard Wanser, northeast by land Wm. Anderson and northwest by land Sarah Van Pelt, Flatlands. Eve Patterson to Alice Johnson. nom

Logan st, w s, 90 s Liberty av, 20x100. Effingham H. Nichols to Josephine Engert. 300

Louis pl, e s, 121.7 n Atlantic av, 23x97. Contract. Mary L. Girvin to Clara V. Thornton. 4,250

Macon st, n s, 184 w Ralph av, 18x100, h & l. George C. Cranford to Russell R. Brown. *Mt.* $5,300. 6,800

Macon st, s s, 155 e Sumner av, 20x100, h & l. John B. Green, Westfield, N. J., to Honora Farrell. 6,750

Macon st, s s, 192 w Ralph av, 18x100. Walter F. Clayton to Amos D. Carver, New York. *Mt.* $5,000. 8,250

Marion st, n e cor Hopkinson av, 20x60; also,
Hopkinson av, e s, 60 n Marion st, runs east to Brooklyn and Jamaica turnpike or plank road, x northwest — to point 80 n from Marion st, x west to Hopkinson av, x south 20 to beginning.
Hannah wife of and Phillip Sullivan to John J. Barry and Daniel B. Mitchell. 2,500

Marion st, s s, 200 e Howard av, 25x100, h & l. John Warmworth to Richard Weise. *Mt.* $1,000. 2,850

McDonough st, s s, 285.8 w Patchen av, 114x 100. John Pierce to Henry B. Hill. 10,290

McDonough st, n s, 285 w Tompkins av, 100x 100. Catharine C. wife of and Daniel Pearsall to Henrietta A. wife of Mortlock Pettit. 35,000

McDonough st, n s, 262.6 w Reid av, 18.9x100. James Comiskey to Catherine T. Lopez. 6,500

McDonough st, s s, 175.5 e Sumner av, 99.7x100. Michael Rofrano to Alberico Caroselli. 40,000

McDonough st, s s, 262.6 e Tompkins av, 20x 100. John W. Newbery to Jenny Von Lyncker. *Mt.* $6,500. 6,500

McKibbin st, s s, 25 w Humboldt st, 25x100. Morres Minden and Simon Spandau to Samuel Karger and Lena his wife, joint tenants. *Mt.* $3,750. 5,000

Melrose st, n w s, 100 n e Knickerbocker av, 125x100. William F. Garrison to Joseph Weidner. 6,500

Melrose st, n w s, 325 n e Broadway, 50x95, hs & ls. John Young to Elizabeth Foruh. *Mt.* $4,500. 7,550

Milford st or av, w s, 210 n Blake av, 60x100. George B. Stoutenburg and Charles F. Hunt to Emily O. Smith. nom

Moffat st, w s, 100 n Central av, 50x100. Harry F. C. Hopkins to John W. Smith. nom

Monroe st, w s, 250 n Liberty av, 25x90. Patrick Lennon to Ellen Lennon. nom

Montague st, No. 130, s s, 26.6 e Henry st, 25x 100. Matilda W. Strouse to Henry Frank. *Mt.* $27,500. nom

Moore st, n s, 250 e Graham av, 25x100, h & l. Michael Krebs to Isaac Greenblatt and Solomon Ellinsohn. *Mt.* $5,000. 6,500

Morton st, s e s, 183.4 s w Bedford av, 21.8x100, h & l. George W. Everitt to William Gaynor. 7,500

Nelson st, n s, 260.6 w Court st, 16.4x100. Margaret wife of John J. Hastings to Hans A. Hansen. 3,500

North Elliott pl, w s, 75.10 s Park av, runs west 80.1 x south 10.4 x southeast 29.4 to centre old Division st, x southwest 10.11 x east 58.8 to North Elliott pl, x north 25 to beginning; also,
North Elliott pl, w s, 125.10 s Park av, runs west 70.4 to centre old Division st, x southwest 8[illegible].6 x east 106 to North Elliott pl, x north 75 to beginning.
James McLaren to John Thatcher. nom

Ocean Parkway, w s, 150 s Av E, 20x100. Release mechanic's lien. John Williams, New York, to Ellen Graham. nom

Osborn st, n w cor Livonia av, 25x100. Adolphus Gload to Annie wife of Joseph Matthews. 1,175

Pacific st, n s, 80 w Stone av, 20x100. Henry P. Kernan to Clara E. Cobb. All liens. 50

Pacific st, s s, 150 e Rockaway av, 16.8x107.2.
Pacific st, s s, 100 e Rockaway av, 33.4x107.2.
Release mort. Edwin O. Phelps to Robert S. Neely. nom

Pacific st, n s, 170 w Albany av, 20x100, h & l. Jennie S. Niles to Mary O'Neill. *Mt.* $4,500. 6,000

Pacific st, s s, 150 e Rockaway av, 16.8x107.2, h & l. Robert S. Neely to John C. Elliott. *Mt.* $1,800. 3,000

Pacific st, s s, 116.8 e Rockaway av, 16.8x107.2, h & l. Same to Henry A. A. Bruhn. *Mt.* $1,833. 3,000

Pacific st, s s, 100 e Rockaway av, 16.8x107.2, h & l. Same to Raynold C. Schreppers. *Mt.* $2,134. 3,000

Palmetto st, s e s, 133 s w Knickerbocker av, 17 x100. Mary E. Koster to Elizabeth wife of and Charles Mason. *Mt.* $3,500. 3,900

Pearl st, No. 256, w s, abt 269.6 s Concord st, 22 x75. William Wilson to John W. Corrigan and Hannah M. his wife. *Mt.* $4,500. 5,500

Powell st, w s, 216.6 n Liberty av, 16.8x100. James E. Seaman, New York, to Emma Shoobert. *Mt.* $2,000. 3,300

President st, n s, 22.6 e 6th av, runs east 17.6 x north 20.11 x east 17.6 x south 95 to st, x west 35. William Brown to James H. McKenna. *Mt.* $13,000. exch

President st, n s, 208.8 w Hoyt st, 16.4x98, h & l. Theodore Smith to Albert Palmer, Cornwall-on-Hudson. *Mt.* $3,000. nom

President st, n s, 22.6 e 6th av, runs north 74.1 x east 17.6 north 20.11 x east 17.6 x south 95 to st, x west 35 to beginning. Release mort. Henry C. M. Ingraham to William Brown. nom

Quincy st, n s, 267.8 e Tompkins av, 19x100. John H. Monteath to Josephine Monteath his wife. *Mt.* $4,000. 1889. nom

Quincy st, s s, 418.9 w Throop av, 18.9x100, h & l. Albert Sibley to William S. and Thomas Ross. *Mt.* $4,000. 7,800

Quincy st, s s, 381.3 w Throop av, 93.9x100. Release mort. Andrew D. Baird to Albert Sibley. nom

Same property. Release mort. Thomas T. Barr to same. 12,500

Quincy st, n s, 309.4 e Stuyvesant av, 20.4x100. Henry Schwarz and Lewis S. Gobel exrs. John Schwarz to Louis Schwarz. 4,000

Quincy st, n s, 248.4 e Stuyvesant av, 20.4x100. Same to William Schwarz. 4,000

Richmond st, e s, 1,250 n 4th st, 50x150. Howard Daisley to George Beach. 1,350

Sands st, s s, 351.5 e Jay st, 20x100, h & l. Patrick H. Funchon to James Hothersall and Catharine his wife. *Mt.* $3,500. 8,000

Seigel st, s s, 100 w Humboldt st, 75x100, hs & ls. David Stern to Joseph S. and Nathan Marcus. *Mt.* $32,937. 39,250

Seigel st, n s, 175 e Graham av, 25x100, h & l. Samuel Parshelsky to Theresa Goodkind, New York. 4,100

Seigel st, s s, adj land of George White on west, 75x100x72x100. John Rueger to Frederick Sprower. 2,000

Smith st, w s, 80 s Butler st, 20x50, h & l. Catharine Buckley to Ann wife of John Ashley. *Mt.* $4,000. 10,000

Stanhope st, s e s, 653 n e Evergreen av, 22x 100. Henrietta Hager widow to Thomas A. Macpherson. 1,450

Stanhope st, s s, 350 w St. Nicholas av, 20x100. Margaretha Bossert to Henry Bossert, Jr. 750

Stanhope st, n s, 310 w St. Nicholas av, 20x100, h & l. William Lenfer to George O. R. Koenig. *Mt.* $1,600. 3,350

Stanhope st, s e s, 360 n e Hamburg av, 20x100. Clara K. wife of and Jacob P. Decker to Theodore F. Jackson. *Mt.* $3,800. 3,300

State st, s w s, 200 s e Henry st, 25x100. Winfield S., formerly George W. Niles, trustee Amanda M. Niles dec'd to Alice L. Stark. in consid. of his appointment

Same property. Alice L. Stark to Winfield S. Niles. in consid. of purposes of trust

Stockholm st, s e s, 350 s w Knickerbocker av, 25x53.2x25x52.5. John S. Ellis and ano. exrs. Lawrence Waterbury to Frederick A. Young. 1,050

Stockton st, s s, 450 w Lewis av, 25x100. Henry Schwarz and Lewis S. Goebel to Elizabeth Schwarz. 7,000

Stockton st, s s, 100 w Throop av, 20x100. Robert Paul, Alice Ruhl and Bertha Becker, of New York City, to Frank A. Lang. nom

Same property. Frank A. Lang to Lillie E. Hughes, of Dennison, Texas. *Mt.* $500. nom

Summit st, n s, 150 e Hicks st, 100x100. Mary Van D. Boyce widow to John W. Moran. nom

Same property. Margaret L. wife of Aries P. Brooke, John W. and George M. Boyce, Mary L. Standerwick widow and Clara L. Boyce heirs John Boyce to same. 11,000

Walworth st, w s, 261.10 s Myrtle av, 18.9x100. Foreclos. John Courtney, sheriff, to Frederick Behrens as trustee Frederick Behrens dec'd. 2,000

Same property. Frederick Behrens as trustee Frederick Behrens to John Ryan. 2,600

Warren st, n s, 25 e 3d av, 25x100. Jennie A. Ives to Margaretha Lewis. *Mt.* $7,500. nom

Warren st, s s, 350 e 4th av, 20x100. Mary Barclay extrx. Alexander Barclay to Peter J. Jacobson. 4,000

Warren st, n s, 25 e 3d av, 25x100, h & l. Margaretha Lewis to Teresa B. Brabe. *Mt.* $8,500. nom

Watkins st, w s, 151.6 s Eastern Parkway, 25x 100. Ada wife of Lewis Parmer to Morris and Rosie Barkovitz. *Mt.* $2,500. 3,800

Watkins st, w s, 100 n Glenmore av, 25x100. Herbert C. Smith to Morris Shatt, New York. 700

Weirfield st, s e s, 240 n e Bushwick av, 20x100, h & l. Emma H. Shipsey to Joseph F. Shipsey. C. a. G. *Mt.* $2,000. nom

Woodbine st, s e s, 228 n e Hamburg av, 18x 100. George W. and Charles H. Francisco to Hester A. wife of George M. Richardson. nom

Woodbine st, s e s, 105 s w Central av, 20x100, h & l. Thomas A. Macpherson to Henrietta Hager widow. *Mt.* $2,800. 4,800

2d st, No. 395, n s, 304 w 6th av, 17.6x100, h & l. Julius Bohn to Oscar Roebsler. *Mt.* $4,500. nom

Same property. Oscar Roebsler to Minnie wife of Julius Bohn. *Mt.* $4,500. nom

2d st, n e s, 895.10 s e 7th av, 137x100. Edward H. Litchfield et al. trustees Edwin C. Litchfield to John Adamson. nom

2d st, s w s, 100 s e 7th av, 188x95,
2d st, n e s, 198.10 s e 7th av, 197x100.
Edward H. Litchfield to John Adamson. Taxes, &c. nom

North 2d st, s s, 124.2 w Havemeyer st, 25.4x 91.3x25.2x92.9, h & l. Thomas P. Kenna to Helena Wulp. *Mt.* $3,000. exch

3d st, s s, 28.6 e Smith st, runs south 53.5 x south 27.4 x east 13.2 x north 80 to 3d st, x west 18.6, h & l. Edward M. Townsend individ. and exr. of Belinda R. Townsend to William O. Sumner. 4,437

4th st, n s, 297.10 w 8th av, 100x95. Roderick Von Graff to Henry B. Spencer. B. & S. 25

East 5th st, w s, 142 n Greenwood av, 25x100, Flatbush. Patrick E. Sheridan to Margaret wife of and John Laing, Paterson, N. J. *Mt.* $1,975. 2,675

North 6th st, n s, 175 w Havemeyer st, runs north 100 x west 25 x south 66 x east .02½ x 34 to North 6th st, x east 24.9 to beginning; also,
North 6th st, s s, 140 e Havemeyer st, runs south 76 x east 21 x north 69 x west 20.
Humphrey Bennett to John Bennett, of New York. 3,000

North 8th st, n s, 150 e Kent av, 25x100, h & l. Mary wife of Joseph Whittaker to Peter and Joseph Young. 2,800

South 8th st, n s, 122.4 e 1st st, 20.2x70x20.8x70, h & l. Charlotte A. wife of Richard E. Jarmain to Adam Mann. C. a. G. nom

Same property. Adam Mann to Richard E. Jarmain. C. a. G. nom

10th st, No. 307. Samuel Stone to Mary J. Stone. nom

North 10th st, s s, 134 w Roebling st, runs west 21.5 x south 33.3 x northeast 39.6. Margaret Clark extrx. Edward J. Clark to Peter Blake. exch

North 10th st, s w s, 237.6 s e Driggs st, 28.6x— x 35, gore. Release mort. Frank S. Bradford et al. exrs. Samuel I. Hunt to Margaret Clark widow. nom

11th st, n s, 296.5 e 5th av, 16.8x100, h & l. Dennis J. Donovan and William H. Heron to Florence J. Donohue and Ellen his wife. *Mt.* $3,750. exch

11th st, n s, 89.5 e 8th av, 54x100. Isabella wife of William Brown to James H. McKenna. *Mt.* $13,000. exch

North 11th st, n e s, 100 n w Bedford av, 25x 100. Frank S. Bradford et al. exrs. Samuel I. Hunt to George Kleinbub. 2,500

12th st, n s, 105.9 w 4th av, 50x100. James H. McKenna to William Brown. *Mt.* $13,000. exch

12th st, n s, 215.11 w 6th av, 16.8x100. David Oakley to Henry J. Holt. *Mt.* $1,500. 3,000

12th st, s s, 181.2 e 4th av, 16.8x100, h & l. Mary Mulcrone widow to Maria Sharpe. B. & S. 1,000

13th st, s s, 138.9 w 4th av, 17.2x100. James C. McEachen to John Watson. 6,000

13th st, s s, 155.11 s w 4th av, 17.2x100, h & l. Mary F. Du Buisson, New York, to Ernest Adler. *Mt.* $5,500. nom

13th st, s s, 173.2 w 4th av, 17.2x100. Frank W. Belmont to Ernest Adler. *Mt* $5,500, taxes, &c. nom

13th st, s s, 347.10 e 5th av, 25x100. Charles Schmidt to Charles Schultz. 6,300

15th st, s w s, 83.10 n w 4th av, 22x100. Contract for property. Bernard Cosgrove to Mary Metcalf. 4,100

West 15th st, w s, adj north line of land New York & Coney Island R. R., runs west 88.8 x north 26.6 x east 86.7 to West 15th st, x south 38.11, Gravesend. Ellen Tilyou to Alfonso Balsamo. 1,000

16th st, s s, 229.4 e 5th av, 44x145.2x44x144.2. Andrew J. Doyle to Ann Doyle. Q. C. nom

18th st, s s, 214 w 4th av, runs south 70 x east 54 x south 30 x west 54 x south 100 to 19th st, x west 10 x north 70 x west 40 x north 130 to 18th st, x east 46. Contract. John Quinn to Maria A. wife of Florian Schneider. 6,000

24th st, s s, 175 e 3d av, 25x99x26x100. Rose A. and William D. Ryan to John T. Bierds. 1,700

Bay 32d st, n w s, 200 n e Benson av, 60x96.8, Bensonhurst. Foreclos. John Courtney to George E. McKenna, New York. 5,110

38th st, n s, 175 e 3d av, 20x100.2. Thomas Brady to Ernest Gerken. 2,000

38th st, n s, 175 e 3d av, 20x100.2. Release mort. Frederick C. Train trustee Virginia W. Blanchard to Thomas Brady. 1,400

40th st, s s, 280 e 5th av, 40x100.2. John S. Lovejoy to William Coburn. *Mt.* $301. 1,050

48th st, n s, 160 w 4th av, 20x100.2. Adrian De Groff to Lewis Lawson. *Mt.* $2,300. 3,900

48th st, n e s, 160 s e 4th av, 20x100.2. Release mort. Emma A. Cantrell to Alexander Waldron. 600

48th st, n s, 160 e 4th av, 20x100.2, with parts of two party walls. John L. Craig and George W. Craig to William R. Rogers. *Mt.* $600. 900

49th st, s s, 360 e 8th av, 20x100.2, New Utrecht. James V. S. Woolley to Arndt H. Olsen. 175

52d st, s w s, 150 s e 14th av, 50x100.2, New Utrecht. West Brooklyn Land and Impt. Co. to Anneva MacCallum. 700

52d st, s w s, 200 s e 14th av, 50x100.2, New Utrecht. Same to Eugenia M. FitzSimons. 700

55th st, n s, 220 e 6th av, 20x100.2. John Mulrenan to Paul Rapp. 300

57th st, s w s, 150 s e 14th av, 75x100.2, New Utrecht. West Brooklyn Land and Improvement Co. to Louise Kuhn. 1,200

59th st, s w s, 160 n w 17th av, 50x100.2, New Utrecht. Release mort. William A. Copp exr. Mary M. Warner to Hans C. Pfalzgraf. 150

60th st, s s, 320 w 12th av, 40x100, New Utrecht. John H. Carlson to John L. Lawson. 500

61st st, n s, 380 w 11th av, 20x100, New Utrecht. John Hall to Henry Seligman. 300

65th st, s s, 86.7 w New Utrecht av, 20x100, Lefferts Park. Effingham H. Nichols to Margaret Eckel. 275

65th st, s s, 440 e 14th av, 20x100, Lefferts Park. Same to same. 275

66th st, n s, 100 w 14th av, 20x100, Lefferts Park. Effingham H. Nichols to Francis Kelly. 220

70th st, s s, 160 e 10th av, 80x100, h & l, Bay Ridge Park. Fred. C. Cochen to The Bay Ridge Park Improvement Co. 4,200

70th st, s s, 350 w 15th av, 20x100, New Utrecht. James V. S. Woolley to Andrew J. Moroney. 260

73d st, n s, 218.8 w 18th av, 20x100, New Utrecht. John H Hanley to Isaiah W. Emaus. 250

73d st, n e s, 180 n w 9th av, 40x100, New Utrecht. Prospect Land and Improvement Co. to James Duff. 530

79th st, n e s, 100 n w 12th av, 80x100, New Utrecht. Hoik D. Campbell to James E. Coane, Hoboken, N. J. 1,000

81st st, n s, 270 w 3d av, 80x109.4, New Utrecht. Milton J. Bennett to William Williamson. *Mt.* $500. 2,000

82d st, s w s, 280 s e 23d av, 60x100, Bensonhurst. James D. Lynch to Fanny M. Leffer. 900

Albany av, e s, 80 n Furnald st, 20x92, Flatbush. Mark B. Knight to Elizabeth Kerz. 350

Atlantic av, n s, 80 w Gunther pl, 15x98.7. Foreclos. J. Wm. Greenwood to John R. Anderson. 450

Atlantic av, s s, 278.11 w Crescent av, lot 5, block 603 assessor's map 26th Ward. Rebecca F. Forman to Hannah Bennett. *Mt.* $250. 600

Bedford av, e s, 65.9 n Grand st, 18x59.2x17.6x61.4, h & l. Bernard and Philip Katz to John J. Dunn. *Mt.* $1,500. 2,000

Belmont av, n s, 100 e Thatford av, 25x100. Dora R. wife of Aaron Bernart to Isaac Schenker. *Mt.* $2,300. 3,800

Blake av, n s, 50 w Christopher av, 50x100. Herbert C. Smith to Samuel Goldberg and Louis Levinson. 1,200

Bushwick av, s e cor Willoughby av, 22.9x77.4x22x83.2, h & l. William Ulmer to Hermann P. Bender. 13,840

Bushwick av, s w s, 107 n w Van Voorhis st, 18x75. Philip Steingotter to Margaretha Koerner. 7,000

Bushwick av, w s, 40 s Woodbine st, 20x80. Edward Michaelis to Charles Lewis. *Mt.* $5,000. 9,400

Bushwick av, w s, at s e cor of Wm. T. Mill's land, 54x—x69.10, gore. Gustav J. L. Doerschuck to The Claus Lipsius Brewing Co. nom

Bushwick av, northerly cor Linden st, 50x85. John L. Heaton to Albert C. Waterman. *Mt.* $6,000. nom

Same property. Albert C. Waterman to Eliza P. Heaton. *Mt.* $6,000. nom

Bushwick av, s w s, 25 s e Covert st, 16.8x75, h & l. Sarah J. Golden formerly Senior to Henry M. Quinn and Mary A. his wife, joint tenants. B. & S. *Mt.* $2,500. nom

Bushwick av, south cor Lafayette av, 30x78.6x30x77.8. Minnie W. Williams, Plainfield, N. J., to Clarence J. Rice and Mary R. Loomis. *Mt.* $6,000. exch

Central av, s w s, 275 s e Troutman st, runs southeast 25 x southwest 72.6 x west — x northwest 12.10x100. Bertha Koester to Frederick Davis. *Mt.* $4,500. 5,600

Central av, No. 382. Contract for property. Bertha Kaufmann to Adolph Berkowitz, of New York. nom

Central av, Weirfield st, Halsey and Old Bushwick road—the block. Newbury H. Frost to Leopold J. Lippmann. *Mt.* $5,000. 10,000

Central av, north cor Starr st, 25x100, h & l. Sebastian Missig to Michael Braun. *Mt.* $1,500. 4,300

Central av, s w s, 100 s e Linden st, 19.1x100x25x100, h & l. David Stern to Bertha Kaufmann, Maspeth, L. I. Q. C. nom

Same property. Bertha Kaufmann to Joseph Berkowitz. *Mt.* $4,300. exch

De Kalb av, s e s, 300 n e Irving av, 25x100, h & l. Louis and Barbara or Babette Best to Emilie Marcellus. *Mt.* $1,400. nom

Same property. Emilie Marcellus to Babette Best. *Mt.* $1,400. nom

De Kalb av, s s, 60 w Sumner av, 20x100, h & l. John O'Connor to Mary C. wife of John O'Connor. B. & S. nom

Driggs late Van Cott av, s s, 75 e Humboldt st, 25x100. John W. Kine to Frances Lutz. Sub. to mort. $3,000. ½ part. 2,000

East New York av, n s, 289.1 e Schenectady av, 20x100. Robert J., Matthew B. and John H. Cain or Kane and Annie wife of Henry Hare heirs John Cain or Kane to Henry Hare. 200

Evergreen av, w s, 50 n Schaeffer st, 25x100.
Evergreen av, e s, 50 n Schaeffer st, 25x100.
Henry Vogel to Charles F. and William G. Wehr. exch

Evergreen av, w s, 50 s Schaeffer st, 25x100. William G. Wehr to Veronika Vogel, New York. *Mt.* $3,500. 7,000

Evergreen av, w s, 125 n Covert st, 39x95x34.10x95. Annie Herzog to Abby J. Bills, Newtown, L. I. *Mt.* $2,400. nom

Flushing av, s s, 337 w Broadway, 20x100. Hedwig Schneider to Gertrude Holzhausen. *Mt.* $2,500. nom

Franklin av, n w cor Flushing av, runs west 120.9 x north 196 x east 24.2 to Wallabout st, x east 106 to Franklin av, x south 200.4.
All title in gore adj on Wallabout st, 23.10x4x—.
Foreclos. George L. Fox to Loftis W. O'Berry. 13,500

Same property. Loftis W. O'Berry to John Macdonald. 21,500

Glenmore av, n e cor Stone av, 50x100. Henry P. Rindskopf to Morris Levy, of New York. 1,800

Greene av, s e s, 203.10 s w Central av, 15x100. Lillie Cohen to Charles Eisenhardt. *Mt.* $1,100. 3,500

Greenwood av, s s, 45 w East 4th st, 30x100, Flatbush. Jennie V. Wilbur to Sarah J. Murphy. 500

Hamburg av, east cor Moffatt st, 100x100. Minnie S. Cornell to Henry Segelke. nom

Jamaica av, n s, 350 e Barbey st, 25x114.11x25x114.10, h & l. George L. Frank, Jr., to Harry A. Du Bois and Carrie A. his wife. *Mt.* $1,200. 2,900

Jamaica av, n s, 200 e Barbey st, 25x114.1x25x114. John E. Milholland to Francis H. Koenig. 825

Jefferson av, n s, 100 w Tompkins av, 19x100. Henrietta A. wife of and Mortlock Pettit to Catherine C. wife of Daniel Pearsall. *Mt.* $5,500. 15,000

Jefferson av, north cor Bushwick av, 100x100. Jacob Bennett to Philip Steingotter. ½ part. 2,400

Jefferson av, n s, 101 w Franklin av, 21x100, h & l. Hannah M. Hendrickson to Phebe C. Hicks. C. a. G. nom

Jefferson av, s s, 290 e Marcy av, 20x100. Arthur G. Stone to Charles S. Buell. *Mt.* $10,000. 16,700

Jefferson av, No. 1143, n w s, 20 s w Evergreen av, 18.9x100. Robert B. Muller to Friederika K. Ernst, New York. *Mt.* $2,850. 5,100

Lawrence av, s e cor Bergen lane, 307.6 to Gravesend av, x— to Washington av, x211.10 to lane, x—, h & ls, New Utrecht. John L. Laidlaw and ano. exrs. Thomas Laidlaw to Frederick Kupfer and Anthony W. Huber, New York. 9,500

Lewis av, n e cor Pulaski st, 40x100, h & l. Richard G. Phelps to The Peoples Trust Co. *Mt.* $9,000. nom

Lexington av, s w s, 50 n w Forest pl, 50x100, New Utrecht. Bernard Cruse to Thomas Taylor. 500

Lexington av, n s, 100 w Clason av, 67.9x100. John Y. Hallock, exr., &c., William H. Waring to Eldred A. Carley. All title. *Mt.* $5,000 and sales for taxes. nom

Same property. Release dower. Anna M. Waring widow to same. nom

Livonia av, s w cor Watkins st, 100x100. Mary E. Cook, Newtown, L. I., to Joseph O. Shinsky. 2,750

Metropolitan av, s s, 275 e Catharine st, 25x100. Release mort. The Williamsburgh Savings Bank to Christian Bott. 500

Montauk av, e s, 150 s Belmont av, 20x100. Charles H. Machin to Donald Laing. 400

Montauk av, e s, 90 n Belmont av, 40x100. Effingham H. Nichols to William T. Goundie. 550

Myrtle av, n s, 20.6 w Himrod st, runs west 28 x north 64.9 x northeast 5.4 x southeast 30.6 x southeast 5.3 x south 42.10. Henry and John Von Glahn to Otto A. Wicke. 9,000

Myrtle av, northerly cor Himrod st, runs northeast 26.11 x northwest 80 x southwest 9.6 x southeast 30.6 x southeast 5.3 x south 42.10 x east 20.6. Same to Dietrich F. Linnemeyer and Edward N. Boback. consid. omitted

Nichols av, w s, 75 n Union av, 275x200. William M. Miller to Alonzo Reed. *Mt.* $4,500. 7,000

Park av, s s, 25 w Carlton st or av, 25x99x25.6x98. Ellen L. Huggins to George W. McKee. *Mt.* $2,500. nom

Park av, s s, 280 w Marcy av, 25x100. Louis Beer and Michael Schaffner to Francis E. Clark. *Mt.* $2,700. nom

Pennsylvania av, w s, 175 n Glenmore av, 25x100. Hulda Hill, of New York, to Rosa Barnett. 1,700

Prospect av, w s, 136 n Greenwood av, 75x150, Flatbush. Catharine B. Aitken widow to William B. Aitken. 2,400

Putnam av, s s, 228.6 e Ralph av, 121.6x100. Charles Lewis to Edward Michaelis. *Mt.* $7,500. 10,500

Putnam av, n s, 120 e Reid av, 20x100. Release mort. John Cassidy to William O. Forrester. 1,000

Same property. William O. Forrester to William Burns. *Mt.* $4,500. 8,600

Putnam av, s s, 343 e Stuyvesant av, 19x100, h & l. Charles Isbill to Lucy T. Barrie. *Mt.* $4,500. 8,700

Putnam av, e s, 300 s Central av, 20x100. Mary V. Lake to Louis Beer. *Mt.* $1,200. exch

Rockaway av, e s, 175 s Belmont av, 50x100.1.
Rockaway av, e s, 300 s Belmont av, 75x100.1.
Marks Jacob and Israel M. Cohen to Isaac Cohen and Jacob K. Singerman. *Mt.* $3,100. nom

Schenectady av, e s, 55.7 s Bergen st, 50x100, hs & ls. David Stern to Simon Danto. *Mt.* $3,100. 5,800

Schenck av, e s, 25 s Van Brunt av, 20x100. Charles Woollam to William Rosbotham. 150

South Portland av, e s, 149.8 n Atlantic av, 21.6x82.6. Leysander W. Manchester to Tinea wife of Emil H. Storms. 2,000

St. Marks av, s w s, 120 s e Vanderbilt av, 16x181, h & l. Foreclos. Francis T. Johnson to Milton B. Belden. 3,000

St. Nicholas av, n e s, 50 s e Troutman st, 25x94; also,
St. Nicholas av, s w s, 25 s e Troutman st, 25x95; also,
St. Nicholas av, n e s, 25 s e Troutman st, 25x94; also,
St. Nicholas av, east cor Troutman st, 25x94.
John Lapp to Charles Miller. *Mt.* $1,600. 4,250

Stone av, e s, 80 n Somers st, 20x90, h & l. George H. Box to Thomas H. Truman. *Mt.* $5,000. 7,500

Sumner av, n e cor Macon st, 30x95, hs & ls. Jeanie Cable to Alexander Cable. *Mt.* $6,000. nom

Sutter av, n s, 50 e Schenck av, 25x100. Charles H. Smith to Mary Hooper. Q. C. 20

Same property. Mary Hooper to Charles B. Hunt. 2,000

Union av, w s, 33.3 s South 4th st, 20x61, h & l. Ferdinand Scheiffer to Betsey wife of Abraham Greenstone. 4,800

Utica av, e s, 75 n St. Marks av, 20.7x106.7. Thomas Garrahan to Patrick Garrahan his son. *Mt.* $750. nom

Van Sielen av, e s, 275 n Blake av, 50x100. Jacob T. Van Sielen to Henry F. Smith. Taxes, &c., from 1889. 700

Vermont av, w s, 200 n Fulton av, 50x100. Release mort. Marvin Cross, Sherlock Austin and John H. Ireland, of Cross, Austin & Co., to Catherine Distler. 1,000

Same property. Catherine wife of George Distler to Henry Distler. *Mt.* $6,500. 7,500

Vernon av, s s, 100 w Sumner av, 75x100. Mary E. Smith to Sigismund Eisenbach. 7,500

Same property. Release mort. Margaret Schauf to Mary E. Smith. nom

Willoughby av, n w s, 325 n e Evergreen av, 25x83x25x87.11. Eleanora Armann individ. and as extrx. Ferdinand Armann to Henrietta Heisingler. 3,750

Willoughby av, s s, 150 e Hamburg av, 25x100. Odile wife of Louis Orthlieb to Joseph J. Stoll. *Mt.* $4,000. 5,600

Wyckoff av, e s, 64.4 n De Kalb av, 19.4x92.8. Jakob Schnurle or Schmerle to Emilie Marcellus. nom

Same property. Emilie Marcellus to Pauline Schnurle. nom

4th av, s w cor 87th st, 8x100x80x100, New Utrecht, error. Domenico Cuccio to Guiseppe Cuccio "Di B." 1,460

5th av, w s, 40 s Butler st, 20x90. Release mort. Marie A. Udall to Florence J. Donohue and Ellen his wife. 1,500

Same property. Florence J. Donohue to Dennis J. Donovan and William Heron. exch

11th av, west cor 54th st, runs southwest 200.4 to 55th st, x northwest 140 x northeast 100.2 x southeast 40 x northeast 100.2 to 54th st, x southeast 100, New Utrecht. Charles C. Stelle to Edward Dougherty, Buffalo. *Mt.* $950. nom

22d av, n w s, 250 n e Cropsey av, 50x96.8, hs & ls, Bensonhurst. J. Bentley Squier to Sadie A. Collins. *Mt.* $4,500. 7,650

23d av, east cor 82d st, 100x80, Gravesend. Adeline E. F. wife of Hubert F. Praeger to Nathan Kaplan. *Mt.* $700. 3,000

Brooklyn and Coney Island plank road, s w cor Johnsons lane, 7 acres, 1 rood, 27 90-100 perches, Gravesend. William Elliott to Isaac H. Young. *Mt.* $1,000. 1878 1,485

Lots 74–77 block 2 and 339 block 8 map No. 1 of 618 lots, Cowenhoven farm, New Utrecht. Effingham H. Nichols, New York, to Henry F. McCarthy. 1,025

Lots 394 and 395 block 9 same map. Same to Robert Peach. 100

Lots 89 and 95–99 block 2 same map. Same to Michael Ajello. 1,170

Lots 447 and 448 block 10 same map. Same to Charles McDonnell. 320

Lots 449–452 same map. Same to Charles E. Hebberd. 620

Lots 09 and 90–94 inclusive block 2 same map. Same to Luigi Capiero. 1,370

Lots 317–321 block 8 same map. Same to Patrick J. McHenry. 1,025

Lots 434 and 435 block 10 same map. Same to Cornelius Murray, New York. 310

Lot at Gravesend, begins at high water mark along Gravesend Bay at intersection with land of James L. Harway, runs northwest 120.2 x northeast 229.6 x northwest 90.9 x northeast 274.5 x southeast 67.7 x southwest 287.9 x southwest 210.8 with land under water. Elizabeth A. Van Wart to Charles E. and Harry C. Van Wart. Reserves life estate. *Mt.* $1,500. nom

Lots 9 and 10 block 1 map of M. J. Bergen's 221 lots, New Utrecht. James V. S. Woolley to Harriet Dilger. 400

Lots 421 and 422 block 10 map 1 of 61 lots, Cowenhoven farm, New Utrecht. Effingham H. Nichols to Alice A. Douglas. 310

Interior lot, 155.5 w Roebling st and 33.3 s North 10th st, runs south 66.9 x west 42.11 x northeast 79.3. Peter Blake to Margaret Clark extrx. Edward F. Clark. exch

Interior lot, 350 s w Knickerbocker av and 100 s e Stockholm st, runs southwest 25 x northwest 46.10x25x47.7. James M. Waterbury to Frederick A. Young. B. & S. nom

Plot begins 14.8 s Sackett st and 350 e New York av, runs southwest 552.10 x south to centre Crown st, x southeast along same 207.8 to centre Brooklyn av, x southwest along same 808.5 to patent line, x east along same 206.10 x northerly 2,188.8 x west 101.11, excepting Sackett st, centre line, 350 w Brooklyn av, runs south to centre Union st, x east to J. Skillman's land, x north to centre Sackett st, x west abt 110. Edward Schell trustee Mary R. Cargill to Frederick A. Brown trustee Mary R. Cargill. C. a. G. nom

Shore road, n w s, adj land W. Bennett, 50x— to bay or river, x52.7x35, New Utrecht. Jacob M. Bergen et al. exrs. Michael Bergen to Jacob M. Bergen, Babylon, L. I. nom

WESTCHESTER COUNTY.

SEPTEMBER 9 TO 15—INCLUSIVE.

CORTLANDT.

Guest, Sarah to Rachel H. Snowden, s s Main st, 203.6 e Field st, 65.6x164.6. $1,310

Jordan, Warren to John N. Tilden, e s Oak Hill st, adj Eliz'h Cramer, 50x—. 2,500

EASTCHESTER.

Barker, Mary A. to John P. O'Brien. 7 acres on road to Reeds Mills and Mill Creek. 5,000

Baxter, Ellen F. to Giovanni Pereto. Lot 4 s e s White Plains road, Washingtonville, 50x 100. 1,000

Blumenberg, John H. to Henrietta Blumenberg, s s Mt. Vernon av, 25.6 e Union st, 22x 88.7. nom

Cunningham, Eliz'h to Margt. E. Downey, lots 18 and 20, Dunham Park. nom

Efferen, Louisa to Cath. L. Haag, s s Bridge st, 100 n 5th av, 42x100. 3,250

Held, Harry to Fred. C. Pinne, part lot 133 n e s Mt. Vernon av, West Mt. Vernon, 50x100. 5,250

Hayes, Regina M. to Margt. Roller, s e s Old Boston road, adj Mead and Howe, 235x127x 234x292. 3,000

Koehler, Margt. to Henry Lebander, part lot 409 n w s Greenwich st, West Mt. Vernon, 30 x125. nom

La Faye, Clara to Arch. Taylor, Jr., w s Fulton av, 445 n Sidney av, 50x115. 6,500

McManus, Mary to Thos. L. Reynolds, e s White Plains road, adj J. B. Dunham, abt 244x247. 7,750

Mager, Fred. to Helen E. Fitch, part lot 902 w s 11th av, Mt. Vernon, 33.4x105. 5,000

Pitman, Oscar V. to Geo. Ullrich, n w cor Kossuth av and Concord st, 50x100. 900

Rich, Geo. E. to Geo. Rich, lots 70 and 72 5th st, Dunham Park. nom

Walcher, Marcus to Chas. Birngruber, lots 8–12 s s Highland av, e Waverly. 4,250

Wheeler, John to Robert Walker, lots 25 and 26 Boulevard, Vernon Park. 340

Same to John H. Kain, lots 19 and 20 Boulevard. 300

Whitmore, Daniel W. to Emilie L. Brown, s e cor 13th av and 3d st, 100x105. 1,475

GREENBURGH.

Brandt, Grace P. to John S. O'Connor, e s Maple av, 596 s Chatterton Hill road, abt 100x 150. 450

Barnhart, John W. to Isabella Dixon, n w cor Elizabeth and John sts, 30x85. 4,625

Blackwell, Wilson H. to Fred. B. Haviland, lots 555 and 556 at Ardsley. 400

Same to Frank M. Beitzung, lots 696 and 697. 350

Biegen, Francis to Chas. Wachenfeld, e s 1st st, 55 s Cedar st, 76.8x120. 2,500

Dobbs Ferry Land Co. to Edw. V. Skinner and ano., lot 54 n w cor McClelland av and Skinner st, 50x100. 750

Same to Gust. G. Lansing and wife, lots 43 and 44 and 53 n s McClelland av. 2,100

Field, Laura B. to Wm. Pullen, lots 55 and 57 n s Ashford av, Belden Park. nom

Huestis, Clinton D. to Clara B. Wright, w s road from Greenville to Tuckahoe, 75x247. 375

Jones, Cyrus P. and ano. to Thos. Williams, lots 186 and 187, Ardsley. 327

Pell, Lillie F. to Dorvah D. Tallman, w s Railroad av, adj grantee, abt 60x80. 800

MAMARONECK.

Coles, Adam G. to Thos. J. Coles, lot 2 s e s Boston road, map property grantor, 25x125. 1,250

Larchmont Manor Co. to Laura Barretto, n e cor Walnut and Circle avs, 217x193x215x217. 3,045

Mutual Life Ins. Co. to Howard N. Bailey, lots 13–22 e s Mamaroneck av, map Barnard property. 15,000

MOUNT PLEASANT.

Smadbeck, Louis to Paul Strieffler, lots 261 and 262, Sherman Park. 200

Same and ano. to Rachel Silverman, lots 81–96, Lakehurst Villa Park. 1,600

NEW ROCHELLE.

Doyle, Cornelia M. to Welcome G. Hitchcock, 144 acres on road to White Plains. 50,000

Manhattan Life Ins. Co. to Margery S. Stewart, lot 5 block F, Rochelle Park. 3,100

Viola, Auth. C. et al. Odle Close ref. to Ange A. Patton, n s Washington av, 300x240, and strip in rear. 2,500

NORTH SALEM.

Mackerer, Rosa to Owen Logan, e s road from s e to Somers, 130x—. 550

OSSINING.

Buckhont, Steph. C. exr. of, to Walter W. Law, n s old Briarcliff road and e s road to Whitsons, 50 acres. 5,250

Conklin, Caroline extrx. of, to Julia W. Wilkins, s s William st, adj W. Washburn, 25x 100. 1,385

Steneck, Chas. H. to Jane Montgomery, e s Linden av, adj Henry Gerlach, 44x182. 2,550

Westchester Town Site Co. to Jos. Krejci, lots 41–45 s w cor Caroline and Clarendon avs, 103x129. 1,550

Same to Alex. Moldenhauer, lots 258 and 259 s s Clarendon av, 50x123. 600

Same to Matthew Butler, lots 35–40 s e cor Highland and Clarendon avs. 1,900

Same to Barbara Porges, lots 27–30 e s Highland av, 100x108. 1,400

Same to Moritz Brockman, lots 90–94 and 134–138 s e cor Maple and Caroline avs, 125x200. 3,100

Same to Jacob Wolf, lots 97, 98, 130 and 131 e s Caroline av, 50x200. 1,200

Same to Anna Seelig, lots 68, 69 and 70 n w cor Maple and Caroline avs, 75x100. 950

Same to Adam Gernand, lots 33 and 34 n e cor Clarendon and Highland avs, 50x100. 750

PELHAM.

Bissell, Wm. W. to Wm. Towner and ano, part lot 67 s s Washington av, Prospect Hill, 150x200. 1,300

Towner, Wm. H. to Parkside Land Co., part lot 69 Prospect Hill. 325

Waterhouse, Wm. W. to Thos. Clongblin, n s Scofield av, 363 e Main st, 50x119. 700

RYE

Merritt, Jas. S. and ano. to Henry Collins, lot 110 n s West William st, Washington Park, 50x150. 200

McCarty, Daniel and ano. to Hannah Flood, n w cor Fairview and Irenhyl avs, 50x100. 350

Same to same, lots 126–129 w s Fairview av. 1,300

WESTCHESTER.

Burlando, Emanuel to Sarah I. Lewis, east ½ lot 365 n s 2d av, Wakefield, 50x114. 3,500

Carter, Emma J. to Jos. Troman and ano., n s Julianna st, 100 e Barker av, 25x100. 2,900

Same to Jas. A. Cunningham, e s Barker av, 67 n Julianna st, 33x100. 3,700

Cooper, Margt. et al. J. B. Lockwood ref. to Arnold D'Epagnier, lots 2, 3 and 4 n s Main st, William Cooper map. 5,000

Cunningham, Jas. A. to Emma J. Carter, n s 5th av, 105 e 5th st, Wakefield, 100x113.6. 1,600

Dexter, Fred. C. to Jennie E. Goetze, lot 999 s s 8th av, Wakefield, 100x114. 2,000

Hahn, Barbara to Gottfried Katz, n s Westchester av, cor old road to West Farms, 100x 32x106. 12,000

Hielman, Eliz'h to Chas. Gunther, n w cor White Plains road and Bridge st, 100x100. 3,000

Same to Theo. H. Allers and ano., w s White Plains road, adj above, 150x100. 3,800

Same to Christian Stellwager, n e cor Bridge st and Elliott av, 50x102. 1,200

Same to Maria Steger, e s Elliott av, adj above, 50x102. 1,000

Mace, Levi H. and ano. to Nathalie Rolet. Lots 259–262, Laconia Park. 800

Oakley, Jos. B. to Jeanette Renwee, lot 137 e s 3d st, New Jerome, 25x112. 700

Oliver, Louisa to Dina Conrad, lot 42 s s 3d st, Unionport, 108x205. 1,000

Smith, Geo. to Francis E. Walkley, n e cor Sackett av and Bear Swamp road, 74x75x161 x115. 3,500

WHITE PLAINS.

Smith, Orlando J. to Longview Co., w s Old Manik road, adj Green Ridge Park, 33 acres. 25,000

YONKERS.

Barnes, Ella L. to Robert Mayer, w s Hyatt av, 513 n Scott av, 104x—. 700

Callahan, Rose to Adolph Haffner and wife, lot 64 w s Riverdale av, Geo. Herriot map, 25x100. 4,600

Cochran, Henry H. to Alex. J. A. Callaghan, w s Palisade av, 250 x to North Broadway. 15,000

Druid Hill Park Co. to Fred Gaus, Jr., lots 383, 384 and 385 Mohegan Park. 555

East Side Land Co. to Robt. D. McGairah, lots 64 and 65 Shearwood Hill. 945

Monrovia Park Co. to Emma D. Ayer, lots 233 and 234 e s Euclid av, 50x100. 200

Parsells, Edw. W. to John Giles, e s Briggs av, 50 s Fort Field av, 25x100. 250

Same to Cath. J. Riley, n w cor Fort Field and Briggs avs, 25x100. 350

Pagan, John to Peter Doerner, s s Main st, adj E. A. Switzer, 25.8x121. 8,000

Valentine, Clara M. to Chas. Bartosch, e s Cook av, 200 s Summerfield st, 50x100. 500

Same to Leopold Schiermbock, e s Cook, 150 s same, 50x100. 500

Same to Patrick McGuire, w s Bennett av, 225 s same, 50x100. 525

Same to Mary Martin, w s Bennett av, 275 s same, 50x100. 525

Whitehead, Rich. J. to Nath. B. Valentine, e s East Main st, 400 s Herriot, 25x98. 3,100

MORTGAGES.

NOTE.—*The arrangement of this list is as follows. The first name is that of the mortgagor, the next that of the mortgagee. The description of the property then follows, then the date of the mortgage, the time for which it was given, and the amount. The general dates used as headings are the dates when the mortgage was handed into the Register's office to be recorded.*

Whenever the letters "P. M." occur, preceded by the name of a street, in these lists of mortgages, they mean that it is a Purchase Money Mortgage, and for fuller particulars see the list of transfers under the corresponding date. Whenever the rate is not given, read it 6 per cent

NEW YORK CITY.

SEPTEMBER 11, 12, 14, 15, 16, 17.

Abraham, Lena and Morris Smoley to Abraham Brown and Isaac Haft. Delancey st. P. M. Sept. 15, 5 years. $3,500

Ackerman, Frederick to Josiah A. Hyland. 32d st, n s, 350 w 6th av, 25x101.7x26.1x108.5. Sept. 12, 5 years or installs. 2,000

Ahern, Maurice to THE FARMERS' LOAN AND TRUST CO. 18th st, n s, 286.6 w 6th av, 20.6x 69x33 6x95. Sept. 14, 3 years, 5 %. 10,500

Algeo, James E. and Eliza J. his wife to The Sun and Evening Sun Building, Mutual Loan and Accumulating Fund Assoc. Ann st, s s, lots 44 and 45 map of Mary S. Shipley, West Farms, 46.6x96 8x69.2x98. Sept. 2, installs., 5 %. 3,678

Arbogast, George P. to Haskell A. Searle. 165th st, s s, 310 w Trinity av, 20.2x100. Aug. 7, 3 years. 4,000

Same to same. 163th st, s s, 330.2 w Trinity av. 19.9x100. Aug. 7, 3 years. 4,000

Aronson, Samuel and Louis Gordon to Louis Leypold. Park st, No. 37. P. M. Sept. 15, 5 years, 5 %. gold, 20,000

Same to same. Park st, No. 39. P. M. Sept. 15, 5 years, 5 %. gold, 20,000

Bernart, Dora R. to Isaac Schencker. Av D. P. M. Sub. to mort. $8,500. Sept. 15, installs. 2,500

Billington, Reno R. to THE NEW YORK SAVINGS BANK. 49th st, s s, 60.1 w 4th av, 19.8x 25.5. Sept. 15, due June 1, 1896, 4½ %. 6,000

Same to Jacob T. Boyle, Alexander D. Stratton and Eugene D. Bergen trustees. Same property. Sept. 15, installs, 5 %. 2,300

Beaudet, John and Ernest P. to David Garrison, George C Renkauff and Edward B. Staggers, of Hall & Garrison. Mt. Morris av, s w cor 121st st, 100.11x100. Sub. to morts. Aug. 25, due March 1, 1892, or sooner. 30,000

Bamberger, Max mortgagor with POUGHKEEPSIE SAVINGS BANK mortgagee. Extension of mort. at 4½ %. Sept. 1. nom

Bugler, Adam and Christina mortgagors with POUGHKEEPSIE SAVINGS BANK mortgagee. Extension of mort. at 4½ %. Sept. 1. nom

Bennett, John to Catharine T. Bennett. West Washington pl, n s, 110 w Macdougal st, 22x 97. Sept. 8, 1 year, 5 %. 3,000

Brady, Patrick and Henry, of Brady Bros., to Bernheimer & Schmid. 3d av, No. 561. Saloon lease. Sept. 10, note, demand. 1,500

Bach, Lewis Z. to Henry de Forest Weekes. 58th st, Nos. 132 and 134, s s, 68.9 w Lexington av, runs south 80.5 x west 11.3 x south 20 x west 26.8 x north 100.5 x east 37.6. Sept. 15, due Oct. 1, 1892. 4,000

Bohm, Rudolph mortgagor with Jacob Schlosser mortgagee. Extension of mort. Sept. 15. nom

Brown, Harriet P. to Elizabeth C. McKibbin. 98th st. P. M. Sept. 8, due Sept. 20, 1892. 19,500

Browning, Harry C. to Julius A. Candee and George M. Smith. Willis av, s w cor 144th st, 50x84 Sept. 15, 1 year. 3,600

Byrne, John H. to The Eureka Co-operative Savings and Loan Assoc. of the City of New York. 135th st, s s, 220 w 3d av, 30x100. Sept. 14, installs, 5 %. 1,600

Corn, Samuel and Henry to THE GERMAN SAVINGS BANK. Broome st, Nos. 492 and 494, n s, 60 e South 5th av, 40x75. Sept. 11, due Sept. 14, 1892. 70,000

Same to same. Waverley pl, No. 12, s s, 25 w Mercer st, 25x82.8. Sept. 11, due Sept. 14, 1892. 55,000

Same to THE TITLE GUARANTEE AND TRUST CO. Mercer st, No. 235, w s, 25x100. Sept. 14, due Dec. 31, 1892. 45,000

Cavinato, Luigi, Natale, Guiseppe and Steffano to THE UNITED STATES SAVINGS BANK of City of New York. 87th st, s s, 35.3 e Lexington av, 27x100. Aug. 28, 1 year, 5 %. 25,000

Same to Edward C. and Patrick Sheehy. 87th st, s s, 35.3 e Lexington av, 27x100.8. Collateral. Sept. 9. 54,622

Same to The Bradley & Currier Co. (Lim.). 87th st, s s, 35.2 e Lexington av, 27x100.8. Sub. to morts. $79,622. Sept. 8, 2 months. 6,000

Campbell, John V. to Joseph L. Buttenwieser. Essex st, No. 169, w s, 200 s Houston st, 25x87.6. Sept. 10, demand. 3,000

Capel, Susan M. to C. Walser & Co. and George Silva & Co. 44th st, s s, 256.3 e 8th av, 18.9x100.5. Lease. Sept. 11, notes. 2,906

Clark, Matthew to The Buffalo Door and Sash Co. 74th st, n s, 400.3 w Columbus av, 149.9x102.2. Sub. to morts. Sept. 5, due Jan. 31, 1892. 34,500

Coutan, Susanna M. widow to THE SEAMEN'S BANK FOR SAVINGS, New York. Franklin st, s s, 191.10 w Broadway, 26.9x75.2x22.4x74.6. Sept. 14, due April 20, 1894, 4½ %. 10,000

Congregation Chasam Sopher to THE MUTUAL LIFE INS. Co. of New York. Clinton st, e s, 100 s Houston st, 75x100.2. Sept. 17, 1 year. 40,000

Same to Sigmund B. Steinman. Same property. Sept. 17, due July 1, 1892. 10,000

Chase, Charles D. and Ella I. his wife to Susan E. Hoyt et al. exrs. Joseph B. Hoyt. Declaration amending description in mort. Sept. 16. nom

Durbrow, Wilson B., East Orange, N. J., to Welcome S. Jarvis, Brooklyn. 30th st, s s, 100 w Lexington av, 17.10x98.9. Sept. 16, 1 year, 5 %. 2,000

Dempsey, William and John Smith to Lee Wolff trustee. 106th st, s s, 200 w 1st av, 25x100.11. Sub. to morts. $15,000. Aug. 31, demand. 431

Donnelly, Mary A. to Elba A. Maring and ano. extrxs. Susan A. Maring. Robbins av, s e cor Beck (Pontiac) st, runs east 105 x south 50 x west 44 x north 25 x west 61 to av, x north 25. Sept. 3, 3 years. 1,000

Downing, Flora E. wife of Albert D. to Harry Berry. Valentine av, s s, 175 e Southern Boulevard. 50x110. Sept. 5, 3 years, 5 %. 2,662

Doyles, Margaret to Bridget M. Olsen. Brook av, s e cor 164th st, runs southeast 32 x southwest — to av, x north —. Sept. 11, 3 years or installs, 3½ %. 700

Downey, Charles and George W. Curry to Frank H. Barr, James Thaw and Alexander Fraser. Park av, s w cor 93d st, 100.8x105. Sub. to morts. $129,904. June 1, due Dec. 15, 1891. 1,900

Duff, Patrick to Howard & Childs. 3d av, No. 679. Saloon lease. Sept. 14, note. 753

De Peyster, General J. Watts, Red Hook, N. Y., to Estelle L. De Peyster and Louis Livingston. 21st st, No. 59, n s, 25 w 4th av, runs north 98.9 x west 50 x south 24 x east 29 x south — to st, x east 21. Aug. 21. Secures annuity to Estelle L. De Peyster of 14,000

Duckler, Adolf to Julius Rosenberg. Lewis st. P. M. Sept. 15, installs. 5,300

Duff, Patrick to George Ehret. 3d av, No. 679. Lease. Sept. 12, demand. 2,000

Eckhardt, Peter C. to Louisa Ungrich. 184th st, n s, 125 e 11th av, 75x99.11. Sept. 15, 3 years, 5 %. 7,000

Eichhorn, Yette to Meta Salberg. Willett st. P. M. Sept. 10, installs. 3,450

Eschwei, George F. to The Bradley & Currier Co. (Lim.). 143d st, s e cor Bradhurst av, 68x99.11x78.11x100.6. Sub. to morts. $50,000. Aug. 17, 3 months. 8,500

Egan, John J. and Daniel Hallecy to THE GERMANIA LIFE INS. Co. 103d st, n s, 200 w West End av, 5 lots, each 20x100.11. 5 morts, each $16,500. Sept. 10, due Sept. 11, 1894, 6 % and 5 %. 82,500

Fay, Michael and William Stacom to John Van D. Reed. Market st, s w cor Henry st, 25x—. Sept. 11, 5 years, 5 %. gold, 47,000

Friedline, Charles W. and Louisa C. wife of Samuel A. Friedline to The Bradley & Currier Co. (Lim.) 93d st, s s, 175 e Columbus av, 100x100.8. Sub. to morts. $96,000. July 24, 4 months. 13,574

Fielbig, George J. to Conrad Aiheidt. 164th st, s s, 250 e 10th av, 25x112.4. Sept. 12, 1 year. 500

Franke, Henry, Brooklyn, to THE TITLE GUARANTEE AND TRUST Co. 113th st, n s, 120 w 5th av, 16x100.11. Sept. 10, 1 year, 5 %. 5,000

Freudenthal, William and Christina M. his wife to Samuel H. Stone. Grand st, Nos. 411 and 413, s s, 25 e Clinton st, runs south 75 x east 25 x south 25 x east 25 x north 100 to Grand st, x west 50 to beginning. Sept. 10, 6 months. 4,000

Faber, Charles P. to Luigi, Guiseppe, Steffano and Natale Cavinato. Willis av and 135th st. P. M. Sept. 15, 1 year or sooner. 2,350

Fash, Ann, Mt. Vernon, N. Y., and Phoebe M. Mariotte to Rosalie M. (Dowager) Lady Steele widow. 16th st, No. 35, n s, 535 w 5th av, 25x92. Sept. 15, 3 years, 5 %. gold, 20,500

Fine, Christopher to George P. Fine. 21st st, No. 230, s s, 416.1 e 8th av, 16x92, 44-120 part. Sept. 15, demand. 1,000

Farley, John T. to William D. Manning. Amsterdam av, Boulevard, 69th and 70th sts, block bounded by above. Sept. 15, 1 year. 5,000

Ferber, Nathan and Seeley his wife to Ignatz Schultz. Pike st, No. 53, e s, 20.1x50.6x19.1x50.6. Sept. 15, 1 year. 1,000

Finkelstein, Bertha to Charlotte Hastorf. Essex st. P. M. Sub. to mort. $12,000. Sept. 15, installs. 14,500

Flagge, Francis H., Rebecca M. wife of Charles Otten and Frederick W. Flagge to George H. Coutts, Brooklyn. 55th st, s s, 200 e 11th av, 25x144.10x25.1x143.4. Sept. 9, 5 years, 5 %. 4,000

Fox, Sarah J. to William A. Klingler and Herman Fox. 133d st, n s, 100 w 7th av, 20x99.11. Sept. 15, 8 years, 4½ %. 6,000

Freedman, Raphael to Jacob Horowitz. East Broadway, No. 204. Sept. 1, 1 year. See Conveys. 1,500

Gano, Jane M. to Caroline M. Coman. 22d st. Leasehold. P. M. Sept. 15, 5 years, 5 %. 6,000

Greene, Josephine T. to Newbury D. Lawton, New Rochelle, N. Y. 166th st. P. M. Aug. 25, 1 year, 5 %. 1,500

Gautier, Marguerite to Percival C. Smith, Brooklyn. 40th st, s s, 214.3 w 7th av, 14.3x98.9. Sept. 16, due July 1, 1894, 5 %. 6,000

Geidel, John to Henry Zeltner. 156th st, No. 654 E., s e cor Melrose av. Sept. 12, demand. 400

Hawkins, George L., Asbury Park, N. J., to THE MUTUAL LIFE INS. Co. of New York. 125th st, s s, 519.4 w 5th av, 15.7x100.11. Sept. 15, 1 year, 5 %. 8,000

Hammer, John to Richard Cummings. 108th st. P. M. Sept. 12, installs., 5 %. 10,500

Hasler, John E. to THE CITIZENS SAVINGS BANK. 2d av, s w cor 112th st, 22.6x83. Aug. 26, 1 year, 5 %. gold, 25,000

Herche, Peter to THE METROPOLITAN LIFE INS. Co. of New York. 87th st. P. M. Sept. 11, 3 years or sooner, 5 %. 12,000

Hirschfelder, Sigmund mortgagor with Mina Le Vino mortgagee. Extension of mort. Sept. 11. nom

Hodgson, William to Henry C. Peters. New York & Harlem R. R. Co., w s, adj land William G. Dunn over which West Vanderbilt av has been laid out but not opened, which point is 116.6 s Samuel st, produced, runs northeast 275.6 x northwest 78 x northwest 546.9 x northwest 222.4 to e s Old Valentine av, x southwest 312.4 x southeast 820.3 to beginning, except part taken for Webster av; Old Valentine av, e s, 12.6 n Folin st, runs southeast 222.4 x southeast 546.9 x northwest 771.11 to e s Old Valentine av, x southwest 32.5 to beginning, except part taken for Webster av. Aug. 27, 5 years or sooner, 5 %. 10,000

Hagan, Thomas with Buffalo Door and Sash Co. both mortgagees. Agreement as to priority of morts. made by Matthew Clark. Sept. 8. nom

Herter, Peter to Abraham Kaufmann. Allen st, n w cor Stanton st, 50x75. Sept. 14, 2 years. 8,000

Henderson, Lillie E. wife of and Andrew A. to THE MUTUAL LIFE INS. Co. Manhattan av, w s, 18.5 n 120th st, 15x80. Sept. 15, 1 year, 5 %. 8,000

Holden, Mary widow and devisee and Horatio N. Holden to Moses Furst. 3d av, e s, 98.9 s 36th st, 24.8x100. Sept. 15, 5 years, 5 %. 5,000

Hunt, Delia C. wife of Abel C. to Isaac L. Kip trustee Adelaide B. Harris. 84th st, s s, 98 w 8th av, runs south 100.4 x west 2 x south 1.10 x west 19 x north 102.2 to st, x east 21. Sept. 15, due March 20, 1895, 5 %. 5,000

Jacobs, Elias to Ignatz Bauer, Jr., and Wilhelmina his wife. 9th st. P. M. Sept. 15, due May 22, 1892, 5 %. 3,850

Jones, Edward to Daniel Riedemann. Summit av, w s, lot 5 map of 16 building lots of K. B. Daly, 23d Ward, 25x95.7x25.2x92.9. Sept. 11, 5 years, 5 %. 2,800

Kelly, Edward J. to Lewis Morris. 143d st. P. M. Sept. 1, demand. gold, 30,000

Same to Charlotte B. Logan, Yonkers, N. Y. Same property. Sept. 1, demand. gold, 3,000

Kelly, Mary A. and Annie E. to Charlotte B. Logan. Av A, w s, 102.2 s 75th st, 85.8x101.3x69.11x100. Lease. Sept. 1. gold, 3,000

Keil, Francis to THE FARMERS' LOAN AND TRUST Co. 162d st, s s, 300 e Morris av, 125x115. Sept. 12, due Sept. 15, 1893, 5 %. 12,500

Kenedy, Patrick J. to Frederick Moeller. 3d av. P. M. Sept. 15, 3 years or installs, 5 %. 30,000

Kauffmann, Pauline M. to THE UNION DIME SAVINGS INST. 21st st. P. M. Sept. 17, due Nov 1, 1894, 5 %. 5,000

Levy, Isaac mortgagor with Jacob Schlosser exr. and trustee Christian L. Nunnenkamp mortgagee. Extension of mort. Sept. 15. nom

Laforge, Isabella to Joseph Corbit. 25th st, s s, 200 e 9th av, 50x98.9. Sept 10. 2,000

Levin, Amelia to Sender Jarmulowsky. Pleasant av. P. M. Sept. 11, installs. 1,200

Lindenfelser, Stephan to Charles F. Klippert. 107th st, No. 232, s s, 175 w 2d av, 25x100.11. Sept. 11, 5 years, 5 %. 5,500

Same to Ernest Goldbacher. Same property. Sub. to last mort. Sept. 11, 5 years or installs., 5 %. 3,500

Lustig, Arnold to THE WASHINGTON LIFE INS. Co. St. Nicholas pl, s e cor Edgecombe av, 104.10x175.4 to av, x north and west 215.1. Aug. 31, due Dec. 1, 1892, 5 %. 40,000

Lyman, William to THE METROPOLITAN LIFE INS. Co. 112th st, n e cor Lexington av, 41.8x100.11. Sept. 9, due Oct. 1, 1896, 5 %. 57,000

Same to Samuel Weil. 113th st, s e cor Lexington av, 50x100.11. Sept. 10, due Jan. 10, 1892, 5 %. 14,797

Mahony, James A. mortgagor with THE METROPOLITAN LIFE INS. Co. Declaration as to time of payment of int. July 24. nom

Monaghan, Mary E. to Ephraim B. Levy. Katonah av. P. M. Sept. 10, due Sept. —, 1894, or sooner, 5 %. 1,200

Martin, Ellen wife of and Hugh to THE UNITED STATES SAVINGS BANK, City of New York. 155th st, n s, 400 e Courtlandt av, 50x100. Sept. 10, 1 year, 5 %. 2,500

Same to same. 156th st, s s, 400 e Courtlandt av, 50x100. Sept. 10, 1 year. 2,500

Masson, Henry J. and Sadie P. his wife to Eleanor H. Decker. Washington av, w s, 50 s 186th st, 50x100. Sept. 14, 5 years, 5 %. 1,400

McNamara, Patrick H. to Beadleston & Woerz, a corporation. South st, No. 260. Store lease. Sept. 12, demand. 500

McGuire, Thomas J. to Maria L. Travers. 102d st, s s, 350.7 w Columbus av, 26x100.11. Sept. 15, 3 years, 5 %. 20,000

Same to Margie B. Lacey extrx. and trustee Frederick Lacey. 102d st, No. 128, s s, 403.7 w Columbus av, 25.3x101.1x30.7x100.11. Sept. 15, 3 years, 5 %. 20,000

McIntyre, Peter to George Ehret. 10th av, n e cor 54th st, 25.9x100. Lease. Sept. 15, demand. 7,000

Mensch, Matthaus to Margaret G. Gerken. 152d st, s s, 300 e Courtlandt av, 25x115. Sept. 14, 5 years, 5 %. 3,500

Muldoon, William H. to Arthur E. Hemmel. 14th st, s s, 250.6 w Av C, 27x91. Sub. to morts. Aug. 15, 6 months. 1,100

Muldoon, William H. to Thomas Hagan. 14th st, s s, 304.6 w Av C, 27.6x103.3. Sub. to all liens. Aug. 31, 1 year. 3,000

Musgrave, Edward G. to The Mount Morris Co-operative Building and Loan Assoc. Madison av, w s, 203 n Kingsbridge road, 25x100. Sept. 11, installs, 5 %. 3,000

McKinley, Duncan C. to John M. Canda and John P. Kane. 72d st, s s, 155 w West End av, 20x102.2. Sub. to morts. $90,000. Sept. 15, due March 1, 1892. 2,500

McManus, Patrick H. to Albert N. Hallgarten. Bleecker st, n w cor South 5th av, 32.3x100. Aug. 19, due Jan. 1, 1895, 5 %. See Conveys. gold, 80,000

Same to Alonzo T. Decker, William A. Murray, Orrin D. Person and William H. Simonson trustees for creditors. Same property. Aug. 12, 1 year. 42,285

Same to Edward Hilson. Same property. Sept. 15, due June 1, 1892. 18,670

Martin, Eli to Herman Freund. 78th st, s s, 106.3 w 9th av, 48x99.2x48x100.6. Sept. 15, due July 1, 1892. 16,000

McGuire, Thomas J. to Albert N. Hallgarten. 102d st, No. 126, s s, 377.7 w Columbus av, 26x100.11. Sept. 17, due Aug. 1, 1895, 5 %. gold, 20,000

Meister, George, Sr., and Louis Meister to Nathan A. Chedsey. 13th st. P. M. Sept. 14, due Sept. 14, 1893. 2,000

Michelson, Isidor to Henrietta Studinski. 118th st. P. M. Sept. 8, 4 months. 3,000

Moriarty, Thaddeus to Elizabeth H. Jordan. Jumel terrace, n w cor 160th st, 94x76.3x—x80; Audubon av, s e cor 167th st, 80x95. Aug. 4, 5 years, 5 %. 26,000

Nichols, Hannah J. wife of Harvey, Orange, N. J., to Sarah A. Brown admrx. Charles W. Brown. 155th st, n s, 183.4 e Willis av, 16.8x100. Sept. 14, installs, 5 %. 4,000

Neis, Ferdinand to James S. Kelly. West st, No. 127. Lease. Sept. 15, notes. 2,500

New York Lumber and Wood Working Co. mortgagee to Welcome R. Steinmetz mortgagor. Agreement to release certain premises from lien of mortgage. Sept. 14. nom

Osborne, Susan M. to The College of St. Francis Xavier. 15th st, s s, 165 e 7th av, runs south 103.3 x east 10 x north 3.3 x east 10 x north 100 to st, x west 20. Aug. 1, due July 1, 1894, 4 %. 15,000

O'Brien, Luke to Michael H. Cashman. Wadsworth av, n w cor 187th st, 189.10x95. Sept. 8, due Dec. 16, 1891. 17,000

Osborn, Kate L. to Justin Wohlfarth. Madison or Bathgate av. P. M. Aug. 31, installs. gold, 1,000

O'Halloran, Edward to THE DRY DOCK SAVINGS INST. Market st, No. 36, e s, bet Madison st and Henry st, 25x86.10x—x86.9. Sept. 17, due Sept. 20, 1892, 5 %. 18,000

Pape, Margaretha to Louis Kaysser. Brook av, w s, 125 n 170th st, 25x90. Sub. to mort. $500. Sept. 11, 3 years, 5 %. 100

Phillips, Hartwig I. to Martha E. wife of Thomas K. Egbert, New Jersey, Catharine L. wife of George Lowthers, Rye, N. Y., and Clara wife of Charles Greer, Rye, N. Y. Boulevard or Broadway and 65th st. P. M. Sept. 8, 3 years or sooner, 5 %. gold, 75,000

Phillips, Josephine to THE HARLEM SAVINGS BANK. 118th st, n s, 187.6 e 3d av, 18.9x100.10. Sub. to morts. Sept. 16, 1 year, 5 %. 250

Rapelye, Pheba C. to Read Gordon and ano. exrs. William H. Dilworth as trustee for Mary D., Alice G. and Edward F. Dilworth. 135th st, n s, 170.8 e Southern Boulevard. P. M. Sept. 17, due Dec. 1, 1894. 3,500

Same to same. 135th st, n s, 187.4 e Southern Boulevard. P. M. Sept. 17, due Dec. 1, 1894. 3,500

Same to Walter Barnes trustee for Mary Barnes. 135th st, n s, 154 e Southern Boulevard. P. M. Sept. 17, due Dec. 1, 1896, 5 %. 3,000

Richter, Frederick A. H. otherwise Herman to Peter Naylor and ano. trustees Peter Naylor dec'd. Elm st, No. 190, w s, 21.3x100. Sept. 17, 5 years, 5 %. 11,100

Rohrs, Frederick to Mary F. Hopkins, Stamford, Conn. 70th st, n s, 248 e Av A, 25x100.5. Sept. 16, 3 years, 5 %. 13,000

Same to Clara Hirsch. Same property. Sub. to mort. $13,000. Sept. 16, 1 year. 1,000

Same to John Q. A. Ward. 70th st, n s, 298 e Av A, 25x100.5. Sept. 16, 5 years, 5 %. gold, 13,000

Same to Clara Rothschild. Same property. Sub. to mort. $13,000. Sept. 16, 1 year. 1,000

Same to Bradley & Currier Co. (Lim.) 70th st,

n s, 248 e Av A, 25x100.5; 70th st, n s, 298 e Av A, 25x100.5. Sub. to morts. $28,000. Sept. 16, 2 months. 4,500

Reiss, Lob to Henry Metz. Delancey st. P. M. Sept. 15, 5 years, 4½ %. 16,000

Reiss, Jetta wife of and Lob to THE BOWERY SAVINGS BANK. 3d st, s s, 69.9 e Av C, 22.11 x87. Sept. 17, 1 year, 5 %. 9,000

Raymond, James to Charles H. Langdon and ano. exrs. Thomas B. Langdon. 124th st, n s, 225 w 1st av, 25x100.11. Sept. 9, 1 year. 2,000

Rettinger, George, Passaic, N. J., to Julius Chatelan. Rivington st, s w cor Clinton st, 25x100. Sept. 14, due Aug. 12, 1892, 5 %. 10,500

Ruck, John M. to Joseph P. Sauer, Jersey City, N. J. 9th av, n e cor 58th st, 100.5x125. Sept. 1, 1 year. 25,000

Rieger, Donatus and Elizabeth mortgagors with THE POUGHKEEPSIE SAVINGS BANK mortgagee. Extension of mort. at 4½ %. Sept. 1. nom

Rothstein, Daniel to John Ochse. Elizabeth st. P. M. Sub. to mort. $26,000. Sept. 14, installs. 14,750

Ritter, Charles to George F. Bristow. 144th st, s s, 387.11 e 3d av or Boston road, 22x100. Sept. 10, 3 years, 5 %. 600

Schneider, Morris and Abraham to THE MECHANICS NATIONAL BANK. 123d st, s s, 240 e 4th av, 75x100.11. Sept. 9, notes. 15,005

Schul, Paul to Peter Doelger. 6th st, No. 217 E. Lease. Sept. 10. 1,000

Spektorsky, Abraham to THE MUTUAL LIFE INS. CO., New York. Eldridge st, e s, 100.8 n Canal st, 25x109. Sept. 11, 1 year, 5 %. 17,000

Steele, Thomas A. to Joel M. Marx. 28th st, No. 141, n s, 247.2 e 7th av, 23.4x98.9x23.5x 98.9. ½ part. Sept. 11, due Dec. 11, 1891. 150

Stumpf, Peter J. and Catherine J. his wife to John L. Daniels. Lyon st, s s, 174 w Fox st, runs south 68.6 x southwest 55.9 x northwest 30 x northeast 44.3 x west 32.2 x north 45.5 to Lyon st, x east 60. Sept. 11, 3 years, 5 %. 2,250

Schaller, Frank L. to Theodora Ernst. Franklin av. P. M. Aug. 26, 1 year or sooner, 5 %. 5,500

Schmeckenbecher, Martin to Julius Weill, Titusville, Pa. Av A, No. 1313, n w cor 70th st, 27.8x94. Sept. 12, due Sept. 14, 1892. 4,000

Same to same. Av A, No. 1315, w s, 27.8 n 70th st, 27.8x94. Sept. 12, due Sept. 14, 1892. 3,000

Schuster, Sophia wife of and Susman to Pauline Schweizer. 1st av, No. 1666, s e cor 87th st, 25.7x74. Sept. 14, due Sept. 15, 1893. 3,000

Simpson, John F., Peekskill, N. Y., and Charles H. Simpson, Quebec, Can., to The General Theological Seminary of the Protestant Episcopal Church in the United States. Park row, No. 225 and No. 63 New Bowery, begins Park row, s s, 72.8 e James st, 28x50.3 to New Bowery, x32.8x77.8. Sept. 1, due Sept. 15, 1896, 5 %. gold, 50,000

Sinnot, Amos J. to George Ehret. Whitehall st, No. 20½. Store lease. Aug. 14, demand. 2,200

Smith, Thomas C. to Charles J. Burke, Rochester, N. Y. 46th st, s s, 350 e 8th av, 18.9x 100.5. Sept. 15, 5 years or installs, 5 %. 4,000

Steinmetz, Welcome R. and Elizabeth wife of and John H. Steinmetz to Walter B. Smith, Yonkers, N. Y. West End av, s w cor 103d st, 20.11x79.3. Aug. 1, 1 year. gold, 28,000

Same to same. West End av, w s, 20.11 s 103d st, 4 lots, each 20x79.3. 4 morts., each $18,-000. Aug. 1, 1 year. gold, 72,000

Same to same. 103d st, s s, 79.3 w West End av, 20x100.11. Aug. 1, 1 year. See Conveys. gold, 17,000

Same to same. 103d st, s s, 99.3 w West End av, 20x100.11. Aug. 1, 1 year. See Conveys. gold, 16,000

Same to same. 103d st, s s, 119.3 w West End av, 20x100.11. Aug. 1, 1 year. See Conveys. gold, 16,000

Same to same. 103d st, s s, 139.3 w West End av, 20.2x100.11. Aug. 1, 1 year. See Conveys. gold, 17,000

Same to Marvin S. Buttles. West End av, s w cor 103d st, 100.11x79.3; 103d st, s s, 139.3 w West End av, 20.4x100.11. Sept. 14, demand. 4,000

Same to same. West End av, s w cor 103d st, 100.11x79.6; 103d st, s s, 139.3 w West End av, 20.4x100.11. Aug. 1, demand. 7,000

Same to The New York Lumber and Wood Working Co. West End av, s w cor 103d st, 100.11x159.6, excepting therefrom 103d st, s s, 119.3 w West End av, 20x100.11. Sub. to morts. $150,000. Sept. 14, due Jan. 1, 1892, or sooner. 13,840

Steinmetz, Welcome R. to Wilbur F. Washburne, Yonkers, N. Y. West End av, s w cor 103d st, 100.11x79.3. Sept. 15, demand. 4,270

Same to same. Same property. Sept. 15, notes. Collateral. 850

Same to same. Same property. Sept. 10, 1 year. Collateral. 6,500

Same to William T. Campbell and Henry B. Weselman. West End av, s w cor 103d st, 100.11x79.6; 103d st, s s, 139.6 w West End av, 20.4x100.11. Sub. to morts. Sept. 14, 1 year. 3,500

Same to Thomas Hagan. 103d st, s s, 139.3 w West End av, 20.4x100.11. Sub. to morts. $16,000. Sept. 15, due Feb. 1, 1892. 1,500

Steinmetz, Welcome R. mortgagor with Wilbur F. Washburn, Yonkers, N. Y. Agreement as to priority of mortgages made by Wilbur F. Washburn. Sept. 15. nom

Stich, John to Lizzie Wagner, Monica Scheffler and Cecilia wife of Augustus N. Mathieu. 46th st. P. M. Aug. 8, due Sept. 15, 1892, or sooner, 5 %. 6,000

Samelson, Moses to Joseph Samelson. 117th st, s s, 100 e Columbus av, 100x100.11. Sept. 14, 1 year. 10,000

Senior, Ida L. wife of and Theodore E. to Elizabeth Stark. Keppler av, n w cor Willard st, 75x100. Building loan. Aug. 1, 3 years or sooner. 3,500

Sackin, Louis to Saul Federman. Allen st, No. 33. P. M. Sept. 15, installs. 3,000

Schmid, Elizabeth otherwise Schmit or Schmidt to The Home Mutual Building and Loan Assoc, New York. 174th st, s s, 13.9 e Webster av, 35x108.8x35.3x107. Sept. 12, installs. 800

Sennhauser, Casper to George F. Bristow. Stebbins av, e s, 413.4 n 165th st, 25x150x25.4 x154.2. Sept. 15, 5 years, 5 %. 2,500

Shulman, Yette wife of and Lazarus to Charles E. Tracy and ano. trustees James Bogert. East Broadway, n s, 104.7 w Jefferson st, 26x 69.6. Sept. 16, 2 months, 5 %. gold, 12,000

Schaller, Frank L. to Leonard Seib. Norfolk st, No. 81, w s, 25x100. Sept. 17, 1 year, 5 %. 1,000

Tripler, Thomas E. to Bernhard Beinecke. West End av, No. 244, e s, 42.8 n 76th st, 19.10 x90. Sept. 17, 3 years. 6,000

Underhill, Francis T. to Henry de F. Weekes. 22d st, n s, 544.8 w 4th av, 25.10x98.9. Sept. 14, due Jan. 1, 1893, 5 %. 5,000

Vander Roest, William G., Mt. Vernon, N. Y., to THE TITLE GUARANTEE AND TRUST CO. Grand st, No. 378, n s, 52 e Norfolk st, 23x80. Sept. 2, due Sept. 14, 1892, 5 %. 15,000

Vander Roest, William to William G. Vander Roest. 9th st, No. 57, n s, 226.4 w Broadway, 26x92.3. Lease. Sept. 2, due Sept. 14, 1896. 15,000

Van Rensselaer, Anna W. widow to The American Bible Society. Grand st, No. 186, n w cor Mulberry st, 25.2x100. Aug. 28, 5 years, 5 %. 30,000

Valentine, Matthias B., New Rochelle, N. Y., to Sarah F. Dunwell. 90th st, s s, 118.9 e 9th av, 15.9x100.8. Aug. 21, 3 years, 5 %. 2,600

Washburn, Wilbur F., Yonkers, N. Y., to FIRST NATIONAL BANK of Yonkers, N. Y. 103d st, s s, 79.3 w West End av, 40x100.11 Sept. 16, 1 year. See Conveys. 12,000

Wood, Frederick to William Hall's Sons. 88th st, n s, 175 w 8th av, 75x100.8. Sub. to mort. $58,500. Sept. 10, 2 months. 9,600

Weiler, Henry mortgagor with THE POUGHKEEPSIE SAVINGS BANK mortgagee. Extension of mort at 4½ %. Sept. 1. nom

Wessell, Otto and Anna C. his wife to Henry Wiener, Philadelphia, Pa. Columbus av, No. 729, e s, 100.8 n 95th st, 25.2x93.3x25.3x90.8. Sept. 17, 5 years, 4 %. 8,000

Westheimer, Jacob H. to John McMillan. Morris av, s w cor 150th st. P. M. Sept. 14, due March 17, 1892, 5 %. 4,250

Wiersch, Johanna wife of and Louis to Henry Fritz. Broome st, No. 204, n s, 75 e Norfolk st, 25x100. Sept. 14, 6 months. 2,000

Wilkes, Lizzie T. to Thomas Tracy. 13?d st, No. 6 E., s s, 125 e 5th av, 25x99.11. Sept. 9, 4 months. 1,500

Zimmerman, Ernest to John and Matthias Haffen. Lewis st, s w cor 5th st, 25x29.8x25x 29.7. All title. Sept. 15, 6 months. 1,532

Zimmermann, Jacob A. to Philip Sammet. 51st st, s s, 484 w 8th av, 40.8x100.5, with all title to strip on w s, 0.4x100.5. Sept. 15, due March 1, 1892. 13,000

KINGS COUNTY.

SEPTEMBER 10, 11, 12, 14, 15, 16.

Adamson, Robert to The Riverhead Savings Bank. Manhattan av, w s, 225 n Nassau av, 25x100. Sept. 8, 5 years, 5 %. $1,000

Adamson, John to Edward H. Litchfield and ano. trustees Edwin C. Litchfield. 2d st, n e s, 298.10 e 7th av. P. M. Sept. 12, due Sept. 15, 1896, 5 %. 13,228

Same to Edward H. Litchfield. 2d st, n e s, 298.10 s e 7th av. P. M. Sept. 12, due Sept. 15, 1896, 5 %. 9,365

Same to same. 2d st, n e s, 198.10 s e 7th av. P. M. Sept. 12, due Sept. 15, 1896, 5 %. 9,655

Same to same. 2d st, s w s, 200 s e 7th av. P. M. Sept. 12, due Sept. 15, 1896, 5 %. 8,497

Same to same. 2d st, s w s, 100 s e 7th av. P. M. Sept. 12, due Sept. 15, 1896, 5 %. 9,655

Aitken, William B. to Gertrude Collins. Prospect av, w s, 154 n Greenwood av, 18x150. Sept. 4, 3 years. 1,750

Same to same. Prospect av, w s, 136 n Greenwood av, 18x150. Sept. 4, 3 years. 1,750

Same to Elizabeth Collins. Prospect av, w s, 172 n Greenwood av, 18x150. Sept. 4, 3 years. 1,500

Ashley, Ann wife of and John to Catharine Buckley. Smith st. P. M. Aug. 31, due Sept. 1, 1896, 5 %. 6,000

Auten, Mary L. to The Title Guarantee and Trust Co. Baltic st, n s, 159.4 w 5th av, 20x 100. Sept. 14, 3 years, 5 %. 2,700

Same to Ebenezer S. James. Same property. Sept. 15, 1 year, 5 %. 2,500

Balsamo, Alfonso to Ellen Tilyou, Coney Island. West 15th st, Coney Island. P. M. Sept. 15, installs. 500

Barnett, Rosa to Michael Minden. Pennsylvania av, w s, 175 n Glenmore av, 25x100. Sept. 8, 3 years, 5 %. 1,700

Barkovitz, Morris and Rosie to Ada Parmer. Watkins st. P. M. July 18, installs. 550

Barth, Emma M. to John A. Lott, Jr. Lots 1 and 2 map 90 lots of Edward Egolf, Bath Beach. P. M. May 14, due June 1, 1894, 5 %. 700

Barth, Maria to Albert V. B. Voorhies. 85th st, e s, at intersection with land of J. E. Lott, runs east 100.3 x north 38.8 x west 100 to st, x south 47, New Utrecht. Sept. 8, 3 years. 1,300

Barrie, Lucy F. to Charles Isbill. Putnam av P. M. Sept. 14, 6 months. 1,765

Bender, Hermann P. to William Ulmer. Bushwick av, s e cor Willoughby av. P. M. Sept. 5, 3 years, 5 %. 4,500

Bennett, Jane L. wife of Rulloff R. to John H. Rowland. Madison st, n s, 85 e Franklin av, 17x100. Sept. 15, 3 years, 5 %. 1,000

Bennett, Hannah to Elizabeth C. Halcott. Atlantic av, s s, 278.11 w Crescent av, 25.4x81.4 x25.4x85.8. Sept. 14, due June 1, 1895. 1,250

Bieier, John to John S. Freese. Harman st, s e s, 325 n e Central av, 25x100. Sept. 11, 2 years, 5 %. 1,500

Bigelow, Anna E. to Frances M. Vibbard. 53d st, s w s, 100 n w 4th av, 20x100.2. Sept. 9, 3 years, 5 %. 2,500

Bills, Abby J. wife of and James A. to The East Brooklyn Savings Bank. Sunnyside av, n s, 200 w Miller av, 50x250 to Highland Boulevard. Sept. 14, due in Sept. 1892. 5,000

Bishop, Gertrude A. G. to The German Savings Bank, Brooklyn. Madison st, n s, 24 e Sumner av, 18x82. Sept. 8, due Dec. 1, 1892, 5 %. 4,500

Brenen, James to William Leahy, Flatlands, L. I. Lot at Gravesend adj John Hettrick, 50x70. Sept. 3, 5 years. 600

Brown, William to Henry C. M. Ingraham. 7th st, s s, 147.10 w 6th av, runs west 225x100 x east 25 x south 100 to 8th st, x east 200 x north 200. P. M. Sept. 19, 1890, demand. 5,000

Brown, Russell R. to George C. Crawford. Macon st. P. M. May 7, due Feb. 24, 1892. 1,100

Brown, Thomas to Mary Copeland. 5th av, e s, 21.6 s Berkeley pl, 18.6x87.4. Sept. 8, 3 years, 5 %. 7,500

Brush, Lucinda H. and Amelia M. to Hannah C. Hawks. Clifton pl, n s, 100 w Marcy av, 25x100. May 28, 1891, 1 year. 1,000

Buckley, Daniel to Albro J. Newton. President st, n s, 117 w 6th av, 100x95. Sept. 15, 1 year, 5 %. 7,500

Bruhn, Henry A. A. to Robert S. Neely. Pacific st. P. M. Sept. 12, installs. 1,038

Burns, William to William O. Forrester. Putnam av. P. M. Sept. 9, installs. 2,000

Burwell, Charles D. to The Dime Savings Bank, Brooklyn. South Oxford st, e s, 44 n Lafayette av, 44x82. Aug. 31, 1 year, 5 %. 50,000

Cable, Alexander to Samuel Gusfield. Sumner av, n e cor Macon st, 30x95. March 6, 2 years. 3,500

Caroselli, Alberico to The Title Guarantee and Trust Co. McDonough st, s s, 175.5 e Sumner av, 4 lots, together 99.7x100. 4 morts., each $6,000. Sept. 9, 3 years, 5 %. 24,000

Same to same. McDougal st, s s, 235.5 e Sumner av, 20x100. Sept. 9, 3 years, 5 %. 6,000

Clark, Augustus G. to The East Brooklyn Savings Bank. Carlton av, e s, 402.11 s Fulton st, 20x100. Sept. 12, 2 years, 5 %. 2,250

Clark, Francis E. to Henry Wills. Park av. P. M. Sept. 15, 2 years, 5 %. 4,000

Clayton, Joseph D. to Harry Clayton. Dean st, s s, 316.8 w Buffalo av, —x107.2x68.8x107.2. Sept. 3, demand. 800

Coane, James E., Hoboken, N. J., to Frank Bailey. 79th st. P. M. Sept. 8, due Sept. 11, 1892. 300

Collins, John H. to Guernsey Sackett. Wyona st, e s, 300 s Fulton st, 25x100. Sept. 15, due Feb. 1, 1892. 100

Colyer, John to Jeremiah Ervin. 9th av, s e s, 80 n e 64th st, runs southeast 80 x northeast 20 x southeast 295.6 to Fort Hamilton av, x northeast 79.3 x northwest 397.11 to 9th av, x southwest 16.10, New Utrecht. Sept. 12, 3 years. 2,200

Cooler, Eloise to Ernest O. Hiltermann, Philadelphia, Pa. Fulton av, n s, 39.5 e Jay st, 30x88.9x18.9x80.3. Sept. 15, 5 years, 5 %. 2,500

Cooper, John mortgagor with John C. Benham. Extension of mort. Aug. 28. nom

Cordts, Henry W. to Luer and George Otten. Broadway, No. 19. Lease. Sept. 10, notes. 5,000

Cordts, Louise wife of and Henry W. to John W. and Ernst A. Haaren and Ernst A. Meinken. Union st, s s, 108.9 e Smith st, 17x98. Sept. 10, 2 years. 2,000

Corwin, Frank L. to John Andreas. Butler st. P. M. Sept. 1, installs. 1,750

Crawford, Mary M. wife of and Bernard to The Title Guarantee and Trust Co. Dean st, s w s, 180 n w 3d av, 20x100. Sept. 10, 3 years, 5 %. 1,000

Danto, Simon to David Stern. Schenectady av. P. M. Sept. 14, due Sept. 1, 1898, 5 %. 1,700

Desmond, Timothy and Johanna his wife to Jeremiah Desmond. Huron st, s s, 225 w Oakland st, 25x100. Sept. 11, 2 years, 5 %. 1,500

Du Bois, Harry A. and Carrie A. his wife to George L. Frank, Jr. Jamaica av. P. M. Sept. 9, installs. 1,050

Duff, James to The Prospect Land and Improvement Co. 73d st. P. M. Sept. 14, due Sept. 15, 1894, 5 %. 318

Dunn, Ellen to Mary Hickey. Hull st, s s, 117.6 w Stone av, 16.3x100. Sept. 9, due Nov. 1, 1894, 5 %. 600

Dunn, John J. to Bernard and Philip Katz, Paterson, N. J. Bedford av, e s, 65.9 n Grand st, 18x59.3x17.6x61.4. Sept. 7, 3 years. 2,000

Eisenhardt, Charles to Lillie Cohen. Greene av, s e s, 203.10 s w Central av, 15x100. Sept. 14, installs, 5 %. 1,100

Elliott, John C. to Robert S. Neely. Pacific st. P. M. Aug. 21, installs. 973

Elssou, John to Esther M. Hedges. 62d st, s s, 100 w 11th av, 20x105x21.4x100. Sept. 10, 5 years. 500

Ernst, Friederka K. wife of and Francis to Robert B. Muller. Jefferson av. P. M. Sept. 15, installs, 5 %. 2,250

Fennel, John mortgagor with W. H. Ames, Hackensack, N. J., mortgagee. Extension of mort. June 30. nom

Fickett, Sophronia M. widow to John Williamson. Franklin av, s e cor Quincy st, 50x110. Sept. 12, 1 year. 30,000

Fitzgerald, Michael and Mary to Daniel Doody. 4th av, w s, 80.2 n 33d st, 20x80. Sept. 10, demand. 2,000

Fitzsimmons, Owen to Timothy Perry. Van Cott av, n e cor Leonard st, 24.10x80.3. Sept. 12, 1 year. 500

Fogel, Jacob and Henry Leiner to Ferdinand Feldblum and Louis Berman. Throop av. P. M. Sept. 15, 4 years, 5 %. 1,100

Fowler, Mary E. wife of and Levi to George W. Blauvelt. St. Marks av, n s, 220 e Franklin av, 20x128.6. Sept. 10, 3 years. 7,500

Same to John Petrie. St. Marks av, n s, 200 e Franklin av, 20x128.6. Sept. 10, 3 years. 7,500

Same to Adolph Vaurcin. St. Marks av, n s, 240 e Franklin av, 20x128.6. Sept. 10, 3 years. 7,500

Franke, Henry to William B. Franke. 6th av, east cor 44th st, 113.5x200x126.3x200. Sept. 5, 1 year. 1,000

Fruh, Elizabeth to John Young. Melrose st. P. M. Aug. 8, due Sept. 1, 1896, or sooner, 5 %. 4,500

Gastmeyer, Ernestine wife of and Charles F. to The Title Guarantee and Trust Co. Eldert st, n w s, 100 n e Evergreen av, 100x100. Sept. 14, demand. 10,000

Gayler, Augustus S. and William F. Stoney to Charles B. Dutton. Gates av, s s, 300 w Tompkins av, 50x100. June 18, 1 year, 5 %. 3,000

Gerken, Ernst to The South Brooklyn Co-operative Building and Loan Assoc. 38th st. P. M. July 28, installs. 2,000

Goodkind, Theresa to Samuel Parsbelsky. Seigel st. P. M. Aug. 1, 1 year, 5 %. 3,100

Goodwin, Jennett C. wife of and John J. to Mary McGovern. Prospect pl, s s, 125 w Vanderbilt av, 18.9x131. Sept. 9, 3 years, 5 %. 2,000

Graham, Ellen wife of and James F. to Laure E. Mills. Ocean Parkway, w s, 100 s Av E, 250x60, Flatbush. Aug. 19, 3 years, 5½ %. 12,000

Greenblatt, Isaac and Solomon to Michael Krebs. Moore st. P. M. Sept. 15, installs. 2,000

Greenstone, Betsey wife of and Abraham to Ferdinand Schieffer. Union av. P. M. Sept. 15, 5 years, 5 %. 4,300

Hansen, Hans A. to Julia A. Schenck. Nelson st. P. M. Sept. 8, installs. 2,500

Heaton, John L. to Cornelia M. Covert, trustee Francis M. Covert and children. Bushwick av, north cor Linden st, 50x85. Sept. 16, 3 years, 5 %. 6,000

Hegeman, Joseph to The Title Guarantee and Trust Co. Irving pl, w s, 115 n Fulton st, runs west 49.4 x south 17 x east 19.6 x again east 39 to pl, x north 20. Sept. 12, 3 years, 5 %. 2,000

Heisinger, Henriette to Eleanora Armann. Myrtle st, n s, 325 e Evergreen av, 25x83.9x25.4x87.11. Sept. 10, 5 years, 5 %. 2,500

Hilditch, Ephraim to Matthew Riley. Locust st, w s, 579.6 s Jamaica turnpike, 37.6x150. Sept. 4, 2 years. 300

Hill, Henry B. to John L. Young exr. Isaac H. Young. McDonough st, s s, 303.8 w Patchen av, 18x100. Sept. 1, 3 years, 5 %. 5,500

Same to same. McDonough st, s s, 285.8 w Patchen av, 18x100. Sept. 1, 3 years, 5 %. 5,500

Same to Pauline Ettlinger. McDonough st, s s, 321.8 w Patchen av, 72x100. Sept. 14, 2 years or sooner. 8,000

Hochspeier, Emil and Annie Corin widow and Carrie wife of Henry Mulleneaux devisees of Helen Hochspeier to Philip L. Balz, Jr. Pacific st, n s, 89.4 e Schenectady av, 18.6x80, due Nov. 1, 1892. 150

Hoffmann, Henry to William Schmitz. Scholes st, s s, 75 w Leonard st, 25x100. Sept. 11, 5 years, 5 %. 6,400

Hopkins, Harry F. C. to R. Cummings Sons. Bleecker st, s s, 20 e Knickerbocker av, 40x80. Sept. 9, 1 year. 736

Same to Rudolph and Otto E. Reimer. Bleecker st, s e s, 60 n e Knickerbocker av, runs southeast 80 x northeast 14.2 x northwest 25.4 x northwest 55.4 to st, x southwest 20. Sub. to mort. $28,500. Sept. 9, 1 year. 1,000

Hothersall, James to Patrick H. Funchon. Sands st. P. M. Sept. 15, 3 years, 5 %. 1,500

Hunt, Charles G. to Clifton L. Goff. Sutter av. P. M. Sept. 14, 3 years. 1,300

Hurley, Catharine A. to Winfield S. Mountguard. Jennie R. and Grace H. Mount. Duffield st, w s, 169.4 n Myrtle av, 19.9x100. Sept. 8, 2 years, 5 %. 2,500

Jones, E. Willard to John Wilson and ano. trustees David Gibson. McDonough st, n s, 270.6 e Lewis av, 19x100. Aug. 21, 5 years, 5 %. 7,000

Jones, John B. to Daniel K. Hall, Jr., Glen Cove, L. I. Hewes st, n w s, 102 s w Harrison av, 20.2x100. Sept. 1, 3 years, 5 %. 2,500

Jones, Richard to Jose Gros, Morristown, N. J. 2d av, e s, 50 n 13th st, 50x97.10. Sept. 5, 3 years. 500

Jones, Maria to John S. Ladd. Dean st, s s, 400 e Rockaway av, 25x107.2. Sept. 15, due Jan. 1, 1891. 250

Joost, Christopher to The South Brooklyn Savings Inst. Hart st, n s, 260 e Tompkins av, 20x100. Sept. 15, 1 year, 5 %. 1,200

Katzmann, Katie wife of and Henry to S. Liebmanns Sons Brewing Co. Harman st. P. M. Sept. 1, 1 year, 5 %. 1,500

Kayser, Theodore to Edward F. Patchen admr. Martha W. Patchen. Graham av, w s, 25 n Scholes st, 25x75; Scholes st, n s, 75 w Graham av, 25x100. June 26, 3 years, 5 %. 10,000

Kenna, Thomas P. to Otto F. Struse. North 2d st, s s, 124.2 w Havemeyer st, 25.4x91.3x25.2x92.9. Sept. 9, 3 years, 5 %. 1,400

Kerr, Peter G. to Eliza Wanmaker. Warwick st, w s, 105.6 n Fulton st, 25x95. Sept. 9, 3 years or installs. 2,200

Kerz, Elizabeth to Mark B. Knight. Albany av, e s, 80 n Furnald st, 20x92. Sept. 12, 3 years, 5 %. 350

Kirby, J. Mason to George C. Hollister, Rochester, N. Y. Decatur st, n s, 340 w Saratoga av, 173.4x100. Sub. to mort. $39,434. Sept. 5, 1 year. 4,000

Klebsch, Gustav to The F. & M. Schaefer Brewing Co. 3d av, n w cor 15th st. Saloon lease. Sept. 15, demand. 1,075

Kleinbul, George to Frank S. Bradford et al. exrs. Samuel I. Hunt. North 11th st. P. M. Sept. 16, due Nov. 1, 1894, 5 %. 2,000

Koenig, George O. R. to William Lenfer and Annie M. his wife. Stanhope st. P. M. Sept. 9, 1 year, 5 %. 200

Korb, Wenzel to Theresa Sebek. Covert st, n w s, 175 s w Evergreen av, 25x100. Sept. 9, 3 years, 5 %. 800

Kuhn, Louise to West Brooklyn Land and Impt. Co. 57th st, New Utrecht. P. M. Sept. 10, 5 years, 5 %. 720

Kupfer, Frederick and Anthony W. Hubner to John L. Laidlaw and ano. exrs. Thomas Laidlaw. Bergen lane, s e cor Lawrence st, New Utrecht. P. M. Sept. 14, 3 years. 5,500

Laing, Donald to William A. Cook trustee Charlotte E. Harris dec'd. Montauk av, e s, 150 s Belmont av, 20x100. Sept. 10, 3 years. 2,000

Le Beau, Theodore M. to Alois Lazansky. Jerome st, also Eastern Parkway and Barbey st. P. M. Sept. 10, due March 10, 1892. 3,800

Lang, Frank A. to The East Brooklyn Savings Bank, Brooklyn. Stockton st, s s, 100 w Throop av, 20x100. Sept. 12, due Sept. 14, 1892, 5 %. 500

Larsen, Peder A. to Warren A. James, New York. 54th st, n s, 140 w 4th av, 20x100.2. Sept. 10, 5 years, 5 %. 2,500

Same to Mary A. Gray. 54th st, n s, 120 w 4th av, 20x100.2. Sept. 10, 5 years, 5 %. 2,500

Law, Mary C. to Almon Gunnison and ano. trustees Curtis B. Lowerre. Lafayette av, s e cor Ashland pl, runs east 22.1 x south 95.1 x east 22.6 x south 20 x west 45 to Ashland pl, x north 115.1. Sept. 2, due Sept. 1, 1894, 5 %. 9,000

Leffer, Fanny M. to James D. Lynch. 82d st, s w s, 280 s e 23d av, 60x100. Sept. 2, due Sept. 10, 1892, 5 %. 600

Levy, Morris to Henry P. Rindskopf. Glenmore av, n e cor Stone av. P. M. Sept. 10, 2 years, 5 %. 1,000

Lewis, Charles to Edward Michaelis. Bushwick av. P. M. Sept. 12, 1 year, 5 %. 1,450

Lewis, Margaretha to Jennie A. Ives. Warren st. P. M. Sept. 15, 1 year, 5 %. 1,000

Linnemeyer, Dietrich F. and Edward N. Boback to The Williamsburgh Savings Bank. Myrtle av, north cor Himrod st, runs northeast 26.11 x northwest 80 x southwest 9.6 x southeast 30.6 x southeast 5.3 x south 42.10 to av, x east 20.6. Sept. 9, 1 year, 5 %. 4,500

Same to Henry and John Von Glahn. Same property. P. M. 2d mort. Sept. 9, 5 years. 5,000

Lobrentz, Christiana E. to Bernhard H. Bulling, Ridgewood, L. I. Railroad av, w s, 100 n Griffin pl, 25x100. Sept. 4. 3 years. 1,750

Lopez, Catherine T. wife of and Ramon to The Title Guarantee and Trust Co. McDonough st. P. M. Sept. 6, 1 year, 5 %. 4,000

Lott, Moe S. to Charles H. Lott. Mackay pl, s s, 150 e River road, 50x90, New Utrecht. Sept. 14, 3 years. 600

Lutz, Frances to Joseph Thum. Driggs av, s s, 50 e Humboldt st, 25x100. Sept. 15, 5 years, 5 %. 2,000

Lyons, Susan T. to The Williamsburgh Savings Bank. Lewis av, e s, 60 n McDonough st, 20x90. Sept. 11, 1 year, 5 %. 1,500

Macdonald, John to Loftis W. O. Berry. Flushing av, n w cor Franklin av. P. M. Aug. 31, due Aug. 1, 1898, 5 %. 21,000

Mafera, Stephen to Bernhard H. Bulling. Railroad av, w s, 75 n Griffin pl, 25x100. Sept. 4, 3 years. 1,750

Mahon, Michael to Guy Loomis. Broadway, s s, 360 w Brooklyn av, 20x100. Sept. 4, 1 year. 133

Major, Anna M. wife of Charles W. H. to The Metropolitan Life Ins. Co., New York. Vernon av, s s, 380.6 w Marcy av, 18x100. Sept. 11, due Oct. 1, 1894, or sooner, 5 %. 2,000

Marber, Victor to Henry A. Latimer. 14th av, n e cor 64th st, 60x100, New Utrecht. Sept. 12, 3 years. 300

Margolin, Morris to Sophie G. Parker. Watkins st, w s, 225 s Sutter av, 25x100. Sept. 16, demand. gold, 1,000

Mason, Elizabeth wife of and Charles to Virginia A. Kleine. Palmetto st. P. M. Sept. 10, 5 years. 1,100

McGuirk, Annie E. wife of and George to Louisa S. Ince. Willoughby av, s s, 100 e Spencer st, 16x90. Sept. 14, 3 years. 300

Matthews, Annie wife of and Joseph to Thomas C. Balderston et al. trustees of the Order of Tonti. Osborn st, n w cor Livonia av, 25x100. Sept. 3, 1 year, 5 %. 5,500

McGrath, Robert to Catharine A. Ferris. Luquer st, s s, 73.6 w Court st, runs south 60 x west 19.6 x south 40 x west 10.3 x north 35.2 x northeast 12.8 x north 56.8 to st, x east 20. Sept. 14, 5 years, 5 %. 3,000

McKinley, Jane R. and Regina Snyder, Elizabeth, N. J., to H. B. Scharmann & Sons. Fulton st, s s, 219.7 w Washington av, 20x100. Aug. 20, 3 years, 5 %. 7,500

Miller, Andrew to The Title Guarantee and Trust Co. St. Marks av, n s, 372 e Rogers av, 28x125.3. Sept. 9, due Sept. 10, 1894, 5 %. 8,500

Same to same. St. Marks av, n s, 332 e Rogers av, 20x125.3. Sept. 9, due Sept. 10, 1894. 8,500

Same to same. St. Marks av, n s, 352.1 e Rogers av, 20x125.3. Sept. 9, due Sept. 10, 1894. 8,500

Moran, John W. to The Title Guarantee and Trust Co. Summit st, n s, 150 e Hicks st, 100x100. Sept. 10, due Sept. 15, 1892. 6,000

Moynahan, Margaret F. wife of and Daniel to James S. Clark trustee Benjamin M. Clark. 48th st, No. 242, s s, 200 e 3d av, 20x100. Sept. 10, installs, 5 %. 1,500

Murphy, John to Elizabeth F. Noble. Sackett st, s s, 178 e Henry st, 28.6x100. Sept. 15, 3 years, 5 %. 9,000

Nelson, John mortgagor with William E. Valentine, Jamaica. Extension mort. Sept. 9. nom

Nichols, Wilhelmina to Cresenz Merk. Bush st, s s, 300 w Hicks st, 20x100. July 1, 2 years, 5 %. 600

Norris, Henry D. to Irene B. Braman. 3d st, s s, 22 w 7th av, 22x90. Aug. 24, 3 years, 5 %. 7,000

O'Brien, Bridget wife of and Patrick to Patrick McMahon and Ellen his wife. India st. P. M. Sept. 1, 3 years, 5 %. 1,500

O'Neill, Mary to Jennie S. Niles. Pacific st. P. M. Sept. 14, installs. 500

Olsen, George to Julia A. Smith. Barbey st, w s, 300 n Blake av, 25x100. Sept. 8, 5 years. 1,500

Paduano, Nicola to James H. Watson and James H. Pittinger, of Watson & Pittinger. 13th av, e s, 40 s 64th st, 20x53.11x20x55.2. Sept. 10, 1 year. 500

Pannwitz, Max to John and Barbara Sherman. Himrod st, s e s, 380.8 w Central av, 20x100. Sept. 11, due Sept. 11, 1894, or installs., 5 %. 500

Parshall, George H. to The Peoples Trust Co. guard. of John Donnelly. 5th av, e s, 25.2 s 53d st, 100x100. Sept. 14, 1 year, 5 %. 2,000

Pettit, Henrietta A wife of and Mortlock to Catharine C. wife of Daniel Pearsall. McDonough st. P. M. Sept. 9, due Sept. 10, 1896, 5 %. 19,000

Pfalzgraf, Hans S. to Cornelius Cowenhoven. 59th st, s w s, 160 n w 17th av, 60x100.2, New Utrecht. Sept. 10, demand. 3,000

Pink, Bernhard J. to John H. Vanderveer. Amboy st, w s, 140.5 s Eastern Parkway. Sept. 14, 3 years, 5 %. See Conveys. 940

Same to same. Amboy st, w s, 90.5 s Eastern Parkway. Sept. 14, 3 years, 5 %. See Conveys. 315

Same to same. Amboy st, w s, 115.5 s Eastern Parkway. Sept. 14, 3 years, 5 %. See Conveys. 315

Same to same. Eastern Parkway, s w cor Amboy st. Sept. 14, 3 years, 5 %. See Conveys. 315

Same to same. Eastern Parkway, s s, 25 w Amboy st. Sept. 14, 3 years, 5 %. See Conveys. 1,260

Prehn, Henry M. to Christiana F. Wallace. Prospect av, w s, 536 n Greenwood av, 12.6x125. Sept. 15, due Nov. 1, 1896. gold, 800

Radcliffe, Thomas H. to Horatio S. Stewart. McDonough st, s s, 81 e Ralph av, 19x90. Sub. to mort. $5,500. Aug. 29, 1 year. 1,000

Ransom, James F. to Charles E. Rogers. 10th st, n e s, 97.10 n w 8th av. 200x100. Sub. to morts. May 27, demand. 10,000

Reynolds, William W. to Charles Seidler. Glenada pl, w s, 50 s Decatur st, 50x85. Sept. 8, 1 year. 15,247

Richardson, Hester A. wife of and George M. to The Title Guarantee and Trust Co. Woodbine st. P. M. Sept. 16, 3 years, 5 %. 2,000

Riechers, Louis to Jacob Zimmer. Skillman av, s s, 82 w Leonard st, 18x100. Sept. 11, 3 years, 5 %. 2,500

Same to same. Skillman av, s s. 64 w Leonard st, 18x100x21.5x100.1. Sept. 11, 3 years, 5 %. 2,500

Rinaldi, Pauline to James and Catharine Hothersall. Jay st. P. M. Sept. 15, 5 years, 5 %. 4,000

Roach, Mary widow to William F. Corwith. Greenpoint av, s s, 93.9 e Eckford st, runs east 25 x south 35.10 x south 24 x west 29.6 x north 67.8. Sept. 10, 3 years. 1,100

Robinson, John to John Dill, Jr. Prospect pl, s s, 150 w Buffalo av, 75x127.9; Buffalo av, w s, 52.9 s Prospect pl, 51x100. Aug. 25, due July 1, 1892. 1,500

Rogers, William R. to Mary E. Seaman, Hempstead, L. I. 48th st, n e s, 160 s e 4th av, 20x100.2. Sept. 1, 3 years, 5 %. 2,800

Rozell, Henry M. to Amelia C. Van Cliff. Clinton av, w s, 103 n Park av, 23x100. Aug. 28, 2 years. 1,000

Ryan, Annie wife of and Edmund to Otto Huber Brewery. Ryerson st, w s, 237 s Myrtle av, 25x100. Sub. to mort. $2,000. Aug. 31, due Oct. 1, 1891, 5 %. 1,200

Ryan, John and Margaret his wife to Frederick Behrens trustee Frederick Behrens dec'd.

Walworth st. P. M. Aug. 28, due Sept. 1, 1892, 5 %. 2,000

Schiner, Adam to Henry Gerhard. Kingsland av, n e cor Division pl, 25.6x103x25x108. Sept. 15, 5 years, 5 %. 500

Schoefer, Henry J. to John Dill, Jr. Gates av, n s, 80 w Vanderbilt av, 20x75. ½ part. Sept. 15, due Nov. 1, 1891. 135

Schreiner, John G. to Henry and Annie Schreiner. Ashford st, e s, 282.6 s Fulton st, 25x100. Sept. 9, due Sept. 1, 1894, 4½ %. 1,000

Schreppers, Raynold C. to Robert S. Neely. Pacific st. P. M. Sept. 12, installs. 486

Schwarz, William to Lewis S. Goebel. Quincy st. P. M. Aug. 1, due Sept. 9, 1894, 5 %. 2,100

Schwerzel, Catharine wife of and Andreas to William Hoffman et al. trustees Daniel Webster Council No. 516 American Legion of Honor. Floyd st, s s, 227.6 w Tompkins av, 19x100. Sept. 8, 1 year, 5 %. 1,500

Seidenbergh, Abraham and Rochmiel Abramovitz to Earl A. Gillespie, Woodhaven, L. I. Livonia av, s e cor Osborn st. 20x100. Sub. to morts. $1,500. Sept. 14, installs. 1,000

Same to Mary W. Smith. Same property. Sept. 5, due Nov. 10, 1891. 500

Seligman, Henry to The Equitable Co-operative Building and Loan Assoc. 61st st, n s, 380 w 11th av, 20x100, New Utrecht. Sept. 4, installs. 2,250

Sgier, Joseph N. to Mary E. James. Harman st, n w s, 375 n e Knickerbocker av, 25x100. Aug. 30, 1 year, 5 %. 700

Shatt, Morris to Herbert C. Smith. Watkins st. P. M. Sept. 8, installs. 400

Shaw, Lizzie A., Finderne, N. J., to Warren B. Sammis, Edgewater, N. J. Winthrop st, n e cor East 45th st, runs north 421.4 x east 200 to East 46th st, x south 423.2 to Winthrop st, x 200; East 46th st, e s, 100 n Winthrop st, runs north 324.1 x east 200 to Schenectady av, x south 328.8 x west 200; Schenectady av, n e cor Winthrop st, runs north 100 x east 100 x west 20 x west 100 to av, x north 40 x east 100 x north 80 x west 100 to av, x north 90.4 x east 200 to East 48th st, x south 434.9 to Winthrop st, x west 200, Flatbush. Sept. 12, 3 years. 2,500

Shoobert, Emma to James E. Seaman. Powell st. P. M. Sept. 14, installs. 600

Sibley, Albert to William S. and Thomas Ross. Quincy st, s s, 437.6 w Throop av, 18.9x100. Sub. to mort. $4,000. Sept. 10, 2 years. 1,500

Same to same. Quincy st, s s, 456.3 w Throop av, 18.5x100. *Mt.* $4,000. Sept. 10, 2 years. 1,500

Same to Andrew D. Baird. Quincy st, s s, 287.6 w Throop av, 7 lots, each 18.9x100. 7 morts., each $500. Sub. to 7 prior morts. aggregating $28,000. Sept. 9, 1 year. 3,500

Sibley, Albert to William and Theodore Kilian, of Kilian Bros. Quincy st, s s, 493.9 w Throop av, 18.9x100. Sub. to mort. $4,500. Sept. 10, 2 years, 5 %. 1,000

Smith, Henry F. to Jacob T. Van Siclen. Van Siclen av, e s, 275 n Blake av, 50x100. Sept. 9, 3 years. 1,600

Smith, Marion C. to Augusta M. Hobe. Bergen st. P. M. Sept. 15, 1 year, 5 %. 1,300

Spaeth, Frank to Jacob Boslet. Jefferson st, s s, 175 e Knickerbocker av. P. M. Sept. 15, due Sept. 11, 1893, 5 %. 1,100

Spangenberg, Caroline E. wife of and Leonard, Plainfield, N. J., to Henry Hentz. Halsey st, n s, 156.3 e Marcy av, 18.9x100. Sept. 5, 6 months, 5 %. 1,000

Stearns, Horace W. to Juliette A. Raymond. Washington av, s e cor De Kalb av, runs south 17.6 x east 82 x south 1.6 x east 23 x north 19 to De Kalb av, x north 105. Sept. 12, 3 years, 5 %. 15,000

Same to same. Washington av, e s, 17.6 s De Kalb av, runs south 28.6 x east 110.5 x north 46 to De Kalb av, x west 5.6 x south 19 x west 23 x north 1.6 x west 82. Sept. 12, 3 years, 5 %. 5,000

Stern, David mortgagor with John Holsten. Extension of mortgage. Sept. 14. nom

Steingotter, Philip to Jacob Kiefer. Bushwick av, s w s, 89 n w Van Voorhis st, 18x75. Sept. 14, due July 1, 1894, 5 %. 4,000

Stichter, Phillip J., Anna, Elizabeth and Barbara to Margaret Stevenson. Bridge st, w s, 16.3 s Tillary st, 21.9x80.8x16.8x80.3. Sept. 3, 3 years. 500

Stoddard, Lucy E. to George Merchant. Degraw st, s s, 217.10 e 3d av, 240x100. Sept. 5, 1 year. 10,000

Stoll, Joseph to Odile Orthlieb. Willoughby av, s s, 150 e Hamburg av, 25x100. Sept. 10, 4 years, 5 %. 1,000

Stone, Arthur G. mortgagor with Thomas H. Lowerre, Jr., mortgagee. Extension of mort. Sept. 14. nom

Storms, Tinea wife of and Emile H. to The Title Guarantee and Trust Co. South Portland av. P. M. Sept. 8, due March 14, 1892. 1,000

Sumner, William O. to Edward M. Townsend exr. Belinda R. Townsend. 3d st. P. M. Sept. 8, due Sept. 9, 1894, 5 %. 3,250

Swimm, Frank C. to The Title Guarantee and Trust Co. Halsey st, s s, 349.4 e Reid av, 50.8x100. Sept. 10, demand. 11,250

Szyszka, Otto to Sarah Chatterley. Bergen st. P. M. Sept. 16, 6 years, 5 %. 2,550

Thatcher, John to James McLaren. Park av, s w cor North Elliott pl, runs west 40.1 x south 85.6 x west 23.10 x south 10.4 x southeast 29.4 to centre old Division st closed, x southwest 10.11 x east 58.3 w North Elliott pl, x north 100.10; North Elliott pl, w s, 125.10 s Park av, 75x106 to centre old Division st, x81.6x70.4; Park av (Tillary st), n s, at intersection with centre line of old Division st, at point 102.6 e Canton st, x north 102.3 x west 25 x south 102.3 to av, x east 25. Sept. 15, 3 years, 5 %. 20,000

Tieleke, Caroline R. wife of August to John Ranken. Madison st, n s, 137.6 e Ralph av, 18.9x100. Sept. 10, 1 year, 5 %. 3,048

Trinity Presbyterian Church to Lili Galschiot, Elsinore, Denmark. Marcy av, s w cor Jefferson av, 100x100. Sept. 9, 3 years, gold, 8,000

Van Deverig, John H. to Thomas C. Balderson et al. Supreme trustee of Order of Tonti. Sackett st, n s, 297.10 e 2d av, 60x100. Sept. 15, 3 years, 5 %. 5,500

Varuna Boat Club to The Peoples Trust Co New York Bay, bet 57th and 58th sts, boat house; also, Atlantic av, Nos. 164–168, gymnasium. Notes. 5,000

Vien, Francis X. to Doris Wilke. Nelson st, s s, 160 e Court st, 40x100. July 1, 3 years, 5 %. 1,800

Vogel, Veronika to William G. and Charles F. Wehr. Evergreen av. P. M. Sept. 10, 3 years. 700

Voorhies, Edmund W. to Gerrit H. Wyckoff. Ocean av, w s, 86.7 s Av Q, 251.7x86.7, Gravesend. Sept. 14, 3 years. 2,000

Vose, Isabel M. to The Dime Savings Bank, Brooklyn. Eastern Parkway, n e s, 70 n w Utica av, 70x220.7 to Degraw st. Sept. 12, 1 year, 5 %. 1,500

Watjen, Anna S. widow and Christopher H. Steinkamp to Louis Stroening and Dorothea his wife. Lewis av, s e cor Hart st, 32x80. Sept. 10, 5 years, 5 %. 2,500

Weidner, Joseph to William F. Garrison. Melrose st. P. M. Aug. 26, due Sept. 21, 1893. 3,000

Weishaupt, Joseph G. and Hermann Thielemann to Caspar Lucke. Herkimer st. P. M. Sept. 15, installs. 1,275

Wells, Fannie E. to Julius Steinwender. Fort Greene pl, w s, 171.6 s Lafayette av, 21.3x100. Aug. 29, 1 year, 5 %. 1,000

Wicke, Otto A. to The Williamsburgh Savings Bank. Myrtle av, n s, 20.6 w Himrod st, runs west 28 x north 64.9 x northeast 5.4 x southeast 30.6 x southeast 5.5 x south 42.10. Sept. 9, due in Sept., 1892, 5 %. 3,500

Same to Henry and John Von Glahn. Same property. P. M. 2d mort. Sept. 9, installs. 4,330

Williams, Susan to The East Brooklyn Savings Bank, Brooklyn. Cumberland st, e s, 187.3 n Myrtle av, 25x100. Sept. 16, 1 year, 5 %. 5,000

Williamson, William V. to Milton J. Bennett. 81st st, n s, 270 w 3d av, New Utrecht. P. M. Sept. 12, 6 months. 900

Wissmuller, Karl K. to Henry Ries. Sterling st, n s, 200 w New York av, runs north 100 x west 70.6 to Canarsie av, x south 101.9 to st, x east 51, Flatbush. Sept. 10, 3 years, 5 %. 650

Zeh, Philip to Edward T. Hunt exr. Thomas Hunt. 5th av, n w cor 23d st, 100x75. Sept. 7, 3 years, 5 %. 11,500

MORTGAGES----ASSIGNMENTS.

NEW YORK CITY.

SEPTEMBER 11 TO 17—INCLUSIVE.

Austin, Joseph E. to Matthew J. Lamarche. $3,500

Same to same. 1,500

Same to same. 1,000

Barnes, William D. as general guard. to John H. Van Antwerp. 2,500

Blackwell, Robert W. exr. and trustee James M. Mills to The Brooklyn Trust Co. trustee for Charlotte A. M. Blackwell. order of Court

Same to Franklin Trust Co. trustee for Ellen M. Blackwell. order of Court

Bonnell, John H. to Robert L. Harrison. nom

Barbour, William D. and ano. exrs. Margaret S. Barbour and Norman Barbour et al. exrs. Elizabeth Huntington to Marie Hoehr. 12,597

Cooper, Robert W. to Ann Boylan. 3,000

Clark, Edward S., Cooperstown, N. Y., to Alfred C. Clark general guard. of Robert S. Clark. 20,000

Cheever, John H. to Arthur P. Heinze guard. of Florence De L. Virginia and Tracy S. Buckingham. 2,700

Dempsey, William to Daniel Haggerty. 1,000

Davenport, William B. and ano. exrs. Samuel Cardwell to John Morris trustee Elizabeth Morris. order of Court

Fisher, Edward, Eastchester, N. Y., to Jessie Gifford, Eastchester, N. Y. 400

Godwin, Joseph H. to Benjamin C. Wetmore admr. William C. Wetmore. 10,000

Gwynne, David E. to Maria N. Anderson, Rondout, N. Y. 1,500

German-American Real Estate Title Guarantee Co. to Anson P. Stokes trustee Elizabeth S. Slade. 18,000

Guggenheimer, Randolph to Moses Weinman. 5,000

Guggenheimer, Randolph to Marie Staats. 3,000

Grabau, Henry and Lizzie to Gustav Lange. 1,700

Henn, Mary to Randolph Guggenheimer. 5,000

Hynard, Halsted C. admr. Eliza T. Hynard to George E. Hoe. 7,500

Hartwig, Dorothea to Edward F. Hassey. 3,000

Hassey, Edward F. to Emile A. Hassey. 3,000

Kirke, Agnes S. to Catharine J. McGuire. 2,000

Le Compte, Frank S. and ano. exrs. Susan Le Compte to Mary A. Easton, Summit, N. J. 10,000

Lansing, George R. to Isabel Eldridge. consid. omitted

Leggett, E. Howard exr. Mary B. Clapp to George L. Prentiss. nom

Livingston, Anna T. and Charles L. beneficiaries of will of Ludlow Livingston to Eugene Kelly & Co. 10,000

McCann, John, Brooklyn, to John McConvill. 15,333

Merrill, Edward B. trustee Ludlow Livingston dec'd to Anna T. and Charles L. Livingston. nom

Middlebrook, Frederick J., Brooklyn, to B. Anna R. Seymour. 1,000

Mayer, Alexander J. to Eliza Jacobs extrx., &c., Aaron Jacobs. 17,430

Morgenthau, Henry to Moses Goldsmith. 2,800

Ottinger, Marx and Moses to George W. Gallinger. 4,555

O'Connor, Thomas H. exr. John F. O'Connor to The Farmers' Loan and Trust Co. trustee John F. O'Connor. nom

Prochazka, Josefa to Joseph Wirth, Brooklyn. 200

Pyke, William C. M. and Etta Forgotston to Margaretta L. Shirley. 2,500

Peck, Edwin H. to Julia E. wife of Edwin H. Peck. 10,000

Potter, Jane guard. Mira A. Bowie formerly Potter to Jessie C. McBride, Arverre, N. Y. 1,000

Real Estate Loan and Trust Co. to William Whitlock. nom

Rieser, Jacob to Jacob Schlosser exr. and trustee Christian L. Nunnenkamp. 6,120

Rosendorff, Morris to George J. Schamberger. 4,066

Same to Jacob Schlosser. 5,041

Simon, Kaufman to George B. Ashley. 400

Smoley, Morris to Abraham Brown and Isaac Hatt. 2,118

Stone, Samuel H. to Lewis Leining. 4,000

Stier, Joseph F. to John J. Hughes. nom

Seybel, Daniel E. to Jane Stammers. 1,800

Same to Anne S. Sclater and ano. trustees for Annie Van Vlack. 1,533

Sheady, Martha M. individ. and as guard. of Anna A., Maria, Martha L., George and Archibald M. Sheady to Anna A. Sheady. nom

Sturges, Isabel V. guard. of Isabel and Thomas K. Sturges to The American Surety Co., of New York. 1,000

The House of Rest for Consumptives to St. Lukes Hospital in the City of New York. Rerecorded. 19,000

Title Guarantee and Trust Co. to The Hudson City Savings Institution. 8,500

Title Guarantee and Trust Co. to The German Society, of New York. 5,000

Title Guarantee and Trust Co. to The American Employers' Liability Ins. Co. 7,500

Winslow, Edward to William N. Crane trustee. nom

Weinman, Rachel to Elkan Levinger. 3,000

Willits, Amy, North Hempstead, L. I., to Mary H. Stone. 600

Washburn, Wilbur F. to The First Nat Bank of Yonkers. nom

KINGS COUNTY

SEPT. 10 TO 16—INCLUSIVE.

Axelrod, Jacob and Davis to Rope & Co. $850

Brush, Mary E. to Mary W. Smith. 1,000

Boldt, Henriette admrx. of John H. or Henry Wicke to Henriette Boldt. 500

Same to same. 1,821

Same to same. 1,000

Brown, George R. to Harry H. Lawson. 1,250

Broadway Bank of Brooklyn to Margaret Schauf. 1,500

Condict, Silas to Daniel S. Arnold. 3,000

Cook, Thomas H. to Louise Cook. 200

Cruse, Bernard to John Pfortner. 1,200

Cowenhoven, Mary E. and Garret exrs. Jacob V. D. Cowenhoven to Mary E. Cowenhoven. 3 assigns. nom

Same to same. 1,500

Dobbin, Robert J. to Agnes Van Hagen. nom

Davison, Charles M. exr. John M. Davison to Sarah W. Davison. 1,016

Dougherty, Mary to Louise Cook. 430

Earle, Ella C. to Ann E. Buckley. 1,515

First Nat. Bank, Brooklyn, to William Laytin et al. exrs. and trustees William Laytin. 5,600

Fortesque, George O., Buffalo, N. Y., to George C. Case. 2,250

Franke, William B. to Henry Frank. 1,000

Greenebaum, Henry to Beinecke & Co. 1,100

Horowitz, Isaac to Louis Bossert. 2,800

Hadden, Crowell, President Long Island Bank to exrs. of estate of Elbert Carll. 1,000

Handler, Moritz to Joseph H. Strauss. 400

Heubach, Amanda W. to Oscar S. Straus. 1,800

Jackson, William H. to Catharine E. Rowland, Woodhaven Junction, L. I. 1,800

James, Mary E. wife of Darwin R. to Anna L. Short and ano. exrs. John J. Pettit. 4,000

Kenedy, Patrick J. to Lawrence A. Whitehill. 2,075

Klees, Annie to William Horst. 550

Konwenhoven, William H. to Susan C. Strain. 4,500

Koehler, Anna B. to Jacob Manneschmidt. 3,000

Livingston, Anna T. and Charles L. to Eugene Kelly & Co. 1,000

Merrill, Edward P. trustee Ludlow Livingston to Anna T. and Charles L. Livingston. nom

Morse, Daniel P. to Annie Fawcett. 2,000

Meyer, Minnie to Joseph Liebmann. nom
Murphy, James to John Teeney. 4,500
Norris, William H. and William Bowers to Albro J. Newton. nom
Pacific Fire Ins. Co. to The Title Guarantee & Trust Co., New York. 3,750
Pearson, Theodore to Albro J. Newton. 1,500
Pettengill, Georgianna H. wife of Samuel M to George W. Banker. 4,000
Powell, Mary and ano. admrs. Richard Powell dec'd to D. Frank Powell. 1,500
Same to same 2,000
Same to John G. Powell. 2,500
Same to same. 2,000
Same to same. 1,500
Same to same. 4,000
Same to Mary Powell. 1,200
Powell, Sarah H. to Hannah Willets, North Hempstead, L. I. 7,500
Reed, Frances M. to Andrew F. Kindberg. 5,000
Rope, William W. to Francis H. Folliard. 900
Rust, Charles D. to The Title Guarantee and Trust Co. 5,500
Reid, David C. to Louisa M. Crane 500
Reynolds, Jennie C. B. to Silas A. Condict. 2,400
Seberry, Anna M. to Marie S. Ring widow. 500
Smith, Henry F. exr. Rosa A. Smith to Charles H. Wadsworth. 800
Smith, Mary W. to Mary E. Brush. 1,650
Stern, David to Leopold Michel. nom
Sweet, Stephen to Virgil Comfort. 600
Stewart, Horatio S. to Grace Hunter. 1,000
Struse, Otto F. to Catherine Kenna. 1,400
Taylor, Henry to John L. Wadsworth. 724
The Brooklyn Methodist Episcopal Church Home to Winifred A. Ingraham. 2,000
The Niagara Fire Ins. Co. to Christine Grote. 700
Title Guarantee and Trust Co. to Brooklyn Trust Co. 8,500
Same to same. 8,500
Same to same. 8,500
Same to Josephine Campbell. 2,000
Same to Wilkins U. Greene. 5,000
Same to John Turner. 1,500
Same to Robert Reiners. 4,000
Same to same. 4,000
Same to same. 4,000
Same to Martha G. Reiners. 5,000
Same to Robert Reiners. 2,000
Same to D. Stuart Dodge. 5 assigns., each $7,500. 37,500
Same to Peekskill Savings Bank. 4,000
Same to same. 3 assigns., each $2,000. 6,000
Same to same. 2,500
Same to same. 1,500
Same to same. 4,500
Same to same. 5,000
Same to same. 4,500
Same to Eunice R. Franke. 5,500
Same to The Brooklyn Trust Co. 6 assigns., each $4,000. 24,000
Same to same. 950
Same to John B. Wade exr. George Wade. 5 assigns., each $4,000. 20,000
Underhill, Edward C. exr. Abraham Underhill to William Crane. 1,100
Vail, John H. to John H. Rowland. 2,500
Van Hagen, Allen to Robert J. Dobbin. nom
Vanderveer, Sarah J., Newtown, L. I., to Lawrence A. Whitehill. nom
Wahl, John to Jacob Manneschmidt. 4,000
Whitehill, Lawrence to Marie L. Linington. 5,1?2
Williamson, John to Grace Giberson. 3,000
Weil, Samuel to Amelia and Babette Plaut. 4,000
Weild, David to James S. Anderson. 700

JUDGMENTS.

In these lists of judgments the names alphabetically arranged, and which are first on each line, are those of the judgment debtor. The letter (D) means judgment for deficiency. (*) means not summoned. (†) signifies that the first name is fictitious, real name being unknown. Judgments entered during the week, and satisfied before day of publication, do not appear in this column, but in list of Satisfied Judgments.

NEW YORK CITY.

Sept.

13 Ainsworth, James—Holmes, Booth & Haydens $169 84
13 Asmus, Charles—Atlantic White Lead and Linseed Oil Co 95 10
14 Alger, Byron—N Y Soap and Chemical Co 82 40
14 Angervine, William—N Y Soap and Chemical Co 101 33
14 Andress, Charles W—C De H Brower 571 34
14 the same——H W Andress, Sr 1,021 34
15*Ansel, Mary—J S Stern 208 80
15 Abraham, Sigismund—W H Thorne 103 02
15 Arthur, Edward—F R Wood 38 37
15 Ames, John F—C D Haines 120 32
18 Alden, John B—Adolph Alexander 154 67
18 Atkinson, John H G—E L Goodsell 1,862 53
12 Backer, Abraham—Isaac Sanger 13,366 29
12 Brook, Charles W—A D Thompson 119 86
14 Bechstedt, Charles F—Ferdinand Sulzberger 362 58
14 the same——N Y Veal and Mutton Co 133 36
14 Barcalow, George B—Joseph Marshall 2,704 63
14 Barry, Michael H—Edison General Electric Co 213 04
15 Beuscher, Henry M—Michael Moloughney 126 84
15 Backer, Abraham—Jacob Pollock 25,019 49
15 Backer, Abraham—Caroline White 6,064 46
15 Barkhausen, Charles—George Schmitt 330 39
15 Backer, Abraham—Alfred Wolf 7,558 89
15 the same——V H Rothschild 16,786 10
16†Borgwardt, Francis—G B Weiss 228 00
16 Butler, Frank—Timothy Harrington 86 38
16 Bowman, James H—G F Lewis 29 18
16 Boulter, William A—T B Harkins Foundry Co 157 45
17 Barcalow, George B—G F Perkins 384 38
17 Baldwin, Theron—J W Mitchell 51 64
17 Bailey, William—William Barr Dry Goods Co 250 37
17 Blake, Patrick J—Marvin Safe Co. costs 57 19
17 Beaudet, George E—Wight Fire Proofing Co 399 94
17 Bonnell, John Harper—Chatham Nat Bank 906 74
17 Bell, William—Peter Benson 29 87
17*Beaumont, George—W T Bradley 1,144 79
18 Blohm, Charles—W H Henneberger 1,238 43
18 Backer, Abraham—S H Eckman 10,054 37
18 the same——Macon Hardware Co, of Macon, Ga 4,512 46
18 Barnes, Oliver W—R J Horner 5,422 43
18 Balcazar, Romulo—T G Thomas 425 80
18 Bonnell, John Harper—Bank of N Y Nat Banking Assoc 1,581 97
18 the same——the same 1,270 21
18 Beck, Francis E—Henry Iden 147 75
12 Conkling, Sarah L—D E Palmer 1,505 58
15 Colgan, George A—J F Spaulding 80 89
15 Cohen, Solomon, as Marshall—W F McDonald 164 13
15 Crennan, Timothy S; Crennan, William J—Pratt & Lambert 212 68
15 Cumins, Patrick; Cummins, James; Cummins, Mary—Julius Schulow, assignee 136 05
16 Cragin, William B—C S Day 73 86
16 Christy, James D—S D Bruce 62 75
16 Cahill, Edward Hamilton—Abraham Siegel 90 00
17 Caulfield, John T—Ignaz Weissenhorn 68 60
17 Crosher, James—Charles Urbanek 126 10
17 Chipman, Albert E—F A Hall 122 24
17†Carroll, James T—J S Ford 83 40
12 Durrand, O Michel—James Simpson costs 34 71
15*Daily, James A—J F Spaulding 80 69
15 Doran, Myles—Hermann Weiller 270 22
16 Donnelly, Edward—H B Claflin Co 1,255 57
16 Dreyer, Henry H—Samuel Maas 122 50
17 Dumont, James A—Walter Scott 29 42
17 De Murguinodo, Carter—J T Bildebrand 61 49
17 De Wolf, David R; De Wolf, Joseph B—W T Bradley 1,144 79
18 David, George G; David, Bertha—A Kremer Brewing Co 259 87
12 Ewing, Justus E—John Canavan 129 85
14 Edelmuth, Louis—Samuel Goodfriend 257 98
14 Eggenberger, Ulrich—J J Niederer 100 37
15 Emerich, Clara—Edward Baker 83 41
16 Eisele, Daniel—F E Haines 248 48
16 Elsbre, William C—C A Morrill 7,978 01
18 Elzer, Louis—Louis Hoopes 155 68
12 Finley, Henry H—Ransom Parker, Jr costs 133 78
12 Freeman, Edward H—Campbell Printing Press and Mfg Co 232 98
14 Fitzgibbon, Maurice—Joseph Marshall 2,704 63
15 Franke, Otto; Franke, John—H W Schloman 109 00
15 the same——O J Eggers 247 58
15 the same——C B Knapp 114 81
15 the same——G H Tobias 223 60
15 the same——Louis Lehn 521 35
15 Fechheimer, Sigmund—Caroline White 6,064 46
15 Franke, Otto; Franke, John—Armin Fritze 415 12
15 Fellows, Franklin J—D A Vanhorne 144 59
15 Franke, Otto; Franke, John—L J Behringer 60 02
15 Frank, Michael—John Fleming 94 33
17 Fitzgibbon, Maurice—G F Perkins 384 38
17 Filkens, Grace—Max Goldsmith 324 00
18 Frank, Herman—G W MacLean, recvr 154 10
12 Gleason, Timothy—Henry Sproessig 28 12
12 Gerth, Frank—C H Unverzagt 760 07
15 Gillet, Marie—J S Stern 208 80
15 Greim, Wilhelmina—Phillippina Suas 64 84
16 Griesmeyer, Charles—W O Wyckoff 283 30
17 Gilmartin, James—G H Averdieck 796 00
17 †*Gunn, John; †Grant, Jan—Dominick Williams 14 00
17 Grady, Joseph; Graynor, John W—Peter Smith 1,454 07
17 Graynor, John W——the same 1,289 79
17 Grady, Joseph; Graynor, John W—the same 896 74
18 Gordon, Benjamin—Horace Galpen 775 37
18 Gorman, John M—D G Yuengling, Jr, Brewing Co 1,202 29
12 Handler, Joseph—J C Geissel 186 15
12 Haas, Carl—Consumers' Cigar Mfg Co 143 24
12 Harvey, Charles T—Solomon Loeb 1,318 08
12 Hessman, John—Mary Innes 418 30
12 Hagar, James W—Campbell Printing Press and Mfg Co 232 98
14 Howell, Eugene N—Importers and Traders' Nat Bank 9,048 95
14 Harris, Isaac K—J G Johnson 403 05
14 Hecker, Maud D—William Walsmann 217 74
15 Hannegan, Mary E—Joseph Schappert 30 09
15 Hutton, John W—Frank Smith 140 44
15 Harper, William D—St Nicholas Bank 944 31
15 the same——Western Nat Bank 822 39
16 Haas, Frank—J L Morgan 81 54
16 Hanover, Henry—John Draher 763 24
16 Holohan, Patrick—Excelsior Dynamite Co 76 16
16 Hillier, Henry E—James Thomson 753 20
16 Hazard, Roland N; *Hazard, John C; *Hazard, Herbert—C W Mulford 33 67
16 Hartung, Lorenzo R—P & F Corbin 118 89
17 Heyman, Leopold—J W Windecker 222 29
17 Harper, William D—Chatham Nat Bank 906 70
17 Heineman, Louis—Katy Fische 103 60
18 Harper, William Durbin—Bank of N Y Nat Banking Assoc 1,581 97
18 the same——the same 1,270 21
17 Irvine, Allan A—W T Bradley 1,144 79
15 Jones, William F—Charles Hurst 329 48
17 Johnson, Susie R—William Resquin, Jr 98 03
14 Krumm, Charles—Leiberger & Oehm Brewing Co 96 44
15 Kelly, Thomas—A B Powell 482 06
16 Koziell, Francis A—Peter Losowski 134 75
16 Kolb, Louise—Mary Bullowa 73 29
16 Kehoe, John—W J Young 69 06
17 Kalisber, Joseph—Francis Hager 102 56
18 Katz, Ferdinand—Lucius Hart 848 36
18 Katz, Sarah——the same 1,961 16
12 Lowe, F Augustus—Ami K Strang 211 40
15 L'Hommedieu, Sylvester Y—J H Lyon 1,210 50
15 Luhring, John H—Emil Krulich 133 82
17 Leverich, Henry M—E F Randolph 205 79
18 Lentz, Henry—Henry Tietjen 49 11
12 Meeker, William B—Charles Seale 153 84
14 Morelli, Felice—Vincenzo De Vito 319 62
14 Muller, Conrad, Jr—John McCormick 97 49
14 Meyer, Gesene—George Gennerich 260 41
14 Mitchell, Charles R—C De H Brower 571 34
14 the same——H W Andress, Sr 1,021 34
14 *Miller, Louis A; Moore, Gilbert—Metropolitan Telephone and Telegraph Co 23 41
14 Munzinger, John C—F C Gleason 155 10
15 Miller, Nathan G—Barstow Stove Co 70 91
15 Meyer, Samuel—Hyatt Co 128 60
15 Miner, Theresa—John Illig 44 55
15 Manners, Charles—John Fleming 94 33
16 Motley, William M—C F Nagel 51 00
16 Mann, William D—Grant Squires 139 55
16 Meagher, James—T J Dunn 897 65
16 Marx, Kossuth; Marx, Jacob; Marx, Adolph—F F Bioren 964 66
16 Mackie, Edward—George Cordner 128 04
16 Morrison, Richard J—C R Flint 4,238 07
17 Murphy, James—E H Van Ingen 1,616 01
17 Malmken, George—Jacob Ruppert 964 50
17 Mattmann, Candid—J D Herklotz 357 58
17 More, Mary J—E C Cockey 321 18
17 Mehrback, Isadore—H M Hitchings, recvr 1,230 62
18 Meagher, John A—G W Venable 52 70
18 Meincke, Frederick—E C Korner 285 43
18 Mason, James H—J H Haaren 94 31
18 Maguire, William—Metropolitan Telephone and Telegraph Co 28 37
12 McCahill, James L—H S Mack 306 28
14 McKenna, Patrick—Metropolitan Telephone and Telegraph Co 25 81
15 McGovern, Peter—C H Evans 70 25
16 Mackie, Edward—George Cordner 128 04
17 McKeever, John—Peter Smith 1,454 07
17 the same——the same 896 74
18 McGlynn, Patrick—Joseph Corcoran 2,376 04
14 Nierenberg, Morris—Gerson Gersbauck 981 32
16 Nesbit, John—Whitfield Terriberry 355 18
16 Neville, James J—Adolph Offenberg 234 50
18 Nesbit, William H—H P Havens 271 49
16 O'Connor, Eleanor—Richard Vom Hofe 472 12
16 O'Neill, Dennis—Lazarus Strauss 139 70
18 O'Loghlen, Thomas—Robert Gordon 114 71
18†O'Keefe, John—A E Barnes 134 88
18 O'Gorman, Mary—O K Dimock 74 17
14 Plump, Louis—F W Mertens 95 05
14 Potter, Lemott M—E M Gattle 422 37
15 Plante, Falconbridge—Matilda Plante 2,767 70
16 Purssell, Kate—James Stroud 36 83
16 Pearsall, Robert—P G Decker 40 00
17*Pearce, John—E F Randolph 205 79
17 Pomeroy, Thomas S—Peter Smith 1,454 07
17 the same——the same 896 74
17 the same——the same 1,289 79
14 Quigley, Hugh J—T J Martin 135 23
15 Rasquin, Kneppler—William Krumbeck 1,027 31
15 Rudolph, Simon—Jacob Fetbrandt 59 50
15 Rau, John—Caroline White 6,064 46
16 Ruck, John—Catskill Nat Bank 327 15
16 Rasquin, Kneppler—C T Pulsifer 510 82
16 Rehberger, Joseph H D—John Draher 763 24
16 Reardon, Michael J—J M Koehler 94 69
17 Ripley, Horace—J D Shotwell 442 94
18 Roberts, John B—Joseph Kahn 97 50
18 Richardson, Frank G—B S Donahue 74 93
18 Rich, William; *Rich, Henry—L M Levy 99 90
18 Romaine, James H—A B Powell 229 74
18 Raubitschek, Katti—Hyman Israel 629 55
18 Raubitschek, Max H——the same 551 97
18 Reynolds, James—John Brosen 170 84
12 Sheerin, Mary—James Simpson costs 34 71
12 Sonin, Solomon—E S Mashbir 30 50
12 Small, Samuel W—J B Cornish 44 15
14 Saunders, Stiles M—Theodore Von Gerichten 25 42
14 Schneider, Louis H—Metropolitan Telephone and Telegraph Co 83 19
14 Stransky, Emanuel—Alois Kohn 1,430 49
15 Stahlnecker, William A—Thomas Rand 359 50
15 Studwell, Dwight—Benjamin Wright 1,191 33
16 Stone, Howard C—L K Prince 110 97
16 Schuster, William—C B Goldthwaite 96 80

Stark, Isidore }
16 Stark, Edward J } Joseph Hirsch..... 268 23
Stark, Gustave }
16 Scott, George H—Whitfield Terriherry 355 18
16 Solscheck, Carl—Stereo Relief Decorative Co. 225 39
17 Schuyler, Samuel—First Nat Bank of Albany 2,536 78
17 Shorter, James H—Mary L Lawrence 591 75
17 Siegel, Hattie—H C F Koch 510 29
17 Speiss, August—James Hart 124 19
17 Spencer, Frank A—Peter Smith 2,482 21
17 Silverman, Robert H—The Hoffman House 335 78
17 Spencer, Frank—Peter Smith 1,454 07
17 Spencer, Frank A—the same 1,289 79
17 the same—the same 896 74
18 Steiner, Emma R—Alfred Van Beuren 153 41
18 Schoemann, Abraham—Hyman Israel 629 55
18 Schoemann, Abraham—Hyman Israel 629 55
Stark, Isidore }
18 Stark, Edward J } Lionel Sutro...... 221 14
Stark, Gustav }
14 Smith, Theophilus G—Metropolitan Telephone and Telegraph Co. 26 26
15 Smith, Waightstill A }
*Smith, Frank F } C D Haines... 120 32
15 Smith, Waightstill A—the same 120 32
17 Smith, Joel B—Northern Nat Bank (D) 16,949 48
18 Smith, Albert F—J E Callinan 479 15
18 Smith, Frederick A—J J Harrington. 104 25
12 The Willard Metal Co—Georgiana I Hotchkiss 503 61
12 The W D Wilson Printing Ink Co (Lim)—A E Ford costs 91 47
14 The Willard Metal Co—J J Zimmele. 598 88
The Manhattan Railway Co }
14 The N Y Elevated R R Co } Edith Kane.... 3,035 28
14 The N Y & Harlem R R Co—Anthony McGarry 6,591 91
15 Kneppler, Rasquin and Porr Lithographing Co—William Krumbeck 1,027 31
15 Brooklyn Consumers' Hygiene Ice Co—B B Kenyon 557 95
15 The Saxony Woolen Mills—Ellen Harrison 20,802 40
15 the same—Melissa Phelps 4,020 00
15 Richensteen Lumber Co (Lim)—J J Cooney 396 44
15 Banker & Campbell Co (Lim)—Aluminum Brass and Bronze Co 300 60
15 The Uptown Paper Co—M H Taylor 778 07
15 J H Bonnell & Co (Lim)—St Nicholas Bank 839 68
15 the same—the same 944 32
15 the same—Western Nat Bank 822 39
16 Porr Lithographing Co—C T Pulsifer. 510 82
16 Columbia Silk Co—A G Turner 152 06
16 Muller Bronze Co—C U Ely 94 90
16 Banker & Campbell Co (Lim)—T H Sweeting 1,644 96
16 The John Bonte Sons Co—J A Johnson 304 03
16 D F Foley & Co—Eberhard Faber 1,071 67
17 Willard Metal Co—W H Atwater 1,814 86
17 the same—the same 581 76
17 The U S Hydroline Co—Neil O'Donnell 1,245 14
17 The Mayor, Aldermen, &c—G W Hunt 750 00
17 Kneppler, Rasquin & Porr Lithographing Co—Albert Gray 158 37
17 J H Bonnell & Co (Lim)—Western Nat Bank 4,036 72
17 the same—the same 481 65
17 the same—the same 905 57
17 the same—St Nicholas Bank 1,528 20
17 The Standard Chemical Co—Commercial Advertiser Assoc 40 90
17 Fibrone Mfg Co—Russell Johnson 156 57
18 The Consolidated Printing and Publishing Co—P W Ostrander 327 93
18 The Mayor, Aldermen, &c—Edward Davy 130 58
18 The Henry G Allen Co—G W Millar. 1,977 56
The N Y Elevated R R Co }
18 The Manhattan Railway Co } William Ritterbusch... 760 80
18 The Mayor, Aldermen, &c—F S Beard 1,847 97
18 The Chaddock & Hickox Co—W H Chappell 213 25
18 J H Bonnell & Co (Lim)—Bank of N Y Nat Banking Assoc 1,581 97
18 the same—the same 1,270 21
18 The Chatthens & Willard Mfg Co—C L Wright 1,364 28
18 Harris & Co—James Biggart 120 60
15 Tigbi, Michael—A B Powell 482 06
15 Tucker, Milton T—D G Yuengling, Jr, Brewing Co 121 32
15 Tietzel, Ernst—William Schweckendieck 755 34
16 Thyer, Henry—J J Froelich 135 00
16 Thompson, James—Marvin Safe Co costs 51 33
17 Travis, Eugene M }
Travis, James M } Henry Schoeffler costs 86 34
17 Tangemann, Richard H—Alphons Dryfoos 114 10
16 Unser, John—G W Venable 298 78
18 Ulmer, Barbetta—Georgiana I Hotchkiss 239 18
16 Valentine, Josephine G—Louis de V Wilder 255 57
16 Viemeister, John B—Moses Weis 627 67
17 Voorhis, Jacob—Long Island City 339 84
12 Wallace, Kiernan A—Cecilia Stanton 227 46
14 Walker, George T }
Willard, Albert B } J H Lee 426 73
14 Wendelschaefer, Lena—P L Ronalds, trustee 262 65
15 Wieck, Frederick G—Thomas Mackellar, exrs and trustees 91 07
16 †Weinstein, James }
†*Weinstein, Henry } Tradesmen's Nat Bank 418 34
16 Whyte, William H—Pasquale Streppone 107 33
17 Wogan, John J—Duparquet, Huot & Monense Co 63 62

KINGS COUNTY.

Sept.

11 Adams, Frank—Tunis Lumber Co $158 28
12 Althuser, Nicholas—T H Phillips 88 77
14 Alcock, Maskalayne—J Baehr 97 00
14 Andress, Charles W—C De H Brower. 571 34
14 the same—H W Andress, Sr 1,021 34
15*Adams, Fannie A—Sims Lumber Co. 381 37
17 Ash, William H—G P & E Jacobs 126 81
12 Bowes, Henry—J G Staib 122 99
14 Bell, George H—J C & G E Gazlay 50 50
14 Bennett, Wm J—J Beck and B Stahl. 393 00
Bushfield, John C }
14 Brady, Mary A, extrx of } F R Welles, trustee.. 352 28
Brady, Philip A }
15 Barker, Adelia—G W Lounsbury, exr. 73 73
16 Bennett, William J—J & N Weser 66 57
16 Bedell, Edwin J and Hiram—T G Chamberlin 350 10
17*Burcher, Walter V—C B Keogh Mfg Co 630 74
17* the same—the same 3,252 73
17* the same—the same 630 74
17* the same—C W A Romer and J H Wilkins 478 23
17* the same—the same 106 54
17* the same—the same 322 44
17 Burns, Dennis J—H Eggers and F Hambrock 52 50
10 Cleery, John—A Worms and S Schwarzmann 126 15
11 Cassidy, Sarah—H & H Sonn 20,241 11
12 Conkling, Sarah L—D E Palmer 1,565 58
12 Cook, Henry—C & F Figge 145 26
15 Caplis, Mary E—F Seaman 33 21
17*Colgan, George A—J F & B Spaulding and J G Tewksbury 80 89
17 Craigan, George J—W R Adams and J R Glover 365 61
17 Christy, James D—S D Bruce 62 75
11 Drew, Samuel H—Title Guarantee and Trust Co 36 73
16 Doran, Myles—H Weiller 270 22
16 Donahue, Margaret F—Sullivan, Drew & Co 870 36
17 Daly, Patrick J—S Wilson 194 99
17*Daily, James A—J F and B Spaulding and J G Tewksbury 80 89
11 Eakins, Wm R—J R Bruce 1,287 88
11 Eiben, John—E Diehl 104 59
14 Ewald, Edward J—S E Ostrander and J B Peck, exrs 78 00
16 Edwards, Margaret F—Sullivan, Drew & Co 870 36
16 Fowler, Lizzie L }
*Fowler, Warren C } Feigenspan Brewing Co 331 46
16 Feigenspan, Augustus—Leibinger & Oehm Brewing Co 405 03
17 Field, William S—J M Field 2,216 89
17 Frosbrey, Henry J—G P and E Jacobs 75 77
12 Gilkinson, James—W K Murray 141 66
16 Good, Samuel R—C Parker 278 72
17 Graves, Horace—The Phenix Ins Co 398 72
17 Grotz, William F—Standard Athletic Co 77 58
17 Good, Samuel R—Ross Bros 370 72
11 Hart, Alexander R—The Chatham National Bank of New York 1,491 09
11 Henderson, Frederick D—W F Severance 134 69
11 Heveler, Hartmann—Elisa Deihl 104 59
11 Huber, August—H W Erichs 344 59
12 Haas, Carl—Consumers Cigar Mfg Co 143 22
15 Hand, Hannah M }
Hand, Parmelia } Geo W Lounsbury, as exr 73 72
16 Hess, Nathan—Commercial Bank 179 21
16 Hiller, George—Leibinger & Oehm Brewing Co 571 41
16 Haefner, Henry—R & O E Reimer 165 35
16 Hanover, Henry—J Draher 763 24
17 Hasse, Emil F—W F Hasse. 510 48
11 Jessup, John C—J R Bunce 1,287 88
11 Johnson, Susie R—W Rasquin, Jr 98 03
12 Jackson, Louis—G Henrike 329 09
16 Judson, Edward—M Bennett 71 56
11*Kirkland, William—Tunis Lumber Co 158 28
15 Kinze, Paul—E Deihe 99 20
15*Kirkland, William—Sims Lumber Co 381 37
17 Kingge, E—C Bischoff 117 57
17 Kehoe, John—W J Young 69 06
17 Kunzweiler, Hermann—King & Adams 150 79
11 Lewey, William J—F J Moulton 68 14
11 Lang, John—G Distler 122 16
15 Lawrence, Atkins—Henry Carson 84 59
16 Lincoln, Clarence—J M Graff 366 05
11 McGuire, Cornelius F—T McGovern 91 81
11 Malleson, Frederick—Randolph & Clowes 1,384 56
11 Marvin, Jr, Charles R—A LaCroix 101 49
11 Mandeville, James M—W R Adams & Co 85 24
11 McCool, Nicholas A—Sonn Bros (D) 20,241 11
11 McLaughlin, Peter F—William Massey Brewing Co 86 53
12 Morrow, James—G H Stege 227 52
14 Moylan, William—M F Phelan 146 00
14 Mitchell, Charles R—C DeHart Brower 571 34
14 the same—the same 1,021 34
15 Mills, James N—A C Haynes 100 00
17 Meyer, Gesene—G Gennerich 260 41
12 Nollman, Charles H—J Knight. 303 04
17 Neuberger, Jacob—A Adams 259 60
12 O'Connor, Peter—A Charret 85 58
15 O'Neill, Dennis—J Shaw 139 70
16 Osborne, Edwin G—Strauss & Kohns. 70 77
16†O'Brien, Daniel—P N Clarke et al, trustees 26 85
12 Pitts, John J—W H Wickham 599 30
15 Poellnitz, Charles B—Elisa Deihl. 99 20
16 Prendergast, George F—Feigenspan B Co 331 46
12 Queen, Montgomery—State Homeopathic Asylum for the Insane 121 53
11 Ross, Alexander W—A La Croix 101 49
11 Raymond, Newman H }
Raymond, Benjamin C } Ross & Snyder 126 78
16 Rehberger, Joseph H D—J Draher 763 24
17 Reynolds, William W—C B Keogh Mfg Co 630 74
17 the same—the same 3,252 73
17 the same—the same 630 74
17 the same—the same 478 23
17 the same—the same 106 54
17 the same—the same 322 44
10 Scott, Ellen E—J A De Camp 55 80
11 Scheppendick, Gustav }
Schlegel, Frederick } E Deihl 104 59
14 Searing, Theodore F—Lawrence Frazier & Co 70 96
14 Sonin, Solomon—E S Mashbir 30 50
14 Steinwedel, Eliza—L T Lazell 332 00
15 Studwell, Dwight—B Wright 1,191 38
16 Stillwell, Andrew—H J Braker. 110 86
17 Stokes, William H—L Hoopes 273 44
17 the same—the same 200 27
11 Tuohey, Michael W—T McGovern 91 31
11 Thompson, James—J Harrison 71 21
14 Terry, Ellsworth L—E L Ropkin 174 33
14 The extrx of Philip H Brady—F R Wells, trustee W B Wells, dec'd 352 28
15 The Banker & Campbell Co (Lim)—Aluminum Brass and Bronze Co 300 60
15 Thompson, James—Saugatuck Iron Works Co 298 17
16 The Brooklyn Consumers' Hygienic Ice Co—B B Kenyon 557 95
16 Thyer, Henry—B B Froehlich 155 00
17 The Muller Bronze Co—C Upham Ely. 94 90
17 Turner, William C—L Hoopes 200 27
17 Travis, Eugene M and James M—H Schoeffler 86 34
11 Van Vorst, George W—J S Dyett 92 59
10 Williams, "Ida" W, "Ida" being fictitious—A Obert 119 79
11 Wolff, William—H Egges 178 21
12 Watson, Prescott L—E Stevens 38 49
12 Walter, Ferdinand—J G Staib 122 99
15 Walker, George T and Albert B—J H Lee et al 426 73
12 Young, Annie V—Occidental Oil Co 283 16
10 Zipprian, George—Dora Ender 213 91
11 Zahler, George—Elisa Deihl 104 59
16 Ziemer, Henry—Leibinger & O B Co. 405 03

SATISFIED JUDGMENTS.

NEW YORK.

September 12 to 18—Inclusive.

Andrews, Wallace C—W H Burnet. (1888) $5,518 15
Same—J V Lewis. (1889) 92 82
Same—same. (1888) 11,190 09
Same—same. (1891) 115 79
Bagott, Richard H—H W Skerry. (1891) 500 66
Baldwin Fertilizer Co—G F Baldwin. (1891) 42,080 00
Behrens, William J—Eppens, Smith & Wieman Co. (1891) 371 94
Beker, Nathan—People State N Y. (1891) 2,000 00
Brooke, Charles W—T E Cable. (1890) 363 74
Brown, William—A B Smith. (1891) 184 20
Brennan, Thomas—Excelsior Elevator Guard and Hatch Cover Co. (1891) 225 78
Same—J A Wilson. (1891) 1,075 16
Caviuato, Luigi, Guiseppe, Natale and Steffano—William Kuhn. (1891) 959 52
*Corcoran, John B—O L Hinds. (1891) 379 42
Cohen, Lena—Charles Jacob. (1887) 527 80
Clover, Bertrand—John Ashley. (1891) 165 15
Denbosky, Morris—People State N Y. (1891) 2,000 00
Easton, William—Frederick Lee. (1885) 2,938 06
Einstein, Benjamin F—G F Baldwin. (1891) 42,080 00
Emmerich, Gustav—F L Glover. (1891) 95 39
Gent, Louis A—J H Klenke. (1891) 369 24
*Grasenauer, John—People State N Y. (1891) 2,000 00
Harstadt, Henry—G W Venable. (1891) 91 50
*Junius, Charles—People State N Y. (1883) 100 00
Kruskop, Carl—Louis Haeberle. (1886) 217 82
Kilpatrick, T Judson—C V Sidell. (1891) 146 00
Lindenborn, David—John Baehr. (1891) 406 00
Lischke, John—T J Crombie. (1888) 79 37
†Lennon, William F—David Conover. (1891) 1,799 08
McManus, Patrick H—W J de Rivera. (1891) 172 17
Mayer, Moritz—Neil McCallam. (1877) 152 12
Miller, Anna J—F M Ackerman. (1891) 95 87
Palmer, Enos C—Nellie K Ranney. (1891) 113 47
Pope, Charles—E G Barrett. (1891) 147 15
Same—same. (1890) 180 66
Slote, Aaron—Julius Stone. (1891) 221 25
Schellhaus, Ferdinand—People State N Y. (1891) 2,100 00
*Spriggs, Robert H—People State N Y. (1883) 100 00
§Same—Mary G Ganie. (1886) 92 73
Staples, Rosalie L—Edith M Davies. (1889) 2,319 96
Steinmetz, Elizabeth—W T Campbell. (1891) 2,881 98
Same—Pierce, Butler & Pierce Mfg Co. (1891) 6,616 40
Same—W F Washburn Brass and Iron Works. (1891) 955 03
Theiss, Gertrude—Josephine Nolan. (1889) 39 50
Thomas, Eddy T—Sarah Wilson. (1889) 5,323 00
Weiss, Nathan and Samuel—F L Glover. ('91). 95 39

*Vacated by order of Court. †Suspended on Appeal. ‡Released. §Reversal. ‖Satisfied by Execution.

KINGS COUNTY.

September 11 to 17—Inclusive.

Anderson, Katharine A, individ and extrx Humphrey S. Anderson—W W Culver. (1889) $88 82
Brown, William—A B Smith. (1891) 184 20
Chase, Henry A—J D Mallone. (1891) 97 19
Coffin, William H—Elliott Dash Stitching Machine Co. (1890) 174 36
Grove, Charles T—L T Lazell. (1891) 454 17
Hunger, Theodore—Elliott Dash Stitching Machine Co. (1890) 174 36
Wider, Charles A—J E Gay. (1888) 76 55
Waring, William—C L Moorehouse. (1890) 202 65
Same—E G W Dietrich. (1891) 708 02
Zeh, Philip and Philip, Jr—J A Scollay. (1890). 307 49

MECHANICS' LIENS.

NEW YORK CITY.

Sept.

14 Amsterdam av, e s, 100 n 194th st, 60x100. Charles Molten agt Louis or C. Wendel, owner, and same and H. Taylor, contractors $627 50

14 One Hundred and Seventeenth st, Nos. 360-366 W., s s, 100x100.11. Luke Highton agt Moses Samelson, owner and contractor... 435 00
14 Same property. T. K. Lemon agt same... 1,810 00
14 Tenth av, n e cor 91st st, 136.4x100. James Matthews & Son agt Edward Smith or Smith & Menken, owners, and Edward Smith, contractor. (Continued from Sept. 15, 1890) 400 00

14 Fifty-sixth st, No. 86, s s, 16.8 w 4th av, 16.8x75. G. W. Smyth and T. C. Gaff agt Ann O. Humphrey, owner, and H. Humphrey, contractor 15 00
14 Valentine av, w s, 300 n 181st st, 100x— to Ryer av. Julius Kaesemeyer agt Margaret and James Murphy, owners and contractors 24 00
14 One Hundred and Sixth st, s s, 200 e 1st av, 25x100. Graham & Burt agt Dempsey & Smith, owners and contractors 350 00
14 One Hundred and Eighteenth st, s s, 35 e Madison av, 100x100.11. Same agt Samuel Harris and Bernard and Levi B. Ginsburg, owners, and Mary Mescha, contractor ... 350 00
14 Waverley pl, No. 116, s s, 170.4 e 6th av, 22x97. Daniel Fields agt James Cunningham, owner, and John Boyle, contractor 17 00
15 One Hundred and Seventeenth st, Nos. 360-366 W., s s, 100x100.11. Albany Venetian Blind Co. agt Moses Samelson, owner and contractor 261 00
15 Same property. Traitel Bros. agt same... 1,268 75
15 Thompson st, No. 21, n w cor Grand st, 60x20.2. Lambert Hahn agt Ernest Franklin, owner and contractor 74 15
15 Madison av, s e cor 134th st, 100x100. C. E. Gates & Co. agt Thos. Jetter, owner, and Thos. B. McCormick, contractor 543 89
15 Columbus av, w s, 75.5 n 97th st, 25.3x100. George Mungo agt John Doe, owner, and John Hatch, contractor 39 50
16 One Hundred and Seventeenth st, Nos. 360-366, s s, 100 e Columbus av, 100x100.11. Joseph Donaldson agt Moses Samuelson, owner and contractor 910 00
16 One Hundred and Twenty-first st, No. 309 E. William Lukas agt Henry Schaeffer, owner and contractor 72 43
16 Claremont av, e s, 100 s Highbridge st, 45x60. Isaac Thompson agt John Doe, owner, and —— Gessiner, contractor.... 25 12
16 Tenth av, No. 490, e s, 74 n 37th st, 25x100. Schoeller & Winbladh agt Georgiana F. Webster, owner, and J. Webster, contractor 325 00

16 Courtlandt av, n e cor 150th st, 50x150. Pasquale Fiore agt Henry and J. M. Muller, owners, and Fred. Koopman, contractor, 189 86
16 Hamilton pl, e s, 38 s 142d st, 85x72. Buess & Co. agt Mary E. Stevens, owner, and Mark S. Stevens, contractor 216 25

16 Amsterdam av, n e cor 91st st, 125x100. James McDonald agt Edward Smith, owner, and George Mayer, contractor 23 00
16 Canal st, No. 503, n e cor Renwick st. Francis Muldoon agt John Lyons and Charles L. Fleming, owners, and Charles L. Fleming, contractor 200 00
16 Sixty-third st, No. 31, n s, 300 w 8th av, 37.6x100.5. J. J. Rich and Herman Goerke agt M. J. Barrow or Mrs. Barrow, owner, and John Riesinger, contractor 30 00

17 Convent av, n w cor 145th st, 100x75. M. H. Scharf agt Jacob Streifler, owner and contractor 150 00
17 Eighty-ninth st, n s, 113.4 w Madison av, 51.1x100.8. Tully & O'Connell agt Thomas Graham, owner and contractor 730 00

17 Ninety-eighth st, n s, 100 w 8th av, 25x—. Canda & Kane agt Edward J. Kelly, owner and contractor 399 00
17 One Hundred and Twentieth st, s s, 125 w 8th av, 75x—. Peter Otto agt James Thompson, owner and contractor 100 00
17 Seventy-eighth st, Nos. 164-170, s s, 200 w 3d av, 100x—. Same agt W. C. Burne, owner and contractor 163 75

17 Davidson av, w s, 130 n Fordham Landing, 50x—. Joiner Planing and Moulding Co. agt Mrs. George W. Yeandle, owner and contractor 158 49
17 Thirty-fourth st, Nos. 126 and 128, s w cor Lexington av, 95x117.6. Edison Electric Illuminating Co. agt The Lexington Improvement Co., owner and contractor.... 4,025 34
17*Morton st, Nos. 47 and 49, n s, 284.8 e Hudson st, 59.6x—. Ferdinand Gehlker agt Victoria F. Dauphinais, owner, and H. MacLaughlin, contractor 110 00
17 Thirty-fifth st, Nos. 241-245, n s, 331 e 8th av, 69x—. Pelham Hod Elevating Co. agt William H. Ramsay, owner, and George Beebe and Thomas Sanderson, contractors 260 00
18 Vandam st, Nos. 4-8, s w cor Macdougal st, 118x—x—x87. Harry McNally agt Downey & Curry, owners and contractors 3,900 00

*Editor Record and Guide:

A person named Gehlker having filed a lien against 47 and 49 Morton street I would like permission to explain the circumstances. That part of his framing contract, done by him, has been outrageously performed. When pointed out to him on this occasion he made use of obscene language, for which he received a sound drubbing—hence his malicious lien. I have a bill against him for over $960, which has been partially paid the carpenter for doing his work.

G. C. MacLaughlin, att'y.

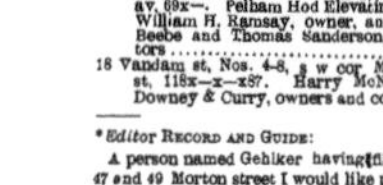

KINGS COUNTY.

Sept.

12 Glenada pl, s w cor Decatur st, 100x85. Philadelphia Fire Proofing and Brick Co. agt William W. Reynolds, owner and contractor $657 50
12 Sixth av, n w cor President st, 100x100. New York Anderson Pressed Brick Co. agt Edward Judson, owner, and Hobby & Doody, contractors 341 07
12 Manhattan av, e s, 50 s Norman av, 40x100. Holbrook Bros. agt Chas. P. Germann, owner, and Walker & Co., contractors.... 275 00
12 Thatford av, e s, 100 s Glenmore av, 50x100. Dannat & Pell agt Samuel Balsam and Maurice Hendler, owners and contractors. 795 04
12 Watkins st, w s, 100 n Sutter av, 25x100. Wyandance Brick and Terra Cotta Co. agt Elias Kaplan, owner and contractor.. 68 00
12 Same property. Potts Bros. agt same owner and contractor 172 96
14 Thatford av, e s, 100 s Glenmore av, 50x100. Michael Meyer agt Moses Hendler and Samuel Balsom, owners and contractors. 600 00
14 Seventh st, n s, 297.6 e 4th av, 50.4x100. William Kerby agt Mary E. Miller, owner, and George E. Miller, contractor...... 121 00
15 Woodbine st, n w s, 45 s w Knickerbocker av, 40x100. Matthew Bosch agt Albert Buckmeier, owner, and Anton Herbst, contractor 20 00
15 Ocean Parkway, cor Johnsons lane, Gravesend, L. I. C. A. Lundine agt J Hamblin, owner and contractor 316 00
16 Sixty-third st, n s, 240 w 14th av, 20x100, New Utrecht. Francis Ryan agt John Healey, owner and contractor 42 05
16 Sixty-sixth st, n s, 375 e 6th av, 20x100, New Utrecht. E. A. Colban agt Peter Johnson, owner and contractor 20 00
16 Belmont av, s s, 100 e Osborn st, 25x100. Martin Pearson agt Joseph Davis, owner, and Abraham Stone, contractor 11 64
16 Christopher av, e s, 200 n Belmont av, 25x100. Katie Horowitz agt Joseph Berger and Samuel Mishel, owners and contractors 26 00
16 Sixty-sixth st, n s, 375 e 6th av, 20x100, New Utrecht. Bernhard Larsen agt Peter Johnson, owner and contractor 45 00
16 Herbert st, s s, extends from North Henry st to Monitor st, 200x100. John J. Kierst agt The Roman Catholic Church of St. Cecelia, owner, and The Blue Ridge Marble Co. and Byrnes & Perry, contractors.. 600 00
16 Patchen st, w s, extends from Macon st to McDonough st, 200x100. James W. McManus agt Thomas H. Robbins, owner and contractor 225 00
16 Marion st, s s, 50 w Rockaway av, 128x100. Same agt same owner and contractor.... 750 00
17 Harrison av, e s, 25 n River st, 25x100. Jacob Willman agt Sarah Taylor, owner, and Lippmann & Taylor, contractors 41 50
17 Hancock st, n s, 90 w Central av, 380x100. Same agt same owner and contractors... 67 20
17 Weirfield st, n s, 81 w Central av, 260x100. Same agt Leopold J. Lippmann and Alexander Taylor, owners and contractors.... 482 76
17 Eighth av, e s, extends from 15th st to 16th st, 200x160. William E. Valentine agt Edward J. Bedell, William J. Fitzpatrick, Thomas McCann and William Martin, owners and contractors 65 00

SATISFIED MECHANICS' LIENS.

NEW YORK CITY.

Sept.

12 Av B, Nos. 1582 and 1584, w s, 102.2 s 82d st, 50x—. R. B. Douglas & Co. agt John Huber. (Lien filed Sept. 18, 1890)........ $637 00
12 Av B, Nos. 1582 and 1584, 50x100. Kirchoff & Brown agt John Huber. (Sept 23, '90) 950 00
14 Honeywell av, e s, 125 s Samuel st. C. E. Gates & Co. agt E. M. Bowman and L. A. Soule and D. Kent. (July 24, 1891)........ 79 20
14 Honeywell av, e s, 95 s Samuel st. Owen Tober agt same. (Aug. 21, 1891) 26 00
14 Honeywell av, e s, 100 s Samuel st. Edward Welsh and Charles Bennett agt Eugene M. Bowman and Daniel Kent. (July 24, 1891) 115 00
15‡Pike st, No. 23 / Henry st, Nos. 108 and 110 { begins Pike st, s e cor Henry st, 25x110. Philip Catlowsky and Barnett Levy agt Louis Goodman. (May 5, 1891). 4,080 00
15 Barrow st, Nos. 52 and 54, 50x100 / Grove st, Nos. 19 and 21, 50x51 } C. E. Dornbusch agt Alphonse Hogenauer and Joseph Gollick. (Sept. 1, '91). 85 00
15 One Hundred and Twenty-third st, Nos. 132-142 W., 100x100.11. Steindler & Hahn agt Elizabeth K. Smith and John Sauer. (Sept. 14, 1891) 700 00
15 West End av, No. 501, n w cor 89th st, 24x90. Jacob Wimmer agt George W. and Henry M Lawrence and The Brinkman Skylight Works. (Sept. 8, 1891) 100 00
16 Willis av, w s, extends from 134th to 135th st, —x100. A. E. Hemmel agt Cavinato Bros. (Jan. 30, 1891) 71 20
16 Thirty-first st, No. 48 E., 25x100. M. C. Foertsch agt Daly & Brung Ullrich. (Sept. 8, 1891) 76 16
16 Fifty-fourth st, No. 144 W., 18.9x100.5. Pasco & Palmer agt Alice A. Stetler or Alice De Forest. (June 19, 1891) 1,000 00
16 West End av, s w cor 103d st, 100.11x159.10. John Bell & Son agt Elizabeth Steinmetz. (Jan. 12, 1891) 912 80
16 Same property. Valentine Moeslein agt same and Welcome R. Steinmetz. (July 16, 1891) 989 50
16 Same property. William Hilgars agt Welcome R. Steinmetz. (July 15, 1891)...... 1,450 00
17 Seventy-ninth st, Nos. 200-206, s w cor Amsterdam av. L. L. Ellsworth agt Susanna H. Hagan and Thomas Osborne. (Sept. 1891) 943 50
17 Eighth av, e s, extends from 118th to 119th sts, 201.10x—. John Fox agt Philip Braender. (May 5, 1891) 776 64
17*One Hundred and Second st, Nos. 120-128 W., 100x—. Ruffus Darrow agt Joseph R. Black and Thomas J. McGuire. (July 28, 1891) 194 76
17*Twenty-sixth st, Nos. 334 and 336 E., 50x—. Isaac Motner agt McCormick & Martin and John Meyer. (Sept. 14, 1891) 11 50
17*Same property. Solomon Rothenberg agt same. (Sept. 14, 1891) 25 00
18‡Park av, Nos. 1807 and 1809, e s, 69.4 s 125th st, 62.8x—. Henry Taylor agt William H. McCarthy and John Sheehy & Son. (Sept. 1, 1891) 1,739 05

*Discharged by depositing amount of lien and interest with County Clerk.
‡Discharged by order of Court on filing bond.

KINGS COUNTY.

Sept.

10 Central av, n w s, extends from Cornelia st to Jacob st, 200x100. Joseph Hopkins agt John T. Barnard, owner and contractor. (Lien filed Aug. 3, 1891) $16,000 00
10 Watkins st, w s, 100 n Sutter av, 25x100. Louis Bossert agt Elias Kaplan, owner and contractor. (Aug. 5, 1891) 515 46
11 Shepherd av, e s, 280 n Ridgewood av, 120x102.7x120x102.5. Henry McShane Mfg. Co. agt Sebastian T. Hollister, owner and Ulysses Brown, contractor. (Sept. 10, 1891) 492 56
11 Warren st, s s, 150 e Smith st, Public School No. 6. James Harley agt Board of Education, owner, and John C. Carlin, contractor. (Sept. 5, 1891) 630 50
11 Columbia st, s e cor Amity st, 100x100. Same agt same owner and contractor. (Sept. 5, 1891) 1,375 00
11 Ralph av, n w cor Macon st, 96x112. Salvatore McCue agt Raymond Bros., owners, and John Connelly, contractor. (May 27, 1891) 63 00
11 Watkins st, e s, 175 n Blake av, 25x100. Emil Reineking agt Mrs. Danancher, owner, and Louis Ratner, contractor. (Sept. 10, 1891) (Deposit) 100 00
11 Dumont av, n w cor Thatford av, 25x100. Same agt —— Goldstein and Abram Wolf, owners, and Louis Ratner, contractor. (Sept. 10, 1891.) (Deposit) 225 00
12 Van Voorhis st, s s, 100 w Bushwick av, 75x100. Bradley & Currier Co. (Lim.) agt Frederick Amman, owner, and Amzi D. Vreeland, contractor. (Sept. 4, 1891)..... 860 00
12 Same property. J. M. Pilcher & Co. agt same owner and contractor. (Sept. 8, 1891) 460 00
12 Van Voorhis st, s e s, 100 s w Bushwick av, 75x100. Lewis Finch agt Frederick Ammon, owner, and Amzi D. Vreeland, contractor. (Sept. 8, 1891) 215 00
12 Same property. G. F. Every agt same owner and contractor. (Sept. 4, 1891).... 70 00
12 Same property. E. Felgenhauer agt same owner and contractor. (Sept. 10, 1891)... 129 00
— Same property. R. G. Phelps agt same owner and contractor. (Aug. 10, 1891)... 609 19
12 Same property. Jacob Manneschmidt agt same owner and contractor. (June 4, 1891) 1,530 00
12 Same property. Hyde & Gload Mfg. Co. agt same owner and contractor. (June 4, 1891) 234 00
12 Howard av, s w cor Macon st, 94x94. Salvatore McCue agt Mr. Lincoln, owner, and John Connelly, contractor. (May 27, 1891.) 40 00
14 Central av, n w s, extending from Cornelia st to Jacob st, 200x100. Guiseppe Cannella agt Joseph Hopkins, owner and contractor. (Aug. 3, 1891) 295 00
14 Cooper st or av, s s, 125 w Evergreen av, 50x100. William Foley agt Henry Corlis, owner and contractor. (July 22, 1891) .. 24 00
15 Van Voorhis st, s s, 100 w Bushwick av, 100x100. Walter T. Klots & Brothers' Sons agt Fred. Ammann, owner, and Amzi D. Vreeland, contractor. (June 5, 1891)..... 465 34
15 Same property. C. H. Reynolds & Sons agt same owner and contractor. (Aug. 1, 1891) 660 06
15 North 7th st, No. 255, n s, 145 w Havemeyer st, 25x100. Edward Burke agt John B. Ferrall, owner and contractor. (Aug. 19, 1891) 150 00
15 Linden Boulevard, section 18 amended map Linden Terrace Beautiful Villa Plots, Flatbush. Ross & Snyder agt Anna Dudley, owner, and Edgar S. Hmoans, contractor. (Aug. 28, 1891) 812 00
15 Finnimore st, s s, 125 w Clove road, 50x80, Flatbush. John Williams agt Gaetano Pranzo, owner, and Alexander Wood, contractor. (June 12, 1891) 21 75
15 Livonia av, s e cor Osborn st, 20x100. George Scheinfeld agt Abraham Seidenberg and Rochmiel Abramovitz, owners and contractors. (Aug. 26, 1891) 1,295 00
15 Same property. Earl A. Gillespie agt same owner and contractor. (Aug. 13, 1891)... 700 00
17 De Kalb av, s s, 150 w Marcy av, 100x100. Isaac Norris agt Elizabeth S. Maitland, owner, and Charles Collins. (Sept. 15, 1891.) (Deposit) 78 25
17 De Kalb av, Nos. 676-682½, s s. Brooklyn Slate Mantel Co. agt E. J. Maitland, owner, and Charles H. Collins, contractor. (Sept. 14, 1891.) (Deposit) 425 00

BUILDINGS PROJECTED.

The first name is that of the owner; ar't stands for architect, m'n for mason, c'r for carpenter and b'r for builder.

NEW YORK CITY.

SOUTH OF 14TH STREET.

Columbia st, s e cor Rivington st, six-story brk flat, 55.6x41.8 and 35.8, tin roof; cost, $26,000; H. Fischel, 55 Norfolk st; ar't, H. Horenburger. Plan 1227.

Ridge st, n e cor Delancey st, three five-story brk flats, one 25.4x96, two 25x88, tin roofs; total cost, $69,000; Fenella Burrell, 100 Pierrepont st, Brooklyn; ar't, F. Baylics. Plan 1222.

12th st, Nos. 22-26 E., six-story brk building, 70.9x96 and 90, tin roof; cost, $35,000; W. T. Van Zandt exr., 12 Highland av, Yonkers, N. Y.; ar't, J. McIntyre. Plan 1226.

Henry st, No. 266, five-story stone flat, 31.1x95.2, tin roof; cost, $22,000; M. Solomon, on premises; ar't, C. Rentz. Plan 1230.

2d st, Nos. 385 and 387 E., frame shed, 75x22, tin roof; cost, $800; J. Rheinfrank and ano., 325 East 4th st; b'r, P. Nies. Plan 1231.

BETWEEN 14TH AND 59TH STREETS.

28th st, No. 335, and part of No. 337 E., one-story brk and stone building, 32.6x100, tin roof; cost, $15,000; E. P. Southwell, Rector, 334 East 29th st; ar't, T. H. Poole. Plan 1219.

BETWEEN 59TH AND 125TH STREETS, EAST OF 5TH AVENUE.

5th av, n e cor 60th st, four-story attic and basement marble and brk club-house, 90x185, tile and copper roof; cost, $750,000; The Metropolitan Club, R. Goelet, chairman building committee, 9 West 17th st; ar'ts, McKim, Mead & White. Plan 1221.

88th st, n s, 296 w Av B, two five-story brk and stone flats, 24.11x77, tin roofs; cost, $17,000 each; J. Schreiner, 110 West 121st st; ar't, J. Bauser. Plan 1241.

115th st, s s, 225 e Pleasant av, brk water-closet, 6x14, gravel roof; cost, $350; Standard Gas Light Co., 2 Cortlandt st; b'rs, J. & L. Weber. Plan 1238.

Av A, s e cor 74th st, four five-story brk flats, 25x73, 25.7 and 26x63, tin roofs; total cost, $65,000; F. J. Schnugg, 129 East 95th st; ar't, L. Eutzer, Jr. Plan 1235.

BETWEEN 59TH AND 125TH STREETS, WEST OF CENTRAL PARK WEST AND 8TH AVENUE.

68th st, s s, 150 e Columbus av, three five-story stone flats, 25x87.6, tin roofs; cost, $20,000 each; ow'r and b'r, P. Wagner, 844 9th av; ar't, J. W. Cole. Plan 1234.

69th st, No. 258 W., rear, one-story brk stable, 35x21, gravel roof; cost, $2,000; G. Thomson, on premises; ar't, C. H. Richter, Jr. Plan 1238.

76th st, n s, 90 w Amsterdam av, two two-story brk and stone stables, 25x95, tin roofs; cost, $12,000 each; W. B. Baldwin, 58 West 74th st; ar't, G. F. Pelham. Plan 1232.

79th st, n s, 175 w Columbus av, four-story and basement brk and stone dwell'g, 25x58, with extensions, tin roof; cost, $30,000; H. Jaeckel Grimes Hill, Staten Island, N. Y.; ar'ts, Schickel & Co. Plan 1229.

110TH TO 125TH STREET, BETWEEN 5TH AND 8TH AVENUES.

123d st, Nos 228 and 230 W., two five-story stone flats, 25x87.6, tin roofs; cost, $30,000 each; Elizabeth K. Smith, 150 West 123d st; ar't, R. R. Davis. Plan 1220.

NORTH OF 125TH STREET.

Kingsbridge road, e s, 175 n Academy st, two-story frame dwell'g, 17.6x39.6, tin roof; cost, $900; J. Corbett, Inwood, N. Y.; ar't, W. S. Berrian. Plan 1237.

132d st, s s, 374.6 e 7th av, five three-story and basement stone dwell'gs, 15x50, tin roof; cost, $8,000 each; W. McReynolds, 158 West 131st st; ar't, W. H. Boylan. Plan 1239.

23D AND 24TH WARDS.

Church st, e s, 300 s Broadway, 24th Ward, two-story frame shop, 14x16, tin roof; cost, $100; ow'r and b'r, F. M. Denton, Kingsbridge, N. Y. Plan 1223.

Courtlandt av, w s, 75 n 156th st, three-story frame dwell'g, 25x55, tin roof; cost, $6,000; H. Hohmann, 747 Courtlandt av; ar't, F. J. Miller. Plan 1224.

Cromwell av, e s, 200 n 150th st, two story frame shed, 150x16, tar and gravel roof; cost, $350; lessees, L. H. Mace & Co., Williamsbridge, N. Y.; ar't, C. T. Mott. Plan 1228.

Union av, w s, 175 n 169th st, two two-story and basement frame dwell'gs, 18x22, tin roofs; cost, $2,200 each; R. D. Barnum, 1314 Boston av; c'r, B. F. Frisbie. Plan 1225.

148th st, s s, 95.5 w Brook av, one-story brk shop, 75x48, tin roof; cost, $4,000; C. E. Hertlein et al., 266 West 127th st; ar'ts, Ogden & Son. Plan 1236.

Fairmount pl, n s, 275 w Marmion av, two-and-a-half-story frame dwell'g, 20x30, shingle roof; cost, $2,500; W. C. Littlewood, West Farms, N. Y.; ar't, J. J. Vreeland. Plan 1242.

Inwood av, n e cor Elliot st, rear, two-story and basement frame dwell'g, 30x25, tin roof; cost, $2,500; Mary Russhan, 4 West 136th st; ar't, C. F. Lohse. Plan 1243.

Vanderbilt av, e s, 100 n 186th st, two story and basement frame dwell'g, 20x35, tin roof; cost, $2,500; W. Wechwerth, 301 East 109th st; ar't, A. Spence. Plan 1240.

KINGS COUNTY.

Plan 1671—Jefferson av, n s, 80 e Bushwick av, one three-story frame (brk filled) tenem't, 20x53, tin roof; cost, $4,500; ow'r and b'r, Phillip Steingotter, 1254 Bushwick av; ar't, T. Engelhardt.

1672—Bushwick av, n e cor Jefferson av, five three-story frame (brk filled) stores, dwell'gs and tenem'ts, 20x53 and 60, tin roofs; total cost, $22,000; ow'r, ar't and b'r, same as last.

1673—Watkins st, w s, 100 n Eastern Parkway, one one-story frame tailor shop, 18x28, tin roof; cost, $400; H. Max, Eastern Parkway, near Thatford av.

1674—Evergreen av, w s, 21 n Hancock st, three three-story frame (brk filled) tenem'ts, 25x62, tin roofs: cost, total, $12,000; Lehmann Bros., 13 Sumner av.

1675—Sutter av, s e cor Hendrix st, one one-story frame store, 26x36, tin roof; cost, $300; William Miller, Sutter av and Hendrix st; ar't, A. J. Warren; b'r, J. King.

1676—Nassau av, s s, 50 e Humboldt st, five three-story frame (brk filled) tenem'ts, 25x60, gravel roofs; cost, each, $4,200; ow'r and b'r, Andrew E. Walker, 97 Milton st; ar't, F. Weber.

1677—18th st, s s, 250 w 3d av, one one-story frame dwell'g, 19x34, tin roof; cost, $850; James Crane, 127 Ellery st.

1678—Stanhope st, No. 88, one two-story frame (brk filled) dwell'g, 22x42, tin roof; cost, $3,600; I. Erhardt, 47 Harman st; ar't, T. J. Keir.

1679—Jefferson av, s s, 100 e Nostrand av, four three-story and basement brk and Lake Superior stone dwell'gs, 20x42, tin roofs, iron cornices; total cost, $33,000; Arthur C. Mason, Hancock st, near Nostrand av; ar't, M. W. Morris; b'rs, P. Cleary and J. Hiller.

1680—Macon st, s s, 62 e Ralph av, two two-story and basement brown stone dwell'gs, 18x45, tin roofs, wooden cornices; cost, each, $4,000; ow'r and ar't, John R. Pitt, 297 Stuyvesant av; m'n, J. Court; c'r, not selected.

1681—Macon st, s s, 26 e Ralph av, two two-and-a-half-story and basement brown and red stone dwell'gs, 18x45, tin roofs, wooden cornices; cost, $10,000; ow'r, ar't and b'r, same as last.

1682—Norman av, s s, 125 e Jewel st, two three-story frame (brk filled) tenem'ts, 25x55, gravel roofs; cost, each, $4,500; Margaret Beaver and Henry Stubbe, Manhattan av, near Dupont st; ar't, P. Tillion; b'rs, J. A. & W. H. Port and C. C. Gately.

1683—Moore st, No. 34, one two-story frame stable, 13.6x25, tin roof; cost, $350; S. Rath, on premises; ar't, R. Von Lehn.

1684—Park pl, n s, 250 e Utica av, one one-story frame dwell'g, 16x20, gravel roof; cost, $75; Wm. Plunkett, 994 Bergen st.

1685—Degraw st, s s, 175 e Utica av, one one-story frame stable, 18x20, gravel roof; cost, $75; Elizabeth Strang, 1004 Atlantic av.

1686—Suydam st, Nos. 168 and 170, s s, 100 e Central av, two one-story frame stables and sheds, 12x18, gravel roofs; cost, $150; Mr. Hennessy, 1070 De Kalb av; b'r, C. Franz.

1687—Huron st, No. 202, 225 w Oakland st, one three-story frame (brk filled) tenem't, 25x55, gravel roof; cost, $4,500; Timothy Desmond, 198 Huron st; ar't, C. Dunkhase; b'r, not selected.

1688—Sigourney st, s s, 100 e Court st, one one-story brk chemical works, 26x61, gravel roof, brk cornice; cost, $1,000; W. H. H. Childs, 388 Washington av; ar't and b'r, J. Waddell.

1689—Court st, e s, bet Hallock and Sigourney sts, one two-story frame (brk filled) factory (tar paper), 200x60, gravel roof; cost, $30,000; ow'r and b'r, same as last.

1690—Linwood st, w s, 75 s Eastern Parkway, one two-story frame dwell'g, 19x40, tin roof; cost, $2,000; John Monseer, Bergen st, near Rockaway av; ar't, O. S. Totten.

1691—Lewis av, s e cor Jefferson av, one four-story brk tenem't, 25x75, tin roof, iron cornice; cost, abt $12,000; ow'r and c'r, David S. Beasley, 187 Van Buren st; ar't, S. Curtis.

1692—Nostrand av, No. 398, w s, 180 s Gates av, one one-story brk greenhouse, 16.6x30, glass roof; cost, $350; ow'r, ar't and b'r, J. Y. Peek, 398 Nostrand av.

1693—Throop av, w s, 75 s Kosciusko st, one six-story brk and stone factory for patterns, 21x80, tin roof, iron cornice; cost, $14,000; Butterick & Co., Franklin av, and Monroe st; ar't and c'r, T. C. Greenland.

1694—Prospect pl, n s, 293 e Utica av, one one-story frame stable, 12x20, gravel roof; cost, $75; Philip Grass, 1427 Prospect pl.

1695—Atlantic av, n s, 25 w Georgia av, one three-story brk store and office building, 50x60, tin roof, iron cornice; cost, $15,000; Jacob W. Erregger, Pennsylvania av; ar't, A. J. Warren.

1696—Marcy av, n e cor Stockton st, one one-story brk stable, 18x16, tin roof, wooden cornice; cost, $445; F. W. Mahland, on premises; ar't and c'r, J. H. Hough; m'n, W. Langridge.

1697—Harman st, n s, 100 e Central av, two three-story frame (brk filled) tenem'ts, 25x60, tin roofs; cost, $9,000; ow'rs, ar'ts and b'rs, A. Berkmeier & Hahn, 101 Ralph st.

1698—Stockholm st, n s, 75 w Evergreen av, one two-story brk laundry, 91x22, tin roof, wooden cornice; cost, $7,000; Little Sisters of the Poor, De Kalb av and Bushwick av; ar'ts, Parfitt Bros.; b'r, not selected.

1699—2d av, s w cor 57th st, one four-story frame store and tenem't, 20x50, tin roof; cost, $5,000; Letitia Barber, 243 45th st; ar't and b'r, W. Barber.

1700—Powell st, w s, 256 n Liberty av, one two-story and basement frame (brk filled) dwell'g, 18.6x37, tin roof; cost, $2,800; ow'r and c'r, John F. Voorman, 20 Powel st; ar't, J. Vorman; m'n, J. Hennessy.

1701—Yates pl, Nos. 16 and 18, two four-story frame (brk filled) tenem'ts, 25x65, tin roofs; cost, each, $5,000; George Bere, 43 McKibbin st; ar't, H. Smith; c'r, F. Herty.

1702—Stanhope st, s s, 95 w Wyckoff av, one-and-a-half-story frame stable, 10x12, gravel roof; cost, $83; Henry Fick, 132 Wyckoff av.

1703—Hancock st, n s, 250 e Marcy av, four three-story and basement sandstone dwell'gs, 20x45, tin roofs, wooden cornices; cost, each, $6,000; Wm. H. Reynolds, Hancock st; ar't, J. D. McAuliffe.

1704—Macon st, n s, 140 w Patchen av, two three-story basement brown and red stone dwellings, 20x45, iron roofs, wooden cornices; cost, each, $5,300; A. L. Beasley, 229 Van Buren st; ar't, F. J. Lessing.

1705—Macon st, n s, 100 and 180 w Patchen av, two two-story and basement brown and red stone dwell'gs, 20x45, tin roofs, wooden cornices; cost, each, $4,500; ow'r and ar't, same as last.

1706—Chestnut st, e s, abt 520 n Fulton av, one two-story frame dwell'g, 20x35, tin roof; cost, $2,600; Margaret Messmer, 219 Somers st; ar't and c'r, C. Messmer; m'n, not selected.

1707—Snediker av, e s, 275 s New Lots road, one two-story frame dwell'g, 20x30, tin roof; cost, $1,800; Anna Leinfelder, New Lots road, near Rockaway av; ar't and b'r, C. Ratner.

1708—Fulton st, s s, 30 e Elton st, one one-story frame real estate office, 15x18, tin roof; cost, $200; A. D. Patterson, 89 Elton st.

1709—Ashford st, e s, 125 n Arlington av, one two-and-a-half-story frame dwell'g, 25x38, tin roof; cost, $3,300; ow'r and ar't, De Witt C. E. Baisley, 1550 Pacific st; W. D. Losee.

1710—Lexington av, s s, 200 e Nostrand av, four four-story brk tenem'ts, 25x52, gravel roofs, wooden cornices; cost, $11,000; ow'r and ar't, H. Toulmin, 752 Marcy av.

1711—Jefferson st, s s, 150 e Knickerbocker av, one three-story frame (brk filled) store and tenement, 25x56, tin roof; cost, $4,000; Conrad Reuter, 150 Jefferson st; ar't, F. Wunder.

1712—Halsey st, n s, 120 e Evergreen av, two two-story and basement frame (brk filled) dwellings, 20x45, tin roofs; cost, $2,500 each; K. E. Monohan, 52 Stockholm st.

1713—Monitor st, e s, 400 s Norman av, one three-story frame (brk filled) tenem't, 20x40, gravel roof; cost, $3,500; ow'r and b'r, J. Iversen, 72 Nassau av; ar't, F. Weber.

1714—Norwood av, w s, 125 s Fulton st, rear, one one-and-a-half-story frame stables, 13x20, tin roof; cost, $80; Nicholas Bourgignon, on premises.

1715—Driggs av, n e cor North 14th st, one one-story frame machine shop, 25x60, iron roof; cost, $200; Novelty Foundry Machine Works; b'r, C. Pomeroy.

1716—48th st, n s, 120 w 4th av, one two-story and basement frame dwell'g, 20x36, tin roof; cost, $1,800; ow'r and b'r, A. De Groff, 298 15th st.

1717—Buffalo av, w s, 18 s Atlantic av, nine two-story and basement frame dwell'gs, 16.4x42, gravel roofs; cost, $2,500; ow'r, ar't and b'r, Thomas Denike, 724 Herkimer st.

1718—Atlantic av, s w cor Buffalo av, one three-story frame store and tenem't, 18x47, gravel roof; cost, $3,000; ow'r and b'r, Thomas Denike, 724 Herkimer st.

1719—Atkins av, e s, 175 s Liberty av, one two-story frame dwell'g, 20x30, tin roof; cost, $1,500; George Grolimund, Liberty av, near Shepherd av; ar't, L. F. Schillinger; b'r, F. Gundermann, Jr.

1720—Warwick st, e s, 100 s Eastern Parkway, one two-story frame dwell'g, 20x30, tin roof; cost, $2,200; Abraham L. Hopkins; ar't and b'r, same as last.

1721—Flushing av, No. 922, w s, bet Bremen st and Evergreen av, one one-story frame saw-filing shop, 12x10, gravel roof; cost, $50; Carl Neeman, on premises.

1722—Warwick st, w s, 20 n Blake av, two two-story frame dwell'gs, 17.6x30, tin roof; cost, $2,000 each; Chas. E. Maguire, 157 Liberty av; ar't, J. H. Maguire.

1723—Linwood st, w s, 231.4 s Fulton av, one one-story frame tailor shop, 18x30, tin roof; cost, $550; Samuel Soudon; ar't, C. G. Schwartz; b'rs, Heyser & Schwartz and Fitzsimmons.

1724—Ellery st, No. 255, one two-story brk upholstering shop, 25x28, tin roof, wooden cornice; cost, $800; Adolph Schlesinger, 166 Ellery st; ar't, H. Smith; b'rs, A. Sachs and J. Rueger.

1725—Cornelia st, s s, 174 e Central av, ten two-story and basement frame (brk filled) dwell'gs, 18x42, tin roofs; cost, $2,500 each; ow'rs and c'rs, Raymond & Donly, 759 Macon st; ar't, C. N. or H. Raymond.

1726—Bergen st, n s, 256.10 e Troy av, two two-story and basement frame (brk filled) dwell'gs, 18.9x48, tin roofs; cost, $2,500 each; Alexander Woods, 1479 Bergen st; ar't, W. Ultzen; b'r, A. Woods.

1727—South 8th st, s s, 66 w Bedford av, one one-story brk store, 25x20, tin roof, wooden cornice; cost, $1,500; Mrs. Hutchings; ar't, H. W. Billard; b'r, J. J. Brennan.

1728—North 10th st, No. 144, one four-story frame (brk filled) tenem't, 25x65, tin roof; cost, $6,400; J. Fischer, 41 Kent av; ar't, A. Herbert; b'r, P. F. Fitzgerald.

1729—St. Marks av, s s, 150 e Howard av, one two-story and attic frame dwell'g, 20x28, tin roof; cost, $1,300; Mrs. Mary A. Dowdell, 1408 St. Marks av.

1730—Graham av, s w cor Newton st, one one-story frame stable, 12x13, gravel roof; cost, $50; Frank Lornez, 320 Maujer st; b'r, C. F. Canfield.

1731—Woodbine st, w s, 24 e Hamburg av, eighteen two-story and basement frame (brk filled) dwell'gs, 19.6x45, tin roofs; cost, each, $3,000; ow'rs, ar'ts and b'rs, Francisco Bros.

1732—Seigel st, No. 121, one four-story frame (brk filled) stores and tenem'ts, 25x60, tin roof; cost, $8,500; S. B. Goodkind, Rochester, N. Y.; a'rt, H. E. Funk.

1733—Herkimer st, n s, 75 w Sackman st, one two-story and basement frame dwell'g, 17x40, tin roof; cost, $2,000; Robert E. Topping estate; b'r, H. S. Hawkins.

1734—Troutman st, n s, 167.1 w Wyckoff av, one two-story frame (brk filled) dwell'g, 25x35, tin roof; cost, $2,500; Edmund Stein, 34 Wyckoff av; ar't, H. E. Funk.

ALTERATIONS NEW YORK CITY.

Plan 1644—55th st, Nos. 71 and 73 E., two-story extension, 8.6x15.6; cost, $1,600; estate Thomas Goadby, 21 West 35th st; ar'ts, Thom & Wilson; m'ns, Dawson & Archer.

1645—10th av, Nos. 28 and 30, interior alterations; cost, $1,300; P. D. Strauch, 342 West 15th st; c'r, W. E. Crofton.

1646—57th st, No. 47 W., extension raised one story and windows altered; cost, $1,000; A. K. Ely, 132 East 23d st; b'rs, Robinson & Wallace.

1647—Boulevard, e s, 75.11 n 104th st, moved to new foundation; cost, $2,000; R. Hartley, secy., 202 West 103d st; ar't, H. F. Kilburn.

1648—48th st, No. 34 W., one-story and basement extension, 8.6x16, interior alterations and walls altered; cost, $3,000; C. W. Cass, on premises; ar'ts, F. & W. E. Bloodgood; c'rs, Smith & Son.

1649—44th st, No. 1 W., raised one story; cost, $1,200; F. Dean, cashier; 262 Division av, Brooklyn; c'r, W. Van Dorn.

1650—50th st, No. 216 W., two-story extension, 20x40, interior alterations and walls altered; cost, $3,000; J. C. Miller, 239 West 50th st; ar'ts, McKim, Mead & White.

1651—3d av, No. 1554, walls altered; cost, $4,000; Catherine A. Deane, 277 West 11th st.

1652—78th st, No. 203 W., wrought iron structure on rear; cost, $250; L. Mendelsohn, on premises; ar'ts, A. B. & W. T. Westervelt.

1653—6th and 7th avs, 50th and 51st sts, extensive alterations to walls and interior changing stable to power house; cost, abt $150,000; Broadway & Seventh Av R. R. Co., 7th av and 50th st; ar't, W. B. Powell; m'n, R. L. Darragh & Co.

1654—Centre st, Nos. 241-249 and Elm st, Nos. 167-171, tank on roof; cost, $325; A. Trenkman, 468 Washington av, Brooklyn; m'n, P. H. Murphy.

1655—170th st, n s, 113.6 e Washington av, rear, moved to new foundation; cost, $300; Mrs. D. Berndt, n e cor Washington av and 170th st; ar't, J. Wolf.

1656—Orchard st, No. 109, new oven under walk; cost, $1,150; P. Fabel, on premises; ar't, H. Horenburger; b'r, H. Wild.

1657—Cannon st, No. 52, interior alterations, walls altered and new front; cost, $1,500; A. Bleistift, 233 East 62d st; ar't, H. Horenburger.

1658—25th st, No. 436 W., interior alterations, walls altered and new front; cost, $1,200; Margarett Heins, on premises; ar't, H. Horenburger; c'r, F. Sackett.

1659—47th st, No. 528 W., new front, cost, $350; Emilie Talbot, 25 East 48th st; ar't, T. M. Fanning.

1660—West Broadway, n e cor Chambers st, walls altered; cost, $1,000; C. F. Wildey, 302 West 88th st; ar'ts, Schweitzer & Diemer.

1661—125th st, Nos. 145 and 147 W., one-story extension, 29x34, interior alterations and walls altered; cost, $2,000; lessees, Harlem Republican Club; ar't, M. J. Fitz-Mahony; b'rs, Westervelt Bros.

1662—3d av, No. 69, alterations for new boiler; cost, $100; Moran & Green, on premises.

1663—Mercer st, No. 135, interior alterations and walls altered; cost, $300; lessee, N. Geries, 94 Prince st; m'n, H. Hassall; c'r, J. M. Dubois.

1664—Irving pl, No. 23, one-story extension, 20x25, interior alterations and walls altered; cost, $300; lessee, C. W. Rosekrans, on premises; ar't, E. W. Greis.

1665—Cherry st, Nos. 468 and 470, tank on roof; cost, abt $800; att'y, A. T. Carroll, 47 West 72d st; m'n, F. Nelson.

1666—Houston st, No. 73 E., interior alterations and walls altered; cost, $1,500; J. H. McGurck, 253 Bowery; ar't, B. McGurck.

1667—Washington av, w s, 288.6 s 175th st, three-story and basement extension, 14.5x8, interior alterations and walls altered; cost, $2,500; Sarah J. Wyckoff, 1773 Washington av; ar't, T. E. Thomson.

1668—Union sq, Nos. 11-15 W., interior alterations; cost, $75; Tiffany & Co., on premises; m'ns, H. & T. Firmey.

1669—69th st, Nos. 163-167 E., walls altered; cost, $150; B. Muldoon, on premises.

1670—Potter pl, n s, 775 e Anthony av, one-story extension, 12x12; cost, $200; D. Banks, on premises; ar't, F. D. Miller.

1671—56th st, No. 206 E., new show window; cost, $450; A. Altmayer, 152d st and St. Nicholas av; ar't, C. C. Churchill; c'rs, Wiswell & O'Brien.

1672—50th st, No. 537 W., interior alterations and walls altered; cost, $400; C. Abele, 456 West 50th st.

1673—129th st, No. 3 E., walls altered; cost, $350; Jean W. Eldredge, on premises; ar'ts, French, Dixon & De Saldern.

1674—Jane st, Nos. 128-132, repair damage by fire; cost, abt $20,000; J. D. Hass, 658 West 34th st; ar't, A. H. Blankenstein.

1675—6th st, No. 618 E., two-story extension, 16.8x49.8, interior alterations and walls altered; cost, $8,000; D. Schmitt, on premises; ar't, F. Ebeling.

1676—14th st, No. 202 W., interior alterations and walls altered; cost, $1,900; lessee and b'r, H. Slevin, 213 Bleecker st; ar't, J. B. Franklin.

1677—Courtlandt av, n e cor 161st st, walls altered; cost, $400; C. Moritz, 679 East 155th st; ar't, C. F. Lohse.

1678—3d av, No. 1607, raised to grade; cost, $300; C. Helle, on premises; ar't, C. F. Lohse.

1679—158th st, No. 641 E., one-story extension, 25x13; cost, $500; F. Zimmermann, on premises; ar't, C. F. Lohse; c'r, T. Jonson.

1680—Union av, w s, 275 n 166th st, to be moved; cost, $1,000; Catherine Love, 1101 Union av; ar't, C. F. Lohse.

1681—14th st, Nos. 430 and 432 W., tank on roof; cost, $240; lessee, H. Inman, Amsterdam, N. Y.; m'n, A. Bross.

KINGS COUNTY.

Plan 874—McKibbin st, No. 65, new store front; cost, $300; Isaac Greenblat, 119 Boerum st.

875—Gold st, No. 412, flat tin roof; cost, $400; J. J. Hennessy, on premises; b'rs, J. Hanig and W. Mahler.

876—Moore st, No. 103, new store front; cost, $600; J. Greenblatt, 119 Boerum st; ar't, H. E. Funk.

877—Atlantic av, No. 2730, new store front; cost, $500; Edward Alt, 2744 Atlantic av; b'rs, H. M. Smith and J. Rudershausen.

878—Cleveland st, No. 214, raised 6 feet on brk wall; cost, $100; Mr. Welte, on premises.

879—Fort Greene pl, No. 169, two-story brk extension, 20x51.6, gravel or tin roof, front and interior alterations; cost, $4,500; J. and P. and M. Scanlan, 613 West 40th st, New York; ar't, J. G. Glover; m'ns, A. Farrell and B. McLaughlin.

880—Atlantic av, No. 51, flat tin roof; cost, $1,000; Charles Lehnkuhl, on premises; ar't and c'r, W. O. Donnell; m'n, J. McDermott.

881—Graham av, No. 284, one-story frame extension, 15x30, tin roof; cost, $200; Mrs. J. M. Luther, 286 Graham av; ar't, C. Dunkhase.

882—Atlantic av, n w cor Georgia av, underpin west wall with stone; cost, $200; John Migu; b'r, H. Cook.

883—Gold st, Nos. 171 and 173, add one story, flat tin roof; cost, $2,050; ow'rs and ar'ts, S. & J. C. Burling, 171 Gold st; b'r, S. Rippingale.

884—New Jersey av, e s, 250 n Jamaica av, flat tin roof; also two-story frame extension, 20x19, tin roof; cost, $800; Mrs. A. Jewel, New Jersey av, near Jamaica av; b'r, W. Max.

885—McDougal st, No. 76, flat tin roof; cost, $600; A. S. Bryant, on premises; ar'ts and b'rs, C. L. Johnson's Sons.

886—Gold st, No. 230, add one story, flat tin roof; cost, $500; F. Buse, 404 East 58th st, New York; ar't and c'r, J. W. Thompson; m'ns, J. Kennedy & Son.

887—Prince st, No. 195, flat tin roof; cost, $600; Wm. H. Ludlum, Painsville, Ohio; agent, J. W. Bergen, 199 Fulton st; b'r, J. Wahlman.

888—Moore st, No. 34, new store front; cost, $300; S. Katz, on premises; ar't, R. Von Lehn.

889—Nelson st, No. 108, rebuild areas, lower cellar windows; cost, $40; Patrick McKeon, on premises; b'r, J. Tighe.

890—Henry st, No. 62, one-story and cellar brk extension, 24x14.4, tin roof; cost, $1,500; Garrett Murray, on premises; ar't, T. F. Houghton; b'rs, Spratt Bros.

891—Park pl, No. 1172, raised 5 ft. on brk wall; cost, $150; Mr. Handy, on premises.

892—Lorimer st, No. 513, raised 3 ft. on brk wall, &c., also two-story frame extension, 20x15, gravel roof; cost, $800; Bernard Miss, on premises; b'r, J. W. Moore.

893—Devoe st, No. 197, new stone foundation; cost, $208; B. F. Shevlin, on premises.

894—West 9th st, No. 18, raised 6 feet on brk foundation; cost, $300; George Finkmore, 155 Bridge st; b'r, T. W. Smith.

895—Hamburg av, No. 55, one-story frame extension, 25x20.3, tin roof; cost, $50; L. A. Wardenhauer, on premises; ar't, F. Wunder.

MISCELLANEOUS.

BUSINESS FAILURES.

N. Y. ASSIGNMENTS—BENEFIT CREDITORS.

Sept.

14 Zuckerman, Emanuel and Josef Blumfeld (dealers in shoes, at No. 78 Canal st), to Richard Bergmann; preferences, $1,610.

15 Beck, Frank E. (plumbing, range and furnace business, at No. 999 3d av), to Edward P. Sargent; preferences, $198.

17 Groschee, William (manufacturer of mouldings and picture frames, at No. 82 Bowery), to John J. Sullivan; preferences, $681.

17 Alexander, Rudolph (dealer in leaf tobacco, at No. 211 Pearl st), to Julius Lehmann; preferences, $3,000.

18 Madden, Robert (retail dealer in teas, coffees, groceries, &c.), to Richard I. Brooks; preferences, $250.

18 Turton, Edgar S. and John (composing firm of John Turton & Sons, merchants in Naval stores), to Charles B. Turton; preferences, $10,500.

18 Smith, John W. (coal merchant, at No. 1901 Park av.), to John Dobbins; preferences, $1,100.

KINGS COUNTY.

GENERAL ASSIGNMENTS.

Sept.

Flanagan, Patrick J. to Frank B. Cameron.

PROCEEDINGS OF THE BOARD OF ALDERMEN AFFECTING REAL ESTATE.

APPROVED PAPERS.

Resolutions passed by the Board of Aldermen calling for the following improvements have been signed by the Mayor for the week ending September 12, 1891. *Indicates that the Mayor neither appoved nor objected thereto, therefore the same became adopted.

CURBSTONES SET AND SIDEWALKS FLAGGED.

George st, from Boston av to Prospect av.
Railroad av West, from Morris av to 165th st.

REGULATING, GRADING, ETC.

George st, from Boston av to w s of Prospect av.
Railroad av West, from Morris av to 165th st.

CROSSWALKS LAID.

George st, from Boston av to Prospect av.
Railroad av West, from Morris av to 165th st.

ADVERTISED LEGAL SALES.

REFEREES SALES TO BE HELD AT THE REAL ESTATE EXCHANGE AND AUCTION ROOM (LIMITED), 59 to 65 LIBERTY STREET, EXCEPT WHERE OTHERWISE STATED.

Sept.

3d av, s w cor 170th st, 26x79.9x26.4x82.6........
170th st, s s, 82.6 w 3d av, 40x52.9x40x57.8, ½ part, being all right, title and int. of Matilda Carter to above........
by P. F. Meyer. (Receiver's sale)........ 21

52d st, No. 521, n s, 275 w 10th av, 25x100.5........
52d st, No. 523, n s, 300 w 10th av, 25x100.5........
Two five-story brk tenem'ts........
by Wm. Kennelly........ 21

65th st, No. 138, s s, 458 e 10th av, 20x100.5, four-story stone front dwell'g, by Richard V. Harnett. (Amt due $21,242)........ 21

Av A, Nos. 393 and 395, s w cor 24th st, 49.5x81.5, vacant, all right, title and interest which Daniel D. Conover had on June 10, 1891, by Sheriff at City Hall. (Sale under execution)........ 21

Thompson st, No. 240, e s, 90 n 3d late Amity st, 19x47.10, three-story brk tenem't, by Smyth & Ryan. (Leasehold; amt due $1,963)........ 22

Washington st, No. 765, e s, 20 s 12th st, 15x78x15x76.3, five-story brk store and tenem't, by B. L. Kennelly. (Amt due $12,791)........ 22

51st st, Nos. 602-608, s s, 100 w 11th av, 75x100.5, two-story brk office, one-story frame sheds and vacant, by R. V. Harnett. (Leasehold; receiver's sale)........ 22

67th st, Nos. 228-246, s s, 125 e 11th av, 10 lots, each 25x100.5, ten five-story brk and stone tenements, by J. N. Golding. (Amt due on each abt $9,523)........ 22

88th st, No. 256, s s, 118 w Boulevard, 18x100.8, three-story stone front dwell'g, by J. F. B. Smyth. (Amt due $2,577; prior morts. $——)........ 22

144th st, n e cor Bradhurst av, 32.4x99.11x21.4x100.6, five-story brk store and flat, by Smyth & Ryan. (All right, title and int. which Jacob Striffler had on March 5, 1890)........ 22

27th st, No. 330, s s, 428 e 9th av, 22x98.9, three-story brk dwell'g, by P. F. Meyer. (Amt due $6,479)........ 23

114th st, No. 322, s s, 262.6 e 2d av, 18.9x100.11, four-story brk tenem't, by B. L. Kennelly. (Amt due $9,852)........ 23

87th st, No. 136, s s, 350 w 9th av, 20x100.8, four-story stone front dwell'g, by D. P. Ingraham & Co. (Amt due $24,156)........ 24

87th st, No. 142, s s, 410 w 9th av, 20x100.8, four-story stone front dwell'g, by D. P. Ingraham & Co. (Amt due $26,240)........ 24

115th st, No. 211, n s, 225 w 7th av, 20x100.11, five-story stone front flat, by R. V. Harnett. (Amt due $16,878)........ 24

Av A, Nos. 1314-1320, n e cor 70th st, 100.4x98, four and five-story brk planing mill, &c., by R. V. Harnett & Co. (Amt due $54,331)........ 24

Convent av, w s, 74.11 n 144th st, 25x94.5, three-story brk dwell'g........
Convent av, w s, 49.11 n 144th st, 25x94.5, three-story brk dwell'g........
Convent av, w s, 24.11 n 144th st, 25x94.5, three-story brk dwell'g........
Convent av, n w cor 144th st, 24.11x94.5, three-story brk dwell'g........
144th st, No. 455, n s, 214.2 e Amsterdam av, 20x99.11, three-story brk dwell'g........
144th st, No. 459, n s, 177.8 e Amsterdam av, 20x99.11, four-story brk dwell'g........
144th st, No. 461, n s, 157.8 e Amsterdam av, 20x99.11, four-story brk dwell'g........
144th st, No. 463, n s, 137.8 e Amsterdam av, 20x99.11, three-story brk dwell'g........
144th st, No. 465, n s, 121.2 e Amsterdam av, 16.6x99.11, three-story brk dwell'g........
144th st, No. 467, n s, 100 e Amsterdam av, 21.2x99.11, three-story brk dwell'g........
by A. H. Muller & Son. (Amt due on first 3 lots on Convent av, each $14,909, and $18,891 on cor lot, $11,335 on No. 455, $14,998 on each of Nos. 459 and 461, $13,061 on No. 465, $11,355 on No. 465 and $13,061 on No. 467)........ 24

3d av, No. 714, w s, 24.11 s 45th st, 25.6x95, four-story brk store and tenem't, by William Kennelly. (Amt due $30,819)........ 24

94th st, No. 39, n s, abt 355 w 8th av, 17.9x100.8, three-story brk dwell'g, all right, title and int. of Edward Van Orden which he had on March 21, 1891, by Sheriff at City Hall. (Sale under execution)........ 25

98th st, Nos. 141-169, n s, 100 e 10th av, 325x113.2x—x129.6, fifteen five-story brk flats, by R. V. Harnett........ 25

119th st, No. 408, s s, 94 e 1st av, 17x100.10........
119th st, No. 410, s s, 111 e 1st av, 17x100.10........
119th st, No. 412, s s, 128 e 1st av, 17x100.10........
Three three-story stone front dwell'gs........
by J. C. Lalor. (Amt due on each $5,547)........ 28

KINGS COUNTY.

Sept.

Georgia av, w s, 175 s Fulton av, 50x100, two two-story frame tenem'ts; assessed value, $6,000; partition; by T. A. Kerrigan, at 13 Willoughby st........ 21

Kosciusko st, No. 404, s s, 201.8 w Lewis av, 16.8x100, two-story frame dwell'g; assessed value, $1,600........
Spencer st, No. 87, e s, 275 s Park av, 25x100, two-story frame dwell'g; assessed value, $1,000........
Road from Village of Flatlands to the Neck and to Canarsie, n w s, 182.9 n e Hubbard st, 86.8x534.2x87x518.2, contains 1 acre, 5 36-100 perches, Flatlands, two-story frame dwell'g........
New Utrecht road, e s, adj land of Protestant Dutch Church and Jos. H. Story, except portion taken for Prospect Park & Coney Island

R. R. Co., Flatbush. two-story frame dwell'g; partition

by J. Cole, at 389 Fulton st ... 21

Spencer st, No. 108, w s, 78 n Willoughby av, 22x80, three-story frame dwell'g; assessed value, $2,100; partition ...

Lot at Coney Island known as No. 4 on map of Wyckoff tract of common lands of Gravesend, begins at intersection of south line of lot 3 on same map and lot hereby described, runs south along w s of a road 30 ft. wide — x west to e s of 10-foot way, x north — x east to beginning, except ...

West 5th st, w s, 43.4 s of W. Thompson's land, runs northwest along land of Coney Island Elevated Railroad 70.6 x west along same 52.7 x northeast 134.11 to st, x south 48.4 ...

by T. A. Kerrigan, at 13 Willoughby st ... 22

6th st, s s, 70 w 4th av, 105x100, by T. A. Kerrigan, at 13 Willoughby st ... 23

Cedar st, No. 14, s s, 235 w Evergreen av, 20x91.11x20x91, two-story brk dwell'g; assessed value, $2,100 ...

Decatur st, n s, 350 w Throop av, 18.9x100 ...

Decatur st, n s, 358.9 w Throop av, 18.9x100, error Two three-story brk dwell'gs; assessed value, $6,500 each ...

Decatur st, No. 494, s s, 43.9 w Ralph av, 18.9x100, two-story and basement brk dwell'g; assessed value, $3,700 ...

62d st, s s, 480 w 14th av, 20x100, New Utrecht, frame dwell'g ...

by T. A. Kerrigan, at 13 Willoughby st ... 23

Lexington av, No. 798, n s, 326 e Reid av, 34x100, four-story brk flat; assessed value, $10,500; by Albert W. Seaman, ref., at County Court House. 23

East New York av, s s, 192.6-10 w Albany av, 25x200 to Furnald st, Flatbush; by T. A. Kerrigan, at 13 Willoughby av ... 24

LIS PENDENS, KINGS COUNTY.

Sept.

Bridge st, e s, 375 s Willoughby st, 25x100. Henry S. Gilbert agt Barbara Miller; att'y, Edgar Whitlock ... 11

Prospect st, n s, lot 28 map J. A. Hamilton, 25x75. Same agt same; same att'y ... 11

Bay 26th st, n w s, 345 n e Benson av, 60x96.8, New Utrecht. Sarah Peterson agt Charles W. Anderson; action to set aside deed; att'y, James R. Bowen ... 11

York st, No. 209, n s, 125 e Gold st, 25x100. Brooklyn Elevated R. R. Co. agt Aaron Davidson; action to acquire real estate; att'ys, Hoadly, Lauterbach & Johnson ... 11

Myrtle av, n s, 166.4 e Chesnut st, 25x80.1x27.1x69.7. Louis Rubenstein agt Philip L. Young, Jr.; action to set aside deed; att'y, Isaac N. Miller ... 12

Flatbush av, south cor Prospect pl, runs southeast 123.5 x south 2.6 x southwest 90 x 3.6 to av, x north 120.5 ...

Interior gore, adj. begins at point 120.5 s Flatbush av, runs north 90 x south 40.8 x southwest 50.8 ...

Prospect pl, s s, 105.9 w 6th av, 16.8x100 ...

Prospect pl, s s, 138.9 w 6th av, 31.4x100 ...

Prospect pl, s s, 188.9 w 6th av, 16.8x100 ...

Merritt H. Day agt E. Eliza Knight; action to set aside deeds; att'ys, Peabody, Baker & Peabody ... 12

Herkimer st, s s cor Pleasant pl, 19x90. Elizabeth W. Aldrich agt Robert Valentine et al.; att'y, Spencer Aldrich ... 12

4th pl, s s, 100 w Smith st, 25x100. David W. Binns et al. exrs. Elizabeth Binns agt Michael Daly; att'y, Frank A. Whelan ... 12

40th st, s s, 100 w 6th av, runs south 200.4 to 41st st, x west 50 x north 100.2 x west 25 x north 100 to 40th st, x east 75. Jane A. McKenna and ano. exrs. Wm. T. Gormley agt Mary E. Johnson; action to set aside deed, &c.; att'y, Herman Frank ... 12

Hudson av, No. 207, s e cor Nassau st, 21.5x75. Notice of action premises under condemnation proceedings by Brooklyn Elevated R. R.; att'ys, Hoadly, Lauterbach & Johnson ... 12

Himrod st, n s, 175 e Evergreen av, 25x70.1x—x69.5. John G. Jenkins committee of Henry C. Ely agt William R. Smith; att'ys, Jackson & Burr ... 12

Hicks st, w s, 366.6 n Degraw st, 19.6x97.6. Louise Cook agt Margaret Sweeney et al.; att'y, H. H. Cook ... 12

Lorimer st, s w cor Conselyea st, 50x100 ...

Lorimer st, n e cor Jackson st, 25x100 ...

Frost st, bet Ewen and Graham avs, adj land of Mary Smullen, 25x100, vacant lot ...

Mary J. Cannon agt Francis E. Rogers; action of ejectment; atty's, Rudd, Hunt & Wilder ... 14

North 10th st, s w s, 100 s e Kent av, 25x100. James Murphy agt Margaret Winters; partition; att'y, John P. Donnelly ... 14

1st st, s s, 305 w 5th av, 108x100. William Van Horne agt William S. Hale; foreclos. mech. lien; att'y, James Taylor ... 14

Rodney st, s e s, 140 n e Marcy av, 20x100. Mutual Life Ins. Co. agt Harvey L. Calkin; att'y, Robert Sewell ... 15

Jefferson av, s s, 420 e Howard av, 20x100. Irwin Heasty agt George D. Blydenburg; att'y, Charles S. Taber ... 15

Chauncey st, n s, 350 e Patchen av, 25x50.6 to Jamaica plank road, x26x51.3. Julia M. Smyth agt Frederick M. Trimm; att'y, James P. Philip ... 15

Cambridge pl, No. 40, w s, 325 n Gates av, 25x100. Marie E. Jacobson agt Pauline Storm; att'ys, Wells & Waldo ... 15

Van Voorhis st, s s, 100 e Evergreen av, 200x100. Noah Tebbetts agt Gilbert Haynes; att'y, Noah Tebbetts, in person ... 15

Hull st, n s, 375 e Rockaway av, 18.9x100. George Carll and ano. exrs. Mary A. Carll agt Michael J. Boylan; att'y, Henry W. Gaines ... 16

Pacific st, s s, 160 e Albany av, 20x107.2. George A. Scudder agt John H. Bonnell; same att'y ... 16

Pacific st, s s, 180 e Albany av, 20x107.2. Gertrude S. Davis agt same; same att'y ... 16

Pacific st, s s, 240 e Albany av, 20x107.2. Jesse Carle agt same; same att'y ... 16

Jamaica av, s s, 42.10 e Essex st, 21.5x91.5. Henry Lange agt John A. Davies; att'y, S. A. Underhill ... 16

Jefferson av, s s, 440 e Howard av, 20x100. Josephine D. Powers agt George B. Blydenburgh; att'y, Charles S. Taber ... 16

Hancock st, s s, 150 e Lewis av, 74.7x100. Bradley & Currier Co. (Lim.) agt Melissa D. Franklin; att'y, Geo. F. Alexander ... 16

Junius st, e s, 240 s Dumont av, 40x165. Jane De Wald agt Edmond B. Lewis; action for specific performance; att'y, James P. Campbell ... 16

2d av, west cor 1st st, runs northwest 100 x southwest 166 to channel of Dentons Mill Pond, x south — to st, x southeast 24 to 3d av, x northeast 200 ...

1st st, s w s, 100 n w 3d av, 300x200 to 2d st, x192 x100 ...

1st st, south cor Gowanus Canal, 200 to 2d st, x 285.9x200 to 1st st, x 283.9 ...

John F. Schmadeke agt William T. Pyle; amended partition; atty's, Morris & Whitehead ... 16

Roebling st, e s, 75 n North 5th st, 25x100. William Journeay agt Edward McDonnell; att'ys, Jackson & Burr ... 16

Eastern Parkway, e s, 25 e Thatford av, 25x100. Louis Bossert agt Meyer Marcus; foreclos. mechanic's lien; att'y, Frank Obernier ... 17

Eldert st, n s, 198 w Bushwick av, 54x100. Foroseagean J. Ledoux agt Francis E. O'Connor; att'y, Noah Tebbetts ... 17

Liberty av, n s, 27.6 e Ashford st, 25x100. Henry Taylor agt Gesina Meyer; att'ys, Thornton, Earle & Kiendl ... 17

Prospect st, n s, 100 e Jay st, 25x61 ...

Prospect st, n s, 175 w Bridge st, 25x75 ...

Frances Dixon agt Adelaide B. Stilwell; action to recover possession; att'ys, Agar, Ely & Fulton ... 17

RECORDED LEASES.

NEW YORK. Per Year

Centre st, No. 176. L. P. Hawes to T. M. Hass; from Feb. 1, 1891, to May 1, 1897 ... $2,500, 2,750

Delancey st, No. 214, store and part cellar. Terence P. Rafferty to Samuel M. Kolasky; 5 years, from May 1, 1890 ... 720

Bighbridge st, s s, 10 e Tiebout av, 33x172x36x166. Charles H. McNamara to Thomas G. and John L. Holland; 3 7-12 years, from Sept 1, 1891 ... 360, 420

Madison st, No. 330, stores and basement. David Well to Thomas J. Sullivan; 10 years, from Sept. 1, 1891 ... 300

Monroe st, No. 94. Rachael Sacks to Hanna Judge; 3 years, from Dec. 1, 1890 ... 480

Mott st, No. 141. Michael Lapp to Frank Carlo; 5 years, from Oct. 1, 1891 ... 2,600

South st, No. 260, first floor and cellar. Thomas Hitchcock to Patrick H. McNamara; 1 year, from May 1, 1891 ... 1,060

Stanton st, No. 52. Caroline Muller to Daniel D. Frercks; 5 7-12 years, from Oct. 1, 1891 ... 1,400, 1,500

Stanton st, No. 85. Jacob Cohen to Antonio Graucig; 5 years, from May 1, 1892 ... 300

Thompson st, No. 113. J. R. Mallany, agent for Mary H. Moore, to Angelo Casella; 3 years, from July 1, 1891 ... 750

Water st, No. 171. Charles D. Leverich admr. Charles P. Leverich to G. Falk & Bro.; 3 years, from May 1, 1888 ... 2,000

Whitehall st, No. 20½, store and basement. Elizabeth P. and Emily P. Paulding to Amos J. Sinnot; 4 years 9½ months, from July 15, 1891 ... 1,200

Washington st, n w cor Perry st. Richard S. Newcombe to John F. Doyle; 5 years, from June 1, 1891 ... 1,500

Same property. Assign. lease. John F. Doyle to John Eichler Brewing Co ... nom

6th st, No. 409. Isaac and Jacob Fleischbauer, of Fleischbauer & Brother, to Martin Wuzner; 20 months, from Sept. 1, 1891 ... 1,080

9th st, No. 230 E., all. Hannah M. Tynan, individ. and as guard. Edward and Florence Tynan, to Sarah wife of Ferdinand Katz; 10 years, from May 1, 1889 ... 1,000

Same property. Assign. lease. Sara Katz to Emma Bachmann ... nom

28th st, No. 104 W. Herman L. Kingsbury to Jacob H. Simms; 3 years, from May 1, 1891. 1,100

29th st, No. 44 W. George Schmetzel agent for Catherine L. Schmetzel to Kate Dehnhoff; 5½ years, from Nov 1, 1891 ... 1,800, 2,000

32d st, No. 555 W. Rose Hyman to John Torlia; 3 years, from Sept. 6, 1891 ... 204

45th st, No. 121 W. Pierson E. Sanford, Warwick, N. Y., to Richard J. and John P. Carter; 5 years, from May 1, 1891 ... 3,200

47th st, No. 121 E. / 47th st, No. 119 E. / Lexington av, No. 407. { Charles Wise and Sali Simonson to Maurice V. Freund; 5 7-12 years, from Oct. 1, 1891 ... 6,600, 9,000

48th st, s s, 375 w 11th av, 50x100. Peter Billiemayer to David J. Keefe; 5 years, from May 1, 1892 ... 780

53d st, No. 510 W., s s, 150 w 10th av, saloon floor. Elsworth L. Striver to Nicholas Reasner; 5 years, from Nov. 1, 1891 ... 1,000

54th st, No. 232 E., all. John S. Robinson to Bernard Rank; 5 years, from May 1, 1891 ... 1,100

58th st, No. 230 E. Mary A. McGuire to Bernhard Rank. 4¾ years, from Sept. 1, 1891 ... 1,100

70th st, No. 401½ E., store. Theresia Farciot to Wenzel Keller; 5 years, from May 1, 1891. 420

Same property. Assign. lease. Wenzel Keller to Peter Buckel ... 500

73d st, No. 171 W. Christiana Conklin to Louis A. Lehmaier; 3 years, from Sept. 1, 1891 ... 1,550, 1,625

75th st, No. 403 E., ground floor. Max Peters to Herman and Lena Peters; 10 years, from Sept. 10, 1891 ... 50 cents

76th st, No. 403 E., front and rear buildings. Charles Beutel to William J. Butler; 5 years, from May 1, 1891 ... 900

155th st, No. 654 E., store floor. Regina Nieland and Margaretha Stadta to John Geidel; 5 years, from Sept. 1, 1891 ... 240

Av B, No. 280, store, rear rooms and cellar. Ferdinand Becker to Gottfried Kellerhals; 3¾ years, from Sept. 1, 1891 ... 300

Amsterdam av, No. 693, store and basement floors. George W. Eggers to S. Cushman & Sons; 5½ years, from Nov. 1, 1891 ... 480

Brook av, n w cor 148th st, store. Emma C. Sanguinetti to Charles Seebeck; 5 years, from May 1, 1891 ... 420, 480

Madison av, No. 511. Charles Haight to Charles H. White; 4 years, from May 1, 1897 ... 2,400

1st av, No. 10, store floor and cellar. George Rothman to Julius Hess; 3¾ years, from Sept. 1, 1891 ... 720

1st av, No. 2294, s e cor 118th st. John Furey to Patrick Lynch; from Sept. 7, 1891, to May 1, 1895 ... 1,350

Same property. Assign. lease. Patrick Lynch to The Henry Elias Brewing Co ... nom

2d av, No. 1508, south store. Joseph Cohn to Arnold Fritz; 3 years, from May 1, 1891 ... 600

Same property, south flat on first floor. Same to same; 3 years, from May 1, 1891 ... 240

3d av, No. 1898, store floor and basement. Kaufman Hirsh to Herman Greitner; 1⅔ years, from Sept. 1, 1891 ... 1,000

3d av, No. 617, all. Hyman and Henry Sonn to J. C. G. Hupfel; 10 years, from Aug. 1, 1891 ... 3,600

3d av, No. 1935, all. John G. Lindenberger and Christiana his wife to Eugene Huber; 5 years, from Oct. 1, 1891 ... 1,800

3d av, No. 170, all. Morris Franklin to John C. Junker; 5⅚ years, from Jan. 1, 1891 ... 1,500, 1,600

3d av, No. 861, n e cor 37th st. Mary E. Travis to Patrick and Henry Brady; 3 years, from May 1, 1893 ... 2,400

Same property. Assign. lease. Hannah O'Shaughnessy admrx. John O'Shaughnessy to same ... nom

3d av, No. 1929, store and rear rooms. Richard H. L. Townsend to Richard Sichler; 5 years, from May 1, 1891 ... 1,332

4th av, No. 361, s e cor 26th st. Charles P. Palmer and Mary A. P. Draper trustees C. Palmer to Robert B. Nooney; 5 years, from May 1, 1889 ... 3,000

5th av, Nos. 539–549, lot in rear, 50x100.5 to 45th st, x50x irreg. John M. Hodgson to Henry Gebhard; 9 10-12 years, from July 1, 1888. 3,000, 3,600

6th av, No. 112. Caroline E. Lane, Katherine B. Favre and Jennie L. Pool to Elias Dreyer and Emelia his wife; 3 years, from May 1, 1891 ... 2,500

8th av, No. 2785, store floor and basement. Francis M. Wilmurt to John J. Battell; 5 years, from Oct. 1, 1891 ... 600

8th av, No. 610, all. Julia Lehman to Henry Schwindt; 3 1-12 years, from April 1, 1890 ... 840, 900

9th av, No. 255, store and basement. Margaret Chirney to Thomas E. Anderson; 5 years, from May 1, 1891 ... 540

10th av, No. 819, store and basement. Fred. Bittmann to Otto Merath; 4⅔ years, from Sept. 1, 1891 ... 660

CHATTELS.

NOTE.—The first name, alphabetically arranged, is that of the Mortgagor, or party who gives the Mortgage. The "R" means Renewal Mortgage.

NEW YORK CITY.

SEPTEMBER 11 TO 17.—INCLUSIVE.

SALOON AND RESTAURANT FIXTURES.

Arnold, J. 64 6th av....Hills Union B Co. $416

Azzolio, A. 420 E 113th....D Mayer. 479

Ahlers, Ahrens. 38 Beekman....J Gatjen. (R) 2,000

Bahneth, Anna E. Greene st....I Greenwald. Restaurant Fixtures. (R) 50

Born, Leopold. 2362 3d av....J Eichler. (R) 4,000

Burns, Patrick. 281 Av C....J Ahles B Co. 550

Buttell, J J. 2785 8th av....Hirsch & S. 950

Bauer, C. 811 6th av ...G Ehret. (R) 1,550

Black, John 2079 7th av....R Caterson. 1,600

Blancke, H L. Duane st, n w cor Church st.... G Ehret. (R) 3,000

Born, J. 2331 3d av....J Eichler B Co. (R) 3,200

Brady, H and P. 561 3d av. ...Bernheimer & S. 1,500

Brown, Eugene. 518 6th av....Bernheimer & S. (Satisfied Sept 16, 1891.) (R) 2,500

Burckel, J. 43 E 18th....J Kress B Co. (R) 810

Byrne, J. 15 Madison... T C Lyman & Co. (R) 3,000

Same. 15 Madison....J Kress B Co. (R) 1,000

Same. 33 Oliver ...same. (R) 1,000

Barmbold, F. 103 E 8th....J Kuntz B Co. 400

Blake, J J. 507 Grand....J Ruppert. 300

Boss, Henry Jr. 106th st and Madison av.... Bernheimer & S. (R) 2,600

Brennan, James. 824 7th av....P Doelger. (R) 2,200

Bauer, Gustav. 85 and 87 Chatham....G Ehret. (R) 4,000

Bridenburg, D M. 415 Canal .. J & M Haffen. 4,310

Callahan, Edward. 410 10th av ...H Ferris Son. Saloon Pump. 100

Clark, J J and T J. 179 Varick....J Everard. 5,095

Concannon, Thos. 349 W 52d....Bernheimer & S. (R) 350

Coyle, J F. 323 Delancey....J Hoffman B Co. (R) 350

Cerovsky, J & F. 1391 Av A....Weiz & Z. 2,000

Diehl, J H. 389 7th av....J Kress B Co. (R) 1,991

Deery, M J. 120 Leonard....G Ringler & Co. (R) 1,200

Delicker, Chas. 177th st and Vanderbilt av ... W L Flanagan. 2,000

Doran & McHugh. 177 1st av....S E Boehm & Co. (R) 500

Duff, Patrick. 679 3d av....Howard & Childs. 773

Donoho & Gilligan. 29 and 31 Centre....G Ehret. (R) 3,000

Egan, F J. 837 6th av....G Ehret. 1,500

Eisenbauer, August. 578 Hudson....Bernheimer & S. (R) 650

Flanagan, Patrick. 6 Lawrence... Bernheimer & S. (R) 550

Friedman, Joseph. 245 E 77th....Bavarian B Co. 385

Fauser, J M. 414 E 16th....J Hoffman B Co. 600

Finucan, Mary. 2028 1st av... J Kuntz B Co. (R) 100

Freyknect, Max. 221 Bowery....F Stivers. Pool Table, &c. 500

Geidel, John. 654 E 155th....H Zeltner. 400

Glasstetter, D. 129 Pitt....C Iba. 125

Guilfoyle, R. 204 E 42d....Bavarian B Co. 400

Gottlieb & Kliemeck. 35 Walker .. F & M Schaefer B Co. 2,000

Griffith, T. Lexington av and 33d st....Bernheimer & S. Saloon Pump. 84

Griffith, T. Lexington av and 33d st....Bernheimer & S. Saloon Ice Box. 96

Griffith, Patrick. 23 West....W Herrmann. (R) 400

Hearn, P M. 10th av, s w cor 38th st....D Stevenson. (R) 1,250

Huse, O H. 324 E 32d....J Eichler B Co. (R) 500

Harenburg, Anna C. 188 and 190 Greenwich ... J N Crusius. 10,500

Hinrichs, Henry. 482 E 17th....Bernheimer & S. (R) 700

Hackauff, Gustav. 208 East Houston ...Burr, Son & Co. (R) 1,000

Hoenig, William. 1325 Av A....F Hower B Co. 400

Kingwell, Chas. 3d av and 15th st....Redmond & Sheehy. 2,000

Kundig, J W. 430 W 40th....J Kuntz B Co. 250

Keller, V. 401½ E 70th....P Buckel. 500

Kerls, H. 358 3d av....F & M Schaefer B Co. 2,500

Klein, Rudolph. 102 Nassau....A Brooks. Restaurant Fixtures. 300

Klei, W. 67 Cannon....F Ibert. (R) 400

Koelker, Hugo. 104 1st.. J Ruppert. 950
Kraemer, Louis. 1600 Av B....G Ringler & Co. (R) 1,975
Kunzenman, J. 157 1st av....J Eichler B Co. (R) 1,200
Kuszy, J. 90 Pitt....H B Scharmann & Sons. 300
Kennedy, Patrick. 409 E 124th....Bernheimer & S. (R) 600
Krejci, Josef. 415 E 72d....V Loewers. (R) 300
Lane Bros. 748 10th av....Bernheimer & S. (R) 1,500
Liebel, W and S. 124 Attorney... P Buckel. (R) 300
Lorch, P. 433 E 15th....Lembeck & Betz Eagle B Co. 700
Landthaler, John. 23 Rivington....Rubsam & H B Co. (R) 1,000
Levy, Charles. 4 Cortlandt....J Ruppert. (R) 1,000
Lynch, Patrick. 2294 1st av ...A Gary. 500
Lynch, Patrick. 2294 1st av....H Elias B Co. 1,500
McSchaffry, W E. 317 E 114th....P Doelger. 200
Morgenweck, Wm. 2750 8th av .. J Ruppert. 2,000
Muhs, H F. 186 Monroe....Danenberg & C (R) 350
Mariano, John. 153 Bleecker....Burr B Co. (R) 700
Meyer & Solomon. 2 Bayard and 1 Forsyth....Weiz & Z. 800
Madden, W J. 3d av, s w cor 65th st....S Liebmann's Sons B Co. 20,000
Manny, C J. 166 West Broadway....Bernheimer & S. Saloon Ice House. 100
Masano, Frank. 339 E 109th....Bernheimer & S. (R) 400
McAree, J J. 211 W 16th... J & M Haffen. (R) 275
McGee, M. 11th av, s w cor 60th st....J Kress B Co. 1,000
McLaughlin, D. 11th and Hudson sts....C Iba. (Satisfied Sept 14, 1891.) 1,125
McNenamy, Thos. 231 W 19th....Bernheimer & S. (R) 500
Meehan, M. 1621 2d av....Bernheimer & S. 500
Miller, H. 313 E 60th....P Doelger. 1,200
Muller, A. 2409 2d av....Bernheimer & S. (R) 250
Muller, Carl. 36 Maiden lane....G Ringler & Co. (R) 300
Muller, K. 2110 8th av....J Kress B Co. (R) 1,400
Murphy, D. 188 Park row .. C & A Bereuter. Billiard Table. 260
Murray, J J. 1815 2d av....Bernheimer & S. (R) 2,500
Maisch, Leopold. 384 Pearl....F Oppermann, Jr. (R) 1,574
Marrone & Parnolo. 321 E 111th....Bernheimer & S. (R) 900
McIntyre, Peter. 558 W 51st....G Ehret. 7,000
Meier, George. 326 E 40th....J Feldman. 78
Minder, Conrad. 79 South 5th av....F Oppermann, Jr. 1,025
Myers, J J. 541 10th av....C Iba. 350
Neis, Ferdinand. 127 West....J S Kelly. 2,500
Newman, Chas. 163 E 52d....J H Bereuter. Pool Table. 260
Newmann, S. 161 Attorney... J Kuntz B Co. (R) 749
Nixon, John. 3 1st....J & M Haffen. (R) 250
Nolte, H W. 25 Pearl... Beadleston & W. (R) 3,000
O'Connor, T E. 51 Beach....J Ruppert. (R) 900
O'Neil, M. 505 W 43d....D Stevenson. (R) 250
Riester, Martin. 72 Greenwich....Bernheimer & S. (R) 200
Rocco, Eugene. 165 Elizabeth....F Bachmann. (R) 800
Rohm, H. 128 E 8th....J C G Hupfel B Co. 700
Reitman, Sareck. 240 Stanton ...H B Scharmann & Sons. 1,000
Ritzel, Philippan 524 E 13th....G Ringler & Co. (R) 400
Sauter, John. 406 W 38th....D Bermes. (R) 400
Schudel, Michael. 230 Eldridge....Rubsam & H B Co. (R) 475
Selzam, F and J. 440 Pleasant av....G Ringler & Co. (R) 1,500
Sasse, W. Brook av, n w cor 162d st... H Pohlmann. 1,000
Schlotterbeck, C. 199 Broome....F Ibert. (R) 300
Schroeder, Albert. 448 W 40th Schmitt & S. 400
Schultze, F W. 237 E 10th....P Doelger. (R) 1,500
Schul, P. 217 E 6th....P Doelger. 400
Scott, Jr, J. 2180 3d av....G Ehret. 3,000
Simon, K. 227 10th av....F & M Schaefer B Co. 500
Stephan, W. 2497 3d av... J Eichler B Co. (R) 700
Sternberg, Emilie. 338 E 81st....J Ruppert. 1,200
Steiz, G. 232 E 9th....J Eichler B Co. (R) 500
Summers, F and R. 302 Bowery....Cornish & Co. Restaurant Fixtures. 1,000
Smith, John. 640 8th av....W L Flanagan. (R) 6,313
Stadelberger, Frank. 880 8th av....M Groh's Son. 3,000
Toebing, W. 216 E 126th....P & W Ebling B Co. 800
Troiano, A. 62 Baxter....H Elias B Co. 500
Tiedemann, Claus. 103 Washington ..H P Nordbruch. (R) 1,000
Vladyka & Pokorny. 420 E 59th....E Freund. 2,000
Wiltsie, Susan E. 5 Greenwich av and 2 Christopher st....L Frank. Restaurant Fixtures. 750
Wack, Elizabeth. 445 E 83d....J Eichler B Co. (R) 760
Walsh, R P. 1391 Broadway....G Ehret. (R) 4,500
Weil, A. 2465 8th av ...J Eichler B Co. 800
White, J H. 139½ W 25th....Wagner & S. Billiard Table. (R) 50
Willett, R R. 530 8th av....H Harburger. Restaurant Fixtures. 250
Willy, E. 131 Prince....J Kuntz B Co. (R) 400
Worsnop, Alfred. 699 1st av .. Bernheimer & S. (R) 1,200
Wurslin, F. 335 W 44th....G Ehret. (R) 300
Weygandt, Adolph. 288 Broome ...P Weidmann. 500
Wulf, Christ. 33 Ferry....F Oppermann, Jr. (R) 1,180
Zulberti & Paracca. 144 Bleecker....A Lazzare. Restaurant Fixtures. 1,000
Zarek, S S. 251 Rivington....Beadleston & W. (R) 1,000

HOUSEHOLD FURNITURE.

Alberson, Marion. 409 W 50th....J Baumann. 186
Arnold, Dora. 266 W 39th....J Baumann. 496
Adams, Hattie. 31 E 27th....F G Smith, Piano. (R) 165
Arenal, M. 210 E 25th....Wheelock & Co. Piano. (R) 220
Alcott, E H. 356 W 26th....J Moriarty. 186
Alexander, Tillie. 18 Delancey....H Israel & Sons. 142
Aguais, Josephine. 43 W 29th....J Gregg & Co. 229
Anderson, T J. 109 W 39th... L Baumann. 242
Austin, Moses. 430 W 59th....L Baumann. 132
Baird, Lottie H. 108 W 102d....H E Hunt. 177
Baker, Nellie. 15 St Marks pl....F J Brechtel. 117
Bergerman, Abraham. 140 W 29th....J Gregg & Co. 113
Blaustein, Michael. 65 E 1st....Amer Guar Assoc. 100
Born, Henrietta. 691 E 135th....E Falke. 2,500
Block & Hochstein. 200 Chrystie....S I Herschmann. 170
Bailey, H C. Storage, 124th st and 8th av....E S Baker. 600
Bannum, F A. 256 W 43d....Brooklyn F Co. 614
Bates, Annie. 315 Broome....L Baumann. 225
Beal, W H. 2 W 95th....H Thoesen. 231
Becannon, W H & C. 2067 Madison av....M A Birtles. 145
Berthoef, Ellen. 144 W 10th....J Moriarty. 283
Bewer, Julia. 1629 Av A....Wheelock & Co. Piano. (R) 93
Birdsall, C E. 159 W 129th....W Bettman. 125
Bliss, Hattie W. 89 W 87th....J Pyle. (R) 3,000
Same. 37 W 32d....same. (R) 4,000
Bliss, Harriett W. 10 W 28th....J Pyle. 5,000
Bonback, C F. 527 W 43d....Jordan, M & Co. 197
Brennan, T. 24 Albany....H Israel & Sons. 126
Brown, Annie. 401 E 77th....Wheelock & Co. Piano. (R) 195
Brown, Mrs G. 61 E 122d....Brooklyn F Co. (R) 187
Brown, Henry. 357 E 72d....L Baumann. 379
Brown, T G. 237 W 41st....Wheelock & Co. Piano. (R) 170
Bruce, Elsie M. 53 W 33d....J Pyle (R) 1,500
Bush, G H. 55 W 19th....Brooklyn F Co. 1,267
Butler, J P. 241 W 25th....L Baumann. 145
Button, Miss M. 2053 7th av....S Knapp & Co. (R) 120
Beach, Christina. 550 E 143d....B M Cowperthwait & Co. 113
Bernheim, Leon. 125 Clinton pl ...C R Ruggels 257
Bersick, G M. 493 Lexington av....Cowperthwait & Co. 933
Bligh, Andrew. 133 W 100th....B M Cowperthwait & Co. 115
Braender, F. 2202 8th av... B M Cowperthwait & Co. 584
Brett, G J. 858 9th av.. .B M Cowperthwait & Co. 198
Buckley, W A. 307 W 119th....B M Cowperthwait & Co. 256
Burroughs, Maggie A. 443 E 123d....B M Cowperthwait & Co. 284
Canfield, May E. 114 W 43d....B M Cowperthwait & Co. 886
Carleton, Rita. 143 W 16th....J Baumann. 1,100
Condon, J E. 308 E 28th....B M Cowperthwait & Co. 120
Corr, P R and T A. 61 Grove....E C Hinsdale. 160
Crolius, Grace J. 2202 8th av....J Baumann. 348
Cross, Sadie C. 301 W 21st....J Baumann. 482
Carr, J J. 1911 3d av ...J Moriarty. 100
Cary, R C. 32 Greenwich av....Fanny Cary. 200
Casanges, Constanto....Gately & W. 222
Cochran, Sophia. 110 E 117th....F G Smith. Piano. (R) 178
Collins, Nellie A. 11 Pell....Jordan & M. 164
Crowder, C E. 628 10th av....L Baumann. 113
Curtis, Rose. 151 W 35th....L Baumann. 126
Casey, Marie. 326 E 37th ...J Moriarty. 160
Carson, Christiana. 2396 2d av....Dreisacker & Co. 190
Cleary, Henry. 257 W 32d....L Baumann. 197
Cohen, Mrs Harris. 163 E 87th....H Israel & Sons. 155
Cooper, Maggie. 261 W 39th....L Baumann. (R) 145
Same....same. (R) 245
De Luca, Germaro. 129 Cherry....Fennell & Pye. (R) 105
de Palos, J S. 222 Lexington av....L Baumann. (R) 128
Donohue, Bridget. 311 E 33d....E O'Callahan. 158
Deguizee, Hosanna. 200 W 62d...Jordau & M. 122
Durgan, J L. 8 Greenwich av....H Israel & Son. 204
Daly, J V. 209 Chrystie....R M Walters. Piano. 250
Darling, Florence. 241 E 114th....J Moriarty. 235
Dayton, Lucy. 211 W 53d ...H Israel & Sons. 414
Drumm, Frankie. 124 Macdougal... J Moriarty 275
Duke, Georgie. 220 E 18th....J Gregg. (R) 114
De Tramasure, P A. 125 5th av....J Baumann. 334
Duggan, Denis. 532 W 35th....O'Farrell & Co. 232
Ely, H A. 360 W 116th....J Baumann. 482
Ellis, Cora E. 119 5th av....J Gregg & Co. 316
Eupheat, Louis. 368 W 36th....L Baumann. 232
Eustace, Mary V. 219 W 104th....S J Savin. 1,154
Fay, Mary. 136 W 33d ....L Baumann. 127
Fernendes, John. 168 Monroe....F J Brechtel. 188
Fischer, Max. 345 E 74th....F J Brechtel. 168
Fox, Helena. 219 E 48th....F J Brechtel. 206
Finkelstein, J L. 361 6th av....J P Delehanty. 208
Fisher, G. 566 Columbus av....J G Truelson. Piano. 300
Freedman, A. 16 Sutton pl....Wheelock & Co. Piano. (R) 104
Falk, H and C. 72 Henry....H Israel & Sons. 191
Ferdon, L B. 438 W 55th....B M Cowperthwait & Co. 121
Frendburt, Ernestine. 829 9th av....J Baumann. 138
Grey, G J. 123 W 39th....J Baumann. 215
Garten, H M. 77 E 4th....Fennell & Pye. (R) 154
Gasling, A. 166 E 67th....Jordan, M & Co. 357
George, A. 1730 Madison av....Simpson & P. Piano. (R) 165
Georgine, Gusire. 222 W 13th ...M Myers. 700
Gilbert, C E. 247 E 49th....L Baumann. 352
Hater, Mary....E O'Callahan. 124
Hayward, Susan L. 19 W 84th....L Baumann. 153
Healy, E H. 836 Railroad av....L Baumann. (R) 123
Heinze, Reinbold. 52 Av A....L Baumann. 129
Hewitt, Minnie. 26 Perry....J Moriarty. (R) 167
Hickman, R N. 8th av and 107th st .. L Baumann. 414
Holland, Teresa. 125 E 63d .. L Baumann. 203
Haidmann, Annie. 41 W 65th....Wheelock & Co. Piano. (R) 80
Harison, Katie. 7 Cornelia....Simpson & P. Piano. 275
Hoffman, Dora. 327½ E 122d....Dreisacker & Co. 246
Hoffman, Kate. 338 E 17th....L Baumann. 161
Holz, J B. 209 E 51st .. Wheelock & Co. Piano. (R) 177
Horwitz, Abraham. 22 E 3d....F G Smith. Piano. (R) 255
Hovy, C M. 360 W 41st....F G Smith. Piano. (R) 140
Hagan, Eunice. 79 W 52d....M E Sheve. 500
Hornung, Charles. 345 Pavonia av, Jersey City, N J. Manges Bros. 203
Henry, John. 190 E 96th....B M Cowperthwait & Co. 173
Hogan, Maggie. 128 and 130 Macdougal ...B M Cowperthwait & Co. 150
Holmes, H L. 28 W 18th ...J Baumann 151
Jacobs, Rebecca. 204 W 44th....Amer Guar Assoc. 100
Johnson, Mary E. 176 E 55th....H Eisler. (R) 12
Jennings, Ellen. 455 W 57th....J Baumann. 118
Jackson, Mrs A. 327 W 59th....Brooklyn F Co. (R) 191
Jones, W P. 313 E 128d....Dreisacker & Co 163
Jordan, Elizabeth A. 188 W 27th....R M Walters. Piano. 190
Jacoby, Fanny. 854 2d av... S I Herschmann. 148
Jarvis, Louisa. 193 2d av....S I Herschmann. 204
Kelsing, Sadie. 407 E 85th....J Baumann. 305
Kern, I J. 235 and 237 W 14th....J Baumann. 236
Knapp & Fox. 251 W 42d....J S Rice. 214
Kamery, H. 400 W 39th....H Israel & Sons. 112
Kerby, Mary J. Bathgate av and 179th st....Jordan, M & Co. 279
Killen, Estelle. 959 6th av....Brooklyn F Co. 342
Kirby, Margaret E. 551 Grand....F G Smith. Piano. (R) 143
Kirk, Charlotte A. 249 W 55th....S Knapp & Co. (R) 142
Lambert, Alice. 468 6th av....A Pond. 150
La Porte, F. 235 W 18th....Wheelock & Co. Piano. (R) 201
Lawrence, T H. 233 W 135th... Simpson & P. Piano. 325
Laws, Bertha. 230 W 76th....B Weinstein. 600
Lee, Mrs E F. 209 W 21st ...S Knapp & C. (R) 127
Lewis, H. 312 Broome....H S Eisler. 128
Lichtwitz, F. 353 W 50th....Mary Potts. 500
Lockwood, A L and E W. 151 W 133d....E C Hinsdale. 160
Lathrop, L J. 288 E 126th....L Carle. Piano. 100
Larsen, Christina. 322 Henry....B M Cowperthwait & Co. 121
Lemaire, F B. 164 E 109th....B M Cowperthwait & Co. 211
Logan, Mary. 342 W 18th....B M Cowperthwait & Co. 232
La Finne, Nettie. 204 W 46th....L Baumann. 1,233
Laughna, Rose. 217 W 135th....J Baumann. 252
Lawrence, William. 169 Forsyth....F J Brechtel. 151
Leavout, Minnie. 140 W 32d....H Israel & Sons 280
Lilley, G F. 935 2d av ...Friel & Hand. 358
Lowenthal, Albert. 34 Greenwich av....S Lowenthal. 1,800
McGhee, Chas. 64 E 122d....L Baumann. 215
Meyer, Henry. 22 E 84th....L Baumann. 100
Meyers, Ida. 1838 3d av....Krakauer Bros. Piano. 375
Mills, Margaretta. 745 Amsterdam av....L Baumann. 110
Miller, Christian. 1422 Park av....J Baumann. 180
Morand, Joseph. 335 E 6th....S I Herschmann. 105
Morse, Carrie E. 10, 12 and 14 W 125th....Dreisacker & Co. 437
Muller Alex. 121 E 85th .. Friel & Hand. 179
Mallon, D J. 137 E 50th....F G Smith. Piano. (R) 200
Maxwell, Martha J. 253 W 121st....C L Sears. (R) 200
McCann, G P and E. 196 3d av....E C Hinsdale. 250
McCormack, Johanna. 2 Quincy slip....B M Cowperthwait & Co. 201
Mendelson, Alex. 64 E 114th .H S Eisler. (R) 133
Miller, Elsie. 213 Pearl....B M Cowperthwait & Co. 170
Mackin, Jane. 229 E 70th... L Baumann. 112
Madden, J. 411 E 120th....Dreisacker & Co. 243
Malone, Rose. 408 W 30th....L Baumann. 164
Manzini, A. 707 Columbus av....E Fantini. 110
Mardon, H C, Jr. 502 W 46th....L Baumann. 115
Martinez, C. 911 6th av....J Moriarty. 426
Mayo, Ella....Gately & W. 236
McCabe, Anna L. 2327 1st av....F G Smith. Piano. (R) 130
Mertens, Helene. 225 10th av....L Baumann. 187
Mettler, H C....Gately & W. 132
Myers, Felix. 326 Columbus av....L Baumann. 139
Newbrauch, Andrew. 65 W 99th ...J Baumann. 281
Neuman, Conrad. 325 E 9th... F J Brechtel. 145
O'Brien, J F. 208 W 88th... C E Pierce. 100
O'Connor, H. 234 E 83d....H Israel & Sons. 114
Odon, Laura D. 222 W 48th....C Mooney. 150
Ohrdorf, Louise. 63 W 51st....H Thoesen. 624
O'Connor, Mary. 234 E 59th....Jordan & M. 168
O'Neill, James. 82 Henry....B M Cowperthwait & Co. 151
O'Reilly, Mary A. 274 4th av....Jordan & M. 105
Pinaker, Macher. 231 Broome....H S Eisler. 124
Prentice, C H. 252 W 38th....B M Cowperthwait & Co. 319
Perrett, Ulric. 47 E 105th... L Baumann. 148
Pino, Pasquale. 103 W 108d... J S Rice. 216
Popper, Eliza. 102 W 94th... J Baumann. 288
Rauscher, Ed. 972 5th av....L Baumann. 133
Reagen, J B. 3 Perry ..L Baumann. 240
Reynolds, Mary. 186 Lexington av ...L Baumann. (R) 404
Roux, Felix. 1244 Broadway....J Moriarty. (R) 148
Rosander & Ohlsen. 231 E 45th....J Gregg & Co. 180
Ross, Lotta. 1009 6th av... L Baumann. 939
Ryan, S A. 159 W 62d....H S Eisler. (R) 187
Rath, W C, Jr. 42 Morton....Manges Bros. (R) 124
Rheimsrrom, N. 1235 Lexington av... Jordan, M & Co. 150
Richter, H F. 324 E 90th....H S Eisler. 104
Robbins, A M. 78 W 48th....Wheelock & Co. Piano. (R) 190
Rotondo, Tolia. 256 Broome... L Baumann. 149
Ruge, Emma. 1701 Lexington av....Wheelock & Co. Piano. (R) 180
Rusig, Alice M. 39 E 50th....Wheelock & Co. Piano. (R) 112
Russell, M E. 254 W 38th....Wheelock & Co. Piano. (R) 100
Sellars, Lizzie. 496 7th av ...L Baumann. 125
Simon, J. 310 E 83d....C E Pierce. 130
Smith, W. 228 W 52d ...Wheelock & Co. Piano. (R) 155
Speckelsen, Lena. 41 St Marks pl....J Moriarty. 114
St Clair, Georgia. 161 E 90th....Fennell & P. (R) 121
Strother, Julia. 250 W 41st....O'Farrell & Co. 123
Spitz, Amalia. 525 5th....P Ratzersdorfer. 250
St Clair, Jane M. 307 and 309 W 22d....W C Demorest. 250
Smith, Mrs A. 51 W 98th....B M Cowperthwait & Co. 136
Smith, Mrs C A. 342 E 65th....B M Cowperthwait & Co. 110
Showles, Pearl. 152 E 27th....N Y F Co. 177
St Albe, G. 215 E 69th....B M Cowperthwait & Co. 324
Serrano, C A. 328 E 14th....Dreisacker & Co. 191
Shipman, O A. 100 9th av....J Baumann. 360
Smyth, Samuel. 210 E 57th....J Baumann. 180
Stapleton, T H. 1644 Madison av....J Moriarty. 108
Thiessen, Elizabeth. 351 W 36th....J Baumann. 253
Truchsess, Phillipine D. 162 W 23d....W F Widmayer. 350
Thorp, Marcella. 662 E 142d....Spies Bros. 158
Tubb, Clara. 426 W 46th....H Israel & Sons. 128

Vallis, J M. 1208 Columbus av....Brooklyn F Co. 285
Vaughn, W H. 144 W 53d....L Baumann. 306
Vincent, A. 108 E 87th....Brooklyn F Co 492
Van Wie, Mary E. 41 W 49th....H L Wight. secures rent
Van Wormer, Lizzie. 121 W 43d....Manges Bros. (R) 317
Vossnack, S E. 446 W 24th ..E O'Callahan. 599
Werner, Emil 9 E 3d....F J Brechtel. 180
Wortmann, Sadie L. 228 West st, Hoboken, N J ....Manges Bros. 106
Wall, J J. 93d W 134th....Dreisacker & Co. 286
Walsh, Mary. 345 E 118th... Dreisacker & Co. 171
Webber, F. 347 W 58th....Fennell & Pye. (R) 321
Same...same. 157
White, Mrs H B. 124 Hicks st, Brooklyn....S Knapp & Co. (R) 435
Wicks, I S and I. 17 Debevoise pl, Brooklyn....E C Hinsdale. (R) 190
Wilson, Hattie. 134 W 53d....Wheelock & Co. Piano. (R) 410
Williams, G W. 133 W 24th....B M Cowperthwait & Co. 160
Wisker, Thomas. 70 Oliver ...B M Cowperthwait & Co. 157
Wood, M. 200 W 39th... I Mason. (R) 115
Zukschwerdt, J and M. 145th st and 10th av....M Smith. (R) 115
Zutte, L. 69 Chrystie....H S Eisler. 177

MISCELLANEOUS.

Adams, William. 617 and 619 W 38th. ..J J O'Connell. Horse, Fixtures, &c. 1,000
Augenmeyer, G W. 221 St Nicholas av....G Rieburg. Store Fixtures. 500
Allen, A R. 133 W 31st....Wolff Bros. Wagon, Horse, &c. 125
Anderson, John. 82d st and Western Boulevard ...J Rothschild. Horse, &c. 155
Angevine, W & Co. 1400 Broadway, 133 Waverley pl, 258 W 15th st, 209 W 15th st, 202 E 81st st, 201½ E 39th st and 56th st and Lexington av ...J Rowland, Jr. Laundry Fixtures. (R) 800
Banner, Simon. 161 Broome....S Presler, Store Fixtures. 50
Behringer, Henry. 735 Amsterdam av....Abstein & Schaeffer. Wagon. 100
Berger, Casper. 53 Willett....H Brand. Butcher Fixtures. 87
Bresler, Max. 241 Clinton....A Smith. Drug Fixtures. 400
Brown, J W. 239 and 241 E 115th....B Weill. Horse. 75
Boddy, George. 146 W 17th ...C K Krull. Horse, Ice Wagon, &c. 200
Bowman, G G. 2002 2d av....G T Bowman. Grocery Fixtures. 575
Bunger, Henry. 12 Jane....Wolff Bros. Horse and Coupe. 175
Baum, P J. 535 6th av....A S Leopold. Barber Fixtures. 200
Burnham, E L. 10 E 14th....W H Blain. Books. 227
Blaack, Paul. 129 1st av....Lamson Consol S S Co. Register. 50
Braun, Henry. 323 1st av....J C Klatzl. Bakery Fixtures. 800
Brown, J A. 1212 Broadway....A E Prescott. Office Fixtures. (R) 800
Carsten, H C. 2386 Hoffman....H Ruhe. Horses, &c. 1,500
Clements, Fred. 24 Desbrosses....Duparquet, H & M Co. Range, &c. (R) 20
Call, J. 669 6th av ...A Schwaab & Son. Barber Fixtures. 311
Chroback, O. 76 Orchard....H Gambert. Bakery Fixtures. 150
Cook, T. 247 W 41st....Hincks & J. Coach. 400
Craven, T C. 29 Broadway ...Hall's Safe and Lock Co Safe. 188
Crow, H P. 550 W 52d....J Lasch. Horse and Wagon. 150
Calazzi, Vincenzzo. 86 Carmine... F Malnelli. Barber and Grocery Fixtures. 130
Clark, I S. 230 W 47th....D B Dunham. Coach. (R) 52
Cornet, W H. 511 W 54th....H & W Hartt. Horses, Trucks, &c. (R) 750
Connors, Thomas. 200 E 47th....P A Cassidy. Wagon. 142
Crescenzio, Francesco. 192 Bleecker ...A Petrone. Barber Fixtures. 174
Drewes, John. Western Boulevard and 130th st ....J Winter. Coal Yard Fixtures. 300
Della, L. 441 1st av....A Schwaab & Son. Barber Fixtures. 264
Di Chiara, Pietro. 1434 3d av....A Schwaab. Barber Fixtures. 275
Dallimore, H B. 116 Withers st, Brooklyn....E W Reynolds. Horses and Trucks. 600
Same. 13th av and Horatio st....Same. Horses and Trucks. 900
Deisser, John. 117 Lincoln av....R J Costello. Horse and Ice Wagon. 800
de Preissig, E. 1031 1st av....E Winterbottom. Press. 125
Deery, M J. 120 Leonard....Lamson Consol S S Co. Register. (R) 210
Drummond, L E. Stewart Building....A L Drummond. Office Fixtures. 3,000
Eckhoff, D. 349 1st av....J Mathews Co. Soda Fixtures. 400
Eitel & Umgetter. 176 E 112th....H Dillmann. Horse, &c. 50
Edsell, Frank. 72 Morton....M Borden. Furnished Rooms, &c. 100
Elliott, W. 2351 3d av....Bramhall, Deane & Co. Ranges. 85
Farrell, Margaret. Park av and 101st st....J Glackner. Horses and Wagons. 1,000
Farina, Petrina. 1084 Park av....A M Dolph & Co. Laundry Fixtures. 400
Faust, G A. 300 E 31st ..A Busby. Butcher Fixtures. 500
Framberg, B. 139 Norfolk....C Dierking. Butcher's Ice Box. 50
Fricke, E J. 15 E 12th....C Lebritter. Saloon and Grocery Fixtures. (R) 675
Friedman, M. 228 Stanton...Restaurant F Co. Range. 42
Fergerson, Robert. 2 Strykers lane....G Irving. Horses, Carts, &c. 3,000
Ferera, Michael....Cohen & Mulheiser. Horse and Truck. (R) 161
Fisher, J M. 360 E 79th....J Mathews Co. Soda Fixtures. 275
Grisafi, F and B. 306 E 26th....G Seiniara. Barber Fixtures. 35
Grossman, Max. 275 Delancey....S Weiss. Machines. 200
Granelo & Caramono. 2393 1st av....J Souvay. Barber Fixtures. 120
Guida, E. 145 Baxter....R Fnichi. Confectionery Store. 120
Gunther & Kahn. 763 Columbus av, 1995 3d av, 728 2d av and 242 E 113th st....Lena Gunther. Butcher Shops, Leases, Horses, &c. 12,000
Graham, R H. 75th st and 10th av ..J F Schreyer. Horses, &c. 1,000
Huber, Eugene. 1953 3d av....H Eberhard. Bakery Fixtures. 1,500
Heinzer & Miller. 171 Suffolk .. F Miller. Machinery. 2,000
Heitzman, Geo. 61, Amsterdam av....National C Reg Co Register. 400
Hoanen, L M. 2177 7th av....National C Reg Co. Register. 225
Harwitz, L & A. 280 East Broadway....I Isaacson. Bags, Satchels, &c. 1,000
Henderson, William, Jr. 127 W 32d....W Henderson. Laundry Fixtures. 250
Hoffman House. Broadway and 25th st, 7 Beaver, Exchange pl and New st, 126th st and Riverside Drive ...Farmers' Loan and Trust Co. Hotel Fixtures. (R) 500,000
Hopps, H. 999 6th av....H S Hopps. Boot and Shoe Factory. 389
Haas, Frank. 30 Suffolk....J Mathews Co. Soda Fixtures. 75
Same. 390 Madison... same. Soda Fixtures. (R) 1,785
Hess, G A. 26 W 59th....G Lewandowsky. Barber Fixtures. (R) 313
Hoag, H G. 128 South 5th av....E F Hoag. Machinery. 3,000
Huneke & Lutter. 271 9th av...L Faschen. Grocery Fixtures. 1,275
Hyde, J P. 417 West 24th....T E Stewart. Machinery. 200
Iron Malt Chemical Co. 50 Vesey....J Mathews Co. Soda Fixtures. 402
Illert, George. 609 E 11th....A Raabe. Barber Fixtures. 200
Johnston, J M. 83 Gold....C B Cottrell & Son. Press. 1,500
Jones Printing Co ..Campbell P P and M Co. Press. (R) 1,540
Jannitelli, Luke. 183 7th av....A Schwaab & Son. Barber Fixtures. 250
Knepper, C M. 75 Murray....H E Wagner. Presses, &c. (R) 3,000
Same....J F Wagner. Presses, &c. (R) 3,500
Same....A Kitcheit. Presses, &c. (R) 3,000
Keleher, John. 341 E 11th....J Kennedy. Lumber, &c. 550
Kiley, M. 226 E 38th....Bridget Russell. Horses, Wagons, &c. (R) 1,500
Kuerzlen, G C. 880 11th av....J Roltmann. Butcher Fixtures. 300
Kaminer, N and S....J Kaminer. Horses, Wagons, &c. 500
Kaplan, P & Co. 71 Essex....H J Bierman. Laundry Fixtures. 500
Kelly, B J. 1248 Railroad av....C Kelly. Office Fixtures. 300
Keols, Herman. 26th st and 3d av....National C Reg Co. Register. 175
Koebler, John. Courtlandt av ..W J McMullen. Grocery Fixtures. 250
Koop, Louis. 74 and 76 Little 12th....H J Koop. Horses, Trucks, &c. 850
Lehmann, Max. 102 Av A... A Frey. Machinery. (R) 400
Lord, Exiner & Co. 624 Madison av ...F Exiner. Store Fixtures, &c. 2,500
Leslauer, Albert. 137 Pitt....L Heinsfurter. Butcher Fixtures. 200
Levy, C. 271 East Houston....A Schwaab & Son. Barber Fixtures. 119
Lichtwitz, F. 416 W 32d....Ernest Kaufman. Horse and Wagon. 600
Locurto, C. 1488 Park av....A Schwaab & Son. Barber Fixtures. (R) 194
Lisanti, Antonio. 808 2d av....A Schwaab & Son Barber Fixtures. 451
Luehrmann, Henry. 413 Willis av and 612 E 144th st ..Smith & Sills. Grocery Fixtures, &c. 650
Marose, Alex. 342 2d av....A Schwaab & Son. Barber Fixtures. 375
Mangione & Pistorino. 58 Barclay....A Schwaab & Son. Barber Fixtures. 680
Mayforth, J C. 807 8th....Wilhelmine Kleemann. Horse and Wagon. 400
Messino, Francesco. 516 Canal....A Schwaab. Barber Fixtures. 220
Michel, C. 228 8th av....L Mertens. Barber Fixtures. 175
Murphy, J. 953 Broadway....Sarah Hoey. Cloth. 1,877
McCaffery, John. 3d av and 108th st....National C Reg Co. Register. 200
McCann, Patrick. Highbridge....Korner & S. Horses, Wagons, &c. 748
McNamee, J J. 352 W 25th....P McElduff. Horses and Ice Wagon. 2,000
Miller, Louise. 10th av, bet 183d and 184th sts ....C Weber. Hotel Fixtures. (R) 500
Neiss, Henry. 84 Varick... National C Reg Co. Register. 175
Oliveras, B F. 513 Lexington av ...J Stapleton. Store Fixtures, Lease, &c. 400
Palmer, John. 114 Greenwich av....H Brand. Butcher Fixtures. 75
Petersen & Woltmann. 324 W 53d ...J W Katzenberger. Bottler Fixtures. (R) 3,000
Purcell, Christopher. 2290 8th av....National C Reg Co. Register. 175
Patti, M A. 179 East Houston ...C Generoso. Barber Fixtures. 95
Pepper, David. 681 Amsterdam av... Columbia Wagon Co. Wagon. 150
Peter, J. 165 E 27th....A Schwaab & Son. Barber Fixtures. 197
Ramhorst, W F. 10 Church ...Restaurant F Co. Range. 97
Rosenfeld, Jr, J. Room 10, Times building....Marvin Safe Co. Safe. 200
Rossi, M. 255 Bowery....A Schwaab & Son. Barber Fixtures. 460
Roth, W. 314 E 75th....P Pryibil. Machinery. 110
Rudolph, J A. 581 W 42d....J H Seward. Horse, Milk Wagon, &c. 300
Riehl & Coughlin. 1253 9th av....T Riehl. Butcher Fixtures. (R) 900
Scherer, E C. 193 Greene... M Reimers. Tools, Machinery, &c. 250
Seipel, John. 90 and 92 Park row....K Seipel. Machinery. (R) 880
Schmid, Julius. 616 W 46th....R Reiss. Horses, Trucks, Tools, &c. 1,000
Schmidt, Charles. 579 2d av....Lamson Consol S S Co. Register. 250
Suorrer & Silvermann. 208 Broome....J Mathews Co. Soda Fixtures. 100
Scherman, S. 160 E 45th....G Pius. Barber Fixtures. 300
Sheehan, J L & Co. 247 and 249 W 41st....Hutchinson & Co. Horses, Coaches, &c. 3,000
Sherlock, Mary. 11 Washington...D B Dunham. Coach. (R) 100
Stransky, Emanuel. 5 Clinton....East Side Bank. Jewelry Fixtures. 290
Sanna, Carmine. 147 Mott....Marvin Safe Co. Safe. (R) 250
Schiff, A. 284 East Houston....Duparquet, Huot & Co. Range. 36
Shaeffer, M S. 117 Christopher....R H Downing. Horse, Truck, &c. 500
Steinberg & Barthfeld. 63 Stanton....D Telk. Bakery Fixtures. 70
Steiner, M. 306 E 53d....C Dierking. Butcher's Ice Box. 50
Sullivan & Westervelt. 133 7th av ...Restaurant F Co. Ranges. 97
Telloma, R M. 561 W 42d....A Schwaab & Son. Barber Fixtures. (R) 323
Theil, Selman. 178 Norfolk....F & G Haag & Co. Barber Fixtures. 155
Ulmer, Fred. 617 Greenwich....J Shulles. Bakery Fixtures. 1,000
Ullmann, S. 415 E 113th....Sarah Levy. Horses, Wagon, &c. 450
Utjer, Henry. 2631 8th av....M Peters. Grocery Fixtures. 1,500
Vico & Rocco. 49 Bowery....A Schwaab. Barber Fixtures. 174
Von Lehe, Catherine M. 1118 Forest av....H Corrs. Horses, Wagons, &c. 800
Von Boerio, Emily. 376 7th av....J B Bokens. Grocery Fixtures. 1,000
Weysser, William. 754 6th av....R A Hoffman. Barber Fixtures. 250
Walz, W. 205 Wooster....W S Hewley. Bakery Fixtures. (R) 600
Weinmann, Gustav. 43 Park....L Weinmann. Tools, &c. —
Wheat & Marks. 157 William....Globe Mfg Co. Presses. (R) 400
Wurzweiler, E A. 344 E 12th....E Marscheider. Butcher Fixtures. 176
Wagner Bros. 199 Hester....E Glaser. Butcher Fixtures. 250
Wildes, James. 8 Manhattan....Donigan & Nielson. Wagon. 364
Woslawsky, Simon. 73 Suffolk....S Glazer. Grocery Fixtures. 35
Yorke, W C. 2248 3d av....Lamson Consol S S Co. Register. 210
Zugner, P J....D B Dunham. Coach. (R) 379
Zipser, A. 248 Rivington....M Engel. Barber Fixtures. 80

BILLS OF SALE.

Bartnett, Joseph. 317 E 114th....W E McShaffrey. Saloon. 1,000
Bokens, J B. 376 7th av....E Van Boerie. Grocery Fixtures. 1,500
Castle, J W. 1526 1st av....Sarah A Ashton. Bakery Fixtures. 50
Dryfuss, Mary. 1862 3d av....J & H Rushmeyer. Grocery Fixtures. 1,800
Dobson, G C. 50 W 125th....C B Reed. Office Fixtures, &c. 100
Eckstein, William. In store of J McConvill & Co, Walker st ...R Friedlander. Stock, &c. 1
Ellenbogen, Lipa. 176 Rivington....F Ellenbogen. Butcher Fixtures. 200
Ellis, D F. 165 W 102d....A T Seaman. Grocery Fixtures. 631
Freund, Leopold. 262 Bowery....F Summers. Restaurant Fixtures. 1,500
Ganzenmuller, William. 179 E 106th....H Masemann. Butcher Fixtures. 812
Glaser, Frederick. 95 and 97 Pearl....Henrietta Ziegler. Saloon Fixtures. 2,000
Geoghegan, P. 100 E 109th....H McGuire. Saloon Fixtures. 2,700
Goldberg, Rachel. 124 Delancey....J Milakawsky. Grocery Fixtures. 400
Goldblatt, Hannah P. 116 Broome....N Goldblatt. Grocery Fixtures. nom
Hogan, J F. 2294 1st av....P Lynch. Saloon. —
Hayward & Williamson. 127 West....J S Kelly. Saloon Fixtures. 1
John Kress B Co. 60 Stone....Henrietta Ziegler. Saloon Fixtures. 1,750
Kahrs, Herman. 105th st, near 3d av....J Synnott. Horse, Wagon, &c. 300
Same....J & H Rushmeyer. Horse, Truck, &c. 800
Kelly, J S. 127 West ...F Neis. Saloon Fixtures. 8,500
Kahaly & Weinheim. 40 Howard....D & M Weil. Upholstery Goods. nom
Kleeblatt, S. 305 E 83d....H Kleeblatt. Saloon Fixtures. 400
Klockemeyer, F. 209 E 11th ...J Klockemeyer. Horses and Wagon. 550
Koch, Peter. 2517 8th av....H Koch. Bakery Fixtures. 650
Philbrook, Stella. 7 E 27th....H W Riddle. Furniture. 2,000
Parker, G W. 412 Grand....M Pollack. Soda Water Business. 1,150
Price, S T B. 75th st and Amsterdam av....S Aldrich. Carpenter Work. 1
Rhodes, H J. 36 Liberty....G P Taylor. Furniture. nom
Seaman, C H ...T J Nall. Horse, Wagon, &c. 40
Stein, Lewis. 278 Canal....G D Nichols. Fancy Goods, &c. 1,609
Slote, A. 544 3d av ..J Stone. Cigar Store. 100
Suder, F. 217 E 6th....P Scheel. Saloon Fixtures. 1,950
Schlosser, H....F Summers. Lease. 1
Sherlock, Anna M ..Mrs J T Cox. Furniture. 490
Waldeck, A. 284 2d....E Simon. Butcher Fixtures. 100

ASSIGNMENTS OF CHATTEL MORTGAGES.

Brooks, A L to H Greenbaum. ½ int. (Mort. given by R Klein, Sept. 12, 1891.) 150
Moore, T exr of Mary M Stapleton to C Mooney. (L D Odon, Oct. 7, 1890.) 150
Potter, Helen, to A E and A M Wallace. (W A Maher, Oct 16, 1884). 6,053
Rosenfeld, Emil to A Dinkelmann & Co. (F Freedmann, May 15, 1891.) 1,100

KINGS COUNTY.

SEPTEMBER 10 TO 16.—INCLUSIVE.

SALOON AND RESTAURANT FIXTURES.

Bachert, G C. 88 Central av....J Dewalds. $1,000
Bachmayer, A. Grand st, Maspeth....F Ibert. (R) 400
Bauer, F. 116 Jefferson....J Doelger's Sons. 600

Boehlau, G E. 714 4th av....Claus Lipsius B Co. 250
Bouquet, F. Newtown, L I....J Kress B Co. (R) 300
Christie, A. 133 Hudson av....H B Scharmann & Sons. 500
Coyle, O. 51 Spencer....A Altenbrand. 308
Curran, J J. 99 Columbia....H B Scharmann & Son. (R) 600
Collins, M G. 100 Bridge....Claus Lipsius B Co. (R) 500
Deinhardt, M. 762 Hart. ..L Eppig. 585
Dietz, A and Elise. Schenck av and Fulton st ....C Frese. (R) 500
Duerkes, P. 1081 Myrtle av....Williamsburgh B Co. 1,000
Dempsey, J. 245 North 7th....M Seitz. 300
Deppe, L. 1243 Broadway....D M Koehler & Co. 400
Deering, W. 223 Boerum....J Doelger's Sons. 600
Donnelly, R. 290 Gold .. H B Scharmann & Sons. 600
Egan, T F. 62 Degraw....P Ballantine & Sons. (R) 1,100
Evers & O'Brien. 80 Atlantic av... J Ruppert. 1,900
same. 357 Hicks....same. 1,300
Feeks, J B. 35 Main ...H B Scharmann & Sons. 1,075
Frey, J. 366 Bushwick av.... C Frese. (R) 1,000
Gerdes & Ruge. 9 Nassau....Beadleston & W. (R) 1,000
Greenpoint Turn Verein. Greenpoint av....C Frese. (R) 1,042
Gallagher, F. 677 Driggs....E Ochs. 409
Herriott, T. 99 Canton....J Ruppert. 300
Hervey, C. 959 De Kalb av. Williamsburgh B Co. 450
Hogan, C J. 287 Bond....H B Scharmann & Sons. 650
Harper, J D E, and G Merritt. 528 4th av. . S Liebmann's Sons B Co. 800
Heavy, J. Atlantic av, cor Clason av....Claus Lipsius B Co. (R) 400
Jeanson, C. 228 Conover....M Seitz. 1,302
Jones & Falkenburgh. 7 Leonard....J Kress B Co. 600
Katzmann, Kate. 164 Harman....S Liebmann's Sons B Co. 500
Kinkel, Mary. 578 Court ...H B Scharmann & Sons. 787
Klott, H P. 728 Broadway....Rubsam & Horrmann B Co. 700
Kabelitz, C....L Eppig. 500
Kludt, H. 58 Fulton....W Ulmer. (R) 500
Koechel, J. 288 Flushing av....C Frese. 195
Koschmieder, R. 585 Broadway.. Claus Lipsius B Co. (R) 1,200
Klebsch, G. 1196 3d av....F & M Schaefer Brewing Co. 1,075
Lawley, F J and S L Holden. 714 Grand....T N Halden. Restaurant Fixtures. 300
Lynch, O and R Roe. 328 Flushing av....Otto Huber Brewery. 350
Lang, A. 186 Troutman....M Seitz. 1,000
McCaffrey & McNamee. 62 Columbia....Long Island Brewery. 500
McGreal, P. 325 Bond....W Craft. 400
Muller, J J. 70 Kingsland av....M Seitz. (R) 350
Mooney, J F. 743 Kent av....Obermeyer & L. (R) 500
Mulvaney, J J. 11 Alabama av....J Goetz. 200
Maupai, Elizabeth. 1207 Myrtle av....Weiz & Z. (R) 1,200
McCauley, W. Kent av, s e cor Flushing av... Claus Lipsius B Co. (R) 300
McDermott, C and T. 247 Johnson....Claus Lipsius B Co. (R) 1,000
McFarland, J and T. 510 Manhattan av....S Liebmann's Sons B Co. 1,000
McGuinniss, P. 137 Degraw .... Howard & Childs (R) 300
Meyer, R. 131 Franklin....Claus Lipsius B Co. (R) 1,000
Muller, J. 174 Ewen....Weiz & Z. (R) 1,100
Murphy, E and T F. 4 Howard av....Esther A Crawford. 800
May, A and E....L Epig. 800
Phelan W J and Annie M Malone. 144 Court .... J E Malone. 1,600
Picard, J. 145 Walton .. M Seitz. 735
Ralph, P I. 123 Kent av....O Huber B Co. (R) 125
Rissel, P. 81 Johnson av....J Doelger's Sons. (R) 500
Roberts, W. 218 South 1st....J Kress B Co. (R) 1,000
Reiss, N. 177 Greenpoint av....Claus Lipsius B Co. (R) 1,500
Rohr, J P. 56 Jay....Claus Lipsius B Co. 300
Riley, J. 1020 3d av ...B McMahon. 300
Scherbotz, T. 229 5th....Claus Lipsius B Co. (R) 300
Schloen, J H. 670 Baltic....H & G Monsees. (R) 1,100
Serakog, J. 184 Dupont....S Liebmann's Sons B Co. 280
Shea, W. 190 Meeker av....Claus Lipsius B Co. 1,300
Steffens, C. 1188 Bedford av ...J Kress B Co. (R) 1,500
Stelljes, J. 83 Union av....J Kress B Co. (R) 240
Shannon, T. 129 Harrison....P Ballantine & Sons. (R) 3,750
Smee, R. 363 Hamilton av ...M Seitz. 567
Smith, P T. 501 Humboldt....O Huber B Co. 1,000
Sweeney, D F and W Hughes. 1528 3d av.... Beadleston & Woerz. 500
Tiemers, H F. 493 Manhattan av....Weiz & Z. 1,000
Ulrich, A. Osborn, cor Summit av....F Munch. (R) 75
Van Strydonck, G. 651 5th av....Claus Lipsius B Co. (R) 300
Viemeisler, C. 1765 Broadway....S Liebmann's Sons B Co. 2,500
Witte, G. 166 Palmetto .. W Ulmer. 500
Warholy, S. 84 North 6th....S Liebmann's Sons B Co. 500
Zerrenner, W. 113 Withers....Rubsam & Horrmann B Co. 200
Zimmermann, S. Thatford st and Sutter av.... L Eppig. 360

HOUSEHOLD FURNITURE.

Alford, H A V. 252 Grand av....Brooklyn F Co. 254
Anderson, J. 955 53d....Brooklyn F Co. 185
Anderson, Emma. 25 Manhasset pl....J McEnery & Co. 201
Alzamord, J. 332 8th . . Cowperthwait & Co. 216
Becher, C E. 390 Gates av....W H Myer. 150
Bersick, G M. 493 Lexington av....Cowperthwait & Co. 933
Brennan, Mrs P. 116 Stanhope....I Mason. 180
Banner, W G. 319 Degraw....Brooklyn F Co. 257
Culver, C. 727 Prospect....Brooklyn F Co. 326
Carmer, J R H. 44 Lefferts pl....Brooklyn F Co. 181
Cederberg, A H. 61 Tompkins pl....A C Flatley. 182
Cooper, A. 391 Park pl... Brooklyn F Co. 140
Dawler, Delia. 211 4th av....O'Connor & T. 138
Dederick, E H. 201 W 118th, New York....Nat Loan and Guarantee Co. 150
Dormer, J. 662 Warren ..O'Connor & T. 283
Edwards, Margaret F and William F. 337 Putnam av....J Crombie. 100
Ebrat, M L. 75 1st pl....J McEnery & Co. 136
Falco, C J and Martha T. 66 Grove....Mary A Britles. 145
Hassett, Ann. 289 Hicks....Ellen McMahon. 500
Have, Mrs W. 763 Monroe....Mullins & Sons. 156
Hughes, Kittie. 217 Pearl. ..Mullins & Sons. 127
Hulsoven, T. 92 Washington ...E Driscoll & Bro. 205
Hynes, C. 51 Columbia....I Mason. 115
Higgins, P. 51 Sands....I Mason. 143
Kenney, Maggie. 67 Front....O'Connor & T. 127
La Roza, Lizzie. 222 Freeman....L Baumann. 143
Mackintosh, Anna. 21 St. Marks av.... H Thoesen. 286
McDougall, Emma. 127 McDonough....Brooklyn F Co. 264
McLoughlin, J. 239a Vernon av....Brooklyn F Co. 149
Moore, D. 436 Gates av....Trustee of J A Roberts. 491
Murphy, B. 451 Sackett .. J McEnery & Co. 149
Perrin, H E and Mary F L. 64 Hicks....S W Angel. Piano. 400
Primitive Meth Church, U S A, Eastern Conference. 249 Fulton and 237 Schenck....P Allen, Sr. Printing Office. 6,900
Robinson, Lucy. 439 St Marks av....L Baumann. 129
Rugg, Mrs. E H. 709 Lafayette av....C A Coleman. 128
Rush, E H. 309 Madison....A Pearson. 107
Rutzer, C. 266 Rodney....A Schulz. 265
Raymond, J. 180 McDonough....Lincoln I and G Assoc. 135
Read, Amelia J. 63 Degraw....Jordan & M. 130
Schluter, A. 1443 Broadway....Maria T Hauser. 2.0
Shaw, Matilda. 20 Tompkins pl....Leila Shaw. (R) 4,000
Savarese, F. 244 Bridge....J McEnery & Co. 278
Schields, F and A Reynolds. 12 Glenada pl.... C D Rust. 500
Seeley, I. 379 5th av .. Brooklyn F Co. 111
Selover, Lucy wife of W W. 669 Willoughby av ....C A Selover. (R) 250
Smith, C A. 331 St Marks pl....O'Connor & T. 208
Timmins, E F. 270 St Marks av....L Baumann. 173
Tirsbier, Helena. 86 Throop av....A Schulz. 137
Van, C E. 90 Concord . .Brooklyn F Co. 158
Wall, T E. 175 Meserole av....Jordan, M & Co. 320
Webb, G H and Ellen G. 54 Decatur....E C Hinsdale. 100
Wentworth, T H. 215 Washington av....O'Connor & T. 280
Wicks, I S. 17 Debevoise pl....E C Hinsdale. 190
Woerner, H. 580 Herkimer....O'Connor & T. 181
Wood, E B. 214 Schermerhorn ...R G Lockwood's Sons. (R) 100
West, Maggie. 465 Delmont av . Mullins & Sons. 165
Wieland, F L. 273 Fulton....A B Moore. 803
Waite, A J. 720 Degraw....O'Connor & T. 109
Young, Emily. 251 Duffield....I Mason. 164
Yackly, Eugenia E. 124 Joralemon....Evelyn Miller. 400
Zeriko, Marie A. 87 Cambridge pl....C A Barnett. 368

MISCELLANEOUS.

Bargelini, F. 259 Bond....G Bargelini. Butcher Fixtures. 300
Burger, O. 10 Scholes....B Kern. Butcher Fixtures. 100
Billello, G and A Orlando....M Lamaze. Shoe Store Fixtures. 200
Berthelson, C and E. 122 39th....Eliz Berthelson. Horse and Wagon. (R) 400
Brasse, J M. 616 Fulton....F & G Haag & Co. Barber Fixtures. 871
Cordis, H W. 19 Broadway....L & G Otten. Hotel Fixtures. 5,000
Costilo, J E. 515 Kent av....Prentiss Tool and S Co. Tools. 902
Same....same. Tools. 490
Costilo, J E. 515 Kent av....Prentiss Tool and Supply Co. Tools. 700
Dobbins, Ellen. Varick st, near Meeker av....J Volkommer, Jr, & Co. Horses, &c. 1,000
Drummond, R. New York....Campbell P P and Mfg Co. Press. (R) 2,025
Dowd, M J....Nat Cash Register Co. Register. 175
Fisk, C H. 291 W 11th st, New York....J Monk. Machinery, &c. 500
Forscutt, H E. 81 Fulton....C E Hammett, Jr. Drug Store Fixtures. 1,985
Glinnen, E and D. ..G Dessecker. Hearse. (R) 175
Greiner, H. 520 Graham av....M Ibert. Bakery Fixtures. 300
Giovanni, R. 316 North 2d....Marvin Safe Co. Safe. 300
Hanson, E....W Conrady. Wagon. 150
Hanson, A. 288 Schermerhorn....H A C Dahl. Horses, &c. 230
Hennings, Mary. 4th av and 53d st....Austin, Nichols & Co. Grocery Fixtures. 225
Ireland, T H....G Dessecker. Hearse. (R) 300
Jones, D. 288 Schermerhorn....H A C Dahl. Horse, &c. 110
Junker & Co. 264 Columbia....J P Stein. Horse and Wagon. 200
Kneppler, C M. 75 Murray st, New York....J F Wagner. Printing Office. (R) 3,000
Same....A Kilchelt. Printing Office. (R) 3,000
Same....H E Wagner. Printing Office. (R) 3,000
Kunz, L. 33 Throop av....J Klobutscheck. Barber Fixtures. 100
Lober & Schlim. 390 Tompkins av....Austin, Nichols & Co. Horse and Wagon. 584
Lynch & Roe. 328 Flushing av....M T Garvey. Butcher Fixtures. 200
McCormack, J T. 196 Rockaway av... P H Ahlers. Fixtures, &c. 1,000
Mulhern, T. Benton st....E Rothschild. Cows. 1,082
Murray, J C. 851 Myrtle av....Lamson Store Service Co. Register. 140
Maloney, J. 171 Evergreen av....Arthur & Randel. Horses 140
McCormick, M and J. 628 Fulton....J McCormick, Sr. Bird and Cage Store Fixtures. 1,200
Mochin & Scott. Atlantic av and Ashford st.... J E Vincent. Plumber Fixtures. 90
Mohrmann, F. Patchen av, s w cor Halsey st ....M Brunjes. Grocery Fixtures. 1,442
Mohrmann, F. Patchen av, s w cor Halsey st ....M Brunjes. Grocery Fixtures. 1,442
Malowanczyk, E. 51 Broome. ..R Spahn. Sewing Machine. 125
Max, J. 9th st, 2d and 3d avs....G Ibnken. Horses, &c. 400
Miller, G F. Prospect Park....B Wassermann. Machinery and Ice Cream Manufactory. (R) 1,064
Orthlieb, L. 176 Ainslie....Nat Cash Register Co. Register. 175
Ossman, C. 236 Lee av....G Adler. Store Fixtures. 1,000
Pease, J R. Foot of Division av....C H Lord. Steam Launch. 700
Roberts, S. 369 Pearl....H Rees' Sons. Machinery. (R) 3,763
Rothschild, J H. 230 and 232 10th....C Ficken & Co. Milk Wagon and Horse. 200
Remmeney Bottling Co. 312 Rutledge....S Liebmann's Sons B Co. Bottling Business. 10,000
Ringen, J H and C E Jahn. 1-5 Fulton....F Lemmermann. Hotel Fixtures. (R) 21,000
Simonson, H J. 236 Lafayette av... J Cunningham Son & Co. Coach. 900
Stoddart, W H. 1464 Fulton....Sarah Stoddart. Store Fixtures. 200
Swain, S S. 395 Fulton....National Cash Register Co. Register. 175
Scotto, J....R B Maxwell. Horse and Wagon. (R) 125
Schertt, L and P Schrober. 291 Kent av....H Fricke. Horses, Trucks, &c. 100
Swenson, A. Madison st....J Crombie. Horse. 125
Traugott, H. 1289 Bedford av....J F C Elfers. Store Fixtures. 600
Vonderlieth, W. 1607½ Fulton .... F Dopke. Butcher Fixtures (R) 200
Wiese & Thoenicke. 67 Tillary....H J Haff. Horses, Wagons, &c. 800

BILLS OF SALE.

Barrie, G. 494 5th av.... Helen Barrie. Saloon Fixtures. 2,500
Benzin, A. 88 Central av....G C Bachert. Saloon Fixtures. 1,800
Clark, P. 682 Evergreen av....H Koch. Saloon Fixtures. 75
Gadeka, Dora. 1961 Fulton... A M Drosh. Grocery Fixtures. 90
Golsang, J. 1065 Flushing av....J Golsang. Horses, Wagons, &c. 40
Graf, M M. 886 Park av....J Graf. Machinery. nom
Koehl, J. 100 Buffalo av....J Fulton. Saloon Fixtures. 500
Lapp, J. 25 St Nicholas av....H Flechsenhaar. Pickles. 1,500
Magin, F. 400 Central av....F Kappauf. Barber Fixtures. 200
Merica, A. 65 Morrell....Rachel Merica. Merchandise. 300
Schwarze, Eliz. 79 Gwinnett....W Schwarze. Machinery. 300
Stokes, W H. 187 W 9th....G E Stokes. Tools, Horses and Trucks. 500
Sterbenz, F. 28 Thornton....H Moller. Saloon. 350

NEW JERSEY.

NOTE.—*The arrangement of the Conveyances, Mortgages and Judgments in these lists is as follows; the first name in the Conveyances is the Grantor; in Mortgages, the Mortgagor; in Judgments, the Judgment debtor.*

ESSEX COUNTY.

CONVEYANCES.

Allen, F B—E Schnaft, South 11th st.......... $300
Allen, W H—M H Parkhurst, East Orange...... 1,850
Anderson, I S—C E Borland, Montclair.......... 4,250
Same——H Fear, Montclair.................. 650
Ball, Louis—F J Eddows, Summer av............ 1
Ball, Isaiah—G Brown, East Orange.............. 3,950
Barradale, A F—J F Ehlers, Milburn.............. 300
Beers, Mindwell—J Philippot, e s Mulberry st 83 s Cottage st 7x100x 5x16x8x17x36.......... 5,000
Buermann, August—C Buermann, s s Clinton av 50 s Badger av 25x78x25x65 7,100
Blanchard, W W—E C Earle, East Orange...... 3,650
Buchanan, Paul—W J Kearns, North 4th st 550
Burckhard, C F—P Gengenbach, Court st........ 1,900
Campfield, M E—The Orange Free Library, Orange.................................... 12,000
Carter, K B—C L Albee, Hillside.................. 1,500
Same——F Wisljahn, Johnson av.............. 900
Chace, I C—A C Eastwood, Montclair.......... 1,000
Citizens Gas Light Co—W Titus, w s Lombardy pl adj Halsey court 40x45x48x64x171.......... 8,000
Clarke, Caroline—W H Wood, Montclair.......... 2,200
Condit, E M—J J Haag, West Orange 1,500
Conger, Henry—J L Wells, Spruce st.............. 1,000
Same——L C Parkhurst et al, Thomas st...... 1
Conover, W H—W J Kearns, North 4th st...... 1
Coolbaugh, F W—N Mauger, East Orange........ 1,750
Cort, Thomas—C R Garabrant, w s 7th st 525 s 13th av 25x100.................................... 3,500
Crane, H B—F Condit, Caldwell.................. 790
Crane, J C—W F Pier, Montclair.................. 625
De Witt, M H—D H Bartlett, Montclair.......... 13,000
De Witt, W H—A C Draper, Montclair.............. 1
Dobbins, D F—C W Dobbins, Caldwell.............. 1
Dodd, Amzi et al exrs—M Pfeifer, North 6th st.. 1
Draper, A C—W H Dewitt, Montclair.............. 1
Drexel Improvement Co—J Wood, Montclair.... 400
Same——T R Hart, Montclair.................. 1,200
Duryee, J R—B Krebs, Hecker st.................. 750
Eddowes, Wm—L Ball, Summer av.................. 1
Eastwood, A C—M E ——, Montclair.............. 1,000
Eppley, F M—G Spottiswoode, West Orange.... 1,460
Fischer, C A—E E Muller, Court st.............. 1
Fletcher, A J—H Merz, w s Littleton av 171 n 18th av 50x120.................................... 4,000
Fullerton, Mary—F W Boice, South Orange...... 800
Garabrant, C R—K K Cort, w s South 7th st 525 s 13th st 25x100.................................... 3,500
Gilman, A R—M Bock, Cabinet st.................. 750
Goris, John—F P Grub, South 10th st.............. 700
Grey, Mary—D Kaufhen, Carden st.................. 1,100
Haas, William—L Ombach, Ann st 1
Hartshorne, Stewart—H S Leavitt, Milburn...... 4,500
Hartwick, M C—T T Allen, Livingston.............. 3,000
Hayes, Charles exr—P Ulrich, Fairmount av.... 800
Hayes, Charles exr—W Hill, s w cor Bergen st and 17th av 100x200.................................. 8,500
Headley, C J—H C Benson, Milburn.............. 900
Hill, Wm—C H Muinster, Bergen st.............. 2,800
Same——R Isenmann, Bergen st.................. 2,400
Same——P Ulrich, Bergen st.................. 2,200

Hepburn, Henry—The East Jersey Water Co, Bloomfield........ 1
Hussex, W H—R A Kennedy, East Orange...... 2,437
Jones, A E—I H Ormsby, e s Broad st 50 s Bridge st 26x116........ 20,000
Koehler, Peter et al—J Isaacs, Boyd st........ 1
Lewis, I N—E C Whipple, Dublin........ 1
Lindsley, O W—H Dwyer, East Orange........ 300
Same——M Dwyer, East Orange........ 300
Lister, J C—A Mahon, Albert av........ 500
Same——T Monaghan, Catherine st........ 255
Lowry, Philip—R P Schlegel, w s Livingston st adj C Miller land 35x100........ 4,000
Mackin, Francis—A Wood, Summer av........ 2,500
McCabe, P H—G S Porter, Bloomfield........ 325
Mittnacht, H A—F Wagner, Clinton........ 4,250
Nesler, C L—B A Healey, Lentz av........ 340
Nivin, M W—A E Nivin, Montclair........ 2,840
Same——H F Canedy, Montclair........ 2,535
Same——R C Nivin, Montclair........ 2,840
Osborne, J H—A Decker, Clinton........ 1,000
Same——E G Hotchkiss, Clinton........ 900
Same——H P Cook, Clinton........ 6,000
Otis, H G—R P Myhers, North 11th st........ 1,200
Parkhurst, L C—A Force, Thomas st........ 1,000
Peabody Land and Loan Co—R B Kitchell, Mt Prospect av........ 125
Peloubet, F W—N Snyder, East Orange........ 4,800
Same——J W Ord, East Orange........ 4,800
Pfeifer, August—A I Schaufelberger, South 11th st........ 1,150
Pfeifer, Maria—A Dodd et al, Dickerson st........ 1
Piker, E L B—S O Smith, Richmond st........ 125
Prieth, L J et al—R Kercher, Clinton........ 200
Same——C Selm, Clinton........ 200
Prieth, L J—W Hoffmann, Clinton........ 150
Presbyterian Church, Caldwell—L G Lockward, Caldwell........ 1
Randall, Francis—C M Jennings, Orange........ 400
Rhoades, W L—F W Ussier, n cor Bloomfield av and 7th st 97x44........ 3,500
Richardson, R W—E Whitney, New York av........ 1
Rudman, A M—P Fenster, e s Broome st 25 n Court st 25x100........ 4,500
Rusher, G J trustee—E H Godby, Alpine st........ 1
Sattler, L R—R Sattler, 4 tracts containing abt 8½ acres near what was formerly the "great harbor"........ 5,250
Schuetz, Charles—H W Richardson, s s New York av 389 n Pacific st 25x102........ 6,400
Small, Thomas—A Horn, Waverly pl........ 1,800
Smith, H C L—J McBarron, Clinton........ 300
Snyder, E H—J Nolan, South Orange........ 400
Spottiswoode, George—E E Marcy, West Orange........ 1
State Banking Co—R Salter, South 15th st........ 2,500
Same——Robert Sattler, Springfield av........ 900
Stern, Louis—M Grossner, Bank st........ 1,100
Tichenor, William—M Corcoran, Montclair........ 1
Till, H J—H Heald, South Orange........ 175
Tolman, James—G Dill, Clinton........ 725
Union Building and Loan Assoc—F H Sieger, e s South 8th st, 350 n South Orange av 25x100........ 4,200
Van Revper, A E—R T Young, Belleville........ 700
Van Rensselaer, J H—R Hertzog, n s Fulton st 317 e Broad st 22x160........ 7,000
Wagner, F J—H Bretcher, Orange........ 4,200
Ward, P J—E M Ball, Bloomfield........ 1,500
Wood, Alexander—C F Dana, Verona av........ 1,575

MORTGAGES.

Alben, C L—K B Carter, Hillside av........ 750
Atwater, Samuel—P R Taylor, 9th av........ 900
Baldwin, B M—Eighth Ward B and L Assoc, Garside st........ 300
Bell, Saml—M A Jaggers, West Orange........ 200
Been, Ralph—R Martin, East Orange........ 3,360
Biedermann, William—R Levy, South Orange av........ 1,100
Blaicher, F E—Fidelity Title and Deposit Co, Market st........ 4,600
Boesen, W J—K J Myddleton, Orange........ 1,000
Brady, M E—M S Richards, Adams st........ 600
Brientnall, J H H et al—M Pfeifer, North 6th st. 1
Brockie, John—Mt Pleasant Cemetery Co, Summer av........ 2,000
Brown, Chas—H Goble, South Orange av........ 300
Buermann, Charles—A Buermann, Clinton av........ 7,100
Burns, M J—D H Carpenter, South Orange........ 2,000
Cook, H P—J H Osborne et al, Clinton........ 3,500
Dayton, M A—J R Seaman, Orange........ 200
Decker, Annie—J H Osborne et al, Clinton........ 600
Denglowitz, Merle—The Washington B and L Assoc, Prince st........ 2,000
Dobbins, C W—J H Busk, Caldwell........ 500
Donnelly, Maria—A H Dart, West Orange........ 500
Fenster, Philip—A M Rudman, Broome st........ 3,400
Force, Alice—T Condit, Thomas st........ 1,000
Forman, D H—J Chadsey, Lincoln av........ 1,000
Same——same, Lincoln av........ 1,000
Freeman, Mary—The American Insurance Co, Franklin........ 1,000
Garrity, John—C Bach, Inness st........ 2,200
Glasson, William—J L Blake, Orange........ 1,200
Godby, E H—E A Murphy, Alpine st........ 3,000
Goodell, E B—J E Wilson, Montclair........ 700
Greason, Herbert—E C Greason, 8th av........ 2,000
Guyer, R T—Mutual Benefit Life Ins Co, Summer av........ 900
Hanseling, M H—L W Haussling admrx, Mulberry st........ 1,000
Same——same, Franklin st........ 2,500
Same——same, Summit st........ 1,0.0
Same——same, Liberty st........ 3,500
Harrison, E M—H F Coffin, Montclair........ 3,000
Hart, John—F William Helbig, Roseville av........ 200
Healy, J J—M Gounley, Orange........ 200
Hedenberg, M J—Howard Savings Inst, Broad st........ 17,000
Hills William—Charles Hayes exr, Bergen st........ 1,000
Hinchcliffe, G B—A Buermann, Badger av........ 2,800
Honig, Theresa—J R Duryee, Sussex av........ 1,000
Hotchkiss, E G—The E O B and L Assoc, Clinton 650
Krebs, Bertha—J R Duryee, Hecker st........ 2,500
Lapp, George—Franklin Savings Inst of Newark, South 6th st........ 2,000
Lourie, Solomon—C Meyer, admrx, Academy st. 6,500
Mabey, E J—The American Ins Co, Montclair........ 2,100
Mackey, C E—Knights of Pythias B and L Assoc, Oriental st........ 600
M[illegible]er, Jacob—Woodside B and L Assoc, Elliott st........ 1,700
Miller, J M—S W Rish, East Orange........ 2,000
Same——same, East Orange........ 2,000
Monaghan, Thomas—J C Lister, Catherine st........ 127
Munster, Clara—C Hayes, exr, Bergen st........ 1,000
Myhers, R P—E J Otis, North 11th st........ 600
Nessler, F W—W L Rhoades, Bloomfield av........ 1,500
Ormsby, I H—A E Jones, Broad st........ 9,000
Pardue, C E—J H Flintoft, South Orange av........ 6,200
Peloubet, F W—Wm F Bailey, North 14th st........ 700
Pfeiffer, C F—L D Stern, South 14th st........ 100
Phillippot, Judith—E A Nesler, Mulberry st........ 2,500
Pier, W F—J C Crane, Montclair........ 400
Pollard, G S—M E Dickinson, Summer av........ 1,000
Riley, F E—The Mutual Benefit Life Ins Co, Kearney st........ 500
Rizzolo, Alfonzo—A P Baldwin, Elizabeth av........ 7,000
Rodgers, M N—S Steele et al, South 18th st........ 100
Ryerson, R C—The Prudential Ins Co, Caldwell. 2,750
Schaufelberger, A J—A Pfeifer, South 11th st........ 250
Schlegel, R P—The Workingmen's B and L Assoc, McKenzie st........ 3,200
Schuetz, S F—The Workingmen's B and L Assoc, Johnson av........ 4,500
Starzmann, Julius—G Schoenamsgruber, Alyea st........ 2,500
Sweeny, Daniel—J L Johnson et al trustees, Belleville av........ 3,000
Torrey, H A—The Bloomfield Savings Inst, Montclair........ 4,000
Ulrich, Peter—C Hayes exr, Bergen st........ 700
Same——same, Fairmount av........ 600
Van Houton, Abram—A Buermann, Avon av........ 3,600
Van Houten, J B—The 10th Ward B and L Assoc, Quimby st........ 2,000
Westwood, W H—The Howard B and L Assoc, 8th av........ 4,500
White, Margaret—The Half Dime Savings Bank, Orange........ 1,100
Whitsey, J A—G Hegeman, New York av........ 2,300
Zitzner, J P—D S Crowell exr, Magnolia st........ 700

CHATTEL MORTGAGES.

Barattoni, Cæsar—E M Douglas, oil painting........ 600
Barschow, John—J Walsh, furniture........ 506
Beckmeyer, Henry—C Mueller, stock groceries. 280
Brenner, Adam—J M Hann, furniture........ 180
Burt, B B—M W Riley, furniture........ 700
Campbell, J W—F Beckmeyer, furniture........ 100
Coddington, E M—F Lisiewski, saloon........ 550
C Maiers & Co—The Prentiss Tool and Supply Co, machinery........ 86
De Benedictis, Guiseppe—Lang & Co, horses and wagons........ 85
Fairchild, Jonathan—J S Paulison, furniture........ 350
Greves, E M—P H Hanley, organ........ 35
Haenggle, Jacob—F J Kastner, saloon........ 600
Hatt, Philipp—B Hatt, bakery fixtures........ 215
Hedges, J N—D Harper, milk business........ 150
Herberg, William—H Thierfelder, furniture........ 30
Higgins, Charles—H Higgins, stock groceries........ 535
Kenniss, Ike—Hirschfield & Co, safe........ 80
Maier, William—F Schule, butcher fixtures........ 500
McGuirk, William—M Burne & Co, stock groceries........ 290
McIlravy, Eliza—J Ketcham, furniture........ 65
Milikowsky, Israel et al—J Epstein, stock picture frames........ 200
Perry, B C—Essex Co Brewing Co, saloon........ 475
Risden, W B—C Weigand, barber fixtures........ 50
Servos, Solomon—A Bornstein, horse and wagon 299
Smith, W M—E A Knott, stock jewelry........ 400
Stein, Abraham—L Mendel, furniture........ 110
Wachtel, Charles—The Prentiss Tool and Supply Co, machinery........ 265
Winters, A H—National Cash Register Co, cash register........ 200
Wolf, Anne—J Ketcham, furniture........ 130
Zarillo, Michele—Hills Union Brewing Co, saloon 500

JUDGMENTS.

Arndt, George—C B Smith & Co........ 130
Beck, H C—The State of New Jersey........ 500
Bray, Ard—L W Stephens........ 142
Dykman, August et al—R S Roberts et al........ 569
Heitemeyer, Charles—The Central Glass Co........ 409
Jacobs, H R—J E Seder........ 790
Parker, R V—M C Crane........ 1,178

HUDSON COUNTY.

CONVEYANCES.

Allaire, Rachel H—J Morecraft, Bayonne........ $900
Appleby, Leonard—S H White, J City........ 3,000
Archibald, S A—W S Klene, J City........ 3,800
Arnold, Nicholas—Emil Herz, J City........ 2,250
Ballard, F W—W Ballard, J City........ 1,000
Barnickel, C A—C J Grosel, Hoboken........ 500
Becker, Cecilia—H J Bonn, Union........ 2,500
Bellotte, Henry—Eliz J Bellotte, Weehawken........ nom
Same——Mary L Bellotte, Weehawken........ nom
Same——G A Bellotte, Weehawken........ nom
Berghans, Albert—A Ludwig, Guttenberg........ 750
Blake, Elizabeth M—F S Hoyt, J City........ nom
Board, J M—W K Leicht, Hoboken........ 45
Bonn, H J—O Schultz, West Hoboken........ 1,000
Bornhagen, Fred—W K Leicht, Hoboken........ 1,200
Byrnes, D P—Maggie McGrail, J City........ nom
Cadmus, George—Rachel J Bell, Bayonne........ 855
Cadmus, J R—H Binse, Bayonne........ nom
Same——H Knobloch, Bayonne........ nom
Champney, B F—J Hunt, J City........ 4,500
Combes, Mary E—J Meyers, Bayonne........ nom
Condit, Fillmore—A H Turnbull, Kearney........ 325
Same——same, Kearney........ 150
Same——Sarah Owens, Kearney........ 300
Cooney, Margaret—H Walker, Guttenberg........ 330
Divin, W J—G Walbaum, Hoboken........ 500
Duscher, Chas by exr—G B McIntyre, West Hoboken........ 400
Same——Helen Maupai, West Hoboken........ 1,200
Eniff, H A—J Hurley, Bayonne........ 275
Same——M Ahearn, Bayonne........ 230
Fitzsimmons, John—Catharine F Lentz, J City. 650
Fitch, Harriet—T F Cullas, J City........ 475
Fleming, Walter—Margaret Schumacher, J City........ 5,500
Fugel, Christian—G Gaetz, J City........ 2,325
Furey, Cath E—E Van Hontenas, J City........ nom
Glassford, James—J H N Glassford, J City........ nom
Grob, Dorothea—E G Grob, J City........ nom
Hnup, Rosalie—E Castro, J City........ 3,000
Hoboken Land and Impt Co—H J Bonn, West Hoboken........ 2,700
Hoehne, Oscar—C Timannus, J City........ 4,800
Hoyt, F S—Eugenie T Faunce, J City........ 1,200
Hulshizer, J E, Jr—Catharine Murphy, J City........ nom
Kerrigan, J M—M S Kerrigan, West Hoboken........ nom
Kerrigan, M S—J H Kerrigan, West Hoboken........ nom
Same——Margaret A Dingee, West Hoboken. nom
Krieg, Charles—S Adelstein, Bayonne........ 1,850
Lewis, C A—Lizzie R Feltner, J City........ 700
Marion, J F—J A Wright, Union........ nom
Marron, Patrick—E Marron, J City........ 950
Marvin, F W—Sadie A Marvin, J City........ nom
Marvin, Sadie A—F A Marvin, J City........ nom
Matthews, F J—P Sehnst, J City........ 1,500
Maturin, George by sheriff—D Baumann, J City. 50
McDonald, W F—J K McDonald, J City........ 4,000
McGrail, Maggie—D P Byrnes, J City........ nom
McIntyre, Sarah A by exrs—T McIntyre, Bayonne........ 40
Murphy, T J—J E Hulshiser, Jr, J City........ nom
Mundel, Philip—C Baumann, Guttenberg........ 250
Myers, J L—J J Duffy, Bayonne........ 2,650
Neunsinger, Wilhelmina—W Lee, Hoboken........ 1,000
Ogden, W B by exrs—J S Edwards, J City........ 8,000
Otto, Emma—H Clausen, J City........ 815
Phillips, Alpha—J Neiman, Bayonne........ 500
Same——W Story, Bayonne........ nom
Prigge, Henry—R Gabrielsky, J City........ 350
Rademan, Peter—J F Cordes, J City........ 7,800
Regan, Mary J—J Fitzsimmons, J City........ 650
Schmidt, O R—W B Schmidt, J City........ 1,000
Schumann, Geo—E De Groff, Union........ 876
Seitz, Arthur—Hoboken Land and Improvement Co, Hoboken........ 34,000
Severance, G M—M S Severance, Kearney........ 2,200
Shortell, Stephen—J Paoli, Hoboken........ 1,765
Same——A Borrone, Hoboken........ 1,765
Siegfried, Adam—Annie M Donacker, J City........ 750
Skelley, Joseph V—F Duryea, West Hoboken........ 3,600
The Central New Jersey Land and Improvement Co—W I Coines, Bayonne........ 510
The Equitable Life Assur Soc of the United States—T D Jordan, J City........ 34,000
Urahlers, J T—C H Kopf, J City........ 5,000
Van Wagenen, Christiana by exr—J Van Wagen, J City........ 2,000
Same—J F King, J City........ 1,000
Van Wagenen, Christian by exr—W Pfeiffer, J City........ 700
Van Wagenen, Jacob—J H Leonard, J City........ 650
Vreeland, Maria A—J Meyers, Bayonne........ nom
Walker, Herman—J Reichenback, Guttenberg........ 1,600
Same——Anna Eckert, Guttenberg........ 875
Whelan, J J—Catharine Burns, J City........ 2,125
Will, Albert—C J Cramer, Union........ 200
Wright, Paulina—J F Marion, Union........ nom

MORTGAGES.

Adelstein, Simon—The Industrial Co-operative Building and Loan Assoc, Bayonne, installs. 1,250
Astley, Horatio—F Haggerty, Kearney, 1 year. 1,600
Anshutz, Marie—Schelles Kreuken Nalershutzuug Verein No. 3, J City, 1 year........ 250
Battin, S H—The Provident Inst for Savings, J City, 1 year........ 25,000
Bell, R J—G Cadmus, Bayonne, 2 years........ 427
Bonn, H J—Cecilia Becker, Union, 1 year........ 1,500
Brockel, George—G H Gartman, J City........ 1,200
Brower, J D—Augusta T Vreeland, J City, 5 years........ 2,700
Clausen, Henry—Ann M Elbryoth, J City, 1 year 600
Coleman, Sarah A—H Schumann, J City, 3 years........ 2,200
Cordts, J F—P Rademan, J City, 4 years........ 4,000
Same——same, 3 years........ 2,700
Doherty, James—The New Jersey Title Guarantee and Trust Co, J City, installs........ 2,000
Dorn, Henry—H J Leitzen, J City, 3 years........ 6,500
Dreyer, Fred—J V Skelly, West Hoboken, installs........ 400
Edward, W W—Exrs R W Southmayd, J City, 1 year........ 1,500
Elliott, W H—The North Hudson Co B & L Assoc, J City, installs........ 600
Faulhaber, Caspar—Dorothea Och, J City, 3 years........ 1,558
Fondeville, Eugene B—Hoboken Bank for Savings, West Hoboken, 1 year........ 5,000
Gabrielsky, Richard—H Prigge, J City, 1 year........ 175
Gay, W N—S B Vreeland, Bayonne, 3 years........ 3,500
Gerken, Anna—E J Ducker, Hoboken, 3 years........ 2,500
Goetz, Gottlieb—J Kraemer, J City, 3 years........ 1,000
Grosdorf, Helena—Annie Newkirk, West Hoboken, 5 years........ 2,500
Grosel, C J—C A Barnickel, Hoboken, 1 year........ 100
Growney, Catharine—Hannah L Dood, Kearney, 1 year........ 1,300
Guthur, John—O H Perry, J City, 3 years........ 400
Head, George—Catharine Cary, Kearney, 1 year. 5,000
Herman, R G—R Driemel, J City, 3 years........ 2,000
Hollstein, Henry—The North Hudson Co B and L Assoc, J City, installs........ 4,400
Hoffman, Charles—Mary Kaiser, J City, 5 years. 400
Holling, Henry—Anna Riedemann, J City, 5 years........ 1,500
Jordan, T D—The Equitable Life Assur Soc, J City, 1 year........ 34,000
Same——same, J City, 1 year........ 80,000
Kaysee, Otto—Hoboken Bank for Savings, Hoboken, 1 year........ 8,000
King, J F—Exrs C Van Wagenen, J City, 3 years 500
Laudenthal, Gustav—A Siegfried, North Bergen, 6 years........ 4,750
Same——same, North Bergen, 1 year........ 4,730
Laskewski, Wilhelm—Jane E Birdsall, J City, 3 years........ 330
Leonard, J H—World Co-operative B and L Assoc, J City, installs........ 3,750
Lilliendahl, W A—Billings Slate and Marble Co, J City, mortgage on lease........ 3,000
Lovesey, Mary C—J Harper, Hoboken, 3 years........ 500
Ludwig, Anton—Adelheid Berghaus, Guttenberg, 1 year........ 250
McEwan, Thomas, Jr—Georgianna Theurer, J City, 1 year........ 1,000
McMahon, D F—North Hudson Co B and L Assoc Issue G, J City, installs........ 1,600
Morecraft, James—Industrial Co-operative B and L Assoc, Bayonne, installs........ 750
Mullone, Michael—H H Farrier, J City, 1 year........ 8,000
Murphy, M V—D Daly, J City, 3 years........ 1,200
Numan, Jacob—A Phillips, Bayonne, 3 years........ 400
O'Shea, Denis—Phœnix L and B Assoc, J City, installs........ 1,400
Peterson, Ida E—Rachel Hanna, Kearney, installs........ 1,400
Peltke, Albert—A Heritage, J City, 1 year........ 1,500
Quirk, Richard—The Hoboken Bank for Savings, Hoboken, 3 years........ 12,000
Reichenbach, John—H Walker, Guttenberg, 1 year........ 1,600
Reulbach, George—Sophie Hentze, J City, 1 year 1,175
Saint Mary Catholic Church—The Provident Inst for Savings, J City, 1 year........ 16,000
Salomon, Herman—Emil Hartman, J City, 1 year........ 2,000
Schultz, Otto—G Zurn, West Hoboken, 3 years........ 5,000
Schust, Philopena—F J Matthews, J City, 1 year 1,000
Smyth, Ann J—The New Jersey Title Guarantee and Trust Co, J City, installs........ 4,000
Snedeker, Michael—Cartaret M B and L Assoc, J City, installs........ 4,630
Spengeman, F A—Exrs C Von Wagenen, J City, 3 years........ 1,000
Steinbecker, A H—Provident Inst for Savings, J City, 1 year........ 2,500
Stoddard, E R—The Provident Inst for Savings, J City, 1 year........ 1,000
Taeffner, Jacob—W H Von Ojen, J City, 1 year. 208
Tomfohrde, Martin—N J H Edge, J City, 3 years 8,000
Troy, Thomas—The Provident Inst for Savings, J City, 1 year........ 1,000

Van Emburgh, Annie M—L McCloud, Kearney, 1 year ... 200
Warren, Joseph—The Provident Inst for Savings, J City, 1 year ... 12,000
Westervelt, D P—W Carroll, Hoboken, 5 years.. 2,000
White, Simon—Trustee of L Appleby, J City, 5 years ... 2,400

CHATTEL MORTGAGES.

Bartel, B H, J City—Lembeck & Betz Eagle Brewing Co, saloon and lease ... 852
Behring, Frank, J City——same, saloon and lease ... 350
Boetcher, William, J City—Hoos & Schultz, furniture ... 206
Bryan, J L, Guttenberg—L Bauman, furniture. 106
Cassidy, Susan, J City—F G Smith, piano ... 190
Crawford, R W, Kearney—J Keliol, horses, wagons, harness ... 614
Degerberv, Henry and Elizabeth, Hoboken—Commercial Credit Co, furniture ... 140
Donnelly, Theresa, J City—Hoos & Schultz, furniture ... 210
Doscher, Katie, J City——same, furniture ... 190
Fernstein, Max, J City—Bernheimer & Schmidt, pool table ... 150
Gerst, Edward, J City—Hoos & Schultz, furniture ... 139
Glaser, Frank, West New York—Lembeck & Betz Eagle Brewing Co, saloon and lease.... 251
Hikel, M C, J City—H Thoesen, furniture ... 119
Horman, Morris, J City—L Bauman, furniture.. 106
Jackson, Iredenia, J City—Hoos & Schultz, furniture ... 149
Johnson, Kate M, J City——same, furniture ... 180
Keefe, Julia, J City——same, furniture ... 151
Kemp, C H, J City—C Pesenecker, horses, wagon and harness ... 125
Kept, George, West Hoboken—H Stuhler, bakery ... 1,000
Kretzamer, F, Bayonne—F G Smith, piano .. 320
Loveland, J K, J City—Bernheimer & Schmidt, saloon and lease ... 250
Maloney, Mary A, Hoboken—The William Peter Brewing Co, saloon fixtures ... 500
Marshall, Geo, Bayonne—F G Smith, organ ... 54
Mathison, Sarah, J City——same, piano ... 192
McDonald, John, J City—Bernheimer & Schmidt, saloon ... 500
Mead, D C, J City—T R Gueman, horses, trucks and harness ... 205
Orr, Mary E, J City—F G Smith, piano ... 300
Pilgram, Morris, J City—Emile Hartman, boiler and engine, machinery, &c ... 200
Poley, J H, J City—Hoos & Schultz, furniture... 161
Provost, A A, J City—L Bauman, furniture ... 227
Rachon, Chas—P Ballantine & Son, saloon ... 290
Richards, Etta J W, Hoboken—F G Smith, piano ... 265
Robertson, Mary, J City——same, piano ... 190
Scofield, J L, J City—W Stewart, furniture ... 89
Schwartz, John and Henry Luming, Hoboken—The Manhattan Type Foundry, printing press, &c ... 170
Skillman, W E and C A, partners as William E Skillman Bro, J City—J Skillman, hardware business, goods and fixtures ... 4,000
Snow, J J, Weehawken—E B Bishops, horses... 600
The Hudson River Ice Co, J City—S McBurney, horses, wagons, harness, engine and boiler. 31,500
Tierney, Belle, J City—Hoos & Schultz, furniture ... 181
Tomlins, M C, J City—F G Smith, piano ... 375
Vaughan, W T, Bayonne—H Thoesen, furniture. 142
Viehwig, F E, Union—The William Peter Brewing Co, one pool table ... 175
Wallis, John, J City—Hoes & Schultz, furniture ... 422
Warner, William and Hugo Knabner, J City—W Braband, building and kiln of china decorating establishment ... 150
Wayne, Edith, West Hoboken—L Bauman, furniture ... 90
Wheeler, G E, Bayonne—F G Smith, piano ... 250
Whittan, C A, J City—Hoos & Schultz, furniture ... 175
Welsh, Millor G, J City—L Bauman, furniture.. 266
Winter, C E, J City—Lembeck & Betz Eagle Brewing Co, saloon and lease ... 450
Young, Wilhelmine, Bayonne—F G Smith, piano ... 80

BILLS OF SALE.

Gem, Julius, Union—H Buess, saloon ... 1,400
Korge, Louis, Hoboken—Charlotte Wilcox, saloon 700
Lapham, T C, J City—J H Peloubet, furniture.. nom
Peloubet, J H, J City—Asneath O Lapham, furniture ... nom
Peter, A M, Union—F M Guaragalu, saloon ... 1,200
Pollard, P F, J City—Jane E Wilber, furniture business ... 500
Same——same, horse, wagon and harness ... 300

JUDGMENTS.

Dwyer, Ed—J J Dewitt ... 180
Fonjes, John—W Sturn ... 14
McHugh, James—E Sullivan ... 74
Willsture, Geo—J M Bettam ... 169

MECHANICS' LIENS.

Ashland, Emma A, owner; Walter Ashland, builder; John Brady, claimant, Bayonne... 65
The W J Wilcox Lard and Refining Co, builders; The W J Wilcox Lard Refining Co and American Cotton Oil Co, owners; Wallis Iron Co, claimants, Union ... 4,686

BUILDING MATERIAL MARKET.

BRICKS.—Another addition must be made to the long list of dull and monotonously unchanged markets that have come, week after week, in unbroken sequence throughout the greater portion of the season. Demand certainly has not improved since our last, some of the trade think it worse, and while there are evidences of a slight falling off in the number of shipments, there has nevertheless been plenty of stock and a liberal over-run at all times available. On the general range of quotations we retain about former figures, as they seem to cover about the average views of operators, but when anything over $5.00 per M is obtained, it is for something exceptional, either in the way of quality, delivery or special adaptation for particular work. While the assortment offering has been of a character to permit of any ordinary selection there is a little more complaint regarding quality, and some of the trade have an idea that poor stock will be more plentiful. Favorable weather and extra care in production have turned out a very good run of stock this season, but in view of the unpropitious condition of the market it is feared greater carelessness will now ensue. Pales remain dull and without recovery in value. As to the general prospects of the market most operators incline to be non-committal except to suggest that an improvement in tone can hardly be expected until the pressure of supplies is removed, and that will, of course, depend upon manufacturers. Some of them have already become discouraged and stopped, and it will be some surprise if all do not follow suit within the next two or three weeks, as it is difficult to understand where an inducement to prolong work can be found.

LATH.—By skirmishing around and carefully watching local and out-of-town demand, receivers have managed to place the not over abundant arrivals without making any change in the line of valuation. That is, the bulk of business goes at $2.10 per M with exceptional claims at $2.15 per M for Eastern. No really new features are suggested, the actual consumption and replenishing wants of dealers both running small at the moment, but up to present writing a fair balance found in comparatively moderate offerings, both on spot and to arrive.

LIME.—Cargoes have come to hand coastwise during the week in fair but not liberal quantity, and the report is that most of them found sale without much difficulty. Demand, however, is neither anxious or general and for the present receivers do not care to be bothered with any larger q a y of stock. On prices former figures are quoted without, so far as best makes are concerned.

LUMBER.—On the distributive outlet there is not much change from last week, except that the movement has been a little fuller and more easily managed, as most of the workmen have returned to their labors. Toward bulk parcels, however, attention is turning with greater freedom in many cases, and we commence to encounter reports that show a measure of hope and cheerfulness quite in comparison with the experiences of a few weeks ago. The progress of the season would no doubt have wrought some change for the better, but there is evidence that dealers commence to feel a return of confidence that promises well for business during the balance of fall and early winter. Goods are low in cost in many cases. In others the chances for supplies have somewhat diminished, and even though consumption may not amount to much until spring, there seems to be little danger in accumulating supplies of a thoroughly staple character.

Eastern Spruce hardly comes within the circle of really improving trade and we still hear frequent complaint from receivers over the difficulties in the way of securing prompt custom for the consignments coming forward. A goodly number of specials have been contracted for since the middle of August, and others are under treaty, making buyers feel easy in regard to certain wants, and they still feel inclined to take matters easy regarding such random as may be required to fill in assortments. Out of town custom affords some help and sellers in several instances speak well of the success they have met with Newark trade this season. At primary points the effort is to keep production and shipment within bounds, and manufacturers insist they must shut down much earlier than usual this season unless the market improves.

Piling continues to find a little custom, and some of the trade think demand is increasing, if anything, with about a steady tone to the market, though not strength enough to raise the line of value as yet. Current arrivals have been running about on a balance with the outlet and on these receivers accept former rates, but few if any of them are willing to sell stock from the basin, except at an advance on quotations.

Hemlock is securing fair attention, and the run of reports have a more promising expression throughout. It seems to be here as with other woods, dealers appreciating the progress of the season and admitting necessity for getting together some sort of an assortment, though an increase of actual consuming wants, especially in the outlying districts, helps matters somewhat. Prices generally rule quite steady on all standard cuts, and sellers are talking about an advance not far away.

White Pine unquestionably commences to take a more promising position. For this time of the year there are several accumulations of considerable size, and further arrivals in fulfillment of old contracts are daily taking place, but numerous dealers are scantily supplied and seem to be working up to the propriety of providing for their wants. The gain of tone is most noticeable upon the upper qualities, and clear and finishing lumber especially sought after, with values decidedly stiffer than they were a few weeks ago. Even on the coarser grades there is a greater firmness and it is doubtful if any more $13.00 box can be obtained, though at $13.50 we have heard of business this week. There does not appear to be apprehension of any positive scarcity, but higher freight rates and the materially reduced accumulation of dry lumber in the Ottawa district induce shrewd buyers to believe they have secured all the advantage likely for this season of the year.

Yellow Pine seems to be gaining in tone somewhat, and reports generally are inclined to take a more or less favorable view of the situation. In addition to quite a fair number of special bills placed there is better demand from dealers, both in and out of town, for general yard assortments and prices are firmer. Advices from the South are also shaping up into more confident form with a somewhat methodical effort said to be under way for purpose of controlling the output, and the big contract with Germany, noted in our last, will for a long time occupy a great deal of productive capacity that would otherwise be contributing to the home supply.

Carolina Pine is selling very well, indeed in some cases we hear claims of a movement "nearly" equal to last season with prospects of an increase. Prices, too, are quite generally reported as ruling steady on pretty much all grades of stock, though buyers assert they have occasionally found competition strong enough to enable them to extract moderate advantages.

Hardwoods, so far as immediate consumption is concerned, are not going out to any extent, and the selection made covers simply an ordinary assortment, a sort of routine business. Agents, however, seem to be picking up a little trade among dealers in the city and near by vicinity, and chances favor a gradual improvement in business from this time forward. In the matter of prices there is some doubt as to the figures actually ruling on the various descriptions of stock, but the chances are that quartered oak is selling off somewhat, and while car lot poplar command about $32.00, more liberal sized contracts could probably be negotiated on a lower basis. Latest advices from abroad spoke somewhat discouragingly of American woods, but more owing to momentary surplus of supply than through any antagonism to the stock.

GENERAL LUMBER NOTES.

FOREIGN.

The London *Timber Trades Journal* says:

In pitch pine charters we hear of nothing doing, but it is expected that rates will soon show an upward tendency, especially for steamers, as these latter will, of course, not entertain wood cargoes while there are such good prospects of securing grain.

The Rio *News* reports: Pitch Pine—Receipts nil and the market is still firm at 46$000 a 47$000 per dozen. White Pine—Quotations are advanced to 115 a 120 rs. per foot; market steady. There have been no receipts during the week. Swedish Pine—Receipts are 713 dozen per Sylphide, from Memel, on order. Quotations are nominal. Spruce Pine—Nothing to report.

THE WEST.

The Chicago Northwestern *Lumberman* as follows:

The wholesale dealers in this city have been rather apathetic about stocking up this season. They have also been exacting in selections of stock, and in demanding time for payment. There has been an especial demand for certain kinds of lumber, such as long joists and timbers, good strips and high-grade lumber generally. These conditions have been a drawback on the cargo market, and have been something of a disappointment to the manufacturers. But a heavy trade from now onward, that will call for wholesale yard stocks in abundance, will soon change the attitude of the dealers toward the cargo market. Assortments, not now very even or full, will become badly broken. Then the dealers will seek the market for lumber with which to even up their supplies.

All over the northwest there is a disproportion between stocks of high grade strips and good boards of stock width and coarse lumber. This has necessarily resulted from the increasing disproportion of coarse and small logs to good ones. This year the lack of good lumber is seriously felt, and prices are firm on such stock, and are likely to so continue.

The cargo movement out of Saginaw valley ports is making a better showing than in August. A sufficient number of sales have been made to encourage shippers in the belief that the fall movement will be heavy. It is expected that lake rates will soon advance from valley to Lake Erie points.

Throughout the country the car factories are filling up with work. The vastly increased traffic has necessitated this. Nothing more promising to the lumber trade of the country at large could be presented than the revival of requirement from car shops and railroads

Cargo receipts were considerable during the week, and the market was fairly well supplied. The decline in the price of piece stuff lent new interest to the cargo market. This week the $9.75 basis was touched, and that is all that the commission men pretend to ask for strictly short stuff. Cargoes have been sold this week at $10, but that price was made because there was a sprinkling of long lengths in the tally. It is reported that piece stuff has been sold for less than $9.75 a thousand, but it was in cases where the cargo contained a percentage of lumber that was off grade or of especially undesirable tally. The regular price of short piece stuff can be named $9.75. At this price dealers are taking hold with rather more freedom, as they see a little better chance to get a handling bill out of it. * * *

Low grade boards continue to arrive, but the demand for them is sluggish. But generally speaking the demand for inch lumber is somewhat better than a short time ago. Strips are in special demand. Anything that includes common and upward sells readily at full prices. Cargoes containing a large percentage of such lumber are sought after, and command prices proportionate to the amount appearing on the tally.

Little long dimension is arriving. The manufacturers seem to have determined to hold back their long stuff and sacrifice their short dimension. This can be said, however, the long lumber has been selected out and sold to dealers at the mills or to arrive here, while short has accumulated. Of course, now that the season is drawing toward the close, the short must be sold. Hence, probably, the yielding in price.

In regard to the Chicago hardwood market the *Timberman* says that demand has been a little better the past week than during the previous seven days, and so far September promises to be a much better month than August, although probably not up to the same month last year. Just now there is a strike among the cabinet makers, but as the factories have not been buying a great deal of stock of late its effect upon the yard trade is not particularly noticeable.

There is a difference of opinion in regard to the amount of stock now on hand, and in the absence of any statistics bearing upon the matter, it is difficult to arrive at the true condition. One dealer will report his stock considerably short of a year ago, and many low piles and vacant places in his yard will bear him out in his assertion. Another says his stock is much heavier than a year ago, and points to many towering piles of lumber in evidence of that fact.

But no matter what the condition of stocks in the city may be there is undoubtedly plenty of lumber in pile at interior points to supply any demand that is likely to arise for some months.

With regard to particular woods, nothing new or additional can be said to what has already been stated in previous reports. All classes of hardwoods are moving with more or less freedom, but there is still great room for improvement in prevailing conditions.

Nothing new has developed in the poplar trade locally within the past week, but reports received from the principal manufacturing and distributing centres, south and east, continue to be encouraging and indicated a steady increasing demand and growing strength to the market. Predictions are freely made that prices will be $1 to $2 per thousand higher on the upper grades within sixty days. While there is a considerable accumulation of common and cull in some sections, these grades are by no means as weak as they were during the summer. Box boards have been selling more freely of late, and squares have as usual been in fair demand.

The Mississippi Valley *Lumberman* says that in the Saginaw valley some improvement in trade is reported, but it is evident that there is no rush of demand in any of the markets depending upon the eastern call for lumber. From Muskegon comes the same complaint of light shipments of lumber that is heard in the Saginaw valley towns. During August Muskegon shipped a total of 18,114,000 feet. The shingle shipment reached 520,000 and lath 1,075,000. During July the lumber shipment amounted to 28,-

889,000. All in all, August has been one of the dullest months known in lumbering circles in Muskegon for several years past. The cargo trade is nearly at a standstill. Purchasers seem to have withdrawn from the market for the present, and there is but little demand for lumber. The few demands are based on purchases on long time and at prices entirely unsatisfactory. The total lumber shipments from Muskegon thus far this season reach 136,000,000 feet.

METALS.—COPPER—Ingot is passing into consumption fairly on regular trade orders, and occasionally the market shows some little animation, though generally manufacturers are conservative in their movements. Offerings fairly meet the outlet, though it is understood there is no surplus stock. On an average range of valuations we quote at 12¼@12½c. for Lake, and 11½@12c. for casting brands. Manufactured Copper has been rather more active in some cases, though the claim is that all culls are running only upon basis of natural trade wants, and now and then comes an intimation of quiet cutting on rates. We quote as follows: Sheet, not above 30x72 in., 16 oz. and over, 25c.; do. 14 to 16 oz., 23c.; do. 12 to 14 oz., 24c.; do. 10 to 12 oz., 25c.; do. 8 to 10 oz., 28c.; do under 8 oz. 30c. Sheets longer than 72 inches add 1c. for 12@14 oz., 2c. for 10@12 oz. and 3c. for 8@10 oz. Sheets, not above 36x96 in., 16 oz and over, 22c.; do. 14 to 16 oz. 24c.; do. 12 to 14 oz. 26c.; do. 10 to 12 oz. 30c.; do. 8 to 10 oz. 33c. Sheets longer than 96 inches 22c. for over 32 oz. and add 1c. for 16 to 32 oz.; 3c. 14 to 16 oz.; 5c. 12 to 14 oz. and 13c. for 8 to 10 oz. Sheets, not above 48x96 32 to 64 oz. 22c.; do. 16 to 32 oz. 25c.; do. 14 to 16 oz. 27c.; do. 12 to 14 oz. 29c.; do. 10 to 12 oz. 33c. Sheets wider than 48x96 and longer, 22@25c. for 32 to 64 oz. and over, 27@[illegible]c. for 16 to 32 oz. 29c. for 14 to 16 oz and 34c. for 12 to 14 oz. All bath tub sheets, per lb., 16 oz. 17c.; 14 oz. 29c.; 12 oz 31c.; and 10 oz. 35c. Bolt copper, ⅝ inch diameter and over, 22c. Circles, 60 diameter and less, 3c. above price of sheets of same thickness; circles, 60 to 96 do do, 5c. do; circles, 96 do and over, 6c. do. Segment and pattern sheets, 3c. above price of sheets required to cut them from. Cold or hard rolled copper, 1@2c. per lb. above the foregoing prices. Copper bottoms, 26@32c. per lb. IRON—American Pig of first-class quality is meeting with a fair average demand, enough, it is said, to keep the production well sold up and sustain about former range of values. On the lower grades, however, business is dull and unsettled, with prices fluctuating according to size of deals, though for any respectable parcels buyers are likely to gain advantage. There is quite a general effort to curtail production. We quote at $16.25@18.00 per ton for No. 1 X foundry; [illegible].50@16.50 for No. 2 X do. and $14.00@15.00 for Gray Forge. Old material is valued at about as before, but meets with a slow hesitating sort of demand from most sources and does not show a satisfactory market for any grade of stock. We quote at about $20.50@21.50 for old rails; $20.00@21.00 [illegible] No. 1 wrought scrap; $17.00@18.00 for cast scrap and $17.00@17.50 for car wheels. Manfactured iron from store is not moving with any great amount of freedom and the deals made may be considered as mainly of a regular order. Contracts for special jobs, however, are somewhat more plentiful and in most cases at quite satisfactory rates. We quote Common Merchant Bar ordinary size, at 2.00@2.10c. from store, and refined at 2.30@2.60c; Rods, round and square, 2.20@2.40c. Bands, 2.40@2.60c.; Norway Nail Rods 4@5c., and domestic sheet on the basis of 3.00@3.05c. for common Nos. 10@16. Other descriptions at corresponding prices, with 1-10c. less on large lots from cars. Steel Rails are doing no better and the absence of railroad patronage is felt throughout the entire steel trade and kindred material. Some sales of rails are made from time to time, but only in a jobbing sort of way, and under the dull state of trade manufacturers are inclined to reduce production. We quote standard sections $30 per ton at mill, with usual advance for delivery at tide water. Pig Lead, although handled mainly in moderate sized parcels against immediate natural wants of consumers, is nevertheless going out in fair volume, and shows generally steady rates, with no very abundant supply available. We quote at 4.50@4.52½c. per lb. The manufactures of lead are quoted at 7c. for Pipe, 7¾c. for sheet, 15c. for Tin-lined Pipe, and 37½c. for Block Tin Pipe. Pig Tin shows about the usual fluctuation under speculative manipulation; but consumers are indifferent, and calculate upon advantages to come through the influences of full supply here and to arrive. We quote at about 20.00@20.05c. for round lots, and 20.10@20.20c. for jobbing parcels. Tin Plate has found rather limited sale, with prices showing no great change. The supply seems to be under control with owners not particularly anxious to operate. We quote prices as follows: I. C. Charcoal, ½ cross assortment Melyn grade, $6.40@6.45, each additional X add $1.50; I. C. Charcoal, ½ cross assortment, Allaway grade, $5.90@6.00, each additional X add $1; Charcoal terne, M. F. grade, 14x20, $7.50@7.55; M. F. grade, 20x28, $15.50@15.55; Worcester, 14x20, $5.70@5.75; Worcester 20x28, $11.25@11.30; Dean grade, 14x20, $5.20@5.25; Dean grade, 20x28, $10.40@10.50; D. R. D. grade, 14x20, $5.15@5.20; D. R. D. grade, 20x28, $10.00@10.05; I C. Coke, Penlan grade, $5.40@5.45; J. B. grade, 14x20, $5.45@5.50; I. C. Bessemer steel, squares, $5.75@5.80 basis; I. C. Siemens steel, squares, $5.85@6.00 basis. Spelter has undergone little change, the demand proving light, with business at about former rates. We quote $4.95@5.10c. for Common Western, according to brand.

NAILS.—Scarcely any change is taking place on this market. Wire nails retain their popularity and are taken with considerable freedom by dealers who feel justified in laying them away at the cost, but free offerings prevent any advance in the value line. Cut meet with some demand but it is apparently unsatisfactory and manufacturers generally are grumbling over the situation. We quote Cut at $1.50@1.60 per keg for car lots and $1.75@1.85 per keg for parcels from store, for iron, and add 5@10c. per keg for steel; Wire, $2.00@2.05 at mills, and 2.20@2.35 from store.

PAINTS, OILS, COLORS, ETC.—On immediate local account the demand may be considered as almost wholly of a jobbing character and without tendency to much improvement. From all dependent outside sources, however, the calls show a steady gain, and business is getting into the good shape predicted for it with the approach of fall. A great deal of hope is entertained in the abundant crops as a basis from which the agricultural district are to derive much profit, and this to be reflected in all commodities farmers may need for improvements and repairs. At the present time the selections making are composed principally of thoroughly standard grades, colors and mixed paints, including several specialties that have come to be looked upon as a necessity in all first-class assortments. The market is well supplied and prices generally steady, though the outside element is charged with some cutting on White Lead. Association Corroders' rates stand as follows: Lead in oil in kegs and dry lead in kegs, in lots of less than 500 lbs., 7⅛c. net; in lots of 500 lbs to 5 tons at one purchase, 7c.; 5 tons to 12 tons, one purchase, 5⅞c.; 12 tons and over, one purchase, 6¾c.; dry white lead in bbls. ⅛c. per lb. less than price in kegs. Lead in oil 12½ lb. in tin pails, add 1c.; in 25 and 50 lb. tin pails, add ½c.; and in 1 to 5 lb. tin cans, assorted (100 lbs. in case) add 2½c. per lb. to keg price. Terms on lots on 500 lbs. and over, note or acceptance at sixty days, or 2½ per cent. discount will be allowed for cash paid within fifteen days of invoice date. To make either of the above required quantities any assortment of packages of white lead, red lead and litharge may be counted. The above quotations are free on board cars or boat at corroding point. Linseed Oil has fair demand, the finer makes in particular selling well, and while prices fluctuate at times there seems to be an effort to hold the market in steady position. We quote at general range at 40@45c. for Western, and 44@56c. for City. Spirits Turpentine remains under good control and offered indifferently with a generally firm tone ruling, but the market is not active and buyers appear unwilling to invest beyond immediate wants. We quote at 37½@39c. per gallon, according to quality, delivery, etc.

TAR AND PITCH.—Not much change of a noteworthy character on the general market. Demand shows irregularity and has once or twice of late been pretty dull, but stocks well in hand give holders an advantage and prices are sustained. We quote Pitch at $1.70@1.75 per bbl.; Tar at $2.15@2.50, according to quantity, quality and delivery.

MISCELLANEOUS.

MISCELLANEOUS.

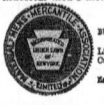

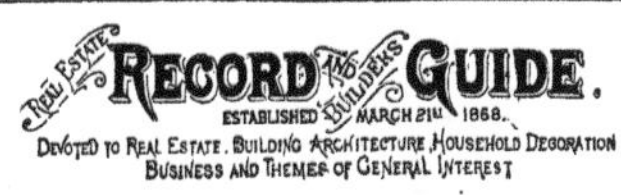

PRICE, PER YEAR IN ADVANCE, SIX DOLLARS.

Published every Saturday.

TELEPHONE - - - - CORTLANDT 1370.

Communications should be addressed to

C. W. SWEET, 14 & 16 Vesey St.

J. T. LINDSEY, Business Manager.

VOL. XLVIII SEPTEMBER 26, 1891. No. 1,228

IMPORTANT NOTICE.

The readers of this journal are invited to visit the handsome exhibition of architects' drawings now on view at the Hall of THE RECORD AND GUIDE, *Nos. 14-16 Vesey street. Nearly 300 designs from the boards of the leading architects in this city and Brooklyn are displayed, offering an opportunity for the study of the best recent architectural work, that rarely occurs. The exhibition is free.*

AT the moment when the ingenious gentlemen who write Wall Street matter for the daily newspapers had discovered that there were no bears, but only reactionists, the public mind has been unsettled by the White failure and the Missouri Pacific troubles, and a bear party very soon showed its face. The result of its operation is not great, except in Missouri Pacific, the grangers especially standing up strong under large selling pressure. Regarded from their action under bad news, stocks so easily discounting all that was unfavorable, the impression is that their prices can only advance. But that is not taking into account the whole situation, in which there are not a few caution signals for the near future; looking beyond that there is no occasion to be anything but bullish. Just now, however, we have to take into consideration the position of those detestibilities known as Gould stocks, particularly Missouri Pacific and Union Pacific. The intimation that Missouri Pacific would pass its dividend for once, because it was not earned was bad enough, but the unofficial hint that it may still pay one under any circumstances is far worse. It is easy to see that certain powerful parties are, notwithstanding their protestations to the contrary, hindering rather than aiding the funding of the Union Pacific floating debt. We are at the time when the demands of the interior for funds are likely to be heaviest. The conflict in the Union Pacific matter, if conflict is inevitable, will be carried on by powerful forces on both sides, actuated by motives which the public will not be asked to share, and in such an event it behooves smaller people to retire to a convenient distance whence they can watch the fight and escape all danger of the blows. The rates for money are hardening and scarcity in that direction would have more influence toward lower prices than any cause we have yet mentioned. A large amount of gold is on its way from Europe to this point and this, with other importations, if speedily made, may offset the crop-moving requirements. The public is so thoroughly convinced of the certainty of ultimately higher prices for American securities that it will not readily part with even its speculative holdings, and if it were not for the knowledge that when the crowd sways it is as a unit, it might be confidently predicted that the many on the bull side would more than outweigh the few, however powerful individually, who are seeking to depress values. Whatever the outcome and in face of all the facts obtainable, caution is in every sense justifiable.

THE stock markets are somewhat stronger all over Europe. In England many of the trades which have been very dull this year are now picking up, and impart something of a stimulus to the whole industrial system. The large quantity of loanable funds and the confidence of financiers is shown by the refusal to raise the rate of discount more than ½ per cent. Foreign trade, however, still remains poor, both in England and France. The imports continue very nearly at the level of the past two years; but the exports in the case of both countries are well below the same figures. There is a good deal of talk concerning the new Russian loan, and in Vienna and elsewhere the reports relating thereto are discredited. In London, however, it is generally believed that a group of French financiers have undertaken to carry through a loan of £20,000,000, the rate of interest having been fixed at 3 per cent. It is not likely that conversion is the principal object of the present loan, for under such circumstances it would scarcely be brought forward at the present time when, owing to the more or less serious falling off in the cereal crops, and to the fears of consequent internal disturbances, Russian credit has been depreciated. It is rather more plausible that the Russian government is compelled to borrow afresh in consequence of the advances which it has already been forced to make to the districts in which the rye crop has been a failure, and of the practical certainty that the next Budget statement will exhibit a very material deficiency. Authorities do not expect that if the loan bears interest at 3 per cent that the price of issue will be much more than 80. If the issue is made, however, the lending ability of the French people will probably be temporarily exhausted, for the Credit Foncier is also about to issue 400 million francs of 3 per cent lottery bonds. It is reasonably certain that borrowing of this kind would not be done unless the managers of the institution were sure of their ground.

THE announcement of a big sale of Washington Heights property, to be held early next month, again calls attention to the present position of that district. During the summer that part of the city, like every other, has escaped anything like activity in real estate; but, unlike some other parts, prices have remained very firm. Pretty nearly all the owners on the hill are holding their property in the expectation of a rise; and their wishes are not likely to be disappointed. Washington Heights is next in line of improvement. Under the stimulus of the cable road some building has been done already, but it is scattered and tentative. So far as the hill is occupied at present, the improvements thereon consist of handsome stone or frame dwellings, erected before the city had stretched above 59th street, beer gardens and picnic grounds which take advantage of the wooded declivity on the Harlem side, and some few houses in rows. These latter are mostly tenements, and are built along the avenues which are more likely than the others to be given over to business. Manifestly, however, almost nothing has yet been done which indicates unequivocally the way in which the classes of buildings will be distributed—what streets and avenues will be given over to trade, what to flats, what to dwellings of moderate dimensions and cost, and what to a more expensive and luxurious dwellings. Hence arises the uncertainty of the future values of realty for the whole region. It is hazardous, if not impossible, to make any sure predictions about matters of this sort. It was fully expected, for instance, that the Boulevard would be the handsomest thoroughfare on the West Side; its width and the possibility of a park in its middle lent plausibility to the assertion that if handsome dwellings were to be built anywhere they would be built along the Boulevard. Well, the West Side became a district of handsome dwellings; but the Boulevard was painfully neglected, partly because it was kept like a pig-pen, partly because it was wretchedly paved during the heat of the West Side movement, partly because the prices of property had become too high. Anticipations of a glorious future ruined it. Builders found that they could buy more cheaply on West End avenue and the side streets, and this they did, beautifying the avenue after purchasing. Meanwhile, but too late, prices on the Boulevard fell off, and it now seems to be pretty well turned over to the builder of flats—of good flats and of bad flats. Thus we may see the difficulty of predicting the future of any particular section or thoroughfare. It all rests with the speculative builder; and he is not guided by the anticipations of other people. Neither is he very much tempted by natural advantages of location—that is, when these natural advantages are very high-priced. He would rather risk less money by buying cheaper property, even if it did not have a river view and an unexceptional breeze. In other words, his object, like that of other men, is to make the most money at the least risk; and what combinations of buildings this object may bring about on Washington Heights no one may yet know. Hence, as we said at the outset, there is a large element of chance in any purchases made at the present time; but the chance turns on the percentage, not on the fact of profit. It is true that prices on Washington Heights are probably double the prices that were obtained on the West Side when that locality was similarly undeveloped; but so certain is the future of this delightful part of the city that at the present time a buyer can buy almost blindfold.

IT would also be difficult to predict when the movement on Washington Heights will start in. That also depends on the speculative builders. To return to our former illustration—that of the West Side—they kept aloof from that district long after the conditions were apparently very favorable for active building operations. During the years 1879, 1880, 1881 and 1882 the property-owners were expecting that the speculative builders would begin to start in west of the park. The elevated roads had long been running and there were no impediments to be overcome save some removable ones, such as squatters, delayed street-opening proceedings, and so on. Consequently, associations were organized, and an immense amount of planning and talking was started and sustained. But meanwhile the builders went very slow. While spending $10,000,000 or more a year in the comparatively well-established East Side, they could not be persuaded to put much more than a tithe of that sum into the experimental district to the west. Indeed, the man who started the movement, and whose success proved to be its greatest stimulus, was not a builder at all, but an investor. And it was not until 1884, until the lapse of five or six years of delay, that something like a large number of houses began to be built. Now there is not the slightest chance that such a delay will take place in the improvement of Washington Heights. What kept the builders back on the West Side was undoubtedly a lack of familiarity with the district; the attempt to build handsome residences well in the western part of the city was experimental and had to be approached gingerly. No such obstacle will interpose on Washington Heights. It is not likely that there will be such a large margin of profit in that district, or that so many fortunes will be made therein; but the opportunity for profit will be secure—just as soon as the Rapid Transit Commissioners can tempt some corporation to build the perfect route of the future. But until then Washington Heights will have to languish. The cable road connecting with the 125th street "L" road station is not tempting, and the district will not have any source of local employment. There are, indeed, some few manufactories up there at the present time, but it is safe to say that they will not increase with time. Every part of the city has been and will be built up to suit the purpose for which it is adapted. Washington Heights is primarily adapted to residences, and it can be hoped, but only hoped, that the residence will be worthy the location. The dwellings and flats will be built when the district becomes accessible, and at least two years must elapse before that time will come. Meanwhile the West Side can fill in, and the streets of Washington Heights can be opened and graded in preparation for an activity that is sure to come.

The Way Out of the Water Front Shoals.

WE have said that, estimating on the receipts, the improved water front property now in the possession of the city would be worth $25,000,000 were it in hands that had caught the trick of making property valuable. We have said further that in such hands it would soon be made worth twice or thrice $25,000,000, and it would then become one of the great tax paying resources of the city. But we have also called attention to the fact that in present hands it is simply a very worthless possibility, and the cause of great material loss. Let us see if there is not an easy way through which the situation can be amended.

The city of New York claims title to the lands under water along many miles of water front, and it would be difficult to estimate at this time the exact marketable value of this property. Much of it is for present uses practically worthless, no commerce reaching it, and no immediate prospect of commerce giving it a speculative value. It would be of use in rounding out the possessions of riparian property-holders were it not for the idiotic practice of building exterior streets along the water front, and could those property-holders feel themselves secure against bisection at some future day it is reasonable to presume that they would gladly pay something to recover a title which their property should never have lost. In many cases, however, they could not afford to pay a great deal.

But there is another large section of unimproved water front in the possession of the city, which it only requires a little enterprise to make very valuable. Take the lumber yard district on the West Side for example. The total area covered by those yards may extend over a square mile, more or less—more likely more than less—and there is not a lumber dealer with sense enough in his head to measure up a pile of boards who would not jump at the chance of locating his yard direct on the river, where he could be served in receiving and shipping lumber at his own piers, and be spared the nuisance and cost of truckage. There are miles of unimproved water front on both sides of the city that could immediately be made productive were the complete riparian franchises in the hands of individuals, and this property could readily be sold at large prices were it offered for sale, without any complicating reservations or entanglements.

Taking the whole batch together, the water front property that has been improved after a fashion, the property that might be advantageously improved, and the property not now to be made productive but which it would be desirable to hold for future contingencies, it might not be an exaggerated estimate to place the total marketable value at $75,000,000. We feel very sure that a syndicate or association composed of the riparian property-holders could very well afford to offer this sum and secure to the city the larger part of the amount in a mortgage at 6 per cent. We believe that with the improvements that could speedily be made the whole of the interest money could be drawn from the property within a very brief period.

The advantages to be gained by the city through such a transaction will be very evident. We have already through pictorial illustrations and statements of fact called attention to the mischievous influences which grow from our present system of water front tenure. All along the water front private property is made almost valueless by its divorce from the lands under water, and commerce, which belongs to the city by right of the original title, is floating away to other shores where it can find greater freedom. Then, see the enormous waste. This property in present hands can be said to have no value. It contributes nothing or next to nothing to the resources of the city. At best it is merely a self-supporting piece of machinery maintained by the labors of a few gentlemen who are entirely competent to find situations where they can do some good. The property itself should be paying about $2,000,000 a year in the form of taxes. Doubtless men will be found who will maintain that the city should go ahead and improve this property, build granite piers, erect warehouses and otherwise add to the beauty and convenience of the water front. Such men for consistency's sake ought not to be found among the men who control the water front to-day; but principles are sometimes forgotten when plums are abundant. But why should the city go ahead and improve? We have already suggested a very simple and every-day means through which the riparian property-holders can command operative resources to an amount in money that should rattle even Edward Bellamy, and make the advocates of unlimited taxation stand aghast. For the end in view the riparian property-holders of New York are stronger than the city with its political parties, its factions, and its rings all pulling at cross purposes and working for indefinite ends. Those property-holders could do all the work needed while the city was holding caucuses and discussing preliminaries.

This water front question in New York is peculiar. We want no decorative work at present. It would be like decorating your house before you have done more than lay the foundations. It is hard perhaps for a man to have to take a lesson from his offspring; but Brooklyn has pointed the way which New York should follow. We may felicitate ourselves, however, that we shall be able to greatly better the instruction.

The water front offers the best field for productive investment to be found in New York. There is no other field where the engineer, the architect, the builder, and the merchant can work so efficiently together. But we must have the subject right. We must get rid of abuses and superstitions, and strangle or drown this old man of the sea whom it is becoming yearly more and more burdensome to carry.

THE officials of the Manhattan Company are not apparently very much disturbed over the renewal of the attack on the occupancy of Battery Park by their structure. In all the hearings before Boards of Commissioners, legislators and Aldermen, which the matter has brought forth, they have been represented by counsel; but the arguments made by the lawyer did not smack very much of apprehension. Nor, indeed, have they any reason for alarm. Were the injury to Battery Park twice as great as it is, and were the legality of the occupancy only one-half as sound, common sense and circumstances would still bar any tampering with the structure. Even if the Park Commissioners could be persuaded to revoke the permit, it is incredible that the revocation would subsist. During the six months at their command the officials of the company would not have time to condemn the private property required for a new terminal, and a loop around State street is said to be impossible. Moreover it would be a far wiser policy on their part simply to sit inactive and confident, and to make no other preparations than those necessary for switching the trains at Rector street. At present, there is an absolute minimum of public interest in the matter, either in favor of the "champions of the people" or the Manhattan Company. It is easy enough for a few "hustlers" to trump up some thousand signatures to a petition for or against the corporation; but as a matter of fact the public are deadly indifferent to the whole controversy. It is safe to say that few besides those directly interested have exhibited the slightest concern as to the outcome of the affair. The "champions of the people" consist of a few misguided citizens and a few cheap and sensational journalists. The pretence that the movement is in any sense a popular one is outrageous, silly, and absolutely false. If the opponents of the Manhattan Company, or their dreary mouthpiece had conducted the controversy in a fair and truthful spirit, their movement might have commanded sympathy if not support, but the disgusting part of the whole business has been their paltry, childish and pretentious methods. On the other hand, no one has taken any active interest in opposing them, but people like Erastus Wiman, whose business would be injured by the removal of the structure, or some of the residents of Harlem who feel indebted to the company and vaguely fear any infringement of its privileges. If, however, the traveling public are hampered and delayed by a removal of the structure, the public opinion, which is now dormant, will awaken to the folly of the disabling a transit service that is already so deplorably weak. It is in this conviction that the Manhattan Company evidently feels secure.

"Who are the leading New York architects and what work have they done recently?" A visit to the exhibition of architects' drawings at THE RECORD AND GUIDE *Hall, Nos.* 14-16 *Vesey street, will answer this question.*

Investments—Good and Bad.

THE GRANGERS.—The indications are that the next upward move, whenever it shall come, will be led by the granger stocks. This assertion looks very much like a novice's bulling of things that have gone up. It is really not so, however. The grangers were the first to advance when a large crop was assured and when the fears of tight money which had existed all the spring and summer were proved to be unfounded or had defeated themselves by creating caution among trading classes. For some weeks the grangers stood almost still, what slight movement they showed was reactive on large realizing sales, and meantime the rest of the market was getting into line. While Rock Island lost 2 points and Burlington & Quincy about the same, Wabash, Missouri, Kansas & Texas, Lake Shore and New York Central made gains of from 5 points and upwards, and many other stocks large or small amounts. Notwithstanding the hesitation and suspicion created in the minds of the public by the White failure and by the action of the management of Missouri Pacific, the grangers have been very strong for the circumstances. The *jeu d'esprit* attributed to Mr. Gould, that Missouri Pacific should not pay an unearned dividend need not necessarily destroy the faith of the public in the dividend-paying power of other granger stocks. Any one familiar with Missouri Pacific and its published reports, would never be surprised to see that remarkable issue classed among the rattletraps at any time. If Missouri Pacific has, as it is authoritatively stated, not earned any money in the first seven months of the year, it is because the property has been always weighted down with fixed obligations imposed and increased from time to time, in order that a few might make large profits out of a weak-sighted and credulous many. Meantime far-sighted people have been building around Missouri Pacific and taking away its rates and business until that road has been almost smothered. The first seven months of this year were bad ones for the Western railroads. That is no secret, it has been proclaimed month by month, by managements honester than that of Missouri Pacific, publishing regular results of operations. But the eighth month of the year has passed and the ninth is closing, and in them some changes for the better may be easily found.

Admitting that the grangers' stocks are to continue the new advance, what are the reasons which will support and maintain that position? They are chiefly to be found in the growing business of the granger properties. Take a look at the figures published by the different granger roads from month to month, and it will be easily seen how their business is improving. Take a few of those figures and test them on the mileage basis, and the fact is brought out still more prominently. For instance, Burlington & Quincy in January last earned $446 on every mile of road it operated, and in July last $530. In the first seven months of the year it earned an average of $480 per mile per month, while in the year 1890 its average gross earnings were only $443 per mile per month. Take another instance, Rock Island's monthly mile-earnings for this year have run between $303 in February to $492 in August, making an average for eight months of $379. This was less than the monthly average for the fiscal year ended March 31st last, during which $427 per mile were earned, but the returns for the fiscal year include all the bad and none of the good months of this year. April earnings per mile showed a satisfactory increase over those of any of the three preceding months and the improvement has been steady and substantial each month since. Northwest answers to this test most satisfactorily. In February earnings per mile were only $400, in July they were $597, for seven months they averaged $489, and for the fiscal year which ended May 31, and as in the case of Rock Island took in the bad and excluded the good months of the year, the average was $542. St. Paul, in the year ended June 30th, earned an average of $401 a mile a month, and in the first eight months of this year an average of $371 a mile a month. January earnings per mile were $341, and those of August $411. Northern Pacific has an average per month per mile for the fiscal year to June 30th of $494, and for eight months of $427. The Atchison figures for the fiscal year are not available for comparison, but taking the earnings per mile for each month of this year on the 6,527 miles of Atchison proper the growth of business is shown to be very large. In March only $247 per mile were earned, as against $469 in August, and an average for the eight months of $378 a mile. These and other details will be found in the subjoined table by those who care for them:

MONTHLY MILEAGE EARNINGS.

1891.	C., B. & Q.	N'w'n.	St. Paul.	N. Pac.	Atch.	Rock Id.
January	$446	$441	$341	$410	$338	$326
February	429	400	329	354	317	303
March	477	471	374	408	247	362
April	476	469	370	449	392	376
May	502	496	368	444	430	381
June	500	554	376	434	410	382
July	530	597	405	451	424	409
August	....	....	411	471	469	492
Totals	$3,360	$3,428	$2,974	$3,421	$3,026	$3,031
Av. 7 or 8 months	480	489	371	427	378	379
Aver. last fiscal y'r	443	542	401	494	....	427

To the foregoing facts must be added the prices at which the several grangers have sold in the past year or two, under circumstances possessing none of the encouragements which are found in the present situation, compared with current figures. It will then be seen that there is every reason to be sanguine about their movements, if not now, in the near future. If Lake Shore is worth the current quotation of 122, what must Northwest be worth in the light of its splendid record in the past and its magnificent prospects for business in the future. Northwest has not been higher than about 117¼ in two years, and in the same time previous to its late advance Lake Shore did not at any time sell as high by a good many points. It is to be borne in mind, too, that the extensions of the grangers have been limited in the way of newly-built road in the last year or two, and there is consequently no new unpaying mileage to discount the benefit coming to the old lines. The managements of these properties have not been free from the blame of large and competitive extensions, but if their properties have discounted their faults during the hard period which closed with the beginning of this summer, they are all the more ready to take advantage of the better traffic and to reflect it in advanced quotations for their stocks.

Rapid Transit Finances.—Difficulties Ahead.

WHY SHOULD NOT THE CITY BUILD THE ROAD?

Although the Rapid Transit Commission has been in possession of the reports of its consulting engineers on the plans of construction of the Broadway-Boulevard line for over a week, the commissioners have been unable to come to any agreement upon them up to the present time. It was said yesterday that diagrams showing the general plan of construction which would be adopted had been prepared by the regular engineers of the board, but that when they came before the board for what was intended to be the final consideration before adoption, some exceptions were taken to them, and they were referred back to the engineers for amendment, with a fair prospect of their being satisfactorily finished to-day or early in the coming week.

The difficulties of the purely mechanical problem are undoubtedly far greater than anybody who has not had it to solve has been able to appreciate, and the commission is pursuing the wisest course in taking all the time necessary for the development of the best possible plan; but, as has been said by one of the engineers, any scheme of construction is so complicated an affair that changes might be made in it every day for a year, many of them with undoubted advantage to the plan, but as there has to be a conclusion reached some time, if ever the road is to be built, it would be well to report the general plan as speedily as possible, leaving the minor details of construction for the time when the detailed plans and specifications, required by section 6 of the act, become necessary. It is highly probable that this will be done, and that the general plans, embracing all that is necessary for the report to the Common Council, will be ready for presentation to the Common Council at its meeting next Tuesday.

But when the mechanical part of the problem shall have been thus disposed of, for the time being, *there will remain the financial scheme*, beset with quite as serious difficulties. President Steinway, who has been giving a great deal of consideration to this feature of the question, said last week that it would be very difficult to float so large an enterprise in the present condition of the finances of the world. Asked if it was not the intention of the commission to apply to the Legislature for some amendment of the law before submitting the franchise to a public auction, he gave no direct reply, but said it would be well if the law would authorize the temporary construction of the lines through the North Side section on the established grade. It would be difficult, he thought, to get capital to construct either an underground or a viaduct road through the North Side, along the routes laid out, because of the great cost of such construction, and especially because it would be four or five years at any rate before the upper sections of the roads would have traffic enough to pay. Still, the aspect of financial affairs was brightening, both in this country and in Europe, and by the time the plans of construction were approved by the Common Council, and the necessary consents of property-owners had been secured, and the scheme was ready to be submitted for the consideration of possible investors, the money markets of the world would probably be in better condition to assimilate so large an enterprise.

Asked whether the commission was considering the feasibility of the proposition that the city should build the road and own the entire system, Mr. Steinway said that whatever opinions the commissioners might entertain on that question could make no difference; the law prescribed their course of action, which was to offer the franchise for sale for such a term of years as it should deem proper, and to sell it to the highest bidder. He agreed to the general proposition that the road could be built by the city at a cost for the capital invested of only 3 per cent, whereas it would cost any corporation or construction company at least 5 per cent for the construction capital, and would therefore burden the road with a much higher and heavier burden of annual fixed charges. But he thought the construction of the road under a guarantee by the city of the fixed charges would be contrary to the constitution of the State, and was therefore out of the question. The provision of the constitution which Mr. Steinway had in mind prohibits the city from lending its credit to any corporation for any such purposes, and when it was suggested to him that the proposition was, not that the city should lend its credit for the purpose, but that it should build and own the rapid transit railroads as it had built and owned the water supply system, he said he had not sufficiently informed himself upon that proposition to give an opinion upon it.

But this is one of the most important auxiliary questions there is connected with the whole general question of adequate rapid transit. To the people whose daily fares, deposited in the coffers of the operating company, are to furnish the cost of maintenance and repairs, to reimburse the original construction company, and to pay the semi-annual dividends of the shareholders, it is by far the most important question connected with the entire subject. And viewed in the light of the future, it is the most important question to the city considered as a municipality. If the road is to cost

$50,000,000, the city can get the money to build it for an annual interest charge of $1,500,000; whereas, any corporation that might buy the franchise at public auction would not expect to raise the money for less than 5 per cent per annum, which would make the annual interest charge $2,500,000 on the bonded indebtedness alone. But besides the bonded indebtedness of $2,500,000, the construction of the road by a private corporation would entail an issue of stock, in such sum as the corporation should require, to represent its idea of the value of the property when completed and in operation. And on all this bonded debt and all this stock the traveling public of New York would be called upon to pay the interest and dividends; and since it would take a much larger annual income to do this than it would to pay the $1,500,000 of fixed charges in case the city should build, the operating corporation could not afford to pay the city so much by several times for the franchise as it could if the road was furnished complete.

One able banker of this city, Mr. Jacob Schiff, early advocated before the commission the construction of the rapid transit railroads by the city. Mr. Schiff has assured THE RECORD AND GUIDE reporter that he was advised by his attorney that there were no legal obstacles in the way of the construction of the road by the city. And as for the financial community, he said, it would much rather have the 3 per cent bonds of the city than the 5 per cent bonds of a private corporation. There was no doubt in his mind of the city being able to get the necessary money to build the roads whenever it should want it, and there was grave doubt in his mind of the road ever being built in any other way.

Colored perspectives of the several great hotels now building in this city are on exhibition at THE RECORD AND GUIDE *rooms, Nos.* 14-16 *Vesey street.*

An Important Decision for Bidders.

THE NATIONAL ASSOCIATION OF BUILDERS.
Office of the Secretary, 164 Devonshire street, Boston, Mass.
September 3d, 1891.

STEPHEN M. WRIGHT, ESQ., Secretary Mechanics' and Traders' Exchange, New York, N. Y.:

DEAR SIR—I take particular pleasure in informing you as to a matter of great interest to the building fraternity, inasmuch as it establishes a valuable precedent in the matter of submission of estimates and the rights of bidders.

You may possibly remember that at the midyear meeting of, as well as in my annual report as Secretary of the National Association, I mentioned the case of McNeill Bros., of Boston, against the Chamber of Commerce, of this city, in a suit for damages, on account of his being refused a contract for a building upon which he was the lowest invited bidder. At the time of my report a verdict had been rendered giving damages to McNeill in the amount of fourteen thousand five hundred dollars ($14,500), but the Judge of the Court carried the case up to the Supreme Bench on questions of law relating to the authority of the building committee of the Chamber of Commerce to award the contract. The Supreme Court of Massachusetts rendered its final decision (from which there is no appeal), to the effect that the damages awarded must be paid by the Chamber of Commerce to the said McNeill Bros.

This decision is of immense importance to builders, inasmuch as it gives a precedent of unquestioned character as to the rights of the lowest bidder.

Yours truly, WM. H. SAYWARD, Secretary.

The Lease of No. 812 Fifth Avenue.

106 BROADWAY, NEW YORK, September 19, 1891.

Editor RECORD AND GUIDE:

Relative to your statement that Bellamy & Winans, V. K. Stevenson and W. P. Seymour have leased for Mrs. Sanford to Col. W. H. Thompson, No. 812 5th avenue, between 62d and 63d streets, at $9,000 per annum, of even date, the facts of the case are, the lady owning the house being inexperienced in this real estate business talked with Messrs. Bellamy & Winans, also with Mr. W. P. Seymour's nephew, but Messrs. Riker & Co., whose office adjoins Messrs. Bellamy & Winans' office, on 5th avenue, is one of the oldest and ablest real estate firms in the city, and in justice to those gentlemen, we trust you will publish this letter, because they insist that neither Bellamy & Winans, nor W. P. Seymour's nephew are entitled to any recognition in this commission, or any credit for this rental. Our firm spent over $100 advertising 812 5th avenue, and the leases were signed here in this office by the tenant, Vice-President Thompson, of the United States National Bank, and as all the brokers claiming the right of recognition in this matter are prominent ones, we are still endeavoring to get as many of them recognized as possible. As long as you made this publication, as your paper has such an immense circulation among rich people, we trust that you will also publish this letter in full, and in justice to

V. K. STEVANSON & CO.

Real Estate Notes.

William R. Martin has traded with Charles E. Runk the four-story stone front office building, Nos. 40 and 42 Exchange place, for a plot containing about twenty-five lots, lying on 138th and 139th streets and Lenox avenue.

Judge Bischoff, in the Court of Common Pleas, on Wednesday last, gave judgments for the plaintiffs in suits against the elevated roads as follows: Charles Golden, South 5th avenue, near Bleecker street, $10,591 for loss of rental and $12,000 damages to the fee; Gordon Cunard, No. 151 Pearl street, $9,000 loss of rental and $12,500 for the fee; Nicholas Hoffman, No. 517 2d avenue, $2,318.77; Morris Blum, No. 974 2d avenue, $2,734.49 damages to fee and rental value.

The United States Government have taken title to Plum Island at Gravesend, in Sheepshead Bay, directly in rear of Manhattan Beach, at Rockaway Inlet. The Island contains fifty acres, and will be used for fortification purposes. The sum of $92,000 was paid to the Engeman estate, the former owners of the property.

John M. Ruck has passed title to Louis E. Oxee, of Brooklyn, to the two five-story brick flats with stores, known as Nos. 1313 and 1315 3d avenue, at an expressed consideration of $160,000.

John T. Williams has taken title at $90,000 to the two vacant lots at Nos. 54 and 56 Franklin street from the Metropolitan Telephone and Telegraph Co.

John Pettit has secured a loan of $300,000 at 5 per cent from the Fayerweather estate on the new office building on Washington street, east side, extending from Liberty to Cedar street.

Personal.

Benjamin Sturges has procured a loan of $15,000 on Emanuel Episcopal Church building, on President street, near Smith street, Brooklyn.

Contractors' Notes.

Sealed bids or estimates will be received by the Commissioner of Street Improvements of the 23d and 24th Wards, at his office, No. 2622 3d avenue, corner of 141st street, until 3 o'clock P. M., on Tuesday, September 29, 1891, for regulating, grading, setting curbstones, flagging the sidewalks and laying crosswalks and building culverts in 173d street, between the New York & Harlem Railroad and Weeks street; also for sewer and appurtenances on the southerly side of the Southern Boulevard, from the end of existing sewer west of Willis avenue to the summit east of Willis avenue.

Bids or estimates, inclosed in a sealed envelope, will be received at the Department of Public Works, No. 31 Chambers street, until 12 o'clock M. on Tuesday, September 29, 1891: For regulating and paving with granite-block pavement the carriageway of 90th street, from 1st to 2d avenue; for regulating and paving with granite-block pavement the roadway of 96th street, from Lexington to 4th avenue; for regulating and paving with granite-block pavement the carriageway of 103d street, from the Boulevard to Riverside Drive; for regulating and paving with granite-block pavement the carriageway of 103d street, from Central Park West to Columbus avenue; for regulating and paving with granite-block pavement the roadway of 119th street, from 7th to Lenox avenue; for regulating and paving with granite-block pavement the carriageway of Bradhurst avenue, from 142d to 145th street; for regulating and paving with asphalt pavement, on concrete foundation, the roadway of Edgecombe avenue, from the south side of 138th street to the north side of 141st street; and from thence north to the south side of 145th street, with granite-block pavement; for alteration and improvement to sewer in 9th street, between Avenues C and D; for repairs to sewers in 26th street, between Avenue A and 1st avenue; for alteration and improvement to sewer in 34th street between 11th and 12th avenues, and new sewer in 12th avenue, between 34th and 35th streets; for sewer in 115th street, between Riverside avenue and Boulevard, with curves into Boulevard.

Estimates for preparing for and building a crib bulkhead from a point about 100 feet north of West 97th street, North River, to a point about 20 feet 6 inches north of West 99th street, North River, and for dredging thereat, will be received by the Board of Commissioners at the head of the Department of Docks, at the office of said department, on Pier "A," foot of Battery place, North River, in the City of New York, until 1 o'clock P. M. of Thursday, October 1, 1891.

Proposals for estimates for furnishing materials and work in the erection of an armory building on the easterly side of 4th avenue, extending from 33d to 34th street; also for estimates for furnishing materials and work for additions, alterations and repairs to the armory buildings for the Eighth, Twelfth and Twenty-second Regiments, N. G. S. N. Y., New York City, will be received by the Armory Board, at the Mayor's office, City Hall, until 10.30 o'clock A. M. of the 9th day of October, 1891.

Sealed bids or estimates for furnishing the materials and work required for building a pavilion for New York City Asylum for Insane, Blackwell's Island, will be received at the office of the Department of Public Charities and Correction, No. 66 3d avenue, in the City of New York, until Thursday, October 8, 1891, until 10 A. M.

New Incorporations.

The Star Union Improvement Company filed a certificate of incorporation in the County Clerk's office on September 22d for the purpose of purchasing and improving real estate and selling material for the construction of buildings. The capital stock is $10,000, divided into 100 shares of $100 each, with privilege to increase to $25,000. The directors are David B. Mitchell and eight others.

Builders and house owners interested in good architecture should visit the exhibition of architects' drawings at Nos. 14-16 *Vesey street.*

Newark News.

Henry J. King has plans for the Warren Street Primary Public School, to be erected at a cost of $20,000. It will be of brick and three stories high, and the main building will be 58x60, while there will be two extensions of 15x40 and 26x44, respectively. Mr. King also has plans for a three-story frame dwelling, 25x54, to be built at the corner of Murray and Broad streets, at a cost of $4,000; for a dwelling on Mount Prospect and 7th avenues, 25x48, to cost $4,000; and for a two-and-a-half-story frame dwelling, to be built at No. 37 South 7th street by Hugh C. Marley at a cost of $3,500.

"Which architect shall I commission?" See the recent work done by the leading members of the profession, in New York, at THE RECORD AND GUIDE *Exhibition Rooms, Nos.* 14-16 *Vesey street.*

Real Estate Department.

The real estate market this week has not shown the improvement that was looked for and confidently expected by brokers. This failure to realize the bright predictions that were made for it is probably due to the unexpected warm weather of the past few days and to the stock market which, up to Thursday, was a rising one. Doubtless both of these reasons, so frequently advanced by brokers, have something to do with the continued quietness all along the line. The unpleasantly warm days we have experienced lately have beyond question delayed the return of many of those who otherwise would have been already in the market and alluring prospects of larger gains in Wall street have also had their share in enticing many other capitalists away from the surer investment, real estate. The lesson that these traders have learned from the stock-jobbing of the last few days, real estate brokers say, will not be without its beneficial effects. It will turn away from Wall street much of the capital that was pouring into stocks and divert it into the safer investment channels of real estate. For it is pointed out with reason that such a drop in the value of real estate, as occurred in a few hours in stocks during the week, is impossible. In the first place real estate is the last thing to be affected either by a rise or a depreciation. It never moves very rapidly either one way or the other, so that the loss of great sums of money in the space of a few hours is unknown to the holders of it. Then, too, the holder of real estate is dependant on no one but himself. He is his own president, secretary, board of directors and executive committee, and it is impossible to manipulate his property against his own interest. When investors have experienced heavy enough losses to make them realize that the irresponsible directors of a railroad or other stock company do not care one way or the other for the interests of stockholders, when those interests are not identical with their own, a great amount of capital that has hitherto found investment in stocks will be turned to real estate.

Renting continues active at fairly good prices and the inquiry in brokers' offices for houses both for sale and to rent is if anything better than it was last week. A great many transactions are now under way, but for a variety of reasons they have not yet been consummated. That those various sales will eventually be closed the brokers engaged on them have no doubt, for buyers talk with considerable confidence. One factor alone is discouraging, and that is the tendency of owners to increase their asking price as soon as a buyer has been secured who will pay the figure previously demanded. This practice of course discourages brokers and disgusts bona fide buyers. The real estate men of this city are congratulating themselves just now on the many prominent people who have lately acquired, or who have evidenced their intention of acquiring, dwelling houses in New York. Among those who have recently purchased or who will shortly do so are Charles T. Yerkes, the many-times-millionaire of Chicago; Daniel O'Day, the Standard oil millionaire of Buffalo; Walter Damrosh and Michael Grace. It will be seen that several of these gentlemen are from other cities, and they are only examples of a large class of residents in other parts of the United States who take up a permanent residence in this city as soon as they have arrived at prominence in their own towns.

THE AUCTION MARKET.

The auction market has not been a particularly satisfactory one this week. Although the advertised list of parcels announced to be sold was longer than it has been for some time, the actual sales were few in number and generally unimportant in character. In the city proper nearly all the real estate announced to be sold was to be offered by order of the courts, so that the outside market had little interest in the bulk of the New York offerings. In the one or two cases where up-town property was voluntarily offered the sales were failures, the owners having to bid the parcels in or withdraw them from sale. Many of the legal sales, too, were adjourned, and the few that took place were of little general interest. There was a larger number of Brooklyn offerings on 'Change this week than often occurs. The attempts to sell the parcels so offered met with very little success, the owners of many of them having to withdraw them or bid them in. Only one parcel out of eighteen that were offered was sold. All of which seems to indicate that New York City is not the place to sell Brooklyn real estate. This fact has been more or less clearly shown in nearly every sale of Brooklyn property that has been held on the New York Exchange. Local buyers are not on the ground to bid and the capitalists whose operations are largely in this city do not care to do so.

The suburban lots offered have sold both well and ill. The sale at South Bensonhurst was not a success, notwithstanding the fact that there was a fairly large crowd present. Out of the 526 lots offered only about forty-seven were sold, and these at prices that were unsatisfactory to the owners. On 26th avenue, near Bath avenue, lots sold at $185; on Bath avenue at $190 to $260, and the corner of Cropsey avenue and 26th avenue at $200, while adjoining lots on Cropsey avenue brought $165 and $175 each. Auctioneer John F. B. Smyth was more successful at Rahway, N. J. Out of 168 lots he managed to dispose of about eighty-five at prices which ranged between $50 and $500. There was a crowd of about three hundred people present, and the prices obtained were generally satisfactory to the owners. Inside lots sold from $50 to $150, while prices for corners were between $200 and $500 each. Many of the other lots were not sold, the auctioneer says, because the owners had not an absolutely clear title to them.

The list of announcements for next week is a very uninteresting one generally. There are a number of foreclosure sales, though none that are very important. A few offerings at public auction, a suburban sale of nearly two hundred lots at Tuckahoe and another of the Ferguson farm near the Ocean Parkway, Kings County. Altogether the outlook for business next week is not particularly bright.

On Tuesday, September 29th, William Kennelly will sell, by order of the Supreme Court, in partition, the three-story and cellar brick building, lot 25x100, No. 155 West Broadway; the four-story dwelling, lot 20x98.9, No. 447 West 22d street, and the three-story brown stone dwelling, lot 16.8 x100.8½, No. 127 West 87th street.

On Tuesday, September 29th, Jere. Johnson, Jr., will sell at 2 o'clock, on the premises, all the 243 desirable lots remaining of the Ferguson farm. The property is situated directly opposite Hiram Howe's famous hotel and between the Coney Island & Brooklyn Electric Railway and the Ocean Parkway, one of the most beautiful Boulevards in the World. The lots may be paid for in monthly installments, and may be reached by the Bridge or the down-town ferries.

On Monday, October 5th, James L. Wells will sell 214 lots at Tremont, comprising the well-known Ryer Homestead—five minutes' walk east of the 177th Elevated road station. Tremont has two rapid transit lines—the 3d avenue Elevated and the 4th avenue depressed roads—with 467 trains arriving and departing daily; a horse-car line, soon to be operated by electricity, parks, drives, sewers, abundant water, gas, and all the conveniences of city life. The lots will be judiciously restricted; liberal terms are offered, and a perfect title will be guaranteed, free of cost, to each purchaser.

On Tuesday, October 6th, Adrian H. Muller & Son will sell 238 choice lots on Kingsbridge road, 10th, 11th, Wadsworth and Audubon avenues, 188th, 189th and 190th streets. This property is just above the new Washington and Highbridge Park; the cable railroad runs within a few blocks of the property on 10th avenue, and the proposed new rapid transit line, will, if the present scheme is carried out, pass immediately through the property. Hence it has a large prospective value. Nothing is more certain than that Washington Heights will be the next district reached by the march of improvement, and the property now offered for sale is situated in the pleasantest part of that region. Seventy per cent of the purchase money may remain on bond and mortgage for one or three years at 5 per cent. The title is guaranteed by the Lawyers' Title Insurance Company free of charge to each purchaser.

On Tuesday, October 6th, D. Phoenix Ingraham & Co. will sell eight lots on the west side of Lenox avenue, being the entire block front from 116th to 117th street; also four lots on the north side of 116th street and four lots on the south side of 117th street, being immediately in the rear of the above Lenox avenue lots. The whole plot is 201.10x200, and is desirable for improvement.

On Monday, October 12th, James L. Wells will sell 196 desirable lots on Jerome terrace, opposite and overlooking Jerome Park. Jerome terrace is an attractive extension of the Bedford Park settlement, and is a very desirable residential section, because of its accessibility, its healthfulness and its city conveniences. Covenants prohibiting nuisances will be inserted in each deed. They are carefully worded so as to be in no way oppressive, and will promote improvements of a good character. The titles will be insured and the terms liberal.

S. F. Jayne & Co., of No. 254 West 23d street and No. 59 Liberty street, offer a very desirable opportunity to manufacturers. They have for lease for a term of years the premises at No. 6 Gansevoort street, near Hudson. The buildings are substantial, the front one being four-story and basement, 25x41, and the rear one three-story and basement, 25x43. It contains a 12 horse-power steam engine and full machinery for wood-working. It is in first-rate order, and would be rented for the purpose of any business. Additional property running through the block can be obtained if wanted.

CONVEYANCES.

	1890. Sept. 19 to 25 inc.	1891. Sept. 18 to 24 inc.
Number	178	174
Amount involved	$2 593,108	$2,424,156
Number nominal	49	59
Number 23d and 24th Wards	46	24
Amount involved	$338,950	$34,835
Number nominal	9	1[illegible]

MORTGAGES.

	1890.	1891.
Number	171	198
Amount involved	$2,160,175	$2,348,291
Number at 5 % or less	79	92
Amount involved	$924,120	$1,779,223
Number at less than 5 per cent	20	13
Amount involved	$454,800	$231,500
Number to Banks, Trust and Ins. Cos	32	31
Amount involved	$826,200	$581,200

PROJECTED BUILDINGS.

	1890. Sept. 20 to 26 inc.	1891. Sept. 19 to 25 inc.
Number of buildings	63	51
Estimated cost	$892,700	$678,100

Gossip of the Week.

SOUTH OF 59TH STREET.

Bellamy & Winans have sold for Hugh R. Garden to Joseph Bostwick No. 14 West 53d street, a four-story brown stone dwelling, on lot 25x 100.5, for $82,000.

Cyrille Carreau has sold for J. B. Wickersham, exr., of Philadelphia, to Well & Mayer the four-story factory, on plot 75x100, Nos. 57 to 61 Lewis street, on private terms.

Ascher Weinstein has purchased from Isaac K. Kahn Nos. 283 and 285 7th avenue, northeast corner of 26th street, a five-story brick and stone hall and stores, on plot 50x100, on private terms; from Virginia Hall No 364 West 32d street, a four-story English basement brown stone dwelling, on lot 16.8x100, on private terms; and No. 193 East Houston street, 22x50, running through to Nos. 85 and 87 1st street, 43x50, with the two and three-story and basement dwellings thereon, on private terms. The seller is Mrs. Marie Oest.

Goodman & Stern have sold for Goodman & Brother the three-story and basement house No. 740 East 5th street for $14,000.

H. V. Mead & Co. have sold the three-story brown stone private house, size 16.8x55x98.9, No. 354 West 20th street, for Casper J. Westervelt to Dr. Jos. F. Gray for $16,000.

.B. Flanagan & Son have sold for John H. McGinu No. 220 West 40th street, a four-story English basement brown stone dwelling, 15x50x100, on private terms.

NORTH OF 59TH STREET.

Jacob Cohn has sold to Michael Grace, brother of ex-Mayor Wm. R. Grace, No. 52 East 79th street, a four-story brick and stone dwelling, 25x 88x100, for $70,000.

W. H. De Forest, Jr., has sold for immediate occupancy three dwellings on the south side of 144th street, between Convent and Amsterdam avenues (Hamilton Grange). A 17-foot house was purchased by F. J. Worcester, a lawyer; the 19-foot house by Major Williamson, the Assistant Superintendent of the New York Post-office, and the 21-foot house by Geo. S. Evans, the lace manufacturer. The terms of sale are private.

Slawson & Hobbs have sold for J. & G. Raddell one of their five uncompleted houses on West 70th street. The house, No. 59 West, is a four-story brown stone, 20x58x102.2, and it was purchased by W. H. Van Allen for $38,000.

McMonegal & Eckerson have sold for Patrick Farley to Edward Davis, the Washington Market butcher, the four-story brown stone dwelling, No. 112 West 76th street, for $37,000.

J. B. Ketcham has sold the four-story brick house and lot on the south east corner of Lenox avenue and 120th street, 19x85, for Henry Morgenthau to C. D. Shephard for $35,000.

P. Fisher has purchased from G. W. Eggers Nos. 17, 19 and 21 West 100th street, three five-story flats, on plot 75x100.11, on private terms.

Ward Belknap has sold for Edward S. Willing, of Philadelphia, No. 287 West 61st street, a five-story brown stone double flat, 25x80x100, to Mrs. Katie Lasher, on private terms.

Jas. L. Libby & Son have sold for Mrs. Wm. J. Merritt No. 402 West End avenue, a three-story and basement private house, 19x52x82, to Rufus D. Pitcher, for $22,500.

Warren & Skillin have sold for Richard G. Platt to A. G. Thompson the three-story English basement brick and stone dwelling, No. 487 West End avenue, on private terms.

Frank L. Fisher & Co. have sold for Dr. Candidus four lots on the north side of 116th street, 90 feet west of 4th avenue, to a West Side builder, on private terms.

Theodore A. Squier has sold his three remaining three and a-half-story houses, 20x55 and extension x 100, on the south side of 90th street, west of West End avenue, as reported in last week's RECORD AND GUIDE. No. 302 West was sold to a Mr. Smith, a lawyer of 55 Liberty street, for $23,750; No. 304 to D. N. Griffin for $24,000, and No. 310 to Mrs. Emma B. Richardson for $23,650.

Harry Content has purchased the four-story brown stone dwelling, on lot 16.8x100.5, No. 62 East 79th street, for $31,000. The seller is Mr. Herman, of L. Levy & Co., the stock brokers.

The Germania Life Insurance Company, it is reported, has sold the four-story dwelling No. 1045 Madison avenue.

L. J. Phillips & Co. have sold through their 23d Ward office for Smith Williamson, to Dr. Rose and Dr. Einhorn, four lots on the north side of Crotona avenue, 100 feet east of Franklin avenue, for $5,000.

The buyer of the four story dwelling No. 56 West 76th street, reported sold last week, is Patrick Smith, of Far Rockaway, L. I.

Scott Bros. have sold for William P. Anderson to Warren W. Brooks No. 140 West 93d street, a four-story dwelling, 20x52 and extension x100.8, on private terms.

H. H. Dreyer has sold for Henry Stube No. 789 Amsterdam avenue, a five-story flat and store, 30x85x100.

LEASES.

Warren & Skillin have leased for W. E. Lanchantin the three-story dwelling No. 309 West 89th street at a yearly rental of $1,600.

E. H. Ludlow & Co. report that they have rented the following houses: No. 18 East 41st street, No. 156 East 38th street, No. 269 Lexington avenue, No. 15 West 47th street, No. 45 West 56th street, No. 51 West 11th street, No. 125 East 39th street, No. 59 West 92d street, No. 522 5th avenue, No. 38 East 57th street, No. 106 East 87th street, No. 74 West 70th street—all four-story private dwellings.

The Real Estate Loan and Trust Co. have leased for Haywood Cutting to August Belmont, No. 101 5th avenue, a four-story brown stone dwelling, between 15th and 16th streets, for two years at $9,000 per annum.

Brooklyn.

J. P. Sloane has sold for Mary McNeill the two-story and basement frame dwelling, 25x30x100, No. 210 Greene street, to Patrick Kieran for $2,700.

Corwith Bros. have sold the property consisting of three-story brick store and dwelling, 25x40, with two-story frame rear dwelling, on lot 25x101, on the north side of Greenpoint avenue, 75 west of Bradley avenue, L. I. City, for Mary McBreene, to William Gallagher for $4,750, and the lot on the north side of Richardson street, 100 feet east of Union avenue, for P. B. Amory, to Jacob Haehler for $700.

William Walsh has sold to Mary J. Lucke a plot, 100x100, on the north side of 32d street, 260 feet west of 5th avenue, for $3,300.

CONVEYANCES.

	1890. Sept. 18 to 24 inc.	1891. Sept. 17 to 23 inc.
Number	293	295
Amount involved	$1,414,224	$993,199
Number nominal	67	67

MORTGAGES.

	1890.	1891.
Number	275	289
Amount involved	$1,002,114	$779,087
Number at 5 per cent. or less	159	116
Amount involved	$583,925	$425,130

PROJECTED BUILDINGS.

	1890. Sept. 19 to 25 inc.	1891. Sept. 18 to 24 inc.
Number of buildings	53	96
Estimated cost	$300,075	$442,580

Out of Town.

TUXEDO PARK, N. Y.—Ames & Co. have sold for John Mack eighty acres of land in the Ramapo Valley, situated equidistant between Millionaire Havemeyer's property and Tuxedo Park, twenty-seven acres of which are in the famous Lake Anthony. The price paid is $18,000. The property was purchased by a syndicate of gentlemen, Messrs. Guernsey, Emerick and Jones, for the purposes of improvement and to lay out villa sites on the border of the lake made famous by Mad Anthony Wayne.

MOUNT VERNON, N. Y.—Lewis & Holder, who sold the McEvoy farm here for J. M. Levy and ex-Mayor Ely, report that the consideration was $100,000.

BREWSTERS, N. Y.—W. H. Drew has sold the Drew Cliffs farm, formerly owned by Daniel Drew, to a Mr. Scheffer, of Newport, R. I., for $75,000. The farm embrances 160 acres, and the sale includes residence, stock, etc. It is said that the property originally cost old Daniel Drew nearly $200,000.

Out Among the Builders.

De Lemos & Cordes have plans on the boards for a seven-story granite, cut stone and terra cotta warehouse, to be built at the southwest corner of Centre and Broome streets, on a plot 54x71.3. The building will be finished with elevators and first-class appointments in all respects, including fire-proof halls and stairs. The basement and first story will be arranged for store purposes. A. Trenkmann is the owner.

J. Averit Webster has plans on the boards for eleven three-story brown stone dwellings, 17.6x50 and extension, to be built on the north side of 93th street, between Central Park West and Columbus avenue. The houses will have all the improvements, and will cost, it is estimated, $139,500. The same architect has plans for two five-story brick and stone flats, 25x85, to be built by Laura J. Stephens on the north side of 115th street, 175 feet west of Lenox avenue, ar a cost of $40,000.

Richard R. Davis is the architect for an extension of five stories, 25x 97, which Jas. Lawlor will make to the Hotel Hamilton restaurant, on the south side of 125th street, 100 feet west of 8th avenue; and for three five-story flats, 25x87.6, to be built by the same owner on 125th street adjoining. The total cost will be $90,000.

G. H. Griebel will furnish plans for a three-story frame dwelling, 30x46, which Oscar Rudolph will build at Prospect avenue and 165th street; cost not estimated.

Out of Town.

JERSEY CITY HEIGHTS, N. J.—F. Ebeling has plans on the boards for a two-story and basement dwelling and school, 25x42, to be built for Emil Guhl on Cambridge avenue, near Bowers street, at a cost of $3,000.

WANTS AND OFFERS.

(Advertisements strictly in accordance with this title will be inserted at the practically nominal rate of 10 CENTS per line (agate). In figuring for themselves advertisers may count seven words for each line, the address to be taken as one line. The object of this department is to bring buyers and sellers into communication with customers. Advertisements must be marked "Wants and Offers Column," and sent to the office of publication, Nos. 14 and 16 Vesey Street, not later than 8 P. M. Friday.)

OFFERS.

60TH ST., NEAR 10TH AV.—Four-story brick tenement, with stores, in fine condition; all rented; 25x100.
T. A. BROWN, 177 Broadway.

FOUR BUILDINGS, near 7th av. and 34th st., 68x100; will be sold at a bargain.
T. A. BROWN, 177 Broadway.

SEVENTH AV., NEAR 120TH.—Five five-story single flats with stores including corner; all rented; paying well; sold at great bargain.
MAINHART & LOWE, 258 West 125th.

TWELVE best-paying five-story single flats, with stores, in Harlem; situated on most prominent avenue in city; all rented; sold at bargain or trade for good down-town property not heavily mortgaged; equity, $200,000.
MAINHART & LOWE, 258 West 125th.

BARGAIN—Four-story private dwelling. 43 West 130th, 20x50x100; newly decorated; excellent order; finest street in Harlem; price $20,000.
MAINHART & LOWE, 258 West 125th.

67 WEST 97TH ST.—Four-story; low figure.
Premises or OWNER, 20 Nassau st., Room 58.

BARGAINS IN WEST SIDE.—Three and four-story dwellings; several furnished houses for sale or rent; also elegant house on 64th st., near 5th av., to close an estate. ISAAC T. MEYER, 111 Broadway.

3D AV., near 74th st., size 50x100.
8th av., near 125th st., size 50x100.
42d st., near 9th av., size 50x100.
41st st., near 8th av., size 25x100.
Above are five-story flats, with stores, well rented; will sell cheap. ISAAC T. MEYER, 111 Broadway.

ATTENTION!—Must be sold; now is your chance to secure a home on the West Side; one of our largest builders, retiring, instructs us to reduce his entire list, and refuse no reasonable offer.
HUNT & WENDELL,
249 Columbus av., southeast corner 72d st.

BARGAINS.—Four-story 18 and 20-foot houses, near Riverside Drive; cabinet trim; all improvements; now offered for the first time at $26,500 and $27,500. Keys with HUNT & WENDELL, 249 Columbus av., southeast corner 72d st.

FOR SALE.—A grand 25-foot four-story brown stone house, 80 feet deep, West 53d st., near 5th av.; at a bargain. Can be seen only by permits of
HUNT & WENDELL,
249 Columbus av., southeast corner 72d st.

BARGAINS.—Five-story single flat, nine rooms, all improvements, on 116th st., near station. Five-story store and tenem't on prominent st., near station; all rented; $23,500; easy terms. Five-story double flat; good investment; well rented; all improvements; near 116th station; $19,500; mortgage, $15,000. Must be sold, three-story and basement brown stone dwelling, ten rooms and bath; decorated; in perfect order; $12,500. WOOD, WHITTLE & KENNELLY, 184 East 116th st.

RENTERS OF FLATS, New York or Brooklyn.—I will give you twice the room for the same rent you pay, and you can own the house.
C. G. DAVISON,
138 Stewart Building, 280 Broadway, New York.

FOR SALE.—Five new first-class four-story and basement private dwellings, Nos. 109, 113 and 119 East 45th st., and Nos. 462 and 464 Lexington av.; all leased to desirable tenants or can arrange to give possession to some of them if desired. For further particulars apply to
THE C. GRAHAM & SONS CO., 309 East 43d st.
Sept.19–1aw8w.

SIX-STORIED BUILDING to sell or lease, 25x72; well-ventilated rooms; in good condition; 76th st., East, New York. Apply to ENGINEER, 17 John st.
Sept. 12-1aw8w

FOR SALE.—At a sacrifice, new five-story double flats, near 125th st. L station. Address,
Aug. 1—1aw-9w. BUILDER, 319 East 125th st.

FOR SALE.—Six new cabinet-trimmed three-story and basement brown stone private dwellings, Nos. 142-152 West 123d st.; prices reasonable and brokers commissions allowed. For further particulars apply at office of
FRED'K. M. LITTLEFIELD, 156 Broadway.
Aug. 29-uf.

FOR SALE.—2443 8th av and 210 and 212 West 105th st.; commission allowed brokers. Apply at
Aug. 29-uf. Room 19, 156 Broadway.

OFFERS.

FOR SALE—2443 8th av.; 26.8½x100; easy terms; commission allowed brokers; apply at
Mar. 28-u-f. ROOM 19, 156 Broadway.

FOR SALE—210 and 212 West 105th st.; five-story apartments; each, 25x89x100; decorated and carpeted; apply at ROOM 19, 156 Broadway.
Mar.28-u-f

Improved Property.

SIXTY feet frontage by 100 in depth, covered with buildings, on 9th av., near 80th st. "L" station; good income; sold to close an estate.
T. A. BROWN, 177 Broadway.

HAGUE ST., near Pearl st.—33 feet frontage, two buildings can be purchased very cheap.
T. A. BROWN, 177 Broadway.

A CORNER BUILDING FOR SALE, suitable for manufactory, Water and Oliver sts.
RULAND & WHITING, 5 Beekman st.

FOR SALE.—A large manufacturing property down town, fronting the East River. Apply to
RULAND & WHITING, 5 Beekman st.

TO INVESTORS.—A large piece of improved property; situation the very best; a guaranteed lease at 4 per cent net for a number of years will be given. For particulars apply to
SCOTT BROS.,
Equitable Building, 120 Broadway.

EXCHANGE.—A Columbus av. front (200 feet), improved for lots on the West Side or in Harlem, above 125th st. Also two blocks of lots on West Side for improved below 59th st
SCOTT BROS.,
Equitable Building, 120 Broadway.

15TH STREET—625 and 627 East; four-story factory building, 50x100; engine, boiler and shafting; immediate possession; rent low.
WM. A. WHITE & SONS, 400 Broadway.

OFFICE OF
FREDERICK SOUTHACK,
471 BROADWAY,
offers for sale some choice pieces
of property on
LEONARD ST., between Broadway and West B'way.
FRANKLIN ST., between B'way and West B'way.
WHITE ST., between B'way and West B'way.
BROADWAY, from Barclay to 14th st.
BLEECKER ST., from B'way to South 5th av.
GREENE ST., Canal to 8th st.
WASHINGTON PLACE, B'way to Wooster.
WAVERLEY PLACE, B'way to Wooster.
APPLY AS ABOVE.
FREDERICK SOUTHACK.

PLANING MILL, branch of my business, for sale.—Is located at 24th st. and 11th av., on four or five city lots, leased ground, and consists of two and three-story brick buildings and adjoining sheds; also 80 horse-power engine and boiler, planers, moulders, saws, etc., all in good running order and now in operation; will leave a portion of value on bond and mortgage three years; this offers splendid opportunity to enlarge wood-working industry or to secure good mill business to add thereto. For further particulars, etc., apply to
EBEN PEEK, 24th st. and 11th av.
Advertiser intends to continue his lumber business now carried on at above address. Sept. 5–1aw4w

TO LET OR TO LEASE.—Two floors of a factory, 25x98 light on all sides, 1st av and 107th st; terms moderate. J. REEBERS' SONS,
Aug. 22-uf. 409 East 107th.

Vacant Lots.

LOTS.—Two vacant lots on East 71st st., between Park and Lexington avs.; to be sold low to close an estate. T. A. BROWN, 177 Broadway.

TWO CHOICE LOTS FOR SALE—Southeast corner 68th st. and 10th av.
ALEX. PATTON & SON, 218 Canal st.

100TH ST., between 2d and 3d avs.; ten lots cheap; all mortgage if improved.
Sept.26-1aw8w. EDWIN A. ELY, 103 Gold st.

40 CHERRY ST., between Roosevelt and Franklin sq., 32x64, vacant; $12,000; accommodating terms. EDWIN A. ELY, 103 Gold st.
Sept.26-1aw8w.

A VALUABLE LOT for sale, with a frontage of 106 feet on Brooklyn Bridge.
RULAND & WHITING, 5 Beekman.

OFFERS.

BLOCK TWENTY-FIVE LOTS, including front on 8th av., near 135th st. elevated station; will be sold at bargain; terms to suit; or will sell front separate to responsible builder with small cash payment.
MAINHART & LOWE, 258 West 125th st.

125TH ST., south side, bet 7th and 8th avs, 150x200, running through to 124th st. This is the only large plot for sale between these avenues. For further particulars apply to or communicate with
MAINHART & LOWE, 258 West 125th st.

FOUR ATTRACTIVE LOTS, 149th st., adjoining southwest corner 7th av., $3,600 each; builders' terms. EDWIN A. ELY, 103 Gold st.
Sept 26-1aw8w.

FOR SALE.—On easy terms, nine first-class lots, ready for immediate improvement, on south side 116th st., commencing about 150 feet east of 7th av. THE C. GRAHAM & SONS CO, 309 East 43d st.
Sept. 19–1aw4w.

FOR SALE.—Five lots, northeast corner Willis av. and 137th st, 100x125; easy terms; all ready for improvement; splendid location. Apply to
Sept. 5—1aw4w. JAMES CARNEY, 167 East 52d st.

EASTERLY FRONT BOULEVARD, with 200 ft. on 86th st. and 264 ft. on 85th st.; one or more plots.
OTTO ERNST,
Aug. 22-1aw-8w. South Amboy, N. J.

Brooklyn Real Estate for Sale.

FOR SALE.—Bargains on easy terms by Benjamin Andrews, 186 Remsen st., Brooklyn; 406 7th av. four-story brick corner; 269A and 271 17th st., frame; 611 and 613 4th av., frame; 143 26th st., frame; 50 Commercial and 13 Clay sts., frame.

BARGAIN.—Store property, 1507 Fulton st.; four-story brown stone; promising business block; must be sold; $2,500 cash required.
Sept.19-26. EDWIN SPARKS, 102 Vesey st.

PLATE-GLASS CORNER on avenue thoroughfare, 17th Ward, Brooklyn, half block from big shipyard; suitable for saloon; price, $3,800; easy terms.
J. P. SLOANE,
Aug. 29-1aw5w. 343 Manhattan av, Brooklyn, E. D.

Country Property.

ATTENTION SPECULATORS AND INVESTORS.—Plot of eleven acres or more to divide into lots; 2d Ward, Yonkers, on Kimball av., adjoining Richmond Park, where lots are rapidly selling and houses being built, and opposite Cedar Plot, Hyatt Farm, which has all been sold in lots and a number of houses erected; high ground, with an extended view from Palisade to Long Island Sound and surrounding country; ½ mile to Washingtonville Station on Harlem Railroad (board walk most all the way), and one mile from either Woodlawn or West Mount Vernon Stations on same Railroad. Terms easy.
A. L. ODELL, 451 Columbus av. and 10 Barclay st.

TWO CHOICE LOTS for sale on 1st st., 100x100, Woodlawn Heights, Hyatt Farm, near station; also 50x169 on Bronx River road.
R. T. MEEKS, 39 Vesey st.

FOR SALE.—In plots to suit; eligible building sites (commanding view of Sound for miles), on North st., Greenwich, Connecticut; price reasonable; terms easy; neighborhood aristocratic and fashionable. Apply to
FRED. J. STONE, owner, 60 Broadway, N. Y.
Sept. 12-uf.

Miscellaneous.

BUILDING MATERIAL EXCHANGE.—Salesman who is a member of above would obtain liberal commission from Y. A., RECORD AND GUIDE.

WE WANT owners, investors and speculators to know that we make a specialty of 12th Ward property; what have you for sale, exchange or rent? what do you wish to purchase? entire charge taken of property; correspondence solicited; established 1881. J. P. & E. J. MURRAY, 2030 3d av., near 112th st. Sept. 26-1aw4w

A PARTY ABOUT TO BUILD A FIVE-STORY factory, 50x98, in Harlem, near water-front, will lease the three upper floors and build to suit tenant. Terms very moderate. Address
May 16 u. f. OWNER, 409 E. 107th St.

PRINTING.—Book, News and Job.
RECORD AND GUIDE PRESS,
14 Barclay, and 14, 16 Vesey sts.

SALES OF THE WEEK.

The following are the sales at the Real Estate Exchange and Auction Room for the week ending Sept. 25.

** Indicates that the property described has been bid in for plaintiff's account.*

R. V. HARNETT & CO.

*115th st, No. 211, n s, 235 s w 7th av, 20x100.11, five-story stone front flat. F. F. Woodward admr. (Amt due $16,878) $17,000

A. H. MULLER & SON.

27th st, No. 330, s s, 428 e 9th av, 22x98.9, three-story brk dwell'g. W. E. Billings. (Amt due $6,479) 14,000

WM. KENNELLY.

*52d st, Nos. 521 and 523, n s, 275 w 10th av, 50x100.5, two five-story brk tenem'ts. John J. Jones et al. exrs 10,000

3d av, No. 714, w s, 24.11 s 45th st, 25.6x95, four-story brk store and tenem't. W. Longman. (Amt due $20,819) 27,800

B. L. KENNELLY.

*Washington st, No. 765, e s, 20 s 12th st, 15x78x15x47.10, five-story brk tenem't and store. Gertrude Jewett et al. exrs. (Amt due $12,791) 10,250

114th st, No. 322, s s, 262.6 e 2d av, 18.9x100.11, four-story brk tenem't. (Amt due $9,852) 11,000

SMYTH & RYAN.

*Thompson st, No. 210, e s, 90 n 3d st, 19x47.10, three-story brk tenem't. John J. Harrington. (Leasehold; amt due $1,965) 2,000

JOHN N. GOLDING.

*67th st Nos. 227-243, s s, 125 e 11th av, 225x100.5, nine five-story brk and stone tenem'ts. Equitable Life Assurance Society. (Amt due on each abt $9,523) 137,850

67th st, No. 223, s s, adj, 25x100.5, five-story brk and stone tenem't. S. H. Denton. (Amt due $9,523) 17,750

J. F. B. SMYTH.

114th st, No. 216 E., 25x100.11, four-story double tenem't. (Bid in) .... —

Total $298,650
Corresponding week, 1890 .... $811,995

BROOKLYN, N. Y.

FOR WEEK ENDING SEPTEMBER 24.

R. V. HARNETT & CO.

Bath av, s e cor Bay 41st st, South Bensonhurst, 28.2x100. J. Keene $650
Bath av, e s, adj, 147x100. Same 1,830
Cropsey av, n e cor 26th av, South Bensonhurst, 28.2x100. M. Dowling 200
Cropsey av, e s, adj, 21x100. Same 175
Cropsey av, e s, adj, 21x100. J. M. Levy 165
26th av, n s, 100 e Bath av, 25 lots. J. Kruc. 6,475
De Kalb av, No. 448, 18.5x71.11, three-story brk dwell'g and store. Geo. King 5,700

JOHN F. B. SMYTH.

Garfield pl, Nos. 169 and 171, 35x100, two three-story and basement brk and stone dwell'gs. (Bid in) .... —

JERE. JOHNSON, JR.

West st, e s, 81 n Av F, 2 lots. Wm. Hartung 600
West st, adj, 4 lots. Louis Camera 1,210
West st, adj, 1 lot. Mrs. Mabady 300
West st, adj, 1 lot. Mrs. Shaw 300
West st, adj, 1 lot. Conrad Bless 305
East 2d st, s w cor Lotts lane, 2 lots. A. J. Cracknell 580

East 2d st, adj. 3 lots. Mrs. O'Brien.......... 915

East 2d st, adj. 2 lots. Oswald Schuesler..... 610

East 2d st, adj. 2 lots. Thos. Farrell.......... 610

East 2d st, adj. 3 lots. Joseph Park.......... 930

East 2d st, adj. 3 lots. John Maloney 915

East 2d st, adj. 4 lots. John M. Gregory...... 1,280

East 2d st, e s, 62 s Lotts lane, 2 lots. Mary Long.......... 640

East 2d st, adj. 4 lots. Rae Impt. Co 1,300

East 2d st, adj. 4 lots. John M. Gregory...... 1,300

East 3d st, w s, 80 s Av F, 2 lots. E. A. Radigan.......... 600

Av E, e s, East 2d to East 3d st, 10 lots. H. C. Beck.......... 3,500

Av F, n w cor Gravesend av, 4 lots. Mrs. M. Murray.......... 1,160

Av F, n e cor West st, 5 lots. J. A. Cracknell. 1,400

Gravesend av, s w cor Lotts lane, Flatbush. 4 lots. Mrs. C. Bolinger.......... 1,280

Gravesend av, w s, adj. 2 lots. A. J. Cracknell.......... 580

OTHER AUCTIONEERS.

Cedar st, No. 14, s s, 235 w Evergreen av, 20x91.11x20x91, two-story brk dwell'g. Dr. H. F. Praeger.......... 2,700

Decatur st, No. 494, s s, 43.9 w Ralph av, 18.9x100, two-story and basement brk dwell'g. John C. Creveling.......... 4,800

Gwinnett st, No. 79, n w s, 85 n e Marcy av, 20x100, one-story frame brass foundry. Frank Schwarze.......... 1,850

Glenada pl, Nos. 12-16 (late Albany av), w s, 100 s Decatur st, 49.9x100, two four-story stone apartment houses..........
Glenada pl, Nos. 18-22 (late Albany av), w s, 149.9 s Decatur st, runs west 100 x south 38.2 x east 24.11½ x south 6.10 x east 77.2½ to Albany av, x north 50.3 to beginning, two four-story apartment houses..........
Charles D. Rust.......... 59,700

*Jackson st, No. 176, s s, 100 e Graham av, 25x100, two-story frame dwell'g on rear. Evadna P. Green.......... 1,400

Kosciusko st, No. 404, s s, 201.8 w Lewis av, 16.8x100, two-story frame dwell'g. Robert Gibbs. 2,675

*Pacific st, s s, 480.8 e Rochester av, 16.8x107.2¾, two-story and basement frame dwell'g. Sarah C. Savage.......... 2,000

Spencer st, No. 87, e s, 275 s Park av, 25x100, two-story frame dwell'g. James D. Andrews.......... 1,825

*Somers st, No. 40, s s, 26 e Rockaway av, 18.6x69.8¼, three-story brk flat. William J. Gaynor.......... 6,000

62d st, s s, 480 w 14th av, 20x100, New Utrecht, frame dwell'g. A. O. Treadwell.......... 500

*East New York av, s s, 192.6-10 w Albany av, 25x200 to Furnald st, two-story frame dwell'g, Flatbush. Elihu Ayres.......... 1,193

Georgia av, w s, 175 s Fulton av, 25x100, two-story frame dwell'g. Bridget McGuire...... 1,350

Georgia av, w s, 200 s Fulton av, 25x100, two-story frame dwell'g. James J. Rogers..... 1,800

Road from Village of Flatlands to the Neck and to Canarsie, n w s, 182.9 n e Hubbard st, 86.8x534.2x87x513.2, contains 1 acre, 5 36-100 perches, Flatlands, two-story frame dwell'g. Louis Worth.......... 3,180

New Utrecht road, e s, adj land of Protestant Dutch Church and Jos. H. Story, except portion taken for Prospect Park & Coney Island R. R. Co., Flatbush two-story frame dwell'g. James Warner.......... 3,500

Lot at Coney Island known as No. 4 on map of Wyckoff tract of common lands of Gravesend, begins at intersection of south line of lot 3 on same map and lot hereby described, runs south along w s of a road 30 ft. wide — x west to e s of 10-foot way, x north — x east to beginning, except.
West 5th st, w s, 43.4 s of W. Thompson's land, runs northwest along land of Coney Island Elevated Railroad 70.6 x west along same 52.7 x northeast 134.11 to st, x south 43.4..........
Andrew Van Opstal.......... 9,800

Total.......... $148,183
Corresponding week, 1890.......... $98,550

CONVEYANCES.

Wherever the letters Q. C., C. a. G. and B. & S occur, preceded by the name of the grantee they mean as follows:

1st—Q. C. is an abbreviation for Quit Claim deed, i. e., a deed in which all the right, title and interest of the grantor is conveyed, omitting all covenants or warranty.

2d—C. a. G. means a deed containing Covenant against Grantor only, in which he covenants that he hath not done any act whereby the estate conveyed may be impeached, charged or encumbered.

3d—B. & S. is an abbreviation for Bargain and Sale deed, wherein, although the seller makes no express covenants, he really grants or conveys the property for a valuable consideration, and thus impliedly claims to be the owner of it.

NEW YORK CITY.

SEPTEMBER 18, 19, 21, 22, 23, 24.

Beekman st, No. 56, n e s, 47.1 n w Gold st, 24.6x87.6x24.2x87.11, five-story stone front store. Stephen F. Shortland and Frances C. his wife to Thomas S. Shortland. ½ part. Sept. 21. nom

Broadway, No 652. Mary Defendorf widow and Matilda wife of and Samuel Cleland and Wilson L. Defendorf to and with Allen D. M. and Winifred I. Defendorf. Mutual agreement whereby parties of 2d and 3d parts do not object to probate of will of Wilson Defendorf and conveyance of 1-6th part of above premises to parties of 3d part. July 17. gift

Canal st, No. 454, s s, 126.6 e Hudson st, runs south 60 x east 4.9 x south 10.5 x southeast 13.3 x northeast 70 to st, x west 24, three-story brk store. Mary Davis widow, Minnie wife of Michael Driscall and Thomas G. Davis and Norah his wife heirs George Davis to The Rector, &c, Trinity Church. C. a. G. *Mt.* $10,000 Aug. 8. nom

Same property. James B. Ryan exr. George Davis to same. *Mt.* $10,000. Aug. 8. $19,000

Cedar st, No. 102, s s, 80 w Temple st, —x56.3x25x50.4, six-story brk store and tenem't. Thomas and Charles J. Cody to Edward T. Cody. Q. C. Sept. 23. nom

Centre Market pl, No. 5, three-story brk tenement with stores.
2d av, Nos. 626 and 628, two four-story stone front tenem'ts with stores.
36th st, No. 318 E., four-story brk store and tenem't.
41st st, No. 339 E., three-story stone front dwell'g.
22d st, No. 466 E., error, should be 446 East 72d st, three-story stone front dwell'g.
2d av, Nos 1929 and 1921, error, also 2d av, s w cor 100th st, two-story frame store and dwell'g and vacant.
97th st, n s, abt 100 e 4th av, 1 lot.
Park av, s w cor 105th st, 5 lots, with two-story brk dwell'g and one-story frame stable thereon.
117th st, n s, 135 w Park av, 1 lot.
1st av, n e cor 108th st, 1 lot.
Av B, n w cor 72d st, 8 lots.
Poplar st, s w cor Henry st, 5 lots, Flatbush, L. I.
Thomas Monaghan, Jr., Eldora, Hardin Co., Iowa, to Mary and Elizabeth Monaghan, Mary Lynch, John Cooney, Rose Bolster, George and Joseph Cooney, Thomas, William J., Mary, John and J. Alfred Monaghan. 12-13 part. July 1. other consid. and nom

Chestnut st, No. 26 } begins Chestnut st, e s,
New Bowery, No. 24 } 23.3 s Madison st, 25.1x44.10 to New Bowery, x35.4x69.10, three-story brk store. Lavinia and John J. Barrett by Charles A. Clark guard. to Joseph Hughes. All title. Sub. to dower of Cath. Barrett. Sept. 22. 167

Clinton pl (8th st), No. 90, s s, 72.10 e Macdougal st, 24.8x100 to alley, with use of alley, three-story brk dwell'g. Thomas D. Day, Jr., to Alice R. wife of J. Archibald Murray. *Mt.* $17,100. Sept. 19. nom

Clinton st, No. 250, e s, abt 20 n Cherry st, 20.1x71.11x19.11x71.11, three-story brk tenem't. Abraham Edelson and Annie his wife to Aaron Kaplan. *Mt.* $11,000. Sept. 15. 13,000

Delancey st, No. 157, s s, 77 w Clinton st, runs south 71.8 x east 7 x south 17.6 x west 30 x north 89.2 to st, x east 23, three-story brk store and tenem't with three-story brk tenem't on rear. Louis Hyman and Henrietta his wife to Louis Greenblatt. *Mt.* $13,500. Sept. 31. See Willett st 19,500

Exchange pl, Nos 40 and 42, s s, 68 w William st, 38.11x102.4x43.9x82.4, two four-story stone front office buildings. William R. Martin and Millicent H. his wife to Charles E. Runk. Sub. to mort. $100,000 and life annuity of $5,000. Sept 17 See 138th st exch

Exchange pl, No 69, n e cor New st, 23.3x24.7x24.10x24.7, three story brk office building. Henry W. Miller, Brooklyn, to Catharine W., Louise F., J. Matilda, Isabella E. and Minnie P. Miller. Sept. 19. nom

Forsyth st, No. 20, e s, abt 130 s Canal st, 22.6x100, three-story brk tenem't with stores. Hyman Blausteyn and Yetta his wife, Simon Freedman and Pesche his wife to Louis Goodman. *Mt.* $11,000. Sept. 18. 18,500

Forsyth st, No. 36, e s, abt 50 n Canal st, 25x100, five-story brk tenem't with stores. James J. Loonie and Mary A. his wife and Eugene Parker and Henrietta his wife to Bessie and Edward Butler. Re-recorded. *Mt.* $27,000. May 21, 1891. 45,500

Franklin st, No. 56, n e cor Courtlandt alley, 25x100, frame shed and vacant. Sub. to mort. $39,250.
Franklin st, No. 54, n s, 25.1 e Courtlandt alley, 25x100.3, vacant. *Mt.* $25,000.
Metropolitan Telephone and Telegraph Co. and The Mercantile Trust Co. as trustee assenting to John T. Williams. Sept. 15. 90,000

Horatio st, No. 81, n s, abt 115 e Washington st, 23x84.3, four-story brk tenem't. William Keys and Sibera his wife, George E. Keys and Julia L. his wife, Richard Keys and Emma T. his wife, Thomas B. Keys, Mary A. Hines, Catharine Harrow and Jane E Mount to John F. Cordes. Sept. 22. 13,000

Houston st, No. 249, s s, 37.6 e Norfolk st, 18.9x75, two-story brk store and tenem't. Frank H. Allen and Susan E. his wife, San Francisco, Cal., to William S. Shepard, Bath, Me. All title Dec 31, 1890. 2,000

Lewis st, No. 87, w s, 140.5 s Stanton st, 18.1x100, four-story brk store and tenem't with six-story brk building on rear. Jonas Weil and Theresa his wife and Bernhard Mayer and Sophia his wife to Benedict A. Klein. Sept. 24. 24,500

Same property. Benedict A. Klein and Karoline his wife to Jonas Weil and Bernhard Mayer. *Mt.* $13,000. Sept. 24. 24,500

Leroy st, No. 14, s s, abt 120 w Bleecker st, 20x80, three-story brk dwell'g. Adaline Miller, East Orange, N. J., to Joseph E Miller. Sept. 21. nom

Same property. Joseph E. Miller and Adelaide R. his wife to William H. Miller, East Orange, N. J. Sept. 21. nom

Madison st, No. 231, n s, 47.8 e Jefferson st, 47.5x100, five-story brk tenem't. Forsclos. George F. Langbein to Tallmadge W. Foster. Sub. to morts. Sept. 8. 23,850

Madison st, No 357, n s, 239.10 e Scammel st, 23.10x90, five-story brk tenem't with stores. Jacob Cohen and Mary his wife, Adolph Hahn and Fannie his wife to Maurice Klinkowstein and Rebecca Heyman. *Mt.* $13,500. Sept. 16. 18,500

Monroe st, s s, 163.4 w Montgomery st, 23.4x98.4x23.4x98.5. Release mort. Hyman Schnitzer to Louis Goodman. Sept. 18. nom

Oliver st, No. 74, e s, 126.2 n Cherry st, 26.2x100.6x25.3x100.6, five-story brk tenem't.
Oliver st, No. 77, w s, abt 100 n Cherry st, 25x100, five-story brk tenem't.
Oliver st, No. 79, w s, abt 100 n Cherry st, 24x100x25x100, five-story brk tenem't.
Louis Edelson and Mary his wife and Abraham Edelson and Annie his wife to Louis Gordon. *Mt.* $98,000. Sept. 28. 100,000

Oliver st, No. 45, w s, abt 135 s Madison st, 25x100, five-story brk tenem't with stores. Charles Malawista and Rebecca his wife to Morris Piatigorsky. *Mt.* $25,500. Sept. 15. 35,250

Park st, No. 37, s s, abt 100 w Pearl st, 25x93.6.
Park st, No. 39, s, abt 75 w Pearl st, 25x95.6
Two six-story brk tenem'ts, store in No. 37 and a six-story brk tenem't on rear of each.
Olivia Christal and Mabel his wife to Henry R. and Kate Christal. *Mt.* $30,000. Sept. 15. (Corrects error in last issue.) 14,400

Park st, No. 37, s s, 25x93.6x25x93.
Park st, No. 39, s s, 25x95.6.
Louis Gordon and Jennie his wife to Herman Fichter. 1-6 part. *Mt.* 1-6 of $40,000. Sept. 15. 10,000

Same property. Same to Aron Levy. 1-6 part. *Mt.* 1-6 of $40,000. Sept. 15. 10,000

Pitt st, No. 55, w s, 168.8 n Delancey st, 18.7x63, three-story brk store and tenem't. Samuel and Theresa Stuller to Henry Gottlieb. C. a. G. *Mt.* $9,000. Aug. 18. 12,000

Rivington st, No. 181, s e cor Attorney st, 50x100, six-story brk store. Stephen F. Shortland and Frances C. his wife to Thomas S. Shortland. ½ part. Sept. 21. nom

Rivington st, No. 231, s w cor Willett st, 25x63, five-story brk tenem't with stores. August F. Schwarzler and Julia H. his wife to Bernard Metzger. Sept. 21. 43,500

Stanton st, No 183, s s, 37.8 w Attorney st, runs west 18.6 x south 63.4 x east 16.5 x north 0.10 x east 2.6 x north 62.6, three-story brk tenem't. Caroline wife of Herman Peters to Solomon Greenbaum. Sept. 24. 11,600

Thompson st, No. 66, e s, abt 192 n Broome st, runs east 94 x north 13.9 x west 4 x north 20 west 90 to Thompson st. x south 33.9, five-story stone front tenem't with store. Louis Edelson and Mary his wife and Abraham Edelson and Annie his wife to Solomon Jacobs. *Mt.* $30,875, judgm't $1,330 and taxes, &c Sept. 18. 35,500

Washington st, Nos. 502, 504 and 506, w s, 80 n Spring st, 62x100x62x97, three-story brk store
Hudson st, No 486, s e cor Morton st, 23x55, four-story brk store and tenem't.
Rachel Olmsted widow to Evelyn wife of George E. Horr, Jr., Charlestown, Mass, formerly Sacchi and Alice Olmsted. June 30. nom

Water st, Nos. 343 and 343½, s s, 129.3 e Roosevelt st, 25.1x75x23.11x75.11, two four-story brk stores and tenem'ts.
Water st, No. 345, s s, 154.4 e Roosevelt st, 19.5x85.5x19.1x85.9, four-story brk store and tenem't.
Morris Berkowitz and Yetta his wife to Louis Goodman. *Mt.* $16,000. Sept. 11. nom

Same property. Louis Goodman and Rachel his wife to Thomas S. Stevenson. *Mt.* $16,000. Sept. 22. 29,000

Willett st, No 6, e s, 103 n Grand st, 25x100, five-story brk tenem't. Lewis Greenblatt and Sarah his wife to Louis Hyman. *Mt.* $22,000. Aug. 31. See Delancey st. 40,000

Wooster st, Nos. 101 and 103, w s, 125.1 n Spring st, runs west 100 x north 24.10 x east 5 x north 25 x east 95 to st, x south 49.10, two three-story frame (brk front) stores with one and three-story brk buildings on rear. Amos R. Eno to Emily Stern. C. a. G. Sept. 11. 57,000

7th st, No. 294, s s, 104.9 w Lewis st, 22x90.10x22x—, three-story brk tenem't. Louis Weiler and Rosa his wife to Sophie Mayer. Sept. 21. nom

Same property. Matt Mayer and Sophie his wife to Louis Weiler. Sept 21. nom

11th st, No 335, n s, 245.4 w Greenwich st, 21.4x95.9x21.5x95.9, four-story brk tenem't. Lambert S. Quackenbush and Alice H. his wife and Abraham Quackenbush, Jr., and Rebecca M. F. his wife to Amelia Mosher. Q C. Sept. 14. nom

16th st, No 251, n s, 209 e 8th av, 17x80, three-story brk dwell'g. Ulrich Schlaeppi and Mary his wife to Victor L. Veyrac. September 21. 12,200

17th st, n s, 125 w 8th av. Party wall agreement. John McSweeney and Mary his wife to Harriet F. Howe Sept. 11. nom

18th st, Nos. 337-341, n s, 275 e 9th av, 75x92, one, two and three-story brk and frame buildings.
19th st, Nos. 338-342, s s, 275 e 9th av, 75x92, three three-story brk dwell'gs.
Louis Lese and Sarah his wife to Ascher Weinstein. Sept. 21. nom

21st st, No. 113, on map No. 157, n s, 180 e 7th av, 20x98.9, four-story stone front dwell'g. John Graham to Mary A. G. McLochlin. Sept. 24. nom

24th st, Nos. 36-50 and 54 W.
22d st, Nos. 409 and 411 W.
22d st, No. 528 W.
8th av, No. 551.
21st st, No. 230 W.

Catharine wife of David Bonner, Buffington, Pa., to Mary Hettrick. ⅙ part. Sept. 19. nom

Same property. Mary Hetrick to David Bonner, Buffington, Pa. ⅙ part. Sept. 19. 25,000

29th st, No. 231, n s, 200 w 2d av, 25x98.9, five-story brk tenem't with stores. Peter F. Rafferty to Bridged Rafferty. Nov. 20, 1890. nom

30th st, No. 102, s s, 60 e 4th av, 20x79, five-story stone front flat. Benjamin Richards and Eliza F. his wife to John B. Pine. *Mt.* $15,000. Sept. 22. 24,500

34th st, Nos. 209 and 211, n s, 125 e 3d av, 25x98.9, two three-story stone front dwell'gs. Henry C. Acker and Emma L. his wife to Mary L. Fettretch. Correction deed. All Liens. Oct. 13, 1890. nom

35th st, No. 36, s s, 475 w 5th av, 20x100, three-story stone front dwell'g. Samuel O. J. Simms to Elizabeth Ann Richards, Evansville, Ind., and William H. Fuller, Brooklyn. Q. C. and C. a. G. Confirmation deed. Aug. 25. nom

35th st, s s, 475 w 5th av, 20x100. Elizabeth A. wife of and David Richards, Evansville, Ind., to William H. Fuller, Brooklyn. All title. Taxes, 1891. Sept. 23. 25,000

35th st, No. 412, s s, 125 w 9th av, 25x98.9, four-story brk store and tenem't with two-story frame and brk dwell'g on rear. Contract. Raoul Dupuy to Hugo E. Distelhurst. July 25. 16,000

39th st, No. 348, s s, 125 e 9th av, 25x98.9, six-story brk tenem't with stores and four-story brk tenem't on rear. Philip Pinkel and Catharine his wife to John F. Schreyer. Q. C. Confirmation deed. Sept. 12. nom

39th st, No. 350, s s, 100 e 9th av, 25x98.9, six-story brk tenem't with stores and four-story brk tenem't on rear. Same to Anna M. Martling. Q. C. Confirmation deed. Sept. 12. nom

42d st, Nos. 552-562, s s, 100 e 11th av, 117x98.9, vacant lots, coke yard, &c. Charles McCready and James P. Campbell exrs. and trustees Hugh Murray, Thomas C. and Henry J., Rose K., Catharine and Hugh Murray by George B. Morris guard. ad litem to Henry Murray. All title. Confirmation deed. July 23, 1886. 9,316

45th st, No. 130, s s, 345 w 6th av, 20x100.4, four-story brk dwell'g. Samuel O. J. Simms to Elizabeth Ann Richards, Evansville, Ind., and William H. Fuller, Brooklyn. B. & S. and C. a. G. Confirmation deed. August 25. nom

45th st, No. 130, s s, 345 w 6th av, 20x100.4, four-story brk dwell'g. Elizabeth Ann wife of David Richards, Evansville, Ind., to William H. Fuller, Brooklyn. All title. Taxes, 1891. Sept. 23. 25,000

45th st, No. 133, n s, 385 w 6th av, 20x100.4, four-story stone front dwell'g. Samuel O. J. Simms to William H. Fuller, Brooklyn, and Willie R. Fuller. Q. C. and C. a. G. Confirmation deed. Aug. 25. nom

47th st, No. 504, s s, 115.4 w 10th av, 15.4x100.4, two-story frame dwell'g and one-story frame shed on rear. William Ferguson, Jersey City, to Peter J. Bresnan. *Mt.* $2,500. Sept. 21. 3,000

47th st, No. 334, s s, 160 w 1st av, 20x100.5, four-story brk store and tenem't. Alexandrina Jordan widow to Michael Cohen. *Mt.* $5,000. Sept. 1. 8,700

47th st, No. 112, s s, 606.3 e 7th av, 18.9x100.5, four-story stone front dwell'g. Ascher Weinstein and Annie his wife to Mordecai S. Kauffman. *Mt.* $13,000, taxes, &c. Sept. 1. 18,800

52d st, No. 523, n s, 300 w 10th av, 25x100.5, five-story brk tenem't. Foreclos. William F. Emmet to John J. Jones and ano. exrs. David Jones. Sept. 22. 10,000

52d st, No. 521, n s, 275 w 10th av, 25x100.5, five-story brk tenem't. Foreclos. Same to same. Sept. 22. 10,000

58th st, Nos. 405-409, n s, 88.5 e 1st av, 51.4x100.4, three three-story brk and stone dwell'gs. Gertrude M. Train to Alfred Dolge. *Mt.* $20,000. June 20. nom

61st st, No. 65, n s, 96 w 4th av, 19x100.5, four-story stone front dwell'g. Elizabeth Ann wife of and David Richards, Evansville, Ind., to William H. Fuller, Brooklyn. All title. Taxes, 1891. Sept. 23. 25,000

61st st, No. 65, n s, 96 w 4th av, 19x100.5, four-story stone front dwell'g. Samuel O. J. Simms to Elizabeth A. Richards, Evansville, Ind., and William H. Fuller, Brooklyn. Q. C. and C. a. G. Confirmation deed. Aug. 25. nom

65th st, No. 53, n s, 100 w 4th av, 17x100.5, four-story stone front dwell'g. Morris Schneider and Grace his wife, of Sherman, Texas, and Abraham Schneider and Julie his wife to Jacob B. Weinberg. All liens. Sept. 21. nom

65th st, No. 136, s s, 458 e 10th av, 20x100.5, four-story stone front dwell'g. Foreclos. William Sulzer to Joseph Wallach. June 11. 21,750

Same property. Joseph Wallach and Matilda his wife to Charles A. Troup and Charles A. Lieb. *Mt.* $15,000. Sept. 18. 26,500

65th st, No. 168, s s, 150 e 10th av, 24x100.5, five-story stone front flat. John H. Clapp and Mary J. his wife, Portchester, N. Y., to Howard S. Hall, Plainfield, N. J. All liens. Sept. 18. 50,000

66th st, No. 217, n s, 275 w Amsterdam av, 25x100.5, five-story stone front tenem't. Foreclos. William N. Armstrong to The Equitable Life Assur. Soc. U. S. *Mt.* $6,500. Sept. 16. 17,000

66th st, No. 219, n s, 300 w Amsterdam av, 25x100.5, five-story stone front tenem't. Foreclos. Same to same. *Mt.* $6,000. Sept. 16. 16,250

66th st, No. 221, n s, 325 w Amsterdam av, 25x100.5, five-story brk tenem't. Foreclos. Same to same. *Mt.* $6,000. Sept. 16. 17,250

67th st, No. 232, s s, 300 e West End av, 25x100.5, five-story brk and stone tenem't. Foreclos. Gilbert M. Speir, Jr., to The Equitable Life Assurance Society, United States. *Mt.* $7,000. Sept. 22. 17,250

67th st, No. 238, s s, 225 e West End av, 25x100.5, five-story brk and stone tenem't. Foreclos. Same to same. *Mt.* $7,000. Sept. 22. 17,500

67th st, No. 234, s s, 275 e West End av, 25x100.5, five-story brk and stone tenem't. Foreclos. Same to same. *Mt.* $7,000. Sept. 22. 17,250

67th st, No. 230, s s, 325 e West End av, 25x100.5, five-story brk and stone tenem't. Foreclos. Same to same. *Mt.* $7,000. Sept. 22. 17,000

67th st, No. 236, s s, 250 e West End av, 25x100.5, five-story brk and stone tenem't. Foreclos. Same to same. *Mt.* $7,000. Sept. 22. 17,000

67th st, No. 240, s s, 200 e West End av, 25x100.5, five-story brk and stone tenem't. Foreclos. William N. Armstrong to same. *Mt.* $7,000. Sept. 22. 17,250

67th st, No. 242, s s, 175 e West End av, 26x100.5, five-story brk and stone tenem't. Foreclos. Same to same. *Mt.* $7,000. Sept. 22. 17,500

67th st, No. 244, s s, 150 e West End av, 25x100.5, five-story brk and stone tenem't. Foreclos. Same to same. *Mt.* $7,000. Sept. 22. 15,000

67th st, No. 246, s s, 125 e West End av, 25x100.5, five-story brk and stone tenem't. Foreclos. Same to same. *Mt.* $7,000. Sept. 22. 17,600

69th st, No. 324, s s, 191.8 e 2d av, 16.8x77.4, three-story stone front dwell'g. Release mort. Henry S. Strauss to Emma wife of Louis Krug. Sept. 14. nom

Same property. Emma wife of Louis Krug to Jennie Arnstein. *Mt.* $7,200. Sept. 15. See 114th st. nom

75th st, No. 18, s s, 275 w Central Park West, 21x100, four-story stone front dwell'g. Frederick Aldhous and Eliza his wife to Emeline T. Kirby. *Mt.* $26,000. Sept 16. See 76th st. 46,250

76th st, No. 108, s s, 100 w Columbus av, 25x102.2, vacant lot. Emeline T. Kirby to Frederick Aldhous. Sept. 18. See 75th st. 14,000

76th st, No. 345, n s, 275 e 2d av, 25x102.2, four-story stone front tenem't. George Hand to Valentine, Johanna, Mary and Rosa Kihn. *Mt.* $9,300. Sept. 22. 12,800

80th st, Nos. 170-182, s s, 105 e 10th av, 145x102.2, seven four-story brk dwell'gs. Morris Schneider and Grace his wife, of Sherman, Texas, and Abraham Schneider and Julie his wife to Jacob B. Weinberg. All liens. Sept. 21. nom

83d st, No. 533, n s, 148 w East End av, 25x102.2, five-story brk tenem't. Joseph Schreiner and Amelia his wife to Frederick Pritz. *Mt.* $16,000. Sept. 24. 22,500

85th st, Nos. 22 and 24, s s, 250 e 5th av, 50x102.2, two two-story frame dwell'gs with one and two-story frame buildings on rear. Margaret P. Barker et al. exrs. Stephen Barker to William Schneider. *Mt.* $14,000. Sept. 15. 10,000

86th st, No. 134, s s, 345 w 9th av, 20x106.10, four-story stone front dwell'g. D. Willis James and Ellen S. his wife to Kate B. O'Hara. Sept. 17. 35,000

86th st, s s, 80 e West End av, 20x83.2, four-story brk dwell'g. William H. Ramsey to Mary J. Stevens. *Mt.* $22,000. Sept. 19. nom

86th st, No. 66, s s, 171.8 w 4th av, 31.11x102.2, five-story stone front flat. Fred. K. Van Court and Mary E. his wife to Benjamin Van Leeuwen. *Mt.* $35,000. Sept. 21. 41,875

87th st, No. 338, s s, 460 w West End av, 20x100.8, four-story stone front dwell'g. John Dunn and Eliza J. his wife and David Dunn and Maggie his wife to Harvey L. Pence. *Mt.* $17,000. Sept. 24. 23,575

89th st, No. 315, n s, 210 w West End av, 20x100, three-story stone front dwell'g. Release mort. Francis M. Jencks to William E. Lanchantin. Sept. 22. 1,000

Same property. William E. Lanchantin and Carriebell D. his wife to Helen D. Adams. *Mt.* $17,500. Sept. 24. nom

90th st, No. 304, s s, 110 w West End av, 20x100.8, four-story stone front dwell'g. Theodore A. Squier and Carrie B. his wife to Anna B. Griffen. *Mt.* $17,000. Sept. 19. nom

91st st, s s, 225 e 5th av, 25x100, vacant. Bertha Volkening to Robert W. Thain. *Mt.* $8,000. Aug. 10. 15,000

93d st, Nos. 203, 205 and 207, n s, 90 e 3d av, 60x100.8, three four-story brk tenem'ts. Anna M. wife of and Edward P. Steers to William J. Mathews. *Mt.* $20,000. Aug. 31. nom

96th st, No. 23, n s, 220 w 8th av, 20x100.11, four-story stone front dwell'g. Edward Kilpatrick and Julia A. S. his wife to Sophia B. Silleck. *Mt.* $22,500. Sept. 21. 34,000

102d st, Nos. 203 and 205, n s, 80 e 3d av, runs north 63.9 x east 25 x north 38.2 x east 25 x south 100.11 x west 50, two five-story brk tenements with stores. John H. Clapp, Portchester, N. Y., and Mary J. his wife to Howard S. Hall, Plainfield, N. J. All liens. Sept. 18. 50,000

102d st, n e cor Park av, 52x100.11. Release mort. The Bradley & Currier Co. (Lim.) to Frederick Rohrs and Louisa his wife. Sept. 24. nom

102d st, n e cor Lexington av, 317.6x100.11. }
103d st, s e cor Lexington av, 209.6x100.11. } vacant.

Margaretta H. Ward to Lewis Z. Bach. Sept. 8. 114,200

103d st, No. 137, n s, 300 w Columbus av, 17x100.11, three-story stone front dwell'g. Kate F. Ritchie to Henry M. Turk. Sub. to mort. $13,000. Sept. 22. 18,500

106th st, s s, 150 w 10th av, 75x100.11, vacant. Ida Meyer et al. exrs. Isaias Meyer to James A. and Orlando W. Norcross, Worcester, Mass. *Mt.* $17,500. Sept. 15. 22,500

111th st, No. 224, s s, 285 e 3d av, 25x100.11, four-story brk tenem't. Emily Beckert to Mary C. Behm widow. *Mt.* $6,000. Sept. 24. 12,000

113th st, No. 81, n s, 75 w 4th av, 25x100.11, five-story brk flat. James Smith to Pauline Staehlen. *Mt.* $14,000. Sept. 23. 20,625

114th st, No. 436, s s, 193 w Av A, 25x100.10, four-story stone front tenem't with two-story brk dwell'g on rear. Jennie wife of George Arnstein to Emma wife of Louis Krug. *Mt.* $14,000. Sept. 14. See 69th st. nom

117th st, No. 443, n s, 410.8 e 1st av, 16.8x100.10, two-story brk dwell'g. Henry S. Moore et al. exrs. Monmouth H. Underhill to Julia A. Tucker. Sept. 21. 7,500

Same property. Clara B. Moore, Monmouth H. Underhill, Jr., and Emily C. Underhill individ. and assignee of Monmouth H. Underhill, Jr., to same. Q. C. Sept. 21. nom

118th st, No. 160, s s, 235.2 w 3d av, 17.1x100.11, five-story brk store and flat. Thomas H. O'Connor exr. and trustee of John F. O'Connor to The Farmers Loan and Trust Co. substituted trustee John F. O'Connor dec'd. Sept. 10. nom

120th st, n s, 100 w Amsterdam av, 25x100.11, vacant. Thomas Butler and Julia his wife, Jeremiah Butler and Alice his wife and Johanna wife of Jeremiah Falconer formerly Butler to William Patchell. Sept. 23. 3,350

121st st, No. 261, n s, 573 w 7th av, 17x100.11, three-story stone front dwell'g. Abraham Schneider and Julia his wife to Jacob B. Weinberg. All liens. Sept. 19. nom

121st st, s s, 100 w 8th av, 175x100.11, vacant. }
121st st, Nos. 309-315, n s, 95 e Manhattan av, 100x100.11. }
Four five-story brk flats. }

Abraham Schneider and Julia his wife to Jacob B. Weinberg. All liens. Sept. 18. nom

123d st, Nos. 124-128, s s, 240 e 4th av, 75x100.11, three five-story stone front flats. Morris Schneider and Grace his wife, of Sherman, Texas, and Abraham Schneider and Julia his wife to Jacob B. Weinberg. All liens. Sept. 21. nom

123d st, No. 348, s s, 212 e 9th av, 16x100.11, three-story stone front dwell'g. Pauline Neustaedter widow to Henriette wife of Joseph H. Senner. *Mt.* $12,000. Sept. 21. 15,000

124th st, Nos. 149 and 151 } begins 124th
Lexington av, Nos. 2151 and 2153 } st, n e cor
Lexington av, 40x100.11; No. 149, five-story brk (stone front) store and flat; No. 151, four-story stone front flat; Nos. 2151 and 2153, five-story brk flat with stores. Adolph M. Bendheim and Henriette his wife to Isidor Herz. Sept. 19. 80,000

124th st, No. 317, n s, 193.9 e 2d av, 18.9x100.11, three-story brk dwell'g. Sarah E. Palmer widow, Jamestown, N. Y., to Anton Larsen. *Mt.* $5,200. Sept. 24. 10,100

126th st, No. 265, n s, 145 e 8th av, 20x99.11, two-story brk dwell'g. Partition. Ladislas Karge to Joseph Bierhoff. *Mt.* $5,000. Sept. 19. 8,800

Same property. Joseph Bierhoff and Julie his wife to Michael Reichert and Elizabeth his wife. *Mt.* $5,000. B. & S. Sept. 17. nom

131st st, No. 58, s s, 212.6 w Park av, 17.6x99.11, three story stone front dwell'g. Mary Cahill to Michael Smith. *Mt.* $9,300. Sept. 15. 10,250

132d st, s s, 200 w Lenox av, 175x99.11, vacant. Henry McAleenan exr. of Hugh McAleenan to William McReynolds. ½ part. Sept. 17. 28,000

Same property. Henry McAleenan and Annie his wife to same. ½ part. Sept. 17. 28,000

138th st } begins 138th st, n s, 75 e Lenox av,
139th st } runs east 250 x north 199.10 to
Lenox av } 139th st, x west 211.8 x southwest
143.6 to av, x south 86.10 x east 75 x south 24.11, vacant. Charles E. Runk and Aurelia E. his wife to William R. Martin. *Mt.* $55,000. Sept. 21. See Exchange pl. exch

141st st, n s, 100 e 11th av and 75 e New Boulevard, 25x100, vacant. Robert P. Lee and Anna M. his wife to William Fanning. Re-recorded. 4-5 part. March 2, 1869. 2,400

150th st, s s, 225 e 11th av or Boulevard, 25x99.11, four-story brk flat. Anne B. Reuschle extrx. Frederick Reuschle to Isabella wife of Frank Koch. *Mt.* $9,500. Sept. 22. 16,200

Same property. Anne B. Reuschle widow to same. 1-3 part. *Mt.* $9,500. Sept. 22. 16,200

165th st, s s, 266.8 e 10th av, 33.4x70.4x33.1x65.8. Release mort. William R. and Charles B. Knapp exrs. Shepherd F. Knapp to Christine Hansson. June 25. nom

Amsterdam av, w s, 25 s 180th st, 25x100. *Mt.* $5,500. }
Kingsbridge road, e s, 25.6 n 178th st, 76.7x81.3x75x96.8. *Mt.* $11,000. }

Caleb M. Hillman and Laura A. his wife to Teresa Wallach. Sept. 22. 24,000

Amsterdam av, w s, 25 s 180th st, 25x100. *Mt.* $5,500.
Kingsbridge road, e s, 25.6 n 178th st, 76.7x 81.3x75x96.8. *Mt.* $11,000.
Teresa wife of Leopold Wallach to Henrietta wife of Solomon Moses. ½ part. Sept. 22. 12,000

Columbus (9th) av, e s, 100.8 n 95th st, 25.2x 93.3x25.3x90.8. Confirmation of release of mort. Martin Klebisch to Henry Bornkamp. Sept. 5. nom

Madison av, w s, 100.5 n 62d st, 20x70. Release dower. Louise A. wife of Albert Block formerly Louise A. Silleck widow to Willy Meyer. Sept. 19. nom

Madison av, No. 811, s e cor 68th st, 22.5x95, four-story brk dwell'g. Josephine A. Van Vorst widow, Nyack, N. Y., Frederick B. Van Vorst and Mary G. his wife and Marie L. Van Vorst, Nyack, N. Y., to George N. Miller. *Mt.* $10,000. Sept. 24. 81,800

Same property John H. Van Vorst by Edward De Witt guard. to George N. Miller. 1-3 part. *Mt.* 1-3 of $10,000, and taxes 1891. Sept. 24. 27,100

St. Nicholas av, Nos. 417–421, e s, 149.11 s 133d st, 60.9x128x60.9x149.1, three five-story brk flats.
Morton st, No. 68, s s, 55 e Hudson st, 25x31, three-story brk store and tenem't.
Florence G. wife of Delos Woolverton to Rachael Olmsted widow. Life Estate. June 30. gift

Same property. Rachel Olmsted widow to Florence G. wife of Delos Woolverton. June 30. gift

West End av, No. 48, e s, 75.5 s 67th st, 25x100, five-story stone front tenem't with stores. Foreclos. Gilbert M. Speir, Jr., to The Equitable Life Assur Soc., United States. *Mt.* $8,000. Sept. 16. 20,500

West End av, No. 42, e s, 25.5 n 66th st, 25x100, five-story stone front tenem't with stores. Foreclos. Same to same. *Mt.* $8,000. Sept 16. 20,000

West End av, No. 44, e s, 50.5 n 66th st, 25x100, five-story stone front tenem't with stores. Foreclos. Same to same. *Mt.* $8,000. Sept. 16. 20,250

West End av, No. 52, e s, 25.5 s 67th st, 25x100, five-story stone front tenem't with stores. Foreclos. Same to same. *Mt.* $8,000. Sept. 16. 20,250

West End av, No. 46, e s, 75.5 n 66th st, 25x100, five-story stone front tenem't with stores. Foreclos. Same to same. *Mt.* $8,000. Sept. 16. 20,250

West End av, No. 50, e s, 50.5 s 67th st, 25x100, five-story stone front tenem't with stores. Foreclos. Same to same. *Mt.* $8,000. Sept. 16. 20,250

West End av, s w cor 85th st, 8 lots. Declaration of Richard G. Platt that yards in connection with above shall always remain open and unbuilt upon. Sept. 8, 1891. nom

2d av, No. 1468, e s, 27.2 s 77th st, 25x88.8x25x 88.7, five-story brk tenem't with stores. Isaac White and Matilda his wife to Elizabeth Morris. *Mt.* $15,000. Sept. 5. 28,000

2d av, No. 2304, e s, 27 n 118th st, 26x80, five-story brk tenem't with stores. Joseph L. Buttenwieser to Benedict A. Klein. *Mt.* $11,500. May 1, 1891. 25,500

3d av, Nos. 1313 and 1315, e s, 27.2 n 75th st, 56.3x105, two five-story brk flats with stores. John M. Ruck and Clara A. his wife to Louis E. Oxee, Brooklyn, N. Y. *Mt.* $110,000. Sept. 15. 160,000

5th av, No. 2127, e s, 50 n 130th st, 16.8x75, four-story stone front dwell'g. Elizabeth Ann wife of and David Richards, Evansville, Ind., to William H. Fuller, Brooklyn. All title. Taxes 1891. Sept. 23. 25,000

5th av, No. 2127, e s, 50 n 130th st, 16.8x75, four-story stone front dwell'g. Samuel O. J. Simms to Elizabeth Ann Richards, Evansville, Ind., and William H. Fuller, Brooklyn. Q. C. and C. a. G. Confirmation deed. Aug. 25. nom

5th av, w s, 80.2 s 19th st. Party wall agreement. Sarah Beadel extrx. Henry Beadel to John A. Cisco exr. John J. Cisco. Sept. 15. nom

All rear part of mortgaged property lying west of line 90 w Boulevard (11th av), 25x10 deep. Release mort. Elizabeth Bloodgood to Francis W. Seagrist, Jr.. Sept. 16. 300

Same property. Release mort. Same to same. Sept. 16. 300

Same property. Release mort. Same to same. Sept. 16. 600

All rear part of mortgaged premises lying west of line 90 w Boulevard, 25x5 deep. Release mort. Nathaniel E. Wood, Norwood, N. J., to same. Sept. 16. 250

All rear part of mortgaged premises lying west of line 90 w Boulevard, 24.11x5 deep. Release mort. Same to same. Sept. 16. 500

All rear part of mortgaged premises lying west of line 90 w Boulevard, 25x5 deep. Release mort. Sarah M. Starr to same. Sept. 16. 250

All rear part of mortgaged premises lying west of line 90 w Boulevard, 25x10 deep. Release mort. Same to same. Sept. 16. 300

All rear part of mortgaged premises lying west of line 90 w Boulevard, 25x5 deep. Release mort. Same to same. Sept. 16. 250

Lot in 12th Ward on s s of lands late of Eliza B. Jumel, 100 w Amsterdam av, runs west 25x100. Andrew A. Henderson and Lillie E. his wife to Margaret Brandreth. Sept. 23. nom

Mill Rock or Gibson's or Leland's Island, being Hell or Hurl Gate, abt 1 acre, with land under water, containing 8 639-1,600 acres. Cecil C. Biggins, of Bartow, N. Y., and Susan R. his wife to William R. Peters. Sept. 22. 6,615

MISCELLANEOUS.

Ante-nuptial agreement whereby party of the second part relinquished claim to dower in real estate and right to personal property not bequeathed by will. John Graham with Theresa Cassidy. July 3. nom

General release, also all right to dower in real estate of Theodore Silleck dec'd. Louisa A. wife of Albert Bloch to Henry G. and Walter Silleck individ. and exrs. Theodore Silleck and Estella Fraser, Oscar Silleck and Lilias Corwin. Sept. 19. 1,000

Release of annuity and of all dower in estate of Robert Gregory dec'd. Charlotte J. Gregory widow and extrx. Robert Gregory to Euphemia Stevenson also extrx. and William B. Charlton, Jr., heir and devisee of said Robert Gregory. Sept. 23. 18,500

23d and 24th WARDS.

Gerard st old, n e s, 230.9 s e Bergen av, 16.9x100 x15.6x100. George J. Grossman and Mathilda his wife to Harry Berry. *Mt.* $3,500. Sept. 14. nom

John st, s w s, lot 17 map East Tremont, 66x 150. Emma wife of Henry B. Hall, Jr., to Evadna H. wife of Daniel Mapes, Jr. Sept. 21. 1,500

Ryer st, w s, 125 s Irving st, 25x100. Ellen Murray heir Mary Murray to James T. Murray. C. a. G. Sept. 21. 150

Same property. Peter H. and Michael J. Murray to James T. Murray. B. & S. Sept. 4. nom

Simpson st, w s, 146.7 n 169th st, 25x74.11, h & l. Joseph F. Leamy, New York, to Mary T. Leamy. Sept. 22. 250

Samuel st, n e s, lot 21 map East Tremont, 66x 150. Emma wife of Henry B. Hall, Jr., to Daniel Mapes, Jr. Sept. 21. 1,500

Tiffany st, e s, lot 1 map 919 block 467 map Lyman Tiffany, part Fox estate, 25.6x98.6x 18.6x100. Mary Meehan to Mary Layden. *Mt.* $300. Dec. 29, 1890. 2,800

134th st, n s, 125 w Alexander av, runs north 100 x west 25 x north 100 to 135th st, x west 25 x south 200 to 134th st, x east 50.
134th st, s s, 125 w Alexander av, 125x100.
Release mort. M. Dasher Wylly, Bayonne, N. J., to Frederick Rohrs. Sept. 3. nom

135th st, n s, 104 e Southern Boulevard, 100.7x 75. Pheba C. Rapelye to R. Clarence Dorsett. *Mt.* $19,000. Sept. 17. nom

151st st, n s, 400 w Courtlandt av, 50x116.7x50x 116.6. Barbara Schneider widow, Carolina Waldeyer and Anna M. Ernst to Michael Velter. *Mt.* $2,100. Sept. 19. 6,500

174th st, s e cor Lexington av, runs east 157 to Prospect av, x south 85 x west 134 to Lexington av, x north 100. Mary J. Donnelly to Susan M. Donnelly. 1-5 part. Sept. 17. nom

Anthony av, e s, 130.9 n 175th st, 95x170x98.11x 142.0, hs & ls. Timothy Donovan and Mary T. his wife to Irene L. Stoeckel. *Mt.* $5,000, taxes 1891. Sept. 4. 7,500

Bathgate av, w s, 216 s 175th st, 24x120. John P. Wenninger and Caroline his wife to Lillie C. O'Connor. Sept. 17. 4,250

Belmont av, s e s, 80.2 n e John st, 35.1x155.6x 35x151.8. Paul A. Hartnett and Ellen his wife to Edward J. O'Gorman. Sept. 25. nom

Belmont av, s e s, 185.6 n e John st, 35.1x168.5x 35x168.11. Hibbert B. Roach and Annie H. his wife to Edward J. O'Gorman. Sept. 24. nom

Berrian av, s e s, lots 163 and 164 map of part of Charles Berrian's farm, Fordham. James W. Amory and Clara his wife, Jersey City, N. J., to Peter B. Amory, Newark, N. J. *Mt.* $300. July 1, 1887. nom

Brook av, w s, 100 s 170th st, 42x90. John F. Lambias, Brooklyn, to Adolph Mueller. Sept. 24. 1,700

Clinton av, s e cor Spring st, 100x100. Foreclos. Leicester Holme to Lanty Ryan and Michael Doherty. Sept. 21. 4,100

Creston av, w s, 225 s Kirk pl, 25x110. John S. Reiner and Margaret A. his wife to Peter Ryan. Sept. 17. 935

Morris av, s e cor 154th st, 25x95.3. Bernhard Stock and Marie his wife to Lillie E. McClusky. Sept. 15. 3,800

Morris av, s w cor 150th st, 50x100. Jacob H. Wertheimer and Ella his wife to Nathan Lemlein and Herman Cottek. ⅔ part. *Mt.* ⅔ of $4,250. Sept. 17. 4,500

Opdyke av, n s, 325 e 3d st, 25x100. Louise E. wife of George E. Daniels, Brooklyn, N. Y., to Caroline wife of Nickolaus Schwarz. Sept. 17. 400

Same property. Angelina M. O. Valentine, Brooklyn, N. Y., to Louise E. Daniels. Dec. 27, 1887. nom

Tinton av, e s, 68 s Denman pl, 17x95, h & l. John C. Fahl and Clara his wife to Charles Hess and Sophie his wife. *Mt.* $2,200. Sept. 23. 4,500

Willis av, s e cor 138th st, 100x74.4. Thomas L. Reynolds to Patrick H. McManus. Q. C. May 28. nom

Same property. Patrick H. McManus to Mary McManus. Sept. 22. nom

3d av, e s, part lot 149 map Morrisania, 16.8x 82.2 to now west line of Boston road or av, x north 16.8 x abt 95. Eliza Prescott widow, New York, to Christiana A. Buckle. *Mt.* $5,500. Sept. 19. 6,500

3d av, e s, 225.11 s 163d st, 25.2x133.5x25x130.4.
Lots 8, 9, 10, 20, 23, 24 and 35 map sub-division Charlotte F. Trowbridge.
Lots, 24, 1, 2, 5, 6, 15–18 map property Isabel T. Perry.
Abraham Schneider and Julia his wife to Jacob B. Weinberg. All liens. Sept. 19. nom

Abraham Schneider and Julia his wife to Jacob B. Weinberg. All liens. Sept. 18. nom

LEASEHOLD CONVEYANCES.

Henry st, s s, 94 e Clinton st, 23.6x100. Assign. lease. Morris Robinson to Tobias Krakower. ½ part. 2,500

Park row, No. 105 Michael T. N. Burke to James Jennings. 14 years 8 months and 16 days, from Aug. 15, 1891, per year, 2,200 to 2,500

Same property. Assign. lease. James Jennings to Nicholas T. Brown. nom

Same property. Assign. lease. Nicholas T. Brown to Michael J. Callahan. 3,500

Pearl st, No. 74, n e cor Coenties slip. Charles F. Kargebehn to Henry Bruggemann and Adam Stecker. 15 years 2 months and 3 days, from Feb. 25, 1891, per year, 2,000, 3,000

Varick st, No. 22. Maria Dolan to Henry McArdle. 21 years, from Aug 1, 1891, per year, taxes, and 1,200

Washington st, Nos. 502, 504 and 506, w s, 80 n Spring st, 62x100x62x97.
Hudson st, No. 426, s e cor Morton st, 23x55.
Evelyn wife of George E. Horr, Jr., and Alice Olmstead to Rachel Olmstead widow. June 30. life lease

4th st, n s, 112.11 e 1st av, 25x96.2. Assign. lease. Charles Obry, Jr., to Charles Obry, Sr. 6,750

18th st, n s, 275 e 9th av, 25x92. Assign. lease. Louis Lese to Ascher Weinstein. nom

32d st, No. 107 W., n s, 84 w 6th av. Agreement to lease for 21 years, from May 1, 1894, per year, $1,500, tenant to have right to remove buildings. Anna M. Miller to Garret D. Rhinehart. Sept. 18. nom

51st st, No. 56, s s, 729 w 5th av, 21x100.5. Trustees of Columbia College to Louisa I. Pendergast. 21 years, from Oct. 1, 1889, per year, taxes and 708

87th st, n s, 300 w 2d av, 25x100.8.
87th st, n s, 275 w 2d av, 25x100.8.
87th st, n s, 250 w 2d av, 25x100.8.
Assign. lease. Joseph Murray to Jacob Dieter. Sept. 16. 2,400

1st av, No. 411. Assign. lease. James Everard to Martin J. Fitzpatrick. nom

2d av, No. 746. Assign. lease. Henry Holcroft to James Fay. nom

8th and 9th avs and 51st and 52d sts. Tax leases. Agreement subordinating above leases to mortgages. Benjamin F. Dunning to John J. Jones and ano., exrs. David Jones. Sept. 21. nom

KINGS COUNTY.

SEPTEMBER 17, 18, 19, 21, 22, 23.

Ashford st, w s, 265 s Vienna av, 20x100. Alfred E. Oldaker to Burton J. Mosier. $112

Ashford st, w s, 245 s Vienna av, 20x100. Alfred E. Oldaker to Watson J. Mosier. 113

Ashland pl, w s, 389.3 n Fulton st, 21x100.6. Henry C. Overing to Ann Muldary. 5,800

Bainbridge st, s e cor Ralph av, 25x100. John Reilly to John H. Kucks. *Mt.* $10,000. 18,000

Baltic st, s s, 200 e Bond st, 25x100. Adrian V., Helen and Eliza W. Martense, Mary M. and Gertrude Prince to James P. Philip. nom

Same property. James P. Philip to Charles Gold. *Mt.* $1,800. nom

Barbey st, w s, 100 n Eastern Parkway, 25x 100. George Tucker to Patrick Brophy. 600

Same property. Release mort. Maria L. Sackett to George Tucker. 300

Bergen st, n s, 175 w Vanderbilt av, 25x110, h & l. Kendall Towne to Samuel Post, Morris Park, L. I. B. & S. nom

Bergen st, n s, 120 w Nevins st, 20x100. Catharine wife of Nicholas McCaul to Mary E. Healy and Julia Gerety. nom

Bergen st, s s, 325 e Rochester av, 40x127.9. Charles J. Schriefer to Alexander J. Hilzinger. 1,475

Berriman st, s w cor New Lots road, 120x— s Van Brunts, x—x—.
Vienna av, Stanley av, Berriman st and Shepherd av.
Shepherd av, s e cor Stanley av, 33.5x110.3x 31x131.1.
Release mort. Catharine E. wife of William H. Rowland to William H. Jackson. 3,447

Bleecker st, s e s, 283.4 s w Knickerbocker av, 16.8x100.
Bleecker st, s e s, 266.8 s w Knickerbocker av, 16.8x100.
Bleecker st, s e s, 233.4 s w Knickerbocker av, 33.4x100.
Hannah F. Street to Herman E. Street, Rockville Centre, L. I. All liens. nom

Boerum st, No. 129, n s, 150 w Graham av, 25x 100. Edward Notter to Marie A. Notter his wife. B. & S. C. a. G. All title. nom

Boerum st, No. 162, 25x100. Contract for property. Israel and Abraham Jarashow to Samuel Cassel. 11,650

Broadway, s w s, 103 n w Willoughby av, runs southwest 65.8 x south 26.6 to av, x west 23.7 x north 31.2 x northeast 79.1 to Broadway, x southeast 20 to beginning. Jacob Mayer, of New York, to Henry Mayer. *Mt.* $2,500. 7,500

Butler st, s s, 374.8 e Nostrand av, 16.8x100. Jennie S. Conklin, Cold Spring, N. Y., to Hannah E. Olmstead. *Mt.* $4,500. 5,350

Butler st, s s, 391.4 e Nostrand av, 16.8x100. Same to same. *Mt.* $4,500. 5,400

Carroll st, n s, 232 e 7th av, 20x100. Cornelius E. Donnellon to Ella L. Donnellon. 10,000

Carroll st, s w s, 70 s e 3d av, 20x81.3x20x1x—. Michael Maber to William J. Conway. *Mt.* $1,250. 3,500

Carroll st, s s, 41.1 e Polhemus pl, 21x103.9x21.1x105.8. Marion wife of and Harry W. Smith to Anna S. wife of Louis H. Amy. *Mt.* $10,000. 16,000

Centre st, s s, 180.1 e Hamilton av, 25x100. Mary J. Parker, of San Francisco, Cal., widow to Jane Lawler. Q. C. 200

Cheever pl, w s, 39 n Degraw st, 20x80; also two leaseholds. Cornelius Coffey to Lillie M. Coffey. All liens. nom

Clifton pl, No. 214, 25x100. All interest. James Creed to John Maxwell. 225

Clinton st, No. 212. Release life estate. Alexander Cochran to John A. Cochran. nom

Clinton st, w s, 80.6 s Atlantic av, runs west 25 x north .06 x west 65 x south 25 x east 90 to st, x north 24.6. John A. Cochran to William H. Cochran. 21,000

Clinton st, s e s, 42 n e State st, 21x90x21.5x—. Margaret P. Bridge to Frank A. Butler. *Mt.* $9,500. 19,000

Columbia st, n e cor Congress st, 25x90. Trustees Brooklyn Benevolent Soc. to Cornelius Coffey. 21 years, from Feb. 1, 1889, per year, 200

Cook st, n s, 75 w Humboldt st, 25x75. Joseph Schmalheiser to Hannah Schmalheiser. ½ part. nom

Cook st, s s, 150 e Morrell st, 25x100. Eva Henlein widow to Leopold, Michel and David Stern. *Mt.* $800. 2,600

Cook st, n s, 275 e Morrell st, 25x100. Jacob Unterreiner to Leopold Michel and David Stern. *Mt.* $1,000. 2,400

Cumberland st, w s, 624.10 s Fulton st, 32x100. Release judgment. Emily C. Underhill, of White Plains, N. Y., to Clara B. Moore. nom

Same property. Julia A. Tucker, of New York, Monmouth H., Jr., and Emily C. Underhill individ. and as assignee Monmouth H. Underhill, Jr., to same. Q. C. nom

Same property. Henry S. and Clara B. Moore and George H. Tucker as exrs. Monmouth H. Underhill, Jr., to same. 5,500

Dean st, s s, 180 w Nostrand av, 20x107.2. Clark W., Courtlandt De L., Louis M. and Annie E. Evans to Maria E. Davis. 14,500

Dean st, s s, 275 w Vanderbilt av, 25x110. Michael Bracken to James P. Stevenson. 2,300

Dean st, s s, 80 w Grand av, runs south 93.1 x southeast 18.2 x west 26.7 x north 110 to st, x east 20. William H. Gardiner, of Southold, N. Y., to David S. Weekes. *Mt.* $650. 1,000

Decatur st, s s, 100 e Ralph av, 18x100. William J. Northridge to William H. Chapman. *Mt.* $4,500. nom

Same property. Release mort. Charles M. Marsh to William J. Northridge. nom

Degraw st, s s, 380 e Buffalo av, 40x78x40x70. Amos S. Lamphear to Harriet E. Greene and S. B. Newbery and Fanny B. Newbery. *Mt.* $600. nom

Degraw st, s s, 380 e Buffalo av, 20x78x20x74. Harriet E. Greene to Fanny B. Newbery. nom

Degraw st, s s, 400 e Buffalo av, 20x74x20x70. Fanny B. Newbery to Harriet E. Greene, of New York. Sub. to taxes, &c. nom

Dresden st, e s, 110.1 n Atlantic av, 25x100. John B. Snook to Charles E. Smith. 750

Driggs st, s w cor Kingsland av, 20x95. Frank A. Koefler to John Mayer. Sub. to mort. nom

Duffield st, e s, 100 n Johnson st, 130 x 100. Foreclos. John Courtney, Sheriff, to Maurice V. Freund, of New York. 5,100

Eagle st, n s, 66.7 w Oakland st, 33.5x50, h & l. Matilda Weinberger and Lena Herskovics to Heinrich Indorf, New York. 2,600

Eastern Parkway, n s, 125 e Christopher av, 25x100. Joseph Solomon to Hyman Goldberg. *Mt.* $3,000. nom

Eastern Parkway, n s, 100 e Christopher av, 25x100. Hyman Goldberg to Joseph Solomon. *Mt.* $3,000. nom

Eastern Parkway, n s, 25.1 e Rockaway av, 25x100. Adolf Landesmann to Aaron Grabosh and Simon Cohen, of New York. *Mt.* $2,050. 2,600

Eastern Parkway, n s, 20 w Logan st, 20x90. Effingham H. Nichols to Frederick C. M. Silveis. 350

Eastern Parkway, n s, 75 e Osborn st, 50x100. Release mort. Herbert C. Smith to Abraham Levine and Jacob Muller. 1,400

Eldert st, n s, 198 w Bushwick av, 54x100. Frances E. O'Connor to Paul W. Ledoux. *Mt.* $16,500, taxes, &c. nom

Elton st, w s, 100 n Dumont av, 75x84. Catherine wife of Bernard Carey to Charles S. Osborn. 825

Essex st, w s, 380 n Arlington av, 20x100.
Essex st, w s, 340 n Arlington av, 20x100.
Edward F. Linton to Thomas Corker. 1,600

Essex st, w s, 90 s Ridgewood av, 20x100. Elizabeth wife of Anthony Geigenheimer to Anthony Geigenheimer. *Mt.* $3,200. nom

Floyd st, n s, 315 e Nostrand av, 25x100. Conrad Schaffner to Balthaser Hohn. *Mt.* $6,000. 1,000

Floyd st, n s, 125 e Sumner av, 25x100. Anna M. Erb formerly Schneider, of Woodhaven, N. Y., to Philippine Grinbeck formerly Schneider. 1-5 part. 1,000

Floyd st, n s, 290 e Nostrand av, 25x100. Louis Beer and Michael Schaffner to Friederich Pape. *Mt.* $4,500. 10,000

Franklin st, w s, 95.3 s Greenpoint av, 23.5x75, Sarah J. Willmott to Mary J. Willmott. Q. C. ½ part. nom

Franklin st, w s, 75 n Java st, 25x95, h & l. Josiah A. Benton to Peter H. Merkens. 6,000

Franklin st, w s, 50 n Java st, 25x95, h & l. George T. Lenton to same. 6,000

Fulton st, s w cor Saratoga av, 100x86. Foreclos. John Courtney, Sheriff, to Noah Tebbets. 8,000

Fulton st, s s, 300 w Albany av, 20x100. Anne L. wife of and Charles E. Rogers to Asa L. Rogers. *Mt* $2,000. nom

George st, s e s, 275 n e Central av, runs northeast 25 x southeast 81.7 x south 27.10 x northwest 94. Nicholas Seagrist to Gottwald Jakob. 1,375

Glenada pl, s w cor Decatur st, 50x85, hs & ls. Mary E. wife of William Reynolds to Charles D. Rusk. *Mt.* $35,000. 3,500

Graham st, e s, 164.7 s Nassau st on old map, 25x85.
Graham st, e s, 75 s Nassau st on old map, 29.7x75.
Contract. John Gillen to Gemario Fortsnato. 5,000

Grattan st, n s, 100 e Morgan av, 25x100. Theodore F. Jackson to Peter Lambertus. 1,300

Hancock st, s s, 175 w Tompkins av, 60x100.
Hancock st, s s, 255 w Tompkins av, 20x100.
Release mort. Title Guarantee and Trust Co. to William H. and William Reynolds. nom

Hancock st, s w cor Marcy av, 20x90. The Bedford Building Co. to Mary E. Price, of Providence, R. I. *Mt.* $13,000. nom

Harman st, s s, 350 e Central av, 50x100. Adam Heinrich to William and Christina Berlinger. 2,800

Hart st, s s, 330 e Sumner av, 20x100. Release dower. Margaret Herwig to Joseph Herwig. 395

Hendrix st, e s, 145 s Hegeman av, 40x100. Louise M. wife of William A. Blakslee, of Hamsport, N. J., to John Winckler. 400

Hendrix st, e s, 325 n Blake av, 25x100. John Sherwood to Michel Devitt. 550

Herbert st, n s, 69 w Humboldt st, 24x100. John E. Bennett to Frank H. Ross. *Mt.* $500, taxes, &c. 1,000

Herkimer st, n w cor Saratoga av, 20x80, h & l. Foreclos. Charles H. Winslow to Thomas Brennan. Sub to morts. 2,550

Herkimer st, No. 1134, s s, 65 w Russell pl, 16.3x85.9. The New York Building Loan Banking Co., New York, to Charles E. Gray. Lease with covenants for warrantee deed, the rent being installments for payment of the property. About 12 years' taxes, &c., and per month, 82

Herkimer st, n s, 145 e Troy av, 20x100. Dorcas E. wife of William H. Randolph to William H. Randolph. *Mt.* $3,100. 4,500

Herkimer st, n s, 240 w Rockaway av, 20x100. Foreclos. Robert Merchant to Stephen G. Williams guard. of Paul F. and Blair S. Williams. Sub. to another foreclosure and sale, also all taxes, &c. Mar. 31. 2,000

Same property. Foreclos. Same to Perry P. Williams exr. John S. Williams. Sub. to foreclosure and sale under mort. and interest $2,303, expenses of sale, taxes, &c. 3,000

Herkimer st, n s, 20 w Saratoga av, 80x80.
Saratoga av, w s, 80 n Herkimer st, 40x100.
Foreclos. Charles H. Winslow ref. to Noah Tebbets. 3,000

Hubbard st, e s, 120 s Centre pl, 66x57.6, Gravesend. Release mort. John Y. McKane to Edward Wilson. nom

Hubbard st, e s, 180 s Centre pl, runs south to high-water line Gravesend Bay, x east 57.5 x north to point 180 s of Centre pl, x west —, Gravesend. Sarah J. and John T. Hinman to John W. and Thomas P. Murphy. 1,505

Same property. Release mort. John Y. McKane to same. nom

Humboldt st, e s, 100 s Driggs av, 25x100, h & l. Charles Engert to Andrew R. Henry. 6,000

Humboldt st, e s, 100 n Scholes st, 25x100, h & l. Theresa Goodkind widow to Harris Seigel and Samuel Nelkin, New York. *Mt.* $2,600. 4,500

Jerome st, e s, 45 n Van Brunt av, 20x200 to Washington st. William B. Nichols to Asher Lewine, of New York. 175

Kane pl, w s, 98 s Herkimer st, 23x110. Washington Sackmann exr. of Jacob H. Sackmann to Kate wife of Antoni Bapst. Correction deed. nom

Kent st, n s, 175 e Oakland st, 25x100, h & l. Margaret Witzki to Anne Poppe widow, New York. 1,200

Kosciusko st, No. 490, 100x100. Contract for property. Frank Raessle to Leopold Michel. 1,700

Lake st; w s, adjoins M. W. Joralemens on north, 58x156 to Van Sicklen st, Gravesend. Martin W. Joralemon to William S. Hasson. *Mt.* $555, taxes, &c. 20

Leonard st, n w cor Boerum st, 22x100, h & l. Nathan Lieber to Ettal wife of Hyman Lieber. ½ part. Sub. to mort. $6,500 on whole premises. 500

Leonard st, w s, 46.6 n Boerum st, 28.6x100. Conrad Valentine to Max Knopf. *Mt.* $6,000. 11,700

Linden st, e s, 335.11 n Evergreen av, 40x100. Aaron Kaplan, of New York, to David Shedorsky. *Mt.* $3,000. 8,500

Logan st, w s, 190 s Glenmore av, 20x100. Bernard Costello to Almon G. Bardin. 350

Louis pl, w s, 98 s Herkimer st, runs west 95 x south 2 x west 2.6 x south 13.4 x east 97.6 to Louis pl, x north 15.4. Frederick Widmann to Gustaf A. Borin. 4,200

Macon st, s s, 170 e Ralph av, 18x100. John R. Pitt to Emily Blackwell. *Mt.* $4,000 7,000

Macon st, s s, 447 e Reid av, 18x100. Contract for property. James G. Roberts and Edwin L. Gwathmey. 8,935

Madison st, s e s, 188 s w Knickerbocker av, 18x100. George A. Craig to Christian F. Hommel. Sub. to mort., &c. nom

Marion st, s s, 16.8 e Hopkinson av, 16.8x75. Henry Weil to John B. Goode. 4,100

Maujer st, s s, 450 e Waterbury st, 25x95. Frank Lorenz to Adolph Reinhardt. *Mt.* $1,500. 3,400

McDonough st, n s, 100 w Hopkinson av, 117.6x100. William H. Chapman to Frederick W. Lawrence. *Mt.* $5,750. nom

McDonough st, n s, 370 e Ralph av, 72x100. Release mort. Julia Young to Wilfred Burr. 9,910

Same property. Release mort. Bernard Levino and Walter F. Clayton and as trustee to same. 1,600

McDougal st, s s, 249.7 e Hopkinson av, 25.5x100. Jessie A. Annin to Catharine M. Manning. 8,750

Melrose st, s s, 325 e Bremen st, 25x100.1. Otto Henkel to Christina Bauer. *Mt.* $4,400. 6,900

Milford st, e s, 190 s Glenmore av, 40x100. Effingham H. Nichols to Almon G. Bardin. 600

Montieth st, n s, 100 e Bremen st, 25x90. Christina Bauer to Henry Roth. *Mt.* $3,000. 5,000

Monroe st, n s, 225 w Stuyvesant av, 20x100. Susan E. wife of and George J. Collins to Claus H. Stelling. 6,750

Navy st, e s, 280 n Myrtle av, 25x100. Annie and Francis C. Garahan exrs. Ann Garahan to Peter Barrett. 3,050

Nelson st, s w cor Henry st, —x75x20x75. Patrick McCarthy to Nicholas Ryan. 2,100

Same property. John Andrews to Patrick McCarthy. 1,200

North Henry st, e s, 101.3 n Van Pelt av, 17x100. Charles Engert to Charles W. Drake. 3,500

North Henry st, w s, 110.8 s Meeker av, 25x75.6x28.10x64.1. Samuel Lord, of Manchester, England, to Michael Lenihan. 600

Ocean Parkway, w s, adj Washington Cemetery, 12 721-1,000 acres, Gravesend. Emile Beneville, New York, to Charles W. Dayton. B. & S. and C. a. G. *Mt.* $11,000. nom

Osborn st, e s, 75 s Sutter av, 25x100. Harris Max to Max Gross. *Mt.* $3,000. 6,200

Osborn st, e s, 200 s Sutter av, 75x100. Henry Jarkowitz and Izar Lowitz to Sophia Blanck, of New York. Sub. to morts. 4,650

Pacific st, s s, 330 e Rochester av, 16.8x107.2, h & l. Foreclos. John Courtney to George G. Hill. 2,000

Pacific st, s s, 247.3 e Rochester av, 16.7x107.2, h & l. Foreclos. Same to same. 2,000

Pacific st, s s, 297.3 e Rochester av, 16.8x107.2, h & l. Foreclos. Same to same. 2,000

Pacific st, s s, 313.11 e Rochester av, 16.8x107.2, h & l. Foreclos. Same to same. 2,000

Pacific st, s s, 480.8 e Rochester av, 16.8x107.2, h & l. Foreclos. Same to same. 2,000

Pacific st, s s, 297.3 e Rochester av, 66.8x107.2.
Pacific st, s s, 408.8 e Rochester av, 16.8x107.2.
George G. Hill to Francis H. Cowdrey, New Rochelle. *Mt.* $10,500. nom

Pacific st, n s, 360 e Rochester av, 16x100. Frederick Dhuy, Jr., to Anton Nehrbas. *Mt.* $1,200. 2,800

Pacific st, n s, 392 e Rochester av, 16x100. Frederick Dhuy, Jr., to Alice Woodburn. *Mt.* $500. 2,800

Pacific st, s s, 305 w Hoyt st, 20x100. Helen D. wife of and J. Ralph Burnett to Walter Dickinson, of New York. 4,000

Palmetto st, n w s, 300 n e Broadway, 20x100. William B. Dugan, of Jamaica, N. Y., to Henry Ruthmann. *Mt.* $4,500. 7,600

Parkway, n s, 350 w Rogers av, runs north 57.9 x west 75.1 x southeast to Eastern Parkway, x east 24.7. Lucius H. Haynes, of Bridgehampton, N. Y., to Emma Quinn. nom

President st, n s, 108 e 7th av, 21x95. William E. D. Stokes, of New York, to Joseph L. Harris. *Mt.* $6,000. 13,000

President st, n s, 80 e 3d av, 163.10x95. Catharine Buckley to Michael Kenny, Jr. *Mt.* $4,500. 9,830

Prince st, e s, 208.9 n Myrtle av, 21.3x85. Partition. James F. McGee ref. to John C. Von Glahn. 4,500

Prospect pl, s s, 350 e Troy av, runs south 102.6 x northeast 25.8 x north 96.8 x west 25. James W. Gillies to Sylvester L. Stearns and David Black. Correction deed. nom

Same property. C. J. King to same. Correction deed. nom

Prospect pl, s s, 150 w Buffalo av, 50x127.9. Sarah Childrey and Thomas H. Robinson to John Robinson. 250

Prospect pl, s s, 105.5 w 6th av, 16.8x100.
Prospect pl, s s, 138.9 w 6th av, 33.4x100.
Prospect pl, s s, 188.9 w 6th av, 16.8x100.
E. Elizabeth Knight, Sparkhill, N. Y., to Mary E. Day, Rapid City, Dakota. *Mt.* $28,000. nom

Pulaski st, s s, 350 e Nostrand av. 18.9x100, h & l. Kate E. wife of James Nevin to Hattie F. Maynard. *Mt.* $3,000. 5,400

Russell pl, w s, 20 n Atlantic av, 17x97. Kate T. wife of Alfred Ogden to Joseph A. Foster. *Mt.* $2,200. nom

Ryerson st, w s, 133.11 n Park av, 40x100. Charles H. Bulkley to Abraham G. Jennings. 7,500

Sackman st, w s, 150 s Blake av, 50x100, h & l. Lena Durchholz to Benjamin Sachs. *Mt.* $2,200. 4,300

Sackman st, s w cor Livonia av, 105.6x100,

Edward R. Jourdan to Alonzo E. De Baun. *Mt.* $800. 1,950

Sands st, No. 172, s s, 100 w Gold st, 19x100. Maria Dugan widow to John Witte. 3,700

Seigel st, s s, 390 e Bushwick av, 25x100. Charles W. Truslow admr. William Wall to Ferdinand A. Reinheimer. 1,100

Smith st, n e cor Warren st, 40x60. John I. Conway to James T. Conway. nom

Somers st, s s, 26 e Rockaway av, 18.6x69.2. Foreclos. John Courtney, Sheriff, to William J. Gaynor as trustee of Andrew McClennen. 6,000

South Elliott pl, w s, 447 s De Kalb av, 20x100. George H. Rice to Betti wife of William Gottlieb and Rezi wife of David Gottlieb. *Mt.* $5,000. 6,500

St. Marks pl, n s, 460 w 5th av, 20x100. Hermann Benke to James A. Walsh. *Mt.* $4,000. 6,200

Stagg st, n s, 200 e Lorimer st, 25x100, h & l. Henry Schulz to Henry C. and Henry M. Brascher. 2,550

Stagg st, n s, 150 w Waterbury st, 25x100. George Kraemer to Frederick Schumacher. Q. C. nom

Stagg st, n s, 150 w Waterbury st, 25x100. Frederick Schumacher to Ernest Holland. nom

Same property. Ernest Holland to Catharine wife of Frederick Schumacher. nom

Steuben st, w s, 245 s Park av, 20x100. Peter Fagan to William Mullin. 1,800

Stockholm st, s e s, 200 n e Irving av, 100x100. William Davison to A. Stewart Walsh. *Mt.* $1,800. exch

Summit st, n s, 150 e Hicks st, 100x100. John W. Moran to Michael T. Kilaby as trustee St. Stephen's R. C. Church. *Mt.* $6,000. 11,000

Vanderveer st, s s, 132 e Bushwick av, 17.6x100. Oscar J. Chase to Betty S. Ludden. *Mt.* $1,500. 2,375

Veret st, n s, 305.6 e Bushwick av, 25x100. John Schaeffer to John Kern. *Mt.* $1,500. 3,125

Walworth st, e s, 290 s Willoughby av, 16.8x100. Ferdinand W. Odell to Valentine Spahn, of New York. *Mt.* $1,500. 3,000

Warwick st, w s, 234.11 s Fulton st, 16.8x95. Emma wife of and James I. Newman to Herman Jacobs, of New York. 3,550

Weirfield st, n w s, 101 s w Central av, 20x100. Release mort. Timothy G. Sellew to David J. Lippman and Alexander Taylor. 2,473

Washington st, w s, 28.2 s Concord st, 53.4x105.9x53.4x105.2. The Brooklyn Inst. to the trustees of the New York and Brooklyn Bridge. 74,000

Windsor pl, s w s, 293.6 s e 7th av, 13.8x100, h & l. Mary A. wife of and Willis B. Goodsell to Elisha Dyer. 2,200

Withers st, s s, 175 e Leonard st, 25x100. Mary E. Frost widow, of Central Islip, N. Y., to Salvatore Larocca, of New York. *Mt.* $600. 1,200

Woodbine st, s e s, 228 n e Hamburg av, 18x100. Release mort. Anna E. Cozine and James Gascoine exrs. Jno. G. Cozine to George W. and Charles H. Francisco. 2,352

Woodbine st, n w s, 45 s w Knickerbocker av, 20x100. Albert Berckmeier to Henry G. Small. nom

Same property. Release mort. Anna E. Cozine and James Gascoine exrs. John G. Cozine and James Gascoine individually to Albert Buckmeier. 2,147

Woodbine st, s e s, 156 n e Hamburg av, 18x100, h & l. George W. and Charles H. Francisco to William Stephens. nom

York st, No. 53, n s, 16.8 e of alley bet Washington and Adams sts, 16.8x75. Samuel Harvey to Antonio and Vincenzo and Clementa Sollitto. *Mt.* $1,000. 4,000

1st st, s w s, 305 n w 5th av, 81x100. William N. Hale, of Westfield, N. J., to Alfred McDonald. *Mt.* $30,000. nom

Same property. Agreement as to completion of building and conveyance, &c. Same with same. nom

2d st, s w s, 100 s e 7th av, 188x95; also, }
2d st, n e s, 198.10 s e 7th av, 234x100. }
John Adamson to Cornelius E. Donnellon. *Mt.* $50,400. nom

2d st, s w s, 197.10 n w 7th av, runs northwest 98.2 x southwest 95 x southeast 32 x southwest 5 x southeast 66.1 x northeast 100 to 2d st. Jennie L. Ross to Donald C. Ross. *Mt.* $42,500. nom

North 2d st, n s, 75 w Lorimer st, runs north to point 100 s Conselyea st, x west 25 x south —to North 2d st, x east — to beginning. David Shedorsky to Aaron Kaplan, of New York. *Mt.* $3,500. 7,000

3d pl, s s, 230 w Clinton st, 19x133.5. Catherine Lee to Michael D. Ryan, New York. 5,700

4th st, s s, 197.10 w 7th av, 18x100, h & l. Louis H. Myers, Jr., to George H. Raymond. *Mt.* $6,250. nom

North 4th st, n s, 104 e Roebling st, 25x113x23.3x121.6. Eugene R. O'Connell to Antonio Dimiere. 4,000

South 4th st, n e s, 128.6 n w 4th st, 25x95. George G. Terrill, of Boston, Mass., to Amelia M. Terrill. *Mt.* $2,600. nom

6th st, n e s, 497.10 n w 5th av, 100x100. Release mort. Edward H. Litchfield to Erwin G. Gollner. 4,058

8th st, n s, 202.4 w 6th av, 18.8x100. Michael Kenney, Jr., to Charles G. Balmann. *Mt.* $4,500. 7,250

North 8th st, n s, 150 e Kent av, 25x100. Annah B. Bush, of Tioga, N. Y., to Peter and Joseph Young. nom

9th st, n w cor 4th av, 20x87. Charles H. Collins to Frank Bailey. *Mt.* $11,000. nom

Same property. Frank Bailey to Charles H. Collins. *Mt.* $11,000. nom

13th st, n s, 156 w 3d av, 20x100; also strip of land adj on e s of above. Annie Youngtob to Philip Youngtob. nom

13th st, n s, 156 w 3d av, 20x100, also strip of land adj east side of above. Phillip Youngtob to Ellis Youngtob. ½ part. *Mt.* $1,650. nom

14th st, n s, 397.10 e 5th av, 18.9x100. Charles A. Leibman to Flora Levine. *Mt.* $2,100. 3,150

15th st, s s, 180.3 w 8th av, 25x43.3. Lavinia E. wife of Benjamin W. Blott to Julia Quinn. Q. C. 600

16th st, s s, 169.4 e 9th av, 19x100, error. John Assip and Timothy J. Buckley to John Cannon. *Mt.* $4,350. 5,650

17th st, s s, 291 w 6th av, 21x100.2. Oscar West to William M. Thomas. 2,500

17th st, n e s, 300 s e 3d av, 18.9x100. George I. Murphy exr. and trustee of Mary McGovern to Mary McGovern heir, &c., of Mary McGovern dec'd. nom

Bay 17th st, e s, 250 s 86th st, 50x96.8. Archibald Young, of New Utrecht, to Sarah A. Haviland. 1,000

East 17th st, e s, gore bounded north by line 850 n of Av B, and southeast by line bet lands of parties hereto, Flatbush. Cornelius J. Bergen exr. of John C. Bergen to John McElvery and Robert Getty. 10

20th st, w s, 100 n Vanderbilt st, 25x100, Flatbush. Thomas Heffernan to Augusta M. Dalton. *Mt.* $1,550. 2,400

44th st, n e s, 275 s e 3d av, 25x100.2. Foreclos. John Courtney, Sheriff, to The Daily News Building and Loan Assoc. 3,500

52d st, n e s, 166.8 n w 4th av, 16.8x100.2. Jeremiah D. Phelan to Lucy wife of Peter Farrell. nom

53d st, s w s, 160 n w 5th av, 40x100.2. John H. Durack to Charles B. Spicer. Q. C. nom

57th st, s s, 240 e 2d av, 20x100.2. Lettia Barber to John Ennis. *Mt.* $200. 800

59th st, n s, 220 w 13th av, 60x100.2. New Utrecht. Edward E. Burrows to Clarissa A. Jackson. 800

64th st, s w s, 240 n w 9th av, 40x100, New Utrecht. Claus Doscher to Charles W. Newton. 250

66th st, s w s, 260 n w 13th av, 40x100.2, New Utrecht. Clarissa A. Jackson to Edward E. Burrows. Sub. to mort. 3,150

67th st, s s, 140 w 13th av, 51.1x130.1x45.7x130, Lefferts Park. Effingham H. Nichols to Frederick W. Miller. 425

72d st, s s, 155.10 w 18th av, 40x100, New Utrecht. John H. Hanley to Hannah Clark. 400

72d st, s s, 555.10 w 18th av, 28.3x100x26.3x100, John H. Hanley to Maurice J. Coughlin. 300

79th st, s w s, 140 n w 12th av, 100x100, New Utrecht. Hoik D. Campbell to Solomon and Max Stern and Samuel Hirshbaum. 1,250

79th st, n e s, 180 n w 12th av, 60x100, New Utrecht. Hoik D. Campbell to Charles W. Emerson, Boston. Sub. to assessm't. 750

80th st, s w s, 160 n w 19th av, 60x200 to 81st st. George B. Stoutenburg to Thomas and Robert Edgerton. 2,100

81st st, s w s, 60 n w 24th av, 60x100, Gravesend. James D. Lynch to Thomas Bell. 900

82d st, n e s, 100 n w 22d av, 80x100, New Utrecht. Edward C. White to James D. Lynch. 1,400

85th st, n e s, 200 s e 23d av, 60x100, New Utrecht. James E. Hedges, of Elizabeth, N. J., to James D. Lynch. 750

Albany av, n e cor East New York av, 200 to Lefferts av, x east 407 x south 100.1 x west 100 x south 100 to East New York av, x west 300. }
Lefferts av, n s, 101.2 e Albany av, 287.6 to land of E. Sinnot x northerly along same to patent line abt 295, x southwest along same to s s of Malbone st, at point 140.5 e of Albany av, x south 99.9 x west 40 x south 142.10, Flatbush. }
David C. Reid to Georgiana Richters, Bayside, L. I. *Mt.* $5,500. exch

Atlantic av, s s, 333.4 w Stone av, 16.8x100. Foreclos. George W. Pearsall ref. to Thomas Everit. consid. omitted

Atlantic av, s s, 150 e Saratoga av, 100x100. George E. Schmoll to Alfred Ogden. nom

Atlantic av, s s, 166.8 e Saratoga av, 16.8x100. Alfred Ogden to Julia Payrleitner, of New York. *Mt.* $2,400. nom

Bedford av, e s, 114.7 n Lynch st, runs east 85 x north 78.4 x east 23 x north 80 to Heyward st, x west 74 to av, x south 120.6. Foreclos. Alfred Wagstaff ref. to Dennis C. Gately, of Newtown, Conn. 1878. Sub. to taxes, &c. 10,000

Bedford av, Nos. 111 and 113, s e cor North 11th st, 50x100, h & l. Contract. Joseph N. Graver to Heinrich Stimper. 6,550

Belmont av, n s, 56 w Schenck av, 50x100. William W. St. John, of Port Jervis, New York, to Frederick Eiermann. 1,500

Blake av, s w cor Williamson av, runs west along Blake av 200 to Ocean av, x south 100 x east 200 x north 100. Bernhard J. Pink to Joseph Morris. *Mt.* $3,500. 6,125

Blake av, s s, 75 w Ocean av, 25x75. Mary wife of and Flavious J. Maynard to Melissa wife of John B. Brewster. 2,000

Bushwick av, n e s, 250 n w De Kalb av, runs northeast 81.5 x northwest 11.8 x west 29.1 x southwest 54 to Bushwick av, x southeast 22. Jacob Bossert to Caroline Kock. *Mt.* $3,500. 9,000

Christopher av, e s, 125 s Blake av, 25x100. Jacob Cohen to Louis Smith. *Mt.* $1,700. 2,500

Clason av, e s, 49.6 n Pacific st, 24x88. Patrick Donohue to Richard Donohue. Q. C. nom

Clinton av, e s, 485.7 s Park av, 20x120. Maria E. Krueder widow, of Long Island City, N. Y., to Robert Woodcock. *Mt.* $3,300. 5,000

Central av, n e s, 50 n w Woodbine st, 25x100. John T. Fisher to Charles Welcher. 1,700

De Kalb av, n s, 72.8 e Kent av, 23.6x100, h & l. William, Thomas S. and Louise E. James and Elizabeth Moore to John H. Rowland. 3,000

De Kalb av, n s, 174.4 e Wyckoff av, 60x100, hs & ls. Crawford Monds to Charles K. Hoerning. *Mt.* $5,650. nom

Dumont av, n s, 75 w Thatford av, 25x100. }
Dumont av, n s, 25 w Thatford av, 25x100. }
Thatford av, w s, 250 n Dumont av, 25x100. }
Release mort. Gilbert S. Thatford to Lewis Hurst. 1,600

Emmons av, n s, 118.6 w Leonard av, runs west 134.4 x northwest 432 x east 144 x south 442.10, Gravesend. James McCormick to Francis J. and Robert J. McManamy, Wm. R. Dougherty and Brian G. Hughes. nom

Evergreen av, s w s, 36.8 s e Van Voorhis st, 16.8x80. August Nickel to Louise Ritzenhoff. *Mt.* $1,400. 2,500

Evergreen av, n e s, 20 s e Weirfield st, 20x100. Release dower. Josephine wife of Francis Fely to Josephine Sweet formerly Uris. nom

Flatbush av, south cor Prospect pl, runs southeast 123.5 x south 2.6 x southwest 90 x 30.6 to av, x north 120.5. }
Interior gore, 120.5 s Prospect pl and 3.6 e Flatbush av, runs north 90 x southerly 40.8 x southwest 50.8. }
E. Eliza Knight, Sparkhill, N. Y., to Mary E. Day, Rapid City, South Dakota. nom

Flushing av, n s, 113.1 e Morgan av, 25x111.2x25.10x117.11. Wilhelm F. Weik, of New York, to Gottfried I Kohlhepp. 7,000

Same property. Gottfried I. Kohlhepp to Elizabethe Weik, of New York. 7,000

Flushing av, No. 922, s s, 150 e Bremen st, 25x67.1. Ellen Cordial and Mary E. A. Daley to Charles Neumann and Mary his wife, joint tenants. 1,800

Franklin av, s s, 892 w 3d st, 89x115.6x89x—, Greenfield, parcel 86 United Freemans Land Assoc., Greenfield. Mary T. Maloney to Catherine Ann Hamerschlag. ½ part. nom

Franklin av, e s, 31.6 s Union st, runs south 99.6 x east 100 x north 131 to s s Union st at 100 e Franklin av, x west 52.4 x southwest — to beginning. Joseph Farrell to Julia A. Thorns. *Mt.* $3,500. nom

Same property. Julia A. Thorns to William H. Kent. *Mt.* $2,000. 3,500

Gates av, n w s, 233.4 n Knickerbocker av, runs northeast 16.8 x northwest 128.6 x southwest 50 x southeast 29.6 x northeast 33.4 x southeast 100 to Gates av. Helen L. Tompkins to Edward MacDonald. *Mt.* $1,800. 1,000

Graham av, south cor Newton st, 25.4x95.10x25x100. John H. Scheidt to Frank Lorenz. *Mt.* $3,000. 9,100

Grand av, e s, 205 s Park av, 25x100. Anne Gorman to Mary A. Gorman. nom

Greene av, n w s, 90 n e Irving av, runs northeast 60 x northwest to land John Troutman, x southwest — x southeast — to beginning; also, }
Greene av, westerly cor Wyckoff av, runs nortewest 119.10 x southwest to land N. Y. & Manhattan Beach R. R., x southeast to Greene av, x northeast 140 to beginning. }
Adolph Koehler and Herman G. Sperl to Darwin R. James. 8,000

Hamburg av, n e s, 25 s e Woodbine st, 18.9x100. Release mort. James Gascoine to Jacob Manneschmidt. 2,053

Same property. Jacob Manneschmidt to Anna B. Koehler widow. nom

Hamburg av, s w s, 25 s e Jefferson st, 25x75. Alois Dillmann to August Siefers. *Mt.* $2,850. 6,800

Hamilton av, n w s, 25 n e Clinton av, runs northeast 50 x northwest 101.3 x northeast 25 x northwest 25 x southwest 100 x southeast 25 x northeast 25 x southeast 100.9, New Utrecht. David Randall to James McGlynn, of Fort Hamilton, N. Y. 75

Hudson av, e s, 23.4 s Plymouth st, 23.4x75. Thomas Wood to Anna Berge, Monmouth, N. J. *Mt.* $2,000. nom

Irving av, easterly cor De Kalb av, 25x100. Philip Tishler, of Jacksonville, Fla., to Edward J. Burns. 1,500

Irving av, westerly cor Himrod st, 100x100. Nathan Levy to Jakob Marquardt. *Mt.* $4,500. 6,500

Jefferson av, s s, 100 e Throop av, 18x100. Charlotte A. Bierds to Joseph C. and George W. Pool. *Mt.* $6,000. nom

Jefferson av, n s, 21 e Lewis av, 77x100. Release mort. Henry Weil to Theodore W. Swimm. 6,800

Jefferson av, s s, 180 w Nostrand av, 20x100. James C. Rogers to Thomas H. Elliott exr. Stephen Pettus. *Mt.* $8,500. nom

Kent av, s w s, 110 s e Taylor st, runs southwest 100 x northwest 10 x southwest 49 x southeast to centre line Wilson st, x northeast 205.3 to av, x northwest 125.3. Thomas F. Taylor exr. Richard Taylor, Joseph L., James R. and Thomas Taylor, Gertrude M. Edwards, Joseph R., William H., Moses and Josie Taylor and Belle Robinson to Thomas F. Taylor. 47,000

Knickerbocker av, easterly cor Suydam st, 25x100; also, }
Knickerbocker av, westerly cor Stockholm st, 50x100. }
John S. Ellis and James M. Waterbury exrs.

Lawrence Waterbury to John Andrew and Joseph G. Wischerth. 6,550

Knickerbocker av, west cor Stockholm st, 50x100. John Andrew and Margaret Wischerth to Amelia Fleischmann. 4,200

Knickerbocker av, westerly cor Stockholm st, 50x100; also,
Hamburg av, southerly cor Stockholm st, 50x100; also,
Hamburg av, s w s, 75 s e Stockholm st, 25x100.
Joseph G. Wischerth to Margaret wife of Frank Wischerth. ½ part. Sub. to morts., &c. nom

Knickerbocker av, southerly cor Madison st, 100x80. Henry G. Small to Albert Berckmeier. *Mt.* $2,500. exch

Lafayette av, w s, 418 n e Broadway, 32x92. Abram P. Fardon, of Washington, D. C., and Alfred A. Fardon to Margaret Young. *Mt.* $4,000. 8,000

Lewis av, w s, 100 n Myrtle av, 25x100, h & l. Salomon Wolf to Gustav Dobler. 4,500

Lexington av, s s, 259 w Nostrand av, 32x100, hs & ls. George Finck to Edward Philips. 15,000

Marcy av, w s, 90 s Hancock st, 20x20. Jane Blauvelt to Mary E. Price, of Providence, R. I. nom

Miller av, w s, 60 s Arlington av, 20x75. George, John W. and Joseph T. Fletcher to Hortense wife of Erdmann F. S. Seifert. *Mt.* $2,500. nom

Myrtle av, n s, 58.7 w Pearl st, 22.2x80. Angeline E. Darling, of Utica, N. Y., to Mathias L. Rosencrans. *Mt.* $7,000. 5

Myrtle av, s s, 29 e Evergreen av, runs east 32.9 x southwest 3.2 x southeast 42.10 x southwest 25 x northwest 65.10, h & l. Crawford Monds to Charles K. Hoerning. *Mt.* $4,300. nom

Myrtle av, n s, 24.1 w North Oxford st, runs north 40 x north 33.4 x west 16.6 x south 31.7 x south 38 to av, x east 20. Gertrude B. and John Z. Lott exrs. Abraham Lott and Gertrude B. Lott widow, John A. Lott, Jr., Marie B. Clarkson and Katharine L. Lott children of Abraham Lott to Henry Longstreth. 1,000

Myrtle av, n e cor Adams st, known as No. 27 Myrtle av. Joseph S. Elliott to The Union Elevated R. R. Co. nom

Nostrand av, n e cor Dean st, 100x100. Release mort. Union Dime Savings Inst. to Frank H. and Fred'k S. Cowperthwait exrs. Mary E. Cowperthwait. 7,500

Same property. Frank H. and Fred. S. Cowperthwait exrs. Mary E. Cowperthwait to Andrew Miller. 17,000

Ocean av, s s, 83.4 e of J. A. Cooks, 29.9x100x26.9x100, Coney Island. Sub. to leases. Mary E. Dibble and Frederick W. Thompson to Mary M. Parker. 1,700

Ovington av, n s, 240.2 w 14th av, 20x124.6, Lefferts Park. Effingham H. Nichols to Martin Larsen. 200

Park av, n s, 25 e Steuben st, 25x100. Maria C. Schnell to Otto and Maria C. Schnell. *Mt.* $3,000. nom

Patchen av, e s, 20 s Putnam av, 80x80. Kate G. wife of and George E. Hyatt to Albert Esmon. *Mt.* $4,140 and taxes. 4,975

Patchen av, e s, 82 s Decatur st, 18x92.8x18x93.3. Rudolph Reimer to Lea Meyer, of New York. *Mt.* $2,850. 5,500

Pennsylvania av, e s, 125 n Eastern Parkway, 25x110. Charles E. Maguire to Richard W. Kaatze. *Mt.* $3,500. 6,500

Prospect av, s w s, 250 s e 5th av, 25x80.2. Dorothea Lang widow to Mary Ann wife of William Pope. 3,600

Putnam av, n s, 65 e Sumner av, 20x100. A. Stewart Walsh to William Davison. *Mt.* $5,000. exch

Putnam av, n s, 300 e Broadway, 20x100. Charles E. Ring to Robert L. Moores and Charles A. Le Quesne. nom

Putnam av, s e s, 120 n e Broadway, 20x100, h & l. The East Brooklyn Co-operative Building Assoc. to Morris Hart. 6,000

Rockaway av, e s, 25 n Baltic av, 18.4x80. Release mort. Joseph Seitz to Michael Sullivan. nom

Saratoga av, e s, 87 n St Marks av, 63x100. Walter R. Parfitt to Aline Oertel. 1,100

Schenck av, w s, 175 n Blake av, 25x100. Peter G. Kerr to Joseph F. Murphy. *Mt.* $1,800. 3,075

Shepherd av, w s, 245 s Union av, 50x100. Amelia P. Robinson to Winfred McLaughlin, of New York. 2,000

Shepherd av, w s, 125 s Eastern Parkway, 25x100, h & l. Thomas Davies to Adolf Muuss. *Mt.* $750. 1,300

Shepherd av, e s, 160 n Ridgewood av, 80x102.5x80x102.4. Edward F. Linton to James Graham. 3,000

Same property. Release mort. Williamsburgh Savings Bank to Edward F. Linton. 1,440

Stone av, e s, 100 n Liberty av, 100x100. Release mort. Mary E Brush as trustee Joseph Petit to Sarah wife of and Barney Tarpey. nom

Stone av, w s, 65.2 n Bergen st, 42x100. William A. Valentine to Joseph Bussy and Aaron Levy. 4 000

St. Marks av, s s, 255 e Clason av, 20x126. Daniel B. L. McCormick to John P. Cranford and David H. Valentine. 1,600

Thatford av, w s, 25 s Livonia av, 75x100. Release mort. Gilbert S. Thatford to Jacob Goldblatt and Marks Rapps. nom

Same property. Jacob Goldblatt and Marks Rapps to Elias Epstein. 2,000

Thatford av, w s, 75 s Belmont av, 25x100. Adolph Feier and Samuel Hirsch, of New York, to Barnet Lipkowitz. *Mt.* $3,000. 4,000

Thatford av, e s, 100 s Sutter av, 25x100. Fanny Restter, of New York, to Isaac Simorvitch. 1,350

Thatford av, w s, 100 n Dumont av, 25x100. Release mort. Gilbert S. Thatford to Lewis Hurst. 400

Throop av, w s, 50 n Stockton st, 25x100. Ferdinand Feldblum and Louis Berman, of New York, to Jacob Fogel and Henry Leiner. *Mt.* $4,900. 6,650

Underhill av, n e cor Dean st, 82.6x77. John F. Richters, of Bayside, N. Y., to David C. Reid. *Mt.* $28,500. nom

Willoughby av, s s, 100 w Lewis av, 50x100. Release dower. Emilie Krauter to Sophie Simon et al. 1,252

Wyckoff av, southerly cor Greene av, 180x100. Adolph Koehler and Hermann G. Speil to Darwin R. James. 9,000

Wythe av, e s, 66.9 n Division av, 21.1x100.4. William J. Rigney to John McLoughlin, of New York. 6,000

3d av, w s, original line, 50 s 94th st, 50x110, New Utrecht. Andrew Lemon to John P. Stenger. 1,250

3d av, e s, 50.2 s 40th st, 0.3½x55.2½x0.2½x55.2½. Release mort. South Brooklyn Co-operative Building and Loan Assoc. to Margaret Campbell. 100

Same property. Margaret Campbell to Herman Coleil. 135

3d av, n w s, 25 s w Wakeman pl, 25x100, New Utrecht. William N. Coates to Elmira M. Reeves. 1,500

4th av, w s, 30 s 13th st, 28x86.10. William H. Norris and William Bowers to William B. Riddle, New York. *Mt.* $9,000. nom

6th av, w s, 100 n Garfield pl, runs west 95.9 x north 16.4 x northwest 33.9 x east 98.11 to av, x south 50. John W. Mason to Peter F. Delaney and Peter J. Collins. 5,500

6th av, northerly cor 5th st, 100x95.9. Edward H. and Grace D. Litchfield individ. and as trustees Edwin C. Litchfield to Louis Bonert. Sub. to taxes, &c. 12,000

11th av, s e s, extends from 78th to 79th st, 200x460.
75th st, s w s, 360 s e 12th av, 80x100, New Utrecht.
Albert Friedlander to Frederick Spiegelberg. 18-50 part. nom

11th av, westerly cor 54th st, runs southwest 200.4 to 55th st, x northwest 140 x northeast 100.2 x southeast 40 x northeast 100.2 to 54th st, x southeast 100 to beginning. Edward Dougherty, of Buffalo, N. Y., to William B. Hurd, Jr. *Mt.* $950. 4,800

11th av, n w cor 62d st, runs north along av 32.4 x west 40 x south 33 10 to 62d st, x east 40, New Utrecht. Axel Anderson to Andrew Erickson. *Mt.* $1,300, taxes, &c. 1,700

13th av, centre line, n w cor 57th st, runs north to centre 56th st, x west to point 100 w 13th av, x south to centre line bet 56th and 57th sts, x west 40 x south to centre line 57th st, x east 140.
13th av, e s, 100.2 s 55th st, runs southwest 200.4 x east 150 to New Utrecht av, x north 223 x west 51.11, New Utrecht.
Release judgment. Richard B. Fithian to Heloise M. L. Allin. nom

18th av, s w cor 72d st, 40x96.5x40x95.10, New Utrecht. John H. Hanley to Richard Slandorff. 900

Interior lot, 98 n e 13th st, 156 n w 3d av, runs southwest 35 x southeast .05 x northeast 35 x northwest .02½. Annie C. Rice to Annie and Philip Youngtob. Q. C. 75

Interior lot, 100 e Underhill av and 14.11 n Warren st, runs east 51.11 x north 25 x west 36.9 x south 28.7. Margaret Dunn widow and Peter Dunn heir of Daniel Dunn to Patrick McArdle. nom

Interior lot, 14.11 n of Prospect pl or Warren st and 101.11 e Underhill av, runs east 100 x north 25 x west 86 9 x south 28.7. Patrick McArdle to Margaret Dunn. nom

Interior lot, 25 n Eagle st and 66.7 w Oakland st, runs north 25 x west 33.5x25x33.5. Release mort. Nickolas Drogo to Matilda Weinberger and Lena Herskowisc. nom

Lots 242, 243 and 248-253 map lands Asa W. Parker, New Utrecht. Augustus Mayers, of New York, to Mathilda Mayers. *Mt.* $3,000. nom

Lots 453 and 454 block 10 map No. 1 of 618 lots Cowenhoven farm, New Utrecht. Effingham H. Nichols to Boroch J. Rapaport. 310

Lots 70-73 block 2; also lots 369-372 block 9 map No. 1, 618 lots Cowenhoven farm, New Utrecht. Effingham H Nichols to Catherine Biehn, of New York. 1,560

Lot 27 block 1 and lots 291 and 292 block 7 same map. Same to Richard Murphy. 670

Parcel in New Utrecht, 1 rood 26 5-6 perches adj V. Cropsey. Francis A. Gunz to Jane E. wife of F. H. Johnson. 300

Parcel, being part of old 8th av, west of centre line of same and contiguous to lot 249 J. Simon property, and all title in plot bounded west 8th av and fronting 422.10 on 14th and 15th sts. A. D. Clutterbuck to Ross C. Browning. Q. C. nom

Plot of land in New Utrecht, bounded north by land of N. Stillwell, east by land heirs of R. J. Stillwell and G. R. and N. R. Stillwell, south by land J. A. Emmons and west by land Helen Sumner. James R. Stillwell and Catharine A. Stillwell widow to Jane E. wife of F. H. Johnson. 800

Plot of land in New Utrecht, bounded north by land now or late of Major De Rusey, east by land heirs S. N. Stillwell, south by land now or late of R. Stillwell and west by a road, contains ⅛ acre. Elias H. Ryder to Jane E. Johnson. 500

Plot of land in New Utrecht, bounded north by land of John I. Stillwell and others and land of formerly S. N. Stillwell, east by land J. R. and C. H. Stillwell, south by land Ira O. Miller and north by land G. R. Stillwell. Ellen J. Voorhies, Anna M. Stillwell and Ida wife of Elias H. Rider to Jane E. wife of F. H. Johnson. 1,000

Plumb Island, Gravesend, parcel contains 50 acres. George H. Engeman trustee William A. Engeman dec'd and George H., William A., Jr., and John Engeman to United States, America. 92,103

New Lots road, s w cor Berriman st, 40x100, hs & ls. William H. Jackson to Ellen M. Donnelly. 1,900

Sheepshead Bay road, s s, part of D. Lake property, 2 acres 1 rood 9 7-10 perches, reserving easement, Gravesend. Catharina Morony to Dennis Morony. 1,500

WESTCHESTER COUNTY.

SEPTEMBER 16 TO 22—INCLUSIVE.

CORTLANDT.

Nelson, Thos. to Clarence H. Frost, e s Washington st, adj Pell S. C. Vought, 88x405. $2,000

EASTCHESTER.

Bard, Wm. H. to Arthur B. Holmes, lot 225 s w s Westchester av, Washingtonville, 50x100. 700

Same to Margt. A. McKenzie, part lot 259 s e s Marian st, Washingtonville, 25x100. 500

Bullard, John E. et al. to Mary H. Gilbert, lots 68-71, w s Johnson st, 120x87. 1,100

Same to Welthea A. Hammond, lots 81 and 82 w s same st, 60x85. 550

Crean, Ellen L. to Wm. H. Bard, lots 245, 227, 259, 187, 225 and 21, Washingtonville. 3,000

Conkling, Mary A. and ano. to Lydia A. Haddock, w s Rich av, 407 n White Plains road, 50x113. 1,750

Cudlipp, Chas. to Ida W. Phillips, lot 26 and north ½ 25 e s Fulton av, Chester Hill. 8,500

Downey, Margt. E. to Annie E. Carney, lots 22 and 24, Dunham Park. nom

Fiske, Samuel to Edwin W. Fiske, w s av, 577 n Sidney av, 50x125. 2,574

Forster, Fred. P. to Edwin S. Young, lots 182 and 183, Chester Hill. 1,500

Nesbitt, Margt. L. to John Berry, n s Monroe st, 309 e Franklin av, 40x91. 600

Berry, John to Geo. W. Bard, same property. 500

Sharkey, John E. et al. to Wm. H. Van Arsdale, lot 19 w s 2d av map 13A adj Mt. Vernon, 50x105. 3,600

Thomas, Fred. to Winslow E. Buzby, part lot 486 e s 6th av, Mt. Vernon, 50x105. 3,000

Wood, Jos. S. to Jas. L. Reynolds, lot 78, Villa Park. nom

Yaker, Chas. to Susan Ray, plot 936 s s 17th av, Wakefield, 50x114. 900

GREENBURGH.

Blackwell, Wilson H. to Edwin J. Freedman, lot 589, Ardsley. 115

Coles, Edw. to Geo. Silver, lot C Coles and Woodland avs, grantors map. 625

Erhardt, Joel B. trustee to John J. Killian, s w cor Livingston and Danforth avs, 25x100. 350

Gillets, Eliza P. to Dundas T. Pratt, s e cor Croton and McKeel avs, 100x108. 4,500

Jones, Cyrus P. and ano. to Geo. Klenck, lot 252, Ardsley. 116

MOUNT PLEASANT.

Bliss, Alb. E. and ano. to John Welsh, n w cor Bedford av and Cottage st, 25x101. 230

Engelke, Barnett H. and ano. to Alf. Lawrence, n s College av, adj Seth Bird, 50x125. 850

Smadbeck, Louis to Sarah Gallagher, lots 34 and 35, Sherman Park. 300

Same and ano. to Arthur Cassot, lots 49 and 50, Lakehurst. 225

Same to Auth. L. Aste and ano., lots 211-240. 5,500

Smith, Wm. R. to Chas. C. Finch, lot 13 block 9, Lake Kensico. 85

Same to Eliz'h Finch, lot 12 block 9. 85

Same to Thomas E. Donlon, lots 27-30 block 9. 440

Same to W. O. Crisman, lots 65-68 block 6. 510

NEW CASTLE.

Crowther, John to Boltis Moore, part lots 66 and 68 e s Lexington av, Union Park, 50x150. 250

Moore, Boltis to Maria L. Hegeman, e s Lexington av, 150 n New st, 92x200. 450

Same to Thomas H. Nicholson, w s Main st, s of Church, 75x250. 600

NEW ROCHELLE.

Carpenter, Rob't. P. to Lisle C. Thomas, lots 3, 4 and 5 w s Clinton av, Huguenot Park, 300x300. 3,500

Disbrow, Susan W. extrx. of, to John F. New, e s Clinton av, 200 s Mayflower, 100x300. 1,200

Johnson, Chas. F. to Barbara Hellmich, n s Winthrop av, 169 w North st, 68x84. 300

New, John F. to Wm. H. Youngs, w s Webster av, 100 n Coligni, abt 101x260. 1,550

Van Court, Chas. W. to Jas. L. Sharp, s w cor Liberty av and Chestnut lane, 70x148. 2,300

Waldorf, Fred. H. to George L. Carlisle, n e cor North st and Winyah av, 100x200. 7,750

Youngs, Wm. H. W. to Annie L. Allen, w s Webster av, 100 n Coligni, abt 50x260. 675

OSSINING.

Sullivan, Annie to Isabell S. Martin, lot 15 s s Ann st, 50x150. 2,?00

Woolsey, Charles W. to Walter W. Law, tract on road to Sing Sing, adj Church lot. 36 acres. 25,000

PELHAM.

Standen, Wm. T. to Grace I. Warner, lot 1, Chester Park. 725

RYE.

Bulkley, Mary E. et al. to John Condon, lot 27 w s Smith av, map Poningo Dale. 600

Greer, Chas. to Clara A. M. Greer, 93 acres on Ridge and Purchase roads, part in Harrison. 20,000

McCarty, Rich'd T. to Pauline E. Brown, lot 61 n s Seymour road map Poningo Dale. 525

Merritt, Jas. S. and ano. to Daniel Murray, n e cor West William and Lyon sts, 150x150. 940

Same to same, s w cor Ellendale av and Lyon st, 50x100. 260

Same to Geo. Grandison, e s Ridge st, 100 s Ellendale av, 100x100. 300

Same to Thos. J. White, lots 18 and 19, n s Ellendale av, Washington Park, 100x150. 520

Sands, Purdy G. to Frank O'Toole, n s Sands st, 225 w Grace Church st, 40x170. 510

SCARSDALE.

Popham, Lewis C. to Adele T. Carstensen, s s road on grantor's farm, adj John Sedgwick, 1½ acres. 1,511

Popham, Annie J. to same, abt ¾ acre, adj above. 741

WESTCHESTER.

Cooper, Margt. et al. J. B. Lockwood, ref., to Ignatz Weisberg, lot 83 e s Cooper av, 25x100. 55

Same to Julia Bible, lots 19 and 20 e s Franklin av, 50x100. 410

Crozier, John to John Thompson, s e cor Thomas and Dock sts, 50x80. 400

Crosby, Florence S. to John McCormack, n s 14th st, 455 e Av B., Unionport, 50x108. 350

Carter, Emma J. to Etta Forgolston, lot 171 n s 5th av, Wakefield, 105x113.5; also, n e cor Barker av and Julianna st, 77x100, and e s Barker av, 133 n Julianna st, 67x125, Olinville. 15,000

Forgolston, Etta to Chas. F. Kelly, same property. 15,000

Davidson, John to Jos. Troman, lot 984, Wakefield. 1,000

Heilman, Elizb. to Alex. Eger, n s Bridge st, 110 w Old White Plains road, 75x160. 1,500

McCracken, Robt. J. and ano to Peter Albrecht, w s Elm, 150 n Maple st, 25x100. 180

Mapes, John S. to Wm. Nagles, Jr., n s Zulette av, 250 w Mapes av, 50x100. 550

Mace, Levi H. and ano. to Bernard Cannon and ano., lots 82 and 83, Laconia Park. 400

Mack, Chas. H. to Madison Scott, west ½ lot 954 n s 7th av, Wakefield, 50x114. 3,700

Mapes, John S. to Mary A. Graham, s s Middleton road, 156 e Mapes av, 25x110. 240

Parsons, Laura M. to Addie Buebler, e s Barker av, 223.4 n Elizabeth st, 28.4x125. 4,500

Rice, Wm. et al., B. J. Tinney ref., to Patrick Murphy, w s 3d st, 100 s 5th av, Wakefield, 57x120. 3,751

Selig, Max to Isidore Simon, lot 289 map McGraw estate. 275

Striegal, Cath. to Sigmund Simon, s w cor 3d av and 4th st, Wakefield, 100x200. 8,750

Simon, Sigmund to Wm. H. Moore, same property. 4,500

Smith, Mathew to John F. Crotty, lot 231 map McGraw estate. 450

Taber, Aug. to John Tuito, n w cor Mapes and Zulette avs, 100x100. 1,200

WHITE PLAINS.

Abrams, Seth R. to Chas. D. Sutton, w s Davis av, adj John R. Smith, 90x120. 1,250

Clowe, Hannah W. to Robt. S. Moore, w s Broadway, 102 n Railroad av, 79x205. 6,700

Combs, Geo. F. to Jas. Hyatt, w s Madison av, 50x100. 175

Reed, John to Phebe H. Capron, n e cor Lake and Warren sts, 55x150. 3,450

Robbins, Russell exr. of, to Jackson Wright, n w cor Lexington av and Charles st, 50x150. 250

Sutton, Chas. D. to Carrie S. Abrams, n s Barker av, 100 e Warren st, 50x100. 2,750

Underhill, Monmouth H. exr. of, to Emily C. Underhill, s w cor Broadway and Hamilton av, 80x310. 7,500

YONKERS.

Barnes, Jerome D. to Marcia F. Butler, lot 17 and east half 16 Pond st map Nodine Hill property, Flagg estate. 7,000

Columbia Land and Impt. C. to Robt. L. Sackett, e s Columbia av, 200 n Hearst st, 150x100; also e s same, 100 n same. 50x100. 3,500

Ferguson, Robt. to Leslie Sutherland, lot 78 w s Beech st, Herriot map. nom

Herriot, J. Groshon exr. of, to Charles Cutbill, lot 91 e s Beech st. 385

Same to Alfred W. Cutbill, lot 90 e s Beech st. 360

Littlefield, Arthur to John Deion, e s 1st st, 144 n Scott av, 25x137.5. 500

Lowerre, Fannie M. to Margt. C. Doran, lots 1, 2 and 3 block 1, e s Park Hill av. 1,350

Miller, Chas. E. to Kate Williams, s w s Grove st, 275 s e Jerome av. 50x119. 400

Parsells, Edw. W. to Mary E. Bailey, n s Fort Field av, 100 e Briggs av, 48x125. 600

White, Arthur to Eliza M. C. White, lot adj A. S. Barnes and ano., 587.6 w North Broadway, 150x581; also lot adj same, 325x to Warburton av. 50,000

MORTGAGES.

NEW YORK CITY.

SEPTEMBER 18, 19, 21, 22, 23, 24.

Aul, Charles A. to Elizabeth Aul. Monroe st, s s, 50.5 w Scammel st, 25.3x69.10x25x71.6. Sept. 17, demand, 5 %. $1,640

Amory, Peter B., Newark, N. J., to Darius G. Crosby, Scarsdale, N. Y. Berrian av, s e s, lots 163 and 164 map of part farm of Charles Berrian, Fordham, —x—. June 14, 1888, 5 years, 5 %. See Conveys. 1,050

Bach, Lewis Z. to Bowes & Coombs. 102d st, n s, 209 6 e Lexington av, 54x100.11. Sept. 22, due Oct. 1, 1892, 5 %. 2,500

Blume, George to Elise de Coppet. Forsyth st, w s, 25 s Hester st, 26.8x50x26.6x50. Sept. 24, 3 years, 5 %. 18,000

Bresnan, Peter J. to William Ferguson, Jersey City, N. J. 47th st. P. M. Sub. to mort. $1,500. Sept. 21, due Aug. 1, 1896, or installs. 1,000

Byrne, Peter J. to Eva Bechtel extrx. George Bechtel. Peck slip, No. 43. Lease. Sept. 24, demand. 1,300

Banta, Mathias, Mamaroneck, N. Y., to Eliza A. Banta. 4th st, Nos. 310 and 312, w s, 51.3 s West 12th st, runs south 86.5 x west 56 9 x north 28.2 x east 16.6 x northeast and east to beginning. Sept. 1, 3 years. note

Barnett, Benjamin to Deborah Freed. Broome st, No. 301, s s, 21.11x87.6. Sept. 17, 3 years. 5,000

Bates, Hester mortgagor with Peter Donald mortgagee. Extension of morts. Sept. 5. nom

Bergener, William to August Bergener. 11th st, n s, 216.4 w Av C, 16.8x103.3. Sept. 15, due Jan. 1, 1893, 5 %. 4,000

Budde, Christiana to Sarah H. Wightman. Courtlandt av, e s, 25 n Gouverneur st, 25x100. Sept. 17, 5 years. 5 %. 4,000

Budde, Christiana A. widow to Eliza Prescott. 3d av, e s, part lot 149 map of Morrisania, 16.8x88.2 to new w s Boston road or av, x 16.8x95. Sept. 19, 1 year, 5 %. 2,000

Burnham, Emily wife of Theodore to Theresa Geggus. Rockfield st, n s, 115 w Williamsbridge road, runs west 50 x north 125.10 x east 46.3 x southeast 6 3 x south 120.7 to beginning. Sept. 11, 5 years, 5 %. 700

Bach, Lewis Z. to Margaretta H. Ward. 102d st, n e cor Lexington av. P. M. Sept. 3, 2 years or sooner, 5 %. 27,900

Same to same. 103d st, s e cor Lexington av. P. M. Sept. 3, 2 years or sooner, 5 %. 27,900

Same to same. 102d st, n s, 101.6 e Lexington av. P. M. Sept. 3, 2 years or sooner, 5 %. 19,600

Same to same. 103d st, s s, 101.6 e Lexington av. P. M. Sept. 3, 2 years or sooner, 5 %. 19,600

Same to same. 102d st, n s, 200.6 e Lexington av. P. M. Sept. 3, 2 years or sooner, 5 %. 18,000

Belsky, Frank to Joseph Vopelak. Stebbins av, e s, 158.9 n Freeman st, 50x126.1x50x127.2. Sept. 23, 3 years or sooner, 5 %. 1,000

Boecher, Gertrude mortgagor with Henrietta Adler mortgagee. Extension of reduced mort. Sept. 21. nom

Brandreth, Margaret wife of John to Elizabeth V. R. de Peyster. Audubon av, e s, 75 n 168th st, 25x95. Already mortgaged to mortgagee. Sept. 22, due Nov. 1, 1894, or installs, 5 %. 1,500

Bickelhoupt, George to John Hardy. 47th st, n s, 325 e 8th av, 50x100.5. Sept. 21, 8 years. 5,000

Casey, Elizabeth widow to Ellen Enright. Arthur st, w s, lot A T map of 70 lots Cedar Hill plot on Powell farm, Fordham, 25x122x25x121.8. Sept. 21, 3 years, 5 %. 500

Cohen, Michael to Alexandrina Jordan. 47th st. P. M. Sept. 1, due Sept. 15, 1894, or installs, 5 %. 2,500

Cooney, Peter J. to Thomas MacKellar. 148th st, n s, 140 w Brook av, 50x100. Sept. 22, due Dec. 21, 1891. 1,000

Cronly, John E. and Mary Emma his wife to Celine Rheinhold. 167th st, s s, 119.4 e Amsterdam av, 39.1x109.3x32.9x131.11. Sept. 21, 1 year. 1,400

Coogan, Matthew to THE FARMERS' LOAN AND TRUST CO. 105th st, No. 311, n s, 175 e 2d av, 25x100.11. Sept. 21, 2 years, 5 %. 15,000

Coogan, Patrick to THE EMIGRANT INDUST. SAVINGS BANK. 109th st, s s, 235 e 3d av, 50x100.10. Sept. 18, 1 year, 4½ %. 6,000

Campbell, John V. to Joseph L. Buttenwieser. Eldridge st, No. 55, w s, 25.2x101x25x101. Sept. 18, demand. 3,400

Congregation Chasam Sopher to Hannah Newberger. Clinton st, e s, 100 s Houston st, 75x100.2. Sept. 18, installs. 6,500

Cordes, John F. and Anna R. his wife to Bessie Collamore. Horatio st, No. 81, n s, 23x84.3. Sept. 23, 4 years, 5 %. 7,000

Donnelly, Bernard E. to Joseph O'Donnell. 20th st, No. 129 W., n s, 22.6x92. Sept. 24, 6 months. 1,500

Drake, Alexander W. to Alice M. Lloyd, East Orange, N. J. Clinton pl, n s, 133.11 w University pl, 25x93.11. Lease. Sept. 22, due May 1, 1897, or sooner, 5 %. 3,000

Dick, Robert to George E. Hyatt, Brooklyn. 90th st, s s, 200 w Columbus av, 3 lots, each 26.6x100.8. 3 morts. each $14,000. Sept. 16, due Sept. 1, 1892, 5 %. 42,000

Same to same. 90th st, s s, 279 6 w Columbus av, 20.6x100.8. Sept. 16, due Sept. 1, 1892, 5 %. 11,000

Same to same. 90th st, s s, 300 w Columbus av, 20.6x100.8. Sept. 16, due Sept. 1, 1892, 5 %. 11,500

Same to same. 90th st, s s, 320.6 w Columbus av, 3 lots, each 26 6x100.8. 3 morts, each $14,000. Sept. 16, due Sept. 1, 1892, 5 %. 42,000

Delabarre, Elizabeth M. to Hugh R. Garden. 22d st, s s, 257 e 6th av, 23x98.9. Sept. 2, due Nov. 4, 1891. 600

Ducey, Jane M. wife of John M. to James H. Case, Newburgh, N. Y. Walton av, w s, 400 n 150th st, 16.8x98.10x16.8x98 9. July 21, due Aug 5, 1893, 5 %. 1,550

Deutermann, William and George to Ida A. W. Siney. Grand st, No. 147, s s, 43.2 w Elm st, 17 9x80.4x18.2x84.4. Sept. 23, due Oct. 1, 1893. 2,500

Fankhauser, Caroline mortgagor with Carl A. Fischer mortgagee. Extension of mortgages at 5 %. Sept 23. nom

Field, Mary E widow, Rome, Italy, to THE UNION TRUST CO of New York trustees Richard M. Hoe dec'd. Burling slip, Nos. 32 and 34, s s, 93.2 w South st, runs west 43 x south 23.1 x west 4.11 x south 28 x east 48 x north 45.3. Aug. 31, due Sept. 1, 1894, 4½ %. 18,000

Finkelstein, Bertha wife of Israel M. to Rosanna Rosenfeld. Essex st, No 12, e s, 144.6 s Hester st, 18.9x100x19x100. Sept. 15, 6 months. 250

Fischer, George and Valentine Fischer and Maria his wife to Valentine Fischer exr. Louis Fischer. Forsyth st, w s, 143 s Houston st, runs south 14 x west 66.10 x south 143 to point 100 n Stanton st, x west 58 3 to point 75 e Chrystie st, x north 224.9 to point 74.3 s Houston st, x east 58.9 x south 68.9 x east 66.10 to beginning. Sept. 14, 1 year, 4½ %. 5,500

Foster, Tallmadge W. to Samuel Weil. Madison st. P. M. Sept. 8, due Jan. 1, 1892. 26,358

Foder, Rosa to Joseph Kepes. Sheriff st, No. 112, e s, 150 n Stanton st, 25x100. Sept. 23, 1 year. 2,000

Geisenheimer, Joseph to Abraham Gruber. 3d av, e s, 20.1 n 59th st, runs north 40.2 x east 100 x south 60.3 to 59th st, x west 20 x north 20.1 x west 80 to beginning. May 21, note. 2,000

Gessner, Margurite to Charles S. Loughurst, Brooklyn. 133d st, No. 160, s s, 183.1 e 7th av, 17.3x99 11. Sept. 24, 1 year. gold, 1,000

Greenbaum, Solomon to George W. Adams Stanton st. P. M. Sept. 24, 5 years, 5 %. 7,000

Same to Caroline Peters. Same property. Sept. 24, 5 years, 5 %. 2,000

Gault, Ella L. to Murray & Hill. Pleasant av, w s, 20 s 118th st, 18.6x75. July 29, 1 year or sooner. 1,000

Greig, Katie to Sarah L. Weir. 20th st, n s, 190 w 7th av, 23x98.9. Sept. 19, due March 19, 1896. 1,000

Ginsberg, Nathan to Cornelius Hayes. 49th st, No. 340, s s, 125 w 1st av, 25x100.5. Sub. to mort. $8,000. Sept. 22, due May 1, 1893, 5 %. 1,000

Greenebaum, Moses to Elise King. 3d av, w s, 72 s 40th st, 24x80. Sept. 21, due Oct. 1, 1893. 4,000

Garrett, Joanna C. wife of and James to Nicholas Luquer exr. Helen F. Watson. 114th st, No. 338, s s, 250 w 1st av, 16.8x100.11. Sept. 21, 2 years, 5 %. 1,500

Gray, Matilda to Elizabeth U. Hitchcock, Poughkeepsie, N. Y. Willis av, e s, 121 n 135th st, 20x92. Sept. 21, 1 year or sooner. 1,000

Gallagher, Kate wife of and Joseph F. to John T. Willets et al. exrs. Robert R. Willets. 114th st, s s, 300 w 1st av, 30x100.10. Sept. 21, 3 years, 5 %. 19,000

Same to Goldchen Adler. Same property. Sub. to last mort. Sept. 22, 1 year. 3,000

Gannon, Ellen F. wife of and James to Jennie L. Simons. Arcularius pl or 163th st, s s, 282 w Walton av, 50x122.3x52.11x112.3. Sept. 1, 2 years. 1,000

Heyer, Maria A. widow to THE HARLEM SAVINGS BANK. Terrace pl or Railroad av, s e cor 157th st, 169.6x169.5x150x90, except part taken for Railroad av. Sept. 18, 1 year, 5 %. 16,000

Hoguet, Robert J. to THE TITLE GUARANTEE AND TRUST CO. 57th st, No. 331, n s, 400 w 8th av, 24.6x100.5. Sept. 17, due Sept. 18, 1896, 5 %. 15,000

Horgan, Arthur J. and Vincent J. Slattery to Samuel S. Sands. Thompson st, w s, 125 n Spring st, 50x100. Sept. 18, 3 months or sooner. 10,000

Hulberg, Frederick to THE GERMAN-AMERICAN REAL ESTATE TITLE GUARANTEE CO. St. Nicholas av, w s, 100.11 n 121st st, 59.3x96.11x50.5x128. Sept. 18, demand. 36,000

Hyman, Louis to Lewis Greenblatt. Willett st. P. M. Aug. 31, installs. 7,000

Same to same. Same property. P. M. Sub. to last mort. Aug. 31, installs. 1,500

Harris, Samuel to Marie Mascho. Assignment of certain monies to grow due on mortgage made by Samuel Harris. July 8. nom

Hafner, William and William, Jr., to A. Hupfel's Sons. 3d av, No. 3027. Lease. Sept. 19, note, demand. 1,000

Hartwell, Louise M. to John Barber, Philadelphia. Convent av, w s, 39.11 n 143d st, 20x100, error. Sub. to morts. Sept. 3, notes. 5,000

Same to Howard A. Stevens. Convent av, w s, 79.11 n 143d st, 20x100. Sub. to morts. $21,282. Sept. 10, 1 year. 2,500

Havens, James H. and Robert C. Winters to George F. Hyatt, Brooklyn. Wooster st, w s, 75 n West Houston st, 49x100. Sept. 14, due Jan. 1, 1893, or sooner, 5 %. 70,000

Same to same. Wooster st, w s, 124 n West Houston st, 49x100. Sept. 14, due Jan. 1, 1892, or sooner, 5 %. 70,000

Herz, Isidor to The Title Guarantee and Trust Co. 124th st and Lexington av. P. M. Sept. 19, 3 years, 5 %. 37,500

Hillman, Caleb M. and Laura A. his wife to Sarah Friedlander and ano. exrs. and trustees Herman Friedlander. Kingsbridge road, e s, 25.6 n 178th st, 76.7x81.3x75x90.8. Sept. 22, 5 years, 5 %. 11,000

Same to Isaac Wallach et al. exrs. and trustees Samson Wallach. Amsterdam av, w s, 25 s 180th st, 25x100. Sept. 22, 5 years, 5 %. 5,500

Hogan, Patrick and Bridget his wife to John P. Kane. 129th st, No. 56, s s, 125 e Lenox av, 27x99.11. Sub. to morts. $23,000. Sept. 18, 1 year or sooner. 3,800

Hughes, Joseph to Frederic J. Middlebrook, Brooklyn. Chestnut st, e s, 23.3 s Madison st, 25.1x44.10 to New Bowery, x—x09.10. ⅓ part. Sept. 22, 1 year. See Conveys. 8,000

Hall, Howard S., Plainfield, N. J., to John H. Clapp trustee William Forgay dec'd. 102d st, No. 205, n s, 80 e 2d av. P. M. Sept. 18, 5 years, 4 %. 16,000

Same to same. 65th st. P. M. Sept. 18, 5 years, 4 %. 16,000

Hess, Charles and Sophia his wife to John C. Fahl. Tinton av. P. M. Sept. 23, installs. 1,800

Hutchinson, John W. and Emma E. his wife to John Brooks exr. Edward S. Brooks. Ridge av, centre line, adj land of William Harrison, runs south along said centre line of Ridge av 50.1 x west 149.10 x south 5.9 x west 150 x north 56.7 x east 287 to beginning; also Ridge av, centre line, adj land of John W. Hutchinson, runs west along s s said Hutchinsons land 149.10 x south 45 x east 150.9 to said centre line, x north 45. Sub. to morts. $15,800. Sept. 22, due Nov. 1, 1894, 5 %. 8,000

Johnsen, Amund to The Bradley & Currier Co. (Lim.) 12th st, Nos. 255 and 257 W., n s, 50x 69.10. Sub. to mort. $44,500. Sept. 9, 3 months. 3,300

Johnston, Elizabeth wife of Richard E. to William T. Lahey. 80th st, No. 75, n s, 30.6 w Park av, 20x82.2. Sub. to mort. $25,000. Sept. 19, 1 month or sooner. 2,000

Kent, Stephen to William H. Bormann. 144th st, n s, w ½ lot 234 map of Mott Haven, 25x 100. Sept. 19, due Jan. 1, 1895. 2,000

Kahn, Leopold to The Germania Life Ins. Co. 104th st, s s, 375 w Columbus av, 32.8x 101.2x37.2x100.11. Sept. 18, 2 years, 6 % and 5 %. 30,000

Klein, Benedict A. to Jacob Klingenstein. 2d av, No. 2304, e s, 27 n 118th st, 26x80. Sept. 17, due Dec. 18, 1891. 9,500

Klein, Benedict A. to George R. McKenzie, Glen Spey, N. Y. Lewis st, No. 87, w s, 140.5 s Stanton st, 18.1x100. Sept. 24, 3 years, 5 %. gold, 13,000

Krug, Emma wife of and Louis to Henry S. Strauss. 114th st, No. 436, s s, 193 w Av A, 25x100.10. Sept. 17, due Sept. 1, 1892. 1,800

Kauffman, Mordecai S. to Ascher Weinstein. 47th st. P. M. Sept. 1, installs. 4,500

Kelly, James S. to James Stokes, West Orange, N. J. 125th st, n s, 175 e 7th av widened, 50x 99.11. Sept. 23, 2 years. 52,500

Kingwell, Charles to The F. & M. Schaefer Brewing Co. 3d av, Nos. 140 and 142; 15th st, No. 144 E. Lease. Sept. 21. 3,000

Klee, Joseph and Wilhelmine his wife to Benjamin Demarest and Lambert S. Quackenbush, joint tenants. 85th st, s s, 131.6 w Av B, 16.6 x102.2. Sept. 24, due Oct. 1, 1894, 5 %. 8,000

Lazinsk, Flora wife of Hyman M., Brooklyn, to Elise de Coppet. Essex st, e s, 50 s Hester st, 25x50. Sept. 24, 3 years, 5 %. 15,000

Lennon, William F. to George E. Hyatt, Brooklyn. Columbus av, w s, 75.6 n 95th st, 25.3x100. Sept. 9, due May 1, 1892, or sooner. 22,500

Same to same. Columbus av, w s, 100.9 n 95th st, 25x100. Sept. 9, due May 1, 1892, or sooner. 22,500

Lesinsky, Charles to The Institution for the Savings of Merchants' Clerks. Warren st, s s, 25 e College pl, 25x70.4x24 9x70.6. Sept. 18, 3 years, 4½ %. gold, 30,000

Mortling, Anna M. wife of Stephen H., Ridgefield, N. J., to The New York Savings Bank. 39th st, s s, 100 e 9th av, 25x95.9. Sept. 17, due Dec. 1, 1892, 4½ %. 7,000

Mathews, William J., Yonkers, N. Y., to Robert H. Mathews. 93d st, n s, 90 e 3d av, 60x 100.8. Sub. to morts. $26,000. Sept. 22, 1 year. 3,000

McGuire, Thomas J. to D. Stuart Dodge exr. Helen P. Dodge. 102d st, No. 122, s s, 325.7 w Columbus av, 26x100.11. Sept. 22, 5 years, 5 %. 20,000

McGuire, Thomas J. to Charles E. Strong trustee for Kate P. Warden. 102d st, s s, 299.7 w Columbus av, 26x100.11. Sept. 23, 3 years, 5 %. 20,000

McReynolds, William to Henry McAleenan. 132d st. P. M. Sept. 17, due Oct. 1, 1892, or sooner. 27,000

Same to Henry McAleenan, exr. Hugh McAleenan. Same property. P. M. Sept. 17, due Oct. 1, 1892, or sooner. 27,000

Morris, Elizabeth to Isaac White and Matilda his wife. 2d av. P. M. Sept. 21, due Oct. 5, 1891, or sooner. 4,000

Mueller, Adolph to John F. Lambias, Brooklyn. Brook av. P. M. Sept. 24, 3 years, 5 %. 540

Murray, Michael and Delia A. his wife with Federal Co-operative Building and Loan Assoc. Agreement modifying morts. Aug. 5. nom

Madigan, Ellen to The Harlem Savings Bank. 151st st, n s, 200 w Courtlandt av, 25x116.1x 25x116. Sept. 22, 1 year, 5 %. 2,500

Mapes, Daniel, Jr., to Emma wife of Henry B. Hall. Samuel st. P. M. Sept. 21, 3 years, 5 %. 750

Mapes, Evadna H. to Emma wife of Henry B. Hall. John st, 24th Ward. P. M. Sept. 21, 3 years, 5 %. 750

Mayer, Rachel wife of and Ferdinand to Marks Levin. Lexington av, s w cor 105th st, 17.7 x55. Secures notes. Sub. to morts. $5,000. Sept. 3, due Dec. 3, 1891. 1,200

Norcross, James A. and Orlando W., Worcester, Mass., to Ida Meyer et al. exrs. Isaias Meyer. 106th st. P. M. Sept. 15, due Sept. 18, 1894, or sooner, 5 %. 17,500

Neresheimer, Emil A. mortgagor with Poughkeepsie Savings Bank mortgagee. Extension of mort. at 4½ %. Sept. 1. nom

Oakes, Thomas to Andrew J. Dalton. 179th st, n s, 75.10 w Vanderbilt av West, proposed, 25.3x92x25x88. Sept. 22, 2 years. 1,500

O'Connor, John J. to George Jaus. 115th st, s s, 175 w 1st av, 25x100.11. Sept. 21, 6 months. 500

Same to same. 115th st, s s, 225 w 1st av, 25x 100.11. Sept. 21, 6 months. 500

O'Connor, Mamie and John J. mortgagors with E. Euphemia Kennedy and ano. extrx. Robert Kennedy mortgagees. Extension of mort. at reduced interest. July 25. nom

Same with Mary E. Winfamute extrx. George Wintamute mortgagee. Extension of mort. at reduced interest. July 25. nom

O'Connor, Lillie C. to The Murray Hill Co-operative Building and Loan Assoc. Bathgate av. P. M. Sept. 17, installs, 5 %. 2,000

Same to John P. Wenninger. Same property. P. M. Sub. to last mort. Sept. 17, 1 month, 5 %. 512

O'Hara, Kate R. to D. Willis James. 86th st. P. M. Sept. 18, 3 years, 4 %. 25,000

Parke, Maria B. wife of and William A. to The Union Dime Savings Inst. 25th st, s s, 300 w 6th av, 25x98.9 Sept. 22, due Nov. 1, 1894, 5 %. 20,000

Pettit, John, East Orange, N. J., to Justus L. Bulkley et al. exrs. and trustees Daniel B. Fayerweather. Washington st, s e cor Liberty st, runs south 113.1 to Cedar st, x east 69.11 x north 53.2 x west 4.8 x north 57.10 to Liberty st, x west 77.6 to beginning. Sept. 23, due Nov. 1, 1894, 5 %. gold, 300,000

Prague, John G. to D. Willis James. 86th st, Nos. 133–141, n s, 355 e Amsterdam av, 115x100.8. Sept. 18, 1 month. 25,000

Putnam, James D., Brooklyn, to The Mutual Life Ins. Co. of New York. Madison av, n e cor 117th st, 100.11x260. Secures bond of mortgagor and John H. Hankinson. Sept. 21, 1 year. 65,000

Pfeiffer, Jacob to John Eichler. Railroad av, s w cor 169th st, —x— to Mill Brook; N. Y. & Harlem R. R., n w s, part lot 162 map of Morrisania, 75x298 to centre of Mill Brook, x 74x301, except part heretofore conveyed to mortgagee. Sept. 17, 5 years, 5 %. 10,000

Plass, Jenni to Samuel Fuld. 51st st, n s, 181.8 e 2d av, 18.9x100.5. Sept. 23, 2 years. gold, 3,000

Platt, Richard G. to The Germania Life Ins. Co. West End av, w s, 86.2 s 85th st, 16x100. Sept. 18, due Aug. 1, 1894. gold, 15,000

Same to same. West End av, w s, 70.2 s 85th st, 16x82. Sept. 18, due Aug. 1, 1894. gold, 14,500

Same to same. West End av, w s, 50.2 s 85th st, 20x64. Sept. 18, due Aug. 1, 1894. gold, 15,500

Same to same. West End av, w s, 30.2 s 85th st, 20x64x30.4x41. Sept. 18, due Aug. 1, 1894. gold, 14,500

Same to same. West End av, s w cor 85th st, 30.2x34. Sept. 18, due Aug. 1, 1894. gold, 19,000

Same to same. 85th st, s s, 34 w West End av, runs south 30.2 x west 7 x southwest 30.4 x north 50.2 to st, x east 30. Sept. 18, due Aug. 1, 1894. gold, 17,000

Same to same. 85th st, s s, 64 w West End av, 18x70.2. Sept 18, due Aug. 1, 1894. gold, 14,500

Same to same. 85th st, s s, 82 w West End av, 18x86.2. Sept. 18, due Aug. 1, 1894. gold, 15,000

Rapelye, Pheba C. to Lewis Atterbury et al. trustees Edward J. C. Atterbury. 135th st, n s, 104 e Southern Boulevard, 3 lots. 3 P. M. morts., each $3,000. Sept. 17, due Dec. 1, 1894, 5 %. gold, 9,000

Reynolds, Catharine F. formerly Pine mortgagor with The Poughkeepsie Savings Bank mortgagee. Extension of mort. at 4½ %. Sept. 1. nom

Rosenthal, Harris to Thomas C. T. Crain as Chamberlain of the City of New York. Pike st, e s, 27x85. Sept. 22, 2 years, 4½ %. 18,000

Ryan, William, Sr., to Henry S. Trenchard, Yonkers, N. Y. 147th st, s s, 40 e Prospect st, 60x100. Sept. 22, 3 years. 2,500

Reichert, Michael and Elizabeth his wife to The Society for Ethical Culture. 126th st. P. M. Sept. 17, 3 years or sooner, 4½ %. gold, 3,000

Reilly, Hugh to The Bradley & Currier Co. (Lim.). 116th st, s s, 100 e 4th av, 100x100.11. Sub. to mort. $79,000. Aug. 17, 4 months. 10,200

Richey, David to John A. Stewart et al. trustees of The Liverpool and London and Globe Ins. Co., in New York. 84th st, n s, 356.8 w 8th av, 17 4x102.2. Sept. 18, 5 years, 5 %. gold, 17,500

Same to same. 84th st, n s, 368 w 8th av, 32x 102.2. Sept. 18, 5 years, 5 %. gold, 32,500

Ruck, Clara A. wife of and John M. to George Roll. 58th st, s s, 187.6 w 9th av, 12.6x100.5. Sept. 17, 6 months or sooner. 3,000

Riker, William B. to The Excelsior Savings Bank, New York. 6th av, w s, 23 s 22d st, 20x65. Secures bond of mortgagor and William H. Riker. Sept. 24, due Oct. 1, 1892. 55,000

Rohrs, Frederick to The Bradley & Currier Co. (Lim.). Av A, s w cor 76th st, 51.1x100. Sub. to mort. $42,000. Sept. 10, 3 months. 5,000

Same to Bradley & Currier Co. (Lim.). 134th st, s s, 150 w Alexander av, 100x100. Sept. 18, 1 month. 10,000

Same to William J. Seaman. 102d st, n s, 103 e Park av, 125.6x100.11; 70th st, n s, 228 e Av A, 100x100 4. Sept. 18, 3 months. 10,000

Rohrs, Frederick to Agnes P. Brown. 102d st, n e cor Park av, 27x100.11. Sept. 24, due Dec. 1, 1894, 5 %. gold, 14,000

Same to Agnes P. and Matilda B. Brown. Same property. Equal lien with last mort. Sept. 24, due Dec. 1, 1894, 5 %. gold, 8,000

Same to The Bradley & Currier Co. (Lim.) Same property. Sub. to morts. $22,000. Sept. 24, 6 months. 5,000

Same to same. 102d st, n s, 27 e Park av, 25x 100.11. Sub. to morts. $14,500. Sept. 24, 6 months. 2,000

Same to Oliver B. Tweedy, Plainfield, N. J., trustee. Same property. Sept. 24, due Dec. 1, 1894. gold, 17,500

Same to Anna J. Wood, Huntington, L. I. Same property. Sub. to mort. $18,000. Sept. 21, due Dec. 1, 1894, 5 %. gold, 2,000

Seuner, Henriette wife of Joseph H. to Pauline Neustaedter. 123d st. P. M. Sept. 21, due Sept. 24, 1894, or sooner, 5 %. 12,000

Simon, Theodore to Magdalena Becker. 3d av, n e cor 83d st, 28.1x77. Sept. 23, 2 years. 1,500

Steventon, Euphemia and William B. Charlton, Jr., heirs and devisees of Robert Gregory to Charlotte J. Gregory. Av C, w s, 23.3 n 6th st, 23x83. Sept. 23, due Oct. 1, 1896, 5 %. 6,500

Stewart, Elizabeth wife of John B. to The Title Guarantee and Trust Co. 17th st, No. 564, s s, 125 e 11th av, 25x95. Sept. 23, 2 years. 3,500

Seagrist, Francis W., Jr., to D. Stuart Dodge exr. of Ellen P. Dodge. 140th st, n s, 90 w Boulevard, 25x199.10 to 141st st. Sept. 21, 5 years, 5 %. 20,000

Seaman, Samuel A. to Harriette E. Dodge, Saddle Rock, N. Y. 87th st, No. 147, n s, 375 w 9th av, 16.8x100.8. Sub. to morts. $13,500. Sept. 17, 1 year. 1,000

Schwartz, Max to John and Henry Stemme. Houston st, s s, 25 w Suffolk st, 25x80. Sept. 19, due Sept. 1, 1893, or sooner. 10,500

Shea, John and Mary A. his wife to Conrad Stein. 2d av, No. 1710, e s, 50.8 s 89th st, 25x 100. Sept. 21, 5 years, 5 %. 17,000

Silleck, Sophia B. to Edward Kilpatrick. 96th st. P. M. Sept. 21, 3 years or installs, 5 %. 6,100

Sneckner, William to Mary S. Van Beuren. Union pl, w s, 26 n 15th st, 26x116.10. Lease. Sept. 21, 5 years. 10,000

Stern, Emily to Amos R. Eno. Wooster st. P. M. Sept. 11, due Sept. 21, 1894, or sooner, 5 %. 48,000

Striker, James A. to John J. Jones and ano. trustees David Jones. 52d st, s s, 317.1 w 8th av, runs southwest abt 100.9 x south 100.5 to 51st st, x west 125 x north 100.5 x east 20 x north 100.5 to 52d st, x east 102.11; 11th av, w s, 96.10 s 54th st, 257.10 to centre line Hoppers lane, x— to Hudson River, x— to s s of 54th st, x —. Sept. 21, 1 year. 80,000

Saladin, Joseph E. to George Ehret. 10th av, No. 703. Store lease. Sept. 15, demand. 1,000

Schneider, William to Margaret P. Barker et al. exrs. Stephen Barker. 85th st, s s, 250 e 5th av, 25x102.2. P. M. Sept. 15, due Sept. 18, 1894, or sooner, 5 %. 3,000

Same to same. 85th st, s s, 275 e 5th av. P. M. Sept. 15, due Sept. 18, 1894, or sooner. 5 %. 3,000

Stelbuszeski, John to The Harlem Savings Bank. Robbins av, s e s, 125 s w Uncas st, 25x103. Sept. 12, 1 year, 5 %. 700

Sweeney, Mary C. to Christopher Kelly. Lexington av, No. 1850, w s, 80.11 n 115th st, 20 x78.10. Sept. 18, 5 years, 5 %. 10,000

Schreyer, John F. to The New York Savings Bank. 39th st, s s, 125 e 9th av, 25x98.9. Sept. 17, due Dec. 1, 1890, 4½ %. 13,000

Simpson, John F. and Charles H. to Sarah F. Herrick, Peekskill, N. Y. Park row, No. 225, s s, 72.8 e James st, 28x56.2 to n s Bowery as extended, x32.8x77.8. Sept. 15, due May 1, 1896. 7,000

Smith, Thomas S. to Maurice Roberts. 3d av, e s, 80.2 s 51st st, 20.1x76. Sub. to mort. $11,000. Sept. 16, 1 year. 4,000

Smith, Jennet wife of John W. to The Bradley & Currier Co. (Lim.) 92d st, n s, 256.6 w 9th av, 18.6x100.8. Sub. to morts. $58,500. Sept. 21, 6 months, 5 %. 4,800

Same to same. 92d st, n s, 238.6 w 9th av, 18x 100.8. Sub. to morts. $57,000. Sept. 21, 6 months, 5 %. 5,000

Same to same. 92d st, n s, 220.6 w 9th av, 18x 100.8 Sub. to morts. $46,500. Sept. 21, 6 months, 5 %. 5,000

Same to same. 92d st, n s, 200 w 9th av, 20.6x 100.8. Sub. to morts. $49,000. Sept. 21, 6 months, 5 %. 5,000

Smith, Tillie E. widow to Maria H. Rider, Brooklyn. 119th st, s s, 460 e Lenox av, 125x100.11. Sept. 14, demand. 5,000

Stevens, Mary E. wife of Mark S. to William M. Holmes and Townsend Bull. Hamilton pl, s e s, 40.8 s 142d st, 67.9x81.5x62.6x55.10. Sub. to morts. $32,600. Sept. 22, demand. 4,000

Tremper, Margaret J. wife of Robert A. to Mount Morris Co-operative Building and Loan Assoc. 177th st, s s, 300 w Monroe av, 50x125. Sept. 23, installs, 5 %. 5,625

Treu, Leopold R. to Estelle V. Bristow. Fox st, w s, 161 n 165th st, 16.8 x 100. Sept. 23, 5 years. 1,800

Same to same. Fox st, w s, 177.9 n 165th st, 16.8x100. Sept. 23, 5 years. 1,800

Same to Alice and Eliza Hall. Fox st, w s, 194.6 n 165th st, 16.8x100. Sept. 23, 5 years. 1,800

Thain, Robert W. to Bertha Volkening. 91st st, s s, 225 e 5th av, 25x100. Aug. 17, due May 1, 1892. 12,000

Same to same. Same property. P. M. Aug. 10, due May 1, 1892. 7,000

Theiss, Gertrud to The German Savings Bank, New York. Lawrence st, s s, 231 e Bloomingdale road, 75x100. Aug. 26, 1 year. 2,000

Same to same. Manhattan st, n s, 39.8 e 10th av, 50x100. Aug. 26, 1 year. 4,000

Tack, Mary A. wife of and Theodore E. to John Campbell. 82d st, s s, 150.11 w 9th av, 17x102.2. Sept. 21, 1 year. 5,000

Talbot, Emilie wife of Marcus H. to The Metropolitan Savings Bank. 117th st, n e cor Lexington av, 16.4x67 to Old Boston Post road, x64.11,x32.10. Aug. 25, 1 year, 4½ %. 7,000

The Bradley & Currier Co. (Lim) with William I. Seaman both mortgagees. Agreement as to priority of morts. made by Frederick Rohrs. Sept. 18. nom

Uihlein, Charles to Isabella G. Francis, Bridgehampton, L. I. Southern Boulevard, e s, 35 s Briggs av, 50x100. Aug. 8, 3 years, 5 %. 5,500

Vakay, George to Charles A. Acton. 144th st, n s, 254 5 e 3d av, 25x100. Sept. 17, 1 year. 700

Wallach, Joseph to The Mutual Life Ins. Co., New York. 65th st, s s, 458 e Amsterdam av, 20x100.5. Sept. 18, 1 year. See Conveys. 15,000

Weixelbaum, Sarah wife of Bernhard to Sophie Seidner. 73d st, n s, 115 w 3d av, 20x102.2. July 15, due July 1, 1894. 5 %. 4,000

Williams, Louise L. to Rebecca and Edward R. Ladew trustees for Rebecca Ladew and remaindermen. 23d st, No. 21, n s, 215.2 w 5th av, runs north 59 x west 4.7 x north 39 8 x west 19.11 x south 98.9 to st, x east 24.6. Sept. 9, due Oct. 1, 1892, 4½ %. 68,000

Weinstein, Ascher to Frederic J. Middlebrook, Brooklyn. 19th st, No. 342, s s, 275 e 9th av. P. M. Sept. 21, 1 year, 5 %. 3,000

Same to same. 19th st, s s, 300 e 9th av. P. M. Sept. 21, 1 year, 5 %. 3,000

Same to same. 19th st, s s, 325 e 9th av. P. M. Sept. 21, 1 year, 5 %. 3,000

Same to same. 18th st, n s, 275 e 9th av. P. M. Sept. 21, 1 year, 5 %. 10,000

Same to same. 18th st, n s, 275 e 9th av. P. M. Sept. 21, 1 year. 2,000

Same to same. 18th st, n s, 300 e 9th av. P. M. Sept. 21, 1 year, 5 %. 3,000

Same to same. 18th st, n s, 325 e 9th av. P. M. Sept. 21, 1 year, 5 %. 3,000

Williams, Richard R. to Ella L. Barnes. Oostdorp av, Walker st, n w s, adj land formerly of Ephraim Seaman now of Mary McKenna and Rose A. Graham, runs northwest 127 to land of Thomas Walker, x northeast 94.7 to land of Joseph Horridge, x southeast 120.6 to st, x southwest 94.3. Sept. 22, 3 years. 3,000

Wilson, Carrie A. wife of and Isaac M. to Marilla Mackenzie, West Haven Conn. 126th st, s s, 206.8 e 4th av, 16.8x99.11. Sept. 23, 3 years, 5 %. 5,000

Consent of stockholders of Parkside Land and Improvement Co. to mortgage. George A. Peters, Charles J. Miller and William W. Bissell to Charles C. Miller trustee. Sept. 23. nom

KINGS COUNTY.

September 17, 18, 19, 21, 22, 23.

Alder, Mary A. to Sarah B. Aikman. Pacific st, s w s, 200 s e Hoyt st, 25.4x100. Sept. 17, due Nov. 1, 1895. $1,000

Asher, James to Theodore F. White, Summit, N. J. President st, s s, 383.4 w Columbia st, 16.8x100. Sept. 18, 1 year, 5 %. 475

Bardin, Almon G. to Bernard Costello. Milford st, e s, 190 s Glenmore av, runs east 200 to Logan st, x south 20 x west 100 x south 20 x west 100 to Milford st, x north 40. Sept. 17, 3 years or installs. 450

Beer, Louis and Michael Schaffner to Kings Co. Savings Inst. Floyd st, n s, 290 e Nostrand av, 25x100. Sept. 21, 1 year, 5 %. 4,500

Bell, Thomas to The Fifth Avenue Co-operative Building and Loan Assoc. Lots 2221-2223 block 35 map Second Addition to Bensonhurst-by-the-Sea. Sept. 21, installs. 8,250

Bendix, Angelica to Williamsburgh Savings Bank. Havemeyer st, s e cor South 5th st, 20x70. Sept. 22, 1 year. 2,000

Berlinger, William and Christina his wife to Phebe E. Leverich extrx. Augustus A. Leverich. Harman st, s e s, 375 n e Central av, 25x100. Sept. 18, 3 years, 5 %. 3,000

Same to William Laytin et al. trustees William Laytin. Harman st, s e s, 350 n e Central av, 25x100. Sept. 18, 3 years, 5 %. 3,000

Balmanno, Charles G. to Michael Dalton. 8th st. P. M. Sept. 21, due Oct. 4, 1894, 5 %. 1,500

Bierds, John T. to James Hart. 24th st. P. M. Sept. 14, 6 months. 1,400

Bischoff, Annie and Elizabeth to Jacob F. Trembig. Fulton st, No 1908, s s, 300 w Ralph av, 28x100. Sept. 24, 1887, demand, 4 %. 2,500

Bishop, Eli H. to The Title Guarantee and Trust Co. Putnam av, s s, 195 w Stuyvesant av, 5 lots, each 20x100. 5 morts., each $7,500. Sept. 19, 3 years, 5 %. 37,500

Blackwell, Emily to John R. Pitt. Macon st. P. M. Aug. 29, due Sept. 22, 1892. 750

Boeckel, William to James A. Roosevelt and ano. trustees for Clarisse Ludwig. Bedford av, w s, 47.6 s South 3d st, 28x103.6. Sept 21, 5 years or installs, 5 %. 12,000

Same to same trustees for Marcia R. Scovel. Bedford av, w s, 75.6 s South 3d st, 19.6x103.6. Sept. 21, 5 years or installs, 5 %. 6,000

Bonert, Louis to Grace D. Litchfield individ. and with Edward H. Litchfield trustees Edwin C. Litchfield. 6th av, n w s, 50 n e 5th st. P. M. Sept. 19, 3 years, 5 %. 4,500

Same to Edward H. Litchfield. 6th av, north cor 5th st. P. M. Sept. 19, 3 years, 5 %. 4,500

Borchers, William to Henry Ruter. Kent av, No. 559. Saloon lease. Aug. 1, note. 2,000

Borin, Gustaf A. to Frederick Widmann. Louis pl. P. M. Sub. to mort. $3,000. Sept. 14, installs. 900

Bourke, Mary E. to Frederick H. Trowbridge. Debevoise st, e s, 59 s Fleet st, runs east 98 x south 8.10 x east 2.1 x south 8 x west 100 to st, x north 16.6. Sept. 10, 2 years. 600

Brascher, Henry C. and Mary his wife and Henry M. Brascher to Margaret E. and Martha A. Farrell. Stagg st. P. M. Sept. 15, 5 years, 5 %. 2,200

Brennan, Thomas to Noah Tebbetts. Saratoga av, n w cor Herkimer st. P. M. Sept. 17, demand. 2,000

Brewster, Melissa wife of John B. to Mary wife of and Flavious J. Maynard. Blake av, s s, 75 w Ocean av. P. M. and security for life maintenance of mortgagees. Sept. 18. 2,000

Bridge, Margaret P. wife of Charles E. to The Brooklyn Trust Co. Clinton st, s e s, 42 n e State st, 21x—x21.5x90. Sept. 19, 1 year, 5 %. 9,500

Brooklyn, Bath & West End R. R. Co. Consent of stockholders to mortgage on company's property for $100,000. June 22. nom

Brown, John to William T. and Percival C. Smith trustees for Alice C. Smith. Fulton st, n s, 128.4 w Clermont av, runs north 54.9 x east 1.1 x north 25 x west 7.7 x south 71.1 to av, x east 20.1. May 26, due May 1, 1896, 5 %. 12,000

Brymer, Adolph to The Star Co-operative Building and Loan Assoc. 77th st, s s, 170 w 3d av, 40x109.4, New Utrecht. Sept. 18, installs. 4,139

Bussy, Joseph and Aaron Levy to William A. Valentine. Stone av. P. M. Sept. 24, 10 years, installs. 3,685

Burr, Wilfred to John C. Schenck. McDonough st, n s, 370 e Ralph av, 3 lots, each 18x100. 3 morts., each $4,500. Sept. 17. 3 years, 5 %. 13,500

Same to Michael Lamm. McDonough st, n s, 424 e Ralph av, 18x100. Sept. 17, 3 years, 5 %. 4,500

Burr, Wilfred to Sarah M. Bulmer. McDonough st, n s, 460 e Ralph av, 18x100. Sept. 22, due Jan. 1, 1893, 5 %. gold, 4,500

Same to Hope H. Conkling. McDonough st, n s, 442 e Ralph av, 18x100. Sept. 22, due Jan. 1, 1893, 5 %. gold, 4,500

Burtis, Nathan W. to Jane Douglass. Chauncey st, n s, 98.11 w Lewis av, 19.9x100. Oct. 16, 1890, due Jan. 21, 1892. 1,550

Cannon, John to John Assip and Timothy J. Buckley. 16th st, s s, 109.4 e 9th av, 19x100. Sub. to mort. $3,500. Sept. 18, due March 15, 1893. 850

Carroll, John D. to John R. Kuhn exr. Annie Rabitte. Schenck av, e s, 200 s Arlington av, 25x100. Sept. 18, 1 year, 5 %. 3,000

Chaplin, George F. to John Cowenhoven. 12th av, n w cor 59th st, 40.2x100; 12th av, w s, 60.2 n 59th st, 40x100; New Utrecht. Sept. 22. 500

Comb, John, Jr., to Rachel M. Gilsey. Pearl st, e s, 43.4 n Tillary st, runs east 53.2 x north 7.8 x east 3.8 x north 13.4 x west 56.10 to st, x south 21. Sept. 21, 2 years. 500

Cornwell, Theodore I. W. to Metropolitan Life Ins. Co. St. Marks av, n s, 265 e Clason av, 26x70. Sept. 17, due Oct. 1, 1896, installs. until Oct. 1, 1892, 6 %; afterwards 5 %. 6,500

Same to same. St. Marks av, n s, 291 e Clason av, 25 6x70. Sept. 17, due Oct. 1, 1896, installs, until Oct. 1, 1892, 6 %; afterwards 5 %. 6,500

Coughlin, Maurice J. to John J. Hanley. 72d st, s s, 555.10 w 18th av, 26.3x100, New Utrecht. Sept. 19, installs. 124

Crilley, Catharine to Maurice Fitzgerald. 8th av, w s, 75.2 s 41st st, 25x100. Sept. 19, 3 years. 500

Daily, William to Tunis G. Bergen. 29th st, s s, 285 w 4th av, 25x100.2. Sept. 17, due Oct. 1, 1892. 600

Daly, Michael to Margaret Keane. Union st, s s, 210 w Smith st, 22x100. Sept. 15, demand. 1,500

Delaney, Peter F. and Peter J. Collins to John W. Mason. 6th av. P. M. Sept. 14, due March 17, 1892, 5 %. 4,500

Duny, John to Albertine J. Lankau. Atlantic av, n s, 73 e Suydam pl, 16x88.10. Sept. 21, 3 years, 5 %. 1,800

Davison, William to A. Stewart Walsh. Putnam av. P. M. Sept. 19, 1 year, 5 %. 1,000

Dickson, Ann wife of James to John N. Eitel. 14th st, n s, 147.4 w 4th av, 20x100. Sept. 16, 3 years, 5½ %. 4,000

Same to same. 14th st, n s, 167.4 w 4th av, 20x100. Sept. 16, 3 years, 5½ %. 4,000

Dimiere, Antonio to Eugene R. O'Connell. North 4th st. P. M. Sept. 21, 5 years, 5 %. 1,400

Dittmar, George to Theodore E. and George W. Green. North 10th st, n s, 100 w Roebling st, 40x100. Sept. 22, 1 year. 200

Dobler, Gustav and Bertha his wife to Salomon Wolf. Lewis av. P. M. Sept. 21, 5 years, 5 %. 3,000

Donnelly, Ellen M. to Winifred McConnell. New Lots road, s w cor Berriman st. P. M. Sept. 5, due Sept. 1, 1896, 5 %. 1,800

Downey, George, Mary A. and Sarah V. to Esther R. Barton. Greene st, s s, 225 w Oakland st, 25x100. Sept. 16, due May 25, 1894. 250

Drake, Charles W. and Ella J. his wife to The Kings County Savings Inst. North Henry st. P. M. Sept. 8, 1 year, 5 %. 1,750

Same to Charles Engert. Same property. 2d mort. Sept. 8, installs, 5 %. 1,250

Dunne, Desmond to Jane H. wife of Joseph S. Thayer. Lefferts pl, n s, 93.10 e Clason av, runs north 90 x west 24.7 x southeast 30.5 x southwest 0.7 x south 59.9 to Lefferts pl, x east 20. Sept. 17, 3 years, 5 %. 5,000

Durban, Martha E. to John B. Remsen, Roslyn, L. I. 63d st, n s, 160 w 14th av, 40x100, New Utrecht. Sept. 19, due Sept. 1, 1894, 5 %. 1,600

Dyer, Elisha to Mary A. wife of Willis B. Goodsell. Windsor pl. P. M. Sept. 18, 3 years, 5 %. 1,400

Eagle, Clarence H., Thomas H. Messenger, Fitch W. Smith and Minerva Eagle exrs. Henry Eagle mortgagees with Mary A. Powell mortgagor. Extension of mort. Sept. 15. nom

Eden, John D to The Dime Savings Bank, Brooklyn. Tompkins av, w s, 80 s Monroe st, 70x100. Sept. 21, 1 year, 5 %. 18,000

Eppstein, Elias to Gilbert S. Thatford. Thatford av, w s, 25 s Livonia av, 75x100. Sept. 9, 4 years, 5 %. 1,500

Erickson, Charles A. to George E. Wicks. 78th st, n e s, 360 n w 4th av, 120x109.4, New Utrecht. Sept. 17, due May 20, 1892. 1,000

Faley, Joseph to Thomas Doran. 39th st, n s, 450 e 4th av, 25x52.7x43.10x88.9. Sept. 21, 3 years, 5 %. 1,000

Falke, Henrietta to Poline Byk. Heyward st, s s, 54 e Bedford av, 20x80. Sept. 15, due March 15, 1894, or sooner. 500

Falvey, Deborah widow to Bedford Co-operative Building Loan Assoc. Park pl, s s, 200 e Rogers av, 25x48.4x25.6x43.8. Sept. 14, installs. 400

Fanning, John B. and Edward T. and Cornelia F. McCoun mortgagors with John H. Powel, Jr., and ano. trustees Samuel Powel mortgagees. Five extensions of morts. Sept. 5. nom

Findlay, Charles E. S. to Mary J. Syme. Clermont av, e s, 265 s Greene av, 20x100. Sept. 18, due June 1, 1894. 2,000

Fitch, Louisa F. to Frederick Yung. Dodworth st, s e s, 116.4 n e Broadway, 36.9x91.6. Sept. 23, 5 years, 5 %. 2,600

Flannigan, Ann to Rulef J. Van Brunt. 96th st, n e s, 360 n w 3d av, 50x100. Sept 15, 3 years. 1,500

Frost, Newbury H. with Emeline E. Brower, both mortgagees. Agreement as to priority of mortgages made by Leopold J. Lippmann. Sept. 14. nom

Foster, Joseph A. to Kate T. Ogden. Russell pl. P. M. Sept. 16, installs, 5 %. 1,900

Giblin, Margaret F. to Bernard Cruse, Jr. Bay 28th st, s e s, 460 s w Benson av, 60x96.8, New Utrecht. Sept. 19, 1 year. 250

Gleason, Louisiana I. to Christopher P. Skelton. Atlantic av, n w cor Bancroft pl, 17x90. July 25. 1,125

Goode, John B. to Henry Weil. Marion st. P. M. Sept. 1, installs, 5 %. 1,850

Graham, James to The Williamsburgh Savings Bank. Shepherd av, e s, 180 n Ridgewood av, 4 lots, together 80x102.4x80x102.5. 4 morts., each $1,500. Sept. 21, 1 year, 5 %. 6,000

Grimm, William to Manly R. Hubbs. Walton st, s e s, 375 n e Marcy av, 25x100. Sept. 15, 3 years, 5 %. 3,000

Gross, Max to Harris Max. Osborn st. P. M. Sept. 16, installs. 2,200

Guilfoyle, Maria to The Williamsburgh Savings Bank. Willoughby av, s s, 200 w Lewis av, 50x100. Sept. 21, 1 year, 5 %. 7,500

Hagele, George to Albert V. B. Voorhees. 85th st, w s, 85.3 s lands J. P. Moore, 40x100, New Utrecht. Sept. 17, 3 years. 1,000

Hancock, Charles to George Covert. Montauk av, e s, 650 n Liberty av, 75x100. Sept. 15, 3 years. 3,000

Hanford, Maria A. widow to The Title Guarantee and Trust Co. Cambridge pl, e s, 40 s Greene av, 20x100. Sept. 22, 3 years, 5 %. 2,000

Hart, Morris to Frank Kelly. Jacob st, s e s, 120 n e Broadway, 20x100. Sept. 14, 1 year, 5 %. 1,500

Harris, Joseph L. to William E. D. Stokes. President st. P. M. Sept. 5, 3 years, 5 %. 10,000

Hall, Sarah M. E. widow to Rebecca F. Sturgis trustee Lawrence Forbes. Meeker av, n w s, 125 s w Varick st, 27.9x25x143x27.9x155.1. Sept. 19, 3 years, 5½ %. 2,000

Harvey, Samuel to The Title Guarantee and Trust Co. York st, No. 58, n s, 16.8 e of alleyway bet Washington and Adams sts, 16.8x75. Sept. 22, 1 year, 5 %. 1,000

Hazard, Elizabeth wife of and William H. to Gilbert S. Thatford. Jefferson av, s s, 148 e Lewis av, 16x100. Sept. 22, 3 years, 5 %. 1,000

Henry, Andrew R. to The Kings Co. Savings Inst. Humboldt st. P. M. Sept. 21, 1 year, 5 %. 3,000

Same to Charles Engert. Same property. Sub. to last mort. Sept. 21, installs, 5 %. 1,500

Hill, George G. to Sarah C. Savage, Philadelphia, Pa. Pacific st, s s, 330.7 e Rochester av. P. M. Sept. 21, 1 year. 2,100

Same to same. Pacific st, s s, 480.8 e Rochester av. P. M. Sept. 21, 1 year. 2,100

Same to same. Pacific st, s s, 347.3 e Rochester av. P. M. Sept. 21, 1 year. 2,100

Same to William Jervis. Florence, Italy. Pacific st, s s, 313.11 e Rochester av. P. M. Sept. 21, 1 year. 2,100

Same to same. Pacific st, s s, 297.3 e Rochester av. P. M. Sept. 21, 1 year. 2,100

Hill, Henry B. to Eldred A. Carley. McDonough st, s s, 249.8 w Patchen av, 18x100. Sept. 15, 3 years, 5 %. 1,000

Same to same. McDonough st, s s, 267.8 w Patchen av, 18x100. Sept. 15, 3 years, 5 %. 1,000

Hilzinger, Alexander J. to Charles J. Schriefer. Bergen st. P. M. Sept. 16, 1 year, 5 %. 475

Hooney, William F. to Samuel D. Morris. Pearl st, s e cor Prospect st, 22x68x22x67.8. Sept. 22, 1 year. 2,000

Hooper, Laura A. to Thomas Everit. 15th st, s w s, 75 s e 6th av, 22.10x50. Sept. 1, 3 years. 300

Hunt, Charles F. to Martin Byrne. Clifton pl, n s, 400 w Nostrand av, 25x100. Sept. 19, 1 year, 5 %. 4,000

Same to same. Clifton pl, n s, 425 w Nostrand av, 25x100. Sept. 19, 1 year, 5 %. 4,000

Hurd, Jr., William B. to John Kempton. Butler st, s w s, 300 s e Smith st, 25x100. Sept. 9, 3 years, 5 %. 2,000

Hyde, Florence E. to The Industrial Co-operative Building and Loan Assoc. Greene av, n s, 125 w Stuyvesant av, 16.4x100. June 30, installs. 6,500

Jacobson, Peter J. to Mary Barclay extrx. Alexander Barclay, Newburgh, N. Y. Warren st. P. M. Sept. 10, 5 years, 5 %. gold, 3,500

James, Darwin R. to John Speri. Wyckoff av, south cor Greene av. P. M. Sept. 22, 3 years, 5 %. 4,500

Same to same. Wyckoff av, west cor Greene av. P. M. Sept. 22, 3 years, 5 %. 4,000

Jarvis, Augusta B. wife of and James O. to The Dime Savings Bank, Brooklyn. Hawthorne st, s s, 2,805.7 e Flatbush av, 50x106, Flatbush. Sept. 22, 1 year, 5 %. 1,700

Jones, Mary D. to Henry J. D. Jones, Media, Pa. De Kalb av, s s, 58 2 w Cumberland st, runs west 21 x southwest 51 x south 47 x east 16 x northwest 94.11. Sept. 23, 3 years. 5 %. 5,500

Kelly, James to Kate wife of and Michael Carroon. Sullivan st. s w s, 253.2 s e Richards st. 21.10x100. Sept. 18, 3 years. 700

Kelty, Mary E. wife of James T. to The Mutual Life Ins. Co., New York. Washington av, e s, 25.1 s Pacific st, 18.3x62.5x17.7x53.1. Sept. 22, 1 year. 2,500

Kentana, Joseph F. to Joseph M. Greenwood. 34th st, n e s, 160 s e 3d av, 100x100.2. Sept. 21, note. 2,000

Kern, John to John Schaeffer. Varet st. P. M. Sept. 17, due Oct. 1, 1892. 500

Klett, Jacob to The German Savings Bank, Brooklyn. Hamburg av, s w s, 55 n w Stockholm st, 25x100. Sept. 11, due Dec. 1, 1892, 5 %. 3,500

Knopf, Max to Conrad Valentine. Leonard st, n w cor Boerum st. P. M. Sept. 21, due May 1, 1893, 5 %. 1,000

Knott, George A. to The Flushing Co-operative Savings and Loan Assoc. Steuben st, e s, 225 s Myrtle av, 25x100. Sept. 15, installs. 10,000

Knorr, Bertha to The Williamsburgh Brewing Co. Bayard st, s s, 96 3 w Graham av, 19.6x100. Sept. 1, 1 year, 5 %. 800

Kock, Caroline to Jacob Bossert. Bushwick av. P. M. Sept. 17, installs, 5 %. 3,000

Kreig, August to David J. Molloy. Hemlock st, e s, 225 n Griffin pl, 25x100. Sept. 1, installs 250

Lamkay, Aaron and Amelia his wife to Thomas C. Balderston et al. trustees Supreme Order of Tonti. Thatford av, e s, 75 n Livonia av, —x100x25x100. Sept. 21, 3 years. 3,200

Lanning, Julia B., Josephine E and Edith A. to Charles Boenan. 4th av, north cor 17th st, 60.2x60. Sept. 18, 3 years, 5 %. 2,000

Lentz, Henry to The Fifth Av Co-operative Building and Loan Assoc. Webster av, s s, 278 e 1st st, 36x106.9x36x106.11, Flatbush. Sept. 21, installs. 1,500

Levine, Abraham to George Schwarz. Eastern Parkway, n s, 75 e Osborn st, 25x100. Sept. 21, 3 years. 3,500

Littman, William to Hamilton Co-operative Building and Loan Assoc. Luquer st, n s, 104.6 e Henry st, 25x100, with all title to strip 2.6 wide adj above. Sept. 23, installs. 3,500

Loehr, Fanny to The Brevoort Building Co. Central av, s e cor Stockholm st, 25x100. Secures rent reserved in lease bet parties hereto. Sept. 17.

Lorenz, Alexander and Martha S. his wife to Ellen M. Moore. Garnet st, n s, 146.6 w Hicks st, 40x100. Sept. 15, due Nov. 1, 1894, 1,000

Lorenz, Frank to John H. Scheidt. Newton st. P. M. Sept. 18, 5 years, 5 %. 4,100

Lippmann, Leopold J. to Emeline E. wife of James C. Brower. Weirfield st, n w s, 81 s w Central av, 20x100. Sept. 12, 1 year. 3,500

Lynch, John and Mary C. his wife to Thomas C. Balderson et al. Supreme trustees of the Order of Tonti. 4th pl, n s, 177.6 e Clinton st, 18.9x100. Sept. 21, 3 years, 5 %. 2,500

Mackenzie, Ann to William F. Corwith. Freeman st, n s, 145.3 e Oakland st, 22.2x100. Sept. 16, 2 years. 500

Maly, James to Isabell Hodgetts. Hancock st, s s, 120 w Lewis av, 20x100. Sept. 17, due July 1, 1894, 5½ %. 1,000

Marquardt, Jakob to Nathan Levy. Himrod st, Irving av. P. M. Sept. 17, 3 years, 5 %. 4,500

Mayer, Henry and Chotilde his wife to Jacob Mayer and Marie his wife. Broadway. P. M. Sept. 21, 5 years or sooner, without int. during life of mortgagee. 2,500

McCadden, James to Earl A. Gillespie and Rudolph Reimer. Hemlock st, w s, 316.10 s Jamaica turnpike, 25x85.1x25x85.5. Sept. 1, demand. 480

McCormack, Mary to John W. Ostrander. St. Marks av, s s, 427.6 e Utica av, 20x127.9. Sept. 18, 3 years. 2,000

McDonald, Thomas to Walter J. Klott. McDonough st, n s, 179 w Howard av, 18x100. July 25, note. 700

McMannis, William to Albert V. B. Voorhies. 18th av, n w cor Bath av, 125x96.8 Sept. 8, 3 years. 1,000

Mead, Thomas H. to John R. Woods. Walworth st, w s, 310 s Willoughby av, 20x100. Sub. to mort. $1,750. Sept. 22, 3 years, 5 %. 1,250

Same to The Title Guarantee and Trust Co. Same property. Sept. 22, 3 years, 5 %. 1,750

Merkle, Catherine M. to George W. Pearsall. 88th st, n e s, 325 n w 4th av, 25x100. Sept. 18, 3 years. 350

Merkens, Peter H. to Josiah H. Benton, Jersey City, N. J. Franklin st, w s, 50 n Java st, 2 lots. P. M. 2 morts., each $3,500. Sept. 2, 5 years, 5 %. 7,000

Meyer, Elizabeth, Charles and William to Emma Wehrmann. Van Brunt st, s w cor Degraw st, —x100. Sept. 15, 1 year. 350

Meyer, Lea to Rudolph and Otto E. Reimer. Patchen av. P. M. Sept. 18, installs. 2,150

Meyerholz, Henry to Phebe E. Sharp. Atlantic av, n s, 250 w Rochester av, 25x99.1. Sept. 12, 3 years. 2,500

Michel, Leopold and David Stern to Eva Herrlein. Cook st, s s, 150 e Morrell st, 25x100. Sub. to morts. Sept. 19, 5 years, 5 %. 1,400

Miller, Andrew to The Title Guarantee and Trust Co. Nostrand av, n e cor Dean st, 100 x100. Aug. 28, demand. 38,000

Miller, Jane to The Brooklyn Door and Sash Co. Macon st, n s, 272 e Patcheu av, 18x100. Sub. to mort. $4,000. Aug. 4, 6 months. 1,875

Miller, Oliver P. to Charles H. Gaus and ano. exrs. and trustees of Henry Oltmans. Keap st, n w s, 100 n e Marcy av, 20x100. Sept. 18, due Jan. 1, 1895, 5 %. 3,500

Morris, Joseph to Bernhard J. Pink. Blake av and Watkins st. P. M. Sept. 17, 1 year. 1,600

Moore, Isabella wife of and Henry B. to The Franklin Trust Co. St. Marks av, n s, 250 e Brooklyn av, runs north 255.7 to Bergen st, x east 40 x south 100 x east 60 x south 155.7 to av, x west 100. Sept. 23, 1 year, 5 %. 11,000

Moores, Robert L. and Charles A. Le Quesne to George F. Alexander. Madison st, south cor Broadway, 21.10x48.2x49.5x18.11. Sept. 11, 2 years. 5,000

Same to Earl A. Gillespie, Woodhaven, L. I. Broadway, s w s, 158.11 s e Madison st, 28x 78.8x28.11x71.6. Sept. 1, 2 years. 3,500

Same to same. Broadway, s w s, 158.11 s e Madison st, 28x78.8x28.11x71.6. Sept. 2, 2 years. 1,500

Same to Thomas H. Rodman trustee of Abijah Mann, Jr. Broadway, s w s, 38.2 n w Putnam av, runs northwest 28 x southwest 50 x south 11.8 to av, x east along same 28x northeast 38.8. Sept. 17, 3 years, 5 %. 10,000

Morrison, Samuel to The Title Guarantee and Trust Co. Smith st, e s, 20 s Huntington st, 20x75. Sept. 23, 1 year, 5 %. 2,000

Murphy, Joseph F. to Peter G. Kerr. Schenck av. P. M. Sept. 17, due Oct. 1, 1897. 725

Murphy, John W. and Thomas P. to Sarah J. Hinman. Hubbard st, e s, 180 s Centre pl, runs south to high-water line of Gravesend Bay, x east 57.5 x north —x—, Gravesend. Nov. 16, 1890, 2 years. 600

Muuss, Adolph to Thomas Davies. Shephard av. P. M. Sept. 18, 3 months. 200

Nebrbas, Anton to Frederick Dhuy, Jr. Pacific st. P. M. Sept. 21, 3 years, 5 %. 1,200

Opp, John to The Title Guarantee and Trust Co. Vernon av, n s, 368.9 e Tompkins av, 18.9x100. Sept. 21, 3 years, 5 %. 3,500

Osborn, Charles S. to Catharine Cary. Elton st. P. M. Sept. 15, 3 years 650

Pape, Friedrich and Margaretta his wife to Louis Beer and Michael Schaffner. Floyd st. P. M. Sept. 22, due Oct. 1, 1892, 5 %. 1,000

Payeleitner, Julia wife of Oscar to Alfred Ogden. Atlantic av. P. M. Sept. 21, installs. 1,500

Parker, Mary M. to Mary E. Dobbie and Frederick W. Thompson. Ocean av, Gravesend. P. M. Sept. 21, 3 years or installs. 1,200

Perego, Ira K. to The Home Life Ins. Co. Flatbush av, n e s, 211.8 n w Lafayette av, 51.6x79.1x50.5x66.10. Sept. 1, due July 1, 1892, 5 %. 20,000

Philips, Edward to Union Dime Savings Inst. Lexington av, s s, 259 w Nostrand av, 16x100. Sept. 21, due Nov. 1, 1894, 5 %. 3,500

Same to same. Lexington av, s s, 275 w Nostrand av, 16x100. Sept. 21, due Nov. 1, 1894, 5 %. 3,500

Pope, Mary A. wife of William to Dorothea Lang widow. Prospect av. P. M. Sept. 17, due January 1, 1898, 5 %. 3,000

Radcliffe, Thomas H. to John C. Schenck. Decatur st, n s, 299.8 w Howard av, 146.8x100. Sept. 18, demand. 5,000

Rector, &c., of Emanuel Church to Jeremiah J. Campion, Jr., New York. President st, n s, 50 w Smith st, runs north 75 x east 26.6 x north 25 x west 99.6 x south 100 to st, x east 72.6. Sept. 18, 1 year. gold, 15,000

Reeves, Elmira M. to William N. Coates. 3d av, New Utrecht. P. M. Sept. 22, 3 years. 700

Reinheimer, Ferdinand A. and Henrietta his wife to Charles W. Truslow trustee of Wm. Wall. Seigel st, s s, 390 e Bushwick av, 25x 100. Sept. 17, 2 years, 5 %. gold, 650

Rice, George H. to John B. O'Donohue et al. exrs. Peter J. O'Donohue. Schermerhorn st, n e cor 3d av, 46.6 to Flatbush av, x southeast 83.2 to st, x west 69. Sept. 16, due Sept. 17, 1894, 5½ %. 14,000

Riddle, William B. to William H. Norris and William Bowers. 4th av, w s, 30 s 13th st, 28 x86.10. Sept. 18, 2 years. 2,500

Riley, Mary to Joseph D. Smyth. 42d st, No. 28; 3d av, No. 1020; 42d st, n s, 300 w 2d av, 25x100.2. Sept. 18, 60 days. 100

Ritzenhoff, Louise to August Nickel. Evergreen av. P. M. July 17, due Sept. 17, 1894, 5 %. 600

Ritzenhoff, Louise to Addison O. Coe and Lena his wife. Cooper st, s s, 155 e Bushwick av, 25x100. Oct. 1, 1891, 5 years, 5 %. 550

Robbert, Friedrich to The Germania Savings Bank, Kings Co. 6th av, w s, 18 n 11th st, 18 x75. Sept. 20, 1 year, 5 %. gold, 2,000

Rosencrans, Mathias L. to Angeline E. Darling, Utica, N. Y. Myrtle av. P. M. Sept. 18, due Sept. 1, 1894, or installs., 5 %. 6,000

Rosemon, Vincent to Susan Dunn widow, Paterson, N. J. Quincy st, n s, 248.8 e Tompkins av, 19x100. June 1, 5 years, 5 %. 1,600

Ross, Frank A. to The Nassau Co-operative Building and Loan Assoc. Herbert st. P. M. Sept. 21, installs. 1,000

Ross, Jennie L. to The Brooklyn Door and Sash Co. Fulton st, s s, 200 w Stone av, 40x 100. Sub. to morts. $19,000. July 21, 1 year. 5,790

Same to same. 2d st, s w s, 117.10 n w 7th av, 39.3x100. Sub. to morts. $12,000. July 21, 1 year. 3,750

Ruth, John and Barbara to Elizabeth Meltzer. North 5th st, s e s, 87 n w 3d st, 25x100. Sept. 19, due Sept. 15, 1894. 600

Sachs, Benjamin to Lena Durchholz. Sackman av. P. M. Sept. 19, due Sept. 15, 1892. 900

Sandhusen, Louis to The Dime Savings Bank, Brooklyn. Lafayette av, n w cor Adelphi st, 25x100. Sept. 11, 1 year, 5 %. 10,000

Sandhusen, Louis to Anna Schmults widow. Lafayette av, n w cor Adelphi st, 25x100. Sept. 21, 1 year, 5 %. 3,500

Schafer, Charles and Eliza his wife to Joseph Wingenfeld. Central av, n e s, 26 n w Magnolia st, 20x80. Sept. 17, 1 year, 5 %. 880

Schneider, George H. to Mary M. Schneider, Schwoon, N. Y. 10th st, s w s, 131 s e 5th av, 18.8x100. Sept. 1, 3 years. 1,700

Schoefer, Henry J. to Terence Jacobson. Gates av, n s, 80 w Vanderbilt av, 20x75. Sept. 17, due Nov. 1, 1891. 200

Seigel, Harris and Samuel Nelken to Theresa Goodkind. Humboldt st, e s, 100 n Scholes st. P. M. Sept. 1, installs. 1,100

Shedorsky, David to Aaron Kaplan. Linden st. P. M. Sub. to mort. $3,000. Sept. 22, due Oct. 1, 1894, or sooner. 2,600

Sheridan, John to Salomon Zeman. 7th av, n w cor 39th st, 100x100. Sept. 18, 1 year. 300

Simorvitch, Isaac to Fanny Restler. Thatford av, e s, 100 s Sutter av, 25x100. P. M. June 4, 6 months, 5 %. 850

Sims, Harriett L. to Allan Stevenson. Cumberland st, e s, 389.11 s Fulton st, 30x100. Sept. 23, 1 year. 500

Small, Henry G. to The Title Guarantee and Trust Co. Woodbine st. P. M. Sept. 21, 3 years, 5 %. 2,000

Smith, Joseph M. to Joseph McKeage. North Oxford st, e s, 161.8 n Myrtle av, 25x100. Sept. 16, 2 years. 600

Speth, Theodore to Elizabeth Kramer. Gates av, s s, 195 w Evergreen av, 26x100. Sept. 17, 1 year. 600

Spicer, Charles B. to The Roslyn Savings Bank. 53d st, s s, 180 w 5th av, 20x100.2. Sept. 17, due Sept. 1, 1894, 5 %. 2,000

Same to Mary S. wife of Calvin S. Denman. 53d st, s s, 160 w 5th av, 20x100.2. Sept. 17, due Sept. 1, 1894, 5 %. 2,000

Stahl, Helena wife of Anton to Philip L. Balz, Jr. Schenectady av, e s, 87.2 s Pacific st, 20 x50. Sept. 17, due July 1, 1893. 500

Stelling, Claus H. to Susan E. wife of George J. Collins. Monroe st. P. M. Sept. 16, 5 years, 5 %. 3,500

Stephens, William to The Title Guarantee and Trust Co. Woodbine st. P. M. Sept. 19, due Sept. 23, 1894, 5 %. 2,000

Same to George W. and Charles H. Francisco. Same property. P. M. Sub. to last mort. Sept. 19, installs. 1,700

Stern, Solomon and Max and Samuel Hirshbaum to Frank Bailey. 79th st, New Utrecht. P. M. Sept. 8, due Sept. 11, 1892. 375

Street, Herman E. to The Title Guarantee and Trust Co. Bleecker st, s s, 233.4 w Knickerbocker av., 2 lots, each 16.8x100. 2 morts., each $2,250. Sept. 23, 1 year. 4,500

Spabn, Valentine to Ferdinand W. Odell. Walworth st. P. M. Sept. 21, installs. 5 %. 500

Struller, Bernbardine S. wife of and Alexis to Luder Seebeck. Rochester av, n w cor Pacific st, runs north 50 x west to centre Old Hunterfly road at point 150 s Atlantic av, x south — to st, x east —; Rochester av, e s. 50 n Pacific st, 50x100. Sept. 21, 1 year. 1,000

Sullivan, Michael and Ellen his wife to Katie wife of John M. Stearns. Rockaway av, e s, 25 n Glenmore av, 18.4x80. Sept. 15, 3 years. 2,500

Sweeney, Daniel F. and William Hughes to Beadleston & Woerz. 3d av, No. 528. Lease. Sept. 12, demand. 500

Sweet, Josephine wife of Charles F. formerly Uris to Blauche E. Smith, East Marion, L. I. Evergreen av, n e s, 20 s e Weirfield st, 20x100. Sept. 15, 1 year, 5 %. 500

Swinm, Theodore W. to The Title Guarantee and Trust Co. Jefferson av, n s, 28 e Lewis av, 77x100. Sept. 19, demand. 80,000

Taber, Charles S. and George C. Case to Mary E. Stone admrx. David Stone. Albany av, n w cor Butler st, 22.3x80. Aug. 26, due Nov. 21, 1891, 5 %. 1,400

Tarpey, Sarah, called Sarah Toffay in the deed of conveyance, wife of and Barney to Horace D. Vandenbergh. Stone av, e s, 100 n Liberty av, 100x100. Sept. 17, 3 years. 1,000

Taylor, Thomas F. to Thomas F. Taylor exr. Richard Taylor. Kent av. P. M. June 1, 10 years. 24,000

Taylor, William H. and Sarah E. his wife to Simeon B. Chittendon, Jr., et al. exrs. Simeon B. Chittenden. Caton av, s s, at intersection with centre line bet. East 14th st and East 15th st, runs south 621.6 to Church lane, x west 187.8 to centre East 14th st, x north 622.10 to Caton av, x east 187.8, contains 1 857-1,000 acres, Flatbush. Sept. 22, 1 year. 2,000

Terrett, Sarah A widow, Harriet M. and Lillian R. Terrett, Sarah L. Holt and Julia A. Holbrook to The Brooklyn Savings Bank. Bedford av, w s, extends from Putnam av to Madison st, 200x80. Sept. 21, 1 year, 5 %. 5,000

The Canarsie Yacht Club to Hermann Lohman, Jamaica. Plot on Bay, 75x200, Flatlands. Aug. 15, due Sept. 1, 1894. 600

Towne, Kendall to William P. Carey. Bergen st, n s, 175 w Vanderbilt av, 25x110. Sept. 21, 3 years. 400

Tybring, Adolph J. mortgagor with Garret J. Garretson exr. Mary E. Waldron. Extentension of mort. Aug. 31. nom

Van Glahn, John C. to James S. Bearns. Prince st, e s, 238.9 n Myrtle av, 21.3x85. Sept. 18, 1 year, 5 %. 1,000

Voell, John to Eliza Wanmaker. Dresden st, e s, 150 n Arlington av, 50x100. Sept. 17, 3 years. 300

Wagner, Sarah E. widow and George A. Davies heirs of George A. Davies to Sarah Davies. Bridge st, w s, 73.9 s High st, runs west 55.8 x north 11.9 x west 10.4 x south 38 to alley, x east 75 to st, x north 26.3; Bridge st, w s, 50 s High st, runs west 50 x south 12 x west 5.8 x south 11.9 x east 55.8 to st, x north 23.9. Sept. 12, due May 1, 1893, 5 %. 3,000

Waldron, Honora wife of and Patrick, formerly Fogarty, to William F. Corwith. Interior lot, begins at point 100 s Huron st and 183 w Manhattan av, runs south 23.10 x northwest 25 x north 36.6 x east 25. Sept. 17, 1 year. 200

Walling, Thomas to James H. Watson and James H. Pittinger, of Watson & Pittinger. Patchen av, n e cor Putnam av, 20x100. Sept. 22, demand. 1,753

Walling, Thomas to John M. Canda and John P. Kane, of Canda & Kane Patchen av, n e cor Putnam av, 20x100. Sept. 22, demand. 2,750

Walsh, Georgia T., Amenia, N. Y., to Louis Getz. Bedford av, e s, 133 s South 4th st, 23 x100. Sept. 1, due April 18, 1896, 5 %. 2,500

Ward, Catherine R. to Otto Huber Brewery. Court st, No. 310. Lease. Sept. 15, due Oct 1, 1891. 1,500

Watkins, Emma L. to George E. Kitching. Greene av, s s, 100 e Cumberland st, 20x80. Sept. 18, 3 years, 5 %. 3,500

Weild, David to The Title Guarantee and Trust Co. Halsey st, s s, 308 w Throop av, 108x100. Sept. 15, demand. 27,000

Werbelovsky, Jacob H. to Francis E. Doughty. Moore st, s s, 50 e Ewen st, 25x100. Sept. 21, 5 years, 5 %. 5,000

Wilde, Clara E. to William Lohmann. East 94th st, s w s, 100 s e Flatlands av, 52.7x½ block, x52.3x—, Canarsie. Aug. 1, 10 years. 1,000

Willant, Friedrich and Mary his wife to The Bushwick Savings Bank. Stagg st, n s, 175 w Bushwick av, 25x100. Aug. 31, due Sept. 1, 1892, 5 %. 3,000

Witte, John to The Emigrant Industrial Savings Bank. York st, s w cor Charles st, 50x 75. Sept. 16, 1 year, 4½ %. 5,900

Wolff, Solomon to Thomas C. Balderston et al. Supreme trustees of the Order of Tonti. Belmont av, s s, 75 e Osborn st, 25x100. Sept. 18, 3 years. gold, 3,500

Same to same. Belmont av, s s, 50 e Osborn st, 25x100. Sept. 18, 3 years. gold, 3,500

Wordburn, Alice to Frederick Dhuy, Jr. Pacific st. P. M. Sept. 10, due Dec. 1, 1895, or installs, 5 %. 500

Youngtoh, Philip or Youngeutoh to Oscar Goerke and Elmer D. Gildersleeve trustees of the Educational Fund of the New York Yearly Meeting of the Society of Friends. 13th st, n s, 156 n w 3d av, 20x100; Interior lot, begins at point 98 n e 13th st and 156 n w 3d av, runs southwest 35 x southeast 0.5 x northeast 35 x northwest 0.2½. Sept. 18, 5 years. 5½ %. 1,650

Yung, Frederick to The Williamsburgh Savings Bank. Broadway, east cor Dodworth st, 22.10x100. Sept. 23, 1 year, 5 %. 2,000

Zahn, Edward to The Daily News Building, Savings and Loan Assoc. 45th st, s s, 460 w 5th av, 20x100.2. Sept. 23, installs. 2,750

MORTGAGES----ASSIGNMENTS.

NEW YORK CITY.

September 18 to 24—Inclusive.

Archer, Oliver H. P. to Clara Bendheim. $3,000

Bendheim, Clara to Bertha Greenebaum widow. 3,000

Boyle, Jacob T., Alexander D. Stratton and Eugene D. Bagen to The Teachers Building and Loan Assoc. nom

Brown, Edward J. and ano. exrs. Margaret Cleland to Elizabeth C. Brown. 7,017

Same to Susan Alvord. 2,516

Boehm, Gustav, Long Island City, to Samuel Riker. 4,600

Bautje, William, Brooklyn, to Henrietta Adler, Brooklyn. 3,000

Chambers, James, John A., Jeanette D. and Katharine Chambers, Morristown, N. J., to William G. De Witt, committee of John T. Housman. nom

Chambers, John A. exr. Helen De W. Chambers to James, John A., Jeanette D. and Katharine Chambers, Morristown, N. J. nom

Colles, James and Sarah R. and Frederick O. Beach admrs. Edward P. Beach to The New York Life Ins. and Trust Co. 33,000

Colles, James to Edward P. Beach. 3,000

Coovey, William to William M. Heagerty, Brooklyn. 450

Cram, Henry A. and ano exrs. and trustees George C. Cram to The Metropolitan Savings Bank. 6,000

Cruger, Stephen V. R. trustee of Mary E. B. Field to The New York Life Ins. and Trust Co. guard. of Mary V. Johnston. 21,000

Same to same. 21,000

Cruger, James P. to The New York Life Ins. and Trust Co. guard. of Mary V. Johnston. 11,500

Dennis, Page C. to William Post committee of John Rogers. Assign. of mort. as collateral. 1,000

De Witt, William G. committee of John T. Housman to James, John A., Jeanette D. and Katharine Chambers, Morristown, N. J. consid. omitted

Eden, John H. to Mary E. Monaghan. 515

Engelhard, Rudolph to Josephine Engelhard. nom

Greenblatt, Lewis to Jacob K. Weiner. 7,000

Gruber, Abraham to C. Fred. Richards and Alphonse Montant, of Townsend & Montant. 2,000

Gregory, Charlotte J and Euphemia Steventon exrs. Robert Gregory to Charlotte J. Gregory. nom

Hyde, Albert G. to David B. Ogden. 15,156

Hickey, John to Sidney H. Stuart. 1,516

Ludwig, Amelia to Ellis B., Maria L. and Mary C. Mundy, Richmond Co., S. I. 3,000

McGovern, James S. to Josiah F. Cadmus. 1,000

Macdonell, Ann, Ottawa, Can., to Emanuel Katz 2,700

Middlebrook, Frederic J., Brooklyn to Mary A. Chisolm. 18,263

Same to William H. Jackson. 14,037

Morgenthau, Henry to Laura A. Hillman. 4,270

Morgenthau, Henry to Andrew J. Connick. nom

Muller, John M. to Walter N. De Grauw, Sr. and Jr., exrs. and trustees James A. De Grauw. 5,000

McMillan, John to William C. Illig exr. and trustee John G. Illig. 4,250

O'Hara, Kate to Mary McManus. 3,342

Peabody, Anna H. to Charles F. Darlington, Newark, N. J. 2,500

Roberts, Maurice to Raphael R. Govin. 4,000

Rintelen, Elizabeth to Adam C. Rintelen. nom

Scudder, Edward M. to Anna J. Wood, Huntington, L. I. 5,000

Scott, John S. to Thomas W. Robinson. 3,000

Starr, Sarah M. to Nathaniel E. Wood, Norwood, N. J. 3 assigns. nom

Same to Elizabeth Bloodgood. 3 assigns. nom

Smith, Theodore to Mortimer Smith. 2,000

The New York Life Ins. and Trust Co. to James Colles. nom

The Lawyers Title Ins. Co. of New York, to Walter N. De Grauw, Sr. 9,066

Title Guarantee and Trust Co. to James Sullivan. 1,200

Title Guarantee and Trust Co. to D. Stuart Dodge. 37,500

Train, Gertrude M. to Alfred Dolge, Dolgeville, N. Y. nom

Union Trust Co. of New York admr. Margaret Langlois to United States Trust Co. committee of Charles A. Langlois. 9,500

Same to same. 15,000

Same to same. 8,000

Same to same. 10,000

Same to same. 8,000

Same to same. 4,500

Same to same. 12,000

Same to same. 5,000

Same to same. 4,500

United States Trust Co. to Francis H. Tobias. nom

Same to Florian Tobias. nom

Same to Edith R. Lewis. nom

Wood, W. Wilton, Huntington, L. I., to M. Dasher, Wylly, Bayonne, N. J. nom

Woolverton, Samuel to Caroline M. Dingee. nom

Washburn, Wilbur F., Yonkers, N. Y., to William W. Scrughan. nom

Whalen, John to Timothy Donovan. nom

Winslow, Edward to Henry W. Ford trustee Augustus H. Ward dec'd. nom

Same to same. nom

Wight, Sophia A. admrx. Danforth P. Wight and George R. Wight. 3,702

Wasserman, Moses to Josiah Lockwood. 275

KINGS COUNTY.

Sept. 17 to 23—Inclusive.

Alexander, George F. to William H. Owen. $1,500

Alexander, George F. to Watson & Pittinger. 5,000

Allin, Heloise M. L. to Stickney, Spencer & Ordway. nom

Arnold, Daniel S. to Harriet A. Joslyn guard. Hattie L. Tucker. 2,811

Barrett, Bridget to Earl A. Gillespie. 900

Beach, George to Cross, Austin & Co. 1,500

Benedict, Erastus D. to Mary A. Miller. 530

Blank, Henrich to Burger & Hower Brewing Co. (Lim.) 700

Brown, Edward J. and James H. Benedict exrs. Margaret Cleland to Elizabeth C. Brown. 2,019

Byk, Poline to Margaret A. wife of James E Young. 1,006

Chapman, William H. guard. Ada. M. Chapman to Ada M. Chapman. nom

Condict, Silas A. to Warren P. Ackerman. 700

Cook, James H. to Francis C. Willis, Tenafly, N. J. 3,050

Dexter, Alice M. to Margaret Young, Westchester, N. Y. nom

Drake, John J. to Walter S. Tuttle. 500

Durchholz, Lena to Ernest H. Blinn. 900

Eiermann, Frederick to William W. St. John. 700

Fink, Amalie to Sigmund Cohn. 500

Fithian, David A. to Mary E. Jackson. 1,000

Frianf, Mayanc admrx. Philipp Frianf to Babette H. Hayman. 4 assigns. nom

Fitzgerald, Maurice to Mary A. Westbury. 500

Gasser, August to Caroline Gasser. nom

Ginsberg, Nathan to Hyman A. Brody. 900

Same to same. 900

Guyer, Eliza to Charles W. Church. 750

Hoffmann, George to Minna Muske. nom

Hubbard, Herman B. and Merwin Rushmore to Jemima N. Dudley. 800

Hinman, Sarah J. to John Y. McKane. nom

Hibben, Harriet F. to Thomas J. Tilney exr. Helen F. Isola. 1,000

Hiltman, Peter J. to Christian W. C. Dreher. 400

Hoagland, Cornelius N. to Clarence H. Eagle et al. exrs. Henry Eagle. 5,000

Hyman, Rebecca to Jacob Cohen and Adolph Hahn. 600

Klots, John T. exr. John Devoo to Willard S. Watson. nom

Kenyon, Whitman to Cornelius E. Donnellon. 7,000

Linton, Edward F. to Thomas Monahan. 2,250

Same to same. 3,000

Levius, Louise K. to The Title Guarantee and Trust Co. 1,000

Losee, Wilmot D. to Earl A. Gillespie. 1,000

Moss, Frank exr. Maltby G. Lane to Charlotte R. Johnson. 4,875

Murphy, George J. to George J. Murphy trustee Mary McGovern. 2,509

Murphy, George J. exr. and trustee Mary McGovern to Mary McGovern. nom

Magilligan, John to Whitman W. Kenyon. 2,600

Maguire, Catharine F. to Martin Bennett. 512

Manneschmidt, Jacob to James Gascoine. 4,000

Marsh, Charles M. to John Andrews, Jr. 684

Miller, Horace W. to Erastus D. Benedict. 2,000

Meise, Henry H. to Elizabeth Meise. nom

Mitchell, Betsey A. to Ringletta Griffith. nom

Nelson, Maud P. to Robert Plaut. 3,500

Oliver, Paul A., Wilkesbarre, Pa., to Susan E Blodgett, Stockbridge, Mass. 18,000

Reilly, Patrick to Edgar W. Youmans. 1,000

Smith, Mary W. to Hamilton Trust Co. nom

Same to Lizzie P. Willis. 250

Sands, Benjamin A. to James W. Gerard and Jenny A. his wife, joint tenants. 8,524

Sands, Frederick to George W. Pearsall. 1,400

Same to same. 1,000

Schmalbeiser, Joseph to Hannah Schmalbeiser. 1,500

The West Brooklyn Land and Improvement Co. to Elizabeth E Butter, Philadelphia, Pa. 7,600

Title Guarantee and Trust Co. to Edward H. R. Lyman trustee. 3,000

Same to Emma L. Knight. 2,700

Same to Kings Co. Trust Co. 6,000

Same to Franklin Trust Co. trustee for Ethelbert I. Low. 1,000

Same to William F. Tooker, Jr. 2,700

Same to Mary A. Knight et al. trustees Henry Knight. 8,000

Same to Franklin Trust Co. trustee Ella C. Ward. 7,000

Same to Brooklyn Society for the Prevention of Cruelty to Children. 1,000

Same to John Lee. 7,500

Union Trust Co. of New York admr. Margaret Langlois to The United States Trust Co., committee Charles A. Langlois. 7,700

Same to same. 4,000
Van Duyne, Theresa to Amy Moody 750
Watson, Willard S. to Lippman Tannenbaum. nom
Wehr, William G. and Charles F. to Louis Bossert. 700
Wemmell, Sallie R. to Catharine F. Maguire. 150
Wilcox, George to Edward A. Quin. 1,000
Watson, William to Barbara Bauer. 200

JUDGMENTS.

In these lists of judgments the names alphabetically arranged, and which are first on each line, are those of the judgment debtor. The letter (D) means judgment for deficiency (*) means not summoned. (†) signifies that the first name is fictitious, real name being unknown. Judgments entered during the week, and satisfied before day of publication, do not appear in this column, but in list of Satisfied Judgments.

NEW YORK CITY.

Sept.
21*Alnelt, William P—Abraham Friedland.......... $173 80
22 Alliger, Richard D—E S Percival.... 117 12
22 Ahlers, George—Leopold Reuther.... 158 33
22 Anderson, Mary I / Anderson, Byron W } Victoria Raymond........ 507 50
23 Allen, William S—D C Burns........ 69 41
23 Asher, Julius—Simon August........ 256 91
24 Alden, John B—Hubley Printing Co (Lim).......... 128 17
24 Arkell, William J—Deyol Lobnas.....1,901 73
25 Ambrose, John K—D D Toal.........1,093 50
25 Anderson, John R—L S Chase........ 620 00
25 Aylward, John W—Richard Vom Hofe.......... 207 15
19 Baumgras, Julius A—Standard Varnish Works.......... 447 10
19 Bailey, William—Helen A Sheriff ... 277 26
19 Blumenthal, Isaac—T H Mulch....... 257 57
19 Bonnell, John H—Nat State Bank of Camden..........4,543 11
21 Borchardt, Ison—W E Trefft......... 180 47
21 Butler, James H—Theodore Wegener 913 06
22 Buckley, John B / Buckley, James J } Robert Gordon... 999 34
22 Blydenburgh, George B—J W Fiske.. 344 00
22 Baumgras, William H—F W Devoe & Co..........1,257 11
22 Brogan, Richard—John Emmons. ... 173 27
22 Burre, William C—Henry McShane Co (Lim).......... 820 33
22 Beck, Frank E—Martin Reynolds.... 375 08
22*Bresinger, Charles—Dundee Chemical Works.......... 41 56
23 Bloomfield, John J—W H Smith......1,172 56
23 the same——the same..........1,210 71
23 the same——Mary A Bloomfield.. 493 81
23 Bacon, William H—J J O'Donohue.. 374 61
23† Burmeister, Mary—J W Hatch, assignee.......... 154 40
23 Baiseley, Albert H—Emeline McEwen.1,551 88
23 Bonnell, John Harper—Bank of N Y Nat Banking Assoc..........1,269 50
23 Beebe, Mary A, admrx Almira Brien—E J McGuire.......... 100 00
23 Bloch, Emily—Solomon Sulzberger.. 242 50
23 Bayer, Frederick W—G W Amsdell.. 208 00
23 Busnitz, Simon—Deborah Rosenzweike..........1,233 93
23 Briggs, William—Charles Brown..... 107 90
24 Beckert, Richard—Lithographing Art Journal Publishing Co.......... 28 80
24 Bohen, Daniel I—Marvin Safe Co.... 51 33
24 Burgess, Robert—Henry Kavanagh.. 103 73
25 Brown, Robert—Gretchen Schwenk.. 411 96
25 Baushman, George—Annie Struve.... 30 00
25 Brennan, Thomas—John Selfridge.... 735 92
25 Ball, Max—Philip Jacobs.......... 822 89
25 Benedict, Henry W—Union Stove Works.......... 562 89
25 Benjamin, Edmund B / Benjamin, Irving J } Joaquin Bishop.... 330 86
25 Brewster, —— —Chatham Nat Bank. 591 52
25 Blake, Patrick J—Edward Tracy.... 525 47
19 Constantine, Charles—Samuel Kohn. 61 63
21 Cohen, Hyman—Thomas Wilson..... 962 20
23 Cox, William C—Eloise Wilder......1,515 74
22 Connor, William M—William Ottman & Co..........5,874 74
23 Cohn, Aaron B—J S Warren......... 183 86
23 Cohn, Walter I / Cohn, William I } Leopold Haas....2,458 07
23 Carter, Richard J / Carter, John P } Rudolph Schmidt 182 51
23 Coit, Edward W—Richard Pancoast. 4,949 83
23 Clark, Beman—Booth Bros.......... 985 27
24 Corson, William—Amelia Westheimer 97 38
24 Carr, Walter / Carr, Delwin B } Robert Krull...... 522 10
24 the same——the same..........1,000 67
24 Caughlin, Emily R—C F Kelly....... 27 80
25 Charpentier, —— —George Hollister. 940 72
25 Chapin, Ezra W—A T Skerry........4,875 88
25 Chaskel, James—C G Burgoyne...... 115 11
25 Connor, William M—Charles Genscher 814 07
19 Demarest, Henry H—Abraham Olmsted.......... 91 52
19 the same——Janet Dunbar....... 189 88
19 Donnelly, Edward—H B Claflin Co..10,123 51
19 the same——the same........costs 68 94
21 Dougherty, Thomas—J L Clarke..... 104 74
21 Dittenhoefer, Meyer—G R Brown.... 478 16
21 Dodge, John S—Benjamin Spier..... 27 50
21 Dunn, John Halstead—W J Leeds.... 182 01
22 Dessau, Simon—Richard Highton....1,968 12
23 Demarest, Henry H—T D Mead...... 591 88
23*Dan, Isaac—Samuel Herrmann....... 120 74
23 Demarest, Henry H—J T Mitchell.... 101 85
23 the same —— Elizabeth Higenbotam.......... 76 98
24 De Peyster, Wilson—F L Requa, assignee..........12,658 28
24 Del Cairo, Francis B—Sidney Marx.. 142 07
24 Donnell, Raymond L—E J Merriam.. 24 13
24 Devantry, Joseph—C P Kalkenbrenner.......... 44 48
25 de Murguiondo, Carter—C A Miller.. 526 72
25 Dolsen, Harriet L—O B Libbey.......1,114 00
25 Dyett, George H—Central Trust Co.. 373 36
25 Doyle, Andrew T—Union Stove Works.......... 563 89
25 Davis, Frederick S—H A Buffum....2,302 40
25 Davis, Lew E—Knickerbocker Printing and Publishing Co.......... 647 20
25 Davidson, George H—Joaquin Bishop. 330 86
25 Devlin, James—G W Venable........ 228 19
19 Eder, Frederick—G P Valentine...... 224 16
21 Ebneter, Johan Jacob—Salomon Ruppel.......... 241 34
21 Eibsen, Herman—Henry Kroger.....1,170 65
22 Ettinger, Charles S—James Whitall.. 197 87
24 Egenberger, Edward—Moses Adler...1,604 58
19 Frost, Fred C—C F Thayer.......... 51 80
19 Farley, Thomas H—Julius Engel..... 262 39
21 Field, William S—J M Field.........2,216 89
21 Fiske, Frederick B—Campbell Printing Press and Mfg Co.......... 76 20
21 the same——the same.......... 131 60
21 Fiske, Frederick B / Fiske, Wilson } the same........ 160 35
23 Fischer, Marie—Frederick Gossweyler 116 50
23 Fuchs, Gustav A——the same....... 26 90
23 Finan, James—Esther Broadbent, extrx.......... 162 07
23 Frank, Nathan—H B Claflin Co...... 186 36
23 Fiske, Wilson—R M Perlee, extrx.... 164 00
23 Freeman, Alfred A—Bank of America 5,468 78
24 Fogg, John C—A J Murray..........3,327 94
25*Freeman, Alfred A—New Britain Nat Bank..........6,025 60
19 Gebhardt, Adolph—E N Tailer....... 429 59
21 Griffin, Charles—J W Ettel.........1,380 16
21 *Gottscho, Isaac / Gottscho, Herman } Thomas Wilson 92 33
21 Goldstein, Moses—H H Muller....... 219 98
21 Greeley, Edward A / *Greeley, William B } Washington Nat Bank.......... 329 00
22 Groschee, William—Eliza Arnold.... 452 75
23 Gordon, Michael—H B Claflin Co.....1,950 04
23 †Guethlein, John / *†Gatzenmeyer, James } Abram Berliner.......... 135 00
24 Goldschmidt, Lottie—D W Dazian... 403 43
24 Gabriel, Michael—Reuben Isaacs..... 436 44
24 Gambee, Isaac T—W H H Childs..... 157 49
25 Goldschmidt, Lottie—D W Dazian ... 191 93
25 Grimes, John—Irene B Roberts, exr. 71 98
19 Howard, Robert—C H Bliss.......... 97 94
19 Hartley, Ray—William Walsmann... 454 42
19 Hall, Thomas J—William Prodgers...2,327 47
19 Hudson, Henry B—F R Utley........ 506 49
19 Harper, William D—Nat State Bank of Camden..........4,543 11
21 Hart, Alexander R—Chatham Nat Bank.......... 868 23
21 *Hendrickson, Richard / Hendrickson, Stephen W } G H Brouwer.....1,024 92
21†Hulse, William L—Mary Bullowa.... 166 60
21 Hirsch, Rosalie—Alfred Lissner...... 528 51
21*Huhn, Henry—J P Murphy......... 346 10
22 Henriques, Alexander F—Abraham Siegel.......... 183 94
22 Hess, George—Metropolitan Telephone and Telegraph Co.......... 77 85
22 Hyers, Samuel V—J W Fiske........ 344 00
22 Hartung, Lorenzo R—C E Pell....... 666 69
22 Hart, Alexander R—Western Nat Bank..........1,250 63
22 Hogue, Camille—M B Edinger........ 163 70
22 Hoyt, Russell P—C G Burgoyne...... 76 18
22 Humphries, Louis G—E M Osborn.... 95 57
22 Harper, William D—Madison Square Bank.......... 699 19
22 Howland, Benjamin T—Unit Co...... 154 16
23 Hart, Alexander R—Bank of N Y Nat Banking Assoc..........1,280 91
23 Harper, William Durbin—Bank of N Y Nat Banking Assoc..........1,260 50
23 the same——Western Nat Bank.. 488 55
23 Hirshhorn, Jacob M—S J Weaver....2,570 97
23 Heineman, Louis—Emanuel Strauss.. 103 60
23 Henriques, Joseph C—John Baehr.... 184 00
23*Haight, Effingham C—Bank of America..........5,468 78
24 Heinzer, Conrad—J R Jackson....... 179 72
24 Hess, Nathan—Commercial Bank.... 179 21
24 Hemsley, Oswald T / Hemsley, Walter } Henry McCready...... 104 82
25 Horowitz, Jacob—Michael Baumgarten.......... 529 04
25*Haight, Effingham C—New Britain Nat Bank..........6,025 60
25 Hopcraft, Alfred—American Artistic Gold Stamping Co.......... 671 75
25 Harvy, James A—E N Crow.......... 85 84
25 Hoffstadt, Isidor—Cyrus Cole........ 109 11
21*Indoe, Walter J—J N Provenzano.... 95 42
23 Ingram, Edwin—A L Dennis......... 254 37
19 Jung, Joe—Quan Ming.............. 241 73
21 Jones, J Dana—Washington Nat Bank.......... 329 00
22 Jacobs, Samuel / Jacobs, Ralph } Henrietta Jacobs...2,517 37
22 Jacobs, Mark—J S Gans............ 306 71
23 Johnson, George—F W Devoe & Co.. 223 31
25 Joeckel, Adam—G F Victor.......... 118 91
25 Jacobson, Frederick—G R Fowler.... 443 41
19 Kelly, Thomas P—Murray Hill Bank. 179 84
21 Kiersted, Guilietta R—Joseph Beck.. 106 69
21 Kalorisky, Moses—H G Marshall, assignee.......... 908 51
22 Kemp, A—Scheuer Bros.............. 37 25
22 Keeney, James C—J H Brewer....... 347 49
23 Kopf, Esther—Edward Siegman..... 273 88
23 Kelly, Thomas F—William Koch..... 96 01
22*Knight, Peter—H R Kelly & Co (Lim) 519 89
23 Koper, Henry—Bank of America....5,468 78
23 Kirsch, John—R B Klussman........ 260 29
24 Kimpton, Edward—T R Hall........ 84 16
24 Knoppler, Charles M—Robert Hoe... 148 37
25 Kierst, John J—A C Jacobson 216 07
25 Kareski, Leo—R B Beaumont Co..... 09 94
25 Kelly, John P / Kelly, Annie } Mount Morris Bank.. 197 82
25 Koper, Henry—New Britain Nat Bank..........6,025 60
25 Kelly, John—W A Fenn............ 175 30
25 Kean, Henry—E N Crow............ 85 84
19 Lohrman, Ernst—F W Davey........ 410 37
21 Lalor, William / Lalor, James C } Jacob Marks....... 381 06
21 Ludwig, Louis—Abraham Friedland. 172 80
21 Low, John W—J H Miller.......... 202 56
21 Lipscher, Herman—Katie Ziegler.... 209 26
21 Lewis, Samuel—H G Marshall, assignee.......... 118 51
22 Lichtwitz, Theodore / Lichtwitz, Frances } N L McCready 105 61
22 Lewis, Jared E—J E Simmons, recvr.10,693 33
22 Levy, Herman L / *Levy, Aaron } Carl Voight.....3,247 90
22 the same——F S Passavant....... 552 73
22 the same——Amory Leland......1,548 44
22 Lester, George—C Kenyon Co........ 178 45
23 Liscomb, Alfred A—F B Russell..... 243 83
23 Laugan, Patrick T / Laugan, Joseph P } C F Droste.....5,580 14
23 Lieke, William—Edward Haeuser... 149 51
23 Lawson, Louise—Ruth A Wallace... 479 43
24 Lassell, William J—Robert Hill.... 637 78
24 Lees, Samuel—C F Webb............ 81 01
25 Lamm, Robert M—Importers' and Trader's Nat Bank..........2,020 10
25†Levy, Charles—Ernest Meyer........ 33 40
19 Morgenweck, William—S C Bohm... 51 67
21 Moen, Edward A—Silas Nourse......2,092 41
21*Martin, Charles E—Alfred Lissner... 538 51
21 Musgrove, Thomas B—J P Murphy... 346 16
22 Main, John—P W Ledoux............ 446 68
23 Moisan, Delphis F—B F Jones....... 109 89
22 Muldoon, William H—William Mullin.......... 164 87
22 Mars, Henrietta A—Edward Davis... 417 98
22 Moses, Max / Moses, Jennie } Julius Bernstein..... 827 24
22 Mauder, Charles T—Rider Engine Co. 571 65
22 Metzner, Harris—Nathan Hutkoff.... 921 94
22 Mutter, Adam—E B Dusenberry..... 51 00
22 Miller, Leopold / Muller, Joseph } Alois Kohn.........1,446 43
23 Marks, Frank R—Washington Nat Bank..........1,843 93
23 Meyer, Siegmund T / Meyer, Arthur L } H N Jarchow..1,477 18
23 the same——the same..........1,086 52
23 the same——W N Coler, Jr......78,365 69
23 the same——the same..........48,361 64
23 the same——the same..........10,700 41
23 the same——H M Coxe..........60,823 73
23 Monachesi, Nicolas—Thomas Tomlinson.......... 68 17
23 Meyer, Siegmund T / Meyer, Arthur L } H N Jarchow.. 595 17
23 Meyer, Frederick—Horace Benjamin. 252 54
24 Muldoon, William H—Max Jakobson. 70 27
24 Maher, Edward—Richard Vom Hofe. 249 29
24 Malone, Neil—Sven Wendein........ 80 18
24*Meyer, John—Amelia Westheimer.... 97 88
24 Mooneliss, Adolph—H C L Peetsch....8,738 98
24 the same——Patrick Cunningham 2,255 17
24 Mars, Henrietta A—David Boyd..... 248 91
25 Meyer, Siegmund T / Meyer, Arthur L } J L Mott Iron Works....11,868 91
25 the same——H N Jarchow......... 232 67
25 Meyer, Arthur L—John Selfridge.... 806 13
25 Mahnken, Henry—F W Mertens..... 546 00
25 Meyer, Arthur L—Northern Nat Bank.......... 731 19
19 McCloskey, Felix—G P Valentine.... 224 16
21 †McKenzie, John / †McPherson, —— } Thomas Wharton.. 35 50
23 McElroy, James—Burr Brewing Co.. 620 55
24 McIntosh, Burr W—H G Hale........ 117 08
24 McKervey, Thomas F / McKervey, John P / exrs and trustees of Mary McGearvey or McKervey } J P McKervey individ and exr and trustee.......... 209 00
24 the same——Mary McKervey et al, exrs and trustees.......... 255 50
24 the same——J H Judge, guard.... 155 75
25 McGilliwie, Alexander L—W J Quinlan, trustee.......... 73 98
25 McCue, Patrick—D M Koehler...... 206 27
25 the same——the same.......... 278 74
25 McEvoy, James—Abram Berliner.... 75 15
25 McFadden, William / *McFadden, George } Peter Barry.. 723 00
25 McCullough, Willis J—W T Kohring. 191 75
21 Neville, James J—Richard Vom Hofe. 99 76
21 the same——David Greenfield.... 88 22
23 Noonan, Lawrence—J W Johnston... 48 50
23 Navarro, Jamie—H R Kelly & Co (Lim).......... 510 82
24 Normoyle, John—W H H Childs..... 157 49
25 Nimmo, Sarah J / *Nimmo, Charles W } Frank Rhoner. 88 74
19 O'Reilly, Michael—Nathaniel Waterbury.......... 193 31
22 Obert, William J—Dundee Chemical Works.......... 41 56
23 O'Brien, John—Booth Bros.......... 983 27
23 O'Meara, Patrick B—Henry McShane Co (Lim).......... 125 33
23 O'Brien, Michael D—Thomas O'Brien. 419 41

23 O'Meara, Patrick B — Lennox Hill Bank........ 276 64
24†O'Gorman, William J—O D Person... 16 44
24 O'Keefe, John D—Jonas Stolts 124 38
24 O'Flaherty, James—H H Schwietering........ 1,149 00
25 Ortmann, Fritz—Elias Hartman...... 187 27
25 O'Flaherty, James—James McCreery. 837 45
19 Pierce, John. Jr—Augusta D Pierce.. 802 82
19 Prodgers, Augustus D—William Prodgers........ 2,327 47
21 Peet, Alexander J—Christian Koenig. 48 73
21 the same——M F Mooney........ 47 20
22 Pierce, John—W A White........ 1,567 83
22 the same——the same........ 1,052 41
22 Perrin, Henry E—S E Harris........ 58 65
22 Percy, Townsend—George Everall.... 565 05
22 Pyle, Alexander—Robert Prentice.... 78 50
23 Pineiro, Modesto—Richard Gurney... 388 93
25 Potts, George—G A Twele........ 258 04
25 Provost, Frederick—Catharine A Provost........ 1,576 12
25 the same——the same........ 1,913 00
25 the same——the same........ 1,778 92
25 Petit, Edward A—Julius Lippman... 186 43
25 Pfister Book Binding Co—T F Gane.. 150 37
21 Roth, Joseph—Katie Ziegler........ 299 26
21 Ress, Janet E Runtz—H B Kimball.. 275 09
21 Rose, Hattie—Joseph Rohman........ 53 41
21 Rutherfoord, John W—J E Simmons, recvr........ 826 07
22 Rosenthal, Sarah—Leo Stein........ 79 17
22 Russell, Mary A—D F Ellis 422 08
22 Ryan, Daniel—W H Flitner, exr..... 192 25
22 Rankin, Jacob—Simon Silverstein.... 67 50
22 Reid, David—E M Osborn........ 95 67
23 Rehm, Stephen—V Loewers Gambrinus Brewery Co........ 75 47
23 Rosenfeld, Bernhard—Samuel Herrmann........ 120 74
23 Rosenthal, Louis—H B Claflin Co.... 1,950 04
23 Ramhorst, William—Thomas Patten. 39 50
23 Rezau, Joseph O—J M Riley........ 382 12
23 Russell, William R—M L Chamberlain........ 91 38
24 Russo, Domenico—Jos Kuntz Brewing Co........ 416 70
24 Reno, Louis—W A White........ 70 94
24 Rasquin, Robert G—Robert Hoe.... 148 37
24 Roberts, Walter J—J E Simmons, recvr........ 10,002 21
24 Reilly, Catharine, admrx Edward Reilly—William Fiss........ costs 120 60
24 Reisenberger, Alexander / Reisenberger, Isidor } Jacob Loewenthal 206 67
24 Ryan, John / Robinson, Thomas D } J P McKervey, individ, exr and trustee. 299 00
24 the same——Mary McKervey et al, exrs and trustees........ 255 50
24 the same——J H Judge........ 155 75
25 Rice, James—W A Fenn........ 175 30
25 Robinson, Morris—J D Eisenstein.. 473 24
25 Ramhorst, William F—P H Meier... 16 07
19 Seidenberg, Henry—D Hirsch & Co.. 99 92
19 Schell, Theodore C—Bowery Savings Bank........ (D) 933 09
19 Sheehan, John—Calvin Tompkins Co. 290 98
21*Sachs, Louis—Abraham Friedland.. 172 80
21 Schneider, Louis H—Press Publishing Co........ 371 11
21 *Sonn, Julius / Sonn, Herman } Thomas Wilson.... 266 69
21 Straus, Louis—Lenox Hill Bank..... 222 14
21 Schierenbeck, John / Schierenbeck, Frederick } Richard Vom Hofe 153 77
21 Sommer, Moritz—O J Boessneck..... 2,667 06
21 Schulhoff, Henry—E B Colby........ 124 00
21 Short, John C—J E Simmons........ 2,345 29
21 Steiner, Emma R—Thomas McIlvaine 141 70
22 Snodgrass, James—Swampmills Excelsior Co........ 130 79
22 St Leon, John—Catharine M Boyd.... 620 14
22 Shoen, Charles A—Eliza Arnold...... 452 75
23 Stampfer, William—Peter Okkerse.. 206 89
22 Scharmann, Frederick—Samuel Robert........ 672 79
23 Solomon, Ephraim—Leopold Haas.. 2,458 07
23 Steinmetz, Elizabeth—J L Mott Iron Works........ 459 44
23*Silberblat, Gerson — Samuel Herrmann........ 120 74
23 Schwab, Gabriel / Schwab, Nathan / Schwab, Abraham / Schwab, Leo L } Amory Leland. 5,829 09
23 Scott, Samuel, Jr—L K Smith....... 425 38
23 Stark, Isidor / Stark, Edward J / Stark, Gustav } Martha L Colby... 520 64
23 Schwarting, Charles W—Richard Uffelman........ 735 30
23 Sonin, Solomon—Arcadius Soltz..... 122 85
23 Seekamp, John H—John Baehr....... 235 00
23 Sieman, William F—Knickerbocker Brewing Co........ 196 00
23 Slattery, Philip M—Pelham Hod Elevating Co........ 150 00
23*Stubenrauch, August—John Baehr... 184 00
24 Schwab, Nathan—A F D'Oench...... 137 30
24 Sturtevant, Edgar F—J W Mangam. 86 71
24 Scribner, Gilbert H / Scribner, Howard } A J Murray.... 3,327 94
24 Sykes, Charles P—G P Rowell........ 171 04
24 Sneckner, William H—Robert Krull. 522 26
24 the same——the same........ 1,006 67
24 Sommer, Moritz—M L Stieglitz....... 708 70
24 Stoddard, Henry L—J E Simmons, recvr........ 9,550 35
24 Stevenson, Vernon K—W O Wyckoff. 36 40
24 Sharkey, Albert G—Brooklyn Union Elevated Railway Advertising Co.. 219 75
25 Stroub, Michael—Herman Gampert.. 554 94
25 Stinson, Daniel—Patrick Mahoney... 100 87
25 Schmidt, Gustave—F W Mertens..... 532 78
19 Smith, George C—Martin Brock...... 82 50
22 Smith, Frank E—Real Estate Record Assoc........ 295 30
19 The Willard Metal Co—William Eddison........ 377 27
21 Welch Fracker Co—H J Weber...... 412 91
22 Fibrone Mfg Co—Metropolitan Telephone and Telegraph Co........ 45 76
22 The American Finance Co—J E Simmons, recvr........ 24,126 45
22 The Willard Metal Co—C F Oxley.... 607 33
22 J H Bonnell & Co (Lim)—Western Nat Bank........ 1,350 62
22 Willard Metal Co—G I Cook........ 83 46
22 The Addressing, Duplicating and Mailing Co (Lim)—Palmer Chemical Co. 107 36
22 the same——the same........ 107 36
22 J H Bonnell & Co (Lim)—Madison Square Bank........ 699 19
23 Marks Adjustable Folding Chair Co—Washington Nat Bank........ 1,843 93
23 The Lexington Improvement Co—H N Jarchow........ 1,086 57
23 The D Frisbie Co—Elizabeth W Chanler........ 837 14
23 J H Bonnell & Co (Lim)—Bank of N Y Nat Banking Assoc........ 1,269 50
23 The Mechanics' and Traders' Bank—Michael Noonan........ 1,610 02
23 J H Bonnell & Co (Lim)—Western Nat Bank........ 817 13
23 the same——the same........ 486 55
24 The Fibrone Mfg Co—Simeon Hartley........ 1,561 59
24 The McWilliams Printing Co—Campbell Printing Press and Mfg Co..... 75 64
24 American Diamond Rock Boring Co—Western Nat Bank........ 1,037 76
24 the same——the same........ 652 83
25 The Metropolitan Railway Co / The Manhattan Railway Co } Sophia Frank.... 1,047 28
25 the same——Rosa Scheier........ 1,118 59
25 the same——Isaac Lubin........ 1,047 28
25 the same——Barbara Fahrbach.. 1,290 84
25 the same——Peter Mager........ 1,407 17
25 the same——Gustav Zimmer...... 1,249 92
25 the same——Eliza A Burggraf et al 143 93
25 the same——Maria L Marshall... 1,129 70
25 Metropolitan Electric Signal Co—W B Pope........ 119 87
25 American Diamond Rock Boring Co—F M Pierce........ 1,113 19
25 Pneumatic Dynamite Gun Co—J E Simmons, recvr........ 42,668 35
21 Tilden, Beverly Bingham—John Patterson........ 109 58
22*Thompson, George W—Robert Gordon 199 34
24 Tompkins, Charles H—Western Nat Bank........ 1,037 76
25 Thompson, James—Patterson Bros... 378 45
25 Tarr, Horace G H—F M Pierce..... 1,113 19
21 Vondy, Thomas D—J N Provenzano.. 95 42
23 Valentine, Robert H C—Chatham Nat Bank........ 702 65
25 *Vlasto, Demetrius / Vlasto, Solon J } Metropolitan Telephone and Telegraph Co...... 54 88
19 Van Tuyl, Andrew P, Jr—J B Bloomingdale........ 408 55
24 Van Cleve, Garret—Charles Schneider 242 34
25 Van Cleve, Garret—Henry McShane Co (Lim)........ 621 24
25 Vandewater, Samuel H—J E Simmons, recvr........ 292 03
21 Walker, John—N Y Gas Fixture Co.. 884 10
21 Winterroth, Joseph M — Benjamin Gillespie........ 80 90
21 Wells, William H—Washington Nat Bank........ 329 00
22 Wiley, John W—P W Ledoux........ 446 08
23 Wilkes, George / Wilkes, Lizzie T } H N Jarchow..... 595 17
23 Weinhauer, Charles F—L K Smith... 69 20
23 Weiss, William—Edward Siegman.... 273 88
23 Williams, May—Kate Williams...... 52 50
23 Wise, Isaac—S J Weaver........ 2,570 97
23 Wood, Henry B—S G Dorland........ 256 63
24 Whitehead, Edward—M J Lasar..... 159 07
24 West, Eleanor S—George Barrie...... 144 13
25 Wetherell, Frederick—J H Doering.. 105 37
25 Whitbed, Marshall—James Slater.... 206 51
25†Wadsworth, Emil M—E M Pritchard 80 00
24 Zimmermann, Henry—Frederick Betz 34 87
24 Zimmerman, Ernest—Thomas Nash.. 189 42
24 Zeidler, Martin—D W Dazian........ 402 43

KINGS COUNTY.

Sept.
18 Adams, Frank E—J C French........ $775 55
19 Atkinson, John H G—E L Goodsell.. 1,862 53
23 Ahlers, George E—L Reuther........ 158 33
18 Boyle, John E—R Vom Hofe........ 48 83
18 Brown, Harvey H—Charlotte A Holcomb........ 60 56
19 Baird, William, Jr—W Smith........ 48 25
22 Blum, Adolph / Blum, George / Blum, Mrs George } W H Juster..... 430 54
22 Blydenburgh, George B—J W Fiske.. 344 00
23 Blazo, Augustus—W H Young....... 2,446 25
23 Brower, George V, assignee Howard, Schackelton & Co—W M Ducker... 283 99
24 Brown, Heyman—First Nat Bank.... 325 18
24 Burtis, Nathaniel H—C Collins....... 482 72
18 Connelly, John—F Norman........ 495 86
21 Collins, William C—H Sugerman.... 27 85
22 Cotte, Augustus S—G T Bowler...... 88 43
23 Cooper, Charles——the same........ 2,446 25
23 Carroll, Gus M—Kate M Carroll, $40 per month on 7th day of each month during natural life of plaintiff, from April 29, 1891........ — —
18 Donnelly, Edward—H B Claflin Co.. 3,803 43
19 Dusenbury, Charles / Dusenbury, Thomas } Elizabeth Dusenbury........ 943 14
22 Deubert, Henry—M Knauth........ 238 94
24 Denton, Frank—Sarah L Denton..... 1,500 00
24 Downs, Peter—Howard & Fuller Brewing Co........ 379 33
18 Finucan, Thomas—G Vander Borgh. 77 87
23 Frank, Edward C—J Leffler........ 272 27
23 Froelich, George—H May........ 174 86
24†Frankenstein, "Morris"—D Block... 37 25
18 Gleichman, William—S S Hatt, assignee........ 116 00
18 Gass, August F—C Koch........ 193 19
19 Glock, Carl—Gans & Miller........ 171 34
19 Good, Samuel R—J Foley........ 439 16
21 Griffin, Charles—J W Ettel........ 1,380 16
21 Gorman, John M—D G Yuengling, Jr, B Co........ 1,202 89
23 Groesbee, William—Eliza Arnold.... 452 75
23 Gibby, George H—N Tebbetts.....(D) 7,019 02
24 Goldschmidt, Lottie—D W Dazian... 402 43
21 Huwer, John W—Homer Brooke.... 10 00
22 Hart, Alexander R—Chatham Nat Bank........ 868 23
22 Herbute, George—W H Juster........ 430 54
22 Hyers, Samuel V—J W Fiske........ 344 00
23 Hants, Benjamin—N Bernstein........ 188 69
23 Hoffman, John E—L Bossert........ 217 72
23 Howard, Schackelton & Co, assignee of—W M Ducker........ 286 99
24 Howard, William B—T W Cummings 120 84
24 Heinemann, Louis—E Strauss........ 103 60
24 Heffner, Conrad / Heffner, his wife Elizabeth } C F Diehlmann... 80 75
21 Jung, Joe—Q Ming........ 241 73
23 Jacobs, Mark—J S Gans........ 396 71
24 Johnson, George—F W Devoe........ 222 31
18 Kemp, A—Scheuer Brothers........ 37 25
18 Kirkland, William—J C French........ 775 55
23 Kellogg, Frederick L—L W Tice.... 50 46
24 Kirsch, John—R B Klussman........ 260 29
21 Lyons, Annie—J Loader........ 70 48
21 Lyon, Thomas—J Mizl........ 53 00
22 Lucas, Melona—N Dannenhofer...... 2,869 74
18 Malhmken, George—J Ruppert........ 964 50
18 †Munger, "Alfred" S / Munger, Louis A } Isaac I Booth.. 132 26
18 Mackie, Edward—Cordner & Williamson........ 128 04
19 Mcinoke, Mary M—E Jackson........ 458 45
18 O'Farrell, Henry P—E E Duryea..... 248 92
19 Oriol, George M—H W Sundermann.. 313 29
24 O'Brien, Daniel—F Adee........ 187 18
24 O'Hara, John T—J V Dubernell...... 42 40
18 Prasse, Henry B—C Krieger........ 51 25
21 Preston, Charles W—T Finan........ 405 00
22 Pierce, John—W A White........ 1,052 41
22 the same——the same........ 1,567 83
18 Rose, Stephen / Rose, George } L Bossert........ 161 90
19 Robbins, Thomas H—Albany Venetian Blind Co........ 43 28
22 Ronginsky, Pincus—S Spero........ 53 35
23 Ravkin, Jacob—S Silverstein........ 67 50
23 Rodegerdts, William A—G J Siemers. 322 68
24 Reno, Louis—W A White........ 70 94
24 Reardon, Michael J—J M Koehler.... 94 69
18 Smith, Herman H—J D Frost........ 143 36
18 Sefferin, Charles—C Koch........ 193 19
19 Schwarze, John / Schwarze, Elizabeth } R H Thomas.. 54 75
19 the same——F M Pierce........ 54 79
19 Stephenson, Anna—Albany Perforated Wrapping Paper Co........ 89 11
19 Schouleber, Charles—N Bernstein.... 259 25
19 Schroeder, Frederick—E H Nearing.. 90 03
22 Samuelson, Samuel——the same...... 53 35
22 Specker, William—C Cohn........ 28 10
23 Schoen, Charles A—Eliza Arnold..... 452 75
23 Schult, Peter M / Schult, Anna } C Sundheim........ 335 90
23 Schackelton, Howard & Co, assignee of—W M Ducker........ 286 99
19 Thomas, Clara—W H Birck, admr... 25 97
19 Thomas, Samuel E—B C Anderson... 384 02
19 Thompson, James—C H Briggs....... 112 42
22 The Eureka Glass Annealing Works—N Dannenhofer........ 2,869 74
23 The assignee of Howard, Schackelton & Co——the same........ 286 99
21 Van Sickle, P A—W A Blauvelt..... 72 52
24 Viemeister, John B—M Weis........ 627 67
22 Wilke, Martha—W H Juster........ 430 54
22 Wilson, Eugene H—Drayton Burrill, exr........(D) 1,854 26
22 the same——the same........(D) 1,976 41
22 the same——the same........(D) 1,885 72
23 Weaver, Isaac N—H Fitzgerald & Co. 13 70
24 Wohlfarth, Charles—H E Kane...... 18 78
24 Ziedler, Martin—D W Dazian........ 402 43

SATISFIED JUDGMENTS.

NEW YORK.

September 19 to 25—Inclusive.

Brown, Frances R—Rose M Sprague. (1886)... $291 99
Same——G F Habb. (1886)........ 261 98
Behrmann, Hermann—S T Willets (G H Behrmann, by assign). (1889)........ 607 18
Same——same. (1889)........ 305 83
Same——same. (1890)........ 173 50
Same——J C B Matthews (same, by assign)... (1890)........ 226 31
Bruner, Joseph C—P G Wisely. (1890)........ 373 41
*Bonnell, John Harper—Chatham Nat Bank. (1891)........ 898 53
Carner, William W—P G Wisely. (1890)........ 373 41
‡Crouk, Justine M, admrx Andrew W Morgan—T F Mason, recvr. (1891)........ 346,284 61
Cairnes, James / Crandall, William E } John Bell. (1887)...... 110 60
Clayton, Michael—Edward Baker. (1891)..... 33 77

Dunn, Thomas and Mary A—Sheppard Knapp. (1885)........ 264 17
Darling, William S—First Nat Bank of Hazleton, Pa. (1890)........5,066 56
Edelson, Abraham—W T Hance. (1891)........1,296 94
Fox, Charles J, Michael and G Louis—S W Kent. (1891)........1,104 16
Geery, David R—Lewis Ferguson. (1888)........ 27 99
*Gillespie, Benjamin—J M Winterroth. (1891). 80 90
Glover, John M—Zerlina Rosenfield. (1891)........ 625 88
Graham, James H—J H Soteroadis. (1891)........ 68 50
Goldstein, Louis—B M Feldman. (1888........ 167 56
Hart, William T A and William J—Andrew Moltzen. (1891)........ 139 61
*Harper, William D—Chatham Nat Bank. (1891)........ 896 58
*Kley, Anna C—Michael Maloughney. (1891). 84 59
Katz, Samuel—Sylvester Swain. (1891)........ 90 01
‡Kilpatrick, Walter F—Highland Nat Bank of Newburgh. (1890)........ 642 40
‡Same——same. (1890)........1,497 12
‡Same——same. (1890)........1,085 31
Lawrence, Charles W—W G Ross. (1887)........12,159 68
Lyons, Thomas—Sheppard Knapp. (1885)........ 254 17
Lane, Belle and Elliot T—E M Earle. (1885)........ 563 88
Mars, Hannah O—J B Kniffin. (1891)........ 99 09
Mars, Henrietta A—Edward Davis. (1891)........1,500 00
Martin, Walter S—Andrew Moltzen. (1891)........ 139 61
Merriam, William S—P G Wisely. (1890)........ 378 41
Monaseh, Fannie—Morris Eschwege. (1891)........ 49 26
*Murphy, Charles—People State N Y. (1888)........1,000 00
*O'Neill, William—People State N Y. (1888)........1,000 00
‡Plummer, John F—New England Co. (1890)........155,055 83
‡Plummer, John F and Albert T——same. (1890)........158,163 41
‡Same——Rockville Nat Bank. (1890)........20,291 91
‡Same——George Leask. (1890)........5,041 78
‡Same——same. (1890)........9,309 48
‡Same——Savings Bank of Rockville. (1890)........5,165 25
‡Same——Mount Vernon Nat Bank of Boston. (1890)........5,201 65
‡Same——Leather Mfrs Nat Bank. (1890)........25,442 25
‡Same——New Britain Nat Bank. (1890)........5,084 17
‡Same——First Nat Bank of Rockville. (1890)........5,096 24
Plummer, John F—First Nat Bank of Hazelton, Pa. (1890)........5,212 77
Plummer, Albert J——same. (1890)........5,066 56
*Quick, Woodward F—C R Willson. (1891)........ 241 46
Robinson, Morris and Isaac—Abraham Zubrinsky. (1891)........ 327 97
Smith, Archibald—Philip Bierschenk. (1891)........ 144 24
Stoddart, George B—Herman Passavant. (1887)........ 389 39
Saul, Julius, Charles and Isidor—J P Cahen. (1889)........ 783 96
Saul, Charles, Isidor and Julius—Frederick Bergner, Jr. (1889)........ 105 25
Same——Philip Voss. (1889)........ 317 33
Same——Henry Rice. (1889)........ 214 76
Same——B H Goodman. (1889)........ 265 41
Same——Henry Lewis. (1889)........ 244 67
Same——Michael Rosenthal. (1889)........ 362 38
Same——G F Vietor. (1889)........ 223 09
Same——Philip Voss. (1889)........ 526 75
Same——Jennie Plouskyer. (1890)........ 223 27
Same——Daniel Miller. (1890)........ 188 77
Same——Julius Sawalsky. (1890)........ 86 62
Same——Isaac Hirsch. (1890)........ 183 20
Same——F C Bill. (1891)........ 250 54
Same——Max Wolff. (1889)........3,550 15
Trimm, Frederick M—J B Hance. (1885)........ 422 66
Tobias, Frank H—W E Phillips. (1891)........ 94 87
Van Eupen, Theodore—Clara Pausewang. (1891)........ 169 18
Van Voorhis, Charles—Sven Wendelin. (1890). 69 96
Weaver, George B and James H—John Elsey. (1889)........ 149 16
Webster, Horace—W G Ross. (1887)........12,159 68

*Vacated by order of Court. †Suspended on Appeal. ‡Released. §Reversal. ‖Satisfied by Execution.

KINGS COUNTY.

September 18 to 24—Inclusive.

Brinkerhoff, Aaron—L I Doyle. (1877)........ $367 13
Caprari, J—J Van Nostrand. (1891)........ 290 43
Clover, Bertrand—J Ashley. (1891)........ 165 15
Gould, Edwin—C F Hommel. (1891.) (Order of Court)........ 494 00
Hoffmann, Henry—Heinbockle & Co. (1888)........ 504 40
Harris, George S——same. (1891.) (Order of Court)........ 494 00
Johnson, Nicholas J—F Ludlam. (1889)........ 296 65
Kinkel, Konrad—H Loeffler. (1891)........ 46 04
O'Shea, George H—Dixon & Hayes. (1891)........ 875 44
Pilcher, Joseph M——same. (1891.) (Order of Court)........ 494 00
Southard, Harry D——same. (1891)........ 875 44
Skelly, John—S Williamson. (1891)........ 46 10
Thomas, Eddy T—Sarah Wilson. (1891)........5,328 00

MECHANICS' LIENS.

NEW YORK CITY.

Sept.

19 One Hundred and Eighteenth st, s s, 240 w 4th av, 100x—. Sims' Lumber Co. agt Samuel Harris, owner, and Bernhard Ginsburg, contractor........$1,552 31
19 Thirteenth st, Nos. 316-326 E., n s, 150x100. Filippo Quaglino agt Raffaele Pasta, owner and contractor........ 32 20
21 Kingsbridge road, e s, 50 s Nindham pl, 40x95. E. C. Schoonmaker agt James Hodge, owner and contractor........1,858 20
21 Davidson av, w s, 165 n Highbridge road, 60x100. C. E. Gates & Co. agt Adelaide A. Yeandle, owner and contractor........ 408 76
21 Park av, Nos. 1169 and 1171, e s, 117.5 n 92d st, 33.7x80. Richardson & Boynton Co. agt Alan D. Kenyon, owner, and The N. Y. Lumber and Wood Working Co., contractor........ 178 00
21 Seventy-eighth st, Nos. 206-212, s s, 100 w Amsterdam av, 75x102.2. Daniel Cooney agt Clegg & Richards, debtors, and Arthur Boehmer, owner........ 6 30
21 Same property. John Hickey agt same........ 22 50
21 Same property. Thomas Byrnes agt same. 5 30
21 Same property. Thomas Hanly agt same.. 21 94
21 Same property. Mathew Lynch agt same. 11 20
2[illegible] Bainbridge av, w s, 452.2 n Travers st, 79x125. J. M. Reid agt Eunice C. Lawrence, owner and contractor........ 74 00

22 West End av, Nos. 40-54; Tenth av, Nos. 902-916; Sixty-sixth st, Nos. 201-247; Sixty-seventh st, Nos. 202-248 } the block. Ritchie & Henrikson agt John Ruck, owner and contractor........5,193 00
22*West End av, n w cor 83d st, 96x100. Frank Falk agt Samuel Colcord, owner, and Gerald L. Schuyler, contractor........8,940 95
22 Park av, Nos. 885 and 887, n e cor 78th st, 75x60. Isaac Goldstein agt August F. Schwarzler, owner and contractor........ 119 50
22 One Hundred and First st, Nos. 75 and 77 W. A. R. Becker agt William M. Walsh, owner and contractor........ 282 90
22 One Hundred and Fifth st, n s, 280 w Park (4th) av, 50x—. Thomas Dixon agt John O'Connor, owner and contractor........ 800 00
22 Fifty-seventh st, s s, 175 w 6th av, 75x100. Nathaniel Wise agt Louis N. Phelps, owner, and Thomas J. and William Walsh, contractors........ 962 95
23 Pelham av, s s, 58.2 e Hoffman st, 25x108. Douglas, Dolan & McMaster agt Ida M. Ayars, owner and contractor........ 73 00
23 Thirty-first st, No 510, s s, 118.9 w 8th av, 16.9x98.9. Cornelius Ford agt Ephraim and Susannah Posner, owners, and Ephraim Posner, contractor........ 144 37
23 One Hundred and Fifteenth st, s s, 275 e 8th av, 200x100. Thomas Halpin agt Conrad Muller, Jr., and Annie Hauff, owners, and Peter S. Halpin, contractor........ 60 00
23 Pearl st, No. 546, n s, 244.8 e Broadway, 24x95. E. H. Ogden & Co. agt —— Leaycraft, owner, and Priebe & Co., contractors........ 210 08
23 Ninety-eighth st, n s, 475 w 8th av, 25x100.11. Steindler & Hahn agt Gregory Leahy and Agnes Reynolds, owners, and Frank Reynolds and —— Foster, contractors........ 58 85
23 Fifty-eighth st, No. 4, s s, 185 w 5th av, 40x100.5. Jacob Winter agt Charles B. Alexander, owner, and George Chase, contractor........ 208 08
23 Thirty-fifth st, No. 41, n s, 375 e 6th av, 18.9x98.9. R. A. Patterson agt Janette Pirsson, owner and contractor........ 96 20
24 Sixty-fifth st, Nos. 29 and 31, n s, 200 w 8th av, 75x100. E. P. Creamer agt James O'Brien, owner; Frederick Rondel and Wallace & George A. Hunter, contractors 38 25
24 Same property. L. W. Lashier agt same.. 35 00
24 Same property. Joseph Treubig agt same. 16 50
24 Same property. August Poline agt same.. 22 67
24 Same property. Frederick Pulvermacher agt same........ 11 50
24 Seventh av, e s, 24.11 s 134th st, 50x—. James Cairnes agt James Riley and Teresa Coogan, owners and contractors. (Continued from Sept. 25, 1890)........1,250 00
24 Twelfth st, n s, 200 e 1st av, 24.4x—. Henry Eugesser agt Jeannette Weil, owner, and Michael Lang, contractor........ 339 35
24 Same property. Michael Lang agt Jeannette Weil, owner and contractor........ 780 35
24 Seventy-fourth st, n s, 275 e Amsterdam av, 150x—. A. R. Ackert and August Schroeder agt John and Joshua Coar, owners and contractors........ 100 00
25 Third av, No. 827, e s, 80.4 s 51st st, 20.1x75.6. James Fay agt Thomas S. Smith, owner and contractor........ 600 00
25 One Hundred and Fourteenth st, n s, 495 w 5th av, 75x100. Martin & Co. agt Peter Biringer and Emil Haenschen, owners and contractors........ 72 00
25 One Hundred and Eighteenth st, s s, 60 e Madison av, 100x100. Graham & Bunt agt Samuel Harris, owner, and same and Mary Mascha, contractors........ 800 00
25 Eighth av, No. 2140, e s, 60 s 116th st, 25x100. Jos. P. Carney & Co., agt J. Heumann, owner and contractor........ 179 70
25 Greenwich av, No. 30, e s, 114.8 n 10th st, 25x—. Samuel and C. H. Nichols agt T. Kelly, owner, and S. I. Acken, contractor, and Phoenix Iron Co. of Trenton, N. J., sub-contractor........ 188 23
25 Sixty-fifth st, Nos. 29 and 31, n s, 200 w 8th av, 50x—. R. H. Gerstle agt James O'Brien, owner, and Rondell & Co., owners and contractors........ 154 28
25 West End av, e s, 25 n 92d st, 50x—. Kaufman Simon agt Jacob B. Tallman, owner, and Thomas J. McLoughlin, contractor........ 250 00

*Editor Record and Guide:

Referring to the lien of Frank Falk against the buildings northwest corner 83d street and West End avenue would state that he has no just claim for such a lien. He made a contract on June 5, 1891, to excavate the lots and sewers in six weeks at certain prices, $1,000 to be paid when that amount of work had been done, the balance to be paid for when all the work was complete. I hold his receipt for the $1,000 paid on July 8, 1891. The balance of the work will not be completed for a month yet if he continues at his present pace. I have a claim against him for damages and for expenses paid on his account. I shall bond the lien and contest his claim to my utmost.

GERALD L. SCHUYLER.

KINGS COUNTY.

Sept.

18 Thatford av, e s, 100 s Glenmore av, 50x100. The Wyandance Brick and Terra Cotta Co. agt Handler & Balsom, owners, and Patrick Creegan, contractor........$151 98
18 Same property. Potts Bros. agt same owners and contractors........ 323 87
18 Bergen st, s s, 100 w Hopkinson av, 25x127.6. George Scheinfeld agt Rosa Rosenfeld, owner and contractor........2,205 00
18 Eighth av, e s, extends from 15th to 16th st, 200x160. Leslie M. Irish agt Edwin J. Bedell, William J. Fitzpatrick, Thomas McCann and William Martin, owners, and Edwin J. Bedell, contractor........ 27 12
18 Bergen st, s s, 100 w Hopkinson av, 25x100. Michael Newman agt Rosa Rosenfeld devisee of Martin G. Johnson, owner and contractor........ 45 01
18 Dumont av, s s, 25 e Thatford av, 25x100. Earl A. Gillespie agt Isaac and Solestina Y. Scheen, owner, and George Shenfeld, contractor........ 279 82
18 Stone av, e s, 200 n Blake av, 50x100. Frank J. Dilzer agt Louis Regenbogen, Samuel Davis, William Schechtel and Louis Cohen, owners and contractors........ 53 00
19 India st, s s, 275 e Oakland st, 25x100. Thomas Davies agt Randall McDonald, owner and contractor........ 368 90
19 Garfield pl, n s, 90 w 7th av, 150x100. Richard K. Cooke agt John M. Styles and Edward L. Beekman, owners, and John Elder, Jr........3,985 00
19 Christopher av, e s, 175 s Eastern Parkway, 25x100. John Schaeble agt Joseph Berger & Co., contractor........ 200 00
19 Second st, n s, 90.7 w 7th av, 80x100. B. S. Phillips agt Roderick Von Graff and John Hallaran, owners, and Roderick Von Graff, contractor........ 91 00
19 Bergen st, s s, 50 w Hopkinson av, 150x130. W. W. Rope & Co. agt Rosa and Jonas Rosenfield and George Schoenfield, owners and contractors........ 490 24
19 Willoughby av, No. 766, s s, 179.6 w Lewis av, 20x100. Jacob Friedmann agt Jacob Bisson, owner, and Fred. J. Clough, contractor........ 240 00
19 Bergen st, s s, 290 e Brooklyn av, 100x100. Curry Mfg. Co. agt Joseph M. Pilcher, owner, and Theodore Dingeldein and Joseph M. Pilcher & Co., contractors........ 880 00
19 Fulton st, s e cor Ashford st, 25x100. John C. Creveling agt Mrs. Liebow, owner, and Charles Liebow, contractor........ 29 15
19 Broadway, n e cor Cooper st, 80x80. Lorillard Brick Works Co. agt John A. Loucks, owner and contractor. (Refiled by order of Court)........1,237 60
19 Glenada pl, s w cor Decatur st, 100x85. William G. Paxton & Co. agt William W. Reynolds, owner and contractor........ 100 00
21 Railroad av, w s, 75 n Griffin pl, 50x100. Wyandance Brick and Terra Cotta Co. agt Charles Lohrentz and Stephen Mafera, owner and contractor........ 160 56
21 Same property. Potts Bros. agt same, owner and contractor........ 59 01
21 Liberty av, s s, 50 w Watkins st, 100x100. Same agt Charles W. Tomlinson and J. Y. Cochran, owner and contractor........ 286 99
21 Eastern Parkway, s s, 75 w Thatford av, 25x100. Same agt —— Kopilauski and ano., owner, and Carl Becker, contractor........ 120 00
21 Watkins st, w s, 250 s Sutter av, 25x100. James O'Connor agt Solomon Morris, owner, and Abraham Stone, contractor.. 200 00
21 First st, s s, 305 w 5th av, three four-story double brick flats. E. F. Hale agt W. S. Hale, owner, and E. F. Hale, contractor.. 168 26
21 St. James pl, w s, 75 s Fulton st, 50x70. Hugh J. Barron agt George R. Brown, owner and contractor........ 600 00
22 Prospect pl, Nos. 729 and 731. Oscar Hammander agt John O'Toole, owner, and Powderly & Murphy and John F. Tilman, contractors........ 22 00
22 Seventh st, s s, 297.6 w 4th av, 50.4x100. Jacob May agt Mary E. Miller, owner, and George M. Miller, contractor........ 223 45
23 Columbia Heights, w s, 188.1 n Pierrepont st, 37.8x100 to Furman st, x27.9x150.3. Edison Electric Illuminating Co. agt Mary S. Hewsey, owner and contractor........ 412 00
23 First st, s s, 305 w 5th av, 108x100. John H. Gass agt William S. Hale, owner, and Miller & Anderson, contractors........ 86 71
23 Sixteenth st, n s, 192.11 w 8th av, 75x100. Same agt William Wingerath, owner, and Miller & Anderson, contractors........ 64 44
23 Second st, e s, 90.7 n 7th av, 80x100. Martin Connaughton agt Roderick Von Graf and John Hollaran, owners and contractors........ 22 00
24 Sheffield av, n e cor Glenmore av, 100x100. Benjamin C. Smith agt John Victory, owner, and Charles Farrell, contractor.. 57 01
24 Pulaski st, n s, 100 w Sumner av, 380.6x100. E. & F. Barbig agt Fred. Hower Brewing Co. (Lim.), owner and contractor........1,577 77
24 Glenada pl, w s, 50 s Decatur st, 50x85. Frederick B. Langston agt Mary E. Reynolds, owner, and William W. Reynolds, contractor........ 312 50
24 Cropsey av, n s, 160 w Bay 19th st, 165.9x415x irreg., New Utrecht. John Regan agt The New York Outing Club, owner and contractor........1,288 00

SATISFIED MECHANICS' LIENS.

NEW YORK CITY.

Sept.

19 Av C, Nos. 217 and 219. Emily Beyel agt Cile Rubenstein. (Lien filed April 22, '90) $144 00
21 West End av, s w cor 103d st, 100.11x79.6; One Hundred and Third st, s s, 79.6 w West End av, 80x—........ Henry Huber & Co. agt Elizabeth Steinmetz. (Nov. 14, 1890)........1,302 95
21 Same property. James McLaughlin agt same and Welcome Steinmetz. (July 8, 1891)........ 777 58
22 West End av, s w cor 103d st, 100.11x159.10. James McLaughlin agt Elizabeth Steinmetz. (July 6, 1891)........ 777 58
23 One Hundred and Fourteenth st, s s, 300 w 1st av, 30x90. Hoopes & Shipman agt Joseph F. Gallagher and George Brietenbach. (Aug. 31, 1891)........ 200 00
23‡Eighty-sixth st, n s, 200 e Riverside Drive, 100x—. H. C. and G. S. Baillie agt W. E. D. Stokes and John N. Franklin. (July 16, 1891)........1,200
23‡Same property. Same agt William E. D. Stokes and Squier & Whipple. (July 16, 1891)........ 775 00
23‡Seventy-second st, n s, 100 e West End av, 125x—. Same agt same. (July 16, 1891).. 750 00
23‡Same property. Same agt William E. D. Stokes and John N. Franklin. (July 16, 1891)........1,560 69
23‡West End av, n w cor 86th st, ½ block x100 Same agt William E. D. Stokes and Squier & Whipple. (July 16, 1891)........1,260 00
23 ‡West End av, w s, extends from 86th to 87th st, block x100; West End av, n e cor 87th st, 100x100........ William Wilkenning agt same. (July 17, 1891)........1,869 49
23‡West End av, s e cor 72d st, 100x100. Thomas Osborne agt same. (Aug. 18, 1891)........5,000 00

‡Eighty-sixth st, n s, 100 e Riverside Drive, 125x100.
23 Eighty-sixth st, s s, 200 e Riverside Drive, 125x100.
Seventy-second st, n s, 100 e West End av, 150x100
West End av, s e cor 72d st, 100x125. Philip Biershenk agt same. (July 13, 1891) ... 4,000 00

23‡West End av, Nos. 441–459, w s. Thomas Osborne agt same and John J. Brewster and Francis M. Jencks (Aug. 7, 1891)... 8,000 00

24 Lexington av, No. 666, w s. Patrick Leddy agt Poline and Morris Byk. (Aug. 25, 1891)... 170 00

24 West End av, s w cor 103d st, 100.11x156. J. J. Brown agt Elizabeth Steinmetz. (July 6, 1891)... 600 00

24 One Hundred and Seventy-seventh st, No. 463 E. Clark Stevens agt Gardiner F. Underhill and Simon P. Saxe. (Jan. 16, 1891)... 165 44

24 Same property. Merritt Stevens agt same. (Jan. 16, 1891)... 68 75

24 One Hundred and Seventy-seventh st, No. 467 E. Samuel Beiter agt same. (Jan. 10, 1891)... 145 75

24 Same property. Byron Brown agt same. (Dec. 26, 1890)... 477 47

24 One Hundred and Fourteenth st, n s, extends from Morningside av to Manhattan av, 68.8x100.11x—x118.9. Canda & Mathews Mfg. Co. (Lim.) agt Hiram Morton Moore. (Aug. 19, 1891)... 6,760 00

25 Hamilton pl, e s, 38 s 142d st, 72x—. Ingbright Mikkelson agt Mary A. and Mark A. Stevens. (Aug. 10, 1891)... 250 00

25 One Hundred and Eighteenth st, s s, 60 e Madison av, 100x100. Graham & Bunt agt Mary Mescha, Bernhard and Leon Ginsburg and Samuel Harris. (Sept. 14, 1891). 350 00

‡Discharged by order of Court on filing bond.

KINGS COUNTY.

Sept.

16 Eastern Parkway, n w cor Osborn st, 45x100. George Covert agt John Power, owner and contractor. (Lien filed Sept. 5, 1891)... $898 00

16 President st, n w cor 6th av, 100x100. New York Anderson Pressed Brick Co. agt Edward Judson, owner, and Hobby & Doody, contractors. (Sept. 12, 1891)... 341 00

18 Walworth st, e s, 390 s Willoughby av, 65x100. Hobby & Doody agt Frank R. Moore, owner, and John Daly and W. P. Rae, contractors. (Aug. 28, 1891)... 619 21

18 Weirfield st, n w s, 81 s w Central av, 260x100. Jacob Willman agt Leopold J. Lippmann and Alexander Taylor, owners and contractors. (Sept. 17, 1891.) (Deposit)... 432 76

18 Hancock st, n w s, 90 s w Central av, 360x100. Same agt Leopold J. Lippmann, owner, and Lippmann & Taylor, contractors. (Sept. 17, 1891.) (Deposit)... 67 20

18 Harrison av, e s, 25 n River st, 25x100. Same agt Sarah Taylor, owner, and same contractors. (Sept. 17, 1891.) (Deposit)... 41 50

19 Osborn st, w s, 150 s Belmont av, 50x100. Karl F. Schmidtt agt Joseph Morris, owner and contractor. (Nov. 1, 1890)... 116 74

21 Navy st, e s, 61.7 n Myrtle av, 50x100. Edward F. Nicoll agt Henrietta Fisk, owner, and William H. H. Glover, contractor. (June 27, 1891)... 1,450 00

21 Navy st, e s, 75 n Myrtle av, 50x100. Thomas Sheffield agt Henrietta Fiske, owner, and Wm. H. H. Glover. (Aug. 1, 1891)... 475 00

22 Bergen st, n s, 100 e Ralph av, 220x107.1. Potts Bros. agt Mary E. Mason, owner, and Isaac D. Mason, contractor. (July 20, 1891)... 285 45

22 Same property. Stephen Delaney agt Paul W. and Foroseajean Ledoux, owners, and Mary E. and Isaac D. Mason, contractors. (July 25, 1891)... 130 00

22 Christopher av, e s, 200 n Belmont av, 25x100. David Levy agt Annie Levy, owner and contractor. (Sept. 3, 1891)... 90 00

23 Willoughby st, No. 136, s s, 42 w Prince st, 25x66. James W. Thompson agt Jacob Rathgeeber, owner, and Marie Rathgeeber, contractor. (Aug. 28, 1891)... 36 73

23 Woodbine st, n w s, 45 s w Knickerbocker av, 40x100. Matthew Posch agt Albert Berckmeier, owner, and Anton Herbst, contractor. (Sept. 15, 1891.) (Deposit)... 20 00

23 Bergen st, s s, 200 w Troy av, 25x119. Robert McKee agt William H. V. Cornell, owner. (Aug. 12, 1891)... 19 94

23 Stuyvesant av, n w cor Decatur st, 100x120. Howell & Saxtan agt James A. Lawrence, owner and contractor. (Dec. 18, 1890)... 379 74

23 Bergen st, s s, 200 w Troy av, 25x119. John Irish agt William H. V. Cornell, owner. (Aug. 12, 1891)... 24 38

24 Glenada pl, s w cor Decatur st, 100x85. Frederick B. Langston agt Calvin C. Church and William W. Reynolds, owners and contractors. (Sept. 19, 1891)... 625 00

24 Rockaway av, w s, 300 n Eastern Parkway, 50x100. James O'Connor agt Samuel Levy, owner, and L. Rattner and Charles F. Harles, contractors. (Aug. 8, 1891)... 50 60

24 Garfield pl, w s, 100 n 8th av, 10?x100. Frank W. Gilbert agt L. Anderson & Bro., owners and contractors. (Sept. 24, 1891. (Deposit)... 39 95

BUILDINGS PROJECTED.

The first name is that of the owner; ar't stands for architect, m'n for mason, c'r for carpenter and b'r for builder.

NEW YORK CITY.

SOUTH OF 14TH STREET.

3d st, No. 25 E., five-story brk and stone flat, 25x88, tin roof; cost, $20,000; Fay & Stacom, 337 Pleasant av; ar't, Chas. Rentz. Plan 1250.

Delancey st, No. 186, five-story brk flat, 26x75.9, tin roof; cost, $22,000; L. Goodman, 217 Henry st; ar't, F. Ebeling. Plan 1256.

Delancey st, No. 188, five-story brk flat, 17.8x75.9, tin roof; cost, $16,000; ow'r and ar't, same as last. Plan 1257.

BETWEEN 14TH AND 59TH STREETS.

25th st, No. 561 W., one-story brk shop, 16x22, brk and cement roof; cost, $900; J. M. Cornell, 29 East 37th st; ar't, G. W. Debevoise. Plan 1246.

7th av, n w cor 56th st, seven-story brk and terra cotta hotel, 78x78 and 100, tin roof; cost, abt $300,000; W. Noble, 246 Central Park West; ar't, E. L. Angell. Plan 1248. (Substituted for plan No. 881, filed in June, 1891.)

BETWEEN 59TH AND 125TH STREETS, WEST OF CENTRAL PARK WEST AND 8TH AVENUE.

91st st, n s, 100 e Amsterdam av, six three-story and basement stone dwell'gs, on plot 100x50 and 52, tin roofs; cost, $15,000 each; J. Brown, 164 West 92d st; ar't, G. F. Pelham. Plan 1249.

NORTH OF 125TH STREET.

129th st, n s, 27.6 w 2d av, one-story iron boiler-house, 70x30, tin roof; cost, $5,000. F. K. Hain, manager, 71 Broadway. Plan 1254.

7th av, s w cor 138th st, twenty-nine three-story and basement brk, stone and terra cotta dwell'gs, irreg. in size, tin roofs; cost, $7,000 each; ow'r and b'r, D. H. King, Jr., 5th av, s w cor 43d st; ar't, James B. Lord. Plan 1258.

23D AND 24TH WARDS.

Reservoir Drive, s s, 340 w Holt pl, two-story and attic frame dwell'g, 18x28, shingle roof; cost, $1,400; Kate Lynch, Williamsbridge, N. Y.; ar't, F. D. Miller. Plan 1244.

Suburban st, n s, 84 w Briggs av, two-story frame dwell'g, 20x40, shingle roof; cost, $2,400; H. McArdle, 2159 8th av; b'rs, T. & W. Greenlees. Plan 1251.

145th st, s s, 225 w Brook av, frame shed, 20x25, gravel roof; cost, $100; lessee, T. Young, 721 East 144th st; ar't, A. Pfeiffer. Plan 1252.

156th st, n s, 325 w Courtlandt av, rear, two-story frame shed, 20x16, tin roof; cost, $300; J. Hoetzel, 563 East 156th st; ar't, C. F. Lohse. Plan 1259.

Elton av, e s, 50 s 157th st, one-story frame stable, 30x25, tin roof; cost, $500; G. Russhan, 4 West 136th st; ar't, C. F. Lohse. Plan 1260.

Locust av, e s, 165 n 168th st, two-story brk shop, 40x125, slate roof; cost, abt $15,000; Central Gas Light Co., Alexander av and 142d st; ar't, H. S. Ihnen. Plan 1247.

Perry av, w s, 661 s Gun Hill road, one-story frame stable, 16x22, shingle roof; cost, $150; J. Curtain, 379 Perry av; ar't, F. D. Miller. Plan 1245.

Spuyten Duyvil Parkway, e s, 40 n Warren av, two-story frame stable, 20x20, tin roof; cost, $550; I. G. Judson, trustee, Spuyten Duyvil, N. Y.; b'r, S. L. Berrian. Plan 1253.

Valentine av, s s, 145 w Southern Boulevard, rear, two-story frame stable, 24x15, tin or gravel roof; cost, $800; T. Everest, 169 East 111th st; ar't, L. Entzer, Jr. Plan 1255.

KINGS COUNTY.

Plan 1735—Commercial st, w s, 25 n Bell st, one one-story frame syrup storage tank, 52x86, gravel roof, sheathed with corrugated iron; cost, $2,000; ow'r, ar't and c'r, American Sugar Refining Co., Commercial st; m'ns, Carpenter & Woodruff.

1736—Stagg st, No. 18, s s, bet Union av and Lorimer st, one four-story frame (brk filled) tenem't, 25x49, tin roof; cost, $4,200; Jacob Nagel, on premises; ar't, H. Vollweiler; b'r, not selected.

1737—Harman st, s s, 100 e Hamburg av, two three-story frame (brk filled) tenem'ts, 25x60, tin roofs; cost, $4,500 each; ow'r and b'r, John J. Hennimann, 18 North Oxford st; ar't, H. Vollweiler.

1738—Morrell st, w s, 50 s Cook st, two four-story frame (brk filled) tenem'ts, 25x65, tin roofs; cost, $5,000 each; Theo. Auhke; ar't, H. Vollweiler; b'r, not selected.

1739—Herkimer st, s s, 125 w Utica av, one four-story frame (brk filled) tenem't, 25x55, tin roof; cost, $4,500; Wm. H. Reynolds, Hancock st; ar't, J. D. McAuliffe.

1740—Jefferson st, s s, 175 e Knickerbocker av, one one-story frame (brk filled) dwell'g, 25x26, tin roof; cost, $400; ow'r, ar't and b'r, Frank Spath, 1120 Willoughby av.

1741—Knickerbocker av, e s, 175 n Melrose st, one two-story frame (brk filled) dwell'g, 25x25, tin roof; cost, $1,500; Max Hilderbrand, 20 Locust st; ar't, H. Vollweiler; b'r, not selected.

1742—Centre st, n s, 140 w Hicks st, one one-story frame dwell'g, 20x25, board roof; cost, $80; Daniel Fitzgerald, 109 Bush st; b'r, J. Fitzgerald.

1743—Grinnell st, n w cor Gowanus Canal, one one-story frame coal storage, 18.6x12, shingle roof; cost, $200; Nelson Bros., on premises; b'r, D. E. Harris.

1744—Calyer st, n w cor Newell st, one one-story frame stable, 25x25, felt roof; cost, $200; Charles S. Jackson, 160 Calyer st; b'r, H. S. Jackson.

1745—Meserole av, n s, 75 w Diamond st, one one-story frame storage shed, 50x110, gravel roof; cost, $1,000; ow'r and ar't, John A. Dowst, 157 Meserole av; b'rs, J. A. & W. H. Port.

1746—24th st, s s, 175 e 3d av, one two-story frame shop, 25x60, tin roof; cost, $1,000; John T. Bierds, 158 24th st; b'r, John J. Salmon.

1747—48th st, n s, 200 e 4th av, one two-story and basement frame (brk filled) dwell'g, 20x40, tin roof; cost, $3,000; ow'rs and c'rs, Mark Hall and Samuel J. Atwater, 1154 3d av; ar't, W. Shaw (?); m'n, M. Robertson.

1748—Stockholm st, n s, 310 w St. Nicholas av, one one-story frame woodshed, 20x20, gravel roof; cost, $100; George Spitzer, 353 Stockholm st; ar't, F. J. Lessing.

1749—Newell st, e s, 222 n Van Cott av, one four-story frame (brk filled) tenem't, 25x65, tin roof; cost, $6,800; ow'r and c'r, George Wittrich, Bushwick av and Varet st; ar'ts, D. Acker & Son.

1750—Evergreen av, s e cor Schaeffer st; Evergreen av, n e cor Hancock st, and Knickerbocker av, n w cor Woodbine st, three three-story frame (brk filled) stores and tenem'ts, 25x60, tin roofs; cost, each, $4,000; ow'rs, ar'ts and b'rs, Cozine & Gascoine, 1223 and 1225 Bushwick av.

1751—14th st, s s, 100 w 2d av, one one-story frame dwell'g, 20x30, gravel roof; cost, $600; P. McCarthy, 91 14th st; b'r, G. Petterson.

1752—48th st, n s, 180 e 4th av, one two-story and basement frame (brk filled) dwell'g, 20x38, tin roof; cost, $3,500; Wm. R. Rogers, 314 48th st; ar't, George Walkenshaw.

1753—Willoughby av, s w cor Waverly av, six three-story and basement brk and Ohio stone dwell'g, 17.6 to 18.4x44.4, tin roof, iron cornice; cost, each, $9,000. Mary C. Osborn; ar'ts, R. H. Robertson and A. J. Manning; b'rs, J. H. Harned & Son.

1754—Stuyvesant av, n e cor McDonough st, six three-story free stone dwell'gs, 20x45, metal roofs and cornices; cost, $42,000; ow'rs, ar'ts and b'rs, W. R. Bell & Co., 185 Chauncey st.

1755—Stanhope st, n s, 100 w Irving av, one three-story brk furniture factory, 25x40, tin roof; cost, $2,500; Pincus Seifters, 1403 Myrtle av; ar't, B. Finkensieper; b'r, not selected.

1756—Clinton av, s e cor Willoughby av, four four-story and basement brk and Ohio stone dwell'gs, 17.8 to 18.2x54, tin and slate roofs, terra cotta and iron cornices; cost, each, $12,000; Mary C. Osborn; ar'ts, R. H. Robertson and A. J. Manning; b'rs, J. B. Harned & Son.

1757—McDonough st, n s, 302 e Reid av, two two-story and basement sandstone dwell'gs, 18.9x42, tin roofs, iron cornices; cost, each, $5,000; Chas. H. Roberts, 243 Reid av; ar't, H. B. Hill.

1758—McDonough st, n s, 240.6 e Reid av, six two-and-a-half-story and basement sandstone dwell'gs, 18x42, tin roofs, iron cornices; cost, each, $7,000; C. H. Roberts, 243 Reid av; ar't, H. B. Hill.

1759—4th av, n s, 60 e President st, one four-story brk store and tenem't, 20x45, gravel roof, wooden cornice; cost, $5,000; D. Fenroff, 246 4th av.

1760—57th st, s s, 180 e 3d av, one two-story basement and cellar frame (brk filled) dwell'g, 20x40, tin roof; cost, $3,000; G. Colby, 3d av and 53d st; ar'ts, H. L. Spicer & Sons; b'r, S. F. Sherwood.

1761—56th st, s s, 220 e 3d av, three two-story basement and cellar frame (brk filled) dwell'gs, 20x40, tin roofs; cost, each, $3,000; J. Marsters and M. C. De Noyelle, 240 47th st; ar'ts, H. L. Spicer & Son; b'r, S. T. Sherwood.

1762—Montauk av, e s, 150 s Belmont av, two two-story frame dwell'gs, 20x30, tin roofs; cost, $4,400; Donald Laing, Belmont, cor Atkins av, and C. H. Machin, Gates, cor Franklin av; b'r, D. Laing.

1763—Bedford av, No. 184, w s, 45 s North 7th st, one four-story brk store and club-house, 20x75, gravel roof, metal cornice; cost, $1,200; E. Scott, 140 North 6th st; ar't, A. Herbert; b'rs, W. J. Moran and J. J. Brennan.

1764—Berriman st, e s, 90 n Stanley av, one two-story frame dwell'g, 19x30; tin roof; cost, $2,000; Jane Ferguson, Montauk av, near New Lots road; b'r, R. Forrest.

1765—Flushing av, No. 806, one three-story frame (brk filled) tenem't, 28x55, tin roof; cost, $6,000; Wm. Wallmann, 33 Fayette st; ar't, H. E. Funk.

1766—Hamburg av, n w cor Stanhope st, four three-story frame (brk filled) stores and tenem'ts, 25x65, tin roofs; cost, total, $18,000; ow'rs and b'rs, F. Eller and F. Kline, 312 Melrose st; ar't, E. Schrempf.

1767—Moore st, No. 33, one four-story frame tailor shop, 25x30, tin roof; cost, $2,500; Mr. Volk, on premises; ar't, H. Smith; b'r, J. Pomeranz.

1768—Belmont av, n s, 50 w Schenck av, two two-story frame dwell'gs, 21x42, tin roofs; cost, each, $2,500; ow'r and b'r, Fred'k Eiermann, 260 Schenck av.

1769—Jewel st, w s, 100 n Nassau av, three three-story frame (brk filled) tenem'ts, 16.8x50, gravel roofs; cost, $9,000; Thomas Thompson, 46 Clay st; ar't, W. Lenwick; b'rs, J. Wilhelm and McGarry & Moran.

1770—Hicks st, e s, 38 n West 9th st, one two-story frame dwell'g, 18x36, tin roof; cost, $1,400; ow'r, ar't and b'r, Chas. Thorsen, 707 Hicks st.

1771—Moore st, No. 95, bet Graham av and Humboldt st, one five-story brk tailor shop, 25x38, tin roof, iron and brk cornice. cost, $4,000; S. Simon, 35 East Broadway, New York; ar't, H. Vollweiler; b'r, not selected.

1772—Humboldt st, e s, 25 s Varet st, one four-story frame (brk filled) store and tenem't, 25x57, tin roof; cost, $5,000; Jacob Nagel, 18 Stagg st; ar't, H. Vollweiler; b'r, not selected.

1773—Humboldt st, s e cor Varet st, one four-story frame (brk filled) store and tenem't, 25x57, tin roof; cost, $6,000; Jacob Nagel, 18 Stagg st; ar't, H. Vollweiler; b'r, not selected.

1774—Ashford st, e s, 350 n Arlington av, two two-story and attic frame dwell'gs, 20x30, shingle roofs; cost, each, $4,000; Theo. M. Le Beau, 68 Van Siclen av; ar't, C. Infanger.

1775—Halsey st, n s, 100 or 160 e Evergreen av, four two-story and basement frame (brk filled) dwell'gs, 20x45, tin roofs; cost, $2,500 each; R. or K. E. Monahan, 52 Stockholm st.

1776—45th st, n s, 300 e 3d av, six two-story and basement frame dwell'gs, 20x38, tin roofs; cost, $2,800 each; James F. O'Rourke, 215 45th st; ar't and b'r, J. H. O'Rourke.

1777—Eckford st, e s, 64 s Greenpoint av, one three-story frame (brk filled) store and tenem't, 24x41, gravel roof; cost, $4,000; Mary A. Brink, 240 East 29th st, New York City; ar't, J. F. Conlon.

1778—Jacob st, n s, 90 e Central av, eight two-story and basement frame (brk filled) dwell'gs, 17.6x36, tin roofs; cost, $25,000; Sarah Hopkins, 794 Halsey st; ar't, F. Holmberg.

1779—Atlantic av, n s, 75.1 e Hendrix st, one one-story frame (brk filled) store, 50.1 and 50x60, tin roof; cost, $2,500; Carsten J. Mehrten, 2767 Atlantic av; ar't, C. Infanger; b'rs, H. Hermann and J. Fench.

1780—Macon st, s s, 160 e Nostrand av, three three-story and basement red and brown stone dwell'gs, 20x45, tin roofs, iron cornices; cost, $6,000 each; S. C. Whitehead, 138 Macon st; ar'ts, I. D. Reynolds & Son.

ALTERATIONS NEW YORK CITY.

Plan 1682—Water st, No. 120, interior alterations and repairs; cost, $650; B. H. Drake, 171 West 71st st; ar't, Snook & Sons; b'r, D. Codington.

1683—57th st, No. 1 W., and 5th av, No. 746, interior connecting doors; cost, $1,000; C. Vanderbilt, on premises; b'rs, Cockett & Weeks.

1684—1st av, Nos. 1217 and 1219, general repairs; cost, $350 to $500; lessee, M. Rosenthal, 208 East 58th st; c'r, J. J. Guirry.

1685—39th st, Nos. 337-341 W., new fronts; cost, $1,100; agent, F. Haffner, 323 West 39th st; c'r, E. M. Hackett.

1686—76th st, No. 505 E., one-story extension, 25x8, and wall altered; cost, $275; P. A. Decker, 179 East 94th st; ar'ts, Kurtzer & Rohl; m'n, A. Brose.

1687—71st st, No. 340 E., interior alterations and walls altered; cost, $1,300; Fannie Froelich, 435 East 120th st; ar't, E. Wenz.

1688—110th st, s s, 100 e 5th av, one-story extension, 36x25; cost, $1,500; F. Blessing, 65 East 110th st; ar'ts, Thom & Wilson.

1689—Park av, No. 1500, interior alterations; cost, $75; H. Tonjes, on premises; ar't, A. R. Duryee.

1690—Bathgate av, w s, 189 n 175th st, moved to new foundation; cost, $500; C. A. Becker, 1872 Washington av; ar't, J. C. Kerby.

1691—14th st, No. 32 E., show windows altered; cost, $1,000; W. J. Demorest, 21 East 57th st; ar't, R. T. Brown; c'r, W. Watts.

1692—Barclay st, No. 37, new skylight in roof; cost, $250; S. R. Van Duzer, Newburgh, N. Y.; ar'ts, D. & J. Jardine.

1693—5th av, n w cor 126th st, two-story extension, 9x9, new bay; cost, $1,500; Dr. S. C. Warner, on premises; ar't, A. B. Jennings.

1694—126th st, n s, 80 w 5th av, one-story extension, 4x22; cost, $500; ow'r and ar't, same as last.

1695—92d st, No. 204 E., raised one story and extensive interior alterations; cost, $6,000; J. Ruppert, s e cor 5th av and 93d st; ar't, J Kastner.

1696—73d st, s s, 300 e Av A, shed repaired; cost, $15; Mrs. M. Connelly, 518 East 73d st.

1697—3d av, e s, 150 s 183d st, rear raised two stories, interior alterations and walls altered; cost, $7,500; Home for Incurables, 182d st and 3d av; b'r, R. E. Rogers. (Substituted for plan No. 1586).

1698—Broadway, e s, bet 44th and 45th sts, interior alterations; cost, not given; R. T. Ford, 2 West 29th st; ar't, Bruce Price.

1699—9th av, No. 502, one-story extension, 11x9; cost, $200; agent, W. Quinn, on premises; b'r, C. Mooney.

1700—Courtlandt av, w s, 50 n 156th st, moved to new foundation; cost, $140; G. Hoffman, 767 Courtlandt av; ar't, F. J. Miller.

1701—Madison av, No. 56, interior alterations and walls altered; cost, $100; A. Iselin, on premises; m'n, T. H. Mulvaney; c'r, S. Lee.

1702—59th st, s s, 130 e 5th av, walls altered; cost, $370; Gentlemen's Riding Club, 7 East 58th st; ar't, B. L. Gilbert; m'ns, Crockett & Weeks.

1703—Park av, No. 1209, extension raised three stories; cost, $1,500; Julia F. Hines, 1192 Park av; ar't, J. Kastner.

1704—Broadway, No. 828, one-story extension, 25x35, interior alterations and walls altered; cost, $3,500; lessee, G. E. Stechert, 7 2d pl, Brooklyn; ar't, J. Kastner.

1705—Monroe st, No. 67, windows altered; cost, $75; Mrs. E. Musgrave, 65 Monroe st; ar't, B. W. Berger.

1706—West st, w s, opposite Park pl, one-story extension, 55x145; cost, $4,100; N. Y. C. & H. R. Railway Co., Grand Central Station.

1707—86th st, No. 519 E., one-story extension, 15x19; cost, $300; D. L. Sturges, exr., on premises.

1708—85th st, No. 342 E., three-story extension, 25x60; cost, $5,000; F. Heins, 1656 Av B; ar't, E. Wenz.

1709—3d av, n e cor 87th st, repair damage by fire; cost, $100; Mrs. S. Smith, 327 East 113th st; ar't, C. V. McConologue.

1710—Mott st, Nos. 216 and 218, entrance alterations; cost, $75; lessee, H. Herrmann, 230 East 15th st; ar'ts, Kurtzer & Rohl.

1711—81st st, No. 100 W., interior alterations, walls altered and new front; cost, $1,000; lessee, H. C. Borger, s w cor 8th av and 71st st; ar'ts, Kurtzer & Rohl.

1712—53d st, No. 510 W., interior alterations, walls altered and new front; cost, $350; E. L. Striker, 502 West 53d st; ar't, W. H. C. Hornun.

1713—3d av, Nos. 2188-2192, one-story extension, 25x63, interior alterations and walls altered; cost, $2,000; lessee, H. Kahn, 171 East 119th st; ar't, W. H. C. Hornun.

1714—Clinton st, No. 57, new front; cost, $900; R. Marten, 234 5th st; ar't, H. Horenburger.

1715—Bleecker st, Nos. 367 and 369, interior alterations; cost, $200; lessee, J. H. Goetchius, 68 Bank st.

1716—Morris av, No. 624, one-story extension, 12.9x10.6; cost, $250; T. Wegener, 630 Morris av; ar't, C. F. Lohse.

1717—143d st, No. 740 E., moved and altered and new foundation; cost, $580; J. Sheridan, 742 East 143d st; ar't, C. F. Lohse.

1718—Morris av, No. 681, raised one story, one-story extension, 21x14.8, new foundation; cost, $1,965; W. Weis, 159 East 121st st; ar't, C. F. Lohse; c'r, H. Jaeger.

1719—Madison av, s e cor 68th st, two-story extension, 10.6x13, interior alterations, new tankhouse on roof, new stoop and bay; cost, abt $5,000; G. N. Miller, 811 Madison av; ar'ts, McKim, Mead & White; m'n, W. W. Owens

1720—175th st, n s, 25 e Webster av, two and three-story extension, 20x10 and 9.7, interior alterations and repairs, front wall altered and new front; cost, $2,000; Georgianna Ruland, on premises; ar't, J. J. Vreeland; m'ns, Ruland & Stone.

KINGS COUNTY.

Plan 896—Stone av, e s, 75 n Glenmore av, raised 2 ft. on stone foundation; cost $250; J. Murphy, 16 Little Hull st.

897—Essex st, e s, 125 n Belmont av, one-story frame extension, 7.6x10; cost, $50; ow'r and ar't, Charles E. Baillee, on premises. b'r, M. Lewis.

898—Grand st, Nos. 363-640, three-story brk and frame extension, 8x12.6, tin roof; cost $1,900; Joseph Carney, 283 Hewes st; ar't and c'r, J. A. Terhune; m'n, G. Quinn.

899—Duffield st, No. 11, rebuild south and rear walls, &c.; cost, $200; George W. Platt, 144 South Oxford st; ar't, H. Case; b'rs, —— Bennett and M. A. Case.

900—Marion st, No. 254, new store front; cost, $575; Lewis Beman, on premises.

901—Woodbine st, No. 176, raised 3 ft. on brk wall; cost, $150; Mr. Fie, on premises.

902—Ross st, No. 31, add one story to extension; cost, $600; ow'r and ar't, James Klots; b'r, W. L. Langridge.

903—Kent av, No. 343, rebuild south wall; cost, $400; ow'rs and ar'ts, Young & Smylie, 51 South 5th st; b'rs, W. J. Moran and Jeukins & Gilles.

904—Frost st, No. 243, n s, 125 w Kingsland av, one one-story frame extension, 11.6x15, tin roof; cost, $75; John Kane, on premises.

905—Throop av, n w cor Lafayette av, underpin north wall with brk; cost, $400; Mr. Pollard; b'r, T. E. Greenland.

906—Milton st, No. 100, cellar under extension; cost, $150; H. Bittmann, on premises; ar't and c'r, S. M. Randal l; m'ns, I. and J. Van Riper & Co.

907—Sumpter st, No. 74, one-story frame extension, 25x35, tin roof; cost, $100; F. W. Eckelkamp, 3 McDougal st; ar't and c'r, C. Rieger.

908—Franklin st, No. 150, one-story frame extension, 18x32.6, gravel roof; cost, $200; Emil Gruber, Long Island City; b'r, C. Wessler.

909—Elm pl, No. 9, front and interior alterations; cost, $600; Thos. F. Corning, on premises; ar't, R. Dixon.

910—India st, No. 84, two-story frame extension, 8.9x8, gravel roof; cost, $375; A. Hinz, 84 India st; ar't and c'r, R. Gasser; m'n, G. Smith.

911—18th st, s s, 100 e 8th av, two-story brk extension, 40x10, tin roof; cost, $300; W. M. Brasher & Co., on premises.

912—Liberty av, s e cor Crescent st, lowered to grade of street; cost, $300; Mrs. M. Koueman, on premises.

913—Berriman st, n e cor Glenmore av, two-story frame extension, 12.4x28, tin roof; cost, $400; Thomas Smith, on premises; ar't, R. Dixon.

914—Halsey st, No. 385, flat tin roof; cost, $1,000; Mrs. E. A. Barr, on premises; ar't, S. Barr; b'r, W. Cable.

915—North 5th st, No. 242, add one frame story, tin roof; cost, 900; Peter Delap, 1622 Fulton st; b'r, J. A. De Camp.

916—Prospect pl, s s, 225 w Buffalo av, raised 7 feet on stone and brk extension; cost, $250; J. Roberson, 1882 Prospect pl.

917—Bergen st, No. 2141, one one-story frame extension, 21x16, tin roof; cost, $150; F. Heddesheimer, on premises; c'r, W. Colcraft.

918—Seigel st, No. 42, new store front, cost, $400; L. Sjakner, on premises; c'rs, Harrison & Galigar.

919—Gates av, No. 1470, one two-story stone and brk extension, 25x18, tin roof, interior alterations; cost, $2,000; Anton Voght, on premises; ar't, Benjamin Finkensieper; b'r, not selected.

920—Wyckoff av, e s, 15 s Troutman st, add one story of frame; cost, $400; ow'r and b'r, Paul Wesphal, on premises.

921—St. Marks av, n e cor Grand av, propose to raise roof and add one story; cost, $600; E. M. Knox, on premises; ar't, Benjamin Finkensieper; b'r, not selected.

922—Atlantic av, No. 2750, add one story, interior alterations; cost, $1,800; James J. Farrell, on premises; ar't, Chas. Infanger; b'r, not selected.

923—Nevins st, e s, 50 n Butler st, add 4 feet to height of present building; cost, $1,500; John S. Loomis, on premises.

924—Clason av, n e cor Flushing av, front altered, iron work; cost, $800; Ed. Faulkner, on premises; b'rs, H. Kroenke and E. Bindewald.

925—Canton st, e s, 250 w Auburn pl, one-story brk extension, 15.9x12, tin roof; cost, $250; Trinity Chapel; b'r, J. Demott & Sons and J. Campbell.

MISCELLANEOUS.

BUSINESS FAILURES.

N. Y. ASSIGNMENTS—BENEFIT CREDITORS.

Sept.

19 Harriman, James, of No. 42 West 58th st (not carrying on any business), to Herman Kobbe; without preferences.

21 Hyman, Annie (boot and shoe store at No. 646 Columbus av), to Louis L. Rolland; preferences, $1,919.

21 Coates, Edward W. (fruit dealer at No. 1288 Broadway), to Thomas W. McWaters; preferences, $528.

21 Pierce, John, Jr. (dealer in books at No. 76 Nassau st), to Charles S. Shivler; preferences, $863.

21 Marks Adjustable Folding Chair Co. (Lim.) (mfg. and selling adjustable folding chairs at No. 930 Broadway), to William S. Kelley; without prefcrenees.

21 Marks, Frank R. (pres't of Marks Adjustable Folding Chair Co. (Lim.), to same; without preferences.

22 White, Stephen V. and Franklin W. Hopkins (composing firm of S. V. White & Co., bankers and brokers at No. 36 Wall st.), to Charles W. Gould; without preferences.

25 The Pfister Book Binding Co. (business of binding books at No. 430 West 14th st), to Robert Avery; preferences $7,703.

PROCEEDINGS OF THE BOARD OF ALDERMEN AFFECTING REAL ESTATE.

APPROVED PAPERS.

Resolutions passed by the Board of Aldermen calling for the following improvements have been signed by the Mayor for the week ending September 19, 1891. *Indicates that the Mayor neither appoved nor objected thereto, therefore the same became adopted.

FENCING VACANT LOTS.

107th st, from Park to Madison av.
Madison av, bet 106th and 107th sts.
Park av, bet 106th and 107th sts.

PAVING.

118th st, bet Madison and Park avs; granite block.*

LAMP-POSTS ERECTED AND LAMPS LIGHTED.

20th st, in front of Nos. 29 and 31 E. } at owners'
125th st, s e cor Madison av. } expense.*
9th av, Nos. 371 and 381, in front of St. Michaels Church; four lamps.*

MAINS.

Boulevard, bet 96th and 145th sts; water.
42d st, bet 2d and 3d avs; water.
101st st, bet 1st and 2d avs; water.*
101st st, bet East River and 2d av; water.
103d st, bet 2d and 5th avs; water.
117th st, bet Madison and 5th avs; water.
Park (4th) av, bet 94th and 100th sts; water.
2d av, from 42d to 105th st; water.

ADVERTISED LEGAL SALES.

REFEREES SALES TO BE HELD AT THE REAL ESTATE EXCHANGE AND AUCTION ROOM (LIMITED), 59 to 65 LIBERTY STREET, EXCEPT WHERE OTHERWISE STATED.

Sept.

119th st, No. 408, s s, 94 e 1st av, 17x100.10
119th st, No. 410, s s, 111 e 1st av, 17x100.10
119th st, No. 412, s s, 128 e 1st av, 17x100.10
Three three-story stone front dwell'gs.
by J. C. Lalor. (Amt due on each $5,547) ... 28

3d av, s w cor 170th st, 26x79.9x26.4x87.6
170th st, s s, 89.6 w 3d av, 40x52.9x40x52.8, ½ part, being all right, title and int. of Matilda Carter to above.
by P. F. Meyer. (Receiver's sale) ... 28

22d st, No. 447, n e s, 410 n w 9th av, 20x98.8, four-story stone front dwell'g
87th st, No. 127, n s, 225 w 9th av, 15.8x100.8, three-story brk front dwell'g
West Broadway, No. 155, e s, 75 n Lispenard st, 25x100, three-story brk store
by William Kennelly. (Partition sale) ... 29

Monroe av, s e s, adj land John Ittner, runs northeast along said av 93.6 x northeast still along av 314.11 x southeast through an old stone wall 723 x still southeast 350 to Valentine av, x southwest along av 381.8 x northwest 356 x again northwest 138.6 to beginning, by W. R. Brown. (Amt due $27,797) ... 29

Duane st, No. 116
Delancey st, No. 53 } begins Delancey st, s
Eldridge st, Nos. 145-151 } w cor Eldridge st, 25x100
Delancey st, No. 51, n s, 25x100
Park row, Nos. 142 and 144, n s, 25x96
Chrystie st, No. 90, e s, 25x100
by J. L. Wells. (Partition sale) ... 30

Southern Boulevard, n w cor Garden av, runs northwest along Garden av, 115.2 x northeast 98 to Kingsbridge road, x south along road 60.2 x south along same 70.9 to Southern Boulevard, x south 22.4 to beginning
Southern Boulevard, w s, 21.3 s Garden av, runs south along w s Southern Boulevard 90.8 x northwest 40.10 x northerly 81 to beginning
West st, s w s, known as lot 14 map of Wardsville, West Farms, 50x126x50.1x129
by R. V. Harnett. (Partition sale) ... 30

67th st, Nos. 206-222, s s, 150 w 10th av, 9 lots, each 25x100.5, Nos. 206, 212, 214, 220 and 222, five five-story brk tenem'ts; Nos. 208, 210, 216 and 218, four five-story stone front tenem'ts, by D. P. Ingraham & Co. (Amt due on each, abt $9,669) ... 30

98th st, s s, 150 e 10th av, 200x100.11, vacant, by Wm. Kennelly. (Amt due $38,511) ... 30

115th st, n s, 400 w 11th av, 50x100.11, vacant, by R. V. Harnett. (Partition sale) ... 30

116th st, n s, 50 e Madison av, 60x100, vacant; also

all right, title and int. of Patrick J. Quinn and Mary F. his wife to a strip of land 10 inches wide on n s of above property, by R. V. Harnett..... 30

127th st, No. 218, s s, 180 e 3d av, 40x99.11, three-story frame dwell'g and vacant, by J. F. B. Smyth. (Amt due $4,102)...... 30

Park av, Nos. 565-569, e s, 75.8 s 63d st, 66.5x100.1x60x100, five-story brk flat, Lonsdale, by William Kennelly. (Amt due $10,967; prior morts. $90,000)...... 30

Oct.

22d st, No. 44, s s, 257 e 6th av, 23x98.9, four-story stone front dwell'g, by William Kennelly. (Amt due $28,960)...... 1

25th st, No. 336, s s, 150 w 1st av, 25x98.9, five-story brk tenem't, by William Kennelly. (Partition sale)...... 1

Madison av, No. 1678, n e cor 111th st, 15x70, three-story brk (stone front) dwell'g, by R. V. Harnett & Co. (Amt due $1,492; prior morts. $7,000; sold May 24, 1890, for $11,500)...... 1

7th av } begins 7th av, n e cor 124th st, 100.11x125, 124th st } two-story brk market, &c., by A. H. Muller & Son. (Leasehold; foreclos. mech. lien) 1

Houston st, No. 331, s s, 18.6 w Washington st, 18.9x60, three-story brk tenem't. 1-5 part.....
Hester st, No. 211, n s, bet Baxter and Centre sts, runs west along st 24.11 x northeast 35.6 x northeast 66.6 x east 21.8 x southwest to beginning, five-story brk tenem't with stores. 1-5 part......
by R. V. Harnett & Co. (Amt due $4,359)...... 2

119th st, No. 7, n s, 95.5 w 5th av, 14x57.9x14.6x58.11, three-story brk dwell'g, by B. L. Kennelly. (Amt due $4,734)...... 5

3d av, Nos. 881 and 883, e s, 50.5 n 53d st, 31.10x100, two five-story brk tenem'ts with stores; all right, title and interest of Dora and Simon Moses which they had on June 29, 1891, by Sheriff, at City Hall. (Sale under execution...) 5

KINGS COUNTY.

Sept.

President st, No. 185, n s, 120 e Henry st, runs north 55 x east 1 x north 45 x east 14.6 x south 10, to beginning, three-story brk dwell'g; assessed value, $5,000; by W. Cole, at 7 Court sq...... 29

Fulton st, s s, 200 e Stone av, 50x100; assessed value, $2,500 each......
Sanford st, No. 212, w s, 283 n De Kalb av, 25x100, two-story brick dwell'g with one-story frame extension; assessed value, $1,400......
by T. A. Kerrigan, at 13 Willoughby st...... 29

Elton st, w s, 175 n Liberty av, 25.2x90, three-story frame dwell'g; assessed value, $2,980; partition; by Edward R. Vollmer, ref. at County Court House...... 30

Oct.

St. Marks av, No. 131, n s, 40 w Carlton av, 20x78.6, three-story brk dwell'g; assessed value, $4,700......
6th st, s s, 70 w 4th av, 105x100......
Lot at Gravesend, begins at Atlantic Ocean at division line bet old lots 22 and 23 on one side and old lots 20 and 21 on the other side, as shown on Kowolski's map of common lands of Gravesend, Coney Island, runs north — x west — x south to ocean, x east to beginning, except strip 40 ft. wide condemned for use of New York & Coney Island R. R. Co., and part lying south of centre of Surf av; partition......
by T. A. Kerrigan, at 13 Willoughby st...... 1

Grove st, n w s, 225 n e Central av, 22x100, by T. A. Kerrigan, at 13 Willoughby st...... 2

LIS PENDENS, KINGS COUNTY.

Sept.

Sackett st, n s, 125 w Van Brunt st, runs west 125 x north 200 to Degraw st, x east 50 x south 100 x east 75 x south 100. The Henry McShane Mfg. Co. agt Rebecca M. Ferry; action to set aside deeds and foreclos. mechanic's lien; att'y, Daniel W. Northup...... 18

Clinton st, e s, 68.6 n 2d pl, 17.3x76.6. Same agt James J. Ferry; action to set aside deed and foreclos. mechanic's lien; same att'y...... 18

President st, s s, 331.6 e 5th av, 17x100. Harry H. Pawson agt Henry Dundas; att'y, Robert F. Rhodes...... 18

Cropsey av, n e s, 100 s e 21st av, 25x100. Conrad Gans agt Catharine F. Monjo; foreclos. mechanic's lien; att'ys, Fisher & Volz...... 18

Ocean pl, e s, 98.7 n Atlantic av, 69x150 to Gunther pl. Leopold Michel agt Oscar H. Doolittle; att'y, Ira L. Bamberger...... 18

Vanderbilt st, s s, 487.6 e Short st, 12.6x108, Flatbush. Hannah C. McCracken agt Ida L. Cheever; att'y's, Carrington & Emerson...... 19

1st st, s w s, 224.3 n w 7th av, 17.6x100. Hans S. Christian agt Hannah Cole; att'y, George V. Brower...... 19

Gates av, n s, 80 w Vanderbilt av, 20x75. Henry J. Schoefer agt Louise Kuhle; partition; att'y, Samuel E. Faron...... 21

?1 av, e s, 67.6 n President st, 22 6x100. Margaret B. Warren et al. exrs. Charles C. Warren agt James C. Jewett; att'ys, Havens & Beebe...... 21

Flushing av, s e cor Sandford st, 25x100. Charles J. Patterson agt William Kaufman; att'y, Chas. J. Patterson in person...... 21

Roebling st, e s, 50 n South 2d st, 25x50. Same agt William E. Butler; same att'y...... 21

South 2d st, s w s, 75 n w 11th st, 25x120. Edgar J. Taylor agt Emma Taiber; att'y, T. J. Taylor...... 21

Coney Island and Sheepshead Bay road, n s, lot 3 on Duck Hills or Supplement C, 129x94.4x129x93.6. John L. Voorhels, Commr. of Investment, Gravesend, agt Sarah P. Birmingham; att'ys, Hubbard & Rushmore...... 22

Vanderbilt st, s s, 437.6 e Short st, 12.6x108, Flatbush. James W. McDermott agt Sophronia M. Pickett; att'ys, Boardman & Boardman...... 22

Throop av, e s, 42.1 s Hancock st, 19.6x81.6. American Baptist Home Mission Society agt Ervin G. Gollner; amended notice; att'y, Edward L. Clinch...... 22

York st, Nos. 145-153, n w cor Bridge st, 95x50.
Bridge st, n e cor York st, 25x100......
York st, n w cor Gold st, 75x127......
York st, No. 215, n s, 150 w Hudson av, 25x75...
Brooklyn Elevated R. R. Co. agt Deha W. Wilson et al.; action to acquire real estate; att'ys, Hoadley, Lauterbach & Johnson...... 22

Hull st, n s, 875 e Rockaway av, 16.9x100. George Carll and ano. exrs. Mary A. Carl agt Margaret McLaughlin; att'y, Henry W. Gaines...... 22

Evergreen av, s w s, 25 s e Covert st, 25x82. Henry A. Moore agt Jane E. Taadle; att'y, John F. Nelson...... 23

Bergen st, n s, 240 w Nevins st, 20x100, Sarah Drew agt Harriet J. Bradley; att'ys, Rolfe & Snedeker...... 23

Patchen av, w s, extends from McDonough st to Macon st, 200x80. Thomas H. Robbins agt Edwin Beers; att'y, Francis S. Turner...... 23

7th av, w s, 40 n 4th st, 30x88. Metropolitan Life Ins. Co. agt Garwood W. Powell; amended notice; att'ys, Arnoux, Ritch & Woodford...... 23

7th av, w s, 21 n 4th st, 19x88. Same agt same; amended notice; same att'ys...... 23

Grand av, both sides, from Myrtle to Lexington av. All lots abutting Brooklyn Elevated R. R. Co. agt Annie Cochran et al.; action to acquire easement; att'ys, Hoadley, Lauterbach & Johnson...... 23

Lots 4461-4660 block 80 map 291 lots Fifth Addition to Bensonhurst-by-the-Sea, Gravesend. William Crouch agt Mathilde H. Desvernine; foreclos. mechanics' lien; att'y, Michael Furst...... 23

President st, n s, 175 e 8th av, 50x100. Orson D. Munn agt Patrick Sheridan; att'y, John H. Betts...... 23

7th av, w s, 50 s Lincoln pl, 100x110. Charles E. Pell agt William S. Hale; notice of attachment; att'y, A. Shiland, Jr...... 24

Butler st, n s, 50 w Bond st, 37.6x100. William O. Moore et al. exrs. Abraham Underhill agt Annie F. Marrin; att'y, Philip L. Balz, Jr...... 24

1st st, s w s, 305 n w 5th av, 81x100. Charles E. Pell agt William S. Hale; notice of attachment; att'y, A. Shiland, Jr...... 24

Pacific st, s s, 260 e Albany av, 20x107.2. Anna L. Owen agt John H. Bonnell; att'y, Henry W. Gaines...... 24

Pacific st, n s, 280 e Albany av, 20x107.2. Lizzie A. Paddock agt John H. Bonnell; att'y, Henry W. Gaines...... 24

Glenada pl, s w cor Decatur st, 100x85. The Philadelphia Fire Proofing and Brick Co. agt William W. Reynolds; foreclos. mechanic's lien; att'y, Alfred H. Page...... 24

Covert st, n w s, 175 s w Evergreen av, 25x100. Thomas Hanlon agt Patrick F. Fitzgerald; foreclos. mechanic's lien; att'y, Theo. Burgmyer...... 24

RECORDED LEASES.

NEW YORK.

Per Year

Centre st, No. 27......
Centre st, No. 31, upper part of......
Mary Goodman to Carlo Barsotti; 5 years, from May 1, 1893...... $2,400

Cornelia st, No. 19. John B. McPherson to Paul Viane; 5 years, from Sept. 1, 1891...... 1,800

Same property. Assign. lease. Paul Viane to The Eastern Dispatch and Delivery Co...... 600

Dover st, Nos. 12 and 14, all. Ju Johnson to James H. Lavelle; 5 years, from Oct. 1, 1891. 1,320

Elm st, No. 191. Mary McKeon to Charles H. Weissert; 9 7-12 years, from Oct. 1, 1891...... 900

Forsyth st, No. 41, all. Mrs. A. L. Ranney to William Armendinger; 3 years, from May 1, 1890...... 950

Gansevoort st, No. 96 } except parts occupied
Gansevoort st, No. 94 } as stable and rear of cigar store in No. 94. Marie K. R. Thumann to Paul Baresel; 7¾ years, from Sept. 1, 1891...... 1,700

Greenwich st, No. 152, except small rear office. Henry Armstrong to Frederick Halem; 5 years, from May 1, 1891...... 1,880

Hester st, No. 148, basement store. John Carstens to Herrman Steffens; 3 years, from May 1, 1891...... 240

Peck slip, No 43. Bridget Kane extx. Nicholas Kane to Peter J. Byrne; 5 years, from Aug. 1, 1891...... 900

Union st, No. 114, s s, bet Ogden av and Lind av. Catharine Schmidt to John Franz; 5 years, from May 1, 1891...... 300, 420

81st st, No. 110 E. Charles Irving to George H. Taylor; 3 years, from Oct. 1, 1891...... 1,450

45th st, No. 548 W., store and cellar. Francis Mensing to Edward J. Murphy; 5 years, from May 1, 1891...... 360

51st st, No. 354 W. Mary H. Cudlipp to Ann Gallagher; 2 years and 11½ months, from Oct. 15, 1891...... 900

2d av, No. 547, store and basement. Paul Kreyling to Henry Hesse; 5 years, from May 1, 1892...... 720

3d av, No. 140, store floor and cellar. Charles Kingwell to Golding Bros.; 6⅔ years, from Oct. 1, 1891...... 1,200

3d av, Nos. 1313 and 1315, front basement and stores on first and second floors. John M. Ruck to Jacob and Samuel Baumann; 3 years, from Sept. 1, 1891...... 4,000

3d av, Nos. 140 and 142 } Dennis Redmond and
15th st, No. 144 E } Patrick Sheehy to Charles Kingwell; 7 years, from May 1, 1893. 7,200

3d av, No. 2444. Brian G. Hughes to Charles Kroegel; 5 years, from May 1, 1891...... 720, 900

3d av, No. 3027, all. William K. Peyton to William Hafner, Sr., and William Hafner, Jr., of Hafner & Son; 3 years, from Aug. 1, 1891...... 840, 900

5th av, No. 252, front room on second floor. Eliza Rallings to John Bartels; 3 years, from May 1, 1891...... 1,500

6th av, No. 847, s w cor 48th st. Nellie R. Lydon to Charles Cunz; 5 years, from May 1, 1896...... 2,808

8th av, No. 224, store and front basement. John Neher to Bernard Courtney; 10 1-6 years, from Mar. 1, 1891...... 2,500

CHATTELS.

Note.—The first name, alphabetically arranged, is that of the Mortgagor, or party who gives the Mortgage. The "R" means Renewal Mortgage.

NEW YORK CITY.

September 18 to 24.—Inclusive.

SALOON AND RESTAURANT FIXTURES.

Beer, Emil. 213 Forsyth....G & V Fischer. $2,000
Begley, Alexander. 615 W 46th....V Loewers. (R) 200
Blane, P J. 146th st and 8th av....W L Flanagan. 217
Boffa, A. 65 Mulberry....Budweiser B Co. (R) 600
Branstaedter, Klein. 71 Mercer ..J Hirschberg. Restaurant Fixtures. 275
Burke, M L. 126 W 50th....J Kress B Co. 1,800
Busse, Ernst. 139 Av A....J & M Haffen. 400
Becker, Peter. 58 Lewis....F Ibert. 400
Bode, Christian. 210 Eldridge....J C G Hupfel B Co. (R) 800
Bolhalter, A. 657 Washington....W Peter B Co. Ice House. 50
Brewster, J A. 425 W 17th....Budweiser B Co. Ice House. 125
Brown, C A and J. 153 East Houston....India Wharf B Co. 560
Byrne, P J. 43 Peck slip.. G Bechtel, exr of. 1,300
Byrne, Peter J. 124 Cherry....S C Boehem & Co. (R) 278
Barry, John. 1681 1st av....B McGuire. (R) secures rent
Bamwoll, Abram. 9½ Essex....Restaurant Furnishing Co. Restaurant Fixtures. 51
Bluhm & Geneis. 323 E 74th....Restaurant Furnishing Co. Restaurant Fixtures. 80
Cordes, William. 198 Lexington av... A Dryfoos & Co. 634
Carroll, F J. 219 Spring....H Elias B Co. (R) 500
Carroll & Kelly. 219 Spring....H Elias B Co. (R) 2,000
Cochran, Patrick. 2 Catharine....P H Brandt. (R) 450
Conway, Mary. 2028 1st av....J Kuntz B Co. 235
Davidson, Isidor. 230 7th av....M Van Rensselaer, Jr. (R) 350
Dreyer, William. 108 Division....Rubsam & H B Co. 900
Durante, Michael. 61 James....Budweiser B Co. (R) 112
Dwyer, J J. 497 Lexington av....C Stein. (R) 2,488
David, George. 342 E 32d....Budweiser B Co. Ice House. 90
Donohue, Kiran. 351 W 11th....D Stevenson. 434
Edler, Jacob, Jr. 529 9th av....J H Bereuter. Pool Table. 125
Elbsen, Hermann. 231 West....Burr B Co. (R) 5,000
Engelke, Henry. 2403 3d av....G T Lawrence. Restaurant Fixtures. 1,000
Flerz, Louisa. 22 1st av....W Kuntz. 830
Fischer, Herman. 368 Alexander av....G Ehret. (R) 1,200
Fox, J P. 1002 2d av....H Elias B Co. (R) 1,700
Gabriel, Barbara. 35 W 43d....J Wallace & Sons. 500
Gordon, David. 193 10th av....J Ruppert. 1,000
Graft, Heiman. 107 Hester....Budweiser B Co. 2,500
Hagen, Ewald. 101 Broad ...D Hollweg. (R) 5,000
Hammel, Franz. 35 1st av....C Stein. 995
Hirschfeld, Isaac. 129 Suffolk....Budweiser B Co. 1,500
Hitchcock, C B. 55 Bowery....W Ottman & Co. Restaurant Fixtures. 1,000
Huber, August. 126 3d....Knickerbocker B Co. 250
Hafner, W and W, Jr. 3027 3d av....A Hupfel's Sons. 1,600
Halim, Frederick. 152 Greenwich....M Eckstein B Co. (R) 500
Herrmann & Nickenig. 152 W 28th .. Bernheimer & S. 1,000
Hoffmann, J M. 431 7th av... V Loewers. 600
Hoffmann, Josef. 1731 3d av....J Eichler B Co. 600
Hughes, Michael. 562 3d av....D Stevenson. 300
Isaac, Abram. 28 East Broadway....F Munch, exr of. (R) 445
Isaac, Abram. 28 East Broadway....F Munch exr of. 445
Jorg, Anton. Elton av and 161st st. ..D Stevenson. 500
Karst, Frank. 582 E 150th....D Stevenson. 400
Kaufmann, H W. 29 Broadway....C Iba. 750
Ketcham, Willington. 794 8th av....H S Ketcham. Restaurant Fixtures. 400
Koster, A E. 1578 Broadway....C H Blancke. 700
Karst, Frank. 582 E 150th....D Stevenson. 400
Kingwell, Chas. 142 3d av ....Redmond & Sheehy. 1,000
Luper, David. 74 Suffolk....Rubsam & H B Co. 650
Lavalio, Pasquale. 113 Mulberry....Budweiser B Co. Ice House. 80
Loeninger, Joe. 319 E 74th....Schmitt & S. 700
Lang, William. 2491 2d av....D Stevenson. (R) 400
Ledr, Josef. 322 E 73d... J Doelger's Sons. 2,000
Malz, T F. 475 Pearl....T Reimer. (R) 1,500
Marcori, Angelo. 15 Baxter....J C G Hupfel B Co. (R) 1,333
Meier, John. 151 Broome....F Ibert. 250
Muller, Gustav. Allen and Houston sts....G Bechtel. (R) 1,954
Maggi, G. 127 South 5th av... Bernheimer & S. Saloon Ice House. 20
Same... same. Saloon Ice House. 85
McCabe, Michael. 588 Hudson....T C Lyman & Co. (R) 1,000
McCool, Thos A. 149 E 42d ...J Doelger's Son. (R) 400
McLaughlin, Daniel. 567 and 569 Hudson....Budweiser B Co. 3,500
Michels, J. 107 Av C....Bernheimer & S. Saloon Pump. 81
Same....same. Saloon Drip Pan. 20
Same....same. Saloon Ice House. 75
Same....same. Saloon Ice House. 85
Myers, J J. 541 10th av....B Wintermeyer. 300
Myers, M L. 152 W 52d....J C G Hupfel B Co. 750
May, Frederick. 1543 Broadway....G Ruppel. 2,500
Madden & Fuss. 884 3d av....J Ahles B Co. 500
McGlynn, John. Greenwich and Laight sts....Budweiser B Co. Ice House. 156
Nicholson & Donnelly. 605 3d av....H Elias B Co. (R) 400
"Ninth Ward Regulars." 12 Abingdon sq....W H Griffith & Co. Pool Table. 325
Neimeyer, August. 779 3d av....Restaurant Furnishing Co. Restaurant Fixtures. 287
O'Brien, James. 329 W 17th....P McCann. 750
O'Reilly, Myles. 69 Gansevoort.... Empire State B Co. 135
Oliveros, B F. 518 Lexington av....J Everard. 846
O'Rourke, Patrick. 1140 1st av....M Livingston. 300
Polak, Samuel. 686 Tremont av ...Brunswick-B-C Co. Pool. 425
Proppe, Louis. 417 West.. .Beadleston & W. (R) 3,000
Payne, Wiltshire. 19 Fulton ...M Duffy. Restaurant Fixtures. 100
Quinn, J F and P E. 131 W 23d....R Chapman. Restaurant Fixtures. 75
Rosenthal, C L. 274 Broome....G Ehret. 2,500
Rettig, J M, Jr. 244 W 32d... C Stein. (R) 830
Richmond, Louis. 636 Bowery....G Ringler & Co. 1,500
Rail, Patrick. 533 6th av....H Elias B Co. 1,500
Ryan, James. 111th st and Boulevard....Bernheimer & S. 150
Roberts, C H. 300 E 96th....A F Hahn. Restaurant Fixtures. 50
Rohlfs, William. 418 W 25th....D Mayer. 1,100
Schaum, John. 110 E 41st ...G Ringler & Co. 500
Schorr, Michael. 1263 3d av....Restaurant Furnishing Co. Restaurant Fixtures. 80

Schererloh, Anna. 20 Delancey....J Everard. 2,547
Shauer, V F. 529 Broadway....D Auerbach. Restaurant Fixtures. 102
Sommer, Ludwig. Elm av and Southern Boulevard....J Eichler B Co. 550
Saladin, J E. 500 W 48th....G Ehret. 1,000
Schuster, George 49 Franklin....J Ruppert. 650
Siemers, F C. 2817 3d av....H Zeltner. (R) 1,000
Tirelli, Louis. 117 Bleecker....Bachmann & Co. (R) 300
Wagner, J A. 1971 Washington av....J Eichler B Co. 500
Walther, Louis. 285 Bowery ..Bishop & Babcock Co. 184
Wettje, John. 81 Lispenard....F Hotze. (R) 6,794
Weygandt, Adolph. 283 Broome....J Ruppert. 500
Wulfus, H A G. 264 and 266 West....J C G Hupfel B Co. (R) 3,000
Weber, Henry. 76 Laight....Bavarian B Co. 1,700
Zoller, John. 548 Courtlandt av... A Hupfel's Son. 200

HOUSEHOLD FURNITURE.

Allport, J G. Highbridge....J C Kennedy. 500
Same ...F G Blaney. 1,500
Apel, Marie. 308 1st av....Simpson & P. Piano. 190
Adler, Josie. 201 W 53d....S Heyman & Co. 239
Abner, J M. 887 Cadwell av....L Baumann. 218
Armstrong, David, Jr. 111 W 44th....J E Armstrong. 2,000
Armstrong, Dora. 267 W 40th....J Moriarty. 315
Arnold, G W, Jr, and C G. 118 W 133d ...F H Ross. 550
Anthes, Wilhelm. 221 E 46th....H Thoesen. 158
Beatty, H A. 467 4th av....J Foulke, Jr. Piano. 140
Bedell, Mrs Thos. 630 6th av....T Leonard. 168
Brionck, P J. 217 W 60th....L Baumann. 257
Bullock, F and M L. 1689 1st av....W H Rogers. 200
Berbeinch, Catherine. 337 E 5th....S Baumann. 317
Banta, Ella. 110 W 45th ...S Baumann. 511
Brady, Carrie. 207 E 22d . H S Eisler. 162
Barnes and Van Dyck. 17 Abingdon sq....J L Rusling. 1,200
Bernard, Mrs L. 117 W 15th....S Heyman & Co. 561
Best, Mrs E. 268 W 39th....O'Connor & T. 129
Bostwick, J O. 180 E 95th. . L Baumann. 200
Bozelle, E J. 303 W 145th....Fennell & P. 102
Brandt, Louisa. 555 E 140th .Fennell & P. (R) 108
Byrne, Nellie. 334 W 17th....D M Brown. 260
Cassidy, Isabel. 33 W 23d....S Baumann. 1,322
Charlotte, Sarah R. 202 W 78th....S Baumann. 243
Cormeier, J E. 324 West....H S Eisler. 119
Callery, P J. 223 E 70th....H Thoesen. 120
Canfield, W de H Q. 8 E 18th....Amer Guar Assoc. 100
Cassenas, M. 116 E 90th....S Heyman & Co. 160
Cavanagh, Maggie. 388 Cherry ...Jordan & M. 126
Cohn, A J. 244 E 20th... S Heyman & Co. 237
Conlon, Jennie E. 535 Union av ...Fennell & P. (R) 106
Charlton, C E. Beach av and 149th st....W E Wheelock & Co. Piano. 275
Cummings, Julia. 216 Chrystie....H S Eisler. 101
Canfield, Mary E. 114 W 43d....T Leonard. 122
Chovin, Carolina. 508 6th av....L Baumann. 136
Cohn, W J. 216 E 104th....R Epstein. 350
Collopy, Thomas. 862 8th av....E D Farrell. 148
Depue, Carrie. 210 W 35th....L Baumann. 114
Doyle, Lizzie. 1897 3d av....L Baumann. 169
De Nicola, Antonio. 57 Mott....H S Eisler. 114
Downing, D P. 1195 3d av....L Baumann. 139
Deborn, Ernst. 388 E 41st....G Fennell & Co. (R) 191
Dempsey, J H. 548 E 84th ...Jordan & M. 167
Doremus, A H and M D. Storage ...P L Van Wagenen. (R) 500
Evans, Maggie. 523 Hudson....H S Eisler. 127
Eaton, G A. 1869 Lexington av....Garvey Bros. 127
Ellis, Louisa H. 642 Columbus av ...T Kelly. 123
Elbers, Gerhard. 98 2d av....M Elbers. 2,000
Earle, Mrs W T. 52 W 22d....H Thoesen. (R) 301
Eckhart, Margaret. 38 and 40 Centre....L Baumann. 277
Eustace, J A and M V. 219 W 104th....Russmann & G. (R) 8,500
Fall, Mary. 13 Michell pl....H Thoesen. 146
Feeney, Delia. 430 Pearl....Jordan & M. 130
Feldman, E K. 315 E 120th....Fennell & P. (R) 114
Fields, Kate. 257 W 39th O'Farrell & Co. 202
Flattwell, Elizabeth. 172 W 97th....S Heyman & Co. 116
Foote, Helen A. 1771 9th av....Fennell & P. (R) 110
Fox, Margaret. 237 W 33d....O'Farrell & Co. 272
Francis, John. 304 W 21st....L Baumann. (R) 145
Franzan, Chas. 306 E 25th....S Heyman & Co. (R) 122
Freer, E B. 330 W 56th....S Heymann & Co. (R) 297
Froehlich, Marina. 1437 Lexington av....S Baumann. 191
Fuhse, Adelia. 110 E 90th....L Baumann. 144
Faulhater, Julius. 1551 2d av....S Baumann. 189
Forstner, William. 305 Columbus av....S Baumann. 650
Graubard, Morris. 189 Chrystie....H S Eisler. 104
Gravel, Louisa. 149 E 38th. ..J Moriarty. (R) 188
Gillvon, Cora. 234 E 64th....D M Brown. 103
Gorman, Anna. 156 St. Anns av....S Baumann. 254
Grate, A H. 361 W 116th....J Moran. 218
Greenbaum, M. 172 W 96th .. L Baumann. 318
Gunson, T J. 305 E 72d....S Heyman & Co. 309
Gillespie, Edward. 990 Jackson av....L Baumann. 227
Greene, E C. 319 W 16th....K Strack. 625
Glass, Stella. 201 W 29th....H Thoesen. 155
Goodwin, Mrs L A. 318 W 34th....H Thossen. 119
Henderson, Mrs M A. 98 E 8th ...D M Brown. 133
Hennessey, J H. 46 W 100th....Jordan & M. 100
Home, Ellen. 244 W 22d . J Moriarty. 107
Hagemeyer, William. 344 E 20th....A Frey. 100
Hartley, Mrs Kay. 158 W 53d....J A Baker. 4,000
Hayes, Mrs Edward. 115 Waverley pl....T Kelly. 149
Heffero, Maggie. 367 W 52d....T Leonard. 165
Hurn, Edward. 210 W 59th ...Garvey Bros. 126
Hammerschmidt, C F. 417 St Nicholas av....S Heyman & Co. 232
Harriet, A F and H M. 2125 8th av....American Guarantee Assoc. 150
Hart, J P. 218 W 32d ...O'Farrell & Co. 204
Heath, Michael. 12 Forsyth....J Rubenstein. 126
Henry, Kate. 595 Grand....D M Brown. 145
Herisse, Marie. 568 7th av... O'Farrell & Co. 124
Hill, Mrs J P. 102 W 50th ...Thomas Kelly. (R) 116
Holland, Teresa. 125 E 63d....L Baumann. 203
Horan, Mrs B. 1000 2d av....D M Brown. 317
Howard, Mary F. 143 W 53d....Alexander Bros. 303
Jones, Laura. 1005 6th av....H Israel & Sons. (R) 158
Jackson, R H. 239 W 41st....L Baumann. 188
Jervis, Ellen. 224 E 27th ...Garvey Bros. 119
Jonson, Edward. 312 W 49th....L Baumann. 132
Kaiser, Mary L. 414 E 81st. ..T Leonard. 255
Kempter, Chas. 524 W. 49th....T Leonard. 167
Klatschke & Bernstein. 183 Orchard ...S I Herschmann. 175
Kean, Julia. 1964 7th av....S Baumann. 140
Kerwin, John. 941 3d av....J Moran. 127
Koch, Otto. 355 W 43d .. D M Brown. 111
Kornhauser, Sam. 108 7th S Heyman & Co. 120
Kendall, Lillian. 189 Lexington av....S Heyman & Co. (R) 176
Kelton, M S. 129 E 90th....L Baumann. 140
King, Annie. 149 W 26th ...H Mannes & Son. 170
Lund & Forst. 108 W 28th....H Mannes & Son. 150
Lacrouts, Amelia. 131 W 3d....J Libretto. 125
Laurent, Edward. 165 Clinton pl....J Gregg & Co. 185
Loring, Mrs L. 111 W 56th....S Heyman & Co. 601
Lovecraft, E G. 2200 8th av....S Baumann. 124
Lauer, Pierre. 165 Prince....M Lauer. 700
Lewis, Mrs Henry. 22 Morton....D M Brown. 207
Loomis, G A. 184 E 76th....D M Brown. 326
Lowrey, J E. 561 Grand....T Willis. 195
Lamarr, Ellner. 231 E 70th....L Baumann. 200
Leve, Robert. 170 E 111th....Krakauer Bros. Piano. 265
Lewis, Alice. 309 W 14th....L Baumann. 214
Maidhoff, Peter. 888 E 165th....T Leonard. 421
Manning, Nellie. 241 W 32d .. O'Farrell & Co. 116
McClellan, Margaret. 285 E 33d....S Baumann. 137
McKenna, W H. 313 E 69th . J Gregg. (R) 354
Mallon, Annie. 429 Grand ...R M Walters. Piano. (R) 133
Mordaunt, Clementine J. 112 W 39th....J Baumann. (R) 378
Mackenzie, A H. 52 E 116th....Simpson & P. Piano. 335
Markowitz, Fritz. 36 Greenwich....D M Brown. 124
Marks, Alfred. 445 W 57th....C F Pierce. 130
Mason, Annie J. 138 W 33d....S Baumann. 234
Manley, Henry. 545 W 158th....Jordan & M. 117
Morse, Carrie E. 10, 12 and 14 W 125th....Fennell & P. (R) 707
Morton, H W. 140 E 48th....J Moran. 162
Myles, W S. 142 W 62d....Jordan & M. 143
Madigan, Michael. 559 E 136th....Jordan & M. 196
Middleton, Virginia. 109 E 128d. . S Baumann. 210
Moser, Lizzie. 521 E 83d....G Fennell & Co. 104
Murray, Kate. 235 E 27th....J Moriarty. 145
Nolan, Nellie. 120 E 93d .. S Baumann. 190
Nisser, Felix. 226 W 17th ...J Gregg & Co. 115
Nixon, Theresa C. 11 E 32d....A C Brown. (R) 2,766
Nace, Mrs A S. 61 W 105th....T Kelly. 225
Needham, Mrs P. 191 Waverley pl....T Kelly. 142
Oliver, Margaret J. 362 W 22d....O'Farrell & Co. 560
Oliver, Margaret. 362 W 22d....A Gillies. 122
Oliver, M G. 362 W 22d....O'Farrell & Co. 505
Olmsted, Fannie B. 108 W 80th....J McEnery & Co. 266
Obenauer, Christina. 9 W 48th....S Obenauer. 5,000
Picket, Eva. 13 Pell....H S Eisler. 114
Post, W C. Hastings... J Moriarty. (R) 256
Pettet, Lillian. 316 W 36th....S Heyman & Co. (R) 152
Perry, E T... Gately & W. 222
Pollack, Gussie. 69 Chrystie....H S Eisler. 159
Plump, Annie. 5 Watt.. E D Farrell. 125
Powell, S A & M. 139, 140 and 142 W 11th....H H Hawkes. (R) 1,000
Powell, S A, Mrs. 138 and 142 W 11th ..T Kelly. 146
Reichelt, Joseph 123 E 90th....T Kelly. 142
Rhoades, F R. 122 W 102d....Garvey Bros. 100
Ratzky, Henrietta 68 E 12th....O'Farrell & Co. 435
Reagen, Mary. 69 W 133d... D M Brown. 118
Reilly, Elizabeth. 719 E 146th....Fennell & P. 160
Renlein, Lillie. 181 W 102d....H Israel & Sons. 116
Robeson, Dora. 311 8th av....O'Farrell & Co. 124
Ross, R S. 36 W 24th....H L Ross. 500
Rothschild, Matilda. 167 E 85th....S Baumann. 139
Rozengrave, Mary. 115 Washington pl....R M Walters. Piano. 220
Rumler, Mrs E. 22 St Marks pl....Alexander Bros. 122
Raymond, Jennie. 214 W 42d... L Baumann. 231
Salotowitz, Solomon. 117 Henry....H S Eisler. 100
Sanvigne, Emil. 239 E 29th... L Baumann. 197
Schultz, Annie. 52 E 4th....S Harris. 336
Sears, Amelia C. 124 W 11th....J Moriarty. (R) 149
Shaffer, Laura E. 85 E 114th....W E Wheelock & Co. Piano. 260
Smith, Margaret. 547 W 125th ...H Mannes & Son. 145
Sturges, J S. 167 West Boulevard ...H Mannes & Son. 110
Sanches, Rafael. 1798 3d av....S Heyman & Co. 259
Schaffer, Michael. 235 W 66th....L Baumann. 127
Schramek, A. 534 8th av... H Thoesen. (R) 445
Schvenberg, Herman. 205 E 72d....M C Hegemann. 128
Seymour, Virginia....Gately & W. 210
Shaw, Clotilda. 305 W 126th... M Garry. 125
Silberstine, Simon. 1627 Madison av....Amer Guar Assoc. 100
Smith, Minnie. 1557 2d av....L Baumann. 176
Smith, Richard. 140 W 99th....L Baumann. 137
Sokolousky, Joseph. 78 Cannon....Alexander Bros. 113
Souza, Julius. 298 E 54th....Fennell & P. 135
St Auges, Mimi. 120 W 35th ...S Baumann. 135
Stark, Philip. 63 Suffolk....J Rubenstein. 165
Sullivan, Catherine. 128 Leonard....Jordan & M. 145
Sullivan, Katie. 22 Oliver....S Baumann. 475
Searing, E J. 207 W 134th ...T Kelly. 340
Spitz, H. 208½ Broome .E D Farrell. 116
Sullivan, M, Mrs. 319 Bowery....E D Farrell. 135
Sandberg, John. 237 E 29th... Jordan & M. 141
Sanders, Julius. 71 Courtlandt av....W E Wheelock & Co. Piano. 200
Scanlon, Margaret. 426 4th av....J J Coogan. (R) 175
Schmidtt, G A. 131 E 7th....J Moriarty. 114
Stoessel, A. 965 3d av....H Thoesen. 119
Sweet, George. 57 W 42d.... J Baumann. (R) 292
Tucker, Elizabeth. 117 W 45th....T Willis. 620
Titcomb, Helen A. 2260 8th av....L Baumann. 129
Tainter, H H. 399 Douglas, Brooklyn....Simpson & P. Piano. 250
Timin, A J. 52 W 47th ...J Moriarty. 124
Thompson, C A. New Rochelle....J Dickson. 450
Timberlake, Nellie. 282 W 115th....J Moriarty. (R) 139
Verplanck, W A. 233 W 135th....S Baumann. 301
Washauer, Gracie. 109 1st....J Moriarty. 119
Weiss, Alexander. 333 E 89th....G Fennell & Co. 394
Whitmore, Charlotte. 9 E 17th....M R Goodwin. 500
Wood, Augusta F 240 E 122d....W H Gillette. (R) 280
Ware, B F. 327 W 87th ..Jordan & M. 100
Warshauer, J C. 219 W 122d ...Fennell & P. 227
Same....same. 330
Warren, Mrs F A. 161 W 33d ...T Kelly. (R) 241
Weidner, Mrs M. 36 E 64th....S Heyman & Co. 160
Weston, M A. 931 Park av....S Heyman & Co. (R) 609
Wheeler, Edmund. 1506 2d av....J Moriarty. 337
Wilson, Ida. 11 Pell....Jordan & M. 108
Woodward, Mrs E S. 107 W 40th....S Heyman & Co. 205
Waterhouse, A E. 1142 Park av....Lincoln I and G Co. 100
Zander, Marie. 90 4th av....Fennell & P. 313

MISCELLANEOUS.

Angelica, Giuseppe. 985 1st av....S Ribaudo. Barber Fixtures. 325
Antoine, F. 189 Bleecker .. National Cash Reg Co. Register. 200
Aul, C A. 216 and 253 Monroe .. E Aul. Bakery Fixtures. 4,640
Amsbry, F M .... Perrin, P & Co. Buggy Wagon. 50
Same... same. Buggy Wagon. 160
Same....same. Buggy Wagon. 63
Beck, Reuben. J Gottsleben. Coach. 650
Bisdorf, Henry. 381 E 10th.... C A Beckers. Butcher Fixtures. 506
Busch, Garrett. 433 W 44th ...D P Nichols & Co. Cab. 275
Birm, William. 102 Clinton....C Speck. Barber Fixtures.
Braun, Geo. 363 10th av... National Cash Reg Co. Register. 200
Caske, David. 1111 2d av....Archer Mfg Co. Barber Fixtures. 65
Chabiss, Herman. 334 Grand....W H Griffin. Photo Fixtures. 100
Coleman, Max. 156 Forsyth....R Rainforth. Barber Fixtures. 57
Carr, J R. 17 1st....M Solomon. Cigar Fixtures. 200
Carroll & Smith....D P Nichols & Co. Cab. 650
Cranston, T L. 39 Gold....Hub Publishing Co. Printing Fixtures. 2,185
Cohn, Solomon & Co. 627 and 629 Broadway.... A Gross. Machinery, &c. 700
Crow, J J. 358 W 38th....J Cunningham Son & Co. Coach. 1,550
Doggett, F W E. 104 John . C P Ayers. Office Fixtures. 150
Dzialka, Markus. 110 Clinton....H Schlamyck. Butcher Fixtures. 30
David, G G. 165 E 122d....J Williams. Bottler Fixtures (R) 556
Davis, Ernest. 206 Bowery....J Sangunitti. Machinery. (R) 600
Deichmiller, F A. 585 E 143d....Archer Mfg Co. Barber Fixtures. 381
Deutsch, Wm. 1331 3d av....Archer Mfg Co. Barber Fixtures. 37
Exiner B Lord & Co. 624 Madison av....E H Van Duzer & Co. Fixtures, Stock, &c. 650
Edelson, Abraham. 38 Jefferson....A Edelson. Butcher Fixtures. 500
Edelson, Louis. 39 Hester....I Glasser. Butcher Fixtures. 500
Fidelbogen, Herman. 48 Ludlow... Duparquet, H & M Co. Ranges, &c. 102
Francia, Luca. 26½ E 42d ...M Russo. Barber Fixtures. 550
Farrell, M E....B Weill. Horses, Trucks, &c. 300
Filipstein, Moses. 102 Allen....Archer Mfg Co. Barber Fixtures. 58
Fitzgerald, J B and E L. 333 and 335 E 60th.... F P Brown. Horses, Ice Wagon, &c. 625
Fraser, T E. 1024 2d av....L A Frasick. Drug Fixtures. 4,800
German Evangelical Church. 339 E 84th... L Goebel. Church Fixtures. (R) 3,000
Gibson, C C. 367 8th av... J W Tufts. Soda Fixtures. 200
Goldberg, Harris. 18 Bowery....S Goldberger. Machines. 150
Greenslade, Edward. 173 E 130th....S E Hoose. Horse, Truck, &c. 150
Grumbler, Simon. 68 Stanton....Archer Mfg Co. Barber Fixtures. 506
Gutkof, Abraham. 17 Chrystie....S Goldberger. Horse, &c. 28
Giss, Joseph. 745 10th av....J Albiez. Barber Fixtures. 200
Goldblatt, Nathan. 116 Broome....H Oppenheim. Grocery Fixtures. 250
Gruenberg, S & Co. 96 East Houston....V Goworowski. Drug Fixtures. 400
Gallon, Edward L. 305-309 W 41st....J Ohlsen. Lumber Business. 3,300
Herzfeld, Herman. 260 7th av....G Hoffmann. Drug Fixtures. 1,000
Holling, J H. 324 W 40th....L Baechle. Milk Wagon. 55
Harding, Frank. 229 Bowery....E J Amor. Presses, &c. (R) 1,500
Hartmann, F J. 1448 2d av....T Austermann. Drug Fixtures. 500
Haas, F X. 30 Suffolk ...M Garry. Horse, Trucks. 250
Haas, Joseph. 93 White....A W Sloggelt. Press, &c. 1,200
Heldy, G & Co .H B Smith & Co. Machinery. 302
Hellman, Ph. 71 Division....W H Butler. Safe. 125
Hendrick, F J... Kean & Lines. Coach. (R) 375
Hess, G and H, 279-285 Rivington ...M Hess. Machinery. 5,408
Hoerth, F L. 541 9th av....R F Harmes. Grocery Fixtures. 1,300
Holmes, W D. 93 Maiden lane....L Freiberge. Machinery, &c. 107
Hopkins, L A. 127 Pearl....National C Reg Co Register. 200
Hart & Co. 2303 2d av .... E Marscheider. Butcher Fixtures. 100
Heimlich, Max. 192 Columbus av....P Westphal. Barber Fixtures. 272
Hofer, L C. 443 W 45th....J Hollings. Milk Wagon, Horse, &c. 450
Hanson, F G & Co. 19 W 3d....W M Ducker. Presses, &c. 1,319
Ironside, C N. 154 and 156 W 27th....E H Bartley. Presses, &c. 186
Isacove, H. 31 Ludlow....Archer Mfg Co. Barber Fixtures. 37
Jaunelli, Antonio. 686 11th av....A Telloche. Barber Fixtures. 75
Kallmeyer, Frederick. 528 E 85th....Archer Mfg Co. Barber Fixtures. 125
Kaplan, Isaac. 161 Varick....Archer Mfg Co. Barber Fixtures. 149
Kile, C. 135th st and 7th av....J W Tufts. Soda Fixtures. 200

Kuhn, Martin. 152 Eldridge....C A Proben. Drug Fixtures. 4,750
Kirchenbauer, E L. 2386 Hoffmann....H C Carstens. Horse, Wagon, Bottles, &c. 550
Knief, Henry. 101 and 103 E 126th....H Luesse. Horse, Wagon, &c. 300
Krause, Otto. Plaza Hotel....Archer Mfg Co. Barber Fixtures. (R) 4,025
Kunz, H....C H Bangs. Drug Fixtures. 650
Kieferdorf, Fred. 75th st and Columbus av....National C Reg Co. Register. 220
King, Charles. Yonkers ...C H W Carter. Machinery. 1,082
Koelsch, Geo. 1181 Broadway....National C Reg Co. Register. 175
Locke, C E. 247 E 99th....J K Emmett, Jr. Scenery, &c. (R) 1,500
Lina, Lorenza. 413 W 40th....R Rainforth. Barber Fixtures. 76
Loerssen, F W. 19 6th....H Ricken. Drug Fixtures. 1,602
Maher, Thos. 52 Centre....Nat Cash Register Co. 50
McWilliams Printing Co. 83 Elm....Van Allens & B. Paper Cutter. (R) 175
Mercur, J G. 198 Chambers....Nathan & K. Cigar Fixtures, &c. 190
Mertens, Louis. 225 10th av....J H Von Glahn. Barber Fixtures. 425
Miller, Elijah. 213 Monroe....O J Ward. Drug Fixtures. 2,200
Miller, Harris. 2306 2d av....J M Winterroth. Butcher Fixtures. 150
Milliken & D'Amour. 151 and 153 Cedar....M Rubens. Machinery. 750
Mooney, Christopher. 134 W 49th ...Hincks & J. Coach. 650
MacCaffery, John. 126th st and Boulevard....T H Rohdenburg. Horses, &c. 250
Mercer, Elizabeth B. 50 Bond ..A B Rice. Fixtures, Furniture, &c. 1,092
Meyers, William. 112 Bank....N Campbell. Horses, Trucks, &c. 125
Monaglean, Edward. 136 E 32d....W B Davis. Coupe. (R) 100
Moss, Charles....W B Davis. Coupe. (R) 36
Murphy, George. 3 E 14th....U S Photo Supply Co. Fixtures, &c. 13,627
Meyer, Elias. 179 Delancey....E Marscheider. Butcher Ice House. 70
Markiewicz, Franks 88 Wall....Archer Mfg Co. Barber Fixture . 187
McArdel, Philip... J Gottsleben. Coach. 275
McDermott, B. 229 Monroe....J McDermott. Horse, &c. 900
Meyer, J M. 418 Lenox av....C F Gennerich. Grocery Fixtures. (R) 500
Niblo, W H. 74 Chambers....F Robinson. Store Fixtures. 70
New York Printing Co. 536 Pearl .. Campbell P P Co. Press. (R) 200
Neal, H J. 386 Columbus av....E W Blinn. Office Fixtures. 200
Owens, John. 512 W 15th....R Hutchinson. Horses, Trucks, &c. 500
Palumbiere, Domenico. 13½ Oliver....Archer Mfg Co. Barber Fixtures. (R) 220
Pine, C H. 216 Church....J Heyman. Office Fixtures. 35
Payne, Robert. 888 11th av....Nat Cash Register Co. Register. 350
Phelan, John. 168 E 73d....W Griffin, Horses, Coaches, &c. 1,000
Politowicz, Frank. 104 Essex....S Prus. Barber Fixtures. 80
Rankin, George .. T M Bower. Wagon. 250
Rosenzweig, Max. 72 Forsyth....Archer Mfg Co. Barber Fixtures. 650
Riniker, Adolph. 2515 8th av....J McLean. Butcher Fixtures. 164
Rapp, Ignatz. 66 Av C....P Reidenbach. Milk Wagon. 50
Reinhard, August. 1561 Av A....W Eichenlaub. Barber Fixtures. 262
Richters, William. 2471 3d av ...C H Crocker. Soda Fixtures. 225
Stern, Leopold. 863 6th av....J Stern. Laundry Fixtures. 500
Schwartz, M. 168 Clinton....Archer Mfg Co. Barber Fixtures. 42
Sinnot, M. 20½ Whitehall....Lamson Consol S S Co. Register. 140
Smith & Horgan. Fulton Market....G Sieman. Stands, &c. (R) 4,300
Schwack, J I. 122 Norfolk....J H Schwack. Horses and Milk Fixtures. 1,000
Schwake, H H. 224 W 20th....G Schuttenberg. Grocery Fixtures. 400
Schleustein, Christian. 1623 2d av....Livermore & Enders. Bakery Fixtures. 280
Seipel, Henry. Bleecker st and Broadway....Archer Mfg Co. Barber Fixtures. 135
Slupsky, Bertha. 80 Sheriff and 77 Willett....M Slupsky. Horse, Wagon, &c. 140
Stossel, A J and A. 265 3d av....W Fritzel. Bakery Fixtures. 1,500
Tolk, Herman. 106 East Broadway....Bennett & G. Soda Fixtures. 825
Townsend, T S. Columbia College....F A Schermerhorn Library. 7,345
Triolo, John. 1494 1st av....Archer Mfg Co. Barber Fixtures. 111
Tams, A W. 416 W 28th....Damon & Peets. Cutter. 55
Vastolo, Lorenzo. 36 Rector....Archer Mfg Co. Barber Fixtures. (R) 712
Valenti, Pietro. 101 2d av....Archer Mfg Co. Barber Fixtures. 198
Van Dine, J R. 17 South....National C Reg Co. Register. 175
Warrill & Govan. 225 W 27th....Archer Mfg Co. Barber Fixtures. 85
Whitten, J W. Long Branch....J Mathews. Soda Fixtures. (R) 715
Weinstein, Jacob. 28 Spring....J T Robinson & Co. Machinery. 300
Weitzman, Jacob. 453 and 455 Water....M Liberman. Machinery. 260
Wm Wicke Co....Central Trust Co. Machinery Fixtures, &c. (R) 400,000
Weitzen, I. 105 Sheriff....Bennett & G. Soda Fixtures. 235
Wendelken, John. 4th av and 24th st....National C Reg Co. Register. 175
Wolinsky, Samuel. 328 E 39th....E Marscheider. Butcher Ice House. 85
Wolff, V S. 15 Washington....Marvin Safe Co. Safe. 120
Zeller, Oscar. 1846 2d av....A Zeeler. Bakery. 400
Zagat, Max. 858 2d av....J K Ambrose. Drug Fixtures. 1,500
Zoeller, F. 2217 Park av....Archer Mfg Co. Barber Fixtures. 590

BILLS OF SALE.

Capel & McNulty....Susan M. Capel. Assets, &c. 1
Duffy, Matthew, 19 Fulton....W Payne. Restaurant Fixtures. 250
Freiberger, R C. 121 Amsterdam av....C S Erb. Drug Fixtures. 2,300
Freund, Clara. 171 Eldridge....J Horowitz. Seltzer Water Fixtures. ½ interest. 800
Germond, C. 445 and 447 E 150th....F G Burk. Machinery, &c. 5,000
Gilman, Aman. 146 Suffolk....Sarah Gilman. Machines, &c. 500
Hirsch, M & Co. 729 E 177th....H Klauber. Saloon Fixtures. 1,700
Hart, E H and F W. 246 E 23d....D Ramsey. Pictures, Photo, &c. 1,339
Kay, Mary J. 684 Columbus av....C Plump. Confectionery Fixtures. 700
Leslie, J H. 178 Varick ...Nancy H B Leslie. Cigar Fixtures, &c. 1
Levandowski, Leib. 191 Rivington....A Hollander. Barber Fixtures. 100
Mallaby, F B ...M A Ferris. Int in Will of E B Seaman. 1,000
McNeilly, Hugh. 298 West Houston....G Weisner. Grocery Fixtures. 697
Schorling, F. 187 6th av ...F D Fricek. Saloon. 5,500
Vetromile, Nicola. 283 Bowery....F Falisi. Barber Fixtures. 230
Walsh, J H. 1777 Columbus av....Margaret Walsh. Grocery Fixtures. 450
Weiss, Mary. 17 1st....J R Carr. Cigar Fixtures. 300

ASSIGNMENTS OF CHATTEL MORTGAGES.

Dinkelmann, A & Co to E Rosenfeldt. (Mort given by F Freedman, May 15, 1891.) 1,100
Eibsen, Hermann to H Kroger & Co. (A Sauerland, Aug 24, 1891.) 1
Sturzemegger, Edmund to C N Martin. (J Ringeisen, Aug 9, 1890.) 50

KINGS COUNTY.

SEPTEMBER 17 TO 23—INCLUSIVE.

SALOON AND RESTAURANT FIXTURES.

Ackerman, H Y. 639 5th av....J H and J C Doyle. $4,000
Adams, R. 335 Driggs av ...Burger & Hower B Co. 1,169
Bellmann, J F. 159 Evergreen av ...F Ibert. 500
Blank, R J. 1391 Broadway....Danenberg & Coles. 1,200
Brossard, T and O A. 4 and 5 Court sq....O Huber. (R) 1,200
Brown, F. 252 Central av....J Doelger's Sons (R) 800
Burke, J F. 1549 Broadway....Olena & Craig. 768
Burke, T. 221 Greene....M Seitz. 500
Barte, F. 75 Meserole....J Fallert B Co. 450
Bermann, L. 951 Grand... Rubsam & H B Co. 165
Coleman, D H. 285 Sackett....G Ringler & Co. 1,457
Carlson, P. 490 Atlantic av....Bachmann B Co. (R) 200
Carroll, R. 270 Humboldt....J Fallert B Co. 550
Connell, J. 131 Imlay....T C Lyman & Co. (R) 1,044
Creighton, G. 670 4th av....T C Lyman & Co. (R) 600
Casey, Patrick. 269 Washington st, 472 Atlantic av and 83 Nevins st....M Van Rensselaer, Jr, trustee. (R) 3,650
Dintelmann, B. 176 Fulton....Higgins & Co. Billiard Table. 150
Dehmann, G. Atlantic av, s e cor Snedeker av ....Leibinger & O B Co. (R) 500
Ebert, Ernestine. 29 Locust....L Eppig. 450
Eagan, J C. 500 Grand....India Wharf B Co. 250
Eichner, K and J Celler. 317 Central av....Elizabeth Metzler. 200
Frischmann, J. 194 Boerum st....Burger & Hower B Co. (R) 500
Freidank, C. 117 Seigel....J Kress B Co. 625
Fraser, A. 134 Fulton....F Bachmann. (R) 200
Freyknecht, M. 221 Bowery, New York....M Freyknecht. Billiard Table. 500
Fitzsimmons, W J. 284 Driggs av....P Doelger. 425
Gasser, A. Atlantic av, s w cor Eaton st....Long Island Brewery. 500
Giacomino, R. 30 Maspeth av .. Budweiser B Co. 450
Gink, P. 129 Graham av....J Fallert B Co. 555
Grafenstein, T. Atlantic av, cor Sheffield av....Budweiser B Co. (R) 1,500
Grasser, J. 25 Lee av....Williamsburgh B Co. 360
Hilpert, J G. 172 Montrose av ...Claus Lipsius B Co. 600
Henry, T. 256 Hamilton av....S Liebmann's Sons B Co. 716
Hrizko, A. 295 Kent av....S Liebmann's Sons B Co. 1,200
Holly, W C. 191 Baltic....T C Lyman & Co. (R) 1,000
Hagmauer, F. 134 Ewen....J Eppig. 1,200
Keegan & Fee. 213 Hamilton av....Welz & Z. (R) 200
Kenny, M. 116 Manhattan av....Leibinger & Oehm B Co. 450
Kavanagh & Duffy. 35 Lafayette av....Budweiser B Co. (R) 400
Keim, F J. 245 Troutman....Burger & H B Co. (R) 500
Kilduff, M B. 87 South 6th....Abbott Brewing Co. 800
Kossmann, M. 217 and 219 Manjer....M Seitz. 550
Layer, J. 1047 Flushing av....Burger & Hower B Co. (R) 450
Leimer, F. 281 Scholes....O Huber. (R) 190
Lanigan, S. 196 Myrtle av....Claus Lipsius B Co. 800
Mack, J. 333 Wyckoff av, cor Myrtle av....Otto Huber Brewery. 2,000
Madigan, J H. 1002 4th av, cor 39th st....T C Lyman & Co. (R) 700
Malone, C. 745 Washington av....Budweiser B Co. 879
McGovern, P. 200 Union av... L Eppig. 625
Murray, M. 650 3d av....India Wharf B Co. 250
McCutcheon, F. 3 Willoughby....E Ochs. 5,000
Marquardt, A. 376 Central av....J Eppig. 300
Morloch, C. 791 Flushing av....Danenberg & C. (R) 450
Nagle, J. 336 Oakland....T C Lyman & Co. (R) 300
O'Neil, J. 227 Plymouth....Budweiser B Co. 500
Peterson, P. 927 Flushing av....S Liebmann's Sons B Co. 350
Peterson, T. 74 Hamilton av....India Wharf B Co. 100
Peters, L. 281 Ainslie....Rubsam & H B Co. 1,000
Rapporte, A. Stone av, cor Blake av....Budweiser B Co. 545
Rommeny, T. 491 Broadway... H Abels & Co. (R) 300
Roberts, J W. 364 Flushing av....Long Island Brewery. 1,050
Schmidt, C. 16 Havemeyer... Long Island Brewery. 822
Seibert, A. 264 Stagg....Burger & Hower B Co. 700
Schnaars, H H. 386 Liberty av....W Ulmer. 400
Schreiber, C and J Jantzen. 1189 Gates av....S Liebmann's Sons B Co 1,350
Schiffmann, W. 97 Scholes....India Wharf B Co. 300
Seeholzer, A J. 114 Weirfield....L Eppig. (R) 655
Shea, J. 73 Bedford av....Claus Lipsius B Co. 150
Schoenberg, A J. 393 Central av....M Seitz. 450
Schwerzel, A. 262 Floyd....J Eppig. 500
Sommers, H. 564 Wythe av....H Breckman. (R) 475
Tiedemann, H. Foot of Court st ....India Wharf B Co. 1,000
Tetzner, F J. 2d av, s w cor 55th st....India Wharf B Co. 900
Winkel, C 1032 Broadway....C Frese. (R) 800
Ward, Cath R. 310 Court....O Huber. 1,500
Wegner, T. 249 Hopkins....W Ulmer. 600
White, F. 200 Hoyt....Danenberg & Coles. (R) 775
White, J J. 199 Tillary....E Ochs. 410
Wolf, J. 251 Powers.... L Eppig. (R) 600
Wulp, T. Rockaway and East New York avs....J Wulp. 800
Zoesch, F. 16 Lewis av....Budweiser B Co. (R) 1,100

HOUSEHOLD FURNITURE.

Brownrigg, Mary. 163 52d....M Bierman. 160
Byrnes, Mary A. 93 Driggs av....Jacob Bros. Piano. 285
Barnum, L L. 65 Monroe....J Hamlin. 380
Brant, G H. 2163 Fulton.... Manges Bros. 120
Campbell, Rosina. 559 Union....A Pearson. 117
Cummings, Nettie. 24 Chapel....Manges Bros. 117
Combs, Mrs E K. 73 South 5th... Jacob Bros. Piano. 225
Connelly, Mamie. 28th st....J Coyne & Co. 211
Dapper, A. 173 Duffield. ..J McEnery & Co. 125
Davis, Eliza. 102 Warren....H Israel & Sons. 100
Devlin, P. 1152 Myrtle av....J McEnery & Co. 121
Driver, A E. 90 Clinton av....Jordan & M. 327
Edwards, L. 50 Concord....A Pearson. 161
Everett, J W. 308 Schermerhorn....Mary A Birtles. 300
Ferrer, Mary O. 12 Hicks... H Israel & Sons. 109
Folsom, Nettie. 725 Driggs....Mullins & Sons. 260
Fullwood, G. 561 Franklin av... Mullins & Sons. 131
Gallagher, M. 330 Jay....J Moriarty. 237
Gardner, Carrie. 229 South 3d....Jacob Bros. Piano. 255
Gowen, Selma. 41 South Oxford....J Baumann. 990
Hyman, F J. 109 Fleet pl....A Pearson. 139
Keiser, Mrs H. Butler st, near Prospect st, Flatbush....Jacob Bros. Piano. 235
Lesser, J. 192 Middleton....J E Murray. 209
Lewis, E B. Junius st . Mary M Webster. (R) 100
Lahey, J. 175 Pearl....H Israel & Sons. 366
Mitchell, Kate L. 541 Willoughby av... A Pearson. 250
Morretti, F. 94 South 1st....H Israel & Sons. 256
McGonagle, Nellie. 150 Lexington av....Mullins & Sons. 100
Mitchell, Kate L. 541 Willoughby av....A Pearson. 266
Neil, Sofia. 112a Nassau av....A Schulz. 228
Olcott, Nettie W. 80 Rockaway av... Mullins & Sons. 177
Palmer, W J. 117 Palmetto....Jacob Bros. Piano. 215
Post, Mrs D. 317 Broadway....Jacob Bros. Piano. 165
Russell, D. 361 16th....L Baumann. 118
Shook, Harriet wife of W H. 65 Division av...Marthe A Munn. 200
Snyder, Mrs W. 301 South 1st....Jacob Bros. Piano. 200
Steubel, E. 36 Grand....A Schulz. 271
Torgerson, E. 20th st ...J McEnery & Co. 237
Thoma, N L. 1070 De Kalb av....Alexander Bros. 158
Totans, P. 165 Reid av....C E Pierce. Piano. 130
Vincent, Rosalie. 319 Grand av....J P Blauvelt. 300
Vogt, E E. 87 Sands....P Ottmann. 125
Van Dusen, J W. 901 Bedford av....Mullins & Sons. (R) 144
Watson, Eliz. 68 E 113th....Jacob Bros. Piano. 190
Watson, J W. 101 Norman av ..J A Schwarz. 117
Wheeler Mercantile and Guar Trust. 35 39th....G C Robinson. 177
Whittaker, Emily E. 111 6th av....Lincoln Ind and Guar Assoc. 100
Watson, J C. 103 Duffield....H S Eisler. 198
Welles, Ada H. 435 Gold....Manges Bros. 256
Whelan, P. 94 North Henry....L Baumann. 110
Williamson, Anna L. 96A Hicks....Mullins & Sons. 142

MISCELLANEOUS.

Adorno, J. 1093 Hancock .... Lizzie Barnett. Drug Fixtures. 1,000
Alt, E. 2744 Atlantic av ...J Matthews Apparatus Co. Soda Water Apparatus. 450
Burke, Catherine. 41 Brooklyn av....W B Davis. Coupe, &c. (R) 550
Drewes, H....Barrett & Brush. Wagon. 282
Billonnand, D. 190 7th av....Archer Mfg Co. Barber Fixtures. 207
Brzezinski, J. 80 Eldert....R A Holcke. Barber Fixtures. 141
Buttner, T. 856 Evergreen av. . C Birk. Horse and Wagon. 800
Callmeyer, F. 499 Myrtle av....R H Rebenklan. Horse and Wagon, Store Fixtures. (R) 2,000
Crudup, P G. 1189 Fulton....Mary Watson. Confectionery Store. 50
Folger, G. 340 Ralph av .... Louisa Folger, Blacksmith Shop. 900
Fisher, F W. 8 and 10 Atlantic av....H Greenfield. Lease and Furniture. (R) 263
Fennikoh & Bockhoff. 143 Lorimer and 48 Maujer....H Fennikoh. Grocery Stores. 2,100
Grimberg, L. 23 Moore ... M Zimmermann. Store Fixtures. 300
Griffin, Mary....P Barrett. Wagon. (R) 150
Hanna, J. Clason av, e s, n of President st....S O'Connor. Frame House, Cow, &c. 290
Hoffman, J. 800 Myrtle av....Archer Mfg Co. Barber Fixtures. 110
Hold, Kate. 213 Central av....H Otterbein. Fancy Goods. 350
Hutchinson, F. 1235 Bedford av....Nat Cash Register Co. Register. 200
Hoepp, W H. 550 8th av....R A Holcke. Barber Fixtures. 175

Helfenburg, Solomon. Essex st, bet Atlantic av and Fulton st....Simon Helfenburg. Window Glass. (R) 800
Heinz, Dorothea. 418 Central av ...V Halet. Grocery Store Fixtures. 100
Johnson, G E....M Armstrong & Co. Coach. 800
Jackson, J B. 4 and 6 New Chambers st, New York....Walker & B. Printing Fixtures. (R) 1,000
John J & G Maniaracina. 91 Manhattan av....Archer Mfg Co. Barber Fixtures. 264
Johnson, Mary A. 201 5th av....S W & J A Haviland. Bakery Fixtures, Horses, Wagons. 1,000
Kuhn, H. 67 39th....J G Meister. Horse and Wagon. 100
Lang, Gesine. 87 Clermont av .... B Weill. Horses. 250
Lamm, H. 492 Graham av....F Klumpp. Horse and Wagon. 550
Leaver, T. 579 Court....Nat Cash Register Co. Register. 170
Lippman, J....P Barrett. Wagons. (R) 150
Leifelts, J J . P Barrett. Truck. 200
Lippman, J and G....P Barrett. Wagon. (R) 100
Leary, Bridget. 38 Liberty....W B Davis. Coupe. 160
Manley, E T. 442 Wythe av....Nat Cash Register Co. Register. 175
McGovern, T. 1438 Fulton....Lamson Consol Store S Co. Register. 210
McCain, J....W B Davis. Horse. (R) 125
Meyer, C E. 1017 3d av....Anna Schlueter. Butcher Fixtures. 200
Moodhe, A S. 52 South 3d....J Petri. Coach. 250
Mollo, V. Myrtle av, cor South 8th st....Archer Mfg Co. Barber Fixtures. 190
Morehart, L. 1532 Gates av .. C J Stoll. Butcher Fixtures. 200
Nordenbrock, J A. 207 Johnson av ....J L Kortright. Drug Fixtures. 2,500
Nelson, J R. 47 Carroll.. .Nat Cash Register Co. Register. 230
Ogulbene, L. 124 Graham av....L Saafina. Barber Fixtures. 182
O'Brien, D. Fulton and St Felix sts....Nat Cash Register Co. Register. 175
Piazza, L. 117 Elizabeth....A Palmentiere. Bakery Fixtures. 100
Rand, Almira M and W J. Bedford av, n e cor Fulton st....H Carson. Organ. 551
Riggs, W B. 2541 Atlantic av....Nat Cash Register Co. Register. 180
Rath, F & R. 59 Stockton....M Ruoff. Butcher Fixtures. 80
Schwaner, E. Atlantic av, near 6th av....C Schwencke. Horses, &c. 100
Sidebotham, Jr, T B....Campbell P P and Mfg Co. Press. (R) 271
Schleuter, A. 1443 Broadway....Archer Mfg Co. Barber Fixtures. 772
Speh, G. 983 Broadway....J Matthews' Apparatus Co. Soda Fountain. 830
Stern, W. 194 Hamburg av....Amalie Ludewig. Drug Fixtures. 615
Schlattenkircher, G. 734 3d av....T & L Krombach. Undertaker Fixtures. 300
Strauss, I. 47 Sackett....T Farrell. Butcher Fixtures 125
Valente, G. 60 Canton....S Imperiale. Second Hand Bottle Shop. 61
Voege, G. 1507 Broadway....Nat Cash Register Co. Register. 175
Winter, G. 497 Atlantic av ...Nat Cash Register Co. Register. 175
Wassett, E J. 216 South 8th....J T Robinson & Co. Machinery. 300
Weber, L and P A. 228 Bushwick av....O J Cameron & Co. Machinery. 747
Weisser, C. 167 Troutman....Deininger & Tienken. Horse and Wagon. 50

BILLS OF SALE.

Abruscato, S. 178 Bridge....Dragotta & Ciraulo. Barber Fixtures. 210
Gallo & Confessore. 121 Navy....Pozzerosso & Contino. Grocery Fixtures. 215
Halet, V. 418 Central av....Doretha Heinz. Delicatessen Store. 260
Heilman, B. 144 Bedford av....J Neidecker. Butcher Fixtures. 500
India Wharf B Co. 650 3d av....M Murray. Saloon Fixtures. 500
Kennedy, Hughey. 42 Bergen....Tumson & Kidd. Horses. 60
Klein, Eliz. 282 Central av....F Brown. Saloon Fixtures. 1,600
Meyer, E. 2577 Atlantic av....K Meyer. Cigar Fixtures. 500
Nellis, J L. 513 5th av....N C Seedorf. Saloon Fixtures. 2,000
Reid, P N. 2545 Atlantic av....Felicita A Garbeer. Drug Fixtures. 390
Riecker, C. 622 Manhattan av....F Schrempf. Butcher Fixtures. 150
Rubinorz, B. 87 Seigel....M Goldfarb. Grocery Fixtures. 145
Unsar, C. 73 Morgan av ...J Herckes. Bakery Fixtures. 100
Zucke, A. 78 Johnson av....Rosie Weinberger. Soda Water Factory. 800

ASSIGNMENTS OF CHATTEL MORTGAGES.

Bennes, T H to India Wharf B Co. (Mort given by A Caemmerer, May 12, 1891.) 1,600
Plunkett, F to B F Gray. (Bernard F Gray, Aug 20, 1891.) nom

NEW JERSEY.

NOTE.—*The arrangement of the Conveyances, Mortgages and Judgments in these lists is as follows: the first name in the Conveyances is the Grantor; in Mortgages, the Mortgagor; in Judgments, the Judgment debtor.*

ESSEX COUNTY.

CONVEYANCES.

Allen, W L—A Denk, Hunterdon st. $700
Anderson, I S—M A Gould, Montclair 625
Armstrong, E R—F Di Menna, Bank st cor J M Gould's land 30x135 5,000
Athearn, E C—A A Raven, Caldwell 500
Atwater, Samuel trustee—J D Brumley, 8th st. 900
Banes, E B—L M Holmes, Milburn 1,000
Banks, Thomas—S Moffett, 1st st. 200
Bayles, C I—P F Hogan, Montclair 2,000
Same——P Wilcox, Montclair 2,375
Becker, Charles—L P Lalor, High st. 1,100
Bennett, C R—A W Bennett, Gold st. 1
Bennett, W S—A W Bennett, Gold st. 1
Binder, Albert et al exrs—E B Fey, Alyea st. 1
Same——A Binder, Ferry st. 1
Blair, J E—J Pettit, West Orange 3,000
Blanchard, W W—D Strachan, East Orange 11,000
Block, William—J O'Bryan, Belleville av 1
Bradley, E A—H I Libbey, Montclair 26,000
Braun, Henry—G Lauer, Kinney st 6,500
Brown, C J—M R Roche, 9th av 900
Buchanan, Paul et al—C W Heilman, South 6th st. 1,900
Buchanan, Paul et al exrs—J Hembauser, Court st. 1,050
Buettner, J C—O Henke, Orange 1,625
Buermann, August—H Ohmeis, North 4th st. 850
Same——M Peipe, southerly cor Hamburgh pl and Lafayette st. 9,000
Canon, W S—J Brown, Crane st. 1
Carson, Margaret—L J Carson, Montclair 650
Cole, M M—M H Jacobs, South Orange 1
Condit, S J—E T Lindsley, Orange 4,500
Same——same, Orange 3,500
Davis, C D—C Van Wagoner, Bloomfield 500
Devine, Arthur—C Trefz, Brenner st. 2,700
Dobbins, Rachel—E Dobbins, Caldwell 1
Dod, Robert—W E McDougall, South 6th st. 1
Dowden, G A—A Redding, Washington av. 1,000
Doyle, Elizabeth—E Allen et al, Clifton av. 725
Eisele, J G—J C Eisele, w s Prince st 50 s Montgomery st 50x100 6,000
Finn, R A—M Illig, s s South Orange av 36 e Rankin st 26x88 7,500
Gahr, Jacob—C Kunzli, Jabez st. 415
Ganghren, Rose—M Hebring, Warren st. 1
Same——W O'Leary, Crane st. 1
Garton, E M—C E Wheeler, East Orange 600
Geissele, H J—J J Burkhardt, Ferry st. 2,800
Gillman, Jacob—East Jersey Water Co, Franklin 900
Gilmartin, Patrick—B Gilmartin, Orange 300
Glorieux, W L—F W Muller, Clinton 1,200
Guthrie, S M—H B Corwin, South Orange 6,000
Hebring, Mary—P Reilly, Warren st. 1,300
Heerwagen, Richard—O Heerwagen, Kinney st. 1
Same——same, Kinney st. 2,500
Same——J Heerwagen, Kinney st. 2,900
Heerwagen, Oscar——same, Kinney st. 1
Harrison, Marcus—E C Athearn, Caldwell 260
Harper, David—W E Van Riper, Bloomfield av. 1,550
Holmes, E M—J Stiegele, Millburn 1,000
Honig, Charles—S A Walsh, Dickerson st. 2,200
Hopper, J E—E B Williams, Quitman st. 850
Hopping, S E—J Colyer, w s Columbia st 122 from Elm st 25x100 4,800
Iee, E J—A Vogel, Bergen st 600
Jacobs, J B—M M Cole, South Orange 1
Jones, W F, Jr—C Lawson, Montclair 2,040
Kane, C J—A A Raven, Caldwell 500
Koelsch, Adelheid—T B Heginbotham, Monroe st. 2,500
Krick, A C—M Durr, West st. 2,050
Krippendorf, Gottfried—W H Stemmermann, Crawford st. 1
Lawrenz, Charles—C Lawrenz, Jr, Plane st. 1
Lewis, D P—A A Raven, Caldwell 300
Lysaght, James—E Pearce, Caldwell 150
Mandeville, H A—The trustees of the First Presbyterian Church, South Orange 1
Manderschied, J J—J N Tuttle, Essex st 1
McCloskey, Mary—C McCloskey, Orange 1
Miller, J W—C Frank, Malvern st. 600
Mitchell, A P—J A Morfit, East Orange 840
Mott, A M—L R Winterton, East Orange 4,500
Meeker, Washington—J Pettit, West Orange 8,000
O'Bryan, John—W Block, rear Belleville av. 1
Orr, James—D D McKoon, Franklin 10
Parkinson, Wm—J F Deary, Orange 784
Pearce, Elisha—W O Dowd, Caldwell 100
Personette, W H—A L Parkhust, Caldwell 1,800
Pfeifer, Maria—J L Pfeifer, w s North 6th st 50 n Dickerson st 150x100 4,200
Reynolds, G L—W A Woodbury, South Orange 1
Rief, George—G Baierle, South 8th st 150
Rich, W S—A K Schambacher, Clinton 2,100
Roediger, Dorothea—J Weber, South 6th st. 400
Ruby Light Company—C Wiebach et al, Av L. 2,000
Rushing, M E—F H Smith, Liberty 2,700
Sargeant, S S et al—F Del Guercio et al, 7th av. 1,000
Schoenman, David—L S Samuel, Jones st. 2,800
Seibert, C L—W R Raab, Bloomfield 400
Seitz, C F—B M Farley, near Prospect av. 1
Shanks, A E—C Mayer, East Orange 6,800
Stemmermann, W H—F Krippendorf, Crawford st 1
Sweet, N D—H L Munden, East Orange 1
The Central New Jersey Land Improvement Co—E N Dwyer, Ferguson st. 800
The Howard Savings Inst—W McManus, n e cor Elizabeth av and Alpine st 100x300 5,000
Thorne, Louisa—C Yule, rear Plane st. 175
Thorne, G W——same, rear Plane st. 150
Trippe, C A—J Kelly, Orange 150
Trusdell, A E—M Doyle, East Orange 800
Same——J Byrne, East Orange 300
Same——S Fulyer, Camden st. 1,350
Tunis, Nehemiah—H Schaeffer, Van Buren st. 900
Tunison, Edward—F Mackin, n w cor Lincoln av and Mary st 125x260x30x40x90x240 18,000
Tuttle, J N—M J Manderschied, Essex st 1
Van Duyne, Harrison—J E Faulkner, Mt Prospect av. 1,100
Wakeman, J P—P A Sexton, Garside st 2,800
Welsh, John—J Swift, Orange 450
Wiedenmayer, Louisa et al—V Burkhard, Garrison st 600
Williams, B S—M A Howard, Orange 250
Williams, James—R Salyer, East Orange 525
Wilson, Henry—M Baxter, Jr, 2d st. 600
Winterton, L R—A M Mott, East Orange 1,500
Wirth, Peter—L Hafner, e s Charlton st 33 n Court st 33x100 6,000
Wood, Alexander—F Mackin, 18th av. 1,200
Woodbury, W A—H T Chapin, South Orange 1
Ziesse, L J—W S Doyle, Gray st 1,800

MORTGAGES.

Alston, C B—A Howell, Columbia st. 3,000
Ballard, L M—Mutual Life Ins Co, N J R R av. 10,000
Barnes, Robert—R Martin, East Orange 2,586
Beck, C L—A F Tillon, South Orange 1,000
Beck, Joseph—J S Schwarz, Lentz av 1,675
Berry, L D—E L Rogers, East Orange 4,000
Binder, Albert—A Binder et al, Ferry st. 1
Branigan, Eliza et al—T S Henry, Cherry st. 150
Bryan, J R—T V Doup, East Orange 750
Burkhardt, J J—The Security B and L Assoc, Ferry st. 2,000
Cadmus, James—Fidelity Title and Deposit Co, Jelliff av. 2,500
Chapin, H T—M Jobs, South Orange 2,200
Candee, D E—Howard B and L Assoc, Mt Prospect av. 2,800
Corwin, H B—S M Guthrie, South Orange 5,500
Chace, M E—E Ordway, Montclair 500
Compressed Barrel Co—A Millard, River road 1,500
Connolly, John—Fraternal B and L Assoc, East Orange 1,200
De Mott, Giles—L D Crane, New st. 1,200
Dent, Adam—W L Allen, Hunterdon st. 425
Di Menna, Fideli—E Armstrong, Bank st. 3,000
Dodd, E L—C V Stoutenburgh, Warren st. 3,000
Durr, Magdalena—Newark B & L Assoc, West st. 2,400
Eich, John—G Stripp, Orange 1,500
Embury, P A—B T Kissam, West Orange 9,350
Fey, E B—A Binder et al, Alyea st. 1
Finger, Fannie—U S Credit System Co, Warren st 10,500
Fitch, Lyndon—D B Coe, Bloomfield 5,500
Fuller, L C—P T Pierpont, cor 4th and Dickerson sts 30,000
Fulyer, Susanna—A E Trusdell, Camden st 1,150
Garabrant, E R—J Wharton, East Orange 4,000
Gile, F A—M M Gile, East Orange 2,500
Gilmartin, Bessie—J W Condit, Orange 1,000
Ginneson, Samuel—S E Ginneson, Clinton 182
Goodell, E B—Montclair B and L Assoc, Montclair 1,000
Grundy, Daniel—C Van Wagoner, Bloomfield 1,500
Hafner, Louisa—P Wirth, Charlton st 5,000
Heake, Otto—F Berg, Orange 1,000
Hembauser, Joseph—P Buchanan, Court st. 700
Herold, O E—C A Feick, Van Buren st. 2,000
Hill, G A—A Somerville, Roseville av. 1,500
Hoeler, P J—A Buermann, 13th av. 3,200
Hopper, J E—I W Tichenor, Quitman st. 1,700
Hertzog, Robert—C C Billhofer, Fulton st. 5,600
Hyeck, Louisa—J J Robrecht, South 11th st. 200
Irish, Anna—F J Love, Montclair 3,300
Jackson, E H—The Woodside B and L Assoc, Summer av. 4,400
Jacobi, Amelia—F Bonykamper, Jr, Walnut st. 2,500
Kelaher, Kate—Savings B and L Assoc, Hudson st. 100
Kronenberger, J J—J Gahr, Bremen st 1,000
Lehmann, Henry, Jr—Montclair B and L Assoc, Montclair 2,000
Lemassena, Lillian—The Mutual Benefit Life Ins Co, Mt Prospect av. 7,000
Libbey, F A—M G Bradley, 3 tracts, Montclair 25,000
Lilly, Henry—R Martin, South Orange 3,000
Lysaght, Martha—C Barkhorn, Bloomfield av. 500
Matthews, Joseph—D B Coe, Bloomfield 1,700
McClatiney, Annie—The American Ins Co, Plane st. 3,200
McDougall, W E—The West End B and L Assoc, South 6th st. 3,000
McMains, R C—R W Parker trustee, Franklin 800
McManus, Walter—Howard Savings Inst, 8th av. 4,000
Mee, John—C J Conrad, Chapel st 1,400
Metzger, Philip—The Security B and L Assoc, Ferry st. 200
Moffet, J R—W Clark, Wakeman av. 1,500
Moffett, Susan—C O Harris, 1st st 350
Muns, R W—J Nash, Montclair 1,000
Ombach, Leopold—W Haas, Ann st. 800
Pain, W J—J Wharton, 3d st. 1,000
Pecott, J G—J Evans, Bloomfield 500
Peipe, Marie—A Buermann, Hamburgh pl. 4,500
Persins, S G—S B Jackson special guard, 8th av 550
Pettit, John—L M Meeker, West Orange 5,450
Reilly, J J—F Bonykamper, Jr, Schalk st. 170
Rindell, M L—Mutual Benefit Life Ins Co, Broad st. 6,000
Rodgers, Thomas—C Porter, Hunterdon st. 1,500
Roe, G M—E E Ball, Prince st. 2,500
Ruggles, J A—J S Ayres, East Orange 2,700
Sayre, W T—C F Harrison, Orange 4,000
Schaaf, F P—Irvington B & L Assoc, Clinton 1,500
Schmidt, Louis—The Security B & L Assoc, Livingston st. 200
Seymour, J A—T A Condit, South 7th st. 600
Sexton, P A—Howard B & L Assoc, Garside st. 2,200
Smith, F H—The 14th Ward B & L Assoc, Liberty st. 1,000
Smith, P E—A Dodd surviving exr, Montclair 5,000
Stager, Jesse—A Haussling, Jefferson st. 500
Stuehlinger, Rosina—Security B & L Assoc, Esther st 2,000
Stubler, Charles—G W Wiedenmeyer, Jabez st. 500
Swift, James—Orange Savings Bank, Orange 350
Theuer, C W—S Doughty et al, exrs, Bergen st. 3,300
Thiessen, Emilie—F Millering, River st. 2,500
Trommer, Caroline—C A Feich, Hawthorne av. 400
Van Clief, Benjamin—T Williams, Warren st. 2,300
Van Riper, G W—Fraternal B and L Assoc, Bloomfield av. 1,400
Vogel, Marie—E J Iee, Bergen st. 350
Voorhees, F I—V Taylor, Clinton 1,780
Walsh, Catharine—E Weitlauf, Elm st. 400
Walsh, M L—First Nat Bank of Jersey City, Franklin 800
Walsh, S A—Reliable B and L Assoc, Dickerson st. 1,600
Wankmuller, Joseph—Home B and L Assoc, Belmont av. 200
Wardell, W S—J W Condit, West Orange 300
Wiebach, Charles et al—Ruby Light Co, Av L. 1,000
Williams, E B—I W Tichenor, Quitman st. 1,700
Yeager, M B—W W Jacobus, East Orange 250

CHATTEL MORTGAGES.

Benbrook, J T—A Steadman, furniture 200
Burns, P J—G Krueger Brewing Co., saloon 315
Carolan, Matt—The National Cash Register Co, cash register 200
Conlin, John—G Krueger Brewing Co, saloon 185
Corbett, W F—J Ketcham, furniture 54
Corcoran, G A——same, furniture 65
Dean, F E—P H Hanley, furniture 67
Dolyn, Mary—M Kane, furniture 26
Falcione, Pasquale—R Ramforth, barber fixtures 187
Falzinger, R L—A T Looker, furniture 1,039
Fetzer, T M—F J Kastner, saloon 1,000
Fulham, Jennie—J Walsh, furniture 234
Fulton, Robert—E M Fulton, kindling wood machinery 9,436
Gibson, Augustus—F J Hull et al, horses and wagons 95
Green, Peter—G Krueger Brewing Co, saloon 175
Griggs, A H—A Finger, furniture 400
Higby, G D—J Ketcham, furniture 65
Hill, Delia—J Northrup, furniture 200
Lang, Adolph—M Burne & Co, bakery 475
Littell, A W—P H Hanley, organ 35
Macklon, M C G—M E Gardner, furniture 500
Malony, John—G Krueger Brewing Co, saloon 177
McFadden, John—H M Irwin, saloon 1,124
Miller, Gussie—A H Van Horn, furniture 151
Moran, Joseph—G Krueger Brewing Co, saloon 175
Moses, Sigmund—E A Kromke, ice box &c. 167
Millkowsky, Israel et al—J Epstein, stock in store 200

Riker, Samuel—A H Van Horn, furniture 151
Ritt, Mary—J Ketcham, furniture 130
Schaefer, Chas—National Cash Register Co, cash register 175
Smith, Louvina—P H Hanley, furniture 33
Stevenson, W H—The Fairlie & Wilson Goal Co, office fixtures, &c 1,000
Wishinsky, Hyman—P Janette, stock in store 75
Witaker, Julia—M Kane, furniture 24
Wyatt, A R—F J Kastner, furniture 1,000
Zimmermann, Charles—M Kane, horses 26
Zipf, Louis—S R Hutchins, furniture 200

JUDGMENTS.

Bailey, Mary—J W Dehart 257
Blake, A S—The Orange Nat'l Bank 250
Davis, F W—T G Barber 842
Dixon, G A—F Iliff et al 469
Higgins, Charles—A Eisenhour 354
Starin's River and Harbor Trans Co—V Holler et al 462
Tappan, E J—T G Knight 296
Thompson, C W et al—J E Lee Company 206
Townley, C H—T Bailey 351
Van Horn, A H—J H Van Horn et al 500
Young, R S—The Orange Nat'l Bank 1,011

HUDSON COUNTY.

CONVEYANCES.

Appleby, Leonard by exr—F Zedliach, J City $500
Argner, Chas—Dorothea Kringel, Guttenberg nom
Baier, Chas—Barbara Baier, J City nom
Battin, S H—The Rector, Wardens and Vestryman Christ Church, J City nom
Behring, C H—S A Ross, J City 3,298
Bove, John—S Brandt, West Hoboken nom
Brandt, Stephen—F Brandt, West Hoboken nom
Brooke, Margaretta L—Saint Mary's Catholic Church, J City 16,000
Brupbe, Robert—C Stoll, West Hoboken 1,575
Bumsted, W G—T H Speir, J City 5,600
Burke, Annie—G P Kate, J City 175
Cadmus, Geo—C Siebach, Bayonne 425
Cole, E F—T H McCann, Hoboken 3,000
Combes, Mary E—C Siebach, Bayonne 1,275
Condit, Fillmore—Elizabeth Cole, Kearney 150
Condit, Fillmore—Isabella Crookall, Kearney 300
Same—J Welsh, Kearney 200
Same—H Dunnell, Kearney 150
Same—Bridget A Caffrey, Kearney 250
Same—W R Ball, Kearney 750
Condon, P J—J J Whelan, J City 1,450
Cox, George—Ann Abbott, North Bergen 300
Currey, Richard—J H Symes, Union nom
Davenport, F M—B L Clark, J City 5,000
Davis, Thomas—The Edison General Electric Co, Harrison 3,300
De R ye, Mary V—Saint Mary's Catholic Church, Jo City nom
Drescher, Chas by exr—F Feistel, West Hoboken 800
Same—F J Loh, West Hoboken 800
Same—Jane Schmidt, West Hoboken 1,900
Duryee, Geo—R W Gleason, Bayonne nom and exch
Eberhard, F N—C J Deehey, Hoboken 500
Eilshemius, H G—C L Eeickert, Kearney 1,100
Same—M Bumstead, Kearney 1,025
Faze, C J—F Condit, Kearney 150
Gardner, John and Chas Pinnelt—R Curry et al, Union nom
Gross, Clara B—Ferger, Becker & Kohl Bavarian Brewing Co, J City 425
Heck, Catharine—F Schwarzer, J City nom
Hetzel, Geo—Mary Hetzel, Guttenberg nom
Hentze, Sophie—G Raubach, J City 1,800
Hill, Laura C—L W Herkstroter, J City 1,000
Hubbert, Minnie—H W Halbohm, J City 1,225
Jacoby, J H—H Riekens, J City 6,900
Kinsey, Samuel exr—L Mesbach, J City 265
Kilroy, John—B Jacobowitz, J City 3,500
Klink, W M—Anna McComb, J City nom
Knerr, John—P Semler, J City 200
Knoblauch, A A—W Hackett, J City 500
Kringel, Dorothea—Ernestine Arguer, Guttenberg nom
Lewis, C A—Meta Gadeburg, J City 5,050
Linn, Clarence—J Warner, J City nom
Lofqvist, J A—A Allaire Crowell, Kearney 7,750
Logan, Martin—C Hoffman, J City 1,000
Markus, Carl—A Markus, West Hoboken 1,000
Mathison, J D—Charlotte A Matthison, J City nom
McComb, John—W M Klink, J City nom
McInerney, Alex—C H Weller, Bayonne nom
McKenzie, G R—The trustees of the John Knox Presbyterian Church, J City nom
Meyer, Elise—C A Barnickel, J City 3,500
Morris, T F—P J Condon, J City 2,620
Nathan, P R by sheriff—J J Nathan, North Bergen 1,000
Neville, Margaret B—Lillie M Neville, J City natural love and affection and nom
Nichols, E H—Matilda Hobbs, J City 175
Nichols, E H—W Corcoran, J City 300
Same—same, J City 300
O'Callahan, Mary by sheriff—Elizabeth D Baker, J City 500
Rademin, Peter—H Behrens, J City 6,300
Randolph, J F—Margaret Brown, J City 1,900
Same—M Kelly, J City 900
Rapp, Jacob—Mathilda S Fuchs, J City 550
Richards, C O—A Siegfried, North Bergen 300
Rittenhouse, Rebecca L—H Z Nibbett, North Bergen 1,200
Rothweiller, J H—D Baumann, J City 50
Schaideler, Caroline—J Schaideler, North Bergen nom
Schlegel, Ottelie—Emma Wagner, Hoboken nom
Schuyler, E O—W J Denton, Bayonne 500
Schwarzer, Fred—Catharine Beck, J City nom
Semard, August—P Tivy, Hoboken 4,000
Semler, Peter—C M Heim, J City 1,450
Silva, Harriet—W T Courtney, West Hoboken 800
Smith, Catharine E—F Angevine, J City 5,000
Smith, William—W Connolly, J City nom
Sofield, S T—W T Sofield, J City 4,000
Sofield, W T—P Sofield, J City 4,000
Spies, W A—J Ortug, West Hoboken 550
Siegfried, Adam—J Willms, North Bergen 400
Swift, E C—Newark Stock Yards, Harrison nom
Taylor, J F—J L Fairnworth, J City 2,175
The Central N J Land and Impt Co—E T Jennings, Bayonne 550
Same—G S Jennings, Bayonne 550
Same—Josephine G French, Bayonne 2,200
The Equitable Life Assur Society—T D Jordan, J City 7,000
The Mallinckrodt Chemical Works—The West Side Connecting R R Co, J City 3,261
Thourot, F L, by exr—J Lemonier, West Hoboken 6,000
Veit, Katie—Julia Weller, Hoboken nom
Vreeland, M D M—J J Sheridan, J City 400
Vreeland, N S by exr—P J Condon, J City nom
Vreeland, Anna H and Peter Baylor individ and exr of Sophia E Baylor—Exrs N S Vreeland, J City nom
Wagner, William—O Schligel, Hoboken nom
Warner, Ann J—C Linn, J City nom
Warren, D F—Elizabeth A Ackerman, J City 1,100
Same—same, J City nom
Wauters, A P—G D Bernina, J City 25,500
Wescott, W P—R M Jarvis, J City 1,000
Weissenberger, Conrad et al by sheriff—C Kamlah, J City 1,000
Weller, C H—A McInerney, Bayonne nom
Yale, C B—The West Side Connecting R R Co, J City 1,200
Zahr, Rosalia—P Lippert, J City 2,250
Zapp, Frederick—R Currey, Union nom

MORTGAGES.

Appmann, J H—Catharine Henken, J City, 5 years 2,000
Barnickel, C A—Elise Meyer, J City, 3 years 1,500
Beck, A W—The American Ins Co, Kearney, 1 year 2,500
Behrens, Herman—P Rademan, J City, 3 years 3,000
Same—same, J City, 3 years 1,500
Bennett, Eliza J—S G Babcock, J City, 1 year 350
Browne, Margaret—J F Randolph, J City, 3 years 1,200
Burke, Maria—Julia Frumbach, Union, 5 years 500
Calam, Cecelia—A Herber, J City, 3 years 1,000
Campbell, Margaret—Phoenix L and B Assoc, J City, installs 4,000
Clark, B L—Lincoln B and L Assoc, J City, installs 8,000
Corcoran, William—W R Cook, J City, 5 years 1,800
Corell, H R—The Provident Inst for Savings, J City, 1 year 3,000
Corcorcan, Martin—F W Franklin, J City, 3 years 400
Coupland, Mary E—Hoboken B and L Assoc, Union, installs 2,000
Crowell, A A—J A Lofqvist, Kearney, 2 years 2,670
Denton, W J—E Q Schuyler, Bayonne, 1 year 250
Flaherty, Edward—The Provident Inst for Savings, J City, 1 year 2,000
French, Joseph G—The Central New Jersey Land and Improvement Co, Bayonne, 3 years 1,600
Fucherl, Christian L—Cecile E Eilshemius, Kearney, 3 years 800
Fuchs, Mahilda S—Susan M Vreeland, J City, 2 years 700
Gadeberg, Meta—C A Lewis, J City, 1 year 200
Green, W H—W S Cann, trustee, Kearney, 1 year 3,000
Gueff, Rudolph—Lafayette M B and L Assoc, J City, installs 3,500
Guaraglia, Rosa—Anna Lagomaisine, Hoboken, 1 year 700
Guff, Wilhelm—Town of Union B and L Assoc, J City, installs 3,000
Heim, C M—P Semler, J City, installs 250
Heikel, Otto—The New Jersey Title Guarantee and Trust Co, Union, installs 9,000
Herkstroter, L W—Laura C Hill, J City, 3 years 800
Hespe, W E—Serial B and L Assoc, J City, installs 1,800
Hoffman, Christian—Bridget McInelry, J City, 3 years 1,500
Hoffman, Filippo—Mary A Holler, Hoboken, 2 years 1,080
Hornkohl, August—Elizabeth Krause, Harrison, 1 year 1,000
Houghlin, Alfred—Lafayette M B and L Assoc, J City, installs 1,600
Jacobowitz, Bernard—J Kilroy, J City, 5 years 2,500
Same—New Jersey Title Guarantee and Trust Co, J City, installs 2,500
Jennings, E T—The Central N J Land and Imp't Co, Bayonne, 3 years 400
Jennings, G J—The Central N J Land and Impt Co, Bayonne, 3 years 400
Johnson, Mary—J M Hillery, J City, 4 years 1,125
Kiersted, Elizabeth T—G E Ward, J City, given as collateral security 7,500
Kruse, Adele M—The Jersey City Galvanizing Co, Kearney, 7 years 1,550
Laux, Emil—Industrial M B and L Assoc, West Hoboken, installs 1,400
Same—same, West Hoboken, installs 200
Marschall, Herman—W Westrum, J City, 1 year 200
McCarthy, James—D McCarthy, J City, 4 years 5,000
McComb, Anna—The Highland M B and L Assoc, J City, installs 3,600
McCormick, J J—Gottfried Krueger Brewing Co, J City, 1 year 1,800
McInerney, Alex—Greenville B and L Assoc, Bayonne, installs 4,280
McKernan, Robert—C G Hoble, Union, installs 400
Miller, Adolph—The Garfield B and L Assoc, J City, installs 900
Muller, Diedrick—The Provident Inst for Savings, J City, 1 year 1,000
O'Connell, Daniel—Provident Inst for Savings, J City, 1 year 3,500
Orteig, Joseph—Emma Pohle, West Hoboken, 1 year 300
Rickens, Henry—A R Meyer, Hoboken, 3 years 1,500
Rieley, Patrick—R R Blackwell, J City, 1 year 500
Ross, F A—C H Behring, J City, 5 years 2,000
Sheridan, J J—Agnes Van Horn, J City, 3 years 300
Skerry, Ann—C H O'Neil, J City, 1 year 212
Smith, Emma G—Electric B and L Assoc, Kearney, installs 3,600
Spangenberg, Chas—Amelia Schmidt, Hoboken, 3 years 500
The Jersey City Printing Co—G R McKenzie, J City, 5 years 16,000
Thomas, T J—Enterprise M B and L Assoc, J City, 1 year 3,000
Troy, Peter—A Semrad, Hoboken, 3 years 2,000
Townsend, Maria—The Provident Inst for Savings, Bayonne, 1 year 1,500
Van Riper, Sarah J—Howard B and L Assoc, J City, installs 4,000
Weiss, Joseph—C Fox, Union, 5 years 3,300
Willims, John—J N Oelschlegel, North Bergen, 3 years 500
Zimmer, Otto—Exrs N S Hibler, J City, 2 years 3,000
Zoellig, Charles—F H Baur, J City, 3 years 1,500

CHATTEL MORTGAGES.

Ae, Otto, J City—Philip Schaefer & Son, saloon 600
Belho, Salvatore, Hoboken—The Archer Mfg Co, barber chair 75
Bondy, S E, Bayonne—J Fries, furniture, surgical instruments, books, &c 300
Brown, James, J City—John Matthews Apparatus Co, one soda water apparatus 525
Campbell, Mary, J City—J Gilken, furniture 185
Chase, S A, J City—Brooklyn Furniture Co, furniture 302
Christie, Elmira, J City—John Mullins & Co, furniture 72
Clark, John and Hugh Coughlin, Harrison—P Hauck, saloon 600
Cromly, Abbie M, J City—Brooklyn Furniture Co, furniture 189
Curtan, Alex, Bayonne—same, furniture 102
Deetjen, Theodore, Hoboken—Lembeck & Betz Eagle Brewing Co, saloon 300
Etzkorn, Wilhelm, J City—J S Wallace, chairs, crockery and cooking utensils 90
Garretson, Frederick, J City—Wolf Bros, horse, wagon, harness 200
Gastingen, Ferdinand, J City—The William Peter Brewing Co, saloon fixtures 1,000
Gehlski, H G, J City—Lembeck and Betz Eagle Brewing Co, saloon and Greenville B & L Assoc stock 575
Glenn, Margaret A, J City—J F Hart, horse, wagon, harness 450
Gudgen, C E, J City—John Mullins & Co, furniture 172
Kavanagh, Peter, New York—W J Robinson, horses 1,700
Kraus, J B, J City—A Fredericks, horse, wagon, one gross glass, milk business 600
Krumm, Martin, J City—The F M Schaefer Brewing Co, saloon fixtures 500
Malliet, W A and E H partners as Malliet Bros, J City—Hayden W Wheeler & Co, jewelry business 394
Mauro, Ignasio, J City—The Archer Mfg Co, barber fixtures 840
McMurray, Geo, J City—Union Brewing Co, saloon fixtures 350
Muller, Anton, Hoboken—Lembeck & Betz Eagle Brewing Co, saloon 165
Stogman, E H, Newark—A H Van Horn, furniture 78
Stellman, Katie H and Henry, Hoboken—A Tunke, horse, wagon, harness 500
The Crescent Watch Club, J City—Hayden W Wheeler, trading as Hayden W Wheeler & Co, jewelry business, stock and fixtures 6,641
Troetler, Henry, Bayonne—The Eagle Brewing Co, saloon 600
Van Drathan, John, J City—P Ballantine & Son, saloon 1,000
Wude, Edward, J City—C Stein, saloon fixtures 185
Young, Fred, Hoboken—The Archer Mfg Co, barber fixtures 214

BILL OF SALE.

Gaddis, James, J City—Fanny McLaughlin, grocery store, horse, wagon, harness 500

JUDGMENTS.

Hauser, C J—C H Smith 15
Hines, Catharine—Assignee J Schwell 74
Lesser, Ulrice—P Murray damages 6 cents
Manker, Rudolph—R Segelken 354
McCue, R A—G W Venable 106
McDonald, Isabella—P E Taylor 112
McHugh, James—E Sullivan 74
O'Donohue, P J—G W Venable et al 182
Meyer, Christian and Herman, partners as C & H Meyer—The William Peter Brewing Co 2,316
Rowe, Annie D otherwise Annie D Gilman and Barney Burns—T C Lyman & Co damages 6 cents
Shanahan, M A—M McShane & Co 528
Veranglia, Camine—India Wharf Brewing Co 336
Wurster, Christian—G W Venable et al 199

MECHANICS' LIENS.

Klabre, Arthur, claimant; Chas Bemhammer, builder; James E Drescher, owner, West Hoboken 444
Rathstein, Rebecca, builder and owner; Augustus Schmidt, Bayonne 81

BUILDING MATERIAL MARKET.

BRICKS.—Efforts to find something cheerful and positively promising in the general market are again fruitless. As a matter of fact some of the ordinarily most hopeful operators appear to have succumbed to the depressing influences and exhaust their stock of expletives in the attempt to characterize the dull and stupid condition of affairs. The demand made is wholly one of positive necessity, with necessity very small, and while we discover a slight difference of opinion as to the volume of arrivals in comparison with previous week there is no disagreement whatever over the claim that there was at all times a very liberal surplus and sufficient anxiety for custom to keep advantage entirely on the side of buyers. No change is necessary on quotations, and for first-class stock of all kinds it may be fair to call the tone about steady, but on ordinary quality it is believed that to make a clean-up sale of stuff they have been carrying for some time holders would allow a pretty decent sort of concession. It is just possible, however, that the market is at its worst and may not be far from the turning point into better conditions. A greater number of manufacturers have already shut down, others are stopping all along the river, and if the various reports and promises are confirmed it looks very much as though 80 to 90 per cent of the working capacity on Haverstraw Bay would wind up operations for the season by the first of October. Whether demand will improve does not appear to come within the line of predictions by receivers, but they do seem to feel that if relieved of the impact of heavy weekly receipts they can shape the market into better form.

GLASS.—For some reason manufacturers have not allowed the annual strike to take place, but after a temporary hitch finally came to an agreement with their workmen, and fires will generally be started on the first of the incoming month. Meanwhile the market is kept in pretty good shape, with comparatively moderate open offerings and a less general inclination to shade values, especially on standard sizes. For imported stock, too, there is a steadier feeling and less pressure to realize. The demand for all kinds of window glass at the moment is only moderately active, but promises to improve, from interior custom at least. Plate is selling in usual relative proportion and sustaining a steady general tone.

HARDWARE.—For pretty much all kinds of staple builders' hardware the line of valuation is well preserved and the production seems to be so well managed as to prevent any surplus offering. On local consuming account the sale of supplies is comparatively moderate at the moment, but interior demand is good and increasing, and promises still greater growth, owing to the excellent and remunerative crops. There is also reported a very satisfactory export trade, present and prospective.

LATH.—There has been a somewhat irregular market since our last report with the final result leaving affairs just about where they stood one week ago. For a time it happened that a little more demand developed while the available supply was short, and receivers lucky enough to have an offering were successful in getting $2.20 per M in several instances. Almost immediately after buyers became supplied, however, arrivals increased and the tone weakened with some inferior stuff sold down to $2.05, but practically $2.10@2.15 per M were the operating rates for standard goods, and figures so remain at the close, though one operator thought he could obtain bids at $2.20 over the telephone. There is the usual claim of small shipments, and further report that production will shut down earlier than usual.

LIME.—The market has become unsettled and finally weakened off a fraction on common, which is now selling at 85c. for Rockland, and somewhat less for other Eastern makes, but finishing is held at $1 per bbl. Demand had no great force, buyers in most cases requiring a little coaxing, and with supplies somewhat fuller a shading became a natural result, especially as in some cases manufacturers were urging a prompt disposal of their cargoes. State stock is also slack and slow of sale.

LUMBER.—Upon what may be considered a really new call from actual consumers it is doubtful if much gain has been made this week, and indeed some dealers manifested a disposition to take us to task for even hinting at such a thing. They complain, however, mainly of the present inaction and have some hope of the early future and possibly a good fair trade should the winter prove open. In any event, however, stocks and assortments must be made up and the move in that direction is keeping alive a line of trade in bulk parcels, some of which proves advantageous to sellers and is giving them the stiffening of value line calculated upon as a natural and probable recovery from the extreme depression under which some lines of stock have labored. Increasing cost of transportation with possible delay in deliveries and the more independent attitudes of operators at some primary points have also acted as contributing factors to stir up buyers who know they must sooner or later be compelled to invest, and are, therefore, disposed to give attention to desirable offerings as they may happen to be presented.

Eastern Spruce continues to show about the most unsatisfactory tone of any wood upon the market and some of the business, within the past fortnight, was upon a lower basis than we had supposed. Naturally, sellers have not felt particularly anxious to reveal the full extent of concessions allowed in the search for custom, but cargoes of narrow stuff are now admitted to have gone as low as $14.50 per M., with some buyers talking as though they were conferring a favor by taking goods at that. On wide and attractive specifications fair steadiness is claimed, and for specials quite decided firmness, indeed in some cases a little more money exacted, as in this line the mills have a fair number of orders booked. There is practically nothing new regarding supplies, the position being very uncertain. Some seventy-five to eighty cargoes have arrived this month and, while manufacturers continue to talk about a cessation of shipments, dealers seem to think stuff will keep coming along until climatic influences interfere.

Piling has not been coming along quite so freely for some little time past, yet receivers have appeared very well satisfied with the quantities they were called upon to handle, and the current demand it is said was met without infringing upon the accumulation in chains. Pretty much the old line of quotations is retained, but with an expressed hope of a little more firmness before long.

Hemlock is coming in on deliveries, but agents say they are not finding much encouragement in new demand at the moment, so far as local custom is concerned. From outside sources fair attention is at times received, and that is helping trade, though not stimulating it sufficiently to give the position any real boom, and well sustained values seems to be about the best that can for the present go upon record.

White Pine retains the progressive inclination noted in our last, and while the market probably stands little chance of becoming really animated or buoyant, a firm feeling is expressed regarding the upper line of quality. Dealers and consumers generally feel that it is time to prepare for their winter wants, and as they look about for supplies discover that offerings are neither so plentiful or so cheap as they had expected, a feature having a natural stiffening influence. Pretty good export orders are being placed for low grades, with hopes of an early call for the better qualities.

Yellow Pine, although still unsettled and neglected by a considerable portion of the local trade, retains some promising general features. Additional heavy contracts have been made for portions of the Southwestern cut, mostly for railway work, and there is still a good f. o. b. trade doing, especially with countries that have accepted the reciprocity treaty. There seems also to be hope of revival of demand with River Plate and some of the States on west coast of South America.

A paragraph has been somewhat freely circulated about the country, claiming a deal at the South valued at $8,000,000. It may be well, therefore, to note the following correction as given in the Galveston *Daily News*:

The Reliance Lumber Company, of Beaumont, Texas, recently closed the contract for what is beyond doubt the largest bill of timbers ever placed with a mill in the South or Southwest, and there have been few of equal size placed with any mill on the American continent. It is for ties, bridge timbers, section houses, platforms, stock-pens, etc., for 1,000 miles of railway, and has been ordered for the completion of the Omaha, Kansas Central & Galveston Railroad, from Lyons, Kan., to Galveston, Tex. The whole aggregates about 100,000,000 feet, amounting in dollars and cents to between $800,000 and $1,000,000, not $8,000,000 as reported.

Carolina Pine while not particularly active on local account is nevertheless finding a fair trade, and a little more demand from outside sources. This shapes reports up into fairly cheerful form, and steady rates are claimed all around. It is understood that production is so well managed as to prevent a surplus.

Hardwoods are somewhat slow on the distributive

outlet and not very active for bulk parcels, though resident and traveling agents by skirmishing around manage to find considerable custom for such staple stock as poplar and oak, and a sprinkling of other woods goes along in somewhat fuller proportion than earlier in the season. In general terms it is fair to call values steady, but there seems to be nothing in the present situation calculated to afford basis for buoyancy. On foreign account the demand is fair for usual assortment at steady rates.

GENERAL LUMBER NOTES.

GREAT BRITAIN.

The *Timber Trades Journal* as follows:

LIVERPOOL.

There is not, nor could there be expected to be, anything doing locally in c. i. f. business for sawn pitch pine. The present state of our stocks entirely precludes the possibility of any contracting for the future being entertained. The stock of upwards of 1,000,000 cubic feet of sawn pitch pine timber will have to be greatly diminished before merchants will feel justified in entering into future engagements in this article. Besides this we have the stock at Fleetwood to take into consideration, and this will be no unimportant quantity. We therefore come to the conclusion that some time must elapse before there is any advance upon present prices to be obtained in this market.

Of Quebec goods there are only three or four cargoes discharging at present.

The customary imports of pine deals, boards and sidings by the steamers from Montreal continue to come forward in moderate quantities for the usual shippers.

Pine deals, in point of fact all descriptions of sawn pine goods, are firmer on the other side, and prices have advanced at least 5s. per standard for 3d quality. No freight transactions have been done here for the Montreal trade, but we learn that two lines of steamers have taken deals and boards at 50s. per standard, Montreal to Liverpool, for a very limited period.

GLASGOW.

Pitch pine is not perceptibly improving, but there is no further decline; the stocks have been somewhat reduced from the abnormal condition they have occupied for some time.

U. S. whitewood logs (canary) have been rather freely imported for some time past, and meantime are not readily salable, and a good many logs have been yarded recently by the brokers.

A consignment of about 10,000 pieces Quebec spruce deals has just been landed at Yorkhill ex ss. Concordia.

Other recent arrivals of Quebec deals per the Allen and Donaldson liners have been mostly disposed of ex quay, but on the whole these arrivals are this season keeping on a smaller scale than usual; a full steamer cargo, it is reported, is shortly expected.

Two cargoes of N. B. pine deals have just arrived at Yorkhill, one of which is to be stored in Yorkhill Yards and the other carted direct to mills.

THE WEST.

The Northwestern *Lumberman*, speaking of improved conditions of trade, says:

Perhaps the most striking and sudden revival has been in Saginaw Valley. In that section of the field there had been complaint all season of a slow demand and an accumulation of unsold stocks. Now the tide has turned. During the week ending on Wednesday 30,000,000 feet had been sold for eastward shipment, and the car-load trade was active. The shipping interest had revived. Rates to Lake Erie points had been advanced 25 cents a thousand. Though there was a large accumulation of lumber on the mill docks, the larger part of it had been sold, and it was thought that all available tonnage would be required to carry the lumber to destination. There is a decidedly better feeling in Saginaw Valley. The World's Fair is drawing on the resources of that district. One order for this purpose amounts to 200 car-loads. Lumber and timber for the World's Fair is also coming from the Huron shore as far north as Alpena.

Good reports come from Mississippi river all the way from Minneapolis to St. Louis, and these are seconded by returns throughout Wisconsin. The prices named at the late Minneapolis meeting are being nearly or quite realized. Advances of 50 cents a thousand are indicated at several places on the river, under the influence of a brisk demand and broken stocks. Many of the mills are short of logs, numerous rafts having been standing along the big stream, while millions of feet of logs are hung up in the tributaries. While the lack of logs is considered a serious thing to the mill operators, advantage of it is being taken to strengthen the market. Some of the loss experienced for lack of logs will be compensated by the rapid sale of lumber on hand and the profitable prices that will be realized for it.

The decline in the selling price of piece stuff on the cargo market does not seem to have caused any appreciable decline in the yards. Evidently the dealers are determined to save the difference in their sales. They have contended all season that the cargo piece stuff market was too stiff. They insisted that they could not raise prices in the yard and meet Wisconsin competition. What they wanted was a drop in cargo prices sufficient to enable them to secure a safe handling bill. Now that they have almost got what they desired they for once appear disposed to hold it by keeping prices in the yards where they were before the drop on the cargo market. If the big fellows will keep from plunging in the country prices may be maintained.

There is a loud call for 18 and 20-foot 12-inch boards. Stocks of such lumber are low, which renders the call particularly urgent.

Though the demand for boards of promiscuous widths has dragged all summer, it is thought that the general increase of the trade in merchandise and packing-house products will stimulate a demand for boxboards, especially those of the No. 2 class.

There is a continual call for high grade stripe. There is a fair demand for thick selects, with the prospect that shop lumber will be in extraordinary request before next spring. Of course, with the rise of trade and the increase in city and suburban building, there is no trouble about the disposition of both No. 1 and No. 2 fencing.

The *Timberman* says:

In the hardwood trade there does not seem to be as much cause for congratulation as in other lines of the lumber business, but the fact that the market has remained reasonably firm in spite of the many discouraging circumstances which have arisen since last spring, shows that confidence in the future is by no means shaken as yet. The revival of demand for some woods is noted in the Eastern markets, and with the anticipated improvement of financial conditions in the West there is no doubt but that a corresponding improvement in demand and prices of hardwoods will be noted. * * *

Oak continues to be the best selling of any of the hardwoods, but supply is in excess of demand and prices are weaker than they were in the early summer. Plain sawed red oak still sells readily, especially Wisconsin stock, which is usually held at from $1 to $2 per thousand higher than southern oak.

There is not a great deal of inquiry for quarter sawed oak and this in connection with the fact that stocks are excessive makes prices very weak. Dealers report free offerings of stocks from interior points at prices from $5 to $10 per thousand lower than they were in the early part of the year. There continues to be a good market, however, for bone dry and extra wide stock which will bring a fancy price. Dealers are paying for quarter sawed oak all the way from $32 to $38 for inch.

NAILS.—Demand is running very much as before as to general volume, and wire nails continue to have precedence over cut. Manufacturers are dissatisfied with prices, and constantly threatening to cut down production, but have made no scarcity as yet, and in some cases the line of action seems to indicate that accumulations are a little toppy. We quote Cut at $1.50@1.60 per keg for car lots and $1.75@1.85 per keg for parcels from store, for iron, and add 5@10c. per keg for steel; Wire, $2.00@2.05 at mills, and 2.20@2.35 from store.

PAINTS, OILS, COLORS, ETC.—The market remains in a somewhat monotonous condition, and it is difficult to discover any feature of a positively interesting character. There are no outside or unusual influences calculated to interest either buyer or seller, and business is in consequence conducted upon conservative lines, with few fluctuations taking place on values for any of the leading articles. Distribution is claimed to be about up to average for the season, with every encouragement to expect a continuation, but nothing of a speculative nature shown. Dry colors adapted to house painters' use and grinders' specialties are getting very fair attention, and outside the local trade have a movement about as full as usual at this season of the year and retain steady prices throughout. Whiting and Paris White receive reasonably full attention and there is some demand for Block Chalk. For Zincs, both domestic and foreign, there is a somewhat slow trade, but no noticeable surplus of supply and values very well sustained. White Lead has been selling somewhat more freely with the cheaper varieties irregular, but the pure pigment ruling pretty steady. Association Corroders' rates stand as follows: Lead in oil in kegs and dry lead in kegs, in lots of less than 500 lbs., 7¼c. net; in lots of 500 lbs to 5 tons at one purchase, 7c.; 5 tons to 12 tons, one purchase, 5⅝c.; 12 tons and over, one purchase, 6¾c.; dry white lead in bbls. ¼c. per lb. less than price in kegs. Lead in oil 12½ lb. in tin pails, add 1c.; in 25 and 50 lb. tin pails, add ½c.; and in 1 to 5 lb. tin cans, assorted (100 lbs. in case) add 2½c. per lb. to keg price. Terms on lots on 500 lbs. and over, note or acceptance at sixty days, or 2½ per cent. discount will be allowed for cash paid within fifteen days of invoice date. To make either of the above required quantities any assortment of packages of white lead, red lead and litharge may be counted. The above quotations are free on board cars or boat at corroding point. Linseed Oil meets with about the average trade and for the present has a pretty steady market, competition from the outside or Western makes proving mild and indifferent and prices ruling about steady. We quote at general range at 40@45c. for Western, and 44@56c. for City. Spirits Turpentine for a while following our last was somewhat firmer in tone, but the demand ran light and of late with less favorable accounts from the South it would require concessions to sell readily. We quote at 38½@39c. per gallon, according to quality, delivery, etc.

TAR AND PITCH.—Demand has been somewhat variable, and not particularly full at any time, with market void of marked features worthy of note. The supply is kept well enough in hand to avoid any movement that would tend to disturb values. We quote Pitch at $1.70@1.75 per bbl.; Tar at $2.15@2.50, according to quantity, quality and delivery.

MISCELLANEOUS.

MISCELLANEOUS.

DEVOTED TO REAL ESTATE, BUILDING ARCHITECTURE, HOUSEHOLD DECORATION, BUSINESS AND THEMES OF GENERAL INTEREST

PRICE, PER YEAR IN ADVANCE, SIX DOLLARS.

Published every Saturday.

TELEPHONE - - - - CORTLANDT 1370.

Communications should be addressed to

C. W. SWEET, 14 & 16 Vesey St.

J. T. LINDSEY, Business Manager.

VOL. XLVIII OCTOBER 3, 1891. No. 1,229

The exhibition of architectural drawings is now open in the exposition rooms of THE RECORD AND GUIDE, *at Nos. 14 to 16 Vesey street, to which the public are cordially invited, free of charge. This display of drawings is one of the finest that has ever been made in New York City. It contains about three hundred works from the boards of the leading architects. Among the perspectives of more than ordinary interest are those of the several large hotels now building in this city, and the designs submitted in competition for the new cathedral of St. John's. No one who wishes to study the principal recent architectural works in the metropolis and the contiguous suburban district should fail to pay a visit to the exposition.*

IT must not be forgotten that while stocks were declining under so many adverse influences as were seen in the last week or two they were the object of the very careful regard of many people who believe in their future. Consequently, as soon as such issues as are most affected by the recent events which have caused so much comment have settled themselves into their places for the time being there will be a new and rapid rise in the general list. Yesterday's movements were very encouraging, showing conclusively that all were not of one mind. If it could be asserted that all stocks had been wholesomely touched by the depression there could be no doubt but that the recovery would be of a very snappy kind. It will be so in some cases, but there are others in which manipulation put prices way above any conceivable merit, and has kept them there. Such instances menace the continuation if not the beginning of a new advance. The time, too, is one in which a considerable enlargement of trading can hardly fail to raise the price of money available here unless gold imports come in even greater than the satisfactory bulk they now show. Nor is it among the railroads themselves all sunshine yet. The storm seems to be passing away, but there continue heavy rumblings which threaten a return and from another direction. The best that can be seen in the market is the way in which it withstood blows showered upon it, and if it has not passed through all the trouble it has to receive for this time, it has certainly had the worst.

THE strength which many of the European markets have recently shown has not been maintained. The tightening of money in all the centres has helped to keep things quiet; and the continued political uncertainty has made financiers very cautious about entering into operations that involve much time. Indeed, it is not too much to say that political conditions are dominating the financial situation. In Berlin, for instance, the market has again become depressed, not only because the economic prospects are so bad, but because the political outlook is considered to be quite cheerless. No one expects immediate war; but people are astounded and dismayed at the extent to which France has been carried by her Philo-Russian craze. They do not attempt to discriminate between a diplomatic alliance and one for war-like purposes. They only appreciate the fact that the close union threatens Germany, and many are preparing to meet the worse possible consequences. This, however, is rather the popular impression than that which exists in well-informed political and financial circles. Bankers are bitterly opposed to hostilities as peculiarly inimical to their interests; and will exercise to their uttermost their large powers towards the maintenance of peace. The coming Russian loan continues to be the main topic of discussion. It is to be issued some time during the present month. All that appears to be decided is, that the loan will be in Three Per Cents, and that it will be contracted for by a syndicate and not be issued direct by the Russian government. The group are said to be endeavoring to interest the Credit Foncier in the issue to the extent of receiving subscriptions; but it is doubtful if that establishment would accede to the request except under pressure from the government. It is considered to be a very grave fact that French investors and financiers, known to be a careful and economical people, should consent again to credit Russia with 500,000,000 roubles when they have already invested 3,000,000,000 roubles at a price that is almost on a par with German stocks—particularly when Russia's debt is not secured by anywhere near as much property as that of Germany. Among minor items it is interesting to note that the scheme of making Paris a seaport by a ship canal has finally received its death blow. The Council-General of Roads and Bridges has adopted unanimously the unfavorable report of the commission charged to examine the plan. The principal objections to the canal were the insufficiency of the practicable dimensions, the frequent intersection of its course with the Western Railway, the trains of which, more than a hundred a day in the section near Paris, would have to be carried over the canal by draw-bridges, the disturbance to the water-courses of the region traversed, and the interruption in the communication between the localities on the two sides of the projected canal.

WE have called attention in these columns several times to the heavy decline in building operations in every district of the city since the first of the year. The labor troubles of the spring were regarded as the chief cause of the dullness, and it was expected that the beginning of the fall would see not only a revival of work, but a hustling activity stimulated and augmented by the inactivity of the early part of the year. These hopes are now proved to have been delusive. There will be no "hustle" this fall. The architects and the "arch-i-tects" of the city are busy at present discharging their draughtsmen for want of work, there are few enterprises of any moment under way, and the speculative builder is busier with "adverse circumstances" than with new plans. A dull, quiet fall and winter in the Building trade is inevitable. Hope has taken herself off to the spring of '92. The fact of the matter is, we are now in the midst of a reaction from the phenomenal activity of the last two or three years. THE RECORD AND GUIDE published figures in 1890 and in 1889, which showed clearly that both the West Side and the East Side had been "overbuilt," and that the development of Harlem was arrested and forced to a pause by inadequate transit facilities.

THE present dullness is one of the best guarantees possible for, and one of the surest precursors of more active and healthier conditions. Both the West Side and the East Side are in a much better state now than they were this time a year ago. There are fewer buildings on the market and stronger hands hold those that are. Besides this, there is now only a tithe of the new structures "under way" or "projected" that there was in the fall of 1890. Our weekly lists of conveyances show that the number of unsold houses is steadily lessening. The financial condition of our builders and speculators is improving, and the conditions for new operations are becoming more and more inviting. The effect of this and the better tone of general business due to the large crops will no doubt be noticeable in the real estate field next spring. The next great building movement, however, will probably not be in the older sections of the West Side and the East Side. Henceforth operations there will be more closely in touch with demand than they have ever been. Land has become too expensive there for the touch-and-go speculator. Many things apparently point to the Washington Heights district as the scene of the next big speculative movement in up-town real estate; but before much can be done in that section it must be made available to residents by comfortable and speedy transit. The future of the district hinges upon that. The next speculative movement in this city will be determined by and will follow the line of improved transportation facilities.

IT is not surprising that the Rapid Transit Commissioners have found so much worthy of consideration in the reports of the experts to which their plans have been submitted, and that considerable time has been occupied in the consideration of these reports. The statement can be made without fear of contradiction that the problem which they are attempting to solve is about as trying and complicated a transit problem as can well be conceived. The best engineering, railroad and financial ability in the country is needed to meet its many diverse requirements and to overcome its many difficulties; and while the commission contains a number of shrewd and ingenious men, and while its engineering counsel are trained experts, still it is obvious that it would be possible to find railroad specialists more peculiarly adapted to the task. Some eighteen months ago, before the Rapid Transit bill was passed, THE RECORD AND GUIDE pointed out how necessary it was that such a class of men should constitute the commission, and this judgment has since been vindicated by events. The commission as appointed was a good one, but it might have been better. It has been studying the problem for something like eight months, has listened to all the suggestions which people interested and people disinterested, people crazy and people sane, could make; it has rejected all of these and has evolved a plan which, so far as the route is concerned, has been considered unexceptionable by the press. Then it set to work and selected a plan of construction which, so far as announced, appeared to be adequate. These plans are sent to a number of experts, and lo! their suggestions are so valuable that the commission is obliged to consider carefully whether changes should not be made. But what if these experts, or men of equally high standing, were themselves commissioners—paid to devote their whole time to the solution of this difficult problem, would not a prolonged study thereof by men so qualified have brought forth a plan more ingenious and more suitable? The chances are that then we should indeed get the perfect system which everybody is looking for. There is, however, no cause for complaint. We have got the next best thing at all events—the benefit of the advice of a number of the best experts, and no doubt the commissioners will need all the "authority" procurable before they finish with their work.

Reform.

THE Gubernatorial contest this fall will not be one over measures, except so far as it is regarded as a skirmish for position in the greater fight to take place next year for the Presidentship. The chief question which Mr. Fassett and his party are forcing upon voters is whether the *morale* of their opponents is such that they can safely be intrusted with the government of the State. From a practical point of view the question is not worth answering. It implies the existence of a choice between the politicians of the two parties, and it is hard to see how, in the estimation of candid persons, there can be a choice. Neither is distinguished by any perceptible superiority over the other in aims, methods, intelligence or decency. The deficiency of both in these matters is lamentable and disheartening. But, though the question unfortunately is at this juncture not worth much attention from the voter, it does deserves the careful consideration of the citizen.

Partly through lack of thought and partly through a habit of thought perhaps forced upon us by our political system we have come somehow to regard good government or bad government as largely a matter of method and machinery. If any governmental activity doesn't produce satisfactory results our first cry is for a change of system. In other words, good government is supposed to be chiefly a matter of good institutions. For instance, in the long, wearisome and fruitless agitation over the costliness, corruption and inefficiency of municipal government in this country, nearly all efforts at reform have taken the direction of effecting some change in the administrative system. Increase the power and the responsibility of the Mayor and better government will ensue, say some Reformers. Home Rule is the sure cure for these evils say others. The Civil Service system is the panacea, we are told in one quarter, and in another that Ballot Reform is the necessary and sufficient remedy. Even so experienced an observer and so astute a student as Mr. Seth Low recently informed us that the way to get a dollar's worth for every dollar spent—the great problem in municipal government—is to increase the power and the responsibility of our Mayors, adopt Civil Service Reform and change the time for holding city elections so that they do not happen upon the same dates as the State and National contests.

Everyone of these suggested reforms, no doubt, would be fruitful in good results. But each and all of them miss the real source of our evils. They might improve our condition, they might even materially improve it, but, in themselves, they would not insure to us good, honest, wholesome and efficient government. The weakness of all these schemes for reformation lies in the fact that good government is not mainly a matter of machinery, while it is largely a matter of men—their character and ability. Honest men will produce honest government be the administrative machinery or system what it may. What is the use of conferring upon a dishonest or an inefficient Mayor greater power and concurrently greater responsibility. We have made a great many systematic changes in our municipal governments in the last ten or fifteen years, but with very trivial results, for we have left the *personnel* of government unchanged. The administration of the affairs of our cities are in the same sort of dirty, inefficient, uneducated hands as ever.

Here, then, is the direction which reform must take if it is ever to result in anything radical and important. Ballot Reform is a good thing worthy of the support and effort of every honest intelligent man; Civil Service Reform, also, is excellent, and so is Home Rule and the concentration of power and responsibility upon the chief officials; but all of these will count for little unless *pari passu* with every effort made for them an equal effort is made to improve the official character.

This task is not an easy matter to accomplish. In the first place the average voter is such a desperate uncompromising partisan. In political matters he is so rarely an unbiassed or even an intelligent creature. Party is to him the paramount phase of government. Add to this the fact that the unintelligence, the inefficiency, the corruption of official life are reflections of and spring from like defects in the national and local character and it is easy to see how vast is the problem before us. Government is *of* the people, it reflects their average. The only sure way to improve government is to heighten this average. This is the task which reformers must undertake if their work is to be real reformation.

THE news about the Chicago Fair continues to be encouraging. Both England and Germany have made a request for a large amount of floor space; the Spanish-American republics will all of them make elaborate exhibits, and the managers of the enterprise are exhibiting great shrewdness and energy in completing the arrangements of detail. They seem to have thought better of a number of the merely sensational "attractions" which have from time to time been announced in the newspapers, and are settling down to the more sensible and fruitful task of organizing the different departments of the Fair and making each of them instructive and illustrative. It is sincerely to be hoped that Congress at its coming session will consent to give to Chicago the additional help which the city needs. The country is committed to making the Exposition representative of its resources and productive capacity. Exhibits and representation have been sought from other nations on the ground that this is a national undertaking. If some money is not advanced the Fair will be hampered by a lack of funds; it will be impossible to make adequate arrangements, expenses will have to be cut down in every direction until the whole undertaking might become cheap and arid. This is not merely a local enterprise. If there is any deficit, let Chicago stand it, because Chicago will be principally benefited; but neither the national nor the State governments should be niggardly in helping that city in every reasonable way.

Every builder in New York City should visit the exhibition of architectural drawings at THE RECORD AND GUIDE *rooms, Nos. 14 to 16 Vesey street.*

Law Answers.

Editor RECORD AND GUIDE:

Will THE RECORD AND GUIDE kindly decide this question: Who is entitled to the $10 deposit to secure a flat, afterwards abandoned or thrown up, the broker, for his services (not a special agent), or the owner?

From the form of the question we assume that the payment was on account of rent. In such case it would belong to the owner and not to the broker.

Editor RECORD AND GUIDE:

If two business buildings are directly opposite one another on the same street, and are the property of one owner, has he the privilege of erecting a bridge between the two at a given height, without conflicting with any regulations of the city government?

H. I. PHILLIPS.

The owner has no power to build such a bridge, and we doubt that the city government, under charter and present laws, has power to permit such a bridge to be erected. (See Farrell *vs.* The Mayor, etc., 20 State Reporter, affirmed 5 N. Y. Supp., 580; O'Reilly *vs.* The Mayor, etc., 59 How. Pr., 277.)

Editor RECORD AND GUIDE:

Will you kindly answer the following in your next Saturday's issue?

1. If A gives a piece of property to a real estate agent to sell at a certain price, and the agent finding a purchaser at A's terms, accepts 10 per cent purchase money; what redress has the purchaser should A refuse to deliver the property? Can A be compelled to deliver, and is he liable for damages should he refuse?

2. What constitutes requisite authority of an agent to sell? Does it mean power of attorney in writing, or can you give him the authority verbally, and are you then bound by his action, supposing, certainly, that your terms are adhered to? Does the fact of your telling him that he may sell the property and his making a memorandum of it and taking a description of the property, give him the requisite authority to sell?

Your answer will greatly oblige one of your subscribers.

VICTOR LEVI.

[Unless a contract to sell has been made, the purchaser's redress is limited to a return of the 10 per cent. In the absence of a contract, A can not be compelled to transfer the property, nor would he be liable for damages. It is assumed, however, that in this case there has been no fraud or deceit practiced.

2. The authority to an agent to sell can be conferred without a writing. Except under special circumstances where the Court acting as a Court of Chancery would grant equitable relief, the law requires the contract of sale to be in writing, and the Statute of our State prescribes that it shall be in writing. This, however, is not the authority to the agent. The authority to, or employment of, the agent precedes the contract of sale. It is not necessary that the agent should have a power of attorney to sell. The authority is often conferred in that manner. Parol authority is sufficient to empower an agent to enter into and execute a contract for the sale

of land, and if such authority be given to the agent, a contract so made is binding upon the principal (Moody *vs.* Smith, 70 N. Y., 595).

No special form of words is required to confer the authority to the agent to sell. If the owner tell the agent to make the sale, naming terms, etc., and to execute the contract in the principal's name, that would be sufficient not only to make the sale but to execute and deliver the contract. The mere authority to produce a purchaser, which is the ordinary and usual authority to a broker to sell, would not include power to execute the contract of sale.]

Facts of General Interest.

The purchasers at the Morgenthau sale last May have begun to improve their property between 178th and 182d streets, Kingsbridge road and 10th avenue. The first house to be erected on these lots is now nearing completion. It is located on Kingsbridge road, near 179th street, and is a three-story structure. The erection of other houses will probably be begun as soon as the streets are actually opened, but this may not be for some time yet. It may be remembered that streets through this property were legally opened before the sale, but apparently nothing has been done since that time looking towards the actual opening of these streets, and of course the improvement of any lots which are not located on the avenues or 181st street which has been open for a long time is out of the question. It is a pity that this property and other vacant lots in the neighborhood are not restricted to a certain class of buildings. The neighborhood is an exceptionally desirable one for private residence, and if it was only restricted to an unobjectionable class of dwellings there is no doubt but that it would be the scene of fine improvement in the next ten years, for on Washington Heights the next great building movement on Manhattan Island will be located. As it is now the large crowds which are attracted to Washington Bridge on Saturdays and Sundays encourage the erection of saloons and other objectionable buildings, and unless some measures of prevention are taken by owners in the vicinity what is destined to be a fine district of attractive houses will be ruined for everything but picnicking.

The Board of Health owes it to residents along the line of upper 3d avenue and intersecting streets to take prompt and radical measures to have some of the dust and dirt and all decayed and decaying odor-producing matter, which now make that avenue a disgrace, removed. The laying of the new cable road is responsible for much of the dust which makes the air along upper 3d avenue white and thick, and doubtless this evil is a necessary accompaniment of the improvement; but this is no excuse for the stench from the gutters which is to be met with at many points along the avenue. Block after block the gutters are filled with papers, decaying vegetables and fruit swept by the grocers into the street, and black, foul water that looks as though it had lain there since the last rainstorm. It is easy to imagine that the gutters, occupied as they are by such refuse, are an offense not only to residents but also to the pedestrians and the passengers on the surface cars. In the present torn-up condition of the avenue it may not be possible to sweep it with the machines, but until it is the disease-producing matter that will collect on this busy avenue should be removed by a patrol of laborers.

Several attempts have been made lately to attract small home-seekers to Staten Island, but before any of these efforts can be attended with much success many improvements in certain districts must be made. In the first place, the train service is not frequent enough nor good enough. Trains are run at intervals of considerable time, and very often they are late. The fares are not very cheap and the accommodations are susceptible of considerable improvement, and added to these discomforts and inconveniences the roads are, nearly all of them, very bad. In this latter respect, however, there will be some improvements before long, several long macadamized roads having been determined upon and partly constructed. With all of these evils, or some of them, corrected Staten Island real estate will be easier to dispose of to people who not only want pleasant homes, but also comfortable, cheap and quick access to them.

The Opinions of Others.

Edmond J. Sause, Jr., said: "It is a peculiar thing about real estate that when general business throughout the country is good the real estate market is inactive, and when other business is dull real estate is active. This is explained, I suppose, by the fact that people engaged in business, as a rule, only put their surplus money into real estate and, of course, when industrial enterprises of all kinds are so successful that they are attracting the overplus of capital real estate is not dealt in to any great extent. On the other hand, when dullness prevails in regular business it is the most natural thing in the world for capital to seek investment in real estate, the surest as well as one of the best paying commodities there is."

"I have been pleased to see that despite every attempt on the part of the daily papers to boom real estate," said an up-town broker, "that THE RECORD AND GUIDE has told the truth about the market right along. The daily papers pay very little attention to real estate anyway, and when they do publish the truth it is not hard to see that their information comes from your paper. I suppose that their object in endeavoring to boom the market is to secure advertisements, but I wonder that they do not see that such a course will only avail them for a little while. It does not take those who are daily in close relation to the real estate market long to find out that such and such a paper is forever presenting a false picture of the situation, and, of course, when that fact is discovered the paper is very properly mistrusted. Then, too—but this is a fact that I don't suppose will appeal to the dailies—they are not only injuring themselves but they are doing a great deal of harm to real estate. By continually presenting a bright picture they, of course, encourage owners to ask extravagant prices which have no foundation in fact, and, of course, when the time for readjustment comes all of those who were foolish enough to be misled lose money, and real estate itself is greatly discredited as a means of investment. When the other papers follow the lead of THE RECORD AND GUIDE and tell the truth about real estate, regardless of consequences, more capital will be invested and greater profits made in real property."

J. J. Plummer said: "Very many sales are prevented by the over-anxiety of owners to dispose of their holdings. If owners would only leave negotiations in the hands of their brokers until called on to act more transactions would be consummated and with less difficulty. Nowadays owners seem to think that by waiting upon a prospective buyer at all times, no matter how inopportune, they will succeed in disposing of their real estate, while as a matter of fact they generally only succeed in frightening off the buyer. By their experience and their position as intermediaries simply, brokers are better able to deal with a buyer than an owner. He has not so much at stake as the latter, and his word will, therefore, have more weight, and from dealing every day with men who are anxious to buy he has learnt what the most convincing arguments are. By all means, then, let owners leave customers to their brokers."

Contractors' Notes.

Estimates for furnishing granite stones for bulkhead or river wall will be received by the Board of Commissioners at the head of the Department of Docks, at the office of said Department, on pier A, foot of Battery place, North River, until 1 o'clock, P. M., of Thursday, October 15, 1891.

Sealed bids or estimates will be received by the Commissioner of Street Improvements of the 23d and 24th Wards, at his office, No. 2322 3d avenue, corner of 141st street, until 3 o'clock P. M., on Tuesday, October 13, 1891: For regulating, grading, setting curb-stones, flagging the sidewalks and laying crosswalks in 138th street, from the Southern Boulevard to a point 330 feet east of Locust avenue; for regulating and paving with granite block pavement the roadway of and laying crosswalks in 149th street, from the New York Central and Hudson River Railroad to Mott avenue; for sewer and appurtenances in 170th street, from 3d avenue to Washington avenue.

The Architectural Quarterly.

"We have very great pleasure in welcoming to architectural journalism one of the most satisfactory periodicals which has yet been devoted to architecture in any country. This newcomer is a quarterly, to be known as the *Architectural Record*, and if it is to fulfill the promise of its first number, we advise those of our readers who like to see architectural subjects of permanent interest treated by writers who understand them, to lose no time in sending one dollar to its publishers, at 14 and 16 Vesey street, New York, for their first year's subscription. In their introductory address, the conductors of the new review say that they have undertaken to enter a field which must be entered with serious purposes, or not at all, and all thorough architects will agree with them that, while the occupation of this field imposes grave responsibilities, it greatly needs to be occupied; and that a magazine which will faithfully fulfill the duties incident to such a position may do incalculable service to the cause of art in this country, and perhaps, later, elsewhere. We believe that architects everywhere are heartily sick of seeing professional periodicals either padded with disquisitions which seem to have been composed by second-year students in the professional schools or devoted to the personal advancement of some small clique of practitioners; and will welcome with much satisfaction a publication from which even the best of them may learn something to help him in his work, while it will offer a still more valuable service, one, too, which it is hardly possible for a weekly journal to render, in the form of honest and intelligent criticism of current architectural work. Not only is it almost impracticable for a weekly journal, which must rather reflect the course of events than comment upon them, to undertake this latter task, but the criticism which will be of most service to architects should generally have something of the lay character which a quarterly review may possess, as distinguished from the intimate connection with the members of the profession more proper to the weekly periodical. In fact the criticism of a well-instructed amateur is perhaps more useful to architects than that of a member of their own profession, who, while he comprehends their difficulties better, is more likely to be biased for or against a particular school, and may have personal relations, which, if they do not warp his judgment, hinder the free expression of it; and if, as we suppose, the new review intends to give a considerable space to such criticism, its value to the profession is assured. The first number contains an article on the Romanesque Revival in New York, by Mr. Montgomery Schuyler, which, we need not say, is a model of conscientious work of the kind, and we hope is only one of a series. We find also, among other things, an interesting article on the New York Building Law, by that most earnest and untiring advocate of improvements in the statute, Mr. William J. Fryer, Jr.; a reprint of a part of Professor Aitchison's admirable Royal Academy lectures on Byzantine Architecture; a very good paper on plumbing, by a contributor who modestly signs his initials only, and a review, much too short, of Professor Moore's book on Gothic Architecture. This last is by far the best review we have yet seen of Professor Moore's book and, it seems to us, the best review of an architectural book that has yet been published in this country."—*American Architect.*

Important to Architects and Builders.

SHEET METAL.

The Architectural Sheet Metal Works, of No. 205 East 99th street, are doing all the copper work on St. Michael's Church, on Amsterdam avenue and 99th street; all the slate roofing and galvanized iron work for the new water-works building in Brooklyn, and the corrugated iron work for Pier 10, East River, which is 500 feet long. Among their other contracts are two police precinct stations in Brooklyn. They are also putting in two new machines, one of which is the largest heavy skylight press in existence, the other being one of Meitor's cutters.

Notice to Property-Owners.

BOARD OF ASSESSORS.

OFFICE OF THE BOARD OF ASSESSORS,
NO. 27 CHAMBERS STREET,
NEW YORK, Sept. 13, 1891.

Notice is given to the owner or owners of all houses and lots, improved or unimproved lands affected thereby, that the following assessments have been completed and are lodged in the office of the Board of Assessors for examination by all persons interested, viz.:

No. 1.—Paving 67th st, from 8th to 9th av, with granite blocks.
No. 2.—Paving 109th st, from Madison to 5th av, with granite blocks.
No. 3.—Repaving 16th st, from Av C to the East River, with asphalt, and laying crosswalks.
No. 4.—Flagging, reflagging, curbing and recurbing e s of West End av, bet 76th and 77th sts.
No. 5.—Laying crosswalks across Lenox av, at the northerly and southerly sides of 132d st.
No. 6.—Laying crosswalks across Lenox av, at the northerly and southerly sides of 118th st.
No. 7.—Fencing the vacant lots on the n s of 99th st, bet 8th and 9th avs.
No. 8.—Fencing the vacant lots on both sides of 88th st, from Central Park West to Riverside Drive.
No. 9.—Flagging and reflagging in front of vacant lots Nos. 10, 12 and 14 West 56th st.
No. 10.—Flagging, curbing and recurbing in front of Nos. 7 and 9 Abingdon square.
No. 11.—Laying a crosswalk across the Western Boulevard at the northerly side of 140th st.
No. 12.—Laying crosswalks across 10th av, from the present line of bridgestone on the easterly house-line of 10th av to the westerly line of 10th av, at the intersection of the southerly line of Kingsbridge road.

[The limits embraced by such assessments include all the several houses and lots of ground, vacant lots, pieces and parcels of land situated on—

No. 1.—Both sides of 67th st, from 8th to 9th av, and to the extent of half the block at the intersecting avs.
No. 2.—Both sides of 109th st, from Madison to 5th av, and to the extent of half the block at the intersecting avs.
No. 3.—Both sides of 16th st, from Av C to the East River, and to the extent of half the block at the intersecting avs.
No. 4.—East side of West End avenue, from a point distant abt 102 ft. 2 ins. south of 77th st to the southerly line of 77th st.
No. 5.—To the extent of half the block from the northerly and southerly intersections of Lenox av and 132d st.
No. 6.—To the extent of half the block from the northerly and southerly sides of Lenox av and 118th st.
No. 7.—Lots known as Block 911, Ward Nos. 10, 11 and 18.
No. 8.—Both sides of 88th st, from Central Park West to Riverside Drive, upon the following described lots: Block 900, Wards Nos. 6, 7, and 8, 12, 13, 14, 15, 16, 17; Block 1014, Ward Nos. 42 to 51, inclusive; Block 1015, Ward Nos. 13, and from 18 to 29, inclusive; Block 1129, Ward No. 29; Block 1244, Ward Nos. 46 to 53, inclusive; Block 1245, Ward Nos. 22 to 25, inclusive.
No. 9.—Block 540, Ward Nos. 46, 47 and 48.
No. 10.—Ward Nos. 2553 and 2554.
No. 11.—To the extent of half the block from the northerly intersection of Boulevard and 140th st.
No. 12.—Farm 9, Ward Nos. 31 to 35, inclusive, and Ward No. 124; Farm 3, Ward Nos. 61 to 64, inclusive.]

All persons whose interests are affected by the above-named assessments, and who are opposed to the same, or either of them, are requested to present their objections in writing to the Chairman of the Board of Assessors, at their office, No. 27 Chambers street, within thirty days from the date of this notice.

The above-described lists will be transmitted, as provided by law, to the Board of Revision and Correction of Assessments for confirmation on the 10th day of October, 1891.

OFFICE OF THE BOARD OF ASSESSORS,
NO. 27 CHAMBERS STREET,
NEW YORK, Sept. 15, 1891.

Notice is given to the owner or owners of all houses and lots, improved or unimproved lands affected thereby, that the following assessments have been completed and are lodged in the office of the Board of Assessors for examination by all persons interested, viz.:

No. 1.—Paving 64th st, from 10th to 11th av, with granite blocks.
No. 2.—Laying a crosswalk across Hamilton pl, at the northerly side of 138th st.
No. 3.—Laying crosswalks across 5th av, at the northerly and southerly sides 119th st.
No. 4.—Laying crosswalks across 175th st, at the easterly and westerly sides of 11th av, and across 11th av, at the northerly and southerly sides of 175th st.
No. 5.—Laying crosswalks across Av A, at the northerly and southerly sides of 71st st.

[The limits embraced by such assessments include all the several houses and lots of ground, vacant lots, pieces and parcels of land situated on—

No. 1.—Both sides of 64th st, from 10th to 11th av, and to the extent of half the block at the intersecting avs.
No. 2.—To the extent of half the block from the northerly intersection of Hamilton pl and 138th st.
No. 3.—To the extent of half the block from the northerly and southerly intersections of 119th st and 5th av.
No. 4.—To the extent of half the block from the easterly and westerly intersections of 11th av and 175th st, and to the extent of half the block from the northerly and southerly intersections of 175th st and 11th av.
No. 5.—To the extent of half the block from the northerly and southerly intersections of 71st st and Av A.]

All persons whose interests are affected by the above-named assessments, and who are opposed to the same, or either of them, are requested to present their objections in writing to the Chairman of the Board of Assessors at their office, No. 27 Chambers street, within thirty days from the date of this notice.

The above-described lists will be transmitted, as provided by law, to the Board of Revision and Correction of Assessments for confirmation on the 16th day of October, 1891.

OFFICE OF THE BOARD OF ASSESSORS,
NO. 27 CHAMBERS STREET,
NEW YORK, Sept. 21, 1891.

Notice is given to the owner or owners of all houses and lots, improved or unimproved lands affected thereby, that the following assessments have been completed and are lodged in the office of the Board of Assessors for examination by all persons interested, viz.:

No. 1.—Laying a crosswalk across Lenox av at the northerly side of 130th st.
No. 2.—Laying crosswalks across Amsterdam av at the northerly side of 155th st, and the northerly and southerly sides of 156th, 157th, 158th, 159th and 160th sts.

[The limits embraced by such assessments include all the several houses and lots of ground, vacant lots, pieces and parcels of land situated on—

No. 1.—To the extent of half the block from the northerly side of 130th st and its intersection with Lenox av.
No. 2.—To the extent of half the block from the northerly side of 155th st, northerly and southerly sides of 156th, 157th, 158th, 159th and 160th sts and Amsterdam av.]

All persons whose interests are affected by the above-named assessments, and who are opposed to the same, or either of them, are requested to present their objections in writing to the Chairman of the Board of Assessors, at their office, within thirty days from the date of this notice.

The above-described lists will be transmitted, as provided by law, to the Board of Revision and Correction of Assessment for confirmation on the 22d day of October, 1891.

FINANCE DEPARTMENT,
COMPTROLLER'S OFFICE, September 28, 1891.

In pursuance of Section 997 of the "New York City Consolidation Act of 1882," the Comptroller of the City of New York gives public notice to all persons, owners of property affected by the assessment list in the matter of acquiring title to Melrose avenue, from 3d avenue to East 163d street, in the 23d Ward of the City of New York, which was confirmed by the Supreme Court, May 1, 1891, and entered on the 22d day of September, 1891, in the Record of Titles of Assessments kept in the "Bureau for the Collection of Assessments and Arrears of Taxes and Assessments and of Water Rents," that unless the amount assessed for benefit on any person or property shall be paid within sixty days after the date of said entry of the assessment, interest will be collected thereon, as provided in section 998 of said "New York City Consolidated Act of 1882."

The above assessment is payable to the Collector of Assessments and Clerk of Arrears, at the "Bureau for the Collection of Assessments and Arrears of Taxes and Assessments and of Water Rents," Room 31, Stewart Building, between the hours of 9 A. M. and 2 P. M., and all payments made thereon on or before November 23, 1891, will be exempt from interest and after that date will be subject to a charge of interest at the rate of 7 per cent per annum from the date of entry in the Record of Titles and Assessments in said Bureau to the date of payment.

Notice is given to all persons, owners of property, affected by the assessment list in the matter of acquiring title to East 172d street, from Vanderbilt avenue, East, to 3d avenue, in the 24th Ward of the City of New York, which was confirmed by the Supreme Court, September 22, 1891, and entered on the 26th day of September, 1891, in the Record of Titles of Assessments kept in the "Bureau for the Collection of Assessments and Arrears of Taxes and Assessments, and of Water Rents," that unless the amount assessed for benefit on any person or property shall be paid within sixty days after the date of said entry of the assessment, interest will be collected thereon as provided in section 998 of said "New York City Consolidation Act of 1882."

The above assessment is payable to the Collector of Assessments and Clerk of Arrears, at the "Bureau for the Collection of Assessments and Arrears of Taxes and Assessments and of Water Rents," Room 31, Stewart Building, between the hours of 9 A. M. and 2 P. M., and all payments made thereon on or before November 28, 1891, will be exempt from interest as above provided, and after that date will be subject to a charge of interest at the rate of 7 per cent per annum from the date of entry in the Record of Titles of Assessments in said Bureau to the date of payment.

The designs submitted in competition for the new Protestant Cathedral of St. John's are on exhibition at Nos. 14 to 16 Vesey street.

ENTRANCE TO MACHINERY HALL.

TRANSPORTATION BUILDING.

The Lease of 812 Fifth Avenue.

Editor RECORD AND GUIDE:

We apologize for asking space to correct the manifold errors in statement of Messrs. V. K. Stevenson & Co. regarding above lease.

We received the particulars of this house from W. P. Seymour, and personally showed the house to Col. Thompson and his family, introducing Col. Thompson to Mrs. Sanford, making an offer for same. The offer was reported to Mr. Seymour, Sr., who sold Mrs. Sanford the house, and at his request we called on Mrs. Sanford and reported same, and the next day we had the second interview.

Mrs. Sanford, desiring Mr. Stevenson's advice, called on him, and he, using his usual well-known methods of persuasion, induced her to let him send for Col. Thompson to meet her. She the more readily did this, as in her presence he telephoned us. His action in the matter should not interfere with our receiving full commission. Col. Thompson came and the lease was effected. Now Mr. Stevenson wishes to recede from his telephonic agreement and "third" the commission.

Another error we might suggest is V. K. Stevenson & Co. did not spend over $100 advertising the house, but by those "methods of persuasion" induced Mrs. Sanford to advance said sum to their firm, and it resulted in absolutely no benefit to the owner.

We might also correct the statement of Messrs. V. K. Stevenson & Co. in your issue of September 19, 1891, as the house northwest corner of Convent avenue and 144th street, reported sold by him, is not yet sold to Gen. Fassett or to Private Anyone Else.

The 5th avenue rental transaction is a minor one to W. P. Seymour, to Riker & Son, and to us; but from the special reports in the daily press by Mr. Stevenson's firm, of the "Important lease of 5th avenue property," we thought it would give Mr. Stevenson pleasure to be mentioned in some other portion of your paper than the column where his name most frequently appears, where the accuracy of its items cannot be questioned.

Respectfully yours, BELLAMY & WINANS.

Editor RECORD AND GUIDE:

We were greatly surprised to see a letter in your issue of Saturday last containing certain statements entirely foreign to us and placing us in a very false position. While we thank Mr. V. K. Stevenson for his complimentary remarks on our ability, way of doing business, etc., we must beg to disclaim any knowledge of the transaction named. It is not our custom to publicly or otherwise criticise the rights of brokers to commissions, and most certainly not where we are disinterested. The only ground we can imagine for Mr. Stevenson's remarks is the fact of our having called Col. Thompson's attention, verbally, to the 5th avenue house about the time he looked at it through (as it now appears) other brokers. Mr. Stevenson must have obtained his information elsewhere, as neither of our firm can recollect having had the pleasure of any communication, either verbal or written, with him for a long period.

Very respectfully yours,

RIKER & SON.

The Brooklyn Exchange.

An informal opening of the Brooklyn Real Estate Exchange will take place Monday evening, October 5th, when the Secretary will throw open its doors and afford all who may feel disposed to enter an opportunity to inspect the building. It will be lighted by electricity, and the elevators will be kept running until 10 P. M.

It is evident that the Secretary intends to make the Exchange a paying institution. His purposes are now fully disclosed, and there is no doubt that he will receive the earnest support of the Committee and the Board of Directors.

Notes.

The property-owners whose land is being taken for the opening of Manhattan avenue, from 12th avenue to the North River, were in the Supreme Court during the week arguing that the awards of the commissioners for the land taken was far below its value. Presiding Justice Van Brunt, before whom the case was heard, took the papers and will shortly render a decision.

The Real Estate Exchange, in its suit to oust James S. McQuillen from the occupancy of the stand which Mr. McQuillen some time ago purchased from Mr. Levy, was this week successful in the Supreme Court. The opinion is written by Judge Barrett and concurred in by Judge Patterson.

Real Estate Department.

The market this week at private sale has been more active than for some time past. The activity, it is true, has been confined almost entirely to private houses, but that an increased business is being done, no matter if it is only in one class of holdings, is cause for congratulation. Naturally, too, the brokers are devoting their attention mainly to private houses, for in a short time the anxiety of buyers to take hold of that class of real estate will be over, and it will be a very much more difficult matter to dispose of them then than it is now. The cooler weather of the past week has induced many large investors who have been anxiously awaited to return, and they will be followed by the others who have been lagging behind. This week many of the well-known buyers made their appearance in business circles for the first time this season, and as a conesquence there is more confident talk of lots and business property. That a great many sales will be closed seems unlikely, notwithstanding all this talk. Owners of real estate in the business districts are very firm in their demands, and will make but very few and then very small concessions from their asking price. The fact of the matter is that the prices asked for business property are so high that there will be very few sales, unless a speculative feeling makes its appearance very shortly. That there will be any speculation until next spring when the profits from the present prosperous business of the country are ready for investment seems in the height unlikely. Arguing from this there will not be much activity in business property unless owners lower their prices considerably. In lots, too, the fall market does not promise very much. Good builders, in the language of the building loan operators, are very scarce just now, so that these latter are not large factors in the business of the present market. The loan operators, without whose aid there would be very little speculative building, fear trouble with the labor unions, and they are distrustful of most builders from the fact that the material men are very much more particular as to whom they will give credit. Many of the good builders, too, seem disposed to sell out their present holdings before taking on new responsibilities, so that until after January 1st next it is not to be expected that there will be either very much building or very much selling of lots. After that date, however, bright times are expected. The market will, to a large extent, be free of the dragging surplus of houses, and both builders and operators will feel more confidence in engaging in new undertakings.

THE SALES OF THE PAST WEEK.

The auction market during the past week has been very generally uneventful. The most interesting sale of the week, that of the Shrady estate, of property on Park row, Delancey, Duane, Eldridge and Chrystie streets, developed nothing of interest to the general market. With the exception of one parcel everything offered was bought by the parties in interest so that the prices are not in themselves significant. Outside of this partition sale the legal sales of the week were of only an ordinary character, unless that of No. 44 West 22d street can be made an exception. After some bidding this house was knocked down to Jos. H. Kane for $38,750. The amount due upon it for mortgages and cost was $28,960. One very satisfactory thing about the foreclosure sales, not only for this but also for the past three or four weeks, is, that so far as can be ascertained the amount of encumbrances in no case exceeded the selling price as was the case, so frequently earlier in the year. The public auction sales, so called, included little of particular interest. The property offered was very ordinary in character and the bidding lacked spirit. Two sales on the Heights, however, may be worthy of attention in view of next Tuesday's sale in the same locality. The lot on the northwest corner of 10th avenue and 185th street sold for $8,000, although the three adjoining lots on the avenue were bid in. On 185th street, between Audubon and 11th avenues, a plot 50x about 55.4 was sold for $3,450. These lots, of course, so few in number, did not attract as large a crowd as the sale on next Tuesday will, but at the same time they were nearer to Washington Bridge, the centre of activity in that section, and consequently the chances for higher prices were in their favor. The suburban sale of the week, that of lots at Mohegan Park, Tuckahoe, was not a success. The auctioneer knocked down perhaps 75 or 100 lots, but he actually sold only twelve at $230 and $290 each.

NEXT WEEK'S ANNOUNCEMENTS.

The auctioneers' bills for next week contain but few announcements of sales where interesting city property is to be offered. There are a few private houses to be offered under legal decrees that will doubtless occasion some bidding, but the voluntary offerings include little property down town and none in the residence districts that will particularly interest the outside speculator and investor. In the way of suburban sales the announcements are very much more interesting. James L. Wells will open the week with a sale of 214 lots at Tremont, part of the old Ryer Homestead that was granted to the Ryer family back in sixteen hundred and something. The same auctioneer will follow this lot sale up by an offering of cottages and vacant property in the 23d and 24th Wards, and near Yonkers, on Thursday. The lot sale, however, that is attracting the most attention, is that of 238 lots on Washington Heights, which will be offered on Tuesday by A. H. Muller & Son. Altogether next week will be interesting enough in the way of undeveloped New York City property and vacant lots in the suburbs, and the experience of those who will come into the market in the next few days will, in all probability, decide the attitude of other holders of like real estate towards the present market. Unless next week's business meets with more success than previous sales where the property offered was of about the same character, the chances are that many large suburban sales already planned will go over to next spring.

On Monday, October 5th, James L. Wells will sell 214 lots at Tremont, comprising the well-known Ryer Homestead—five minutes' walk east of the 177th Elevated road station. Tremont has two rapid transit lines—the 3d avenue Elevated and the 4th avenue depressed roads—with 407 trains arriving and departing daily; a horse-car line, soon to be operated by electricity, parks, drives, sewers, abundant water, gas, and all the conveniences of city life. The lots will be judiciously restricted; liberal terms are offered, and a perfect title will be guaranteed, free of cost, to each purchaser.

On Tuesday, October 6th, D. Phoenix Ingraham & Co. will sell eight lots on the west side of Lenox avenue, being the entire block front from 116th to 117th street; also four lots on the north side of 116th street and four lots on the south side of 117th street, being immediately in the rear of the above Lenox avenue lots. The whole plot is 201.10x200, and is desirable for improvement.

On Tuesday, October 6th, Adrian H. Muller Son will sell 238 choice lots on Kingsbridge road, 10th, 11th, Wadsworth and Audubon avenues, 188th, 189th and 190th streets. This property is just above the new Washington and Highbridge Park; the cable railroad runs within a few blocks of the property on 10th avenue, and the proposed new rapid transit line, will, if the present scheme is carried out, pass immediately through the property. Hence it has a large prospective value. Nothing is more certain than that Washington Heights will be the next district reached by the march of improvement, and the property now offered for sale is situated in the pleasantest part of that region. Seventy per cent of the purchase money remain on bond and mortgage for one or three years at 5 per cent. The title is guaranteed by the Lawyers' Title Insurance Company free of charge to each purchaser.

On Tuesday, October 6th, Richard V. Harnett & Co. will sell the Astor leasehold, bounded by 9th avenue, West 13th street and Hudson street.

On Wednesday, October 7th, Richard V. Harnett & Co. will sell the four-story tenement, No. 640 East 5th street, and the three-story brick tenement, No. 126 East 95th street.

On Monday, October 12th, James L. Wells will sell 196 desirable lots on Jerome terrace, opposite and overlooking Jerome Park. Jerome terrace is an attractive extension of the Bedford Park settlement, and is a very desirable residential section, because of its accessibility, its healthfulness and its city conveniences. Covenants prohibiting nuisances will be inserted in each deed. They are carefully worded so as to be in no way oppressive, and will promote improvements of a good character. The titles will be insured and the terms liberal.

On Wednesday, October 14th, John F. B. Smyth will sell some valuable improved and unimproved property, situated at Melrose, in the 23d Ward. These lots are located on 157th, 158th, 159th streets and Railroad avenue, East. Melrose can be reached by the 3d avenue Elevated road station, at 156th street, and by the Melrose station, 161st street and Railroad avenue. The terms are 10 per cent and the auctioneer's fee on the day of sale, 20 per cent on the passing of title, November 9, 1891, and 70 per cent on bond and mortgage, for one or three years, at 5 per cent.

S. F. Jayne & Co., of No. 254 West 23d street and No. 59 Liberty street, offer a very desirable opportunity to manufacturers. They have for lease for a term of years the premises at No. 6 Gansevoort street, near Hudson. The buildings are substantial, the front one being four-story and basement, 25x41, and the rear one three-story and basement, 25x43. It contains a 12-horse power steam engine and full machinery for wood-working. It is in first-rate order, and would be rented for the purpose of any business. Additional property running through the block can be obtained if wanted.

CONVEYANCES.

	1890. Sept. 26 to Oct. 2 inc.	1891. Sept. 25 to Oct. 1 inc.
Number	303	236
Amount involved	$5,120,340	$4,227,312
Number nominal	77	68
Number 23d and 24th Wards	48	44
Amount involved	$200,950	$298,918
Number nominal	8	15

MORTGAGES.

	1890.	1891.
Number	296	290
Amount involved	$4,260,632	$2,321,047
Number at 5% or less	145	143
Amount involved	$2,446,310	$1,611,872
Number at less than 5 per cent	44	16
Amount involved	$753,650	$299,900
Number to Banks, Trust and Ins. Cos	68	34
Amount involved	$1,553,175	$722,200

PROJECTED BUILDINGS.

	1890. Sept. 27 to Oct. 3 inc.	1891. Sept. 26 to Oct. 2 inc.
Number of buildings	55	62
Estimated cost	$524,275	$703,700

Gossip of the Week.

SOUTH OF 59TH STREET.

As the season advances the rumors of large and important sales become more numerous and persistent. Investigation generally proves that there is little or no truth in them, as was the case in two stories which found a limited circulation in real estate circles this week. One of these stories had it that William Astor had sold to William Waldorf Astor the southwest corner of 5th avenue and 34th street, together with a depth on 34th street equal to that of the hotel now being erected on the corner of 33d street and 5th avenue. It was said that the purchaser would remove the dwelling houses now occupying the ground and extend his hotel through to 34th street, thus securing a block front on 5th avenue and a large depth on each street. Mr. Bartlett, William Waldorf Astor's manager, was seen yesterday morning in relation to the story. He said that there was absolutely no truth in the rumor, that the only thing that had been done in regard to the corner in question was a private matter concerning only the family of Mr. William Astor. He said the latter had no intention of selling the property to any one, and that no hotel would be erected on the ground at all.

The other story concerned the Broadway Tabernacle property, northeast corner of Broadway and 34th street. It was said that this corner had been sold by the church people presumably for the erection of a business building. A reporter for THE RECORD AND GUIDE saw Dr. Taylor, the pastor of the church, and questioned him as to the truth of the matter. The Doctor said that although he was not one of the trustees of the church he would certainly have known if the property had been sold. He had heard nothing about the matter, he said, and furthermore he had not even heard talk of any contemplated sale.

The contract of sale of the southwest corner of Nassau and Fulton streets, 57x113, the site of the old *Commercial Advertiser* building recently destroyed by fire, has been filed this week. The seller was the estate of Moses Y. Beach, the purchaser Lewis S. Wolff and the price $375,000. Brokers, L. J. Phillips & Co.

Bellamy & Winans have sold for Alfred H. Smith to Benjamin Knower the four-story high stoop dwelling No. 48 West 40th street, 17.6x98.9, for $48,000.

Riker & Son have sold for C. T. Barney No. 110 West 58th street, a four-story brick and stone dwelling, for about $40,000.

Charles Gregor has sold for Sonn Bros. to Frederic Hackman No. 29 South street for $32,500 and this year's taxes. Sonn Bros. purchased this property at auction on May 27th for $23,250.

Mrs. H. N. Humphreys has sold to Wm. D. Barnes No. 86 East 56th street, a four-story brown stone dwelling, 16.8x55x75, for about $24,000.

Miss Abbie N. Allen has sold No. 75 West 55th street, a four-story brown stone dwelling, 16.8x50x100.5, for about $25,000.

Wm. S. Patten has sold No. 133 West 47th street, a four-story high stoop brown stone dwelling, 20x52x100.5, on private terms.

Plunkitt & McKenna have sold for Annie Norton to Mary Holliday No. 325 West 48th street, a three-story brown stone dwelling, 18x45x100, for $12,550.

Fairchild & Yoran have sold for Potter Bros. No. 324 East 33d street, being a four-story brick tenement, 25x55x98.9, for $12,000.

Ascher Weinstein has sold to John M. Baldwin No. 152 West 27th street, a three-story old building, on lot 22.6x98.9, on private terms.

NORTH OF 59TH STREET.

L. J. Phillips & Co. have sold for the Arkenburgh estate to Wm. B. Baldwin, for improvement, two lots on the north side of 76th street, 125 feet west of 10th avenue, for $24,000, and for Francis Crawford to S. Emrich No. 122 West 72d street, a four-story brown stone dwelling, 25x60 and extension x102.2, for about $80,000. Mr. Crawford has also sold to Oliver Jones, one of the former owners of the White Elephant property at 31st street and Broadway, No. 118 West 72d street, a similar dwelling, for about $78,000.

Chas. E. Schuyler has sold for Lamb & Rich to A. P. Ralli, of Ralli Bros., No. 251 West End avenue, a four-story brick and stone dwelling, 20x58x82, for $40,000, and for the same owners No. 306 West 77th street, a four-story brick and stone dwelling, 18x60x88, for $32,000. This makes three houses that Lamb & Rich have sold out of an uncompleted block of fourteen. Mr. Schuyler has also sold for Francis Crawford to John S. Hawley, for improvement, the lot on the south side of 71st street, 100 feet east of Columbus avenue, for $16,000.

Jesse C. Bennett has sold for Breen & Nason to a Mrs. Price No. 113 West 75th street, a four-story brown stone dwelling, 20x60x100, with a three-story extension, for $35,000.

Louis H. Hallen has sold for Le Roy Dewey the four-story brick building, size 21x100, No. 108 East 126th street, to Wm. Bloodgood for $11,000.

C. W. Luyster has sold the four-story brown stone dwelling, 25x60x100, on the south side of 74th street, 200 feet west of Central Park West, on private terms. The house is not yet completed.

Dore Lyon has sold to a Mr. Roosevelt, No. 1032 5th avenue, between 84th and 85th streets, a four-story brown stone French basement dwelling, 20x72x100.8, on private terms.

McMonegal & Eckerson have sold for Wm. E. Lanchantin to Wm. M. Leslie, No. 307 West 89th street, a three-story dwelling, 20x53 and extension x100, for $24,000; and for Walden P. Anderson to Charles A. Esler, No. 160 West 93d street, a three-story brown stone dwelling, 17x52x100, on private terms.

Francis J. Hillenbrand has sold to Joseph Schneider a five-story brick flat, 25x85x100, on the north side of 94th street, 100 feet west of Columbus avenue, on private terms.

Wilson H. Blackwell & Co. have sold for Dr. A. W. Lozier to I. O. Woodruff, No. 152 West 78th street, a four-story Ohio stone front dwelling, for about $33,000.

Machette & Kenyon have sold for W. P. Anderson, No. 152 West 93d street, a three-story high stoop brown stone dwelling, to Nicholas Brewer, on private terms.

W. E. Jackson has sold for Patrick Farley to John S. Silver No. 118 West 76th street, a four-story brown stone dwelling, 20x55 and extension x102.2, for about $37,000.

F. Zittel has sold for Geo. W. Ruddell to Mrs. C. A. Wessel No. 63 West 70th street, a four-story brown stone dwelling, 20x60 and extension x102.2, for about $38,000.

C. G. Martin & Bro. have sold No. 233 East 99th street, a five-story tenement, on lot 26x100, on private terms.

Gunn & Grant have sold to H. Ramsell Moore, the stock broker, No. 309 West 88th street, a four-story dwelling, 19x50x100, on private terms.

Slawson & Hobbs have sold for David Richey to a Mrs. McLeod No. 23 West 84th street, a five-story brown stone flat, 18x90x102.2, for $32,000.

David T. Kennedy has sold to Miss A. C. Stevens No. 17 West 74th street, a four-story brick and brown stone dwelling, 19.6x57 and extension x102.2, for about $45,000.

Hunt & Wendell have sold for Gunn & Grant to Frederick G. Cunningham No. 311 West 88th street, a four-story brown stone dwelling, 18x56x102.2, on private terms.

M. Kayser has sold for Hirsch & Victorius the two five-story apartment houses, Nos. 151 and 153 East 97th street, being 54 feet in front by 100 feet in depth, for $48,000; for A. Spadone to F. A. Seitz the four-story dwelling, No. 7 West 82d street, 25 feet front by 102 feet in depth, for $45,000; for Daniel Hennessy four lots, 100x100, north side of 118th street, west of 5th avenue, on private terms, to Hy. Hirsch; for Henry Hirsch the above-mentioned lots to F. A. Seitz, and for F. A. Seitz to Spadone & Warner the same property for $40,000.

Otto Pullich has sold for Lowen & Halliday and Hayes & Hessels No. 142 West 62d street, a five-story tenement, 25x90x100, to a Mr. Ritterbusch for $30,500.

Slawson & Hobbs have sold for Ferris Thompson two lots on the north side of 84th street, about 250 feet west of Central Park West, for $30,000.

LEASES.

E. H. Ludlow & Co. report that they have leased the following four-story dwellings: No. 10 East 57th street, furnished; No. 235 Madison avenue, furnished; and No. 106 East 37th street, partly furnished.

Riker & Son report the following leases: No. 112 West 58th street, a four-story 20-foot dwelling, for Chas. T. Barney to a Mr. Stanton; No. 118 West 55th street, a four-story 17-foot house, to Dr. Withaus; No. 127 East 40th street, a four-story 20-foot furnished dwelling, to a Mrs. Thurston; No. 72 West 55th street, a four-story 17-foot dwelling, to Dr. Rau; and No. 44 East 65th street, a four-story 20-foot dwelling, for J. B. Pinard to a Mr. Kane, of Larchmont.

S. M. Blakely has rented the following private dwellings; 117 West 45th street, 122 West 47th street, 66 West 47th street, 202 West 46th street, 133 West 43d street, 1545 Broadway, 206 West 46th street, 208 West 43d street, 251 West 50th street, 145 West 48th street, 152 West 48th street, 107 West 45th street, 103 West 48th street, 145 West 43d street, 163 West 47th street, 126 West 47th street and 126 West 44th street.

Chas. E. Schuyler reports the following leases: No. 259 West 71st street, a three-story 18-foot front dwelling, for three years at $1,800 per annum, for Mrs. Van Loon to John B. Middleton; No. 153 West 70th street, a four-story dwelling, for Thomas W. Bracher to a Miss Coos for one year at $1,800 per annum; No. 235 West 74th street, a three-story 20-foot dwelling, for E. J. Woolsey to E. P. Goodwin for two years at $1,600 per year; No. 263 West 70th street, a three-story 17-foot dwelling, for Michael Giblin to M. Somborn for three years at $1,100 per year; and No. 314 West 70th street, a three-story dwelling, for Jas. Scott to Wm. A. Gillette for three years at $800 per annum.

Slawson & Hobbs have made the following leases: No. 242 West 73d street, a four-story 20-foot dwelling, for Dwight H. Olmstead to Mrs. T. H. Leonard for two years at $2,400 per annum; No. 160 West 76th street, a four-story 21-foot dwelling, for Mrs. Carrie Levy to Wm. Livingston for three years at $2,000 per annum; No. 37 West 91st street, a three-story 19-foot dwelling, for Wm. Scott to Henry D. Meyers for three years at $1,700 per year; No. 142 West 94th street, a three-story 18-foot dwelling, for B. F. Romaine to Dr. H. F. Hatherway for three years at $1,700 per year.

Hunt & Wendell have leased for W. E. D. Stokes to G. B. Smith No. 244 West 76th street, a four-story 20-foot dwelling, for five years at $2,000 per annum.

Brooklyn.

Corwith Bros. have sold the two-story and basement frame dwelling, 25x20x100, No. 178 Eagle street, for Bridget O'Brien to Andrew Blochle for $2,400, and the three-story frame double tenement, 25x55x100, No. 88 Manhattan avenue, for Frank J. Kelly to Abraham Weiss for $6,475.

J. P. Sloane has sold for the Sparrow estate the four-story brick dwelling and store, 25x65x95, No. 95 Greenpoint avenue, to Simon Lipsky for $13,500.

CONVEYANCES.

	1890. Sept. 25 to Oct. 1 inc.	1891. Sept. 24 to 30 inc.
Number	367	345
Amount involved	$1,293,081	$1,762,073
Number nominal	100	81

MORTGAGES.

	1890.	1891.
Number	207	272
Amount involved	$1,898,974	$848,015
Number at 5 per cent. or less	179	133
Amount involved	$1,526,190	$490,460

PROJECTED BUILDINGS.

	1890. Sept. 26 to Oct. 2 inc.	1891. Sept. 25 to Oct. 1 inc.
Number of buildings	78	95
Estimated cost	$309,875	$803,050

Out Among the Builders.

Andrew Spence has plans on the boards for two five-story brick and stone double flats, 25x85, to be built on the south side of 135th street, 200 feet east of 7th avenue, by Richard White, at a cost of $40,000.

John S. Hawley will erect a four-story brown stone dwelling on the lot he has just purchased, on the south side of 71st street, 100 feet east of Columbus avenue.

The designs for the several large hotels now building in New York City may be seen at THE RECORD AND GUIDE *rooms, Nos. 14 to 16 Vesey street.*

WANTS AND OFFERS.

(Advertisements strictly in accordance with this title will be inserted at the practically nominal rate of 10 CENTS *per line (agate). In figuring for themselves advertisers may count seven words for each line, the address to be taken as one line. The object of this department is to bring buyers and sellers into communication with customers. Advertisements must be marked "Wants and Offers Column," and sent to the office of publication, Nos. 14 and 16 Vesey Street, not later than 3 P. M. Friday.)*

WANTS.

WANTED.—Foreman or shop superintendent, thoroughly familiar with iron construction work, engineers' detail drawings, &c. Permanent position guaranteed to right man. Address,
IRON WORKS, 29 Broadway, N. Y. City.

ADVERTISER would like to purchase the good-will of a fire insurance business. An excellent chance for a real estate man who finds it impracticable to give the insurance his proper attention.
INSURANCE, care of RECORD AND GUIDE.
Sept. 19—1aw4w.

BUILDERS.—Ten years' experience as practical builder; desires position as foreman or superintendent. Address, BUSINESS, 122 7th avenue.

WANTED, by a bright, active young man, a position in a real estate office; can furnish undoubted references and security if desired. Address,
SECURITY, RECORD AND GUIDE.

Real Estate Wanted.

OFFICE OF
FREDERICK SOUTHACK,
401 BROADWAY, N. Y.
WANTED, PROPERTY on 5TH AVENUE, between 14th and 42d sts.; pieces that have been altered or improved for business purposes preferred.
Oct. 8 uf.

OFFERS.

Dwellings and Flats.

HOUSE AND LOT.—195 West 10th st., between Bleecker and West 4th sts. Address, OWNER.

FOUR-STORY private stable and flat, near 79th st. entrance to Park; flats rent for $1,000; stable entire depth of lot.
Oct.3-10. JOHN G. BORGSTEDE, 207 East 54th st.

NEAR 53d st. "L" Station.—Five-story apartment; fifteen families; ranges, hot and cold water and two closets on each floor; windows in every room; rent, nearly $4,000; elegant order.
Oct. 3-10. JOHN G. BORGSTEDE, 207 East 54th st.

FOR SALE.—Detached frame house, 20x54, built by day labor; two stories; light high cellar; furnace, sewer, water, gas; 600 feet from Melrose station, Harlem Railroad, near 161st st. station Suburban "L" road; lot 24x110, paved street; walks, front and side, flagged; price, $7,500. Address,
Owner, SIDNEY WHITE, 963 Fleetwood av.

FIRST CLASS 4-story bay window brown stone high stoop house, 20x55x102.2, No. 116 West 71st st., with butler's pantry and bath-room extensions. Inquire on premises.

FOR SALE—At a bargain, no better investment; two houses, with all improvements; eight rooms; sold on account of owner going to Denver. Apply to GEO. E. SHERWOOD, 3473, above 167th st., 3d av. Ten per cent on investment.

OFFERS.

FOR SALE.—A newly-built double flat in Essex st., now fully tenanted and returning 7 per cent net on p[rice] asked, or 9½ per cent on investment required. Full particulars and accounts. FULLER & FROTHINGHAM, 945 Broadway, cor. 22d st.

FOR SALE.—North side of 22d st., between 6th and 7th avenues, 24x55x100, three-story and basement; price reasonable. Permits of FULLER & FROTHINGHAM, 945 Broadway, cor. 22d st.

A—At reasonable prices and easy terms, three and four-story residences, with three-story extensions; all improvements. Call and examine or inquire of the owner and builder, on the premises.
S. O. WRIGHT, 128 West 121st st., open daily.
Oct. 3 uf.

FOR SALE.—A private house on East 110th st., near Lexington av., $10,000; a private house on Lexington av., $18,000; tenement on West 27th st., rents for $3,600, $35,000; a private house on East 5th st., $17,000. HIRAM MERRITT, 53 3d av.

FOR SALE.—Five new first-class four-story and basement private dwellings, Nos. 109 113 and 119 East 45th st., and Nos. 402 and 404 Lexington av.; all leased to desirable tenants or can arrange to give possession to some of them if desired. For further particulars apply to
THE C. GRAHAM & SONS CO., 309 East 43d st.
Sept 19-1aw8w.

FOR SALE.—Six new cabinet-trimmed three-story and basement brown stone private dwellings, Nos. 142-152 West 123d st.; prices reasonable and brokers commissions allowed. For further particulars apply at office of
FRED'K. M. LITTLEFIELD, 156 Broadway.
Aug. 29-uf.

FOR SALE.—2443 8th av and 210 and 212 West 105th st.; commission allowed brokers. Apply at
Aug. 29-uf. Room 19, 156 Broadway.

FOR SALE—2443 8th av.; 26.3½x100; easy terms; commission allowed brokers; apply at
Mar. 28-u-f. ROOM 19, 156 Broadway.

FOR SALE—210 and 212 West 105th st.; five-story apartments; each, 25x89x100; decorated and carpeted; apply at ROOM 19, 156 Broadway.
Mar. 28-u-f

Improved Property.

OFFICE OF
FREDERICK SOUTHACK,
401 BROADWAY,
offers for sale some choice pieces
of property on
LEONARD ST., between Broadway and West B'way.
FRANKLIN ST., between B'way and West B'way.
WHITE ST., between B'way and West B'way.
BROADWAY, from Barclay to 14th st.
BLEECKER ST., from B'way to South 5th av.
GREENE ST., Canal to 8th st.
WASHINGTON PLACE, B'way to Wooster.
WAVERLEY PLACE, B'way to Wooster.
APPLY AS ABOVE.
FREDERICK SOUTHACK.
Oct. 8 uf.

ANOTHER SUPERIOR INVESTMENT.—9th av. business property, below 59th st.; assured enhancement. COADY'S, 922 9th av.

OFFERS.

TO LET OR TO LEASE.—Two floors of a factory, 25x98 light on all sides, 1st av and 107th st; terms moderate. J. REEBERS' SONS,
Aug. 22-uf. 409 East 107th.

FOR SALE.—A large manufacturing property down town, fronting the East River. Apply to
RULAND & WHITING, 5 Beekman st.

A BLEECKER ST. CORNER, near Broadway; also five-story (iron front) building on Grand st.; no brokers. JOHN E. PYE, 140 Nassau st.

Vacant Lots.

O. I. C. THERE ARE BARGAINS ON THE FOX estate yet. Lots for sale. Apply to GEO. E. SHERWOOD, Agent, 3473 3d av. Never sold a lot but what the buyer could make money out of it.

ATTENTION CAPITALISTS.—We have a desirable corner plot, south of 14th st., for sale; also an amply responsible firm ready to take a long lease of a building on above site, at a rental netting 7 per cent on total cost, $370,000.
WM. A. WHITE & SONS, 409 Broadway.

A DESIRABLE LOT for sale, with a frontage of 106 feet on Brooklyn Bridge.
RULAND & WHITING, 5 Beekman st.

100TH ST., between 2d and 3d avs.; ten lots cheap; all mortgage if improved.
Sept.26-1aw8w. EDWIN A. ELY, 103 Gold st.

40 CHERRY ST., between Roosevelt and Franklin sq., 32x64, vacant; $12,000; accommodating terms. EDWIN A. ELY, 103 Gold st.
Sept.26-1aw8w.

FOUR ATTRACTIVE LOTS, 140th st., adjoining southwest corner 7th av., $3,600 each; builders' terms. EDWIN A. ELY, 103 Gold st.
Sept 26-1aw8w.

FOR SALE.—On easy terms, nine first-class lots, ready for immediate improvement, on south side 116th st., commencing about 150 feet east of 7th av. THE C. GRAHAM & SONS CO., 309 East 43d st.
Sept. 19-1aw4w.

EASTERLY FRONT BOULEVARD, with 200 ft. on 86th st. and 264 ft. on 85th st.; one or more plots.
OTTO ERNST,
Aug. 22-1aw-8w. South Amboy, N. J.

Brooklyn Real Estate for Sale.

BROOKLYN.—FOR SALE, HOUSE 770 PUTNAM, two-story and extension brick, with rough brown stone trimmings; fancy front; nine rooms and bath; fifteen closets; parlors and hall frescoed; decorated throughout; built for and occupied by owner; lot, 20x100; will be sold at a bargain, as owner desires to leave the city. Inquire on premises. House not shown on Sunday.

Country Property.

TO EXCHANGE.—Ten room cottage, north Asbury Park; furnished complete; $4,500; for small house up-town, west side; will add some cash.
OWNER, 25 West 55th st.

SALES OF THE WEEK.

The following are the sales at the Real Estate Exchange and Auction Room for the week ending Oct. 2.

** Indicates that the property described has been bid in for plaintiff's account:*

R. V. HARNETT & CO.

115th st, n s, 400 w 11th av, 50x100.11, vacant. J. H. Waydell $9,000

116th st, n s, 50 e Madison av, 60x100, vacant; also all right, title and int. of Pat'k J. Quinn and Mary F. his wife to a strip of land 10 inches wide on n s of above property. Simon Arendt 44,730

*Madison av, No. 1673, n e cor 111th st, 15x70, three-story stone front dwell'g. (Amt due $1,492; prior morts. $7,000; sold May 24, 1890, for $11,500). J. G. Flammer 11,850

WM. KENNELLY.

West Broadway, No. 155, e s, 75 n Lispenard st, 25x100, three-story brk store. John Boyd. 30,200

22d st, No. 447, n e s, 410 n w 9th av, 20x98.8, four-story stone front dwell'g. Ascher Weinstein 15,700

87th st, No. 127, n s, 225 w 9th av, 16.8x100.8, three-story brk (stone front) dwell'g. Sarah D. McDonald 16,900

*98th st, s s, 150 e Amsterdam av, 206x100.11, vacant. Julius Lipman 57,000

22d st, No. 44, s s, 257 e 6th av, 23x98.9, four-story stone front dwell'g. Jos. H. Kane. (Amt. due $28,960) 38,750

25th st, No. 336, s s, 150 w 1st av, 25x98.9, five-story brk tenem't. A. F. Kruse 21,200

JAMES L. WELLS.

Ash st, n s, 150.2 w Morris av, 50x94.4, vacant. Wm. Hodgson 2,000

Ash st, s s, 125.6 w Morris av, 50x100, vacant. J. M. Erlick 2,400

Chrystie st, No. 90, e s, 25x100. Martha M. Shrady et al. party in interest 23,500

Delancey st, Nos. 51 and 53, s w cor Eldridge st, Nos. 145-151. Benj. F. Cohen 54,500

Duane st, No. 116. Wm. B. Lynch, party in interest 83,000

Park row, Nos. 142 and 144, n s, 25x96. Martha M. Shrady et al., party in interest 39,600

Morris av, s w cor Ash st, 25x125.6, vacant M. J Wiley 2,250

Morris av, w s, 25 s Ash st, 75x126.1, vacant. Same 4,800

Washington av, w s, 102 s 180th st, 46x73.10x62.2x80.5, vacant. F. Ryan 2,425

10th av, n w cor 184th st, 24.11x100, vacant. J. McClenahan 8,000

10th av, w s, adj, 75x100, vacant. (Bid in) .... —

JOHN F. B. SMYTH.

*127th st, No. 218, s s, 180 e 3d av, 40x99.11, three-story frame dwell'g and vacant. Fred'k. Aldhous. (Amt due $4,102) 11,225

185th st, n s, 100 w Audubon av, 50x55.4, vacant. Jacob Gottgen 3,450

J. C. LALOR.

12th st, No. 435 E., 24.2x103.3, four-story brk house and one-story sheds. Max C. Sewygen 11,300

OTHER AUCTIONEERS.

67th st, No. 206, s s, 150 w 10th av, 25x100.5, five-story brown stone flat. J. W. Haaren.. 18,750

*67th st, Nos. 208-220, s s, adj, 175x100.5, seven five-story brown stone flats. Equitable Life Assur. Soc 126,050

67th st, No. 222, adj, 25x100.5, similar flat. S. Denton 18,800

Total $658,480
Corresponding week 1890 .... $340,914

BROOKLYN, N. Y.

FOR WEEK ENDING OCTOBER 1.

JERE. JOHNSON, JR.

Coney Island av, w s, 40 s Av M, 1 lot. L. Camera $140

Coney Island av, adj, 2 lots. James S. Packard 265

Coney Island av, adj, 1 lot. Same 130

Coney Island av, adj, 2 lots. John G. Anderson 250

Coney Island av, adj, 1 lot. James Hoyne 128

Coney Island av, adj, 2 lots. Mrs. M. Rodman 200

Coney Island av, adj, 1 lot. M. Carroll 130

Coney Island av, n w cor Av M, 6 lots. James S. Packard 1,155

Coney Island av, adj, 2 lots. Alfred Ball 270

Coney Island av, adj, 2 lots. H. F. Brill 290

Coney Island av, adj, 2 lots. Harry Metz 290

Coney Island av, adj, 2 lots. J. Tinsley 260

Coney Island av, w s, 80 s Av L, 6 lots. James S. Packard 780

East 8th st, w s, 340 s Av M, 2 lots. C. F. Schleussner 300

East 8th st, adj, 2 lots. Kate Mooney 300

East 8th st, adj, 2 lots. Mrs. M. Rodman 290

East 8th st, adj, 1 lot. James S. Packard 145

East 8th st, e s, 140 s Av M, 2 lots. Same 804

East 8th st, adj, 4 lots. C. Barberie 560

East 8th st, adj, 2 lots. Frank Burrill 290

East 9th st, w s, 260 s Av M, 3 lots. James S. Packard 435

East 9th st, e s, 300 s Av M, 2 lots. Eliz. J. Hartley 260

East 9th st, adj, 4 lots. Henry Metz 560

East 9th st, adj, 2 lots. Kate Brennen 260

East 10th st, e s, 70.9 n Ryder av, 1 lot. C. J. Bates 135

East 10th st, adj, 2 lots. P. F. Kay 250

East 10th st, e s, 360 n Av M, 4 lots. C. J. Bates 540

East 10th st, e s, 80 s Av L 1 lot. E. H. Hall. 125

East 10th st, adj, 1 lot. T. F. Quackenbush 125

TAYLOR & FOX.

Berry st, n e cor South 6th st, two-story brk dwell'g and store. P. F. Fitzgerald 7,600

Boerum st, n w Bogert st, 1 lot. Mark Mayer. 2,900

Boerum st, adj, 1 lot. Same 1,350

Boerum st, adj, 1 lot. Mark Neutstunge 1,400

Boerum st, adj, 1 lot. Henry Roth 875

Boerum st, adj, 2 gore lots. Same 720

Boerum st, s s, 111.10 w Bogert st, 100x100. Max Levy 2,600

Bogert st, s w cor Boerum st, 1 lot. Herman Gerdes 1,825

Bogert st, adj, 3 lots. Henry Roth 3,000

Bogert st, adj, 2 lots. Same 2,050

Bogert st, adj, 1 lot. Same 1,100

Bogert st, n w cor McKibbin st, 1 lot. Same.. 1,860

Bogert st, n e cor Ingraham st, 1 lot. Ph. Warth 1,675

Bogert st, adj, 1 lot. —— Linsky 1,200

Bogert st, adj, 2 lots. Jos. Erich 2,300

Harrison pl, s s, 100 e Bogert st, 3 lots. Henry Schiachter 3,225

Harrison pl, adj, 1 lot. Michael Olikus 1,100

Harrison pl, adj, 2 lots. Fred. Stern 1,150

Harrison pl, adj, 1 lot. Peter Fritz 1,050

Ingraham st, n s, 100 e Bogert st, 2 lots. L. Erk 2,350

McKibbin st, n s, 104.4 w Bogert st, 4 lots. Henry Schlachter and John Singer 2,800

McKibbin st, adj, 2 lots. Ernst Ochner 1,250

McKibbin st, adj, 4 lots. Chas. A. Keppler 3,600

Moore st, n s, 279.5½ w White st, 50x100. Chas. Diemer 2,900

Moore st, adj, 50x100. Fred. Elflein 2,850

Moore st, adj, 75x100. Chas. Diemer 3,675

Seigel st, s s, 190.0½ e Bushwick av, 25x100. John Ketterle 1,000

Seigel st, adj, 25x100. Same 1,100

Seigel st, adj, 25x100. H. Christman 1,075

Seigel st, adj, 25x100. John Ketterle 1,075

Seigel st, adj, 25x100. Same 1,025

Seigel st, adj, 25x100. J. Hemming 1,025

Seigel st, s s, 279.5½ w White st, 25x100. L. Weil 650

Seigel st, s s, adj, 25x100. M. Kratzer 625

Seigel st, s s, adj, 25x100. Jos. Hermann 625

Seigel st, s s, adj, 75x100. Chas Diemer 1,975

Seigel st, s s, adj, 25x100. J. Hemming 750

Seigel st, s s, adj, 25x100. M. Ketterle 825

Seigel st, s s, adj, 25x100. M. Taylor 925

Seigel st, s s, adj, 100x100. Michael Mayer 3,700

Johnson av, s e cor Bogert st, 1 lot. Mark Mayer 2,100

Johnson av, adj, 3 lots. Mark Hermann 3,750

Johnson av, adj, 3 lots. Chas. Buntky 3,675

Johnson av, n e cor Bogart st, 1 lot. Henry Roth 2,150

Johnson av, adj, 2 lots. Same 1,275

Johnson av, adj, 2 lots. Sebastian Hoh 1,325

Johnson av, adj, 2 lots. Same 1,425

Johnson av, adj, 2 lots. Charles Keppler 1,500

Johnson av, adj, 1 lot. Jos. Hermann 1,125

Johnson av, adj, 1 lot. Charles Keppler 1,700

Montrose av, s s, — e Bogert st, 2 lots. Charles Keppler 1,250

South 2d st, No. 186, three-story frame dwell'g. W. J. Abbott 5,300

A. H. MULLER & SON.

Kent av, No. 829, 25x200, two three-story buildings. James Feely 5,000

OTHER AUCTIONEERS.

Amity st, No. 170, s s, 165 e Clinton st, 25x100, three-story and basement brk dwell'g. A. J. Heney 9,200

Dean st, No. 1697. John W. Gaster 2,475

Dean st, No. 1699. Geo. H. Crawford 2,365

Dean st, No. 1701. David J. Molloy 2,370

Dean st, No. 1703. G. H. Cranford 2,350

Dean st, No. 1705. David J. Molloy 2,425

*Fulton st, s s, 200 e Stone av, 50x100. David H. Bayea 7,300

Sandford st, No. 212, w s, 283 n De Kalb av, 25x100, two-story brick dwell'g with one-story frame extension. John C. Tracy 1,600

Gates av, No. 11, n s, 80 w Vanderbilt av, 20x78, three-story brk flat and store. Maximillian Lang. (Rents $684 per annum) 7,750

St. Marks av, No. 131, n s, 40 w Carlton av, 20x78.6, three-story brk dwell'g. H. V. Raymond 6,410

Total $157,687
Corresponding week, 1890 .... $195,080

CONVEYANCES.

NEW YORK CITY.

SEPTEMBER 25, 26, 28, 29, 30, OCTOBER 1.

Allen st, No. 165, w s, 150.6 s Stanton st, runs west 46 x north 0.6 x west 41.6 x south 25 x east 87.6 to Allen st, x north 24.6, five-story brk store and tenem't with three-story brk tenem't on rear. Simon Sigel and Fannie his wife to Aaron Walder. *Mt.* $21,000. Sept. 30. $25,000

Attorney st, Nos. 155 and 157, w s, 200 s Houston st, 50x100, two six-story brk tenem'ts with stores and two four and five-story brk buildings on rear. Sarah Feiner to Libet Stern. Sub. to all liens, also lis pendens. Aug. 21. nom

Bleecker st, Nos. 26-30 } begins Bleecker st,
Mott st, Nos. 318 and 320 } s e cor Mott st,
runs east 69 x south 69.9 x east 12.3 x south 19.9 x west 81.4 to Mott st, x north 90, three two-story and three-story brk dwell'gs on Bleecker st, and two three and four-story brk stores and tenem'ts on Mott st. Jonas G. Godsmith and Hannah his wife to Gabriel Goldsmith. All liens. Sept. 21. nom

Boulevard, n w cor 122d st, runs north 15.3 x west to former centre line old Bloomingdale road, x south along same to 122d st, x east 149.3, vacant. William M. and Chas. R. Stilwell exrs. Harriet L. Stilwell to Henry Boschen and Anna his wife. Sept. 15. 10,000

Broadway No. 1455, w s, 40.9 n 41st st, 20.11x58.4x20.3x56 5, four-story brk store. Edward Morrison and Zipporah his wife to Julian B., David B. and John I. Hart individ. and as exrs. of Mary H. Dessau extrx. of Benjamin J. Hart. C. a. G. ½ part. Mort. on whole property $12,000. Sept. 22. nom

Broome st, No. 520, n w cor Thompson st, 20.1 x 75 to alley, two three and four-story brk tenem't with stores. Simon P. Flannery and Mary E. his wife to Alesandro Bellando and Mary his wife. Sept. 26. *Mt.* $16,000. nom

Broome st, No. 296, n s, abt 50 w Eldridge st, 25x100, five-story brk tenem't. Louis Spero to Sarah R. Spero. *Mt.* $36,000. September 29. nom

Broome st, No. 192, n s, abt 25 e Suffolk st, 25.1x75.1x24.11x75.5, five-story brk store and tenem't with three-story brk tenem't on rear. Morris Shapiro and Rachel his wife to John Solomon. *Mt.* $18,250. Sept. 30. 29,000

Cannon st, Nos. 92-100, e s, 75 s Stanton st, 102.6x100.6; Nos 92, 94, 98 and 100, four three-story brk tenem'ts; No. 96, six-story brk factery with six-story brk factory covering rear of entire plot. Sophie wife of Charles A. Goff to Amelia Robison. *Mt.* $64,000. Oct. 1. 73,000

Charles st, No. 42, s s, 241.7 e 4th st, 24x95, three-story brk dwell'g. Ann A. S. Blauvelt et al. trustees George E. Sage and Lesa L his wife and Truman H. Baldwin and Peter Van V. Sage and Carrie T. his wife to Ann A. S. wife of Cornelius R. Blauvelt, East Orange, N. J. C. a. G. Re-recorded Aug. 13, 1880. 7,500

Central Park West (8th av), s w cor 94th st, 25 8x100, vacant. Julia L. wife of Charles J. Nourse, Jr., formerly Peabody to Edward Hirsh. Sept. 25. nom

Cherry st, No. 2 8 } begins Cherry st, n w
Pelham st, Nos. 7 and 8 } cor Pelham st, runs
north 135 x west 39.3 x south 38.6 x east 10 x south 100 to Cherry st, x east 29, six-story brk store on Cherry st and six-story brk store on Pelham st. Karl M. Wallach to Max Inkeles. *Mt.* $63,000. Sept. 25. 65,000

Downing st, No. 48, s s, abt 245 e Varick st, 20x87.3x20.9x82.2, two-story brk dwell'g. John A. Deraismes and Margaret L. his wife to Samuel W. B. Smith. Sub. to taxes for 1891. Sept. 28. 9,000

Delancey st, Nos. 233 and 235, s s, 26.6 e Willett st, 48x87.6, two and three-story frame tenem'ts with two-story frame and four-story brk tenem'ts on rear. Pincus Lowenfeld and Celia his wife and Samuel Goldstein and Dora his wife to Mark Ash. *Mt.* $16,000. Oct. 1. See Sheriff st. nom

Delancey st, No. 233, s s, 26.6 e Willett st, 23.6x87.6. Samuel Kempner to Pincus Lowenfeld and Samuel Goldstein. Taxes 1891. Oct. 1. 14,750

East Broadway, No. 141, s s, 260 9 e Pike st, 25 4x105x25.3x105, five-story brk tenem't with stores. Louis Bernstein and Annie his wife to Florentine Isaacs. *Mt.* $47,000. Sept. 28. 52,000

Goerck st, No. 31, w s, 125 n Broome st, 25x100, five-story brk tenem't. Emanuel Glauber, Sigmund Glauber and Minnie his wife and Hulda Wittner to Rebecca I. Hurwitz and Harris Levy. *Mt.* $20,000. Oct. 1. 28,000

Goerck st, w s, 124.9 n Broome st, 0.3x100, with all title to strip 0 5x25x0.6x25 in rear. Emanuel Glauber, Sigmund Glauber and Hulda Wittner to same. Q. C. All title. Oct. 1. nom

Gold st, No 38, s e cor Edens alley, 24.8x54.6 to Ryder alley, x25.3x58.8, five-story brk store. Henry W. McMann and Sarah L. his wife to Lewis S. Wolff. *Mt.* $20,000. Sept. 30. 24,000

Henry st, No. 43, n s, 315 w Market st, 25x100, five-story brk tenem't, James J. Toomie and

Mary A. his wife and Eugene Parker and Henrietta his wife to Simon Shapiro and Abram Baruatt. *Mt.* $27,000. Sept 29. 42,500

Henry st, No. 215, n s, abt 69 e Clinton st, 25 4 x85, five-story brk tenem't. Max Cohen and Esther his wife to Louis Goodman. *Mt.* $32,-500. Sept. 30. 39,000

Jane st, No. 55, n s, 59.10 e Hudson st, runs north 56 x east 20 x south 16 x south 39 to Jane st, x west 19.5, three-story brk dwell'g. Melville Sutphen and Margaret his wife to James Lennen. Taxes 1891. Oct. 1. 9,600

Jumel terrace } in deed Jumel terrace,
Sylvan terrace, No. 19 } w s, 140.6 n 160th st, 34.6x20.8 on map, Sylvan terrace, n w cor Jumel terrace, 20.8x34.6, two-story frame dwell'g. William Thompson and Margaret A. his wife to J. Oscar Goetz. Sept. 23. 4,500

Lewis st, No. 35, w s, 125 s Delancey st, 25x75, five-story brk store and tenem't. Charles Hahn to David Greenberg. Taxes, 1891. Sept. 28. 18,500

Ludlow st, No. 93, w s, 137.6 s Delancey st, 25x87 6, five-story brk tenem't with stores. Anna wife of and Florian Schmitt to Theresa Schmeidler. *Mt.* $11,000. Sept. 30. 27,100

Maiden lane, Nos. 48 and 50 } begins Maiden
Liberty st, No 88 } lane, s w s, abt 155 n w William st, runs southwest 78.11 x southeast 24 x southeast 39 to Liberty st, x southeast 24 8 x north 100.9 to Maiden lane, x northwest 47.10.
Liberty st, No 86, n e s, 24x39.8x24x38.6.
Five-story brk stores.
Herman Wronkow and Serena his wife to Randolph Euler. *Mt.* $250,000. Oct. 1. exch

Macdougal st, Nos. 24 and 26, e s, 103.2 s Prince st, 50x100, two two-story brk dwell'gs. George Schuster and Emma his wife and August Reiff and Mena his wife to The Mayor, &c., New York. Sept. 1. 40,000

Madison st, s s, 184 w Montgomery st, 1.1x100. James E. Dougherty and Mary A. his wife to William Rankin. Q. C. Sept. 28. nom

Same property. Fisher Lewine and Esther his wife to same. Q. C. Sept. 30. nom

Madison st, Nos. 278-282, s s, 115 w Montgomery st, 60x100, one and two-story frame and brk buildings. James E. Dougherty and Mary A. his wife to Fisher Lewine. *Mt.* $19,000. Sept. 28. 50,000

Same property. Fisher Lewine and Esther his wife to William Rankin. *Mt.* $40,000. Sept. 30. See 18th st. 60,000

Madison st, No. 223, n s, 26.1 w Jefferson st, 26 1x100, three-story brk tenem't. John Manning to Joseph L. Buttenwieser. *Mt.* $12,000. Oct. 1. 21,000

Maiden lane. No. 30, s s, 15.11 e Nassau st, runs south 89 8 x east 6 7 x north 1 x east 10.2 x north 84 3 to Maiden lane, x west 18, four-story brk store. Adele S. Bass and Frank A. Otis exrs., &c., Uriah J. Smith, James Andariese and Mattie W. Lee exrs. Cornelius S Lee and Margaret M. his wife, Philip H. Williams and Mary A. his wife, Wesley Harper, James Harriman, Jr., to John Wilson and Sophia his wife. Q. C. and release covenant. July 17. 300

Same property. John Wilson and Sophia his wife to Helen Langdon. April 30. 100

Market st, Nos. 26 and 28, e s, 21.3 s Henry st, 44.6x86.8x44.6x86 6, two three-story brk tenements with stores. Mary Finkelstein to Morris Simonson. *Mt.* $25,250. Sept. 29. 34,000

Same property. Morris Simonson and Rachel his wife to Jacob Finkelstein. *Mt.* $25,250. Sept. 29. 34,500

Monroe st, No. 235, n s, 168 e Scammel st, 23.8 x96x24x96, five-story brk tenem't with stores. Jenny Diamant to Benedict A. Klein. Sept. 25. 20,500

Monroe st, No. 175, n s, abt 90 w Montgomery st, 23x100, four-story brk store and tenem't. Barnett Levy and Sarah his wife, Louis Gordon and Jennie his wife and Sophia Gruenstein to Moses Blumberg and Ida Epstein. *Mt.* $12,000. Sept. 24. 20,000

Mott st, No. 193, w s, abt 270 n Broome st, 25x 100, three-story brk tenem't with four-story brk tenem't on rear. Maurice Propper to James Palumbo. *Mt.* $12,000. Oct. 1. 19,500

Mulberry st, No. 243, w s, abt 143 s Prince st, 25x100, five-story brk store and tenem't with five-story brk tenem't on rear. Leonore Rosenthal to Harris Rosenthal. *Mt.* $23,667. Oct. 1. 34,500

Oliver st, Nos. 42 and 44, e s, 58 8 s Madison st, 60.2x69x61x75, two five-story brk tenem'ts with stores. Louis Lese and Sarah his wife to Max Cohen. *Mt.* $40,000. Sept. 18. 64,750

Same property. Max Cohen, 96 Av C, and Esther his wife to Max Cohen, 240 Clinton st. *Mt.* $45,000. Sept. 30. 61,000

Pitt st, No 15, w s, 80 s Broome st, 20x100, two-story frame (brk front) tenem't with six-story brk building on rear. Max Cohen, No. 96 Av C, to Max Cohen, No. 240 Clinton st. *Mt.* $16,000 Sept. 30. 25,000

Rivington st, No 284, n w cor Willett st, 24.10 x100, five-story brk tenem't with stores. Benjamin Light and Annie his wife to John Kafka. All title. *Mt.* $45,000. Sept. 30. 5,000

Sheriff st, No 86, e s, 175.4 n Rivington st, 25x 100, five-story brk tenem't with stores. Mark Ash and Rose his wife to Pincus Lowenfeld and Samuel Goldstein. *Mt.* $18,000. Oct. 1. See Delancey st. 32,000

Sheriff st, No. 77, w s, 81 n Rivington st, runs north 19 x west 50 x south 21 x east 25 x north 2 x east 25, six-story brk building. Charles Lowen and Sarah E. his wife and Edward F. Halliday and Mary J. his wife to Louis Aaron. *Mt.* $10,000. Sept. 28. nom

Sheriff st, No. 73. Agreement as to easement for light and air. Charles Lowen and Edward F. Halliday with Louis Aaron. Sept. 28. nom

Sheriff st, No. 77. Agreement not to build up side window or take away light. Louis Aaron with Charles Lowen and Edward F. Halliday. Sept. 28. nom

South st, No. 29, n w cor Cuylers alley, 19 1x 85.2x19.2x84.7, four-story brk store. Hyman Sonn and Rosa his wife and Henry Sonn and Eva his wife to Frederick Hackmann. *Mt.* $15,000. Oct. 1. 32,500

Stanton st, No. 318, n s, 25 w Goerck st, 24.5x 75, five-story brk tenem't with stores. Moses Blumberg and Sarah his wife and Ida Epstein to Barnett Levy, Louis Gordon and Sophia Gruenstein. *Mt.* $12,750. Sept. 24. 20,500

Stanton st, No. 189, s e cor Attorney st, 16.8 x64.
Stanton st, No. 191, s s, 33.4 e Attorney st, 16 8x64.
Attorney st, Nos. 140 and 142, e s, 64 s Stanton st, 36x50.
Three and five-story brk moulding mill, &c.
Charles A. Bernhardt to Louise Bromhorst and Mary J. Bernhardt. Q. C. and confirmation of release. Sept. 26. nom

Suffolk st No. 57, w s, abt 50 s Broome st, 25x 75, five-story brk tenem't with stores. Frederick Muller, Sr., to Frederick Muller, Jr. Oct. 1. nom

Varick st, Nos. 69 and 71, s w cor Vestry st, runs south 46.6 x west 62.3 x north 22 x west 6.6 x north 24.6 to Vestry st, x68.9, four and five-story brk stores. Mary A. Palmer formerly Eagle extrx. and trustee of William Eagle to Charles H. Simmons. Aug. 10. 43,000

2d st, No 266, n s, 102.10 e Av C, 20x106, three-story frame (brk front) store and tenem't with three story brk tenem't on rear. John Losel and Theresia his wife to Louis Solomon Oct. 1. 13,500

4th st, No 234 } begins 4th st, n w cor West
10th st, No. 189 } 10th st, 29 7x88, three-story brk store and tenem't on 4th st and two-story brk dwell'g on 10th st. Harriet A. wife of Robert Armour to William S. Cooper. Taxes 1891. Sept. 1. 30,000

4th st, No. 383, n s, 296.6 w Av D, 20 3x96, three-story brk tenem't. Meyer Kleiner and Julia his wife to Charles Seligman. *Mt.* $6,500. Sept. 29. 14,000

5th st, No. 746, s s, 102 w Av D, 22x95, four-story brk tenem't. Jacob Goldberg and Henrietta his wife to Adolph Finkenberg. *Mt.* $7,500. Sept. 30. 16,250

5th st, No. 733, n s, 264 w Av D, 27x75, five-story brk tenem't with stores. Ernest E. W. Schneider and Henry Herter and Henrietta his wife to Max Landesmann. *Mt.* $25,500. Sept. 28. 30,000

6th st, No. 719, n s, 253.6 e Av C, 25.5x90 10, five-story brk tenem't with stores. David Friedman to Marks Levin. *Mt.* $27,000. Sept. 29. 31,000

7th st, No. 97, n s, 118.2 e 1st av, 24.2x97.6, five-story brk tenem't. George Hornberger and Louisa his wife to Friederich Weber. *Mt.* $29,000. Oct. 1. 43,000

7th st, No. 260, s s, 297.6 w Av D, 23 8x90.10, three-story brk tenem't. Lina Rossman individ. and as extrx. Nathan Rossman, Mary wife of Nathaniel L. Nathan, Pauline wife of Jacob Eichenbroner, Carrie Meyers. Hannah wife of Gustavus A. Wolfe, Sarah wife of Edward Kaufmann heirs Nathan Rossman to Sigmund Kraus. Sept. 22. 16,500

10th st, No. 10, n s, 151.10 w 5th av, 25x94 10, three story brk dwell'g. Henry L. Slade to Jarvis Slade. B. & S. and C. a. G.. Sub. to mort. Sept. 24. nom

10th st, No. 149, n s, 44 e Waverley pl, 22x72.11, three-story brk dwell'g. James Muir to Frederick Warnecke and Martha his wife Oct. 1. 11,700

11th st, No. 519, n s, 245 6 e Av A, 25x103.3, five-story brk tenem't with stores. Thomas J. Johnston and Marion A. his wife to Charles W. Meyer. *Mt.* $24,000. Sept. 29. nom

11th st, No. 335, n s, 245.4 w Greenwich st, 21.4x 95.9x21.5x95.9, four-story brk tenem't. Amelia Mosher widow to Joseph T. Hackett and Mary A. his wife. Sept. 30. 15,000

12th st, No. 711, n s, 158 e Av C, 23.10x103.3, five-story brk tenem't. Joseph Matzke and Caroline his wife, College Point, L. I., to Daniel Kohn. *Mt.* $11,000. Sept. 8. 14,800

13th st. No. 642, s s, 298 e Av B, 25x103.3., five-story brk tenem't with four-story brk tenement on rear. Michael Wielandt and Lizzie his wife and Johanna Pfenning to Anna C. Storrier. *Mt.* $10,000. Oct. 1. See 48th st. 21,500

13th st, No. 546, s s, 95 w Av B, 17.7x70, three-story brk store and tenem't John Eichler and Annie M. his wife to Christian Regelmann. Sub. to mort. Sept. 23. nom

Same property. Anna M. M. wife of Christian Regelmann to John Eichler. Sub. to mort. Sept. 28. nom

15th st, No. 611, n s, 163 e Av B, 25x103.3, one-story frame building with two-story brk building on rear. Charles Deeny to Thomas Cunningham. Sept. 1. 7,500

17th st, No. 446, s s, 198.11 e 10th av, 30.4x92, three-story brk dwell'g. Partition. William N. Armstrong to James C. Cady. Aug. 4. 10,500

17th st, No 405, n s, 94 e 1st av, 25x92, four-story brk tenem't with stores. Engenia Pecare to Frank F. Leman. *Mt.* $9,000. Sept. 26. nom

18th st, No. 330, s s, 260 w 1st av, 21x92, three-story brk dwell'g. Frederick Rietzel and Christina A. his wife to George Kilian. *Mt.* $5,500. Sept. 28. 10,750

18th st, No. 235, n s, 450 w 7th av, 25x92, five-story brk tenem't. John Rankin and Mary his wife to Fisher Lewine. *Mt.* $18,000. Sept. 30. See Madison st. 35,000

Same property Fisher Lewine and Esther his wife to Marks Kirshbaum and Harris Rosenthal. *Mt.* $18,000. Sept. 30. nom

18th st, No. 412, s s, 150 w 9th av, 20.7x92, three-story brk dwell'g. Emily D. wife of Seth R. Johnson to Edward Reilly. Taxes 1891. Oct. 1. 11,000

18th st, No. 342, s s, 300 e 9th av, 25x92, five-story stone front flat. Harris Rosenthal and Sarah his wife to Leondre Rosenthal. *Mt.* $22,000. Sept. 30. 40,000

21st st, No. 32, s s, 350 w 4th av, 25x92, four-story stone front dwell'g. Louise D. Charvet extrx. and trustee Louise E. Riffard to W. Jennings Demorest. Sept. 30. 38,000

21st st, No. 232, s s, 211.6 w 2d av, 26.3x92, five-story brk tenem't. Charles Ruff and Maria his wife to Robert C. Schnitzer. *Mt.* $22,-500. Sept. 29. 37,000

21st st, No. 208, s s, 118.1 w 7th av, 23.7x102.3, three-story brk dwell'g. The Farmers Loan and Trust Co guard. of Anna H. Hudson to said Anna H. Hudson, Washington, D. C. B. & S. June 25. nom

Same property. Anna H. Hudson, Washington, D. C., to Mary J. Gordon. C. a. G. June 25. 17,500

22d st, No 448, s s, 345 e 10th av, 15x72, four-story brk dwell'g. Ernestena C. Unger to Caroline A. Overton. *Mt.* $6,500. Sept. 24. nom

23d st, No. 326, s s, 253.1 w 8th av, 21.10x98 8, five-story stone front dwell'g. Thomas Stokes and Eliza his wife to Luke Fitzgerald. *Mt.* $14,460. Sept. 30. 25,000

25th st, s s, 375 e 11th av, 25x98 9, vacant. Warren M. Merrill and Henrietta his wife, F. Joseph Wehrle and Johanna his wife to William Holden, Clifton, N. J. Sept. 30. 19,500

26th st, No. 234, s s, 384.11 e 8th av, 21.3x98 8x 21.4x98.9, three-story brk dwell'g. Katie wife of and Bernard Boyle formerly Doyle to Bridget Doyle. *Mt.* $5,000. Sept. 15. nom

27th st, No. 502, s s, 60 w 10th av, 15.5x24.8, three-story brk store and tenem't. Peter O'Neil and Bridget his wife, Union Hill, N. J., to Adolph Schaefler. Sept. 8. 1,400

Same property. Bridget F. Swann to same. Q. C. Sept. 8. nom

29th st, No. 354, s s, 566.8 w 8th av, 16 8x98.9, four-story stone front dwell'g. Casper J. Westervelt and Annie C. his wife to Joseph F. Gray. *Mt.* $11,000. Oct 1. 16,000

30th st, No. 356, s s, 172.8 e 9th av, 18.4x98 9, three-story brk dwell'g. Francis P. Burke exr. Michael Donnelly to Ellen Donnelly. Sept. 29. 12,000

31st st, No. 337, n s, 230 w 1st av, 20x98.9.
31st st, No. 341, n s, 190 w 1st av, 20x98.9.
Two four-story brk tenem'ts, stores in No. 337.
Bernard Galewski and Helene his wife to Samuel Goldstein. Oct. 1. 23,500

37th st, No. 124, s s, 56.6 w Lexington av, runs south 49 x west 18.6 x north 15.4 x west 0.6 x north 34.1 to st, x east 19, four-story stone front dwell'g. James C Fargo and Fannie S. his wife to Frank B. Martin. Sept. 22. nom

37th st, No 324, s s, 450 e 9th av, 25x98.9, five-story brk tenem't. James Thompson to Eleanor P. and Thomas F. Wentworth exrs. George W. Parsons. *Mt.* $17,500. Sept. 25. 29,000

40th st, No. 220, s s, 228 6 w 7th av, 14.3x98.9, four-story brk dwell'g. John H. McGinn to Fannie Eisfeld. *Mt.* $8,000. Oct. 1. 12,500

43d st, No. 242, s s, 380 e 8th av, 20x100.4, five-story stone front flat. J. Augustus Randel and Mary A. his wife to Araminta Rockwood. *Mt.* $22,000. Sept. 12. 22,000

48th st, No. 4, s s, 125 e 5th av, 25x100.5, four-story stone front dwell'g. Harrison D. Kerr and Mary S. his wife to Arthur V. Briesen. *Mt.* $30,000. Oct. 1. 77,000

48th st, No. 402, s s, 75 e 1st av, 25x75.4, five-story brk tenem't with stores. Anna C. Storrier formerly Miller to Michael Wielandt and Johanna Pfenning. *Mt.* $12,000. Oct. 1. See 13th st. exch

49th st, No. 157, n s, 140 w 3d av, 20x100.5, four-story stone front dwell'g. Charles Broglie, West Brighton, S. I., to Michael McGovern. *Mt.* $6,000. Sept. 30. 23,500

50th st, No 311, n s, 120 8 e 2d av, 16.4x100.5. four-story stone front dwell'g. Matilda Henry to Leo Friedman. *Mt.* $5,450. Oct. 1. 11,000

53d st, Nos. 528-536, s s, 275 e 11th av, 125x 100.5, five five-story brk tenem'ts, stores in No. 536. James O'Donelan and Margaret his wife to Alice Davis. B. & S. Aug. 24. nom

54th st, No. 209, n s, 115 e 3d av, 20x75.4, four-story brk dwell'g. Adam E. Schatz and Anna J. his wife, Sophia Hoelzle, Katie Ellinghausen, Anna Schatz, Margaretha Kranich and George Schatz to John Kress Brewing Co. *Mt.* $5,000. Sept. 30. 17,000

54th st, No 41, s s, 460 w 5th av, 25x100.5, four-story brk dwell'g. James H. Young and Sophie D. his wife to Sarah B. wife of Fritz Hoeninghaus. *Mt.* $32,500. Sept. 10. 55,000

54th st, No. 8 E., s s, 161 e 5th av, 20x100.5, four-story stone front dwell'g. George W. Montgomery and Hester A. his wife to Childs H. Childs. *Mt.* $30,000. Oct. 1. 58,500

54th st, No. 540, s s, 325 e 11th av, 25x159.7x25.3 x156, four-story brk store and tenem't. John Foersch and Theodora his wife to The Central Park North and East River R. R. Co. *Mt.* $6,350. Sept. 22. 14,750

55th st, No. 137, n s, 60 e Lexington av, 20x 100.5, four-story stone front dwell'g. William H. Van Allen and Emma A. his wife to Angela R. Holahan. Oct. 1. 22,000

58th st, No. 353, n s, 75 w 1st av, 25x100.2, three-story brk building. George Schmechenbecher and Pauline his wife and John G. Schmechenbecher and Sarah E. his wife to Martin Schmechenbecher. *Mt.* $14,000. Aug. 27. 21,000

61st st, No. 347, n s, 182.4 w 1st av, 23x100.5, five-story brk flat. Foreclos. Edward T. Wood to Henrietta Cohn. Sept. 25. 10,000

66th st, s s, 96.1 w Grand Boulevard, 25x100.4. Certificate of payment under party wall agreement. Margaret Shannon to William L. Flanagan. Sept. 25. 660

66th st, n s, 90 w Amsterdam av, 10x100.5, vacant. John M. Ruck and Clara A. his wife to Peter Doyle. All liens. Sept. 1. 500

67th st, No. 202, s s, 100 w 10th av, 25x100.5, five-story stone front tenem't. Clara A. wife of John M. Ruck to Emma Ulmer. *Mt.* $15,-000. Oct. 1. 22,000

67th st, No. 220, s s, 325 w Amsterdam av, 25x 100.5, five-story brk tenem't. Foreclos. Gilbert M. Squier, Jr., to The Equitable Life Assur. Soc., United States. *Mt.* $7,000. Sept. 30. 17,500

67th st, No. 212, s s, 225 w Amsterdam av, 25 x100.5, five-story brk tenem't. Foreclos. Same to same. *Mt.* $7,500. Sept. 30. 18,250

67th st, No. 210, s s, 200 w Amsterdam av, 25x100.5, five-story stone front tenem't. Foreclos. Same to same. *Mt.* $7,500. Sept. 30. 18,000

67th st, No. 216, s s, 275 w Amsterdam av, 25x 100.5, five-story stone front tenem't. Foreclos. Same to same. *Mt.* $7,500. Sept. 30. 18,000

67th st, No. 218, s s, 300 w Amsterdam av, 25x 100.5, five-story stone front tenem't. Foreclos. Same to same. *Mt.* $7,500. Sept. 30. 18,000

67th st, No. 208, s s, 175 w Amsterdam av, 25x 100.5, five-story stone front tenem't. Foreclos. Same to same. *Mt.* $7,500. Sept. 30. 18,050

67th st, No. 214, s s, 250 w Amsterdam av, 25x 100.5, five-story brk tenem't. Foreclos. Same to same. *Mt.* $7,500. Sept. 30. 18,250

69th st, No. 327, n s, 375 e 2d av, 25x100.5, four-story stone front tenem't. Josephine D. wife of Edmund W. McClave to Moses Esberg. *Mt.* $14,500. Sept. 25. 18,500

69th st, No. 335, n s, 150 w 1st av, 25.1x100.5, four-story stone front tenem't. Max Frankenheim to Mary Bier. *Mt.* $17,000. October 1. 19,500

69th st, No. 337, n s, 125 w 1st av, 25x100.5, four-story stone front tenem't. Same to Sarah Wertheimer. *Mt.* $12,000. Oct. 1. 19,500

73d st, Nos. 433 and 435, n s, 100 w Av A, 50x 102.2, two five-story brk tenem'ts. Karl M. Wallach to Caroline Cahn. *Mt.* $32,000. Oct. 1. 42,000

73d st, No. 418, s s, 300 w Av A, 25x102.2, five-story brk tenem't with stores. Vaclav Nemecek to John Nemecek. All liens. Sept. 28. nom

74th st, No. 315, n s, 200 e 2d av, 25x102.2, five-story brk tenem't with stores. Charles Weisberger and Mary his wife and Max C. Baum and Minnie his wife to Jacob Cohen. *Mt.* $15,000. Sept. 28. 19,000

76th st, No. 46, s s, 182 w 4th av, 18.9x102.2, four-story stone front dwell'g. R. S. Jordan, Jersey City, to Henry C. Jordan. *Mt.* $25,-000. Dec. 2, 1890. nom

76th st, n s, 100 w 8th av, 25x102.2, vacant. Contract. William T. Evans to Robert Schell treasurer of New York Historical Soc. Feb. 28. 17,000

76th st, No. 133, n s, 325 w 9th av, 19x102.2, four-story stone front dwell'g. Annie M. Good to Brent Good trustee. B. & S. Sept. 30. nom

77th st, No. 233, n s, 305 e 3d av, 12.6x102.2, three-story brk dwell'g. Edward Oppenheimer and Mathilde his wife and Edward Hirsh and Flora his wife to Albert C. Henderson. All liens Sept. 24. nom

80th st, Nos. 164-168, s s, 250 e Amsterdam av, 60x102.2, three four-story stone front dwellings. George J. Cohen and Hattie V. his wife to Frederick F. Woodward. *Mt.* $89,000 Oct. 1. nom

80th st, No. 341, n s, 80 w 1st av, 20x66.3, four-story stone front tenem't. Virginia B. Gibbs, Newport, R. I., to Julia Elsbach. Sept. 26. 9,700

80th st, No. 323, n s, 200 w 1st av, 25x102.2, four-story stone front dwell'g. Bertha Pasternak to Matilda Levy. *Mt.* $12,000. Sept. 25. 15,500

80th st, No. 145, n s, 387.9 w Columbus av, 21x 102.2, four-story brk dwell'g. Michael Giblin and Catherine his wife and James W. Taylor and Mary E. his wife to Robert G. Irving. *Mt.* $22,000. Sept. 29. nom

82d st, No. 238, s s, 200 w 1st av, 25x102.2, four-story stone front tenem't. Frederick Graf and Maria his wife to Samuel Levy and Lina his wife. *Mt.* $9,000. Sept. 30. 18,275

83d st, No. 525, n s, 373 e Av A, 25x102.2, five-story brk tenem't. Anton Scheuermann and Louisa his wife to Mathias Goeren and Sophia his wife. *Mt.* $14,000. Sept. 29. 21,800

83d st, No. 18, s s, 219.6 w Central Park West, 18x102.2, four-story stone front dwell'g. John Livingston and Eliza his wife to John S. Sutphen, Jr. *Mt.* $16,000. Oct. 1. 30,000

84th st, No. 410, s s, 100 e 1st av, 19.11x102.2, four-story stone front tenem't. William Stern and Caroline his wife to Elise Forster. *Mt.* $7,500. Oct. 1. nom

85th st, No. 224, s s, 304.9 e 3d av, 24.9x102.2 two-story frame dwell'g. Joseph McNamara and Evelina his wife to John W. French. *Mt.* $5,000. Oct. 1. 12,000

86th st, No. 138, s s, 385 w Columbus av, 21.8x 106.10, four-story brk dwell'g. D. Willis James and Ellen S. his wife to Silvanus F. Jenkins. Sept. 17. 40,000

86th st, No. 332, s s, 305 w 1st av, 20x102.2, four-story stone front tenem't. Max Danziger and Virginia his wife to Max Leve and Jacob Lauchheimer. Q. C. Sept. 29. nom

Same property. Max Leve and Jacob Lauchheimer to John Dippold and Lena his wife. *Mt.* $9,000. Sept. 29. 16,050

87th st, No. 151, n s, 383.4 w 3d av, 16.6x100.8, two-story brk dwell'g. Katharine wife of Joseph Bollarth to Henrietta wife of Samuel Blum. *Mt.* $4,000. Sept. 28. 7,500

89th st, Nos. 312-320, s s, 180 w West End av, 102x100.8, five four-story brk dwell'gs. Elmore D. Alvord, Fairfield, Conn., to Francis M. Wilmurt. B. & S. All liens. July 29. nom

90th st, No. 114, s s, 163.6 w Lexington av, 27.6 x100.8, four-story stone front flat. Louis Spero to Sarah R. Spero. Sept. 29. nom

93d st, n s, 335 w West End av, 50x100.8, vacant. William H. Myer and Harriet F. his wife to Peter Herche. *Mt.* $10,000. Sept. 29. nom

93d st, No. 161 on map No. 163, n s, 356 w 3d av, 14x61, three-story brk dwell'g. Jennie N. Zucker in her own right and Alfred J. R. E. Zucker her husband to Arnold and Edmund Kohn. *Mt.* $4,000. Sept. 28. 10,500

94th st, No. 44, s s, 396.6 w Central Park West, 17x100.8, three-story brk dwell'g. Increase M. Grenell and Jeannette T. his wife to Emma Ambler. *Mt.* $14,000. Oct. 1. 21,000

94th st, No. 53, n s, 465 w Central Park West, 20x100.8, three-story stone front dwell'g. Same to John A. Mapes. *Mt.* $17,000. Oct. 1. 27,000

Same property. Release mort. Edward Oppenheimer and Isaac Metzger to Increase M. Grenell. Sept. 30. 1,500

94th st, No. 63, n s, 200 e Columbus av, 18x100.8, three-story stone front dwell'g. Frank Lugar and Charlotte his wife to Albert Gerstendörfer. *Mt.* $18,000. Oct. 1. nom

96th st, n s, 200 e 10th av, 75x100.11. Release mort. Sarah H. Powell to Alexander Cameron. Sept 21. nom

Same property Release mort. Edmund S. Bailey to same. Sept. 22. nom

102d st, No. 234, s s, 99.8 w 2d av, runs south 65 x west 0.4 x south 35.11 x west 25 x north 100.11 to 102d st, x east 25.4, four-story brk tenem't with stores. Elizabeth F. Albert to Henry Heuser. *Mt.* $10,000. Sept. 28. 17,000

102d st, No. 215, n s, 230 e 3d av, 25x100.11, five-story brk tenem't. Aaron Kaplan and Rachel his wife to Morris and Abraham Lipman. *Mt.* $16,000. Sept. 29. 22,100

103d st, No. 107-113, n s, 150 w 9th av, 75x100.11 x74.6x— on curved line, four five-story stone front flats. Jonas G. Goldsmith to Matilda Salomon All liens. Sept. 21. nom

104th st, No. 250, s s, 118 e West End av, 19x 100.11, three-story stone front dwell'g. Ellen M. Harlow to Sophia M. S. Stallman. *Mt.* $14,500. Sept. 22. 21,000

104th st, No. 236, s s, 212.6 w 2d av, 18.9x100.11, three-story stone front dwell'g. Babette Geib widow to Henry Aronson. *Mt.* $4,000. Re-recorded. July 2, 1891. 10,500

107th st, s s, 100 w Madison av, 100x100.11. }
106th st, n s, 100 w Madison av, 100x100.11. }
Release mort. Mutual Life Ins. Co. to James McCreery. Sept. 29. 30,000

108th st, No. 104, s s, 25.6 e 4th av, 25.6x50, four-story brk tenem't. Francis Mitchell and Ann his wife to Malchan Schoenthal. *Mt.* $6,000. Sept. 25. 12,500

108th st, n s, 100 w Boulevard, runs north 100.11 x west 90 x south 35 x west 75 x south 65 to 108th st, x east 165.
108th st, s s, 100 w Boulevard, 165x100.11. The Atlas Improvement Co., owner.
Riverside Drive, s e cor 108th st., 50x110. Emily Bayne, owner.
Riverside Drive, n e cor 108th st, 50x100. William H. Riker, owner, who with above owners create a restriction as to character of buildings to be erected on their property.
Sept. 24. nom

110th st, No. 234, s s, 385 e 3d av, 25x110, four-story brk tenem't. Annie J. McDowell, Green Village, N. J., to Kate F. Boyle. *Mt.* $6,000. Sept 22. 12,000

113th st, No. 68, s s, 230 w 4th av, 25x100.11, five-story brk flat. Frederick Kirchhoff to Mary E. Kirchhoff. All title. Sub. to mort. Sept. 25. 3,000

114th st, No. 221, n s, 310 e 3d av, 25x100.11, five-story stone front flat. Lazarus Mannheimer and Bonnete his wife to Peter Hermann. *Mt.* $17,000. Oct. 1. 22,000

115th st, s s, 150 e 3d av, 50x100.11. Release mort. William H. Jackson to Frederick Schuck. Sept. 29. 32,000

115th st, s s, 200 e 3d av, 50x100.11. Release mort. Same to same. Sept. 29. 30,000

115th st, Nos. 212 and 214, s s, 200 e 3d av, 50x 100.11, two five-story stone front flats. Frederick Schuck and Mary his wife to Maria Wehdebrock. Oct. 1. 50,500

115th st, Nos. 208 and 210, s s, 150 e 3d av, 50x 100.11, two five-story stone front flats. Same to Gustav and Catharina Wittenborg. Oct. 1. 50,750

115th st, n s, 175 w Lenox av, 50x100.11, vacant. Benjamin F. Raynor, Jr., and Ida his wife to Laura J. Stephens, Yonkers. Sept. 24. 17,000

116th st, Nos. 67 and 69, n e cor Madison av, 50 x100, two seven-story brk flats, store in No. 67. Edward Smith and Mary his wife to John R. Maguire. *Mt.* $60,000. Sept. 16 nom

118th st, s s, 219 w 5th av, 22x100.11, vacant. Henry Franke and Eunice R his wife, Brooklyn, to Matilda M. Strouse. *Mt.* $2,400. Sept. 5. 7,000

Same property. Matilda M. Strouse to Frances L. Manners. *Mt.* $24,000. Sept. 10. nom

119th st, No. 449, n s, 113 w Pleasant av, 20x 100.11, three-story frame dwell'g. George W. Thurber and ano. exrs. Mary Davis to Jacob F. Fisher. Sept. 29. 7,200

120th st, No. 233, n s, 255 e 3d av, 20x100.11, four-story brk tenem't. Bertha Unger to Mary Ward. Oct. 1. 10,250

121st st, No. 408, s s, 150 e 1st av, 25x100.11, five-story brk flat. Michael L. Goetz and Elizabeth his wife to Harriet Robeck. *Mt.* $12,000. Sept. 26. 19,000

122d st, No. 141, n s, 441.8 w Lenox av, 16.8x 100.11, four-story brk dwell'g. John H. Day to Ernestine Day. ⅙ part. All liens. Aug. 27. nom

Same property. Clifford W. Day to same. ⅙ part. B. & S. All liens. Aug. 21. nom

Same property. Ernestine Day, Baltimore, Md., to Charles Mayne. Sub. to mort. Aug. 21. 17,500

122d st, No. 173, n s, 180 w 3d av, runs north 87.4 x west 20 to point 200 w 3d av, x south 88 to 122d st, x east —, three-story frame dwelling. John F. McGowan and Mary F. his wife, Mary Rudd, Elizabeth Corey and Catharine McGowan to Frederica Brettell. Taxes 1891. Sept. 16. 8,000

123d st, No. 146, s e cor Lexington av, 35x100.11, five-story brk flat with stores. Frank McCormick to Alexander A. Jordan. Sub. to mort. Sept. 30. nom

Same property. Alexander A. Jordan and Gertrude his wife to Frank McCormick. Sub. to mort. Sept. 12. nom

124th st, No. 259, n s, 125 e 8th av, 25x100.11, four-story stone front flat. William A. Martin and Margaret T. his wife to Lillie H. Rogers. *Mt.* $40,000. Sept. 30. 27,000

124th st, No. 261, n s, 100 e 8th av, 25x100.11, four-story stone front flat. Same to John M. Hogencamp. *Mt.* $40,000. Sept. 30. 27,000

126th st, No. 108, s s, 168.6 e 4th av, 21.6x99.11, four-story brk store with two-story frame building on rear. Le Roy S. Dewey and Isabella M. his wife to William Bloodgood. *Mt.* $10,000. Sept. 29. 11,000

132d st, No. 233, n s, 291 w 7th av, 15x99.11, three-story stone front dwell'g. Mary S. Davis to William E. Parsons, Jr., trustee Florence A. and Mary A. Parsons. *Mt.* $8,-500. Sept. 25. 12,375

132d st, s s, 250 w 4th av, 150x99.11, vacant. Grace T. Wells, Franklin township, N. J., to Frederick Rohrs. Taxes, &c. Sept. 24. 46,000

133d st, No. 200, s s, 150 e 8th av, 16.8x99.11, three-story stone front dwell'g. Marietta P. Cooke to George J. Cohen. Oct 1. See 7th av. nom

134th st, No. 59, n s, 347.6 e Lenox av, 18.9x 99.11, three-story brk dwell'g. Frederick Wm. Jockel and Helena B. his wife to Ophelia Weeks. *Mt.* $8,500. Sept. 25. 14,000

134th st, No. 232, s s, 375 e 8th av, 25x99.11, five-story brk flat. Foreclos. Henry W. Johnson to Louis C. Elterich. Sept. 25. 24,500

156th st, n s, 175 e 10th av, 25x99.11, five-story brk tenem't. Charles H. Holland and Juliet his wife to Isabella Koch. *Mt.* $16,000. Sept. 30. 21,000

Av A, No. 1370, n e cor 73d st, 27x98, five-story brk store and tenem't. Release judgment. Charles H. Bunn to Margaret M. Lett. Sept. 28. nom

Same property. Margaret M. wife of William F. Lett, Brooklyn, to Isaac Sneider. *Mt.* $33,000. Sept. 25. nom

Av A, No. 1370, n e cor 73d st, 27x98. Isaac Sneider and Ida his wife to Adam Moran. *Mt.* $32,000. Sept. 30. nom

Av A, No. 1394 } begins Av A, n e cor 74th
74th st, Nos. 501-505 } st, 22.2x98, one two and three-story brk stores and tenem'ts. Samuel Kempner to Robert Moser. *Mt.* $8,000. Oct. 1. 13,275

Av A, No. 1640, e s, 60 n 86th st, 20x75, four-story stone front tenem't. Frederick Abendschein and Margaretha his wife to Caroline Gutteutag. *Mt.* $7,000. Sept. 30. 14,500

Av A, No 1642, e s, 80 n 86th st, 20x75, four-story stone front tenem't. Same to Theresa Repp. *Mt.* $7,000. Sept. 30. nom

Amsterdam av, No. 585, e s, 53.10 n 88th st. 28.4 x100, five-story brk flat with stores. The New York Life Ins. Co. to Edmund Dodge. Sept. 25. 25,000

Amsterdam (10th) av, s w cor 189th st, runs west along s s 189th st 800 to 11th av, x north 60 to n s 189th st, x east 800 to Amsterdam av, x south 60.
11th av, s w cor 189th st, runs west 300 along s s 189th st to e s Wadsworth av, x north 60 to n s 189th st, x east 300 to 11th av, x south 60.
Emily A. Smith widow to The Mayor, &c., New York, for street purposes. Sept. 30. nom

Columbus av, No. 324, w s, 51.2 n 75th st, 25.6x100, five-story brk flat with stores. Jacob M. Newman to Gustav and Benjamin Gomprecht. Taxes, 1891. Oct. 1. other consid. and 1,000

Columbus av, No. 326, w s, 76.8 n 75th st, 25.6x100, five-story brk flat with stores. Benjamin Gomprecht to Gustav Gomprecht. ½ part. Mt. $22,500. Aug. 20. nom

Lexington av, No. 1462, w s, 109.8 n 94th st, 18x80, three-story stone front dwell'g. William E. Japhe to Christopher Byrnes. Mt. $7,500. Oct. 1. 14,000

Lexington av, No. 1730, w s, 51 n 108th st, 25x75, five-story stone front store and flat. Jacob Weiss and Lizzie his wife to Frederick Winter. Mt. $14,000. Sept. 24. 24,000

Madison av, No. 315 } 42d st, Nos. 26½ and 28 } begins Madison av, s e cor 42d st, runs east 118.6 x south 74.1 x west 18.6 x south 4.2 x west 5 x north 52.6 x west 95 to av, x north 25.9, five-story brk (stone front) dwell'g on av and two three-story brk stores and dwellings on st. William S. Allen and Ellen wife of George D. Allen, Moses A. Allen and Mary A. his wife, John H. Allen and Elenora W. his wife, Elam S. Allen and Helen S. his wife, Harriet E. wife of Elliott Johnson, Frances A. Allen and E. Jennie Allen heirs Benjamin W. Allen to William M. Fliess. B. & S. C. a. G. June 1, 1887. nom

Madison av, No. 1657, e s, 75.4 n 110th st, 25.6x75, five-story stone front flat with stores. Elizabeth M. wife of John C. Borges to Nathan Stern and Leopold Altmayer. Mt. $17,500. Sept. 30. 25,000

Madison av, No. 1673, n e cor 111th st, 15x70, three-story brk stone front dwell'g. Foreclos. William Irwin to J. George Flammer. Mt. $7,000 and judgment $3,140. Oct. 1. 1,500

Park av, No. 1050, w s, 75.8 s 87th st, 25x80.11, five-story brk flat with stores. Abraham Steers and Susan C. his wife to Joseph McNamara and Evelina his wife, joint tenants. Mt $20,000. Sept. 30. 29,000

Same property. Release mort. Henry F. Wells to same. Sept. 30. nom

Park av, No. 1213, e s, 80.8 s 95th st, 20x100, three-story brk dwell'g. Frederick Braender and Emily his wife to Julia F. Henes. Mt. $16,000. Oct. 1. 23,000

Riverside av or Drive, n e cor 108th st, 50x100, three-story brk dwell'g. Minnie M. Pullman widow to William H. Riker. Mt. $50,000. July 17. 107,000

West End av, n w cor 83d st, 96x100, new buildings in course of erection. Samuel Colcord and Alice B. his wife to Gerald L. Schuyler. Mt. $44,000. May 19. 54,000

West End av, No. 441, n w cor 86th st, 22.8x98, four-story brk dwell'g. William E. D. Stokes to Belle M. wife of Albert F. Sawyer. C. a. G. Sept. 15. 75,000

1st av, No. 940, e s, 50.2 s 52d st, 25.1x74, four-story brk tenem't with stores. Susanna Strauss to Feist Samuels. Mt. $8,000. Oct. 1. 16,500

1st av, No. 1491, w s, 25 s 78th st, 25x100, five-story brk store and tenem't. Isaac Bitterman and Ida W. his wife to Leopold Yankauer. Mt. $20,000, taxes 1891, and assessm't for East River Park. Sept. 25. 31,500

2d av, No. 1319, w s, 75.5 n 69th st, 25.1x80, five-story stone front tenem't with stores. Margaret wife of Stephen Pendergast to Peter J. Schneider and Emilia L. his wife. Mt. $14,100. Oct. 1. 22,000

2d av, No 1109, w s, 60 n 58th st, 20x63, four-story stone front store and tenem't. Michael Wachtel and Lotta his wife to Henry Aronson. Mt. $4,500. Oct. 1. 16,000

2d av, No. 1326, s e cor 70th st, 25.5x70, five-story brk (stone front) store and tenem't. William Beneke and Emma his wife to Christopher Rooney. Mt. $18,000. Sept. 30. 41,500

2d av, No. 740, e s, 49.4 s 40th st, 24.8x100, five-story brk tenem't with stores and three-story brk tenem't on rear. Louisa Fischer to Samuel Strauss. Mt. $10,000. Sept. 30. 31,500

3d av, No. 2024, w s, 50.6 n 111th st, 25x70, four-story stone front flat with stores. Toni wife of Joseph B. Koplik to Philip Bernhardt. Mt. $10,000. Sept. 30. 28,500

3d av, No. 2197, e s, 95 s 120th st, runs south 31 x east 125 x north 26 x west 25 x north 25 x west 10 x south 20 x west 90, four-story brk store. Partition. Ladislas Karge to Richard Webber. Mt. $32,500 and int. from Jan. 1, 1891. Aug. 19. 60,400

3d av, e s, 100 s 120th st, 26x125. John J. Wilson and Sarah E. his wife to same. Q. C. Aug. 28. nom

5th av, n w cor 114th st, 50.5x100, vacant. Moses and Philip Schloss to Max Barnett. Sept. 4. other consid. and 100

5th av, No. 2087, e s, 104.11 n 128th st, 20x100, four-story stone front dwell'g. Henry H. Brown and Mary A. his wife to John H. Rogan. B. & S. Sept. 26. nom

Same property. John H. Rogan to Mary A. wife of Henry H. Brown. B. & S. Sept. 26. nom

5th av, No. 1414, w s, 51 s 116th st, 29.11x100, five-story stone front flat. John J. Sheehan and Mary R. his wife to Michael Stern. Mt. $28,000. Sept. 30. 34,000

5th av, No. 607, e s, 28 s 49th st, 25x100, four-story stone front dwell'g. Robert H. Neilson and ano. exrs. and trustees Mary A. McClelland to Alexander B. Simonds. Taxes, 1891. 100,000

Same property. Charles A. Van Deursen, New Brunswick, N. J., to same. Q. C. Aug. 14. nom

Same property. Alexander B. Simonds to Eliza W. White, Litchfield, Conn. C. a. G. Mt. $50,000. Sept. 25. 100,000

5th av, n e cor 98th st, 50.11x100, vacant. Alfred Roe and Elizabeth M. his wife to Michael H. Gillespie. Mt. $30,000. Sept. 29. 35,000

5th av, No. 1032, e s, 44.2 n 84th st, 20x125, with use of right of way, &c., five-story stone front dwell'g with two-story brk stable on rear. Dore Lyon and Anna E. his wife to Samuel M. Roosevelt. Mt. $35,000. Oct. 1. nom

7th av, Nos. 1985 and 1987, e s, 27 n 119th st, 53.11x98, two five-story brk flats with stores. Frederick F. Woodward and Ellen his wife to George J. Cohen. Mt. $52,000. Sept. 30. nom

7th av, No. 1987, e s, 54 n 119th st, 26.11x98. George J. Cohen and Hattie V. his wife to Marietta P. Cooke. Mt. $26,000. Oct. 1. See 133d st. 42,000

8th av, No. 2196, e s, 75.11 n 118th st, 25x80, five-story brk flat with stores. Philip Braender and Lizzie his wife to Jacob Weiss. Mt. $16,000. Sept. 28. 25,500

10th av, No. 559, w s, 24.9 n 41st st, 18.6x100, four-story brk store and tenem't. Sophia Oppenheimer to Michael T. Joyce. Mt. $6,000. Oct. 1. 14,000

Mill Rock or Gibson's or Leland's Island, abt 1 acre, with land under water, containing 8 639-1,000 acres. Cecil C. Higgins, Bartow, N. Y., and Susan R. his wife to William R. Peters. Re-recorded. June 9, 1890. 6,615

MISCELLANEOUS.

All real estate now owned by Joseph H. Hawes or which he may hereafter acquire and wheresoever the same may be. Release dower. Lucretia A. wife of Joseph H. Hawes to said Joseph H. Hawes. Oct. 16, 1889. nom

23d and 24th WARDS.

Bristow st, w s, 150 n Jennings st, runs north 22.6 x west 59.3 x west again 28 x south 24.2 x east 87.3, h & l. Mary Miller to Elizabeth M. wife of George Walter. Sept. 28. 2,100

Evelyn pl, s s, 175 w Jerome av, 50x100, hs & ls. Joseph F. Stier to Thomas J. Robinson B. & S. and C. a. G. July 30. nom

Frederick st, w s, lots 415 and 416 map S. Cambreling et al., Fordham, 50x87.6. Timothy Donovan and Mary P. his wife to Harry P. Clary, Jersey City. Sept. 28. nom

Fairmount pl, s s, 99.9 w Marmion av, 24x83.10 x24x85.6. Philip Geisendorfer and Katherina his wife to John Darmody. Sept. 29. 862

Field st, w s, 100 s Beech st, runs south 175 x west 100 x north 175 x east 100.
Field st, e s, 150 s Beech st, runs south 375 to Rock st, x east 200 to Forest st, x north 425 x west 100 x south 50 x west 100.
Rock st, s e cor Forest st, runs south 315 x east 100 x north 250 x east 100 to Hill st, x north — to Rock st, x southwest 275.
Rock st, s e cor Hill st, runs south 350 x northeast — to Rock st, x west 575.
Beech st, n s, 540 e Riverdale av, runs northeast 238.6 x southwest 121 x southeast 44 x southeast 289 x southeast 144 x again southeast 75 x south — to Rock st, x west 475 to Hill st, x north 412 to Beach st, x west 210.
Thomas C. Cornell and Jane E. his wife to James F. and Patrick H. Sheridan and James S. Hegrave. Aug. 21. 28,000

Forest st, w s, 150 n Rock st, 100x100. James Stewart, Yonkers, and Mary E. his wife to Jane E. wife of Thomas C. Cornell. B. & S. Aug. 26, 1886. nom

Jennings st, s s, 95.2 e Union av, 19.11x107.2x18.5x114.8. William H. Wright and Arena A. his wife, William J. Pragnell and Agnes M. his wife to Edmund Schnabel. Aug. 28. 4,200

Rockfield st, n s, 500 e Marion av, runs north 126.11 x west 100 x south 27.9 x east 75 x south 100 to Rockfield st, x east 25. William S. and Charles W. Opdyke to John E. Murgatroyd. Sept. 5. 650

Rock st, s e cor Hill st, 550x600 to Hill st, x 250. James C Bell, Jr., and Eliza D. his wife to Thomas C. Cornell. Q. C. Aug. 28. nom

Rock st, s s, 140 e from range of Hill st, runs east 250 x south 100 x — to point 100 s of Rock st, x west 225 x north 100. Thomas Coyle, Yonkers, and Rose his wife to Thomas C. Cornell, Yonkers. C. a. G. Nov. 27, 1878. nom

Suburban st, n s, 83.11 w Briggs av, 50x100. James M. Peebles and Agnes his wife and William J. McPherson to Henry McArdle and Catherine his wife. Sept. 29. 2,100

Tiffany st and Burnett pl, lots 218 and 224-230 inclusive map of Springhurst, made by C. B. Taylor. Ellen M. Maverick to Edward J. Churchill. All morts. April 8. nom

Waverley pl, n e s, part of lot 110 map Fairmount, &c., 50x200, h & ls. Joseph Ferri and Annie his wife to Edward Sheridan. Sept. 25. 4,000

134th st, s s, 250 w Alexander av, 150x100. The New York Lumber and Wood Working Co. to Wallace C. Andrews. Mt. $20,000. Sept. 25. nom

138th st, s s, 310 e Southern Boulevard, runs east 30 to e s of Willow av, x south 460 to 136th st, x west 30 to Centre Willow av, x 460; also,
All of mortgaged premises bet 137th and 138th sts, lying east of a line 200 e from e s of Willow av; also,
All of mortgaged premises bet 136th and 137th sts, lying east of line 175 e of e s Willow av; also,
All of mortgaged premises lying within the lines of 137th st, being a strip 60 feet wide.
Release mort. Michael H. Hagerty et al. trustees for Mary, Margaret and Catherine McConvill to William R. Brown, White Plains, N. Y. Sept. 8. nom

151st st, n s, 375 w Courtlandt av, 25x116.6x25x116.5 Herman Herold to Anna M. wife of said Herman Herold. All liens. Sept. 22. nom

162d st, s s, 363.6 w Elton av, 100x189.8 to 161st st, x100x187.11. Franklin W. and Edward S. Gilley, Brooklyn, to Lawrence V. Conover. Q. C. and release tax sale. Sept. 24. 6

164th st, n s, 46.3 e Grant av, 23x95. Eliza F. Balmford to Alice K. Bowen. Sept. 23. 5,300

Belmont av, s e s, lot 4 map East Tremont, 60.5 x176x60x168.5. John H. Morrison, Jr., and Mary W. his wife to Edward J. O'Gorman. Sept. 25. nom

Belmont av, s e s, 115.3 n e John st, 35.1x159.5x35x155.6. James D. Mahoney to Edward J. O'Gorman. Sept. 24. nom

Boston av, n e cor 169th st, runs east 100 x north 0.8 x west 100, being parcel 19 on damage map for widening 169th st from Franklin av to 167th st. Release mort. The Metropolitan Savings Bank to Henrietta Barnum. April 24. nom

Brook av, n w cor 134th st, 100x45.1. Robert H. Mathews and Fannie C. his wife to Edward P. Steers. Mt. $3,850. Sept. 16. nom

Cauldwell av, n w cor Clifton st, 19x100. Modification of covenant. John W. Decker with Philip Luther. Sept. 29. nom

Clinton av proposed, w s, 95 n Tremont av, 140 x100. Mary Seiferd to John J. Brady. Sept. 23. nom

Creston av proposed, w s, centre line Donnybrook st, 30x140, error. The Twenty-fourth Ward Real Estate Association of New York to John C. Wood. Sept. 15. nom

Crotona av, n s, 110.10 e Franklin av, 50x101. Smith Williamson and Sarah A. his wife to Max Einhorn. Mt. $1,050, tax 1891. Oct. 1. 2,400

Crotona av, n s, 160.10 e Franklin av, 50x101.2x 50x101. Same to Achilles Rose. Mt. $960. Oct. 1. 2,400

Hull av, w s, 250 s Scott av, 50x110. Ida Keck to Joseph H. Lee. Mt. $480. Oct. 1. 1,400

Keppler av, e s, 50 s Willard st, 50x100. Adelbert J. Howe and Mary L. his wife to Henry Franz. Sept. 25. nom

Lexington av, e s, 100 s Spring st, 25x— to Prospect av, x25x134. Charles Leonard to Lida Matthews. Sept. 23. nom

Locust or Tremont av, n w cor Prospect av, runs north 951 x west 1,012.8 x south 875.10 x east 105.8 to Franklin av, x south 100 x east 52 x south 100 to Tremont av, x east 600 to beginning, except parts conveyed by said Lucy A. Mason to Mary Seiferd. Isabell M. Blood and John Leddy and Lena and Rose Seiferd, Lucy A. Mason widow to John J. Brady. Aug. 12. nom

Monroe av, n w cor Columbia st, 75x100. Release mort. The American Savings Bank to Margaret Stonebridge. Sept. 22. 1,600

Same property. Margaret wife of Charles Stonebridge to The Board of Domestic Missions of the Reformed Church of America. Sept. 23. 4,000

Ryer av, e s, 125 s 2d st, 25x100. Edward D. McCabe and Isabella H. his wife to Joseph R. Zubrod. Mt. $3,734. Sept. 25. 4,000

Sedgwick av, n w s, 269.6 n e Perot st, 49x120x 43.11x131. George T. Lorigan and Eva P. his wife to Arthur Berry. Q. C. Sept. 21. nom

Strong av, s e cor Forest av, 300x189.4, excepting portion taken for Tinton av. John W. Decker to Annie Ormiston. Mt. $17,000. May 27. nom

Trinity av, e s, 100 n 161st st, 50x100. Helena Pittoll formerly Helena Jaacksch widow and devisee Henry Jaacksch, L. I. City, to Gustavus Emil and Edward Robitzek, of G. Robitzek & Bros. Mt. $2,300. Sept. 30. 3,600

Tinton av, s e s, 175 s w 151st st, 25x105. John Heerot and Louise his wife to Conrad Weicker. Sept. 29. 2,000

Washington av, w s, 96.6 n 166th st, 77.8x150; also all title of grantor in his father's estate. William C. Hammond to Mary A. Hammond. B. & S. Oct. 1. val. consid

Bronx River road, n w cor Willard av, 53.3x 114.5x50x96.1. William H. Barney and Ruth his wife, Scranton, Pa., to Mary E. Monaghan. Sept. 26. nom

Lot AD map 70 lots Cedar Hill plot Powell farm. Mary Burns to Catherine Burns. B. & S. July 15, 1890. nom

Lots 282, 283, 326 and 327 map Woodlawn Heights, 24th Ward. Mt. $550.
Plot 3 map of land of Thomas M. Partridge and Robert Craighead, 24th Ward. Mt. $1,400.
Plot 11 map W. O. Giles property, 24th Ward. Mt. $2,500.
Elizabeth wife of Lorenz Reich to Goldchen Adler. Sept. 29. nom

Parcel 15 on damage map for opening 159th st from Railroad av East to 3d av. Release mort. Jacob Neuscheler to Mayor, &c., New York. June 8. nom

Long Island Sound, lots 1 and 2 map of Hunts Point, West Farms, runs southwest along shore 1,330.6 to line of P. N. Spofford farm if extended, x southwest 68.7 x north 21.9 and 28.4 and 103 and 264 and 58.9 x north 421.7 x northeast crossing Bronx av 1,057.6 to beginning, 12 345-1,000 acres; also land under water 23 25-100 acres. Addie Metzgar to East Harbor of New York Land Co. Sept. 25. nom

Long Island Sound, first parcel above 12 845-1,000 acres. William H. Caswell and Harriet A. his wife to Addie Metzgar. *Mt.* $50,000, for above and other premises. July 30. 80,000

Parcel 22 25-100 acres land under water, same as second parcel in deed above. William H. Caswell and Harriet A. his wife to Addie Metzgar. B. & S. and C. a. G. *Mt.* $50,000, for above and other premises. July 30. 80,000

LEASEHOLD CONVEYANCES.

Broadway or Union pl, w s, 26 n 15th st, 26x116 10. Assign. lease. William Sneckner with consent of Mary S. Van Beuren to Bank of the Metropolis. Sept. 24. nom

Broad st, No. 91, s w cor Stone st. Assign. lease. Charles Schwarm to William Aufenanger. nom

Warren st, No. 767. Assign. lease. Louis W. Dusing to James Everard. 5,000

5th st, n s, 150 e 1st av, 25x97. Assign. lease. Martin A. Furchtenicht to Elizabeth Peters. 14,000

9th st. n s, 174.4 w Broadway, 26x92.3. Assign. lease. Archibald J. C. Anderson to Edward L. Kellogg. 7,400

48th st. No. 34, s s, 452.6 w 5th av, 20.6x100.5. Assign. lease. Harriet E. W. wife of George A. Strong to Katharine D. wife of Charles W. Cass. 25,000

55th st, s s, 212.6 w 9th av, 20.10x81.3x21x83.11. Assign. lease. Katie Dooley to Mary Dooley. 10,000

Same property. Assign. lease. Virgilio Del Genovese to Katie Dooley. nom

55th st, s s, 237.9 w 8th av, 17.3x100.5. Assign. lease Lewis Ash to John G. Jenny. 5,800

1st av, No. 1075. Assign. lease. George and John G. Schmechenbecher to Pauline and Sarah E. Schmechenbecher. 3,000

1st av, No. 2003, w s, 20 n 103d st, 20x75. John Simon to George T. Diefentbaler. 20 7-12 years, from Oct. 1, 1891, per year, taxes and 300

2d av. No. 794. Assign. lease. Henry Hillert and Margaretha his wife to John Schmitt. 1,500

3d av, No. 701. Assign. lease. Patrick J. O'Keefe to John J. Hickey. nom

3d av, s e cor 44th st. 27x80. Assign. lease. John J. Hickey to Peter Doelger. nom

Same property. Assign. lease. Patrick J. O'Keefe to John J. Hickey. nom

3d av, No. 1843, s e cor 102d st. Assign. lease. Thomas F. Gillin to Daniel Fitzpatrick. 1,000

8th av, No. 830. Assign. lease. Frank Stadelberger to M. Groh's Sons. Sept. 16 nom

Same property. Patrick Giles to Frank Stadelberger. Sept. 16. nom

11th av, s w cor 22d st, 24.8x75. Assign. lease. Anton Schultz exr. Henry W. Hencke and Anna C. Blase legatee to Thomas Farrell. 2,500

KINGS COUNTY.

SEPTEMBER 24, 25, 26, 28, 29, 30.

Adams st, s s, 842.1 w Coney Island plank road, 34x103.7x34x103.5, Flatbush. Benjamin Meakin to Rebecca Roberts. *Mt.* $1,700. $3,500

Aberdeen st, n w s, 100 s w Bushwick av, 20.2x100. George W. Adams, of Hempstead, N. Y., to Rebecca E. Cring. Sub. to morts. nom

Adelphi st, w s, 761.10 s Park av, 25.4x100. Ida M. Myers individ. and as extrx. of Henry V. Myers, Leon G. and Jacob C. Reakirt and Walter B. Knighton and H. C. Huckel to William K. Shryock, of Philadelphia, Pa. 4,000

Adelphi st, e s, 161.1 s De Kalb av, 20x126.8. Release judgment. Trumon A. Brown to Eliza L. Phillips. nom

Ainslie st, s s, 161 w Lorimer st, 23.5x100, h & l. Mary wife of Jacob Roch to James Hayden. 9,500

Anthony st, w s, 40.8 n Emmons av, runs northwest 141 x west 133 to Dooley st, x south 138 x southwest 37.2 x east 127 to beginning, Gravesend. Martha McKane widow to James McKene. 6,000

Ashford st, e s, 200 n Arlington av, 20x100. Anna M. Beach to Edward O. Bragdon. 880

Bainbridge st, n e cor Saratoga av, 23x100. Kate S. wife of Samuel R. Good to Victor J. Dowling, New York. *Mt.* $8,000. 15,000

Barbey st, w s, 225 s Blake av, 50x100. Albert H. W. Van Sielen to Henry C. Heyser. Sub. to taxes, &c. 900

Baltic st, n e s, 98 s e Henry st, 25x99.10. John Earl to Jeremiah Costello. 7,000

Bergen st, s s, 100 w Hopkinson av, 25x127.9. Release mort. Catherine Molloy to Rose Rosenfeld. 400

Bergen st, s s, 100 w Hopkinson av, 50x127.9. Release mort. John D. and Catherine Ditmis and Georgiania J. Bussen, of Jamaica, N. Y., to Charles M. Thompson. 400

Bergen st, s s, 200 w Troy av, 25x127.9. William H. Cornell to Isaac Halstead. *Mt.* $5,000. 6,250

Bergen st, s s, 75 w Hoyt st, 16.8x100. Laura N. Richards, of Stratford, Conn., to George J. Mulholland. 4,625

Bleecker st, n s, 362.6 n e Evergreen av, 27.6x100. Lewis J. Worth to Adam Henrich. 1,800

Boerum pl, w s, 73.2 s Livingston st, runs northwest 86.4 x south 24.3 x west — x southeast 85 x northeast 27.4. Thomas F. Stevenson to Morris Berkowitz. *Mt.* $15,000 and taxes. 28,000

Bogart st, e s, 81 s Rock st. runs east 100 x south 19 x west 25.11 x south 3 x west 74.1 x north 22. Henry Hebenstreit to Louis Rubenstein, of New York. 2,750

Boerum st, n s, 59.9 e Bushwick av, 25x42.8x8.10x15.1x52.5. Henry Roth to Anna Oster. *Mt.* $1,200. 2,200

Bond st, w s, 100 s Warren st, 25x75, h & l. Samuel Harris to Thomas Meehan. Sub. to mort. 1,225

Broadway, s w s, 27 s e Reid av, runs southwest 50.9 x south 10.3 x west 20 to Reid av, x south 40 x east 49.10 x northeast 3.6 x northwest 31.11 x northeast 60 to Broadway, x northwest 25. William T. and P. C. Smith exrs. Thomas T. Smith to Adeline E. F. wife of Hubert F. Praeger. 10,500

Broadway, northerly corner Vanderveer st, 75x100. Edwin O. Phelps to Henry H. Cochran. *Mt.* $19,000. 28,500

Broadway, north cor Vanderveer st, 75x100. Foreclos John Courtney to Edwin O. Phelps. *Mt.* $19,000 and interest from March 1, 1890. 1,000

Butler st, n s, 273.4 w Nostrand av, 16.8x127.9. Elizabeth Rohrschreider to George P. Klockert. *Mt.* $2,100. 4,500

Butler st, n s, 150 w Clason av, 25x131x13 and 12.8x126 9, h & l. Herman W. Meyer to Orson W. Sheldon, Fort Ann, N. Y. *Mt.* $2,500. nom

Butler st, s w s, 300 s e Smith st, 25x100. William B. Hurd to Edward Dougherty *Mt.* $2,000. exch

Carroll st, n s, 140 w Columbia st, 20x100. Jacob Bernstein to Hyman Schimkowitz. *Mt.* $2,500. 1,000

Carroll st, n s, 372 e 7th av, 20 6x100. James B. Henry to Emma E. Taylor. *Mt.* $7,500. 17,500

Cedar st, s s, 255 w Evergreen av, 20x91.11x20x—. Foreclos. John Courtney to Adeline E. F. Praeger. 2,700

Chauncey st, s s, 325 e Stuyvesant av, 125x100. Foreclos. John Courtney, Sheriff, to Sarah J. Morgans. *Mt.* $7,000. 250

Clarkson st, s s, 1,300 e Main st, 25x200, hs & ls, Flatbush. Sarah E. Bennett to John F. Battermann. *Mt.* $2,500. 4,250

Clinton st, e s, 50 n President st, 20x95. James H. Snow to Teresa De Gregori. *Mt.* $5,000. 9,500

Cook st, n s, 100 w Morrell st. 25x100. Thomas H. and Michael O'Neill to Mary A. wife of Henry Tracy. 2-7 part. 500

Cornelia st, n w s, 100 n e Broadway, 60x100. John Tennant to Edward E. Kelly. 6,000

Crown st, n s, 336 w New York av, 10x100. Release mort. Hans S. Christian to Mary McG. and Jeremiah Reagan. nom

Crown st, n s, 336 w New York av, 10x100. Release mort. Sarah F. Mead to same. exch and nom

Crown st, n s, 336 w New York av, 10x100. Mary McG. and Jeremiah Reagan to Loretta J. Mead. 250

Crown st, n s, 364 w New York av, 11x100. Right of way agreement. Loretta J. Mead to Sarah F. Mead. nom

Crown st, n s, 364 w New York av. 11x100. Loretta J. Mead to Mary McG. Reagan. 250

Crown st, n s, 318 w New York av, 28x100. Loretta J. Mead to Annie E. wife of Michael Fox. 1,750

Crown st, n s, 300 w New York av, 18x100. Loretta J. and George W. Mead to Peter Fox. 1,750

Dean st, s s, 213.4 w 5th av, 20x100. Charles J. Maguire to Julia E. Carroll. nom

Dean st, s s, 180 w Nostrand av, 20x107.2. Release mort. Lyman D. Calkins to Asa C. Brownell. 1,000

Dupont st, s s, 250 w Oakland st, 25x100. Catherine and Josephine Galvinny, Michael Mangan guard. to William Mangan. 1,200

Dumont st, n s, 25 w Thatford av, 25x100. Lewis Hurst to Joseph Morris. 900

Dumont st, n s, 75 w Thatford av, 25x100. Lewis Hurst to same. 900

Eagle st, n s, 300 e Oakland st, 25x100. William W. Campbell to John Griffin. 1,000

Eastern Parkway, s s, 25.1 w Thatford av, 25x100. Charles Ratner and Israel Zagalovitz to William Schlossberg, of New York. *Mt.* $3,500. 6,000

Eastern Parkway, s s, 25 w Amboy st, 100x90.5. Bernhard J. Pink to Annie wife of William Schwarz. 2,260

Eckford st, e s, 125 s Meserole av, 25x100, h & l. Alfred T. Frost to Joseph Doherty. 2,800

Eldert st, n w s, 240 n e Evergreen av, 19x100. Leopold J. Lippmann to Marie Pfaefflin. nom

Same property. Release mort. Anna E. Cozine and ano. exrs. J. G. Cozine and J. Gascoine individ. to Leopold J. Lippmann. 2,570

Eldert st, n w s, 146 s w Bushwick av, 18x100. Margaret A. Tostevin to Nathan Rittermann and Hirsch Wilkenfeld. *Mt.* $5,400. exch

Ellery st, s s, 225 w Marcy av, 150x100; also factory, boilers, &c. James S. Willet assignee Hooper & Gore to Rachel A. Cooper and Calvin Gore. nom

Franklin st, e s, 47.4 n Greenpoint av, 23.4x80. Mary E. Kramer widow to Adolph Mahler. *Mt.* $6,750. 7,400

Franklin st, w s, 50 n Noble st, runs north 50 x west 95 x south 100 to Noble st, x east 25 x north 50 x east 70 to beginning. Foreclos. John Courtney, Sheriff, to John C. Orr. All right, title, &c. 100

Frost st, s s, 125 w Leonard st, 25x100. Dennis Carroll to Peter Pierri. *Mt.* $650. 2,000

Frost st, s s, 225 w Kingsland av, 25x100. John Gillespie, New York, to John Pfleging, Jr. 1,025

Garden st, n e s, 345.1 s e Flushing av, 20x50x52.2 to Bushwick av, x20x58.8x56.4. Alois Fensch to Christian W. C. Dreher. 2,000

Granite st, n w s, 100 n e Broadway, 360x100. Contract for property. Thomas and John Morgan to Nathan Levy. 23,400

Grant st, n s, 54.3 w land of Protestant Reformed Dutch Church, 25x122.5x25x132.2, Flatbush. George Kerswill to James Lyons. 1,000

Greene st, s s, 150 w Oakland st, 25x100. Mary wife of Robert McNeill to Patrick Kiernan. 2,700

Grove st, n s, 110 w St. Nicholas av, 40x100. Frederick Erhardt to Emil Kieser. 1,500

Gwinnett st, n w s, 85 n e Marcy av, 20x100. Foreclos. John Courtney, Sheriff, to Frank Schwarze. 650

Halsey st, s e s, 100 n e Central av, 180x100. William Duryea to George A. Craig. 10,800

Hancock st, n s, 190 e Throop av, 300x100. David C. Lyall to John F. Saddington. 34,500

Hancock st, s s, 150 w Patchen av, 50x100. Foreclos. John Courtney to Denis Hayes. *Mt.* $4,000. 2,300

Hancock st, n s, 389 w Marcy av. 20x100, h & l. Marion A. wife of Thomas J. Johnston to Charles W. Meyer. *Mt.* $7,000. nom

Hancock st, s s, 450 e Reid av. 25x100. Mary wife of Henry Schmalstich to Alfred L. Beasley. *Mt.* $5,800. 9,250

Harman st, s e s, 200 n e Central av, 25x100. Christian and Andrew Hahn to Anna C. Cibulsky. *Mt.* $3,500. 7,500

Harman st, n w s, 200 s w Central av, 20x100. Emil Kieser to Frederick Erhardt. *Mt.* $1,800. 4,000

Harman st, n w s, 100 n e Evergreen av, 20x100. Frederick Erhardt to Julius Metzger and Elizabeth Studt. *Mt.* $3,000. exch

Harrison st, n s, 174 6 e Henry st, 24.9x99.10. Thomas Norton to Christine wife of Thomas Norton. ½ part. nom

Hart st, n s, 362.11 w Evergreen av, 18.11x95. Cordelia M. Seaman formerly Wright extrx. Henry F. Wright to Bushwick Democratic Club. 3,100

Same property. Release mort. Cordelia M. Seaman formerly Wright widow to same. nom

Hart st, s e s, 142 6 n e Central av, 20x75. William Lindemann to Louise Boegel. 4,900

Hart st, s e s, 225 n e Knickerbocker av, 100x100. Charles A. Cross to Julia Hobby. *Mt.* $2,400. nom

Henry st, s e s, 40 n e Harrison st, 20x83, h & l. William S., John, Alexander, Robert and Margaret Stewart heirs of James Stewart to Ellen Moran. 6,200

Heyward st, s e s, 86 n e Harrison av, runs northeast 30 x southeast 100 x southwest 10 x northwest 11 x southwest 20 x northwest 89. Margaretha Wolf to Charles Lippmann, of Hartford, Conn. *Mt.* $8,500. 12,350

Hicks st, e s, 25.3 n Poplar st. 25.3x100. Contract for property. John Cottrell to William H. Mattocks, of Jersey City, N. J. 6,250

Himrod st, s s, 110 w St. Nicholas av, 50x100. Edward MacDonald to Richard Meyerrose. 1,600

Hopkins st, n s, 175 w Throop av, 25x100, h & l. Nicolaus Kerzner to August Gomer and Jacob Wollpert. *Mt.* $2,000. 3,050

Hopkins st, s s, 105 e Marcy av, 20x100. Joseph Werner to August Nile. 2,500

Hopkins st, s s, 425 e Marcy av, 25x100. David Klein, of New York, to Juda Rozenblub, of New York. 6,087

Humboldt st, e s, 41.8 n Ainslie st, 16.8x60, h & l. Catharine Nohar widow, Jane wife of Patrick Jordan, Bernard and Patrick Daily and Rose wife of Peter Daily heirs Michael Daily to Maria E. L. wife of John F. Werner. 2,700

Humboldt st, e s, 50 n Powers st, 25x100, h & l. Peter Garms, Jr., to Leopold Brown, New York. 11,250

Humboldt st late Smith st, e s, 50 s Debevoise st, 25x75. Henry Huhn to Henry Weinrauch and Jacob Schaefer. *Mt.* $1,500. 3,300

India st, s s, 150 e Manhattan av, 25x100, h & l. John Carroll, Centreville, N. J., Patrick and Timothy Carroll heirs Timothy Carroll to James McGuckin. 2,350

India st, s s. 150 e West st, 25x100. William Shields, of New York, to Susie Crossou. nom

Jerome st, w s, 20 s Dumont av, 40x100. Charles Smith to Ellen Regan, of New York. 650

Jerome st, s w cor Dumont av, 20x100. William W. Clayton, of New York, to Ellen Regan, of New York. 450

Jerome st, e s, 80 s Dumont av, 20x100, h & l. James H. and Susie Brundage to Lorentz R. Seaholm. *Mt.* $1,800. 2,590

Jerome st, e s, 60 n Dumont av, 20x100. James Smith to William McElroy. 830

Jerome st, e s, lots 150, 151 and 154-157 map Michael G. Duryea property, 26th Ward. Lucinda H. Jones to Francis H. Koenig. 2,100

John st, n e cor Jay st, 195x— to East River, x — to e s of Jay st if extended, x south along the e s Jay st — to beginning, with land under water, &c. Charles and John Arbuckle to Arbuckle Bros. Coffee Co. B. & S. 1884. 200,000

Same property. Arbuckle Brothers Coffee Co. to Arbuckle Bros., composed of John Arbuckle, William V. R. Smith, James N. Jarvis and William A. Jamison. 200,000

Kosciusko st, s s, 300 w Reid av, runs west 25 x south 200 to Lafayette av. x east 100 x north 100 x west 75 x north 100. Elizabeth E. Hutchins widow, New York, to George Fletcher. 10,000

Lombardy st, n s, 175 w Morgan av, 25x150. Jeremiah V. Meserole to Henry Bindrim. 500

Lawrence st, s e cor Tillary st, 20x56.6. Eliza J. Sniffen, Westport, Conn., to William T. Sniffen. ½ part. *Mt.* ½ of $1,200. 800

Linwood st e s, 100 s Liberty av, 25x100, h & l. Patrick O'Hanlon to Michael Bulger. 2,200

Linwood st, w s, 122.6 s Eastern Parkway, 22.6 x90. John M. Stearns to Mary J. wife of John Monsees. 700

Logan st, w s, 150 s Vienna av, 50x100. Charles A. Canavello, of Englewood, N. J., to Henry Josephowitz, of New York. 300

Logan st, w s, 130 n Glenmore av, 40x100. Effingham H. Nichols to Joseph Dart. 600

Lynch st, s s, 158.1 e Lee av, 25.9x100. Sarah A. and Martha R. World to Conrad F. Kromm. *Mt.* $3,000. 6,800

Macon st, n s, 164 e Ralph av, 18x100. F. Augustus Conkling to Frederick W. Rowe. *Mt.* $5,000. 6,900

Macon st, n s, 200 4 e Ralph av, 18x100. Frances Holland to Otto F. Struse. 6,500

Macon st, n s, 340 e Throop av, 20x100. Frederick M. Trimm to Mary E. wife of Frederick M. Trimm. *Mt.* $3,000. 8,000

Macon st, s s, 429 e Reid av, 18x100, h & l. James G. Roberts to John C. Berges, New York. *Mt.* $5,500. 8,900

Macon st, s s, 308 e Patchen av, 18x100. Walter F. Clayton to Eugene A. Egan. *Mt.* $4,500. 7,800

Madison st, s e s, 367.8 s w Knickerbocker av, 18x100. Sophie wife of Louis Gelb to George A. Craig. *Mt.* $4,000. nom

Madison st, No. 1244, s e s, 367.8 s w Knickerbocker av, 18x100. George A. Craig to David Roy. *Mt.* $3,280. 4,300

McDougal st, n s, 133 11 w Howard av, runs north 100.2 x west 47.2 x south 100 to st, x east 41.1 to beginning. Franz Ganen to Martha Blank, New York. *Mt.* $2,400. 3,200

McDonough st, s s, 55.2 w Ralph av, 35.2x80. Joshua L. Barton, New York, to Maria W. Barton. *Mt.* $7,000. 13,200

McDonough st, s s, 350 e Reid av, 114.4x100. Release mort. Joseph C. Hoagland to John Peirce, of New York 7,700

McDonough st, s s, 102 e Lewis av, 19x100, h & l. John F. Ryan to Emanuel Katz. *Mt.* $6,200. 12,500

Milford st, w s, 225 n Liberty av, 25x100. James W. King to Mary Fitzgerald. 3,000

Monroe st, n s, 133.4 e Patchen av, 16.8x100. Alice wife of and Virgil Comfort to Absalom W. Dieter. *Mt.* $4,000. exch

Monroe st, No. 186, s s, 325 w Nostrand av, 20x63.6x20x61.6.
Monroe st, No. 184, s s, 345 w Nostrand av, 20x65.6x20x63.6.
Arthur A. Van Kleeck to Jean G. Van Kleeck. 1886. nom

Monroe st, n s, 165 w Reid av, 20x100. Rolla S. Marsh to Emma J. Bradshaw. nom

Same property. Emma J. Bradshaw to Caroline A. Marsh. nom

Monteith st, n s, 100 e Bremen st, 25x90, h & l. Henry Roth to David Schneider and Catharina his wife, joint tenants. *Mt.* $2,000. 4,100

Moore st, s s, 50 e Leonard st, runs south 57.7 x northeast 45.4 x southeast — x north 74.2 to st, x west 50. Henry Roth to Ray Riesenberger. *Mt.* $4,000. 8,500

Noll st, s s, 125 e Central av, 25x100. Franklin E. O'Reilly as recvr. of Gustav Schoepfer to Gustav Schoepfer. Q. C. and release judgment. nom

Same property. Gustav Schoepfer to Joseph Wendel. *Mt.* $600. 2,200

Osborn st, w s, 150 n Glenmore av, 25x100. Contract for property. Louis Lebewohl and Abraham Ruth to Maggie Fischer and Katy Dugan. 5,800

Osborn st, w s, 75 s Livonia av, 25x100. Release mort. Albert W. S. Proctor guard. of William J., Evaline F., Hebert and Arthur Magrath to Hirsh Wilkenfeld and Nathan Ritterman. 100

Pacific st, n s, 68 e Rockaway av, 16x80, h & l. Francois J. G. Ladd to Frank E. Francisco. *Mt.* $2,000, taxes, &c. nom

Palmetto st, northerly cor Central av, 25x75. Gustav Feigenspan, of Newtown, N. Y., to Charles Gundluch. *Mt.* $4,000. 10,200

Plymouth st, n s, 150 e Jay st, 45x100. John Arbuckle, Kate A. Jamison widow and Christina Arbuckle, both of Alleghany City, Penn., being heirs of Charles Arbuckle to Arbuckle Bros. 9,638

President st, n s, 357.6 w 9th av, 21x95. William J. Hazlewood to Katie wife of William J. Hazlewood. gift

Prospect pl, n s, 275 e Franklin av, 65 6x128.6. William E. Cox to Minnie A. Cox. Q. C. nom

Richardson st, n s, 100 e Union av, 25x100. John M. Amory to Jacob Haehler. 700

Richardson st, n s, 95 w Herbert st, runs north 59 x west 15.11 x north 15 x west 0.10 x south 62.5 to Richardson st, x east 22.1 to beginning. Anna G. Schiel to Mary E. Graham. *Mt.* $1,200. exch

Schaeffer st, s s, 100 w Bushwick av, 0.2x100x 0.3x100. Charles Kappelman to George Schwartz. 100

South Oxford st, w s, 277 n Lafayette av, 22x 100, h & l. William G. Jones, of Temple, Texas, Anna M., Ette O. and Henrietta O. Jones, Saratoga Springs, to Adelia K. Broome. *Mt.* $8,000. 13,500

Stanhope st, n w s, 100 n e Hamburg av, 25x 100. Wilhelmine Schwenk to Helene Lungeshausen. *Mt.* $3,000. 6,050

Stanhope st, s e s, 175 n e Irving av, 25x100. James P. Brown, Bayonne, N. J., to Christian F. Homel. 700

Stanhope st, n w s, 125 n e Hamburg av, 25x 100, h & l. Josephine wife of Peter Eisemann to Frederick H. Horchler. B. & S. and C. a. G. 6,050

State st, s s, 195 w Nevins st, 20x90. Benjamin F. Tyler to William H. and Horace H. Tyler. All title. 2,000

State st, n s, 44.10 w Nevins st, 105.1x100.
Lafayette av, n s, 325 e Reid av, 125x100.
Patchen av, s e cor Van Buren st, runs east 280 x south 100 x west 180 x south 75 x west 100 to av, x north 175.
Spencer st, e s, bet Myrtle and Park avs, 50x 100. All title.
Myrtle av, s s, 460.8 e Lewis av, 19.11x100.
Francis Jezek to Augusta B. Jezek. All liens. nom

Sterling pl, s w s, 0.11 n Flatbush av, runs southwest 135.8 x east 45 x northeast 82 to av, x north 28.11 to Sterling pl, x northwest 0.11 to beginning. John Adamson to Francis Hart, of New York. *Mt.* $4,500. 8,000

St. Marks pl, n s, 380 w 5th av, 20x100. Louise Kathe to Greenleaf W. Crossmann, of New York. *Mt.* $3,000. 6,600

Stockholm st, s e s, 350 s w Knickerbocker av, 25 x100. Frederick A. Young to Albert Tremmel. 1,150

Stockholm st, n s, 101.1 e Wyckoff av, 20x100. Release mort. James C. Brower to George Blank. nom

Same p pe ty. George Blank to James Ledwith.ro r 800

Summit st, s s, 250 w Columbia st, 25x58.8x27x 48.4. Francis Gibrson to James Conway. 6,000

Summit st, n s, 400 w Columbia st, runs north 69 x southwest 69 to Hamilton av, x southeast 29 8 to Summit st, x east 28.1. James Calvert to Hamilton Bank of Brooklyn. 15,000

Thornton st, s s, 71.5 from southerly cor Broadway, 25x87.6x28.6x103.10, h & l. Henry Meis to Edward Michaelis. 7,000

Truxton st, n s, 60 w Stone av, 40x80, hs & ls. Augusta A. Roby to John Fallon. nom

Vanderveer st, s e s, 276.6 n e Broadway, 16.6 x100. Anna H. wife of and Jacob E. Olsen to Charles E. Hegstrom and Betty his wife, joint tenants. *Mt.* $1,800, assessm'ts, &c. 3,100

Vandyke st, n e s, 135 s e Van Brunt st, 25x100. Margaret Kentler to William Kentler, Jr. Sub. to mort. 8,000

Vandyke st, s s, 180 e Conover st, 20x100. Ellen Morgan formerly Walsh widow to William Krause. *Mt.* $1,500. 2,900

Vanderbilt st, s s, 450 e Short st, 12.6x108, Flatbush. Jane wife of and Hugh Moffat to Alexander Cherrie. *Mt.* $1,250. 2,500

Vanderbilt st, s s, 462.6 e Short st, 12.6x108, Flatbush. Anna wife of Henry Richter to said Henry Richter. *Mt.* $2,300. gift

Van Voorhis st, n w s, 200 s w Evergreen av, 70x100. Release mechanic's lien. Venetian Blind Co. to Edwin J. Bedell. nom

Van Voorhis st, n w s, 202 w Evergreen av, 17 x100. Alice B. Bedell to Annie F. Marrin. exch

Varet st, s s, 150 e Ewen st, 25x100. Samuel Harris to Isaac Horowitz. 3,500

Warren st, s s, 158.4 w 5th av, 20x100. Theresa Vidal to Carl Vollmann. *Mt.* $3,500. 4,500

Wallabout st, s s, 250 w Throop av, 25x100. Pincus Seifter to Max Engelstein. *Mt.* $5,500. 7,800

Same property. Max Engelstein, of New York, to Maver Levinsky, of New York. ½ part. Sub to mort. nom

Weirfield st, s e s, 200 n e Bushwick av, 20x100, h & l. Robert Gillies to William H. Hasselbrook. *Mt.* $2,500. 4,600

West st, e s, 425 s Sackett st, runs along West st 150 x east 100 x north 150 x west 100; also,
Chester st, w s, 575 s Sackett st, 100x100; also,
Chester st, w s, 425 s Sackett st, 100x100; also,
Rockaway av, w s, 300 s Sackett st, 50x100.
Philip Spencer to Annie Spencer. nom

Willoughby st, n s, 72.9 w Prince st, runs west 24.6 x north 78.4 x northeast 25 x east 10 7 x south 100. Peter Mallon to Frank C. Joslin. *Mt.* $3,500. 6,000

Wyona st, w s, 75 n Fulton av, 75x100 John D. Bennett to John W. Fleck, New York. 3,000

1st st, s w s, 202.10 n w 8th av, 20x100. Joseph B. Stilwell to Joseph J. Burk. *Mt.* $8,000. 13,500

1st st, n e s, 197.8 n w 6th av, 2.4x100. Release mort. John A. P. Ingoldsby and Henry J. Adkin, London, Eng., to Peter Larsen. 250

North 1st st, n s, abt 70 e Berry st, 25x ½ block, h & l. Joseph A., Isaac B. and William H. Maslen to Frank Joa and Agnes his wife. 1,800

North 1st st, s e cor Berry st, 44x55x50x84.9. Silas L. Lawless, of Brookhaven, N. Y., to James F. Lawless, of same place. ½ part. nom

Same property. James F. Lawless to Elizabeth M. Lawless. ½ part. nom

North 1st st, s w s, 141.6 s e 1st st, 25x142.8x25x 142.11. Foreclos. John Courtney to Huntington Page. 2,700

Same property. Huntington Page to Archibald Graham. 4,000

2d st, n e s, 259.9 n w 7th av, 18x100. Alice G. wife of Daniel M. Waterman to Charles G. Peterson. *Mt.* $2,000. exch. and 2,500

North 4th st, n s, 175 e Berry st, 25x100. Mary Lennon widow and Annie T., Patrick J. and Mary J. Lennon heirs Charles Lennon to Jacob Woessner and Sophie his wife. 4,275

4th st, s s, 291.10 w 7th av, 20x100. Annie J. Dynes to Charles L. Peacock, of Hoboken, N. J. nom

4th st, s s, 215.10 w 7th av, 18x100. Sadie F. Morse to Guilford R. Barteaux. *Mt.* $6,250. nom

North 5th st, n e s, 175 n w Havemeyer st, 25x 100. Hugh McCann, Rock Lake, Pa., to Mary Costello. nom

5th st, n s, 260 e 5th av, 20x100. Julia E. Cohen widow to Maria E. Sturgess. *Mt.* $3,500. 6,000

South 6th st, s e cor Wythe av, 25x100. Henry Mahnken to Mary C. Mahnken his wife. nom

East 8th st, w s, 360 n Av D, 40x120.6, Flatbush. Jane wife of Albert Spikesman to George M. Eddy. 577

9th st, n e s, 273 w 3d av, 25x100. Hamlet Edwin Forrest to Francis H. Stillman. 9,000

9th st, s s, intersection e s Gowanus Canal, runs east along st 230 x south 200 x west 40 x south 300 x west 100 to canal, x north 490 to st at beginning; also land under water adj. Daniel Doody to Asa W. Parker, of Hempstead, N Y. *Mt.* $30,500. 13,000

10th st, No. 307, n s. Mary J. Stone to Samuel Stone. nom

North 10th st, Nos. 70–74, s s, 69.9 w Wythe av, 55.3x100.
North 10th st, Nos. 58–62, s s, 200 w Wythe av, 50x100.
Cornelius J. and Edward F. Duggan and Millie wife of Frederick Mabbett heirs Edward H. Duggan to John Kerwin. All title. 6,000

Same property. Homan V. Duggan by Julia Duggan guard. to same. Infant's share. 2,000

North 10th st, s s, 69.9 w Wythe av, 55.3x100.
North 10th st, s s, 200 w Wythe av, 50x100.
Release mort. John S. Ellis exr. Julia Waterbury to John Kerwin. 7,000

11th st, n s, 344.7 e 8th av, 18.11x100. Frank O. Peterson to Emily Rauppius. *Mt.* $4,000. 7,250

11th st, n s, 148.10 w 9th av, 18.6x100. Charles G. Petersen to Daniel M. Waterman. *Mt.* $6,000. 10,500

12th st, s s, 99 w 4th av, 18x100. Stephen B. Shepherd to Michael Bergen. *Mt.* $2,300. 3,100

East 13th st, lots 14 and 15 map of 57 lots M. Healey, Sheepshead Bay, 50x100. Margaret Healy, Margaret A. Boyle and Ellen M. Hall to Mary A. Thibault. 150

14th st, n s, 308.10 w 9th av, 18.6x100. Christopher C. Firth to Esaias Mahner. *Mt.* $3,500. 6,600

16th st, No. 553. Contract. Eliza Culyer to James Hutchison. 1,400

16th st, s s, 190.3 e 4th av, 17x100. Charles L. Prindle, of Sharon, Conn., to Alexander Hodge. 3,300

16th st, n e s, 208.2 s e 4th av, 19.3x100. George Keymer to Mary Fox. *Mt.* $4,000. 6,500

Bay 16th st, centre line, e s, 100 n 86th st, 40x 130, New Utrecht. Ella L. Hutter to George Hutter. 650

18th st, s s, 80.4 w 10th av, 20x100.2. Charles Hart to Ellen wife of Henry Mangan. 650

20th st, n s, 140 w 5th av, 19.8x100, h & l. William D. C. Scheelje to Anna Jacobi. 2,500

East 21st st, w s, 160 n Voorhies av, 20x100, Gravesend. Alouson Tredwell and Alonzo Slote to William J. Gladding. 400

22d st, n e s, 160 n w 4th av, 25x100. Dudley S. Steele and Nathan W. Condict, Jr., to B'Nai Jacobs. 2,000

Bay 25th st, s e s, 160 s w Benson av, 60x96.8, Bensonhurst. James D Lynch to Allie Hillyer, of Helena, Montana. 1,650

27th st, n s, 138.4 e 3d av, 18.4x101.2x18.4x—. Anna E. Jenks to James O'Neill. 1,100

27th st, n s, 140 e 3d av, 18.4x101.2. James O'Neill to Isaac Newcomb and Ellen his wife, joint tenants. 1,400

Bay 29th st, n w s, 390 s w Benson av, 70x96 8, Bensonhurst. Anna M. Leinfelon to Rebecca F. Forman. *Mt.* $1,620. nom

30th st, s s, 125 e 3d av, 25x100.2. Michael Fleisch to Christian Fleisch. nom

30th st, s s, 150 e 3d av, 25x100.2. Same to Katie Fleisch. nom

Bay 35th st, s e s, adj land John B. Denyse, 25x 98.6, Gravesend. Margaret R. Bateman to George H. Gilmour. 1,250

39th st, s s, 220 w 4th av, 20x100.2. Johanna, Jeremiah and Kate Roach by guard. to Robert and Mary Catland. 1,285

Same property. Daniel J. Roach one heir of Daniel Roach to same. 428

39th st, s s, 258.4 w 3d av, 16.8x100.2. Frances J. Pierret and Anne Reppel to Johanna wife of Edward Pierret. *Mt.* $1,000. 2,600

Same property. Jacob Schaefer exr. Julia Roach to same. 1,285

39th st, n s, 450 e 4th av, 25x88.9x43.10x52.7. Joseph Foley to Michael W. Costello. *Mt.* $1,000. 2,000

39th st, n e s, 100 s e 8th av, 25x100.2, h & l. Annie McJohn, formerly Tupper, to Edward J McCarty. ½ part. nom

Same property. Edward J. McCarty to Thomas J. McJohn. ½ part. Q. C. nom

49th st, n s, 100 e 6th av, 20x100.2. Release mort. Edward T. Hunt exr. and trustee of Thos. Hunt to Francesco Alessi. 140

55th st, n e s, 620 s e 8th av, 21x104.1x50.2x100.2, partly in New Utrecht. Stephen McMahon, of Jersey City, N. J., to Catherine Millane. 500

55th st, n e s, 375 n w 14th av, 50x100, New Utrecht. Amelia L. wife of Henry C. Bull to Alexander Wilson. *Mt.* $2,000. 3,600

55th st, s w s, 500 s e 8th av, 40x100.2, New Utrecht. Antonio Colosimo to Francesco Scarmato. 500

55th st, n s, 125 w 2d av, 25x100.2, 8th Ward. Louis H. Schenck to Ida L. De Nyse. nom

57th st, s s, 300 e 6th av, 20x100.4. Ann Meehan to Catherine C. McMahon. Sub. to mort. nom

57th st, n e s, 100 s e 15th av, 50x100.2, New Utrecht. The West Brooklyn Land and Impt. Co. to Blanche E. Clark. 700

58th st, n e s, 160 n w 17th av, 80x100.2, New

Utrecht. Hans C. Pfalzgraf to Peter Kraeger and Elisabeth his wife, New York. 4,625

60th st. n s, 240 w 13th av, 20x100.2, New Utrecht. John P. Free to Bridget Dundon. B. & S. nom

66th st, n s, 100 e 12th av, 40x100, New Utrecht. James V. S. Woolley to Clans J. H. Semken. 350

66th st, s s, 140 w 13th av, 20x100, Lefferts Park. Effingham H. Nichols to Annie V. Benson, New York. 175

67th st, s s, 140 e 11th av, 20x130, New Utrecht. Anna B. Sorenson to George R. Lund and Paul C. Forst, New York. 450

67th st, n s, 100 e 13th av, 40x100, Lefferts Park. Effingham H. Nichols to Michael J. Smith. 370

67th st, s s, 160 e 11th av, 20x150, New Utrecht. Sarah E. and Christian N. Brown to Catherine Kleinbub. 250

68th st. east cor 1st av, 29.11x147x44.9x147.7, Bay Ridge. Release mort. Catharine Carman to George Kidney. consid. omitted

Same property. George Kidney to Elipalet W. Bliss. 5,000

75th st, s w s, 190 s e 3d av, 100x½ block, New Utrecht. Release mort. A. Gertrude Van Brunt et al. to James A. Townsend. 450

75th st, s w s, 250 s e 3d av, 40x107.2, New Utrecht. Release mort. James A. Townsend to Benjamin Letcher. nom

Same property. Benjamin Letcher to Phebe R. Derby. 950

76th st. n e s, 190 s e 3d av, original line, 50x107.2, New Utrecht. Bay Ridge Mfg. Co. to George P. Rockwell. 4,700

83d st, n e s, 280 s e 22d av, 60x100, New Utrecht. William Watson to Emily S. Andrews, East Orange, N. J. *Mt.* $3,100. 7,500

East 93d st, s w s, runs southwest 100 along land R. L. Baisley, x southeast 50 along land. John J. Morrison, x northeast 100 x northwest 50 to beginning, Flatlands. Matilda Seelars to John T. Ford. 275

East 93d st, s w s, bet Avs J and K, runs southwest along land C. V. R. Ludington 100, x northwest along land grantor 31x6, x northeast 100 x southeast 31 to beginning, Flatlands. John J. Morrison to John T. Ford. 189

East 93d st, n e s, runs northeast along land Abram Vooris, x southeast 31.6 along land of grantor, x southwest 100 along land Clinton Ludington, x northwest 31.6 to beginning, Flatlands. Same to Elizabeth Ford. 189

East 98th st, e s, 150 s Av G, 30.8x100, Canarsie. John H. Ireland to James Warner. Correction deed. nom

Atlantic av, s s, 200 e Saratoga av, 16.8x100, h & l. Alfred Ogden to Goodman Grodjinski. nom

Atlantic av, n e s, 382.6 s e Grove av, 106.6x208 x100.7x227, New Utrecht. John M. D. Head to Alexander Mellville. 800

Atlantic av, s s, 65.4 w Utica av, 16.8x83 4. Mary W. Prior to Mary E. Prior. *Mt.* $1,500. nom

Atlantic av, s s, 233.4 e Saratoga av, 16.8x100, h & l. Alfred Ogden to Anna Pierce. Sub. to mort. $2,400. nom

Bedford av, w s, 125 s on old De Kalb st, now closed, being north one half of lot 577 J. Skillman map, 12.6x100. Charles W. Sloane, of Sands Point, N. Y., to Simon Jackson. 2,000

Bedford av, s e cor North 11th st, 50x100. Frank S. Bradford et al. exrs. Samuel I. Hunt, of Morristown, N. J., to Joseph N. Graver. Correction deed. *Mt.* $3,000. nom

Same property. Joseph N. Graver to Heinrich Stimper. *Mt.* $3,000. 6,550

Belmont av, s s. 25 w Christopher st, 25x100. Barney Quinto, of New York, to Israel Rubenstein. 800

Belmont av, s s, 25 e Thatford av, 25x100. Charles Feltman to Jacob Goldblatt, New York. *Mt.* $2,903. val. consid. and 500

Buffalo av, e s, 157.10 n Atlantic av, 19.3x100. Herman J. Wasner to Lawrence O'Reilly. *Mt.* $2,000. 4,500

Bushwick av, northerly cor Furman av, 20x82. Charles D. Reynolds to Fannie Walsh. *Mt.* $4,600. 6,600

Central av, w s, 24.6 s Myrtle st, 24.6x100.4x 23.9x94.4. Fridrich Kirschenheiter to Mary A. wife of and Valentine Ullrich. 2,975

Central av, n e s, 50 n w Harman st, 25x100. Julius Metzger and Elizabeth Studt to Frederick Erhardt. *Mt.* $3,500. exch

Clason av, e s. 650 s Myrtle av, 25x105. Alexander McKnight to James P. Heary. *Mt.* $2,000. 3,500

Clason av, e s, 49.6 s Pacific st, 24x88. Francis Plunkett to Lucrezia wife of Frank Pugano. *Mt.* $1,000. 1,725

Clermont av, w s, 62 s De Kalb av, 30x79.8 in two courses, x30.7x63.7. Patrick O. Dougherty to Mary A. wife of William Hughes. *Mt.* $4,000. gift

De Kalb av, n s, 475 e Throop av, 25x100. Frank H. Tyler to George A. Berry. *Mt.* $8,500. exch

Evergreen av, s w s, 25 s e Ivy st, 25x100. Elizabeth Wilkins to William Andrews. 1,700

Flatlands av, south cor East 94th st, 50x—x50x 131.9, Canarsie. Henry L. Schmeelk to Gustaf Nystrom. 550

Flushing av, n s, 121.11 e Bushwick av, runs east 127.7 x west 127.5 x south 9 to beginning. Sarah D. Vandervoort, of Falsington, Pa., to Nicholas Dietz, Jr. nom

Same property. Francis and William O. and Frederick J. Vandervoort by Arthur H. Ely guard. to same. 1-16 part. 70

Same property. Caroline M. Knapp, of New York, and Andrew E. Burr individ. and as exr., &c., Ida V. Burr to Joseph A. Burr, Jr. nom

Same property. Joseph A. Burr, Jr., to Nichlas Dietz, Jr. 70

Flushing av, n s, 146.11 e Bushwick av, runs east 27.7 x north 5.4 x west 27.6 x south 7.3. Nicholas Dietz, Jr., to William Thalen. 270

Flushing av, n s, 224.6 e Bushwick av, runs east 25 x west 25 x south 1.10 to beginning. Same to Cynthia F. Cass. 120

Flushing av, n s, 174.6 e Bushwick av, runs east 25 x north 3.7 x west 25 x south 5.4. Same to Philip L. Balz, Jr. 220

Flushing av, n s, adj land of A. D. Moore, 125x 100. Foreclos. Albert Daggett to Thomas I. Morrell and Cornelius H. Tiebout. Sub. to mort. $10,000. Sept. 2, 1878. 100

Flushing av, s s, 25.4 w Steuben st, 25x93.5x25x 94.10. John Jackson to Alonzo E. De Baun. 100

Flushing av, n s, 121 11 e Bushwick av, 25 1x7.3 x25x9. Nicholas Dietz, Jr., to Martha Voelk. Q C. 330

Flushing av, n s, 199.6 e Bushwick av, 25x1.10x 25x3.7. Same to Harriet A. McVicar. Q. C. 170

Gates av, n s, 146 e Franklin av, 16x100. Emma J. wife of Frank H. Phillips to Walter S. Jarvis. *Mt.* $4,250. 6,850

Gates av, n s, 166 e Nostrand av, 19x100. Morris Bolstein to Joseph Mentz. *Mt.* $3,000. 5,150

Gates av, n s, 130 e Franklin av, 16x100. J. Russell Taber to Edward Hooker. 6,717

Glenmore av, n s, 75 w Warwick st, 25x100. George Schmidt to Edward Schmidt. nom

Glenmore av, n s, 526 e Adams st, 25x100. Michael Bulger to Patrick O'Hanlon. 2,800

Grand av, e s, 50 s Greene av, 25x100. Elbert Snedeker to William H. Tunison. exch

Grand av, e s, 50 s Greene av, 25x100. Release mort. William W. Clark and ano. exrs. James W. Clark to Elbert Snediker. 1,000

Greene av, s s, 41.8 e Carlton av, 20.10x75. Emma J. wife of Frank H. Phillips to Alfred D. Ingram. 6,750

Greene av, s e cor Lewis av, 200x100. Foreclos. John Courtney to Spencer Aldrich. 55,300

Greene av, s s, 100 e Grand av, 25x100. William H. Tunison to Elbert Snediker. exch

Hamburg av, southerly cor Jefferson st, 25x75. August Seefris to John Bernard. *Mt.* $2,700. 10,000

Hamburg av, w s, 20 n Troutman st, 20x60. Carl F. W. Borchert to Louis Koch. *Mt.* $2,000. 4,800

Hamilton av, s w s, 43 s Summit st, runs west 95.4 x southeast 21.3 x east 91.2 to av, x north 20.10. Mary L. Godfrey wife of and Edward K. Godfrey to Wm. H. Kutscher. 7,600

Hegeman av, n e cor Hinsdale av, 100x90.
Vienna av, s e cor Williams av, —x99.11x100 x66.6.
Warehouse st, n s, 105.7 w Louisiana av, 40x 90.
Rebecca F. Forman to Anna M. Leinfelder. *Mt.* $600. exch

Hopkinson av, w s, 150 s Baltic st, runs west 100 x north ½ block x west 25 x south 127.9 x east to East New York av, x northeast to Hopkinson av, x north —. Peter Van Cott to Anna G. Williams. Q. C. 50

Howard av, n w cor Chauncey st, 17.8 to Brooklyn and Jamaica pike, x200.1x23.1x200. Jacob, Frederick and John Enders and Margarete Sharkey to David C. Lyall. Correction deed. Q. C. nom

Kent av, southerly cor North 7th st, 75x75. Patrick J. Carlin to Mary J. Lennon. nom

Kingsland av, w s, 184.5 n Nassau av, 37.11x 100. Morris Lipman and Abraham Lipman to Aaron Kaplan. Sub. to morts. 11,000

Kingsland av, s e cor Lombardy st, runs east 191.1 x southeast 200.8 to Beadel st, x west 232 9 to point 16.6 e Kingsland av, x northwest 20 6 to said av, x north 159.2. Jeremiah V. Meserole to Phillip H. Schoenig. 8,750

Knickerbocker av, s w s, 25 s e George st, 25x 100; also,
Stuyvesant av, e s, 50 s Quincy st, 25x90; also,
Knickerbocker av, w s, 75 n Harman st, 75x 100.
Rosa Deppe to Julius F. Wiegel. *Mt.* $11,-000. 35,000

Livonia av, s w cor Osborn st, 50x100. Hirsch Wilkenfeld and Nathan Rittermann to Margaret A. Tostevin. *Mt.* $2 0. exch. and 400

Lafayette av, n s, 187.6 w Nostrand av, 18.9x 100. David J. Blauvelt, of Nyack, N. Y., to Evilder S. Blauvelt, of Nyack, N. Y. nom

Lafayette av. n s, 86 w St. Felix st, 21x100. Cornelia J. Knowles, of Passaic, N. J., to Cornelia K. wife of Francis E. Fitch, of same place. *Mt.* $8,500. 13,500

Lafayette av, s s, 40 w South Portland av, 20 x80. Patrick O'Dougherty to Catharine E McLaughlin. gift

Lewis av, e s, 66.8 n Kosciusko st, 16.8x75, h & l. Mary E. Graham to Annie G. Schiel. *Mt.* $5,500 and tax 1890. exch

Lexington av, n s, 230 e Throop av, 15x100. David S. Beasley to Eugene Brush. 4,700

Lexington av, n s, 295 w Reid av, 20x100. William Bates, New York, to Samuel M. Fitch. 6,400

Lexington av, s s, 340 w Nostrand av, 15x100. George A. Berry to Frank H. Tyler. *Mt.* $4,000. exch

Lexington av, s s, 210 w Nostrand av, 16x100. Same to same. *Mt.* $1,200. exch

Lexington av, s s, 100 w Nostrand av, 15x100. Same to same. *Mt* $4,000. exch

Marcy av, e s, 36 s Gwinnett st, 18x85. Susan E. Miller to Emma J. wife of Frank H. Phillips. nom

Marcy av, e s, 34.8 n Lexington av, 16.4x66.11. Clara A. wife of and C. W. Millen to Elizabeth J. Bishop. 5,050

Marcy av, s w s, intersection n s Flushing av, runs west 65.4 x north 100 x east 8.5 to Marcy av, x southeast 117.7. Peter Thomas, of Hempstead, N. Y., to Morris Grauer. *Mt.* $11,000. 15,800

Marcy av, e s, 150 s Flushing av, 25x100. Moritz Grauer to Peter Thomas, of Hempstead, N. Y. *Mt.* $2,200. 5,000

Ocean av, e s, 331.1 n Fenimore st, 29.3x150 to Brooklyn, Flatbush & Coney Island R. R., Flatbush. Release mort. William T. Hudson to William Schwarzwaelder. 1,000

Same property. William Schwarzwaelder to Louis Von Wallmerich. 1,500

Myrtle av, s s, at w s John Skillman's land, 7th Ward, 25x162. William H. and James F. Fitzpatrick to Margaret Fitzpatrick. 1,058

Myrtle av, s w cor Sumner av, 50x100. Henry Bielenberg to J. Henry Blohme. *Mt.* $15,000. 35,000

Park av, n s, 37 w Delmonico pl. runs north 62.6 to Delmonico pl, x northwest 54 8 x southwest 26.4 x south 50.8 to av, x east 20, h & l. David Ungerleider to Moritz Scharfman. *Mt.* $3,500. 6,000

Patchen av, n e cor Madison st, 20x80. William Bornkamp to Louisa wife of Charles Bruning. 6,000

Prospect av, s e cor Greenwood av, 46.7x96.6x 75.4x76.4, Flatbush. Anna M. Ferris to James T. Kelly. 1,450

Putnam av, s s, 130 e Ralph av. 24.6x100. Alfred L. Beasley to Mary Schmalstich. *Mt.* $9,050. 13,500

Ridgewood av, s s, 20 e Essex st, 20x90, h & l. Wilmot D. Losee to William C. Lane. *Mt.* $1,600. 3,200

Rochester av, s w cor Bergen st, 43.9x75. Herman Kahrs to Ernst A. Grote. 2,500

Schenck av, w s, 165 s Hegeman av, 20x100. George Cring to George W. Adams, Hempstead, L. I. nom

Schenectady av, s e cor Garrison av, centre lines, runs south to south line of the Remsen farm, x northeast along same to centre Garrison av, x southwest to beginning. George S. Wheeler exr. of Nancy B. Wheeler to Isaac Halstead. B. & S. All liens. 100

Schenectady av, n e cor Atlantic av, 16.6x80. Emil Gormann to Matthew Healey. *Mt.* $2,-000. 3,725

Shepherd av, e s, 420 n Arlington av, 80x102x 80x131.11. Charles Lewis to Jacob Wills and James I. Newman. 2,800

Stillwell av, e s, 340 s Av S, 60x100, Bensonhurst. James D. Lynch to Katherine Rober, Boston, Mass. 900

Stone av, w s, 275 s Blake av, 25x100. Release mort. J. C. & H. Smith & Koepke to Mary E. Cook. 62

Same to same. Mary E. Cook, of Newtown, N. Y., to Benjamin Finkelstein. *Mt.* $2,000. 3,000

Stuyvesant av, e s, 20 s Lexington av, 20x90. Francis D. Jackson to John P. Gallagher, of Sullivan Co., N. Y. 6,500

Thatford av, w s, 50 n Blake av, 25x90. Barnet Levin to Morris Levin. *Mt.* $1,600. 3,400

Thatford av, w s, 125 n Dumont av, 25x100. Lewis Hurst to Joseph Morris. 900

Thatford av, 250 n Dumont av, 25x100. Same to same. 900

Throop av, w s, 44 6 n Pulaski st, 55.6x84 9. Release mort. Francis P. Furnald, Jr., of New York, to George B. Stoutenburg. 16,000

Throop av, w s, 26 n Pulaski st, 18.6x84.9. Release mort Frances P. Furnald, Jr., of New York, to George B. Stoutenburg. 5,000

United States av, n w s. 100 n e Washington st, 100x116.3, New Utrecht. Eliza Wilson widow and Abraham D. Wilson et al heirs of Abraham D. Wilson to James Lake. 1804. 765

Union av, n e cor Richardson st, 25x100. John H. and Mary A. McGarry to Guiseppe Deperino. 1,700

Union av, e s, 25 n Richardson st, 25x100. Same to Alfonzo and Antonio Deperino. 1,70

Vanderbilt av, w s, 81 s Bergen st, runs west 95 x south 50 x west 5 x south 56 x east 100 to av, x north 106. James D. Putnam to Daniel O'Connell. 8,750

Wyckoff av, n w cor Ralph st, 25x100. Gustav Feigenspan, of Newtown, N. Y., to Charles Gundlich. *Mt.* $4,000. 9,500

3d av, e s, 40.2 n 47th st, 30x85. Release mort. Jacob Heim to Frederick Seiferd and Frederick Gommel. 2,635

Same property. Release mort. Mary G. Manning to same. 4,000

Same property. Frederick Gommel to Frederick M. Seiferd. B. & S. nom

4th av, northerly cor 17th st, 60.2x60. Charlotte A. A. Sands widow, East Greenwich, R. I., to Julia B. Lanning. nom

4th av, w s, 100 s 6th st. 100x100. Henry Putzel to Charles S. Kendall. *Mt.* $5,000. nom

4th av, w s, 121.9 s 15th st, 21x90x20x90. Simon J. Harding to Catharine T. Jamison, of New York. *Mt.* $2,000. 3,700

6th av, e s, 40 n Park pl, 20x74.7. Benjamin Atha, of Newark, N. J., to Stephen W. McKeever. *Mt.* $1,000. 9,500

7th av, Nos. 151-155, e s, 40 9 n Garfield pl, 59.3 x80, h & l. George T. Riley to William A. Armstrong, Patchogue, L. I. *Mt.* $30,-000. exch

Same property. William A. Armstrong to Margaretta Armstrong. *Mt.* $30,000. 45,000

8th av, s w cor Windsor pl, 21x79.10, h & l. Thomas Brown to William Ebeling. *Mt.* $6,000. 11,500

8th av, n w s, 80 s w 16th st, 20x97.5. Nassau Land and Improvement Co. to Henry Leopold. 6,250
9th av, s e s, 50 n e 16th st, 50x97.10. Israel Muller to George F. Muller. 13,000
15th av, easterly cor 57th st, 50.2x100, New Utrecht. The West Brooklyn Land and Improvement Co. to Blanche E. Clark. 1,125
20th av, s e s, 540 n e Benson av, 60x96.8, New Utrecht. Edwin H. Kowing, of Stamford, Conn., to Arnett G. Smith. 1,500
Indefinite plot on Coney Island. Ovid A. Hyde to Chauncey W. Clark. nom
Interior lot, 83.7 s St. Marks av and 60 w Bedford av, runs south 23.5 x west 40 x north 24 x east 40; also,
St. Marks av, s s, 60 w Bedford av, 20x83.4x 20x83.7.
Mary W. wife of and John G. McAuley to Mary L. Stacy, of West Springfield, Mass. *Mt.* $7,500. 14,000
Interior parcel, 100 n w Adams st and 314 n e Washington st now Bremen st, on old map, runs northwest 100 x northeast 99 x southeast — x southwest 96. Conrad Diem to Julius Radecke. 1,500
Lot 4 block 17 map No. 2 First Section or Manufacturing District, East New York. Edward Wemple, State Comptroller, to Emily C. Siemon. Tax deed. 5
Lots 7 and 8 block 1 map 618 lots Couwenhoven farm, New Utrecht. Effingham H. Nichols to Owen Lynam. 450
Lots 81 block 2 and 426 and 427 block 10 same map. Same to Martha J. Buhsen. 495
Lots 423, 424 and 425 block 10 same map. Same to Annie Norman. 465
Lots 22, 23 and 24 map Joseph Stehlin property, New Utrecht. Release mort. Joseph C. Levi trustee to Joseph Stehlin. 500
Lot 172 block F map Vanderveer Homestead. John H. Vanderveer to John Murtaugh. 670
Lots 233 and 234 block 10 map 1,197 lots belonging to William Ziegler, New Utrecht. Richard Hawley to Delic P. Hawley. *Mt* $300. 500
Lots 377 and 378 block 9 map No. 1 of 618 lots Cowenhoven property, New Utrecht. Effingham H. Nichols to William A. French. 340
Lot 578 block 11 same map. Same to Jennie R. Worthington. 150
Lots 21-25 block 17 map 660 lots part Cowenhoven farm, belonging to Effingham H. Nicholas, New Utrecht. Effingham H. Nichols to Katharina F. Unkelbach. 975
Lots 198, 199 and 200 block 21 same map. Same to Peter Conroy. 565
Lots 281 and 282 block 22 map 2 of 660 lots Cowenhoven farm, New Utrecht. Effingham H. Nichols to Mary Gallagher. 370
Lot 114 block 19 map No. 2 of 660 Cowenhoven farm lots belonging to E. H. Nichols, New Utrecht. Effingham H. Nichols to Peter Egan, of New York. 130
Lot 289 block 7; also lots 381 and 382 block 9 same map. Same to Mott L. Brock. 460
Lots 105-107 block 19 same map. Same to same. 795
Lots 115-119 blocks 19, and 220, 221 and 222 block 21 map No. 2 660 lots Cowenhoven farm, belonging to Effingham H. Nichols, New Utrecht. Effingham H. Nichols to Martin Hayden. 1,165
Lots 212 and 213 block 21 map 2 of 660 lots Cowenhoven farm, New Utrecht. Effingham H. Nichols to Samuel Ibbotson. 370
Lots 21-28 block 17, 57-59 and 71-78 block 18, 105-109, 114-119 and 135-139 block 19, 143, 159, 160-164, 165 and 167 block 20, 188-192, 198-200, 213, 214, 218, 220, 221, 222, 227, 228 and 258-269 block 21; also 270-274 and 280-287 block 22, 488-492, 494, 495, 503, 504, 507, 508 and 513-530 block 25 map 2 of 660 lots of E. H. Nichols, Cowenhoven farm, New Utrecht. Release mort. Magdalene Cowenhoven admrx. of Garret Cowenhoven to Effingham H. Nichols. 12,000
Lot 86 map made by Noyes F. Palmer for the Brooklyn & Rockaway Beach R. R., Flatlands, contains 16,650 sq. ft. Adaline F. Bromley widow to The Brooklyn & Rockaway Beach R. R. Co. 1-24 part. nom
Lots 509 and 510 block K map of Zabriskie homestead, Flatbush. William J. Kaiser, John H. Vanderveer and George W. Dalton to Harriet wife of John G. Richardson. 800
Lots 336 and 347 block 8 map 1 of 618 lots, Cowenhoven farm, New Utrecht. Effingham H. Nichols to Frederick Jensen. 175
Lot at New Utrecht, begins at s e cor of land of George Kidney on south line of grantors land, runs south 146.9 to n s 68th st, x west 50 x north 146 9 x east 50. Eliphalet W. Bliss to George Kidney. 5,000
Parcel begins at north line of land of grantee at point 200 n w of 11th av, runs northeast to s s of S. N. Stillwells land, x east to centre line bet 83d and 84th sts, in block bet 10th and 11th avs, x southeast along same to centre 11th av, x northeast to s s of N. R. Stillwells land, x east to centre 83d st, x southeast to point 200 n e from centre 11th av, x north to s s of N. R. Stillwells land, x east to land of Val. Cropsey, x south to land of grantee, x west —.
Parcel begins at land of G. R. Stillwell, runs north along same to land of E H. Ryder, x east to centre 84th st, x east to north line of grantees land, x west —, New Utrecht.
Jane E. wife of Frederick H. Johnson to Ira O. Miller. 3,368
Brooklyn & Rockaway Beach R. R., e s, 506.2 s Atlantic av, 50x100. Edward R. Vollmer to Abraham H. Dailey and Elihu J. Granger, rather vague. 674
Canarsie road, e s, adj land Christian Holm, runs north 290.10 x east 986.1 x south 595.3 x west 515.11, contains 4 8-10 acres, Canarsie. Charles M. Marsh, of Morris Plains, N. J., to Michael Sullivan, of Flatbush. 17,500
Canarsie road, e s, adj north line of C. Hohns land, 900.10x1,049.9x595 3x517.11, being 11 69-100 acres, Flatlands. Michael Sullivan to William Herod, Charles Taber and George C. Case. *Mt.* $12,500. nom
Sheepshead Bay road, e s, adj land Geo. D. Bradley, 35x100, Gravesend. Charles M. Snow to Ida M. Head. nom
Assignment of judgment. John I. Waterbury and Isaac N. Waterbury to Freeman A. A. Brown. See Adelphi st. 200

WESTCHESTER COUNTY.

SEPTEMBER 23 TO 29 —INCLUSIVE.

BEDFORD.

Fish, Martha J. to Martha T. Horton, e s Main st, adj C. F. Pelton, 100x170. $575
Miller, Jos. O. to Aug. Bartholdi and wife, s s Main st, adj Theresa Crist, 20x200. 2,875

CORTLANDT.

Brown, Eliz'h to Jas. Clancey, n s Lincoln terrace, adj Mich. Dunn, 50x130. 250
Douglass, John W. to Chas. H. Chase, n e cor Central and Nelson avs, 58x75. 1,800
Lent, Weldon H. to Hannah F. Lent, e s old road, from Post road to Furnace Woods, 82 acres. 5,000

EASTCHESTER.

Crowe, Cath. A. to Edwin J. Lucas, lots 238-243, Chester Hill, Forster property, 150x230. 6,050
Gay, Margt. C. to Robt Ferguson, part lot 973 s s 21st av, Wakefield, 50x114. 800
Ferguson, Robt. to Adolph Greeder, part same property, 25x114. 400
Henneberger, Herman to Jay L. Oldham, s e cor Villa av and Urban st, 100x100. 2,200
Lane, John S. to Annie E. Dickinson, w s Glen av, 188 n Prospect av, 63x109. 7,700
Mutual Life Ins Co. to Fred. W. Ellenberger, s e cor Pelham road and Fulton av, 50x—. 1,000
Mandrey, Lucy W. to Doris Mandrey, lot 429 s e s Garden pl, Washingtonville, 40x122. 2,650
Smith, Marion to Louis N. Smith, s c cor 11th av and 2d st, Mt. Vernon, 100x105. 4,000
Thorn, Thomas to Annie M. Smith, lots 3-6 and 22-25 Boulevard and West st, grantor's map. 5,000
Wallach, Adolph to Lucy W. Mandrey, lots 311, 313, 315 and South Washingtonville. 1,700
Mandrey, Lucy W. to Wm. W. Penfield, same property. 3,100
Weeks, Mary M., exrs. of, to John H. Murphy and ano., lot 18 w s Rich av, Chester Hill, 50x125. 1,700
Wheeler, Dwight E. to Lewis W. Sageman, n s 2d st, centre block bet 1st and 2d avs, 50x 120. 6,000
Wise, Cath. et al. to Mertil Lickert, s w cor White Plains road and road to Quarry, 56x 120. 3,100
Whitmore, Daniel W. to Fred. Mager, lot 924 e s 12th av, Mt. Vernon, 100x105. 2,000

GREENBURGH.

Blackwell, Wilson H. to Elizb. J. Millett, lots 681-684, Ardsley. 700
Same to Owen Ward, Jr., lot 701. 175
Same to Alfred J. Shaw, lots 559 and 560. 360
Equitable Life Assurance Society to Emma L. Milderberger, n s Church st, 124.9 w Broadway, 100x152. 1,500
Mathews, Wm. J. to Edw. P. Steers, tract on New Tarrytown road adj And. Martine. nom
Quinby, Annie B. to Wm. C. Hanson, lots 52 and 54 e s Washington av, Chatterton Hill, 66x125. 200
Tole, Rev. Wm. H. to The Church of St. John, White Plains, 2 tracts road from Fair Grounds to Kensico, abt 50 acres. nom

MOUNT PLEASANT.

Cashman, Maggie to Josephine Foot, lot 10 s s Beekman av, 55x125. nom
Smadbeck, Louis and ano. to Louis Berger, lots 31 and 32, Lakehurst. 200
Same to Ferd. Chabie and ano., lots 437-440. 550
Smith, Wm. R. to John H. Laskarn, Jr., lots 1 and 2 block 5, Lake Kensico. 350
Soltz, Arcadius to Samuel Ashman, e s Lenox av, 125 n Broadway, 25x100. 100
Wood, Emily et al. S. S. Marshall ref., to Mutual Life Ins. Co., plot North End, Wood Court. 5,000

NEW ROCHELLE.

Diehl, Adam to Wm. C. Ryan, s s Winyah av, 401 — North st, 25x100. 315
Disbrow, Susan W. exrs. of, to Aug. Mohr, n s Horton av, 100 w Brook st, 100x180. 650
Gregg, Jas. A. S. to Wm. E. Mulligan, lot 8 map property grantor, 100x200. 3,000
Hudson, Alex. B. to Wm. Keveloh, n e s Beechwood av, 378 n w Main st, 51.6x150. 375
Lambden, Jos. to Benj. F. Renoud, n w cor Hillside and Mayflower avs 30x140. 450
Manhattan Life Ins. to Albion T. Stevens, lot 9 block I, Rochelle Park. 1,300

OSSINING.

Buckley, Bartholomew to Annie Buckley, n s Division st, adj Jas. Shute, 50x80. nom
Lent, Smith to Ann E. Leary, w s Prospect st, adj Rev. J. B. Gibson, 50x100. 1,000

PELHAM.

Black, Robt. C. to Josephine C. Cuppia, plot Manor Circle road, abt 1 acre. 3,423
Lockyer, Jas. to Wm. Roberts, n s Scofield av, adj grantee, 50x119. 700
Standen, William T. to Ida Stoetzel, lot 25, Chester Park. 1,800

RYE.

Merritt, Jas. S. and ano. to Wigtor Neilson, lot 8 n s Ellendale av, Washington Park, 50 x150. 202
Same to Wm. Duncan, lot 68 s s same av. 202
Same to Chas. Park, lots 27, 28 and 29 n s same av. 185
Same to same, lots 79, 80 and 81 n e cor Ridge and West William sts. 400
Same to Clarence S. Willson, lot 55 s w cor Ellendale av and Merritt st. 340
Schmaling, Chas. H. to Halsey K. Smith, s e cor Hawthorne and Irenbyl avs, 198x55x186x 126. 550

WESTCHESTER.

Cash, Daniel to Magdalena Odell, w s 3d st, 100 s 10th av, Wakefield, 25x100. 1,000
Camp, Hugh N. to Wm. Briggs et al., lot 235 map McGraw estate. 200
Dexter, Fred. C. to Sarah W. Vail, lot 898 n s 13th av, Wakefield, 105x114. nom
Davis, Daniel to Fred. C. Dexter, east ½ lot 311 s s 12th av, Wakefield, 50x114. nom
Hellman, Elizh. to Jahn Knewitz, w s Old Boston road, 211.6 n Juliana st, abt 40x105. 3,500
Hughes, Miles to Thos. H. Wright, e s Deane pl, 125 s Pierce av, 65x100. 545
Jetter, Thos. to Chas. A. Axtmann, e s Westchester road adj Frank Buckel, abt 109x300. 1,000
Jones, Betsey E. to Alex. U. Mayer, e s Barker av, 100 s Elizabeth st, 100x125. 2,500
Lorenz, Henry to Franz Engel, lot 39 s e cor Av B and 2d st, Unionport, 108x200. 500
Lyon, Dore to Maria H. Potts, e s Doris av, 200 n Westchester av, 25x100. 575
Mace, Levi H. to Chas D. Shirmer, lots 5-10, 84-88, 120-126, 180-185, 245-250, Laconia Park, ½ int. nom
Same and ano. to Carrie Wyburn, lots 32 and 33 n s Ash av, Laconia Park. 400
Waters, Wm. to Edw. G. Williams, lot 367 s s 14th st, Unionport, 105xx108. 1,000
Weekes, Harriet A. to G. De Witt Clocke and wife, lot 107 s s 14th av, Wakefield, 100x 114. 800

WHITE PLAINS.

Ferris, Jas. M. to Vincenzo Balletto, w s Madison av, 50x120. 100
Ferris, Kath. to Clarence Leviness, lot 17 e s Brookfield st, Fisher map, 40x125. 300
Moran, Jas. H. to F. Herbert Norvil, n e Railroad av, adj Edw. Baxter, 50.6x126. 10,250

YONKERS.

Armour Villa Park Assoc. to Angie Beery, lots 296 and 297. nom
Barnes, Ella L. to Victor Lingert, lot 73 e s Hyatt av, map Hyatt farm, 55x100. 595
Cain, Jos. H. to Jerome D. Barnes, lots 36-40 block 19½ and lots 17 and 18 block 19 Lowerre Station. 3,400
Edwards, Jas. J. to John L. Pool, lots 15-18 n s Cornell av, Lowerre Station. 2,500
Gramatan Park Co. to Jas L. Stewart, lots 168, 169, 170, 207, 208 and 209. nom
Jones, Cyrus P. and ano. to Chas. A. Wright and ano., lots 16 and 17 block A grantor's map. 550
North End Land Co. to Nath. B. Valentine, s e cor Yonkers av and Alida st, 125x100. 2,725
Parsells, Edw. W. to Martin J. Quinn, w s Briggs av, 100 n Fort Fieldav, 25x100. 250
Shannon, Patrick to Arthur J. Burns, No. 219 w s Buena Vista av, City map, 25.1x120.6. 1,500
Shonnard, Fred. to Mary J. Papasian, lot 3.8 Edward pl, City map. 125
Valentine, Clara M. to Jas. McKone and ano., w s Bennett av, 325 n Summerfield st, 25x 100. 210
Waring, Jeanette P. to John F. Leonard, e s Nepperhan av, 200 n Lake av, 50x100. 600
Yonkers Savings Bank to Howard Carroll, n w cor Post st and Livingston av, 108.6x219. 8,000

MORTGAGES.

NOTE.—*The arrangement of this list is as follows. The first name is that of the mortgagor, the next that of the mortgagee. The description of the property then follows, then the date of the mortgage, the time for which it was given, and the amount. The general dates used as headings are the dates when the mortgage was handed into the Register's office to be recorded.*

Whenever the letters "P. M." occur, preceded by the name of a street, in these lists of mortgages, they mean that it is a Purchase Money Mortgage, and for fuller particulars see the list of transfers under the corresponding date. Whenever the rate is not given, read as 6 per cent.

NEW YORK CITY.

SEPTEMBER 25, 26, 28, 29, 30, OCTOBER 1.

Anderson, Pehr S. to Martha E. Randall, West st, n e s, west ½ lot 29 map of Wardsville, West Farms, 25x100. Sept. 26, 3 yrs, 5%. $200

Andrews, Wallace C. and Margaret M. St. J. his wife to Ferdinand McKeige, Hempstead, L. I. 134th st, s s, 250 w Alexander av, 150x100. Sept. 25, 1 year. 6,000

Angel, Addie B. wife of James R. to THE EAST RIVER SAVINGS INST. Franklin av, s e s, 142 s w 169th st, 50x185.5, except part taken for opening 169th st. Sept. 23, 1 year, 5 %. 4,500

Alsfeld, Christian and Margaretha mortgagees to Mark Ash present owner. Acknowledgment of payment of $4,000 on account of mortgage made by Hyman Goldberg and extension for balance. Oct. 1. nom

Ambler, Emma to Increase M. Grenell. 94th st. P. M. Sub. to mort. $14,000. Oct. 1, 3 years or installs. 4,500

Anwander, John to The Prospect Home Building and Loan Assoc. of Brooklyn. Forest av, e s. 125 n Cedar pl, 18.3x103 to lane. Sept. 28, installs, 5 %. 2,750

Aronson, Henry to Lotta Wachtel. 2d av. P. M. Oct. 1, 1 year, 5 %. 1,500

Banks, David and Annie H. G. his wife to Eva C. Glover widow, Lakewood, N. J. Potter pl, n s, 625 w st not named in 24th Ward, 25x100, being lot 417 map No. 3 of New York City private park. Sept. 30, 3 years. 2,000

Beisner, Behrend to Peter Doelger. 10th st, No. 351 E. Store lease. Oct. 1, demand. 1,200

Bier, Mary to Max Frankenheim. 69th st, No. 335 E. P. M. Sub. to mort. $12,000. Oct. 1, installs, 5 %. 5,000

Same to Sigmund Cohn. Same property. Sub. to morts. $17,000. Oct. 1, 9 mouths. 750

Briesen, Arthur V. to Harrison D Kerr. 48th st. P. M. Oct. 1, 3 years or sooner, 5 %. 32,000

Barclay, Annie E. to THE TITLE GUARANTEE AND TRUST CO. Barrow st, No. 4, n s, 75.4 w 4th st, runs north 22.7 x west 4 x north 22.7 x west 18 x south 45.2 to Barrow st, x east 22. ½ part. Sept. 24, 4 years. 700

Barnett, Max to Moses and Phillip Schloss. 5th av and 114th st. P. M. Sept. 4, 2 years or sooner, 5 %. 16,000

Barnett, Nancy, Jr., sister of Jane McDonald to William J. Roome. 24th st, Nos. 36-54 W.; 21st st, No. 230 W.; 22d st, Nos. 409 and 411 W.; 22d st, No. 528 W.; 8th av, No. 551. ⅙ part. Sept. 26, demand. 600

Bloomfield, Mary A. wife of John J. to THE EMIGRANT INDUST. SAVINGS BANK. 52d st, s s, 162.6 e 8th av, 20.10x100.5. Sept. 28, 1 year, 4½ %. 2,000

Bowen, Alice K. to Hannah M. Balmford. 164th st. P. M. Sept. 23, due Sept. 24, 1896, 5 %. 3,000

Same to Joseph Balmford. Same property. P. M. Sub. to last mort. Sept. 23, due Sept. 24, 1896, 5 %. 1,300

Bremeier, Friedrich to George Steinbrecher. 7th st, s s, 216 w Av B, 25x90.10. Lease. June 20, due July 1, 1894, or sooner, 5 %. 1,500

Brettell, Frederica to Agnes W. Seaton. 122d st. P. M. Sept. 16, 3 years, 5 %. 6,000

BANK OF THE METROPOLIS with William Saeckner. Declaration that assignment of lease was intended as mortgage. Sept. 24. nom

Banta, Nancy E. wife of and William, Brooklyn, to Joshua Hendricks, exr. and trustee Rebecca Tobias. Canal st, No. 361, n s, 41.7 w Wooster st, 18.11x64.2x19.4x66.11. Sept. 25, due Mar. 31, 1896, 5 %. gold, 3,000

Brennan, Margaret wife of and Patrick to John Livingston. 88th st, n s, 86 e 1st av, 20x125.10. Sept. 25, due Oct. 1, 1893, or sooner. 2,000

Same to Benigno S. Suarez. Same property. Sept. 25, due Oct. 1, 1896, 5 %. gold, 15,000

Beach, Moses S., Peekskill, to Lewis S. Wolff. Fulton st, s w cor Nassau st, 113.9x50.3x110.9x57.10. Contract to sell for $375,000. Recorded as a mort. Sept. 28. Deposit secured 10,000

Bernhardt, Philip to Toni Kopitk. 3d av. P. M. Sept. 30, 5 years or installs, 5 %. 5,500

Boschen, Henry and Anna his wife to William M. and Charles R. Stilwell exrs. Harriet L. Stilwell. Boulevard and 122d st. P. M. Sept. 15, due Oct. 1, 1896, 4½ %. 5,000

Bradley, Miles to Samuel Weeks. Cherry st, No. 412, n s, 21.5x97.4. Sept. 30, 1 year, 5 %. 500

Christie, James to J. Chr. G. Hupfel Brewing Co. 1st av, No. 605. Store lease. Sept. 28, demand. 600

Churchill, Edward J. to Josephine L. Peyton. Tiffany st, w s, bet Burnett pl and Lafayette road, plots 224-230 "Springhurst" property of Mrs. Corinne Churchill. Sept. 28, notes. 441

Clary, Harry P., Jersey City, N. J., to Timothy Donovan and Alethea V. Harris. Frederick st. P. M. Sept. 28, 1 year. 400

Cohen, Max, of 96 Av C, to Max Cohen, 240 Clinton st. Oliver st, Nos. 42 and 44. P. M. Sept. 29, 1 year. 1,750

Cohen, Max to Louis Lese. Oliver st, e s, 58.8 s Madison st. P. M. Sub. to mort. $20,000. Sept. 18, due Oct. 1, 1896, or installs. 2,500

Same to same. Oliver st, e s, 88.9 s Madison st. P. M. Sub. to mort. $20,000. Sept. 18, due Oct. 1, 1896, or installs. 2,500

Cunningham, Thomas to Charles Deeny. 15th st. P. M. Sept. 1, 3 years or installs, 5 %. 4,000

Cady, James C. to THE EAST RIVER SAVINGS INST. 17th st, s s, 198.11 e 10th av, 30.4x92. P. M. Aug. 4, 1 year, 5 %. 5,000

Cameron, Alexander to Sarah N. Hallock, East Orange, N. J. 96th st, n s, 200 e Amsterdam av, 25x100.11. Sept. 29, due Oct. 1, 1894, 5 %. gold, 20,000

Same to Peter Donald. 96th st, n s, 225 e Amsterdam av, 25x100.11. Sept. 29, due Oct. 1, 1894, 5 %. gold, 20,000

Same to Randolph W. Townsend. 96th st, n s, 250 e Amsterdam av. 25x100.11. Sept. 29, due Oct. 1, 1894, 5 %. gold, 22,000

Cavinato, Natale, Luigi, Guiseppe and Steffano to Jacob New. South 5th av, e s, 100 n Houston st, 24x100. Secures contract for purchase. Sept. 28. 2,500

Corn, Samuel and Henry to THE TITLE GUARANTEE AND TRUST CO. Waverley pl, No. 18, s s, 50 e Greene st, 33.4x81.10x33.4x81.8. Sept. 28, due Dec. 31, 1892. 75,000

Cahn, Caroline to Karl M. Wallach. 73d st, n s, 100 w Av A. P. M. Oct. 1, 5 years, 5½ %. 3,000

Same to same. 73d st, n s, 125 w Av A. P. M. Oct. 1, 5 years, 5½ %. 3,000

Cammeyer, Catherine M. to THE DRY DOCK SAVINGS INST. Bleecker st, n e cor Carmine st, 60x75. June 27, due July 1, 1892, 5 %. 35,000

Camp, Antoinette to Christian F. Tietjen. 7th av, e s, 78 s 26th st, runs east 70 x south 0.9 x east 42 x south 40 x west 112 to av, x north 40.9. Sub. to mort. $35,000. Sept. 30, due Oct. 1, 1894, or installs, 5 %. 5,000

Camp, Elizabeth D. wife of and Hugh N. to THE MUTUAL LIFE INS. CO. Macombs Dam road, n w s, at south cor land of Mrs. Dashwood, West Farms, runs west along said road 239.6 x west still along road 163.5 to centre of private road or lane, x northwest 789 to an angle in said road, x north still along centre of private road 160 x north along same 178 x southwest 64 x north 161.5 to land of Mrs. Dashwood, x southeast 1,219 to beginning, contains 9 7-100 acres, except part released to Mayor, &c., of New York, for st purposes. Already mortgaged to mortgagee for $40,000. Sept. 30, due Oct. 1, 1892. 20,000

Cass, Katharine D. wife of Charles W. to Harriet E. W. wife of George A. Strong. 48th st, No. 34, s s, 452.6 w 5th av, 20.6x100.5. Leasehold. P. M. Sept. 29, installs, 5 %. 22,500

Childs, Childe H. to George W. Montgomery. 54th st. P. M. Oct. 1, 2 years or sooner, 5 %. 10,000

Cohen, George J. to Frederic J. Middlebrook, Brooklyn. 133d st. P. M. Oct. 1, 3 years, 5 %. 8,000

Same to same. Same property. P. M. Sub. to last mort. Oct. 1, 1 year. 1,500

Cooper, William S. to Harriet A. wife of Robert Armour, Newark, N. J. 4th and 10th sts. P. M. Sept. 1, 1 year, 5 %. 25,000

Same to Meyer L. Sire. Same property. Oct. 1, installs, 5 %. 6,500

Davies, Alice to Otto Volkening. 53d st, s s, 275 e 11th av, 125x100.5. Sept 1, 6 months. 33,500

Doherty, Michael to Sarah Farley, Weeks st, s e cor 174th st, 100x100. Sept. 21, 3 years, 5 %. 2,000

Donnelly, John F. to Marie Staats. 75th st, n s, 300 e 2d av, 25x102.2. Sept. 25, 3 years. 2,000

Dunn, Margaret to Abraham H. Sonn. 44th st, n s, 327 e 3d av, runs north 43 x west 22 x north 57.6 x east 25 x south 100.6 to st, x west 3; 44th st, n s, 305 e 3d av, 22x43. Sept. 24, 1 year. 1,047

Dippold, John and Lena his wife to Max Leve and Jacob Lauchheimer. 86th st. P. M. Sept. 20, due Jan. 15, 1893, or sooner. 3,000

Dodge, Edmund, Bayonne, N. J., to THE NEW LIFE INS CO. Amsterdam av. P. M. Sept. 25, due Oct. 1, 1894, 5 %. 20,000

Dooley, Mary to Katie Dooley. 55th st, s s, 212.6 w 9th av, 20.10x81.3x21x83.11. Leasehold. Sept. 29, 5 years. 5,500

Darmody, John to Philipp Geisendorfer. Fairmount pl. P. M. Sept. 29, 1 year, 5 %. 369

Demorest, W. Jennings to George H. Byrd. 21st st. P. M. Sept. 30, due Oct. 1, 1894, 5 %. gold, 28,000

Donnelly, Ellen to Francis P. Burke exr., &c., Michael Donnelly. 30th st. P. M. Sept. 29, 1 year, 5 %. 3,000

Dunning, Edgar F. to THE EMIGRANT IMDUST. SAVINGS BANK. 128th st, n s, 35 e Madison av, 37.6x99.11. Oct. 1, 1 year, 4½ %. 6,000

Durr, John George to Magdalena Frees widow. Courtlandt av. w s, 125 n 151st st, 25x100. Sept. 30, 3 years, 5 %. 3,000

Einhorn, Max to Smith Williamson. Crotona av. P. M. Oct. 1, 1 year, 5 %. 200

Elsbach, Julia to Virginia B. Gibbs, Newport, R. I. 80th st. P. M. Oct. 1, 3 years or installs., 4 %. 7,000

Engelking, Henry and Minnie his wife to Lewis Morris. 10th av, e s, 49.10 s 130th st, 25x100. Sept. 1, 4 years, 5 %. gold, 4,000

Same to Frederick V. Osthoff. Same property. Sept. 1, 1 year. gold, 2,000

Euler, Rudolph to Herman Wronkow. Maiden lane and Liberty st. P. M. Oct. 1, installs, 4½ %. 50,000

Elterich, Louis C. to The American Baptist Home Mission Soc. 134th st. P. M. Sept. 25, 1 year, 5 %. 22,000

Fisher, Jacob F. to THE METROPOLITAN LIFE INS. CO. of New York. 119th st. P. M. Sept. 29, due Oct. 1, 1896, or sooner, 5 %. 3,000

Ferguson, Edwin H. to George Hillen. 125th st, s e cor 7th av, 25x100. Lease. Sept. 29, note. gold, 17,000

Fitzgerald, Luke to Thomas Stokes. 23d st. P. M. Sept. 30, due Oct. 1, 1894, or installs. 7,540

Fitzgerald, Luke to THE UNION DIME SAVINGS INST. 23d st, s s, 350 w 8th av, 25x98.8. Sept. 29, due Nov. 1, 1892, 5 %. 17,000

Florence, Mary to David McClure. 123d st, No. 147, n s, 500 w Lenox av, 25x100.11. Sept. 23, due Sept. 25, 1893, 5 %. 8,500

Same to William Heuermann, Stapleton, S. I. Same p p y. Sept. 24, 1 year. 500

Foley, Elizabeth widow to THE MUTUAL LIFE INS. CO. of New York. 10th st, s s, 200 e 2d av, 25x92.4. Sept. 28, due Sept. 29, 1892. 12,000

Foley, Ellen to Josephine L. Horton, Brooklyn. Southern Boulevard, n w cor Lyon st, 25x103.6x36.8x100. Sept. 26, due Feb. 1, 1892. 400

Franz, Henry to Adelbert J. Howe. Keppler av. P. M. Sept. 25, 3 years or sooner, 5 %. 600

Fuller, Charles A. to David Mitchell. Columbus av, w s, extends from 81st to 82d st, 204.4x134. Sub. to mort. $300,000. July 29, demand. 25,000

Fay, Michael and William Stacom to THE FARMERS' LOAN AND TRUST CO. Grand st, No. 468, n w cor Pitt st, 25x100. Oct. 1, 3 years, 5 %. 51,000

Forster, Elise widow to William Stern. 84th st. P. M. Oct. 1, 3 years or installs, 5 %. 3,250

Friedman, Leo to Matilda Henry. 50th st. P. M. Oct. 1, 1 year or sooner, 5 %. 1,500

Froman, Julia wife of and Jacob to Phebe Pearsall. 79th st, No. 333, n s, 181.10 w 1st av, 27x102.2. Sub. to mort. Oct. 1, 2 years. gold, 3,500

Gillespie, Michael H. to Alfred Roe. 5th av, n e cor 98th st, 50.11x100. Sept. 29, due Oct. 1, 1892, 5 %. 3,000

Gillie, James B. to James Reilly. 21st st, n s, 400.3¾ e 9th av, 24.11x98.9, all; 21st st, n s, 400 e 9th av, 0.3¾x98.9, all title (all being known as No. 327 West 21st st). Oct. 1, 5 years, 5 %. 24,000

Goeren, Mathias and Sophia his wife to Anton Scheuermann. 83d st. P. M. Sept. 29, due Oct. 1, 1894, or installs, 5 %. 3,300

Goldstein, Samuel to The Hahnemann Hospital of the City of New York. 31st st, No. 341, n s, 190 w 1st av. P. M. Oct. 1, 5 years, 5 %. 6,500

Same to same. 31st st, No. 337, n s, 230 w 1st av. P. M. Oct. 1, 5 years, 5 %. 6,500

Same to Bernard Galewski. 31st st, No. 337, n s, 230 w 1st av; 31st st, No. 341, n s, 190 w 1st av. P. M. Sub. to morts. $13,000. Oct. 1, 2 years or sooner. 5,000

Gomprecht, Gustav and Benjamin to THE GREENWICH SAVINGS BANK. Columbus av. P. M. Oct. 1, due May 1, 1894, 5 %. 22,500

Same to Jacob M. Newman. Columbus av. P. M. Sub. to mort. $22,500. Oct. 1, installs, 5 %. 9,000

Gray, Joseph F. to Casper J. Westervelt. 29th st. P. M. Oct. 1, 3 years, 5 %. 11,000

Gilmore, William J. to The Bradley & Currier Co. (Lim.) 134th st, n s, 200 e 7th av, 50x99.11. Sub. to morts. Sept. 18, 3 mouths or sooner. 4,000

Goldbacher, Joseph N. to Henry Durk, Niagara Falls City, New York. 3d av, s s, 75 w Port Morris Branch of N. Y. & Harlem R. R., 25x77x22x91. Sept. 24, 1 year or sooner. 2,091

Guttentag, Caroline wife of and Erhardt to THE NEW YORK SAVINGS BANK. Av A, n e cor 86th st, 20x75. Sept. 25, due Dec. 1, 1896, 4½ %. 10,000

Same to same. Av A, e s, 20 n 86th st, 20x75. Sept. 25, due Dec. 1, 1896, 4½ %. 7,000

Greenberg, David to Charles Hahn. Lewis st. P. M. Sept. 28, due Jan. 1, 1897, 5 %. 13,000

Gault, Mary wife of James to Vassar College, Poughkeepsie, N. Y. 120th st, s s, 125 e 5th av, 37x100.10. Sept. 29, 3 years, 5 %. 35,500

Gault, Mary to Mary McManus. 120th st, s s, 125 e 5th av, 37x100.11. Sub. to morts. $35,500. Sept. 29, 6 months or sooner. 3,290

Same to Peter Patry. Same property. Sub. to morts. $38,720. Sept. 29, 6 months or sooner. 538

Same to Patrick Cassidy and I. Richard Adler, of Cassidy & Adler. Same property. Sub. to morts. $39,258. Sept. 29, due April 1, 1892. 500

Gordon, Mary J. to Anna H. Hudson, Washington, D. C. 21st st. P. M. June 25, due Sept. 30, 1894, 5 %. 12,500

Goetz, J. Oscar to The Mount Morris Co-operative Building and Loan Assoc. Jumel terrace. P. M. Sept. 29, installs, 5 %. 3,000

Same to William Thompson. Same property. P. M. 2d mort. Sept. 28, installs. 1,000

Haydon, James to THE EMIGRANT INDUSTRIAL SAVINGS BANK. 32d st, s s, 56.6 w 9th av, 21.10x49.4. Sept. 29, 1 year, 4½ %. 5,000

Hamann, George to Thomas L. Concklin. 21st st, n s, 60 e 9th av, 17.6x74. Sept. 28, 3 years, 5 %. 5,000

Henderson, Albert C. to Edward Oppenheimer and Edward Hirsh. 77th st. P. M. Sept. 24, 6 months or sooner. 842

Hess, Ida to Sigmund Cohn. 121st st, s s, 300 w 4th av, 17x100.11. Sept. 24, installs. 400

Hughes, John mortgagor with Henry W. Strauss mortgagee. Extension of mort. at 5 %. Sept. 25. nom

Hackett, Joseph T. and Mary A. to Amelia Mosher. West 11th st. P. M. Sept. 30, 3 years or installs, 5 %. 3,000

Hickey, John J. to Peter Doelger. 2d av, No. 564, n e cor 31st st. Lease. Sept. 29, demand. 1,800

Hamma, Maria individ. and extrx. Gregor Hamma to THE GERMAN SAVINGS BANK, New York. West 10th st, n s, 137.6 e Bleecker st, 37.6x95. Sept. 30, due Oct. 1, 1892. 27,000

Hermann, Peter to Lazarus Mannheimer. 114th st. P. M. Oct. 1, 1 year. 1,000

Holahan, Angelo R. wife of and Maurice F. to THE EQUITABLE LIFE ASSUR. SOC, United States. 55th st. n s, 80 e Lexington av, 20x100.5. Oct. 1, due Jan. 1, 1893. gold, 15,000

Same to Rosina Boll. 55th st. P. M. Oct. 1, 3 years. 1,500

Houck, Amelia to Mary A. and Mary E. Van Zandt. Boston Post road, s e s, 100 s w West Farms to Westchester road, 25x100. Sept. 30, due Jan. 1, 1895, 5 %. 1,000

Howell, Annabella wife of George C. to Nathaniel Reynolds, Unionville, Westchester County, N. Y. Garden st, n s, 220 w 3d av, 24.6x100. Sept. 30, 3 years, 5 %. 2,000

Hurwitz, Rebecca J. and Harris Levy to Hulda Wittner, Sigmund and Emanuel Glauber. Georck st, No. 31. P. M. Oct. 1, 5 years or installs. 4,000

Israel, Hyman and Simon Bing. Jr., to THE GERMAN-AMERICAN REAL ESTATE TITLE GUARANTEE CO. 121st st, n s, 150 w 1st av, 25x100.11. Sept. 23, 3 years, 5 %. 10,000

Inkeles, Max to Karl M. Wallach. Cherry st. P. M. Sept. 25, demand. 8,000

Jones, Ella L., Rockville Centre, L. I., to THE WEST SIDE SAVINGS BANK. 48th st, No. 331, n s, 332 w 8th av, 18x100.5. Sept. 22, due Nov. 1, 1892, 5 %. 5,000

Jenkins, Thomas J. and George to George E. Hyatt, Brooklyn. 118th st, s s, 100 e 8th av, 200x100.11. Sept. 28, due May 25, 1892, or sooner. 5,000

Joseph, Fanny mortgagor with Tarrant Putnam and ano. trustees for Geraldine W. Goddard mortgagees. Extension of mort. Dec. 9, 1890. nom

Joseph, Fanny to Solomon Barnett. 94th st, n s, 137.6 w 3d av, 18.9x100.8. Sept. 30, due Dec. 1, 1893, or sooner. gold, 2,500

Jenkins, Silvanus F. to D. Willis James 86th st, No. 138 W. P. M. Sept. 30, 3 years, 4 %. 27,500

Kern, Henry to John D. Jones (Marine underwriter). 104th st, s s, 125 w 2d av, 25x100.11. Oct. 1, 1 year, 5 %. 5,000

King, Will L., Brooklyn, to Anna M. Z. wife of Count Charles F. de Mountsaulnin, Paris. 170th st, s w cor Brook av, 25x100. Sept. 28, 3 years, 5 %. 1,200

Klett, John C. to Cecilia wife of Martin Keppler 170th st, s s, 150 e 11th av, 25x95. Oct. 1, 3 years, 5 %. 2,000

Kohn, Daniel to Joseph Matzke and Caroline his wife, College Point, L. I. 12th st, n s. P. M. Sept. 8, due Oct. 1, 1894, 5 %. 11,000

Kuebler, William F. to Catharina Bescher. 104th st, No. 246, s s, 100 w 2d av, 25x100.11. Sept. 30, due Jan. 1, 1893. 1,000

Kaplan, Aaron mortgagor with Bernhard Silberstein mortgagee. Agreement to postpone date for payment of first installment. Sept. 29. nom

Kirshbaum, Marks and Harris Rosenthal to Fisher Lewine. 18th st. P. M. Sept. 30, 6 months or sooner. 3,000

Kraus, Sigmund to Lina Rossman extrx. Nathan Rossman. 7th st. P. M. Sept. 22, 5 years, 5 %. 10,000

Kaiser, John and Mary his wife to Mary Kraser. Elton av, s w cor 155th st, 25x100. Sept. 28, 3 years, 5 %. 1,000

Knight, Kate P. wife of Azariah L., Orange, N. J., to George W. Van Slyck. Spruce st, n w cor Gold st. 21.5x27.5x23.11x27.1, with strip 0.3x27.1 on Gold st. Sept. 26, 3 years. 8,000

Kohn, Arnold and Edmund to Jennie N. Zucker. 93d st. P. M. Sept. 28, due Oct. 1, 1896, or installs, 5 %. 5,000

Keil, Francis to Adolph G. Hupfel. 162d st, s s, 300 e Morris av, 125x115. Sept. 24, 1 year. 4,500

Klein, Benedict A. to Jenny Diamant. Monroe st. P. M. Sub. to mort. $12,000. Sept. 25, due Oct. 1, 1896, or sooner. 5,500

Lee, Joseph H. to Ida Keck. Hull av. P. M. Oct. 1, 1 year, 5 %. 420

Lennen, James to Euphemia A. Nichols. Jane st. P. M. Oct. 1, 5 years, 4½ %. 4,000

Lowenfeld, Pincus and Samuel Goldstein to Samuel Kempner. Delancey st. P. M. Oct. 1, 1 year, 5 %. 13,000

Same to Israel L. Prager. Sheriff st. P. M. Oct. 1, 1 year. 2,500

Lee, Franklin, Buffalo, N. Y., to THE ALBANY SAVINGS BANK Columbus (9th) av, e s, extends from 119th to 120th st, 201.10x100. Aug. 19, 5 years, 4½ %. 120,000

Luyster, Cornelius W. to THE TITLE GUARANTEE AND TRUST CO. 74th st, s s, 150 w Central Park West, 25x102.2. Sept. 26, due Sept. 28, 1894, 5 %. 32,500

Same to same. 74th st, s s, 175 w Central Park West, 25x102.2. Sept. 26, due Sept. 28, 1894, 5 %. 32,500

Same to same. 74th st, s s, 200 w Central Park West, 25x102.2. Sept. 26, due Sept. 28, 1894, 5 %. 25,000

Same to same. 74th st, s s, 225 w Central Park West, 25x102.2. Sept. 26, due Sept. 28, 1894, 5 %. 32,500

Landers, Edward J. to Fritz Bachmann, Clifton, S. I. South st, n e cor Moore st, 11.9x99.10x11.8x100.1. Sept. 17, 1 year. gold, 5,600

Langdon, Helen to THE MUTUAL LIFE INS CO., New York. Maiden lane. P. M. April 30, due Oct. 1, 1892, 5 %. 45,000

Lewine, Fisher to James E. Dougherty. Madison st. P. M. Sept. 25, due Sept. 29, 1892, 5 %. 21,000

Luckey, Christian to Beadleston & Woerz. Broad st, No 50, basement. Lease. Sept. 30, demand. 893

Levy, Samuel and Lina his wife to Frederick Graf and Maria his wife. 82d st. P. M. Sub. to mort. $9,000. Sept. 30, due Oct. 1, 1890, or installs. 7,000

McArdle, Henry to The Railroad Co-operative Building and Loan Assoc. Suburban st. P. M. Sept. 29, installs, 5 %. 4,500

McCormick, Frank to THE METROPOLITAN LIFE INS. CO. of New York. 123d st, s e cor Lexington av, 35x100.11. Sept. 29, due Oct. 1, 1896, 5 %. 55,000

Metzgar, Addie to William H. Caswell. Long Island Sound, &c., near Hunts Points. P. M. July 30, due May 1, 1894, 5 %. 50,000

McVitty, James to Peter Doelger. Spring st. No. 333. Store lease. Sept. 28, demand. 5,000

Meyer, John H. and Peter F. to Dorathea Meyer. 146th st, n s, 325 e Willis av, 75x100. Aug. 15, 5 years, 5 %. 2,500

Marks, Samuel and Harris Needle to Lazarus Levy. Jefferson st, No. 34, w s, 25 n Monroe st, 25x104.4. Collateral for notes. Sept. 25. 2,500

Marks, Elizabeth wife of Gabriel to Solomon Friend. East Broadway, No. 217, s s, 24x87.6. Sub. to mort. $13,000. Sept. 28, 1 year. 2,500

McComb, Jane P. to Charlotte M. Rullmann. Washington st, No. 831. Leasehold. Sept. 19 2 years or sooner. 2,000

McDonald, Mary M. and John mortgagors with Charles Earle mortgagee. Extension of mort. July 27. nom

McGurran, Arthur J. to Thomas J. McKee. 2d av, n e cor 37th st, 24.8x64.3. All title. Aug. 31, 1 year, 5 %. 500

McGirr, Peter to Jacob Rieser. 11th av, n w cor 37th st, 49.4x100. Sept. 25, demand. 3,500

Monaghan, Martin C. and Ann his wife to Edward and Henry Hirsh. 93d st, s s, 325 e Columbus av, 75x100.8. June 5, due June 1, 1892. 27,000

Morse, Sidney E. to Matilda C. McVicker. Nassau st, n e cor Beekman st, 85.3x69.11x85.2x69.6. Sub. to morts. Sept. 3, 1890, demand, 5 %. 30,000

Myers, Eva wife of and Lewis to Adolph S. Kalischer. Broome st, s e cor Norfolk st, 25x51.7. Sept. 1, 4 months. 6,000

Martin, John and Robert to Kate A. Wetherill widow, Garden City, L. I. Canal st, No. 383, n s, 21.6 w South 5th av, 21.6x78.7x21.7x80. Oct. 1, 5 years, 4½ %. gold, 15,000

McCarthy, William H. to Arthur D. Weekes and ano. exrs. Arthur M. Jones. Park av, e s, 75.8 s 125th st, 63.2x90. Aug. 6, due Sept. 1, 1892, 5 %. gold, 24,000

McKenzie, Alexander devisee Alexander McKenzie dec'd, Washington, D. C., to Angelo Morello. 4th st, No. 16, s w cor Mercer st, 25x91.1x25x91.2; 4th st, No. 35, n w cor Greene st, 25x94; Broadway, No. 765, leasehold; 9th st, No. 74 E., leasehold. All title. May 28, installs. 3,000

Monaghan, Mary E. widow to William H. Barney, Scranton, Pa. Bronx River road, n w cor Willard av. Sept. 26, 1 year, 5 %. See Conveys. 400

Moser, Robert to Samuel Kempner. Av A and 74th st. P. M. Oct. 1, installs, 5 %. 1,275

Nathan, Marcus, Samuel Cohen and Clarence M. Fowler to Annie M. Harrison. 161st st, n s, 200 e Morris pl or av, 3 lots, each 16.8x146. 3 morts., each $500. Sept. 15, 1 year. 1,500

O'Gorman, Edward J. to David Webster exr. Caroline Webster. Belmont av, s e s, 185.6 n e John st. P. M. Sept. 24, 2 years, 5½ %. 700

Same to same. Belmont av, s e s, 80.2 n e John st. P. M. Sept. 24, 2 years, 5½ %. 1,400

Ottiwell, Sarah C. to Anna M. Z. wife of Count Charles F. de Montsaulnin, Paris. Webster av, w s, 100x84 to Crestline av, x100.6x74.6, being lots 7, 8, 9 and 10 map W. E. M. Zborowsky property, 23d and 24th Wards. Sept. 28, 3 years, 5 %. 1,000

Palumbo, James to Morris Propper. Mott st, No. 193. P. M. Oct. 1, 4 years. 3,500

Same to Morris Kerner and Marcus Jalien. Same property. Oct. 1, 1 year. 1,000

Parsons, William E., Jr., trustee for Florence A. and Mary A. Parsons to Mary S. Davis. 132d st. P. M. Sept. 25, 2 years, 5 %. 1,875

Pitt, Alfred S. to THE GERMAN SAVINGS BANK, City New York. 4th av, n e cor 28th st, 23.5x80. Sept. 25, 1 year. 4,000

Posthoff, Frederick W. to Miriam H. C. Cannon. Forest av, w s, 49 n 161st st, 21x90. Sept. 25, 3 years, 5 %. gold, 1,500

Person, Lars J. to Martha B. Randall. West st, n e s, east ½ lot 29 map of Wardsville, West Farms, 25x100. Sept. 26, 3 years, 5 % 200

Piatigorsky, Morris to Charles Malawista. Oliver st. P. M. Sept. 15, 3 years or sooner. 2,000

Padula, Francesco to Hervey D. La Coste. 149th st, n s, 250.3 e Morris av, 25x100. Sept. 29, 3 months. 300

Peebles, James M. to New York & Wakefield Co-operative Building and Loan Association. Rockfield st, n s, 825 e Marion av, 25x126.4. Sept. 29, installs, 5 %. 2,750

Pinckney, Harry C. to George Ehret. 105th st, No. 175 E. Lease. Sept. 29, demand. 1,500

Powers, Jesse W. and Abraham Steers with Maria H. Rider all mortgagees. Agreement as to priority of morts. made by Tillie E. Smith. Sept. 30. nom

Quinn, Elizabeth widow to John J. Gleason, Flushing, L. I. 79th st, s s, 194 e 1st av, 25x102.2. Sept. 25, 1 year. 1,500

Reeder, Augusta and Edward F. to Michael J. Walsh. South st, No. 391, n s, 75 e Jackson st, 25x90. Sept. 25, due Feb. 6, 1893, or sooner. 350

Ramsey, Peter N. to Joseph F. Stier. Madison av, Nos. 136 and 138, n w cor 31st st, 49.7x95. Sept. 25, demand. 6,400

Riker, William H. to Minnie M. Pullman widow. Riverside Drive and 108th st. P. M. Sub. to mort. $50,000. July 17, installs, 5 %. 52,000

Rosen, Lena wife of Meyer to Rachel Purdy. 11th av, e s, 20 n 171st st, 25x100. Sept. 25, 3 years. 1,200

Rosenbaum, Louis to August Hassey. Av B, w s, 40.2 s 6th st, 47.1x69.6x13x60.1. Aug. 12, due July 1, 1894. 3,000

Robinson, Thomas J. to Joseph F. Stier. Evelyn pl. P. M. Sept. 28, due Sept. 1, 1894, or sooner, 5 %. 2,000

Same to Francis J. Thomson. Same property. P. M. Sub. to last mort. September 28, 1 year. 1,000

Rosendorf, Morris with Solomon Stern. Agreement that an assignment of mortgage made by party first part to party second is given as collateral security for $9,000 to be absolute power if said sum is not duly paid, &c. Feb. 19, 1891.

Reidy, Michael and Mary E. his wife to THE CO-OPERATIVE BUILDING BANK, New York. Columbia av, s s, 25 e Jefferson av, 25x75. June 30, installs, 5 1-5 %. 1,600

Rahill, James to Sophia wife of Carl G. A. Hoble. 169th st, n s, 150 e 11th av, 25x81.7. Sept. 30, due Oct. 1, 1894, 5 %. gold, 2,750

Reilly, Edward to THE EMIGRANT INDUST. SAVINGS BANK. 18th st, s s, 150 w 9th av, 20.7x92. P. M. Oct. 1, 1 year, 4½ %. 6,000

Roberts, Arthur mortgagor with Gustav H. Schwab and ano. exrs. Gustav Schwab mortgagees. Extension of reduced mort. in gold. Oct. 1. nom

Rockwood, Araminta wife of and George G. to Edward Kaiser. 43d st, s s, 380 e 8th av, 20x100.4. 2d mort. Oct. 1, 2 years. 7,000

Rockwood, Arminta to Joseph F. Feitner, Carlstadt, N. J. Same property. Oct. 1, 3 years, 5 %. gold, 21,000

Rogers, Josiah to Sarah Farley Goerck st, No. 72, e s, 275 n Delancey st, 25x99.4. Sept. 24, due Sept. 30, 1894, 5 %. 10,000

Rohrs, Frederick to Grace T. Wells, Franklin, N. J. Madison av, s s cor 132d st. P. M. Sept. 24, 6 months. gold, 10,000

Same to same. Madison av, e s, 25 s 132d st. P. M. Sept. 24, 6 months. gold, 8,000

Same to same. Madison av, e s, 50 s 132d st. P. M. Sept. 24, 6 months. gold, 8,000

Same to same. Madison av, e s, 74.11 s 132d st. P. M. Sept. 24, 6 months. gold, 8,000

Same to same. 132d st, s s, 96 e Madison av. P. M. Sept. 24, 6 months. gold, 6,000

Same to same. 132d st, s s, 123 e Madison av. P. M. Sept. 24, 6 months. gold, 6,000

Same to Eliza S. Bibby, Baltimore, Md. Madison av, s e cor 132d st. P. M. Sept. 24, 1 year. gold, 1,500

Rooney, Christopher to George Ehret. 2d av, s e cor 70th st. P. M. Sept. 30, due Oct 1, 1892, 5 %. 13,500

Rose, Achilles to Smith Williamson. Crotona av. P. M. Oct. 1, 1 year, 5 %. 290

Rosenthal, Leonore to Harris Rosenthal. 18th st. P. M. Sept 30, due Oct 1, 1895. 6,500

Roosevelt, Samuel M. to Dore Lyon. 5th av. P. M. Sub. to mort. $35,000. Oct. 1, installs. 11,750

Sawyer, Belle M. wife of and Albert F. to William E. D. Stokes. West End av, n w cor 86th st. P. M. Sept. 15, 3 years, 5 %. 50,000

Same to same. Same property. P. M. Sept. 15, installs, 5 %. 25,000

Schafer, Mary wife of and Simon to Joseph Holl and Anna his wife. 121st st. No. 445, n s, 125 w Av A, 25x100.10. Sept. 30, due Feb. 10, 1892. 2,000

Schnabel, Edmund to The Eureka Co-operative Savings and Loan Assoc., New York. Jennings st. P. M. Aug. 28, installs. 5 %. 3,600

Schnitzer, Robert C. to Peter Schupp. 21st st, s s, 211.6 w 2d av. P. M. Sub. to mort. $4,500. Sept. 29, due Jan. 1, 1892, 5 %. 4,000

Same to Charles Ruff. Same property. P. M. Sept. 29, due Oct. 1, 1894, or installs. 4,500

Schuyler, Gerald L. to Samuel Colcord. West End av and 83d st. May 19, due March 30, 1892. See Conveys. 50,000

Same to same. Same property. P. M. May 19, 1891, due March 30, 1894. 10,000

Seabold, Caroline wife of Jacob to Mary A. Halloran. 134th st, No. 688, s s, 317 e Willis av, 16.8x100 in two courses. Sept. 28, 3 years, 5 %. 6,000

Shepard, Richard and Annie his wife to Thomas L. Concklin. 49th st, n s, 500 w 10th av, 25x100.5. Sept. 30, 3 years, 5 %. 12,000

Screven, John H., Westchester, N. Y., to Robert Winthrop. 110th st, n s, 275 e 7th av, 75x100.11. Sept. 22, due Sept. 29, 1894, 5 %. 20,000

Smith, Elizabeth K. to William Wilkening. 123d st, s s, 190.6 e 7th av, 74.6x100.11. Sept. 28, 1 year or sooner. 1,450

Stephens, Laura J., Yonkers, N. Y., to Benjamin F. Raynor, Jr. 115th st. P. M. Sept. 24, due Oct. 1, 1893, or sooner, 5 %. 17,000

Same to same. Same property. Sept. 24, due Oct. 1, 1892, or sooner. 23,000

Smith, Kate A. to Alfred C. Cheney trustee for holders of notes. 135th st, s s, 168.4 w 7th av, 17.6x99.11. Sub. to mort. $11,000. Sept. 25, note. 5,000

Smith, Samuel W. B. to John A. Deraismes. Downing st. P. M. Sept. 28, due Sept. 30, 1892, or sooner, 5 %. 9,000

Schmitt, Louis to William J. McPherson. Suburban st, n s, 83.11 w Briggs av, 25x100. Sept. 29, 5 years. 500

Schmitt, George to William J. McPherson. Suburban st. P. M. Sept. 29, 1 year. 500

Strauss, Samuel to Louisa Fischer. 2d av, e s, 49 4 s 40th st. P. M. Sub. to mort. $10,000. Sept. 30, installs, 5 % 17,500

Strauss, Emanuel to Thomas C. T. Crain, as Chamberlain of City of New York. 3d st, s s, 160.9 w Av D, 22.7x106. Sept. 29, 2 years, 4½ %. 7,400

Streeter, Emma A. to Caroline M. Phraner, Summit, N. J. 72d st, n s, 210 e 3d av, 15x102.2. Sept. 28, due Dec. 1, 1894, 5 %. gold, 1,000

Scherding, Christian to THE HARLEM SAVINGS BANK. 3d av, e s, 112 n 140th st, 28x111x25x123.8. Already mortgaged to mortgagee. Sept. 25, 1 year, 5 % 2,000

Stellman, Sophia M. C. to Ellen M. Harlow. 104th st. P. M. Sept. 22, installs, 5 %. 3,500

Stern, Libet to Sarah Feiner. Attorney st. P. M. Sept. 28, 2 years. 12,000

Schoenthal, Malchan to Francis Mitchell. 108th st, s s, 25.6 e 4th av. P. M. Sept. 25, 5 years, 5 % 4,500

Schwarzler, August F. to Francis C. Devlin. Broome st, n w cor Tompkins st, 125x75. March 10, demand. 836

Sheridan, Edward to Joseph Ferri. Waverley pl. P. M. Sept. 25, 5 years, 5 %. 2,000

Shipman, Herbert A. to William E. M. Zborowski, Melton Mowbray, Eng. Webster av, e s, 105 8 n Anna pl, 15.4x90. Sept. 15, 3 years or sooner, 5 %. 3,500

Silberberg, Simon and Hannah his wife to Jacob Abrahams. Broome st, No. 171, s s, 120 w Attorney st, 20x75. Sept. 24, 2 years. 1,000

Simmons, Charles H., Brooklyn, to Harmon W. Hendricks. Varick st, w s, 24 s Vestry st, 22x62 3. Sept. 25, due Feb. 1, 1893, 5 % 3,000

Simon, Moritz, Denver, Col., to THE TITLE GUARANTEE AND TRUST CO. Park row, No. 98, s s, 119.10 w New Chambers st, runs west 19 x south 31 x still south 44.2 x east 18.6 x northwest 1.1 x east 3.4 x north 44 1 x still north 29 4 to beginning. Sept. 15, due Sept. 24, 1896, 4½ %. gold, 15,000

Simonds, Alexander B. to Robert H. Neilson and ano. trustees Mary A. McClelland. 5th av. P. M. Sept. 10, due Sept. 25, 1892, 5 %. 50,000

Schenectady Street Railway Co. to THE CENTRAL TRUST CO., New York. Railway property in Schenectady, N. Y., with all rights and franchises, by consent of stockholders. Issues bonds. Sept. 1. 300,000

Sheridan, James F. and Patrick H. and James S. Segrave to Thomas C. Cornell, Yonkers, N. Y. Field st, Rock st, Forest st, Hill st and Beech st. P. M. Aug 21, 1 year, 5 %. 27,000

Smith, Archibald to William Rankin. 35th st, No. 440, s s, 475 w 9th av, 25x98.9. Sub. mort. $20,000. Oct. 1, 1 year. 4,800

Same to Ernest H. Herb. Same property. Oct. 1, 5 years, 5 %. 20,000

Solomon, Louis to John Losel and Theresia his wife. 2d st. P. M. Oct. 1, installs, 5 %. 2,500

Same to same. Same property P. M. Oct. 1, 8 years, 5 %. 8,000

Stoehr, Christian to Herman F. Kanenbley et al. exrs. August Kanenbley. 38th st, n s, 125 e 2d av, 25x87.6x27.7x99.1. Oct. 1, 3 years, 5 %. 14,000

Same to George H. Droste. 38th st, No. 311, n s, 175 e 2d av, 25x64.4x27.7x75.11. Oct. 1, 3 years, 5 %. 10,000

Same to same. 38th st, No. 309, n s, 150 e 2d av, 25x75.11x27.3x87.6. Oct. 1, 3 years, 5 %. 10,000

Stoeper, Anna C. to Michael Wielandt and Johanna Pfenning. 13th st. P. M. Oct. 1, 4 years, 5 %. 4,500

Sutphen, Jr., John S. to John Livingston. 83d st. P. M. Oct. 1, 1 year, 5 %. 5,000

Thorn, Julia A. wife of Thomas H. to Robert A. B. Dayton trustee for Mary M. Martindale. Edenwood late 6th av, centre line, 95 n Highbridge st, 50x133 to Croton aqueduct. Oct. 1, 5 years or installs, 5 %. 1,700

Trinkans, William to Margaretha Speckhardt. Av A, w s, 76.10 n 82d st, 25.4x80.5. Oct. 1, 3 years, 5 %. 1,000

Trainor, John to John S. Reiner. Av B, s e s, part lot 102 map of Prospect Hill Estate, Fordham, 25x125. Sept. 28, 3 years. 200

The First Reformed Presbyterian Congregation of the City of New York to Eliza L. Edgar widow. 119th st, n s, 306 w 5th av, 70x100.11. Sept. 30, 3 years, 5 %. 20,000

Thompson, Margaret A. wife of and Hugh B. to THE GREENWICH SAVINGS BANK. 35th st, n s, 200 w Lexington av, 12.6x98.9. Sept. 15, due Oct. 1, 1894, 5 %. 5,000

Thompson, William W., Peil, Mary G. and Clendinen heirs Mary C. Thompson to Henry De F. Weekes. Pearl st, No. 168, s e cor Pine st, 20.7x—x20.7x47.3. Sept. 29, due Oct. 1, 1893. 1,500

Same also Alice W. wife of Clendinen Thompson to THE INSTITUTION FOR THE SAVINGS OF MERCHANTS' CLERKS. Same property. Sept. 25, due Aug. 15, 1894, 4½ %. 16,000

Van Brunt, Thomas C. to Alfred C. Cheney trustee. 136th st, s s, 100 e 8th av, 152.6x99 11; 136th st, s s, 269.2 e 8th av, 33.4x99.11; 136th st, s s, 336.8 e 8th av, 34.2x99.11. Sub. to morts. $185,859. Sept. 25, notes. 25,000

Van Cleve, Kathrine to Thomas Hagan. Walton av, n e cor 149th st, 79.11x54 1x86.10x48. Sub. to morts. $49,627. Sept. 24, demand. 1,000

Same to Bradley & Currier Co. (Lim.) Same property. Sub. to morts. $25,694. Sept. 24, 6 months. 3,985

Same to William Ormiston. Same property. Sub. to mort. $20,000. Sept. 24, demand. 5,692

Same to Susan W. Duncan. Same property. Sept. 24, due Dec. 1, 1894. 20,000

Woods, Thomas to Lydia S. Horn. 132d st, n s, 150 w Lenox av, 25x99.11. Sub. to mort. $5,250. Sept. 30, 5 years, 5 %. gold, 5,750

Walter, Elizabeth M. wife of George to The Mount Morris Co-operative Building and Loan Assoc. Bristow st, w s, 150 n Jennings st, runs north 22.6 x west 59 3 x west again 28 x south 24.2 x east 87.2. P. M. Sept. 28, installs. 5 %. 2,000

Winter, Frederick to Claus Karsten. Lexington av, w s, 51 n 108th st, 25x75. Sept. 24, 2 years, 5 %. 3,000

Same to John C. Fayen. Same property. Sept 24, 2 years, 5 %. 5,000

Wood, Mary Y. to Mary A. D. Lange and ano. exrs. John H. Lange. 129th st, n s, 300 w Lenox av, 75x99.11. Sept. 28, 1 year. 17,000

Weber, Caroline A. wife of and William F. to New York Produce Exchange. 3d av, s e s, 51.4 s w Rose st, runs south 188 to Bergen av, x southwest 25 x northwest 100 x southwest 25 x northwest 88 to 3d av, x northeast 50 to beginning. Sept. 25, 1 year, 5 %. 15,000

Walder, Aaron to Simon Sigel. Allen st. P. M. Sept. 30, due Aug. 1, 1892. 2,000

Ward, Mary to Bertha Unger. 120th st. P. M. Oct. 1, 3 years, 5 %. 7,500

Warnecke, Frederick and Martha his wife to James Muir. West 10th st. P. M. Oct. 1, 2 years or sooner, 5½ %. 6,000

Wehcebrock, Maria to William H. Jackson. 115th st, s s, 235 e 3d av. P. M. Oct. 1, 5 years, 5 %. 15,000

Same to same. 115th st, s s, 200 e 3d av P. M. Oct. 1, 5 years, 5 %. 15,000

Weicker, Conrad to The Model Building and Loan Assoc., Mott Haven. Tinton av, s e s, 175 s w Pontiac st, 25x105. P. M. Sept. 29, installs. 2,000

Weinberg, Joseph to Anita P. Echeverria. Av A, e s, 38.9 n 14th st, 19.1x72.4. Oct. 1, 5 years, 5 %. 5,000

Wertheimer, Sarah to Max Frankenheim. 69th st, No. 337 E. P. M. Sub. to mort. $12,000. Oct. 1, installs, 5 %. 4,000

White, Charles J. to Bernheimer & Schmid. Southern Boulevard, No. 508, s e cor Lincoln av. Saloon lease. Sept. 10, note, demand. 3,500

Wittenborg, Gustav and Catharina to William H. Jackson. 115th st, s s, 175 e 3d av. P. M. Oct. 1, 5 years, 5 %. 16,000

Same to same. 115th st, s s, 150 e 3d av. P. M. Oct. 1, 5 years, 5 %. 16,000

Same to Frederick Schuck. 115th st, s s, 175 e 3d av. P. M. Oct. 1, 3 years, 5 %. 5,000

Same to same. 115th st, s s, 150 e 3d av. P. M. Oct. 1, 3 years, 5 %. 5,000

Zickler, Ignatz to Peter Doelger. Av D, No. 42. Store lease. Oct. 1, demand. 1,000

KINGS COUNTY.

SEPTEMBER 24, 25, 26, 28, 29, 30.

Arnold, Konrad to Michael Roth. Hopkinson av, e s, 125 s McDougal st, 20x100. July 1, 3 years, 5 %. $1,000

Axelrod, Jacob, David and Isaac to Charles J. Bobe. Stone av, e s, 150 n Sutter av, 25x100. Sept. 25, 5 years 2,000

Arens, Henry mortgagor with Milton A. Straw mortgagee. Extension of mort. Sept. 29. nom

Bannon, Patrick to Julia Costello. Fulton st. P. M. June 7, 1890, demand. 1,000

Battermann, John F. to Henry Battermann. Clarkson st, s s, 1,700 e Main st, 25x200. Sept. 29, due Oct. 1, 1896, 5 % 2,000

Beasley, David S. to The Title Guarantee and Trust Co. Lexington av, n s, 200 e Throop av, 2 lots, each 15x100. 2 morts., each $2,000. Sept. 25, 3 years, 5 %. 4,000

Same to same. Lexington av, n s, 245 e Throop av, 15x100. Sept. 25, 3 years, 5 %. 2,000

Bernard, John to August Siefers. Hamburg av, south cor Jefferson st, 25x75. Aug. 31, 1 year, 5 %. 1,000

Same to Mathias Bernard. Same property. Aug. 31, 1 year, 5 %. 1,000

Same to Peter Bernard. Same property. Aug. 31, 1 year, 5 %. 1,000

Bird, Sarah to Hannah Pritchard and Elizabeth Wiseburn. De Kalb av, n s, 38.8 e Schenck st, 18.9x80x20.1x80. Sept. 23, 1 year. 800

Bishop, Eli H. to The Title Guarantee and Trust Co. Putnam av, s s, 95 w Stuyvesant av, 100x100. Sept. 24, demand. 37,500

Bishop, Elizabeth J. to The German Savings Bank, Brooklyn. Marcy av, e s, 34.8 n Lexington av, 16.4x66.11. Sept. 29, due Dec. 1, 1892, 5 %. 1,000

Blanke, Martha to Franz Gauen. McDougal st, n s, 133.11 w Howard av, 41.1x100x47.2x100.2. Sept. 23, 5 years or installs, 5 %. 1,300

Blohme, J. Henry to Henry Bielenberg. Myrtle av, s w cor Sumner av. P. M. Sept. 23, due Sept. 23, 1896, 5 %. gold, 24,500

Boegol, Louise to William Lindemann. Hart st. P. M. Sept. 26, due Oct. 1, 1896, or sooner, 5 %. 2,900

Bragdon, Edward O. to Anna M. Beach. Ashford st. P. M. Sept. 23, 1 year. 350

Bryant, Thomas B. to The Title Guarantee and Trust Co. Greene av, s w cor Sumner av, 27x100. Sept. 28, 1 year, 5 %. 17,500

Brown, Leopold to Peter Garms, Jr. Humboldt st. P. M. Sept. 25, installs, 5 %. 7,000

Burke, Richard to T. C. Lyman & Co. North 7th st, s w cor Berry st, 25x100. Sept. 26, 1 year, 5 %. 1,941

Bloodgood, Joseph to James McKane. East 22d st, e s, 382.2 n Voorhees av, 40x85.2 to Anthony st, 42.3x98.10, Gravesend. Aug. 12, 5 years. 1,500

Burke, Joseph J. to Joseph B. Stillwell. 1st st. P. M. Sept. 28, installs. 4,500

Benedict, Emma H. to Ann P. Benedict. Monroe st, s s, 134.4 e Lewis av, 16.4x100. May 7, 1 year, 5 %. 1,000

Berger, Joseph and Samuel Michel to Mary L. Berry. Christopher av, e s, 175 s Eastern Parkway, 25x100. Sept. 25, 3 years. 2,000

Berlinger, William and Christian to Adam Henrich. Harman st, s s, 350 e Central av, 25x100 Sept. 11, 1 year. 1,000

Bernard, John to The Williamsburgh Savings Bank. Hamburg av, south cor Jefferson st, 25x75. Aug. 21, 1 year, 5 %. 5,000

Beryman, Charles P. to Nellie A. Hiers. 67th st, e s, 100 5 n 5th av, 25x100.2, New Utrecht. Sept. 30, 2 years. 1,000

Bierds, William H. to The Mechanics' Bank, Brooklyn. President st, s s, 100 e 3d av, 100x100. Sept. 29, note. 3,000

Booden, Patrick to Cornelius N. Hoagland. Nostrand av, w s, 106 n Madison st, 20x100. Sept. 29, due Nov. 1, 1894, 5 %. gold, 3,730

Booth, Isabelle B. wife of and John N. to Paul W. Ledoux. Covert st, s s, 90 e Central av. 6 lots, each 18x100. 6 morts., each $3,000. Sept. 15, 1 year, 5 %. 18,000

Brownell, Asa C. to Frank A. Barnaby. State st, n s, 250 e Hoyt st, 100x100. Builders loan. Sept. 25, demand. 55,650

Caulfield, Thomas to Jacob W. Erregger. Hale av, e s, at intersection with n e line of centre line from air chamber to mouth-piece, as shown on map entitled Brooklyn Water Works, Location of Water Works and Force Tubes, runs north 75 x east 100 x south 220 x northwest 175. Sept. 23, 3 years. 250

Same to Phebe E. wife of George B. Sharpe. Same property. Sept. 4, 5 years. 1,500

Cochran, Henry H. to Edwin O. Phelps. Broadway and Vanderveer st. P. M. Sept. 22, due Jan. 1, 1892. 8,500

Connor, Katy wife of Michael to Jennie L. Burton. Wallabout st, s s, 225 e Bedford av, 20x75. Sept. 29, due Sept. 1, 1892. gold, 250

Craig, George A. to William Duryea, Nyack, N. Y. Halsey st, s e s, 100 n e Central av, 180x100. Sept. 30, 6 months. 22,800

Catland, Mary wife of and Robert to Mary E. Schaefer guard. of Johanna, Jeremiah and Kate Roach. 39th st, s s. P. M. Sept. 21, 5 years or sooner, 5 %. 1,000

Cherrie, Alexander to Jane Moffat. Vanderbilt st, Flatbush. P. M. Sept. 28, due Jan. 28, 1899, 5 %. 1,050

Chidwick, Richard to Reuben R. and Warren L. Brush, Huntington, L. I. 5th av, s e s, 41.8 s w 22d st, 16.8x100. Sept. 25, 3 years, 5 %. 1,500

Same to Smith Sammis, Huntington, L. I. 5th av, e s, 25 s w 22d st, 16.8x100. Sept. 25, 3 years, 5 %. 1,500

Clark, Blanche E. to The West Brooklyn Land and Improvement Co. 15th av, east cor 57th st. P. M. April 21, due March 24, 1895, 5 %. 787

Same to same. 57th st, n e s, 100 s e 15th av. P. M. Sept. 19, due July 1, 1895, 5 %. 490

Collins, Patrick to Frederick W. Hearn. Hendrix st, w s, 150 s Belmont av, 25x100. Sept. 21, 3 years. 1,500

Colyer, John to Nellie A. Hiers. 9th av, s e s, 80 n e 64th st, runs southeast 80 x northeast 20 x southeast 295.6 to Fort Hamilton av, x northeast 79 3 x northwest 397.11 to av, x southwest 16.10, New Utrecht. Sept. 25, 1 year. 200

Costello, Jeremiah to The Equitable Co-operative Building and Loan Assoc. Baltic st. P. M. Sept 22, installs. 6,750

Cring, Rebecca E. to George W. Adams, Hempstead, L. I. Aberdeen st, n w s, 100 s w Bushwick av, 20.2x106. Sept. 22, installs. 1,000

Crossmann, Greenleaf W. to Louise Kathe. St. Marks pl. P. M. Sept. 23, 5 years, 5 %. 2,600

Cuming, Elizabeth to Abraham Mandeville. 56th st, n e s, 420 n w 3d av, 80x100.2. Sept. 1, due Sept. 10, 1894. 1,800

Daly, Michael to Margaret Keane. Union st, s s, 210 w Smith st, 22x100. Sept. 24, 3 years or installs. 500

Daly, Michael to John S. Ryder, Gravesend. Gravesend av, n e cor Woodside av, runs east 136 x north 100 x west 50 x south 50 x west 86 to Graveaed av, x south 50, Gravesend. Sept. 28. 500

Deverell, Thomas R. to Nellie A. Hiers. 44th st, n s, 152 w 4th av, 18x100.2. Sept. 25, 1 year. 250

Dillon, Frank to Patrick O'Brien. Lafayette av. P. M. Sept. 24, 1 year. 300

Same to The Title Guarantee and Trust Co. Same property. Sept. 24, 3 years, 5 %. 4,500

Dittrich, John and Mary his wife to John Wygand. Humboldt st, w s, 75 n Stagg st, 25x100. Sept. 25, due Oct. 1, 1894, 5 %. 5,500

Dreher, Christian W. C. to Alois Fensch. Garden st. P. M. March 4, 1891, 5 years. 1,100

Derby, Phebe R. to Benjamin Letcher. 75th st, New Utrecht. P. M. Sept. 30, 3 years, 5 %. 350

Dwelle, Vernon to Cornelius N. Hoagland, Willoughby av, s s, 74.3 w Clason av, 17x66.9x17x66.7. Sept. 29, due Nov. 1, 1894, 5 %. gold, 4,000

Eiermann, Frederick to Emeline Gallup. Jerome st, w s, 240 s Blake av, 20x100. Sept. 22, due Aug. 15, 1894. 200

Egan, Eugene A. to Walter F. Clayton. Macon st. P. M. Sept. 24, installs. 2,700

Edminster, Minnie wife of and Frank S. to The Title Guarantee and Trust Co. Gates av, s s, 489 w Nostrand av, 18x100. Sept. 25, 3 years, 5 %. 5,000

Engelstein, Max to Mary E James. Wallabout st, s s, 250 w Throop av, 25x100. Sept. 28, due Oct. 1, 1895, or installs. 1,300

Fallon, John to Charles Griffen et al. trustees Samuel Willets dec'd. Truxton st, n s, 80 w Stone av. P. M. Sept. 28, 3 years, 5 %. 5,000

Same to same. Truxton st, n s, 60 w Stone av. P. M. Sept. 28, 3 years, 5 % 5,000

Ficken, Richard to the trustees of the Reformed Prot. Dutch Church, Flatbush. East 19th st, w s, 200 n Av A, 100x100, Flatbush. Sept. 1, 5 years, 5 %. 5,000

Ficken, Richard to William C. F. Mangels guard. Walter B. A. and Dora A. Mangels. Av A, n e cor Brooklyn, Flatbush & Coney Island Railway, runs east 64.7 to East 17th st, x north to Railway, x southwest 177.3; Av A, n e cor East 17th st, runs east 200 to 18th st. x north 683.3 x northwest 117 to Brooklyn, Flatbush & Coney Island Railway, x southwest 465 to st. x south 368.10, Flatbush. Sept. 17, due after 6 months notice, 4 %. 10,000

Finkelstein, Benjamin to Mary E. Cook, Newtown, L. I. Stone av. P. M. June 9, installs. 700

Fisher, John to William H. Hanna. Atlantic av, s s, 206.10 e Schenectady av, 30.10x100x 30.8x100. Sept. 28, due Sept. 1, 1893. 1,000

Fitzgibbon, James to George W. Pearsall. Woodbine st, e s, 150 n Central av, 25x100. Sept 23, installs. 300

Fletcher, Joshua to Gilbert S. Thatford. Rockaway av, e s, 200 n Linington av, 25x100. Sept. 24, 5 years. 1,500

Fletcher, George to Phebe R. Kissam. Lafayette av, n s, 307 w Reid av. P. M. Sept. 29, 3 years. 4,000

Same to same. Lafayette av, n s, 289 w Reid av. P. M. Sept. 29, 3 years. 4,000

Same to W. Ryerson Kissam. Lafayette av, n s, 271 w Reid av. P. M. Sept. 29, 3 years. 4,000

Same to same. Lafayette av, n s, 253 w Reid av. P. M. Sept. 29, 3 years. 4,000

Same to Elizabeth E. Hutchins. Kosciusko st, s s, 300 w Reid av; Lafayette av, n s, 225 w Reid av. P. M. Sept. 29, 1 year, 5 %. 4,090

Flood, Catherine to The Equitable Co-operative Building and Loan Assoc. Tremont st, n e s, 160 n w Richards st, 40x100. Sept. 23, installs. 4,000

Flynn, Maria E to The Bushwick Savings Bank. Pulaski st, n s, 260 e Stuyvesant av, 20x100. Sept. 25, 1 year, 5 %. 2,000

Forrester, William O. to Edward Hincken. Putnam av, n s, 200 e Reid av, 100x100. Sept. 26, due Jan. 1, 1892, 5 %. 5,750

Fox, Annie E. wife of and Michael to Sarah F. Mead. Crown st, n s, 318 w New York av. P. M. Sept. 18, installs. 550

Same to Hans S. Christian. Same property. Sept. 18, installs. 100

Same to Florence C. Mead. Same property. P. M. Sept. 18, due Nov. 1, 1896. 800

Fox, Peter to Elizabeth B. Mead. Crown st, n s, 300 w New York av. P. M. Sept. 18, due Nov. 1, 1896. 800

Same to Sarah F. Mead. Same property. P. M. Sept. 18, installs. 550

Same to Hans S. Christian. Same property. Sept. 18, installs. 100

Froehlich, Charles and Annie his wife to Peter B. Bracken. 16th st. P. M. Sept 26, 5 years. 1,500

Fuller, Margaret B. to Matthew Hooker. Putnam av, n s, 175 e Marcy av, 25x100. Sept. 24, 3 years. 250

Fowler, Mary wife of and Levi to James D. Rankin and James Ross. Prospect pl, n s, 140 e Franklin av, 20x131. Sept. 28, due Oct. 1, 1892. 1,000

Gair, Estella to George W. Prankard. Van Voorhis st, n w s, 385 s w Evergreen av, 30x 100. Sept. 29, 1 year. 500

Gallagher, John P. to Edward V. Gallagher. Stuyvesant av, e s, 20 s Lexington av, 20x 90. Sept. 24, 5 years, 5 %. 4,500

Gibson, Francis to Baldwin F. Strauss. Carroll st, s s, 22.3 w Bond st, 22.3x62.6x22.2x62.6. Sept. 29, 3 years. 750

Giller, Elizabeth A. wife of and Henry W. to The Title Guarantee and Trust Co. Willoughby av, s s, 265 w Throop av, 20x100. Sept. 24, 3 years, 5 %. 4,000

Goldblatt, Jacob and Betty to Ferdinand Eherlich, New York. Belmont av, s s, 25 e Thatford av, 25x100. Sept 26, 4 years. 900

Goodwin, Mary A. to The East Brooklyn Savings Bank. Bedford av, e s, 350 n Park av, 25x100. Sept. 24, 1 year, 5 %. 2,000

Gordon, John to Mary A. Sproule trustee James Sproule. Decatur st, n s, 75 w Throop av, 20x100. Sept. 24, due Oct. 1, 1804, 5 %. 4,500

Same to same. Decatur st, n s, 95 w Throop av, 20x100. Sept. 24, due Oct. 1, 1894, 5 %. 4,500

Same to William H. Hazzard et al. trustees James Brady dec'd. Decatur st, n s, 135 w Throop av, 20x100. Sept. 24, due Oct. 1, 1894, 5 %. 4,500

Same to same. Decatur st, n s, 115 w Throop av, 20x100. Sept. 24, due Oct. 1, 1894, 5 %. 4,500

Gilmour, George H. to Margaret R. Bateman. Bay 35th st, s e s, adj land John B. Denyse, Gravesend. P. M. Sept. 28, due Oct. 1, 1896, 5 %. 600

Grodjinski, Goodman to Alfred Ogden. Atlantic av. P. M. Sept. 23, installs. 1,600

Grauer, Moritz to Peter Thomas, Hempstead. Marcy av and Flushing av. P. M. Sept. 30, 3 years or installs, 5 %. 1,000

Griffin, John to Timothy Perry. Eagle st. P. M. Sept. 15, due Sept. 29, 1893. 500

Hillyer, Allie, Helena, Mont., to James D. Lynch. Bay 25th st, New Utrecht. P. M. Aug. 13, due Aug. 31, 1892, 5 %. 1,150

Hooker, Edward to The Title Guarantee and Trust Co. Gates av. P. M. Sept. 30, 3 years, 5 %. 4,000

Holt, H. Jasper and Annie S. wife of and Emily F. Holt to Rosa P. Atwater. 10th st, n e s, 387.6 s e 6th av, 18.9x100. Already mortgaged to party of second part for $3,000. Sept. 24, due Sept. 9, 1894, 5 %. 1,000

Hooper, Rachel A. wife of and Nicholas B. and Calvin Gore to Seaman L. Pettit, Hempstead, L. I. Ellery st, s s, 225 w Marcy av, 150x100. Sept. 29, 1 year. 10,000

Hadding, William J. to Alonson Tredewell and Alonzo Slote. East 21st st, w s, 160 n Voorhies av as narrowed, 20x100. Sept. 14, 3 years. 300

Hagstrom, Charles E. to Alfred Ogden. Vanderveer st, s e s, 276.6 n e Broadway, 16.6x 100. Sept. 26, installs. 800

Hart, Frances to D. and M. Chauncey Real Estate Co. (Lim) Sterling pl, s w s, 0.11 n w Flatbush av, runs southwest 135.8 x east 45 x northeast 82 to Flatbush av, x north 28.11 to Sterling pl, x northwest 0.11. Aug. 13, demand. 8,000

Hart, Frances to John Adamson. Sterling pl, &c. P. M. Aug. 13, 1 year. 3,500

Hart, William J. to P. Ballantine & Sons, a corporation. Middagh st, s s, 72.5 w Hicks st, 28.4x50.4. Sept. 26, note. 4,000

Hatton, Thomas to James McKane. Kouwenhovens lane, w s, 200 n Gravesend Neck road, 25x176.7x25x176.9, Gravesend. Sept. 16, 5 years. 1,000

Hayes, Denis to Patrick Hayes. Hancock st, s s, 150 w Patchen av, 50x100. Sept. 8, due Sept. 29, 1892, 5 %. 3,000

Heary, James P. and Annie J. his wife to Mary McKnight. Clason av, e s, abt 50 s Willoughby av, 25x105.2. Sept. 24, 5 years, 5 %. 1,500

Heiselmann, John A. to Charles A. Braun. Myrtle av, s s, 161 w Grove st, 25x77.10x77.10 to Grove st, x25x67.4x67.4. Sept. 21, 1 year. 2,000

Heyser, Henry C. to Jacob T. Van Sielen. Barbey st, w s, 225 s Blake av, 3 lots, each 16.8x100. 3 morts., each $1,000. Sept. 24, 3 years. 3,000

Heyzer, John to George G. Reynolds. New York av, Nostrand av, Douglass st and Degraw st—block. Sept. 25, 1 year. 1,500

Hill, Henry B. to John Peirer. McDonough st, s s, 321.8 w Patchen av, 72x100. Sept. 15, 1 year. 2,833

Homan, Edgar S. to Sarah E. Van Wyck, East Fishkill, N. Y. Tulip st, n s, 100 e Nostrand av, 80x100, Flatbush. Sub. to mort. $1,000. Sept. 24, due Oct. 1, 1892, 5 %. 1,000

Same to Sarah E. Van Wyck extrx. Anna L. Van Vechten. Tulip st, n s, 100 e Nostrand av, 80x100, Flatbush. Sub. to mort. $1,000. Sept. 24, due Oct. 1, 1892, 5 %. 1,000

Horchler, Frederick and Louise his wife to Josephine Eiseman. Stanhope st. P. M. July 27, due July 1, 1894, 5 %. 2,500

Horowitz, Isaac to Annie Bailey widow. Varet st. P. M. Sept. 25, due Oct. 1, 1894, 5 %. 2,000

Houlahan, John and Mary to Jane L. Smith. Fulton st, st, s s, 75 w Miller av. P. M. Sub. to mort. $1,500. Sept. 21, installs. 900

Howard, William B. to Rudolph Reimer. Sunnyside av, n s, 150 e Barbey st, 50x200 to Laurel st. Sept. 23, due Oct. 1, 1891, per year, 170

Same to The Hall Sash and Door Co, Same property. Sept. 23, due Oct. 1, 1891. 320

Hunter, Mary wife of and James to William A. Wright. 4th av, east cor Carroll st, 20x 100. Sept. 28, 5 years. 600

Ingram, Alfred D. to The Title Guarantee and Trust Co. Greene av. P. M. Sept. 26, 1 year, 5 %. 1,500

Jamison, Catharine T. to The Emigrant Indust. Savings Bank. 4th av. P. M. Sept. 30, 1 year, 4½ %. 1,000

Josephowitz, Henry to Rachel A. Wenzenburger. Logan st. P. M. Sept. 9, 1 year or installs. 350

Jacob, B'Nai to Dudley S. Steele and Nathan W. Condict, Jr. 22d st. P. M. Aug. 31, installs, 5 %. 1,500

Jacobs, Herman and Caroline his wife to George Jacobs. Warwick st, w s, 234.11 s Fulton st, 16.8x95. Sept. 21, 5 years, 5 %. 1,000

Jamer, Jacob to Russie M. L. Strange. South 6th st, n s, 95.3 w Bedford av, 24x78. Sept. 24, 5 years. gold, 8,000

Jones, Mary A. D. to Charles Donohue and Albert Cardoza. De Kalb av, s s, 58.2 w Cumberland st, runs west 21 x southwest 51 x south 47 x east 16 x northwest 94 11. Sub. to mort. $5,500. Sept. 25, due Sept. 24, 1892, 5 %. 2,600

Judson, Edward to Jennie W. Brown. 6th av, n w cor President st, 100x92. Sept. 23, demand. 1,650

Kaplan, Aaron to Joseph M. Greenwood. Linden st, n w s, 315.11 n e Evergreen av, 20 x100. Sept. 28, due Nov. 1, 1894. 2,000

Same to same. Linden st, n w s, 295.11 n e Evergreen av, 20x100. Sept. 28, due Nov. 1, 1894. 2,000

Klein, Max to Adolph I. Namm. Wyckoff st, s s, 100 w 3d av, 20x100. Sept. 29, 1 year. 1,500

Keating, Ellen formerly Kottmann to Sallie R. Wemmell. Moffat st, n w s, 482.6 n e Hamburg av, 17.6x100. Sept. 26, 3 years. 300

Kekut, Frederick to Michael Seitz. Metropolitan av, s s, 250 e Catharine st, 25x100. July 1, 3 years, 5 %. 500

Kelly, Elizabeth to Sarah A. Cowenhoven. 57th st, s w s, 350 n w 15th av, 50x100.2, New Utrecht. Sept. 28, 3 years. 1,700

Kelly, James T. to Anna M. Ferris, all of Flatbush. Prospect av, s e cor Greenwood av, Flatbush. P. M. Sept. 10, 5 years, 5 %. 1,000

Kerzner, Nicolaus to John Frank. Troutman st, n w s, 102.8 s w Wyckoff av, 25x173 to Old Newtown turnpike (closed), x25 11x166. Sept. 23, 5 years, 5 %. 2,000

Knight, Alexander W. to The Brooklyn Savings Bank. Prospect st, n s, 25 e Charles st, 50x100. Sept. 26, 1 year, 5 %. 2,500

Koch, George and Frederick Korner to Louis Beer. Knickerbocker av, east cor De Kalb av, 75x100. Sept. 25, due Oct. 24, 1891, 5½ %. 6,302

Krause, William and Maria to Ellen Morgan. Vandyke st. P. M. Sept. 28, 3 years, 5 %. 500

Kreuder, Daniel to Bernhard Haussner. McKibbin st, n s, 50 w Leonard st, 25x100. Sept. 28, due Oct. 1, 1894, 5 %. 1,000

Kreuder, Daniel and Helena his wife to Bernhard Haussner. McKibbin st, n s, 25 w Leonard st, 25x100. Sept. 28, due Oct. 1, 1894, 5 %. 3,500

Kutscher, William H. to Mary L. Godfrey. Hamilton av. P. M. Sept. 24, 3 years, 5 %. 4,000

Same to same. Same property. P. M. Sub. to last mort. Sept. 24, 1 year, 5 %. 600

Kaminski, Lawrence to John H. Shults Co-operative Building and Loan Assoc. Diamond st, e s, 115.6 n Driggs st, 25x86.6x25 x79.4 in two courses. Sept. 30, installs. 2,400

Kidney, George to Eliphalet W. Bliss. Lot at New Utrecht, begins at northwest cor land of George Kidney on south line of land of Eliphalet W. Bliss, runs south 146.9 to 68th st. P. M. April 30, 1891, due May 9, 1892, 5 %. 1,500

Kiernan, Patrick to John McCarthy. Greene st. P. M. Sept. 29, 5 years, 5 %. 1,600

Klockert, George P. to Elizabeth Rohrschneider. Butler st. P. M. Sub. to mort. $2,100. Sept. 28, 3 years, 5 %. 1,000

Knight, Mark B. to Henry H. Adams, County Treasurer. Webster st, n s, 100 e Albany av, 20x100, Flatbush. Sept. 23, 1 year, 5 %. 500

Kozenblub, Juda to David Klein. Hopkins st. P. M. Sept. 29, due Feb. 1, 1892. 300

Kraemer, Augusta wife of and Charles to The Title Guarantee and Trust Co. Monroe st, s s, 340 w Marcy av, 20x100. Sept. 30, 3 years, 5 %. 4,000

Kromm, Conrad to Sarah A. and Martha R. World. Lynch st. P. M. Sept. 28, 4 years, 5 %. 800

Lansing, Charles W. to John W. C. Leveridge. 55th st, s w s, 100 n w 3d av, 25x100. Sept. 28, 3 years, 5 %. 1,500

Lipman, Morris and Abraham to Aaron Kaplan. 102d st. P. M. Sept. 29, due Nov. 20, 1893 1,400

Lamb, James W. and Albert J. to William Laytin et al. trustees William Laytin. Putnam av, n w s, 100 s w Central av, 17.6x100. Sept. 25, 3 years, 5 %. 1,800

Same to same. Putnam av, n w s, 117.6 s w Central av, 4 lots, each 17.6x100. 4 morts., each $1,500. Sept. 25, 3 years, 5 %. 6,000

Lamb, James W. and Albert J. to William Baltz. Putnam av, n w s, 187.6 s w Central av, 17.6x100. Sept. 25, 3 years, 5 %. 1,500

Same to same. Putnam av, n w s, 205.5 s w Central av, 17.6x100. Sept. 25, 3 years, 5 %. 1,500

Lase, William C. to Wilmot D. Losee. Ridgewood av. P. M. Sub. to mort. $1,600. Sept 28, installs. 1,100

Last, John A., Tarrytown, N. Y., to Mary A. Lawton. Java st, n s, 220 e Franklin st, 25x 100. Sept. 24, 2 years, 5 %. 1,400

Ledwith, James to William W. Browning trustee William Browning. Stockholm st, n s, 161.1 e Wyckoff av, 20x100. Sept. 28, 3 years, 5 %. 300

Leopold, Henry to The Title Guarantee and Trust Co. 8th av, w s, 80 s 16th st, 20x97.5. Sept. 21, due Sept. 28, 1892, 5 %. 3,000

Levin, Morris to Barnet Levin. Thatford av. P. M. Sept. 23, installs. 800

Same to same. Same property. Sept. 23, due Oct. 1, 1894. 800

Lippman, Charles and Rachel his wife, Hartford, Conn., to Margaretha Wolf. Heyward st. P. M. Sept. 28, 5 years, 5 %. 3,500

Loper, James H. to Lauretta Gill. Halsey st, n s, 250 w Howard av, 16.8x100. July 24, 2 years. 638

Lynch, Owen to Bedford Co-operative Building and Loan Assoc. Clason av, w s, 150 s Baltic st, 35x106x100, gore. July 6, installs. 250

Lyons, James to George Kerswill. Grant st, Flatbush. P. M. Sept 25, 2 years, 5½ %. 500

Maas, William F. to Libbie Brown. Glenmore av, s e cor Schenck av, 31.6x60. Sept. 16, 3 years, 5 %. 1,000

Manning, Ellen to M. Gibbons & Son. Conover st, west cor Vandyke st, 20x80. Sept. 25, due Sept. 1, 1894. 1,000

Mason, Emma J. to The Title Guarantee and Trust Co. Van Buren st, n s, 201 w Throop av, 20x100. July 13, 3 years, 5 %. 2,500

Mathews, Arthur J. to The Emigrant Indust. Savings Bank. Union st, n s, 20 e Hoyt st, 20x100. Sept. 23, 1 year, 4½ %. 3,000

Malmar, Esaias to Christopher C. Firth. 14th st. P. M. Sept. 16, 2 years. 1,500

McGuckin, James to George H. Gerard. India st. P. M. Sept. 28, due Jan. 1, 1895. 1,400

McElroy, William to James Smith. Jerome st. e s, 60 n Dumont av, 20x100. Sept. 28, 2 years. 400

McKay, Henry J. mortgagor with Lillian Berry mortgagee. Extension of mort. July 12. nom

McKnight, John F. to Terence Jacobson. Columbia st, s e s, 60 s w Summit st, 20x80. Sept. 25, due Nov. 1, 1893. 550

Mentz, Joseph and Lena to Lena and Morris Bolstein. Gates av. P. M. Sept. 25, installs. 1,000

Meybert, Peter to James McKane. Lots 19 and 20 map Garrett Stryker dec'd, Gravesend. Sept. 23, 3 years. 350

Monsees, John to Joseph Seitz, Dobbs Ferry, L. I. Linwood st, w s, 122.6 s Eastern Parkway, 22.6x90. Sept. 21, 3 years. 1,500

Moores, Robert L. and Charles A. Le Quesne to Earl A. Gillespie. Broadway, s w s, 38 2 n w Putnam av, runs northwest 28 x southwest 50.4 x south 11.8 to Putnam av, x east 28 x northeast 38.8. Sept. 24, 2 years. 4,000

Morris, Joseph to Jane M. Oakley, Milton, N. Y. Dumont av, n s, 25 w Thatford av, 25x100. Aug. 26, 3 years. 2,000

Same to Esther Hillick, Newburg, N. Y. Dumont av, n s, 75 w Thatford av, 25x100. Aug. 26, 3 years. 1,800

Same to same. Thatford av, w s, 250 n Dumont av, 25x100. Aug. 26, 3 years. 2,000

Same to same. Thatford av, w s, 125 n Dumont av, 25x100. Aug. 26, 3 years. 2,000

Muller, George F. to Israel Muller. 9th av. P. M. Sept. 23, demand, 5 %. gold, 9,000

Murray, James to Lewis S. Goebel, New York. 9th st, n s, 85 w 4th av, 25x100. Sept. 22, due Sept. 22, 1890, 5 %. 500

Mangan, Ellen to Charles Hart. 18th st, s s, 80.4 w 10th av, 20x100.2. P. M. May 27, 5 years. 625

Maynard, Hattie F. wife of and William to George Whitlock Pulaski st, s s, 350 e Nostrand av, 18.9x100. Sept. 21, due Sept. 22, 1891, 5 %. 5,400

Michaelis, Edward to Henry Meis. Thornton st P. M. Sept. 29, 3 years, 5½ %. 5,000

Miller, Jane to Theodore and William Killian, of Killian Bros. Macon st, n s, 25 e Patchen av, 18.9x100. Sub. to morts. $5,700. Sept. 29, 6 months. 320

Same to same. Macon st, n s, 254 e Patchen av, 18x100. Sept. 29, 6 months. 320

Moadinger, Charles F. to John H. Rowland. Kosciusko st, n s, 201 e Tompkins av, 18.9x85. Sept. 30, 3 years. 3,000

Mousees, Mary J. wife of and John to Earl A. Gillespie, Woodhaven, L. I. Linwood st, w s, 122 6 s Eastern Parkway, 22.6x90. Sept 26, demand. 800

Mulholland, George J. to The Title Guarantee and Trust Co. Bergen st. P. M. Sept. 18, due Sept. 30, 1894, 5 %. 3,500

Muller, Herman D. M. to Eva Bechtel extrx. George Bechtel. Sands st, No. 81. Lease. Sept. 30, demand. 800

Newcomb, Isaac to James O'Neill. 27th st, n s, 120 e 3d av, 18.4x101.2. Sept. 28, 3 years, 5 %. 700

Nill, August and Regina his wife to Joseph Werner. Hopkins st. P. M. Sept. 26, 3 years, 5 %. 2,000

Nolan, Patrick mortgagor with Franklin Lodge No. 182 Independent Order of Odd Fellows. Extension of mort. Sept. 8. nom

Nystrom, Gustaf to Anna Schmeelk, both of Canarsie, L. I. Flatlands av, south cor East 94th st. 100x131.7, Canarsie. Sept. 26, due Jan. 1, 1897. 2,000

Nicoll, Fanny A. W. to Edgar E. Duryea, Glen Cove, L. I. Livingston st, s s, 100 w Smith st, 25x100. Sept. 30, due Nov. 1, 1892. 500

Oates, Patrick to William J. Gaynor. Newkirk av, s e cor Brooklyn, Flatbush & Coney Island Railway Co., 209x125x265.1x136.11; also parcel adj land John A. Lott, at point 941.1 w land of R. R. Fox, runs west 159.5 x north 468.4 x east 159.5 x south 468.4, Flatbush. Sept. 29, due Oct. 1, 1894. 5,000

O'Connell, Daniel to The Title Guarantee and Trust Co. Vanderbilt av, s w cor Bergen st, 73x95. Sept. 28, 2 years, 5 %. 15,000

O'Reilly, Lawrence to Edward J. Smith. Dean st, n s, 162 w Ralph av, 18x107.2. Sept. 25, due Oct. 1, 1894. 1,500

Parmer, Ada wife of Lewis to Mary W. Smith. Watkins st, w s, 100 s Eastern Parkway, 51.6 x100. Sept. 23, demand. 100

Pleissner, Guido to Caroline M. Butterfield. Lincoln pl, s s, 100 e 8th av, runs south 100 x east 73.10 to Prospect Park plaza, x north to Lincoln pl, x west 34.3. Sept. 25, due Oct. 1, 1894, 5 %. 30,000

Pollard, Patrick to Sarah H. Pippey and Wm. M. Fliess trustees Robt. A. Fliess dec'd. Harrison st, s w cor Hicks st, 41.2x70. Sub. to mort. $5,000. Sept. 28, 5 years, 5½ %. 8,000

Power, John to Mary W. Smith. Eastern Parkway, n w cor Osborn st, 46.5x100. Sept. 24, demand. 1,000

Praeger, Adeline E. F. wife of and Herbert F. to William T. Smith and ano. exrs. Thomas T. Smith. Reid av, e s, 150 n De Kalb av, runs east 49.9 x northeast 2.11 x northwest 22.10 x west 34.2 to Reid av, x south 20. Sept. 28, due Oct. 1, 1894, or installs, 5 %. 1,800

Same to same. Reid av, e s, 170 n De Kalb av, runs east 34.2 x northwest 7.10 x northeast 8. x northwest 11.4 x west 25.7 to av, x south 20. Sept. 28, due Oct. 1, 1894, 5 %. 1,800

Same to same. Broadway, s w s, 27 s e Reid av, runs southwest 47.5 x south 12.2 x east 5.7 x southeast 11.4 x northeast 5.2 to Broadway, x northwest 25. Sept. 28, due Oct. 1, 1895, 5 %. 6,400

Puels, Joseph P. to The Title Guarantee and Trust Co. Decatur st, n s, 100 w Howard av, 199.8x100. Sept. 23, demand. 4,200

Putzel, Henry to Frank C. Elliott. 4th av, w s, 100 s 6th st, runs west 160 x south 100 to 7th st, x east 100 x north 50 x east 60 to av, x north 50. Sept. 18, due April 1, 1892. 1,500

Pfaefflin, Marie wife of Edward to Leopold J. Lippmann. Eldert st. n w s, 240 n e Evergreen av. P. M. *Mt.* $2,500. Sept. 1, installs. 1,500

Same to Thomas C. Balderston et al. Supreme trustees of the Order of Tonti. Same property. Sept. 1, due Sept. 30, 1894, 5 %. 2,500

Pierri, Michael and Peter to Martha C. Jennings, New Brunswick, N. J. Frost st, s s, 275 e Lorimer st, 25x100. Sept. 15, 5 years, 5 %. 500

Pierce, Anna to Alfred Ogden. Atlantic av. P. M. Sept. 28, installs. 1,400

Rober, Katherine to James D. Lynch. Stillwell av, Gravesend. P. M. Sept. 4, due Sept. 15, 1893, 5 %. 630

Rubinstein, Louis to Henry Hebenstreit and Charles Butzgy. Bogart st, e s, 81 s Rock st. P. M. Sept. 29, due Sept. 22, 1894, or installs, 5 %. 2,250

Rapalje, Williamson to H. H. Petty. Liberty av, s w cor Sackman st, 27.10x89x29.10x89. Sept 25, 3 years, 5 %. 4,500

Ray, David to George A. Craig. Madison st, s e s, 367.8 s w Knickerbocker av, 18x100. Sept. 28, 5 years. 500

Raymond, John to John N. Eitel. Rockaway av, w s, 17 s Hull st, 16.8x75. Sept. 28, due Sept. 14, 1894. 2,750

Reagan, Mary McG. wife of and Jeremiah to Sarah F. Mead. Crown st. P. M. Sept. 18, due May 1, 1894, installs. 265

Rickard, Peter to Adrian M. Suydam. Palmetto st, n w s, 500 s w Central av, 25x100. Sept. 23, due Sept. 22, 1892, 5 %. 200

Reibling, Wilhelm and Catherina his wife to Mathias Neger. Floyd st, No. 238, s s, 125 e Throop av, 25x100. Sept. 28, 5 years, 5 %. 1,800

Reichert, Constantine to Louis Bahrs. Palmetto st, s s, 240 e Hamburg av, 20x100. Sept. 1, 3 years, 5 %. 2,000

Riesenberger, Ray to Henry Roth. Moore st. P. M. Aug. 1, 5 years, 5 %. 1,800

Robinson, John to Isaac Embree. Buffalo av, w s, 52.8 s Prospect pl, 17.11x100; Buffalo av, w s, 127.9 s Prospect pl, 25x100. Sept. 24, due Nov. 1, 1894. 1,700

Same to Elizabeth A. Pratt, Essex, Conn. Buffalo av, w s, 70.7 s Prospect pl, 33.2x100. Sept. 24, due Nov. 1, 1894. 1,800

Rosenfeld, Rosa wife of Jonas to Carrie Engs. Bergen st, s s, 100 w Hopkinson av, 25x127.9. Sept. 14, 2 years. 2,000

Rugen, John F. to The F. & M. Schaefer Brewing Co. 7th av, No. 361. Saloon lease. Sept. 26, demand. 800

Ryder, Catharine to Janetta and Cornelia White. Washington av, w s, 128.7 s Myrtle av, 16.1x100. Sept. 29, due Nov. 1, 1893, 5 %. 500

Sackmann, Frederick A. to E. Otto Sackmann and ano. trustees for Amalia C. Gross. Wyona st, w s, 86.11 n Atlantic av, runs north 100 x west 100 x south 56.8 x west 25 x south 25 x east 45 x south 17.3 x east 80. Sept. 24, due Oct. 1, 1896. 2,750

Scharfman, Moritz to David Ungerleider and Lena his wife. Park av. P. M. Sept. 28, 10 years, 5 %. 1,500

Schlossberg, William to Charles Ratner and Israel Zagalovitz. Eastern Parkway. P. M. Sept. 26, installs. 1,500

Schneider, David and Katharina his wife to Henry Roth. Montieth st. P. M. Sept. 26, installs, 5 %. 1,500

Schrenig, Philip H. to Jeremiah V. Meserole. Kingsland av, s e cor Lombardy st. P. M. Sept. 28, 5 years. 6,250

Schroeder, Margaret A. wife of and Albert J. mortgagors with James Hall and ano. exrs. Thomas C. Moore. Extension of mort. Sept. 26. nom

Seaholm, Lorentz R. to James H. Brundage. Jerome st. P. M. Sept. 25, installs. 390

Seifried, Frederick to William J. Gaynor exr. Andrew McClennen. 3d av, e s, 40.2 n 47th st. 30x85. Sept. 28, due Oct. 1, 1894. 9,000

Smith, John to Frederick and Minna Schuermann. 53d st, n s, 217.3 e 3d av, 18x100.2. Sept. 1, 1 year. 1,760

Stabler, Elizabetha to Peter Schmidt. 4th av, west cor 23d st, 50x60. Sept. 26, due Jan. 1, 1895. 2,500

Stevenson, James P. to Adeline W. Jewett, Keyport, N. J. Dean st. P. M. Sept. 22, 3 years, 5 %. 1,500

Stewart, Augusta wife of and Albert to Albert Friedrich. North 2d st, n s, 150 w Humboldt st, 50x100. Sept. 25, 1 year, 5 %. 1,000

St. Johns College, Brooklyn, to The Emigrant Industrial Savings Bank. Stuyvesant av, w s, extends from Willoughby av to Hart st, 200x565. Sept. 28, 1 year, 4½ %. 50,000

Stoutenburg, George B. to Charles W. Thomas. Throop av, w s, 44.6 n Pulaski st, 18.6x84.9. Sept. 23, due Nov. 1. 1894. 5 %. 5,500

Same to William Mackenzie, Bowden, England. Throop av, w s, 63 n Pulaski st, 18.6x 84.9. Sept. 23, due Nov. 1, 1894, 5 %. 5,500

Stoutenburg, George B. to William A. De Long and ano. exrs. &c., Charlotte A. Schlim, Throop av, w s, 26 n Pulaski st, 18.6x84.9x 17.6x34.9x1x50. Sept. 24, 3 years, 5 %. 5,500

Same to same. Throop av, w s, 81.6 n Pulaski st, 18.6x84.9. Sept. 23, due Nov. 1, 1894, 5 %. 5,500

Stratton, Edward, Jr., to Edward P. Day. Bay 16th st, w s, 332 n Bath av, 50x96.8, New Utrecht. Sept. 17, due May 1, 1892, or installs. 250

Stubley, Harry to Gilbert S. Thatford. Rockaway av, e s, 50 n Bergen st, 25x100. Sept. 29, due Oct. 1, 1895. 700

Sturgess, Maria E. to Julia E. Cohen. 5th st, n s, 260 e 5th av, 20x100. Sept. 26, installs. 500

Sullivan, Michael to Charles M. Marsh, Morris Plains, N. J. Road leading to Canarsie, Flatlands. P. M. Sept. 10, 2 years, 5 %. 12,500

Swezey, Joseph B. and Ida W. J. his wife to Edwin A. Pitt, Bay Shore, L. I. Lefferts st, s e s, 494.7 n e Brooklyn av, 120x100. Sept. 15, 3 years. 800

Saddington, John F. to David C. Lyall. Hancock st. P. M. Sept. 28, 2 years, 5 %. 3,150

Schiel, Anna G. to John Schaefer. Lewis av, e s, 66.8 n Kosciusko st, 16.8x75. Sept. 26, 2 years, 5 %. 500

Taylor, Emma E. to James B. Henry. Carroll st. P. M. Sept. 30, due May 1, 1892, 5 %. 5,000

Traub, Frederick to William G. Peirson. De Kalb av, n s, 84.1 w Vanderbilt av, runs north 40 x north again 28.8 x west 19.7 x south 24 8 x south 40 to av, x east 20. Sept. 28, due Oct. 1, 1893. 1,000

Taylor, Arthur to Henry Albers, Jersey City, N. J. Macon st, s s, 216.8 e Stuyvesant av, 19.2x100. Sept. 24, due Jan. 1, 1894, 5 %. 4,000

The Congregation and Charitable and Benevolent Assoc. Anschi Serbnaer, New York, to Louis Levene. Lots 136-140 and 146-149 map Washington Cemetery, New York. Sept. 17, 2 years. 365

Trapp, George F. to Dennis Reardon and George P. Doremus, Jersey City, N. J. North 4th st, s s, 50 e Berry st, 25x60. Sept. 21, 2 years, 5 %. 1,500

Treacy, Eliza to Samuel W. Sayres exr. Abigail Sayres. Buffalo av, s w cor Butler st, 30x100. Sept. 26, due Nov. 1, 1893, 5 %. 500

Ullrich, Mary A. wife of and Valentine to Friedrich Kirschenbeiter and Elizabetha his wife. Central av. P. M. Sept. 25, due Oct. 1, 1896, 5 %. 1,450

Van Dolah, Sarah and Ann M. Beam to Mary Latimer. Halsey st, s s, 440 e Throop av, 20 x100. Sept. 24, 3 years, 5½ %. 3,500

Wisely, Peter G. to Edward Wisely, West New Brighton, S. I. Saratoga av, s e cor McDougal st, 25x75. Lease. Sept. 22, 1 year. 500

Woessner, Jacob and Sophie his wife to Fredericka Lichtenfels. North 4th st. Sept. 25, due July 1, 1893, 5 %. See Conveys. 3,000

Waldron, Alexander to Anna M. Bennett and ano. exrs. Cornelius Bennett. 47th st, s w s, 240 s e 4th av, 20x100.2. Sept. 25, 3 years, 5 %. 3,500

Same to Elizabeth H. Taylor. 47th st, s w s, 160 s e 4th av, 80x100.2. Sept. 25, 6 months, 5 %. 6,000

Wilkenfeld, Hirsch and Nathan Rittermann to Reuhamay Proctor. Osborn st, w s, 75 s Livonia av, 25x100. Sept. 29, due May 1, 1892. 100

MORTGAGES----ASSIGNMENTS.

NEW YORK CITY.

SEPTEMBER 25 TO OCTOBER 1—INCLUSIVE.

Anderson, Isaac to Sarah E. Palmer. $900

Barnes, Frederick E. to Henry Nobel. 2,150

Bell, John to Frances E. Bell. nom

Brush, Walter F. to John E. Roosevelt admr. Amos Cotting. 22,000

Brady, John J. to Sarah E. Palmer. 600

Bailey, James S. and ano exrs. Solomon Freeman to Joseph R. Conklin. 3,000

Baker, Laura S., East Orange, N. J., to William D. Brooks, Washingtonville, N. Y. consid. omitted

Bowes, John and John Coombs, of Bowes & Coombs, to Henry Greenebaum. 2,300

Colgate, Bowles and ano. exrs. Frances E. Colgate to Bowles Colgate. nom

Carroll, Kate to Charles O. Shay. 3,000

Campbell, John V. to Joseph L. Buttenwieser. 5,000

Cohen, Max, 96 Av C, New York, to Louis Lese. 1,750

Same to Max Cohen, of 240 Clinton st, New York. 5,250

Crane, William N. trustee to The Mercantile Trust Co. 25,000

Cassidy, Margaret J. to Alice d'Aguiar. 1,666

Dexter, Walter F. admr. Lucie E. Dexter, Brooklyn, to David Stevenson. 600

Dorsett, R. Clarence to Charles Unangst. nom

Same to same. nom

Dazian, Wolf and Henry, of W. Dazian, to Asa Heineman et al. trustees for children of Justina Spiegel. 10,000

Ford, Henry W. trustee Augustus H. Ward dec'd to William N. Crane trustee. consid. omitted

Same to same. consid. omitted

Gleason, John J., Flushing, L. I., to Tobias Silverstone. 1,400

Goeren, Mathias and Sophia his wife to Sigmund Cohn. 2,278

Same to Morris and Henry Kahn. 2,538

Gormly, James to Henry W. de Forest, Oyster Bay, L. I. 16,000

Galewski, Bernhard to Pasquale Caponigri. 3,042
Huntington, Sarah E. and ano. exrs. Benjamin F. Curtis to George W. Mercer. nom
Henriques, Louis N. to Raphael R. Govin. 14,000
Hassey, August to Helene Gillman, Mamaroneck, N. Y. 3,000
Hogencamp, John M. to Stephen E. Garretson and ano. trustees for Jane Irwin. nom
Hogencamp, John M. to Lillie H. Rogers. 10,167
Hyatt, George E. to Henry W. Ford trustee Augustus H. Ward. nom
Same to same. nom
Hershfield, Samuel to Anna wife of Levi Epstein, Sheffield, Pa. 6,060
Hagan, Thomas to Hugo Weil. 4,000
Howe, Robie S. to Title Guarantee and Trust Co. 3,000
Jackson, Charles A. to Robert L. Harrison trustee. Re-recorded. 5,000
Jackson, Charles A. to Robert L. Harrison trustee. 5,000
Josephthal, Louis to Moriz Josephthal. 8,124
Jencks, Francis M. to The Equitable Life Assurance Society of the U. S. 10,000
Kalischer, Adolph S. to Marks Rinaldo. 6,000
Kraner, Abraham and Israel Krakower to Tobias Krakower. 5,000
Krakower, Tobias to Charlotte Hastorf. 5,000
Keeler, Caroline E. widow and Carrie K. wife of William H. Shaw and Theodore Keeler to David McClure. 2,500
Klingenstein, Jacob to Jacob and Regina Mandelbaum. 4,000
Levin, Marks to David Freedman. 2,795
Lewine, Fisher to The Corn Exchange Bank. 14,400
Ladew, Rebecca et al. exrs. and trustees Harvey S Ladew to Rebecca and Edward R. Ladew as trustees. 28,000
Same to same. 2 assigns., each $50,000. 100,000
Same to same. 5,000
Same to same. 8,000
Le Compte, Frank S. and William J. exrs. Susan Le Compte to The Title Guarantee and Trust Co. 2 assigns. each $6,000. 12,000
Same to same. 8,000
Same to same. 10,000
Levy, Abraham and Matilda to Bernard Pasternak. 1,350
Middlebrook, Frederic J., Brooklyn, to August Limbert trustee Frederick C. Gebbard dec'd. 9,019
Same to same. 12,193
Same to same. 9,049
Middlebrook, Frederic J., Brooklyn, to George Riehl. 12,674
Middlebrook, Frederic J., Brooklyn, to Frederick W. Lockwood, New Canaan, Conn. 4,635
Morgenthau, Henry to R. Clarence Dorsett. 2 assigns. nom
McKee, Thomas J. to Sarah A. Lott. 500
McShane, William to Adelia F. Philp. nom
Mitchell, David to Charles Frazier. 25,000
Murray, Russell to Rosalie Steinhardt. 1,279
McMurror, Cornelius and ano. exrs. Bridget McKenna to Isabella M. Hayes et al. extrxs. Stephen Hayes. 5,000
Nathan, Julian exr. Rosalie Florance to United States Trust Co., of New York, trustee Rosalie Florance dec'd. order of Court
Ormiston, Annie to Sumner R. Stone and ano. exrs. Caroline M Hitchcock. 16,216
Pietz, Charles to Anna Zimmermann. 8,000
Rogers, Archibald, Hyde Park, N. Y., to Robert H. Coleman trustee for Anne C. Rogers 4,066
Same to same. 6,118
Schuster, Sophia to Emilio del Pino. 3,000
Stern, Abraham to Bernhard Grunbut. 1,500
Studinski, Henrietta to John V. Campbell. 5,000
Steers, Abraham to Jesse W. Powers. nom
Sire, Meyer L. to Edward F. Browning. 6,500
Schuster, David K. to Julia M. Bowerman and ano. exrs. and trustees William D. Bowerman. 3,030
Seybel, Daniel E. to Antony Wallach. consid. omitted
Title Guarantee and Trust Co. to Alfred Wagstaff guard. of Alice Barnard. 700
Title Guarantee and Trust Co. to Maurice M. Sternberger exr. Mayer Sternberger. 32,500
Title Guarantee and Trust Co. to Robie S. Howe. 1,000
Same to Phillips and Lloyd Phoenix trustees Stephen W. Phoenix dec'd. 15,000
Same to George F. Hussey, East Orange, N. J. 3,000
Title Guarantee and Trust Co. to Thomas E. Rochford. 3,500
Same to The American Employers' Liability Ins. Co. 10,000
Same to same. 8,000
Same to same. 2 assigns., each $6,000. 12,000
Same to Annie G. Paddock. 3,000
Towle, Louise O. wife of Henry B. formerly Odell to Samuel Riker. 5,000
Taylor, Charles E., Brooklyn, to Laurence Pottier. Collateral. 4,000
The Bradley & Currier Co. (Lim.) to John W. Haaren. 5,047
Same to same. 4,637
Union Square Bank of the City of New York, to Louis Kreuder. 20,000
Walsh, Richard M. L. to Elizabeth R. Walsh. 9,500
Weil, Jonas and Bernhard Mayer to Samuel Weil. 9,333
Weil, August M. to Sigmund Cohn. 2,000
Wolf, Ernst et al. exrs. &c., Katharina Schwarzott to Joseph Baum. 7,000
Washburn, Willord W. to Alfred Q. Elgar. nom
Winslow, Edward to John E. Roosevelt admr. Amos Cotting. 30,000

KINGS COUNTY.

SEPT. 24 TO 30—INCLUSIVE.

Andrews, William to Juan B. C. Phillips. $1,000
Austin, John C. to George Mohrmann. 650
Andrews, Jr., John to John Andrews. 1,500
Ashcroft, Mary K. to Joseph C. Hoagland. 5,000
Benjamin, Joseph to Leopold Michel. 500
Same to same. 1,000
Beach, Anna M. to Hannah D. White. 350
Betts, Charles A. to The Hamilton Trust Co. 4,000
Blinn, Henriette to Edward W. Blinn. 4,500
Barnaby, Frank A. to Hamilton Trust Co. 26,000
Burrows, Mary A. to Whitman W. Kenyon. 1,332
Bossert, Louis to Christine Gross. 1,984
Clements, Nathaniel H. to James F. Morgans. 2,000
Canavello, Charles A. to Mary J. wife of William Smith. 800
Collins, Stephen W. guard. Minturn and Charles Collins to Minturn P. Collins. 2,036
Draper, Elizabeth A. to James W. Smith trustee for Elizabeth Draper. 8,000
De Bevoise, John C. and ano. exrs. Gertrude Calyer to Mary Bennett. 4,000
Dunn, Harriet E. to Phebe R. Kissam. 1,500
Dunning, Eliza A. to Florence H. Dunning. 330
Foote, Margaret L. to The Title Guarantee and Trust Co. 1,700
Frazer, Janet to Grace C. Halstead. consid. omitted
Gibbins, Mary E. to James P. Campbell. 15,000
Gordon, John to Adam Ohlweiler. 1,000
Goldblatt, Jacob to Ferdinand Eberlich. 525
Gay, John to Augusta H. Wyand. 3,000
Geyer, Charles T. exr. Reuben T. Pollard to Blanche Alexander. 507
Hoagland, Cornelius N. to Clara D. Carpenter. 5,000
Hardrich, Friedrich to Christian W. C. Dreher. 2,000
Hirsch, Louis and Joseph Cohen to Jacob Goldblatt. 250
Howe, Rose to Arthur C. Salmon. gift
Hutchins, Elizabeth E. to Metropolitan Savings Bank. 9,300
Hyde & Gload Mfg. Co. to Alfred P. Tostevin. 900
Jackson, Theodore F. exr. Maryett Hodgetts to Sarah H Hodgetts. 413
Jackson, Theodore F. to Theodore F. Jackson et al. trustees Loftis Wood. 12,600
James, Darwin R. and Mary E. his wife to The Broadway Bank of Brooklyn. 8,500
Krumb, Faustus to Mary Preston. 1,000
Lubs, Henrietta S. to Elizabeth M. Willson. 1,600
Lockwood, Georgiana to James Hall and ano. trustees Thomas C. Moore. 2,500
Lippmann, Leopold J. to Conrad Wasserman. nom
Moss, Frank exr. Maltby G. Lane to Ella R. Van Buskirk, Bloomfield, N. J. 1,800
Marsh, Charles M., Morris Plains, N. J., to Archibald C. Shenstone. 2,000
McKane, James to John Y. McKane. 1,550
Same to same. 1,000
Same to same. 700
Same to same. 1,050
Same to same. 1,500
Same to same. 1,000
Same to same. 500
Monsees, John to John M. Stearns. 700
Miller, James to Michael and Theresa Nuber. 700
Monaghan, Frank J. to Annie E. and Henry A. Monaghan. nom
Morgan, Ellen to Mamie E. Cruse. val. consid
Moran, John to John Kerwin. 3,000
Nostrand, George E. to Eliza S. Farran and ano. exrs. John S. Farran. 500
Olena, Alfred H. to David S. Jones. 7,550
Ostrom, Edward to Isaac P. Rogers. 3,000
Porterfield, Robert and ano. exrs. Allen Alexander to Blanch Alexander. 7,525
Same to same. 5,118
Same to same. 5,007
Rausch, Benjamin to Mirabeau L. Towns. 600
Reineking, Emil to Bernhard J. Pink. 700
Rome, Frederick W. to William H. Doremus. nom
Sullivan, Michael to Charles S. Taber and George C. Case, all of Flatbush. 400
Stobbe, Henry and Annie to John R. Sargeant. 3,200
Title Guarantee and Trust Co. to John Lee. 2,500
Same to Samuel Lee. 2,500
Same to same. 2,500
Same to George B. Forrester. 1,000
Same to George C. Blanke. 4,000
Same to same. 4,000
Same to Lizzie F. Kretschmar extrx. Francis A. Moran. 1,500
Same to The Atlantic Trust Co. trustee. 10,000
Same to Elizabeth F. R. Laing. 7,500
Same to same. 7,500
Same to The Northfield Seminary. 1,000
Same to The Franklin Trust Co. guard. Evelyn M. A., Henry A., Edward M. and Lawrence C. Dalley. 8,000
Same to same as trustee for children of Cornelia S. Dow. 8,000
Same to The Northfield Seminary. 5,500
Same to Charles T. Geyer guard. Caro L., Walter F., Marguerite and Anna R. Engs. 3,500
Same to Hattie B. Uhler. 7,500
Same to The Franklin Trust Co. guard. Evelyn M. A., Henry A., Edward M. and Lawrence C. Dalley. 6,000
Same to same as trustee Ella C. Ward. 5,000
Same to The Brooklyn Trust Co. 4,500
Same to same. 4 assigns., each $2,000. 8,000
Same to same. 4,000
United States Savings Bank, New York, to R Rosalie P. Mendes. 12,567
Van Reypen, Nellie C. to Selina Cocks, Flushing, L. I. 1,000
Van Reypen, Nellie C. to Elizabeth M. St. Amant. 2,500
Wever, Josephine F. to Mary B. Weaver, Hudson, N. Y. 1,541

JUDGMENTS.

In these lists of judgments the names alphabetically arranged, and which are first on each line, are those of the judgment debtor. The letter (D) means judgment for deficiency (*) means not summoned. (†) signifies that the first name is fictitious, real name being unknown. Judgments entered during the week, and satisfied before day of publication, do not appear in this column, but in list of Satisfied Judgments.

NEW YORK CITY.

Sept. and Oct.

26 Alton, Henry—H W Benedict....... $1,358 96
28 Ames, Julia M—William Walsmann. 549 02
29 Andress, Charles W—William Campbell. 646 58
29 Armstrong, William A—George Everson, exr.................. 275 16
29 the same——the same.......... 556 75
1 Almy, Edwin R—Nat Bank of North America.................. 868 96
1 the same——the same........... 823 74
1 Audsay, Nathan A—Winslow Robinson....................3,776 02
2 Apollonio, Samuel T—B J Ludwig.. 222 55
26 Beyel, Emilie—J S Jacobs........... 77 02
26 Blank, Joseph C—Jacob Ruppert.... 1,762 56
28 Bopp, Andrew—J W Lauterbach 155 20
28 Beh, Mary A—J G Johnson.......... 190 09
29 Beacham, John—J S Virtue & Co (Lim)...................... 208 26
29 Bonnell, John Harper—Bank of N Y Nat Banking Assoc............... 1,494 20
29 Bauer, John—Annie E Otto.......... 79 42
29 Boyne, William C—Henry McShane Co (Lim)..................... 1,779 69
29 Backer, Abraham—S H Eckman.... 22,023 03
29 Bonnell, J Harper—Poland Paper Co. 1,158 56
29 Bonnell, John Harper / Bonnell, Tammisiu H } Second Nat Bank of Red Bank....... 2,757 30
29 Bonnell, John Harper——the same.... 531 52
29*Baker, Peter—G W Childs........... 315 50
30 Bonnell, J Harper—Second Nat Bank of Red Bank...................... 994 25
30 Baird, James Henry / Baird, Robert B } Liebig Mfg Co. 437 74
30 Burrows, John P / Burrows, James C } Harry McBride.. 870 41
30 Bonnell, John Harper / Bonnell, Tammisin H } Nat Bank of Republic... 3,051 50
30 Barton, William E—Sackett & Wilhelms Lithographing Co........... 256 45
30 the same——the same.............. 224 88
1 Black, Joseph R—Phœnix Iron Works Co.......................... 569 35
1 Brett, William—Mannheim Stern.... 139 07
1 Bernstein, Phillip—J C Wilmerding.. 1,501 12
1 Buethe, Jacob—Seligman Trier...... 156 01
1 Busley, James R, Jr—W F Lyman... 108 99
1 the same——the same 118 05
1 Bessell, John W—James Murray..... 4 9 41
1 Black, Joseph R—Thomas Maddock.. 134 87
1 Bidman, Mary—People State N Y.. 2,000 00
1 Brunon, Marie C—Hannah Birdsell.. 41 00
1 Bates, Charles R—R M Gilmour...... 41 20
1 Butler, Jay F—Toledo Metal Wheel Co.......................... 926 29
2 Bloomfield, John J—Edward Kimpton 300 57
2 Beshwater, Abraham—Ameen Batal. 790 46
2 Byrne, Patrick—Marvin Safe Co. costs 53 00
2 Birnbaum, Sigmund—Columbus Market Co.......................... 118 75
2 Brady, Lucy A—Albert Shumway... 195 72
2 Brennan, Michael—G W Venable..... 93 95
2 Blaack, August—G C Berthold........ 157 74
2 Base, Joachim—Emma M Ackley...... 271 39
2 Burton, Joseph L—Thomas Brown.... 120 06
2 Bolger, Martin—Emil Heller......... 317 74
26*Crain, W E S—Ebeneazer Beals...... 105 21
26 Cook, Frank—August Muller.......... 171 79
28 Colhoun, William—Thomas Vernon.. 601 95
28 Coersmeyer, Charles F—Lewis Sylvester........................ 142 53
29 Cohen, Moses—Harris Samilson...... 716 38
29 Cram, J Sergeant, comm'r Dock Dep't—Michael Magee................ 164 32
29 Cohen, Moses—Samuel Firuski....... 299 66
29 Coffin, Frederick R—Poland Paper Co......................... 1,158 56
29 Compton, Melvin D—Joseph Hammitt...................... 168 72
30 Callaghan, Annie—David Jones Co.. 469 99
30 Cullen, Richard J—Catharine Siedento............................ 125 51
30 Cornell, Alonzo B—J A Cocke........ 338 97
30 Couch, Albert C—Elizabeth L Couch ....costs 86 43
30 Carter, Richard J / Carter, John P } C F Pitney..... 289 61
30 the same——J W Pitney........ 247 85
1 Cohen, Wolf—People State N Y...... 2,000 00
1†Caulfield, John T—G D Royston..... 150 00
1 Campbell, James E—Davids Machine Works.......................... 271 93
1 Campbell, Neil—A A Grant.......... 133 96

1 Cohn, Walter I / Cohn, William I } Amory Leland... 2,662 47
1 Cargill, Livingston H—Winslow Robinson.... .... 3,776 02
2 Crandell, E y D—K A Illch........ 81 50
2 Carr, Walter / Carr, Delwin B } James Carroll...... 228 74
2 Camp, W Stanley—John Gleason 192 75
2 Corey, John—Sigmund Ashner....... 817 14
2 Carmiencke, John H—J B Ladd..... . 106 58
2 Callaghan, Annie—David Jones Co... 145 29
2 Chancellor, Mary A—Louis Hoopes... ,86 44
2 Crossley, Charles A—Nat Pipe Bending Co............................ 135 87
2 Carr, Walter / *Carr, Delevin B } Henry Hanson..... 629 18
26 Donnell, Raymond L—Walter Hering 2,886 46
28 Donnell, Raymond L—C H Pepper... 121 61
28 Donohue, Daniel J—M R Cook........ 127 08
28 Dexheimer, John—Emil Steffens..... 179 50
28 Davis, George H—C H Raymond..... 174 42
29 Donovan, William—Albert Busch.... 86 40
30 De Lavalette, Adelaide M — Kate Terry, extrx.... ....costs 79 61
2 Davis, Charles—William Roggenstein. 28 50
2 Dugan, Denis—J F Paulsen.......... 185 82
2 Dreyfuss, Bernard—H W Grindal.... 172 13
26 Eitzen, William—J M Underhill..... 153 55
29 Egenberger, Edward—Morris Green. 891 21
30 Evans, Frederick—Philip and William Ebling Brewing Co................ 110 06
1 Edelson, Abraham—G Z Hawk...... 1,896 79
1 Edelson, Louis——the same.......... 519 07
2 Eble, Andreas—F W Flaacke......... 127 00
2 Erlanger, George S—Calixto Lopez.. 144 00
26 Faulkner, John H—Israel Lewis...... 117 76
26 Foster, William H—J G Mitchell..... 421 90
29 Fischman, Joseph—Rubsam & Horrmann Brewing Co.................. 760 33
29 Farron, Thomas J—G W Childs...... 315 50
30 Fischer, William—J H Mohlman Co. 1,143 35
30 Fischer, George—U S Net and Twine Co................................ 112 16
30*Ferguson, Robert L—A Baertsorn.... 2,460 35
1 Flynn, Florence C, extrx—C W Dickel................................. 902 15
1 Finn, Sidney H—J M Favill......... 254 24
1 Feldman, Benson M—Phillip Howell. 323 96
1 Fursman, Annie H—H T Slosson..... 578 41
1 Fay, J Rockwell / Fries, Louis K } Winslow Robinson............ 3,776 02
2 Franke, Johan / Franke, Otto M } Monopol Tobacco Works............1,304 85
2 Frey, Moritz—Julius Sewalsky....... 147 58
2 Florence, Mary—William Drucker... 265 36
2 Fursman, Annie H—H T Slosson..... 618 59
2 Fruchteuicht, John—Bernard Heim.. 324 99
2 French, Patrick J—Richard Vom Hofe................................ 190 92
28 Goldsmith, Charles—Samuel Levine.. 2,517 74
29 Groschee, William—J B Huntting.... 25 95
29 Guilfoyle, Dennis—George Everson, exr................................ 275 16
29 Gates, Leonard H—Cook & Bernheimer Co............................ 507 47
30 Guenard, Lionie—Henry Witson..... 73 45
30 Giesecke, Ramien—Martin Schroeder. 191 52
30 Grimes, John—Charles Stone, trustee. 100 86
30 Garrow, John F—P & W Ebling Brewing Co............................ 110 06
30 Grinspan, Abraham—H B Claflin Co. 167 82
1 Graeve, Henry W—Gramercy Co.... 322 28
1 Gliues, Moses K—Emily G Ellingwood................................ 127 42
1 Griswold, Margaret D—J R Churchill, trustee............................ 419 93
1 Gardner, Charles E / *Gardner, George I } E D Howes..... 540 72
1 Gedney, Wm H / Gregg, Joshua } Winslow Robinson 3,776 02
1 Glor, Hippolyte—J L Pettit.......... 137 50
2 Grad, Osios—Frederick Kaffeman.... 199 56
2 Gollner, Ada F M—Mary Pratt..... .. 86 65
26 *Humphrey, Theodore F / Humphrey, James H / Humphrey, Correl..... } Union Nat Bank of Troy...... 6,994 32
26 Hirsch, Rosalie—S S Stern.......... 70 92
26 Hoops, Frederick—J J Matthews..... 481 13
28 Haan, Rudolph M—G L Hoffman.... 372 38
28 Hickey, Frances—S H Hayt.......... 39 67
28 Heiland, Mary C—Robert Blissert ....costs 22 47
28 Herrell, George—S L Eisner.......... 78 50
29*Hirsch, Rosalia—H C Howell, Jr..... 95 19
29 Harper, William Durbin—Bank of N Y Nat Banking Assoc............. 1,494 20
29 Hallet, Theodore—Edwin Ives........ 35 20
30 Harper, William D—Second Nat Bank of Red Bank...................... 994 25
30 Hanley, James—George Unger....... 139 37
30 Howe, Bridget / Howe, Michael } W H Sage......... 154 14
30 Heffron, Thomas H—H E Dewey..... 85 01
30 Harper, William D / Harper, Tacie McD } Nat Bank of Republic.... 3,051 50
30 Hess, George / Hess, Henry } Henry Herrmann.... 312 50
1 Hefner, Joseph—J S Piza............ 249 23
1 Huber, Theresa—Chester Billings..... 176 62
1 Huner, John F—James Kane......... 44 39
1 Heinemann, Simon D—Mary Keckeisen, exr.............................. 606 52
2 Hale, Joseph W—The Chelsea........ 444 36
2 Henderson, Juliette C—Fenwick Hall Co................................ 455 06
2 Hirsch, Rosalia—C H Bruel......... 504 43
2 Hockstadter, Sigmund / Honeywell, Edward } E P Tysen. 448 17
2 Hanse, James—W B Tatham....... . 447 38
2 Immig, Charles H—W P Tatham ... 447 38
26 Jordan, Frank M—J D Aspinwall.... 118 93
28 Jensen, Harold—W E D Vincent..... 80 89
30 Junior, William—Jeweler's Weekly Publishing Co. 142 34

1 Johnson, Fanny—J P Delehanty...... 160 97
26 Kimball, Dennison W / Kimball, Maria } James Gilmartin.......... 118 89
26*Kirshbaum, Jacob—Louis Rosenberg. 99 85
26 Kitchel, Charles H—W H O'Dell..... 10 80
26 Keller, Joseph—Samuel Marx........ 124 73
26 Kaplan, Joseph—D H Roberts....... 1,225 35
28 Kirchoff, Fred—P D Armour.......... 609 44
28 Kolb, Henry—Lorenz Zeller.......... 72 74
29 Kleneo, Martin—Robert Gordon...... 77 33
29 Kelly, Michael J / Kelly, Thomas P } J T Nevin......... 45 34
29 Knox, J Armoy—D H Van Name..... 300 20
29*Kendrick, Frank M / Kendrick, Adele } Lawrence Marston.......... 1,019 75
30 Klein, John—J J Phillips............ 86 52
30 Kelly, Joseph T—Marvin Safe Co.... ....costs 37 79
30 Kiernan, Thomas—N Y and Brooklyn Brewing Co........................ 216 56
1 Khuner, Norbert C—Nineteenth Ward Bank.............................. . 184 86
2 Kloffar, Anna—Paul Domeyer....... 109 66
2 Kirby, Thomas E—Western Nat Bank 1,940 15
26 Lubring, John H—Henry Ruhl...... 1,539 64
26 Leikowitz, Mary—Lewis Sylvester... 176 58
28 Lee, Mon—Chu Kwai.............. 1,633 97
28 Lang, Julia—Thomas Sullivan........ 227 92
28 Locke, Charles E—E C Hedmondt.... 1,270 56
28 the same——the same........... 3,176 90
29†Levine, Hyman—F M Lowenstein.... 112 87
29 Leavitt, Rufus W—Wright & Co (Lim)................................. 102 69
29 Lens, Albert—David Greenfield...... 185 00
30 Lippman, Leonard—Nancy Viano.... 191 61
30 Lackes, Christopher — V Loewer's Gambrinus Brewery Co........... 123 40
30 Lynch, James F—Eisner & Medelson Co................................. 140 80
1 Ludden, Julius E—Sigmund Haubenstock............................. 40 50
1 Lemlein, Benjamin—Joseph Kahn.... 92 84
1 Leverich, Henry M—C G Cornell, Jr.. 61 11
1 Lovejoy, John F—R M Gilmour...... 41 20
2 Loeb, Frederick—William Drucker... 265 36
2 Litzinger, Charles / Litzinger, Emile A } John Eichler Brewing Co.... 241 50
26 Meyers, Jacob J—Louis Rosenberg... 99 85
26 Meyer, Arthur L / Moore, John } N Y Nat Exchange Bank........... 225 33
26 Menken, Mortimer M—H W Benedict.............................. 1,637 77
26*Martin, Charles A—S S Stern........ 70 92
28 Morton, William O—W H H James.. 301 26
28 Mackintosh, Louis A—Mitchell Packard................................. 86 64
28 Marvan, Jennie—George Watson..... 102 41
28 Millhauser, Napthali—William Silverman............................... 62 10
28 Maas, Henry—Nathalie F Reynal.... 103 04
28 Muller, John—F W Mertens.......... 314 13
28 Muller, Katie — Edward Sanders ....costs 23 96
29 Martin, Charles E—H C Howells, Jr. 95 19
29 Mitchell, Charles R—William Campbell.............................. 646 58
29 Meyer, Arthur L—D W Moran 241 82
29 Mannkopf, Charles—Gretchen Defren 96 13
29 Meyer, Henry—Theodore Lewis...... 49 25
29 Meyer, Regina—Diederich Stelling... 243 42
29 Matthews, James, Comm'r Dock Dep't —Michael Magee.......... . ... 164 32
29 Murphy, James—W P Willis......... 298 76
29 Montgomery, Edward L—B E Hall.. 71 45
29 Murphy, James—T F Schumann..... 171 12
29 Mars, Henrietta A—Jacob Raichle... 164 87
29 Munger, Alfred S / Munger, Louis A } New Haven Clock Co............ 454 29
1 Murray, John E—Martin Schrenkeisen.............................. 148 62
1 Mallet, Adrian—P G Sabatie......... 1,341 44
1 Metcalf, Benjamin F—D F Wood.... 77 00
1 Mahon, Dennis—F & M Schaefer Brewing Co.... .... 284 53
1 Mott, Samuel C—Winslow Robinson. 3,776 02
1 Myers, Henry J—M M Govan......... 779 60
2 Martin, Charles E—C H Bruel....... 504 43
2 Myberg, Maude—F G Hertee......... 72 90
2 Meyer, Frederick—Edwin Bennett... 287 15
2 Munch, Adam—W P Tatham...... . 447 38
2 Mayer, Morris S—Columbus Market Co.................................. 118 75
26 McCullough, Willis J—G D Pohalski. 189 16
26 McManus, Patrick H—Bradley & Currier Co (Lim)....................... 370 74
26 McGrath, Patrick J—Max Stiner..... 105 75
28 McDonald, William H / McDonald, Blanche A } T F McDonald.........9,677 40
28 Mackintosh, Louis A—Mitchell Packard 86 64
30 McGowan, Hugh C—Sophia Strauss.. 226 00
30 McRae, Virginia H—H C Jenkins.... 325 74
30 McLaughlin, John—G E Ketcham... 831 67
1 McCarty, Frank J—J W Post........ 208 99
2 McAleer, John—Archibald Fraser.... 268 48
2 McKenna, Patrick / McKenna, Margaret } William Drucker............ 265 36
2 McLaughlin, Lizzie—C E Colsey...... 518 48
28 Nightengale, James—H J Gaddum... 1,190 96
28 Neuburger, Jacob—R S Gould Co.... 126 00
30 Newton, Thomas—J H Berry........ 197 13
2 Nimmo, Sarah J / *Nimmo, Charles W } Charles Weinberg.......... 246 35
28 O'Sullivan, John / O'Sullivan, Margaret } Henrietta Cohn..(D) 8,509 78
29 Osborn, Charles S—M L Ernst... .... 221 45
30 O'Neill, Hugh J—B F Morningstar... 96 30
26 Purdy, Jonathan S—John de Rivera.. 196 53
26†Pratt, Samuel G—Leopold Bergfield.. 32 50
28 Patton, James J / Patton, William J } Joseph Cabus, Jr....... . .. 146 98
29 Price, Jesse—Chatham Nat Bank..... 126 56
29 Price, Jesse—Market and Fulton Nat Bank.... .... 820 42

29 Post, Edwin A, comm'r Dock Dep't—Michael Magee........ .... 164 32
30 Potter, La Motte—W E Lown........1,132 20
1*Pearce, John—C G Cornell, Jr........ 61 11
2 Prediger, William—Christian Striffler 246 66
2 Poole, Sidney G—Mary Pratt..... .... 86 65
26*Redington, W E—Ebeneazer Beals... 106 20
26 Rogers, Lilian—H W Benedict....... 1,358 91
26 Ross, George—Joseph Bierhoff....... 147 56
28 Ross, James Stewart—Bryant Building Co (Lim)....................... 409 30
29 Roberts, Austin J—Thomson-Houston Electric Co.... .... 6,641 43
1 Rogers, John B—N P Rogers.........25,081 23
1 Root, James H—Nat Bank of North America.............................. 868 96
1 the same——the same 623 74
1 Reineman, Soloman — New Britain Knitting Co......................... 319 22
2 Robitscher, Joseph—R J Dean...... ... 461 00
2 Robinson, Austin R—Western Nat Bank.............................. 1,940 15
2 Reed, James C—Maria W Livingston. 922 63
2 Ryan, Michael—J E Lassig.... ...... 1,808 02
2 Robinson, Morris—S I Kepelman..... 359 03
26 Schaefer, John E—Ebeneezer Beals.. 106 21
26 Schultz, Gustav / Schultz, John } William Stroube.. 822 35
26 Schwartz, Charles—Leopold Bergfield 32 50
28 Schmidt, Frederick—James Mooney.. 56 50
28 Schumacher, William—F W Mertens. 314 13
29 Schwartz, Julius / *Schwartz, David P } Emanuel Kleinmann......... 169 47
29 the same——the same 365 24
29 Streeseman, John F—G F Swift...... 394 40
29 Spiwak, Louis—Rubsam & Horrmann Brewing Co........ .... 760 33
29 Stark, Isador / Stark, Edward J / Stark, Gustav } H W T Mali 1,565 96
30 Sherwin, Frank R—H K Thurber.... 2,060 26
1 Streifler, Jacob—Union Stove Works 358 74
1 Sardy, John L—N P Rogers.........25,081 23
1†Steinhardt, John—F H Brummer.... 51 00
1 Sulzer, Alfred—Nat Bank of North America.............................. 868 96
1 the same——the same... .... 623 74
1 Solomon, Walter B—G R Hill........ 73 50
1 Solomon, Ephraim—Amory Leland.. 2,662 47
1 Scott, Archibald / Scott, Walter E / Scott, Archibald T } Merchants' Nat Bank.........3,372 28
1 Shepard, Charles D—Winslow Robinson.................................3,776 02
2 Sterling, Richard—R K Fox......... 85 00
2 Sneckner, William H—James Carroll. 228 74
2 Simmons, James A—Ashbury Park Nat Bank...........................7,511 55
2 Solomon, David / Solomon, Bernhard } Clara Rosenthal 796 39
2*Sutton, James F—Western Nat Bank. 1,940 15
2 Schaper, Albert—Sarah E Bussell.... 321 60
2 Stricker, Frederick—Joseph Pur..... 1,209 89
2 Styles, Clara—Emma Breitenbach, admrx............................. 332 75
2 Schmeckenbecker, George / *Schmeckenbecker, John G } Patrick Callaghan 110 50
2*Sneckner, William H—Henry Hanson 629 18
26 Smith, Edward—H W Benedict..... 1,637 77
26 Smith, John—Miguel Llano.......... 128 96
26 Smith, Albert E / Smith, Elizabeth K } Joseph Bierhoff. 147 50
30 Smith, C Howard—T M Barnes...... 376 00
26 The Mayor, Aldermen, &c — M B Brown...............................4,970 04
26 The Fioune Mfg Co—T C Burrows.... 152 52
26 The Metropolitan Railway Co / The Manhattan Railway Co } Mary L Jones et al.... .... 132 34
26 the same——Maria L Marshall.... 923 85
26 the same——J E Ahrens.......... 952 48
26 the same——Charles Ludovici.... 1,047 28
28 The Federal Valley Coal Co—Moses Strauss.............................1,032 81
28 Lodi Chemical Co—G W McLean, recvr.......... .... 271 00
28 The Railway Directory Publishing Co —C H Pepper.... .... 121 61
28 The Mascotte Invalids Lifting Chair Co—Kate A Tingley........ .... 578 13
28 the same——F B Tingley......... 565 64
28 The Pelham Bay Park Electric Light Power and Storage Co — Jane Franklin............................. 145 24
29 Riverside Wheelman—Hermann Korff 32 00
29 J H Bonnell & Co (Lim)—Bank of N Y Nat Banking Assoc 1,494 20
29 Ellenville Gas Light Co—Nason Mfg Co.................... .... 87 11
29 Suburban Electric Construction Co—Thomson-Houston Electric Co......6,641 43
29 J H Bonnell & Co (Lim)—Market and Fulton Nat Bank... .... 820 42
29 The Willard Metal Co—A H Love & Co.................................. 705 42
29 The J H Bonnell & Co (Lim)—Second Nat Bank of Red Bank............ 531 52
29 the same——the same.............2,757 30
30 The Metropolitan Elevated Railway Co / The Manhattan Railway Co } Samuel Weiss.. 878 31
30 the same——the same et al........ 132 43
30 The J H Bonnell & Co (Lim)—Second Nat Bank of Red Bank 994 25
30 The Manhattan Railway Co / N Y Elevated Railway Co } Gordon Cunard.10,109 83
30 J H Bonnell & Co (Lim)—Nat Bank of Republic 3,051 50
30 Mark's Adjustable Folding Chair Co (Lim)—Washington Nat Bank......1,228 61

30 The Willard Metal Co—H B Claflin Co.......... 167 82
1 The Metropolitan Elevated Railway Co / The Manhattan Railway Co } J M Otter.....1,782 76
1 the same——Alexandrina Jordan.1,757 99
1 the same——Gretchen Seebach, individ and extrx.......... 294 43
1 the same——the same, individ.... 712 00
1 the same——the same, extrx..... 512 00
1 The American Electric Exercise Machine Co—W A Simmons..........1,332 11
1 The Pennsylvania Railroad Co—Thomas Keck..........1,500 00
2 J Dewing Publishing Co—T J Gagney Binding Co.......... 276 30
2 Banker & Campbell Co—John Baehr. 372 40
2 The Mayor, Aldermen, &c—G L Greene.......... 103 73
2 Porr Lithographing Co—Konrad Schmidt.......... 267 00
2 Barr Electric Mfg Co—Electrical Engineer.......... 91 77
2 Fred Hower Brewing Co (Lim)—De La Vergne Refrigerating Machine Co. 5,464 89
26 Tiernan, Hugh P—Charles Schlesinger.......... 104 81
26 Todd, Edward Farnham—D F Harris 261 93
26 Taylor, Charles R / Taylor, Frank } A S Moore..... 866 47
26 Thayer, Stephen H / Thayer, Horace H exrs and trustees } J H Valentine, admr.........4,403 15
30 Titus, Herbert B—George Degenhardt 129 79
30 Trigg, Henry S—G A Wilson....... 95 45
1 Thie, Otto—W L Glorieux..........1,011 05
2 Townsend, Solomon S / Townsend, Maurice E / Townsend, Edward N } Gregory & Coe Lumber Co.......... 193 72
2 Tucker, William G—Germania Bank. 1,099 22
28 Utley, William R—Moses Strauss....1,032 81
2 Ullrich, Charles A—Bernard Heim.. 324 99
29 Vette, John / *Vette, Dederick } W C Cushman..... 204 00
29 Valentine, Robert H C—Second Nat Bank of Red Bank.......... 581 52
30 Vernon, Edward—E M Beardsley ... 272 51
30 Vernam, Remington / Vernam, Florence G } Phoenix Furniture Co......3,530 91
2 Valentine, Robert H C—Chatham Nat Bank.......... 832 82
2 Valentine, Robert H C—Bank of N Y Nat Banking Assoc.......... 976 82
2 the same——the same..........1,718 48
30 Van Cleve, Garret—John Walsh..... 123 87
28 Ward, William—Martin Reynolds... 288 71
29 Waters, John / Waters, Adolph } T M Ansdell...... 537 88
29 Wolfgram, Louis—F C Mainhart..... 47 50
29 Whipple, Frederick H—John Baehr.. 375 00
29 Whitecar, William A—Lawrence Marston..........1,019 75
29 Walter, James N—Morris Wasel..... 109 51
29 Wilson, S Franklin—Violet Cheesman 54 49
30 Wendt, Charles M—J H Mohlman....1,143 35
30 Willoughby, Norman G—O L Hinds. 166 88
30*Walsh, James—B F Morningstar..... 96 30
30 Webster, Thomas—Thomas Kendel... 62 00
30 Webb, Susan E—Julia Adam......... 242 63
30 Weiler, Charles H—A Baertsorn.....2,460 35
1 Waterman, Franklin—Wallace Muller & Co (Lim)..........2,617 93
1 Wah, Wing—Sam Lee.......... 96 53
1†Waitzfelder, Samuel—Henry Grubb. 47 00
1 Wyckoff, Jacob V D—L F Sass....... 156 52
1 Walker, Herbert H—Simon Wright.. 146 92
1 West, Charles G—Winslow Robinson. 3,776 02
2 White, Robert J—Richard Vom Hofe. 192 95
2 Wognum, John H—Philip Treanor... 392 41
2 Yale, Maude—F G Herter.......... 72 90
1 Zimmerman, Ernest—Isaac Rosskam. 180 50

KINGS COUNTY.

Sept. and Oct.

26 Allen, Thomas—G I Amsdell.......... $394 00
30 Armstrong, William A—G Everson, exr J Wilkinson.......... 275 16
25 Bennett, William J—B H Brow...... 243 35
25 Breen, Martin—P O'Dowd..........5,342 31
29 Benjamin, Edward B / Benjamin, Irving J } Bishop & Cox........ 330 86
30 Brownell, John E—Catherine Cleary. 69 85
30 Bailey, William T—D Winant....... 173 06
1 Blohm, Charles—W H Henneberger. 1,228 42
25 Cusick, Rose—J M Droge.......... 114 92
25 Chapman, Louisa W—J A Smith..... 131 72
25 Countryman, Alfred—J B Sweeting.. 719 55
25 Carr, Walter / Carr, Delwin B } Krull & Volger.... 522 26
25 the same——the same..........1,000 67
26 Carpenter, G Storms—J Loader...... 78 93
28 Cook, Frank—A Muller.......... 171 79
28 Congro, Frank—J T M Brewster...... 28 10
28 Curtis, James—T Curtis.......... 247 40
29 Coers, Meyer Charles T—L Sylvester. 142 53
29 Cullen, Edward J—Fishel & Levy.... 84 85
30 Cozzens, Charles E—J Cunivan...... 198 74
30 the same——J F Heydinger...... 243 66
25 Danielson, Josie—Fannie S Hedges... 176 10
25 Duffy, Hugh—J Andrews.......... 32 60
26 Davis, Lew E—Knickerbocker Printing and Pub Co.......... 647 29
26 Dunham, "William" L—Thurber, Whyland & Co.......... 43 77
28 Delmar, A—J H Sand.......... 102 19
29 Downey, William—Wechsler & Abraham..........1,161 16
29 Donohue, Maggie F—W T Ramsey & Co.......... 78 81
29 Davidson, George H—Bishop & Cox. 330 86
29 Dexheimer, John—E Steffens........ 179 50
30 Drinkhammer, Charles—M Stevskel. 35 80
1 Delmar, Mary—Fulton Bank, Brooklyn..........2,041 91
26 Freund, Theodore F—John C Orr & Co.......... 704 85
28 Fedden, George L—J C C Gatje...... 237 96
28 Fish, Isabel C / Fish, James H } W H Sage......(D) 1,162 92
30 Ferry, Rebecca M—T Silk.......... 783 50
30 Ferry, James J—T Silk.......... 285 39
1 Ferry, Daniel——Fulton Bank.......2,041 91
1 Fellows, Franklyn J—M Rofrano.... 680 29
26 Gross, Henry A / Gross, Margaret } F D Bailey....... 72 79
28 Gregory, John—T W Cummings..... 215 00
28 Garguillo, Luigi—G Mennella........ 68 85
28 Goldman, Abraham J—J O Shinsky.. 192 13
30 Gill, Lauretta—T Kelly.......... 123 06
30 Guilfoyle, Dennis—J Everson, exr J Wilkinson.......... 275 16
30 Guenard, Lionie—H Witson.......... 73 45
25 Hawkins, William M / *Hawkins, Elias H } Watson & Pittinger....1,115 54
26 Hall, Thomas H—Lissette Hall....... 101 62
29 Holywell, William C—Wechsler & Abraham..........1,161 16
30 Heffron, Thomas H—H E Dewey.... 85 01
1†Hurlbut, "Addie A"—Robert Thomas 84 78
28 Iverson, Carl—C M Anderson........ 107 94
29 Imperiole, Salvatore—Schiaffino & Co 10 90
29 Imperiale, Salvatore / Imperiale, Rosario } the same...... 64 88
1 Ithill, George—Cross, Austin & Co... 58 78
25 Jacobson, Frederick—G R Fowler.... 442 41
25 Jacobs, Julius—B Rapaport.......... 46 80
26*Jackson, Charles—The Bergner & Engel Brewing Co.......... 40 40
26 Jewett, James C—H F Ogden.....(D) 5,018 65
26 the same——the same.........(D) 5,018 75
26 the same——the same.........(D) 5,018 89
26 Kunzweiler, Maria—W Natelson..... 52 75
29 Krause, George H—D L McDonald... 69 80
29 Knebel, Charles E—W Wright.......3,016 59
29 King, John—J Gleason.......... 131 53
30 Klein, John—J J Phillips.......... 86 52
28 Lang, Julia—T Sullivan.......... 227 92
25 McGilliwie, Alexander L—W J Quinlan.......... 73 98
25 Meyer, Siegmund T / Meyer, Arthur L } H N Jarchow... 232 63
26 McNeill, Henry—G I Amsdell........ 394 00
26 Manning, Michael J—Moore & Sinnott.......... 182 50
28 Meyer, Arthur L—J Selfridge........ 806 17
28 McAveney, Bernard J / *McAveney, John / *McAveney, Bryant } J Siebert..... 51 50
28 Maguire, John—I Mason.......... 300 17
28 Metzger, David—Knickerbocker Ice Co.......... 116 26
28 Muller, Charles H——the same........ 75 33
29 McManus, Patrick—The Christian Moerlein B Co.......... 70 50
29 Mowlem, Gideon / Mowlem, Edward } C S Lynan....... 149 75
30 McKenzie, Murdock W—W H Ammerman.......... 196 69
30 Moore, Marcus D—A M Moore........ 428 75
30 Miesel, Jacob—S T Willets.......... 459 26
30 McEathrow, James E—C S Higgins Co.......... 83 43
30 Muller, Adolph—Anna Meixner...... 241 08
1 Meyer, Gesene—D Lyon.......... 53 41
1 Monahan, Patrick—Central Gas and Electric Fixture Co.......... 166 46
1 Murray, John E—M Schrenkeisen.... 148 69
1 Muenker, Maria A—H Vogel........ 12 25
26 Nolan, John J—G Von Januschowsky. 192 98
29 Newman, John—D Lippmann........ 63 96
29 Nichols, Charles A—J Aronson....... 70 11
29 Neuburger, Jacob S—Robert S Gould Co.......... 126 00
25 O'Neill, Dennis—Gaus & Miller...... 397 00
26 O'Keefe, John D—J Stolts.......... 124 38
30 Poillon, Richard H—H E Roehr..... 200 83
1 Price, George F—A Meurer & Co.... 33 66
26 Quantin, Edward H—Edison Electric Illuminating Co, Brooklyn.......... 110 61
25 Rose, Henry—J Andrews.......... 94 49
28 Rosenbaum, Joseph—H Liepmann.... 153 61
29 Riggs, Walter B—J Hickey.......... 129 43
30 Ross, James S—Bryant Building Co (Lim).......... 409 30
30 Ritter, Maria L—W H Amerman.... 196 69
30 Roesel, John—J Currivan.......... 198 74
30 the same——J F Heydinger...... 243 66
1 Rommeney, Frederick—H W Biffar.. 42 25
25 Schlansky, Moses—H F Burroughs....1,306 44
25 Sueckner, William H—Krull & Volger.......... 522 26
25 the same——the same..........1,000 67
26 Seekamp, John H—J Baehr.......... 235 00
28 Sharkey, Albert G—Brooklyn Union Elevated Railway Advertising Co. 219 75
28 Seidenberg, Henry—D Hirsch & Co.. 99 92
29 Stapleton, Martin J—G E P Howard. 42 60
30 Sheridan, Thomas J—New York and New Jersey Telephone Co.......... 102 40
1 Stewart, Theodore L—R Bennett..... 274 14
26 The Chadwick Two-wheeler Co—Brooklyn Medical Journal.......... 154 51
28 Tietje, Henry—H M Bischoff........ 68 90
28 The Hunt Engineering Co—B R Western.......... 142 70
30 Tracy, Harriet R—Lyon & Smith.... 537 04
30 The Adams & Bishop Co—N Hawkins 2,038 23
25 Walling, Thomas—Watson & Pittinger..........1,115 54
25 Wetherell, Frederick—J H Doering.. 105 37
26 Whigan, Cornelius J—Bergner & Engel Brewing Co.......... 40 40
30 Windrum, Emma—W W Windrum.. 80 94
1 Warshaur, Lewis—D M Koehler & Co 54 83
1 Weitting, Christian—N Y and N J Telephone Co.......... 74 80

SATISFIED JUDGMENTS.

NEW YORK.

September 26 to October 2—Inclusive.

Amerman, Jacob B—George Snyder. (1883).. $178 08
Blake, Sarah F—Thomas Kitson. (1890)......1,442 81
Brown, Frances R Sprague—J C Miller. (1887) 519 19
Brown, Samuel H—Dennis McMahon, Jr. ('82) 94 19
Caughlin, Emily R—C F Kelly. (1891)......... 27 50
Carpenter, Robert B / Cornell, Joseph and Samuel } Rudolph Ranow. (1891)..1,124 62
§Carroll, Joseph W—C J Cronin. (1891)...... 650 50
Campbell, Andrew J—Thomas McPartland. (1891)..........2,500 00
Columbia Jurist Publishing Co—Emma T Corning. (1887).......... 501 67
Colleran, John and Michael—J C Conover (1891)..........1,087 91
*Derrickson, Samuel G—Dennis McMahon. (1891).......... 144 86
‡Darlington, John H—Charles Frazier. (1881).1,956 32
*Ewing, Justus E—John Canavan. (1891).... 129 85
Fischer, William—J H Mohlman Co. (1891)...1,143 35
Farley, Thomas H—Herrmann Weiller. (1891). 265 72
Foley, John—Michael Noonan. (1890).......5,963 37
Same——D F Foley. (1890).......... 634 69
Fitzgerald, Frank T—John Sloane. (1882).... 108 32
Goldschmidt, Lottie—D W Dazian. (1891).... 402 43
Gore, Calvin—L A Jones. (1891).......... 741 02
Same——Michael Meyberg. (1891)..........1,133 58
Gleason, Timothy—Henry Sproessig. (1891).. 28 12
Harris, George S, George T and William T—Samuel Josephs. (1890)..........6,640 58
Haws, William E / Hallin, Henry E } A T Adams. (1891)...... 488 29
Hooper, Rachel A—L A Jones. (1891).......... 741 02
Same——Michael Meyberg. (1891)..........1,133 58
*Hay, James, Sr, James, Jr, John and Archibald Hay—Sylvester Sawyer. (1891)...... 195 92
Home Ins Co—J J Gorman, sheriff. (1891)....1,058 64
Higgins, Thomas—Joseph Weber. (1889)...... 324 01
Hudson Wagon Co—N Y News Publishing Co. (1891).......... 14 96
Hughes, George W—J S Conover. (1891).....1,087 91
Hood, Joseph—Edward Fisher. (1890)........1,054 51
Johnson, Susie R—William Rasquin, Jr. ('91). 98 03
‡Kilpatrick, James—F H Palmer. (1889)......2,029 88
Kenyon, Norman S—Real Estate Record Assoc. (1891).......... 71 81
Kearney, Peter—Frederick Lange. (1888)..... 866 34
Same——same. (1889).......... 94 27
Kenney, George W—A T Adams. (1891)..... 438 29
Lang, Lorenz—John Drohan. (1890).......... 139 61
Laserowitch, Marie—O A Krauss. (1887)..... 95 16
Loechner, George—Virginia Paper Co. (1891). 231 56
Livingston, Harry B / Lovejoy, Josiah T } A T Adams. (1891)... 438 29
Lentz, Henry—Henry Tietjen. (1891).......... 49 11
McMahon, Dennis—Henry Nichols. (1890).... 126 07
*McCabe, James—People State N Y. (1888).. 100 00
Machette, Edwin V—Real Estate Record Assoc. (1891).......... 71 81
Murdock, Harvey—J V Schaefer. (1890)...... 91 71
Same——same. (1890)..........1,081 13
Miller, Peter—Virginia Paper Co. (1891)..... 231 56
Mortimer, William—G W Venable. (1891)..... 94 53
Meyer, Charles T—J A Lantz. (1888).......... 136 18
Marcher, John—Frederick Cook. (1891)....... 189 45
Meyers, Merrick—Leopold Weil. (1891)....... 440 53
†Myers, Lewis—M A Brokman. (1890)..........3,767 70
†Same——same. (1891).......... 86 78
McCormack, Peter and Francis—Robert Stewart. (1890).......... 221 86
‖O'Shaughnessy, John F—Nat Commercial Bank of Albany. (1891).......... 528 37
Ormes, James M—T W Shreve. (1890)........ 378 89
Oppenheimer, Jacob and Bertha—H A Mott. (1891).......... 93 75
Plant, Henry W / Pearce, Willard A } A T Adams. (1891)....... 438 29
*Robinson, Morris—J D Eisenstein. (1891).... 473 24
Schmidtke, Carl—Central Park, North & East River R R Co.......... 119 38
Spriggs, Robert H—John Boyle. (1889)....... 159 50
*Sheehy, Patrick—People State N Y. (1888).. 100 00
Schatz, Adam E—J S Warren. (1885)........ 774 81
Trimm, Frederick M—R W McMaster. (1885).1,095 39
Truman, James O—J K Cilley. (1884)........1,387 86
Same——A R Hammond. (1885).......... 317 85
Thompson, William W—Francis Lynch. (1889). 79 12
Same——same (1889).......... 129 56
Travis, Eugene M and James M—Henry Schoeffler. (1891).......... 86 34
*Thompson, William W—Katharine E Kipp. (1889).......... 92 54
The American Fibre Assoc / The Tompkins Paper Stock Co } Nat Commercial Bank of Albany. (1891)....... 528 37
Van Hoesen, George W—Joseph Weber. (1889) 324 01
Van Tassell, William H—Thomas McPartland. (1891)..........2,500 00
Wendt, Charles M—J H Mohlman Co. (1891)..1,143 35
Wallace, George S—C F Nagel. (1890)........ 107 81
Woods, Thomas—T F Tone. (1890).......... 79 16
Winans, Benjamin W / Ward, Moses W / Wilson, Edward S } A T Adams. (1891)... 438 29
Zeidler, Martin—D W Dazian. (1891)......... 402 43

*Vacated by order of Court. †Suspended on Appeal. ‡Released. §Reversal. ‖Satisfied by Execution.

KINGS COUNTY.

September 25 to October 1—Inclusive.

Andrews, William D / Andrews, George H } J Brooks. (1883).......$2,336 99
Cozzens, Walter—J Hancock Mutual Life Ins Co. (1890).......... 91 63
Collins, Herbert E, individ and admr Sarah E Collins / Conway, William F } H Weil. (1891.) (Release).......... 430 28
Graves, Horace—Phenix Ins Co. (1891)....... 398 72
Lubben, John H—J H Schutte. (1891)....... 821 48
McCann, Thomas J—J Hancock Mutual Life Ins Co. (1890).......... 91 63
Raymond, Newman H / Raymond, Benjamin C } Ross & Snyder. ('91) 126 78
Renton, John R—M Reynolds. (1891)......... 410 81
Trimm, Frederick M—J B Hance. (1885)...... 422 66
Walsh, Thomas / Grabber, Edward } S B Krause. (1890)........ 86 43
Same——same. (1890).......... 169 76
Youngentob, Emma—J Solomon. (1889)...... 28 95

MECHANICS' LIENS.

NEW YORK CITY.

Sept.

26 Union av, No. 1054, e s, 25 s 166th st, 22x40. John Hanson agt Phillip Eckstein, owner, and Frederick Kemlein, contractor...... $56 52

26 Sixth av, No. 691, w s, 80 s 40th st, 20x50. Michael and Richards Gibbons agt Pompeo Maresi, owner and contractor 2,105 06

26 Sixty-fifth st, Nos. 9 and 11, n s, 200 w 8th av, 50x100. Frank E. Truax agt James O'Brien, owner, and W. B. Hunter, assignee of Rondel & Hunter, contractors. 28 00

26 Twenty-second st, No. 448 W., s s, 20x70. Allison & Smith agt Mrs. Ernestena Unger, owner and contractor........... 300 00

26 Boulevard, s w cor 85th st, 400x400. R. J. Cullen agt Homer J. Beaudet, owner and contractor............ .... 109 20

28 Sixty-fifth st, Nos. 29 and 31, n s, 200 w 8th av, 75x100. Joseph McCloskey agt James O'Brien, owner, and Frederick Rondel and Wallace and George A. Hunter, contractors.......... .... 22 00

28 Pearl st, No. 546, n s, 224 e Broadway, 25x100. Architectural Sheet Metal Works agt Anna E. Leaycraft, owner, and Priebe & Co. contractors 198 20

28 One Hundred and Ninth st, No. 341 E., n s, 25x100. Philippe Quaglino agt Frank Rofiri, owner; —— Smith, contractor, and Guiseppe Cobuccio, sub-contractor....... 25 00

28 Same property. Bennardo Cinino agt same.............................. .... 25 00

28 Same property. Johanno Binenti agt same.................. .... 25 00

28 Fifty-third st, s s, 250 w 10th av, 150x100. Michael Tobin agt John Crawley, owner and contractor............ .. .. 184 00

29 Eighty-seventh st, n s, 100 w West End av, 90x100. F. A. Clarke agt John Henney, owner, and James Sullivan, contractor.. 155 60

29 Ninety-ninth st, s s, 260 w 8th av, 50x100. Same agt Hugh McDowell, owner, and James Sullivan, contractor............... 161 25

29 Pearl st, No. 546, n s, 224.8 e Broadway, 24x95. W. J. Peck agt Robert J. Leaycraft, owner, and Priebe & Co., contractors.... 372 20

29 Madison av, s e cor 134th st, 100x50. Philip Dutz and Thomas Kelly agt Thomas Yetter, owner, and Thomas B. McCormack, contractor.............................. 1,000 00

30 Sixty-third st, n s, 300 w 8th av, 37.6x100.5. Henry Iden agt Esther E. Baron, owner, and Robert Carey, contractor........... 334 00

30 One Hundred and Twenty-fourth st, Nos. 166-172 E., s s. Alexander Kenney agt Henry E. Fox, debtor, and Webster White and Stephen P Anderson, owners. 65 00

30 Forty-eighth st, No. 324, s s, 300 e 2d av, 25x100. Hausen & Christensen agt Henry Holck, owner and contractor... . ... 234 75

30 Twenty-seventh st, Nos. 431-435, n s, 400 e 10th av, 75x100. R. J. Cullen agt Homer J. Beaudet, owner and contractor........ 80 60

Oct.

1 Ninety-eighth st, Nos. 220-224, s s, 225 e 3d av, 75x100. P. Blumenthal agt Dempsey & Smith, owners and contractors. .. . 383 00

1 Sixty-fifth st, Nos. 29 and 31, n s, 200 w 8th av, 50x100.5. W. N. Gordon agt J. O'Brien, owner, and George A. Hunter, contractor....... ... . 25 50

1 Seventy-ninth st, No. 153, n s, 393 w Columbus av, 19x102.2. J. T. Hall Building and Decorative Co. agt George A. Denig, owner, and William Nimmo & Son, contractors.................................. 555 00

1 Forty-eighth st, No. 324, s s, 300 e 2d av, 25x100.5. Jacob Rubin agt Henry Holck, owner and contractor....................... 47 65

1 Same property. Richard Dorre agt Nathan Federgreen, owner, and Henry Holck, contractor.......................... .... 711 66

1 Twenty-sixth st, Nos. 328 and 330, s s, 225 w 1st av, 50x100. Charles Wein agt John Matthews, owner, and Peter Graber and R. S. Ferguson, contractors.... .. .. 201 25

1 Forty-eighth st, s s, 300 e 2d av, 25x100. Frank Lenz agt Nathan Federgreen, owner, and Henry Holck, contractor......... 280 00

1 Tenth av, Nos. 488 and 490, e s, 49.5 n 37th st, 49.4x—. A. E. Hemmel agt Georgiana W. Webster, owner, and Thomas Webster, contractor... .... 220 00

2 Tenth st, No. 238, s s, 125 w 1st av, 25x100. W. H. Schmohl agt John P. Schuchman, owner, Fred. Daiber, contractor, and Jacob Schneider, sub-contractor. (Continued from Oct. 19, 1890)..................... 182 00

2 Ninety-sixth st, n s, 70 e Lexington av, 125x100. John Clark agt Owen, Jr., and William McElroy, owners, and Clark & Dolan, contractors 50 00

2 Ninth av, s e cor 56th st, 24x70. P. G. Banks agt Charles Plault, owner, and Benjamin Steinhardt, contractor.... .... 124 00

KINGS COUNTY.

Sept.

25 Bainbridge st, n s, 115.6 e Saratoga av, 180x100. Berkmeier Bros. agt J. Mason Kirby, owner and contractor........................ $150 60

25 Bergen st, n s, 170.11 w Rockaway av, 29x107.2. Earl A. Gillespie agt George H. Rhodes and John Monsees, owners and contractors.............................. .... 517 95

25 Fulton st, s e cor Ashford st, 25x100. George Rehn agt Anna Libone, owner, and Anna Libone and Charles Libone, contractors.................................. 161 76

26 Eastern Parkway, s s, 75 w Thatford av, 25x100. Hall Sash and Door Co. agt Solomon Koenstein, owner, and S Kopalanski & Co., contractors........ .... 726 00

26 Schermerhorn st, n s, 150 w 3d av, 160x100. Paul Rofrano agt Roderick Von Graff, owner and contractor....................... 500 00

26 Seventh st, n s, 297.6 e 4th av, 50.4x100. Frank D. Creamer agt Mary E. Miller, owner, and George Miller, contractor.... 119 05

26 De Kalb av, s s, 150 w Marcy av, 100x100. William R. Rountree agt Elizabeth S. Maitland, owner, and Charles H. Collins, contractor.................................... 484 00

26 Seigel st, No. 61, n s, 98.6 w Ewen st, 24x100.................................. }
Seigel st, Nos. 55-57, n s, 146.6 w Ewen st, 48x100.................................. }
Charles Hofer & Son agt Henry Meyer, Jonas Feldberg and Sarah Barasch, owners and contractors........................ 341 37

26 Flushing av, n w cor Vandervoort av, 25x100. George D. Koch agt Peter Johnson, owner and contractor........ .... 355 00

26 Sumpter st, n s, 300 w Howard av, 25x100. Jacob Steinbreaher agt Albert Otto, owner, and John J. Pirrung, contractor.. 54 00

28 Liberty av, s s, 100 w Watkins st, six houses. Salvatore Bove agt Charles W. Tomlinson, owner, and George Treville, contractor... 340 40

28 Livonia av, s e cor Osborn st, 25x100. James O'Connor agt Abraham Seidenbergh and Rochmiel Abramovitz, owners and contractors. 280 00

28 Macon st, s s, 93.6 w Howard av, 108x100. Raeburn Latourette & Co. agt Charles Lincoln, owner and contractor........... 1,276 12

28 Stagg st, n s, 50 e Bogart st, runs east 50 x north 200 to Meadow st, x west 100 to Bogart st, x south 100 x east 50 x south 100. Gustav Hesse agt Henry Berau, owner, and George Engelhardt, Frank Ibert and George Bruens, contractors.......... 431 25

28 Christopher av, e s, 200 n Belmont av, 25x100. James O'Connor agt Annie Levy, owner, and Reichert Bros., contractors.. 108 00

28 Grand av, s w cor St. Marks av, 26x90. The N. Y. Anderson Pressed Brick Co. agt W. J. Conway, owner and contractor........ 299 09

28 Twenty-third st, s w cor 4th av, 20x50. Hobby & Doody agt John Staebler, owner and contractor... .... 467 00

29 Herkimer st, n s, 200 e Howard av, 16.8x100. Jacob Steinbrecher agt William Wiedeson, owner, and James M. Fraser, contractor 18 25

29 Ferris st, e s, extends from Dikeman st to Wolcott st, 200x150. Charles M. Detlefsen agt The Brooklyn Consumers Hygenia Ice Co., owners and contractors........ .. 917 31

29 Ninth st, n s, 100 e Hicks st, 25x100. James Sullivan agt —— Cosgrove, owner, and —— McCulpin, contractor.. .... 21 00

29 McDougal st, n s, 325 e Saratoga av, 20x100. Charles Ratner agt D. Davison, owner, and Joseph Davison, contractor.......... 605 00

30 Gates av, n s, 80 w Vanderbilt av, 20x75. Thomas Read agt William Schoefer, owner and contractor........................ . 18 78

30 Bay 22d st, n s, 370 w 86th st, 40x96.8, New Utrecht. Halsted Bros. agt Agnes M. Bruns, owner, and Louis Larsen, contractor..... .... 300 00

30 Eastern Parkway, n w cor Osborn st, 45x100. William Gormley agt John Powers, owner and contractor.................. 425 00

30 Bedford av, No. 186, w s, 80 n North 9th st, 20.3x80. Jacob Sternbrecher agt W. H. Myers, owner, and James M. Fraser, contractor.................................. 449 00

30 Eastern Parkway, n w cor Osborn st, 50x100. Hall Sash and Door Co. agt Elizabeth C. and John Powers, owners and contractors 825 00

Oct.

1 Marion st, n s, 350 e Stuyvesant av, 100x100. The Bradley & Currier Co. (Lim.) agt Josiah Morgans and Catharine Whalen, owner and contractor...................... 1,100 00

SATISFIED MECHANICS' LIENS.

NEW YORK CITY.

Sept.

26*West End av, n w cor 85th st, 96x100. Frank Falk agt Samuel Colcord and Gerald L. Schuyler. (Lien filed Sept. 22, 1891) $3,940 95

28*One Hundred and Twentieth st, No. 14 E. John Dempsey agt Mrs. James Gault and Nicholas L. Demorest. (July 10, 1891)... 150 00

28*Same property. Same agt same. (July 28, 1891)............. .... 150 00

29 Greenwich av, No. 30, e s, 114.8 n 10th st, 25x—. Samuel Nichols & Son agt T. Kielley, S. I. Acken and Phœnix Iron Co. (Sept. 25, 1891)............................. .... 188 48

29 Seventy-fourth st, No. 323 E. Minna Mueller agt —— Federgreen. (July 11, 1891).. 48 49

29 Eighty-ninth st, s s, 180 w West End av, 140x100.8. Graff & Co. agt Garret Van Cleve. (Nov. 11, 1890)......... .. .. 1,186 80

29 Same property. Zimmerman & Biershenk agt same. (Nov. 10, 1890)................. 801 80

30‡Thirty-fifth st, Nos. 241-245 W., 69x—. Pelham Hod Elevating Co. agt William H. Ramsay and George Beebe and Thomas Sanderson. (Sept. 17, 1891)............... 260 00

Oct.

1*Twenty-sixth st, Nos. 334 and 336 E., 50x—. Patrick Malony agt Michael McCormack, —— Madden and —— Myer. (Sept. 30, 1891)........... .... 18 00

2 Fox st, w s, 75 n 165th st, 50x100. C. E. Gates & Co. agt Leopold R. Trew. (Aug. 17, 1891).................................. 63 18

2 Fox st, w s, 135 n 165th st, 50x—. A. S. Nichols agt same. (Aug. 22, 1891)........ 90 00

2 Fox st, w s, 151 n 165th st, 50x—. P. G. Decker agt same. (Aug. 14, 1891).... .... 563 60

2 Same property, Wilson, Adams & Co. agt same. (Aug. 20, 1891)................ .... 303 38

2 Same property. E. T. Hawkins agt same. (Aug. 16, 1891)............................ 105 80

2 Fox st, w s, 161.1 n 165th st, 50x—. C. H. Kirk agt same. (Aug. 18, 1891)........... 146 00

2 Fox st, w s, 200 n 165th st. H. G. McClelland agt same. (Aug. 13, 1891) 285 00

*Discharged by depositing amount of lien and interest with County Clerk.

‡Discharged by order of Court on filing bond.

KINGS COUNTY.

Sept.

25 Woodbine st, n w s, 25 s w Knickerbocker av, 200x100. Michael Mayer agt Albert Berckmier, owner and contractor. (Lien filed Aug. 14, 1891)........................ $1,246 45

25 Bergen st, s s, 100 w Hopkinson av, 25x127.9, George Scheinfeld agt Rosa Rosenfeld owner and contractor. (Sept. 18, 1891)... 2,305 00

25 Bergen st, s s, 50 w Hopkinson av, 150x130. W. W. Rope & Co. agt same owner and contractor. (Sept. 19, 1891)............... 45 01

26 De Kalb av, s s, 150 w Marcy av, 100x100. Isaac Norris agt Elizabeth S. Maitland, owner, and Charles Collins, contractor. (Sept. 18, 1891)................ .... 78 96

26 Liberty av, s s, 50 w Watkins st, 100x100. Potts Bros. agt Charles W. Tomlinson and J. Y. Cochran, owner and contractor. (Sept. 21, 1891).............................. 295 99

28 Bergen st, s s, 100 w Hopkinson av, 25x100. Michael Neumann agt Rosa Rosenfeld, owner and contractor. (Sept. 18, 1891)... 45 01

28 Navy st, s w cor Nassau st, 25x78. Palmer Mfg. Co. agt John Ryan, owner and contractor. (Aug. 29, 1891)................... 220 00

28 Navy st, s w cor Nassau st, 25x78. Palmer Mfg. Co. agt John Ryan, owner and contractor. (Aug. 29, 1891).... .... 220 00

28 Chestnut st, w s, 158 s Fulton av, 75x100. Earl A. Gillespie agt The Solidarity Watch Case Co., owner, and J. Le Clair & Son, contractors. (May 18, 1891)....... 687 02

29 Lewis av, s e cor Hancock st, 150x100. Jacob Lazarowitz agt Aaronson & McWhinney, owners and contrators. (Sept. 29, 1891).. 1,340 00

29 Same property. Albert J. Felty agt same owners and contractors (Sept. 28, 1891).. 3,050 00

29 Hancock st, s s, 25 e Lewis av, 180x100. Burke & Garrahan agt same owners and contractors. (Sept. 28, 1891)......... ... 1,970 75

29 Railroad av. w s, 75 n Griffin pl, 50x100. Wyandance Brick and Terra Cotta Co. agt Charles Lohrentz and Stephen Mafera, owners and contractors. (Sept. 21, 1891)....... .... 160 56

29 Same property. Potts Bros. agt same owners and contractors. (Sept. 21, 1891)..... 59 01

Oct.

1 Fourth st, s s, 100 e 6th av, 440x100. Paul Rofrano agt Moses & Fanton, owners and contractors. (Aug. 31, 1891)............. 215 00

1 Third st, n s, 431.9 e 6th av, 44x90. Paul Rofrano and Louis Sanders agt same owners and contractors. (Aug. 31, 1891). 751 56

1 Fourth st, s s, 97.10 e 6th av, 440x100. Charles E. Rogers & Co. agt Moses & Fanton, H J. Dynes, S. F. Moses, Eliza A. Fanton, F. M. Moses, Henry B. Fanton, M. L. Moses, Lewis H. Meyers, Jr., and Charles W. Moses, owners, and Moses & Fanton, contractors. (Aug. 31, 1891).. 1,100 39

BUILDINGS PROJECTED.

The first name is that of the owner; ar't stands for architect, m'n for mason, c'r for carpenter and b'r for builder.

NEW YORK CITY.

SOUTH OF 14TH STREET.

Division st, No. 81, five-story brk flat, 25x40, tin roof; cost, abt $10,000; ar'ts, Snook & Sons. Plan 1268.

William st, No. 79, eight-story brk and iron building, 44.4x36.8 and 38.7, asphalt and cement roof; cost, $80,000; agent, J. M. Thomas, 640 Madison av; ar'ts, Macgregor & Son; m'n, J. D. Murphy; iron, Wallis Iron Works. Plan 1275.

13th st, No. 5 E., three-story brk, iron and glass building, 19.9x70.2, tin roof; cost, $12,000; W. J. Demorest, 21 East 57th st; ar'ts, Bunce & Co. Plan 1277.

BETWEEN 14TH AND 59TH STREETS.

31st st, n s, 53 w Park av, one-story brk building, 28.9x21.7, tin roof; cost, $2,000; J. M. Lohse 3d av, s e cor 17th st; ar't, J. P. Walther. Plan 1270.

56th st, n s, 60 w 9th av, one-story brk building, 15x25, tin roof; cost, $1,000; J. A. Bernholz, 225 West 128th st; ar't, J. W. Cole. Plan 1261.

57th st, s s, 80 e Lexington av, five-story brk flat, 20x40.5, tin roof; cost, $18,000; T. Kieley, 11 West 13th st; ar't, L. C. Holden. Plan 1265.

BETWEEN 59TH AND 125TH STREETS, EAST OF 5TH AVENUE.

102d st, No. 316 E., two-story brk dwell'g, 18x28, gravel roof; cost, $1,000; J. Schmitt, 311 East 101st st; ar't, O. Wirz; b'r, F. Freese. Plan 1269.

117th st, Nos. 535 and 537 E., frame horse run and coal bins, 50 and 75x100; cost, $4,000; Crotty & Lally, on premises. Plan 1263.

2d av, n w cor 101st st, four five-story brk flats, three 25x89, one 25.11x96, tin roofs; cost, $20,000 each; Jessie Mark, Roselle, N. J.; ar't, L. J. Phyfe. Plan 1274.

3d av, No. 1554, four-story brk shop, 25x90, tin roof; cost, $4,000; Catherine A. Deane, 277 West 11th st. Plan 1279.

BETWEEN 59TH AND 125TH STREETS, WEST OF CENTRAL PARK WEST AND 8TH AVENUE.

76th st, n s, 140 w Amsterdam av, two-story brk and stone stable, 25x95, tin roof; cost, $12,000; W. H. Clark, 152 West 86th st; ar't, G. F. Pelham; m'n, J. Began. Plan 1267.

96th st, s s, 205 w Central Park West, six four-story and basement stone dwell'gs, 20x57, with 12x16 extension, tin roofs; cost, $18,000 each; ow'r and b'r, E. Kilpatrick, 42 West 67th st. Plan 1288.

103d st, s s, 80 e West End av, three-story and basement stone dwell'g, 20x55, with 10x15 extension, tin roof; cost, $16,000; ow'r and ar't, same as last. Plan 1286.

West End av, s e cor 103d st, five stone dwellings, one four stories, 20.11x54 with 15 ft. extension, four 20x54 with 10x15 extension, tin roofs; total cost, $86,000; Carew & Drought, 243 West 42d st; ar't, M. V. B. Ferdon. Plan 1285.

110TH TO 125TH STREET, BETWEEN 5TH AND 8TH AVENUES.

St. Nicholas av, n w cor 118th st, five five-story brk and stone flats, irreg. in size, tin roofs; cost, $20,000 each; P. Braender, 120 East 86th st; ar't, W. W. Luyster. Plan 1287.

NORTH OF 125TH STREET.

132d st, s s, 460 w 5th av, two five-story brk and stone flats, 25x76, tin roofs; cost, $20,000 each; A. L. Judge, 164 St. Nicholas av; ar't, J. C. Burne. Plan 1276.

178th st, n s, 125 w 11th av, two-story frame dwell'g, 18x24, tin roof; cost, $1,200; agent, C. G. Haggerty, 244 West 143d st. Plan 1266.

135th st, s s, 200 e 7th av, two five-story brk and stone flats, 25x85, tin roofs; cost, $19,000 each; R. White, 71 West 124th st; ar't, A. Spence. Plan 1284.

23D AND 24TH WARDS.

163d st, s s, Tinton and Forest avs, sixteen three-and-a-half-story frame dwell'gs, 18.5 and 18x44, tin roofs; cost, $3,800 each; J. W. Decker, 841 Forest av. Plan 1264.

Creston av, w s, 700 s Fordham Landing road, one one-story frame greenhouse, 18x60, glass roof; cost, $600; Mary E. Bixby, Fordham, N. Y.; m'n, T. Johnston; c'r, S. H. Mapes. Plan 1278.

Forest av, e s, 47 n 161st st, two-story frame stable, 29x26, gravel roof; cost, $550; A. Rinschler, on premises; ar't, A. Pfeiffer. Plan 1272.

Morris av, s w cor 150th st, two three-story frame dwell'gs, 25x60, tin roofs; cost, $5,000 each; J. H. Westheimer et al., 242 West 130th st; ar't, A. Pfeiffer. Plan 1271.

River av, w s, 250 n 150th st, two-story brk stable, 51x38, tar and gravel roof; cost, $2,500; L. H. Mace, Williamsbridge, N. Y.; ar't, C. T. Mott. Plan 1262.

Washington av, e s, 84 s 182d st, two-story and basement frame dwell'g, 18x40, tin roof; cost, $3,-700; W. J Sheppard, 2427 1st av; ar't, E. N. Unruh. Plan 1273.

Arcularius pl, n s, 325 e Jerome av, two-story and basement frame dwell'g, 20x42, tin roof; cost, $3,000; Elizabeth McPherson, on premises; ar't, J. Spindler. Plan 1282.

Creston av, w s, 200 n 183d st, two-story frame dwell'g, 16x25, shingle roof; cost, $1,100; P. Ryan, Valentine av; ar't and c'r, C. W. Vreeland; m'n, T. Johnston. Plan 1281.

Tiebout av, e s, 80 s Highbridge road, two-story frame building, 17x18, tin roof; cost, $250; ow'r and c'r, C. W. Vreeland, 2500 Tiebout av; m'n, J. P. Levetch. Plan 1280.

3d av, e s, 150 s 183d st, three-story brk shop, 56x30, tin roof; cost, $8,000; B. H. Field, pres't, 21 North Madison sq; ar't, R. E. Rogers; b'r, J. Spears. Plan 1283. (Substituted for alteration Plan No. 1697 filed last week.)

KINGS COUNTY.

Plan 1781—Ralph and Howard avs and Dean and Pacific sts, one two-story and attic brk and slate orphan asylum, 130x105, and extension, 60x146, slate and tin roof, iron cornice; cost, abt $75,000; trustees Hebrew Orphan Asylum, by Moses May, 500 Bedford av; ar'ts, J. B. Snook & Son; b'r, not selected.

1782—North 10th st, North 11th st and Berry st, four one-story and one four-story brk buildings for factory, pattern shop, foundry, &c., 107x52, gravel roofs, iron cornices; total cost, $30,000; Poulson & Egar; ar't, S. Constable; b'rs, W. & T. Lamb and Libbey & Keese.

1783—6th av, n w cor 5th st, five four-story brk and brown stone apartment houses, 19.10 and 20.8x19.10 and 21.8x55 and 60, tin roofs, wooden cornices; total cost, $35,000; ow'r and b'r, L. Bonert, 528 10th st; ar't, W. M. Coots.

1784—3d st, n s, 290 e 7th av, five three-story and basement brown stone dwell'gs, 20x45, tin roofs, iron cornices; cost, $10,000 each; ow'r, ar't and b'r, E. H. Mowbray, Garfield pl, bet 5th and 6th avs.

1785—Willoughby av, s s, 175 e Sumner av, one two-story and attic brk dwell'g, 22x45, and extension, 14x35.8, tin roof, wooden cornice; cost, $10,000; Aug. Grill, Jefferson av, near Bushwick av; ar'ts, D. Acker & Son; b'r, W. Auer.

1786—57th st, s s, 240 e 2d av, one two-story frame dwell'g, 18x25, tin roof; cost, $500; ow'r and b'r, John Ennis, 55th st and 2d av; ar'ts, M. Freeman & Sons.

1787—6th av, n e cor 15th st, two four-story brk stores and tenem'ts, 27 and 28x99 and 60.6, tin roofs, iron cornices; total cost, $30,000; G. O. Van Orden, 428 5th st.

1788—Osborn st, n s, 150 n Livonia av, three two-story frame (brk filled) dwell'gs, 16.8x32, tin roofs; cost, each, $3,000; Sam Tostevin; ar'ts, D. Acker & Son.

1789—Stone av, e s, 240 n Dumont st, three two-story frame (brk filled) dwell'gs, 16.8x32, tin roofs; cost, each, $3,000; ow'r and b'r, Al. Tostevin; ar'ts, D. Acker & Son.

1790—Livonia av, s w cor Osborn st, two three-story frame (brk filled) stores and tenem'ts, 25x67, tin roofs; cost, each, $6,000; ow'r and b'r, Ann Matthews, 1466 Broadway; ar'ts, D. Acker & Son.

1791—Bradford av, e s, 150 s Liberty av, one two-story frame dwell'g, 21x32, tin roof; cost, $2,500; Patrick Brophy, Liberty av, near Miller av; ar't, C. Infanger.

1792—Dean st, n s, 200 e Nostrand av, five three-story and basement brk and brown stone dwell'gs, 20x48.8, tin roofs, iron cornices; cost, each, $6,500; ow'r and b'r, J. A. Bliss, 204 McDonough st; ar't, A. E. White.

1793—Watkins st, e s, 150 n Livonia st, one two-story brk dwell'g, 20x32, tin roof, wooden cornice; cost, $1,500; Michael Sullivan, 1888 Atlantic av; ar't, O. E. Hoffses.

1794—Dumont st, s s, 75 w Watkins st, one two-story brk dwell'g, 20x32, tin roof, wooden cornice; cost, $1,500; ow'r and ar't, same as last.

1795—De Kalb av, s s, 43 e Graham st, one three-story brk store and tenem't, 22x50, tin roof, tin cornice; cost, $5,000; Wm. Vaughn, 444 De Kalb av; ar't, J. Hauser.

1796—Vanderbilt av, w s, 80 s Bergen st, six four-story brk tenem'ts, 19x50, tin roofs, wooden cornices; cost, each, $6,000; Daniel O'Connell, 596 Dean st; ar't and b'r, T. Remson.

1797—Butler st, s s, 129 e Bedford av, one two-story and basement brown stone dwell'g, 20x40, tin roof, iron cornice; cost, $3,800; Mrs. G. F. Beatty, 745 Franklin av; ar't, I. L. Quesenbury; b'r, G. F. Beatty.

1798—Pacific st, s s, 83.4 e Utica av, five two-story frame dwell'gs, 17x38, tin roofs; cost, each, $2,000; ow'r, ar't and b'r, Chas. D. Terry, 1694 Dean st.

1799—Lorimer st, e s, 60 s Conselyea st, one three-story frame tenem't, 15x60, tin roof; cost, $3,000; Jacob Hoffmann, on premises; ar't, F. J. Berlenbach, Jr.; b'r, not selected.

1800—Rochester av, s w cor Bergen st, one three-story frame store and dwell'g, 23.9x50, tin roof; cost, $3,000; Ernst A. Grote, 62 Albany av; b'r, not selected.

1801—Rochester av, s w cor Bergen st, one two-story frame stable, 15x23.9, tin roof; cost, $1,000; ow'r, &c., same as last.

1802—Belmont av, n s, 60 w Fountain av, and Logan st, e s, 90 n Belmont av, eight two-story frame dwell'gs, 20x44, tin roofs; cost, each, $2,500; Richard Geary, 470 Madison st; ar't and br, W. Godfrey.

1803—Nichols av, w s, 225 n Sutter av, five two-story and attic frame dwell'gs, 16.6 and 20.6x28.6, shingle and tin roofs; cost, each, $2,000; Ch. Lobrent and H. Mafna, 2921 Atlantic av; ar'ts, Danmar & Fischer; b'r, not selected.

1804—Evergreen av, e s, 250 s Madison st, one two-story frame (brk filled) stable and dwell'g, 25x50, tin roof; cost, $500; ow'r, ar't and b'r, Wm. Andrews, 1076 Bushwick av.

1805—Arlington av, n w cor Hale av, one three-story frame store and tenem't, 25x60, tin roof; cost, $5,500; J. Grube, 2921 Atlantic av; ar'ts, Danmar & Fischer; b'r, not selected.

1806—Jamaica av, n s, 200 e Barbey st, one two-story and attic frame dwell'g, 20x32, shingle roof; cost, $3,000; ow'r and b'r, F. H. Kolnig, 2921 Atlantic av; ar'ts, Danmar & Fischer.

1807—Tillary st, s w cor Adams st, one one-story brk theatre, 99x153, gravel and metallic tile roof, metal cornice; cost, $100,000; Liebman Bros.; ar'ts, Parfitt Bros.; b'rs, Flynt Construction and Building Co., of Palmer, Mass.

1808—1st st, s s, 272.10 e 7th av, four three-story and basement brown stone dwell'gs, 20x47, tin roofs, wooden cornices; total cost, $28,000; John Magilligan & Son, 56 Berkely pl.

1809—Ralph st, s e s, 115 n e Wyckoff av, two three-story frame (brk filled) tenem'ts, 25 and 15x57, tin roofs; cost, $2,500 and $3,500; Dora Miller, 116 Himrod st; ar't, R. B. Miller; c'r, J. G. Humnel; m'n, not selected.

1810—North 11th st, n s, 100 w Bedford av, one three-story frame (brk filled) store and dwell'g, 25x60, tin roof; cost, $5,000; ow'r and b'r, G. Kleinbub; ar'ts, D. Acker & Son.

1811—Broadway, e s, 62 s Fairfax st, one three-story brk store and dwell'g, 19x45, tin roof, iron cornice; cost, $7,000; H. W. and I. Schwall, 205 Leonard st; ar't, J. Burns; b'r, not selected.

1812—Sheffield av, No. 167, one one-story frame stable, 18x22, shingle roof; cost, $100; Philip Heyer, on premises; b'r, W. Heyer.

1813—Carroll st, s e cor Fiske pl, five three-story and basement brk and brown stone dwellings, 20.1 and 20x50, tin roofs, iron cornices; total cost, $60,000; Wm. Irvine, 395 9th st; ar't, J. C. Burne, m'n, not selected; c'r, day's work.

1814—Jay st, e s, 100 n Willoughby st, one five-story brk, granite and Lake Superior stone Fire Department Headquarters, 50 and 42x103, tile and tin roof, terra cotta and copper cornice; cost, $137,650; City of Brooklyn; ar't, F. Freeman; b'rs, P. J. Carlin & Co. and J. Lees & Sons.

1815—4th av, n e cor Carroll st, one one-story brk stable, 20x35, tin roof, wooden cornice; cost, $300; Mary Hunter, 4th av and Garfield pl.

1816—St. Marks av, No. 691, one two-story brk stable, &c., 40 and 25.4x46.6, slate roof; cost, $7,-500; A. Schwarzmann, 600 St. Marks av; ar't, J. A. Sinclair; b'r, A. W. Blazo.

1817—Central av, e s, 50 n Woodbine st, one three-story frame (brk filled) store and tenem't, 25x57, tin roof; cost, $4,000; ow'r and b'r, Chas. Welcher, 65 Grove st; ar't, H. Vollweiler.

1818—Grand st, Nos. 1197-1203, being 5 e of Stewart av, one one-story coal shed, 61.6x112, gravel roof; cost, $700; ow'r, ar't and b'r, Chas. H. Reynolds, 810 Bushwick av.

1819—Van Voorhis st, s s, 100 e Bushwick av, five three-story frame (brk filled) tenem'ts, 25x63, tin roofs; cost, $4,500 each; ow'r and br, Ch. A. Wehr, Bushwick av, cor Covert st; ar't, B. Finkensieper.

1820—McKibben st, No. 65, one four-story frame (brk filled) tailor shop, 25x32, tin roof; cost, $2,000; J. Greenblat, 119 Boerum st; ar't, H. Vollweiler; b'r, not selected.

1821—Moore st, No. 103, one two-story frame (brk filled) tailor shop, 25x30, tin roof; cost, $1,000; ow'r and ar't, same as last; c'rs, Rosenberg & Fineberg.

ALTERATIONS NEW YORK CITY.

Plan 1721—Liberty st, No. 21, roof raised 3.6, new iron and brk front; cost, $8,000; agent, W. B. Nichols, 16 East 74th st; ar'ts, MacGregor & Son; m'n, J. J. Cody; c'r, G. McKenzie; iron, Cook & Radley.

1722—81st st, s s, 100 e West End av, walls altered; cost, abt $250; Dr. C. F. Hoffman, 51 West 53d st; ar'ts, Snook & Sons; m'n, C. T. Wills.

1723—10th st, Nos. 465-475 E., rear, two-story extension, 19.6x34.8, and walls altered; cost, not given; W. E. Uptegrove, 1180 Dean st, Brooklyn; ar't, J. W. Moulton.

1724—117th st, No. 535 E., repaired; cost, $300; Crotty & Lally, on premises; c'r, J. Regan.

1725—12th av, w s, 260 n 132d st, portion of building raised one story, two-story extension, 24x46; cost, $1,500; T. H. Wheeler, pres't, 43 West 95th st; ar't, J. T. Pennycork; b'rs, Smith & Co.

1726—Lexington av, s e cor 57th st, raised one story, four-story and basement extension, 20.5x23.5, interior alterations and walls altered; cost, $15,000; T. Kieley, 11 West 13th st; ar't, L. C. Holden.

1727—Reade st, Nos. 2-10, interior alterations; cost, $1,350; agents, W. A. White & Sons, 115 Broadway; ar't, H. O. Chapman; m'ns, Darragh & Co.

1728—Greene st, Nos. 204 and 206, raised one story, one-story extension, 24.6x24, new elevator and shaft, walls altered and new front; cost, $18,-000; L. Schultz, 34 West 19th st; ar't, H. Gilvarry.

1729—33d st, No. 13 W., interior alterations, walls altered and roof changed; cost, $7,500; W. W. Astor, 8 East 33d st; ar't, H. J. Hardenbergh; b'r, J. Downey.

1730—35th st, No. 133 E., interior alterations; cost, $700; Rev. Dr. C. H. Parkhurst, on premises; ar't, H. J. Hardenbergh; b'rs, Jeans & Taylor.

1731—9th av, No. 74, new front and doors; cost, $300; lessee, G. Leiebberger, on premises; b'r, J. L. Lowny.

1732—Broad st, Nos. 111 and 113, interior alterations and walls altered; cost, $3,000; L. N. & J. M. Levy, 66 East 34th st; ar't, C. H. Israels.

1733—14th st, No. 520 E., interior alterations, new front and doors; cost, $1,200; Bridget Golden, on premises; ar't, F. Wandelt; b'r, P. J. Connor.

1734—22d st, Nos. 523 and 525, W., interior alterations; cost, abt $300; F. S. Kinney, Butler, N. J.; ar't, W. W. Howe; c'r, A. Ravekes.

1735—Elm st, No. 194, roof altered, rear raised one story; cost, $1,600; C. M. Boland, Woodbridge, N. J.; ar't, I. Cammeau; c'r, T. Cammean.

1736—2d av, No. 190, one-story extension, 21x5.3; cost, $1,000; F. C. Hahn, on premises; b'r, C. W. White.

1737—37th st, No. 18 W., two-story extension, 10x7, and interior alterations; cost, $10,000; Anna C. McCreery, Victoria Hotel; ar't, J. B. Lord; b'rs, Smith & Bell.

1738—Canal st, No. 41, interior alterations and new front; cost, $1,200; L. Cahen, 129 East 92d st; ar't, M. Muller.

1739—Charles st, Nos. 98-104, raised one story in part, one and two-story extension, 64.4x81 and 80, and walls altered; cost, $15,000; C. Hall, 111 East 64th st; ar't, F. Baylies.

1740—108th st, s s, 330 w 9th av, interior alterations; cost, $1,000; Bernheimer & Schmid, 107 West 57th st; ar't, Lederle & Co.

1741—3d av, No. 1251, interior alterations and walls altered; cost, $350; H. S. Strauss, 155 West 57th st; ar't, G. Huttmann.

1742—7th av, s e cor 26th st, walls altered and new front; cost, $2,800; P. Hynes, 108 West 26th st; ar't, G. G. Youngs; b'rs, Spearing & Son.

1743—Greenwich st, s e cor Vandam st, interior alterations; cost, $750; E. May, 236 East 67th st; ar't, J. Munckowitz; m'n, J. C. Lyons.

1744—Nassau st, No. 85, repair damage by fire; cost, $7,600; agent, J. Birchett, 341 West 32d st; ar't, M. F. Pinney; c'r, J. W. Clark.

1745—50th st, Nos. 138 and 140 E., one-story and basement extension, 40x58, interior alterations and walls altered; cost, $20,000; D. Metzger, pres't, 1044 2d av; ar't, L. F. Heinecke.

1746—Wall st, Nos. 49 and 51, walls repaired; cost, $18,000; Atlantic Mutual Ins. Co., on premises; ar't, J. Sexton; m'n, C. Callahan.

1747—25th st, Nos. 165 and 167 W., interior alterations and walls altered; cost, $5,000; The Geo. C. Flint Co., 104 West 14th st; ar't, F. C. Merry.

1748—Lexington av, s e cor 60th st, five-story extension, 21.6x41.5, roof changed, interior alterations, walls altered and new front; cost, $30,000; H. B. Stein, 143 East 49th st; ar't, T. S. Godwin.

1749—Broadway, No. 1241, front alterations; cost, $90; C. D. Shepard, on premises; c'r, J. Leslie.

1750—147th st, s s, 200 w Brook av, raised to grade; Bridget Lennon, on premises.

1751—5th st, No. 816, new boiler stack; cost, $300; Mary A. Young, 607 Carlton av, Brooklyn; m'ns, Van Riper & Co.

1752—Eldridge st, Nos. 209 and 211, walls altered; cost, abt $1,000; Emily R. Kipp, Mt. Vernon, N. Y.; ar't, J. W. Moulton.

1753—27th st, No. 502 W., interior alterations, walls altered; cost, $1,200; A. Schaefle, 323 10th av; ar'ts, Thom & Wilson.

1754—47th st, Nos. 243 and 245 W., two-story extension, 50x22; cost, $1,500; G. Bickelhoupt, 747 West End av; ar'ts, Thom & Wilson.

1755—German pl, e s, 350 n Westchester av, moved to new foundation; cost, $500; G. Dure, 627 Courtlandt av; ar't, F. J. Miller.

1756—169th st, s s, 42 w Vanderbilt av, moved 8½ ft. rear to new foundation, three-story and cellar extension, 30x15, interior alterations and walls altered; cost, $3,500; J. Pfeiffer, on premises; ar't, F. J. Miller.

KINGS COUNTY.

Plan 926—Washington st, s e cor Tillary st, erect division wall; cost, $180; Liebman Bros.; ar'ts, Parfitt Bros.; b'r, Flynt Construction and Building Co., Palmer, Mass.

927—Hancock st, s e cor Bedford av, interior alterations; cost, $200; J. A. Dillard, on premises; b'r, H. J. Smith.

928—Stockholm st, No. 18, door and window openings, excavate cellar, &c.; cost, $500; Emma V. Schmidt, on premises; b'r, J. O'Sullivan.

929—Ryerson st, No. 124, flat tin roof; cost, $500; Mary H. Whitenack, on premises; ar't, J. Whitenack.

930—22d st, No. 332, raised 16 feet on stone and brk wall; cost, $500; Mr. Mullaley, on premises.

931—Lawrence st, No. 114, add one story; cost, $700; Chas. Ruhlman, —— Adams st; b'r, B. J. Kolle.

932—Bowne st, s s, 140 w Richards st, rebuild part front wall, portion of upper stories removed; cost, $2,000; ow'r and ar't, Henry R. Worthington, Hydraulic Works.

933—Bayard st, No. 182, one-story frame extension, 20x5, tin roof, part of front wall taken out; cost, $200; ow'r, and ar't, M. Spinner, on premises; b'r, J. Rueger.

934—Varet st, No. 201, one-story frame extension, 25x5, tin roof, part of front wall removed; cost, $100; ow'r, ar't and b'r, Mr. J. Kern, 192 Varet st.

935—Kent av, Hewes and Penn sts, foundation for water tanks on roofs, &c.; cost, $1,000; D. Appleton & Co.; ar't and b'r, Harkness Fire Extinguishing Co.

936—Hancock st, No. 704, new stone stoop, new doorway and interior alterations; cost, $300; Denis Hayes, 782 Monroe st.

937—Hart st, No. 547, two-story frame extension, 8.11x7.6, gravel roof; cost, $250; Margaret Kaffy, on premises; ar'ts, Langston & Dahlander.

938—Hope st, Nos. 11-17, rear, add one story, also four-story brk extension, 78x13 to 17, cement roof, interior alterations, rebuild rear wall, &c.; cost, $1,500; James Cavanagh, on premises; ar't, M. J. Morrill; b'r, not selected.

939—Schenck av, No. 187, two-story frame extension, 16x20, tin roof; cost, $140; George Lohmann, on premises; ar't, R. Von Lehn.

940—Cleveland st, No. 226, raised 4 feet on brk wall; cost, $200; Mr. Walters, on premises.

941—Frost st, No 74, one-story frame extension, 12x13, tin roof; cost, $200; Peter Pierce, on premises.

942—Lafayette av, s s, 140 w Bushwick av, add one story to main building and two stories to extension, also three-story frame extension, 12.6x16, tin roof; cost, $1,000; A. Jobum, on premises; ar't, H. Vollweiler; b'r, not selected.

943—Kingsland av, e s, 200 s Nassau av, one-story brk and frame extension, 20x40, gravel roof; cost, $1,500; ow'r and b'r, Alfred Sheffler, 248 Kingsland av; ar't, J. F. Conlon.

944—Johnson av, s w cor Lorimer st, add two stories, also four-story frame extension, 25x16.6, tin roof; cost, $3,000; Frank Hess, on premises; ar't, H. Vollweiler; b'r, not selected.

MISCELLANEOUS.

BUSINESS FAILURES.

N. Y. ASSIGNMENTS—BENEFIT CREDITORS.

Sept.

30 Nimmo, Sarah J. and Charles W. (composing firm of Wilson, Nimmo & Son, upholstery and decorations, at No. 336 Columbus av and No. 8 East 60th st), to James C. McEachen; without preferences.

30 Rich, Aquila B. and Willis B. Troy (Aquila B. Rich & Co., buying, selling, etc., and otherwise dealing in bicycles and similar machines, at No. 1790 Broadway), to Willard N. Baylis; preferences, $7,000.

PROCEEDINGS OF THE BOARD OF ALDERMEN AFFECTING REAL ESTATE.

* Under the different headings indicates that a resolution has been introduced and referred to the appropriate committee. † Indicates that the resolution has passed and has been sent to the Mayor for approval. ‡ Passed over the Mayor's veto.

New York, September 29, 1891.

REGULATING, GRADING, ETC.

Southern Boulevard, from Home st south to Hunts Point road.†
101st st, from 2d av to East River.†
141st st, from e s Alexander av to w s Willis av.†
141st st, from w s Brook av to e s Willis av, at expense of Wm. O'Gorman.†
148th st, from Boulevard to 12th av.†
149th st, from Boulevard to 12th av.†

CURBING AND FLAGGING.

Southern Boulevard, from Home st south to Hunts Point road and crosswalks laid at intersecting and terminating sts and avs.†
28th st, from 9th to 10th av.†
37th st, from 8th to 9th av.†
99th st, both sides, bet 2d and 3d avs.†
101st st, both sides, from 2d av to East River.†
115th st, from 3d to Lexington av.†
136th st, n e cor 2d av, extending east abt 100 ft.†
141st st, both sides, from Alexander to Willis av.†
148th st, from Boulevard to 12th av, and crosswalks laid at the intersecting avs.†
149th st, from Boulevard to 12th av, and crosswalks laid at the intersecting avs.†
Jerome av, both sides, from McCombs Dam Bridge to Southern Boulevard.†
Madison av, both sides, bet 131st and 132d sts.†
Mount Morris av, n w cor 120th st, abt 100 on av and 300 on st.†
10th av, in front of Nos. 390 and 392.†
10th av, e s, from 28th to 29th st.†

GAS-LAMPS ERECTED AND LIGHTED.

Broadway, s e cor 41st st, two on Broadway and one on 41st st, at expense of L. L. Todd.†
Henry st, in front of Nos. 38 and 40, two lights.†
Madison Square Garden, in front of, two lights.†
Union sq, in front of No. 5, at expense of A. Brentano.†
91st st, from Columbus to Amsterdam av.†
101st st, from 2d av to East River.†
117th st, from Madison to 5th av.†
142d st, from Boulevard to 12th av.†
Amsterdam av, from 110th to 114th st.†

PAVING.

57th st, from 11th av to w s of 12th av, and crosswalks laid at each side of each intersecting avs.†
90th st, from 1st to 2d av, and crosswalks laid at terminating avs.†
141st st, from e s Alexander av to w s Willis av, trap blockro
141st st, from w s Brook av to e s Willis av, trap block, at expense of Wm. O'Gorman.†
154th st, from w s Courtlandt av to w s Morris av, granite block.†

MAINS LAID.

91st st, from Columbus to Amsterdam av, gas.†
101st st, from 2d av to East River, gas.†
117th st, from Madison to 5th av, gas.†
138th st, from 7th to 8th av, water.†
139th st, from 7th to 8th av, water.†
142d st, from Boulevard to 12th av, water.†
142d st, from Boulevard to 12th av, gas.†
Amsterdam av, from 110th to 114th sts, gas.†
Tinton av, from 161st to 163d st, water.†

CROSSWALKS.

Broadway, from No. 60 to opposite No. 61, at expense of New York Consolidated Exchange.†

APPROVED PAPERS.

Resolutions passed by the Board of Aldermen calling for the following improvements have been signed by the Mayor for the week ending September 26, 1891. *Indicates that the Mayor neither appoved nor objected thereto, therefore the same became adopted.

CURBSTONES SET AND SIDEWALKS FLAGGED.

Birch st, from Wolf st to Marcher av.*
157th st, from 3d to Railroad av.*

CROSSWALKS LAID.

Birch st, from Wolf st to Marcher av.*
157th st, from 3d to Railroad av.*
170th st, from 3d to Fulton av, at expense of Henry Zeltner.*

REGULATING, GRADING, ETC.

Birch st, from Wolf st to Marcher av.*
167th st, from 3d to Railroad av.*
170th st, from 3d to Fulton av, at expense of Henry Zeltner.*

PAVING.

170th st, from 3d to Fulton av, at expense of Henry Zeltner; granite block.*

ADVERTISED LEGAL SALES.

REFEREES SALES TO BE HELD AT THE REAL ESTATE EXCHANGE AND AUCTION ROOM (LIMITED), 59 to 65 LIBERTY STREET, EXCEPT WHERE OTHERWISE STATED.

Oct.

119th st, No. 7, n s, 95.5 w 5th av, 14x57.9x14.6x53.11, three-story brk dwell'g, by B. L. Kennelly. (Amt due $4,732)........ 5

3d av, Nos. 881 and 883, e s, 50.5 n 53d st, 32.10x100, two five-story brk tenem'ts with stores; all right, title and interest of Dora and Simon Moses which they had on June 29, 1891, by Sheriff, at City Hall. (Sale under execution).... 5

Av A, Nos. 393 and 395, s w cor 24th st, 49.5x81.5, vacant, all right, title and interest which Daniel D. Conover had on June 10, 1891, by Sheriff at City Hall. (Sale under execution)........ 5

Carmine st, No. 79, n s, abt 300 w Bedford st, 24x—, three-story brk store and tenem't..........
Houston st, No. 228 / Downing st, No. 64 } begins Houston st, n s, 68.6 e Varick st, 23x84.8 to Downing st, x25x71.8, five-story brk tenem't with stores. (Leasehold)..........
Downing st, Nos. 57 and 59, n s, 221 w Bedford st, 39.1x90, three and five-story brk tenem'ts with stores and two-story brk building on rear.
49th st, No. 134, s s, 449.6 w 6th av, 25.6x100, three-story brk stable, all right, title and int of Alfred H. Senior had on July 7, 1868........
by Sheriff, at City Hall. (Sale under execution). 6

Willett st, No. 58, e s, 180 n Delancey st, 25x100, five-story brk building, by D. P. Ingraham & Co. (Leasehold; amt due $4,302)........ 6

Convent av, No. 61, e s, 599.6 n 141st st, 20x100, three-story brk dwell'g, by William Kennelly. (Amt due $15,269)........ 6

Lenox av, w s, extends from 116th to 117th st, 201.10x100, vacant..........
116th st, n s, 100 w Lenox av, 100x100.11, vacant.
117th st, s s, 100 w Lenox av, 100x100.11, vacant.
by D. P. Ingraham & Co. (Amt due $25,231).... 6

Monroe av, s e s, adj land John Ittner, runs northeast along said av 98.6 x northeast still along av 814.11 x southeast through an old stone wall 723 x still southeast 350 to Valentine av, x southwest along av 381.3 x northwest 856 x again northwest 738.6 to beginning, by W. R. Brown. (Amt due $27,797)........ 6

Southern Boulevard, n w cor Garden av, runs northwest along Garden av 115.4 x northeast 95 to Kingsbridge road, x south along road 60.2 x south along same 70.9 to Southern Boulevard, x south 22.4 to beginning..........
Southern Boulevard, w s, 21.3 s Garden av, runs south along w s Southern Boulevard 90.8 x northwest 40.10 x northerly 81 to beginning....
West st, s w s, known as lot 14 map of Wardsville, West Farms, 50x126x50.1x120..........
by R. V. Harnett. (Partition sale).......... 7

57th st, Nos. 110 and 114, s s, 175 w 6th av, 75x100.5, five-story brk flats, by R. V. Harnett. (Amt due $19,413; prior morts, $70,000).......... 7

76th st, Nos. 311, 341 and 343 (?), n s, 200 e 2d av, 75x102.2, three five-story brk tenem'ts, stores in Nos. 311 and 341, by D. P. Ingraham & Co. (Amt due $12,950).......... 7

123d st, No. 268, s s, 100 e 8th av, 25x100.8, five-story stone front flat, by A. H. Muller & Son. (Amt due $16,056).......... 7

2d av, Nos. 747 and 749, n w cor 40th st, 39.8x75, two four-story brk tenem't's with stores......
40th st, Nos. 237-241, n s, 75 w 2d av, 80x98.9, one and two-story brk and frame buildings ....
79th st, No. 179, n s, 112 w 3d av, 22x102, three-story stone front dwell'g..........
by R. V. Harnett & Co. (Partition sale)........ 7

8th av, No. 2140, e s, 51.4 s 116th st, 25.5x100, one-story brk stores, by James L. Wells. (Amt due $3,330).......... 7

123d st, No. 264, s s, 150 e 8th av, 25x100.11........
123d st, No. 262, s s, 175 e 8th av, 25x100.11........
Two five-story stone front flats..........
by William Kennelly. (Amt on each $4,866; prior morts, $30,000).......... 8

148th st, n s, 90 w Brook av, 50x100, by R. V. Harnett & Co. (Partition sale).......... 8

Convent av, w s, 74.11 n 144th st, 25x94.5, three-story brk dwell'g..........
Convent av, w s, 49.11 n 144th st, 25x94.5, three-story brk dwell'g..........
Convent av, w s, 24.11 n 144th st, 25x94.5, three-story brk dwell'g..........
Convent av, n w cor 144th st, 24.11x94.5, three-story brk dwell'g..........
144th st, No. 455, n s, 214.2 e Amsterdam av, 20x99.11, three-story brk dwell'g..........
144th st, No. 459, n s, 177.8 e Amsterdam av, 20x99.11, four-story brk dwell'g..........
144th st, No. 461, n s, 157.8 e Amsterdam av, 20x99.11, four-story brk dwell'g..........
144th st, No. 463, n s, 137.8 e Amsterdam av, 20x99.11, three-story brk dwell'g..........
144th st, No. 465, n s, 121.2 e Amsterdam av, 16.6x99.11, three-story brk dwell'g..........
144th st, No. 467, n s, 100 e Amsterdam av, 21.2x99.11, three-story brk dwell'g..........
by A. H. Muller & Son. (Amt due on first 3 lots on Convent av, each $14,909, and $18,891 on cor lot, $11,335 on No. 455, $14,998 on each of Nos. 459 and 461, $13,061 on No. 463, $11,355 on No. 465 and $18,061 on No. 467).......... 8

Madison av, No. 801, e s, 82.5 n 67th st, 18x84, four-story stone front dwell'g, by B. L. Kennelly. (Amt due $12,551).......... 8

119th st, No. 408, s s, 94 e 1st av, 17x100.10........
119th st, No. 410, s s, 111 e 1st av, 17x100.10........
119th st, No. 412, s s, 128 e 1st av, 17x100.10........
Three three-story stone front dwell'gs........
by J. C. Lalor. (Amt due on each $5,547)........ 8

Houston st, No. 331, s s, 18.6 w Washington st, 18.9x50, three-story brk tenem't. 1-5 part.....
Hester st, No. 211, n s, bet Baxter and Centre sts, runs west along st 24.11 x northeast 35.6 x northeast 66.6 x east 21.8 x southwest to beginning, five-story brk tenem't with stores. 1-5 part..........
by R. V. Harnett & Co. (Amt due $4,359)........ 9

114th st, No. 418, s s, 240 e 1st av, 30x100.11, four-story stone front tenem't, by B. L. Kennelly. (Amt due $1,711).......... 9

Boulevard, e s, 24.11 n 139th st, 75x100, vacant, by D. P. Ingraham & Co. (Amt due $31,451)........ 12

60th st, No. 100 / Park (4th) av, No. 511 } begins 60th st, s e cor 4th av, 20x100.5, four-story brk (stone front) dwell'g on 60th st and one-story brk store on av, by William Kennelly. (Amt due $16,360).......... 12

KINGS COUNTY.

Oct

Pacific st, s s, 75 w Utica av, 298.8x107.2½, two-story and basement frame dwell'gs..........
Spencer st, No. 168, w s, 78 n Willoughby av, 22x80, three-story frame dwell'g; assessed value, $2,100; partition..........
Van Voorhis st, n w s, 100 s w Evergreen av, 17x100..........
Van Voorhis st, n w s, 117 s w Evergreen av, 17x100..........
Van Voorhis st, n w s, 134 s w Evergreen av, runs northwest 100 x southwest 16 x southeast 51.9 x southwest 1 x southeast 48.1¾ to Van Voorhis st, x northwest 17 to beginning, unfinished frame dwell'gs; assessed value, $2,000 each..........
26th st, centre line, 300 n w 3d av, runs northwest to exterior line, x southwest to centre 27th st if continued, x southeast to point 300 n w 3d av, x northeast to centre 26th st, with all docks, wharves, piers, cribs and erections, and land under water to centre of channel in front of above and right of way..........
by T. A. Kerrigan, at 13 Willoughby st.......... 6

Ashland pl, No. 149, e s, 90.0½ n Hanson pl, 15.0¼x79.6½x15x80.2, three-story brk dwell'g; assessed value, $4,000..........
Decatur st, n s, 350 w Throop av, 18.9x100........
Decatur st, n s, 358.9 w Throop av, 18.9x100, error. Two three-story brk dwell'gs; assessed value, $6,500 each..........
43d st, No. 212, s s, 100 w 4th av, 25x100.2, two-story frame dwell'g on rear; assessed value, $800; all right, title and interest..........
by T. A. Kerrigan, at 13 Willoughby st.......... 7

Dresden st, w s, 270.5 n Atlantic av, 75x108.11½x75x104, vacant; assessed value, $120 each..........
Williams av, w s, 100 n Eastern Parkway, 100x100, vacant; assessed value, $200 each..........
by W. B. Thomas, at 2786 Atlantic av.......... 7

Collins st, n s, 567.5 e Schenectady av, 100x100, Flatbush..........
Douglass st, n s, 400 w Franklin av, 140x131........
Quincy st, No. 841, n s, 85.6 w Ralph av, 20x100.
Quincy st, No. 839, n s, 105.6 w Ralph av, 20x100. Two three-story brk dwell'gs; assessed value, $7,000 each..........
Ridgewood st, s s, 33.6 w Clove road, 150x117.6, Flatbush..........
Gates av, n s, 224 e Lewis av, 96x100, four-story brk flat and store; assessed value, $7,350........
6th st, s s, 70 w 4th av, 105x100..........
by T. A. Kerrigan, at 13 Willoughby st.......... 8

26th st, centre line, 300 n w 3d av, runs northwest to exterior line, x southwest to centre 27th st if continued, x southeast to point 300 n w 3d av, x northeast to centre 26th st, with all docks, wharves, piers, cribs and erections and land under water to centre of channel in front of above and right of way, by William Hughes, ref., at Real Estate Exchange.......... 8

Pacific st, Nos. 1105 and 1107, n s, 379.8 w Franklin av, runs north 186.8 x west 150 x south 19.9 x east 120 x south 100 to Pacific st, x east 30 to beginning; assessed value, $1,600, by T. A. Kerrigan, at 13 Willoughby st.......... 9

Withers st, n e cor North 9th st, 38.7x50.8x62.5x10; assessed value, $600..........
Howard av, e s, 98 s Herkimer st, 35x98, frame church, by T. A. Kerrigan, at 13 Willoughby st.. 12

4th st, n e s, 297.10½ n w 8th av, 100x93; by Alfred F. Britton, ref., at County Court House........ 12

LIS PENDENS, KINGS COUNTY.

Sept.

Prospect av, n s, 110.6 w Webster av, 18.5x80. John S. Griffith exr. Lewis Griffith agt Thomas F. Regan; a t'y, Albert Prentice 25

St. Johns pl, s s, 100 w 8th av, 18.10x100 Emma Stevens exr. Robert F. Stevens agt Carman E. Anderson; notice of attachment; att'y, John F. Foley 25

Same property. Same agt same; notice of attachment; same att'y 25

Jefferson av, e s, 462 n Broadway, 18x100. Elizabeth L. Studwell et al exrs. John J. Studwell agt George Walker; att'y, George W. Mead 25

Herkimer st, s s, 51 e Saratoga av, 15.6x87. Amelia A. Van Hoesen agt William H. H. Robbins; att'y, Benjamin Estes 26

5th av, No. 585, e s, 106 s 16th st, 15.4x97.4. William Tuttle agt John A. Schilling; att'ys, Wells & Waldo 26

State st, n s, 44.10 w Nevins st, 106.1x100 ....
Lafayette av, n s, 325 e Reid av, 125x100 ....
Patchen av, s e cor Van Buren st, runs south 180 x east 99.9 x north 80 x east 180.3 x north 100 to st, x west 280 ....
James Williamson agt Francis Jezek; att'y, Rufus T. Griggs 26

Lafayette av, n s, 325 e Reid av, 125x100. Same agt same; same att'y 26

State st, n s, 44.10 w Nevins st, 106.1x100. Same agt same; same att'y 26

Moore st, n s, 150 w Ewen st, 25x100. Peter Kunzweiler agt Meyer Rich; foreclos. mechanic's lien; att'y, Max Brill 26

Pearl st, w s, 50.1 n High st, 27.7x103. David Jordan agt Anna A. Jordan; att'y, Wm. J. Carr.. 26

Coney Island av, e s, adj land John H. Watson, runs northeast 842.2 x southeast 20 x northeast 372.7 to land of Brooklyn and Brighton Beach R. R. Co., x southeast 403.5 x southwest 415.6 x northeast 124.2 x southwest 754.6 to av, x northwest 300, contains 8 23-100 acres ....
Manhattan Beach R. R. Co.'s land, e s, at intersection with above, 3 20-100 acres, Gravesend.
Edward T. Hunt exr. Thomas Hunt agt Frank Pettit; att'ys, Bergen & Dykman 26

Clermont av, No. 87, e s, 636.11 n Myrtle av, runs east 100 x north 50 x west 25 x south 19 x west 75 to av, x south 31. O. A. Reich agt James Shannon; notice of attachment; att'ys, Carter, Hughes & Kellogg 26

4th av, s w cor President st, 20x100. Frank Feurey agt Michelo Salvato; action for an accounting, &c.; att'ys, Birsh & Rasquin 26

Ocean Parkway, w s, 424 s Coney Island and Sheepshead Bay road, 100x250, Coney Island. John L. Voorhies, Comm'r of Investment, Gravesend, agt William H. Wallace; att'ys, Hubbard & Rushmore 26

Halsey st, s s, 149 w Arlington pl, 17.6x100. Russell S. Walker agt Kate G. Farrington; att'y, John N. Townell 28

Lafayette av, n s, 425 e Nostrand av, 25x100. M. Ella Devoy agt Susan Burton; partition; att'y, Isaac S. Catlin 28

6th av, s w cor Pacific st, runs south 142.6 x west 125 x north 32.6 x east 25 x north 110 to Pacific st, x east 100. John L. Voorhies, Comm'r of Investment, Gravesend, agt The Niagara Meter Co.; att'ys, Hubbard & Rushmore 28

Atlantic av, s s, 25 w Clinton st, 21.8x30. The Mutual Life Ins. Co. agt Thomas F. Regan; att'y, Robert Sewell 28

2d st, s s, 108.3 e 5th av, 30x100 ....
2d st, s s, 138.3 e 5th av, 30x100 ....
Stephen B. Sturges agt John L. Lansdell; att'ys, Sturges & Roby 29

1st st, s w s, 306 n w 5th av, 81x100. Cornelius E. Donnellon agt William S. Hale; att'ys, Johnson & Lamb 29

Willow st, Nos. 147 and 149, e s, 218.11 n Pierrepont st, 42x101.3. Charles H. Collins agt David Kearr; foreclos. mechanic's lien; att'ys, Rochfort & Stavton 29

Cumberland st, e s, 93.4 n Atlantic av, 20x100. Josephine L. Weiss agt Catherine T. Welsh; att'ys, Wells & Waldo 29

Prospect st, No. 123, n s, 175 w Bridge st, 25x75..
Prospect st, No. 105, n s, 100 e Jay st, 25x61 ....
William L. Whiting agt Adelaide S. Stilwell; J. A. Balestier 29

Schaeffer st, n s, 204 w Hamburg av, 48x93.9. Orson W. Sheldon agt Herman W. Meyer; att'y, Noah Tebbetts 29

Saratoga av, s e cor Decatur st, 100x115.6. Joseph P. Puels agt Samuel R. Good; att'y, Charles R. Halsey 29

Sands st, s s, 50.4 e Jay st, 25x103.10x25x103.7. Mary J. Leeds agt Ann F. Clark; att'y, A. Prentice 29

Rockaway av, e s, 100 s Duryea av, 125x100 ....
Eastern Parkway, s w cor Powell st, 50x100...
William Livingston agt Leon Weltfish; notice of attachment; att'y, Louis Levene 30

Hicks st, n e cor Poplar st, 25.3x99.9. Joseph H. Colyer agt Ida M. Edwards; foreclos. mechanic's lien; att'y, Samuel P. Potter 30

Lafayette av, n s, 425 e Nostrand av, 25x100. E. B. Drummond agt David B. Drummond; partition; att'ys, Robertson & Bull 30

Clinton st, centre line, 170 s w Bryant st, runs northwest 338 to centre Henry st slip, x southwest 1,241.3 to bulkhead line Gowanus Bay Channel if extended, x northeast 464.1 to centre line of Clinton st if extended, x945.10. Jeremiah P. Robinson et al. exrs. Jeremiah P. Robinson agt Mary W. Poillon and ano. exrs. Richard Poillon; att'ys, Sullivan & Cromwell 30

Oct.

Clason av, w s, 75 s Gates av, 25x100. George W. Montgomery agt James E. Slight; att'y, Edward F. Brown 1

Adelphi st, e s, 280 n Atlantic av, 50x100. Antonio Muguo agt Vincenzo De Clemento; partition; att'ys, Magner & Hughes 1

Av B, n s, 118 w Coney Island road, 40x110, Flatbush. Denslo D. Hamlin agt Louisa K. Wright; foreclos mechanic's lien; att'y, Henry B. Davenport 1

RECORDED LEASES.

NEW YORK. — Per Year

Abingdon sq, Nos. 7 and 9, stores, basements and vaults. Louis N. Phelps to James J. Lutkin; 5 years, from Oct. 1, 1891 .... $4,000

Broad st, No. 50, basement. Jeronemus S. Underhill to Christian Luckey; 2 years, from May 1, 1892 1,500

Fulton st, No. 140, store floor, basement and cellar. Marguerita Salembia by Louis Spader guard. to Lazarus Spero; 3¾ years, from Aug. 1, 1891 4,500

Greene st, No. 151, first floor and basement. Stephen V. R. Cruger trustee to Frederick Cook; 10 years, from Jan. 1, 1892 .... 7,500, 8,000

Pearl st, No. 481, all. Robert Boyd to John Manthe; 5 years, from May 1, 1891 900

Rivington st, No. 7 W., store and two rear rooms and part cellar. Catharina Odendhal and John C. Oscar to Charles Carter; 6 years, from Oct. 1, 1891 750

Thompson st, No. 66, store. Louis Edelson to John G. White; 5½ years, from Nov. 1, 1890. 840, 900

Vesey st, No. 45, basement. Annie Sheehy to Scudder V. Lewis; 1 year, from May 1, 1891. 420

10th st, No. 351 E., whole store floor and cellar. Heinrich Junck to Behrend Beisner; 5 years, from Oct. 1, 1891 720

13th st, No. 426 E., front and rear. John Hurley to Vincenzo Poppitu; 3 years, from Oct. 1, 1891 1,380

14th st, No. 28 W. Frank J. Gaynor to George Heather and Elwood Carpenter, of Heather & Co.; 5½ years, from Sept. 1, 1890 11,000

18th st, Nos. 145, 147 and 149 W., all. Roosevelt & Son, agents, to Adam Schwaab & Son; 4½ years, from Oct. 1, 1891 4,000

23d st, Nos. 273, 275 and 277 / 8th av, No. 258, cor } all. John Corse and ano exrs. and trustees Henry Corse to Jacob Appell; 5 years, from May 1, 1893 7,000

23d st, s s, bet 7th and 8th avs, The Chelsea apartment, No. 98. Henry R. Tredwell to Rowse Babcock; 1 year, from Oct. 1, 1891, per year, $1,700, with privilege of renewal in 4 years at 1,800

29th st, No. 265 E., all. George Brown committee for Henry Brown to Marianna Amen; 4 years 10½ months, from June 15, 1891. ... 900

37th st, No. 37 W. Martha M. Weyman to Frederick Von Bernuth; 3 years, from Oct. 1, 1891 3,000

38th st, No 114 E. Randolph W. Townsend to Margaret G. Kopper; 3 years, from May 1, 1892 1,400

38th st, No. 344 W., store and back rooms on first floor. Michael Bischoff to Karl T. Erhard; 5 years, from May 1, 1890 420

Same property. Assign. lease. Charles Nehring to Fred. Hower Brewing Co. (Lim) .... nom

44th st, No. 341 W., one story and half upper story. Wilhelmina D. C. Josenhaus to John C. Klett; 5 years, from Oct. 1, 1891 240

58th st, Nos. 202, 204 and 206 W., all. Thomas Canary to Kelsie Fullagar; 10 years, from Aug. 15, 1891 6,500

76th st, No. 46 E. Jessie Meyer to Morris Rossin; 1 year, from Oct. 1, 189 2,100

105th st, No. 175 E., store and four back rooms and front cellar. Jennie L. Denig to Harry C. Pinckney; 3 7-12 years, from Oct. 1, 1891.. 900

120th st, No. 14 E. Mary Gault to Mary McManus; 1½ years, from Oct 1, 1891 540

125th st, s e cor 7th av, 25x100, all. George Hillen to Edwin H. Ferguson; 3 7-12 years, from Sept. 29, 1891 10,000

Av B, No. 1615, n e cor 83d st, store floor and part cellar. Tousmann & Muchler to John Knobloch; 5 years, from May 1, 1891 .... 600, 720

Lincoln av, s e cor Southern Boulevard or 133d st, store and cellar room. Henry Spies to Charles J. White; 10 years, from March 1, 1889 2,600

1st av, n e cor 10th st, being No. 164 1st av and 245 East 10th st, all. William J. Morris to Timothy Burns; 5 years, from May 1, 1890.. 2,400

1st av, No. 605, store floor and part cellar. Andrew Steinmuller to Francis McGuire; 4 11-12 years, from June 1, 1890 .... 480, 540

1st av, No. 605. Assign. lease. Michael McLoughlin to James Christie .... nom

1st av, No. 805, n w cor 45th st, first floor and part cellar. Mary Irving to Peter Dunn; 5 years, from May 1, 1890 924

2d av, No. 564, all. Christopher Donleavy to John J. Hickey; 5 years, from May 1, 1888... 2,160

2d av, No. 839, store floor and part basement. Charles Boyce to William Osterholz; 5 years, from Nov. 1, 1887 1,620

3d av, n e cor 86th st (Parepa Hall), all above first story and part cellar. Hyman and Henry Sonn and Augustus C. Bechstein to Louis Harris; 10 years, to commence 28 days after written notice. See lease 5,000

Same property. The store on n e cor and store on 3d av adj, with three basements fronting on av. Same to Jacob Lauchheimer and Isaac Harris; 5 years, to commence 3 days after written notice. See lease. 4,000

3d av, n e cor 84th st, store. Heyman Vogel to Claus Ohlhaver; 5 years, from May 1, 1890.. 2,000

6th av, No. 798, store and basement. Abraham Thacker to John Walker; 3 years, from May 1, 1891 1,200

6th av, No. 187. Elizabeth Hawthorn to Frederick D. Fricke; 10 7-12 years, from Oct. 1, 1891 .... 4,000, 4,500

6th av, No. 483, s w cor 29th st. John Noonan to Adolph Luhrs; 5 years, from May 1, 1889. .... 4,000, 4,500

8th av, No. 2140, store and cellar. John Heumann to Hugh M. Hawkins; 5 years, from Oct. 1, 1891 1,200

10th av, No. 576, n e cor 42d st. Catherine and Anna M. Aspell, Mary R. wife of John F Brennan, James, Edward J., Thomas J. and John Aspell individ. and heirs James Aspell to Frank Daly; 10 7-12 years, from Oct. 1, 1891 2,250

Same property. Assign. lease. Francis Daly to James Everard .... nom

CHATTELS.

NOTE.—The first name, alphabetically arranged, is that of the Mortgagor, or party who gives the Mortgage. The "R" means Renewal Mortgage.

NEW YORK CITY.

SEPTEMBER 25 TO OCTOBER 1.—INCLUSIVE.

SALOON AND RESTAURANT FIXTURES.

Alpenburg, Victor. 713 Vernon av....G Ehret. $1,000
Blath, Emma. 242 W 30th... Stuner & Murioll. 1,500
Burke, Joseph. 197 Crosby....J Eichler B Co. (R) 1,200
Behrmann, Adolph. 926 6th av....J Ruppert. 200
Brandamour, John. 38 East Houston....P Bolender. Restaurant Fixtures. 3,000
Baust, Karl. 448 E 72d....G Ehret. 1,560
Berger, Henry. 153 Forsyth....J Ruppert. 1,000
Blass, Karl. 417 E 9th....Knickerbocker B Co. Tables, &c. 60
Same....same. Bar Fixtures. 100
Braun, G C T. 363 10th av....J Kress B Co. 2,000
Buchmann, John. 2 Chrystie ..M F Hoepfner. (R) 3,400
Carter, Charles. 7 Rivington....J Eichler B Co. 500
Connor, Edward. 2027 3d av....J Eichler B Co. (R) 500
Cannon, J B. 1734 Madison av....F & M Schaefer B Co. (R) 2,000
Christie, James. 605 1st av....J C G Hupfel B Co. 600
Cody, William. 118 Christopher....Bernheimer & S. 2,500
Dempsey, P J. 84 Centre....W Craft. 815
Daly, Francis. 42d st and 10th av....J Everard. 8,130
Di Marco, Domenico. 246 Elizabeth....Bernheimer & S. Pool Table. 150
Doyle, J F. 702 Washington....J Eichler B Co. 2,000
Dickemann, Martin. 154 Allen....A Hupfel's Sons. 450
Duesing, L W. 67 Warren....J Everard. 5,085
Eule, Paul. 308 6th....Schmitt & S. (R) 400
Ewald, Geo. 501 E 80th....J Ables B Co. 300
Eibsen, Louis. 45 West....Burr B Co. (R) 5,000
Erzer, Louis. 623 E 16th....J Eichler B Co. (R) 650
Faber, C P. 374 Willis av....D Mayer. 2,000
Fitzpatrick, Daniel. 1695 3d av....H Koehler & Co. 1,200
Ferguson, E H. 7th av and 125th st. ..G Hillen. 17,000
Foster, W E. 177 Hudson....Wagner & Co. Pool Table. 150
Farr, Jacob. 52 Av D....J Wallace & Son. 450
Florio, Antonio. 307 E 104th....J Ruppert. 300
Fritz, Frans. 245 W 19th....J Everard. (R) 359
Ficken, H E. 61 Clinton pl....Brunswick-B-C Co. Pool Table. 300
Gerner, William. 215 E 4th .. P Doelger. (R) 800
Goldberg, Hyman. 247 Delancey....Williamsburgh B Co. 1,000
Glasstetler, F D. 129 Pitt... J C G Hupfel B Co. 800
Galbraith, Martin. 318 and 320 Canal ...F D Fricke. 6,400
Hauser, John. 161 Chrystie....J Hoffmann B Co. (R) 350
Haack, Auguste. 222 Chrystie....F & M Schaefer B Co. (R) 320
Herrenschmidt, Gus. 25 Platt....Beadleston & W. 800
Hilbert, F H. 705 E 12th... G Ringler & Co. 600
Hafner, Jacob. 415 E 106th....G Ehret. (R) 700
Hayes, Patrick. 545 3d av....Wagner & S. Pool Table. 240
Hickey, J J. 701 3d av ...P Doelger. 1,500
Same. 564 2d av... same 1,800
Hintz, Ernst. 161 E 4th. ..P Weidmann. 800
Jacob, Katharina. 217 7th... G Ringler & Co. 565
Junker, Joseph. 1323 2d av... V Loewers. 400
Klotschkof & Bernstein. 182 Orchard....A B Marx. Pool. 200
King, August. 212 Spring... P Buckel. 200
Krause, Katie. 212 Spring....P Buckel. (R) 150
Kiernan, Thomas. 2049 2d av....B Kiernan. 900
Killer, Geo. 1621 1st av....Wagner & S. Pool Table. (R) 50
Kiwent, Philip. 86 Suffolk....H Koehler & Co. 425
Klein, Bernhard. 71 Mercer....G Sommer. Restaurant Fixtures. ½ int. 600
Kurtz, John. 414 6th av....G Ehret. (R) 6,000
Krieg, Fred. 142 Essex... J Doelger's Sons. 1,100
Krudner, George. 2032 1st av....J Eichler B Co. (R) 800
Kassebohm, F A. 2322 2d av....P Doelger. (R) 1,000
Kelly & Cummings. 2103 3d av....W L Flanagan. 3,000
Kelly, Philip. 28th st and 10th av. ..D Stevenson. (R) 1,200
Kladgen, John. 318 4th av....Brunswick-B-C Co. Pool Table. 390
Luckey, Christian. 50 Broad ...Beadleston & W. 893
Lynch, James. 253 Rivington....P Doelger. (R) 1,500
Lamuro, Vincenzo. 2224 1st av....Bernheimer & S. Saloon Ice House. 75
Lawson, Harry. 107 Cherry....E Meltzer. 200
Lynch, Joseph. 2687 3d av....J Eichler B Co. (R) 1,200
Lenz, Charles. 185 Greenwich....B Boyle. 6,000
Lincke & Faller. 163 E 4th....G Ringler & Co. 1,100
Mansmann, John. 635 W 42d....V Loewers. 1,000
McLaughlin, Michael. 849 10th av....J C G Hupfel B Co. 3,000
McVitty, James. 233 Spring....P Doelger. 5,000
Maxey, C J. 168 West Broadway....Bernheimer & S. 350
Magio & Guerrieri. 340 E 115th....Bernheimer & S. Pool Table. (R) 125
Same....same. (R) 250
McCusker, C H. 342 West ...M Regan. (R) 4,000
McGirr, Terence. 438 11th av....J Everard. 3,252
McGowan, J W. 417 W 26th....F & M Schaefer B Co. (R) 600
McLaughlin, Michael. 849 10th av....J Christie. 500
Mitchell & O'Connell. 1512 2d av....P Doelger. (R) 2,500
Mueller, Louis. 1319 Av A....Schmitt & S. (R) 400
Naw, John. 2087 2d av....G Ehret. 875
Needham, M J. 378 1st av....O'Reilly, Skelly & Fogarty. 1,700
Niven, D C. 199 Bleecker....G C Woolsey. Restaurant Fixtures. 700
Ney, Edmund....M Knorrn. 200
O'Brien, J J. 1031 Washington av....J Eichler B Co. (R) 550
O'Connell, Michael. 922 2d av....Bernheimer & S. (R) 1,500
Olpp, E C. 216 E 98th....J Kuntz B Co. 500
Powers, Christopher. 499 6th av....Consumers' B Co. 2,000
Pfaff, Henry. 505 W 51st....C Stein. (R) 397
Pokorny, Joseph. 1091 1st av....V Masin. 500
Pinckney, H C. 175 E 105th... G Ehret. 1,500
Roeder, George. 608 E 151st....J & M Haffen. 300
Riepe & Fagen. 158 Canal....F Munch exr of. (R) 995
Roberts, Thomas. 470 W 23d....G Ringler & Co. 1,500
Rump, C & M. 108 4th av....D Mayer. (R) 600
Rettig, Philip. 1422 Av A.... Schmitt & S. (R) 400
Rusciana, Winifried. 241 E 111th....P Buckel. (R) 200
Sabatel, Juan. 522 3d av....J Wallace & Son. (R) 2,900

Schuster, Paulus. 116 Chrystie....J Ruppert. (R) 1,550
Siegel, Christian. 246 11th av ...P Doelger. (R) 5,000
Stroh, Michael. 10th av, bet 157th and 158th sts ....Bernheimer & S. (R) 550
Sauer, G W. 1 Chambers....G Ehret. (R) 4,500
Scharninghaus, Diederich. 815 10th av....J Eichler B Co. 8,500
Schmidt, H P. 117 Wooster....V Loewer B Co. (R) 268
Schneider, Ignatz. 98 Cannon....Claus Lipsius B Co. 500
Schoenberg, Joseph. 278 East Houston....I Berkowitz. Restaurant Fixtures and Billiard Tables. 250
Schwarm, Charles. 58 Fulton....W Aufenanger. Restaurant Fixtures. 2,400
Schiffer, Andrew. 2706 8th av....G Ehret. 1,900
Silberschmidt, Rudoelph. 339 E 6th....J Hoffmann B Co. 350
Schmitt, Adam. 338 E 9th....J Ruppert. 300
Schmitt, Frederick. 156 1st av....F & M Schaefer B Co. (R) 350
Scovill, L M. 2491 2d av....A Van Dusen. Restaurant Fixtures 100
Specht, L W. 117 Pitt....F Ibert. 400
Staab, William. 1 and 2 State....E Unger & Co. (R) 2,000
Stronezer, Stephan. 249 E 2d....Long Island Brewery. 800
Talasco, Josef. 215 E 73d....Schmitt & S. 400
Ungemach, Adolph. 72 1st av....J & M Haffen. 600
Vassollo, Pietro. 53 Mulberry....Burger & H B Co. 300
Vaupel, P F. 694 Courtlandt av....A Hupfel's Sons. (R) 1,300
Volk, Eberhard. 44 Gold....G Ehret. (R) 2,500
Vollmer, Mary. 42 Forsyth....Schmitt & S. (R) 291
Walther, Louis. 285 Bowery ...W Peter B Co. 850
White, Chas I. 568 Southern Boulevard....Bernheimer & S. 8,500
Wavra, Josef. 318 E 71st....Long Island Brewery. 1,500
Wendel, C O. 195th st and 10th av....C Iba. 650
Wendelken, John. 35 E 24th....J Ruppert. (R) 2,000
Wiessenberg, Karl. 335 W 39th....A Finck & Son. 1,200
Wilkinson & Gordon. 40 Howard....G Ringler & Co. 700
Wilzig, Paul. 85 E 4th....Wagner & S. Pool Table. (R) 35
Walfers, J and H. 72 University pl... F D Fricke. (R) 9,400
White & Ralph. 456 Washington ...Bernheimer & S. Saloon Ice House. 85
Zimmer, Jacob. 29 Vandewater....P & W Ebling. (R) 195
Zickler, Ignatz. 42 Av D....P Doelger. 1,000

HOUSEHOLD FURNITURE.

Alexander, W J. 1797 Lexington av.. .J Baumann. (R) 224
Anglebart, J M. 103d st and 2d av....Dreisacker & Co. 138
Allen, Alice S. 157 W 44th....Jordan & M. 150
Adlum, Lizzie P. 426 E 57th....W E Wheelock & Co. Piano. (R) 200
Adolphi, Hattie. 238 W 13th....J Moriarty. 264
Bingham, J M. 275 Lenox av....J Baumann. (R) 119
Bloom, J M & S. 226 Rivington....L Molsky. 337
Bond, Caroline C. 139 E 21st....W E Wheelock & Co. Piano. 350
Booze, Carrie. 187 Chrystie....B M Cowperthwait & Co. 101
Britton, Fannie. 156 E 47th....C E Pierce. 1,850
Brownlee, Annie. 227 E 30th....Garvey Bros. 122
Bamberg, Isaac. 154 W 103d....T Kelly. 327
Bassey, Albertine. 131 W 40th....O'Farrell & Co. 124
Beggs, Grace. 261 W 110th....T Kelly. 115
Buthman, Kate. 317 10th av....O'Farrell & Co. 171
Bageley, Annie M. 124 W 29th....L Baumann. 176
Becker, Julius. 446 E 11th ...R Silverman. (R) 200
Bibyram, Mamel. 6 E 14th....Fennell & Pye. (R) 119
Bird, Annie. 254 E 10th....L Baumann. 173
Burke, Ray. 142 E 48th....L Baumann. 420
Burns, Thomas. 850 Columbus av....L Baumann. 303
Blake, Mary E. 149 W 16th....J Baumann. 438
Blanden, Jos. 458 9th av....J Early. 110
Cozzins, S D. 238 W 134d....J Baumann. (R) 203
Craig, R R. 70 W 90th....J Early. 104
Clodio, Victor. 829 Park av....Dreisacker & Co. 245
Covington, T H. 145 W 41st....O'Farrell & Co. 539
Clark, Hattie M. 256 W 38th....J Gregg & Co. 182
Clayton, Emma. 322 W 17th....B M Cowperthwait & Co. 159
Colt, M m. 9 Jackson ...B M Cowperthwait & Co. 187
Connolly, Elizabeth....213 W 49th....Jordan & M. 100
Cooke, Ellen M. 133 W 101st....B M Cowperthwait & Co. 111
Cronauer, Mrs J. 167 E 77th....H Thoesen 110
Cahill, J F. 1225 Intervale av....W E Wheelock & Co. Piano. 175
Carrol, Mary. 470 Pearl....S Sachs. 209
Claton, Eliza. 247 E 14th....B M Cowperthwait & Co. 125
Cook, Sarah. 108 W 61st....C E Pierce. 130
Cornet Pleasure Circle. 290 Henry....H Rosen & Son. 123
Cozzens, S D. 238 W 32d....J Baumann. (R) 574
Cyne, B dget. 421 E 25th....B M Cowperthwait & Co. 113
De la Barre, Marie. 31 Delancey....Manges Bros. 341
Del Valle, J M. 3 E 84th....Lincoln I & G Assoc. 150
Duggan, S P. 307 E 56th....Garvey Bros. 156
Dexter, Mrs E E. 129 W 103d....T Kelly. 206
Diossy, Josie. 126 W 47th ...J Moriarty. (R) 387
Douglass, Mrs M J. 153 Lexington av....T Kelly. 144
Same....same. 336
Dunn, Ellen. 346 W 52d....B M Cowperthwait & Co. 148
Deshauriers, A E. 24 Grove....J Early. 174
Doerrzoff, George. 341 E 81st....J Baumann. 156
Dean, Fred. 81 W 65th....J H Little. 170
De Mandeville, James. 486 St Nicholas av....J Baumann. (R) 142
Demorest, Geo. 1209 Woodruff av ...Dreisacker & Co. 134
Dewitt, Mrs A. 174 E 81st....H Isenberg. 138
Dorff, L K. 100 W 103d....Brooklyn F Co. 213
Dunham, Mrs A E. 74 Madison av....S Knapp & Co. 1,384
Eisinger, M N. 1194 Park av....L Baumann. 171
Emes, V H. 319 W 14th....N Y F Co. 147
Eaton, Sadie M. 158 W 13th....J Gregg & Co. 514
Eurelle, Mrs A. 153 Lexington av....T Kelly. 142
Eustice, Nellie. 421 E 25th....Garvey Bros. 121
Evans, J F. 8 W 134th....B Molony. 350
Fay, Edith. 2495 2d av....W E Wheelock & Co. Piano. 250
Folkart, Flora. 57 E 106th....Krakauer Bros. Piano. 155
Frankenstein, L. 527 E 83d....D M Brown. 114
Fleming, Geo H. 136 W 16th....T Kelly. 362
Flockhart, H H. 672 Degraw st, Brooklyn....J Moriarty. (R) 420
Foster, V A. 61 and 63 W 92d....Amer Guar Assoc. 150
Fox, Mary. 187 Lawrence. ..B M Cowperthwait & Co. 158
Fagan, Julia. 319 E 14th....J A Moss. (R) 145
Frey, R G. 334 E 77th.... Jordan & M. 158
Goddard, Carrie L. 183 Lexington av....J Baumann. 342
Granert, Ellen. 118 E 27th .. J Baumann. 131
Gabel, Jacob. 301 E 76th ..L Baumann. 184
Gedalge, Julius. 654 E 6th.. .G Reubel. 181
Gottshall, Ed. 183 E 116th....L Baumann. 656
Griffen, Mrs T. 125 W 56th....J H Little. 1,085
Grotaloup, Louise. 236 W 13th....J Baumann. (R) 224
Gustavsen, Marie. 438 W 39d....L Baumann. 112
Gaerschuer, Hugo. 301 E 102d.... L Baumann. 127
Garrison, F C. 41 or 43 W 125th....B M Cowperthwait & Co. 481
Goldman, Nathan. 54 Pike....H S Eisler. 160
Gulick, Geo. 107 W 100th....T Kelly. 181
Galvin, Delia. Hudson st....W E Wheelock & Co. Piano. (R) 171
Garvey, Isaac. 675 Greenwich....J Garvey. (R) 450
Gill, Catharin. 8 King....Manges Bros. 117
Goldfeld, Bertha. 316 E 82d....H Israel & Son. (R) 104
Goolder, Ella. 170 E 122d....Manges Bros. 126
Hagemeister, Grace. 148 W 24th....W E Wheelock & Co. Piano. (R) 241
Hay, Mrs C C. 2?5 W 39th. ..H Thoesen. 496
Higgins, Margaret J. 2068 Madison av... American Guarantee Assoc. 200
Hill, G E. 42 Broadway....B M Cowperthwait & Co. 126
Hoffman, J M. 619 8th av....J Baumann. (R) 235
Hunter, F A. 10 Lafayette pl... W E Wheelock & Co. Piano. 225
Harding, Margaret. 360 W 117th....B M Cowperthwait & Co. 358
Hilbrandt, John. 534 E 85th....J Moriarty. 153
Hirschfield, Mrs R. 683 Lexington av....T Kelly. 148
Hoffman, Elizabeth. 403 E 13d....L Baumann. 321
Howard, Mary L. 241 W 32d....O'Farrell & Co. 160
Haddon, Dora. 2283 7th av ...E D Mills. 500
Havens, Mamie. 317 W 36th....Jordan & M. 223
Hagan, Mrs C V. 136 W 47th....N Y F Co. 558
Hamill, Mrs C L. 226 W 43d....Brooklyn F Co. 159
Hammond, Florence. 155 E 47th....F G Smith. Piano. (R) 300
Hannegan, Mary E. 358 W 36th....F T Higgins. (R) 185
Hartman, Mrs F. 230 E 86th....J H Little. 149
Hasting, Caroline A. 16 W 24th....J & J Dobson. Carpets. 178
Haughtaling, Mary. 2073 7th av... J Baumann. (R) 314
Hayes, Alice S. 2066 Madison av....American Guarantee Assoc. 100
Heilbroner, Gertrude. 242 E 60th....Krakauer Bros. Piano. 250
Higgins, Mrs W. 660 E 144th....J H Little. 158
Hobby, Mrs C. 25 Broad .. L Baumann. 136
Home, F. 414 E 81st....L Baumann. 205
Hubert, Albert. 286 E 56th....L Baumann. 165
Jackson, Dora. 252 W 30th....O'Farrell & Co. (R) 221
Jacobs, Leah. 235 E 54th.... L Baumann. 121
Joel, H M. 18 E 120th....J Gregg & Co. 178
Journeay, Mrs S E. 60 W 25th....B M Cowperthwait & Co. 187
Knell, Emily. 122 W 61st ..L Baumann. 188
Kelley, Emma. 217 E 80th....L Baumann. 154
Kilroy, Katie. 209 W 21st....J Baumann. (R) 184
Klemme, Anna. 52 E 104th....Krakauer Bros. Piano. 250
Kornicker, Felix. 23 Delancey .... Krakauer Bros. Piano. 225
Kallies, Frederick. 217 W 64d....Jordan & M. 212
Kelly, Mary. 123 W 54th....J Baumann. (R) 121
Kemble, Mrs A. 107 W 106th....W E Wheelock & Co. Piano. (R) 216
Kennedy, Annie. 1866 9th av....W E Wheelock & Co. Piano. (R) 120
Kirby, John. 2688 3d av....R M Walters. Piano. 115
Klabold, Frank. 362 9th av ...W E Wheelock & Co. Piano. (R) 139
Kuchenmeister, Fred. 691 8th av .... F J Brechtel. 547
Leadbitter, H N. 40 W 65th.. J Baumann. (R) 125
Le Count, Mary H. 193 W 134th....Toles Bros. 250
Lynch, Thomas. 304 E 12th....W E Wheelock & Co. Piano. 100
Lyon, H T. Church st....J Baumann. 409
Lampey, William. 200 8th av....L Baumann. 478
Lancaster, Mary. 749 E 143d....J Moriarty. 182
Lang, T J. 223 W 36th....L Baumann. 192
Lange, I C F. 6 Spring ...J H Little. 505
Lewis, B H. 207 W 118th....J H Little. 147
Loewy, Albert. 558 Lexington av... J Baumann. (R) 128
Lopatnikoff, Rebecca. 43 Henry....Simpson & P. Piano. 225
Leads, Lottie A. 125 W 28th....J Baumann. 213
Lahm, Alice H. 25 E 21st....Jordan & M. 2,436
Lasker, Abraham. Lexington av....S I Herschmann. 623
Leamond, James. 31 Charles....L Baumann. 132
Leidberg, Mary. 539 10th av ...L Baumann. 178
Levy, Amanda. 123 W 46th....R Glanz. 210
Lunt, C T. 141 E 19th....De Graaf & Taylor Co. 450
Lyles, Mrs W B. 127 W 17th....T Kelly. 362
Maule, Agnes. 979 6th....O'Farrell & Co. 619
Meissner, Albert. 14 Broome....L Baumann. 110
Mooney, Neil. 310 W 116th ...B M Cowperthwait & Co. 249
Moore, Bessie. 226 W 16th.... S I Herschmann. 154
Maddeforg, W G. 266 E 29th....L Baumann. 147
Madden, John. 411 E 120th....Dreisacker & Co. 272
Mahon, Agnes G. 429 Pleasant av....W J Ruddell. 200
McCauley, C F, Mrs. 131 E 30th ...J H Little. 438
McClellan, L C. 121st st and Manhattan av....Brooklyn F Co. 260
Meilbold, Marian....J Williams. 147
Minchin, Elizabeth. 252 W 30th....O'Farrell & Co. 110
Moise, Mary T. 209 W 43d....Lincoln I and G Co. 100
Mooney, Maggie. 120 W 49th ...L Baumann. 118
Morris, Maggie. 292 Willis av....L Baumann. 116
Muirtha, Mrs. 132 W 25th....J P Delehanty. 184
Mulady, Mary. 251 E 32d....L Baumann. 111
Mulcahy, Daniel. 2660 8th av....J Baumann. (R) 225
Mace, J P. 455 9th av....J Early. 178
McDonald, Mary. 345 W 50th....J Baumann. 125
McKee, Emma. 117 E 24th....J Baumann. 244
Monteverde, Aldine. 54 W 35th....J Baumann. (R) 114
Morse, Carrie E. 10, 12 and 14 W 125th, ..Lincoln I and G Co. 500
Mahon, Mrs J E. 429 Pleasant av....D M Brown. 180
Martin, Mrs J. 221 W 14th....W E Wheelock & Co. Piano. 390
Mauss, Julia....J Williams. 187
Maxheimer, L P. 245 Broadway....H Israel & Son. 258
McAmney, Ellen. 135 W 26th....W E Wheelock & Co. Piano. (R) 145
McWhinney, Emma. 219 E 104th....W E Wheelock & Co. Piano. (R) 110
Mordaunt, Jessie C. 112 W 39th....J Baumann. (R) 159
Nickolsby, R B. 223 E 84th....W E Wheelock & Co. Piano. 275
Norris, R J....J Williams. 150
Nelson, C A. 717 9th av .. F T Higgins. 172
Niedenwiesen, Josephine. 1634 Madison av....B M Cowperthwait & Co. 150
Naylor, William. 885 2d av....J Early. 174
Owen, Mrs C. 59th st and Broadway... J Bauman. (R) 350
Owens, H E, Mrs. 81st st and 9th av....Fennell & Pye. (R) 167
O'Keefe, Lillie E. 179 Waverley pl....Manges Bros. 138
Pratt, John. 56 Goerck....D M Brown. 103
Pyne, Kathleen. 8th av and 93d and 94th sts ....J J McGrorty. 338
Paige, W E. 236 E 118th....Manges Bros. 268
Perine, Samuel, Mrs. 1124 3d av.... H Thoesen. 177
Phillips, Carrie. 263 W 39th.... J Moriarty. 223
Pinies, Eli. 130 E 93d.... J Kauffmann. 125
Porter, Leroy. 102 W 102d ...J Gregg. 327
Pinkham, Mary E. 128 W 96th....B M Cowperthwait & Co. 121
Prescott, Mrs J. 385 W 58th....B M Cowperthwait & Co. 202
Randall, Fred. 1157 3d av.. H S Eisler. 116
Read, Henry. 112 E 11th....J Moriarty. (R) 204
Rosenberg, J. 2017 2d av....H Thoesen. 125
Rossheim, D and C. 1414 5th av....Amer Guar Assoc. 150
Russell, H C. 173 W 81st ...B M Cowperthwait & Co. 918
Reed, James. 17 Lexington av....Jordan & M. 120
Robinson, Laurine. 208 W 119th....J Baumann. 130
Rosenberg, Lucy. 61 E 122d....J Baumann. (R) 241
Rabold, Catherine. 402 W 58th.... J Baumann. (R) 403
Randolph, Mrs S. 148 W 4th....J H Little. 144
Reilly, Bridget. 12 Amsterdam av....L Baumann. 128
Reisig, Mrs A. 205 W 50th....J H Little. 160
Reneiro, C J....J Williams. 263
Robertson, Agnes. 315 W 134th....J Baumann. (R) 112
Robinson, W J. 161 W 102d.... J Baumann. (R) 138
Roumegous, August. 1300 Broadway....G Pons. Paintings. 900
Redmond, May. 94 W 104th....B M Cowperthwait & Co. 128
Rominger, Emily. 326 W 87th....W E Wheelock & Co. Piano. (R) 195
Rosengrave, J F. 58 E 11th....R M Walters. Piano. (R) 132
Rush, Hattie. 110 W 52d ...S Sachs (R) 400
Ryerson, M V. 85 W 104th.. .J Mullin & Co. 186
Schaefer, Annie. 2783 8th av....W E Wheelock & Co. Piano. 250
Shea, Kate. 173 E 93d....B M Cowperthwait & Co 170
Silberstein, Davis. 450 Grand.... W E Wheelock & Co. Piano. 300
Soulleyet, Kate L. 625 E 136th....R M Walters. Piano. (R) 160
Schwartz, Fany. 127 Cannon....Krakauer Bros. Piano. 260
Sellen, Mrs M E. 106 W 40th.... J H Little. 348
Shandley, Marion. 148 W 105th.... O'Farrell & Co. 209
Sharkey, Libbie. 112 W 104th....J Baumann. (R) 222
Simmons, H P. 38 Gramercy Park ...F G Smith. Piano. (R) 375
Simon, Annie. 538 E 83d ...Alexander Bros. 120
Smith, F H. 206 E 20th....H Thoesen. 102
Stark, Moses L. 436 W 48th....L Baumann. 111
St Clair, G. 162 E 46th.... Fennell & Pye. (R) 190
St Clair, Georgia. 162 E 46th....Fennell & Pye. (R) 205
Shepard, Nellie. 224 W 16th....T Kelly. 204
Sherwood, Flora. 1055 Lexington av....J Moriarty. 304
Simonson, Annie. 1181 2d av....B M Cowperthwait & Co. 119
Smith, M Emily. 121 W 21st....E H Kerner. 1,000
Spagat, Simon. 77 Ludlow....H S Eisler. 1?9
Sands, C D and C F. 229 E 109th....L Stern. 300
Schwandey, George 323 W 17th .. J Baumann. 127
Sparrow, Ida. 55 E 122d....J Baumann. 284
Staats, Homer. 25 E 119th....J Baumann. 120
Sullivan, H and E. 326 W 37th....J Early. 104
Spencer, Goldie. 156 W 36th....H Israel. 630
Stanton, Thos. 422 E 27th.. Garvey Bros. 179
Tracey, Mrs P J. 15 Jones....J P Delehanty. 151
Tebbutt, Samuel. 158 W 119th....T Kelly. 187
Toner, J F. 152 W 63d....B M Cowperthwait & Co. 182
Tanco, Mrs B. 115 E 92d....J H Little. 248
Thorne, Sara. 110 W 38th....D Neuman. 524
Thoronton, Mary. 155 W 51st....Alexander Bros. 164
Trout, Mrs C R. 256 W 22d....Brooklyn F Co. 240
Uhl, C I. 10 W 136th....L Baumann. 112
Van Wyk, David. 100 W 97th....W J Ruddell. 100
Von Bello, E. 168 E 96th. ..J H Little. 216
Weber, Theo. 152 W 25th....J Baumann. (R) 170
Wendel, Libbie A. 1420 Park av....J Baumann. (R) 196
Westing, Charles....J Williams. 190
Westlake, I S. 208 E 103d....J H Little. 150
Wheeler, G M. 174th st and St Nicholas av....J Baumann. (R) 276
Whittaker, Thos. 143 W 30th ...L Baumann. 145
Wicks, Isabella....J Williams. 410
Wilkins, G A. 59 W 105th .. J H Little. 15?
Williams, Frank. 151 E 26th....L Baumann. 200
Werdenschlag, Abe. 497 Lexington av ...J Baumann. 347
Wilson, Mary. 324 E 82d....L Baumann. 132
Wormser, Esther. 509 E 83d ...J Moriarty. 203
Wilson, Florence K. 101 W 52d....H Israel & Son. 152
Same....same. 150

Zarnick, Caroline. 224 Chrystie....A Schaklinsky. Furnished Room House. 328

Zimmermann, Nettie. 101½ E 30th....J Moriarty (R) 100

Zutte, Leon. 161 Rivington....S I Herschmann. 507

MISCELLANEOUS.

Abbott, C B and S A. 436 W 57th.... H Killam Co. Coach. 1,152

Ashbey, N R. 118 Macdougal....A R Conklin. Horse, Ice Wagon, &c. 300

Anastasi, Francesco. 2432 8th av....A Schwaab. Barber Fixtures. 272

Arnold, Andrew ...I Arnold. Horse, Wagon. 200

Biekhart, M & Co ...Kean & Lines. Coach. (R) 400

Buckley, J and J. 425 Western Boulevard....M A Gordon. Machinery, &c. 2,500

Baierd, Alexander. 315½ W 24th....J Freeman. Coupe. (R) 40

Blum, Nicolaus. Railroad av, 167th and 168th sts....F A Ranson Dyestuff Co. Machinery. 586

Brauner, Max. 65 St. Marks pl. ..A Brauner. Store Fixtures 600

Bruns, Frederick. 193 Spring.....C Fischer. Confectionery Fixtures. (R) 1,000

Babcock, Jennie N....E A Thayer. Clocks, &c. (R) 3,000

Belmonte, D. 525 Canal....J Souvay. Barber Fixtures. 20

Christie, C W. 552 and 554 Washington....G H Richardson. Horses, Trucks. (R) 3,435

Cahill, Maggie....E Willis. Coupe. (R) 421

Castaldo, Luigi. 228 Av B....A Schwaab. Barber Fixtures. 44

Contozi, Leopold. 836 1st av....A Schwaab. Barber Fixtures. 81

Caffarello, Chas. 1451 1st av....F and G Haag & Co. Barber Fixtures. 73

Carter, R J and J P. 121 and 123 W 45th... Wolff Bros. Horse. 150

Same....same. Horses, &c. 1,530

Conciaidi, Salvator. 1 Horatio....L Ognibene. Barber Fixtures. 85

De Bouis, Francesco. 1743 1st av....A Schwaab & Son. Barber Fixtures. 38

Dunham Mfg Co. 75 E 10th....Mosler Safe Co. Safe. 142

Di Conga, Frank. 26 Albany....A Schwaab. Barber Fixtures. 140

Dickmann, Ernst. 855 1st av. ..G F Weldon. Bakery Fixtures. 308

Driscoll, J P. 156 E 105th....D Shea. Undertaker Wagon. 350

Ezechel, B and A. 27 Union sq....J C Fiuch. Flower Fixtures. 350

Ehrlich, M....J Stewart. Machines. 360

F H Whipple Co. Temple Court....D V Whipple. Office Fixtures, &c. 3,948

Feineman & Weitzman. 326 Church....J Stewart. Machines. 392

Fitzgerald, Michael. 133 W 31st....Wolff Bros. Horse, &c. 400

Faller, W M. 50 W 14th....J F Adams. Press, &c 500

Faracy, A W. 8th av, bet 74th and 75th sts.... A Schwaab & Son. Barber Fixtures. 189

Farrell, Eliza H....J F Galvin. Horses, Carts, &c. 170

Ferguson, G & Co. 154 W 27th....Michle P P Co. Press. 7,600

Freidberg, Michael. 71 Forsyth ...Archer Mfg Co. Barber Fixtures. 400

Friedman, Morris. 206 Forsyth... I Friedman. Machines. 250

Fuchs Bros. 134 Pitt...F Wesel Mfg Co. Printing Fixtures. 568

Freund & Horovitz. 171 Eldridge....I Margarethen. Bottling Fixtures. 390

Freund, O & Co. 11 Lispenard....M L Hiller. Machines. 100

Furber, C W. Produce Exchange Building and 11 and 13 Waverley pl....O F Gleason. Office Fixtures. (R) 275

Fischerer, Guiseppe. 1927 3d av... A Schwaab. Barber Fixtures. 618

Fiuhu, Geo, Jr. 1½ Rivington ...P Reidenbach. Truck. (R) 105

Gallo, Salvatore. 539 9th av....A Schwaab. Barber Fixtures. 151

Goetting, E C. 100th st and Amsterdam av....J Mathews. Soda Fixtures. 500

Garms, Henry. 160 Eldridge....J D Hanson. Horses, Trucks. 650

Garms, Henry. 160 Eldridge....F A Straus. Wagon. 250

Gay & Hays. 314 W 59th....Manhattan Type Foundry Co. Press, &c. 106

Gleason, M J. 2121 2d av... National C Reg Co. Register. 225

Goodman, Aaron. 111 Norfolk....P Reidinbach. Wagon. 124

Gayetty Paper Co. 42 West Broadway ..Mosler Safe Co. Safe. 185

Geanatasio, Rozario. 819 9th av....A Schwaab & Son. Barber Fixtures. 701

Georgi, Jacob. 143 Liberty....S Klingler. Barber Fixtures. 2,285

Godby, R L. 427 W 42d....Chappell-Chase-Maxwell Co. Undertaker Fixtures. 518

Goldner, S. 96 Fulton....W H Butler. Safe. 300

Goldstein, Isaac. 175 Monroe... C Dierking. Butcher Fixtures. 98

Goldwater, A L. 2571 3d av....C Kervan. Drug Fixtures. 5,330

Grey, Rose. 123 Chambers....B N Smith. Machinery. 123

Same....A Lowy. Machinery. 400

Grotte, C A. 958 8th av....Wolff Bros. Horses. 250

Haber, John. 556 W 36th....C Striffler. Machinery. 600

Hagan, Frederick. 328 E 104th ...C Doyle. Horse, Truck, &c. 400

Hamann, L F. 526 W 47th ...H Hellriegel. Press, &c. 100

Hausen & Schiek. 169 Eldridge ...Manhattan Type Co. Press, &c. 1,004

Hieatt, N B. 37th st and Broadway....Columbia Wagon Co. Wagon. 100

Hlawatsch, Joseph. 901 Forest av....L Hlawatsch. Plumbing Fixtures. 750

Hoffernan, Thomas. 165 E 35th....J Cunningham Son & Co. Undertaker Wagon. 425

Horvitz & Seibel. 641 Broadway....A Schwaab & Son. Barber Fixtures. 56

Hamacher, Jos. 881 3d av....A Glaser. Confectionery Fixtures. 250

Haskin, S E. Avoca, N Y....H H Cook. Horses, Cattle, &c. (R) 27,058

Haupt, Hermann. 165 W 31st....A Feulner. Barber Fixtures. 200

Hiller, Heyman. 24 Pitt....E Hiller. Machines. 150

Holmes, Joseph. 4 Pearl....Manhattan Type Co. Press. 290

Heins, J J. 446 Water....G A Young. Machinery. 150

Herzfeld, Jacob. 81 East Houston....G Herzfeld. Machines. 350

Jones, W F. 47 Broad....D Welch. Press, &c. (R) 400

Jonas, Bernhard. 647 1st av ...S Freiler. Cigar Fixtures. 200

Joseph, W and M. 246 E 80th... A Steinhardt. Laundry Fixtures. 400

Kirsch, Christian. 391 Bleecker....J Goebel. Butcher Fixtures. 500

Koehler, Jacob 175 E 114th ...P Westphal. Barber Fixtures. (R) 78

Kunz, Daniel. 205 Broadway .. Goodyear's India Rubber Co. Barber Fixtures. 450

Khuen, Frank. 155 Amsterdam av....National C Reg Co. Register. 225

Klee, Emil. 98 Rivington....J Ottmann. Butcher Fixtures. 65

Kohkohl, Louis. 815 W 145th....P A Cassidy. Wagon. 55

Kress, O & Co. 918 6th av... J Matthews. Soda Fixtures. 600

Kleine, August. 15 E 134th....Warren & Stratton. Bakery Fixtures. (R) 468

Koch, Henry. 444 E 77th G Devermann. Coach, &c. 300

Kallman, M & Son. 49 2d. ..Mosler Safe Co. Safe. 175

Kayser, J J. 78 Amsterdam av....McKesson & R. Drug Fixtures. 1,000

Kelly, P J. 34 North Moore....Van Allens & B. Press. 2,700

Khuen, Frank, 155 Amsterdam av....Nat Cash Register Co. Register. 220

Klaus, W J. 734 11th av....C Groll. Butcher Fixtures. 100

Locchse, J. 322 E 54th....A Schwaab. Barber Fixtures 23

Losee, L H. 358 W 48th....J W Hatch. Office Fixtures. 111

Larkin, M J. 2340 10th av....Lamson C S S Co. Register. (R) 210

Laux, W A. 27 and 29 E 3d....W McCrudden. Horse, Wagon, &c. 19

Lemon, G D. 10th av, 156th and 157th sts.... Mosler Safe Co. Safe. (R) 105

Lenz, Katie. 494 Amsterdam av....Bernheimer & S. Pool. 175

Levy, Max. 580 E 5th and 160 Stanton....American Guarantee Assoc. Hat Fixtures and Furniture. 100

Lewis, L. 2444 8th av ...Mosler Safe Co. Safe. 167

Liebler & Maass. 224 Centre. ..R E Emmerich. Lithographic Press. 5,735

Same. 224 Centre....P Adams & Co. Lithographic Press. 15,929

Liquri, Stefannia. 350 E 115th....A Schwaab & Son. Barber Fixtures. 227

Lowey Printing and Stationery Co. 85 Nassau ....Winthrop Press. Press, &c. 950

Lowey Printing and Stationery Co. 85 Nassau ....Winthrop Press. Type, &c. 429

Machauer & Lehman. 100 Orchard....C Kiehl. Presses, &c. (R) 400

Maher, Patrick. 8 West End av...T Maher. Horses, Trucks, &c. 425

Maher, W S. 22 Union sq....H St Ormond. Presses. (R) 12,000

Marino, A & P. 71 Mulberry....B Antico. Barber Fixtures. 160

McAllister, J F....J Stolts. Wagon. 350

McDermott, Peter. 734 10th av....National Cash Register Co. Register. 175

McDonald, James....Kean & Lines. Coupe. 450

McDermott, Peter. 734 10th....National C Reg Co. Register. 175

Menzell, Ida. 57th st and 6th av....National C Reg Co. Register. 175

Mooney, Christopher. 134 W 49th ....Hincks & J. Coach. 425

Moroso, A....J Souvay. Barber Fixtures. 24

Martin, C S. 436 11th av....W T Martin. Drug Fixtures. 900

McDermott, John. 134 W 49th....Wolff Bros. Horse, &c. 267

Meltzer & Pierken. 90 Henry....L Rodensky. Butcher Fixtures. 80

Newwelt, Ignatz. 23 Av A ...Duparquet, H & M Co. Ranges. 118

Nice, T H. 1st st and 1st av....F Goll. Horse, Truck, &c. 100

Nielsen, M V. 110 E 125th....A Dupont. Photo Fixtures. 550

N Y Steam Co....Union Trust Co. Franchise, &c. (R) 1,000,000

Osgood, L, Mrs. 362 Canal....J Stewart. Machines. 200

Ostroosky, Antonio. 45 Clinton....E Marscheider. Butcher Fixtures. 187

Ohlsen, J D. 350½ W 24th .. H Von der Lieth. Grocery Fixtures. 2,000

Pantiel, Theodore. 60 Broome .... I Flam. Butcher Fixtures. 30

Pfeffer, Solomon. 134 Norfolk ....S Becker. Machines. 236

Piening, Otto. 151 Forsyth ...F Oschmann. Bakery Fixtures. 500

Plaut, I S. 41st st....H A Wolf & Son. Horses, &c. (R) 1,841

Parrish, B, Mrs. 62 East Broadway....Bennett & G. Soda Fixtures. 170

Perley, E M, Jr. 59 Pelham av....P A Cassidy. Wagon. 49

Peters, Sophia, 136 7th ...W Schmidt. Store Fixtures. 300

Photo Color Print and Engraving Co. 341 E 11th ....Mieble P P Co. Press. 7,000

Prucha, Barbara, 528 E 68th... V Masin. Horses, Ice Wagon, &c. 250

Ringeisen, Jacob. 600 E 154th....C N Martin. Machines. 130

Romer, G A & Co. 31 and 33 Broadway....Marvin Safe Co. Safe. 218

Roos, P A .. J Cunningham Son & Co. Coach. 200

Rubin, Myer. 53 Spring....S Goldstein. Machines. 150

Roe, F N. 402 4th av....E C Wolcott. Store Fixtures. 500

Rosenfeld & Silberblatt. 308 E 110th....A D Sugarman. Bedding Stock. 38

Roth & Geiss. 519 10th av....A Roth. Painter Fixtures. 207

Sauerbrey, A H. 1519 1st av .. J F Bruning. Drug Fixtures. 1,550

Scarpinato, Giosippe. 223 E 73d....A Schwaab & Son. Barber Fixtures. 265

Sardy, Coles & Co....N P Rogers. General Assignment. 25,063

Schneider, Adolph. 501 E 72d....P A Cassidy. Wagon. 116

Straub, M and A. 546 W 54th....H Gampert. Bakery Fixtures. 100

Sutherland, Irene. 193 6th av....W H Owen. Office Fixtures, &c. (R) 138

Schneiz, Hugo. 576 3d av....J Matthews. Soda Fixtures. 400

Schwartz, Max. 263 East Houston....Otis Bros. Elevator. 2,750

Scott, A & Sons.. 543 and 545 E 21st....J Scott exr of. Horses, Ice Wagon, &c. 6,930

Siersema, Arno ...D P Nichols Co. Cab. 900

Schenectady Street Railway Co....Central Trust Co. Bonds, &c. 300,000

Simon, T M. 268 Henry....V Kallman. Drug Fixtures. 1,000

Simpson, S W. 89 W 14th....C B Cottrell & Son. Press. (R) 540

Sloan, Ella L. 775 Broadway....E Gribbon & Son trustee of. Machines. 372

Smith, Thomas. 430 2d av....J Burke. Cab. (R) 600

Spall, Emil. 358 W 53d ...L Boettger. Store Fixtures, Horse, &c. 500

Stafford, C B and A G 508 3d av... A D Puffer & Sons. Soda Fixtures. 100

Stewart, Alexander....Kean & Lines. Coupe. 425

T asi, Raphael. Gouverneur slip....Couper, Zimmermann & Co. Machinery. 1,325

Terris & Linsensburg. 59 Rutgers....H Jacot. Barber Fixtures. 125

Taylor, A E. 57 and 59 W 122d .. A Losey. Horse and Milk Wagon. 160

Volpe, Sebastiano. 140 Mulberry....G Costellano. Grocery Fixtures. 500

Varney, Frederick. 707 Amsterdam av ...Breher & Rogers. Barber Fixtures. 125

Walter, J. World Building....Mosler Safe Co. Safe. 385

Warnke, Henry. 626 E 12th... M Schneider. Bottling Fixtures. 150

Williams & Co. 44 Gold....M H Semple. Book Machine. 250

Weiher, A C and L F. 2756 Amsterdam av... Schwarzschild & S. Butcher Fixtures. 1,700

Zagat, Mendel. 858 2d av....J K Ambrose. Drug Fixtures. 672

BILLS OF SALE.

Atkinson, M B. 96 John and 19 Platt....W G Bates. Press, &c. 376

Asmus, Charles....W Sussmann. Horse, Fixtures and Furniture. 1,800

Barcia, Francesco. 196 Elizabeth....S Schillizel. Grocery Fixtures. 220

Boettger, Louis. 358 W 53d....E Spall. Store Fixtures, Horse, &c. 1,000

Brayton, F H. 279 Church....H R Laskamp. Horses, Trucks, &c. 1,000

Cicerone, Pasquale. 350 E 115th....S Siguori. Barber Fixtures. 75

Disbrow, F I. Storage....A E Pressinger. Furniture, &c. 1

Doyle, Cathrine....F Hagan. Horse, Truck, &c. 1

Freudenthal, Lotta. 2051 3d av and 287 Centre ....Laura Freudenthal. Machinery, &c. 2,000

Gold, J and H....S Horowitz. Clothing Stock. 1,000

Gillen, T F. 1843 3d av....D Fitzpatrick. Saloon Fixtures. 1,000

Greenberg, Harris. 21 Willett....H Oppenheim. Butcher Fixtures. 50

Holtermann, F A. 123 Av D....C Runke. Grocery Fixtures. 200

Hunter & Osborn. 492 E 138th....H S Baker. Horses, Trucks, &c. 300

Hillen, Geo. 7th av and 125th st....E H Ferguson. Saloon Fixtures. 1

Helnig, Paul E. 238 Canal....Anna M Ortmann. Restaurant Fixtures. 4,000

Horowitz, Samuel....J S Gold. Clothing Stock. 893

Joiner Planing and Moulding Co. 480 E 139th ....N Y Exhaust and Blow Pipe Co. Machinery. 152

Klussmann, R B. 4 9th av....H D Klussmann. Grocery Fixtures. 5,825

Koch, Peter. Burling slip....Bridget Rug. Store Fixtures. 175

Leasenfeld, Charles. 902 Columbus av....W H Kleinfelder. Butcher Fixtures. 2,000

Meyer, F I....C J Weigald. Horses, Wagon. 400

Mueller, Adolph. 141 8th .. Emma Mueller. Restaurant Fixtures. 100

Marafini, Francesco. 170 Mulberry ...A Tannini. Saloon, ½ interest 290

McKiernan, Peter....J McKiernan. Horses, Coal Carts, &c. 450

O'Keefe, P J. 701 3d av....J J Hickey. Saloon Fixtures. —

Ring, Pauline ..C J and M T Weigold. Express Fixtures. 100

Rossi, Raffaele. 55 Mott....Cajazzo & Caroselli. Barber Fixtures 265

Schmidt, G C. 831 1st av....G Schmidt. Bakery Fixtures. 1,000

Stern, Sam. 2264 8th av....H Hamburger. Butcher Fixtures. 165

Stuckenschmidt, Sophie. 420 Greenwich... F Brauer. Grocery Fixtures. 1,000

Steiner, Emma R Helen Stuart. Costumes. 500

Sussmann, William... M Asmus. Horse, Wagon, Furniture, &c. 2,000

Stritzky, M & G. 618 5th....C Stritzky. Tools, &c. 150

Thompson, Mary E. 940 Broadway ...J W Thompson. Hair Store Fixtures. 2,540

Wendt & Fischer. 404 8th av....J H Mohlman Co. Store Fixtures. 1,202

Zeller, Oscar. 1846 2d av ...S Zeller. Bakery Fixtures. 1

ASSIGNMENTS OF CHATTEL MORTGAGES.

Ambrose, J K to J C Childs & Co. (Mort given by M Zagat, Sept 24, 1891). 550

Byrnes, M T to L Collins. (M Chappell, May 15, 1891.) 300

Coglianese, Frank to Ella Murich. (Antonio Murich, May 6, 1891). 2,500

Cossin, Adeline to H C Schrader. (Fruchtenicht & Ulrich, Jan 26, 1891). 451

Cody, William to H Weiler. (W J Knoud, July 2, 1890). 1

Gronwoldt, Emma to O Koster. (G Buck, Feb 20, 1891).

KINGS COUNTY.

SEPTEMBER 24 TO 30.—INCLUSIVE.

SALOON AND RESTAURANT FIXTURES.

Bertuch M. 157 Fulton....J Brown. 1,050

Black, A C. East New York Hotel, 28 Jamaica av....Feigenspan B Co. Saloon and Hotel. 350

Botty, F. 306 Adams....Obermeyer & L. 125

Bright, I G. 115 Atlantic av....S Liebmann's Sons B Co. (R) 1,000

Burke, R. North 5th st, cor Berry st....Williamsburgh B Co. (R) 300
Carnochan, Lucy J. 174 Grand....S Liebmann's Sons B Co. 1,000
Carle, W and A Haack. 1081 Gates av... Williamsburgh B Co. 925
Clark, J. 168 Bridge ..W Ulmer. (R) 1,000
Cleary, J. 164 Columbia....Burger & Hower B Co. 1,700
Cosgrove, J. 935 3d av....Danenberg & Coles. (R) 250
Carlsen, L. 214 Columbia....Margaret Dobrowsky. 1,500
Dowd, F M and J J. Hoyt st, s e cor Butler st ....W L Flanagan, Managing Director. (R) 8,448
Dorn, J. 58 Lorimer....S Liebmann's Sons B Co. 1,200
Flynn, T R. 782 Fulton ....S Leibmann's Sons B Co. 2,000
Frank, Margt. 167 Boerum....Burger & H B Co. 900
Gallen, J.. 456 De Kalb av....Danenberg & Coles. (R) 350
Graf, H and J H Bertram. 1418 Fulton....P Ballantine & Sons. 3,500
Gaffney, J. 1064 Atlantic av....Williamsburgh B Co. (R) 350
Grote, E. 112 Utica av....S Liebmann's Sons B Co. 1,000
Hagendorn, V. 185 Ten Eyck....S Liebmann's Sons B Co. (R) 300
Heuns, J H. Cypress av, Old Mill....L Eppig. 410
Hopf, C. 88 Ewen... Claus Lipsius B Co. 115
Huschle, F. 426 Bushwick av....S Liebmann's Sons B Co. (R) 500
Hodgkiss, G and T Stevenson. 472 6th av. S Liebmann's B Co. 1,200
Hoffmann, H C. 567 Manhattan av....J C G Hupfel B Co. (R) nom
Hafner, C H. 190 Johnson av....Burger & Hower B Co. 525
Johanson, M. 1280 Myrtle av....Williamsburgh B Co. (R) 700
Konenkamp, H. 9 Woodhull....Williamsburgh B Co. (R) 1,500
Keller, J H. 958 Herkimer....E Ochs. 800
Keller, R. 25 Lorimer....Burger & H B Co. 900
Kelly, P. 7th av, n w cor 13th st....E Ochs. 1,000
Kenna, M. 399 Van Brunt....H B Scharmann & Sons. 350
Kuiest, M. 203 Driggs av .. Feigenspan B Co. 1,000
Lewis, J. 186 Throop av....E Ochs. 600
Lanigan, J J. 72 Huntington....India Wharf B Co. 550
Martin, Pauline. 1156 Myrtle av....J Ruppert. 800
McCahill, L. 723 5th av ...W Purcell. 1,500
McElhatton, M. 1 95 Broadway...Williamsburgh B Co. 600
McLindon, A and E. 91 Franklin....Danenberg & Coles. 200
McTiernan, M. 2 State....M Seitz. 265
Murphy, M and D F Sweeney. 270 and 270A 5th av....Schmitt & S. (R) 1,210
Mahlmann, C. 667 Myrtle av....Margaret Hartough. Restaurant Fixtures. 650
McGuire, P. 168 4th av....S Liebmann's Sons B Co. (R) 260
Miller, J. 898 Fulton....S Liebmann's Sons B Co. 1,200
Muller, H D. 81 Sands....Eva Bechtel extrx. 800
Nelson, J. 426 Prospect av....Danenberg & Coles. 636
Oldenburg, R. 257 Greenpoint av....Claus Lipsius B Co. 400
Planer, A A. 695 Flushing av. H B Scharmann & Sons. 478
Rudd, Mary A. 241 Bushwick av... Eliz Zeiser. 300
Rugen, J F. 363 7th av. ..F & M Schaefer B Co. 800
Rugen, J T. 361 7th av....F & M Schaefer B Co. Saloon Ice Box. 70
Roden, A. 66 Freeman....J Kress B Co. 500
Ruehle, J. 115 Knickerbocker av....L Eppig. (R) 700
Schechtel, W & Bro. Watkins st and Belmont av ....Williamsburgh B Co. (R) 250
Shaffer, G A. 36 Broadway....F & M Schaefer B Co. (R) 1,580
Stewart, A. 89 Ralph av....Welz & Z. 1,200
Swithenbank, R. 181 Pearl....Leary & B B Co. 1,068
Schwab, W. 395 Melrose....Claus Lipsius B Co. 500
Stein, L. 2021 Fulton....H Stoff. 800
Strober, A. 659 Flushing av....H B Scharmann & Sons. 750
Taylor, S T. 224 Franklin....W Ulmer. (R) 4,000
Same. 349 Manhattan av....same. (R) 1,600
Uttendorfer, G. 206 Stagg st....Burger & H B Co (Lim). (R) 500
Wogan, T F. 774 3d av....H Clausen & Son B Co. (R) 1,500
Wagenblast, J. 258 Metropolitan av....M Seitz. 400
Werner, J. 177 Sackett....W H Werner. 1,575
Zapp, J. 74 North 5th st....P Weidmann. 400
Zerrenner, C. 1836½ Fulton....S Liebmann's Sons B Co. (R) 600

HOUSEHOLD FURNITURE.

Aims, A C. Washington st, cor Concord st.... J Hegeman & Co. 393
Boecher, Lena. 30 Throop av....A Schulz. 186
Brown, Mary. 100 Johnson . I Mason. 339
Banackowsky, M. 176 New Jersey av....J H Little. 246
Cottrell, C E. 385 Bridge....C C Coutrell. 188
Case, Jr, S. 1094 Bedford av....J T Sherwood. 150
Cody, Mary A. 39 Maujer....F J Brechtel. 100
Corr, Lizzie I. 276 Ainslie....J Gregg. 213
De Mott, L. 852 Livingston....Brooklyn F Co. 324
Drew, J. New Utrecht....W C Woodbine. (R) 245
Degan, Eliz A and Thos S. 487 6th av....M O'Keefe. 200
Elbert, Minnie. 128 Withers....Brooklyn F Co. 160
English, Mary J. 64 Greene av....Brooklyn F Co. 1,584
Farrell, Sadie. 579 Driggs....S Baumann. 124
Fooks, H. 79 South 5th....Brooklyn F Co. 102
Fowler, G W. 374 14th....R Silverman. 185
Fuller, F H. 330 Sackett....J Michaels. 300
Gardner, C. 448 State....Brooklyn F Co. 213
Giraud, Jennie. 884 Gates av....L Baumann. 182
Gould, A S and Edith. 149 Keap... E C Hinsdale. 100
Grobner, C. 175 Harrison....L Baumann. 148
Grossman, V. 197 Floyd... Simpson & P. Piano. 110
Halpern, Ester. 28 Middagh....H S Eisler. 178
Hanrahan, Ellen. 931 Dean....Brooklyn F Co. 206
Hanson, E. 518 6th av ...Brooklyn F Co. 149
Hartmann, P. 216 Nassau....Brooklyn F Co. 166
Hay, P. 1440 Broadway. A Pearson. 112
Ingram, J. 60 Columbia pl....J McEnery & Co. 181
Jayson, N. 491 Pacific....T F Ryan. 176
Johnson, E N. 151 Waverly av....Simpson & P. Piano. 300
Karkella, J and Kate D. 1065 3d av.....E C Hinsdale. 100
Kelly, P J. 34 North Moore st, New York... Van Allens & B. Press. 2,700
Kessel, H A. 535 Madison av....J G Truelson. Piano. 850
Kuster, Fannie A. 190 Degraw....R Silverman. 200
King, Evelyn A. 58 Decatur....M M Webster. 150
Lynch, N J. 87 Summit....J M Marcus. 164
Littlejohn, G M S. 89 Pineapple....Brooklyn F Co. 140
Madden, Pauline. 1187 Herkimer....Brooklyn F Co. 285
Mansfield, J H. Atlantic av....Brooklyn F Co. 124
Martin, C. 60 Clinton av . I Mason. 179
Masshall, W E. 622 President ...J Baumann. 118
Marshall, Stella. 184 South Oxford....W Battermann. (R) 724
McCormack, E J. 77 Degraw....Brooklyn F Co. 171
McKennee, Anna B. 582 10th ...C W McKennee. Piano. 126
McMahon, Mary. 29 Withers ... Alexander Bros. 140
Miss, S. 518 Lorimer....M M Webster. 100
Musgrave, Lucy. 320 Clason av .... Ellen M Dunn. 300
Maddock, H. 1855 Pacific....O'Connor & T. 344
May, Rose. 202 Hamburg av ...O'Connor & T. 215
Noonan, T. 966 Myrtle av....O'Connor & T. 150
Nelson, H. Smith st, south cor 4th st....J Michaels. 126
Newhall, A H. 98 Heyward ...Brooklyn F Co. 139
Noll, E. 192 Hudson av....Brooklyn F Co. 160
O'Neil, Ida. 660 Bergen....Brooklyn F Co. 143
Packer, E. 511 Willoughby av....Brooklyn F Co. 405
Pearson, C F. 485 Washington av....Brooklyn F Co. 385
Phillips, W G. 194 Vernon av....Brooklyn F Co. 142
Potts, Ann. Glenmore av, near Sackman st ... C S Lacey. 167
Reynolds, W W. 20 Glenada pl....C D Rust. 450
Robinson, J. 668 6th av....J Michaels. 143
Rabelo, C. 185 Washington....M Diaz. 100
Rich, J A. 420 St Marks av . O'Connor & T. 186
Shuttleworth, J E. 999 Greene av ...I Mason. 154
Schellam, C. 16 Lee av....H Hudtwalker. (R) 700
Sawkins, S E. 201 Baltic....Brooklyn F Co. 187
Schambacher, C F and L M. 340 Clinton....M H Campbell. 1,100
Schroeder, H A. 1022 Putnam av....I Mason. 188
Smith, T H. 654 Carroll....Brooklyn F Co. 357
Staats, Anna C. 312 Macon....A Pearson. 109
Stauk, A. 67 North 8th....Alexander Bros. 131
St George, J. 29 Conselyea. ..A Schulz. 107
Stinson, R L. 134 Nelson....I Mason. 155
Tainter, H C. 399 Douglass....Simpson & P. Piano. 250
Thompson, W S. 806 Franklin av....Mullins & Sons. 170
Welch, Alida. 801 Keap....E Driscoll & Bros. 116
Wilson, J. 181 Sands....E Driscoll & Bros. 140
Walker, Annie. 14 Folsom pl....S Baumann. 172
Waring, H F. 53 Schermerhorn....Brooklyn F Co. 127
Welch, M F. 1318 Fulton... Brooklyn F Co. 467
Weisfold, A. 165 Greene av....M Brock. Piano. 250
Whitbeck, Mrs H M. 815 President....Brooklyn F Co. 118
Wynne, T D. 9 Stuyvesant av....E C Hinsdale. 250
Williams, J C. 167 Wyckoff av....O'Connor & T. 225

MISCELLANEOUS.

Abernethy, E T....Knickerbocker Ice Co. Horse and Wagon. (R) 165
Alazzio, L. 219 Hoyt....G Campilonzo. Shoe Store Fixtures. 112
Ash, Rachel B. 8th av and 42d st....P McCabe. Farming Stock. 234
Bell, G H. 41 Park row....O L Caldwell, Horse and Wagon. 450
Betzel, G and Benjamin B. 11-17 Humboldt.... J Benjamin. Steam Carousel, &c. 1,000
Bieling, A C. 1147 De Kalb av.. .R A Demill and ano exrs Richard M Demill. Tools, Horse, Wagon, &c. 500
Blauthorne, L K. 18 Jefferson....C E Blauthorne. Horses, Ice Wagon, &c. 1,200
Bindrim, J. 712-724 Bedford av....North Side Bank, Brooklyn. Horses, Coaches, &c. 3,550
Behrens, C. 45 Brooklyn av....J Biot. Horse and Wagon. 150
Bergen, Maria W. New Lots av and Wyona st.... A V Suydam. Farming Stock. 200
Burk, Catherine. 41 Brooklyn av....D B Dunham. Coach. (R) 436
Cartolano, P. 550 7th av....G Campilonzo. Shoe Store Fixtures. 112
Corrigan, J S. 212 5th av....Marvin Safe Co. Safe. 120
Dallimore, H S. 116 Withers....E W Reynolds. Horses. 600
Doe, W S. 619 3d av....J Strathan. Store Fixtures. 550
Dolbrazia, A M. 800 Myrtle av... A Schwaab & Son. Barber Fixtures. 190
Dressel, W. 72 Varet....R Spahu. Sewing Machine. 110
Ehrichs & Berry. 1467 Broadway... Mosler Safe Co. Safe. 180
Gallagher, M J. 5th av, cor President st....National Cash Register Co. Register. 175
Groenwoldt, C. 2154 Fulton....B Fischer & Co. Groceries. 1,000
Green, H S. 23 Carlton av....G D Knight & Co. Brass Foundry. 100
Grecco, A and R. 112 Livingston....V Grande. Barber Fixtures. (R) 285
Grote, W. 503 Liberty av....W Seuling. Grocery Fixtures. 200
Heineman, G D. 301 Bedford av....T Westing. Tailor Fixtures. 200
Hill, H. Williams and Atlantic avs ...National C Reg Co. Register. 175
Hesse, E W. 70 Boerum pl and 216 Pacific st.... A J Foren. Store and Factory Fixtures. (R) 230
Hill, Harry. Williams av, cor Atlantic av. National Cash Register Co. Register. 175
Hopkins, T. 306 Prince....Wolff Bros. Horse and Cab. 300
Kranz, C. 305 Stagg....P Dieffenbach. Milk Business. 400
Kent, R. 45 Jay....J G Meyers. Machinery. 400
Liebler & Maas. 224 Centre st, New York....R F Emmerich. Presses, &c. 5,785
Liebler & Maas. 224 Centre st, New York....P Adams Co. Presses, &c. 15,929
Luca, J W. 2624 Atlantic av....Flora C Fleisch. Butcher Fixtures. 200
Leary, P. 129 Congress....Wolff Bros. Horses and Coach. (R) 167
Marrs, T H. 255 Atlantic av....Nat Cash Register Co. Register. 175
Martens, H and P. 1111½ Bedford av....O W Van Campen & Son. Grocery Fixtures. 352
McGowan, P J. Woodbine st, near Evergreen av.. A M Suydam. Horse. 90
Musculino, O. 57 Bergen....A Schwaab & Son. Barber Fixtures. 365
Nielsen, L. 248 Smith....C Menken. Grocery Fixtures. 700
Paulsen, H. 124 Park av....Nat Cash Register Co. Register. 175
Ritzheimer, G H. 72 Myrtle av....H Ritzheimer. Butcher Fixtures 600
Scherr, A. 122 Franklin....J Matthews. Soda Apparatus. 400
Schmidt, A W. 310 Graham av....Nat Cash Register Co. Register. 225
Schott, W. 15 Monitor .. F Schieffer. Machinery. 200
Shaughnessy, T. Flatbush, L I....Nat Cash Register Co. Register. 175
Streck, W. 686 4th av... Roberts & C. Bakery Fixtures. 150
Strome, A. 1124 Bedford av....J Matthews' Apparatus Co. Soda Apparatus. 199
Steinam, A. 65 and 67 Union av....L E Nicot. Drugs. (R) 1,100
Same....same. Drugs. (R) 162
Schmidt, A W. 310 Graham av....National Cash Register Co. Register. 225
Underhill, L. Flatbush....Cunningham Son & Co. Wagon. 400
Weiner, C. 167 Troutman....M Wertheimer. Horse, &c. 150
Winhelman, A. 1058 3d av....P Ballantine & Sons. Bottling Business. 350
Wahlers, J A. 93 Harrison av ...J Sackmann. Horse and Wagon. 270
Wilson, Eliza and J. 77 York....Wolff Bros. Horse and Carts. (R) 130
Woelber, C. 249 De Kalb av....National Cash Register Co. Register. 175

BILLS OF SALE.

Badger, Robert E. 27 Kossuth pl... J Frazer. Milk Route. 500
Beckroge, J... J Durenberg. Milk Business. 250
Cooney, P. 4th av, cor 12th st.... Bridget Cooney. Horse. 72
Denton, F and D. 51 West av, Wallabout Market....Sarah L Denton. Produce Business. 300
Eagan, J. 1081 Gates av....W Carlo and ano. Saloon Fixtures. 1,125
Fischer, B & Co. 2154 Fulton....C Groenwoldt. Grocery Fixtures. 500
Hartough, Margaret. 667 Myrtle av....C Mahlmann. Restaurant Fixtures. 800
Herlich, J. 87 Graham av....L C Starke. Grocery Fixtures. 1,500
Huttle, F....A Deim. Horses and Rolling Stock. nom
Komel, A. 57 Moore....J Goldberg. Fish, &c, Business. 50
Kranz, C. 305 Stagg... P Dieffenbach. Milk Business. 450
Ossman, C. 296 Lee av... W Wenzel. *Dry Goods.* Sub to mort $1,000. 800
Plough, D H. 393A 6th av....F H Parsons. Furniture. 234
Stauch, V. 190 Union av....F Caruso. Grocery Fixtures. 140
Straub, A. 987 Flushing av....C Dewald. Butcher Fixtures. 250
Zahrt, Caroline. 81 Sands....H D M Muller. Saloon Fixtures. 1,500

ASSIGNMENTS OF CHATTEL MORTGAGES.

Benjamin, J to J Rueger. (Mort given by G Betzel and B Benjamin, Sept 28, 1890). nom
Silverman, R to S J Goldsmith. (Assign mort by Fannie A Kuster, Oct. 29, 1890) See Kuster, in furniture. nom

NEW JERSEY.

NOTE.—*The arrangement of the Conveyances, Mortgages and Judgments in these lists is as follows: the first name in the Conveyances is the Grantor; in Mortgages, the Mortgagor; in Judgments, the Judgment debtor.*

ESSEX COUNTY.

CONVEYANCES.

Annilly, Annie—W H Bellis, 14th av.............. $1
Batterson, T H—J J Gaffney, South 7th st....... 640
Beach, A E—E L Jaeger, Montclair.............. 1,525
Bellis, W H—E Annilly, 14th av 1
Boulton, W R—T K Gardner, Lincoln av.......... 5
Brant, S O—T Cushman, Millburn.................. 6,000
Bub, Barbara—C A Feick, McWhorter st......... 1,800
Bullock, J R—S M Mintonye, Montclair............ 1
Cadmus, E J—M A Smith, n s Market st 75 e Chambers st 50x100.......................... 6,500
Carter, X B—C A Rindell, Ridgewood av.......... 500
Cassidy, Patrick—T D Richards, East Orange... 200
Christian, C A—M C Aymar, East Orange....... 12,000
Clark, Mary—J Clark, Orange...................... 2,000
Condit, Fillmore—C M Bloxham, Caldwell....... 1
Farley, B M—E Reeve, Clinton...................... 1
Francis, Daniel—B Fletcher, South Orange...... 1
Garabrant, C R—N I Surges, Jr, s s Ferry st ... 5,000
Gardner, T K—L K Boulton, Orange.............. 5
Glorieux, W L—F F Johnson, Irvington.......... 1
Guentber, J G—P J Kull, Hawkins............... 575
Hartshorne, Charles—Newark and Roselle Ry Co, Clinton...................................... 1
Same—same, Clinton 1
Same—same, Clinton...................... 1
Same—same, Clinton...................... 1
Same—same, Clinton...................... 1
Same—same, Clinton...................... 1
Same—same, Clinton...................... 1
Headley, W C—T O'Keefe, Millburn.............. 114
Higbie, A T—The Lincoln B and L Assoc, Irvington.. 1,200
Hutton, C G—C A Babcock, West Orange...... 4,000
Jamison, John—O Miller, Franklin.............. 1,100
Johnson, Emery—C C Chamberlain, Clinton.... 100
Johnson, F T—W L Glorieux et al, Irvington.... 1
Kitchell, G F—J W Straban, Hunterdon st...... 1,450

Kreig, M A—J R Frederick, East Orange 1
Kussy, Meyer—H Stiegler, s e cor Morris and 15th avs 50x100 3,300
Kunzendorf, Elizabeth—E Tresch, Hunterdon st. 5,900
Lehman, A M—S D Miller et al, East Orange 860
Lemassena, Lillian—E A Van Ness, Winthrop st. 1,000
Liebstein, Mary—P Lowy, Livingston st 1
Lister, J C—W P Dunn, Esther st 300
McCaskie, John, Jr—A Newkirk, East Orange .. 1
McLagan, J F et al—J Archer, Clifton av 230
Same—J E Janes, Clifton av 558
McQuilkin, John—D McQuilkin, Millburn 500
Mitchell, A P—M Vandunker, East Orange 1,250
Mitchell, A P et al—W C Gross, 6th av 1,000
Newkirk, Annin—E McCaskie, East Orange 1
Otis, A W—H Mills, East Orange 5,625
Palmer, A E—J T Palmer, Orange 1
Palmer, Jane—A E Palmer, Orange 1
Pope, W C—J Nessler, South Orange 1
Reeve, Ezra—B M Farley, Clinton 1
Rowe, Michael—W C Jones, South 8th st 3,200
Rutan, Letitia—S Reynolds, Franklin 870
Sargeant, S S et al—A Del Guercio, 7th av 1,250
Scofield, Cyrus—G Negro, Adams st 1
Selby, W B—J T C Selby, Clay st 1,380
Selby, J T C—E G Selby, Clay st 1,380
Selby, W B—J T C Selby, Clay st 1,610
Selby, J T C—W B Selby, Clay st 1,610
Sharwell, W G—A M Jamouneau, South 7th st .. 310
Snyder, E H—S B Schneider, South Orange 490
Surges, M E—C R Garabrant, s s Ferry 5,000
Taylor, A E—C H Eaton, Montclair 4,025
The Mutual Homestead Assoc—J A Becker, Jr, Clinton 34
Same—same, Clinton 36
Same—same, Clinton 34
The Peabody Land and Loan Co—J Archer, Clifton av 469
Same—J E Janes, Clifton av 700
Same—C A Bennett, Mt Prospect av 750
Towne, J W et al—C E Lyon, East Orange 5,900
Van Ness, E A—L Lemassena, w s Summer av 457 n Fredonia av 25x123 3,600
Van Order, M B—F W Lestrade, Caldwell 900
Wade, I H—W C Headley, Millburn 1
Wadsworth, E M—F Chandler, East Orange 3,000
Same—same, East Orange 3,000
Walters, John—S Griffin, 7th st 312
Same—W J Osgood, 7th st 312
Ward, C W—A M Jamouneau, North 7th st 550
Whitney, G W S—E W Whitney, East Orange .. 1
Whitty, M C—G Negro, Adams st 500
Williams, E C—C H Early, West Orange 2,500
Wood, Andrew—A Bowden, Caldwell 450

MORTGAGES.

Agens, G W—Roseville B and L Assoc, Sussex av 200
Allen, William—S E Richards, State st 1,500
Alston, C B—Merchants Ins Co, Orchard st 2,000
Bauer, Gottlieb—J C Smith, Kinney st 3,000
Banta, C W—F O Pierson, Orange 350
Betts, E J—S Crump, Montclair 350
Betz, Katherina—Central B and L Assoc, North 5th st 2,200
Blewitt, Daniel—F Bonykamper, Jr, Van Buren st 1,000
Broadbent, Minerva—M Broadbent, Franklin 800
Bruen, Anna—M E Kilburn, Pennington st 500
Burke, R P—M J Williams, Orange 500
Carlson, J S—J A Keyler, Montclair 2,500
Chandler, Forester—L Wadsworth, East Orange 2,000
Same—same, East Orange 2,000
Curtis, W F—A C Bogie, Montclair 500
Cushman, Townsend—S O Brant, Millburn 4,000
Devine, Arthur—E C Robertson, Clinton 4,000
Duerr, John—Excelsior B and L Assoc, Magazine st 3,500
Dwyer, G B—J Jackson, Washington st 2,250
Early, C H—E C Williams, West Orange 2,400
Eisele, J C—The Lincoln B and L Assoc, Prince st 5,000
Emens, E F—L D Berry, East Orange 5,000
Faith, E A—The Franklin B and L Assoc, Franklin 400
Forman, D H—F Whitney, Lincoln av 1,000
Gates, A A—W N Lewis, North 3d st 1,500
George, M L—J Jackson exr, Central av 500
Grogan, John—J Colyer, Willet st 250
Guercio, A Del—C S Stockton, 7th av 1,000
Hall, W H—The Half Dime Savings Bank, Orange 11,500
Hedges, S M—C Williams, Orange 1,500
Helbig, F W—The Franklin Savings Inst, Roseville av 10,000
Hooley, F H—Roseville B and L Assoc, North 9th st 200
Jacobus, L C—The Eighth Ward B and L Assoc, Clifton av 400
James, J E—A Hitchcock, Washington av 500
Jerolemon, C E—M P Hennion, East Orange 2,000
Jones, S E—E R Bradford admr, West Orange ... 1,000
Jones, W C—G Neff, South 6th st 4,000
Joachim, Benjamin—Standard B and L Assoc, Boyd st 400
Liebstein, Mary—Excelsior B and L Assoc, Wallace st 6,000
Livingston, J L—Orange Savings Bank, East Orange 1,000
Lyon, C E—J W Towne et al, East Orange 2,500
McCredy, W E—F R Condert, Livingston 7,500
McLagan, J F—Howard B and L Assoc, Summer av 2,500
McManus, Patrick—H T Brumley, Condit st 250
Mills, Henry—A W Otis, East Orange 2,000
Nolte, Eva—The Franklin Savings Inst, Belmont av 4,500
Oppermann, L H—J J Brown, East Orange 1,000
Ord, John—F W Peloubet, East Orange 1,000
Ord, J W—L H Calvin, East Orange 3,000
Pope, W C—Fireside B and L Assoc, Joseph st .. 600
Same—same, Joseph st 600
Same—same, Joseph st 650
Radofsky, Charles—M H Pennington, Broome st 2,200
Richards, T D—P Cassidy, East Orange 100
Rueger, John—Unabhaengige Germania Schuetzen Bund, Bank st 1,400
Schliep, L C—W J Slinkard, South Orange 500
Schumacher, Margaretha—M Holsten, South 6th st 1,100
Sheldon, W H—Howard Savings Inst, Bloomfield 6,000
Sherman, M A—D O Brown, East Orange 3,500
Sliker, M J—J P Condit, West Orange 1,500
Snyder, Nellie—F W Peloubet, East Orange 1,000
Snyder, Nellie—L H Calvin, East Orange 3,000
St Augustine Roman Catholic Church—S Koellhoffer, Sussex av 8,000
Truesdell, Thomas—J H Worden, Montclair 1,500
Vail, H J—F Whiteley, North 7th st 2,006
Van Riper, W E—Fraternal B and L Assoc, Bloomfield av 200
Vernieri, Francesco—J M Trimble, Adams st 2,400
Wade, John—The American Insurance Co, Montclair 700
Ward, S E—The Orange Savings Bank, West Orange 6,000
Zeh, Charles—L F Crowell, South 7th st 1,500

CHATTEL MORTGAGES.

Allin, T W E—F J Kastner, saloon 265
Baker, J M—A Steadman, furniture 100
Beldon, J M—E D Knower, horses and wagons .. 2,500
Same—H A Fluck, coach 328
Blackburn, James—J Ketcham, furniture 130
Brennan, Jeannette—S Brennan, furniture 70
Buchanan, J R—Brooklyn Furniture Co, furniture 295
Daly, Thomas—Lyon & Sons Brewing Co, saloon 257
Dempsey, J F—J Cromwell, stock fruits 1,246
Doremus, F T—J K Doremus, groceries 642
Same—S M Doremus, groceries 2,700
Eitz, Anthony—Lyon & Sons Brewing Co, saloon 150
Girado, Pasquale—F Lisiewski, saloon 180
Jessup, C H—P Ballantine & Sons, saloon 200
Joralemon, S L—Hirschfield & Co, safe 62
Lee, J J—E E Spence & Co, machinery 270
Marsh, M B—M E Leonard, butcher fixtures 382
Meyer, Otto—J & J Dobson, carpets 184
Mollet, Sophia—F C Edwards, piano 350
Muller, N A—C Bierman, furniture 130
Neill, James—S A Woods Machine Co, machinery 450
Oschwald, Hermann—F Lisiewski, wagon 150
Parbery, F A—J Ketcham, piano 130
Pierce, Nellie—J M Hann, furniture 65
Rizzolo, Donato—F Lisiewski, saloon 475
Rowan, W T—F G Cope, wagonette 40
Studer, A C—Marvin Safe Co, safe 75
Tea and Portrait Co—same, safe 60
Wantoch, L J—J Meyer, horse 60
Young, J W—F McCormick, groceries 366

JUDGMENTS.

Barclay, J D—J O'Rourke 556
Dempsey, J F—J Tur et al 583
Dougherty, Andrew—Wilkinson, Gaddis & Co 469
Farley, Thomas—Wilkinson, Gaddis & Co 193
Gedicke, M A—A Ward et al 294
Hedden, I C—W B Whitney 764
Moll, L M—W G Hainski 248
Taylor, I V—C Biermann 118
Wyatt, Irving—C Festermann 1,068

HUDSON COUNTY.

CONVEYANCES.

Allen, Robert—A E Wright, Kearney $4,000
Allen, Robert and M M Forrest—Jessie M Perkins, Kearney 500
Same—Mary L Haley, Kearney 900
Aiken, W B—Elizabeth Evarts, J City .... nom
Barnickel, C A—O Frommel, Hoboken 545
Banta, Aaron—Sophia D Smith, Kearney 300
Beck, Andrew—The Flower Hill Cemetery Co, North Bergen 8,000
Black, C C—B McEneary, J City 2,000
Same—Henrietta Godfrey, J City 1,100
Brinkerhoff, William—W E Korth, J City 3,500
Bonn, J H—The Flower Hill Cemetery Co, North Bergen .... nom
Bonn, H J—O Schultz, West Hoboken .... —
Brady, Maggie N—J N Long, J City 2,000
Brett, W G—E N Little, West Hoboken 1,800
Burr, J Brown—E L Brown, J City 3,000
Cadmus, Andrew—S McElmiel, Bayonne 1,000
Clark, James—J Russell, J City 1,150
Condit, Filmore—Ann Riley, Kearney 450
Same—W Trautz, Kearney 600
Same—W F Hongin, Kearney 150
Conlon, Jane by master—H Thompson, J City .. 525
Connor, J P—Margaret Connor, J City .... nom
Dalton, Frank—W McIlroy, J City 765
Daucet, Lulu E—Belle Lafter, J City 195
Downs, S C—J Means, J City 3,000
Dulam, Anna C—E Hoosit, J City 7,250
Earle, F H—H Thompson, J City 700
Eberhard, F N—Louisa Rosa, Hoboken 380
Same—A Rosa, Hoboken 1,000
Faber, John—A Siegfried, West Hoboken .... nom
Faber, Veronica—same, West Hoboken 900
Fitzgerald, Marie E—H R Powley, West Hoboken 3,000
Fugel, Christian—G Wolf, J City 1,075
Fugger, Robert—E Tist, J City 200
Gilligan, Rosanna—S Herzog, West Hoboken 2,550
Glantzmann, Peter—A Wehausen, J City .... nom
Goodchild, Bertha B exr R W Goodchild—J Hollyer, Bayonne 500
Harriott, Geo—J King trustee, J City .... nom
Harney, William by exrs—P E Martin, J City ... 6,000
Harney, W A—same, J City .... nom
Hatch, A S—T Flanagan, J City .... nom
Same—A J Howard, J City .... nom
Same—C C Black, J City .... nom
Hatch, A S by assignee—same, J City 4,545
Hatch, A S by assignee—T Flanagan, J City 205
Hatch, A S by assignee—A J Howard, J City ... 605
Hennion, Abram—F Hennion, Hoboken, 7 deeds nom
Hennion, F C—Mary Hennion, Hoboken, 6 deeds nom
Hille, F W—F C Hausen, Union 2,625
Hoboken Land and Impt Co—J C Carr, Hoboken ... 5,000
Same—G Hauser, Hoboken 15,594
Same—T Kirchgesner, West Hoboken 270
Hudson, Hannah—Annie Hayes, J City 2,000
Indian Spring Land Co—F Luchio, West Hoboken 1,300
Kemp, G W—J J Duffy, J City 4,500
Lutz, John—Caroline Lutz, J City .... nom
Luxton, Susan—Sarah Murray, West Hoboken .. 700
MacLean, Mary M—C D Ridgway, J City 2,700
Newbery, I L—Sarah J Wright, Kearney .... nom
Nichols, E H—B J Reilly, J City 125
Same—M Lynch, J City 2,000
Same—Lulu E Dancet, J City 100
Same—J J Ward, J City 225
O'Neil, J F—A Lennox, Harrison 500
Pyne, Emily—R Allewetal, Kearney 900
Rademan, Peter—C Deppisch, J City 3,950
Raggu, Giovanni—J Lang, Hoboken 3,500
Rector, Julia R—L A Brooks, J City 8,000
Ridgway, C D—J H Watson, Jr, J City 100
Roake, J D—A W Anderson, Bayonne 800
Russell, William—Ada Stevens, J City 3,750
Schulz, Chas—Eliz Walt, Union .... nom
Siegfried, Adam—T A Kennedy, West Hoboken. 625
Simons, C D—W Williams, J City 6,000
Silva, Harriet—Susan Pous, West Hoboken 800
Suryock, Allen—Annie E Huckle, Bayonne .... nom
Sulfusch, Margaretha—Maria Schillinger, Union 1,200
Tewkesbury, H A—Tillie K Williams, Hoboken. nom
The North Jersey Land Co—J Anderson, Kearney 950
Tici, Minetta L—C O Tice, J City 5,000
Tierney, Myles—F McDonald, Hoboken 5,800
Same—W Bradford, Hoboken 5,800
Same—F P McMahon, Hoboken 5,600
Same—B McGovern, Hoboken 5,800
Trask, Martha C—Irene W Trask, Bayonne .... nom
Trask, N W—Martha C Trask, Bayonne .... nom
Wallis, Eliz—L A Dodworth, North Bergen .... nom
Watson, J H, Jr—Julia W Ridgway, J City 100
Watt, Eliz—P Bonden, Union .... nom
Wehausen, August—P Glanzmann, J City .... nom
Wedemeyer, Claus—W Hons, Guttenberg 300
Wetterer, August—G E Thomas, West Hoboken. 3,000
Williams, J B—D D Bryan, Kearney 3,100
Williams, James—H A Tewkesbury, Hoboken ... nom
Wright, A E—I L Newbery, Kearney .... nom

MORTGAGES.

Ahles, Josie—A Wetterer, West Hoboken, 1 year 3,000
Appenzeller, Fred—Union B and L Assoc, Union, installs 1,000
Arnold, Mary—Peoples B and L Assoc, Kearney, installs 1,000
Atkins, S DeH—People's B and L Assoc, Kearney, installs 2,400
Bettcher, L F—Susan J Wortendyke, J City, 1 year 500
Bradford, William—M Tierney, Hoboken, 5 yrs. 2,500
Brendli, Herman—J G Hintze, West Hoboken, 5 years 1,000
Deppisch, Carl—P Rademan, J City, 3 years 2,000
Same—same, J City, 3 years 1,350
Furey, Catharine E—Howard B and L Assoc, J City, installs 250
Furey, Maria L—same, J City, installs 3,000
Same—same, J City, installs 1,250
Gregor, E A R—F W De Groff, Union, 3 years ... 2,000
Haley, Mary L—R Allen et al, Kearney, 3 years 550
Hauser, Gustav—The Hudson Trust and Savings Inst, Hoboken, installs 14,500
Hayes, Annie—The Erie B and L Assoc, J City, installs 2,000
Hermann, Sophie L—K Kern, J City, 3 years 1,000
Herz, Jacob—L Emmerick, Union, 5 years 1,800
Horn, August—A Wiese, Union, 4 years 1,800
Hoos, Edward and Adam Schultz—Ann C Derlam, J City, 1 year 4,000
Howard, A J—Assoc of A S Hatch, J City, 3 years 300
Hunna, J B—G W Luseh, Kearney, 1 year 3,000
Kennedy, T A—A Siegfried, West Hoboken, 7 years 425
Kopf, C H—C G Groenwoldt, J City, 1 year 4,500
Korth, W C—Hester L Combes, J City, 5 years .. 2,000
Kolebuhler, Maggie—Susan M Vreeland, J City, 3 years 1,800
Kull, J W—J T McBride, J City, 1 year 800
Lang, John—G Raggio, Hoboken, 1 year 1,000
Lanton, J M—Z E Ten Broeck, Bayonne, 1 year. 700
Long, J N—A Franck, J City, 1 year 1,300
Lutz, John—Rachel Lutz, J City, installs 2,336
Mackie, Mary J—The American Ins Co, Kearney, 1 year 1,000
Mahon, Francis—J Collins, J City, 5 years 2,500
Martin, P E—New Jersey Title Guarantee and Trust Co, J City, installs 4,000
McDonald, Francis—M Tierney, Hoboken, 5 years 2,500
McGovern, Bernard—M Tierney, Hoboken, 5 years 2,500
Same—same, Hoboken, 5 years 2,300
McKee, Rosanna—D R Dunham, J City, 1 year. 500
McMahon, F P—M Tierney, Hoboken, 5 years ... 2,500
Same—same, 5 years 2,500
Middleton, J H—Charlotte Sherwood, West Hoboken, 5 years 4,000
Miller, William—A Roen, West Hoboken, 1 year. 1,300
Moebus, Charlotte—Elizabeth Bajer, J City, 5 years 250
Murphy, Sarah A—Hudson Trust and Savings Inst, West Hoboken, 3 morts, each $2,000, 5 years 6,000
O'Brien, Mary A—The Hudson Trust and Savings Inst, Hoboken, 4 years 1,000
Olson, A P—Ella M Crowell, Kearney, 1 year 600
Paulus, Wilhelm—F Killian, Union, 1 year 1,800
Pau, R A—P E Brockway, Kearney, 1 year 75
Perkins, Jessie M—Exr W Veitch, Kearney, 3 years 2,000
Powley, H R—B Fitzgerald, West Hoboken, 5 years 2,800
Pyne, Edmund—R Allen et al, Kearney, 3 years. 900
Roncoroni, Luigi—W H Beadleston, West Hoboken, 1 year 800
Russell, James—J Clark, J City, 1 year 550
Stanton, Martin—R Johnston, J City, 2 years ... 100
Schultz, Otto—F Schimper, West Hoboken, 5 years 4,000
Same—same, West Hoboken, 5 years 4,000
Same—C F Ruh, West Hoboken, 5 years 3,500
Same—same, West Hoboken, 5 years 3,500
Same—same, West Hoboken, 5 years 4,000
Smith, John—C Stevens, J City, 5 years 800
Stagen, G H, Jr—Hudson Trust and Savings Inst, West Hoboken, 4 years 1,400
Stevens, Ada—J Baird, J City, 1 year 3,250
The First Methodist Episcopal Church—The Provident Inst for Savings, Bayonne, 1 year 3,500
Tivy, Peter—L Becker, Hoboken, 2 years 2,500
Trask, Irene W—W A Buckle, Bayonne, 1 year, 1,500
Van Emburgh, Annie M—The People's B and L Assoc, Kearney, installs 1,000
Williams, William—W Hanks, J City, 5 years .. 3,000
Wolf, Geo—Hudson County Caledonian B and L Assoc, J City, installs 1,896
Wright, Andrew E—Jessie Seidel, Kearney, 3 years 1,800
Yeury, S J—Union B and L Assoc, J City, installs 3,400

CHATTEL MORTGAGES.

Baade, Matthews, West Hoboken—D Bermes, saloon fixtures 500
Bates, I C, J City—Marvin Safe Co, safe 196
Bennett, J C, Hoboken—Berheimer & Schmidt, saloon and lease 700
Bergeman, Louisa J, Guttenberg—C F Walters, piano 255
Boland, R E, Kearney—H Thoesen, furniture ... 121
Brachel, William, J City—A Friedrichs, horse, wagon and harness 1,311
Brede, Herman, J City—J Ryan, grocery store. 300
Colville, C M, Bayonne—Marvin Safe Co, safe ... 60
Crawford, Mary B, J City—C Birdsall, furniture 100
Debarburo & Savaggi, West Hoboken—William Peter, ice box 135
Dunn, Frederick, J City—C Birdsall, furniture .. 100
Durr, Marie, J City—J Hautsch, grocery store fixtures 550
Dusinbire, J Frank, J City—W J Dusinberre, horses, wagon, harness, stock and fixtures store 800

Eastern Plaster Board Co, Bayonne—F Forbes, trustee, machinery and implements used in the mfg of plaster board.......................25,000
Fahey, John, J City—The William Peter Brewing Co, saloon fixtures.......................... 487
Farrand, W C, Kearney—C Birdsall, furniture.. 250
Foley, J H, J City—Marvin Safe Co, safe 60
Hague, Lottie, J City—C Birdsall, furniture 99
Hahner, Moritz, J City—Marvin Safe Co, safe... 25
Halsey, Julia, J City—C Birdsall, furniture..... 130
Hart, D J, J City——same, furniture............ 130
Hushion, M J, J City—Beadleston & Woerz, saloon fixtures.................................. 300
Jost, R A, Bayonne—Marvin Safe Co, safe...... 120
Kohls, Charles, Hoboken—H Eggert, horses, wagon and harness............................ 200
Kopf, Albert, West Hoboken—G Fieberling, horse, wagon, harness and butcher fixtures. 125
Krieg, G F, J City—Marvin Safe Co, safe......... 80
Laine, Margaret, J City—John Mullins & Co, furniture.. 196
Lambert, T J, J City—Marvin Safe Co, safe...... 55
Landminer, Phil, J City—M Brown, horses, wagons, harness.................................. 100
Langan, Patrick, J City—Mary Lanagan, tinner and plumbing business......................... 100
Liebermann, Jacob, Secaucus—L Heilbrum, 130 cows, 41 horses, trucks.......................... 1,800
Loscheid, Carl, J City—C Birdsall, furniture ... 100
MacDonald, J D, J City—Marvin Safe Co, safe.. 30
Meyer, W F, Hoboken—Lembeck and Betz Eagle Brewing Co, saloon 1,212
Murphy, Mary, J City—C Birdsall, furniture.... 130
Pace, J W, J City——same, furniture........... 130
Perley, Fanny, J City——same, furniture....... 130
Rothwell, Margaret, J City—John Mullins & Co, furniture 222
Roth Bro, Bayonne—Marvin Safe Co, safe... .. 33
Rubacki, Joseph, J City——same, safe.......... 44
Salladin, John, Hoboken — Bernheimer & Schmidt, pool table.................................. 150
Schwan, Jacob, J City—C Birdsall, furniture.... 130
Schurenbech, F H, Hoboken—Korner & Schwaldant, horse, wagon, harness....................... 341
Spitzmas, William, J City—C Birdsall, furniture. 100
Waday, Annie, J City——same, furniture 190

BILLS OF SALE.

O'Connor, Jas, J City—E C Corley, saloon fixtures 700
Reid, W T, Bayonne—Seeman Bros, grocery store, horse, wagon, harness....................... 542

MECHANICS' LIENS.

Burrows, T J, claimant; Margaret Connors, builder and owner, Bayonne....................... 20
Jaeger & Dressell, claimant; Margaret Connors, builder and owner, Bayonne....................... 16

JUDGMENTS.

Keating, James—Susan A Hanks and Alfred A Hanks, partners as Hanks & Co 143
Miber, Albert—H Klein............................ 344

BUILDING MATERIAL MARKET.

BRICKS.—Investigating the condition of the market for Common Hards affords but a poor return in the way of fresh and important information. Receivers very generally agree that about former quotations may be retained as prices certainly have not advanced and are too low to expect further shrinkage, especially at this season, while the form and volume of demand show just about the same as for some time past, except that there has been one move since our last a trifle out of the ordinary run. The collection of medium and poor stuff spoken of one week ago has been about all worked off principally at $4.00 per M downward, and it is given out that it was purchased to pile away on chance of being able to use it during the winter months. Arrivals have probably been a little lighter in the aggregate, yet there was plenty and to spare at all times for the outlet waiting and sellers do not as yet appear to find it in their power to get rid of the surplus, a consummation that must undoubtedly be reached before foundation for a stronger tone can be laid. Current receipts show generally good quality, and it is calculated that the average will be very well preserved during balance of the season. With the colder weather and the unfavorable condition of the market it is believed that moulding will be practically suspended along the entire river with the ending of this week, and it is claimed that around Haverstraw Bay work came to end last Saturday, though a couple of manufacturers in that district who ceased shipments during August have again commenced seeking sale for some of their stock. As the season draws to close operators commence to speculate upon the probable production, amounts likely to be carried over and the chances for finding custom, but opinions are considerably mixed at the moncur, and very few operators have arrived at any very pronounced conclusion. We do not learn that any one claims to have discovered profit in the business this year.

LATH.—The market has had another stroke of too much stock and went down under the blow Arrivals following our last came in with much freedom from Maine and the Provinces, "unexpectedly" of course, they always come that way according to report of receivers, and not finding custom calling for a supply, it required not only the making of a more attractive line of value but a great deal of bustling among the local and outside trade to find dealers willing to handle the offering. After getting down to $2.00 per M the supply seems to have been placed and once more sellers are dusting off and setting up the "hope" that the market will strengthen. Recovery depends as much upon supply as anything, the demand promising little or no expansion after dealers have added so liberally to their stocks as of late.

LIME.—In the matter of price the market is no worse than a week ago, but conditions are evidently unsatisfactory. Without rush of supplies at any time, dealers have gradually accumulated a pretty good stock, against which there is but a poor compensating outlet, and the cargoes now coming to hand from the Eastward are difficult to place. From other sources offerings are said to be moderate and careful in the face of ruling unpropitious conditions.

LUMBER.—Distribution does not increase to any extent but is gaining somewhat, and dealers evidently try to feel as cheerful over the situation as circumstances will admit. At all events most of them are giving some attention to first hand supplies, and along the line of standard grades may be found more or less demand daily, with now and then some pretty good sized invoices closed. The effect is sufficient to keep the market about steady, with here and there an exceptional inclination to buoyancy where very desirable quality may happen to be sought after. All culls, however, are free from speculation except that some of the larger dealers, with ample financial carrying ability, are taking in out of the cold all the first-class lots drifting their way and available at about the rates current for some time past. The export movement is footing up well, and a considerable portion of the recent increase of foreign orders is attributed to the influence of the new reciprocity treaties with West Indies and Brazil.

Eastern Spruce has continued unsettled as usual, without evolving any really new features. Even the most optimistic of receivers seem willing to admit that it is practically useless to expect any really anxious demand this season, especially as so many customers have about placed their orders for specials, and such advantage as may accrue will have to come through moderate offerings. Manufacturers promise that the supply shall be curtailed, but so they did before the last full arrivals under which prices dropped off, and vessels can make several trips again before winter storms commence to blow. Prices are somewhat firmer than last week and may creep higher awaiting next arrivals. All the commission houses have sent in their application for membership in the Lumber Trade Association, "by request." That, of course, tends to strengthen the organization.

Piling is without much animation and cannot be sold at any higher rates, the current market as a whole ruling somewhat stupid. Receivers and dealers, however, console themselves with the smaller run of arrivals and the probability that two or three big jobs will soon be calling for supplies.

Hemlock presents no change of an important character. An absence of activity is admitted by the largest operators, yet they report some little growth of business both local and outside and seem to have faith in further expansion as the fall progresses. Manufacturers still exercise very good control over the output and by preventing pressure to realize preserve values upon about a steady basis.

White Pine has a generally steady market, without further real gain since our last, indeed some salesmen express a little dissatisfaction over the result of their efforts to place contracts. It may be, and possibly is, only a temporary lapse of demand, however, for while there does not seem to be the least prospect of any really liberal deal, it is pretty certain that a great many small dealers in this vicinity are still in want of stock, and some of the larger ones will not object to investment when they can get hold of desirable parcels "just right." Export chances continue among the promising features of the situation.

Yellow Pine, it is claimed, will be gradually whipped into better form at the primary end of the market. Here most buyers appear sluggish and indifferent, and the competition to secure such custom as may be extant has a tendency to keep rates easy, but there are growing railroad calls and very fair export orders, with good prospect for an increase of the latter, and that forms basis for considerable hope.

Carolina Pine has somewhat increased demand, with here and there an agent reporting a really good full run of trade, including orders from dealers, who have returned to partially duplicate former orders consequent upon a fuller distribution than they had calculated. The market is well in hand, and on all standard stock values preserved without difficulty.

Hardwoods show essentially the same general features as for some weeks past. Putting oak and poplar as leaders, all the various grades are getting some attention from dealers and manufacturers who are getting up stocks and assortments, and there is said to be a little better prospect for consumption within a few weeks. Quartered oak is unsettled in value, with the pitch in favor of buyers, but other woods of standard quality rule pretty steady. Exporters are heard from occasionally, and as usual they must have fine quality to fill orders, though some poor stuff goes out on commission.

The exports of lumber, exclusive of hardwood, from the port of New York during the month of September were as follows:

	1890. Feet.	1891. Feet.
To West Indies	3,146,000	3,076,000
To South America	1,760,000	1,781,000
To East Indies	1,391,000	1,846,000
To Europe	393,000	77,000
Total feet	6,690,000	7,280,000
Previously reported	56,794,000	57,212,000
Total since Jan. 1	63,484,000	64,442,000

GENERAL LUMBER NOTES.

STATE.

The report of Albany market by the *Argus* is as follows:

While trade in this market cannot unequivocally be called dull as a whole, the actual situation is not far from that condition, it being an undeniable fact that business is much lighter than is unusually expected during this season of the year. The fall trade is usually looked forward to to partially make up for dullness in the preceding months, but unless the general demand picks up rapidly in the near future, the market will scarcely show as good business for the season as was done last year, and even that was scarcely up to the average. The building troubles in New York have made themselves felt throughout the year thus far, and their influence will not be eradicated until another season shall have set in.

Except with a few houses and in certain lines of stock the pine trade at present is undeniably slow and the stocks on hand are full. Receipts of Western pine are light, dealers having on hand about all they want to carry under the conditions of the present demand, while from Canada but little is coming forward, a condition attributable largely to the strike among the boatmen at Ottawa for higher freights.

In spruce the market is doing only fairly, and good lumber is having a better sale than culls at present. No spruce to speak of is arriving from the northern mills, as they are now all shut down. From Canada a moderate quantity is being received. Hemlock, with the exception of 13-foot boards, is also dull. The standard hardwoods are doing moderately well, while shingles of which there is an ample supply (contrary to some statements), are doing about as well as anything in the market.

CANADA.

A Montreal journal publishes the following significant figures:

There is a marked decline in the export of the square timber from Quebec this year compared with 1889 and 1890. The following statement in cubic feet, of timber measured and culled up to the 1st of September, at Quebec this year, as compared with the two preceding years, shows how this branch of the lumbering industry has declined:

	1889.	1890.	1891.
Waney white pine	2,811,842	2,868,730	1,339,358
Red pine	612,175	97,808	34,269
White pine	3,477,910	2,147,793	842,149
Oak	960,188	843,086	653,358
Elm	705,480	486,053	471,340
Ash	229,540	92,787	76,240
Birch and maple	385,980	163,377	126,606

THE WEST.

The *Timberman*, on the subject of White Pine, has the following:

While there has been no united attempt to secure higher prices, other than the action taken by the manufacturers and dealers of Iowa, Wisconsin and Minnesota, at a recent meeting, the conditions in all sections of the country favor a general advance. In most of the leading markets white pine lumber is in ample supply at the present time, but there is every indication that many items will be scarce before spring. No one seems to have a doubt but that the fall and spring trade will be unusually active, because of the abundant crops and improved financial condition of the country at large, but still there are dealers to be found who persist in making the same prices to the trade that were current during the dullest season of the year.

Wholesale dealers should remember that they are not going to have the same sharp competition from the manufacturers that they have had in times past, because the latter have not the lumber with which to maintain the fight. A large number of mills have already shut down, with but little lumber on hand, and the fact that the logs down are pretty generally cut out indicates that they will be late in starting up next season. Surely there is every reason to advance the prices of white pine, and *The Timberman* looks to see this done in other sections of the country, as has already been done in the Northwest.

At Chicago, the cargo market is somewhat firmer than it was a week ago, and inquiry a little more urgent from such dealers as have dock room to receive stock, but still prices cannot be said to have advanced. Receipts have not been heavy, but there has been something in every day, and commission men say they have had all they wanted to do during the hot weather.

Short piece stuff is again firm at $10, but no sales are reported at more than figure. The longer lengths have kept up to very nearly the figures current all season, the present range being between $12.50 and $14.50. Cull piece stuff is quoted at from $6.50 to $8, but is in very light demand. Hemlock is ready sale at $7.50 to $8.

Receipts of good timber are below the average, if anything, and there is ready sale for all that arrives at prices quoted.

Several dealers are still receiving oak quite freely, but a great deal of it is going into pile. Plain sawed red oak is quite ready sale, but as the supply is somewhat in excess of demand, prices are not particularly firm and quotations are from $1 to $2 per thousand lower than they were two or three months ago.

Quarter-sawed oak shows no improvement. The market has been flooded with stock, good, bad and indifferent, and prices show no present indication of recovering from the tumble of $5 to $8 per thousand which they took some months ago.

The Northwestern *Lumberman*, reviewing the Chicago wholesale market, says:

The yard men begin to feel that there is not much risk in buying lumber at current prices, and are dipping in with more freedom. Besides, there are numerous world's fair and special bills that require sorts, and resort is had to the cargo market in search of what is required.

Short piece stuff has sold more readily for a few days. The drop in price from $10 to $9.75 probably stimulated the demand. The fact that trade has considerably picked up in the yards has also helped matters. It is easier to sell lumber than it was, and there is little attempt to beat down prices on fair lots. The yard dealer has but little object in the present stage of the game in bearing the market, for that means a cut in the value of what he has on hand. It is likely that there will be no further decline this fall.

It is a peculiar phase of the market these days that thick selects are wanted less than almost any other sort. Such stuff will lie around the docks, while nobody will ask for it. This is directly opposite from the condition that prevailed last season, or even last year. It is partly explained by the habit the dealers have acquired of buying their high grade lumber at the mills, which they have piled, to be brought forward dry. When a few thousand feet is sent forward to the market in a cargo, dealers do not care to buy it and pile it green on top of their dry stuff of a like grade. Hence it is neglected. It would be different, however, if there was as much of a scarcity as prevailed last year. Then everything in the shape of thick selects was eagerly taken, green or dry. The condition of the select market is an example of the flip-flap of trade. A scarcity in any description of stock is usually followed by plenty, and vice versa. The way to make money is to hang on to the tail of a pronounced condition and get ready to catch on when the new one comes along. Or perhaps the better way is to keep fairly stocked with all sorts of lumber, and follow the trade wherever it goes.

Cargoes containing a good percentage of strips continue to be salable, though it is said that loads of high-grade inch have sometimes been neglected of late. This is another case of flip-flap. Early in the season everybody wanted good strips, especially; now common and No. 2 strips and piece stuff are becoming more active. It would not be surprising to see a great demand for coarse promiscuous boards before long, which would only be following out the rule that one extreme follows another. It is certain that there is to be a great demand for packing boxes for a year to come, and that will absorb a lot of coarse inch.

And also reports as follows on the Saginaw Valley:

Trading in the cargo market has been fairly active, fair to good lots having the call, and transactions being chiefly for small cargoes, running from 200,000 to 500,000 feet. The situation seems to have visibly improved, although holders of coarse lumber are grumbling at the dullness in that kind of stock. Prices are steady and firm. Under inspection sales are on a basis of $9 to $9.50 for shipping culls, $13 to $19.50 for common, and $38 for uppers. Several good cargoes sold at $18 and $19 straight. Coarse lumber, straight measure, is quoted at $10.50 and upwards, box being held at $9.50 to $10. Norway bill stuff is firm for ordinary dimension at $9, and boards and strips at $11 to $11.50. Long Norway sells at $12 to $16. Mill culls are quoted at $3.50 to $6.

The Mississippi Valley *Lumberman* as follows:

Some of the Wisconsin Valley mills have got under way again, but low water still prevails in all the lumbering streams, and fully half the mills are idle. Every day adds to the number. The streams are so low that it will require very heavy rains to put them in condition for driving out many more logs this season. Some of the mill men at Middle Mississippi points, dependent upon the logs being got out of the West Newton rafting works have already reached the conclusion that the chances are slim for getting out any more logs this season. The Minneapolis mills are, however, buzzing away and making a plentitude of lumber.

The evidence is at hand that the recent advance made in the Mississippi Valley is being very generally maintained. Buyers accept the prices named without question. Some of the down river dealers have even advanced their prices beyond the association schedule and it has been suggested that a corresponding advance upon other certain items in the list may not be outside of the possibilities.

METALS.—COPPER—Ingot has reached an improved position since our last report. At least one million pounds of Lake have been taken by the home trade, on immediate shipment and for balance of year at fractionally higher rates, with additional demand at the advance not readily accommodated. On an average range of valuations we quote at 12¼@12½c. for Lake, and 11½@12c. for casting brands. Manufactured Copper is also doing somewhat better. The demand cannot be called active or even anxious, but the number of buyers is increasing and a greater variety of stock called for. Values are well sustained at full former figures all around. We quote as follows: Sheets, not above 30x72 in., 16 oz. and over, 25c.; do, 14 to 16 oz., 23c.; do, 12 to 14 oz., 24c.; do, 10 to 12 oz., 25c.; do, 8 to 10 oz., 28c.; do under 8 oz. 30c. Sheets longer than 72 inches add 1c. for 12@14 oz., 2c. for 10@12 oz. and 3c. for 8@10 oz. Sheets, not above 36x96 in., 16 oz and over, 22c.; do, 14 to 16 oz. 24c.; do, 12 to 14 oz. 26c.; do, 10 to 12 oz. 30c.; do, 8 to 10 oz. 33c. Sheets longer than 96 inches 2½c. for over 32 oz. and add 1c. for 16 to 32 oz.; 3c. 14 to 16 oz.; 5c. 12 to 14 oz. and 13c. for 8 to 10 oz. Sheets, not above 48x96 32 to 64 oz. 22c.; do, 16 to 32 oz. 25c.; do, 14 to 16 oz. 27c. do, 12 to 14 oz. 29c.; do, 10 to 12 oz. 33c. Sheets wider than 48x96 and longer, 22@25c. for 32 to 64 oz. and over, 27@[illegible]c. for 16 to 32 oz. [illegible]c. for 14 to 16 oz and 34c. for 12 to 14 oz. All bath tub sheets, per lb., 16 oz. [illegible]; 14 oz. 29c.; 12 oz [illegible]; and 10 oz. [illegible]. Bolt copper, ¾ inch diameter and over, 22c. Circles, 60 diameter and less, 3c. above price of sheets of same thickness; circles, 60 to 96 do do, 5c. do; circles, 96 do and over, 6c. do. Segment and pattern sheets, 3c. above price of sheets required to cut them from. Cold or hard rolled copper, 1@2c. per lb. above the foregoing prices. Copper bottoms, 26@32c. per lb. IRON—American Pig for foundry use has secured fair attention and mill grades are reported as going somewhat better than a few weeks ago, with operators more or less inclined to entertain a hopeful view of the outlook. There is nothing particularly speculative in the situation, but a belief in growing consumptive wants prevails, and sellers feel correspondingly encouraged, so far as the better grades are concerned at least. We quote at $17.00@18.00 per ton for No. 1 X foundry; $1[illegible].50@16.50 for No. 2 X do. and $14.00@15.00 for Gray Forge. Old material has, as a rule, been quiet and barren of marked or significant feature, unless it be in the pretty firm and determined manner in which holders clung to their stocks and expect full previous rates. We quote at about $21.[illegible]0@21.50 for old rails; $20.00@[illegible]1.00 for No. 1 wrought scrap; $17.00@18.00 for cast scrap and $17.00@17.50 for car wheels. Manufactured iron has been selling somewhat irregularly, with the demand in the main on regular trade account, so far as open market is concerned, but reports are made of an increased call on special contract for later delivery. We quote Common Merchant Bar ordinary size, at 2.00@2.10c. from store, and refined at 2.30@2.60c; Rods, round and square, 2.20@2.40c. Bands, 2.40@2.60c.; Norway Nail Rods 4@5c., and domestic sheet on the basis of 3.00@3.05c. for common Nos. 10@16. Other descriptions at corresponding prices, with 1-10c. less on large lots from cars. Steel Rails have been meeting with somewhat increased attention in all localities, and while the orders placed were not particularly liberal the renewal of interest among buyers bring with it a feeling of greater cheerfulness and hope. It is also generally understood that the old combine valuation was strictly adhered to, and that is an additional element of satisfaction. We quote standard sections $30 per ton at mill, with usual advance for delivery at tide water. Pig Lead has retained a firm position and buyers could not, as a rule, invest until they were willing to pay a slight advance over figures last noted. Submission has been fair and business satisfactory. We quote at 4.50@4.55c. per lb. The manufactures of lead are quoted at 7c. for Pipe, 7¾c. for sheet, 15c. for Tin-lined Pipe, and 37½c. for Block Tin Pipe. Pig Tin is still subject, in the main, to speculative influences; but there is, on the whole, somewhat better call for consumption and it improves the tone of the market. We quote at about 20.10@20.15c. for round lots, and 20.35@20.45c. for jobbing parcels. Tin Plate meets with about the usual trade demand, with few important changes in values, and the market is practically without new features. Supplies are ample. We quote prices as follows: I. C. Charcoal, ½ cross assortment Melyn grade, $6.50@6.55, each additional X add $1 50; I. C. Charcoal, ½ cross assortment, Allaway grade, $5.85@5.90, each additional X add $1; Charcoal terne, M. F. grade, 14x20, $7.50@7.55; M. F. grade, 20x28, $15.30@15.55; Worcester, 14x20, $5.70@5.75; Worcester, 20x28, $11.25@11.30; Dean grade, 14x20, $5.40@5.45; Dean grade, 20x28, $10.60@10.65; D. R. D. grade, 14x20, $5.25@5.30; D. R. D. grade, 20x28, $10.00@10.05; I. C. Coke, Penlan grade, $5.35@5.40; J. B. grade, 14x20, $5.45@5.50; I. C. Bessemer steel, squares, $5.75@5.80 basis; I. C. Siemens steel, squares, $5.85@6.00 basis. Spelter has improved in value and, while no large lots are handled, there is a good steady trade demand from regular sources. We quote $5.00@5.10c. for Common Western, according to brand

NAILS.—The market as a rule is more or less unsatisfactory to the selling side. Wire nails do very well, including some pretty good calls for export; but the rate has to be kept low to retain custom. For cut no ordinary reduction in cost would stir up much addition to the indifferent call prevailing, and manufacturers find no satisfaction except in grumbling. We quote Cut at $1.50@1.60 per keg for car lots and $1.75@1.85 per keg for parcels from store, for iron, and add 5@10c. per keg for steel; Wire, $2.00@2.05 at mills, and 2.20@2.35 from store.

PAINTS, OILS, COLORS, ETC.—So far as the general run of supplies may be concerned there are practically no new suggestions of this market. Demand has run off a little in some cases during the week, owing mainly to the change from one month into another, but it is assumed that there will be a prompt recovery and a gain if anything in the volume of business. The current call covers pretty much everything in the way of staple goods, and while buyers have not the speculative feeling sufficient to greatly anticipate their wants they find a place for some pretty good-sized invoices. No quotable changes have been made in price on any of the leading descriptions of stock, but some evidences of irregularity now and then show themselves, with a fear expressed that White Lead may be influenced toward a lower range owing to the break in oil. Old figures for the present, however, remain current. Association Corroders' rates stand as follows: Lead in oil in kegs and dry lead in kegs, in lots of less than 500 lbs., 7½c. net; in lots of 500 lbs to 5 tons at one purchase, 7c.; 5 tons to 12 tons, one purchase, 5⅞c.; 12 tons and over, one purchase, 6¾c.; dry white lead in bbls. ½c per lb. less than price in kegs. Lead in oil 12½ lb. in tin pails, add 1c.; in 25 and 50 lb. tin pails, add ½c.; and in 1 to 5 lb. tin cans, assorted (100 lbs. in case) add 2½c. per lb. to keg price. Terms on lots on 500 lbs. and over, note or acceptance at sixty days, or 2½ per cent. discount will be allowed for cash paid within fifteen days of invoice date. To make either of the above required quantities any assortment of packages of white lead, red lead and litharge may be counted. The above quotations are free on board cars or boat at corroding point. Linseed Oil has struck an unsettled market again. For the local product a fair measure of steadiness is shown, but the Western manufacturers are on the rampage and seem determined to take up the old policy of cutting and slashing values. The close is more or less nominal, but mainly inclined to favor the buyer. We quote at general range at 36@40c. for Western, and 40@56c. for City. Spirits Turpentine sells in ordinary routine way to jobbers and small consumers and commands about former rates, with market assisted by steady accounts from the south. Large parcels, however, could hardly be placed except at a concession. We quote at 37½@39c. per gallon, according to quality, delivery, etc.

TAR AND PITCH.—The run of demand does not vary much from week to week, and the market shows a pretty even sort of movement. Supplies in the meanwhile appear to be regulated to the outlet, and values held steadily. We quote Pitch at $1.70@1.75 per bbl.; Tar at $2.15@2.50, according to quantity, quality and delivery.

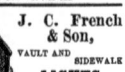

MISCELLANEOUS.

MISCELLANEOUS

MISCELLANEOUS.

PRICE, PER YEAR IN ADVANCE, SIX DOLLARS.

Published every Saturday.

TELEPHONE - - - - CORTLANDT 1370.

Communications should be addressed to

C. W. SWEET, 14 & 16 Vesey St.

J. T. LINDSEY, Business Manager.

VOL. XLVIII OCTOBER 10, 1891. NO. 1,280

The exhibition of architectural drawings is now open in the exposition rooms of THE RECORD AND GUIDE, *at Nos. 14 to 16 Vesey street, to which the public are cordially invited, free of charge. This display of drawings is one of the finest that has ever been made in New York City. It contains about three hundred works from the boards of the leading architects. Among the perspectives of more than ordinary interest are those of the several large hotels now building in this city, and the designs submitted in competition for the new cathedral of St. John's. No one who wishes to study the principal recent architectural works in the metropolis and the contiguous suburban district should fail to pay a visit to the exposition.*

CONSERVATIVE owners of stocks have no reason to feel dissatisfied with the dullness which has overtaken the market and with the comparative immovability of quotations. The prices of securities have advanced smartly in response to a manifest improvement of conditions, but they have not advanced too much, and it is better that they should not. It seems likely that in spite of daily fluctuations the present level of prices will be maintained until some substantial effects of the increased prosperity are shown. Already there is beginning to be talk about a higher rate of dividend on many lines of securities, while in some cases it appears probable that stocks which have long been non-dividend payers will take their place on the dividend list. When this time comes, or when these events are umistakably foreshadowed, it will be time for a further advance. Nothing of the kind is likely to take place this fall; and very shortly Congress will make a disturbing element. If stocks, however, are about as high as they should be at present, the same is not true of bonds. In the beginning there was some improvement in many good mortgages: but it soon ceased, and many excellent issues are still selling at very low prices. Evidently, the buying has been of a speculative, but not of an investment character; and if there should be a further advance in stocks, without a corresponding one in bonds, it would be a sign of an empty and precarious rather than a stable and legitimate movement.

IN Europe the financial situation remains unchanged. France is still cheerful and sanguine in spite of her bad crops, while in Berlin the bears still control the market. In the latter place the strength displayed by Paris is both inexplicable and a matter for envy. Comparisons are drawn between and comments made as to the high market prices of the French Three Per Cent Rente, and the low quotations of the Imperial and Prussian three per cent loans. Some Germans do justice to the energy displayed by the French nation in the reconstruction of her political, economic and financial position; others argue that it is all a bubble and will burst some day. But even those who take this view frequently betray a trace of admiration for France, though as soon as they talk on political questions, they are as emphatic as anybody in denouncing the exuberant mood of the French, which prompts them to advance any amount of money to Russia. They pretend that Russia at the present wants only the money of the French; and that in order to get this money, the Muscovite statesmen are making security out of France's hatred of Germany. Nevertheless, according to one well-informed authority, many people are preparing for grave international emergencies. The subdued anxiety is naturally a big impediment to all attempts to impart new life to the stagnant markets. It is feared that one day France will discover that she is unable to support the present market price of Russian loans, that the latter will give way, and that a disastrous crisis in Paris will be the result. The change of German opinion in regard to Russia is curious and instructive. In the midst of the rise in Russian notes and loans a year and a-half ago the Empire was designated as the "country of the future," and unmeasured praise was bestowed on its progress. The bad crops, the meeting at Cronstadt, and perhaps some part of Russia's domestic policy has put a quietus on this hypocritical enthusiasm. The country is now believed to be on the verge of ruin.

IT will be remembered that the bill constituting the present Commissioner of Street Openings in North New York provided that within two years and a-half from the first of last January the new commissioner must complete a survey of the streets in his district, and arrange them according to some fitting plan—a plan which will subsequently be submitted to the Board of Street Opening and Improvement for approval. If the Board finds the plan satisfactory it will settle for all time the general street system of that part of the city. Local changes may and probably will be made here and there; but a stable determination of street lines is so essential to property-owners that no other general alteration will ever be attempted. It is consequently very necessary no mistake should be made either in the general system or in the details. What a mistake brings with it we have an ample experience in that part of the city south of 14th street. The commissioners who laid out the city in the early part of this century stuck very largely to the lines of the old roads, and consequently the municipality has since been obliged to go to a very heavy expense in cutting through blocks and widening streets to meet the traffic requirements. At the present time two expensive improvements of this kind are under way, that of Bethune street and that of College place, while one other, that of Elm street, is imperatively required. North of 14th street another egregious error was committed. In a city like New York, which is far longer than it is broad, the traffic naturally runs up and down town more than across town. Consequently the avenues ought to have been placed nearer together than the streets—that is provided a rectilinear plan was adopted. With singular foolishness, however, exactly the opposite course was taken, and the consequence is a totally unnecessary concentration of traffic on comparatively few thoroughfares. Of course no errors of this character could be made at present, although the uncertainty which attends any anticipation of local development of the 23d and 24th Wards makes it probable that some errors in detail will be made. There are, however, other conditions to be met than those of traffic requirements, and these can be anticipated with exactitude. When the present maps were made, the street lines were planned on the supposition that the North Side would be given over mainly to villa sites, and that consequently winding roads would meet all requirements and be more picturesque than straight ones. Mr. Heintz finds, however, that the demand is not for villa plots, but for the usual rectilinear parcels on which city houses are built. Consequently he intends, so far as possible, to reform the street lines of the district on the checker-board plan, so common in this country, and in doing this he will undoubtedly have the support of the property-owners and brokers in his district. In the southern part thereof the demand will certainly be for the same kind of parcels as those needed in the lower wards, but it may be doubted whether the northern part of the North Side will not take rather a suburban form. However that may be, the property-owners of that section may well consider whether they will not lose more than they gain by the adoption of a checker-board plan. Is that dead level of uniformity, the East Side of this city, no lesson to them? In Europe cities are not built so quickly as here, but they are built more enduringly—and more effectively. It is, however, waste time to advocate the creation of a street system on any plan which would subordinate the individual to the general interest.

WE regard the *Evening Post* as one of the very few "influences" in this city that make for decency and intelligence in public matters. It is an excellent fighter and its cause is usually a good one, or at any rate a strong one, from its point of view. The paper is particularly noticeable, in the present degraded state of "journalism," for the lack of the fictitious in its columns—the sensational, the trumped-up opinion or argument, and all the other insincerities, devices and subterfuges practised by the showmen and fakirs who "run" the local press at present. Consequently few of the *Post's* readers can follow with satisfaction its utterances recently about the Rapid Transit Commission and the Greathead system. Clearly, the paper has said either too little or too much on that score. If the *Post* is in possession of any positive information that the Commission—composed, as we all know it is, of citizens who have hitherto and do still occupy a high place in commercial and social estimation—is rejecting plans and concocting others so that a sordid lot of scurvy politicians may plunder the community, why does not the *Post* make the facts public? Or is it that the *Post* is allowing a political bias or, if one prefers, a just antipathy to a not over estimable organization, to overthrow its poise, judgment and adherence to truth? Is the *Post* thoroughly informed as to the requirements for an adequate rapid transit service? Is it certain that the Greathead system will surely meet these requirements, and meet them, on the whole, to a greater extent and degree than the Worthen plan (with modifications) which we understand will be reported favorably next week? And even though the *Post* answer these interrogatories in the affirmative, what just reason has it for saying, even by implication only and innuendo, that the Commission is playing into Tammany's hands. It may charge the Commission with not giving proper attention to certain systems of construction; it may prove that other systems than the one adopted would have been better and financially more attractive; but between these matters and the *intention* of aiding and abetting political schemers there is a great and weighty difference.

As It Might Have Been and May Be.

A VOYAGER from Europe, who had formerly been a citizen of New York, but who had not seen his native city in more than twenty years, recently found himself steaming up the bay on a visit to his ancient home. As he approached the Battery he saw from the deck of the steamer the Field Building, the Produce Exchange, the Cotton Exchange, the Standard Oil Building, the Welles Building, the Potter Building, the *Tribune* Building, the towering dome of the new *World* Building and the numerous other tall structures that had transformed the lower part of the city during the period of his absence. Naturally enough, he was struck with a very considerable feeling of surprise. "Surely," he thought, "this cannot be New York. The ship has not been true to this new-fangled steering machinery. We have made some other port." But the doubt was of short duration. The steamer soon ran in alongside her pier, and the traveler landed on the water front. "Ah!" he exclaimed, still mentally, of course, "I see that I am at home after all." There had been no change on the water front except the change that could be wrought by ruin. There, all along shore, were the same tumble-down rookeries that he had known in boyhood, transformed only in the direction of the increased dilapidation that a quarter of a century could bring. He had indeed discovered the New York of almost two generations ago, and strange to relate, the emotions raised were not pleasurable. On the contrary, he was possessed with a feeling of humiliation. Was his youth indeed passed amid such barbaric surroundings?

But our traveler is not the only man who has observed the anomalous situation along the water front. Everywhere else during the last seventy-five years the city has advanced like a giant. It has worn its seven-leagued boots for its movement northward, and save where its march was broken by a second anomaly, created by the founder of the Sailors' Snug Harbor, it has moved with a steady and firm tread. Our architects have not all the genius of Greece; but when we make our observations away from the water front we find that we have a very decent city, a city for which no responsible resident has reason to blush. Our financial and office buildings, mercantile warehouses, hotels, apartment houses, and many even of our private dwellings, are just sources of pride, and our buildings devoted to educational, religious, artistic and benevolent uses are always respectable and sometimes admirable. But whenever a New Yorker feels a disposition to unduly exalt himself he should take a walk along the water front and cool off his head. He will find there, and in the neighborhood of the water front where all property is suffering under a common blight, streets which expose the fact that he is not a resident of a city which is universally advancing, but of one that is in part retrograding. Can it be for a moment conceived, however, that this situation is necessary?

Let us forget the disagreeable fact for a few moments and indulge in a little romance. Let us suppose that in the infancy of its career the city of New York had had no Governor Dongan. There never was another man on earth who conceived the idea of robbing riparian property-holders of their common law right to the lands under water; and it is conceivable that New York might have escaped the rule of the one man who was capable of the fatuity. We can suppose, then, that this city may have had no Governor Dongan, and if there had been no Dongan there would have been no Legislature at Albany to complete and perpetuate the robbery. To confess the truth, however, there would be a good *a priori* reason to suspect that the old Governor himself never intended to commit a robbery. We never saw his deed of gift to the city, and would probably decline to read it were it offered for our perusal, because the reading might cause a loss of faith in human nature, and we have no excess of such faith to risk. But at the period of his rule the colony of New York exercised no legislative functions worth mentioning, and in giving the lands under water into the hands of the city it would be a fair supposition to presume that he only intended to make the city the direct local representative of the Crown, in the belief that the authority of eminent domain would be exercised in accordance with the principles of the common law. This we say is a fair supposition, for it is hardly conceivable that a man of sufficient character to be appointed to a responsible office deliberately intended to rob the riparian property-holders of their common law rights. But, however this may be, the deed was done as the result of a succession of either blunders or crimes, and we can now only speculate on what might have been had it not been done.

We will suppose, then, that all the riparian property-holders on Manhattan Island had always maintained their right to a grant of the lands under water whenever it pleased them to make an application, and on this supposition what could we have looked to see follow? New York has had a very considerable commerce ever since the completion of the Erie Canal, now more than fifty years ago; and at the time of its completion no terminal works of any importance had been undertaken at the port. Then we have had for the period of a half century the best field in the world probably for lucrative investment in terminal machinery, and knowing the character of our people what could we not reasonably have expected had the riparian property-holders been at liberty to go forward and increase the value of their property by making the needed improvements?

Here is a capital opportunity to draw a companion picture for Bellamy's "Looking Backward." On this supposition imagine a system of basins, piers, and water front warehouses extending all the way from the elevators of the New York Central Railroad on the North River to some point on the East River nearly opposite, passing around by way of the Battery. Had our water front property-holders been at liberty all the storage warehouses built in Brooklyn would have been built in New York, and our sister city, though still large in population, would not have grown stiff-necked enough to not only refuse all flattering offers of annexation but to anticipate the day when she will wear the commercial crown and wield the commercial sceptre of the port. Neither would Jersey City ever have dreamed of becoming much more than a home for the overflowing population of New York, for every Jersey railway would long since have had its tunnel under the river, and this city, instead of finding itself surrounded by rivals, would be able to discover nothing in view but satellites. Why, the very holders of riparian property in New York have gone to Brooklyn to make the improvements which they were not permitted to make on their own possessions at home.

We doubt if there is a man in New York who will undertake at this late day to defend the system of water front land tenure that has obtained all around Manhattan Island. Or, considering human frailties and eccentricities, it would be better to say, perhaps, that if there be any such person he is an excellent subject for an examination by a board of what we will delicately call psychological experts. He is crazy without doubt. We know what may be said, and perhaps what will be said. It can be maintained that the city could make a better use of its title to the land under water than it is making; that it might build better piers and rear warehouses upon them that could be serviceable to commerce. But this would be a very shallow view of the subject, and it is also a very unrepublican view. The tenure of the lands under water by the city has already caused a loss or relinquishment of many hundreds of millions of dollars on the assessed valuation of adjacent property, and nothing that the city can do, except to get out of the way, can prevent a continuance of the sacrifice. The city has recently been making some improvements in the 8th Ward on the North River. It is at the seat of the heaviest commerce in New York; yet a glance at the tax books shows that the West street property in the ward is assessed at about an average of $7,000 a lot, more lots with their buildings running down to $5,000 than rising to $10,000. Almost all property in the neighborhood, too, is rated ridiculously low. The trouble is radical and fundamental. The property has been cut in two; and you might as well have a gun without a trigger as riparian lands without the franchises that belong to such lands.

Here is at once the secret of all our terminal disabilities and our disgraceful water-front spectacles. The city stands in the attitude of an obstructor instead of a promoter of its own prosperity. Were it to announce to-morrow that it was ready to make the use of its right of eminent domain which the State is making, and to grant a clear title to the lands under water to any riparian property-holders who choose to make the application for purposes of improvement, we cannot say that the riparian lands would rise $100,000,000 in value before the day after to-morrow. The announcement of the new policy would be too stunning. It would paralyze the property-holders and they might not be able to appreciate so suddenly the extent of their good fortune. But their wits would soon be sharpened by the extraordinary pressure that would be brought to bear to gain possession of their lands, and there would soon be no more assessment rolls bearing at $5,000 property which ought to be worth $50,000 or even more.

IF the new municipal building is to be situated outside of City Hall Park the site reported to be chosen, that of the *Staats Zeitung* building is as convenient and as fit a one as can be selected. A location on Broadway is practically out of the question, because of the expense; the city officials would gain nothing in convenience in return for the enormous cost. Of the two remaining feasible sites, that on Chambers street and the *Staats Zeitung* building, the latter is preferable because it gives more opportunity for effective architectural treatment. The expense, however, in any case will run up into several million dollars, and it is an outrage that the city should be obliged to spend this large sum principally for the purpose of keeping three or four newspaper offices well surrounded by air. A park site would be more desirable in every way; it would be more convenient and would not cost anything at all. But confessedly the city officials are afraid to proceed on these lines because of the newspaper opposition, which they would inevitably have to face. Hence the City Hall Park, which is utterly useless save to a few tramps, will remain as it is; enough money will be spent to provide park space three or four times its size in the crowded portions where park space is needed; and our municipal buildings will ramble inconsequently over a large area, whereas they might be bunched to the great convenience of public business within a comparatively small space. If it is impossibble, however, to arrange the matter on some proper business principle, there are certain alterations to the present City Hall which ought to be made. Since the shell is worthy to stand, let it stand; but the interior should be repaired and made to present a bright and pleasant appearance. At present the halls are cheap, as sordid and as dirty as the entrance to a Bowery theatre. The new office buildings offer instructive examples of the way to make halls look attractive; and the city can afford to do what any private individual can afford. The Equitable building is far more frequented than the City Hall (though by a better class of people), yet the arcade always looks tidy and presentable. Politicians, however, do not seem to be offended by dirt, either in the streets or in the passageways.

The designs submitted by Wm. A. Potter and R. H. Robertson, R. W. Gibson and Huss & Buck are now on exhibition at THE RECORD AND GUIDE *Hall. This is the most important architectural work yet contemplated in this country.*

Rapid Transit Plans.

People who have read the published reports of the consulting engineers on the plans of construction of the Rapid Transit engineers, have gained new ideas of the immense labor there is involved in the task of the Commissioners. Those whose patience has been strained to the breaking point, over the seeming dilatoriness of the Commissioners, are now able to contain their souls in patience a little longer. It was comparatively easy to designate the general routes and the system—whether viaduct, elevated or underground. And these points were quickly settled by the Commissioners; but after that the real labor, the discussion and settlement of the infinite details—details of engineering, mechanical details, legal details, financial details—lay before them.

The engineers have in general reported in favor of the Worthen plan, with modifications, as THE RECORD AND GUIDE has hereotfore predicted they would. In general they recommend a single track loop through State and Whitehall streets, meeting at Bowling Green, and extending in two tracks on a level through Broadway to City Hall Park. Here there is to be a two-track loop through Mail street, Park row and Chambers street, uniting with the two other Broadway tracks, and forming a four-track road from Mail street to the Harlem River. Between Mail and 12th streets it is recommended that the Parsons' "double deck" plan be employed in order to get all four tracks between the curb walls, which at some points would be too narrow to contain all four tracks on the same level. But from 12th street the tracks should spread out to a single level. Through the Boulevard to 124th street it is suggested that they divide into two tunnels, one on either side of the central grass plots, with stations in the middle of the Boulevard, between the tracks.

Messrs. Octave Chanut and Theodore Cooper suggest that the conduit for sub-surface works be provided for the business district, but do not insist upon it; Mr. Cooper holding that it should be kept separate from the underground railroad project. THE RECORD AND GUIDE is assured that the Commission will be ready with a report adopting the modified Worthen plan some time during the coming week.

Lumber Handlers Causing Trouble.

THE ANNUAL ELECTION OF OFFICERS.

The Lumber Handlers' Union are evidently trying to stir up strife once more between the lumber handlers and their employers. Last week the union made a demand on Rapp & Johnson's men that they pay their back dues and come into the union again as full-fledged members. This the men declined to do, so the story goes, stating that they did not care whether they had anything to do with the union or not. The delegates then tried to argue Rapp & Johnson into urging their men to come forward with their back dues, the employers to pay the dues in case the men were unable to do so. This the employors also declined. Nonplussed, the union went to the Board of Delegates, who, through their Framers' Union, ordered out on strike the framers who were working on Cook's warehouse on 125th street near 3d avenue, and Wilson's factory on Bank and Hudson streets, both buildings to which Rapp & Johnson are supplying lumber. The framers returned to work on Thursday, their union being indisposed to keep them idle under the circumstances, an occurrence which, of itself, is a condemnation of the Lumber Handlers by their fellow-workers in the framing line. At present all is smooth-sailing, but, should the Lumber Handlers' Union order any more strikes of so unreasonable a character, they may find that they have tampered with fire that will not be quenched until their organization is either thoroughly demoralized or ruined. For, it is not improbable, that at the very first wanton strike at any of the lumber yards, every yard in New York, Brooklyn and vicinity will again be shut down, and this time there will be no quarter offered.

THE FORTHCOMING ANNUAL ELECTION.

The election of officers of the Lumber Trade Association for the ensuing year will take place on Wednesday next, the 14th inst. The committee appointed by the President, which is composed of Messrs. Wm. H. Simonson, Wilson Godfrey and Walter G. Schuyler, have submitted the following ticket:

For President, Mr. Charles H. Willson; for First Vice-President, Mr. John H. Voorhees; for Second Vice-President, Mr. I. I. Vanderbeek; for Treasurer, Mr. Charles E. Pell; for Secretary, Mr. E. H. Ogden; for Trustees for one year, Messrs. John F. Steeves, Abraham Steers, W. W. Kenyon, John Ireland, Russel Johnson, Charles K. Sparks, Charles L. Bucki, James H. Pittinger, Thomas Williams, Charles A. Meigs.

There may possibly be a change in one of the names of the candidates for the vice-presidency. Otherwise the ticket will stand and probably be elected in toto.

Merchants and others intending to build should visit the display of architectural drawings at the exhibition halls of THE RECORD AND GUIDE, *Nos.* 14 *to* 16 *Vesey street.*

Special Notice.

The firm of G. L. Schuyler & Co. is the oldest in the lumber business in this city, having been established in 1835 by the grandfather of the members of the present energetic firm, and has been continued from that time to the present. Owing to the model system of handling material which this firm has instituted, together with the additional advantage of the largest dock facilities by far in the business (being equal to four city blocks), they are enabled to handle and deliver lumber at the lowest market prices, and allow a satisfactory margin. They have recently added to their other regular lines of stock an assortment of the principal hardwoods, and are also prepared to deliver Georgia pine of any description. All dressing on lumber is performed on their premises. Kiln-dried North Carolina, of all descriptions, especially high grade vertical grain lumber, is constantly in stock and always kept under cover.

Two Forthcoming Auction Sales.

THREE HUNDRED AND FORTY-NINE WELL-LOCATED LOTS TO BE OFFERED AT FORDHAM AND KINGSBRIDGE HEIGHTS, IN THE TWENTY-FOURTH WARD.

[COMMUNICATED.]

Two important parcels of property are to be offered at public auction by James L. Wells, the well-known real estate auctioneer, one on Monday next, October 12th, and the other on Monday week, October 19th. They comprise a parcel of 196 choice lots at Fordham and 153 select lots at Kingsbridge Heights.

THE FORDHAM PROPERTY.

The Fordham parcel is situated on Jerome Terrace, opposite and overlooking Jerome Park, in the 24th Ward. Jerome Terrace is practically an extension—and a somewhat attractive one—of the Bedford Park development. It is comprised in that part of Fordham which is so admirably located for the erection of homes. It is on the easterly side of Jerome avenue, between Kingsbridge road and Travers street, overlooking the picturesque scenery to the west.

IMPROVEMENTS.

Jerome avenue and Kingsbridge road are macadamized thoroughfares, and are lighted by gas and supplied with water. The road has a flagged sidewalk direct to Fordham station. The property to be auctioned off is situated on Jerome avenue, Park View Terrace, Kirkside and Crescent avenues, Wellesley and Travers streets and Kingsbridge road. The important point to investors is that all these streets and avenues are graded and have gas and water pipes laid. All these improvements have been paid for, and a guaranteed title will be given with each lot sold.

NEIGHBORING ATTRACTIONS.

The property fronts directly on Jerome Park and leads to Van Cortlandt Park. It has splendid views of the Harlem valley and in the vicinity is St. John's College, with its costly buildings, magnificent lawns, elm groves, etc., and its statue of Archbishop Hughes. Mount St. Ursula, with its attractive park and new academy, the latter erected at a cost of over $150,000, is near by; while "The Home," Grammar School No. 64, the picturesque St. James' Church, with its ivy-covered walls, its fine memorial windows, its cosy rectory and stone chapel, now being erected, are within easy distance. Other neighboring places of interest include the historic Dutch Reformed Church of the Ancient Manor of Fordham, founded in 1696; the Church of Our Lady of Mercy, with its Gothic walls, belfried tower, stained-glass windows and art treasures; the cottage which was once the home of Edgar Allen Poe, Rose Hill Manor House, and old forts and earthworks recalling the days of the Revolution.

MEANS OF ACCESS.

Fordham depot, which is near the property, is reached from the elevated road platform at 155th street, via the New York & Northern Road, in about five minutes. It is about forty-two minutes in time from Wall street, via the express trains of the Manhattan Road; about thirty-one minutes from 14th street, and about fifteen minutes from 125th street. It is also reached from the Grand Central depot at 42d street, via the Harlem Road, which, since its four tracks have been depressed, provides a quick and efficient service. Sixty-seven trains stop daily at Fordham station. A line of horse cars, now being changed into an electric road, runs from Harlem Bridge to Fordham, and connects with the elevated stations running from 129th street to 177th street.

THE KINGSBRIDGE HEIGHTS SALE.

The sale of the property at Kingsbridge Heights will take place on the 19th inst., and the 153 lots to be sold are situated on Sedgwick, Elwood and Graham avenues, Old Boston Post road, Perot, Knowlton, Malcolm and Lasher avenues and Oakley place. All these thoroughfares are laid with sewer, water and gas pipes, Sedgwick avenue, in addition, being macadamized. This avenue, which is 80 feet wide, forms a most delightful drive along the eastern bank of the Harlem River, from Macomb's Dam, High and Washington Bridges to Van Cortlandt Park. All the improvements made on the property have been paid for up to date, and purchasers will receive a guaranteed title with each parcel sold.

Oak Ridge Club. This is a very popular organization, composed of prominent residents in the neighborhood, as well as many outsiders—chiefly New York business men. The site of the club was once a portion of the estate to be sold. It consists of about ninety city lots, in the midst of which stands the large and attractive residence now used as the club-house. It is always a great advantage to a locality of a semi-rural character to have a club like this in its midst, for it brings together the neighbors from time to time and creates a pleasant social life which would otherwise not be engendered.

HISTORIC ASSOCIATIONS.

Kingsbridge has historic associations dating back over two-and-a-half centuries. Some of the streets and avenues are named after heroes of days gone by, such as the brave Lasher, the daring Knowlton, Malcolm and

Oak Ridge Club, Kingsbridge Heights.

THE VIEW.

Those who have driven along Kingsbridge Heights know how beautiful is the view. It is about 125 feet above tide water. The air is pure and salubrious and the panorama takes in the Harlem Valley, the hills and heights of upper Manhattan Island and the Palisades on the west bank of the Hudson River.

other gallant men who fought for their country's liberty. Every road is full of reminiscences of Washington, Howe and the other generals of last century. The post road over which Paul Revere traveled from Boston to New York with the news from the Battle of Lexington, and over which the American Army marched in 1776 to occupy Fort Independence, is now owned by Mr. Ogden Giles. The child seen in the accompanying illustration is a descendant of Gen. Giles, one of Washington's aides. Among local magnates who own historic ground are Nathaniel P. Bailey, John Claflin, Samuel W. Fairchild and other well-known New Yorkers.

1776-1891. *Revolutionary Cannon on Bastion of Fort Independence, Kingsbridge.*

RESTRICTIONS.

The sellers have restricted the property. All nuisances are excluded and a neighborhood will thus be created that will be ornate and attractive. A restriction of this kind gives buyers a sense of security against factories and other structures objectionable in a residential locality, and gives additional value to every lot.

CHURCHES AND SCHOOLS.

In the neighborhood is the Episcopal Church of the Mediator, St. John's Roman Catholic Church, St. Stephen's Methodist Episcopal Church and the historic Reformed (Dutch) Church of the Manor of Fordham. One of the best grammar schools in the city (No. 66) is in the vicinity. St. John's College, the Ursuline Academy and other institutions of learning are also within easy distance.

THE OAK RIDGE CLUB.

One of the most prominent and interesting features of the locality is the

SPLENDID TRAIN SERVICE.

One hundred and seventeen trains run daily to Kingsbridge, via the New York & Northern Road and the New York Central Road. Monthly tickets on the former, including the elevated road fare, average 9¼ cents per ride, and by the latter about 6 5-6 cents per ride. The property to be sold is within earshot of the depot. The time is twenty-one minutes from 42d street, thirty-three from 14th street, and forty-five from Rector street.

PROSPECTIVE VALUES.

The future of property along Fordham and Kingsbridge Heights is assured. New York, it need hardly be repeated, is moving northward continuously. As the tide of population advances it must, of necessity, flow in the channels alon g which the steam roads run. This is exactly in the territory named, and it is no exaggeration to say that—just as the values of vacant lots have doubled, trebled and quadrupled in several sections of the city north and west of the Central Park during the last decade—so will the value of lots north of Washington Bridge increase during the next five or ten years. When a building lot costs $7,000 to $10,000, more or less, in a fairly good street between Lexington and 2d avenues, in Harlem and further south, people who want to build their own homes will scarcely hesitate to pay as many hundreds for lots that can be reached by steam from points down town in just as quick time as they can be reached on the 2d or 3d avenue road by the ordinary trains that leave the City Hall. It is possible, indeed, to get from the Stock Exchange to Fordham or Kingsbridge by West Side connections in much less time than it takes to journey to 125th street by the East Side lines of the elevated road.

OBSERVER.

Real Estate Exchange Matters.

The Board of Directors held their regular monthly meeting on Tuesday. The only business of importance transacted was the appointment of the following Nomination Committee: James Rufus Smith, Franklin B. Lord and J. Edgar Leaycraft. This committee is made up of the same gentlemen who acted last year.

The following names have been posted for membership: G. R. Katzenmeyer by E. L. King, and S. Frothingham by E. A. Cruikshank.

Real Estate Department.

The market this week has not been as active as it was last week. Dullness has been the prevailing feature and the prospects are that it will be very quiet, comparatively speaking, until next spring. Brokers and real estate men generally are trying to keep up one another's courage as to the prospects for a busy season during the remaining months of the year, but it is rather a hard task that they have set themselves. Substantial results bearing out the bright views that have been in the recent past and that even at the present time are being expressed more or less freely, are lacking. There is, of course, business being done, but it is neither large nor important, and while the talk about the large deals that are under way continues it is impossible to obtain definite information in regard to them. The large list of sales which we were enabled to present last week is more or less misleading. After closely inquiring we find that what appeared as last week's work really dated back for some time, several of the negotiations having been commenced as far back as five months ago. While this does not take away the satisfaction that accompanies actual consummation of the transactions it is still to be regretted that so little of it was really new business. As to the general features of the market there is little new to report. Owners of all kinds of property continue firm in their asking prices, which buyers seem to consider are altogether too high. The buyers, while not scarce, are, on the other hand, not numerous. In the money market it is still difficult to place loans on flat property, although private-house mortgages are more easily secured.

A SUCCESSFUL LOT SALE AT TREMONT.

The week opened auspiciously on Monday with an auction sale of 227 lots, comprising the Ryer Homestead at Tremont. It will be remembered that this property was purchased last October by the syndicate who sold it on Monday from Ex-Congressman Haskin and Judge A. B. Tappan. Miss Agnes K. Murphy, who was the broker in the sale to the syndicate and who was herself financially interested in this lot sale, conducted the whole affair. It is stated by the syndicate that the property cost them $115,000, but that they only paid down $25,000 in cash. They sold a portion of the property for $17,000 and realized $187,000 from the lot sale, a total of $204,000, showing a gross profit of $89,000. Deducting the amount of expenses there is a net profit of $71,000 on an actual investment of only $25,000 cash. These figures give some idea of the success of the sale, and it was a success. The sale commenced at 12 o'clock and was not concluded until after 5 o'clock, and yet so anxious were those present to buy that up to the time the last lot was sold the auctioneer, James L. Wells, must have had an audience of 100 men and women still present. The crowd which attended the sale was one of the best, from an auctioneer's standpoint, that has been in the auction room for some time. It was made up of men and women, and the latter were not infrequently the most persistent bidders. At the sale's start the audience must have numbered over 300 people and very few of these were spectators. The bidding throughout, while showing no great enthusiasm, was steady and responsive enough and altogether the managers of the sale have good cause to feel satisfied with the result. There is only one large lot sale with which this sale can fairly be compared, that of the Stony Estate, on Decoration Day, 1890. At that time of course there was no Elevated station at 177th street, although it was projected. On Monday, Tremont avenue (177th street) corners sold at $2,300 and $2,400 apiece, while at the Stony Estate corners almost opposite brought but $1,600 and $1,900 each. Inside lots on Tremont avenue sold at the Ryer sale at from $1,600 to $1,900 each, while at the Stony sale they brought only from $1,175 to $1,300 each. The other lots on less important streets do not show the same degree of improvement in the matter of prices, but that is hardly to be expected. 177th street is the main street of Tremont, and in the matter of values it is, as it were, the standard for the neighborhood. Some of the other prices at the Ryer sale were as follows: Prospect avenue corners from $910 to $1,050, inside lots from $525 to $1,000; Clinton avenue corners from $800 to $1,425, inside lots from $525 to $1,175; Crotona avenue corners from $775 to $1,409, inside lots from $540 to $1,350. The details of the sale will be found in another column. The average price per lot for the whole sale was $900, the auctioneer says.

WASHINGTON HEIGHTS SALE.

When the bell rang for the sales to begin on Tuesday the auction room presented a crowded appearance that was second only to the attendance last May, when Auctioneer Peter F. Meyer sold the Morgenthau syndicate property on Washington Heights. In front of the central stand which had been placed in the middle of the room there was an immense crowd of spectators, home-seekers and speculators, and crowded on the various auctioneers' stands about the room were others who had taken these elevated positions in order to get a better view of the proceedings. Even up in the gallery there were interested persons, both men and women, who wished to avoid the crowd on the floor. The management of the Exchange had arranged to close the "Information Bureau," expecting that all the available space would be needed, and indeed everything looked as though there would be a successful sale. The bidding at first was not particularly spirited, but those who remembered how slowly the first offers for the Morgenthau lots came thought this fact of little significance. The first lot offered, the northwest corner of Amsterdam avenue and 188th street, was started at $5,000 and disposed of finally for $8,000. The general verdict of those who ought to know was that this was a very good figure. The cable road at present stops three blocks south of the property; it is seven blocks away from the Washington Bridge and 181st street, the centre of activity on the Heights, and it is also down hill from the Morgenthau property. All these things had to be taken into consideration in the bidding, and $8,000 for one corner of 10th avenue, and $7,500 for that at 189th street on the same avenue, with from $4,100 to $4,600 for the lots in between were considered good prices. On 188th street, west of Amsterdam avenue, lots sold at $2,200 each, while in the rear, on 189th street, they brought from $1,875 to $2,100. On Audubon avenue, between 188th and 189th streets, corners sold at from $3,000 to $3,200, while inside lots were disposed of at prices between $1,780 and $1,900. It was plain to see that these prices, which when the advantages of the Morgenthau property are considered do not compare unfavorably with the figures at that sale, were unsatisfactory to those in charge of the sale. The auctioneer said that unless there was a decided improvement in the bidding he would withdraw the remaining lots. The lots on 188th street, west of Audubon avenue, were then sold at $1,900 and $1,975, which prices were not better than those previously obtained. The auctioneer consulted with the owners and then offered the northeast corner of 11th avenue and 188th street, for which he obtained $4,475, and the adjoining avenue lot, for which $2,975 was paid. After declaring that he was not there to give the lots away the auctioneer withdrew the remainder of the property. As has been said, it was the opinion of those who are versed in neighboring values that the prices obtained were good, and certainly, if appearances count for anything, the crowd that was present stood ready to take most of the lots offered at prices that were proportionately the same as those which were paid at the beginning of the sale. This Washington Heights property failed to sell therefore, because the owner's figures were too high.

OTHER SALES.

The other sales of the week developed little that was of interest. A significant fact, however, is that the city property offered in many instances failed of success in selling. The owners in several cases were so discouraged at the dispirited bidding that they withdrew their properties from sale, and in other instances where they thought there was a possibility of its selling they allowed the auctioneer to knock it down, and they themselves bought it in. This indifferent success, of course, is largely traceable to the fact that most of the property offered was of a very unimportant kind, practically nothing being offered that was in itself likely to attract outsiders to the Exchange. In addition to the city parcels offered at public auction Jas. L. Wells, on Thursday, successfully sold a miscellaneous list of holdings in Northern New York and in Westchester County. The foreclosure sales, too, offer little that is worthy of remark. So far as can be ascertained all the parcels sold for more than the amount due for mortgages and costs, and about the only parcel sold that was above the ordinary in character was No. 801 Madison avenue, which J. A. Mahony, the plaintiff in the legal action, bought for $42,400.

On Monday, October 12th, James L. Wells will sell 196 desirable lots on Jerome terrace, opposite and overlooking Jerome Park. Jerome terrace is an attractive extension of the Bedford Park settlement, and is a very desirable residential section, because of its accessibility, its healthfulness and its city conveniences. Covenants prohibiting nuisances will be inserted in each deed. They are carefully worded so as to be in no way oppressive, and will promote improvements of a good character. The titles will be insured and the terms liberal.

On Tuesday, October 13th, Smyth & Ryan will sell twenty-four valuable lots in the 23d Ward, situated as follows: Four lots on the southeast corner of St. Ann's avenue and 134th street; ten lots on 134th street, east of St. Ann's avenue; three lots on 135th street, west of Brown place; one lot on 135th street, east of St. Ann's avenue; a gore on 149th street, west of Brook avenue: one lot on 158th street, near 3d avenue; four lots on Marsher avenue, north of Highbridge street, and one lot with dwelling thereon at No. 508 Wales avenue.

On Wednesday, October 14th, Richard V. Harnett & Co. will sell three three-story brown stone dwellings, Nos. 224, 226 and 228 West 82d street, and the three-story dwelling, No. 303 West 136th street.

On Thursday, October 15th, Richard V. Harnett & Co. will sell the three-story brick house (leasehold), No. 109 East 12th street; the six three-story and basement brown stone dwellings, Nos. 1648–1658 Lexington avenue, and the three-story brown stone building, No. 1062 2d avenue.

On Thursday, October 15th, Adrian H. Muller & Son will sell 121 desirable lots on 3d, Washington, Eagle, Cauldwell, Tinton, Concord and Jackson avenues, Teasdale place, 156th, 161st and 163d streets, all in the 23d Ward.

S. F. Jayne & Co., of No. 254 West 23d street and No. 59 Liberty street, offer a very desirable opportunity to manufacturers. They have for lease for a term of years the premises at No. 6 Gansevoort street, near Hudson. The buildings are substantial, the front one being four-story and basement, 25x41, and the rear one three-story and basement, 25x43. It contains a 12-horse power steam engine and full machinery for wood-working. It is in first-rate order and would be rented for the purpose of any business. Additional property running through the block can be obtained if wanted.

CONVEYANCES.

	1889. Oct. 4 to 10 inc.	1890. Oct. 3 to 9 inc.	1891. Oct. 2 to 8 inc.
Number	181	218	214
Amount involved	$1,969,8?5	$3,912,375	$3,552,081
Number nominal	56	58	47
Number 23d and 24th Wards	37	56	55
Amount involved	$154,835	$148,264	$215,716
Number nominal	8	7	10

MORTGAGES.

	1889.	1890.	1891.
Number	218	240	222
Amount involved	$3,195,430	$2,812,693	$2,881,420
Number at 5 per cent	81	130	119
Amount involved	$1,717,100	$1,615,317	$1,291,690
Number at less than 5 per cent.	27	12	12
Amount involved	$412,000	$134,612	$369,457
Number to Banks, Trust and Insurance Companies	31	40	32
Amount involved	$1,298,000	$1,143,800	$647,200

PROJECTED BUILDINGS.

	1889. Oct. 5 to 11 inc.	1890. Oct. 4 to 10 inc.	1891. Oct. 3 to 9 inc
Number of buildings	58	45	68
Estimated cost	$1,171,748	$1,179,700	$742,050

Gossip of the Week.

SOUTH OF 59TH STREET.

Geo. R. Read has sold for James G. Wallace to Harris Mandelbaum, Nos. 126 and 128 Ludlow street and Nos. 101 and 103 Rivington street, being the southeast corner of the two streets, 43.9x100, with the old buildings thereon, on private terms.

Hiram Merritt has sold the house, 20x50, No. 242 East 5th street for Michael Springer, for $16,000.

Harris Mandelbaum has purchased from the Ranney estate No. 41 Forsyth street, 25.7x100, with the old buildings thereon, on private terms.

B. Flanagan & Son have sold for John H. McGinn No. 242 West 49th street, a three-story brown stone dwelling, 20x50x100, for $17,500.

Weil & Mayer have sold to Fisher Levine No. 769 3d avenue, a four-story brick flat and store, on private terms.

D. Kempner & Son have sold for Mrs. Miller No. 405 West 50th street, a five-story brown stone apartment house, 25x85x100, for $30,000.

Fisher Levine has sold to Weil & Mayer Nos. 746 and 748 9th avenue, a plot 50x100, with the old buildings thereon, on private terms.

H. C. Bryan & Co. have sold for Dr. Geo. V. Foster to the Rhinelander estate the apartment house, 25x90, 132 West 12th street, for $49,500.

John M. Knox has sold to William Brenton Welling No. 107 East 40th street, a three-story dwelling, on lot 21x98.9, for about $25,000.

NORTH OF 59TH STREET.

Mayer Kahn has purchased from R. T. Wilson the six four-story brown stone flats, on plot 150x100, on the north side of 59th street, 150 feet east of 5th avenue, on private terms.

F. Zittel has sold for Peter J. McCoy to Oppenheimer & Metzger the three lots on the north side of 70th street, 300 feet west of Central Park West, and has resold them for the purchasers to John D. Taylor, for improvement. The price in the first sale is said to have been $15,000 for each lot, and in the second $17,000. The same broker has sold for Julius Kohn, the banker, to a Mr. Scott, two lots on the north side of 72d street, 200 feet east of Columbus avenue, for $6?,000, for improvement.

Charles Gahren has sold to Patrick Farley four lots on the north side of 87th street, 250 feet west of Central Park West, for $60,000, for improvement.

Frederick P. Foster has sold to B. G. Oppenheim the five lots on the northeast corner of West End avenue and 86th street, on private terms, for improvement.

Slawson & Hobbs have sold for David Richard to H. Kenny, No. 27 West 84th street, a five-story brown stone flat, 32x90x102.2, for $51,750.

Otto Pullich has sold for James B. Gillie his two-story and basement private house, 34x40 on plot x50x100 on the south side of 152d street, 112 feet west of St. Nicholas avenue, to a Mr. Scheffer, on private contract.

F. A. Condit has sold for F. W. Wilman, of Pelham Manor, to Henry Dale, No. 316 West ??th street, a four-story dwelling, for $30,000.

F. Zittel has sold for Mrs. Del Risco to a Mr. Foster No 113 East 59th street, a three-story brown stone, high stoop dwelling, on private terms.

J. S. Robinson has sold to Edward J. Kelly and Thomas Sturgeon the four lots on the south side of 142d street, 75 feet east of Lenox avenue, for $20,500, for improvement.

Ames & Co. have sold for Col. Oliver L. Shepherd to John and Phillippina Unger, 100x200 on the south side of 141st street, 125 feet west of the Boulevard, consisting of four lots on 140th street and four lots on 141st street, with the old family mansion and stable. This property was purchased by the Colonel in 1863, and adjoins the Hoguet estate property on Washington Heights.

J. W. Stevens has sold for George F. Johnson to Mrs. Delia Zinke No. 129 West 97th street, a four-story brick and stone dwelling, 16x60x100, on private terms.

Adler & Hermann have sold the plot, 75x100, on the east side of Washington avenue, 300 feet north of 169th street, on private terms.

Hunt & Wendell have sold for John E. Kaughran to A. A. Andruss & Son two lots on the south side of 68th street, 275 feet east of West End avenue, on private terms, for improvement.

LEASES.

Frederick Winant reports that he has leased the following houses: No. 44 West 48th street, for Mrs. V. M. Moore to Dr. Griffin; No. 71 East 52d street, for Mrs. J. L. Martin to C. R. Thorn; No. 557 Madison avenue, for C. R. Hickox to Mme. A. Sp.ess; No. 61 East 56th street, for W. P. Esterbrook to Thornton N. Motley; No. 43 East 59th street, for Mrs. G. H. Hickok to Miss M. H. Baldwin; No. 45 East 59th street, for William E. Keys to Dr. ?. N. Bradley; No. 38 East 63d street, for Miss A. S. Stephens to Mrs. F. Cutting.

Ames & Co. have leased the following private houses: No. 122 West 85th street, a three-story and basement dwelling, for Arturo Cuyas to W. J McIndoe, for two years, at $1,400 per annum; No. 128 West 82d street, four-story and basement dwelling, for John J. Brown to Mrs. Howland, for three years, at $1,600 per annum; and No. 102 West 81st street, a three-story and basement dwelling, for Mrs. C. L. Beekman to Mrs. J. L. Crawford, one year, at $1,350.

E. H. Ludlow & Co. have leased No. 37 Park avenue, a four-story unfurnished dwelling, and No. 41 East 74th street, a four-story furnished dwelling.

Brooklyn.

Corwith Bros. have sold the three-story frame double tenement, 25x60x100 No. 19 Oakland street, for Andrew E. Walker, to Chas. F. Neidig for $7,250.

CONVEYANCES.

	1889. Oct. 3 to 9 inc.	1890. Oct. 2 to 8 inc.	1891. Oct. 1 to 7 inc.
Number	284	365	474
Amount involved	$1,041,207	$1,447,584	$1,584,648
Number nominal	65	80	141

MORTGAGES.

	1889.	1890.	1891.
Number	299	355	419
Amount involved	$1,050,083	$1,106,481	$1,355,952
Number at 5 per cent. or less	156	200	255
Amount involved	$657,151	$633,533	$1,012,031

PROJECTED BUILDINGS.

	1889. Oct. 4 to 10 inc.	1890. Oct. 3 to 9 inc.	1891. Oct. 2 to 8 inc.
Number of buildings	1?7	79	95
Estimated cost	$626,255	$363,950	$814,075

Out of Town.

ORANGE MOUNTAIN, N. J.—J. S. Robinson has sold to Chas. E. Rogers the Pearson Place, of two acres and dwelling, taking in part payment some property in Brooklyn.

Out Among the Builders.

B. Gerson Oppenheim, the lawyer, who this week purchased the five lots on the northeast corner of West End avenue and 86th street, it is said, will build upon the site a thirteen-story fire-proof apartment hotel.

J. Monroe Taylor will build at Nos. 49 and 51 Cortlandt street a twelve-story and basement office building, 51.6x128 in size. The frame work is to be of iron construction. The first three stories of the front of stone entire and the upper portion done in brick and terra cotta. The main entrance will be placed in the centre of the front, and is to be elaborately carved and finished with ornamental iron-work. All the stairs throughout are to be of iron, with marble treads and wainscoting. The building is to have three elevators, steam heat and electric light. It is to be finished in hard woods, and in all its appointments will be thoroughly equipped and strictly first-class. Oswald Wirz is the architect.

Charles Gahren will improve the plot, 100x100, on the northeast corner of 9?d street and Columbus avenue, by the erection of first-class flats. The corner flat will have a frontage of 40 feet and will have stores on the first floor.

John Hauser has plans on the boards for three five-story tenements and stores, 25x70, which John Schreiner, Jr., will build on the east side of Avenue A, 25 feet south of 88th street, at a cost of $48,000; and for the same owner, plans for a five-story tenement to be built on the south side of 88th street, 100 feet east of Avenue A, at a cost of $16,000. The fronts will be of brick and stone, and each floor will have accommodations for two families.

A. A. Andruss & Son will improve the two lots on the south side of 68th street, 275 feet east of West End avenue.

John D. Taylor will improve the three lots on the north side of 70th street, 300 feet west of Central Park West, by the erection of four-story brown stone dwellings.

It is said that the Mr. Scott, who this week purchased the two lots on the north side of 72d street, 200 feet east of Columbus avenue, will improve the same by the erection of two first-class four-story brown stone 25-foot dwellings.

Patrick Farley will build five four-story brown stone 20-foot dwellings on the north side of 87th street, 250 feet west of Central Park West.

Kurtzer & Rohl have plans under way for a five-story brick, stone and terra cotta flat, 25x88.8, to be built at No. 76 Suffolk street, at a cost of $20,000, for August Ruff, and for a $10,000 alteration to be made in the building in 6th avenue, at the southwest corner of 13th street. The interior is to be altered and redecorated extensively, the front roof changed and a one-story extension, 15x25, built at the rear for a store opening on the street. F. D. Fricke is the owner.

D. P. Chesebro will build, from plans drawn by O. Wirz, a six-story brick and iron warehouse, 25x92, at No. 49 Crosby street. The building will be supplied with elevator and steam heat, and is to cost $20,?00.

Edward J. Kelly and Thomas Sturgeon will build four five-story brick and stone flats on the south side of 142d street, 75 feet east of Lenox avenue.

Visiting the Camp Cement Works.

An excursion of engineers, architects and others to the Allen Cement Works will take place on Tuesday at the invitation of Hugh N. Camp & Sons. Many interested in the manufacture of cement have accepted invitations.

New Incorporations.

The New York State Mortgage Bank and Savings Association filed articles of association in the County Clerk's office, on October 5th, for the purpose of purchasing and improving real estate. The incorporators are J. B. Sabine and fifteen others.

WANTS AND OFFERS.

(Advertisements strictly in accordance with this title will be inserted at the practically nominal rate of 10 CENTS per line (agate). In figuring for themselves advertisers may count seven words for each line, the address to be taken as one line. The object of this department is to bring buyers and sellers into communication with customers. Advertisements must be marked "Wants and Offers Column," and sent to the office of publication, Nos. 14 and 16 Vesey Street, not later than 3 P. M. Friday.)

WANTS.

SITUATION WANTED.—Does any real estate man desire a strictly honest young man for active employment at $5 or $6 per week with prospects? If so please address,
EDWARDS, care of McCormick, 54 New st., N. Y.

A YOUNG WOMAN DESIRES POSITION AS REAL estate collector. References and security. Address. E. L., RECORD office.

WANTED.—Position to figure for building contractor by a man with 8 years' experience in architect's office; thorough knowedge of plans.
Address, D, RECORD AND GUIDE.

ADVERTISER would like to purchase the good-will of a fire insurance business. An excellent chance for a real estate man who finds it impracticable to give the insurance his proper attention.
INSURANCE, care of RECORD AND GUIDE.
Sept. 19—1aw4w.

Real Estate Wanted.

WANTED.—At Bedford Park or vicinity, house; limit $10,000; or one to four lots.
H. T. SCHELLHASS, 171 Broadway.

OFFICE OF
FREDERICK SOUTHACK,
401 BROADWAY, N. Y.
WANTED, PROPERTY on 5TH AVENUE, between 14th and 42d sts.; pieces that have been altered or improved for business purposes preferred.
Oct. 3 uf.

OFFERS.

Dwellings and Flats.

A BLOCK OF PRIVATE DWELLINGS being completed on West End av., between 97th and 98th sts.; inspection invited; various sizes and prices. Apply, E. KILPATRICK, Owner and Builder, 60 West 67th.

A VERY CHOICE HOUSE, 79 West 70th st.; last of six; 20 feet wide; pantry and bath-room extension; parlor, music-room and dining-room; extra large library, with bay window on second story; price only $39,000; always open. Apply on premises, or to
CHARLES BUEK & CO., Owners,
Columbus av. and 72d st.

FOR SALE.—Five new first-class four-story and basement private dwellings, Nos. 109 113 and 119 East 45th st., and Nos. 462 and 464 Lexington av.; all leased to desirable tenants or can arrange to give possession to some of them if desired. For further particulars apply to
THE C. GRAHAM & SONS CO., 309 East 43d st.
Sept 19—1aw6w.

FOR SALE.—2443 8th av and 210 and 212 West 105th st.; commission allowed brokers. Apply at
Aug. 29-uf. Room 19, 155 Broadway.

OFFERS.

FOUR-STORY private stable and flat, near 79th st. entrance to Park; flats rent for $1,000; stable entire depth of lot.
Oct. 3-10. JOHN G. BORGSTEDE, 207 East 54th st.

NEAR 53d st. "L" Station.—Five-story apartment; fifteen families; ranges, hot and cold water and two closets on each floor; windows in every room; rent, nearly $4,000; elegant order.
Oct. 3-10. JOHN G. BORGSTEDE, 207 East 54th st.

A—At reasonable prices and easy terms, three and four-story residences, with three-story extensions; all improvements. Call and examine or inquire of the owner and builder, on the premises.
S. O. WRIGHT, 128 West 121st st., open daily.
Oct. 3 uf.

FOR SALE.—Six new cabinet-trimmed three-story and basement brown stone private dwellings, Nos. 142-148 West 123d st.; prices reasonable and brokers commissions allowed. For further particulars apply at office of
FRED'K. M. LITTLEFIELD, 156 Broadway.
Aug. 29-uf.

FOR SALE—2443 8th av.; 26.8½x100; easy terms; commission allowed brokers; apply at
Mar. 28-u-f. ROOM 19, 156 Broadway.

FOR SALE—210 and 212 West 105th st.; five-story apartments; each, 25x89x100; decorated and carpeted; apply at ROOM 19, 156 Broadway.
Mar. 28-u-f

Improved Property.

OFFICE OF
FREDERICK SOUTHACK,
401 BROADWAY,
offers for sale some choice pieces
of property on
LEONARD ST., between Broadway and West B'way.
FRANKLIN ST., between B'way and West B'way.
WHITE ST., between B'way and West B'way.
BROADWAY, from Barclay to 14th st.
BLEECKER ST., from B'way to South 5th av.
GREENE ST., Canal to 8th st.
WASHINGTON PLACE, B'way to Wooster.
WAVERLEY PLACE, B'way to Wooster.
APPLY AS ABOVE.
FREDERICK SOUTHACK.
Oct. 3 uf.

TO LET OR TO LEASE.—Two floors of a factory, 25x98 light on all sides, 1st av and 107th st; terms moderate. J. REEBERS' SONS,
Aug. 22-uf. 409 East 107th.

Vacant Lots.

100TH ST., between 2d and 3d avs.; ten lots cheap; all mortgage if improved.
Sept. 26-1aw8w. EDWIN A. ELY, 103 Gold st.

40 CHERRY ST., between Roosevelt and Franklin sq., 32x64, vacant; $12,000; accommodating terms. EDWIN A. ELY, 103 Gold st.
Sept. 26-1aw8w.

FOUR ATTRACTIVE LOTS, 149th st., adjoining southwest corner 7th av., $3,600 each; builders' terms. EDWIN A. ELY, 103 Gold st.
Sept 26-1aw8w.

EASTERLY FRONT BOULEVARD, with 200 ft. on 86th st. and 264 ft. on 85th st.; one or more plots.
OTTO ERNST,
Aug. 22-1aw-8w. South Amboy, N. J.

OFFERS.

FOR SALE—On easy terms, nine first-class lots, ready for immediate improvement, on south side 116th st., commencing about 150 feet east of 7th av. THE C. GRAHAM & SONS CO, 309 East 43d st.
Sept. 19—1aw4w.

Brooklyn Real Estate for Sale.

FOR SALE IN BROOKLYN.—Three blocks from 39th st ferry, one full block of seventy lots for factory purposes; unsurpassed; terms easy; inquire of the owner, S. McDOUGALL,
Oct. 10—1aw4w. 242 and 243 Washington Market.

SEVEN TWO-STORY AND BASEMENT HOUSES, renting for over $1,250 per year; expenses low. Particulars from EXECUTRIX, RECORD AND GUIDE.

$3,300.—DETACHED two-story house, six large rooms; lot 25x100; parlor richly papered. Terms easy. 55 Powell st., near Manhattan Junction.

AT A BARGAIN, because of death in the family, 116 Clinton av., Brooklyn, fine three-story and basement brick residence, in first-class condition, on lots 50x125 feet, with fruit trees, flower and vegetable garden; is an excellent and convenient location for a New York business man. Apply on premises.

Country Property.

FOR SALE.
A LARGE MODERN RESIDENCE, WITH GROUNDS,
in Flatbush, near Prospect Park, Brooklyn. Every way desirable for continuous summer and winter residence. Address,
Oct. 3-10. BOX 2974, New York Post-office.

FOR SALE—In plots to suit; eligible building sites (commanding view of sound for miles), on North st., Greenwich, Connecticut; price reasonable; terms easy; neighborhood aristocratic and fashionable. Apply to
FRED. J. STONE, owner, 60 Broadway, N. Y.
Sept. 12-uf.

Miscellaneous.

WE WANT owners, investors and speculators to know that we make a specialty of 12th Ward property; what have you for sale, exchange or rent? what do you wish to purchase? entire charge taken of property; correspondence solicited; established 1881. J. P. & E. J. MURRAY, 2030 3d av., near 112th st.
Sept. 26-1aw4w

A PARTY ABOUT TO BUILD A FIVE-STORY factory, 50x98, in Harlem, near water-front, will lease the three upper floors and build to suit tenant. Terms very moderate. Address
May 16 u. f. OWNER, 409 E. 107th St.

PRINTING.—Book, News and Job.
RECORD AND GUIDE PRESS,
14 Barclay, and 14, 16 Vesey sts.

SALES OF THE WEEK.

The following are the sales at the Real Estate Exchange and Auction Room for the week ending Oct. 9.

** Indicates that the property described has been bid in for plaintiff's account:*

R. V. HARNETT & CO.

*Hester st, No. 211, n s, bet Baxter and Centre sts, runs west along st 24.11 x northeast 35.6 x northeast 66.6 x east 21.8 x southwest to beginning, five-story brk tenem't with stores. 1-5 part. Same. (Amt due $4,359) $2,075
*Houston st, No. 331, s s, 18.6 w Washington st, 18.9x50, three-story brk tenem't, 1-5 part. Louis M. Jones 975
Southern Boulevard, n w cor Garden av, runs northwest along Garden av 115.. x northeast 98 to Kingsbridge road, x south along road 60.2 x south along same 70.9 to Southern Boulevard, x south 22.4 to beginning. Bridget Nagle 3,850
Southern Boulevard, w s, 21.3 s Garden av, runs south along w s Southern Boulevard 90.8 x northwest 40.10 x northerly 81 to beginning. Same 1,025
West st, s w s, known as lot 14 map of Wardsville, West Farms, 50x126x50.1x129. Same.. 1,425
5th st, No. 640 E., four-story brk tenem't and stores. (Bid in) .... —
40th st, Nos. 237-241, n s, 75 w 2d av, 80x98.9, frame buildings. J. Cloherty, party in interest 45,050
79th st, No. 179, n s, 112 w 3d av, 22x102, three-story stone front dwell'g. J. Cloherty 17,100
95th st, No. 126 E., 18x100.8, three-story English basement brk dwell'g. Mrs. Sarah Harris. 14,750
2d av, Nos. 747 and 749, n w cor 40th st, 39.8x76, two four-story brk tenem'ts. J. Cloherty. 33,300

A. H. MULLER & SON.

24th st, No. 411, n s, 125 w 9th av, 25x98.9, three-story brk dwell'g and two-story brk stable. Chas. A. Robinson 15,350
123d st, No. 268, s s, 100 e 8th av, 25x100.8, three-story stone front flat. Richard Cummings. (Amt due $16,056) 20,000
144th st, No. 455, n s, 214.2 e Amsterdam av, 20x99.11, three-story brk dwell'g. B. Lyon. (Amt due $11,385) 12,200
144th st, Nos. 459 and 461, n s, 157.8 e Amsterdam av, 40x99.11, two three-story brk dwell'gs. B. Lyon. (Amt due, each $14,998) 30,200
144th st, No. 463, n s, 137.8 e Amsterdam av, 20x99.11, three-story brk dwell'g. P. A. Nevins. (Amt due $11,355) 14,025
144th st, Nos 465 and 467, n s, 100 e Amsterdam av, 47.8x99.11, two three-story brk dwell'gs. Robt. Young. (Amt due $24,416) 28,300
188th st, n s, 100 w Amsterdam av, 75x99.11, vacant. L. C. Regener 8,600
188th st, n s, adj. 95x99.11. Rob't Goeller 8,500
188th st, n s, 100 w Amsterdam av, 6 lots. P. J. Ryan 11,615
189th st, s s, 100 w Amsterdam av, 3 lots. P. J. Ryan 6,075
189th st, s s, adj, 95x99.11. J. J. Quinn 7,400
Amsterdam av, n w cor 188th st, 24.11x100, vacant. L. C. Regener 8,000
Amsterdam av, w s, adj, 50x100. Same 9,200
Amsterdam av, adj, 25x100. Melton Lee 4,175
Amsterdam av, adj, 75x100. August Ritter 12,300
Amsterdam av, s w cor 189th st. J. Baldenstein 7,500
Audubon av, n e cor 188th st, 24.11x100, vacant. Robt. Goeller 8,200
Audubon av, e s, adj, 50x100. Same 8,900
Audubon av, adj, 75x100. B. P. Fairchild 5,400
Audubon av, adj, 25x100. E. M. Cronin 1,900
Audubon av, s e cor 189th st, 24.11x100. Same 3,000
Audubon av, n w cor 188th st, 24.11x100. Walton Storms 3,050
Audubon av, w s, adj, 75x100. Leonard Zeh 5,400
Audubon av, s w cor 189th st, 24.11x100. Otto Geiss 3,000
Audubon av, w s, adj, 25x100. R. Caway 1,800
Audubon av, adj, 50x100. J. Moheimer 3,550
Convent av, n w cor 144th st, 24.11x94.5, three-story brk dwell'g. B. Lyon. (Amt due $18,891) 20,000
Convent av, w s, adj, 75x94.5, three three-story brk dwell'gs. Same. (Amt due on each $14,969) 47,550
11th av, n e cor 188th st, 24.11x100. P. J. Ryan. 4,475
11th av, e s, adj. Same 2,975

JOHN F. B. SMYTH.

Oliver st, No. 69, 24.6x100, four-story brk building and store and four-story brk building in rear. (Bid in) .... —
38th st, No. 322 E., five-story brown stone and brk tenem't. (Bid in) .... —
127th st, No. 148 E., three-story brown stone dwell'g. (Bid in) .... —

B. L. KENNELLY.

74th st, s s, 173 e Av A, 50x100, vacant. Frank X. Rauley 3,400
*Madison av, No. 801, e s, 82.5 n 67th st, 18x84, four-story stone front dwell'g. John A. Mahony. (Amt due $12,551) 42,400

WM. KENNELLY.

78th st, No. 179 E., five-story tenem't with stores. (Bid in) .... —
Convent av, No. 61, e s, 599.6 n 141st st, 20x100, three-story brk dwell'g. C. R. Rawlings 19,000
92d st, No. 58 W., 17.6x100.8, four-story brown stone dwell'g. (Bid in) .... —
*123d st, Nos. 262 and 264, s s, 150 e 8th av, 50x150.11, two five-story stone front flats. John S. McWilliam, plaintiff. Amt due on each $4,866; prior morts. $30,000) 40,700

J. C. LALOR.

119th st, Nos. 408-412, s s, 94 e 1st av, 51x100.11, three three-story stone front dwell'gs. (Amt due on each, $5,547.) Wm. H. Harrison 16,000

JAMES L. WELLS.

Armand pl, s w cor Perot st, 22x80, vacant. E. B. Leroy ... 1,200
Buchanan pl, n s, 150 e Grand av, 25x100, two-story frame dwell'g. H. D. Clark ... 2,950
Elmwood pl, s s, 96.11 e Crotona av, 75.1x123. Mrs. Fox ... 3,000
Elmwood pl, s s, 100 e Clinton av, 70x145. F. Boss ... 2,715
Elmwood pl, adj, 28x120. J. A. Gray ... 825
Elmwood pl, n s, 100 w Prospect av, 72x95. H. Knock ... 2,250
Elmwood pl, adj, 21.8x95. Chas. Brorkegram. 700
Lebanon st, s s, 100 w Crotona av, gore lot. M. J. Klug ... 910
Lebanon st, n s, 100 w Crotona av, 70 6x100x irreg. John H. Maurer ... 1,500
Lebanon st, n s, 100 e Crotona av, 73,2x100. C. A. Becker ... 2,250
Lebanon st, s s, 100 e Crotona av, 22.8x95. John Armstrong ... 690
Lebanon st, adj, 50x95. Andrew Lemon ... 1,520
Lebanon st, s s, 100 e Clinton av, 21.8x95. Wm. Boffman ... 630
Lebanon st, adj, 72x95. H. Knock ... 2,145
Lebanon st, n s, 100 e Clinton av, 21.10x100. W. J. Powers ... 580
Lebanon st, adj, 24x100. C. A. Becker ... 6'0
Lebanon st, adj, 24x100. J. Armstrong ... 625
Lebanon st, adj, 24x100. T. J. Reilly ... 620
Mosholu Parkway, near Bainbridge av, 30x124 to Niles st. E. B. Leroy ... 1,125
Mosholu Parkway and Niles st, adj, gore plot. W. H. Niles ... 1,925
Oakland pl, s s, 100 e Clinton av, 94.5x100. C. A. Becker ... 2,240
Oakland pl, s s, 100 w Crotona av, 75x100. C. A. Becker ... 1,260
Oakland pl, adj, 31.3x100x irreg. W. Katzbrowski ... 540
Oakland pl, n s, 100 w Crotona av, 92x98.5. C. A. Becker ... 1,500
Oakland pl, adj, 19.6x98x irreg. B. P. Fairchild ... 400
Oakland pl, n s, 100 w Clinton av, 74.9x128. C. A. Becker ... 1,900
Oakland pl, s s, 100 w Clinton av, 74.5x100. Same ... 1,890
Oakland pl, n s, 100 e Clinton av, 22.6x109. J. Healy ... 500
Oakland pl, adj, 24x108. John O'Brien ... 540
Oakland pl, adj, 24x107. Wm. J. Caviner ... '40
Oakland pl, adj, 24x106. John Quigley ... 555
Southern Boulevard, n w cor Penford av, 25x 100, vacant. I. B. Brook ... 1,350
Travers st, n s, 87.10 w Webster av, 25.3x92. Albert Smith ... 950
Arthur av, e s, 298 s Kingsbridge road, 50x100. Wm. B. Kufman ... 1,950
160th st, No. 529, 44x55, three-story frame dwell'g. M. Cohen ... 5,850
Boston av, s s, 295 e Perot st, 24x108. R Smadbeck ... 1,150
Bainbridge av, e s, 200 s Scott av, 75x100. E. B. Leroy ... 1,675
Bainbridge av, n e cor Mosholu Parkway, 62.8 x103.8x irreg. G. W. Taylor ... 1,000
Cambreleng av, e s, 98 n Oakland pl, 82.5x99x irreg. Wm. Bloodgood ... 1,050
Clinton av, n e cor Lebanon st, 1 lot. A. V. Harris ... 1,030
Clinton av, e s, adj, 1 lot. B. P. Fairchild ... 710
Clinton av, n w cor Lebanon st, 1 lot. J. Dixon ... 1,150
Clinton av, w s, 2 lots. Peter A. Engelson ... 1,620
Clinton av, 1 lot. L. Eickwort ... 775
Clinton av, 3 lots. B. P. Fairchild ... 2,325
Clinton av, s w cor Oakland pl, 1 lot. Same ... 1,100
Clinton av, s w Lebanon st, 1 lot. Andrew Lemon ... 985
Clinton av, w s, adj, 3 lots. B. P. Fairchild ... 2,655
Clinton av, adj, 2 lots. W. H. Barkmeier ... 1,750
Clinton av, adj, 1 lot. Henry Rivett ... 900
Clinton av, n w cor Elmwood pl, 1 lot. L. Koerner ... 1,175
Clinton av, n e cor Elmwood pl, 1 lot. N. Smith, Jr ... 1,000
Clinton av, e s, adj, 2 lots. J. Dixon ... 1,390
Clinton av, adj, 4 lots. A. Lemon ... 3,600
Clinton av, s e cor Elmwood pl, 1 lot. Same ... 1,210
Clinton av, s w cor Elmwood pl, 1 lot. J. Grebbin ... 1,425
Clinton av, e s, adj, 2 lots. Mrs. L. Seiferd ... 2,250
Clinton av, adj, 1 lot. Mary Seiferd ... 1,100
Clinton av, e s, 100 n Tremont av, 1 lot. B P. Fairchild ... 970
Clinton av, adj, 1 lot. H. C. Weyand ... 975
Clinton av, w s, 100 n Tremont av, 1 lot. H. Ruf ... 990
Clinton av, adj, 1 lot. G. A. Castle ... 975
Clinton av, w s, 25 s Elmwood pl, 2 lots. Mary Seiferd ... 2,150
Clinton av, n w cor Oakland pl, 5 lots. B. P. Fairchild ... 2,900
Clinton av, n e cor Oakland pl, 1 lot. P. Coughlin ... 825
Clinton av, e s, adj, 4 lots. B. P. Fairchild ... 2,360
Clinton av, s e cor Oakland pl, 1 lot. A. V. Harris ... 1,000
Clinton av, e s, adj, 1 lot. Jas. O'Brien ... 655
Clinton av, adj, 3 lots. M. J. Klug ... 2,070
Clinton av, adj, 1 lot. J. Dixon ... 690
Creston av, No. 2692, 40x75, three-story frame dwell'g. A. J. Paris ... 6,000
Crotona av, s e cor Elmwood pl, 24.4x98.11. M. Duffy ... 1,400
Crotona av, e s, adj, 25x100. Same ... 1,125
Crotona av, adj, 2 lots. Mary Seiferd ... 2,050
Crotona av, adj, 1 lot. J. J. Devins ... 1,075
Crotona av, adj, 2 lots. Jas. Bracken ... 2,600
Crotona av, adj, 1 lot. Mary Malone ... 1,000
Crotona av, n e cor Elmwood pl, 1 lot. M. Sorese ... 1,425
Crotona av, e s, adj, 2 lots. R. Bray ... 2,080
Crotona av, adj, 1 lot. Caroline Weyand ... 1,015
Crotona av, n e cor Lebanon st, 1 lot. Jas. Mallon ... 1,325
Crotona av, e s, adj, 2 lots. B. P. Fairchild ... 1,950
Crotona av, adj, 3 lots. Nelson Smith, Jr ... 2,870
Crotona av, adj, 1 lot. G Bofingen ... 925
Crotona av, s e cor Oakland pl, 1 lot. J. Dixon 1,100
Crotona av, n e cor Oakland pl, 2 lots. N. Smith, Jr ... 1,550
Crotona av, e s, adj, 1 lot. J. Reinschmitt ... 700
Crotona av, adj, 1 lot. E. J. Cronin ... 695
Crotona av, adj, 1 lot. B. P. Fairchild ... 685
Crotona av, adj, 1 lot. L. Eickwort ... 385
Crotona av, n w cor Oakland pl, 3 lots N. Smith, Jr ... 1,975
Crotona av, w s, adj, 3 lots M. E. Monahan ... 1,905
Crotona av, s w cor Oakland pl, 2 lots. N. Smith, Jr ... 1,675
Crotone av, w s, adj, 3 lots. Rob't Chapman, [illegible]
Crotona av, adj, 2 lots. W. Bloodgood ... 1,550
Crotona av, n w cor Lebanon st, 1 lot. P. Coughlin ... 1,025
Crotona av, s w cor Lebanon st, 1 lot. R. Chapman ... 1,125
Crotona av, w s, adj, 1 lot. C. Weyand ... 940
Crotona av, adj, 2 lots. Wm. Bloodgood ... 1,900
Crotona av, adj, 1 lot. Jeremiah O'Brien ... 950
Crotona av, adj, 2 lots. J. Balmford ... 1,800
Crotona av, adj, 2 lots. Spencer Barron ... 1,610
Crotona av, adj, 1 lot. Patrick Foy ... 725
Crotona av, adj, 1 lot. Mary Mullen ... 600
Crotona av, adj, 2 lots. C. P. Roos ... 1,290
Jerome av, w s, 175 n Wolf pl, 75 6x145.9x35.8x 140, vacant. Wm. C. Mead ... 3,800
Kingsbridge road, n s, 194 e Marion av, 40.10x irreg., vacant. W. W. Edwards ... 2,500
Prospect av, w s, 95 n Tremont av, 3 lots. F. Amabile, Jr ... 2,775
Prospect av, w s, adj, 3 lots. A. Smith, Jr ... 2,475
Prospect av, adj, 1 lot. P. Coughlin ... 1,000
Prospect av, s w cor Elmwood pl, 1 lot. Same. 1,050
Prospect av, n w cor Elmwood pl, 1 lot. Same. 1,030
Prospect av, w s, adj, 2 lots. Same ... 1,660
Prospect av, s w cor Lebanon st, 1 lot. R. E. Holder ... 1,000
Prospect av, w s, adj F. Amabile, Jr ... 2,295
Prospect av, n w cor Lebanon st, 2 lots. Thos. J. Reilly ... 1,900
Prospect av, w s, adj, 2 lots. H. Beecher ... 1,600
Prospect av, adj, 1 lot. L. Eickwort ... 800
Prospect av, adj, 1 lot. John Sheridan ... 800
Prospect av, adj, 1 lot. Thos. Graham ... 830
Prospect av, s w cor Oakland pl. A. Lemon ... 1,025
Prospect av, n w cor Oakland pl, 1 lot. P. Coughlin ... 910
Prospect av, w s, adj, 2 lots. A. L. French ... 1,200
Prospect av, adj, 1 lot. M. Kelly ... 585
Prospect av, adj, 1 lot. Theo. P. Farrell ... 525
Tremont av (177th st), n s, 46.11 e Crotona av, 25x90.6, vacant. W. Bloodgood ... 1,600
Tremont av, n s, adj, 25x90.6. Nelson Smith, Jr ... 1,600
Tremont av, adj, 50.3x117.5. Mary Seiferd ... 3,800
Tremont av, adj, 28x117.5. I. Modry ... 1,675
Tremont av, adj, 75x100. Peter Coughlin ... 4,920
Tremont av, n w cor Clinton av, 25x100. Same. 2,400
Tremont av, n e cor Clinton av, 25x100. J. Paulin ... 2,300
Tremont av, n s, adj, 75x100. I. Modry ... 4,850
Tremont av, adj, 50x145. J. A. Boss ... 3,500
Tremont av, adj, 25x145. F. Boss ... 1,725
Tremont av, adj, 50x95. J. A. Gray ... 3,200
Tremont av, adj, 25x95. L. Eickwort ... 1,600
Tremont av, adj, 22x95. J. Dixon ... 1,800
Tremont av, n w cor Prospect av, 22x95. Same. 2,300
Vanderbilt av, e s, 10.2 n 180th st, 25x100, vacant. R. E. Holder ... 1,250
Vanderbilt av, e s, adj, 75x100. H. W. Shipman ... 3,750
Vanderbilt av, e s, 225 s 182d st, 25x150. Joseph Weber ... 1,300

OTHER AUCTIONERRS.

Willett st, No. 58, e s, 130 n Delancey st, 25x 100, five-story brk building. Max Tanenbaum. (Leasehold; amt due $4,302) ... 5,000
69th st, No. 50 E, 19x104.5, four-story and basement brown stone dwell'g. (Bid in) ... ——
*76th st, Nos. 311, 341 and 343 (?), n s, 200 e 2d av, 75x102.2, three five-story brk tenem'ts, stores in Nos. 311 and 341. Lewis Morris. (Amt due $12,950) ... 14,947
119th st, No. 134 E., 22x100.11, three-story brk and frame house. Edw. Laube ... 6,750
*Lenox av, w s, extends from 116th to 117th st, 201.11x100, vacant ...
116th st, n s, 100 w Lenox av, 100x100.11, vacant ...
117th st, s s, 100 w Lenox av, 100x100.11, vacant ...
Bertha Smith ... 180,125

Total ... $982,887
Corresponding week 1890 ... $695,722

BROOKLYN, N. Y.

FOR WEEK ENDING OCTOBER 8.

J. F. B. SMYTH.

4th st, No. 28, 20x100.2, two-story and basement frame dwell'g Ferd. Eysel ... $1,900
42d st, n s, 300 w 2d av, 25x100.2, vacant. John Wichem ... 800
3d av, No. 1020, 25x100, one-story frame store. Otto Betz ... 4,400

JERE. JOHNSON, JR.

73d st, s s, 100 e 12th av, 25 lots, Bay Ridge William Lalor ... 4,500
74th st, n s, 100 e 12th av, 23 lots. Same ... 4,370
74th st, n s, 100 w 13th av, 2 lots. G. W. Hanley & Co ... 350
75th st, s s, 100 e 11th av, 3 lots. Same ... 450
75th st, s s, 100 w 11th av, 6 lots. William Lalor ... 1,290
75th st, adj, 5 lots. J. N. Scott ... 1,175
Washington av, e s, 189.1 s Greene av, 18.1½x 120, vacant. G. B. Bretz ... 5,000
Washington av, No. 415, adj, 54.0½x120, two-story frame dwell'g. William Lalor ... 15,000
11th av, s e cor 75th st, 5 lots. G. W. Hanley & Co ... 950
13th av, w s, 73d to 74th st, 10 lots. Same ... 2,900

OTHER AUCTIONEERS.

*Ashland pl, No. 149, e s, 90.0½ n Hanson pl, 15.0½x79.6½x15x80.2, three-story brk dwell'g. Charles Dennis ... 4,000
*Collins st, n s, 477.6 e Schenectady av, 100x100, Flatbush. William M. Tebo ... 500
*Douglass st, n s, 400 w Franklin av, 140x131. George Wilcox ... 5,000
Decatur st, n s, 350 w Throop av, 18.9x100 ...
Decatur st, n s, 358 9 w Throop av, 18.9x100, error ...
Two three-story brk dwell'gs ...
Francis B. Wright ... 14,050
Elton st, w s, 175 n Liberty av, 25.2x90, three-story frame dwell'g. Sarah Lipskey ... 3,730
*Grove st, n w s, 225 n e Central av, 22½x100, Virginia A. Kleine and Frank Bailey ... 19,019
*Pacific st, s s, 75 w Utica av, 298.8x107.1½, two-story and basement frame dwell'gs. Henry Weil ... 31,000
Quincy st, No. 841, n s, 85.6 w Ralph av, 20x 100 ...
Quincy st, No. 839, n s, 105.6 w Ralph av, 20x 100 ...
Two three-story brk dwell'gs ...
Moores & Le Quesne ... 15,100
*Ridgewood st, s s, 33.6 w Clove road, 150x 117.6, Flatbush. William M. Tebo ... 600
Spencer st, No. 168, w s, 78 n Willoughby av, 22 x80, three-story frame dwell'g. John Schliemann ... 2,000
*Van Voorhis st, n w s, 100 s w Evergreen av, 17x100 ...
Van Voorhis st, n w s, 117 s w Evergreen av, 17x100 ...
Van Voorhis st, n w s, runs northwest 100 x southwest 16 x southeast 51.9 x southwest 1 x southeast 48.1¾ to Van Voorhis st, x northwest 17 to beginning, unfinished frame dwell'gs ...
Moses P. Prout ... 9,600
*26th st, centre line, 300 n w 3d av, runs northwest to exterior line, x southwest to centre 27th st if continued, x southeast to point 300 n w 3d av, x northeast to centre 26th st, with all docks, wharves, piers, cribs and erections and land under water to centre of channel in front of above and right of way. Union Trust Co., of New York ... 25,000
43d st, No. 212, s s, 100 w 4th av, 25x100.2, two-story frame dwell'g on rear. Chas. W. and Peter Backus. (All right, title and interest) ... N ... 10

Total ... $169,694
Corresponding week, 1890 ... $127,341

CONVEYANCES.

Wherever the letters Q. C., C. a. G. and B. & S occur, preceded by the name of the grantee they mean as follows:

1st—Q. C. is an abbreviation for Quit Claim deed, i. e., a deed in which all the right, title and interest of the grantor is conveyed, omitting all covenants or warranty.

2d—C. a. G. means a deed containing Covenant against Grantor only, in which he covenants that he hath not done any act whereby the estate conveyd may be impeached, charged or encumbered.

3d—B. & S. is an abbreviation for Bargain and Sale deed, wherein, although the seller makes no express covenants, he really grants or conveys the property for a valuable consideration, and thus impliedly claims to be the owner of it.

NEW YORK CITY.

OCTOBER 2, 3, 5, 6, 7, 8.

Bridge st, Nos 3 and 5, n s, abt 61 w Whitehall st, 52x126 6x45 4x126.6.
Water st, No. 30, n s, 74.5 e Broad st, 19x43.
4th av, s e cor 49th st, 98.9x100.
4th av, n e cor 48th st, 98.9x1^5.
Peter De Witt to William G. De Witt. All title. Oct. 1. nom

Broome st, No 416 | begins Broome st, n w cor Elm st, No. 186 | Elm st, runs north along Elm st 115 x west 75.3 x south 15.1 x east 50.2 x south 101.5 to Broome st. x east 25.4, three-story brk store and tenem't on Broome st and three-story brk store and tenem't on Elm st. John E. Kaugbran to Joseph Steiner. B. & S. Oct. 1. $60,000

Broome st, Nos. 77 and 77½, s s, 55 e Columbia st, 24.8x100, five-story brk tenem't with stores. John Solomon and Dina his wife to Morris Shapiro. *Mt.* $22,500. Oct. 1. 29,500

Same property. Morris Shapiro and Rachel his wife to Michael Fay and William Stacom. *Mt.* $22,500 Oct 2 See Henry st. 27,750

Broome st, No. 496. Certificate of payment of ½ part cost of party wall. Sarah F. Cotheal to Samuel and Henry Cohn. Oct. 2. 613

Broome st, Nos. 496–494. Party wall agreement. Joseph Bach to Richard Berg and William Gebhard. Re-recorded. Oct. 25, 1884. nom

Canal st, No. 41, n s, 21.10 w Ludlow st, 21.10x 50, four-story brk store and tenem't. Dolz Frey to Hannah wife of Leon Cahen. ½ part. ½ mort. $10,000. Oct. 1. 10,000

Central Park West (8th av), Nos 335 and 336, w s, 25.8 s 94th st, 50x100, two five-story brk flats. Julia L. wife of Charles J. Nourse, Jr., formerly Peabody, to Bernard Cohen. Sept. 25. nom

Columbia st, No. 28, e s, 100 n Broome st, 25x 100, five-story brk tenem't with stores. Abraham Schlesinger and Pauline his wife to Max Cohen. *Mt.* $25,000 Sept. 30. 32,000

Columbia st, No. 56, e s, 120 n Delancey st, 20x 100, three-story brk tenem't. Isaac Levy and Dora his wife to Joseph Goldstein. *Mt.* $10,-850. Sept. 30. See Suffolk st. 15,000

Charles st, No. 7, n s, 104 2 w Greenwich av, 22 x95, four-story brk dwell'g. John B. Howser and Martha E. his wife to Madeline Pierce. Aug. 31. 17,500

Same property. Madeline Pierce to St. Agnes Nursery Church of the Ascension. *Mt.* $5,-000. Aug. 31. 17,500

Crosby st, No. 49, e s, abt 185 n Broome st, 25x 100, two-story brk store. Jacob Korn to Denison P. Chesebro and Harry McNally. *Mt.* $12,500, tax 1891. Oct. 5. 25,000

Cannon st, No. 113, w s, 95.9 n Stanton st, 20.9 x100, three-story brk tenem't. Morris Kraus and Jennie his wife to Ignatz Gluck. Tax 1891. Oct. 1. 11,500

Same property. Ignatz Gluck and Hannah his wife to Ignatz Kaufmann. *Mt.* $9,500. Oct. 6. 13,500

Delancey st, No. 147, s w cor Suffolk st, 25x62, five-story brk store and tenem't. Aaron Goodman and Fannie his wife to Pincus Low eufeld, Morris Goldstein and Mark Blumenthal. *Mt.* $24,500. Sept. 30. See Madison st. 35,500

Delancey st, No. 192½, n s, 41.10 w Ridge st, 25x51.10, five-story brk tenem't with stores. Samuel Weil and Rachel his wife to Simon Bollt. *Mt.* $17,400. Sept. 29. 23,000

Delancey st, No. 104, n s, 38.7 e Ludlow st, 25x75, five-story brk tenem't with stores. John Hess and Anna his wife to Simon Hoffmann. Oct. 1. 24,500

Delancey st, No. 241, s s, 50 w Sheriff st, 25x87.6, five-story brk tenem't with stores. Rachel Moses to Hyman Berliner. *Mt.* $23,500 and tax 1891. Oct. 1. 33,000

Delancey st, No. 225, s s, 50 w Willett st, 25x87.6, four-story brk tenem't with stores. Sarah Lese wife of Louis Lese to George Siezefsky. *Mt.* $19,000. Oct. 1. 24,800

Downing st, No. 46, s s, 175.1 w Bedford st, 19.9 x 87.4 x 20.9 x 92.4, two-story brk dwell'g. Charles F. Henke and Catharina M. his wife to Samuel W. B. Smith. *Mt.* $9,000. Oct. 8. 10,500

Gramercy Park, Nos. 35 and 36, otherwise East Gramercy Park, 44x83. Release of contract and discontinuance of suit. Mary F. King to Francis A. Clark. Oct. 5, 1891. nom

Henry st, No. 96, s s, 110 w Pike st, 25x100, five-story brk tenem't. Michael Fay and Mary his wife and William Stacom and Catherine his wife to Morris Shapiro. *Mt.* $25,000. Oct. 2. See Broome st. 45,000

Henry st, No. 306, s s, 239 8 e Scammel st, 24x½ block, five-story brk tenem't. Lizzie wife of Max Sturtz to Louis Gordon. *Mt.* $16,500. Oct. 1. See Lewis st. 25,000

Same property. Louis Gordon and Jennie his wife to Abraham Schlesinger. *Mt.* $16,500. Oct. 6. 28,000

Henry st, No. 29, n s, 174.10 e Catharine st, 25x100, five-story brk tenem't with stores. Harris Ratkowsky and Fannie his wife to Joseph and Abraham Kojawsky. *Mt.* $20,000. Oct. 1. 32,000

Henry st, No. 45, n s, 290 w Market st, 25x100.8, excepting part taken for widening Henry st, five-story brk store and tenem't with four-story brk tenem't on rear. William Hodge et al. exrs. Eliza Hodge to Betsey Wolf. Oct. 1. See Ludlow st. 23,250

Henry st, No. 249, n e cor Montgomery st, 19x85.8x19.1x86 9. Jacob Korn to Theresa wife of Leopold Schmeldler. Oct. 23, 1890. other consid. and 100

Jefferson st, No. 27, e s, 80 n Madison st, 20x47.8, five-story brk tenem't. Henry Pasinsky and Rachel his wife to Bertha Epter. Oct. 1. 20,000

Jefferson st, Nos. 25 and 27. Agreement as to encroachment and release. Abraham Goldberg to Henry Pasinsky. Oct. 7. nom

Kingsbridge road, e s, 25.6 n 180th st, runs east 99.11 x north 50 x east 10 x north 44.6 x west 90.6 to road, x south 96.6.
Amsterdam av, s w cor 179th st, 25x100.
Kingsbridge road, s e cor 179th st, 25.6x90.10 x25x85.9.
Amsterdam av, s w cor 178th st, 25x100.
Emanuel Heilner and Moses J. Wolf and Katie his wife to Morris Mayer. ½ part. Oct. 3. nom

Laight st, No. 57, s w cor Collister st, 25x87.6, two and three-story brk and frame stores. Milton M. Ford, Galva, Ill., to Carrie I. Rowell formerly Young, Rutland, Vt. Q. C. Re-recorded. May 14, 1888. 300

Ludlow st, Nos. 13 and 15, w s, 137.10 n Canal or Walker st, 37.7x83, two five-story brk tenements, store in No. 13, and two-story brk building on rear of both. Fannie M. Updike to Samuel Aronson and Morris Denbosky. ½ part. Oct. 2. 19,500

Ludlow st, No. 121, w s, abt 135 s Rivington st, 19x87.6, three-story frame (brk front) tenement. Joseph Kojawsky and Abraham Kojawsky and Sarah his wife to Harris Ratkowsky. *Mt.* $8,000. Oct. 1. See Henry st. 15,000

Lewis st, No. 118, e s, 123 s Houston st, 25x100, five-story brk tenem't. Herman Fichter and Kedy his wife, Barnett Levy and Sarah his wife, Louis Gordon and Jennie his wife and Sophia Mayer to Lizzie wife of Max Sturtz. *Mt.* $26,600. Oct. 1. See Henry st. 38,000

Madison st, No. 336, s s, 56 e Scammel st, 19.5x37x19.5x36, four-story brk tenem't. Pincus Lowenfeld and Celia his wife to Aaron Goodman, Brooklyn. *Mt.* $6,000. Sept. 30. See Delancey st. 10,000

Monroe st, No. 175, n s, abt 95 w Montgomery st, 23x100, four-story brk store and tenem't. Moses I. Blumberg to Sarah L. Blumberg his wife. ½ part. All liens. Oct. 2. nom

Madison st, s s, 184 w Montgomery st, 1.1x100. William Rankin and Elizabeth his wife to William and Thomas Morton and David Brown. Q. C. Oct. 1. nom

Madison st, Nos. 278–282, s s, 115 w Mongomery st, 69x100, one and two-story frame and brk buildings, coal yard, &c. Same to same. *Mt.* $40,000. Oct. 1. 60,000

Maiden lane, Nos. 48 and 50 } begins Maiden
Liberty st, No. 33 } lane, s w s, abt 150 n w William st, runs southwest 78.11 x southeast 24 x 39 to n e s Liberty st x southeast 24.3 x northeast 109.9 to Maiden lane, x northwest 47.10.
Liberty st, No. 35, n e s, 24x39.8x24x38.6.
Five-story brk stores.
Rudolph Euler and Ida his wife to Charles E. Runk. All liens. Oct. 6. 365,000

Orchard st, No. 109, w s, abt 75 s Delancey st, 25x87.6, five-story brk tenem't with stores. Philipp Fabel and Elizabeth his wife to Otto Stubmer. ½ part. Sub. to mort. $21,000. Oct. 1. 15,500

Suffolk st, No. 76, e s, 150 n Broome st, 25.8x100 x25.5x100, three and four-story brk and frame tenem'ts with three-story brk building on rear. George W. Adams to August Ruff. Oct. 6. 21,400

Suffolk st, No. 30, e s, 80.1 s Grand st, 20x100, six-story brk factory. Joseph Goldstein and Sarah his wife to Isaac Levy. *Mt.* $25,000. Oct. 1. See Columbia st. 40,000

6th st, No. 226, s s, 230.3 w 2d av, 25x97, five-story brk flat. Jobst Hoffmann and Anna his wife to Louisa Fischer. *Mt.* $28,000. Oct. 1. 45,000

9th st, No. 402, s s, 60 e 1st av, 20x50, three-story brk tenem't. Achille Lentz and Therese his wife to Jacob Kleinhans and Phillipina his wife. All title and dower. Sept. 28. nom

Same property. Eugene Lentz and Susie, his wife, Brooklyn, N. Y., to same. All title. Sept. 28. nom

Same property. Emilie S. or Emeline Lentz widow to same. Oct. 1. 10,825

Same property. Eugenie wife of and Jules Weber to same. All title. Sept. 28. nom

10th st, No. 208, s s, 150 e 2d av, 25x92.4, four-story brk tenem't. Frederick Hildebrandt and Margaret J. his wife to Jacob Wiebe and Magdalena Endholz. *Mt.* $10,000. Sept. 28. 20,500

12th st, Nos. 307 and 309, n s, 120 e 2d av, 40.6x103.3, two three-story brk tenem'ts. Emily M. Wheeler to Children's Aid Society. C. a. G. July 13, 1891. nom

14th st, No. 40 } begins 14th st, s s, 53.1 e
University pl, No. 79 } University pl, runs south 130.4 x west 62.3 to University pl, x north 26 x east 33 6 x north 102.8 to 14th st, x east 26.10, five-story brk store. Helen M. wife of and William S. Haseltine, Rome, Italy, an heir of Charles H. Marshall to John Downey. Sept. 17. nom

23d st, No. 312, s s, 100 w 8th av, 20.7x28.9, five-story stone front dwell'g. Leopoldine Frankenheimer widow to Luke Fitzgerald. *Mt.* $23,000. Oct. 6. 26,000

24th st, Nos. 207–211, n s, 125.3 e 3d av, 68.4x98 8, two and four-story brk and frame stables. John B. Doerr and Mary A. his wife to William A. Darling prest. Murray Hill Bank. C. a. G. *Mt.* $26,000. Sept. 30. 60,000

25th st, No. 208, s s, 146.5 e 3d av, 24.5x98.9, five-story brk tenem't. Augustus M. Herring to Frederick W. Sherman. *Mt.* $20,000. Oct. 5. 31,500

26th st, No. 167, n s, 100 e 7th av, 44x98.9, brk church. Trustees of the Presbytery, New York, to The George C. Flint Co. *Mt.* $10,000. Oct. 2. 30,000

31st st, No. 305, n s, 86 e 2d av, 14x98.9, four-story brk tenem't. Sophie S. wife of and Charles W. Rose, Hamptonburgh, N. Y., to Mary J. Mitchell. *Mt.* $4,000. Oct. 8. 6,500

31st st, No. 346, s s, 460 w 8th av, 20x98.9, three-story brk dwell'g. John Curry and Eliza his wife to Thomas H. Fox and Mary E. his wife tenants in common. *Mt.* $11,000 and taxes 1881. Oct. 7. 16,250

32d st, No. 364, s s, 250 e 9th av, 16.8x98.9, four-story stone front dwell'g. Virginia Hall to Ascher Weinstein, New York. *Mt.* $6,000. Oct. 2. 12,000

34th st, No. 211, n s, 137.6 e 3d av, 12.6x98.9, three-story stone front dwell'g. Foreclos. George B. Newell to L. Napoleon Levy. Aug. 31. 1,225

38th st, No. 42, s s, 525 w 5th av, 21x98.9, four-story stone front dwell'g. Harriet S. wife of Theodore M. Burton to Albert J. Milbank. Oct. 7. 48,700

44th st, No. 29, n s, 23 w Madison av, 17.10x85.5, four-story brk dwell'g. Menco Stern to Signion M. Stern. Sub. to mort. B. & S. All title. Oct. 1. nom

47th st, No. 133, n s, 460 e 7th av, 20x100.5, five-story stone front dwell'g. Mary E. wife of William S. Patten to Samuel J Murphy and Serena D. his wife, joint tenants. *Mt.* $10,000. Oct. 8. 30,000

48th st, No. 149, n s, 260 e 7th av, 20x100 5, four-story stone front dwell'g. Leopold Kahn to Michael Murray. *Mt.* $12,000. Oct. 5. 23,000

Same property. Declaration as to payment of legacies under will of Lucinda J. Kitching. William C. Flanagan to Leopold Kahn and Michael Murray. Oct. 2. nom

50th st, in deed Nos. 413, 415 and 417, on map Nos. 415–421, n s, 500 e 10th av, 78x98.9, four four-story brk dwell'gs with three-story brk building on rear of No. 415. Elias Jacobs and Bertha his wife, Jersey City, to Max Borger. *Mt.* $45,000. Sept. 30. 67,500

50th st, No. 537, n s, 475 w 10th av, 25x100.5, four-story stone front tenem't with three-story brk building on rear. Jacob Schneider and Emma his wife to Christian Abele. Sept. 1. 19,250

53d st, No. 14, s s, 247.6 w 5th av, 25x100.4, four-story stone front dwell'g. Hugh R. Garden and Lucy R. his wife to Mary A. wife of Joseph S. Bosworth. Oct. 8. 82,000

53d st, Nos. 208–214, s s, 68 w 7th av, 68x50.5, four four-story stone front dwell'gs. Foreclos. John H. Judge to Aaron D. Farmer. *Mt.* $35,000 and expenses, interest, &c. Sept. 11. 16,000

54th st, No. 319, n s, 200 e 2d av, 25x100.5, four-story brk tenem't. Fredericka and Lena Otto, Fredericka Schaefer and Catherine Hungerbuehler heirs John Otto to Margaret Woersching. *Mt.* $7,000. Oct. 1. 15,100

56th st, No. 86, s s, 16 8 w 4th av, 16.8x75, four-story stone front dwell'g. Ann O. Humphrey, Brooklyn, to William D. Barnes. *Mt.* $15,000. Oct. 6. nom

60th st, No. 233, n s, 325 e 11th av, 25x100 5, four-story brk tenem't with stores. Release mort. David Weisburger to Jacob Knecht and Louisa his wife. Sept. 30. nom

Same property. Jacob Knecht and Louisa his wife to Charles Kilpatrick. *Mt.* $8,000. Oct. 2. 11,500

63d st, No. 31, n s, 300 w Central Park West, 37.6x100.5, five-story stone front flat. Esther E wife of Martin J. Barron to Frederick Buse. *Mt.* $40,000 Sept. 15. See 8th av. 64,000

65th st, No. 24, s s, 225 w 8th av, 25x100.5, five-story stone front flat. Foreclos. Charles W. Dayton to Katherine M. Mahley Sub. to mort. $27,000 and interest from June 1, 1891. Sept. 8. 9,000

65th st, No. 22, s s, 200 w 8th av, 25x100.5, five-story stone front flat. Foreclos. Same to same. Sub. to mort. $27,000 and interest June 1, 1891. Sept. 8. 9,000

67th st, No. 228, s s, 350 e West End av, 25x100.5, five-story brk tenem't. Foreclos. Gilbert M. Speir, Jr., to Samuel H. Denton. *Mt.* $7,000. Oct 6. 17,750

69th st, Nos. 251 and 253, n s, 215 e West End av, 40x100.5, two-story brk dwell'g. Robert I. Brown to George Thomson. Oct. 1. 13,000

69th st, No. 327, n s, 375 e 2d av, 25x100.5, four-story stone front flat. Moses Esberg and Carrie his wife to Max Frankenheim. *Mt.* $14,500. Oct. 5. 19,000

69th st, No. 339, n s, 99.6 w 1st av, 25.6x100.5, four-story stone front tenem't. Max Frankenheim to Morris Zucker and David Hochner. *Mt.* $12,000. Oct 1. 19,900

72d st, n s, 200 e 9th av, 75x102.2, vacant. John E. Huking and Florence D. his wife to Julius A. Kohn. *Mt.* $55,000 and judgment $439. Oct. 27, 1890. nom

74th st, No. 122, s s, 222 w 9th av, 20x102.2, four-story stone front dwell'g. William H. Riker and Lillie A. his wife to William B. Riker. *Mt.* $26,000. Sept. 30. 45,000

74th st, No. 522, s s, 323 e Av A, 25x102.2, two-story frame dwe'l'g on rear of lot. Clara V. Le Gendre to Hugh Fitzpatrick. Oct. 2. 5,500

74th st, No. 17, n s, 241.6 w 8th av, 19.6x102.2, four-story brk dwell'g. Carrie S. wife of and David T. Kennedy to Catherine A. Stevens. Oct. 6. 43,000

75th st, No. 115, n s, 220 w Columbus av, 20x102.2, four-story stone front dwell'g. James R. Breen and Bathsheba his wife and Alfred G. Nason and Mary A. his wife to Agnes R. Wilcox. Sept. 30. 35,000

76th st, No. 159, n s, 219 e Amsterdam av, 19x102.2, four-story stone front dwell'g. Duncan C. McKinlay and Elizabeth his wife to Adelaide L. and Mary E. Beekman. Sept. 16. nom

76th st, No. 159, n s, 219 e Amsterdam av, 19x102.2. Release mort. John P. Kane to Duncan C. McKinlay. Sept. 15. nom

Same property Release mort. John P. Huggins to same. Sept. 30. nom

Same property. Release mort. Same to same. Sept. 30. nom

Same property. Release mort. The Bradley & Currier Co. (Lim.) to Duncan C. McKinlay and Elizabeth his wife. Sept. 14. nom

Same property. Release mort. Same to same. Sept. 14. nom

76th st, No. 112, s s, 145.1 w Columbus av, 20x102.2, four-story stone front dwell'g. Patrick Farley to Edward Davis. *Mt.* $25,000. Oct. 5. 33,250

78th st, No. 14, s s, 221 e 5th av, 20x102.2, four-story stone front dwell'g. Madlon Morganstern to Albert G. Morganstern. ½ part. *Mt.* ½ $20,000. Oct. 6. 22,500

81st st, No. 407, n s, 156.6 e 1st av, 25x102.2, five-story brk tenem't with stores. Elias Jacobs and Bertha his wife to Kate Bremer. Oct. 8. 23,000

82d st, No. 345, n s, 175 w 1st av, 22.4x100.2, two-story frame dwell'g. Samuel J. K. Adler and Carrie his wife to Louis Plant, Long Island City. *Mt.* $9,000. Aug. 24. 24,000

83d st, No. 128, s s, 300 w Columbus av, 32.4x102.2, four-story brk flat. Eugene D. Miller to Henry J. Batchelder. *Mt.* $33,000. Oct. 3. 40,000

83d st, No. 515, n s, 248 e Av A, 25x102.2, five-story brk tenem't. Joseph Schreiner and Amelia his wife to William Dauth and Kate his wife. *Mt.* $14,000. Sept. 30. 22,000

83d st, No. 523, n s, 348 e Av A, 25x102.2, five-story brk tenem't. Same to Maurice Rapp. *Mt.* $14,000. Oct. 1. 22,000

83d st, No. 529, n s, 108 w Av B, 25x102.2, five-story brk tenem't. Same to Friederich Otterstedt and Henriette his wife. *Mt.* $14,000. Oct. 2. 22,000

85th st, n s, 250.10 e 3d av, 0.8½x102.1x0.2½x102.1. Charles T. Cromwell, Manersing Island, Westchester Co., to Lizzie McGuiness. Q. C. Sept. 14. 100

85th st, n s, 276.5 e 3d av. Party wall agreement. Henry Purnhagen to same. June 10. nom

86th st, No. 73, n s, 114.6 e Columbus av, 20.6x100.8, four-story brk dwell'g. Thomas Reid and Jane M. his wife to Carrie A. W. wife of Royal C. Vilas. *Mt.* $30,000. Sept. 21. 43,000

88th st, No. 318, s s, 265 w West End av, 20x100.8, three-story brk dwell'g. Antoinette

C. wife of Charles E. Hughes, Ithaca, N. Y., to Daniel L. Sturges. *Mt.* $18,500. Taxes 1891. Oct. 3. 24,250

88th st, No. 449, n s, 107 w Av A, 20x100.8, three-story frame dwell'g. John I. Tilton, Paterson, N. J., to Susan M. Vail. Q. C. Sept. 30. 1,067

88th st, No. 155, n s, 325.6 e Amsterdam av, 16 6 x100.8, three-story stone front dwell'g. Sigismund B. Steinmann and Theresa his wife to Ferdinand Mayer. *Mt.* $14,000. Oct. 2. 19,500

89th st, No. 306, s s, 150 e 2d av, 25x100.8, five-story brk tenem't. George Esswein and Katharina his wife to Jacob Johann and Margaretha his wife. *Mt.* $12,000. Sept. 30. 21,400

89th st, No. 345, n s, 200 w 1st av, 25x100.8, five-story brk tenem't. Elizabeth M. wife of Conrad A. Kerner, formerly Uihlein, Rochester, N. Y., to Frank A. Uihlein. 1-5 part. B. & S. and C. a. G. Sept. 30. 4,600

Same property. Catherine A. wife of Valentine Maickel, formerly Uihlein, Mary E. wife of Henry Peters, Jr., formerly Uihlein, and Anna C. Uihlein to same. 3-5 part. B. & S. C. a. G. Sept. 30. 13,800

89th st, No. 339, n s, 275 w 1st av, 25x100.8, five-story brk tenem't. Elizabeth M. wife of Conrad A. Kerner to Mary E. Peters. 1-5 part. Sub. to 1-5 part of mort. $10,000. B. & S. and C. a. G. Sept. 30. 4,600

89th st, No. 345, n s, 250 w 1st av, 25x100.8, five-story brk tenem't. Same to Catherine A. Maickel. 1-5 part. Sub. to 1-5 part of mort. $10,000. B. & S. and C. a. G. Sept. 30. 4,600

89th st, No. 343, n s, 225 w 1st av, 25x100.8, five-story brk tenem't. Same to Anna C. Uihlein. 1-5 part. Sub. to 1-5 part of mort. $10,000. B. & S. and C. a. G. Sept. 30. 4,600

Same property. Frank A. Uihlein and Mary J. his wife, Catherine A. wife of Valentine Maickel formerly Uihlein and Mary E. wife of Henry Peters, Jr., formerly Uihlein to Same. 3-5 part. Sept. 30. 13,800

89th st, n s, 275 w 1st av, 25x100.8. Frank A. Uihlein and Mary J. his wife. Catherine A. wife of Valentine Maickel formerly Uihlein and Anna C. Uihlein to Mary E. Peters. 3-5 part. B. & S. and C. a. G. *Mt.* 3-5 of $10,000. Sept 30. 13,800

89th st, n s, 250 w 1st av, 25x100.8. Frank A. Uihlein and Mary J. his wife and Mary E. wife of Henry Peters, Jr., formerly Uihlein and Anna E. Uihlein to Catherine A. Maickel. 3-5 part. C. a. G. Sub. to 3-5 part of mort. $10,000. Sept. 30. 13,800

89th st, n s, 200 w 9th av, 100x100.8, vacant. Robert Dick and Kate his wife to Lida A. Brown. *Mt.* $28,500. Oct. 5. nom

93d st, Nos. 175 and 177, n s, 220.6 w 3d av, 59.10x100 8, two four-story stone front flats. Charles R. Lauterjung and Wilhelmina his wife to Amelia Friedman. B. & S. and C. a. G. June 2, 1888. 75,000

94th st, No. 14, s s, 125 w 8th av, 18.9x100.8, four-story stone front dwell'g. Ella L. Gault to William B. Baldwin. *Mt.* $21,000. Sept. 1. nom

96th st, No. 128, s s, 300 w Columbus av, 25x 100.8, five-story stone front flat. Alexander Cameron and Margaret his wife to Elizabetha Hauck. *Mt.* $22,000 Aug. 14 35,000

96th st, s s, 150 e 10th av, 100x101.5, error, vacant. Amy E. wife of and Bernard Cohn to Amsterdam Improvement Co. Q. C. Oct. 1. 44,000

96th st, n s, 250 e Amsterdam av, 25x100.11, five-story stone front flat. Alexander Cameron to Valentine F. Hauck. *Mt.* $22,000. Oct. 5. 35,000

98th st, s s, 175 e 2d av, 25x100 9. Release mort. Mutual Life Ins. Co., New York, to Matthew Mullen. Oct. 7. 2,000

98th st, s s, 150 e Amsterdam av, 200x100.11, vacant. Foreclos. Thomas F. Gilroy, Jr., to George Stone *Mt.* $23,000. Sept. 30. 57,000

101st st, n s, 175 e 9th av. Party wall agreement. Frank Davis to William M. Walsh. Jan. 1, 1891. nom

101st st, No. 73, n s, 150 e Columbus av, 25x 100.11, five-story brk flat. William M. Walsh and Mary A. his wife to Sophia Oppenheimer. *Mt.* $20,000. Sept 26. 30,000

105th st, Nos. 65 and 67, n s, 170 e Madison av, 50x100 11, two five-story brk flats John J. Feehan and Matilda his wife and Ernest Hammer and Catherine his wife to William Laue, Brooklyn. *Mt.* $30,000. Oct. 2. 50,000

111th st, No. 12, s s, 119 e 5th av, 18x100.11, five-story stone front flat. John Hickey and Ann his wife to Samuel H. Goodenough. *Mt.* $15,000. Oct. 6. 19,000

111th st, No 130, s s, 182.2 w Lexington av, and being 627.2 w 3d av, 17.10x100.11, three-story frame dwell'g. Hannah J. wife of Frank E. Stephens to Catherine Neumann. Oct. 3. 7,500

Same property. Edward Green and Susan Hitchcock widow, both of Albany, N. Y., to Hannah J. Stephens. Oct. 2. 6,500

112th st, s s, 250 w 7th av, 25x100.11, vacant. William M. Rider and Emma L. his wife, Dunellen, N. J., to Anthony H. Brennan. *Mt.* $5,316. Oct. 1. 6,500

113th st, No. 445, n s, 93 w Av A, 25x100.10, five-story stone front tenem't.
106th st, No. 323, n s, 275 w 1st av, 25x100.11, four-story brk tenem't.
Nettie Kolben to Joseph Steiner. All liens. Oct. 6. nom

114th st, No. 154, s s, w253.4 3d av, 16.8x 100.10.
114th st, No. 168, s s, 220 w 3d av, 16.8x 100.10.
Two three-story brk dwell'gs.
Sarah A., Harriet M. and Lillian R. Terrett and Sarah L. Holt to Julia A. wife of Dudley B. Holbrook, Sing Sing. Oct. 1. nom

115th st, Nos. 323 and 325, n s, 300 w 1st av, 50 x100.11, two four-story brk tenem'ts with stores. Ann O. Humphrey, Brooklyn, to William D. Barnes. *Mt.* $20,000. Oct. 6. 2,400

115th st, No. 211, n s, 225 w 7th av, 20x100.11, five-story stone front flat. Foreclos. Edward H. Schell to Frederick F. Woodward admr. Samuel A. Woodward. Sept. 30. 17,600

115th st, No. 280, s s, 80 e 8th av, 20x100.11, five-story stone front flat.
110th st, No. 56, s s, 36.8 e Madison av, 16.8x 100.11, three-story stone front dwell'g.
Louisa, Thomas K. and Arthur E. Moore and Hiram Moore and Ida E. his wife to Marion E. Moore. C. a. G. June 25. nom

120th st, No. 14, s s, 125 e 5th av, 37x100.11, five-story brk flat Mary wife of James Gault to Ella L. Gault. *Mt.* $39,750. Oct. 3. nom

122d st, No. 215, n s, 180 e 3d av, 25x100.11, four-story brk tenem't. Joseph B. Bissell and Josephine his wife to Fanny Nugent. *Mt.* $13,500. Oct. 1. 17,000

123d st, No. 111, n s, 205 w Lenox av, 20x100.11, three-story stone front dwell'g. Robert Simpson to George S. Simpson, Brooklyn. Trust deed. July 21. nom

123d st, No. 69, n s, 40 w 4th av, 20x100.11, four-story brk flat. Amanda Basch to Edward Loewenberg. *Mt.* $12,500. Oct. 1. exch

126th st, n s, 100 w 9th av, runs north 99.11 x west 25 x south 95.8 to Lawrence st, x southeast 9.2 to 126th st, x east 16.10, vacant. *Mt.* $4,500.
Lawrence st, No. 2, s s, 14.10 n w 126th st, runs southwest 100 x southeast 25 x northeast 104.7 to 126th st, x west 9.9 to Lawrence st, x northwest 14 10, one-story frame store with two-story frame dwell'g on rear. *Mt.* $4,100
Charles C. Schildwachter and Friedericka his wife to Mary wife of Anton Liebler. C. a. G. Taxes 1891. Oct. 6. 11,100

127th st, No. 218, s s, 180 e 3d av, 40x99.11, three-story frame dwell'g and vacant. Foreclos. James F. Swanton to Frederick Aldhous. *Mt.* $9,000 and int. Oct. 6. 2,000

127th st, Nos 105 and 107, n s, 95 e Park av, 50 x99.11, two five-story brk flats. Mary E. Yost to Mary Emeline wife of Fernando Yost. Sub. to morts. Sept. 30. nom

128th st, No. 59, n s, 198.4 w Park av, 16.8x99.11, three-story frame dwell'g. Patrick Keirns and Adelia his wife to James Martin. Sept. 25. nom

129th st, No. 145, n s, 308 4 e 7th av, 16.8x99.4, three-story stone front dwell'g. Henrietta F. Hansen to Benjamin B. Hoffman, Red Hook, N. Y. Oct. 8. 15,000

151st st, s s, 150 e Boulevard, 50x99.11, one-story frame sheds, &c William A. Shelton and Minnie T. his wife to Frederick C. Dexter, Brooklyn, N. Y. ½ part. ½ morts. $4,500. Oct. 1. nom

167th st, s s, 100 w 10th av, 25x85, vacant. William Hogg and Mary his wife to Charles A. Kinne. *Mt.* $1,700. Oct. 5. 2,500

Amsterdam av, No 855, e s, 58.10 n 88th st, 28.4 x100, five-story brk flat with stores. Edmund Dodge and Sarah J. his wife to Henry F. Miller. *Mt.* $20,000. Oct. 1. nom

Amsterdam (10th) av, No. 307, e s, 70 4 n 74th st, 17x81, four-story brk dwell'g. Foreclos. John B. Whiting to William Bryan. Aug. 17. 15,350

Av A, No. 1098, e s, 38.8 n 59th st, 19.4x80, four-story stone front flat. Herman Wronkow and Serena his wife to Margaret Pendargast. *Mt.* $6,000. Oct. 6. 11,750

Av B, No. 178, w s, 23.3 n 11th st, 20x90.6, five-story brk store and tenem't. Solomon Appel and Hannah his wife to Abraham Katz and Louis Maier. *Mt.* $6,000. Oct. 8. 20,000

Av B, No. 289, e s, 22 s 17th st, 20x68, five-story brk store and tenem't. Henry M. Sendheim and Clara his wife to Mary J. Kelly. *Mt.* $12,500. Oct. 1. nom

Av D, Nos. 143 and 145, s w cor 10th st, 50x 93, five-story brk cigarette factory.
10th st, No. 444, s s, 93 w Av D, 25x92.3, four-story brk cigar factory.
Interior lot, 72 s 10th st and 73 w Av D, runs west 25 x south 22 x east 20 x north 22.
10th st, No. 442, s s, 118 w Av D, 21x92.3, four-story brk cigar factory with two-story brk building on rear.
10th st, s s, 139 w Av D, 1.4x92.3. All title.
Interior strip, 92.3 s 10th st and 93 w Av D, runs south 1.9 x west 25x1.9x25.
Elias Spingarn and Sarah his wife to Alexander Lichtenstein. C. a. G. Oct. 5. nom

Bradhurst av, w s, centre line bet 147th and 148th sts, runs west 75 x south 129.11 x east 75 to av, x north 129.11, vacant. Henry H. Lloyd to Joseph H. T. Martin, Woodbridge, N. J. *Mt.* $10,500. Aug. 1. nom

Lexington av, No. 157, e s, 22.8 s 30th st, runs east 42 x south 2.5 x east 49 x south 14.1 x west 91 to av, x north 16 6, four-story stone front dwell'g. Emma G. Galway to Mary C. Burke. Oct 5. 17,000

Lexington av, No. 609, e s, 60.5 s 53d st, 20x80, three-story stone front dwell'g. Patrick Leamy to Ellen V. Kinneary, Cincinnati, Thomas F. Leamy and Mary F. Morgan. Q. C. Dec. 5, 1889. nom

Lenox av, No. 198, s e cor 120th st, 19 8x85, four-story brk dwell'g. Henry Morgenthau and Josephine his wife to Clara V. wife of Charles D. Shepard. *Mt.* $20,000. Sept. 30. 35,000

Madison av, No. 222, w s, 106.8 s 37th st, 25x95, four-story stone front school. Albert C. Mears to Louise D. Mears. Sub. to mort. Oct. 7. nom

Madison av, Nos. 1736 and 1738, w s, 25.11 n 114th st, 50x100, two five-story stone front flats. Anna S. Cohen to Joseph Gottlieb. C. a. G. May 8. 52,000

Madison av, n w cor 98th st, 45.11x— to st, x 10.6, vacant. Warren Ferris, Orangetown, N. Y., to L. Napoleon Levy. Oct. 7. 2,500

Madison av, w s, at centre line bet 98th and 99th sts, runs west to w s of old Boston Post road, x southerly along same to 98th st, x east along st 35.10 to centre said old road, x north along same to w s Madison av, x north —, vacant. Same to same. Q. C. Oct. 7. 1,000

Pleasant av, No. 407, w s, 75.7 n 121st st, 25.2x 100, three-story frame dwell'g. Bernard Reynolds to Mary J. O'Neill. Oct. 6. nom

Pleasant av, s w cor 115th st, 75.8x74, vacant. Release judgment. Eugene Kelly individ. and Eugene and Edward Kelly and William Farrell and Joseph A. Donahue, of Eugene Kelly & Co., to William T. Washburn and ano. exrs. Benjamin Richardson. Sept. 30. nom

Same property William T. Washburn and Emma Richardson exrs. and trustees of Benjamin Richardson to Thomas F. Shannon. *Mt.* $11,000 Oct. 2. nom

Prescott av, east cor Bolton road, 114.2x82.3x 81.9 to Seaman av, x138.8 to Bolton road, x north 128.6. Daniel E. Seybel to Frank Koch. Oct. 3. 10,500

South 5th av, No. 55, s e s, 150 s w Bleecker st, 25x100, vacant lot. Patrick J. Kelly and Robert H. Ramsgate to Denison P. Chesebro. *Mt.* $23,000. Oct. 5. 27,000

West End av, n e cor 77th st, 102.2x100.
77th st, n s, 100 e West End av, 75x102.2, vacant.
Theophilus A. Brouwer and Elizabeth his wife to the Ministers, &c., Reformed Prot. Dutch Church. *Mt.* $53,400. Feb. 10. 89,000

West End av, s e cor 103d st, 100.11x100, vacant. Alexander Walker and Margaret H. his wife and Judson Lawson and Martha A. his wife to William Drought, New York, and Charles J. Carew, Norwich, Conn. *Mt.* $27,500. Oct. 1. nom

West End av, n e cor 97th st, runs north 19.11 x east 89 x north 72 x east 36 x south 91.11 to 97th st, x west 125.
West End av, e s, 55.11 n 97th st, 18x89.
West End av, e s, 91.11 n 97th st, 18x100.
Release mort. Harriet Overhiser to Edward Kilpatrick. Oct. 7. 25,000

West End av, No. 469, w s, 80.6 n 87th st, 20.2x 100, three-story stone front dwell'g. Thomas P. Kelly and Mary J. his wife to Bertha Davis. *Mt.* $30,000. Oct. 1. nom

3d av, Nos. 1645-1649, n e cor 92d st, 75.6x100, one and two-story frame and brk stores. Charles Rieger and Maria his wife to George Ringler & Co. *Mt.* $50,000. Oct. 1. 72,500

7th av, No. 890, w s, 75.5 n 56th st, 25x100, four-story frame store and tenem't. Elizabeth wife of William Noble to William Noble. Oct. 2. nom

7th av, Nos. 2018 and 2020, s w cor 121st st, 40x 85, two five-story brk flats with stores. John D. Taylor and Hannah his wife to Gustave A. Jenny and Helene G. his wife. *Mt.* $45,000. Sept. 29. 70,000

8th av, Nos 2192 and 2194, e s, 25.11 n 118th st, 50x80, two five-story brk flats with stores. Philip Braender and Lizzie his wife to Peter Diehl. *Mt.* $16,000. Sept. 28. 50,000

8th av, w s, 24.11 n 154th st, 50x100, vacant. *Mt.* $7,000
Bradhurst av, w s, 346.6 s 155th st, 25.6x97.2x 25x92.2, vacant.
Frederick Buse and Martha his wife to Esther E. Barron. Sept. 15. See 63d st. 31,000

8th av, No. 2200, e s, 50.11 s 119th st, 25x80, five-story brk flat with stores. Philip Braender and Lizzie his wife to William E. Burkhardt. *Mt.* $16,000. Sept. 16. 25,000

8th av, w s, 25 n 126th st, 25x100.
Fleetwood av, n s, 83.7 w Popham st, 30x100.
Anastasia Power to Mary Power. Q. C. June 6 nom

9th av, No. 738, e s, 22 s 50th st, 22x80, three-story frame store and tenem't. Louis Linnemann to Henry Linnemann. All title. *Mt.* $2,000. Oct. 8. 1,300

11th av, e s, 25 n 173d st, 25x100. Susan Bunce to John A. Lachner. *Mt.* $2,000. Oct. 6. 3,700

Interior lot, 328 w of Central Park West and 100 n 74th st, runs north 2.2 x west 22 x south 2.2x22. Frederick Aldhous and Eliza his wife to Elizabeth L. Goodnow. June 17. 123

MISCELLANEOUS.

All title in estate Valentine Euler dec'd. Catharine Grom heir and legatee Valentine Euler to Juliane Siegel. June 27, 1891. nom

Appointment of George C. Magoun, of the City of New York, as trustee of The Sun Fire Office Co The Sun Fire Office Co. to George C. Magoun. Sept. 28. nom

Appointment of new trustee under deed by Maria R. Bartow. William A. Bartow and Henry E. Duncan, Jr., with concurrence of Catharine B. Duncan, Clarina B. Morgan and Henrietta B. Jackson to William H. Jackson. Sept. 28. nom

23d and 24th WARDS.

Cornell pl, e s, 100 n Rock st, 25x100. James F Sheridan, Patrick H. Sheridan and Kate his wife and James S. Segrave and Catharine A. his wife to Lena Cirker. Sept. 30. 400

Cordova pl, e s, 234.3 n St. Georges Crescent, 25x100. Conrad Brencher to Carl Hanson and Christina his wife, joint tenants. Oct. 5. 640

Field st, e s, 150 s Beech st, 25x100. James F. Sheridan, Patrick H. Sheridan and Kate his wife and James S. Segrave and Catharine A. his wife to Manuel H. Heatly. Sept. 30. 550

Field st, w s, 200 s Beech st, 77.7x100. Same to Elmer E. Woolson. Sept. 30. 1,371

Field st, w s, 100 s Beech st, 100x100. Same to John A. Woolson. Sept. 30. 1,829

Field st, e s, 175 s Beech st, 25x100. Same to Valentine H. Muller Sept. 30. 550

Forest st, w s, 100 n Rock st, 50x100. James F. Sheridan, Patrick H. Sheridan and Kate his wife and James S. Segrave and Catharine A. his wife to Joseph F. Gombert. Sept. 30. 1,100

Fox st, w s, 194.5 n 165th st, 16.8x100, h & l. Leopold R. Treu to The Hollister Mfg. Co. *Mt.* $1,800. Sept. 30. 298

Field st, e s, 150 s Beech st, 50x100.
Hill st, west cor Rock st, 72.2x91.7x116.5.
Release mort. Thomas C. Cornell to James F. and Patrick H. Sheridan and James S. Segrave. Sept. 30. 2,850

Gerard st, n e s, 129 s e Bergen av, 25x100; also ½ of Gerard st. George B. Bond and Lilian L. his wife, Tacoma, Washington, to Irene A. Bond, Brooklyn June 1. 500

Gambril st or Suburban st, n e s, 496.8 s e Marion av, 60x100. John E. Murgatroyd to John Ovens. Aug. 15. 2,200

Hill st, e s, 100 n Rock st, 100x100.
Hill st, e s, 200 n Rock st, runs north 150 x east 64.8 x southeast — x south 75.9 x west 25 x south 25 x west 100.
Hill st, s e cor Rock st, 75x100.
Field st, e s, 150 s Bleech st, 25x100.
Release mort. Same to same. Sept. 30. 7,425

Hill st, e s, 100 n Rock st, 100x100. James F. Sheridan, Patrick H. Sheridan and Kate his wife and James S. Segrave and Catharine A. his wife to Charles M. Edwards. Sept. 30. 1,500

Hall pl, e s, 149.11 n 167th st, 26.5x126.3x26.3x127.3. Hannah wife of Edward E. Levi to James Farley. Sub. to taxes 1891. Oct. 6. 757

Mount Hope pl, n e s, 100 n w Fleetwood or Madison av, 19x125, h & l. Arthur Boehmer to Anthony M. Clegg. *Mt.* $4,400 and tax for 1 year. Oct. 1. 6,000

Mount Hope pl, n s, 100 w Monroe av, 50x125. Caleb C. Dusenbury and Amelia W. his wife, Carmel, N. Y., to Frederick M. Ulrich. Oct. 6. 4,000

Rock st, n w cor Forest st, 200 to Field st, x—x200 to Forest st, x250.
Rock st, n e cor Hill st, 475x— to n s Beech st, x— to Hill st, x412.
Anna M. C. Barnes widow, Toledo, Ohio, and Jane E. wife of Thomas C. Cornell to said Thomas C. Cornell. Aug. 8. nom

Rock st, n w cor Forest st, 100x100. James F. Sheridan, Patrick H. Sheridan and Kate his wife and James S. Segrave and Catharine A. his wife to Francis X. Werner and Catharine his wife. Sept. 30. 2,200

Rock st, s w cor Hill st, 116.5x91.7x72.2. Same to Julius Fischler. Sept. 30. 800

Rogers pl, s e s, 642.4 n e Westchester av, 30x78.11x23.1x81.8. James McCarthy and Mary his wife to Mary E. Burrell. *Mt.* $450. Sept. 30. 1,200

Walker st, north cor Centre st, 21.3x126.5x—x —. Henrietta and Mary E. Speke to Richard D. Williams and Lillian M. his wife. Oct. 5. 3,500

133d st, s s, 225 e St. Anns av, 25x100. Release mort. T. Gaillard Thomas to John Entwistle. Oct. 1. 2,460

134th st, s s, 100 w Alexander av, 25x100. Release mort. The Bradley & Currier Co. (Lim.) to Frederick Rohrs and Louisa his wife. Oct. 1. nom

Same property. Frederick Rohrs and Louisa his wife to Frederick Grafelmann and Margaretha his wife, Newtown, N. Y. *Mt.* $14,500. Oct. 2. 19,500

135th st, s s, 225 e St. Anns av, 25x100. John Entwistle and Lucy E. his wife to Annie Derleth. Oct. 3. 2,650

137th st, s s, 225 e Willis av, 100x100. James Brown and Eliza M. his wife to the trustees of the Presbytery N. Y. April 25, 1871. nom

150th st, s s, 98 w Mott av, runs south 100 x west 2 x south 100 x west 12 x north 200 to 150th st, x east 14. Mary A. More, Catskill, N. Y., formerly Turner to Anna T. wife of James S. Dale. Sub. to right of way; also to paving assessm't and taxes 1891. Sept. 23. nom

150th st, s s, 73.10 e Railroad av East, 20x100. Edward Callahan and Margaret his wife to Joseph Frank and Ellen his wife. Sept. 30. 2,300

163d st, s w cor Brook av, 79.3x217.9x67.2x154.3. Mary E. Yost to Mary Emeline wife of Fernando Yost. *Mt.* $5,000. Oct. 3. nom

165th st, s w cor Tiffany st, runs west 55.3 x south 73.1 x south 22.3 x east 50 x north 98.11. Hannah Levi to Nestor Berman, Port Henry, N. Y. Oct. 6. nom

173d st, n w cor of a tract formerly known as Brook st, 100x93x100x89. Barbara Ranchfuss, Brooklyn, to George H. Purser, Yonkers. Oct. 1. 2,000

176th st, s s, 315.2 e Fleetwood av, 59.10x125x36.4x127.2 Lewis G. Morris to Theodore Roehrs. Oct. 1. 1,750

Anthony av, w s, 796 n Southern Boulevard, 44.10x78.5x39.11x79.10. Michael Kirwan and Mary S. his wife to Michael Clayton. Oct. 1. 5,000

Av A, e s, 132 s Highbridge road, 75x131.6x75x129.6. George Lockyer and John Daly to John J. Curtin. Oct. 5. 3,750

Bainbridge av, s s, 243.3 w Suburban st, 73.2x227.3x73.2x231.1. Ferdinand J. Frerichs and Dorothea F. M. his wife to Alfred J. R. E. Zucker. *Mt.* $3,860. Sept. 30. nom

Bainbridge av, s e s, 208.7 s w Travers st, 25x115.
Bainbridge av, s e s, 155 s w Travers st, 26.9x114x18.3x111.
Benjamin F. De Klyn to Walter J. Lea. Sept. 26. 2,500

Briggs av, n w s, 327.4 n e Travers st, 50x100. Margaret Watt to Thomas Everest. Oct. 2. 1,400

Bathgate av, s e s, 243 s w Fitch st, 27x113.3x27x112.2. John B. Smith and Bertha his wife to William Fernschild. Oct 5. nom

Courtlandt av, e s, 75 s 15?th st, 25x100. John Lutz and Anna his wife to Christopher Kubner and Annie his wife. Oct. 5. 5,500

Elton av, n s, 63.8 w 162d st, 31.10x105.4x25x124.8. Frederick W. Ehrsam and Louise his wife to George D. Pointner. Oct. 3. 1,600

Elton av, s e cor 158th st, 75x100. Henry Bobleo, Newark, N. J., to the trustees of the First German Methodist Episcopal Church of Morrisania. B. & S. and C. a. G. Sub. to taxes and assessm'ts. March 10, 1890. nom

Forest av, s w cor Cedar st, 20x100. John W. Decker to Anna wife of Henry Cramer. Sept. 29. 6,650

Jefferson av, s e s, lots 199, 200 and 201 map S. Ryer homestead, 75x100 to Ryer pl. James W. McBarron and Eliza B. his wife to Edward J. O'Gorman. Sept. 25. 2,800

Monroe av, s e s, adj land John Ittner, runs northeast 93.6 x northeast again 814.11 x southeast 723 x again southeast 350 to Valentine av, x southwest 881.2 x northwest 356 x northwest 738.6. Walter S., Arthur W., Wm. Lesley and Henry Schaefer exrs. Peter W. Schaefer to Benjamin R. Miller. Q. C. July 20. nom

Monroe av, e s, 410 n from s w cor of tract conveyed to John Ittner by Peter Buckhout, 63.6x320.7x still along said av 1,066.7 to w s Valentine av, x 364.1x1,085.11, contains 9 17-100 acres. Benjamin R. Miller to William H. Lawson, Brooklyn. Oct. 8. 51,728

Nathalie av, w s, lot 85 map of 16 villa sites and 80 lots part of Anthony estate, Kingsbridge, 24th Ward, 25x121.11x25.2x118.11. Perry P. Williams and Maria L. C. his wife to Augustus S. Frazee. Sept. 12. 1,000

Opdyke av, n s, 200 w 4th st, 230x148.3x211x151.6. W. R. Lamberton to Matilda Culver. Sept. 24. 3,900

Penfold av, n s, 100 w Southern Boulevard, 25x100. Charles Bradley and Catharine his wife and Henry Kelly and Catharine his wife to August J. Besson, Jersey City. Oct. 5. 700

Pelham av, s e cor Hoffman st. 58.2x108x59.2x108. John Ovens to Michael Duffy. Aug. 27. 6,000

Robbins av, s e s, 75 n e 150th st, 25x105. Helene Spengler widow to Peter Knauf and Maria his wife. Oct. 3. 2,375

Ryer av, e s, 100 s 2d st, runs south 25 x east 100 x south 25 x east 97.3 x north 50.3 x west 191.0. Thomas White to Kate E. Goodenough. Sept. 26. 2,000

Railroad av, s e s, lot 54 map Village Morrisania, 25x150. Charles Zimmermann and Marie his wife to Henry Wuest. Sept. 10. 3,900

Scott av, n s, 26.2 e Perry av, 26.2x105.4x25x97.8. George Heather to Annie C. Bischoff. Oct. 5. 775

Sedgwick av, w s, 410 n north line of proposed st as monumented, 20 ft. wide, extdg. to the westward from Sedgwick av, runs west 170.7 to proposed st 40 ft. wide, x north 42.11 x east 196.9 to Sedgwick av, x south 157.6. Alfred J. Taylor and Kathleen K. his wife and William D. Peck to Roma L. wife of Robert L. Niles. Sept. 10. 7,750

Tinton av, e s, 126.9 s 168th st, 17.6x132.6x15.6x132.6. Margaret A. O'Rorke to Julius Grossmann. *Mt.* $1,500. Oct. 6. 4,650

Webster av, s e cor Scott av, 50x100x80.9x104.7. George V. Krauss and Louisa R. his wife to Emile Pidoux. *Mt.* $685. Oct. 7. 2,250

Washington av, north cor 169th st, 98x150. Robert R. Sherwood, Westchester, N. Y., to Ann Mapelsden, Brooklyn, N. Y. Q. C. Aug. 3. nom

Washington av, w s, 475 s 171st st, 25x150. Mary A. wife of and Peter C. Ritchie to August Berbert. Oct. 1. 3,000

Washington av, w s, 400 s 171st st, runs west 300 to Railroad av, x south 100 x east 150 x north 75 x east 150 to Washington av, x north 25, with all right to strip 1 3x10, whereon is situated the s e cor factory, fronting on Railroad av, so long as same is in its present position. Same to Richard F. Otto. Oct. 1. 12,000

Plot in 24th Ward, bounded northeast by New York and Yonkers line, southeast and south by creek bet premises and Hyatt farm and west by 2d st and road from South Yonkers to Mile Square, excepting any part taken for streets, also excepting 16 lots numbered 906 to 911 and 954 to 958 and 1096 to 1100 inclusive, on map E. K. Willard property, Woodlawn Heights. John C. Ely to Lucy S. Ely. *Mt.* $5,500. Jan. 8. 27,350

Interior lot, begins at point 146.8 s 168th st and 100 e Tinton av, runs east 32.6 x north 15.6 x west 32.7 x south 15.6. Release mort. Joseph L. Hewlett, Great Neck, L. I., to Margaret A. O'Rorke. Sept. 30. nom

Release of right of way over strip of land in town of West Farms, 24th Ward, on n e s of land owned by John Ittner and on the s e s of land owned by Peter Buckhout, 10 feet wide. Myer Finn and Sarah his wife and Abraham Levy and Amelia his wife to Benjamin R. Miller. Oct. 6. nom

LEASEHOLD CONVEYANCES.

Bayard st, n s, 100 e Pyne st, 42.10x100.3x49.6x100. Release mort. Mary E. Cumming to Eliza Prescott. Oct. 7. 950

Same property. Eliza Prescott to William D. Carroll. Oct. 7. 1,400

Cherry st, No. 448, n s, 100 e Jackson st, 25x100, Leasehold. Foreclos. Theodore F. Miller to Alexander T. Watson trustee for Helen K. Watson. Sept. 24. 3,000

Grand st, No. 226. Assign. lease. Theodore Timpe to Michael Bolz. nom

Same property. Assign. lease. Michael Boltz to Charles Lortcher. nom

Mott st, No. 227. Assign. lease. Henry J. and William Wirth to Peter Thomas. 1,700

Warren st, No. 167. Assign. lease. Louis W. Dusing to James Everard. (Corrects error in last issue) 5,000

3d st, No. 222, n s, 100 e Av A, 22.6x96.2. William Astor to Barbara Palm. 20 years, from Feb. 1, 1880, per year, taxes, &c., and 550

Same property. Assign. lease. Henry Schmid exr. and trustee Barbara Palm to John Losel and Theresia his wife. 5,150

8th st, n s, 125 w 1st av, 25x85.10. Assign. lease. Edward Lowenberg to Amanda Basch. *Mt.* $2,000. exch

21st st, s s, 250 w 8th av, 25x91.11. Consent to assign. lease. Francis L. Ogden to David L. Price. nom

67th st, Nos. 60 and 62, s s, 100 e Columbus av, 50x100.5. Edward Kilpatrick to Charles R. Saul. 14 7-12 years, from Oct. 1, 1891, per year, 6,120, 6,624

106th st, No. 419 E. Assign. lease. Frederick Neus to Joseph Hartnett. 2,500

1st av, No. 1512. Assign. lease. William O'Hara to James E. Clifford. nom

KINGS COUNTY.

OCTOBER 1, 2, 3, 5, 6, 7.

Ainslie st, n s, 200 e Marcy av. 25x100, h & l. Martin D. Meyers to George W. Meyers. B. & S. nom

Ainslie st, n s, 175 e Marcy av, 25x131.8x27.8x119.9, h & l. Martin D. Meyers to Edward E. Meyers. B & S. nom

Apollo st, w s, 242.11 n Meeker av, runs north 20.6 x northwest 79 x southwest 162.6 to Hausman st, x south 17.8 x east 100 x south 25 x east 100; also,
Van Cott av, s e cor Sutton st, 25x113x28.6x136.8.
Jeremiah V. Meserole to Kings County Improvement Co. $816

Bainbridge st, n s, 41.6 e Saratoga av, 18.6x100, h & l. William H. Good to John R. Hughes. *Mt.* $4,400. nom

Bainbridge st, n s, 151 e Saratoga av, 18x100.
Bainbridge st, n s, 205 e Saratoga av, 72x100.
Franklin Trust Co. to J. Mason Kirby. 18,300

Same property. Release mort. Joseph P. Fuels to J. Mason Kirby. nom

Bainbridge st, n s, 169 e Saratoga av, 36x100. Release mort. Same to same. nom

Same property. Release mort. Franklin Trust Co. to same. 7,700

Bainbridge st, n s, 187.3 e Saratoga av, 17.9x100. Release mort. Joseph P. Puels to J. Mason Kirby. nom

Bainbridge st, s s, 128.8 w Patchen av, runs south to the line which was the n s of the Brooklyn and Jamaica turnpike road, x west to point 143 from Patchen av, x north to Bainbridge st, x east 14.4, with all title in road. Jesse Price to Thomas D. Hurst. 2,750

Baltic st, n s, 172.10 w Clinton st, 20x100. Patrick J. Gunn to Charles H. C. Schild. *Mt.* $4,000. 7,500

Baltic st, s s, 125 w Bond st, 25x100. Annie Lamb individ. and as extrx. Mary Lamb to Patrick Connors. 2,100

Bancroft pl, e s, 98.7 n Atlantic av, 69x90. Alton H. Fancher to Frank Hyde. *Mt.* $1,500. nom

Barbey st, e s, 60 n Blake av, 20x100. George Dehn to Andrew Siegling. 350

Beaver st, s s, 25 s e Fayette st, 25x100, h & l. Simon K. Saenger to Richard A. Berger. *Mt.* $4,500. 6,500

Beaver st, s w s, 80 n w Park av, 20x91.6. Louis Beer and Michael Shaffner to Henry Levy. 3,450

Bergen st, s s, 125 w Hopkinson av, 50x127.9. Rose wife of Jonas Rosenfeld to Mary Hurley. *Mt.* $900. 1,300

Bergen st, n s, 200 w Stone av, 25x107.2.
Bergen st, n s, 100 e Stone av, 25x101.4x37.10 x—.
Solomon Beck to Alexander Spitzer. ½ part. 3,000

Bergen st, s w s, 100 s e Nevins st, 25x100. Mary C. or Kate Cahill to Mary F. Kelly. 4,700

Boerum st, s s, 150 w Graham av, 25x100. Barbara Wagner widow to Samuel Frankel. 5,000

Bristol st late West st, e s, 125 n Sackett st, 25x100, 20th Ward. Bridget Gibney widow to John Steuer and Karolina his wife, joint tenants. 1,000

Broadway, n e s, 42.3 s e Palmetto st, 19.3x90. Abraham and Aaron Kodziesen to Henry Sahlfeld. Mt. $5,000. nom

Broadway, s s, 120 w Brooklyn av, 40x100, Flatbush. Antonio Montraperto or Montaperlo, of Flatbush, to Luigi Marchesana. 1,100

Broadway, s s, 56 e of road formerly leading to south entrance of Evergreens Cemetery, 28x— to Brooklyn and Jamaica plank road, x23x—. Sarah Gallagher widow and devisee George Moore to Giuliano Craparella. Mt. $2,200. 2,800

Broadway, n e s, 80 n w Ivy st, 40x100, hs & ls. Jacob Mayer to Henry W. and George J. Schreiber. Mt. $9,250. 17,000

Broadway, s s, 420 w Brooklyn av, 40x100, Flatbush. Peter Carolin and May Hayes to Pasquale and Vincenza la Fiatare. 600

Butler st, s s, 458 e Nostrand av, 16.8x100. Sabra A. Wobbe widow to Charles M. Marsh, of Morris Plains, N. J. Mt. $3,750. nom

Cambridge pl, e s, 174 n Gates av, 17.6x100. Blanche M. wife of Clarence Creighton to Sarah A. Terrett. nom

Chester st, e s, 500 s Sackett st, 50x100. Jeremiah Ervin to Francis J. Rice. 1,700

Cleveland st, w s, 210 s New Lots road, 20x100. Christopher or Christian Nicklaus to Arthur Musy. 290

Cleveland st, e s, 205 s Hegeman av, 60x100.
Cleveland st, w s, 225 s Hegeman av, 20x100.
Henry R. Fechtmann to Eliza M. Stackhouse. exch

Clinton st, s e s, 42 n e State st, 21x—x21.5x90, h & l. Frank A. Butler to Alexander J. C. Skene. Mt. $9,500. 19,500

College pl, e s, 127.11 n Love lane, 20x50. Partition. George W. Roderick ref. to Carrie Shay, of Montclair, N. J. 2,900

Conover st, s e s, 20.3 n e Partition st, 19.9x75. Katharine E. Finkeldey to Anna M. Wolf. nom

Conover st, w s, 20 s Vandyke st, 20x80, h & l. Catherine Oswald to Martin Hansen. Q. C. and C. a. G. nom

Same property. Henry W. Oswald to Martin Hansen. Q. C. and C. a. G. nom

Cooper st or av, n w s, 159.7 n e Broadway, 19.7x100. Hermann Reiche to Sophia Reiche. All liens. nom

Cooper st, n w s, 125 s w Bushwick av, 25x100. Edward E. Kelly to Thomas Halloran. 8,400

Cooper st, s e s, 367 n e Evergreen av, 19.6x100, h & l. Hannah M. Rose to John Ock, New York. Mt. $3,200 and assessm't. 3,700

Cornelia st, n w s, 100 s w Evergreen av, 75x100. August Todebush to Christian Reiner. Mt. $4,000. nom

Cornelia st, s e s, 155 s w Evergreen av, 20x100. Richard Dreyer to Antonia wife of John Ernst. Mt. $3,200. 6,500

Cornelia st, s e s, 35 s w Evergreen av, 40x100; also,
Cornelia st, s e s, 155 s w Evergeen av, 20x100.
Release mort. Eburn F. Haight to Richard Dreyer. 4,500

Covert st, n w s, 130 n e Broadway, 20x100. Salome wife of and Peter Johnson to Moolusene Riedemann, of New York. Mt. $4,000. 6,850

Covert st, s e s, 90 n e Central av, 108x100. Release mort. Ida L. T. Ledoux to Isabelle B. Booth. nom

Covert st, s s, 126 e Central av, 18x100, h & l. Isabelle B. wife of John N. Booth to Rudolph and Otto E. Reimer. Mt. $3,000. 4,750

Cumberland st, w s, 177.3 n Myrtle av, 25x100. Partition. George F. Elliott to Alvan H. Williamson. 3,600

Dean st, n s, 157.4 w Grand av, 16.5x110, h & l. Clara Murdock to Andrew Anderson. 4,100

Dean st, w s, 100 e Albany av, 40x80. Frances J. Helfrich widow, of Jersey City, N. J., to Catharine M. Manning widow. Mt. $1,200 9,000

Dean st, s s, 200 w Classon av, 50x110, hs & ls. James Dunn, New York, to Edward E. Bergen. Mt. $7,000. nom

Same property. Edward E. Bergen to Silas A. Condict. Mt. $7,000. nom

Same property. Silas A. Condict to Samuel L. Bailey. Mt. $7,000. exch

Dean st, n s, 300 e Rockaway av, 25x107.2. John P. Schofield to Charles Leuchtmann. 750

Same property. Brooklyn City Co-operative Building and Loan Assoc. to John P. Schofield —

Dean st, s w s, 283.4 s e Smith st, 20.10x100. Cynthia M. Lewis widow, North Adams, Mass., to John McNamara. 5,000

Dean st, n s, 240 e Stone av, 40x107.2, hs & ls. Henry Meyer to James O'Halloran. Mt. $2,000. 4,250

Dean st, n s, 168.3 e Utica av, 84.11x107.2. Henry Weil to Charles A. Martin. 4,000

Decatur st, s e s, 58 e Patchen av, 18x82. William M. Seymour to Louis Hoelzle. Mt. $2,850. 5,250

Decatur st, s s, 40 e Patchen av, 18x82, h & l. Hyde & Gioad Mfg. Co. (Lim.) to George Schatz and Anna his wife, joint tenants. Mt. $2,850. nom

Decatur st, n s, 299.8 w Howard av, 0.4x100. Joseph P. Fuels to Thomas H Radcliffe. nom

Dikeman st, s w s, 125 n w Richards st, 25x100. Friedrich Kohlberger to Thornwald Olsen. 2,400

Douglass st, s s, 293.4 w 5th av, 16.8x100. John S. Loomis to Hannah Greve, of New York. Mt. $2,500. 4,100

Dresden st, e s, 110.1 n Atlantic av, 25x100. Charles E. Smith to Carll S. Burr, Jr., of Huntington, N. Y. exch

Eagle st, s s, 250 w Oakland st, 25x100. Mary McCluskey or Comasky widow to Bridget O'Brien. Q. C. nom

Eagle st, s s, 250 w Oakland st, 25x100, h & l. Bridget O'Brien widow to Andrew Blochle. 2,400

Eastern Parkway, s w cor Powell st, 50x100. Leon Weltfisch to Feige Kuverska. 1,500

Eastern Parkway, n e cor Atkins av, runs north 400 to Glenmore av, x east 200 to Montauk av, x south 200 x west 100 x south 20 x east 100 to Montauk av, x south 180 to Eastern Parkway, x west 200 to beginning. Marenus J. Goodenough to Bentley F. Adams. 17,000

Eastern Parkway, n s, 50 e Schenck av, 50x100. August Moll to Adolph Krueger, of New York. Mt. $2,500. 4,500

Eldert st, n s, 198 w Bushwick av, 54x100. Paul W. Ledoux to Margaretha Lewis. Mt. $13,500. nom

Eldert st, n w s, 198 s w Bushwick av, 54x100. Margaretha Lewis to Frank Hyde. Sub. to all liens. nom

Essex st, e s, 200 n Ridgewood av, 20x100. Henry W. Harding to W. Ryerson Kissam. Sub. to morts. 3,000

Floyd st, No. 247, n s, 350 w Sumner av, 25x100. Philipp Schoenbardt to William Funk. 3,000

Fort Greene pl, e s, 293.6 s Hanson pl, 20.6x100. Hendrich Haste to Annie A. wife of Jacob Klinck. Mt. $4,000. 7,600

Freeman st, s s, 145 w Franklin st, 25x100. Elizabeth Gash to Henry Ahlborn. Mt. $2,400. 3,250

Frost st, n s, 375 w Kingsland av, 25x100, h & l. Philip Taggert to Mary wife of said Philip Taggert. B. & S. gift

Fulton st, s s, 200 e Stone av, 50x100. David H. Beyer or Beyea to Edmund R. Collins. nom

Fulton st, n s, 42.4 e Irving pl, 18.8x122x20.5x113.8. Charles M. Howell to George Howell. Mt. $2,000. nom

Fulton st, No. 1442, s s, 200 e Brooklyn av, 20x100; also,
Fulton st, s s, 240 e Brooklyn av, 20x100.
Nathan Kaplan to George C. Jeffery. Mt. $16,000. nom

Same property. George C. Jeffery to Sarah E. Kaplan. Mt. $16,000. nom

Fulton st, s s, 300 w Albany av, 20x100. Asa L. Rogers to Joseph Hilton, Nyack, N. Y. Mt. $2,000. 4,315

Same property. Release judgment. Charles E. Rogers to Asa L. Rogers. nom

Fulton st, s s, 200 e Stone av, 50x100. Foreclos. John Courtney, Sheriff, to David H. Beyea. Mt. $6,000. 500

Fulton pl, w s, 120 n Livingston st, 22.11x50. Azel D., James, Georgianna H. and Gardiner D. Matthews to Frederick and Gustav Loeser and Howard and John Gibb. Mt. $2,500. nom

Fulton pl or alley running from Fulton to Livingston st, e s thereof and distant 125 w from Bond st and 70 n Livingston st, runs east 42 x north 10 x east 16 x north 20 x west 58 to alley, x south 30. Azel D., James, Georgianna H and Gardiner D. Matthews to Aaron S. Robbins. Mt. $3,000. nom

Gallatin pl, w s, 165.11 s Fulton st or av, 22.6x95.10, h & l. Josephine G. wife of Lewis M. Holton and Mary E. wife of Joseph Benedict to Azel D., James and Gardiner D. Matthews, of A. D. Matthews & Sons. nom

Garfield pl, n s, 227.6 e 5th av, 20x99.11x20x98.10. Elmira E. Christian to Mary F. Barry. Mt. $6,000. 8,050

Grand st, s s, 274.1 w Lorimer st, 24.5x110. William Ginste to Adolph Schmidt. Mt. $10,000. 11,300

Guernsey st, e s, 52.2 s Bedford av, 150x100. David Rice, of West Troy, N. Y., to The Builders' Wood Working Co. Mt. $6,500. transfer of stock

Guernsey st, s w s, 525 n w Nassau av, 42.10x100.2x37.2x100. The People's Trust Co. to Minnie, Ada and Gertrude Kuster by The People's Trust Co. guards. to John J. Leibfried. 3,750

Hall st, e s, 256.4 s Flushing av, 20x100. Melville Brown, of Hackensack, N. J., to James Kearney, of New York. Sub. to all liens. exch

Halsey st, n s, 84.8 e Sumner av, 20x85.11x20.1x84.1. Edward Driscoll to Asa W. Parker, of Hempstead, N. Y. 5,500

Halsey st, s e s, 120 s w Central av, 20x100. James Gascoine to Frances wife of John H. Quail. nom

Halsey st, s e s, 140 s w Central av, 20x100, h & l. James Gascoine to John T. Maxwell. nom

Halsey st, n s, 164 w Patchen av, 36x100, hs & ls. R Levy to Emma H. Hudson. Mt. $5,300 nom

Halsey st, No. 985, n w s, 125 n e Broadway, 20x100, h & l. Mary E. Metcalf to Greenleaf W. Crossman, New York. Mt. $2,300. 5,000

Hancock st, n s, 95 e Tompkins av, 18x100. Samuel Cregar to F. Marion McAllister, of Elizabeth, N. J. Mt. $5,000. nom

Hancock st, n w cor Lewis av, 30x100. Benjamin Wright to Frank G. Fardon Q. C. nom

Hancock st, s s, 195 w Tompkins av, 20x100. William H. and William Reynolds to Ella M. Jewett. Mt. $9,000. 15,000

Hancock st, n s, 99 e Sumner av, 18x100. Joel F. Tyler to Bellangee D. Paulin. Mt. $4,000. 7,300

Hancock st, n s, 145 w Ralph av, 16.8x85. Isreal Meyers to Adele F. Emmerson. Mt. $1,500. 3,200

Hancock st, s s, 275 w Tompkins av, 20x100, h & l. Title Guarantee and Trust Co. to William H. and William Reynolds. Release mort. 8,000

Same property. William H. Reynolds to John Dohse. exch

Hancock st, n s, 63 e Sumner av, 18x100 Joel F. Tyler to Robert Dunlap. Mt. $4,000. 7,500

Hancock st, s s, 255 w Tompkins av, 20x100, h & l. William H. Reynolds to Emily B. wife of Thomas B. Smith. Mt. $8,000. exch

Hancock st, s s, 20 e Sumner av, 17.6x80. Mary W. Prior, of Oyster Bay, N. Y., to Charles W. Hayes, of Rockville Centre, N. Y. Mt. $3,550. exch

Hancock st, n w s, 520 n e Bushwick av, 20x100. Henry Longman, of New York, to Constance Evans. Mt. $2,500. 4,500

Hancock st, n w cor Lewis av, 30x100. Frank G. Fardon, of Washington, D. C., to Josie wife of Frank S. Bonny. Mt. $1,850. nom

Harman st, n w s, 100 n e Central av, 50x100. Mary Haas to Andrew and Christian Hahn. nom

Harman st, No. 17, n w s, 180 s w Evergreen av, 20x100, h & l. Claus Heinbockel to Kresensia Baumann. Mt. $2,500. 5,100

Hart st, n s, 306 w Lewis av, 16x100. Miriam Rockwell to Annie S. Ennis. 5,750

Hendrix st, e s, 99.6 s Arlington av, 25x100. Arthur E. Sumner, of New York, to Emma A. Sumner. Mt. $2,500. 5,500

Hendrix st, e s, 100 n Belmont av, 25x100. Joseph Burley to Henry Shaddock. 2,800

Hendrix st, w s, 125 n Dumont av, 25x100. Jacob T. Van Siclen to John F. Wallberg. Sub. to taxes. 450

Herkimer st, s s, 50 w Howard av, 21x75. Edwin F. Corey, of New York, to Caleb S. Fordham. 3,000

Herkimer st, s s, 50 e Howard av, 16x98. Caspar Lucke to Jacob Pohs, New York. Mt. $2,350. 4,850

Herkimer st, n s, 150 w Ralph av, 25x100. Elizabeth wife of Adam Dauernheim to Johann Ebel. 2,300

Same property. Johann Ebel to The Roman Catholic Church St. Benedict. 2,300

Herkimer st, s s, 350 w Utica av, 36x92. Whitman Kenyon and Albro J. Newton to Maria E. Wachter. See Nevins st. exch

Hewes st, n s, 80 e Marcy av, 20x80, h & l. Augustus Wenzel to Thomas McGarry. 7,000

Hewes st, s s, 23.6 e Wythe av, 19x100, h & l. Richard Healy to William Wright and Ann his wife. Mt. $4,000. 8,600

Hicks st, No. 23. Assign. of contract. William H. Matlocks to Lewis A. Mitchell. nom

Hicks st, e s, 25.3 n Poplar st, 25.3x100. John Cottrell to Lewis A. Mitchell. nom

Hicks st, n e cor Poplar st, 25x100. Ida W. Edwards to Duncan Edwards. nom

Hopkins st, s s, 600 w Marcy av, 25x100. Johanna Rohlfs to David Mayer. Mt. $4,550. 1,100

Hopkins st, No. 226, s s, 150 w Sumner av, 25x100. Christian Huber to Hugo Basler. Mt. $2,500. 6,500

Hopkins st, n s, 325.4 e Throop av, 20x100. Franz Kautler to Christian Eppler and Theresa his wife Mt. $2,500. 4,600

Hull st, s s, 240 e Rockaway av, 15x100. Nathaniel F. Jones to Virginia Tenney. Mt. $3,500. 4,200

Hull st, n s, 337.6 e Rockaway av, 18.9x100, h & l. John H. Elfers to George Evans. Mt. $4,000. 4,600

Humboldt st, s w s, 81.2 n w Meeker av, 40.6x40.3x41x33.7. William Curtin to John D. Deetjen. 1,450

Huntington st, s s, 225 w Court st, 16.8x100. Michael J. McGuire to George C. M. Bander. Mt. $1,800. 3,000

Huntington st, s s, 100 e Hicks st, 20x200 to West 9th st; also,
39th st, s s, 175 e 5th av, 50x100.2; also,
½ part lots 406-409 map of heirs of George Marteuse, Flatbush, 100x100.
Joseph Foley to Thomas McGrath. nom

Huntington st, s s, 258.4 w Court st, 16.8x100, h & l. Adrienna I. Stevenson to Michael J. McGuire. 1,950

Huntington st, s s, 225 w Court st, 16.8x100. William H. Burroughs individ. exr. and trustee Sophia M. Burroughs to Michael J. McGuire. nom

Huron st, n s, 345 e Franklin st, 25x100. Peter Russell to Henry Kahn. Mt. $3,150. 3,800

Jefferson st, s e s, 280 n e Evergreen av, 20x100. John W. Stolzenberg to Charles F. W. Borchert. Mt. $1,800. 4,500

Jefferson st, n s, 100 w Knickerbocker av, 25x100, h & l. Johann G. and Edwart Dietz to Christian Mussler. Mt. $3,000. 5,800

Jerome st, w s, 175 s Atlantic av, 25x100. Release mort. Nina and Louise P. Jordan to Jacob Wien. 200

Same property. Jacob Wien to George Ott. 800

Johnson st, n s, 175 w Leonard st, 25x100. Margaretha Stoecker with Pauline Kohlmeyer. Agreement as to disposal of property. nom

Kosciusko st, n w s, 381.8 s w Bushwick av, 18x98.9. Emily M. wife of and John Herbold to Charles A. Liebman. 4,000

Kosciusko st, s s, 152.6 e Lewis av, 17.3x100, h & l. James S. and George F. Simpson to George B. Read. Mt. $4,500. 5,500

Kosciusko st, s s, 124.6 w Reid av, 25.6x100. Mathias Hauser to James and Martha Anderson. Mt. $7,700. exch

Kosciusko st, n s, 166.8 w Stuyvesant av, 16.8x100. Herman Stuetzer, Jr., to James P. Murphy. 4,100

Lawton st, n w s, 102.6 n e Bushwick av, runs northwest 90 x west 50 x southeast 90 to st, x east 50. Catherine T. Shay widow to Agnes A. McCormick. ½ part. nom

Leonard st, e s, 25 s McKibbin st, 25x100. H Cohn to Simon Brookman. Mt. $4,900. exch 9,000

Lincoln pl, n s, 100 e 5th av, 44x118.8. Israel W. Lyon to Henry B. Lyons. 5,600

Lincoln pl, westerly cor 7th av, runs southwest 80 x northwest 90 x southwest 20 x northwest 20 x northeast 50 to Lincoln pl, x southeast 110 to beginning. Thomas E. Warman, of North Plainfield, N. J., to Albert Scott. Mt. $15,000. exch and 2,000

Same property. Albert Scott to Hosmer B. Parsons. Mt. $15,000. 20,000

Linden st, s e s, 325 s w Central av, 25x100. Mary wife of Joseph F. Miller to Robert B. Muller. Mt. $600. 1,500

Same property Josephine Bowron extrx. Watson Bowron to same. om

Linden st, Nos. 106 and 108, e s, 175.11 n Evergreen av, 40x100, error, course omitted. Morris Piatigorsky to Charles Malawista, New York. Mt. $3,000. 8,000

Lorimer st, w s, 276.7 n Van Cott av, 25x100, h & l. Peter Lippert to Andrew Schuhlein. 2,500

Louis pl, e s, 20 n Atlantic av, 17x97.6. Gertrude Simon, of New York, to Mary A. Buckley. Mt. $3,550. 4,000

Lynch st, s s, 261.1 e Lee av, 25x100. Sarah A. and Martha R. World to Edmund J. Walsh. 6,850

Macon st, s s, 272.6 w Stuyvesant av, 17.6x100. Foreclos. John Courtney to Arthur Taylor. Mt. $4,500. 3,000

Macon st, n s, 76 w Ralph av, 18x100, h & l. Benjamin C. Raymond to Henry B. Snow. Mt. $5,500. 6,800

Macon st, n s, 58 w Ralph av, 18x100. Benjamin C. Raymond to Heydon Starrett. Mt. $5,500. 7,000

Macon st, n s, 175 w Lewis av, 20.9x100. Daniel B. Norris to Susie D. wife of Frederick B. Norris. nom

Macon st, n s, 215.6 w Lewis av, 19.9x100. Daniel B. Norris to Eliza W. Mason. Mt. $4,200. 9,000

Macon st, s s, 194.6 w Lewis av, 0.6x100. Mary E. Ross to Daniel B. Norris. 250

Madison st, n s, 310 e Nostrand av, 20x100, h & l. Emily B. wife of Thomas B. Smith to William H. Reynolds. 7,000

Madison st, n s, 200 w Lewis av, 20x100. Rufus L. Scott to Robert P. Wilson. 8,000

Magenta st, s s, 125 w Railroad av, 25x100, h & l. George Bennett to Charles F. Cramer. 1,100

Main st or State road, n e s, 200.8 n w 16th av, 251.9x203.8 to centre 83d st, x 250x202.10, New Utrecht. Albert V. B. Voorhies to Cornelia E. Voorhees. B & S. nom

McDonough st, s s, 175.4 e Ralph av, 18.5x100. Thomas H. Radcliff to John A. Lamphear. Mt. $4,500. 6,800

McDonough st, s s, 216.8 e Reid av, 16.8x100. Henry B. Hill to Sarah A. Short. Mt. $4,000. 6,300

McDougal st, No. 198, s s, 249.7 e Hopkinson av, 25.5x100. Catherine M. Manning to Francis J. Helfrich, of Jersey City, N. J. Mt. $5,500. 10,000

Melrose st, n w s, 325 n e Broadway, 25x95. Elizabeth Fruh to John Young. om

Midwood st, s s, 180 e Albany av, 20x100, Flatbush. Anna G. wife of and Sidney Williams to John Thomas Cody. 175

Same property. Release mort. Christopher C. Walson to Anna G. Williams. 100

Milford st, e s, 150 n Liberty av, 25x100. Stephen W. Stoothoff to Jacob J. Knox. Mt. $1,600. 2,500

Monroe st, s s, 345 w Nostrand av, 20x65.6x20 x63.6, h & l. Jean G. Van Kleeck to Owen Morgan. 2,900

Monroe st, s s, 325 w Nostrand av, 20x63.6x20x 61.6, h & l. Jean G. Van Kleeck to Alfred Morgan, Jr. 2,900

Monroe st, n s, 199 w Reid av, 18.4x100. Mary F. Creney to Mary M. Webster. Mt. $2,250. 3,600

Monroe st, s s, 345 e Bedford av, 20x87.6x20.1x 89.6. George Ingraham, Flushing, L. I., to Daniel P. Morse. 8,500

Monroe st, s s, 486.6 w Throop av, 19.3x100, h & l. Martha J. wife of William H. Vogell to Jennie L. Storm. Mt. $3,000. 7,900

Moore st, s s, 63.6 w Smith st on old map now Humboldt st, 11.6x100x46x104.6. Margaret Fifer to Lawrence White. ⅙ part. 1886. 125

Moore st, n s, 225 e Graham av, 25x100, h & l. Margaretha Appel to David Stern and Solomon Blatteis. 7,000

Montague st, s s, 179 e Hicks st, 25x100. Charles M. Clarke to John Boyle. Q. C. nom

Nassau st, w s, 50 n 1st st, 25x150, 26th Ward. Mahala E. Morris, Mary E. Mapes, Jane M. Beatty and George W. Von Volkenburgh to Margaret Blood. 2,700

Nevins st, e s, 40 s Sackett st, 20x80. Thomas Wilson to Michael Farrell. 1,615

Nevins st, n e cor President st, 40x80. Maria E. Wachter widow and devisee John Wachter to Whitman Kenyon and Albro J. Newton. See Herkimer st. exch

New Lots road, n s, 21.1 w John st, 42.2x87x 40x73.8. Albert Sibley to William W. Clayton. 400

Oakland st, w s, 190.6 n Van Cott av, 25x100. Andrew E. Walker to Charles F. Neidig. Mt. $3,500. 7,250

Oakland st, e s, 75 s Nassau av, 25x75. Conrad Meyer to Maurice G Quinlan. 5,050

Osborn st, e s, 225 s Dumont av, 25x100. Catharine L. Babcock to James O'Halloran. 350

Pacific st, s s, 56 e Hicks st, 18x100. William Holzapfel to John F. Boyn or Bayne. Mt. $4,200. 5,200

Pacific st, s w s, 50 s e Hoyt st, 25x100. Mary J. Halstead widow to Joseph J. Zapf and Julius Lobel, of New York. 6,200

Palmetto st, n w s, 200 n e Irving av, 25x100. Frank Duffrin to Lucinda Ellingworth. Mt. $2,500. exch

Park pl, n s, 96.6 e 5th av, 17.8x100. Henry B. Lyon to Hattie Dreyfus. Mt. $5,500. 8,000

Park pl, s s, 334.7 e 6th av, 20x100. John T. Rockwell, of East Orange, N. J., to Mary A. C. Atmuller. 8,750

Penn st, n s, 151.4 e Bedford av, 21.7x100. Helen F. Burnett extrx. James P. Burnett to Edmund W. Burnett. 4,000.

Pilling st, w s, 428.7 n Broadway, 16.5x100, h & l. Henry R. Fechtmann to Eliza M. Stackhouse. Mt. $2,100. exch

President st, n s, 115 w Bond st, 20x100. Herman Wronkow to Richard O'Brien. Mt. $3,000. 3,800

Prospect pl, s s, 100 w Vanderbilt av, 25x131. Edward M. Clark to Charles McDonnell. 4,600

Prospect st, n s, 150 w Bridge st, 25x74. Ellen Dougherty to James Sullivan, of New York. 4,600

Quincy st, s s, 208.4 e Patchen av, 16.8x100. Ada E. Bedell to Lydia M. Howard. Mt. $2,700. exch

Ralph st, n w s, 100 n e Hamburg av, 200x100. John D. Fish, of Hempstead, N. Y., to Edward Vanderkar. Mt. $3,900, taxes 1890. 10,500

Raymond st, w s, 125 s Bolivar st, 25x75. }
Stone av, w s, 25 s Somers st, 25x80. }
Charles S. Kendall, of New York, to Henry Putzel. Mt. $11,000. nom

Richardson st, n s, 120 w Lorimer st, 20x100. Maria Casella to Sarah Schindel. Mt. $500. 1,800

Sackman st, w s, 150 n Belmont av, 50x100. Samuel Tepfer to Rosie wife of said Samuel Tepfer. Mt. $2,700. 450

Schaeffer st, n s, 156 w Hamburg av, 16x100. Katharine Piehl to Gustav Hagel. Sub. to liens. nom

Schermerhorn st, s s, 24.10 w Nevins st, 18.9x 100. Frank Audemars to Florian Grosjean. 8,500

Seigel st, s s, 125 w Graham av, 25x100, h & l. Morris Berger to Mary Jarashow. All liens. 4,500

Skillman st, e s, 36 s Willoughby av, 18x50. Harold L. Crane to Katie Tresham. 2,500

Somers st, s s, 44.6 e Rockaway av, runs east 18.6 x south 72.8 x west 16 x north 3 x west 2.6 x north 69.3. John S. Ladd to Eliza A. Palmer. Mt. $8,000. 10,000

Starr st, s e s, 75 s w Hamburg av, 25x100. Patrick Tuohy to August Dess. Mt. $2,500. 6,050

Steuben st, e s, 175 s De Kalb av, 22.4x100. Peter Herche, of New York, to Adelaide E. Jobston. Mt. $11,000. nom

Steuben st, w s, 245 s Park av, 20x100. William Mullin to Frank Colgan. nom

Stewart st, n s, 199 e Bushwick av, 17x100. Henry Weil to Josephine wife of William P. Dunham. 1,600

Strong pl, e s, 260 s Harrison st, 17.5x98x16.8x 98. John T. Mygatt trustee of grantees to Grace A. Birdsall formerly Trubee and Frank C. Trubee. nom

Strong pl, e s, 352.11 s Harrison st, runs east 50 x east 56.2 x south 47 x northwest 114.2 to Strong pl, x north 8.1. Benjamin A. Hegeman exr. Charles Kelsey to Louis Lehn. nom

Strong pl, e s, 282.6 n Degraw st, runs east 106.2 x north 13.6 x west 56.4 x west 50 to pl, x south 16.9. Louis Lehn to Bessie O. wife of Harry N. Covell. 7,750

Stockton st, s s, 200 w Lewis av, 25x100. James Anderson to Mathias Hauser. Mt. $1,000. exch

Stockholm st, n w s, 241.8 n e Evergreen av, 16.8x100. Oscar J. Chase to William F. Ryan. Mt. $1,400. 3,000

Stockholm st, s e s. 200 n e Evergreen av, runs southeast 100 x southwest 18.9 x northwest 57.5 x northeast 0.4½ x northwest to st, x northeast 18.7, h & l. James A. Caufield or Canfield to Oscar J. Chase. 5,000

St. Johns pl, s s, 339.7 e 6th av, runs east 20 x south 100 x west 9.7 x north 8.8 x west 10.5 x north 91.9. William Flanagan to James Wood, New York. 15,200

St. Marks pl, n s, 400 w 5th av, 20x100. Louis Kathe to Edgar W. Young. 6,600

Sumpter st, s s, 120 w Rockaway av, runs south 100 x west 20.4 x north — x west .02 to point 140.6 w Rockaway av, thence to Sumpter st, thence along Sumpter st 20.6 to beginning. Foreclos. John Courtney, Sheriff, to Joseph Liebman. 2,000

Taylor st, s e s, 406 s w Wythe av, runs southeast 25 x southwest 102.11 to Kent av, x northwest 25.1 to st, x northeast 104.3. Sarah E. Kirk to Frederick G. Feldbusch. Mt. $11,000. 17,000

Ten Eyck st, s s, 60 e Lorimer st, 30x100, h & l. Francis J. Rodney, Nanuet, N. Y., to Mary Noonan. 4,100

Tillary st, n s, 99.8 e Raymond st, 26.7x100. John Gardello to Catherine Gardello. ½ part. Mt. $10,000. 1,000

Same property. Catharine Green admrx. of Thos. Green, Catharine and William Green and Emma F. wife of James McGough to Peter Jahnsen or Johnson, John Gardella, Enrico Garwazzio and Salvator Guarnieri. Mt $9,000. 18,300

Troutman st, n s, bet Wyckoff and Irving avs, being lot 12 block 896 assessment map 18th Ward. John C. McGuire, Registrar, to Peter Comerford. 3[illegible]

Same property. Peter Comerford to James Carroll. 375

Truxton st, n s, 60 w Stone av, 40x80. John Fallon to Stephen P. Sturges. Mt. $5,000 nom

Union st, n s, 331.3 w 8th av, 18.9x90. Foreclos. Frank Pettit ref. to Henry F. Ogden. 7,000

Union st, n s, 312.6 w 8th av, 18.9x90. Foreclos. Same to same. 7,000

Union st, n s, 200 w 8th av, 18.9x90. Foreclos. Same to same. 7,000

Van Brunt st, s e s, 70.2 s w King st, 20x90, h & l. Margaret Gorman to Martin Flanigan. 8,000

Van Buren st, n s, 400 w Patchen av, 25x100. George W. Van Hoesen heir Martha Van Hoesen to Abram H. Van Hoesen. nom

Van Voorhis st, n w s, 269.11 s w Evergreen av, 17x100. Foreclos. John Courtney, Sheriff, to Julian Lucas. 3,500

Warren st, s s, 200 w Buffalo av, 25x127.9. Foreclos. Samuel N. Garrison to John Robinson. 1,200

Warren st, n s, 50 e 3d av, 25x100. Frank Hyde to Margaretha Lewis. Sub. to all liens. nom

Watkins st, w s, 126.6 s Eastern Parkway, 25x 100. Release mort. Mary W. Smith to Ada wife of Lewis Parmer. nom

Same property. Release mort. Herbert C. Smith to same. 875

Watkins st, e s, 100 s Dumont av, 25x100. Catharine L. Babcock to James O'Halloran. 300

Same property. Release mort. Charles R. Lynde to Catharine L. Babcock. nom

Watkins st, w s, 126 s Eastern Parkway, 25x 100. Ada wife of Lewis Parmer to William Smolinsky. Mt. $2,500. 4,500

Weirfield st, n w s, 201.2 s w Central av, 20x 100. Leopold J. Lippman to Annie C. wife of Howard D. Allen. nom

Same property. Release mort. Oliver W. Coe, of New York, to Leopold J. Lippman. 2,477

Weirfield st, n w s, 261 s w Central av, 20x100. Release mort. Oliver W. Coe, of New York, to Leopold J. Lippman. 2,477

Same property. Leopold J. Lippman to John Ruppel. nom

Weirfield st, n w s, 141.2 s w Central av, 20x 100. Leopold J. Lippmann to John Brady, Jr. 4,600

Same property. Release mort. Oliver W. Coe to Leopold J. Lippmann. 2,475

Weirfield st, n w s, 181.2 s w Central av, 20x 100. Release mort. Oliver W. Coe to Leopold J. Lippmann. 2,475

Same property. Leopold J. Lippmann to Mary Lennon. nom

West st, e s, 160 s Av I, 60x100, New Utrecht. James Cropsey to Annie Keefe, New York. Mt. $2,250. 4,200

Windsor pl, s s, 279.10 e 7th av, 13.8x100, h & l. Mary A. wife of Willis B. Goodsell to Thomas J. Griffin. Mt. $1,100. 2,300

2d st, n e s, 277.9 n w 7th av, 18x100. Erik G. P. Wern to Charles G. Peterson. Mt. $6,158. exch

North 2d st, s s, 125 w Humboldt st, 25x100, h & l. Jacob Geist to Ludwig Asmus. 4,000

South 2d st, s s, 45 e Havemeyer st, 20x78. Charles Bernard, of Chicago, Ill., to Charles H. Bernard, Eleanor T. Baker, Annie L. Fink, and Florence M. Bernard and Julie B. Gorman, of Evanston, Ill., and Edward W. Bernard, of Indiana. nom

Same property. Charles H. Bernard et al. to Martha Davids. 4,800

3d st, n s, 20 w Bond st, 20x74.6. Julia Tepe widow to James J. and Thomas F. Reilly. 3,500

East 3d st, e s, 105.7 n Fort Hamilton av, 45.4x 100x11.2x105.7, Flatbush. Jennie V. Wilbur to Mary A. Hogan. 275

South 3d st, s s, 150 w Havemeyer st, 25x95. Evadna P. Green to Ellen wife of Francis Kelly. 4,625

4th st, s s, 233.10 w 7th av, 19x100, h & l. Eliza A. Fanton to Louis H. Myers, Jr. Mt. $6,600. nom

4th st, s s, 252.10 w 7th av, 19x100. Fannie M. Moses to Louis H. Myers, Jr. Mt. $6,600. nom

South 4th st, n e s, 300 s e Keap st, 25x95. Matthaus Beck to Charles Keil. 14,800

South 4th st, s s, 171.6 w 4th st, 23x100. Release mort. James L. Truslow and Gilbert Potter exrs. Gilbert Potter to Samuel L. Hill. 3,500

Same property. Samuel L. Hill to Thomas Smith. 4,850

South 4th st, s w s, 25 n w Hewes st, 25x76.4. Michael Jaeger to Charles Lewis. Mt. $1,000. 3,200

5th st, s s, 197.10 w 5th av, 20x100. Charles H. Denison to Charles D. Burwell and Frank A. Barnaby. Mt. $4,500. nom

Same property. Release mort. The Title Guarantee and Trust Co. to same. nom

Same property. Charles D. Burwell and Frank A. Barnaby to Charles H. Denison. nom

North 6th st, n s, 25 w Wythe av, 25x100. William Gross by Emil Kuhl guard. to Ernest Erdmann. 198

Same property. Magdalena Gross to same. 2,801

7th st, n e s, 166.7 s e 4th av, 18.9x100. Louis H. Muller to Louis Bonert. Mt. $3,000. exch

East 9th st, w s, 320 s Av M, 120x100, Gravesend. Thomas Ferguson to The Reformed Protestant Dutch Church of Gravesend nom

10th st, n e s, 97.10 n w 8th av, 20x100. James F. Ransom to Kate Newman. 9,000

Same property. Release mort. Charles E. Rogers to James F. Ransom. nom

10th st, s w s, 131 s e 5th av, 18.8x100. George H. Schneider to Frank M. Davis. *Mt.* $1,700. 5,500

10th st, n e s, 60 s e 4th av, 20x80. John Hatton to Frederick A. Phillips, Jr. *Mt.* $5,000. 7,500

11th st, n e s, 130.4 n w 9th av, 18.6x100. Charles G. Peterson to Erik G. P. Wern. *Mt.* $6,000. exch

11th st, n e s, 295.11 n w 5th av, 16.8x100. Virginia D. wife of Willis Halstead to Clayton E. Wood. *Mt.* $3,500. 4,950

12th st, n s, 229.9 e 5th av, 16.8x75. Charlotte E. Lundequist, of East Orange, N. J., to John Gosling. 3,300

13th st, s s, 97.10 e 5th av, 25x100. John E. Green to Mary A. Bennet. 4,000

West 13th st, w s, 160 s Av S, 60x100, Bensonhurst. James D. Lynch to H. Augusta Wilcox. 750

14th st, No. 441, n s, 97.6 from 8th av, 26x100. Contract. Martha S. Hawkins to Isaac Spiero. 6,600

14th st, s s, 157.10 w 5th av, 20x100. Release dower. Annie L. Hyland widow to William Cleverley. 658

Same property. Christopher, Denis and Sarah Hyland by Annie L. Hyland guard. to same, infant's share. 3,250

14th st, s s, 83.4 e 6th av, 14.6x71. Louis A. Emich to Claudius H. Dumahut. 2,725

14th st, s s, 376.10 w 5th av, 18x100. John McDowell, of New York, to James Heaney. nom

Same property. James Heaney to Annie wife of John McDowell. nom

15th st, s s, 65.10 w 4th av, 22x100. Bernard Cosgrove to Mary M. wife of John W. Metcalf. 4,100

15th st, s s, 232.2 w 5th av, 12.6x100. Joseph W. Ray to Joanna B. Barkeloo. *Mt.* $420. 1,600

15th st, s s, 122.10 e 7th av, runs south 100 x east 25 x 65.3 x west 8.8 x north 34.8 to st, x west 17.2. Adrian Degraff to Charlotte A. Bierds. *Mt.* $500. 900

16th st, s w s, 242.10 s e 10th av, 21x100. Peter B. Bracken to Charles Froehlich. *Mt.* $1,500. 2,100

16th st, s s, 224.3 e 4th av, 17x100. Charles L. Prindle to Margaret L. Smith. 3,300

Bay 17th st, w s, 125 n Bath av, 96.8x100, New Utrecht. Elisha Kingsland to Charlotte M. Johnston. 5,500

18th st, s w s, 142.8 s e 5th av, 17.8x100. John A. Williams to Samuel J. Thatcher. 3,400

19th st, s s, 250 e 3d av. 25x100. Frances wife of C. Fleuter to Charles E. Parsons. *Mt.* $1,200. nom

19th st, s s, 303 w 8th av, 15.6x100.2. Henry C. Bull, of Blythebourne, N. Y., to Claude V. Gentry. *Mt.* $1,500. 2,650

19th st, s s, 287.6 w 8th av, 15.6x100.2. Same to same. *Mt.* $1,500. 2,650

19th st, s s, 272 w 8th av, 15.6x100.2. Same to same. *Mt.* $1,500. 2,650

Bay 20th st, n w s, 280 s w 86th st, 40x96.8, New Utrecht. John V. Van Pelt to Margaret Costello, of New York. 800

Bay 20th st, n w s, 240 s w 86th st, 40x96.8, New Utrecht. Same to Sarah McDonald, of New York. 800

Bay 22d st, n w s, 165 n e Bath av, 60x96.8, New Utrecht. Joseph Stehlin to James Devlin. 1,650

Bay 25th st, s e s, 420 n e Benson av, 60x96.8, New Utrecht. Lillian M. and Alfred Farrar to Nathaniel Tuttle, New York. 7,000

Bay 26th st, w s, 292.6 n Cropsey av, 60x96.8, New Utrecht. Edwina W. wife of William C. Brose to Mary L. Ruger. *Mt.* $1,000. 1,650

32d st, n s, 260 w 5th av, 100x100.2. Ernest Sass, New York, to William Walsh. *Mt.* $2,500. 3,000

Same property. William Walsh to Mary J. Lucke. *Mt* $2,500. 3,300

Bay 35th st, n w s, 140 s w 86th st, 60x96.8, Gravesend. Franklin B. Case widower to Theodore B. Case. 1,000

38th st, n s, 85 w 5th av, 40x100.2. Release mort. The South Brooklyn Co-operative Building and Loan Assoc. to Annie Wiggins. 800

42d st, n e s, 94.4 n w Fort Hamilton av, 100x100.2, New Utrecht. Richard Hawley to Noe Trahan. 4,200

43d st, s s, 325 e 5th av, runs south 78.8 x west — x north 74.2 to 43d st, x east 25 to beginning. William Butler, of San Diego, Cal., to James W. White. Sub. to mort. 500

45th st, s w s, 140 n w 4th av, 20x80. Jane A. MacDowell to Caroline Winarski. *Mt.* $3,500. 4,500

47th st. s w s, 100 s e 4th av. Party wall agreement. Alexander Waldron with Annie Israel. nom

50th st, n s, 120 w 4th av, 60x100.2. John Koski to John Lindner. Sub. to all liens. 425

52d st, s s, 160 w 5th av, 20x100.2. George H. Parshall to Louis Bradfisch and Clarence E. Hopkins. 700

52d st, s s, 180 w 5th av, 20x100.2. John Ennis to same. 800

53d st, n s, 160 w 5th av, 60x100.2. Rutherford W. Woodhead by guard. to Louis Bradfisch and Clarence E. Hopkins. 2,250

53d st, s s, 100 w 6th av, 100x100.2, 8th Ward. Robert W. Firth to Sarah Burgess. *Mt.* $420. 2,000

54th st, n s, 100 w 4th av, 140x100.2. Daniel, Abraham, Sivert, Lene B. and Lars Larsen, Berthe L. Tomesen widow and Sarah wife of Tormes Olsen heirs Andreas B. Larsen to Peder A. Larsen. B. & S. nom

56th st, n e s, 100 s e 14th av, 50x100.2, New Utrecht. West Brooklyn Land and Improvement Co. to Helena Fuchs, New York. 1,000

62d st, s s, 440 w 14th av, 20x100, New Utrecht. James V. S. Woolley to Nils P. Johnson. 175

66th st, s s, 220 e 13th av, 40x100, New Utrecht. Effingham H. Nichols to Helen McL. Abbott. 460

67th st, s s, 180 e 13th av, 20x125, New Utrecht. Effingham H. Nichols to Joseph B. Nosworthy. 185

67th st, s s, 100 e 11th av, 40x130, New Utrecht. Brooklyn City Co-operative Building and Loan Assoc. to Samuel Loring. 2,967

67th st, s s, 500 e 4th av, 60x100, New Utrecht. James W. Murphy and Michael McCormick to Flora wife of Emil Knopp. 1,350

67th st, s s, 140 e 14th av, 60x120, Lefferts Park. Effingham H. Nichols to John Hurley, New York. 825

72d st, n s, 390 w 15th av, 40x100, Lefferts Park. James V. S. Woolley to John Elliott. 400

73d st, s w s, 310 s e 3d av, 60x100, hs & ls. John A. Lindsey to Thomas Gillespie. nom

74th st, s s, 410 w 15th av, 40x100, Lefferts Park. James V. S. Woolley to Robert Brown. 320

74th st, s s, 503.2 w 18th av, 40x100, New Utrecht, John H. Hanley to Nels M. Nelson. 550

74th st, s s, 130 w 15th av, 20x100, New Utrecht. Maria J. Stokes to David C. Beatty. 250

75th st, centre line, at centre line 11th av, runs northeast 234.3 x west 496.1 x southwest 43 to centre 75th st, x southeast 507.4.
Interior lot, on centre line, bet 76th and 77th sts, at point 480 n w 11th av, runs northwest 22.7 x northeast 264.10 x southwest 263.10.
Interior lot, on line bet lands of parties hereto, bet 72d and 73d sts, 120 n w 13th av, runs northeast 110.4 x east 12.2 x southwest 116.2, New Utrecht.
Franklin Allen to The Bay Ridge Park Improvement Co. exch

76th st, s s, 90 w 15th av, 20x74.11x20x75.6, Lefferts Park. James V. S. Woolley to James Lindsay. 175

76th st, centre line, at north line of grantor's land, runs west 74.6 x southwest 27.7 x east 79.6.
Interior lot, on centre line, bet 75th and 76th sts, 160 n w 11th av, runs southwest 98.4 x east 282.10 x northwest 265.2
Interior lot, on north line of land of grantee, at point 160 s e 11th av, runs east 286.10 to centre 75th st, x northwest 268 11 x southwest 99.8, New Utrecht.
Franklin Allen to Hoik D. Campbell. exch

76th st, s s, 110 w 15th av, 20x75.6, Lefferts Park. James V. S. Woolley to Mary A. L. Lindsay. 125

81st st, s s, 240 w 1st av, runs west to line bet R. J. and C. B. Van Brunt's property, x southeast along same to point 240 w of 1st av, x north — to beginning, New Utrecht. Rulef J. Van Brunt to Cornelius B. Van Brunt. nom

82d st, n s, 200 w 1st av, runs north to line bet C. B. and R. J. Van Brunt's property, runs northwest to point 240 w of 1st av, x south to 82d st, x east 40, New Utrecht. Cornelius B. Van Brunt to Rulef J. Van Brunt. nom

Alabama av, e s, 125 s Liberty av, 25x100. Charles Ries to Henry Ries. ½ part. *Mt.* $1,500. 1,500

Albany av, w s, 88.11 n Butler st, 16.8x85. George C. Case to George O. Fortescue, of Buffalo, N. Y. *Mt.* $3,800. 6,000

Atlantic av, n s, 150 e Utica av, 225x99.1 to Brooklyn & Jamaica R. R. Joseph B. Philson to Henry J. Davison, New York. C. a. G. nom

Atlantic av, n s, 89 e Suydam pl, 15x88.10. John Dhuy to Leopold de Arrastia. *Mt.* $1,700. 3,300

Atlantic av, n s, 80.7 e Georgia av, 20.3x80.2x20x82.10. Abraham Schlank, of Jamaica, L. I., to Lewis Krieger. Sub. to liens. 7,000

Atlantic av, s s, 225 w Bond st, 25x90, h & l. Lottie N. Palmer to Thomas Green. nom

Atlantic av, s s, 133 e Rockaway av, 16 8x100. John S. Ladd to Eliza A. Palmer, of Babylon, L. I. *Mt.* $2,000. 4,000

Arlington av, n e cor Essex st, 50x100. Charles J. Laderer, of Newtown, N. Y., to Christian A. Keppler. *Mt.* $3,050. 6,000

Bedford av, e s, 40.3 n South 1st st, 20.3x81x18.6x81. Foreclos. John Courtney to John F. Werner. 4,900

Bedford av, e s, 140 s Halsey st, 201.3x75.6. Annie Y. wife of and David H. Fowler to Michael McNamee. *Mt.* $1,500. nom

Bedford av, n w cor Putnam av, runs west 80 x north 200 to Madison st, x east 80 x south 200 to beginning; also,
Fulton st, s s, 40 w South Oxford st, runs west 40 x south 60 x southeast 30 to Hanson pl, x east 33 x northwest 26.2 x northeast 14 x north 35.1 to beginning; also,
Hanson pl, n e cor Portland av, runs north 69.11 x east 31 x northeast 68.3 to Fulton st, x southeast 40 x southwest 39.5 x south 72.2 to Hanson pl, x west 80; also,
Fulton st, s w s, 68.5 s e Portland av, runs southwest 59.1 x west 20 to Portland av, x south 20 x east 31 x northeast 68.3 to Fulton st, x northwest 20; also,
Franklin av, w s, 40 s Madison st, runs west 80 x south 60 x east 80 to Franklin av, x north 60; also,
Lexington av, n s, 234.5 w Franklin av, 30x121.7.
Julia A. wife of Dudley B. Holrook to Sarah A., Lillian B. and Harriet M. Terrett and Sarah L. Holt. 1-27 part. nom

Buffalo av, w s, 52.8 e Prospect pl, .01½x52. William L. Beers to John Robinson. nom

Bushwick av, e s, 82.11 s Jackson st, 25x100. Daniel Godfrey, John, Louisa and Frederick Haupert by Godfrey Haupert guard. to Frank and Concreta Otto. 1-3 part. 532

Bushwick av, e s, 82.11 s Jackson st, 25x100, h & l. Theresa A. wife of John McNichol and Sarah C. wife of Frank Vandeweldt to Frank and Concreta Otto, joint tenants. ⅔ part. 1,118

Central av, w s, 24.6 s Myrtle st, 24.6x100.4x23.9x94.4. Friedrich Kirschenheiter to Mary A. wife of and Valentine Ulirich, joint tenants. Correction deed. 2,975

Central av, e s, 25 s Hart st, 7.1x102.11x31.5x100. William O'Dwyer to Michael J. Mulhern. 900

Central av, westerly cor Palmetto st, 25x100. Adam Schneider to Johann H. Maasz, of New York. 10,500

Christopher av, n e cor Eastern Parkway, 100x100. Joseph Solomon and Hyman Goldberg to Constant Liegedis. *Mt.* $2,200. 3,400

Clason av. w s, 145 n Lafayette av, 15x100. Mary widow Richard Powell, of North Hempstead, N. Y., and John G. Powell, of Cocoa, Fla., heirs Richard Powell to D. Frank Powell, of Roslyn, N. Y. nom

De Kalb av. s s, 50 e Evergreen av, 25x79.6. Anna Frey to George Covert. 7,000

De Kalb av, n s, 42 w Waverly av, 27x83.6, h & l. George E. Fahys to Antoinette G. H. Fahys. nom

Division av, n s, 40.4 w 7th st, now Havemeyer st, 20.2x70. Clark D. Rhinehart, late Sheriff, to James Rowland and Walter Burt. 40

East New York av, s s, 192.7 w Albany av, 25x200 to Furnald st, Flatbush. Foreclos. John Courtney, Sheriff, to Elihu Ayres, of New York. 1,193

Evergreen av, w s, 100 n Willoughby av, 25x100, h & l. Jane Peffers widow to Jakob Freist. 8,500

Evergreen av, w s, 75 s Schaeffer st, 25x100. William G. Wehr to Sophie J. Krause. *Mt.* $3,500. nom

Evergreen av, e s, 100 s Stanhope st, 35 5x100x32.7x100. John Griffin, Jr., to Carl A. Evertz 2,400

Evergreen av, e s, 58.9 n Cedar st, 18.9x75. William Coar to Mary Bell. *Mt.* $200. nom

Same property. Mary Bell to Grace wife of William Coar. *Mt.* $200. nom

Flushing av, n w s, 315.7 s w Knickerbocker av, 25x87.8x25.11x80.11, h & l. Catherine Weber to Nanni Straus. *Mt.* $3,500. 6,300

Flushing av, s w cor Marcy av, 25x100. Partition deed. William B. Hurd, Jr., to Peter Feeley. 9,900

Franklin av, No. 443, e s, 80 s Madison st, 20x90. Sarah A., Lillian R. and Herriet M. Terrett and Sarah L. Holt to Julia A. wife of Dudley B. Holbrook, Sing Sing, N. Y. 26-27 part. nom

Same property. George Howell to Mary L. wife of Charles M. Howell. *Mt.* $2,000. nom

Gates av, s s, 125 e Bedford av, 100x100. Peter De Witt to William G. De Witt. All title as an heir of G. G. De Witt. nom

Gates av, n w s, 140.3 n e Broadway, runs northwest 100 x northeast 19.9 x southeast 37.7 x northeast 0.4 x southeast 10 x southwest 0.4 x southeast 45.1 to av, x southwest 19.9. Charles J. Nielsen to Charles A. Cross. *Mt.* $6,500. nom

Gates av, n w s, 250 s w Irving av, 25x125.10x25x125.3, h & l. Andrew Schmidt to John Hirn. 4,500

Glenmore av, n s, 100 e Thatford av, 25x100, h & l. James Asher to Jacob Strauss. *Mt.* $1,900. 3,300

Graham av, s w cor Boerum st, 50x25. Valentin Zimmerman to Barbara Wagner. 6,200

Graham av, e s, 40.5 s Van Pelt av, 70.2x75.
Van Pelt av, s s, 80.10 e Graham av, 27x70.2x25x80.4.
Charles Engert to Anton Mehling. 5,800

Greene av, n w cor Patchen av, 20x81.9, h & l. John Von Olsen to William Stolzenberg. *Mt.* $3,000. 14,500

Greene av, n s, 50 w Stuyvesant av, 25x100, h & l. Letitia McC. Hartell to Richard F. Magau. *Mt.* $3,500. 4,000

Greene av, s s, 100 e Reid av, 40x100, hs & ls. Sarah E. wife of Nathan Kaplan to Oliver Markham, Middletown, Conn. *Mt.* $11,000. 18,500

Hale av, w s, 275 n Arlington av, 25x100. Contract for property. Ellen J. A. wife of Peter J. Fitzsimmons to Menna Weidlich, of New York. 2,400

Hamburg av, n e s, 43.9 s e Woodbine st, 18.9x100. Jacob Manneschmidt to Alois Wabenbauer. exch

Hamburg av, n e s, 43.9 s e Woodbine st, 18.9x100. Release mort. James Gascoine to Jacob Manneschmidt. 2,061

Same property. Same to same. 2,061

Hamburg av, n e s, 43.9 n w Madison st, 18.9x80, h & l. Jacob Manneschmidt to George Uihlein. nom

Same property. Release mort. James Gascoine to Jacob Manneschmidt. 2,062

Hamburg av, east cor Woodbine st, 175x80.
Woodbine st, s e s, 80 n e Hamburg av, 20x100.

James Gascoine individ. and with ano. exrs. John G. Cozine to James Gascoine. Correction deed. nom

Hamburg av, n e s, 62.6 s e Weodbine st, 18.9x100, h & l. Jacob Manneschmidt to Martin Gebhardt. nom

Hamburg av, n e s, 62.6 n w Madison st, 18.9x80. Jacob Manneschmidt to Ludwig Petry. nom

Harrison av, n e cor Gerry st, 25x100. Mary E. Ecker extrx. Elizabeth Brunagel to Andreas Meth. 9,400

Jefferson av, No. 1133, n w s, 115 s w Evergreen av, 20x100, h & l. Mary C. wife of John H Meyers, Meriden, Conn., to Elizabeth Hachmeister, New York. *Mt.* $2,500. 5,200

Jefferson av, s s, 330 w Nostrand av, 40x100. Sarah M. Bussing, of Mount Kisco, N. Y., to David Martling. *Mt.* $13,000. 500

Johnson av, s s, 200 e Humboldt st, 25x100. Levy Clar to Gerson Krakauer and Nathan Goldberg, of New York. *Mt.* $2,000. 5,800

Knickerbocker av, s e cor De Kalb av, 25x90. Christian A. Keppler to Charles J. Laderer, of Newtown, N. Y. *Mt.* $4,500. 12,000

Knickerbocker av, n e s, 180 n w Putnam av, 40x88. Louis Keller to Henry Rauch. 1,050

Lafayette av, n s, 175 e Sumner av, 20x100, h & l. John Dohse to Margaret J. Reynolds. nom

Lafayette av, s e cor Navy st, runs east 20.6x85-10x20.6x85. Julia wife of J. Josef Stuehler to Ira Perego. *Mt.* $15,000. 25,000

Lafayette av, n s, 60 w Franklin av, 20x76. Amelia T. Rowley to Kate E. wife of James Nevin. 5,000

Lewis av, e s, 20 n Lexington av, 20x80. Charles H. Heimburg to Gustave J. Wiederholdt. *Mt.* $5,000. 6,700

Lewis av, s w cor Willoughby av, 50x100. George Covert to Isaas Ginsburg, of New York. 13,000

Lewis av, e s, 32 s Hart st, 17x80, h & l. Elizabeth wife of Timothy L. Brophy to Fredericka Zimmermann. *Mt.* $2,500. 4,500

Lewis av, w s, 60 n Pulaski st, 20x79.10. Bridget Byrne widow to Frank Bayersdorfer. 4,500

Lewis av, e s, 60 s Lexington av, 20x80. Frank Hyde to Helen A. wife of Alton H. Fancher. *Mt.* $6,700. ex b

Lewis av, e s, 33.4 n Kosciusko st, 16.8x75. The General Synod of the Reformed Church to Joseph Burley. 6,400

Lexington av, n s, 316.8 e Bedford av, 33.4x100. Charles H. Heimburg, of New York, to Peter P. McLaughlin. *Mt.* $6,700. 10,500

Lexington av, n s, 327 w Bedford av, 22.4x100. Kate L. wife of and John F. Petry formerly Hoeft to Richard R. Lane or Laue. *Mt.* $2,000. 3,500

Lexington av, n e cor Patchen av, 95x100x9x20x86x120. John B. Altmann to Isabella Brinkenhoff. *Mt.* $10,000. 18,500

Liberty av, n s, 100 w Orient av, 25x100.
Liberty av, n s, 125 w Orient av, 25x100.
Bay av, n s, 25 e Sackman av, 25x100.
Bay av, n e cor Sackman av, 25x100.
Jeannette V. S. and Maria H. Lott, of New York, committee of estate Christopher I. Lott to Simon C. Wilson, Baldwins, L. I. 2,575

Manhattan av, e s, 124.3 s Nassau av, runs south 24.3 x east 100 x north 20.3 x northwest to point 82.3 e Manhattan av and 125 s Nassau av, x east 17.9 x north 1.9 x west 100, h & l. Frank J. Kelly to Abraham Weiss, New York. *Mt.* $1,500. 6,475

Marcy av, s w cor Middleton st, 25x80.4x25x80.8. Julius Nulle to William Weimann. *Mt.* $4,250. 6,000

Meeker av, n w cor Sutton st, runs north 69.1 x west 100 x south 20.6 x east 18.9 x southeast 82.1 to Meeker av, x northeast 36.3, h & l. Kings Co. Improvement Co. to Henry Offerman. nom

Myrtle av, n s, 200 w Lewis av, runs north 100 x west 25 x north 20 x west 25 x south 120 x east 50. Rebecca Lewis to Esther Hallheimer. nom

Myrtle av, s s, 425 e Nostrand av, 25x100. George Covert to Anna Frey. 13,500

Myrtle av, s s, 26.3 s e Cumberland st, runs east 19.11 x south 77.4 x west 18.4 x north — to beginning. George Wilson to Charles L. Behlert. 7,400

New York av, w s, 70 s Herkimer st, 17x76.6, h & l. Hannah wife of Henry J. Green to Mabel L. wife of David B. Conklin. *Mt.* $4,000. 7,200

New York av, s w cor Park pl, 50x100. Release mort. John Bentley to Robert W. Gleason. 1,000

Same property. Robert W. Gleason to Mary B wife of Joseph D. Huggins. See 9th av. exch

Park av, n s, 40.3 w North Elliott pl, 20.7x49.5x14.10x45.3. George W. Heatley to Domenico Molinelli, of New York. *Mt.* $2,500. 3,400

Park av, s s, 225 e Tompkins av, 25x100, h & l. Sarah C. Savage trustee of Elihu Chauncey dec'd to John, Jr., d Dorothea Bauer. B. and S. and C. a. Gan 4,300

Pennsylvania av, n e cor Eastern Parkway, 100x100. Frederick Hornby to Emilie Kehle, of New York. *Mt.* $4,500. 7,000

Pennsylvania av, e s, 75 s Fulton av. 75x110, hs & ls. Abraham Schlank to Lewis Krieger. Sub. to all liens. 15,500

Pennsylvania av, e s, 100.1 s Atlantic av, 25x100. Same to same. Sub. to all liens. 7,000

Putnam av, s e s, 180 n e Broadway, 20x100. Michael Mulvihill to Anna Ohrig. *Mt.* $3,000. 6,500

Putnam av, n s, 194.1 e Patchen av, 18.9x100. Fannie J. Mugford to John Campbell. 5,900

Putnam av, n s, 175.4 e Patchen av, 75x100. Release mort. John Truslow to Fannie J. Mugford. 2,700

Putnam av, n s, 95 e Stuyvesant av, 18.10x100. John Mitchell and Charles Herr to Elizabeth D. wife of Isaac N. Odell. nom

Putnam av, s e s, 200 n e Broadway, 20x100. Michael Mulvihill to Louisa Haupert. 6,550

Ralph av, n s, 150 w St. Nicholas av, 100x100. Richard A. Berger to Louisa Saenger. *Mt.* $2,000. exch

Reid av, e s, 22 s Quincy st, 19.6x77, h & l. William Johnston to Louis Hirsch. *Mt.* $6,000. 11,000

Reid av, e s, 150 n De Kalb av, runs east 47 x northeast 3.6 x northwest 24 x west 34.2 to Reid av, x south 20. Adeline E. F. wife of Hubert F. Praeger to Charles W. Evans. *Mt.* $1,800. 2,800

Reid av, e s, 99 n Macon st, runs east 90 x north 1 x east 35 x north 25 x west 125 to av, x south 26. Louis W. Fischer to Lucy G. wife of Henry J. Lawes. *Mt.* $5,000. 12,500

Reid av, e s, 73 n Macon st, 26x90. John H. Elfers to Claus Quadt. *Mt.* $9,000. 12,200

Ridgewood av, s s, 40 e Essex st, 20x90. Wilmot D. Losee to William M. Offutt, of New York. 3,300

Rockaway av, e s, 110 n Glenmore av, 30x100.1. Barnet L. Price and Barnet L. Price two of same name to Israel Radar. 6,000

Saratoga av, w s, 75 s Sumpter st, 25x75. Catherine Molloy to Henry R. Fechtmann. *Mt.* $3,750. exch

Schenectady av, s w cor Pacific st, 49.6x100. Eliza J. Smith to Sarah Evers. 3,800

Schenectady av, e s, 80 n Pacific st, 16.8x85. Annie wife of Oscar C. Hamlet, Boston, Mass., to Mary T. J. Caddell. *Mt.* $2,000. 3,100

Sheridan av, e s, 425 n Adams av, 25x100. Otto F. Struse to Rudolph Reimer. nom

Shepherd av, e s, 250 s Ridgewood av, 20x101.10x20x101.11. William R. Josiah to Joseph R. Le Poidevin. *Mt.* $1,800. 2,800

Stone av, w s, 112 n Blake av, 23x100. Boozy Spevack to Jacob Steinberg. *Mt.* $1,700. 2,600

Stone av, w s, 50 s Blake av, 50x100. Mary E. Cook, Newtown, L. I., to Gussie Volinsky. 4,550

St. Marks av, n s, 20 e Rogers av, 20x100, h & l. Mallie L. Clapp, Albany, N. Y., to George E. Glines, New York. *Mt.* $6,000. 9,500

Stuyvesant av, e s, 121 n Halsey st, 19x100. Walter F. Clayton to Bernard Levino. *Mt.* $6,500. 12,000

Sumner av, w s, 20 n Van Buren st, 20x100. Mary McDougall to Johanna Madden. 4,800

Throop av, s w cor Wallabout st, 25x75, h & l. Henry Heymann to Myer Bach and Albert Sokolski. *Mt.* $3,750. 7,600

Utica av, n w cor Fernald st, 100x200, Flatbush. Jacob Strauss to James Asher. 2,300

Union av, e s, 26.3 n Conselyea st, 25x100, h & l. George Peth trustee for Geo. J. W. Peth and Louisa F. Stoss to George J. W. Peth and Louisa F. Stoss. nom

Van Cott av, s w cor Morgan av, runs west 100 x south 82.2 to Meeker av, x northeast 113.10 to Morgan av, x north 27.8. Jeremiah V. Meserole to Martin Rourke and Robert H. Barry. 3,000

Van Siclen av, e s, 125 n Sutter av, 25x100. John H. Ives sole devisee Elizabeth A. Ives to Mary A. wife of John H. Stoker. *Mt.* $600. 1,900

Van Siclen av, w s, 100 s Arlington av, 25x100; also,
Miller av, e s, 125 s Arlington av, 40x100.
Wilmer C. Smith to Alfred Stygall. *Mt.* $2,000. 4,000

Van Sielen av, w s, 125 s Arlington av, 25x100. Wilmer C. Smith to Arthur Taylor. 1,000

Voorhies av, s w cor 16th st, runs west 50 x 100, Gravesend. Elizabeth Clute to Amelia Miller. 1,450

Voorhies av, n s, 107.2 e of centre line proposed East 18th st, 40x100, Gravesend. James McKane to Ida R. Jones. 1,000

Washington av, s s, 300 e 2d st, 100x100, Flatbush. Jacob Contrie to William H. Contrie. C. a. G. nom

Willoughby av, s e s, 225 s w Knickerbocker av, 25x100. Anton and John Amann to Christoph Derr. *Mt.* $3,500. nom

1st av, e s, extends from 42d to 43d st, 200.4x300. Stewart McDougall to The National Meter Co. 28,500

4th av, south cor 11th st, 60x97.10. John J. Lynch to Alexander G. Calder. *Mt.* $4,233. 6,500

4th av, n e cor 47th st, 40.2x100. Benjamin Shreve to James G. Carroll. 3,100

6th av, s s, 74 w 14th st, 13.9x97.10x13.11x97.10, h & l. Henry M. Noe, New York, to Claudins H. Dumabut. 2,600

6th av, w s, 26.4 n Middle st, 18x80. Eliza Goodman widow to Fanny Schlesinger. 4,700

6th av, w s, 84.2 s Carroll st, 8x89.5x8x88.8. Theodore P. Cooper to Peter F. Delaney and Peter J. Collins. 850

6th av, e s, 20 s 1st st, 40x90. John D. Hallaren to Robert Miller, Jr. *Mt.* $1,112. nom

7th av, s w s, 25 s e 16th st, 50x97.10. James Jack to Alexander Ogilvie, Philadelphia, Pa. *Mt.* $14,000. 22,500

7th av, w s, 60 s 2d st, 20x80. Lydia M. Howard to George H. Doughty. *Mt.* $3,000. exch and 600

7th av, w s, 80.6 s 12th st, runs west 22.4 x north 0.6 x west 75.6 x south 20 x east 97.10 to 7th av, x north 19.6. Louis Bonert to Louis H. Muller, New York. *Mt.* $5,000. exch

7th av, e s, 50.2 s 50th st, 25x100. Israel D. Velsor to Augusta M. Guilmartin. 300

8th av, s e cor 11th st, 100x120. William C. Turner to Allison V. B. Norris. Sub. to morts. nom

9th av, s e s, 80 s w 18th st, 20x85. Mary B. wife of Joseph D. Huggins to Robert W. Gleason. *Mt.* $3,500. See New York av. exch

13th av, e s, 40 n 67th st, 40x100, New Utrecht. Effingham H. Nichols to Albert Eberg, of New York. 500

13th av, north cor 74th st, centre lines, runs northeast 60 to centre 73d st, x northwest 160 x northeast 115.4 x southwest 328.8 x west 107.4 x southwest 11.11 to centre 74th st, x southeast 300.
75th st, centre line at n w line of lands of grantees, runs northwest 12.8 x southwest 146.2 x northeast 146.9, New Utrecht.
Bay Ridge Park Improvement Co. to Franklin Allen. nom

15th av, n w s, 64 s w 67th st, 46x88x46x89.3, New Utrecht. John H. Gutheil to Henry Schmidt. *Mt.* $1,200. 2,800

15th av, s e s, 31.9 n e 82d st, runs southeast 383.10 x southwest 242.7 x southeast 113.3 x southwest 295.3 to Main st, x northwest 16.10 x northeast 202.10 to centre 83d st, x northwest 125 x northeast 130 x northwest 275 x northeast 130 to 82d st, x northwest 100 to 15th av, x northeast 61.9, New Utrecht. Cornelia Voorheis to John L. and George E. Nostrand. nom

15th av, east cor Main st or State road, 269.2x southeast 100 x southwest 25 to centre line bet 82d and 83d sts, x southeast 275 x southwest 130 to centre 83d st, x northwest 125 x southwest 203.8 to Main st, x northwest 265.10, New Utrecht. Cornelia E. Voorhees to John E. Nash. 4,000

Same property. Cornelia Voorheis to Cornelia E. Voorhees. Q. C. nom

Same property. John E. Nash to John L. and George E. Nostrand. *Mt.* $2,000. 4,000

15th av, east cor Main st or State road, runs northeast 269.2 x southeast 100 x northeast 105 to centre 82d st, x northwest 100 to s e s 15th av, x northeast 61.9 x southeast 383.10 x southwest 242.7 x southeast 113.3 x southwest 295.3 to Main st, x northwest 16.10 x northeast 202.10 to centre 83d st, x northwest 250 x southwest 203.8 to Main st, x northwest 265.10, New Utrecht. Albert V. B. Voorhies to John L. and George E. Nostrand. B. & S. nom

15th av, n w cor Bay Ridge av, 40x90, Lefferts Park. James V. S. Woolley to Charles Johnson, New York. 750

17th av, w s, 350 s Bath av, 214.9 to Cropsey av, x 108.7x222.3x108.4, hs & ls, New Utrecht. Jeannette wife of Louis A. Lanthier to Albert V. B. Voorhies. *Mt.* $3,000. 17,000

24th av, south cor 83d st, 100x80, Bensonhurst. James D. Lynch to Adolph C. Wenzel. 1,600

Interior lot, 80 n Atlantic av, and 17 w Bancroft pl, runs west 16 x north 10 x east 16 x south 10. Christopher P. Skelton to Julia F. Fuller. Q. C. nom

Interior lot, 61.6 s Debevoise st, and 49.5 e Morrell st, runs south to n s Newtown and Bushwick turnpike road at point 50 e Morrell st, x east 31 to land of Lewis F. Varet, x north along said land to point east of place of beginning, x — to beginning. Lucinda Ellingworth widow to Frank Duffrin. exch

Interior lot, on centre line bet 72d and 73d sts, 100 s e 12th av, runs southwest 86.6 to land of grantee, x east to said centre line, x northwest 227.6.
73d st, centre line, s w s, 100 n w 12th av, runs southwest 62.10 to land of grantee, x east to centre 73d st, x northwest 165.6
Interior lot, on centre line bet 73d and 74th sts, 240 s e 11th av, runs southwest 69.5 to land of grantee, x east to centre of block, x northwest 183.
11th av, centre line at centre line of 74th st, runs southwest along av 45.9 to land of grantee, x east to centre of 74th st, x northwest 120.5, New Utrecht.
William Spence to Franklin Allen. exch

Interior lot, on centre line bet 76th and 77th sts, 320 n w 11th av, runs north 102.4 to land of grantee, x west 191.7 x southwest 35.7 to said centre block, x southeast 182.7.
76th st, centre line, n e s, 160 n w 11th av, runs northeast 31.8 to land of grantee, x west 91.2 to centre 76th st, x southeast 85.5.
Interior lot, bet 75th and 76th sts, 160 s e 11th av, runs northeast 50.4 x west 143.9 to centre of block, x southeast 134.10.
75th st, centre line at south line of lands of grantee, runs southeast along st 246.2 to land of grantee, x north 85.6 x west 228.5, New Utrecht.
Holk D. Campbell to Franklin Allen. exch

Interior lot, on centre line bet 72d and 73d sts at point 327.6 s e 12th av, runs southeast 252.6 x northeast 95.9 to land of grantee, x west —.
73d st, centre line, n e s, 100 s e 12th av, runs northeast 43.5 to land of grantee, x west to centre 73d st, x southeast 114.6.
Interior lot, on centre line bet 73d and 74th sts, 100 n w 12th av, runs northeast 67.2 to land of grantee, x west to centre of block, x southeast along same 177.
74th st, centre line, n e s, 240 s e 11th av, runs northeast 60.7 to land of grantee, x west to centre 74th st, x southeast 159.6, New Utrecht.
Franklin Allen to William Spence. exch

Lot 43 block 1 map of M. J. Bergen's 221 lots, New Utrecht. James V. S. Woolley to Sophie M. Olsen. 175

Lot 44 (north half of) block 1 same map. Sophie M. Olsen to Arndt H. Olsen. 87

Lots 508 block 25 map 2 of 660 lots Cowenhoven farm, New Utrecht. Effingham H. Nichols to Anna A. Kelly. 160

Lots 334 and 335 block 8 and lots 392 and 393 block 9 map No. 1 of 618 lots Cowenhoven farm, New Utrecht. Same to Maria Donovan. 355

Lot 507 block 25 map 2 of 660 lots Cowenhoven farm, New Utrecht. Same to Henry P. Kelly. 160

Lots 494 and 495 block 25 same map. Same to William R. Pope. 320

Lots 283 and 284 block 22 same map. Same to Dennis Murphy. 360

Lots F and G and parts of lots 28 and 29 on map common lands, Coney Island. Albert J. Burtis, of New York, to James A. Johnson 500

Lot No. 15 portion of 40 ft. wide map property Jane Smith, New Utrecht. Mary A. wife of Michael Walsh to James Keegan. nom

Same property. Sarah M. wife of James T. Simpson to Mary A. wife of Michael Walsh. ½ part. *Mt.* $1,600. 3,000

Same property. James Keegan to Michael Walsh. nom

Lots 68-70, 79-81 and 101 block 18; also lots 110-113, 120-127 and 129-134 block 19 map No. 2 of 660 lots Cowenhoven farm, owned by E. H. Nichols, New Utrecht. Effingham H. Nichols to Hans C. Pfalzgraf. 5,281

Lots 18-20, 43-49 block 1, lots 255-286 block 6, lots 293-316 block 7 map 618 lots Cowenhoven farm, New Utrecht. Same to same. 10,073

Lot 218 block 21 map No. 2 660 lots property E. H. Nichols, New Utrecht. Same to Alpheus Rollins. 180

Lots 54-67 and 71-78 block 18 same map. Same to George and Gustave A. Helm. 5,000

Lots 1-20 and 41-44 block 17 same map. Same to Lawrence Weber and John Quinn. 4,203

Lots 164 and 165 block 20 map 2 of 660 lots, Cowenhoven farm, New Utrecht. Effingham H. Nichols to Jane Hevie. 300

Lotts lane. East 4th and East 5th sts, lots 15-20 and 71, 72 block 6, town of Flatbush. Leander V. M. Blakeman, Mt. Vernon, to Mary A. Conkling. 2,400

Lots 215 and 216 map A. W. Parker, Bath Beach. Frederick O. Miller to Segred wife of Frederick O. Miller. nom

Lots 374-376 block 7 map 597 lots Wm. Ziegler, Gravesend. William Ziegler to Thomas Ferguson. nom

Lots 10 and 18 block 20 assessment map 21st Ward. Max Hallheimer to Rebecca Lewis, of New York. nom

Same property. Rebecca Lewis to Esther Hallheimer. nom

Lots 502-506 block K map Zabriskie homestead, Flatbush. Wm. J. Kaiser, John H. Vanderveer and George W. Dalton to Alice E. wife of William H. Goldey. 2,000

Parcel in New Utrecht, begins at intersection of south line of F. Allen's land with n w line of land of Bay Ridge Park Improvement Co., runs southwest 1,087.1 to point 440 s e of 12th av, x northeast 1,044.6 to land of F. Allen, x east 107.4, New Utrecht. Graham K. Anderson to The Bay Ridge Park Improvement Co. nom

Amberstrand road, adj J. Holland, Gravesend Neck, 25x120. Edmund Williams to Anna and John W. Greenwood. C. a. G. 100

Brooklyn, Flatbush and Coney Island Railway Co. land, w s, 456.2 s Ocean av, 40x110, Flatbush. Kate E. wife of and Chas. A. Von Wallmenich to Gottfried Bungarz. *Mt.* $2,000. 4,250

Coney Island and Sheepshead Bay road, n s, lot 3 on Duck Hills, supplemental map C common lands, Gravesend, 129x94.4 to Coney Island plank road, x129x93.6. Robert Brown to Samuel M. Hubbard. B. & S. 25

Same property. Samuel M. Hubbard to John Birmingham. B. & S. *Mt.* $333, taxes, &c. 100

WESTCHESTER COUNTY.

SEPTEMBER 30 TO OCTOBER 6—INCLUSIVE.

BEDFORD.

O'Leary, Anne to Margt. Curran, w s road from Mt. Kisco to Geo. Hubbels, 130x—. $830

Secor, Amelia C. to Alf. J. Tharp, n s road to Baptist Church, cor road to Cherry st, 5 acres. 250

CORTLANDT.

Bauer, Cacilie et al., S. S. Marshall ref., to Henry P. Graaf, tract e s Cortlandt st, Crugers. 10,000

Buck, Grace L. to Clemence R. Wilson, s s Park st, adj Ida C. Brown, 44.6x154. 1,400

Ferry, Alice exr. of, to Geo. Tandy, s s 7th st, Verplancks, 25x95. 425

Murphy, Patrick D. to Hugh Kennedy, n e cor Bay and South sts, 150x159x168x108. 825

Welch, John to Thos. Welch, lot 50 s w s 6th st, Verplancks, 25x95. 50

EASTCHESTER.

Arvidson, And. to Edw. J. Chapman, lots 655 and 611 s w cor 21st av and Old Kingsbridge road, Wakefield. 5,000

Bard, Wm H. to Benj. De F. Curtis, lot 245 s e s Catharine st, Washingtonville. nom

Cappelmann, Emma L. B. to Michael J. Phelan, lot 1 e s White Plains road, Central Mt. Vernon, 34.2x150. 1,700

Conkling, Mary A. et al., H. T. Dykman ref., to Emma A. Blakeman, s e cor 4th st and 11th av, abt 284x144. 10,775

Forster, Fred P. to Martha T. Bodden, lot 230 Chester Hill, 50x115. 1,000

Gay, Margt. C. to Leah F. Fitzgerald, east ½ lot 1018 n s 21st av, Wakefield, 50x114. 800

Horton, Sarah V. to Daniel B. Horton, w s Union av, 199 s 2d st. 35.4x78.8. 500

Lucas, Mary E. to Emma A. Blakeman, e s 11th av, 254 s 4th st, abt 127.9x200. 4,000

McDonald, Belinda C. to Wm. H. Bard, lots 586 and 310, Washingtonville. other consid. and 200

Patterson, Ella J. to Lillie L. Cahaskie and ano., lot 108 s e s Fulton st, Washingtonville, 33x151. 675

Phipps, Edw. L. E. to C. Stacey Clark, n s Mt. Vernon av, 113.6 w Bleecker st, 50x88. 5,000

Roe, Elizn. L. to Geo Schuster, east ½ lot 1040 n s Stevens av, Mt. Vernon, 50x105. 8,250

Wood, Jos. to Fried Petereit, lot 90 Primrose Park, 50x100. 1,000

GREENBURGH.

Blackwell, Wilson H. to Adelia L. Gould, lots 553 and 544, Ardsley. 400

Same to Thos. F. Conlon, lots 649 and 650. 240

Dederer, Henry to Carrie Whitsun, e s Central av, adj grantee, abt ½ acre. 180

Elmsford Impt. Co. to Eliza J. Ketchale, lots 39-48 block 19, Elmsford Park. 450

Gardner, Eleanor to Julia A. Maxwell, e s road from Hartsdale to Dobbs Ferry, 50x200. 550

Goodman, Rachel to Moses Oppenheimer, n s Main st, adj Martin Smith, 24x134.6. 7,500

Jones, Cyrus P. and ano. to Wm. Bode and wife, lots 91 and 92, Ardsley. 275

Leviness, Martha D. to Rosa K. Smith, w s N. Y. C. & N. R. R., adj Thos. Cortlett, 34x188. ——

Same to Emma J. Knapp, n w s Saw Mill River road, 5 acres. 500

Morris, Geo. H. et al. Edgar Logan ref. to Henry Hirsch, 332 acres e s Sprain road, part in Yonkers. 48,000

Moran, Jas. H. and ano. to Aug. Russe, e s Maple av, 446 s Chatterton Hill road, 50x160. 400

Nalty, John to Mary M. Harwood, 3 acres on Peter Bond road, adj Henry Drisler. nom

Popham, Lewis C. to Sylvester M. Leviness, e s road from Tuckahoe to Greenville, 1 acre. 500

Tracey, Wm. to Peter Geis, 2 tracts adj S. G. Losee and S. L. Acker, 25¼ acres. 3,500

Van Tassel, Bruce et al. W. M. Skinner ref. to Thos. Howitt, w s Central av, adj W. I. Smith, 65x292. 2,450

MAMARONECK.

Kane, Michael A. to Richard Restore, n s St. Clare av, 150 w Beech av, 50x100. 600

MOUNT PLEASANT.

Smadbeck, Louis to Agnes Haines, lots 87 and 1064 Sherman Park. 425

Same to Fred. Nands, lot 100. 100

Same to Thomas Crosley, lot 155. 200

Same to Henry Lohman, lots 1004 and 1005. 300

Same to Phillip Smithson, lots 1104 and 1105. 250

Same and ano. to Chas. Lasinsky, lots 305, 306, 315 and 316 Lakehurst. 540

Same to Bernhard Poctmann and ano., lots 417 and 418. 250

Schofield, Leona E. to Maurice Blanckensee, lot 1017 Sherman Park. 100

NEW CASTLE.

Hunt, Geo. to Chas. W. Cornell, e s road from Conklins Mills to Chappaqua Meeting House, 1 acre. 500

Piersall, Jas. S. to Jas. Reynolds, exr. of, s s Smith av, adj Emily B. Adams, 100x—. 3,450

NEW ROCHELLE.

Condon, Edw. B. to Thos. H. Hall, s w cor Meadow lane and Field av, abt 162x150. nom

Huguenot Park Land Assoc. to Geo. P. Govers, n e cor Clinton and Mayflower avs, 300x300. 663

Lacey, Wm. J. to Mary J. Lacey, n s Mayflower av, 312 w North st, 100x125x140x132. nom

Lambden, John F. to Abby S. Baldwin, s s Poplar pl, 150 e Liberty av, 50x150. 1,400

Lorenzen, Fred. to Horace Crosby, s e cor Hickory and Church sts, 150x185. 4,550

Same to John E. Bong, n e cor same, 50x100. 1,400

Same to S. Terry Hudson, e s Church st, 50 n Hickory, 50x100; also n s Hickory, adj, 87x150. 5,200

Same to Chas. W. Kirchhoff, e s Church st, 100 n Hickory, 50x100. 1,200

Same to Jas. A. Grenzebach, n s Hickory, 186 e Church, 100x150. 4,000

Same to John F. New, s s same, 185 e Church, 97x149. 1,800

Mayer, Wilhelmina to Carl Goewitz, n s Pelham road, 305x to L. I. Sound. 15,500

Nicholas, Mary S. to Fred. Lorenzen, e s Church st, adj John Dyott, 355.6x288.4. 12,500

NORTH CASTLE.

Crespo, Lizzie to Middle Patent M. E. Church. "The Round House," ¾ acre. 1,300

OSSINING.

Brown Memorial Assoc. to Minnie B. Lober, lots 1, 5, 6, 14 and 15, map Duntcomb property; also 75 acres adj Benj. Brandreth, part in New Castle. 7,000

Westchester Town Site Co. to Mich. Kelly and wife, s e cor Highland and Maple avs, 50x103. 750

PELHAM.

Deveaugh, Jos. C. to Chas. A. Tier, e s Main st, adj Jas. Hyatt, 25x100. 3,400

Holman, Sarah J. to Jas. Howie, s e cor Jackson av and Peace st, 200x400. 2,550

POUNDRIDGE.

Hoyt, Mary E. to Jas. N. Hoyt, 58 acres w s Stamford road. 2,500

Platt, Stephen to Edw. F. Brush, 80 acres adj Enoch Avery and John Knox. 2,000

RYE

Brooks, John to Fred. J. Selzer, lot 34 w s Davis av map Hayward, 50x151. 100

Same to John O. Reardon, n e cor Meadow and Goldwin sts, 100x144. 150

Same to Mary A. McGeary, s e cor same, 100x144. 150

Merritt, Jas. S. and ano. to Wm. E. Merritt, lot 125 s s West William st, Washington Park, 50x114. 180

Same to Emma A. Shea, lots 1-4 n e cor Ellendale av and Ridge st, 125x150. 545

Same to same, lots 97, 99 and 100 n w cor West William and Merritt sts. 766

Scoffin, John exr. of, to Jas. McClenahan, 77 acres on Harrison st, part in Harrison. 7,500

Woods, Jas. to Sarah Kaiser and ano., e s Willett av, 125 n Rectory st, 40x125. 1,850

WESTCHESTER.

Brady, Jas. to Basilia Bottinelli and wife, w s 2d av, 200 n 1st st, Olinville, 100x100. 2,350

Camp, Hugh N. to Geo. S. Springsteel, lots 149 and 150 map McGraw estate. 540

Cooper, Margt. et al., J. B. Lockwood ref., to Edw. Secor, lots 49, 50 and 51 e s Cooper av. 120

Same to Samuel G. Derrickson, lots 53-58 n s Grant st. 105

Same to Wm. E. Ferguson, lots 39-41 e s Cooper av. 200

Same to Thos. S. Ryan, lot 35 e s Cooper av. 200

Dexter, Fred. C. to John P. Ott and ano., east ½ lot 954 s s 8th av, Wakefield, 50x114. 4,500

Same to Raymond C. Kayser, part lot 610 n s 4th av, Wakefield, 25x114. 2,700

Duncan, Wm. F. to Jos. F. Dean, lots 71 and 72 map property grantor. 1,200

Same to Chas. E. Dobson, Jr., lots 69 and 70. 1,200

Hall, Jas. to Annabella Howell, west ½ lot 497 n s 6th av, Wakefield, 50x114. 3,200

Hughes, Miles to Jennie Lynch, s w cor Sackett av and Deane pl, 50x100. 585

Same to John J. Foley, s s Pierce av, 250 e Deane pl, 25x192. 260

Johnston, Jas. to Mary A. Thompson, lot 288 n e cor 11th st and Av C, Unionport, 105x108. 1,400

Kendrick, Samuel to Thos. R. Thorn, n s 7th st, 305 w Av A, Unionport, 108x—. 400

Klunder, John to Jas. Hall, n w cor 4th st and 5th av, Wakefield, 50x105. 1,050

Low, Jacob to Eliza K. Sandford, lots 90, A B, map 2, Olinville, abt 107x125. 4,000

Myers, Sinclair, W. M. Lyddy ref., to Helen M. Chisolm, lot 137 s s 7th st, Unionport, 200x108. 430

Seton, Alfred trustee of, to Adrian Iselin, s e cor Seton and 3d sts, 30x100. 200

Wilhelm, Kath. M. to Philip H. Smith, lot 162 s s 5th av, Wakefield, 100x114. 1,000

WHITE PLAINS.

Dick, Isabella to Benoni Platt et al., e s North st, adj Henry Welsh, 73 acres. 10,750

Moore, Henry S. to Clara B. Moore, s s Railroad av, adj grantee, 45x240. 3,500

YONKERS.

Ackerman, John W. to Gert. F. Bell, e s Warburton av, 118 s Quincey pl. 6,500

Butler, Marcia F. to Florence Frazee, lots 37, 39, 45 and 47 n s Yonkers av, Nodine Hill. 12,000

Cain, Joseph H. to Marcia F. Butler, n s Fairview st, 275 e Park av, 75x200. 4,000

Codington, Mary E. to Titus C. White, s w cor Maple and Waverly sts, 22.10x100. 4,500

Deane, Cath. to The Deane Plaster Co. lots 33, 34 and 35 e s Willow st, Herriot map, 75x100. 1,650

Gramatan Park Co. to A. G. Cattell, Jr., lots 74, 75 and 76 Armour Villa Park. 7,100

Keppel, Fred. to Nellie R. Smith, s e cor Irving pl and Warburton av, abt 42x119. 7,000

Jones, Cyrus P. and ano. to Sarah Judge, lots 6 and 7 block E and lot 22 block F, grantor's map. 710

Same to Mary A. Heaton, lot 22 block G. 225

Same to Annie Laregy, lot 24 block F. 270

Laugshore, Wm. J. to Ellis B. Edwards, w s Van Sice av, 25 n Landscape av, 25x125. 700

Murray, Frank E. to Theo. Chatterton, lots 32 and 33, Sherwood Park. 1,100

Shearwood Hill Land Co. to Clarence M. Fowler, lot 133, Shearwood Hill. nom

Scully, David H. to Clarence W. Gaylor, s s Rauford st, 75 e Florence, 25x100. 500

Valentine, Nath. B. to Peter J. Sullivan, lots 229, 231 and 233 w s South Broadway, Flagg map, 78.4x113. 6,300

Yonkers, Teutonia to The Congregation of the Sons of Israel No. 230, e s new Main st, City map. 6,500

MORTGAGES.

NOTE.—The arrangement of this list is as follows. The first name is that of the mortgagor, the next that of the mortgagee. The description of the property then follows, then the date of the mortgage, the time for which it was given, and the amount. The general dates used as headings are the dates when the mortgage was handed into the Register's office to be recorded.

Whenever the letters "P. M." occur, preceded by the name of a street, in these lists of mortgages, they mean that it is a Purchase Money Mortgage, and for fuller particulars see the list of transfers under the corresponding date. Whenever the rate is not given, read as 6 per cent.

NEW YORK CITY.

OCTOBER 2, 3, 5, 6, 7, 8.

Aronson, Samuel and Morris Denbosky to The Greenwood Cemetery, Brooklyn. Ludlow st, Nos. 13 and 15, w s, 137.10 n Walker st now Canal st, 37.7x88.3. Oct. 1, due Nov. 1, 1896, 5 %. See Conveys. $35,000

Ash, Mark to Leon Sternberger. St. Nicholas av, n w cor 156th st, 25.10x92.10x24.11x99.9. Oct. 1, 1 year or sooner, 5½ %. 11,000

Abele, Christian to Jacob Schneider. 50th st. P. M. Sept. 1, 1 year, 5 %. 10,000

Bremer, Kate to Elias Jacobs. 81st st. P. M. Sub. to mort. $18,000. Oct. 8, 5 years or sooner. 4,000

Same to The Teachers' Co-operative Building and Loan Assoc. Same property. P. M. Oct. 8, installs, 5 %. 18,000

Byk, Poline wife of and Morris to Simon R. Weil. Lexington av, w s, 75.11 s 50th st, 24.6 x90. Oct 8, demand. 1,000

Berbert, August to Mary A. Ritchie. Washington av. P. M. Oct. 1, 1 year, 5 %. 2,000

Bloomer, Edward M. to Elizabeth V. Irwin. 143d st, s s, 400 e Boulevard, 18.9x99.11. Oct. 2, 2 years. 600

Bollt, Simon to Samuel Weil. Delancey st. P. M. Sept. 29, installs. 8,475

Borger, Max to Elias Jacobs. 40th st. P. M. Sept. 30, due Oct. 1, 1893, 5 %. 3,000

Breen, James R. and Alfred G. Nason to Henry M. Alexander et al. trustees for THE SUN FIRE OFFICE Co. 75th st, n s, 240 w Columbus av, 20x102.2. Sept. 30, due Nov. 1, 1894, 5 %. gold, 24,000

Same to same. 75th st, n s, 200 w Columbus av, 20x102.2. Sept. 30, due Nov. 1, 1894, 5 %. gold, 24,000

Same to Louis Clark, Jr. 75th st, n s, 200 w 9th av, 20x102.2; 75th st, n s, 240 w 9th av, 60 x102.2. Sub. to morts. $96,000. Sept. 30, due May 12, 1892. 12,000

Same to Caroline W. Whiton. 75th st, n s, 280 w Columbus av, 20x102.2. Sept. 30, due July 10, 1894, 5 %. 25,000

Same to same. 75th st, n s, 260 w Columbus av, 20x102.2. Sept. 30, due July 10, 1894, 5 % 25,000

Brodek, Solomon to Ann E. McCaddin, Brooklyn. 9th av, n e cor 29th st, 20.9x70. Oct. 2, 5 years, 4½ %. gold, 8,000

Burrell, Mary E. to James McCarthy. Rogers pl. P. M. Sept. 30, 2 years. 400

Barron, Esther E. to Frederick Buse. 8th av. P. M. Sept. 15, due April 14, 1893, or sooner. 1,000

Bischoff, Annie C. to George Heather. Scott av, n s, 26.2 e Perry av, 26.2x105.4x25x97.8. Oct. 5, 3 years, 5 %. 375

Buse, Frederick to Augusta U. von Kleinck, Laura J. D. L. d'Aveuel and Nina A. de la Tournelle. Bradhurst av, w s, 295.6 s 155th st, runs west 87.1 x south 25 x east 5 x south 25 x east 92.2 to av, x north 51 to beginning. Sept. 15, 1 year, 5 %. 2,500

Beekman, Adelaide L. and Mary E. his wife to THE TITLE GUARANTEE AND TRUST Co. 76th st. P. M. Sept. 16, due Sept. 19, 1892, 5 %. 17,000

Bryan, William to Charles Lanier trustee for Alexander C. Lanier. Amsterdam or 10th av, e s, 70.4 n 74th st, 17x81. Aug. 17, due Aug. 1, 1894, 5 % See Conveys. 18,000

Buckley, Michael to THE MUTUAL LIFE INS. Co. of New York. 5th av, e s, 75.11 s 115th st, 25x100. Already mortgaged to mortgagee. Oct. 7, 1 year. 1,500

Burke, Mary C. to Mary Harrison. Lexington av. P. M. Oct. 5, 3 years, 5 %. 12,500

Cannon, John B. to The Bradley & Currier Co. (Lim.) 114th st, s w cor Park av, 30x100.11. Sub. to morts. $26,000. Sept. 8, 3 months. 3,779

Cirker, Lena to James F. and Patrick H. Sheridan and James S. Segrave. Cornell pl. P. M. Sept. 30, 3 years, 5 %. 265

Clayton, Michael to Michael Kirwan. Anthony av. P. M. Oct. 1, 1 year, 5 %. 200

Clock, Jesse M. to THE HARLEM SAVINGS BANK, New York. Willis av, w s, 50 s 142d st, 30x 80. Oct. 1, 1 year, 5 %. 4,000

Cannon, Bartley to Frances H. Johnson, Yonkers, N. Y. Van Courtlandt av, s s, 29.7 w Villa av, 88.10x74.11x75x122.6. June 20, 5 years. 500

Cotter, John and Nicholas to The Bradley & Currier Co. (Lim.) Willis av, w s, extends from 135th st to 136th st, 200x131.6. Sub. to morts. $175,000. Sept. 8, 3 months. 21,210

Same to same. 138th st, s s, 156.6 e Alexander av, 175x100. Sub. to morts. $100,000. Sept. 8, 3 months. 14,000

Cunningham, Michael to The Society of the Lying-In Hospital of the City of New York. Columbus av, e s, 75.8 n 94th st, 25x80. Oct. 5, due Feb. 1, 1897, or sooner, 5 %. 17,000

Carlew, James to THE TITLE GUARANTEE AND TRUST Co. 74th st, s s, 300 w Columbus av, 100x102.2. Building loan. Oct. 6, demand, 5 %. 100,000

Chesebro, Denison P. and Harry McNally to Jacob Korn. Crosby st, No. 49. P. M. Oct. 5, 1 year or sooner. 10,500

Curtin, John J. to George Lockyer and John Daly. Av A. P. M. Oct. 5, 2 years, 5 %. 1,875

Carroll, William D. to Mary E. Cumming. Bayard st, 24th Ward. P. M. Oct. 7, 5 years or sooner, 5 %. 950

Cohen, Matilda wife of and Samuel A. to THE FARMERS' LOAN AND TRUST Co. 115th st, No. 205, n s, 98 e 3d av, 18x100.11. Oct. 7, 3 years, 5 %. 9,000

Cornet, William H. to The Bradley & Currier Co. (Lim.) 21st st, n s, 425.2 e 9th av, 24.10x 98.9. Sub. to morts. $22,000. Sept. 24, 3 months. 2,450

Cunningham, David and Mary A. to Elizabeth C. Forsyth. Ernescliffe pl, s s, lot 492 map of G. F. and H. B. Opdyke adj New York City private park, 25.4x107.3x25x103. Oct. 1, 5 years. 1,300

Cohen, Alfred N. mortgagor with THE METROPOLITAN LIFE INS. Co. of New York mortgagee. Extension of reduced mortgage at reduced interest. Oct. 7. nom

Cumming, William and Robert Ferguson to THE TITLE GUARANTEE AND TRUST Co. 21st st, n s, 200 e 11th av, 25x98.9, except strip 0.1¼x—x0.2¼x— on west. Oct. 2, 1 year, 5 %. 25,000

Dauphinais, Victoria F. to Zoller Lumber Co., Fort Plain, N. Y. Morton st, Nos. 47 and 49, n s, 284.4 e Hudson st, 59x79.5x21.8x57. Sub. to morts. $86,004. Oct. 3, installs. 6,917

Davis, Alice wife of David T. to James O'Donelan. 53d st, s s, 275 e 11th av, —x 100.5x125x100.5. Aug. 24, 3 months. 600

Diehl, Peter to Philip Braender. 8th av. P. M. Oct. 1, installs, 5 %. 4,000

Drought, William, New York, and Charles J. Carew, Norwich, Conn., to Alexander Walker and Judson Lawson. West End av, 103d st. P. M. Oct. 1, due April 1, 1892. 36,500

Donnelly, Frank to J. Homer Hildreth. Valentine av, e s, 280 n land of Thomas Bassford, being lot 35 map of south part of farm of Peter Valentine, Fordham, 100x167.4x101.2x 152.3. Oct. 1, 1 year or sooner. 250

Edwards, Charles M. to James F. and Patrick H. Sheridan and James S. Segrave. Hill st. P. M. Sept. 30, due Oct. 1, 1894, 5 %. 1,000

Essig, Henry to Friedrich Graf. 14th st, No. 436, s s, 122 w Av A, 22x78.3x26.3x63.10. Oct. 1, 2 years, installs. 3,000

Same to Anna Meisel. Same property. Oct. 1, 5 years, 5 %. 9,000

Epter, Bertha wife of and Benjamin to Louis S. Brush. Jefferson st. P. M. Oct. 1, 5 years, 5 %. gold, 11,500

Epter, Bertha to Henry Pasinsky. Same property. P. M. Sub. to last mort. Oct. 1, installs. 3,500

Esper, Frederick to Richard F. Carman. 150th st, n s, 275 e 10th av, 75x99.11. Oct. 8, due March 2, 1894, 5 %. 12,000

Feehan, John J. and Ernest Hammer to THE GERMAN-AMERICAN REAL ESTATE TITLE GUARANTEE Co. 105th st, n s, 195 e Madison av, 25x100.11. Oct. 1, 3 years, 5 %. 15,000

Same to Charles Laue. 105th st, n s, 170 e Madison av. P. M. Nov. 17, 1890, due Dec. 15, 1891. 18,000

Same to James Gormly, Parkville, L. I. Same property. Oct. 1, 3 years, 5 %. 15,000

Fischler, Julius to James F. and Patrick H. Sheridan and James S. Segrave. Rock and Hill sts. P. M. Sept. 30, due Oct. 1, 1894, 5 %. 500

Frank, Joseph and Ellen his wife to Edward Callahan. 150th st, s s, 73.10 e Railroad av E., 20x100. Sept. 30, due Oct. 1, 1896, 5 %. 1,300

Fountain, Alfred E. and Alfred E., Jr., to THE HARLEM SAVINGS BANK. 128th st, n s, 374.6 w 5th av, 12.6x99.11. Oct. 1, 1 year, 5 %. 7,000

Same to same. 128th st, n s, 360 w 5th av, 12.6x99.11. Oct. 1, 1 year, 5 %. 7,000

Frank, Marcus A. mortgagor with Fannie Hoexter mortgagee. Extension of mort. Oct. 2. nom

Feehan, John J. and Ernest Hammer to THE GERMAN-AMERICAN REAL ESTATE TITLE GUARANTEE Co. 105th st, n s, 220 e Madison av, 25x100.11. Oct. 1, 3 years, 5 %. 15,000

Fischer, Louisa to John Schmitt and Christina his wife. 6th st. P. M. Oct. 1, 3 years, 5 %. 8,000

Same to Jobst Hoffmann. Same property. P. M. Sub. to morts. $36,000. Oct. 1, 9 months, 5 %. 1,450

Fisher, Elizabeth T. wife of and Charles W. to THE MUTUAL LIFE INS. Co. of New York. 76th st, No 47, n s, 107.6 e Madison av, 12.6x 102.2. Oct. 6, 1 year, 5 %. 4,000

Fine, Simon and Lena his wife and Harris Boskey and Rosie his wife to Solomon Bachrach. Elizabeth st, No. 242, e s, 331.7 s Houston st, 20x91.4x19.6x91.4. Oct. 5, due Jan. 6, 1893. 4,000

Fitzpatrick, Hugh to Waldron P. Brown and ano. trustees for Julia E. Soutter. 74th st. P. M. Oct. 2, 3 years. gold, 4,000

Fitzgerald, Luke to Leopoldine Frankenheimer. 23d st. P. M. Oct. 6, 5 years, installs, 5 %. 23,000

Frazee, Augustus L. to Perry P. Williams. Nathalie av. P. M. Sept. 10, due Sept. 1, 1894, 5 %. 600

Fox, Thomas H. and Mary E. his wife to THE LAWYERS' TITLE INS. Co. of New York. 31st st. P. M. Oct. 7, due Oct. 8, 1894, 5 %. 9,000

Goldstein, Isaac to Louis Goldberg. Broome st, No. 147, s s, 55 w Ridge st, 20x41.6. Sept. 16, due Oct. 16, 1893, or installs. 1,500

Grossman, Julius, Jr., to Thomas O'Rorke. Tinton av. P. M. Oct. 6, installs, 5 %. 2,600

Grube, Charles to Bernheimer & Schmid. 1st av, No. 1616, s e cor 84th st. Saloon lease. Oct. 5, note, demand. 4,000

Gallagher, Kate wife of and Joseph F. to Robert Froese. 114th st, No. 332, s s, 300 w 1st av, 30x100.11. Sub. to morts. $22,000. Oct. 2, 1 year. 1,025

Goodenough, Kate E. to Thomas White. Ryer av. P. M. Sept. 26, due Oct. 2, 1896, 5 %. 1,000

Gombert, Joseph F. to James F. and Patrick H. Sheridan and James S. Segrave. Forest st. P. M. Sept. 30, due Oct. 1, 1894, 5 %. 700

Greenwood, Lester J., Syracuse, N. Y., to John E. Lockwood, Long Island City. 102d st, s s, 125 w 11th av, 25x100.11. Sept. 26, 3 years, 5 %. 5,000

Geisenheimer, Joseph to Samuel Louis. 3d av, e s, 20.1 n 59th st, runs north 40.2 x east 100 x south 60.3 to 59th st, x west 20 x north 20.1 x west 80 to beginning. Oct. 2, due Oct. 5, 1892, note. 4,350

Ginsburg, Leon B. with Buffalo Door and Sash Co. both mortgagees. Agreement as to priority of mortgages made by Samuel Harris and Jennie his wife. Sept. 21. nom

Gilsey, Lucy wife of and Henry to Charles E. Miller. Broadway, Nos. 1195, 1197, 1199, 1201 and 1203, s w cor 29th st, —x—x98.9 to st, x72.5. Sub. to mort. $45,000. Oct. 7, 1 year, 5 %. 10,000

Gluck, Ignatz to Morris Kraus. Cannon st. P. M. Sub. to mort. $8,000. Oct. 1, 2 years or sooner. 1,500

Hallam, Charles F. and Mary A. his wife to Carl R. Eberth. Webster av. P. M. July 1, due Oct. 1, 1893, 5 %. 1,600

Haase, Henry W. A. and Minnie his wife, Jersey City, to Helen A. wife of George N. Phelps, Aurora, Ill. 21st st, n s, 325 e 9th av, 25x98.9. Oct 2, due Oct. 1, 1894. 5,000

Heatly, Manuel H. to James F. and Patrick H. Sheridan and James S. Segrave. Field st. P. M. Sept. 30, due Oct. 1, 1894, 5 %. 375

Henderson, James to John F. Thompson. 122d st, s s, 202 w 3d av, 26.3x70.3x26.3x71.4. Oct. 1, 2 months. 12,000

Same to John Burke, Llewellyn Park, N. J. 122d st, s s, 175 w 3d av, 26x74.9x26x74.11. Oct. 1, 5 years, 5 %. gold, 16,000

Same to Joseph B. Kaiser. 122d st, s s, 150 w 3d av, 26x74.11x26x75.1. Oct. 1, 5 years, 5 %. 16,000

Horowitz, Moses to Peter Doelger. Forsyth st, No. 69. Store lease. Sept. 30, demand. 1,850

Harms, Richard and John, of Harms Brothers, to Edward Koehler. Warren st, No. 61. Store lease. Oct. 5, notes. 10,000

Harris, Samuel to The Buffalo Door and Sash Co. 118th st, n s, 60 e Madison av, 100x100.11. Sub. to morts. $68,000. Sept. 21, 3 months. 20,000

Hauck, Valentin F. to Alexander Cameron. 96th st. P. M. Oct. 5, due Oct. 1, 1892, or sooner. 1,000

Haupt, Louis and Frances Haupt widow to THE MUTUAL LIFE INS. Co. of New York. 14th st, s s, 344 e 1st av, 25x115, with all title to old Stuyvesant st in rear. Oct. 6, 1 year. 13,000

Hickey, John to Alice S. H. Davies, New Haven, Conn. 116th st, s e cor Lexington av, 25x100.11, being No. 150 East 116th st and Nos. 1863, 1865, 1867 and 1869 Lexington av. Oct. 1, 5 years, 5 %. gold, 40,000

Hoffmann, Simon to John Hess. Delancey st. P. M. Oct. 1, 5 years, 5 %. 14,000

Honigsberger, Caroline wife of Daniel to Regine Bunzl. 78th st, No. 155, n s, 562.6 e 4th av, 12.6x102.2. Oct. 6, 5 years, 5 %. gold, 6,000

Houston, Charlotte A. widow, Frederick K. and Henrietta A., Ridgewood, N. ., to THE MANHATTAN SAVINGS INST. 19th st, n s, 195 w 5th av, 25x92. Oct. 6, 1 year, 5 %. 6,000

Hunt, Emily C. and Susan H. wife of Albert M. Cudner to Charles H. Chumar. 20th st, No. 325, n s, 350 w 8th av, 25x91.11. Oct. 5, due Oct. 1, 1894, 4½ %. 8,000

Hasell, Clemence L. widow and Amelia W., Annette B. and Clemence L. Boardman and Margaret W. Boardman by Richard A. Brown special guard. to THE INST. FOR THE SAVINGS OF MERCHANTS' CLERKS. 3d av, No. 325, e s, 49.4 n 24th st, 24.8x97.7; 3d av, Nos. 310, 312 and 314, w s, 98.9 n 23d st, 49.4x84. Oct. 5, 5 years, 4½ %. gold, 35,000

Hasell, Clemence L. widow and Amelia W., Annette B., Clemence L. and Margaret W. Boardman infant by Richard A. Brown guard. to Albert N. Hallgarten. Broadway, No. 654, e s, 29x130. Oct. 5, 5 years, 4½ %. gold, 90,000

Hoffman, Benjamin B., Red Hook, N. Y., to John R. Tresidder exr. Hedwig Roesler. 129th st. P. M. Oct. 8, due Jan. 1, 1893, 5 %. 5,000

Horner, Edward H. to Albert A. Kraetzer. 85th st, No. 124, s s, 275.9 e 4th av, 20.11x 102.2. Sub. to morts. $20,000. Oct. 7, 1 year. 4,000

Hickey, John J. to Peter Doelger. 3d av, No. 701, s e cor 44th st. Saloon lease. Sept. 29, demand. 1,500

Hagan, Susanna V. to Russell Sage. Amsterdam av, s w cor 79th st, 102.2x100. Oct 5, 6 months. 100,000

Same to Julius Lipman and William Cohen. Same property. Sub. to last mort. Oct. 5, due May 1, 1892. 30,148

Same to same. Same property. Sub. to mort. $100,000. Oct. 5, due May 1, 1892. 53,520

Same to Burrows & Smith. 79th st, s s, 40 w 10th av, 40x102.2. Sub. to morts. $183,668 on this and other property. Oct. 7, demand. 7,445

Same to Paul Gautert & Son. Amsterdam av, s w cor 79th st, 102.2x100. Sub. to morts. $183,668. Oct. 7, note. 1,268

Same to Ernest F. Amsler. Same property. Sub. to morts. $183,668. Oct. 5, demand. 1,000

Hall, John T. to Aaron Ogden. 5th av, No. 398, w s, 76.11 n 36th st, runs north 27.7 x west 120 x south 5.9 x west 5 x south 21.10 x east 125. ½ part. Sept. 26, 3 years. 6,000

Hayes, Amelia E. wife of and William B. to George A. Barker et al. exrs. and trustees George Bell. Lenox av, n e cor 131st st, 17x85. Sept. 28, 3 years, 5 %. 16,000

Janeway, Hugh H. to Sarah R. N. wife of Willard P. Voorhees, New Brunswick, N. J. City Hall pl, No. 6; Centre st, No. 20, begins Centre st, s e s, 12.8 s w Reade st, 41.7x35.3 to City Hall pl, x23.10x55.4. Oct. 1, due May 1, 1893. 2,000

Johann, Jacob and Margaretha to George Esswein and Katharina his wife. 89th st. P. M. Sept. 30, due Oct. 1, 1896, 5 %. 3,500

Jordan, Alexander A. to Alexandrina Jordan. 123d st, s e cor Lexington av, 35x100.11. Sub. to mort. $55,000. 5Oct. 1, years. 10,000

Kervan, Matthew C. and Charles to The Bradley & Currier Co. (Lim.) Amsterdam av, e s, 275 s 133d st, 75x100. Sub. to mort. $42,000. Sept. 4, 3 months. 7,450

Kilpatrick, Charles to David Weisburger. 60th st. P. M. Oct. 2, due Oct. 15, 1893. 1,000

Kilpatrick, James to Edgar S. Appelby. 95th st. s s, 200 e 2d av, 100x100.8. *Mt.* $12,500. Oct. 1, due Oct. 2, 1892. 10,000

Kleinhans, Jacob and Phillipina his wife to Emilie S. Lentz. 9th st. P. M. Oct. 1, due Jan. 1, 1897, 5 %. 5,000

Krapp, Nicholaus and Theresa his wife to Otto N. J. Egner. West End av, s e cor 69th st, 25.5x100. Sept. 30, 1 year, 5 %. 2,000

Knauf, Peter and Maria his wife to Helene Spengler. Robbins av. P. M. Oct. 3, 3 years, 5 %. 1,000

Koch, Frank to John J. Brown et al. exrs. George Brown. Prescott av and Bolton road. P. M. Oct. 3, 3 years, 5 %. 6,000

Kroenke, Henry to Henry Staats. Av A, n e cor 18th st, 23x64. Lease. Oct. 3, due Oct. 1, 1896, 5½ %. 5,000

Kennedy, Carrie S. wife of Daniel T. to The Germania Life Ins. Co., City New York. 71st st, s s, 125 w Central Park West, 5 lots, each 20x99.5. 5 morts., each $25,000. Oct. 6, 3 years, 6 and 5 %. gold, 125,000

Koelle, Louis to The Sun and Evening Sun Building, Mutual Loan and Accumulating Fund Assoc. Briggs av. P. M. Oct. 1, installs, 5 %. 5,400

Katz, Abraham and Louis Maier to August Hassey. Av B. P. M. Oct. 8, 5 years, 5 %. 13,000

Kaufmann, Ignatz to Louis Kircher, Mt. Vernon, N. Y. Cannon st. P. M. Oct. 6, due Oct 7, 1894, 5 %. 8,000

Kelly, Mary J. wife of and Thomas P. to Henry M. Bendheim. Av B, e s, 22 s 17th st, 20x68. Oct. 1, 1 year or sooner. 556

Same to Bertha Davis. Same property. Oct. 1, demand. See Conveys. 2,000

Kilpatrick, Edward to William M. Kingsland, Mt. Pleasant, N. Y. West End av, n e cor 97th st, 19.11x89. Oct. 7, 3 years, 5 %. 23,000

Same to Cornelius F. Kingsland, Mt. Pleasant, N. Y. West End av, e s, 91.11 s 98th st, 18x100. Oct. 7, 3 years, 5 %. 15,000

Same to Louisa Minturn, Lenox, Mass. West End av, e s, 55.11 n 97th st, 18x89. Oct. 7, 3 years, 5 %. 15,000

Same to John A. Aspinwall and ano. trustees of Katharine A. Kingsland. 97th st, n s, 89 e West End av, 18x91.11. Oct. 7, 3 years, 5 %. 11,200

Same to John A. Aspinwall and ano. trustees of Louisa Minturn. 97th st, n s, 107 e West End av, 18x91.11. Oct. 7, 3 years, 5 %. 11,200

Klebisch, Charles W. to Anton Schwarz. 106th st, n s, 150 e Madison av, 24.9x100.11. Sub. to mort. $17,000. Oct. 5, 2 years, 5 %. 3,000

Levy, Isaac to Joseph Goldstein. Suffolk st. P. M. Sub. to morts. $25,000. Oct. 1, installs. 7,850

Loehr, Barbara to Theresa Seifeiling. 55th st, s s, 340 7 w 9th av, 21.10x100.5. Aug. 5, due Jan. 15, 1895, 5 %. 6,000

Lowenfeld, Pincus, Morris Goldstein and Mark Blumenthal to Aaron Goodman. Delancey st and Suffolk st. P. M. Sept. 30, due April 1, 1893. 2,000

Levy, Nathan and Marx Meyer to Daniel Dressner, Brooklyn. Essex st, e s, abt 125 s Hester st, 19.3x100x19.6x100. Aug. 10, 5 years. 19,000

Lee, Walter J. to John S. Huyler. Bainbridge av, e s, 208.7 s Travers st. P. M. Sept. 26, due Oct. 1, 1892. 5,000

Same to same. Bainbridge av, e s, 155 s Travers st. P. M. Sept. 26, due Oct. 1, 1892. 5,000

Lennon, William F. to George E. Hyatt, Brooklyn. Columbus av, w s, 125.9 n 95th st. 25.2x100. Sept. 9, due May 1, 1892. 22,500

Lipman, Morris, New York, and Abraham, Oil City, Pa., to Aaron Kaplan. 102d st, n s, 230 e 3d av, 25x100.11. P. M. Sept. 29, due Nov. 20, 1893. 1,400

Louis, Lavinia widow with Regine Bunzfl both mortgagees. Agreement as to priority of mortgages made by Caroline wife of and Daniel Honigsberger. Oct. 5. nom

Lawson, William H., Brooklyn, to Benjamin R. Miller. Monroe av. P. M. Oct. 8, 1 year, 5 %. 20,200

Lockman, Mary R. to The Harlem Savings Bank. Madison av, s w cor Grove st, 135x157x135.2x162. Oct. 1, 1 year, 5 %. 2,700

Loewenberg, Edward to Alexander T. Watson trustee Helen K. Watson. 8th st. Sept. 26. 2 years. See Leasehold Conveys. 2,000

Loewy, Joseph to The Harlem Savings Bank. North 3d av, s e s, 362.11 n e Grove st, 36x180 to n w s Mill Brook, x36x164. Oct. 2, 1 year, 5 %. 10,000

Lowenberg, Edward to Amanda Basch. 123d st. P. M. Oct. 1, 5 years or installs, 5 %. 2,000

Lynch, Thomas J. to James D. Lynch. Amsterdam or 10th av, s e cor 68th st, 50.5x100. Sept. 29, 1 year, 5 %. 2,450

Muller, Valentine H. to James F. and Patrick H. Sheridan and James S. Segrave. Field st. P. M. Sept. 30, due Oct. 1, 1894, 5 %. 350

McCarthy, Mary E. wife of Frederick to John V. Fenchere. Prospect av, e s, 200 n of lot 67 map of Woodstock, 16.8x100. Oct. 1, due Jan. 1, 1895, 5 %. 3,000

Same to Mary A. Handes. Prospect av, e s, 216.8 n lot 67 same map, 16.8x100. Oct. 1, due Jan. 1, 1895, 5 %. 2,500

Same to Louisa Widder. Prospect av, e s, 233.4 n lot 67 same map, 16.8x100. Oct. 1, due Jan. 1, 1895, 5 %. 2,500

Morison, Rachel S., Margaret A. and Stella A. devisees Frederick S. Morison to Eugenia D. wife of Henry Wiener, Philadelphia. 42d st, No. 143, n s, 137.10 e Broadway, 25x100.5. Oct. 6, 7 years, 4½ %. 4,000

Morton, William and Thomas and David Brown to William Rankin. Madison st. P. M. Oct. 1, 1 year or sooner. 20,000

Same to same. Same property. Oct. 1, demand. 30,500

Mullen, Matthew to The Mt. St. Vincent Co-operative Building and Loan Assoc. 98th st, s s, 175 e 2d av, 25x100.9. Oct. 6, installs, 5 %. 5,000

Martin, Henry to Eva Bechtel extrx. George Bechtel. 1st av, No. 489. Store lease. Oct. 7, demand. 362

Martin, James to Patrick Keirns. 128th st. P. M. Sept. 25, due Oct. 1, 1893, 5 %. 5,500

McGrory, Anna to Isaac Danenburg. 93d st, No. 185, n s, 100 w 3d av, runs north 94.8 x west abt 10 x north — to centre line block, x west 20.6 x south 100.8 to st, x east 30.6. Oct. 7, 1 year, 5 %. 9,000

Morrison, Sarah to Edith Jayne. 128th st, n s, 183.4 w 7th av widened, 16.8x99.11. Sept. 30, due Oct. 8, 1892. 2,500

Muller, Michael to Bernheimer & Schmid. 1st av, No. 1549, s w cor 81st st. Saloon lease. Oct. 8, note, demand. 4,000

Nelson, Charles E. to James S. Stearns, Brooklyn. 35th st, n s, 142.6 e Park av, 18.9x98.9. Oct. 5, due Jan. 1, 1896, or sooner, 5 %. 850

O'Gorman, Edward J. to John H. Morrison, Jr. Belmont av, s e s, lot 4 map East Tremont, 60.5x176x60x168.5. Sept. 24, 3 years or sooner. 1,000

O'Gorman, Edward J. to David Webster exr. Caroline Webster. Jefferson av. P. M. Sept. 24, 2 years, 5½ %. 1,500

Otto, Richard F. to Mary A. Ritchie. Washington av, w s, 400 s 171st st. P. M. Oct. 1, 5 years or installs, 5 %. 8,000

O'Halloran, Patrick D. to Peter Doelger. Christopher st, No. 185. Store lease. Oct. 2, demand. 475

Pendergast, Louisa I. wife of Charles H. to William P. Woodcock, Bedford, N. Y. 51st st, s s, 729 w 5th av, 21x100.5. Lease. Sub. to morts. $7,000. Oct. 2, 3 years, 5 %. 2,000

Pentz, Margaret C. wife of George B. to Rufus L. Todd exr. of Mary L. Todd. Grand st. n s, 50 e Forsyth st, 25x87.6. 1-6 part. July 9, 1 year, 5 %. 1,000

Pierce, Madeline to The Title Guarantee and Trust Co. Charles st. P. M. Aug. 31, due Sept. 1, 1896, 4½ %. 5,000

Phoenix, Phillips & Lloyd trustees S. Whitney Phoenix mortgagees with Morris Goldberg and Nathan Shancupp, present owners Agreement subordinating mortgage to party wall agreement. Sept. 15. nom

Same with same. Agreement subordinating mortgage to party wall agreement. Oct. 2. nom

Reilly, John J. to George E. Hyatt, Brooklyn. 2d av, e s, 50.2 n 59th st, 25.3x76.7. Oct. 2, due Jan. 15, 1892. 1,500

Regan, John to James and Mary A. O'Neill. 38th st, No 452, s s, 125 e 10th av, 25x98.9. Oct. 5, 3 years, 5 %. 3,000

Reckendorfer, Louis J., present owner, to The Germania Life Ins. Co. Certificate of validity of mortgage made by George H. Purser and that amount due thereon is 30,000

Ruff, August to George W. Adams. Suffolk st. P. M. Oct. 6, 1 year or sooner, 5 %. 10,000

Regnier, Elise otherwise Lena de Merville to Delilah L. Shorb. 50th st, Nos. 106 and 108 W. Leasehold. Secures notes. Sept. 8. 3,000

Ritchie, Mary A. wife of Peter C. to William Cauldwell. Washington av, w s, 425 s 171st st, 50x150. Oct. 1, 2 years, 5 %. 4,100

Rohrs, Frederick to The Bradley & Currier Co. (Lim.) 134th st, s s, 100 w Alexander av, 25x100. Sub. to mort. $13,000. Sept. 30, 1 year. 1,500

Ratkowsky, Harris to Joseph Kojawsky. Ludlow st. P. M. Oct. 1, 6 months. 1,000

Rutherfurd, Winthrop C. to Douglas Robinson, Herkimer Co., N. Y. 18th st, s s, 265 w 2d av, 18x80. Oct. 8, due Nov. 1, 1893, 5½ %. 6,000

Riker, William B. to George F. Martens. 6th av, w s, 23 s 22d st, 20x65; 74th st, s s, 222 w 9th av, 20x102.2. Oct. 2, demand. 16,000

Shepard, Clara V. wife of and Charles D. to Henry Morgenthau. Lenox av, s e cor 120th st, 19.8x85. Sept. 30, installs, 5 %. 15,000

Steinhardt, Benjamin to Minnie Bayer guard. of Stephen A. and Edwin M. Bayer. Boulevard, w s, 57.6 n 77th st, 19.2x—. Oct. 5, 1 year, 5 %. 14,000

Sauter, John G. mortgagor with Harriet G. Benson, Brooklyn mortgagee. Extension of mort. Sept. 30. nom

Shapiro, Morris to Charles Dexheimer. Henry st, No. 96. P. M. Oct. 2, due April 1, 1892. 1,000

Shapiro, Morris to Michael Fey and William Stacom. Henry st. P. M. Oct. 2, installs, 9,750

Sherman, Frederick W. to Augustus M. Herring. 25th st, No. 208, s s, 146.5 e 3d av, 24.5x98.9. Oct. 5, notes. 6,500

Smith, Frank C. to Douglas Robinson. 185th st, s s, 225 w Amsterdam av, 25x179.10 to 184th st. Oct. 3, due Oct. 1, 1896, 5 %. 5,400

Smith, William C. to Henry Burden trustee Henry Burden dec'd. Watts st, Nos. 34, 36 and 38, n s, 69.7 w Varick st, runs north along alley 63.6 x west 9.10 x north 17 x west along another alley 9 ft. wide running into Watts st, 50.4 x south 80 to Watts st, x east 60.6, with all title to alley. Oct. 1, 1 year, 4½ %. 27,457

Stadecker, Leopold and Jacob Emsheimer to Justus L. Bulkley et al. exrs., &c., Daniel B. Fayerweather. Thompson st, Nos. 34, 36 and 38, e s, 162 8 n Grand st, 61.10x94; South 5th av, Nos. 190, 192 and 194, w s, 125.3 s Broome st, 59.5x68.7x59.5x68.3. July 27, due Nov 1, 1894, 4½ %. 80,000

Sauervein, John L. to Isaac Fry. 8th av, No. 882, e s, 61 2 s 53d st, 19.7x80. Oct. 7, 5 years, 4½ %. 15,000

Slezefsky, George to Sarah Lese. Delancey st, No. 225, s w s. Oct. 5, installs. See Conveys. 3,800

Smith, John B. to The Mutual Life Ins. Co., New York. Bedford st, No. 35, w s, 75 n Downing st, 15x62.6; Downing st, Nos. 41 and 43, n s, 62.6 w Bedford st, 30.1x90. Oct. 5, due Oct. 7, 1892, 5 %. 15,000

Spiel, Bertha wife of Otto to Annie Ormiston. Forest av, e s, 180 5 n Cedar st, 18.7x110 to lane, x18.7x110. Oct. 7, due Dec. 1, 1894. 2,100

Sturges, Daniel L. to Antoinette C. wife of Charles E. Hughes, Ithaca, N. Y. 88th st. P. M. Oct. 5, installs. 5,250

Sturtz, Lizzie wife of Max to Herman Fichter, Barnett Levy, Louis Gordon and Sophia Mayer. Lewis st, No. 118. P. M. Oct. 1, 3 years. 2,900

Schloss, Nathan J. mortgagor with Henry A. C. Taylor, Newport, R. I., mortgagee. Extension of mort. Sept. 24. nom

Shannon, Thomas F. and Mary his wife to William T. Washburn and ano. exrs. Benjamin Richardson. Pleasant av and 115th st. P. M. Oct. 2, due Dec. 31, 1891, 5 %. 11,000

Smith, Jennet wife of John W. to Ryan & Rawnsley. 92d st, n s, 238.6 w 9th av, 36.6x100.8. Sub. to morts. Sept. 16, 1 year, 5 %. 4,000

Steiner, Joseph to The Baron de Hirsch Fund. Broome and Elm sts. P. M. Oct. 1, 3 years, 5 %. 40,000

Sauervein, John L. and Sarah his wife to John H. V. Arnold. South 5th av, No. 60, w s, 25x75. Oct. 7. Collateral to mort. on No. 882 8th av, due June 1, 1892, for 4,000

Smith, Samuel W. R. to Charles F. Henke. Downing st, s s, 175.1 w Bedford st, 19.9x87.4x20.9x92.4. Oct. 8, due March 1, 1892, 5 %. 6,500

Stephens, Laura J., Yonkers, N. Y., to Abraham Steers. 115th st, n s, 175 w Lenox av, 50x100.11. Sept. 30, demand. 1,000

Same to George W. Morrow, Jersey City, N. J. Same property Sept. 30, demand. 1,000

Stubmer, Otto to Louis P. Mahler. Orchard st, No. 109, w s, 25x87.6. Oct. 1, due Jan. 1, 1895. See Conveys. 3,000

Thomas, Samuel A. to Hebrew Relief Society. Mott av, e s, 205.2 s 149th st, 18x108. Oct. 5, 5 years, 5 %. gold, 5,000

Thomson, George to Alexander Hadden. 69th st. P. M. Oct. 1, 3 years, 5 %. 7,000

Same to same. Same property. Oct. 1, 8 months. 2,000

Thurber, Horace K. to The Title Guarantee and Trust Co. Renwick st, w s, 131.4 s Spring st, runs west 36.2 x south 8.3 x northwest 28.4 x west 17.4 x south 57.1 x east 5 x south 25.4 x east 70 to st, x north 72.8. Oct. 2, due Oct. 6, 1894, 5 %. 35,000

The Church of St. Francis of Assisi to The Emigrant Indust. Savings Bank. 31st st, n s, 275 e 7th av, runs north 126 x east 25 x north 71.6 to 32d st, x east 25 x south 49 x east 75 x south 148.6 to 31st st, x west 125; 31st st, n s, 275 w 6th av, 24.6x98.9. Oct. 7, 1 year, 4½ %. 60,000

The Bradley & Currier Co. (Lim.) with Ryan & Rawnsley both mortgagees. Agreement as to priority of mortgages made by Jennet and John W. Smith. Sept. 26. nom

Tilden, Lilian E. F. widow to George W. H. Iago mortgagors, ½ share in late Milano C. Tilden's share of his father's (William Tilden) state, real and personal. Sept. 25, due March 25, 1892. £300

Same to Harry Mear and George J. Fowler. Same property. Sept. 25. secures atty's costs and expenses

Ueckermann, Marie wife of and William to Lambert Suydam. 87th st, s s, 107.9 w Park av, 51.1x100.8. Oct. 6, due Jan. 1, 1892. 3,000

Uhlig, Caroline to Wilbur F. Washburn, Yonkers, N. Y. 97th st. P. M. Sept. 15, due March 15, 1895, or installs, 5 %. 3,500

Uihlein, Frank A. to Elisabeth Appel. 89th st, n s, 200 w 1st av, 25x100.8. Sept. 30, due Oct. 1, 1894, 5 %. 10,000

Uihlein, Anna C. to Joseph Grunder and Elisabetha his wife. 89th st, n s, 225 w 1st av, 25x100.8. Sept. 30, due Oct. 1, 1896, 5 %. 10 000

Viebrock, Henry C. to Henry Gaffken. 6th av. No. 813. Saloon lease. Oct. 1, installs, note, 5 %. 16,000

Voellmeke, Franz to The Knickerbocker Trust Co. 85th st, s s, 256 e 1st av, 25x100.8, Oct. 5, 1 year, 5 %. 10,000

Weiss, Rosa to Henry Braun. East Houston st, No. 387, s s, 57.5 e Willett st, 20.6x100. Oct. 5, due Oct. 1, 1894. 2,000

Williams, Richard D. and Lillian M. to Henrietta and Mary E. Speke. Centre st and Walker st, 24th Ward. P. M. Oct. 5, 3 years. 2,000

Wilkes, Lizzie T. to Thomas Tracy. 132d st, No. 6, s s, 125 e 5th av, 25x99.11. Sept. 29, 2 months. 1,500

Wilkes, Lizzie T. wife of George S. to George S. Wilkes. 132d st, s s, 125 e 5th av, 85x99.11. June 1, 3 months. 3,000

Wilson, Mary wife of John A. to The Metropolitan Life Ins. Co. 31st st, n s. 175 w 7th av, 25x98.9. Oct. 6, due Oct. 1, 1896, or part sooner, 6 % and 5 % 25,000

Wilson, Mary wife of and John to Reuben Ross. Same property. Sub. to last mort. Oct. 6, 1 year. 3,500

Wuest, Henry to John Andreas and Marie his wife. Railroad av. P. M. Sept. 10, 3 years, 5 %. 2,000

Wood, Philip to David McClure. West End av, No. 63, w s, 25.5 n 67th st, 25x80. Oct. 7, 3 years, 5 %. 12,000

Weinstein, Ascher to Virginia Hall. 32d st, s s, 250 e 9th av, 16.8x98.9. Oct. 2, 3 years or sooner. 3,000

Whiting, Jennie N. wife of and Holland S. to Hyman Sylvester. 35th st, n s, 289.3 e 6th av, 21.5x98.9. Aug. 10, due Aug. 12, 1892. 1,000

Walker, Frederick H. to George W. R. Matteson et al. trustees John C. Brown dec'd Columbus av, w s, 25.8 n 82d st, 25.6x100. Oct. 2, 5 years, 5 %. 18,000

Walker, Mary A. to Anna N. Rogers. Riverview terrace, e s, lot 22 map of Mary A. Walker, Morris Dock, 24th Ward, 241.1 n Fordham Morris' land, 87x125. Oct. 2, 3 months. 1,500

Walters, Louisa M. formerly Cregier to John A. Weekes, Jr. 116th st, n s, 159 e 1st av, 18x100.11. Oct. 2, due Nov. 1, 1892. gold, 500

Werner, Francis X. and Catharine his wife to James F. and Patrick H. Sheridan and James S. Segrave. Rock and Forest sts. P. M. Sept. 30, due Oct. 1, 1894, 5 %. 1,350

Wiehe, Jacob and Magdalena Endholz to Margaret Hildebrandt. 10th st. P. M. Sub. to mort. $10,000. Oct. 1, 3 years, 5 %. 4,000

Wilcox, Agnes R. wife of Clermont H. to The Title Guarantee and Trust Co. 75th st. P. M. Sept. 30, due Oct. 2, 1894, 4½ %. 15,000

Wolf, Betsey to William Hodge et al. exrs. Eliza Hodge. Henry st. P. M. Oct. 1, 3 years, 5 %. 20,000

Same to Isaac Cohen. Same property. Sub. to last mort. Oct. 1, 1 year. 1,000

Woolson, Elmer E. to James F. and Patrick H. Sheridan and James S. Segrave. Field st. P. M. Sept. 30, due Oct. 1, 1894, 5 %. 930

Woolson, John A. to James F. and Patrick H. Sheridan and James S. Segrave. Field st. P. M. Sept. 30, due Oct. 1, 1894, 5 %. 1,220

Wood, Philip to Lenore H. Garretson. West End av, w s, 25 5 n 67th st, 25x80. Oct. 7, due Oct. 1, 1892. 1,500

Yale, William H. to The Inst. for Savings of Merchants' Clerks. Warren av, w s, 285.2 from point of intersection of the prolongation of the e s of the Spuyten Duyvil Parkway, runs southwest 204.2 x southwest 181.9 x southwest 114.1 to e s Johnson av, x southeast 188.6 x northeast 82.3 x southeast 319 x northeast 150 x northeast 102.6 x northwest 105 x southwest 48.8 to Warren av, x north following curves and courses 383.6. Secures bond of mortgagor and Henry C. Yale. Oct. 7, 5 years, 4½ %. gold, 15,000

Zucker, Morris and David Hoschner or Hochner to Max Frankenheim. 69th st, No. 339, n s, 99.6 w 1st av, 25.6x100.5. P. M. Oct. 1, installs. 4,700

Zucker, Alfred J. R. E. mortgagor with Miln P. Palmer trustee Frances B. Hegeman dec'd. Extension of reduced mort. Oct. 1. nom

KINGS COUNTY.

OCTOBER 1, 2, 3, 5, 6, 7.

Ackerman, Sarah A. widow to Cornelius N. Hoagland. Madison st, n s, 96 e Sumner av, 18x100. Sept. 30, due Nov. 1, 1894, 5 %. gold, $5,000

Abbe, Ida P. wife of and Walter to The Title Guarantee and Trust Co. St. Marks av, n s, 80 e Carlton av, 20x90. Oct. 6, due Sept. 30, 1894, 5 %. 4,500

Adams, Bentley F. to The Title Guarantee and Trust Co. Eastern Parkway, Atkins av, Glenmore av, Montauk av. P. M. Oct. 2, 1 year, 5 %. 5,000

Allen, Annie C. wife of Howard D. to William Laytin et al. trustees William Laytin. Weirfield st, n w s, 201.2 s w Central av, 20x100. Oct. 5, 3 years, 5 %. 2,800

Same to Leopold J. Lippmann. Same property. P. M. Sub. to last mort. Oct. 5, installs. 1,700

Allen, Franklin to Albert Van Brunt Voorhees. 73d st, n e s, 120 n w 13th av, 480x100; 12th av, west cor 73d st, 200 to 74th st, x northwest 460 x northeast 100 x southeast 360 x northeast to 73d st, x southeast 100; 12th av and 13th av, 73d and 74th sts—the block; 11th av and 12th av, 74th st and 75th st—the block; 12th av, south cor 74th st, 100x180; 11th av, west cor 75th st, runs northwest 480 x southwest 100 x southeast 20 x southwest 100 to 76th st, x southeast 300 x northeast 100 x southeast 160 to 11th av, x northeast 100; 11th av, south cor 75th st, 100x160; 76th st, s w s, 320 n w 11th av, 160x100, New Utrecht. Sept. 23, due Nov. 7, 1891, 5 %. 16,000

Altmuller, Mary A. C. widow to The Brooklyn Trust Co. Park pl, No. 118, s s, 334.7 e 6th av, 20x100. Oct. 6, 3 years, 5 %. 2,000

Anderson, James to Mathias Hauser. Kosciusko st. P. M. Oct. 1, 5 years, 5 %. 3,200

Anderson, Robert H. to Andrew D. Baird. Vernon av, s s, 220 w Throop av, 160x100. Sub. to morts. $17,600. Sept. 11, due Nov. 1, 1891. 2,000

Antrobus, Mary A. and Thomas mortgagors with Lucy R. Blancke mortgagee. Extension of mort. Sept. 31. nom

Asher, James to Jacob Strauss. Utica av and Furnald st. P. M. Oct. 1, 5 years, 5 % 1,000

Asmus, Ludwig to Jacob Geist. North 2d st. P. M. Oct. 1, due Nov. 1, 1896, 5 %. 3,200

Atwell, Josephine B. wife of Amos M. to Alvin Graff, Spring Valley, N. Y. Dean st, s s, 380 e Franklin av, 20x110. Sub. to morts. $2,550. Oct. 1, 1 year. 500

Avery, Edward W. to The Title Guarantee and Trust Co. Prospect pl, s s, 200 w Kingston av, 80x255.7 to Park pl. Oct. 6, 1 year. 6,000

Bach, Meyer and Albert Sokolski to Henry Heymann. Throop av, s w cor Wallabout st, 25x75 Sept. 29, installs, 5 %. 2,600

Bates, Jerome E. to Albert Delafield et al. trustees Richard Delafield. Washington av, w s, 176.3 s Lafayette av, 25x211.1 to Waverly av. Sept. 30, due Nov. 15, 1894, 4½ %. 10,000

Baker, Albert G. to Lottie N. Palmer. Poplar st, n e s, 51.5 s e Buckbees alley, 51x67.8x57.10x95.6. Oct. 1, due March 1, 1892. 3,000

Baker, Janet wife of and Lewis H. to A. Maria Brown. Verona pl, e s, 270 n Fulton st, 19x78.2x19.6x82.5. Oct. 5, 5 years, 5 %. 4,000

Barber, Letitia wife of and William H. to Bridget Ward. 48th st, s s, 240 e 3d av, 20x100.2. Sept. 15, 3 years, 5 %. 2,000

Barre, Adelaide P. to Florence E. Morris. Hanson pl, s s, 20 e Elliott pl, 20x90. Sept. 30, 2 years. 1,000

Barschow, Frederick C. to Frederick Black. Conover st, n w s, 75 n e Dikeman st, 25x100. July 29, 3 years. 1,000

Basler, Hugo to Christian and Christina Huber. Hopkins st. P. M. Oct. 1, 3 years, 5 %. 2,500

Bauer, John, Jr., and Dorothea to Sarah C. Savage trustee Elihu Chauncey dec'd. Park av. P. M. Oct. 1, 1 year, 5 %. 3,300

Bayerdoefer, Frank to Henry Ginnel. Lewis av. P. M. Oct. 1, 3 years, 5 %. 3,500

Bayn, John F. to Wilhelmine Holzapfel. Pacific st. P. M. Oct. 5, 1 year. 900

Behlert, Charles L. to George Wilson. Myrtle av. P. M. Oct. 1, 3 years, 5 %. 5,000

Bennett, Mary L. to The East New York Savings Bank. Norwood av, w s, 1,025 n Hatton pl, 45.6x150. Sept. 30, 1 year. 1,800

Benziger, Louis heir Joseph to John Gratzer. Jefferson st, s e s, 200 s w Hamburg av, 24.10x100. Oct. 5, due Nov. 1, 1893, 5 %. 600

Bergen, Edward E. to James Dunn, New York. Dean st, s s, 200 w Clason av, 25x110. Oct. 1, 2 years. 1,000

Same to same. Dean st, s s, 225 w Clason av, 25x110. Oct. 1, 2 years. 1,000

Berger, Richard A. to Louisa wife of Simon K. Saenger. Beaver st, s w s, 25 s e Fayette st, 25x100. Oct. 1, 5 years, 5 %. 4,500

Berri, Eugene D. to The Title Guarantee and Trust Co. Bedford av, w s, 80 n Butler st, 79x—x—x100. Oct. 6, 2 years. 4,000

Bertram, John H. to William Graf. St. Marks av, s s, 440 e Troy av, 22.8x127.9x22.8x127.9. Sept. 21, demand. 1,000

Betts, Cordelia E. wife of Henry L., Philadelphia, Pa., to Mary L. Phipard. Herkimer st, s s, 375.7 e Nostrand av, 20x85.6. Oct. 1, 1 year. 4,500

Bigelow, Anna E. to Clarence Creighton and ano. exrs. Christopher Risley. 53d st, s w s, 130 n w 4th av, 80x100.2. Sept. 24, 3 years, 5 %. 2,500

Blaser, Josephine to Julia E. Soutter trustee for Ellen M. B. and James T. Soutter. Bay 32d st, s e s, 100 s w Benson av, 100x96.8, New Utrecht. Sept. 15, 3 years, 5 %. gold, 3,000

Blochle, Andrew to Joseph Riecker. Eagle st. P. M. Sept. 30, 3 years, 5 %. 1,000

Bolles, Matilda L., Bayport, Conn., to Frank E. Hart. Atlantic av, s s, 81.6 w Williams av, 20x104.11x20x101.3. Sept. 18, 3 years. 1,400

Same to same. Atlantic av, s s, 61.2 w Williams av, 20.4x101.1x20x97.2. Sept. 18, 3 years. 1,450

Bollmann, John H. to Otto W. P. Westervelt trustee Andreas F. Meineke. Fulton st, No. 1169, n s, 105.7 w Spencer pl, 20x75.8x21.11x84.7. Oct. 1, 3 years, 5 %. 9,000

Bonert, Louis to The Title Guarantee and Trust Co. 10th st, s s, 399.8 e 7th av, 4 lots, each 20x100. 4 morts., each $5,000. Oct. 1, 3 years, 5 %. 20,000

Bradshaw, Nathan F. to Margaret R. Bateman. Mill road, south cor old road to shore, runs southeast 30 x southwest 92 x northwest 41 x northeast 82, New Utrecht. Oct. 1, 3 years, 5 %. 1,200

Bonny, Josie wife of and Frank S. to Frank G. Pardou. Lewis av, n w cor Hancock st, 80x100. Sept. 9, due Sept. 30, 1892, 5 %. 1,050

Brady, John, Jr., to The Title Guarantee and Trust Co. Weirfield st. P. M. Oct. 1, 3 years, 5 % 2,500

Same to Leopold J. Lippmann. Same property. P. M. 2d mort. Oct. 1, 5 years. 2,100

Breitenstein, Frederick to The East New York Savings Bank. Snediker av, w s, 350 s Newport av, runs west 100 x south 50 x west 100 to Vesta av, x south 100 to Lott av, x east to New Lots road, x northeast to Snediker av, x north —. Sept 16, 1 year. 1,500

Brennan, John J. to James D. Lynch. Benson av, east cor Bay 32d st, 96.8x100. Sept. 12, demand, 5 %. 1,500

Brookman, Simon to Henry Cohn. Leonard st, e s, 25 s McKibbin st, 25x100. Oct. 1, 1 year, 5 %. 550

Brown, Thomas to Jane Copeland admrx. George Copeland. 5th av, e s, 40 s Berkeley pl, 27.6x87.2. Sept. 28, 3 years, 5 %. 10,000

Brown, William to Max Bottstein. 12th st, n s, 105 9 w 4th av, 25x100. Sub. to mort. $6,500. Sept. 30, 1 year. 1,500

Same to same. 12th st, n s, 130.9 w 4th av, 25x100. Sub. to mort. $6,500. Sept. 30, 1 year. 1,500

Burke, Catharine wife of and Francis to Susan Ward. Lot in 8th Ward, begins at west cor of land of Thomas Hunt, runs northeast — x southeast to line 400 e 6th av, x south 449 x northwest —, indeft. Oct. 1, 5 years, 5 %. 1,700

Burley, Joseph to The General Synod of the Reformed Church in America. Lewis av, e s, 33.4 n Kosciusko st. P. M. Oct. 2, installs, 5 %. 4,000

Bush, Wesley C. to Henry Weil. Hancock st, n s, 325 e Lewis av, 100x100. Oct. 1, 1 year, 5 %. 10,000

Byk, Poline wife of and Morris to Artlissa V. wife of Miles Gearon. Hancock st, No. 501, – s, 30 w Lewis av, 18x100. Oct. 6, 6 months. 1,500

Caddell, Mary T. J. to Oscar C. Hamlet and Annie his wife, Boston, Mass. Schenectady av. P. M. Sept. 24, due Oct. 1, 1895. 900

Campbell, John to The Title Guarantee and Trust Co. Putnam av, n s, 194.1 e Patchen av, 18.9x100. Oct. 2, 3 years, 5 %. 3,500

Carroll, James G. to Benjamin Shreve. 4th av, n e cor 47th st. P. M. Oct. 6, 1 year, 5 %. 2,500

Cassidy, Josephine A. to The Brooklyn Savings Bank. Nassau st, n w cor Navy st, 18.9x77. Oct. 1, 1 year, 5 %. 500

Chase, Oscar J. to James A Canfield. Stockholm st. P. M. Oct. 2, 3 years. 1,950

Cheesman, Phebe A. widow to Cornelius N. Hoagland. Putnam av, n s, 235 e Tompkins av, 20x100. Oct. 1, due Nov. 1, 1894, 5 %. gold, 5,000

Clausen, Mary A. to John Hayes and Ann his wife. 65th st, n s, 100 w 13th av, 60x100, New Utrecht. Sept. 30, 5 years. 1,000

Clementson, James D., Philadelphia, Pa., to Samuel Riker. Clarkson st, s s, 367 w Irving pl, 175x250 to Crooke av, Flatbush. Sept. 24, due May 1, 1892, 5 %. 2,500

Cleverley, William to George W. Pearsall. 14th st. P. M. Oct. 5, 1 month. 800

Same to Annie L. Hyland. Same property. P. M Oct 5, due Oct. 1, 1892. 400

Cochran, John C. to Cornelius N. Hoagland. Monroe st, s s, 90 w Sumner av, 20x100. Sept. 30, due Nov. 1, 1894, 5 %. gold, 4,000

Colgan, Frank to Mary J. Colgan. Steuben st, w s, 215 s Park av, 30x100. Oct. 6, 5 years, 5 %. 3,000

Collins, Edmund R. to Margaret Demarest, Belleville, N. J. Fulton st, s s, 225 e Stone av, 25x100. Oct. 2, due Dec. 1, 1894. 5,000

Same to Charles M. Demarest et al. exrs. Cornelius H. Demarest. Fulton st, s s, 200 e Stone av, 25x100. Oct. 2, due Dec. 1, 1894. 5,000

Same to Watson & Pittinger. Fulton st, s s, 200 e Stone av, 50x100. Oct. 2, demand. 2,500

Collins, Mary to Theodore E. and George W. Green. Roebling st, e s, 25 s North 6th st, 25x50. Oct. 1, 1 year. 250

Conklin, Mabel wife of and David H. to Hannah Green. New York av, w s, 70 s Herkimer st, 17x76.6. Oct. 1, due May 1, 1895, or installs. 2,700

Conlin, Margaret wife of Richard A. to Frederick M. Alles. Hooper st, s e s, 57 3 s w South 3d st, 22.2x50. Sept. 16, 5 years, 5½ %. 4,000

Cornwell, Theodore I. W. to The Metropolitan Life Ins. Co. St. Marks av, n s, 316.6 e Clason av, 26x70. Sept. 29, due Oct. 1, 1896, installs; until Oct. 1, 1892, 6 %; after, 5 %. 6,500

Same to same. St. Marks av, n s, 368 e Clason av, runs east to point 375 w Franklin av, x north 126 x west 31.11 to centre Clason av, x northwest 44.11 x west to point 265 e Clason av, present line, x south 1.4 x east 103 x south 70. Sept. 29, due Oct. 1, 1896, installs; until Oct. 1, 1892, 6 %; after, 5 %. 5,000

Same to same. St Marks av, n s, 342.6 e Clason av, 25.6x70. Sept. 29, due Oct. 1, 1896, installs; until Oct. 1, 1892, 6 %; after, 5 %. 6,500

Costello, Margaret to John V. Van Pelt. Bay 20th st, New Utrecht. P. M. Oct. 6, 3 years, 5 %. 550

Cramer, Charles F. to Louis A. Mueller, Queens, L. I. Magenta st. P. M. Oct. 1, 3 years, 5 %. 600

Craparella, Giuliano to Sarah Gallagher, Far Rockaway, widow and devisee of George Moore. Broadway. P. M. Oct. 1, installs, 5 %. 1,000

Cross, Charles A. to Charles J. Nielsen. Gates av. P. M. Oct. 1, due Jan. 1, 1893. 1,500

Crosson, Clarissa A. wife of Joel to Catharine J. Westervelt, Newark, N. J. India st, s s, 175 e West st. 25x100. Oct. 1, 3 years, 5 %. 2,000

Cunningham, Lawrence J. to James S. Bearns. Smith st, n e cor State st, 20x78.2x19.11x77. Oct. 1, due July 1, 1892, 5 %. 3,000

Carl, George mortgagor with Barbara Carl mortgagee. Extension of mort. Oct. 7. 1,000

Clauss, Christian to Margaretha Boehm. Jefferson av, n s, 106.7 w Saratoga av, runs northwest 24.7 x northeast 100 to Broadway, x southeast 75 to Saratoga av, x south 34.5 to Jefferson av, x west 106.7. Oct. 6, 1 yr. 1,500

Connors, Patrick to Ellen Hallahan. Baltic st. P. M. Oct 7, 3 years, 5 %. 1,000

Crossman, Greenleaf W. to Mary E. Metcalf. Halsey st. P. M. Oct. 6, installs, 5 %. 2,200

Curran, Mary to The Title Guarantee and Trust Co. Wyckoff st, n s, 660 w Smith st, 25x100. Oct. 6, due Oct. 7, 1892, 5 %. 2,500

Derr, Cristoph and Mary his wife to Anton and John Amann. Willoughby av. P. M. Oct. 3, 3 years, 5 %. 1,250

Daly, Morris to Oscar Abrams. 2d av, w s, — s 41st st, 50x100, error. Sept. 4, 5 years, 5 %. 4,000

Davis, Frank M. to George H. Schneider. 10th st. P. M. Oct. 1, 5 years or installs. 3,200

De Arrastia, Leopoldo to John Dbuy. Atlantic av. P. M.. Oct. 1, 5 years, 5 %. 1,700

Dehn, George to Andrew Siegling and Barbara his wife. Schenck av, w s, 125 n Union av, 25x100. Aug. 24, due July 1, 1896, 5 %. 600

De la Rionde, Bernard to Magin Jauer. Lafayette av, n s, 60 e Nostrand av, 20x70. Oct. 1, 1 year. gold, 4,000

Denison, Charles H. to Ann Ketcham. 5th st. P. M. Oct. 2, due Oct. 3, 1894, 5 %. 4,500

Dobse, John and Alice E. his wife to The Franklin Trust Co. Hancock st. P. M. Oct. 1, due April 1, 1892. 7,500

Dreyfus, Hattie to Henry B. Lyons, Flatbush, L. I. Park pl. P. M. Oct. 1, 2 years. 1,200

Duffy, James S exr. John Grace to Louis DeB. Kuhn. Smith st, s e s, 40 s w Sackett st, 20x80. Sept. 30, 3 years. 1,200

Dumahut, Claudius H. to Charles Hart. 14th st. P. M. Oct. 2, 3 years, 5 %. 2,650

Same to The Emigrant Industrial Savings Bank. 6th av. P. M. Oct. 2, 1 year, 4½ %. 1,200

Same to Henry M. Noa. Same property. Sub. to last mort. Oct. 2, due April 2, 1893, 5 %. 800

Dunham, Josephine wife of William P. to Henry Weil. Stewart st. P. M. Oct. 1, 3 years, 5 %. 1,200

Eirich, Joseph to John A. Bachmann. Hart st, n s, 310 w St. Nicholas av, 20x81.3x20x80.10. Oct. 1, 3 years, 5 %. 1,900

Ennis, Annie S. wife of and William H. to The Title Guarantee and Trust Co. Hart st, n s, 366 w Lewis av. P. M. Oct. 3, 3 years, 5 %. 3,750

Same to George S. Rockwell. Same property. Sub. to last mort. Oct. 3, 1 year, 5 %. 250

Ennis, John to Gertrude Prince, Flatbush, L. I. 57th st, s s, 240 e 2d av, 20x100.2. Oct. 5, 5 years, 5 %. 500

Eppler, Christian and Theresia his wife to Franz Kantler. Hopkins st. P. M. Oct. 1, 5 years, 5 %. 1,100

Erdmann, Ernest to The Kings County Co-operative Building and Loan Assoc. North 6th st. P. M. Sept. 30, installs. 3,000

Erickson, Charles A. to Bernard Larzelere. 96th st, s s, 170.2 e Shore road, 25x100. Oct. 1, 1 year. 3,000

Ernst, Antonia to Amelia Keppes. Cornelia st. P. M. Sept. 29, due Oct. 1, 1892, 5 %. 2,000

Evans, Charles W. to Elizabeth Gerbeth. Reid av. P. M. Oct. 1, 5 %. 900

Evans, Constance to Henry Longman. Hancock st, n w s. 520 n e Bushwick av. P. M. Sept. 30, installs. 1,400

Evers, Sarah to Eliza J. Smith. Schenectady av, s w cor Pacific st, 49.6x100. Sept. 30, 5 years, 5 %. 3,300

Fagans, George W. to John C. Schenck. Jerome st, e s, 137.6 s Arlington av, 37.6x95. Sept. 30, due Oct. 17, 1897, 5 %. 300

Farrell, Michael to Thomas Wilson. Nevins st, e s, 40 s Sackett st, 20x80. Oct. 5, 1 year, 5 %. 1,100

Feeley, Peter to Joseph Liebmann and Theodore Obermeyer. Flushing av, s w cor Marcy av, 25x100; Wyckoff av, north cor Elm st, 40x86.6x40x87.7. Sub. to mort. $5,000 on first parcel. Oct. 1, installs. 5,000

Same to Joseph Liebmann and Theodore Obermeyer. Flushing av, s w cor Marcy av. P. M. Oct. 1, 3 years. 5,000

Feldberg, Johannes to Marie E. Jacobson. Osborn st, n e cor Glenmore av, 50x100. Oct. 2, due April 1, 1892. gold, 4,500

Fenney, Virginia to Nathaniel F. Jones. Hull st, s s, 240 e Rockaway av, 15x100. Sub to mort. $2,750. Oct. 1, due July 1, 1893, 5 %. 750

Ficken, Diedrich F. to The South Brooklyn Savings Inst. 5th av, s e s, 40 n e 10th st, 20x70. Oct. 2, 1 year, 5 %. 4,000

Finken, Elizabeth to Martin Eselgroth. North 8th st, n s, 175 w Wythe av, 25x100. Oct. 5, 3 years, 5 %. 6,000

Fitch, Cornelia K. wife of and Francis E. to Thomas H. Messenger exr. Thomas Messenger. Lafayette av, n s, 86 w St. Felix st, 21.6x100.1x21x100. Sept. 30, 3 years, 5 %. 7,000

Flanigan, Martin to Annie Price. Van Brunt st, s e s, 70.2 w King st, 20x90. Sept. 30, 2 years, 5 %. 2,500

Same to Margaret Gorman heir of Michael and Anna Gorman. Van Brunt st, s e s, 70.2 s w King st, 20x90. Sept. 30, 5 years, 5 %. 5,500

Follmer, Xavier and Elizabeth to Edwin Haase. Broadway, south cor Sumpter st, 19.4x68x61x35. Oct. 2, 3 years, 5 %. 1,000

Ford, Mary wife of and James to Cornelius N. Hoagland. Lafayette av, n s, 187 e Lewis av, 19x100. Sept. 30, due Nov. 1, 1894, 5 %. gold, 5,000

Frankel, Samuel to Barbara Wagner. Boerum st. P. M. Sept. 30, due Oct. 1, 1897, 5 %. 4,000

Freist, Jakob and Maria his wife to Michael Hartmann. Evergreen av, w s, 100 n Willoughby av, 25x100. Oct. 3, due Oct. 1, 1894. 900

Same to Elizabeth Manpai. Same property. P. M. Oct. 1, 1 year, 5 %. 1,500

Frey, Anna to George Covert. Myrtle av. P. M. Oct. 1, 5 years, 5 %. 5,500

Frische, Frederick to Joseph J. Hess. Lorimer st, w s, 100 s Ten Eyck st, 24x89.7. July 1, 2 years, 5 %. 1,000

Fruh, Elizabeth to John Young and Katharina his wife. Melrose st. P. M. Aug. 28, due Sept. 1, 1891, 5 %. 4,500

Fuchs, Helena to The West Brooklyn Land and Imp't Co. 56th st, New Utrecht. P. M. Sept. 24, due Dec. 24, 1895, or installs, 5 %. 600

Fitzpatrick, Margaret and Catharine A. wife of and Francis Owens and Margaret R. and Mary A. Fitzpatrick to Bernard O'Donnell. Myrtle av, s s, adj land John Skillman, 25x162. Sept. 19, 3 years. 1,000

Goering, Jacob to Peter J. Levendecker. Johnson av, s s, 60 e Graham av, 20x50. Oct. 1, 3 years, 5 %. 1,600

Grossman, Frank to Henry Licht and Elizabeth his wife. Hemlock st, n e cor Griffin pl, 50x100. Oct. 1, 3 years. 350

Grasman, Henry to Thomas Shepherd. Monroe st, s s, 152.6 w Stuyvesant av, 17.6x100. Oct. 7, 3 years, 5 %. 3,500

Same to same. Monroe st, s w cor Stuyvesant av, 17.6x100. Oct. 7, 3 years, 5 %. 3,500

Same to same. Monroe st, s s, 175 w Stuyvesant av, 17.6x100. Oct. 7, 3 years, 5 %. 3,500

Gebhardt, Martin to Jacob Manneschmidt. Hamburg av. P. M. Sub. to mort. $2,000. Oct. 2, installs, 5½ %. 1,000

Same to The Title Guarantee and Trust Co. Same property. P. M. Oct. 2, due Oct. 6, 1894, 5 %. 2,000

Ginsburg, Isaac to George Covert. Lewis av, s w cor Willoughby av. P. M. Oct. 1, 5 years or installs, 5 %. 11,000

Gillespie, Thomas to Ernest T. M. Boenke. 73d st, s s, 310 e 3d av, 60x100, New Utrecht. Oct. 1, 3 years. 4,000

Goldey, Alice E to William J. Kaiser, John H. Vanderveer and George W. Dalton. Lots 502, 503, 504, 505 and 506 map Zabriskie Homestead, Flatbush. Sept. 29, 3 years. 2,000

Goldey, Alice E. wife of and William H. to Magdalene Cowenhoven. Av C and East 19th st, Flatbush. Sept. 29, 3 years. 2,500

Gosling, John to Charles E. Parsons. 12th st. P. M. Oct. 1, 3 years, 5 %. 800

Gould, John to Ann S. wife of Isaac E. Bergen. Lot at north boundary line of William H. Waring, 300 e 2d av, 50x114.5, New Utrecht. Oct. 1, 3 years, 5½ %. 3,000

Green, Frederick G. to The South Brooklyn Co-operative Building and Loan Assoc. 59th st, New Utrecht. P. M. Sept. 22, installs. 2,000

Green, Hannah to Catharine E. L. Duryee. New York av, w s, 70 s Herkimer st, 17x76.6. Oct. 1, 3 years, 5 %. 4,000

Green, Thomas to Anna C. Eden. Atlantic av. P. M. Oct. 1, 3 years, 5 %. 4,000

Greve, Hannah to Sherman and Guy Loomis. Douglass st. P. M. Oct. 1, installs. 1,100

Griffin, Thomas J. to Mary A. wife of Willis B. Goodsell. Windsor pl. P. M. Oct. 1, installs, 5 %. 200

Guilfoyle, Maria to Julia Kennedy. Willoughby av, s s, 200 w Lewis av, 50x100. Sept. 24, 5 years or sooner, 5 %. 400

Halloran, Thomas to The Williamsburgh Savings Bank. Cooper st, n w s, 125 s w Bushwick av, 25x100. Oct. 1, 1 year, 5 %. 4,000

Same to Edward E. Kelly. Cooper st. P. M. Sub. to mort. $4,000. Oct. 1, installs, 5 %. 2,000

Haradon, Herbert H. to Don A. and Theodore L. Beck, of Beck Brothers. Linwood st, w s, 375 n Liberty av, 25x90. Sept. 30, installs, 5 %. 2,000

Haussman, Gottlob to George Schwab. Woodbine st, n s, 100 e Central av, 25x100. July 6, 2 years. 1,000

Hawsen, Martin to John F. Waldorf. Conover st, w s, 20 s Vandyke st, 20x60. Oct. 2, 3 years, 5 %. 3,000

Heig, Rudolph to Louis W. Holste. 53d st, n s, 117.3 w 3d av, 17.3x100.2. Sept. 29, 5 years. 2,000

Hein, Ferdinand R. to The Title Guarantee and Trust Co. Ross st, n s, 275 e Lee av, 2 lots, each 25x100. 2 morts., each $8,000. Oct. 2, 1 year, 5 %. 16,000

Helm, George and Gustave A. to Effingham H. Nichols. Lots 50-67 and 71-78 block 18 map No. 2 of 660 lots, Cowenhoven farm, New Utrecht. Sept. 24, 3 years, 5 %. 3,500

Henchel, Simon to Mary L. Fraser. Prospect av, s w s, 160 n w 8th av, 20x90.4. Sept. 11, due Sept. 1, 1894, 5 %. 3,750

Same to Ida F. wife of James H. Fraser. Prospect av, s w s, 180 n w 8th av, 20x90.4. Sept. 11, due Sept. 1, 1894, 5 %. 3,750

Hobart, Agnes V. wife of and John W., East Orange, N. J., to Susan W. Talmage. Livingston st, s s, 204.2 e Bond st, 21.8x100.9. Oct. 3, 3 years, 5 %. 6,000

Hall, John mortgagor with Margaret L. Foote mortgagee. Extension of mort. Sept. 24. nom

Hoelemann, Frank to William Hoffman et al. trustees of Daniel Webster Council No. 516, American Legion of Honor. Tompkins av, w s, 46.8 n Stockton st, 21.8x90. Oct. 1, 1 year, 5 %. 4,000

Holbrook, Julia A. wife of and Henry to Sarah A., Harriett M. and Lillian R. Terrett and Sarah L. Holt. Franklin av, e s, 80 s Madison st, 20x90. Oct. 1, 3 years, 5 %. 1,400

Homann, Casper to Frank Emmerick. Glenmore av, s w cor Jerome st, 25x100. Sept. 15, 2 years, 5 %. 1,200

Housman or Hausman to Flora A. Gordon. 18th st, Nos. 101 and 103, n s, 125 w 3d av, 50x100. Oct. 1, 2 years. 5,500

Hurley, Mary to Rose Rosenfeld. Bergen st, s s, 125 w Hopkinson av, 50x127.9. Oct. 1, installs. 200

Hudson, Emma H. to Rosa Levy. Halsey st. P. M. Oct. 5, installs, 5 %. 1,800

Jackson, Edward, Stonington, Conn., to Melvin Brown. Fort Greene pl, w s, 90.6 s De Kalb av, 20x85. Oct. 3, 1 year, 5 %. 1,000

Jahnsen or Johnsen, Peter, John Gardello, Enrico Garevazzi and Salvator Guarnieri to Rose Barcoco. Tillary st, n s, 99.8 e Raymond st, 26.7x—x26.7x100. Error. Oct. 1, 1 year, 5 %. 1,000

James, Wilhelmina wife of Charles to Mary W. Heartt, New York. New Utrecht av, w s, 44.9 n 57th st, 22.3x99x20x108.9, New Utrecht. Oct. 2, 1 year, 5 %. 2,500

Jewett, Ella M. to William H. Reynolds. Hancock st. P. M. Sept. 28, installs, 5 %. 3,700

Johnson, William F. to The Mutual Life Ins. Co., New York. Herkimer st, n s, 120 w Rochester av, 20x100. Oct. 1, 1 year, 5 %. 1,500

Johnson, James A. to Albert G. Burtis. New York & Manhattan Beach R. R. Co., Gravesend. P. M. Oct. 3, installs. 375

Jarashow, Mary wife of and Israel to Morris Berger. Seigel st. P. M. Oct. 5, due Oct. 1, 1894, 5 %. 1,500

Same to Charles A. Johnson. Same property. P. M. Oct 5, due July 1, 1894. 2,300

James, Wilhelmina to The Blythebourne Improvement Co. New Utrecht av, w s, 44.9 n 57th st, 22.3x99x20x108.9, New Utrecht. June 23, 2 years. 520

Johnson, John P. to John Dill, Jr. 16th st, s s, 145.8 e 6th av, 16.8x80. Oct. 6, due Oct. 1, 1894, 5 %. 600

Klett, Jacob to The German Savings Bank, Brooklyn. Hamburg av, s w s, 50 n w Stockholm st, 25x100. Oct. 7, due Dec. 1, 1893, 5 %. 300

Knapf, Flora wife of and Emil to James W. Murphy and Michael McCormack. 67th st, New Utrecht. P. M. Oct. 1, due Jan. 1, 1893, 5 %. 900

Kaplan, Aaron to Aaron Levy. Linden st, e s, 295.11 n Evergreen av, 20x100. Sept. 30, due Oct. 1, 1894. 500

Same to same. Linden st, e s, 315.11 n Evergreen av, 20x100. Sept. 30, due Oct. 1, 1894. 500

Keefe, Annie to James Cropsey. West st. P. M. Sub. to morts. $2,250. Oct. 1, installs. 1,450

Keeley, John and Mary his wife to Edward D. White and ano. exrs. John S. Thorne. Van Brunt st, east cor Elizabeth st, runs southeast 90 x northeast 75 x northwest 20 x southwest 50 x northwest 70 to Van Brunt st, x southwest 25. Oct. 5, due Nov. 1, 1894, 5 %. 3,000

Keble, Emilie to Frederick Hornby. Pennsylvania av, n e cor Eastern Parkway. Sept. 28, due Oct. 1, 1894, 5 %. 4,500

Kehoe, John to John McNamee. Clymer st, n e cor Wythe av, 18x60. ½ part. Oct. 5, 1 year. 1,500

Kell, Charles and Elizabeth his wife to Matthaus Beck. South 4th st. P. M. Oct. 5, 3 years, 5 %. 5,800

Kern, Michael and George to Theodore F. Jackson. Knickerbocker av and Grattan st. P. M. Sept. 22, due Oct. 1, 1893. 5,000

Kirby, J. Mason to Susan Watson. Bainbridge st, n s, 169 e Saratoga av, 18x100. Oct. 1, 3 years, 5 %. 4,000

Same to same. Bainbridge st, n s, 187 e Saratoga av, 18x100. Oct. 1, 3 years, 5 %. 4,000

Same to William and William H. Bradley. Bainbridge st, n s, 187 e Saratoga av, 18x100. 2d mort. Oct. 1, 1 year. 1,000

Same to James Keenan. Bainbridge st, n s, 169 e Saratoga av, 18x100. 2d mort. Oct. 1, 1 year. 1,000

Kirby, Joseph M. to Helen K. Sumner extrx., &c., Adams C. Sumner. Bainbridge st, n s, 151 e Saratoga av, 18x100. Oct. 1, 2 years, 5 %. 4,000

Kirby, J. Mason to John S. Cameron trustee. Bainbridge st, n s, 259 e Saratoga av, 18x100. Oct. 1, 3 years, 5 %. 4,050

Same to Francis F. Murray et al. exrs. Ellen M. Murray. Bainbridge st, n s, 241 e Saratoga av, 18x100. Oct. 1, 3 years, 5 %. 4,000

Same to Edward A. Price et al. exrs. Frederick Butterfield. Bainbridge st, n s, 223 e Saratoga av, 18x100. Oct. 1, 3 years, 5 %. 4,000

Same to same. Bainbridge st, n s, 205 e Saratoga av, 18x100. Oct. 1, 3 years, 5 %. 4,000

Kluber, John C. to George E. Kitching trustee John H. Kitching. Lafayette av, s e s, 330 n e Broadway, 20x103. Oct. 3, 3 years, 5 %. 3,000

Krakauer, Gerson and Nathan Goldberg New York, to Levy Clar. Johnson av. P. M. Oct. 1, 2 years, 5 %. 1,000

Kraus, Anna wife of and John to Mary K. Kerz. Sumpter st. P. M. Oct. 3, 3 years, 5 %. 1,100

Laing, Mary E. wife of and Donald to Louisa W. Taylor, Boston, Mass. Belmont av, s e cor Atkins st, 40x90. Oct. 3, 3 years. 3,000

Lamphear, John A. to Thomas N. Radcliffe. McDonough st. P. M. Oct. 1, 1 year. 1,700

Le Beau, Theodore M. to Edward F. Linton. Ridgewood av, s e cor Ashford st, 100x100, Sept. 18, 1 year. 2,000

Lebrett, William J. and Frances C. his wife to Susan A. Baldwin. 54th st, s w s, 80 s e 8th avenue, 20x100.2, New Utrecht. Sept. 16, due Sept. 3, 1896. 650

Lehmann, Clara to Caspar Blass. Sheffield av, e s, 75 s Glenmore av, 25x100. Aug. 1, 3 years, 5 %. 500

Leibfried, John J. to The Metropolitan Co-operative Building and Loan Assoc. Guernsey st, s w s, 525 n w Nassau av, 42.10x100.2x37.2 x100. Oct. 1, installs. 3,000

Leibman, Charles A. to Emily M. Herbold. Kosciusko st. P. M. Oct. 2, 2 years. 1,000

Levine, Abraham to George Schwarz Eastern Parkway, n s, 100 e Osborn st, 25x100. Sept. 21, due Oct. 1, 1894. 3,500

Levy, Henry to Louis Beer and Michael Schaffner. Beaver st. P. M. Oct. 1, 5 years, 5 %. 1,900

Lewis, Margaretha to Paul W. Ledoux. Eldert st, n s, 198 w Bushwick av, 3 lots. 3 morts., each $900. P. M. Sept. 25, due Jan. 1, 1894, or installs. 2,700

Lewis, Margaretha to Frank Hyde. Warren st. P. M. July 15, 1 year. 1,000

Lober, Cunigunda to Theodore D. Dimon exr. Hannah S. Dimon. North 8th st, n e s, 100 n w Berry st, 25x100. Sept. 30, 2 years. 500

Loring, Samuel to Brooklyn City Co-operative Building and Loan Assoc. 67th st, New Utrecht. P. M. Oct. 3, 3 years. 2,100

Lott, Moe S. to Charles H. Lott. Mackay pl, s s, 150 e River road, 50x90x50x95, New Utrecht. Oct. 1, 3 years. 1,000

Lummis, Elizabeth formerly Coleman to Anna M. Jager. Frost st, s s, 100 e Lorimer st, 100 x100. Sept. 25, due Sept. 28, 1893. 1,700

Lyons, Henry B to Israel W. Lyon. Lincoln pl. P. M. Oct. 1, due Nov. 30, 1891, 5 %. 4,850

Lucas, Julian to George Carll, Suffolk Co., L. I. Van Voorhis st. P. M. Sept. 30, due Nov. 1, 1894. 2,500

Maasz, Johann H. to Adam Schneider and Mina his wife. Central av, west cor Palmetto st. P. M. Oct. 1, 5 years or installs, 5 %. 6,500

Madden, Johanna to Bridget Ware. Sumner av, w s, 20 n Van Buren st, 20x100. Oct. 1, 3 years, 5 %. 1,500

Same to Mary McDougall. Same property Oct. 1, 3 years, 5 %. 2,800

Magan, Richard F. to Emilie Huber. Greene av, n s, 50 w Stuyvesant av, 25x100. Oct. 2, 1 year, 5 %. 500

Mannel, Anton to The Kings Co. Savings Inst. Bedford av, n w s, 25 n e North 10th st, 3 lots, each 25x100. 3 morts., each $3,000. Oct. 2, 1 year, 5 %. 9,000

Manning, Catharine M. to The Title Guarantee and Trust Co. Dean st. P. M. Sept. 30, 1 year, 5 %. 1,500

Martens, Claus H. with Sophia H. Howard both mortgagees. Agreement as to priority of mort. by Henry W Hoffmann. Aug. 28. nom

Martling, David, Hackensack, N. J., to Sarah M. wife of Peter Bussing, Mount Kisco, N. Y. Jefferson av, No. 146. P. M. Sept. 26, due Oct 1, 1893. 1,000

Same to same. Jefferson av, No. 148. P. M. Sept. 26, due Oct. 1, 1893. 1,000

Martin, Charles A. to Henry Weil. Dean st, n s, 168.3 e Utica av, 84.11x107.2. Oct. 1, 1 year. 6,000

Same to same. Same property. P. M. Oct. 1, 1 year. 4,000

Mason, Eliza W. to Daniel B. Norris. Macon st. P. M. Oct. 1, installs, 5 %. 1,800

Mathews, Susan wife of and Owen to James Gormly. East 7th st and Ocean Parkway, lots 6, 7 and 8 and 74, 75 and 24 map Ocean Parkway and Park lots, Flatbush. Oct. 5, 1 year. 2,000

Matthews, Azel D., James and Gardiner D., of A. D. Matthews & Sons to Josephine G. Hatton. Gallatin pl. P. M. Oct. 1, due Nov. 1, 1896, 5 %. 10,000

Maxwell, John T. to James Gascoine, Halsey st. P. M. Sept. 28, installs. 2,100

McCloskey, Mary A. to Cornelius N. Hoagland. Steuben st, e s, 175 s Myrtle av, 25x100. Sept. 30, due Nov. 1, 1894, 5 %. gold, 6,500

McCormack, Rosanna to Percies S. Pearsall. Bergen st, n s, 300 w Rockaway av, 25x107.2. Sept. 29, 1 year. 100

McDonald, Sarah to John V. Van Pelt. Bay 20th st, New Utrecht. P. M. Oct. 6, 3 years, 5 %. 550

McDonald, William to George H. Roberts. Cranberry st, n s, 61.11 e Henry st, runs north 50 x east 12.5 x south 25 x south again 25.4 to Cranberry st, x west 15.1. Oct. 2, 2 years. 1,000

McDonnell, Charles to The Title Guarantee and Trust Co. Prospect pl. P. M. Sept. 29, due Oct. 1, 1894, 5 %. 2,500

McEveney, Bryan to Joseph W. Campbell. Washington av, e s, 308.5 s Park av, 3 lots, each 20x100. 3 morts., each $500. Oct. 1, 1 year, 5 %. 1,500

McGarry, Thomas to Augustus Wenzel. Hewes st. P. M. Oct. 1, 10 years or installs, 5 %. 6,000

McGinn, John G. to Mary Grimes. 43d st, n s, 90 w 4th av, 40x100.2. July 1, 3 years. 1,000

McGuire, Michael J. to Mary E. Young, Cornwall, N. Y. Huntington st, s s, 265 w Court st, 16.8x100. Sept. 30, due Nov. 1, 1894. 1,800

Same to William O. Moore et al. exrs. Abraham Underhill. Huntington st. P. M. Oct. 1, 3 years, 5 %. 1,800

McKelvey, John to George B. Forrester. Underhill av, w s, 20 n Pacific st, runs west 80 x north 20 x west 30 x south 0.2 x east 50 to Underhill av, x south 19.10. Oct. 3, 1 year. gold, 600

McKeon, John S. to James W. Smith trustee for Helen A. Kent. South 6th st, s s, 59.8 e 3d st, runs southwest 36x— to point 44 e of 3d st and 40 n South 7th st, x south 40 to South 7th st, x west 24 x north 29.8 x southeast abt 2.4 x northeast 67.9 to South 6th st, x east 17.6. Oct. 1, due Oct. 2, 1894, 5 %. gold, 15,000

McLaughlin, Peter to Charles H. Heimburg. Lexington av, n s, 316.8 e Bedford av, 33.4x 100. Sept. 30, due July 1, 1892. 700

McNamara, John to The Orphan Asylum Society of the City of Brooklyn. Dean st. P. M. Sept. 11, due Oct. 1, 1894, 5 %. 3,000

Mehling, Anton to Charles Engert. Graham av. P. M. Sept. 15, 2 years, 5 %. 4,300

Merschoff, Adam to Thekle Merschoff. Aberdeen st, s e s, 210 s w Bushwick av, 20x100. Sept. 3, installs. 2,000

Metcalf, Mary M. wife of and John W. to Bernard Cosgrove and Anne his wife. 15th st. P. M. Oct. 1, 5 years, 5 %. 3,000

Meyer, Simon G. to Peter Kraemer. Hamburg av, e s, 50 s Suydam st, 25x100. Sept. 23, due Oct. 1, 1894, 5 %. 3,500

Micieli, Michael to James and Joseph D. Huggins, of James Huggins & Brothers. Greene av, n s, 370 w St. Nicholas av, 20x100. Oct. 1, 2 years. 300

Mildner, Charles to Anna K. Strom. Adams st, w s, 100 s Liberty av, 25x90. Oct. 2, 5 years. 1,200

Miller, Amelia to Elizabeth Clute, Gravesend, L. I. Voorhis av, s w cor East 10th st, 50x 100, Gravesend. Oct. 1, 5 years. 1,200

Mitchell, Lewis A. to George H. Coutts. Hicks st. P. M. Sept 30, 5 years, 5½ %. 5,000

Monahan, Thomas to The East Brooklyn Savings Bank. Madison st, n s, 200 w Sumner av, 87.6x100. Sept 30, 1 year, 5 %. 10,000

Moran, Thomas to Mary A. Moran. Grand av, w s, 82.6 s Pacific st, 27.6x50; interior lot, 50 w Grand av and 110 s Pacific st, runs west 50 x north 27 6 x east 50 x south 27.6. Oct. 1, 5 years, 5 %. 1,000

Moran, Ellen to William S. Stewart. Henry st. P. M. Sept. 7, due Jan. 1, 1897, 5 %. 3,200

Morgan, Owen to The Title Guarantee and Trust Co. Monroe st, s s, 345 w Nostrand av. P. M. Oct. 1, 1 year, 5 %. 1,200

Morgan, Alfred, Jr., to same. Monroe st. P. M. Oct. 1, 1 year, 5 %. 1,200

Morris, Joseph to Carrie Engs. Dumont av, n e Thatford av, 25x100. Sept. 29, due Sept. 15, 1893. 4,000

Morris, Jane E T. wife of and Henry J., Freehold, N. J., to Sarah M. B. Mitchell, Flushing, L. I. Ross st, No. 81, n s, 116.3 e Wythe av, 19.4x100. Sept. 1, 3 years. 410

Morse, Daniel P. to George Ingraham, Flushing, L. I. Monroe st. P. M. Sept. 28, 3 years, 5 %. 5,000

Mowbray, Edward H. to The Title Guarantee and Trust Co. 3d st, n s, 197.4 e 7th av, 5 lots, each 25x95. 5 morts., each $9,000. Oct. 5, 1 year, 5 %. 45,000

Mugford, Fannie J. to The Title Guarantee and Trust Co. Putnam av, n s, 175.4 e Patchen av, 18 9x100. Oct. 2, 3 years, 5 %. 3,500

Same to same. Putnam av, n s, 212.10 e Patchen av, 2 lots, each 18.9x100. 2 morts., each $3,500. Oct. 2, 3 years, 5 %. 7,000

Mulhern, Michael J. to William O'Dwyer. Central av, e s, 25 s Hart st, runs east 100 x south 31.5 x west 102.11 to av, x north 7.1. Sept. 17, 2 years. 400

Muller, Louis H. to Louis Bonert. 7th av. P. M. Sept. 30, 1 year. 1,500

Mullowney, Richard to A. S. Nichols. Halsey st, s s, 40 w Ralph av, 18x100. Sub. to morts. $4,000. Sept 28, 1 year. 1,000

Musy, Arthur to Christian Nicklaus. Cleveland st. P. M. Sept. 23, 3 years. 140

Madn, Francisca wife of and Louis to Mary Mandery. Throop av, s e cor Vernon av, 40 x85. Oct. 1, 3 years, 5 %. 2,000

Marquart, Charles and Frederick to Henry Kiep. Madison st, s s, 225 w Howard av, 25 x100. Oct. 7, due Oct. 1, 1896, 5 %. 5,500

McConnell, Catharine J. wife of James to Isabella Andrews. Monroe st, s s, 22.6 w Lewis av, 19.6x81. Oct. 6, demand, 5 %. 1,500

McCormick, Mary A. to Richard W. and Mary P. Titus, Oyster Bay, N. Y. Prospect av, s s, 178 e 4th av, 28x75. Oct. 7, 3 years, 5 %. 4,000

Montauk Club to The Franklin Trust Co. trustee. 8th av, n e cor Lincoln pl, 100x99.6 to Prospect Park, 101.7 to Lincoln pl, x117.5. Oct. 1, due July 1, 1911. issue of 5 % bond for 100,000

Murphy, James P. to The Title Guarantee and Trust Co. Kosciusko st. P. M. Oct. 5, due Oct. 7, 1892, 5 %. 2,000

Nash, John E. to Cornelia E. Voorhees. Main st or State road and 15th av, New Utrecht. P. M. May 18, 1891, due May 1, 1896, 5 %. 2,000

National Meter Co. to Stewart McDougall. 42d st. P. M Oct. 1, 10 years, 5 %. 27,000

Nelson, Thomas to Cornelius N. Hoagland. Lefferts pl, n w cor Clason av, runs west 36.8 x northeast 59 x north 56.2 x east 7.2 to Clason av, x south 124.11. Oct. 1, due Nov. 1, 1892, 5 %. gold, 2,000

Same to same. Same property. Oct. 1, due Nov. 1, 1894, 5 %. gold, 7,500

Nevin, Kate E. to Amelia T. Rowley. Lafayette av, n s, 60 w Franklin av, 20x75. Oct. 5, 5 years, 5 %. 3,000

Newcombe, Helen E. to The Brooklyn Trust Co. State st, s w s, 175 e Hicks st, 25x100. Oct 3, 1 year, 5 %. 5,500

Newman, Kate and Patrick to The Mutual Life Ins. Co., New York. 16th st, n s, 251.3 e 5th av, 25x100. Oct. 1, 1 year, 5 %. 1,500

Noonan, Mary to Margaret E. and Martha A. Farrell. South 2d st, s s, 100 e Rodney st, 22 x72. Oct. 3, 3 years, 5 %. 2,500

Nordstrom, Olof to The German Savings Bank, Brooklyn. Park av, n s, 100 e Throop av, 125 x100. Oct. 1, due Dec. 1, 1892, 5 %. 10,500

Nulle, Julius and William Weimann to Anton Riedmann and Maria his wife. Marcy av, s w cor Middleton st, 25x80.4x25x80.8. Oct. 1, due April 1, 1896, 5½ %. 4,500

O'Brien, Maria to The Fifth Avenue Co-operative Building and Loan Assoc. 5th st, n s, 280 e Smith st, 22x100. Oct. 1, installs. 1,000

O'Brien, Richard to Herman Wronkow. President st. P. M. Oct. 1, 5 years, 5 % 300

Ohrig, Anna to Michael Mulvihill. Putnam av. P. M. Oct. 1, 1 year, 5 %. 2,500

Ock, John to Hannah M. Rose. Cooper st. P. M. Oct. 1, due April 27, 1892. 700

Odell, Elizabeth D. to The Williamsburgh Savings Bank. Putnam av, n s, 95 e Stuyvesant st, 18.10x100. Oct. 1, 1 year, 5 %. 4,500

Same to John Mitchell and Charles Herr. Same property. Sub. to last mort. Oct. 1, installs. 1,550

O'Halloran, James to Lewis Du Bois. Watkins st, e s, 100 s Dumont av, 25x100. Oct. 6, due Nov. 1, 1894. 2,000

O'Halloran, James to Henry Meyer. Dean st. P. M. Oct 3, due Oct. 1, 1894, 5 %. 1,250

Offutt, William M. to The Nassau Co-operative Building and Loan Assoc. Ridgewood av. P. M. Sept. 29, installs. 3,000

Otto, Frank and Concreta to Godfrey Haupert. Bushwick av, e s, 82.11 s Jackson st, 25x100. Sept. 29, installs, 5 %. See Conveys. 800

Olsen, Thorvald to The Hamilton Co-operative Building and Loan Assoc. Dikeman st, s w s, 125 n w Richards st, 25x100. Sept. 30, installs, 5 1-5 %. 2,000

Parmer, Ada wife of and Lewis to Sarah L. Hodgetts. Watkins st. P. M. Oct. 1, 3 years. 2,500

Paulin, Bellangee D. to Joel F. Tyler. Hancock st. P. M. Oct. 1, installs. 2,300

Perego, Ira to Julia wife of J. Josef Stuebler. Lafayette av, s e cor Navy st. P. M. Oct. 1, 3 years, 5 %. 15,000

Petry, Ludwig to Jacob Manneschmidt. Hamburg av. P. M. Sub. to mort. $2,000. Oct. 5, installs. 1,600

Same to The Title Guarantee and Trust Co. Same property. P. M. Oct. 6, due Oct. 5, 1893, 5 %. 2,000

Pfalzgraf, Hans C. to Effingham H. Nichols. Lots 68–70 and 79–81 and 84–101 blocks 18 and 110–118 and 120–134 block 19 map No 2 of Cowenhoven farm, New Utrecht. Sept. 24, 3 years, 5 %. 5,000

Same to same. Lots 18, 19, 20 and 43–49 block 1 and 255–286 block 6 and 293–306 and 309–316 block 7 and lot 337 block 8 map No. 1 of 618 lots Cowenhoven farm, New Utrecht. Sept. 24, 3 years, 5 %. 9,340

Pobs, Jacob to Caspar Lucke. Herkimer st. P. M. Sub. to mort. $2,350. Sept. 30, installs. 1,100

Poillon, John E. to Marie E. Jacobson. John st, centre line, 160 w Gold st if extended, runs west 196.1 x north to point 87 n John st, x west to centre Bridge st, x north to centre Marshall st, x west to point 120 w of w s Bridge st, x north to East River at pier line, x east along same to point 160 w of w s Gold st if extended, x south —, with land under water, docks, etc. All title. Sept. 30, due Nov. 1, 1894. 3,000

Potashinski, Wolf to Kunigunde Buhn. Eastern Parkway, s s, 75 e Christopher av, 25x100. Oct. 1, 3 years. 3,000

Same to Francis Miller. Eastern Parkway, s s, 50 e Christopher av, 25x100. Sept. 21, 3 years. 3,000

Pugano, Lucrezia wife of and Frank to Francis Plunkett. Classon av. P. M. Sept. 25, due Oct. 1, 1894, 5 %. 200

Parmer, Ada wife of and Louis to William Rope. Watkins st, w s, 126.6 s Eastern Parkway, 25x100. Oct. 7, 1 year. 500

Peck, John B. to Sarah E. Ostrander. De Kalb av, n s, 150 e Johnson av, 25x100. July 1, 1 year. 5,000

Same to Sarah E. Ostrander. De Kalb av, n s, 125 e Johnson av, 25x100. July 1, 1 year. 5,000

Quadt, Claus to John H. Elfers. Reid av. P. M. Sept. 13, due Oct. 1, 1893, 5 %. 2,000

Quinlan, Maurice G. and Rosanna his wife to Conrad Meyer. Oakland st. P. M. Oct. 1, 3 years or sooner, 5 %. 3,000

Quinlan, Maurice G. to Matilda and Mary E. Calder. Eagle st, s s, 225 w Manhattan av, 25x100. Oct. 1, 5 years, 5 %. 2,500

Radar, Israel to Barnett L. and Barnett L. Price (two persons), of Barnett L. Price & Co. Rockaway av. P. M. Oct. 5, installs. 500

Randel, Elias C. to Elizabeth Decker. Ditmars st, s e s, 256.3 n e Broadway, 18.9x95. Oct. 1, 3 years, 5 %. 3,000

Reynolds, William H. to Emily B. wife of and Thomas B. Smith. Madison st. P. M. Oct. 1, 3 years, 5 %. 4,500

Rice, Francis J. to Jeremiah Erwin. Centre st, e s, 500 s Sackett st, 50x100. Oct. 1, 5 years. 1,200

Rich, Jane wife of Theodore W. to Samuel Loyd trustee, &c. Quincy st, n s, 145 w Bedford av, runs north 105 x west 10 x south 5 x west 10 x south 100 to st, x east 20. Sept. 30, due Oct. 1, 1894. 1,500

Ries, Bertha to Fernandine Jung. Myrtle av, n s, abt 314 w Central av, 60x39.6x71.6, gore. Oct. 1, 3 years, 5 %. 1,500

Robertson, John F. to George H. Roberts. State st, s s, 100 e Henry st, 25x100. Sept. 28, 3 years. 1,650

Robinson, John to John Dill, Jr. Prospect pl, s s, 150 w Buffalo av, 75x127.9; Buffalo av, w s, 127.9 s Prospect pl, 25x100; Buffalo av, w s, 52.8 s Prospect pl, runs west 52 x south 0.1½ x west 48 x south 51 x east 100 to av, x north 51.1. Oct. 1, 1 year. 1,200

Rockliff, Emily G. wife of Charles to Cornelius N. Hoagland. Willoughby av, s s, 91.3 w Clason av, 17x66 11x17x66.9. Sept. 28, due Nov. 1, 1894, 5 %. gold, 4,200

Rose, Henrich T. and Matilda to Fred. Wittich. Parcel in Canarsie adj B. Afler and late B. Lohmann and R. Schenck, 127x96x211x96. Sept. 29, 5 years. 400

Roth, Henry to Louis P. Walton and ano. exrs. Georgiana J. Trim. Myrtle av, n s, 375 w Lewis av, 25x100. Oct. 1, 5 years. gold, 9,500

Rourke, Martin and Robert H. Barry to Jeremiah V. Meserole. Van Cott and Morgan avs. P. M. Sept. 27, 3 years. 2,000

Ruger, Mary L. to Edwina W. Brose. Bay 26th st, New Utrecht. P. M. Oct. 1, 1 year, 5 %. gold, 1,000

Ruppel, John to William Laytin et al. trustees William Laytin. Weirfield st, n w s, 261 s w Central av, 20x100. Oct. 5, 3 years, 5 %. 2,300

Same to Leopold J. Lippmann. Same property. P. M. Sub. to last mort. Oct. 5, installs. 2,100

Rust, Charles D. to The Metropolitan Life Ins. Co. Glenada pl, w s, 149.9 s Decatur st, runs west 100 x south 38.2 x east 24.11 x south 6.10 x east 77.2 to pl, x 50.3. Oct. 5, due Oct. 1, 1894, installs, 6 % to Oct. 1, 1892, after 5 %. 25,000

Same to same. Glenada pl, w s, 100 s Decatur st, 49.9x100. Oct. 5, due Oct. 1, 1894, installs, 6 % to Oct. 1, 1892, after 5 %. 25,000

Ryan, William F. to Oscar J. Chase. Stockholm st. P. M. Sept. 30, 5 years. 1,200

Ryder, Isaac to Joseph Brennan. Neck road, east cor Ryders lane, 35 acres, Gravesend. Sept. 30, 1 year. 900

Raymond, Benjamin C. to Lottie N. Palmer. Macon st, n w cor Ralph av, 22x100. Oct. 3, due Nov. 1, 1891. 1,050

Reynolds, Mary J. widow to George H. Gerard. Manhattan av, e s, 75 s Nassau av, 25x75. Oct. 5, 5 years. 3,000

Saalfield, Ada L. wife of Arthur J. to Israel Minor, Jr., exr. Jane V. C. Cooper. Stuyvesant av, s w cor Putnam av, 20x95. Sept. 25, 3 years, 5 %. 7,000

Sarles, Carrie to Lucy R. wife of George C. Blanke. Lafayette av, s s, 452 e Bedford av, 23x100. Oct. 1, 2 years. 400

Sattler, George to Christian Mayer. Van Sicle n av, w s, 100 s Liberty av, 25x100. Oct 1, 5 years. 3,000

Schindel, Sarah to Edward S. McVey. Richardson st. P. M. Sept. 30, 3 years. 300

Schmidt, Henry to Townsend C. Van Pelt. 15th av. P. M. Sept. 30, due May 1, 1893. 300

Schmidt, Adolph to Sarah Ginste. Grand st, s w, 274 1 w Lorimer st, 24.5x110. Oct. 1, 10 years, 5 %. 10,000

Schmonsees, Gevert to Jost Moller. Broadway, n e cor Havemeyer st, 20x71.6. Sept. 29, due Jan. 1, 1896, 5 %. 7,000

Schoefer, Henry J. to John Dill, Jr. Gates av, n s, 80 w Vanderbilt av, 20x75. Oct. 2, due Nov. 1, 1891. 125

Schublein, Andrew to Peter Lippert. Lorimer st. P. M. Oct 5, 5 years, 5 %. 1,700

Schworn, Maria A. to Leonhard Eppig. Warwick st late Washington st, n e cor Glenmore av, 31x100x32x100; Glenmore av, n s, 125 w Ashford st, 21x100. Sept. 30, due Oct. 1, 1894, 5 %. 2,300

Sears, Norman C., Fanwood, N. J., to Mary W. Smith. Glenmore av, s e cor Thatford av, 50x100. Oct. 1, 2 years. 750

Seafe, Sarah D. to The Triennial Benefit League. Bergen st, n s, 233.6 w Buffalo av, 16.6x100. Oct. 1, 3 years, 5 %. 1,700

Shaddock, Henry to Lawrence Frank. Hendrix st. P. M. Oct. 2, due Oct. 2, 1894, 5 %. 1,500

Shaw, Mary E. wife of William B. to Elizabeth C. Bailey. Dean st, s s, 433.4 e 3d av, 20.10x100. Oct. 5, 2 years. 1,800

Simon, Isaac to George F. Bliel and Louisa his wife. Park av, No. 692, s s, 300 w Tompkins av, 20x100. Oct. 1, 5 years, 5 %. 2,500

Simon, Rosina to Theresa Gauter. Humboldt st, e s, 75 s Ten Eyck st, 25x100. Oct. 1, 5 years, 5 %. 2,000

Sokolski, Albert to Myer Bach. Throop av, s w cor Wallabout st, 25x75. Sept. 29, 1 year, 5 %. 194

Solomon, Charles W. to Cornelius N. Hoagland. Willoughby av, s s, 125.3 w Clason av, 17x67.3x17x67.1. Sept. 28, due Nov. 1, 1894, 5 %. gold, 3,000

Smith, Margaret L. to Charles L. Prindle, Shasron, Conn. 16th st. P. M. Oct. 2, due Oct. 1, 1896, 5 %. 2,800

Smith, Oscar G. and Edgar P. to The East Brooklyn Savings Bank. Monroe st, s s, 219.7 e Lewis av, 19.11x100. Sept. 30, 1 year, 5 %. 2,000

Smith, Mary wife of Nathan to Emily Huber. 5th st, n w cor North 12th st, 100x100. Oct. 6, 1 year, 5 %. 3,500

Smith, Thomas to George W. Conselyea. South 4th st. P. M. Oct. 2, 3 years, 5 %. 2,200

Stackhouse, Eliza M. to Lizzie B. Tollmon. Cleveland st, e s, 205 s Hegeman av, 60x100. Sept. 29, 3 years. 500

Same to Joseph La Fumee. Pilling st, w s, 428.7 n Broadway, 16.5x100. Sept. 29, installs. 700

Stanche, Charles to The Citizens' Co-operative Building and Loan Assoc., New York. Bay 11th st, s e s, 220 s w Bath av, 40x96.8, New Utrecht. Aug. 17, installs. 250

Starrett, Heydon to Benjamin C. Raymond. Macon st. P. M. Sept. 30, installs. 825

Stern, David and Solomon Blatteis to Margaretha Appel. Moore st. P. M. Oct. 1, 5 years, 5 %. 5,000

Stoker, Mary A. wife of John H. to Clara H. Ives. Van Siclen av. P. M. Sub. to mort. $600 Sept. 29, 1 year. 250

Sullivan, James to Ellen Dougherty. Prospect st. P. M. Oct. 1, 3 years, 5 %. 1,500

Stahl, Bernhard mortgagor with Anna F. P. Knight mortgagee. Extension of mort. Oct. 5. nom

Taylor, James to The Brooklyn Savings Bank. 5th av, e s, 25.2 n 46th st, 25x100. Oct. 1, 1 year, 5 %. 1,200

Telfer, George to Leonard W. Lott, Lonsdale, R. I. 14th st, n e s, 187.4 n w 4th av, 20.6x100. Oct. 2, 3 years, 5 %. 4,000

Tepe, Sophia wife of and William, Gravesend, L. I., to Alletta A. Stillwell. Ocean av, s w cor Neck road, 70x125.9x25x125.9, Gravesend, Oct. 1, 1891, 3 years, 5 %. gold, 3,000

Thatcher, Samuel J. to John A. Williams. 18th st. P. M. Sept. 30, due Oct. 1, 1894, 5 %. 2,000

The Rector, &c., of the Protestant Episcopal Church of the Holy Spirit, Bath Beach, N. Y., to The People's Trust Co. Bay 17th st, e s, 50 s 86th st, 100x96.8. Sept. 30, 1 year, 5 %. 3,100

Tinney, Edward to Cornelius N. Hoagland. Willoughby av, s s, 57.3 w Clason av, 17x66.7 x17x66.5. Sept. 28, due Nov. 1, 1894, 5 %. 4,200

Terrett, Sarah A., Harriet M. and Lillian R. and Sarah L. Holt to Hattie Lovejoy. Franklin av, w s, 40 s Madison st, 60x80. Oct. 1, 3 years, 5 %. 8,000

Tobin, Thomas J. to Cornelius N. Hoagland. Van Buren st, s s, 165.9 w Throop av, 18x100. Oct. 5, due Nov. 1, 1894, 5 %. gold, 2,000

Trahan, Noe to Richard Hawley. 42d st, n e s, 94.4 n w Fort Hamilton av. P. M. Oct. 1, 2 years. 2,400

Same to same. 42d st. P. M. 2d mort. Oct. 1, note. 800

Tresham, Katie to Harold L. Crane. Skillman st. P. M. Oct. 3, due Oct. 5, 1896. 1,000

Trimm, Mary E. wife of and Frederick M. to Madison Co-operative Building and Loan Assoc. Macon st, n s, 340 e Throop av, 20x100. Oct. 5, installs. 3,000

Uihlein, George and Mary R. his wife to The Title Guarantee and Trust Co. Hamburg av, e s, 43.9 n Madison st, 18.9x80. Oct. 5, 3 years, 5 %. 1,800

Urso, Michael and Peter Cazza to Watson & Pittinger. 14th av, e s, 20 s 66th st, 20x100, New Utrecht. Sept. 30, demand. 421

Vanderkar, Edward to James D. Fish, Hempstead, L. I. Ralph st, n w s, 100 n e Hamburg av. P. M. Sept. 24, due Oct. 1, 1893, 5 %. 3,200

Same to same. Ralph st, n w s, 200 n e Hamburg av. P. M. Sept. 24, due Oct. 1, 1893, 5 %. 3,000

Van Sielen, Ernst J. to Hope M. Voorhies. Coney Island road, s e cor West 6th st, runs south 300 x east 50 x north 50 x east 50 x north 250 to Coney Island road, x west 100; Cortlandt st, w s, 250 n from land of other parties, runs west 300 to Prospect Park and Coney Island R. R. Co., x south 250 x east 300 to st, x 250, Coney Island. March 28, demand. 300

Varian, Anna M. wife of and Isaac C. to Cornelius N. Hoagland. Monroe st, s s, 110 w Sumner av, 20x100. Oct. 5, due Nov. 1, 1894, 5 %. gold, 4,000

Voorhies, Albert V. B. to Jeannette wife of Louis A. Lanthier. 17th av. P. M. Oct. 1, due Dec. 1, 1891. 8,000

Vail, Caroline wife of and Henry C. to Caroline E. Hotchkiss. Bay 29th st, n w s, 100 n e Cropsey av, runs northwest 63.3 x northeast 12.6 x northwest 31.10 x northeast 47.6 x southeast 96.8 to Bay 29th st, x southwest 60; Bay 29th st, n w s, 160 n e Cropsey av, 60x96.8, New Utrecht. Oct. 6, due Oct. 7, 1892 600

Van Duyne, Elizabeth W., Myra, Ga., to Charles C. Cummings. Warren st, n e s, 75 n w Smith st, 25x75. Sept. 19, 3 years, 5 %. 1,200

Volinsky, Gussie to Mary E. Cook, Newtown, L. I. Stone av. P. M. June 24, installs. 1,050

Vollweiler, Henry to The Williamsburgh Savings Bank. Driggs st, east cor North 5th st, 20x75. Oct. 7, 1 year, 5 %. 5,000

Walsh, Edmund J. to Sarah A. and Martha R. World. Lynch st, s s, 261.1 e Lee av, 25x100. Oct. 2, due Oct. 1, 1896, or installs, 5 %. 4,850

Wilhelm, Carolina to Christian Huber. Garden st, n e s, 205.10 s e Flushing av, 20x103.8 x20.3x103.11. Oct. 1, 3 years, 5 %. 500

Same mortgagor with same mortgagee. Extension of mort. Oct. 1. nom

Wagner, Barbara to Valentin Zimmermann. Graham av, Boerum st. P. M. Oct. 1, 5 years, 5 %. 4,200

Waring, William H. to John Y. Hallock, New York. Clason av, w s, 43 n Lexington av, runs north 32 x west 100 x north 25 x west 67.9 x south 100 to Lexington av, x east 67.9 x north 43 x east 100. Oct. 28, 1877, 5 years, 7 %. 5,000

Webenbauer, Alois to The Title Guarantee and Trust Co. Hamburg av. P. M. Oct. 2, 3 years, 5 %. 2,000

Same to Jacob Manneschmidt. Same property. P. M. 2d mort. Oct. 2, installs. 700

Weber, Lawrence and John Quinn to Effingham H. Nichols. Lots 1-20 and 40-44 block 17 map No. 2 of 660 lots Cowenhoven farm, New Utrecht. Sept. 21, 3 years, 5 %. 2,941

Weidner, Joseph and Elizabeth his wife to Caroline Broistedt. Melrose st, n s, 200 e Knickerbocker av, 25x100. Oct. 1, 3 years, 5 %. 3,000

Same to same. Melrose st, n s, 175 e Knickerbocker av, 25x100. Oct. 1, 3 years, 5 %. 3,000

Weiss, Abraham to Frank J. Kelly. Manhattan av. P. M. Sept. 30, due May 1, 1892, 5 %. 2,200

Wern, Erik G. P. to Charles G. Peterson. 11th st. P. M. Oct. 5, installs, 5 % 2,150

Wheelan, Elizabeth to The Title Guarantee and Trust Co. Hicks st, w s, 40.3 n Warren st, 19.10x72.5x19.10x73.5. Oct. 2, 3 years, 5 %. 2,500

Whitlock, Julia J. to John Brommer et al. exrs. Frederick Ring. Wyona st, w s, 225 n Fulton av, 75x103. Oct. 1, 2 years. 1,750

Winarski, Caroline to Jane A. MacDowell. 45th st s w s, 140 n w 4th av, 20x80. Sept. 30, due Oct. 1, 1896. 1,805

Wolf, Anna M. wife of John formerly Finkeldey to Emeline Davison, Rockville Centre, L. I. Conover st, s e s, 20.3 n e Partition st, 19.9x75 Oct. 5, due Nov. 1, 1894, 5 %. 3,000

Woodford, Emma C. to Cornelius N. Hoagland. Monroe st, s s, 133.4 e Tompkins av, 33.4x100. Sept. 29, due Nov. 1, 1894, 5 %. gold, 4,700

Young, Edgar W. to Louise Kathe. St. Marks pl. P. M. Oct. 7, due Jan. 1, 1897, 5 %. 2,600

Zapf, Joseph J. and Julius Lobel to Mary J. Halsted. Pacific st. P. M. Sept. 30, due Oct. 1, 1896, 5 %. 5,000

Zeyhle, Mary L. to Albin Warth, Middleton, N. Y. 17th st, s s, 200 e 5th av, 25x100.2. May 1, 5 years, 5 % 2,000

Same to Peter A. Warth, Middleton, N. Y. Same property. July 1, 2 years, 5 %. 1,000

Zoellner, Joseph and Helena his wife to Jean Schneider. Elm st, s s, 340 e Broadway, 25x68.8x20x69.1.

MORTGAGES----ASSIGNMENTS.

NEW YORK CITY.

October 2 to 8—Inclusive.

Bloch, Israel to Sender Jarmulowsky. $3,000

Borger, Max to Joseph Fox. 8,000

Same to Solomon B. Solomon and ano. exrs. Phoebe M. Davies 6,000

Backhaus, Mary and Eliza and Gertrude Hoellebolt to James H. McCormick, Coney Island, L. I. 3,000

Burke, Martin to Townsend & Mahan. 2,053

Cohen, Isaac to Morris Berger. 1,000

Cohen, Max to Leopold S. Weiner. 4,262

Same to Abraham Schlesinger. 4,000

Cruger, James P., Newburg, N. Y., to Jeannie Marie Camille de Vatry. 14,000

Callender, William E. to David H. Fowler. 3,000

Dann, William to Henrietta Adler, Brooklyn. 6,000

Denmark, William S. to Rachel M. Gilsey 462

Ford, Henry W. trustee Augustus H. Ward dec'd to Walter F. Brush. nom

Gebhard, William H. exr. Frederick C. Gebhard to August Limbert trustee for Mary I. Neilson. nom

Hegemann, Emil H. to Reuben Mapelsden, Brooklyn. 1,075

Hagen, Eunice to Charles E. Campbell. 3,000

Hagan, Thomas to Hugo Weil. 1,500

Hart, Harmon H. admr. Julia Higgins to Mary J. Platt, Bayonne City, N. J. nom

Halstead, Pearson exr. Annie Joy to George Jeremiah exr. George A. Jeremiah. 7,656

Same to same. 6,554

Same to Louise F. Runk. 5,000

Heilner, Emanuel and Moses J. Wolf to Morris Mayer. nom

Hyatt, George E., Brooklyn, to Henry W. Ford trustee Augustus H. Ward dec'd. 4 assigns. nom

Haydock, Robert and ano. exrs. Joseph D. Thurston to Joseph Wharton exrs. Joseph D. Thurston. Assign. 7 morts. order of Court

Hyatt, George E., Brooklyn, to Edward Winslow. Assign. 7 morts. nom

Joy, Joseph F. and ano. exrs. Annie Joy to Joseph F. Joy and ano. exrs. Annie Joy. 2 assigns. nom

Knapp, David H. to Judson Lawson. 1,500

Kerwin, Andrew J. to Samuel Woolverton. nom

Kojawsky, Joseph to Meyer Landsberger. 1,000

Levers, William to Caroline R. Gihon, Tarrytown, N. Y. 12,000

Low, William G., Brooklyn, individ. and trustee for his children to The Brooklyn Hospital. 10,000

Middlebrook, Frederic J., Brooklyn, to John M. Bowers trustee Franklin Osgood dec'd. 8,134

Middlebrook, Frederic J., Brooklyn, to August Limbert trustee Frederick C. Gebhard dec'd. 20,283

Same to same. 3,006

Mayer, Morris to Emanuel Heilner and Moses J. Wolf, of Heilner & Wolf. nom

Macdonald, Sarah E. wife of Norman to Sarah E. Macdonald committee of Sophia Ely. 3,000

Mott, Jordan L. to The J. L. Mott Iron Works. nom

Morgenthau, Henry to The Title Guarantee and Trust Co. nom

Morris, Fordham and Albon P. and William Man trustees to Julia E. Rodman, Montclair, N. J. nom

Manning, William D. to William Hall's Sons. nom

Myers, Anna F. wife of and Charles to Charles Myers. 5,000

Moen, Philip W. admr. Philip L. Moen to Marie G. Moen, Worcester, Mass. 30,000

Morrison, George A. to John Herriman. 2,000

Newman, Jacob M. to William Hall's Sons. nom

O'Donelan, James to Margaret O'Donelan. nom

Parsons, John E. and ano. exrs. Eliza Clark to John E. Parsons trustee. 7,067

Pirnie, Sarah F. widow to William G. De Witt committee of John T. Housman. 10,000

Same to George G. De Witt et al. exrs. George G. De Witt. 4,000

Platt, Mary J., Bayonne City, N. J., to Josephine L. Tobias. nom

Palmer, Franklin G., Philadelphia, to Charles Ritchie. 930

Ritchie, Mary A. to William Cauldwell. 8,000

Same to same. 2,000

Roosevelt, James exr. Isaac Roosevelt to James Roosevelt. nom

Rosenbach, Moses S. to Henry C. Copeland. 4,500

Rasines, Antonio to Lydia F. Martin, Woodbridge, N. J. nom

Rosenberg, William to James B. Vredenburgh, Jersey City, N. J. 9,000

Randell, Charles H. exr. Betsey A. Randell to Mary L. Randell, guard. of Harry M. Randell. 4,000

Same to same. 500

Same to same. 8,000

Sackett, Sarah E. extrx. Adam T. Sackett to Susanna P. Titus, Brooklyn. 10,208

Schnugg, Francis J. to Lippmann Meyer. 8,400

Steel, Hannah C. admrx. Mary E. Thompson to Emily W. Thompson. 4,500

Schlemmer, Mathilda admrx. Martha Loos to Mathilda Schlemmer extrx. Conrad Loos. nom

Schuyler, Philip and ano. trustees Gertrude L. Lowndes dec'd to Philip J. Sands as trustee. 5,000

Shaw, Charles R. to Edwin F. Payne. 4,000

Sheridan, James F. and Patrick H. and James S. Segrave to Thomas C. Cornell. 265

Same to same. 1,000

Same to same. 500

Same to same. 700

Same to same. 375

Same to same. 350

Same to same. 930

Same to same. 1,220

Same to same. 1,350

Stedman, Ernest G. to Sarah Taylor. 5,000

Stix, Otto L. to William Rosenberg. nom

Stix, Louis to James B. Vredenburgh, Jersey City. 6,000

Snyder, Augusta to James H. McCormick, Coney Island, L. I. 2,000

Thomas, Peter, Hempstead, L. I., to Henry J. and William Wirth. 1,000

Todd, Paul P. to Terence Jacobson. 5,000

The United States Fire Ins. Co. to John J. Brown et al. exrs. George Brown. 14,000

Title Guarantee and Trust Co. to Ambrose K. Ely et al. executors. 30,000

Title Guarantee and Trust Co. to John Polhemus, Flushing, L. I. 17,000

Title Guarantee and Trust Co. to Armand Levy and ano. exrs. and trustees Theodore Levy. 11,000

Title Guarantee and Trust Co. to Leander Horton, Portchester, N. Y. 15,000

Same to The Excelsior Savings Bank. 25,000

Union Trust Co of N. Y. as depositary and trustee for Anna R. Cuming the younger and others to Kate A. Peck. 5,000

Von Bernuth, Emily F. to The Germania Life Ins. Co. 30,000

Winslow, Edward to Henry W. Ford trustee Augustus H. Ward. nom

Whalen, John to William J. Donald, Norfolk, Va. 7,500

Washburn, Wilbur F., Yonkers, N. Y., to John E. Andrews, Yonkers, N. Y. 3,500

Wehle, Theodore to Mila P. Palmer trustee Frances B. Hegeman. 50,000

Weil, Jonas and Bernhard Mayer to Leah Buttenwieser. nom

KINGS COUNTY.

OCT. 1 TO 7—INCLUSIVE.

Adams, Bentley F. to Marenus J. Goodenough. $12,000

Allen, Mary E. to John L. Voorhies, Commissioner of Investment, Town Gravesend. 1,000

Beer, Louis and Michael Schaffner to Adrianna Miller. 1,900

Betts, Charles A. to Hamilton Trust Co. 2,640

Bossert, Jacob to John Auer. 3,000

Barnard, John T. to William Warner. 3,000

Behrens, Frederick trustee Frederick Behrens dec'd to James H. McCormick. 1,537

Chapman, William H. exr. Samuel Wanser to Gertrude L. Gottsch. 4,000

Comfort, Virgil to William Andrews. 600

Corey, Charles to James Gascoine. 575

Cole, Randolph H. to Charles Skidmore, Jamaica, L. I. 4,000

Cortis, Mary E. wife of Arthur M. to Hamilton Trust Co. nom

Chapman, George F. to The Williamsburgh Savings Bank. 1,600

Dill, John, Jr., to John Dill. 850

Davenport, Julius exr. Ann Wilson to William Harkness. 3,000

Dess, August and Wallburga to The German Savings Bank, Brooklyn. 3,000

Du Bois, Lewis to Maria L. Linington. 4,000

Evans, George to John H. Elfers. 600

Finkeldey, Henry guard Kath. E. Finkeldey to Katharine E Finkeldey. nom

Gottsch, Gertrude L. to John Schliemann. 2,000

Greenfield, Henry to Lembeck & Betz Eagle Brewing Co. 1,581

Hachemeister, Elisa extrx. Charles Hachemeister to Robert B. Muller. 1,500

Holton, Josephine G. to Mary E. wife of Joseph Benedict. 5,000

Hagemeyer, Garetta P. admr. F. E. Hagemeyer who was trustee of Alwina A. C. Hagedorn to The Guarantee Trust and Safe Deposit Co., Philadelphia, as trustee of A. A. C. Hagedorn. nom

Halstead, Pearson exr. Annie Joy to George A. Jeremiah exr. George A. Jeremiah. 2,015

Ingraham, Richard to George W. Underhill. 4,500

Joy, Joseph F. surviving exr. Annie Joy to Joseph F. Joy and Pearson Halstead substituted exrs. of said Annie Joy. nom

Klemlein, Dorothea to Anna M. Schuster. 1,000

Kaplan, Aaron to Samuel L. Brody. 2,800

Linton, Edward F. to Anna M. Beach. 1,520

Longman, Henry to James Gascoine. 1,400

Loines, William H. and ano. exrs. Sarah Loines to Mary B. wife of Robert F. Mathews. 2,500

Lyons, Henry B. to George H. Roberts. nom

Lott, Charles F., Troy, N. Y., to Cynthia Lott, New Utrecht, L. I. 4,500

Lott, Cynthia to John S. Denton, Jamaica, L. I. 2,000

Lacey, Margie B. extrx. Frederick Lacey to William and Henry H. Man. 4,000

Laidlaw, John L. and ano. exrs. Thomas Laidlaw to John L. Laidlaw and ano. trustees Elizabeth Mann. 5,500

Levino, Bernard to Walter F Clayton. 1,200

McChesney, Sarah M. to Marion S. Sheldon. 3,000

McShane, Henry & Co. to The Henry McShane Mfg. Co., Baltimore, Md. nom

Meyer, Henry to Barbara Meyer. 1,250

Miller, Hannah E., Philadelphia, Pa., to Robert I. Miller. 5,000

Mott, Eliza A. to Sarah A. Howell. 3,587

Meller, Christian H. to Charles J. Patterson. 2,000

Meth, Andrew to Peter Stebe. 3,000

Same to same. 3,000

Same to Bernhard Heussner. 2,000

Meth, Andreas to John N. Wirth. 1,500

Muller, Robert B. to Mary Miller. 650

Man, William and Henry H. to Margie B., Jr., and Anna M. Lacey. 4,000

Molloy, David J. to Hall Sash and Door Co. 250

Newton, Albro J. to Constantia A. P. Duppen. 3,000

Planten, John R. to Henry Blatchford. 2,400

Painter, Adelaide L. admrx. Thomas A. Painter to Frederick D. Somers, Montclair, N. J. 3 assigns., each $1,750. 5,250

Same to same. 2 assigns., each $750. 1,500

Raymond, Henry V. to Flora A. Gorden. 4,088

Ries, Henry to Charles Ries. 650

Robbins, Eugenia B. to Triennial Benefit League. 2,000

Roberts, Charles H. to O. W. Thomas. 1,800

Suydam, Evert to John L. Voorhies, Commissioner of Investment for Gravesend. 1,000

Seliew, Timothy G. to Oliver W. Coe. 35,969

Schwarz, William to Bernhard J. Pink. 1,300

The Farmers Loan and Trust Co. trustee Nathaniel L McCready to The Farmers Loan and Trust Co. guard. Francis M. Whaley. nom

Title Guarantee and Trust Co. to The Brooklyn Trust Co. 4,000

Same to same. 1,750

Same to same. 1,500

Same to Pauline May et al. exrs. Mary May. 7,500

Same to J. Kelsey Burr. 5,000

Same to Robert W. Cooper. 3,500

Same to Stephen D. Horton trustee William J. Horton. 1,700

Same to Rachel and Phebe J. Valentine. 1,200

Same to Annie G. Paddock. 2,000

Same to Brooklyn Trust Co. 2,500

Same to Garetta P. Hagemeyer. 5,000

Same to Jane A. Aikman. 1,200

Same to Rebecca G. Leger. 4,500

Same to Brooklyn Trust Co. 5 assigns., each 9,000. 45,000

Same to Elizabeth F. R. Laing. 800

Turner, George V. exr. Catharine A. Benson to Mary M. Turner and Mary H. Bush. 4,500

Tyson, George I. and ano. exrs. and trustees John Hamilton to Oscar Hamilton. 4,000

Truslow, Charles W. admr. William Wall to Williamsburgh Savings Bank. 2,400

Underhill, Edward C. exr. Abraham Underhill to Richard R. Jordan. 1,000

Underhill, George W. exr. James Underhill to Richard Ingraham, Hempstead, L. I. 4,500

Weinig, Michael to Roman Catholic Church Holy Trinity. 500

Watson, Willard S. to Lippman Tannenbaum. nom

Whalen, Harriet S. to Samuel Ayres. 2,000

Whitlock, Julia J. to Emma A. Sumner. 400

Wood, Gertrude P. to Melvin Brown. 600

JUDGMENTS.

In these lists of judgments the names alphabetically arranged, and which are first on each line, are those of the judgment debtor. The letter (D) means judgment for deficiency (*) means not summoned. (†) signifies that the first name is fictitious, real name being unknown. Judgments entered during the week, and satisfied before day of publication, do not appear in this column, but in list of Satisfied Judgments.

NEW YORK CITY.

Oct.

8 Alden, John B—Hubley Printing Co (Lim) $730 76

6 Almy, Edwin R—W R McClellan 838 24

6 Abrahams, Sigismund—H B Claflin Co 283 26

7 Aquilera, Miguel L—Homer Lee Bank Note Co 1,813 69

7 Atwell, Edwin—Anna M V Gildersleeve 313 02

7 Alexander, Samuel—A H Masten 88 66

7 Arden, Henry—J M Gove 68 50

8 Asmus, Charles—Daniel Morgan 231 50

8 Aylward, John W—Richard Vom Hofe 258 08

9 Ayres, Charles H—M F Schrenkeisen 571 80

3 Ball, Max—George Simon 680 56

3 Banker, Albert C—R R Haydock 275 60

3 Borchardt, Ison—H B Claflin Co 300 14

3† Bene, Richard T—J H Weimers 88 44

5 Barron, Mary A—John Carroll 145 84

5 B . T m —Nathan Lewis 1,045 75

5 Brennan, James } Brennan, Thomas } J J FitzGerald 79 54

5 Bedell, George C } Bedell, Edwin } A W Lindsay Type Foundry 211 65

5 Benjamin, Mary—W F Clemmons 458 19

5 Bernstein, Samuel—Hulda J Bernstein 4,127 47

5 the same—Elizabeth A Bernstein 2,894 32

5 the same—B F Bernstein 2,320 37

5 Brennan, Thomas—Northern Nat Bank 642 44

6 Beardsley, Charles S—Susan C Crossman 78 15

6 Beno, Joseph—Max Hurvich 1,958 22

6 the same—the same 1,674 39

6 Bailey, William T—R E Dietz Co 152 78

6 Beno, Joseph—G F Vietor 1,334 56

6 Bernstein, Samuel—Elizabeth A Bernstein 1,698 04

6* Berger, John—Hughes Fawcett 154 00

6* Barcalow, George B—W T Bradley 775 10

6 Blake, Patrick J—W M Leslie 109 45

6 Brown, Christopher—G W Brown 226 69

6 Bonnell, John Harper—Bank of N Y Nat Banking Assoc 1,500 54

6 the same—the same 1,456 40

6 Bensel, Rebecca—S V Constant 119 07

6 Brennan, Thomas } *Brennan, Winifried } Lilly Hertzberg 485 20

6 Brennan, Thomas—Peter Walls 163 90

7 Burkart, Joseph H } *Burkart, William J } D P Morse 379 22

7 Bodenheimer, Max—Max Lichtenstadler 30 70

7 Boyd, William J—Frederick Lutz 52 29

7* Bonnell, J Harper—Webster Paper Co 1,167 80

7* Burger, Lewis—Joseph Sawyer 394 28

7 Backer, Abraham—Morris Schneider 51,541 77

8 Brown, Thomas, Jr—N Y Wall Paper Co (Lim) 170 64

8 Behrend, Edward—F A Bohm 1,466 12

8 Bonnell, John H—Nat State Bank of Camden 1,014 84

8 Buell, Henry—Mary Brockman 430 99

8 Bachrach, Nathan—New Haven Clock Co 90 60

8 Burke, Joseph P—Beadleston & Woerz 171 00

8 Bennett, Philo S } Blendermann, Albert } C E Burke, assignee 455 17

8 Beno, Joseph—Carl Schefer 1,226 97

8 Beardsley, Henry W—Martha E Willis 566 05

8 Backer, Abraham—M S Fechheimer 20,296 38

9 Brady, Edward J—P G Moloney 191 55

9 Blanchard, Charles A—M F Schrenkeisen 571 80

9 Butcher, Edward C—W H Sage 134 78

9 Boyd, George Banks—Alfred Corley 94 33

9 Beblmer, John F—Henry McCready 353 00

9 Blohm, Charles—W H Henneberger 394 00

9 Belvin, Mary—Jacob Appel 538 11

9 the same—Aaron Kohn 4,617 99

9 Birnbaum, Charles Z—George Bleistein 1,081 16

9 the same—the same costs 65 65

9 Belagh, Frank } Balop, Andor } Carl Berger 654 39

9 Bauer, Anton—Abraham Bernheim 29 22

9 Buonsignore, Giovanni } Buonsignore, Filomena } Vincenzo Farenga 654 39

3 Cameron, James W—J A Fleischer 132 22

3 Campbell, William S } Campbell, Neil } R R Haydock 275 60

5 Cohn, Walter J } Cohn, William I } Liberty Woollen Mfg Co 1,066 69

5 the same—William Whitman 1,208 95

5 the same—Delhi Woolen Mills 1,075 42

5 Conforti, Nicholas—J G Goldsmith 1,742 40

6 Cooper, John H—David Mayer 238 00

6 Coffin, Frederick R—Nonotuck Paper Co 411 04

6 Cohn, Louis—J D Eisenstein.........196 69
7 Coplon, Morris—G A Le Blanc.......305 06
7 Cohen, Moses—Samuel Firnski.......299 66
7 Canavella, Benjamin J—E M Aguirre 298 68
7 Cohn, Walter J / Cohn, William I } H W T Mali.......2,5?2 87
7 Craft, Henry S—D G Yuengling, Jr Brewing Co.......120 70
7 Curtis, Louis—C N Moulton..........164 50
8 Canavello, Benjamin J—Benoit Wasserman.......121 29
8 Costello, Lawrence—J H Strong, trustee.......325 00
8 Collis, Charles H T—G W McLean, recvr.......139 94
8 Callahan, Thomas F—Hugo Heyman.123 66
8 Coffey, John F—O K Dimock.........131 28
9 Conrad, August—Susan Martin.......99 27
9 Conklin, Ellen C L—Edward Boote..306 58
9 Colllag, Alex—Carl Berger..........654 39
9 Campbell, John V—Henry McShane Co (Lim).......170 00
9 Cragin, Aaron, Jr—E H Reynolds...115 07
9 Cohen, Morris—F G Kenney..........186 85
5 Dwyer, Thomas H—Isabella Rummens.......67 80
5 Davis, John C—L D Hosford..........785 49
5 Dodd, Cortland H, treas of Dodd & Childs' Express—Fannie Grossman.1,707 50
6 de Kraft, William R—J B Saalmann. 231 60
6+Doe, John—Leopold Zimmermann...8,299 98
7 Dempsey, William—H F Gundrum..173 72
7 Dunn, Mary A—Frederick Aldhous.......(D) 2,215 72
7 Desant, William F Z—Louis Hanneman, recvr.......5,073 55
7 Donoho, Constantine—Empire State Brewing Co.......239 47
7 Damner, Hermann—the same.......78 24
9 Dampf, Fanny P—J G Flammer......446 37
9 Dreyfuss, Bernard—F E Russell......612 72
9*Doe, John—F E Russell.............116 53
9 Dreyfuss, Bernard—Moses Tanenbaum 824 95
9 Demarest, Francis E, an infant, by Wm E Demarest, her guard—J A Fleck.......costs 153 29
9 De Florez, Robert—Oscar Unz.......16 19
9 Demarest, Henry H—W H Salt.......273 84
9*de Occhvary, Adalbert—Carl Berger. 654 39
3 Edick, James—David McCosker......160 33
6 Epstin, Solomon D—Equitable Life Assurance Society of U S..........225 00
6 Eastman, Richard B—Frederick Keppel.......1,277 20
6 Elkan, Siegfried—Thurber, Whyland Co.......345 58
7 Egan, John—Empire State Brewing Co.......77 92
8 Eller, Maurice, Jr—Wakefield Rattan Co.......28 44
9 Eick, Gross—Carl Berger............654 39
3 Frost, Fred C—C F Thayer...........103 35
3 Fursman, Annie H—W J Wainwright.......321 24
5 Fay, Anna B—L D Hosford...........785 47
5*Fruchtenicht, John—W F Redlich...745 09
5*Fried, Louis / Foder, Sigmund } Herman Price....206 02
5 Faeger, Adam—Joseph Hoffmann....478 00
5 Fublrott, Otto—C M Marsh..........608 88
6 Flasch, Julius—Jeanne Flasch........773 10
6*Farrington, John A / Farrington, Jonas A } Joseph Schwarzschild.......1,700 00
6 Fitzgibbon, Maurice—W T Bradley .775 10
6 Fricke, Ernst J—Charles Lehritter...923 78
6 Ferguson, John—J E Stewart.........211 33
6 Fleisch, Benjamin—C V Fornes......179 11
7 Fischer, William—G W Smith........529 22
8 Franks, Isaac—W W McNaught.....77 92
9 Fischer, William—J E Armstrong...550 04
9 Fuller, Carrie W—Title Guarantee and Trust Co.......1,052 50
5 Gregory, Richard A—Jane Howes...1,834 15
6 Glesch, John N—Maria Martin......281 34
6 Green, Philip A—Anna H Gerding...84 18
6 Gunning, Alexander P—C F Tietjen..323 68
7 Goss, Henry—Robert Hill...........85 28
7 Gerdts, Frederick W—D G Yuengling, Jr, Brewing Co.......1,426 37
8 Grohbrugge, John—Cord Mahnken...2,133 70
8 Glover, Howard N—Magdelaine Ranchfuss.......79 90
8 Graff, Charles H—J H Lane..........92 74
8 Gelbe, Edward A—J E Nichols.......150 89
9+Gutenstein, Henry—Solomon Deutz..175 30
9 Goodkind, Moses—Harriette Strong..298 84
9 Griffith, Charles E—J P Mones.......193 37
3 Honey, John J—Robert Macbeth....414 35
3 Holmes, Joseph—W L Hyde.........31 00
5 Hitchcock, Jacob W—A P W Kinnan.......1,716 50
5 Haiss, Henry—Knickerbocker Ice Co. 182 83
5 Henderson, Juliette C—Herman Kuhnast.......624 22
5 Hore, Peter—Burr Brewing Co......256 65
5 Harper, William D—Madison Square Bank.......1,281 45
the same—the same.............981 49
the same—the same 571 14
5 Hester, Eugene W—Bank of Commerce in Buffalo.......448 26
6 the same—the same.......costs 64 52
6 Howard, Robert—W B Roe..........103 00
6 Harper, William D—Market and Fulton Nat Bank.......1,028 34
the same—the same.............125 96
6 the same—the same.............1,473 51
6 Harper, William Durbin—Bank of N Y Nat Banking Assoc.......1,456 40
6 the same—the same.......1,500 54
6 Harper, William D—Chatham Nat Bank.......921 50
6 Howe, Charles M / Howe, Adelaide C } E M Gattle.......385 78

6 Hess, George / Hess, Henry } George Hagemeyer....365 29
6 the same—the same.............460 54
7 Hanover, Henry—John Draher......323 76
7 Holcke, Henry—Martin Reynolds.....735 47
7 Henkel, Charles A—L H Allen........666 15
7 Hart, Alexander R / Harper, William D } Market and Fulton Nat Bank.1,428 85
7 the same—the same............946 97
7 Hart, Alexander R—the same......1,121 81
7 Hammacher, Gustav—A J Koehler...110 44
7 Harper, William D—Webster Paper Co.......1,167 80
7 Haas, Joseph—Louis De Jonge.......153 75
7 Hyatt, George E / Hyatt, Kate G } Annie Melley, extrx.......428 04
8 Harper, William D—Nat State Bank of Camden.......1,014 84
8+Hayden, Martin M—Vitalis Himmer. 201 00
8 Heney, George T—P J Barthel......101 79
8 Hickey, Francis—Marcus Beckmann. 27 23
8 Hammerstein, Jacob—Cornelius Evans.......87 42
8 Hawley, Oscar F—M B Tidey, Jr....315 88
9 Hardenbrook, Frank M—Equitable Life Assurance Society of U S.....141 15
9 Hubay, Bela—Carl Berger...........654 39
9*Hastings, William—Barzella Grover. 1,086 38
9 Hirsch, Louis—Joseph Sawyer.......253 79
9 Harper, William D—Madison Square Bank.......371 71
9 Halpin, Peter—Patrick Cassidy......326 80
9 Rusted, Sabina—Leon Tanenbaum...1,638 28
6 Isaak, Max—Benjamin Raphael 149 50
7 Isselbacher, Simon—H A Claflin.....599 13
9 Iglauer, Simon—E S Levi...........342 34
5 Jackman, Michael—John Brosen.....66 16
6 Johnson, Luman W—Leopold Zimmermann.......8,299 95
9 Joszy, Symmezi / Joszy, Gross } Carl Berger......654 39
3 Kelly, Michael J—Murray Hill Bank. 203 58
3 Kennedy, Daniel R—Albertype Co....63 57
3 Klee, Henry W—John Stout.........316 10
5 Kasschan, John—Alfred Greenbaum. 264 05
6 Krauss, Jean K—William Neumann..110 50
6*Kirshbaum, Jacob—Samuel Wolff....142 97
6*Krouder, Frank / Kreuder, Adolph / Kline, Charles } Frederick Leschhorn.......516 49
6 Kuntz, Joseph A—Solomon Berliner. 519 51
6 Kelly, Michael J—F A Burnham.....293 98
6*Kepes, Joseph—August Marshall.....851 78
7 Klein, Peter, Jr—Christopher Schunemann.......96 15
7 Katz, Sarah—Lucius Hart...........117 55
8 Kips, John—A G Hupfel.............758 60
9 Kohner, Maurice M—C M Buckman..993 63
9 Kahn, Louis—Solomon Deutz.........100 04
9 Klussmann, Rudolph B—A B Cooper. 240 31
9 Kleeblatt, Max—M R Cook..........82 20
9 Kahl, John E—Hanover Fire Ins Co..2,172 15
3 Lawson, John—Conrad Diehl.........368 58
5 Lucey, Gerald—Henry Eggers........405 54
6 Lee, George C—J W Ackerman 869 32
6 Loonie, John J—Crawford Maxwell..100 78
6 Locke, Charles E—W G Shuyler.....170 39
7 Lowenstein, Joseph H—A S Hyman..201 88
7 the same—the same.......102 91
7*Levy, Morris / Levy, Marcus } Isaac Elkins..........2,936 07
7 Lowenstein, Joseph—A S Hyman....90 56
8 Levi, Morris—A I Mayerson 85 56
8*Lyon, Edward / Lyon, Katherine } T E Conklin.......1,295 27
8 Lederer, Benjamin—James Boiles, Jr 107 00
9 Lilly, George—Mary James..........632 03
9 Lustig, Samuel—Carl Berger........654 39
3+Mercur, John G—Abraham Winegarden.......44 87
3 Maher, Edward—John Dimond......323 18
5 Murphy, Jeremiah A—Aaron Strauss 119 87
5 Mandel, Elias—Alois Kohn...........161 58
5 Miller, Robert H—Madison Square Bank.......981 49
5 Moore, Joseph S—W E Coffin........231 73
5 Miller, Frank W—Metropolitan Telephone and Telegraph Co..........83 62
6 Meyers, Jacob J—Samuel Wolff.......142 97
6 Mehrback, Isidor—H W Haas.........104 98
6 Mayer, Regina—Babette Blumenthal. 199 02
6 Mollers, Joseph—Henry Eggers......186 22
6 Muller, William—G F Warner.......95 14
6 Muller, Louis—Marvin Safe Co......47 02
6 Molleson, George E—M R Winchell..370 60
8 the same—P C Richardson.....310 80
6 Miller, Robert H—Market and Fulton Nat Bank.......1,473 51
7 Meyerson, Chana—Harry Levene....106 16
7 Mooney, Peter W—W P Baker..costs 40 24
7 Meyer, Philip L—F G W Beard......5,803 55
7 Megargee, Louis N—F J Allen.......147 44
8 Mushcovitz, Mayer—Adolph Edelmuth.......71 87
8 Meyer, Henry—J L Rees.............397 29
8*Moore, John—A L Lowenthal........78 90
8 Meyer, Siegmund T / Meyer, Arthur L } C F Estwick....490 68
8 Mead, Sarah F—David Miller....costs 124 57
9*Meyer, Gesine / Meyer, Anna } Henry Eggers........1,164 65
9*Meyer, Siegmund T / Meyer, Arthur L } C L Marshall...6,369 46
9 Margowski, Max—Max Jokinsky.....213 90
9 Morro, August T—Hodgman Rubber Co.......304 41
9 Morris, Henry O—G R Brown.......647 51
9 Menyus, Sarkozy—Carl Berger.......654 39
9 Moeller, Henry—G T Lawrence......70 70
9 Michel, Valentin—Henry Eggers.....115 47
9 Mead, Barron A—Provident Fund Society.......75 81
9 Mills, Emma D—A F W Leslie.......75 27
9 Morehead, Franklin C—J F Peavey..4,681 77

9 Mitchell, John J—Nat Park Bank....533 82
3 McLean, James—Merchant Bank of Rochester.......858 21
5 McDonald, Samuel—Henry Herrmann 66 85
6 McKean, Thomas—Thomas Lenane..506 00
6 McNab, George R—John Boyle........550 85
6*McIndoe, Walter J—T G Palmer.....193 92
6 McNichle, Andrew F—B W Traitel..38 83
9 McNamara, Daniel—P J Galligan....1,086 44
9 McEntee, Francis M—Patrick Cassidy 326 80
5 Newhall, Richard W—J C de La Mare.......59 50
5 Nolte, Kirschner H—Robert Hill.....82 41
5 Osborn, William—J M Young, assignee 83 99
6 O'Connell, Maurice—Union Blue Stone Co.......495 82
6 O'Hanlon, Philip F—Benjamin Altman.......230 96
7 Orbendorfer, Nathaniel—A S Hyman 201 88
7 the same—the same...........102 91
7 the same—the same...........90 56
9 Overin, Henry C—Barzella Grover...1,086 38
9 Olmstead, Charles—F E Russell......116 53
9 Ogden, John R—J F Peavey.........4,681 77
3 Parrett, Arthur C—J L Mott Iron Works.......424 16
5 Pidgeon, Frank—Thompson Nat Bank of Thompson, Conn 406 51
5 Pine, Charles H—F C Linde..........47 41
6 Ponti, Edward—G W Venable.......1,932 68
6 Palmer, George W—J T Bruen.......863 63
6*Pratt, Charles E—M R Winchell.....370 60
7 Payne, George A—Murray Hill Bank 203 43
7 Pauritsch, Joseph—North Bass Island Wine Co.......343 97
8 Price, Jesse—Western Nat Bank.....1,047 63
8 Pettchaft, Bernard—Semon Dittman. 763 79
8 Price, Jesse—Western Nat Bank.....499 40
8 the same—the same...........225 30
9 Pearlman, Morris—Louis Rothschild. 199 81
9 Petchir, Istvan—Carl Berger.........654 39
9 Park, Charles H—Knickerbocker Ice Co.......53 48
9 Picaza, John—Oscar Unz 16 19
3 Quimby, Thomas W—Boston Buckboard and Carriage Co............255 21
5 Randall, Maggie M—C M Marsh.....608 88
5 Ryan, Patrick—Hecla Powder Co....212 04
6 Root, James H—Market and Fulton Nat Bank.......1,028 34
6 the same—the same...........947 70
6 Rametta, Francesco—Guiseppa Rametta.......109 25
7 Rehberger, Joseph H D—John Draher 323 76
7 Ross, Ivison M—A H Masten........71 21
7 Ritz, Nicholas—Empire State Brewing Co.......98 04
7 Rosenstein, George—C G Rives......707 17
8 Root, James H—Nat State Bank of Camden.......1,014 84
9 Reim, Charles—Annie Carr, extrx...131 34
3 Seibel, George F—Merchants' Bank of Rochester.......858 21
3 Scharff, Hyman—A F Gardner.......246 30
3 Sparks, Alfred M—E P Gleason Mfg Co.......544 39
5 Shandley, Kate—F W Angel. 267 50
5 Sheehan, John—C H Rose...........614 59
5 Solomon, Ephraim—Liberty Woolen Mfg Co.......1,306 69
5 the same—William Whitman...1,208 95
5 the same—Delhi Woolen Mills..1,075 42
5 Schwiefert, Frederick—Seyfried Cigar Mfg Co.......76 30
5 Stayert, Peter—Joseph Weishaupt...221 70
5 Stalps, Theodore—E R Leavitt.......398 24
5*Spaulding, Charles W / *Stein, Alexander } Metropolitan Telephone and Telegraph Co. 83 62
5 Sotscheck, Carl—Charles Lersch.....420 68
6 Schneider, Louis H—Frederick Jenkins.......134 45
6 Styles, Clara—Leopold Schwartz.....471 65
6 the same—the same.......costs 67 52
6*Schultz, Maurice—Jeanne Flasch.....773 10
6 Sulzer, Alfred—W R McClellan......838 24
6 Schlachter, John—Patterson Bros....182 55
6 Schaupert, Lorenz J—Libanio Sarre. 177 46
6 the same—the same...........178 09
6 Swick, John J—L T Hepburn........253 71
6 Squires, Newton—Franco-American Food Co.......81 24
6 Seward, Thomas J—Baltimore Copper and Smelting and Roller Co....costs 24 01
6 Singer, Marlon—Joseph Wehrle.......61 87
6 Spofford, Joseph L—T B Starr.......194 56
6*Steinfeld, David—Lilly Hertzberg....485 20
6 Schmidt, Edmund P—C F Tietjen....323 68
7 Schlansky, Moses / Schlansky, Sarah } East Side Bank..427 27
7 Simon, Isaac—Joseph Sawyer.........894 28
7 Solomon, Ephraim—H W T Mali....2,582 87
7 Schewning, Charles—Morris Spiegel..10 00
7 Smoot, Samuel S—C K Sherwood.......costs 111 60
8 Sicherman, Louis—Adolph Edelmuth 152 02
8 Schlansky, Moses—Benjamin Dearing 124 29
8 Stewart, Matthew C—Joseph Bierhoff 162 50
8 Stephenson, Helen S—F W Seybel...631 28
8 Stuckenschmidt, Sophie—C H Luedeke.......303 90
8 Silberstein, Simon—People State N Y 1,000 00
8 Spengler, William—John Sackett ...279 99
9 Springer, Jacob—O W. Buckingham. 1,461 66
9 the same—C M Bucknam.......992 65
9 *Slater, William G / Slater, Howard P / *Slater, Seymour D } H C Graves.....384 08
9 Slater, William G / Slater, Seymour D / Slater, Howard P } Franklin Stetson 543 07
9 Stone, Howard C—F W Rockfellow..119 81
9 Stewart, James E—O B Potter.......77 64

9†Seaman, John C—E S Mailler........ 269 15
9 Stemmerman, Henry—Martin Cook.. 194 41
7 Smith, John—Empire State Brewing Co........ 88 49
3 The Thomas Murray Co—Merchants Bank of Rochester........ 858 21
3 The Chadwick Two Wheeler Co—C N Lockwood........ 423 64
3 The Willard Metal Co—G A Higgins. 68 94
3 The Alden Publishing Co—Hubley Printing Co (Lim)........ 730 76
3 Teachers Publishing Co—J S Edwards 193 19
5 Eastman & Krauss Razor Co—T E Jones........ 24 50
5 J H Bonnell & Co (Lim)—Madison Square Bank........ 571 14
5 the same——the same........ 1,281 45
5 the same——the same........ 981 49
5 Barr Electric Mfg Co—Electrical Review Publishing Co........ 87 91
5 The Consumers Gas and Electric Light Co—Tucker Electrical Construction Co........ 135 26
6 Belford Co—American Photo-Engraving Co........ 121 00
6 Fibrone Mfg Co—Patterson Bros..... 49 78
6 U S Volta Electric Battery Co—Timothy Hurley........ 1,789 99
6 J H Bonnell & Co (Lim)—Market & Fulton Nat Bank........ 1,028 34
6 the same——the same........ 947 70
6 the same——the same........ 125 96
6 the same——the same........ 1,473 51
6 the same——Bank of N Y Nat Banking Assoc........ 1,456 40
6 the same——the same........ 1,500 54
6 National Vulcan Burner Co—T N Motley........ 64 19
7 The Manhattan Railway Co / N Y Elevated Railroad Co } J H F Ubleubaut 3,264 18
7 J H Bonnell & Co (Lim)—Market and Fulton Nat Bank........ 1,428 85
7 the same——the same........ 940 97
7 the same——the same........ 1,121 81
7 The Mayor, Aldermen, &c—J W Franklin........ 355 91
7 Ducker Portable House Co—Annetta Villari........ 150 00
7 N Y Steamship Co—David Kahnweiler........ 135 36
7 The Mayor, Aldermen, &c—P E Donlin........ 524 95
7 The Hudson River Boot and Shoe Mfg Co—E R Ladew........ 806 90
8 J H Bonnell & Co (Lim)—Nat State Bank of Camden........ 1,014 84
8 The Sonneborn Rubber Comb and Novelty Co—W E Zabriskie........ 72,086 47
8 The Uptown Paper Co—Byron Ross.. 881 93
8 The Lawton Mfg Co—Eugene Gerbeveux........ 67 22
8 N Y Steamship Co—William Parter, Jr........ 235 90
8 The C S Phillips Patent Process Tobacco Growing and Curing Co—Judge Publishing Co........ 644 32
8 The Mayor, Aldermen, &c—C L Dana 436 17
9 The Germania Fire Ins Co—Hanover Fire Ins Co........ 2,172 15
9 The Mayor, Aldermen, &c—M D Cassidy........ 159 50
9 Belford's Magazine Co—Adams & Bishop Co........ 1,697 56
9 the same——the same........ 1,679 11
9 J H Bonnell & Co (Lim)—Madison Square Bank........ 371 71
9 American Musician Publishing Co—Americo Gori........ 183 41
9 Pierce Artesian and Oil Well Supply Co—Joseph Icenhower........ 199 33
3 Tuttle, William M B—Catharine E Skidmore........ 27 07
5 Thorne, George W—R F Baxter........ 189 14
6 Thierfelder, James—Hughes Fawcett. 154 00
6 Taylor, George R—Robert Gordon.... 100 58
8 Teets, George—J C Cook........ 1,020 61
8 Tollner, Henry—Nathan Stern........ 109 14
8 Tuft, John B / Tuft, Annie C } John Early........ 474 87
9 Teale, Robert E J C—Hodgman Rubber Co........ 304 41
9 Truman, David H—Mason Au & Magenheimer Confectionery Co........ 336 50
5 Ullrich, Carl—W F Redlich........ 745 09
5 Valentine, Robert H C—Western Nat Bank........ 1,133 09
5 the same——the same........ 1,759 04
5 the same——the same........ 498 45
5 the same——the same........ 1,219 20
5 the same——the same........ 317 84
5 the same——Madison Square Bank........ 571 14
5 Von Lehn, Richard—Alexander Hanneman........ 249 32
6 Voudy, Thomas D—T G Palmer...... 193 92
8 Von Tobel, Rudolph H—A G Hupfel. 758 60
9 Vaast, Jules—Faience Mfg Co........ 273 46
3 Wendt, Charles W—J Caroline Loudon........ 124 06
3*Welsh, Frank M—Albertype Co...... 63 57
3 Waddell, Hamilton—James Fitzpatrick........ 243 42
5 White, John J—Boston Boot Co...... 334 71
5 Webster, Hanson S—J H Lee........ 536 32
5 Wachtol, Jacob, admr Solomon Klein—William Dattelbaum........ 57 97
5 the same——Max Freund & Co... 565 54
6 Walthr, John W / †Walter, Ralphi } Max Steiner........ 216 29
6 Weser, George W—L F Hepburn.... 253 71
6 Wormser, Edward—August Marshall. 851 78
6 Wyatt, George S—C W Wells........ 250 07
7 Wendt, Charles M—G W Smith........ 529 22
7 Walton, Ray—Charles Rehme........ 104 08
7 Warrin, Frank L—F A Lord........ 371 12
7 Walsh, Thomas J—D W Moran........ 1,063 64
8 Wallace, William—A L Lowenthal.. 78 90
8 Weiss, Rosa—People State N Y........ 1,000 00
8 Willard, Samuel H—W H Atwater... 2,381 19
8 Wanmaker, William—Susan Wanmaker........ costs 43 02
9 Walker, Charles E—George Whitaker 712 08
9 Whiting, Walter B—Lucien Baer.... 189 33
9 Wachenheimer, Isaac—Solomon Levy 837 63
9 Wendt, Charles M—J E Armstrong.. 550 04
9 Waters, Archibald O—Knickerbocker Ice Co........ 58 48
9 Wheeler, William A—Manhattan Oil Co........ 140 32
9 Watkins, James O—L A Thole....(D) 434 30
9 the same——J D Ottiwell......(D) 1,364 33
9 Wicht, William—A B Cooper........ 240 31
9 Walling, Edward P—Shepard & Morse Lumber Co........ 1,066 58
7 Yeaton, Charles C—F G W Beard.... 5,803 55
6 Zinsheimer, Louis—John Baehr..... 165 00
6 Zimmerman, Ernst—Ludwig Kurzschenkel........ 138 84

KINGS COUNTY.

Oct.
5*Adams, Francis H—Superior Lumber Co........ $331 75
5* the same——the same........ 287 83
5 Andress, Charles W—C Dehler........ 607 25
7 Aldom, Charles W—A C Macoduck.. 226 88
1 Burton, Joseph L—T Brown........ 120 06
2 Bennett, William J—G W Venable... 100 66
2 Baumgarten, Karl A / Baumgarten, Margaretha } F Bauer.. 115 71
2 Bauer, Henry—Burger & Hower B Co (Lim)........ 113 38
3 Baker, Henry C—L Snethen & Stoney 321 66
3 Bennett, William J—Leibinger & Oehm B Co........ 120 04
3 Burrows, Harry B—W M Wilcox..... 122 60
3 Bowers, Alfred—Metallic Relief Mfg Co........ 622 47
5 Bedell, Edwin J—Superior Lumber Co........ 335 75
5 Buell, Henry—Mary Brockman........ 430 99
5 Blohm, August—C H Eggert & Bro.. 33 58
5 Barry, William J—A Underhill...... 65 55
6 Burcher, Walter V—L Schwartz..... 377 15
6 Blanchard, Ben—H P Kirkham...... 7,604 89
6 Berger, Ferdinand—H Limp........ 675 57
7 Baird, William—E F Kent........ 182 05
7 Bennett, Philo S / Blendermann, Albert } C E Burke, assignee........ 455 17
7 Bowers, Henry H, admr Michael J Hynes—W A Campbell........ 158 19
8 Burkart, Joseph H / *Burkart, William J } D P Morse.... 379 22
8 Broach, John H—G Stryker........ 58 50
3 Covert, Kate—W B Townsend........ 716 88
3 Cargill, Livingston H / Chedsey, Nathan A } W Robinson.. 3,776 02
7 Campbell, William A—M Hynes...... 88 00
2 Defiebre, Conrad—Burger & Hower Brewing Co (Lim)........ 113 38
2 Du Bois, Ithamut—A Saulpaugh..... 337 51
5 Denton, Frank—Sarah L Denton..... 1,516 71
5 Davies, James R—C W Barnard...... 227 87
6 Eastman, Richard B—F Keppel...... 1,277 20
2 Ferry, James J / Ferry, Daniel } Fulton Bank of Brooklyn........ 5,022 21
2 Ferry, Rebecca M / Ferry, Daniel } the same........ 6,016 46
3 Freuenthal, Joseph—E M Travis...... 123 19
3 Fay, J Rockwell / Fries, Louis K } W Robinson...... 3,776 02
5 Funk, Frederick—C G Covert's Sons.. 190 78
6 Flasch, Julius—J Flasch........ 773 10
2 Graham, Charles W—J Bowes........ 542 93
2 Gibbons, John W—E McNamara..... 209 40
3 Gedney, William H / Gregg, Joshua } W Robinson... 3,776 02
6 Gailing, William—J H Hoeft........ 113 35
7 Griebel, Henry—C D Rhinehart..... 146 27
3 Hanse, James—W P Tatham........ 447 38
3 Hopkins, Jr, Joseph—J Gleason...... 220 08
5 Hurst, Celena—F S Van Horne...... 280 54
6 Hintze, Julius E—Bettie Hochstadter 235 83
6 Hanlon, Thomas—H F Burroughs.... 307 19
6 Hardenburg, Henry R—R W Johnson 705 05
7 Hanover, Henry—J Draher........ 323 76
7 Howard, Harriet H—M Ryan........ 185 77
7 Holmes, Mary E—G A Williams...... 270 48
7 Heney, George T—P J Barthel...... 101 79
7 Hyatt, George E / Hyatt, Kate G } Annie Melley, extrx 158 19
7 Hynes, Margaret, admrx / 8 Hynes, Michael J, dec'd } W A Campbell...... 177 92
3 Immig, Charles H—W P Tatham.... 447 38
7 Jarvis, Jr, Nathaniel—Sarah Lynch. 1,179 64
2 Knee, Henry—Kate Carney........ 94 28
3 Kingman, Richard S—H Heywood... 856 11
3 Kenney, Rosanna—Ellen Creamer... 2,169 46
5 Kirkland, William—Superior Lumber Co........ 335 75
5 the same——the same........ 287 83
5 Klee, Henry W—J Stout........ 316 10
3 Levy, Julius / Levy, Augustus H / Levy, Moses S } L Muhlhauser... 2,598 13
3 Leach, George T—H E Kirchner..... 748 08
5 Lehnert, Peter—C G Covert's Sons... 190 78
5 Larkin, Christopher—National Cash Register Co........ 136 10
6 Lucey, Gerald—H Eggers........ 405 54
6 Lansdell, Henry—Fuller & Warren Co........ 283 68
2†McBean, "Andrew" N—W P Rae.... 43 60
2 Munger, Alfred S / Munger, Louis A } New Haven Clock Co........ 454 29
2 McAleer, John—A Fraser........ 268 43
3 Munch, Adam—W P Tatham........ 447 38
3 Mann, Ernst G—L J Keim........ 169 30
3 Mott, Samuel C—W Robbins........ 3,776 02
3 Meguire, Michael B—J Jamer........ 174 52
5 Mitchell, Charles R—C Dehler...... 667 25
5 Mason, James H—Safe Insulated Wire and Cable Co........ 121 71
6 Mohlenhoff, Henry—Bettie Hochstadter........ 187 97
7 Murphy, Patrick—H Kettelbodt...... 207 39
7 Meyer, John—J Burzer........ 41 75
8 Maroney, Patrick F—D Mulholland.. 785 76
2 Noll, Jacob—Burger & Hower Brewing Co (Lim)........ 113 38
5 Newhall, Richard W—J C de La Mare. 59 50
6 Norris, Allison—N Schneider........ 389 64
2 O'Sullivan, John / O'Sullivan, Margaret } Henrietta Cohn........ (D) 8,509 73
2 Potts, George—The Marietta, Columbus, Northern R R Co........ (D) 8,851 08
7 Pletsch, Jacob—J Gardes, exr........ 113 25
3 Quimby, Thomas W—Boston Buckboard Carriage Co........ 255 21
8 Queen, Montgomery—Arthur & Randall........ 601 48
2 Ryerson, James A—T W Cummings.. 48 51
6 Reynolds, Wm W—L Schwartz...... 377 15
6 Reichenbach, Gustave—J Cook...... 98 17
6 Rametta, Francesco—G Rametta..... 109 25
7 Rehberger, Joseph H D—J Draher... 323 76
1 Sidebotham, Thomas B—R N Flagg.. 160 13
2 Spear, George W—J Bowes........ 542 93
2 Stout, Charles S—T W Cummings... 330 92
2 Stokes, William H—A Hormann..... 68 57
3 Shepard, Charles D—W Robinson.... 3,776 02
3 Sheldon, Cevedra B—The New York and New Jersey Telephone Co...... 48 45
3 Sheridan, Owen—B Morris........ 9 60
3 Searing, Sarah J—C U Wing.....(D) 404 90
3 Sherwood, William / Sherwood, Milton } J Wise........ 2,202 95
6 Schultz, Maurice—Jeanne Flasch..... 773 10
7 Sweet, Annie E—M Ryan........ 185 57
7 Sagar, Alonzo M—J Kopke........ 90 34
8 Schneider, Louis H—F Jenkins...... 134 45
8 Smith, Thomas—J Q Maynard....... 108 85
8 Singer, Marion—J Wehrle........ 61 87
3 Timony, Thomas K—The N Y & N J Telephone Co........ 38 53
3 The Fred Hower B Co (Lim)—The De La Vergne Refrigerating Machine Co........ 5,464 89
5 The Prudential Ins Co—Maria Armet 80 56
5 The City of Brooklyn—J E W Sanderson........ 192 07
5 the same——L W Pearson........ 192 07
5 the same——G Wieseckel........ 193 0
5 the same——T D MacRae........ 192 07
5 the same——P F Hogan........ 192 07
5 the same——F J Bruce........ 193 07
5 the same——J E Walsh........ 192 07
5 the same——V A Robertson...... 192 07
5 the same——P J Genthner........ 192 07
5 the same——R J Bell........ 192 07
5 the same——A F Carroll........ 192 07
5 the same——J J O'Connell........ 192 07
5 the same——G G Cochran........ 192 07
5 the same——C F Newman........ 192 07
5 the same——H Euton........ 192 07
5 the same——F E Boyden........ 192 07
5 the same——E F Pearce........ 193 07
6*Turner, William—N Schneider...... 389 64
6 The County of Kings—J Denyse...... 60 80
6 Tilman, John F—B R Sage, Jr........ 121 23
6 The Fred Hower Brewing Co (Lim)—H Limp........ 675 57
7†Taft, "Amos B"—M Ryan........ 185 77
7 The New York Soap and Chemical Co—J S Thompson........ 220 24
7 The admrs of Michael J Haynes, dec'd—W A Campbell........ 158 19
2 Utley, William R—The Marietta, Columbus, Northern R R Co....(D) 8,851 08
6 Von Lehn, Richard—A Hannemann. 249 32
1 Watson, Christopher—H Lennart.... 95 75
2 Walter, Ferdinand—Burger & Hower B Co (Lim)........ 113 38
3 West, Charles G—W Robinson........ 3,776 02
3 Wilhams, Henry F / Williams, Jane E } C O West........ 262 24
6 White, John J—Boston Boot Co...... 334 71
7 Webster, Harrison S—J H Lee....... 536 82
3 Zimmermann, Abraham—G L Hardy. 80 54

SATISFIED JUDGMENTS.

NEW YORK.

October 3 to 9—inclusive.

Abbott, Adeline—John S Tilton. (1891)........ $44 15
Benedict, Henry W—Union Stove Works. (1891)........ 562 89
Blair, Charles H—A B Van Gausbeck. (1885).. 1,137 12
Barton, William E—Sackett & Wilhelms Lithographing Co. (1891)........ 256 45
Brown, Henry C—Augustus Prentice. (1891). 217 87
Blank, Heinrich—David Mayer. (1891)........ 72 58
*Brown, William—Samuel Kessler. (1891).... 198 06
Colleran, Michael and John—First Nat Bank of Yonkers. (1891)........ 2,545 42
Cornell, Oliver H P—A B Van Gausbeek. (1885) 1,137 12
Cullen, Richard J—Catharine E Sidentop. (1891)........ 125 51
Cohen, Solomon—Henry Meyer. (1891)........ 35 82
Donihee, William B—J J Hopper. (1888)...... 233 22
Doyle, Andrew T—Union Stove Works. ('91).. 562 89
De Richmond, Albert—Leopold Lithauer. (1881)........ 457 89
Same——Robert King. (1881)........ 519 34
Same——W J Doremus. (1884)........ 260 63
Donovan, Daniel E—Hecla Powder Co. (1891). 326 24
*Emrich, Joseph, Jr—James Murray. (1891).. 802 16
Fay, Michael—Henry Muhlker. (1881)........ 715 01
Hood, Joseph—Solomon Stein. (1888)........ 1,185 29
*Hillson, Thomas—Franklin Stebbins. (1884). 50 85
Irvine, Allen A—G B Brown. (1891)........ 420 82

Same——same. (1890)........ 446 93
Jacocks, Joseph F and George M—Second Nat Bank, Patterson. (1891)........ 443 78
Kelly, Thomas P—George Cook. (1891)........ 95 08
Same and John A——T P Huffman. (1891)..1,218 85
Same——N Y Horse Manure Co. (1890) 173 23
Lawrence, Henry C—W E Conway. (1891).... 233 25
London Toilet Bazaar Co—William Albrecht. (1891)........ 188 98
Lowerre, George H—Henry Chauncey. ('91) 157 55
Lowenstein, Joseph H—Isaac Harmen. ('91). 91 70
Macmichael, Samuel—J W Hatch, assignee. (1891)........ 129 08
McDonald, Theodore F—A H Allen. (1891)...1,431 75
†Moonelis, Adolph—Simon Auerbach. (1891)..1,489 66
Molleson, George E—M R Winchell. (1890).. 120 68
Manhattan Railway Co—Adolphus Koffmann. (1890)........2,565 70
Same——Aaron Altmayer. (1891)........ 517 70
Same——Margaretha Rupp. (1891)........ 184 98
N Y Elevated R R Co—Margareth Rupp. (1891) 184 98
Same——Adolphus Koffman. (1890)........ 2,565 70
Same——Aaron Altmayer. (1891)........ 517 70
Oberndorfer, Nathaniel—Isaac Harman. ('91) 91 70
†Peetsch, Henry C L—Simon Auerbach. ('91).1,489 66
†Same——same. (1891)........ 96 23
Pratt, Charles E—M R Winchell. (1890)........ 120 68
Pennsylvania R R Co—Thomas Keck. (1891)..1,500 00
Ramsgate, Robert H—Simon Dessau. (1884). 181 85
Rabbiner, Fanny—J D Solomon. (1890)........ 109 50
Romaine, Alice P—G W Berrey. (1890) 170 22
Rosenbaum, Louis—Rachel Kroops. (1888)... 675 22
Schneider, Henry—G B Brown. (1890)........ 446 93
Same——same. (1891)........ 420 82
Sxelly, Peter A—J R Anderson. (1887)........ 244 19
Same——Hannah M Bainbridge. (1887)........ 182 36
Schwarzler, August—William King. (1891)... 35 00
Saul, Isadore, Julius and Charles—J D Eisenstein. (1889)........ 52 74
Same——Rebecca Saul. (1889)........1,620 06
Sweet, E Nathan—A H Van Hausbeek. (1885).1,187 12
Sheehy, Patrick—Health Dep't. (1890)........ 209 87
Same——same. (1889) 59 87
Same——same. (1889)........ 59 87
Sreiber, Morris—Moses Mendelsohn. (1891).... 575 68
Truman, James C—A M Wright. (1885)........ 128 10
Taylor, Charles R and Frank—A S Moore. (1891)........ 866 47
Van Schauwenberge, Desire—W J Doremus. (1884)........ 260 63
Same——Robert King. (1881)........ 519 84
Same——Leopold Lithauer. (1881)........ 457 89
Van Volkenburgh, Philip, Jr, admr A J Moderno—Percival Knauth. (1891)........ 184 87
Vail, Susan M and John R—J S Tilton. (1891). 44 15
Wood, Thomas—Health Dept. (1890) 209 87
Wilson, Mary—West Side Bank. (1891)........ 83 09
Weinstein, Morris—William Solomon. (1883). 22 85
Weil, Samuel—Health Dep't. (1889)........ 59 87

*Vacated by order of Court. †Suspended on Appeal. ‡Released. §Reversal. ‖Satisfied by Execution.

KINGS COUNTY.

October 2 to 8—Inclusive.

Bailey, William T—C D Archer. (1890)........$1,082 27
Same——same. (1890)........ 373 59
Same——L T Mulhearn. (1891)........ 97 88
Cordial, Michael—N Patterson. (1889) 178 49
Culver, Weeks W—J B Leverich. (1890)........2,233 18
Davenport, William R, Public Admr, as admr of Mary Devine, dec'd—Mary Clark. (1891) 202 78
Gore, Calvin—L A Jonas. (1891)........ 741 02
Same——M Meyberg. (1891)........1,133 58
Hooper, Rachel A—L A Jonas. (1891) 741 02
Same——M Meyberg. (1891)........1,133 59
Horton, Theodore K / Horton, Franklin M } J M Smith. (1891)........4,845 66
Hood, Joseph—E Fisher. (1890)........1,064 81
Same——S Stein. (1888)........1,185 29
Higgins, Thomas—J Weber. (1891)........ 824 01
Same——A H Van Hoesen. (1889)........1,821 78
Johnson, Susie R—W Hasquin, Jr. (1891) ... 98 08
Krieger, Rachel—J Pirrung. (1891)........ 371 44
Koehler, Bertha—Kate Minter. (1891)........ 292 83
Maguire, John—I Mason. (1891)........ 800 17
Roche, Edward—J Stewart. (1891)........1,141 89
The Anglo-American Dry Dock and Warehouse Co—J Moore. (1890)........3,667 09
Trimm, Frederick M—R W McMaster. (1885)..1,095 89
Van Hoesen, George W—A H Van Hoesen. (1889)........1,821 78
Same——J Weber. (1889)........ 824 01
Van Kleeck, Arthur A—J G Van Kleeck. (1889)........20,016 47
Wright, Benjamin—J B Leverich. (1890)........2,233 18
Walsh, Thomas—Kate E Greek. (1890)........ 252 00
Same——J D Green. (1891)........ 752 26
Wallace, Gustavus S—A Barrie. (1891)........ 264 14

MECHANICS' LIENS.

NEW YORK CITY.

Oct.

3 Forty-eighth st, No 324, s s, 300 e 2d av, 25x100.5. Charles Lehmann agt Henry Holk, owner, and Henry Holck, contractor........ $67 20

3 Ninety-fourth st, Nos. 105 and 107, n s, 100 w Columbus av, 50x100.8 .... / Ninety-fifth st, Nos. 104 and 106, s s, 100 w Columbus av, 50x100.8 .... } William Auk agt Francis J. Hillenbrand, owner and contractor........ 147 00

3 Fourteenth st, s s, 88 w Av C, 225x100. Charles Molton agt William H. Muldoon, owner and contractor........2,478 40

5 Forty-eighth st, No. 324, s s, 300 e 2d av, 25x100. Slevin & Sheeran agt Henry Holcke, owner and contractor........ 253 02

5 Third av, e s, 106 n Powell st, 35x100. W. W. Taylor agt John R. Shea, owner and contractor........ 210 00

5 Ninth av, w s, 100 s 94th st, one house. Frank Koch agt Albert Flake, owner, and Percy Jacobs, contractor........ 78 00

5 Fifty-second st, Nos. 527-531, n s, 300 w 10th av, 75x100. Canda & Kane agt James A. Linscott, owner and contractor........ 953 84

5 Ninth av, w s, 100 s 94th st, 20x100. Frederick Brandt agt Albert Flake, owner, and M. Schmeckenbecker & Sons, contractors. 136 00

6 Ninety-fifth st, No. 171 W., n s, 50x100.... / Ninety-sixth st, No. 166 W., s s, 0x100.... } James Taylor agt S. M. Styles, owner and contractor........ 118 00

6 One Hundred and Sixth st, No. 338, s s, 225 w 1st av, 25x100. Vermont Marble Co. agt Dempsey and Smith, owners and contractors........ 160 41

6 Sixty-fifth st, Nos. 29 and 31, n s, 200 w 5th av, 75x100. Joseph Treubig agt James O'Brien, owner, and George A. Hunter, contractor........ 18 00

6 Same property. Magnus Fox agt same ... 9 00

6 Columbus av, No. 688, w s, 100 s 94th st 20.7x—. Samuel Pollack agt Albert Flake, owner; Percy Jacobs, contractor, and M. Schmeckenbecher's Sons, sub-contractors........ 258 78

6 Same property. Joseph Braun agt Albert Flake, owner, and M. Schmeckenbecher's Sons, contractors........ 150 00

6 Same property. George Pfister agt same. 100 00

6 Same property. M. Schmeckenbecher's Sons agt Albert Flake, owner, and Percy Jacobs, contractor 1,000 00

6 Sam property. East River Mill and Lumber Co. agt same and M. Schmeckenbecher's Sons, sub-contractors 372 60

6 Lexington av, No. 666, w s, 75.10 s 56th st, 24.6x90. Folmer & Schwing Mfg. Co. agt Morris and Pauline Byk, owners and contractors 214 28

6 Eighteenth st, n s, 194 e Av A, 200x92...... / Nineteenth st, s s, 194 e Av A, 200x92...... } Goubert Mfg. Co. agt N. Y. Steam Co., owner and contractor........ 300 00

6 One Hundred and Twenty-ninth st, n s, 100 e 5th av. Harry Orr agt Francis Eldridge or Eldredge, owner, and Albert T. Lum, contractor. (Continued from Oct. 6, 1890)........ 105 00

6 One Hundred and Sixth st, n s, 175 w 8th av, 50x100. James Maloney agt Antonio Gallo, owner and contractor. (Continued from Oct. 7, 1890)........ 227 00

9 One Hundred and Fifth st, s s, 149.10 e Columbus av. 21.6x100.11. J. & T. Donellon agt Samuel L. Schultz, debtor and owner........2,230 00

6 Fifty-first st, Nos. 235 and 237, n s, 200 w 2d av, 88.6x100. Henry McShane Co. agt James Graham, owner, and same and Charles R. Dey, contractor........ 1,007 68

6 Seventeenth st, n s, 100 e Broadway, 25x—........ / Eighteenth st, s s, 100 e Broadway, 25x—. } Nals Bensen agt William H. Jackson, owner, and Lewis & Jones and William Metz, contractors........ 959 00

7 One Hundred and Forty-fourth st, s w cor Convent av, 50x100. Daniel Fitzpatrick agt James T. Hoy and George McCletchey, debtors, and William H. De Forest, Jr., owners........ 80 00

7 Thirty-sixth st, No. 361, n s, 125 e 9th av, 16.8x99.9. Abraham Melzer and Abraham Tobias agt John Curry, owner and contractor 280 00

7 Amsterdam av, n e cor 194th st, 100x— to Harlem River. L. Rosenbaum agt Chas. C. Wendel, owner, and Henry Taylor, contractor 184 00

7 Columbus (9th) av, w s, 127 n 80th st, 25.6x119. August Kissling agt William Eisenberg, owner and contractor 49 20

7 Forty-eighth st, No. 234, s s, 300 e 2d av, 25x100. Louis Kramer agt Henry Holk, owner and contractor........ 255 00

7 Amsterdam av, e s, extends from 194th to 195th st, 104.5x480 to Harlem River, x134x405. Henry Taylor agt Charles C. Wen. owners and contractors........ 104 45

7 Manhattan av, n e cor 121st st, 100x100. Mosher Bros. agt Allan A. Irvine and Henry Schneider, owners and contractors 335 65

8 Andrews pl, n s, 400 w Jerome av, 50x100. O. E. Gates & Co. agt Henry M. Greenberg, owner and contractor. (Continued from Oct. 8, 1890)........ 594 09

8 Eighteenth st, No. 333, n s, 423.2 w 8th av, 21.5x98.9. Howden & Campbell agt David Mackey, owner, and Peter Wagner, contractor........ 38 50

8 Twenty-fourth st, Nos. 341-345, n s, 271.7 e 9th av, 78.4x100. Joseph Marren agt Joseph McFarland, owner, and Thomas H. Snape, sub-contractor, and Frederick Wood, contractor........ 550 80

8 Eighty-fifth st, Nos. 73-77, n s, 70 w 4th av, 60x102.2. E. J. Rogers agt Martin J. Hackett, owner and contractor........ 284 69

8 One Hundred and Thirty-third st, s s, 250 w 7th av, 150x—. Wm. Buess & Co. agt F. A. Thurston, owner, and George and Francis L. Morrell, contractors........ 124 00

9 Convent av, w s, bet 143d and 144th sts, indeft. Culbert Bros. agt Louisa M. Hartwell, owner and contractor........ 295 00

9 One Hundred and Twentieth st, s s, 125 w 8th av, 75x100. Fort Plain Furniture Co. agt James Thompson, owner and contractor........ 570 00

9 Division st, No. 193, s s, 156 11 e Jefferson st, 27x46. Barrow & Bass agt Louis Cohen, owner and contractor........ 647 50

9 Baxter st, No. 64, s w cor Franklin st, 25x50. Isaac Hoffman agt Louis Levy, owner, and Samuel Chodicor, contractor. 41 50

9 One Hundred and Fifth st, No. 228, n s, 225 w Amsterdam av. 25x100.11. J. O. Shumway agt Christian H. Schultheis, owner, and Matthesius & Valloria, contractors.. 500 00

9 Simpson st, w s, 171.7 n 109th st, 25x—. Henry Sproessig agt John Walsh, owner and contractor 273 65

9 Thirty-first st, Nos. 135-141, n s, 300 e 7th av, 100x138.6. Patrick Maher agt St. Francis Assisi Church, F. Ludger Beck, rector, owner, and Henry H. Amberg, contractor........ 350 00

9 Lexington av, s w cor 103d st, 56x100. Frank Wennemer agt Frederick Willenbrook and Egbert Winkler and The Blair Memorial Methodist Episcopal Church, owners, and The Blair Memorial Methodist Episcopal Church, contractor........ 160 00

9 One Hundred and Forty-seventh st, n e cor Convent av, 25x61. James Slavin agt —— Southworth, owner, and John and Thomas Donnellon, contractors........ 187 72

9 Thirty-ninth st, Nos. 509 and 511 W., n s. Same agt —— Coster, owner, and John and Thomas Donnellon........ 58 10

KINGS COUNTY.

Oct.

2 Cropsey av, s w cor 17th av, 150x100 ...... / Cropsey av, s s, 150 w 17th av, 125x500 to Gowanus Bay, New Utrecht........ } Anson Squires agt Joseph H. Horton, owner and contractor........ $314 54

3 Liberty av, s s, 50 w Watkins st, 100x100. James O'Connor agt Tomlinson & Cochran, owner, and Salvatore Bove, contractor........ 85 15

3 Glenmore av, n e cor Sheffield av, 100x100. Erickson & Karlson agt John Victory, owner, and Allen Gordon, contractor ... 300 00

3 Decatur st, n s, 100 e Howard av, 250x100. Martin Walsh agt Mason Kirby, owner and contractor........ 150 00

5 Bay 22d st, n s, 370 w 86th st, 40x96.8, New Utrecht. Isaacson & Pearson agt Agnes M. Bruns, owner, and Louis Larsen, contractor........ 40 00

5 West 9th st, No. 63, n s, 200 e Hick st, 20x100. John F. McCuelpin agt Stephen Cosgrove, owner and contractor 180 00

5 Hemlock st, w s, 310.10 s Jamaica turnpike, 25x85.1. John Comaskey agt James McCadden, owner and contractor........ 30 00

5 Douglass st, n s, 410 w Franklin av, 131x150. S. C. Prescott & Son agt William Ruland and Thomas H. Robbins, owners and contractors........2,625 00

5 Sixth av, s e cor 1st st, 100x100. Morgan Bros. agt Roderick Von Graff and John O'Halleron, owners and contractors 700 00

5 Navy st, e s, 100 n Myrtle av, 50x100. Peter Feeley agt Henrietta Fisk, owner, and William H. Glover, contractor........ 374 00

6 Saratoga av, s e cor Decatur st, 100x115.6. John R. Hughes agt —— Good, owner, and William H. Good, contractor........ 263 25

6 Same property. James J. McCue agt same owner and contractor........ 450 00

6 Same property. John C. Creveling agt same owner and contractor........ 762 00

6 Tompkins av, s w cor Vernon av, 100x137. Sanford A. Peterson agt Thomas Walling, Morris Hawkins and —— Pratt, owner and contractor........ 252 87

6 Putnam av, s e cor Patchen av, 20x100. Same agt same owner and contractor.... 283 00

6 Hancock st, n s, 162 w Marcy av, 22x100. The Mitchell Vance Co. agt Emma F. Carey, owner, and James F. Carey, contractor........ 850 73

7 Hancock st, s s, 168.9 w Reid av, 48.9x98.11. James J. McCue agt Mrs. S. M. Stilson, owner, and S. J. Stilson, contractor...... 375 00

7 Liberty av, s s, 50 e Osborn st, 100x100. Henry Konemann agt Charles Tomlinson and Israel Y. Cockran, owners, and John Barnes, contractor........ 81 00

7 De Kalb av, s s, 150 w Marcy av, 100x100. Jacob H. Werbelovsky agt Elizabeth S. Maitland, owner, and Charles H. Collins, contractor........ 510 00

7 Eastern Parkway, s s, 100.1 e Rockaway av, 25x100. Earl A. Gillespie agt Solomon Kringstin and S. Kopalansky, owner, and S. Kopalansky, contractor........ 460 00

8 Christopher av, e s, 175 s Eastern Parkway, 25x100. John Schwaeble agt Joseph Berger & Co., owner and contractor........ 150 00

8 Hancock st, s e cor Lewis av, 150x100. The New York Anderson Pressed Brick Co. agt McWhinney & Aronson, owners and contractors........ 607 55

8 Clymer st, n s cor Wythe av, 25x100. Washington Bulkley agt John E. Bulwinkle and John Kehoe, owners, and J. E. Williams and Charles Collins, contractors..... 98 60

8 Dean st, n s, 75 e Utica av, 160x100. Rudolph Reimer & Co. agt Frank P. Martin. 678 83

SATISFIED MECHANICS' LIENS.

NEW YORK CITY.

Oct.

3 One Hundred and Forty-ninth st, n e cor Walton av, 53x86.9x54.9x79.9. Fenn & Braxmar agt Kathrine and Garret Van Cleve. (Lien filed May 26, 1891)........ $125 00

3‡Sixty-third st, n s, 300 w 8th av, 75x100.5. Hardwood Decorative Co. agt Richard Everett and Robert Cary. (June 20, 1891)........ 200 00

3‡Same property. Same agt same. (June 20, 1891)........2,000 00

3 Sixty-third st, n s, 300 w 8th av, 37.6x—. Same agt same and Esther E. Barron. (June 24, 1891.) (Released)........ ——

3 Same property. Same agt same. (June 14, 1891.) (Released) .... ——

5 One Hundred and Sixty-ninth st, s w cor Vanderbilt av, 31x98. John Diehl agt Jacob Pfeiffer. (July 24, 1891)........2,600 00

5 One Hundred and Twenty-fifth st, Nos. 243 and 235 W. I. E. Marsh agt Lippman Toplitz and John Ryan. (Sept. 4, 1891)........ 97 50

5 Sixty-third st, n s, 300 w 8th av, 75x100.5. J. L. Mott Iron Works agt Richard Everett, Esther E. and Martin J. Barron and Robert Carey. (July 25, 1891)........ 180 00

5 Sixty-third st, n s, 300 w 8th av, 37.6x100.5. Same agt Esther E Barron and Robert Carey. (Aug. 1, 1891)........ 180 00

5 Same property. Benedict, McIlroy & Fowler agt Martin J. Barron and John J. Carey. (Aug. 10, 1891)........ 520 53

5*Sixty-third st, n s, 300 w 8th av, 37.6x—. Henry Iden agt Esther E Barron and Robert Carey. (Sept. 30, 1891)........ 331 00

5*Same property. J. J. Rich and Herman Goerke agt M. J. or Mrs. Barron and John Riesinger. (Sept. 16, 1891)........ 30 00

5*Sixty-third st, n s, 300 w 8th av, 75x—. Maxwell & Dempsey agt Barron Bros. and Thomas F. Fallon. (May 14, 1891)........ 78 75

6*One Hundred and Twenty-fourth st, Nos. 166-172 E. Alexander Kenney agt Henry E. Fox, Webster White and Stephen P. Anderson. (Sept. 30, 1891)........ 65 00

6 One Hundred and Eighteenth st, s s, 240 w 4th av, 100x—. Sims Lumber Co. agt Simon Sulton, Samuel Harris and Bernhard Ginsburg. (Sept. 19, 1891)........1,552 31

6 Home st, s s, 176 e Stebbins av, 75x—. Bengt Bengtson agt Triffler H. Allard and Alexander McCone. (July 13, 1891)...... 125 00

6 Fourth st, Nos. 23-29, n s, 75 w Mercer st, 100x—. Clinton Harris assignee agt Louis and Samuel Sachs. (April 24, 1891)......10,116 75

6 Washington pl, No. 9, n s, 25x—. Same agt same. (April 24, 1891).......... 2,049 06

7 Park av, No. 1167. Richardson & Boynton Co. agt George Cody. (Oct. 8, 1891) 178 50

7*Fourth st, Nos. 21-29, n s, 25 e Greene st, 100x—. F. C. Potter and nine others agt L. Sachs & Bro. and John F. Moore; 10 liens. (May 11, 1891) ....total, 804 45

7*Same property. Hugh Lawson agt same. (April 27, 1891).......... 38 50

7*Same property. Fred. Grau and ano. agt same; 2 liens. (April 17, 1891)........total, 97 63

8 Park av, No. 1148, w s. Jacob Winter agt Mrs. Lacy. (Jan. 23, 1889) 66 30

8*Ninetieth st, n s, 150 w West End av, seven dwell'gs. Henry McShane Mfg. Co. agt Thomas J. Sheriden and James E. Hurne to W. Otis Monroe's Son & Co. (Oct. 6, 1891).......... 1,076 39

8‡Catharine st, Nos. 53 and 55, e s, 27.6x104.6. Frederick Jenth agt Eliza Louis Miller. (Aug 14, 1891).......... 483 45

9 Simpson st, w s, 171.7 n 169th st, 25x—. Abraham Steers agt John Welsh and Thomas A. Lynch. (Sept. 4, 1891)...... 120 74

9 Third av, No. 2318, e s, 90.11 n 125th st. Same agt Louis J. Kahn and Percy Jacobs. (Oct. 7, 1891).......... 1,334 15

9 Rockfield st, n s, 325 e Jerome av, 28x100. Charles E. Rogers & Co. agt Jennie Michelena and C. W. Rabadan. (Oct. 21, 1889). 875 00

9‡One Hundred and Eighteenth st, s s, 60 e Madison av, 100x—. Graham & Bunt agt Samuel Harris and Henry Masche. (Sept. 25, 1891).......... 300 00

9 Sixty-third st, n s, 300 w Central Park West. J. F. Pease Furnace Co. agt Richard Evarts, Robert Carey and Esther E. Barron. (July 10, 1891).......... 500 00

9 One Hundred and Thirty-third st, n s, 86 w Park av, 50x100. Thomas Dixon agt Addison Brown and Amelia and William Bell. (July 22, 1891).......... 125 15

9 Park av, n w cor 133d st, ½ block x—. Same agt Amelia and William Bell. (July 21, 1891) 570 00

9 Fifty-eighth st, No. 4 W, s s, 135 w 5th av. Jacob Winter agt Charles B. Alexander and George Chase. (Sept. 23, 1891)...... 208 98

9*Twenty-sixth st, Nos. 334 and 336 E., 50x—. Charles Wein agt Michael McCormick and Henry Madden. (Oct. 7, 1891).......... 104 45

*Discharged by depositing amount of lien and interest with County Clerk.

‡Discharged by order of Court on filing bond.

KINGS COUNTY.

Oct.

2 Bainbridge st, Nos. 505-528, n s, 115.6 e Saratoga av, 180x100. Berkmeier Bros. agt J. Mason Kirby, owner and contractor. (Lien filed Sept. 25, 1891).......... $150 00

2 Henry st, n e cor State st, 25x100. Wright L. Glidden agt Charles H. Collins, owner, and William Killey, contractor. (Aug. 20, 1891).......... 47 36

2 Watkins st, e s, 175 n Blake av, 25x100. Emil Reineking agt Mrs. Danancher, owner, and Louis Ratner, contractor. (Sept. 10, 1891).......... 100 00

2 Dumont av, n w cor Thatford av, 25x100. Same agt Abram Wolff and —— Goldstein, owners, and same contractor. (Sept. 10, 1891).......... 225 00

2 Harrison av, e s, 45 n Wallabout st, 25x100. Jacob Willman agt Sarah Taylor, owner, and Leopold J. Lippmann and Alexander Taylor, contractors. (Sept. 17, 1891)...... 41 50

2 Hancock st, n w s, 99 s w Central av, 360x100. Same agt Leopold J. Lippmann, owner, and same contractor. (Sept. 17, 1891).......... 67 20

2 Weirfield st, n w s, 81 s w Central av, 260x100. Jacob Willman agt Leopold J. Lippmann and Alexander Taylor, owner and contractors. (Sept. 17, 1891).......... 432 76

3 Fulton st, s s, 76.7 w Linwood st, 25x90. Earl A. Gillespie agt William Reuss, owner, and R. F. Schmidt, contractor. (Aug. 21, 1891) 1,000 00

5 Patchen av, w s, 25 n Putnam av, 85x100. Graf & Seitz agt Earnest D. Yarber, owner and contractor. (June 5, 1891) 635 00

5 Grand av, s w cor St. Marks av, 26x90. New York Anderson Pressed Brick Co. agt W. J. Conway, owner and contractor. (Sept. 28, 1891).......... 299 09

5 Livonia av, s e cor Osborn st, 25x100. James O'Connor agt Rachel Abramovitz and Abraham Siedenbergh, owners and contractors. (Sept. 28, 1891.) (Deposit)..... 280 00

6 Sixteenth st, Nos. 386-391, n s, 192.11 w 8th av, 75x100. John H. Gross agt Wm. Wingerath, owner, and Meller & Anderson, contractor. (Sept. 23, 1891).......... 64 44

6 Fourth st, s s, 97.10 e 5th av, 440x100. Thomas McCann agt Moses & Fanton, owners and contractors. (Aug. 25, 1891). 1,000 00

6 Osborn st, n w cor Eastern Parkway, 45x100. William Gormley agt John Powers. (Sept. 30, 1891).......... 425 00

6 Stone av, e s, 200 n Blake av. Frank J. Dilzer agt Louis Regenbogen, Samuel Davis, William Schechtel and Louis Cohen, owners, and J. and H. McGarrick, contractors. (Sept. 18, 1891).......... 53 00

BUILDINGS PROJECTED.

The first name is that of the owner; ar't stands for architect, m'n for mason, c'r for carpenter and b'r for builder.

NEW YORK CITY.

SOUTH OF 14TH STREET.

Madison st, s s, 115 w Montgomery st, three five-story stone flats, two 25x88.8, one 20.1x88.8, tin roofs; total cost, $55,000; ow'r and b'r, W. Rankin, 163d st and North River; ar't, J. W. Cole. Plan 1292.

Centre st, s w cor Broome st, seven-story brk and terra cotta warehouse, 71.3x54, tin roof; cost, $55,000; A. Trenkmann, 241 Centre st; ar'ts, De Lemos & Cordes. Plan 1302.

Madison st, No. 223, five-story brk and stone flat, 26.1x89, tin roof; cost, $22,000; ow'r and b'r, J. V. Campbell, 426 West 27th st; ar't, M. V. B. Ferdon. Plan 1306.

BETWEEN 14TH AND 59TH STREETS.

41st st, No. 217 E., two-story brk and stone shop, 25x84, tin roof; cost, $3,500; J. Mitchell, on premises; b'r, W. McGrath. Plan 1289.

54th st, s s, 200 e 10th av, five-story brk flat, 25x89, tin roof; cost, $18,000; ow'r and b'r, W. Rankin, 163d st and North River; ar't, J. W. Cole. Plan 1291.

BETWEEN 59TH AND 125TH STREETS, WEST OF CENTRAL PARK WEST AND 8TH AVENUE.

78th st, s s, 50 e Boulevard, frame shed, 75x15, tin roof; cost, $400; lessee, W. J. Carlin, on premises. Plan 1305.

110TH TO 125TH STREET, BETWEEN 5TH AND 8TH AVENUES.

St. Nicholas av, s w cor 119th st, five five-story brk, stone and frame flats, irreg. in size, tin roofs; cost, $20,000 each; P. Braender, 120 East 86th st; ar't, W. W. Luyster. Plan 1290.

NORTH OF 125TH STREET.

7th av, s w cor 138th st, twenty-nine three-story and basement dwell'gs; read cost each $12,000 instead of $7,000 as altered in plan No. 1258.

7th av, n w cor 139th st, four-story brk and terra cotta stone dwell'g, 20x74.10, tin roof, cost, $15,000; ow'r and b'r, D. H. King, Jr., 514 5th av; ar'ts, McKim, Mead & White. Plan 1296.

7th av, w s, 20 n 139th st, four four-story brown stone and terra cotta dwell'gs, three 16.8x50, one 17.6x52, tin roofs; cost, $10,750 each; ow'r and ar'ts, same as last. Plan 1297.

139th st, n s, 79 w 7th av, thirty-two four-story brown stone and terra cotta dwell'gs, irreg. in size, tin roofs; total cost, $346,000; ow'r and arts, same as last. Plan 1298.

8th av, n e cor 139th st, four-story brown stone and terra cotta flat, 87.5x43.1, tin roof; cost, $50,000; ow'r and ar'ts, same as last. Plan 1299.

23D AND 24TH WARDS.

Fairmount pl, No. 111, two-story frame dwell'g, 20x30, tin roof; cost, $2,500; Caroline A. Blair, 2030 Bathgate av; c'r, T. J. Blair. Plan 1293.

135th st, s s, 225 e St. Anns av, three-story brk and stone dwell'g, 21x50, tin roof; cost, $6,000; Annie Derleth, 535 East 134th st; ar't, A. E. Davis. Plan 1295.

150th st, s s, 75 w Morris av, three-story frame dwell'g, 25x45, tin roof; cost, $5,000; J. H. Westheimer et al., 242 West 130th st; ar't, A. Pfeiffer. Plan 1300.

Clinton av, n s, 275 w 2d st, Woodlawn, two-story frame dwell'g, 16x26, shingle roof; cost, $1,250; A. G. More, Woodlawn Heights; b'r, S. L. Berrian. Plan 1294.

Hyatt st, n s, 60 e Kingsbridge road, frame shed, 100x20, shingle roof; cost, $700; H. N. Camp, Morris Heights; b'rs, Tolin & Son. Plan 1303.

Southern Boulevard, s s, 50 e 136th st, frame shed, 12x45, tin roof; cost, $200; lessee, J. Murtaugh, on premises; ar't, A. Spence. Plan 1301.

Kingsbridge road, e s, 81 s Nindham pl, two-story and attic frame dwell'g, 27.6x80, shingle roof; cost, $4,000; agent and b'r, N. M. Whipple, 61 West 96th st. Plan 1308.

158th st, n s, 250 e Courtlandt av, four two-story frame dwell'gs, 18.9x46, tin roofs; cost, $4,000 each; ow'rs and b'rs, S. & K. Kramer, 651 East 158th st. Plan 1307.

Cambrelling av, e s, 107 s Pelham av, two-story frame dwell'g, 20x30, tin roof; cost, $2,000; J. J. Palmer, 18 Minetta lane; b'r, F. Ludford. Plan 1304.

KINGS COUNTY.

Plan 1822—Amboy st, w s, 90 s Eastern Parkway, two two-story and basement frame dwell'gs, 20x30, tin roofs; cost, $1,600 each; Emil Reinking, Liberty av and Alabama av; ar't, A. J. Warren.

1823—Logan st, e s, 100 s Jamaica av, two two-story frame dwell'gs, 20x32, tin roofs; cost, $1,500 each; Henry T. Smith, Logan st; ar't, A. J. Warren.

1824—Dresden st, e s, 150 n Arlington av, one one-and-a-half-story frame stable, 20x19, tin roof; cost, $300; John Norel, 50 Dresden st; b'r, P. G. Kerr.

1825—9th st, n s, 75 e Hamilton av, one three-story and basement brk tenem't, 16.8x45, tin roof, wooden cornice; cost, $4,000; M. Kelly, on premises.

1826—Flatbush av, s w cor Sterling pl, one five-story brk store and tenem't, 25.6x66 and 80, tin roof, iron cornice; cost, $10,000, Peter Hart, 236 West 42d st, New York; ar't, H. Vollweiler; b'r, not selected.

1827—Lewis av, n e cor Jefferson av, one four-story brk flat, 23x92, tin roof, iron cornice; cost, $18,000; Geo. W. Bryant, Van Buren st; ar'ts, I. D. Reynolds & Son; b'r, not selected.

1828—Lexington av, n s, 150 w Throop av, two two-story and basement brk and brown stone dwell'gs, 10x40, tin roofs; wooden cornices; cost, each, $2,500; John Kearns, 924 Greene av; ar't, I. D. Reynolds; b'r, not selected.

1829—8th av, w s, bet 14th and 15th sts, one three-story front and one-story rear brk armory, 200x363, tin roof, brk and stone cornice; cost, $342,000, County of Kings, N. Y.; ar't, W. A. Mundell; b'rs, T. B. Rutan and L. W. Seaman.

1830—6th av, w s, 11 s Carroll st, three three-story and basement brown stone dwell'gs, 19.4x45, tin roofs, wooden cornices; cost, each, $6,000; ow'rs and c'rs, P. F. Delancy and —— Collins, 930 Pacific st and 67 Clermont av; ar't, P. F. Delancy; m'n, not selected.

1831—Railroad av, e s, 150 from Fulton st, one two-story frame dwell'g, 19x32, tin roof; cost, $1,200; George W. Epworth, 825 Herkimer st; m'n, E. L. Hurley.

1832—Union av, n e cor Richardson st, three four-story frame (brk filled) stores and tenem'ts, 25x50, tin roofs; cost, $18,000; Deperiro Bros., on premises; ar'ts, H. L. Spicer & Son; b'rs, D. Madeo & Son.

1833—Halsey st, s s, 100 e Central av, ten two-story and basement frame (brk filled) dwell'gs, 18x45, tin roofs; cost, each, $3,000; ow'r, ar't and b'r, Geo. A. Craig, 1270 Madison st.

1834—Stanhope st, n s, 375 e Hamburg av, two three-story frame (brk filled) tenem'ts, 25x58, tin roofs; cost, $16,000; George Gess, 183 Stanhope st; ar't, F. Holmberg.

1835—Thatford av, e s, 100 s Liberty av, five two-story frame (brk filled) dwell'gs, 16x38, tin roofs; cost, each, $1,500; ow'r, ar't and b'r, Oscar W. Velsor.

1836—Blake av, n s, 50 w Barbey st, two two-story frame dwell'gs, 20x40, tin roofs; cost, each, $2,300; Lauer & Kiesel, Blake av.

1837—St. James pl, w s, 250 s Lafayette av, two four-story brown stone tenem'ts, 40x72, tin roofs, wooden cornices; cost, each, $20,000; J. Gray, 323 Washington av; ar't, S. Peden.

1838—Warwick st, w s, 200 s Sutter av, one two-story and attic frame dwell'g, 20x28, tin roof; cost, $1,400; Frank Hess, Glenmore av, near Elton st; ar't, L. F. Schillinger; b'r, F. Gunderman, Jr.

1839—Jerome st, w s, 125 s Glenmore av, one two-story frame stable, 13x18, tin roof; cost, $100; H. Stander, Jerome st, near Glenmore av; b'r, F. Gundermann, Jr.

1840—St. Marks av, n s, 317 w Vanderbilt av, one four-story brk tenem't, 30x52, tin roof, wooden cornice; cost, $6,500; Wm. Gane, 263 St. Marks av; ar't, W. H. Wirth; b'r, Erick Soderstrom.

1841—Atlantic av, n e cor Kane pl, six two-story brk dwell'gs, 17.4x33.6, and one-story extension, 12x14, tin roofs, wooden cornices; cost, $14,000 each; N. Hamblin, 106 St. James pl; ar'ts, Firth & Grewey; b'r, not selected.

1842—Wyona st, w s, 75 n Fulton av, three three-story frame tenem'ts, 25x57, tin roofs; total cost, $12,000; ow'r, ar't and b'r, Charles Ries, 80 Alabama av.

1843—Jerome st, w s, 125 s Fulton av, three two-story and attic frame dwell'gs, 16.8x39, tin roofs; cost, $2,000 each; ow'r and b'r, James J. Newman, Warwick st, near Fulton av; ar'ts, Danmar & Fischer.

1844—Dean st, s s, 50 w Utica av, twelve two-story frame (brk filled) dwell'gs, 17x40, tin roofs; cost, each, $1,500; ow'r, ar't and b'r, Christopher P. Skelton, 296 6th av.

1845—Railroad av, w s, 100 n Griffing pl, one two-story frame dwell'g, 20x38, shingle roof; cost, $2,000; Betsey Reichert, Eastern Parkway, cor Eldert st; ar't and b'r, T. C. Reichert.

1846—Conover st, w s, 20 s Vandyke st, one four-story frame tenem't, 20x42, tin roof; cost, $2,500; Martin Hanson, 240 Conover st; b'rs, G. Hansen and F. Spratt.

1847—38th st, n s, 85 e 5th av, one one-story frame carpet cleaning factory, 39x18, tin roof; cost, $250; Adelina Holmgren, 377 Bergen st; ar't and b'r, J. Stanley.

1848—21st st, s s, 225 w 5th av, one three-story frame tenem't, 25x52, tin roof; cost, $3,500; ow'r, ar't and c'r, John Anderson; m'n, A. Sundell.

1849—Liberty av, n s, 50 e Sackman st, two three-story frame (brk filled) tenem'ts, 25x60, tin roofs; cost, $3,000 each; ow'r, ar't and b'r, S. C. Wilson, 2499 Atlantic av.

1850—Himrod st, s s, 100 e Knickerbocker av, two three-story frame (brk filled) tenem'ts, 25x58, tin roofs; cost, $5,000 each; ow'r and b'r, E. Augustine.

1851—Moore st, n w cor Bushwick av, one four-story frame (brk filled) store and tenem't, 25x50 and 65, tin roof; cost, $8,000; Jos. Pandar, Cook st; ar'ts, D. Acker & Son.

1852—Varet st, No. 192, one three-story frame (brk filled) store and tenem't, 25x57, tin roof; cost, $5,000; Dora Neubert, on premises; ar'ts, D. Acker & Son.

1853—Harrison pl, s s, 100 e Bogart st, three three-story frame (brk filled) tenem'ts, 25x57, tin roof; cost, $15,000; H. Schlachter & Co.

1854—52d st, s s, 160 w 5th av, one three-story frame paper coating factory, 40x198, tin roof; cost, $16,000; Brodfish & Hopking; ar'ts, H. L. Spicer & Son.

1855—Schenck av, e s, 235 n Arlington av, one one-story frame stable, 22x16, shingle roof; cost, $150; ow'r, ar't and b'r, S. T. Hollister, 166 Barbey st.

1856—2d av, w s, 150 n 9th st, one one-story frame shed, 25x15, felt roof; cost, $100; Patrick E. Quinn, 170 Wyckoff st.

1857—Willoughby av, n s, 350 w Wyckoff av, one one-story frame (brk filled) dwell'g, 25x25, tin roof, cost, $350; ow'r, ar'ts and b'rs, A. Schunk and C. J. Schmidt, 1137 Willoughby av.

1858—32d st, n s, 100 e 3d av, one three-story frame tenem't, 25x54, tin roof; cost, $3,300; John Boeurland, 145 27th st; b'r, C. Sroberg.

1859—47th st, n s, 120 w 3d av, one one-story frame blacksmith shop, 20x50, gravel roof; cost, $250; Henry Kruscher, 143 23d st; ar'ts, H. L. Spicer & Son.

1860—6th av, w s, 80 s 20th st, one one-story frame stable, 13x18, felt roof; cost, $75; John Healy, on premises.

1861—32d st, n s, 260 w 5th av, two three-story frame (brk filled) tenem'ts, 20x50, tin roofs; cost, each, $2,000; Mary J. Lucke, 202 32d st; ar't and b'r, H. Lucke.

1862—Lincoln pl, n s, 100 e 5th av, one three-brk apartment house, 26 and 21.6x70, tin roof, wooden cornice; cost, $10,000; ow'r and b'r, H. B. Lyons, Flatbush, ar't, W. M. Coots.

1863—Lincoln pl, n s, 126 e 5th av, one three-story brk apartment house, 18x45, tin roof, wooden cornice; cost, $6,000; ow'r, ar't and b'r, same as last.

1864—Jefferson av, n s, 255 e Stuyvesant av, 2 two-story basement and attic brown stone dwell'gs, 20x45, tin roofs, wooden cornices; cost, each, $4,500; Charles Isbill, 749 Putnam av; ar'ts, D. Acker & Son.

1865—Van Siclen av, e s, 303 n Fulton av, one two-story frame dwell'g, 21.6x47, tin roof; cost, $3,000; William G. Carr, 65 Van Siclen av; ar't, C. Meins; b'rs, J. J. Bennett and H. Cook.

1866—Stagg st, No. 132, s s, 125 e Ewen st, one two-story frame store and dwell'g, 24.10x40, tin roof, brk cornice; cost, $3,000; J. G. Lutz, 134 Stagg st; ar't, T. Engelhardt; b'r, not selected.

1867—Bleecker st, n s, 150 e Hamburg av, one two-story brk stable, 32x74.4, gravel roof, brk cornice; cost, $4,000; C. Heinbockel & Co., Hamburg and Greene avs; ar't, T. Engelhardt; m'n, J. Auer; c'r, not selected.

ALTERATIONS NEW YORK CITY.

Plan 1757—25th st, Nos. 18 and 20 W., interior alterations; cost, $1,500; lessees, New York Southern Society, on premises; ar't, J. S. Barney.

1758—150th st, No. 582 E., new store front; cost, $350; Mary Nimpkins, on premises; ar't, C. F. Lohse.

1759—Bergen av, No. 666, raised one story, extended two stories, 22.6x14; cost, $1,800; W. Gerhardt, on premises; ar't, C. F. Lohse.

1760—3d av, No. 138, one-story extension, 16.6x45; cost, $1,900; H. F. Helpt, on premises; ar'ts, Boekell & Son; b'r, A. G. Imhoff.

1761—44th st, No. 122 E., windows altered; cost, bet $25 and $40; lessee, Mrs. R. Reed, on premises.

1762—Madison av, No. 202, two-story extension, 18x14.6, and walls altered; cost, $2,500; agent, C. W. Baldwin, Orange, N. J.; b'r, J. W. Downey.

1763—143d st, No. 274 W., interior alterations and windows altered; cost, $200; S. Charig, 351 West 40th st; ar't, J. B. Franklin; b'r, N. Connor.

1764—Broadway, No. 848 and 850, interior alterations; cost, $150; lessee, J. G. Mackie, 123 East 15th st; ar't, J. B. Franklin.

1765—3d av, No. 2191, 120th st, No. 208 E., one-story extension, 26x5, interior alterations and walls altered; cost, $5,000; R. Webber, 1871 Madison av; ar't, W. H. C. Hornum.

1766—Pier No. 24, East River, one-story extension, 60x50; cost, $3,250; lessee, Hartford and New York Transportation Co., on premises; ar't, J. B. Arol.

1767—Boston av, s e cor 168th st, one-story extension, 5x11; cost, $150; G. S. Bell, on premises; ar't, C. C. Churchill; c'r, H. Berry.

1768—21st st, No. 332 W., raised one story; cost, $1,500; T. Orr, 215 West 15th st; ar'ts, Thayer & Robinson.

1769—Central Park West, No. 248, one-story extension, 11x11; cost, $200; R. Lathers, on premises; c'r, T. H. Johnston.

1770—Lenox av, e s, bet 113th and 114th sts, one-story extension, 22x50, front walls altered, new portico, new elevator and extensive interior alterations for hotel purposes; cost, $175,000; Mary E. McGuckin, 124 East 122d st; ar'ts, French, Dixon & De Saldern.

1771—9th st, No. 615 E., repair damage by fire; cost, $275; agent, G. W. Fanning, 315 Madison av; ar't, W. Havenstile; m'n, J. M. Barnes; c'r, W. H. Vanderpool.

1772—Broome st, No. 520, interior alterations and repairs, new roof and new front; cost, $3,500; A. Bellando, 510 Broome st; ar't, J. De Martini; c'r, A. Amolia.

1773—Columbia st, No. 26, interior alterations; cost, $500; att'y, J. F. Dettmar, 212 Rodney st, Brooklyn; ar't, F. Baylies.

1774—Amsterdam av, No. 585, interior alterations and new show windows; cost, $400; H. F. Miller, 491 West End av; ar't, C. W. Miller.

1775—Amsterdam av, s w cor 130th st, moved to new foundation; cost, abt $75; Mary Larkin, on premises; m'n, T. J. Larkin.

1776—Weeks st, w s, 100 n 173d st, roof raised 4 feet, two-story extension, 16x18.6, interior alterations and repairs; cost, $1,325; Anna Horacek, on premises; ar't, J. J. Vreeland; b'rs, Lally & Co.

1777—4th av, No. 112, rear, raised one story; cost, $1,500; estate S. I. Hunt, 171 Broadway; ar't, B. W. Berger.

1778—29th st, No. 10 E., interior alterations and walls altered; cost, $1,000; T. Hitchcock, 8 East 29th st; m'ns, W. A. & F. E. Conover; c'rs, Hoe's Sons.

1779—119th st, No. 227 E., interior alterations, new entrance and skylight; cost, $600; T. E. Tripler, 301 Av B; ar't, C. E. Rentz.

1780—Cherry st, No. 19, walls altered; cost, $250; J. W. Healy, 17 Cherry st; m'n, H. Read.

1781—Great Jones st, No. 45, two-story extension, 27x50, and interior alterations; cost, $4,000; J. B. Miller, agent, 58 West 9th st; art, M. C. Merritt.

1782—Doyer st, Nos. 5 and 7, interior alterations and walls altered; cost, $3,000; lessee, R. Kerr, 9 Chatham sq.; ar't, F. Ebeling; c'r, A. Rosenberg. (Substituted for alterations, plan No. 1047.)

1783—Washington st, No. 550, repair damage by fire, interior alterations and walls altered for stable purposes; cost, $1,200; lessee, G. R. Chrystie, 228 Greenwich st; m'n, J. Terhune; c'r, J. F. Johnson.

1784—166th st, Nos. 703 and 705 E., raised one story; cost, $1,650; R. Walker, 130 West 57th st.

KINGS COUNTY.

Plan 945—Franklin st, No. 24, one-story frame extension, 25x12, gravel roof; cost, $200; William S. Doig, 153 Eckford st; b'r, J. C. Williamson.

946—Graham st, w s, 120 s Flushing av, front altered; cost, $900; Tucker & Carter Cordage Co., 98 Pine st, New York; ar't, A. V. B. Brush.

947—Broadway, Nos. 282 and 284, interior alterations; cost, $1,000; Dugan Bros., on premises; ar't, P. B. Marryott; b'r, S. Parks.

948—Park av, n w cor Sandford st, interior alterations; cost, 2,000; A. J. Dawer, on premises; ar't, R. Dixon.

949—Myrtle av, No. 37, add one story, flat tin roof; cost, $400; Brooklyn Trust Co., trustees; b'r, H. V. Terboss.

950—Marcy av, east cor Ellery st, new store front; cost, $600; H. Ruppel, 63 Ewen st; ar't, H. E. Funk; b'r, L. Hess.

951—Conover st, n w cor Partition st, new store front; cost, $600; H. Finkeldey, on premises; ar't and b'r, C. M. Detlefsen.

952—Van Brunt st, n w cor William st, front altered; cost, $500; Mrs. Brennan, 671 10th st; ar't and b'r, C. M. Detlefsen.

953—Leonard st, s e cor Powers st, add one story, flat tin roof; cost, $500; Mrs. Witty; ar't and b'r, G. H. Garrison.

954—Bushwick av, No. 1387, one-story frame extension, 14x20, tin roof; cost, $200; John Prehn, 87 and 89 Allen st, New York; b'r, C. Doerfler.

955—Johnson av, No. 139, flat tin roof; cost, $200; William Gross, on premises; b'rs, Becker & Rueger.

956—Berriman st, w s, 125 s Eastern Parkway, brk wall beneath building; cost, $120; E. Wood, on premises; b'r, C. E. Baldwin.

957—Park av, n w cor Sandford st, rebuild rear wall, altered for store and flats; cost, $460; A. J. Dower, 380 Union st; ar't, R. Dixon; b'r, O. Nolan.

958—Morrell st, No. 42, new store front; cost, $200; Peter E. Zimmer, on premises.

959—3d av, No. 549, flat tin roof; cost, $300; J. Kurtz, 173 Smith st; b'r, L. R. Harsha.

960—Greenpoint av, No. 328, raised 7 feet on posts; cost, $100; Michael Mahoney, on premises; house raiser, J. A. Weaver.

961—Rockaway av, s w cor Chauncey st, one-story frame extension, 56x14, gravel roof; cost, $100; Pickett & Tenny, Broadway, s e cor Fulton st, New York.

962—Ainslie st, No. 238, two-story frame extension, 15x8, gravel roof; cost, $250; ow'r and ar't, Mr. Hand, 633 Grand st; b'r, J. W. Moore.

963—Power st, No. 105, one-story frame extension, 12x13, tin roof; cost, $300; H. J. Moore, on premises; b'rs, J. P. McQuaid and G. Schaedle.

964—Huntington st, No. 72, one-story frame extension, 20x45, gravel roof; cost, $200; James Lanigan.

965—West 9th st, No. 18, add one story, gravel roof; cost, $300; G. B. Finkenauer, 155 Bridge st; b'rs, T. W. Smith and T. Cooper.

966—Cleveland st, No. 206, raised 4 ft. on brk wall; cost, $175; M. Light, on premises.

967—Lee av, No. 97, two-story brk extension, 13x15, tin roof; cost, $500; D. Simmons, on premises; b'r, W. Kinder.

968—Reid av, No. 3, new store front; cost, $300; H. F. Praeger, 703 Bushwick av; ar't, H. Vollweiler; b'r, A. Floyd and J. Kirchner.

969—Fulton st, No. 484, five-story brk and iron extension, 125 and 124 x104 and 82, gravel roof, iron cornice; cost, $60,000; Aaron S. Robbins, 114 6th av; ar't, G. L. Morse.

970—Broadway, n e cor Furman st, one-story frame extension, 20x48, tin roof; cost, $800; Xaver Tollner, on premises; b'r, W. G. Dillingham.

971—Atlantic av, n e cor Linwood st, extension on a brk wall; cost, $100; Jos. F. Ulzheimer, on premises.

972—Bushwick av, No. 18, two-story frame extension, 10x41, gravel roof; cost, $700; V. J. Kleine, on premises; ar't and c'r, E. A. Schottel; m'ns, Ermak & Veit.

973—Warren st, No. 330, add two stories; cost, $4,000; Joseph Pruzma, on premises; b'r, J. O'Connor.

974—Broadway, Nos. 282 and 284, one-story frame extension, 46.8 and 22.11x37, tin roof; cost, $1,400; Dugan Bros., on premises; ar't, P. B. Marryott; b'rs, S. Parks and J. W. Bedell.

975—Myrtle av, No. 1332, one-story frame extension, 20x4.6, glass and wood roof; cost, $175; John Hanna, on premises; ar't, E. Dennis; b'rs, B. J. Dennis & Son.

MISCELLANEOUS.

BUSINESS FAILURES.

N. Y. ASSIGNMENTS—BENEFIT CREDITORS.

Oct.

5 Rosenblieth, Jacob and Isaac Katz (composing firm of Rosenblieth & Katz, manufacturers and dealers in gent's hats, at No. 103 Clinton st), to Abraham Schulder; without preferences.

6 Worthley, Peter A. (dealer in hats, caps and straw goods, at No. 143 Greene st), to George W. Dunn; without preferences.

7 Chatfield, Thomas B. and Charles D. (Chatfield Bros., wall papers, at No. 874 8th av), to Peter Wagner; without preferences.

8 Poulter, Alfred (heating engineer, at No. 234 Water st), to William M. Mackay; preferences, $400.

PROCEEDINGS OF THE BOARD OF ALDERMEN AFFECTING REAL ESTATE.

* Under the different headings indicates that a resolution has been introduced and referred to the appropriate committee. † Indicates that the resolution has passed and has been sent to the Mayor for approval ‡ Passed over the Mayor's veto.

NEW YORK, October 6, 1891.

REGULATING, GRADING, ETC.

Boulevard, from 156th st to Inwood st now Dyckman st and crosswalks laid in certain portions thereof.†
German pl, from Westchester av to 156th st.†
162d st, from 11th av to Kingsbridge road.†

PAVING.

133d st, from Broadway to Amsterdam av; granite block and crosswalks laid at intersection and terminating st and av.†

FLAGGING AND CURBING.

Boulevard, w s, from 155th st to Inwood st now Dyckman st.†
Christopher st, in front of Nos. 4 and 6.†
German pl, from Westchester av to 156th st and crosswalks laid at intersecting sts.†
Pearl st, in front of No. 419; relaid, &c.†
26th st, n s, west of 3d av / 27th st, s s, west of 3d av } in front of Broadway alley.†
78th st, n s, bet 2d and 3d avs.
89th st, s s, in front of vacant lots bet 2d and 3d avs.†
102d st, n s, from Columbus to Amsterdam avs.†
117th st, both sides, from 8th to St. Nicholas av.†
133d st, n s, from Lenox to 7th av.†
162d st, from 11th av to Kingsbridge road.†
Madison av, e s, from 93d to 100th st.†
Madison av, both sides, from 116th to 120th st.†
Manhattan and St. Nicholas avs, 122d and 123d sts, the block.†
St. Nicholas av, w s, from 117th to 119th st.†

ELECTRIC LIGHTS.

1st av, from 14th to 59th st.†

MAINS.

West Farms road, from Main st to Southern Boulevard; gas.†
91st st, bet 9th and 10th avs; water.†
161st st, from 3d to Railroad av E.; water.†
12th av, from 133d to 134th st; gas.†

FENCING VACANT LOTS.

98th st, n s, bet Columbus and Amsterdam avs.†
138th, 139th and 14th sts, Lenox and 5th avs, the blocks, where not already done.†
Amsterdam av, s w cor 81st st, 100 on av and 110 on st.†
Madison and 5th avs, 89th and 90th sts, the block.†

LAMP POSTS ERECTED AND LIGHTED.

Essex st, in front of eastern entrance to Essex Market building.†
Houston st, in front of No. 286 E., at expense of S. I. Kohn.†
West Farms road, from Main st to Southern Boulevard.†
12th av, bet 133d and 134th sts.†

CROSSWALKS.

28th st, in front of No. 28 W., at expense of John McGrath.†

BROOKLYN BOARD OF ALDERMEN.

BROOKLYN, Oct. 5, 1891.

CROSSWALKS.

Clermont av, 186 ft. n Park av.†

ELECTRIC LIGHTING.

Broadway, e s, at junction of Myrtle av and Jefferson st.
Nostrand av, s e cor Butler st.
Rogers av, n w cor Butler st.
} †

FENCING VACANT LOTS.

Marion st, n s, bet Reid and Patchen avs.
18th st, n s, bet 6th and 7th avs.
Clason av, w s, bet Butler and Douglass sts.
} †

FLAGGING.

Barbey st, e s, bet Atlantic av and Fulton st.
Park pl, bet Bedford and Rogers avs.
Warren st, n s, bet Bond and Hoyt sts.
18th st, n s, bet 6th and 7th avs.
Underhill av, n w cor St. Marks av.
5th av, bet 27th and 39th sts.
} †

GAS LAMPS, ETC.

Brooklyn Homeopathic Hospital, in front of.†
Broadway, n w cor Kent av, at owners' expense.
Halsey st, bet Evergreen and Knickerbocker avs.†
Harrison pl, bet Morgan av and Bogart st.
Hart st, bet Knickerbocker and Hamburg avs.
Ingraham st, bet Morgan av and Bogart st.
Macon st, bet Ralph and Howard avs
} at owners' expense.†
Sackett st, bet 3d and 4th avs.
Schaeffer st, bet Central and Bushwick avs.
} †
2d st, bet 7th and 8th avs, at owners' expense.†
4th st, bet 7th and 8th avs.
52d st, bet 3d and 4th avs.
55th st, bet 3d and 4th avs.
} †
Evergreen av, bet Hancock and Jefferson sts.
Lexington av, No. 26, in front of.
} at owners expense.†

GRADING, PAVING, ETC.

Degraw st, n s, bet Schenectady and Utica avs.
Louis pl, bet Herkimer st and Atlantic av.
Pacific st, bet Rochester and Ralph avs.
Pacific st, bet Howard and Hopkinson avs.
11th st, s s, bet 8th and 9th avs.
12th st, n s, bet 8th and 9th avs.
St. Marks av, bet Ralph and Saratoga avs.
St. Marks av, bet Buffalo and Ralph avs.
4th av, e s, bet 51st and 52d sts.
} †

STREET OPENING.

Barbey st, bet Highland Boulevard and Eastern Parkway.
Bayard st, bet Union av and Humboldt st.
Highland Boulevard, bet Hendrix and Warwick sts.
43d st, bet 3d and 4th avs. †

STREET CLOSING.

Old Bushwick road, s e of Vigelins to Weirfield st.*

SEWERS.

Dean st, from Utica av East to midway bet Utica and Rochester avs, at owners' expense.
Park pl, bet Bedford and Nostrand avs.
Pacific st, from Utica av East to midway bet Utica and Rochester avs, at owners' expense. †
Lewis av, n w cor Hancock st.†

ADVERTISED LEGAL SALES.

REFEREES SALES TO BE HELD AT THE REAL ESTATE EXCHANGE AND AUCTION ROOM (LIMITED), 59 to 65 LIBERTY STREET, EXCEPT WHERE OTHERWISE STATED.

Oct

Boulevard, e s, 24.11 n 189th st, 75x100, vacant, by D. P. Ingraham & Co. (Amt due $31,451)..... 12

60th st, No. 100 / Park (4th) av, No. 511 { begins 60th st, s e cor 4th av, 20x100.5, four-story brk (stone front) dwell'g on 60th st and one-story brk store on av, by William Kennelly. (Amt due $16,360).... 12

51st st, Nos. 602-606, s s, 100 w 11th av, 75x100.5, two-story brk office, one-story frame sheds and vacant, by R. V. Harnett. (Leasehold; receiver's sale).... 13

115th st, Nos. 221-227, n s, 325 w 7th av, runs west along st 75 x north 100.11 x east 25 x south 10.7 x northeast — x east 24 x south 100.11 to beginning, four five-story brk flats, by J. C. Lalor. (Amt due $50,939).... 13

Monroe av, s e s, adj land John Ittner, runs northeast along said av 93.6 x northeast still along av 314.11 x southeast through an old stone wall 728 x still southeast 350 to Valentine av, x southwest along av 381.8 x northwest 356 x again northwest 738.6 to beginning, by W. R. Brown. (Amt due $27,797).... 13

52d st, No 315, n s, 204.6 e 2d av, 20x100.5, four-story stone front dwell'g, by William Kennelly. 14

Av A, Nos. 393 and 395, s w cor 24th st, 49.5x81.5, vacant, all right, title and interest which Daniel D. Conover had on June 10, 1891, by sheriff at City Hall. (Sale under execution).... 14

8th av, No. 2140, e s, 51.4 s 116th st, 25.5x100, one-story brk stores, by James L. Wells. (Amt due $3,380).... 14

49th st (Mitchell pl, No. 9), n s, 144 e 1st av, 18x 80.10, four-story stone front dwell'g, by D. P. Ingraham & Co. (Amt due $6,117).... 15

79th st, No. 442, s s, 75 w Av A, 19x79, five-story brk flat, by B. L. Kennelly. (Amt due $5,189; prior morts $11,500).... 15

87th st, No. 166, s s, 350 w 9th av, 20x100.8, four-story stone front dwell'g, by D. P. Ingraham & Co. (Amt due $24,156).... 15

97th st, No. 142, s s, 410 w 9th av, 20x100.8, four-story stone front dwell'g, by D. P. Ingraham & Co. (Amt due $26,340).... 15

103d st, No. 206, s s, 118 w Amsterdam av, 20x76 to Clendenning lane, x20x77.2, five-story brk flat....
103d st, No. 208, s s, 138 w Amsterdam av, 20x75 to Clendenning lane, x20x76, five-story brk flat....
103d st, No. 210, s s, 158 w Amsterdam av, 20x74 to Clendenning lane, x20x75, five-story brk flat
103d st, No. 212, s s, 175 w Amsterdam av, 20x73 to Clendenning lane, x20x74, five-story brk flat....
by William Kennelly. (Amt due $17,686 on each) 15

114th st, No. 418, s s, 240 e 1st av, 30x100.11, four-story stone front tenem't, by B. L. Kennelly. (Amt due $1,711).... 16

92d st, No. 148, s s, 342 w 3d av, 33x100.8, three-story brk dwell'g, by B. L. Kennelly. (Amt due $19,807).... 16

119th st, No. 7, n s, 95.5 w 5th av, 14x57.9x14.6x 58.11, three-story brk dwell'g, by B. L. Kennelly. (Amt due $4,732).... 19

133d st, Nos. 248 and 250, s s, 416.8 w 7th av, 33.4x 99.11, two three-story brk (stone front) dwell'gs, by J. C. Lalor. (Amt due $30,367).... 19

Park (4th) av, No. 886, w s, 69.2 n 78th st, 15x75, four-story brk dwell'g, by D. P. Ingraham & Co. (Amt. due $18,905).... 19

KINGS COUNTY.

Oct.

Withers st, n e cor North 9th st, 38.7x40.3x62.5 x10; assessed value, $600....
Howard av, e s, 98 s Herkimer st, 35x98, frame church....
by T. A. Kerrigan, at 13 Willoughby st.... 12

4th st, n e s, 297.10½ n w 8th av, 100x95, by Alfred F. Britton, ref., at County Court House.... 12

Marion st, Nos. 29-35, n s, 350 e Stuyvesant av, 100 x100, three four-story double brk flats, by T. A. Kerrigan, at 13 Willoughby st.... 13

President st, No. 185, n s, 120 e Henry st, runs north 55 x east 1 x north 45 x east 14.6 x south 10 to beginning, three-story brk dwell'g; assessed value, $5,000; by W. Cole, at 7 and 8 Court sq.... 13

6th st, s s, 75 w 4th av, 105x100, by T. A. Kerrigan, at 13 Willoughby st.... 14

Decatur st, No. 49, n s, 229 w Throop av, 18x100.
Decatur st, No. 51, n s, 211 w Throop av, 18x100, two three-story brk dwell'gs; assessed value, $6,500 each....
Pacific st, Nos. 1450 and 1452, s s, 50 w Kingston av, 50x107, two-story brk dwell'g on plot; assessed value, $6,000....
Lot at Gravesend, begins at Atlantic Ocean at division line bet old lots 22 and 23 on one side and old lots 20 and 21 on the other side, as shown on Kowolski's map of common lands of Gravesend, Coney Island, runs north — x west — x south to ocean, x east to beginning, except strip 40 ft. wide condemned for use of New York & Coney Island R. R. Co., and part lying south of centre of Surf av; partition....
by T. A. Kerrigan, at 13 Willoughby st.... 15

Vanderveer st, Nos. 15-19, n w s, 119.5 n e Broadway, 56.3x100, three three-story frame (brk lined) dwell'gs; assessed value, $2,500 each; by Stephen B. Jacobs, ref., at County Court House.... 15

President st, s s, 470.8 e 8th av, 25.10x100, three-and-a-half-story brk dwell'g; assessed value, $10,500....
3d pl, No. 5, n s, 40 e Henry st, 20x80, two-story brk dwell'g; assessed value, $4,000; also all right, title and int. in courtyard in front, 20x 33.5¼....
by T. A. Kerrigan, at 13 Willoughby st.... 16

Kingsland av, Nos. 89 and 91, w s, 50 n Richardson st, 50x100, one-story frame dwell'g on plot; assessed value, $900; partition; by Howard J. Forker, ref., at County Court House.... 19

LIS PENDENS. KINGS COUNTY.

Oct.

Thatford av, e s, 100 s Glenmore av, runs east 154.8 x south 25 x west 54.8 x south 25 x west 100 to av, x north 50. Charles E. Pell and ano. agt Morris Handler; foreclos. mechanic's lien; att'y, A. Shiland, Jr.... 1

Carroll st, s s, 94.5 w 9th av, runs south 94.10 x south 94.10 to Montgomery st, x west 50 x north 92.7 x north 92.7 to Carroll st, x east 50. ½ part. Andrew J. Dwinelle agt Carsten W. Riecks et al.; att'y, J. H. Betts.... 1

Madison st, No. 1266, s s, 188 w Knickerbocker av, 18x100. Lydie H. Gleason, extrx. Hugh Hutchison agt George A. Craig et al.; att'y, J. A. Anderson.... 2

6th av, s w cor 45th st, 100.2x240. Samuel Morrison agt William E. Crist et al.; att'y, C. R. Halsey.... 2

14th av, west cor 56th st, 50.2x100. Elizabeth E. Hutter agt Clara B. Dederick and ano.; att'ys, Hubbard & Rushmore.... 2

East New York av, s s, 70 w Troy av, 35.5x160.1x 31.3x100, Flatbush. Annie C. Bennett agt Henry M. W. Tragman et al.; att'y, Geo. C. Case.... 2

De Kalb av, west cor Bushwick av, 80x90. Charles N. Peed agt Cedar Street Methodist Episcopal Church; att'y, W. H. Kent.... 2

Pulaski st, s s, 580.2 e Throop av, 101.10x100. Charles D. King agt Maria Roberts; att'y, Frederick Cobb.... 2

Strong pl, e s, 260 s Harrison st, 17.5x98x16.8x98. Grace A. Birdsall agt Frank C. Trubee; partition; att'y, George H. Yeaman.... 3

Fort Hamilton av, n e cor 65th st, runs east 188.6 x north to s s Cowenhovens lane, x west 160.7 to av, x south 166.8 to beginning, New Utrecht. Elisha G. Selchow agt John M. Baldwin; action for specific performance; att'y, Edward S. Clinch.... 3

Lot of woodland situate at Bushwick, bounded east by Wyckoff av, south by road leading to Union Cemetery, west by said cemetery and north by land late of William Furman, 12 79-100 acres. Frederic Cromwell and ano. exrs. William H. Husted agt Margaret Coats; att'y, Thomas L. Moore.... 3

Ocean Parkway, s w cor West av, runs west 200 to Brighton pl, x north 40 x east 100 x north 40 x east 100 to Parkway, x south 80, Gravesend. Erastus F. Brown and ano. exrs. John S. Kenyon agt Mary Clinton; att'y, Edgar K. Brown.. 5

Jefferson av, s s, 420 e Howard av, 20x100. Irwin Beasty agt George B. Blydenburgh; amended notice; att'y, Chas. S. Taber.... 5

Ocean Parkway, w s, 424 s Coney Island and Sheepshead Bay road, 100x250 to roadway, Gravesend. John L. Voorhies, Commissioner of Investment, Gravesend, agt William H. Wallace; amended notice; att'ys, Hubbard & Rushmore. 5

Middle st, n s, 375 e 3d av, 25x52.6x25.1x50.7. Josephine A. Walsh agt Daniel Foley; amended partition; att'y, Willard S. Pladwell.... 5

Carroll st, s w s, 260 s e 4th av, 40x67.4x40x65.5. Mutual Life Ins. Co., New York, agt John E. Swetzer; att'y, Robert Sewell.... 6

Kosciusko st, n s, 442.9 w Stuyvesant av, 14.3x100. Hannah E. Miller trustee Hannah M. Lovett agt Joseph H. Ford; att'y, Kennard Buxton.... 6

South 9th st, n s, 75 w Roebling st, runs north 131.6 x west 75 x south 31.6 x east 50 x south 101.6 to st, x east 25. The Williamsburgh Savings Bank agt Lorenzo Burbans; att'ys, S. M. & D. E. Meeker.... 6

Greene av, s s, 125 w Central av, 63x100....
Greene av, s s, 233.10 w Central av, 16.2x100....
Virginia A. Kleine agt Virgil R. Case; att'y, Charles R. Halsey.... 6

Newell st, e s, 111.8 n Norman av, 16.8x100. Charlotte Hoar agt William H. H. Hoar; att'ys, Dittenhoefer & Gerber.... 6

Sumpter st, No. 172, s s, 330 e Howard av, 25x100. Isidor Blatt agt Minnie Finklestein; notice of attachment; att'y, Henry Wehle.... 6

Putnam av, n e cor Howard av, 20x100. The Kings Co. Savings Inst. agt Robert L. Moores and ano.; att'ys, Bearns & Brenner.... 6

Madison st, s e cor Howard av, 20x100. Same agt same; same att'ys.... 6

Pearl st, n e cor Water st, 50x90.8. Margaret J. Billet agt William Sherwood; action to recover ½ interest; att'y, John J. Leary.... 6

Hicks st, e s, 80 n President st, runs east 75 x south 11 x east 25 x north 11 x east 75 x north 20 x west 175 to st, x south 20. The Equitable Life Assur. Society of the U. S. agt John Egan; att'y, Henry Day.... 6

Graham st, e s, against lot 6 map Jeremiah Johnson, runs east 85 to point 100 w Kent av, x 25 x northwest 85 to st, x south 25....
Graham st, e s, lot 4 same map, 29.7x75....
Germario Fortenato agt John Gillen; action for specific performance; att'y, Henry E. Heisted. 6

Eckford st, e s, 200 n Norman av, 25x100....
Java st, n s, 370 e Franklin st, 25x100....
Lorimer st, w s, 290 s Norman av, 15x100....
Andrew J. Hennion, Jr., agt Deborah A. Chandler; partition; att'y, A. B. Chalmers.... 7

Flatbush av, east cor Prospect pl, runs south 60.4 x northeast 48.6 to Prospect pl, x northwest 63.4. Metropolitan Life Ins. Co. agt James Finlay; att'ys, Arnoux, Ritch & Woodford.... 7

Flatbush av, e s, 60.4 s Prospect pl, runs south 20.1 x northeast 64 to Prospect pl, x northwest 20.1 x southwest 48.6. Same agt same; same att'ys.... 7

Flatbush av, e s, 85.5 s Prospect pl, runs south 20 x northeast 79.6 to Prospect pl, x northwest 20.1 x southwest 64. Same agt same; same att'ys.... 7

Flatbush av, e s, 100.5 s Prospect pl, runs northeast 79.6 to Prospect pl, x southeast 20 x south 2.6 x southwest 90 x 3.6 to av, x north 20; also, Gore adj above, 120.5 south cor Flatbush av and Prospect pl and 3.6 e Flatbush av, runs northeast 90 x south 40.8 x southwest 90....
Same agt same; same att'ys.... 7

50th st, n s, 120 w 4th av, 60x102.2. Marteuse B. Story trustee Isaac Orr agt John Koski; att'y, George G. Dutcher.... 7

Decatur st, s s, 365 w Saratoga av, 95x100. Edwin M. Keiser agt Kate L. Pardonner; att'y, James P. Philip.... 8

Union av, e s, 25 s Bayard st, 25x99.4. Guiseppe Miele agt Joseph Depermo; action for specific performance; att'y, Daniel W. Northup.... 8

61st st, s w s, 160 s e 7th av, 20x— to New York & Sea Beach R. R., x—x—, New Utrecht. Hamilton Co-operative Building and Loan Assoc. agt Michael Fitzgerald; att'ys, Treadwell & Catlin. 8

RECORDED LEASES.

NEW YORK. Per Year

Bowery, No. 273, all. Robert M. Weed to Abraham Cohn; 3 years, from May 1, 1892.. $2,100

East Broadway, No. 290. Ann P. Hilliard, Jersey City, to Elizabeth Galvin; 5 years, from Aug. 1, 1889.... 1,080

Forsyth st, No. 69, store and part cellar. James B. Brady to Moses Horowitz; 3 years, from Aug. 1, 1891.... 720

Goerck st, Nos. 127 to 135. Richard Lathers to William H. Miller; 5 years, from May 1, 1891. (Renewal).... 3,000

Harrison st, Nos. 52-56. Thomas Patten trustee to Charles L. Rickerson; 3 years, from May 1, 1891.... 5,000

Houston st, No. 186 E., corner store and basement. Carl Franck to John P. Yunk; 5 years, from Oct. 1, 1891.... 1,800, 1,000

Pearl st, No. 104, restaurant. George F. Langenbacher to H. Schlossheimer; 1 year, from May 1, 1891.... 900

Park row, No 169, basement. Thomas Maher to Antonio V. Viegiano; 2 7-12 years, from Oct. 1, 1891.... 420

Warren st, No. 61, s e cor College pl, store floor, basement and sub-basement. Mary J. McWhorter and ano. exrs. and trustees John E. McWhorter to Edward Koehler; 7 years, from May 1, 1891.... 3,250

Same property. Assign. lease. Edward Koehler to Richard and John Harms; Oct. 5.... nom

Warren st, No. 61, front part of basement as partitioned off. Richard and John Harms to Max Weber; 7 years, from May 1, 1891.... 600

West st, No. 404, store and cellar. George J. Lecher to Max Ullmann; 4 7-12 years, from Oct. 1, 1891.... 1,200

Washington st, No. 489, all. John B. Ginnochio to Edward H. Gallagher; 3 years, from May 1, 1892.... 500

Willett st, Nos. 41 and 43, blacksmith shop. Patrick Ruddy to Henry Goellner; 5 years, from May 1, 1891.... 444

1st st, No. 20, all. Augusta Herwig to Julius Stelzner; 2 7-12 years, from Oct. 1, 1891.... 650

25th st, Nos. 18 and 20 W. Coles Morris and ano. exrs. J. Joseph Neill to New York Southern Society; 5 7-12 years, from Oct. 1, 1891.... 7,100

28th st, No. 527 W., store floor and cellar. Frank Farrell to Peter Fitzpatrick; 5 years, from Nov. 1, 1891.... 360

33d st, No. 346 E., store floor and cellar. Edward Gaynor to Adeline Christoffers; 5 7-12 years, from Oct. 1, 1891.... 360

58th st, Nos. 221 and 223 W. Andrew S. Bennett to William H. Van Cott; 5 years, from Feb. 1, 1892.... 3,200

64th st, No. 404 E., store floor and part cellar and second floor. Max Strumpf to Anton Masin; 5¾ years, from Aug. 1, 1891.... 960

109th st, No. 100 E., store, cellar and second floor. Jacob Indorf to Patrick Cumiskey; 5½ years, from Nov. 1, 1891.... 960, 1,080

125th st, No. 377 W. Carl G. A. Hoble to Theresa Gertenbach; 3 years, from May 1, 1891. 1,284

Av A, No. 48, third and fourth floors....
3d st, No. 143 E., second, third and fourth floors....
Anthony Engelbrecht admr. George Arend to Henry Schoerry; 5 years, from May 1, 1892.... 1,488

Madison av, n e cor 106th st, corner store. Mary Fash to Henry Boss, Jr.; 5 years, from May 1, 1894.... 1,400

Pleasant av, No. 298, s e cor 116th st, store and basement....
116th st, No. 500 E., first floor....
Richard Lathers, New Rochelle, N. Y., to Lawrence E. Kaim; 3 years, from Nov. 1, 1891.... 804, 840

Park (4th) av, s w cor 119th st, store and five rooms on first floor. Henne Metzger to Henry Michaelis; 5 years, from Sept. 1, 1890.... 1,500

South 5th av, No. 201, store floor and cellar and part of second and third floors. Mary Myers to Joseph Bloechlinger; 5 years, from May 1, 1890.... 1,110

Willis av, s e cor 138th st, corner store floor and part cellar. P. H. McManus to John Siegmann. 5 years, from Sept. 1, 1891.... 1,000, 1,100 1,200

Willis av, No. 441, store and first flat. John W. Cavanagh to Hugh Duffy; 3 years and 2 years extension, from Nov. 1, 1891.... 900

West End av, No. 246. Dore Lyon to Adolph Rusch; 2 10-12 years, from Nov. 1, 1891.... 2,800

1st av, No. 489, north store and cellar. Andrew Koch to Henry Martin; 1 year, from Oct. 1, 1891.... 360

2d av, No. 1559, store floor and basement. William Lausen to Kehlenbeck & Emigholz; 5 7-12 years, from Oct. 1, 1891.... 1,000, 1,100

2d av, No. 2055, store. Morris Moses to August Schneider; 2 7-12 years, from Oct. 1, 1891.... 384

3d av, No. 467, s e cor 32d st, all. Francis J. Keogh, Philadelphia, to John Savage; 5 years, from May 1, 1892.... 3,000

3d av, No. 1953, store floor and basement. John G. Lindenberger and Christiana his wife to Charles Coy; 4 years, 6 months and 18 days, from Oct. 12, 1891.... 1,440

3d av, No. 835, s e cor 51st st, 30x50. Philip M. Smith to Henry K. Meyer; 10 years, from May 1, 1892.... 3,500, 3,800

3d av, No. 1569. Sarah Irvine to George Ringler & Co; 10 7-12 years, from Oct. 1, 1891.. 1,500, 1,700

3d av, No. 701, s e cor 44th st. George R. Burris and Florence A. Voss to Patrick J. O'Keeffe; 8 years, from July 15, 1891.... 2,200

Same property. Assign. lease. Patrick J. O'Keefe to John J. Hickey.... nom

6th av, No. 813, s w cor 46th st, all. Henry Gaffken to Henry C. Viebrock; 10 years, from Oct. 1, 1891.... 6,000

10th av, No. 861. Michael E. Carley to Michael J. Lawlor; 10 years, from Oct. 1, 1891.... 1,500

11th av, No. 438, n e cor 36th st. Felix McKenna to Terence McGirr; 10 years, 7 months and 15 days, from Sept. 15, 1891.... 2,500

12th av, s e cor 130th st, store and cellar. George Ehret to Henry Streib; 5 years, from May 1, 1892.... 1,000

CHATTELS.

Note.—The first name, alphabetically arranged, is that of the Mortgagor, or party who gives the Mortgage. The "R" means Renewal Mortgage.

NEW YORK CITY.

October 2 to 8.—Inclusive.

SALOON AND RESTAURANT FIXTURES.

Ahrens, Henry. 258 Av A....Rubsam & H B Co. $2,900
Arnold & Schwalenberg. 1805 10th av....Bernheimer & S. (R) 2,000
Albert, Samuel. 65 Hester....D Mayer. 1,000
Amthor, Gustav. 210 E 28d ..J Ruppert 1,000
Baier, Konigunda. 1754 Park av....Bernheimer & S. (R) 1,500
Baudendistel, Fritz. 347 E 54th ...P Doelger. 500
Bergen, James....J H Berenter. Pool Tables. 550
Braase, William. 92 Washington....Beadleston & W. 1,500
Braun, Rudolph. 848 11th av....V Loewers. (R) 150
Battan, Charles. 2398 Arthur av....F & M Schaefer B Co. 500
Baylis, Mary. 133 Lincoln av....G Ehret. 350
Bellezza, Pietro. 94 Park....Burr B Co. (R) 368
Bittong, Louis. 178 Spring... H Zeltner. (R) 449
Byrne, Peter. 122 Cherry....J Kress B Co. (R) 900
Bachmann, Ella. 53 1st.. Budweiser B Co. (R) 1,500
Buss, Reinhard. 154 E 22d....G F Gwinder. 2,750
Casciotti & Margarito. 156 Mott....Budweiser B Co. (R) 700
Collins, Maria. 100 E 102d....Mutual B Co. 829
Cangro, Antonio. 353 E 118th....D Mayer. 900
Caton, W T. 2162 3d av....M Glogan. Restaurant Fixtures. 1,200
Cohn, Nathan. 176 Madison....C Frese. 725
Crucci, Felice. 583 Broome....H Plohr. 3,0
Cardine, Antonio. 203 Elizabeth....H B Scharmann & Sons. 400
Cohrs, H J. 55 Rutgers....Lembeck & Betz. 1,100
Carty, James. 218 Av A....Bernheimer & S. (R) 1,000
Same. 1848 3d av ...same. (R) 2,000
Doran, Myles. 148 Washington....S C Boehm & Co. (R) 535
Dean, Adelaide. 434 8th av....G C Woolsey. Restaurant Fixtures. 600
Dieterlein, Fritz. 1543 Av A....V Loewers. (R) 740
Early, Frank. 74th st and 1st av....E Tracy. (R) 834
Eggers, Richard. 2261 2d av....H Zeltner. (R) 2,000
Englert, Maria A. 525 Courtlandt av ...H Zeltner. 1,300
Ehlers, Luer. 100 E 125th... G Snyder. (R) 1,427
Fassott, J A. 187 Monroe....F Oppermann, Jr. (R) 1,925
Fuchs & Schneider. 346 1st av....S Liebmann's Sons B Co. (R) 400
Fischer, William. 144 Ludlow....V Loewers. (R) 336
Fitzpatrick, John. 1098 1st av....Bernheimer & S. (R) 2,350
Fitzpatrick, M J. 380 2d av....J Everard. 1,532
Flannery, Catharine. 586 Hudson. C Stern. 3,745
Fuchs, J G. 1110 2d av....J Failert B Co. 600
Geller, Joseph. 129 Broome, new No 123....H B Scharmann & Sons. 1,300
Gardner, J B. 129 Suffolk....Budweiser B Co. 1,500
Georges, Chr. 51 Elm S Liebmann's Sons B Co. (R) 3,000
Gleason & Boland. 532 Broome....P Ballentine & Sons. (R) 1,000
Grenz, C F. 228 E 74th....V Loewers. 600
Groll, Barbara. 163 E 53d....J Ruppert. 1,000
Grube, Charles. 1616 1st av....Bernheimer & S. 4,000
Harms, R and J. 61 Warren....E Koehler. 10,000
Hanrahan, J J. 429 6th av....J Kress B Co. (R) 1,100
Havranek, Vadar. 1395 2d av ...Schmitt & S. 680
Hazard, O L. 85 E 113th....Bavarian B Co. 1,000
Hickson, Mary. 238 Av B... Bernheimer & S. (R) 1,000
Horowitz, Moses. 69 Forsyth....P Doelger. 1,350
Harding, John. 192 South....Bernheimer & S. (R) 200
Herbst, Frederick. 204 Hester....Restaurant Furniture Co. Restaurant Fixtures. 35
Holian & Maul. 411 Broadway....G E W Stivers. Restaurant Fixtures. (R) 2,250
Hornberger, Frederick. 199 Lewis...G Ringler & Co. 615
Jarkovsky, Wenzel. 1432 1st av....P Doelger's Son. (R) 1,000
Kearney, T E. 10 Chrystie... P Weidmann. 100
Kuschel, O A and T. 49½ 1st av and 99 E 3d st ....Long Island Brewery. 1,427
Konrath, Heinrich. 274 E 10th... Wagner & S. Pool Table. 135
Kramm, Henry. 332 E 53d....F Oppermann, Jr. 800
Krienz, Adolph. 1621 2d av... J Gundlach. (R) 1,075
Kraemer, Hermann. 202 E 6th... J Ruppert. 450
Kraft, August. 517 W 47th....C Stein. 1,700
Koch, Cora. 726 11th av... Consumers' B Co. 2,100
Same... J H & H Wellbrock. 425
Krug, August. 212 Spring....G Bechtel, exr of. 500
Langer, Isaac. 66 Essex....H B Scharmann (R) 3,500
Lockley, P C. 329 4th av....L Bradt. Restaurant Fixtures. 100
Lohr, Chas. 416 E 84th.. E Jackson. (R) 300
Larsen, Emanuel. 88 Cherry....Fitzgerald B Co. 500
Lurssen, Christel. 355 Broome....Rubsam & H B Co. 1,000
Lauber, Charles. 111 Av C ...S Liebmann's Sons B Co. (R) 500
Ling, C P. 59 East Houston....S Liebmann's Sons B Co. (R) 500
Levy, J and A. 69 Ludlow....H Zeltner. 2,000
Matto, J E. 56 South 5th av....J Kress B Co. (R) 1,500
McDermott, J F. 315 E 35th....Williamsburgh B Co. 400
McManus, James. 250 Grand and 105-109 Chrystie... D Mayer. 3,000
Meyer, C S. 118 Hester....F Metzer. 60
Meyer & Mohrmann. 135 4th av....J Kress B Co. (R) 674
Miller, E H. 765 1st av....Bernheimer & S. Pool Table. (R) 140
Miller, W J. 358 Bleecker....Brunswick-B-C Co. Pool. 425
Mistele, Albert. 154 Forsyth....India Wharf B Co. 600
Moran, John. 194 Av A... J Kress B Co. (R) 1,789
Muller, Robert. 317 W 41st....G Ehret. (R) 150
McCloskey, Bernard. 425 W 17th....Budweiser B Co. (R) 150
Martin, Henry. 489 1st av....G Bechtel, exr of. 362
Marron, Patrick. 553 11th av....J Ruppert. (R) 2,550
Myers, Philip. 209 Western Boulevard....H Vogel. 250
Massett, Lawrence. 447 W 27th....Danenberg & C. 300
Matthai, F O. 236 Av A ...G Bechtel exr of. (R) 350
Maures, G C. 319 W 17th....J C G Hupfel B Co. 800
Muller, Michael. 1549 1st av....Bernheimer & S. 4,000
O'Halloran, P D. 183 Christopher ...P Doelger. 475
O'Hara, William. 1509 Av A....Bernheimer & S. (R) 2,700
Pryor, Elizabeth. Greenwich and Cortlandt sts ....J Morgan. (R) 5,000
Park, Robert. Grand and Mott sts....J Everard. 2,185
Same. 18 6th av....same. 1,740
Porein, William. 2491 3d av....P & W Ebling B C. (R) 1,990
Pinckney, Chas. 175 E 105th....Wagner & S. Pool Table. 150
Pulsifer & Co. 190 3d av....M E Pulsifer. Restaurant Fixtures. 1,000
Perless, Dora. 84 Eldridge Sekosky Bros. 140
Plischke & Galdun. 217 E 3d ...P Doelger. (R) 300
Quinn, J F & P E. 131 W 23d....T E Quinn. Restaurant Fixtures. 80
Reese, Alexander. 104 2d av ...G Ehret. 1,700
Rackebrandt, Henry. 38 and 40 Reade ...J V Halk. 1,000
Reddy, Patrick. 97 Walker....J Kress B Co. (R) 2,300
Reeves, Francis. 1779 3d av. ..E Roberts. Restaurant Fixtures. 440
Reich, B and L. 50 Essex....D Mayer. 1,418
Rump, Anton. 225 E 44th... D Mayer. (R) 500
Ryan, Michael. 704 Grand Boulevard....G Ehret. (R) 1,500
Schlichter, George. 330 E 11th....D G Yuengling, Jr. (R) 400
Schneider, George. 339 W 39th.. D Mayer. (R) 400
Shaler, N E. 52 W 125th....Restaurant F Co. Restaurant Fixtures. 50
Smith, C J. 181 Av C J Kress B Co. (R) 1,750
Same. 298 E 10th....same. (R) 1,750
Smith, John. 304 E 28th....Bernheimer & S. (R) 900
Sommer, John. 433 W 45th....P Schaefer & Son. 900
Stehle, Adolf. 9 West ...Rubsam & H B Co. 1,000
Schulz, Julius. 540 E 15th....Budweiser B Co. 500
Shaler, N E. 52 W 125th....Restaurant F Co. Restaurant Fixtures. 75
Spitz, Samuel. 379 East Houston....Budweiser B Co. (R) 1,000
Schopbach, Jacob. 272 Spring....V Loewers. 450
Spengler, Andreas. 76 Stanton....P Weidmann. 665
Schaefer, Remiguis. 1 1st av....Bernheimer & S. (R) 900
Schakowitz, Salomon. 101 Norfolk....H B Scharmann & Son. 500
Tangney, Patrick. 56 Market....R Von Hofe. (R) 650
Toemblom, Emil. 132 Church....S Liebmann's Sons B Co. (R) 600
Tanck, Herman. 100 Forsyth....Rubsam & H B Co. 1,500
Thompson, John. 48 New....Bernheimer & S. (R) 500
Ulliceni, Johan. 224 2d....Budweiser B Co. 500
Viebrock, H C. 813 6th av....H Gaffken. 16,000
Vielbauer, Rudolph. 101 E 106th....Fitzgerald B Co. 400
Vissichio, Viscenzo. 299 Mott....H B Scharmann. (R) 300
Wolf, Isaac. 171 Stanton and 436 Clinton....Burger & H B Co. 1,000
Wood, I D. 78 Beaver....G Ehret. (R) 600
Wagner, William. 23 Chatham sq....O Huber Brewery. 5,300
Winter, Moses. 247 Division... Sekosky Bros. Bar Fixtures. 307
Witte, Hermann. 7 3d av....Budweiser B Co. (R) 1,500
Wagner, Leonhard. 1741 9th av... Bernheimer & S. (R) 600
Walsh & McKnight. 117 4th av....K Rupp. (R) 600
Waul, Michael. 2341 Bathgate av. ..H Zeltner. (R) 500
Wedemeyer, G H and G H. 1521 9th av....Bernheimer & S. (R) 2,000
Wicht, Christopher. 1407 Av A .. J Ruppert 2,000
Wirz, Emil. 54 West End av....C Stein. (R) 3,500
Wollerman, A H & C T. 354 W 14th....Brunswick-Balke-Collender Co. Billiard Table. 130
Zambory, Paul. 217 E 3d....P Doelger. 1,500
Zerbarini, Charles. 265 Bowery....Wagner & S. Pool Table. 250
Zipf, Charles. 30 Rector....Rubsam & H B Co. 400

HOUSEHOLD FURNITURE.

Ambler, J G and E M. 40 W 45th....W H Kelsey. (R) 192
Austin, Moses. 430 W 57th....L Baumann. 123
August, Marie. 109 Shepherd av, Brooklyn....McClain, S & Co. 179
Ayres, M W. 261 W 88th....L Baumann. 158
Balfouy, Sidney. 253 W 15th....S Baumann. 127
Baier, Katie. 105 E 109th....Manges Bros. 186
Baiseley, Jennie. 274 W 118th... Manges Bros. 243
Barnett, Mary. 60 W 35th....J C Devereaux. 500
Beach, Julia A. 437 5th av and 11 W 34th st .. J A Gallagher. 6,000
Bernstein, Rachel. 149 W 130th....S Baumann. 277
Britton, Fannie. 156 E 47th....E C Pierce. 1,600
Brodsky, Benjamin. 8 Attorney....J Rubenstein. 472
Brooks, G T. 517 W 146th....H S Eisler. 302
Brundage, Ida. 79 E 119th....Manges Bros. 175
Brown, Lizzie. 1702 2d av....S Baumann. 216
Burns, John. 140 W 49th. ..R M Walters. Piano. 60
Burt, Ella T. 69th and 70th sts and Boulevard ...S Baumann. 1,062
Besto, J G. 66 5th av ...M Jackson. 100
Bithom, Harriet. 108 E 56th... J Moriarty. 469
Bleezard, G W. 207 W 33th....L Baumann. 186
Bunayn, Theodore. 204 E 38th....L Baumann. 137
Bacon, Ellen M. 114 W 16th... J Gregg. 140
Baer, Selina. 769 Lexington av... L Baumann. 1,302
Ballinger, S L. 154 W 34th....H B Cohn. 1,569
Baumann, Catherine. 302 E 65th....L Baumann. (R) 252
Bills, Mamie 315 W 36th.. L Baumann. (R) 187
Blafield, Martha S. 949 8th av....Simpson & P. Piano. (R) 143
Bolton, Edward. 237 E 56th....L Baumann. 130
Brett, M H. 751 9th av ...A Pearson. 179
Brotherton, Geo. 300 W 126th... L Baumann. 206
Conden, J E. 125 E 27th... L Baumann. (R) 203
Chatfield, A W. 287 W 39th....Krakauer Bros. Piano. 225
Chaves, L M. 130 W 44th....J Gregg. (R) 288
Checks, Orlando. 144 Madison av ...N W Carpenter. 2,000
Cohen, Harriet. 348 E 118th....H Thoesen 128
Cohn, C L. 45 W 60th L Baumann. (R) 181
Cooper, Maggie. 261 W 39th....L Baumann. (R) 145
Cox, Rose. 521 W 48th....L Baumann. 190
Curtis, Bernice. 49 W 98th....L Baumann. 279
Cashin, Matilda F. 783 6th av....J Gregg & Co. 930
Coursen, Annie. 4 Hanover... Jordan & M. 100
Charlesmith, C A. 68 Macdougal....C E Pierce. 100
Conklin, E T. 128 W 53d....Brooklyn F Co. 851
Craig, W L. 210 W 4th....American Guarantee Assoc. 200
Candano, Antonio. 565 Amsterdam av....C R Ruegger. 100
Carrillo, Irene. 73 W 88th....S Baumann. 238
Cates, Geo. 51 Washington....J Moriarty. 277
Chrystal, Kate L. 176 W 81st....S Baumann. 247
Corson, Mary. 107 E 85th....Spies Bros. 210
Dailey, Annie. 592 3d av....H S Eisler. 222
Davis, H S. 527 E 83d....S I Herschmann. (R) 179
Davis, Mattie. 232 W 43d....S Baumann. (R) 340
Denny, Marguerite. 30 Bayard....Manges Bros. 191
Dessar, L A. 102 W 44th....S Baumann. (R) 287
Dietterlen, E A. 212 E 20th... S Baumann. (R) 494
Dophin, Mary....J Williams. 163
Doherty, J J. 240 W 35th....S Baumann. 198
Draper, J A. 68 E 121st. ..Manges Bros. 194
Dupont, L A. 912 6th av....S Baumann. (R) 260
Dillon, C C. 200 E 27th Jordan, M & Co. 110
de Leon, G W. 101 W 93d....Brooklyn F Co. 415
Doody, Minnie A. 65 E 129th....L Baumann. 121
Duryea, Carrie. 118 W 83d... Jordan & M. 315
Edgeton, Herbert. 1045 Bedford av, Brooklyn ... McClain, S & Co. 262
Emerson, I Ross. 920 9th av ...L Baumann. (R) 115
Erstein, Louisa A. 336 W 59th....J Gregg & Co. (R) 123
Edwards, Jennie. 1864 3d av ...S Baumann. 113
Fahrenholz, Amelia. 133 W 45th....S Baumann. (R) 891
Fanieg, Leonora C. 41 W 126th....S Baumann. 258
Finkenstein, Leopold. 237 E 114th....J Rubenstein. 416
Finn, J T Y. 107 7th av ...R M Walters. Piano. (R) 190
Fell, Eva. 5 W 135th....Frank Holt. 100
Finster, Elizabeth. 432 W 58th....O'Farrell & Co. 180
Fisher, Charles. 121 E 108th.. L Baumann. 162
Ford, Mary J. 77 Sullivan ...L Baumann. 161
Finkenstein, K J. 54 W 24th ...H Coghlan. (R) 1,000
Fletcher, Susan. 144 W 27th....Jordan & M. (R) 100
Fottenbacher, Dora. 877 10th av....F T Higgins. 189
Fulforth, Henrietta. 517 E 82d....L Baumann. 113
Gibbons, T F. 236 W 17th ...W J Ruddell. 132
Green, Mary. 370 W 58th ...L Baumann. 155
Gantier, Marguerite. 218 W 40th....L Baumann. 780
Gaudin, H and J. 27 Cottage pl....A Blane et al. 440
Gener, F E. 213 E 5th....L Baumann. 186
Gleitz, Stephonie. 613 11th av ...L Baumann. (R) 100
Gordon, Minnie. 12 Pell....Jordan & M. 122
Graham, Eliza. 44 Beach....I Mason. 116
Gannon, Catherine. 84 Madison .... Garvey Bros. 200
Geelan, Michael. 1980 2d av....L Baumann. 113
Goldner, Herman. 216 7th ...G Schwartz. 100
Green, H W. 409-415 W 22d....S Knapp & Co. (R) 700
Grodinsky, Eva. 205 E 69th....M Richmond. (R) 107
Gable, John. 20 Downing....C R Rugger. 187
Gaultier, Andre. 163 Clinton pl....M D Favier. 800
Gaynor, J P. 340 E 55th....H Thoesen. 109
Goldman, H. 59 Bayard... H S Eisler. 164
Greenwood, Edna. 120 W 49th....S Baumann. (R) 443
Heuser, Stella S. 119 W 50th....S Baumann. 805
Hookins, Mary. 131 W 78th....B Robinson. Carpets. 450
Hopkins, P H. 217 W 38th .S Baumann. (R) 514
Harkins, Rebecca O. 207 W 40th....J Gregg. (R) 108
Harney, Mary L. 321 and 323 W 23d....Jordan, M & Co. 272
Hatten, Alice. 7 Pell....Jordan & M. 100
Head, Azelie. 142 W 33d....W J Ruddell. 433
Hogan, Maria. 228 W 37th....J F Doherty & Co. 149
Hall, Park. 200 W 132d .L Baumann. 449
Haven, Nellie. 160 W 49th....L Baumann. 271
Isaacson, H B. 155 Madison....J Rubenstein. 117
Johnston, C E L. 1011 Park av....S Baumann. 164
Johnston, Horace. 150 E 49th....J Baumann. (R) 157
Jacques, A M. 140 W 63d....H Thoesen. 506
Jordan, Rein. 211 E 11th....L Baumann. 149
Jussen, Carl. 122d st and 7th av....American Guarantee Assoc. 400
Keegan, William. 417 E 77th....L Baumann. 165
Kendall, Carrie S. 115 W 62d. ..L Baumann. 194
Kenny, Catharine. 1202 3d av....Jordan, M & Co. 158
Kerrens, Thomas. 442 E 23d ...L Baumann. (R) 140
Kiefer, Fred'k. 222 Lexington av....L Baumann. (R) 258
Kircher, H E. 330 E 84th....Krakauer Bros. Piano. 200
Kleinhart, K. 192 Stanton... Fennell & P. (R) 162
Ketcham, J W and A. 125 E 106th....Commercial Credit Co. 300
Kendall, Mrs E K. 205 W 44th....S Knapp & Co. (R) 728
Kingsbury, Floy. 125 W 28th... Garvey Bros. 261
Krieg, Mrs R F. 1967 and 1969 7th av....Brooklyn F Co. 248
Kaufman, I. 378 Grand....H S Eisler. 250
Kinnear, S O. 44 W 17th....J S Van Cleef. (R) 300
Leonie, Mary. 422 E 66th....J Baumann. 122
Linde, Emma. 78 2d av.. .J Gregg. (R) 236
Lyman, Lida. 81 W 91st....S Baumann. 200
Lehm, Alice S. 25 E 91st....Jordan, M & Co. 388
Ledoux, Alexander. 341 E 14th....J Moriarty. 146
La Finne, Nettie. 204 W 46th....L Baumann. (R) 744
Latschaw, Zacariah. 241 W 34th....C S Brown. (R) 200
Laughton, E C, Mrs. 301 W 55th....L Baumann. (R) 100
Levien, Jane T. 778 Madison av....L Baumann. 706
Levy, G & A. 27 Cannon ..W H Griffin. 100
Mansion, Michel. 118 W 31st... F S Webb. (R) 1,000
Mayer, Lulu. 998 1st av Jordan & M. 124
McKae, Virginia H. 8 W 116th. ..Spies Bros. (R) 169
Mellon, Philip. 173 Bleecker....H Israel & Sons. 183
Melville, Jane A. 109 E 88th....E Ward. 130

Meyer, George. 326 W 40th....Abstein & Schaeffer. 185
Meyer, Henry. 22 St Marks pl....L Baumann. (R) 165
Morrell, Nellie. 328 W 37th....J F Manges. (R) 282
Moses, Benjamine. 1831 3d av....L Baumann. 112
Mahoney, Mamie. 307 E 28th....J Moriarty. 184
Marlow, James. 230 Clinton.... Jordan & M. 170
Mayer, Edward. 208 E 88th....L Baumann. 179
McLoughlin, O. 1809 Lexington av....L Baumann. 165
Mehigan, Kitty. 178 W 98th....Jordan & M. 269
Mulford, Randolph. 42 New.... L Baumann. 157
Mahoney, Mary. 304 E 11th....Jordan & M. 283
McLean, Geo. 144 W 62d.... Brooklyn F Co. 184
Marshall, M M....J Williams. 128
McCarthy, Julia. 204 E 20th.. W H Griffin. 135
McCollum, P R. 216 E 85th Spies Bros. 173
Milton, Anna. 249 W 21st....Manges Bros. 266
Mordant, J J. 570 5th av and 112 W 39th st ... J Baumann. (R) 264
Munger, Alphonzo. 120 W 44th....S Baumann. 499
Nichols, W J. 513 Greenwich.... F T Higgins. (R) 115
Nolan, Mathew. 125 W 28th....J F Manges. (R) 201
Odou, L D. 222 W 48th....M M Stapleton, exr of. (R) 150
Ohrdorf, Mrs L. 65 W 51st....H Thoesen. 813
O'Neill, Lottie. 18 Bleecker.... J Moriarty. 203
O'Hanlon, P F. 321 E 29th ...C E Pierce. 100
Peterson, H W. 218 E 25th....L Baumann. 133
Potter, C E. 5 W 82d....S Baumann. 472
Peterson, Annie. Greenwich and Leroy sts....L Baumann. 164
Pirrie, Marjory. 529 W 52d .. F T Higgins. 158
Perine, Mary L. 335 W 35th....L Baumann. (R) 168
Perless, Dora. 84 Eldridge ...S I Herschmann. 116
Petit, Isabella. 235 W 74th....Brooklyn F Co. (R) 620
Powell, S A and M. 128-142 W 11th....M H Howell. 600
Pitt, Mrs Wm. 88 Charles.... H Thoesen. 260
Pohl, Auguste. 207 E 21st....A C Nau. 170
Quinn, G W. 290 8th av....L Baumann. 170
Regnier, Elise. 106 and 108 W 50th....D L Shorb. 1,000
Rochall, Bertha. 140 E 87th....O'Farrell & Co. (R) 120
Ramirez, James. 102d st and Amsterdam av.... O'Farrell & Co. 218
Reid, J W. 17 E 113th.. Alexander Bros. (R) 225
Reyen, Lizzie. 145 W 16th .. H Israel & Sons 105
Reddich, Helen. — W 29th....J & J Dobson. (R) 381
Reid, Emily. 439 W 57th....J Baumann. 161
Riordan, W L. 74 W 100th....S Baumann. 141
Rosenbaum, Rose. 207 E 34th....J Baumann. 207
Santzky, Isaac. 184 Chrystie....J Rubenstein. 213
Schneer, Martha. 217 E 34th....J Moriarty (R) 492
Shinkman, Paulina. 364 Grand....J Rubenstein. 747
Siegelstein, P A. 85 Rivington....S I Herschmann. 137
Silberman, Elizabeth. 13 Suffolk.. H S Eisler. 104
Sinnott, Elizabeth. 116 W 47th....S Baumann. 266
Sinnott, John. 227 E 121st....McClain, S & Co. 189
Simons, G L. 315 W 25th....L Baumann. 147
Strauss, Max. 491 2d av....J Moriarty. 168
Saksen, Louis. 214 E 29th....L Baumann. 116
Schreiber, Clara. 570 7th av....P Bechstein. 197
Scully, Kate. 518 E 83d....L Baumann. (R) 212
Sievers, Lina. 184 E 70th....H Thoesen. 196
Smith, Julia M. 303 10th av....L Baumann. 228
Smith, Maggie. 140 W 27th....L Baumann. (R) 102
Smith, W D. 230 Varick....R M Walters. Piano. 215
Schneider, J G, Jr. 140 W 129th .. S Baumann. 189
Schwarz, H F. 151 E 124th....F Coster. 410
Swensonn, John. 311 E 27th....Garvey Bros. 150
Soarnois, Jennie. 200 E 25th....L Baumann. 126
Tauszky, Henry. 62 E 108th ...American Guarantee Assoc. 200
Thurnblaser, Wilhelm. 301 W 147th....Jordan, M & Co. 175
Taylor, Sarah. 258 W 121st....Dreisacker & Co. (R) 221
Thompson, Peter. 205 E 100th....Jordan & M. 100
Tiedemann, F. 970 3d av....H Brenzel. 110
Tiffany, Frank. 10 Le Roy....Mullins & Co. 152
Tonnesen, Martin. 11 W 133d... Simpson & P. Piano. (R) 190
Torayer, Josef. 170 W 81st....L Baumann. 457
Tetu, A L....J Williams. 250
Valentine, Anne. 592 3d av....H S Eisler. 222
Vanderberg, Mrs F. 326 W 59th....J Moriarty. (R) 160
Vincent, C T. 1 W 87th... S Baumann. 615
Von Meckel, Minnie. 254 W 38th....J F Doherty & Co. 186
Van Wyk, David. 100 W 97th....W J Ruddell. 1,400
Varian, Bertha. 277 W 128th....Jordan & M. (R) 145
Vincent, L C. 52 W 26th....H Q Brooks. 512
White, W W. 670 E 142d....Brooklyn F Co. 465
Wilson, Rose. 84 E 118th....Garvey Bros. 164
Wall, Joseph. 101 Madison....J Rubenstein. 133
Westfield, Margaret. 54 W 47th....J Baumann. (R) 395
Wormsley, Mary. Storage .. H Israel. 400
Wall, Ellen. 303 E 14th....J F Conley. 1,500
Ward, Agnes S. 211 E 11th....R M Walters. Piano. 290
Watts, Marion. 217 W 40th....L Baumann. (R) 101
Weinstock, Annie. 1683 Lexington av ...Manges Bros. 147
Worth, Emma L. 313 W 26th....G Beck. 148
Williams, Annie. 126 Leroy....F T Higgins. (R) 225
Wollermann, A H and C F. 354 W 14th....L Baumann. 479
Yost, Mary E. 319 E 125th....A Yost. 235
Same....A Mattyetschek. Organ. 350
Zander, Marie. 10 4th av....Fennell & Pye. 210

MISCELLANEOUS.

Aronson, Harris. 111 Hester....C Dierking. Ice box. 115
Adams, Hattie. 393 4th av....H J Myers. Horses and Stable Fixtures. 1,800
Anderson, W H, and A Giraldi. 452 6th av....M L Giraldi. Press, &c. 200
Abrams & Co. 6 Pell .. Marvin Safe Co. Safe. 192
Bass, J C. 14th st, bet 9th and 10th avs....E Cole. Horses and Ice Wagon. 450
Broderick, John. 149 Madison....McAdams & D. Undertaker Fixtures. (R) 324
Bowles, Lilian. 33d st and Lexington av....G Meyer. Coupe. 906
Botjer, H M. 1641 Broadway....D B Hunter. Billiard Room Fixtures. (R) 1,197
Bowles, Lillie. 156 Lexington av....J R Reynolds. Horses, Carriages, &c. 5,000
Briggs, J E. 111 W 33d....E H Benn. Drug Fixtures. 870
Baxt, Max. 178 Suffolk....N Bloch. Horse, Truck, &c. 220
Bennett, Charles. 163 Hudson....Nat Cash Register Co. Register. 200
Berry, J J or Van Campen Bros & Co. 5 and 7 Dey....Hastings Card Co. Office Fixtures. 2,378
Bittermann, Joseph. 168 Allen....C Frerich. Horse, Truck, &c. 100
Blees, Max. 575 2d av....C Dorscher. Confectionery Fixtures. 500
Bobker, Harris. 101 Attorney....R Spahn. Machine. 55
Bonnell, F G and Co. 40 Catharine....Lamson Consol S S Co. Register. (R) 250
Buttell, J J. 2785 8th av....Nat Cash Register Co. Register. 200
Beyer, George. 621 E 16th....K Beyer. Horse and Milk Fixtures. 400
Buchholz, H A. 24 Clinton pl....L Z Buchholz. Tools, &c. (R) 500
Cohn, Samuel. 86 Columbia.....H Rosner. Tailor Fixtures. 100
Cordes, Frederick. 216 Cherry .... A Cordes. Horses, Trucks, &c. 800
Daggett & Ramsdell. 328 8th av....J W Tufts. Soda Fixtures (R) 475
David, G G and B. 342 and 344 E 32d....Hahn & Seligman. Horses, &c. 315
Dauman, Eva. 146 Orchard....J Weiss. Barber Fixtures. 125
De La Mare, A T & Co. 169 and 170 Fulton.... J S Browne, exr of. Presses, &c. 8,000
Dempsey & Carroll. 36 E 14th ...G B Hurd & Co. Presses, &c. (R) 48,312
Dietz & Stolzenburg. 1462 2d av....C W Roux. Drug Fixtures. 1,500
Feely, B F. 720 Tremont av....J J Feely. Undertaker Fixtures. 2,000
Fettroter, John. Amsterdam av, bet 155th and 156th sts....W F Naegele. Butcher Fixtures. 1,200
Finck, Henry. 136th st and 6th av....M Finck. Horses, Wagon, &c. 1,000
Fritzel, Ludwig. 289 Rivington....H C Mendell. Bottling Fixtures. (R) 2,027
Fitzgerald, Michael....D P Nichols & Co. Cab. 800
Fink, Abraham. 81 Suffolk .... H Zewald. Horse, Wagon, &c. 100
Friss & Meyer. 736 8th av ...Jaburg Bros. Bakery Fixtures. 500
Gordon, R A. 193 8th av ...J Stewart. Machines. 135
Green, B P. 433 and rear of 429 2d av....C Green. Laundry Fixtures. 800
Goisong, Anna. 240 Stanton....F Lutz. Butcher Fixtures. 600
Gallivan, M J and Mary J. 82 and 84 W 43d....E Blackburne. Horses, Coach, &c. 215
Gerlach, A. W. 714 Columbus av....C F Gerlach. Butcher Fixtures. 100
Goldenitz, Auguste. 1050 Av A....G T Lawrence. Horse, Wagons, &c. 500
Gurwitch, Isidor. 74 East Broadway....A Silvermann. Drug Fixtures. (R) 1,640
Gordon, A. William and Fulton sts....Archer Mfg Co. Barber Fixtures. (R) 88
Hansen, H C. 1976 3d av....J W Tufts. Soda Fixtures. (R) 200
Hess, Adolph. 12 Maiden lane ...A Goldsmith. Office Fixtures and Safe. 468
Hoffmann, G B. 305 and 307 W 128th .... P Brinckmann. Horses, &c. 668
Handler, Moritz. 294 Stanton....M Blux. Machines. 300
Henery, Jeremiah .... M Armstrong & Co. Coach. (R) 410
Heyman, Joseph. 736 8th av....Jaburg Bros. Bakery Fixtures. 500
Hill & Walch. 42 Dey....Campbell P P Co. Press. (R) 25
Hohmeier, Wilhelm. 612 E 88d....H Spegel. Horse, Milk Wagon, &c. 100
Hartshorn, J W. 141 E 59th....Hincks & J. Coach. (R) 325
Hawthorn, J B....P Barrett. Truck. 240
H B Douglass Mfg Co. 484 E 139th....P Pryibil. Machinery. 285
Henry, Kennedy. 543 W 27th....J McDonald. Machinery, &c. 135
Huff, F P....C A Drews. Ice Wagon. 100
Itzschlan, Rebecca. 526 1st av ...D Bottger. Grocery Fixtures. 300
Keely, James. 536 W 43d....J H Lippe. Coach. 332
Kestenbaum, Clara. 101 Av C ....J H Westheimer. Barber Fixtures. 275
Kopp, Robert. 69 6th av....H Rieken. Drug Fixtures. 2,000
Kreiner, Peter. 217 W 36th....T T Reid. Horse, Wagon, &c 500
Kaim, L E. 298 Pleasant av....R Lucke. Drug Fixtures. 3,000
Kahn, Bernhard. 175 7th av....Jackson & Co. Butcher's Ice House. 140
Kessel, L W. 321 W 145th....National C Reg Co. Register. 175
Kiesel, William. 1695 1st av.... J Weiss. Barber Fixtures. 27
Lange, J H ...J Werlein. Truck. 215
Lichtwitz, Ida M. 416 W 32d....P A Cassidy. Wagon. 80
La Rabier, Vito. 25 Clinton....G Montel. Barber Fixtures. 55
Lappert, D. 4 Walker....A Schrader. Machinery. 400
Leuchtenburg, Gerhard. 111th st, near 7th av ... H Cramer. Frame House and Garden Fixtures. 1,000
Lashewer, Louis. 127 Stanton ...Archer Mfg Co. Barber Fixtures. 120
Lederer, S & Co....Kean & Lines. Coach. 700
Levin, Sam. 76 Ludlow....Archer Mfg Co. Barber Fixtures. (R) 128
Lippiott, Thomas. 90 Fulton....S B Stifter. Machinery. (R) 42
McFarland & Judge. 1799 3d av....National Cash Reg Co. Register. 175
McGowan, George. 630 Greenwich....E H Gallagher. Horse. 175
Miller, O. 234 E 81st... H Miller. Horse. 75
Morche, Ernest, Jr. 606 E 17th. Koenig & Schuster. Horses, &c. 3,000
Same....same. Horses, &c. 2,750
Mach, Louis. 1026 Av A... C Hauk. Grocery Fixtures. 126
Mahler, Henry. 1784 Amsterdam av...Gennérich & Voo B. Grocery Fixtures. (R) 580
Mahon, J F. 181 Pearl....J W Walters. Printing Press, &c. 150
Marks Adjustable Folding Chair Co. 930 Broadway and 403-407 E 23d....Washington Nat Bank of New York. Machinery, &c. 5,588
Martin, John....M Armstrong & Co. Coach. (R) 225
McKeon, Thomas. 1807 and 1809 Washington av .. P Goodman. Horses, Trucks, &c. 2,728
Meehan, M J .. M Armstrong & Co. Coach (R) 190
Muhm, Henry. 159 E 53d... J Weiss. Barber Fixtures. 28
Murphy, J A. 44 Chatham....National C Reg Co. Register. 175
Marcus & Leibowitz. 66 Eldridge....Mosler Safe Co. Safe. 120
Mayer, Gottlieb. 1906 2d av... E Marscheider. Butcher Fixtures. 75
Mechler, W M and E. 2978 Broadway....W Neely & Co. Horse, Wagon, &c. (R) 245
Munch, George. 187th st and Arthur av....E Marscheider. Butcher Fixtures. (R) 85
Moses, Rachel. 30 Essex....S Fleck. Butcher Fixtures. 800
Mackey, Joseph....Campbell P P Co. Press. 1,279
McLeod & Co. 9th av and 86th st....W W Scott. Drug Fixtures. (R) 600
Neidlinger, John. 501 W 59th....S Littman. Barber Fixtures. 305
Nelson, Fleming. 138th st and Rider av....Halsey & Co. Horses, Trucks, &c. 350
Nobis, John. 258 W 28th ...A Nobis. Machinery. 750
National Gas Investment Co.....J H Corwin. Franchises, &c. 100,000
Oldenbuttel, Louis. 135 Washington....C F Bruggemann. Grocery Fixtures. 150
Ossenbenggen, Matthias. 1664 Columbus av ... J W Tufts. Soda Fixtures. (R) 280
O'Gorman, Edward. 3d av and 156th st....Lamson Consol S S Co. Register. 210
Orbel, H A. 237 E 100th....E Gilch. Butcher Fixtures. 273
Platte, J & Co. 571 Courtland av....R Hill. Grocery Fixtures. 471
Postill, R H and T ...W G Watkins. Horse and Milk Fixtures. 300
Praeses, Isidor. 381 6th av and 60 W 22d st.... S Zipser. Hair Fixtures, &c. 120
Price, Jesse. 65 Rutgers slip ...T D Hurst. Press, &c. 2,052
Palumbo, P. 252 E 125th....Archer Mfg Co. Barber Fixtures. 309
Paris, G. 3d av and 121st st....Archer Mfg Co. Barber Fixtures. (R) 591
Peattie, C E. ..A Peattie. Vans, &c. 2,000
Philips, J E and C S. 188 Pearl st and 251 Macon st, Brooklyn....J Davis. Machinery and Furniture. 2,257
Perkinson, L C....M Armstrong & Co. Coach. (R) 150
Perless, Dora. 84 Eldridge ...Sekosky Bros. Ice House, &c. 63
Quinlan, Edward.... M Armstrong & Co. Coach. 400
Rankin & Fifield. 2270 7th av ...Varney & Farley. Milk and Butter Fixtures. 250
Reynolds, M H. 147 Horatio....S P Dunn. Horses, Trucks, &c. 425
Runkel, C F. 378 7th av....M L Wood. Drug Fixtures. 2,300
Riccio, Nicola. Madison and James sts ...Jackson & Co. Butcher Ice House. 64
Sandrowich, Barney. 107 Columbia ...M Newmen. Bottling Fixtures. 400
Stratton, E & Son. 61 Broadway....Manhattan Type Co. Cutter. 40
Sweetser, C S. 525 Hudson, foot Bank....F A Potts & Co. Coal Yard Fixtures. (R) 5,000
Sachse, Henry. 2164 8th av....Archer Mfg Co. Barber Fixtures. 500
Saracena, Michael. Pulitzer Building....Archer Mfg Co. Barber Fixtures. (R) 1,088
Saracena & Struth. 82d st and Lexington av ....Archer Mfg Co. Barber Fixtures. 1,650
Schmidt, S. Park av and 89th st... J W Tufts. Soda Fixtures. (R) 250
Schweitzer, Andrew. 67 New....Archer Mfg Co. Barber Fixtures. 235
Schlueter & Bartholdi. 341 E 11th....E C Reinhardt. Printing Fixtures. 2,500
Schneider, John. 679 9th av....Gennerich & H. Bakery Fixtures. (R) 800
Senger, M, Jr, and J. 732 9th av and 427 W 50th st....M Senger. Undertaker Fixtures. 5,000
Springmeyer, W H E. 522 E 119th...M C Koerth. Bottler Fixtures, &c. 4,000
Straub, Anton. 540 W 54th and 511 W 54th....E J McCarthy. Store Fixtures, Horse, &c. 500
Smith, Martin H. Lexington av and 76th st.... G F Tausig. Drug Fixtures. 3,116
Sohn, William. 582 Grand....Mosler Safe Co. Safe. 150
Strauss, Michael. 63 Maiden lane....Marvin Safe Co. Safe. 285
Trehaler, Clementine. 1829 3d av.. .J Doyle & Co. Bakery Fixtures. 230
Traubmann, R. 62 Stanton....N Brown. Bakery Fixtures. 200
Taylor & Son. 19 Dey... J R Holcomb. Machinery. 243
Tilden, Lilian E F....Isaacs & Edwards. Int in Wills of M C Tilden and W Tilden. (R) £300
Trapani, Gaetano 487 5th av....L Tavolace. Barber Fixtures. 150
Vaast, C L or Vaust, C L. 190 William . Conner Bros. Press. 228
Vanden Houten & Co. 249 Pearl.... J G Day. Press, &c. 2,500
Van Steenbergh, B. 58 Broadway....Alice A Woods. Office Fixtures. 840
Watson, Oliver. 69 John....T Burnier. Press. 1,250
Wyatt, G N. 123 Warren....C W Wells. Grocery Fixtures. 256
Wallach & Co. 40 Columbia....Bennett & G. Soda Fixtures. 150
Walters, J H. Washington Market....A E McCarthy. Stands, &c. 2,500
Weller, J L. 223 Grand....J W Tufts. Soda Fixtures. 450
Wettlaufer, W L. 597 9th av....E Wettlaufer. Store Fixtures. 200
Williams, R H....M Armstrong & Co. Coach. (R) 150
Willis, Henry....Kean & Lines. Coach. (R) 525
Wodiska, Julius. 49 Maiden lane....J R Planten. Machinery. 4,500
Worzberger, F J. 244 Canal....C Berrien. Cigar Moulds. 300
Wellman, W C. 1949 2d av....W J Mitchell. Butcher Fixtures. 188

BILLS OF SALE.

Adler, S J K. 1933 2d av....L Plaut. Butcher Fixtures. 10,000
Avato, Giovanni. 43 Mott .... V Parantelli. Butcher Fixtures. ½ int. 180
Bonaventure, E F. 2 Barclay... H Mischke. Store Fixtures, &c. 600
Cuccia, Mrs Francesco. 230 E 2d....A Bisulca. Barber Fixtures. 250
Daino, Giro. 2151 3d av....S Torretto. Barber Fixtures. ½ int. 20

D G Yuengling, Jr, B Co. 2393 8th av... T F Lyons. Saloon Fixtures. 250
Firth, G W, 530 W 34th....Winklemeyer & Lutz. Sadler Fixtures. 150
Graff, C H....H B Claflin Co. Horse Covers. 1
Gardner, George. 909 Columbus av....E Donahue. Restaurant Fixtures. 900
Grant, Robert. 758 6th av....Carrie Grant. Glass. 800
Gerhard, Jettie. 121 Pitt....H Gluck. Store Fixtures, &c. 350
Hunter & Osborn. 492 E 138th....J B Simpson. Horses, Trucks, &c. 500
Keris, Hermann. 835 3d av....H K Meyer. Saloon Fixtures. 2,750
Lichtenau, August. 151st st and Courtlandt av ....E Muller. Wagon. 120
Lucke, Reinhard. 298 Pleasant av....L E Kaim. Drug Fixtures. 3,000
Mathews, J J. 154 3d av....C A Mathews. Restaurant Fixtures. 500
Neff, Edward. Jerome av and 162d st....K Neff. Saloon, House, &c. 3,000
Neus, Frederick. 419 E 106th .. J Bartnett. Saloon Fixtures. 2,500
Riecker, F H. 2433 2d av....Josephine Riecker. Saloon Fixtures. 1
Rose, John. 859 9th av....J Neumann. Restaurant Fixtures. 90
Robinson, Bessie. 131 W 78th....M Hopkins. Carpets. 450
Schutt, Henry. Washington and Rector sts.... W Brase. Saloon Fixtures. 2,150
Sullivan, J E. 2393 3d av ...W F Getgood. Restaurant Fixtures. 5,500
Schreiber, Max. 69 Forsyth ...M Horowitz. Saloon Fixtures. 800
Traver, J P. "Auctioneer." 116 Wall....Jennie Payne. Fixtures. 450
Wolff, Simon. 556 Broadway....Dora Kelter. Fur Manufacturing Fixtures. 2,000
Wagler, John. 122 W 25th ...Theresa Wagler. Machinery, &c. 2,000

ASSIGNMENTS OF CHATTEL MORTGAGES.

Boyle, Bernard to B McFarland. (Mort given by C Lenz, Sept 26, 1891.) 1
Brinckmann, Peter to J C Watson Co. (G B Hoffman, Oct 5, 1891.) 1
Coon, Fred to C Y Num. (Chong C Kong, July 31, 1891.) 1
Ducker, W M to M Rubens. (F G Hanson & Co, Nov 8, 1890.) 1
Finance Accommodation Co to L Cohen. (M C Jantzen, March 5, 1891.) 400
J Eichler B Co to Bernheimer & S. (C J White, March 27, 1889.) 2,527
Mayer, Jenny R to B Brand. (T H Allard, July 15, 1891.) 25
Same to same. (M Byrne, May 14, 1891.) 40
Rosenfeld, Emil to A Dinkelman & Co. (F Freedman, May 15, 1891.) 1,566
Steencken, Christian to A Dinkelman & Co. (I Neuwelt, May 15, 1891.) 750
Shimberg, S to J Irving. (W O Laughna, Nov 14, 1890.) 1
Volkenning, Otto to J W Cryan. (T L Duffy, Oct 2, 1889.) 1,800
Zipser, Solomon to M Reith. (F X Haas, May 8, 1891.) 500
Same to same. (K Steinhardt, Feb 21, 1891.) 115

KINGS COUNTY.

OCTOBER 1 TO 7.—INCLUSIVE.

SALOON AND RESTAURANT FIXTURES.

Alt, J A. 251 Rockaway av....Welz & Z. $425
Beuhler, J. 504 E 12th st, New York....J Eppig. (R) 650
Brown, J. 377 South 5th....Welz & Z. 700
Buck & Heissenbuttel. 442 Grand ...Welz & Z. 1,500
Barte, F. 75 Meserole....J Fallert B Co. 450
Benzin, A. 247 Ellery....J Eppig. 230
Boettcher, M A. 288 Atlantic av ...R Oelsner. 500
Broen, J. 5th av, east cor 11th st....J Kane. 8,799
Cain, W. 81 Ferris....Beadleston & W. 200
Conoely, W H. 233 North 5th....L I Brewery. 600
Cassidy, J J. 1013 De Kalb av....F Ibert. 350
Degnan, P. 380 Hudson av ...Budweiser B Co. (R) 304
Dewey, Mary D. 469 Fulton .. J H Albohn. Restaurant Fixtures. 1,000
Fagan, B. 411 Hamilton av....L I Brewery. 600
Fischer, A. 2450 Fulton....Leibinger & Oehm B Co. 1,000
Frayne, E J. 212 Hamilton av....T C Lyman & Co. (R) 1,500
Frey, P. 62 Montrose av....J Doelger's Sons. 600
Garser, A. 99 Morrell .. J Eppig. 350
Gibbs, D E. 672 Atlantic av....E Ochs. 950
Gordon, J H. 210 3d av....Rubsam & H B Co. 320
Guntersdorf, P J. 608 Grand....F Fedderke. Pool Table. 160
Haesloop, J. 108 Reid av....L I Brewery. 997
Haley & Young. Berry st.. .Elizabetha Meltzer. (R) 850
Hanrahan, P. 1300 3d av....M Seitz. (R) 550
Hartmann, J and Julie. 483 20th....W Ulmer. 400
Hassenkamp, P. 566 10th av....F X Obermeier. 600
Heisenbuttel, H. 108 3d av. ..J Kress B Co. 2,000
Henry, C. 577 Driggs....E Ochs. 1,000
Heubel, V. 108 Ewen... J Eppig. 900
Hommell, L. East New York av and Sackmann st .. Williamsburgh B Co. (R) 325
Hahnle, Karoline. 223 Hopkins....F Ibert. (R) 400
Hassler, W. 636 6th av....H Kludt. 315
Hensler, G. 216 Throop....F Munch. (R) 700
Jager, J and Babette. 37 Schaeffer....H B Scharmann & Sons. 400
Keegan, J. 213 Hamilton av....Welz & Zerweck. 350
Koehler, C. 356 Oakland....O Huber Brewery. 750
Koehnken, M. 479 Liberty av....J Fallert B Co. 600
Kojan, E. 1414 Bergen . Burger & H B Co. (R) 300
Kretschmar, C and B. 1460 Gates av....L I Brewery. 450
Kleinlein, G. 171 Boerum....J Eppig. (R) 450
Laderer, G. 98 Ewen....J Eppig. 900
Levy, M. 37 Bridge ...H B Scharmann & Sons. 400
Lewis, B G. 773 3d av....Claus Lipsius B Co. 1,000
Lober, J. 169 Bedford av....Obermeyer & L. 700
Lyman, J. 706 Atlantic av....H Koehler & Co. 500
Maher, E. 335 Lorimer....M Early. (R) 1,500
McLaughlin, J. 203 9th....M Seitz. (R) 600
Meyer, K. 121 Franklin....G Siems. (R) 2,050
Millard, J J, and M C Heenan. 217 Hoyt....M Seitz. (R) 718
Murphy, D. 227 North 8th....J Fallert B Co. 417
Manersbach, A. 1608 Bushwick av ...F Ibert. 700
Nikols, F. 287 Kingsland av....F Munch Brewery. 600
Pressler, L. 25 Seigel....M Annenberg. 60
Quigley, J F. 311 Bedford av ...J Murtaugh. 2,000
Same ...O Huber Brewery. 2,000
Schaefer & Neidhart. 892 Broadway....J Doelger's Sons. 2,500
Schnorr, C. 341 Melrose....F Munch Brewery. 500
Schorn, L. 993 Flushing av....Welz & Z. 675
Schott, F. 351 Kent av....P Doelger. (R) 4,000
Savarese, M. Foot Columbia st ...W Ulmer. (R) 500
Scholl, J. 1597 Atlantic av....J Fallert B Co. 1,000
Schopp, L. 50 Leonard....J Eppig. 600
Sisto, J and R Speranzo. 525 Carroll....Budweiser B Co. Pool Table. 150
Stroub, F A. 37 Broadway... W Danisaer. Restaurant Fixtures. 400
Walsh, J. 121 Harrison....M Seitz. (R) 500
Wohlfarth, C. 179 Richards....P Weidmann. 450
Zimmermann, A. 90 Alabama av....Welz & Zerwick. (R) 600

HOUSEHOLD FURNITURE.

Alcock, M. 274 Grand....J T Runcie. (R) 800
Billman, Sophia E. 742 4th av....R Q Quick. (R) 500
Breen, T W. 85 Sands... A Pearson. 141
Brossard Bros....P Strobel & Sons. 175
Burke, Katie. 87 Sands....Mullins & Sons. 160
Butler, M S. 792 Gates av....Mullins & Sons. 203
Berry, Mrs J T. 464 Belmont av....J McEnery & Co. 120
Champney, Annie. 721 Macon....L Baumann. 195
Cohn, Annie 142 Grand....Simpson & P, Piano. 220
Collins, Mary E. 239 9th....Brooklyn F Co. 402
Cowden, Amelia. 112 Harrison av....L Baumann. 185
Davidson, W. 414 Myrtle av....M Bottstein. 140
Dillon, J J. 157 Nassau av....J F Doherty & Co. 209
Dunn, F A. 136 Lawrence....D Moriarty. 109
Diehl, S. 139 South Elliott pl ...Mullins & Sons. 125
Dillon, H. 92 Myrtle av....J Michaelis. 156
Doggett, F W E, Jr. 473 and 475 Clermont av ....Anna Tarbell. 400
Donaldson, Anna M....J Williams. 158
Dunn, F A. 36 Lawrence....W O'Neill. 164
Edinburg, C D. 24 McDonough....Brooklyn F Co. 358
Ellery, Sarah M. 165 Waverley av....H P Eldridge. 200
Forbes, Anna B. 137 4th av ...Manges Bros. 125
Fry, G. 744 Driggs av....A Schulz. 217
Faubach, L. 253 46th....J F Doherty & Co. 235
Ford, T P. 130 Willoughby av....Brooklyn F Co. 225
Grippentrog, Kath. 437-445 Carlton av....Emma Miller. Furniture in storage. 250
Grossert, Martha. 111 North Oxford. ..A Pearson. 159
Grosbeck, J. 79 Tillary....J McEnery & Co. 118
Haas, Julia. 12 Belvidere....J McEnery & Co. 162
Heath, Mary. 98 Bond.. L Baumann. 138
Hecker, J P. 982 Myrtle av....C T Kendrick & Co. 203
Heddenkamp, Meta C. 199, South 9th....A Schulz. 200
Hellpick, L. 693 Park av . .J A Schwarz. 179
Herbert, E. 16 Liberty....O'Connor & Treacy. 125
Housmain, Mathilde. 221 Roebling .... J A Schwarz. 175
Hanley, M. 92 Amity....O'Connor & Treacy. 174
Heyne, R. 380 Central av....O'Connor & Treacy. 132
Johnson, L H. 151 Waverly av....Brooklyn F Co. 431
Keller, F. 242 Hamburg av....J A Schwarz. 284
Knapp, E R. 168 Jefferson av... L Baumann. 114
Keyer, Jennie M. 106 4th av... M Schulz & Bros. 113
Lathrop, F G. 281 Clifton pl....Brooklyn F Co. 221
Levy, M. 129 North Oxford....Brooklyn F Co. 157
Ladd, Charlotte. 145 Nassau....M Bottstein. 150
MacGregor, Amelia G. 105 Hewes....L Baumann. 125
Mason, W A. Blake and Van Sielen avs....J Moriarty. 214
McCook, Mary. 128 Bedford av....A Schulz. 124
McInerney, J. 42 North Oxford....A Dudley. 135
Meier, G F. 1080 Herkimer....J A Schwarz. 252
Meineke, Mary M. 200 St Johns pl... O W B Westervelt. 2,029
Morton, Bertha. 1210 Gates av....H Thoesen. 106
Murphy, J A. 49 Concord....J B Eccelsine. 275
Marshall, E. 34 South Oxford....Brooklyn F Co. 198
Martin, Julia M. 1012 Lafayette av....Simpson & P. Piano. 365
Mayer, J. 61 Driggs av .. Fritz & Hummel. 227
McCleery, J. 112 Calyer....Jordan, Moriarty & Co. 168
Morriss, Carrie A. 101 Montague... Brooklyn F Co. 440
Morris, G S. 203 Amity....O'Connor & Treacy. 179
O'Higgins, Mrs H E. 417 10th....M Bottstein. 106
Parsbley, F E. 70 Hicks....Simpson & P. Piano. 270
Renard, Clara. 124 McDougal....L Baumann. 152
Raymond, F S. 385 Pacific....A W Whittelsey. 243
Schomburg, G. 80 Clifton pl... J N Smith. 200
Schwalbach, Sarah E. 426 Kosciusko....A Waeldin. (R) 200
Simpson, C. 861 Greene av .. Brooklyn F Co. 278
Stevens, Sophia. 250 Clifton pl. ..M Schulz & Bro. 138
Sarach, C F. 80 Leonard....A Levy. 187
Simon, H. 489 7th....Manges Bros. 208
Smith, Helen M. 250 Washington av ...D Crowell. 100
Steele, B. 260 Myrtle av....C T Kendrick & Co. 215
Sullivan, M. 81 Amity....A Pearson. 152
Tiner, Jennie. 29 Ocean pl....M Schulz & Bro. 281
Tainter, Margaret J. 309 Douglass .Simpson & P. Piano. 250
Thorne, Bella S. 80 North Elliott pl....Brooklyn F Co. 187
Weeden, A M. 109 South Oxford....Brooklyn F Co. 151
Wright, B. 356 Lafayette av ...M Schulz & Bro. 233
Washburn, W. 71st st and 14th av....J Moriarty. 365
Wood, A J and Annie D. 199 Amity....H A Robinson. (R) 100
Zeh, O. 722 5th av....M Bottstein. 210

MISCELLANEOUS.

Adamy, C. 1001 3d av....C Bach. Barber Fixtures. (R) 170
Abbruzio, F. 342 Flushing av ...Archer Mfg Co. Barber Fixtures. 111
Arbuckle, Cora B. 260 Rutledge....O W Van Campen & Son. Grocery Fixtures. 417
Artale, L. 336 Flushing av....Archer Mfg Co. Barber Fixtures. 111
Borrmann, W F. 418 17th....F H Hutwelker. Horse and Wagon. 700
Bourne, W G. 373 Lewis av....A S Leonard. Drug Fixtures. 1,500
Bringman, G. 885 Fulton....National Cash Register Co. Register. 200
Brown, H. 177 Hudson av ...Mary Cowan. Grocery Fixtures. 100
Batsford, W F....Barrett & Brush. Wagon. 143
Baur, J. Rockaway av .... J E Monahan. Wagons, Tools, &c. (R) 290
Cohen, A. 902 Manhattan av....Mosler Safe Co. Safe. 100
Covert, F M. 194 Moore....Cornelia M Covert. Coaches. 600
Campbell, F R. 196 5th av....H McShane Mfg Co. Plumber Fixtures. 466
Same....Eliza A. Campbell. Store Fixtures, Tools, &c. 200
Case, H and Magt A. 109 and 111 Skillman .. G W Platt. Machinery, &c. (R) 7,552
Cordes, H and J Bargfrede. 439 Hicks....J Siems. Grocery Fixtures, Horses, Wagons. 3,300
Craw, J H. 7 Reid av....J Metz. Printing Press. 292
Cain, J. 38 Havemeyer....M D Meyers. Horse and Wagon. 100
Doscher, H. 1097 Broadway.. .G W Blauvelt. Ice Cream Manufactory. 550
Deissig & Sessions. 448 Grand....D Engel. Fixtures. 300
Deitz, C J. 754 3d av....D M Ford. Drugs. (R) 750
Dix, T H. Douglass st, near 3d av ...Marvin Safe Co. Safe. 120
D'Abramo, R. 89 North 2d .. Mosler Safe Co. Safe. 100
Edwards, L R. 197 Hamilton av....Mary A Edwards. Drug Fixtures. 3,000
Same. 315 5th av . same. Drug Fixtures. 3,000
Freeman, F B. 1073 Putnam av....Rathbun & Co. Presses, &c. 100
Field, F C. 861½ Middleton....S Field. Express Business. 100
Fitzpatrick, J S. 153 Lawrence....F and G Haag & Co. Barber Fixtures. 387
Gallagher, H. 1244 3d av....C Bach. Barber Fixtures. (R) 120
Geutzlinger, Henrietta, 459 Graham av. 454 Graham av....Lamson Consolidated Store Service Co. Register. 130
Gibbs, D S. 6th av and Atlantic av.. .National Cash Register Co. Register. 175
Graf, F. 517 Graham av ..Lizette Muhlfeith. Grocery Fixtures. 175
Grannemann, C F W. 89 Nassau....Anna M Schachr admrx. Butcher Fixtures. (R) 800
Greenf H. 171 Myrtle av....Mosler Safe Co. Safe. 100
Havnor, G N. Coles st, cor Columbia st....D Kelly. Horse and Wagon. 150
Hilton, A P....J N Smith. Organ. 341
Horwitz, M 177 Hoyt....Archer Mfg Co. Barber Fixtures. 121
Haddon, E G. 358 Bainbridge....National Cash Register Co. Register. 200
Harvey, E. Atlantic av and Logan st....Mary Harvey. Machinery. 600
Heissenbottle, H. 118 3d av....Lamson Consol S S Co. Register. 165
Heumann, R. 160 William st, New York.... Campbell Printing Press and Mfg Co. Presses. (R) 504
Hertzler, Rachel A. 819 Gates av....A T Bam. Grocery Fixtures. 150
Hunter, W B. 1948 Fulton.. .Elizabeth Hunter. Cigar Fixtures. 100
Jerd, J E. 1536 Gates av... F H Butters. Soda Apparatus. 100
Joa, F. 70 Grand... National Cash Register Co. Register. 225
Kelly, J M & Co. 211 Canal st, New York....D N Peak. Stock and Credits. 6,639
Koor, J and A. 269 South 2d .. L Hassebauer. Tailor Fixtures. 144
Kruger, C. 153 9th....E E Johnson. Horse, &c. 112
Krebs, W and F Maehlker. 205 Wallabout....F Reckmeyer. Coal, Wood and Ice Business. 475
Lederman, M. 1226 De Kalb av....M Gussibel. Horses, &c. 300
Lang, G & Co. 186 5th av....Lamson C S S Co. Register. 235
Lee, A. 3d and Bay Ridge avs....National Cash Register Co. 200
Loftus, E....Royal Horse Assoc (Lim.) Brown Gelding. 85
Linker, J. 16 Metropolitan av....J Matthews Apparatus Co. Soda Water Apparatus. 450
Marcucci, C. 291½ Main st, Flushing....B Repetti. Fruit Store. 300
McElheny, M. 18 Flushing av ...National Cash Register Co. Cash Register. 175
Mollo, V. Wythe av, cor South 8th st....Archer Mfg Co. Barber Fixtures. 290
McLeod, J T. 116 Norman av....R R Whiting. Drug Fixtures. (R) 1,500
Meyer, F. 287 Columbia .... National Cash Register Co. Register. 200
Moadinger, C F. Pennsylvania av, near Atlantic av....W F Moore. Horses, Carriages. 1,500
Moore, J. 182 Jay .. National Cash Register Co. Register. 175
Morrison, Ellen. 400 5th av....G H K White. Fixtures and Furniture. 210
Muller, F, F Hillmann, W Delmeyer, H Monsees, and W Mehl, of Hillmann, Muller & Co. 487 South 5th....G Wieber. Soda Water Manufactory. (R) 20,000
Mathias, C. 136 Evergreen av. ..Gaus & M. Grocery. 240
Neder, G. 26 Monteith....Elise and Cath Neder. Ice Business, &c. 225
Philips, Julia E and C S. 183 Pearl and 251 Macon....J Davis. Machinery, &c., also Furniture. 2,557
Rumpf, W. 911 Broadway ...Archer Mfg Co. Barber Fixtures. 221
Rosenson, L. 115 North 2d....Mosler Safe Co. Safe. 130
Robertson, A H. 50 Hicks....J G Staib. Fish store. 123
Romanelli, J. 124 Court....Archer Mfg Co. Barber Fixtures. 308
Savarese Bros. 11 Union and 50 Irving....Cath Barano. Paste Factory, &c. 3,000
Searle, W S. 104 Henry ...M L Filley. Furniture, also Horse, &c. 3,009
Slattery, D & Son. 136 Columbia....Wolff Bros. Horses, &c. (R) 525
Simonson, H J. 236 Lafayette av....B Weill. Horses. 600
Smith, J. 105 Franklin....M T Garvey. Store Fixtures. 155

Smith, Lucy V. 1545 Fulton....W E Wheelock & Co. Piano. 250
Stollberg, G. Bergen st, near East New York av....L E Hommel. Tools, &c. 150
Schwicker, Theresa C. East New York av....W De.erling. Butcher Fixtures. 400
Sunddrmann. H W... M Armstrong & Co. Coach. 350
Simon, H. 489 7th av....D Atkin. Drug Fixtures. 400
Sturges, E. 1060 3d av....J Matthews Apparatus Co. Soda Water Apparatus. 555
Terrence, C....P B Bracken. Horses, &c. 271
Tower, Ellen. King st, cor Columbia st....P B Bracken. Live Stock. (R) 129
Weisser, C. 1058 Willoughby av....P Brandmeier. Horse and Wagon. 225
Wohlke, E. 1242 St Marks av....Lamson Consolidated S S Co. Register. 140
Webster, H S. Carlton av and Bergen st....M M Webster. Horse. 500
Whitlock, Julia J. 42 Wyona....J Brommer et al exrs. F Ring. Machinery. 1,750
Willenbrock, J C. 1046 Willoughby av....H Rosenbrook, Jr. Grocery Store Fixtures. 600
Wilson, C J and W F Stoney. 108 Livingston....T A Wilson. Printing Fixtures. 500

BILLS OF SALE.

Brandner, Eliz. 76 Gerry....S Bauer. Carpenter's Tools and Stock. 450
Britton, W A and J 408 Bedford av....Eliza Britton. Cigar Store. 1,597
Doellinger, H A. 1900 Fulton....W J Ryan. Millinery Store. nom
Dowling, G J S. 459 Fulton....R T Flynn. Restaurant. nom
Eveling, W. 120 3d av.... J H Gatje. Grocery. 3,500
Edwards, Mary A. 197 Hamilton av....L R Edwards. Drug Fixtures. 2,500
Flynn, R T. 459 Fulton....Mary D. Dewey. Restaurant. 2,000
Good, S R. 214 Ralph av....W H Good. Office Furniture. 500
Halling, Karoline. 719 Flushing av....Lina Aronholt. Grocery. 195
Lynch, J. 674 Marcy av....C Hecker. Horse. 220
Lewry, S D. 575 Washington av.. Margaret McSorley. Fish Business. 50
Marquart, F. 1228 De Kalb av....M Lederman. Bakery. 200
Payne, Jennie and Hulbert. 106 Livingston....Wilson & Stoney. Printing Office. 1,000
Pruden, A B. 770 Broadway... Mary L Pruden. Cracker Store. 600
Schmidt, A. 1465 Gates av....J Hirn. Blacksmith Business. nom

NEW JERSEY.

NOTE.—*The arrangement of the Conveyances, Mortgages and Judgments in these lists is as follows: the first name in the Conveyances is the Grantor; in Mortgages, the Mortgagor; in Judgments, the Judgment debtor.*

ESSEX COUNTY.

CONVEYANCES.

Allen, F B—W L Allen, South 12th st.......... $1
Same——W H Lauck, South 14th st.......... 550
Allen, W L—A S Allen, South 12th st.......... 1
Allen, William—M Gerrigan, Hudson st.......... 2,350
Alling, I A—M L Dana, n s Pennington st, 178 w Mulberry st, 22x79.......... 3,500
Alling, I A, dec'd, by exrs—L A Lipps, n s Wright st, 175 e Hanover pl, 25x100.......... 4,000
Arnold, M A—J Crikculey, State st.......... 1
Aymar, E R—J Herter, East Orange.......... 1
Bach, Charles—G H Bach, Caldwell.......... 100
Bailey, William—A Devine, s w cor Lawrence and Commerce st, 97x69x16x109x71.......... 25,000
Bannister, A P—C L D Smith, Bergen st.......... 1
Barnes, Robert—C M Decker, East Orange.......... 4,500
Baum, Philip—W H F Fiedler, South 15th st.......... 500
Bedell, A E—E C Robertson, n s Chestnut st, 100 w McWhorter st, 100x100.......... 8,000
Berg, Frederick—C Sauer, Orange.......... 620
Bingham, L A—J L Strahan, Orange.......... 1
Blake, J L—L C Matthews, Orange.......... 1
Bonykamper, Frederick, Jr—W W Collyer, 9th av.......... 1,210
Breakenridge, J H et al—B Frith, Clinton.......... 175
Cadmus, G K—E White, Orange.......... 3,075
Carle, J S—H Jerolaman, Newark Meadows.......... 100
Cavanagh, Garret—P McMahon, Bergen st.......... 1
Condit, B S—E R Armstrong, South Orange.......... 3,700
Condit, E M—W H Fleming et al, West Orange.......... 1,000
Cone, E M—M C Muller, South 6th st.......... 500
Cook, H P—J W Read, s s Nelson pl 289 w High st 25x100.......... 8,000
Colyer, Charles—C Raquet, s s Cottage 261 e Mulberry st 27x111.......... 6,500
Cowell, C E—G H Smyth, East Orange.......... 10,000
Coyne, Edward—E Coyne, Orange.......... 150
Crane A J—M J Lyon, Montclair.......... 6,400
Crane, G D et al—L A Brugler, Caldwell.......... 1,500
Critchley, John—C P Young, Nassau st.......... 2,200
Denman, J C—D Rutherford, East Orange.......... 500
Denninger, Joseph—E Storsberg, 16th av.......... 1,400
Diem, Frederick—J Kasilke, Magazine st.......... 2,640
Devine, Arthur—J Tynan, South Orange.......... 175
Devine, Arthur—D Vollweiler, Central av.......... 1,830
Same——A E Ryerson, North 3d st.......... 750
Diem, Frederick—C G Maier, Magazine st.......... 2,500
Dobbins, D F—S A Vedder, Caldwell.......... 2,500
Dobbins, Rachel—W N Dobbins, Caldwell.......... 1
Dodd, A V—H B Demarest, w s Cutler st 262 s 5th av 25x100.......... 3,200
Dodd, N M—The Bethel Presbyterian Church, East Orange.......... 5
Doering, Otto—S Weber, s s 18th av 258 w High st 25x47.......... 5,100
Dow, F L—J Heany, Camp st.......... 1
Doremus, Philip—J L Andrus, Montclair.......... 1
Dye, J W—E S Flohn, e s Summer av 225 s Nursery st 25x110.......... 4,300
Escalante, F H—E A Howell, Orange.......... 4,500
Farley, B M et al—C F Seitz, Prospect av.......... 1
Flannery, Thomas et al, exrs—M Konoy, Bloomfield.......... 1,000
Frey, Robert—P Schwing, Ferry st.......... 1,800
Graw, J J—J Miller, Jr, Clinton.......... 1,425
Hallock, E L—W Watson, East Orange.......... 12,000
Hamilton, E P—S Marquet, Orange.......... 4,250
Harris, Marx—S Einhorn et al, e s Prince st 124 e Court st 24x100.......... 7,000
Harrison, C J—E Schott, West Orange.......... 125
Same——H Schott, Jr, West Orange.......... 250
Hayes, Charles—O Doering, Fairmount av.......... 750
Hayes, T O—H Jerolaman, Newark Meadows.......... 100
Hartpence, J P—D E Moore, East Orange.......... 160
Heaney, John—F E Dow, Camp st.......... 1
Hill, William—J Abeles, 18th av.......... 2,100
Same——same, Bergen st.......... 2,100
Howell, Ambrose—C B Alston, Liberty st 30x100.......... 5,800
Howell, J E, special master—C F Seitz, Holland st.......... 1,225
Holzhauer, Mary—G V Aschenbach, East Orange.......... 600
Hull, Harriet—R Clark, East Orange.......... 1,000
Jeffs, M B—The East Jersey Water Co, Belleville.......... 1,800
Jerolaman, Nicholas—H Jerolaman, Grant st.......... 1,700
Jerolaman, Henry—E J Rothery, Grant st.......... 850
Jimmerson, Nehemiah—C M Ryman, North 11th st.......... 550
Johnson, C H—A H W Johnson, Montclair.......... 1,200
Keasbey, A Q—A Blair, South 10th st.......... 1,440
Keefe, E J—J J Daly, e s Mt Pleasant av 75 n land M L Ward 87x200.......... 4,000
Klement, Michael—E F Klement, Union.......... 1
Same——same, undivided ½ s s Fair st 119.8 e Broad st 48x164.......... 6,650
Klink, Minnie—F L Salmon, Parker st.......... 1
Kierstead, M J—J Kierstead, Montclair.......... 1
King, M L—J Tuers, Montclair.......... 1,050
Koelsch, Mary—F E Charpentier, O'Connell st.......... 1
Kopf, Joseph—J Keller, South 6th st.......... 915
Krug, John—E Beyer, Spruce st.......... 1,300
Kull, Louis—C Conradi, Clinton.......... 2,600
Lum, M L et al—J Heany, n s Camp st 100 w Mulberry st 33x108.......... 4,900
Mackin, Francis—E Tunison, 1st tract n s Branford st, 2d tract w s Sherman av.......... 5,490
Same——same, 1st tract s s Bremen st 350 e Hamburgh pl 80x100, 2d tract s s Bremen st 450 e Hamburgh pl 75x100.......... 17,880
Martin, Renne—R Barnes, East Orange.......... 1,100
Same——same, East Orange.......... 4,360
Matthews, A L—H G Cortis, Orange.......... 11,000
Matthews, J H—J L Blake, Orange.......... 1
Mayfield, Robert—R A Finn, s s Crawford st 287 e High st 50x96.......... 5,500
McEvoy, Patrick—G A Richards, Downing st.......... 1,250
McKenna, Owen—T Fitzpatrick, Chestnut st.......... 100
McMahon, Patrick—G J Cavanagh, Bergen st.......... 1
Miller, H D—W D Haws, South Orange.......... 1
Nesler, C L—O Staeger, Ferry st.......... 680
Paling, A E—G Wilkinson recvr, Caroline st.......... 1
Parker, R W—R C McManus, Franklin.......... 1,000
Parkinson, Wm—M C Marsh, Orange.......... 800
Peck, L M—J McKinley, East Orange.......... 1,225
Pfeifer, Nanette—W Nickolaus, s s Darcy st 325 e Niagara st 25x81.......... 3,000
Reynolds, John—W J Kearns, e s Madison st, 275 s Downing st, 30x95.......... 3,000
Righter, W A—M A Benjamin, Clifton av.......... 1,050
Salmon, F L—H J Klink, Parker st.......... 1
Salomon, R G—G F Reeve, Sussex av.......... 1
Same——same, East Orange.......... 5,000
Sanger, R M—S T Drake, East Orange.......... 5,000
Sauvalle, M L—W A Bode, Orange.......... 1,500
Satterthwaite, J F—J Stirrat, Franklin.......... 1,085
Sayre, F F—P E Smith, Montclair.......... 9,300
Scarlett, William—Scarlett & Scarlett, Irvington.......... 2,000
Seaver, W R—S Hartshorne, Milburn.......... 2,514
Sipp, J Wilhelm—F A Fischer, South 14th st.......... 400
Same——M Wenner, South 14th st.......... 800
Smith, C L D—A P Bannister, Hunterdon st.......... 1
Smith, George—W Smith, Ferry st.......... 1
Smith, T J—M Reid, East Orange.......... 2,950
Snyder, E H—M L Causse, South Orange.......... 1,413
Same——same, South Orange.......... 200
Stanton, Thomas—W Decker, South Orange.......... 75
Stephens, M A—A H Stephens, Belleville.......... 1,000
Stirrat, Ellenor—J Needzinski, Franklin.......... 500
Strahan, J L—A M Bingham, Orange.......... 1
Sullevain, M F—A B Wilson, West Orange.......... 325
Taylor, S C—E E Taylor, Caldwell.......... 1
The Peabody Land and Loan Co of America—M Leith, Parker st.......... 450
Thomson, William—S A McCracken, e s Lincoln av 107 s Delavan av 87x110.......... 3,000
The First Baptist Church—G F Hatt, East Orange.......... 4,000
Tichenor, J F—H W Carpenter, Clinton.......... 1
Tuers, Joseph—M L King, Montclair.......... 750
Tompkins, S L—J C Taylor, South Orange.......... 2,500
Van Name, M J B—E R Carhuff, w s Orchard st 175.5 n Pennington st 36x133.......... 9,900
Van Wagoner, Cornelius—D Grundy, Bloomfield.......... 700
Vogel, John—W Beekman, South Orange.......... 2,200
Walsh, Michael—J Byrne, e s Plane st 18 s Bleeker st 17x77.......... 3,800
Ward, J F—J C Ward, Bloomfield.......... 150
Ward, W C—H Hemsath, Clinton.......... 550
Watson, William—K F Ritchie, East Orange.......... 15,000
Weidersum, P H—R A Finn, Crawford st.......... 1
Wettyen, Conrad—S C Taylor, Caldwell.......... 3,650
Wiedenmayer, G W—A Huber, Market st.......... 1,900
Williams, B S et al—M A Howard, Orange.......... 250
Williams, J A—W R Scudder, Belleville road.......... 5,000
Williams, Augusta—E W Hine, Orange.......... 4,500
Williams, J R—L C Parkhurst, Caldwell.......... 2,500
Williams, I M—J Hoey, Montclair.......... 5,000
Wilkinson, Maurice—M A Benjamin, 2d av.......... 2,500
Same——W A Righter, Clifton av.......... 750
Young, C P—J Critchley, n s Mulberry pl 202 from Mulberry pl 26x100.......... 3,800

MORTGAGES.

Ackeman, K H—I E Woodruff, East Orange.......... 800
Almquist, Victor—A W Almquist, Bloomfield.......... 5,000
Allen, J H—M M Allen, South Orange.......... 4,000
Anderhub, Anton—J Idland, Hunterdon st.......... 5,700
Beckmann, William—J Vogel, South Orange.......... 1,700
Benjamin, M A—M Wilkinson, 2d av.......... 2,250
Blatt, J A—G H Doane, Academy st.......... 3,000
Bliss, M K—J A Lebknecher, Vanderpool st.......... 1,000
Bode, W A—M L Sauvalle, Orange.......... 1,000
Bohlen, Catharine—M Jacobus, Littleton av.......... 2,000
Brady, W T—Franklin Savings Inst, 5th av.......... 3,000
Byrne, James—North End B and L Assoc, Plane st.......... 2,800
Cadmus, M J—E J Cadmus, East Orange.......... 1,500
Chew, C P—F H Smith, Jr, Mt Pleasant av.......... 1,000
Clark, Robert—East Orange B and L Assoc, East Orange.......... 1,000
Clark, S E—E McCormick, Clinton.......... 1,400
Colyer, W W—F Bonykamper, 9th av.......... 600
Combe, Jacob—Central B and L Assoc, South 11th st.......... 1,400
Condit, O E—Security Savings Bank, East Orange.......... 3,000
Cook, H P—H J Cook, Pennington st.......... 3,500
Coppersmith, John—Phœnix B and L Assoc, Chester st.......... 500
Corrigan, J F—J Radel, Market st.......... 5,000
Cozzens, H A—J Huebel, Summer av.......... 1,000
Cramer, J M—S Johnson, Bathgate pl.......... 190
Crane, I S—Montclair B and L Assoc, Montclair.......... 6,000
Critchley, John—J A Flintoft, Mulberry pl.......... 700
Crook, W A—A M McDonald, Prince st.......... 1,000
Dalrymple, D L—People's B and L Assoc, 3d st.......... 3,000
Dawson, O B—M B Lindsley, Caldwell.......... 1,000
Demarest, H B—Knights of Pythias B and L Assoc, Cutler st.......... 2,400
Denney, J J—Enterprise, Orange.......... 2,000
Dimmick, Wm—C W English, Montclair.......... 540
Drake, S T—M G Sanger, East Orange.......... 2,000
Ebbinghausen, Augusta—G F Reeve, Spring st.......... 1,500
Einhorn, Sam'l—Excelsior B and L Assoc, Prince st.......... 5,600
Same——M Harris, Prince st.......... 600
Eisele, Charles—E F Randolph, Clifton st.......... 400
Ford, F M—Fidelity Title and Deposit Co, Berkey av.......... 7,000
Fritz, William—M Fleich, Bloomfield.......... 200
Gehring, Frederick—M Meller, Johnson st.......... 1,000
Gemperli, J G—J E Terhune, Boyd st.......... 5,500
Glass, John—M A Wharton, Fairview av.......... 2,000
Gregory, Bridget—O T Casebolt, Murray st.......... 500
Hartshorn, Stewart—W R Seavey, Milburn.......... 2,200
Hart, John—E S Hand, North 7th st.......... 2,000
Heany, John....M Holmes, Camp st.......... 1,000
Heitman, William—R F Ballantine, Springfield av.......... 9,500
Huber, August—J F Bitz, South Market st.......... 1,300
Hughes, M E—G A Richard, Charlton st.......... 200
Haira, Alfonso—Union B and L Assoc, Borden st.......... 6,500
Same——same, Boyden st.......... 2,000
Jacobus, S B—M Vanderhoof, Caldwell.......... 250
Jaques, M A—Mutual Benefit Life Ins Co, Beaver st.......... 2,500
Jennings, Oscar—J H Robinson, East Orange.......... 2,100
Kasilke, Julianna—F Millerring, Magazine st.......... 1,500
Keonoy, Michael—Essex County B and L Assoc, Bloomfield.......... 1,500
Kinney, Theodore—Eighth Ward B and L Assoc, Summer av.......... 500
Klemmert, E F—American Ins Co, Fair st.......... 4,500
La Sala, Anna—Mutual B and L Assoc, 8th av.......... 500
Same——same, 8th av.......... 2,000
Lauch, William—F B Allen exr, South 14th st.......... 250
Lehman, Leser—Mutual Benefit Life Ins Co, Broad st.......... 15,000
Mahoney, Edward—P E Smith, Orange.......... 800
Maier, C G—F Diem, Magazine st.......... 400
Same——S A Bonykamper, Magazine st.......... 1,500
Mandeville, Isaac—H M Dunn, East Orange.......... 1,000
McCracken, S A—W Thomson, Lincoln av.......... 2,400
Miller, I M—M S Ward, Mt Prospect av.......... 3,500
Mills, A D—J D Cleaver, New York av.......... 150
Morfilt, J A—Newark Fire Ins Co, East Orange.......... 2,000
Nichols, H W—E H Green, Marshall st.......... 500
Nicholaus, Wilhelmina—N Pfeifer, Darcy st.......... 800
Niedziuski, Joseph—E Stiratt, Franklin.......... 100
North, Annie—S S Edmonston, Montclair.......... 6,000
Parkhurst, W A—J R Williams, Caldwell.......... 1,500
Paul, William, Jr—Mary Paul, Wright st.......... 1,000
Peppel, M J—M Schuebel, Lang st.......... 2,000
Pfeifer, Nanette—G A Richards, Darcy st.......... 500
Raquet, Carl—C Colyer, Cottage st.......... 5,000
Same——M B Spencer, Cottage st.......... 5,000
Read, J W—R Dod, Nelson pl.......... 2,500
Reid, Mary—S E Tappen, East Orange.......... 1,600
Rudolph, G F—W R Trippe, East Orange.......... 2,000
Ryerson, A E—W L Flohn, Newark st.......... 1,000
Scudder, W R—O M Lydecker, Belleville road.......... 2,500
Same——J A Williams, Belleville av.......... 2,500
Schulz, Herman—J H Kase, Franklin st.......... 2,500
Schwing, Peter—R Frey, Ferry st.......... 1,800
Same——O McCabe, Ferry st.......... 1,000
Searle, F M—E Martin, Franklin.......... 1,500
Sharkey, James—B Sharkey, Orange.......... 1,000
Shrump, F W—A J Harrison, West Orange.......... 2,000
Silvey, J A—D P Dusenbury, High st.......... 2,000
Sipps, L A—G A Reeve et al exrs, Wright st.......... 2,000
Smith, C L D—A P Bannister, Hunterdon st.......... 300
Smith, Margaret—H F Backus, Caldwell.......... 1,100
Same——same, Caldwell.......... 600
Strachan, David—W W Blanchard, East Orange.......... 3,500
Taylor, E E—S C Taylor, Caldwell.......... 2,500
Taylor, L P—T Burnet, South Orange.......... 1,500
Tegen, Frederick—A Hupfel, Badger av.......... 7,000
Townsend, A S—M E Finnegan, East Orange.......... 800
Trusdell, J G, Jr—M Noll, Jr, Bryant st.......... 1,590
Van Nostrand, H T—J Van Nostrand, Orange.......... 4,000
Wagner, W F—The Howard Savings Inst, Orange st.......... 4,000
Walter, David—F Bonykamper, Jr, South Orange.......... 1,000
Ward, F S—F Frelinghuysen, Roseville av.......... 6,500
Weber, Sebastian—The Mercer B and L Assoc, 13th av.......... 4,500
Wickes, F R—W W Jacobus, East Orange.......... 3,200
Young, Charles—J J Weld, State st.......... 1,400

CHATTEL MORTGAGES.

Bailey, Theodore—W Allen, coaches.......... 2,400
Belzler, J—The National Cash Register Co, cash register.......... 310
Beullesa, Esther—Hamilton & Co, furniture.......... 375
Bennett, L L—T S Carley, machinery.......... 2,045
Breming, Ernest—F J Kastner, saloon.......... 1,000
Cohen, D J—C W Clayton, furniture.......... 195
Dunning, A W——same, household furniture.......... 1,400
Dussler, Samuel—L Bloomer, furniture.......... 65
Foe, W T—The Brunswick-Balke-Collender Co, pool tables.......... 325
Gaskin, Patrick—P Gaskin, Jr, bakery.......... 500
Henderson, Wm—Christian Feigenspan, saloon.......... 500
Herrmann, Karl—H Dengler, furniture.......... 98
Huhn, George—L Bloomer, furniture.......... 36
Koellhoffer, A A—R Koellhoffer, stock groceries.......... 850
Kynor, C A et al—J P Howard, stock in store.......... 400
Same——M E Kynor, stock in store.......... 400
Same——M A Cook, stock in store.......... 400
Same——A C Kynor, horses and wagons.......... 216
Law, J A—S Green, machinery.......... 1,000
McKinnon, Angus—P Ballantine & Sons, saloon.......... 300
Moran, Austin—H Koch, groceries.......... 400
Neuvohner & Freu—The Brunswick-Balke-Collender Co, billiard table.......... 190
Reinhard, G F—Wilkinson, Gaddis & Co, grocery fixtures.......... 695
Richards, M I—J Ketcham, furniture.......... 48
Rogers, M E—J M Hann, furniture.......... 65
Schneider, Leopold—F Lisiewski, saloon.......... 627
Schwager, Bernhard——same, chairs.......... 360
Schwing, Peter—R Frey, machinery.......... 700
Stine, Walter et al—E E Osborn, horses and wagons.......... 1,800
Struble, William—A H Van Horn, furniture.......... 225
Thompson, E M—The National Cash Register Co, cash register.......... 175
Tower, G W—R M Stiles, horses.......... 175
Worley, Joseph—G Krueger Brewing Co, saloon.......... 500

JUDGMENTS.

Belden, J M—I C Williams et al.......... 1,694
Dalessio, Joseph—T Wolfe.......... 195
Hedden, I C—A Lesage.......... 336
Same——W H Graef.......... 791
Hedden, S A—E P Backus.......... 164
Mennen, Gerhard—G Staehling et al.......... 274

Raphael, Morris—A Zabriski ... 915
Seabury & Johnson—W Healey ... 1,500
Stone, Thomas et al—G Green ... 1,071
Trandt, Alexander—E Gould et al ... 84

HUDSON COUNTY.

CONVEYANCES.

Anderson, Amelia—T F Wollenharpt, Kearney ... $800
Anderson, John——same, Kearney ... 2,700
Barthels, G A—C Rosin, J City ... 2,650
Barrett, M T—M Lawless, Harrison ... 850
Behm, Louisa—Ephraim De Groff, Union ... nom
Bessell, J W and Henrietta Bartlett, by sheriff—Henrietta Bartlett, J City ... 1,000
Bissell, J W—J Schasser, J City ... 1,500
Black, C C—C A King, J City ... 2,600
Boon, H J—O Schultz, West Hoboken ... nom
Bostwick, Frances M—Reni Henry, J City ... 1,500
Britten, E F—B F Butte, J City ... 4,000
Britten, B F—E F Britten, J City ... 6,000
Brown, Kate—Mary L Mitzemius, Bayonne ... 3,500
Buechler, C W—A F Buehler, Union ... 800
Burns, P J—Mary Powers, Kearney ... 100
Bruemmer, Herman—J N Braden, J City ... 3,500
Cadmus, Andrew, by special master—J Eppinger, Bayonne ... 775
Condit, Fillmore—Mary Welloughley, Kearney ... 800
Condict, J D—E H De l'Orme, J City ... 2,500
Colton, Catharine and S V A Van Horne—The West Side Connecting R R Co, J City ... 3,858
Converse, Ellen—J Nicholls, J City ... 1,200
Couper, Chas—G W Scales, J City ... 800
Cruyer, Charles—Arsenic Costa, J City ... 9,400
Currie, James—W P Stoecklein, Bayonne ... nom
Danbeck, Joseph—O Roessler, J City ... 7,850
Dixon, Hugh—Augusta Dede, Kearney ... 1,200
Donnell, Gertrude A—Anna K Fitzgerald, Bayonne ... 1,200
Dowden, Benj—Gesine Hausen, Hoboken ... 4,100
Du Puget, Marinda—W Asmack, Hoboken ... 5,000
Eberhard, F N—Susan Luxton, Hoboken ... 3,000
Same——same, Hoboken ... 1,500
Egan, Margaret—J Ambrey, J City ... 1,000
Farrant, H W—J H Farrant, Bayonne ... 3,000
Foye, A J C—H W Ehlbeck, J City ... 950
Glass, W H—Catharine Kauffman, West Hoboken ... 1,700
Godfrey, Joseph—G Terry, J City ... 900
Gray, James—Dorothea Gordon, J City ... 1,900
Haines, Mary L—H L Fritze, J City ... 900
Halsey, H F—T F O'Brien, J City ... 2,700
Hatch, A S—J P Crystal, J City ... nom
Hatch, A S by assignee—J P Crystal, J City ... 1,125
Hauck, Peter—Catharine Huck, J City ... nom
Henley, Henriette E—P F Uhlemeyer, West Hoboken ... 1,800
Henn, H S—A Morpeth, Harrison ... 450
Hillery, J M—Mary Johnston, J City ... 2,250
Hinrichsen, Lorenz—J Perry, West Hoboken ... 3,000
Hinrichsen, Marie—J Perry, West Hoboken ... nom
Hoboken Land and Impt Co—Jessie Borthwick, Hoboken ... 1,980
Same——A Seitz, Hoboken ... 11,825
Lahey, Richard—Eva Moller, J City ... 1,900
Lovejoy, Susan C—W D Peck as recvr, Harrison ... ——
Meagher, Jeremiah—Mary Mulvahill, J City ... 775
McMakin, James—P J Burns, Kearney ... nom
Miller, George—Catharine Dengler, J City ... 8,900
Mount, Samuel W—S M Odell, Jr, Bayonne ... 500
Merseles, Maggie L—E F Emmons, J City ... 750
Mulbeas, Ida—A Semrad, Jr, Hoboken ... 500
Munchert, Antoine—F Heintze, Hoboken ... 1,200
Murray, Catharine—Augusta C Knack, Union ... 2,000
Nixon, Robert—R Confessore, Harrison ... 2,000
O'Brien, James—Sarah A Murphy, West Hoboken ... nom
O'Leary, Louis by Collector—A Voorhees, Bayonne ... 100
Otto, Emma—P Meincke, J City ... 215
Reich, Emma—G Pape, Hoboken ... 4,174
Ross, J A—Augusta Tapper, Union ... nom
Rowe, H R—Gertrude A Fradeigh, Bayonne ... 575
Schultz, Otto—Johanna A Brogelmann, West Hoboken ... 6,500
Same——G Schiffer, West Hoboken ... 10,000
Same——P Siegfried, West Hoboken ... 4,800
Same——Katharine Siefred, West Hoboken ... 1,800
Same——Malentine Welzel, West Hoboken ... 700
Semrad, August, Jr—A Semrad, Sr, Hoboken ... 500
Semrad, August, Sr—A Hirchberg, Hoboken ... 500
Simonds, A B—Bridget Donnelly, Harrison ... 500
Smith, J G—D Etling, J City ... nom
Stevenson, Eugene—Sarah Havens, J City ... nom
Stoeckiein, W P—J Currie, Bayonne ... nom
Stuart, John—Caroline Dwyer, North Bergen ... 132
Same——J Blatz, North Bergen ... 132
Stuhr, Henry—J Haberstock, J City ... 446
Tapper, Augusta—J A Ross, Union ... nom
The Hoboken Land and Imp't Co—J G Zur Lage, Hoboken ... 5,523
The Provident Inst for Savings—Benj Ritter, J City ... 8,100
Thompson, Mary C—C J Baltzer, J City ... 3,200
The Kearney Land Co—T Lillis, Kearney ... 825
Union Fire Dep't, by trustee—Trustee of Weehawken Fire Dep't, Union ... nom
Voohis, Arthur—J Cassidy, Bayonne ... 600
Vreeland, C M—G F Schulze, J City ... 1,900
Vreeland, Marie A—S L Norman, Bayonne ... 900
Wahming, Karl—Theresa Reinach, West Hoboken ... 5,215
Wallace, Hiram—H L Fritze, J City ... 900
Washburn, J T—A Mackey, J City ... 3,500
Wheeler, H W—A Obringe, West Hoboken ... 700
Wilkins, Rosa—C G Rode, J City ... nom

MORTGAGES.

Ambrey, John—J Manners, J City, 1 year ... 500
Appel, C P—V Bonget, J City, 2 years ... 2,000
Baader, Mattaeus—O Schultz, West Hoboken, 5 year ... 2,000
Baltzer, C J—Madison B and L Assoc, J City, installs ... 2,600
Bartsch, Herman, North Bergen—F C Hansen, greenhouse and hot water apparatus ... 200
Becroft, W B—J Wirtz, West Hoboken, 5 years ... 2,000
Braden, J N—Communipaw B & L Assoc, J City, installs ... 2,600
Brenziew, Conrad—O Schultz, West Hoboken, installs ... 500
Brogelmann, Johanna A—O Schultz, West Hoboken, 5 years ... 2,500
Brown, Pauline C—Hoboken B & L Assoc, Hoboken, installs ... 6,000
Buckwedel, E A—G H Stueck, J City, 3 years ... 2,700
Bremer, August—Guisseppe Gruffra, Hoboken, 3 years ... 1,000
Carr, J C—New Jersey Title Guarantee and Trust Co, Hoboken, installs ... 10,000
Cash, Meyer—O Schultz, West Hoboken, installs ... 1,000
Cassidy, James—A Voorhis, Bayonne, 1 year ... 1,000
Castra, Edward—Hudson City Savings Bank, J City, 1 year ... 1,400
Centanni, Gaetano—I J Thompson, Harrison, 1 year ... 2,000
Confessore, Raffaelo—The People's B and L Assoc, Harrison, installs ... 1,500
Cooper, G W—North Jersey Land Co, Kearney, 5 years ... 2,250
Cost, Arsenio—P Schaefer, Bayonne, 1 year ... 2,500
Cunningham, Richard—The Provident Inst for Savings, J City, 1 year ... 2,000
Cutley, Mary—Hudson City M B and L Assoc, J City, installs ... 600
Dengler, Catharine—Mary M Miller, J City, 3 years ... 1,900
Depenbrock, Martin—Exrs Eliz Kesterman, J City, 3 years ... 1,500
Ettleng, David—N Campbell, J City, 5 years ... 1,000
Same——same, J City, 5 years ... 1,000
Fagin, Joseph—Harrison and Kearney B and L Assoc, Kearney, installs ... 1,300
Feistel, Fred—O Haars, Union, 3 years ... 1,500
Frank, Magdalena—Industrial Co-operative B and L Assoc, Bayonne, installs ... 5,000
Frank, Philip——same, Bayonne, installs ... 6,000
Fritze, Henry L—H Wallace, J City, 3 years ... 500
Same——Mary L Haines, J City, 1 year ... 400
Gillespie, James—Mutual Life Ins Co, J City, 1 year ... 1,000
Hansen, Georine—B Dowden, Hoboken, 5 years ... 2,300
Hardy, Horatio N—E Meail, Bayonne, 3 years ... 1,800
Heidt, H A—The Provident Inst for Savings, J City, 1 year ... 10,000
Henry, Reni, Jr—Frances M Bostwick, J City, 5 years ... 1,250
Hirchberg, Augusta—A Semrad, Jr, Hoboken, 5 years ... 6,000
Holon, Philip—L Abbett, Hoboken, 5 years ... 3,000
Kemble, J P—N C Van Buskirk, Bayonne, 1 year ... 300
Kenney, Mary L—Annie Berningham, J City, 1 year ... 728
King, McL, William—W J Daly, J City, 5 years ... 2,000
Kling, C A—Mary E Ahrens, J City, 5 years ... 1,000
Same——same, J City, installs ... 500
Knapp, Kate A—I Cadmus, Bayonne, 5 years ... 500
Lawless, Martin—M T Barrett, Harrison, 3 years ... 250
Mackey, Arthur—New Jersey Title Guarantee and Trust Co, J City, installs ... 2,000
Same——J T Washburn, J City, 1 year ... 500
McElmeel, John—Greenville B and L Assoc, Bayonne, installs ... 5,110
McEneany, Bernard—Mary E Ahrens, J City, 5 years ... 1,000
Same——C C Black, J City, installs ... 300
McKiernan, Patrick—D Stevensen, saloon ... 500
Merkl, Anna—Barbara Merkl, Union, 5 years ... 1,800
Mitzemno, Mary L—Kate Brown, Bayonne, 1 year ... 900
Mollman, Emil C—E G Burdgess, Bayonne, 3 years ... 3,000
Nichols, Jas—Ella Converse, J City, 5 years ... 950
Nimmo, James—Union B and L Assoc, J City, installs ... 2,200
Noredenholtz, Anna—Industrial M B and L Assoc, West Hoboken, installs ... 3,000
O'Brien, T F—Garfield B and B Assoc, J City, installs ... 2,400
Obringer, Adam—H W Wheeler, West Hoboken, 1 year ... 500
Odell, S M, Jr—Industrial Co-op B and L Assoc, Bayonne, installs ... 2,000
Pape, John, Union—A Wellner, furniture ... 32
Parker, Joseph, Jr—Kearney B and L Assoc, Kearney, installs ... 2,000
Pierce, Alice W—Julia Crowley, J City, 5 years ... 500
Plavano, Lena—Exrs H Von Drehle, West Hoboken, 3 years ... 2,100
Quensel, August—O Schultz, West Hoboken, installs ... 700
Reushan, Chas—Eva L Smyth, West Hoboken, 3 years ... 375
Righter, W A—Caroline Miller, West Hoboken, 5 years ... 2,500
Ritter, Benjamin—The Provident Inst for Savings, J City, 1 year ... 6,600
Rissel, C B—R Steinworth, Hoboken, 2 years ... 1,000
Roesler, Otto—J Danbeck, J City, 5 years ... 1,000
Rufle, Joseph—L Linnewerth, Union, 5 years ... 3,500
Ryan, William—Centreville B and L Assoc, Bayonne, installs ... 1,400
Same——Mary Ryan, Bayonne, installs ... 528
Savary, Eugene A—Industrial M B and L Assoc, West Hoboken, 1 year ... 1,000
Schiffer, Geo—O Schultz, West Hoboken, 5 years ... 2,500
Schoch, Gottfried—J Morgan, Union, 3 years ... 1,000
Schulze, G F—C M Vreeland, J City, 3 years ... 600
Schultz, Jacob—M B Linn, J City, 5 years ... 2,500
Schultz, Otto—Hoboken Bank for Savings, West Hoboken, 1 year ... 6,500
Same——same, West Hoboken, 2 years ... 3,500
Simonds, J C—Greenville B and L Assoc No 2, J City, installs ... 2,269
Smith, Grace—J H Cook, Kearney, 1 year ... 225
Sorenitz, Matilda—Rebecca Von Drehle, West Hoboken, 3 years ... 900
Staecklin, W T—Pamrapo B & L Assoc, Bayonne, installs ... 6,300
Steinbach, Emil—O Schultz, West Hoboken, installs ... 500
Terry, George—Amelia R Godfrey, J City, installs ... 750
The Congregation Beth Abraham Church—H Richards, Bayonne, 3 years ... 6,000
The First Presbyterian Church—New Jersey Title Guarantee and Trust Co, J City, 3 years ... 10,000
The trustees of the First German Evangelical Lutheran Church—H W Kuhl, J City, 1 year ... 1,000
Vreeland, Mary C—Suetta L Shea, J City, 2 years ... 300
Wetzel, Valentine—O Schultz, West Hoboken, installs ... 1,000
Wollenhaupt, T F—M Gorman, Kearney, 2 yrs ... 1,600

CHATTEL MORTGAGES.

Baumann, Michael, West Hoboken—J Hirstman, bakery ... 200
Bonnell, G H, J City—Gustav Dessecker, coffin wagon ... 225
Buckridge, William, J City—I Moran, horse, wagon, &c ... 85
Buess, Henry and Harry Oslerty otherwise Henry Smith, Union—C Buess, saloon fixtures ... 800
Clarke, Mary, J City—J Mullins & Co, furniture ... 216
Farrell, Bernard, J City—Bernheimer & Schmidt, saloon ... 1,000
Gallagher, D J and Sarah, J City—C Birdsall, furniture ... 124
Gloch, George, J City——same, furniture, horse, wagon, &c ... 115
Heinsdorf, E O, Hoboken—J Bauman, furniture ... 218
Jonas, Frank, J City—J Gregg, furniture ... 106
Kessler, Frederick, J City—S Kessler, butcher shop fixtures, horse, &c ... 150
Kuhn, Peter, Secaucus—E Eckert, pigs, horses, wagons, &c ... 100
Leibemann, Simon, Secaucus—M L Rickerson, cows, horses, trucks, &c ... 2,500
Link, Jeremiah—J Oreswick et al, horse, wagon ... 100
Long, John, Bayonne—F Krech, J City, saloon ... 500
Malliet, William, J City—J Palmer, jewelry business ... 320
Meyerhoff, Gustav, Hoboken—The F & M Schaefer Brewing Co, saloon ... 450
Monaco, George, J City—M Balestrom, barber shop fixtures ... 125
Montgomery, James, J City—Marvin Safe Co, safe ... 50
Muller, C J, Hoboken—J A Allers, saloon ... 900
Norton, Michael, J City—D Stevenson, saloon and grocery fixtures ... 200
O'Brien, Thomas, J City—J Mullins & Co, furniture ... 248
Powers, Harry, J City—C Birdsall, cigar store ... 130
Prasser, Bruno, J City—P Schaefer & Son, saloon fixtures and furniture ... 800
Reilly, Joseph, J City—The Bavarian Brewing Co, saloon ... 400
Rideout, H M and Addie his wife, J City—T M Moore, piano ... 410
Richetta, F H, J City—Knickerbocker Brewing Co, saloon fixtures ... 950
Rosa, Frank, Hoboken—Lembeck & Betz Eagle Brewing Co, pool table, ice box ... 440
Rubatsky, J V, J City—The Bavarian Brewing Co, saloon ... 700
Seymour, G S, Hoboken—C Birdsall, furniture ... 100
Shaffer, Charles, North Bergen—J H Berenter, pool table ... 100
Slockbower, Susan E, J City—J S Sheldon, horse, wagon, store fixtures ... 600
Smith, Jane Mrs, J City—C Birdsall, furniture ... 250
Smith, W L, West Hoboken—A B Johnston, furniture ... 46
Sutton, Lawrence, J City—The Brunswick-Balke-Collender Co, pool table ... 250
Volpe, Simon, Hoboken—J H Berenter, pool table ... 105
Wake, C A and G H, partners as Wake Bros, Bayonne—Lembeck & Betz Eagle Brewing Co, saloon ... 500
Wangersheim, George, Hoboken—A Cordts, furniture ... 700
Webber, James, J City—D Bermes, saloon fixtures ... 250

BILLS OF SALE.

Frisch, Frederick by John Graham, att'y, mortgagee, J City—M Latz, cigar store ... 1,000
Latz, Mack, J City—R Frisch, cigar store ... nom
Wahnung, Karl, West Hoboken—Theresa Reinach, saloon ... 595

JUDGMENTS.

Edwards, J W and E J, partners as Edwards Bros, and John, Thomas and Frank English, firm John English & Sons—The Cleveland Stone Co ... 679
Engel, Louis—J Scholz ... 559
Flavin, John—G W Venable et al, partners ... 95
Fuller, Edwin—H Hanks ... 124
Hage, Adolph and G T Butts—The U S Watch Co ... 248
Malliet Bros—Hodenpyl & Son ... 297
McCrea, L T and C R Kelly, partners—W N Goddard et al, partners ... 544
Same——Lesher, Whitman & Co ... 653
Same——S Stein et al ... 352
Mills, Mary C—C S Schultz ... 10,000
Moriarty, Margaret—D O'Brien ... 35

BUILDING MATERIAL MARKET.

BRICKS.—Pretty much anything that has been written about the brick market during the past two or three months will apply again this week. The arrivals to be sure have been smaller, but that is the one sole new feature, and as demand seems to have fallen off correspondingly the general conditions are practically unchanged. Of course a little stock is selling all the while as wants may arise, but buyers operating from necessity rather than choice do not furnish a healthy satisfactory inquiry, and receivers are simply compelled to wait until custom comes to them. Taking the ruling price and the season into consideration it might be expected that more or less stock would be bought to pile away, but scarcely anything of the kind is going on and business simply drags in the old listless manner. We make no change in quotations, leaving $2.25 as a top open market rate; but now that so many yards have stopped shipping, buyers insisting upon having any special or favorite maker's production would have to pay an advance on the above figure to obtain accommodation. Although there is possibly a little desultory work going on yet, it is only of a finishing up character and the season may be considered as closed. Shipments also are reported as gradually falling off from most localities, and those manufacturers who can afford it have ceased sending forward anything whatever for the present.

GLASS.—Generally the demand for window glass is lacking in volume and spirit. There has been some little gain in trade during the past week or so, but the movement is not altogether satisfactory and more or less complaint may be heard on all sides. The supply of imported stock, however, appears to be very well in hand and dealers rather more determined in taking a steady position with full rates quite generally insisted upon, the figures asked being slightly in excess of last month. On domestic glass there is considerable irregularity. Western manufacturers competing and cutting down cost accordingly. That action, however, does not prove successful in drawing much trade or inducing buyers to depart from the policy of confining investments to the immediate wants of the moment. It is estimated that present run of trade is at least 100,000 boxes less than one year ago, but that is in a measure neutralized by about a corresponding reduction in the output occasioned by the failure of natural gas in many localities and the necessary changes that must be made for the use of other combustibles. Plates are selling a little slowly, but the market kept well in hand and the old line of discounts preserved.

LATH.—Since our last report there has been a gradual recovery of tone, and the general market is now in better shape, with $2.10 inside and more money asked on the comparatively small quantities offering to arrive. The heavy supply under which the market broke some ten days or so ago, has, in disappearing, pretty well filled up the present requirements of a great many dealers, but not all, as was shown by the attendance of buyers this week, especially from out of town, who came in looking for bargains and found they had arrived just a little too late. With that development and a belief that they have encountered the last heavy arrivals for the season, receivers are inclined to feel much encouraged. Some of the Eastern ports are said to have ceased shipments entirely for the year, while the quantity to come from other localities will, it is asserted, be curtailed and rendered more costly by the scarcity of transportation facilities and advance in freight charges. Altogether, while bullish talk is always a little dubious on this market, it seems to have better foundation than ordinary at the moment.

LIME.—Supplies still appear quite plenty enough for the current run of demand, and there is not much of a market to report at the moment. Receivers tender the cargoes as they came in coastwise at about old rates, and the product of other sections is also available at previous valuation, while buyers so far as wants may exist respond, but show no anxiety and have no speculative feeling inducing them to invest against the future.

LUMBER.—It appears to be pretty well concluded among dealers that the chances for more than an ordinary trade for building consumption during balance of calendar year are meagre. There is a certain amount of work, as we have previously intimated, that will come in after awhile, but not enough to create any special animation within the city limits proper or the immediately contiguous suburban districts. A comparatively slow distribution has, therefore, come to be looked upon as a matter of course, and reports upon the condition of yard trade return a dull tone. It does not do, however, to neglect getting together assortments and supplies. On the contrary, many look upon such course as a prime necessity and action in that direction proceeds fairly well, with a feeling of reasonable confidence over investments at present, in view of a belief that unless some new and unexpected influence should in the meanwhile arise the spring trade will open well and probably reach a point of sharp animation during the summer, with all leading woods participating. Offerings of late have proven ample for current calls in the majority of cases, but were carefully made with prices sustained and here and there a hardening. The Lumber Trade Association is gradually increasing its membership and expects to have all classes of operators upon its rolls before long and to so arrange rules and regulations as to bring full and satisfactory benefits to all.

Eastern Spruce promise better, and if the market escapes another free, full arrival the chances are that values will gain somewhat. Buyers are not displaying real anxiety and a great many of them continue to talk offish, yet there has been a noticeable increase of suggestive inquiries as to when desirable cargoes may be expected forward, and it is thought that any ordinary supply can now be taken care of without much difficulty or depressing influence upon the line of values. The commission houses have gone into the association with the understanding that dealers are not to purchase direct from primary points, and if faith is kept in the matter it is likely to prove an additional supporting factor. Eastern manufacturers are still talking about an early shut down, and some mills claim to have about all the orders on their books they can attend to during balance of the sawing season. Some little Northern thirteen feet stock is offered and finds very good sale.

Piling remains about as before in price, but tends toward an increase of business, deals having already been made for planned jobs, with indications of more demand to come. Arrivals have been running comparatively light for some time past, but there is an ample supply in the basins to draw upon whenever wanted.

Hemlock remains steady in price and finds a very fair average run of trade with the ordinary line of customs, though some of the agents confess to a measure of disappointment in not obtaining a larger number of orders of late. Of Pennsylvania stock the tenders are fair and can be increased if desired, but the Northern product is still scant and the market is fortunate in not having the usual fall experience of irregular offerings from boat captains, etc., who take small ventures of their own and generally manage to undersell regular rates in order to realize promptly.

White Pine retains the promising features to which we were the first to call attention some little time ago, and the market is probably pretty solid for balance of the season. It is becoming quite evident that the medium and better qualities, if not really scarce, will be far from plenty in all sections, and local buyers are therefore inclined to place their orders as rapidly as they can reach desirable parcels adapted to their wants and promptly meet sellers upon the basis of valuation for some time prevailing. The coarser grades are called steady, but are in good supply either here or to come, and not many additions wanted.

Yellow Pine retains an appearance of quietness, and occasional tales are told of stuff available at very low rates. Leading operators, however, deny that the market is being seriously slaughtered at the moment, but on the contrary speak more encouragingly of the call for special bills and hopefully of the prospects for random. There seems to be also something moving looking to doing away with senseless competition, and the chances on the whole are favorable for the general market.

Carolina Pine retains attention from a fair amount of custom, and is proportionately as active as any lumber on the market. Buyers cannot be hurried, because they see no need of it, but when a quantity or assortment is decided upon as necessary the call is made promptly enough, and without objection to about former cost.

Harwoods meet with more or less demand for consumption, principally in the way of small lots, but nevertheless reaching a very good general total, and it costs about as much as for some time past to obtain a really desirable assortment of stock. Reasonable attention is also given to bulk lots, and dealers are adding to their accumulations from time to time. There seems to be a little difference of opinion about poplar, some operators suggesting that it may be somewhat neglected on account of the increased attention given white pine, but others contend the latter is too scarce and hardly cheap enough on the better grades to prove much of a competitor. From sources of supply advices are steady, but without special developments at the moment.

The following decision has just been given by the Board of United States General Appraisers:

W. H. Horn Cedar and Lumber Co. vs. Collector at Chicago, Ill.—"Cedar posts." May 16, 1891. The merchandise consisted of 11,658 cedar paving posts, valued at 7c. each, and 9,657 cedar fence posts, valued at 2¼ cents each. Duty was assessed upon both kinds at 20 per cent ad valorem as cedar paving posts, under paragraph 219, new Tariff. The importers claimed that the 9,657 posts, valued at 2¼ cents each, were entitled to free entry as "cedar fence posts" under paragraph 755, and were sustained.

GENERAL LUMBER NOTES.

STATE.

The Albany market is reported by the *Argus* as follows:

Generally speaking the market shows a very quiet trade, with no present indications that the remainder of the month is to bring any improvement in the demand. In medium and common grades of pine there is but very little activity. There is some demand, it is true, for box and shipping boards, but it is not so urgent that it cannot be easily satisfied. The best movement in pine at present is in the uppers, many grades of thick lumber from 1¼-inch up being in very fair request, with a very firm feeling in prices. Receipts for the past week have not been large and in nearly all cases the stocks on hand are ample. With spruce about the same conditions prevail as previously reported. There is much less than the usual supply on hand, and again there is much less than the usual demand, while receipts are light even from Canada. The northern Hudson mills are now all shut down, and but one is reported running in the Black River country. Hemlock boards are the only thing in that line which sell, and those are in fair request and stocks are light. Hardwoods continue to do about as well as anything. Good dry stock is wanted and the supply of oak, ash and cherry is none too large. Shingles are also selling fairly.

THE WEST.

The Northwestern *Lumberman*, as follows:

There is apparently more energy and life in trade on the Mississippi River than anywhere else in the country. This is because the bountiful yield of the crops has given the people of the grain growing region a purchasing power that is beginning to be felt. Besides the hitherto reported shortage of logs, and the consequent shutting down of numerous mills, has tendered to the strengthening of prices in the Mississippi Valley, and a sharper looking about for supplies than elsewhere. The full effect of a curtailment of product, that seems now a foregone conclusion, will not be felt this fall. About the outset of the new year, when holders of lumber begin to cast up their resources for the spring trade, it will be realized what the shortage is, and then an advance of prices may be looked for. As things now are the feeling in respect to values is much stronger on the river than further eastward.

The cargo movement on the great lakes is necessarily heavy at this season of the year, but there is less spirit in the market than was anticipated would arise after the crop outcome was rounded up to a full success by the security of the corn yield. Apparently, the wholesale yard dealers do not fear an advance in prices, for they are buying carefully and are manifesting no more eagerness than when the prospect for trade was doubtful. This is partly owing, no doubt, to the facts that dealers, as a rule, are not overstocked with funds, and margins between bulk stock and yard prices are so close that there is no great temptation for dealers to anticipate trade very far in advance. They are in something of a doubt as to whether they had better follow the market or stock up for an advance. We need not look for a marked activity in the cargo demand until the requirement in the country shall have reached such proportions that it will be easier to obtain a profit margin in sales than it now is.

In cargo lots at Chicago the price of short piece stuff is still $9.75 a thousand, with variations dependent on tally and the amount of long length in the cargo.

There is a frequent inquiry for good strips—all strips in fact. Boards, unless running well to stock widths, are somewhat neglected. Cargoes of No. 1 lumber containing a large percentage of thick stuff do not sell readily. Thick selects are not wanted as much as earlier in the season. A cargo lay on the market Thursday that was cut from selected logs, and was held at $15 a thousand. It was composed of inch and thicker, but nobody seemed eager to buy it.

GREAT BRITAIN.

The London *Timber Trades Journal* as follows on the Glasgow market:

Of the Quebec deals, mentioned in the Glasgow import list for the past week, nearly all have gone into consumers' hands, so that it may be said these arrivals represent no addition to yarded stock. Other imports here for the week have been light, consisting of parcels of U. S. logs and planks, staves, etc. The ss Washington City, from Newport News, has landed several consignments of walnut and whitewood logs, chiefly the latter, though for some time lately the imports of whitewood have been more than ample.

Walnut of good quality and sizes meets with ready demand. And referring to an auction sale says: There was a large attendance, but transactions were limited to a few lots, owing to the difference between the ideas of buyers and sellers as to prices. Holders are naturally very firm and look for good prices, as supplies of Quebec deals have been light and stocks now moderate, and on the other hand purchasers, though at Thursday's sale they seemed to want the goods, were not disposed to give the figures expected by the exposers.

NAILS.—The market still fails to work into really first-class shape, and there is a great deal of fault-finding to be heard all around. Wire nails sell freely enough to prevent an accumulation of stock, but cannot get a stimulus on value, and cut, though offered freely on a low basis of cost, fail to attract more than passing attention. There are thought to be very good chances for the export trade. We quote Cut at $1.50@1.60 per keg for car lots and $1.75@1.85 per keg for parcels from store, for iron, and add 5@10c. per keg for steel; Wire, $2.00@2.05 at mills, and 2.20@2.35 from store.

PAINTS, OILS, COLORS, ETC.—The market as a rule presents somewhat monotonous features, yet they are not of a discouraging character by any means, but on the contrary rather tend to make progressive the gains before advised. In short, without speculation or disposition to dip in freely, buyers are inclined to make up invoices to full extent of known or probable wants, so far as first-class standard goods are concerned and leading specialties, and manufacturers together with importers feel satisfied that no trade is being lost at the moment. Those who serve the export outlet are speaking well of present business and the indications they receive of further calls likely to follow. Supplies have been plenty enough but not up to a point of liberality calculated to induce any pressure to find a market and consequently prices generally retained a steady position. There are the usual rumors about White Lead but no official changes made in cost. Association Corroders' rates stand as follows: Lead in oil in kegs and dry lead in kegs, in lots of less than 500 lbs., 7½c. net; in lots of 500 lbs to 5 tons at one purchase, 7c.; 5 tons to 12 tons, one purchase, 5¾c.; 12 tons and over, one purchase, 6¾c.; dry white lead in bbls. ½c. per lb. less than price in kegs. Lead in oil 12½ lb. in tin pails, add 1c.; in 25 and 50 lb. tin pails, add ½c.; and in 1 to 5 lb. tin cans, assorted (100 lbs. in case) add 2½c. per lb. to keg price. Terms on lots on 500 lbs. and over, note or acceptance at sixty days, or 2½ per cent. discount will be allowed for cash paid within fifteen days of invoice date. To make either of the above required quantities any assortment of packages of white lead, red lead and litharge may be counted. The above quotations are free on board cars or boat at corroding point. Linseed Oil remains in an irregular and unsatisfactory condition, owing to antics of Western makers, but city crushers as a rule endeavor to maintain steadiness on the product of imported seed and offer carefully. We quote at general range at 35@40c. for Western, and 40@56c. for City. Spirits Turpentine finds very little demand outside the ordinary run of jobbing orders, and shows a dull market. The supply, however, appears to be well in hand and prices are sustained upon a steady basis. We quote at 37½@39c. per gallon, according to quality, delivery, etc.

TAR AND PITCH.—Buyers and sellers meet without much friction upon a basis of about former rates, and in a general way it may be called a steady market. The present movement of supplies is a little irregular, but making on the whole a seasonable average. We quote Pitch at $1.70@1.75 per bbl.; Tar at $2.15@4.50, according to quantity, quality and delivery.

MISCELLANEOUS

MISCELLANEOUS.

BLINDS

MISCELLANEOUS.

Real Estate Record and Builders' Guide.
Established March 21st 1868.
Devoted to Real Estate, Building Architecture, Household Decoration, Business and Themes of General Interest

PRICE, PER YEAR IN ADVANCE, SIX DOLLARS.

Published every Saturday.

TELEPHONE - - - - CORTLANDT 1370.

Communications should be addressed to

C. W. SWEET, 14 & 16 Vescy St.

J. T. LINDSEY, Business Manager.

VOL. XLVIII OCTOBER 17, 1891. No. 1,281

The second number of THE ARCHITECTURAL RECORD *is published to-day, and may be procured on the elevated railroad stands or at the offices of publication. Articles appear in this issue from the pens of such well-known writers on architecture as Prof. A. D. F. Hamlin, Barr Ferree and Montgomery Schuyler, the first of whom points out the "Difficulties of Modern Architecture," the second discusses the question of "What is Architecture?" and the third continues his critical account of the "Romanesque Revival in America." A paper by William J. Fryer, Jr., on "Skeleton Construction," one by Harry W. Desmond, a second part of Prof. Aitchison's lecture on "Byzantine Architecture," and the regular departments complete a very interesting number. The magazine is, as usual, profusely illustrated, and in matter and appearance is fully up to the high standard set by the first issue. Subscription for one year, one dollar; single copies, 25 cents.*

THE stock market ended a dull week with an upward turn; but the changes have been circumscribed and not particularly significant. The feeling, however, is slightly better than it was a week ago, and an exposure such as that contained in the charges against John Hoey, reflecting as they did on the management of conservative investment property produced absolutely no effect on prices. What is particularly noticeable about the railroad earnings is the way in which the income of the branch lines of the Grangers are picking up. A company like the St. Joseph & Grand Island, which last year was injured by the short crops, has during the month of September increased its gross about $20,000, and its net $25,000. But the most encouraging feature of the immediate financial situation is the renewed buying of bonds. The purchasing is of a discriminating order, and is concerned mainly with the many good investment bonds at present selling at cheap prices.

THE state of trade in the most prosperous of European countries at the present time, Great Britain, continues to be far from satisfactory. The downward movement in which the prices of nearly all commodities participated during the first half of this year has been continued throughout the third quarter. It is not a very marked downward movement, but it has been steady and almost universal. Business suffered somewhat from the financial crisis of last autumn, and in certain cases the spasmodic stimulus given to trade before the passage of the McKinley bill has been followed by a severe reaction. This is shown by every known method of testing trade. The freight receipts of the railroads are falling off, and the returns for foreign trade are by no means favorable. For the first eight months of the present year imports showed an increase over the same period last year of 2½ per cent, but on the other hand exports decreased 4¾ per cent. Most of this falling off has taken place in the last quarter. The returns for bankers' clearings in London to September 30th are less by 13 per cent than during the same interval in 1890. This, however, is testimony rather to the decrease in speculation than to the decrease in general business, so that it is well to add that the same story is told by the clearings of such centres as Manchester. In this connection it is interesting to note that the public revenue, particularly that large portion derived from the excise, is increasing, which, taken together with the increase of imports, indicates that, although trade is not as active as it was, the public have not as yet begun to moderate their expenditure. The domestic demand is just as good as ever; it is the consumption of foreign countries which is falling off. Manifestly, however, this state of things will not continue. In time the home consumption of home and foreign products will decrease also, and business will become far less prosperous than it is at present. The labor situation is already said to be very bad—large numbers of men are unemployed and wages are being cut down in every direction. The siuation may end by being far more serious than it is at present.

THE "position" which the Press of this city has taken concerning the World's Fair and Chicago is an unfortunate piece of folly. The policy they are pursuing is reflecting injuriously upon this city's and even this State's reputation for generosity, magnanimity and patriotism in the estimation of the many millions of people of this country, whose local interests are not confined to Manhattan Island. Despite the sour-grapes cry of the *Evening Post*, that after all the Fair would have been a sort of calamity to the city, the loss of the Exposition was a real misfortune to New York and a gain of incalculable value to Chicago. New York has undoubtedly lost something of its former pre-eminent and uncontested metropolitan reputation, and that which New York lost Chicago gained. Be the Exposition in the end a noteworthy success, or be it the dismal "country fair" failure which our great journalists prophecy, the Exposition is a *national* undertaking. No amount of talk can make it out to be a little "local celebration;" and it is ridiculous for New York to think that the people of the country and those abroad have valued the fact that this city was superseded by Chicago in a matter of national importance quite according to our own estimation. People have not done anything of the kind. Opinion is not altogether an unimportant factor in the affairs of men, and in this particular affair opinion is not entirely favorable to New York.

BUT the loss of the Fair is now a secondary matter. The thing is done. The lamentable part of the business is that instead of coming forward in a broad-spirited way and giving Chicago a hearty support in an undertaking in which the reputation of the whole nation is concerned, the Press of this city persists in a mean policy of disparagement. Chicago and the Exposition have been turned over to that sad crowd, the funny men, though the most comic efforts of all are the supercilious editorials which appear once in a while to keep New Yorkers informed of the great national enterprise which is progressing steadily in Illinois. The effect of this policy is not only that readers in this city are befogged, for they know no more of what has been done and is to be done in Jackson Park than they do of the local affairs of Honolulu, but it is creating a nasty spirit of resentment against New York throughout the entire West. A Western merchant said the other day: "New York has acted so meanly in this matter that I'd rather pay a little more for my goods than trade in New York." Of course statements of this kind need not be taken at their face value, and we do not give this one as more than an indication of the unfriendly spirit towards New York of which any one traveling in the West just now can find plenty of evidence. And the worst of all is the people of this city have not moved a finger to do the slightest thing that might remove or lessen the unfriendly feeling. While other cities and other States are in some way showing an interest in the Fair, New York has scarcely stirred, has not done a tithe of what London and Paris and Berlin have done—cities which our "brainy" editors have been telling us will have nothing to do with a "way-side show." First and last this Fair business has been a discreditable thing for New York.

THE report of the Manhattan Railway Company for the year ending June 30, 1891, is an impressive tribute to the growth both of the corporation and the City of New York. During the past year the elevated roads earned gross $9,959,710, against $9,388,681 for the year previous, an increase of $571,029. During the same period its increase in operating expenses was only about $150,000, so that a handsome expansion of net earnings is shown. Few corporations in the country have to spend less in order to meet their increase of traffic. During the past four years, while the gross earnings have been increasing something like $1,100,000, the operating expenses have increased only $250,000. The fixed charges have, however, undergone a very heavy augmentation during the past year—increasing about $300,000, and the capital stock is also larger by $4,000,000 than it was; consequently, although the same rate of dividend has been continued, the surplus is only $50,000 more than it was at the end of the last fiscal year. As this surplus amounts to $976,586, it will be seen that the Manhattan Company is not poor in consequence. Indeed, the way in which Mr. Gould manages some of his properties is so different from the way he manages others that an investor may well be puzzled and ask himself whether book-keeping has not a good deal to do with the apparent difference. The Missouri Pacific pays dividends which it does not earn, while the Manhattan and Western Union earn dividends which are not paid. Ostensibly these second two are among the most conservatively managed corporations in the country. In the case of the Manhattan, however, the wisdom of accumulating a surplus is very obvious. With all these damage suits hanging over the company, payments on many of which cannot be long postponed, if, indeed, they are not already being made, the management is obliged to be conservative. Never, however, was the business of any corporation safer. Notice the increase in passengers and earnings since 1878:

Year ending Sept. 30.	Passengers.	Earnings.	Year ending Sept. 30.	Passengers.	Earnings.
1878–79....	46,045,181	$3,526,825	1886–87....	158,963,"32	$8,1'2,662
1879–80....	60,831,757	4,612,976	1887–88....	171,529,789	8,673,871
1880–81....	75,585,778	5,311,076	1888–89....	179,497,433	9,080,881
1881–82....	86,361,029	5,973,633	Year ending June 30.		
1882–83....	92,124,943	6,386,506			
1883–84....	96,702,620	6,723,832	1888–90....	185,833,632	9,388,081
1884–85....	103,354,729	7,000,566	1890–91 .	196,714,199	9,959,710
1885–86....	115,109,591	7,426,216			

How many corporations in the country could show such a percentage of increase with such enormous totals. Nearly 11,000,000 more passengers were carried during the past year than during the year before. This increase has been very unevenly distributed among the different lines of the company. The 2d avenue shows a small decrease, the 3d avenue an increase of about 4,500,000, the 6th avenue an increase of 6,000,000, and the 9th avenue an increase of 1,000,000. At present the 3d avenue line carries nearly nine million more passengers than the 6th, but the latter has been gaining for years and eventually will outstrip the East Side road. It should be remembered, also, that all this increase has been made in the face of conditions that rendered traveling on the elevated lines very unpleasant. If the company was free to develop all the possible business and increase its service even these stupendous totals given could be enlarged by at least 25 per cent.

Parks and Morals.

OPEN places and small parks in the crowded districts of large cities are universally recognized as essential to the maintenance of general health. Statisticians by their figures, not less than theorists by their arguments, have so concentrated public opinion upon this point that not only do new cities expressly provide for parks in their original plans, but old ones, where the problem is one of much greater difficulty, are with scarcely an exception engaged in providing breathing places for the masses. It is, in fact, a condition, not a theory, which confronts every municipal body, and it is one that is daily growing more and more important. Yet the creating of open places is not the only question to be considered; it is necessary not only to supply fresh air, but to provide the means of enabling the people to enjoy it in a suitable manner.

Theoretically, of course, both these functions are performed by every public park, but practically, in New York at least, the public are so far the losers as to render the parks of very doubtful value.

In some respects New York has an advantage over other cities in being tolerably well supplied with parks in the older portions of the city, but this advantage is largely counteracted by the removal of the centres of population to other districts where the parks are not so numerous. The result is well known; instead of being real pleasure grounds for the people they are given over almost exclusively to the most worthless and disreputable part of the population. Battery Park, City Hall Park, Union and Madison squares and many others are the recognized resting places of the great army of hangers-on and people out of work with which New York is infested. This is especially the case with the two lower parks, the crowd of men and boys that fill their benches all day and much of the night, if not composed of the worst of the city are sufficiently bad to make them unpleasant and undesirable to well-behaved people.

The value of these places to the city at large thus becomes a serious question and one that is seldom treated with the importance it deserves. They have not yet lost their whole value as breathing places for the multitude, though they have been deprived of much of it, and are rapidly being transformed into sinks of iniquity for the dissemination of all manner of evil. Every city needs breathing spots and small parks scattered through thickly-built districts have an unquestioned hygienic value, but when they become useless as places of resort for the people and children because they are monopolized by loafers and disreputable characters, it becomes the plain duty of the authorities to take such steps as may be needful to return them to their original purposes or abolish them altogether. And in this consists the great problem of municipal parks. If they are wanting their absence is a serious detriment to the health of the city if they are present they may become sources of moral danger which may more than offset their health-giving qualities. They are most needed in the crowded portions of the city, where the population is densest and most vicious. These do not hesitate to appropriate anything intended for the general public, and thus the parks become the means of spreading all manner of evil with an ease and freedom that would be impossible without them.

The moral element, therefore, enters into the maintenance of public parks as well as the physical. No useful purpose is served by providing open places which cannot be used by those for whom they are primarily intended. The benches of the Battery and of City Hall Park can be much more profitably employed than supporting the bodies of those who now most make use of them, and these ever-present and useless members of society had much better be otherwise taken care of by the authorities if it is necessary for the city to look after them than by being permitted to be the sole beneficiaries of our expensive park system. The same condition is to be observed in other parks, though perhaps best illustrated in the lower part of the city, so that it is scarcely an exaggeration to maintain that the public parks of New York are very far from fulfilling their natural functions and conferring those benefits upon the masses for which they were designed.

The situation is one that merits careful attention on the part of the authorities. The law cannot make people moral or well-behaved, but the concentration of vice in any form is an evil that calls for public remedies. With proper and judicious police regulations it would be possible to restore the parks to their legitimate uses and very much increase their value. It is true, judiciousness is a quality not always well developed in the average policeman, but it is not wholly extinct in the average man. At all events the attempt is worth a trial, for notwithstanding the changes in the density of the population there are many thousands who would gladly make use of the lower parks if they were respectable places to visit. The city has recently expended large sums of money in acquiring lands for parks in the new districts, but unless some method is adopted to secure these to the people their history will be that of the older parks and the money worse than wasted. Tammany is not perhaps an organization given to studying questions of public morality, but the moral value of parks cannot be overlooked by the intelligent part of the community. The question may be no graver in New York than elsewhere, but it is sufficiently pressing here to call for earnest consideration and energetic reform.

Nine Months of Real Estate.

IT is encouraging to be able to report slightly better totals for the month of September than for any recent month. There is still a material decrease from the figures of 1890; but the decrease fails to reach those serious proportions which characterized it during August. In the September of the present year 702 conveyances were recorded, involving an aggregate value of $10,585,186; in the September of 1890, 757 conveyances were recorded, involving $12,987,659—a decrease of 55 or 7 per cent in number, and $2,402,473 or 19 in amount. That this is encouraging may be gathered from the fact that in August the decreases amounted to 26 per cent in number and 41 per cent in amount. It will be seen that the falling off still consists rather in the large transfers than in the small ones. The figures, however, for the whole nine months are far from stimulating. The year 1891, up to the first of October, can count 10,689 conveyances, involving $180,416,195, while, during the same period in 1890, 12,230 transfers were recorded, involving $223,326,413, a decrease of 1,541 in number and $42,909,218 in amount. The mortgage filings preserve about the same characteristics as they have exhibited for the past few months, the small change being in the direction of greater activity. The building figures for September present a marked improvement. Compared with the figures of 1890 the decrease is slight, but it should be added that the figures for 1890 show a heavy falling off from those of 1889. In September of the present year plans were filed for 185 buildings, to cost $3,122,635, against 191, to cost $3,589,725, for the same month in 1890. A monthly total, however, in the matter of buildings, means very little. One-third of the expenditure involved in the plans filed during last month is necessitated by two buildings.

NINE MONTHS OF REAL ESTATE.

NEW YORK CONVEYANCES.

	No. Conveys.	Amount.	No. Nom.	No. 23d & 24th W.	Amount.	No. Nom.
1891.						
Jan.-Aug., inc.	9,987	$169,831,027	2,854	1,826	$7,862,794	456
Sept	702	10,585,168	240	143	534,728	57
Total.......	10,689	$180,416,195	3,094	1,969	$8,397,522	513
1890.						
Jan.-Aug., inc	11,473	$210,338,754	2,869	1,888	$9,386,589	478
September....	757	12,987,659	196	157	656,135	.35
Total.......	12,230	$223,326,413	3,065	2,045	$10,242,724	513
1889						
Jan.Aug., inc.	10,658	$193,258,121	2,361	1,952	$8,626,758	479
September....	743	13,035,222	191	151	463,385	37
Total.......	11,401	$206,293,343	2,552	2,103	$9,090,138	516

MORTGAGES.

	No. Morts.	Amount.	No. at 5 p. c.	Amount.	No. at less than 5 p. c.	Amount.	No. to B. T. & I. Cos.	Amount.
1891.								
Jan.-Aug., inc.	10,070	$122,032,618	5,119	$62,926,045	888	$40,020,089	1,457	$36,740,886
September....	823	8,394,408	383	4,568,430	38	726,350	117	2,306,400
Total.......	10,893	$130,427,021	5,502	$67,494,475	926	$40,746,439	1,574	$39,047,286
1890.								
Jan.-Aug., inc.	10,640	$183,297,308	5,124	$75,881,657	4,220	$65,261,680	1,541	$84,015,416
September....	782	16,781,391	379	10,042,327	73	1,740,656	153	10,364,200
Total.......	11,422	$200,078,699	5,503	$85,923,984	1,293	$67,002,336	1,694	$94,379,616

1889.								
Jan.-Aug., inc.	9,874	$124,975,620	4,617	$57,617,474	1,231	$26,107,714	1,369	$32,568,968
September....	752	8,916,809	369	3,852,540	96	1,976,488	121	3,117,550
Total......	10,626	$133,892,429	4,986	$61,470,014	1,327	$28,084,202	1,490	$35,686,518

Includes mortgage given in February, 1890, by the Manhattan and Metropolitan Elevated Railway Companies on real and personal property to The Central Trust Co. for $40,000,000; mort. given in March, 1890, by the Edison Illuminating Co. to The Central Trust Co. for $5,000,000; mort. given in August, 1890, by the Mount Morris Electric Light Co. to the Central Trust Co. for $4,000,000; morts. given in September by the United States Electric Light and Power Co. to the Union Trust Co. for $5,000,000, and the Standard Gas Light Co. to The Mercantile Trust Co. for $1,500,000.

NEW YORK BUILDINGS PROJECTED DURING NINE MONTHS, GIVEN BY DISTRICTS.

	1889. Jan. to Sept., inc.	1890. Jan. to Sept., inc.	1891. Jan. to Sept., inc.
Total No. of plans filed	1,644	1,636	1,278
Total No. of buildings projected	2,988	2,835	2,139
Estimated cost	$56,644,212	$60,902,126	$43,966,569
No south of 14th st	389	358	313
Cost	$12,812,895	$15,296,700	$11,358,835
No. bet 14th and 59th sts	255	331	235
Cost	$7,308,375	$13,581,470	$7,750,820
No. bet 59th and 125th sts, east of 5th av	491	465	294
Cost	$7,817,830	$8,424,480	$6,795,918
No bet 59th and 125th sts, west of 8th av	726	651	494
Cost	$17,553,550	$14,600,850	$11,722,180
No. bet 110th and 125th sts, 5th and 8th avs	84	103	42
Cost	$1,947,850	$2,044,625	$903,000
No. north of 125th st	360	286	187
Cost	$5,525,895	$3,497,908	$2,499,693
No. 23d and 24th Wards	687	641	574
Cost	$3,880,717	$3,456,593	$2,936,088

NEW YORK BUILDINGS PROJECTED DURING SEPTEMBER, GIVEN BY DISTRICTS.

	1889. September.	1890. September.	1891. September.
Total No. of buildings projected	211	191	185
Estimated cost	$4,826,540	$3,589,725	$3,122,635
No. south of 14th st	22	16	16
Cost	$437,000	$625,500	$398,800
No. bet 14th and 59th sts	11	20	8
Cost	$1,827,000	$1,342,000	$360,900
No. bet 59th and 125th sts, east of 5th av.	18	20	15
Cost	$505,750	$261,425	$994,350
No. bet 59th and 125th sts, west of 8th av.	63	32	36
Cost	$1,800,000	$705,550	$571,500
No. bet 110th and 125th sts, 5th and 8th avs	13	6	2
Cost	$204,000	$84,000	$60,000
No. north of 125th st	16	24	41
Cost	$212,000	$293,900	$463,100
No. 23d and 24th Wards	68	73	67
Cost	$340,790	$277,350	$273,985

	1889 No. b'ld'gs.	1889 Cost.	1890 No. b'ld'gs.	1890 Cost.	1891 No. b'ld'gs.	1891 Cost.
Jan.-Aug., inc.	2,777	$51,817,672	2,644	$57,312,401	1,954	$40,843,934
September	211	4,826,540	191	3,589,725	185	3,122,635
Total	2,988	$56,644,212	2,835	$60,902,126	2,139	$43,966,569

FOR THE MONTH OF SEPTEMBER, 1891, CLASSIFIED.

	Flats and Tenem'ts No.	Flats and Tenem'ts Cost.	Private Dwell'gs No.	Private Dwell'gs Cost.	Hotels, Stores, Churches, Office Build'gs, &c. No.	Hotels, Stores, Churches, Office Build'gs, &c. Cost.	Miscellaneous, Stables, Shops, &c. No.	Miscellaneous, Stables, Shops, &c. Cost.
South of 14th st	9	$185,000	..	....	4	$162,000	3	$51,800
Bet 14th and 59th sts	2	41,000	..	....	1	$300,000	5	19,900
Bet 59th and 125th sts, east of 5th av.	10	179,000	2	$61,000	1	750,000	2	4,350
Bet 59th and 125th sts, west of 8th av	3	60,000	29	473,500	.	....	4	38,000
Bet 110th and 125th sts, 5th & 8th avs	2	60,000	..	....	..	....	..	....
North of 125th st	4	68,000	36	390,100	..	....	1	5,000
23d & 24th Wards	..	..	46	184,710	..	....	21	89,275
Total for Sept. 1891	30	$593,000	113	$1,109,310	6	$1,212,000	36	$208,325
Total for Sept, 1890	55	$1,208,000	87	$535,450	11	$1,571,500	38	$254,775

THE COSTLIEST BUILDINGS FILED DURING SEPTEMBER, 1891.

Location and Character.	Owners.	Cost.
William st, No. 79, eight-story office building.	J. M. Thomas	$90,000
Rivery av, n w cor 150th st, three-story factor	L. H. Mace	60,000
5th av, No. 852, four and five-story dwelling	H. O. Havemeyer	60,000
5th av, n e cor 60th st, four-story club-house	The Metropolitan Club.	750,000
7th av, n w cor 56th st, seven-story hotel (substituted for plan filed in June last)	Wm. Noble	$3:0,000
Five buildings, to cost		$1,250,000

FLATS AND DWELLINGS IN ROWS.

70th st, n s, 325 e 9th av, five four-story dwellings	J. Ruddell	$100,000
76th st, n s, 151 w West End av, four five-story dwellings	Reuben Skinner	72,000
91st st, n s, 100 e Amsterdam av, six three-story dwellings	J. Brown	90,000
121st st, s s, 80 w Manhattan av, eleven three-story dwellings	A. A. Teets	137,500
163d st, s s, bet Tinton and Forest avs, sixteen three-and-a-half-story dwellings	J. W. Decker	60,800
2d av, n w cor 101st st, four five-story flats	Jessie Marks, Roselle, N. J.	80,000
7th av, s w cor 138th st, twenty-nine three-story dwellings	D. H. King, Jr.	348,000
Seventy-five buildings, to cost		$888,300

KINGS COUNTY CONVEYANCES.

	1890. Number.	1890. Am't involved.	1890. Nom.	1891. Number.	1891. Am't involved.	1891. Nom.
January	1,342	$5,816,826	341	1,429	*$7,878,196	412
February	1,293	6,137,587	344	1,219	4,704,985	390
March	1,685	7,608,870	423	1,602	6,245,195	475
April	2,176	11,587,703	490	1,998	9,042,227	490
May	1,882	9,317,270	437	1,802	7,230,963	482
June	1,515	5,920,270	357	1,731	6,233,014	406
July	1,738	7,729,816	351	1,680	6,020,359	402
August	1,274	4,606,970	322	1,238	4,251,552	327
September	1,224	4,519,766	305	1,324	5,004,534	345
Total	14,129	$62,335,084	3,870	14,023	$56,611,025	3,728

KINGS COUNTY MORTGAGES.

	1890. No.	1890. Am't involved.	1890. No. at 5 per cent. or less.	1890. Am't involved.	1891. No.	1891. Am't involved.	1891. No. at 5 per cent. or less.	1891. Am't involved.
Jan.	1,264	$4,994,740	793	$3,455,240	1,182	†$14,007,748	620	$2,417,480
Feb.	960	4,117,787	553	2,659,475	1,082	4,123,056	615	2,802,984
March	1,272	5,648,729	780	3,916,105	1,229	5,147,777	662	3,072,480
April	1,679	6,575,719	1,067	4,586,146	1,581	6,871,680	917	4,16?,699
May	1,516	6,042,149	927	4,233,752	1,272	5,059,644	680	2,941,830
June	1,322	5,488,301	772	3,987,174	1,460	5,664,829	792	3,727,914
July	1,446	5,785,961	901	3,879,466	1,468	5,050,339	777	3,014,425
August	1,091	4,576,404	622	3,076,165	1,057	3,438,058	568	2,160,599
Sept.	1,067	4,091,156	611	2,639,688	1,090	3,623,546	583	1,972,690
Total	11,617	$47,315,985	7,026	$32,338,211	11,421	$52,971,672	6,184	$26,276,100

*Includes seven deeds at a total of $2,560,000 given by the various sugar companies in Brooklyn to The American Sugar Refining Co. of New Jersey.

†Includes mortgage given by The American Sugar Refining Co. of New Jersey to The Central Trust Co. of New York, for $10,000,000.

KINGS COUNTY PROJECTED BUILDINGS.

	1890. Total No. b'gs.	1890. No. of brk, stone and iron b'gs.	1890. No. of frame b'gs.	1891. Total No. b'gs.	1891. No. of brk, stone and iron b'gs.	1891. No. of frame b'gs.	1890. Cost.	1891. Cost.
Jan	344	108	236	268	61	207	$1,407,615	$1,108,295
Feb.	388	158	230	350	160	190	1,816,425	1,545,895
March	484	215	269	427	185	242	2,829,661	2,170,100
April	525	249	276	563	305	258	2,406,950	3,177,972
May	426	193	233	427	205	222	2,469,985	2,455,380
June	547	274	273	299	122	177	2,632,739	1,873,275
July	369	133	236	270	94	176	2,653,540	1,185,580
August	347	136	211	308	102	206	1,747,245	1,344,700
Sept.	323	106	217	408	145	263	1,553,265	2,324,112
Total	3,753	1,572	2,181	3,320	1,379	1,941	$19,517,375	$17,685,179

IN attempting to re-plot the 23d and 24th Wards, Commissioner Heintz is accomplishing a work of the greatest importance to the future of this city, and yet the public discussion of the matter has practically amounted to nothing. The immediate wishes and interests of the property-owners, brokers and builders of the district have been alone consulted; those of the rest of the city will, according to all accounts, be totally disregarded. It is comforting to see that at all events one daily journal has seen fit to take the matter up. The *Times* has very properly deplored the adoption of a system of plotting on the North Side similar to that used south of the Harlem. New York City for every æsthetic purpose and for the convenience of living in is one of the worst planned cities in the world; and if the North Side is to be made as ugly, those who are responsible for the step ought to be very certain that the conditions which partially justify the uniformity south of the Harlem are going to prevail north of that river. Manhattan Island has of necessity been given over to 25x100 lots. As in other cities these lots might have been grouped more effectively for architectural purposes and arranged more conveniently for domestic purposes—that is, the street system might have been more organic and less mechanical, while the running of an alleyway between the back yards of two rows of houses would have been a decided convenience. But against the practice of uniform sub-divisions, it would have been and is futile to protest. The pressure of population on space has rendered them necessary. Furthermore, in a city wherein the pressure is as severe as it is in New York, it may be doubted whether any arrangement of the street system would have helped to make the larger part of the city any more attractive than it is; only in those quarters where the well-to-do live, work or play, would the difference have been noticeable. It is a very questionable matter, however, whether the same pressure of population on space will exist in the 23d and 24th Wards as in the lower portions of the city. On Manhattan Island itself people are forced to live; they have not the time to make the necessary journey from a suburb or they cannot afford to do so. But the same circumstances will not obtain north of the Harlem. As soon as the island is left population will distribute, as indeed it has already begun to distribute, in every direction instead of only one direction. Consequently there will be a similar distribution of pressure, and a similar distribution of value, an enlargement of space which a man of average means will have to live on, and an absence of those conditions which partially justify a rigidly mechanical and uniform street system. Commissioner Heintz would do well to consider whether he is wise in giving way entirely to the 25x100 lot man. In the northern part of the district that pushing and necessary person may have no place.

The Report at Last.

The Rapid Transit Commission has at last reached a final and definite conclusion on the important question relating to the plans of construction, and has announced as a positive fact that the formal report with elaborate diagrams will be presented to the Board of Aldermen on Tuesday.

The report, the commissioners say, will be as elaborate and complete as anything short of working drawings and specifications can be, and the illustrations will be numerous and complete. They are being guarded from the enterprising newspaper reporters with anxious concern, lest the public should be made acquainted with their contents before they are formally reported to the Board of Aldermen.

From such casual hints and expressions as have been made by the commissioners, however, the fact is apparent that the Worthen plan for a shallow tunnel road, with all four tracks on the same level, with a two-track loop around the City Hall square and a two-track extension from the City Hall square to Bowling Green, and a single-track loop through State and Whitehall streets, will be the plan reported. The commission, having thoroughly investigated the merits of the deep tunnel, or so-called Greathead system, has found sufficient reasons for preferring the shallow tunnel system. One of the principal of these reasons is that the road will have to compete with the cable and elevated roads for the short distance traffic, which is the cream of the intermural transit business, and with a deep tunnel requiring elevators to get travelers to and from the station platforms it would be at a great disadvantage. Most of the other agreeable features claimed for the Greathead system, it is declared by Engineer Wm. Barclay Parsons, will be found in the plans which the commission has adopted.

North Side Improvements.

A very important part of the work cut out for the Commissioner of Street Improvements for the 23d and 24th Wards, by the act of the Legislature creating that office, is that which requires him, within two years from next New Years, to prepare new maps of the entire district. Commissioner Heintz inherited from the Park Board, as an unfinished work, the requirement to prepare tax maps of the district, in order to complete the records of the Tax Department; but the new maps of the district required by the act of 1890 are quite different from the tax maps.

The tax maps, upon which Chief Engineer Risse and his assistants are engaged, require only the bringing down to date of the maps of the district as it was, when annexed to the city—a mere matter of skillful draughting, with the maps in the records at White Plains as a basis. But the new maps required by the act of 1890 are designed to serve as the land maps of the district, and in this respect to supersede all previous records.

Their preparation would not involve so great labor and expense but for the fact that as a preliminary work the greater part of the entire north side will first have to be resurveyed and monumented and replotted. It was rather an attractive scheme of the Park Department, which first had jurisdiction of the matter, to lay out a large part of the north side in the semblance of a park, with winding streets and avenues, marking off villa sites and irregular-shaped plots, which in its prophetic eye should become the sites for the residences of the millionaires of the business end of Manhattan Island. It was believed, when this scheme was adopted, that within the portions of the district so plotted there would never be any other species of building constructed than the villa homestead of the wealthy New Yorker.

But the scheme, attractive as it was in the abstract, has been found impracticable. Owners of the property in question have found that the demand for villa sites was exceedingly limited. At the prices at which the property was held there was small prospect of the owners ever realizing, while it was offered in these villa plots. There was opportunity for trading in smaller parcels—building sites, plots for rows of city houses, and for business blocks, but for no villa sites. Then, too, the winding streets and avenues did not prove as convenient in practice as they had seemed attractive on paper. It was found that they would increase distances, and would vastly increase the cost of street improvements.

Commissioner Heintz has therefore undertaken the replotting of the entire district. Owners of the property involved, very soon after his election, gave him to understand that they wanted to be able to sub-divide their land into parcels of a size and shape assimilating with city blocks and lots and capable of the same class of improvements. The prospect of direct rapid transit connection with the lower end of the city has induced inquiries by speculative builders, whose expressed intention it is to extend their operations into these districts as soon as the "first low wash of the waves where soon shall roll a human sea" is heard beating upon their frontiers. Accordingly, the villa style of improvement has been abandoned as a "barren ideality," and the style of improvement characteristic of the rest of the city is being provided for, as far as public improvement, street and avenue lines and the reshaping of the blocks can provide for them.

In order to prepare for the remapping of the district, therefore, the replotting of all the district north of the Kingsbridge road in the 24th Ward; all that part of the north side west of the Harlem Railroad, including West Morrisania, Highbridge, Mt. Hope, South Fordham and Fordham Heights; and on the east side of the 23d Ward, the Hunt's Point District, is to be replotted. Out of the meagre appropriation allowed him by the Board of Estimate and Apportionment last year Commissioner Heintz has already surveyed the Hunt's Point district, and made the preliminary maps. But in discussion with some of the property-owners it has been recommended to him to alter the plan of the redistricting in a significant manner. As originally laid out, Edgewater avenue skirts the Bronx River and the Dutch Kills in the same manner in which West and South streets skirt the North and East Rivers. But the property-owners, profiting by the ill experience of New York, have asked to have Edgewater avenue located 150 feet back from the water front, so that there shall be a strip of land 150 feet wide extending from the avenue down to the water front, capable of improvement for commercial purposes, by the erection of warehouses and sheltered wharves where merchandise can be unloaded direct from vessels without extra cartage—an expensive item—to get it under shelter. To this the commissioner has consented, and the maps will be altered accordingly.

A meeting of interested property-owners has been called for the 19th instant, at 10 o'clock, at Commissioner Heintz's offices, 2622 3d avenue, to examine the changes and revision of the maps thus far outlined as follows: (1) Change of grade of Willow avenue, from Long Island Sound to East 138th street. (2) Change of location of Dawson street, west of Prospect avenue and the discontinuance of Hewitt place, from Robbins avenue and Westchester avenue to Prospect avenue. (3) The discontinuance of the unnamed avenue between Brook and 3d avenues along the west side of the Port Morris Railroad, and the widening of German place, between East 156th street and John street. (4) A new sewerage plan for district "33 U," bound by Brook, Webster, Pelham, 3d and Washington avenues and 165th street. (5) A new sewerage plan for district "37 A," bound between 144th street, the Harlem River, River avenue, 161st street, Walton avenue, 165th street and Mott avenue. (6) A new sewerage plan for district "33 V," bound by 160th street, Morris avenue, 164th and 165th streets and Railroad avenue West. All of these changes of the grades and lines of streets and of the drainage of the streets are made necessary by the depression of the tracks of the Harlem and Port Morris Railroads. Since in nearly every instance they will have some effect upon the pocket-books of the adjoining property-owners, there will probably be no lack of interest in the meeting.

Commissioner Heintz expects to have three sections of the redistricting maps ready for submission to the Board of Street Opening and Improvement for its approval by the 1st of January, showing the changes of street lines and grades. The profile maps will show the present grades and the grades as they will be when the depression of the tracks of the Port Morris Railroad is completed. Every street will cross the railroad either above or below the tracks. There are to be no railroad crossings of the streets at grade. All the depression of the tracks west of Westchester avenue has been completed, and the plans are ready for the work east of Westchester avenue.

Notice was sent to Commissioner Heintz last week of the confirmation by the Supreme Court of the report of the commissioners opening Melrose avenue, from 149th to 163th street, through the already densely-populated Melrose district. This is one of the most important improvements in the district. It has been long and anxiously awaited, and now that it is definitely settled, will lead to an extensive system of much-needed street improvements. Plans are being prepared for the sewering of Melrose, Courtlandt and Railroad avenue East, and for all the side streets between 154th and 161st streets inclusive. Work will be commenced on this system as soon this fall as the contracts can be advertised and let. The grading and paving of all the streets mentioned will follow immediately upon the sewering. Work was begun last week upon the pavement of Morris avenue, from 139th to 152d street.

Before the Melrose avenue improvement will begin, however, there will be an interesting sale of some sixty frame cottages and dwelling houses, now located on property taken for the street, which have become the property of the city under the condemnation proceedings. Commissioner Heintz will soon advertise them, and they will be sold at auction, for spot cash, and must be removed within thirty days after the sale.

Bids were opened on the 15th instant for three improvements—the regulating, grading, curbing, flagging and constructing of crosswalks in 138th street, from the Southern Boulevard to a point 330 feet east of Locust avenue; regulating and paving with granite blocks 149th street, from the Central Railroad to Mott avenue: and sewering 170th street, from 3d to Washington avenue. Including these, there will have been awarded since January 1 last fifty-nine contracts for street improvements. Besides these the commissioner has in the hands of the printer the specifications for eleven other contracts, the most important of which are the regulating, grading, curbing and flagging of Burnside avenue, over two miles in length, and the regulating, grading, curbing and flagging of 184th street, from Jerome to Webster avenue.

Since August 27th there have been awarded twelve contracts, aggregating in amount over $101,000, as follows:

No. 1. For furnishing and delivering where required, broken trap-rock stone and trap-rock screenings and Tompkins Cove blue stone, along certain roads, avenues and streets in the 23d and 24th Wards, in the city of New York	$26,010 00
No. 2. For constructing sewer and appurtenances in 132d street, from Brook avenue to summit west of Trinity avenue, and branch in St Ann's avenue, between 132d street and Southern Boulevard	6,456 25
No. 3. For regulating, grading, setting curb-stones, flagging the sidewalks and laying crosswalks in College avenue, between Morris avenue and 146th street	2,761 43
No. 4. For readjusting curb-stone and laying crosswalks in and paving with trap block pavement the roadway of 153d street, between 3d and Courtlandt avenues	5,164 63
No. 5. For constructing sewer and appurtenances in Wales avenue, from summit south of 149th to Kelly street, and in Kelly street easterly to existing sewer	9,059 80
No. 6. For regulating, grading, settting curb-stones, flagging the sidewalks and laying crosswalks in 173d street, between 3d avenue and Vanderbilt avenue, East	5,691 50
No. 7. For regulating, grading, setting curb-stones, flagging the sidewalks and laying crosswalks in 163d street, between Brook and 3d avenues	5,123 00
No. 8. For regulating, paving with trap block pavement and laying crosswalks on 134th street, from the easterly crosswalk of Brook avenue to the westerly crosswalk of the Southern Boulevard	8,153 40
No. 9. For regulating and paving with trap block pavement the roadway of 135th street, and laying crosswalks, between the easterly crosswalk of Brook avenue and the westerly crosswalk of Cypress avenue	8,722 00
No. 10. For regulating, grading, setting curb-stones, flagging the sidewalks and laying crosswalks in and paving with granite block pavement the roadway of 143d street, between 3d avenue and 144th street	6,951 75
No. 11. For regulating, grading, curbing and flagging 173d street, between the Harlem Railroad and Weeks street	16,578 90
No. 12. For constructing a sewer and appurtenances in the south side of the Southern Boulevard, from a point west of Willis avenue to the eminence east of Willis avenue	2,888 50

An important feature of the redistricting plan contemplated by Commissioner Heintz is the widening of the Southern Boulevard throughout its entire length by taking 30 feet off the blocks on the south and east sides of the Boulevard.

Obituary.

NATHANIEL PLATT BAILEY.

In the decease of Nathaniel P. Bailey the real estate community loses one of the largest owners of vacant property in the metropolis.

Mr. Bailey died at his country house, "The King's Redoubt," Fordham Heights, on Monday last. In this place he had lived for over forty years, the house being situated in the midst of about 100 acres of ground, purchased by him nearly half a century ago.

Mr. Bailey was for many years a member of the Real Estate Exchange, the Union and Union League Clubs, and the St. Nicholas Club, of which he was once president. He was the senior-governor of the Society of the New York Hospital, and at the time of his death was vice-president of that institution.

The deceased, who was eighty-two years of age, was the son of Judge William Bailey, one of the earliest settlers of Plattsburg, N. Y., and a brother of the late Rear Admiral Theodorus Bailey. He was related to the Lorillard, Edgar, Strong, Morris, Cammann and other New York families, and was an uncle of Hermann H. Cammann, ex-president of the Real Estate Exchange.

The funeral services took place on Thursday morning at Trinity Chapel, of which the deceased was for many years a vestryman. The Union League Club and other organizations of which the deceased was a member were represented, and members of many of the oldest families in New York and vicinity were present.

Cumulative Voting Abolished.

The following circular has been forwarded to members of the Real Estate Exchange:

NEW YORK, October 16, 1891.

To the Stockholders in the Real Estate Exchange and Auction Room (Limited):

GENTLEMEN—The Business Corporation Act of 1875, under which this Exchange was registered, having been amended, the next election will take place under the new law, under which votes cannot be cumulated on any one candidate. The law also forbids the purchase or sale of proxies, or any voting by persons who are not bona fide owners of the stock on which they claim to vote. Nor can any stockholder vote on stock that has not been registered in his name thirty days prior to the date of the meeting.

The directors desire that you be notified in due time of this alteration of the law which came into force May 1, 1891. GEO. R. READ, President.

The effect of the measure is to abolish the system of cumulative voting and to give each member one vote for every director at an election of officers instead of ten.

About the Projected Broadway Theatres.

It has been currently reported during the week that Abbey, Schoeffel & Grau would build a theatre of their own at the northeast corner of 38th street and Broadway. In the daily newspaper reports it was stated that the firm would not lease the proposed theatre, but would purchase the site and improve it themselves. Inquiry at the offices of Abbey, Schoeffel & Grau, yesterday morning, elicited the information that the firm had not even begun negotiations for the purchase of a site. It was said that they had looked at several available Broadway corners, but that as yet absolutely nothing had been done looking to the purchase of any of them or the erection of a theatre. Mr. Abbey had just returned from Chicago, where he had been since March, and Mr. Grau is still in Paris, and it is not likely that anything definite will be done until the firm is able to come together. It is hardly likely anyhow that the corner of 38th street and Broadway would be improved, except by the lessees of the ground, for the fee is owned by Ogden Goelet, who is not given to selling his holdings In connection with this report, a remark made by a member of the firm of J. B. McElfatrick & Sons, the theatre architects, to a RECORD AND GUIDE reporter, may be of interest. It was stated by this gentleman that he was pretty certain that at least two theatres would be built on Broadway this fall, between 30th and 40th streets. No further particulars in regard to them could be obtained.

The Lumber Dealers' Association.

ANNUAL MEETING ON WEDNESDAY.

The annual meeting of the New York Lumber Trade Association took place on Wednesday at 3 P. M. There was an unusually large attendance of members from the Metropolis and vicinity.

Several amendments were made to the by-laws, one being that the present number of trustees, instead of being elected for one year should be increased to thirty and be elected as follows: Ten for one year, ten for two years and ten for three years.

The treasurer's report was read and showed a balance of about $3,500. The membership is now about 140, about double what it was last year, the increase being due to the co-operation engendered during the recent labor troubles in the lumber yards.

The officers elected are as follows:

One-Year Term: For President—Mr. Charles H. Willson; for First Vice-President—Mr. James H. Pittinger; for Second Vice-President—Mr. I. P. Vanderbeek; for Treasurer—Mr. Charles E. Pell; for Secretary—Mr. E. Hudson Ogden; for Trustees—Messrs. John F. Steeves, Abraham Steers, W. W. Kenyon, John Ireland, Russel Johnson, Charles K. Sparks, Charles L. Bucki, John H. Voorhees, Thomas Williams and Charles A. Meigs.

Two-Year Term: Trustees—David M. Ressiguie, J. T. E. Litchfield, C. K. Buckley, W. H. Simonson, Alfd. W. Booth, H. E. Stevens, Geo. Hagemeyer, Jr., Geo. Wanmaker, E. M. Price and Lowell Talbot.

Three-Year Term: Trustees—Sylvester Ross, John S. Loomis, Louis Bossert, Walter G. Schuyler, E. W. McClave, D. J. Carroll, Thos. T. Reid, Louis C. Small, H. D. Steers and W. E. Marsh.

A New Hotel for the West Side.

The rumor in last week's issue of THE RECORD AND GUIDE to the effect that B. G. Oppenheim, the lawyer, who purchased the northeast corner of West End avenue and 86th street, would improve the same by the erection of a thirteen-story fire-proof hotel turns out to be correct. Mr. Oppenheim, when seen in relation to the matter, said that he was organizing a stock company to carry out the project, but that he could give none of the names of those interested at the present time. The hotel will cost, it is estimated, $1,000,000. It will have a front of brick, stone and terra cotta, and will be absolutely fire-proof. There will be four passenger elevators in the building, and bachelors suites of two and three rooms, as well as family suites of fifteen rooms and less. There will be Turkish and Russian, as well as plunge baths on the top floor. Both public and private dining-rooms are to be provided for, and altogether the hotel will contain every conceivable improvement. In the rear of the hotel the management intends to build stables for the use of the occupants of the house. No architect has yet been selected.

Colonial Club.

The new building for the Colonial Club on the southwest corner of 72d street and the Boulevard is fast approaching completion. The first social meeting of members for the season takes place this evening at the present home of the club, No. 127 West 72d street.

Our Letter Bag.

Editor RECORD AND GUIDE:

On examining title it appears that the lot in question, located in Westchester County, was sold for taxes some years ago to a stranger, A, who in due time received his lease for 1,000 years. At the tax sale the following year A again bought it and received a second lease, same term. The taxes being subsequently unpaid the lot was sold again some years later and bought by B, who in due time received his lease for 1,000 years. A cannot be found. B is friendly to the owner of the fee and will do anything to aid him to make the title marketable. What would you advise?

A SUBSCRIBER.

[In the case of sales for unpaid taxes, if the requirements of the law were complied with in the levying of the tax, etc., and in the sale, the lease on the last sale would be the better title; in other words, B, if his lease be valid, would be entitled to the possession of the property for the term of 1,000 years granted to him, as against A, and as such 1,000 years will expire after each of the terms granted to A, the effect of the lease to B, if valid, is practically to cut off A, and, therefore, if the owner obtain an assignment of the lease B, taking it so as not to merge the lease in the fee, he can, if that lease be valid, successfully defend against any effort made to obtain possession under either of the leases to A. This, however would not clear the record title of the leases to it. If the owner investigate the tax sales on which leases were given to A he may find enough to justify proceedings to set aside those leases. In the absence of an assignment from A of his leases, or a quit claim from him, or a decree of the court setting aside those sales and the leases granted to him thereon, we think it best to obtain an assignment of B's tax lease, but so as not to merge in the fee, and thus, while not relieving the title of the tax leases to A, practically cutting off those leases by obtaining a title which, if the proceedings and tax sale were regular, will give to the owner a title paramount to the title under A's lease for a term expiring beyond the terms in those leases.—LAW ED.]

Editor RECORD AND GUIDE:

Would you kindly reply to the following in your next issue:

Should a person renting a floor in a flat for a definite period and in the meantime be subject to the following annoyances, such as the parties on the floor above shaking their mats from their windows over our freshly-washed clothes and violently closing our windows in the light shaft by means of a broom and numerous other annoyances of the same character; and should these acts be repeated could the landlord hold said tenant for the unexpired term in case he should at any time vacate, in view of these facts as above stated?

TENANT.

[The acts complained of by "Tenant" were committed by another tenant occupying apartments in the house. The landlord does not warrant against such acts, nor is he responsible for them. They constitute a trespass, and being committed by such other tenant, and for which an action can be brought, and which if persisted in could be enjoined.

The landlord would be entitled to his rent notwithstanding such annoyances.—LAW ED.]

Visiting the Camp Cement Works.

This past week a large party of architects, builders and others interested in building and building materials visited the Portland and Rosendale Cement Works in the Lehigh Valley. They were guests of Hugh N. Camp & Sons, of this city, and started on Tuesday, reaching Allentown, Pa., in time for a hearty dinner, which was enjoyed by all. A thorough inspection was made of the Allen Cement Works owned and operated by Hugh N. Camp & Sons, and after lunch the party were driven to the Coplay Cement Mill, one of the largest Portland mills in this country. But a few years ago American Portland Cement was unheard of, and the little that was manufactured previous to 1885 was used with the greatest of care and precaution by a few builders only. A glance at immense mills, high ledges of rock and acres of quarry soon satisfied the party that things are different. American Portland Cement is now used in the most important engineering work, and is called for by many prominent architects and engineers in their specifications. Thousands of barrels of Portland and Rosendale Cements are shipped from the Lehigh Valley mills each week, and the production and consumption is being increased each year. Among the party were: Chas. Andruss, David Stroud, Dan'l Herbert, A. J. Robinson, Frank N. Howland, of Candee & Smith, Allen Conover, J. H. Deeves, J. J. Bell, of John Bell & Son, J. G. Van Horn, David K. Young, E. Moneek, Rob't Treffenberg, Wm. Brennan and John M. Canda. On arrival in New York, all expressed themselves well pleased with their visit, and each in turn admitted they were astonished at the magnitude of the cement industry in this section of the country.

Estimates for the Coming Year.

The Board of Estimate and Apportionment has received the preliminary estimates of expenses from all the departments of the city and county government for 1892, except from the Police Department. Compared with the appropriations for 1890 and 1891 they are as indicated in the following table:

Department.	Amount allowed for 1890.	Amount allowed for 1891.	Amount asked for 1892.
Law	$199,200	$192,650	$218,600
Public Works	8,216,215	8,124,470	8,490,176
Parks	1,190,700	991,500	1,074,645
Charities and Corrections	1,949,100	2,166,287	2,877,245
Health	392,200	419,400	444,288
Police	4,647,791	4,777,515	...
Street Cleaning	1,255,885	1,584,250	2,658,233
Fire	2,138,543	2,145,868	2,977,997
Education	4,294,417	4,267,367	4,627,832
Streets (Annexed District)	....	260,200	480,866

The board has prepared its programme for the consideration of these estimates as follows:

Monday—Department of Public Works, Department of Charities and Correction.

Tuesday—Health Department, Department of Public Parks.

Wednesday—Police Department, Bureau of Elections, Commissioners of Accounts.

Thursday—Board of Education, Fire Department.

Friday—Commissioners of Street Improvements, Annexed District, Civil Service Commissioners, Commissioner of Street Cleaning.

Monday—Sheriff, Coroners, District Attorney.

The most remarkable increase in the estimates is in the Departments of Street Cleaning, and the requirements of that Department, as shown by the Mayor's Advisory Commission, afford ample explanation therefor. The increase in the estimates for the North Side Commissioner of Street Improvements is made necessary by the work of redistricting the North Side, as described in another column of this issue.

Real Estate Exchange Matters.

The Auction Room of the Exchange is to be lighted on dark days by means of incandescent electric light. The manner of the lighting has not yet been determined upon by the Auction Room Committee, who have the matter in charge, but it will probably be fashioned after the dining-room of the Hotel Imperial, where the lights are placed at intervals all over the ceiling. The number of lamps used will probably be in the neighborhood of one hundred.

Contractors' Notes.

Bids or proposals for grading, improving and fencing the grounds at several of the shafts of the New Croton Aqueduct, as called for in the approved forms of contract and specifications on file in the office of the Aqueduct Commissioners, will be received until 3 o'clock P. M. on Wednesday, October 21, 1891, at the Aqueduct Commissioners' Office, Room 209, Stewart Building.

Bids or estimates will be received at the Commissioner's office, Department of Public Works, No. 31 Chambers street, until 12 o'clock M., on Tuesday, October 20, 1891: For alteration and improvement to sewer in 95th street, between 1st and 3d avenues, and in 2d avenue, east and west sides, between 95th and 96th streets, and curve in 2d avenue, south of 95th street; for sewer in 125th street, between present sewer and bulkhead wall at 125th street and Harlem River; for sewer in 185th street, between Amsterdam and Audubon avenues; for sewer in 1st avenue, between 43d and 44th streets; for sewer in 1st avenue, between 42d and 43d streets, connecting with present sewer in 43d street, east of 1st avenue; for sewer in 1st avenue, between 89th and 90th streets; for sewer in Park avenue, east side, between 115th and 116th streets; for connecting new gate-house at 135th street and Convent avenue with the old aqueduct on 10th avenue and the removal of the gate-houses on 10th avenue at 134th and 142d streets; for necessary materials and labor for repairing sidewalks and fencing around the corporation yard, Mangin, Rivington and Tompkins streets; for regulating and paving with granite block pavement, with concrete foundation, the carriageway of 19th street, from Avenue A to 1st avenue, so far as the same is within the limits of grants of land under water; for regulating and paving with granite block pavement, with concrete foundation, the carriageway of 52d street, from the easterly side of 12th avenue to bulkhead line of Hudson River; for regulating and paving with granite block pavement the roadway of 58th street, from 11th avenue to a line about 360 feet westerly; for regulating and paving with granite block pavement the roadway of 58th street, from a line about 360 feet west of 11th avenue to the Hudson River, so far as the same is within the limits of grants of land under water; for regulating and paving with granite block pavement, with concrete foundation, the roadway of 103d street, from 1st avenue to East River; for flagging and reflagging, curbing and recurbing the sidewalks on the east side of 10th avenue, from 29th to 30th street, and on the south side of 30th street, from 9th to 10th avenue; for flagging full width and reflagging the sidewalks on 19th street, from Avenue A to 1st avenue; for flagging full width and reflagging, curbing and recurbing the sidewalks on 116th street, from Madison to 8th avenue; for regulating and grading 127th street, from St. Nicholas avenue to Lawrence street, and setting curbstones and flagging sidewalks therein; for regulating and grading Amsterdam avenue, from 194th street to Fort George avenue, and setting curbstones and flagging sidewalks therein, and for flagging and reflagging, curbing and recurbing the sidewalks on the northeast corner of 5th avenue and 86th street.

Estimates for dredging at sundry-named places on the North and East rivers will be received by the Board of Commissioners, at the head of the Department of Docks, at the office of said department, on Pier A, foot of Battery place, North River, in the City of New York, until 1 o'clock P. M., of Thursday, October 22, 1891.

Sealed estimates for altering the station-houses, lodging-houses and prisons on the ground and premises situated in the City of New York, at No. 160 East 35th street, No. 137 West 30th street, No. 146 East 126th street, No. 221 Mercer street, and the Thirteenth Precinct Station-house known as "Union Market," will be received at the Central Office of the Department of Police, No. 300 Mulberry street, in the City of New York, until 12 o'clock M. of Friday, the 23d day of October, 1891.

Notice to Property-Owners.

Owners of property affected by the taking of land for the easterly approach to the proposed bridge over the Harlem River, at 155th street (to replace the old McComb's Dam bridge) are requested to attend a hearing before the Board of Commissioners of Public Parks, No. 49 Chambers street, on Wednesday, October 21, 1891, at 10 o'clock A. M., with reference to the value of the land to be taken for such purpose.

THE WEST SIDE INDEX.

All persons interested in West Side real estate should possess an Index of Ten Years' Conveyances affecting property between the north side of 59th and south side of 125th streets, from west side 8th avenue to Hudson River. This Index is published by THE RECORD AND GUIDE, *and the period covered is the ten years prior to June 30th, 1884, to which has been added a list of the conveyances up to January 1st, 1885. Every transfer of real estate in that section, made between those years, is recorded in the Index, with a description of the property, the price paid for it, the liber and page in which the conveyances are recorded in the Register's Office, and the name of the seller and the purchaser. The volume is of the utmost value to conveyancers, lawyers, real estate brokers, agents and dealers in real estate generally, and we will supply the Index to our readers, if ordered before January 1st next, at the reduced price of $5.*

Special Notices.

We notice that Isaac Serven, the old-established grate and fender manufacturer, of 1479 Broadway, has taken a partner and the business will henceforth be carried on under the firm name of Serven & Irwin. Isaac Serven was one of the pioneers of the grate and fender trade in this city. During his almost sixty years experience he has witnessed many changes in the arrangement and style of fire-place fittings. The old-fashioned black grate of our fathers has given place to the modern open fire-place surrounded by enamelled tiles of almost every conceivable tint and with designs so varied as to suit all classes of decoration. The artistic improvements during the last few years in this necessary adjunct to our homes have been remarkable, and that they are well abreast of the times a visit to the show-room of the new firm will convince.

Ogden & Clark, of No. 11 Pine street, call the attention of investing syndicates to 143 acres at Mount Vernon, which they are able to offer at such a low price that a handsome return would be yielded. The property is adapted to subdividing into lots.

In another column will be found the advertisement of the well-known firm of Ridley's, on Grand street, of this city. This firm calls attention to its window-shade department. Shades are made to order to suit any kind of apartment, and are guaranteed to be first-class. On all shades they use none but the best quality of Hartshorn's spring rollers. Lettering of the shades is made a specialty.

One of the most reliable firms engaged in the building material business in New York is that of Traitel Brothers, of No. 499 5th avenue, next to 42d street. These gentlemen have on hand at all times a large and attractive stock of tiles— wall tiles, floor tiles, hearth and facing tiles. Consequently there is no delay about securing the execution of an order or obtaining satisfaction for a most exacting taste. Close estimates are cheerfully furnished and all the work is promptly executed.

The Providence Steam Engine Co., Providence, is changing the drums of the Moore boilers (which were recently set up at the Narragansett Electric Light Co.'s station by the National Water Tube Boiler Co., of New Brunswick, N. J.) to the Babcock & Wilcox system. The Babcock & Wilcox Co., of New York, has the contract for the alterations, which have been delayed until the job of putting in of 1,120-horse power of its own boilers was completed.

The designs submitted in competition for the new Protestant Cathedral of St. John's are on exhibition at Nos. 14 to 16 Vesey street.

Newark News.

The following is a list of the plans filed with the Superintendent of Btild. ings recently: Peter Badewitz, 1-sty fr factory, 14x35, 170 Boyd st; C. Horner, 2-sty fr store, 18x24, 596 Central av; Atha & Hughes, 5-sty brk warehouse, 110x50, Sussex av; W. S. Richardson, 2½-sty fr dwell,g, 26x34, 83 South 10th st; Geo. Price, 1-sty factory, 25x30, 104 Johnson st; F. J. Kastner, 1-sty fr extension, 17x27, 144 16th av; Edward Wagner, 3-sty brk store and dwell'g, 30x59, 15th av and 10th st; D. J. Edwards, 1½-sty fr stable, 18x16, 232 South 7th st; J. Choppa, 2-sty fr dwell'g, 20x27, 298 Broome st; E. G. Heller, t-sty fr dwell'g, 56x63, Elwood av; William Block, 1-sty fr bowling alley, 12x100, 85 Belleville av; H. B. Doremus, 3-sty fr stores, 36x38, Bloomfield av and Garside st; John Eviness, 3-sty fr dwell'g, 24x40, 43 Jacob st; J. Knorr, 1-sty fr shop, 12x20, 245 Ferry st; C. Olston, 3-sty fr store, 22x64, 101 7th av; W. H. Brown, 2½-sty fr dwell'g, 27x34, 123 3d av; E. S. Shawger, 1-sty brk stores, 12x35, Roseville av and Orange st; Jos. Denman, 1-sty fr shop, 15x36, 257 New York av; Helen Camm, 1½-sty fr carriage-house, 27x15, rear, 306 South 9th st; E. J. Baldwin, 2-sty fr dwell'g, 16x42, 211 and 213 Chestnut st.

Real Estate Department.

This has been a dull week in real estate circles, a very dull week for this season of the year, and the worst of it is that it promises to continue for some time yet. Not many sales have been actually consummated and but an insignificant number of transactions are under way. In other words, the market, although strong enough as to the matter of prices, too strong perhaps, is very inactive, and the prospects are that it will not improve materially until the spring. The real estate men are trying to account for the quietness of the fall market in various ways, many of them attributing it to the excitement incident to the election. Other reasons more local in their application are advanced, all tending to show that the market is only temporarily at a standstill. The truth of the matter is, however, that owners are holding their real estate at figures that are above what is warranted by the present condition of the market, and until they make concessions there will be no activity. This state of affairs is not at all a new one. Prices have been too high for a year or more past, and during the same period there has been a most persistent inactivity. Owners, quite satisfied that by waiting they would secure their figure, have held on, refusing all offers that did not almost meet their real asking price, and they are still holding on to their property at figures that have not changed to a lower plane. This policy is all well enough in a brisk, lively speculative market, when buyers are quite as numerous as the sellers and very much more anxious, but in a market where there is, comparatively speaking, no speculation going on, and where the buyers, like the sellers, are inclined to wait for prices to run their way, it must be admitted that it is a very poor policy, especially if a man is at all anxious to dispose of his holdings. Taking it altogether the present real estate market is one of the most peculiar that has been seen in years. Of the really good property not very much of it is on the market, and where it is for sale the owners are in no hurry to dispose of it, and so they are asking figures that in many cases are above the real value of their property, while buyers, uninfluenced by the confident position of the present holders of real estate, are offering only what they consider fair prices, content to wait for a market of lower prices.

THE AUCTION MARKET.

The past week has been an uneventful one in the auction room. Holders of Manhattan Island property apparently do not look to the auctioneers to dispose of their holdings, for the list of offerings is as small and generally uninteresting as it well can be at this season of the year. The parcels that are voluntarily offered, at what is known as public auction, include only real estate that is located in "off color" districts. The consequence is that the outside public who, after all, make the high prices at an auction sale, are not attracted to the Exchange and the bidding is left almost entirely to the dealers and speculators who don't want anything that is not a bargain. The owners do not intend to sacrifice their property, so that they either allow the sale to be concluded and then buy their property in or else, as soon as they see the general feeling, they withdraw it. This happened several times during the week and the present state of affairs is not unlikely to continue. Altogether the auction market for this fall, for which so much was confidently predicted, by those who ought to know, looks exceedingly as though it would amount to nothing, if we except perhaps a few successful lot sales in North New York and the suburbs.

FORDHAM LOTS SELL WELL.

Monday again saw the conclusion of a successful lot sale, and those who were present at it predicted a pleasant reception for the hundreds of other lots that were to be thrown upon the market later on during the week. The sale on Monday was of what are known as Jerome terrace lots, some of them situated on Jerome avenue and overlooking the racing park of the same name. It forms an outlying section of the 24th Ward settlement known as Bedford Park, where so many successful lot sales have been held. The auctioneer, James L. Wells, had a very good crowd in front of him when he commenced the sale. It was made up of both men and women (and the latter in not a very great minority either) who looked as though they might be people of moderate circumstances. The bidding throughout was not as spirited as that at the Ryer Homestead sale on the previous Monday, but it was nevertheless satisfactory, as the prices quoted in full in another column show. The women present were among the most regular bidders, and some of the best lots were purchased by persons of their sex. This fact calls attention to new a departure in real estate speculation. Heretofore the only real estate held by women has been held simply as an investment. This is changing now, and women are coming into the market in strong numbers as speculators on a small scale. Numerous examples could be quoted in corroboration of this statement, but they are not necessary, the fact is already generally recognized by brokers, and especially by those doing business in the outlying wards and in the suburbs.

These Jerome terrace lots, 196 in number, are situated about 15 feet above Jerome avenue and separated from the same by a retaining stone wall, which is surmounted by a driveway. The highest-priced lots, of course, were those on what is known as Parkview terrace, immediately overlooking the park. Here inside lots sold from $875 to $1,350, while the corners were disposed of at $1,625 and $2,050 respectively. Immediately in the rear on Kirkside avenue inside lots brought from $525 to $800 each, while similar lots on the opposite side of the street brought from $460 to $600. The corners on this avenue brought $1,050 and $1,075 each. Inside lots on Creston avenue from $430 to $775, while the corners brought from $950 to $1,025 each. The prices quoted will give a very fair idea of the way the property sold. Competent judges of neighboring values said the prices were very good, and this is especially satisfactory considering the fact that all the lots were sold. The buyers included a great number and variety of outsiders—most of the lots being sold in plots of two or three—with only a few speculators and dealers among them.

OTHER LOT SALES.

Besides the Jerome terrace lot sale there were four other sales similar in character. Three of them were in North New York, while the fourth was situated in Flatbush. The largest of the sales in the 23d and 24th Wards was of 121 lots in the neighborhood of 156th and 163d streets, off 3d avenue. There was a large crowd present, but the auctioneer had difficulty in inducing them to bid, and after selling nine or ten lots at only fair prices he withdrew the rest. The other sales were of a smaller number of parcels and were more successful. The first one on Tuesday, by Smyth & Ryan, was of twenty-four lots, between 134th and 158th streets and on St. Ann's and Marsher avenues. Considering the number of lots offered there was a very good attendance, and if all the lots were really sold, and they appeared to be, they brought very good figures. Auctioneer John F. B. Smyth's small sale of houses and lots at Melrose was also fairly successful. The bidding was perhaps not quite so spirited as in the other 23d Ward sale, but the prices obtained were as good, and that after all is the essential point. These four sales, three of which were successful, strikingly illustrate the vitality and activity of the two wards above the Harlem known as North New York. For a long time now, and when business in the city proper has been as dull as it well could be, there was selling and trading above the Harlem, and the auctioneers have had more success in that section, of late, than in any of the suburbs, or in fact any other part of the city, if we except perhaps the remarkable sale of lots on the Heights last spring. It will be interesting to see whether this comparatively new section of the city will bear up under the flood of vacant lots that is and has for some time been coming in upon the market. The Zabriskie Homestead sale of 350 lots at Flatbush was decidedly not a success. Out of the total number of lots offered only about thirty-five were sold. The inside avenue lots sold at $230 and $235, while the corners brought $240 and $250 and the street lots were disposed of at $140 and $145 each.

THE CITY PROPERTY SOLD.

The parcels in the city proper that were disposed of this week were of the most uninteresting kind. The list of offerings announced in the first place was short, and it included holdings that had probably been everywhere else in the market before they came to the auction room. Like last week's list, none of it was of the kind calculated to attract outsiders, and the speculators and dealers did not care to take hold of it unless they could secure bargains. The owners were not prepared to sacrifice their holdings, and so the natural consequence of no great anxiety to buy or no pressing need to sell was that some of the property was withdrawn while other parcels were bid in by their owners in order to protect themselves. Some few of the parcels voluntarily offered were sold, it is true, but they mean nothing to the general market. They were unimportant in themselves and the prices obtained for them were in no case remarkable. The details of the several sales will be found as usual in our "Sales of the Week" column. The legal sales dwindled down this week to four or five in number and they were in no case interesting enough to call for special remark. The only instance where the amount due in a foreclosure sale exceeded the selling price was in a house on 92d street, west of 3d avenue, which sold for $19,550, as against $19,807 due for mortgages and costs.

WHAT IS TO BE OFFERED NEXT WEEK.

Next week opens, as the past two weeks have done, with a large suburban sale by Auctioneer James L. Wells. On Monday he will offer 153 lots at Kingsbridge, and this sale will be watched with considerable interest, in view of the number of building plots in North New York that have changed hands recently at auction and otherwise. The list of offerings in the way of city property for next week is very much more interesting than it has been for some time. It includes the Ferrigan estate sale on Thursday by A. H. Muller & Son, when No. 80 Duane street will be offered among numerous other parcels. Then, too, Richard V. Harnett & Co. will sell two plots on Riverside Drive on the same day, and they will doubtless draw an interested audience. The first of these is a lot on the Drive, near 104th street, while the second includes two lots north of 122d street, and about opposite the site of the Grant monument. On Wednesday John F. B. Smyth promises to sell No. 40 West 29th street. The other advertised offerings are very ordinary in character.

On Monday, October 19th, James L. Wells will sell 153 lots, all desirably located on and adjacent to Sedgwick avenue on Kingsbridge Heights in the 24th Ward. Sewer, water and gas pipes are laid, and all city conveniences can be obtained. Two railroad stations are within a few minutes' walk from the property, and 117 trains a day furnish quick transit. The ground is high and healthy, and the location has many advantages. The terms are easy and the title guaranteed.

On Tuesday, Oct. 20th, Jere. Johnson, Jr., will sell, by order of William Zeigler, 150 remaining lots on the Ferguson farm, directly opposite Hiram Howe's and between the Coney Island & Brooklyn Electric Railroad and the Ocean Parkway. The property is easily accessible and has many advantages. The lots may be paid for in monthly installments.

On Tuesday, October 20th, Richard V. Harnett & Co. will sell, by order of trustees, Nos. 210, 212 and 214 West 4th street, three seven-story brick flats; Nos. 70 and 72 Christopher and Nos. 65 and 67 Grove street, with five-story flats thereon, and No. 424 East 48th street, a two-story brick building.

On Wednesday, October 21st, Richard V. Harnett & Co. will sell the two four-story brown stone flats, Nos. 175 and 177 East 93d street, and by order of executors, the two six-story tenements, at Nos. 91 and 93 Sheriff street, and the three-story brown stone dwelling, No. 154 East 78th street.

On Wednesday, October 21st, John F. B. Smyth will sell, by order of the Supreme Court, the five six-story brown stone double flats, on the northwest corner of 3d avenue and 91st street. Four of these buildings, lots 25.2x75, are situated on the avenue, and two lots, 25x100.8½ each, on the street.

On Thursday, October 22d, Richard V. Harnett & Co. will sell a lot, 26x100, on Riverside Drive, north of 104th street, and the plot, 50x100, on Riverside Drive, 550 north of 122d street.

On Thursday, October 22d, Adrian H. Muller & Son will sell, by order of the executors of Hugh Ferrigan, some valuable improved and unimproved property, situated in various parts of the city. The parcels offered comprise the business buildings at No. 80 Duane street and at No 3505 3d avenue, and fifty-seven desirable lots, situated on 167th and 173d streets, Fulton, Franklin, Washington, Central, Gerard and Inwood avenues and Arcularius place—all of them in the 23d and 24th Wards.

CONVEYANCES.

	1890. Oct. 10 to 16 inc.	1891. Oct. 9 to 15 inc.
Number	284	246
Amount involved	$3,506,996	$3,959,509
Number nominal	63	81
Number 23d and 24th Wards	64	52
Amount involved	$288,365	$160,401
Number nominal	15	16

MORTGAGES.

	1890.	1891.
Number	245	244
Amount involved	$2,745,178	$2,260,425
Number at 5 % or less	109	122
Amount involved	$1,363,660	$1,205,087
Number at less than 5 per cent	25	20
Amount involved	$336,000	$268,000
Number to Banks, Trust and Ins. Cos	27	33
Amount involved	$721,200	$574,540

PROJECTED BUILDINGS.

	1890. Oct. 11 to 17 inc.	1891. Oct. 10 to 16 inc.
Number of buildings	39	43
Estimated cost	$606,613	$1,195,185

Gossip of the Week.

SOUTH OF 59TH STREET.

Christian F. Schramme has sold to O. T. Zollikoffer Nos. 77 and 79 Broad street, running through to Nos. 32 and 34 South William street, with the buildings thereon, for a figure in the neighborhood of $110,000. Mr. Schramme purchased this property in 1869 for $90,000. Broker, J. Freedman.

Geo. R. Read has sold for the Presbyterian Hospital Nos. 113 and 115 Cedar street, two three-story brick buildings, on plot 37.6x60, for $37,500.

Monaghan & Co. have sold for C. T. Barney, No. 108 West 58th street, a four-story dwelling, lot 20x100.5, to Mrs. Danforth for $39,000.

Robert Auld & Co. have sold for George Rauchfuss the five-story flat and store property on the northwest corner of 53d street and 7th avenue, for $75,000.

Peter Herter has purchased from Harris Mandelbaum the plot, 43.9x100, southeast corner of Rivington and Ludlow streets, with the old buildings thereon, for improvement.

M. Kayser has sold for the estate of Samuel J. Solomon to Joseph Beran the lot, 25x100, with the old building thereon, No. 25 West Houston street, 50 feet west of Mercer street, for $46,500.

Bernard Cohen has purchased No. 14 Morton street, old buildings, on lot 25x90, on private terms.

Benjamin F. Cohen has purchased No. 56 Morton street, a lot 25x100, with the old buildings thereon, on private terms, and No. 308 West 26th street, a three-story dwelling, on lot 18.9x98.9, also on private terms. Mr. Cohen recently purchased Nos. 310 and 312 West 26th street, adjoining, so that he is now the owner of the three houses.

Harris Mandelbaum has purchased from Louis Bernstein No. 111 Henry street, 25x100, with the old buildings thereon, on private terms.

H. Rinaldo & Bro. have sold to Fay & Stacom for H. Mandelbaum the house and lot No. 111 Henry street, on private terms. The purchasers will build a six-story tenement on the plot.

Morris B. Baer & Co. have sold for Joseph Strauss No. 218 West 25th street, a four-story brick and brown stone English basement dwelling, on lot 15.4x98.9, for $11,500.

NORTH OF 59TH STREET.

Oppenheimer & Metzger have purchased from the estate of Acton Civill the five lots on the southeast corner of Columbus avenue and 84th street for $85,000.

Robt. Auld & Co. have sold for Mark Brennen the two five-story flat houses known as "The Chetwood," Nos. 133 and 135 West 83d street, for $80,000.

D. B. Freedman has sold to W. F. Havemeyer, the sugar refiner, a tract of land on the west side of Kingsbridge road, north of Academy street. The plot has a frontage of 300 feet on Kingsbridge road and runs through to the street in the rear. Mr. Freedman has also sold nine lots on Vermilyea avenue, near Hawthorne street, on private terms.

Oppenheimer & Metzger have sold to James A. Breen their remaining four lots on the south side of 87th street, 150 feet west of Central Park West, on private terms, for improvement.

Judge George L. Ingraham has sold to W. B. Isham No. 15 East 66th street, a four-story brown stone dwelling, on lot 20x100, on private terms.

Frederick Wiznant has sold for Baron Jerzmannowski the four-story brown stone dwelling, 16.8x50x60, No. 741 Madison avenue, for $80,000.

J. W. Stevens has sold for Chas. F. Bauerdorff to Robt. Hanna the lot, 31.6x75.6x37.6x—, on the south side of 95th street, 100 feet east of the Boulevard, on private terms.

F. Zittel has sold for Dr. Edmund Guilbert to William Orr No. 50 West 76th street, a four-story brown stone dwelling, 19x55x100, on private terms, and for Russell Sage to John D. Taylor the lot on the north side of 70th street, 275 feet west of Central Park West, for $16,000.

Henry Morgenthau has purchased the four-story brown stone dwelling, 20x58 and extension x102 2, No. 33 West 74th street, on private terms. The house is decorated and completely furnished.

Bryan L. Kennelly has sold for the estate of Robert Crowley to Maurice Aaron, No. 58 West 92d street, a four-story, high stoop, brown stone dwelling, 17.6x52 and extension x100.8, for $24,500.

John D. Dent has sold for Tichborne & Wilson to Mrs. Ella Sugden the three-story and extension terra cotta and brown stone dwelling, No. 179 West 87th street, on private terms.

Geo. W. Ruddell has sold to a Mrs. Lester the four-story dwelling, No. 61 West 70th street, on private terms. This is the third house which Mr. Ruddell has sold out of an uncompleted row of five.

Wm. H. Scott has sold to Wm. M. Walsh the southeast corner of Columbus avenue and 65th street, 26.2x100x25x86.10, on private terms, for improvement.

Wm. M. Walsh has sold one of his three five-story flats on the north side of 101st street, east of Columbus avenue.

Wood, Whittle & Kennelly have sold for Eva Muller No. 314 East 116th street, a five-story flat, to Babeth Doctor, of Albany, for $23,000.

W. H. De Forest has sold to J. H. Morrison, Jr., the three-story and basement brick and stone dwelling, 16.6x55x100, on the north side of 144th street, the second house east of Amsterdam avenue, for about $17,000. Brokers, V. K. Stevenson & Co.

Monaghan & Co. have sold for Mrs. Gordon to Jacob Aberle, No. 169 West 118th street, a four-story brick flat, on lot 25x100, for $25,000; and for J. B. Bissell to Francis Nugent, No. 115 East 122d street, a four-story flat on lot 25x100.11, for $17,000.

LEASES.

E. H. Ludlow & Co. have leased No. 10 West 37th street and No. 125 East 34th street, two four-story unfurnished houses, on private terms.

T. A. Burnett has leased No. 53 East 65th street, a four-story dwelling, for A. Schneider, at $1,800 per annum, and for Alex. McSorley, the four-story dwelling No. 54 East 67th street, at $2,400 per year.

Brooklyn.

Corwith Bros. have sold the house and lot, No. 198 Oakland street, for Walter Smith for $1,100, and the three-story and basement frame dwelling, 22x36, on lot 25x100, No. 166 Calyer street, for Ephraim A. Walker to Sedgwick and Sarah F. Barnett for $6,500.

J. P. Sloane has sold for General J. V. Meserole the plot of ground, 50x100, on the east side of Diamond street, 75 feet south of Calyer street, to Evind Axland for $800.

CONVEYANCES.

	1890. Oct. 9 to 15 inc.	1891. Oct. 8 to 14 inc.
Number	334	314
Amount involved	$1,291,484	$1,164,682
Number nominal	77	81

MORTGAGES.

	1890.	1891.
Number	298	262
Amount involved	$1,476,239	$1,066,566
Number at 5 per cent. or less	171	125
Amount involved	$792,810	$455,800

PROJECTED BUILDINGS.

	1890. Oct. 10 to 16 inc.	1891. Oct. 9 to 15 inc.
Number of buildings	120	75
Estimated cost	$449,055	$489,070

Out of Town.

WHITE PLAINS, N. Y.—The Westchester County Society of Agriculture and Horticulture have bought from Wm. P. Uptegrove the property known for twenty-five years as "The Fair Grounds," on the Tarrytown road, about one mile west of White Plans, where they will continue to hold the County Fair, which has this year been made such a success. Mr. Uptegrove bought this property in 1885 from the estate of Wm. D. Warren for $16,500, and sells it to the society for $30,500.

YONKERS, N. Y.—Jos. W. Archer has sold for the Ware estate to James Shipman, of Hartford, Conn., eight acres of land on Kimball avenue, in the 2d Ward, on private terms.

Out Among the Builders.

John C. Burne has plans on the boards for a four-story and basement brown stone front dwelling, 25x60, with an 18-foot extension, which Frederick Aldhous will build at No. 108 West 76th street, at a cost of $35,000. The same architect will furnish plans for five five-story brick, stone and terra cotta front flats, to be built on the north side of 103d street, 180 feet west of Park avenue, at a cost of $100,000; the size will be 25x69, with a 13x6 extension.

Wm. M. Walsh will improve the lot on the southeast corner of Columbus avenue and 65th street, probably by the erection of a flat and stores.

James A. Breen will build five four-story brown stone front dwellings on the four lots he has just acquired on the south side of 87th street, 150 feet west of Central Park West.

Ogden & Fountain intend to build two five-story brick and stone flats, one 25x63 and extension, and one 25x71 in size, on the southeast corner of Brook avenue and 149th street, at an estimated cost of $33,000.

Peter Herter will improve the plot 43.9x100, on the southeast corner of Rivington and Ludlow streets, probably by the erection of a six-story tenement.

Fay & Stacom will improve the lot 25x100, No. 111 Henry street, by the erection of a six-story tenement.

F. Ebeling has plans on the boards for a six-story factory, 25x90, to be built at No. 20 Forsyth street, at a cost of $24,000; and for a four-story and basement extension, 16x35, to be built to the house No. 217 Henry street for the same owner, at a cost of $12,000.

Thomas C. Van Brunt will build thirty-five three-story brick and stone dwellings on the north side of 136th street, between 7th and 8th avenues. Architects, Thayer & Robinson.

We are informed that Cyrus L. W. Eidlitz has been commissioned to draw the plans for the Texas State Building at the Columbian Exposition.

Two five-story tenements, 25x80.6, are to be erected for Theodore Van Eupen at Nos. 331 and 333 West 16th street. Max Muller has the plans.

Kurtzer & Rohl have plans on the boards for a six-story brick, stone and terra cotta apartment house with stores. The building is to be 37.6x95.6, and is to be finished with all modern improvements at a cost of $40,000. Geo. Hornberger is the owner.

J. C. Burne is the architect for the $25,000 apartment house to be built for J. W. French on the south side of 85th street, 304.6 east of 3d avenue. The building is to be of brown stone and terra cotta, and will be 25x90 in size.

Out of Town.

BELLEHAVEN, CONN.—Boring, Tilton & Mellen have drawn plans for a two-story and attic frame dwelling, to be built here for James McCutcheon at a cost of $10,000, and for a similar dwelling to be built for S. B. Tyler at a cost of $9,000. Both these houses will be Colonial in style. The same architects will have supervision of the interior alterations to be made in the residence of Charles Moore, the plans for which were originally drawn by them. The billiard-room is to be converted into a library, and the first story supplied with hardwood floors and oak wainscoting throughout. This house has been regarded as a model of its class, and when the improvements in hand are completed it will be one of the most attractive of its kind in this section.

GREENWICH, CONN.—Wm. Cutajar has ordered plans drawn by Boring, Tilton & Mellen for a two-story and attic frame Colonial dwelling, to cost $10,000. The lot on which this house will stand is irregular in size and shape, calling for considerable ingenuity and skill in the interior arrangement of the dwelling.

NEWARK, N. J.—H. E. Reeves has plans for a two-and-a-half-story frame dwelling for Marie Eisile, corner Madison and Belmont avenues, size 28x40; cost, $7,500.

The designs for the several large hotels now building in New York City may be seen at THE RECORD AND GUIDE *rooms, Nos. 14 to 16 Vesey street.*

WANTS AND OFFERS.

OFFERS.

I HAVE several choice designs on hand for city and suburban residences which I would dispose of at a low figure, or would undertake any work of that class on moderate commission

C. W. MULLIN, architect,
35 Schermerhorn st, Brooklyn.

OFFERS.

A PARTY ABOUT TO BUILD A FIVE-STORY factory, 50x98, in Harlem, near water-front, will lease the three upper floors and build to suit tenant. Terms very moderate. Address
May 16 u. f. OWNER, 409 E. 107th St.

OFFERS.

PRINTING.—Book, News and Job.

RECORD AND GUIDE PRESS,
14 Barclay, and 14, 16 Vesey sts.

SALES OF THE WEEK.

The following are the sales at the Real Estate Exchange and Auction Room for the week ending Oct. 16.

** Indicates that the property described has been bid in for plaintiff's account:*

JAMES L. WELLS.

Kingsbridge road, n e cor Kirkside av, 1 lot. C. Man	$1,950
Park View terrace, s e cor Travers st, 1 lot. H. Frank	1,125
Park View terrace, e s, adj. E. F. Mallahan	2,175
Park View terrace, s e cor Wellesley st, 1 lot. F. Jauss	2,050
Park View terrace, e s, adj, 3 lots. E. Ehrlich	3,845
Park View terrace, adj, 4 lots. B. F. Cromwell	5,150
Park View terrace, adj, 3 lots. Geo. V. Krauss	3,600
Park View terrace, adj, 2 lots. E. A. Freystadt	2,000
Park View terrace, adj, 2 lots. Jas. Bradley	2,050
Park View terrace, adj, 1 lot. A. A. Levy	1,025
Park View terrace, adj, 4 lots. Mary V. Kronenbitter	4,100
Park View terrace, adj, 1 lot. Thos. Hill	1,035
Park View terrace, adj, 2 lots. Harlow & Meens	2,000
Park View terrace, adj, 1 lot. J. D. Mahoney	1,000
Park View terrace, adj, 2 lots. H. J. Abels	1,900
Park View terrace, adj, 1 lot. E. Ehrlich	845
Park View terrace, adj, 3 lots. D. Stiugier	3,325
Park View terrace, s e cor Kirkside av, 1 lot. Same	1,625
Park View terrace, n e cor Kirkside av, 1 lot. H. Frank	850
Park View terrace, e s, adj, 3 lots. J. F. Toussaint	1,575
Travers st, s w Creston av, 1 lot. H. Frank	1,025
Travers st, s s, adj, 1 lot. G. V. Krauss	600
Travers st, adj. 6 lots. B F Cromwell	3,450
Travers st, adj. 1 lot. J. F. Toussaint	580
Wellesley st, n s, 47.9 w Kirkside av, 3 lots. A. A. Crawford	2,400
Wellesley st, s e cor Kirkside av, 1 lot. C. W. Spooner	1,075
Wellesley st, s s, adj, 1 lot. J. Neuberry	725
Wellesley st, adj, 1 lot. F. Edgar	675
Wellesley st, n e cor Creston av, 1 lot. Wm. C. Marks	1,000
Wellesley st, n s, adj, 2 lots. Mrs. Watts	1,240
Wellesley st, n w cor Creston av, 1 lot. J. J. Mabedy	1,900
Wellesley st, n s, adj, 3 lots. Mrs. Watt	2,100
Wellesley st, adj. 3 lots. Fred Allen	2,100
Wellesley st, n e cor Kirkside av. C. W. Spooner	1,030
Wellesley st, n w cor Kirkside av. I. M. Toussaint	1,030
Wellesley st, n s, 1 lot. Same	875
Creston av, e s, 107.9 n Wellesley st, 25x69, vacant. Elizabeth McCabe	430
Creston av, e s, adj, 225x43x—x69. S. M. Daniels	2,500
Creston av, adj, 75x35x—x43. W. L. Hartley	690
Creston av, adj. 25x36. R. M. Rosell	185
Creston av, adj. 58x33. B. F. Cromwell	235
Creston av, adj, 50x27. R. M. Rosell	400
Creston av, adj. 15x24. B. F. Cromwell	125
Creston av, adj. irreg. strip. M. Simons	2,945
Creston av, w s, 99.7 s Travers st. 4 lots. B. F. Cromwell	2,800
Creston av, adj, 5 lots. J. J. Bannon	2,150
Creston av, adj 5 lots. B. F. Cromwell	2,875
Creston av, adj, 2 lots. G. W. Moore	1,200
Creston av, adj, 2 lots. Mrs. C. R. Mosher	1,150
Creston av, adj, 2 lots. Luke Gleason	1,160
Creston av, adj, 4 lots. J. J. Bannon	2,345
Creston av, adj, 2 lots. W. C. Monks	1,200
Creston av, adj, 1 lot. Jos. Mallan	675
Creston av, adj, 1 lot. W. S. Carey	725
Creston av, adj, 2 lots. W. Grune	1,450
Creston av, adj, 1 lot. A. Spindler	750
Creston av, adj, 1 lot. D. B. Wyckoff	775
Kirkside av, w s, 100 n Wellesley st, 2 lots. L. G. Hahn	1,550
Kirkside av, adj. 2 lots. G. E. Shepperd	1,550
Kirkside av, adj. 2 lots. Wm. Wheltan	1,600
Kirkside av, adj. 2 lots. F. E. Kohl	1,500
Kirkside av, adj. 2 lots. J. F. Toussaint	1,450
Kirkside av, adj. 2 lots. W. B. Berkmeier	1,420
Kirkside av, adj. 4 lots. J. F. Toussaint	2,740
Kirkside av, adj. 2 lots. Jas. McBride	1,290
Kirkside av, adj. 2 lots. J. F. Toussaint	1,240
Kirkside av, adj, 2 lots. Mrs. Watt	1,050
Kirkside av, adj. 2 lots. T. Hill	1,625
Kirkside av, e s, 103 s Wellesley st, 5 lots. B. P. Fairchild	2,475
Kirkside av, adj, 1 lot. M. F. Wilhelm	900
Kirkside av, adj, 1 lot. C. H. Babcock	925
Kirkside av, adj, 4 lots. Geo. Desoye	4,000
Kirkside av, adj, 1 lot. B. P. Fairchild	1,025
Kirkside av, adj, 1 lot. F. Edgar	1,000
Kirkside av, adj. 3 lots. B. P. Fairchild	2,475
Kirkside av, adj. 2 lots. Geo. S. Shepperd	2,050
Kirkside av, adj. 2 lots. J. C. Holmes	2,300
Kirkside av, e s, 94 n Wellesley st, 2 lots. A. F. Crawford	1,200
Kirkside av, adj, 2 lots. J. F. Toussaint	1,140
Kirkside av, adj. 2 lots. Alfred Sharp	1,110
Kirkside av, adj. 2 lots. J. F. Toussaint	1,100
Kirkside av, adj. 2 lots. Mrs. H. F. Tuthill	1,110
Kirkside av, adj, 2 lots. L. G. Robertson	1,090
Kirkside av, adj. 2 lots. Jas. McBride	1,070
Kirkside av, adj, 1 lot. M. P. Campbell	520
Kirkside av, adj, 4 lots. B. F. Cromwell	2,000
Kirkside av, adj, 2 lots. T. B. Mesick	1,000
Kirkside av, adj, 1 lot. T. M. Trainor	470
Kirkside av, adj. 2 lots. T. B. Mesick	920
Kirkside av. adj. 4 lots. J. J. Bannon	1,880
Kirkside av, adj, 1 lot. M. L. Burke	630
Kirkside av, adj. 1 lot. Fanny Taylor	630
Kirkside av, adj, 1 lot. J. F. Toussaint	1,445

SMYTH & RYAN.

134th st, s s, 250 e St. Anns av, 50x70, vacant. P. W. Ehrsam	4,850
134th st, adj, 50x70, vacant. J. A. Hamilton	4,750
138th st, s s, 45 w Brown pl, 75x100, vacant. Dr. Galavan	9,975
140th st, s s, 215.6 w Brook av, gore, 20.9x irreg. J. A. Hamilton	5,000
158th st, s s, 123 w 3d av, 23.4x100. M. D. Burke	2,250
Marsher (3d) av, near Devoe st, 100x100. Jos. Mahan	3,500
St. Anns av, s e cor 134th st, 100x80, vacant. J. A. Hamilton	13,000
Wales av, No. 608, e s, 83 n 147th st, 17x100, two-story frame dwell'g. J. A. Hamilton	4,425

R. V. HARNETT & CO.

51st st, Nos. 602-606, s s, 100 w 11th av, 75x100.5, two-story brk office, &c. N. O'Donnell. (Leasehold; receiver's sale)	275
62d st, No. 226 W., 16.8x102.2, three-story brown stone dwell'g. A. Finelite	19,250
12th st, No. 109 E., 25x103.3, three-story brk dwell'g. Wm. G. Gardner	6,750
Lexington av, No. 1652, 16.8x55, three-story brown stone dwell'g. M. Levine	8,900
2d av, No. 1062, s e cor 56th st, three-story building and store. Wm. and Frank Herzog	25,000

A. H. MULLER & SON.

29th st, No. 333 E., 22.6x98.9, four-story brk tenem't. (Bid in)	—
156th st, cor Jackson av, 25.3x100.5. B. P. Fairchild	1,075
163d st, s e cor Cauldwell av, 1 lot. B. P. Fairchild	1,000
Jackson av, w s, near Cedar av, 4 lots. B. P. Fairchild	1,940
Washington av, e s, 117.8 n 163d st, 4 lots. Chas. E. O'Connor	9,900
2d av, No. 1591, three-story brk building and store. (Bid in)	—
3d av, e s, 150.2 n 161st st, 25x125. B. P. Fairchild	5,350

WM. KENNELLY.

6th st, No 734 E., 25x119x50x49x—x70 to beginning, five-story tenem't and two-story stable. G. Groo	34,100
52d st, No. 315, n s, 201.6 e 2d av, 20x100.5, four-story stone front dwell'g. Geo. Hall	10,800
60th st, s e cor 4th av, 20x100.5, four-story brown stone dwell'g. J. A. Lane	29,000

JOHN F. B. SMYTH.

29th st, No. 136 E., 20x98.9, four-story brown stone dwell'g. Cornelius Callahan	20,200
157th st, n s, 132.7 e Railroad av, 1 lot. C. Neundorff	1,940
157th st, adj, 1 lot and house. G. Scheffler	5,000
157th st, n s, — e Railroad av, 4 lots. O. L. Mosher	6,400
158th st, s s, 795 e Railroad av, 1 lot and two-story frame dwell'g. M. Geismann	5,925
158th st, adj, 1 lot. Same	1,710
158th st, adj, 2 lots. J Kubsam	3,245
158th st, adj, 1 lot. O. L. Mosher	1,610
158th st, n s, 97.9 e Railroad av, 3 lots with three two-story frame dwell'gs thereon. Wm. E. Dunn	17,100
158th st, adj, 1 lot, two-story frame dwell'g. —— Wilson	,475
Av A, No. 97, w s, 22.10 n 6th st, 22.8x100, four-story brk building. C. Klenin. (Leasehold)	10,100
Madison av, No. 1847, 17.7x83, three-story brown stone dwell'g. (Bid in)	—
Railroad av East, n e cor 159th st, 1 lot. E. Nass	2,700
Railroad av East, e s, adj, 2 lots. W. E. Dunn	3,775
Railroad av East, adj, 1 lot with three-story brk dwell'g. G. Scheffler	4,825
Railroad av East, n e cor 158th st, 1 lot. J. Kubsam	3,145
Railroad av East, e s, adj, 1 lot. —— Schumann	2,000
Railroad av East, s e cor 157th st, 21x70, —— Rolette	540
Railroad av East, s e cor 158th st, 55x79.5x48x106. M. Geismann	5,000
Railroad av East, e s, adj, 2 lots. —— McGinn	3,575
Railroad av East, n e cor 157th st, 2 lots. W. Devine	4,050
Railroad av East, e s, adj, 1 lot. —— Leehane	1,625

J. C. LALOR.

115th st, Nos. 221 and 223, n s, 325 w 7th av, two five-story brk flats M. McDermott. (Amt due on this and adj flats $50,939)	29,800
115th st, No. 225 W., adj. G. Boehm	14,900
115th st, No. 227 W., adj. R. Cummings	14,900

OTHER AUCTIONEERS.

Bayard st, Nos. 16 and 18, n e cor Chrystie st, 31.10x49.9, three-story brk store and two-story brk tenem't. (Bid in)	—
49th st, n s, 144 e 1st av, 18x80.10, four-story stone front dwelling. Jas. V. McManus. (Amt due $6,117)	8,750

B. L. KENNELLY.

92d st, No. 148, s s, 342 w 3d av, 33x100.8, three-story brk dwell'g. Geo. Ehret. (Amt. due $19,807)	19,550
Total	$541,015
Corresponding week 1890	$741,495

BROOKLYN, N. Y.

For Week Ending October 15.

TAYLOR & FOX.

Broadway, Nos. 1006-1010, 65.2x—, three two-story frame dwell'gs and stores. Simon Ash	$12,000
Broadway, Nos. 1013-1021, 72x80, five one-story frame stores. Fanny Jacobs. (Rent $960 per annum)	2,450
Broadway, No. 1028, 23x—, three-story brk flat and store. C. H. Moller. (Rent $876 per annum)	15,450
Broadway, No. 994, 21x—, three-story brk flat and store. John M. Otto	9,525
Broadway, No. 996, 20.4x—, three-story brk flat and store. Henry Ruthmann	9,425
Broadway, No. 998, 20x—, three-story brk flat and store. Same	9,275
Broadway, No. 1050, 20x—, four-story brk flat with stores. John Mitchell	10,100
Knickerbocker av, s cor Linden st, 20x100, vacant. B. S. Naub	2,350
Myrtle av, s e cor Central av, 150x105.4x117.5, gore, vacant. H. B. & J. F. Dreyer	6,800

JERE. JOHNSON, JR.

Quincy st, No. 294, s s, 365 e N strand av, 20x100, frame dwell'g. John E. Aldridge. (Rent $540 per annum)	5,500
Clark st, No. 58, s s, 175 e Hicks st, 25x185.5, four-story brk dwell'g. Henry L. Meyer	13,500
47th st, s s, 120 w 3d av, 1 lot. Frank D. Creamer	550
47th st, s s, 220 w 3d av, 2 lots. Henry D. Wylie	1,050
47th st, adj, 4 lots. W. J. Morrison	1,800
47th st, adj, 1 lot. Chas. Whitehead	430
47th st, adj 1 lot. B. J. Kruider	410
47th st, adj, 1 lot. Thos. Courtney	360
47th st, adj, 2 lots. F. D. Van Pelt	490
3d av, w s, 25 s 47th st, 3 lots. S. Martin	6,000

J. F. B. SMYTH.

Degraw st, No. 84, 19.6x100, three-story brk tenem't. A. Sessa	4,275
52d st, No. 290, 18.4x100.2, two-story brk and frame dwell'g. P. McDermott	1,700

OTHER AUCTIONEERS.

Clinton st, No 346, 20x106, three-story brown stone dwell'g. Thos. Wilson	10,000
Dresden st, w s, 279.5 n Atlantic av, 75x103.11½x75x104, vacant. Jane L. Smith	1,100
*Decatur st, No. 51, n s, 211 w Throop av, 18x100, three-story brk dwell'g. Moses Sablein	6,000
Grand st, No. 626, 20x100, two-story frame dwell'g. H. C. Conrady	5,250
Gold st, No. 127, 15x39 / York st, No. 208, s e cor Gold st, 19.6x75 / York st, No. 210, 19.6x75. Three two-story frame dwell'gs and stores. Andrew Mulaney	9,100
Marion st, Nos. 29-35, n s, 330 e Stuyvesant av, 100x100, three four-story double brk flats. Geo. H. Gerard	32,225
Pacific st, Nos. 1450 and 1452, s s, 50 w Kingston av, 50x107, two-story brk dwell'g on plot. L. Montgomery	9,500
*Pacific st, Nos. 1105 and 1107, 379.8 w Franklin av, runs north 136.8 x west 150 x south 19.9 x east 120 x south 100 to Pacific st, x east 30 to beginning. John Devlin	50
Prince st, No. 73, 23.3x86, two-story frame dwell'g. Wm. F. Wright	2,650
6th st, No. 309, 20x100, three-story brick flat. L. Froskey	5,850
6th st, s s, 75 w 4th av, 105x100. James P. Phillips	3,000
East 11th st, e s, 85 s Av C, 10 lots, Flatbush. J. Schoenwald	1,450
East 12th st, w s, 127.5 s Av C, 6 lots. C. J. Curtin	840
Av C, s w cor East 11th st, Flatbush, 1 lot. H. Kidd	240
Av C, s w cor East 12th st, 1 lot. J. Schoenwald	250
Av C, s s, adj, 3 lots. C. J. Curtin	510
Av C, s e cor East 11th st, 1 lot. C. L. Lang	240
Av C, s s, adj. 4 lots. H. T. Meyer	940
Av C, adj. 4 lots. W. H. Gouldie	920
East 12th st, adj, 4 lots. J. Woolley	570
Atlantic av, n s, 150 e Utica av, 225x99.1. Israel F. Fisher. (Bid in)	7,700
Williams av, w s, 100 n Eastern Parkway, 100x100, vacant. John I. Davies	1,500
Total	$225,415
Corresponding week, 1890	$395,680

CONVEYANCES.

NEW YORK CITY.

October 9, 10, 12, 13, 14, 15.

Boulevard, Nos. 501-507, s w cor 85th st, 100.5x93.7x100.2x100.10, four five-story brk flats, store in No. 507. Homer J. Beaudet to Albert C Henderson. Oct. 13. $175,000

Boulevard / Amsterdam av / 87th st } begins 87th st, s s, extends from Grand Boulevard to Amsterdam av, —x108x332.10x108, vacant. Frederick Haberman and Eva his wife to John O. Baker, Newark, N. J. *Mt.* $76,000. Oct. 9. 135,000

Broadway, No. 1133, the St. James Hotel, City New York; also real and leasehold property in block bet Washington and West sts and Hubert and Leight sts. Order of Court that Paul N. and Jos. L. Spofford convey above property to Thomas W. Pearsall and Everitt P. Wheeler trustees under will of Paul Spofford dec'd, also adjudging No. 4 East 14th st relieved of charges that are otherwise provided for, &c.

Broome st, No. 74, n s, 103 e Columbia st, 22x75, four-story frame (brk front) store and tenement with three-story brk building on rear. William Rosenbush and Henrietta his wife to Moritz Feldman. *Mt.* $9,500. Oct. 1. 12,000

Bowery, No. 30 / Bayard st, Nos. 42-48 } begins Bowery, n w cor Bayard st, runs north 26 x west 100 x north 49 x west 51 x south 75 to Bayard st, x east 151, four and five-story brk New England hotel. Ferdinand R. Minrath to Third Av R. R. Co. B. & S. All liens. Oct. 10. 150,000

Catharine st, No. 28, w s, abt 19 s Henry st, 24.6x100x25.8x100, four-story brk tenem't. Moses Lubolsky and Esther his wife to John V. Campbell. Mt. $18,000. Oct. 1. See Monroe st. 26,000

Cherry st, No. 427, s s, 100.4 w Jackson st, 25.1x90.7x25x92.6, five-story brk tenem't. Joseph Gru and Rachel his wife to Augusta Pottlitzer, Fort Wayne, Ind. Mt. $23,500. Oct. 5. 26,000

Charlton st, No. 40, s s, 156.7 e Varick st 28x100, three-story brk tenem't. Conveyance and release mort. Elizabeth L. Lees to Harriet Loveridge. Oct. 15. 6,500

Same property. Harriet Loveridge and Elizabeth his wife to Denis F. Gerbereux. Oct. 5. 20,500

Delancey st, Nos. 142–146 } Declaration of trust.
Suffolk st, Nos. 89 and 91 } James H. Gilbert to William T. Gilbert. June 30, 1888. nom

Elizabeth st, No. 157, w s, abt 225 n Broome st, 25x93.8, two-story frame store and tenem't with three-story brk tenem't on rear. George Heyman and Hannah his wife to Serafino Magliola. Mt. $12,500. Oct. 13. 15,500

Essex st, No. 116, e s, 141 s Rivington st, 16x60, three-story brk store and tenem't. Max Jokinsky and Celia his wife to Jacob Ordman. Mt. $8,500 Oct. 14. 12,800

Essex st, No. 81, w s, abt 130 n Broome st, 22x87.6, five-story brk store and tenem't. Adolf Mayer and Emma his wife to Harris Gudwitzki. Mt. $13,000. Oct. 12. 24,750

Same property. Harris Gudwitzki and Betsey his wife to Bernard Harris. ½ part. Mt. $20,000. Oct. 15. 12,375

Goerck st, Nos. 104–108 } begins Goerck st, e s,
Mangin st, Nos. 95–99 } 246.7 n Rivington st, runs east 100 x north 34.10 x east 100 to Mangin st, x north 65.9 x west 100 x south 26 x west 100 to Goerck st, x south 75, three five-story brk tenem'ts with stores on Goerck st and vacant lots on Mangin st. Samuel Goetz and Julia his wife to William F. Lennon. Mt. $60,000. Oct. 9. See Lexington av. nom

Same property. Moses Weinman to Samuel Goetz Mt. $50,800. Oct. 8. nom

Grand st, No. 428, s w cor Attorney st, —x60x20x60, four-story brk store and tenem't. Florence L. Richards, Brooklyn, to James O. Clark. ½ part. C. a. G. March 11. nom

Same property. Robert Hartmann exr. Henry F. Hartman and admr. Henrietta Hartmann to same. B. & S. Q. C. Re-recorded. Nov. 21, 1890. nom

Hamilton st, No. 39 } begins Hamilton st, n s,
Monroe st, No. 34 } abt 175 w Market st, 16.10x82.9 to Monroe st, x19.7x77.4, two-story frame (brk front) tenem't on Hamilton st and two-story frame tenem't on Monroe st. Randolph Guggenheimer and Eliza his wife and Solomon Marx and Betche his wife to The Amsterdam Improvement Co. Mt. $10,000. Oct. 9. See 96th st, also 1st av. 15,000

Henry st, No. 55, n s, abt 165 w Market st, 25x100, five-story brk tenem't. James J. Loonie and Mary A. his wife and Eugene Parker and Henrietta his wife to Annie wife of Nathan Roggen. Mt. $27,000. Sept. 29. 42,500

Hester st, No. 194, s s, 50 e Baxter st, 25x75.4, five-story brk tenem't with stores. }
Cherry st, No. 174, n s, abt 85 e Market st, 25x114, five-story brk store and tenem't. }
Michael Rofrano and Alessandrina his wife to Alberico Caroselli. All liens. June 5. 45,000

Hudson st, No. 282, n e cor Dominick st, 20x55.6 to alley with use of same, four-story brk tenem't with stores. John H. Heaselden to John Dauenhauer. Q. C. and correction deed. Sept. 29. nom

Same property. John Dauenhauer and Marie L. his wife to Edward Knowlton. Oct. 14. 25,000

Jefferson st, No. 32, w s, 50 n Monroe st, 25x104.4, five-story brk tenem't. Abraham M. Levy and Fanny his wife to Solomon Cohen. Mt. $30,500. Oct. 15. See Norfolk st. 42,000

Laight st, No. 57, s w cor Collister st, 25x87.6, two and three-story frame store and tenem't. Du Bois Smith and Fannie E. his wife, Smithtown, L. I., to Vincent J. Slattery. Mt. $15,000 Aug. 3. 2,500

Ludlow st, No. 170, e s, 75.10 n Stanton st, 24.10x90, five-story brk tenem't with stores. John A. Frey and Ellen his wife to George B. Christman. ½ part. Mt. ½ of $15,000. May 11. 10,000

Madison st, No. 336, s s, 56 e Scammel st, 19.5x87x19.5x86, four-story brk tenem't. Aaron Goodman and Fannie his wife to Aaron Kaplan. Mt. $6,000. Sept. 30. exch

Same property. Aaron Kaplan and Rachel his wife to Nathan and Marks Rosenberg. Mt. $6,000. Oct. 8. See Suffolk st. 10,000

Madison st, Nos. 313 and 315, n s, 58.3 w Gouverneur st, runs west 53.2 x north 87.4 x east 56.1 x south 5.7 x west 2.4 x south 78.7, two five-story brk tenem'ts. Michael J. Mahony and Anne E. his wife and Daniel F. Mahony and Mary C. his wife to Harry and Harris Newcorn. Mt. $30,000. Sept. 5. 58,500

Maiden lane, No 134 } begins Maiden lane, e s,
Fletcher st, No. 19 } abt 53 s Water st, 17x the block to Fletcher st, five-story brk store. William H. Field and Lottie E. his wife to James W. McCaffrey. C. a. G. Mt. $11,000. Sept. 14. 28,000

Monroe st, No. 244, s s, 269.3 e Scammel st, 24.9x97.8, five-story brk tenem't with stores. Release mort. Joseph L. Buttenwieser to John V. Campbell. Oct. 1. nom

Same property. John V. Campbell and Elizabeth M. C. his wife to Moses Lubelsky. Mt. $29,000. Oct. 1. See Catharine st. 38,000

Mott st, No. 110, e s, 43.2 s Hester st, runs east 45.11 x south 6.10 x east 22 x south 16 x west 68.5 to Mott st, x north 22.10, three-story frame (brk front) store and tenem't. William S. Cooper to Benjamin Sirb. Mt. $12,500. June 13. 18,000

Norfolk st, No. 119, w s, 80 s Rivington st, 20x50, three-story brk store and tenem't. Solomon Cohen and Katie his wife to Abraham M. Levy. Mt. $8,600. Oct. 15. See Jefferson st. 13,000

Suffolk st, No. 12, e s, abt 75 n Hester st, 25x50, five-story brk tenem't with stores. Nathan Rosenberg and Sarah his wife and Marks Rosenberg to Aaron Kaplan and Aaron Goodman. Mt. $21,500. Oct. 8. See Madison st. 27,000

Suffolk st, No. 12, e s, abt 75 n Hester st, 25x50, five-story brk tenem't with stores. Aaron Goodman and Fannie his wife, Brooklyn, to Aaron Kaplan. ½ part. Sub. to morts. Oct. 8. 13,500

Water st, No. 230, n s, abt 25 e Beekman st, 24.11x81.8x24.7x82.4, four-story brk store. Clemence L. Hasell widow, Georgetown, S. C., Amelia W., Annette B. and Clemence L. Boardman and Margaret W. Boardman an infant by Richard A. Brown guard. to H. Eugene Holdridge. Oct. 5. 22,500

Water st, No. 230, n s, abt 25 e Beekman st, 24.11x81.8x24.7x82.4, four-story brk store. H. Eugene Holdridge to Charles F., Jr., and William M. V. Hoffman. Mt. $11,000. Oct. 13. 22,500

18th st, No. 325 n s, abt 310 w 8th av, 21.10x92, three-story brk dwell'g. James Harrison to Joseph Doyle. Mt. $8,000. Oct. 13. other consid. and 15,000

20th st, No. 161, n s, 80 e 7th av, 20x92. }
20th st, No. 159, n s, 100 e 7th av, 26.1x92. }
Two four-story brk tenem'ts with two three-story brk tenem'ts on rear. }
George A. Heaney to Ada, Mary and Grace E. Ingersoll. B. & S. Dec. 28, 1887. 112

23d st, No. 244, s s, 462.6 w 7th av, 18.9x98.9, four-story stone front dwell'g. William H. Field and Lottie E. his wife to James W. McCaffrey. C. a. G. Mt. $9,000. Sept. 14. 21,250

24th st, No. 142, s s, 262.6 e 7th av, 18.9x98.9, three-story brk dwell'g. Cora Belle Cornwall to Eliza G. Kennison. Mt. $9,000. Oct. 14. 14,750

31st st, Nos. 239–243, n s, 250 e 8th av, 75x98.9, three three-story brk tenem'ts with two three-story brk buildings on rear. Thomas H. Moffatt to Meelissa G. Moffatt. B. & S. All title. All liens. May 11, 1891. nom

39th st Nos. 266 and 268, s s, 100 e 8th av, 61.6x98.9, two five-story stone front flats. Margaret Devlin widow to Jacob Korn and Thomas B. Chatfield, joint tenants. Oct. 13. In trust for benefit creditors to sell for not less than 110,000

40th st, Nos. 310 and 312, s s, 200 w 8th av, 50x98.9, two five-story brk stores and tenem'ts with three-story brk building on rear. Max Borger to Richard Stacpoole and Laura his wife. Mt. $28,000. Oct. 15. 41,000

41st st, No. 329, n s, 375 w 8th av, 25x98.9, four-story brk store and tenem't with three-story frame building on rear. Issac Mannheimer and Rebecca his wife to Joseph Brucker. Mt. $10,000. Oct. 5. See 99th st. 13,500

45th st, No. 342, s s, 70 w 1st av, 30x100.5, four-story brk building. Charles Weiland and Melaine his wife to Henry, Jr., and Paul P. Zubille, of H. Zubiller's Sons. Mt. $10,000. Oct. 13. 13,750

45th st, No. 238, s s, 150 w 2d av, 22x82.1x25x94.2, extends to lane, four-story brk store and tenem't. Helen F. wife of and William E. Clark, Independence, Kan., and Harriet M. Williams, Rahway, N. J., to John H. Williams, Rahway, N. J. Mt. $2,000. B. & S. Re-recorded. June 10, 1887. 7,000

46th st, No. 433, n s, 349.8 w 9th av, runs west 26.4 x north 100.5 x east 31 x southwest 13.10 x south 87.1, five-story stone front flat. John P. Kane and Mary T. his wife to James Cassin, Brooklyn. Q. C. Oct. 9. nom

Same property. John P. Ryan to same. Mt. $16,000. Oct 10. 21,000

54th st, No. 543, n s, 500 w 10th av, 25x51.1x25.2x48.4, two-story frame store and dwell'g. Charles F. Herrmann and Annie his wife to Jacob New. Q. C. Oct. 9. nom

54th st, No. 351, n s, 80 w 1st av, 20x100.5, four-story brk tenem't. Xaver and Elizabeth Pacher to Pauline Frank. Mt. $9,000 and int. and taxes 1891. Oct. 6. 14,000

55th st, No. 75, n s, 83.4 w 4th av, 16.8x100.5, four-story stone front dwell'g. Abbie M. Allen to William L. Turner. Mt. $11,000. Oct. 15. nom

55th st, No. 250, s s, 158.4 e 8th av, 16.8x100, four-story stone front dwell'g. Leah Hackett, Littleton, N. C., and Cornelius R. Waterbury and Coralyn B. his wife to Eunice R. Waterbury and Eloise B. Crothers formerly Waterbury. All title. Q. C. Sept. 17. 11,000

57th st, No. 320, s s, 200 e 2d av, 25x100.5, five-story brk flat. Henry Stengel and Lillian his wife to Sophia, Maria J., Katharine F. and John C. or Jean C. de Krom. Mt. $20,000. Oct. 15. See 2d av. 40,000

57th st, No. 56, s s, 28 w Park av, 22x100.5, four-story brk dwell'g. Sarah R. Beach widow to Fanny E. wife of John H. Harris. Mt. $51,250. Sept. 14. 63,750

59th st, Nos. 9–19, n s, 175 e 5th av, 150x100.5, six four-story stone front flats. Richard T. Wilson and Melissa C. his wife to Mayer Kahn and Marcus Kohner. Mt. $108,000. Oct. 14. val. consid

61st st, No. 303, n s, 75 e 2d av, 25x75, five-story brk tenem't. Gustav Wenzel to Fanny B. Clarke. ½ part. Mt. $13,000. Oct. 15. 15,000

61st st, No. 303, n s, 75 e 2d av, 25x75, five-story brk tenem't. Fanny B. wife of Daniel A. Clarke to Gustav Wenzel. ½ part. Mt. $13,000. April 4. nom

62d st, No. 142, s s, 475 w Columbus av, 25x100.5, five-story brk flat. Charles Lowen and Sarah E his wife, Edward F. Halliday and Mary J. his wife, Michael Hayes and Caroline M his wife, and George Hessels and Mary his wife to William Ritterbusch. Mt. $18,000. Oct. 14. 30,500

63d st, No. 340, s s, 125 w 1st av, 25x100.5, five-story brk tenem't with stores. Jacob Geisenheimer to Bernard Klein. Mt. $12,500. Oct. 5. 16,500

65th st, No. 138, s s, 438 e 10th av, 20x100.5, four-story stone front dwell'g. Lee Wolff trustee to The Amsterdam Impt. Co. Sept. 28. nom

66th st, No. 229, n s, 350 e West End av, 25x100.5, five-story brk tenem't. George F. Betts and Ellen P. his wife to Thomas R. Hughes, Weehawken, N. J. Mt. $17,500. Oct. 15. nom

66th st, No 231, n s, 325 e West End av, 25x100.5, five-story brk tenem't. Same to same. Mt. $15,000. Oct. 15. nom

67th st, No 206, s s, 150 w Amsterdam av, 25x100.5, five-story brk tenem't. Foreclos. Gilbert M. Speir, Jr., to Samuel H. Denton. Oct. 13. 18,800

70th st, No. 33, n s, 375 w 8th av, 25x100.5, one-story frame building. Aaron Holbrook, Winchester, Mass., and Julia R. his wife to John Bates, Cohasset, Norfolk Co., Mass. Re-recorded. Nov 18, 1884. nom

Same property. Sarah R., Ann M., Georgiana H. and Jonathan Bates, Boston, Mass., Susan E. wife of Royal S. Warren, Colorado Springs, Col., Ella S. and Mary W. and C. Francis Bates, New York, to Charles S. Bates, Boston, Mass. B. & S. March 2, 1889. nom

Same property. Charles S. Bates, Boston, Mass., to John Ruddell. B. & S. July 17. 15,000

70th st, No. 59, n s, 305 e Columbus av, 20x100.5, four-story stone front dwell'g. George W. Ruddell to William H. Van Allen. Mt. $22,500. Oct. 14. 37,000

70th st, No. 63, n s, 265 e Columbus av, 20x100.5, four-story stone front dwell'g. George W. Ruddell to Anna C. wife of Otto Wessell. Mt. $22,500. Oct. 15. nom

71st st, No. 233, n s, 432 e 11th av, 18x102.2, three-story stone front dwell'g. W. W. Flannagan to Frances J. Flannagan. Mt. $12,500. Sept. 17. nom

71st st, s s, 100 e Columbus av, 25x100.5, vacant lot. Francis Crawford and Margaret his wife to John S. Hawley. Mt. $9,000. Oct. 13. 15,750

72d st, No. 122, s s, 200 w Columbus av, 25x102.2, four-story stone front dwell'g. Francis Crawford and Margaret his wife to Charles G. Emery. Oct. 13. 75,000

73d st, No. 432, s s, 125 w Av A, 25x102.2, five-story brk tenem't. Joseph Stang and Rebecca his wife and David Hittner and Dora his wife to Joseph Berkowitz. Mt. $20,590. Oct. 9. 26,450

74th st, No. 12, s s, 200 w Central Park West, 25x102.2, four-story stone front dwell'g. Cornelius W. Luyster and Mary W. his wife to Seamen Lichtenstein. Mt. $25,000. Oct. 10. nom

74th st, No 5, n s, 120 w Central Park West, 20x102.2, four-story brk dwell'g. Carrie S. wife of David T. Kennedy to Hester A. Montgomery. Mt. $27,500. Oct. 14. 50,000

75th st, No. 28, s s, 400 e Columbus av, 20x95, four-story stone front dwell'g. Release mort. Gideon Fountain to John C. Umberfield. Oct. 14. 5,000

Same property. John C. Umberfield and Mary W. his wife to Joseph wife of Albrecht Graef. Mt. $25,000. Oct. 13. nom

75th st, No. 113, n s, 200 w 9th av, 20x102.2, four-story stone front dwell'g. Release mort. Louis Clark, Jr., to James R. Breen and Alfred G. Nason. Oct. 8. 3,000

Same property. James R. Breen and Bathsheba his wife and Alfred G Nason and Mary A. his wife to Mathilda Price. Mt. $24,000. Sept. 30. 35,000

75th st, No. 408, s s, 138 e 1st av, 25x116.11x25.4x118, four-story stone front tenem't. Charlotte Ehrlinger widow to Sigmund Lewy and Moritz Weiss. Mt. $9,000. Oct. 15. 17,500

Same property. Charles Ehrlinger and Louisa C. his wife to Christian Ehrlinger and Charlotte Beck heirs Christian Ehrlinger to same. Q. C. Oct. 14. nom

76th st, No. 56, s s, 100 e 9th av, 18x102.2, four-story stone front dwell'g. Edmund Guilbert and Minnie I. his wife to Patrick Smith. Mt. $22,500. Oct. 15. nom

76th st, No. 135, n s, 344 w 9th av, 19x102.2, three-story stone front dwell'g. Florence I. wife of and John S. Silver to Camille Weidenfeld. Mt. $17,000 and all liens. Oct. 15. 30,000

76th st, n s, 90 w Amsterdam av, 50x102.2, vacant. Eliza J. and Oliver M. Arkenburgh exrs. Robert H. Arkenburgh to William B. Baldwin. Oct. 2. 22,250

76th st, Nos. 312–320, s s, 200 w 11th av, 100x102.2x100x104.2, five three-story brk dwell'gs. Susan D., John P. and Ruth Huntington heirs James M. Huntington to William F. Buckley. Q C. July 14. nom

Same property. Anna B. and Emily B. Lathrop and Mary L. wife of De Lancey Rochester heirs of John P. P. Lathrop and Anna B. Lathrop widow to same. Q. C. July 14. nom

Same property. Elizabeth R. Huntington widow and guard. of Susan D., John P. and Ruth Huntington, also James M., Elizabeth B., Mary and Roscoe Huntington to same. July 14. nom

Same property. Mary L. Bartow widow, Francis C. Lathrop and Fanny C. his wife. Priscilla A. Lathrop widow, Thomas Lathrop, Joshua Lathrop and Emily R. his wife and Lydia H. Pierson widow to same. Sept. 29. nom

Same property. Charles P. Huntington to same. Q. C. July 14. nom

Same property. George De N. Gillespie to same. Q. C. July 14. nom

Same property. Benjamin F. Huntington, Henry R. Bond and William H. and Mary P. Huntington to same. Q. C. July 24. nom

77th st, No. 233, n s, 305 e 3d av, 12.6x102.2, three-story brk dwell'g. Albert C. Henderson to William C. Lesster. *Mt.* $5,300, taxes, &c. Oct. 8. nom

79th st, Nos. 171-175, n s, 205 e Amsterdam av, 45x102.2, three three-story stone front unfinished dwellings. John O. Baker and Lucy D. W. his wife, Newark, N. J., to Amelia wife of William Bell. C. a. G. Oct. 12. 40,000

81st st, No. 413, n s, 231.6 e 1st av, 25x102.2, five-story brk tenem't. Jacob Schlosser and Margaret his wife to Catharina E. Birkenbauer. *Mt.* $14,000. Oct. 13. 22,000

82d st, No. 524, s s, 329 e Av A, 18.9x102.2, four-story stone front tenem't. Louis Newberger and Jennette his wife to Adolph Helmus. *Mt.* $7,000. Oct. 13. 13,000

83d st. No. 527, n s, 398 e Av A, 25x102.2, five-story brk tenem't. Louis Lese and Sarah his wife to Joseph Demmer. *Mt.* $16,000. Oct. 14. 22,500

83d st, No. 527, n s, 398 e Av A, 25x102.2, five-story brk tenem't. Morris Goldstein and Pauline his wife to Louis Lese. ½ part. *Mt.* $16,000. Aug. 4. nom

84th st, No. 124, s s, 92.9 w Lexington av, and being 587.9 w 3d av, 25.7x102.2, three-story frame building. Anna J. Lennon to William F. Lennon. Oct. 10. nom

85th st, No. 214, s s, 180 e 3d av, 25x102, five-story brk flat. Louis Wirth and Barbara his wife to Michael Gebhard. *Mt.* $15,000. Oct. 15. 29,500

85th st, No. 6, s s, 144 e 5th av, 20.6x102.2, four-story stone front dwell'g. Jacob New and Esther his wife to Agostino Cavinato. *Mt.* $18,000. Oct. 12. See South 5th av. 30,000

85th st, No. 44, s s, 375 e 9th av, 25x102.2, four-story stone front dwell'g. Foreclos. Henry V. Sackett to Thomas R. Hughes, Weehawken, N. J. Oct. 9. 35,150

Same property. Thomas R. Hughes, Weehawken, N. J., to Henry J. Braker. *Mt.* $38,000. Oct. 9. 55,000

85th st, No. 156, s s, 300 e Amsterdam av, 25x59.10x25.4x58.9, two-story brk dwell'g. John Campbell and Anne L. his wife to Mary Walbridge, Brooklyn. *Mt.* $4,500. Oct. 13. 12,000

86th st, No. 137, n s, 401 e Amsterdam av, 23x100.8. Release mort. D. Willis James to John G. Prague. Oct. 6. nom

86th st, No. 77, n s, 72.6 e Columbus av, 20x100.8, four-story brk dwell'g. John G. Prague to Caroline Stine. *Mt.* $30,000, taxes, &c. Oct. 9. nom

86th st, Nos. 269 and 271, n s, 100 e West End av, 125x100.8, two-story frame, three-story brk livery stable and two vacant lots. Mary A. Jordan widow, Eleanor P. wife of Wellesley W. Gage to William W. Brower. Q. C. All liens. Dec. 30, 1890. nom

88th st, No. 309, n s, 119 w West End av, 19x100.8, four-story brk dwell'g. Release mort. The Bradley & Currier Co. (Lim.) to Andrew Grant and William Gunn. Oct. 14. nom

Same property. William Gunn and Martha his wife and Andrew Grant and Janet his wife to H. Ramsdell Moore. *Mt.* $21,000. Oct. 14. 26,500

89th st, No. 309, n s, 150 w West End av, 20x100, three-story stone front dwell'g. Release mort. Francis M. Jencks to William E. Lanchantin. Oct. 15. 1,000

Same property. William E. Lanchantin and Carriebell D. his wife to William M. Leslie. *Mt.* $17,500. Oct. 13. nom

89th st, No. 262, s s, 82 e West End av, 18x100.8, four-story brk dwell'g.
West End av, No. 490, e s, 81.8 s 89th st, 19x82, three-story brk dwell'g.
West End av, No. 498, s e cor 89th st, 24.8x52, three-story brk dwell'g.
West End av, Nos. 494 and 496, e s, 24.8 s 89th st, 38x64, two three-story brk dwell'gs.
Jacob Brandt to Joseph E. Weed, Brooklyn. Oct. 7. nom

Same property, excepting therefrom No. 494 West End av. Joseph E. Weed, Brooklyn, to Arminthia Merritt. *Mt.* $72,000. Oct. 8. nom

90th st, n s, 240 w West End av, 35x100.8, vacant. Charles T. Barney and Lilly W. his wife to John O. Baker, Newark, N. J. C. a. G. Oct. 1. 20,000

Same property. John O. Baker, Newark, N. J., and Lucy D. W. his wife to Thomas J. Sheridan and James E. Byrne. Oct. 5. 20,000

90th st, No. 310, s s, 160 w West End av, 20x100.8, four-story stone front dwell'g. Theodore A. Squier and Carrie B. his wife to Emma B. Richardson. *Mt.* $17,000. Oct. 1. nom

91st st, n s, 175 e 5th av, 25x100, vacant.
91st st, No. 11, n s, 204.5 e 5th av, 25.7x100.8, one-story frame store and three-story frame dwell'g on rear.
Thomas Graham and Jennie his wife to Isaac Untermyer. All liens. Oct. 13. nom

96th st, s s, 150 e Amsterdam av, 100x101.5. Amy E. wife of and Bernard Cohn to The Amsterdam Imp't Co. All liens. Oct. 9. nom

96th st, s s, 150 e Amsterdam av, 200x101.5, vacant. The Amsterdam Imp't Co. to Randolph Guggenheimer and Salomon Marx. *Mt.* $63,000. Oct. 9. See Hamilton st also 1st av. 98,720

99th st, No. 71, n s, 75 e 9th av, 24.6x100.11, five-story brk flat. Joseph Brucker and Louise his wife to Isaac Mannheimer. *Mt.* $11,000. Oct. 6. See 41st st. 21,500

99th st, No. 233, n s, 79 w 2d av, 26x101, five-story brk tenem't. William C. Martin and Alice L. B. his wife to Waldemar Faehndrich. *Mt.* $12,500. Oct. 9. 18,750

100th st, n s, 200 e 5th av, 50x100, vacant, also out-of-town property. Edward A. Carley to William P. Hill. Q. C. Oct. 7. nom

100th st, 162, s s, 200 w 3d av, 25x100.11, five-story brk tenem't. Herman Vehstedt to Frederick Dittman. *Mt.* $18,000. Oct. 15. 20,000

101st st, No. 194, s s, 96 w 3d av, 27x100.11, four-story brk tenem't. Valentine Pressler and Louisa his wife to William J. Gilmore. *Mt.* $14,500. Oct. 15. See 133d st. 18,000

102d st, n s, 52 e Park av, 50x100.11. Release mort. The Bradley & Currier Co. (Lim.) to Frederick Rohrs and Louisa his wife. Oct. 8. nom

103d st, n s, 250 w 4th av old line, 25x100.11. Release of covenant. James F. Stansbury and Catharine N. his wife, Elizabeth, N. J., to Margaret J. wife of Terence P. Smith. Oct. 6. 30

103d st, n s, 230 w 4th av, 25x100, vacant. Margaret J. wife of Terence P. Smith to J. Allen Townsend. *Mt.* $4,000. Oct. 7. nom

105th st, No. 69, n s, 220 e Madison av, 25x100.11, five-story brk flat. John J. Feehan and Matilda his wife and Ernest Hammer and Catherine his wife to William Laue, Brooklyn. *Mt.* $15,000. Oct. 6. 25,000

105th st, No. 305, n s, 100 e 2d av, 25x100.11, five-story brk store and flat. Matthew Coogan and Teresa his wife to Peter V. Stocky. *Mt.* $15,000. Oct. 2. 21,000

105th st, Nos. 55 and 57, n s, 280 w 4th av, 50x100.11, two five-story brk flats. John and Margaret O'Connor to Joseph Hoffman. All liens. B. & S. Oct. 13. 4,000

106th st, No. 338, s s, 200 w 1st av, 25x100.11, five-story brk tenem't. William Dempsey and John Smith to Mary Ann Duffy. *Mt.* $15,400 and all liens. Oct. 10. 2,600

111th st, No. 99, n e cor 4th av, 16x100.11.
111th st, No. 111, n s, 95.8 e 4th av, 15.11x100.11.
111th st, No. 139, n s, 239 e 4th av, 15.11x100.11.
Three three-story stone front dwell'gs.
John H. Bloodgood and Elizabeth his wife to George W. Bryant. *Mt.* $2,500. Re-recorded. May 29, 1891. nom

113th st, n s, 100 e Lenox av, 25x100.11, vacant.
114th st, s s, 100 e Lenox av, 25x100.11, vacant.
Johanna wife of Julius Hirschberg to Mary E. wife of Henry J. McGuckin. All liens. Oct. 7. exch and 15,000

114th st, Nos. 14 and 16, s s, 150 e 5th av, 50x100.11, two five-story brk flats. Jacob Mohr to Andrew Pfeiffer. *Mt.* $36,000. Oct. 12. See Av A. 50,500

116th st, s s, 175 e 4th av, 25x100.11, vacant. Hugh Reilly and Elizabeth his wife to John P. Kane. All liens. Oct. 12. nom

116th st, No. 412, s s, 462.1 w Pleasant av, 18.7x100.11, three-story stone front dwell'g. Alice wife of Martin Stettiner to James B. and Kate F. Dolan. *Mt.* $8,000. Oct. 14. 11,000

120th st, No. 57, n s, 250.2 w 4th av, 16.8x100.11.
120th st, No. 53, n s, 283.5 w 4th av, 16.6x100.11.
Two three-story stone front dwell'gs.
Michael Cain and Bridget his wife to Johanna wife of Julius Hirschberg. *Mt* $24,000. Oct. 7. 35,000

120th st, n s, 283.5 w 4th av, runs east 0.2x100.11. Michael Cain and Bridget his wife to Mary J. Raynor. Q. C. Oct. 9. nom

121st st, No. 4, s s, 100 w Mount Morris av, 20x100.11, four-story stone front dwell'g. Samuel O. Wright and Maria T. his wife, Rockville Centre, L. I., to Carrie A. Taylor. *Mt.* $25,000. Re-recorded. July 2. 40,000

121st st, No. 6, s s, 120 w Mount Morris av, 20x100.11, four-story stone front dwell'g. Same to Edgar Lockwood. *Mt.* $25,000. Re recorded. Aug. 20. 39,000

123d st, No. 262, s s, 175 e 8th av, 25x100.11, five-story stone front flat. Foreclos. William H. Ricketts to Joseph F. Stier. Sub. to mort. $15,000. Oct. 12. 5,000

123d st, No. 264, s s, 150 e 8th av, 25x100.11, five-story stone front flat. Foreclos. Same to same. Sub. to mort. $15,000. Oct. 12. 5,700

123d st, No. 436, s s, 218.9 w Pleasant av, 18.9x100, three-story stone front dwell'g. Hannah wife of Herman Weinberg to Peter E. Sheridan. *Mt.* $3,250. Oct. 13. 4,750

127th st, No. 254, s s, 333.4 e 8th av, 16.8x99.11, three-story stone front dwell'g. Frederick Aldhous and Eliza his wife to Annie V. and Emily C. Fox. *Mt.* $10,000. Oct. 9. 14,500

133d st, No. 153, n s, 300 e 7th av, 25x99.11, five-story brk flat. William J. Gilmore and Julia A. his wife to Valentine Pressler. *Mt.* $19,500. Oct. 15. See 101st st. 28,000

135th st, s s, 300 e 7th av, —x99.11x50x99.11, vacant. Ethelbert Wilson and Adelaide E. his wife to Richard White. *Mt.* $14,000. Oct. 13. 22,000

137th st, s s, 430 w Lenox av, runs south 99.11 x west 20 x north 48 x west 22 x north 51.11 to 137th st, x east 42, three-story brk dwell'g. Foreclos. Martin T. McMahon to Patrick Farley. Sept. 2. 17,000

Same property. Lucy A. Kneeland widow to same. Q. C. Oct. 13. nom

Same property. Sarah E. Le Compte to same. Q. C. Oct. 13. nom

144th st, No. 456, s s, 195 e 10th av, 19x99.11, three-story brk dwell'g. Release mort. Alfred P. Dix and John J. Phyfe individ. and of Dix & Phyfe to Harriet De Forest. Oct. 12. nom

Same property. Release judgment. Samuel Clark to Harriet and William H. De Forest, Jr. Oct. 13. 150

Same property. Release judgment. Emma H. Worcester to same. Oct. 12. nom

Same property. Harriet wife of William H. De Forest, Jr., to Anna Williamson. *Mt.* $6,500. Oct. 15. other consid. and 1,600

152d st, s s, 425 e Amsterdam av, 50x99.11, two-story brk dwell'g. James B. Gillie to Philip Schaefer. *Mt.* $13,000. Oct. 15. nom

Amsterdam av, No 789, e s, 104.8 n 98th st, 29.11x—x24.10x100, five-story brk flat with stores. Henry Stube and Elizabeth his wife to Margaret Dreyer. *Mt.* $17,000. Oct. 15. nom

Amsterdam av } begins Amsterdam av,
184th st (original line) } e s, 99.11 n 183d st, 259.10 crossing 184th st, x150. Charles E. Runk and Aurelia E. his wife to Herman Wronkow. *Mt.* $55,000. Oct. 1. nom

Amsterdam av } begins Ams-
Broadway or Kingsbridge road } terdam av, w s, 139.10 s 164th st, 39.11x182.5 to Broadway or Kingsbridge road, x 42.8x197.4, two-story brk dwell'g. Francis H. Weeks and Louisa B. his wife to Andrew J. McCormack. Oct. 7. 12,500

Av A, No. 1333, n w cor 71st st, 29.4x75, five-story brk tenem't with stores. Andrew Pfeiffer and Christina his wife to Jacob Mohr. *Mt.* $20,000. Oct. 12. See 114th st. nom

Av A, Nos. 28 and 30, e s, 88.6 s 3d st, 44x120, five and three-story brk assembly rooms. Foreclos. Delano C. Calvin to David M. Kellogg. Aug. 25. 60,000

Same property. Charles J. Forster and Matilda his wife to Moritz Bauer. Re-recorded. Sub. to morts. Sept. 27, 1884. 90,000

Av A, No. 293, w s, 22 n 18th st, 20x90, four-story brk store and tenem't with four-story brk tenem't on rear. Jacob Mayer and Celestine his wife to J. H. Ludwig Reinemann. *Mt.* $8,000. Oct. 15. 15,250

Columbus av, No. 465, e s, 51.10 n 82d st, 25.2x100, five-story brk store and flat. George F. Betts and Ellen P. his wife to Jacob Winkler. *Mt.* $30,000. Oct. 15. 34,250

Columbus av, No. 467, e s, 77 n 82d st, 25.2x100, five-story brk store and flat. Same to Michael J. Wolf. *Mt.* $29,000. Oct. 15. 34,250

Lenox av, Nos. 334 and 336, e s, 34 s 127th st, 33x85, four-story stone front school. Andrew Zerbau to Mary Zerbau his wife. *Mt.* $22,000. Oct. 14. nom

Lenox av, w s, extends from 116th to 117th st, 201.10x100, vacant.
116th st, n s, 100 w Lenox av, 100x100.11, vacant.
117th st, s s, 100 w Lenox av, 100x100.11, vacant.
Foreclos. Edward F. O'Dwyer to Bertha Smith. *Mt.* $165,000. Oct. 14. 11,000

Lenox av, Nos. 60-70, e s, extends from 113th to 114th st, 201.10x100, six five-story brk flats, stores in corners, buildings will be altered for hotel purposes. Johanna wife of and Julius Hirschberg to Mary E. wife of Henry J. McGuckin. *Mt.* $126,500 and taxes. Oct. 7. exch. and 216,000

Lexington av, No. 616, n w cor 53d st, 21x68, five-story brk (stone front) store and flat. William S. Cooper to Benjemen Sire. Sub. to morts. April 28. 38,000

Lexington av, Nos. 1636 and 1638, n w cor 104th st, 33.11x55.
Lexington av, No. 1642, w s, 50.7 n 104th st, 16.8x55.
Lexington av, Nos. 1648-1658, w s, 100.7 n 104th st, being the s w cor 105th st, 100.7x55.
Nine three-story brk and stone front dwellings.

Rachel wife of Ferdinand Mayer to Louis Cohen. All liens. Recorded Sept. 23, 1891. Sept. 18. nom

Lexington av, No. 874, w s, 80.5 n 65th st, 20x70, four-story stone front dwell'g. John Higgins devisee of Ann C. Higgins to Simon P. Flannery. Oct. 12. nom

Lexington av, Nos. 1029 and 1031, e s, 68.2 s 74th st, 34x93.9, two three-story stone front dwell'gs. William F. Lennon and Anna J. his wife to Samuel Goetz. Sub. to morts. Oct. 9. See Goerck st. nom

Same property. Samuel Goetz and Julia his wife to Randolph Guggenheimer and Salomon Marx. Sub. to morts. Oct. 9. nom

Madison av, No. 811, s e cor 68th st, 22.5x95, four-story brk dwell'g. Edwin R. Allen,

Brooklyn, to George N. Miller and Martha Le R. his wife. B. & S. Oct. 9. nom

Same property. George N. Miller, Rhinebeck, N. Y., to Edwin R. Allen. B. & S. Oct. 9. nom

Park av. No. 1301, n e cor 94th st, 17.8x66, three-story brk dwell'g. Adolph M. Bendheim and Henrietta his wife to Henry Hachmeister. *Mt.* $17,000. Oct. 13. 22,400

Pleasant av } begins Pleasant av, w s, 150.10
113th st, No. 438 } s 113th st, runs west 93 x north 50 x west 50 x north 100.10 to 113th st, x east 143 to Pleasant av, x south 150.10, with machinery, &c., one and two-story frame and brk buildings, stone works, &c. William Dempsey and John Smith, of Dempsey & Smith, to The Brainerd Quarry Co. *Mt.* $32,800. April 24. 87,000

South 5th av, No. 65, s e s, 100 n e Houston st, 24x100, six-story brk tenem't. Natale, Luigi, Guiseppe and Steffano Cavinato to Jacob New. *Mt.* $35,000. Oct. 12. See 85th st. 60,000

West End av, No. 494, e s, 43.8 s 89th st, 19x64, three-story brk dwell'g. Joseph E. Weed, Brooklyn, to Sara R. Foote. *Mt.* $16,000. Oct. 8. 20,750

West End av, No. 492, e s, 62.8 s 89th st, runs east 64 x south 5 x east 18 x south 14 x west 82 to av, x north 19, three-story brk dwell'g. Jacob Brandt to Rufus D. Pitcher. *Mt.* $17,000. Oct. 9. 25,000

West End av, s e cor 98th st, 19.11x100. }
West End av, e s, 55.11 s 98th st, 18x100. }
Release mort. Harriet Overhiser to Edward Kilpatrick. Oct. 14. 20,000

1st av, e s, 50 s 94th st, 50.8x94. Release mort. James D. Shipman exr. Asa L. Shipman to Frederick Willenbrock and Hancke Hencke. Oct. 12. nom

1st av, No. 549, w s, 49.4 s 32d st, 24.8x100, four-story brk tenem't with stores. Randolph Guggenheimer and Eliza his wife and Salomon Marx and Betche his wife to The Amsterdam Improvement Co. *Mt.* $10,500. Oct. 9. See Hamilton st and 96th st. 15,000

1st av, Nos. 1140 and 1142, e s, 25 s 63d st, 50x81.5, two five-story brk tenem'ts with stores. Michael Rofrano and Alessandrina his wife to Alberico Caroselli. All liens. June 5. 45,000

2d av, No. 2422, e s, 20.11 n 124th st, 20x80, three-story stone front dwell'g. Isidor Alkus and Carry his wife to Agnes Yost. Oct. 14. 10,900

2d av, No. 1012, e s, 80.5 n 53d st, 20x70, five-story brk store and tenem't. Anna Catharine or Catherine Gerhards widow trustee and extrx. Charles Gerhards, Anna Lackwitz, Henry and Albert Gerhards and Emily Daeschler heirs Charles Gerhards to Ignatz Zickler. *Mt.* $8,500. Oct. 7. 18,300

2d av, No. 555, w s, 59.4 s 31st st, 19.8x77, four-story brk store and tenem't. William H. Newschafer and Amelia S. his wife to Charles E. Lansing. Sept. 2. 15,000

Same property. Charles E. Lansing to Amelia S. Newschafer. Oct. 12. 15,000

2d av, No 92, e s, 48.6 n 5th st, 24.8x100, four-story brk store and tenem't. Sophia, Maria J., Katharine F., John C. or Jean C. de Krom widow and heirs Jean de Krom to Henry Stengel. *Mt.* $13,500. Oct. 5. See 57th st. 25,000

2d av, No. 1066, n e cor 56th st, 21.3x70, four-story brk store and tenem't. John McSweeney and Mary E. his wife to John Vollmer. *Mt.* $26,000. Oct. 15. 32,500

3d av, No. 805, e s, 81 s 50th st, 21x90, with the right to build over the alley adjoining the premises on the south, 6.5x90, five-story brk store and tenem't. George A. Just heir George Just to Christina Just. *Mt.* $14,000. Oct. 5. nom

5th av, No. 95 } begins 5th av, s e cor 17th st,
17th st, No. 4 } runs southeast 116.10 to alleyway, x southwest 20 x northwest 54.2 x west — x northwest 60 to av, x north 22.8, five-story brk store on av and one and three-story brk stores on st. Wolf Dazian to Henry Dazian. *Mt* $100,000. June 27. 145,000

5th av, n w cor 114th st, 50.5x100, vacant. Max Barnett and Rosa his wife to Max S. Korn. All liens. Oct. 9 nom

7th av, Nos. 283 and 285, n e cor 26th st, 49.5x100, four-story brk stores. Isaac K. Cohn to Ascher Weinstein. *Mt.* $22,500. Oct. 15. 59,000

8th av, n e cor 139th st, 99.11x42.7. Agreement as to easement for light and air. David H. King, Jr., with said David H. King, Jr., trustee and Board of Health, New York. Oct. 10. nom

8th av, No. 2353, w s, 25 n 126th st, 25x100, five-story brk store and flat. }
Fleetwood av, n s, 33.7 w Popham st, 30x100. }
Norah Power sister of Margt. Power to Mary Power. June 6. nom

Same property. Hannah Power sister of Margt. Power to same. June 6. nom

Same property. Julia Power sister of Margt. Power to same. June 6. om

8th av, No. 2202, e s. 25.11 s 119th st, 25x80, five-story brk tenem't with stores. Philip Braender and Lizzie his wife to John Effinger. *Mt.* $16,000. Oct. 15. 25,000

9th av, Nos. 453 and 455, w s, 24.9 n 35th st, 49.4x100, two five-story brk tenem'ts with stores. Patrick Collins and Catherine his wife to Herman Joveshof. *Mt.* $42,000. Oct. 15.— nom

9th av, No. 738, e s, 22 s 50th st, 22x80, three-story frame store and tenem't. George Linnemann to Henry Linnemann. All title. *Mt.* $2,000. Oct. 13. 1,300

10th av, No. 313 } begins 10th av, n w cor 28th
28th st, No. 505 } st, 24.8x100, three-story brk store and tenem't on av and two-story brk stable on st. Catharine wife of and John McCauley to said John McCauley. Q. C. Oct. 1. nom

12th av, the plot is bounded on north by centre line of 87th st, east by west line of 12th av, south by centre line of 86th st, and west and southwest by west line of land or right of way of New York Central & Hudson River R. R. Co. as the same now runs. Wallace C. Andrews and Margaret M. St. J. his wife to Ellen R. Randall. Q. C. Oct. 6. nom

MISCELLANEOUS.

General release, especially as to estate of John Gibney and individ. J. W. Mitchell, William W. Stetson and Everett L. Mower to John McMillan and Robert McWilliam trustees John Gibney. Aug. 5. 258

Similar general release. Agnes Gibney to same. Aug. 8. 258

Similar general release. Grace Riddell to same. Aug. 8. 1,058

Similar ge ra release. Mary McLeod to same. Aug. 8. ne l 1 058

23d and 24th WARDS.

Church st, w s, 128 n from n s of proposed st, which point is the n e cor of S. W. Richards' lot, 50x100, Kingsbridge. Catharine Connelly widow to William Connelly. *Mt.* $1,500. Oct. 9. nom

Cordova pl, w s, 198.5 n St. Georges crescent, 25x100. Michael Morowske to Juliana Morowske his wife. Oct. 14. gift

Denman pl, n w cor Tinton av, 120x145.2. Allen Dodworth and Calanthe E. his wife, Pasadena, Cal., to Emily Fogal and George W. Harris. Oct. 10. 4,800

Same property. George W. Harris and Sarah A. his wife and Emily Fogal to Peter Herche. *Mt.* $3,000. Oct. 13. nom

Forest st, w s, 175 n Rock st, 25x100. James F. Sheridan, Patrick H. Sheridan and Kate his wife and James S. Segrave and Catharine A. his wife to Charles Lohr. October 15. 550

Forrest st, e s, 215 s Rock st, 100x100. }
Rock st, s s, 150 e Hill st, 50x154.6x54.8x177.4. }
Hill st, e s, 275 n Rock st, 25x125. }
Rock st, n e cor Hill st, 75x100. }
Rock st, n s, 75 e Hill st, 25x100. }
Rock st, n s, 100 e Hill st, 50x100. }
Forrest st, w s, 250 s Beach st, 52.7x100. }
Release mort. Thomas C. Cornell to James F. and Patrick H. Sheridan and James S. Segrave. Oct. 1. 7,925

Forrest st, w s, 150 n Rock st, 25x100. James F. Sheridan, Patrick H. Sheridan and Kate his wife and James S. Segrave and Catharine A. his wife to Ida M. Lichtwitz. Oct. 2. 550

Forrest st, e s, 215 s Rock st, 100x100. Same to James C. Croviel and Catharine A. his wife. Oct. 1. 1,750

Forrest st, w s, 250 s Beech st, 52.7x100. Same to Peter Herrmann and Caroline his wife. Oct. 1. 1 000

Forrest st, w s, 200 s Beech st, 50x100. Same to Alois Geiger and Johanna his wife. Oct. 1. 1,100

Hill st, w s, 122.2 s Rock st, 50x100. James F. Sheridan, Patrick H. Sheridan and Kate his wife and James S. Segrave and Catharine A. his wife to John H. Cook. Oct. 2. 850

Hill st, e s, 275 n Rock st, 25x125. Same to Patrick M. Dorgan. Oct. 1. 475

Hill st, e s, 25 s Rock st, 25x100. Same to Delia A. Moclair. Oct. 3. 425

Hill st, e s, 50 s Rock st, 50x100. Same to Amelia A. wife of Frederick S. Rockwell. Oct. 3. 850

Hill st, w s, 172.2 s Rock st, 50x100. Same to Mathew T. Kenealy. Oct. 2. 850

Hill st, e s, 200 n Rock st, runs east 100 x north 25 x east 25 x north 25 x west 125 to Hill st, x south 50. Same to Joseph Reilly. Oct. 1. 850

Hill st, s e cor Rock st, 25x100. Same to Kate A. Moclair. Oct. 3. 575

Hill st, w s, 122.2 s Rock st, 50x100. }
Hill st, w s, 172.2 s Rock st, 50x100. }
Rock st, n e cor Field st, 100x100. }
Release mort. Thomas C. Cornell, Yonkers, to James F. and Patrick H. Sheridan and James S. Segrave. Oct. 2. 4,450

Hill st, s e cor Rock st, 25x100. }
Hill st, e s, 50 s Rock st, 50x100. }
Release mort. Same to same. Oct. 3. 1,550

Main st, n e s, lot 231 map Village Mott Haven, 50x100. Alexander Johnry and Ellen E. his wife to Michael O'Neil. Oct. 13. 5,500

Mount Hope pl, n s, 150 w Morris av, 25x125. Caleb C. and Amelia W. Dusenbury, Carmel, N. Y., to Robert N. Cleverdon. Oct. 12. 2,000

Rock st, n s, 100 e Hill st, 50x100. James F. Sheridan, Patrick H. Sheridan and Kate his wife and James S. Segrave and Catharine A. his wife to James Leitch. Oct. 1. 850

Rock st, n s, 75 e Hill st, 25x100. Same to Mary M. Alheit. Oct. 1. 500

Rock st, s s, 150 e Hill st, 50x154.6x54.8x177.4. Same to Carl Kreutzer and Katharina E. his wife. Oct. 1. 900

Rock st, n e cor Hill st, 75x100. Same to Louise Muth. Oct. 1. 1,500

Rock st, n e cor Field st, 100x100. Same to Bernhard Armbruster and Karolina his wife. Oct. 2. 2,200

Spring st, old west line, 124.2 s 161st st, runs west 24.9 to w s Sheridan av at point 125 s 161st st, x west 95.9 x north 24.7 x east 96 to w s Sheridan av as laid down on Park Department map at point 100 s from s w cor 161st st and new line of Sheridan av, x again east 23.11 to said w s Spring st, x south — to beginning. Mary Corsa to Samuel G. Revans. B. & S. Oct. 12. 6,000

Waverly st, n s, east ½ of lot 78 map Melrose, 25x100, h & l. Anna Uebel heir of Conrad and Elizabeth Uebel both dec'd to Ferdinand Bohmer, Jr. *Mt.* $1,500. Sept. 30. 2,700

2d st, s w s, lot 42 map Prospect Hill estate, 50x100. Gottfried Schultz and Louisa his wife to Jennie Lyons. Aug. 10. 4,400

134th st, s s, 175 w Alexander av, 50x100, error. Release mort. The Bradley & Currier Co. (Lim.) to Frederick Rohrs and Louisa his wife. Oct. 8. nom

Same property. Release mort. Same to same. Oct. 8. nom

Same property. Frederick Rohrs and Louisa his wife to Edward M. Scudder. *Mt.* $28,000. Oct. 8. nom

134th st, n s, 341.8 e St. Anns av, 16.8x100, h & l. James Morrow and Anna his wife to Mary E. Whitney. *Mt.* $4,500. Oct. 10. 8,000

138th st, No. 632, s s, 106.6 w Willis av, 25x100. Release mort. Edward and Henry Hirsh to John and Nicholas Cotter. Oct. 8. 4,000

Same property. Release mort. The Bradley & Currier Co. (Lim.) to same. Oct. 14. nom

Same property. John Cotter and Sarah his wife and Nicholas Cotter and Eliza his wife to John M. Tracy. *Mt.* $13,500. Oct. 15. nom

141st st, s s, 123.1 e 3d av, runs east 100 to Alexander av, x south 75 x west 75 x south 25 x west 25 x north 100. Foreclos. John Fennel to Henry Muller and Herman Oetjen. Oct. 9. 23,300

143d st, s s, 150 w Clifton av, 25x100. George Schneider to Jules Schneider. Q. C. and release of all claim. Oct. 10. nom

144th st, s w cor Rider av, 25.4x114x25x118, h & l. Richard C. Fellows, of Warren Co., N. J., to Michael O'Neil. Q. C. Oct. 8. nom

Same property. William E. Rider to same. Q. C. Oct. 12. nom

148th st, n s, 200.3 e Morris av, 25x106.6. John Hayden, Jr., and Catherine his wife to Timothy Toohig. Jan. 26. 3,000

149th st, s s, part of lots 21 and 22 map Melrose, runs south 6.10 x east 100 x north 51.9 to st, x west 109.7. }
149th st, s s, part lot 23 same map, 17.2x7x15.7, gore. }
Charles Q. Freeman and Evelyn W. his wife to Frederick Folz. Taxes, &c. Oct. 5. nom

184th st, s e s, 113.3 s w Bainbridge av following curve of st, 28.8x83.7x25x96.7, h & ls. Foreclos. Augustus H. Vanderpoel to Thomas J. Falls. Sept. 16. 2,525

184th st, s e s, 141.11 s w Bainbridge st, 26.1x77.1x25x83.7. Foreclos. Same to same. Sept. 16. 2,500

Anthony av, e s, 144 s intersection e s Anthony av and w s Burnside av, runs south 50x100. Abram T. Buckhout and Martha his wife and James Buckhout and Sarah E. his wife to Marietta McTerney. Oct. 1. 3,000

Bathgate av, w s, 270 s 175th st, 1.8x75. }
Bathgate av, w s, 265.4 s 175th st, 1.8x75. }
Agreement granting rights of way. William Fernschild and Dora his wife with John P. Wenninger and Caroline his wife. Sept. 8. nom

Clinton av, n w cor 2d st, 100x100. George Lockyer and John Daly to Henry Franz. Oct. 10. nom

Decatur av, s s, 125 e Mosholu Parkway, 25x120. Lewis Moore and Sarah E. his wife to Paul Bremer. Oct. 13. nom

Franklin av, s e s, lots 101 and 104 map Village Morrisania, runs northeast 36.4 x southeast 150 x southwest 61.4 x northwest 150 to av, x northeast 25. Joseph Kleinschnittger and Elizabeth his wife to Elizabeth M. Barry. Oct. 12. 8,150

Harrison av, w s, 75 n Morton pl, 25x99.11x25x98.10. Hugh N. Camp and Elizabeth D. his wife to Jeane L. Morgan. June 15. 975

Jerome av, e s, 85.6 s Southern Boulevard, runs southeast 93.5 x southwest 25 x southeast 25 x southwest 25 x northwest 91 to av, x north 57. Louis and Albert L. Lowenstein to Julius Westheimer. Oct. 14. 1,475

Lafontaine av, w s, part lot 119 and all of lot 120 map Upper Morrisania, commonly called Monterey. Charles Hartmann to Robert E. Davis. *Mt.* $1,050. Oct. 10. 3,500

Marion av, n w s, lot 178 map East Tremont, 66x150. }
Marion av, n w s, lot 176 same map, 66x150. }
Abraham Schneider and Julia his wife to Henry Schneider. ½ part. All liens. Oct. 2. nom

Mohegan av, e s, 645 s Samuel st, 82x150. Siman Unger and Bertha his wife to Abraham Nathan. Sub. to mort. Oct. 13. 100

Mohegan av, w s, 529 s Samuel st, runs west 47.10 to Crotona Parkway, x southeast 72.5 x east 19.1 to Grant av, x north 66. William J. Reynolds and Jennie his wife to Michael P. Casey and Mary A. his wife, joint tenants. Oct. 8. 1,500

Morris av, n e cor 183d st, 100x100. Stephen T. Ray and Elizabeth his wife to Richard H. Troy. Oct. 9. nom

Same property. Richard H. Troy to Stephen T. Ray and Elizabeth his wife, joint tenants. Oct. 9. nom

Palisade av, south east cor River av, 153x385x150 to River av, x382 on straight line and 44 on curve to beginning. Edmund Titus and Esther C. his wife, Riverdale, N. Y., to Henry W. Sackett. Oct. 10. 21,000

Perry av, w s, 75 s Holt pl, 25x100. Sarah A. wife of Francis Bourne formerly Rawlings to Frank Rawlings. July 2. 450

Prospect av, e s, 156.2 n Home st, —x113.5x116.8, gore. Laura A. Thompson widow, Brooklyn, to William W. Buckley, Tenafly, N. J. C. a. G. Dec. 12, 1890. nom

Same property. Henry D. Tiffany and Caroline C. his wife to Laura A. Thompson. June 25, 1890. 3,000

Retreat av, s s, 100 e Henry st, runs south 242 to Mill Brook, x east 162 x north 251 to av, x south 100, except part taken for 149th st. Charles C. Holcombe and Elizabeth D. his wife, Lee, Mass., to Frederick Folz. Taxes and assessm'ts. Oct. 5. nom

Washington av, No. 1325, n w s, 242.3 n e 169th st, 24.2x150. George and Marinna Hey and Rosina Hurd to Christian Kuenneth. *Mt.* $4,000. Oct. 1. 6,000

Webster av, e s, 275 s Anna pl, 32x149x15.4x151.5. Sarah C. Ottiwell to Moses Green. Oct. 14. 1,800

Lots 3076-3084 inclusive in sections 4 and 9 map grantors property, contains 8,988 sq. ft. The Woodlawn Cemetery to Collis P. Huntington and Elizabeth P. his wife. May 8, 1876. 17,976

Lots 7364-7374 in section 9 same map, contains 3,306 sq. ft. Same to same. Oct. 6, 1891. 6,000

Lots 5, 6, 7 and 124-128 inclusive map of property opposite Jerome Park, 24th Ward, of The Metropolitan Real Estate Assoc., Fordham Ridge. Max Silberstein and Gussie his wife to Martin Simons. *Mt.* $5,000. Oct 9. 1,000

Lots 142, 143, 144, 187 and 188 map Edward K. Willard map Woodlawn Heights, in block bet 2d and 3d avs and 2d and 3d sts, each lot 26x100. Ephraim B. Levy to George Lockyer and John Daly. Oct. 8. 875

Plot salt meadow on Bronx River or West Farms Creek, adj north end of Plaintain Neck, bet Eliz. Willetts and C. Thorn, 7 acres, 23d Ward. David Lydig and ano. exrs. Philip M. Lydig to Leslie M. Daniel, Plainfield, N. J. Aug. 5. 500

Plot begins where south line of premises heretofore conveyed to Alfred J. Taylor by the exrs. of Loring Andrews intersects a line 87.8 s of Hampden st and 95.9 e intended Andrews av, runs east 134.3 x north 63.9 x west 148.7. Release mort. The Seamen's Bank for Savings, New York, to The New York Skin and Cancer Hospital, New York. Oct. 8. nom

Plot begins at point where south line of premises heretofore conveyed to A. J. Taylor, &c., intersects line drawn parallel to and 87.8 s of Hampden st formerly East 184th st and which point is 95.9 e of Andrews av, runs east along said parallel line 134.3 x north 63.9 to said south boundary line, x west 148.7 to beginning. The New York Skin and Cancer Hospital to Alfred J. Taylor ⅘ parts and William D. Peck ⅕ part. July 21. 3,000

LEASEHOLD CONVEYANCES.

Broadway, No. 175, basement and cellar. Assign. lease. Frederick Semken to Mary E. White and Lewis A. Olsen. Oct. 6. nom

Centre st, No. 253. Assign lease. Henry Ruhl to The A. Kremer Brewing Co., of Guttenburg, N. J. Oct. 12. 500

Clinton pl, n s, 35.6 e University pl, 28.11x93.11 x29x93.11. Assign. lease. Marquis. L. and Octavius M. Hawley, Binghampton, N. Y., to Matilda Gebhardt. Aug. 1. 13,500

Hester st, No. 161. Assign. lease. Daniel B. Curtin to David Ryan. 4,000

Thompson st, e s, 95 n 3d late Amity st, 19x47.10. Leasehold, 990 years. Foreclos. Royal S. Crane to John J. Harrington. Oct. 7. 2,900

Warren st, No. 67. Assign lease. Louis W. Dusing to James Everard. (Corrects error in issue of Oct. 3.) 5,000

West st, n e cor Franklin st, 43.10x80x43.9x80. Mary A. Burbans to Carsten H. Meyer. 21 years, from May 1, 1892, per year, taxes, and 2,500

11th st, No. 323 W., n s, 163 w Greenwich st, 25x95. Leasehold. John L. N. Hunt ref. to George T., Mary and Isabella C. Stewart, Catharine S. Herrmann and Matilda Haddock. Oct. 9. 4,100

14th st, No. 201 W. Ophelia A. Byrnes to Hugh Slevin. 20 years, from Nov. 15, 1891, per year, 6,000, 7,000

Same property. Agreement modifying terms of lease. Same to same. Oct. 13. nom

41st st, n s, 224.11 e Lexington av. Assign. lease. John P. Lein to William R. Stymus, Adam Markel and Frank R. Pentz trustees Pottier. Stymus & Co. 1,000

Same property. Assign. lease. Abram R. Briggs to same. nom

42d st, No. 25, n s, 354.2 w 5th av, 20.4x100.5, four-story stone front store and dwell'g. Foreclos. Jerome Buck to Henry C Demorest. Oct. 12. 20,000

47th st, No. 3 W. Assign. lease. Helen B. Van Emburgh to John W. Sierling and Edwin S. Chapin trustees. Oct. 12. 47,500

105th st, No. 305 E. Assign. lease. Sigmund Schulhof to Peter Buckel. Oct. 10. nom

142d st, n s, near Willis av, 25x100. Assign. indeft. lease made by F. A. Wilcox, Jan. 21, 1891. John P. Johnson to James D. Robinson. Oct. 13. nom

Amsterdam av, No. 160. Assign. lease Joseph J. Fay to Conrad Stein. July 20. nom

Same property Assign. lease. Conrad Stein to Joseph J. Fay. Aug. 12. nom

Same property. Joseph J. Fay to James Everard. Aug. 18. 3,000

Amsterdam av, No. 2756. Assign. lease. August C. and Louis F. Weiber to Schwarzschild & Sulzberger. 1,000

1st av } begins 1st av, e s, 67.9 n 119th st, runs
119th st } north 78.8 x east 100 x south 50.6 x east 25 x south 50.5 x west 45 x south 49.11 to 119th st, x northwest — to beginning, being lots 45, 49, 2, 3, 4, 4½ and north ½ 6 block 149 tax map for 12th Ward. William Austin to Henry Berghorn. 16⅔ years, from Nov. 1, 1891. per year, 2,050

2d av, No. 817. Assign. lease. Diedrich Arberg to John Bazant. 1,500

Same property. Assign. lease. John Bazant to Jacob and Anthony Doelger. 1,000

5th av, No. 224. Assign. lease. Mary E. Thompson to Harriet Lindley. 500

10th av, e s, 80.4 n 49th st, 25x100. }
10th av, e s, 105.4 n 49th st, 15.2x100. }
7th av, w s, 49.5 n 40th st, 24.8x60.11. }
Assign. lease. Josephine N. Porr to Christian Abele. Trust deed. Sept. 30. nom

11th av, No. 736. Assign. lease. Dora Koch to The Consumers' Brewing Co. of New York. Oct. 5. nom

KINGS COUNTY.

OCTOBER 8, 9, 10, 12, 13, 14.

Aberdeen st, w s, 140.4 s Bushwick av, 20.1x100. Louise and Theresa Leimbach to Sarah Tooker. *Mt.* $3,000. $3,900

Amboy st, w s, 90.5 s Eastern Parkway, 25x100. Bernhard J. Pink to Emil Reineking. *Mt.* $315. 550

Ashford st, e s, 100 s Ridgewood av, 100x100. Release mort. The Williamsburgh Savings Bank to Edward F. Linton. 1,400

Ashford st, e s, 100 s Ridgewood av, 100x100. Edward F. Linton to Frederick E. and W. Lincoln Scofield. 4,000

Bayard st, n s, 20 w Graham av, 18.9x100. William Bedford to Mathilda Weinberger and Lena Herskovics. 1,800

Bergen st, s s, 370 e 6th av, 30x131. }
St. Marks av, n s, 415 w Carlton av, 21 x131. }
Jasper H. and Leander C. Adams to Sarah B. Adams. B. & S. nom

Bergen st, s s, 310 w Kingston av, 40x105.7. Joseph M. Pilcher to Rachel A. Finch. Sub. to mort. 14,000

Bergen st, s s, 245 e Vanderbilt av, 25x131. John F. Hill exr. John F. Hill to George O. Hill. 2,200

Bergen st, s s, 195 e Vanderbilt av, 25x131. John F. Hill exr. John F. Hill to Charles P. Hill. 1,400

Berry st, e s, 60 s South 8th st, 20x69. William B. Thompson to Eliza Thompson. All title. nom

Boerum st, s s, 175 w Humboldt st, 25x100, h & l. Israel and Abraham Jarathow to Samuel Cassel. *Mt.* $3,700. 11,650

Boerum st, n s, 175 w Leonard st, 25x100. Frederick Moll to Morris Levine. *Mt.* $4,700. 7,075

Bond st, w s, 60 s President st, 20x75, h & l. }
Bond st, w s, 80 s President st, 20x75, h & l. }
Caroline Van Nostrand widow, Jersey City, to George L. Herrick. 2,500

Butler st, n s, 75 e Franklin av, 25x131. George and Catharine Damen to Christian Baur. *Mt.* $1,100. 1,900

Butler st, n s, 177.9 w Troy av and at centre line of Old Pine st, runs north along said centre line to centre line Old Van Voorhis av, x along same 133 x south to Butler st, x east —. Melvin Brown to William Herod. 5,000

Calyer st, s s, 75 w Manhattan av, 25x100, h & l. Ephraim A. Walker to Sedgwick Barnett. 6,500

Cedar st, s s, 420.7 e Evergreen av, runs east 20 x south 77 x west 20.1 x north 79.3. Charles Breitkopf to Abbie C. Smith. *Mt.* $2,700. nom

Cleveland st, e s, 205 s Vienna av, 20x100. James Gallo, of New York, to Angelo Palladino. 175

Clifton pl, No. 248, s s, 135 e Bedford av, 15x100, h & l. Howard McWilliams to James Langmuir. *Mt.* $5,000. nom

Cook st, n s, 99 e Humboldt st, 23.9x77.5x38.4x69.10. William Loughlin to Valentine Zimmermann. *Mt.* $4,650. 5,550

Cook st, s s, 175 e Morrell st, 25x100. Thomas Bardmann to Dora Tuchman. 3,400

Covert st, n w s, 347 n e Evergreen av, 18x100, h & l Lizzie wife of Peter W. Sylvester to Edward J. Lonergan. B. & S. Sub. to mort. $3,000. nom

Same property. Edward J. Lonergan to Peter W. Sylvester and Lizzie his wife. B. & S. *Mt.* $3,000. nom

Dean st, s s, 213.4 w 5th av, 20x100. Jullia E. Carroll to Agnes J. wife of Charles J. Maguire. nom

Dean st, s s, 310 w Ralph av, runs south 73.1 x southwest — x north 76 to Dean st, x east 20. Theresa wife of Rudolf Berkmeier to Rudolf Berkmeier. *Mt.* $396. 25

Decatur st, n s, 100 w Howard av, 199.8x100. Ansel H. Van Buren to Joseph P. Fuels. *Mt.* $50,000. nom

Same property. Joseph P. Fuels to Ansel H. Van Buren. nom

Decatur st, s s, 22 e Patchen av, 18x82, h & l. Charles H. Reynolds to Charles C. Goodell. *Mt.* $2,850. 4,500

Degraw st, n s, 130 w 5th av, 20x98.6. Peter Kelly to Patrick Coffey. *Mt.* $4,000. 7,200

Degraw st, n s, 90 w 5th av, 20x98.6. Peter Kelly to Margaretha Schoen. *Mt.* $4,000. nom

Degraw st, n s, 110 w 5th av, 20x98.6. Same to George Rauscher. *Mt.* $3,000. 7,200

Devoe st, n s, 94.7 w Bushwick av, runs north 35 x north 12 x north 16.9 x west 20 x south 57.6 to Devoe st, x east 22.6. Charles W. Cooper, of New York, to Mary T. wife of Bernard F. Shevlin. 1,850

Dumont st, s s, 75 w Watkins st, 25x100. }
Watkins st, e s, 150 n Livonia av, 25x100. }
Elizabeth Taber individ. and with others exrs. Franklin W. Taber to Michael Sullivan. 1,000

Dupont st, No. 132, s s, 125 e Manhattan av, 25 x100. Lizzie Levi heir Jacob Goldberg, of New York, to Lawrence Kaminsky. 1-5 part. *Mt.* $3,500. 438

Same property. Moses Goldberg and Sarah, Amelia and David Goldberg by Rosa Goldberg and ano. guards. to Lawrence Kaminsky. 6,450

Elm st, s s, 425 e Central av, 25x100. Sarah J. Smith to Henry Weber. 3,350

Elton st, e s, 125 s Arlington av, 25x100. Release from covenant. Edward F. Linton to James W. Crawford. 5

Elton st, w s, 275 n Arlington av, 25x100. Edward F. Linton to Howard N. Acker. 1,000

Elton st, w s, 350 s Ridgewood av, 25x100. }
Essex st, e s, 140 n Arlington av, 40x100. }
Release mort. Williamsburgh Savings Bank to Edward F. Linton. 1,050

Essex st, e s, 140 n Arlington av, 40x100. Edward F. Linton to Jennie H. Smith. 1,600

Essex st late Eldert av, e s, 45 s Belmont av, 45 x100. Samuel Shaw to John G. MacMahon. 2,000

Floyd st, No. 124, s s, 335 e Marcy av, —x100x 20x100. Louisa C. wife of John J. Muller to The Board of Education, Brooklyn. 5,250

Floyd st, s s, 315 e Marcy av, 20x100, h & l. Balthasar Rauch to same. 5,250

Fulton st, n w cor Crescent av, 105.9x102.6x 105x89.8. Marenus J. Goodenough to John H. Ives. 3,500

Fulton st, s w cor Stone av, 200x100. Charles C. Stelle to Hoik D. Campbell. All title. nom

Fulton st, s s, 75 w Miller av, 25x100, h & l. Jane L. Smith to John Houlahan and Mary his wife, joint tenants. *Mt.* $1,500. 2,900

Fulton st, Nos. 1010, 1012 and 1014, s s, 294.2 e Grand av, 60.6x102. Mary B. D. wife of Fordyce S. Caldwell to Henry W. Sherrill. *Mt.* $25,500. nom

Glenada pl, w s, s of Decatur st. Release of covenant. William W. Reynolds to Charles D. Rust. nom

Glen st, s s, 25 w Crescent st, 23x100. Charles S. Taber and George C. Case to Grace C. Taber. *Mt.* $1,500, and taxes 1890. 2,100

Grand st, south cor Driggs av, 23x80x20.3x80.6. Joseph McKee exr. Lydia McKee to Solomon May. *Mt.* $7,000. 18,000

Guernsey st, w s, 1.5 s Bedford av, runs south 100 x west 48.5 x northwest to Bedford av, x northeast 87.11 x east 2.9. Samuel Self, Smithville, L. I., to Edward P. Self. Sub. to morts. nom

Halsey st, s s, 100 w Marcy av, 20x100. Mary Colton widow to Pomeroy P. Dickinson, of New York. *Mt.* $4,000. 8,750

Hancock st, n s, 347 e Tompkins av, 18x100. Catharine Quin to William H. Reynolds. *Mt.* $5,000. 8,500

Hancock st, n w s, 210 n e Evergreen av, 40x 100. Leopold J. Lippmann to Louis Beer. *Mt.* $4,900. nom

Hancock st, s s, 235 w Tompkins av, 20x100. William H. Reynolds to Marietta wife of James Harkness. nom

Hancock st, n w s, 210 n e Evergreen av, 40x 100. Louis Beer to Theodore L. Schultze. *Mt.* $4,960. nom

Hancock st, n s, 253.11 e Stuyvesant av, runs northeast 9.6 x south 1.6 to Hancock st, x west 9.5. Israel Minor, Jr., exr. Catherine S. Cooper to Charles Isbill. 125

Same property. Israel Minor, Jr., as exr. Jane V. C. Cooper to same. 125

Hancock st, s e cor Lewis av, 150x100. Thomas A. McWhinney to Jacob Aronson. ½ part. *Mt.* $51,875. nom

Harman st, s e s, 220 s w Central av, 20x100, h & l. Edward Nichols to Henry Roth. *Mt.* $2,000. 4,500

Harman st, s s, 202.11 e Wyckoff av, 20x100. John Rudert to Charles Loffler. 700

Henry st, n e cor State st, 25x89.1. Charles H. Collins to Frank A. Barnaby. *Mt.* $28,250. nom

Henry st (old line before widening), n e cor State st, 25x96.7. Frank A. Barnaby to Mary L. Ward, of Richmond, Va. *Mt.* $27,-250. nom

Herkimer st, n s, 184.8 e Howard av, 15.4x100, h & l. James J. Smith to William E. Griffin. *Mt.* $2,000. 4,000

Herkimer st, n e cor Troy av, 50x100. Emanuel Swedish Methodist Episcopal Church to The Swedish Bethany Methodist Episcopal Church. *Mt.* $4,500. nom

Hicks st, n w cor Cranberry st, 24.6x65. William Court to Thomas W. Matthews. *Mt.* $10,000. nom

Hopkins st, No. 181, 25x100. Contract. Michael Schenck to Andrew Wohlgermuth and Marie his wife, joint tenants 3,700

Hoyt st, w s, 74 s Carroll st, 22.10x47.10x22.10x 45.9, h & l. Sophia P. wife of and Ashley C. Morrill, Little Falls, Minn., to David F. Manning. 2,500

India st, s s, 195 e Franklin st, 25x100, h & l. Frederick J. Thomas to Louisa H. Hintz, Louisa Lenz, Augusta Brethicker and John H. Belter. Q. C. and release from charges. 500

Jerome st, w s, 20 n Blake av, 20x100. Annie Schroeter to William Haug. 400

Jerome st, n w cor Blake av, 20x100. Charles L. Schroeter to William Haug. 550

Jerome st, e s, 100 n Division av, 25x95. John C. Schenck to Helen Pickering. 909

Lawrence st, e s, 125 n Tillary st, 25x114.6. Alice A. Bedell and William G. Low exrs.,

&c., Mott Bedell to William H. McDonald. 7,000

Linden st, e s, 315.11 n Evergreen av, 20x100. Aaron Kapjan to Aaron Goodman. *Mt.* $2,500. 4,500

Linden st, e s, 275.11 n Evergreen av, 20x100. Aaron Kaplan, of New York, to Kusche Idelsohn and Max Tempkin. *Mt.* $1,500. 4,000

Linwood st, w s, 100 s Eastern Parkway, 22.6x 90. John M. Stearns to Will A. Brown. 1,950

Logan st, e s, 94 s Jamaica av, 50x100. Catherine Molloy to Magdalena B. wife of Henry T. Smith. 1,600

Logan st, w s, 1,575 n 2d st, 50x150, h & l. George W. Stone to Carrie A. Vollmer. *Mt.* $1,500, taxes, &c. 2,400

Macon st, n s, 100 w Patchen av, 100x100. John Cassidy to Alfred L. Beasley. 10,000

Macon st, n s, 290 e Patchen av, 110x100. Release mort. William Ziegler to Jane Miller. 8,250

McDonough st, s s, 302.6 e Tompkins av, 19.6x 100, h & l. Barbara Bliss to Edward H. Wilson. *Mt.* $6,000. nom

McDonough st, n s, 270.6 e Lewis av, 19.6x100. E. Willard Jones to Henry R. King, Far Rockaway, L. I. *Mt.* $5,000. nom

McDonough st, s s, 195 w Hopkinson av, 20x100. Julius Schwarz to Balthasar Rauch. 4,500

McDonough st, n s, 250 e Lewis av, 20.6x100, h & l. E. Willard Jones to Lucie E. Klatte. *Mt.* $8,000. 13,000

McDonough st, n s, 80 e Reid av, 19.6x100. Ransom F. Clayton to Catherine M. S. Bremer. *Mt.* $4,000. 6,500

McKibbin st, n s, 100 e Ewen st, 25x100. John C. Wirth to Charles Hutwelker and Fred'k. Figge. 5,800

McKibbin st, s s, 125 w Morrell st, runs east 0.7½x50. Sarah E. wife of and Philip Worth to Elizabeth Kern. 40

Middleton st, n w s, 130 n e Lee av, 50x100. Isaac H w t to Johanna Horowitz. *Mt.* $14,000. oro i z 24,000

Milford st, e s, 100 n Liberty av, 25x100. Stephen W. Stoothoff to Herman Kramer. *Mt.* $1,600. 2,500

Monitor st, w s, 101.3 s Driggs av, 18x100, h & l. Charles Engert to Henry Vollner and Joseph P. Driesel. 3,800

Moore st, n s, 84.10 w Bogert st, 25x the block to Seigel st. Release dower. Eliza A. Wall widow to Ferdinand Hosch. ⅙ part. 215

Same property. Louise B. W. wife of and Edward R. Ladew to same. 1-6 part. 387

Same property. Eliza A. Wall extrx. William Wall to same. 1-6 part. 386

Same property. Frank T. Wall and Edwin R. Brinckerhoff trustees and exrs. Michael W. Wall to same. ⅓ part. 1,375

Same property. Eliza A. Wall widow to same. 1-6 part. 387

Moore st, n s, 500 w White st, 25x100. Release mort. Charles W. Truslow admr. William Wall to Michael Mayer. 1,400

Same property. Michael Mayer to Emilie Huber. 7,600

Monroe st, n s, 620 w Ralph av, 30x100. Richard D. Robbins to Elizabeth W. Aldrich, of New York. *Mt.* $9,000. exch

Oakland st, e s; 32 n Calyer st, runs north 25.3 x east 64 11 x southwest 51 x southeast — x west 25, h & l. Walter Smith to John M. Fowler. *Mt.* $450. 1,100

Oakland st, e s, 150 n Nassau av, 25x100, h & l. John C. Bremer to Susan C. Smith. 4,700

Oakland st, s w cor Huron st, 50x100, hs & ls. Stephen A. Donlon to Johanna wife of Stephen A. Donlon. *Mt.* $3,500. nom

Pacific st, n s, 60 e Brooklyn av, 20x100. Release mort. William H. Lyon to James O. Carpenter. 2,500

Same property. James O. Carpenter to James F. McCaffrey. *Mt.* $7,000. 10,100

Pacific st, s s, 69.6 e Flatbush av, runs south 29 x southwest 30 to Flatbush av, x southeast 19.1 x northeast 38.7 x north 26.10 to st, x 19.4. John Kelly to Lawrence MacNaughton. 9,250

Pacific st, s s, 75 w Utica av, 298.8x107.2. Foreclos. John Courtney to Henry Weil. *Mt.* $30,000. 1,000

Pacific st, n s, 456 e Rochester av, 16x100, h & l. Frederick Dhuy, Jr., to Robert R. Colfax, New York. 3,500

Parkway, n s, 350 w Rogers av, 24.7x—x75.1x 57.9. Henry P. Haynes, Bridgehampton, L. I., to Emma Quinn. Q. C. 10

Penn st, n s, 151.4 e Bedford av, 21.7x100. Edmund W. Barnett to Albert E. Martin. 6,000

Poplar st, n s, 77 4 e Hicks st, 22.8x25. Duncan Edwards to Charles W. Smith. nom

Same property. Release mort. Clarence W. Hillyer, of New York, to Duncan Edwards. nom

President st, s s, 416.8 w Columbia st, 16.8x100. Rosa Horowitz to Maria Rapuzzi, New York. 4,500

President st, n s, 80 w 4th av, 162x95. Catharine Buckley to John Heinlein and William Rexer. *Mt.* $5,000. 9,600

Prospect pl, s s, 154.1 e 6th av, 20.6x100. Martin L. Bamman, of Asbury Park, N. J., to Ella Reynolds. *Mt.* $3,000. 6,400

Quincy st, s e cor Ralph av, runs south 100 x east 66 x north 22 x west 21.4 x north 78 to st, x west 44.8. Edward Hendrickson to Ada F. Hendrickson. nom

Quincy st, s w cor Lewis av, 44x100. Frederick C. Loeble to Margaret Wilson. All title. C. a. G. nom

Same property. Margaret Wilson to Minnie wife of Frederick C. Loeble. nom

Quincy st, s s, 231.3 w Throop av, 18.9x100. Contract for property. Albert Sibley to Harriet F. wife of William M. Geeke. 5,500

Richardson st, s s, 100 e Graham av, 20.6x75, h & l. Nickolaus Hardt, New York, to Elizabeth wife of Adam Parthesius. *Mt.* $1,800. 2,700

Ross st, n w s, 255.1 n e Bedford av, 19.11x100. John W. Sullivan to John H. Mowen. *Mt.* $5,000. 8,950

Rutledge st, s s, 116 e Lee av, 19x100. Andrew Mander to Agnes Weygandt. 5,750

Rutledge st, s e s, 328 s w Harrison av, 28x100, h & l. August Muller to John Wilhelm. *Mt.* $5,000. 10,500

Rutledge st, No. 108, s s, 153.1 w Bedford av, 18.5x100. Eli H. Bishop to Mary Roch. *Mt.* $3,000. nom

Sackett st, s s, 75 w 4th av, 25x75, h & l. George R. Brown to John S. Ashley. All liens. 1,200

Sackman st, w s, 150 s Blake av, 50x100. Benjamin Sachs to Jacob Betsky. *Mt.* $3,100. 4,300

Sackman st, w s, 75 n Belmont av, 25x100, h & l. Simon C. Wilson to James H. Saunders. *Mt.* $1,500. 2,800

Schermerhorn st, n e s, 93.1 n w Boerum pl, runs northeast 78.5 x southeast 3 5 x northeast 26.10 x northwest 23.1 x southwest 104 3 to street, x southeast 19.7. Heinrich and Louis Herbold and ano. admrs. Elizabeth Schweitzer to Henry Werner. 6,750

Sedgwick pl, e s, 80 s Wakeman pl, 80x100, New Utrecht. Release mort. Phillip H. Gill to Charles A. Erickson. 1,920

Sedgwick pl, e s, 80 s Wakeman pl, 100x100. Philip H. Gill to Charles A. Erickson. Correction deed. 2,500

Seigel st, s s, 620 w White st, 25x100. Michael A. and Thos. F. Delaney to Frank Dumpeck. 1,250

Smith st, e s, 19.7 s Carroll st, 19.4x75.5x19.3x 77.3, h & l. John Heim to Louis T. Heim. 7,000

South Oxford st, w s, 207.6 s De Kalb av, 22x 100. The Brooklyn Trust Co. exr. Reuben W. Ropes to Byron De Witt. 8,250

Stagg st, n e cor Bogert st, 50x100. John A. Eppig to Henry Bereau. 5,500

Starr st, s e s, 188.5 s w Wyckoff av, 25x100. Albert Nugent to Jacob J. Velter. nom

Same property. Jacob J. Velten to Adoph Mayer. nom

Starr st, s e s, 188.5 s w Wyckoff av, 25x100. Frederick J. Grace, Sr., of Bergen County, N. J., to Albert Nugent, of New York. 50

Summit st, n s, 150 e Hicks st, 100x100. Michael Kilaby trustee St. Stephens R. C. Church to Right Rev. John Loughlin. *Mt.* $6,000. 11,000

Sumpter st, s s, 350 e Howard av, 25x100. Joseph and Israel Fatowsky to Minnie and Betze Finkelstein. *Mt.* $4,500. 6,500

Same property. Minnie wife of Charles Finkelstein and Betze wife of Abraham Finkelstein to Mendel Levin. *Mt.* $4,500. 6,300

Suydam st, s s, 350 w Evergreen av, 25x95. William Kaiser to Anna M. Deublein. *Mt.* $1,500. 5,000

Union st, n s, 268 e Smith st, 22x90, h & l. Peter Nostrand to Sarah A. Nostrand. gift

Vanderveer st, s e s, 227 n e Broadway, 16.6x 100, h & l. Caleb Elliott to Charlotte A. Holdredge. *Mt.* $1,800. 3,200

Walton st, n s, 73 e Harrison av, 22x100. Michael Sommer to Caroline wife of Michael Sommer. ½ part. Sub. to mort. nom

Walworth st, w s, 142.3 s Flushing av, 25x50. Magnus Berk to Peter Berk. nom

Same property. Peter Berk to Magnus Berk and Katharina his wife. C. a. G. nom

Warren st, s s, 100.10 w 4th av, 20x100. Frederick A. Farley trustee Augustus Graham to Grindall Reynolds and Isaac H. Cary as trustees. nom

Washington st, w s, 522 s Concord st, runs west 76 9 x south 9.9 x west 3.3 x south 13.3 x east 80 to Washington st, x north 25. Bernard McCaffrey to The Trustees of the New York and Brooklyn Bridge. 22,500

Washington st, No. 254, w s, 547 s Concord st, runs west 80 x south 36 1 to Tillery st, x northeast 80 3 to Washington st, x north 25. Same to same. 40,000

Washington st, w s, 108 s Concord st, 25x105. David W. Stein to New York and Brooklyn Bridge. 27,500

Watkins st, e s, 150 s Dumont av, 50x100. }
Watkins st, e s, 225 s Dumont av, 50x100. }
Jacob Manheim to Isaac Harris and Solomon Lasher. Sub. to mort. 2,900

Watkins st, e s, 25 n Riverdale av, 25x100. Sara Burstein to Bertha Luwer or Luwei. *Mt.* $2,200. 2,650

Watkins st, w s, 175 s Sutter av, 25x100, h & l. Mary wife of Abraham Goldstein to Abraham Lifschitz. Sub. to mort. 625

Weirfield st, n w s, 241 s w Central av, 20x100. Louis Beer to Theodore L. Schultze. *Mt.* $4,480. nom

Weirfield st, n w s, 223.8 n e Evergreen av, 17.8 x100. Samuel Blackwell to Annie Herzog. *Mt.* $4,000. nom

Weirfield st, n w s, 117.8 n e Evergreen av, 141.4x100. Annie wife of John Herzog to Richard Goodwin. nom

Same property. Release mort. Richard Goodwin to Annie Herzog. nom

Weirfield st, n w s, 241.4 n e Evergreen av, 17.8x100. Robert Bayles to Annie Herzog. B. & S. nom

Weirfield st, n w s, 241 s w Central av, 20x100. Leopold J. Lippmann to Louis Beer. *Mt.* $4,480. nom

Weldon st, n s, 100 w Crescent st, 50x100. Israel W. Littell to Louis E. Littell. *Mt.* $1,000. nom

Same property. Louis E. Littell to Sarah W. Littell. nom

Winthrop st, n s, 1,955.7 e Flatbush av, 700x 437.8 crossing a st, x700x438.9. }
Winthrop st, n s, 3,105.7 e Flatbush av, 469 to Canarsie av, x northwest 445 x west 383.10 x south 437.1, crossing a st to Winthrop st point of beginning, excepting indeft. portions thereout. Flatbush. }
John F. Hart to Daniel Doody. nom

Wilson st, n w s, 70 s w Wythe av, 15x100. William H. Griffin to Augustine M. O'Neil. *Mt.* $2,500. Error. 3,800

Woodbine st, n w s, 300 n e Central av, 50x100. Herman and Christian Kellerman to William C. Herbert. 1,900

Same property. William C. Herbert to Christian Nickel. 2,000

North 1st st, s s, 128 w Roebling st, 20x60, h & l. Abraham Blum to Henry Blum. ½ part. 2,500

1st st, n s, 212.10 w 7th av, 100x100. Daniel Doody to James Mills. *Mt.* $6,000. 16,000

Same property. William S , Jr., to Daniel Doody. *Mt.* $6,000. pencer exch

1st st, s w s, 272 s e 7th av. Party wall agreement. John Magilligan with John Adamson. nom

North 2d st, n s, 100 w Lorimer st, runs north to point 75 s from Conselyea st, x west 25 x south to North 2d st, x east — to beginning. }
North 2d st, n s, 125 w Lorimer st, runs north 78 x west 0.6 x south — x east 0.6 to beginning. }
Kusche Idelsohn and Max Tempkin to Aaron Kaplan, of New York. Sub. to mort. 5,000

3d st, s s, 66 e Smith st, 38x80, h & l. William O. Sumner to Margaritta Ritterbusch. *Mt.* $3,250. 9,400

South 3d st, s w s, 43 n w Roebling st, 21x71.3. Mary A. wife of George Shear to Joseph Dimes. 3,550

South 3d st, s s, 103.6 e Berry st, 25x95. Thomas Smith to William Lamb. *Mt.* $2,400. 4,250

Same property. William Lamb to The Brooklyn E. D. Dispensary and Hospital. *Mt.* $2,400. 4,250

4th st, s s, 102.6 e 5th av, 16.8x100. Rufus T. Griggs to Mary C. Macfarlan. 6,600

6th st, s s, 177.10 e 6th av, 85x100. Release of mortgage or any other interest. Sophie G. Parker to George W. Powell, Absalom W. Dieter, Edwin C. Stimson and George A. Devnell. nom

East 7th st, w s, 105.8 s Greenwood av, runs west 90.6 x west 14.4 x south 20 x east 100 to East 7th st, x north 49.3, Flatbush. Anna M. Ferris to Frederick Crane. 575

North 8th st, n e cor Kent av, runs north 105 x east 100 x south 5 x east 50 x south 100 to North 8th st, x west 150. The Sts. Peter and Paul Church to Joseph Young. ½ part. 14,000

Same property. The R. C. Church of St. Vincent de Paul to same. ½ part. 14,000

Same property. Joseph Young to Peter Young. nom

South 9th st, n s, 200 e 5th st, 25x110. Fanny Sussman, of New York, to Israel Sussmann. *Mt.* $3,000. 4,000

10th st, s s, 263.4 w 3d av, 120x100. Release mort. Asa W. Parker, of New Hamburgh, N. Y., to John F. Hart. nom

Same property. John F. Hart to William Spencer, Jr. *Mt.* $10,000. exch

10th st, s s, 459.8 e 7th av, 20.4x100. Louis Bonert to Robert C. Lynch. *Mt.* $5,000. 9,250

10th st, s s, 399.8 e 7th av, 20x100. Same to Henry E. Ludder. *Mt.* $5,000. 9,250

10th st, s s, 419.8 e 7th av, 20x100. Same to same. *Mt.* $5,000. 9,250

10th st, s s, 150 w 8th av, 16.8x100. Ida M. wife of and James F. Ransom to Henrietta Dukeshire. *Mt.* $5,500. 6,200

11th st, n s, 17.10 w 4th av, 17.4x100. Laura S. wife of Samuel Carey to Ann Cosgrove. 3,350

12th st, s w s, 322.10 s e 6th av, 53x100. }
12th st, s w s, 400.10 s e 6th av, 22x100. }
Sarah L. Jackson, of New York, to William Killey. 7,500

14th st, n s, 242.11 e 7th av, 17.6x100. Henry Ward, of Mamaroneck, N. Y., to James F. Tierney and Francis J. Beattie. *Mt.* $2,000. 4,000

20th st, n s, 100 e 6th av, 20x100.2. Ira O. Miller to Nels Nelson. 1,000

22d st, s s, 60 w 4th av, 22x100. Ella A., George and Lily C. Linssen or Linssina heirs Cecilia Linssen or Linssina to Charles D. Bergman, of New York. nom

22d st, s s, 250 e 6th av, 50x100. George Wilson to Mary Donnelly. Taxes and assessm'ts. 1,400

Bay 22d st, n w s, 225 n e Bath av, 56.10x—x 48.11x96.8, Bath Beach. Joseph Stehlin to Mary F. wife of George Zurdt. B. & S. nom

42d st, e s, 150 s 12th av, 25x100, New Utrecht. William J. Kiernan to Daniel C. McIntosh. 350

44th st, s s, 80 w 4th av, 108x100.2. Daniel F. Doody to John F. Hart. *Mt.* $15,450. 24,000

47th st, n e s, 275 n w 13th av, 75x100.2, New Utrecht. The West Brooklyn Land and Improvement Co. to Emma E. Baker. 1,125

48th st, n s, 260 w 4th av, 20x100.2. Albert J. Driver to Adrian De Groff. 1,100

57th st, s s, 140 w 3d av, 20x100.2. William S. Hassan to G. W. Crossman, New York. *Mt.* $2,700. 4,600

63d st, n s, 440 w 14th av, 20x100, Bath Junction. James V. S. Woolley to Sarah M. wife of Frank V. Reilly, Far Rockaway, L. I. 225

64th st, s w s, 320 n w 7th av, 20x81.7; also, Fort Hamilton av, southerly cor 64th st, runs southwest 4.6 to Cowenhoven lane, x east 22.8 to 64th st, x northwest 21.1, New Utrecht. }
Claus Doscher to Elizabeth McDonald. 170

66th st, s s, 420 e 14th av, 20x100, New Utrecht.

Effingham H. Nichols to George F. and Charles Pigott. 250

72d st, s s, 530 w 15th av, 20x100, Lefferts Park. James V. S. Woolley to Felipe Rodriguez, New York. 200

83d st, s w s, 220 s e 23d av, 60x100, Bensonhurst. James D Lynch to Fanny M. wife of William H. Leffler. 900

East 95th st, w s, 150 s Av G, 27.3x100, Canarsie. John H. Ireland to Henry Van Houten. 225

Albany av, w s, 88.11 n Butler st, 16.8x85. George O. Fortesque, Buffalo, N. Y., to George C. Case. *Mt.* $3,500. 5,500

Arlington av, s e cor Elton st, runs east 50 x south 100 x east 50 x south 25 x west 100 to Elton st. x north 125 to beginning. Release mort. The Williamsburgh Savings Bank, to Edward F. Linton. 1,050

Same property. Edward F. Linton to James F. Bidstrup. *Mt.* $2,100. 3,600

Atlantic av, n s, 48.2 w 3d av, 18.2x80. Ann E. Morrison to George W. Rudkin. *Mt.* $2,500. 3,950

Atlantic av, s s, 150 e Rockaway av, 16.8x100. John S. Ladd to Eliza A. Palmer. *Mt.* $2,000. 4,000

Same property. Eliza A. Palmer, of Babylon, to Sadie S. Dauphinee, of New York. *Mt.* $2,000. 4,000

Atlantic av, s w s, 100.2 s e Court st, 21.8x73.5x19.1x73.5. Gordon L. Ford to Henry Hyams. 5,000

Av E, n w cor East 5th st, 100x100, Flatbush. Joseph Wechsler to Sarah wife of William Neidlinger. 1,725

Bedford av, n w s, 60 s w North 7th st, 20x80. August Koch to William J. Dornan. 7,300

Belmont av, s s, 125 e Thatford av, 25x100. Jennie Loewenthal, New York, to Rebecca Hyman. 950

Belmont av, n s, 125 e Thatford av, runs north 100 x west 25 x north 25 x east 52.10 x south 25 x west 2.9 x south 100 to Belmont av, x west 25 Joseph Davis to Hyman Silverman. *Mt.* $1,600. 6,000

Belmont av, s s, 75 e Osborn st, 25x100. Solomon Wolff to Levy Duchman and Louis Greenberg. *Mt.* $3,500. 6,000

Blake av, n s, 50 w Sackman st, 50x100. Wolff Lewis to Lazarus Feit. *Mt.* $700. 1,425

Blake av, n w cor Sackman st, 25x100. Benjamin Rothbel and Bernard Kreiger to Moritz Rosenthal. *Mt.* $700. 1,000

Buffalo av, w s, 36.8 s Pacific st, 16.8x85. Thomas S. Denike to Anna and August Miller. *Mt.* $2,000 and tax 1890. 3,500

Bushwick av, south cor Lafayette av, 30x78.6x30x77.8. Clarence J. Rice and Mary R. wife of Edwin Loomis, North Plainfield, N. J., to Louese Lowenstein. *Mt.* $6,000. 12,000

Carlton av, w s, 117.7 s Fulton av, 25x100. Edward J. Fearon, of Port Washington, N. Y., trustee to Hattie A. Allen. nom

Same property. Hattie A. wife of Sherwood R. Allen to William S. and James S. Wright. 4,000

Carlton av, No. 552, w s, 80.6 n Bergen st, 19.6x85.
Carlton av, No. 554, w s, 61 n Bergen st, 19.6 x85.
Mary Skelly to Mary A. McGivern. All liens. 12,000

Central av, s w s, 100 s e Linden st, 18.1x100x25 x100, h & l. Joseph Berkowitz to Joseph Stang and David Hittner. *Mt.* $4,800. 10,000

Central av, s w s, 77.4 s e Hart st, 25.9x100.9x 25x100.10, h & l. Henry Schneider to William Litzebauer. *Mt.* $2,500. 9,800

Christopher av, w s, 250 s Blake av, 50x100. E. Christian Korner and Henry Schwabeland to Jacob Goldstein. 1,000

Coney Island av, e s, adj J. H. Watton on south, abt 8 23-100 acres.
Parcel adj above on west at intersection of e s of land of Manhattan Beach R. R. and south line of Margaret Goodfellows land, 8 21-100 acres, Gravesend.
Daniel T. Lewis to Patrick H. Flynn. nom

De Kalb av, s e s, 125 n e Knickerbocker av, 50 x100. Charles A. Wagner to George Gutting. ½ part. Sub. to mort. $1,200. nom

Evergreen av, s w s, 50 s e Jefferson av, 50x100, h & l. John H. Hilnker, Richmond Hill, L. I., to George D. Meyran. ½ part. Sub. to morts $7,000. nom

Flushing av, s s, 50 w Marcy av, 25x100. Martha L. wife of and Peter Feeley to Conrad Mets. 1,950

Flushing av, n s, 75 e Vandervoort pl, 25x80.11. Charles A. Wagner to George Gutting. ½ part. *Mt.* $3,500. nom

Flushing av, s s, 50 e Bremen st, 25x81.9. Wilhelmina Henje to Gustav Luley. *Mt.* $4,000. 5,250

Fountain av, w s, 725 n Liberty av, 25x100. Lucy A. Quin to Amelia F. Robinson. 1,900

Same property. Release mort. Laura F. Beecher to William E. Smith. nom

Franklin av, s e cor Crown st, 131x100. Josiah A. Hersey as trustee to Alonzo E. De Baun. Q. C. 1890. nom

Graham av, e s, 75 s Varet st, 25x100, h & l. Margaretha Sauerle to Otto N. Braun. 12,400

Gates av, s e s, 275 n e Hamburg av, 25x100. Marie T. wife of John J. Brennan to John Badenhoop. *Mt.* $3,500. 7,250

Gates av, s e s, 250 n e Hamburg av, 25x100. Same to Charles Asmus. *Mt.* $3,500. 7,000

Gates av, s e s, 275 n e Irving av, 25x100. Matharina wife of Charles Motschenbacher to William Nagel. *Mt.* $3,500. 8,000

Gates av, n w s, 100.6 n e Evergreen av, 25x 100. William Baumgarten to Wilhelm Lohr. *Mt.* $5,000. 7,500

Gates av, No. 949, n s, 100 w Patchen av, 20x 100. John C. Remick to Marshall J. Couch. exch. and 2,300

Georgia av, s e cor Brooklyn and Jamaica turnpike road now Jamaica av, runs south to Virginia now Fulton av, x east 50 x north 78 x west 0.4 x north to Jamaica av, x southwest — to beginning. Martin Bennett, Jr., to Lena wife of Frederick Koch. 20,000

Gravesend av, n w cor 60th st, 1 642-1,000 acres, Gravesend. Kate L wife of Alfred D. Hicks to James H McCormick. 3,250

Greene av, s e cor Lewis av, 200x100. Spencer Aldrich to William W. Owen, of Stamford, Conn. 63,000

Greene av, n w s, 100 s w Evergreen av, 40x 100, h & l. John W., Edmund O., Stella I., and George C. Phelps and Adeline B. Saddington legatee John M. Phelps to Richard G. Phelps. nom

Greene av, s e s, 270 s w Irving av, 20x100, h & l. Jacob Blank to Rachel Frey. *Mt.* $2,200. nom

Greene av, n s, 45 e Carlton av, 21.6x80. Noah Tebbutts to Robert Murphy. *Mt.* $5,000. 8,000

Hamburg av, s e cor Suydam st, 50x100, h & ls. Catharine wife of Jacob Klein and widow of Henry Dietz, Mary A. wife of August Baumgarten, formerly Dietz, and George H. Dietz to Louisa Lintner. Q. C. and C. a. G. nom

Same property. Louisa Lintner widow to George Dittrich and Lippman Reizenstein. *Mt.* $1,000. 6,000

Irving av, h e s, 25 n w Stanhope st, 25x100. Levi Blumenau to Charles Kucherer. 1,000

Jefferson av, s s, 175 e Stuyvesant av, runs south 80 x east 25 x south 20 x east 50 x north 100 to Jefferson av, x west 75 to beginning. William Carey to John Collins. Correction deed. nom

Same property. John Collins to Catharine Carey. Correction deed. nom

Jefferson av, No. 328, n s, 155 w Tompkins av, 16.8x100. Ann, Frank K. and Joseph C. Taylor exrs. William Taylor to Charles H. Bellows, of Summit, N. J. 7,300

Knickerbocker av, west cor Himrod st, 100x150. Charles A. Wagner to George Gutting. ½ part. *Mt.* $3,000. nom

Knickerbocker av, west cor Linden st, 40x100. Julia B. F. wife of John D. Fish, Hempstead, L. I., to Anna G. Schiel. *Mt.* $800. exch

Kent and Wythe avs, North 8th and North 9th sts. Annah B. Brush to George L. Fox, James Hoey, Sophie Bender, and other grantees of property in above block, Confirmation deed of release, &c. nom

Kent av, e s, 450 n Myrtle av, 25x200. John Dawson exr. Isabella Dawson to Jane Dawson, of Bay Shore, L. I. *Mt.* $1,050. Dated 1878. 2,800

Same property. Jane Dawson to John Dawson, of Islip, N. Y. 3,-00

Lexington av, n s, 325 e Reid av, 34x100, h & l. Foreclos. Albert W. Seaman to Edwin S. Updike, Sr., New York. *Mt.* $11,500. 5,000

Lexington av, n s, 280 e Stuyvesant av, 20x100. Frank L. Corwin to Peter J. Brady. *Mt.* $6,100. 7,500

Liberty av, s s, 50 e Crescent st, 25x100. Valentine Novac to William Stemmler and Lena his wife, joint tenants. 500

Liberty av, s s, 20 w Logan st, 60x90. Effingham H. Nichols to Almon G. Bardin. 1,800

Maspeth av, Orient av, Morgan av and Vandervoort av—the block. Julia, Margaret A., Henrietta and Geo C. Cooper heirs William Cooper to Charles W. Cooper 9,000

Montauk av, s e cor Belmont av, 90x100. Albert W. Sprott to Donald Laing. 2,100

Myrtle av, s s, 26.3 e Cumberland st, runs east 19.11 x south 77.4 x west 18.4 x north — to beginning. Release judgment. The Union Elevated R. R. Co. to George Wilson. nom

Myrtle av, s w cor Suydam st, 88.8x44.11x76.
Myrtle av, s s, 268 w Suydam st, runs south 78.1 x east abt 45 x southeast 57.8 to Suydam st, x northeast 126 x northwest 59.8 to av, x west 150.8.
Edward Hendrickson to Jacob May. Sub. to mort. nom

North Portland av, w s, 127.10 n Park av, 25x 100. Andrew J. Fester to Christina T. Fester. nom

Park av, s s, 280 w Marcy av, 25x100. Francis E. Clark to Charles K. Davies. *Mt.* $4,000. exch

Patchen av, n e cor Macon st, 25x100. William W. and Charles R Rope and George W. McChesney to Jane Miller. Q C. nom

Pennsylvania av, e s, 125 s Glenmore av, 25.9x 110. Stanislaus Lohmiller to Louis E. Liedtke. 1,275

Putnam av, n s, 188.2 e Stuyvesant av, 18.7x 100. John Mitchell and Charles Herr to William H. Timmons. *Mt.* $4,500. nom

Ralph av, e s, 100 s Butler st, 20x100.
Degraw st, s s, 140 e Buffalo av, 20x220.7 to Parkway.
Emma Davis to The Harwinton Land Co. All liens. 1,500

Riverdale av, s w cor Stone av, 25x100. Ellen Gilmer to Harris Tishkofski and Louis Hankin. 700

Rockaway av, w s, 52 s Marion st, 16x50, h & l. James W. McManus to Lina S. Blatt. *Mt.* $2,900. 3,500

Saratoga av, e s, 30 n Pacific st, 20x100. John W. Eckelkamp to Mary Erickson. nom

Shepherd av, e s, 225 s Blake av, 25x100. Michael Davitt to Elizabeth I. Taylor. 2,000

Shepherd av, e s, 100 n Duryea av, 25x100. Thomas E. Pennell to Mary E. Laing. 2,100

Shepherd av, n e cor Dumont av late Duryea av, 100x100. Same to same. 800

Skillman av, s s, 125 w Graham av, 25x100 Charles Majer, Charles Majer, Jr., Elizabeth wife of John Rauscher and Bertha Majer, Fredericka wife of John Kuntz, of Jersey City, heirs of Elizabeth Majer to William Meyers. *Mt.* $1,000. 687

Same property. Charles Majer special guard. of Emma and Louisa and William Majer to same. 513

St. Marks av, s s, 20 w Carlton av, 20x81. J. Spencer Hosford, of Stuyvesant, N. Y., exr. Frederic J. Hosford to Fannie E. Hosford. 12,500

St. Marks av, n s, 350 e Brooklyn av, runs north 145 x east 40 x north 5.7 x east 60 x south 150.7 to St. Marks av, x west 100 to beginning. Edward H. Wilson to Barbara Bliss. *Mt.* $11,000. nom

St. Marks av, s s, 100 e Rockaway av, 25x92.4x 26.2x100. George Leykauf to Eva Barie widow. *Mt.* $1,000. nom

Same property. Eva Barie widow to George Leykauf and Anna C. his wife. *Mt.* $1,000. nom

Stone av, e s, 150 n Sutter av, 25x100. Davis and Jacob Axelrod and Isaac Levenson to Louis and Philip Friedberg. *Mt.* $2,000. 4,150

Stone av, w s, 80 n Truxton st, 20x100. Augusta A. Roby to Robert B Montgomery. nom

Stone av, e s, 100 s Newport av, 100x100; also,
Newport av, s w cor Christopher av, 100x 125; also,
Stone av, n e cor Newport av, 50x100.
Eliza A. Dunning widow to Caroline Belfer. 3,750

Stone av, e s, 150 n Blake av, 100x100. Release mort. Williamson R. Selover to Herbert C. Smith. 1,200

Thatford av, w s, 75 n Blake av, 25x90. Barnet Levin and Max Gittelsohn to Abram J. Littmann, of New York. *Mt.* $1,600. 3,400

Throop av, e s, abt 25 n Wallabout st, 25x68.8x 26.9x59.2. Pinkas Ganz, of New York, to Wolf Lewis. *Mt.* $3,550. 2,875

Union av, w s, 75 s South 1st st, 25x100, h & l. Margaret E. and Martha A. Farrell to Mary A. Keenan. 4,000

Same property. Joseph E. Foley and Mary E. McCann heirs Gerald Farrell to Mary A. Keenan. Q. C. nom

Washington av, n e cor Union st, runs east 68.10 x north 37 x west 34.3 x southwest 46.3 to av, x south 20 to beginning. Ann wife of and John I. Alston to Elizabetha wife of George J. Muller. 1,000

Waverly av, w s, 107.6 e Greene av, 20x75. Elizabeth L. Chinnock to William Gannon. 5,500

Willoughby av, s e s, 100 s w Knickerbocker av, 75x100. Caroline Belfer to Rebecca F. Forman and Martha J. Withers. *Mt.* $2,000. 4,500

Willoughby av, s s, 150 e Evergreen av, 75x95, h & l. John H. Scheidt to Daniel Kreuder. 10,000

Wyckoff av, s w s, 75 n w Himrod st, 25x89.5x 25x88.4. George Dittrich and Lippman Reizenstein to Louisa Lentner. *Mt.* $3,000. 6,300

3d av, e s, 70.2 n 47th st, 30x85. Frederick Seifried to Frederick Gommel. B. & S. nom

3d av, w s, 100.2 n 48th st, 0.2x100.
Interior lot on centre line bet 47th and 48th st, 120 w 3d av, runs west 20 x north 0.2x20 x0.2.
Interior lot on centre line bet 47th and 48th sts, 240 w 3d av, runs north 0.2 x west to centre old Gowanus road, x south to centre of block, x east —.
David J. Tingley to David J. Tingley and ano. exrs. Margt. M. Van Pelt. nom

3d av, s e s, 55 s w 14th st, 18.4x80. Martha Wakefield widow, Middletown, N. Y., to Millie C. Roger. 3,700

4th av, n w cor 20th st, runs north 22 x west 35.1 x north 0.7 x west 19.11 x south 22.7 to 20th st, x east 55, h & l. Annie and Michael T. Green to Patrick J. and Ellen M. Gunn. 6,300

4th av, w s, 133.4 s Warren st, 16.8x80.10, h & l. John H. Ruwe to Joseph Raven. *Mt.* $2,600. 3,600

5th av, No. 203, e s, 43 n Union st, 20x92.6.
Flatbush av, No. 97, e s, 249.10 n Hanson pl, 20x64.7x20.1x62.6.
6th av, No. 207, n e cor Union st, 23x92.6.
Francis H. and Peter A. Skelly to Mary Skelly. All title. All liens. 8,834

6th av, n e cor 21st st, 123x100. Thomas P. Payne to Nathan Kaplan. *Mt.* $6,327. 12,000

7th av, e s, 80.3 n Garfield pl, 19.9x80, h & l. Margaretta Armstrong, New York, to James A. Armstrong, New York. *Mt.* $10,000. 18,650

8th av, n w s, 19.5 n e Prospect av, 13x87.7x14x 89. Sophronia M. Fickett widow to Mary J. Dye. *Mt.* $1,600. 2,450

19th av, south cor 84th st, 100x100, New Utrecht. John Lott Nostrand to William Dittmar, Jr. 2,500

Same property. Release mort. Daniel Barre and Phebe M. wife of Charles E. Amerman to John L. Nostrand. 1,000

24th av, s e s, 180 n e Benson av, 60x96.8, Bensonhurst. James D. Lynch to Sarah A. Moore. 1,050

Interior lot, 48.10 n Grand st, on line which at n s Grand st is 128.11 e of Vandervoort av, runs east 22.3 x south 31.6 x northwest 41.2. Theodore R. Chapman to John J. Gallagher and Anna M. McCann. 260

Interior lot, 90 s McDonough st, 62 e Ralph av., runs east 38x10x38x10. Release mort. Asa W. Tenney to Thomas H. Radcliffe. nom

Lots 201 and 202 block 21, lots 338, 339 and 340 block 23, lots 418-420 and 441 block 24, lot 539 block 26, and lot 575-580 and 598, 599, 608 and 609 block 27, map No. 2 of 660 lots Cowenhoven farm, New Utrecht. Magdalene Cowenboven admrx. Garret Cowenhoven to Effingham H. Nichols. 5,100

Lots 79, 80, 81 and 84–101 block 18, and 110–118 and 120–134 block 19, and 212 block 21, same map. Same to same as last. 4,100

Lots 206, 207, 241–245, 273, 333, 334, 632, 633, 600, 601, 882, 899, 900, 901 and 910 in blocks 5, 6, 7, 11 and 15, map 937 lots belonging to The New Utrecht Improvement Co. Release mort. William Ziegler to The New Utrecht Improvement Co. 2,700

Lots 322–326 and 338 block 8, and 359–362 block 9, map No. 1 of 618 lots Cowenhoven farm, New Utrecht. Effingham H. Nichols to Nicholas E. Thill. 1,960

Lots 50–53 block 2, and 373–376 block 9, same map. Same to Elizabeth Thile 1,500

Lots 503 and 504 block 25 map No. 2 of 660 lots Cowenhoven farm, New Utrecht. Effingham H. Nichols to Thomas H. Lomas. 320

Lots 286 and 287 block 22 same map. Same to Martin McNamara. 370

Lots 600 and 601 block 11 map 937 lots New Utrecht Improvement Co. The New Utrecht Improvement Co. to Mary A. G. English. 250

Lots 881 and 910 block 15 map of 937 lots of the New Utrecht Improvement Co. New Utrecht Improvement Co. to Louis Camera. 340

Lots 241–245 inclus. and 273 block 6 same map. Same to John F. Duffy. 900

Lots 632 and 633 block 11 same map. Same to James Wasson. 250

Lots 899, 900 and 901 block 15 map 937 lots property New Utrecht Improvement Co. The New Utrecht Improvement Co. to Elizabeth F. Fuller, of Blythebourne, N. Y. 420

Lots 278–282, 310, 311, 297–302, 337–340, 365, 367, 394–398, 404–411 and 423 426, all inclus., map Worth & Strawson, Flatbush. Jacob Worth to Henry Newman and James H. Holmes. 4,680

Lots 502–506, 509 and 510 map Zabriskie homestead, Flatbush. Release mort. Jeremiah L., John L. and N. Lansing Zabriskie exrs. Abby L. Zabriskie to William J. Kaiser, John H. Vanderveer and George W. Dalton. consid. omitted

Lot 28 block 17 map 2 of 660 lots Cowenhoven farm, New Utrecht. Effingham H. Nichols to Andrew J. Flood. 195

Lots 333 and 334 block 7 map 937 lots of New Utrecht Improvement Co. The New Utrecht Improvement Co. to Charles Boylhart. 250

Plots No. four = one (4 = 1), also plot No. four = two (4 = 2) map heirs Garret Stryker, Gravesend, contains 6 1-10 acres. John H. Scheidt to Rebecca Lewis. 500

New Utrecht road, e s, adj Protestant Dutch Church land on south and bounded south by J. H. Storys, excepting part taken for Prospect Park & Coney Island R. R., Flatbush. Partition. John H. Kemble to James Warner. 3,500

Canarsie Landing road, plot begins 225 of said road F. A. and J. C. Mathews, 50x100, Canarsie. Fanny and John C. Mathews to Stephen M. McNamara. 300

Kings County Elevated Railroad in the 1st Ward. John C. McGuire, Registrar of Arrears, to City of Brooklyn. 7,909

Union Elevated Railroad in the 11th Ward. John C. McGuire, Registrar of Arrears, to The City of Brooklyn. 9,980

WESTCHESTER COUNTY.

OCTOBER 7 TO 13—INCLUSIVE.

BEDFORD.

Barrett, Emma R. to Wm. B. Timberman, w s road from village to Hoyt's Mills, abt 11 acres. $3,800

CORTLANDT.

Depew, Martha M., exr. of, and ano. to Edgar Roake, w s Chauncey st 237 n Elm st, 40x115. 240

Hill, Uriah, Jr., to Chas. K. Free, n s Orchard st, 610 w Highland, 50x200. 800

White, Benj. R. to John R. Richards, n s Howard st, adj Isaac Seymour, 72x—. 25

EASTCHESTER.

Almirall, Ida to Wm. W. Penfield, lots 242, 334 and U map Washingtonville. 1,000

Allerton, Rachel W. to Walter S. Allerton, lot 51 s s Wartburg av, map Tamerton. nom

Acker, Dorothea to Henry Acker, lot 45, cor Union and Bridge sts, West Mt. Vernon. nom

Same to same, part lot 173, West Mt. Vernon, 40x125. nom

Carroll, Mary to Patrick Carroll, lot 455 w s 4th av, Central Mt. Vernon, 50x100. 1,000

Chivois, Mary A. trustee of, to Mary A. Chivois, e s Rich av. 270 n w P. road, 50x110. 6,500

Chivois, Ferd W. to same, same property. 6,500

Chivois, Mary A. to Edith M. Storey, same property. 6,500

Conkling, Mary A. to Maria Law, s s 1st st, 82.5 e 10th av, 31x89.3. 2,075

Clarey, John, Jr., to Lucy N. Mandrey, lot 15 s e s Garden pl, South Mt. Vernon, 25x140. 3,750

Mandrey, Lucy W. to Giacchino Oricchio, same property. 375

Doell, Paulina to Chas. Stahl, plot 8 n s Washington st, 89.7x80. 2,250

Eayrs, Wm. L. to Winslow E. Buzby, plot 238 n w s High st, West Mt. Vernon, 33.4x100. 4,150

Emmeleith, John, Jr., to John P. Nelson, south ½ lot 468 e s 6th av, Mt. Vernon, 50x105. 5,600

Finn, Josephine S. to Theo. Baier, part lot 885 e s 11th av Mt. Vernon, 33.4x105. 4,750

Gescheidt, Mary to Wm. L. Eayrs, part lot 947 w s 12th av, Mt. Vernon, 33.4x105. 1,100

Glover, Frank N. to Chas. A. Tier, lots 648 and 655 w s 7th av, Mt. Vernon; also 466 w s 4th av, Central Mt. Vernon, 50x100. 10,300

McNolty, Mary to Patrick Havey, part lot 606 s s 6th st, Mt. Vernon, 25x100. 500

Havey, Patrick to Barth. McGrane, same property. nom

Mace, Levi H. to Mary F. Creney, lot 512 n s 16th av, Wakefield, 100x114. 1,200

Miller, Thos. L. to Fred. Trott, lot 31 e s 10th av, Henneberger's map, 25x105. 450

Nelson, John P. to John Emmeluth, Jr., part 278 e s 4th av, Mt. Vernon, 30x105. 4,600

Penfield, Geo. J. to John T. Kubarsik, lot 157, cor W. P. Boulevard and De Milt av. 1,200

Penfield, Wm. W. to Wm. D. Miller, lots 334 and U map Washingtonville. 1,000

Phelan, Mich. J. to Wm. F. Ebeling, part lot 223 s w s Mt. Vernon av, West Mt. Vernon, 44x88. 2,800

Primrose, Emma J. to Wm. B. Gillette, w s Cottage av, 265 n Oakley, 56x110. 2,240

Turner, Mary G. to Rich. W. Turner, n s Prospect av, 175 w Cottage, 25x100, also e s Park av, 300 s Sidney. 13,000

Walter, Richard to Jas. Wilkinson, lot 279 s e s Marian st, Washingtonville, 50x100. 550

GREENBURGH.

Blackwell, Wilson H. to Owen Jones, lots 653, 654 and 655, Ardsley. 275

Caruthers, Amelia A. to Eugene Jones, w s Broadway, 243.5 n Wildey st, abt 100x297. 10,000

Erhardt, Joel B. trustee to Michael F. Shelley, s s Danforth av, 150 w Maple, 50x100, also s e cor same and Orchard st. 1,250

Jones, Cyrus P. and ano. to Herman Dichting, lots 289 and 290, Ardsley Heights. 400

Same to Freuda C. Schutts, lots 275 and 276. 350

Same to Peter F. Schutts, lots 261, 264, 265, 268, 269, 273 and 274. 1,116

Same to John Allen, lots 2, 3, 4 and 5, Ardsley. 1,200

King, Ellen to Mary Lewis, n e cor Broadway and Prospect avs, 25x100. 2,750

Mullan, Peter to Mary F. Ryan, lot 11 map lots Rich. Humphreys. 750

Uptegrove, Wm. P. to Jas. H. Moran et al., The Fair Grounds, w s Tarrytown road, 104 acres. 30,500

Wilson, Francis F. et al. guards. of, to Bernard Huston, s s Clinton av, 132 e old Post road, 66x120. 1,850

MAMARONECK.

Daymon, Wm. D. et al. to Cath. Hayes et al., lots 43 and 44 n w cor Mamaroneck and Bedford avs, 100x100. 1,400

Same to Sarah Franklin, lots 1–7 n w cor Mamaroneck and Elliott avs, 324x100. 8,250

Same to Richard H. Moran, lots 12–17 n e cor Mamaroneck and Denman avs, 200x150. 2,000

MOUNT PLEASANT.

Smadbeck, Louis to John Murray, lots 1276 and 1277, Sherman Park. 400

Same to John Ketz, lot 282. 150

Same to Mark Jaloneck, lots 1752 and 1753. 400

Same to Patrick Leavy and ano., lots 1367 and 1368. 350

Same to Jos. Lombardo, lots 1526. 200

Same to Kate McDonald, lots 1573–1576. 750

Same to Robt. Sloane and ano., lot 1603. 175

Same to Sarah Callon, lot 25. 150

Same to Annie T. Wallace, lots 792 and 793. 200

Same to Thos. Walsh, lot 554. 100

Same to Mary McCarthy, lots 1644 and 1645. 300

Same to Henry Balze, lots 1747–1751 and 1792–1809. 3,200

Same and ano. to Joanna Sullivan, lots 5–8, Lakehurst. 475

Same to Fred. Chable and ano., lots 768 and 769, Lakehurst. 425

NEW CASTLE.

Moore, Geo. W. to Siegfried Gruenewald, s w cor South st and Lexington av, 100x—. 1,000

NEW ROCHELLE.

Manhattan Life Ins. Co. to Julie W. Darling, lot 15 block F, Rochelle Park. 1,600

Schleyer, Marie et al. and C. H. Roosevelt to Peter Krayer et al., s s Main st, 211 e Church st, abt 55x234. 6,000

White, Thos. to Cornelius M. Vander Lee, lot 32 n e s Locust av, Jackson property, abt 65x150. 2,150

Williamson, Lizzie to Estcort Dickerson, n e cor Clinton and Coligni avs, 125x300. 1,600

OSSINING.

Adcock, Edith to Leonard R. Turner, n s Everett av, 311.3 w Post road, 30x186.6. 2,800

Westchester Town Site Co. to Adolph F. Lucker, lots 1 and 2 s e cor Orison and Highland avs, abt 62x102; also 77 and 78 s w cor same and Caroline avs, abt 42x102. 1,400

PELHAM.

Bell, Nathan to Adrian Iselin, lot 12, map property Levina E. Bell, 30x104. 300

Townsend, Jas. M., Jr., and ano. to Alex. A. Jordan, lots 47, 48 and 49 w s Highland av, map Chestnut Grove, &c. 1,850

RYE.

Bulkley, Mary E. and ano. to Wilfred P. Purdy and ano., lot 28 w s Smith av, Poningo Dale. 550

McCarty, Richard T. to Daniel E. Cosgrove and ano., e s Centre st, 651 s Westchester av, 100x196. 2,250

Merritt, Jas. S. and ano., to George Rutland, lot 39 s w cor Ellendale av and Regent st, 50x100. 500

Same to same, lot 42 s s Ellendale av, adj above, 43x150. —

WESTCHESTER.

Bull, Charlotte to Chas. Miller, n e cor Union and Railroad avs, 50x87. 900

Camp, Hugh N. to Gustav Strohhaker, lots 353 and 354, map McGraw estate. 420

Casey, Michael to Mary A. Casey, lots 119 and 120, map McGraw estate. 550

Carlock, Geo., Jr., to Peter Kiefer, part lot 1128 e s Bronx terrace, Wakefield, 25x105. nom

Dexter, Fred. C. to Wm. A. Shelton, lot 610 n s 4th av, Wakefield, 25x100. nom

Gilbert, Henry W. to Eliza McHugh, w s Washington av, 100 n 2d st, abt 24x100. 300

McHugh, Eliza to Henry B. Howell, same property. 300

Hendricks, Emma L. to Aaron V. Hendricks, s s 7th st, 255 w Av A, Unionport, 50x108. nom

Hendricks, Aaron V. to Emma L. Hendricks, s s 7th st, adj above, 50x108. nom

Heilman, Elizh. to Fred. Ackerman, w s old Boston road, 258 n Elizabeth st, 50x140. 7,000

Same to Jacob Binninger and ano., lot 4 s e cor 3d st and Av A, Jerome, 25x106. 4,500

Hughes, Miles to John White, e s Deane pl, 100 s Pierce av, 25x100. 240

Mace, Levi H. and ano. to Martin J. Keogh, lots 69–73 and 135–139 Lacoma Park. 2,000

Sprague, Louisa to Jonas Peterson, s s 2d st, 100 w Union av, 50x100. 1,100

Shirmer, Chas. D. to Eliz'h C. Hadley, lot 43 s s North Oak Drive, Bronxwood Park. 10,000

YONKERS.

Barnes, Jerome D. to Cath. C. MacFarland, lots 17 and 18 block 19 Lowerre Station. 700

Butler, Wm. A., Jr., to same, lots 15, 16 and 24 block 19 Lowerre Station. 1,150

Dickson, John to John Duke, n s Ash st, 350 e Oak st, 50x100. 1,250

East Side Land Co. to Daniel Murray, lots 72 and 73 Shearwood Hill. 1,000

Same to Samuel R. Free, lot 35. 500

Edwards, Adah to Sarah McCord, lot 24 block 3 Lowerre Station. 700

Eddy, Obadiah C. to Ophelia A. Brewer, s s Poplar st, 50 w Oak st, 25x100. 900

Morris, Nicholas J., Jr., to Fred. A. Garnjost, part lot 208 e s Riverdale av, City map, 100x100. 4,400

Sullivan, Peter J. to Alice Ryan, lot 236 e s South Broadway, Geo. Heriot map, 25x100. 6,500

MORTGAGES.

NEW YORK CITY.

OCTOBER 9 10, 12, 13, 14, 15.

Appel, Joseph and Pepi his wife to George H. McCabe. Delancey st. P. M. Oct. 9, due May 1, 1895. $1,500

Aborn, Louise L. wife of and Robert W. to THE UNITED STATES TRUST CO. of New York. 39th st, No. 43, n s, 648 w 5th av, 22x98.9. Oct. 12, due Oct. 1, 1892, 5 %. 30,000

Alheit, Mary M. to James F. and Patrick H. Sheridan and James S. Segrave. Rock st. P. M. Oct. 1, 5 years, 5 %. 250

Armbruster, Bernhard and Karolina his wife to James F. and Patrick H. Sheridan and James S. Segrave. Rock and Field sts. P. M. Oct. 2, due Oct. 1, 1894, 5 %. 1,450

Anderson, Walden P. to Robinson Gill. 93d st, s s, 325 e Amsterdam av, 80x100.8. Oct. 10, demand. 10,000

Bailey, Thomas to THE TITLE GUARANTEE AND TRUST CO. 151st st, n s, 75 w Amsterdam av, 25x74.11. Oct. 12, due Oct. 15, 1892. 2,500

Bell, Amelia wife of William to John O. Baker, Newark, N. J. 79th st. P. M. Oct. 12, demand. gold, 40,000

Same to same. Same property. Building loan to finish incomplete buildings. Oct. 12, demand. gold, 13,500

Bach, Lewis Z. to John Bowes and John Coombs, of Bowes & Coombs. 102d st, n s, 129.6 w 3d av, 27x100.11. Oct. 9, 1 year, 5 %. gold, 1,500

Beaudet, John and Ernest P. to Robinson Gill. Mt. Morris av, s w cor 121st st, 100.11x100. Sub. to morts. Oct. 8, 1 year or sooner. 12,000

Brockner, Isabel to Katharine C. Griswold. 3d av, n e cor 40th st, 24.8x80. Oct. 12, due Nov. 1, 1892, 4½ %. gold, 7,500

Barron, Mary A. wife of Joseph S. to Martha Williams. 42d st, n s, 100 e 11th av, 25x100. Oct. 10, notes. 475

Byrne, Mary T. to THE EMIGRANT INDUST. SAVINGS BANK. 137th st, s s, 530.5 e Southern Boulevard, 25x100. Oct. 12, 1 year, 4½ %. 1,500

Baldwin, William B. to Eliza J. Arkenburgh and ano. exrs. Robert H. Arkenburgh. 76th st, n s, 90 w Amsterdam av. P. M. Oct. 2, due Oct. 10, 1892, 5 %. 10,625

Same to same. 76th st, n s, 115 w Amsterdam av. P. M. Oct. 2, due Oct. 10, 1892, 5 %. 10,625

Brasse, William to Beadleston & Woerz. Washington st, No. 92, s w cor Rector st. lease. Oct. 6, demand. 1,500

Brennan, Thomas to The McElwee Mfg. Co. of New York. Water st, s e cor Market st, 26x80. Oct. 13, 2 months. 2,500

Brown, John to Laura F. Van Riper. Fairmount av or 175th st, n s, 79.6 e Waterloo pl proposed, 26.6x91.3x26x96.5. Oct. 6, due Oct. 8, 1894. gold, 2,500

Brown, Frances S. formerly Sprague to Mary M. Baldwin, Newport, R. I. 104th st, s s, 250 w Columbus av, 25x100.11. Sept. 19, due Oct. 1, 1896, or sooner, 5 %. 18,500

Cameron, Alexander to Sarah H. Powell. 96th st, n s, 150 e Amsterdam av, 25x100.11. Oct. 14, 5 years, 5 %. 20,000

Same to same. 96th st, n s, 175 e Amsterdam av, 25x100.11. Oct. 14, 5 years, 5 %. 20,000

Campbell, John V. to Laemmlein Buttenwieser. Catharine st. P. M. Oct. 1, demand. 2,400

Canda, John M. and John P. Kane, individ. and of firm of Canda & Kane, and George Crawford with Duncan C. McKinlay. Agreement as to priority of mortgages. Sept. 22. nom

Crawford, Chas. A. to Henrietta wife of George Starr. West 10th st, n s, 121.8 e 4th st, 20x95. Oct. 8, due Oct. 4, 1892, 5 %. 1,000

Cleverdon, Robert N. and Lillie B. his wife to The Serial Building Loan and Savings Inst. Mt. Hope pl, n s, 150 w Morris av, 25x125. Oct. 13, installs. 2,000

Cohn, Georgia E. mortgagor with John N. Brown et al. trustees of Sophia A. wife of William W. Sherman. Extension of mort. Oct. 7. nom

Cook, John H. to James F. and Patrick H. Sheridan and James S. Segrave. Hill st. P. M. Oct. 2, due Oct. 1, 1894, 5 %. 650

Cook, Valentine E. N. mortgagor with Mary H. Moore mortgagee. Extension of mort. at increased interest. Oct. 10. nom

Croviel, James C. and Catharine A. his wife to James F. and Patrick H. Sheridan and James S. Segrave. Forest st. P. M. Oct. 1, 3 years, 5 %. 1,170

Cammann, Isabelle wife of Henry J. formerly De Barre to Maria Banks, New Hamburgh, N. Y. 51st st, No. 439, n s, 360 e 10th av, 19x100.5. Oct. 15, 3 years, 5 %. 1,600

Clark, Mary wife of and William to THE HARLEM SAVINGS BANK. 123d st, s w cor Lexington av, 23.4x100.11, excepting a piece on Lexington av, 35x24. Sub. to mort. $5,000. Oct. 15, 1 year, 5 %. 1,000

Cohen, Solomon to Abraham M. Levy. Jefferson st. P. M. Sub. to mort. $45,000. Oct. 15, installs. 6,600

Conklin, Franklin, Newark, N. J., to the trustees of the New York Universalist Relief Fund. Trinity av, s e cor 155th st, runs south 47.1 x east 57.5 x north 0.6 x east 42.7 x north 46.6 to st, x west 100. Oct. 15, 2 years, 5 %. 5,000

Costello, Mary A. D. wife of and Michael to William Fisher. 70th st, s s, 120.6 e Lexington av, 19.7x100.5. Oct. 1, 3 years, 5 %. 15,000

Same to Peter E. Duffy. Same property. Sub. to last mort. Oct. 1, 2 years, 5 %. 2,000

de Krom, Sophia, Maria J., Katharine F. and John C. otherwise Jean C. to Henry Stengel. 57th st, s s, 200 e 2d av, 25x100.5. Oct. 5, due Oct. 15, 1894, 5 %. 7,500

Dixon, Charlotte A. to Paul L. Thebaud. Monroe st, s s, 176 e Corlears st, 22x70. Oct. 15, 5 years. 2,000

Dolan, James B. and Kate F. his wife to Alice Stettiner. 116th st. P. M. Oct. 15, 1 year. 1,000

Dreyer, Margaret to Henry Stube. Amsterdam av. P. M. Oct. 15, 2 years, 5 %. 2,000

Deutsche Evangelische St. Paulis Gemeinde In Ost Harlem to Elizabeth wife of Frederick Storck. 112th st, No. 159, n s, 270 w 3d av, 25x100.2. Sub. to mort. $7,000. Oct. 12, 3 years. 2,500

Dorgan, Patrick M. to James F. and Patrick H. Sheridan and James S. Segrave. Hill st. P. M. Oct. 1, 3 years, 5 %. 300

Demorest, W. Jennings to Frederick T. Van Beuren. 14th st, n s, 175 w 5th av, 25x103.3. Lease. Oct. 10, 3 years. 12,000

Devlin, Margaret widow to THE UNITED STATES TRUST CO. of New York. 39th st, No. 268, s s, 100 e 8th av, 30.9x98.9. Oct. 13, due Oct. 1, 1894, 5 %. 30,000

Same to same. 39th st, No. 266, s s, 130.9 e 8th av, 30.9x98.9. Oct. 13, due Oct. 1, 1894, 5 %. 30,000

Same to The Middlesex Quarry Co., of Portland, Conn. Same property. Oct. 13, 6 months. 1,500

Same to same. Same property. Oct. 13, 6 months. 5,000

Same to G. L. Schuyler & Co. 39th st, s s, 100 e 8th av, 30.9x98.9. Oct. 13, demand. 1,675

Same to The Bradley & Currier Co. (Lim.) Same property. Oct. 12, 6 months. 5,532

Same to Isaac Schmeidler. 39th st, s s, 100 e 8th av, 61.6x98.9. Sub. to morts. $60,000. Oct. 13, 6 months. 26,189

Same to Cassidy & Adler. Same property. Oct. 13, due Jan. 15, 1892. 2,400

Deyerberg, Henry H. to John R. Perlhefter. 10th av, No. 27. Store lease. Oct. 7, installs. 600

Dunbar, Mary B. to THE EMIGRANT INDUST. SAVINGS BANK. 36th st, No. 248, s s, 285 e 8th av, 19.2x98.9. Oct. 9, 1 year, 4½ %. 2,000

Dunker, Herrman to Bernheimer & Schmid. 1st av, No. 1697, s w cor 88th st. Saloon lease. Oct. 9, note, demand. 1,500

Dugan, Dennis to Barbara Eckert. Bathgate av, n e cor 178th st, 54x92x54x94. Oct. 10, 4 years, 5 %. 3,000

Eckes, Mary K. to Katharine Singer. Courtlandt av, n w cor 148th st, 27.3x100. July 12, 2 years, 5 %. 2,000

Eichler, John F. otherwise Frederick and Mary M. his wife to William E. Amos. Inwood av, e s, 175 s Wolf pl, 50x130. Oct. 13, 3 years. 4,000

Effinger, John to Philip Braender. 8th av. P. M. Oct. 15, 2 years or installs, 5 %. 3,000

Fogal, Emily and George W. Harris to Allen Dodworth, Pasadena, Cal. Denman pl and Tinton av. P. M. Sept. 10, due Oct. 15, 1894, or sooner, 5 %. 3,000

Foley, Ellen to Josephine L. Horton, Brooklyn. Southern Boulevard, n w cor Lyon st, 25x108.6x36.7x100. Re-recorded. Sept. 26, due Feb. 1, 1892. 400

Faehudrich, Waldemar to William C. Martin. 99th st. P. M. Oct. 10, installs. 2,000

Fagan, Edward B. to THE EMIGRANT INDUSTRIAL SAVINGS BANK. 117th st, n s, 394 e 1st av, 16.8x100.10. Oct. 9. 1 year, 4½ %. 500

Feldman, Moritz to William Rosenbush. Broome st. P. M. Oct. 1, 1½ years. 500

Folz, Frederick to Charles C. Holcombe, Lee, Mass. 149th st and Retreat av. P. M. Oct. 5, 1 year. 18,000

Franz, Henry to George Lockyer and John Daly. Clinton av and 2d st, 24th Ward. P. M. Oct. 10, 3 years or sooner, 5 %. 1,200

Flannery, Simon P. to John Higgins. Lexington av. P. M. Oct. 12, installs, 5 %. 13,000

Farley, Patrick to Elizabeth D. Chaloner. 137th st, s s, 430 w Lenox av, runs south 99.11 x west 20 x north 48 x west 22 x north 51.11 to st, x east 42. P. M. Sept. 2, 3 years, 5 %. 14,750

Foy, Thomas to Letitia wife of David H. King. 104th st, n s, 18 w 4th av, runs north 57 x west 0.6 x north 18 x west 15.1 x south 75 to st, x east 15.7, with all title to land lying bet rear of premises and a line 75.8 n of 104th st. Oct. 12, due Oct. 13, 1896, 5 %. 5,000

Fanning, George W. and Mary L. his wife, Robert Fanning and Delia his wife, Emilie wife of and Marcus H. Talbot, William Fanning and Kate his wife, Thomas M. Fanning and Mary A. his wife, Frances A. wife of and Stephen V. A. Hunter, and Mary L. wife of and Charles J. Bishop to THE EMIGRANT INDUST SAVINGS BANK. 11th av or Boulevard, n e cor 141st st, 99.11x100. Sept. 22, 1 year, 4½ %. 15,000

Fisher, Philip mortgagor with THE POUGHKEEPSIE SAVINGS BANK mortgagee. Extension of mort. at 4½ %. Sept. 1. nom

Grodjinsky, Samuel and Lena his wife and Golde Lubelsky to Louis Seigel. Henry st, No. 91, n s, 25x100. Sub. to mort. $20,250. Oct. 13, installs. 9,000

Goeller, Charles J. mortgagor with Samuel P. Dunn et al. trustees, &c. Extension of mort. Aug. 18. nom

Goetz, Samuel to Randolph Guggenheimer and Salomon Marx. Goerck st, e s, 246.7 n Rivington st, runs east 100 x north 34.10 x east 100 to Mangin st, x north 65.9 x west 100 x south 26 x west 100 to Goerck st, x south 75 to beginning. Oct. 9, due Nov. 1, 1891. 9,200

Goetz, Samuel, present owner, with William F. Lennon mortgagor. Agreement as to amount to be paid on morts. made by William F. Lennon. Oct. 10. nom

Gebhardt, Matilde to Marquis L. and Octavius M. Hawley, Binghampton. Clinton pl, n s, 35.6 e University pl, 28.11x93.11x29x93.11. Leasehold. P. M. Aug. 1, installs. 8,500

Gerbereux, Denis F. to John Hare Powel, Jr., and ano. exrs. and trustees Samuel Powel. Charlton st. P. M. Oct. 5, 3 years, 5 %. gold, 12,000

Gudwitzki, Harris to Adolf Mayer. Essex st, No. 81. P. M. Sub. to mort. $13,000. Oct. 12, installs. 7,000

Gueli, Domenico and Mary E. his wife to Eva B. Moss. 119th st, No. 509, n s, 177.6 e Pleasant av, 20.6x100.11. Oct. 14, 6 months. 1,000

Haberman, Simon to Maurice S. Bondy. 7th av, s e cor 116th st, runs east 150 x south 100.11 x west — to e s St Nicholas av, x northwest — to 7th av, x north — to beginning. Oct. 15, 6 months. 10,000

Hammond, Thomas S. to Anna R. Connor. Greenwich av, Nos. 97-101, s w cor West 12th st, 67.5x119, Leasehold. Oct. 7, installs. 4,740

Harris, Bertha wife of and Abraham to Henrietta Wimpfheimer extrx. Marx Wimpfheimer. Columbia st, e s, 68.3 n Stanton st, runs east 75.4 x north 6.9 x east 24.8 x north 14.11 x west 100 to Columbia st, x south 21.8. Oct. 15, 3 years, 5 %. 13,500

Same to Bernard Loth. Same property. Oct. 15, demand. 1,500

Herdtfelder, Elizabeth to Oscar Purdy. Eldridge st, e s, 104.1 n Rivington st, 24x87.6. Oct. 15, 3 years, 5 %. 12,500

Hernz, Lily C. M. to Emilio Del Pino. 73d st, s s, 200 w 9th av, 16.8x102.2. April 1, 1890, 1 year. 1,500

Hillier, Mary to THE MUTUAL LIFE INS. CO. of New York. 40th st, Nos. 225 and 227, n s, 217.6 w 2d av, 37.6x98.9. Already mortgaged to mortgagee. 1 year, 5 %. 500

Holdridge, H. Eugene to THE INST. FOR SAVINGS OF MERCHANTS' CLERKS. Water st, No. 280. P. M. Oct. 5, 3 years, 4½ %. gold, 11,000

Hughes, Thomas R., Weehawken, N. J., to George F. Betts. 66th st, No. 229, n s, 350 e West End av. P. M. Sub. to mort. $15,000. Oct. 15, 1 year or sooner, 5 %. 2,500

Same to same. 66th st, No. 231, n s, 325 e West End av. P. M. Sub. to mort. $15,000. Oct. 15, 1 year or sooner, 5 %. 2,500

Hylan, Ellen wife of and John T. to The John Eichler Brewing Co. 144th st, s s, 85 n w from the angle point in said st, 150 from s w cor 144th st and College av, runs northwest 20 x southwest 42.3 x still southwest 37.9 x northeast 40.8 x still northeast 47.2 to beginning. Oct. 14, 1 year. 800

Hanley, John F. to Alfred B. Scott general guard., &c. 23d st, s s, 394 e 1st av, 25x98.9; 22d st, n s, 354.6 e 1st av, 47x98.9. Oct. 6, 3 years, 5 %. 15,000

Hartwell, Louise M. certifies that mortgage made by her to William J. Bailey Aug. 25, 1891, was without consideration and is not good as a lien on property therein described, &c. Oct. 13.

Hencken, Hancke and Frederick Willenbrock to THE DRY DOCK SAVINGS INST. 1st av, w s, 25.2 s 95th st, 75.6x100; 1st av, s e cor 94th st, 100.8x194. Sept. 23, due Oct. 1, 1892, 5 %. 25,000

Herrmann, Peter and Carolina his wife to James F. and Patrick H. Sheridan and James S. Segrave. Forest st. P. M. Oct. 1, 3 years, 5 %. 670

Hoffman, Aaron to Catharine A. Taylor et al. trustees for Albertina S. Pyne, Kate W. Winthrop, Mary Lewis and George C. and Henry A. C. Taylor. 124th st, s s, 339.8 w 3d av, 21.4x100.11; 124th st, s s, 318.4 w 3d av, 21.4x100.11. Oct. 13, 1 year, 4½ %. 10,000

Horgan, Arthur J. and Vincent J. Slattery to Jacob A. Geissenhainer and ano. trustees Henry Elsworth, dec'd. Thompson st, Nos. 91 and 93, w s, 125 n Spring st, 50x100. Oct. 12, 3 years, 5 %. 55,000

Same to Du Bois Smith, Smithtown, L. I. Laight st, s w cor Collister st, 25x87.6. P. M. Aug. 3, 1 year, 5 %. 2,500

Harris, Fanny E. wife of John H. to Sarah R. Beach widow. 57th st, No. 56 E. P. M. Secures bond of mortgagor and John H. Harris. Sept. 14, due Oct. 12, 1894, 5 %. 20,250

Hoeck, Catharine widow to Hermann Weber, Hoboken, N. J. 114th st, No. 320, s s, 243.9 e 2d av, 18.9x100.10. Oct. 9, 1 year, 5 %. 500

Howe, Samuel to THE EMIGRANT INDUSTRIAL SAVINGS BANK. 2d av, No. 576, e s, 149.9 n 31st st, 25.6x72. Oct. 12, 1 year, 4½ %. 8,000

Hasell, Clemence L. widow to Richard A. Brown admr. Margaret W. Boardman. Broadway, No. 854, e s, 29x130; 3d av, No. 325, e s, 49.4 n 24th st, 24.8x97.7; 3d av, Nos. 310, 312 and 314, w s, 98.9 n 23d st, 49.4x84. ⅝ part. Sub. morts. $125,000. Oct. 5, demand, 5 %. 23,041

Hirschberg, Johanna wife of Julius to Michael Cain. 120th st, n s, 250.2 w 4th av. P. M. Oct. 7, 1 year. 2,000

Same to same. 120th st, n s, 283.5 e 4th av. P. M. Oct. 7, 1 year. 2,000

Hughes, Thomas R. to THE CENTRAL TRUST CO. of New York trustee of trust deed by Carl Wiechers et al. 85th st. P. M. Oct. 9, due March 1, 1895, 5 %. gold, 33,000

Hamilton, Ida M. to William Gauld. Amsterdam av, n e cor 90th st, 100.2x100. Sub. to morts. $32,000. Oct. 8, due Mar. 1, 1892, or sooner. 1,300

Heinlein, Moses and Elias to Leopold Bleier. Walnut st, s e cor 2d av, runs east 50 x south 100 x east 50 to centre line of block, x south 50 x west 100 to av, x north 150. Nov. 8, 1883, demand. 800

Same to same. 6th av, w s, lots 69 and 70 map of Mount Eden, 100x100; Walnut st, n w cor Grove av, 37x189x73x178. Nov. 8, 1883, demand. 1,300

Hockstaetter, Katherina W. wife of and Charles W. to Mary E. Hewlett extrx. J. A. Hewlett. 119th st. P. M. Oct. 13, 3 years, 5 %. 7,500

Holly, William A. to John W. Baird and ano. exrs. John Baird. 122d st, n s, 178 w 7th av, 22x100.8. Oct. 13, 1 year, 5 %. 1,000

Joveshof, Herman to Patrick Collins. 9th av, No. 453. P. M. Oct. 15, due Dec. 1, 1893, 5 %. 3,000

Same to same. 9th av, No. 455. P. M. Oct. 15, due Dec. 1, 1893, 5 %. 3,000

Joseph, Annie mortgagee to Wolf Cohen, present owner. Statement that $750 has been paid on account of mort. made by Wolf Cohen to Aaron Levy and Solomon Fluberg April 1, 1891, and that there is now due on account thereof 4,750

Jordan, William G. to The Bradley & Currier Co. (Lim.) 44th st, n s, 300 e 10th av, 40x100.4. Sub. to morts. $40,000. Oct. 8, 4 months. 2,993

Jacob, August to Mabel Slade, East Orange, N. J. 80th st, s s, 225 w 3d av, 25x102.2. Oct. 13, 3 years, 5 %. 20,000

Jessup, Frederick J. to Charles B. Bech. Convent av, e s, 539.6 n 141st st, 20x100. Oct. 12, 5 years, 5 %. 6,500

Kee, Frank T. to Emily L. Wiggins. Wadsworth av, w s, 25 n 179th st, 25x100. Oct. 1, 3 years, 5 %. 3,500

Kenealy, Matthew T. to James F. and Patrick H. Sheridan and James S. Segrave. Hill st. P. M. Oct. 2, due Oct. 1, 1894, 5 %. 570

King, David H. to Matthew Hetrick. Madison st, No. 184, s s, 225.8 w Rutgers st, 21.2x100; Pell st, No. 21, s s, 21x56.8x21x58.4. All title. Sept. 8, 1888, demand. 20,000

Kreutzer, Carl and Katharina E. his wife to James F. and Patrick H. Sheridan and James S. Segrave. Rock st. P. M. Oct. 1, 3 years, 5 %. 600

Kehoe, John mortgagor with William P. Esterbrook mortgagee, Rahway, N. J. Extension of mort. Oct. 30, 1890. nom

Kelly, Adeline C. wife of John P. to Thomas E. Crimmins. 119th st, n s, 36 e 4th av, 18x75.7. Oct. 1, 1 year, 5 %. 800

Krug, August to Eva Bechtel, extrx. George Bechtel. Spring st, No. 212. Store lease. Oct. 7, demand. 500

Kahn, Mayer and Marcus Kohner to Richard T. Wilson. 59th st, Nos. 9-19, n s, 175 e 5th av, 6 lots. 6 P. M. morts., each $12,000. Oct. 14, 3 years, 5 %. 72,000

Kellogg, David M. to The Central Trust Co. of New York. Av A. P. M. Aug. 25, due Sept. 15, 1892, or sooner, 5 %. gold, 40,000

Kilpatrick, Edward to Cornelius F. Kingsland, Mt. Pleasant, N. Y. West End av, s e cor 98th st, 19.11x100. Oct. 14, 3 years, 5 %. 23,000

Same to William M. Kingsland, Mt. Pleasant, N. Y. West End av, e s, 55.11 s 98th st, 18x100. Oct. 14, 3 years, 5 %. 15,000

Kingsland, Albert A., Brooklyn, to Mitchel Valentine. Assignment of all title as legatee or devisee of Daniel C. Kingsland. Oct. 13. 10,000

Knowlton, Edward to John Dauenhauer. Hudson st. P. M. Oct. 14, 2 years, 5 %. 13,000

Krekeler, Thomas, Brooklyn, to The Emigrant Indust. Savings Bank. 17th st, s s, 143 e Av A, 23.9x92. Oct. 14, 1 year, 4½ %. 8,000

Lewy, Sigmund and Moritz Weiss to Charlotte Ehrlinger. 75th st. P. M. Sub. to mort. $9,000. Oct 15, 2 years or installs, 5 %. 2,000

Lennon, William F. to Samuel Goetz. 84th st, s s, 587.9 w 3d av, 25.7x102.2. Oct. 10, demand. 6,000

Lutster, Cornelius W. to The Title Guarantee and Trust Co. 74th st. s s, 225 w Central Park West, 25x102.2. Oct. 10, due Oct. 12, 1892, 5 %. 32,500

Lyons, George W. and Jennie his wife to Gottfried Schulz. 2d st, 24th Ward. P. M. Aug. 10, 10 years or installs, 5 %. 3,400

Levy, Joseph and Annie his wife to Lazarus Levy. Orchard st, No. 22, e s, 28.1x88, all; Forsyth st, No. 145, w s, 24x100. ½ part. Oct 5, demand. 5,000

Lockyer, George and John Daly to Ephraim B. Levy. Lots 142, 143, 144, 187, 188 map of Edward K. Willard, Fordham. P. M. Oct. 8, due Oct. 10, 1894, or sooner, 5 %. 1,000

Lubelsky, Moses to John V. Campbell. Monroe st. P. M. Oct. 1, installs. 8,000

Leitch, James to James F. and Patrick H. Sheridan and James S. Segrave. Rock st. P. M. Oct. 1, 3 years, 5 %. 570

Levy, Bernard S. to William Rosenberg. 134th st, n s, 197 6 e 6th av, original line, 87.6x199.7 to 135th st, x87.6x199.10. Oct. 12, 6 months. 45,000

Lichtwitz, Ida M. to James F. and Patrick H. Sheridan and James S. Segrave. Forest st. P. M. Oct. 2, due Oct. 1, 1894, 5 %. 350

Lindenberger, John G. and Christiana his wife to Elisabeth Reinhardt. 3d av, e s, 106 2 s 108th st, 17.8x100. Oct. 14, 5 years, 5 %. 10,000

Luther, Philip to Henry Broessler, Brooklyn. 3d st, No. 234 E., s s, bet Avs B and C, 24.9x105.11. Oct. 1, 1 year, 5 %. 5,000

Marsily, Emma S. wife of and Ferdinand A. to The Title Guarantee and Trust Co. 59th st, s s, 150 w 1st av, 50x100.4. Oct. 13, 3 years, 5 %. 8,000

McGuckin, Mary E. wife of Henry J. to Johanna wife of Julius Hirschberg. Lenox av, 113th and 114th sts. P. M. Oct. 7, due July 1, 1892. 86,500

Same to Johanna Hirschberg. Same property. Oct. 7, due July 1, 1892. 49,000

Same to same. Lenox av, e s, extends from 113th to 114th st. P. M. Sub. to morts. $15,000. Oct. 7, due July 1, 1892. 15,000

McTerney, Marietta wife of Charles H. to Abram T. and James Buckhout. Anthony av. P. M. Oct. 1, 10 years, 5 %. 2,500

Moclair, Delia A. to James F. and Patrick H. Sheridan and James S. Segrave. Hill st. P. M. Oct. 3, due Oct. 1, 1894, 5 %. 285

Moclair, Kate A. to same. Rock and Hill sts. P. M. Oct. 3, due Oct. 1, 1894, 5 %. 385

Muth, Louise to James F. and Patrick H. Sheridan and James S. Segrave. Rock and Hill sts. P. M. Oct. 1, 5 years, 5 %. 750

Morgan, Jeane L. to Hugh N. Camp. Harrison av, w s, 75 n Morton pl, 25x99.11x25x98.10. P. M. June 15, 3 years or sooner, 5 %. 585

McCormack, Andrew J. to The New York Orthopaedic Dispensary and Hospital. Amsterdam av. P. M. Oct. 7, due Nov. 1, 1894, 5 %. 8,000

McReynolds, William to Emilie J. Murray. 123d st, s s, 200 w Lenox av, 175x99.11. Oct. 6, 1 year or sooner. 25,000

Meyer, Abraham E. to Rachel Behrens. 101st st, n s, 150 w 2d av, 25x100.11. Oct. 9, due Oct. 1, 1892. 1,000

Muller, Henry and Herman Oetjen to Hermann Bruns and Bernard French. 141st st. P. M. Oct. 9, 1 year, 5 %. 15,500

Marrin, William J. exr. Hortense V. Marrin to The Mutual Life Ins. Co., New York. 79th st, n s, 210 e Madison av, 18.4x102.2. Oct. 15, 1 year, 5 %. 8,500

McSweeney, John mortgagor with Abiel M. Hawkins, Brooklyn, mortgagee. Extension of mort. Oct. 6. nom

Michel, Henry to Henry Strasbourger. Delancey st, No. 218, n s, 76.3 e from n w cor of Pitt and Delancey sts, runs north 73 x west 26.3 x south 73 to Delancey st, x east 26 3. Oct. 15, 3 years. 2,500

Morris, James J. to The Emigrant Indust. Savings Bank. 71st st, No. 112, s s, 125 e Park av, 25x100.5. Oct. 15, 1 year, 4½ %. 13,000

New, Jacob to Morris Abrahams. 85th st, No. 6, s s, 144 e 5th av, 20.6x102.2. Sub. to mort. $13,500. Oct. 15, 2 years, 5 %. 4,500

Same with like consent to Jacob H. Purdy et al. exrs. Jacob Halsted. Amsterdam av, w s, 25.5 s 71st st, 75x100. Sub. to mort. $56,800. Oct. 15, due Jan. 10, 1893, 5 %. 14,200

Newman, Jacob M. to Henry A. Barling et al. trustees Edward M. Robinson. 78th st, No. 211, n s, 179 w Amsterdam av, 21x102.2. Oct. 12, 5 years, 4½ %. 15,000

Same to same. 78th st, No. 207, n s, 139 w Amsterdam av, 20x102.2. Oct. 12, 5 years, 4½ %. 14,000

Same to same. 78th st, No. 219, n s, 261 w Amsterdam av, 20x102.2. Oct. 12, 5 years, 4½ %. 14,000

Same to same. 78th st, No. 205, n s, 119 w Amsterdam av, 20x102.2. Oct. 12, 5 years, 4½ %. 14,000

Newcorn, Harry and Harris to Michael J. and Daniel F. Mahony. Madison st, No. 313. P. M. Sub. to mort. $15,000. Sept. 5, 5 years. 6,750

Same to same. Madison st, No. 315. P. M. Sub. to mort. $15,000. Sept. 5, 5 years, 5 %. 6,750

New York Realty Co., with consent of stockholders, to Catharine Purdy. Amsterdam av or Sherman sq, s w cor 71st st, 25.5x100. Sub. to mort. $27,200. Oct. 15, due Jan. 10, 1893, 5 %. 6,800

O'Neil, Michael to The Harlem Savings Bank. 144th st, s w cor Rider av, 25.4x114x25x118. Oct. 13, 1 year, 5 %. 5,000

O'Connor, Mary to The Emigrant Indust. Savings Bank. 145th st, s s, 250 w St. Anns av, 28x100. Oct. 10, 1 year, 4½ %. 500

Oldenbuttel, John C. to George Ehret. Houston st, No. 29 East. Lease. Oct. 14, demand. 1,856

Same to same. 145th st, s s, 278 w St. Anns av, 22x100. Oct. 10, 1 year. 500

Ott, Maria to William A. Cauldwell trustee for Mary B. Cauldwell. 51st st, n s, 100 w 9th av, 25x100.5. Oct. 8, 5 years, 4½ %. gold, 17,000

Ordman, Jacob to Max Jokinsky. Essex st. P. M. Sub. to mort. $8,500. Oct. 15, installs. 1,300

Ott, Maria to Andrew Ewald. 51st st, n s, 100 w 9th av, 25x100.5. Oct. 15, due April 15, 1893. 1,500

Pressler, Valentine to August F. Wiggers. 133d st, n s, 300 e 7th av, 25x99.11. Oct. 15, 2 years. 2,200

Pendargast, Margaret to Herman Wronkow. Av A. P. M. Oct. 6, installs, 5 %. 4,000

Pitcher, Rufus D. to Jacob Brandt. West End av. P. M. Sub. to mort. $17,000. Oct. 9, 3 years or sooner, 5 %. 1,500

Prague, John G. to John C. Tomlinson. 86th st, No. 137, n s, 376 w 9th av, 23x100.8. Sub. to mort. $40,000. Oct. 8, due Aug. 31, 1892, or installs, 5 %. 10,000

Reilly, Joseph to James F. and Patrick H. Sheridan and James S. Segrave. Hill st. P. M. Oct. 1, 3 years, 5 %. 600

Reville, Nicholas J. to Julia A. Vesey. 95th st, n s, 100 w Park av, 75x100.8. July 1, 1 year. 15,000

Richardson, Emma B. to Theodore A. Squier. 90th st, s s, 160 w West End av. P. M. Oct. 1, 1 year. 3,500

Rockwell, Amelia A. wife of Frederick S. to James F. and Patrick H. Sheridan and James S. Segrave. Hill st. P. M. Oct. 3, due Oct. 1, 1894, 5 %. 550

Rooney, Thomas mortgagee to Jeannie L. Taylor, present owner. Certificate of payment of $3,000 on account of mortgage made by Jeannie L. Taylor May 1, 1889. May 11.

Ransom, Nannie G. wife of and William H. to John S. Huyler. 131st st, n s, 305 e 7th av, 20x99.11. Oct. 1, 1 year. 6,000

Roggen, Annie wife of and Nathan to James J. Loonie and Eugene Parker. Henry st, No. 55. P. M. Oct 1, installs. 2,000

Rohrs, Frederick to The Bradley & Currier Co. (Lim.) 134th st, s s, 175 w Alexander av, 25x100. Sub. to mort. $1,300. Oct. 8, 1 year. 1,000

Same to same. 134th st, s s, 200 w Alexander av, 25x100. Sub. to mort. $13,000. Oct. 8, 1 year. 1,000

Same to same. 102d st, n s, 77 e Park av, 25x100.11. Sub. to mort. $14,000. Oct. 8, 6 months. 2,000

Same to same. 102d st, n s, 52 e Park av, 25x100.11. Sub. to mort. $14,500. Oct. 8, 6 months. 2,000

Same to William J. Seaman, New Dorp, S. I. 102d st, n s, 52 e Park av, 25x100.11. Oct. 8, due Nov. 1, 1892. 14,500

Same to same. 102d st, n s, 77 e Park av, 25x100.11. Oct. 8, due Nov. 1, 1892. 14,000

Ruddell, John to Charles S. Bates, Boston, Mass. 70th st. P. M. July 17, due Oct. 9, 1892, 5 %. 11,000

Regan, John to The Bradley & Currier Co. (Lim.). 36th st, s s, 125 e 10th av, 24.11x99.8. Sub. to morts. $17,000. Oct. 6, 1 year or sooner. 2,510

Robinson, Thomas J. to A. C. Monson, Astoria, L. I. 127th st, No. 224, s s, 305 w 2d av, 25x99.11. Oct 14, 3 years, 5 %. gold, 18,000

Same to Abraham Steers. Same property. 2d mort. Oct. 14, 1 year. 3,000

Same to Emma Knapp, East Orange, N. J. 127th st, No. 226, s s, 280 w 2d av, 25x99.11. Oct. 14, 3 years, 5 %. 18,000

Same to Abraham Steers. 127th st, No. 226 E. 2d mort. Oct. 14, 1 year. 3,000

Same to The Farmers' Loan and Trust Co. 127th st, No. 228, s s, 255 w 2d av, 25x99.11. Oct. 14, 3 years, 5 %. gold, 18,000

Same to Abraham Steers. Same property. 2d mort. Oct. 14, 1 year. 3,000

Reilly, Hugh to The Bradley & Currier Co. (Lim.) 117th st, s w cor Lexington av, 24x100. Sub. to morts. Oct. 9, 2 months. 3,165

Reinemann, J. H. Ludwig to Jacob Mayer. Av A, w s, 22 n 18th st. P. M. Oct. 15, 3 years, with privilege of extension for 2 years, 5 %. 8,000

Same to Catharina H. Hagemeyer. Same property. P. M. Oct. 15, 3 years, 5 %. 3,000

Riley, James to The Bradley & Currier Co. (Lim.) 8th av, n w cor 120th st, 25.3x100. Sub. to morts. $32,100. Oct. 5, 2 months. 5,466

Roloff, Ernest to The Irving Savings Inst. 56th st, n s, 83.4 e 9th av, 16.8x100.5. Oct. 15, 1 year, 5 %. 10,000

Schaefer, Philip mortgagor with Eliza J. Buskey mortgagee. Extension of mort. Oct. 14. nom

Schaefer, Philip to James B. Gillie. 152d st. P. M. Oct. 15, installs, 5 %. 7,000

Silber, Catharine T. wife of William H. to Annie M. Good. 22d st, s s, 404.2 e 7th av, 20.10x98.9. Oct. 14, 3 years, 5 %. 13,500

Spencer, Lorillard to Julic Harmony. Catharine slip, No. 6, w s, 20.6x40. Oct. 14, due Nov. 1, 1896, 5 %. gold, 10,000

Stark, Arnim to Fanny Schwabe. 9th st, n s, 83 e Av C, 25x92.3. Oct. 14, due Nov. 1, 1894. 3,500

Schmitter, Louisa F. and Frank A. to Gertie Josephy. 108th st, s s, 82 e Lexington av, 17x100.11. Oct. 13, 3 years, 5 %. 7,500

Seiler, Rosie wife of Bernhard to Henry T. Dressner, Brooklyn. 3d st, n s, 189 e Av C, 20.8x96. Oct. 13, 3 years, 5 %. 4,000

Sheridan, Thomas J. and James E. Byrne to John O. Baker, Newark, N. J. 90th st. P. M. Oct. 5, demand. gold, 20,000

Same to same. Same property. Building loan. Sub. to last mort. Oct. 5. gold, 15,000

Silberstein, Max to Charles Schwed. Lots 5, 6, 7 and 124, 125, 126, 127 and 128 map Metropolitan Real Estate Assoc. Oct. 7, due Nov. 1, 1891. 3,000

Slosson, Harrison T., Bedford, N. Y., with The German-American Real Estate Title Guarantee Co. both mortgagees. Agreement as to priority of morts. made by Elizabeth K. Smith. Oct. 9. nom

Smith, Elizabeth K. to The German-American Real Estate Title Guarantee Co. 123d st, s s, 425 e 8th av, 50x100.11. Oct. 9, demand. 30,000

Sackett, Henry W. to Edmund Titus. River av, s e cor Palisade av. P. M. Oct. 10, 3 years, 5 %. 15,000

Schneider, William mortgagor with the Count Charles de Montsaulnin and Walker Fearn trustees proposed assignees. Declaration as to validity of mortgage made by William Schneider to John H. Harbeck. Oct. 27, 1890. nom

Same with same. Declaration as to validity of mortgage made by William Schneider to John H. Harbeck. Oct. 27, 1890. nom

Sonn, Hyman and Henry mortgagors with The Poughkeepsie Savings Bank mortgagee. Extension of mort. at 4½ %. Sept. 1. nom

Spencer, Bertha H. C. to Olena & Craig. 100th st, s s, 447.2 w 8th av, 19.4x100.11. Oct. 8. 632

Stevens, Frank A. and Adolphus E. to John Larkin. 84th st, s s, 275 e Amsterdam av, 100x102.2. Aug. 31, demand. 500

Streifler, Jacob to Edward B. Holborow. 145th st, No. 473, n s, 275 e Amsterdam av, 75x99.11. Oct. 8, due April 11, 1892. 1,132

Sullivan, Thomas J. to Beadleston & Woerz. Madison st, No. 390, s s, 100 e Jackson st, 25x95. Lease. Oct. 8, demand. 1,000

Sniffin, Catharine widow to The Bowery Savings Bank. 42d st, n s, 173 e 5th av, 30x100.5. Oct. 14, 1 year, 4½ %. 62,000

Thomson, Catharine A. widow to Townsend Wandell trustee for Maria Meylor. 91st st, n s, 210 w Park av, 17x100.8. Oct. 12, due Oct. 13, 1896, 5 %. 7,000

Twomey, Catharine C. to The Emigrant Industrial Savings Bank. 137th st, s s, 355.5 e Southern Boulevard, 75x100. Oct. 12, 1 year, 4½ %. 4,500

The Hebrew Free School Assoc. and Aguilar Free Library Soc. to The Baron de Hirsch Fund. Division st, Nos. 195 and 195½, s s, 153.11 e Jefferson st, 26x43.7; East Broadway, No. 206, n s, 183.6 e Jefferson st, 26.2x69.11x26x69.11. Oct. 5, due Jan. 1, 1893, 5 %. 25,000

The Hebrew Free School Assoc. with The Baron de Hirsch Fund. Agreement as to priority of morts. made by The Hebrew Free School A . and Aguilar Free Library Soc. Oct. 5.ssoc nom

Tuttle, Anna E. wife of and Ezra A. to Sarah H. Powell. 82d st, s s, 305 w Columbus av, 20x102.2. June 24, 1 year. 3,000

Same to Samuel P. Dunn et al. trustees Jacob Travis dec'd. Same property. June 24, 3 years, 5 %. 20,000

United States Feather Down Co. mortgagor with Edward H. Coster committee of John G. Coster. 4 extensions of morts. Oct. 9. nom

Vett, John to Julius Hoffman. 153d st, s s, 125 w Courtlandt av, 25x100. Oct 14, 3 years, 5 %. 500

Same to John Hoffman. Same property. Oct. 14, 3 years, 5 %. 1,000

Walsh, Henry V. to The Harlem Savings Bank. Forest av, w s, 219 s 166th st, 20x87.6. Oct. 15, 1 year, 5 %. 1,800

Weinstein, Ascher to Isaac K. Cohn. 7th av, n e cor 26th st. P. M. Oct. 15, due May 1, 1893, 5 %. 22,500

Westheimer, Julius to Louis and Albert L. Lowenstein. Jerome av. P. M. Oct. 14, 3 years, 5 %. 975

Winkler, Jacob to George F. Betts. Columbus av. P. M. Oct. 15, 3 years or installs, 5 %. 15,000

Winston, Gustavus S. to The Mutual Life Ins. Co., New York. 39th st, s s, 340 e 6th av, 20x98.9. Oct. 15, 1 year, 5 %. 10,000

Walsh, John to Lucy R. Comfort. Simpson st, w s, 171.8 n 169th st, runs north 25 x west 107.11 x south 10.4 x southeast 25 x east 87.8. Oct. 8, 3 years. 1,200

Same to Margaret A. Sheridan. Same property Oct. 8, 2 years. 50

Walsh, William M. to Henry Woods. 101st st, No. 77, n s, 100 e Columbus av, 25x100.11 Oct. 8, 1 year. 3,000

Walsh, William M. to Herbert Coop. 101st st, No. 75, n s, 125 e Columbus av, 25x100.11. Sub. to mort. $22,000. Sept. 26, 1 year, 5 %. 3,000

Same to Peter Patry. 101st st, Nos. 75 and 77, n s, 100 e Columbus av, 50x100.11. Oct. 13, 6 months. 2,650

Wolf, Michael J. to George F. Betts. Columbus av. P. M. Oct. 15, 3 years or installs, 5 %. 12,250

Weed, Joseph E. to THE METROPOLITAN LIFE INS. CO. West End av, s e cor 89th st, 24.8x52. Oct. 7, due Oct. 1, 1894, 5 %. See Conveys. 22,000

Same to same. 89th st, s s, 82 e West End av, 18x100.8. Oct. 7, due Oct. 1, 1894, 5 %. See Conveys. 16,000

Same to same. West End av, e s, 24.8 s 89th st, 19x64. Oct. 7, due Oct. 1, 1894, 5 %. 17,000

Same to same. West End av, e s, 81.8 s 89th st, 19x82. Oct. 7, due Oct. 1, 1894, 5 %. 17,000

Same to same. West End av, e s, 43.8 s 89th st, 19x64. Oct. 7, due Oct. 1, 1894, 5 %. 16,000

Weed, Joseph E. to Francis M. Jencks. West End av, s e cor 89th st, runs east 52 x south 24.8 x east 12 x south 19 x west 64 to av, x north 43.8; West End av, e s, 81.8 s 89th st, 19x82. Oct. 8, demand. See Conveys. 7,000

Weil, David, Palisades, N. J., to Beadleston & Woerz, a corporation. Madison st, s s, 100 e Jackson st, 24.10x95.8x25x95.8. Oct. 7, demand. 1,000

Weinstein, Morris and Morris Morgovitz to Garafelia O. Chickering widow. Division st, No. 243, s s, 46 w Montgomery st, 23x48.6 x23x48.7 Oct. 7, due Nov. 1, 1896, 5 %. 14,000

White, Mary E. and Lewis A. Olsen to Beadleston & Woerz. Broadway, No. 175, w s, 20 n Courtlandt st, 25x100. Lease of basement and cellar. Oct. 7, demand. 3,500

Same to Frederick Semkens. Same property. Lease. Oct. 6, notes. 11,500

Whitlock, Charles W. to Jennie Marston guard. Catharine W. Taylor. 13th st, n s, 220.10 w 7th av, 20.10x75. Sept. 28, demand. 1,500

Walbridge, Mary, Brooklyn, N. Y., to John Campbell. 85th st. P. M. Oct. 13, 1 year. 3,000

White, Richard to Ethelbert Wilson. 135th st. P. M. Oct. 13, 1 year. 7,500

Waterbury, Eunice R. and Eloise B. Crothers to THE EMIGRANT INDUST. SAVINGS BANK. 55th st, s s, 158.4 e 8th av, 16.8x100.5. Oct. 13, 1 year, 4½ %. 10,000

Wilson, Peter M. to THE IRVING SAVINGS INST. Greenwich st, n e cor Bank st, runs east 140.5 to Hudson st, x north 77.8 x west 126 to Greenwich st, x south 120.5. Oct. 13, 1 year, 4½ %. 60,000

Wood, Philip to Mary K. Brooks, Brooklyn. West End av, w s, 25.5 n 67th st, 25x80. Oct. 8, due Oct. 1, 1892. 6,000

Yost, Agnes to Isidor Alkus. 2d av. P. M. Oct. 14, 5 years, 5 %. 5,000

Zickler, Ignatz and Regina his wife to Anna C. Gerhards. 2d av, e s, 80.5 n 52d st, 20x70, Oct. 7, due Oct. 1, 1893, 5 %. 2,000

KINGS COUNTY.

OCTOBER 8, 9, 10, 12, 13, 14.

Acker, Howard N. to E. Otto Sackmann and ano. trustees for Amalia C. Gross. Elton st. P. M. Oct. 1, due Nov. 1, 1894. $3,000

Adams, William H. to James H. Watson and James H. Pittinger. 1st st, s w s, 186 n w 5th av, 53.11x100. Sub. to mort. $8,000, Oct. 14, demand. 1,500

Allan, John T. and Nathaniel Proskey to Fannie M. E. Ensell. 4th st, n e s, 197.10 n w 8th av, 20x95; 4th st, n e s, 235.10 n w 8th av, 62x95. Oct. 8, demand. 2,000

Allen, John T. and Nathaniel Proskey to Charlotte O'Donohue. 4th st, n e s, 277.10 n w 8th av, 20x95. Oct. 8, 3 years, 5 %. 7,000

Same to same. 4th st, n e s, 256.10 n w 8th av, 21x95. Oct. 8, 3 years, 5 %. 8,000

Same to same. 4th st, n e s, 235.10 n w 8th av, 21x95. Oct. 8, 3 years, 5 %. 8,000

Same to same. 4th st, n e s, 197.10 n w 8th av, 20x95. Oct. 8, 3 years, 5 %. 7,000

Anderson, Andrew to Scandinavian Building and Mutual Loan Assoc. Dean st, n s, 157.4 w Grand av, 16.5x110. Oct. 6, installs. 4,000

Andrews, William to Valentin Kettenring. Evergreen av, s w s, 25 s e Madison st, 25x100. Oct. 8, 3 years, 5 %. 2,000

Andrews, William H. to Ellen King, Tarrytown, N. Y. 12th st, s s, 197.10 w 5th av, 100x100. Oct. 12, due Nov. 1, 1892. 2,000

Apiustille, Albert G. to The Daily News Building, Savings and Loan Assoc. East 5th st, Flatbush. Sept. 24, installs. 1,800

Asmes, Charles to Marie T. wife of John J. Brennan. Gates av, s e s, 250 n e Hamburg av. P. M. Oct. 8, installs, 5 %. 2,500

Badenhoop, John to Marie T. wife of John J. Brennan. Gates av, s e s, 275 n e Hamburg av. P. M. Oct. 8, installs, 5 %. 2,750

Banker, Evelina to The Bushwick Savings Bank. Quincy st, n s, 188.3 e Stuyvesant av, 20x100. Oct. 12, due May 19, 1894, 5 %. 500

Baker, Emma E. to The West Brooklyn Land and Improvement Co. 47th st, New Utrecht. P. M. Oct. 7, 5 years, 5 %. 725

Baker, Margaret I. wife of and Amos to Cornelius N. Hoagland. Willoughby av, s s, 142.3 w Clason av, 17x67.5x17x67.3. Oct. 7, due Nov. 1, 1894, 5 %. gold, 4,100

Baker, William F. to The Serial Building, Loan and Savings Inst. Herkimer pl, s s, 185 1 w Nostrand av, 50x49.1. Sept. 15, installs. 600

Balsam, Samuel and Moritz or Morris Handler, Newark, N. J., to Terence Jacobson. Thetford av, e s, 100 s Glenmore av, runs south 50 x east 100 x north 25 x east 54.2 x north 25 x west 154.3. Oct. 7, due Nov. 1, 1892. gold, 4,500

Banta, Theodore M. to The Mutual Life Ins. Co., New York. Marcy av, s w cor Monroe st, 100x162. Oct. 12, 1 year. 12,000

Bardin, Almon G. to Effingham H. Nichols. Liberty av, s s, 20 w Logan st, 60x90. Oct. 10, 2 years or installs, 5 %. 900

Barnett, Sedgwick and Sarah R. his wife to Ephraim A. Walker. Calyer st. P. M. Oct. 1, 5 years, 5 %. 5,500

Beasley, Alfred L. to John Cassidy. Macon st. P. M. Oct. 1, 6 months. 10,000

Belfer, Caroline to Eliza A. Dunning. Stone av, Newport av and Christopher st, &c. P. M. Sept. 30, 2 years. 2,000

Bellows, Charles H. to Ann Taylor et al. exrs. William Taylor. Jefferson av, n s, 195 w Tompkins av. P. M. Sub. to mort. $4,000, Oct. 8, installs, 5 %. 2,300

Same to The Title Guarantee and Trust Co. Same property. Oct. 8, due Oct. 14, 1894, 5 %. 4,000

Betsky, Jacob to Benjamin Sachs. Sackmann av or st. P. M. Sept. 21, installs. 500

Bidstrup, James F. to Edward F. Linton. Arlington av, s e cor Elton st. P. M. Oct. 12, due Nov. 1, 1893. 2,100

Bierds, Eliza A. wife of John T. to Elizabeth B. Hall. 5th st, s s, 248.8 w 7th av, 19.11x100. Oct. 13, 6 months. 1,000

Blatt, Lina S. wife of and Isidor to James W. McManus. Rockaway av, w s, 52 s Marion st, 16x50. Oct. 5, installs. 700

Berau, Henry to John A. Eppig. Stagg st, n e cor Bogart st. P. M. Oct. 5, 1 year, 5 %. 2,500

Bliss, Barbara to Edward H. Wilson. St. Marks av. P. M. Oct. 9, due Oct. 10, 1892. 2,250

Boekee, Isabella S. widow to South Brooklyn Savings Inst. 1st pl, s s, 24 w Clinton st, 24x133.5. Oct. 8, 1 year, 5 %. 4,000

Brindley, Emma wife of and Charles W. to Cornelius N. Hoagland. Madison st, n s, 251 w Nostrand av, 22x110. Oct. 8, due Nov. 1, 1894, 5 %. gold, 1,000

Brown, George R. to The Title Guarantee and Trust Co. Washington av, e s, 120.8 s Fulton st, runs east 100 x south 25 x east 17.8 x south 25 x west 117.8 to av, x north 50. Oct. 9, demand. 24,000

Brown, Mary to William E. Kay. 57th st, n e s, 160 s e 14th av, 50x100.2, New Utrecht. June 1, installs. 1,600

Brown, Will A. to Charles P. Gilson. Linwood st. P. M. Oct. 1, 5 years. 1,100

Same to John M. Stearns. Same property. P. M. 2d mort. Oct. 1, 5 years. 750

Brown, Melvin to Anna R. Reilly, Trenton, N. J. Howard av, n e cor St. Marks av, 83.11x610.9x119.1x— to St. Marks av, x417. May 15, due Nov. 15, 1894, 5 %. 5,000

Buckley, Catharine to Orson D. Munn. Union st, s s, 80 w 4th av, 102x95. Oct. 9, due Dec. 15, 1892, 5 %. 6,500

Same to same. President st, n s, 80 w 4th av, 163x95. Oct. 9, due Dec. 15, 1892, 5 %. 5,000

Buckley, George P. to The Dime Savings Bank, Brooklyn. Pacific st, n s, 192.3 w Clason av, 20x100. Oct. 8, 1 year, 5 %. 2,500

Burr, Moses P. to Alice L. Burr, Comac, L. I. Graham av, n w cor Conselyea st, 25x94. Mar. 1, 7 years, 5 %. 13,000

Carpenter, James O. to William H. Lyon. St. Marks av, n s, 214 e Brooklyn av, 36x150.7. Oct. 13, due Mar. 1, 1892. 2,500

Cassel, Samuel to Israel Jarashow. Boerum st. P. M. Oct. 8, 4 years, 5 %. 5,300

Coffey, Patrick to Peter Kelly. Dwight st, n e cor Vandyke st, 25x100; Nostrand av, west cor Midwood st, 100x100. Oct. 9, 3 years, 5 %. 3,000

Colfax, Robert R. to Frederick Dhuy, Jr. Pacific st. P. M. Oct. 10, 9 months, 5 %. 1,500

Comer, Anna E. wife of John H. to Martha J. Stevenson, New Brunswick, N. J. Decatur st, s s, 340 w Patchen av, 20x100. Oct. 9, due Jan. 1, 1893, 5 %. 2,000

Conklin, Frank M. to Caroline Weber. Livingston st, s s, 375 e Smith st, 25x101.6. Oct. 8, due Oct. 1, 1894, 5 %. 2,000

Cook, Mary widow to Henry Vonderleith in mort. Vonderleith. 28th st, s s, 150 w 5th av, 25x100.2. Oct. 12, 3 years, 5 %. 300

Cosgrove, Anne to Mary Carey widow. 11th st. P. M. Oct. 1, 3 years, 5 %. 1,000

Couch, Marshall J. to The Title Guarantee and Trust Co. Gates av. P. M. Oct. 14, 3 years, 5 %. 2,000

Crimmins, Emma wife of and David L. to India Wharf Brewing Co. Lots 27 and 28 block 27 map Ocean Parkway and Park lots. Oct. 6, demand. 100

Crane, Frederick to Anna M. Ferris, Flatbush, L. I. East 7th st, w s, 165.8 s Greenwood av, runs west 90.6 x again west 14.4 x south 20 x east 100 to st, x north 49.3, Flatbush. Oct. 5, 3 years, 5 %. 1,500

Crossman, G. W. to William S. Hassan. 57th st. P. M. Oct. 7, due Oct. 1, 1894, 5 %. 1,400

Davis, Laura M. to George H. Roberts. Carroll st, No. 726, s s, 430.3 w 7th av, 17.5x123x17.5x124.7. Oct. 8, 1 year. 500

De Groff, Adrian to Clara F. Lang, Andover, Mass. 48th st, n s, 260 w 4th av, 20x100.2. Oct. 10, 3 years, 5 %. 2,300

Deublein, Anna M. to William Kaiser. Suydam st. P. M. Oct. 9, due Oct. 1, 1893, 5 %. 1,000

Dillon, John to Jane V. H. Scranton extrx. Edwin K. Scranton. Willow pl, w s, 148 n State st, 25x80. Oct. 8, 5 years, 5 %. 3,100

Dittmar, William, Jr., to The Safety Co-operative Building, Loan and Savings Assoc. 19th av, south cor 84th st, 100x100. Building loan. Oct. 3, installs. 5,000

Duchman, Levy and Louis Greenberg to Solomon Wolff. Belmont av. P. M. Oct. 8, installs. 1,500

Dumpeck, Frank to The Title Guarantee and Trust Co., New York. Seigel st, s s, 650 w White st, 25x100. Oct. 10, due Oct. 12, 1892. 400

Dunlay, Patrick to The Brooklyn City Co-operative Building and Loan Assoc. Park pl, s s, 419 w Clason av, 22x131. Oct. 13, installs. 500

Eiermann, Frederick to Maria E. Schneider. Belmont av, n s, 75 w Schenck av, 25x100. Sept. 12, 3 years. 2,000

Elliott, Elizabeth mortgagor with Henry Sahlfeld. Extension of mort. Oct. 8. nom

Erickson, Charles A. to Mary A. Lentz. Lots 127-130 map Theodore Sedgwick, New Utrecht; also lots 129 and 130 Michael Bergen, New Utrecht. Oct. 8, 3 years. 5,500

Erickson, Mary wife of and Erick to John W. Eckelkamp. Saratoga av, e s, 30 n Pacific st, 20x100. Oct. 13, 3 years, 5 %. 1,000

Flynn, Patrick H. to Daniel F. Lewis. Coney Island av and Manhattan Beach R. R. Co.'s land, Gravesend. P. M. Oct. 8, 1 year. 15,000

Fowler, John N. to William F. Corwith. Oakland st. P. M. Oct. 7, 1 year. 300

Franke, Henry to William H. Lyon. St. Marks av, n e cor Brooklyn av, runs east 140 x north 150.7 x west 30 x north 20 x west 110 to Brooklyn av, x south 170.7. Oct. 1, 1 year. 8,000

Same to The Title Guarantee and Trust Co. Imlay st, east cor William st, runs northeast 175 x southeast 110 x southwest 125 x northwest 20 x southwest 50 to William st, x northwest 90. Oct. 12, 1 year, 5 %. 9,000

Fogarty, John to Emma Haug. Verona st, s s, 100 w Richards st, 25x100. Oct. 10, due July 1, 1893. 400

Frey, Rachel to Jacob Blank. Greene av. P. M. Oct. 5, installs, 5 %. 1,250

Friedberg, Louis and Philip to David Axelrod. Stone av. P. M. Oct. 1, installs. 1,150

Garrison, Edward H. to John A. Latimer and ano. trustees for Anne M. Vought. 8th av, w s, 22 s Lincoln pl, 20x100. Oct. 13, 1 year, 5 %. 6,000

Glines, George E. to Caroline C. Barnes, Albany, N. Y. St. Marks av, n s, 20 e Rogers av, 20x100. Oct. 1, 5 years, 5 %. 2,000

Gommel, Frederick to Bay Ridge Mfg. Co. 3d av, e s, 70.2 n 47th st, 30x85. Sub. to mort. $9,000. Oct. 13, due Oct. 1, 1892. 1,500

Same to Evert Suydam. Same property. Oct. 13, due Nov. 1, 1894. 9,000

Goodwin, Richard mortgagee with Annie Herzog mortgagor. Extension of mort. Oct. 9. nom

Gunn, Patrick J. and Ellen M. to Eliza J. Smith. 4th av, n w cor 20th st. P. M. Oct. 10, 5 years. 3,500

Griffin, William E. and Mary A. his wife to James J. Smith. Herkimer st. P. M. Oct. 12, 5 years, 4 %. 1,500

Griggs, Stephen C. to Laura and Jessie Benedict. Lefferts pl, n s, 112.10 e Clason av, 20x125. Oct. 1, 3 years, 5 %. gold, 7,000

Hagedorn, Charles to John Konvalinka. 16th st, s w s, 168.9 s e 3d av, 6 lots, together 113.1x90. 6 morts., each $3,750. Oct. 14, 3 years, 5 %. 22,500

Harrison, Charles to Mary Harrison. 59th st, s s, 280 w 13th av, 20x100.2. Oct. 7, 2 years. 250

Hart, John F. to Ralph G. Packard. 44th st, s s, 80 w 4th av, 108x100.2. Oct. 8, demand. 5,000

Hebenstreit, Henry and Mary his wife to George Gutting and Charles A. Wagner. Knickerbocker av, s w s, 75 s e Stanhope st, 25x100. June 23, 1 year, 5 %. 1,000

Heinlein, John and William Rexer to Catharine Buckley. President st. P. M. Oct. 9, 3 years, 5 %. 3,100

Herod, William to Melvin Brown. Butler st. P. M. Oct. 1, 3 years. 3,500

Hollister, Sebastian to Edward F. Linton. Shepherd av, e s, 280 n Ridgewood av, 17.2x102.6x17.2x102.5. 2d mort. Oct. 7, 1 year. 400

Same to same. Shepherd av, e s, 297.2 n Ridgewood av, 17.2x102.6. 2d mort. Oct. 7, 1 year. 400

Same to same. Shepherd av, e s, 314.3 n Ridgewood av, 17.2x102.6. 2d mort. Oct. 7, 1 year. 400

Hopkins, Harry F. C. to Rudolph and Otto E. Reimer. Myrtle av, s s, 20 e Bleecker st, runs south 50 x southeast — x east 7 x northwest — x north 50 to Myrtle av, x west 20. Sub. to mort. Oct. 8, 1 year. 800

Same to same. Myrtle av, s s, 60 e Bleecker st, runs south 80 x west 7 x northwest — x north 50 to av, x east 20. Sub. to mort. Oct. 8, 1 year. 800

Hosey, Michael to William J. Gelston. Bond st, n w cor President st, 20x75. Oct. 9, 3 years. 2,000

Hosford, Fannie E. wife of Henry to Hamilton Trust Co. St. Marks av, s s, 20 w Carlton av, 20x81. Oct. 3, due Nov. 1, 1892, 5 %. 4,000

Hutwelker, Charles and Frederick Figge, of Charles Hutwelker & Co. to John C. Worth. McKibbin st. P. M. Oct. 9, 5 years, 5 %. 3,800

Hyams, Henry to The Title Guarantee and Trust Co. Atlantic av. P. M. Oct. 1, due Oct. 12, 1894, 5 %. 3,000

Herche, Peter to The Bowery Savings Bank. King st, north cor alley leading to south pier Atlantic Dock, 101.6x234.10x100x217.5, with rights in alley, &c. Oct. 8, 1 year, 5 %. 25,000

Idelsohn, Kusche and Max Tempkin to Aaron Kaplan. Linden st, e s, 275.11 n Evergreen av. P. M. Oct. 13, due Oct. 1, 1894. 1,200

Ives, John H. to Marenus J. Goodenough. Fulton st. Crescent av. P. M. May 7, due in May, 1893, 5 %. 1,750

Johnson, John E. to Hiram H. Lamport. Van Buren st, s s, 188.8 e Stuyvesant av, 14.8x100. Oct. 6, due Oct. 1, 1894. 1,300

Kaplan, Aaron to Aaron Levy. Linden st, e s, 255.11 n Evergreen av, 20x100. Oct. 1, 1 year. 1,000

Keenan, Mary to Margaret E. and Martha A. Farrell. Union av. P. M. Oct. 9, 5 years, 5 %. 700

Kelly, Peter to The Title Guarantee and Trust Co. Degraw st, n s, 90 w 5th av, 5 lots, each 20x98.6. 5 morts., each $4,000. Oct. 9, 3 years, 5 %. 20,000

Kern, Elisabeth widow to Jacob H. Bernkopf. McKibbin st, s s, 100 w Morrell st, 25x100. Oct. 1, 2 years, 5 %. 600

Kettering, Jacob to Obermeyer & Liebmann. Stagg st, No. 111. Lease. Oct. 10, demand. 900

Killey, William to Sarah L. Jackson, New York. 12th st. P. M. Oct. 8, 9 months. 7,500

Same to same. Same property. Oct. 8, 9 months. 13,000

Klobge, Wilhelm and Kathrine his wife to John A. Wiechmann. 49th st, s w s, 260 n w 4th av, 20x100.2. Oct. 8, due Oct. 1, 1894, 5 %. 2,000

Kirby, J. Mason to Thomas Monohan. Bainbridge st, n s, 205 e Saratoga av, 18x100. Sub. to mort. $4,000. Oct. 1, 1 year. 1,000

Same to Rudolph and Otto E. Reimer. Bainbridge st, n s, 151 e Saratoga av, 18x100. Sub. to mort. $4,000. Oct. 1, 1 year. 1,000

Same to Joseph P. Puels. Bainbridge st, n s, 259 e Saratoga av, 18x100. Sub. to mort. $4,050. Oct. 1, 1 year. 1,000

Same to same. Bainbridge st, n s, 241 e Saratoga av, 18x100. Sub. to mort. $4,000. Oct. 1, 1 year. 1,000

Same to same. Bainbridge st, n s, 223 e Saratoga av, 18x100. Sub. to mort. $4,000. Oct. 1, 1 year. 1,000

Kayser, Julius to Elizabeth Bache et al. exrs. Semon Bache. Graham st, w s, 165 n De Kalb av, 275x110x272.6x110. Oct. 1, 5 years, 5½ %. 15,000

Kirkman, Ralphina to The Bradley and Currier Co (Lim.). 7th av, e s, 20 s 16th st, 80x73.10. Oct. 8, 1 year. 1,000

Klatte, Lucie E. to E. Willard Jones. McDonough st. P. M. Oct. 12, 2 years. 2,000

Koch, Lena to Martin Bennett, Jr. Georgia av, s e cor Jamaica av, runs south to Fulton av, x east 50 x north 78 x west 0.4 x north to Jamaica av, x southwest —. Oct. 12, 10 years, 5 %. 17,000

Koechler, Joseph to Charles W. Engelhardt. Fulton av, s e s, 102 s w Adams st, 25.6x94x25x99.4. Aug. 1, 1 year. 330

Koehler, Henry J. mortgagee with Frank F. Koehler mortgagor. Extension of mort. Oct. 8. nom

Kreuder, Daniel to John H. Scheidt. Willoughby av. P. M. Oct. 10, due Nov. 1, 1896, 5 %. 8,000

Lacey, Cornelia A. wife of and Richard to The South Brooklyn Savings Inst. Amity st, n s, 165.8 w Clinton st, 16.8x100. Oct. 12, 1 year, 5 %. 1,000

Laing, Mary E. wife of and Donald to Louisa W. Taylor, Boston, Mass. Shepherd av. P. M. Oct. 13, 1 year. 1,500

Langmuir, James to Daniel W. McWilliams. Clifton pl. P. M. Oct. 1, installs. 1,271

Langston, Frederick B. to William Langston. Herkimer st, n s, 411 e Nostrand av, 20x100. Mt. $8,300. July 23, 2 years. 3,000

Leffer, Fanny M. to James D. Lynch. 82d st, s w s, 220 s e 23d av, 60x100. Oct. 2, due Oct. 7, 1893, 5 %. 600

Lehmann, Charles and Catharine his wife and William Lehmann and Barbara his wife to Rosalie Bayer. Evergreen av, n e s, 50 n w Hancock st, 25x100. Oct. 13, 3 years, 5 %. 3,500

Levino, Bernard to Horatio S. Stewart. President st, n s, 257 e Henry st, 40x100. Oct. 1, 1 year, 5 %. 5,000

Same to same. Carroll st, s s, 122 e Henry st, 45x100. Oct 1, 1 year, 5 %. 5,000

Levine, Morris and Nancy his wife to Gerson Kakower. Bocrum st, n s, 175 w Leonard st. P. M. Oct. 13, 3 years or installs, 5 %. 2,800

Lewis, Rebecca to John H. Scheidt. Lots 4—1 and 4—2 map of heirs G. Stryker, &c. P. M. Oct. 1, 3 years. 500

Lippman, Leopold J. to John E. Tweed. Eldert st, n w s, 259 n e Evergreen av, 38x100; Eldert st, n w s, 373 n e Evergreen av, 38x100. Sept. 18, demand. 825

Littmann, Abram J. to Barnet Levin and Max Gittelsohn. Thatford av. P. M. Oct. 6, installs. 900

Litzebauer, William to Henry Schneider and Katharina his wife. Central av, s w s, 77.4 s e Hart st. P. M. Oct. 12, 2 years. 1,200

Loeble, Minnie wife of Frederick C. to George E. Kitching. Quincy st, s w cor Lewis av, 64x100. Oct. 9, 3 years, 5 %. 7,000

Loffler, Charles and Katharina his wife to August Hartmann. Harman st, s e s, 182.11 n e Wyckoff av, 40x100. Oct. 7, 2 years, 5 %. 1,000

Lucius, Frederick L. to Barbara Dudenhoeffer, New York. Van Buren st, n s, 171 e Reid av, 18.2x100 (?), error. Oct. 1, 3 years, 5 %. 3,000

Ludder, Henry E. to Louis Bonert. 10th st, s s, 419.8 e 7th av. P. M. Oct. 10, 2 years, 5 %. 2,000

Same to same. 10th st, s s, 399.8 e 7th av. P. M. Oct. 10, 2 years, 5 %. 2,000

Magrath, Jemima to Ann E. wife of Joseph Boyes. Bergen st, s s, 180 w Clason av, 20x100. Oct 7, installs. 1,500

Maguire, Michael to Mary Totten. 8th st, s s, 135 w 4th av, 50x100. Oct. 7, 3 years, 5 %. 7,000

MacMahon, J. Grattan to Henry C. Richmond. Essex st, e s, 45 s Belmont av, 45x100. Oct. 10, 3 years. 1,500

MacNaughton, Lawrence to John Kelly. Pacific st. P. M. Sept. 29, 5 years, 5 %. 7,000

Martin, Charles A. to Lillie Cohen. Dean st, n s, 83.4 e Utica av, 109.9x107.2. Oct. 2, demand. 2,000

Martin, Albert E. to Edmund W. Barnett. Penn st. P. M. Oct. 12, 5 years, 5 %. 4,500

McDonald, William H. to D. & M. Chauncey Real Estate Co. (Lim.) Lawrence st. P. M. Sub. to mort. $5,000. Oct. 9, due Oct. 1, 1894. 1,000

Same to William G. Low individ. and trustee for his children. Same property. Oct. 9, due Oct. 1, 1896, 5 %. 5,000

Megginson, John W. C. to Ann W. Lambert. Cumberland st, e s, 466.9 s Park av, 14.6x100. Oct. 8, 3 years, 5 %. 500

Michaelis, Edward to The Title Guarantee and Trust Co. Bushwick av, s w cor Woodbine st, 20x80. Oct. 13, 1 year. 2,000

Michel, Leopold to The New York Security and Trust Co. Moore st, n s, 50 e Leonard st, 25x100. Oct. 12, due Oct. 13, 1894, 5 %. 5,000

Miles, Helen to Annagusta B. Darling. Dean st, s s, 188 w Stone av, 43.6x107.2. Oct. 1, 3 years, 5 %. 1,500

Miller, August to Thomas S. Denike. Buffalo av. P. M. Aug. 22, installs. 1,050

Mills, James to Asa W. Parker, New Hamburgh, N. Y. 1st st. P. M. Oct. 9, demand. 10,000

Montgomery, Robert B. to Stephen B. Sturges. Stone av, w s, 80 n Truxton st, 20x100. Oct. 9, demand. 4,500

Moore, Sarah A. to James D. Lynch. 24th av, s e s, 180 n e Benson av, 60x96.8, Gravesend. Oct. 1, due Oct. 7, 1892, 5 %. 700

Moore Margaret to Hannah Worth widow. Little st, w s, 64.6 n Plymouth st, 21.6x63.9x20x56. Oct. 14, due Nov. 1, 1894. 500

Moore, Sarah A. to Agnes N. Lake. East 5th st, e s, 320 s Av W, 64.2x104.11 to Ocean Parkway, x132.10x126.1. Oct. 14, 5 years, 5 %. 400

Muller, Elizabeth wife of and George J. to Anna K. Bock. Washington av, n e cor Union st. P. M. Oct. 8, due Oct. 1, 1894, 5 %. 900

Murphy, Sarah A. to The South Brooklyn Co-operative Building and Loan Assoc. 18th st. P. M. Oct. 13, installs. 1,375

Nagel, William to Katherine Motschenbacher. Gates av, s e s, 275 n e Irving av, 25x100. Oct. 7, due Oct. 1, 1894, 5 %. 2,000

Neidlinger, Sarah wife of William to Joseph Wechsler. Av E and East 5th st. P. M. Aug. 29, installs, 5 %. 1,525

O'Brien, John, mortgagor with John R. Sargeant. Extension of mort. Oct. 8.

O'Neil, Augustine to Lawrence Hurlburt. Wilson st, n w s, 235 s w Wythe av, 15x100; Willoughby av, s s, 270 w Lewis av. 20x100. Oct. 8, 2 years. 1,200

O'Neil, Augustine M. to William H. Griffin. Wilson st. P. M. Oct. 1, 1 year, 5 %. 300

Owen, William W. to Spencer Aldrich. Greene av, s e cor Lewis av, 200x100. Sept. 15, demand. 78,000

Pitcher, Joseph M. to Ernest M. Elmore. Bergen st, s s, 310 w Kingston av, runs west 100 x south 100 x east 60 x south 5.7 x east 40 x north 105.7. Sub. to mort. $30,000. Oct. 9, 1 year. 5,000

Pollard, Patrick to Michael O'Keeffe. Harrison st, s w cor Hicks st, 41.2x70. Oct. 1, 3 years, 5 %. 1,500

Rapuzzi, Maria to Rosa Horwitz. President st. P. M. Sept. 30, installs, 5 %. 2,500

Rathkamp, Laura to Margaretha Waldbauer. Halsey st, s s, 161.2 e Ralph av, 19.5x100. Oct. 8, 3 years, 5 %. 4,500

Rausch, Michael to Leonhard Eppig. Central av, w s, 75 n Melrose st, 25x100. Oct. 12, 5 years, 5 %. 4,000

Raymond, Benjamin C. to Adelbert S. Nichols. Ralph av, n w cor Macon st, 22x100. Oct. 8, due Oct. 1, 1892. 1,240

Rehbein, Adolph to The Title Guarantee and Trust Co. 4th av, s e cor 22d st, 39.2x70x39.3x70. Oct. 10, demand 10,000

Resoft, Frederick and Henrietta his wife to Hannah L. Burroughs. North 2d st, n s, abt 175 w 2d st, 25x95. Oct. 13, 5 years, 5 %. 1,500

Reynolds, Ella to Martin L. Bamman, Asbury Park, N J. Prospect pl. P. M. Oct. 6, due Oct. 1, 1892. 1,400

Robinson, Thomas to The Daily News Building, Savings and Loan Assoc. Freeman st, s w cor Oakland st, 25x100; Elm st, s e s, 278.8 s w Wyckoff av, 50x100. July 23, installs. 7,500

Roger, Millie C. to Martha Wakefield, Middletown, N. Y. 3d av. P. M. Sept. 30, 10 years, 5 %. 2,700

Rosenfeld, Rosa wife of Jonas to Lewis Hurst. Bergen st, s s, 100 w Hopkinson av, 25x100. Oct. 9, due Feb 1, 1892. 200

Rosenthal, Moritz to Benjamin Rothbell and Bernard Kreiger. Blake av, n w cor Sackman st. P. M. July 7, 2 years. 700

Rudderman, Rosa and Sarah Cohn to Ernest and Christine Henken. Stone av, e s, 125 s Belmont av, 25x100. Oct. 1, 3 years. 2,000

Sand, John A. and Catharine his wife, Canarsie, to Frederick Hube. 80th st, w s, bet Matthews & Young, 50x130, with a 12-foot right of way, Canarsie. Oct. 1, 6 years. 500

Saunders, James H. to Simon C. Wilson. Sackman st. P. M. Sept. 1, installs. 800

Schaefer, John mortgagee with Auna G. Schieb mortgagor. Extension of mort. Oct. 6. nom

Scheen, Isaac and Solestina Y. his wife to The Serial Building Loan and Savings Inst. Dumont av, s s, 250 e Thatford av, 25x100. Nov. 17, installs. 2,800

Schlachter, Henry to Frank Dahlbender and Barbara Gross. Stockholm st, n w s, 225 n e Hamburg av, 25x100. Oct. 14, 3 years, 5 %. 2,000

Schmidt, Edward to George Schmidt. Glenmore av, n s, 75 w Warwick st, 25x100. Oct. 9, 5 years, 5 %. 2,000

Scheeu, Margaretha wife of and Carl A. to The Title Guarantee and Trust Co. Atlantic av, s s, 225 e Smith st, 25x90. Oct. 9, 3 years, 5 %. 8,000

Schofield, Albert B. to The Title Guarantee and Trust Co. 7th st, n e s, 283.4 n w 9th av, 19x100. Oct. 12, 1 year, 5 %. 5,000

Schultze, Theodore L. to Louis Beer. Hancock st. P. M. Oct. 12, 1 year 4,000

Same to The Kings Co. Savings Inst. Same property. Oct. 13, 1 year, 5 %. 1,500

Schultze, Theodore L. to Louis Beer. Weirfield st. P. M. Oct. 12, 1 year. 2,000

Schwall, Henry, William and Joseph to Louisa I. Fischer. Broadway, n e s, 63 s e Fairfax st, 19x95. Oct 7, demand. 6,000

Seifried, Frederick to Frederick W. Starr. 3d av, e s, 40.2 n 47th st, 30x85. Oct. 13, due Oct. 1, 1892. 1,200

Seliger, Jr., Frank to Alonzo T. Welch and Samuel Lawson. Powell st, e s, 125 s Liberty av, 45x100. Sub. to mort. $1,500. Oct. 1, installs. 300

Shreve, Benjamin to The Hamilton Trust Co. 4th av, s e cor 46th st, 160x100. Oct. 10, due Nov. 1, 1892. 4,500

Sibley, Albert to J. and T. Charlton, Tonawanda, N. Y. Quincy st, s s, 325 w Throop av, 3 lots, each 18.9x100. 3 morts., each $1,500. Sub. to mort. on each of $4,500. Oct. 7, 8 months. 4,500

Same to same. Quincy st, s s, 400 w Throop av, 18.9x100. Sub. to mort. $4,500. Oct. 7, 8 months. 1,500

Sibley, Albert to Andrew D. Baird. Quincy st, s s, 100 w Throop av, 187.6x100. Oct. 14, demand. 36,000

Same to same. Same property Building loan. Oct. 14, demand. 33,000

Smith, Charles W. to Mary B. Van Beuren. Poplar st, n s, 77.4 e Hicks st, 22.8x25. Oct. 14, due Jan. 1, 1897. 1,500

Smith, Magdalena B. to Earl A. Gillespie. Logan st, e s, 94 s Jamaica av, 50x100. Oct. 13, demand. 600

Smith, Magdalena B. wife of Henry F. to Joseph Seitz, Dobbs Ferry, N. Y. Logan st, e s, 119 s Jamaica av, 25x100. Oct. 1, .. years. 2,000

Smith, Magdalena B. wife of Henry T. to same. Logan st, e s, 94 s Jamaica av, 25x100. Oct. 1, 3 years. 4,000

Smith, Susan C. to John C. Bremer. Oakland st. P. M.; also indemnity agt judgment. Oct. 13, due Jan. 1, 1898, 5½ %. 2,700

Speir, Henry to The South Brooklyn Co-operative Building and Loan Assoc. 53d st, n s, 200 e 4th av, 20x100.2. Oct. 6, installs. 2,000

Stimpson, Edwin E. and George A. Devnell, Haverhill, Mass., to The Metropolitan Life Ins. Co., New York. 6th st, s s, 177.10 e 6th av, 3 lots, each 17x100. 3 morts., each $6,000. Sept. 28, due Oct. 1, 1894, or part sooner. 18,000

Stimpson, Edwin C. and Helen M. his wife and George A. Devnell and Alice E. his wife, all of Haverhill, Mass., to Edward J. McCarty. 6th st, s s, 177.10 e 6th av, 3 lots, each 17x100. 3 morts., each $500. Aug. 29, due Sept. 30, 1894. 1,500

Stoutenburg, George B. to Francis P. Furnald, Jr. Throop av, n w cor Pulaski st, runs north 26 x west 50 x north 1 x west 34.9 x south 27 to st, x east 84.9. Oct. 9, due Oct. 1, 1893. 15,000

Sullivan, Michael to Elizabeth Taber et al. exrs. Franklin W. Taber. Dumont st, s s, 75 w Watkins st, 25x100; Watkins st, e s, 150 n Livonia av, 25x100. Sept. 29, 6 months. 1,200

Same to Joseph D. Powers. Same property. Sept. 29, 6 months. 2,000

Thompson, Jane mortgagee with Jacob Goldberg mortgagor. Extension of mort. Oct. 13. nom

Tilden, Lilian E. F. widow to Harry Mear and George J. Fowler. All title in estates of William and Milano C. Tilden, dec'd. Sept. 25, 4 %. secures attorney's lien

Same to George W. H. Iago. Same property. Sept. 25, 6 months. sterling £300

Toujes, Rose wife of and Diedrich H. to Marie Obry. Willoughby av, s e s, 275 s w Evergreen av, runs south 34 to Myrtle av, x west 67 to Willoughby av, x east 57.7 to beginning. Oct. 6, 3 years, 5 %. 6,000

Tooker, Sarah to Louise and Theresa Leimbach. Aberdeen st. P. M. Oct. 7, due Oct. 1, 1896. 1,000

Tuchman, Dora to Thomas Bardimann and Mary his wife. Cook st. P. M. Sept. 21, 5 years, 5 %. 2,000

Tunison, William H. to Mary E. Dorian. Grand av, e s, 50 s Greene av, 25x100. Oct. 13, 3 years, 5 %. 2,000

Urban, Frederick C. to Frederick Hower. 15th st, s w s, 221.4 s e 3d av, 75x110.7x72.8x107.11. Sept. 24, due Sept. 1, 1892. 8,000

Same to same. Pulaski st, n s, 125 e Throop av, 169 6x100. Sept. 24, due Jan. 27, 1892. 6,000

Same to same. Same property. Sept. 24, due Sept. 1, 1892. 15,000

Van Buren, Ansel H. to The Title Guarantee and Trust Co. Decatur st, n s, 100 w Howard av, 10 lots, each 20x100. 10 morts., each $5,000. Oct. 10, 3 years, 5 %. 50,000

Van Houten, Henry to John H. Ireland. East 95th st. P. M. Sept. 30, 1 year. 100

Vollmer, Henry and Joseph P. Driesel to The Kings County Savings Inst. Monitor st. P. M. Oct. 1, 1 year, 5 %. 1,900

Same to Charles Engert. Same property. 2d mort. Oct. 1, installs. 1,300

Von Oehsen, Henry to The Williamsburgh Savings Bank. Powers st, s w cor Olive st, 25x100. Oct. 12, 1 year, 5 %. 3,000

Vose, Isabel M. to The Dime Savings Bank, Brooklyn. Eastern Parkway, n s, 70 w Utica av, 70x220.7. Oct. 14, 1 year, 5 %. 3,900

Walbridge, Mary to Sidney Wintringham. 10th st, n e s, 106.1 s e 7th av, 18x100. Oct. 13, due May 1, 1892. 2,500

Walker, Mary A. to Charles F. Hitzelberger. Bergen st, n s, 123 e Hopkinson av, 17x107x—x—. Sub. to mort. $1,500. Oct. 8, 5 years. 1,500

Walker, Andrew E. to Rebecca F. Sturgis trustee Lawrence Forbes. Nassau av, s s, 75 w Russell st, 3 lots, each 25x100. 3 morts., each $4,000. Oct. 14, 5 years, 5½ %. 12,000

Warner, James to John M. Rich. 8th av, w s, 52 n 19th st, 32x80. Oct. 5, 3 years, 5 %. 2,000

Watkins, Percy W. to The South Brooklyn Building and Loan Assoc. 39th st. P. M. Oct. 6, installs. 2,750

Weber, Henry to Wilhelmina M. Bruns. Elm st, s s, 425 e Central av, 25x100. Oct. 12, 5 years, 5 %. 1,500

Weinberger, Mathilda and Lena Herskovics to William Bedford. Bayard st. P. M. Oct. 10, 5 years. 1,300

Werner, Henry to Louis Heinrich Herbald and Sophia Schilback. Schermerhorn st. P. M. Oct. 7, due Oct. 9, 1892, 5 %. 1,000

Same to Minerva A. Ketcham. Same property. P. M. Oct. 7, due Oct. 9, 1894, 5 %. 5,500

Werner, John F. to Ella E. wife of Frank W. Werner. Bedford av, e s, 40.3 n South 1st st, 18.6x81. Oct. 1, due Jan. 1, 1893. 3,000

Williams, Mary A. C. to Thomas Stratton. 53d st, n s, 151.9 w 3d av, 17.3x100.2. Sub. to mort. $1,700. Oct. 9, 2 years. 8,000

Wilson, Alexander to Amelia L. Bull. 55th st, New Utrecht. P. M. Sept. 28, installs, 5 %. 600

Winslow, Harriet A. widow to Cornelius Cowenhoven, New Utrecht. Lafayette av, s s, 158.5 e Tompkins av, 19.4x100. Oct. 12, 3 years, 5 %. 4,000

Winterwerb, Charles to Edmund A. Gearon. Butler st, s s, 309 w Clason av, 25x131. Aug. 15, due Oct. 4, 1891. 250

Wood, Herman H. to The Title Guarantee and Trust Co. 8th st, n s, 147.10 w 7th av, 2 lots, each 18.9x100. 2 morts., each $3,500. Oct. 5, due Oct. 9, 1894, 5 %. 7,000

Wood, James, New York, to William Flanagan. St. Johns pl. P. M. Oct. 7, 2 years, 5 %. 10,000

Wright, William S. and James S. to Hattie A. Allen. Carlton av. P. M. Oct. 12, 3 years. 3,000

Young, Peter and Joseph to William M. Ingraham. North 8th st, n e cor Kent av, runs north 105 x east 100 x south 5 x east 75 x south 100 to st, x west 175. Oct. 8, 2 years. 15,000

Zoellner, Joseph and Helena his wife to Jean Schneider. Elm st, s s, 340 e Broadway, 25x68.8x20x69.1. Oct. 2, due Oct. 1, 1896, 5 %. 1,900

MORTGAGES----ASSIGNMENTS.

NEW YORK CITY.

OCTOBER 9 TO 15—INCLUSIVE.

Abrahams, Ellen individ. and admrx. Alfred Abrahams to Nathan Federgreen, Monticello, N. Y. $5,000

Baker, John O., Newark, N. J., to Samuel N. Hoyt et al. trustees for Mary I. Hoyt. 50,000

Brock, Charles exr. Morton Brock to Jane M. Aspinwall extrx. John L. Aspinwall. 15,000

Byrne, John J. to Franklin Seymour. 175

Bell, Enoch C. to Sarah M. Williams, South Oyster Bay, L. I. 10,000

Bowes, John and John Coombs, of Bowes & Coombs, to Henry Greenebaum. 1,400

Bright, Adele, Philadelphia, Pa., to The Title Guarantee and Trust Co. 3,000

Berrick, Abraham H. to Xaver Pacher. nom

Chegnay, Henri to Isaac N. Hebberd. 925

Chambers, John A. exr. Helena De Witt Chambers to James, John A., Jeanette D. and Katharine Chambers, Morristown, N. J. Re-recorded. nom

Chambers, James, John A., Jeanette D. and Katharine, Morristown, N. J., to William G. De Witt committee of John T. Housman. Re-recorded. 8,521

Campbell, John V. to Joseph L. Buttenwieser. nom

Davis, Eugene H., Montreal, Can., to Hyman Sylvester. 2,000

De-Witt, William G. committee of John T. Housmen to James, John A., Jeanette D. and Katharine Chambers. Re-recorded. 10,143

Fisher, Frank L. to The Hudson River Bank. 10,000

Flake, Albert to Frederic J. Middlebrook, Brooklyn. 6,167

Fairchild, Clara to Ella L. Barnes. 1,100

Guggenheimer, Randolph and Salomon Marx to The Amsterdam Impt. Co. 4 assigns. nom

Goetz, Samuel to Randolph Guggenheimer and Salomon Marx. nom

Gebhard, Michael to Louis Wirth. 6,000

Gafney, John H. exr. Arthur J. Donnelly to Peter Donnelly. 430

Hall, Thomas R. A. and William H., of William Hall's Sons, to Henry A. Barling and Edward H. Green and ano. trustees Edward M. Robinson. 14,000

Hassey, August to Hermann Schneider. 5,000

Same to Henrietta Schneider. 8,000

Hoyt, Alfred M. et al. trustees for Mary I. Hoyt to Charles T. Barney, Francis M. Jencks and William E. D. Stokes. nom

Harbeck, John H. to The Count Charles de Montsaulnin and Walker Fearn trustees. 30,617

Same to same. 30,617

Ivison, Sarah B., Rutherford, N. J., to David B. Ivison. 2,500

Kammerer, Robert C. et al. exrs. Louis Kammerer to Robert C. and Lucy Kammerer and Adelheid Liebert. nom

Kammerer, Robert C. and Lucy and Adelheid Liebert to Adelheid Liebert. nom

Kraetzer, Albert A. to Solomon Jacobs. 4,000

Lambias, John F., Brooklyn, to Ada A. Shipman. 546

Lambert, Isaac S. and David S. and Arthur and Julius G. Miller, of Lambert Bros. and Miller, Paterson, N. J., to Eva Lambert. 3,500

Landon, Charles G. and ano. exrs. Benjamin H. Hutton to Adele Hutton, Marquise de Portes. 14,280

Same to same. 24,000

Levy, L. Napoleon to William H. Gibson. 1,000

Lewis, John A. et al. exrs. Benjamin B. Sherman to John A. Lewis et al. trustees for Cornelia M. Sherman. nom

Lyman, William to Margaret O'Connor. Re-recorded. 5,000

Lyman, William to Margaret O'Connor. 5,000

Moore, Amelia R., New York, and Maria K. Hegeman, Mt. Kisco, N. Y., to Boltis Moore, Mt. Kisco, N. Y. 3,000

Mickle, Andrew H. and George B., Flushing, L. I., to J. Albert Lane. 5,237

Marbury, Francis F. exr. Caroline D. Langlois to Johann G. Schlingloff. 8,017

Same to same. 6,081

Murray, Emilie J. to Fannie Metzger. 3,000

Middlebrook, Frederic J., Brooklyn, to J. Harsen Purdy et al. exrs. Jacob Halsted. 12,062

Mills, Alfred and ano. exrs. and trustees Stephen Vail to Robert Cockcroft, Brooklyn. 5,000

Petersen, James, Copenhagen, Denmark, to Waldemar Petersen, New York, and Amanda Wengel, Copenhagen, Denmark. nom

Ross, Reuben to Robert W. Stuart. 3,500

Rankin, William to Mary S. Good, Brooklyn. 6,000

Rogers, Archibald, Hyde Park, N. Y., to Susan C. Herriman et al. exrs. John Herriman. 33,649

Rogers, Archibald, Hyde Park, N. Y., to Robert H. Coleman trustee for Anne C. Rogers. 9,169

Same to same. 6,135

Same to same. 18,337

Seaman, Albert W. trustee of Eliza Eagle dec'd to Matilda McLean, Brooklyn. 3,375

Serr, Charles and Catharina his wife to Charles G. Neumann. 2,000

Sheridan, James F. and Patrick H. and James S. Segrave to Thomas C. Cornell. 250

Same to same. 1,450

Same to same. 1,170

Same to same. 650

Same to same. 300

Same to same. 670

Same to same. 570

Same to same. 600

Same to same. 350

Same to same. 570

Same to same. 385

Same to same. 285

Same to same. 750

Same to same. 550

Same to same. 600

Schermerhorn, William H. and ano. exrs. and trustees Samuel Leggett to Rebecca F. Willets, Queens Co., L. I. 5,382

Schlosser, Jacob to Louis P. Bach. 3,500

Steers, Abraham to Maretta W. Howard. 3,000

Same to same. 3,000

Spratley, Henry to Annie R. Whitney. 25,312

Title Guarantee and Trust Co. to Jonas B. Kissam. 8,000

Title Guarantee and Trust Co. to The Teachers' Building and Loan Assoc. of New York City. 32,500

The East River Savings Inst. to Letitia King. 15,000

Same to same. 25,000

The Lawyers Title Ins. Co. of New York to Charles E. Appleb . 35,513

The Lawyers' Title Ins. Co. of New York to Robert S. Bowne et al. trustees Eliza R. Bowne. 9,000

The Peoples' Trust Co. to Michael F. Dwyer, Brooklyn. 2 assigns. nom

Union Trust Co., of New York, admr. Margaret Langlois to F. F. Marbury et al. exrs. Caroline D. Langlois. 6,000

Same to same. 10,000

Wise, Nathan to Julius G. Miller. 3,000

Weyler, Rudolph or Rudolf to Leon B. Ginsburg. nom

Winters, Robert C. to James H. Havens. 2,000

Yost, Agnes to Isidor Alkus. 3,000

KINGS COUNTY.

OCT. 8 TO 14—INCLUSIVE.

Andrews, John to Hannah W. Andrews, Newark, N. J. $5,000

Bearns, William J. G. to Ellen McAree. 800

Brouwer, Theophilus A. in trust for Margaret M. Brouwer to Mary T. Suydam. 4,700

Same to same. 3,090

Beals, Sarah J. to Oliver Moore et al. exrs. Abraham Underhill. 1,000

Bisson, Mary E. to The Nassau Trust Co., Brooklyn. 7,500

Baird, Andrew D. to The People's Trust Co. 32,000

Cook, Mary E., Newtown L. I., to William M. Miller. 1,370

Cook, Mary E. to John C. and Herbert C. Smith and Herman F. Koepke, of J. C. and H. C. Smith & Koepke. nom

Collins, Benjamin to Mary O'Connor trustee John Purcell. 5,000

Cooper, Charles W., Jr., and ano. exrs. William Cooper to Charles W. Cooper. 15,540

Dittmar, Jr., William, to John L. Nostrand. nom

Doody, Daniel F. to Sophie G. Parker. 4,157

Everit, Edward A. to Henry Sahlfeld. 700

Egolf, Edward to Henry D. Lott. 1,400

Emmerich, Rudolph F. to Auguste C. Barker. 1,000

Festl, Joseph to Rudolph F. Emmerich. 1,000

Farley, Frederick A. trustee Augustus Graham dec'd to Grindall Reynolds and ano. trustees of same. nom

Frothingham, John B. exr. Margaret Cavendy to Mary J. Frothingham legatee Margaret Cavendy. 4,000

Grening, Paul C. to Adolph Simis, Jr. 1,500

Gutierrez, Alonzo R. to Laura E. Mills. 3,007

Gutting, George to Charles A. Wagner. 3 assigns. nom

Same to Bertha Wagner. 3 assigns. nom

Graue, Sarah to Mary W. Smith. 750

Halstead, Isaac to William H. Dill. 1,500

Hewlett, Van W. and ano. exrs. Elizabeth Hewlett to Mary V. W. Pearsall. 2,000

Hazzard, William H. et al. trustees James Brady dec'd to Edward L. Spencer. 8,069

Hower, Frederick to Leopold Kahn. nom

Same to same. nom

Hoyt, Alfred, Stamford, Conn., to Daniel F. Doody. 4,157

Kinkel, Louisa M. to Henry J. Koehler. 1,600

Kleine, Virginia A. to Thomas T. Barr. 9,000

Krebs, Barbara and George to Ignatz Martin. 3,350

Kelly, Eugene & Co., New York, to Michael Fennelly. 1,030

Ledoux, Paul W. to The Hamilton Trust Co. nom

Lemmi, Carmina to Maria G. L. Lemmi. nom

Lewis, Daniel F. to Thomas T. Barr. 1,000

Lott, John A., Jr., to Abby L. Wells. 1,400

Lyons, Catharine to William J. Weldon. 7,000

Marbury, Francis F. exr. Caroline D. Langlois to Johann G. Schlingloff. 2,047

Meller, Christian H. to Charles J. Patterson. 1,000

Martin, Ignatz to The Title Guarantee and Trust Co. 3,350

McMillan, Mary J. to Daniel K. Hall, Glen Cove. 2,000

Montgomery, Emily F. trustee George C. Montgomery to Charles Michenfelder. 650

Menahan, John to William H. Hamilton. 625

Nassau Trust Co. to Mary E. Bisson. nom

Newman, Henry to Jacob Worth. 2,200

Norris, William H. and William Bowers to Albro J. Newton. nom

Preston, Sarah J. extrx. John Preston to William H. Preston, Newark, N. J. 1,000

Same to William H. Preston, Newark, N. J. 3,500

Same to Harriett Card, Newark, N. J. 3,000

Same to same. 2,000

Pierrepont, Henry E., Jr., as trustee to Anne L. Pierrepont. 3 assigns. nom

Post, Stephen R. to Martha W. Post, Westbury, L. I. 2,500

Raymond, Benjamin C. to Adelbert S. Nichols. 825

Rosenfeld, Rose to Lewis Hurst. 200

Roth, Henry to The Hyde & Gload Mfg. Co. 1,100

Ryan, Phebe to Laura E. Reynolds, Brewsters, N. Y. 4,000

Rogers, John C. to Henry McShane Mfg. Co. nom

Rose, Kate to Louise Fehlinger. 900

Reges, Frederick exr. Barbara Reges to Frank Peterkin. 9,135

Stern, David to Nathaniel Conklin, Jr. nom

Sackett, Sarah E. extrx. Adam P. Sackett to Florentine Pettelier, Plainfield, N. J. 1,423

Same to same. 2,042

Shreve, Benjamin to Stephen and Ellen Martin. 2,500

Simis, Adolph, Jr., to Cornelius N. Hoagland. 1,500

Skelly, Mary to Mary A. McGivern. 5,000

Smith, Mary W. to Julia A. Swan. 750

Smith, Warren E. to Harriet B. Fiester. 5,000

Smith, Robert J. to Rebecca Magner. 1,500

Sperl, Hermann G. to Albert Keck. 500

Stearns, John M. to Charles P. Giiron. 1,000

The Brooklyn City Mission and Tract Society to The East Brooklyn Savings Bank. 1,500

Title Guarantee and Trust Co. to Atlantic Trust Co. trustee. 3,000

Same to Brooklyn Young Men's Christian Assoc. 1,000

Same to John R. Willis trustee Mary F. Willis dec'd. 5,000

Same to Martin Fallon. 5,000
Same to Robert W. Cooper. 4,000
Same to The Brooklyn Savings Bank. 110,000
Same to James Sullivan. 2,250
Same to Mary E. Udell. .400
Union Trust Co., New York, admr. Margaret Langlois to F. F. Marbury et al. exrs. Caroline D. Langlois. 3,000
Weldon, William J. to Edmund F. Buckley trustee Amon Buckley. 3,000
Wood, Gertrude P. to Melvin Brown. 1,280
Wheeler, George S. exr. Nancy B. Wheeler to The Peoples' Trust Co. 1.500
Wagner, Charles A. to George Gutting. All title in 3 morts. nom

JUDGMENTS.

NEW YORK CITY.

Oct.
10 Albright, Charles H—George Tilles..$6,749 05
10 Ayers, Charles H—Charles Perceval..1,153 17
10 Abbott, Warren G—J L Mott........ 722 52
10 Ackermann, Bernard L, Jr—Jacob Hays, individ and exr 124 33
12 Archer, Frank M—D J Bannatyne... 669 36
13 Ayres, Charles H—A C Rodriguez... 416 57
13 Abrahams, Mina—Henry Newman.... 4,744 23
13 Abry, Helen M—E A Moret.......... 479 57
13 Aul, Charles A—J S Foster.... .....1,077 20
13 Adelman, Adolph—Simon Ottenberg. 5,567 80
14 Almy, Edwin R—H E Bowns........ 358 53
14 Atkinson, Maurice B—J W Todd....1,766 30
14†Altman, Oscar—Herman Mandelbaum.... ... . 74 11
14 Aldis, Charles Ambrose, an infant by Edward S Savage—J B Simpson ....costs 112 34
15 Albaum, Franz—L C King.......... 162 69
15 Ainsworth, James—E F Randolph.... 170 40
15 Alexander, John V—H S Force...... 120 28
16 Andress, Charles W—Vanderbeck Iron Works Co.................... 278 69
16 Axt, Louis—Philip Smith............ 548 57
16 Adelman, Adolph—Peter McQuade... 904 23
10 Blanchard, Charles A—Charles Perceval..........................1,153 17
10 Bowles, Benjamin L—David Carlisle.14,252 47
10 Bell, George H—Twenty-third Ward Bank............................ 417 31
10 Betts, Carlton H—W H Griffing..... 216 02
10 Bassett, J Fremont—U S Illuminating Co.... .... 79 32
10 Broughton, David F—American Steam Boiler Ins Co.................... 190 33
10†Brockway, Emil—J T Scott.......... 254 69
10 Barcalow, George B—Louis Van Wagoner............................. 479 14
10 Bullock, Samuel R—E F Corey....... 197 74
10 Bourne, Charles R—H G Simmons... 39 68
10 Bell, William R—Isaac Lewis........ 167 27
12†Bleyer, Jacob Mount—George Robinson.............................. 125 93
12 Beaudet, Homer J—Charles MacEvoy 1,536 79
12 the same——Bank of Harlem .. 1,530 84
12 Benedix, Gustav—Edward Regensburg............................. 94 07
12 Blanchard, Charles A—A C Rodriguez.............................. 416 57
12 Beach, Julia A—Marianna de Pepster..............................2,523 83
12 Browne, Henry Huffman—Henry Senior...............................1,380 60
13 Barry, Michael H—Henry Schomberg 7,638 10
13 Belvin, Mary—Jacob Appel.......... 538 11
13 the same——Aaron Kohn........ 4.617 99
13 Bailey, John J—H W Johns Mfg Co.. 385 09
13 Bayer, George—J W Percival........ 97 06
14 Brannigan, John—W M Leslie........ 136 11
14*Baas, Joachim—Emma M Ackley..... 271 36
14 Brown, Egbert G / Brown, Benjamin } F W Devoe & Co............ 100 51
14 Brady, Ellen—Bavarian Brewing Co. 1,548 00
14 Bonnell, J Harper—Lehigh Valley Coal Co.............................1,591 71
14 Beacham, John—W H Appleton...... 144 89
14 Ball, Max—Amory Leland........... 656 63
14 Beacham, John—International Book Co 258 32
15 Bruce, William M—Ella Tredwell 1,535 18
15 Boyle, Mary—Joseph Walsh.......... 281 80
15 Brockmann, William—C H Evans.... 71 50
15 Brewster, Charles—Market and Fulton Nat Bank...................... 495 60
15 the same——the same............ 679 43
15 Berman, Abraham—S J Weaver..... 629 75
15 Backer, Abraham—G W Vultee.....13,443 68
15 Bernstein, Julius—Brooklyn Varnish Mfg Co........ .... 89 97
16†Bright, Isaac O—Julius Engel........ 231 82
16 Barry, Michael H—Butler Hardware Co.................................. 320 91
16 Bales, Walter M—Joseph Hammett.. 173 54
16 Byrne, Elizabeth—James Adair...... 93 18
16*†Baxberger, John—Sidney New...... 153 25
9 Cameron, Roderick W—J S Cameron .. . .costs 170 88
10 Cross, William—W H Dike.......... 148 14
10 Carr, Walter / Carr, Delvin B } W R Peters........2,273 15
10 Casler, Philo W—American Steam Boiler Ins Co........................ 190 33
10 Conner, William M—T W Pearsall, trustee...............................3,048 69
12 Curry, George W—M L Filley....... 364 42
12 the same——the same............ 576 79
12 Crane, Thomas—George Hasenpflug ....costs 170 52
12 Cohn, Walter G / Cohn, William I } B M Ewing....... 723 49
12 Clark, Jacob E—James Phillips, Jr.. 1,028 27
13 Cummiskey, Mary—Abraham Worms 92 50
13 Cabrey, Edmund J—Erastus Brainerd 796 34
13 Carpenter, Robert B—Washington Nat Bank..............................1,019 59
13 the same——the same...... ..... 549 95
13 Clark, Robert P—Peter Neary....... 405 97
14 Casselberry, Jacob R—Julia P Warren..............................10,535 93
14 *Cavinato, Luigi / Cavinato, Guiseppe / *Cavinato, Steffano / Cavinato, Natale } Simon Adler.... 321 99
14 Cawley, Patrick J—G W Smith...... 453 75
14 Clinton, Henry F—J C McEachen.... 160 36
14 Chase, Emily—J B Simpson, exr ....costs 112 34
15 Coughlin, Mary A—H T Terry...... 426 03
15 Chadwick, Helen E—Delamater Iron Works............................. 178 61
15 Carter, John / Carter, Mary Jane } William McIlroy........1,249 39
15 Crawford, Arthur F—J W Arthur... 83 53
15 *Cunningham, John J / Cunningham, Daniel } C G Cornell, Jr.......... 187 71
15 Christie, William—F W Hofele, recvr 1,622 39
15 Coatsworth, Caleb J—John Simmons Co................................. 214 58
15 ¶Cavinato, Luigi / *Cavinato, Steffano / *Cavinato, Guiseppe / Cavinato, Natale } Northern Nat Bank.... ....1,535 49
16 Cone, Thomas R—A G Belden...... . 276 57
16 Clark, Herman—B F Martin, comm'r. 110 00
16 Cranston, Henry—G W Venable...... 228 44
16 Carroll, James—Michael Maguire.... 196 21
9 Doorley, John—F C Combes...... ... 89 50
10*David, Albert A—F W Otheman..... 868 28
10 the same——A D Juilliard........ 469 56
12 Dempsey, William—Louis Schoonmaker............................... 70 17
12 Downey, Charles—M L Filly...... ... 364 42
12 the same——the same............. 576 79
12 Deutschberger, Frederick—C F Lawrence.............................. 223 43
12 Dow, Lorenzo—Theodore Berdell..... 2,805 49
13 Duffy, Thomas L—Bertha Glaser..... 264 11
13 De Veau, John W—Theador Riehl.... 87 18
13 Daniels, Lilyon D—H M Raborg, admr............................... 634 44
13 Dolan, Hugh—Peter Neary.......... 405 97
14 Dempsey, William—G H Flynn...... 295 96
14 Dempsey, John—First Nat Bank of Middletown, N Y.................. 202 55
14 David, Albert A—Siegfried Rosenberg.............................. 658 68
15 De Mitkiewicz, Eugene—James Gamble.............................. 828 26
15 Douglass, Hiram A—O L Hinds...... 282 16
15†Doe, John—S J Weaver............. 358 25
15 Develin, Charles S—Tiffany & Co.... 158 38
15 Diffley, Cecilia F / *†Diffley, John } James Hamill.... 144 77
15†Dallwig, Henry G—Germania Bank.. 175 25
16 Dunn, Thomas F—Nathaniel Wise.... 136 86
16 Demarest, Daniel—T P Galligan...... 499 52
16 Deane, George H—J G Van Camp... 91 53
12 Ewing, Justus E—J R Conkey.......6,039 43
12 Edwards, James H—Frederick Thileman, Jr............................ 134 85
13 Engel, Leopold—State Bank.......... 123 56
13 Edelson, Abraham—Samuel Fleck.... 671 72
14 Eustace, James A—L R Smith....... 518 59
15 Eddy, Robert T—John Simmons Co.. 214 58
16 Emley, Fletcher J—E S McClellan...1,026 07
9 Farrell, Henry—Boynton Furnace Co. 25 01
10 Fitzgibbon, Maurice—Louis Van Wagoner............................. 479 14
12 Fritz, Egbert—R L Coleman......... 484 22
13 Findal, Martin—Peter Rost, Jr....... 114 58
14 Fogerty, James J—F J Allen........ 508 00
14 Freund, Getzel—Arnold Kohn, assignee..... .... 63 47
15 Frankish, Joseph / *Frankish, John K } James Boiles, Jr 331 56
15 Fay, Henry A—J G Fay............. 406 40
15 Fink, Henry—Theodore Agor........ 243 75
15 Fiske, Wilson—F W Eardley........ 116 90
16 Finn, Jerome—Bertha Glaser........ 181 97
16 Farquhar, George—Ernest Cotterill.. 134 17
16 Felter, Samuel—T B Kniffin......... 248 56
16 Fruchtenicht, John—W F Redlich... 746 90
9 Gerken, Anna—Henry Eggers........1,164 65
10 Goebel, Julius—Lennox Hill Bank.... 295 64
12 Gormley, James—Patrick McCann... 279 44
12 Grout, Edward Livermore—Bank of Harlem............................1,530 84
13 Gru, Joseph—Bertha Zolinsky 1,217 25
13 Goodsell, Edward L—Enrico Casabianca..........................costs 73 06
13 Griffith, Ella M—J S McWilliams..... 413 49
13 the same——the same.............1,113 49
13 Gobber, John—John Magenheimer. ....costs 69 57
14 Gondalfo, Joseph—Henry Hahnenfeld 237 76
14 Giddings, Everitt / Giddings, Edith / Giddings, Emily C } J B Simpson.costs 112 34
15 Gebhardt, Adolph—J S Rosenfeld.... 131 52
15†Goldman, Bernard—Alexander Davidoff....... .... 169 00
15 Groschee, William—Germania Bank. 175 25
16 Grant, D Lewis—E A Gross.......... 172 19

¶*Editor* RECORD AND GUIDE:

We have satisfied the two judgments for $1,535.49 in favor of the Northern National Bank, and for $321.99 in favor of Simon Adler and another, but received the certificate of the Clerk of the City Court too late to have them marked off the docket in the County Clerk's office.

Oct. 16, 1891. CAVINATO BROTHERS.

10 Harper, William D—Market and Fulton Nat Bank 469 42
10 the same——the same............ 451 26
10 Hoag, Henry G, individ and / *Hoeg, Emma F composing firm H G Hoag & Co } W H Graef 120 27
12 Hess, Adolph—David Marx.......... 157 50
12 the same——the same............ 162 03
12 Holly, John I—James Phillips, Jr....1,028 27
13 Hayward, Calvin D—John Ganet.... 206 41
13 Hartung, Lorenzo R—J H Heroy....1,024 54
13 Hill, Charles M—David Kearr....... 270 47
13 Haynes, George F—Manhattan Athletic Club............................ 120 24
14 Harper, William D—Lehigh Valley Coal Co.............................1,591 71
14 Hunter, George W—George Scofield.. 44 65
14†Hohmann, Mary—William Campioni. 94 37
14 Hunsicker, Jacob—Chretien Probst...2,873 30
15 Harper, William D—Market & Fulton Nat Bank....................... 679 43
15 Hablo, William F—S J Weaver...... 637 50
15 Harris, Jacob——the same. 358 25
15 Hirschbein, Nathan—Germicide Co... 115 38
16 Hirsch, Max—Julius Saul....... .... 748 65
16 Hilliard, Robert C—Warren Chichester.......................... ...... 177 98
16 Healey, Frank B—G W Venable...... 166 10
16 Hafner, Annie—J W Nicholson....... 116 69
16 Hubbell, Frederick E—F H Leggett.. 309 32
16 Hornby, Frank A—W F Redlich..... 111 95
16 Herod, William—Bowery Bank...... 627 73
10 Jerkowski, Marcus—F W Otheman..1,229 16
10 the same——A D Juillard..... ..1,351 76
10 the same——F W Otheman....... 868 28
10 the same——A D Juilliard........ 469 56
10 the same——H J Hinck.......... 917 11
10 the same——J B Case............1,191 24
10 the same——E A Price...........1,040 86
10 the same——Carl Voight... .....1,494 93
12 Jordan, Joseph V—John Dobson..... 657 58
12 Jumps, John T R / Jumps, John } Oil, Paint and Drug Publishing Co... ....1,154 40
14 Jerkowski, Marcus—Siegfried Rosenberg....... .... 658 68
14 Johnston, James D—Joe Spota....... 465 04
16*Jerkowsky, Marcus—Theodore Wernwag............................... 724 37
16 Jack, Lizzie—R C Johnson........... 99 00
9 Kuntz, Lena, extrx Joseph Kuntz—Mary H Arnold.......................1,330 06
9*Kenzel, William J—Mount Morris Electric Light Co................. 39 08
10 Kennell, Joseph A—Twenty-third Ward Bank........................ 417 31
10 Kelly, Andrew—J E McLarney 101 70
12 Knupfer, Max—J R Berbling......... 97 06
13 Kane, Catherine—J S Barnet......... 280 53
13 Knapp, Shepard—Erastus Brainerd.. 796 34
14 Klotz, Frederick—Sigmund Sternman 76 02
14 Kohlsaat, John W—F O Matthiessen, exr...........................costs 78 31
14 Kaiser, Alexander—Chretien Probst..2,873 30
14 Kelly, John A—A H Leathern....... 110 01
15 Krug, Louis—William Smith........ 119 87
16 Knight, Thomas H—W D Stewart.... 133 95
9 Leeds, William H—Mount Morris Electric Light Co 39 08
10 Lauer, Peter—Leon Hirsh..... ...... 327 06
12 Lederer, Bernard W—W E Smith.... 282 08
12 Lowerre, William H—Jennett Y Lowerre...............................1,051 27
12 Lecher, George—G T Stewart, individ and admr......................(D) 1,191 57
13 Lowerre, William H—J M Cleveland. 408 14
13 the same——Jacob New..........1,050 81
13 the same——E E McCargo........ 597 01
13*Lober, Albert—E L Snyder.......... 99 16
13 Lawson, Jacob—W F Morris.......... 219 61
13 Laughna, William O—Charles Soblesinger............................. 200 70
14 Lowell, Samuel J—D E Seybel....... 295 73
14 Lennon, James / Lennon, James } James McNulty.....1,193 52
15 Light, Philip—S J Weaver..........1,575 07
15 Loveday, Edwin—Essex County Nat Bank.............................. 349 37
15 Landman, Max—S C Howard........ 112 43
15 Lugo, Orazio—G A Raftery.......... 790 90
16 Lyon, Robert—James Adair.......... 95 81
16 Lippmann, Martin—Louis Grunhut..2,134 63
16 the same——the same.. ....7,539 96
16 Leopold, Lewis—Sidney New......... 92 95
16 the same——the same............ 183 25
10 Molloy, John J—Long Island R R Co. 627 69
10 Myers, Alice E—R W Townsend...... 855 68
10 Meyer, Siegmund T / *Meyer, Arthur L } Charles Donohue.........5,094 62
12 Meyer, Siegmund T / Meyer, Arthur L / Meyer, Philip L } Nat Bank of Deposit........14,383 10
12 Morris, Charles B—J L Miller.... ... 673 89
12 Miller, Elijah—A W Balch........... 126 98
12 Munn, Archibald B—C E Johnson.... 141 13
13 Meyer, Esther—Pena Solomon......... 877 25
13 Micieli, Michael—Edwin Wallace.... 134 01
13 Muller, Lewis M—J H Swift.......... 366 06
13 Muller, Louis / Muller, Mary R } J H O'Rourke...... 54 49
13 the same——the same............ 56 97
14 Muench, Egid—W L Douglas Shoe Co.................................... 21 44
14 Marluk, Marcus—Louis Alexander... 118 91
14 Munzinger, John C—J W Hogencamp 179 96
14 Meyer, Siegmund T / Meyer, Arthur L } Abraham Steers 735 12
14 Mayer, Elias—Arnold Kohn, assignee. 104 39
14 Mitchell, Jane—C W Vreeland..costs 10 00
14 Muller, Lewis M—Albert Lang....... 348 11
14 Moore, William O—Henry Hahnenfeld.................................. 287 76
15 Myers, Sinclair—Western Nat Bank.. 562 31

15	Mansfield, Amelia—T F Bush	524 32
15	Monoghan, Margaret—H T Terry	426 03
15	Mezey, Martin / Myers, Marks } S J Weaver	782 95
15	Moeller, Carl—Hipp Didesheim	118 13
15	Meyer, Siegmund T / Meyer, Arthur L / Meyer, Philip L } G B Ashley	530 58
15	Moore, Hiram—Henry McDougall	391 75
15	Mackie, Charles Powell—J S Rosenthal	14,122 74
15	Morse, G Livingston—Holmes & Griggs Mfg Co	128 60
15	Miller, Robert B—Chatham Nat Bank	891 73
16	Mattes, Edward A—E A Hervey	200 57
16	Moisan, Delphis F—Simonds Mfg Co.	337 01
16	Mitchell, Charles R—Vanderbeck Iron Works Co	278 69
16	Meyerson, Chana—Harry Levene	39 93
16	Megargee, Louis N—John Wanamaker	70 81
16	Martin, Harry—F C Neale	370 00
16	Mathews, Fanny Aymar—Daniel Frohman	626 86
16	Monahan, Patrick—Henry Eggers	96 97
12	McCullagh, Matilda—C W Lamb	41 93
12	McNiece, James—E E Ensley	258 30
14	McDermott, Thomas—David Jones Co	369 76
14	McLean, Donald—H B Fullencamp	546 94
14	McDonald, Phillip—H W Matthews	155 37
15	McTeague, Joseph P—Charles McTeague	140 25
15	Mackie, Charles Povell—J S Rosenthal	14,122 74
16	McEntee, William F—S A Brooker	41 54
16	McGuckin, Henry J—Hyatt Co	648 85
13	Newmuller, Franz—Robert Jones	89 54
16	Nelsons, John A—Frederick Arnold	33 94
16	Nealis, Thomas J—Henry Witson	200 39
10	O'Connor, John—Eugene Cushman	124 86
10	O'Keefe, John D—J W Stolts	135 71
13	O'Neill, Dennis—H B Claflin Co	445 86
14	Osborne, Robert E—George Scofield	44 65
13	Petrus, Samuel—Knickerbocker Brewing Co	423 00
14	Pomeroy, Lemuel—Tiffany & Co	698 26
14	Perless, Leon—Bavarian brewing Co.	509 88
14	Palmer, William W—A B Powell	2,394 01
14	Platt, William B—Eloise I Chace, extrx	367 05
14	Payne, Frances E—Marian M Carhart	1,538 25
15	Peck, Nellie E—John Macdonald	11,961 54
15	Praeger, Jacob E—Morris Schwerin	89 74
15	Platte, Joseph—Joseph Staubach	115 19
15	Powers, Edward H—Bavarian Brewing Co	124 46
16	Phelps, Louis N—J O Hern	136 35
16	Price, Jesse—Henry Lindenmeyr	559 50
16	Pierce, Mary J—Adolph Reisenberg ...costs	133 50
10	Roberts, Austin J / Roberts, Walter J } R E Webber	231 12
10	Roemer, Henrietta L—J A Striker	165 43
13	Reilly, Solomon—J S Nathan	203 56
13	Roberts, William H H—Emil Mouthemont	179 87
14	Root, James H—H E Bowns	358 53
14	Rubenstein, Samuel—Arnold Kohn, assignee	32 92
15	Roberts, Austin J—T F Bush	524 32
15	Rubens, Nathan—Michael Barchardt	68 50
15	Roberts, William H H—Daniel Kane	162 52
15	Rosenbecker, Philip—W B Smith	116 85
15	Rothbaum, Mayer H—Boatman's Fire and Marine Ins Co of Pittsburgh, Pa ...costs	111 95
15	the same—People's Ins Co of Pittsburgh, Pa	111 95
16	Ryan, Patrick—David Kennedy	70 53
16	Robinson, John—Fifth Nat Bank of Pittsburgh	10,264 00
16	Rolker, Frederick—Pres't, &c, Manhattan Co	1,311 54
16	Roberts, Austin J / Roberts, Walter J } G C Clark	382 31
16	Richmond, Louis—B E Hicks	312 68
9	Street, William A—J S Cameron	170 88
9	Shaw, Charles P—Lizzie R G Shaw	4,000 00
9	the same—the same ...costs	1,115 80
10	Steindler, Joseph—George Tilles	6,749 05
10	Schuyler, Van Rensselaer—Chemical Nat Bank	1,408 43
10	Sneckner, William H—W R Peters	2,273 15
10	Seaman, Charles H—Twenty-third Ward Bank	417 31
10	Stuckenschmidt, Sophie—J E Nichols	108 93
10	Stevenson, Vernon K—U S Illuminating Co	79 32
10*	Schiff, John—F W Otheman	1,229 16
10	the same—A D Juilliard	1,351 76
10	the same—F W Otheman	868 28
10	the same—A D Juilliard	469 56
10	the same—H J Hinck	917 11
10	the same—J B Case	1,191 24
10	the same—E A Price	1,040 86
10	the same—Carl Voight	1,494 93
12	Stuckenschmidt, Sophia—Benedickt Fischer	213 52
12	Solomon, Ephraim—B M Ewing	723 49
12	See, Amos L / See, E Garnier } Jennet Y Lowerre	1,051 27
12	Schmitt, Robert—A C Manning	333 97
13	See, Amos L / See, E Garnier } J M Cleveland	408 14
13	the same—Jacob New	1,050 81
13	Sommer, Moritz—G E Hicks	1,596 61
13	Shumsky, Morris—Jacob Loewenthal	388 19
13	Stern, Max—State Bank	123 56
13	Schlim, William H—E L Snyder	99 16
13	See, Amos L / See, Edward G } E E McCargo	597 01
13	Schelberg, John / Schelberg, Lena } J Chr G Hupfel Brewing Co	374 03
13	Schmid, Martin A—John Egan	162 69
13	Sturges, Daniel L—James Brand	1,044 31
14	Senior, John W—F J Allen	508 00
14	Stein, Myer J—Charles Whitlock ...costs	108 32
14	Sulzer, Alfred—H E Bowns	358 53
14*	Schiff, John—Siegfried Rosenberg	658 68
14	Savage, Edward S, as guard ad litem—J B Simpson ...costs	112 34
15	Stafford, William H—Western Nat Bank	562 81
15	Schnabell, William—Michael Barchardt	68 50
15	Schwerkolt, Adolph—Mount Morris Electric Light Co	72 63
15	Symons, Henry, Jr—S J Weaver	443 75
15	Schulman, Bernhard / Shapiro, Selig } the same	405 48
15	Salberg, Isaac—the same	637 50
15	Sussman, Samuel—Morris Schwerin	89 74
15	Sherick, Mark—G H Richards, Jr	82 81
15	Streiffer, Jacob—Charles Beckmann	173 08
15	Shonnard, Frederick—Holmes & Griggs Mfg Co ...costs	128 60
16	Schiff, John—Theodore Wernwag	724 37
16	Sommers, Henry—Herrmann Weiller	198 90
16	Sullivan, James J—Mary C Sullivan ...costs	516 40
16	Solinsky, Max—C M Partridge	234 89
16	Sterm, Isaac—Importers and Traders' Nat Bank	1,181 37
16	Sidebotham, Thomas B, Jr—I C Ogden, Jr	147 71
16	the same—Campbell Printing Press and Mfg Co	149 10
16	the same—I C Ogden, Jr	147 73
16	Sulzbach, Jacob—Prest, &c, Manhattan Co	1,311 54
16	Stafford, Edward—John Mitchell	123 54
16	Scheuer, Simon—B F Martin, comm'r	60 00
16	Sauter, Louis—the same	110 00
9	Smith, James H—J S Cameron ...costs	170 86
10	Smith, Anna—John Wanamaker	491 99
12	Smith, John—Louis Schoonmaker	70 17
15	Smith, Henry C—J S Caldwell	223 68
16	Smith, Philip—W F Redlich	111 95
16	Smith, James J—F W Devoe ...costs	367 64
10	The J Dewing Publishing Co—Albert Gray	192 46
10	J H Bonnell & Co (Lim)—Market and Fulton Nat Bank	469 42
10	the same—the same	451 23
10	Standard White Lead Mfg Co—Metropolitan Telephone and Telegraph Co	74 50
10	Manhattan Railway Co—C M Smith	1,429 93
10	The Mayor, Aldermen, &c—William Anderson	284 00
12	The Lexington Improvement Co—August Noel	1,148 26
12	U S Gas and Water Works Construction Co—C F Lawrence	274 21
12	Barriett Electric Co—J L Howe	80 29
12	N Y Concert Co (Lim)—Julian T Davies, recvr ...costs	142 80
12	The Fonda Lake Paper Co—M M Belding	1,675 15
13	The Barnegat Park Co—J R Purcell	359 77
13	The Broadway & Seventh Av R R Co—W F Pyne	5,278 55
14	Joseph B Tiffany Co—G C Boldt	115 70
14	Metropolitan Elevated Railway Co / Manhattan Railway Co } J M Knox, exr ...costs	190 72
14	the same—James Galway ...costs	143 28
14	the same—T E Macy ...costs	136 46
14	The Mayor, Aldermen, &c—Edward Fitzgerald	351 00
14	The Sheet Metal Machine Co—I C Johnson	1,101 26
14	The Sheet Metal Machine Co, of Newark, N J—the same	1,050 98
14	The Metal Seaming Co, of Baltimore City—Walton Ferguson	1,358 05
15	D F Foley & Co—G A Treadwell	3,505 61
15	J H Bonnell & Co (Lim)—Market and Fulton Nat Bank	679 43
15	the same—the same	495 60
15	The N Y Elevated Railroad Co / The Manhattan Railway Co } Mary T Corbitt, individ and admrx	642 33
15	Mark Mayer Mfg Co—John Baehr	151 00
15	The Hoboken Turtle Club—R R Brooks	74 81
15	The Maritime Register Publishing Co (Lim)—H W Jones	103 40
15	Holmes, Booth & Haydens—S H Willard	32,098 44
15	The Holmes & Wessell Metal Co—Holmes & Griggs Mfg Co ...costs	128 60
15	The Suburban Rapid Transit Co—Mary Murphy ...costs	126 99
15	The Mayor, Aldermen, &c—J C Schoonover	115 00
16	The Thomas Murray Co—P G Monroe	117 03
16	The Family Fund Society—People State N Y ...costs	50 00
16	The Metropolitan Elevated Railway Co / The Manhattan Railway Co } Lena Pappenheim	130 78
16	The N Y Elevated R R Co / The Manhattan Railway Co } Joseph Strouse	2,442 25
16	The Manhattan Railway Co / The Metropolitan Elevated Railway Co } John Slater	2,893 79
16	John Bonte, Sons & Co—Lily J Church, admr	464 47
16	D F Foley & Co—W M Hicks	761 60
16	Joseph B Tiffany & Co—C H Nicoll	221 18
16	J H Bonnell & Co (Lim)—Henry Lindenmeyer	559 50
12	Thompson, James—Sangetuck Iron Works Co	298 17
14	Thompson, Ambrose—J B Simpson ...costs	112 34
16	Taylor, Morris—E H Van Ingen	2,461 52
16*	Turner, William / Turner, William J } Henry McShane Co (Lim)	192 87
13	Urban, Conrad / Urban, Robert W } Anna M Eglinger	422 75
13	the same—the same	935 25
10	Valentine, Robert H C—Market and Fulton Nat Bank	469 42
10	the same—the same	451 23
15	Vix, Jacob / Vix, George } P J Dolan	661 98
13	Van Cleve, Garrett—John Theall	247 12
14	Van H t , Charles S—B G Oppenheimou en	120 62
16	Van Holland, John—William Spalding	924 58
16	Van Epps, Barney W—W E Edmonds	78 01
16	Van Zandt, Luke S—Martin Furlong ...costs	108 75
16	the same—the same	25 00
12	Wersebe, Diederich H—Broadway and Seventh Avenue R R Co ...costs	171 40
13	Woodbridge, Eunie C—M B Baer ...costs	69 47
13	Wigdor, Max—State Bank	123 56
13	Wolffe, Fred—S B Solomon	272 66
13	Weeks, George—Michael Rowen	39 75
13	Wells, James S—St Nicholas Bank	6,074 89
14	Walling, Edward P—L J Bovee	163 67
14	Wagner, Jacob—E A Crowninshield	30 44
14	Willershausen, George—G P Cron	82 68
14	Ward, Edwin C, guard ad litem—J B Simpson ...costs	112 34
15	Wyatt, Irving—William McIlroy	2,126 71
15	the same—the same	622 56
15	Webster, Thomas / Wyatt, Irving } William McIlroy	1,249 39
15	Wynkoop, Henry M—A L Root	293 74
16	Wenzel, Charles—V Loewer's Gambrinus Brewery Co	1,040 25
16	Wenzel, William—the same	1,040 25
16	Wilkes, George / Wilkes, Lizzie T } Abraham Steers	635 57
16	Whalen, Patrick—E F Anderson	227 37
16	Wells, William H—Bowery Bank	627 73
16	Wenige, Oscar—Pres't, &c, Manhattan Co	1,311 54
16	Yost, Abraham—L M Feel ...costs	126 76
10	Zweck, Sophie—J E Nichols	108 93

KINGS COUNTY.

Oct.		
19	Abbott, Warren G—J L Mott	$722 52
12	Armstrong, William A—G Everson, exr	566 75
12	Andress, Charles W—W Campbell	646 53
14	Allen, Samuel H—J W Buckley	189 17
9	Bevelacqua, Antonio—G Bevelacqua	202 60
9	Bailey, William T—R E Dietz Co	152 78
9	Blaney, Daniel F—J Boslet	50 64
10	Brossard, Otto / Brossard, Theodore } Thurber, Whyland & Co	56 71
12	Bell, George H—Twenty-third Ward Bank, New York	417 31
13	Bonnell, John H / Bonnell, Tammisin H } Nat Bank of the Republic, N Y	3,051 50
13	the same—the same	3,055 89
13	Bonnell, John H—the same	922 77
13	Bonnell, Tammisin H / Bonnell, John H } the same	8,101 39
13	Bailey, William T—C H Marsh	414 32
13	the same—J W Powell	370 53
14	Bright, Isaac O—J Engel	281 82
14*	Burcher, Walter V—J May	875 52
9	Coutant, Richard—A E Edwards & Co	517 31
10	Conklin, Ellen C L—E Boote	336 53
12	Cohen, Henry N—W A Sherman	417 90
13	Collins, Charles H—Central Gas and Electric Fixture Co	887 95
14	Curry, William—H Kahrs	143 58
14	De Shetley, William—Mary Leece	369 29
12	Ewing, Justus E—J R Conkey	6,039 43
12	Foerster, George A, otherwise Anton—New York & New Jersey Telephone Co	30 26
12	Findal, Martin—P Rost, Jr	114 58
13	Facie, Harper McD—National Bank of the Republic, N Y	3,051 50
13†	Fedden, "William"—J R Doscher	201 87
14	Fahlbusch, Charles—Claus Lipsius B Co	2,652 72
14	Forbes, Edwin—D D Forbes	98 72
10	Griffith, Charles E—J P Mones	193 37
12	Gumpert, Louis D—National Cash Register Co	293 29
14	Good, Samuel R—Central Gas and Electric Fixture Co	1,473 76
15	Grafendinkel, William, Sr—G H Alexander	27 50
15	Grafendinkel, William, Jr—G H Alexander	27 50
10	Hennessey, William J—Anna J Hagerty	474 10
12	Heaney, Frank—W Farrell	88 79
13	Harper, William D—National Bank of the Republic, N Y	3,051 50
13	Harper, William D / Harper, McD Tacie } the same	3,055 89
15	Hale, William S—F W Gilbert	430 93
15	Heffernan, Bernard—Norman & O'Brien	300 62
15	Hennessey, William—L Christenson	210 33
10	Iverson, Iven F—H P O'Farrell	33 10
14	Irwin, George—Claus Lipsius B Co	236 83
12	Kennell, Joseph A—Twenty-third Ward Bank, N Y	417 31
12	Klein, John—C Pape	128 95

14 Kornobis, Theodor—J Gesywienski... 218 49
12 Lord, Joseph B—J Machell........... 72 10
13*Lober, Albert—E L Snyder.......... 99 16
13 Lang, Louis—A Levy.............. 555 43
13 the same——J Levy............... 385 24
14 Larson, Orloff—India Wharf Brewing Co.............. 20 60
9 Mars, Henrietta A—J Raichle........ 164 87
9 Mead, Sarah F—D Miller.......... 124 87
9 Malone, Bernard J—Brooklyn Daily Eagle.............. 20 06
10 McKeown, John, dec'd, exr of—M McCambridge.............. 124 32
12 Mitchell, Charles R—W Campbell.... 646 53
12 Mezick, William B; Mezick, John B } E Jackson, recvr 105 61
12 Morro, August T—Hodgman Rubber Co.............. 304 41
13 Muller, Lewis M—A Lang........... 348 11
13 McCabe, Agnes A—2d Nat Bank N Y. 453 96
13 Muller, Lewis M—J H Swift......... 366 06
13 Mandeville, James—J Langell........ 115 16
13†Meyers, "Henry"—J R Doscher...... 201 87
15 Malone, Joseph; Malone, Margaret } L E Rosenham... 424 87
9 Neukirchen, John H—T New.......... 451 09
14 Nichols, Peter—H Breman........... 52 25
10 Officer, John, exr John McKeown—M McCambridge.............. 124 32
13 O'Keefe, John D—J W Stoltz........ 135 71
9 Pearlman, Morris—L Rothschild..... 199 81
10 Powers, Lawrence—J Wild.......... 100 70
13 Pengel, Henry S; Pengel, William C; Pengel, Elva } F G Mix.......... 492 80
14 Palmer, James L—J O Friel......... 510 79
14 Parnson, Samuel—H Kahrs.......... 143 58
15 Peck, Nellie E—J Macdonald........11,961 54
9 Quigley, James F—A Zimmerman... 45 50
9 Raymond Frank—E Hayward...... 87 95
10 Reim, Charles—Annie Carr, extrx... 131 34
13 Ray, William H—National Bank of the Republic, N Y.............. 922 77
14 Reynolds, William W—J May........ 875 52
14 Reichart, Jennie—T F Schumann.... 134 93
14 Ringe, Herman; Rathjen, Herman } H Eggers........ 25 75
15 Reiss, John A—D Reiss.............. 68 79
15 Ramm, August—P Weidmann.... .. 91 57
15 Rathje, John—L Christenson......... 210 33
8 Seidensticker, Henry—J McMahon... 53 10
9 Schlansky, Moses—S Dearing......... 124 29
9 Simpson, William B—H Hamilton... 35 75
12 Seaman, Charles H—Twenty-third Ward Bank, N Y.............. 417 31
13 Scott, Ellen E—C M Handover...... 148 90
13 Schlichting, George—J H Hoeft...... 92 65
13 Schaum, Louis—H W Cropsey....... 278 41
13 Schlim, William H—E L Snyder..... 99 16
14†Staebler, "John"—J P Nawarath & Co.............. 32 41
14 Stone, George W; Stone, Henrietta L } J P Teale...... 52 75
8 Tilman, John F—A Raeburn.......... 738 32
9 The Brooslyn Fastener Co—Hopedale Elastic Fabric Co.............. 282 58
9 Thebowles Engineering Co—O K Whitney.............. 172 86
9 Tobias, Louis S—Sarah Coben.......1,089 88
10 Taylor, J. Monroe—H Flynn......... 95 72
10 The exr, &c, John McKeown, dec'd; The Board of Home Missions of the United Presbyterian Church of North America, and The Board of Extensions of the United Presbyterian Church of North America } M McCambridge.. 124 32
13 The J H Bonnell & Co (Lim)—Nat Bank of the Republic, N Y.......... 964 80
13 the same——the same............3,055 89
13 the same——the same............3,051 50
13 the same——the same............ 922 77
13 the same——the same............8,101 39
13 Tormey, Thomas; Tormey, Michael } D M Koehler...... 136 37
13 The Excelsior Dynamite Co—Rosina Imperiale.............. 154 58
13 The Williamsburgh Gas Light Co—J J Hennessey..............2,202 97
13 Tyrrell, Martin B—J P Crawford.... 103 09
14 Trotter, David—A W Neumann...... 97 93
13 Teale, Robert E J C—Hodgman Rubber Co.............. 304 41
13 Valentine, Robert H C—National Bank of the Republic, N Y.......... 964 80
15 Van Wyck Philip V R—St Nicholas Bank, N Y.............. 135 06
9 Whiting, Walter B—L Baer.......... 189 33
12 Washington, Thomas M—National Cash Register Co.............. 298 22
13 Warshaur, Louis—D M Koehler.... 82 95
13 Wardrobe, Thomas—Henney Buggy Co.............. 349 42
13 the same——Emerson & Fisher Co.............. 287 40
14 Walling, Edward P—L J Bovee...... 162 67
15 Weber, Daniel—St Nicholas Bank, N Y.............. 135 06
14 Zang, Mathias—J Lucas............. 348 13

SATISFIED JUDGMENTS.

NEW YORK.

October 10 to 16—Inclusive.

‡Allan, John—G N Manchester. (1888)......$1,387 76
Alexander, Joseph—James Talcott. (1875)....1,095 72
Abbott, Adeline M—J I Tilton. (1889)...... 65 50
Ball, Edward—Jacob Loeb. (1878)..........1,881 62
*Belvin, Mary—Jacob Appel. (1891)......... 538 11
*Same——Aaron Kohn. (1891)...............4,617 99
Book, George W—J W Mack. (1891).......... 181 20
Bonner, Catharine—Charles Hauselt. (1889).. 79 55
Barker, William H—J C Shaw. (1887)....... 146 96
Same——Thomas Gill. (1886)............... 353 46
Cavinato, Luigi, Guisseppi, Natale and Steffano—Union Stove Works. (1891)......... 331 31
Claflin, John—Philander Derby. (1891)...... 73 60
Same——Andresen & Blatt Folding Bed Co. (1891).............. 73 60
Same——O O Clark. (1891).............. 73 60
Same——Martin Eckhardt. (1890)........... 99 89
*Coleman, Robert H—Beals' Railway Brake Co. (1891).............. 333 31
Chenowith, Henry—J S Simpson. (1890)...... 427 61
Campbell, John V—Henry McShane Co (Lim). (1891).............. 170 00
Day, George W—Jane McCulloch. (1890)..... 84 58
Eames, Edward E—Philander Derby. (1891).. 73 60
Same——Andresen & Blatt Folding Bed Co. (1891).............. 73 60
Same——O O Clark. (1891).............. 73 60
Same and Simon and Isaac Epstein—Martin Eckhardt. (1890).............. 99 89
Fairchild, Horace J; Force, Dexter N } Philander Derby. (1891) 73 60
Same——Andresen & Blatt Folding Bed Co. (1891).............. 73 60
Same——O O Clark (1891).............. 73 60
Same——Martin Eckhardt. (1890)........... 99 89
‡Fraser, Mary J—L N Levy. (1884)......... 447 05
Fleischer, Jacob A—Market and Fulton Nat Bank. (1891).............. 361 66
Same——same. (1891).............. 361 68
Gray, Laudon Carter—Louisa K Merril. (1880) 1,602 96
Graham, Emma—J S Simpson. (1890)......... 427 61
*Haan, Rudolph M—G L Hoffman. (1891)...... 872 38
Hopecraft, Alfred—American Artistic Gold Stamping Co. (1871).............. 671 75
Heller, Frederick—Prosper Monnet. (1888)..13,328 73
Same——same. (1889).............. 94 82
J Parker Reed Co—Samuel Lees. (1891)......2,036 21
Kirky, Martin—Herman Asher. (1885)........ 42 50
Latham, George—J M Leopold. (1891)........1,881 58
*Mutual Reserve Fund Life Assoc—J H Stuart. (1891)..............13,830 43
Mansmann, John—William Peters. (1891).... 961 59
Marks, Morris—German Exchange Bank. (1888)..............1,489 95
Same——same. (1889)..............5,662 89
Same——same. (1888)..............1,167 06
Mooney, Peter W—W P Baker. (1891)........ 40 24
Merz, Henry—Prosper Monnet. (1888)........13,328 73
Same——same. (1889).............. 94 82
McGowan, William H—W G Fox. (1891)...... 713 81
Patterson, Elizabeth—Charles Hauselt. (1889) 79 55
Petri, Conrad—People State N Y. (1884)....1,000 00
Same——same. (1884)..............1,000 00
Same——same. (1884)..............1,000 00
Robinson, Daniel—Martin Eckhardt. (1890).. 99 89
Same——O O Clark. (1891).............. 73 60
Same——Andresen & Blatt Folding Bed Co. (1891).............. 73 60
Same——Philander Derby. (1891)............ 73 60
Reynolds, Michael—E C Heerwagen. (1891).. 419 89
Runkle, Max—Market and Fulton Nat Bank. (1891).............. 361 66
Same——same. (1891).............. 361 68
Ross, George—Joseph Bierhoff. (1891)...... 147 50
†Smith, Robert J—Michael O'Brien. (1890)..2,472 29
†Same——same. (1891).............. 96 74
Slater, William S, Semour D and Howard P—Franklin Stetson. (1891).............. 543 67
*Schwarting, Charles W—R D Uffelman. (1891) 659 88
Stevenson, Preston, trustee Jane McDonald—Charles Hauselt. (1889).............. 79 55
Smith, Albert E and Elizabeth R—Joseph Bierhoff. (1891).............. 147 50
Spreng, Justus J, exr Catharine Lenihan—Mary F McGowan. (1891).............. 125 26
Schloss, Nathan J and Henry J—S A Ryan. (1891).............. 68 99
‖Simons, Joseph—Berthold Nathan. (1891)....1,199 16
Stonde, Herman—People State N Y. (1884)...1,000 00
Same——same. (1884)..............1,000 00
Same——same. (1884)..............1,000 00
Shannon, Michael—Samuel McMillan. (1891).. 87 50
Thomson, John—F S Selover. (1882)......... 92 22
Thompson, George K—C P H Gilbert. (1885).. 220 73
Todd, Rufus L, exr Mary L Todd—Union Dime Savings Inst. (1890).............. 509 89
Same——same. (1891).............. 102 09
Same——same. (1891).............. 88 92
Vail, Susan M and John R—J I Tilton. (1889) 65 50
White, John J—Boston Boot Co. (1891)....... 334 71
§Wendel, Louis—John Wasilensky. (1886).... 155 47
*Same—J W Hatch, assignee. (1891)......... 158 71
Warrin, Frank L—F A Lord. (1891).......... 371 12
Wood, Joseph L and Fernando, exrs Fernando Wood—J L R Wood. (1890)..............8,048 68
Williams, Mary—Sidney Genung. (1887)...... 221 34
Zweig, Herman—Benedict Grotta. (1883)....1,501 46
Same——Philip Goldman. (1878)..............1,112 12
Same——A A Strohn. (1885).............. 384 44
Same——E M Scheider (1880).............. 364 77
Same——Herman Harris. (1879).............. 89 80
Same——Frederick Giebel. (1880)........... 918 83

*Vacated by order of Court. †Suspended on Appeal. ‡Released. §Reversal. ‖Satisfied by Execution.

KINGS COUNTY.

October 9 to 15—Inclusive.

Abbott, Warren G—Susan T Williams. (1891). $75 08
Bailey, William T—C D Archer, exr. (1890)... 373 59
Campbell, William A—Margaret Hynes. ('91). 88 00
Kenney, Rosanna—Ellen Creamer. (1891).....2,169 46
McSwyny, Bryan G—H Brown. (1890)........2,016 24
Mutual Reserve Fund Life Assoc—J H Stuart. (1891). (Order of Court)..............18,330 43
Philips, Charles S; Philips, Julia E } C H Johnson, recvr. (1888)..............1,008 33
Rommel, John—C Frese. (1890).............. 407 19
Schall, Magdalena—E Lasche. (1890)......... 78 89
Skelly, Peter A—J R Anderson. (1887)........ 224 19
Same——Hannah M Bainbridge. (1887)..... 182 36
Same——H G Alford. (1887).............. 141 56
Same——G B Hurd & Co (1887).............. 135 94
Same——R Sneider. (1887).............. 43 95
Tarpey, Bernhard; Tarpey, Sarah A } H Luhrs. (1891)......... 185 39
Von Dreele, Philip H; Von Dreele, Annie M } H Von Dreele. (1891)..5,049 61

MECHANICS' LIENS.

NEW YORK CITY.

Oct.
10 Kingsbridge road, e s, 50 s Nindham pl, 40x95, William McMahon agt James Hodge, owner, and Elmer C. Schoonmaker, contractor.............. $100 00
10*One Hundred and First st, Nos. 75 and 77, n s, 100 e Columbus av, 50x100. Marcus Murray agt William M. Walsh, owner and contractor.............. 455 71
10 Forty-eighth st, No. 324, s s, 300 e 2d av, 25x100.5. David Miller agt Nathan Federgrun, owner, and Henry Holck, contractor.............. 125 00
10 Thirty-first st, No. 215, n s, 175 w 7th av, 25x98.9. John Sheridan agt Mary Wilson, owner and contractor..............4,000 00
12 Madison av, n w cor 31st st, 49.7x87.6x—x89. Valentine Moeslein agt Peter N. Ramsey, owner and contractor..............5,602 00
12 Amsterdam av, e s, extends from 194th to 195th st, 104x430 to Harlem River, x130x405. J. W. Taylor agt Charles C. Wendel, owner, and Henry Taylor, contractor.... 54 00
12 Seventy-ninth st, No. 448, s s, 65 w Av A, 19x75. J. H. Kilpatrick agt the heirs of John Muldoon and William H. Muldoon et al., owners, and William H. Muldoon, contractor.............. 238 50
12 Ninety-second st, No. 161, n s, 210 w 3d av, 15x100 8. N. Y. Architectural Terra Cotta Co. agt Leopold S. Friedberger, owner, and George Thompson, contractor........ 295 00
12 Lexington av, s e cor 87th st, 100.8x62.2. Pierce Butler and Pierce Mfg. Co. agt Cavinato Bros., owners and contractors..2,458 00
12 One Hundred and First st, Nos. 75 and 77, n s, 100 e Columbus av, 50x100.11. W. & J. Forbes agt William M. Walsh, owner and contractor.............. 700 00
13 Tenth av, No. 605, w s, 25 s 44th st, 25x100. H. A. Templer agt Louis Becker, owner, and William L. Hinrichs, contractor. (Continued from Oct. 14, 1890).............. 83 80
13 Boulevard, s w cor 85th st, 105x100. Ackert & Schroeder agt Homer J. Beaudet, owner and contractor..............1,948 60
13 Eleventh av, 13th av, 27th and 28th sts—the block. Horace Howser agt William W. Rossiter, owner, and Cofrode & Saylor, incorporated, contractors..............7,430 46
13 Third av, Nos. 1912 and 1914, w s, 100 n 105th st, 50x—. Cook & Radley agt Moses Sulzberger, owner, and George Thompson.............. 111 00
14 Eleventh st, Nos. 814 and 816, s s, 300 e 2d av, 46x100. W. R Bell agt John O'Connor, owner and contractor.............. 174 00
14 Madison av, s e cor 134th st, 100x100. N. Y. Anderson Pressed Brick Co. agt Thomas B. McCormick and Thomas Jetter, owner, and Thomas B. McCormick, contractor...2,242 57
14 One Hundred and Twenty-ninth st, No. 205, n s, 125 e 3d av, 25x75. J. A. Baines agt Henry De Forest, owner, and Boes Bros., contractors.............. 174 00
14 Sixty-fifth st, Nos. 29 and 31, s s, 200 w Central Park West, 50x100.5. J. F. Gibbons agt James O'Brien, owner, and George A. Hunter, contractor.............. 211 97
14 One Hundred and Sixty-first st, No. 622, s s, — e Courtlandt av, 25x100. Peyrons Bros. agt Christian Schaefer, owner and contractor.............. 175 00
14 One Hundred and Twenty-third st, Nos. 142-152 W., s s. Burtis Gliddon agt Elizabeth K. Smith, owner and contractor.......... 63 75
15 One Hundred and Sixteenth st, No. 112 W., s s. F. W. Geller agt Sterling E. Edmunds, DeWitt C. and Wells H. Bates, owners and contractors.............. 160
15 One Hundred and Sixteenth st, No. 104 W., s s. Same agt same.............. 171
15 Av C, e s, 72.9 n 5th st, 74.9x103. George Nolan agt Hebrew Congregation Menachen Zion, owner, and Louis Farber, contractor.............. 720
15 Norfolk st, Nos. 56 and 58, e s. G. H. Robbins & Co. agt David Abraham, debtor and owner.............. 107
16 Kingsbridge road, junction of Nathalie av, 85.5x92.5. Crockett & Weeks agt Perry P. Williams and T. Judson Kilpatrick, owners, and T. Judson Kilpatrick, contractor..............4,100
16 Bradhurst av, s e cor 143d st, 100x70. L. & J. Kelly agt Fernando Yost, owner and contractor.............. 904 94
16 Eighth av, s e cor 128th st, 49.11x100. Kirtland, Andrews & Co. (Lim.) agt Christian Andersen, owner and debtor. (Continued from Oct. 25, 1890).............. 750
16 Twenty-seventh st, Nos. 431-435, n s, 368 w 9th av, 82.11x98.9. Ackert Schroeder agt Homer J. Beaudet, owner and contractor..............1,185 06
16 Boston av, s e cor 164th st, 115x115x100x76.4. A. D. Knapp agt Georgiana F. Webster, owner and contractor.......... 942
16 Seventy-eighth st, s s, 100 w Amsterdam av, 75x—. J. F. McLaughlin agt Arthur Boehmer, owner, and Anthony M. Clegg and John Doe, contractors.............. 29 1
16 Eighty-second st, Nos. 157-167, n w s, 200 n e 10th av, 150x105. Emilio Vigno and Rudolph Orrigoni agt Andrew J. Kirwin, owner, and John Askey, contractor....... 188
16 Seventy-eighth st, s s, 100 w Amsterdam av, 75x102.2. Thomas Cilligan agt Clegg & Co., debtors, and Arthur Boehmer, contractor.............. 47 70
16 Ninety-fourth st, n s, 150 w Columbus av, 103.6x100. J. F. McLaughlin agt same debtors and James B. Brady, owner...... 30 00
16 One Hundred and Sixth st, No. 69, n s, 75 e Columbus av, 25x—; One Hundred and Seventh st, No. 70, s s, 75 e Columbus av, 25x— } A. E. Hemmel agt Wm. Cohn et al., owners, and Wm. Cohn, contractor..... 35 00

*Editor Record and Guide:

I beg to call attention to the injustice of Marcus Murray's lien. The entire amount of his contract with me is $2,400, $1,950 of which I paid in cash and the balance a note for $450—which matures on the 9th day of November next. I also obtained for him in the meantime, on his promissory note and for his accommodation, a discount of $300, which I have since been obliged to pay, he having allowed it to be protested. This note is dated August 4th and payable at the Twelfth Ward Bank, this city, October 7th, 1891; besides, Mr. Murray's work is not finished.

Wm. M. Walsh.

KINGS COUNTY.

Oct.

9 Second st, Nos. 466-474, s s, 800 e 6th av, 100x100. David D. Forbes agt Julia A. Skidmore, owner, and Joel E. Skidmore, contractor $50 00

9 Christopher st, e s, 200 n Belmont av, 25x100. Dugan Mfg Co. agt Joseph Berger, Samuel Meschel and Anne Levy, owners and contractors 350 00

9 Bainbridge st, n s, 115.3 e Saratoga av, 188x100. Rudolph Reimer & Co. agt J. Mason Kirby, owner and contractor 440 00

9 Livonia av, s e cor Osborn st, 25x100. Post Bros. agt Abraham Seidenberg and Rochmiel Abramovitz and George Seidenberg, owners and contractors 146 53

9 Atlantic av, n w cor Williams pl, 60x100. Charles Swanson agt Herbert Smith, owner, and John King, contractor 30 00

10 Myrtle av, No. 1309. Henry Israel agt Max Hallheimer, owner and contractor 28 00

10 Saratoga av, s e cor Decatur st, 100x115. Charles Rieger agt William H. Good, owner and contractor 175 00

12 Flushing av, n e cor Vandervoort av, 25x100. George D. Koch agt Mrs. Johnson, owner, and Peter Johnson, contractor 355 00

12 Knickerbocker av, n w cor Moffat st, 100x120. Jeremiah Hackett agt Isabelle Petit, owner, and A. B. Petit, contractor 1,000 00

12 Saratoga av, s e cor Decatur st, 100x1,115, Same agt William H. Good, owner, and Samuel R. Good, contractor 700 00

12 Howard av, e s, 98 s Herkimer st, 69x98. Patrick C. Finn agt Eliza Reed, owner, and Ernest D. Taiber, contractor 75 00

12 Decatur st, n s, 100 e Howard av, 250x100. Louis Bossert agt J. Mason Kerby, owner and contractor 125 84

12 Pulaski st, n s, 100 w Sumner av, 150x100. J. Q. Maynard agt E. Roberts, contractor 240 00

13 Fourth av, w s, 54 s President st, 20x45. James Walsh agt Domencio and Francesco Furo, owners and contractors 192 50

13 Fort Hamilton av, n e cor 59th st, one house. McNulty Bros. agt Ole Gunston, owner, and Trustees District School No. 2, New Utrecht, contractors 105 00

13 Saratoga av, s e cor Decatur st, 100x115.6. Jacob Guthy agt William H. Good, owner and contractor 168 42

13 De Kalb av, s s, 150 e Marcy av, 100x100. Charles E. Ring agt Elizabeth A. Maitland, owner, and Charles H. Collins, contractor 322 00

13 De Kalb av, s s, 150 w Marcy av, 100x100. Nils Olsen agt Elizabeth S. Maitland, owner, and Charles H. Collins, contractor. 210 00

14 Same property. Jacob May agt same owner and contractor 111 60

14 Same property. William H. H. Young agt same owner and contractor 38 00

12 Arlington av, s w cor Dresden st, runs west 108.7 x south — to Fulton av, x east — to Dresden st, x north —. John R. Hughes agt —— Hallahan, owner, and John H. Jennings, contractor. (Redocket) 121 19

14 State st, s s, 100 e Henry st, 30x100. Hans S. Christian agt John F. Robertson and Charles M. Collins, owners and contractors 481 54

15 De Kalb av, s s, 600 e Nostrand av, 100x100. J. M. Pilcher & Co. agt Elizabeth L. Maitland, owner, and Charles H. Collins, contractor 100 40

15 Arlington av, s s, 30 e Hendrix st, 30x100. William J. Ray agt Isidore Warren, owner, and A. J. Warren, contractor 73 26

15 Arlington av, s e cor Hendrix st, 30x100. Same agt same 121 66

15 Watkins st, e s, 175 n Blake av, 25x100. Louis Ratner agt Dora Danancher, owner and contractor 1,300 00

SATISFIED MECHANICS' LIENS

NEW YORK CITY.

Oct.

12 Eighty-fifth st, Nos. 73-77 E., 65x—. Jesse Reynolds agt Martin J. Hackett. (Lien filed June 4, 1891) $600 00

12 Forty-second st, No. 559 W. Martha Williams agt Mary A. Barrow. (July 6, 1891) 1,036 00

13* Thirty-first st, Nos. 341-345 W., 78.4x—. Patrick Maher agt St. Francis Assisi Church and Henry H. Amberg. (Oct. 9, 1891) 350 00

13* Forty-third st, No. 321 W., 25x—. N. Y. Architectural Terra Cotta Co agt Richard J. Keeffe and Thomas Farrell. (Aug. 25, 1891) 1,340 00

14 Greene st, Nos. 192½-200, e s, 200 s 3d st. H. J. Barron agt Meyer Guggenheim and Jonas Sonneborn. (May 2, 1891) 3,240 14

14‡ One Hundred and Eighteenth st, s s, 240 w 4th av, 100x—. Burrows & Smith agt Samuel Harris, Herman and Mary Masche and Bernhard Ginsburg. (Aug. 25, 1891) .. 250 00

14 Thirty-ninth st, Nos. 266 and 268 W., 60.6x100. McCreery & Prendergast agt James Devlin. (May 18, 1891) 270 00

14 Same property. N. Y. Gas Fixture Co. agt same. (May 11, 1891) 351 35

14 Same property. Brooklyn Slate Mantel Co. agt same. (April 24, 1891) 495 00

14 Same property. Henry Bayer agt same. (April 7, 1891) 199 00

14 Same property. Peter Kearney agt same. (April 1, 1891) 49 00

14 Same property. Manchester & Philbrick agt same. (Mar. 24, 1891) 1,883 72

14 Same property. L. E. Mansfield agt same. (Mar. 25, 1891) 90 00

14 Same property. G. B. Robbins & Co. agt same. (Mar. 27, 1891) 109 88

15 Seventy-fourth st, n s, 400 w 9th av, 150x102. Robert Stewart agt Matthew Clark and John Coar. (Jan. 12, 1891) 504 00

15* Seventy-seventh st, s s, 201 e 10th av, 115x—. Hugo Kampff agt —— Kennedy & Edwin Shuttleworth. (Oct. 14, 1891) 150 00

16 One Hundred and Forty-first st, n s, 300 e Boulevard, 50x100. J. and W. C. Spears agt Carns & Hewlett. (July 29, 1891.) 3,048 00

16‡ Chambers st, No. 129, n e cor West Broadway, 100x76.1. P. G. Lough agt Charles F. Wildey and Central Complete Combustion Co. (Aug. 25, 1891) 464 62

16* One Hundred and Fourth st, s s, 175 w 8th av, 25x—. Phillip & Charles Bierschank agt Robertson & Gammie. (Aug. 13, 1891) 285 00

*Discharged by depositing amount of lien and interest with County Clerk.
‡Discharged by order of Court on filing bond.

KINGS COUNTY.

Oct.

9 Bergen st, s s, 290 e Brooklyn av, 100x100. The Curry Mfg. Co. agt Joseph M. Pilcher, owner, and Theodore Dingledein and J. M. Pilcher & Co., contractors. (Sept. 19, 1891.) (Order of Court) $880 00

9 Willow st, Nos. 147 and 149, e s, 218.11 n Pierrepont st, 42x101.3. Charles H. Collins agt David Kearr. (Lien filed Feb. 5, 1891) 378 00

12 Garfield pl, n s, 90 w 7th av, 150x100. Richard K. Cooke agt Edward L. Beekman and John H. Styles, owners, and John Elder, Jr., contractor. (Sept. 19, 1891) 3,985 00

12 Bergen st, No. 267, n s, 225 e Nevins st, 25x100. L. Anderson & Bro. agt David Schwartz, owner and contractor. (July 10, 1891) 155 00

12 Watkins st, e s, 175 n Blake av, 25x100. Charles Tirelli agt Eliza Dannegar, owner, and John King, contractor. (April 16, 1891) 92 68

14 Thatford av, e s, 100 s Glenmore av, 50x100. Michael Mayer agt Moses Handler and Samuel Balsam, owners and contractors. (Sept. 14, 1891) 600 00

14 Schermerhorn st, 3d av and Flatbush av—triangular block. Charles S. Buell agt George H. Rice, owner, and J. F. Richartz & Bro., contractors. (Sept. 10, 1891). 180 35

14 Ocean Parkway, w s, 150 s Av E, 50x100, Parkville. John Williams agt Mrs. Fannie Leslie, owner, and Richartz Bros., contractors. (July 23, 1891) 330 00

14 Thatford av, e s, 100 s Glenmore av, 50x100. Potts Bros. agt Morris Handler and —— Balsom, owners, and Patrick Creegan, contractor. (Sept. 18, 1891) 323 37

14 Same property. The Wyandance Brick and Terra Cotta Co. agt same owners and contractor. (Sept. 18, 1891) 161 93

BUILDINGS PROJECTED.

NEW YORK CITY.

SOUTH OF 14TH STREET.

Cortlandt st, Nos. 39 and 41, twelve-story brk and stone building, 51.6x117, asphalt roof; cost, $200,000; M. Taylor, 34 Gramercy Park; ar't, O. Wirz; b'r, J. G. Wallace. Plan 1336.

Crosby st, No. 49, six-story brk warehouse, 25x92, tin roof; cost, $30,000; D. P. Chesebro, Southern Boulevard, near 167th st; ar't, O. Wirz; b'r, H. McNally. Plan 1335.

Orchard st, No. 35, five-story and basement brk building, 25.4x63 and 44.6, tin roof; cost, $16,000; L. Goodman, 217 Henry st; ar't, F. Ebeling. Plan 1333.

Suffolk st, No. 76, five-story brk flat, 25x88.8, tin roof; cost, $18,000; A. Ruff, 78 East 4th st; ar'ts, Kurtzer & Rohl. Plan 1337.

BETWEEN 14TH AND 59TH STREETS.

21st st West, foot of, on pier, one-story iron and terra cotta freight shed, 58x525, tin roof; cost, $55,000; agent, R. Baldwin, 8 West 32d st; ar't, R. P. Staats. Plan 1314.

50th st, Nos. 138 and 140 E., one-story and basement stone church, 40x94, tin roof; cost, $20,000; D. Metzger, president, 1044 2d avenue; ar't, L. F. Heinecke. Plan 1311.

57th st, Nos. 211-215 W., four-story and basement stone building, 75x143, with extension, asphalt and tile roof; cost, $150,000; American Fine Arts Society, 47 West 42d st; ar'ts, H. J. Hardenbergh, W. C. Hunting and J. C. Jacobsen; contractor, C. F. Wills. Plan 1309.

7th av, No. 281, five-story brown stone and terra cotta flat, 20.9x65 and 70, tin roof; cost, $20,000; P. Hynes, 108 West 26th st; ar't, H. A. Reeves. Plan 1330.

BETWEEN 59TH AND 125TH STREETS, EAST OF 5TH AVENUE.

100th st, n s, 100 w 2d av, two-story brk shop, 10x90, gravel roof; cost, $1,800; T. J. Oates, 224 East 104th st; ar't, M. L. Ungrich; b'r, T. Quinn. Plan 1331.

103d st, s s, 101.6 e Lexington av, four five-story stone flats, 27x75, tin roofs; cost, $16,000 each; ow'r and b'r, F. Braender, 503 East 83d st; ar't, F. Wennemer. Plan 1322.

120th st, n s, 34.3 w Sylvan pl, two-story brk building, 60.9x25.2, tin roof; cost, $7,000; lessees, Lambert & Farrell, 94 East 114th st; ar't, J. C. Burns. Plan 1321.

Lexington av, n w cor 110th st, one-story brk building, 25x54.11, tin roof; cost, $3,000; lessee, W. Lyman, 51 East 122d st; ar't, J. Hauser, Plan 1332.

BETWEEN 59TH AND 125TH STREETS, WEST OF CENTRAL PARK WEST AND 8TH AVENUE.

125th st, s s, 75 w 8th av, three five-story brk and stone flats, 25x87.6, tin roofs; cost, $24,000 each; lessee, J. Lawlor, Hotel Hamilton, 8th av and 125th st; ar't, R. R. Davis. Plan 1317.

Columbus av, s w cor 75th st, seven-story brk and stone flat, 123.8x100, tin or cement roof; cost, $200,000; S. Banner, 68 West 55th st; ar't, G. A. Schellenger; m'n, J. H. Parker. Plan 1312.

Columbus av, n e cor 92d st, five-story brk and stone flat, 40x96.8, tin roof; cost, $60,000; C. Gabren, 71 West 92d st; ar'ts, Thom & Wilson. Plan 1323.

92d st, n s, 40 e Columbus av, five-story brk and stone flat, 20x90.8, tin roof; cost, $25,000; ow'r and ar't, same as last. Plan 1324.

92d st, n s, 60 e Columbus av, five-story brk and stone flat, 40x90.8, tin roof; cost, $50,000; ow'r and ar't, same as last. Plan 1325.

West End av, s e cor 77th st, seven three-story stone dwell'gs, irreg. in size, tin roof; total cost, $118,000; F. M. Jencks, 8 East 45th st; ar't, C. True. Plan 1320.

NORTH OF 125TH STREET.

143d st, n s, 150 w 8th av, two five-story brk and stone flats, 25x72, tin roofs; cost, $20,000 each; E. J. Kelly, 69 East 100th st; ar't, G. A. Schellenger. Plan 1318.

23D AND 24TH WARDS.

Potter pl, n s, 614 e Anthony av, one-story frame stable, 14x15, gravel roof; cost, $65; J. Defino, Bedford Park; ar't, F. D. Miller. Plan 1310.

Brook av, e s, 75 n 148th st, one-story frame shop, 25x35, tin roof; cost, $500; Mary M. Brierly, 777 East 148th st; ar't, M. J. Garvin. Plan 1316.

Decatur av, w s, 150 n Mosholu Parkway, two-story and attic frame dwell'g, 33x51, shingle roof; cost, $3,000; T. Conlon, 309 East 37th st; ar't, H. S. Baker. Plan 1315.

Kingsbridge road, s s, 100 e Ridge st, rear, two-story frame stable, 12x15, shingle roof; cost, $200; W. Delamater on premises. Plan 1326.

184th st, n s, 225 e Lincoln av, two five-story brk flats, 25x69, with extension, tin roofs; cost, $12,000 each; B. Fien, 142 Lincoln av; ar't, F. S. Barus. Plan 1319.

Anthony av, e s, 144 s Burnside av, two-story frame dwell'g, 21x35, tin roof; cost, $2,500; agent, C. H. McTerney, 139th st and Locust av. Plan 1318.

Grant av, e s, 192.8 n 164th st, two-story and attic frame dwell'g, 20x40, tin roof; cost, $3,400; E. Biele, College av, s e cor 164th st; ar't, F. J. Miller. Plan 1328.

St. Anns av, n w cor 160th st, one-story frame church, 42x68, shingle roof; cost, $5,000; Rev. T. Gregg, pastor, Franklin av, n e cor 170th st; ar't, J. McIntyre; b'r, J. Murtha. Plan 1327.

Vanderbilt av, e s, 238 s 169th st, two two-story and basement frame dwell'gs, 14x51, tin roofs; cost, $3,000 each; K. Hartmann, on premises; ar't, F. J. Miller. Plan 1329.

Vanderbilt av, e s, 400 s 171st st, rear, two-story frame stable, 24x18, tin roof; cost, $400; R. F. Otto, 172 East 91st st; ar't, C. C. Churchill. Plan 1334.

KINGS COUNTY.

Plan 1868—Dikeman st, s s, 100 w Conover st, two four-story brk tenem'ts, 25x60, tin roofs, iron cornices; total cost, $17,000; Claus Hohorst, Myrtle av, cor Pearl st; ar't, M. J. Morrill; c'rs, Long & Barnes.

1869—Chestnut st, w s, 125 n Ridgewood av, one two-story and attic frame (brk filled) dwell'g, 16 and 20x32, and extension, 13x14, shingle roof; cost, $2,300; George Beach.

1870—Himrod st, s s, 201 e Evergreen av, three three-story frame (brk filled) tenem'ts, 26.5x60, tin roofs; cost, each, $4,800; ow'rs and b'rs, A. Dillman & Co., 72 Hamburg av; ar't, Th. Engelhardt.

1871—Snediker av, e s, 275 s New Lots road, one one-story frame carriage house, 16x20, shingle roof; cost, $150; Annie Linfelder, New Lots road.

1872—Starr st, No. 106, n w s, near Knickerbocker av, one four-story frame (brk filled) store and tenem't, 25x52, tin roof; cost, $8,500; Henry Mehrhoff, on premises; ar't, H. E. Funk.

1873—Rockaway av, e s, 200 n Livonia av, one two-story frame carpenter shop, 20x30, tin roof; cost, $400; J. C. Fletcher.

1874—Powell st, w s, 150 s Glenmore av, one two-story frame tenem't, 25x52, tin roof; cost, $2,500; Lucinda H. Jones, Powell st, near Glenmore av; ar't, C. M. Thompson; b'r, T. Jones.

1875—Stockholm st, n e cor Knickerbocker av, two three-story frame (brk filled) stores and tenem'ts, 25x60, tin roofs; total cost, $12,000; A. Fleischmann, 149 Bushwick av; ar't, H. E. Funk.

1876—5th st, n s, 77 w 6th av, one three-story brk and brown stone apartment house, 18.9x55, tin roof, wooden cornice; cost, $5,000; ow'r and b'r, Louis Bonnert, 528 10th st; ar't, W. M. Coots.

1877—South 1st st, n s, 65 e Hooper st, one two-story brk bottling factory, 31.6 and 60x40, tin roof, brk cornice; cost, $2,000; Henry Segelke, 391 South 1st st; ar't, H. W. Billard; b'r, not selected.

1878—Varet st, s s, 50 w Ewen st, one one-story brk store, 50x71.4, tin roof, iron cornice; cost, $8,000; Charles Gomers' Sons, on premises; ar't, Th. Engelhardt; m'ns, Doenecke & Bros; c'r, not selected.

1879—4th av, n e cor 47th st, two three-story brk stores and dwell'gs and tenem'ts, 20x55 and 50, tin roofs, wooden cornices; total cost, $14,000; James G. Carroll, 45th st, near 3d av; ar'ts, H. L. Spicer & Son.

1880—Myrtle av, s s, 117.4 w Suydam st, one four-story frame (brk filled) store and tenem't, 25x58, tin roof; cost, $5,500; ow'r and b'r, Chas. A. Wagner, 24 Belvidere st; ar't, Th. Engelhardt.

1881—Myrtle av, s s, 147.2 w Suydam st, three one-story frame dwell'gs and stores, 31.9 and 14 and 25x48 and 17.2x25, tin roofs; total cost, $2,000; ow'r and b'r, Chas. A. Wagner, 24 Belvidere st; ar't, Th. Engelhardt.

1882—Ralph av, w s, 100 n Park pl, one one-story frame dwell'g, 20x30, tin roof; cost, $300; Joseph Keever, cor Ralph av and Park pl; ar't, Patrick Fanning; m'n, Thomas Fanning.

1883—Linwood st, w s, 165 n Wortman av, one two-story frame dwell'g, peak roof; cost, $1,200;

Chas. H. Dahl, Linwood st; c'r, D. A. Smith: m'n, W. Barnes; ar't, D. A. Smith.

1884—Stone av, e s, 125 s Sutter av, one three-story frame store and dwell'g, 20x40, tin roof; cost, $4,500; ow'r and b'r, J. Axelrod, Thatford av.

1885—Ralph av, s w cor Bergen st, one one-story frame wagon shed, 13x14, felt roof; cost, $30; ow'r and b'r, C. Schilds, on premises.

1886—Eastern Parkway, n s, 75 e Bchenek av, one one-story frame store and stable, 25x49, wood and tin roof; cost, $400; A. Kruger, 528 Eastern Parkway; ar't, G. Schwarz.

1887—Halsey st, s s, 160 e Evergreen av, and Eldert st, n s, 200 e Evergreen av, six two-story and basement frame dwell'gs, each 20x45, tin roofs; cost, each, $2,500; ow'r and b'r, C. Gastmeyer, cor Evergreen av and Eldert st.

1888—Bushwick av, No. 15, one two-story frame stable, 16.9x26, tin and gravel roof; cost, $300; V. J. Kleine. 15 Bushwick av; ar't and c'r, E. A. Schoettel: m'ns, Ermak & Veit.

1889—Wyona st, e s, 100 s Atlantic av, one one-story frame carriage house, 25x16, tin roof; cost, $150; Phillip Gardins, cor Atlantic av and Wyona st; c'r, William Max.

1890—South 9th st, s w cor Driggs st, one four-story brk flat, 24x60, tin roof and iron cornice; cost, $14,000; Wm. Dick, on premises; ar't, W. H. Gaylor; b'rs, M. Smith and S. L. Hough.

1891—Bushwick av, No. 303, one five-story brk tailor shop, 28.5x50, tin roof, brk cornice; cost, $15,000; S. Friedmann, 303 Bushwick av; ar't, H. E. Funk.

1892—Van Buren st, s s, 270 e Lewis av, two two-story and basement brown and red stone dwell'gs, 18.6x45, tin roofs and wooden cornices; cost, $4,500 each; T. B. Bryant, 372 Lewis av; ar'ts, I. D. Reynolds & Son.

1893—6th av, s w cor 4th st, five four-story brown stone apartment houses, 19.10x55 and 20.8 x60, tin roofs and wooden cornices; cost, $35,000; ow'r and b'r, L. Bonnert, 528 10th st; ar't, W. M. Coots.

1894—Driggs st, s w s, 75 s e South 9th st, one three-story brk flat, 25x46.6, tin roof, iron cornice; cost, $9,000; Wm. Dick, South 9th st, cor Driggs st; ar't, W. H. Gaylor; b'rs, M. Smith and S. L. Hough.

1895—Himrod st, n s, 250 e Evergreen av, two three-story brk tenem'ts, 25x62, tin roofs, iron cornices; cost, $6,000 each; ow'r, ar't and b'r, Ernst Loerch, 61 Himrod st.

1896—Dean st, n s, 550 w Franklin av, one two-story brk blacksmith shop, 25x95, gravel roof, iron cornice; cost, $5,000; Chas. Bartsch, 655 Clason av; ar't, Th. Engelhardt; b'r, not selected.

1897—Van Buren st, s s, 252 e Lewis av, one two-story and basement brk and red stone dwell'g, 18.6x42; cost, $4,500: T. B. Bryant, 272 Lewis av; ar'ts, I. D. Reynolds & Son.

1898—Knickerbocker av, n w cor Himrod st, one two-story frame stable, 25x18, tin roof; cost, $300; George Gutting, 1331 Greene av; ar't, F. J. Lessing.

1899—Frost st, n s, 150 w Leonard st, one one-story brk brass warehouse, 75x25, gravel roof, wooden cornice; cost, $1,000; Martin Reynolds, 70–82 Richardson st; ar't, H. Vollweiler; b'r, J. Schoch.

1900—Berry st. Nos. 341–345, rear of, one two-story brick stable, &c., 44x43, tin roof, iron cornice; cost, $10,000; City of Brooklyn; ar'ts, Thayer & Wallace; b'rs, T. Nolan and M. C. Rush.

1901—Berry st, Nos. 341–345, one one and two-story brk and stone building for repair shop, &c., of Water Purveyor's Bureau, 47.3 and 34x161, tin roof, iron cornice; cost, $36,500; ow'rs, ar'ts and b'rs, same as last.

1902—Jefferson st, s s, 150 e Knickerbocker av, one three-story frame (brk filled) tenem't, 25x57; cost, $4,000; ow'r and b'r, Chas. Hermann; ar't, H. Vollweiler.

1903—Elton st, No. 37, one one-story frame tailor shop, 14x26, tin roof; cost, $100; Mary Morgan, on premises.

1904—Willoughby av, s s, 376.10 w Wyckoff av, one two-story frame (brk filled) dwell'g, 25x30, tin roof; cost, $2,000; J. Brodsky, 32 Stagg st; c'r, Mr. Boesh.

1905—Evergreen av, e s, 25 s Halsey st, eight three-story frame tenem'ts, 19.4x55, tin roofs; cost, each, $4,000; C. F. Gastmeyer, Evergreen av, cor Eldert av.

1906—Atlantic av, s s, 50 w Pennsylvania av. two three-story brk stores and flats, 25.9 and 24.9 and 24.6 and 25.6x68.2 and 65.2 and 62.2, water-closet extension, 4x8.4, tin roofs, wooden cornices; cost, total, $15,000; M. J. Gibbons, Pennsylvania and Atlantic avs; ar't, J. W. Bailey; b'rs, D. Cook and H. Reis.

1907—Jay st, n s, 25 s Plymouth st, one one-story brk shed, 25x90, gravel roof, iron cornice; cost, $800; J. W. Masury & Son; b'rs, G. H. Stone & Son.

1908—Stockholm st, s s, 150 e Central av, one one-story brk blacksmith shop, 24x48, tin roof, brk cornice; cost, $1,500; Christ Frische, 209 Central av; ar't, F. J. Lessing.

1909—Liberty av, s s, 50 e Crescent st, one two-story frame store and dwell'g, 20x30, tin roof; cost, $1,000; William Stemler, 2153 Bergen st; ar't, C. Infanger.

1910—Quay st, n s, 75 e West st, one one-story frame shed, 12x18, felt roof; cost, $50; ow'r, ar't and b'r, William Kay, Greenpoint.

1911—Seigel st, No. 34, one three-story frame storehouse, 25x30, tin roof; cost, $2,500; Jacob Schwartz, on premises; ar't, H. Smith.

1912—Lorimer st, No. 41, one four-story frame (brk filled) store and tenem't, 25x65, tin roof; cost, $6,500; David Stern, 36 Seigel st; ar't, H. Smith; b'r, not selected.

1913—Scholes st, No. 106, s s, 100 w Ewen st, one four-story frame (brk filled) tenem't, 25x67, tin roof; cost, $6,000; Charles K. Hoerning, on premises; ar't, F. J. Berlenbach, Jr.; b'r, not selected.

1914—Scholes st, No. 104, s s, 125 w Ewen st, one four-story frame (brk filled) tenem't, 25x67, tin roof; cost, $6,000; J. Stadtmueller, 149 Ewen st; ar't, F. J. Berlenbach, Jr.; b'r, not selected.

1915—Bleecker st, s s, 425 e Evergreen av, one four-story frame (brk filled) store and tenem't, 25 x57, tin roof; cost, $4,500; Paul H. Gottschald, 68 Graham av; ar't, F. J. Berlenbach, Jr., b'r, not selected.

ALTERATIONS NEW YORK CITY.

Plan 1785—1st av, s w cor 74th st, interior alterations, new front; cost, $300; Sarah Harris, 102 East 78th st; ar't, W. Graul.

1786—West 4th st, n w cor 10th st, raised two stories, five-story extension, 29.6x42.10, interior alterations, floors raised, walls altered; cost, $30,000; W. H. Cooper, 52 Catharine st; ar't, T. S. Godwin.

1787—181st st, s s, 150 e Ryer av, two-story extension, 13x15; cost, $500; Mrs. C. Carr, Fordham; b'rs, Tolin & Son.

1788—Broadway, n w cor 41st st, walls altered, entire first story and basement rebuilt, interior alterations for hotel purposes; cost, $20,000; M. L. Sire, 61 West 51st st; ar'ts, Radley & Greenough.

1789—77th st, Nos. 332 and 334 E., repair damage by fire; cost, $2,249; W. H. Burroughs, Hotel St. George, Clark st, Brooklyn; b'r, L. C. Webster.

1790—170th st, No. 756 E., lowered to grade; cost, $600; Matilda B. Carter, on premises.

1791—149th st, No 545 E., one-story extension, 16x9; cost, $1,100 (?); R. Fiorella. on premises; c'r, A. J. Tepp.

1792—Pearl st, No. 308, walls altered; cost, $200; W. G. Hoople, 82 Gold st; b'r, J. G. Porter, agent.

1793—54th st, Nos. 207–209 E., interior alterations and walls altered; cost, $4,500; H. M. Haar, 450 West 152d st; ar't, C. Rentz.

1794—13th st, Nos. 100 and 102 W., roof raised and altered, one-story extension, 15x25, interior alterations, walls altered and new front; cost, $6,000; lessee, F. D. Fricke, 341 West 134th st; ar'ts, Kurtzer & Rohl.

1795—Elizabeth st, Nos. 204 and 206, walls altered; cost, $100; agent, H. A. Ackershausen, 65 Madison av, Jersey City; m'ns, Burton & Nichol.

1796—Av D, No. 158, interior alterations and new front: cost, $3,000; R. Maggs, 172 1st st; ar't, F. Ebeling.

1797—8th av, s w cor 125th st, party wall raised one story, five-story extension, 25x57.6, and interior alterations; cost, $28,000; lessee, J. Lawlor, Hotel Hamilton, 8th av and 125th st; ar't, R. R. Davis.

1798—Washington av, s e cor 163d st, raised to grade; cost, $1,000; F. Cordes, 930 Washington av; ar't, M. J. Garvin.

1799—Courtlandt av, w s, 75 s 153d st, one-story extension, 16x14; cost, $350; G. Gebe, 649 Courtlandt av; ar't, E. Stichler.

1800—8th av, Nos. 144 and 144½, new store front; cost, $600; Knickerbocker Brewing Co., 149 East 114th st; c'r, P. A. Ash.

1801—Forest av, No. 890, roof altered: cost, $150; Ann Tyrrell, on premises; c'r, J. Anderson.

1802—Washington, West, Hubert and Laight sts, three-story extension, 110.1x31, tin roof over driveway and coal shed, walls relined; cost, $10,000; P. N. Spofford, exr., Elmwood, Hunters Point, N. Y.; ar't, B. W. Berger.

1803—78th st, No. 304 E., interior alterations; cost, $700; A. Davey, 1522 1st av; c'r, J. A. O'Connor.

1804—1st av, No. 2012, repair damage by fire; cost, $5,500; Catherine Reilly, 305 East 79th st; ar't, J. E. Terhune.

1805—Grand st, No. 57, interior alterations and walls altered; cost, $1,200; W. Haas, on premises; b'r, D. Tyrrel.

1806—11th av, No. 163, interior alterations and walls altered; cost, $1,600; H. Heins. 300 East 86th st; ar't, H. Horenburger.

1807—Pitt st, No. 51, two-story and basement extension, 28x27; cost, $6,000; F. Weintraub, 140 Rivington st; ar't, H. Horenburger.

1808—Elm st, No. 191 and Marion st, No. 8, interior alterations and walls altered; cost, $500; lessee, C. H. Weissert, on premises; ar't, L. F. Heinecke.

1809—9th st, Nos. 103–107 E., rear, three-story extension, 45x23.4; cost, $5,000; B. Fitch, Norton, Conn.; ar't, B. W. Berger.

1810—56th st, No. 83 E., walls altered; cost, $175; F. M. Weiler, 550 Park av; ar't, J. Munckwitz.

1811—Cauldwell av, n w cor 161st st, four-story extension, 19x38; cost, $3,000; P. Luther, on premises: ar't, G. Keister.

1812—46th st, Nos. 339 and 341 E., two extensions, one and one-and-a-half stories high, 20x53 and 30 each; cost, abt $5,000; E. Keil, on premises; ar't, J. Hauser.

1813—Bond st, No. 91, interior alterations; cost, $300; H. Gomez et al.; 152 West 123d st; b'r, E. Smith.

1814—Av A, s e cor 92d st, one-story extension, 45x68; cost, $3,000; A. M. Jarvis, supterintendent for lessees, 685 Leonard st, Brooklyn.

1815—Main st, No. 1777, two-and-a-half-story extension; 22.8x14; cost, abt $400; Martha A. Bolton, on premises; ar't, C. S. Clark.

1816—162d st, n s, 285 w Elton av, raised 5 ft. to grade and moved to new foundation; cost, $1,800; H. Wilson, 123 West 48th st; c'r, B. F. Frisbie.

1817—Sedgwick av, No. 1745, wall and chimney altered; cost, $50; Jennie E. Wiley, 1741 Sedgwick av; ar't, J. J. Vreeland; m'ns, Vreeland & Stone.

KINGS COUNTY.

Plan 976—5th av, No. 79, one one-story brk extension, 33.6x20, tin roof; cost, $675; Henry C. Kucks, on premises; ar't and m'n, Albert E. Kleinert.

977—19th st, s s, 85 w 4th av, one one-story frame extension, 22x12, tin roof; cost, $200; Richard Rippe, on premises; c'r, L. Bollmann.

978—Prospect pl, No. 1568, one one-story frame extension, 10x26, felt roof; cost, $25; ow'r and b'r, Samuel J. Brown, on premises.

979—Bergen st, No. 375, substitute flat for peak roof; cost, $100; ow'r, &c., James Cunningham, on premises.

980—Sumner av, s e cor Livingston or Irvington av, one one-story brk extension, 20x5, tin roof, interior alterations; cost, $1,200; P. Kunzinger, 1 Gold st; m'n, H. King; c'r, W. Mahler.

981—Van Sielen av, n e cor Glenmore av, one two-story frame extension, 10x10, shingle roof; cost, $500; George W. Palmer. 356 Glenmore av; m'n, H. M. Smith; c'r, H. F. Smith.

982—Forest st, n s, 100 w Evergreen av, raise and relay roof and 6x8 girders on top; cost, $700; S. Liebmann's Sons B. Co., Forest and Bremen sts; ar't, Th. Engelhardt.

983—56th st, s s, 200 w 3d av, one one-story frame extension, 12x12, tin roof; cost, $300; E. W. Rogers, 117 56th st; c'r, C. B. Mount.

984—Keap st, No. 214, one two-story brk extension, 14x27.10, tin roof; cost, $2,000; A. H. Creagh, on premises; ar't, N. Le Brun & Sons; m'ns, W. and T. Lamb, Jr.

985—Seigel st, s w cor Bogart st, one one-story brk extension, 43.4x23.6, tin roof; cost, $500; Ferdinand Hosch, on premises; ar't, Th. Engelhardt, b'r, not selected.

986—Jay st, No. 385, interior alterations; cost, $75; Julius Coleberg, on premises; ar't, C. F. Eisenach; m'n, Mr. King.

987—Van Buren st, No. 14, add one story; cost, $1,000; D. F. W. Bowren, 259 Tompkins av; m'ns, Lippmann & Co.

988—20th st, No. 95, substitute flat for peak roof; cost, $2,000; ow'r and b'r, Thomas Coulum, on premises.

989—Somers st, No. 129, new plate-glass store front; cost, $250; Konrad Arnold, 57 Hopkinson av; c'r, C. Wuttke.

990—Park av, No. 57, interior alterations; cost, $900; Domenico Molinelli, 25 Pell st, New York; c'r, John Callareto.

991—Atlantic av, No. 2549, one one-story frame extension, 16x23, tin roof; cost, $200; Mr. Marr, on premises; c'r, Wm. Max.

992—Bristol st, e s, 125 e New York av, one one-story frame extension, 13x13, tin roof; cost, $125; ow'r and b'r, William Caulbidcb, on premises.

993—Stockton st, No. 20½, one one-story brk extension, 17 and 17x4 and 11, tin roof, interior alterations; cost, $250; Sarah F. Mead, Monroe pl; ar't, J. C. Hooper; c'rs, S. C. Prescott & Sons.

994—Johnson st, s w cor Hudson av, iron column under corner; cost, $175; John Flynn, 180 Adelphi st.

995—Irving st, n w cor Columbia st, rebuild gable wall: cost, $1,000; Jas. O'Brien, Hicks st, cor Degraw st; b'rs, M. Gibbons & Sons.

996—Reid av, No. 5, new store front; cost, $150; Chas. W. Evans. 7 Reid av; b'r, D. Williams.

997—Cumberland st, No. 140, flat tin roof; cost, $800; A. H. Williamson, 119 Cumberland st; ar't, C. F. Eisenach; b'r, not selected.

998—Box st, n s, 75 w Oakland st, repair damage by fire: cost, $700: ow'rs and ar'ts, Church & Co., 36 Ash st.

999—Glenmore av, n s, 125 w Elton st, two-story brk and frame extension, 10x16, tin roof; cost, $500; August Boehm, Glenmore av, near Elton st; ar't, L. F. Schillinger; b'r, F. Gundermann.

1000—Stanhope st, No. 45, excavate rear cellar and build brk foundation; cost, 250; Mr. Goldsmith, 48 Stockholm st: b'rs, W. A. & S. J. Griffin.

1001—18th st, s s, 350 w 7th av, three-story frame and brk extension, 11x15, tin roof, front alteration, from store to dwell'g; cost, $600: Mr. Cracknell. 338 18th st; ar't, W. H. Wirth; b'rs, P. Kyle and J. Sutherland.

1002—Park av, No. 826, raised 7 ft. on brk wall; cost, $1,500; —— Hartmann, on premises; b'rs, M. Armendinger and C. Hestermann.

1003—Atlantic av, s s, 25 w Pennsylvania av, three-story brk extension, 25x10, tin roof; cost, $980; M. J. Gibbons, Penna av; ar't, J. W. Bailey; b'rs, D. Cook and H. Reis.

1004—McDougal st, No. 21, add one story to extension; cost, $40; S. Merz, on premises.

MISCELLANEOUS.

BUSINESS FAILURES.

N. Y. ASSIGNMENTS—BENEFIT CREDITORS.

Oct.

13 Kronthal, Louis and Charles (composing firm of Kronthal Bros., selling ribbons at No. 314 Church st), to Abraham S. Jessurun; preferences, $3,001.

14 Simon, Benjamin (feather manufacturer, at No. 12 Bond st), to Julian B. Shope; preferences, $3,450.

15 Stern, Isaac (commission merchant, at No. 70 Pine st), to Ascher Osterman; preferences, $5,168.

16 Lewis, Edwin G. (dealer in salt and smoked provisions, at No. 210 Front st), to Stephen B. Pettit; preferences, $1,000.

KINGS COUNTY.

GENERAL ASSIGNMENTS.

Oct.

8 Colgan, George A. to John A. Clarry.

13 Daly, James A. to same.

PROCEEDINGS OF THE BOARD OF ALDERMEN AFFECTING REAL ESTATE.

* Under the different headings indicates that a resolution has been introduced and referred to the appropriate committee. † Indicates that the resolution has passed and has been sent to the Mayor for approval ‡ Passed over the Mayor's veto.

NEW YORK, October 13, 1891.

MAINS.

Samuel st, from Southern Boulevard West to Prospect, thence on Prospect av to Elm st; water.†

Samuel st, from Prospect st to Southern Boulevard; gas.†

Travers st, from Creston to Jerome av; water.†

Travers st, from Creston to Jerome av; gas.†

179th st, from Webster to Railroad av; gas.†

Bainbridge av, from Travers st to Southern Boulevard; gas.†

Bathgate av, from 188th st to 3d av; gas †

Bathgate av, from 188th st to 3d av; water.†

Briggs av, from Garfield to Travers st; gas.†

Creston av, from Donnybrook to Travers st; water.†

Creston av, from Donnybrook to Travers st; gas.†

Kirkside av, from Kingsbridge road to Donnybrook st; gas.†

Madison av, from Kingsbridge road to Columbine av; water.†

Mapes av, from Samuel to Elm st; gas.†

Prospect av, from Samuel to Elm st; gas.†

Railroad av, from 178th to 179th st; gas.†

Villa av, from Potter pl to Van Courtlandt av; water.†

Villa av, from Potter pl to Southern Boulevard; gas.†

Villa av, from Van Courtland av to Southern Boulevard; water.†

FLAGGING AND CURBING.

114th st, both sides, from 5th to Madison av.†

116th st, n s, from 2d av extending east 100 feet.†

129th st, from 3d to Lexington av.†

150th st, from w s Walton av to e s River av.†

155th st, from 3d to Elton av.†

Columbus av, s w cor 75th st, 100 ft. on av and 200 ft. on st.†

Park av, n e cor 117th st, 150 ft. on av and 100 ft. on st.†

5th av, n e cor 114th st. 100 ft. on av and 150 ft. on st.†

5th av, both sides, from 114th to 115th st.†

LAMP POSTS ERECTED AND LIGHTED.

Samuel st. from Prospect st to Southern Boulevard.†

Travers st, from Creston to Jerome av.†

179th st. from Webster to Railroad av.†

Bainbridge av, from Travers st to Southern Boulevard.†

Bathgate av. from 188th st to 3d av.†

Briggs av, from Garfield to Travers st.†

Creston av. from Donnybrook to Travers st.†

Kirkside av. from Kingsbridge road to Donnybrook st.†

Mapes av, from Samuel to Elm st.†

Prospect av, from Samuel to Elm st.†

Railroad av, from 178th to 179th st.†

Villa av, from Southern Boulevard to Potter pl.†

CROSSWALKS.

150th st. from w s Walton av to e s River av.†

155th st, from 3d to Elton av.†

156th st, from 3d to Elton av.†

158th st. from 3d to Elton av.†

Elton av, from 3d av to 161st st.†

5th av, in front of No. 214, at expense of J. F. De Lury.†

REGULATING, GRADING, ETC.

150th st, from w s Walton av to e s River av, culverts buil ; also where necessary.†

155th st, from 3d to Elton av.†

156th st, from 3d to Elton av.†

158th st, from 3d to Elton av.†

Elton av, from 3d av to 161st st.†

FENCING VACANT LOTS.

1st and 2d avs, 92d and 93d sts—the block.†

PAVING.

156th st, from 3d to Elton av, trap block.†

158th st. from 3d to Elton av, trap block.†

Elton av, from 3d av to 161st st, granite block.†

APPROVED PAPERS.

Resolutions passed by the Board of Aldermen calling for the following improvements have been signed by the Mayor for the week ending October 10, 1891. *Indicates that the Mayor neither appoved nor objected thereto, therefore the same became adopted.

CURBSTONES SET AND SIDEWALKS FLAGGED.

28th st, from 9th to 10th av.

37th st, from 8th to 9th av.

115th st, from 3d to Lexington av.

116th st, n e cor 2d av, extending east abt 100 ft.

Madison av, both sides, bet 131st and 132d sts.

Mount Morris av, n w cor 120th st, abt 100 on av and 300 on st.

10th av, in front of Nos. 390 and 392.

10th av, e s, from 28th to 29th st.

BROOKLYN BOARD OF ALDERMEN.

BROOKLYN, Oct. 12, 1891.

CULVERTS.

Moffat st, s w cor Central av. }*
Van Pelt st, n w cor Graham av. }

28th st, s e cor 3d av.†

Flushing av, s w cor Steuben st. }*
Irving av, n e cor Harmon st. }

Prospect av, n w cor 3d av.†

FLAGGING.

St. Marks av, bet Nostrand and Rogers avs.†

FENCING VACANT LOTS.

Hopkinson av, w s, bet McDougal and Hull sts. }†
Liberty av, n s, bet Linwood and Elton sts. }

GAS LAMPS, ETC.

Cooper st, bet Broadway and Evergreen av.†

GRADING, PAVING, ETC.

Charles pl, north from Willoughby av.*

REGULATE GRADE.

Bradford st, bet Eastern Parkway and New Lots av.
89th st, bet 4th and 8th avs.
Blake av, bet Pennsylvania and Van Sielen avs.
Belmont av, bet Pennsylvania and Van Sielen avs.
Dumont av, bet Pennsylvania and Van Siclen avs.
New Jersey av, bet Belmont and New Lots avs.
Pennsylvania av bet Belmont and New Lots avs.
Sutter av, bet Pennsylvania and Van Siclen avs.
Willis av, bet Eastern Parkway and New Lots av. }†

SEWERS.

Harrison pl, bet Bogert st and Morgan av. }†
Moffat st, bet Central and Hamburg avs. }

STREET OPENING.

Harrison pl, bet Bogert st and Morgan av, at owners' expense.†

WATER MAINS.

Park pl, bet Bedford and Nostrand avs.†

ADVERTISED LEGAL SALES.

REFEREES SALES TO BE HELD AT THE REAL ESTATE EXCHANGE AND AUCTION ROOM (LIMITED), 59 to 65 LIBERTY STREET, EXCEPT WHERE OTHERWISE STATED.

Oct.

119th st, No. 7, n s, 95.5 w 5th av, 14x57.9x14.0x 58.11, three-story brk dwell'g, by B. L. Kennelly. (Amt due $4,732) 19

133d st, Nos. 248 and 250, s s, 416.8 w 7th av, 33.4x 99.11, two three-story brk (stone front) dwell'gs, by J. C. Lalor. (Amt due $30,867) 19

Park (4th) av, No. 8-5, w s, 69.2 n 78th st, 15x75, four-story brk dwell'g, by D. P. Ingraham & Co. (Amt. due $18,908) 19

Norfolk st, No. 78 formerly 66, e s, abt 125 n Broome st, 25x100, three-story frame (brk front) store and tenem't with two-story brk building on rear, by P. F. Meyer. (Amt due $12,570) 20

69th st, No. 302, s s, 100 w 11th av, 25x100.5, five-story brk tenem't, by William Kennelly. (Amt due $19,446) 20

138th st, s s, 75 e Southern Boulevard, 25x100, by J. F. B. Smyth. (Amt due $4,007) 20

8th st, No. 109, n e s, 331.5 n w 5th av, 23x93.11, three-story brk dwell'g, by William Kennelly. (Partition sale) 21

133d st, No. 256, s s, 183.4 e 8th av, 16.8x99.11, three-story stone front dwell'g, by R. V. Harnett & Co. (Amt due $10,226) 21

3d av, Nos. 1622-1628 } begins 3d av, n w
91st st, Nos. 171, 173 and 173½ } cor 91st st, 100.8 x125, four five story stone front stores and tenements on av and two five-story stone front tenements and one-story brk stable on st, by J. F. B. Smyth. (Dower rights, &c.) 21

8th av, No. 2140, e s, 51.4 s 116th st, 25.5x100, one-story brk stores, by James L. Wells. (Amt due $3,390) 21

79th st, No. 442, s s, 75 w Av A, 19x79, five-story brk flat, by B. L. Kennelly. (Amt due $5,189; prior morts $11,500) 22

87th st, No. 138, s s, 350 w 9th av, 20x100.8, four-story stone front dwell'g, by D. P. Ingraham & Co. (Amt due $24,156) 22

97th st, No. 142, s s, 410 w 9th av, 20x100.8, four-story stone front dwell'g, by D. P. Ingraham & Co. (Amt due $26,940) 22

Rivington st, No. 161, s s, 25 w Clinton st, 25x100, five-story brk tenem't with stores, by J. A. Berrian. (Amt due $3,518; prior morts, $——) 22

120th st, Nos. 239-243, n s, 375 w 7th av, 50x100.11, three three-story brk dwell'gs, by P. A. Smyth. 22

143d st, Nos. 227-235, n s, 150 w 7th av, 125x99.11, five five-story brick flats .... }
144th st, Nos. 228-236, s s, 150 w 7th av, 125x99.11, five five-story brk flats .... }
by D. P. Ingraham & Co. (Amt due $27,502; sub. to morts. $35,000) 22

148th st, n s, 90 w Brook av, 50x100, by R. V. Harnett & Co. (Partition sale) 22

8th av, Nos. 2342 and 2344, s e cor 126th st, 49.11x 100, two six-story brk flats with stores, by D. P. Ingraham & Co. (Amt due $7,497; prior morts. $70,000) 23

114th st, No. 418, s s, 240 e 1st av, 30x100.11, four-story stone front tenem't, by B. L. Kennelly. (Amt due $1,711) 23

Canal st, No. 119, n s, old No. 216 Walker st, formerly known as No. 74 Pump st, 18.9x50 old measurement, by D. P. Ingraham & Co. (Partition sale) 26

Boulevard, e s, 24.11 n 139th st, 75x100, vacant, by D. P. Ingraham & Co. (Amt due $31,451) 26

Av A, Nos. 393 and 395, s w cor 24th st, 49.5x81.8, vacant, all right, title and interest which Daniel D. Conover had on June 10, 1891, by sheriff at City Hall. (Sale under execution) 26

KINGS COUNTY.

Oct.

Withers st, n s, 38.7 e North 9th st, runs north 50.8 x southwest 62.5 to North 9th st, x southeast along same 10 to Withers st, x east 38.7 to beginning; assessed value, $600 .... }
Howard av, e s, 98 s Herkimer st, 35x98, frame church .... }
by T. A. Kerrigan, at 13 Willoughby st 19

Kingsland av, Nos. 89 and 91, w s, 50 n Richardson st, 50x100, one-story frame dwell'g on plot; assessed value, $900; by Howard J. Forker, ref., at County Court House 19

Lafayette av, No. 866, s s, 302.6 w Lewis av, 20 x 100, two-story and basement brk dwell'g; assessed value, $4,500 .... }
4th av, No. 177, s e s, 34.8 s w Degraw st, 16.4x75, four-story brk tenem't and store; assessed value, $4,500 .... }
by T. A. Kerrigan, at 13 Willoughby st 20

Glen st, s w cor Crescent av, 25x100, three-story frame tenem't and store; assessed value, $3,000 .... }
Jefferson av late Jefferson st, No. 156, s s, 280 w Nostrand av, 20x100, four-story brk flat; assessed value, $6,500 .... }
Jefferson av late Jefferson st, No. 154, s s, 300 w Nostrand av, 20x100, four-story brk flat; assessed value, $6,500 .... }
by T. A. Kerrigan, at 13 Willoughby st 21

McDonough st, No. 499, n w cor Reid av, 25.6x100, foundation laid; assessed value, $1,800; by W. Cole, at 7 and 8 Court sq 21

President st, No. 185, n s, 120 e Henry st, runs north 55 x east 1 x north 45 x east 14.6 x south 100 x west 15.6 to beginning, three-story brk dwelling; assessed value, $5,000 .... }
Taylor st, No. 39, n s, 173.8 e Kent av, 19.11x80, three-story brk dwell'g; assessed value, $2,500; partition .... }
by W. Cole, at 7 and 8 Court sq 22

President st, No. 185, n s, 121 e Henry st, 14.6x100, three-story brk dwell'g; assessed value, $5,000; by T. A. Kerrigan, at 13 Willoughby st 23

Eastern Parkway late Sackett st, s s, 350 e New York av, runs south 220.7 to Union st, x east along same 180.6 x north 228 to Eastern Parkway, x west 119.3 to beginning, vacant; assessed value, $1,800; by Edward J. Dooley ref., at County Court House 23

Decatur st, No. 49, n s, 229 w Throop av, 18x100, three-story brk dwell'g; assessed value, $6,500 }
Raymond st, w s, 175 s Bolivar st, runs west 75 x south — to Willoughby st, x east — to Raymond st, x north 26 to beginning, four-story brk tenem't and store; assessed value, $8,400 }
Raymond st, w s, 150 s Bolivar st, 27x75, four-story brk tenem't; assessed value, $7,000 .... }
Union st, Nos. 279-291, n s, 247.6 w Clinton st, 140x100, five five-story double brk and stone flats; assessed value, $50,000 .... }
by T. A. Kerrigan, at 13 Willoughby st 26

Van Siclen av, e s, 125 s Blake av, 25x100, vacant, by J. Cole, at 389 Fulton st 26

LIS PENDENS, KINGS COUNTY.

Oct.

Centre st, n s, 175 w Smith st, 25x100. Michael Grady and ano, exrs. Elizabeth Grady agt Marie M. Simonson; att'y, John H. Stoutenburgh 8

Quincy st, n s, 105 w Ralph av, 20x100 .... }
Quincy st, n s, 145 w Ralph av, 20x100 .... }
Quincy st, n s, 185 w Ralph av, 20x100 .... }
William H. Newschafer exr. Catharine Newschafer agt Mal M. Schwenk; att'y, George F. Alexander 9

Monroe st, s s, 141.8 w Tompkins av, 16.8x100. Stillman Soule agt Sarah J. Thistle; foreclos. mechanic's lien; att'y, William J. Courtney 9

Pulaski st, n s, 204.6 e Throop av, 100x90. Adaline H. Saddington agt Frederick C. Urban; att'y, Frederick Cobb 9

19th st, n s, 100 e 10th av, 100x100.2. John E. Bullwinkel agt Frank Hanratty; partition; att'y, John E. Bullwinkel, in person 9

Hancock st, s s, 81 e Throop av, runs south 84.4 x east 9 x south 16.8 x east 89.6 x north 100 to st, x west 89.8. Henry W. Thorpe agt Robert S. Neely; foreclos. mechanic's lien; att'y, Thos. H. Williams 9

50th st, n s, 167 e 3d av, 20x100.2. Mary E. De Wint agt Maria Koski; att'y, George G. Dutcher. 9

Bushwick av, n e s, 20.2 n w Stewart st, 60x79.6. Henry Weil agt Harold B. Kelley; att'y, P. Murray 9

15th st, s s, lot 98 map Dimon Tract of A. W. Benson, 25x100. Fulton Bank of Brooklyn agt James J. Ferry; action to set aside deed; att'ys, Bergen & Dykman 10

Sackett st, s s, 70 w Bond st, 70x100. Elizabeth H. Bache agt James H. Porter; att'ys, Rolfe & Snedeker 10

3d av, s e cor Schermerhorn st, 46.6 to Flatbush av, x88.2 to st, x68. John F. Richartz agt George H. Rice; foreclos. mechanic's lien; att'y, John S. Griffith 10

McDonough st, s s, 175.5 e Sumner av, 99.7x100. Stephen B. Sturges agt Michael Sotrano; att'ys, Sturges & Roby 10

27th st, n s, 225 e 4th av, 40x100. Sophie G. Parker agt Matilda Goodwin; att'y, A. W. Parker 10

Broadway, s s, 25 w Bennett av, 25x100. The Union Mission Chapel Assoc. agt James C. Friel; att'y, John H. Stearns 10

Clinton st, w s, 50.9 n Harrison st, 24.3x46x25x 46.10. William Darton agt Anna Byrne; att'ys, Strong, Harmon & Mathewson 10

Madison st, n s, 155.5 e Ralph av, 18.9x100. Benjamin Downer agt Emily N. Brown; action to set aside deed; att'ys, Esselstyn, Ketcham & Safford 12

Gates av, s s, 275 e Tompkins av, 100x100. Mary A. Manning agt Edward D. Mullen; att'ys, Boardman & Boardman 12

South 2d st, n s, 216 e 3d st, 16.8x100. Henry R. Hatfield agt James T. Hatfield; partition; att'y, Wm. L. Whiting 12

Union st, n s, 90 w Clinton st, 22.11x100. Jose P. del Castillo guard. Maria de Carmen agt Margaretha Pfeiffer; att'y, Josi G. Morales 13

Graham av, e s, 25 n Scholes st, 25x100. Ferdinand M. Thieriot exr. Marie T. March agt Jacob J. Seelbach; att'y, E. Louis Lowe 13

Eldert av, e s, 225 s Blake av, 50x200 to Shepherd av. Sarah E. Mcsherry agt Ruth M. Perry; partition; att'y, Lamont McLoughlin 13

Wyckoff av, n e s, 25 n w Starr st, 25x95 .... }
Troutman st, s e s, 147.2 n e Wyckoff av, 25x100. }
Boerum st, n s, 100 w Ewen st, 25x100 .... }
Jacob Nasel agt Edmund Stein; foreclos. mechanic's lien; att'ys, Moffett & Kramer 13

McDonough st, n s, 280 w Stuyvesant av, 20x100. Emma F. Martin agt John J. De Revere; att'ys, Hubbard & Rushmore 13

Clason av, w s, 75 s Gates av, 25x100. George W. Montgomery agt James E. Sleight; att'y, Edward F. Brown 14

East 19th st, w s, 200 s Av A, 50x100, Flatbush. William Crozier agt Margaret E. Chatfield; foreclos. mechanic's lien; att'y, William J. Gaynor. 14

2d st, n s, 110.9 w 7th av, 20x100. William L. Dowling agt Roderick Von Graff; att'y, Cornelius Doremus 14

Clinton st, e s, 65.6 n 2d pl, 34.0x76.6. Donovan Bros. agt James J. Ferry; foreclos. mechanic's lien; att'ys, Tredwell & Catlin 14

Sackett st, n s, 125 w Van Brunt st, runs west 125 x north 200 to Degraw st, x east 50 x south 100 x east 75 x south 100. Same agt Rebecca M. Ferry; same att'ys 14

Lotts lane, s e cor Flatbush av and extdg. to Rogers av and land of John Vanderveer's heirs, Flatbush. Robert K. Story agt Vincent A. Strawson and Jacob Worth; action for accounting; att'ys, J. W. & C. W. Ridgway 14

Av C, Coney Island av, land of John Ditmas and Flatbush plank road, tract at Flatbush bounded as above. Same agt same; action for an accounting; same att'ys 14

Somers st, n s, 39 e Hopkinson av, 18.6x85. Henry C. Mecklen exr. William Waterman agt Thomas Donohue; att'y, James E. Carpenter 14

Myrtle av, n e cor Lewis av, runs east 125 x north —x northwest — x west 93 to Lewis av, x south 100. The Henry McShane Mfg. Co. agt Max Hallheimer; att'y, D. W. Northup.............. 14

Chauncey st, n s, 93.11 w Lewis av, 19.9x100. Jane Douglass agt Nathaniel W. Burtis; att'y, J. R. Allaben................................ 15

RECORDED LEASES.

NEW YORK. Per Year

Bleecker st, No. 127, basement and first floor. Mitchell A. C. Levy to J. B. Basset; 5 years, from Nov. 25, 1890........................ $1,500

Boulevard, s w cor 85th st, corner store. Homer J. Beaudet to John H. Kahrs; 3 years, from Nov. 1, 1891....................1,000, 1,200

Carmine st, No. 37, store floor and front basement. J. Garrison De Mott to David and Hannah Mendes; 5 years, from May 1, 1892.. 900

Duane st, No. 80. Hugh Ferrigan to Patrick F. Ferrigan and Patrick Smith; 10 years, from May 1, 1884.............................. 4,000

Houston st, No. 29 E., basement. Edmund Heinecke to Charles H. Schminke; 3 years, from May 1, 1891............................ 1,200

Same property. Consent to assign above lease. Same to same; Oct. 13............................ nom

Same property. Assign lease. Charles H. Schminke to John C. Oldenbuttel; Oct. 14... 2,356

Kingsbridge road, n s, abt 50 w Berrian av. Catharine F. Meyer, Saratoga, N. Y., to John J. Dalton; 5 years, from May 1, 1892........ 600

Mott st, No. 133, store and basement room. John G. Payntar to Frank and Catherine O'Neill; 5 years, from May 1, 1891........... 420

Park st, Nos. 37 and 39. Samuel Aronson, Louis Gordon, Aaron Levy and Herman Fichter to Vincenzo Settedocati; 4½ years, from Nov. 1, 1891............................ 5,400

Monroe st, Nos. 160, 162, 164 and 166, s s, all. Martin, Henry G., Anna C., Catherine A. and Arthur Schreukeisen to Frank C. Swan (Wallace & Co.); 10 years, from May 1, 1892. 7,000

Rutgers st, No. 20, store and back room and basement. Emil T. Holthusen to Haim Ornstein; 4 years 7½ months, from Oct. 15, 1891.. 720

Spring st, No. 212, store floor and basement. Frederick D. Mahoney to Auguste Krug; 2 years 9 months and 13 days, from July 18, 1891.. 480

Washington st, No. 92. Benjamin S. Welles to Henry Schutt; 2 years, from May 1, 1891. 1,740

Same property. Consent to assign lease. Same to same.............................. nom

Same property. Assign lease. Henry Schutt to William Braase............................ nom

West st, No. 425, s e cor West 11th st, all. Louis Schortemeier to John Tietjen; 5 years, from May 1, 1893.............................. 1,600

Same property. John Tietjen to Charles H. Zw k; 6½ years and 20 days, from Oct. 10, 1891....................................1,400, 1,600

West st, No. 145, store building. Emeline C. Young, Lena A. and Mary Y. Crocheron, Jersey City, N. J., to Jordan L., Abraham and Elephelet Snedecor; 10 years, from May 1, 1891....................................1,800, 2,000

14th st, No. 46 W., all. Abraham Wolff to William Comyns; 10 years, from May 1, 1893 ....gold, 9,000

28th st, No. 32 W. Edward P. Dickie to John J. McGrath; extension of lease for 5 years.. 6,000

39th st, No. 335 W., store and second floor. Ludwig Zimmer to Karl Wiesenberg; 3 7-12 years, from Oct. 1, 1891...................... 1,200

42d st, Nos. 157 and 159 E. George Rothmann to John W. Lang; 11½ years, from Nov. 1, 1891 ....3,300, 3,360

113th st, No. 414 E., all front and rear. John Argenziana to Federico Annucci and Angiolina Ferrento his wife; 5¼ years, from Feb. 1, 1891.. 1,140

Amsterdam av, No. 146 south store and three rooms on south second floor. Frederick P. and Horatio C. Klenke to Rudolph Wagner; 2 years, from Oct. 1, 1892.................... 636

1st av, s w cor 88th st, store and cellar. Thomas Leamy to Herman Dunker; 5 years, from May 1, 1892.............................. 1,200

2d av, s w cor 112th st, first floor and bowling alleys. John E. Hasler to Susan Murray; 10 years, from Oct. 1, 1891........................ 2,500

3d av, No. 1550 } s a. George W. Archer to 87th st, No. 177 E. } Thomas B. Whiffen; 10 years, from May 1, 1890..................2,400, 3,000

6th av, No. 36, s e cor West 4th st. John J. Worden to George Ringler & Co.; 5 years, from May 1, 1898.............................. 1,800

8th av, No. 918. Catharine Eckert to Theodore R. Westermann; 8 months, with privilege of renewal for 3 years, from April 30, 1892..... 800

11th av, No. 740, store floor, east side. Frederick Ehlenburg to Daniel J. Malchow; 3 7-12 years, from Oct. 1, 1891.........................600, 720

CHATTELS.

NEW YORK CITY.

OCTOBER 9 TO 15.—INCLUSIVE.

SALOON AND RESTAURANT FIXTURES.

Arnold, Conrad. 175 Ludlow ...Feigenspan B Co. (R) $300

Bauman & Graber. 44 Orchard....Burger & H B Co. 550

Burns, Jos. 340 Bowery....J Hoffmann B Co. 1,500

Bazant, John. 817 2d av....J Doelger's Sons. 1,000

Beisner, B. 851 E 10th....J H Bereuter. Pool Table. 130

Bernstein, Morris. 80 Norfolk....Welz & Z. 500

Bloch, Emil. 256 East Houston....J & M Haffen. (R) 400

Boffa, Amibalé. 65 Mulberry....Budweiser B Co. 800

Bolarowsky, Anna. 190 E 3d....F Ibert. 500

Brady, Mathew. 231 E 111th....A Hupfel's Son. 600

Bankauf, Adolph. 98 Forsyth....G D Meimen. (R) 3,930

Broderick, M J. 579 Morris av....D Stevenson. 800

Becker, P H. 89 1st av....V Loewers. 1,500

Beck, Christ. 241 Eldridge ...F Oppermann, Jr. (R) 250

Beubler, John. 504 E 12th....J Eppig. (R) 650

Bisinger, Martin. 108 Greenwich av.. C Stein. (R) 600

Brady & Farrell. 62 West Broadway....Bernheimer & S. (R) 1,000

Brehmer, Rudolph. 7 Albany....Danenberg & C. (R) 1,000

Brosnan & Bro. 600 3d av....Bernheimer & S. (R) 1,560

Same....J J Reilly. (R) 500

Baines, J A. 141 E 130th....G Ebret. 650

Bock, Geo. 301 E 81st....G Ehret. 1,000

Coughlin, Matthew. 403 1st av....C Stein. 600

Carroll, Geo. 2136 2d av....D Mayer. 1,000

Carney, Michael. 8 Jones....J C G Hupfel B Co. 200

Cortello, T. 27 Bridge....Monroe Eckstein B Co. 480

Cuzze & Florio. 322 E 104th....Bernheimer & S. (R) 500

Collon, Michael. 639 E 9th....M Seitz. 600

Degnan, John. 119 E 108th....Bavarian B Co. 500

De Cario, G. 59½ Mulberry ..Abbott B Co. (R) 400

Drawski, A. 527 1st av....J Kuszy. Restaurant Fixtures. 220

Dunker, H. 1697 1st av....Bernheimer & S. 1,500

Dunne, J. 609 11th av....D Stevenson. 1,600

Dewinder, John. 613 9th av... Bernheimer & S. (R) 750

Diffley, T J. 549 Washington....Bernheimer & S. (R) 250

Dunn, Patrick. 10th av and 196th st....D G Yuengling, Jr. 396

Early, M. 683 Hudson....J Ruppert. 5,000

Ege, D. 231 46th ...D Stevenson. 600

Eisenberg, P. 203 Stanton....V Loewer's G B Co. 1,000

Finne, Joseph. 175 Thompson....Bernheimer & S. (R) 140

Favilla, Giuseppe. 89 South William and 29 Stone....J Woods. Restaurant Fixtures. 300

Form, George. 329 W 67th....J Ahles B Co. (R) 614

Freund, Alfred. 1446 2d av....G Ringler & Co. 300

Felleman, Flora. 126 Division....J Levine. 1,500

Friedrichsen, Asmus. 7 Harrison....C Stein. 1,000

Gerhard, Theodora. 1322 2d av....V Loewers. 400

Gluck, Chas. 708 E 13th....C Frese. 450

Gottfried & Zeeck. 198 Av A....J Eppig. 500

Gelb, Adolph. 104 Cannon....F Ibert. 600

Germann, Friedrich. 422 E 66th....J Doelger's Sons. (R) 500

Grob, John. 427 W 53d....J Ahles B Co. (R) 400

Graley, A B. 205 E 9th....J Ruppert. 900

Geib, P. 1746 1st av....V Loewer's G B Co. 224

Gerdes, J H. 2024 2d av....J Everard. 1,015

Giacini, Santo. 2163 1st av....Bernheimer & S. Saloon Beer Pump. 87

Same....same. Saloon Ice House. 85

Same....same. Saloon Ice House. 85

Hiller, G. 146 Orchard....A G Hupfel. (R) 350

Hines, M J. Amsterdam av and 165th st....D Stevenson. (R) 428

Hausmann, August. 197 South....Bernheimer & S. (R) 2,500

Hickson, Mary. 233 Av B....J J Reilly. (R) 500

Holldick, Frederick. 1748 Madison av....Bernheimer & S. (R) 2,500

Hanley, James. 2236 1st av... G Ehret. 700

Hohenstein, Robert. 88 2d av....J Ruppert. (R) 1,500

Kuehn, Leo. 19 Manhattan ...G Ehret. 2,200

Krause, H F, Jr. 3 Irving pl....Beadleston & W. (R) 10,000

Kruger, August. 976 E 163d....A Hupfel's Sons. (R) 200

Kuper, Conrad. 26 2d av ..J Doelger's Sons. 750

Kern, Michael. 331 Bowery....W H Griffith & Co. Pool Table. 400

Kitsell, W T. 613 and 615 3d av ...J Everard. 1,532

Kleber, John. 181 Mott....Budweiser B Co. 1,100

Kolmer & Herman. 178 Rivington.. S Reiser. 1,000

Koster & Jachens. 41 Rose....S Liebmann's Sons B Co. 1,100

Kundig, J W. 480 W 40th....J Ahles B Co. 400

Kunkel, Otto. 32 and 34 Division....Obermeyer & L. 430

Kepes, J. 304 East Houston....Brunswick-B-C Co. Pool Table. (R) 15

Kohlweg, Diedrich. 17 Rivington....J Wallace & Son. 1,000

Laub, Julius. 101 E 53d....J Doelger's Sons. 1,500

Lindenkohl, Gustav. 516 E 5th....P Buckel. 475

Lenz, H J. 2009 3d av....G Ehret. (R) 450

Lutz, Adolph. 67 Grand ..J Hederich. Restaurant Fixtures. 500

Linneman, G and L. 193 Reade and 201 Chambers....I Rosskam et al. 450

McCoy, E J. 208 Av A....Bernheimer & S. (R) 1,000

Murphy, Henry. 136 Liberty... I Roth. 1,200

Mahony, W O. 6 Jones....Bernheimer & S. (R) 200

McGee, J H. 645 1st av....Bernheimer & S. (R) 1,500

Meier, W. 59 North Moore....O Heitz. 500

Michel, J. Western Boulevard and 82d st....D Stevenson. (R) 300

Morrissey, D. 1631 1st av....G Ehret. (R) 2,500

Muller, Henry. 338 6th ...J Doelger's Sons. 300

Murray, J J. 1815 2d av....Bernheimer & S. Pool Table. (R) 150

Machen & Byrne. 888 8th av....J Higgins. 17,000

Maglio, Francesco. 252 Elizabeth....Budweiser B Co. 500

Malchow, Charles. 740 11th av....Budweiser B Co. 140

McCarty, F J. 298 Hudson....J W Post. 208

Micklass, Nic. 300 E 14th....J Rapf. Restaurant Fixtures. 900

Moeller, George. 1599 Av A....J Doelger's Sons. 1,500

Millett, J F and T M. 2077 7th av....E C Hinsdale. Restaurant Fixtures. 150

Neuwohner & Schwartz. 50 Clinton....Bachmann B Co. (R) 800

Oshmsky, Solomon. 185 Rivington....Feigenspan B Co. (R) 700

O'Toole, James. 411 10th av....Budweiser B Co. 2,000

Ochsenreither, J. 32 Norfolk....A Stauf. (R) 300

O'Grady, J. 1886 2d av....D Stevenson. 1,350

Palmer, T F. 434 W 46th....D Stevenson. (R) 150

Pandolfi, Gaetano. 329 E 106th....Bernheimer & S. (R) 375

Petersen, J C & E. 284 8th av. . Burr B Co. (R) 2,450

Pfeiffer, Charles. 439 E 23d ...M Seitz. 925

Prange, P H. 985 2d av....F Oppermann, Jr. 500

Polak, Samuel. Vanderbilt av ...Brunswick-B-C Co. Pool Table. (R) 95

Phillips, Mike. 176 Madison... C Frese. 725

Proops, S G. 431 E 86th....G Ringler & Co. (R) 600

Quick, August. 258 West....Clausen & Price B Co. 2,400

Reeves, Elmira M. 199 Bleecker... G C Wookey. Restaurant Fixtures. 600

Ress, J G. 45 and 47 New Chambers....G Bechtel, exr of. 600

Redican, Annie. 106 Roosevelt....Feigenspan B Co. (R) 700

Rossler, George. 711 E 9th....J Ruppert. 700

Rimrod, William. 872 Forest av... H Hupfel's Son. (R) 1,100

Rosenhain, M. 1232 2d av....G Ringler & Co. 1,800

Roche, Cornelius. 2188 1st av....H Elias B Co. 700

Rickenberg, Henry. 662 9th av....Bernheimer & S. (R) 1,600

Rosenthal, Marcus. 62 Norfolk....H M Rosenthal. 800

Schillberg, J F. 307 8th....G Bechtel, exr of. (R) 850

Schoenfeld, Carl. 1334 2d av....M Koehler. 650

Schuler, Eugene. 1583 1st av....H Elias B Co. 700

Stillgebauer, Otto. 452 W 48th....Bernheimer & S. (R) 1,000

Schoenberger, P. 61 Cannon....D Stevenson. 125

Smith, P. 1495 1st av....G Ehret. (R) 2,000

Sullivan, J J. 666 Water....V Loewer's G B Co. 681

Sullivan, T J. 390 Madison....Beadleston & W. 1,000

Schorling, Frederick. 84 3d av....G Wendelken. 9,000

Sarbacher, Jacob. 346 W 41st....G Ehret. (R) 400

Schmidt, John. 765 1st av....Bernheimer & S. 1,000

Schnath, Frederick. 41st st and 1st av....G Ehret. (R) 3,000

Schneller, Henry. 322 E 29th....M Seitz. 700

Schroeder, John. 50 Lewis....M Seitz. 800

Schwartz, Jacob. 785 1st av....F Oppermann, Jr. 2,300

Schulhof, Sigmund. 305 E 105th....P Buckel. 1,200

Schroder, E J. 1642 2d av....G Ehret. (R) 1,200

Simon, Simon. 73 Ludlow....D Mayer. (R) 5,150

Stader, M G. 782 9th av....G Ehret. (R) 2,200

Truckenbrodt, Martin. 947 Washington av....A Hupfel's Sons. 800

Trautman, D L and T. 24 New Chambers ... Rochester B Co. 170

Turner & McElroy. 571 3d av....J Ruppert. 600

Urnstein, M and O. 54 Rivington....Sonn Bros. (R) 285

Ullmann & Lebright. 76 Essex....Bernheimer & S. (R) 500

Van Wyck, David. 1671 9th av....C F Collender. (R) 3,505

Walger, Henry. 3 Barclay....C Stein. 2,500

Weniger, Louis. 1567 1st av....J Kress B Co. 550

Wilson & O'Connor. 304 Bowery....S Buttner. 2,250

Welsh, J. 319 E 59th....D Stevenson. (R) 200

White, Mary E and L A Olsen....F Semken. 11,500

White & Olsen. 175 Broadway ...Beadleston & W. 3,500

Wislot, F. 1663 1st av....V Loewer's G B Co. 500

Waters, John. 1479 1st av....G Ringler & Co. 1,300

Wallace, T J & J P. 36 6th av....G Ringler & Co. 2,500

Weinert, Fedor. 496 1st av.. J Hoffmann B Co. 550

Williams & Freeman. 1027 6th av....J W Dolliver. Restaurant Fixtures. 800

Woelky, Carl. 454 W 40th....G Bechtel exr of. 500

Zweck, C H. 425 West....J Tietjen. 4,000

Zaccagnino, Giuseppe. 521 Broome ... Bernheimer & S. (R) 150

HOUSEHOLD FURNITURE.

Alberga, Z. E. 72 E 124th....G Fennell & Co. (R) 136

Anderson, A. 563 9th av....O'Farrell & H. 103

Austin, H. 23 W 131st....S Baumann. 290

Ashleigh, Lillian. 118 E 27th....T Kelly. 382

Allen, Dollie. 229 W 16th ...J Baumann. 231

Ames, Mary. 987 6th av... J Baumann. 384

Anderson, Sarah. 204 W 23d....J Baumann. 121

Bacheler, Rufus. 179 W 102d ...J Baumann. 226

Bass, Alice. 303 W 21st J Baumann. 438

Benham, L M. 405 Amsterdam av....J Baumann. 120

Benson, May. 308 W 43d... J Baumann. 164

Bullich, Martha. 511 W 50th... J Baumann. 197

Ball, Thomas. 146 W 37th....W Guinevan. (R) 563

Belford, Minnie. 1244 Broadway....T Kelly. 483

Bischoff, Mrs A. 29 W 61st....W E Wheelock & Co. Piano. (R) 180

Blanchard, Ada. 142 W 98th....L Baumann. (R) 106

Brachner, Victoria. 134 W 45th....L Baumann. (R) 210

Briggs, T G. 155 E 96th....W E Wheelock & Co. Piano. (R) 125

Brown, Elizabeth. 117 W 31st....S Baumann. 600

Brooks, Matilda F. 1672 3d av....R M Walters. Piano. (R) 135

Baldwin, Bessie G. 275 W 38th....H Mannes & Son. 681

Bones, J H. 438 W 20th ...O'Farrell & H. 138

Burmeister, H, and J Wacker. 300 E 70th....S Baumann. 306

Butler, J. 330 W 49th....W Schechter. 179

Baetzer, Catherine. 279 W 84th....L Baumann. 247

Brown, C A. 153 East Houston....J Moriarty. 111

Bull, Julia T. Powell pl, Morris Heights.... L Baumann. 261

Baker, Horace. 208 E 17th....Brooklyn F Co. 215

Bentham, Meyer. 650 9th av....J Baumann. (R) 304

Bissell, L F. 102 W 84th....W Weed. 160

Blum, Harriet. 384 Grand....R M Walters. Piano. (R) 190

Bohrer, Louise. 258 W 35th.. O'Farrell & Co. 144

Callan, Chas. 401 E 113th st and 2200 1st av.... J Moriarty. 265

Carmen, Sylva. 184 W 32d....R H Ramsgate. 1,000

Carter, M C. 238 W 43d....J Baumann. (R) 100

Chamberlain, G W. 172 W 96th....J Baumann. (R) 140

Chenowith, Annie. Roslyn, L I....J S & G F Simpson. 587

Clifton, Helen....J Williams. 161

Cowman, Thos. 274, 276 and 278 W 119th....S Knapp & Co. 315

Crisp, H H. 68 E 49th....Delta Club. (R) 297

Crowley, Rose. 305 W 119th....Dreisacker & Co. 286

Canfield, George. 2309 2d av....L Baumann. 165

Cushin, John. 201 E 38th ..J Moran. 229

Cary, Mary. 447 E 117th....Amer Guar Assoc. 200

Casey, Mrs. 339 E 24th....Jordan, M & Co. 120

Cashman, J C. 255 W 38th ...J Early. 350

Conlon, M. 69 Morton .... Wheelock & Co. Piano. 260

Casey, Mary E. 219 Bleecker....S I Herschmann. 140

Cass, Fannie A. 330 W 24th ...L Baumann. (R) 146

Chamberlain, A B. 8th av and 124th st....E C Hinsdale. 134

Connor, L S. 1095 Tremont av....W E Wheelock & Co. Piano. 275

Conrad, E E. 264 W 34th....S Heyman & Co. 700

Cross, R E. 2253 Fordham av....R M Walters. Piano. 325

Curry, Isabella. 152 E 97th....W E Wheelock & Co. Piano. (R) 180

Curry, Mrs James. 338 E 25th....D M Brown. 160

Cadwell, John. 226 W 123d....J Baumann. 194

Career, Amy. 424 E 110th .. J Baumann. 116

Cohen, Annie. 87 1st av....J Baumann. 209

Collier, Ella. 161 W 132d....J Baumann. 291

Costello, Winefred. 725 Washington ...J Baumann. 125

Cox, Sarah. 350 Lenox av....J Baumann. 190

Davis, M L. 1009 6th av ...J Baumann. 102
Same....same. 860
Donnelly, Anthony. 462 W 53d....J Baumann. 117
De Palos, J S. 222 Lexington av....L Baumann. (R) 128
Dore, Jean. 634 8th av....W Guinevan. (R) 182
Duffy, T L. 1622 Lexington av....E J Post. (R) 309
Dale, Theodore. 156 W 35th....L Baumann. 361
Day, R P. 112 W 47th....L Baumann. 788
Day, Sarah. 39 7th av. ..H Haviland. 2,075
Duffy, Kate. 11 Pell....Jordan & M. 143
Durkee, Mary E. 46 Bank... Wheelock & Co. Piano. 250
Dennison, Mary A. 88 E 21st....L Baumann. 115
Dreithall, Edward. 1107 3d av....S Heyman & Co. 155
Dale, W O. 357 4th av....T Kelly. (R) 104
Ellis, Florence A. 81 W 101st....J Baumann. (R) 320
Same... same. (R) 320
Evans, Catherine. 140 E 16th... J Baumann. 186
Femant, J H. 219 W 20th....J Baumann. 189
Foster, Mrs L. 738 6th av....D M Brown. 361
Fry, T H. 170 W 98th ...L Baumann. (R) 147
Feldan, R. 212 E 35th... Baumann. 486
Frecker, G N. 222 W 23d....Wheelock & Co. Piano. 475
Farnham, T G. 225 W 11th....T Kelly. (R) 102
Fay, John. 257 Greenwich....Simpson & P. Piano. (R) 220
Fletcher, Julia P. 217 Lenox av....B H Ball. 500
Forde, Clyde. 108 W 49th....J Baumann. (R) 181
Francis, John. 304 W 21st....L Baumann. (R) 216
Fitzsimmons, Jas. 304 W 21st....L Baumann. 227
Flynn, Mary. 132 Henry....S Heyman & Co. 184
Goldsmith, Henry. 155 W 28th....L Baumann. 397
Gordon, Jennie. 50 Grove... L Baumann. 134
Gilman, W. 100 W 94th....J Baumann. (R) 1,175
Gottschalk, B W. 116 E 59th....Krakauer Bros. Piano. 300
Gardner, J R. 42 W 65th ...Wheelock & Co. Piano. 300
Gibbons, Mary E. 236 W 17th ...L Baumann. 115
Gilbert, Emma. 257 W 39th....O'Farrell & H. 135
Gilman, L M. 243 W 45th....H Mannes & Son. 326
Goldstein, M. 222 Henry....Wheelock & Co. Piano. 275
Goodrich, G G. 540 W 58th....American Guarantee Assoc. 200
Goring, Clara. 396 4th av....Jordan & M. 110
Germond, John. 420 E 88th....L Baumann. 223
Graeser, Wiggo....Jordan, M & Co. 183
Graves, Olivia. 860 9th av....J Moriarty. 140
Gray, Francis....J Gregg & Co. 164
Greenwood, Edna. 120 W 49th....J Baumann. (R) 1,474
Groves, Anne E. 1067 Lexington av....Wheelock & Co. Piano. 275
Goldstein, Jenny. 171 Eldridge....S I Herschmann. (R) 116
Gross, Amelia. 34 2d av....E Wolf. 105
Gafney, J E. 200 W 96th....J Baumann. 328
Gleason, Jennie. 98 W 103d....J Baumann. 140
Gofney, J E. 200 W 96th....J Baumann. 358
Grant, Anna. 27 W 39th....J Baumann. 568
Hammond, C. 300 W 53d....J Baumann. 809
Haynes, A B. 319 W 34th....J Baumann. 151
Hills, L H. 81 Columbus av....J Baumann. 177
Hills, L H. 81st st and Columbus av....J Baumann. 284
Hobbs, B F. 360 W 46th....J Baumann. 180
Hartman, Geo. 502 W 21st....L Baumann. (R) 118
Hassan, J F. 238 W 15th....T Kelly. 156
Healy, Julia F....E J Dunphy. 1,155
Hiller, Jacob. 204 E 7th....Philipe & Berliner. 125
Hodge, Sarah C. 156 W 10th... W E Wheelock & Co. Piano. (R) 138
Hutchinson, Jennie S. 39 W 60th ...S Heyman & Co. 124
Hadley, F C. 204 E 11th ..J Moriarty. 248
Hartwick, Mary. 501 W 31st....J Early. 211
Hart, M. 251 W 39th....Wheelock & Co. Piano. 375
Hatrel, J E. 260 W 122d....J Moriarty. 320
Hazen, Amy M. 688 3d av....J Baumann. (R) 129
Hazen, Almy. 172 E 51st....J Baumann. (R) 129
Henderson, Mary J. 1520 10th av....J Baumann. (R) 180
Herrmann, Lottie. 108 W 17th....J Moriarty. 446
Hillard, Thos. 527 W 52d....L Baumann. 147
Hornbacker, Carrie. 639 6th....L Baumann. 122
Houghtaling, Mary. 2078 7th av....J Baumann. (R) 209
Humpreys, J. 313 W 20th....J Moriarty. 174
Hunter, Lillian. 268 W 39th....H Mannes & Son. 482
Huth, G & C. 60 Thomas....R Gaptzberg. 350
Hannaford, Sarah. 157 E 37th... .W J Gottlieb. 1,000
Hausman, Belle. 175 W 12th....J Baumann. (R) 112
Heldt & Knight. 18 W 22d... W & J Sloane. 1,230
Hill, Mrs J P. 152 W 50th....T Kelly. (R) 116
Hoelzer, Selma. 47 E 3d....O'Farrell & Co. 590
Harris, Abbie. 79 W 52d ....J Moriarty. (R) 112
Higgins, S C. 166 W 103d....L Baumann. 147
Hurd, Elizabeth L. 313 W 26th....J Moriarty. 326
Immergluck, Bertha. 199 Orchard....S Heyman & Co. 112
Ing, Henry. 221 5th av....L Baumann. 179
Jacobs, I D. 62 E 118th....Lincoln I and G Assoc. 100
Jinatauson, Jonas. 157 Orchard....H Thoesen. 256
Jackson, Addie. 254 W 38th....L Baumann. 274
Jackson, Ida. 350 8th av....W H Griffin. 100
Jacobs, Rebecca and Eva K. 204 W 44th....J Baumann. (R) 2,087
Jacobs, Tessie. 154 E 56th....J Moriarty. 155
Jaenick, Ellen. 172 E 72d....S Baumann. 680
Jane, Emily J. 124 W 102d....J Moriarty. 307
Jensen, Margaret. 162 W 103d... L Baumann. 138
Jaeger, Susie. 535 E 82d ...S Heyman & Co. 143
Johnson, Mrs Edgar. 363 W 57th....T Kelly. (R) 238
Jones, Mrs A. 336 W 4th....J Moriarty. 517
Jellison, Isabella. 247 W 50th....J Baumann. 224
Judge, Margaret. 480 W 46th....J Baumann. 142
Kemp, Minnie. 315 W 26th....L Baumann. 148
Klugmann, Julius. 327 E 52d....S Heyman & Co. 111
Kennedy, Margaret. 449 Canal. ..Simpson & P. Piano. 225
King, Frances M. 136 E 48th....H Thoesen. 204
Kane, Judith. 354 W 46th. ..Wheelock & Co. Piano. 250
Kennedy, Mary. 894 8th av....J Early. 156
King, F L. 165 W 129th....Wheelock & Co. Piano. 275
Knight, May. 19 W 22d....Jordan, Moriarty & Co. 152
Same....same. 125
Lasker, A. 965 Lexington av....S Baumann. 202
Lassiter, Hugh. 663 E 160th....L Baumann. 194
Lauterbach, W. 152 E 27th ...H Mannes & Son. 348
Levy, Mrs E. 661 E 134th....Jordan, M & Co. 184

Livermore, Ella W. 157 Madison av....A C Peck. (R) 1,500
Lobmeyer, Cora. 853 7th av....J Baumann. (R) 100
Lomax, Annie. 2274 8th av....Wheelock & Co. Piano. 250
Lusk, O L. 201½ West 24th....J Baumann. (R) 579
Lynch, Rose. 151 E 40th ..J Moriarty. 131
Lansberg, Edward. West Farms....Dreisacker & Co. 271
Lemien, Louisa. Fleetwood av and 173d st....Dreisacker & Co. 127
Lutz, Henrietta. 343 W 49th....O'Farrell & Co. (R) 124
Levy, Mrs S B. 166 W 102d....J Moriarty. 600
Lighthall, Harry. 200 E 72d ...S Heyman & Co. 134
Leake, Elizabeth. 820 3d av....J Baumann. 121
Lockwood, Lena. 258 W 10th....J Baumann. 208
Lohmeyer, Cora. 170 W 88d....J Baumann. 214
Looney, Mary. 40 E 47th....J Baumann. 232
Lima, Lorenze. 556 W 48th....J Baumann. 247
McCabe, Mary. 227 E 47th....J Baumann. 240
McCormack, Bessie. 84 Amsterdam av....J Baumann. 124
McNeill, Jennie. 62 E 122d....J Baumann. 136
Merkel, Rose. 125 W 28th....J Baumann. 483
Same....same. 638
Morton, Lottie. 227 W 40th....J Baumann. 174
Mure, T G. 148 W 4th ..J Baumann. 288
Manzee, Chas. 207 E 104th....L Baumann. 218
Mardon, Henry, Jr. 502 W 146th....L Baumann. 189
Mayer, William. 497 3d av ...J Moran. 116
McDermott, E E. 682 Water....L Baumann. 124
McMillan, Mary. 61 W 104th....J Baumann. (R) 190
Melick, Mary. 28 W 133d....Dreisacker & Co. 114
Moore, E P and E S. 175 W 45th....N L C Kaenumacher. (R) 1,475
Moore, Mrs S T. 120 W 102d....Brooklyn F Co. 286
Morse, Carrie E. 10-14 W 125th....Dreisacker & Co. (R) 210
Maloney, R J. 155 E 50th... S Baumann. 102
Mansfield, Emma A. 314 W 59th....O'Farrell & H. 278
Manning, T J. 18 E 32d....J A Snyder. (R) 110
Masterson, Sue. 182 W 82d....J Baumann. (R) 617
Mayo, P. 335 E 23d....Wheelock & Co. Piano. 260
McCabe, Bridget A. 366 9th av ..R M Walters. Piano. (R) 138
McClellan, Mrs A. 224 E 14th....Thos Willis. (R) 205
McCormick, M E. 150 E 40th....L Baumann. 120
McDonald, J J. 177 W 94th....L Baumann. 157
Meyer, Jessie B. 341 W 59th....S Baumann. 217
Mitchell, Susie L. 217 Sullivan....J Moriarty. 131
Mosher, Jessie L. 112 E 27th....D Coddington. (R) 1,200
Murphy, Mamie. 9 Pell....Jordan & M. 120
McFall, Chrissie. 201 E 22d....M Coyle. 500
McTeague, Susan. 511 E 119th....J Gregg & Co. 164
Merritt, C A E. 39 E 12th ...E A Merritt. 2,316
Miller, Carrie. 319 W 18th....L Baumann. (R) 171
Mott, H A, Jr. 68 W 45th....T Kelly. 244
Neu, Marion. 127 E 58th....S Fishblate. 2,500
Neu, Marion. 127 E 58th....S H Fishblate. (R) 2,500
Nelson, August. 170 W 65th....J Baumann. 115
O'Brien, Mary. 635 E 138th....Wheelock & Co. Piano. 190
O'Neill, J J. 208 Henry....Jordan, M & Co. 274
O'Neill, Mrs. J. 253 E 78th....Brooklyn F Co. 147
O'Rourke, C A. 225 Willis av ..Dreisacker & Co. 182
Paris, Jacob. 358 W 42d....J Baumann. 156
Potter, Esse. 223 W 43d....J Baumann. 446
Pollak, Lena, 177th st, Mt. Hope....Dreisacker & Co. 127
Price, Charles. 261 W 16th....J Gregg & Co. 147
Pederson, Berndt. 49 E 106th....J F Doherty & Co. 298
Pollock, Mrs A. 101 W 52d... I Mason. 122
Pierce, Mina. 281 W 41st....L Baumann. 184
Plunket, Annie. 279 W 128th....L Baumann. 167
Porter, Mary. 539 10th av....L Baumann. 117
Quinn, Margaret A. 323 E 84th....R M Walters. Piano. (R) 143
Quinn, John. 325 E 16th....J Moran. 213
Quackenbush, Theresa. 151 8th av....J & J Dobson. Carpets. 206
Runkle, L G. Hunter, N. Y....H Martin. 1,000
Reichling, Henry. 424 W 85th....L Baumann. 186
Robertson, Ellen. 326 E 123d....L Baumann. 165
Roe, A E. 406 W 46th....L Baumann. 188
Reardon, Mary E. 217 W 43d....J Baumann. (R) 186
Reed, Marie. 252 W 43d....H Mannes & Son. 879
Reynolds, Julia. 110 E 54th....L Baumann. 257
Richardson, E S. 864 W 117th....Jordan, M & Co. 229
Rickard, K O. Bellevue Hospital....Wheelock & Co. Piano. 375
Robinson, Carrie. 361 W 22d....J A Hyland. 172
Rosenbaum, Rose. 207 E 69th....J Baumann. 181
Rossheim, David. 1414 5th av....L Baumann. 121
Rushton, B A trustee. 41 E 41st....A E & W F Barnes. 776
Richter, Herman. 1513 2d av....Philips & Berliner. 104
Rosen, Ike. 340 E 116th....S Heyman & Co. 455
Rudolph, Augusta. 314 W 116th....T Kelly. 230
Rosenburg, Lucy. 64 E 122d .. J Baumann. 686
Rowland, Ella. 229 W 16th....J Baumann. 272
Russell, Margaret. 124 W 36th....J Baumann. 213
Schebella, John. 225 E 70th....J Baumann. 186
Sharp, Madeline. 2366 7th av....J Baumann. 149
Solomon, B. 2572 8th av....J Baumann. 257
Scott, Anna. 432 W 47th....L Baumann. (R) 113
Shandon, A F. 355 W 58th ...J Gregg & Co 730
Sheddin, Mrs M. 102 E 7th....D M Brown. 130
Shirley, Mrs A F. 140 W 49th....T Kelly. 162
Siegel, Amelia. 58 E 122d....W E Wheelock & Co. Piano. (R) 115
Simon, Louis. 23 E 111th....D M Brown. 125
Spiegel, Chas. 450 7th av....H Spiwak. 166
Stafford, Mary. 779 2d av....S Heyman & Co. 208
St Clair, Jane M. 317 W 22d....J Van Valkenbergh. 200
Stickert, Chas. 528 E 154th....J Gregg & Co. 130
Sabath, Minnie. 330 E 58th....Wheelock & Co. Piano. 300
Sayles, Mary. 255 W 32d....S Baumann. 129
Scanlon, J J. 105 E 89th....L Baumann. 131
Scheffe, Louis. 430 E 9th....L Baumann. 147
Shaw, Annie. 1591 1st av....J Baumann. (R) 111
Shaw, Emma. 62 South 3d st, Brooklyn....Jordan & M. 149
Shaw, Sarah B. 164 W 23d....H Mannes & Son. (R) 241
Shumar, J B. 326 W 32d....O'Farrell & Co. 487
Simon, Annie. 538 E 83d....Alexander Bros. 115
Smith, Fred. 134 Willis av....L Baumann. 146
Smith, May. 519 W 18th....S Baumann. 153
Spohr, Emma. 306 E 11th....J Moriarty. 110
Stafford, E B. 8 E 27th....L Baumann. 102
Stein, Anthony. 142 Willis av....L Baumann. 142
St George, Annie. 138 E 48th....J Baumann. (R) 217
Still, A. E. 26 Christopher....Wheelock & Co. Piano. 250

Subert, C A. 252 E 74th....Wheelock & Co. Piano. 378
Suvage, H. H. 118 E 119th....L Baumann. 300
Sabath, Mrs J. 169 E 74th....H Thoesen. 198
Schwarz, Ralph. 117 E 112th ...Simpson & P. Piano. 250
Sherry, Nellie....J Williams. 150
Steinecke, G D. 278 W 115th....C Hartman. 184
Stockenberg, Christ. 198 Elm....J Baumann. (R) 106
Sweet, Martha E. 47 W 42d....J Baumann. (R) 267
Thompson, Clarence. 703 9th av....L Baumann. 113
Toursaint, Costa. 244 W 22d....L Baumann. 167
Treadwell, Mary T. 153 E 106th....J Moriarty. (R) 266
Turtle, O J. 172 W 94th....T Kelly. (R) 191
Thorn, Ellen J. 48 E 60th....J Baumann. (R) 295
Tobias, Cassie. 401 E 72d....J Baumann. (R) 130
Tucker, George. 501 W 31st....J Early. 149
Turk, Hattie. 109 E 65th....J Baumann. (R) 149
Topfer, Ernst. 856 9th av....S Heyman & Co. 287
Temey, Mary. 304 W 39th....J Baumann. 265
Thompson, Minnie. 457 W 52th ...J Baumann. 142
Trapp, Cornelius. 556 9th av....J Baumann. 188
Van Gilder, C A. 15 W 99th ...J Baumann. 175
Van Wagner, Phoebe. 266 W 117th....J Baumann. 124
Vesley, Rosa. 402 E 56th ..J Baumann. 127
Van Campen, Mary R. 2 W 29th....Havana National Bank, Havana, N Y. (R) 17,732
Voss, Annie A. 101 W 101st ...Wheelock & Co. Piano. 350
Walter, A A. 164 E 79th....A Schoemann. 1,000
Wendell, Libbie. 1420 Park av .. J Baumann. (R) 187
Weiss, Ludwig. 853 E 72d....H S Eisler. (R) 206
Weiss, Regina. 829 E 82d....H S Eisler. (R) 124
White, R T. 818 Myrtle av, Brooklyn....C H Ten Eyck. 100
Wilmer, Chas. 264 3d av....J Baumann. (R) 146
Wilson, Esther L. 402 W 58th....J Baumann. (R) 130
Woodman, Anna. 217 W 24th....J Baumann. (R) 1,039
Wood, J A. 9 1st av....J Moriarty. 138
Wade, R A. 226 W 37th....Doherty & Co. 140
Walker, S P and M P. 202 W 103d ...Lincoln I and G Co. 300
West, Mabel. 19 Pell.. Jordan & M. 237
Winslow, Ella C. 121 W 97th ...C F Gunckel. 300
Same ...same. (R) 1,195
Walker, Annie. 320 E 57th....J Moriarty. (R) 171
Williams, Melissa A. 45 E 22d....E W Holt. 1,500
Wilson, A G....J Williams. 180
Weld, O W. 13 W 26th....J Baumann. 523
Whelan, Nellie. 324 W 47th... J Baumann. 156
Watt, Mrs G. 1770 Columbus av ...W E Wheelock & Co. Piano. (R) 102
Wood, Allen. 125 W 27th ...J Early. 141
Zeisler, Joseph. 70 E 116th....S Heyman & Co. 240

MISCELLANEOUS.

Altorfer, E. 161st st and Courtlandt av ...A D Puffer & Sons. Soda Fixtures. (R) 270
Auchtertonie & Co. 86 Elm....W Cumming. Machinery. (R) 618
Barth, John. 35 2d.. J Krieger. Butcher Fixtures. 100
Berg & Dix. 108 Clinton....Liberty Machine Works. Press. 135
Brautigam, A W. 2452 2d av....R C Lorch. Cigar Fixtures. 600
Browne, H H. 115 Nassau....D E Durham. Office Fixtures. 3,275
Brownell & Co. 87 Centre ...Whitlock Machine Co. Cutter. 600
Blayer, S H. 74 Canal... B Wolf. Press, &c. 500
Bacht, Eliza. 351 E 99th....H & J Colgrove. Horses, &c. 66
Bowers & Coombs. 431-435 E 77th....W & M Coombs. Machinery. (R) 4,000
Corbett, E J. 159 E 54th....R W Buckley. Machinery. 482
Considine, M P. 19 W 26th....National Cash Reg Co. Register. 175
Cranston, T L. 39 Gold....A L Phillips. Printing Fixtures. 2,500
Christie, Walter. 173 Christopher ...Manning & Co. Machinery. 1,025
Crowley, Timothy. 131st st and 10th av....D B Dunham. Cab. (R) 106
Carroll, J W. 78 Duane....A W Clapp. Machinery, &c. 2,000
Calhane, C. 141 Amsterdam av....National C Reg Co. Register. 175
Cooley, John. 207 W 42d....Wolff Bros. Horse and Cab. 190
Condon & Davenport. 4 Liberty....Walker & B. Type, &c. (R) 2,002
Conner, W M. St James Hotel....P Spofford, exr of. Hotel Fixtures. (R) secures rent
Cranston, T L. 39 Gold....A L Phillips. Presses. 2,500
Callahan, W J. 25 Washington....A D Puffer & Sons. Soda Fixtures. (R) 420
Chesley, Ellen E....H Thurm. Mangle. 95
Claussen, A F. 118th st and 8th av. ..National C Reg Co. Register. 225
De Leo, Rosi. 16 Franklin....A Schwaab & Son. Barber Fixtures. 247
Devan, John....J A Hyland. Canal Boat T L Skiff. 250
Dillon, M. United States Warehouse, Washington, etc ...Q A Shaw. Machinery. (R) 350,000
Drobkin, Leon. 74 Suffolk .... G Goldman. Butcher Fixtures. 90
Darby, Geo. 128 W 52d....H Killam Co. Coach. 1,800
Dierberg, Arnold. 124 E 6th....E S Weimann & Co. Horse, Wagon, &c. 86
Donahue, D J. 42 Park row....Lamson Consol S S Co. Register. (R) ——
Dunn, James. 14 W 62d....J T Nevin. Horses, Trucks, &c. 360
Elliott, G H. 18 Charles....D F Fox. Furniture and Dental Fixtures. 125
Franklin, J N & A F. 308 W 13th and 1012 Fulton, Brooklyn....Mary A Ladd. Plumber Fixtures. 1,500
Freisen, George. 247 and 249 Centre....C G Freidmann. Machinery, &c. 1,500
Same... C Freidman. Machinery. 2,500
Fridman, Muli. 422 Canal .. I Goldstein. Machines. 900
Fless & Ridge Printing Co. 5th av and 16th st ....Campbell P P Co. Folding Machine. 800
Same....same. Folding Machine. 1,400
Gilday, Patrick. 3d av, cor 51st st....Kruse C and A Machine Co. Register. (R) 210
Godby, R L. 422 W 43d....National Casket Co. Wagon. 800
Goodwin, Amelia. 958 Gates av, Brooklyn....C H Ten Eyck. Confectionery Fixtures. 34
Goldberger & Simonson....J O Sanford. Printing Office Fixtures. 330
Gunther & Baye. 428 E 19th....A D Puffer & Sons. Soda Water Apparatus. 3,790

Grundlach, Heinrich. 65 Spring ...A Lampe. Bakery Fixtures. 500

Hadley, S H 404 Pearl....W F Brush. Lodging House. (R) 3,500

Hart, Peter. 415 Greenwich....National C Reg Co. Register. 200

Holthusen, R C. 420 E 75th....A C Holthusen. Bottling Fixtures. (R) 4,400

Heins & Stahlhut. 96 Gold....Lamson Con S S Co. Register. 165

Herb, Marcus. 1875 2d av....A F Hahn. Butcher Fixtures. 100

Herrick, Sam. 70 Montgomery....H Dillon. Barber Fixtures. 100

Hopkins, Wood & Hopkins. 2173 7th av....W H Butler. Safe. 153

Heller, Hermann. 858 2d av .... H Haas. Wagon. (R) 58

Hemmer, P A. Webster av, bet 179th and 180th ....L Schmidt. Horses, &c. 2,100

Herschkowitz & Klein. 201 E 47th....L Heintzfurter. Butcher Fixtures. 150

Interchangeable Tool Co....American L and T Co. Machinery, &c. (R) 16,000

Jack, Lizzie. 823 Amsterdam av ...T Gross. Bakery Fixtures. 500

Kane, George. 4 W 186th....Wolff Bros. Horse. 125

Ketchum, H S. 128 W 23d....Lamson Con S S Co. Register. (R) 210

Kirchner & Frickmann. 155 E 128th....M B Tidey, Jr. Machinery. 93

Kramer, Albert. 240 E 3d....A Kramer. Machines. 600

Kennedy, W J. — W 26th.....D B Dunham. Cab. (R) 672

Kreusser, Arthur. 1215 3d av....M Dorothea. Jewelry Fixtures, &c. 3,780

Kelly, P J. 34 North Moore....Van Allens & B. Press. (R) 2,250

Klein, Gustav. 695 6th av....A Schwaab & Son. Barber Fixtures. 176

Kern, Chas. 128 Wooster....National C Reg Co. Register. 200

Levy, Maurice. 135 and 137 Division .. A C Manning & Co. Machinery. 1,250

Linger, Wolf. 85 Monroe. ..Welz & Zerweck. Bottling Fixtures. 200

Landan, Saloman. 119 E 4th....B Frohlich. Horse, Wagon and Milk Fixtures. 150

Lane, F S. 50 Exchange pl....Manhattan Type Co. Press. 30

Lifschitz, Isaac. 146 2d av....G H Wheeler. Drug Fixtures. (R) 1,302

Lankin, John....J A Hyland. Canal Boat Mike Dovan. 60

Lemm, R W. 187 E 23d....J Metz. Printing Office. 400

Lewis, J....J O Hadden. Horses, Trucks. 1,000

McKenzie & McPherson. 162d st and Morris av ....Thos W Weathered & Sons. Machinery. (R) 797

Minard Bros. 271 W 87th....Hincks & J. Coach. (R) 825

Multhaupt, E. 2036 1st av....F Hill. Store Fixtures. 100

McDonnell, Alexander. 98 and 100 Washington ....P McDonnell. Coal Yard Fixtures, Horses, Carts, &c. 749

McEntee, Dan. 631 6th av....Kruse C and A Machine Co. Register. (R) 210

Manhattan Medical and Chemical Co. 163 Pearl ....L E Walter. Office Fixtures, Tools, &c. 200

McCloskey, John. 21 and 23 Hoyt st, Brooklyn ....D B Dunham & Son. Cab. (R) 288

McGuire, Michael. 215 E 36th....M McGuire. Horses, Cabs, &c. 600

Mooney & Douglass. 40 W 18th....J Cunningham Son & Co. Coach. 275

Meinke, John. 306 W 145th....Columbia Wagon Co. Wagon. 75

Monahan, John. 340 E 117th....Wolff Bros. Horses. 450

Muller, A J. 1419 3d av....J C Jeager. Store Fixtures, &c. 150

Maccracken, W H. 710 Greenwich....C E Locke. Horses, Trucks, &c. 200

Matthews, J C. Sturtevant House....A P Sturtevant. Hotel Fixtures. 85,700

Same....same. Hotel Fixtures. 89,371

McCalister, J F. 587 Lexington av....National Casket Co. Undertaker Fixtures. 481

Moran & Green. 69 3d av....J F Bragg. Machinery. 3,000

Morrison, Wm, Jr....Damon & Peets. Press. 66

Muller, Claus. 2655 10th av....H Eggers & Co. Grocery Fixtures. 558

Murphy, M J. 363 South....W Walsh. Ship Chandler Fixtures. 250

Naef, Chas. 39 Maiden lane....G Dilly. Machinery. 150

Newton, C W. 231 E 43d....J Carroll. Horse and Cab. 350

New York City Ice Co....M F Winch, exr of. Horses, Wagons, &c. (R) 29,250

New York Bicycle Club....F W Kitching and J M Adreini trustees. Club Fixtures. 2,000

Ornstein, Haim. 20 Rutgers....E T Holthusen. Drug Fixtures. 1,200

O'Brien, J J. 93 Liberty....A A Jordan et al. Press, &c. (R) 400

Palmer, G W. 115 Broadway....A H Man. Office Fixtures. 100

Puls, F C. 415 Bowery....Damon & Peets. Press. 150

Purcell, Jane. 62d st and 11th av....A L Thompson & Co. Horses, &c. 450

Perona, James. 615 2d av....P Perona. Barber Fixtures. 200

Polizzano & Barcia. 15 Marion....A Feluecia. Bakery Fixtures. 81

Price, Isidor. 81 Delancey....I Ponker. Barber Fixtures. 45

Purviance, W E & Co....E & H T Anthony & Co. Photo Fixtures. (R) 920

Peterson, J H. 14 Platt... Damon & Peets. Printing Press. 106

Plunk, Louis. 307 Spring....National Cash Reg Co. Register. 200

Porcasi, Emanuel. 88 Cortland....A Schwaab & Son. Barber Fixtures. 395

Prosnitz, W. 1670 1st av....A Greenbaum. Bakery Fixtures. 1,000

Reitz, Charles. 922 9th av....S Moeslein. Jewelers Fixtures and Furniture. 1,000

Rooney, M J. 1329 Broadway....H Lindenmeyr. Press, &c. (R) 5,000

Rosenfeld, Sigismund. Thatford av, Brooklyn ....Liberty Machine Works. Press. 700

Rosenthal, Albert. 301 E 63d ...J Metz. Press, &c. 75

Rosenthal, Joseph....P Barrett. Truck. 311

Rosenstock, Leon. 110 Essex....L Kuhen. Barber Fixtures. 55

Schweizer & Walder. 665 10th av....C Kahle. Butcher Fixtures. 125

Scott, J. M A, W, E J and R....A C Cheney et al. Ice Barges, &c. 91,750

Sturtevant, Helen. 519 W 38th....E B Dusenbery. Horses, &c. 2,000

Sturtevant Co. 90 Walker....Johnson Peerless Works. Cutter. (R) 100

Suling, Chas. 2315 2d av... F Schofield. Grocery Fixtures. 200

Schaffner, G & G. 488 2d av....C Stegman's Son & Co. Butcher Fixtures. 650

Singer, M. 206 Rivington....Liberty Machine Works. Press. (R) 230

Smith, M A. 1361 Columbus av....A Raymond. Bottling Fixtures. (R) 5,000

Schaffner, G and G. 488 2d av....L Beer et al. Butter Store Fixtures. 680

Sudovitz, Max. 65 Monroe....Welz & Zerweck. Bottling Fixtures. 250

Sabella, Joseph. 314 E 60th... A Schwaab & Son. Barber Fixtures. 72

Samilson, L. 49 East Broadway....D Brener. Soda Water Factory. 600

Schafer, C. 706 Washington....Phebe Schafer. Horses, Trucks. 2,000

Schatzkin Bros. 177 Monroe....J Kramer & Son. Wagon. 245

Schraner, L. 212 E 34th ...Educational Supply Co. Machinery. (R) 725

Searle, G N....A Hengsbach. Horse, Milk Wagon, &c. 1,000

Sisti, Ginseppi. 166 Mulberry... A Schwaab & Son. Barber Fixtures. 252

Soricro, Antonio. Hudson st.. .A Schwaab. Barber Fixtures. 50

Spreen, D & H. 464 W 51st....C Krumwiede. Grocery Fixtures. 700

Staubach, J. 571 Courtlandt av....R Hill. Grocery Fixtures, Horse and Wagons. 400

Sternberg & Kornblum. 15 Ludlow....E Marscheider. Butcher Fixtures. 95

Towle, F S....P Barrett. Truck. 303

Thompson, Geo. 102 E 41st....D B Dunham. Cab. (R) 134

Tietjen, Hy. 1454 2d av ..National C Reg Co. Register. 225

"Thos Murry Co." 136 Liberty....Pierce & Thomas. Office Fixtures. 300

Van Ordens, C H. 1074 1st av....National C Reg Co Register. 175

Volkmar, & Enste....Kean & Lines. Coach. 400

White, John. 158 E 23d... E Willis. Coupe. 510

Winter, M. Montgomery st, cor Division st.... E Ehrich. Machinery. 98

Wood, Susan A. 142 W 39th....J Dahlman. Horse. 150

Woolf, O H. 2730 Marion av....M Walter. Horse and Cart. 300

Wahlers, John. 607 10th av....C F Gennerich & Co. Grocery Fixtures. 1,600

Weisskopf, S. 1393 2d av....Kruse C & A Mach Co. Register. (R) 210

Woerdemann, George. 1649 1st av....C Kluver. Store Fixtures. 400

Weiss, Joseph. 607 W 52d... A Weiss. Dyeing Fixtures. 400

Wolverton, Chester. 4 Warren....E V Parry. Office Fixtures. 300

Zimmer, Louis. 43 1st av....C Schwarzkopf. Cigar Fixtures. 300

BILLS OF SALE.

Gardner, E C. 122 Clinton pl....H A Lima. Saloon Fixtures. 1,500

Goldblatt, Nathan. 116 Broome....Esther Goldblatt. Grocery Fixtures. 475

Higgins, J B. 1301 Amsterdam av....Margaret Carroll. Grocery Fixtures. 900

Hill, R. 571 Courtland av ...J Staubach. Grocery Fixtures. 475

Krieger, Julia. 35 2d....J Barth. Butcher Fixtures. 300

Lescow, Albert. 1301 Amsterdam av....J B & M Higgins. Grocery Fixtures. 900

Lazarus, Jacob. 2 Av D....L Ewartz. Cigar Fixtures. 150

Lubin, Louis. 112 Broome....H Silberstein. Cigar Fixtures. 250

Michel, Valentine. 462 E 144th... H Eggers & Co. Grocery Fixtures. 100

Miller, Elijah. 213 Monroe....Emma L Miller. Drug Fixtures. 119

Mayers, Mark. 2400 3d av and 3d av bet 130th st and Harlem River ...A B Strauss. Saloon Fixtures, &c. 350

Nicolaus, John. 631 Greenwich....G Cramer. Butcher Fixtures. 340

Platte, Joseph. 571 Courtland av....R Hill. Grocery Fixtures. 470

Reed, C B. 50 W 125th... S E Dobson. Banjo Fixtures. 100

Richter, William. 303 E 19th....M Richter. Furniture, &c. 500

Rienbow, Jos. 27 Ludlow .... Beky Rienbow. Sewing Machines. 300

Schaeler, A. 765 3d av....Eugenia Schaeler. Jewelry Fixtures. 600

Tillotson, W W... O Selleck. All Title in Tillotson Opera Co. 500

Tremer, A. 452 W 38th....Josephine Tremer. Saloon Fixtures. 150

ASSIGNMENT OF CHATTEL MORTGAGE.

Hirschberg, J to S Gordon. (Mort given by Brandsteter & Klein, Sept. 15, 1891.) 275

KINGS COUNTY.

OCTOBER 8 TO 14.—INCLUSIVE.

SALOON AND RESTAURANT FIXTURES.

Agster, J. 29 Locust....L Eppig. $450

Bottjer, H. 19 Adams .. J Ruppert. 1,600

Browne, N. 720 Hancock....Claus Lipsius B Co. 500

Benson, W H. 633 Fulton....C Martin. Restaurant Fixtures. 1,000

Comer, E. 307 Livingston....S B Jones. (R) 2,400

Chambers, J. 28 Broadway....D G Yuengling, Jr, B Co. (R) 500

Cronin, T. Vernon av, Flatbush....S Liebmann's Sons B Co. 350

Cain, J J. 322 Van Brunt....J Ruppert. 2,000

Drangel, P A. 78 Grand....Budweiser B Co. 260

Dreves, C. 255 Clinton....Beadleston & W. (R) 1,600

Elberling, K. 98 Debevoise....L Eppig. 500

Feldmann, G. 1357 Greene av....Claus Lipsius B Co. 500

Foley, J. 197 Greenpoint av....M Seitz. (R) 530

Fuchs, P. 822 Central av....M Seitz. 500

Fitzgerald, J E. 51 Raymond....Budweiser B Co. 110

Gentzlinger, W H. 454 Graham av....Leibinger & O B Co. (R) 600

Gutmann, H. 319 Glenmore av....Leibinger & O B Co. (R) 600

Grube, C. 15 Broadway....H Peters. (R) 2,000

Haasch, W. 11 Myrtle av....Claus Lipsius B Co. 200

Haas, E. 19 Meserole....J Fallert B Co. (R) 400

Hogan, E A. 1426 Bergen....E Ochs. 750

Hughes, M. 562 3d av....D Stevenson. 300

Helling, L and L Varenhold. 765 Wythe av.... Claus Lipsius B Co. 800

Hildemann, K. 1693 Fulton....Danenberg & C. (R) 1,087

Janssen, E. 168 Gwinnett....C Frese. 450

Kettering, J. 111 Stagg....Obermeyer & L. 900

Keller, M J. 202 Graham av....Leibinger & O B Co. 700

Kirchner, L. Rockaway av, n w cor Sackett st ....L I Brewery. 250

Koch, Lena. Fulton and Georgia avs....M Bennett. 500

Lemmi, C. 107 Navy....G L Lemmi. 400

Mangels, H. 703 and 705 Wythe av....Rubsam & H B Co. 3,000

Mapes, W E. 47 Grand. ..P Weidmann. 1,500

Manning, J. 162 Park av ...W Ulmer. 1,369

McCahey, M. 4th av, cor 7th st....H Vogel. 750

Meyer, C L. 270 Cooper. ..M Seitz. 350

Meyer, E D. 720 Grand ..J R Thonsen. 2,000

Same ...P Ballentine & Sons. 3,000

McDonald, M. 937 Atlantic av... Claus Lipsius B Co. 400

Morris, J. Belmont av, west cor Osborn st ... Danenberg & C. (R) 939

O'Donnell, Edward. 178 Hull....Claus Lipsius B Co. 900

O'Brien, D. 697 and 699 Fulton....Budweiser B Co. 4,500

O'Connor, R. 224 Franklin....W Ulmer. 2,000

Quaid, Jr, J. 1 9th....Obermeyer & L. (R) 500

Schaeffler, A. 248 Kingsland av....Burger & H B Co. 500

Schroeder, E. Ralph av, cor Madison st....Fred Hower B Co. 825

Stanton, T. 717 Wythe av....Obermeyer & L. 150

Sweet, J. 1941 Broadway.. .M Seitz. 441

Schilt, A. 99 Johnson av....Claus Lipsius B Co. 800

Ulmer, J. 116 Ellery ..Leibinger & O B Co. 900

Walch, J. 645 Atlantic av... Obermeyer & L. (R) 704

Wagner, G. 173 Smith....G & J Zipp. (R) 600

Wayne, J. 112 Rockaway av....Obermeyer & L. (R) 1,000

Werner, J. 177 Sackett....J H Bereuter. Pool Tables. 180

Wildprett, F. 165 Throop av....F Steurer. 200

Wood, I D. 78 Beaver....G Ehret. (R) 600

Webb, J. 673 Hicks....Budweiser B Co. 125

Yud, J. 166 Lynch....Leibinger & O B Co. 450

HOUSEHOLD FURNITURE.

Ackley, W. C. 579 Putnam av....Brooklyn F C. 197

Adler, J. 127A Calyer....Jacob Bros. Piano. 225

Aldridge, Eliz M. 117 Lawrence....Mary W Harman. 1,500

Ayers, A M. 373 16th....Brooklyn F Co. 350

Bird, Henrietta. 184 Glenmore av....Jacob Bros. Piano. 190

Black, D. 64 Linden....Brooklyn F Co. 580

Brush, S M. 141 Jefferson av....Brooklyn F Co. 131

Brunner, Mrs M. 190 Bergen....R M Walters. Piano. 200

Buckholder, A. 64 Jefferson av... Brooklyn F Co. 163

Barrett, May. 194 Pearl....Brooklyn F Co. 286

Bernard, C L. 1643 Atlantic av....L Baumann. 117

Branigan, J. 964 Myrtle av....C T Kendrick & Co. 140

Cooke, Mrs F. 191 Moffatt . C T Kendrick & Co. 180

Cagney, T J. 171 Stuyvesant av....American Guar Assoc. 200

Cohn, B. 85 Jamaica av....Jacob Bros. Piano. 945

Corrales, P. 150 Adams....J McEnery & Co. 227

Cosgrove, C. 629 Union....I Mason. 111

De Baun, D H. 583 Lafayette av....Brooklyn F Co. 213

Devine, M J. 118 Wythe av....Jacob Bros. Piano. 215

De Witt, Annie. 169 Skillman....Krakauer Bros. 110

Douglas, W H. 295 7th av ...Brooklyn F Co. 325

Dunn, Emma. 100 Willoughby ..Brooklyn F Co. 197

Decker, L P. 48 Ellery ...C T Kendrick & Co. 210

Dooley, C A. 30 Bergen....I Mason. 173

Earl, Jennie J. 582 Kosciusko....J Michaels. 176

Gates, Henrietta L. 18 Oakland....Jacob Bros. Piano. 155

Gibson, Annie M. Broadway, cor Gates av.... Jacob Bros. Piano. 240

Gilson, F W. 328 Clermont av....P Canavello. 135

Golden, Mary. 335 Grand....A Schulz. 147

Gould, Mrs H E. 65 Pineapple....I Mason. 278

Graham, J H. 961 Bushwick av ...W R Willis. 240

Harrison, Lilian. 85 Clinton av... Brooklyn F Co. 421

Heney, G F. 65 St Johns pl....C E Pierce. 100

Henning, M. 178 12th....Manges Bros. 246

Hauekost, Margt. 117 Prospect ...L Baumann. 115

Hanson, F. 430 Carlton av....A Pearson. 125

Holt, Delia. 509 Bedford av....L Baumann. 217

Hill, E L. 670 Quincy....Simpson & P. Piano. 275

Julio, A. 184 Columbia....J Rubenstein. 172

Kerr, J. H. 423 Bedford av ...Jacob Bros. Piano. 207

Klock, J C. 232 15th ...Brooklyn F Co. 180

Knoche, Bertha. 42 Broome....L Baumann. 371

Lattemer, W. 634 Kosciusko....A Schulz. 400

Laviolette, J. 331 Ralph av....G Dompierre. 196

Lazarus, J S. 213 Lorimer....Jacob Bros. Piano. 235

Martin, Abbie. 250 Keap....Manges Bros. 274

Martin, Kab. 144 North 8th....Jacob Bros. Piano. 205

Micholes, C. 438 Gold....Brooklyn F Co. 188

Mueller, B G. 65 Newell....Brooklyn F Co. 190

Murphy, W. 150 Spencer....G L Grove. 141

Marshall, G W L. 526 11th....O Wissner. Piano. 305

Merrell, Mrs P M. 834 Halsey....Brooklyn F Co. 104

Muller, Amelia. 207 Lee av....C T Kendrick & Co. 227

Marquart, F. 1069 Willoughby av....A Zimmermann. 200

Mason, E G. 1251 De Kalb av....Simpson & P. Piano. 209

Matignon, Sophie and Alcide. 2172 Fulton....B Holleneider. 7

McGinn, Mrs J. 118 President ...I Mason. 195
McSwyney, Mary. 1115 Greene av....Jordan, Moriarty & Co. 164
Ossman, Mrs C. 17 Troutman ...I Mason. 118
O'Keefe, M. 117 Prospect ...L Baumann. 384
Olton, Harriet C. 388 Degraw....G H Brockway. 177
Patrick, Mrs E. 49 Pulaski....Mullins' Sons. 114
Pearce, A. 394 Sackett....C A Barnett. 200
Pike, C S. 19 4th av....Brooklyn F Co. 138
Quigley, J F. 198 Driggs....Jacob Bros. Piano. 191
Rich, J. 157 52d ...Manges Bros. 159
Rieley, Miss Frances. 24 Atlantic av....L Baumann. 146
Rourke, Sarah. 16 Tallman....J McEnery & Co. 100
Rozand, Mrs I. 246 Stockton....C T Kendrick & Co. 112
Rymer, J F. 17 Cooper pl....C T Kendrick & Co. 192
Reis, W....I Mason. 100
Stevens, Annie. 34 Tallman....H S Eisler. 148
Schwarzbaum, R. 164 Court...Brooklyn F Co. 156
Simss, D W. 55 Jefferson av... Brooklyn F Co. 259
Spencer, C B. Driggs av, cor Sutton st....Brooklyn F Co. 145
Thym, L A J. 1238 Pacific ...E C Hinsdale. 625
Trautb, W. 255 Jefferson ...A Schulz. 104
Thompson, H B. 918 Madison....J McEnery & Co. 131
Unangust, Emma. 45 Floyd....J Rubenstein. 109
Van Dervoort, Anna. 1156 Fulton....Manges Bros. 366
Weis, L. 106 Devoe....A Schulz. 198
Woodward, F E. 710A Jefferson av...I Mason. 151
Yereance, A. 596 McDonough....Brooklyn F Co. 144

MISCELLANEOUS.

Bergen, V. 2048 Fulton....W H Cornwell. Grocery Fixtures. 265
Bernhard, V ...G Dessecker. Coach. 625
Burkhardt, R. 1256 Broadway... G Hagemeyer. Store Fixtures. (R) 1,000
Brown, S T. 1568 Prospect pl. O Wissner. Horse, &c. 276
Bennett, R R. Greene av .... W B Davis. Coaches. (R) 1,000
Campbell & Schmidt....P Parrett. Wagon. (R) 187
Charters, A. 165 Clifton pl....A Armstrong. Horses, Wagons, &c. 3,000
Condon & Davenport. 4 Liberty st. New York . Walker & B. Printing Office Fixtures. (R) 2,003
Dillon, M. Washington st. &c, United States Warehouse, New York....Q A Shaw. Machinery. (R) 350,000
Donovan, T T. 1030 Broadway....Henrietta Schlim. Printing Office Fixtures. 250
Duffy, I. Myrtle av and Adams st....F J Minck. Horses. 600
Davis, C E. 555 Hamilton av....H J Hoff. Machinery. secures rent and covenants in lease
Gallagher, M. 172 Pacific .... W B Davis. Coach. 400
Grubert, A. Central av. s e cor Troutman st.... A J Plauding. Butcher Fixtures. 200
Geiss, E. 84 Raymond....J Ruppert. Blacksmith Fixtures. 500
Heise, Fredericke. 150 Central av .... Mag Schwarz. Dry Goods Fixtures. 1,050
Hefferan, B and J....H Ungerland. Horses, &c. 500
Helfst, J N. 169 Manhattan av....P N Meincke. Grocery Fixtures. 2,000
Horton, J W & Son. 20 Dougherty... Eunice V K Horton. Horses, &c. 1,000
Hoyt, W R. 45 Clermont av ...E Stevens. Buggy in Storage. (R) 125
Kelly, P J. 37 North Moore st, New York... Van Allens & B. Printing Press. 2,700
Kissam, W S. 410 Broadway....H Douglass. Drug Fixtures. 1,800
Kane, J A. 266 5th av....I C Jersey. Fixtures. 163
Kozlay, C M. 349 Adams ...Whitlock Machine Co. Press, &c. 1,700
Kallert, G. 699 Myrtle av....G Prozesky. Barber Fixtures. 300
Kennedy, D J. 446 Grand....National Cash Register Co. Register. 175
Lutz, Amy A. 624 Wythe av ...Swezey's Sons & Co. Bakery Fixtures. 500
Langhirt, J. 153 Meserole....J Roeller. Candy Store Fixtures. 90
McClain, J. 221 York....W B Davis. ..Coupe. (R) 300
McClain, J....same. Coupe. (R) 300
McLane, J ...W B Davis. Coupe. (R) 450
Murray, R. 88 Willoughby....National Cash Register Co. Register 175
McGuckin, J E. 383 Oakland....J H Murphy. Horses, Coaches, &c. 3,000
Metsch, F B. 685 4th av....J Mulsoft. Barber Fixtures. 50
Neudecker, W. 101 Floyd....E Marscheider. Butcher Fixtures. 188
Noonan, J B. 418 South 4th....J H & M Cooney. Sewing Machines, &c. 100
O'Brien, J. 569 Flushing av....Minnie Kromer. Wagon. 150
Peloubet, S S. 78 Greenwich st, New York....C D Rust. Stereotype Plates. 1,600
Pine G W ...W Conrady. Wagon. 160
Pumphrey & Co ....Barrett & B. Wagon. 145
Rosenfeld, S. Thatford av ...Liberty Machine Works. Presses. 700
Reichert, Rosalie. 2200 Fulton ...O Volk. Candy Store Fixtures. 500
Reinheimer, J. 360 Gold .... J Reinheimer. Horses, &c. 450
Rothang, C. 195 Sumpter....Nat Cash Register Co. Register. 175
Schaefer, P. 49th av....R B Klussmann. Grocery Fixtures. 46
Schorr, J. 1924 Fulton....May, Levy & May. Butcher Fixtures. (R) 282
Selner, J. 350 Leonard....E Zimmer. Butcher Fixtures. 250
Timms, R. 542 Union....W B Davis. Coach. (R) 200
Timper, A. 1906 Atlantic av ...A Immig. Bottling Business. (R) 350
Unadulterated Spice Co....P Barrett. Wagon. 73
Watson, O. 69 John ...T Burnjer. Presses, &c. 1,250
Weidner, Fanny. 105 Meserole....W Scott & Co. Printing Press. 900
Winnett, G W. 61 Orient av....R F Gillin. Horse. 190
Wrede, H L. 37 Chauncey....G H Brede. Store Fixtures. 600

BILLS OF SALE.

Collins, Charles H. 486 4th av....Mary E Collins. Carpenter Fixtures, &c. 500

Cordes, H and J Bargfriede. 111 Smith....H Bargefriede. Grocery Fixtures. 2,600
Dahl, R. 11th av and 61st st, New Utrecht.... Ann Dahl. Horses and Wagons. nom
Grove, G L. 150 Spencer....W Murphy. Furniture. 166
Giuseppe, M. 211 Hudson av....F Pascaelli. Barber Fixtures 130
Kirsch, J. 722 Evergreen av....Louise Kirsch. Grocery Fixtures. 175
Lipkowitsch, H. 85 Court....Josephine Niebel. Furniture and Fixtures. 1,750
Limberger, P. 870 Grand ..E Schmidt. ½ of Blacksmith Shop and Tools. 325
Mathews, W. 74 Grand....J H Pulshen. Saloon Fixtures. 700
Muller, J D. 252 5th av....J M Keane. Store Fixtures. nom
Mallon, R. Pearl and Concord sts....T Bracken. Saloon Fixtures. 1,050
North, W C. 93 Quincy....Emile Moore. Furniture. nom
Rein, M. 4 Monitor....Margaretha Rein. Willow Ware. 80
Schwarz, Magdalena. 150 Central av....Frederick Heise. Dry Goods Fixtures. 1,300
Shea, T J. 179 Franklin....W. Shea. Saloon Fixtures. 600
Starke, L. 87 Graham av....J Herlich. Grocery Fixtures 600
Thermann, A. 121 Macon... J H Woltmann. Grocery Fixtures. 4,000
Tobias, M. 1417 Broadway....T Pink. Butcher Fixtures. 450

ASSIGNMENTS OF CHATTEL MORTGAGES.

Klobutscheck, J to Eliz Goetting. (Mort given by L. Kunz, Sept 15, 1891.) 100
Ulmer, W to E Ochs. (W C Fowler, July 1, 1890.) 900
Walker, Barbara A to John C Valentine. (Feb 21, 1891.) 200

NEW JERSEY.

NOTE.—*The arrangement of the Conveyances, Mortgages and Judgments in these lists is as follows: the first name in the Conveyances is the Grantor; in Mortgages, the Mortgagor; in Judgments, the Judgment debtor.*

ESSEX COUNTY.

CONVEYANCES.

Arcularius, W A—E R Arcularius, South Orange $1
Arnold, T L—B Pearse, Thomas st 1
Ball, Charles—H E Johnson, Bloomfield.......... 1
Rall, Isaiah—D McKeever, South Orange.......... 3,500
Ball, R M—C Ball, Bloomfield 1
Barkhorn, Catharina—C J Solomon, Springfield av.......... 2,900
Barnet, J G—A Wiley, Warick st.......... 2 200
Barrett, M T—The Belleville B and L Assoc, Grafton av 550
Barry, Michael—D Quinlan, Orange.......... 500
Battle, G G—A P Johnson, Montclair 1
Black, E S—J Rummell, Pennington st 575
Brady, P J—F L Corwin, West Orange.......... 17,500
Brown, James—H L Baimmer, Newark st.......... 1,200
Cavanagh, E T—O Naumann, South 14th st.......... 710
Clancey, J J—R M Decker et al, Miller st.......... 1,100
Close, Susan—C A Potter, Montclair 5,500
Condit, Fillmore—J B Voorhees, Caldwell.......... 300
Connall, Elizabeth—A Lloyd, Belleville.......... 800
Dean, E A—J R Pitcher, Milburn.......... 1
Dodd, S E—P H Campbell, South Orange.......... 4,250
Dosa, G H—L W Hand, Clinton.......... 318
Drexel Improvement Co—J F Vogelius, Montclair.......... 657
Same—J C Valentine, Montclair.......... 087
Eberle, Addie—J F Otterbein, West Orange.......... 6,000
Same—M J Sliker, West Orange.......... 1
Same—S F Sliker, West Orange 850
Einwachter, Mary—W J Hughes, Littleton av.. 1,800
Eisele, Charles—R Eisele, Bergen st.......... 1,200
Eifinger, William—E Z Lambertsen, 7th st.......... 275
Fererro, Joseph—C L Nesler, Vanderpool st.......... 1,500
Fischer, H W—J C Eisele, Prince st.......... 1,600
Gerbert, Peter—A Day, Bloomfield 8,000
Graves, W H—E Ziehr, Clifton av.......... 2,300
Gray, T J—L Lesser, n Pennington st 316 e N J R R av 30x80 4,100
Hamilton, E P—A Lee, South Orange.......... 14,000
Hand, L B—J B Partington, Milburn.......... 450
Heyden, Edward—J Mason, Clinton.......... 875
Hoey, John—J M Williams, East Orange.......... 8,000
Howell, N P—A Wood, Walnut st.......... 1,000
Same—S M Thomas, Walnut st.......... 1
Jacobus, W W—J Ferreira et al, Clinton.......... 1
Johnson, C H, Jr—G G Battle, Montclair 1
Knight, W J special master—A Heron, West Kinney st.......... 2,000
Kolbenschlag, G F—C E Schuckai, Barclay st.. 1
Lehrman, Henry, Jr—Francis Leist, Montclair.. 200
Lieberman, Hanne—A J Rosenstein, w s Monmouth st 293 n Spruce st 25x94 3,600
Lord, Francis—S Storms, Montclair.......... 1,500
Lowenstein, Jacob—H V Wort, Charlton st.......... 1,250
Maclay, I W—W Schneider, Orange.......... 335
Meeker, S A—A Connelly, Morris Canal.......... 1,300
Miller, T H—W F Keegan, Clinton 180
Mitchell, A P—R H Butterworth, Bloomfield .. 280
O'Neill, F J—V Andreolo, South Orange.......... 650
Philip, Mary—J S Philip, Franklin 1
Pierson, H S—A E J Morrison, Green st.......... 1
Plum, S H—J Ward, Jr, 1st tract e s Plane st 30x100, 2d tract w s Essex st 227 from New st 30x52.......... 7,250
Richardson, H M—D McKeever, w s South 19th st 150 n 16th av 175x100.......... 5,000
Riker, Frederick—O E C Fentzlaff, Montclair.......... 1,660
Ritchie, J J—H C Marley, South 7th st.......... 650
Rowe, Michael—T W Dalton, Central av.......... 1
Sanford, Joseph B—B M Farley, Sanford av 1
Schneider, William—L A Maclay, Orange.......... 335
Schuhmann, Theresa—T J Regan, Court st.......... 1
Schnellbach, M E—H McGee, s s Kinney st 150 e West st 25x100.......... 3,400
Sliker, M J—A Eberle, West Orange.......... 1
Smith, C L D—J Staats, Hunterdon st.......... 100
Smith, H W—S D Day, Orange.......... 10,250
Smith, P E—E Mahoney, Orange.......... 900
Snyder, E H—J Picot, South Orange 1,140
Sorhagen, Mary—A Sorhagen, Clinton.......... 250
Spottiswoode, George—H C Duffy, Orange.......... 375
Tallmadge, W D—M Harrigan, East Orange.......... 640
The Essex and Hudson Land Impt Co—J C Wilson, Murray st.......... 500
The Howard Savings Institution—P H Mueller, s e cor Elizabeth av and Earl st 200x100.......... 6,300
Thomas, S M—A Wood, rear Elm st.......... 1,000
Tichenor, W T—V Denoth, Montclair.......... 250
Trimble, J M—W I Soverel, Montclair.......... 400
Vogel, Theresa—A Connolly, Lock st.......... 1,200
Wakeman, J P—F P Jaques, e s Mt Prospect av 245 n Bloomfield av 30x150.......... 6,500
Weatherby, Harry et al—A P Sharp, Franklin.......... 650
Same—E N Griswold, Franklin 150
Wiebach, Charles—H Gerhard, Av L.......... 1,300
Wiedenmayer, G W—S Morris, Market st 2,500
Williams, I A—E Gibbons, s s 13th av 388 w High st 25x42 4,600
Williams, I M—E McDermott, Orange.......... 800
Wills, T W—G B Clark, Clinton.......... 800

MORTGAGES.

Allen, Joseph—J H Osborne, Bloomfield.......... 3,000
Austin, William—The Belleville B and L Assoc, Belleville.......... 1,200
Beck, W F—J S Riker, Orange.......... 2,600
Burke, Henry—C Stickler, Orange.......... 8,000
Chittenden, H A—Rev T Carter, Montclair.......... 5,000
Connolly, Thomas—L Leverich, Belleville.......... 1,500
Courter, G W—J H Alsworth, Montclair.......... 1,500
Curtis, T A—W H Graves, Clifton av.......... 1,500
Day, Abraham—P Gerbert, Bloomfield.......... 1,000
Day, S D—H W Smith et al, Orange.......... 7,000
Dodd, H P—G A Oakes, Bloomfield.......... 3,000
Doyle, Matthew—J Grace, Oxford st.......... 2,000
Du Bois, C D—H J Chase et al exrs, Montclair... 10,000
Duffy, H C—G Spottiswoode, Orange 325
Duths, C E—D H Wood, Montclair.......... 2,000
Eisele, J C—The Washington B and L Assoc, Prince st.......... 1,200
English, C W—The American Ins Co, Montclair. 2,000
English, M J—Montclair B and L Assoc, Montclair.......... 7,030
Farash, Thomas—The American Ins Co, Montclair.......... 1,100
Fletcher, Bertha—J McMorrow, South Orange.. 200
Fletcher, Rosanna—S B Jackson, Clinton st.......... 400
Frederick, J R—M Reinhardt, East Orange.......... 3,300
Garduer, A D—J M Ward, Clinton av 5,000
Gavitt, Elizabeth—C Akers, Bloomfield.......... 500
Gemperli, J G—A Ahrrus, Boyd st.......... 1,000
Hand, L W—S F Hand, Clinton.......... 325
Harrigan, Mary—C O Harris, East Orange.......... 350
Helmstaetter, William—C Bader, Baldwin st .. 200
Heron, Archibald—Howard B and L Assoc, West Kinney st.......... 2,400
Jaques, F P—J P Wakemans, Mt Prospect av... 4,000
Johnson, W M—The Norfolk B and L Assoc, Bank st 600
Keegan, W F—F Bonykamper, Jr, Clinton.......... 100
Kelly, Peter—W Una, Catharine st.......... 300
Kingsley, G P—W Mason, Orange.......... 3,000
Kolb, J F—J Stumpf, Waverly pl.......... 1,000
Mason, Joseph—E Heyden, Clinton.......... 150
Mattia, A M—A Ilaria, State st.......... 1,050
McGee, Hannah—C Barkhorn, Kinney st.......... 400
Moller, John—M C Van Ness, East Orange .. 3,000
Morris, Samuel—Phoenix B and L Assoc, Market st.......... 2,500
Mueller, P H—The Howard Savings Inst, Elizabeth av 5,300
Mnester, H L—The United States Industrial Ins Co, Orange.......... 500
Mirzwicki, Frank—B S Stiles, Somerset st.......... 7,500
Oatman, W F—East Orange B and L Assoc, East Orange.......... 1,800
O'Connor, Mary—Belleville B and L Assoc, Belleville.......... 1,000
O'Gorman, S C—E W Crane, Broad st.......... 5,000
Otterbein, J F—A Eberle, West Orange.......... 4,000
Parker, William—E H Snyder, South Orange... 1,850
Peck, L M—Prudential Ins Co, East Orange.... 4,000
Pfister, J D—D Rudolph, Waverley pl.......... 1,000
Proffin, A H—L A Dodd, Montclair.......... 400
Putenlopek, John—Essex Co B and L Assoc, Bloomfield 1,000
Reilly, John—The Mutual B and L Assoc, Vesey st.......... 600
Rindell, C A—K B Carter, Ridgewood av 250
Roegels, Helen—W N Trusdell, Aqueduct st.... 800
Rosenstein, A J—Savings B and L Assoc, Monmouth 2,800
Rowe, W H—F T Johnson et al, East Orange.... 850
Scaine, John—Belleville B and L Assoc, Belleville.......... 100
Sikorra, Andreas—W Hill, Fairview av 1,000
Simonin, P H—C E V C Mershon trustee, Green st 400
Singer, Bartholomaus—W Kraus, Orange.......... 2,200
Skinner, M C—S Hopper, Belleville 1,000
Soverel, W J—C D Soverel, Montclair.......... 400
Spagnuolo, Anelli—14th Ward B and L Assoc, Monroe st.......... 1,600
Stoops, James—L Leverich, Parker st.......... 3,000
Ward, P H et al—W N Trusdel, North 4th st.... 100
Weiss, Markus—The Newark German B and L Assoc, Prince st 400
Wiley, Addison—J G Barnet, Warwick st.......... 1,100
Wood, Alexander—S Doughty et al exrs, Walnut st.......... 1,000
Zelliff, Garry—A Hupfel, Belleville av.......... 1,800

CHATTEL MORTGAGES.

Ackerman, E D—Marvin Safe Co, safe 80
Barber, G W—G Weigand, butcher fixtures.......... 350
Bloch, Sander—Muller & Schmidt, furniture.......... 69
Blum, August—C Feigenspan, saloon 400
Bock, F J—J M Moore, horses and wagons.......... 1,500
Carter, J L—J Ketcham, furniture 100
Crump, J M—W Van Steenburgh et al, horses and wagon.......... 350
Curtis, C H—L H Colvin, piano 130
Forman, George—S Steele et al, furniture.......... 150
Haase, L H B—Hirschfield & Co, safe.......... 125
Handley, W J—The National Cash Register Co, register 125
Helles, Louis et al—T J Schweitzer, stock, wines 500
Heinzinger, John—J Buthmacher, furniture.... 220
Horle, J J—The National Cash Register Co, register 200
Lane, J F—J Ketcham, furniture.......... 130
Law, J A—S Green, machinery 1,000
Lundequist, Ed—Marvin Safe Co, safe.......... 75
Marcell, W H—Marvin Safe Co, safe.......... 100
Mead, Aaron—E S Lyon, horse.......... 115
Myers, Agnes—W M Smith, drugs.......... 1,360
Perkins, T W—F C Edwards, furniture.......... 195
Reinhard, G F—Wilkinson, Gaddis & Co, groceries 595
Ruckel & Newman—H Way, furniture.......... 250
Samell, Nathan—J Hornstein, machinery 30
Scarlett, William—S B Scarlett, furniture.......... 100
Scholz, Theodore—T Voigt, bakery 500
Shebley, Frank—M H Simmons, book accounts. 400
Sleight, C H—Marvin Safe Co, safe.......... 75
Stager, Warren—E B Budd, horses and wagons. 125
Thompson, C H—L H Colvin, piano.......... 210
Webb, W J—P H Hanley, piano.......... 67

Wolfensberger, Charles—G Kaegl, barber fixtures 140
Wiegand, Joseph—Lyon & Sons Brewing Co, pool table 197

JUDGMENTS.

Babendrier, Gustav—W W Muchmore 2,785
Dane, W P—M Wheaton 362
Evans, W H—A Campfield 654
Kynor, C A—Wilkinson, Gaddis & Co 913
Lyon, E S—J R Johnson et al 185
Seymour, J C—F W Moore 2,287
Trefz, Charles—Jane Campfield 663
Same——M A Peiffer 1,042
Wright, Simon—C E Potter 504

HUDSON COUNTY.

CONVEYANCES.

Allen, Robert and Michael Forrest—E Pyne, Kearney $1,800
Same——J Penn, Kearney 400
Andrews, H C—Caroline L Leake, J City nom
Ayres, C D—Catharine W Henny, Bayonne 2,000
Same——J Henny, Bayonne nom
Ballard, Catharine A—R S Smith, Bayonne 5,250
Bergen, Ida E—Mary A Searle, J City 1,000
Booraem, C V V—Josephine B Zabriskie J City nom
Bowes, Michael—Hoboken Land and Improvement Co, Hoboken 3,000
Same——same, Hoboken 9,000
Bramhall, W E—A A Parker, J City 800
Cadmus, George—C J Somers, Bayonne 600
Same——P Muldoon, Bayonne 600
Clear, Catharine—E R Riehl, J City 550
Colgan, Sarah E—E McGonnell, J City nom
Condit, Fillmore—H F Coffin, Kearney 400
Same——M Bonath, Kearney 150
Converse, Ella—M Hesnau, J City 1,000
Cross, R S by sheriff—G P Howell, J City 800
Cunningham, J H—H Laiterbauch, J City 6 5
Doran, Mary J—F Mandler, J City 1,000
Dreyer, Fred—Anna L Ruser, Union 125
Edelstein, John—T W Cappon, J City 600
Ferens, J R—S Chapman, Union 1,100
Fitch, Harriet—C Fitzsimmons, J City 800
Fischer, Lewis—A Fischer, J City 1,500
Fitzgerald, Pat—J S Nolan, J City 800
Gardner, Jno—R E Gardner, North Bergen 950
Gardner, R E—H J Gellen, North Bergen 1,050
Garretson, Mary A—Ellen C Kelly, J City 4,9 0
Same——same, J City 1,250
Gobel, Ellen—W Glenfield, J City 500
Hageberg, William—A Sydow, Kearney 1,650
Hamilton, W H—Catharine A Ballard, Bayonne nom
Havens, Sarah—G Lindenthal, J City 3,000
Hellmer, Betty—Julia A Pierson, J City 4,010
Hilliard, Ann P—Hoboken Land and Impt Co, West Hoboken 2,333
Hoboken Coal Co—Catharine A Ballard, Bayonne nom
Hoboken Land and Impt Co—J D Stover, Hoboken 4,021
Same——M Bowes, Hoboken 22,000
Holste, Maria—C Junge, J City 2,300
Howell, G P—C A Ormsly, J City 4,540
Hudson Co Land and Impt Co—I Morecraft, J City 410
Hulshizer, J E, Jr—Catharine A Tracy, J City nom
Jones, J M—E R Stodd, J City nom
Kattell, C W—W H Cummings, J City 10,500
Kelly, Andrew—W Farrell, J City 200
Same——same, J City 500
Kuhlen, William—W Smith, J City 2,100
Lake, T W—H C Andrews, J City nom
Lawrence, D W—J Hoffman, J City 400
Lehmann, Frances—H Spillner, J City nom
Lowe, Margt W—J Jewkes, J City 1,500
Ludewig, John—H Ludewig, West Hoboken 2,000
Luxton, Susan—H Haskmann, West Hoboken 700
Masterson, Thos—J Reynolds, J City 700
Mathison, Charlotte A—Sarah G Mathison, J City nom
Mausberdt, Fred—Catharine Smith, J City nom
McCall, T F—R Clark, Kearney 300
Mulcahy, Geo by exrs—H Rathyen, J City 800
Mulcahy, Jas and Jno—H Rathyen, J City 800
Nichols, E H—J Golden, J City 185
Same——J H Cunningham, J City 300
Nolan, Clara—T R Hughes, North Bergen nom
Obermier, Fred—W Mould, North Bergen 325
Peer, Kate—T A King, J City 2,400
Peter, Chas—E J Jackel, J City 2,100
Post, Maria F—Eliza Van Emburgh, Kearney nom
Post, Sarah P—F Smith, Hoboken 300
Roche, James—T W Cappon, J City 500
Schultz, Otto—S Dorfmuller, West Hoboken 14,000
Same——J Dedrich, West Hoboken 9,000
Siegfried, Adam—A Kennedy, West Hoboken 375
Simonds, A B—J Connolly, Harrison 1,500
Smith, Fred—F Mausbendt, J City nom
Smith, M L—W D Alston, Bayonne 2,000
Spillner, Henry—F Lehmann, J City nom
The Board of Trustees of the Knox Presbyterian Church—E Sargent, Kearney 650
The Equitable Life Ins Co—T H Smith, J City 7,000
The Jersey City Terminal R R—R H Sayre, J City nom
Toffey, W V—Catharine Barr, J City 1,425
Tracy, J A—J E Hulshizer, Jr, J City nom
Tracey, Michael—C Cullen, J City 1,4.0
Traphagen, W C—Hoboken Land and Improvement Co, West Hoboken 1,333
Van Horne, Marie M—C Wrege, J City 400
Vreeland, Elizabeth by guard—Carl Wrege, J City 400
Vogler, Christianna—J Vogler, J City nom
Washburn, W F—F J Donaghue, J City 3,000
Watson, G E—L Conti, J City 4,500
Weller, Julia—J W Stuart, Hoboken 1,500
Williams, J B—Emma Williams, Union 550
Weston, Mary A by sheriff—Pavonia B & L Assoc, J City 1,000
Wood, Anna F and Florence Lembeck by special master—J Gorman, Bayonne 285
Same, by master—R Hayford, Bayonne 410
Wood, Anna F and Florence Lembeck by master—C Murphy, Bayonne 435
Same——F Straus, Bayonne 8 6
Same——C Murphy, Bayonne 200
Same——R Malloy, Bayonne 200
Same——C Malloy, Bayonne 205
Same——P McGinty, Bayonne 200
Same——J McMahon, Bayonne 235
Same——J J Healy, Bayonne 285
Same——Mary Cady, Bayonne 235
Same——H Dugan, Bayonne 200
Same——C Jaekel, Bayonne 810
Same——T Gormley, Bayonne 200
Same——Emma Scholls, Bayonne 260
Same——G Kurz, Bayonne 200

MORTGAGES.

Alston, W D—The Mechanics' Trust Co, Bayonne, 1 year 2,500
Bowes, Michael—J O Besson, Hoboken, 3 years 4,000
Same——Hoboken Land and Impt Co, Hoboken, 1 year 1,475
Same——Hoboken Bank for Savings, Hoboken, 1 year 10,000
Burke, Timothy—J E Andrus, J City, 2 years 500
Cappon, T W—J Edelstein, J City, 5 years 800
Same——J Roche, J City, 5 years 400
Castro, Edward—Rosalie Hinip, J City, 1 year 1,000
Clarke, William—W H Kenzel, J City, 3 years 10,000
Conklin, Delia—M Ward, J City, 5 years 1,000
Conti, Luigi—G E Watson, J City, 5 years 2,000
Crouse, E J—Charlotte Sherwood, Union, 5 years 2,000
Cullen, Chas—M Tracey, J City, installs 1,200
Deduch, John—Sebastian Dorfmuller, West Hoboken, 2 years 1 800
Same——O Schultz, West Hoboken, 3 years 4,001
De Orme, E H—J D Condit, J City, 1 year 887
De Sandi, Leonard—Eli Teeter, Kearney, 1 year 1,400
Doefmuller, Sebastian—O Schultz, West Hoboken, 1 year 1,000
Doherty, Mary—A A Lutkins, J City, 5 years 6,500
Donaghue, F J—Manhattan M Co-operative B and L Assoc, J City, installs 3,200
Dorfmuller, Sebastian—O Schultz, West Hoboken, 1 year 1,000
Driscoll, Maria C—Julia Van Vorst, J City, 3 years 1,000
Dutcher, Sarah E—Delia A Bumsted, Bayonne, 1 year 4,000
Ely, E B—Bayonne B Assoc No 2, Bayonne, installs 3,000
Fitzgerald, Anna K—New Jersey Title Guar and Trust Co, Bayonne, installs 2,400
Fitzsimmons, Chas—Harriet Fitch, J City, 3 years 675
Furey, Catharine E and J J—C H O'Neil, J City, 1 year 1,000
Getlen, H J—R E Gardner, North Bergen, 2 years 4,000
Gilbert, Maggie A—Lousa Angle, J City, 1 year 1,000
Glenfield, William—T McEwan, Jr, J City, 2 years 350
Goold, Thomas—Kearney B and L Assoc, Kearney, installs 1,000
Gregory, D F—Minnie H Sinn, J City, 1 year 3,000
Gubelman, Theodore—New Jersey Title Guarantee and Trust Co, J City, installs 7,600
Halsey, H F—Garfield B and L Assoc, J City, installs 3,200
Hennan, Mathew—Ella Converse, J City, 3 years 500
Holton, Charlotte—Excelsior M B and L Assoc No 2 issue 4, J City, installs 2,000
Hudson Electric Light Co—State Street Safe and Deposit and Trust Co, Hoboken and elsewhere, 30 years 150,000
Husse, Oscar—Excelsior M B and L Assoc No 2 issue 4, J City, 1 year 8,000
King, T A—Eliza K Buck, J City, 3 years 1,800
Kirchgesner, Theo—guard of Margaretha S A Bishoff, West Hoboken, 5 years 4,500
Klein, Valentine—T Melchior, West Hoboken, 4 years 800
Knox Presbyterian Church—The Provident Inst for Savings, Kearney, 1 year 11,500
Jackel, E J—C Peter, J City, 3 years 1,700
Johnson, Carl—Florida De Groff, Union, 3 years 1,800
Jones, Anna H—H J Braker, J City, 3 years 500
Lampa, R R—New Jersey Title Guarantee and Trust Co, West Hoboken, installs 2,000
Leonard, Catharine—Elizabeth W Chanler, Hoboken, 5 years 1,500
Lindenthal, Gustav—Sarah Havens, J City, 3 years 1,500
Ludlow, C A—C F Ruh, Jr, Union, 5 years 1,000
Ludewig, Herman—J Ludewig, West Hoboken, 5 years 1,500
Mahnken, F C—A H McFadden, Bayonne, 5 yrs 3,000
Maslin, Lucy—C W Fisk, J City, 5 years 1,500
McGonnell, Edward—The Fifth Ward Savings Bank, J City, 1 year 600
Mills, S R—Bayonne B Assoc No 2, Bayonne, installs 200
Molter, Eva—R Lobey, J City, 3 years 1,000
Mueller, Maria—A Krabnke, Union, 3 years 2,000
Nolan, James—Industrial M B and L Assoc, J City, installs 1,800
Numbers, Chas, Jr—A Zabriskie, J City, 5 years 2,000
Newmann, Auguste—F C Hansen, Union, 1 year 100
Ormsly, C A—Howard B and L Assoc, J City, installs 5,400
See, Mary J—New Jersey Title Guarantee and Trust Co, Bayonne, installs 3,500
Simpson, Jane—Elizabeth French, J City, 1 year 2,000
Smith, R A—Catharine A Ballard, Bayonne, 5 years 3,700
Smith, T H—The Equitable Life Assur Society of U S, J City, 2 years 5,000
Sydow, Axel—W Hagberg, Kearney, 3 years 850
Thieman, Marie—Exrs H K Van Horn, West Hoboken, 3 years 1,500
Thom, J K—G R McKenzie, J City, 5 years 5,000
Topps, J A—Union B and L Assoc, J City, installs 2,000
Umbach, Catharine—Martha L Deraisenes, Guttenberg, 3 years 1,000
Van Emburgh, Eliza—L McCloud, Kearney, 1 year 800
Walter, W J—W Kiefer, Union, 5 years 1,000
Walling, Josiah—J W Hansen, J City, 4 years 1,000
Weisnagel, Jacob—Pamrapo B and L Assoc, Bayonne, installs 2,100
Wells, Geo—Provident Inst for Savings, J City, 1 year 500
Wiehl, Christopher—W H Parmley, J City, 3 years 3,500
Wreye, Chas—Marie Weymann, J City, 5 years 400
Wittreich, Chas—Hudson Trust and Savings Inst, J City, 2 years 4,500
Zeiller, Casper—Provident Inst for Savings, Bayonne, 1 year 5,600

CHATTEL MORTGAGES.

Baker, G E, J City—L Bauman, furniture 176
Bria, Adrian, J City—Budweiser Brewing Co, saloon 625
Browning, J J, J City—C E Pierce, furniture 65
Butler, Mary, Bayonne—J Mullins & Co, furniture 156
Chamberlain, H F, J City—Marcy Stove Repair Co, stove repair supplies 1,500
Chaudron, August, J City—Jordan & Moriarty, furniture 125
Same——same, furniture 61
Christiansen, Fritz and Anna his wife, Hoboken—Bachman Brewing Co, saloon 450
Corey, E C and T F McGrath, J City—Lembech & Betz Eagle Brewing Co, saloon 1,025
Cutley, Mary, J City—W H Britton, furniture 400
Dege, A F W, Bayonne—Seeman Bros, grocery and meat business 1,500
Dent, W C, Hoboken—Financial Credit Co, furniture 195
Fisher, Susan, J City—L Bauman, furniture 111
Flanagan, John and James Smith, partners as Flanagan & Smith, J City—Bernheimer & Schmidt, saloon 700
Grasser, John, West New York—L Bauman, furniture 135
Gilroy, Mary, J City——same, furniture 91
Habner, Moritz, J City—D Stevenson, saloon 1,050
Hammer, Carl, J City—Bernheimer & Schmidt, saloon 600
Harrison, G J, Hoboken—J A Heaths, machinery 100
Higham, J T and I, Hoboken—The Marvin Safe Co, safe 41
Hofstetter, Karl, West Hoboken—S Moos, cows, horse, wagon, &c 1,142
Hunt, Madison, J City—Brooklyn Furniture Co, furniture 155
Kenny, Mary, J City—D Steele, furniture 283
Kimmerly, Louis, J City—The Home Brewing Co, saloon 500
Kortlang, Henry, Hoboken—P Pryebil, 4 side moulders 400
MacDaniel, Dirk, and Emil Tirgrath, partners as McDaniel & Co, Hoboken—Rulsam & Hoorman, saloon 1,000
Meyerhoff, Gustav, Hoboken—The F & M Schaefer Brewing Co, saloon fixtures 450
Moran, W A, J City—L Bauman, furniture 268
Mullone, M, J City—Marvin Safe Co, safe 170
Rector, &c, Grace Church, Greenville, J City—J G Hoffman trustee, organ, pulpit, furniture 1,000
Richter, Kate, J City—Jordan & Moriarty, furniture 72
Ruthtein, Valentine, J City—The Marvin Safe Co, safe 55
Schenk, Wilhelm, Hoboken—Bachman Brewing Co, saloon 900
Styles, Daniel, J City—Jordan & Moriarty, furniture 113
The Hudson Electric Light Co of Hoboken—The State Street Safe Deposit and Trust Co, engine, boilers, machinery, plant, &c 150,000
Thom, J K, J City—G R McKenzie, engine, boiler, &c 6,000
Van Antwerp, Cornelius, J City—D B Dunham, coach 1,525
Wagner, George and John Tangeman, J City—L H Bellamy, horse, wagon, &c 25
Walsh, G M, J City—The Brooklyn Furniture Co, furniture 99
Zeik, Peter, Bayonne—Hoos & Schulz, furniture 210

BILLS OF SALE.

Bellamy, L H, J City—G Wagner, milk business 675
Mahnken, A C, Jr, Bayonne—A F W Dege, grocery and butcher business, stock and fixtures 2,000

JUDGMENTS.

Harrison, George—Douglass L Whlyte & Co 406
Huber, Henry—The F & M Schaefer Brewing Co 358
Hutler, William and Henry—The Watts-Campbell Co 1,962
McCloskey, J P—J R Bowen 89
Same——F McCullough 254
McKee, J F—The National Casket Co 199
Moore, Mrs L—D L Whyte & Co 149
Pohley, George, Jr—H Lange 103
Riley, James and Thomas Murtha—D Bauman 155
Strothmann, Henry—Gerken & Baumeister 61

BUILDING MATERIAL MARKET.

BRICKS.—As compared with last week, the week before, and, indeed, for many weeks preceding, the market might be reported with a ditto. We have, to be sure, found some operators claiming a slight increase of business, but even this small comfort is not sufficiently universal to make a solid, compact position, nor has the outlet broadened to a level of the supply. Buyers have no fault to find either with the cost or the quality presented for their selection, but simply no use for any more stock than they are handling and still abstain from piling away to any extent against the future. All leading operators still agree that $5.25 (not $2.5 as the types had it last week) is high enough for an established quotation, and the bulk of business is done at a lower range, but as before advised special calls for any one particular make, and especially if a yard has stopped regular shipments, would not be met until buyers agreed to pay a premium. In contradiction of some previous reports we now learn that some manufacturers of even the very best makes are still moulding, but with the frosty inclination of the weather it is getting to be dangerous work, and production cannot last much longer. From all accounts there is a full accumulation of stock all along the river, and the season is likely to close with quite as many brick on hand as last year. Sales are also dull just now and more or less nominal on a basis of about the quotations for some time given.

LATH.—The market has continued somewhat unsettled with business ranging along from $2.05 up to $2.15 per M, but latterly nothing has been available for less than $2.10, and some receivers refuse to accept that. Arrivals were not very plentiful and some of them come to hand under contract, which, in conjunction with a good general demand, made sellers somewhat independent. Local custom was very well represented and the outside element from quite a broad circle of dependent territory has again been heard from. Light shipments from the Eastward and none from the North are still reported, with little probability of an increase.

LIME.—The market is shaky. Arrivals would not ordinarily be called liberal, but as matters stand the indifferent tone of buyers makes a surplus of a very few cargoes and it is an extremely difficult matter to secure a prompt outlet for stock. Receivers do what they can to sustain already quite low line of valuation and have been nominally successful up to the close, but there is a suspicion that on common at least some favors have been shown with an understanding that no publicity is to be given the matter.

LUMBER.—The market as a whole moves slowly, and there are few, if any, new features of a pronounced character to suggest. The call for goods to enter into consumption is of an irregular character and satisfied with small parcels, though some dealers

REGULAR

Democratic Nominations

FOR GOVERNOR,
Roswell P. Flower.

FOR LIEUTENANT-GOVERNOR,
William F. Sheehan.

FOR SECRETARY OF STATE,
Frank Rice.

FOR COMPTROLLER,
Frank Campbell.

FOR ATTORNEY GENERAL,
Simon W. Rosendale.

FOR STATE TREASURER,
Elliot F. Danforth.

FOR STATE ENGINEER,
Martin Schenck.

FOR SUPREME COURT JUDGE,
George L. Ingraham.

FOR SUPERIOR COURT JUDGE,
Henry A. Gildersleeve.

FOR JUDGE OF THE COURT OF COMMON PLEAS,
Roger A. Pryor.

FOR CITY COURT JUDGES,
Simon M. Ehrlich.
John Henry McCarthy.

FOR JUDGE OF THE TENTH DISTRICT COURT,
Christopher C. Clarke.

FOR CORONERS,
Louis W. Schultze.
John B. Shea.
Ferdinand Levy.

FOR CONGRESSMEN,
Dist
10 W. BOURKE COCKRAN
12 JOSEPH J. LITTLE

FOR SENATORS,
Dist
5 WILLIAM L. BROWN
6 JOHN F. AHEARN
7 GEORGE F. ROESCH
8 MARTIN T. McMAHON
9 EDWARD P. HAGAN
10 JACOB A. CANTOR
11 GEORGE W. PLUNKITT

FOR ASSEMBLYMEN,

Dist.
1. PATRICK H. DUFFY.
2. TIMOTHY D. SULLIVAN.
3. PERCIVAL FARQUHAR.
4. PATRICK H. ROCHE.
5. DOMINICK F. MULLANEY.
6. SAMUEL J. FOLEY.
7. JENKINS VAN SCHAICK.
8. PHILIP WISSIG.
9. WILLIAM H. WALKER.
10. WILLIAM SOHMER.
11. HENRY C. JUDSON.
12. MOSES DINKELSPIEL.
13. JAMES H. SOUTHWORTH.
14. WILLIAM SULZER.
15. LOUIS DRYPOLCHER.
16. WALTER G. BYRNE.
17. THOMAS McMAHON.
18. DANIEL F. MARTIN.
19. JOHN CONNELLY.
20. MYER J. STEIN.
21. LOUIS H. HAHLO.
22. JOSEPH BLUMENTHAL.
23. GEORGE P. WEBSTER.
24. THOMAS J. BYRNES.

FOR ALDERMEN,

Dist.
1. CORNELIUS FLYNN.
2. NICHOLAS T. BROWN.
3. PATRICK J. O'BEIRNE.
4. ANDREW A. NOONAN.
5. PATRICK J. RYDER.
6. WILLIAM CLANCY.
7. JOHN MORRIS.
8. CHARLES S. SMITH.
9. ABRAHAM MEAD.
10. JOSEPH MARTIN.
11. JAMES M. MOOREHEAD.
12. WILLIAM TAIT.
13. CHARLES W. FERRIS.
14. CHARLES J. SMITH.
15. FRANK ROGERS.
16. WILLIAM H. MURPHY.
17. PETER J. DOOLING.
18. JACOB C. WUND.
19. HORATIO S. HARRIS.
20. DAVID J. ROCHE.
21. ROLLIN M. MORGAN.
22. HENRY C. HART.
23. SAMUEL H. BAILEY.

Ward.
23. AUGUST MOEBUS.
24. THOMAS M. LYNCH.

claim to have evidence that there will be somewhat larger amounts wanted for building and dockage purposes within a comparatively short time. For yard stocks more or less stuff is inquired after, but with none of the avidity of former seasons, and advices from tributary markets complaining of dull business for most kinds of stock indicate that dealers are not reaching around the tenders brought to their doors in an effort to secure supplies. Conditions prevailing prevent any buoyancy on values, but a fair general measure of steadiness is preserved, and prices on all leading kinds of stock are preserved at last week's level.

Eastern Spruce shows little, if any, change on random cargoes. Buyers generally are evidently indifferent at the best, and if they can catch receivers with a trifle excess of stock on hand, they are very apt to promptly take advantage of them by crowding the price. We quote at about former general range, but it makes a difference of 50c. to $1.00 per M in cost, up or down, whether the buyer or seller opens negotiations. Specials, however, are pretty firm. Quite a number of them have of late been placed, and manufacturers do not evince much desire to take additional orders, especially as vessels are commencing to haul off, and freights are likely to advance.

Piling has only moderate attention at the moment, and some operators talk as though they rather despaired of gaining the improvement recently calculated upon. Arrivals are limited, but whatever comes to hand is promptly offered, and in common with stock in chains can be reached at about former rates.

Hemlock does not find much attention on local account, but outside custom wants a little more stock for winter accumulation, and now and then quite a respectable sized order can be booked. Buyers find all the supply they require available, and can reach it upon bids at about former figures.

White Pine shows little or no change of a positive character. Demand for the better qualities has continued fair and at steady rates, and there has rather unexpectedly developed an increased amount of attention toward box, though this latter call is a little scattered and apparently mainly to round off the assortments of dealers and manufacturers who have miscalculated as to probable wants. Export chances continue very good and that is causing a somewhat increased demand for shippers, several agents claiming to have secured quite large orders since first of month.

Yellow Pine offered random on open market would in all probability receive only very indifferent attention; but there is some call for specials for yard assortment, and on single jobs that help the tone in a measure, though as yet without lifting the line of values. The market also shows signs of being placed in better form by more harmonious action among operators, and if culmination of present efforts are reached as hoped for the chances are we shall have a healthier market next year.

Carolina Pine is selling very well, and indeed seems to have a rather more snappy movement toward all outlets, local and Eastward. Offerings are full enough to satisfy the developed demand, but not allowed to become excessive, and on all standard stock, kiln-dried stock rough or dressed, prices are fully sustained.

Hardwoods are not active on the movement into consumption, nor is there exhibition of anxiety to secure stock on part of dealers. The latter, however, are picking up such desirable stock as may come under their notice from time to time without increase of cost or may be tendered at a little shading. The latter as compared with last season is most noticeable on quartered oak which at $52.50 is quoted quite up to the average and for nicely cut stock too. Poplar is steady at $32.00 by car lot, and finding fair custom. Nothing specially noteworthy in other woods.

Shingles are still without much animation and the market fails to recover decided strength. Nevertheless receivers speak a little more cheerfully over the chances and prospects and some are hopeful of a fair winter trade. The arrivals of Cypress stock have been cut down a little, but additions can be reached when it is necessary they should come forward.

GENERAL LUMBER NOTES.

THE EAST.

The following is a statement of the amount of lumber surveyed at the port of Bangor from July 1 to October 1, 1891, as compared with the amount surveyed in 1889 and 1890 for the same period:

	1889.	1890.	1891.
Dry pine	4,397,048	4,754,707	4,179,069
Green pine	3,746,011	3,304,271	2,009,970
Spruce	48,197,438	57,032,314	55,128,592
Hemlock	7,661,726	8,172,085	7,319,429
Total	64,002,223	74,163,397	68,727,060

THE WEST.

The Northwestern *Lumberman* says of the Chicago market:

The commission men announce without reserve that the market is more active than a short time ago. Piece stuff sells on arrival, and there is a good demand for strips, shingles and lath. Shingles have been in good form for some time, and the rising fall trade, with more western demand than has prevailed for two or three years past, is stimulating the requirement. Receipts thus far this season have been much less than last year, which induces a firm condition of prices. There is a new call for medium p[illegible]ed shingles, standards being wanted in excess of the supply. Cedars of a grade that correspond to standards are selling well at a price somewhat better than a short time ago.

Piece stuff is still selling at $9.75 for short lengths. Slim jims are perhaps a little firmer than recent market reports would indicate.

In inch lumber strips are still wanted, while boards are of slower sale. Cargoes that contain a good percentage of either strips or stock width boards sell quickly enough. But such lumber is mainly sold at the mill or in advance of arrival.

On the whole the market is looking better than in September. Dealers are beginning to have more confidence in lumber than in the summer. They see a good trade ahead, and want to stock up for the winter and spring trade. They certainly do not anticipate any lower prices this fall. Besides recent good sales have put them in funds, and they now feel justified in getting in more stock.

Lake freight rates have been advanced 12½ cents a thousand from all the leading ports on Lakes Michigan and Huron. This is in accordance with what usually takes place about the first of October.

Referring to Chicago Hardwood trade the *Timberman* says:

The more conservative dealers do not look for any marked improvement before next spring, but all are confident that prices are as low now as they will go nd are showing confidence in the future by continuing o buy all staples and piling the same against the time of need. But after all it does not appear that there is much of a surplus stock of hardwoods in this city. Dealers have been accustomed to sell their oak direct from the cars for so long that they imagine a surplus on hand just as soon as a few cars go into the yard. It must be admitted that the supply of quarter sawed white oak is more than ample for all present requirements, for the demand is by no means heavy, but it should be remembered that the mills have no longer any particular inducement to manufacture quarter-sawed stock, as prices are but little better than for plain-sawed. Therefore a few weeks of the same active demand that prevailed a year ago this fall would soon make a hole in present stocks, and while there is not much prospect for a scarcity of quartered oak next year, the *Timberman* confidently expects that prices will be some little higher than they have been this season. Dealers are at present paying $36 to $38 f. o. b. Chicago for inch quarter-sawed, but are still willing to pay a bonus over these prices for extra wide and well manufactured stock.

Demand for plain-sawed red oak kept well up to the supply until well on into the summer, but for the past two months or so receipts of this wood have been somewhat in excess of rates. Prices weakened somewhat for a time, but an improvement is now noted, and selling prices are about restored to the former basis. Manufacturers are also holding firmer than they did a couple of months since, showing that they also have confidence in the future. Prices are within the range of $24 to $26 for green inch and $26 to $28 for dry, both white and red.

With respect to the other hardwoods there has been little if any changes. Basswood and elm continue to be free sellers, but at low prices, and the same may be said of maple, particularly such stock as is suitable for flooring.

The Mississippi Valley *Lumberman* furnishes the following items:

A modest estimate puts the cut of the mills below Minneapolis and in the Chippewa and St. Croix valleys at 400,000,000 feet less than it was last year. At Minneapolis there will be an increase of about 100,000,000 feet —to offset the large decrease at other points. This is one of the facts that the bears in the lumber market cannot get over. * * *

Will the mills along the Mississippi river already shut down be operated again this year? The probabilities are that they will not be. Every week the mills are idle now adds to this probability. There has as yet been no rise on the Chippewa river sufficient to carry out logs. Even if rafting is resumed at West Newton this season, the mill men will take advantage of the circumstance to get logs down to their mills for an early start next spring rather than to set the wheels moving again this fall. The sawing season of fully one half of the mills in the Mississippi Valley may be said to be over. * * *

One of the surprising features to the dealers in white pine is the fact that the call for their lumber has been generous along the very border line of the field supplied for a year or two past by the yellow pine men. Upper Mississippi valley lumbermen have had a good trade in southern Illinois and Missouri. The burden laid upon the railroads is in part responsible for this condition. The northwestern railroad system practically terminates at St. Louis and Kansas City. These cities form also the northern terminus of the southwestern system. The railroads have in their anxiety to get the best results from their equipment restricted the movement of their rolling stock to their own lines. The southern lumbermen are, therefore, practically barred out of fields into which the railroads have permitted them to get in times of light traffic.

METALS.—COPPER—Ingot has weakened in price and general tone under an unloading effort on the part of speculators said to have several million pounds coming to them on contract at 13c. They had no use for it themselves, nor could they find any of the regular outlets hankering after the supply, and an attempt to secure custom brought them face to face with the necessity for modification on value. At the close the market is unsettled and somewhat nominal. On an average range of valuations we quote at 12⅝@12¾c. for Lake, and 11⅝@12c. for casting brands. Manufactured Copper is without much if any change of a pronounced character. General demand is said to be fair, probably up to average for the season and, so far as known, no variations from list rates are made. We quote as follows: Sheet, not above 30x72 in., 16 oz. and over, 25c.; do, 14 to 16 oz., 23c.; do, 12 to 14 oz., 24c.; do, 10 to 12 oz., 26c.; do, 8 to 10 oz., 28c.; do under 8 oz, 30c. Sheets longer than 72 inches add 1c. for 12@14 oz., 2c. for 10@12 oz, and 3c. for 8@10 oz. Sheets, not above 36x96 in., 16 oz and over, 22c.; do, 14 to 16 oz, 24c.; do, 12 to 14 oz, 26c.; do, 10 to 12 oz, 30c.; do, 8 to 10 oz, 33c. Sheets longer than 96 inches 22c. for over 32 oz, and add 1c. for 16 to 32 oz.; 3c. 14 to 16 oz.; 5c. 12 to 14 oz. and 13c. for 8 to 10 oz. Sheets, not above 48x96 32 to 64 oz, 22c.; do, 16 to 32 oz, 25c.; do, 14 to 16 oz, 27c. do 12 to 14 oz, 29c.; do, 10 to 12 oz. 33c. Sheets wider than 48x96 and longer, 22@25c. for 32 to 64 oz. and over. 27@[illegible]c. for 16 to 32 oz, 29c. for 14 to 16 oz and 34c. for 12 to 14 oz. All bath tub sheets, per lb., 16 oz. 7[illegible]c.; 14 oz, 29c.; 12 oz 3[illegible]c.; and 10 oz, 35c. Bolt copper, ⅝ inch diameter and over, 22c. Circles, 60 diameter and less, 3c. above price of sheets of same thickness; circles, 60 to 96 do do, 5c. do; circles, 96 do and over, 6c. do. Segment and pattern sheets, 3c. above price of sheets required to cut them from. Cold or hard rolled copper, 1@2c. per lb. above the foregoing prices. Copper bottoms, 26@32c. per lb. IRON—American Pig has no unusual demand, but nevertheless appears to find steady custom full enough to exhaust all the better portion of the supply, and give sellers an advantage upon which a firm tone is preserved without much apparent difficulty. Here and there a weak spot appears to be shown in the market, but it is generally traceable to inferior stock, for which there is no special use at the moment. We quote at $17.00@18.00 per ton for No. 1 X foundry; [illegible].50@16.50 for No. 2 X do. and $14.00 @15.00 for Gray Forge. Old material finds little attention outside the general ordinary run of regular orders, and the market is free from particularly noteworthy features at the moment. Supplies do not appear large enough to be forced into notice. We quote at about $21.50@22.00 for old rails; $19.50@[illegible]1.00 [illegible] No. 1 wrought scrap; $17.00@18.00 for cast scrap and $17.00@17.50 for car wheels. Manufactured iron is getting rather tardy demand from pretty much all quarters and furnishes some cause for complaint among sellers. They do not weaken on price, however, and the old line of figures is retained. We quote Common Merchant Bar ordinary size, at 2.00@2.10c. from store, and refined at 2.30@2.60c; Rods, round and square, 2.20@2.40c.; Bands, 2.40@2.60c.; Norway Nail Rods 4@5c., and domestic sheet on the basis of 3.00@3.05c. for common Nos. 10@16. Other descriptions at corresponding prices, with 1-10c. less on large lots from cars. Steel Rails do not meet with continuous favor, and the general character of trade is slow. There has been an idea that two or three of the large railroads would be in the market before this endeavoring to fix contracts for quite a bunch of stock, but it seems to be rumor only, and ordinary small parcels cover all the perfected sales. We quote standard sections $30 per ton at mill, with usual advance for delivery at tide water. Pig Lead not much sought after, and with somewhat greater freedom in the offering there was a loss of tone on prices, with slight irregularity at the close. We quote at 4.40@4.45c. per lb. The manufactures of lead are quoted at 7c. for Pipe, 7¾c. for sheet, 15c. for Tin-lined Pipe, and 37½c. for Block Tin Pipe. Pig Tin meets with only moderate and uncertain demand from trade sources, but is well under control, and a fairly steady undertone preserved throughout. We quote at about 20.10@20.15c. for round lots, and 20.20@20¼c. for jobbing parcels. Tin Plate has ruled pretty dull of late, and under the circumstances to some extent nominal, but owners' views are confident enough to ask about former figures. We quote prices as follows: I. C. Charcoal, ½ cross assortment Melyn grade, $6.50@6.55, each additional X add $1.50; I. C. Charcoal, ½ cross assortment, Allaway grade, $5.85@5.90, each additional X add $1; Charcoal terne, M. F. grade, 14x20, $7.50@7.55; M. F. grade, 20x28, $15.30@15.55; Worcester, 14x20, $5.70@5.75; Worcester 20x28, $11.25@11.30; Dean grade, 14x20, $5.40@5.45; Dean grade, 20x28, $10.60@10.65; D. R. D. grade, 14x20, $5.25@5.30; D. R. D. grade, 20x28, $10.00@10.05; I. C. Coke, Penlan grade, $5.35@5.40; J. B. grade, 14x20, $5.45@5.50; I. C. Bessemer steel, squares, $5.75@5.80 basis; I. C. Siemens steel, squares, $5.85@6.00 basis. Spelter has been pretty slow of sale, and in not unnatural sequence the turn of prices was in buyers' favor. We quote $4.95@5.05c. for Common Western, according to brand.

NAILS.—Business continues disappointing and complaint is quite general. As for some time noted wire nails get the most direct attention, and now and then secure pretty full orders, but even for those the market lacks solidity and on cut seems to have no real strength whatever. We quote Cut at $1.50@1.60 per keg for car lots and $1.75@1.85 per keg for parcels from store, for iron, and add 5@10c. per keg for steel; Wire, $2.60@2.05 at mills, and 2.20@2.35 from store.

PAINTS, OILS, COLORS, ETC.—General trade is working along without much, if any, friction, and although some operators occasionally admit a trifling measure of disappointment in number of orders booked they manifest no discouragement. Dry colors have secured a very fair proportion of the passing trade, and Colors in oil do pretty well, while in the general line of ready mixed paints the claim is for a movement well up to natural season average. Paris White and Whiting get due share of attention, but Block Chalk has been dull with buyers and sellers apart on the value line. Putty has found good trade demand, but with the reduction in cost of oil a little quiet cutting on rates has been going on for some time by outside workers which is now likely to localize. Zincs sell fairly well, but the call not liberal and no inducement given to bring out much imported stock. White Lead meeting with good satisfactory demand from all quarters, and manufacturers are adhering to price list with steadiness. Association Corroders' rates stand as follows: Lead in oil in kegs and dry lead in kegs, in lots of less than 500 lbs., 7½c. net; in lots of 500 lbs to 5 tons at one purchase, 7c.; 5 tons to 12 tons, one purchase, 6⅞c.; 12 tons and over, one purchase, 6¾c.; dry white lead in bbls. ½c per lb. less than price in kegs. Lead in oil 12½ lb. in tin pails, add 1c.; in 25 and 50 lb. tin pails, add ½c.; and in 1 to 5 lb. tin cans, assorted (100 lbs. in case) add 2½c. per lb. to keg price. Terms on lots on 500 lbs. and over, note or acceptance at sixty days, or 2½ per cent. discount will be allowed for cash paid within fifteen days of invoice date. To make either of the above required quantities any assortment of packages of white lead, red lead and litharge may be counted. The above quotations are free on board cars or boat at corroding point. Linseed Oil still showing a more or less uncertain market. City crushers remain fairly steady in their position, but the Western product continues to be knocked about with average inclination in buyers' favor. We quote at general range at 35@40c. for Western, and 40@56c. for City. Spirits Turpentine has remained quiet and on the whole rather tame. For small lots holders ask about former figures, but in a large way investment could probably be made at some concession. We quote at 37@38½c. per gallon, according to quality, delivery, etc.

TAR AND PITCH.—Demand is not active beyond ordinary lines of trade wants, and the market as a whole undergoes little or no change. Offerings fair and available at about rates for some time current. We quote Pitch at $1.70@1.75 per bbl.; Tar at $2.15@4.50, according to quantity, quality and delivery.

MISCELLANEOUS.

MISCELLANEOUS.

BUILDING MATERIAL PRICES

LUMBER.

Appended quotations are based almost wholly upon prices obtained for goods from first hands. Yard rates necessarily range much higher owing to the expenses attending sorting out and grading cargo and even car lots, besides which must be added the cost of handling and carrying until consumers are ready to invest. Terms of sale also prove important factors and, altogether, it is impossible to give a line of retail quotations thoroughly reliable n character.

SPRUCE—Eastern—special cargoes delivered N. Y.	$16 00	@	18 00
Random cargoes, narrow	12 00	@	13 00
Random cargoes, wide	13 50	@	15 00
PILING—Eastern—cargo rates:			
Ranging 30@40 per cent 12 inch butt, 35 to 40 ft average length	4	@	—
Ranging 45@50 per cent 12 inch butt, 35 to 40 ft average length	4¼	@	4½
Ranging 50@60 per cent One-half 12 inch butt, 38 to 40 ft average length	4¾	@	5
Two-thirds 12 inch butt, 38 to 42 ft average length	5½	@	6
Three-fourths 12 inch butt, 40 to 45 ft average length	5¾	@	6
All 12 inch butt and up, 40 to 45 ft average length	6	@	6¼
Piece stick, 40 feet each	4 00	@	—
do. 45	6 00	@	—
do. 50	8 00	@	—
do. 55	12 00	@	—
Inch spars, per inch	20	@	22
Scaffolding poles, each	80	@	1 00
Clothes poles, 45 to 55 feet, each	3 00	@	6 00
HEMLOCK:			
Penn. joist	12 00	@	12 50
do. boards	13 00	@	13 50
do. timber, 20 ft and under	12 50	@	13 00
do. do. 22 to 24 ft	13 00	@	13 50
do. do. 26 to 28 ft	13 50	@	14 00
do. do. 30 to 32 ft	14 00	@	15 50
do. do. 34 to 36 ft	15 50	@	16 00
do. do. 38 to 40 ft	16 50	@	17 50
WHITE PINE—Good uppers and select, 1 to 2 inch	40 00	@	48 00
Upper and select, 2½ to 4 inch	50 00	@	58 00
Shelving	26 00	@	31 00
Pickings, 1 inch	33 00	@	35 00
Cutting-up, 1 inch	25 00	@	28 00
Bracket plank	30 00	@	35 00
Dressing-boards	18 00	@	22 00
Box, inch	13 50	@	14 00
Box, thick	14 50	@	15 50
West India shippers	16 00	@	19 00
Rio Janeiro do.	20 00	@	21 00
River Plate do.	29 00	@	30 00
Australia do.	25 00	@	30 00
YELLOW PINE—Random cargoes delivered N. Y.	18 00	@	19 00
Ordered cargoes	19 50	@	21 00
Flooring	23 00	@	24 00
Step plank	26 00	@	28 00
Common siding	15 00	@	16 00
Heart face boards	24 00	@	28 00
Car orders	21 00	@	23 00
At Atlantic ports, f. o. b.	12 00	@	12 50
At Gulf ports, f. o. b.	11 50	@	12 50
North Caroline pine timber	13 50	@	15 00
do. flooring 1 inch	16 00	@	22 00
do. do. 1¼	16 50	@	22 50
do. do. 1½@2 inch.	24 00	@	25 00
do Shipping culls or box	12 00	@	14 00
do Plain and mottled ½@1½ inch.	18 50	@	25 50
Ash, white	36 00	@	43 00
Elm	20 00	@	22 50
Oak, plain	37 00	@	41 00
Oak, quarter sawed	52 00	@	55 00
Oak, quarter sawed, extra thick	56 00	@	60 00
Redwood	45 00	@	52 50
Maple, clear	28 00	@	33 00
Chestnut, clear	33 00	@	35 50
Cypress, clear	30 00	@	32 50
Black Walnut, good to choice	130 00	@	140 00
Black Walnut, ordinary to fair	100 00	@	120 00
Black Walnut, ⅝	78 00	@	88 00
Black Walnut, selected and seasoned	150 00	@	155 00
Black Walnut counters	110 00	@	150 00
Black Walnut, culls	35 00	@	40 00
Black Walnut, rejects	50 00	@	58 00
Cherry, wide	110 00	@	115 00
Cherry, good	85 00	@	100 00
Cherry, ordinary	65 00	@	80 00
Whitewood, inch	30 50	@	32 50
Whitewood, ⅝ inch	24 50	@	26 00
Whitewood, 1¼ to 2½ inch	32 00	@	34 00
Shingles, Pine, 16 inch, extra	2 75	@	3 10
do 18 inch, extra	4 10	@	4 30
do 18 inch, clear butt	2 90	@	3 10
do 16 inch, stocks	4 50	@	4 60
do 18 inch, stocks	5 30	@	5 40
Shingles, Cypress, 6x20	8 00	@	10 00
do larger sizes	11 00	@	16 00
do sawed	6 00	@	9 00
Cedar—Medium to large	6¼	@	7¼
do. —Extra large	7¾	@	8
Mahogany—small	4½	@	7½
do —Medium	8	@	8½
do. —Large	9½	@	12
do. —Extra Large	12½	@	14

REAL ESTATE RECORD AND BUILDERS' GUIDE.
ESTABLISHED MARCH 21st 1868.
DEVOTED TO REAL ESTATE. BUILDING ARCHITECTURE, HOUSEHOLD DECORATION. BUSINESS AND THEMES OF GENERAL INTEREST

PRICE, PER YEAR IN ADVANCE, SIX DOLLARS.

Published every Saturday.

TELEPHONE - - - - CORTLANDT 1370.

Communications should be addressed to

C. W. SWEET, 14 & 16 Vesey St.

J. T. LINDSEY, Business Manager.

VOL. XLVIII OCTOBER 24, 1891. No. 1,232

Have you read the second number of THE ARCHITECTURAL RECORD *yet? Nobody interested in good building should be without it. Articles appear in this issue from the pens of such well-known writers on architecture as Prof. A. D. F. Hamlin, Barr Ferree and Montgomery Schuyler; the first of whom points out the "Difficulties of Modern Architecture;" the second discusses "What is Architecture?" and the third continues his critical account of the "Romanesque Revival in America." A paper by William J. Fryer, Jr., on "Skeleton Construction," others by Harry W. Desmond and Herbert D. Croly; a second part of Prof. Atchison's lecture on "Byzantine Architecture," and the regular departments complete a very interesting number. The magazine is, as usual, profusely illustrated, and in matter and appearance is fully equal to the first number. The publisher takes pleasure in announcing that the issue immediately following this one will be of unusual interest to architects and of great value to the general reader. Among the contributors will be Prof. E. A. Freeman, the English historian, G. Lindenthal, L. De Coppet Berg. Prof. Kerr and other authorities equally high.*

WHEN one considers the thousand agencies that are at work, not only in informing the public what has taken place respecting large railroads, but in ferreting out any contemplated action which might influence the price of its securities, it is possible to realize with what secrecy the management of the Lake Erie & Western Road has acted in authorizing the issue of a second mortgage increasing the funded debt of the company by 50 per cent. The meeting at which the action is supposed to have been taken was called to be held at Bloomington, Ill., on June 25, 1890, although the proceedings authorizing the mortgage were probably taken at an adjournment of the meeting held several days afterwards, which would be a convenient way of disposing of any stockholders who might chance to be present the first day, but unable or unwilling to remain indefinitely in Bloomington, even if it were known that such action was intended. That the proxies solicited at that time by officers of the company gave no intimation of such a purpose, is shown by the shock the news gives, and the fact that the proxies had been so used has been so adroitly suppressed that Wall Street knew absolutely nothing about it until last Monday. Printed reports of the company have meanwhile been issued, as well as Poor's Manual for 1891, but no mention of a second mortgage occurs therein. Just fancy, for a moment, that the men doing these acts in the dark are sworn directors or trustees performing with their *cestuis qui* trust in this perfectly remarkable manner. The entire proceedings have a most disagreeable and suspicious look. Stockholders in railroad companies have been accustomed to moral looseness in the directors and to performances technically within the law, but so perilously near the edge of the penitentiary that ordinary men look on in amazement; but proceedings relating to placing additional mortgages on the property have generally been carefully taken. When directors come to play boldly with the validity of an issue of bonds to be offered to investors, it illustrates how reckless men may become after a long course of defiance of (let us put it) business decencies.

WHY should trustees strain a proxy to put a mortgage on property without notice to their *cestuis qui* trust and then, having done so, conceal the facts for sixteen months? It does seem to us that a respectable banking house should hesitate before standing sponsor for a security so created and offering the same to its clients. There is a fear that the bonds have been sold or an option given on them to a syndicate made up of the trustees or parties representing them, and this, as well as the further fear of the use the proceeds may be put to, adds to the disquietude of stockholders. This business may yet prove awkward for that redoubtable partnership, Brice & Thomas, if an attempt is made to push it through. If it is necessary to put a mortgage on the property to acquire additional needed equipment, let the facts relating thereto be put before the shareholders; then if they choose they can authorize a mortgage for that purpose with reasonable restrictions as to the delivery of the bonds by the trustee under the mortgage and the uses to which the proceeds can be put. Stockholders are informed that the company is earning over 6 per cent. on the preferred stock but is paying only 4 per cent. because the remainder is required for new equipment. Very well, if investors will not take the new bonds at par let dividends be declared to the preferred stock for the full 6 per cent earned, payable in scrip and exchangeable into bonds at par, and the company will have nearly three-quarters of a million dollars available this year for equipment, full value will be realized for the bonds and the dividends to the preferred shares will be practically increased 50 per cent; but alas—there is no money in that kind of financiering for the average director. It is grand for the company and its stockholders; but our readers will notice there are no discounts and commissions in this method, and so we suppose that the result will be that the bonds will net the company, say, 80 odd per cent, the proceeds to be administered on by the trustees who created them in secret. The dividend on the preferred stock will remain at 4 per cent, the price of the stock reflecting neither that dividend nor the hope of an increase, but rather the state of terror of the shareholder wondering what new trick the trustees have in store for him.

THE Rapid Transit Commissioners' report has proved to be worth waiting for. The demand for better transit facilities which caused the Commission to be constituted was specifically a demand for a system which would not only meet the varying requirements of the present but would be capable of almost indefinite expansion as the city grew northward. These requirements were many and exacting. The length of the city has made express trains drawn at a very high rate of speed quite indispensable, and at the same time local trains in great numbers have to be provided for. This service has to be furnished in competition with a road that charges 5 cents alike for long and short distant traffic. Consequently it was necessary that the system should be so planned as to give the greatest possible comfort to the maximum of passengers obtainable at the smallest cost. It is the great and paramount virtue of the plan of the Commissioners that these difficult requirements have been satisfactorily met. The routes on both the East and the West sides will undoubtedly originate more traffic than any two practicable routes of the same length that could have been selected, and their coalescence at 14th street is an ingenious device, which will save a great deal of money and be rather a convenience than an inconvenience to the public. The line of Broadway from one end of the city to the other is the line of traffic on the West Side; the line of 3d avenue on the East Side would be the best in that section, but that thoroughfare is in the hands of the Manhattan Company. Next to 3d avenue, 4th and Madison avenues are the lines of the most profitable traffic. Again a shallow tunnel, although more expensive than a deep tunnel, would undoubtedly compete more effectually for local traffic than would the latter. Furthermore, the loops at Battery and City Hall Parks and at Union square are skilifully designed to provide an immense capability at a comparatively small expense. So it is with all the details of the elaborate plans; they show a thorough knowledge of the conditions of the problems, and considerable inventiveness in adapting the system to meet these conditions. If the system proposed by the Commission can not be constructed, then no comprehensive system is feasible in this city at the present time.

THE Commissioner's plan is essentially the Arcade plan, and its adoption is a vindication of the shrewdness of the originators of that excellent scheme. If the system is ever constructed, what a thoroughfare Broadway will be! At present it is traveled on more than any other street in the city; and this is so in spite of the fact that the present West Side rapid transit line is always one and is sometimes three or four blocks away. But in the future the current of traffic, instead of reaching its destination around by another avenue, will flow directly up and down Broadway; and the increasing accessibility, which that thoroughfare will so obtain will enhance the high price which property thereon already commands. South of 14th street the tendency of late has been for investors to erect large buildings on the streets running parallel and at right angles to Broadway; but the completion of this plan will forever determine the supremacy of that thoroughfare. The few parcels that are not as yet improved with high buildings will soon be covered with structures taller than any we have yet seen. Above 14th street retail trade, hotels and theatres will cling to it even more firmly than at present. It is above 42d street, however that the thoroughfare may be particularly benefited. Up to this time this part of Broadway has been neglected because it is not sufficiently in the line of traffic, but under the new conditions the pressure of travel, instead of being switched off, will be continued up Broadway, and in the place of the old buildings that are at present so common thereabouts will be erected improvements of the highest class. The Boulevard, too, which hitherto has not been favored of builders, will attain to a sudden and enormous popularity. New York is of such a unique formation that its chief longitudinal thoroughfare should be the greatest in the world—the greatest in the variety of spectacle it offers, the greatest in traffic, the greatest in its signs of wealth, prosperity and activity. Such is what Broadway will become.

THE newspapers have been discussing at length the question whether the money to build the proposed system will be forthcoming, and they have succeeded in showing — the utter futility of their efforts. Since no one can tell how much the road is going to cost until the specifications are prepared, it will be wise of the editors to exercise themselves on questions more easily solved. The estimates made thus far have ranged between $55,000,000 and $90,000,000; and it will be rather important for any corporation which intends to bid on the franchise to know which of the two extremes is nearer correct. On the other hand, it is a matter of great practical importance that we should know how long an interval must elapse before the new system will be completed. Mr. Worthen's calculation that it can be done in eighteen months presupposes that there will be no delays, no impediments, no accidents and no mistakes, whereas we all know that unforseen obstacles are the worst foes of the speedy execution of such complicated and difficult projects. Assuming that the Commissioners will be successful in selling the franchise; and that the construction company will be able to raise the money, it is safe to say that three or four years is low estimate for the completion of this stupendous scheme. What are the traveling public of New York to do meanwhile? Must they continue to suffer the intolerable discomfort at present unavoidable from a residence well up town? Must the property interests of this city watch for another half a dozen years the phenomenal growth of Brooklyn and New Jersey at the expense of our population? The future has been well provided for; is it not time to pay a little attention to the needs of the present? Our pot has been boiling over for some time, and we have gone on preparing our dinner regardless of the loss. Why not stop the pot boiling over? It can be done in three or four months; it can be done for the expenditure of a few hundred thousand dollars. Why is it not done? Mainly because Jay Gould is a very wicked man, a monopolist and so on; and we hate to give any more privileges to so bad a person. Let us cease this silly chatter, and look the situation squarely in the face. If a merchant finds his place of business too small, the first thing he does is to get more space in the same building, if possible; he does not tolerate the present inconvenience because he is erecting an enormous warehouse to be completed when times are good. The transit service between New York and Brooklyn is very inadequate; but the people interested have not made the improvement of the present bridge wait on the construction of another bridge. They have gone ahead to satisfy the pressing requirements of the situation. That is what New York ought to do. In any European city a corporation occupying the position of the Manhattan Company would long ago have been forced into improving its service. The municipal officials with jurisdiction would have met the managers of the road, and in return for the additional privileges they would have exacted more and quicker trains. But New York, which is ruled by editorial clap-trap and political ignorance and cowardice, goes on building for twenty years ahead and will not even stuff up a cold crevice in its present structure.

LATELY a traction company in Baltimore paralleled a number of the most important routes of horse cars operated by the City Passenger Railway Company; and the competition thus instituted was so effectual that at the present rate of decrease the horse car corporation will fail to earn very much net income during the present year. Hence it will be forced to meet good service with good service and introduce a cable system on its own lines. This is interesting to New Yorkers, because it indicates the probable effect of the cable traction now being adopted by the 3d avenue and Broadway companies. Corporations running horse cars that come into competition with either of these lines will not be able to delay very much longer the adoption of a quicker and more capable motive power. It is well known that these and other companies have been long considering the comparative desirability of the various improved methods of traction, and the delay in coming to any conclusion has been caused by the fact that the only feasible motor power which the officials of this city will approve is the cable. The street car lines would any or all of them gladly put in the trolley system costing only about $60,000 a mile, but they are obliged to think a long time before putting in a cable plant costing more than $200,000 a mile. They know, however, that any proposal to introduce the trolley would be howled down by the daily journals; and before adding to their capitalization the large initial cost of the cable plan, they want to be very sure that no subsequent improvement will bring into the market a cheaper and more efficient system. So the matter is put off; and New York is obliged to accept a slow transit that would not be tolerated in a Western city. When the cable on the 3d avenue and the Broadway lines begins to work, an additional stimulus will be given to the hesitating corporations, and they will hasten their own improvements. It is sincerely to be hoped that by the time they come to this action, such improvements in electrical traction will be made that no plausible objections to its introduction can be brought forward. The cheaper the motive power, the better in the end it will be for the city.

An Outbreak of Hotel Building.

A RESIDENT of Chicago strolling up 5th avenue and noting on the one hand the great number of new hotels that are being erected, and on the other hand the frequency of announcements that on and after a certain date some old family mansion will be opened as a hotel, might well wonder whether New York had not in the past been pitifully deficient in accommodations of that character. He could count buildings, without any trouble, that contained prospective living space for thousands of people. Why should all of these improvements and transformations be making at once? he might very well ask. Is any great change taking place in the customs of New Yorkers? Is the metropolis becoming increasingly popular with the residents of other parts of the country? And if his westernism was very aggressive, he might compare the dimensions of the Auditorium with those of our new hotels, and feel a local pride when the comparison resulted in favor of Chicago.

Superficially the number of new hotels either recently opened, or soon to be opened in this city, is certainly inexplicable. Within a year past the Imperial and the Plaza, two very large buildings, have begun offering accommodations for guests, and both are seemingly in a most prosperous condition. Inside of a few months the Holland House on 5th avenue and 30th street will also throw open its doors, following the recent example of the Hotel Renaissance. Judge Dugro's Hotel Savoy is rapidly approaching completion; and the two new Astor hotels are also proceeding steadily on their skyward career. In addition to these there are a number of others less centrally located—such as the Hotel Majestic on 72d street, William Noble's new building, at 56th street and 7th avenue, and a number of other smaller ones. All those specifically mentioned are buildings of the largest description—designed to accommodate many hundred people. Furthermore, if we wished to go back a year we could mention a number of West Side hotels, all recently opened; the Brockholst, the San Remo, and the Endicott. In addition to these new buildings, an observer can count no less than five or six old mansions on lower 5th avenue which are to be changed into family hotels. Now all this will bear a little explanation. Two or three years ago New York's hotels may have been inadequate. Those existing certainly were and are exceedingly prosperous. But there was and is no increase of transients in this city which would warrant this enormous increment of accommodations to meet their needs. Neither has there arisen any sudden love for hotel life as such in the bosoms of our residents. How, then, is the phenomenon to be explained?

It is the effect of a number of causes. In the first place, there is the undoubted fact mentioned above that the hotel business in New York is one in which a great deal of money has been and is being made. Consequently there was room for a certain increase in the number of caravansaries. With this fact to start with it is easy to understand why the old family mansions on lower 5th avenue are being changed into harborages for several families instead of one. The predominantly business character of the thoroughfare has, of course, tended to displace the exclusive people that formerly occupied the avenue, and when they moved out it at once became a problem in what way to use the houses. Many of them have from time to time been turned into stores and office buildings, and eventually it is probable that all of them will be so used. But meanwhile there are certain obstacles in the way of their immediate adaptation to business purposes. The kind of trade which is finding its home on the avenue is of a very excellent character, but the firms who can afford to pay the high rentals are comparatively limited in number. Consequently the demand for new stores is not enormous. Furthermore a mansion needs very expensive changes before it can be used for trade, and not everybody cares to make them. We know of one gentleman who bought a corner on lower 5th avenue, intending to alter it to suit his business, but he discovered subsequently that the expense required for a suitable alteration would be quite as much as that required to erect a new building—more than he cared to pay. Consequently he resold his purchase, which has since been turned into a family hotel. And so it has been in other cases. These hotels are simply makeshifts to tide over the period that must elapse before the business of the avenue becomes large enough to fill its buildings.

A very different explanation serves to account for the large increase in new hotel buildings. Some part of it is undoubtedly accounted for by the greater number of transient visitors to this city. There is more wealth in the country at present, more widely distributed than at any previous time. Consequently there are more people who can afford to visit the metropolis for pleasure, and many of them take advantage of their opportunities. Business also undoubtedly brings a greater number of people to New York now than formerly; this city is becoming increasingly the centre of the country. Local causes, too, contribute much to the prosperity of hotels, and consequently help to make an increase of numbers possible. No small part of the revenue of the best hotels is derived from their restaurants—a room upon which interior decorators are lavishing "taste" and "ideas" with eastern prodigality. They can afford to do this, because New Yorkers themselves dine out oftener than they used to, and patronize a good *cuisine* and a gaudy room. Lastly, New York's suburbs, increasing as they are in number and population, help New York's hotels, because when a family living twenty miles or so outside of the city wishes to go to a theatre, it is frequently more convenient for them to lodge for the night at a hotel around the corner than to go back to the country on some sleepy midnight train.

All these causes fail to explain the singular increase in hotel accommodations in this city, and now perhaps it is time to say that this increase is more apparent than real. Most of these new hotels are called apartment hotels—which is simply another name for the old apartment houses. The building law restricts the height of large flats, but not of hotels. Consequently, any one wishing to erect a building that is really an apartment house, calls it by the name of an apartment hotel. This fact is significant in a number of different ways. As most of our readers will remember, the fever for building enormous apartment houses came to an end back in 1884 and 1885. About before this time the clause above mentioned was inserted in the building law, and the provision certainly tended to stop the erection of these enormous flats—which are probably the most unique feature of New York's building. The law, however, was not the only reason for the disfavor into which such enterprises fell. Several of the largest of them failed of success and nearly ruined their projectors; consequently capitalists became disinclined to invest more money in that way. Then about this time the West Side boom started in, and the attention of speculators and investors was directed to that fertile field. At present, however, there is one very good reason for the increase of apartment houses—or their recent equivalent, apartment hotels. A long journey on the elevated roads is becoming so unpleasant that there is, of course, a constant tendency for people to decrease it so far as they can; consequently they prefer a dwelling place in what is now the lower part of the city. Concurrent with this, a diminution of available dwellings in these lower wards is taking place—owing to their alteration for business purposes. It is quite natural that such conditions should tend to increase the average dwelling space erected at each lot. We look for a continuance of this process until the new rapid transit lines begin to operate. There may, however, be cessation in the immediate future—until it is seen how far successful are the present ventures.

The popularity of apartment hotels may not be entirely due to the building law. It has been noticed recently that well-to-do people are beginning to remain in the country somewhat longer than they used to. It is quite common for them to leave the city in May and not to return until November. It has also been observed that an increasing number of people are forsaking boarding-houses and hotels and taking to cottages during the hot weather. This, of course, means a longer period of house-keeping for the family; and house-keeping of a trying character, because there are more temptations to entertain in the country than in the city. Hence it is very frequently the case that people prefer to avoid the fatigue and the bother of keeping house during the winter; and find it easier to live in an apartment hotel for the few cold months—one in which the cooking and service are all that can be desired. It is certainly an easy and pleasant mode of living for a rich family. Complete privacy can be obtained; and conveniences secured which would be out of the question save in the most elaborate residence.

EVERY friend of France will be sorry to hear that the new Russian loan has been successful. There can be no doubt that it was issued in Paris just at this time so as to take advantage of the Gallic enthusiasm over France's new ally, and that every political prejudice was tickled and flattered in order to make the borrowing an easier matter. The French frequently carry so much sentiment into their finances that no one need be surprised to hear the loan was largely over-subscribed. Indeed, it was predicted by good authorities that, in spite of the adverse conditions, the loan would be the success which it has been. The other financial centres left it from the beginning severely alone, and no wonder, for who would care to advance money to a country whose past, present and future unite to give deep cause for distrust. The following is the ordinary Budget for the last ten years;

	Revenue.	Expenditure.	Surplus.	Deficit.
1890	£94,170,000	£89,500,000	£4,670,000	....
1889	92,704,000	85,788,000	6,916,000	....
1888	89,853,000	84,042,000	5,811,000	....
1887	82,966,000	83,585,000	....	£619,000
1886	77,055,000	83,239,000	....	6,184,000
1885	76,448,000	80,661,000	....	4,213,000
1884	70,627,000	72,790,000	....	2,163,000
1883	70,041,000	72,367,000	....	2,326,000
1882	70,605,000	70,905,000	....	300,000
1881	65,419,000	73,426,000	....	8,007,000
1880	65,101,000	69,555,000	....	4,454,000

It will be seen that the years 1888, 1889 and 1890 were apparently years of handsome surpluses, but unfortunately they were obtained by a deceptive system of book-keeping, which credited to extraordinary expenditure to be paid for out of loans a great many public works. Russia's public debt is increasing more rapidly than that of France, and she is a far poorer country. Furthermore it is asserted that the items in the Budget are falsified. However this may be there can be no doubt that the nominal surpluses of the past three years have been obtained by a series of devices, such as are resorted to by a hopelessly bankrupt merchant. These three years were all years of enormous crops, so that if the government is ever to make both ends of its national finances meet, it should have done so then. It certainly made frantic efforts to do so; and during the process rung from the impoverished peasants their last rouble. Even before the failure of the crops of this year, the farmers of the country, both nobles and common people, were practically bankrupt, the latter having passed through sufferings that paralleled the trials of the French peasantry previous to the Revolution. In what condition, then, were they in to take on the burden of the present disastrous shortage? The destitution of the poor Russians during the coming winter will produce effects terrible to contemplate. Foreshadowings of what will come have already been published; and we may be sure that the worst has been held back by the Russian government. Undoubtedly the imperial revenue will be largely decreased, while at the same time the necessary expenditure will be largely increased. The country has been issuing swads of its inconvertible paper, causing a heavy fall therein, and it will be forced to renew this expedient in the future. All these conditions will, of course, bring about a severe decline in its securities, accompanied by the possibility of a panic in Paris, where they are principally held.

Real Estate as a Quick Asset.

A MAN who invests in improved real estate demands a larger gross return than a man who invests in stocks or bonds, because of the greater difficulty in the former case of collecting the income and realizing on the property. Consequently any means that are taken to make real estate more speedily negotiable will also make it a more popular form of property—that is, the number of possible purchasers at any one time will be enlarged, and this enlargement will be particularly effective under the commercial conditions which obtain in this country. The most prolific source of failures to American business men is their tendency to conduct a larger trade than their capital warrants; they want to get rich too soon. No doubt this tendency is on the decrease rather than the increase, for if the fittest are going to survive in the commercial conflict that element of fitness constituted by an ample capital must be of great avail. But even so there can be no doubt that a large majority of our business men carry on so large a trade in proportion to their capital that they cannot afford to invest as much money in permanent improvements as they should, a disability which prevents our trade from being as highly organized as that of Great Britain. Hence it also inhibits them from putting any part of their capital in real estate; they frequently cannot afford to own their own buildings. Or, assuming that a merchant's business is in a sufficiently sound condition to enable him to accumulate property outside thereof, he will not dare, unless he feels very secure, to make that property real estate. He will prefer securities because he can meet an emergency with them, whereas real estate would be of no use in a flurry. But if landed property were readily negotiable it would be so far on precisely the same footing as personal property. It would be in increased demand, and consequently would attain a higher level of values.

One radical and permanent difference, it is scarcely necessary to state, will always subsist between real and personal property. The latter represents a divided or shared ownership, every part of which is just as good as every other part; real estate is sold not in shares but in parcels, each of which has some particular characteristics. Hence, even if it took only five minutes to pass a title, the difficulty would still remain of finding a purchaser for a parcel so located and selling at such a price. But, although no facility of title-passing would very much decrease the difficulty of finding a buyer, it would make mortgaging a very much simpler process. In Australia, a cattle raiser who lacks money at the end of the month, can come to the city with his certificate of title in his pocket and raise the needed cash in fifteen minutes. Suppose the same were true of New York; suppose every merchant could use at his bank (a change in the banking laws would be necessary) as collateral his business building and his residence, what an enormous difference this would make? A mortgage, instead of being the serious, protracted, tiresome matter which it is at present, would become an every-day affair, with no more fuss about it than there is about borrowing money on a hundred shares of New York Central. There would, of course, be this difference between the two transactions: the value of the shares of Central stock would be exactly ascertainable, whereas the difficulty amounting to an impossibility of accurately appraising real estate might tend to make lenders cautious. Nevertheless there would be an ample margin on which money-lenders could make their advances. Thus the operating capital of the city would be largely increased; the real estate market would be powerfully leavened; an additional stimulus would be imparted to transactions in that kind of property, and a smart increase of values would assuredly result.

The slow negotiability of real estate is felt more severely at some times than at others. The present year is distinctly one in which it has been felt very severely, as an analysis of the mortgage filings for the first nine months conclusively demonstrates. During the first half of the present year very little money was to be had on time. In the early months the lenders were wary from their scare of the previous December; then came the gold shipments and uncertainty as regards the future, and finally a popular speculation on the Stock Exchange absorbed largely the loanable funds Meanwhile a marked decrease had taken place in the activity of real estate, and accompanying this a far smaller decrease in the number of mortgages given—figures which showed that only a few people cared to buy real property, while a good many wanted to borrow money thereon. In order to get the money they were quite willing to pay good prices. Thus, excluding five large general mortgages, the significance of which is quite different from that of ordinary papers, the money loaned on real estate during the first nine months of 1890 was $16,141,678, more than the money loaned on real estate during the same period in 1891. Of this decrease, mortgages bearing interest at 5 per cent are responsible for $8,439,509; and to mortgages bearing interest at less than 5 per cent may be traced $6,255,897 of the residue. This leaves only about $1,500,000 of the decrease to mortgages bearing interest at 6 per cent. So it will be seen that nearly all the falling off took place in papers expressing the lower rates of interest, while there was a relative increase in papers bearing a high rate of interest. Many people, then, needed money very badly; and in order to get it had to pay roundly for it. At the same time large capitalists were disinclined to buy real estate, because in trying times quick assets are far more valuable than slow assets. In case real estate had been more readily negotiable, the market during the present year would undoubtedly have been more active. At any rate, all business men owning large or small amounts of real property should remember that it is perfectly possible to convert it from a slow to a quick asset; and that any time in the past when their money had been tied up, and they felt dubious about pulling through, they would never be troubled by this anxiety in case the land laws of this State were all that they might be.

It is not surprising that the West has bitten at land transfer reform with avidity. The assets of Westerners consists so much of real estate of present or prospective value, that any system which pretends to make this asset more available is eagerly welcomed. Within the past year commissions from several Western States have been appointed to inquire into the feasibility of the Torrens system, and it looks very much as if Australian methods of land transfer would be adopted hastily and without sufficient examination. They are also dazzled by the idea of a sudden perfecting of clouded titles, for in all the newspaper discussions of the matter which have come within our notice it has been assumed that all adverse interests could be incontinently cut off within a short interval by the simple service of a general notice through the press. Such a process could, indeed, be made legal, but unless care was taken it would be profoundly unjust. We presume that some statute of limitations cutting off all adverse claimants after the lapsing of a definite period would be the inevitable accompaniment of any thorough-going reforms in land transfer, but the period named should be long enough to minimize a possible injustice that might be done. New York City can safely proceed on the lines already laid down by the block-indexing law now in operation, and that is really the only safe way it can proceed. The immediate adoption of the Torrens system intoct would, with the innumerable and complicated titles in this city, be quite impossible. The Register's Court would be swamped by the thousands of titles thrown in for adjudication and guarantee. It will be a far safer operation to re-index the present records on the block plan, the work being done under the supervision of a commission of conveyancers, whose duty it shall also be to make suggestions for further reforms. It is encouraging to notice that this more conservative method of procedure is apparently commending to the Massachusetts Commission which is inquiring into the matter.

What the Report does not tell.

A NEW SUBTERRANEAN STREET—WHAT RAPID TRANSIT WILL DO FOR BROADWAY—FEATURES OF THE PLANS NOT SPECIFIED IN THE REPORT OF THE COMMISSION—A SCHEME OF GREAT MAGNITUDE, COSTING OVER $55,000,000, BUT OF IMPERATIVE AND PRESSING NECESSITY.

How well the confidence of the public in the Rapid Transit Commission has been justified is shown by the report of the commission published herewith. THE RECORD AND GUIDE, with a full appreciation of the importance of haste and the dangers of delay in providing rapid transit for this city, has always asked for the commission the indulgence of the public until, in a time consistent with the magnitude of their task, the Commissioners should present their report. Reasonable criticism of the work of the commission could only begin with the presentation of its report, showing the general plan of construction of the proposed roads.

Now the plan is before the public. It bears internal evidence of intelligent and painstaking application to the task that lay before the Commissioners, and as much by what it avoids as by what it proposes, illustrates in some measure the vastness of the work and the difficulties that have attended it. The tangible evidences, included in sixty independent drawings and a report, with exhibits, that would more than fill a copy of THE RECORD AND GUIDE of the usual size, were presented to the Board of Aldermen on Wednesday. The report was made ready for presentation on Tuesday, but a fire in the printing office destroyed a considerable part of it and the work destroyed had to be done over again.

While the report is an exhaustive defense of the conclusions of the commission on the general plan of construction it perhaps properly does not show many things in which the public curiosity is deeply involved. Nothing is said regarding the methods of construction; nor the number and location of stations; nor the extent to which private property and vested rights will be encroached upon; nor the time required for construction; nor the character of the equipment; nor the cost of the enterprise. Neither is the all-important question answered, "What are the chances that it will be built?"

Several of these questions, and some others relating to the details of construction, have been the subjects of a special inquiry by a RECORD AND GUIDE reporter. The plan is essentially that recommended by Wm. E. Worthen, chief engineer of the commission, as predicted by THE RECORD AND GUIDE of last week. It has been improved in several particulars since the reports of the consulting engineers were received, in some important respects against Mr. Worthen's judgment—as, for instance, in confining the downtown section, south of City Hall Park, entirely between the curb-walls, instead of running one track along under the sidewalks, as proposed by Mr. Worthen. Instead of a single-track loop at the Battery, there is a double-track loop, and instead of two tracks between the City Hall Park and Bowling Green there are three tracks.

Upon the middle of the three tracks south of City Hall Park there will be no station, the trains running through to Bowling Green. Along the entire line there will be no encroachments upon sidewalk vaults except at the stations. All local stations in Broadway and Madison avenue will be just beneath the sidewalks, which will have to be reconstructed for that purpose; and at the express stations the way tracks will diverge from the direct line on both sides, so as to run under the sidewalks, and the station platform will be just outside the curb, between the way and express tracks. All down trains will run on the westerly tracks; all up trains on the easterly.

Of the possibilities of street improvement under this plan there has as yet been no adequate conception. Property-owners along Broadway will be given some insight of these facts when the commission sends around its agents to invite their consent to the use of the street. THE RECORD AND GUIDE will anticipate them so far as its readers are concerned. The vaults under the sidewalks in Broadway are for the most part dark, damp, noisome and worthless spaces. Assume, for example, that a station will be constructed at the corner of Bleecker street, with an entrance to the stairway in the corner building. The platform must be long enough to afford quick exit for the passengers from a ten-car train. The train will be 300 feet long. That will be just a block and a-half. Therefore the platform must be at least 300 feet long. Practically it must be nearer 400 feet, or two blocks long. This will make a new sidewalk underneath the upper sidewalk, and from which passengers can pass directly into the basement of any building along the length of the platform. It is intended to have local stations every quarter of a mile apart. That would take 1,600 out of every 5,280 feet of vault space along the line. Storekeepers will find uses for their basements never before dreamed of. The entrances fronting on the platforms would be attractively improved; the basements would be in demand at good rentals for every variety of retail trade and many other kinds of business, and before long the owners of property between the stations would be wanting the station platforms extended throughout the entire line of vaults along Broadway on both sides. Thus before the ancient Knickerbockers are aware of it there will be an entirely new subterranean street in Broadway, light, of equable temperature winter and summer, sheltered from the inclement weather, the roadway occupied exclusively by an ideal system of rapid transit, and the sidewalks secure to pedestrians. Improvements would continue until the sidewalks would be unbroken from station to station throughout the length of Broadway, and wherever else desired in the business section of the city. How vastly this would add to the value of property in Broadway staggers conjecture. Every storekeeper will readily realize how great a card it will be for him if there is a convenient and sheltered passage through the basement of his store to the platforms of the new railway. The possibilities of store and building improvements along this line of suggestion are almost unlimited.

It is promised that with the possible exception of the crossing at Canal street and down at the Battery, where the tunnel will extend below the level of tide water, the tunnel will be excavated and the iron construction put in without disturbing the surface of the street. In order to do this four shields will be employed, each excavating about a quarter of the roadway and following each other say half a block apart on different parallel sections of the work. The shield, which Mr. Worthen is designing, will be operated by hydraulic rams. Beginning at a given point excavating will be begun, say, along the easterly side of Broadway, for the full width of the curb-walls and the supports of the roadway between the way and express tracks, and as soon as the excavation is made a temporary construction to support the roadway will be put in, to be followed immediately by the permanent construction. Half a block further down town another shield will be worked along the parallel section in which the up tracks of the express trains are to run, and still another half block away another shield will be working on the third parallel section, and still another half block distant the fourth shield will be working up along the line, and so on until the entire roadway is excavated and the tunnel constructed.

The commission has not designated the number nor places of the stations, but has left that to be considered in treating with the property-owners for their consents to the construction of the railroads. Still, it is said by them that this is a feature which will largely adjust itself. There are certain points at or very near which stations must be established. Then, when it is stated that the local stations must be a quarter of a mile distant from each other, the proper location of the stations can be determined with close approximation by almost anybody. Some of the stations will be of such great advantage to property at some points that it is believed there will be a sharp competition for the privilege, for which, instead of demanding compensation, some owners will be willing to pay. The news, cigar, restaurant and other privileges at the stations will also be large sources of revenue to the company that shall acquire the franchise.

Engineer Worthen has said that if the money to pay for the construction of the road is provided promptly, he could build the road in eighteen months, and that under ordinary circumstances he could build it in two years. The cars are to be of special design and of large seating capacity, with no windows except such of an ornamental character as may be provided in the plans. While only tentatively adopted, there is no doubt but that the motive and illuminating power will be electricity.

The estimated cost of the road and equipment is $55,500,000. Its entire length is twenty-six miles. The Broadway section, from the South Ferry to 34th street, three and one-half miles long, will cost $3,000,000 a mile, or $10,500,000 in the aggregate; the West Side section, from 34th street to Yonkers, is twelve miles, long and the East Side line, from Union square to Jerome Park, is ten and one-half miles long, making twenty-two and one-half miles in the two. These sections, at the estimated cost of $2,000,000 a mile, will cost $45,000,000, which, added to the cost of the Broadway section, will make the entire system cost $55,500,000.

LOCAL STATION IN BROADWAY

At this cost, will the capital required for the construction of the road be forthcoming? That is the question of greatest importance with which the Commissioners will still have to contend with. President Steinway says he has every reason to believe it will, if not at once, then as soon as the finances of the world have reached their normal tone and elasticity. The Board of Aldermen has set next Wednesday for the consideration of the report. After it has been passed upon the commission will endeavor to obtain the consent of property-owners along the lines designated to the construction of the road. When these are obtained and the specifications and working plans are completed, the commission will have to consider the question of the terms of sale of the franchise, whether it shall be sold for twenty-five or fifty or a hundred years, and what upset price shall be put upon it.

But before that point is reached in the development of the general plan there will be another session of the Legislature, and there is no doubt but that some amendment of the law will be proposed. President Steinway said that he was in favor of giving the purchaser the privilege of waiting to construct the sections of the road above the Harlem River, where population is sparse and there would be but little traffic for the road. Alderman Morris has declared that he proposes to ask the board to memorialize the Legislature in favor of authorizing the city to construct and own the road, selling the privilege of operating at a public auction for a term of years. If it should be offered for sale according to the provisions of the present law, there is reason to believe, President Steinway said, that there will be a lively competition for the franchise. Inquiries have been made of him by the representatives of foreign English and German capitalists, which lead him to believe that they are keeping track of the work of the commission with a view to invest-

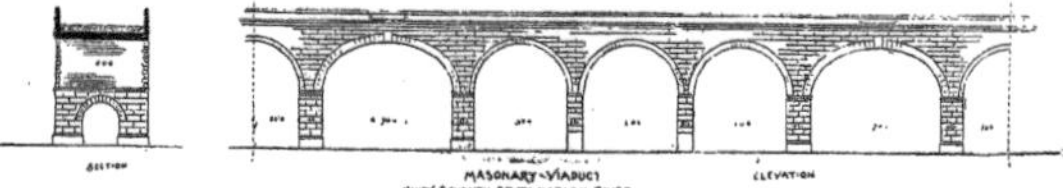

MASONARY VIADUCT
NINTY SEVENTH ST TO HARLEM RIVER

ment when the right time comes. Altogether, New York City is in fairer prospects of securing adequate rapid transit than ever before.

WHAT REAL ESTATE OWNERS, BROKERS AND OTHERS SAY ABOUT THE COMMISSIONERS' REPORT.

A number of prominent real estate owners, etc., were seen. Among the questions asked were: 1. Do you favor the shallow underground road proposed by the Commissioners in preference to a deep tunnel? 2. Do you favor the granting of extra facilities to the Manhattan Road for the convenience of the public as a temporary expedient during the construction of the road as outlined by the Commissioners? Several were asked if there was likely to be opposition on the part of property-owners affected, particularly along Broadway.

Geo. R. Read, President of the Real Estate Exchange, said: "I am not as capable of judging of the merits of a deep or shallow underground road as the Commissioners, who constitute a body of gentlemen known to the community for their position and integrity, and who have made the

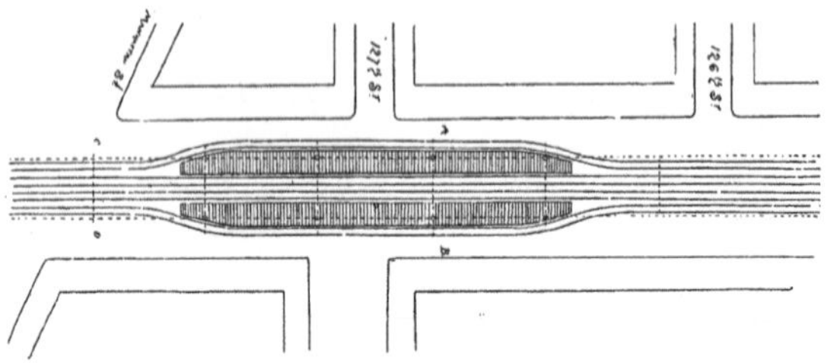

matter a deep study for months past. I am willing to follow them in preference to any opinions which I may hold. On the face of it, it appears to me that a shallow tunnel is undoubtedly superior to a deep tunnel, because it is easily accessible and saves the time and inconvenience of getting up and down in a deep tunnel with elevators. The time lost in the latter way would be sufficient to enable passengers to ride several blocks, and it would be detrimental to short trips. If the road is a few feet below the surface passengers can quickly descend and ascend, and it would be a saving of time and more desirable in every way. As to allowing the present railroad facilities to be increased, speaking as a private individual and as a citizen, I would say that any improvements in that direction that will help the people of this city to travel quickly up and down town, while the more complete road laid out by the Commissioners is being built, would have my support."

J. Romaine Brown, who is not only one of the oldest brokers in the city, but is also a large owner of vacant property in the upper wards, said: "I

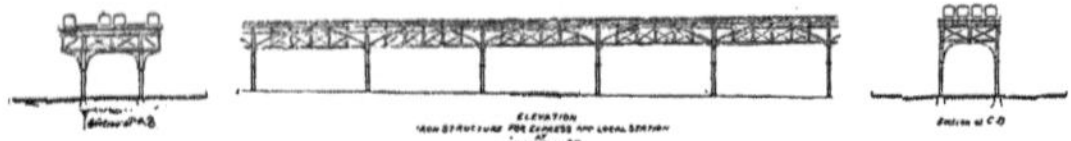

am undoubtedly in favor of a shallow tunnel. There ought to be no two questions about it. When finished it will be far superior to the London Underground Railway, because it will have the advantage of being built a generation later, with all the improvements of the last twenty years to be utilized, including electric motors, which will avoid coal dust, smoke, steam, etc. With the aid of the electric propulsion the proposed underground road will be practically perfection. As to granting further facilities to the Manhattan Road or anyone else, I would say that it would e imprudent to do so, unless we were to receiv a positive assurance that it

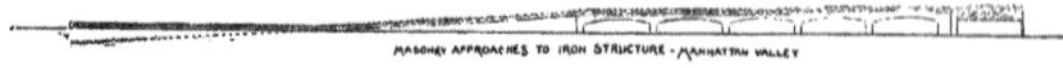

would not jeopardize the Commissioners' road financially. If it would, then I would strongly oppose it, and much prefer to put up with all the inconveniences of deficient transit until the Commissioners' road is built. We ought to bend our energies toward carrying out the plans proposed by them, which are admirable."

J. C. R. Eckerson, of Thomas & Eckerson, real estate brokers, said: "If you can get a tunnel free from gas smells, etc., I would say go ahead. I think an underground road very near the surface preferable to a deep tunnel on many grounds. Yes, I would permit the elevated roads to be extended and given other facilities for increasing the transit service, making it a condition, however, that they should use electric or cable power on such extensions, so as to do away with smoke, cinders, etc., which are a great nuisance."

Geo. Jardine, of D. & J. Jardine, architects, said: "Of course we all favor rapid transit, but the statement that the plan proposed by the Commissioners can be carried out in two years is a big mistake. It is physically impossible. It will take at least nearly double that time, and work will have to proceed vigorously, day and night. Three obstacles will stand in the way of an early completion: 1. The almost inextricable tangle of underground sewer, gas and water pipes, wires, etc. 2. The rock met with very near the surface everywhere north of 11th and 12th streets; and we have found in our experience of a generation in building that rock is nearly always found close to the surface north of those streets. 3. The probable opposition of property-owners at various points."

A gentleman who represents one of the largest estates in New York, an estate which owns considerable property along the lines of the proposed routes, said: "While I am strongly in favor of a comprehensive system of rapid transit which will solve the problem for our city for many years to come, I very much fear that no plan can be carried out without Messrs. Gould & Sage and the Vanderbilts, with their allied interests, have their hand in it. The interests of those people, and the corporations they represent, are too vast for them to permit any new system of roads to be built that will seriously injure their existing lines. I do not know in what direction those interests will get their grip on the situation, but you may depend upon it that it will make itself apparent somewhere when we get further along with the project. If Wm. H. Vanderbilt had lived, we would no doubt by this time have seen a road built from the neighborhood of the City Hall to the Grand Central Depot, with stations half a mile or more apart. This would have given to the people of our city rapid transit of the most approved kind from down town as far north as Westchester County to places on the line of all the steam roads running out of New York City. It would also have relieved the Grand Central Depot, which is now overcrowded, and made the Mott Haven Depot the great entrepot. My belief is that the Vanderbilt interests will eventually get control of the East Side rapid transit route, and that the Manhattan Road interests will obtain control of the West Side route. As to a tunnel, I think that, whether it be shallow or deep, it will not be free from smells. I would give the elevated roads every facility to improve the public service during the five to ten years that I think it is likely to take before a plan such as outlined by the Commissioners can possibly be carried into effect."

Daniel Birdsall, of D. Birdsall & Co., the Broadway real estate brokers and agents, said: "I am not in favor of a tunnel, whether it be deep or shallow. I think it better to travel in the open air and this could be done by viaducts through the yards in the rear of buildings. The cost of acquiring property and the time consumed in doing so, as well as the opposition from property-owners, are sources of delay and financial danger that would alone reconcile people to an underground road. I would favor any extension of the Manhattan system in the meanwhile; for whatever will give us relief from the annoyances of overcrowded trains and long, tedious journeys, will be welcome. As to opposition from property-owners on Broadway, I think there will undoubtedly be opposition in many quarters, while others will favor the plan."

S. Van Rensselaer Cruger, manager for Trinity Corporation, said: "Speaking for myself and not for the corporation which I represent, I may say that I am not in favor of an underground road. We should long since have taken 'the bull by the horns' and built a viaduct road, in the open air, with daylight around us. It will have to be conclusively shown by the engineers that the foundations and walls of buildings along Broadway will absolutely be safe if the Commissioners wish their plan to be free from opposition by property-owners along the lines of their proposed routes. I do not think the elevated roads should be allowed to be extended. They have served their purpose and more structures of the kind are not desirable."

Dwight H. Olmstead, who was chairman of the Citizens' Committee which met for two years at the Murray Hill Hotel, and through which the agitation arose that resulted in the appointment of the present commission, said: "I think the general plan of the Commissioners is good. It is really the Arcade plan which, among various others, was presented to us at the Murray Hill, which I have always felt, in its essential features, was the best proposed. I think a road near the surface of the ground is most desirable, but I think the Commissioners have made a great error in not suggesting an open cut on the Grand Boulevard, north of 64th street. This would have solved the problem of rapid transit for the West Side within about a year's time. Let me explain. When the Citizens' Committee had completed its meetings an open cut was recommended. A gentleman promised me that he would guarantee the money to build such a road on the Boulevard, from 64th to 155th street or beyond up to Kingsbridge. The Manhattan Road unofficially agreed that it would transfer our passengers via the Boulevard cut to its road at 64th street, giving them transport to down-town points by a traffic arrangement with us. The open cut was to be as near the surface as the cars and engines would make it possible, and was to be bridged over at each street, the sides of the cut to be fenced in with attractive and ornamental railings. There is no reason to doubt that such an arrangement could still be entered into with the Manhattan Road, and, if so, we could have rapid transit on the West Side five or six years earlier than we will get it under the Commissioners' plans.

Fred'k Southack said: "I am opposed to all forms of rapid transit on Broadway, but if we are to have any the deep tunnel is the only one that should be allowed and not a shallow one. If they propose to tunnel Broadway and not dig up the road-bed, nor have any designs of using the road-bed or vaults for ventilating purposes in future, I do not see why a deep tunnel, even if they had to go down 100 feet, would not answer, and of course be less damaging to property. (1) In the shallow tunnel the vibration of the running trains could be easily felt in the adjoining property. (2) There is always danger of the company at some future time, on account of the possible non-success of the road, which they might attribute to bad ventilation, wanting to ventilate the tunnel either through the streets or the vaults of the adjoining buildings. A railroad company that represents $90,000,000, and backed by a large portion of the public who are in no way interested in the value of property, thinking that all that was necessary to make the tunnel a success was to ventilate it, could carry out their ideas in spite of what all the property-holders might say. A company of $90,000,000 acting as a unit, and the property-holders, of course, being a number and residing at distant places, could not cope in any way with them as a body. Any company operating should be compelled to compensate property-owners for any damage that may ensue, due to construction. I favor granting the Manhattan Road the third tracks and other additional facilities to carry on their business, but they should be made to pay for the same."

Richard V. Harnett said: "I am content to follow the Commissioners, in whom I have implicit confidence. I would certainly allow the Manhattan Road to use their tracks and otherwise give the people of this city better accommodations until the new road is built, particularly as that road is being compelled to pay heavy damages to property-owners along the line of their structure."

J. H. Hunt, of Hunt & Wendell, said: "I think Westsiders are all satisfied with the proposed routes. Still, Westsiders would prefer to see the Boulevard part of the road commenced at once, the elevated road doing duty south of that thoroughfare."

A member of the Real Estate Exchange said: "I am not a believer in underground travel if it can at all be avoided. If the Commissioners had recommended an elevated road over the routes they have proposed we would have had rapid transit in two years. The structure could have been built of steel, of a neat and artistic design, altogether different from the cumbrous and ungainly roads that we now travel over. Broadway merchants and storekeepers would have been greatly benefited, not to speak of the general public, and people would in a very short time have gotten used to the appearance of the structure, which would have been attractive rather than an eyesore."

Francis Crawford said: "I think the plan of the Rapid Transit Commissioners is a capital one, and so far as the West Side, at least, is concerned, I do not see where it can be improved upon. Of course, very much will depend on how and by whom the plan is carried out, but the plan itself is a very good one. There is only one improvement that suggests itself to me, and that is that there should have been a third route away over on the East Side. Really, the route that runs under and near Madison avenue is not an East Side but a central route. There is a vast territory to the east of it, and a very populous territory too, that it seems to me has been entirely neglected."

Charles Buek said: "I have read the report with the greatest interest and attention, and think it comprises a thoroughly studied and well-digested plan. I was in hopes that above 59th street, on the Boulevard, there would be an open cut or something of that kind, but the commission have evidently had good reason to decide otherwise, and I have confidence enough in the gentlemen composing that commission to believe that they decided as they did because it was for the best interests of all concerned. Of course, below 59th street, a sunken road was the only thing possible, but I fear that the fact of the entire system being practically underground will interfere very materially with the successful disposal of the franchise. There is, without doubt, a decided prejudice against underground roads, and capitalists may hesitate before putting money into the new road for fear that because of this prejudice satisfactory dividends will not be forthcoming."

Chas. E. Schuyler said: "I am heartily in favor of the report as presented. I think if the road is really built up the Boulevard as it has been laid out, it will be the grandest possible thing for the West Side. The only thing I have to ask of the commission is not to change it, and not to let the newspapers or anyone else talk them out of it."

Full Report of the Commission.

OFFICE OF THE
RAPID TRANSIT RAILROAD COMMISSIONERS
FOR THE CITY OF NEW YORK,
22 William street.

To the Honorable the Common Council of the City of New York:

The Board of Rapid Transit Railroad Commissioners for the City of New York, appointed by the provisions of chapter 4 of the Laws of 1891, having determined upon the route or routes and general plan of construction of a rapid transit railway for the conveyance and transportation of persons and property to be established in the said city, in addition to the already existing lines, respectfully represent

The Board in entering upon the duties imposed upon it by the statutes of this State, determined at the outset that it must lay the foundation for such a broad and comprehensive system of rapid transit as would meet the needs of the city at present and be capable of expansion in the future.

That both express and way service should be provided, and that the construction should be effected with a minimum of street obstruction.

The Board, by advertisement, invited the submission to it, at public meetings, of suggestions as to routes, plans and manner of construction. These public meetings were largely attended, and plans submitted in great variety and number, which were carefully examined and considered.

The commissioners made personal investigation as to the exact needs of the city in its several localities. Statistics were gathered as to population, present lines of transit, and the number and destination of passengers carried on such lines.

The members of the Board personally went over all routes suggested, as well as over others laid out by the Board, including the ones now presented for your consideration.

It was appreciated that any system devised with a view to permanency and the capacity requisite for the future would be very costly, and the route therefore should be along main arteries of travel, in order to give relief where most needed and to command the necessary traffic to make the line remunerative.

Well known statistics established the fact that the existing north and south lines of transit nearest the centre of the city absorbed the greater traffic, and that the relative pressure upon them was substantially in proportion to their proximity to Broadway.

These considerations demanded the location of the lower part of the proposed route on or near that thoroughfare. Such a route could be continued by diverging lines above 14th street on the East and West sides of the city respectively, reaching the largest centres of population, now least provided with transit facilities, and avoiding the necessity of more than one route below 14th street.

With this much determined, the two governing questions remaining were the general plan of the structure and the motive power to be used.

Appreciating that a viaduct of masonry would be the most desirable means of transit, the commission considered many plans for such a route.

An elevated structure on Broadway below 33d street was prohibited by the Statute. A viaduct of masonry was manifestly impossible on any adjacent street.

A viaduct through the blocks in the lower part of the city, the Commission believed, after searching investigation, to be too costly, and subject to too many delays in the acquisition of property rights, to be within reasonable hope of attainment.

It was therefore unavoidable that rapid transit, in the lower part of the city, must be secured by an underground structure.

The location of such an underground structure through blocks near the surface was considered.

This system had some advantages.

The stations could be conveniently placed, and the amount of excavation would be reduced, which is a material item where the earth has to be removed through crowded streets.

Many of the objections, however, to the viaduct system, as to cost and long delay in the acquisition of vast amounts of real estate, applied with almost equal force to this plan, and the Commission considered its adoption unwise.

It would extend this report beyond proper limits to lay before you all the reasons which influenced the selection of the line under Broadway. The determination to adopt such a line was communicated to the public in the resolutions of the 27th day of May, 1891, and generally approved.

A line under Broadway being decided upon, the question was narrowed to the character of the structure and its distance below the surface; whether it should be deep or shallow; whether in providing for the four tracks necessary, the entire width of the street or only a portion should be used; and whether the surface of the street and existing pipes should be again disturbed.

The impression prevailed to some extent that a tunnel could be driven under Broadway entirely through rock, within reasonable distance of the surface, thereby obtaining a stable roof and thus avoiding many difficulties in construction.

The Commission caused careful and accurate borings to be made on Whitehall street and Broadway, at every cross street from Front street to 33d street. The results are shown on Exhibit 1, and are indicated generally by the following table, giving the depths of the rock below the street surface at the streets named:

Front street	20 feet.
Pearl street	16 "

Stone street	21 feet.
Beaver street	34 "
Rector street	63 "
Fulton street	83 "
Park place	112 "
Chambers street	100 "
Duane street	103 "
Leonard street	95 "
Walker street	107 "
Canal street	87 "
Broome street	47 "
Houston street	105 "
Washington place	24 "
Clinton place	65 "
Fourteenth street	13 "
Thirty-third street	4 "

Exhibit 1, also shows the material overlying the rock to be sand of different degrees of coarseness.

The difficulties of final decision related especially to that portion of Broadway covered by these test borings. North of 33d street the width of the street was greater, and the rock formation was at such height as to admit of excavation in almost any desired form without endangering foundations. This was also the case with the East Side line above 14th street finally adopted.

These borings conclusively disposed of the idea of a continuous rock roof for a tunnel, except at such depth or with such grades as to be almost, if not quite prohibitory.

It followed then that a tunnel for a considerable portion of its length—and that probably under the portion of Broadway where questions of property rights would present the greatest difficulties—must be driven through sand.

The question was whether this could be best accomplished near the surface or at a considerable distance below, and, if the latter, what that distance should be.

A decision depended upon a variety of complex considerations. Some related to the convenience and cost of construction; others, and the more important ones, to operation when completed.

The cost of tunneling at such depth as to avoid all question of property rights might be cheaper, but the extent of the cheapening would depend upon the depth and might be easily exaggerated.

Much would depend upon the number and depth of shafts used.

The mere cost of excavating below ground would be but a small proportion of the whole when it is considered that all the excavated material for a commodious four-track structure, with ample station and platform facilities, must be raised to the surface through shafts opening on or near crowded streets.

The question also arose as to what depth would secure immunity from damages when the material to be excavated was sand, liable to be wet and to run, with this liability increasing with the depth, and when the pressure from above was that of Broadway's heaviest buildings.

To this nothing but trial and experience could give an answer.

The difficulties of ventilation and drainage increase with every foot of depth.

A deep tunnel would require elevators as a means of access, and stairways would be necessary in addition, which, except for emergencies, would be practically useless, and to properly provide for emergencies must be broad and costly.

Modern and improved elevators in sufficient numbers would doubtless provide for the regular volume of traffic at ordinary stations, but they are not believed to be adapted for large crowds such as must frequently gather on a line of transit under Broadway. Stairways one hundred feet more or less in vertical height would be of no avail as sources of relief for crowds moving upward, and would be extremely dangerous to crowds moving downward.

Moreover, it is not believed that a deep, subterranean line of transit, with elevators, would attract short trip passengers, and the short trip business is absolutely essential for the success of any line the cost of which at all approximates that of a four-track tunnel in New York City.

It is admitted by the strongest advocates of underground transit that other things being equal, the nearer the station platforms are to the surface the more attractive the line.

Conceding, however, that there are some advantages in deep tunneling for lower Broadway, it is seen that they apply entirely during the time of construction and to the first cost of the structure. These, while important, cannot weigh against permanent advantages to be derived in comfort and convenience to the public, facility of operation and the securing of patronage after completion.

Ready accessibility by means of short, broad, and commodious stairways, supplemented where necessary by elevators, better light and better ventilation at stations; light and air at intermediate points if necessary, and the feeling of greater security on the part of the public with a structure which can be more readily reached in time of accident or other emergency, are too potent to be surrendered to mere temporary difficulties of construction.

These and other considerations led to the decision upon the part of the commission to place the underground structure as near the surface of the street as possible, and the Engineers of the Board were directed to submit two separate plans, one for four tracks on a single level, the other for a double deck tunnel with two tracks upon each deck.

These plans were prepared, the one providing for four tracks on a level at the minimum distance below the surface to admit of the non-disturbance of existing pipes, conduits and other underground structures, and occupying substantially the entire width of Broadway from curb to curb, but not at such depth as to require excavation below the foundations of the heaviest and most costly structures abutting on the street. This it was believed would eliminate to a large degree the difficulties to be encountered in protecting abutting property during construction. This plan also provided for carrying on the work of excavation without disturbance of the street surface except for short distances at points of exceptional difficulty.

The other plan of double deck tunnel would occupy less width of the street, and presented the advantage of the removal and replacement in galleries of the pipes and other existing underground structures.

A disturbance of the street surface would be unavoidable in this case, but a great and permanent benefit would be derived from the fact that such disturbance would not be repeated in the future for any cause except the relaying of the pavement, as the pipes in galleries would be accessible at all times for purposes of repair.

The excavation required by this plan was about 4 feet more in depth than by the other. The length of stairway to the local stations would be less, but to the express stations greater than in the other plan.

These plans when matured were submitted separately for separate reports to four distinguished Consulting Engineers, to wit: Messrs. Octave Chanute, of Chicago: Joseph M. Wilson, of Philadelphia; Theodore Cooper, of New York, and John Bogart, State Engineer of New York, with instructions that they were submitted not only for approval or disapproval, but for such general discussion and such suggestions as to alterations and additions as might in their judgments be regarded as necessary or desirable to accomplish in the best manner possible the objects sought to be obtained upon the routes and under the general plans outlined in the resolutions of this commission of May 27th and July 22d, Exhibits 2 and 3.

The Engineers of the Commission were instructed to render such assistance and to give such information as the Consulting Engineers might desire, and to give them access to all records of the commission, and all plans and suggestions which had been placed before the Board by any person.

In accordance with these instructions, full and elaborate reports were received from each of the consulting engineers, copies of which are submitted herewith marked Exhibits 4, 5, 6 and 7.

The surveys which were essential to the exact location of the line in the upper portion of the Island and in the Annexed District were completed during the present month.

All the necessary information for a final conclusion was thus in the hands of the commission.

While the double deck plan provided for subways or galleries for the pipes and other underground structures, and the Rapid Transit Act authorized the Board to make such provision, yet the Board felt that the intent of the Act was that such power should be exercised only when necessary for the proper construction of any proposed railway.

The adoption of such plan would not only again require the disturbance of Broadway, but might expose the railway and passengers to great annoyance, if not serious danger, from escaping gas and steam; it was open also to the objection of greater noise and possibly inferior ventilation.

The double deck plan moreover burdened the enterprise with the heavy additional expense of pipe galleries and removal of pipes.

Another and most serious question which the commission was obliged to consider was facility of movement between the different tracks in emergencies causing congestion and delay. No system of rapid transit would be complete that did not provide on its main trunk line at numerous points for the movement of trains from either track to any other, and the transfer of passengers from disabled trains, if need be, at any point between stations.

This in the double deck plan could be but partially accomplished, while with four tracks on one level the entire blockade of the system would be almost an impossibility.

So important is this consideration that the commission would be loth to recommend any plan wanting in this feature.

It would have been regarded as essential even had the commission adopted a plan for a tunnel at greater depth than the one now reported.

The commission, after weighing carefully all these considerations, together with the recommendations of its own Engineers and of the Consulting Engineers, and the various suggestions presented to it, thereupon determined, by unanimous vote, on the 19th day of October, 1891, that the route or routes and general plan of construction of a Rapid Transit Railway for the conveyance and transportation of persons and property should be established in this city, as follows:

THE ROUTE.

A route, the centre line, commencing at a point under the westerly side of Whitehall street, distant along the same 62.5 feet north from the northerly line of South street produced; thence by diverging lines under Whitehall street and Battery Park and State street, respectively, forming a loop line, the tracks converging to parallelism at a point under Broadway between Bowling Green and Morris street; thence under Broadway and Union square to 59th street; thence under the Boulevard to 121st street; thence by viaduct to 134th street; thence under the Boulevard to the south line of 156th street; thence by viaduct to the north line of 159th street; thence under the Boulevard to 169th street; thence under 11th avenue to a point 1,460 feet north of the centre line of 190th street; thence by a viaduct on the same straight line produced to a point 442 feet north from the intersection of said straight line with the centre line of the Kingsbridge road; thence to the right on a curve with a radius of 1,910 feet and in tunnel a distance of 860.6 feet; thence by tangent 138 feet; thence by curve to the left with a radius of 1,910 feet a distance of 350 feet in tunnel and a distance of 510.6 feet by viaduct to a point on a line coincident with the centre line of Audubon avenue produced and distant 425 feet north from the centre line of 217th street; thence by viaduct and on a tangent coincident with the centre line of Audubon avenue produced across the Government Ship Canal, and thence by the same tangent and in depressed structure 670 feet; thence on the same tangent and by viaduct to and across Spuyten Duyvil Creek; and thence on the same tangent by viaduct, depressed structure and tunnel, as the contour of the lands may require to a point 100 feet north of the centre line of Delafield lane; thence to the left on a curve with a radius of 1,910 feet to a point 30 feet south from the centre line of Delafield's old lane; thence by a tangent to a point 112.4 feet south from the south line of Rock street; thence to the right by a curve with a radius of 500 feet for a distance of 220.8 feet to a point in the centre line of Forest street 112.4 feet north of the south line of Rock street; thence by tangent coincident with the centre line of Forest street to the city limits.

Also, a loop from Broadway, under Mail street, City Hall Park, Park row, and Chambers street, and again connecting with the Broadway line.

Also, a route, the centre line, diverging from the Broadway line at or near 14th street, running under Union square to 4th avenue; thence under 4th and Park avenues to a point 112.15 feet north from the north line of 40th street; thence to the left on a curve with a radius of 250 feet for a distance of 154.55 feet; thence by tangent a distance of 292.18 feet to a point 40.1 feet north from the south line of 42d street, and 215.7 feet west from the centre line of 4th avenue; thence to the right on a curve with a radius of 250 feet a distance of 124.23 feet; thence by tangent 46.39 feet; thence to the left on a curve with a radius of 250 feet a distance of 182.37 feet to a point 4.4 feet north from the north line of 431 street and 159.5 feet east from the centre line of Madison avenue; thence by tangent 39.53 feet; thence to the right on a curve with a radius of 400 feet a distance of 332.28 feet to a point in the centre line of Madison avenue 65.6 feet north from the north line of 44th street; thence under Madison avenue to the south line of 96th street; thence to the right on a curve with a radius of 400 feet for a distance of 240.07 feet; thence by tanget a distance of 132.98 feet; thence to the left on a curve with a radius of 400 feet a distance of 240.07 feet to the south line of 98th street at a point distant 175 feet east from the easterly line of Madison avenue; running thence by viadact parallel with Madison avenue, the centre line, distant 175 feet east from the easterly line thereof across streets and private property to a point 124.6 feet north from the north line of 134th street, and distant 175 feet east from the easterly line of Madison avenue; thence to the right on a curve with a radius of 357.15 feet a distance of 408.6 feet to a point on the west line of River street 54 feet 11 inches south from the south line of 136th street; thence by tangent across the Harlem River a distance of 400 feet; thence to the left on a curve to the south line of 138th street at its intersection with the centre line of Walton avenue, as the same is laid down upon the topographical maps of the 23d and 24th Wards of the City of New York, issued from the office of the Commissioner of Street Improvements of the 23d and 24th Wards; thence, according to said maps, by viaduct, depressed structure and tunnel, as the contour of the lands may require, along the line of Walton avenue to Stebbins place; thence to the intersection of the centre lines of Sylvan avenue and Belmont place; thence along the line of Sylvan avenue to its terminus at Orchard street; thence in a straight line to the centre line of Berrian avenue at the southerly point thereof; thence along the centre line of Berrian avenue to 1st street; thence in a straight line to the intersection of the centre lines of Kirkside avenue and Croton avenue; thence along Kirkside avenue to Trevers street, and thence by straight line to and under Jerome avenue to the north line thereof.

The general plan of construction of the loop under Battery Park, State and Whitehall streets shall be double track; from the Morris street junction to near Vesey street shall be three parallel tracks on the same level with suitable switches and connections between them; from Vesey street to 190th street on the west side line shall be four parallel tracks on the same level; and thence across the Government Ship Canal and Spuyten Duyvil Creek to the city limits shall be two parallel tracks on the same level. On the east side line from 14th street to the Harlem River shall be four parallel tracks on the same level, and thence to the city limits shall be two parallel tracks on the same level. The tunnels shall be not less than 11 feet 6 inches in height in the clear, and 11 feet in width for each track. Whenever necessary for the proper support of the surface of the street, the roof of the tunnel shall be of iron girders with solid plate iron covering supported by suitable iron columns between each of the tracks, and supporting walls on the outside. The roof of the tunnel shall be as near the surface of the street as the pipes and underground structures now laid therein and the street grades will permit. Viaducts shall be of masonry or iron, or both combined. The Government Ship Canal and the Harlem River shall be crossed by double track drawbridges not less than 50 feet in the clear above mean high water mark, with clear spans of not less than 125 feet between the centre piers and bulkhead line. North of the Harlem River the construction shall be by viaduct, depressed structure and tunnel as the grades of the land upon the proposed routes shall require. The junction of the tracks near 14th street shall be effected by dividing them around Union square, raising one pair and depressing the other, so that trains going in opposite directions shall not cross on the same level. All station approaches shall be as far as possible through private property to be acquired for that purpose, except that on the Boulevard, station approaches may be in the centre of the street.

A footway shall be provided the whole length of the line between the centre tracks, and refuge niches shall be built in the side walls at proper intervals for the convenience and protection of employes.

The motive power shall be electricity, or some other power not requiring combustion within the tunnel; and the motor or motors shall be capable of a uniform speed for long distances of not less than forty miles per hour, exclusive of stops.

The manner of construction from South Ferry to about 34th street shall be by underground tunnelling without disturbing the surface of the street. In case of necessity the excavations below Beaver street, and in the neighborhood of Canal street, and at such other special points as this commission may, during the progress of the work determine, may be made by excavation from the street surface, and all excavations in 4th avenue above 14th street and in all other streets and avenues above 34th street may be made in the same manner.

The loop at Battery Park is adopted as furnishing the best and most convenient method for the terminal handling of the trains, both way and express.

The three tracks between Bowling Green Junction and Vesey street provide amply for the volume of traffic below the City Hall, and avoid encroachment beyond the curb line in Broadway at its narrowest points.

The introduction of a loop at City Hall Park by which trains may be stopped, turned and dispatched up town continuously and without switching and, as shown by the drawings, without grade crossings, for trains in opposite directions, furnishes the best means of a second down-town terminus at the most important point, and the best means of connecting with the Brooklyn Bridge.

At Union square, as shown in the accompanying drawings, a system of tracks has been devised by which all trains on the Broadway and Madison avenue line are accommodated at a single station, and all grade crossings between trains in opposite directions are avoided, thus facilitating high speed and eliminating in the best manner possible the dangers and delays incident to such crossings.

At 96th street the contour of the ground necessitates the termination of the tunnel. It therefore became necessary to deflect the line from Madison avenue and occupy private property, thence to the Harlem River, on account of the prohibition in the Rapid Transit Act against the use of Madison avenue for an elevated structure.

The stations on the route selectefi have not been located, for the reason that the Board was advised that they constitute part of the detailed plans which the commission are required to complete after the general plan shall have received the approval of your Honorable Body.

Detailed plans and specifications for the construction of the railway, including stations, devices and appurtenances deemed necessary to secure the greatest efficiency, public convenience and safety, will be prepared by the commission, in accordance with the provisions of the Act, if this report is approved.

The commission make no recommendations as to the method of construction. These matters the commission will deem it wise to leave, so far as permitted by the Act, to the judgment of the purchaser, subject always, as the Act requires, to the control of this Board. The particular shield, if any, to be used in excavating under the streets, the details as to materials and form of walls and other interior surface should, as far as consistent with the requirements of the Act, be subject to his selection. Any attempted determination of the method of construction in advance might narrow the field of possible competition to such an extent as to endanger the success of the enterprise.

When the commission decided to adopt an underground route, it also decided that the motive power must be secured without combustion in the tunnel.

Much attention has been devoted to the consideration of electricity as a motive power. Consultations have been held with eminent electricians; experiments have been witnessed; electric roads in operation have been examined.

While the Board is convinced that electricity as a motive power is available for the purposes of the railway recommended by this report, it is not deemed wise at the present time to exclude other forms of power answering the essential conditions of speed and non-combustion in the tunnel, or to attempt to direct the exact method of application of such power as shall finally be adopted.

Attached hereto will be found certified copies of our several appointments as Commissioners of Rapid Transit by his Honor, Mayor Grant, together with certified copies of our oaths of office, both those taken before the passage of the Rapid Transit Act of 1891, upon which this report is based, and those taken after we had become Commissioners of Rapid Transit in pursuance of the provisions of such Act.

The commission also certifies to you, that within thirty days after the passage of such Act, it duly met and organized as a Board and framed and adopted by-laws and established rules and regulations for the proper exercise of the powers and duties thereby conferred; and adopted a seal and kept a record of its proceedings, which has been open to public inspection at all reasonable times; and of its own motion conducted an inquest and investigation as to whether it was for the interest of the public and of the City of New York that a rapid transit railway or railways for the conveyance and transportation of persons and property should be established therein, and determined that such railway or railways, in addition to those already existing was necessary. Maps and drawings accompanying this Report show the route or routes and general plan of construction. They are marked Exhibits 8 to 60.

With this general statement of the proceedings of this Board, and in accordance with the provisions of section 5 of the Rapid Transit Act of 1891, we now submit the route or routes and general plan of construction thus determined upon, for your consideration.

Done under the signatures of the respective Commissioners, and the seal of the Board at the City of New York this 20th day of October, 1891.

[SEAL]

WILLIAM STEINWAY,
JOHN H. STARIN,
SAMUEL SPENCER,
JOHN H. INMAN,
EUGENE L. BUSHE,
Commissioners.

Real Estate Exchange Matters.

The following names have been proposed for membership: Samuel Frothingham, by E. A. Cruikshank, and Thomas McGuire, by H. P. De Graaf.

Tarrytown-on-Hudson.

F. P. Perkins has purchased from Frederick J. Stone about six acres of ground, adjoining the Sigafus place, the seller taking in exchange therefor the four-story hotel in Wendell Park, recently used as a sanitarium by Dr. Morgan. Mr. Stone proposes to enlarge and improve the building and lease it. A first-class hotel is very much needed at Tarrytown and would be well patronized.

Over the Harlem.

THE PROGRESS OF THE 23D AND 24TH WARDS—MANY PUBLIC IMPROVEMENTS COMPLETED AND OTHERS UNDER WAY—BETTER ACCESS TO AND FROM RAILROADS THAN FORMERLY—SMALL INVESTORS BUILDING HOMES—OTHER ITEMS OF INTEREST—THE REAL ESTATE SITUATION.

So many changes for the better have taken place in the 23d and 24th Wards during the current year, that a running glance at some of the most important improvements will interest many readers.

Among the most valuable of these is the paving of Brook avenue, with granite pavement, from the Harlem River to 156th street. This work is nearly ready, its completion being expected before December.

Many of the side streets have been paved, some with trap block and some with granite.

More has been done in the way of sewering than for many years past.

Most of the leading avenues are now lighted by electricity in the 23d Ward, viz.: 3d, Lincoln, Alexander, Willis, Brook, St. Ann's and Morris avenues and 138th street. The 24th Ward is deficient in this direction, but it is intended to extend the wires in that section soon.

One Hundred and Thirty-eighth street is being regulated and graded and will be paved between Madison avenue bridge and 3d avenue. This will give better access to the Grand Union Station at Mott Haven. This station, which is at 138th street, is fast becoming a very important one, being used by most of the up-town residents south of the Harlem, as well as those in the 23d and 24th Wards, for traveling to various points in the United States. A long, tedious and expensive journey down to the Grand Central Depot, at 42d street, is thus avoided, for passengers can engage sleeping berths, check their baggage through and obtain all the other conveniences at the Mott Haven station that they can obtain at the Grand Central Depot.

Morris avenue is being paved with granite from its junction with 3d avenue to 156th street and the Harlem Railway. This will give improved access to the new freight yards of the Harlem Road at that point. The difficulty in the past has been that the bad condition of the avenue leading up to the freight yards has been an impediment to the sending of freight. Now a good granite pavement will lead up to it. In connection with this freight yard it may be important to note that the receipts and shipments of freight have largely increased, as well as at the freight yard of the New Haven Road at the Harlem River. Manufacturers can now locate on both sides of the Harlem and have ample railroad facilities on the spot to all parts of the United States.

The Suburban Rapid Transit Road's business is increasing. The road now has a depot at 177th street and 3d avenue, and will soon be running further north. Travel is increasing on the line all the time. The Court of Appeals has just decided that the company will not violate any existing law if it passes through the new parks in the 23d and 24th Wards This is important in several ways, one being that the road will now be able to build its eastern line without making an expensive detour around St. Mary's Park. They will now run through a strip of the Park, as outlined in their original plans. The eastern branch has not yet been commenced and this is the reason why property through which it is to run has not been as active as it has been on the line of 3d avenue. A "Y" has been constructed at 144th street, between 3d and Willis avenues, to show how the eastern line will branch out. This line will no doubt be commenced earlier than has been anticipated.

The suburban service of the Harlem River Branch of the New Haven Road to New Rochelle is helping Westchester County and its environs greatly.

The fact that passengers can now come by the New Haven Road to 3d avenue and 129th street is helping all the places on the line of the New Haven Road. It is also helping New York City, inasmuch as it has so saved time and inconvenience in travel as to keep many people from going to reside in New Jersey and Long Island who would have done so but for the improved transit facilities over the Harlem River. It is not as generally known as it should be among New Yorkers that it is possible now to take trains from any point on the New Haven Road and come right into the 3d avenue and 129th street elevated road station.

It is interesting to note that, contrary to the general belief, the surface roads are doing more business since the suburban road has been extended. Ex-Senator Cauldwell, one of the chief officers of the road, is responsible for the statement that his surface road will have carried from 20 to 25 per cent more passengers in 1891 than during 1890. The principle seems to be that steam roads attract population and surface roads get the benefit of these people when they take short trips.

Private sales of vacant and improved property have not been as large as during the corresponding period last year. Auction sales have done fairly well, though it is evidently time for a little relaxation to be given to the market. Too much property has been thrown overboard, and there always comes a time when the man who has saved his money and put every dollar he could scrape together into vacant lots with future value, has got to stop for want of more dollars to put into more lots. That is just the position, and it is the opinion of an old and shrewd dealer that a rest should be given the market until next spring.

The figures show that 1,969 conveyances of real estate have been made in the 23d and 24th Wards this year up to the last day in September, at a total of $8,397,522, against 2,045, at a total of $10,243,724, in the same nine months last year. In 1889 there were 2,163 conveyances, at a total of $9,090,138. There has also been a decrease in building, 574 structures having been projected during the first nine months of this year, at an estimated cost of $2,930,083, while in 1890 there were 641 projected, at an estimated cost of $3,456,593, and the year before 687, at an estimated cost of $3,88[illegible],717.

A feature of the recent building movement is the erection of small and attractive houses by purchasers of lots at auction.

James L. Wells is authority for the statement that an unusually large number of buyers at recent auction sales decline to take advantage of the easy terms of mortgage offered by sellers by paying all cash. This is a hopeful sign, and places the properties in strong hands. Mr. Wells also thinks that building is not being overdone in the 23d and 24th Wards, and that the buildings erected, where not for personal occupation, are generally very quickly rented.

St. Luke's Hospital to Move.

It has been definitely settled upon that St. Luke's Hospital is to move, and the change will in all probability be up town, possibly near the northern limit of Central Park.

A reporter of THE RECORD AND GUIDE called on Geo. Maccullough Miller, President of the Hospital, to ascertain the facts in the matter. In reply to inquiries Mr. Miller said: "We are now placing our property on the market for sale. Our price is $2,500,000. We prefer to sell it as a whole. There are thirty-two lots, with a frontage of 200.10 feet on 5th avenue, 400 feet on 54th street, and 400 feet on 55th street. We will not wait until the property is sold before we move our hospital elsewhere. Nor is it necessary for us to wait, for we have about $1,000,000 on hand now; besides which there are gentlemen in the board who would be prepared to form a corporation and subscribe whatever money might be necessary to buy a site and build and equip a new hospital.".

"Has the Union Club made any offer to you for part of the property?" asked the reporter.

"Not yet; we have offered them a site of about 100 feet on the avenue and 200 feet on the street, the northwest corner of 54th street, for a figure which I am not at liberty to disclose. They are now, I understand, considering the matter. We cannot sell any of the ground on which the hospital building stands, unless it be with a proviso that it shall not be required before a certain date—sufficient time to enable us to get ground and build elsewhere. Should the Union Club or any other parties purchase, they could build on the vacant part of the property on 54th street. The hospital is nearer the 55th street side, and, of course, it could not be touched until we had one new building completed."

In reply to further inquiries, Mr. Miller said: "We have received several offers of sites for our new hospital, but will not make a selection for some time yet. When we build it will be a hospital superior in equipment to anything in this country. We propose, also, to place our hospital in the front rank as a scientific institution. With this object we will engage the very ablest physicians, etc., who will study the causes and prevention of disease, as well as their remedy."

Since the above was written it is ascertained that the hospital offered to take $1,000,000 for the eight lots wanted by the club. The latter have settled upon that site as the best, and it is said they offered $750,000, which was declined. President Miller, when seen yesterday afternoon, said that no agreement had as yet been arrived at.

LOT VALUES.

In view of the price placed on the St. Luke's Hospital lots, quotations of sales of unimproved property in the vicinity may be of interest. The figure asked for the hospital lots—which are thirty-two in number—would give an average of $78,125 per lot. There are eight lots with a front on the west side of the avenue, twelve lots on 54th street, and twelve lots on 55th street. The 5th avenue front, it is estimated, is worth about $1,000,000, and if this is so, the average for the remaining twenty-four lots on the two streets would be $62,500 each. Whether these prices are a little high all round is a matter for consideration. There is only one such plot of lots now vacant below 59th street on 5th avenue, and fancy prices may be established by those who want them, particularly as they are superbly situated.

Wm. H. Vanderbilt paid $400,000 for the four lots, 100.5x100, on the southwest corner of 5th avenue and 54th street, just opposite the hospital property, on April 10, 1882, an average of $100,000 each.

William Astor paid $500,000 for 75.5x100 on the southeast corner of 5th avenue and 55th street, and 50.5x100, adjoining on the street, five lots, on February 16, 1891, an average of $100,000 per lot.

Wm. Waldorf Astor paid $325,000 for the three lots, 50x150, on the northeast corner of 5th avenue and 56th street, on July 15, 1889, an average of $108,333 each.

Collis P. Huntington paid $450,000 for five and three-quarter lots, on the southeast corner of 5th avenue and 57th street, on May 31, 1889, an average of about $78,000 each.

Ph. H. Dugro and others paid $200,000 for two lots on the southeast corner of 5th avenue and 59th street, April 9, 1890, an average of $100,000 per lot, and $75,000 for the lot adjoining on the avenue, May 24, 1890.

Wm. Waldorf Astor paid $390,000 for five lots on the northeast corner of 5th avenue and 59th street, April 2, 1890, an average of $78,000 each.

Cornelius Vanderbilt and others paid $480,000 for eight lots on the northeast corner of 5th avenue and 60th street, April 9, 1891, an average of $60,000 each.

Eldridge T. Gerry paid $450,000 for six lots on the southeast corner of 5th avenue and 61st street, April 9, 1891, an average of $75,000 each. Mrs. Gerry subsequently took title to a lot adjoining on the street, May 26, 1891, at $40,000.

The St. Luke's Hospital lots are, if anything, choicer than any of the above lots, with the exception of those purchased by Wm. H. Vanderbilt, and on which he built the residences of his two daughters now on the site. All the other sales, also, are on the easterly side of the avenue, and on 5th avenue it is no exception to the general rule that the West Side is more valuable than the East Side.

Trans-Harlem Electric Surface Roads.

Workmen are busy on the foundations for the poles to hold the trolley wires for the new electric surface roads in the 23d and 24th Wards. Work is progressing on Westchester avenue, from 3d avenue and thence in a northeasterly direction, and on 138th street, from 3d avenue to Port Morris avenue.

CHICAGO.

The statement of a veracious Western "boomer" that his town grew so fast tuat he lost his way home one night from a neighboring drug store is perhaps truer of Chicago than of any other large city on the continent. The New York builder has impressed his existence conspicuously enough on his city, but the Chicagoan has a capacity for covering ground quite unknown in the East. The fact is, Chicago has grown a long way beyond the knowledge of any one whose last acquaintance with it dates ten or even seven or *sir* years back. Within that short space of time the place has advanced, in some respects, to the position of the greatest city of the country.

It goes far beyond the conception of the untraveled Gothamite. There are in fact two Chicagoes; one, the real, existent, solid hustling, smoky Chicago; the other, the Chicago of the New York myth—a windy Western city, quite non-existent, of large and unstable boundaries running over the country prairie-ways; a loosely-built city where frame buildings straggle out along dreary suburban streets to the circumference; a city at the centre of which may be found its redemption—a few stores, some hotels, and a score or two of "fine residences"—pale, thousand-mile-away reflections of the real New York article. This myth and the many variations and modifications of it is surely the ground-work of the New York superstition that the Columbian Exposition will surely be a failure as a great International show, whatever it may be as a county fair of liberal dimensions. Dare I prophesy, reader, in opposition to your prejudice? At any rate let me say this: If you are busy just now pooh-poohing the idea that Chicago can make the World's Fair a success, and disseminating among your neighbors the weighty opinion that New York would have done the thing in a so much more superior metropolitan way, put your opinions on paper, put them away in an envelope, keep them and bring them with you here in 1893 for verification.

What from drawings and models, and from what can be seen of the buildings now erecting a sufficient idea of what the exterior appearance of the Exposition will be can easily be formed. The exhibition structures are of enormous dimensions grouped picturesquely and promiscuously rather than in relation to one another or with subordination to a systematic plan. The architecture is respectable and adequate, though it offers little I think that is of especial merit or attractiveness. As to the location of the Fair there is nothing available like it in New York. The lake waters wash the shores of Jackson Park as the ocean does Brighton Beach, and the Fair buildings will face them surrounded by lawns, trees, flowers (Chicagoans are very lavish with flowers in public places) and the lagoons. The city here is full of "the Fair." Over everything, the great coming event casts its sh—(nothing of the kind, sir)—its golden light, light with millions in it, from its gilded domes. No single idea of the kind ever dominated a people as this idea of the Fair dominates Chicago. Success! Why, over a million very energetic people have determined that the Exposition shall be a success. The entire West is with them heart and pocket, and before long, as building after building rises on the Lake front, as difficulty after difficulty is conquered, the entire country will fall into line to support the Western metropolis, and I do not think it will become New York or be particularly to her advantage if she does so sulkily or tardily.

But, after all, the greatest part of the Fair will be the city itself. Its streets, boulevards and superb parks, its really vast commercial buildings and its miles and miles of solid, pretty homes—there is absolutely nothing like them, alas! in New York. These will be the chief attractions. Perhaps the first thing—it is so pervasive—that strikes a New Yorker upon entering, or for that matter, approaching Chicago after an absence of a few years is what is locally called the "smoke nuisance." It is every bit as bad as in Pittsburgh or in London. The smoke hangs like a cloud over the city; the soot penetrates everywhere and destroys completely the "new" appearance which all but the very oldest buildings wear in New York. Thus to the eye the city seems to be considerably older than the Eastern metropolis, and the "moderness," the very thing which the visitor most expects is nowhere visible, not even in the newest residential parts. Another effect of this "smoke nuisance" is the impression which it enforces of "industry." One feels instantly that one is in a great manufacturing centre where furnace fires are let to good purpose and the whirl of machinery goes on night and day, counting, perhaps, as is usually the case, for more in the sum of Life than it really is, while man counts for less. One has to look around in New York for evidences of the fact that the city is the seat of vast manufactories; in Chicago the fact is one of the most obvious; indeed, it is taken in through the nose.

The next thing, I think, that strikes the returning visitor, is that during his absence the streets of the city have acquired that indefinable aspect, that characteristic which belongs to only a few cities on the face of the globe—the metropolitan air. The local and provincial atmosphere is quite gone. One feels directly one touches the streets as the city unfolds itself thoroughfare after thoroughfare, that one is in contact with a vast overmastering activity. The streets in the "business section" are everywhere thronged quite as densely as those of New York are. There is the same bustle, the same hurrying tide of men, the same indifference to the individual. As to the buildings they are on the whole higher, if not larger, than those down town in New York, all of them have been erected since 1882 or 1883; they are all fire-proof, built upon the iron skeleton construction system, and in practically every case they are built of brick or in greater part of brick. Stone is not employed to anything like the extent it is in New York. There are no buildings here similar to the Equitable Building or the ornate stone structures of Wall street. The buildings, too, are very much plainer; indeed most of those erecting to-day are nothing but huge piles of brick thirteen to twenty stories and over in height, marked by window upon window. The facades have scarcely any horizontal sub-division into parts, and vertically there is little more division than what is obtained by the projection of angular bays extending almost from the top story to the ground. The aspect is severely practical. The Rookery, the Owings building and a few other structures are more ornate, but even in these cases there is a restraint in ornamentation which is very far from what one sees in New York. There is a movement on foot here to limit the height of these "sky scrapers." Medical opinion favors it and popular opinion, I fancy, is inclined to run with the doctors, though perhaps "run" is too fast a word for the pace that has been set so far. At present the "movement" is not very energetic and is troubled with its own weight. In time, however, no doubt some restriction will be put on builders' aspirations, when they reach to twenty and thirty stories high.

There are a great many contradictions in Chicago for the New Yorker. He runs against one of them when he leaves the "business section" with its colossi for the residential districts. Unlike New York, these are close at hand. They lie in segments of a circle instead of at the end of a line. Here the dwellings are rarely as high as they are on Manhattan Island. Three stories are the rule, and two stories are commoner than four. Then, too (what a benign mercy), there are, practically speaking, no long rows, no whole blocks of homes by the slice. Every building differeth from its neighbor, declareth positively that it was produced by different hands. In New York, even on the West Side, an architectural idea is seldom less than 100 feet long. Here it seldom runs over 30. Each house stands for itself and—better still—by itself, surrounded by at least a few feet of green lawn. And how agreeable the medley of design and material—brick, red and yellow, granite, brown stone, serpentine, marble, limestone, stucco and painted brick. Romanesque (the favorite style here or at least the widest vogue), Renaissance, Gothic (fearful and wonderful productions sometimes), Queen Anne, old Colonial conglomerates and styles which only the rampant fancy of the inventor could properly name. There is very much good architectural work, however, along these miles and miles of pleasant homelike houses, on the whole much more than in New York. A great deal of it is Romanesque, indeed Chicago is a city of "Romanesqueness" if not Romanesque. The greater number of these houses, especially in the newer and better quarters, are of stone, solid structures with heavy arched and capitaled entrances, towered bays, broad windows and porte cocheres, houses in short that resemble the solitary two on the corners of 108th street and Riverside Drive. I hope by and by to show the readers of THE RECORD AND GUIDE some examples of these dwellings which may be counted literally by the hundred.

By the way, there are scarcely any houses for sale in Chicago. The leading brokers have only a few on their lists, and this state of affairs is very striking to any one fresh from the West Side and Harlem. It seems to me there is a great opportunity here for Eastern capital in the hands of an experienced builder. There is plenty of good lots for sale and still more for lease, for curiously the practice of leasing vacant land for a long term of years is very common here. The sign "For lease for ninety-nine years without revaluation" meets one on every second unoccupied lot, and appears to be quite as frequent as "For Sale." By the way, the average depth of lots here is 125 feet, and flats are few and far between.

Real estate just now is quiet but firm. The "boomers" are leaving the city. When Congress decided that Chicago should have the World's Fair these gentry come here with bands and flying colors by the hundreds—and "boomed" outlying acres beyond the reach of anything legitimate. Acres were taken up and "sub-divided" and were then sold on the installment plan, they say, for fifty cents a week per lot and upwards. The strength of advertising was tested—and broke. The printing presses should have been made of brass. And what promising circulars! Some of them, in more senses than one, *lie* before me now. Oh! the prospects of these prospectuses. Every word promises gold. But *that* business is all over now. The sequel is easily told—six hundred "boomers" recently departed from the city.

Real estate in Chicago has got beyond these tricks. One might as well try to "boom" lots on West 72d street. Chicago property is in good hands, men who know its value and demand its legitimate price. As to the real estate agents, their offices are a surprise to the New Yorker. They have offices like bankers, full of clerks, with a constant stream of business.

H. W. D.

WORLD'S FAIR NOTES.

Florida, at its recent World's Fair Convention, decided to raise $100,000 for its representation at Chicago in 1893.

The Associated Press has applied to the Grounds and Buildings Committtee of the Exposition for suitable space, either in the press quarters on the grounds or in a separate building, where its reports can be prepared and dispatched during the Fair. It is certain that the Exposition authorities will provide extensive press and telegraph facilities, but the details are not yet determined.

The Ways and Means Committee has granted W. L. Libby & Son Company, of Toledo, Ohio, a concession for the operation of a big cut-glass factory. The company will invest between $50,000 and $75,000 on its plant, which will be located at 59th street, in the Midway Plaisance, on a plot of land 150 by 250,

---

The magnitude of the building operations now going on at Jackson Park can be surmised from the fact that an average of from thirty-five to forty car-loads of construction material arrives daily. The Exposition buildings are rising with wonderful rapidity.

A mammoth labor congress is to be held in Chicago in 1893, under the auspices of the World's Congress Auxiliary of the World's Columbian Exposition. John Burns and Tom Mann, who led the great London dock strike to a successful issue in 1889, have promised to be present, as have many other prominent labor leaders. Wm. E. Gladstone and Cardinal

Manning have accepted honorary membership, and will submit their views in writing. T. V. Powderly, Carroll D. Wright, and numerous others deeply interested in labor questions, are earnestly supporting the movement.

Transportation rates on articles intended for exhibits at the World's Fair will be the regular tariff rates of the railroads, plus 8 cents per 100 pounds for switching charges at Jackson Park. This will bring the rates from the various Atlantic seaports all the way from 28 to 83 cents per 100 pounds, according to the class of freight in which the goods fall, and the port from which they are shipped. The goods will be returned to starting point free of expense, except for the switching charges at Jackson Park. Of the 8 cents per 100 pounds switching charges, 3 go to the Illinois Central, and 5 to the Exposition Company. Freight charges on exceptionally fine goods, such as statuary, paintings, china, etc., and on horses and other fancy animals, will be somewhat higher than indicated above.

The New Fourth Avenue Bridge.

AN IMPORTANT RUMOR.

THE RECORD AND GUIDE is informed from a most credible source that the New York Central Road authorities have made arrangements with the Lackawanna Steel and Iron Company for the construction of a bridge over the Harlem at 4th avenue, to be 28 feet above the level of high spring tide. The contract, it is presumed, is to be carried out when the Legislature passes a bill to give authority to the New York Central people to build their land approaches on both sides of the Harlem River.

It may be remembered that the officials of the New York Central Road endeavored to pass a bill through the Legislature giving them authority to construct a new bridge over the Harlem to conform with the requirements of the Federal Act which makes it necessary that all bridges over the Harlem at an elevation of less than 24 feet above high spring tide shall be raised to that height. The Road also endeavored to get authority to raise the grade of their road on 4th avenue to meet the increased height of the bridge, commencing at about 125th street on the Manhattan Island side and about one-third to one-half of a mile from the Harlem River on the 23d Ward side. This measure actually passed both Houses of the Legislature in 1890, but did not become a law, owing to the opposition of owners of property on 4th avenue, between 125th street and the Harlem River, who feared that the up-grade approaches would damage the value of their realty.

If the New York Central Road has arranged for the building of the bridge it points to the fact that they anticipate passing their bill during the coming session of the Legislature. The construction of the bridge would be of great advantage to residents both north and south of the Harlem, particularly north of the Harlem, for it would save the delays which now occur through the passage of shipping at the 4th avenue bridge and Harlem River.

F. Loomis, counsel to the New York Central, says that he has not heard of any arrangement having been made such as is outlined above.

An Inspector Exonerated.

Commissioner Platt, of the Department of Buildings for Brooklyn, investigated, on Thursday, the insinuation that Inspector Hugh O'Donnell had received a bribe for permitting a violation of the building laws by Donald C. Ross, a builder. Inspector O'Donnell testified that he had been approached, but refused to be bribed. As no testimony was produced to contradict this statement, but rather confirmed it, the Commissioner promptly exonerated the Inspector.

An Echo of the Morgenthau Sale.

On Thursday evening last the gentlemen composing the syndicate that purchased and so successfully resold the Morton-Bliss property on Washington Heights visited Mr. Henry Morgenthau at his new home, No. 33 West 74th street, and presented him with a handsome service of silver plate in appreciation of his services as chief manager of the sale last May. Among those present were John Whalen, Moses Goldsmith, Simon Adler, Henry S. Herrman, George Lachman and R. C. Dorsett, who made the presentation speech. Mr. Morgenthau responded and the party then sat down to an elaborate supper.

Candidate Wells.

James L. Wells, the real estate broker and auctioneer, who has rendered signal services to the 23d and 24th Wards during his career, has accepted the candidature for the Twenty-fourth Assembly District at the request of friends from all parties. He has been nominated by the Citizens' Local Improvement Party and has been indorsed by the County Democracy, the Republican Party and the People's Municipal League, the latter, in a circular, recommending him particularly. He has also received strong assurances of support from independent Tammanyites and Democrats.

New Incorporation.

The Metropolitan Homestead Investment Company filed a certificate of incorporation in the County Clerk's office on October 20th, for the purpose of purchasing and improving real estate in New York and elsewhere. The capital stock is $3,000, divided into 120 shares at $25 each. The names of the directors are Israel Lipochiz, Louis Solomon, Harris Bobier, Israel Farjeon and Jacob Rosenkranz.

Obituary.

Joseph A. Macdonald, the well-known plumber, was buried on last Wednesday from the Fourth Presbyterian Church on West 34th street. The funeral services, which commenced at one o'clock, were attended by members of the Society of Mechanics and Tradesmen and by a committee from the Real Estate Exchange, consisting of R. V. Harnett, S. F. Jayne, A. M. Cudner, J. H. Woods and W. J. Roome. Mr Macdonald was a respected member of both these organizations. Mr. Macdonald died at his residence on Sunday last, aged 52 years, after a life spent in the plumbing business, in which he not only achieved success from a commercial point of view but won and retained the respect of those with whom he came in contact as a man of uprightness and fair dealing.

Special Notice.

F. R. Houghton offers for sale the very valuable plot of 102.2x100, on the southwest corner of 72d street and Columbus avenue. The plot is splendidly adapted for a savings bank, dry-goods store, apartment hotel or amusement building. This particular part of 72d street must always remain a most central portion of the West Side, and there is no doubt that the rapid transit road to be built will involve a depot at that street. A real need of the West Side is a large dry-goods emporium, and no better site could be found.

Important to Property-Holders.

BOARD OF ASSESSORS.

OFFICE OF THE BOARD OF ASSESSORS,
NO. 27 CHAMBERS STREET,
NEW YORK, Oct. 12, 1891.

Notice is given to the owner or owners, occupant or occupants, of all houses and lots, improved or unimproved lands affected thereby, that the following assessments have been completed and are lodged in the office of the Board of Assessors for examination by all persons interested, viz.:

No. 1.—Paving 87th st, from Madison to 5th av, with granite blocks.

No. 2.—Paving 80th st, from Amsterdam av to the Boulevard, with granite blocks, and laying crosswalks.

No. 3.—Repaving 13th av, from 17th to 18th st (so far as the same is within the limits of grants of land under water), with granite blocks, and laying crosswalks.

No. 4.—Flagging, reflagging, curbing and recurbing both sides of 77th st, from Boulevard to West End av.

No. 5.—Flagging, reflagging, curbing and recurbing south side of 51st st, from 11th to 12th av.

No. 6.—Flagging, reflagging and recurbing both sides of 77th st, from Av A to the East River.

No. 7.—Laying crosswalks across 10th av, at the northerly side of 162d st and across 10th av and Avenue St. Nicholas, at the southerly side of 162d st.

No. 8.—Laying crosswalks across Amsterdam av, at the northerly side of 155th st and the northerly and southerly sides of 156th, 157th, 158th, 159th and 160th sts.

No. 9.—Regulating and grading, setting curb-stones and flagging 111th st, from 8th to Manhattan av.

No. 10.—Extension of sewer in 28th st, between East River and 1st av, connecting with present sewer built by Department of Docks.

No. 11.—Sewer in 12th av, east side, between 35th and 37th sts, with outlet through pier at 36th st, North River, and connections to present sewers in 36th and 37th sts.

No. 12.—Sewer in Park av, east side, between 124th and 125th sts.

No. 13.—Alteration and improvement to sewer in Essex st, between Delancey and Broome sts.

No. 14.—Sewer in 1st av, between 44th and 45th sts.

No. 15.—Alteration and improvement to sewer in 55th st, between 8th and 9th avs.

No. 16.—Receiving basin on the northwest corner of 146th st and 8th av.

[The limits embraced by such assessments include all the several houses and lots of ground, vacant lots, pieces and parcels of land situated on—

No. 1.—Both sides of 87th st, from Madison to 5th av, and to the extent of half the block at the intersecting avs.

No. 2.—Both sides of 80th st, from Amsterdam av to the Boulevard, and to the extent of half the block at the intersecting avs.

No. 3.—Both sides of 13th av, from 17th to 18th st, and the piers at foot of 17th and 18th sts, North River.

No. 4.—South side of 77th st, from Boulevard to West End av.

No. 5.—South side of 51st st, from 11th to 12th av.

No. 6.—Both sides of 77th st, from Av A to the East River.

No. 7.—Farm No. 58, Ward Nos. 34-40, inclusive; also Ward Nos. 57-61, inclusive, and 66-78, inclusive; also Farm No 31-35, inclusive, and Ward No. 124 and Farm No. 53A, Ward Nos. 32-38, inclusive.

No. 8.—Both sides of Amsterdam av, from 155th to 160th st, and to the extent of half the block at the intersecting sts.

No. 9—Both sides of 111th st, from 8th to Manhattan av.

No. 10—East side of 1st av, from 26th to 30th st; west side of 1st av, from 27th st to one-half the distance between 30th and 31st sts; both sides of 2d av, from 27th to 29th st, and east side of 2d av, from 29th st to one-half the distance between 30th and 31st sts; both sides of 30th st, from 1st to 2d av; both sides of 29th st, from 1st to 2d av; south side of 29th st, from 2d to 3d av; both sides of 28th st, from 3d av to the East River; north side of 27th st, from 2d to 1st av, and north side of 26th st, from 1st av to East River.

No. 11—Property bounded by 33d and 39th sts, 10th av and the Hudson River, and east side of 10th av, from 34th to 35th st, both sides of 34th st and south side of 35th st, extending about 225 feet easterly from 10th av.

No. 12.—East side of Park av, from 124th to 125th st.

No. 13.—Both sides of Essex st, from Broome to Delancey st.

No. 14.—Both sides of 1st av, from 44th to 45th st.

No. 15.—Both sides of 35th st, from 8th to 9th av.

No. 16.—North side of 146th st, from 8th to Bradhurst av.]

All persons whose interests are affected by the above-named assessments, and who are opposed to the same, or either of them, are requested to present their objections in writing to the Chairman of the Board of Assessors, at their office, No. 27 Chambers street, within thirty days from the date of this notice.

The above-described lists will be transmitted, as provided by law, to the Board of Revision and Correction of Assessment for confirmation on the 13th day of November, 1891.

In the matter of the application of the Board of Street Opening and Improvement, relative to acquiring title (wherever the same has not been heretofore acquired) to Albany road, from Bailey avenue to Van Cortlandt Park, 24th Ward; Willis avenue, from Harlem River to 147th street, 23d Ward, and Boscobel avenue (although not yet named by proper authority), extending from the easterly approach to the bridge over the Harlem River at West 181st street to Jerome avenue, in the 23d and 24th Wards of the City of New York, as the same has been heretofore laid out and designated as a first-class street or road by the Department of Public Parks; also in the matter of the application of the Board of Street Opening and Improvement of the City of New York, for and on behalf of the Mayor, Aldermen and Commonalty of the City of New York, relative to the opening of Avenue B, from 80th street to the marginal street, bulkhead line, Harlem River, in the 12th Ward of the City of New York. The Commissioners of Estimate and Assessment in the above-entitled matters, give notice to all persons interested in these proceedings, and to the owner or owners, occupant or occupants, of all houses and lots and improved or unimproved lands affected thereby, that they have completed their estimate and assessment, and that all persons interested in this proceeding, or in any of the lands affected thereby, and having objections thereto, do present their said objections in writing, duly verified, to office, No. 200 Broadway (fifth floor), on or before the 23d day of November, 1891, and that the said Commissioners will hear parties so objecting within the ten week days next after the said 23d day of November, 1891, and for that purpose will be in attendance at said office on each of said ten days at 1 o'clock P. M.

Notice to Property-Owners.

CITY OF NEW YORK, FINANCE DEPARTMENT,
COMPTROLLER'S OFFICE, October 24, 1891.

In pursuance of Section 997 of the "New York City Consolidation Act of 1882," the Comptroller of the City of New York gives notice to all persons, owners of property affected by the assessment list in the matter of acquiring title to 165th street, from Union avenue to Westchester avenue, which was confirmed by the Supreme Court, June 3, 1891, and entered on the 10th day of October, 1891, in the Record of Titles of Assessments kept in the "Bureau for the Collection of Assessments and Arrears of Taxes and Assessments and of Water Rents," that unless the amount assessed for benefit on any person or property shall be paid within sixty days after the date of said entry of the assessment, interest will be collected thereon, as provided in section 998 of said "New York City Consolidated Act of 1882."

Contractors' Notes.

Estimates for extending the existing pier at the foot of Jane street, North River, to the pier-head line of 1890 will be received by the Board of Commissioners of the Department of Docks, at the office on Pier "A," foot of Battery place, North River, until 1 o'clock P. M. of Thursday, October 29, 1891.

Bids or estimates will be received at the Department of Public Works, No. 31 Chambers street, until 12 o'clock M. on Wednesday, October 28, 1891, for regulating and paving with granite block pavement the roadway of 100th street, from 3d to Lexington avenue; for regulating and paving with granite block pavement the roadway of 101st street, from 3d to Lexington avenue; for regulating and paving with granite block pavement the roadway of 101st street, from 1st to 2d avenue; for regulating and paving with granite block pavement the roadway of 117th street, from Madison to 5th avenue; for regulating and paving with granite block pavement the roadway of 122d street, from Avenue A to Harlem River; for regulating and paving with asphalt pavement, on the present foundation, the carriageway of 12th street, from a line about 98 feet east of 7th avenue, and running easterly about 136 feet, and for flagging and reflagging, curbing and recurbing the sidewalks on northeast corner of 5th avenue and 85th street.

Sealed bids or estimates will be received by the Commissioner of Street Improvements of the 23d and 24th Wards, at his office, No. 2622 3d avenue, corner of 141st street, until 3 o'clock P. M., on Friday, October 30, 1891, for regulating, grading, curbing and flagging Juliet street, from Mott to Walton avenue; for regulating, grading, setting curb-stones and laying flag-stones and crosswalks in Burnside avenue, from Sedgwick to Webster avenue; for regulating, grading, setting curb-stones, flagging the sidewalks and laying crosswalks in Teasdale place, from 3d to Trinity avenue; for regulating, grading, setting curb-stones, flagging the sidewalks and laying crosswalks in 146th street, between 3d and Railroad avenue East, and for regulating, grading, setting curb-stones, flagging the sidewalks and laying crosswalks in 152d street, between Courtlandt avenue and the easterly curb-line of Railroad avenue East.

Bids or estimates will be received at the Department of Public Works, No. 31 Chambers street, until 12 o'clock M., on Thursday, November 5, 1891, for regulating and paving with granite-block pavement with concrete foundation, the carriageway of 52d street, from the easterly side of 12th avenue to bulkhead line of Hudson River.

The Opinions of Others.

E. P. Steers, President of the Twelfth Ward Bank, in a talk the other day, said: "As a barometer as to the soundness of business in Harlem I think the balances of depositors in bank ought to be an evidence. And if that is true business among Harlemites is good, for both our deposits and balances are larger than usual. As to the talk of overbuilding, I have heard that since I was a boy. They have always talked of there being too many houses and flats in Harlem, but somehow they get tenanted, more or less, for people are moving up our way all the time. I look more cheerfully at the future than many people, and I think that the conditions warrant it."

J. H. Hunt, of the firm of Hunt & Wendell, in a conversation with the writer, said: "There are more buyers in the market for houses, and especially high-priced houses, than I have seen in several years, and prices are paid that could not have been obtained six months ago. There is also inquiry for building lots by first-class builders, which has not been the case for nearly a year. I think the chances for rapid transit, as well as abundant crops and a rising stock market, have had something to do with the improvement.

C. F. Hoffman, Jr., said: "The real estate market at the present time is very unsatisfactory to me as a broker, but as an owner it is all that I can desire. There is little or nothing in the way of salable down-town property that is upon the market; everyone seems very well satisfied with what they hold and they show no anxiety to sell even at full figures." Apropos of a down-town parcel which was to be offered at auction, Mr. Hoffman said: "The property you refer to is located on a street that is devoted to no particular line of business and I do not care to buy very much in such a street. It has been my experience that an owner who holds property on a street that is mainly occupied by the merchants engaged in one line of business is generally very much better satisfied than the man whose holdings are on a thoroughfare the character of which is not settled. This fact is so well established that on some of the side streets given up almost entirely to one trade the value per front foot of the real estate is greater than the value of property on Broadway. Take Maiden lane, for instance, where I happen to own some property, on that street, between Broadway and Nassau street, occupied, as it is, almost entirely by the jewelers, prices are probably higher than on Broadway, between Maiden lane and John street. This street is a fair example of what I mean when I say that property on a street that is given up to one line of business is, after all, the most satisfactory to hold."

James L. Wells said: "Have you noticed the large increase in the number of women who attend the sales in the Real Estate Exchange? It is not very long ago since the presence of a woman in the Auction Room created quite a sensation. It was so rare an occurrence then that everyone noticed it, but nowadays when nearly every day women attend the sales no one thinks of remarking it. And it is not only that they attend the sales and look on; they purchase nowadays and speculate and generally quite as successfully as men. The dealings of the women I refer to have been confined mainly to North New York, where they have purchased lots and sold at good profits. Miss Murphy is the only woman broker, but she is not by any means the only woman who speculates in real estate."

J. C. R. Eckerson, of Thomas & Eckerson, said: "The surface railroad companies should be compelled, every time they replace worn-out rails, to lay down a rail similar to that used in the construction of the cable road on Broadway. Those who drive considerably in New York have already found out what a comfort it is to drive on Broadway compared with what it used to be, not to speak of the danger avoided of broken wheels, etc. It is estimated that a surface road is relaid every five to ten years, and if the improved rail were inforced we would at least have the streets in fair condition in a decade or less. All new surface roads built should also have a rail similar to that of the Broadway cable."

Geo. M. Huss, the architect whose plans were among the four selected for the Cathedral, speaks in high praise of *The Architectural Record*. "I am glad that you have had the independence and courage to criticise peculiar architecture such as that of the Edison Building. Such articles will do good to the profession and will make men careful as to what plans they draw in future. The tone of the magazine is good. The articles show an improvement in the quality of criticism. Any one may criticise, and we have too much of criticism to fill space. The writers in your magazine show quality not quantity, and the illustrations are excellent and very useful to members of our profession. I wish also to express my belief that the criticisms of New York architecture which have appeared in THE RECORD AND GUIDE since 1883 have done very much to improve the standard of designs planned during the last six or seven years. We may not all have agreed with all the criticisms made, but they have more or less been well taken."

The exhibition of architectural drawings is now open in the exposition rooms of THE RECORD AND GUIDE, *at Nos.* 14 *to* 16 *Vesey street, to which the public are cordially invited, free of charge. This display of drawings is one of the finest that has ever been made in New York City. It contains about three hundred works from the boards of the leading architects. Among the perspectives of more than ordinary interest are those of the several large hotels now building in this city, and the designs submitted in competition for the new cathedral of St. John's. No one who wishes to study the principal recent architectural works in the metropolis and the contiguous suburban district should fail to pay a visit to the exposition.*

Newark News.

The following plans have been filed with the Superintendent of Buildings during the past week: Wm S. Brown, 2-sty fr addition dwg, 10x27, 123 Adams st; W. F. Taylor, 1-sty fr extension, 11x14, 82 Webster st; Henry Schaeffer, 3-sty fr dwg, 22x42, 150 Van Buren st; W. C. Hadley, 2-sty fr dwg, 19x38, 81 North 11th st; L. B Heath, two 2-sty fr dwgs, 15x30, 83 Goble st; H. M Van Sant, 1½-sty fr barn, 14x21, 3?9 7th st; A. Schaeffer, 2-sty fr factory, 22x18, 57 and 59 Bergen st; Saml. F. Bailey, 2½-sty fr dwg, 28x44, 18 Mt. Prospect pl; Wm H. Ast, 4-sty brk store and warerooms, 25x50, 7? Springfield av; Gerger Bros., 4-sty brk store and warerooms, 26x46, extension 19x24, 77 Springfield av; Paul W. Roder, 4-sty brk dwg, 3?x52, 21 West st; Newark Turn Verein, 4 sty brk school and gymnasium, 30x60, extension 57x80, 180 and 188 William st; John Merz, 4-sty fr dwg, 28x50, Spruce, cor Prince st; Elizabeth Devling, 2-sty fr dwg, 27x32, 8?9 Parker st; Joseph Gaunt, 2-sty fr dwg, 18x32, 259 Sussex av; J. Jigaro, 1-sty fr hall, 22x40, 699 Bergen st; Terence Reilly, 3-sty fr dwg, 22x40, 25 Norfolk st; Trivitt & Waters, 3-sty fr dwg, 27x55, cor Norfolk and Bond sts; Board of Education, 3-sty brk public school, 57x59, 208-212 Warren st; H. Goble, 1-sty fr store, 20x 8, 298 N. J. R. R. av; Newark Sanitary and Mfg. Co., 2-sty fr stable, 30x30, Roseville av; Board of Freeholders, 1-sty fr boiler house of jail, 3?x3?, rear 106 Newark st; Board of Education, 3-sty brk public school, 6?x30, 44 and 46 Ann st; Board of Education 3-sty brk public school, 50x70, 13th av and Richmond st; James Perry, 2-sty brk drying room, 40x36, 3?0 Norfolk st; C. J. Byles, 2-sty fr dwg, 24x3?, 239 Garside st; Abraham Jenkinson, 3-sty fr dwg, 20x43, 33 Howard st; J. S Mundy, 4-sty brk factory, 3?x105, 21 and 23 Prospect st; Gregor Armbruster, 2-sty fr dwg, 36x24, 446 South 19th st; H. F. Osborne, 1-sty fr express office, 36x4?, Marshall st; Mark S. Clark, 2½-sty fr dwg, 20x43, 399 Washington av; John Bonnet, 3-sty brk dwg, 19x3?, 178 Newton st; E. J. Anderson, 2-sty fr dwg, 26x28, Riverside av; Chester R. White, 1-sty fr wagon house, 11x21, 570 Orange st; George M. White, 2-sty fr dwg, 1?x28, 6th st; Alfonso Del Guercio, 4-sty fr dwg, 30x5?, 105 7th av; George Leith, 2½-sty fr dwg, 20x28, 819 Parker st; Timothy A. Curtis, 3-sty fr dwg, 21x32, 250 Clifton av; Mass & Waldstein, 1-sty brk factory, 74x20, Riverside av; Arthur Haslam, Jr., 2-sty fr dwg, 22x14, 93 Summer av.

THE WEST SIDE INDEX.

All persons interested in West Side real estate should possess an Index of Ten Years' Conveyances affecting property between the north side of 59th and south side of 125th streets, from west side 8th avenue to Hudson River. This Index is published by THE RECORD AND GUIDE, *and the period covered is the ten years prior to June 30th,* 1884, *to which has been added a list of the conveyances up to January* 1st, 1885. *Every transfer of real estate in that section, made between those years, is recorded in the Index, with a description of the property, the price paid for it, the liber and page in which the conveyances are recorded in the Register's Office, and the name of the seller and the purchaser. The volume is of the utmost value to conveyancers, lawyers, real estate brokers, agents and dealers in real estate generally, and we will supply the Index to our readers, if ordered before January* 1st *next, at the reduced price of* $5.

Real Estate Department.

The past week in real estate circles has shown no improvement over its predecessor in the matter of business done. The market is remarkably dull for this season of the year and the fact that Election Day is drawing near does not by any means satisfactorily explain it. During the corresponding weeks last year and the year before fully twice as much business was done as has been accomplished during the past week, and even then the brokers complained. But this year the record for an almost stagnant market is surpassed; little or nothing is being done. In many of the brokers' offices matters are fully as quiet as they are during midsummer, and even the busiest offices at the present time do not come up to their records for previous years. This dullness is explained by the firm, high prices that resist every attack that is made upon them. As we remarked last week, prices are now and for a year past have been too high and until they come down to their true level there can be no activity. A large owner this week placed, with several brokers, a piece of business property in only a fair renting district that does not yield 5 per cent. gross on his asking price, and he is confident, he says, that he will get his figure. This owner is a type of many who are offering and expecting to sell property on these same terms, and yet as buyers they are standing out for the largest possible percentages on their investments. With this extraordinary state of affairs it is small wonder that the real estate market is dull—it could not be otherwise, and the sooner present holders of real estate realize this the sooner will there be a change for the better. A large real estate dealer of experience, who at the present time holds too much property to have any object in talking down the market, said this week that he intended to unload as fast as possible. In his opinion the wisest course for owners who are not investors to pursue is to sell out their real estate for the best price now obtainable, for within the next eighteen or twenty months, he says, prices are bound to come down far below what owners now believe possible. It may be just as well for holders of real estate who are in the market to sell to at once realize the truth contained in the above warning. It is easier for them and much more satisfactory all round to make slight concessions now than to wait until they are forced to make large advances to unwilling buyers, and this is not at all unlikely if the tension under which the market labors at present continues. Unless sellers will consent to make concessions they must be content to have the market remain just as quiet as it is now, for in their present mood would-be buyers are not disposed to advance a step. And if this dullness continues in consequence of the high prices the market may take a sudden turn and right itself at the expense of the present holders, and perhaps very much to their surprise. Added to this now rather old difficulty of high prices is a newer and less important, because only temporary one, and that is the scarcity of money. The money will of course come back to New York in the spring; but in the meantime the temporary scarcity of it in the business centres is a factor in the quiet of the real estate market.

The only special sign which it is worth while calling attention to is the investment movement on Washington Heights. Lately several large capitalists connected with the great trusts have acquired property in the upper part of the 12th Ward, and they are not through yet. Last week Wm. F. Havemeyer, of the sugar trust, bought a large tract on upper Kingsbridge road, and another capitalist, whose name has been zealously kept secret, acquired a plot of lots not far from that thoroughfare. In addition to these purchases reported last week our readers will recall the purchases by officials of the Standard Oil Company earlier in the year on Kingsbridge road and adjoining streets. Several transactions in this same vicinity are even now under way, and if all goes well we may have the satisfaction of reporting some of them in the near future. The point to be kept in mind is that these rich men who are buying up this property are not purchasing with the idea of making a quick and profitable turn, but rather with an eye to holding it for ten or fifteen years, when New York's remarkable march of improvement shall have reached this at present inaccessible region.

This has been a very disappointing week in the Auction Room. The list of offerings was more attractive than it has been for some time, and this fact encouraged the hope that some business would be transacted on the Exchange floor, even if nothing was done at private contract. The week has closed, and there is very little to show as the result of the auctioneers hard work. It is true that on several days the Auction Room presented that crowded appearance that is only to be seen when the season is at its height, or when some valuable property is offered, but that is about all the satisfaction that a constant attendant at the daily sales has had for his trouble. The sales themselves have been in the main very discouraging. They have developed nothing, and have simply emphasized the indifference of buyers and the unyielding firmness of present holders. All over the city, parcels voluntarily offered have been bid in by the owners or withdrawn from sale While on the other side, outside of the legal sales, there are only a few parcels that sold, and these at only fair prices. The week opened badly with two rather unfortunate events. On Monday, when an attempt was made to sell a large plot (Astor leasehold) on West 13th and Hudson streets and 9th avenue there was so little demand for the property that it was withdrawn without a single bid having been made for it. On the same day, though from a different cause, the North New York section received a setback. James L. Wells had advertised that he would sell 158 lots on Kingsbridge Heights and a large crowd of anxious buyers was present. Mr. Wells made the statement that the contractors who were grading and making the streets had disappointed the owners and that many of the lots were therefore not in good enough condition to be put up on the market The sale of the ungraded lots was, therefore, postponed and the auctioneer proceeded to sell about thirty five lots upon which the contractors have finished work. The prices, so far as they went, were good, and the spirit of the bidding warrants the belief that the other lots would have been sold had they been offered. The down-town property offered met with a rather discouraging reception. The plot on 4th street, running from Grove to Christopher street and covered by seven-story brick flats was withdrawn because the bidders did not come forward, and while the adjoining lot in the rear No 70 Christopher and 67 Grove street, with the five-story flat thereon, sold for $36,750, the third parcel in this lot, No. 72 Christopher and 65 Grove street, had also to be withdrawn. Following in the wake of this failure came that of the executors of the Ferrigan estate, when they offered the celebrated "Cobweb Hall," No. 80 Duane street. When this property was offered there was a large crowd of prominent real estate men present, and yet the only bid that was made, $60,000, was offered by a representative of the estate, Peter J. McCoy. The Riverside Drive lots, in the sale of which so much interest it was expected would develop, were not marked successes. The lot on the Drive just north of 104th street was greeted with a first bid of $10,000, and knocked down to a representative of the owner for $13,600, while further up the two lots with the two-story stable on the rear, north of 122d street, were sold for $20,800. The legal sales of the week present no special features worthy of remark. Out of the foreclosure sales which took place there was only one case and that on West 133d street west of 8th avenue, where the amount due exceeded the selling price.

NEXT WEEK'S OFFERINGS.

The list of parcels to be offered at auction next week is neither a long nor imposing one. It includes no properties of great importance, and but few that are of more than ordinary interest, so that the Auction Room next week will not amount to much as a factor in the week's activity. Among the parcels that will probably have the greatest attractions for real estate men generally are No. 259 Canal street, near Broadway, which Auctioneer R. V. Harnett will offer on Tuesday; Nos. 246, 248 261 4th avenue, which Jas. L. Wells will offer on Wednesday, and Nos. 459 and 461 3d avenue, which Thomas C. Smith advertises that he will sell. In the way of suburban offerings, A. H. Muller & Son announce ninety lots in the 2d Ward, Yonkers, to be sold on Tuesday.

On Tuesday, October 27th, John F. B. Smyth will sell the two-story brick and frame dwelling No. 290 West 52d street, Brooklyn; the two lots on the west side of 8th avenue, 24.11 north of 154th street; two lots on the south side of 63d street, 150 feet east of West End avenue; and a lot at No. 1713 Sedgwick avenue, three minutes from the Morris Heights Station.

On Tuesday, October 27th, Richard V. Harnett & Co. will sell the three-story brick dwelling, No. 411 East 122d street, and the six-story and basement marble store, No. 259 Canal street.

On Tuesday, October 27th, Adrian H. Muller & Son will sell by order of James Condie, trustee, ninety desirable lots on Elm, Chestnut, Beach Oak and Linden avenues, in the 2d Ward of the City of Yonkers. This is known as the D. C. Newell property. Sixty per cent of the purchase money can remain on bond and mortgage at 5 per cent.

On Wednesday, October 28th Adrian H. Muller & Son will sell by order of the executors of the estate of Jeremiah P. Robinson, deceased, the four-story brown stone mansion, on lot 34x200, No 6 Montague terrace, Brooklyn Heights This dwelling overlooks the Wall Street Ferry and has a desirable view of New York Harbor.

On Wednesday, October 28th, Richard V. Harnett & Co. will sell the two five-story brown stone apartment houses, Nos. 114 and 116 West 104th street, and the two five-story brick apartment houses, Nos. 302 and 304 West 129th street.

On Thursday, October 29th, Richard V. Harnett & Co. will sell the five-story brick tenement, No. 423 West 26th street; the two five-story brown stone flats, Nos. 2146 and 2148 7th avenue; the six three-story brown stone dwellings, Nos. 107 to 117 West 133d street, and the brown stone dwellings on the northwest corner of Lexington avenue and 1 4th street.

On Thursday, October 29th, Smyth & Ryan will sell the five-story brick flat on the southeast corner of Willis avenue and 146th street.

On Thursday, October 29th, John F. B. Smyth will sell the five-story brick flat (leasehold), No. 533 West 29th street.

On Friday, October 30th, John F. B. Smyth will sell the three-story brick house No. 22 East 130th street.

On Wednesday, November 11th, John F. B. Smyth will sell the five-story flat at No. 173 West 64th street, the brick tenements at Nos. 1842 to 1850 2d avenue, and seven lots on 96th street, east of 2d avenue.

CONVEYANCES.

	1890. Oct. 17 to 23 inc.	1891. Oct. 16 to 22 inc.
Number	190	179
Amount involved	$2,460,566	$3,344,373
Number nominal	54	54
Number 23d and 24th Wards	43	51
Amount involved	$128,045	$87,890
Number nominal	10	11

MORTGAGES.

	1890.	1891.
Number	243	223
Amount involved	$2,782,801	$3,085,406
Number at 5 % or less	110	109
Amount involved	$1,407,0?0	$1,668,020
Number at less than 5 per cent	19	14
Amount involved	$476,500	$167,000
Number to Banks, Trust and Ins. Cos	57	46
Amount involved	$1,025,900	$1,495,174

PROJECTED BUILDINGS.

	1890. Oct. 18 to 24 inc.	1891. Oct. 17 to 23 inc.
Number of buildings	142	44
Estimated cost	$1,720,495	$499,075

Gossip of the Week.

SOUTH OF 59TH STREET.

Julius Friend has sold for William T. Lee to Daniel Rosenbaum the old buildings known as Nos. 137 and 139 Wooster street, size 50x100, on private terms for improvement.

Mrs. Frances E. Ogden has sold the four-story brown stone front dwelling, on lot 24.8x80, No. 74 Park avenue, for $70,000. The purchaser is reported to be Mrs. C. D. Jones. Mrs. Ogden purchased this house in 1884 for $58,000.

P. C. Eckhardt has sold for Lowen & Halliday to Dr. Daniel Galvan the two five-story three-family apartment houses, Nos. 154 and 156 West 35th street, for $9?,000.

John F. B. Smyth has sold at private contract the following houses which failed to sell when offered at auction: No. 40 West 29th street, a five-story and basement brick house with a four-story brick building on the rear of the lot, which was 20.6 98.9, for Dr. John Friedrich to Wm. Sperb, Jr., on private terms; No. 322 East 35th street, a five-story brick and stone tenement, on lot 25x100, for Robert K. Downey to James E. Dougherty, on private terms; and No. 158 West 53d street, a three-story and basement brown stone dwelling for George MacIntosh to a colored organization, of which V. C. Murray is the treasurer, also on private terms.

The estate of Dr. Bayard has sold to Dr. J. J. Hanna, No 8 West 40th street, a four-story, high stoop, brown stone dwelling, 19.6x70x100, for $50,000. Brokers, John N Golding and Charles S. Brown.

Alfred H. Tompkins has sold for Elmira D. Rapp the three-story and basement brick building, 20x50x100, No. 213 East 55th street, to Hiram Slocum for $16,000.

Ascher Weinstein has purchased from Henry T Cutter No. 75 West 45th street, a four-story brown stone dwelling, 20x60x100.5, on private terms, and from Wm. J. McRae No 350 West 34d street, a four-story and basement brown stone dwelling, 19x55x98.9, also on private terms.

L. Froehlich has sold for Mrs. McCabe No. 736 Lexington avenue, between 58th and 59th streets, a four-story stone front dwelling, on lot 20x75, for $2?,000.

Ethelinda V. Allen has sold to Charles Broadway Rouse the four-story brown stone front dwelling (Columbia College leasehold), No. 632 5th avenue, on private terms.

E. H. Ludlow & Co. have sold for Charles Miller to A. Lanfer Norrie, No. 26 West 44th street, a three-story private stable on a full lot, on private terms.

Celia B. Norton, executrix, has sold to a Mr. Meyer, No. 223 West 14th street, a four-story brown stone, high stoop dwelling, for about $26,250.

Ascher Weinstein has purchased from the executors of the estate of Elizabeth Hodge, No. 28 Henry street, a four-story and basement brick dwelling, 25x60x100, on private terms.

NORTH OF 59TH STREET.

John G. Prague, it is reported, has sold the "Brockholst" apartment hotel, on the northwest corner of Columbus avenue and 85th street, for about $472,000. The hotel is six stories in height, and it has a front of Tiffany brick and brown stone. It covers a plot that fronts 102.2 on the avenue by about 125 feet on 85th street. The ground floor on the avenue front is occupied by stores. Mr. Prague could not be seen yesterday in relation to the report, and his attorney, Mr. Comstock, of Adams & Comstock, would only say that admitting that the story was true he had no authority to give any information in regard to the private affairs of his client. It was reported that the sale was not entirely for cash, but that Mr. Prague had taken in exchange some other property, the location of which could not be ascertained.

Charles E. Schuyler has sold for Charles Buek to the devisees of Benjamin F. Romaine the six-story buff brick and brown stone front flat with stores, known as the "Westport," on the southeast corner of Columbus avenue and 73d street, size 5?x9?x100, and the six-story brick and stone front flat, known as the "Greenfield," on 73d street, adjoining the above, to the same purchasers, on private terms. The same broker has sold for Van Wagenen & Card to A. Loisette No. 3?6 West 70th street, a three-story brick and stone stable, 25x90x100, on private terms.

John R. Foley & Son have sold, through the Real Estate Loan and Trust Company, for E. H. Van Ingen, Nos. 525, 527 and 529 West 125th street, three five-story brick and brown stone flats, each 25x75x99.11, for $?,000, and a lot 25x100.8, on the north side of 89th street, west of Central Park West, for $15,000, and one on the south side of 90th street, 25x100.8, west of Central Park West; also for $15,000.

Hall J. How & Co. have sold for the Schreimer estate to J. Allen Townsend five lots on the north side of 103d street, 180 feet west of Park avenue, on private terms.

Lewis Z. Bach has sold to Thomas J. McLaughlin, for improvement, the four lots on the south side of 103d street, 100 feet west of 3d avenue, for $8?,000; and to Frederick Braender, also for improvement, the four lots adjoining the above, for $35,500. Mr. Bach has also sold to J. J. Reilly two lots on the north side of 102d street, 102 feet west of 3d avenue, for $1?,500.

F. A. Condit has sold for Frank W. Wilman, of Pelhamville, New York, to Francis Skiddy Marden No. 3?4 West 59th street for $?5,500.

L. Froehlich has sold for Mrs. Aron No. 146 East 65th street, a three-story brown stone dwelling, on lot 20x100, for $18,?00.

George W. Ruddell has sold another four-story brown stone dwelling on the north side of 70th street, near Central Park West. This leaves Mr. Ruddell only one house out of an uncompleted row of five. The buyer is Radcliffe Baldwin and the house No. 65.

Lewis Z. Bach has sold to Wm. S. Patton the lot on the north side of 89th street, 100 feet west of Central Park West, for $11,000.

John S. Scott has purchased from J. Allen Townsend the five lots on the north side of 103d street, 180 feet west of Park avenue, for improvement. Brokers, Hall J. How & Co.

LEASES.

E. H. Ludlow & Co. have leased the four-story unfurnished dwelling, No. 50 West 51st street; they have also rented the four-story dwelling, furnished, No. 547 5th avenue, to W. Watts Sherman, on private terms.

Chas. E. Schuyler has leased for G. L. Schuyler to Mrs. J. M. Stamm, of Brooklyn, No. 133 East 60th street, a four-story dwelling, 21x58x100, for three years at $1,?00 per annum.

Brooklyn.

Alfred H. Tompkins has sold for Otto Chils, of New York, the block bounded by New Lots road, Stone, Christopher, and Lott avenues; also the plot on the north side of Lott avenue, running 140 feet north on Stone avenue and 140 feet north on Christopher avenue, in the 26th Ward, Brooklyn, to S. P. Sturges, of New York. Mr. Sturges gives in exchange the four flat houses, Nos. 15, 17, 19 and 21 Truxton street, and the three dwellings, Nos. 31, 33 and 35 Gunther place, Brooklyn.

Corwith Bros. have sold the three-story and basement frame dwelling, 22x4?, on lot 25x100, No. 76 Oakland street, for John C. Bremer to Susan Smith for $4,700.

J. P. Sloane has sold the two-story flat house, 22x36, with extension 14x18, lot 25x100, No. 96 Oakland street, for the Ciebulsky estate for $4,500.

Out of Town.

NEWTOWN, L. I.—Walter H. Sherwood has sold to Mayor Patrick J. Gleason, of Long Island City, 1,?03 lots for $3?,500. Broker, S. E. Renner.

WEEHAWKEN, N. J.—S. E. Renner has sold for Florida W. De Groff to J. G. Gerber, of New York, the Schmitt estate of over eight acres at this place for $50,000.

CONVEYANCES.

	1890. Oct. 16 to 22 inc.	1891. Oct. 15 to 21 inc.
Number	384	378
Amount involved	$1,347,291	$1,861,964
Number nominal	82	103

MORTGAGES.

Number	18	322
Amount involved	$1,033,936	$1,262,298
Number at 5 per cent. or less	191	151
Amount involved	$720,465	$651,800

PROJECTED BUILDINGS.

	1890. Oct. 17 to 23 inc.	1891. Oct. 16 to 22 inc.
Number of buildings	113	87
Estimated cost	$487,140	$431,700

Out Among the Builders.

If those of our readers who are interested in the news items of this department have followed the filings of the past few weeks at the Building Department they will not need to be told that the gathering of facts and figures for this column has been much like trying to find " figs on thistles." Not since 1884 have the filings for new work in the month of September been so few and unimportant as this year. Among architects generally very little is being talked of for immediate development, though the feeling is confident for plenty of important work after the holidays. It is a significant fact that many good draftsmen are out of work, having been "laid off" by those in charge of the offices of some of the leading firms in the profession. Much new work is in prospect and talked of, both for New York and Brooklyn; but at the moment matters with the architects is seemingly at a standstill and, so far as we can learn, likely to remain so for the next two months. The reasons for this are variously stated. None of them, however, seem to be sufficiently broad to carry the weight imposed upon them. It is said that the building material trade is not extending the same line of credit as formerly, and that in consequence the Building Loan associations are not supporting speculative ventures. This goes for so much, but is not all sufficient for the cessation of building operations, which is very general and by no means confined to the speculative class. The hope which is abroad for better things seems to be well born. We trust it may be fully and speedily realized, not only for the satisfaction of architects themselves, but for the sake of all who are concerned directly and indirectly in the building operations of the city.

Graul & Frohm have plans under way for a seven-story stone and terra cotta piano factories with show-rooms in first and second stories. The building will have a frontage on 2d avenue of 25 feet, and on 23d street of 50 feet. It will have metal ceilings throughout, two elevators, and be finished in hardwoods through the first two stories. Kranich & Bach are the owners, and the cost is estimated at $100,000.

O. Wirz has plan under way for four five-story brick, stone and terra cotta flats to be built in Avenue B at the northeast corner of 88th street. The corner building will be 25x92 in size and the remaining three 25x70 each with extensions. Geo. G. Banzer is the owner and the cost has been estimated at $60,000.

Schneider & Herter have plans on the boards for a six-story brick, stone and terra cotta flat, to be built at Nos. 186 and 188 Delancey street, on plot 43.4x86.9. The building will have fire-proof stairs throughout and is to cost the owner, Chas. Ruff, $45,000.

Wm. F. Lennon will build at Nos. 95-99 Mangin street a six-story brick and stone building, 65.9x100 to be arranged for stable and manufacturing purposes. The building is estimated to cost $40,000.

Charles Rentz has plans on the boards for a five-story and basement brick, stone and terra cotta flat, 25x99, to be built at No. 29 Market street at a cost of $24,000. Fay and Stacom are the owners. Also for the same owners at No. 111 Henry street, a similar flat, 25x88.6 in size, to cost $23,000.

John S. Hawley will build at No. 80 West 71st street a brick and stone residence, 25x57 in size. J. R. Thomas is the architect.

Plans were filed some months ago for altering No. 118 West 23d street, so as to convert the first two stories and basement into business rooms, and the floors above into apartments. The work was not undertaken at the time, but is now to be proceeded with at a cost of $14,000. The Excelsior Savings Bank has vacated the first floor which it occupied in this house. D. & J. Jardine are the architects. The latter also have plans for several alterations and additions to the building of the Little Sisters of the Poor on 70th street, near —— avenue.

Daniel Rosenbaum will improve the plot, 50x100, Nos. 137 and 139 Wooster street, with a six-story brick store. The architect and builder has not as yet been selected.

Thos. J. McLaughlin will build four five-story brick and stone flats on the south side of 103d street, 100 feet west of 3d avenue.

J. J. Reilly will improve the two lots on the north side of 102d street, 102 feet west of 2d avenue, by the erection of five-story flats.

Frederick Braender intends to build four five-story brick and stone flats on the south side of 103d street, 200 feet west of 3d avenue.

W. H. Hume, the architect for the New Netherlands Hotel, in 5th avenue has contracts ready for signing as follows: For the mason-work, by Brown & Co., of Newark: for the stone-work, by Whalen & Mahoney Bros., and for the iron-work, by the Jackson Architectural Works. Contracts are not yet let for the electric lighting or the marble and onyx to be used in this building. The specifications call for American and African marble and for Mexican onyx. The details have not been fully determined upon as to these decorative materials and the matter of lighting will be put off to the utmost limit of time in order to take advantage of the very latest improvements which may come into the market. Mr. Hume has also let the contracts as given below for the $250,000 building at Pearl and William streets. The Jackson Architectural Works will supply the iron-work and Moran & Armstrong are the masons. The carpenter work is not yet determined.

Out of Town.

WEST BROOKLYN, N. Y.—P. F. Higgs has completed plans for a two story frame Colonial cottage, 20x41, to be built for G. A. Helm at a cost of $5,000.

RIDGEWOOD, N. J.—H. McG. Davis has drawn plans for a two-story and attic frame cottage, 29x32, to cost about $3,300.

HACKENSACK, N. J.—Fred. P. Washburn intends to build a two-and-a-half-story villa, to cost about $6,000, from plans by E. T. Hapgood, of New York.

WANTS AND OFFERS.

(Advertisements strictly in accordance with this title will be inserted at the practically nominal rate of 10 CENTS *per line (agate). In figuring for themselves advertisers may count seven words for each line, the address to be taken as one line. The object of this department is to bring buyers and sellers into communication with customers. Advertisements must be marked "Wants and Offers Column," and sent to the office of publication, Nos. 14 and 16 Vesey Street, not later than 3 P. M. Friday.)*

OFFERS.

OFFICE OF
FREDERICK SOUTHACK,
401 BROADWAY,
offers for sale some choice pieces
of property on
LEONARD ST., between Broadway and Wes B'way.
FRANKLIN ST., between B'way and West B'way.
WHITE ST., between B'way and West B'way.
BROADWAY, from Barclay to 14th st.
BLEECKER ST., from B'way to South 5th av.
GREENE ST., Canal to 8th st.
WASHINGTON PLACE, B'way to Wooster.
WAVERLEY PLACE, B'way to Wooster.
APPLY AS ABOVE.
FREDERICK SOUTHACK.
Oct. 3 uf.

Vacant Lots.

GOOD CHANCE FOR A SYNDICATE.
$600,000 will buy Plot of 150 Lots five minutes walk 125th street Eighth avenue elevated station; this offer can't possibly be duplicated south of 155th st.
MAINHART & LOWE, 258 West 125th.

ENTIRE easterly front of Boulevard, by 130 ft. on 86th st. and 144 ft. on 87th st.
Oct. 24-1aw6w. OTTO ERNST, South Amboy, N. J.

FOR SALE.—Boulevard and 98th st., southwest corner, 100 feet 11 inches on the Boulevard by 75 feet on 98th st.; one of the finest plots on the Boulevard; terms easy. BERNARD SMYTH, 59 Liberty st.

PLOT OF VERY CHEAP LOTS NEAR 10TH AV. and 23d st; bargain.
FRANK HOUGHTON, 145 Broadway.

FIFTH AV.—Plots of six full lots, including a corner, near the 59th st. entrance to the Park, will be sold to a prompt buyer at a great bargain.
BERNARD SMYTH, 59 Liberty st.

EIGHT LOTS on 98th st., bet Amsterdam and Columbus avs.; excavated ready for building; terms easy. Apply or address,
GEORGE STONE, 81 West 87th st.

40 CHERRY ST., between Roosevelt and Franklin sq., 32x61, vacant; $17,000; accommodating terms. EDWIN A. ELY, 103 Gold st.
Sept.26-1aw8w.

OFFERS.

FOR SALE.—Six choice lots, West 88th st., south side. 125 feet west of Central Park; excavated; unrestricted. AUG. BLUMENSTEIN, 210 West 89th st.

SITE for Institution, Factory or Tenements, 263x100; 65th st., near 1st av.; might exchange for improved property.
CRUMBIE, 50 Broadway.

100TH ST., between 2d and 3d avs.; ten lots cheap; all mortgage if improved.
Sept.26-1aw8w. EDWIN A. ELY, 103 Gold st.

FOUR ATTRACTIVE LOTS, 149th st., adjoining southwest corner 7th av., $3,600 each; builders' terms. EDWIN A. ELY, 103 Gold st.
Sept 26-1aw8w.

Brooklyn Real Estate for Sale.

VALUABLE WATER-FRONT PROPERTY FOR SALE.—From 30th st. to 40th st., Brooklyn, adjoining the ferry to New York, 697 feet in length, with the right to extend 623 feet further to the new bulkhead line; very convenient for manufacturing or storage purposes; also the 2d av. front from 30th st. to 40th st., 594 feet in length. Maps and particulars can be had on application at the office of
PHENIX CHEMICAL WORKS,
96 Maiden lane, New York.

$2.500 WILL PURCHASE A PLOT 50x130, ON a corner on a prominent thoroughfare near the ferries, suitable for manufacturing purposes. Apply to CORWITH BROS., 300 Manhattan ave., Brooklyn, E. D. Oct. 24-31.

FOR SALE IN BROOKLYN.—Three blocks from 39th st ferry, one full block of seventy lots for factory purposes; unsurpassed; terms easy; inquire of the owner. S. McDOUGALL,
Oct. 10-1aw4w. 242 and 243 Washington Market.

OFFERS.

SEVEN TWO-STORY AND BASEMENT HOUSES, renting for over $4,250 per year; expenses low. Particulars from EXECUTRIX, RECORD AND GUIDE.
Oct. 24-31.

AT A BARGAIN, because of death in the family 113 Clinton av, Brooklyn, fine three-story and basement brick residence, in first-class condition, on lots 50x125 feet, with fruit trees, flower and vegetable garden; is an excellent and convenient location for a New York business man. Apply on premises.

Country Property.

FOR SALE—White Plains, N. Y., house 40 rooms and 3 acres ground, particularly adapted for hotel; can be filled with paying boarders at once. Inquire DOUGLAS MURRAY, REGISTER'S OFFICE, White Plains, N. Y.

FOR SALE.—In plots to suit; eligible building sites (commanding view of sound for miles), on North st., Greenwich, Connecticut; price reasonable; terms easy; neighborhood aristocratic and fashionable. Apply to
FRED. J. STONE, owner, 60 Broadway, N. Y.
Sept. 12-uf.

Miscellaneous.

THOMAS & ECKERSON, 35 West 30th st., have a large assortment of houses for sale, from 25th st. to 133d st.; ranging in price from $13,000 to $125,000, and on easy terms.
Oct. 24-1aw4w.

SET OF NEW YORK CITY DIRECTORIES FOR sale cheap.
E. A. TREDWELL, Times Building.

A PARTY ABOUT TO BUILD A FIVE-STORY factory, 50x98, in Harlem, near water-front, will lease the three upper floors and build to suit tenant. Terms very moderate. Address
May 16 u. f. OWNER, 409 E. 107th St.

PRINTING.—Book, News and Job.
RECORD AND GUIDE PRESS,
14 Barclay, and 14, 16 Vesey sts.

SALES OF THE WEEK.

The following are the sales at the Real Estate Exchange and Auction Room for the week ending Oct 23.

** Indicates that the property described has been bid in for plaintiff's account:*

JAMES L. WELLS.

Oakley pl, s s, 109.5 e Sedgwick av, 2 lots. W. K. Peyton $1,700
Oakley pl, adj, 2 lots. Patrick Ryan 1,700
Oakley pl, adj, 1 lot. A. Gellrith 850
Perot st. n s, 100.8 e Sedgwick av, 2 lots. W. P. Wight 1,700
Perot st, adj, 4 lots. B. F. Cromwell 3,400
Elwood av, n w cor Perot st, 1 lot. S. N. Daniels 1,150
Elwood av, w s, adj, 4 lots. Same 3,400
Elwood av, adj, 2 lots. Jas. McGinty 1,750
Elwood av, s w cor Oakley pl, 1 lot. Wm. J. Chestnut 1,175
Elwood av, n w cor Oakley pl, 1 lot. B. F. Cromwell 1,200
Elwood av, w s, adj, 3 lots. F. E. Edgar 2,225
Sedgwick av, n e cor Perot st, 1 lot. W. P. Wight 1,450
Sedgwick av, e s, adj, 2 lots. A. F. Fairchild 2,100
Sedgwick av, adj, 1 lot. Mary D. Franklin 1,000
Sedgwick av, adj, 1 lot. F. G. Brouson 1,080
Sedgwick av, adj, 2 lots. W. K. Peyton 2,175
Sedgwick av, s e cor Oakley pl, 1 lot. Same 1,450
Sedgwick av, n e cor Oakley pl, 1 lot. H. Reimer 1,350
Sedgwick av, e s, adj, 1 lot. Wm. Strachan 1,025
Sedgwick av, adj, 1 lot. Chas. Blyth 1,000
Sedgwick av, adj, 1 lot. F. Koster 1,000
Sedgwick av, adj, 3 lots. I. M. Brown 3,000
Sedgwick av, s e cor Knowlton st. Same 1,275
8th av, No. 2140, e s, 51.4 s 116th st, 25.5x100, one-story brk store. Henry Vonder Leith. (Amt due $3,330) 18,760

R. V. HARNETT & CO.

Riverside Drive, e s, 36.11 n 104th st, 26x100, vacant. (Bid in) .... —
Riverside Drive, e s, 550 n 122d st, vacant, 50x100, vacant, and two-story brk and stone stable on rear. Chas. Blauvelt 20,800
Christopher st, No. 70 } 26x77.6x27x82.4, five-
Grove st, No. 67 } story brk flat. Robert V. Stocky 36,750
Sheriff st, Nos. 91 and 93, 50x100, two six-story brk tenem'ts. E. Jacobs 50,000
78th st, No. 154 E., 18.9x102.2, three-story and basement brown stone dwell'g. Gustave Lange 13,000
93d st, Nos. 175 and 177 E., 59.10x100.8, two four-story stone front flats. (Bid in) .... —
*133d st, No 256, s s, 184.4 e 8th av, 16.8x99.11, three-story stone front dwell'g. Cecile Rusch, extrx. (Amt due $10,226) 6,000
148th st, n s, 90 w Brook av, 25x100, vacant. F. W. Mieske 2,600
148th st, adj, 25x100, vacant. John Fryes 2,050

JOHN F. B. SMYTH.

Bank st, Nos. 117-121, three five-story brk flats. (Bid in) .... —
29th st, No. 40 W., 20.6x98.9, five-story and basement brk house and four-story building on rear. (Bid in) .... —
73d st, No. 135 W., 20x102.2, four-story brown stone dwell'g. (Bid in) .... —
91st st, No. 173 E., n s, 75 w 3d av, 25x100.8, five-story stone front flat. R. Ausner 18,000
91st st, No. 171, adj, 25x100.8, five-story similar flat. T. A. Campbell 24,000
106th st, No. 69 W .... }
107th st, No. 70 W .... }
Two five-story brk and stone flats, each 25x 85x100.11. (Bid in) .... —
138th st, s s, 75 e Southern Boulevard, 25x100. Della Gibson. (Amt due $4,607) 6,125
3d av, No. 1622, n w cor 91st st, 25.2x75, five-story flat and stores. Jacob Ruppert 41,500
3d av, Nos. 1624 and 1626, w s, adj 26.2x75, two five-story flats and stores. Adler Herman 49,800
3d av, No. 1628, adj, 25.2x75, five-story flat and stores. Theo. Hesberg 27,000

WM. KENNELLY.

8th st, No. 100 W., 28x98.11, three-story and basement brk building. Francis H. Weeks 16,850
8th st, No. 109, n e s, 531.5 n w 5th av, 23x98.11, three-story brk dwell'g. Francis H. Weeks, for party in interest 16,550
60th st, No. 802, s s, 100 w 11th av, 25x100.5, five-story brk tenem't. H. C. Johnson. (Amt due $19,446) 20,400

A. H. MULLER & SON.

Arcularius pl, s s, 209.3 e Gerard av, runs east 50 x south 100 x east 5 x south — x west 102 x north 197.3 to beginning, vacant. A. A. Jordan 4,025
Duane st, No. 80, s s, 136.7 e Broadway, 25.1x 77.3x25.7x79.2, three and four-story brk Cobweb Hall. Peter J. McCoy 60,000
Norfolk st, No. 78 formerly No. 66, e s abt 125 n Broome st, 25x100, three-story frame (brk front) tenem't and two-story frame building on rear. Loonie & Parker. (Amt due $13,576) 21,400
7th st, No. 32, 24.5x90.10, three-story brk house. Julius Lauterbach 10,000
3d av, No. 38.5, 25x97.5x25x99.7, three-story stone front dwell'g. Robt. Hughes 8,500
Washington av, n w cor 173d st, 100x150, two-story brk dwell'g. Louis Lese 17,000
Central av, n w cor Gerard av, 50x12.10x100x15 x88.11 to beginning, vacant. B. F. Kearns 3,000
Central av, w s, adj, 2 lots. Mary Gallagher 4,850
Central av, adj, 5 lots. Robt. Hughes 9,125
Inwood av, n e cor Gerard av, 29x87.6x—x100 to beginning. A. A. Jordan 2,550
Inwood av, e s, adj, 4 lots. Robt. Hughes 3,900
Gerard av, n s, 100 e Inwood av, 1 lot. B. F. Kearns 1,075

L. J. PHILLIPS & CO.

46th st, No. 343 W., 19.6x100.5, four-story brown stone dwell'g. (Bid in) .... —

J. C. LALOR.

133d st, Nos. 248 and 250, s s, 416.8 w 7th av, 33.4x99.11, two three-story stone front dwellings. Robinson & Gill. (Amt due $30,867) 33,000

B. L. KENNELLY.

*79th st, No. 412, s s, 75 w Av A, 19x75, five-story brk flat. Henry Greenebaum. (Amt due $5,189; prior morts. $11,500) 14,600
*114th st, No. 418, s s, 240 e 1st av, 30x100.11, four-story stone front tenem't. Mary Meyers. (Amt due $1,711) 14,800

SMYTH & RYAN.

*120th st, Nos. 230-248, n s, 375 w 7th av, 50x 100.11, three three-story brk dwell'gs. Stephen H. Wartling 46,500

OTHER AUCTIONEERS.

*Rivington st, No. 161, s s, 25 w Clinton st, 25x 100, five-story brk tenem't with stores. Jane M. Noyes. (Amt due $8,518) 28,000
87th st, No. 136, s s, 350 w 9th av, 20x100.8, four-story stone front dwell'g. Wm. Brennan. (Amt due $24,156) 25,500
*143d st, Nos. 227-235, n s, 150 w 7th av, 125x 99.11, five five-story brick flats .... }
144th st, Nos. 228-236, s s, 150 w 7th av, 125x 99.11, five five-story brk flats .... }
Bradley & Currier Co. (Lim.) (Amt due $27,502; sub. to morts. $80,000) 140,500
*Park (4th) av, No. 885, w s, 60.2 n 78th st, 15 x75, four-story brk dwell'g. Edith N. Wharton. (Amt due $18,900) 19,675
8th av, Nos. 2842 and 2844, s e cor 128th st, 49.11 x100, two six-story brk flats with stores. Henry B. Kerr. (Amt due abt $104,500) 114,500

Total $1,002,840
Corresponding week, 1890 .... $888,800

BROOKLYN, N. Y.

FOR WEEK ENDING OCTOBER 22.

JERE. JOHNSON, JR.

Ocean Parkway, n e cor Av M, 4 lots. Wm. Warton $2,000
Ocean Parkway, e s, 180 n Av M, 2 lots. Mary Gallagher 910
Ocean Parkway, e s, 300 n Av M, 2 lots. E. Freschmann 800
East 7th st, e s, 240 n Av M, 3 lots. C. Schiffmann 510
East 7th st, adj, 1 lot. J. Core 100
East 7th st, adj, 4 lots. Mrs. M. D. Kelly 620
East 8th st, w s, 160 n Av M, 1 lot. A. Hamburger 155
East 8th st, w s, 220 n Av M, 4 lots. W. H. Contana 580
East 8th st, adj, 3 lots. Mrs. Carroll 405
East 8th st, e s, 200 n Av M, 2 lots. L. Stamper 255
East 9th st, w s, 300 n Av M, 2 lots. Mrs. Anderson 280
East 9th st, adj, 2 lots. Mrs. Mary Gallagher 280
East 9th st, adj, 1 lot. Mrs. Burns 135
East 9th st, adj, 2 lots. E. Carhart 270
East 9th st, adj, 1 lot. Mrs. Murphy 140
East 9th st, adj, 2 lots. E. Freschmann 310
East 9th st, e s, 80 n Av M, 2 lots. Mrs. M. D Kelly 200
East 9th st, adj, 2 lots. W. D. Leary 260
East 9th st, adj, 1 lot. Mrs. Grant 135
East 9th st, adj, 2 lots. L. D. Sutley 280
East 9th st, adj, 2 lots. Mrs. Smith 280
East 9th st, adj, 2 lots. Mary Gallagher 290
East 9th st, adj, 2 lots. E. Freschmann 270
East 9th st, adj, 1 lot. A. Hamburger 135
East 9th st, adj, 2 lots. C. Schiffmann 270
East 9th st, adj, 1 lot. A. Dougherty 135
East 9th st, adj, 1 lot. Jos. Marshall 135
East 9th st, adj, 2 lots. F. P. Miller 280
East 9th st, adj, 2 lots. A. Miller 280
Av L, s e cor East 9th st, 5 lots. C. Schiffmann 700
Av M, n w cor East 7th st, 5 lots. Thos. O'Connor 1,525

OTHER AUCTIONEERS.

*Glen st, s w cor Crescent av, 25x100, three-story frame tenem't and store. Charles W. Osborne 4,000
McDonough st, No. 429, n w cor Reid av, 25.6x 100, foundation laid. Charles G. Reynolds 1,600
*President st, s s, 430.8 e 8th av, 25.10x100, three-and-a-half-story brk dwell'g. The Met. Life Ins. Co 11,500
Prospect pl, near Utica av, 66x127.9, vacant. Philip Goss $755
Taylor st, No. 39, n s, 173.8 e Kent av, 19.11x 80, three-story brk dwell'g. Honig & Klein 3,575
*Withers st, n s, 38.7 e North 9th st, runs north 50.3 x southwest 62.5 to North 9th st, x southeast along same 10 to Withers st, x east 38.7 to beginning. Thomas P. Graham 960
3d pl, No. 5, n s, 40 e Henry st, 20x60, two-story brk dwell'g; also all right, title and int. in courtyard in front, 20x33.6¼. Michael H. Hagerty 3,500
Howard av, e s, 98 s Herkimer st, 55x98, frame church. S. & J. C. Burling 6,400
*Jefferson av late Jefferson st, No. 156, s s, 280 w Nostrand av, 20x100, four-story brk flat. Thomas C. Van Hoesen 5,500
*Jefferson av late Jefferson st, No. 154, s s, 300 w Nostrand av, 20x100, four-story brk flat. Eliz. V. H. Nicholson 5,500
Prospect av, Nos. 228 and 230, 38x80.9, four-story brk building. (Bid in) .... —
4th av, No. 177, s e s, 34.8 s w Degraw st, 18.4x 75, four-story brk tenem't and store. Geo. R. Brown .... ,800

Total $58,75
Corresponding week 1890 .... $344,246

CONVEYANCES.

NEW YORK CITY.

OCTOBER 16, 17, 19, 20, 21, 22.

Allen st, No. 165, w s, 150.6 s Stanton st, runs west 46 x north 0.6 x west 41.6 x south 25 x east 87.6 to Allen st, x north 24.6, five-story brk store and tenem't with three-story brk tenem't on rear. Aaron Walder and Jennie his wife to William Slote, Jersey City. *Mt.* $21,000. Oct. 15. $25,000

Bedford st, No. 49, w s, 28 n Leroy st, 22x75 x south 29 x east 12.4 x northeast 12 x east —, with use of alley in rear, two-story brk dwelling with two-story brk building on rear. Release curtesy. Henry J. Herring to Catharine Miller. Oct. 20. 127

Same property David and James H. Anderson exrs. Jane Anderson to same. ½ part. Oct. 20. 4,750

Same property. Jennie A. wife of Stephen L. Birdsall, of Oradelt, N. J., to same. 2-16 part. Oct. 20. 1,124

Same property. Eva Herring by Henry J. Herring committee to same. 2-16 part. Oct. 20. 1,124

Same property. James H. Anderson, Bogota, N. J., to same. 4-16 part. Oct. 20. 2,375

Same property. Release. Catharine Miller to David and James H. Anderson exrs. Jane Anderson, James H. Anderson and Jennie A. Birdsall individ. and Henry J. Herring individ. and committee Eva Herring. Oct. 20. 150

Boulevard, s e cor 152d st, 74.11x100, vacant. Hester A. wife of George W. Montgomery to Carrie S. Kennedy. *Mt.* $7,500. Oct. 14. 25,000

Delancey st, No. 44, n s, 75.2 w Eldridge st, 25.1 x100x25.2x100, five-story brk tenem't with stores. Betsey wife of and Harris Cohen to Lewis Levy. *Mt.* $20,000. Sept. 20. 38,250

East Broadway, No. 293, s s, 43.2 e Gouverneur st, 21.7x110.10 to 12 foot alley, x21.4x110.8 with all title in alley, four-story brk store and tenem't with two-story brk stable on rear. Daniel Galvan to Mary P. Galvan. ½ part. Oct. 16. 12,000

Essex st, No. 101, w s, 77.6 n Delancey st, 24.6x 43.9, five-story brk store and tenem't. Nathan Cohen and Ester his wife to Laemmlein Buttenwieser. *Mt.* $13,000. Oct. 21. See Monroe st. 18,000

Essex st, No. 146, e s, 225 n Rivington st, 25x 100, five-story brk tenem't with stores and five-story brk tenem't on rear. Jacob Wiehe and Christina his wife and Magdalena Endholz widow to Sarah wife of Louis Lese. *Mt.* $10,000. Oct. 20. 35,600

Frankfort st, No. 9, s s, abt 115 e Nassau st, 28.8 x103.9x32x104 3, four-story brk stores with two-story frame and three-story brk buildings on rear. Elenora Frederick, Brooklyn, to Louis W. Duesing. 1-12 part. C. a. G. July 22. 5,000

Same property. Louis W. Duesing and Mary H. his wife, Brooklyn, to Julia R. Foley. 1-12 part. C. a. G. Sept. 15. 4,750

Same property. Excelsior Steam Power Co. to Elenora Frederick. 1-12 part. Q. C. and C. a. G. July 11. 4,750

Same property. Assign. contract. Michael Foley to Julia R. Foley. Oct. 6. nom

Hague st, Nos. 4 and 6, s s, 83.8 w Pearl st, 33.10x25.6x51.6x35.6, two three-story brk tenements, store in No. 6. William Lyman and Jennie his wife to Francis Lawton. *Mt.* $6,-000. Oct. 14. nom

Henry st, No. 154, s s, 82.6 e Rutgers st, 22x100, three-story stone front tenem't with one-story brk building on rear. Robert E. Walsh and Annie E. his wife to Bernard and Louis Blumberg. Oct. 15. 21,250

Houston st, Nos. 367 and 369 East. Agreement as to easement for light and air. Nathan Frankenthaler and Jacob Asch with Adolph and Samuel Ullman. Oct. 16. 500

Jefferson st, No. 16, w s, abt 75 s East Broadway, 20x52.2, two-story brk dwell'g. Max Cohen and Esther his wife to Harry Fischel. Correction deed. Oct. 15. nom

Leroy st, No. 56, s s, 150 w Bedford st, 25x 85, five-story brk tenem't with stores. George B. Marx and Alice his wife to William J. Rauch. *Mt.* $15,000. Sept. 10. 28,400

Lewis st, Nos. 57-61, w s, 125 s Rivington st, 75 x100, four-story brk machine shop. John B. Wickersham and Annie T. his wife, Amos Wickersham and Sarah J. his wife, Ellen S. wife of Edward Lippincott, Philadelphia, Pa., heirs Ellen De B. Wickersham to Samuel Weil. C. a. G. Oct. 19. nom

Same property. John B. Wickersham individ. and exr. of Ellen De B. Wickersham to same. *Mt.* $15,000. Oct. 19. 38,000

Ludlow st, No. 170, e s, 75.10 n Stanton st, 24.10 x90, five-story brk tenem't with stores. Michael C. Gross and H. J. Bertha his wife to George B. Christman. ½ part. *Mt.* ½ of $15,000. Oct. 7. 10,000

Madison st, No. 355, n s, 216 e Scammel st, 23.10 x96, five-story brk tenem't with stores. Abraham Kassel and Ida his wife to Moris Bloch. *Mt.* $17,250. Oct. 20. See Rivington st. 24,000

Madison st, No. 223, n s, 26.1 w Jefferson st, 26.1x100, three-story brk tenem't. Joseph L. Buttenwieser to John V. Campbell. B. & S. *Mt.* $——. Oct. 1. nom

Monroe st, No. 11, s s, abt 175 e Catharine st, 25x100, five-story brk tenem't. Laemmlein Buttenwieser and Leah his wife to Nathan Cohen. Oct. 22. See Essex st. 38,500

Marion st, Nos. 7, 9 and 11, e s, abt 142 n Broome st, 50x100, six-story brk factory. Simon Goldenberg and Mary his wife to Julius L. Goldenberg, Paris, France. *Mt.* $40,000. Oct. 15. 95,000

Nassau st, No. 61, w s, 52.1 n Maiden lane, 23.4x47.11, four-story brk store. Harriet C. wife of Dorman T. Warren to Mary D. and Elizabeth S. Van Winkle. *Mt.* $30,000. Oct. 14. 75,000

Prospect pl, No. 8, w s, 126.3 s 41st st, 17.1x75, four-story stone front dwell'g. Georgiana A. and Florence Merritt to Thomas Bolger. *Mt.* $4,000. Oct. 22. 8,000

Rivington st, Nos. 19 and 21 } begins Rivington
Chrystie st, No. 178 } st, s e cor Chrystie st, 50x81; No. 19, six-story brk tenem't with stores; No. 21, three-story brk store and tenem't; No. 178, six-story brk tenem't with stores. Moris Bloch and Mali his wife to Abraham Kassel. *Mt.* $63,910. Oct. 20. See Madison st. 83,000

Roosevelt st, No. 14, e s, abt 195 s Park row, 26x132, four-story brk store and tenem't with two five-story brk tenem'ts on rear. Mary G. Wood to Domenico Rovegno and Pietro Capevari. *Mt.* $17,500. Oct. 20. 33,000

Sheriff st, No. 87, w s, abt 175 s Stanton st, 20x 100, five-story brk tenem't. Isidor Goldmann to Sarah Dobroczynski. ½ part. All liens. Oct. 5. nom

Same property. Oscar Dobroczynski and Sarah his wife to Isidor Goldmann. ½ part. All liens. Oct. 5. nom

Suiffin court, No. 5, w s, 39.6 s 36th st and being 159 w of 3d av, 19.9x41, with ½ of alley or court, two-story brk stable. Jacob F. Wyckoff and Emily F. his wife to Elizabeth H. Wyckoff, Hightown, N. J. Sub. to morts. Feb. 21, 1884. nom

Stanton st, No. 191, s s, 16.8 e Attorney st, 16.8 x64, portion of three-story brk moulding mill. Marie J. Bernhardt widow to Charles A. Bernhardt and Emma M. Meilert. Life estate in ½ part. B. & S. Oct. 19. nom

Teunissen pl, south cor Terrace View av, 120.1 x69.2 to av, x90.11. Joseph H. Cain and Susan his wife to Anna M. wife of Herbert A. Sherman, Rye, N. Y. *Mt.* $825. Sept. 21. 1,775

Washington st, No. 161, e s, 129.1 s Cortlandt st, 25.1x92.10x25x93.7, seven-story brk store. Joseph D. Eldredge and Henrietta his wife to John Pettit, East Orange, N. J. *Mt.* $50,000. Oct. 21. nom

White st, No. 25, s s, 75.1 w Church st, 25.1x 72.11x25.1x72.10. Release mort. Rebecca Ladew and ano. trustees Harvey S. Ladew to Louise L. wife of John T. Williams. Sept. 16. 31,000

Willett st, No. 121, w s, 193.5 n Stanton st, 18.9 x75, four-story brk store and tenem't. Amalie Cohn to Rachel Bornstein. *Mt.* $10,-100. Oct. 15. 12,000

4th st, No. 234 } begins 4th st, n w cor West
10th st, No. 159 } 10th st, 29.7x88, three-story brk store and tenem't on 4th st and two-story brk stable on 10th st. William S. Cooper to Walton C. Dupignac. All liens. Oct. 1. 42,000

5th st, No. 731, n s, 291 w Av D, 27x75, five-story brk tenem't with stores. Ernest E. W. Schneider and Henry Herter and Henrietta his wife to Isaac and Moritz Klein. *Mt.* $25,-500. Oct. 22. 30,000

7th st, No. 77, n s, 150 w 1st av, 20x90.8, said lot being 6.10 less deep than represented in original map, four-story brk tenem't. Herman Cohen and Bella his wife to Samuel Kahn. *Mt.* $10,000. Oct. 20. 25,500

8th st, No. 314, s s, 263.9 e Av B, 24.9x97.6, four-story brk tenem't with stores. Conrad Witt and Carolina his wife to Magdalena Alff. *Mt.* $8,000. Oct. 15. 17,600

10th st, No. 5, n s, 124.6 e 5th av, 24.6x94.9, five-story brk flat. Martha R. wife of James R. Townsend to Frances Johnston. *Mt.* $25,000. Oct. 9. 55,000

15th st, No. 302, s s, 597.4 w 1st av, 22.1x128.3, five-story stone front tenem't. William Elliott to George L. Elliott. ½ part. January 10, 1890. nom

15th st, Nos. 219 and 221, n s, 227.2 w 7th av, 40.2x103.1, two four-story brk dwell'gs with two-story brk building on rear. William D. Stewart to Maria Stewart. All liens. Aug. 26. nom

Same property. Maria Stewart to William Rankin. *Mt.* $25,500. Sept. 30. See 96th st. 40,000

16th st, Nos. 331 and 333, n s, 350 w 8th av, 50x 92, two two and three-story frame and brk dwellings. Release mort. George Young to John Totten. Oct. 19. nom

Same property. John Totten and Emma A. his wife to Benjamin F. Cohen. Oct. 19. nom

16th st, n s, 350 w 8th av, 50x92. Benjamin F. Cohen and Annie his wife to Theodore Van Eupen. *Mt.* $25,000. Oct. 19. 35,000

16th st, No. 344, s s, abt 250 e 9th av, 25x63.3x 25x64.7, five-story brk tenem't with stores. Gottlieb F. Rapp to John T. Stanley. *Mt.* $10,600. Oct. 1. 17,775

19th st, No. 411, n s, 146.5 w 9th av, 21.5x80, three-story brk dwell'g. James S. Cushman to Francis P. Prial. Oct. 16. 12,900

27th st, No. 504, s s, 75 w 10th av, 25x24.8, three-story frame tenem't. Bridget F. Swan formerly Finn daughter of James O'Neil to Mary A. Cahill another daughter of James O'Neil. Q. C. Sept. 28. 300

32d st, No. 407, n s, 82 w 9th av, 18x74.1, three-story brk dwell'g. Annie T. Harris widow to Mary C. Wentworth. *Mt.* $5,000. Oct. 14. nom

33d st, Nos. 140 and 142, s s, 187.6 e 7th av, 62.6 x143.2 x 49 x 144, two five-story brk flats. Charles G. Martin and Maria M. his wife to William C. Martin. C. a. G. ½ part. April 8. val. consid

Same property. William C. Martin and Alice L. H. his wife to Samuel S. Abbott, Brooklyn, N. Y. Sept. 8. val. consid

35th st, Nos. 241-245, n s. 331 e 8th av, 69x98.9, three four-story brk dwell'gs. William H. Ramsey to Asa R. Davison. *Mt.* $64,500. Sept. 11. 115,000

38th st, Nos. 40 and 42 W. Party wall agreement. Albert J. Milbank to American Surety Co., New York. Oct. 22. nom

46th st, No. 127, n s, 100 e Lexington av, 20x 100.5, five-story stone front dwell'g. John H. Riker, Trappe, Md., to Joseph and Margaret A. Kerr. Oct. 16. 20,000

48th st, No. 325, n s, 278 w 8th av, 18x100.8, four-story stone front dwell'g. Annie Norton to Mary J. wife of John Holliday. Oct. 20. 15,000

49th st, No. 232, s s, 249 w 2d av, 19x100.5, four-story stone front dwell'g. Charlotte wife of Lazarus Friedberger to George Reid. Oct. 19. See 91st st. 15,000

49th st, No. 235, n s, 239 e 8th av, 18x100.5, four-story stone front dwell'g. Samuel Stewart and Isabella his wife to Mary T. Carroll. Oct. 15. 19,250

50th st, No. 543, n s, 225 e 11th av, 25x74.6, four-story stone front tenem't. Sadie Hurson extrx. Myles Hurson to Hugh King. Oct. 19. 23,000

51st st, No. 544, s s, 225 e 11th av, 25x126.4, two-story frame dwell'g on rear of lot. Sadie Hurson extrx. Myles Hurson to Hugh King. Oct. 19. 2,000

52d st, Nos. 413 and 415, n s, 194 e 1st av, 41.8x 85.1x42.3x92.8, two four-story stone front tenements. John Murray and Margaret E. his wife to Lewis A. London. *Mt.* $18,000. Oct. 16. 26,000

53d st, Nos. 200 and 202, s w cor 7th av, 34x50.5, two four and five-story brk (stone front) flats with stores. Louis Weil to Fanny Hoffman. ½ part. *Mt.* $32,000. Oct. 13. nom

54th st, No. 115, n s, 225 w 6th av, 25.6x100.5, three-story brk stable. Olivia M. wife of William B. Cutting to John McL. Nash. Oct. 16. 31,250

Same property. John McL. Nash to Olivia M. Cutting. *Mt.* $15,000. Oct. 16. 31,250

54th st, s s, 200 e 10th av, 25x28.11x25.8x25. Alfred Roe heir of Charles S. Roe and Elizabeth M. his wife, and Louisa A. Roe widow to Peter Gallagher. Q. C. Oct. 9. nom

54th st, No. 448, s s, 200 e 10th av, 25x100.5, three-story frame store and tenem't. Peter Gallagher to William Rankin. Oct. 22. nom

57th st, No. 430, n s, 241.6 w Av A, 20x100.5, three-story stone front dwell'g. }
Lexington av, No. 979, e s, 36.5 s 71st st, 16x 69, four-story stone front dwell'g. }
Owen Moran to Margaret Moran. Sept. 22. nom

59th st, No. 335, n s, 200 w 1st av, 25x100.5, four-story brk building. Bernhard Kolb and Elizabeth F. his wife to Edward Bolger. Oct. 20. 10,500

60th st, No. 211, n s, 200 w 10th av, 25x100.5, five story brk tenem't. Sarah T. Bolger to Bertha Young. All liens. Oct. 15. 25,000

61st st, No. 303, n s, 75 e 2d av, 25x75, five-story brk tenem't. Fanny B. wife of Daniel A. Clarke to Antonia Wenzel. *Mt.* $13,000. Oct. 15. 15,000

62d st, No. 331, n s, 303 e 2d av, 17x100.5, three-story brk dwell'g. Bridget Nealy to Elizabeth A. McKay. Oct. 13. nom

66th st, No. 426, s s, 325 e 1st av, 25x100.5, five-story brk tenem't. Sophie Schmidt widow to Jacob Mohr. *Mt.* $10,000. Oct. 15. nom

66th st, Nos. 229 and 231, n s, 325 e West End av, 50x100.5, two five-story brk tenem'ts. Thomas R. Hughes, Weekawken, N. J., to John Heyzer, Brooklyn. *Mt.* $35,000. Oct. 15. See South 5th av. 50,000

69th st, No. 307, n s, 150 w West End av, 25x 100.5, five-story brk tenem't with stores. Patrick Roache and Margaret his wife to Percival S. Menken. B. & S. June 3. 25,000

Same property. Percival S. Menken to Randolph Guggenheimer. B. & S. Oct. 16. nom

69th st, s s, 125 e West End av, 100x100.5, vacant. Simon Sultan and Ada E. his wife to Robert Wallace. *Mt.* $28,000. Oct. 22. See 124th st. exch

74th st, No. 33, n s, 360 e Columbus av, 20x102.2, four-story stone front dwell'g. Minnie Hayman to Josephine wife of Henry Morgenthau. *Mt.* $28,000. Oct. 17. 45,000

77th st, s s, 100 e West End av, 0.6x102.2. Release mort. The Equitable Life Assurance Soc. of the United States to Dore Lyon. Oct. 9. nom

Same property. Dore Lyon and Anna E. his wife to Francis M. Jencks. Oct. 12. 800

77th st, s s, 100.6 e West End av. Party wall agreement. Same to same. Oct. 13. nom

79th st, No. 52, s s, 75 e Madison av, 25x102.2, four-story brk dwell'g. Jacob Cohen, Samuel Cohen and Rebecca his wife to Mary wife of John W. Grace, Great Neck, L. I. *Mt.* $25,000. Oct. 16. 70,000

79th st, No. 410, s s, 169 e 1st av, 25x102.2, four-story brk tenem't. Patrick J. McLoughlin, Guttenberg, N. J., to William Hasselberger. Oct. 15. 14,000

81st st, Nos. 168 and 170, s s, 158 e Amsterdam av, 42x102.2, two five-story brk flats. John Casey and Kate his wife to Mary E. McCabe. Oct. 1. See Lexington av. 80,000

81st st, s s, 116 e Amsterdam av, 84x102.2. Release mort. Morris Steinhardt to John Casey. Oct. 16. nom

82d st, No. 203, n s, 85.6 e 3d av, 18.3x82.2, three-story stone front dwell'g. J. C. Julius Langbein and Emma J. his wife to Fannie wife of Adolph Bernstein. *Mt.* $5,000. Oct. 1. 13,350

83d st, No. 334, s s, 150 w 1st av, 25x102.2, five-story stone front tenem't. Sophia wife of George Seelig to Gustav A. F. Seelig. ½ part. Sub. to mort. $17,000, Oct. 19. 11,250

83d st, No. 128, s s, 300 w Columbus av, 32.4x102.2, four-story brk dwell'g. Eugene D. Miller to Margaret wife of Stephen Pendergast. Q. C. Oct. 19. nom

Same property. Henry Jones Batchelder to same. *Mt.* $28,000. Oct. 12. 40,000

83d st, No. 508, s s, 148 e Av A. 25x102.2, five-story brk tenem't. George Herbener and Henrietta his wife to Carolina Peters. *Mt.* $10,000. Oct. 19. 20,300

83d st, No. 331, n s, 275 w 1st av, 25x102.2, five-story stone front tenem't. Thomas Moore and Annie his wife and John McLaughlin and Margaret his wife to Franz Gerstner and Frieda his wife. *Mt.* $15,000. Oct. 15. 25,800

85th st, No. 46, s s, 425 w Central Park West, 25x102.2, four-story stone front dwell'g. William Schneider to William F. Havemeyer. *Mt.* $32,500. May 1. nom

86th st, No. 337 n s, 440 w West End av, 20x100.8, four-story brk dwell'g. William E. D. Stokes to Horatio N. Fraser. Sept. 1. 40,000

87th st, No. 134, s s, 330 w Columbus av, 20x100.8.
87th st, No. 142, s s, 410 w Columbus av, 20x100.8.
Two four-story stone front dwell'gs.
Charles D. Milliken to Ralph D. P. Brown. *Mt.* $51,500. Sept. 14. 66,000

87th st, s s, 250 w Central Park West. Party wall agreement. Edward Oppenheimer and Isaac Metzger to James A. Frame. June 5. nom

87th st, s s, 150 w Central Park West, 100x100.8, vacant. Edward Oppenheimer and Mathilde his wife and Isaac Metzger and Bertha his wife to James R. and D. Allison Breen. *Mt.* $36,000. Oct. 2. nom

88th st, No. 149, n s, 374 e Amsterdam av, 17x100.8, three-story stone front dwell'g. Release mort. Francis M. Jencks to John C. Heney. Oct. 15. 2,750

Same property. John C. Heney and Sarah his wife to Harriet Loveridge. *Mt.* $14,500. Oct. 16. nom

88th st, No. 311, n s, 138 w West End av, 18x100.8, four-story brk dwell'g. William Gunn and Martha his wife, Andrew Grant and Janet his wife to Clara L. Cunningham. *Mt.* $20,000. Oct. 21. 26,500

88th st, No. 145, n s, 408 e Amsterdam av, 17x100.8, three-story stone front dwell'g. Hugh McDowell and Julia F. his wife to Therese Steinmann. *Mt.* $20,000. Oct. 8. 18,500

90th st, No. 302, s s, 90 w West End av, 20x100.8, four-story stone front dwell'g. Theodore A. Squier and Carrie B. his wife to Du Bois Smith, Smithtown, L. I. *Mt.* $17,500. Oct. 15. 28,000

91st st, n s, 30 e 5th av. Receipt in payment under party wall agreement. Benjamin A. and George N. Williams, Jr., to George Reid. Oct. 15. 670

91st st, No. 13, n s, 230 e 5th av, 17.1x100.8, four-story stone front dwell'g. George Reid and Henrietta F. his wife to Charlotte Friedberger. *Mt.* $8,000. Oct. 19. See 49th st. 28,500

93d st, No. 112, s s, 105 e 4th av, 14x100.8, three-story stone front dwell'g. Arthur Gorsch and Sophia his wife to Martin Lankenau, Brooklyn. *Mt.* $10,000. Oct. 1. 16,500

93d st, Nos. 161-165, n s, 168 e Amsterdam av, 51x86.8 to Apthorpes lane, x51.1x88.8, with all title in lane, three three-story stone front dwell'gs. Frederick W. Bowne to Henry C. Coe. *Mt.* $46,500. June 13. nom

93d st, s s, 375.1 w Columbus av, 20x100.8. Release mort. Adelia F. Philp to Walden P. Anderson. Sept. 30. nom

94th st, s s, 202 e Amsterdam av, 51x98.2 to Apthorpes lane, x51x96. Release morts. John A. Gwynne to Walden P. Anderson. Oct. 16. 5,000

96th st, No. 58, s s, 200 e Columbus av, 20x100.8, four-story brk dwell'g. William Rankin and Elisabeth his wife to Maria Stewart. Oct. 19. See 15th st nom

97th st, Nos. 151 and 153, n s, 171 w 3d av, 54x100.11, two five-story stone front flats. Henry Hirsch and Ella his wife, Morris Victorius and Rachel his wife and Julius Hirsch and Bella his wife to Daniel Hennessy. *Mt.* $26,000 and tax 1891. Oct. 14. 48,000

97th st, No. 129, n s, 524 e Amsterdam av, 16x100.11, four-story brk dwell'g. George F. Johnson and Emma his wife to Delia Sink. *Mt.* $14,000 and int., July 1, 1891. Oct. 20. 17,500

97th st, No. 155, n s, 154 w 3d av, 17x100.11, five-story brk flat. Henry Dale and Kate L. his wife to Thomas R. Hughes. *Mt.* $10,000. Oct. 19. 10,000

106th st, Nos. 106 and 108, s s, 125 w Columbus av, 50x100.11, two five-story brk flats. John C. Barth and Mary G. his wife to Bertha Candidus, Brooklyn. *Mt.* $42,000. Oct. 16. See 116th st. nom

107th st, Nos. 67-75, n s, 97 w 4th av, 81x100.11, five three-story brk and stone dwell'gs. William S. Cooper to Meyer L. Sire. All liens. Sept. 21. nom

111th st, No. 12, s s, 119 e 5th av, 18x100.11, five-story stone front flat. Samuel H. Goodenough to Carrie wife of Ellis Morris. *Mt.* $15,000. Oct. 21. See 116th st. 19,000

115th st, Nos. 216 and 218, s s, 250 e 3d av, 50x100.11, two five-story stone front flats. Frederick Schuck and Mary his wife to George Schuck. Oct. 21. nom

115th st, n s, 400 w 11th av, 50x100.11, vacant. Partition. William B. Winterton referee to John H. Waydell. Oct. 21. 9,000

116th st, No. 323, n s, 266.6 e 2d av, 16.6x100.11, three-story stone front dwell'g. Carrie wife of Ellis Morris to Samuel H. Goodenough. *Mt.* $7,500. Oct. 20. See 111th st. 12,500

Same property. Samuel H. Goodenough to Isabella M. wife of John B. Johnson. *Mt.* $7,500. Oct. 21. 12,500

116th st, Nos. 6 and 8, s s, 50 w 5th av, 50x51, five-story brk flat. Release mort. Morris Steinhardt to William Radebold and Edward Wenz. Oct. 19. 3,000

Same property. William Radebold and Albertine his wife and Edward Wenz and Anna his wife to Matilda Henry. *Mt.* $22,000. Oct. 14. 35,000

116th st, n s, 90 w Park av, 100.10x100, two-story frame buildings and vacant. Bertha wife of Pantaleon Candidus, Brooklyn, to John C. Barth. *Mt.* $22,000. Oct. 15. See 106th st. nom

118th st, Nos. 52-60, s s, 240 w 4th av. 100x100.11, five five-story brk flats. Release. Marie Masche to Samuel Harris and Bernhard Ginsburg. July 14. nom

118th st, n s, 210 w 5th av, 100x100.11, vacant. Daniel Hennessey to Frank A. Seitz. *Mt.* $12,000. Oct. 15. nom

119th st, No. 408, s s, 94 e 1st av, 17x100.10, three-story stone front dwell'g. Forec'os. Benjamin W. Franklin to William H. Harrison trustee James Harrison dec'd. Oct 16. 5,600

119th st, No. 412, s s, 128 e 1st av, 17x100.10, three-story stone front dwell'g. Foreclos. Same to same. Oct. 16. 5,400

119th st, No. 410, s s, 111 e 1st av, 17x100.10, three-story stone front dwell'g. Foreclos. Same to same. Oct. 16. 5,000

122d st, No. 254, s s, 86 w 2d av, 14x75, three-story stone front dwell'g. Matilda wife of Newbury R. Minor to Hedwig Volgenan or Volgenau. *Mt.* $5,000. Oct. 15. 8,000

124th st, No. 100, s e cor 4th av, 30x100.11, five-story brk flat. Robert Wallace and Mary his wife to Simon Sultan and Leon B. Ginsberg. *Mt.* $40,000. Oct. 22. See 69th st. exch

127th st, Nos. 256, 258, 260, 266 and 268, s s, bet 7th and 8th avs. Release from trust deed with consent of judgment creditors appended. Hiram R. Steele, Brooklyn, Henry S. Redmond, New York, S. Hedding Fitch, Yonkers, to John K. Sloane and Lizzie T. Wray heirs of John Sloane. Sept. 19. nom

130th st, No. 20, s s, 143.4 w Madison av, 16.10x99.11, three-story brk dwell'g. John W. Aitken and Helen P. his wife to Matilda Minor. *Mt.* $11,500. Taxes 1891. Oct. 17. 15,000

131st st, No. 23, n s, 285 w 5th av, 25x99.11, five-story brk flat. Henry Hawkes and Flora A. his wife, Greenwich, Conn., to Charles Bitz and Elizabeth his wife. *Mt.* $17,000. Oct. 16. 25,000

131st st, No. 25, n s, 310 w 5th av, 25x99.11, five-story brk flat. Same to Karl Mueller. *Mt.* $17,000. Oct. 16. 25,250

Same property. Release mort. Emeline Johnston to Henry Hawkes. Oct. 19. nom

Same property. Release mort. Timothy Flood and Edward Frederich to same. Oct. 17. consid. omitted

132d st, s s, 460 w 5th av, 50x99.11, vacant. George F. Johnson and Emma his wife to Andrew T. Judge. Oct. 16. 14,500

133d st, No. 157, n s, 250 e 7th av, 25x99.11, five-story brk flat. Charles F. Schultz and Sarah his wife to Daniel Rabold. *Mt.* $19,000. Oct. 9. other consid. and 3,000

133d st, Nos. 222 and 224, s s, 416.8 w 7th av, 33.4x99.11, two five-story brk flats. Foreclos. John H. V. Arnold to Wallace R. Eickhoff. Oct. 21. 35,200

Same property. Wallace R. Eickhoff to Robinson Gill. *Mt.* $30,000. Oct. 21. nom

135th st, Nos. 21-33 } begins 135th
Madison av, Nos. 2162 and 2164 } st, n w cor Madison av, 150x99.11, seven three-story brk stores and dwell'gs on 135th st and two three-story brk stores and dwell'gs on av. Henry A. Cram and Kathrine S. his wife to John S. Cram. Q. C. Oct. 10. nom

136th st, n s, 90 e 8th av, 585x99.11, one and two-story building, rest vacant. George R. Hamilton and Irene F. his wife to Thomas C. Van Brunt. C. a. G. Oct. 17. 187,200

136th st, Nos. 154-162, s s, 150 e 7th av, 83.4x99.11, five three-story stone front dwell'gs. Stephen J. Wright and Susan A. his wife to Jarvis B. Smith. July 30. nom

138th st, s s, 550 e 6th av, 73.2x69.1x134.8x136.2, vacant. J. Seaver, Edward A. and George B. Page exrs. Thomas Page to James McClenahan. Oct. 21. 8,000

144th st, No. 466, s s, 100 e Amsterdam av, 21x99.11, three-story brk dwell'g. Release judgment. Emma H. Worcester to Harriet De Forest. Oct. 12. nom

Same property. Release judgment. Samuel Clark to Harriet and William H. De Forest, Jr. Oct. 13. 250

Same property. Release mort. Alfred P. Dix and John J. Phyfe, of Dix and Phyfe, to Harriet De Forest. Oct. 12. nom

Same property. Harriet wife of William H. De Forest, Jr., to George S. Evans. *Mt.* $13,000. Oct. 18. 18,250

147th st, No. 455, n s, 231.3 e 10th av, 18.9x99.11, three-story brk dwell'g. Rosanna Havanagh, Newcastle, N. Y., to Ann J. Carroll. *Mt.* $9,000. Oct 21. nom

147th st, No. 467, n s, 669.11 e Amsterdam av, 14.10x99.11, three-story stone front dwell'g. Charles S. Andrews and Mary J. his wife to Edward K. Billings. *Mt.* $7,000. Oct. 22. 17,000

165th st, n s, 270 e 10th av, 20x60.1x20.3x63.4, three-story frame (brk front) dwell'g. Mary Duggan to Casper Muller and Anna his wife, joint tenants. *Mt.* $3,500. Sept. 29. 5,000

182d st, n s, 150 w 10th av, 25x150.
Amsterdam (10th) av, e s, opposite 182d st, runs north 36 x east 150 x south 37 x west 150.
Mary L. Snowden, Fairfield, Conn., to Susan A. Van Tagen. June 30. nom

Amsterdam av } begins Amsterdam av, s w cor
Boulevard } 87th st, runs south to centre
87th st } line bet 86th and 87th sts, x west 332.10 to Grand Boulevard, x north along same to 87th st, x east — to beginning, one and two-story brk and frame buildings and vacant. John O. Baker and Lucy D. W. his wife, Newark, N. J., to Alfred M. Hoyt. *Mt.* $76,000. Oct. 19. nom

Amsterdam av, No. 72, w s, 25.5 s 63d st, 25x100, five-story stone front tenem't with stores. Henry Schweitzer to Christina wife of Henry Schweitzer. *Mt.* $20,000. Oct. 16. nom

Av B, No. 251, e s, 88.3 s 16th st, 26.6x88, five-story brk tenem't with stores. Rose wife of Charles F. McCabe to said Charles F. McCabe. Oct. 10. gift

Av D, Nos. 130 and 132, e s, 26.8 n 9th st, 52.10x101.11, two five-story brk tenem'ts with stores. David Michelson and Lena his wife and Abraham Michelson and Sarah his wife to Simon M. Bernstein. All liens. Oct. 19. nom

Lenox av, No. 196, e s, 19.8 s 120th st, 17.6x85, three-story brk dwell'g. Terence J. Duffy and Jane E. his wife to Isaac White. Oct. 16. 24,000

Lexington av, No. 736, w s, 40.5 s 59th st, 20x75, four-story stone front dwell'g. *Mt.* $10,000.
Lexington av, No. 725, e s, 32 n 58th st, 18.5x76, four-story stone front dwell'g.
Mary E. McCabe to John Casey. Oct. 10. See 81st st. 45,000

Madison av, No. 1035, e s, 22.2 n 79th st, 20x77, four-story stone front dwell'g. E. Clifford Potter and Margaret S. his wife to Henry Dale. *Mt.* $29,500. Oct. 21. 36,000

Madison av, No. 801, e s, 82.5 n 67th st, 18x84, four-story stone front dwell'g. Foreclos. Eugene S. Ives to James A. Mahoney. Sub. to mort. Oct. 15. 8,400

Pleasant av (Av A), No. 361, s w cor 119th st, 17.7x75, four-story brk (stone front) flat with stores. Sarah T. Boulger to Moses Lehmann. *Mt.* $10,000. Oct. 20. 15,000

South 5th av, No. 185, e s, 64.8 s Broome st, 21.2x62.6x20.5x62.6, two-story brk store.
Broome st, No. 495, s s, 41.8 e South 5th av, 21x64.10x21x64.9, three-story brk store.
John Heyzer and Elizabeth his wife, Brooklyn, to Thomas R. Hughes. *Mt.* $34,000. Oct. 15. See 66th st. 50,000

Same property. Thomas R. Hughes, Weehawken, N. J., to George F. Betts. *Mt.* $34,000. Oct. 16. consid. omitted

South 5th av, No. 185 } begins Broome st, s s,
Broome st, No. 495 } 41.8 e South 5th av, runs south 64.9 x west 41.6 to South 5th av, x south 21.2 x east 62.6 x north 85.3 to Broome st, x west 21. Thomas R. Hughes, Weehawken, N. J., to George F. Betts. *Mt.* $34,000. Oct. 16. val. consid

Vermilyea av, e s, 100 s Hawthorne st, 125x150. Julius J. Lyons and Constance H. his wife to Martin Schrenkeisen. *Mt.* $4,050. Oct. 16. nom

West End av } begins West End av, n e cor
97th st } 97th st, runs north 200.4 to
98th st } 98th st, x east 100 x south 100.2 x east 25 x south 102.2 to 97th st, x west 125. Release mort. William W. Scott exr. Ann E. Walker. Charles, Adrian, William, Matthias, Daniel, Charles H., Lucinda W., Mary L. and Margaret J. Feltner to Edward Kilpatrick. Oct. 2. 90

West End av, Nos. 771-779, s w cor 103d st, 100.11x79.3, five three-story brk and stone dwell'gs.
103d st, No. 308, s s, 139.3 w West End av, 20.2x100.11, three-story brk dwell'g.
Welcome R. Steinmetz to Celia M. wife of Edward P. Schell. All liens. Oct. 15. nom

West End av, Nos. 485-489, w s, 50.8 n 88th st, 50x100, three four-story brk dwell'gs. Frank L. Smith and Magdalene his wife to Richard G. Platt. *Mt.* $——. March 12. 85,000

West End av, No. 487, w s, 66.8 n 88th st, 18x100, four-story brk dwell'g. Richard G. Platt to Alonzo Kimball. Oct. 21. 25,000

1st av, Nos. 778-784, s e cor 44th st, 100.5x150.
44th st, s s, 150 e 1st av, 200x100.5.
43d st, n s, 150 e 1st av, 200x100.5.
One, two and three-story frame and brk cattle sheds, slaughter-houses and stables.
Justus L. Bulkley and Laura E. his wife, Thomas G. Ritch and Maria E. his wife and Henry B. Vaughan and Lucy M. his wife to Sidney Ward, Brooklyn. Q. C. Oct. 1. nom

Same property. Justus L. Bulkley et al. exrs. Daniel B. Fayerweather to same. Oct. 1. 190,000

Same property. Release dower. Lucy Fayerweather widow to same. Oct. 9. nom

1st av, No. 603, w s, 74.1 n 34th st, 24.8x70, four-story brk tenem't with stores. John Brodbeck and Johanna his wife to Peter Gauss. *Mt.* $11,000. Oct. 19. 14,000

2d av, No. 1602, s e cor 50th st, 20.5x63, three-story brk (stone front) store and tenem't. Hermen Uher exr. Esther Herzog to Frank and William Herzog. Oct. 16. 25,000

2d av, No. 1687, w s, 100.8 s 88th st, 25x75, five-story stone front tenem't with stores. James Higgins and Annie his wife to Meta Haack and Henry Gerken exrs. Johann C. Haack. All liens. Oct. 12. nom

2d av, No. 2454, e s, 40.7 s 126th st, 20.8x100, five-story stone front tenem't with stores. Rosa wife of and Godfrey Isaacs to Rosalie Seligman. *Mt.* $20,000. Oct. 20. 25,250

3d av, No. 714, w s, 24.11 s 45th st, 25.6x95, four-story brk store and tenem't. Foreclos. Thomas F. Donnelly to Walter Longman. Oct. 22. 27,200

11th av, No. 898, e s, 50.5 s 62d st, 25x100, five-story brk tenem't with stores. Bertha wife of and John B. Smith to James E. Hoctor. *Mt.* $15,000. Oct. 21. nom

Interior lot, 200 e 10th av and 100.5 n 53d st, runs north 75.5 x east 25.3 x south 71.6 x west 25. Catharina Mehlig widow and devisee of John Mehlig to Peter Gallagher. Q. C. Oct. 15. nom

The Hyatt property, Kingsbridge, adj Isaac Dyckmans and lying on Spuyten Duyvil Creek and Harlem River, abt 80 acres.

Meadow land and land under waters of Harlem River and Spuyten Duyvil Creek and which is bounded as follows, n s of inlet to Dyckmans Canal, at point 182 w of 9th av and 51 n 222d st, runs east and north along exterior line to Kingsbridge, x northwest to point in exterior line opposite east cor of I. Dyckmans land, and which point is 276.1 w of w s of 9th av if extended, x south 68.9 to common high water line, x — following curves of high water line to s s of 222d st, and at point 202 w of w s 9th av on Randalls map, x south 150 2 to beginning.

Land under Water Spuyten Duyvil Creek at point 65.2 s of 228th st, runs southwest along said line to point 92.10 n of n s 226th st, x east 97.8 to high water mark, x east to south cor Isaac Dyckmans land at point 65.2 s of 228th st, x west 224.

Parcel of meadow on Spuyten Duyvil Creek, late part of Isaac Dyckman property, 57 to upland of grantees, x97x150x116x130x167 along creek, x220, contains 3 roods, 5 perches.

George H. McLean and ano. exrs. James M. McLean to John McK. Camp. 1-2 part. July 7. 130,000

Same property. John McK. Camp to Hugh N. Camp and Daniel E. Seybel. B. & S. *Mt.* $200,000. Sept. 19. nom

Same property. Joseph H. Godwin and Phebe A. his wife to John McK. Camp. ½ part. July 7. 130,000

MISCELLANEOUS.

All part of mortgaged lands lying east of a line drawn parallel with Amsterdam av and 116 east therefrom. Release mort. Morris Steinhardt to John Casey. Oct. 10. nom

23d and 24th WARDS.

Arcularius pl, n s, 499.6 e Gerard av, 25x100. Thomas W. Surridge to Harvey S. Armstrong. Sept. 1. 1,000

Arcularius pl, n s, 474.6 e Gerard av, 25x100. Same to William H. Fearns. Sept. 1. 1,000

Arcularius pl, n s, 474.6 e Gerard av, 75x100. Eliza Sutcliffe widow to Thomas W. Surridge. Aug. 31. 2,550

Arcularius pl, n s, 524.6 e Gerard av, 25x100. Thomas W. Surridge to John P. Hogan. Sept. 1. 1,000

Broadway, e s, 100 n Columbine st, 100x100. Elizabeth Stricker formerly Messmer, Albert Edward Stricker and Alwine his wife and Matilda Stricker heirs Robert Stricker to Carl E. Randrup. Sept. 1. 3,000

Clifton st, s s, 53.5 w Tinton av, 21.9x76.2. Richard F. Kennellie to Jacob Joung. *Mt.* $1,825. Oct. 14. 2,500

Forest st, w s, 200 n Rock st, 25x100. James F. Sheridan, Patrick H. Sheridan and Kate his wife, James S. Segrave and Catharine A. his wife to Mary E. wife of John H. O'Brien. Oct. 1. 550

Forest st, w s, 352.7 n Rock st, 25x100. Same to Amaziah Lockwood. Oct. 15. 550

Forest st, w s, 175 s Beech st, 25x100. Same to John Schwartz. Oct. 1. 550

Frederick st, w s, 203 s Pelham av, 50x87.6. Mary E. Murphy to Harry P. Clary, Jersey City. Oct. 20. nom

Holly st, n s, 140 w Katonah av, 40x100. David H. Lenox, Plainfield, N. J., to Amanda Warner, Ludlow, Vt. *Mt.* $400. October 16. nom

Jacob st, s w cor Frederick st, 25x100. Edward Reilly and Maria A. his wife to Thomas Kane. Sept. 28. 1,000

Mott st, s s, 61.10 e Terrace pl, 25x100, h & l. William Cohen to Joseph Gottlieb. *Mt.* $900. Oct. 15. 4,000

Oakley st, s s, 100 w Kepler av, 50x100. Release mort. Annie R. Weeks to Andrew Arvidson. Oct. 15. 400

Rock st, n s, 100 e Cornell pl, runs north 125 x east 19.3 x southeast 9 x south 117.8 to st, x west 25. James F. Sheridan, Patrick H. Sheridan and Kate his wife and James S. Segrave and Catharine A. his wife to George Mink. Oct. 1. 540

Summit st, s s, 168.4 e Marion av, 25x100. James H. Havens to Walter E. Andrews. Oct 12. 850

Ursula or Pond pl late 3d av, w s, lot 85 map of part John Cromwell farm, Fordham, 81x137.6x27x125. James Wood and Hariett his wife to Herman H. Maack. Oct. 20. 2,500

Woolf st, s e cor Sedgwick av, 25x80. Matthew Kyle and Sarah his wife to Smith W. Devoe. Oct. 13. 700

134th st, s s, 150 w Alexander av, 25x100. Release mort. The Bradley & Currier Co. (Lim.) to Frederick Rohrs and Louisa his wife. Oct. 16. 1,750

Same property. Release mort. Catherine Hasselbach to same. Oct. 16. nom

Same property. Release mort. Bradley & Currier Co (Lim.) to same. Oct. 16. nom

Same property. Frederick Rohrs and Louisa his wife to M. Dasher Wylly, Bayonne, N. J. *Mt* $12,000. Oct. 16. nom

145th st, s s, 125 w Brook av, 25x100. John Schramm heir John Schramm dec'd to Annie E. Volderauer. Oct. 10. 1,200

154th st, n s, 170 w Washington av, 25x100. Catherine Wurz to Lizzie Wurz. ½ part. Aug. 31. 200

165th st, n s, 50.4 w Sheridan av, 25.8x109, h & l. Janet wife of and George W. McAdam to Peter Benz. Oct. 20. 5,000

170th st, s s, 119.9 w Franklin av, 18.11x128x18.10x124. Jacob Seabold and Carolina his wife to Arthur Arctander. ½ part. All liens. Sept. 30. nom

173d st, n s, 100 e Jerome av, 50x100. Contract. Julius Kasmeyer to Emma Seitz. Oct. 8. 4,500

Av B, s s, 300 n Cedar st, 25x100, error. William Cohen to Joseph Gottlieb. *Mt.* $1,500. Oct. 15. 4,500

Anthony av, w s, 720.6 n Southern Boulevard, 25.1x82.4x25x83.8. Michael Kirwan and Mary T. his wife to George A. Noonan. Oct. 19. 400

Anthony av, w s, 745.9 n Southern Boulevard, 25.1x81.1x25x82.4. Same to James F. Geoghegan. Oct. 17. 400

Anthony av, w s, 770.10 n Southern Boulevard, 25.1x79.10x25x81.1. Same to Olof W. Chell. Oct. 17. 400

Arthur av, s e s, north ½ of lot 68 map of N. Jarvis, Jr., Upper Morrisania, 25x102. John McKnight and Mary his wife to Robert Koch and Caroline his wife, joint tenants. *Mt.* $850. Oct. 10. 2,500

Crotona av, w s, 50 s Lebanon st, 50x100.
Crotona av, w s, 25 n Lebanon st, 50x100.
Prospect av, s w cor Oakland pl, 25x100x25.1x100.
John J. Brady and Jennie M. his wife to John Owens. Oct. 19. 4,475

Fordham or 3d av, e s, south ½ lot 7 map of Monterey, &c., 25.1x265x25x—, except part taken for widening the av. Honora Grogan widow and devisee Owen Grogan to Mary Selford. Oct. 21. 3,000

Franklin av, No. 1315. Grant of easement in sewer pipes. Lucy R. Comfort to Alice F. Randall. Oct. 17. nom

Jefferson av, s e s, lot 196 map of S. Ryer homestead, 24th Ward, 25x105 to Ryer pl, x 25x100. Jacob Rumsteck and Louise A. his wife to Frank Ranisteck. Oct. 19. 1,200

Madison av, e s, 270 s Fitch st, 54x115x54x112. Phinny and Samuel E. Ayres and Kate L. Watkins to William Ferschild. Oct. 14. nom

Marian av, lot 161 and s e part lot 160 map B. Berrian farm, Fordham, 76x150 to right of way, x76x148. Clarissa A. Ennis, Brooklyn, to Joseph E. Ennis. Sept. 1. 3,500

Opdyke av, s w cor 1st st, runs south 83.7 x west 117.7 x south 25 x west 25 x north 100 to av, x east 177.3. Henry Franz and Mary his wife to Laura T. Keller, South Mt. Vernon. *Mt.* $1,800. Oct. 21. nom

Perry av, n w cor Mosbolu Parkway, 89.6 to lands of Jerome Park R. R. Co., x137 to Parkway, x144.7. Emanuel C. Bach and Ephraim B. Levy to Charles F. Langschmidt. *Mt.* $265. Oct. 15. 1,200

Prospect av, e s, 300 n from n w cor lot 67 map of Woodstock, abt ½ mile from railroad depot, 25x142.1x28.8x150.8. John Donohue to James J. Hart. Oct. 20. 1,400

Same property. John H. W. Killeen and Katrina his wife to John Donohue. Q. C. Aug. 4. nom

Sheridan av, e s, lots 221 and 222 map Inwood, 50x110.2x51.1x12.0. Release mort. Joseph O. Brown trustee to Thomas L. Reynolds. Oct. 8. 1,400

Same property. Thomas L. Reynolds to Isidor Grayhead. Oct. 14. 2,000

Same property. Kate O'Hara to Thomas L. Reynolds. Confirmation deed. Sept. 24. nom

Tinton av, e s, 126.9 s 168th st, 17.6x132.6x15.6x132.6. Julius Grossmann, Jr., and Adeline his wife to Julius Krus. Oct. 10. nom

Same property. Julius Krus to Julius Grossmann, Jr., and Adeline his wife. B. & S. Oct. 17. nom

Tremont av, n w cor Prospect av, 44x103.4. John J. Brady and Jennie M. his wife to Henry Gerken. Sub. to proceeding to change line of st. Oct. 19. 3,600

Tremont av proposed, n s, 25 e Clinton av, 75x100, with land bet proposed n s Tremont av and present old north line of Locust av, &c. Same to Ignaz Modry. Oct. 19. 4,850

Tremont av proposed, n s, 60 w Prospect av, 50x95.
Elmwood pl, s s, 100 w Prospect av, 23x120.1.
John J. Brady and Jennie M. his wife to John A. Gray. Oct. 19. 4,025

Walton av, n e cor 149th st, 70.11x54.10x80.10x43. Release mort. Mary A. T. More to William Ormiston. Oct. 10. nom

Webster av, proposed, s w cor Travers st, 28.6x93.10x45.3x91.11. Mary E. Monoghan widow to Mary Conlon. Oct. 19. 2,750

Webster av, s w cor 174th st, 25x86. Martha wife of Eugene Schaefer to Georg Baumann. *Mt.* $1,800. Oct. 17. 1,500

Willard av or st, n s, 275 e 2d st or Katonah av, 50x100. Walter C. Bellows and Lydia A. his wife to Abram G. More. Oct. 14. 800

1st av, s e s, 237.6 n e Highbridge st, 75x200 to brook, x 78.8x210.
1st av, s e s, 200 n e Highbridge st, 37.6x210 to brook, x 37.6x200.
Adam Keefer, Westfield, N. J., and Regina E. wife of James H. Noyes, Orange, N. J., Alice L. wife of Ernest C. Brown, Minneapolis, Minn., and Doris A. Keefer, Minneapolis, Minn., to Charles H. Dietz. Aug. 25. 4,500

8th av, lot 25 map Mount Eden, 50x100. Contract. Julius Kasmeyer to Louisa Labro. Oct. 2. 7,000

Highbridge road, n w s, 87.9 s w Kingsbridge road, 45x5 still along road, x 106.6 x 1.9x43.3 x106 6. Rose wife of Charles F. McCabe to said Charles F. McCabe. Oct. 10. gift

LEASEHOLD CONVEYANCES.

Attorney st, e s, 175 s Delancey st, 25x100. Assign. lease. Sarah Hodes to Hulda Hirschberg, of Hirschberg & Co. nom

Broadway, No. 765. Assign. lease. Jane McKenzie to Jane McKenzie and Alice J. Jones trustees Alexander McKenzie. nom

Division st, No. 8. Assign. lease. Henry J. Arons to Bavarian Brewing Co. nom

East Broadway and Henry st, lot 2620 tax map 1877, 1878 and 1879. Mayor, &c., New York to George B. Vanderpoel. 1,000 years. 331

Same property. Assign. lease. George B. Vanderpoel to A. K. Ely. 331

Same property Assign. lease. Ambrose K. Ely to George C. Gould exr. 560

Same property. Assign. lease. George C. Gould to Max Cohen. 607

Grand st, No. 470. Assign. lease. Julius Valenstein, Morris Valenstein and Abraham Nevins formerly Nevinsky to Hamilton McLaughlin. 10,500

Grand st, No. 470. Leasehold. Julius Valenstein and Jennie his wife and Morris Valenstein and Fannie his wife, Abraham Nevins formerly Nevinsky and Leah his wife to Hamilton McLaughlin. Q. C. July 28, 1891. nom

Maiden lane, No. 63. Assign. lease. Jonathan S. Purdy to Adolph Goebel. nom

Willett st, No. 62. Assign. lease. Budweiser Brewing Co to Bertha Hirschfeld. nom

9th st, No. 74 E. Assign. lease. Jane McKenzie to Jane McKenzie and Alice J. Jones trustees Alexander McKenzie. nom

13th st, Nos. 47-49 W. Assign. lease. Julia Chaffaujon, Charles and Eugene Lichtenberg heirs Eugenie Lichtenberg to Charles Lichtenberg the elder. nom

23d st, n s, 228 w 9th av, 22x117.6. Assign. lease. Rosella M. Kemp admr. John A. Kemp to John Kemp. 10,000

25th st, No. 142, s s, 250 w 3d av, 22x98.9. Gideon Fountain to Hugh Quinn; 21 years, from May 1, 1892, per year, 800

42d st, n s, 354.2 w 5th av, 20.4x100.5. Consent to assign. lease. Charles F. Hoffman to Henry C. Demorest. nom

45th st, n s, 190 e 8th av, 20x100.5. Charles F. Southmayd and ano. trustees for Henry Astor to Edward H. Clarke. 20 years, from Aug. 1, 1891, per year, taxes, &c., and 480

48th st, s s, 225 w 10th av, 25x100.5. Assign. lease. Lizzie G. Purcell to Mary T. wife of Michael J. Casey. ½ part. nom

Same property. Assign. lease. Michael J. Casey to Lizzie G. Purcell. nom

81st st, No. 301 E. Assign. lease. Ambrose Buechler to George Bock. nom

Amsterdam (10th) av, No. 1090. Assign. lease. John Donohue to Edward A. Fraser. nom

Amsterdam av, s e cor 102d st, store and cellar. Assign. lease. John S. Molony to William A. Armstrong. nom

3d av, n e cor 64th st, store. Assign. lease. Matthew Smith to Matthew Bruce. nom

3d av, No. 543. Assign. lease. Henry Siemering to The Clausen & Price Brewing Co. nom

8d av, No. 825. Assign. lease. H. K. Meyer to The F. & M. Schaefer Brewing Co. nom

5th av, No. 632, w s, 86.1 n 50th st, 28.8x131. Assign. lease. Burritt W. Horton and Franklin W. Allen exrs. Ethelinda V. Allen to Charles B. Rouss. nom

7th av, No. 568. Assign. lease. John Kennedy to Samuel Rosenzweig. nom

Same property. Assign. lease. The D. G. Yuengling Brewing Co. to John Kennedy. nom

KINGS COUNTY.

OCTOBER 15, 16, 17, 19, 20, 21.

Ainslie st, s s, 125 w Graham av, 25x100, h & l. Contract. Harry W. Bassett to Thomas J. Hand. $3,400

Same property. Same to same. *Mt.* $2,800. 3,400

Bainbridge st, n s, 133 e Saratoga av, 18x100.
Bainbridge st, n s, 237 e Saratoga av, 18x100,

Release mort. Joseph P. Puels to J. Mason Kirby. nom

Bainbridge st, n s, 220 e Howard av, 40x100. Charles M. Le Furge to William J. Howard. *Mt.* $1,200. 2,800

Beattie st, n e s, 375 n w New Utrecht to Flatbush road, 25x100, New Utrecht. Release mort. Henry L. Nostrand exr. George Nostrand to Jacob Brock. nom

Same property. Jacob Brock to Frederick Bareis and Maria his wife, joint tenants 1,200

Bergen st, s s, 220 e Vanderbilt av, 25x131. John F. Hill exr. John F. Hill to Robert A. Hill. 8,200

Bergen st, n s, 20 e Stone av, 18x107.2.
Bergen st, n s, 219 e Stone av, runs east 9.2 x northeast 17.5 x northwest 100 x west 2.2 x south 107.2.
Arthur H. Lowerre to George B. Lane. nom

Boerum st, n s, 422.9 e Bushwick av, 25x62.11x 25.1x64.8, h & l. George H. Dietz to Samuel Cohan. *Mt.* $2,000. 3,000

Bogert st, n e cor Ingraham st, 25x100. Charles W. Truslow admr. Wm. Wall to Margaret S. Koch. 1,875

Braxton st, s s, 97.10 e 10th av, 80x100.
18th st, s s, 240 e 10th av, 60x100.2.
Nathaniel W. Burtis to William B. Davenport. *Mt.* $2,200. nom

Broadway, north cor Vandeveer st, 75x100x75x 100.8. Henry H. Cochran to Frank A. Barnaby. *Mt.* $27,500. nom

Broadway, e s, 45 s Lawton st, 22.6x100. Fanny wife of Lewis Jacobs to Adolphus A. Newman. *Mt.* $4,500. 8,500

Carroll st, s s, 123 e Henry st, runs south 70 x east 4 x south 30 x east 41 x north 100 to Carroll st, x west 45.
President st, n s, 257 e Henry st, 40x100.
Bernard Levino to Walter F. Clayton. *Mt.* $47,000. 70,000

Cedar pl, w s, 117.11 n Malbone st, runs north 37.8 x west 86.4 x south 20.10 x southeast 24.11 x east 65.6. Amanda M. Ahlquist to Mary J. H. wife of Seaman R. Fowler, of Vineland, N. J. *Mt.* $2,000. exch

Cedar st, n s, 475 e Evergreen av, 25x81.9 to Myrtle av, x29x95.6, h & l. Herman Lonzer to Maria wife of George Heid. *Mt.* $7,-500. exch

Chauncey st, s s, 173 e Saratoga av, 19x100. Jacob Aronson to Thomas A. McWhinney. nom

Chauncey st, s s, 135 e Saratoga av, 38x100. Thomas A. McWhinney and Jacob Aronson to John Dodge, of Hempstead, N. Y. *Mt.* $10,000. nom

Chauncey st, n s, 133.4 e Stuyvesant av, 16.8x 100. Mortimer E. Weldon, of Bristol, Conn., to Alvah C. Haff. *Mt.* $4,000. 6,600

Chauncey st, n s, 150 e Stuyvesant av, 16.8x100. Same to James C. Wells. *Mt.* $4,000. 6,600

Clinton st, w s, 80.6 s Atlantic av, runs west 25 x north 0.6 x west 65 x south 25 x east 90 to st, x north 24.6. William H. Cochran to John A. Cochran. 21,000

Clinton st, e s, bet Huntington st and Hamilton av, being lot 4 block 256 on assessor's map 12th Ward. Ella Daw, of Des Moines, Iowa, to Richard Cronin. 25

Clarkson st, n s, part of lot 26 map M. Clarkson property, Flatbush, 13.9x249.10x14.4x249.9. Release mort. Brooklyn Life Ins. Co. to Eleazer S. Vaughn. nom

Collins st, n s, 86.1 e Canarsie av, 80x100, Flatbush. John E. Tousey to Sven Lewis. 900

Columbia st, w s, 80 n Carroll st, 20x80, h & l. Perico A. Canavello and Donald F. Ayres his assignee to Sarah E. Stevens. All title. *Mt.* $6,000. 3,561

Conselyea st, n s, 100 w Ewen st, 25x125. Dorothea Wakleck to John Magaw and Alice Kelly. 8,000

Covert st, s s, 144 e Central av, 36x100, hs & ls. Isabella B. wife of John N. Booth to George C. Cranford. *Mt.* $6,000. nom

Covert st, s s, 90 e Central av, 18x100, h & l. Isabelle B. wife of John N. Booth to Joseph A. Cross. *Mt.* $3,000. nom

Dean st, n s, 110 w Sackmann st, 30x107.2. Stephen W. Stoothoff to Eliza M. Stackhouse. *Mt.* $2,750 and taxes 1890. exch

Dean st, s s, 260 w New York av, 20x100. Sarah E. Fisher widow to Mamie J. Runyon. *Mt.* $8,000. 13,500

Devoe st, n s, 74.7 w Bushwick av, runs north 37 x west 4.5 x north 13.4 x west 12.5 x south 12 x south 35 to Devoe st, x east 20 to beginning, h & l. Charles W. Cooper, of New York, to Cornelia F. Bedell. nom

Degraw st, n s, 150 w 5th av, 20x98.6. Peter Kelly to Jane J. Kenzel. *Mt.* $8,000. 7,128

Decatur st, s s, 43.9 w Ralph av, 18.9x100. Foreclos. John Courtney to John C. Creveling. 4,800

Diamond st, s s, 2,193.4 e Main st, 40x177.9x40x 177.4, Flatbush. Lyman D., Julia C. and Lydia C. Calkins heirs of Lydia C. Calkins to Sarah E. Bennett. 1,120

Diamond st, s s, 2,183.4 e Main st, 10x177.4x10x 177.2, Flatbush. Same to T. Morris Terry. 280

Dumont st, n w cor Christopher av, 100x100. Johann C. Gottschaldt to Jacob Cohen. 2,200

Same property. Jacob Cohen to Harris Hellman. *Mt.* $1,400. 2,600

Eagle st, n s, 560 w Manhattan av, 75x200 to Dupont st. Theresa T. Hicks, of Alexandria, Minn., to Thomas Anderson. Q. C. nom

Eagle st, n s, 150 e Manhattan av, 25x100. George Grassick, of Maywood, N. J., to Bridget O'Brien. 4,000

Eagle st, n s, 200 e Oakland st, 25x100. Release mort. Trustees Union College to William W. Campbell. 1,000

Eastern Parkway, s s, 25 e Jerome st, 25x100, h & l. Union Real Estate Co., New York, to Wilhelmina Thompson. 3,400

Eastern Parkway, s s, 75 e Thatford av, 25x100. Andrew R. Culver to Hyman Goldberg. Taxes, &c., from 1889. 500

Eastern Parkway, n s, 25 e Thatford av, 25x100, h & l. Louis Ratner to Harris Neublatt. *Mt.* $3,500. 6,000

Elton st, w s, 300 s Sutter av, 54.4x85x50.7x85. Earl A. Gillespie, Woodhaven, L. I., to John Dowling. *Mt.* $1,300. nom

Elton st, w s, 275 s Ridgewood av, 50x100. William S. Stubbs to Rebecca A. Browne. *Mt.* $3,700. 4,200

Same property. Rebecca A. Browne to Susie W. Stubbs. *Mt.* $3,700. 4,200

Enfield st, w s, 400 n Union av, 75x314x75x315, 26th Ward. Irene Plummer, of Oyster Bay, to Charles M. Thompson. 750

Essex st, e s, 750 s Gay st, 25x100. Catharine Brown widow, Maria F. Philcox, William, Jane and George Brown and Carrie L. Schultz heirs James H. Brown to Frederick Kalb. 1,200

Essex st, w s, 200 s Ridgewood av, 20x100. Christian H. W. Lueders to Juliana wife of Christian H. W. Lueders. nom

Essex st, w s, 280 n Ridgewood av, 20x100, h & l. Adolph Weymar to Murdina B. Weymar. *Mt.* $2,800. 3,300

Ewen st, w s, 100 n Withers st, 25x100. Ida M. Voorhis to Katie Mausling. *Mt.* $1,200. 2,750

Floyd st, n s, 350 w Sumner av, 25x100, h & l. William Funk to Heinrich Stor. 3,300

Freeman st, n s, 170 e Franklin st, 25x100. Thomas Murray, of Grassy Point, N. Y., to Charlotte A. Allen. *Mt.* $1,000. 2,800

Fulton st, s s, 160.6 w Stone av, 20x100. Hoik D. Campbell and Henry G. Munger to Jennie A. Ives. *Mt.* $10,000. exch

Fulton st, s s, 180.6 w Stone av, 19.6x100. Same to same. *Mt.* $10,000. exch

Fulton st, s s, 800 w Albany av, 20x100. Release judgment. Charles E. Rogers to Asa L. Rogers. nom

Fulton st, n s, 24 w Ashford st, 24x88.5x82.6x 78. Charles Drasser to Lucy A. Fitch, of Old Chatham, N. Y. Correction deed. nom

Same property. Lucy A. Fitch to Frank J. Kunzinger. *Mt.* $3,000. 6,000

Fulton st, n e cor Elton st, 25.6x108.4x25x108.0. Mathilde Lehmann to Christian F. Nolte. 3,000

Garfield pl, n s, 143.9 w 5th av, 16x77.2x16x 77.11, h & l. Julia A. Johson formerly England, of Buffalo, to William B. Ames. *Mt.* $3,000. exch

George st, n s, 129 e Evergreen av, runs north 67.5 x due north 28.9 x southerly 80.9 to George st, x west 25.6. Henry Sauerbrunn to Charles Hoeckele. *Mt.* $2,200. 5,000

Gold st, e s, 20 n Front st, 20x54.3. Bridget A. Keyburn, of New York, to Bridget A. widow Geo. Keyburn. 530

Graham st, No. 121, e s, 25x—, h & l. Jane A. McKenna to John Warmworth. 8,000

Grove st, s e s, 525 s w Central av, 20x100. Horace Hart, of New York, to Frank Ibert. *Mt.* $500. 775

Halsey st, n s, 85 w Marcy av, 40x90. Bedford Building Co. to Melvin Smith. *Mt.* $14,000. exch

Hancock st, n s, 380 e Nostrand av, 21x100. Cornelius H. Ticbout to Frank H. Tyler. 5,800

Same property. Frank H. Tyler to Frederick B. Langston nom

Hancock st, s e s, 250 n e Broadway, 17x100, h & l. Adam Kaiser to Simon A. Weber. *Mt.* $2,500. nom

Hancock st, n s, 81 e Sumner av, 18x100, h & l. Joel F. Tyler to George A. Williams, Sharon Springs, N. Y. *Mt.* $4,000. 7,300

Hawthorne st, n s, 500.6 w Nostrand av, 40x 166.7, Flatbush. Release mort. Stephen B. Sturges to John F. Hart. nom

Same property. Release mort. Asa W. Parker to same. nom

Same property. Daniel Doody to Francis Kuhn. *Mt.* $2,500. 4,750

Hendrix st, e s, 240 n Hegeman av, 40x100. Jonathan Bicknell to John F. Bullenkamp. *Mt.* $200. 400

Henry st, e s, 60 n Union st, 20x94. George W. Leeds to Florence L. Leeds. *Mt.* $3,500. gift

Herkimer st, s s, 200 w Nostrand av, 50x185.5 to Herkimer pl. Stephen P. Sturges to George R. Brown. nom

Herkimer st, s e cor Gunther pl, 20x86. Charles Hoeckele to Henry Sauerbrunn. *Mt.* $5,800. 8,150

Herkimer st, n s, 20 w Saratoga av, 80x80.
Saratoga av, w s, 80 n Herkimer st, 40x100.
Noah Tebbets to Albert Johnston. 24,000

Same property. Release mort. Same to same. 14,200

Herkimer st, No. 28, s s, 700 w Nostrand av, 20 x92.9. George M. Rackcliffe to Henry F. Clark, Bloomfield, N. J. 3,000

Hicks st, w s, 40 n Lorraine st, runs north 60 x west 100 x south 20 x east 20 x south 40 x east 80. Joseph Foley to Thomas McGrath. *Mt.* $400. nom

Himrod st, n w s, 118.9 n e Evergreen av, 18x 68.9. George W. Chapman to Henry Knoke. 3,000

Hinsdale st, e s, 100 n Vienna av, 60x100. Edward B. Lilly, Newtown, L. I., to Annie L. wife of Maurice Quinlan. 300

Hopkins st, n s, 234.5 e Throop av, 28.4x100. Henry Roth and Joseph E. Middle to Sophie W. Steffan. *Mt.* $5,000. 10,000

Hopkins st, n s, 150 w Throop av, 25x100, h & l. Michael Schenck to Andrew Wohlgermuth and Marie his wife. 3,700

Hooper st, s e s, 234.4 s w Marcy av, 22.4x100. Abraham Mayer to Lewis A. McMillan. *Mt.* $5,000. 9,500

Hooper st, w s, 95 s South 3d st, runs west 75 x north 20 x east 25 x north 3.6 x east 50 to Hooper st, x south 23.6, h & l. Charles K. Davies to Francis E. Clark. *Mt.* $1,000. exch

Hoyt st, e s, 40 s Douglass st, runs east 60 x south 20 x west 60 x north 20; also,
Atlantic av, s s, 215.4 w Utica av, 16.8x100.
Jennie A. Ives to Hoik D. Campbell. *Mt.* $4,350. nom

Humboldt st, w s, 73 n Johnson av, 25x100. Daniel J. O'Brien and James O'Donohue exrs., &c., Daniel O'Conor, of New York, to William Meyer. 3,000

Humboldt st, e s, 50 s Cook st, 50x100, hs & ls. Franz Borowiak to Isaac Goodman and Max Karol. 11,200

Humboldt st, e s, 50 s Cook st, 25x100. Isaac Goodman and Max Karol to Meier Raff, of New York. *Mt.* $5,000. 6,300

Huntington st, s e, 258.4 w Court st, 16.8x100, h & l. Michael J. McGuire to John S. Huyler, New York. 3,500

Huron st, n s, 315 e Franklin av, 25x100. Henry Kahn to Adaline Neumann. 4,200

Jerome st, w s, 240 s Blake av, 20x100, h & l. Frederick Eiermann to Bernard Cunningham, New York. *Mt.* $1,200. 2,200

Keap st, s s, 221.4 w Marcy av. Party wall agreement. Anthony H. Creagh with James M. Richard.

Kosciusko st, s s, 285 e Nostrand av, 15x100, h & l. George P. Rowell to Caroline E. Cook. 3,500

Lorimer st, w s, 25 s Johnson av, 25x100. Release mort. Emily Oberujer to Frank Hess. nom

Same property. Release mort. Ernst Kreusler to same. nom

Same property. Frank Hess to David Stern. 2,500

Linwood st, w s, 175 s Sutter av, 25x90. George W. Ferguson to John Keenan. 500

Logan st, w s, 280 n Blake av, 20x100. William Heuss to Ehrgott Zettler. 275

Macon st, s s, 315 w Lewis av, 40x100. Release morts John F. Saddington to E. Willard Jones. 7,200

Macon st, No. 737, n s, 254.10 e Ralph av, 18x 100. James S. Johnston and Ferdinand Flatuer to Greenleaf W. Crossman, of New York. *Mt.* $4,000. 6,550

Macon st, n s, 256 w Marcy av, 19.6x100. William H. Reynolds to Arthur Boynton. *Mt.* $7,500. 18,750

Macon st, s s, 174 w Ralph av, 18x100. Walter F. Clayton to Alexander Burn. *Mt.* $4,000. 7,300

Macon st, n s, 43.9 e Patchen av, 18.9x100. Irene wife of Frederick Miller to Christiana Grau, of New York. *Mt.* $4,500. nom

Macon st, n e cor Patchen av, 25x100. Jane Miller to Edward A. Woolley. *Mt.* $14,000. 16,000

Macon st, s s, 16.8 e Marcy av, 16.8x100. Sophie W. Steffen, of New York, to Henry Roth and Joseph Middle. 7,000

Macon st, n s, 237.6 w Marcy av, 19.6x100. William H. Reynolds to William H. and Lillian Bridgman. *Mt.* $7,500. 13,750

Madison st, n w s, 200 n e Hamburg av, 20x100, h & l. Adolphus Gload to John E. Stadtmiller. 4,400

Same property. Release mort. James Gascoine individ. and with Anna E. Cozine exrs. John G. Cozine to Adolphus Gload. 1,241

Madison st, s s, 471 e Lewis av, 19x100, h & l. William G. Horton to Mary G. wife of William G. Horton. *Mt.* $4,000. nom

Madison st, n s, 350 w Ralph av, 18x100, h & l. Margaret Bossert to Patk. Brophy, of New York. 2,000

Madison st, No. 1240, s e s, 403.8 s w Knickerbocker av, 18x100. Elizabeth E. wife of Henry Wade, of Jamaica, N. Y., to Robert Schleicher. *Mt.* $2,300. 4,200

Madison st, s s, 190 e Marcy av, 20x100. Samuel D. Kelly to Charles H. Lock. *Mt.* $2,000. 3,500

Madison st, s s, 830 w Franklin av, 22.3x84 to Bedford road, x southeast 5 x northeast 27 x north 72, with all title in that part of the northeast ½ of Bedford road lying east of line 352.5 w of Franklin av, h & l. Elmira J. wife of James Young to Margaret J. Fitzpatrick. *Mt.* $2,500. 3,000

Market st, w s, 542 s Brooklyn and Jamaica turnpike, 100x150. Ferdinand Krooss to Matilda Rutzbach. nom

Maujer st, n s, 150 e Ewen st, 25x100, h & l. Salomon Herrmann, New York, to Otto Saalfeld. 6,850

Same property. Otto Saalfeld to Morris Roth. *Mt.* $4,500. 8,200

McDonough st, s s, 393.8 w Patchen av, 6.4x100. Henry B. Hill to Charles G. Reynolds. 683

McDonough st, s s, 62 e Ralph av, 19x100. Thomas H. Radcliffe to J. Paul Bonner. *Mt.* $5,500. 9,000

McKibbin st, n s, 25 w Leonard st, 25x100. Daniel Kreuder to Max Dassau. 7,200

Monmouth st, s e s, 150 s w Lexington av, 50x 125, New Utrecht. Virginia Massonnean formerly Molini, Raffaele A. and Horatio G. Molini to Joseph H. Mahan. nom

Montgomery pl, n s, 352.11 e 8th av, 17.6x84x 17.6x83.4. William B. Martin and Patrick J. Lee to Florence H. wife of Frederic B. Cochran. *Mt.* $10,000. 15,500

Monitor st, w s, 155.3 s Van Cott av, 18x100. Charles Engert to Ambrose Gasson. 3,800

Monitor st, w s, 119.3 s Driggs av, 18x100, h & l. Charles Engert to John C. Wallace. 3,800

Monitor st, w s, 191.8 s Driggs av, 18x100, h & l. Same to James H. Christie. 3,600

Monitor st, w s, 119.3 s Driggs av, 18x100, h & l. John C. Wallace to William J. Wallace. *Mt.* $1,200. nom

Monroe pl, w s, 275 s Clark st, 48.4x100, h & l. Contract. John H. Recknagle to Henry Richardson. 40,000

Monroe pl, n s, 214 6 w Pierrepont st, runs northwest 26.6x100. Clement S. Parsons, Jr., of New York, Sallie H. widow John H. Parsons, Henry C. Parsons, of Stratford, Conn., and Edward Parsons, of New Brighton, N. Y., to Mary E. P. Tood widow. 4-5 part. *Mt.* $18,000. 5,600

Monroe st, n s, 275 e Nostrand av, 16.8x100. Joseph B. Stillwell to James J. Gallagher. *Mt.* $4,500. 7,200

Monroe st, n s, 590 w Ralph av, 30x100. Richard D. Robbins to Charles Lewis. *Mt.* $10,-350. each

Monroe st, s s, 138.4 e Ralph av, 16.8x100, h & l. Elizabeth Shannon widow to Henry Holzer. *Mt.* $1,500. 4 100

Moore st, s s, 50 w Humboldt st, 25x100. Margaretha Weith to Elek Sundel, Gerson Krakower and Nathan Goldberg, of New York. 6,200

Navy st, No. 107. Assignment contract. Carmino Lemmi to Grazia L. Lemmi. nom

Newport st, n s, 75 e Osborn st, 25x100. Release mort. Gilbert S. Thatford to William Hartmann. nom

Osborn st, w s, 175 n Riverdale av, 50x100. Gilbert S. Thatford to Sarah wife of Jacob Cohen, of New York. 350

Pacific st. Nos. 387 and 389. Agreement as to encroachments. Thadeus K. Chutkowski with Belene wife of K. Lind. nom

Pacific st, s s, 83 4 e Utica av, 84.11x107.2. Henry Weil to Michael Giblin. 4,000

Pacific st, n s, 350 w 6th av, 20.1x90.11x24.11x76.2, h & l. Samuel H. Newby to Bothilda Peterson. *Mt.* $3,000. 6,000

Pacific st. No. 2295A, n s, 333 4 w Stone av, 16.8x100. James McKenna to James Cocks. *Mt.* $1,890. 2,500

President st, s s, 450.8 e 8th av, 25x100, h & l. Foreclos. John Courtney to The Metropolitan Life Ins. Co. 11,500

Pine st, w s, 90.7 n Fulton st, 25x100. Frank Ehlers to Frederick, Richard and Otto Kampf. 650

Poplar st, No. 55, n s, 77.4 e Hicks st, 22.8x25. Charles W. Smith to Ella M. Pelletreau. nom

Same property. Ella M. Pelletreau to Frank L. Tapscott. nom

Powell st, w s, 125 s Glenmore av. 25x100. John Guth to Elizabeth Augusty. *Mt.* $2,000. 3,500

Powell st late Orient av, w s. 250 n Liberty av, 25x100. Daniel Mapes, Jr., New York, to John F. Vrooman. 750

Pulaski st, s s, 100 w Reid av, 25x91.7x12x17.6x100. Mary J. Renton widow to William S. Richardson. *Mt.* $1,600. nom

Pulaski st, n s, 2 3 e Nostrand av, 18x100, h & l. Thomas R. Greenland to Anna M. wife of Peter Mangels. Q. C. Correction deed. nom

Quincy st, n s, 309.4 e Stuyvesant av, 20.4x100. Henry, John A., Edward, William and Elizabeth Schwarz and Mary Schmolze heirs John Schwarz to Louis Schwarz. Q. C. nom

Quincy st, n s, 248.4 e Stuyvesant av, 20.4x100. Henry Schwarz et al, see above, to William Schwarz. Q. C. nom

Richardson st, n s, 100 e Union av, 25x100. Jacob Hoeller to Raffaelo and Angele Depernio. 950

Rodney st, n s, 215.1 w Bedford av, 18.5x100. William H. Harrison to Ambrose M. Morgan in trust for life benefit of Sarah B. Harrison. nom

Ross st, n s, 100 e Bedford av, 19.11x100. Nellie H. Malleson to Francis Vail. 11,000

Sands st, n w cor Charles st, 25x97.6. Mary P. Haviland to George J. McFadden. *Mt.* $5,000. 10,250

Sandford st, w s, 283 n De Kalb av, 25x100. Foreclos. John Courtney, Sheriff, to John C. Tracy. 1,600

Schenck st, e s, 323 s Willoughby av, 25x67.10x25x66.11. Farenus Jackson to Benjamin Andrews. All title. B. & S. 25

Schermerhorn st, s s, 145 e 3d av, 13.6 to Flatbush av, x south 110 x west 89.7 x northwest 63 x north 108.10. George Beach, Hartford, Conn., to Percy G. Williams. 55,500

Seeley st, s e cor 20th st, 50x100, Flatbush. William E. Murphy exr. Thomas Murphy to Elias J. Reynolds, Catskill. 500

Seigel st, s s, 75 w Leonard st, 25x100. Felix Hessberg to Michael Hessberg. nom

Somers st, s s, 220 w Stone av, 15x100. Charles H. Reynolds to Morris Jacobs. consid. not given

Starr st, s e s, 288.5 s w Wyckoff av, 75x100. John Gillen to Emma Cavanaugh. 1,425

Sterling pl, s s, 204.7 e 6th av, 20x100. Eleanor G. T. wife of Edwin J. Taylor to Noah Tebbetts. *Mt.* $9,000. exch

Steuben st, e s, 157.8 s De Kalb av, 22x100. Peter Herche to Henry Baruch. *Mt.* $10,000. nom

St. Marks pl, s w s, 182.2 s e 4th av, 20x100. Amalia Grupe to Hannah Abrahams. *Mt.* $3,550. 5,050

Stanhope st, n s, 445 e Evergreen av, 20x100. Elizabeth, Albert and Mathilde Stricker and Anna L. wife of Giovanni Huber heirs Robert Stricker to Louise wife of George Newkomm 3,600

Stockholm st, s e s, 275 n e Evergreen av, 25x100, h & l. William Schildknecht, Fairfield, Conn., to Dorathea O'Hara. nom

Stockton st, s s, 450 w Lewis av, 25x100. Henry, William, John A., Louis and Edward Schwarz and Mary Schmolze heirs John Schwarz to Elizabeth Schwarz Q. C. nom

Sumpter st, Nos. 393 and 346. Release mort. Felix Kaufman to James A. Bills 500

Truxton st, n s, 283 6 e Stone av, 19 6x100. Margaret Ryan widow to Mary Barcen. 3,000

Union st, s s, 122 w Columbia st, 20.6x100, h & l. Michael and Jeremiah A. Brosnan to Timothy J. Brosnan. Q. C. gift

Same property. Timothy J. Brosnan to John Esola and James Nicholas, of New York. 4,500

Van Buren st, s s, 185 7 w Reid av, 14.5x100, h & l. Darwin R. James to Thomas F. Maguire. 3,150

Van Buren st, No. 282, s s, 251 e Lewis av, 18.6x100. Thomas B. Bryant to Anna M. Redlefsen. 6,700

Van Buren st, s s, 185.7 w Reid av, 14.5x100. Release mort. Hannah E Miller, Philadelphia, Pa., to Darwin R. James. 1,500

Verandah pl, s s, 116.1 w Clinton st, 24 6x69.9. John W. Frothingham to Edward Driscoll. nom

Warren st, n s, 50 e 3d av, 25x100. Margaretha Lewis to Hoik D. Campbell. *Mt.* $8,500. nom

Warren st, n w s, 100 n e Lexington av, 100x125, New Utrecht. Mary O'Neill to Henry Adler. 1,550

Willoughby st, n s, 107.7 e Jay st, 22.11x100. Gordon L. Ford to Joseph Wechsler. 8,000

Windsor pl, s s, 147.10 w 8th av, 16.8x100, h & l. William E. Kay to Edward F. Bulger. 3,500

Woodbine st, n w s, 25 n e Bamburg av, 350x100. James Gascoine to George W. and Charles H. Francisco. ½ part. nom

Same property. Anne E. Cozine widow individ. and with ano. exrs. John G. Cozine to same. ½ part. 9,957

Woodbine st, n w s, 145 s w Knickerbocker av, 20x100, h & l. Albert Beckmeier to Patrick Maloney and Mary E. his wife. 4,500

Same property. Release mort. James Gascoine individ. and with ano. exrs. John G. Cozine to Albert Berckmeier. 2,457

York st, s e cor Gold st, 58x75. Eliza Wood to Adelaide C. Meyers. B. & S. 10,000

2d st, n e s, 259.9 n w 7th av, 18x100. Charles G. Peterson to William E. Douglass. *Mt.* $2,000. nom

South 2d st, s w cor Havemeyer st, 18.6x84, William Quail, of New York, to James T. Quail. 5,000

South 3d st, s w s, 25 n w Wythe av, 25x65.6x25x65. Elizabeth Buchanan heir Thomas Wildman to Martin Nowak. 5,000

4th st, n e s, 297.10 n w 8th av, 100x95, h & l. Foreclos. Alfred F. Britton to Henry B. Spencer. 1,000

East 5th st, e s, 320 s Av W, 64.2x126x132.9x105, Gravesend. Agnes N. Lake to Sarah A. Moore. 1,400

North 5th st, n s, 180 w Bedford av, 20x100, h & l. Richard Schlepegrell, Rockville Centre, L. I., to Patrick Murray. 3,300

6th st, s s, 245.10 e 6th av, 17x100, h & l. George W. Powell to Harriet Powell. *Mt.* $6,000. nom

7th st, n e s, 166.7 s e 4th av, 18.9x100. Louis Bonert to Julia Hickey widow. *Mt.* $3,000. 6,100

7th st, s s, 129.10 w 7th av, 17.8x100. Nellie M. wife of Frederick O. Ernesty to Jane E. wife of James N. Richards, of Montclair, N. J. *Mt.* $5,000. 8,300

8th st, s s, 115.4 w 8th av, 17x100, h & l. Margaret S. Elliott, West Woodstock, Conn., to James Johnson. *Mt.* $5,000. 7,500

East 8th st, w s, 240 n Av E, 100x120.6, Flatbush. Joseph W. Wechsler to Margaret Doheny. 1,265

South 8th st, n s, 74.6 w Bedford av, 0.6x80. John C. C. Gatje and Ida C. Fedden exrs. Olchior L. Fedden and Ide C. Fedden individ. to Jacob S. Van Wyck. 500

10th st, s s, 210 e 3d av, 20x100. Thomas A. Kerrigan to Emilie A. Giese. *Mt.* $3,500 4,500

10th st, s s, 210 e 3d av, 20x100. Emilie A. Giese to Ewald F. Giese. *Mt.* $3,500. 4,500

13th st, n s, 196 w 3d av, 20x100. John Howard to Charles E. Brown. 1,325

13th st, s s, 497.10 e 5th av, 25x100, h & l. }
13th st, s s, 522.10 e 5th av, 0.2¼x100. }
Elizabeth A. wife of William Lundequist to Frances A. Van Wart, New York. 4,000

14th st, s w s, 273 n w 3d av, 16x90. Joseph Smith to Hugo Hoffmann. 1,760

14th st, s w cor 9th av, runs west to 8th av, x south 189.1 x east to 9th av, x north 194.9, except the s e cor thereof taken by commissioners of Prospect Park. Clarissa M. Baker widow, George, Thomas D., Harvey J., Joseph D., Emily J. and Clara Baker, Annie E. wife of Wilbur F. Smith, all of New York. William Baker, of Montclair, N. J., heirs of Harvey Baker to Ross C. Browning, of Orange, N. J. ¼ part. nom

18th st, s s, 391.8 e 6th av, 20x100. Annie wife of and Thomas A. Gallagher, of New York, to Maria Carroll. ½ part. 1,000

19th st, s s, 241 w 5th av, 15.6x100.2. Henry C. Bull to Thomas N. Bowles. *Mt.* $1,500. 2,750

19th st, s s, 85 e 5th av, 40x100.2. Ralph Kirkman to Peter Thomas, of Hempstead, N. Y. *Mt.* $4,750. exch

East 19th st, w s. 425 n Av B, runs south to land late of Stapleton, x—, gore, Flatbush. Cornelius J. Bergen exr. John C. Bergen to William Matthews. 10

20th st, n s, 85 e 5th av, 40x200.4 to 19th st. Frank A. Mulford and James R. Robb to Ralph Kirkman. Sub. to all liens. Correction deed. nom

21st st, s s, 225 w 5th av, 25x100.2. Ellen Gilmartin widow to John Anderson and Andrew Sundell. 1,200

Same property. Release mort. Catharine C. Spies to Ellen Gilmartin 1,000

24th st, s s, 300 e 3d av, 50x—. Patrick Murphy to James Devlin. 2,100

27th st, n e s, 125 n w 5th av, 25x100.2 Foreclos. John F. Bullwinkel to Louise Parrot. 1,500

Bay 31st st, s e s, 260 n e Benson av, 60x96.8, New Utrecht. Mary J. Brown, Elizabeth, N. J., to Frederick B. Opper. *Mt.* $840. 1,450

32d st, No 214, s w s, 133 4 n w 5th av, 16.8x100.2. Henry Klee to Conrad Ericson. 2,800

38th st, n s, 85 e 5th av, 40x100.2. Annie Wiggin to Catherine A. H. Holmgren nom

39th st, s s, 400 w 3d av, 16.8x100.2, h & l. Lizzie M. wife of John G. Burke to Olive A. Williamson. *Mt.* $2 000 3,500

40th st, n s, 120 w 4th av, 20x100 2. Catharine L. McCollum to Thomas Brady. 3,300

42d st, s s, 168.8 e 3d av, 16.8x100 2. Pierre Rocier to Marcelino wife of William Werner. 2,400

43d st, n e s, 250 s e 12th av, 50x100.2, New Utrecht. George W. Stevens to Mary J. Conklin. *Mt.* $270. 700

48th st, n s, 200 e 4th av, 20x100.2. John L. and George W. Craig to Mary Hall. *Mt.* $600. 1,100

50th st, s w s, 160 n w 8th av, 20x100.2. Charles A. Larson to Peter F. Holmgren and Peter O. Wahlman. 200

50th st, n s, 240 e 3d av. 100x100.2. Bessie A. Foley, of New York, to Henry Manue. *Mt.* $3,170. 3,750

52d st, n s, 384 w 3d av, 18x100.2. William S. Hasson to Sarah A. Tibbitts. *Mt.* $2,500. 4,300

53d st, s s, 117 6 w 3d av, 17.6x100.2, h & l. Harriet Martin widow to John Anderson. *Mt.* $2,000. 3,050

54th st, n s, 120 w 4th av, 40x100 2. Release mort. James G. Carroll to Peder A. Larsen 1,000

54th st, n s, 80 w 4th av, 20x100.2. Peder A. Larsen to Raphael Klucken. 4,850

56th st, s s, 180 e 3d av, 20x100.2. Charles Mount to Richard McCurdy. *Mt.* $2,500. 4,500

56th st, s w s, 175 n w 14th av, 175x100.2, New Utrecht. West Brooklyn Land and Improvement Co. to William E Kay 3,500

56th st, n e s, 360 n w 13th av, 40x100.2. Margaret A. Killaughey to George H. Barber. 650

57th st, s s, 200 e 3d av, 20x100.2. Thomas Dunn to Michael Meehan. Sub. to mort. 825

57th st, s w s, 420 n w 8th av, 20x100.2, New Utrecht. Charles W. Lundqvist to Dorothea F. Gundberg. 200

57th st, s s, 220 w 2d av, 40x100 2. Release mort. Edward T. Hunt to Christina Gillman. 378

Same property Christina Gillman to John H. French. 1,300

67th st, s s, 380 e 14th av, 20x120, Lefferts Park. Effingham H. Nichols to Louise F Coates. 275

67th st, s s, 140 e 11th av, 20x130, New Utrecht. George R. and Eva Lund, Paul C. and Emilie Forst to Samuel Loring. 100

73d st, n e s, 170 s e 15th av, 40x100, New Utrecht. Sarah J. Butler, New York, to Abraham C. Lutkins. 600

75th st, n s, 610 w 15th av, 40x200 to 74th st, New Utrecht. James V. S. Woolley to John S. Hamilton. 670

75th st, s s, 450 w 15th av, 40x100. James V. S. Woolley to Martha E Lawson. 350

76th st, n e s, 180 s e 12th av, 260x100, New Utrecht. Hoik D. Campbell to Murray W. Ferris, of Roselle, N. J. 2,925

80th st, s w s, 380 s e 12th av, 60x100; also, }
74th st, s w s, 400 s e 12th av, 40x100, New Utrecht. }
Hoik D. Campbell to James W. Ferguson. 1,125

83d st, n e s, 280 s e 23d av, 60x100, Bensonhurst. James D. Lynch to Mary C. Hamilton, New York. 900

83d st, north cor 24th av, 60x100. Bensonhurst. James D. Lynch to Elbert H. Gammans. 1,200

83d st, n e s, 100 s e 19th av, 60x100, Van Pelt Manor. John L. Nostrand to Louis K. Taylor. 1,050

83d st, s w s, 370 n w 22d av, 60x100, New Utrecht. James D. Lynch, of New York, to Edwin L. Faris. 1,050

84th st, centre line, gore, bounded west or northwest by Second Division line of New Utrecht woodlands formerly J. C. Stillwell's, and south by heirs of N. Stillwell.

Interior gore, bounded northwesterly by line 300 northwest of centre line 11th av, northeast by centre line bet 83d and 84th sts, and south by land late of N. Stillwell's heirs.

11th av, south cor 83d st, centre lines, gore lot, bounded south by land late of Court and Maria Stillwell.

Lot bounded northwest by line 100 northeast (?) of 11th av, southerly by land late of Court and Maria Stillwell and F. A. Guuz, east by land late of V. Cropsey and north by land late of Caroline M. Stiles, New Utrecht.

Jane E. wife of Frederick H. Johnson to Ira O. Miller, New York. 1,677

84th st, s w s, 150 n w 23d av, 60x100, Bensonhurst. James D. Lynch to Lewis H. Lipman. 1,050

93d st, n e s, 185 n w 3d av, 25x100, New Utrecht. William Bell, Sr., to William Bell, Jr. 425

Alabama av, n w cor Glenmore av, 100x200 to Williams av. William Kammann exr. Henry Kammann, of Jamaica, to Louis L. Happ and Bernhard J. Pink. 6,000

Albany av, w s, 72.3 n Butler st, 16.8x85.

Charles S. Taber and George C. Case to Mary A. Henderson. *Mt.* $8,500. exch

Arlington av, s e cor Ashford st, 40x100. Emily Keith to Matilda L. Bolles, of Bayport, Conn. *Mt.* $5,000. 9,000

Atlantic av, s s, 20.6 w Williams av, 20.4x93.4x20x89.5. Matilda L. Boiles, of Bayport, Conn., to Emily Keith. *Mt.* $4,000. 8,000

Bay Ridge av, s s, 590 w 15th av, 20x100, Lefferts Park. James V. S. Woolley to Oscar Johnson. 280

Bedford av, n e cor Jefferson av, 21.1x100. Peter W. Hoeft to Robert J. Smith. *Mt.* $8,000. 25,000

Bedford av, s e cor Degraw st, runs east 134.8 x south 127.9 x west 135 x northwest 30.10 to av, x north 107.2.

Bedford av, e s, 22 n Degraw st, runs north 108.4 x east 102.11 x south 127.9 to Degraw st, x west 40 x north 21.6 x west 84.1 to beginning.

Rogers av, w s, 21.6 n Degraw st, 106.3x100. Charles J. Maguire to Julia E. Carroll. ⅚ part. Sub. to morts. $6,000. nom

Belmont av, n e cor Osborn st, 50x100. Semche Simon, of New York, to Solomon Wolff and Louis Ratner. *Mt.* $875. 2,700

Blake av, n s, 100 e Schenck av, 25x100. Jared J. Chambers to Irving J. Smith, New York 250

Bushwick av, southerly cor Aberdeen st, runs southwest 90 x southeast 20 to Hull st, x northeast 79.2 to Manhattan Branch R. R., x north 28.1 to av, x northwest 190.6. Louisa F. wife of John Reilly to Dennis Sheehan. Sub. to all liens. nom

Bushwick av, e s, 28.1 n McKibbin st, 28.1x100x26.7x98.9. William Fassnacht to Anton and Helena Stahl. *Mt.* $12,500. 13,250

Bushwick av, s w s, 72 s e Lawton st, 18x73.11. Ann wife of and John Officer to John Pack. 6,800

Bushwick av, southerly cor Cornelia st, 40x90. William P. Clark to Abram Cooke. nom

Central av, s w s, 25 s e Jefferson st, 25x100. Henry Eppig to Joseph Theiling. 6,100

Central av, n e s, 70 n w Himrod st, 38.7x100x40x100. William H. O'Hara to Edward Houston. *Mt.* $3,000. 4,500

Christopher av, e s, 200 n Belmont av, 25x100, h & l. Joseph Berger to Samuel Meshel. 160

Christopher av, e s, 100 s Blake av, 25x100. Peter Lawrence to Jacob Cohen. 500

Christopher av, e s, 100 s Blake av, 25x100. Jacob Cohen to Solomon Pfeffer. 550

Clinton av, n e s, 281.2 s e 3d av, 25x100, New Utrecht. Thomas Henry to Margaret wife of Thomas Henry. ½ part. nom

De Kalb av, n s, 50 e Throop av, 25x100. May A. Lyon to Michael K. Wilson. *Mt.* $9,300. exch

De Kalb av, n s, 72.8 e Kent av, 22x100. John H. Rowland to Benjamin J. Brown nom

Flushing av, n s, 75 e Vandervoort pl, 25x80.11. George Gutting to Michael Lehmann. *Mt.* $5,500. nom

Flushing av, s s, 250 e Nostrand av, 25x100, h & l. Harriet Hershatsky to Pincus Mendelsohn. *Mt.* $5,000. 10,300

Franklin av, w s, 325 s Park av, 25x108.4. Sarah Huggins to Frances Ferguson. 4,900

Franklin av, w s, 57 n Jefferson av, 17.2x80. Hannah Horn to Jemima Horn. *Mt.* $2,500. nom

Gates av, s s, 135 e Sumner av, 20x100. Edward Michaelis to Alfred L. Beasley. *Mt.* $4,500. 7,500

Gates av, s s, 285 w Marcy av, 20x100. William S. Ames to Julia A. Johnson, Buffalo *Mt.* $5,000. other consid. and 1,000

Gates av, n s, 126 w Reid av, 20x100. Julius A. Tonner, of New York, to A. Stewart Walsh. Sub. to mort. nom

Graham av, e s, 50 n Seigel st, 25x100. Elise Hesselberg to Louis Kaufman and Benjamin Benjamin. 9,500

Same property. Louis Kaufman and Benjamin Benjamin to Bertha Zeiser. *Mt.* $7,000. 10,500

Grand av, w s, 311.9 n Lafayette av, 16.2x100. Partition. Walter G. Rooney ref. to Margaret W. Loeble formerly Wilson. 4,450

Gravesend av, n e cor Woodside av, runs north 100 x west 10 x south 50 x west 86 to Gravesend av, x south 50, Gravesend. John S. Ryder to Michael Daly. 1,000

Gravesend av, e s, adj B. Doyle on south, 50x86, h & ls, Gravesend. George W. Bennett to Michael Daly. 2,000

Greene av, s s, 235 e Central av, 25x100, h & l. George Lovett to Patrick Maguire. 6,500

Greene av, n s, 310 w St Nicholas av, 20x100. Mary E. Maloney to Albert Berckmeier. nom

Greene av, s s, 100.8 e Wyckoff av, 20x100. Theodore Aubke to Joseph Schneider. 900

Hamburg av, e s, 75 s Suydam st, 25x100. Catharine Meyer formerly Schmelzer, Valentine and Sophia Schmelzer to John Eich. Q. C. nom

Hamilton av, s e s, 100 s w Lexington av, 25x116.3, New Utrecht. Charles Krauss to John McNaught. 400

Hopkinson av, w s, 150 s Baltic st, runs west 100 x north to centre of block bet Baltic and Butler sts, x west 25 x south 127.9 to n s Butler st, x east to n s East New York av, x northeast to w s Hopkinson av, x north —. Anna G. wife of Sidney Williams to Rebecca F. Furman. 2,000

Same property. Release mort. John E. Lovely to Anna G. Williams. nom

Hudson av, w s, 75 n Front st, 25x80. Jane McLeat to Robert Gair. 8,000

Irving av, n e s, 50 n w Greene av, runs northeast 90 x northwest 39.10 x northeast 10 x northwest 5.4 x southwest 100 to av, x southeast 50. Charles A. Cross to Heinrich Schneider and Catharine his wife, joint tenants. 2,950

Jefferson av, n e cor Tompkins av, 23x80.3, h & l. Ernst Hinck to Christian Cornehlsen. *Mt.* $8,000. 21,000

Jefferson av, s s, 308.4 e Reid av, 16.8x100. Marshall J. Couch to John Mitchell and Charles Herr. exch

Jefferson av, No. 1057. Contract. Henry Fuehrer to Alexander H. Mathesius. nom

Jefferson av, n s, 122 w Franklin av, 21x100. David Taylor to John D. Taylor. *Mt.* $4,000. 1880. 8,000

Jefferson av, n s, 250 w Stuyvesant av, 100x100. Adaline B. wife of Thomas B. Saddington to Daniel B. Norris. nom

Kent av, n e s, 150.1 n w Wilson st, 25x102.11x25x101.7. Alfred Hodges and John Rawson to Frederick G. Feldhus. 3,000

Kent av, e s, 525 n Myrtle av, 25x100. Benjamin W. Winans et al. exrs. William W. Winans to James Feeley. 5,000

Kingsland av, e s, 76.7 s Bennett st, runs east 97.11 x south 25 x west 25 x south 50 x west 34 x north 17 x west 51.1 to av, x north 61.3, h & l. Peter J. Hoffman to August Speth and Mina his wife, joint tenants. *Mt.* $1,000. 3,200

Kingsland av, w s, 125 s Herbert st, 25x100. George W. Sammis to Daniel J. Collins. 1,600

Lafayette av, n e s, 600 s e United States av, 50 x abt 170.4x50.1x abt 170.2, New Utrecht. Theodore F. Hascall to Owen Brady. 800

Lafayette av, n s, 350 e Tompkins av, 25x100. Charlotte B. Cogswell to George W. Heatley. 3,000

Lafayette av, s s, 375 e Reid av, 16.8x100. Hattie L. wife of and Wm. F. Berner to Matthias Johnston. 2,800

Lafayette av, s s, 147.10 e Throop av, 18.9x100, h & l. Waldemar Zimmermann to Walter G. Rogers. *Mt.* $3,000. 5,550

Lexington av, Nos. 280 and 282, s s, 100 e Nostrand av, 40x100, hs & ls. Clarissa A. Ennis to Joseph E. Ennis. *Mt.* $3,500. 5,000

Lexington av, n s, 326 e Reid av, 34x100. Edwin S. Updike, Sr., of New York, to Bertha M. Ensley. *Mt.* $11,500. 15,750

Liberty av, s s, 40 e Milford st, 80x90. Effingham H. Nichols to Courtland V. Anable, Castleton, S. I. 1,800

Liberty av, n w cor Christopher av, 50x100, h & l. Charles H. Cowan to Herman Stahl, Newtown, L. I. 2,420

Liberty av, s w cor Van Siclen av, 20x100. George Schwarz and Henry Seiler to George Sommers, of New York. 100

Livonia av, s w cor Christopher av, 100x229.6. Bernard J. Pink to Nathan Nelson, New York. *Mt.* $1,800. 3,800

Metropolitan av, s s, 75 e Catharine st, 25x100. Adolphus D. Pape, of New York, to Richard P. Monzani. ⅓ part. nom

Same property. Julian T. Monzani to Richard P. Monzani. 1,800

Same property. Richard P. Monzani to John H. Pape, of New York. *Mt.* $3,000. 3,500

Montauk av, e s, 150 s Hegeman av, 20x100. William H. Jackson to Joseph Abrahams, New York. 175

Montauk av, w s, 140 s New Lots road, 40x100. Jeremiah O'Brien to Mary E. O'Brien. nom

Same property. Mary E. O'Brien to Ellen C. wife of Jeremiah O'Brien. nom

Morgan av, w s, 50 s Harrison pl, 25x100. Catharine wife of Nicholas Dannenhoffer to John Herckes. *Mt.* $3,500. 7,100

Myrtle av, n s, 350 e Sumner av, 25x100. Henry Roth to Louise Wagner. *Mt.* $9,500. exch

Myrtle av, s s, 225.2 e Broadway, 25x103.1x27x94.9, h & l. Charles Drebold to William F. Gruesser. 8,100

Myrtle av, s s, 250.2 e Broadway, 25x113.2x26.8x103.3. Salomon Wolf to Carl J. M. Berendsen. 8,400

Myrtle av, s s, 155.3 e Willoughby av, runs east 100.7 x southeast 59.10 to Suydam st, x southwest 125.11 x northwest 56.9 x east 4.10 x northeast 64.6 to beginning. Release mort. Henry W. T. Mali, of New York, to Edward Hendrickson. 9,000

Same property. Jacob May to Charles Wagner. 10,650

Nassau av, n s, 40 e Monitor st, 30x80. James D. Lynch to Martin Harnist. 5,600

Nichols av, w s, 75 n Union av, 85.9x90. Alonzo Reed, of Quogue, N. Y., to Thomas D. Wills. 2,400

Norman av, s e cor Jewel st, 75x95. Thomas Ross to John J. Cashmann. 4,000

Park av, s s, 39.9 w Adelphi st, runs south 29.10 x west 20.5 x north to Park av, x east 20.11. John J. Drake to Emma R. Glading. 2,650

Putnam av, n s, 42.6 w Sumner av, 17.6x100. Harriet S. Cooke to E. Willard Jones. *Mt.* $6,250. Taxes, &c. nom

Putnam av, s s, 154.6 e Ralph av, 24.6x100. Alfred L. Beasley to Edward Michaelis. *Mt.* $9,000. 13,500

Putnam av, s s, 305 e Stuyvesant av, 19x100. Charles Isbill to Albert Morris. *Mt.* $4,500. 8,700

Putnam av, s s, 275.6 e Reid av, 19.6x100. Charles Lewis to Richard D. Robbins. *Mt.* $4,500. nom

Putnam av, s s, 210 e Stuyvesant av, 95x100. Charles Herr to John Mitchell ½ part. B. & S. nom

Putnam av, n s, 151 e Stuyvesant av, 18.7x100, h & l. Same to same. ½ part. nom

Putnam av, n s, 169.7 e Stuyvesant av, 18.7x100. John Mitchell and Charles Herr to John C. Remick. nom

Putnam av, s s, 22 e Tompkins av, 18.6x100. Sophia wife of and William Egginton to Charles F. Herbert. *Mt.* $4,500. exch

Ridgewood av, s s, 75 e Cleveland st, 25x100. James E. Vincent to Elizabeth Hewitt. 3,400

Saratoga av, s w cor Fulton st, 80x100. Noah Tebbetts to Albert Muir. 25,750

Saratoga av, e s, 22 n Marion st, 19x78. Release mort. John W. Phelps to Eva Hyers. 6,063

Schenectady av, s w s, abt 60 s e Fulton st, 18x50, h & l. Clarissa A. Ennis to Joseph E. Ennis. 1,500

Schenck av, e s, 192 n Arlington av, 41x100. Release mort. Frederick Middendorf to Sebastian T. Hollister. nom

Same property. Sebastian T. Hollister to Mary C. Hollister. 2,300

Schenck av, e s, 162 n Arlington av, 70x100. Release mort. Elizabeth M. Rapalje to Sebastian T. Hollister. 2,000

Schenck av, e s, 162 n Arlington av, 30x100. Sebastian T. Hollister to Frank C. Lang. nom

Shepherd av, w s, 55 n Blake av, 50x100. M. Annetta wife of and Frank G. Davison to L. A. Shattuck, of New York. *Mt.* $1,750. 900

Shepherd av, e s, 175 n Stanley av, 40x100. William H. Jackson to Henry Farrer or Fauer or Faner. 353

Shepherd av, e s, 95 n Stanley av, 40x100. Same to Limothea King. 303

Shepherd av, w s, 200 n Liberty av, 25x100. John Lynch to Jacob Buhrer. 700

Skillman av, s s, 125 w Graham av, 25x100. William Meyers to James Farrell. *Mt.* $1,000. 2,300

Snediker av, e s, 225 s Glenmore av, late Baltic av, 25x100. Ellen wife of John Taylor to John A. Johnson, New York. C. a. G. exch

St. Marks av, n s, 240 e Rochester av, 85x127.9. William H. Dill to Charles J. Schriefer. *Mt.* $500 3,200

St. Marks av, n s, 200 w Nostrand av, 40x125. Jacob G. Dettmer to Stephen M. Randall. 8,250

St. Marks av, n s, 40 w Carlton av, 20x78.6. Foreclos. John Courtney to Henry V. Raymond. 6,419

Stanley av, n e cor Berriman st, 20x95. Robert B. Logan to Francesco Margaruci. 225

Stewart av, s s, 33 w Denyse st, runs west to Shore road, x south 48 x south 57.3 x south 66.10 x east 289.6 x east 29.3 x north 39.11 x west 98.9.

Stewart av, s s, 319 w Denyse st, and being the intersection with w s Shore road, runs along said road 38 x south 160.10 x south 35 x west 62.9 to high-water mark New York Bay, x north 239.7 x east 24.9 x east 42.6, with all title to land under water, beginning at Stewart av, s s, at high-water line New York Bay, runs southwest 311.10 x south along pier line x 234.4 northeast 772.3 to high-water line x 239.7, with Grand View Hotel furnished.

Brooklyn City R. R. Co. to Adolph Ruehl. *Mt.* $70,000. 8,

Same property. Release mort. Kings Co. Trust Co to Brooklyn City R. R. Co. nom

Stone av, e s, 125 n Sutter av, 25x100. Herbert C. Smith to Jacob Axelrod and Isaac Levingson. 600

Sutter av, n w cor Linwood st, 90x100. Jane Holehouse to Thomas Doyle. *Mt.* $450. 2,050

Sutter av, s w cor Essex st, 24.7x100x24.1x100. William A. Northridge to Henry Riekers, of New York. 4,200

Sutter av, n s, 50 e Hinsdale st, 75x100; also, Christopher av, w s, 125 n Sutter av, 75x100. John F. Smith to Medad Smith. Sub. to morts. nom

Thatford av, e s, 150 s Livonia av, 50x100. Gilbert S. Thatford to Walentan Nowak. 600

Thatford av, w s, 200 n Glenmore av, 100x100.1. Thomas F. Maguire to Darwin R. James. *Mt.* $1,500. nom

Thatford av, e s, 200 n Riverdale av, 25x100. Pauline and William Hartmann to Frank Grosshart. *Mt.* $1,375. 1,675

Throop av, e s, 23 s Hancock st, 19.1x81, h & l. Charles F. Herbert to Sophia Egginton. *Mt.* $8,000. exch

Union av, e s, 26.3 n Conselyea st, 25x100. William H. Treyz and Herman Schumacher exrs. Louisa F. Treyz to George I. W. Peth. nom

Vanderbilt av, w s, 42.7 s Fulton st, 18.9x100. Alexander H. Shipley, of Rockwood, Cal., to Emma J., Elizabeth and Samuel H. Shipley. All title. 1,500

Van Siclen av, w s, 175 n Glenmore av, 25x100, h & l. Alfred Wegner to James A. Henry. 2,300

Vernon av, s s, 162.6 e Throop av, 18.9x80. Christiana Grau to Hartman Bernhart. *Mt.* $3,900. 7,145

Willoughby av, s w cor Clason av, 23.3x66.11x23.3x65.11. Edward M. Parmelee, Catskill, New York, to William L. Van Alstyne, Troy, N. Y. *Mt.* $8,000 and taxes 1891. exch

3d av, s e s, bet 15th and 16th sts, 23x106 to Gowanus road, x27.6x116. Minnie C. wife of Henry Nelson to John D. Jordens. *Mt.* $2,400. 2,500

5th av, s e s, 39.7 n e 7th st, runs southeast 70 x southwest 19 x northwest 17.10 x southwest 0.2 x northwest 18.2 x southwest 0.6½ x northwest 54 to av, x northeast 19.9. Mary Martin widow to Smith S. Brown. *Mt.* $5,000 8,000

6th av, east cor 5th st, 100x87.10. Edward H. and Grace D. Litchfield individ. and as trustees for Henry P. Litchfield to Louis Bonert. 11,500

6th av, west cor 4th st, 100x80. Same to same. 11,000

6th av, w s, 84 s 6th st, 16x78.10. Henry Roth to James F. G lien. Mt. $5,000. nom

6th av, w s, 36 s 6th st, 16x78.10. Same to same. Mt. $5,000. nom

6th av, s w cor 6th st, 20x78.10. Noah Tebbetts to Eleanor G. T. Taylor. Mt. $7,000. exch

6th av, n w s, 86 s w 6th st, 16x78.10; also, 6th av, n w s, 68 s w 6th st, 32x78.10. William P. Wagner to Henry Roth. Mt. $15,000. exch

6th av, w s, 25.2 s 52d st, 75x100. James W. Manson to James G. Carroll. 1,400

7th av, Nos. 153 and 155, e s, 40.9 n Garfield pl, 57.6x80. Margaretta Armstrong, Patchogue, L. I., to Margaret Herrick. Mt. $30,000. 31,000

8th av, e s, extends from 14th to 15th st, 200x 422.10. John L. Blake, of Orange, N. J., and Henry D. White, of New Haven, Conn., to Ross C. Browning, of Orange, N. J. B. & S. nom

Same property. Ross C. Browning to Nassau Land and Impt. Co. 57,000

9th av, e s, 20 s 18th st, 20x85. Mary E. wife of Joseph D. Huggins to Daniel L. Bennett. Mt. $3,500. 4,500

10th av, n e cor 72d st, 100x100, New Utrecht. The Bay Ridge Park Improvement Co. to Lydia O. Remy. 2,000

11th av, e s, 120 s 67th st, 40x100, Bath Junction. James V. S. Woolley to Henry T. Endom. 350

14th av, north cor 70th st, 60x100, New Utrecht. Release mort. Claus Doscher and Henry Offerman to Irving R. Williams. 500

14th av, n w s, 60 n e 72d st, 60x100, New Utrecht. Release mort. Same to same. 390

14th av, west cor 73d st, 60x100, New Utrecht. Release mort. Same to same. 390

14th av, north cor 70th st, 60x100, New Utrecht. Irving R. Williams to Henry U. Cochran nom

14th av, westerly cor 73d st, 60x100, New Utrecht. Same to same. nom

14th av, n w s, 60 n e 72d st, 60x100, New Utrecht. Same to same. nom

Interior lot, 76 2 n Pacific st and 250 w 6th av, runs north 28.9 x west 20.2 x south 9.1 to s w s old Flatbush pike, x southeast —. Samuel H. Newby to Bathilda Peterson. nom

Lot 441 block 24 map No. 2 of 660 lots Cowenhoven farm, New Utrecht. Effingham H. Nichols to Annie M. Barnett. 155

Lots 575–580 inclusive block 27 same map. Same to Henry F. Risch. 780

Lot 530 block 26 same map. Same to Charles Weber. 125

Lots 608 and 609 block 27 same map. Same to Owen Lynam. 250

Lots 201 and 202 block 21 map 2 of 660 lots Cowenhoven farm, New Utrecht. Effingham H. Nichols to Max Schmidt, New York. 360

Lots 214, 227 and 228 block 21 map 2 of 660 lots Cowenhoven farm, New Utrecht. Effingham H. Nichols to James Wasson. 575

Lot 520 block 12 map 520 lots part of the homestead Peter Rapelje. Release mort. Jane E., Samuel M. and A. L. Meeker exrs., &c., Samuel M. Meeker to Julia E. Browne. nom

Lot 332 block 23 map 2 of 660 lots Cowenhoven farm, New Utrecht. Effingham H. Nichols to Laliah Shearman, Long Island City. 180

Two parcels of land in New Utrecht. Mary E. and S. D. Stillwell exrs. N. R. Stillwell and Mary E. Stillwell individ. to Jane E. Johnson. 1,000

Four parcels of land in New Utrecht. William H. Stillwell et al. legal representatives of Stephen N. Stillwell dec'd to Jane E. Johnson. nom

Parcel in New Utrecht, adj V. Cropsey, 1 rood 20 5-6 perches. James R., Catharine A. widow, George and Anna M. Stillwell, Ellen J. Voorhees, Ida wife of Elias H. Ryder to Jane E. wife of F. H. Johnson. Q. C. nom

Road from Flatlands to The Neck and Canarsie, n w s, 182.9 n e Hubbard st, 86.3x524 2x87x 513.2, being 1 acre 5 36-100 perches, Flatlands. Partition. John H. Kemble to Lewis J. Worth. 3,180

Same property. John J. Hegeman trustee for Rosa Hegeman to Lewis J. Worth. B. & S. nom

Bay or Narrows high water mark, adj T. T. Cortelyou, 130 acres, with water rights, fisheries, &c., New Utrecht. Catharine M. Morrison to The Dyker Meadow Land Improvement Co. nom

Shore road, e s, lots 30 and 31 map of N. L. Martin Bennett and others, Bay Ridge, 82.3 x89.6x118.10.
Shore road, e s, lots 36, 37 and 38 same map, 60x209.11x84x153.10.
Henry Mackay to Isabella D. wife of Henry Mackay. nom

Skidmores lane, east cor Brooklyn & Rockaway Beach R. R., 50x353x55.8x353.4, Canarsie. Hermann Lohmann to Herman G. Boedicker. Mt. $2,500. 4,500

Strip for highway which lies bet the w s of the Main road in Flatbush and the w s of Flatbush av as laid out, &c. Amelia or Emilie Doerrer to The Town of Flatbush. 4,733

Mean high water mark on line, bet lands under water of W. H. Perkinson and grantor herein, which points is 507.2 w of w s Narrows av, runs west 1,017.10 to pier line, x south 186.4 x east 1,199 2 to n s of T. G. Bergen's property, x north 52.6 to right of way, x east 144.2 to w s Shore road, x north following curves of road, — x west 130.10 x north to point opposite point of beginning, x west —, being land under water New York Bay. George J. Bryan to David S. Beasley. nom

Coney Island road, n s, 60 w West 1st st, 40x 109.4x40x110.11, Gravesend. Lena Frederick to Ida A. Keechler. 1,200

Rockaway Inlet, n s, 95.11x715x95.1x750, with use of road adj premises on north, Barren Island.
Tract on Barren Island, on n s Rockaway Inlet, 95 11x750, with use of road as above, with docks, &c.
John J. White to Henry B. White. ½ part. nom

Plot in Canarsie on line bet I. Skidmore and J. Johnson, runs southeast along Johnson land to land of George Biggs, x northeast — to H. Lohmann's, x northwest to land of Skidmore, x southwest —, with right of way to East 92d st. Timothy V. Anderson to Hermann Lohmann. 125

Plot bounded west by Stone av, north by Eastern Parkway as now reduced to 80 feet wide, east by Christopher av and south by line 275 south from s s Eastern Parkway. George W. Palmer to James A. and Henry F. Shepherd, of New York. Mt. $12,000. 18,000

Plot in New Utrecht bounded north by land Catherine M. Stiles and grantee, west by the Second Division line of Woodlands and land Zebulon Furman and land G. R. Stillwell, south by land Ira O. Miller, east by land The Bay Ridge Park Improvement Co. Charles M. and M. Louise Stillwell widow to Jane E. Johnson wife of Frederick. Q. C. nom

Same property. John S. Ryder and Maria and Phebe Stillwell and Ann Cortelyou to same. nom

General release and receipt in full for legacy. Magdalena Pfeiff et al. heirs Christian and Magdalena Sailer to Christian Pfeiff exr., &c. nom

General release. Margaret McNamara individ. and as extrx. Daniel McNamara to St. Joseph's Institute for the Improved Instruction of Deaf Mutes. 25,000

General release, especially from legacy. Peter Hess to Frank Hess. 530

WESTCHESTER COUNTY.

OCTOBER 14 TO 20—INCLUSIVE.

EASTCHESTER.

Bard, Wm. H. to Jas. A. Varian, lot 21 map Washingtonville. $1,200

Berry, John to Wm. H. Burkelman, n s Mt. Vernon av, 75 e Bond st, 48 6x100. 3,800

Brown, Wm. I. to Emilie L. Brown, lots 17 and 18 Vernon Park and 24 map Northwest Mt. Vernon. nom

Cranford, Kenneth to Geo. Leier, lot 97 s Vernon Park, 25x134. 1,000

Chivvis, Ferd. W. to John C. Crevier, e s Fulton av, 388 n W. P. road, 100x113. nom

Grey, Sarah E. to Geo. W. Corson, lots 35 and 36 map Wright property, Tuckahoe. 800

Jennings, Maria to Frances L. Ferris, lot 515 w s 6th av, Mt. Vernon, 100x105. 2,000

Tier, Jennie L. to Frank N. Glover, lot 78 n s Valentine st, Central Mt. Vernon, 50x100. 7,000

Underhill, Henry M. to Sarah F. Daniels, lots 70, 71, 74 and part 73 map lots at Tuckahoe. 2,100

Walkley, Geo. to Teresa Saporita, lot 1 s e s W. P. road map 17 lots South Mt. Vernon. 1,250

Wright, Kate L. to Robt. T. Grey, lot 19 map Wright property, Tuckahoe. 400

Wilkinson, Jas. to Geo. H. Walker and ano., lot 295, West Mt. Vernon, abt 87x200. 975

GREENBURGH.

Linke, Theo. to Gustav A. Linke, s s Spring Park av, adj I. H. Barker. nom

Same to same, n s same av. nom

Same to same, 1 acre on Saw Mill River road, adj Ph. Conrad. nom

Same to same, abt 8¾ acres adj Herman Linke. nom

LEWISBORO.

Lawrence, Jane A. to Wm. H. Banks, 100 acres adj Jas. F. Lawrence. 6,000

MAMARONECK.

Bradley, And. R. to Henry Winter, s w cor Railroad and Ward avs, 25x97. 1,450

Gedney, Jos. H. exr. of, to Wm. H. Gedney, e s 3d av, adj Jas. B. Gedney, 50x—. nom

Rooke, Mathew F. to Frank A. Rooke, lot 71 Spencer map. 500

Rooke, Frank A. to Elmira Rooke, same property. 500

Southwick, Minnie B. to Annie L. McCabill, n s Oak av, 116 e Prospect, 128x100. 6,000

MOUNT PLEASANT.

Blackwell, Wilson H. to Kate E. Hatch, lots 40–46 and 65 map Mallory estate. nom

Egan, Jos. P. to Penina Hunter, e s Washington st, adj Sarah Mabie, 54 7x190. 2,000

Mallory, Frank B. to Wilson H. Blackwell, w s Bedford road, 23 acres. nom

Smith, Wm. R. to Walter M. Knox, lots 58 and 59 block 3 map Lake Kensico. 260

Smadbeck, Louis to Sarah May and ano., lots 1788 and 1789, Sherman Park. 336

Same to Hugh M. Byron, lot 2284. 200

Same to Anton Aurada, lots 1660 and 1661. 350

Same to Frank Aurada, lot 1662. 200

Same to Wm. Rosenbusch, lot 1205. 250

Same to Americo Rodriquez, lot 1288. 175

Same to Cath. Donohue, lots 253 and 254. 250

Same to Chas. Betz, lot 547. 100

Same to Conrad Beier, lot 550. 100

Same to Louise Weigert, lot 1708. 200

Same to Harriet E. Torrence, lots 1222 and 1223. 300

Same to Annie Schumann, lot 1704. 200

Same to Patrick O'Sullivan, lots 1700 and 1701. 450

Same to Annie Meir, lots 88, 89 and 90. 375

Same to Hugh Logan, lot 1325. 150

Same to J. H. Stankler, lots 1227 and 2230. 345

Same to Wm. H. Seebeck, lots 1086, 1087 and 1088. 375

Same to Gustav Wenzler, lots 39–42. 400

Same to Wm. Richardson, lots 1836 and 1837. 300

Sames to Jas. H. Gannon, lots 1186 and 1187. 300

Same and ano. to John Lichtman, lots 185 and 186, Lakehurst. 400

NEW ROCHELLE.

Gregg, Jas. A. S. to Wm. Reddy, lot 49 grantor's map, 50x125. 500

Hudson, Alex. B. to Maurice Kingsley, lot 29 e s Highland av, 50x234. 500

Iselin, Adrian, Jr., to Robt. P. Carpenter, lot 28 e s Neptune av, 70x135. 1,500

Latour, Jerome B., Jr., to Wm. L. Sanders, s w s Clinton av, 50 s e Bancker pl, 50x150. 2,300

Miller, Mary E. to Florence N. Knowles, s e s Bancker pl, 150 s w Centre av, 50x150. 2,000

Morgan, Susan M. to Arthur W. Sherman, s w cor Division st and Washington av, 150x250. 7,675

Porter, Sarah M. to Kate Eusinger, lot 10 n s Morris st. 800

Ryley, Madeline L. to Francis Wilson, part lot 67 n e s Meadow lane, Residence Park, 50x 205. 3,000

PELHAM.

Belden, Wm. to The Belden Point Co., all grantors property at City Island. 200,000

POUNDRIDGE.

Dixon, Aug. exr. of, to Jacob Siebert, 151 acres s s Bedford road. 3,750

RYE.

Melarkey, Daniel to Julie E. Peck, lot 2 map estate Laban Russell. nom

Merritt, Jas. S. to Patrick O'Malley, n w cor Prospect and William sts, 100x100. 575

Same and ano. to Conrad F. Ingman, lot 35 n s Ellendale av, Washington Park, 50x150. 187

Same to Alfred F. Osborn, lot 90 n w cor West William and Lyon sts, 50x100. 245

Same to same, lot 103 n e cor West William and Merritt sts, 50x100. 227

SCARSDALE.

Hayes, Amelia E. to Geo. W. Lyons, 108 acres on Hutchinsons River. 65,000

WESTCHESTER.

Bussing, John, Jr., to Thos. R. Thorn, lots 499 and 500 s s 7th and n s 6th sts, Unionport, 100 x216. 350

Camp, Hugh N. to Francis Hagen, lot 338 map McGraw estate. 235

Cooper, Margt. et al., J. B. Lockwood ref., to Jos. Newman, lots 38 and 37 e s Cooper av, 50x100. 210

Same to Jos. Gallagher, lots 26–29 e s Franklin av, 100x100. 1,820

Dexter, Fred. C. to John Young, part lot 610 n s 4th av, Wakefield, 25x114. nom

Young, John to Margt. Young, same property. nom

Harlem Building and Loan Assoc. to Wm. B. Morrison, e s 3d av, 150 n 1st st, Olinville, 50 x100. 3,650

Hughes, Miles to John Groverk, w s Dean pl, 75 n Hilton av, 50x100. 400

King, Martin J. to Herman H. Fiedderman, lots 181–186 map McGraw estate. 2,500

Lowenstein, Louis to John A. Wesp, e s Ferris av, Throggs Neck, 6 acres. 4,600

Mapes, John S. to Longin Fries, s s Maitland av, 330 w Mapes, 25x140. 255

Mace, Levi H. to Dennis R. Sheil, lots 515 and 551, Wakefield. nom

Same and ano. to Mary F. Creney, lots 34 and 35 n s Ash av, Laconia Park. 500

Same to Lavinia Cudlipp, lots 39–43. 800

Same to Emma L. Shirmer, lots 36, 37 and 38. 600

Newman, Jos. and ano. to Henry Dauer and ano., s s 4th st, 205 w Av B, Unionport, 100 x216. 1,200

Shirmer, Chas. D. to Geo. H. Love, lots 79 and 80, Bronxwood Park. 3,200

Same to Chas. H. Love, lot 81. 1,500

Williams, Henrietta to Wm. Callaghan, e s 1st av, 200 n 1st st, Olinville, 100x100. 3,000

WHITE PLAINS.

Moore, Wm. to John H. McArdle, e s Court st, 97.6 s Quarroppas st, 48.9x125. 5,000

YONKERS.

Briggs, Chas. C. to Chas. Bescher, w s Willow st, 225 s Poplar, 50x103. 1,650

Bruce, Geo. W. to Hungarian, &c., Church of St. Nicholas, n s Ash st, 150 e Oak, 50x100. 1,400

Curtiss, John E. to Fred. B. Knowlton, e s Belleville av, 614.6 n Robert av, 100x326. 900

Drinkwater, Jane to Wm. J. McLester and ano., s s Ash st, 310 e Oak, 50x100. 650

Gramatan Park Co. to Theo. S. Todd, lots 85, 86 and 87. 2,250

Shounard, Fred. to Mary T. Kiely, lots 227 and 196 Woodland av, City map. 330

Same to Jos. T. White, lot 157 Lake av. 300

Scott, Jane exr. of, to Fanny Scott, s s Morris st, 149 e Riverdale av, 40x75. 7,500

Sutherland, Leslie to Thos. A. Kettleman, lot 75 w s Beech st, 25x100. 400

YORKTOWN.

Degnau, Jas. E. to Barney D. Millen. n s New York & Boston R. R., adj Gen'l Montrose, 490x240x290. 725

Sammis, Warren B. to Labolt Richard, 82 acres, adj Ezra J. Palmer. 2,500

MORTGAGES.

NOTE.—*The arrangement of this list is as follows. The first name is that of the mortgagor, the next that of the mortgagee. The description of the property then follows, then the date of the mortgage, the time for which it was given, and the amount. The general dates used as headings are the dates when the mortgage was handed into the Register's office to be recorded.*

Whenever the letters "P. M." occur, preceded by the name of a street, in these lists of mortgages, they mean that it is a Purchase Money Mortgage, and for fuller particulars see the list of transfers under the corresponding date. Whenever the rate is not given, read as 6 per cent.

NEW YORK CITY.

OCTOBER 16, 17, 19, 20, 21, 22.

Alff, Magdalena to Conrad Witt. 8th st. P. M. Oct. 15, due May 14, 1894, or installs, 5 %. $2,000

Ainslie, George H., Brooklyn, to THE FIRST NATIONAL BANK, Brooklyn. South st, n s, 79.5 e Catharine st, 110x145x110x145.6, with all title to piers 35 and 35½ and bulkhead, East River. 1-14 part. Sub. to mort. Sept. 5, demand, 5 %. 5,000

Armstrong, Harvey S. to People's Co-operative Building and Loan Assoc. Arcularius pl, n s, 490.6 e Gerard av, 25x100. Sept. 1, installs, 5 %. 1,000

Arnold, William to Gertrude Schoonmaker, Montclair, N. J. 123d st. n s, 200 w 10th av, 200x201.10 to 124th st. Oct. 20, 3 years, 5 %. 12,000

Aldhous, Frederick to Richard A. Cunningham and William H. Taylor. 76th st, s s, 100 w Columbus av, 25x102.2. Oct. 17, due April 10, 1892, or sooner. 16,000

Baker, John E. to Marcy M. Baker widow, East Greenwich. R. I. 134th st, n s, 175 e Lincoln av, 50x100. Sub. to mort. $4,500. July 29, 1891, 1 year, 5 %. 1,000

Bruce, Matthew to Conrad Stein. 3d av, n e cor 64th st. Saloon lease. Oct. 16, demand. 2,600

Banner, Peter to THE EQUITABLE LIFE ASSUR. SOC. of the United States. Broadway, No. 648, e s, 30.3x150x30.8x150, with all title to Cross lane. Sept. 9, due Jan. 1, 1893, or installs. gold, 250,000

Berg, Henry W. mortgagor with Leon Hirsh mortgagee. Extension of mort. at 5 %. Oct. 15. nom

Binswanger, Hyman P. to Joseph M. Arkush. Manhattan av, No. 469, w s, 84.3 s 120th st, 16.8x82; 63d st, No. 118, n s, 170.10 w 9th av, 16.8x100.5. Sub. to morts. Secures notes. Oct. 5. 4,000

Binswanger, Hyman P. to Jacques E. Karelsen et al. exrs. Rosetta Karelsen. Manhattan av, No. 469, w s, 84.3 s 120th st, 16.8x82. Sub. to mort. $10,000. Nov. 19, 1890, due Dec. 1, 1893. 2,500

Same to Jacques E. Karelsen et al. exrs. Ephraim Karelsen. 63d st, n s, 170.10 w 9th av, 16.8x100.5. Sub. to mort. $12,000. Nov. 19, 1890, due Dec. 1, 1893. 2,500

Bornstein, Rachel to Amalie Cohn. Willett st. P. M. Oct. 15, installs. 900

Breen, James R. and D. Allison Breen to Edward Oppenheimer and Isaac Metzger. 87th st. P. M. Oct. 2, 1 year. 26,500

Blumberg, Bernard and Louis to Robert E. Walsh. Henry st. P. M. Oct. 15, 3 years. 5 %. 15,000

Same to Edith Jayne. Same property. P. M. Sub. to last mort. Oct. 15, 2 years. 3,000

Bolger, Edward to Bernhard Kolb. 59th st, n s, 200 w 1st av, 25x100.5, error. Oct. 20, 5 years or installs, 5 %. 10,000

Broderick, John F. to Frederic J. Middlebrook, Brooklyn. 26th st, s s, 80.6 w 8th av, runs south 88.2 x west 9.10 x south 10.9 x west 8.4 x north 98.9 to st, x east 18. Oct. 20, 3 years, 5 %. 7,000

Bach, Lewis Z. to Benjamin Nathan. 103d st, s s, 102.6 w 3d av, 108x100.11. Oct. 15, 1 year or sooner, 5 %. 6,000

Same to John Bowes and John Coombs. 102d st, n s, 102.6 w 3d av, 27x100.11. Oct. 21, 1 year or sooner, 5 %. 1,500

Benz, Peter to Janet McAdam. 165th st. P. M. Oct. 20, 3 years, 5 %. 2,500

Same to same. Same property. P. M. Oct. 20, installs, 5 %. 1,200

Bernstein, Fannie wife of Adolph to J. C. Julius Langbein. 82d st, No. 203, n s, 85.6 e 3d av, 18.3x82.2. Oct. 22, due Oct. 15, 1894, or sooner, 5 %. See Conveys. 5,000

Bishop, Richard and Auguste his wife mortgagors with Anna R. Fairchild mortgagee. Extension of mort. Oct. 7. nom

Bock, George to George Ehret. 81st st, No. 301 E. Lease. Oct. 14, demand. 1,000

Buttell, John J. to Bernheimer & Schmid. 8th av, No. 2785, s w cor 148th st. Saloon lease. Oct. 22, note, demand. 1,500

Coffey, John to James G. Coffey. 51st st, n s, bet 2d and 3d avs, ward block No. 255, indeft. Oct. 19, due Jan. 1, 1892. 6,000

Cohen, Nathan to The Baron de Hirsch Fund. Monroe st. P. M. Oct. 22, 5 years, 5 %. 28,000

Same to Laemmlein Buttenwieser. Same property. P. M. Sub. to last mort. Oct. 22, installs 9,500

Same to same. Same property. P. M. Sub. to same mort. Oct. 22, 3 months. 500

Cram, John Sergeant to THE MUTUAL LIFE INS. Co., of New York. Madison av, Nos. 2162 and 2164; 135th st, Nos. 21-31 E., begins Madison av, n w cor 135th st, 99.11x150. Oct. 16, 1 year. See Conveys. 50,000

Cusack, Jane E., Brooklyn, and Auguste L. Sevestre to Emil Gabler et al. trustees Ernst Gabler dec'd. 4th st, No. 60, s s, 325 w 2d av, runs south 112.4 x west 12.6 x north 7.4 x west 12.6 x north 105 to 4th st, x east 25. Sept. 28, due Oct. 22, 1894, 5 %. gold, 80,000

Same to same. Bayard st, No. 61, s s, 272.2 w Bowery, 25x90. Sept. 28, due Oct. 22, 1894, 5 %. gold, 24,000

Campbell, John V. to Joseph L. Buttenwieser. Madison st. P. M. Oct. 1, 5 months. 13,000

Same to same. Same property. Building loan. Oct. 1, 5 months. 12,000

Carlo, Frank to Bernheimer & Schmid. Mott st, No. 141. Saloon lease. Oct. 6, note, demand. 800

Cary, Ellen F. wife of and Ralph H. to Mary R. Purdy. 156d st, s s, 145 w Elton av, 25x100. Oct. 20, due Nov. 1, 1892. 800

Christman, George B. to Elizabeth Betz, Queens County, N. Y. Ludlow st, e s, 75.10 n Stanton st, 24.10x90. Oct. 15, 3 years, 4½ %. See Conveys. 15,000

Clarke, William to William H. Hewlett, Manhasset, L. I. Washington av, n w cor Tremont av, runs north 131 x west 94 x south 25 x east 22.11 x south 20 x east 41.1 x south 90.5 to Tremont av, x east 30.4. Oct. 20, 3 years, 5 %. 10,000

Callahan, Richard J. to The New York Co-operative Building and Loan Assoc 165th st, n s, 99.8 e Trinity av, 25.1x71. Oct. 10, installs, 5 %. 2,705

Carroll, Ann Jane to James J. Thomson. 124th st, n s, 225 w Lenox av, 25x100.11. Oct. 21, 1 year. 2,000

Colahan, Agnes B. widow to THE BOWERY SAVINGS BANK. 35th st, s s, 289.6 w 2d av, 41x100x57x98.9. Oct. 20, 1 year, 4½ %. 10,500

Crawford, John J. to Laemmlein Buttenwieser. 11th st, No. 53, n s, 309 e 6th av, 24x103.3. Oct. 19, 5 years, 5 %. 30,000

Same to Joseph L. Buttenwieser. Same property. Sub. to last mort. Oct. 19, demand. 9,579

Candidus, Bertha wife of and Pantaleon to Martha Schluter. 106th st, s s, 125 w Columbus av, 50x100.11. Oct. 15, 1 year. See Conveys. 2,000

Cavinato, Luigi, Natale, Guiseppe and Stefano to Pierce, Butler & Pierce Mfg. Co. 87th st, s s, 85.3 e Lexington av, 27x100. Oct. 15, due Oct. 9, 1892, or sooner. 2,400

Cohen, William to Simon R. Weil. 166th st, n s, 75 e Columbus av, 25x100.11. Oct. 17, 1 year. 1,000

Same to Charles S. Robert, Mastic, L. I. 167th st, s s, 75 e Columbus av, 25x100.11. Oct. 17, 1 year. 1,000

Cooper, William S. to Meyer L. Sire. 4th st, n w cor West 10th st, 29.7x88. Oct. 1, installs, 5 % See Conveys. 6,000

Camp, John McK. to Joseph H. Godwin individ. and George H. McLean and Edward A. Walton exrs. James M. McLean. Kingsbridge road, &c. P. M. July 7, 3 years or installs, 5 %. 200,000

Carroll, Mary T. to THE TITLE GUARANTEE AND TRUST Co. 49th st. P. M. Oct. 15, due Oct. 19, 1892, 5 %. 7,000

Casey, John to Morris Steinhardt. Lexington av. P. M. Oct. 19, due Dec. 1, 1891, 5 %. 10,000

Same to The Baron de Hirsch Fund. 81st st, No 172, s s, 137 e Amsterdam av, 21x102.2. Oct. 16, due Oct. 19, 1894, 5 %. 20,000

Same to Solomon Loeb and ano. exrs. and trustees William Meyer. 81st st, No. 174, s s. 116 e Amsterdam av, 21x102.2. Oct. 16, due Oct. 19, 1894, 5 %. 20,000

Chell, Olof W. to Michael Kirwan. Anthony av, w s, 770.10 n Southern Boulevard, 25.1x79.10x25x81.1. Oct. 17, 3 years or sooner, 5 %. 200

Cohen, Benjamin F. to George Young. 16th st. P. M. Oct. 19, 1 year or sooner. 25,000

Donald, Peter mortgagee with William L. Strong present owner. Extension of morts. Oct. 6. nom

Dayton, Emma M. to THE MUTUAL LIFE INS. Co., of New York. 11th st, n s, 176.6 w 4th st, 25x111.8. Oct. 13, 1 year, 5 %. 5,000

Dryer, Caroline L., Brooklyn, to THE CONNECTICUT MUTUAL LIFE INS. Co., of Hartford, Conn. Pearl st, No. 294, s e s, abt 76.10 n e Beekman st, 26.8x86.2x26.2x84.9. Oct. 16, 3 years, 5 %. 4,000

Davison, Asa R. to THE METROPOLITAN LIFE INS. Co. of New York. 35th st, n s, 331 e 8th av, 19x98.9. Oct. 21, due Oct. 1, 1894, 5 %. 21,000

Same to same. 35th st, n s, 350 e 8th av, 25x98.8. Oct. 21, due Oct. 1, 1894, 5 %. 27,000

Same to same. 35th st, n s, 375 e 8th av, 25x98.9. Oct. 21, due Oct. 1, 1894, 5 %. 27,000

Same to George Crawford. 35th st, n s, 331 e 8th av, 60x98.9. Oct. 21, due Jan. 1, 1892. 9,000

Day, Amasa T. to Henry C. Carter. Nathalie av, e s, villa site P, map of 16 villa sites and 80 lots, portion of the Anthony estate on Heights of Kingsbridge, 29.7x125x64.8x129.10. Oct. 20, 3 years. 6,000

Eisenberg, Meyer to THE STATE BANK. Houston st, s s, 40 e Goerck st, 20x75; 47th st, s s, 69 w 1st av, 20x65. Secures credits. Oct. 19. 1,200

Egler, Frederick, Jr., to Charles J. Warner and Amos B. Stratton. 11th av, n e cor 62d st, 100.5x100. Oct. 19, 1 year. 10,000

Eickhoff, Wallace R. to Edwin F. Raynor. 133d st. P. M. Oct. 21, 3 years, 5 %. 30,000

Evans, George S. to Morris Mayer. 144th st. P. M. Oct. 15, 1 year. 3,000

Edgar, Thomas C. to THE METROPOLITAN LIFE INS. Co., of New York. 78th st, n s, 400 w Columbus av, 5 lots, each 20x102.2. 5 morts., each $24,000. Oct. 16, due Oct. 1, 1894, or installs, 6 % to Jan. 1, 1892, and 5 % thereafter. 120,000

Flood, Rosie to Michael Cain. 114th st, s s, 100 e 4th av, 25x100.10. April 22, due May 1, 1899, or installs, 5 %. 7,000

Fearns, William H. to The People's Co-operative Building and Loan Assoc. Arcularius pl, n s, 474.6 e Gerard av, 25x100. Sept. 1, installs, 5 %. 1,000

Foley, Julia R. to Louis W. Duesing, Brooklyn. Frankfort st, No. 9. P. M. Sept. 15, 1 year, without interest. 4,750

Fischel, Harry to The Home for Incurables. Jefferson st, No. 16, w s Oct. 19, due Nov. 1, 1896, 5 %. See Conveys. 12,000

Franck, Carl to THE FARMERS' LOAN AND TRUST Co. Houston st, s w cor Orchard st. 25x97. Oct. 20, 3 years, 5 %. 35,000

Fraser, Horatio N. to William E. D. Stokes. 86th st. P. M. Sept. 1, 5 years, 5 %. 25,000

Same to same. Same property. P. M. Sept. 1, installs, 5 %. 13,500

Fuller, Charles A. to Ellen Quinn. Amsterdam av, n w cor 103d st, 75.11x100. Sub. to mort. $125,000. Oct. 19, 1 year. 3,000

Forbrich, Charles to Herman Wendt. Tinton av, w s, 263.3 s 168th st, runs west 135 x south 6.7 x east 68.8 x south 11.3 x east 66.6 to av, x north 18.6. Oct 21, 3 years. 2,600

Fraser, Edward A. to Beadleston & Woerz, a corporation. Amsterdam av, No. 185. Store lease. Oct. 21 demand. 2,000

Fry, Karoline wife of Bernhard J. to THE TITLE GUARANTEE AND TRUST Co. 62d st, No. 211, n s, 155.9 e 3d av, 18.7x100.5. Oct 22, 5 years, 5 % gold, 16,000

Goldenberg, Simon to THE MUTUAL LIFE INS. Co., of New York. Waverley pl, s e cor Greene st, 56x81.11x50x81.8. Oct. 21, due Oct. 22, 1892, 5 %. 150,000

Garner, Harris to Sophia wife of Mordecai Levy. Chrystie st, No. 40, e s, 25x60x27x60. Oct. 21, 5 years, 5 %. gold, 15,000

Gerken, Henry to John J. Brady. Tremont and Prospect avs. P. M. Oct. 19, 3 years, 5 %. 2,000

Galvan, Mary P. to Frederic J. Middlebrook, Brooklyn. East Broadway, s s, 43.2 e Gouverneur st, 21.7x110.10 to alley, x21.4x110.8, with all title to alley. Oct. 16, 5 years, 5 %. 12,000

Gerstner, Franz and Frieda his wife to Thomas Moore and John McLaughlin. 83d st. P. M. Oct. 15, 3 years or sooner, 5 %. 2,800

Gunn, William and Andrew Grant to The Bradley & Currier Co. (Lim.) Amsterdam or 10th av, n w cor 78th st, 102.2x100. Sub. to morts $157,000. Oct. 14, 4 months. 18,000

Gibney, James H. heir James to The John Eichler Brewing Co. 152d st, s s, 400.3 e Morris av, 50x116.7x50x116.9. Oct. 15, 1 year, 5 %. 1,500

Geissmann, Henrietta to THE TITLE GUARANTEE AND TRUST Co. Brook av, w s, 25 n 147th st, 50x90. Sub. to mort. $2,000. Oct. 19, 1 year, 5 %. 400

Geoghegan, James F. to Michael Kirwan. Anthony av, w s, 745.8 n Southern Boulevard. 25.1x81.1x25x81.4. Oct. 17, 3 years, 5 %. 300

Goetz, Samuel to Salomon Marx. Roosevelt st, No 76, and No. 68 New Chambers st, begins Roosevelt st, e s, 23.9 n Batavia st, 27x56.2 to New Chambers st, x36.3x81.2. Sept. 30, due April 1, 1892, or sooner, 5 %. 25,000

Haas, H. M. and Emma, William and Anna Forster, Martin H. and Ida Hartmann, Henry and Charles Gunther to John Kress Brewing Co. Consent of stockholders to mortgage. Oct. 5. ——

Hogan, John P. to The People's Co-operative Building and Loan Assoc. Arcularius pl, n s, 524.6 e Gerard av, 25x100. Sept. 1, installs. 5 %. 1,000

Hughes, Thomas R., Weehawken, N. J., to Henry Dale. 97th st. P. M. Sub. to mort. $10,000. Oct. 19, due Oct. 21, 1893, 5 %. 4,000

Harris, Samuel to James Nunan. 118th st, s s, 320 e 4th av, 20x100.11. Sub. to morts. $88,000. Oct. 19. 2,350

Hoctor, James E. to Julia A. Low. 11th av, e s, 50.5 s 62d st, 25x100. Oct. 21, 5 years or sooner, 5 %. 15,000

Hasselberger, William to THE EMIGRANT INDUST. SAVINGS BANK. 70th st. P. M. Oct. 15, 1 year, 4½ %. 7,000

Henry, Matilda to William Radebold and Edward Wenz. 116th st, Nos. 6 and 8 W. P. M. Oct. 14, due June 1, 1896, or sooner, 5 %. 6,000

Same to same. Same property. P. M. Sub to last mort. Oct. 14, due Oct. 19, 1893, or sooner. 1,000

Hitchcock, Margaret wife of Frederick to Andrew Stoeckel. 142d st, s s, 406.6 e Alexander av, 25x100. Oct. 17, 2 years. 500

Herberger, Topetus L. to Adam Jung. 19th st, s s, 70 e 1st av, 20x55. Lease. Oct. 15, 3 years. 1,000

Herzog, Frank and William to Hermann Uber guard. of Anna Herzog. 2d av, s e cor 56th st, 20.5x63. Oct. 16, 10 years, 5 %. 8,000

Jesser, Arthur to Knud Franzen. Bush st, n s, 200 w Anthony av, 50x96.2x50x99.4. Oct. 1, 5 years, 5 %. 2,500

Johnston, Frances to Martha R. wife of James R. Townsend. 10th st. P. M. Sub. to morts. $86,000. Oct. 9, due Oct. 15, 1896, or installs, 5 %. gold, 19,000

Same to Caroline B. Townsend. Same property. P. M. Sub. to morts. $25,000. Oct. 9, due Oct. 15, 1896, 5 %. gold, 11,000

Judge, Andrew T. to George F. Johnson. 132d st. P. M. Oct. 16, due May 3, 1892, or sooner. 5 %. 14,500

Same to same. Same property. Building loan. Oct. 16, due May 3, 1892, or sooner, 5 %. 18,000

Same to The Bradley & Currier Co. (Lim.) Same property. Oct. 16, 6 months or sooner. 3,400

Same to Henry Nobel. Same property. Oct. 16, 6 months or sooner. 2,500

Same to John W. Haaren. 128th st, n s, 244.6 w 5th av, runs north 85 x west 15.6 x north 14.11 x west 5 x south 99.11 to st, x east 20.6. Aug. 6, 8 months or sooner. 10,000

Same to The Bradley & Currier Co. (Lim.) Same property. Oct. 16, 6 months or sooner. 2,000

Jones, Annie widow to Cornelia Prime, Huntington, L. I. 36th st, n s, 80 w 1st av, 26.8x98.9. Oct. 21, 3 years, 5 %. 8,000

Koenig, August and Annie his wife, Jersey City, and Carl Schuster and Emma his wife to Mary F. Davidson. 17th st, s s, 138 e Av B, 25x92. Oct. 20, due Jan. 1, 1897, 5 %. 6,000

Kohn, Theodore A. to Moses G. Rosenblatt guard. of Jennie M. Dreyfus. 3d av, No. 1007, e s, 156.8 n 59th st, 18.11x105. Oct. 20, due Oct. 21, 1896, 4½ %. 8,000

Korner, Frederick to Matthew Farrell. Tiffany st, e s, 200 n 165th st. 50x100. Oct. 15, 5 years or installs. 2,000

Kassel, Abraham to Moris Bloch. Rivington and Chrystie sts. P. M. Sub. to mort. $1,750. Oct. 20, due July 1, 1894, or sooner. 7,375

Kerr, Joseph and Margaret A. his wife to John H. Riser, Trappe, Md. 46th st. P. M. Oct. 16, due Oct. 20, 1892, 5 %. 3,000

Koch, Robert and Caroline his wife to John McKnight. Arthur av. P. M. Oct. 19, 2 years or installs, 5 %. 700

Kirchner, Michael to Thomas Schwind. Webster av, w s, lot 39 map of W. E. M. Zborowski, 25x90. Oct. 16, due Oct. 15, 1894, 5 %. 1,000

King, Hugh to THE EMIGRANT INDUST. SAVINGS BANK. Hudson st, Nos. 630 and 632, e s, 56 n Jane st, runs north 45 x east 88.5 x south 25 x west 13.7 x south 20.1 x west 74.1 to beginning. Oct. 19, 1 year, 4½ %. 25,000

Same to same. 50th st. P. M. Oct. 19, 1 year, 4½ %. 8,000

Lally, John to John Halloran. 131st st, n s, 53.11 w 2d av, 31x65.11. Sub. to mort. $5,000. Oct. 15, due Sept. 17, 1894, or sooner, 5 %. 3,000

Lefler, Harriet wife of and Charles to Annie L. Horn. 21st st. s s, 695 w 5th av, 15x92x15.3x92. Sub to mort. $6,000. Oct. 16, due Sept. 18, 1895, or sooner. 4½ %. 2,000

Lerch, Henry to John Paul. 3d av, w s, 82.3 s 155th st, 20.7x72.6x20x75. Oct. 15, 5 years, 5 %. 5,500

Lesinsky, Charles mortgagor with John McKee mortgagee. Extension of mort. Oct. 16. nom

Lankenau, Martin to Arthur Gorsch. 93d st, s s, 105 e 4th av, 14x100.8. Oct. 6, due Oct. 1, 1893. 1,500

Leary, Annie M. wife of Samuel B. to George C. Winkenbach. Home st, s s, 103 e Stebbins av, 25x106.4x26.9x116. Oct. 21, 3 years, 5 %. 2,000

Levenson, Sarah wife of Michael to THE GERMAN SAVINGS BANK. 72d st, n w cor Lexington av, 30x102.2. Oct. 19, 1 year. 12,500

Levy, Lewis to Betsey wife of Harris Cohen. Delancey st. P. M. Sept. 29, due May 1, 1893. 6,000

Lese, Sarah wife of Louis to THE EMIGRANT INDUSTRIAL SAVINGS BANK. Essex st. P. M. Oct. 10, 1 year, 4½ %. 14,000

Same to Jacob Wiebe and Magdalena Endholz. Same property. P. M. Sub. to last mort. Oct. 20, 3 years or sooner. 5,000

Lockwood, Amaziah to James F. and Patrick H. Sheridan and James S. Segrave. Forest st. P. M. Oct. 15, 3 years, 5 %. 370

Lindheim, Celia wife of and Robert to THE UNITED STATES TRUST Co., New York. Madison av, e s, 17.8 n 91st st, 17x68. Oct. 21, due Nov. 1, 1892, 4½ %. 10,000

McDowell, Hugh to The Bradley & Currier Co. (Lim.) 99th st, s s, 225 w 8th av, 50x100.11. Sub. to morts. $45,000. Oct. 1, due Jan. 3, 1892. 3,600

Modry, Ignaz to John J. Brady. Tremont av. P. M. Oct. 19, due Nov. 5, 1894, or sooner, 5 %. 2,910

Mueller, Karl to Henry Hawkes. 131st st. P. M. Sub. to mort. $17,000. Oct. 20, 3 years or installs. 2,000

Muller, Henry to Peter Doelger. 60th st, No. 313 E. Store lease. Aug. 22, demand. 1,200

Maack, Herman H. to Elizabeth Decker. Ursula pl (or Pond pl), w s, 93.1 s Travers st, runs west 48.7 x southwest 83.4 x south 27 x east 125 x north 60. Oct. 6, 3 years, 5 %. See Conveys. 1,000

Maresi, Giovanna, Sophia A. Mazzetti, Rosa L. Lechten, Lucie Sears and Gasper and Henry L. Ughetta heirs Maria Ughetta to Henry L. Ughetta exr. Maria Ughetta. Request of heirs to executor to make assignment of mortgage. Oct. 6.

Muller, Valentine to John Wetzel. 56th st, s s, 200 w 10th av, 25x100.5. Lease. Nov. 24, 1886, demand, 4 %. 6,000

Marsh, Rebecca widow to W. Emlen Roosevelt guard. of William O. Roosevelt. 56th st, n s, 650 w 5th av, 22.8x100.5. Oct. 21, 3 years, 4½ %. 6,000

Michelson, David and Abraham to Samuel Michelson. Av D, e s, 26.3 n 9th st, 26.5x101.11. Oct. 16, demand. 2,500

Michelson, David and Abraham to Samuel Michelson. Av D, e s, 53.1 n 9th st, 26.5x101.11. Oct. 16, demand. 2,500

Miller, Jacob and Ida his wife, Long Island City, and John Fish and Catharine M. his wife to William Danth and Kate his wife. 29th st, No. 237, n s, 125 w 2d av, 25x98.9. Sub. to mort. $22,500. Oct. 17, 1 year or sooner. 4,000

Mohr, Jacob to Sophie Schmidt. 66th st. P. M. Sub. to mort. $10,000. Oct. 15, 3 years or installs, 5 %. 3,000

Mallon, Patrick to Henry Schumacher. 45th st, n s, 100 w 3d av, 20x100.5. Oct. 17, 1 year. gold, 1,000

McCabe, Mary E. to The Baron de Hirsch Fund. 81st st, No. 168, s s, 179 e Amsterdam av. P. M. Oct. 1, 5 years, 5 %. 20,000

Same to same. 81st st, No. 170, s s, 158 e Amsterdam av. P. M. Oct. 1, 5 years, 5 %. 20,000

McKinlay, Duncan C. to The Bradley & Currier Co. (Lim.) 73d st, s s, 95 w West End av, runs west 80 x south 102.2 x east 60 x north 77.10 x east 20 x north 24.4. Sub. to morts. $90,000. Oct. 14, 6 months. 14,500

Michel, Simon mortgagee with William Hennessy, present owner. Extension of mort. Oct. 19. nom

Minor, Matilda to William Gee. 130th st, s s, 143.4 w Madison av, 16.10x99.11. Oct. 17, 1 year, 5 %. 1,300

Mulholland, James to THE UNITED STATES TRUST Co. of New York. 44th st, s s, 175 e 11th av, 25x100.5. Oct. 17, due Nov. 1, 1892, or sooner, 5 %. 9,000

McCabe, Charles F. to William Krais. Av B, e s, 83.3 s 16th st, 26.6x88. Oct. 20, due Jan. 1, 1894. 1,000

Nash, John McL to Julia H. and Jas. A. Billings exrs. and trustees James M. Billings. 54th st. P. M. Oct. 16, due Oct. 22, 1893, 4 %. 15,000

Neus, John and Henry, of Neus Bros., to The F. & M. Schaefer Brewing Co. 10th av, No. 96. Saloon lease. Oct. 19, demand. 3,000

Nordstrom, Elizabeth to John and Anna Hakansson. Suburban st, e s, 63.7 n Bainbridge av, 33.4x100. Oct. 14, 5 years or installs, 5 %. 2,300

Noonan, George A. to Michael Kirwan. Anthony av, w s, 720.7 n Southern Boulevard, 25.2x82.5x25x83.8. Oct. 17, 3 years, 5 %. 145

Nelligan, Rose widow to James and Anna Ellis. Fulton av, s e s, 201 s w 168th st, 16.8x100. Re-recorded. Nov. 1, 1886, 5 years, 5 %. 1,000

Nelson, Samuel to Denis Moloney. Amsterdam or 10th av, s w cor 131st st, 24.11x100; 52d st, No. 416 W. Indemnifies surety to bail bond. Oct. 16. 10,000

Nones, Alexander H. to David C. Anderson exr. Serena Nones. Mercer st, No. 71. Leasehold. Oct. 21, 3 months. 5,000

Olmstead, Dwight H. to THE MUTUAL LIFE INS. Co. of New York. Morningside av, n w cor 118th st, 100.11x150. Oct. 21, 1 year, 5 %. 35,000

O'Neill, Francis to THE CONNECTICUT MUTUAL LIFE INS. Co., Hartford, Conn. Madison av, w s, 74.1 s 29th st, 49.4x95. Oct. 21, 3 years, 5 %. 45,000

O'Brien, Mary E. wife of John H. to James F. and Patrick H. Sheridan and James S. Segrave. Forest st, w s, 200 n Rock st, 25x100. Oct. 1, 3 years, 5 %. 370

O'Connor, Lillie C. to The Murray Hill Co-operative Building and Loan Assoc. Bathgate av, w s, 216 s 175th st, 24x120. Oct. 16, installs, 5 %. 1,750

Ovens, John to John J. Brady. Crotona av, Prospect av and Oakland pl. P. M. Oct. 19, due Nov. 5, 1894, 5 %. 2,200

Picken, George F. to THE NEW YORK LIFE INS Co. 135th st, s s, 450 e Willis av, 16.6x100. Sept. 25, 3 years, 5 %. 7,000

Same to same. 135th st, s s, 466.6 e Willis av, 4 lots, each 16x100. 4 morts., each $7,000. Sept. 25, 3 years, 5 %. 28,000

Pond, Harriet L. to THE IRVING SAVINGS INST. 101st st, n s, 125 w 11th av, 25x100.11. Oct. 15, 1 year, 4½ %. 2,500

Prial, Francis P. to Elizabeth Aymar. 19th st. P. M. Oct. 16, 1 year, 5 %. 7,900

Pettit, John, East Orange, N. J., to Charles E. Tracy and ano. trustees James Bogert dec'd. Washington st, No. 161, e s, 129.1 s Cortlandt st, 25.1x92.10x25x93.7. Oct. 21, due Nov. 1, 1892, or sooner, 5 %. gold, 65,000

Peters, Carolina to George Herbener. 83d st, No. 508 E., s s, 148 e Av A, 25x102.2. Oct. 19, 1 year or sooner. 2,800

Plum, James R. trustee for Elias Plum, Jr., mortgagee with William L. Strong, present owner. Extension of mort. Oct. 6. nom

Plum, Anna L. et al. exrs. Mary G. Willard mortgagees with William L. Strong, present owner. Extension of morts. Oct. 6. nom

Rohrs, Frederick to Enoch C. Bell. Madison av, s e cor 132d st, 99.11x150. Oct. 19, demand. 5,000

Riggs, Karrick mortgagee with John E. Powers mortgagor. Extension of mort. Sept. 15. nom

Rabold, Daniel to Enoch C. Bell. 133d st, n s, 250 e 7th av, 25x99.11. P. M. Oct. 9, due Nov. 1, 1891. 3,000

Rapp, Eva M. to James Williams. 94th st, n s, 250 e 2d av, 75x100.8. Oct. 15, 1 year. 2,000

Read, Catharine G., Summit, N. J., to THE GREENWICH SAVINGS BANK. 16th st, No. 184, s s, 177.5 e Irving pl, 25x103.3. Oct. 20, due Nov. 1, 1892, 5 %. 6,000

Robertson, John and William Gammie and Maggie his wife to Bessie Collamore. 104th st, No. 10, s s, 175 e Manhattan av, 26.1x101.1x22x100.11. Oct. 16, 3 years, 5 %. 21,000

Rouss, Charles Broadway to Burritt W. Horton and ano. exrs. Ethelinda V. Allen. 5th av, No. 632, w s, 86.1 n 50th st, 28.8x131. Leasehold. Oct. 21, 5 years or installs, 4½ %. 38,000

Robertson, John and William Gammie to William Rankin. 104th st, No. 10, s s, 175 e Manhattan av, 26.1x101.1x22x100.11. Oct. 16, 1 year. 4,300

Rothschild, Jacob to THE MUTUAL LIFE INS. Co., New York. 14th st, s s, 125 e 6th av, 25x103.3. Oct. 16, 1 year, 5 %. 45,000

Randrup, Carl E. to Elizabeth Stricker nee Messmer, Albert E. and Matilda Stricker, of St. Gall, Switzerland, and Anna L. Huber, of Lecco, Italy. Broadway. P. M. Oct. 20, 3 years, 5 %. 1,400

Reid, George to THE MUTUAL LIFE INS. Co., New York. 91st st, n s, 264.1 e 5th av, 17x100.8. Oct. 19, due Oct. 1, 1892, 5 %. 16,000

Same to same. 91st st, n s, 247.1 e 5th av, 17x100.8. Oct. 19, due Oct. 1, 1892, 5 %. 16,000

Same to same. 91st st, n s, 230 e 5th av, 17.1x100.8. Oct. 19, due Oct. 1, 1892, 5 %. See Conveys. 8,000

Same to Rosalie King widow. 49th st, s s, 249 w 2d av, 19x100.5. Oct. 19, due Oct. 20, 1894, 5 %. See Conveys. 8,000

Rosensweig, Samuel to Beadleston & Woerz, a corporation. 7th av, No. 568. Store lease. Oct. 20, demand. 1,500

Sackman, Peter to THE TITLE GUARANTEE AND TRUST Co. Amsterdam av, n w cor 147th st, 40x100. Sub. to mort. $30,000. Oct. 20, 1 year. 5,000

Schramm, John and Annie E. Volderauer individ. and exrs. John Schramm to John H. Troll. 145th st, s s, 125 w Brook av, 25x100. Oct. 10, 2 years. 1,500

Schwartz, John to James F. and Patrick H. Sheridan and James S. Segrave. Forest st. P. M. Oct. 1, 3 years, 5 %. 370

Sooysmith, Charles to J. Hood Wright exr. and trustee Sarah Palmer dec'd. Line bet lands of Institute for Blind and property formerly of Harrison & Ackerman at point 870 w Kingsbridge road, runs west 250 x north 195 x east 250 x south 197.10, excepting land taken for Fort Washington ridge road. Oct. 14, due Oct. 19, 1896. 6,000

Sooysmith, Charles and William to the Count Charles de Montsaulnin and ano. trustees under deed of trust, &c. Line bet lands of Institute for Blind and B. L. Ackermans at point 520 w Kingsbridge road, runs west 350 x north 197.10 x east 350 x south 201.7 excepting any land taken for sts. Oct. 12, due Oct. 15, 1896. 15,000

Stepbach, Gustav and Sophie his wife to Annie J. Walkley. 144th st, n s, 400 e Willis av, 25x100; 144th st, n s, 425 e Willis av, runs north 41.6 x west 0.8 x southeast to 144th st, x east 0.4¾. Oct. 19, due Aug. 22, 1896, 5 %. 4,000

Stewart, Maria to William Rankin. 96th st. P. M. Oct. 19, 3 years. 7,481

Strauss, Nathan F. to Maurice S. Bondy admr. will annexed of Solomon Bondy. Lexington av, w s, 51.2 n 81st st, 17x55. Oct. 13, 1 year, 5 %. 8,000

Schmeckenbecher, Sarah E. to August L. Nosser. 56th st, s s, 170 e 2d av, 20x100.5. Oct. 19, 3 years, 5 %. 6,000

Schuck, George to William H. Jackson. 115th st, s s, 250 e 3d av. P. M. Oct. 21, 5 years, 5 %. 14,000

Same to same. 115th st, s s, 275 e 3d av. P. M. Oct. 21, 5 years, 5 %. 14,000

Schnugg, Francis J. to Lambert Suydam. Av A, s e cor 74th st, 102.2x77. Oct. 15, due Nov. 1, 1892. 40,000

Smith, Du Bois, Smithtown, L. I., to Theodore A. Squier. 90th st. P. M. Oct. 15, due July 15, 1894, 5 %. 2,700

Small, Agnes A. to Joanna H. Purdy. 62d st, n s, 68 e Madison av, 16x100.5. Oct. 16, 3 years, 5 %. 6,000

Stewart, Margery S. wife of and Robert A. to THE MANHATTAN LIFE INS. Co. 141st st, n s, 114.4 e Alexander av, 17.2x100. Oct. 16, 1 year, 5 %. 45,000

Stewart, Maria wife of and John to THE UNION TRUST Co. trustee Fanny E. Clark et al. 96th st. P. M. Oct. 19, due Nov. 1, 1894, 5 %. 18,000

Sauter, Anna M. wife of Louis to Silas D. Gifford guard. of Edith M. Lee. 156th st, s s, 350 e Courtlandt av, 25x100. Oct. 15, 1 year. 600

Seiferd, Mary to Helen A. Peck. Fordham or 3d av. P. M. Oct. 21, 3 years. 2,000

Stubberfield, Walter and Marie S. his wife to Edward F. Murray. Villa av, w s 221.3 n Potter pl, 50x100. Oct. 20, 1 year. 117

Troaey, Anne E. to Peter Sackman. Amsterdam or 10th av, w s, 60 n 147th st, 19.11x100. Oct. 15, 1 year. 720

Thompson, Samuel A. to Harry Held. 3d av, No. 1488, s w cor 84th st, 24.2x93.6. Lease. Oct. 19, installs. 750

Tuttle, Anna E. wife of Ezra A. to Joseph F. Stier. 82d st, s s, 305 w Columbus av, 20x102.2. Sub. to morts. $23,000. Oct. 19, due June 1, 1892. 2,000

Tuke, Henry C. to THE METROPOLITAN LIFE INS. Co., New York. 121st st, s w cor Lexington av, 40x100.11. Oct. 19, due Oct. 1, 1894, installs, 5 %. 52,500

Varian, Juliaett wife of and George W. to John H. Thorn. Kingsbridge to Williamsbridge road, n w s, part lot 62 map Charles Darke, Yonkers, 75x184.6x75x191.6. Aug. 28, due May 1, 1892. 1,000

Verdon, William to Cassidy & Adler. 135th st, Nos. 13 and 15, n s, 181.4 w 5th av. 35x99.11. Sub. to morts. $25,000. Oct. 19, demand. 5,000

Van Brunt, Thomas C. to THE EQUITABLE LIFE ASSUR. SOC. of the United States. 136th st. P. M. Oct, 17, due Jan. 1, 1893. gold, 187,200

Van Derveer, Rachel E. to Frederick C. McCormack. 19th st, s s, 277.10 w 5th av, 21.5x93. Oct. 10, 1 year or sooner. 2,500

Van Eupen, Theodore to Benjamin F. Cohen. 16th st, n s, 350 w 8th av, 50x92. Oct. 19, due May 1, 1892. 18,000

Same to same. Same property. P. M. Oct. 19, due May 1, 1892. 10,000

Ward. Sidney, Brooklyn, to James L. Bulkley et al. exrs. Daniel B. Fayerweather. 1st av, 44th st, 43d st. P. M. Oct. 1, 5 years, 5 %. 130,000

Watson, Thomas to James C. McEachen. 35th st, n s, 100 e 11th av. 50x98.9. Oct. 22, 2 years. 5,500

White, Isaac to THE UNITED STATES TRUST Co. of New York. Lenox av. P. M. Oct. 16, due Nov. 1, 1892, 5 %. 12,000

Same to Terence J. Duffy. Same property. P. M. Sub. to mort. $12,000. Oct. 16, due Jan 1, 1893, 5 %. 3,000

Wilson, Catherine S. J. wife of Augustine J. to Philip Geisendorfer and Katrina his wife. Bainbridge av, s e s, 47 n e 184th st, —x127x25x127; lot 2 map Peter Handibode property 24th Ward. Oct. 20, due July 22, 1893, 5 %. 400

Williams, Mary E. widow to Lizzie W. Johnson, Yonkers, N. Y. 46th st, s s, 350 e 8th av, 18.9x100.5. Leasehold. Oct. 19, due April 19, 1893. gold, 2,000

Winter, Moses to Bernheimer & Schmid. Division st, No. 247. Saloon lease. Oct. 20, note, demand. 900

Walton, George A., Frank Koewing and Reuben H. Donnelly to The Standard Fashion Co. Consent of stockholders to mortgage. Aug. 20.

Weinstein, Morris and Morris Margovitz to Sender Jarmulowsky. Division st No. 243, s s, 46 w Montgomery st, 32x48.6x23x48.7. Oct. 16, 1 year. 2,000

Winters, Lawrence to Matilda Rothschild. 129th st, Nos. 306, 308 and 310, s s, 125 w 8th av, 75x99.11. Sub. to morts. $63,000. Oct. 16, 6 months. 1,200

Weinberg, Jacob B. to THE CHEMICAL NATIONAL BANK, THE TRADESMAN'S NATIONAL BANK, THE IMPORTERS AND TRADERS' NATIONAL BANK, New York, THE AMERICAN EXCHANGE NATIONAL BANK, THE NATIONAL NEWARK BANKING CO., THE HARTFORD NATIONAL BANK and H. B. Claflin Co. 121st st, n s, 95 e Manhattan av, 100x100.11, sub. to mort. $86,000; 121st st, n s, 573 w 7th av, 17x100.11, sub. to mort. $10,000; 65th st, n s, 100 w 4th av, 17x100.5, sub. to mort. $18,000; 80th st, s s, 105 e 10th av, 145x102.2, sub. to mort. $158,000; 123d st, s s, 240 e 4th av, 75x100.11, sub. to mort. $65,005; 3d av, e s, 229.11 s 163d st, 25.2x133.3, sub. to mort. $1,500; Intervale av, e s, 194.3 n 165th st, 75x100; Kelly st, s w cor 167th st, 30x75; Kelly st, w s, 90 s 167th st, 75x100; Fox st, w s, 29.6 s 169th st, 25x130.1x25.4x131.10; 167th st, n e cor Kelly st, 23.7x97.6x15.4x99.2; Kelly st, e s, 92.2 n 167th st, 50x106.3x50.3x105.8; Intervale av, e s, 57.5 n Kelly st, 100x80x irreg. x 80.3, sub. to mort. $1,500; 121st st, s s, 100 w 8th av, 175x100.11, sub. to mort, $87,000. Sept. 22, notes. 168,874

Wright, Samuel O., Rockville Centre, L. I., to Reuben Ross 121st st, s s, 260 w Lenox av. 140x100.11. Oct. 16, 3 months. 5,000

Zubiller, Henry, Jr., and Paul P., of H. Zubiller's Sons, to Henry Zubiller. 45th st, s s, 70 w 1st av, 30x100.5. Oct. 17, due Jan. 1, 1895. 4,000

KINGS COUNTY.

OCTOBER 15, 16, 17, 19, 20, 21.

Ahlquist, Amanda M. to George H. Roberts. Clove road or Cedar pl, w s, 117.11 n Malbone st, 37.8x86.4x20.10x65.6, Flatbush. Oct. 15, 2 years. $2,000

Same to same. Clove road or Cedar pl, w s, 59.3 n Malbone st, 132.8x—x54.3x111.1, except portion covered by last mort.; Franklin av, e s, 650 s Montgomery st, 75x100, Flatbush. Oct. 15, 1 year. 2,700

Adler, Henry to The Town of New Utrecht Co-operative Building and Loan Assoc. Warren st, n w s, 100 n e Lexington av, 100x125, Fort Hamilton. Sept. 1, installs, 5 %. 1,750

Alieeky, Charles F. to Mary S. Baker. Penn st, n w s, 314.6 n e Marcy av, 21x100. Oct. 15, 3 years, 5 %. 2,000

Allen, Charlotte A. to Thomas Murray, Grassy Point, N. Y. Freeman st. P. M. Oct. 5, installs, 5 %. 400

Anable, Courtland V. to Effingham H. Nichols. Liberty av, s s, 40 e Milford st, 80x90. Oct. 12, 2 years. 1,000

Andres, Andreas to The German Savings Bank, Brooklyn. Bushwick av, s e cor Troutman st, 55x48.10x50x71.10. Oct. 9, due Dec. 1, 1892, 5 %. 1,000

Ashcroft, Mary K. mortgagor with Clara D. Carpenter mortgagee. Extension of mort. Sept. 25. nom

Bulger, Edward F. to William E. Kay. Windsor pl. P. M. Oct. 17, installs. 500

Bulwer, Jacob to John Lynch. Shepherd av. P. M. Oct. 20, 2 years. 600

Blazo, Augustus W. to Edwin C. Low. Putnam av, s s, 90 w Lewis av, 180x200 to Jefferson av. May 12, 1 year, 5 %. 7,500

Bagley, Dennis J. to Mary S. Baker. Woodbine st, n w s, 75 s w Bushwick av, 20x100. Oct. 14, 3 years, 5 %. 1,500

Barden, Mary to Eugene R. Judge. Truxton st. P. M. Oct. 15, 3 years, 5 %. 600

Bareis, Frederick to Henrietta Cohen. Beattie st. P. M. Oct. 1, 4 years. 750

Bartlett, Ida E. to David C. Bennett. 20th st, n w s, 172.7 s w Benson av. 60x63.9 to De Bruyn's lane, x60x62.9, New Utrecht. Oct. 15, 3 years. 2,500

Beasley, David S. to George J. Bryan. Lot of land and land under water adj lands of William H. Parkinson or Pleasant Home Co. in New York Bay, Gravesend, indeft. Oct. 15, 3 years. 15,000

Bechtel, Anna E. to August W. Muller. Hart st, s s, 169.2 e Wyckoff av, 20x100. Oct. 4, due Oct. 12, 1894. 1,000

Bell, Laura A. and William R. to The Title Guarantee and Trust Co. Gates av, n s, 262 e Nostrand av, 20x100. Oct. 17, 3 years, 5 %. 3,000

Same to same. Chauncey st, n s, 225 e Reid av, 25x99.2x25.5x104. Oct. 17, 1 year. 1,500

Bonert, Louis to The Title Guarantee and Trust Co. 7th av, east cor 15th st, 25x97.10. Oct. 16, 1 year. 3,000

Bonert, Louis to Edward H. Litchfield. 6th av, east cor 5th st. P. M. Sub. to morts. Oct. 19, 3 years, 5 %. 3,833

Same to same. 6th av, west cor 4th st. P. M. Oct. 19, 3 years, 5 %. 3,667

Same to Grace D. Litchfield individ. and with Edward H. Litchfield trustee Henry P. Litchfield. 6th av, n w s, 50 s w 4th st. P. M. Sub. to taxes. Oct. 19. 3 years, 5 %. 3,667

Same to same. 6th av, s e s, 50 n e 5th st. P. M. Sub. to taxes. Oct. 19, 3 years, 5 %. 3,833

Brady, Owen to Theodore F. Hascoll. Lafayette av, n e s, 600 e United States av, 50x170.4x50.1x170.2. Oct. 7, due Nov. 1, 1894, 5 %. 900

Brady, Thomas to Catharine L. McCollum. 40th st. P. M. Oct. 15, 5 years. 3,000

Brady, Bridget T. to George W. Green guard. Clarence S. Green. North 8th st, n s, 275 e Wythe av, 25x100. Oct. 15, 2 years. 800

Brennan, Margaret to Evelina K. Meserole. South 4th st, s s, 248.9 e Roebling st, 21.8x100. Oct. 14, due May 1, 1892. 1,000

Brennan, Marrie T. wife of and John J. to The Kings Co. Savings Inst. Marcy av, west cor Lynch st, 20x80. Oct. 19, 1 year, 5 %. 10,000

Brophy, Patrick to The South Brooklyn Co-operative Building and Loan Assoc. Madison st. P. M. Oct. 13, installs. 2,000

Brown, George R. to Stephen B. Sturges. Herkimer st, s s, 200 w Nostrand av, 50x185.6 to Herkimer pl. Oct. 15, demand. 41,500

Brundage, James H. to Catharine E. Rowland, Jamaica, L. I. Jerome st, e s, 100 s Dumont av, 20x100. Oct. 15, 3 years. 1,500

Buch, Elizabeth mortgagee with John F. Bassett mortgagor. Extension of mort. Oct. 9. nom

Berendsen, Carl J. M. to Salomon Wolf. Myrtle av. P. M. Oct. 15, 3 years, 5 %. 6,000

Bridgman, William H. to William H. Reynolds. Macon st. P. M. Oct. 15, 3 years, 5 %. 2,200

Boedicker, Hermann G. to Hermann Lohmann. Brooklyn & Rockaway R. R., Canarsie. P. M. Oct. 1, 5 years, 5 %. 2,500

Bowles, Thomas N. to Henry C. Bull. 19th st. P. M. Oct. 15, installs. 950

Brown, Benjamin J. to John H. Rowland. De Kalb av. P. M. Oct. 19, 1 year, 5 %. 2,500

Collins, Daniel J. to George W. Sammis. Kingsland av. P. M. Oct. 10, due Oct. 19, 1894, 5 %. 1,100

Cushman, John J. to Thomas Ross. Norman av, s e cor Jewel st. P. M. Oct. 19, 3 years, 5 %. 3,500

Christie, James H. to Charles Engert. Monitor st. P. M. Sub. to mort. $1,900. Oct. 1, installs, 5 %. 1,400

Same to The Kings County Savings Inst. Same property. P. M. Oct. 1, 1 year, 5 %. 1,900

Cohen, Jacob to Peter B. Koechlein and ano. exrs. John Koechlein. Christopher av, n w cor Dumont av. P. M. Oct. 14, 3 years. 1,400

Cohan, Samuel to George H. Dietz. Boerum st. P. M. Oct. 8, 5 years, 5 %. 500

Creveling, John C. to The Title Guarantee and Trust Co. Decatur st. P. M. Oct. 19, 3 years, 5 %. 3,500

Crossman, Greenleaf W. to Johnston & Platner. Macon st. P. M. Oct. 1, 3 years, 5 %. 1,500

Cunningham, Bernard to Frederick Eiermann. Jerome st. P. M. Oct. 19, installs. 400

Cush, Adelia A. to Owen Carroll. Henry st, w s, 40 n West 9th st, 20x84. Oct. 20, due Nov. 1, 1896. 450

Carey, Marianne widow formerly Martin widow to Ellen J. Quackinbush, New York. Dresden st, e s, 400 n Ridgewood av, 50x100. Oct. 16, 2 years. 365

Chinnock, Elizabeth L. to The Title Guarantee and Trust Co. 7th av, w s, 19.3 s 16th st, 18.4x75.1. Oct. 15, 3 years, 5 %. 2,500

Coombs, Ann E. wife of Thomas to John P. Rolfe. Myrtle av, n e cor Adelphi st, 44.1x74.11x28.5x82.3. Oct. 16, 1 year, 5 %. 3,000

Cavanaugh, Emma to John Gillen. Starr st. P. M. Oct. 15, 3 months. 925

Craig, George A. to Bulmer Lumber Co. (Lim.) Halsey st, s e s, 100 n e Central av, 126x100. Sub. to morts. Oct. 15, demand. 3,500

Cochran, Henry H. to The People's Trust Co. trustee Mary Mulloy, 14th av, south cor 73d st. P. M. Oct. 20, 1 year. 3,300

Same to same as committee Julia Heinemann. 14th av, north cor 70th st. P. M. Oct. 20, 1 year. 3,300

Same to same individ. 14th av, n w s, 60 n e 72d st. P. M. Oct. 20, 1 year. 3,300

Cocks, James to James McKenna. Pacific st. P. M. Oct. 20, installs. 460

Danancher, Elise to Louis Ratner. Watkins st, e s, 100 n Blake av, 75x100. Oct. 15, installs. 200

Devlin, James to Patrick Murphy. 29th st. P. M. Oct. 16, 2 years. 1,000

Dawson, James H. P. to The Title Guarantee and Trust Co. Halsey st, s s, 141.9 e Ralph av, 19.5x100. Oct 15, 3 years, 5 %. 1,000

Denike, Thomas S. to Joseph M. Greenwood. Buffalo av, w s, 148.8 s Atlantic av, 16.4x75. Oct. 6, due Nov. 1, 1894. 2,000

Same to same. Buffalo av, w s, 132.4 s Atlantic av, 16.4x75. Oct. 6, due Nov. 1, 1894. 2,000

Same to Susan P. Embury. Buffalo av, w s, 116 s Atlantic av, 16.4x75. Oct. 6, due Nov. 1, 1894. 2,000

Same to Helen Embury. Buffalo av, w s, 99.8 s Atlantic av, 16.4x75. Oct. 6, due Nov. 1, 1894. 2,000

Same to Harriet Aymar. Buffalo av, w s, 83.4 s Atlantic av, 2 lots, each 16.4x75. 2 morts., each $2,000. Oct. 6, due Nov. 1, 1894. 4,000

Same to Marie A. Udall. Buffalo av, w s, 50.8 s Atlantic av. 16.4x75. Oct. 6, due Nov. 1, 1894. 2,050

Same to Wallace W. Williams. Buffalo av, s w cor Atlantic av, 18x75. Oct. 6, due Nov. 1, 1894. 3,000

Same to same. Buffalo av, w s, 18 s Atlantic av, 2 lots, each 16.4x75. 2 morts., each $2,000. Oct. 6, due Nov. 1, 1894. 4,000

Dobeny, Margaret to Joseph Wechsler. East 8th st. P. M. Oct. 16, 3 years, 5 %. 765

Donavan, Cornelius to Mary Latimer. Brooklyn and Jamaica plank road, s s, 106.2 e Sheffield av, 44.1x74x40x61.2. Oct. 15, 3 years. gold, 3,000

Endom, Henry T. to John Ahern. 11th av, e s, 120 s 67th st. 40x100, New Utrecht. Oct. 14, 2 years, 5 %. 500

Ericson, Conrad to Henry Klee. 32d st. P. M. Oct. 15, installs. 1,650

Ernst, John to Obermeyer & Liebmann. Union av, No. 62. Lease. Oct. 15, demand. 750

Evans, George C., Plainfield, N. J., to George G. Reynolds. Blake av, s w cor Williams av, 100x200. Oct. 15, 3 years or sooner, 5 %. gold, 2,500

Same to same. Hinsdale st, e s, 200 s Blake av, 200x100. Oct. 15, 3 years or sooner, 5 %. gold, 2,500

Same to same. Williams av, w s, 200 s Blake av, 200x100. Oct. 15, 3 years or sooner, 5 %. 2,500

Same to same. Williams av, n w cor Dumont av, 100x200 to Hinsdale st. Oct. 15, 3 years or sooner, 5 %. 2,500

Same to same. Blake av, s e cor Hinsdale st, 100x200. Oct. 15, 3 years or sooner. 2,500

Evans, Rebecca I. to Phebe A. Davis. Walworth st, e s, 211.10 s Myrtle av, 20x100. Oct. 13, 1 year. 200

Erslev, Bertha M. to Edwin S. Updike, Sr., New York. Lexington av. P. M. Oct. 8, 1 year. 5,000

Everit, Thomas to Mary Fitzgerald. Atlantic av. P. M. Oct. 16, 3 years. 1,500

Edwards, Corlies to Charles E. Rogers. 53d st, n s, 200 w 3d av, 20x102.2; 53d st, n s, 340 w 3d av, 20x100.2; 52d st, n s, 220 e 3d av, 20x100.2; 52d st, n s, 260 e 3d av, 20x100.2. Oct. 21, due April 1, 1892. 530

Farrell, James P. to Charles W. Voorhis. Skillman av. P. M. Oct. 20, due Jan. 1, 1895. 300

Ferguson, James W. to Frank Bailey. 80th st, 74th st, New Utrecht. P. M. Oct. 15, 1 year. 375

Ferguson, Francis to Sarah Huggins. Franklin av. P. M. Oct. 20, due Nov. 1, 1894, 5 %. 2,500

Francisco, George W. and Charles H. to James Gascoine individ. and with Anna E. Cozine exrs. John G. Cozine. Woodbine st. P. M. Oct. 17, 6 months. 19,915

Same to same. Same property. P. M. Oct. 17, demand. 23,400

Feldhus, Frederick G. to John Rawson and Alfred Hodges. Kent av. P. M. Oct. 15, 3 years, 5 %. 2,000

Faris, Edwin L. to James D. Lynch. 83d st, New Utrecht. P. M. Oct. 12, 1 year, 5 %. 700

Feeley, James to Benjamin W. Winans et al. exrs. William W. Winans. Kent av. P. M. Oct. 16, 3 years, 5 %. 2,500

Fields, Robert to P. Ballantine & Sons. Willoughby st, No. 176. Saloon lease. Oct. 16, demand. 600

Friedman, Julius to Elise Danancher. Watkins st. Oct. 1, installs. 2,000

Fry, Evan to Helvetia B. Dutcher. 19th st, n e s, 209.2 n w 6th av, 17.8x100. Oct. 12, 1 year. 700

Goldberg, Hyman to Andrew R. Culver. Eastern Parkway. P. M. May 22, installs. 300

Gload, Adolphus to James Gascoine individ. and with ano. exrs. of John G. Cozine. Madison st, n w s, 260 n e Hamburg av, 100x100. Sept. 22, demand. 4,000

Gompert, Gottfried to The East New York Savings Bank. Evergreen pl, n s, 100 w New Jersey av, 25x200. Oct. 14, 1 year. 200

Giese, Emilie A. to Thomas H. Kerrigan. 10th st. P. M. Oct. 16, 3 years, 5 %. 3,500

Goodman, Isaac and Max Karol to Franz Borowiak and Pauline his wife. Humboldt st, e s, 75 s Cook st. P. M. Oct. 16, due Oct. 1, 1896, 5 %. 4,000

Same to same. Humboldt st, e s, 50 s Cook st. P. M. Oct. 16, due Oct. 1, 1896, 5 %. 4,000

Same to Leopold Michel. Same property as last. Oct. 16, due Oct. 1, 1896, 5 %. 1,000

Same to same. Humboldt st, e s, 75 s Cook st. 25x100. Oct. 16, due Oct. 1, 1896, 5 %. 1,100

Grasman, Henry to Phebe E. Leverich extrx. Augustus A. Leverich. Monroe st, s s, 100 w Stuyvesant av, 17.6x100. Oct. 15, 3 years, 5 %. 3,000

Gallin, John W. to The Young Men's East Side Benevolent Assoc. South 1st st, n e s, 112.11 n w Berry st, runs north 20 x west 2.6 x north to point 100 s of Grand st, x west 20 x south to South 1st st, x east 22.6. Oct. 17, 1 year, 5 %. 800

Gibbs, Anna De C. wife of Henry J. to Charles Stoll. South 3d st, s s, 108 e Driggs av, 22x 95. Oct. 16, 3 years, 5 %. 2,500

Gruesser, William to Charles Diebold and Katharina his wife. Myrtle av. P. M. Oct. 15, 2 years, 5 %. 2,300

Gammans, Elbert H. to James D. Lynch. 24th av and 83d st, Gravesend. P. M. Oct. 8, due Oct. 9, 1893, 5 %. 840

German Evangelical Church of New Lots to Manly R. Hubbs, Comac, L. I. Wyona st, w s, 175 n Fulton av, 50x100. Oct. 20, 3 years, 5 %. 3,000

Gerken, John to Ira Pettit, Queens Co., L. I. Union st, n s, 378 w 4th av, 26x95. Oct. 20, due Nov. 1, 1894, 5 %. 5,500

Same to Harriet E. Tunison. Union st, n s, 430.10 w 4th av, 26.8x95. Oct. 20, due Nov. 1, 1894, 5 %. 5,500

Gasson, Ambrose to Charles Engert. Monitor st. P. M. Sub. to mort. $1,900. Oct. 1, installs, 5 %. 1,600

Same to The Kings Co. Savings Inst. Same property. Oct. 1, 1 year, 5 %. 1,900

Giblen, Michael to Henry Weil. Pacific st, s s, 83.4 e Utica av. P. M. Oct. 1, 4 months. 4,000

Same to same. Same property. Oct. 1, 4 months. 5,250

Graham, James to Eliza G. and Mary Hampton and John C. Creveling. Shepherd av, e s, 140 n Ridgewood av, 120x102.5x120x102.4. Sub. to mort $9,600. Oct. 6, 2 years. 1,500

Glading, Emma R. to The Title Guarantee and Trust Co. Park av. P. M. Oct. 19, due Oct. 21, 1894, 5 %. 1,500

Grossbart, Frank to Pauline and William Hartmann. Thatford av. P. M. Sub. to mort. $1,200. Oct. 16, installs. 175

Hamilton, Mary E. to James D. Lynch. 83d st, New Utrecht. P. M. Oct. 15, due Oct. 20, 1893, 5 %. 600

Heyzer, John to Maria T. King. Jefferson av, n s, 20 e Nostrand av, 80x100. Oct. 1, 5 years, 5 %. 3,500

Haslam, Thomas to William M. Hull. Eckford st, e s, 336 n Van Cott av, 25x100. Oct. 17, due Jan. 1, 1895, 5 %. 3,000

Helgans, Elias to John Fensch. Van Siclen av, n e cor Belmont av, 50x100. Aug. 24, 3 years, 5 %. 4,000

Hamilton, John S. to Laura J. Sydney. 74th st, New Utrecht. P. M. March 9, due Oct. 16, 1894. 500

Happ, Louis L. and Bernard J. Pink to William Kammann exr. Henry Kammann. Alabama av. P. M. Oct. 15, 3 years, 5 %. 400

Hoeckele, Charles and Susannah his wife to Henry Sauerbrunn. George st. Oct. 16, 2 years, 5 %. See Conveys. 245

Hoyt, Frances G. to Harmon W. Hendricks. Barbey st, w s, 100 n Sunnyside av, 25x124x 25.1x127. Oct. 19, 1 year. 2,750

Hyers, Eva to Frederick Cobb. Saratoga av, e s, 22 n Marion st, 19x79. Oct. 19, due May 1, 1892. 260

Same to Phebe Ryan. Saratoga av, e s, 22 n Marion st, 19x78. Oct. 16, 3 years. 6,000

Hartmann, William to Gilbert S. Thatford. Newport av, n s, 75 e Osborn st, 25x100. Oct. 16, 5 years. 800

Hastings, Catharine and James C. Lake to Susan H. Wells. United States av, n w s, 100 n e Washington st, 100x116.3, New Utrecht. Oct. 16, due Nov. 1, 1896. 2,000

Heatley, George W. to John H. Canfield. Lafayette av, n s, 350 e Tompkins av. P. M. Oct. 15, 3 years, 5 %. 1,800

Henry, Margaret to The Town of New Utrecht Co-operative Building and Loan Assoc. Clinton av, n e s, 281.2 s e 3d av, 25x100. Oct. 5, installs. 1,000

Heury, James A. to John J. Brady. Van Siclen av, w s, 175 n Glenmore av, 25x100. Oct. 12, 3 years. 1,200

Herrick, George to Caroline Van Nostrand, Jersey City. Bond st, w s, 60 s President st, 20x75; Bond st, w s, 80 s President st, 20x75. Oct. 12, 3 years, 5 %. 1,000

Hewitt, Elizabeth widow to Elizabeth M. Vincent. Ridgewood av, s s, 75 e Cleveland st, 25x100. Oct. 15, installs. 870

Hoffmann, Hugo to The New York Co-operative Building and Loan Assoc. 14th st, s w s, 272 n w 3d av, 16x90. Oct. 2, installs, 5 %. See Conveys. 1,800

Hollister, Mary C. to Hannah Hitchings exr. Charles F. Hitchings. Schenck st. P. M. Oct. 8, due Oct. 1, 1894, 5 %. 4,400

Hickey, Julia to Louis Bonert. 7th st. P. M. Oct. 13, 1 year, 5 %. 1,900

Hower, Mary E. to Maria M. Mehrmann. Leonard st, n e cor Frost st, 25x100. July 1, 3 years. 3,000

Irvine, William to The Title Guarantee and Trust Co. Nostrand av, n w cor Monroe st, 60x85. Oct. 20, demand, 5 %. 25,000

Isbell, Charles to Sarah E. Ostrander. Hancock st. n s, 266.10 e Stuyvesant av, 16.4x100. Oct. 15, 3 years, 5 %. 4,500

Same to same. Jefferson st, s s, 283.1 e Stuyvesant av, 16.11x100. Oct. 15, 3 years, 5 %. 4,500

Isbill, Charles to William Entwistle. Hancock st, n s, 300 e Stuyvesant av, 16.10x100. Oct. 15, 3 years, 5 %. 4,500

Jacobs, Morris to Henry Weil. Somers st, s s, 230 w Stone av. P. M. Oct. 12, 3 years 3,000

Same to Charles H. Reynolds. Same property. 2d mort. Oct. 12, 1 year. 600

Joerdens, Lina or Carolina wife of and John F. M. to Jane V. H. Scranton. Summit st, s s, 80 w Hicks st, 20x100. Oct. 16, 3 years, 5 %. 2,800

Johnston, Matthias to The Union Co-operative Building and Loan Assoc. Lafayette av. P. M. Oct. 15, installs. 3,000

Judson, Edward to Carsten H. Meyer. 6th av, n w cor President st, 92x100. Oct. 17, 3 months. 3,500

Johnston, Albert to Noah Tebbetts. Herkimer st and Saratoga av. P. M. Oct. 3, demand. 24,000

Jones, E. Willard to The Title Guarantee and Trust Co. Macon st, s s, 315 w Lewis av, 40x 100. Oct. 20, demand. 15,000

Jordens, John D. and Louise his wife to Charles Bischoff. Gowanus road. P. M. Oct. 20, due May 1, 1893, 5 %. 700

Koch, George D. and Frederick H. Koerner to Goswin Schmitt. Knickerbocker av, s w s, 50 s e De Kalb av, 25x80. Sept. 15, 3 years, 5 %. 3,500

Same to Charles Cutter. Knickerbocker av, south cor De Kalb av, 25x80. Sept. 15, 3 years, 5 %. 4,500

Same to John Young. Knickerbocker av, s w s, 25 s e De Kalb av, 25x80. Sept. 15, 3 years, 5 %. 3,500

Kordes, Henry to The German Savings Bank, Brooklyn. Cooper st, s e s, 125 s w Evergreen av, 18.4x100. Oct. 20, due Dec. 1, 1893, 5 %. 2,000

Same to same. Cooper st, s e s, 143.4 s w Evergreen av, 18.4x100. Oct. 20, due Dec. 1, 1893, 5 %. 2,000

Kalb, Frederick to Adolph Kiendl guard. Charles Kalb. Essex st, e s, 750 s Gay st, 25 x100. Oct. 15, 3 years. 750

Kaplan, Aaron to Bernhard Silberstein. Linden st, e s, 285.11 n Evergreen av, 20x100. Sept. 29, installs. 1,100

Kaufman, Louis and Benjamin Benjamin to Elise Hessenberg, New York. Graham av. P. M. Oct. 15, 3 years, 5 %. 7,000

Keechler, Ida A. to Magdalena Becher, New York. Coney Island road, n s, 60 w West 1st st, 40x109.4x40x110.11. Oct. 14, 5 %. 1,000

Kenna, James to S. H. Apple. Harway av, n w cor Hubbard st, one-story frame store property, Gravesend. Oct. 9, 3 years. 330

Klucken, Raphael to The East Brooklyn Cooperative Building Assoc. 54th st. P. M. Oct. 15, installs. 4,750

Knoke, Henry to George W. Chapman. Himrod st. P. M. Oct. 15, demand, 5 %. 500

Same to The Title Guarantee and Trust Co. Himrod st. P. M. Oct. 15, 3 years, 5 %. 1,500

Kuhlmann, Henry to Carline Kossmann. Central av, north cor Linden st, 25x95. Oct. 16, demand. 300

Kuntz, John F. to The German Savings Bank, Brooklyn. Varet st, s s, 175 w Humboldt st, 25x100. Oct. 8, due Dec. 1, 1892, 5 %. 4,000

Kiefer, Theresa to Henry Doscher. Bushwick av, n e s, 50.6 n w Cedar st, runs northwest 50.7 x northeast 102.6 x southeast 25 x southwest 6.6 x south 22.6 x southeast 6 x southwest 69.8 to beginning, with all title to courtyard in front. Oct. 12, due Nov. 1, 1893. 8,500

Kirkman, Ralph to Henry D. Lott. 20th st, n s, 85 e 5th av, 40x100.2. Oct. 7, 1 year. 1,700

Kappelman, Charles to Charles J. Hauck. Schaeffer st, s s, 99.10 w Bushwick av, 24.9x 100. Oct. 17, 4 years, 5 %. 4,500

Kirby, J. Mason to Joseph P. Puels. Bainbridge st, n s, 277 e Saratoga av, 18x100. Oct. 19, 1 year. 1,500

Same to same. Bainbridge st, n s, 133 e Saratoga av, 18x100. Sub. to mort. $35,000. Oct. 19, 1 year. 1,500

Same to The Title Guarantee and Trust Co. Bainbridge st, n s, 277.7 e Saratoga av, 18x 100. Oct. 19, 3 years, 5 %. 3,500

Same to same. Bainbridge st, n s, 133 e Saratoga av, 18x100. Oct. 19, 3 years, 5 %. 3,500

Kay, William E. to The Roslyn Savings Bank. 56th st, s w s, 175 n w 14th av, 175x102.2, New Utrecht. Oct. 15, due Nov. 1, 1894, 5 %. 4,000

Linson, William to Frank B. Waterman and George D. Beatty. Dean st, s s, 100 w Schenectady av, 16x107. Oct. 1, 3 years. 700

Lock, Charles H. to The Title Guarantee and Trust Co. Madison st. P. M. Oct. 20, 3 years, 5 %. 1,500

Lanzer, Hermann to Emilie Huber. 9th av, s w cor 20th st, being Nos. 322-330 9th av. Lease. Oct. 13, note. 4,000

Levin, Barnet and Max Gittelsohn to Julius Beirach. Thatford av, w s, 100 n Blake av, 25x90. Oct. 14, installs. 1,000

Lehmann, Michael and Anna his wife to George Gutting. Flushing av. P. M. Oct. 17, 3 years, 5 %. 1,700

Lemmermann, Henry L. to Herman Lins. Broadway, No. 1988, s w cor Vesta av. Oct. 7, note. 1,000

Lewis, Sven to John E. Tousey. Collins st. P. M. Oct. 14, 5 years, 5 %. 700

Laing, Donald to William A. Cook trustee Charlotte E. Harries. Belmont av, s s, 80 e Montauk av, 20x90. Oct. 15, 3 years. 2,000

Leiufelder, Anna to Albert G. McDonald. Rockaway av, e s, 100 n Sutter av, 75x100.1. Oct. 5, demand. 1,000

Lloyd, Ida I. to Louis Isenburger. Belmont av, n s, 25 e Vesta av, 25x100. Sept. 30, due Sept. 1, 1893, installs. 250

Loeble, Margaret W. to The Williamsburgh Savings Bank. Grand av, w s, 311.9 n Lafayette av, 16.2x100. Oct. 15, 1 year, 5 %. 2,600

Lipman, Lewis H. to James D. Lynch. 84th st, New Utrecht. P. M. Oct. 16, due Oct. 23, 1893, 5 %. 500

McCormick, George W. to Mathias Grossarth. Reid av, w s, 75 n Halsey st, 25x100. Oct. 20, 1 year. 1,000

Same to same. Reid av, w s, 50 n Halsey st, 25 x100. Oct. 20, 1 year. 1,000

Minto, Robert F. to W. L. Clark, Linden st, s s, 84 e Central av, 16x75. Oct. 21, 6 months. 500

Maguire, Thomas F, to Hannah E. Miller, Philadelphia, Pa. Van Buren st. P. M. Oct. 20, due Nov. 1, 1894, 5 %. 1,500

Maguire, Charles E. to Catharine Von Dreele. Warwick st, w s, 20 n Blake av, 20x100. Oct. 15, 3 years. 1,500

Same to same. Warwick st, w s, 40 n Blake av, 20x100. Oct. 15, 3 years. 1,500

Maguire, Patrick to George Covert. Greene av. P. M. Oct. 13, due Oct. 15, 1896, 5 %. 4,500

Mandell, Adolf to Emilio del Pino exr. Marcos del Pino. Dupont st, n s, 225 e Oakland st, 50x100. Oct. 19, 3 years, 5 %. 4,000

Mason, Mary E. wife of and Isaac D. to Orson W. Sheldon and Paul W. Ledoux. Bergen st, n s, 185.4 e Ralph av, 16.8x107.2. Oct. 1, 1 year. 2,000

Same to same. Bergen st, n s, 304 e Ralph av, 16x107.2. Oct. 15, 1 year, 5 %. 1,800

Same to Paul W. Ledoux. Bergen st, n s, 270 e Ralph av, 17x107.2. Oct. 15, 1 year, 5 %. 1,800

Same to same. Bergen st, n s, 151.4 e Ralph av, 17x107.2. Oct. 1, 1 year. 2,000

Same to same. Bergen st, n s, 168.4 e Ralph av, 17x107.2. Oct. 1, 1 year. 2,000

Same to Orson W. Sheldon. Bergen st, n s, 287 e Ralph av, 17x107.2. Oct. 15, 1 year, 5 %. 1,800

Same to same. Bergen st, n s, 134.4 e Ralph av, 17x107.2. Oct. 1, 1 year. 2,000

Same to same. Bergen st, n s, 100 e Ralph av, 17x107.2. Oct. 1, 1 year. 2,000

Maurer, Ulrich, Adolph Jacobson and Christian H. Meller to Frederick Kremeier and Frederick Becker. 3d av, e s, at intersection with n e s 96th st if continued, runs north 104 x southeast 167.2 x southwest 100 to 96th st, x northwest 138.8, New Utrecht. Oct. 2, notes. 3,500

Martin, George W. to The Mutual Life Ins. Co. (Lim.) 18th st, s s, 85 w 8th av, 2 lots, each 18x100. 2 morts., each $3,000. Oct. 19, 1 year. 6,000

Martin, Mary to John Miner. 5th av, s e s, 39.7 n e 7th st, runs southeast 70 x southwest 19 x northwest 17.10 x southwest 0.2 x northwest 18.2 x southwest 0.6½ x northwest 34 to 5th av, x northeast 19.9. Oct. 16, due Nov. 1, 1894. 5,000

Maloney, Patrick to The Bushwick Co-operative Building and Loan Assoc. Woodbine st. P. M. Oct. 16, installs. 3,750

Magaw, John and Alice Kelly to Dorathea Waldeck. Conselyea st. P. M. Oct. 15, 5 years, 5 %. 1,500

Margolin, Morris to Thomas and Augustin Walsh. Watkins st, w s, 225 s Sutter av, 25x 100. Oct. 15, 3 years. 2,000

Martin, Charles A. to James B. McKewan. Dean st, n s, 133.4 e Utica av, 33.4x100. Oct. 16, 3 months. Sub. to morts. 600

McCurdy, Richard to Charles B. Mount. 56th st. P. M. Oct. 15, due Oct. 1, 1894, 5 %. 1,000

McGowan, Mary to Mary J. Moe. Concord st. P. M. Oct. 3, due in Oct., 1893, 5 %. 500

McDonnell, Charles to Mary M. Webster. Prospect pl, s s, 100 w Vanderbilt av, 25x131. Oct. 14, 1 year. 500

Mendelsohn, Pincus to Barnet Bershatsky. Flushing av. P. M. Oct. 1, installs. 1,200

Muir, Albert to Noah Tebetts. Fulton st, s w cor Saratoga av. P. M. Oct. 3, due Feb. 1, 1892. 24,750

Same to same. Same property. Oct. 3, due Feb. 1, 1892. 15,000

Monzani, Richard P. to Samuel W. Strickland trustee John McNeil. Metropolitan av, s s, 75 e Catharine st, 25x100. Oct. 14, due Oct. 19, 1894, 5 %. 2,000

Meyer, William to Daniel J. O'Conor and ano. exrs. Daniel O'Conor. Humboldt st. P. M. Oct. 15, 2 years. 1,500

Miobel, Leopold to Sophia Loffler and ano. exrs. George Loffler. Cook st, n s, 200 e Ewen st, 25x100. Oct. 15, 5 years, 5 %. 5,000

Mitchell, Frank to Beadleston & Woerz. Grand st, No. 214. Saloon lease. Oct. 14, demand. 750

Moloney, William to The Brooklyn City Cooperative Building and Loan Assoc. 17th st, n s, 324.5 w 5th av, runs north 75 x west 0.2¾ x north 25.2 x west 25 x south 100.2 to st, x east 25.7. Oct. 15, installs. 3,750

Murray, Patrick to Richard Schlepegrell, Rockville Centre, L. I. North 5th st, n s, 180 w Bedford av, 20x100. Oct. 15, 3 years, 5 %. 2,300

Moore, John to The Title Guarantee and Trust Co. 9th st, s s, 218.1 w 8th av, 20.5x72.6x20.4 x72.6; 9th st, s s, 277.6 w 8th av, 18.8x72.6x 18.10x72.6; 9th st, s s, 335.4 w 8th av, 40.3x 82.6x40.3x82.6; 9th st, s s, 415.8 w 8th av, 40.6 x82 6x40.5x82.6. Oct. 15, demand. 30,000

Same to Daniel Doody. 9th st, s s, 100 w 8th av, 18.10x72.6; 9th st, s s, 218.1 w 8th av, 20.5 x72.6x20.4x72.6; 9th st, s s, 277 6 w 8th av, 18.8x72.6x18.10x72.6; 9th st, s s, 335.4 w 8th av, 40.3x82.6x40.3x82.6; 9th st, s s, 415.8 w 8th av, 40.6x82.6x40.5x82.6. Oct. 15, demand. 27,000

Mostkowitz, Hymon to Thomas and Augustin Walsh. Sutter av, s s, 25 w Watkins st, 25x 100. Oct. 13, due Oct. 1, 1894. gold, 3,000

Muir, Albert to Frank A. Barnaby. Fulton st and Saratoga av. P. M. Oct. 15, demand. 11,250

Muller, Bernard mortgagor with Ernest J. F. Risch. Extension of mort. Oct. 15. nom

Naeber, C. to Loftus Hollingsworth, Scotch Plains, N. J. Boerum st, s s, 150 w Leonard st, 50x100. Oct. 1, 3 years, 5 %. 6,000

Neublatt, Harris to Louis Ratner. Eastern Parkway. P. M. Oct. 17, installs. 1,500

Nassau Land and Improvement Co. to Ross C. Browning, West Orange, N. J. 8th av, 15th st. P. M. Oct. 14, due Oct. 16, 1896, 5 % 37,000

Neilson, Samuel H. to George W. Pearsall. 53d st, n s, 80 e 2d av, 20x100.2. Oct. 13, 1 year. 100

Newman, Adolphus A. to Fanny Jacobs. Broadway. P. M. Oct. 5, 1 year, 5 %. 1,000

Niles, Nathaniel to Henry B. Johnson. 2d st, n s, 190 e 6th av, 60x100. Oct. 1, 2 years. 5,000

Norris, Daniel B. to Adaline B. Saddington. Jefferson av. P. M. Oct. 21, 1 year, 5 %. 11,000

Nowak, Martin to Elizabeth Buchanan. South 3d st. P. M. Oct. 20, 5 years, 5 %. 2,000

O'Donohue, Thomas to East New York Savings Bank. Hendrix st, e s, 200 n Glenmore av, 50x100. Oct. 14, 1 year. 2,000

O'Hara, Dorathea to William Schildknecht. Stockholm st, s e s, 275 n e Evergreen av. 25x 100. Oct. 1, 3 years, 5 %. 3,000

O'Brien, Bridget to George Grassick, Maywood, N. J. Eagle st. P. M. Oct. 15, 5 years, 5 %. 3,000

Overlander, Caroline to Helena Wulfing. Tompkins av, n e cor Floyd st, 20x100. May 15, 5 years, 5 %. 500

Pack, John to John Officer. Bushwick av. P. M. Oct. 15, 2 years, 5 %. 2,500

Pendrill, Annie M. wife of and George W. to Cornelia Camman and ano. extrx. William Camman. Lafayette av, s s, 217.3 e Tompkins av, 20x100x17.10x100. Oct. 1, 3 years, 5 %. 3,500

Peterson, Bothilda to Samuel H. Newby. Pacific st. P. M. Oct. 15, 3 years. 1,500

Philips, Julia E. wife of Charles S. to George L. Ronalds. Macon st, n s, 567.2 e Tompkins av, 19.4x100. Sept. 24, due April 1, 1892. 2,150

Palmer, George W. to William L. Palmer, of Norvell, Mich. Van Sielen av, n e cor Glenmore av, 100x100. July 1, 5 years. 6,000

Proctor, Albert W. S. mortgagee with Hannah and Philip Sullivan mortgagors. Extension of mort. Oct. 17. nom

Parish, John L to The Daily News Building, Savings and Loan Assoc 45th st, n e s, 300 s e 5th av, 40x100.2. Oct. 24, installs. 4,000

Parshall, George H. to Susan M. Kissam extrx. Daniel T. Kissam. 17th st, n s, 40 e 3d av, 20 x100.2. Oct. 19, due Nov. 1, 1894, 5 %. 3,000

Quinn, Patrick E. to The South Brooklyn Savings Inst. Wyckoff st, s s, 235 w Bond st, 20 x100. Oct. 16, 1 year, 5 %. 1,000

Radcliffe, Thomas H. to David Barnett. Decatur st, n s, 299.8 w Howard av, 46.8x100. Oct. 17, demand. 3,000

Ranson, James F. to Hans S. Christian. 10th st, n s, 137.10 w 8th av, 100x100. Oct. 12, due Dec. 1, 1891. 2,568

Remick, John C. to Williamsburgh Savings Bank. Putnam av, n s, 169.7 e Stuyvesant av, 18.7x100. Oct. 14, 1 year, 5 %. 14,500

Reynolds, Charles H. to Henry Weil. Somers st, s s, 200 w Stone av, 15x100. Oct. 12, 3 years. 3,000

Same to same. Somers st, s s, 260 w Stone av, 15x100. Oct. 12, 3 years. 3,000

Same to same. Somers st, s s, 315 w Stone av, 15x100. Oct. 12, 3 years. 3,000

Same to same. Somers st, s s, 245 w Stone av, 15x100. Oct. 12, 3 years. 3,000

Richardson, William S. and Jennie L. his wife to Henry Ginnel. Pulaski st. P. M. Oct. 16, 3 years, 5 %. 900

Riekers, Henry to Charlotte E. Northridge. Sutter av, s w cor Essex st. P. M. Oct. 6, due Oct. 15, 1896. 2,500

Raff, Meier, New York, to Isaac Goodman and Max Karol. Humboldt st. P. M. Oct. 16, due Oct. 15, 1895, 5 %. 200

Randall, Stephen M. to Jacob G. Dettmer. St. Marks av. P. M. Oct. 16, 2 years, 5 %. 7,500

Remy, Lydia O. to The Bay Ridge Park Improvement Co. 10th av, n e cor 72d st, 100 x100. P. M. Oct. 7, 2 years, 5 %. 1,000

Renz, Charles to Laurens Darde. Tompkins av, w s, 60 n Ellery st, 20x100. Oct. 17, 5 years, 5 %. 5,000

Roberts, William to Obermeyer & Liebman. Atlantic av, No. 645. Lease. Oct. 17, demand. 700

Rockwell, Gertrude P. to Samuel R. Hawley, New York. Myrtle av, n s, 60.3 w Gold st, 20x100. Aug. 26, note. 2,000

Richards, Jane E. wife of James N., Montclair, N. J., to Nellie M. wife of Frederick O. Ernesty. 7th st, s s, 129.10 w 7th av, 17.8x100. Oct. 20, notes. 2,300

Roth, Morris to Otto Saalfeld. Manjer st. P. M. 2d mort. Oct. 15, 5 years, 5 %. 3,700

Rosse, Augusta to Julius Lehrenkrauss. Hamilton av, w s, 201.4 n Atlantic av, 25x87.6. Oct. 1, due Jan. 1, 1897. 1,000

Reilly, Louisa F. wife of and John to George W. Adams. Bushwick av, south cor Aberdeen st, runs south 90 x southeast 200 to Hull st, x north 79.2 x north 221 to av, x northwest 180.6. Oct. 12, 1 year. 1,075

Reuss, William to Weiz & Zerwick. Fulton av, s s, 76.7 w Linwood st, 25.6x85.9x25x90.11. Oct. 19, due Jan. 1, 1893, 5 %. 1,700

Reynolds, Charles G. to Clementine S. Patchen. McDonough st, s s, 250 e Reid av, 106.4x100. Oct. 20, demand. 6,000

Reynolds, Elias J. to William E. Murphy exr. Thomas Murphy. Seeley and 20th sts, Flatbush. P. M. Aug. 3, 3 years, 5 %. 475

Raymond, Henry V. to The Title Guarantee and Trust Co. St. Marks av, n s, 40 w Carlton av. P. M. Oct. 21, 1 year, 5 %. 3,000

Rosenfeld, Rosa wife of and Jonas to Lena Rosenfeld. Bergen st, s s, 100 w Hopkinson av, 25x127.9. Oct. 17, 3 years. 1,000

Ruehl, Adolph to The Brooklyn City R.R. Co. Stewart av, s s, 32.11 w Denyse st, runs southwest 247.2 to River or Shore road, x southeast 4.8 x again southeast 57.3 x still southeast 66.10 x northeast 289.5 x still northeast 29.3 x northwest 39.11 x northwest again 96.9; Stewart av, s s, 319.1 w Denyse st, runs southeast along River or Shore road 38 x again southeast 160.10 x southeast along River or Shore road 35 x still along same southwest 62.8 to high-water line of New York York Bay, x northwest 239.5 x northeast 24.9 x again northeast 42.5; Stewart av, s s, at intersection of New York Bay at point 388 w Denyse st, runs southwest 811.10 to pier line, x southeast 234 x northeast 772.3 to high-water line New York Bay, x west 239.8 to beginning, New Utrecht. Oct. 1, installs, 5 %. 70,000

Schafer, John to Carolina Kloetman. Halsey st, s s, 180.7 e Ralph av, 18x100. Oct. 19, 5 years, 5 %. 3,500

Sibley, Albert to John and Thomas Charlton, Tonawanda, N. Y. Quincy st, s s, 381.3 w Throop av, 18.9x100. Oct. 7, 8 years. 1,500

Sommers, George A. to George Schwarz. Liberty av, s w cor Van Siclen av. P. M. Oct. 21, 5 years, 5 %. 2,500

Stelzner, Charles W. J. to Edward C. Reinhardt. Bushwick av, w s, 50 s McKibbin st, 25x100. Oct. 20, 3 years, 5 %. 3,500

Smith, Robert J. to Charles T. Harbeck et al. exrs. Ella S. Flagg. State st, s w cor Columbia st, 75x45. Oct. 12, 1 year. 5,000

Schechtel, William, Samuel Davis, Louis Cohen and Louis Regensbogen to Josiah O. Ward guard. to Isabel G. Ward. Stone av, e s, 275 s Sutter av, 25x100. Oct. 14, 2 years. 3,000

Same to same. Stone av, e s, 250 s Sutter av, 25x100. Oct. 14, 2 years. 3,000

Scheen, Isaac to N. Willard Curtis. Dumont av, s s, 25 e Thatford av, 25x100. Oct. 14, 9 months. 100

Sior, Heinrich to William and Ferdinand Funk. Floyd st. P. M. Oct. 12, 1 year. 2,700

Smeaton, Robert to The Metropolitan Savings Bank. 5th st, n s, 24 w 7th av, 17.6x100. Oct. 19, 1 year, 5 %. 2,500

Spangenbehr, Maria to Anna E. Anderson. Palmetto st, n w s, 175 s w Central av, 25x100. Oct. 19, due Jan. 1, 1892, 5 %. 100

Stoddard, Lucy E. wife of and John H. to The Brooklyn Savings Bank. Fulton st, s w cor Hoyt st, 19x100. Oct. 19, 1 year, 5 %. 50,000

Sullivan, Hannah wife of and Philip to Sarah J. wife of Henry S. Vanderveer. Vanderbilt av, w s, 75 n Pacific st, 25x75. Oct. 17, due May 1, 1892, or sooner. 1,000

Schmelze, Mina E. to Owen Carroll. Hicks st, n w cor Garnett st, 25x106.6. Oct. 14, 1 year. 200

Schmitt, Johann J. to August Kromann. Russell st, w s, 120 n Nassau av, 40x100. Oct. 1, 5 years, 5 %. 500

Schoefer, Henry J. to John Dill, Jr. Gates av, n s, 80 w Vanderbilt av, 20x75. Oct. 16, due Nov. 1, 1891. 125

Schwarz, Louis to Mary Schmolze. Quincy st. P. M. Aug. 1, 5 %. 2,000

Serrand, Marguerite to Thomas Minnis. 3d av, w s, 75.2 n 51st st, 20x100. Oct. 14, 3 years. 500

Sheffield, Edward to The Citizen's Savings Bank, New York. Kosciusko st, n s, 300 w Marcy av, 25x100. Oct. 16, 1 year, 5 %. 1,800

Shephard, James A. and Henry F. to George W. Palmer. Stone av and Eastern Parkway and Christopher av. P. M. Oct. 15, 4 years, 5 %. 6,000

Same to same. Same property. P. M. Oct. 15, 4 years, 5 %. 6,000

Smith, James to Obermeyer & Liebman. 5th av, s e cor Prospect av. Saloon lease. Oct. 13, demand. 2,500

Stadtmiller, John E. to William J. Kerrigan. Madison st. P. M. Oct. 15, 3 years, 5 %. 2,500

Same to Adolphus Gload. Same property. Oct. 15, installs. 1,150

Steinfeld, Minna to Charles F. Hitzelberger. Rockaway av, e s, 225 n Belmont av, 25x100.1. Oct. 10, 5 years. 3,000

Stock, Christian J. to Jacob Leeser. Ewen st, w s, 125 n Scholes st, 25x100. Oct. 15, 2 years. 2,000

Stern, David to Sebastian Hohn. Lorimer st, w s, 25 s Johnson av, 25x100. Oct. 20, due May 1, 1892, 5 %. 1,250

Taate, John P. to The Germania Savings Bank, Kings Co. Sands st, n w cor Jay st, 30.4x72. Oct. 12, 1 year. 20,000

Templeman, Charles B. to Frederick D. Colcord. 47th st, n s, 280 w 3d av, 20x100.2. Oct. 16, 3 years, 5 %. 700

Theiling, Joseph to Henry Eppig. Central av. P. M. Oct. 13, due Jan. 1, 1897, 5 %. 4,000

Tebbetts, Noah to Paul W. Ledoux. Herkimer st, n s, 20 w Saratoga av, 80x80; Saratoga av, w s, 80 n Herkimer st, 40x100. Oct. 14, demand. 10,000

Thompson, Wilhelmina to Simon H. Stern. Eastern Parkway, s s, 25 e Jerome st, 25x100. Oct. 13, 3 years. 1,700

Turner, Mary to George A. Hughes. Driggs av, w s, 81 n Division av, 21x101.1x24.2x101.1. Oct. 16, 3 years. 500

Tibbits, Sarah A. to William S. Hassan. 52d st, n s, 384 w 3d av, 18x100.2. Oct. 17, due Nov. 1, 1896. 1,500

Toury or Tonry, James to Phebe A. Davis. Rock st, n s, 200 w Morgan av, 25x100. Oct. 16, 3 years. 300

Teurey, Dominica to Walli W. Zipp. 4th av, w s, 60 s President st, 20x100. Oct. 19, 3 years. gold, 4,000

Tyler, Frank H. and Frederick B. Langston to The Title Guarantee and Trust Co. Hancock st, n s, 380 e Nostrand av, 21x100. Oct. 19, demand. 8,000

Vanderveer, Ada B. to Minnie L. Uhler. 39th st, s s, 150.6 e 3d av, 24.6x100.2. Oct. 16, due Oct. 1, 1894, 5 %. 6,500

Van Wart, Frances A. to Elizabeth A. Lundequist. 13th st, s s, 497.10 e 5th av, 25x100; 13th st, s s, 522.10 e 5th av, 0.2½x100. Oct. 15, 3 years, 5 %. 500

Vrooman, John F. to Rosalie H. Murphy. Powell st, w s, 250 n Liberty av, 25x100. Oct. 15, 3 months. 1,500

Van Deusen, Annie A. wife of and Henry to The Title Guarantee and Trust Co. Hancock st, s s, 257.6 e Tompkins av, 17.6x100. Oct. 20, due Oct. 21, 1894, 5 %. 1,500

Voorhis, Charles mortgagee with James P. Farrell mortgagor. Extension of mort. Oct. 20. nom

Werner, Marceline wife of William to Pierre Rodier. 42d st. P. M. Oct. 1, 10 years, 5 %. 1,400

Wallace, John C. and Emma J. his wife to Dorothea Zerr. Monitor st. P. M. Oct. 1, 1891, 3 years, 5 %. 1,200

Walsh, John to Kate Gottschalk. Hart st, s s, 225 e Evergreen av, 25x97.6. Oct. 15, 3 years, 5 %. 2,000

Wallmann, Raimund and Sibillia his wife to The German Savings Bank, Brooklyn. Flushing av, s w cor Beaver st, runs northwest 129.6 x southwest 73 11 x southeast —x south 9.3 x east 77.8 to st, x north 19.9. Oct. 12, due Dec. 1, 1892, 5 %. 7,000

Warmworth, John and Marianne his wife to Jane A. McKenna. Graham st, No. 121, 25 x—. Oct. 14, 3 years, 5 %. 2,000

Willets, Mary E. to Jemima Seaman, Wantogh, L. I. Washington av, e s, 127 s Myrtle av, 20x100. Oct. 15, due Nov. 1, 1892. 1,000

Wills, Thomas D. to Alonzo Reed, Quogue, L. I. Nichols av. P. M. Sept. 28, demand. 4,000

Wood, Frederic to The United States Trust Co., New York. Baltic st, s s, 192.3 w Columbia st, 141.4x104.10. Oct. 12, due Nov. 1, 1892, 5 %. 10,000

Woodhull, Caleb S. to The Title Guarantee and Trust Co. Fulton st, s w s, 80.7 n w South Oxford st, 20x66.7x33.8x39.5. Sept. 30, 1 year, 5 %. 5,000

Wechsler, Joseph to William J. Gaynor trustee Andrew McClennen dec'd. Willoughby st. P. M. Oct. 19, 1 year, 5 %. 6,000

Weis, Philip to Louis Braun. McKibbin st, s s, 125 w Graham av, 25x100. Oct. 11, due July 1, 1894, 5 %. 4,000

Williams, George, Sharon Springs, N. Y., to Joel F. Tyler. Hancock st. P. M. Oct. 19, installs. 2,800

Williams, Percy G. to George Beach, Hartford, Conn. Schermerhorn st. P. M. Oct. 12, due Oct. 19, 1896, 5 %. 47,175

Zeiser, Bertha to Louis Kaufman and Benjamin Benjamin. Graham av. P. M. Oct. 17, 1 year, 5 %. 1,000

MORTGAGES----ASSIGNMENTS.

NEW YORK CITY.

OCTOBER 16 TO 22—INCLUSIVE

Alten, John C. to The Title Guarantee and Trust Co. $5,000

Bleistift, Jeannette to George and Emma Kocher. 2,000

Bogert, Henry A. trustee for the children of Charles L. Bogert to Henry A. Bogert guard. of Mary E. Bogert. Re-recorded. 3,005

Boss, Frederick to Emily C. Ditchett. 1,600

Baker, John O., Newark, N. J., to Alfred M. Hoyt. 40,000

Bleier, Leopold to William Reichman. nom

Same to same. nom

Bowes, John and John Ccombs to Henry Greenebaum. 1,400

Baer, Morris B. as guard., &c., to Jessie Rosenfeld. 2 assigns. nom

Bickel, Emma W. formerly Safft to Ida C. Safft. consid. omitted

Callender, William E. to Eliza S. Bibby, Baltimore, Md. 1,400

Cornell, John, Nice, France, to Lyman G. and Joseph B. Bloomingdale exrs. and trustees William M. Weil. 9,000

Delafield, Francis and ano. exrs. Edward

Delafield to Catherine D. Wright, Stamford, Conn. nom
Dwyer, Michael F., Brooklyn, to The People's Trust Co. 25,000
Same to same. 15,000
Eggert, Henry admr. Heinrich Kopp to Wilhelm Recke. 3,750
Ersler, Victor P. P. and Bertha M., Brooklyn, to Edwin S. Updike, Sr. nom
Falk, Fannie wife of Arnold to Gustav and Arnold Falk. 12,000
Falk, Gustav to Moses Wallach et al. exrs. Arnold Falk. nom
Falk, Gustav survivor of G. Falk & Brother to Moses Wallach et al. exrs. Arnold Falk. nom
Frank, John and ano. exrs. Lewis S. Frank to Louisa Frank, Brooklyn. 12,000
Same to same. 3,000
Ford, Henry W. trustee Augustus H. Ward to Charles Lanier trustee for Alexander C. Lanier. 16,000
Same to same. 16,000
Gebhard, Michael to Louis Wirth. 5,700
Green, Catherine, Orange, N. J., to Garret E. Green. Re-recorded. nom
German-American Real Estate Title Guarantee Co. to Henry S. Blake and ano. trustees John E. Blake dec'd. 14,000
Grotzinger, Rosina to Magdalena B. Keller. 900
Germania Life Ins. Co. of New York to James F. Pierce as Supt. of the Insurance Dept. of the State of New York. nom
Gorsch, Arthur to Catherine Bode, Brooklyn. 1,500
Gottgetreu, Henry to Dora Kierski. 5,570
Gottgetreu, William to Henry Gottgetreu. 5,500
Gwynne, Mary E. to John A. Gwynne. 30,000
Gershel, Heiman et al. exrs. Henry Gershel to Levi N. Hershfield. 7,150
Gordon, Katie admrx. Stephen T. Gordon to Kittie Wiley, Brooklyn. 15,000
Gordon, Katie to Sarah E. Platt 4,500
Huebsch, Julia admrx. Adolphus Huebsch to William A. Gans et al. trustees of Manhattan Lodge No. 156 I. O. B. B. 4,000
Hyatt, George E. Brooklyn, to Henry W. Ford trustee Augustus H. Ward. nom
Same to same. nom
Hawkes, Henry, Riverside, Conn., to John W. Haaren. 2,000
Hyatt, George E., Brooklyn, to Henry W. Ford trustee Augustus H. Ward dec'd. nom
Isear, Rebecca to Annie F. Leverich trustee. 6,000
Kilpatrick, Edward to John C. Overhiser. 6,100
Kurzman, Ferdinand exr. Babette Myer to The Farmers' Loan and Trust Co. nom
Kelly, Eugene and Edward and Joseph A. Donohue, of Eugene Kelly & Co., to Harriet V. Ogden. 10,000
Leupp, William H. New Brunswick, N. J., to Francis Delafield and ano. trustees Edward Delafield dec'd. 14,000
Middlebrook, Frederic J., Brooklyn, to Charlotte O. Schetter, Brooklyn. 5,605
Middlebrook, Frederic J., Brooklyn, to The Farmers' Loan and Trust Co. 12,684
Morgenthau, Henry to Minnie Hayman. nom
Mahony, Michael J. and Daniel F. to Jonas Weil and Bernhard Mayer. 1,660
Miller, J. Bleecker to The Title Guarantee and Trust Co. 2,000
Nineteenth Ward Bank to Prosnitz & Greenebaum. 5,000
Purser, Priscilla S., Yonkers, N. Y., to Priscilla S. and George H. Purser, Jr., exrs. George H. Purser. 3,000
Radebold, William and Edward Wenz to Willis H. Young, George H. Gerard and Adolphus F. Quick, of Young, Gerard & Co. nom
Riker, Silvanus S. to Samuel Riker. 31,183
Ramsteck, Jacob to Louise A. Ramsteck. nom
Razen, Mary A. to Rosina Riegelman. 3,000
Smith, H. Allen to Charles B. de Barril. nom
Schneider, Louis exr. Anna Schwarz to Bertha Haegele. 800
Sheridan, James F. and Patrick H. and James S. Segrave to Thomas C. Cornell. 3 assigns., each $370. 1,110
Spooner, Charles W. to William H. Kenagh. 1,250
Studwell, William J. and George S. to Henry Hart. 6,650
Stevens, Howard A. to James Thomson. 2,500
Scott, William W. exr. Ann E. Walker to Edward Kilpatrick. 155
Stedman, Ernest G. to Sarah Taylor. Re-recorded. 5,000
The Bradley & Currier Co. (Lim.) to James C. Gulick. 6,065
The Lawyers' Title Ins. Co. of New York to The Twelfth Ward Savings Bank. 13,500
Title Guarantee and Trust Co. to George N. Earl. 2,500
Same to Eliza M. Zerega. 400
Title Guarantee and Trust Co. to Isabel Holmes, Seymour, Conn. 5,000
Same to same. 5,000
Title Guarantee and Trust Co. to Thomas E. Rochford. 5,000
Title Guarantee and Trust Co. to Phebe C. Lawrence, Lawrence, L. I. 2,000
Ughetta, Henry L. exr. and trustee Maria Ughetta to Henry L. Ughetta, Brooklyn. 10,000
Winkler, Jacob and Elizabeth his wife to Margaret Hurley, Brooklyn. 1,400
Whalen, John to John Halloran. 13,000
Wright, Catharine D. to Margaret L. King. 14,000
Wood, Mary L. formerly Randell guard. of Henry M. Randell to Henry M. Randell. 12,500
Wallach, Moses and ano. exrs. Arnold Falk to Fannie Falk widow. nom
Zucker, Jennie N. to Joseph W. Sandford, Jr., Plainfield, N. J. 4,000

KINGS COUNTY.

Oct. 15 to 21—Inclusive.

Anderson, William S. and William L. Dowling to William J. Donald. $5,015
Arnold, Daniel S. and Silas A. Condict to John Townshend et al. trustees William G. Patterson dec'd. 4,200
Boogher, Simson L. and ano. exrs. Mary Plummer to The Title Guarantee and Trust Co. 5,000
Burroughs, William H. to Louis De B. Kuhn. 600
Bennett, Jr., Martin to Minnie Bennett. nom
Burger, Anna M., Mary A. Gilner and Martin Schoeffel to Mary Schoppa. 2,500
Burton, Wingfield G. to Frank P. Ward. nom
Barthman, Eleanora M. to Helen D. Isaacs extrx. Jane C. Moore. 2,750
Bailey, Frank to The Title Guarantee and Trust Co. consid. omitted
Same to same. nom
Same to same. 40,000
Burrows, Mary A. to Samuel Dean. 1,400
Cohn, Amalie to Nathan Levy. 750
Conger, Clarence R. to Susan A. Babcock. 12,303
Case, George C. to Elizabeth Taber. 2,250
Cross, Elizabeth to John H. Schutte. 6,000
Cellars, George to William C. Edwards. 1,000
De Bevoise, John C. and ano. exrs. Gertrude Colyer to Walter M. Cook, Pittston, Pa. 3,700
Same to Mary E. Cook, Pittston, Pa. 1,600
Same to same. 1,000
Same to Arthur Cook, Pittson, Pa. 2,500
Same to same. 3,000
Same to same. 1,000
Doody, Daniel and David Stone to Charles Hagedorn. nom
Driscoll, Edward to Asa W. Parker. 15,800
Dieter, Absalom W. to Hans S. Christian. 14,845
Davenport, Julius exr. Ann Wilson to The Title Guarantee and Trust Co. 2,800
Everit, Thomas to Harriet E. Dunn. 750
Fischer, Jacob to John Fensch. 810
Forrester, William O. to Hans S. Christian. 2,000
Franke, Eunice R. to Otto J. Bueh. 5,159
Flanagan, William to William H. Hazzar et al. trustees James Brady. 10,000
Gillespie, Earl A., Woodhaven, L. I., to Maud P. Nelson. 3,500
Gardner, Jennie to James W. Smith, Yaphank, L. I. 4,000
Germania Life Ins. Co., New York, to James F. Pierce, Sup't of the Ins. Department, New York. nom
Hendrickson, Edward to Ada F. Hendrickson. nom
Hulst, Hannah to Theodore F. Jackson exr. Guy C. Hotchkiss. 2,000
Halstead, Pearson exr. Annie Joy to Pearson Halstead trustee Annie Joy. nom
Same to same. nom
Joost, Magdalena and ano. exrs. Magdalena Joost to Elizabeth Cross. nom
Jacoby, Robert P. to Absalom W. Dieter. 14,845
Jarashow, Israel to Leopold Michel. 3,000
Jarashow, Israel to Mary Jarashow. nom
Keck, Albert to Augustus Ziegler. 500
Kaufman, Louis and Benjamin Benjamin to Joseph Benjamin. 1,200
Kent, Phebe V. to Virginia P. Kent. nom
Kleinlein, Anna D. extrx. John Kleinlein to Margaretha Lutter. 1,000
Koehler, Franklin and ano. exrs. Margaret A. Tietjen to Robert A. B. Dayton trustee Anson Blake. 952
Le Bean, Maria to Julius Lehrenkrauss. 300
Lane, George B. to Herman Hartjen. 1,000
Lemon, Andrew to William Andrews and August Nickel. 1,950
Levin, Barnet and Max Gittelsohn to Julius Beirach. 900
Lippmann, Leopold J. to Frank W. Koch & Co. nom
Lewis, Margaretha to George H. Smith. nom
Low, Edwin C. to Charles Cooper. nom
Marsh, Ettie, formerly Townshend, to Mary A. Townshend. nom
Nafis, William H. to John N. Eitel. 1,500
Nostrand, John L. to Henry L. Nostrand. 1,000
Same to same. 500
Same to same. 500
Oakley, John B. H., New York, to Robert W. Scharf. 8,000
Powell, Sarah H. to The Women's Prison Assoc. and Home. 3,500
Pearce, Nancy and ano. exrs. Hosea O. Pearce to Elizabeth Cross. 2,800
Same to Albert G. McDonald. 2,800
Pillen, Mary J. to Jacob H. Werbelovsky. 200
Rushmore, Isaac W., Plainfield, N. J., to The Children's Home Assoc., Plainfield, N. J. 1,000
Robley, James admr. Christopher to James Robley. 2,800
Same to same. 1,500
Ray, William J. to Maria Le Beau. 500
Stewart, Horatio S. to Bernard Levino. 5,000
Same to same. 5,000
Struse, Henry J. and ano. exrs. Conrad Goebl to Martha C. Jennings, New Brunswick, N. J. 4,000
Simon, Semche to Joseph Newborg. nom
Sink, Delia to George Tiefel. 900
Title Guarantee and Trust Co. to John Morton. 8,000
Same to Elizabeth Cross. 6,000
Same to Matilda S. Taylor. 5,000
Same to The Long Island Historical Society. 17,500
Same to Mary A. Wood. 3,000
Same to The Brooklyn Trust Co. 15,000
Same to Mary H. Powers trustee Elijah P. Woodruff dec'd. 8,000
Same to Sarah M. Mygart and ano. trustees Jacob A. Robertson. 1,500
Same to Edward De Witt Mason. 13,000
Same to Mary M. Webster. 2,500
Same to Brooklyn Society for the Prevention of Cruelty to Children. 5,000
The Sterling Fire Ins. Co. to Clarence R. Conger. 12,303
Watson, James H. and James H. Pittinger, of Watson & Pittinger, to Maud P. Nelson. 2,000
Westfall, George F. and ano. exrs., &c., Diedrich Westfall to Rebecca Stemmermann extrx. of Claus Stemmerman. 6,000
Willets, Samuel to Mary W. wife of Aron Wright, Springboro, Ohio. 1869. 3,000

JUDGMENTS.

In these lists of judgments the names alphabetically arranged, and which are first on each line, are those of the judgment debtor. The letter (D) means judgment for deficiency (*) means not summoned. (†) signifies that the first name is fictitious, real name being unknown. Judgments entered during the week, and satisfied before day of publication, do not appear in this column, but in list of Satisfied Judgments.

NEW YORK CITY.

Oct.
17 Adams, Florence L—A L David...... $119 15
19 Anderson, Rodolphus W—D L Newborg........ 478 45
20 Aldridge, Arthur F—Hettie M Tenney........ 459 98
20 Abbe, Charles C—Robert Dawson...., 304 77
20 Alexander, Robert—Fernando Solinger........ 720 00
22* Albright, Charles H—G C Andrae... 1,183 86
22 the same——G C Andreae........1,758 25
22 the same——Henry Abegg........1,587 09
22 Altschul, Emil—M L Simon.......... 252 42
22 Asselta, Guiseppe—Vincenzo Barone di Jacome........ 244 93
22 Astor, William W—J W Holloway ....costs 216 64
22 the same—the same........costs 216 64
17 Bour, Nicholas A—Williams Silk Mfg Co........ 93 19
17 Bennett, Andrew S—Peter Mitchell.. 356 12
17 Beacham, John—John Gag........ 88 62
17 Bonnell, Tammisie H—Chatham Nat Bank........5,040 45
19 Barnes, Oliver W—Maverick Nat Bank........ 950 63
19 Broderick, Michael J—George Ehret. 250 72
19 Butler, George B—Judge Publishing Co........ 817 76
19 Bonforte, Salvatore—J C Moore..... 105 29
20 Benedict, Edward E—Chemical Nat Bank........ 823 52
20 Busbfield, John H; Brady, Mary A, extrx; Philip H Brady—Moses Sahlein....(D) 1,889 49
20 Black, Joseph R—Patrick Cassidy.... 629 13
20 Burtis, Nathaniel W—Commercial Bank........ 534 33
20 Burlington, Albert S; Bonnell, John Harper—Second Nat Bank of Red Bank....... 537 14
21 Bleiman, Arrah—S C Huntington.... 117 04
21 Bonnell, John Harper—Market and Fulton Nat Bank........2,148 01
21 the same——H E Bowns.......... 682 10
21 Bates, Wilbut Melville—August Heckscher........ 490 26
21 Blanck, George B—Mary A Pomroy.. 234 10
21 Bernard, Franklin B, admr Charles Bernard—J H Screven, exr........ 633 46
21 Byrne, William J—Edward Fisher.... 1,179 43
21 Babson, George F—John Fox........ 152 27
21 Bonnell, John Harper—Chatham Nat Bank........5,048 76
21 Biel, Susan—Mary McKeon.......... 85 13
21 Brickwedel, Charles—Esther Moses.. 452 21
21 Blair, Thomas J—E C Gates.......... 270 78
21 Buek, Gustave H; Buek, Charles—P R Weiler...... 943 13
21 Behrman, Abraham—T G Palmer.... 302 13
22 Beyrich, Richard M—P W Myer.... 10,915 87
22 Brunder, Carl B—Charles Mildenberger........ 209 25
22 Boyle, Joseph W—Dori Lyon........ 195 65
22 Bloch, William—R H Gerstel........ 137 66
22 Burroughs, Horace F, Jr—J C Carney........52,564 83
23 Berliner, Julius—Abraham Goldstein 67 87
23 Bedell, Daniel M—G R Brown........ 123 48
23 Braumgras, William H—F W Devoe & Co........5,100 52
23 Bridges, Francis J—James Falvey.... 84 16
23 Baldwin, Theron—Washington Nat Bank........ 520 74
23* Bailey, John F—H G Cordley........ 51 46
23 Broder, Benjamin—Frederick Gutter. 518 41
23 Beaudet, Homer J—Walter Scott.... 2,784 52
23 Bernheimer, Charles M; Bernheimer, Abraham C; Bernheimer, Julius C; Bauer, Felix L—Simon Kierstein.....costs 89 71
23 Beno, Joseph—M L Stieglitz........ 744 96
23 the same——H H Kahn.......... 553 53
23 Butler, Charles T—Essex Co Nat Bank........ 1,227 64

23 Beno, Joseph—W H Graef.......... 1,088 86
17 Cronin, Daniel J—D G Yuengling, Jr, Brewing Co.......... 224 67
17 Campbell, Reau—C K Alley.......... 563 73
19*Comegys, Henry C—John Maxwell... 333 34
19 Collins, Frank S—John Patterson. ... 150 93
19 Cootey, Harriet G—Julia A Chapman, exr.......... 629 77
19 Campbell, William F—Henry Irwin.. 105 50
19 Caulfield, John—J P Hearne.......... 22 75
19 Cavinato, Luigi; *Cavinato, Guisseppi; *Cavinato, Natale; *Cavinato, Steffano } F G Moore. 585 00
20 Couch, William; Couch, Caroline } Ludwig Ohlbaum.. 84 50
20 Crotty, John—F W Blossom.......... 189 72
20 Cullen, Edward J—W G Ross.......... 113 58
21 Cranston, Henry—R J Anderton..... 395 10
21 the same——the same.......... 278 85
21 Cody, Patrick J—W H Harrison.costs 77 13
21 Chosch, Aaron—N J Waldman....... 618 81
21 Cranston, Henry—H E Bowns........ 569 76
21 Castle, James H—Thurber, Whyland & Co.......... 329 23
21 Carr, John—Lamson Consolidated Store Service Co.......... 78 47
21 Carroll, Robert C—Edward Fisher... 417 26
21 Corzilius, Otto H—Hugo Reisinger... 48 87
21 Collin, N Park—Marie Schuler...... 2,254 46
21 Clark, Samuel; Clark, Alexander; Conover, James S; Conover, Alonzo E; Conover, William E } John Fox...... 152 27
21 Clark, Samuel; Clark, Alexander } John Fox....costs 54 95
21 the same——P B Worrall....costs 356 04
22 Celi, Peter—C A Rinaldi.......... 283 91
22 Carmel, Joseph—Emanuel Gips...... 227 98
22 Cornell, Alonzo B—Merchants' Nat Bank of Newtown, N J.......... 2,863 77
22 Curtis, Francis B D—Robert Milbank 34 67
22 Cohn, William N—A H Dirkes....... 89 63
22 Cranston, Henry—E M Travis....... 161 04
22 Coffin, Frederick R—Western Nat Bank.......... 515 83
22 Caswell, William C—Rayffaele Magnotti.......... 324 12
22 Cranston, Henry—Milton Rathbun... 599 01
22 Cornell, Alonzo B—Third Nat Bank.. 5,643 80
23 Carroll, Michael, Jr—C B Vedder.... 122 55
23 Conkling, Marcus M—P J Moran..... 213 37
23 Comstock, Alexander—Rose Beckett. 166 50
23 Clark, Heman—Painesville Nat Bank 3,549 21
23†Crawley, William K—William Johansen.......... 169 00
23 Craig, William—Adamant Mfg Co... 129 72
23 Commeau, Theodore—J B Coste...... 532 18
17 De Raismes, John A—William Rankin.......... 431 84
17 Dittenhoefer, Meyer—G R Brown.... 456 53
17 De Waard, Quintin—C L Heusner.... 22 40
19 Dodge, Cheever K—Anna M Galbraith.......... 119 97
19 Donovan, James—Elizabeth Donovan 1,661 78
19 Dempsey, William—Leopold Friesen.. 302 48
19 Demarest, Frank P—Theodore Diebold.......... 352 37
19 Dreyfuss, Bernard—Metropolitan Telephone and Telegraph Co.......... 36 83
21 Demarest, Daniel—Edmund Anderson 313 88
21 Doyle, Edward P—August Heckscher 490 26
21 de Rivera, Henry C—Charles Darrow, exr.......... 35,551 62
21 the same——Robert Olyphant.... 2,115 37
21 Dean, Frederick M—G W Stephens... 72 68
22 Davis, Joseph—W A Sherman........ 121 19
22 Dennison, James A—Thomas Russell. 935 42
23 Day, Henry, trustee—J W Holoway..........costs 216 64
23 the same——the same.........costs 216 64
23 Delano, Franklin H——the same.costs 216 64
23 the same——the same.........costs 216 64
23*Drake, John—Terence Kane.......... 1,531 47
23 Davis, Leonard—Bernard Fiero...... 103 00
23 Dunn, James R—P J Moran.......... 213 37
17 Edwards, Ellis B—R A Welcke...... 255 77
19 Elliott, George H—Samuel Aronson.. 372 98
19 Ewing, Thomas—Twenty-third Ward Bank.......... 2,717 74
21 Ertell, William H—Samuel Clark.... 1,248 88
21 Elmendorf, Julia L; Elmendorf, James H } C H Lovett.. 149 85
22 Erlenkoetter, Frederick — Charles Mildenberger.......... 269 25
23 Eustace, Mark S—W H Hallock...... 199 88
19 Frischman, Ignatz—Jacob Fromme.. 74 15
19 Fink, Alois—Henrietta Rice.......... 77 14
19 French, Hamlin Q—Edward Lambden.......... 790 57
19 the same——J F New.......... 132 06
19 Fox, Frederick—Benjamin Hyams... 298 55
19 Foster, David M G—N T Parker...... 289 49
19 Frankish, Joseph; Frankish, John K } O K Eldredge.... 987 25
19 the same——the same.......... 1,651 94
19 the same——the same.......... 1,648 94
20 Fowler, Jacob W—Mary E Lockwood 79 90
20 Flynn, Peter H—Joseph Beck....... 174 00
20 Fitzpatrick, James T—Frank Lucks. 36 25
20 the same——Giovanni Benenti... 38 75
21 Fountain, Inez—Phoebe A Smith..... 293 53
21 Farrell, James H—Henry Sonn....... 82 50
22 Falconi, Cesare—C A Rinaldi........ 283 91
22 Fink, Henry—Edward Bennett....... 94 74
22 Fish, James H—W O Wyckoff....... 107 98
23 Fursman, Annie H—Carrie A Fursman.......... 3,677 20
23 Ficke, William—Gustav Menninger.. 125 88
24 Fogarty, Katie L—Ellen Hynes...... 326 27
17 Greenthal, Frank B—Isaac Raphael.. 319 88
17 Gardner, John—Beadleston & Woerz. 202 43
19 Griffing, Melville S—P J Bresman..... 114 87
19 Gault, Mary—Archibald Culbert..... 267 15
20 Goldstein, Morris—Mendel Diamond, admr.......... 2,064 58
20 Graham, Cornelius W—Queen City Bank.......... 2,545 31
20*Gould, Edmund—Samuel Coles....... 206 11
20 Goold, Michael—Ferdinand Lowenthal.......... 93 93
20 Goldstein, Jeremiah — Phillip Goldstein.......... 532 87
21 Godwin, Parke—Frank Walton...... 4,944 85
21 Gorman, John J, as Sheriff—Marie Schuler.......... 2,254 46
22 Ghetti, Giovanni—C A Rinaldi....... 283 91
22 Glaatstein, Morris—W A Sherman.... 139 54
22 Gebhardt, Adolph—F A Straus....... 228 79
22 Giannelli, Antonio Z—G A Franchi.. 100 14
22 Grant, Hugh J, as Sheriff—Emanuel Neuman.......... 955 65
22 Goldstein, Jeremiah — Harris Goldstein.......... 1,032 74
22 the same——Isaac Goldstein..... 337 62
23 Griswold, Margaret D—Fourteenth Street Bank.......... 1,099 29
23 Goldman, Jackson—T M Dougherty.. 89 70
23 Griswold, Margaret D—Washington Nat Bank.......... 547 99
23 Gifford, Jesse G—H G Cordley........ 51 46
23 Goodwin, Henry J—Hugh O'Neill.... 649 41
17 Haremakar, Peter—Adeline E Haremakar..........costs 42 31
17 Harper, Tacie McD—Chatham Nat Bank.......... 5,046 45
19 Hescote, Henry—Anion Hug......... 34 87
19 Hunt, William H—Emil Dieckerhoff. 731 26
19†Hodes, Morris Nash—S G Hirschberg 1,248 10
19 Holborow, Edward B—William McShane.......... 248 43
19 Hilton, Arthur P—Tribune Assoc.... 160 47
19 Hoppock, Moses—J B Low.......... 121 15
20 Holly, John I—J R Smith.......... 830 29
20 Harris, George S—Samuel Coles...... 206 11
20 *Hedden, William M; Hedden, Joseph E } Metropolitan Life Ins Co.......... 68 13
20 Haas, William—Joseph Zimmerman. 385 20
20 Hyams, Joel E—Harris Friedman.... 155 65
20 Hoag, Harry G—Isaac Landman..... 785 08
20 Hurlbut, Edward N—Herman Schaffner.......... 348 37
21 Harper, William D—Market and Fulton Nat Bank.......... 2,148 01
21 the same——H E Bowns.......... 682 10
21 Hanus, Gustavus C—August Heckscher.......... 490 26
21 Haughey, Edward—A E Massman.... 409 04
21 Hartigan, Dennis—Edward Fisher.... 1,179 48
21 Harper, William D—Chatham Nat Bank.......... 5,048 76
21 Harmon, Ernest H—John Fox......... 152 27
21 Hearn, Frank D V; Hearn, Mary S } L M Ernst....... 888 48
21 Hale, William S—C E Pell.......... 1,048 02
21 Hungerford, Egbert H—R T Pierce... 322 08
21 Hoye, Richard W—Herman Schlosser..........costs 69 12
21 Hornborg, Axel G—M Louise Jeanson 201 74
21 Horowitz, Louis—T G Palmer........ 302 13
22 Hashagen, Julius—H R Rothe........ 449 12
22 Hoffman, Ferdinand G—G H Schmedes 90 68
22 Harper, William D—Western Nat Bank.......... 1,874 94
22 Hughes, Thomas P—J A Lyon........ 27 50
23 Hoornbeck, Rachel, admrx—Bernard & Fiero.......... 103 00
23 Holterbach, Xavier—J F Jacocks.... 119 19
23 Hunerbein, Julius—Shepard & Morse Lumber Co.......... 122 48
23 Higgins, Francis, recvr—Helen McMillan..........costs 79 81
23 Hargreaves, Maggie—O G Staples... 98 23
23 Harper, William D—Market and Fulton Nat Bank.......... 1,240 67
23 Hoebermann, August—John McGee.. 54 30
23 Hartford, Arthur J—W W Astor.... 335 38
23†Herman, Alexander — E P Gleason Mfg Co.......... 419 00
23 Hernin, Martin J—Society of N Y Hospital.......... 107 55
20 Irvine, Allan A—American Encaustic Tiling Co (Lim).......... 88 18
21 Ingraham, Marvin—C A Smith...... 104 84
17 Jacobs, Samuel; *Jacobs, Ralph } H B Claflin Co..... 1,446 96
19 Jones, Joseph R—J A Flomerfelt.... 178 65
22 Jacobs, Samuel—Charles Jackson.... 49 00
22 the same——Moses Goldberg..... 83 23
22 Jordan, Louis, assignee—Mary Israel. 111 47
22 Jaffray, Joseph M—H P Hubbard.... 148 67
23 Joyce, Edward—S M Rosenblatt...... 146 52
23 Jacobs, Asher, by J Allen Townsend guard—Central Stamping Co...... 128 88
17 Kraus, Joseph; Kraus, Julius C } Robert Froese.... 81 20
20 Kelly, Thomas—Joseph Kahn.......... 3,277 45
20 Kahn, Samuel—Brainerd & Armstrong Co.......... 947 40
20 Krollman, Carl — Julius Robertson..........costs 150 85
21 King, Percy R—Charles Darrow, exr. 35,551 62
21 the same——Robert Olyphant.... 2,115 37
21 Kreling, John; Kroling, William } Leo Goldmark... 6,721 73
21 Kaplan, Adolph H—Hugo Reisinger.. 48 87
22 Krumm, Charles—Charles Wanzer... 111 00
22 Kemp, Abraham—W H Lee.......... 38 92
22*Kirschbaum, Jacob—Louis Kessel.... 192 63
23 Kissam, Philip—J W Holloway.costs. 216 64
23 Koerner, John—H F Gundrum....... 99 92
23 Keene, James R—E H Harriman..... 6,537 53
23 Kissam, Philip—J W Holloway..costs 216 64
23 Knab, Charles J—N Y Life Ins Co... 30 68
17 Lawrence, Charles W—Laura K Lawrence.......... 2,766 70
17 Litchhult, Gilbert A—George Singer.. 1,837 07
17 Lowerre, George H—R A Welcke.... 255 77
19 Levy, Copple—Harris Cohen.......... 5,258 93
19 Lusk, O Latham—Isabella S Butler.. 152 87
19 Lewis, Jared E—John Maxwell....... 333 34
19 Luce, Alfred J—T A Knowlton..costs 86 85
19 Lett, Margaret M—C H Bunn.......... 1,388 42
20 Lyon, Harry H—C P Sherwood...... 174 74
20 Loeb, Sigmund—Julius Oberndorf..........costs 123 28
20 Lefkowitz, Louis—Adolf Prince..... 288 39
20 Lippman, Albert—Lorenz Weiher... 222 14
21 Loucks, Frank H—Edwin Wallace... 95 46
21 Lecuyer, Charles G—Hathaway Soule 349 72
21 Lowenstein, Mayer—Mina Solinger.. 81 34
21 Lockwood, John S—B H Tuthill...... 136 31
21 Lawrence, James H—E C Gates...... 270 78
21 Lipschitz, Louis; Lipschitz, Abram } David Mayer. ... 81 87
22 Levy, Elias—S J Weaver.......... 81 33
22 Levy, James C—Charles Reiner...... 204 76
22 Lazard, Felix—Joseph Stern.......... 284 18
23 Lunardini, Angelo—Domenicco Casassa 431 91
23 Leavitt, Edward—Minna L Schack, admrx.......... 18,869 47
23 Liscomb, Alfred A—Sarah K Agate.. 2,065 09
17 Muhlenberg, Emil—W H Jeffers..... 123 09
17 Metzner, Harris—Sigmund Ashner... 1,172 72
17 the same——M L Simon.......... 293 26
19 Michelson, Abraham; Michelson, David } Max Bearlinsky.......... 323 22
19 the same——Samuel Michelson... 697 97
19*Martin, Daniel A—T G Palmer....... 79 78
20 Mittge, Charles—J M Canda.......... 322 04
20 Minuse, John P; Minnse, Carrie D } Emil Calman...... 276 90
20 Murray, John E—G A Le Blanc...... 267 36
21 Mersereau, Joseph W; Moore, Robert } August Heckscher....... 490 26
21 Mars, Henrietta A—E M Van Buren. 147 63
21 Mars, Henrietta A; Mars, James W } the same........ 172 07
21 Murphy, Patrick—J T Harris........ 256 00
21 Morgan, Gwendolyn—Edward Fisher 417 26
21 Mercier, Louis—J E Callinan........ 314 20
21 Muldoon, William H—Joseph Marren 291 20
21 Meyer, Louis; Meyer, Maurice; Meyer, Michael } Bessie Loucheim.... 128 27
21 Morton, Levi P—Mayor, &c.......... 599 03
21 Montgomery, Henry—Importers' and Traders' Nat Bank.......... 624 33
21 Miller, George—Mary Ohl.......... 136 74
21 Mayo, John B—Evening Post Publishing Co.......... 69 73
21 Martin, Robert W—Hyman Rubenstone.......... 35 87
22 Murray, John E—W C Doscher Mfg Co 149 66
22 Madeira, Finnell D—Vittoria Cremers 480 80
22 Meyer, Esther—Mathilde Warnecke. 121 70
22 Muldoon, William—Frank Ross...... 26 50
22 Mills, Henry; *MacDonald, Allen G } M B Wynkoop...... 136 83
22 Meyers, Jacob J—Louis Kessel....... 192 63
22 Mulligan, John J—G W Venable 512 75
23 Mackey, Joseph—Morris Rosenberg. 28 00
23 Murray, Thomas—Mitchell-Vance Co. 169 95
23 Meyer, Siegmund T; Meyer, Arthur L } Raritan Hollow and Porous Brick Co...... 957 18
23 Martin, Leon—Jacob Wicks, Jr.......... 1,879 96
23 Moss, Charles—J A Wilmore.......... 2,727 69
23 Moller, George H—Samuel Valleau... 105 34
23 Mark, Jacob—Elizabeth A L Hyatt..........costs 79 92
20 McNiece, James — Delamater Iron Works.......... 152 28
22 McCullough, Willis J—J V Halk..... 955 86
22*MacDonald, Allen G—M B Wynkoop. 136 83
23 McKinney, Lemuel K—W E Hering.. 171 92
23 McMurray, Charles E — Charles Schlesinger.......... 120 14
23 Mackey, Joseph—Morris Rosenberg. 28 00
23 McSwyny, Bryan G—E E Spencer.. 84 00
19 Newman, John—Louis Mettel........ 36 99
20 Nolan, Henry W—Herman Schaffner 348 37
22 Newman, William M—E H Van Ingen 694 22
23 Nobis, Agnes—Anthony McOwen.... 118 44
23 Newwitter, Nathan J, as assigueee—Henry Fera..........costs 88 87
19 O'Shea, Ann T—D H Carroll........ 662 85
19 O'Brien, Abbie E—S H Richards..... 211 10
20 O'Connor, William—Ephraim Howe.. 346 71
20†O'Conner, John—John Finigan....... 46 00
20 O'Brien, James—J W Brewster & Co. 646 26
20 O'Connor, John—Philip Stein........ 147 38
22 Onetto, Luigi—G A Franchi.......... 94 57
23 O'Shaugnessy, James F—Virginia C Harrison.......... 2,873 06
23*O'Brien, John—Painesville Nat Bank. 3,549 21
17 Prosnitz, William—Robert Froese..........costs 81 20
17 Parsons, Henry E—B F Dalton....... 846 07
19 Phyfe, Jane; Phyfe, John D } George Roll......... 801 74
19 the same——the same.......... 293 73
19 Palmer, Henry D—T G Palmer...... 79 78
19 Prichard, John H—Mary E Wickstead.......... 247 63
20 Palmer, William A—C F Ketcham... 1,839 39
20 Parisio, Gasper—Jose Tur.......... 499 45
20 Plaut, Isaac S; Plaut, Ralph P } Brainerd & Armstrong Co......... 947 40
20 Pilcher, Joseph M—Samuel Coles..... 206 11
20 Paine, William L—J M Brown...... 1,597 27
21 Potter, Henry A—Mary A St John..........costs 68 08
21 Provost, Frederick—F H Graf........ 340 80
22 Parker, Samuel Webber — Charles Blandy.......... 1,949 86
22 Post, George W; Post, Virginius W } F M Jencks.... 855 72
23 Pollard, Martha E—J A Wilmore.... 2,727 69
17 Rofrano, Michael—Patrick Keegan.. 234 54
17 Rieser, Jacob—Jennie Cornelius.costs 22 68

17 Rigsby, R ert—Nat Blank Book Co. 223 64
19 Reinhardt, Aaron / Reinhardt, Henry } Matilda Berg... 409 08
19 Reilly, William B—John McCormick 393 68
19 Rossi, C Talamo—Empire Warehouse Co (Lim)........................ 247 33
20 Remantan, Antonio—David Mayer... 1,424 00
20 Rule, William G—William Hendrickson........................ 265 94
21 Richter, Louis A—E P Chichester.... 117 15
21 Richardson, Emma—J F Markham ....costs 88 74
21 Root, James H—H E Bowns......... 569 76
21 the same——the same............ 682 10
21*Ross, Salvador—Charles Darrow.....35,551 62
21 the same——Robert Olyphant.... 2,115 37
21 Roberts, George H, Jr — Marie Schuler........................ 2,284 46
22 Reynolds, Hugh M—Abraham Steers. 5,936 48
23 Roberts, Austin J / Roberts, Walter J } Luke McHenry, 628 94
23 the same——J W Yale........... 521 91
17 Spiegel, Robert, admr Elsa Spiegel—G K Swinburn................costs 23 72
17 Steiner, Nathan M—Nathan Hellman 676 96
19 Simone, Luella E—Nashawannuck Mfg Co........................ 80 30
19 Streifler, Jacob—William McShane.. 248 43
19 Stono, Louis—Herrmann Weiller.costs 100 63
19 Shelansky, Jacob—G V Keen......... 215 21
19 Snyder, Mesier R—O K Eldredge..... 987 25
19 the same——the same.............1,651 94
19 the same——the same.............1,648 94
20 Schenck, Daniel S—C H Self.......... 83 64
20 Siebert, William M—H C Graves..... 307 56
20 Servis, Peter V—Moses Sahlein....(D)1.889 49
20 Swift, George F—E R Shipman......1,001 92
20 Simon, Falk—Sarah J Lewis.......... 253 36
20 Schneider, Louis H—Morning Journal Assoc........................ 222 00
20 Sheridan, John—H F Burchard....... 235 90
20 Shea, Dennis—F F Lovell............ 745 69
20 Schaum, Louis—H W Cropsey....... 278 41
20 Schellenberger, Ferdinand L—Julius Robertson........................ 150 85
21 Steinmetz, Elizabeth / Steinmetz, John H } Delamater Iron Works......1,920 73
21 Silvie, Isaac A—August Heckscher... 490 25
21 Stables, John J / Stables, Rosalie L / Stables, Ernest / *Stables, Charlotte A } H K Thurber. 151 84
21 Strasburg, John J—F W Devoe & Co. 48 38
21 Stewart, James E—Mayor, &c........ 81 78
21 Stahl, Jacob—Morris Rosenberg...... 73 59
21 Stewart, Robert B—E H Gato......... 95 47
21 Stevens, Adolphus E— Catherine Holtz........................ 173 20
21*Steiger, Joseph—T G Palmer......... 302 13
22 Steindler, Joseph—G C Andrae... ...1,188 86
22 the same——G C Andreae.........1,758 25
22 the same——Henry Abegg... ....1,587 09
22 Schwarts, Abram—J B Fitzgerald... 30 73
22 Schmeckenbecher, George / Schmeckenbecher, John G } C H Wilson.... 458 60
22 Sudowsky, Louis—Moses Goldberg... 88 96
22 Schaffner, Ernestine — Madeline E Hawes........................1,092 53
22 Simon, Kaspar—Charles Mildenberger 269 95
22 Sharpe, Clements—Truman Parsons.. 321 24
22 Salisbury, John, Jr—Milton Rathbun. 354 29
22 Saxton, Josiah C—Washington Nat Bank........................ 521 74
23 Stephens, Harry T—P J Moran 213 37
23 Southmayd, Charles F, trustee William Astor—J W Holloway....costs 216 64
23 the same——the same........costs 216 64
23 the same——the same........costs 216 64
23 the same——the same........costs 216 64
23 Schwartzwold, Abraham—J J Heins. 259 50
23 Schindler, Anthony—H F Gundrum. 99 92
23 Stohrs, John E—P D Armour......... 132 00
23 Subitzky, Louis—Ruben Spitelnik.... 102 69
23 Scharles, John / *Seidel, Ferdinand } N Y Life Ins Co............ 30 68
23 Schwab, Gabriel / *Schwab, Nathan / *Schwab, Abraham / *Schwab, Leo } James Lennon... 262 00
19 Smith, Luella E—Nashawannuck Mfg Co........................ 80 30
19 Smith, John—Leopold Friesen......... 302 48
23 Smith, Justus J—Terence Kane......1,531 47
17 J & J W Ellsworth Co—A J Myer... 36 94
17 The Seeger & Guernsey Co—Charles Kruse........................costs 89 83
17 Saranac Improvement Co (Lim) — Mary Herter........................ 520 95
17 The Thomas Murray Co—Benedict & Burnham Mfg Co........................1,603 28
17 Hudson River Boot and Shoe Mfg Co—R G Solomon........................1,451 36
17 the same——the same............1,295 19
17 the same——the same............1,233 50
17 the same——the same............1,517 47
17 the same——Ferdinand Blumenthal........................2,118 21
17 the same——the same............1,175 18
17 the same——the same............2,137 14
17 The N Y, New Haven & Hartford R R Co—People State N Y...........7,479 81
19 The Barriett Electric Co—A G Hawkins........................ 211 76
19 The Pfister Bookbinding Co—E M Hotchkiss........................10,158 27
19 Rapid Printing Co—C S Connor......1,011 92
19 Manhattan Railway Co—A D M Defendorf........................ 759 80
19 Dunlaps Cable News Co—D M Stone, as pres't........................costs 104 27
20 The Sheet Metal Machine Co of Newar, N J—I C Johnson............ 351 50
20 NewYork Life Ins Credit Co—L W Ahrens........................ 73 45

20 The Mayor, Aldermen, &c—Frank Moss........................ 250 00
20 The N Y Elevated R R Co / Manhattan Railway Co } Mary T Corbett, admrx....... 358 33
20 J H Bonnell & Co (Lim)—Western Nat Bank........................1,206 55
20 The McWilliams Printing Co—J K Wright........................ 413 64
20 E G Blakelee's Sons Iron Works—Robert Robertson................. 820 97
20 J H Bonnell Co (Lim)—Second Nat Bank of Red Bank................. 537 14
21 the same——Market and Fulton Nat Bank........................2,148 01
21 American Tree Guard Co—L W Ahrens........................ 111 94
21 Metropolitan Elevated Railway Co / Manhattan Railway Co } Nancy L Sherwood..costs 140 87
21 The Mayor, Aldermen, &c — Henry Zeltner........................ 325 00
21 North and South American Construction Co—Charles Macdonald..32,369 43
21 J H Bonnell & Co (Lim)—Western Nat Bank........................ 363 13
21 the same——Nat Bank of Republic. 651 37
21 The Mountain Summit House Co—O G Rafferty........................ 241 04
22 Pennsylvania R R Co—Josephine Blakeslee........................ 225 00
22 The Brooklyn (Lim)—Brooklyn Union Elevated Railway Advertising Co.. 211 05
22 Newell Bros Mfg Co—Emanuel Neuman........................ 955 65
22 J H Bonnell & Co (Lim)—Western Nat Bank........................1,874 94
22 the same——the same............ 515 88
22 Manhattan Railway Co—M E Haviland, exr........................costs 101 27
23 The American Musician Publishing Co—V S Flechter................. 367 88
23 Church Publishing Co (Lim)—J R Angel........................ 84 43
23 The College of St Francis Xavier—W S Gridley........................ 708 82
23 Postal Telegraph Cable Co — H J Grant, as sheriff................costs 114 68
23 The Richensteen Lumber Co—Shepard & Morse Lumber Co........... 122 48
23 J H Bonnell & Co (Lim)—Market and Fulton Nat Bank................1,240 67
23 The Mayor, Aldermen, &c—E A Kingsley........................ 40 32
19†Thayer, Horace H—R A Berger...... 95 06
19 Tangeman, Richard—G J Fielbig.... 38 55
19 Tonolla, George C—J N Holden...... 59 45
19 Tuft, Annie—Charles Wiesbecker.... 74 44
19 the same——Meyer Corn......... 140 52
21 Thompson, Joseph A—August Heckscher........................ 490 26
21 Tucker, Preble—Cornelia Gilman.... 681 61
21 the same——the same........costs 111 44
21 the same——the same........costs 40 13
21 Trainer, John B—A T Docherty...... 170 49
21 Turkheimer, Adolph—Mina Solinger. 49 93
22 Tramer, John B / Tramer, Alicia F } W D Woods....... 50 54
22 Thompson, James—H C Steul......... 84 70
22 Trintz, Annie—A J Ridley............ 23 25
22 Taylor, Theodore B / Taylor, William B } Nat Park Bank. 27 75
23 Terrall, Park—P J Moran............ 273 37
23 Train, Henry W—W F Geissel. 1,235 13
21 Ullmann, Raphael R—Bartholomew Cunningham........................ 201 91
22 Ullman, Leopold—Samson Toplitz....1,205 32
17 Valentine, Robert H C—Chatham Nat Bank........................1,267 65
19 Vogel, Albert D—Manhattan Beef Co (Lim)........................ 212 81
23 Videtto, Charles H—J B Caste........ 532 18
17 Wilkens, Christian—C W Wells...... 105 41
17 Winner, Benjamin W—Manhattan Hotel Co........................1,080 85
19 Weiner, Minnie—G H McCoy......... 142 24
19 Weiss, Frederick L—D M Koehler.... 166 50
19 Waggoner, Ralph H—John Simmons. 1,241 35
20 Walton, Arthur H—Commercial Bank 534 33
21 Washburn, William T—J F Markham ....costs 88 74
21 Walter, James N—August Heckscher 490 26
21 Woodman, Nathaniel H—G W Kidd. 1,165 23
21 Wells, Alfred L—Mary A Pomroy.... 234 10
21 Wild, Edward C—Mary Thomas...... 110 50
21 Wyatt, George S, Jr—James Olwell.. 468 18
21 Wilmurt, Jefferson—T A Wilmurt...2,346 32
22 Waring, John T—J R Everall......... 245 10
22 Weston, George N—M B Wynkoop... 136 83
22 Westervelt, B V Allen—Milton Rathbun........................ 599 01
23 Wakeley, Esther A—J G Grissler.... 700 85
23 Wilson, John C, Jr—P J Moran...... 213 37
21 Young, Hugh—John Fox............. 152 27
20†Zarr, Emily—R C Williams.......... 764 32
23 Zuber, Quirin—Frederick Buss..costs 113 52

KINGS COUNTY.

Oct.
15 Albaum, Franz—L C King........... $102 69
16 Allen, Charles—L Isenburger......... 106 37
17 Alexander, Robert—E Frank......... 122 98
17 the same——J H Seed............. 108 00
17 the same——F Solinger........... 720 00
19 Atwood, James—Prudential Ins Co of America........................ 36 97
20 Abbe, Charles C—R Dawson.......... 304 77
22 Adams, Frank H—Third Nat Bank of Buffalo........................ 315 94
15 Bonnell, John H—C Coepel..........5,281 59
16 Burtis, Nathaniel W — Commercial Bank........................ 678 06
16 Berkson, Henry—F Bergner & Co.... 55 85
17 Baisley, Albert H—Emeline McEwen. 1,561 88
17 Blaney, Daniel F—N Ryan........... 318 23
17 the same——the same............ 191 87
17 Brielman, Jr, Emil—G W Piper...... 196 33
19 Bushfield, John C / Brady, Mary A, extrx / Brady, Philip H } M Sablein (D) 1,869 49
20 Brockmann, William—C H Evans... 71 50
20 Burtis, Nathaniel W — Commercial Bank........................ 534 33
20*Burcher, Walter V—W Berri....... 670 98
20 Bullwinkle, Martin—A J Smith...... 354 10
20 Beers, Rollin E—D G Mulford....... 735 18
21 Baur, John—Canda & Kane......... 254 83
21 Bonnell, John H—H E Beers......... 682 10
21 Birdsall, Henry D—G H Fisher...... 423 98
22 Barnes, Oliver W — Maverick Nat Bank........................ 950 43
22 Bolles, Thomas N—Essex Co Nat Bank of Newark........................21,016 64
22 Brown, Junior Thomas—New York Wall Paper Co (Lim)............... 170 64
17 Cummings, George—W E Hall....... 401 16
19 Came, Thomas—I S Vought.......... 28 20
19 the same——the same............ 71 15
19 Collins, Charles H—M McGrath...... 313 04
19 Conkling, Augustus—F P Williams . 128 00
19 Cootey, Harriet G—J A Chapman.... 629 77
20 Cullen, Edward J—W G Ross........ 113 53
21 Cranston, Henry—H E Bowns........ 569 76
21 Chaffee, George—Evangeline C Preble........................ 114 31
21 Collins, Charles H—Abendroth Bros . 526 24
21 the same——the same............ 526 24
15 Dresdner, Solomon—H Herz......... 226 90
15 Duffy, Michael—R H Howard........ 366 03
16 Denike, Thomas S—G W Melvin..... 91 95
16 the same——the same............ 228 47
21 Donovan, James—Eliz Donovan......1,661 78
20 Elford, Charles E—D G Mulford..... 735 18
16 Farr, Jacob—J Fallert B Co.......... 122 23
16 Fogarty, James J—J Goetz.......... 318 95
19 Fullwood, James H—Prudential Ins Co........................ 36 97
20 Frischman, Ignatz—J Fromme....... 74 15
20 Friedman, Louis—C Lewis........... 99 52
20 Fitzpatrick, John—Ella F Austin..... 58 10
20 Fleming, Elizabeth E—J Kelly, admr. 224 49
20 Foster, David M G—N T Parker...... 289 49
20 Frankish, Joseph / Frankish, John K } O K Edredge..... 987 25
20 the same——the same.............1,651 94
20 the same——the same.............1,648 94
21 Franklin, Adelaide F—A J Stewart.. 300 14
16 Geibe, Edward A—J E Nichols....... 150 89
16 Golding, Jr, "William" H—F S Van Horn........................ 96 98
19 Griggs, James M—J H Seims........ 71 29
20 Glashoff, Peter H—J N Starin....... 220 31
20 Graham, Martin—J D Leary......... 120 19
21*Gould, Edward—S Coles........... 206 11
21 Gilgan, John—G Henricke........... 47 25
21 Griffith, William——the same........ 25 90
22 Griffiths, Thomas W / Griffiths, Margaret Theresa } H A Bunker... 296 80
15 Harper, William D—C Goepel........5,281 59
16 Haug, John—H F Burroughs......... 121 28
16 Herod, William—Commercial Bank.. 678 06
16 Hartmann, Max—Cook & Bernheimer Co........................ 94 81
16 Herod, William—Bowery Bank, N Y. 627 73
17 Hogan, John / Hogan, Mary / Hogan, Patrick } F Manno............ 18 10
20 Horn, Ch—L Schuetz................ 138 39
21 Harper, William D—H E Bowns.... 682 10
21 Haas, William—J Zimmeran. 385 20
21 Harris, George S—S Coles.... ...... 206 11
21 Harrison, Ole—F W Koch 246 60
22 Hunt, Joseph F—H I Kniffen.... .... 493 07
19 Jewett, James C—Mary E Parsons ....(D) 1,224 99
19 the same——Laura C Crane...(D) 677 81
19 Jones, Joseph R—J A Flomerfelt..... 178 65
16 Kilcoyne, Patrick—E McDonald..... 143 23
19 Koenig, John—C A Friberg.......... 147 80
20 Kemp, Abraham—W H Lee.......... 38 92
21 Koch, Henry—G H Mahler.......... 211 75
21 Katzmann, Henry—C Loffler........ 114 75
21 Kuckuk, Frederick—H F Burroughs. 238 70
16 Luther, Ella F—F Miller 82 53
19 Leisenheuner, Charles—C A Freiberg. 147 80
19 Levy, Copple—H Cohen 5,258 93
19 Lawson, Jacob—W F Morris......... 219 61
20 Lynch, Francis H—M Mayer......... 84 65
20 Leary, John J—F G Smith... .... 387 56
22 Lett, Margaret M—C H Bunn........1,388 42
23 Lewry, Samuel D—Eliza Lewry 250 46
15 Mallon, Patrick—R H Howard.. .... 484 75
16 McNeil, Henry—L Isenburger........ 106 37
16 Martin, Harry—F C Neale... .... 370 00
16 MacGarrity, James H—F Miller..... 82 53
17 Mason, James H—E V Crandall..... 88 31
17 Monahan, Patrick—H Eggers........ 96 97
17 Martin, Charles—C Scherfig.......... 99 07
17†Maynard, "Olivia"—Martha G Weber. 148 75
17 Mooney, James—Catharine Gregaire. 614 79
19 McBean, Archibald N—J Z Maynard. 220 69
19 McChesney, Joseph—J B Lung...... 98 69
20 McGovern, Peter—C H Evans........ 70 25
20 McKeon, Patrick—J Andrews........ 47 60
20 Moesmer, Frank A—Kellogg, Johnson & Co........................ 817 30
20 Murray, John E—G A Le Blanc...... 267 36
21 Mason, John L—D Van Degrau...... 830 77
21 the same——the same.............2,023 77
22 Murray, John E—W C Doscher Mfg Co........................ 149 66
16 O'Connor, John—W Koller........... 209 75
19 O'Neill, Dennis—H B Claflin Co..... 445 86

19 Fuels, Joseph P—C Bott.............. 149 44
19 Paton, James—Betty Frank.......... 149 55
20 Pentz, John C—M L Brock........... 173 66
21 Pitcher, Joseph M—S Coles........... 206 11
16 Reid, John J—L Isenberger.......... 180 79
16 the same——the same............. 146 95
16 Rogers, Frederick K—D S Yeoman.. 117 14
16 Richter Brothers—J Patterson....... 119 80
16 Rofrano, Michael—P Keegan.......... 224 54
16 Robinson, John—Fifth Nat Bank, Pittsburgh.................10,264 00
20 Reynolds, William W—W Berri...... 670 93
20 Ryan, John—J Andrews 149 60
21 Root, James H—H E Bowns......... 682 10
21 the same——the same............ 569 76
21 Rose, Stephen B / Rose, George W / Rose, Wesley } F W Koch......... 219 67
21 Rose, Stephen B / Rose, George W / Rose, Wesley } F W Koch........ 246 60
21 Ross, J Stewart—F Keller............ 170 72
22 Reed, Charles C—Essex County Nat Bank of Newark...............21,016 64
22 Rathje, John—Annie J Hagerty...... 475 00
15 Schlansky, Sarah—Sophia Sewards(D) 601 54
16 Smith, Jacob—G W Melvin........... 68 74
17 Slavin, Lawrence—W E Hall........ 401 16
17 Styles, John E—G P Jacobs.......... 407 48
17 Sloat, Henry V—E Stearns........... 47 60
19 Servis, Peter V—M Sahlein......(D) 1,889 49
19 Simons, Luella E / Smith, Luella E } Nashawannuck Mfg Co......... 80 30
19 Schumm, Frederick—D M Koehler... 44 06
20 Siegel, Jacob—C Lewis.............. 99 52
20 Snyder, Meiser R—O K Eldredge.... 987 25
20 the same——the same............1,651 94
20 the same——the same............1,648 94
21 Sommers, Henry—H Weiller......... 198 90
21 Stevens, Adolph E—C Holtz.......... 173 20
21 Silberman, Abraham—H Simon...... 322 36
22 Skinner, Edgar—H W Skerry....... 80 05
15 The J H Bonnell & Co—C Goepel....5,281 59
15 The Mark Mayer Mfg Co—J Baehr... 151 00
16 The Germania Savings Bank of Kings Co—C Kummel 140 02
17 The trustees of The New York and Brooklyn Bridge—J L Kimball ...30,700 00
17 The Edison United Mfg Co—A H Rennie.............................1,331 63
19 Thornwell, Charles—I S Voight...... 71 15
19 The Covered Tube Cable Railway Co —A H Mathesius...................25,517 97
19 The extrx Philip H Brady, dec'd—M Sahlein......................(D) 1,889 49
21 The Light House Machine and Selling Co—Berry & Houston Co.......... 178 21
17 Van Buren, Frank W—A Keck...... 65 94
20 Von Graff, Roderick—H Ginnel..(D) 2,075 15
17 Wells, William H—Bowery Bank, N Y.............................. 627 73
19 Waggoner, Ralph H—J Simmons....1,741 35
20 Walton, Arthur H—Commercial Bank 534 33
20 Wingert, Charles W—J Harley...... 66 06
20 Wood, John—Brooklyn City R R Co. 66 44
21 Wildfoerster, Hulda—J C Rocker.... 541 87

SATISFIED JUDGMENTS.

NEW YORK.

October 17 to 23—Inclusive.

Alexander, John V—Harry Force. (1891)..... $120 28
Bierabenk, Peter F—William Rankin. (1891)...5,452 03
Bell, George H—E A Hind (1891)............ 446 56
Brown, Wyman L—C W Dayton. (1875)....... 197 87
Bliss, Archibald M—N L Archer, (1889) 382 81
Cook, Martin—J F Wilson. (1891)............ 218 49
Cragin, Aaron, Jr—E H Raynolds. (1891)..... 115 07
Cavinato, Luigi, Guiseppe, Steffano and Natale —Northern Nat Bank. (1891)..............1,535 49
Same——Simon Adler. (1891).............. 321 99
Clementson, James D—George Allen. (1889).. 143 77
Same——J T Murphy. (1890) 384 90
Cone, Henry W, Abraham and George—S R Lesher. (1884)..............................1,183 39
Cane, H W and George—F D Rogers. (1884).. 228 71
Same and Abraham and William——J M Valentine. (1884)......................... 933 20
Cane, Henry W, Abraham and George—C G Ross. (1884) 1,619 00
Same——Charles Barnes. (1884)............ 351 65
Same——Donald MacLeod. (1885).........2,102 35
Same——C H Joy. (1886)....................1,987 71
Same——J M Valentine. (1885)..............8,387 79
Cavinato, Luigi, Guiseppe, Natale and Stefano —R E Thibaut. (1891)..................... 481 18
Crotty, John—Victoria Paper Mills Co. (1891). 792 46
Carroll, Joseph W—Isaac Berg. (1891)........ 117 00
Cane, Abraham and Henry W—William Woods. (1886) 7,902 97
Same and George W——E C Dillingham (1885) 1,376 11
Same——William Wood. (1886)...............7,844 26
Colwell, Frank W—Garfield Nat Bank. (1891).6,399 40
Delbongue, Henry—Tobias Silverstone. (1884). 538 55
Dolan, John S—Cornelius Callahan. (1889)... 139 44
Dewey, Leroy S—Elizabeth Diamond. (1890) 79 50
*De Lano, George W—H W Grindal. (1891)... 840 03
Davis, John C—G J Schnatz. (1891)........ 163 67
Eastman & Krauss Razor Co—T E Jones. (1891).. 24 80
Fail, Anna—G J Schnatz. (1891)............... 163 87
Fisher, Henry J and Charles N—Abraham Quackenbush. (1891) 279 42
Goerlitz, Philip—East River Lead Co. (1891).. 524 70
Grant, Hugh J, as Sheriff—Sterns Paper Co. (1890) 552 77
Holmes, Booth & Haydens—S H Willard. ('91)32,098 44
Hansberger, Louis—W J Madden. (1890)...... 232 69
Hessman, John—Mary Jones. (1891) 418 30
Howes, Reuben W and Leander T—G F Bailey, individ and trustee. (1885)...............27,012 98
Same——same. (1885)........................2,985 44
Hennessey, Daniel—William Moore. (1885)... 119 75
Holroyd, Electa R—James Talcott. (1877 .... 442 00
Jersey City Iron Works—James Brahn. (1891)2,019 60
*Jordan, Joseph V—A L Heyer. (1891)........ 848 25
Lyon, Dora—J W Boughton. (1891) 2,547 62
Landon, Henry H—G F Bailey. (1885)........2,985 44
Same——same. (1885)........................27,012 28
La Badie, Joseph E—J A McElhinny. (1891).. 259 50

*McLaughlin, John—G E Ketcham. (1891).... 881 67
McCaffrey, William J—F D Rogers. (1884).... 228 71
Same——J M Valentine. (1884)............ 933 20
Same——C G Ross. (1884) 1,619 00
Same——Charles Barnes. (1884)............ 351 65
Same——Donald MacLeod. (1885)..........2,102 35
Same——C H Joy. (1886)....................1,987 71
Same——J M Valentine. (1885)..............3,387 79
Same——E C Dillingham. (1885).............1,376 11
Same——William Wood. (1886)..............7,844 26
Metropolitan Elevated Railway Co / Manhattan Railway Co } James Galway. ('90) 1,108 65
Mayor, &c—J F Page. (1891)...................13,406 28
McCaffrey, William J—S R Lesher. (1884)...1,183 89
National Ice Co—Florence Sullivan. (1891)... 150 71
*Osborn, William—J M Young, assignee. (1891).. 83 99
Pierce Artesian and Oil Well Supply Co—Joseph Icenhower. (1891)..................... 199 83
Phelps, Louis N—J O Hern. (1891)............ 135 25
Russell, William R—M L Chamberlain. (1891). 91 38
Roberts, Joseph D—E A Hind. (1891)......... 445 56
Roach, William F—P O Reilly. (1891)........ 238 94
Ricart, Thomas L—A R Maicas, recv'r. (1891) 587 92
Slater, William G, Howard P and Seymour D—F G Smedley. (1888)................... 250 64
Schwabeland, John—Revere Rubber Co. (1891) 102 91
Same——John Simmons. (1891)............ 393 97
Stewart, John—Sarah Fowler, extrx. (1890).. 582 34
Smith, Frank Leon—William Rankin. (1891)..5,452 03
Smith, Albert F—J E Callinan. (1891) 479 15
Smith, Matthew—David Jones Co. (1891).... 214 94
Same——Solomon Pritz. (1891).............. 337 00
Squires, Newton—Franco-American Food Co. (1891).. 81 24
Terry, Henry T—Isaac Nebenzahl. (1891).... 220 45
Tilson, James—Alexander Wilson. (1891).... 162 45
Wendel, Louis Jr—C S Storms. (1891)......... 82 58
Same——same. (1890) 334 82
Same——Fire Dep't. (1887)...................... 59 50
Same——same. (1887) 59 50

*Vacated by order of Court. †Suspended on Appeal. ‡Released. §Reversal. ‖Satisfied by Execution.

KINGS COUNTY.

October 16 to 22—Inclusive.

Brown, Wyman S—C W Dayton. (1875)...... $197 85
Campbell, William A—M Hynes. (1891)....... 158 19
Donahue, Jacob—M Mayer. (1890)............ 209 75
Feigenspan, Gustav—Leibinger & Oehm B Co. (1891).. 405 08
Fischer, Charles—M Mayer. (1890)........... 209 75
Greine, George—H S Christensen. (1891)..... 96 57
Crotz, William F—Standard Athletic Club. (1891).. 77 50
Gang, John—J W Bott. (1891) 84 98
Judson, Edward—F O Pierce. (1891).......... 91 48
Same——M Bennett. (1891)................... 71 56
Same——J H Lee. (1891) 214 74
Keymer, Reuben—C Furgueson, Jr. (1891).... 380 60
McAveney, John A—P Bohen. (1891).......... 121 92
McCormick, George W—L H Gentes (1891).. 115 28
McLaughlin, Margaret, admr John McLaughlin—Lucy E Grover. (1890) 3,999 85
Potter, Samuel P—F H Smith. (1891).......... 82 28
Russell, Thomas—M Gibbons. (1890).......... 946 60
Same——same. (1891)........................... 89 82
Roche, John J—D R Garniss. (1888)..........1,708 76
Rogers, Andrew L—H E Stillman. (1891)..... 324 65
Smith, Robert J—M O'Brien. (1891) 96 74
Same——same. (1890.) (Suspended)..........2,472 29
Tonjes, Frederick H—H Ritting. (1891.) (Execution)... 60 12
Van Winkle, Daniel—M Hynes. (1891) 158 19
Zienner, Henry—Leibinger & Oehm B Co. (1891).. 405 08

MECHANICS' LIENS.

NEW YORK CITY.

Oct.
17 Anthony av, e s, 200 s Gray st, 25x112. James Smith agt H. Masche, owner and contractor.. $12 50
17 One Hundred and First st, Nos. 75 and 77, n s, 50 e Columbus av, 50x100.11. N. Y. Roofing Co. agt William M. Walsh, owner and contractor.. 400 00
19 Suburban st, n s, 346.8 e Anthony av, 25x100. Edward McCabe agt John Kinney, owner; William Rose, contractor, and William Hoff, sub-contractor............. 22 50
19 Same property. John McCabe agt same... 7 75
19 Twenty-seventh st, Nos. 431-435, n s, 368 w 9th av, 82.11x98.9. Albany Venetian Blind Co. agt Homer J. Beaudet, owner and contractor.. 270 00
19 Forty-ninth st, No. 122 W., s s. P. McGunnigle & Son agt Prescott & McLaughlin, owners, and Priebee & Co., contractors.. 49 50
19 Eighty-fifth st, n s, 70 w 4th av, 65x102.2. Jesse Reynolds agt Martin J. Hackett, owner and contractor.......................1,900 00
19 Anthony av, e s, 80 n 175th st, 50x125. J. A. & E. T. Woolf agt Fanny E. Lawrence, owner, and Herman Masche, contractor. 457 00
19 Crotona av, n s, 128.6 e Broad st, 25x90.9. Charles Pitchie agt Otis Wallace Boyden, owner and contractor.......................1,600 00
20 Waverley pl, No. 114, s s, 170 e 6th av, 22x97. Candee & Smith agt James Cunningham, owner and contractor.............. 372 15
20 Ninety-second st, s s, 100 e 5th av, 150x100. J. D. & T. E. Crimmins agt Thomas Graham, owner and contractor.............1,091 50
20 Fifth av, s e cor 76th st, 100x150. Leopold Freund agt Congregation of Temple Beth El, represented by Messrs. David Mayer, John Fleisch, owner, and Abe Schwarzwald, contractor.............................. 315 00
20 One Hundred and Second st, s s, 100 e Boulevard, 50x160. G. C. McLaughlin agt Lewis Muller and N. A. McBride, owners, and Lewis Muller, contractor.............8,000 00
20 One Hundred and Thirty-fifth st, n s, 60 w 5th av, 100x100. J. W. Binney agt William H. Verdon, owner and contractor .. 159 25
21 One Hundred and Sixth st, n s, 100 w Madison av, 125x100. Dimock, Fink & Co. agt J. J. and P. A. Fitzpatrick, owners, and Thompson & Leithauser, contractor...... 128 09
21 Jones st, No. 23, w s, 100 n Bleecker st, 25x100. Salvator Panella agt Th. Van Eupen, owner and contractor........................ 283 30
21 Amsterdam av, Nos. 633-641, n e cor 91st st, 125x—. David Shuldiner agt Edward Smith, owner and contractor 97 50
22*Lexington av, s e cor 87th st, 100x65. Louis Roller agt Cavinato Bros., owner and contractor...2,402 90
22 Amsterdam av, n e cor 91st st, 130x100. J. T. Mooney agt Edward Smith, owner and contractor.............................. 420 00
22 Pike st, No. 53, e s, 34.10 n Monroe st, 19.11x50. Lazarus Black and Abraham Rochemowitz agt Nathan Farber, owner and contractor....................................1,063 00
22 Sixth av, No. 735 / Forty-second st, No. 61 } begins 6th av, n e cor 42d st, 20.6x62. William Campbell & Co. agt James Wakely, owner and contractor 11,681 10
22 Eagle av, e s, 262.8 n Westchester av, 50x115.1. Adam Gebhardt agt John and Carl Flachbart and Louis Treisner, owner, and John Laugermann, contractor............2,087 69
22 One Hundred and Second st, Nos. 202 and 204, s s, 100 e 3d av, 35x100. A. B. & W. T. Westervelt agt James Duffy, owner and contractor.............................. 183 00
22 Twelfth st, n s, 173 e 1st av, 24.4x—. Michael Lang agt Jeanette Weil, owner and contractor.............................. 789 85
22 Same property. Henry Engesser agt same owner and Michael Lang, contractor..... 339 85
22 Eighth av, s e cor 126th st, 50x100. Adolph Pfaltz agt Christian Andersen, owner and contractor.............................. 750 00
23 One Hundred and Second st, s s, 100 e Boulevard, 50x100. Zoller Lumber Co. agt N. S. McBride, owner, and George C. McLaughlin, contractor 3,500 00
23 Leroy st, Nos. 55 and 57, n s, — w Bedford st, 60x65. Carucci & Co. agt Stevens, McElroy & Co., owners and contractors... 525 00
23 Twenty-third st, No. 130, s s, 150 w 6th av, 25x100. Lewis & Jones agt Henry Lescote, owner and contractor........................ 104 14

*Editor Record and Guide:

We beg to call your attention to the injustice of a mechanic's lien filed against us by one Louis Roller for $2,402.90 for work not yet done, he having been paid for all work done as per contract and specifications.

Cavinato Bros.

KINGS COUNTY.

Oct.
16 State st, n s, 100 w Henry st, 25x100. Herman Becker agt John H. Robertson, owner, and Charles H. Collins, contractor.... $125 00
16 Bergen st, s s, 350 w Kingsland av, 60x100. F. G. Clarke Blue Stone Co. agt Joseph M. Pilcher & Co., owners and contractors....2,647 17
16 Gates av, s s, 250 w Knickerbocker av, 25x100. Joseph Smalheiser agt John Lyons, owners and contractors..................... 85 00
16 De Kalb av, s s, 150 w Marcy av, 100x100. Builders Wood Working Co. agt Elizabeth S. Maitland, owner, and Charles H. Collins, contractor........................ 540 20
17 Seventeenth st, s s, 100 w 10th av, 40x100.2. Michael McCadden agt Thomas Croak, owner and contractor..................... 365 00
17 Boerum st, No. 162, s s, 175 w Humboldt st, 25x100. Louis Bossert agt Israel Javasbow, owner, and S. F. Hayner, contractor 2,221 32
17 State st, s s, 100 e Henry st, 30x100. Charles E. Ring agt John F. Robertson, owner, and Charles H. Collins, contractor........ 22 95
17 De Kalb av, s s, 150 w Marcy av, —x—. Nolan & Kearns agt Elizabeth S. Maitland, owner, and Charles H. Collins, contractor 125 00
17 State st, s s, 100 e Henry st, 30x100. Watson & Pittinger agt James K. Robertson, owner, and Charles H. Collins, contractor 632 00
19 Bergen st, s s, 106 w Hopkinson av, 25x100. Potts Bros. agt Rosa Rosenfeld, owner, and Carl Becker, contractor.............. 42 37
19 Same property. Wyandance Brick and Terra Co. agt Rosa Rosenfeld, owner, and Carl Becker, contractor.................. 131 22
19 Rockaway av, e s, 50 n Bergen st, 25x100. Potts Bros. agt Harry Stubley, owner, and Carl Becker, contractor................ 20 00
19 Gates av, w s, 325 n Hamburg av, —x—. Jacob Lang agt John Lyons, owner, and Joseph Dohmann, contractor 60 00
19 Sixty-sixth st, s s, 350 w 10th av, 53.3x100x60.5x100.2, New Utrecht. Abram C. Shelley agt Margaretha and Gustaf Reichenback, owners and contractors............ 54 49
19 Porter av, s w cor Maspeth av, 400x400. Phoenix Iron Co. agt The Equity Gas Light Co., owner, and Eugene B. Hedden, contractor.....................................4,033 97
19 Bushwick av, w s, 58 s Kossuth pl, 20x84. George Kuhn agt Ludwig Levy, owner and contractor.............................. 536 50
19 State st, s s, 100 e Henry st, 30x100. A. B. See Mfg. Co. agt John F. Robertson, owner, and Charles H. Collins, contractor. 108 36
19 Ovington av, n s, 75 w Stewart av, 25x100. Frank D. Creamer agt Mr. Pade, owner, and Dennington, Connolly & Smyth, contractors.. 138 74
19 Fifty-seventh st, n s, 175 e 11th av, 25x100, New Utrecht. Frank D. Creamer agt M. Umbar, owner, and Emil Kehler, contractor.. 131 00
19 Sixty-fourth st, s e cor 11th av, 20x100, New Utrecht. Same agt M. Sandman, owner, and Emil Kehler, contractor.............. 114 52
20 De Kalb av, s s, 150 w Marcy av, 100x100. William Camp agt Elizabeth S. Maitland, owner, and Charles H. Collins, contractor 17 00
20 Bushwick av, w s, 58 s Kossuth pl, 20x84. Philip Dugro agt Ludwig Levy, owner, and George Kuhn, contractor 132 00
20 Same property. Hyde & Gload Mfg Co. agt same owner and contractor.............. 136 00
20 De Kalb av, s s, 150 w Marcy av, 100x100. John Brockman agt Elizabeth S. Maitland, owner, and Charles H. Collins, contractor 391 00
20 De Kalb av, s s, 150 w Marcy av, 100x100. Christian Olsen agt Elizabeth S. Maitland, owner, and Charles H. Collins, contractor.. 35 00
20 Braxton st, s s, 97.10 e 10th av, 80x100. Thomas McCann agt the estate of Nathaniel W. Burtis, owner and contractor......1,000 00
20 Watkins st, Nos. 493 and 494, w s, 175 n Sutter av, 50x100. Nathan Cohen agt Elias Kaplan, owner and contractor.............. 25 00
20 Watkins st, w s, 175 n Sutter av, 25x100. Same agt same owner and contractor ... 245 00
20 Porter av, s w cor Maspeth av, 400x400.

Eugene B. Hedden agt The Equity Gas Light Co., owners, and William C. Whyte, contractor 13,917 14

20 Eastern Parkway, s s, 50 e Christopher st, 50x100. Henry McShane Mfg. Co. agt Wolf Potashinski, owner, and Pasco & McCormick, contractors 164 31

20 Eastern Parkway, n s, 50 e Christopher st, 50x100. Same agt same owner and contractors 164 31

21 Third av, e s, 40.2 n 47th st, 60x85. Ernst G. Jaehne agt Frederick Seifried and Frederick Gummel, owners and contractors 297 18

21 Bedford av, w s, extends from Pacific st to Atlantic av, 216.11x501.9x400x412.2, Twenty-third Regiment N. G. S. N. Y. Armory. William Ring agt The People of the State of New York, owner, and Bernard McAveney, contractor 36 72

21 Putnam av, n e cor Patchen av, 20x100. Bernhard Schubert agt Thomas Walling and Morris Hawkins, owners, and Thomas Walling, contractor 400 00

21 Gates av, s s, 326 e Hamburg av, 25x100. J. W. Van Ostrand agt John or William Lyons, owner, and John Reilley, contractor. 132 50

21 Gates av, s s, 250 w Knickerbocker av, 25x100. John Newman agt John Lyons, owner, and John Reilley, contractor 175 00

22 Hamburg av, w s, 50 n Stockholm st, 25x100. Martin Deinhardt agt Jacob Klett, owner and contractor 175 00

22 Same property. Gottfried Walter agt same owner and contractor 663 50

22 Saratoga av, Nos. 151-161. Charles Ebel agt J. Aronson, owner and contractor 99 00

22 Reid av, w s, 50 n Halsey st, 50x100. Van Wagner & Co. agt George W. McCormick, owner and contractor 480 60

22 Twelfth st, n s, 222.10 w 5th av, 25x100. Robert M. Warren agt Louise Obert, owner, and August Obert, contractor 80 00

22 Sixth st, s s, 180 w 4th av, 115x100. James W. Ellis agt H. Becker, owner, and P. Malony, contractor 197 20

SATISFIED MECHANICS' LIENS

NEW YORK CITY.

Oct.

17 Fort Independence st, w s, 424 s Bailey av. A. S. Wright agt John H. Kline and William C. Connell. (Lien filed May 14, 1891). $52 00

19 Inwood av, e s, 175 s Wolf pl, 50x130. Klemens Mueller agt John F. Eichler. (Aug. 17, 1891) 40 00

19 Same property. Abraham Steers agt same and Maria his wife. (July 2, 1891) 616 38

19 Convent av, s w cor 144th st, 99.11x250. The Passaic Rolling Mill Co. agt William E. Mowbray (Jan. 23, 1888) 164 40

19 Pleasant av, No. 361, s w cor 119th st, 17.6x60.1. Hermann Perlaud agt Thomas H. Young. (May 28, 1890) 594 50

20 Eighty-second st, Nos. 137-167. Vigna & Orrigoni agt Andrew J. Kirwin. (Oct. 16, 1891) 188 00

21 Eighty-third st, s s, 175 w 9th av, 25x—. James Thomson agt John Chisholm. (July 18, 1891) 1,150 00

21 Same property. Canda & Kane agt same. (July 24, 1891) 1,142 35

21 Same property. Anton Larson agt same. (July 27, 1891) 100 00

21 Same property. J. R Black agt same. (July 28, 1891) 400 00

21 Same property. Morton Bros. & Co. agt same. (July 21, 1891) 1,150 00

21‡ West End av, s w cor 102d st. Charles Hillemeier agt Elizabeth and Welcome M. Steinmetz. (July 6, 1891) 3,250 00

22 Eighty-ninth st, Nos. 438 and 440, s s, 157 w Av A, 50x100.8. Arthur Gorsch agt Mrs. Bertha Von Barker. (July 30, 1891) 464 11

22* Eighty-third st, s s, 175 w Columbus av, 25x—. John Normoyle agt John Chisholm and M. Normoyle. (July 21, 1891) 28 00

22* Same property. Thomas Normoyle agt same. (July 21, 1891) 35 00

22 Ninety-second st, n s, 210 w 3d av, 15x100.8. N. Y. Architectural Terra Cotta Co. agt Leopold S. Friedberger and George Thompson. (Oct. 12, 1891) 295 00

23 Twelfth st, No. 413 E., 26.9x—. Michael Laug agt Jeanette Weil. (Sept. 24, 1891). 789 35

22 Same property. Henry Eugesser agt same and Michael Lang. (Sept. 24, 1891) 339 35

*Discharged by depositing amount of lien and interest with County Clerk.

‡Discharged by order of Court on filing bond.

KINGS COUNTY.

Oct.

16 Gates av, No. 11, n s, 80 w Vanderbilt av, 20x75. Thomas Reade agt William Schoefer, owner and contractor. (Lien filed Sept. 30, 1891) $18 78

17 Chapel st, s s, 250 e Jay st. Paul Ayres & Co. agt Ann O'Connor, owner and contractor (March 13, 1891) 490 00

17 Pacific st, s s, 109 e Rockaway av, 102x107.2. Samuel Glazer agt Robert S. Neely, owner and contractor. (Aug. 18, 1891) 250 00

17 Fourth av, s w cor 23d st, 20x50. Hobby & Doody agt John and Elizabetha Staebler, owner and contractor. Sept. 29, 1891) 467 10

17 Dean st, n s, 75 e Utica av, 160x100. Rudolph Reimer & Co. agt Frank P. Martin, owner and contractor. (Oct. 8, 1891) 678 83

19 Lewis av, s e cor Hancock st, 100x150. The New York Pressed Brick Co. agt McWhinney & Aronson, owners and contractors. (Aug. 8, 1891) 607 55

‡Watkins st, e s, 175 n Blake av, 25x100. Anne Delaney agt Eliza Danaucher, owner and contractor. (April 9, 1891) 265 13

20 Same property. Louis Ratner agt same owner and contractor. (Oct. 15, 1891) 1,300 00

20 Schenck av, e s, 162 n Arlington av. Danmar & Fischer agt Mrs. Thomas F. Parker extrx. and Elizabeth J. Rapelje, owner and contractor. (July 3, 1891) 100 00

21 Arlington av, s s, 30 e Hendrix st, 30x100. William J. Ray agt Isidore Warren, owner, and A. J. Warren, contractor. (Oct. 15, 1891) 73 26

21 Arlington av, s e cor Hendrix st, 30x100. Same agt same owner and contractor. (Oct. 15, 1891) 121 66

21 Flushing av, north cor Vandervoort st, 25x100. George D. Koch agt Peter Johnson, owner and contractor. (Sept. 26, 1891) 355 00

21 East 31st st, w s, lots 50 and 51 block 3 map Reformed Dutch Church property, Flatbush. Peter J. Beffron agt Richard Peyton, owner, and George J. Cragin, contractor. (July 22, 1891) 49 90

21 West 9th st, n s, 100 e Hicks st, 25x100. James Sullivan agt —— Cosgrove, owner, and —— McCulpen, contractor. (Sept. 29, 1891). (Order of Court) 21 00

BUILDINGS PROJECTED.

The first name is that of the owner; ar't stands for architect, m'n for mason, c'r for carpenter and b'r for builder.

NEW YORK CITY.

SOUTH OF 14TH STREET.

Cherry st, No. 274, five-story and basement brk and stone flat, 26.2x98, tin roof; cost, $23,000; Weil & Mayer, 227 East 60th st; ar't, G. F. Pelham; m'n, J. Van Dolsen. Plan 1340.

Sullivan st, Nos. 219 and 221, five-story brk and stone school, 39x82, tile, slate and tin roof; cost, $44,000; Children's Aid Society, 24 St. Marks pl; ar'ts, Vaux & Radford; b'r, R. Deeves. Plan 1339.

4th st, n w cor 10th st, five-story brk flat, 29.6x88, tin roof; cost, $30,000; W. H. Cooper, 52 Catharine st; ar't, T. S. Godwin. Plan 1345. (Substituted for alteration plan No. 1786 filed last week.)

7th st, Nos. 199 and 201, five-story brk flat, 40x71 and 84.6, tin roof; cost, $23,000; L. Adler, 93 St. Marks pl; ar't, E. W. Greis. Plan 1342.

Goerck st, w s, 100 s Houston st, three five-story brk and stone flats, 25x89, tin roofs; cost, $20,000 each; Weil & Mayer, 227 East 60th st; ar't, G. F. Pelham; m'n, J. Van Dolsen. Plan 1361.

BETWEEN 14TH AND 59TH STREETS.

52d st, No. 212 E., two-story brk stable, 20x40, tin roof; cost, $3,800; O. W. Horton, on premises; ar't, G. F. Pelham. Plan 1362.

BETWEEN 59TH AND 125TH STREETS, EAST OF 5TH AVENUE.

95th st, n s, 90 e Park av, nine three-story and basement stone dwell'gs, three 18x52, six 16x52, tin roofs; cost, $12,000 each; F. J. Schnugg, 129 East 95th st; ar't, L. Eutzer, Jr. Plan 1357.

Park av, No. 1843, one-story brk building, 25x36, gravel roof; cost, $500; J. Townshend, 22 West 52d st; b'r, C. W. H. Ebling. Plan 1355.

BETWEEN 59TH AND 125TH STREETS, WEST OF CENTRAL PARK WEST AND 8TH AVENUE.

Central Park W. (8th av), w s, 25.11 n 106th st, two five-story brk and stone flats, 32x88 and 18x88, tin roofs; total cost, $55,000; ow'r and ar't, same as last. Plan 1258.

98th st, n s, 275 w 8th av, two-story brk building, 25x49, tin roof; cost, $3,000; lessee, V. Wille, 215 Av A; ar't, J. W. Cole. Plan 1360.

110TH TO 125TH STREET, BETWEEN 5TH AND 8TH AVENUES.

115th st, n s, 175 w Lenox av, two five-story brk flats, 25x88, tin roofs; cost, $20,000 each; Laura J. Stephens, Yonkers, N. Y.; ar't, J. A. Webster. Plan 1348.

124th st, n s, 125 e 7th av, two-story brk and stone building, 50x100, tin roof; cost, $20,000; lessee and ow'r, W. S. Jennings, 159 Broadway. Plan 1353.

NORTH OF 125TH STREET.

131st st, n s, 200 w Boulevard, one-story brk building, 42x37, tin and gravel roof; cost, $3,600; Standard Gas Light Co., 2 Cortlandt st; ar't, F. Egner; m'ns, J. & L. Weber. Plan 1349.

152d st, s s, McCombs Dam road to 8th av, two-story brk stable, 86x236.10, tar and gravel roof; cost, $25,000; George Law, prest., 259 5th av; ar't, J. W. Cole; m'n, P. Dromesbauser; c'r, G. A. Haag. Plan 1341.

159th st, n s, 300 w Amsterdam av, two-story frame dwell'g, 25x50, tin roof; cost, $4,500; J. H. Banks, Amsterdam av, n w cor 160th st; ar't, H. Fouchaux. Plan 1364.

23D AND 24TH WARDS.

Beech terrace, n s, 111.5 e Crimmins av. }
Oak terrace, s s, 100 w Beekman av. }
Four two-story frame dwell'gs, 20 x 53.6, shingle roofs; cost, $4,500 each; A. B. Hall, Secretary, 193 Alexander av; ar't, C. C. Churchill; c'r, H. Berry. Plan 1350.

Beekman av, w s, 50 s Beech terrace } two two-
Beekman av, w s, 25 s Oak terrace } story
frame dwell'gs, 19.6x100, shingle roofs; cost, $5,000 each; ow'r, ar't and c'r, same as last. Plan 1351.

Suburban st, n s, 35 e Briggs av, frame shed, 16x12, gravel roof; cost, $50; Isabell Merritt, Bedford Park; ar't, F. D. Miller. Plan 1346.

183d st, n s, 100 e Valentine av, two-story frame stable, 18x35, shingle roof; cost, $425; Minna Bresler, Valentine av and 184th st; ar'ts, King & Symond; b'r, A. Sauer. Plan 1344.

184th st, s s, 50 w Andrews av, two-story and attic frame dwell'g, 26.8x35.2, shingle roof; cost, $3,500; Mary L. Adriance, 184th st, near Andrews av; ar't, A. L. C. Marsh; c'rs, Tolin & Son. Plan 1338. (Substituted for N. B. plan No. 894 filed in June, 1891.)

Aqueduct av, w s, 281 n Hampden st, one-story frame stable, 14.9x20.10, shingle roof; cost, $400; F. S. Moore, 342 East 69th st. Plan 1343.

Jefferson av, e s, 130 n Kingsbridge road, two-story frame stable, 24x24, tin roof; cost, $400; H. Budelmann, Kingsbridge road, Belmont; ar't, C. S. Clark. Plan 1352.

Prospect av, w s, 105 s 165th st, two-story frame dwell'g, 27x39, shingle roof; cost, $4,200; O. Rudolph, 1092 Franklyn av; ar't, G. H. Griebell. Plan 1347.

Briggs av, w s, 327 n Travers st, two two-story frame dwell'gs, 16.8x46, tin roofs; cost, $2,500 each; T. Everest, Valentine av, near Southern Boulevard; ar't, L. Eutzer, Jr. Plan 1363.

Cauldwell av, e s, 125 s 166th st, two-story frame dwell'g, 25x48 with extension, shingle roof; cost, $6,000; Phoebe E. Holden, 1074 Boston av; ar't, C. C. Churchill. Plan 1356.

Marmion av, w s, 330 n Tremont av, two-story frame dwell'g, 22x44, tin roof; cost, $3,200; F. Homann, 254 East 53d st; ar't, C. S. Clark. Plan 1359.

Sedgwick av, w s, 400 s Giles st, two story frame stable, 17x21, shingle roof; cost, $500; N. F. Vought and ano., Kingsbridge, N. Y.; ar't, F. Tyrrell. Plan 1354.

KINGS COUNTY.

Plan 1916—Arlington av, n e cor Essex st, one three-story frame (brk filled) store and tenem't, 25x66, tin roof; cost, $7,500; A. Keppler; ar't, F. Holmberg.

1917—Vermont st, w s, 200 n Fulton st, one two-story and attic frame (brk filled) dwell'g, 20x39, tin roof; cost, $5,500; ow'r and b'r, G. Distler, 45 Vermont st; ar't, F. Holmberg.

1918—Sunnyside av, s s, 75 e Barbey st, one three-story frame tenem't, 30x64, tin roof; cost, $5,000; Rosa Peiffer, Sunnyside av, near Barbey st; ar't, C. Infanger; c'r, C. Schneider.

1919—Hamburg av, n w cor Hart st, two three-story frame (brk filled) stores and tenem'ts, 25x58, tin roofs; cost, $4,800 each; ow'r and b'r, Henry Roth, 1091 Myrtle av; ar't, Th. Engelhardt.

1920—Jefferson av, n s, 190 w Stuyvesant av, two three-story and basement brown and red stone dwell'g.s 20x48, tin roofs and wooden cornices; cost, $5,000 each; ow'r and b'r, D. B. Norris, 617 Putnam av; ar'ts, I. D. Reynolds & Son.

1921—Bergen st, s s, 100 e Rogers av, seven three-story brk dwell'gs, 18.11x45, slate and tin mansard roofs, wooden cornice; cost, each, $6,500; A. C. Brownell, Dean st and Rogers av; ar't, G. P. Chappell.

1922—St. Marks av, No. 669, n s, 200 w Nostrand av, one two-story and mansard, brk dwell'g, 30x51, slate and gravel roof, iron cornice; cost, $8,000; ow'r, ar't and c'r, Stephen M. Randall, 154 Manhattan av.

1923—St. Marks av, No. 669, n s, 200 w Nostrand av, one one-story and attic brk stable, 33.6x17 and 26, tin roof, iron cornice; cost, $600; ow'r, ar't and b'r, same as last.

1924—Macon st, s s, 210 w Lewis av, four three-story and basement brk and red and brown stone dwell'gs, 20x45, tin roofs, iron cornices; cost, each, $7,000; E. Willard Jones, 49 Nassau st, New York.

1925—Jefferson av, n s, 250 w Stuyvesant av, three two-and-a-half-story and basement brown and red stone dwell'gs, 20x45, tin roofs, wooden cornices; cost, each, $5,000; D. B. Norris, 617 Putnam av; ar't, I. D. Reynolds.

1926—Willoughby av, s s, 150 e Evergreen av, one four-story frame (brk filled) tenem't, 25x62, tin roof; cost $5,600; ow'r and b'r, Daniel Kreuder, 149 McKibbin st; ar't, Th. Engelbardt.

1927—Jay st, Nos. 351 and 353, one seven-story brk factory, 50 and 47x100, tin roof, iron cornice; cost, $35,000; ow'r and b'r, J. W. Birkett, 120 Lawrence st; ar't, R. B. Eastman.

1928—McDonough st, s s, 43.3 e Ralph av, one three-story and basement brown and Dorchester stone dwell'g, 18.9x45.6, tin roof, iron cornice; cost, $5,000; ow'r and ar't, Thos. H. Radcliffe, 826 Fulton st; b'r, J. Court.

1929—McDonough st, s s, 24.6 e Ralph av, one three-story and basement brown stone dwell'g, 18.9x50, tin roof, iron cornice; cost, $5,000; ow'r and b'r, same as last.

1930—Court st, e s, 25 s 4th pl, one four-story brk store and flat, 25x60, tin roof, iron cornice; cost, $8,000; Thomas Wynne, on premises; ar't, R. Dixon; b'r, P. J. Carlin.

1931—Driggs av, s e cor Sutton st, one three-story frame (brk filled) store and family, 25x49, gravel roof; cost, $5,000; Paul C. Grening, 420 Gates av; ar't, F. Weber; b'r, O. W. Humphrey.

1932—Irving av, e s, 50 n Greene av, two three-story frame (brk filled) tenem'ts, 25x58, tin roofs; cost, total $8,000; Henry Schneider, 239 Irving av; ar't, H. Vollweiler; b'r, not selected.

1933—Warwick st, n w cor Livonia av, one two-story frame store and dwell'g, 20x36, tin roof; cost, $2,000; no names given for ow'r, ar't or b'r.

1934—Linwood st, w s, 241 s Fulton av, one three-story frame tenem't, 25x61.6, gravel roof; cost, $5,400; Julia J. Whitlock, 113 Hendrix st; ar't and b'r, W. H. Whitlock.

1935—Weirfield st, n s, 120 e Evergreen av, eight buildings; Halsey st, n s, 240 e Evergreen av, three buildings—making eleven two-story and basement frame (brk filled) dwell'gs, 20x56, tin roofs; cost, $3,000 each; ow'rs, ar'ts and b'rs, Farrell, Hommel & Co., Weirfield st and Evergreen av.

1936—Richardson st, n s, 75 e Lorimer st, one two-story frame (brk filled) tenem't, 25x30, tin roof; cost, $800; Martin Reynolds, 78 Richardson st; ar't, H. Vollweiler; b'r, J. Shoeb.

1937—Meeker av, n e cor Sutton st, one three-story frame (brk filled) store and tenem't, 25x54 and 65, gravel roof; cost, $5,800; Paul C. Greening; ar't, F. Weber; b'r, O. W. Humphrey.

1938—Belmont av, s e cor Montauk av, five two-story frame dwell'gs, 20x30, tin roofs; cost, total, $11,000; ow'r and b'r, Donald Laing, Belmont av, cor Atkins av.

1939—Flushing av, Nos. 584 and 586, one one-story brk storehouse, 50x45, gravel roof; cost, $800; Knapp & Merces, 584 Flushing av.

1940—Windsor pl, s s, 60 w 8th av, one two-story brk stable, 20x21, tin roof, wooden cornice; cost, $800; Wm. Ebeling, on premises; ar't, W. M. Coots; b'r, T. Brown.

1941—Prospect av, s s, 206 e 4th av, one three-story brk tenem't, 19x48, tin roof, wooden cornice; cost, $4,000; ow'r, art and c'r, Thos. McCormick, 138A 16th st; m'n, D. Landon.

1942—Halsey st, n s, 325 e Sumner av, one two-story brk truck house for Fire Department, 25x71.6, tin roof, brk cornice; cost, $10,000; City of Brooklyn; b'r, R. A. Langdon.

1943—Irving pl, w s, 300 n Putnam av, one three-story brk flat, 22x80, tin roof, iron cornice; cost, $9,000; C. W. and E. M. Barlow, 16 and 18 Irving pl; ar'ts, I. D. Reynolds & Son; b'r, not selected.

1944—Atlantic av, n s, 75.1 e Hendrix st, two two-story frame (brk filled) stores and dwell'gs, 25x61.6 and 60 and 58.6, tin roofs; cost, $4,000 each; Carsten J. Mehrtens, 2767 Atlantic av; ar't, C. Infanger; b'rs, H. Hermann and J. Fensch.

1945—Jerome st, w s, 100 n Eastern Parkway, five two-story and attic frame dwell'gs, 17.8x28, tin roofs; cost $2,500 each; Theo. M. Le Beau, 126 Van Sicien av; ar't, C. Infanger.

1946—Bergen st, s s, 222 e Schenectady av, eight two-story frame (brk filled) dwell'gs, 17x36, tin roofs; cost, $1,600 each; ow'r and b'r, F. Duffy, Jr., 1693 Pacific st.

1947—Jerome st, w s, 45 s Hegeman av, one two-story frame dwell'g, 17x26, tin roof; cost, $2,500; ow'r, ar't and b'r, F. Marritt, Milford st, bet Sutter and Belmont avs.

1948—Saratoga av, e s, 30 n Pacific st, one two-story and basement frame (brk filled) dwell'g, 20x40, gravel roof; cost, $3,000; M. Erickson, 197 McDougal st.

1949—Jefferson st, s s, 175 e Knickerbocker av, one one-story frame (brk filled) stable, 16x10, tin roof; cost, $50; ow'rs, ar'ts and b'rs, Spath & Saenger, on premises.

1950—Knickerbocker av, n e cor Melrose st, one three-story frame (brk filled) store and tenement, 25x57, tin roof; cost, $6,500; ow'r and b'r, Ignatz Wolf, Dupont st; ar'ts, D. Acker & Son.

1951—Myrtle av, n w cor Wyckoff av, one three-story frame (brk filled) store and dwell'g, 37.2 and 54.5x43 and 60, tin roof; cost, $4,800; Meyerose & Brunjes, 1579 Myrtle av; ar't, T. Engelhardt; b'r, not selected.

1952—Chauncey st, s s, 325 w Patchen av, one two-story frame (brk filled) dwell'g, 20x45, tin roof; cost, $2,400; Mr. Bedland, 168 9th av; b'r, G. F. Chapman.

1953—Seigel st, Nos. 104 and 106, two four-story frame (brk filled) tenem'ts, 25x80, tin roofs; cost, $8,000 each; Maria Kort, 104 Seigel st; ar't, H. Smith; b'r, not selected.

1954—Lewis av, s e cor Putnam av, one four-story brk and Lake Superior flat, 25x71.10, tin roof, iron cornice; cost, $10,000; ow'r and ar't, John F. Ryan, 215 Hewes st.

1955—Kingsland av, w s, 100 s Meserole av, one two-story frame (brk filled) stable, 50x60, gravel roof; cost, $2,000; ow'rs, ar't and c'rs, Sone & Fleming Mfg Co., Kingsland and Meserole avs; m'n, J. T. Woodruff.

1956—South 8th st, n s, 75 w Bedford av, one four-story brk store and tenem't, 25x18x80, tin roof, iron cornice; cost, $9,000; Jacob S. Van Wyck, 161 Taylor st; ar't, B. Finkenseiper; b'rs, W. L. Langridge and J. Trevor.

1957—Greene av, s s, 70 e Hamburg av, one five-story brk brewery, 58x38 and 42, gravel roof, brk and stone cornice; cost, $13,000; C. Heinbockel & Co., Hamburg and Greene avs; ar't, T. Engelhardt; m'n, J. Auer; c'r, not selected.

1958—Greene av, s s, 146 e Hamburg av, one four-story brk beer storehouse, 55x53.6, gravel roof, brk and stone cornice; cost, $20,000; ow'rs, ar't and b'r, same as last.

1959—Dean st, n s, 300 w Utica av, two four-story brk tenem'ts, 25x52, tin roofs, wooden cornices; cost, $6,000 each; ow'r, ar't and b'r, John Downie, 283 Flatbush av.

1960—41st st, s s, 100 e 3d av, one frame storage house, 14x—, tin roof; cost, $250; Mary J. Stanley, 144 41st st; ar't and b'r, J. Stanley.

ALTERATIONS NEW YORK CITY.

Plan 1818—Nassau st, Nos 75 and 77, rear, walls altered; cost, $500; C. F. Kingsland, Tarrytown, N. Y.; m'n, J. J. Murdoch; c'r, J. H. McCullough.

1819—Bowery, No. 103, building to be extended 43 ft. in rear and 3 ft. in front, interior repairs; cost, $600; agent, H. Trowbridge, 33 Howard st; ar't, L. F. Heinecke; m'ns, P. & J. Schaeffler; c'r, C. Leyh.

1820—72d st, No. 49 E., three-story extension, 13x9.6, and interior alterations; cost, abt $3,000; J. Wagner, on premises; ar'ts, Rossiter & Wright.

1821—6th av, No. 244, new front; cost, $650; lessee, C. F. Hanson, on premises; c'r, J. Schuster.

1822—28th st, No. 40 W., one-story extension, 12x18; cost, $600; lessee, J. Ulber, on premises; b'r, F. W. Moore.

1823—11th av, s w cor 30th st, new store front; cost, $250; lessee, F. Dehmann, on premises; ar't, J. W. Cole.

1824—Allen st, Nos. 42 and 44, repair damage by fire; cost, $1,000; D. L. Braine, 67 1st pl, Brooklyn.

1825—Barclay st and North River, pier 25, one-story extension, 37x144; cost, $10,000; N. Y. C. & H. R. R. Co., Grand Central Depot.

1826—41st st, Nos. 430-436 W., new roof; cost, $75; lessee, G. W. Thedford, 129 West 87th st; c'r, P. Haugbey.

1827—2d av, No. 1315, front alterations; cost, $50; M. H. Stern, 132 East 80th st; c'r, F. Beinhauer.

1828—1st av, No. 2258, one-story extension, 20x26, and front alterations; cost, $2,560; J. F. Wetler, on premises; ar't, M. L. Ungrich; c'rs, Hollenth & Son.

1829—Dominick st, No. 21, new show window; cost, $15; J. M. Horton, 112 West 120th st; c'r, L. Sibley.

1830—22d st, No. 323 E., one-story extension, 20.8x39.4; cost, $1,000; J. S. Piza, 247 West 45th st; ar't, T. R. Jackson.

1831—47th st, No. 133 W., two-story extension, 9x12; cost, $1,000; S. J. Murphy, on premises; ar't, R. A. Shay; m'n, J. T. Smith; c'r, E. Outwater.

1832—23d st, No. 312 W., walls altered; cost, $60; L. Fitzgerald, on premises; m'n, L. Marcellus; c'r, A. Henderson.

1833—72d st, No. 122 W., one-story extension, 18x56, rear, extension raised two stories, interior alterations and walls altered; cost, $5,000; C. G. Emery, The Belgravia, 5th av; ar't, Van Campen Taylor.

1834—Elm st, No. 194, rear, raised one story; cost, $1,600; C. M. Boland, Woodbridge, N. J.; ar't, T. Commeau.

1835—1st av, No. 2390, interior alterations and new store front; cost, $400; E. Colgate exr., 13 East 69th st; ar't, J. E. Darragh.

1836—West st, No. 69, one-story extension, 25x16.6; cost, $1,700; agent, W. Cruikshank, 113 West 76th st; b'r, J. Downey.

1837—15th st, No 20 W., tank on roof; cost, abt $500; Laura F. Hearn, 46 East 69th st; ar'ts, Snook & Sons.

1838—Union sq, No. 31 W., skylight removed, wall and roof altered; cost, abt $350; agent, C. T. Galloway, 646 Hudson st; ar't, J. E. Nicholsen; m'n, J. V. Meyers; c'rs, Hoe's Sons.

1839—10th st, No. 434 E., walls altered; cost, $400; W. F. Youngs, 153 Rodney st, Brooklyn; ar't, F. Wennemer

1840—Grand st, No. 147, interior alterations and new store front; cost, $1,500; W. Deutermann, on premises; ar'ts, Boekell & Son.

1841—2d av, No. 794, new show windows; cost, $350; S. Adelsberger, exr., 56 West 126th st; ar't, C. Ziegler.

1842—11th av, No. 511, new front and cornice; cost, $275; lessee, J. I. Nolan, 506 West 42d st; c'r, P. Haugbey.

1843—13th st, No. 13 W., front alterations; cost, $1,500; H. Mandelbaum, 181 Henry st; ar't, H. Horenburger; c'r, H. Fischel.

1844—Ridge st, No. 24, new store front; cost, $300; L. Levy, 191 Division st; ar't, H. Horenburger.

1845—27th st, No. 154 E., one-story extension, 15x9; cost, $300; G. G. Minder, 320 East 27th st; ar't, H. Horenburger.

1846—Av A, No. 220, new show window; cost, $600; Anna Hashagen, on premises; ar't, B. W. Berger.

1847—3d av, No. 143, one-story extension, 18x20, interior alterations and walls altered; cost, $900; lessee, S. Hausen, on premises; ar't, W. W. Howe.

1848—33d st, No. 34 E., two-story extension, 7x19.6; cost, $1,300; L. A. Stimson, on premises; b'r, W. S. Miller.

1849—7th av, s e cor 57th st, asbestos curtain on stage; cost, $200; Music Hall Co., on premises, ar't, W. B. Tuthill.

1850—38th st, No. 120 E., roof altered; cost, $250; Jane J. Smith, on premises; ar't, J. Sexton; c'r, J. J. Greville.

1851—52d st, No. 212 E., raised one story and alterations for driveway; cost, $800; O. W. Horton, on premises; ar't, G. F. Pelham.

KINGS COUNTY.

Plan 1005—Liberty av, s e cor Crescent st, flat tin roof, interior alterations; cost, $3,000; Metha Konemann, on premises; ar't, L. F. Schillinger; b'r, F. Gunderman, Jr.

1006—North 4th st, n s, 75 e Driggs st, add one story; cost, $1,000; Thomas Cantwell, 187 North 4th st; ar't, H. Smith; b'r, A. Sachs.

1007—Stagg st, No. 134, door in gable wall and interior alterations; cost, $50; J. G. Lutz, on premises; ar't, T. Engelhardt; b'r, not selected.

1008—Prospect pl, n s, 270 e New York av, add one story, new brk wall; cost, $1,500; J. E. Searles, Jr., 810 St. Marks av; ar'ts, J. C. Cady & Co.; b'r, G. D. Partridge.

1009—Jamaica av, s e cor Logan st, one-story frame extension, 20x12.6, tin roof; cost, $1,000; D. J. Molloy, 2507 Atlantic av; ar'ts, Danmar & Fischer; b'r, not selected.

1010—South 3d st, No. 327, one-story and basement brk extension, 15x11, tin roof; cost, $400; b'rs, Emak & Veit and G. W. Williams.

1011—Jerome st, w s, 125 s Glenmore av, one-story frame extension, 8x16, tin roof; cost, $250; J. Stander, on premises; b'r, F. Gundermann, Jr.

1012—Broadway, No. 1395, interior alterations; cost, $100; A. Kodziezer, 74 Beaver st; ar't, T. Engelhardt; b'r, not selected.

1013—32d st, n s, 225 e 3d av, raised 9 feet on frame story; cost, $400; H Carl, 125 32d st.

1014—Vandyke st, No. 159, new brk foundation; cost, $800; Mrs. N. Redfield, on premises.

1015—44th st, n s, 125 e 4th av, raised 20 feet on brk story; cost, $200; James Grimes, on premises.

1016—Boerum st, No. 163, new store front; cost, $200; Abraham Strasswinski, on premises.

1017—4th pl, s e cor Court st, add one story, also four-story brk extension, 12x4.6, tin roof; cost, $7,000; Thos. Wynne, on premises; ar't, R. Dixon; b'r, P. J. Carlin.

1018—Tillary st, n e cor Raymond st, new store front; cost, $200; Stephen Molishnelli, 51 Mulberry st, New York.

1019—Madison st, No. 586, two-story and basement brk extension, 8 6x16, interior alterations; cost, $1,000; Robert Burns, on premises; b'rs, W. Dixon and J. H. Stone.

1020—Graham av, No. 214, four-story frame extension, 5.9x5, tin roof; cost, $400; Jos. J. Froehlich, Graham av, s e cor Stegg st; ar't, Th. Engelhardt; b'r, not selected.

1021—Broadway, s e cor Van Buren st, one-story frame extension, 20x40, tin roof; cost, $1,100; Jost Moeller, Bedford av and South 9th st; ar't, R. Von Lehn.

1022—Kent av, No. 836, repair damage by fire; cost, $1,000; James Feeley, 525 Park av; b'r, not selected.

1023—Buffalo av, s e cor Herkimer st, two-story frame extension, 18x25, tin roof; cost, $500; H. J. Meyer, on premises; b'rs, C. Baur and J. Frederickson.

1024—De Kalb av, No. 204, one-story brk extension, 12 and 12.3x29.10 and 32, tin roof; cost, $350; L. Goldsmith, on premises; ar'ts, F. W. & C. J. Dodge; b'r, J. McKeefrey.

1025—Lincoln pl, No. 232, one-story brk extension, 25x14, tin roof; cost, $400; Wm. Spence, on premises; b'r, M. Ryan.

1026—Cedar st, No. 14, one-story brk extension, 5.7x4.6, tin roof; cost, $75; Mr. Praeger, 703 Bushwick av; ar't, H. Vollweiler; b'r, not selected.

1027—Grand st, s s, 274.1 w Lorimer st, one-story frame extension, 24.5x30, tin roof; cost, $1,000; Adolph Schmidt, 538 Grand st; ar't, T. Engelhardt; b'r, not selected.

MISCELLANEOUS.

BUSINESS FAILURES.

Schedule of assignments for the seven weeks ending Oct. 23, 1891:

	Liabilities.	Nominal Assets.	Real Assets.
Alexander Rudolph..	$29,706 22	$15,180 84	$7,056 14
Beck, Frank E.......	3,146 47	4,336 66	2,183 78
Black, Joseph R.....	54,058 08	44,432 12	22,664 72
Buckerman, Emanuel. / Blumenfeld, Joseph	5,193 98	3,895 61	3,116 49
Crossley, Charles A..	23,438 29	17,157 78	3,931 50
Carr, Walter. / Snecker, William H. / Carr, Delwin R.	152,574 52	30,801 40	8,606 36
Cohen, Lipman......	9,498 83	11,562 78	4,209 63
Dane, William P.....	75,793 94	81,198 45	45,178 95
Groschee, William...	8,924 88	1,943 88	1,887 00
Hyde, Eugene M.....	8,248 97	4,012 51	1,927 49
Hyman, Annie.......	4,864 18	2,695 42	2,695 42
Jellenek, Morris.....	1,006 16	638 70	282 25
Kerr, Howard D. / Leaman, William S / Newkirk, Edgar	8,553 82	4,152 54	2,357 85
Lewis, Edwin G	10,747 39	5,556 51	3,570 49
North River Lumber Co....	26,087 79	49,149 40	31,373 17
Nimmo, Sarah J. and Charles W.....	8,911 96	4,399 67	2,454 11
Petreins, Charles A..	7,833 71	5,790 47	2,669 90
Poulter, Alfred.......	1,407 14	515 27	515 27
Pierce, John, Jr.....	10,881 22	5,375 00	5,375 00
Rich, Aquila B / Troy, Willis B	22,167 15	6,954 88	5,281 63
Smith, John W.......	4,813 49	1,341 00	1,055 22
Turton, Edgar G. and John....	23,398 88	15,158 04	3,016 69
Wallace, F. R. & Co. / Smith, Morris H	690,940 83	1,312,109 64	28,513 04

N. Y. ASSIGNMENTS—BENEFIT CREDITORS.

Oct.

20 Alexander, Robert (dealer in hardware and specialties, at No. 5 Vesey st), to Joseph Henry Seed; preferences, $188.32.

20 Jelleneck, Morris (gents' furnishing goods, at No. 503 8th av), to George Peyser; preferences, $325.

21 Hoag, Harry G. (hat specialties, at No. 128 South 5th av), to Louis Lowenstein; without preferences.

21 Davis, John (wholesale jobber in millinery goods, at No. 599 Broadway), to Edwin Davis; without preferences

22 Carter, Richard J. and John P. (composing firm of R. J. & J. P. Carter, livery and boarding stable keepers, at No. 121 West 45th st), to Lewis H. Losee; without preferences.

PROCEEDINGS OF THE BOARD OF ALDERMEN AFFECTING REAL ESTATE.

* Under the different headings indicates that a resolution has been introduced and referred to the appropriate committee. † Indicates that the resolution has passed and has been sent to the Mayor for approval. ‡ Passed over the Mayor's veto.

NEW YORK, October 20, 1891.

CROSSWALKS.

West st, in front of No. 209, at expense of Stephen Rockfeller.†

LAMP-POSTS ERECTED AND LIGHTED.

29th st, in front of No. 30 W., at expense of Samuel T. Young.†

Park av, from 96th to 105th st.†

147th st, from Boulevard to a point 500 feet west therefrom.†

MAINS.

75th st, bet West End and Riverside avs; water.†
147th st, from Boulevard to a point 800 feet west therefrom; gas.†
Park av, from 96th to 105th st; gas.†

FENCING VACANT LOTS.

77th st, s s, abt 150 e Columbus av, runs east abt 100 feet.†
1st av, n e cor 90th st, 50 on av and 100 on st.†

APPROVED PAPERS.

Resolutions passed by the Board of Aldermen calling for the following improvements have been signed by the Mayor for the week ending October 17, 1891. *Indicates that the Mayor neither appoved nor objected thereto, therefore the same became adopted.

CURBSTONES SET AND SIDEWALKS FLAGGED.

Boulevard, w s, from 165th st to Inwood st now Dyckman st.
Christopher st, in front of Nos. 4 and 6.
Pearl st, in front of No. 419; relaid, &c.
26th st, n s, west of 3d av } in front of Broadway
27th st, s s, west of 3d av } alley.
78th st, n s, bet 2d and 3d avs.
89th st, s s, in front of vacant lots bet 2d and 3d avs.
102d st, n s, from Columbus to Amsterdam avs.
117th st, both sides, from 8th to St. Nicholas av.
133d st, n s, from Lenox to 7th av.
162d st, from 11th av to Kingsbridge road.
Madison av, e s, from 98d to 100th st.
Madison av, both sides, from 116th to 120th st.
Manhattan and St. Nicholas avs, 122d and 123d sts, the block.
St. Nicholas av, w s, from 117th to 119th st.
Southern Boulevard, from Home st south to Hunts Point road and crosswalks laid at intersecting and terminating sts and avs.*
101st st, both sides, from 1st av to East River.
141st st, both sides, from Alexander to Willis av.*
148th st, from Boulevard to 12th av, and crosswalks laid at the intersecting avs.
149th st, from Boulevard to 12th av, and crosswalks laid at the intersecting avs.
114th st, both sides, from 5th to Madison av.
116th st, n s, from 2d av extending east 100 feet.
129th st, from 3d to Lexington av.
Columbus av, s w cor 75th st, 100 ft. on av and 200 ft. on st.
Park av, n e cor 117th st, 150 ft. on av and 100 ft. on st.
5th av, n e cor 114th st, 100 ft. on av and 150 ft. on st.
5th av, both sides, from 114th to 115th st.

REGULATING, GRADING, ETC.

Boulevard, from 156th st to Inwood st now Dyckman st and crosswalks laid and retaining walls built in certain portions thereof.
162d st, from 11th av to Kingsbridge road.
Southern Boulevard, from Home st south to Hunts Point road.*
101st st, from 1st av to East River.
141st st, from e s Alexander av to w s Willis av.*
141st st, from w s Brook av to e s Willis av, at expense of Wm. O'Gorman.*
148th st, from Boulevard to 12th av.
149th st, from Boulevard to 12th av.

LAMP POSTS ERECTED AND LIGHTED.

Essex st, in front of eastern entrance to Essex Market building.
Henston st, in front of No. 286 E., at expense of S. I. Kohn.
West Farms road, from Main st to Southern Boulevard.
12th av, bet 133d and 134th sts.
Broadway, s e cor 41st st, two on Broadway and one on 41st st, at expense of L. L. Todd.
Henry st, in front of Nos. 38 and 40, two lights.
91st st, from Columbus to Amsterdam av.
101st st, from 2d av to East River.
117th st, from Madison to 5th av.
142d st, from Boulevard to 12th av.
Amsterdam av, from 110th to 114th st.

PAVING.

90th st, from 1st to 2d av, and crosswalks laid at terminating avs.
141st , from e s Alexander av to w s Willis av, trap block.*
141st st, from w s Brook av to e s Willis av, trap block, at expense of Wm. O'Gorman.*
154th st, from w s Courtlandt av to w s Morris av, granite block.
133d st, from Broadway to Amsterdam av; granite block and crosswalks laid at intersection and terminating st and av.

MAINS LAID.

91st st, from Columbus to Amsterdam av, gas.
101st st, from 2d av to East River, gas.
117th st, from Madison to 5th av, gas.
188th st, from 7th to 8th av, water.
189th st, from 7th to 8th av, water.
142d st, from Boulevard to 12th av, water.
142d st, from Boulevard to 12th av, gas.
Amsterdam av, from 110th to 114th sts, gas.
Tinton av, from 161st to 163d st, water.
West Farms road, from Main st to Southern Boulevard; gas.
91st st, bet 9th and 10th avs; water.
161st st, from 3d to Railroad av E.; water.
12th av, from 133d to 134th st; gas.

FENCING VACANT LOTS.

98th st, n s, bet Columbus and Amsterdam avs.*
138th, 139th and 14th sts, Lenox and 5th avs, the blocks, where not already done.*
Amsterdam av, s w cor 81st st, 100 on av and 110 on st.*
Madison and 5th avs, 89th and 90th sts, the block.*

CROSSWALKS.

28th st, in front of No. 28 W., at expense of John McGrath.
8th av, in front of No. 214, at expense of J. F. De Lury.

ADVERTISED LEGAL SALES.

REFEREES SALES TO BE HELD AT THE REAL ESTATE EXCHANGE AND AUCTION ROOM (LIMITED), 59 to 65 LIBERTY STREET, EXCEPT WHERE OTHERWISE STATED.

Oct.

Canal st, No. 119, n s, old No. 216 Walker st, formerly known as No. 74 Pump st, 18.9x50 old measurement, by D. P. Ingraham & Co. (Partition sale) 26
Boulevard, e s, 24.11 n 189th st, 75x100, vacant, by D. P. Ingraham & Co. (Amt due $31,451)..... 26
Av A, Nos. 393 and 395, s w cor 24th st, 49.5x81.5, vacant, all right, title and interest which Daniel D. Conover had on June 10, 1891, by Sheriff at City Hall. (Sale under execution) 26
9th st, No. 747, n s, 93.2 w Av D, 24.8x92.3, four-story brk tenem't with stores, by B. L. Kennelly. (Amt due $5,089; prior morts. $——)............ 27
46th st, No. 517, n s, 275 w 10th av, 25x100.4, five-story brk tenem't with two-story brk building on rear, by D. P. Ingraham & Co. (Amt due $9,991)........ 27
57th st, No. 49, n s, 19 w 4th av, 20x80.5, four-story stone front dwell'g, by R. V. Harnett....... 27
124th st, No. 104, s s, 60 e 4th av as widened, 80x100.11, five-story brk flat, by A. H. Muller & Son. (Amt due $26,887)........ 27
133d st, No. 220, s s, 400 w 7th av, 16.8x99.11, five-story brk flat, by D. P. Ingraham & Co. (Amt due $2,492; prior morts. $16,000)........ 27
Monroe st, No. 87, n s, abt 110 e Pike st, 25x100, four-story brk store and tenem't with five-story brk tenem't on rear, by J. S. McQuillen. (Amt due $7,352)........ 28
131st st, No. 18, s s, 205 w 5th av, 15x84.11........ }
131st st, No. 22, s s, 295 w 5th av, 15x84.11........ }
Two three-story stone front dwell'gs........ }
by R. V. Harnett & Co. (Amt due on No. 18 $1,978, $1,941 on No. 22; prior morts. $17,000)... 28
Rider av, w s, 768 s 144th st, 75x125 to Mott Haven Canal, also all machinery, &c., by William Kennelly. (Amt due $105,429)........ 28
Willis av, s e cor 146th st, 25x100, by Smyth & Ryan. (Amt due $19,864)........ 28
4th av, No. 251, s e s, 46 s w 21st st, 23x90, portion of four-story brk hotel........ }
4th av, Nos. 246 and 248, w s, 20 s 20th st, 40x64, two four-story brk stores and tenem'ts... }
by J. L. Wells. (Amt due $39,374)........ 28
3d st, No. 230, s s, 288.7 e Av B, 24.9x105.11, leasehold, three-story brk tenem't with stores and four-story brk tenem't on rear........ }
4th st, No. 216, s s, 342.9 e Av A, 24.9x96.2, leasehold, four-story brk store and tenem't with four-story brk tenem't on rear........ }
by R. V. Harnett & Co. (Partition sale)........ 29
20th st, No. 205, n e s, 517.6 n w 2d av, 17.6x92, four-story brk tenem't, by J. C. Lalor. (Leasehold; amt due $3,836)........ 29
57th st, Nos. 110 and 114, s s, 175 w 6th av, 75x100.5, five-story brk flats, by R. V. Harnett. (Amt due $19,418; prior morts. $70,000)........ 29
61st st, No. 303, n s, 75 e 2d av, 25x75, five-story brk tenem't, by D. P. Ingraham & Co. (Amt due $2,109; prior morts. $9,000; sold Oct. 15, 1891, for $15,000)........ 29
103d st, No. 206, s s, 118 w 10th av, 99.6x72 to Clendenning lane, x99.7x77.2, five-story brk flat, by J. T. Boyd. (Amt due $12,852)........ 29
1st av, No. 2317, w s, 75.7 s 119th st, 25.2x100, five-story brk tenem't with stores, by J. C. Lalor. (Amt due $16,289)........ 29
1st av, No. 2319, w s, 50.5 s 119th st, 25.2x100, five-story brk tenem't with stores, by J. C. Lalor. (Amt due $16,279)........ 29
Broome st, No. 2, n w cor Tompkins st, 25x75, five-story stone front tenem't with stores, by D. P. Ingraham & Co. (Amt due $40,149)........ 30
Forsyth st, No. 153, w s, 125 s Rivington st, 25x100, five-story stone front store and tenem't, by D. P. Ingraham & Co. (Amt due $15,165)........ 30
50th st, No. 204, s s, 75 e 3d av, 15x60, three-story brk dwell'g, by S. De Walltearss. (Partition sale)........ 30
100th st, Nos. 155-169, n s, 95 e Lexington av, 200x100.11, eight five-story brk flats........ }
101st st, Nos. 154-168, s s, 95 e Lexington av, 200x100.11, eight five-story brk flats........ }
by D. P. Ingraham & Co. (Amt due on each $26,308)........ 30
127th st, No. 148, s s, 350.9 w 3d av, 16.3x99.11, three-story stone front dwell'g, by J. F. B. Smyth. (Amt due $3,736; prior morts. $8,000; sold Sept. 25, 1890, for $12,400)........ 30
130th st, No. 22, s s, 126.8 w Madison av, 16.8x99.11, three-story brk dwell'g, by J. F. B. Smyth. (Amt due $2,712; prior morts. $11,000)........ 30

Nov.

119th st, No. 7, n s, 95.5 w 5th av, 14x57.9x14.6x53.11, three-story brk dwell'g, by B. L. Kennelly. (Amt due $4,732)........ 2

KINGS COUNTY.

Oct.

Decatur st, No. 49, n s, 229 w Throop av, 18x100, three-story brk dwell'g; assessed value, $6,500 }
Raymond st, w s, 175 s Bolivar st, runs west 75 x south — to Willoughby st, x east — to Raymond st, x north 26 to beginning, four-story brk tenem't and store; assessed value, $8,400. }
Raymond st, w s, 150 s Bolivar st, 25x75, four-story brk tenem't; assessed value, $7,000 }
Union st, Nos. 221-229, n s, 227.6 w Clinton st, 140x100, five five-story double brk and stone flats; assessed value, $60,000........ }
by T. A. Kerrigan, at 13 Willoughby st........ 26
Van Siclen av, e s, 125 s Blake av, 25x100, vacant, by J. Cole, at 389 Fulton st........ 26
Monroe st, No. 320, s s, 405.3 w Tompkins av, 19.9x100, two-story and basement frame dwelling; assessed value $2,800........ }
Albany av, s e cor Park pl, 20x80, three-story brk dwell'g and store........ }
Albany av, n e cor Butler st, 235.7x80, thirteen three-story brk dwell'gs, corner with store... }
by T. A. Kerrigan, at 13 Willoughby st........ 27
Caton av, n s, 95.6½ w Ocean av, runs west 176.1½ x northeast 370.7 to Crooke av, x east 12.5½ x south 203.10 to beginning, Flatbush; partition; by J. Cole, at 389 Fulton st........ 27
1st pl, No. 120, s s, 225 e Court st, 25x133.5¼, five-story brk flat; assessed value, $5,000; by Jere. Johnson, Jr., at Real Estate Exchange, 189 and 191 Montague st........ 27
Washington Park late Cumberland st, No. 204, e s, 114.0¼ n De Kalb av, 28x100, four-story brk dwell'g; assessed value, $13,400; partition; by J. Cole, at 389 Fulton st........ 28
Glenmore av, Nos. 449 and 451, n s, 56 w Wyona av, 44x25, two-story frame dwell'g on plot; assessed value, $950; by T. A. Kerrigan, at 13 Willoughby st........ 28
Fulton st, n e cor Somers st, 127.4x27.11¾x124.2⅞, gore; assessed value, $9,000........ }
Garfield pl, No. 174½, s s, 312.6¼ w 7th av, 12.5¼x100, three-story brk dwell'g; assessed value, $3,000........ }
McDonough st, No. 415, n s, 135 w Reid av, 16.8x100, two-story and basement brick dwell'g; assessed value, $3,500........ }
Raymond st, No. 122, w s, 25 s Bolivar st, 25x75, four-story brk tenem't; assessed value, $7,000. }
Raymond st, No. 124, w s, 50 s Bolivar st, 25x75, four-story brk tenem't; assessed value, $7,000. }
Gates av, n s, 224 e Lewis av, 25x100, four-story double brk flat and store; assessed value, $7,850........ }
by T. A. Kerrigan, at 13 Willoughby st........ 29
Madison st, Nos. 916 and 918, s s, 20 e Howard av, 40x100, four-story double brk flat; assessed value, $14,000........ }
Oliver st, n s, 100 w Marine av, runs north 193.7 x northwest 25.3 to 1st av, x west — x south 200 to Oliver st, x east 50, New Utrecht........ }
Oliver st, n s, 300 w Marine av, 150x200 to 1st av, New Utrecht........ }
Marine av, w s, 100 n Oliver st, 50x100, New Utrecht........ }
3d av, n w cor 91st st, 50.2x112.6x irreg., New Utrecht, except........ }
Oliver st, n s, 200.6 w Shore road, 25x200 to 1st av, New Utrecht........ }
by J. Cole, at 389 Fulton st........ 30
Graham av, No. 206 e s, 50 n Scholes st, 25x100, four-story brk dwell'g and store and three-story frame dwell'g in rear; assessed value, $6,000; by T. A. Kerrigan, at 13 Willoughby st........ 30

Nov.

Atlantic av, Nos. 870-874, s s, 340 w Underhill av, 60x100, two four-story double brk flats; assessed value, $14,000........ }
Willoughby av, n w cor Tompkins av, runs north 77.6 x west 80 x north 22.6 x west 45 x south 100 to Willoughby av, x east 125 to beginning, Reformed Presbyterian Church........ }
by T. A. Kerrigan, at 13 Willoughby st........ 2
South 9th st, Nos. 167 and 169, n e cor Driggs st, 50x78x50x76.4, two three-story brk dwell'gs, corner with store; assessed valua, $16,000; partition; by W. Cole, at 7 and 8 Court sq........ 1

LIS PENDENS, KINGS COUNTY.

Oct.

Sidney pl, w s, 125.6 n State st, 21.1x104.5x28.9x100. William L. Culbert to Mary L. Van Slooten; att'y, J. C. Palmer........ 15
Orient av, w s, 150 s Blake av, 100x100. Lucy F. Ronyon extrx. Alphonse Ronyon agt Augusta Koch; att'y, Washington Sackmann........ 15
South 3d st, s e cor 8th st, 50x55. Phoebe M. Adams agt Milton Wooley; att'ys, Smith & Perkins........ 15
2d st, s s, 300 w Hoyt st, 20x90. Margaret Young agt Bertrand Clover; att'y, Alexander U. Mayer........ 16
McDonough st, s s, 385.6 e Throop av, 19.6x100. Israel Minor, Jr., exr. Jane V. C. Cooper agt Virginia L. Raymond; att'y, Emile Bemoille........ 16
Willow pl, Nos. 38 and 40, n w s, 100.7 n e State st, 47.5x80x irreg. Carsten H. Meyer agt Morris Valenstein; att'y, Charles F. Holm........ 16
Gold st, n w cor Johnson st, 25x100. Mary V. M. Johnson agt Henry Green; att'y, James P. Philip........ 16
Withers st, s s, 150 e Union av, 25x70. Nicola Cetera agt Nicolo Bianculli; att'ys, Judge & Durack........ 16
York st, No. 41, n s, 31.4 e from alley, 16.4x75... }
Carll st, e s, 62.10 n Johnson st, 13x43.7x13x43.6.. }
John King agt Mary Trainor; att'y, M. F. McGoldrick........ 17
Jay st, w s, 260 n Myrtle av, 20x100. William Casey admr. James Casey agt William Casey; att'y, Wm. Sullivan........ 17
Dean st, n s, 160 e Albany av, 20x80. Laura S. Baker agt Robert Valentine; att'ys, Cannon & Atwater........ 19
Dean st, n s, 140 e Albany av, 20x80. Same agt same; same att'ys........ 19
Sheffield av, w s, 25 s Fulton st, 50x100. The Nassau Co-operative Building and Loan Assoc. agt Belle F. Capron; att'ys, Judge & Durack........ 19
Hancock st, s s, 145 e Sumner av, 20x100. Farmers' Loan and Trust Co. guard. Francis M. Whaley agt William A. Taylor; att'ys, Turner, McClure & Rolston........ 19
Richardson st, s s, 150 e Graham av, 25x75. David Springsteen exr. Michael Springsteen agt James Gallagher; att'y, Otto F. Struse........ 19
Lot Canarsie adj land Bennett, 5 acres........ }
Flatbush to Canarsie Landing road, s w s, adj land Daniel Walker, 1 acre; also........ }
3 acres, 6 perches of land adj George Kouwenhoven........ }
Harriet E. Volckening agt Jane E. Rogers; partition; att'ys, J. C. & H. C. Smith & Koepke........ 19
York st, No. 132, s s, 175 e Jay st, 25x123. Brooklyn Elevated R. R. Co. agt Benjamin S. Hitchings; action to acquire real estate; att'ys, Hoadley, Lauterbach & Johnston........ 20
Patchen av, w s, extends from McDonough st to Macon st, 200x80. Edward L. Spencer agt Edwin Beers; att'y, Edward L. Spencer, in person. 20
7th st, s s, 118.8 e 7th av, 19.3x100. Maggie M. Trimble agt Joseph Trimble; action for admeasurement of dower; att'y, James W. Glendenning........ 21
5th av, No. 611, e s, 60.2 s Prospect av, 20x79.5. Mary K. E. Monk to Frank A. J. Kestermann; partition; att'y, Charles Hagedorn........ 21
South 3d st, s e cor 8th st, 50x55. Pheoebe M. Adams agt Milton Woolley; att'ys, Smith & Perkins........ 21
15th st, s s, lot 98 map A. M. Benson, 25x100........ }
Clinton st, e s, 65.6 n 2d pl, 17.3x76.6........ }
Thomas Silk agt James J. Ferry; action to set aside deeds; att'y, Willard S. Pladwell........ 21
Lewis av, s w cor Putnam av, 22x90........ }
Putnam av, s s, 90 w Lewis av, 180x200 to Jefferson av........ }
Charles Cooper agt Augustus W. Blazo; att'ys, McGuire & Low........ 22
Stockton st, n s, 195 w Sumner av, 25x100. Robert B. Jackson trustee Samuel T. Jackson agt Thomas C. Jackson; att'y, Edward Jackson........ 22
24th st, s s, 225 e 3d av, 20x—. Lawrence V. Cortelyou and ano. exrs. Jaques Cortelyou agt James Lambert; att'ys, Hubbard & Rushmore. 22
14th st, s w s, lots 400-405 map Richard Berry farm, 198x100. Charles T. Corwin agt Veronica F. Gibbins; att'y, William M. Benedict........ 22

RECORDED LEASES.

NEW YORK. Per Year

Bleecker st, No. 379, store. Frederick Egler, Jr., to John Lohrmann; 5 years, from May 1, 1891........ $900

Broadway, No. 768, three upper floors. Albert Wagner to Frank Sachse; 3 years, from May 1, 1892 ... 2,000

Carmine st, Nos. 18 and 20, store floors and basements. Catherine M. Cammeyer to Joseph Beck and Bernard Stahl, of Joseph Beck & Co; 5 7-12 years, from Oct. 1, 1891 ... 4,800

Centre st, No. 120, all. Anthony Miller, Brooklyn, to Frederick Rabbe; 9 5-6 years, from July 1, 1891 ... 3,000, 4,000

Cornelia st, s w cor 4th st, store and basement. Charles E. Runk to John, Mariano and James F. Hunt, of Mariano & Hunt; 5 years, from Oct. 1, 1891 ... 1,200, 1,300

Chrystie st, No. 2 } Michael Wolbach to John Division st, No. 46 } Buchmann; 5½ years, from Nov. 1, 1891 ... 2,220

Division st, No. 247, cor Montgomery st, store and basement. Wolf Boroschek and Julius H. Gross to Moses Winter; 2½ years, from Nov. 1, 1891 ... 480

Forsyth st, No. 60, cor store. George L. Balheimer to Marks Epstein; 3 years, from May 1, 1891 ... 900

Grand st, No. 69, store and building. Frederick Siefke to John Soehl; 3 years, from May 1, 1892 ... 2,400

Hester st No. 189, store and front cellar. J. H. Strodl to Domenico Russo; 5 years, from May 1, 1891 ... 840

Same property. Assign. lease. Domenico Russo to James Lanza ... 900

Same property. Assign. lease. James Lanza to Henry Elias Brewing Co ... nom

Mercer st, No. 71, all. James P. Kernochan et al., exrs. and trustees Lorillard Spencer to Leon A. Nones; 6 years, from Jan. 1, 1889, taxes, &c., and ... 2,000

Same property. Assign. lease. Leon A. Nones to Alexander H. Nones ... 5,670

Mott st, No. 161, store and three rooms on ground floor. Simon Fine and Harris Boskey to Joseph Ketzlik; 4 years, from May 1, 1891 ... 840

Willett st, No. 62, store floor and cellar. Kleiman Hirsch to Sam Hirschfeld; 4 years, from Nov. 1, 1890 ... 420

Same property. Assign. lease. Samuel Hirschfeld to Budweiser Brewing Co ... nom

William st, No. 198, store floor. Julius Levy agent to Max L. Jackson; 5 years, from May 1, 1893 ... 2,400

William st, No. 29, basement and first floor.. } Exchange pl, No. 38, first and second floors. } The estate of Charles Lord to Messrs. Heidelbach & Ickelheimer & Co. 4½ years, from Nov. 1, 1891 ... 6,800

Washington st, No. 700. Abbie S. Howell to John H. O'Brien 5 years, from May 1, 1891.. 900

86th st, No. 556 W., ground floor. Florian, Charles, Jr, Robe and Charles F. Bauerdorf exrs. Charles Robe to John Haber; 5 years, from Aug. 1, 1891 ... 660, 780

49th st, No. 122 W., store and basement. Thomas J. McLaughlin and Lewis Z. Bach to John Jaegeler; 5 years, from Nov. 1, 1891 ... 840

60th st, No. 318 E., store and rear rooms. Rachel S. Goritz to Henry Miller; 5 years, from May 1, 1891 ... 600

86th st, Nos. 519 and 521, n s, 175 e Av A, 50x138. Daniel L. Sturges to Philip Rheinwald; 10 years, from Nov. 1, 1891 ... 1,800

110th st, No. 170 E. John Eichler to Peter Neuer; 5 years, from Dec. 1, 1890 ... 480

114th st, No. 87 E., corner store, otherwise Park av, No. 1602, with cellar. Lewis C. Tufts to John J. Neary; 5 years, from April 1, 1891 ... 1,200

133d st, No. 57 W., all. Henry Duchardt to Charles Trueman; 4½ years and 15 days, from Oct. 15, 1891 ... 660

Lexington av, No. 1719, s e cor 108th st, store and part cellar. Bridget Laughlin to Louis Hansberger; 3 years, from May 1, 1895 ... 1,200

Madison av, No. 625, Scotia building, first floor, store and cellar. George M. Miller to Francesco Fabbrini; 5 1 6 years, from March 1, 1891 ... 2,000

Manhattan av, n e cor 121st st, store and cellar room. Henry Schneider to McCellan & Patton; 5 years, from Sept. 1, 1891 ... 750, 1,000

Pleasant av, No. 361, cor store and floor over. Sarah T. Bolger to Edward Holt; 2 years, from May 1, 1891, with privilege of extension for same term ... 600

Westchester av, No. 886, store and stable. Natalie Cambies to John Delventhal; 1 year, from May 1, 1891 ... 360

1st av, No. 1442, store and front part. S. Frank to John Jost and Anton Kunz, of Jost & Kunz; 2 years, from May 1, 1891 ... 1,820

2d av, s w cor 76th st, store floor, cellar, &c. Herman Wellbrock to Christian H. Ordemann; 5 years, from May 1, 1894 ... 2,000

3d av, No. 2027, s e cor 111th st, store and four rooms over store. G. W. Bryant to Edward Connor; 5½ years, from Nov. 1, 1890 ... 1,200

Same property. Consent to assign. lease. G. W. Bryant to Peter Coleman. Sept. 28 ... —

Same property. Assign. lease. Edward Connor to Peter Coleman ... nom

3d av, No. 1674, store, rear rooms and basement. Julius Livingston to Michael and John J. Manning; 4 years, from Oct 1, 1891 ... 900, 1,020

8th av, No. 166, store floor and basement. John A. Whittet to John A. Weber; 5 years, from May 1, 1892 ... 1,080

8th av, No. 2211, store and basement. Albert Baumann to William Murphy and Jeremiah Healy; 5 years, from May 1, 1891 ... 1,400, 1,800

10th av, No. 546, store floor. Dirk C. F. Janssen to Martin Schuster; 3½ years, from Nov. 1, 1891 ... 480

CHATTELS.

Note.—The first name, alphabetically arranged, is that of the Mortgagor, or party who gives the Mortgage. The "R" means Renewal Mortgage.

NEW YORK CITY.

October 16 to 22.—Inclusive.

SALOON AND RESTAURANT FIXTURES.

Antinozzi, Antonio. 70½ James ....P Weidmann. $700
Aylevard, J W. 1828 9th av ...D G Yuengling, Jr., B Co. (R) 1,500
Arons, H J. 8 Division.. Bavarian B B Co. 750
Astor, Carl. 510 W 80th....India Wharf B Co. (R) 450
Beisler, J F. 424 E 10th....Mutual Brewing Co. 600
Brophy, John. 313 E 38th .. V Loewers. 285
Buttell, J J. 2765 8th av....Bernheimer & S. 1,500
Becker, F W. 939 E 149th....J & M Haffen. (R) 700
Beyer, Oscar. 179 East Houston....F Oppermann, Jr. 400
Bruce, Matthew. 3d av and 64th st....C Stein. 2,600
Burkley, Jacob. 125 Amsterdam av....A Finck & Son. 1,500
Berger, L M. 44 Attorney ...H B Scharmann & Son. 690
Beyer, Oscar. 179 East Houston....J Kuntz B Co. 400
Behan, Cornelius. 2775 8th av ...J Everard. (R) 800
Bohan, Patrick. 521 W 49th....J Everard. (R) 2,855
Brodie, Stephen. 355 Bowery....Feigenspan B Co. 500
Bauer, J T. 1151 3d av....Bauer & Boland. 6,000
Bendt, J E W. 716 9th av....Bachmann B Co. (R) 3,000
Bischoff & Hannewald. 118 Leonard....F & M Schaefer B Co. (R) 1,000
Brotherton, G C. 2348 8th av .. J Roth. 220
Bruner, Maria L. 141 E 17th ..J Ruppert. (R) 3,000
Colve & Gavan. 1451 2d av....D Stevenson. 900
Couzoniero, Peter. 11 Varick pl....H B Scharmann & Son. (R) 500
Coyle, P J. 25 Ludlow....P A Fogarty, exr of. (R) 2,000
Cunningham, H F. 647 W 42d....D Stevenson. 2,500
Cario, Frank. 141 Mott....Bernheimer & S. 800
Clark, John. 806 8th av....F A Clark. (R) 3,000
Dowd, M O. 402 W 14th....G Sieburg. 2,500
Dreves, Charles. 255 Clinton....Beadleston & W. (R) 1,600
Drout, J J. 122 Varick....J Everard. (R) 817
Day, Nathaniel. 7 Greenwich av....Wagner & S. Pool Table. 405
Duff, Patrick. 679 3d av....J C G Hupfel B Co. 3,000
De Vito, Vincenzo. 44 Mulberry....H B Scharmann & Sons 750
Same. 88 Mulberry....same. 750
Early, Frank. 74th st and 1st av....I Sommers. (R) 920
Engelfried, Frank. 2712 3d av. ..P & W Ebling B Co. (R) 1,950
Engenhoefer, Henry. 654 9th av....Bernheimer & S. 600
Epstein, M and I. 38 Essex....H B Scharmann. (R) 1,200
Feist, Abraham. 718 6th... J Ruppert. 1,300
Ficken & Weichman. 133 Maiden lane....M Steljes. (R) 3,500
Fitzpatrick, John. 1098 1st av....J J Reilly. (R) 100
Flanagan, Michael. 2218 2d av....D Stevenson. 203
Flynn, T F. 309 W 69th....J J Reilly. (R) 600
Fuchslocher, William. 110 Rivington....Rubsam & H B Co. 500
Fellermann, A & F. 126 Division....Weiz & Z. (R) 400
Forst & Taustein. 212 East Houston....W H Griffin. Restaurant Fixtures. 175
Fritz, Jacob. 684 E 11th ....F Oppermann, Jr. (R) 1,000
Fruhsorge, Richard. 514 W 44th....F Oppermann, Jr. (R) 250
Farley, M F. 35 10th av ...S F Bingay. 6,500
Fraser, E A. 183 Amsterdam av....Beadleston & W. 2,000
Flannery, P J. 141 E 41st....G Ehret. (R) 855
Gerstenberger, R G. 406 and 408 7th av.. .G Ehret. 800
Gombossy, Jacob. 294 Bowery....Rubsam & H B Co. 1,500
"Gotham Wheelman." 54 E 79th....Brunswick-B-C Co. Pool Table. 225
Gutschon, George. 10 Stanton ...G Bechtel. (R) 1,000
Guzzi, Vincenzo. 156 Mott ...Sekosky Bros. 205
Gerstl, Sophia. 5 St Marks pl....Hirsch & S. 358
Gessner, John. 1957 3d av....G Ehret. (R) 1,300
Hagen, Ewald. 56 Pearl....G Ehret. (R) 14,000
Heuer, Edward. 87 Stanton....H B Scharmann & Sons. (R) 800
Hopfengartner, J. 90th st and 1st av....Bernheimer & S. Saloon Ice House. 120
Halohan, James. 852 11th av....H Wagner & Co. Pool Table. (R) 41
Hansberger, Louis. Lexington av and 108th st ....W L Flanagan. 1,500
Hamilton, Patrick. 85 Carmine ...J C G Hupfel B Co. 300
Jordan, Rebecca. 100 Broome....D Stevenson. 800
Kaplan, Adolph. 120 W 17th....P & W Ebling B Co. 13,665
Karst, Frank. 582 E 150th....D Stevenson. 700
Korff & Langerfeld. 328 Broome....G Ehret. (R) 800
Kraemer, E & A. 1681 3d av....India Wharf B Co. 200
Krug, Louis. 1251 3d av....D Mayer. Saloon Pump. (R) 75
Kaufman, H W. 6 Morris....P Ballantine & Sons. 600
Kennedy, George. 81 Lexington av....J Ruppert. 2,000
Klinger, John. 504 6th....J & M Haffen. 300
Kruse, Henry. 1275 3d av....G Ringler & Co. 800
Koeb, Louis. 12 W 4th....S Liebmann's Sons B Co. 1,000
Luhrs, L H M. 1312 2d av....J Kress B Co. 800
Laemmle, John. 1061 10th av....F Oppermann, Jr. (R) 500
Leer, Henry. 108 Av B....C Iba. 175
Loud, F E. 285 Bowery....W F Whitehouse, &c. Restaurant Fixtures. (R) 3,563
Lubring, J H. 238 Centre....H Ruhl. (R) 1,089
Lanza, James. 189 Hester....H Elias B Co. 500
McGivney, Owen. 721 11th av....J McGivney. (R) 1,800
McKallen, Felix. 385 10th av....G Ehret. 500
Meyer, August. 106 Prince....C Tobaben. 800
Miller, Samuel. 851 W 37th....J Kress B Co. 600
Mariano, John. 516 and 518 Broome....Burr B Co. (R) 700
May, Fred. 1543 Broadway....J Everard. 2,243
McPartlan, J and P. 1491 Av A. ..H Elias B Co. 2,000
Mokrank, Vincenz. 425 E 72d....Schmitt & S. 200
Mortimer, Thomas. 685 1st av....J C G Hupfel B Co. 2,500
Murphy, Jeremiah. 2298 8th av....J C G Hupfel B Co. (R) 862
Muller, Philip. 392 11th av....G Ehret. (R) 1,400
Neus Bros. 96 10th av....F & M Schaefer B Co. 3,000
Ney, Edmund. 138 Bowery....H Peltz. Billiard Saloon. 500
Nolan, J J. 59th st and 2d Av....Bernheimer & S. Beer Pump. 139
N Y Turn Verein. Bloomingdale, 54th st and 8th av....G Ehret. (R) 10,000
Nurnberg, John. 390 Willis av ...H C Schrader. 1,750
O'Shea, John. 621 1st av....F & M Schaefer B Co. (R) 250
O'Gorman, Edward. 3042 3d av....J & M Haffen. 2,460
O'Brien, James. 329 W 17th....V Loewers. 600
Petrucelli, Angelo. 340 E 110th....D Mayer. (R) 200
Poole, M R. 470 6th av....H Wagner & Co. Pool Table. (R) 16
Parys, Charles. 32 Greenwich....M Seitz. (R) 300
Paul, Mary F. 744 6th av....M C Mead. Restaurant Fixtures. 757
Pereira, F C. 21 Greenwich av....A W Schmidt. 5,000
Quinn, G W. 290 8th av....A B Mark. Pool Table. 420
Raimmonto, Frank. 34 Mulberry....Budweiser B Co. 500
Rambousek, Chas. 1497 Av A... Long Island Brewery. 1,000
Reiss, Berman. 80 Allen .. C Schwelke. Restaurant Fixtures. 800
Ripp, Henry. 29 W 3d....Rubsam & H B Co. (R) 1,500
Rosenfeld, Leo. 57 2d av....A Heinzen. Restaurant Fixtures. 2,125
Rosenzweig, Saml. 508 7th av....Beadleston & W. 1,500
Rosseau, J P and J E. Pulitzer Building....C Boinay. Restaurant Fixtures. 100
Same....same. Restaurant Fixtures. 60
Rahl, Matthew. 558 W 51st....P McIntyre. 3,000
Schmitt, Joseph. 2353 3d av....India Wharf B Co. (R) 1,200
Stocker, Ottman. 73 Broome....J Ruppert. 500
Sigler & Reizler. 96 Willett....E Walker. Pool Table. 75
Stillgelauer, Otto. 542 W 48th....A & S Boehm. (R) 500
Sugerman & Rosal. 101 Allen....E Walker. Pool Table. 90
Sandy, E J. 77 Jackson....F Ibert. 800
Saito, K. 65 Oliver .. F Feddorke. Pool, &c. 165
Schauer, V F. 91 Spring ..S Schauer. 800
Schneider, N J. 43 Grand....G Ringler & Co. (R) 500
Schosser, Geo. 611 Columbus av ...D Stevenson. 800
Schroder, F E. 1618 1st av....G Sieburg. 2,300
Smith, Amanda 495 E 10th....M Seitz. (R) 400
Speckmann, Henry. 44 Goerck....H Kroger. 1,100
Stepezynski, Joseph. 2375 8th av....G Ehret. (R) 3,000
Sulzmann, Jacob. 324½ E 8th....Budweiser B Co. 850
Siemering, Henry. 542 3d av ...Clausen & P B Co. 1,500
Tvelia, John. 555 W 32d....Knickerbocker B Co. 160
Torre, Giuseppe. 73 Thompson....J C G Hupfel B Co. (R) 100
Tschantre, Ernest. 279 Broadway....A H Hawkins. Restaurant Fixtures. 800
Wellmann, H. 118th st and 1st av....Bernheimer & S. Saloon Ice House. 145
Same....same. Saloon Ice House. 80
Winter, Moses. 247 Division....Bernheimer & S. 900
Wagner, Fred. 271 Av A.... Budweiser B Co. 400
Woolley, Peter. 87th st and East River....G Ehret. (R) 1,000
Waiblinger, Julius. 27½ Chrystie....Gluck & S. (R) 388
Zerbarini, Chas. 265 Bowery....Wagner & S. Pool Table. 390
Zimmerman, Ernest. 188 Lewis ...H Koehler & Co. 300
Zimmerman, Jakob. 90 Lewis.. J H Rosenfeld. Pool Table. 70
Zweig & Susskind. 91 Spring st and 529 and 531 Broadway....Martha Wolff et al. Restaurant Fixtures. 600

HOUSEHOLD FURNITURE.

Altman, Jennie. 227 E 70th....Jordan & M. 105
Ashleigh, Lillian. 118 E 27th....T Kelly. 125
Ahner, J M. 887 Caldwell av....L Baumann. 218
Archer, Jeanet. 125 W 64th....J Baumann. 181
Arnold, Dora. 226 W 39th....J Baumann. 568
Ames, K M. 138 E 84th....M T Gudeman. 2,100
Aiken, Mary. 35 Cornelia....Simpson & P. Piano. (R) 157
Adler, Henry. 117 E 40th....S Bachman. 4,512
Amodeo, Antonio. 458 W 36th....B M Cowperthwait & Co. 149
Aronson, M & E. 1958 Madison av....Lincoln I and G Assoc. 400
Arveschow, Albert. 515 Lexington av....C E Tracy. (R) 250
Beaney, Sarah. 224 W 135th... B M Cowperthwait & Co. 102
Benners, Fred. 601 10th av....Garvey Bros. 157
Benninger, Ray. 434 E 14th....B M Cowperthwait & Co. 115
Berrian, J. 240 E 127th....B M Cowperthwait & Co. 178
Brown, Albert. 452 W 29th....B M Cowperthwait & Co. 139
Byrne, J T 429 W 51st....M Fall. 500
Banta, Dora B. 78 5th av... J Gregg & Co. (R) 677
Behr, Fred. 402 W 48th....W J Ruddell. 133
Bell, Anna E. 26 E 111th....E Bell. 1,000
Borchardt, Isadore. 519 E 84th ...Spies Bros. (R) 142
Barrett, Kate. 226 E 20th....L Baumann. (R) 137
Benham, Alice E. 270 W 118th ..J Baumann. 150
Blackburn, Maude. 142 W 53d....D Schwarzkopf. 190
Bollas, R A & E. 2121 8th av....E C Hinsdale. 180
Breen, Henrietta. 411 W 48th....L Baumann. 188
Broome, Maud. 119 Macdougal....J Moriarty. 256
Bailey, Anna M. 141 E 44th....S Baumann. 189
Banks, George. 1590 2d av....L Baumann. 133
Beauchamp, Henri. 1186 Lexington av....B H De Boes & Co. 589
Benedict, Mrs W N. 103 W 102d....T Kelly. 209
Blaine, Mrs J D. 264 W 116th....T Kelly. 354
Boyle, K F. 234 E 110th....S Baumann. 510
Brady, Carrie. 219 E 32d....Manges Bros. 123
Branch, Lena. 122 W 17th....T Kelly. 156
Browne, Mary C. 8 E 47th....H A Strobridge. 3,000
Brown, P G. 217 W 46th....G W Nathan. 260
Burke, Cora. 137 W 46th....O'Farrell & Co. 181
Burns, G A. 528 W 48th....L Baumann. 124
Callahan, Susan H. 116th st and 7th av....J Gregg & Co. 110
Cassel, Jean. 110 W 61st....S Baumann. 166

Chatwood, Carrie. 167 W 29th....T Kelly. 177
Clifton, E. Mrs. 314 W 70th....T Kelly. 404
Cohen, Lena. 237 E 77th....H S Eisler. (R) 109
Connell, Richard. 107 W 32d... S Heyman & Co. (R) 151
Cornelius, E E, Mrs. 368 W 116th....T Kelly. 121
Cowles, E J, Mrs. 3 W 103d....T Kelly. 161
Cromelien, Lottie C. 333 W 21st....R M Walters. Piano. (R) 114
Conklin, Belle M. 149 W 125th....J Heyman. 205
Chaves, Leopoldina. 130 W 44th... J Gregg & Co. (R) 128
Closson, N A. Rochester, N Y....S J Cushman. 250
Clusman, Emily. 176 E 117th... J Baumann. 132
Campbell, H R. 119 9th av....B M Cowperthwait & Co. 126
Chapman, Jennie. 201 E 42d....B M Cowperthwait & Co. 191
Clench, C A, Mrs. 402 W 58th....B M Cowperthwait & Co. 469
Clerihen, A C. 404 W 57th....B M Cowperthwait & Co. 219
Denovitz, Philip. 160 Henry....B M Cowperthwait & Co. 166
Durbin, W H. 604 St Anns av....W E Wheelock & Co. Piano. 215
De Lisser, Esther. 1713 Lexington av... J Moriarty. 283
Davis, Minnie S. 1009 6th av....J Baumann. 740
Davis, W D... J Stewart. (R) 814
Doherty, Eliza. 616 Lexington av... Jordan, M & Co. 136
Donahue, Elizabeth. 909 Columbus av....J Gregg & Co. 187
Doyle, Eloise. 62 E 114th... S Baumann. 204
Danna, Mary. 2476 8th av....H S Eisler. 111
Dempewolf, Arnold. 506 E 162d....L Baumann. 321
Denisson, C E. 131 Charles....N Y F Co. 160
Dezendorf, Hannah V. 211 E 45th....S Baumann. 168
Douglass, M J, Mrs. 153 Lexington av....T Kelly. 251
Dowdell, James. 163 Amsterdam av....J Moriarty. 228
Dupont, Etta. 574 5th av....L Baumann. 171
Dupre, Meta. 13 Prospect pl....L Baumann. 436
Eggers, Wilhelm. 501 E 83d....J Gregg & Co. 102
Ellis, C E. 119 5th av....J Gregg & Co. 138
Everett, Allie S. 235 E 14th....N Y F Co. (R) 105
Erb, Margaret. 856 6th av....J Baumann. 115
Eik, F E. 231 E 10th....B M Cowperthwait & Co. 100
Evans, W H. 43 W 131st....J Moriarty. 110
Fisher, Mrs Henry. 50 Rivington.. B M Cowperthwait & Co. 137
Freeman, Lillian. 248 and 250 W 47th....B M Cowperthwait & Co. 117
Fitch, Florence. 150 W 16th....J T Ackerman. 225
Fitch, Mary L. 67 W 11th....Manges Bros. 194
Friedman, Sarah V. 234 W 51st....J Baumann. 566
Same....same. 566
Furet, W W. 156 W 84th....Jordan, M & Co. 422
Fisher, Kate. 1243 Columbus av....L Baumann. (R) 146
Fortescue, Viola. 346 W 18th....L Baumann. (R) 117
Friedman, Sarah. 234 W 53d....J Baumann. 625
Fuchs, Nanette. 344 E 4th... R Rosenheim. 122
Fountain, Inez. 110 W 33th....E M Saul. 2,500
Freeman, F H. 167 W 60th....H S Eisler. 131
Fredberg, Sam. 137 Essex....H S Eisler. 146
Friedman, Ernest. 301 E 83d....S Heyman & Co. (R) 146
Gallagher, J J. 338 W 51st....L Baumann. 337
Garaghty, Fannie. 507 E 82d....S Heyman & Co. (R) 205
Geon, O M. 123 W 58th....J Gregg & Co. 151
Gorman, L C. 104 W 8th....S Baumann. 271
Goulding, Ada. 1035 Madison av.... A V Smith. 130
Geisenheimer, Herman. 722 6th....R Rosenheim. 141
Garner, Chas. 222 W 4th....J Baumann. 196
Gilbert, S. 119 W 6th....J Moriarty. 800
Gay, S D. 50 E 86th... P Wilkens. (R) 350
Ghioldi, Lizzie. 3 New Chambers....Krakauer Bros. Piano. 245
Ghiold, Mrs Louis. 31 New Chambers....B M Cowperthwait & Co. 189
Glover, H N. 109 E 105th....B M Cowperthwait & Co. 196
Goodwin, Mary W. 211 E 14th...B M Cowperthwait & Co. 443
Gray, F L. 5 and 7 Murray....B M Cowperthwait & Co. 122
Griscom, Sarah C. 239 E 20th....B M Cowperthwait & Co. 140
Gross, L and A. 22 Bond... A Dinkelman. Restaurant Fixtures. 200
Hallberg, Evelyn. 285 Lenox av...L Baumann. 211
Hebner, F J. 513 E 75th....B M Cowperthwait & Co. 119
Hyland, Elizabeth. 311 E 40th...B M Cowperthwait & Co. 112
Haas, Emil. 222 E 86th....S I Herschmann. 177
Harris, Esther. 109 Attorney....B M Cowperthwait & Co. 150
Hayes, Mary. 220 Chrystie.. J Moriarty. 139
Hommedieu, Minnie. 29 Perry...J Moriarty. 138
Howard, Mary. 217 E 70th....S I Herschmann. 205
Hawkinson, Hannah G. 109 E 87th....J Baumann. 115
Helmolt, Jeanette. 324 E 128th....J Baumann. 141
Hackert, Henry. 65 E 106th....L Baumann. 588
Harby, J D. 5 W 87th....J Gregg & Co. 121
Hardenbrook, Mrs F M. 539 W 51st...T Kelly. 266
Hausrath, Anna B. 1591 Washington av.. Dreisacker & Co. 159
Heller, R M. 31 E 97th... S Baumann. 147
Hayes, Dollie. 258 W 2d....L Baumann. 133
Hoffman, Mary E....J Williams. 121
Hilkeman, Theodore. 26 Grove....J Gregg & Co. 125
Hulse, Helen. 272 W 117th....S Baumann. 118
Jackson, Lizzie. 134 W 26th....J Moriarty. 154
Jimmerson, W W. 112 Cannon...A H Mangold. Piano. 140
Joppe, B. 141 Division....H Thoesen. 250
Jonassen, Emily. 253 E 10th....S Baumann. 133
Jaeger, Clara. 59 E 20th... J Gregg & Co. 909
Johnson, Addie H. 244 W 53d....E A Heaney. 450
Kane, Catherine. 354 W 46th....Krakauer Bros. Piano. 425
Killard, Mary M. 3 W 46th....B M Cowperthwait & Co. 456
Keeler, Louise. 143 E 20th...A M Crosby. 100
Kerrews, Thomas. 412 E 23d....L Baumann. (R) 128
Kirchenbauer, Helen....208 E 104th....Fennell & P. (R) 185
Kuphal, Otto. 156 W 83d....L Dolan. 912
Kaufman, Julius. 100 W 74th....J Gregg & Co. 588
Kaye, Emma T. 224 W 59th....J Gregg & Co. 290
Kearney, Mrs J P. 410 W 46th....T Kelly. 150
Keim, Freda. 231 E 10th...Jordan & M. 118
Kendall, Lillian. 169 Lexington av....H Israel. 1,500
Kilbin, Estelle. 210 W 41st....J Moriarty. (R) 211
Kilpatrick, Jno. 139 E 96th... H S Eisler. 183
King, A G. 49 E 75th.. J Gregg & Co. 367
Kobler, Auguste. 162 E 88th....F Struvy. 1,000
Leist, Mrs L. 207 Lexington av...Krakauer Bros. Piano. 182
Lenet, Virginia. 222 W 17th....L Baumann. 191
Lowenberg, Rose. 77 W 47th.... Amer Guar Assoc. 180
Lubsky, Jennie. 155 E 84th....S Baumann. 139
Lasell, Lizzie S. 207 E 48th....Manges Bros. 234
Law, James. 121 Charles....R M Walters. Piano. (R) 125
Lemon, Alice. 297 10th av....L Baumann. 128
McCormick, E. 529 W 40th....L Baumann. 146
McGuire, Elizabeth. Railroad av, bet Danforth st and Ridgewood av, Brooklyn....H Thoesen. 861
Misell, David. 78 W 82d....B M Cowperthwait & Co. 364
Morris, Annie. 50 Oliver....B M Cowperthwait & Co. 117
Macon, Jennie. 317 W 21st....W J Ruddell. 210
Mack, Blanche. 161 W 89th... J Baumann. 368
Mansfield, J P. 928 2d av... J Moriarty. 228
Manwell, Kate. 493 9th av....J F Doherty & Co. 191
McCavin, Kate. 126 W 52d....N Y Furn Co. (R) 200
McDonald, T D. 414 W 49th....J Baumann. 209
Moore, Elbertine. 83 W 21st....A Vandyke. 200
Mussen, Minnie. 170 E 100th....Manges Bros. 222
Mayer, Henry. 246 W 14th....L Baumann. 128
Martin, Catherine. 80 E 116th....J Baumann. 139
McCarty, J A. 229 Mulberry.... J Moriarty. 156
McCarthy, Maggie. 213 E 56th....Fell & Van Ness. 122
McCloy, Fred. 104 W 40th....D Schwarzkopf. 645
McConnell, Mollie. 259 W 39th...Jordan, M & Co. 400
Macdonald, Mrs. M. 157 W 49th....T Kelly. 166
Magee, James. 172 W 81st....S Baumann. 782
Mankin, G B. 63 Bank....B H De Boes & Co. 382
Martin, Henry. 319 2d av....L Baumann. 188
McDonald, Donald. 91 Bedford....L Baumann. 139
McEvily, Catharine. 134 E 50th....H Thoesen. 100
Mearson, Angelina. 315 W 26th....O'Farrell & Co. 179
Meyers, Agnes. 591 9th av....L Baumann. 161
Milne, Mary. 168 W 98th....L Baumann. 159
Moore, Jennie. 12 Leroy....Manges Bros. 204
Morse, Carrie E. 10, 12 and 14 W 125th....Dreisacker & Co. (R) 210
Musica, Anthony. 2255 2d av....Krakauer Bros. Piano. (R) 110
Normann, Lottie. 123 W 67th....L Baumann. 118
Nussbaum, L. 667 E 139th....D Schwarzkopf. 321
Newman, W H. 527 W 51st....L Baumann. 196
Nugent, Catherine. 251 W 14th....L Baumann. 137
Nulty, T F. 207 E 37th....L Baumann. 193
Nunberg, Solomon. 2053 2d av....S Heyman & Co. (R) 118
Nathan, Charles. 60 W 22d....G Fennell & Co. 390
Nunes, Leopoldo. 128 E 97th....B M Cowperthwait & Co. 111
Olfans, John. 321 E 119th....B M Cowperthwait & Co. 192
O'Brien, W S. 966 E 162th....Jordan & M. (R) 175
Ossmann, V L. 9 W 125th...Jordan & M. (R) 112
Oginz, Elias. 179 Madison...H Thoesen. 150
Ohrdorf, Mrs L. 68 W 51st....H Thoesen. 125
Same....same. 555
Pietscher, Pauline. 305 E 69th....F J Brechtel. 201
Paulson, Emma J. 355 W 2th....J Baumann. 218
Pepper, Halsey. 364 W 58th....J Baumann. 226
Perry, Isabella J. 214 W 42d....Morris & Haddock. 149
Pinkham, Mary E. 128 W 96th....J Baumann. 231
Pond, Annie. 114 W 32d....C Beers. (R) 1,000
Price, Charles. 261 W 16th.... J Gregg & Co. 109
Perley, Mamie. 158 W 20th....L Baumann. 328
Perdue, R L. 212 W 28th....B M Cowperthwait & Co. 104
Platz, Ellen. 242 W 128th....L Baumann. 172
Rezansky, L. 1573 1st av....B M Cowperthwait & Co. 118
Rizzuto, Mrs Alexander. 2218 1st av... B M Cowperthwait & Co. 140
Rose, H O. 81 Warren....B M Cowperthwait & Co. 105
Ross, Miss M. 222 E 86th....B M Cowperthwait & Co. 118
Ross, Ruth S. 43 E 21st... L S Kuroski. 1,350
Richardson, A A and B....C C Richardson. 550
Robertson, W E. 322 Columbus av... W W Gage. 125
Robinson, Gertie. 306 E 86th....Jordan, M & Co. 166
Rosen, Ike. 340 E 116th....S Baumann. 223
Redfern, W W. 534 E 164th... L Baumann. 218
Reinl, John. 544 E 163d....J Gregg & Co. 333
Rietmann, G H. 401 W 43th...F J Brechtel. 231
Sloan, Mrs H P. 139 W 60th...S Heymann & Co (R) 100
Suppel, Mrs E. 282 W 132d....T Kelly. 148
Spaulding, E B and I M. Storage....Commercial Credit Co. 360
Schneer, Martha. 217 E 34th....J Moriarty. (R) 492
Sprague, S H and A. 515 W 138th... E T Lee. 100
Siebens, J J. 443 E 88th.. Fennell & Pye. 109
Schopp, H J. 613 2d av....O'Farrell & Co. 194
Shaw, Emilie B. 401 St Nicholas av....L Baumann. 164
Samuel, M W. 15 E 85th...C S Samuel. 1,000
Sauer, Emma. 32 Bayard.. G H Orange. 4,500
Schwarz, Z. 715 E 5th....R Rosenheim. 106
Smith, F. 10 W 104th....D Schwarzkopf. 241
Strassburger, L and S. 304 E 118th....M Pareira. 183
Sweitzer, Joseph. 327 East Houston....R Rosenheim. 165
Sherwood, Charity M. 13 W 20th...G Beck. 200
Simons, Lizzie. 1126 Columbus av....Jordan & M. (R) 138
Smith, F B. 50 E 23d...E Parmily. (R) 3,200
Stanolt, Minnie. 122 W 103d...J Moriarty. 210
Samuel, Montague. 122 W 102d... L Baumann. 815
Samuels, Sadie. 142 W 28th....Garvey Bros. 135
Sanderson, J C. 212 W 61st...B M Cowperthwait & Co. 132
Seaton, Mrs Chas. 224 E 10th....B M Cowperthwait & Co. 125
Shea, H. Kingsbridge....B M Cowperthwait & Co. 315
Somers, Richard. 115 Chrystie....B M Cowperthwait & Co. 147
Sparta, John. 118 Chrystie....B M Cowperthwait & Co. 135
Stephenson, Mrs Wm. 307 E 18th...B M Cowperthwait & Co. 191
Sutcliff, Hattie. 234 E 24th....Krakauer Bros. Piano. 350
Thorn, Elizabeth. 867 Park av....B M Cowperthwait & Co. 291
Treadwell, Mary T. 158 E 116th.... J Moriarty. 349
Tribolet, Albert. 530 5th....G Fennell & Co. 140
Tuck, Fannie. 34 Market....B M Cowperthwait & Co. 110
Tissier, Armand. 37 Marion...H S Eisler. 18
Taylor, A S. 214 Lexington av....American Guarantee Assoc. 100
Todd, Sarah E. 402 West End av....Manges Bros. (R) 359
Tabbs, Rosanna. 207 E 97th....O'Farrell & Co. 128
Taylor, Mary. 221 E 59th.. Jordan & M. 227
Thomas, Mrs O V. 367 W 48th....N Y F Co. 177
Thorpe, M. 155 E 54th....S Heyman & Co. 159
Same....same. 123
Frischet, Anna. 134 E 58th... Krakauer Bros. Piano. 310
Tugwell, Mary E. 218 W 21st....S Baumann. 117
Valeria, Gracia. 322 W 47th....S Baumann. 150
Vance, A St C. 204 W 7th...L Baumann. 813
Vitole, Andrew. 99 Macdougall....H S Eisler. (R) 123
Voss, Eliza. 24 Bayard.... S Roberts. 700
Vanderbeek, Mrs M. 107 W 104th....Garvey Bros. 150
Vandervoort, Jennie. 417 E 114th....B M Cowperthwait & Co. 287
Winter, Wm. 107 W 106th....B M Cowperthwait & Co. 118
Woodward, Helene. 58 W 129th....B M Cowperthwait & Co. 208
Wolff, Otto. 207 E 59d.. L Baumann. 223
Worden, Annie. 128 W 63d....B M Cowperthwait & Co. 141
Weiner, Minnie. 13 Bleecker...H C Jacobs. 2,500
Wiertz, Charles. 112 E 1th....S I Herschmann. 240
Williams, Nellie. 252 W 84th....J Baumann. 111
Wood, S S. 254 W 55th....B M Cowperthwait & Co. 257
Same....same. 115
Same....same. 164
Walcott, B S. 327 W 21st.... Manges Bros. 129
Walter, Tillie. 165 E 54th....L Bazousky. 1,600
Wellner, Clara. 190 Hester....Fennell & Pye. 107
White, Lillian. 8 St. Marks pl....Jordan & M. 125
Willard, Georgia. 53 E 29th.. F G Rindell. 365
Williams, J E. 72 W 125th. L Baumann. 192
Williams, Maggie. 125 E 97th....L Baumann. 127
Wood, W T. 405 St Nicholas av....Fennell & Pye. 165
Winkler, Fannie. 260 2d....R Rosenheim. 184
Winnie, Alice. 242 W 55th....D Schwarzkopf. 1,042
Woodbridge, Annie. 254 W 16th.. L Baumann. 169
Yedock, Anna C. 60 W 25th....T Kelly. 118
Zimmerman, Benton. 246 W 124th....B M Cowperthwait & Co. 212

MISCELLANEOUS.

Adams, Anton. 437 W 41st.... O Shmith. Horse, Wagon, &c. 200
Antoine, F. 159 Bleecker....Nat Cash Reg Co. Register. 200
Armus, C....Rothschild Bros. Horse. 125
Adams, F R. 180 Prince....Racine Wagon Co. Wagon. 100
Auerbach & Bloch. 1834 Park av....J Strauss. Butcher Fixtures. 1,000
Bertram, C N....L A Bertram. Scenery, &c. 3,500
Blumenthal, Louis. 560 8th av....F Mandelbaum. Butcher Fixtures. 500
Bradley, P E. 458 Hudson....Racine Wagon Co. Wagon. 90
Broder, Benjamin. 14 Bond....A Unger. Machines. 125
Brown, Isaac. 2077 3d av....L Heinsfurter. Butcher Fixtures. 300
Bannan, Frederick. 203 E 118th.... J F Paulsen. Horse, Wagon, &c. (R) 400
Bernara, Giuseppe. 208 E 38th....S Ribarero. Barber Fixtures. 375
Brown, David. 79 Nassau....L Weil & Co. Machinery. 400
Brown, James....Armstrong & Co. Coach. 750
Beckett, James. 35 and 37 Vesey....R J Bradford, exr of. Machinery. (R) 2,400
Benedict, Raffaele. 42 Madison....C E Pierce. Confectionery Fixtures. 50
Burmeister, Henry. 376 Willis av....D Leibe. Drug Fixtures. 2,000
Baldinger, M and J. 222 2d....P Birn. Grocery Fixtures. 90
Baslan, Abel. 71 Norfolk....A Neides. Drug Fixtures. 550
Bassford, W K, Jr. 136 Liberty...C Conti. Machinery. 50
Batzdorf, R A. 174 3d av....G Portefee. Laundry Fixtures. 375
Bauer, Valentine. 357 Bowery....Nat Cash Reg Co. Register. 200
Bickhardt, Peter. 1323 4th av....S Loeb. Cows. 102
Brown, J W. 239 and 241 E 115th....B Weill. Horse, &c. 160
Cahill, Mrs M. 9 Greenwich....Nuffer & L. Coach. (R) 159
Casiragh, Aug. 733 and 735 1st av....P Prybil. Machinery. 90
Cohen, Israel. 65 Sheriff....A Berlensky. Bath Fixtures, &c. 500
Coleman, Daniel. 102 E 41st....H Killam Co. Coach. (R) 400
Cohrs, H J. 411 E 15th....H Koehler & Co. Bottling Fixtures. 100
Central Safe Deposit Co.. W I Worrell. Fixtures, &c. (R) 30,000
Cohen & Goldberg. 405 7th av.. J Cohen. Clothing Store Fixtures. 805
Cohn, Martin. 357 Canal....Naday & Fleisher. Machines. 1,000
Columbia Slate Co. Pawlet, Vermont....S E Burr. Machinery, &c. (R) 6,518
Cornish, G H. 108 E 38th....I Griggs. Horses, Coaches, &c. (R) 3,350
De Gaetano, Jesse. 258 E 125th....A Schwaab & Son. Barber Fixtures. 55
Delany, William. 229 Western Boulevard... E B Gardner. Butcher Fixtures. 400
Digasquale, Rocco. 290 3d av....A Schwaab & Son. Barber Fixtures. 119
Dimino, Giuseppe. 1534 and 1584 2d av....A Schwaab & Son. Barber Fixtures. 102
Dieffenbach, Philip. 500 W 125th... S Dieffenbach. Butcher Fixtures. (R) 1,000
Delany Bros. 377 2d av....National Casket Co. Undertaker Fixtures. 1,000
Delinsky, Hyman. 4 Hester.... N Barchan. Store Fixtures, &c. 150
Demarest, Daniel. 27 Barrow. M Larkin. Horse, Cart and Mason Fixtures. 650
Doering, O A. 304 E 95th....Prentiss Tool Co. Machinery. 250
Doyle, J J. 164 W 10th... Nat Cash Reg Co. Register. 200

Darby, Geo. 128 W 53d....H Killam Co. Coach. 1,000
Duggan, Jno. 87th st and 3d av.... Nat Cash Reg Co. Register. 175
Echhoff, D. 349 1st av....Blauvelt & Co. Confectionery Fixtures 630
Elfect, Christian. 71st st and Av A....J Rothschild. Horse. &c. 165
Excelsior Button Hole Works. 102-110 Attorney ....F Welsh. Machinery 350
Fayman & Sprague. Grand Central Hotel.... Beinecke & Co. Hotel Fixtures. 7,638
Feek, E L. 114 Centre....W Scott & Co. Press, &c. 1,100
Fink, Charles, 291 Willis av....J J Carey. Barber Fixtures. 180
Freidman, Herman. 1298 Lexington av and 149 E 87th st....M Schuster. Barber Fixtures. 150
Facklamm, John. Lexington av and 26th st.... Nat Cash Reg Co. Register. 175
Fox, M & H. 2194 7th av....Frasse & Co. Machinery. 176
Frommer, Johanna. 616 Hudson....J N Heubner. Bakery Fixtures. (R) 600
Gallin, J W. 22 Chrystie and 11 Canal....Young Men's East Side Benevolent Assoc. Painters Fixtures 800
Gee Long & Co. 847 Broadway....Astor Place Bank. Merchandise. 3,000
Greco, Francesco. 219 Park row ....G Posillo. Barber Fixtures. (R) 165
Grenthal, Benjamin. 572 7th av....W Grenthal. Grocery Fixtures. 700
Grobe, William. 132 Hamburg av, Brooklyn.... F X Baumert & Co. Fixtures (R) 154
Grogan, M A. 181 William....C B Cottrell & Sons. Press. 1,500
Garlick, Henry. 143 Ridge .... R Garlick. Butcher Fixtures. 500
Giordano, Vincenzo. 1969 1st av....A Schwaab & Son. Barber Fixtures. 60
Goldthwaite, J C. 80 John....S Goldthwaite. Office Fixtures, Books, &c. 2,800
Gintzberger, Simon. 396 W 37th....T Farrell. Butcher Fixtures. 75
Goodman, Henry. 1807 Park av ...T Farrell. Butcher Fixtures. 138
Hazard, R. N. 163½ and 165 W 18th .. Fuller Wood Electric Co. Machinery. (R) secures rent
Heide, H and A. 864 3d av....F Happersberger. Milk Fixtures, &c. 153
Hackett, M J. 75-77 E 85th....Albany Venetian Blind Co. Blinds, &c. 285
Hartshorn, J W. 142 and 144 E 59th....Hincks & J. Coach. 600
Held, Emil. 171 Attorney....W Frieder. Printing Fixtures. 200
Henckel, G and L. 3547 3d av....Roberts & Collin. Bakery Fixtures. (R) 200
Jenkins & McCowan....Campbell P P Co. Press. (R) 2,000
Jennings, Thomas. 3 Willett ...J H Lippe. Coach (R) 323
Jewell, R L 321 Bleecker....A M Sachs. Cigar Fixtures. 125
Kirchner, Michael. 148th st and Brook av....A Rinschler. Horses, Trucks, &c. 2,500
Kochmann, J. 41 Ridge .... P Reidenbach. Wagon. (R) 69
Kropp, J and W. 902 Amsterdam av....Couper, Z & Co. Bakery Fixtures 500
Kile, C U. 2821 7th av....S J Maltaby. Drug Fixtures. 500
Locke, C E. 28 Union sq....F R Lawrence. Costumes, Scenery, &c. (R) 34,500
Lubliner, J. 226½ Bowery....Marvin Safe Co. Safe. 200
Launey, J A. Anderson av and Orchard st.... J E Connolly. Truck, &c. 150
Lavey Printing and Stationery Co. 6 Barclay ....Babcock P P Co. Press. 2,600
Lipman, I and S. 246 E 76th .. J Ruppert. Bottling Fixtures. 811
Marie, J B ...M V Maderia. Horse, Coach, &c. (R) 2,000
McClellan & Pallon....C H Bangs. Drug Fixtures. 956
Miebert, Leonard. 8 and 10 Manhattan....J C Geissel. Milk Wagon, &c. 150
Miller, G C. 27 Centre....Bramhall, D & Co. Range. 43
Mortimer, Geo. 369 Canal....M Jung. Trunks. 984
Mullen, J J. 158 Centre....W J Broderick. Presses. (R) 916
McAdams, J J... G Dessecker. Hearse. 825
McVay, G P H. 258 W 125th....Manhattan Type Co. Press, &c. 200
Mewing, Adolph. 1640 2d av....J H Evers. Grocery Fixtures. (R) 500
Mohr, George. 147 Amsterdam av....A Weisser. Butcher Fixtures. 150
Marino, Antonio. 290 3d av....F Recora. Barber Fixtures. 130
Milbut, L. 100 Lewis.. J Probst. Wagon. 44
Munsell, H M. 148 Liberty....Marvin Safe Co. Safe. 140
Nebenzahl, Abe. 88 Pitt....M Goldstein. Machines. 600
"Old Homestead Dairy," 339 and 341 W 52d.... H M Holly et al. Horses, Wagon, &c. 8,000
Oberhauser, Charles. 477 Cherry....J Oberhauser. Horses, Trucks, &c. 900
Palmer, J H. 151st st and Mott av....Warren & Stratton. Machinery. (R) 2,700
Pariser, M and A. 65 East Broadway....Bennett & G. Bottling Fixtures. 850
Pasquino & Dovie. 67 Sullivan .... A Cini. Butcher Fixtures. 60
Pause & Guadt. 173 and 175 Grand....McKee & Harrington. Machinery. 1,500
Porter, M D. 178 Greenwich . Marvin Safe Co. Safe. 210
Price, Jesse....Campbell P P Co. Press. (R) 2,006
Peccoraca, Frank. 27 Bowery....A Schwaab & Son. Barber Fixtures. (R) 30
Post, N A. 584 9th av....Canton Surgical Chair Co. Chair. 100
Reardon, D & B. 96th st and 1st av... M Smith. Horses, &c. (R) 150
Rotchford, W H. 420 Cherry....Racine Wagon Co. Wagon. 115
Reutlinger, Samson. 317 E 77th....G Clemens et al. Wagon. 225
Robinson, C L. 87 W 42d and 61 W 42d....M J Evans. Dental Fixtures and Furniture. (R) 1,500
Rooney, A. 4 th st and 3d av....Nat Cash Reg Co. Register. 175
Rothman, Herman. 322 E 8th....S Schwartz. Grocery Fixtures. 150
Rosdzi J. Regina. 2704 3d av....W Schmidt. Barber Fixtures. (R) 40
Romain, W G. 156 and 158 W 127th....J J Hayes. Livery Stable Fixtures. (R) 1,500
Seide, Joseph. 103 Clinton....Damon & Peets. Cutter. 35

Simon, Samuel. 107 Barclay....C E Weis. Barber Fixtures. (R) 225
Singhi, H U. 2099 3d av....Lamson Consol S S Co. Register. (R) 285
South Publishing Co. 22 College pl....Babcock P P Co. Press. 4,700
Spellman, M J. 354 E 10th....Bernheimer & S. Saloon Ice House. 100
Spiegel & Held. 171 Attorney ...S I Hoffman. Press, &c. 200
Standard Fashion Co.. .S M Tallman. Letters Patent, &c. 2,500
Same.. .E J Walton. Letters Patents, &c. 2,500
Stapff, R and C. 537 W 54th....Wellmann & Holste. Bottler Fixtures. 2,400
Schaefer, George. 22 Av B....L Georgens. Barber Fixtures. (R) 103
Standfast, John. 2490 Valentine av....L Hanneman. Horse, Wagon, &c. 323
Schaefer, John. 443 W 39th....J Grundler. Butcher Fixtures. 150
Smith, F B. 50 E 23d....E Parmley. Dental Fixtures. (R) 1,500
Sopere, Frank. 125 Clinton pl....A Schwaab & Son. Barber Fixtures. (R) 124
Sovieri, Luigi. 74 West . A Schwaab & Son. Barber Fixtures. (R) 29
Schiel, Fritz. 154 William....National Cash Register Co. Register. 175
Schoenberger, Louis. 28 Elm....Manhattan Type Co. Press, &c. 200
Schumm, M A. 327 E 47th ..Couper, Zimmermann & Co. Bakery Fixtures. 500
Stabile & Co. 74 Mulberry... Mosler Safe Co. Safe. (R) 125
Taylor, J O. 1279 Franklin av....Canton Surgical Chair Co. Chair. 160
Tancredi, Ludovicio. 1968 3d av....A Schwaab & Son. Barber Fixtures. 103
Taylor, J, P S Terhune and Boland & Co. 711 1st av.. J McCormick. Carriage Maker Fixtures. 600
Tocchi, Ernesto. 197 South 5th av... Eardley & W. Cutter. 90
Treutler, Paul. 125th st and 2d av... G Freygang. Drug Fixtures. 8,000
Union Ferry Co....New York and Brooklyn Central Trust Co. Boats, &c. (R) 2,200,000
Union Bottling Co and P P Krummerich. 240 and 242 E 20th... M C Moran et al. Bottler Fixtures. 7,000
Vermilyea, H M. 1st av and 37th st....F A Potts & Co et al. Coal Yard Fixtures. 4,570
Vodermaier, Chas. 57 Av B....C Buhler. Butcher Fixtures. 100
Van Buren, H C. 2116 8th av....C Hollingworth. Butter and Egg Fixtures. 200
Vorwold, Joseph. 85 Christopher....M Gottlieb & Son. Horse, Wagon, &c. 100
Vanderbilt, I T 96 Spring....E H Hotchkiss. Office Fixtures. 421
Volz, Henry. 538 W 49th... J Gilbert. Horse, Wagon, &c. 200
Winkopp, Alex. Wall st and Broadway, Brooklyn....National Cash Register Co. Register. 225
Wheaton, F W & Co. 216 W 42d....Marvin Safe Co. Safe. 219
Wartenberg, Emma. 129 Hudson... O Wartenberg. Office Fixtures. 100
Weiss, Adolph. 108 and 110 Attorney....H Goldberger. Tailor Fixtures, &c. 800
Weller, J L. 223 Grand....S Kurinsky. Bottler Fixtures. (R) 3,000
West Indies Asphalt Co....Wattson & Farr. Agreement to purchase asphalt.

BILLS OF SALE.

Ashley, E W. 106 Mulberry....M Mooney. Saloon Fixtures. 1,000
Broadbent, R C. 18 Cortlandt....W H Johnson. Office Fixtures. 1
Bellotte, H A. 828 and 830 6th av....L I Bellotte. Confectionery Fixtures. 5,750
Clifford, H B. 64th st and 2d av....T P M Bennett. Horses, &c. 1,800
Cohen, Israel. 168½ Delancey ...B Cohen. Tailor Fixtures. 1,050
Same ...M Berlinsky. Church Scroll. 100
Cuff, J M. 73 W 133d ...J E Cuff. Furniture. 1
Cohen, Solomon. 201 Delancey....M Levine. Cigar Store Fixtures. 350
Cortiss, Sarah. Bayonne, N J, and 588 Av B.... J F Walsh. Furniture. 1
Cory, E V. 4 E 133d ...J Ennis. Furniture. 100
Eureka Cigar Machine Co. 144 Centre O C Frost. Machinery, &c. 2,255
Fountain, Inez. 17 W 34th....Kurtz & Graham. Furniture, &c. 1
Frost, O C. 144 Centre....E H Miller. Machinery, &c. 1,250
Flasch, Julius. 108 W 28th....J U Flasch. Furniture and Fixtures. 1
Guinan, Thos. 77 Bayard....M Feinberg. Saloon Fixtures. 750
Grenz, C F. 328 E 74th ...Dora Grenz. Furniture. 1
Grundler, Joseph. 443 W 39th.....J Schaefer. Butcher Fixtures. 350
Hellen, Harris. 105 Essex .. S Solomon. Shoe Store Fixtures. 500
Layman, J M and H A. 367 W 116th....D M Smith. Piano. 200
McIntyre, Peter. 558 W 51st....M Rohl. Saloon. 4,000
Mahon, C C. 18 Coventies slip....M H Murphy. Saloon Fixtures. 2,000
Melam, J W. 3d av and 161st st....L & J Hammer. Frame Building, &c. 500
McKeon, J H....H L Morris. Store Fixtures 149
Nones, L A. 71 Mercer....A H Nones. Building, &c. 1
Russo, Domenico. 189 Hester....J Lanza. Saloon Fixtures. 900
Solomon, Simon. 105 Essex....S Hellen. Shoe Store Fixtures. 500
Specht, Louis. 117 Pitt....J Kreittner. Saloon Fixtures. 900
Schuster & Koenig. 63 Av D....G Brinck. Grocery Fixtures. 1
Siemon, W F & J E. 76 Spring .A W Egle. Saloon Fixtures 705
Schlebensied, A. 738 11th av....C W Roux. Drug Fixtures. 6,000
Wicks, A E .. Rose & Beck. Machinery. 117

ASSIGNMENTS OF CHATTEL MORTGAGES.

Loewenthal, Emil to S Eilanger. (Mort given by H Tranguilini, Aug 10, 1891.) 240
Mayer, Jenny R to B Loeb. (G E & E Romaine, Sept. 14, 1891.) 10
Same to D Uhlfeld. (T. Meighan, Sept. 12, 1891.) 12

KINGS COUNTY.

OCTOBER 15 TO 21.—INCLUSIVE.

SALOON AND RESTAURANT FIXTURES.

Allen, G W, of Allen Bros. 2130 Fulton....Claus Lipsius B Co. (R) $375
Blooman, J. 156 Berry....Williamsburgh B Co. 300
Brossard Bros. 4 and 5 Court sq....G Siebling. (R) 567
Behrens, W. 250 Kent av....P Weidmann. 400
Burke, J F. 1551 Broadway....Claus Lipsius B Co. (R) 1,500
Butt, H C. 9 Bergen....M Seitz. (R) 600
Callan, J. 146 Hoyt....W Ulmer. (R) 600
Coar, W. 16 Seigel....H B Scharmann & Sons. 400
Cosselo, M. 205 Johnson st, 316 Hudson av.... Claus Lipsius B Co. (R) 500
Coyne, P. 508 Flushing av....W L Flanagan. 750
Dressell, N. 160 Harrison av....Eliz A Meltzer. (R) 650
Ebert, E. 284 Devoe....E Ochs. 550
Ernst, J. 62 Union av... Obermeyer & L. 750
Fassnacht, W. 791 Flushing av....Burger & H B Co. 450
Feeney, O. 211 Bedford av... S Liebmann's Sons B Co. 500
Fields, R. 176 Willoughby....P Ballantine & Sons. 600
Fitz Gibbon, J J. 602 Myrtle av....Claus Lipsius B Co. (R) 1,000
Frey, G. 232 Ewen....H B Scharmann. (R) 1,000
Fulton, J. 100 Buffalo av....C Freese. 384
Fulton, Annie. 50 Broadway....Williamsburgh B Co. 1,200
Gabriel, J. 315 Maujer....M Seitz. (R) 684
Gallagher, J. 104 Park av....Claus Lipsius B Co. (R) 1,322
Goldenberg, S. Livonia av, cor Osborn st... Budweiser B Co. 80
Hilburger, J. 250 Ellery....Claus Lipsius B Co. 900
Hobenkamp, H H. 19 Woodhull....Williamsburgh B Co. (R) 1,500
Haffner, P. 826 Lorimer ...J Fallert B Co. (R) 400
Kehr, Bertha. 13 Tompkins av....Claus Lipsius B Co. (R) 400
Koelmel, W. 117 Hopkins....Burger & H B Co. 450
Kaiser, J. 84 Central av....Claus Lipsius B Co. 700
Kemnitzer, H. 1258 De Kalb av....Leibinger & O B Co. (R) 700
Lyons, M J. 22 Brooklyn av ..Claus Lipsius B Co. 700
Lucas, H J. 572 Wythe av....W Ulmer. 4,500
Malone, C. Washington av and Butler st....Budweiser B Co. 45
Manning, M J. 228 Tillary....Claus Lipsius B Co. (R) 500
Maier, A. 1039 Flushing av....Williamsburgh B Co. 415
McIntyre, F. 134 North 6th ... Williamsburgh B Co. 350
McLaughlin, P. 3d av and 33d st....F Hower B Co. 800
McCauley, W Kent and Flushing avs....H Koehler & Co. 1,500
McPhee, J H. 58 Meeker av....Claus Lipsius B Co. (R) 400
Mehling, A. 174 Leonard....J Fallert B Co. (R) 600
Meyer, E G. 31 Greenpoint av....Otto Huber Brewery. 2,000
Miller, C. 51 Graham av....E Ochs. 693
Mitchell, F. 214 Grand Beadleston & W. 750
Mohrman, J F. 401 Gates av ...F Martens. (R) 950
Niebuhr, L. 172 Grand ...Claus Lipsius B Co. 1,500
O'Connell, R. 396 Warren....W L Flanagan. 1,700
Rhein, J. 55 Central av....Claus Lipsius B Co. (R) 500
Roberts, W. 645 Atlantic av....Obermeyer & L. 700
Rowland, W. 54 Fulton....R F Crawford. Restaurant Fixtures. 200
Rugen, H D. 221 4th av....T F Martin. 3,250
Scheibel, E. 158 McKibbin....Claus Lipsius B Co. (R) 550
Schlib, J. 40 Floyd....S Liebmann's Sons B Co. 600
Schmidt, J C. 260 Columbia....Obermeyer & L. (R) 900
Schoenborn, J. 115 Knickerbocker av ...L Eppig. 700
Smith, J. 605 5th av ...Obermeyer & L. 2,500
Steiges, G W. 68 Union....Bachmann B Co. 910
Stoecker A. 125 Fulton... P Moller. 1,700
Schechtel, W & Bro. Belmont av and Watkins st ...Williamsburgh B Co. (R) 250
Schwarzmuller, F. 76 Monteith .. Leibinger & O B Co. 350
Tarpey, B. East New York av, s e cor Stone av ....H B Scharmann. (R) 1,200
Touzer, H. 322-330 9th av....E Huber. 4,000
Van Dollen, P. 111 Furman....J Fallert B Co. (R) 1,500
Wolf, H. 260 Reid av....F Ibert. 600
York, T. 164 5th av....G Mason. 750
Same....D P Morey. 250
Zeisner, S. 238 Hopkins....J Kress B Co. (R) 200
Zweygardt, F. 1056 Myrtle av....Leibinger & O B Co. 100

HOUSEHOLD FURNITURE.

Applegate, Mrs. 55 Lincoln pl ...I Mason. 155
Bogardus, L. 99 Cornelia....J Baumann. 163
Broussen, Meta. 102 Huron....A Schulz. 184
Brosball, I. 126 Bergen....J Baumann. 121
Carruthers, C. 30 South 9th .. Fennell & P. 123
Chaplu, Mrs L A. 178 Sterling pl....J McEnery & Co. 158
Christianson, Mrs E. 1079 Bushwick av....J McEnery & Co. 190
Coe, J H. 71 Keap....A Schulz. 125
Cooke, Fannie L. 37 Schermerhorn....A Pearson. 120
Corwin, E. 70 Union av....J A Schwarz. 134
Criscallo, L. 357 Jay....J Hegeman & Co. 275
Cutts, C F. 1116 Gates av....D M Brown. 372
Clark, F. 42 Sands....O'Connor & Treacy. 238
Cornell, J A. 624 Monroe....Mary M Webster. 150
Davidge, E M. 24 Lefferts pl....Brooklyn F Co. 294
Donohue, M. 11 Dunham pl....J Wolf & Son. 161
Daykin, H E. 430 Bedford av....A S Phelps. (R) 400
De Costa, B. 22 Stockholm....J Baumann. 125
Deitz, Ida. 876 Driggs av....A Schulz. 191
Evans, N B and Margt H. 18 Berkeley pl....Augusta V Smith. 165
Farrell, H T. Fulton st, n e cor Essex st.. W Basler. 250
Farrell, Winifred. 130 Bridge....A Pearson. 108

Follenus, C. 380 Tompkins av....C S Lacey. 139
Gravel, A. 445 5th....Brooklyn F Co. 202
Gray, Mrs. Saratoga av, cor Prospect pl....Brooklyn F Co. 136
Hann, Mrs. S. 210 Conover....Mullins Sons. 123
Hartwig, E. 57½ Vernon av....W H Griffin. 100
Herlis, G A. 832 Flushing av....S Jacoby. 100
Higginson, G. 73 Van Voorhis ...Fennell & P. 110
Harvey, J L. 287 Myrtle av....L Baumann. 128
Ings, H D. 221 5th av....L Baumann. 179
Juhass, Annie. 158½ Central av....Josephine Wens. 209
Kaiser, A. 188 Stanhope....Fennell & P. 189
Ludeman, R A. 268 South 3d ...A Schulz. 224
Lewis, Ella. 285 South 5th....L Baumann. 110
McLaughlin, Mrs E. Jr. 320 Carlton av....J McEnery & Co. 204
Monaghan, A. 99 Sumpter....A H King & Co. (R) 166
Mullens, Mrs. 98 2d....O'Connor & Treacy. 115
Ostrander, G W. 167 Navy... A Pearson. 152
O'Connor, Kate. 9 Ellery....A Pearson. 106
Redfield, F L and Carrie E. 156 Greene av....H Valentine. 110
Rogers, J. 800 Monroe .. J McEnery & Co. 164
Schneider, Elizabeth. 497A Kosciusko....J McEnery & Co. 133
Simmons, Eliza. 1359 Broadway....Brooklyn F Co. 215
Taylor, Mary. 274 Pearl....A Pearson. 828
Thompson, F M. 149 Jefferson av....O'Connor & Treacy. 157
Vredenburgh, Elizabeth. 871 Herkimer....Mullin's sons. 159
White, E S. 587 McDonough....Mullin's Sons. 150
Walters, Mary L. 369 Tompkins av....S D Boggs. 100

MISCELLANEOUS.

Adams, A....P Barrett. Truck. 325
Bailey, Antoinette. 67-73 Kent av....J W Kay. Bottling Business. 12,000
Bathford, W F....Royal Horse Assoc. Horse. 100
Berkevitz, K. Gravesend....J F Heinbockel & Co. Frame Building. (R) 600
Beyrer, C W. 150 Sackett... J Hahn. Barber Fixtures. (R) 240
Blum, M. 819 Bedford av E Marscheider. Butcher Fixtures. 191
Bunker, B H. 30 McDonough....H H Copeland. Library. (R) 142
Bartroff, C. 832 Bedford av .... M Vosseler. Bakery Fixtures. (R) 150
Beckett, J. 85 and 87 Vesey st, New York... W O Platt exr R J Bradford. Tools, Stock, &c. (R) 2,400
Bengert, J F. 1544 Fulton....Marvin Safe Co. Safe. 115
Dohrmann, W H....Wolf Bros. Horse. 115
Dunn, H and J Murcott. 10 and 12 Richardson ....J Murcott. Factory. 1,000
Fischer & Crawford. Baltic st, near Smith st. Horse, &c. 300
Ferris, J P. 338 18th .... Bath & Hayward. Horses. 400
Frank, S. 265 Roebling....F Ellmers. Butcher Fixtures. 500
Franklin, J N and Adelaide F. 81 8th av and 308 W 13th st, New York .... Mary A Ladd. Plumber Fixtures. 1,500
Glas, C, Jr. 18 Howard st, New York ...Johnson Peerless Works. Engine, Press, &c. (R) 240
Hendrickson, J E. Nassau st, near Jamaica av ....Eliz Mister. Milk Business, Cows, &c. 600
Hess, G & H. 279-285 Rivington st, New York ....Maria Hess. Machinery, Tools, &c. 5,408
Isaacs, H. 630 5th av... J H & J C Doyle. Cigar Fixtures. 700
Jenkins & McCowan .. Campbell Press and Mfg Co. Press. (R) 2,000
Joose, C F. 105 Smith....A D Puffer & Sons Mfg Co. Soda Apparatus. 500
King, F. 167 Jefferson... J Staat. Horses. (R) 500
Kuhl, L P. 819 Broadway, New York....Johnson Peerless Works. Presses, &c. (R) 1,320
Linke, O. 2 Sumner av....Eimer & Amend. Drug Fixtures. (R) 630
Mehrtens, D. 442 Humboldt....J Kriete. Tobacco Route. 400
McIntyre & Deitz. 48 and 50 Ross....J Cunningham Son & Co. Coach. 750
Nielsen, L. 242 and 244 Smith and 56 Douglass ....J H Kraut. Grocery Fixtures, &c. 1,400
Nolting, W F. 669 Myrtle av....Lamson C S S Co. Register. 255
O'Connor, J. 28 Chapel .... J F O'Connor. Horses, Wagons. (R) 300
Pink, T. 1417 Broadway....M Tobias. Butcher Fixtures. 325
Pettit, F. 310 Broadway and 11 Ralph av....Salzer & Wolf. Machinery. 1,697
Renz, C. 774 Broadway....L Darde. Fixtures. 1,000
Rubino, A, and G Noschese. 91 Bridge....A Zottarelli. Barber Fixtures. 120
Sauer, Kate. 275 Stagg....Wolff Bros. Horse. 125
Schmutte, F. 523 Fulton....J A Dieckmann. Cigar Factory, &c. 1,000
Sheffield, E & Co....Campbell Press and Mfg Co. Press. (R) 1,050
Summerfield, Eliz A. 757 Gates av....Jennie Dieringer. Drug Fixtures. 500
Schwaner, F. 181 Wyckoff av ...P Koeber. Wagon. 100
Stokes, R T & W L and H G Schoff. 462 Bedford av ...May, Levy & May. Butcher Fixtures. (R) 700
Union Ferry Co. New York and Brooklyn....Central Trust Co, New York. All Property, Rights and Franchise. (R) 2,800,000
Van Woert, F T. 355 Manhattan av....W E Balsey. Dental Tools and Stock. 600
Wahlers, H B. 292 Stagg ...J H Albohm. Grocery Fixtures. (R) 600
Wittmann, J. 729 Flushing av....G Ringler & Co. Bottling Business. 1,200
Young, W B and J H Keeler... J W Garrison. Floating Hoisting Engines, &c. 1,700

BILLS OF SALE.

Beasley, W. 508 Flushing av....P Coyne. Saloon Fixtures. Sub to mort $400. 350
Bodkin, J. 214 Grand....F Mitchell. Saloon Fixtures. nom
Doyle, J H & J C. 630 5th av....H Isaacs. Cigar Fixtures. 800
Donnelly, C J. 172 Grand....L Niebuhr. Saloon Fixtures. 1,800
Faella, A. 794 Grand....R Neumann. Saloon Fixtures. 900
Froehlich, L. 400 Atlantic av....Karoline Papel. Saloon Fixtures. nom
Gallo, L. 108 Navy....Celeste Confessore. Grocery Fixtures. 125
Hurych, J. 1339 Greene av....Anna Hurych. Pulley Business, Tools, &c. nom
Johannsen, C. 918 Flushing av....C Mienert. Grocery Fixtures. 1,550
Lepp, H. 13 McDougal....J Scholl. Saloon Fixtures. 900
Lewry, S D. 375 Washington av....Margt McSorley. Fish Business. 25
O Connell, J. 396 Warren....R O'Connell. Saloon Fixtures. 2,500
O'Connor, P J. 144 Park av....W F O'Connor. Grocery Fixtures. 500
Papel, L. 400 Atlantic av... L Froehlich. Saloon Fixtures. nom
Riedmann, Cath. 368 Atlantic av .... Margt Schultz. Employment Office. nom
Scherer, P. 546 Broadway....Mary Anderson. Restaurant Fixtures. 350
Welch, A M....W L Welch. Cat Boat Alda. 150

NEW JERSEY.

NOTE.—The arrangement of the Conveyances, Mortgages and Judgments in these lists is as follows: the first name in the Conveyances is the Grantor; in Mortgages, the Mortgagor; in Judgments, the Judgment debtor.

ESSEX COUNTY.

CONVEYANCES.

Abernethy, Hamilton—W H Hennion, South Orange.... $100
Adams, John—M Miko, Clinton.... 1
Allen, F H et al—W Allen, State st.... 358
Allen, I E—P J Dunning, Court st.... 50
Alling, Horace—J L Kessler, South 18th st.... 1,600
Ames, Catharine—W J Knight, Orange st.... 1
Austin, M H—T W E Allin, Hudson st.... 2,200
Ball, Charles—L M Cadmus, Bloomfield.... 500
Ball, Isaiah—A Romine, North th st.... 1,500
Bayles, C J—M H Wilcox, Montclair.... 3,800
Belfatto, E V A—C Sears, Montclair.... 1
Bensmann, Caroline—W S Wade, South 15th st. 5
Berry, J A—The Church of St Rose of Lima, n w cor Warren and Gray sts 119x79x90x84.... 5,500
Bloemecke, Henry, Jr—G O Scherer, 1st tract s s 13th av 458 w High st 25x59, 2d tract s s 13th av 433 w High st 25x59.... 11,000
Boerger, Ernest—E Rohrschneider, w s Sidney pl 60 s Bank st 40x80.... 4,280
Bradley, Martha—H H Gallien, East Orange.... 1,350
Cannon, W S—D Ames, Orange st.... 1
Carty, Mary—C Garry, Bridge st.... 2,750
Chandler, H L—Orange Heights Land Co, West Orange.... 1
Chambliss, J A—G E Huebner, East Orange.... 8,500
Clark, C L exr—F T Bey, Washington av.... 1,600
Coe, Abby dec'd by exrs—C M Coe, Prince st.... 2,500
Same—B J Coe, South 7th st.... 750
Same—L F Crowell, Broome st.... 2,500
Same—C A Coe, South 8th st.... 1,400
Same—M A Holden, South 8th st.... 1,400
Same—S E Parkhurst et al, Broome st.... 2,000
Same—H Pierson, s e cor Court st and Coes pl, 50x85.... 7,150
Same—S E Parkhurst et al, Prince st.... 2,500
Same—E J Osborne, Court st.... 1,920
Same—C A Coe et al, Prince st.... 2,500
Same—J L Grover, Coes pl.... 2,400
Coe, C A—T Coe, South 8th st.... 1,400
Corby, W H—A D Brundage, Montclair.... 5,500
Cowell, C E—S Levi, East Orange.... 6,775
Devine, Arthur—F Stuberoth, South Orange.... 150
Dodd, G F—J McGonigal, Orange.... 300
Same—J McGarry, Orange.... 300
Donnelly, Timothy—P H Harrison, South 12th st 1
Drexel Improvement Co—A Schantz, Montclair. 150
Same—F Lord et al, Montclair.... 810
Dunning, E W—A D Taylor, Court st.... 1
Eisele, J C—D McCance, Johnson av.... 800
Farley, B M—J H Sanford, Clinton.... 1
Feick, C A—S Viegler, Boyd st.... 2,400
Francisco, L F—M Haddon, Montclair.... 12,500
Fried, S A—M E Oelkers, s s Mechanic st n e cor C N Lockwood 5x90.... 17,000
Garrabrant, P S et al—The East Jersey Water Co, Bloomfield.... 6,025
Garrigan, B M—H Schuman et al, e s Lush st 125 s Bank st 30x96x25x51x5x45.... 5,300
Guthrie, P F—J Davis, Franklin.... 750
Hagamann, Sophia—J Dubois, South 9th st.... 2,000
Hauck, Agnes—J Merck, Niagara st.... 1
Harrison, P H—T Donnelly, 9th av.... 1
Hawkins, W C—T Lally, Belleville.... 575
Heller, G E—F F Minton, Montclair av.... 1,800
Hoffman, William—J Haug, Clinton.... 125
Jacobus, C H—G E Taylor, Caldwell.... 300
Jerring, Alfred—S Wolfe, East Orange.... 750
Keenan, Margaret—P E Keenan, Academy st.... 1
Same—same, Boyden st.... 1
Kingsley, G P—A H Root, Orange.... 7,500
Lambert, G H—M A Decker, w s Washington av adj J C McGeragle land 31x90.... 4,000
Lawrence, Nathaniel—W Neill, East Orange.... 350
Lister, J C et al—F Walsh, e s Belleville av, 255 s Isaac Van Wagenen 47x90.... 5,235
Lowy, Philip—F Sauer, Quitman st.... 2,700
Lum, Henrietta—H Jerolaman, Salt Meadow.... 89
Maurer, Frederick—C E Sharp, East Orange.. 5,500
Maynard, O H—J Jenkins, Montclair.... 8,200
McGowan, Catharine—T McGrath, Belleville.... ——
McGowan, John—W Haase, Napoleon st.... 500
McLoud, George—B S Williams et al, Orange.... 450
Metzger, Philip—M Reilly, Lentz av.... 350
Mersereau, W T—W T Mersereau Co, cor East Mechanic st and N J R R av.... 1
Miller, G C—F Woodruff, East Orange.... 1
Mitchell, A P et al—F Maurer, East Orange.... 1,200
Mitchell, A P—M Vandunker, East Orange.... 1,250
Mintonye, S M—J Jenkins, Montclair.... 5,500
Morehouse, Delia—E J Smith, Orange.... 1
Morris, Charlotte—F Vogel, South 7th st.... 900
Osborne, J H et al—E L Heath, Clinton.... 1,000
Peck, Cyrus—J A Gries, 3d st.... 2,400
Peloubet, F W—A D Trimpi, East Orange.... 1,350
Pippert, Frederick—B Mayer, e s Broome st 550 s Montgomery st 25x116.... 3,700
Price, Matthias—L E Price, Pennington st.... 1,600
Pruden, P S—A Kalisch, s s Bleecker st 325 w Plane st 25x106.... 3,800
Rehber, Margaretha—A Steines, s w s Market st, 100 n Mott st, 28x62x49x112x57x72.... 3,500
Roediger, Dorothea—J Weber, South 6th st.... 1
Roseville M E Church—J A Berry, n w cor Warren and Gray sts, 119x79x90x81.... 5,500
Ryan, E M—W M Wigger, w s Washington st, 88 n New st, 22x82.... 5,000
Scheerer, G O—E F Sloe, Clinton.... 225
Same—H Bloemecke, Jr, Clinton.... 4,500
Sears, W H—E V A Belfatto, Montclair.... 1
Sheridan, Mary—P Sheridan, Morris av.... 5
Skinkle, Jacob—G Conradi, South 14th st.... 550
Smith, J C—N Horowitz, e s Boyd st, 225 s Kinney st, 25x100.... 5,000
Spottiswoode, George—A Flaherty, Orange.... 450
Same—C E Jones, Orange.... 1,356
Same—E J Duffy, Orange.... 1,125
Same—H L Chandler, West Orange.... 1
Stanton, Thomas—T J O'Brien, South Orange.. 25
Stemmler, Emilie—F X Loy, Oraton st.... 350
Stewart, H C—B W Taylor, East Orange.... 1
Taylor, A D—P J Dunning, Court st.... 1
Taylor, Jerome—C V Stoutenburgh, Chestnut st 300
The Central New Jersey Land Impt Co—R C Boice Co, Van Buren st.... 500
Thompson, I F—F E Thompson, s s Academy st 51x84.... 4,500
Tichenor, Dr Hiram—W A Knorr, Littleton av.. 2,300
Torrey, Willard—F Hogen, Montclair.... 275
Towler, Lewis—I J Bedell, South Orange.... 1
Tucker, Warren dec'd by heirs—C S Tucker, Elm st.... 1
Van Duyne, Harrison—A M Case, Mt Prospect av.... 1,500
Van Reyper, A E—J P Tonsor, Belleville.... 250
Same—C Ortholf, Belleville.... 250
Weatherby, Barry et al—W Hilton, Franklin.... 250
Wiesmann, John—Tobias Velden, Bloomfield.... 400
Williams, I M—M Macchia, Orange.... 1,900
Same—M Potter, Bloomfield.... 700
Woodruff, Frederick—K A Miller, East Orange.. 1
Wright, E E—O H Maynard, Montclair.... 1
Wright, G S—S M Shanley, Grubart st.... 800
Young, M E—F M McDermit, North 7th st.... 2,950

MORTGAGES.

Allen, T W—J Leverguard, Hudson st.... 3,800
Barlet, M J—J H Breakenridge et al, Clinton.... 100
Barrett, J F—West End B and L Assoc, Summit st.... 8,000
Bellew, Patrick—C E Barnard, Broome st.... 100
Bennett, E H—Chosen Friends' Home, Loan and Savings League, East Orange.... 1,000
Binn, Mary—M Betz, Bank st.... 2,300
Blanchard, I H—Greenville B and L Assoc, Frelinghuysen av.... 6,052
Bloemecke, Henry, Jr—B Ellermann, Clinton.... 300
Brown, Georgiana—I Ball, East Orange.... 1,100
Byles, C J—A Davis, Garside st.... 2,400
Carroll, James—J F Shanley, Market st.... 1,000
Carson, S J—F J Love, Montclair.... 2,200
Case, A M—H Van Duyne, Mt Prospect av.... 1,000
Chieheny, James—G Krueger, Clifton av.... 5,500
Condit, E M—C Zulauf, West Orange.... 700
Conover, W H—F Moses, 5th av.... 2,500
Cornisky, Patrick—R S Gould, Aqueduct st.... 100
Dubois, Joseph—S Hagamann, South 9th st.... 17,000
Duff, Theresa—A E Wright, Warren st.... 1,000
Ebert, Emil—G Schoenamsgruber, Academy st. 2,000
England, E H—C N Lockwood, Clinton.... 4,800
Faitoute, E C—J H Baldwin, Summer av.... 2,000
Flanagan, J F—Belleville B and L Assoc, Belleville.... 200
Fletcher, George—E J Brockett, North 7th st.... 1,100
Fray, Albert—West End B and L Assoc, South Orange av.... 4,000
Fuerth, Bertha—Woodside B and L Assoc, Carteret st.... 1,900
Gallien, H H—M Bradley, East Orange.... 1,150
Garry, Catherine—J O H Pitney guard, Cross st. 2,750
Gerberich, Bernard—I H Bachman, Pond st.... 500
Goman, Chas—A Hobley, Montclair.... 300
Graham, Amelia—Belleville B and L Assoc, Belleville.... 200
Grom, Catharine—Newark German B and L Assoc, Academy st.... 3,000
Guild, C H—C D Hayes, Chadwick av.... 2,000
Haase, William—C A Feick, Napoleon st.... 300
Harth, Joseph—S Scheuer, Camden st.... 700
Healy, A E—W Pierson, Orange.... 1,000
Horwitz, Nehtin—J C Smith, Boyd st.... 900
Howard, Thomas A—E M Condit, Orange.... 1,000
Jackson, T W—C M Lillie, Mt Prospect av.... 800
Jones, C E—G Spottiswoode, Orange.... 700
Kattenstroth, M F—D B Stearns, East Orange.... 1,000
Kalisch, Abner—Newark B and L Assoc, Bleecker st.... 2,800
Krueger, Nathan—Essex Co Brewing Co, Montgomery st.... 1,000
Lambert, G H trustee—Trustees of First Presbyterian Church, Newark, Washington av.... 3,500
Longua, Paul—Franz Berg, Orange.... 700
Loy, F X—E Stemmler, Washington av.... 350
Macchia, Michael—I M Williams, Orange.... 950
Mac Rorie, Daniel—M Mac Rorie, Orange.... 500
Mallet, Severo—C F Davis, Orange.... 1,500
Marlatt, James—Wilkinson, Gaddis & Co, Elm st.... 1,600
Mayer, Adolph—Savings B and L Assoc, Broome st.... 3,500
McDermit, Frank—Enterprise B and L Assoc, 7th av.... 3,000
McGinty, Patrick—E Geppert, Walnut st.... 1,500
McGrath, Thomas—Belleville B and L Assoc, Belleville.... 1,200
McGrath, James—E Mulford Orange.... 2,400
McNolty, Michael—S Scheuer et al, Belleville.... 300
Meeker, Robert—Central B and L Assoc, Mt Prospect av.... 2,400
Merck, John—G Krueger, Niagara st.... 600
Nereid Boat Club—Home B and L Assoc, Belleville.... 800
Oelkers, M E—S A Fried, Mechanic st.... 16,000
Owen, J A—Montclair B and L Assoc, Montclair.... 3,000
Peters, C W—S M Peters, Broad st.... 20,000
Peters, G W—Prudential Ins Co, Broad st.... 35,000
Picot, John—E H Snyder, South Orange.... 500
Post, E M—B M Shanley, Goble st.... 1,500
Potter, Maynes—H J Thatcher, Bloomfield.... 1,900
Rachlin, Morris—S Doughty et al exrs, Broome st.... 3,300
Richards, Elizabeth—American Ins Co, Pennington st.... 2,500
Roesch, William—L A Baxter, Bloomfield.... 800
Robinson, A E—Orange Memorial Hospital, West Orange.... 2,100
Salmon, James—M S Richards, Ferry st.... 1,200
Sauer, Frank—The Aetna B and L Assoc, Quitman st.... 1,700
Schmidt, Christian—The Washington B and L Assoc, Littleton av.... 5,200
Schunk, M L—The Enterprise B and L Assoc, Quitman st.... 200
Smith, A W—The East Orange B and L Assoc, East Orange.... 2,500
Smith, C H—The American Ins Co, Milburn.... 5,000
Steines, Anton—M Klement, Market st.... 2,000
Same—M Rehberger, Market st.... 500
St John, Burr—E F Tichenor, Halleck st.... 200
Taylor, C A—M McRorie, Orange.... 400

Thieme, F J—H S Pfeil, Gold st 150
Thieringer, J M—The Montclair B and L Assoc, Montclair 600
Thompson, F E—A M Keen, Academy st 3,000
Trimpi, A H—The Fraternal B and L Assoc, East Orange 4,200
Tucker, C C—B W Tucker, Elm st 2,008
Van Iderstine, W H—The Chosen Friends' Home Loan and Savings League, South Orange 2,500
Viegler, Sarah—C A Feick, Boyd st 1,900
Vogel, Frederick—C Morris, 16th av 650
Wadsworth, E M—I Ball, East Orange 7,000
Waldron, Michael—Montclair B and L Assoc, Montclair 1,400
Wilcox, Paul—Charles I Bayles, Montclair 1,700
Williams, John—Woodside B and L Assoc, South Orange 2,000
Wilson, James—Orange Valley B and L Assoc, Orange 1,500
Woenitzer, Max—Thirteenth Ward B and L Assoc, Prince st 800
Zarra, Filomena—Fourteenth Ward B and L Assoc, Lock st 12,000

CHATTEL MORTGAGES.

Blinn, George—G Kahn, horses and wagon 135
Bose, W F—P H Hanley, furniture 245
Brisius, Catharine—F Lisiewski, pool table 2'0
Carolan, Matt—Nat Cash Reg Co, register 200
Dey, L H—C Feigenspan, saloon 320
Franzblau, Sarah—A Hahn, stock of hats 250
Griffin, John—C Weigand, furniture 250
Jones, T S R—Nat Cash Reg Co, register 200
Lance, G M—M Minton, furniture 203
Meiers, Charles—J C Kohant, machinery 100
Meusel, John—Hirschfield & Co, safe 25
Mey, Charles—J Ketcham, furniture 86
Marden, J S—J Ketcham, furniture 65
Noonan, M C—W K Rankin, groceries 280
Presdee, J G—The J H Mohlman Co, groceries 500
Smith, H L—A Steadman, furniture 200
Stuhlinger, J G—P Ballantine & Sons, saloon 120
The South Orange Field Club—R M Miles, bowling alley, &c 2,000
Thompson, John—J Matthews Apparatus Co, soda apparatus 295
Von Possinger, Louis—A Blum, saloon 208
Wolfarth, Albert—M Kane, furniture 40

JUDGMENTS.

Kearney, Margaret—G Riker 150
Lehman, Charles—A M Allegaert 116
Meeker, L M et al—G Pearce 337
Rhodes, Wm—A L Tiplin 181

HUDSON COUNTY.

CONVEYANCES.

Baker, Elizabeth D—A F Smith $375
Banta, W S—L Fader, Harrison 800
Bescher, Chas—W Crannston, Hoboken nom
Same——same, Hoboken nom
Blauvelt, J J—C B Lawson nom
Bloch, Valentine—H Pilz, Union 3,350
Briden, Frank—Rosetta A Barbour, Kearney 800
Brown, Juliette L—H N Lang, Bayonne 700
Brown, Samuel—H Sharf 550
Buck, T W and C H—W Buck, Hoboken nom
Britten, Virginia F—T H Love 1,600
Burrows, Waters—J Nist 1,600
Carscallen, J D—R M Jarvis 800
Chaddock, J W—W H Chaddock 23,000
Clark, Alice and Mary A, by sheriff—H Harney 3,200
Cogan, Thomas—W Fleming 900
Coster, Henrietta T—T Featherston, Hoboken 250
Crane, Clarissa L, devisee of Thomas—Mary C Haskard, Bayonne 600
Crannston, William—Margaret Bescher, Hoboken —
Same——same, Hoboken nom
Cummings, Joseph—J D Leary, Hoboken 7,000
Curry, J H—J Kennedy 750
Dorr, Caroline D—Gustave F Schepeler nom
Same to Ida E Schepeler nom
Egbert, T K—G L Bettcher 1,500
Ellshemius, H G—Martha E Munn, Kearney 1,450
Elliot, D G—Dorothea M Fahr 3,000
Ettinger, Moritz—G M Behrmann, Hoboken 6,250
Eoff, Rachel A—J Lindsay 5,500
Ford, Geo—H D Magee, Bayonne 1,650
Same——Mary L Thomas, Bayonne 2,400
Gardner, R E—W H Murphy, Union 1,400
Gillen, Michael—P McArdle 1,100
Glaser, Theobald—A Rebholz, North Bergen nom
Godfrey, H H—R J B Lutz, Bayonne 600
Heckingbotham, J C—J Wilson 3,500
Hensing, Chas—Ellen B Wecht 4,000
Hertgen, Jno—T Flynn 1,800
Hoboken Land and Impt Co—The Mayor and Councilmen, Hoboken 1,190
Holmes, H B—W Fleming 900
Hudson, J H and Hannah—C Martens 1,666
Hughes, T R—J Usher, Guttenberg nom
Jacoby, Theodore—J F Hoops 3,600
Kannard, William, by sheriff—D S Naylor 500
Keegan, Cornelius—Mary J McCoy, Guttenberg 588
Kneale, Edward—Mary Maines nom
Maines, Mary—Ella Kneale nom
McClue, Arthur—Sarah Williams 1,600
Mehl, John—E A Brickwedel 1,200
Monson, Penmah, by sheriff—Provident Institution for Savings 1,500
Muirhead, W G—I I Vanderbeck nom
Naylor, D S—J F Kenney 2,100
Nichols, E H—L Benois 600
North Jersey Land Co—Augusta C Larson, Kearney 250
Oakley, Margaret—F Oakley, North Bergen nom
Same——W Oakley, North Bergen nom
Pane, Mifflen by exrs—D W Bedford, Weehawken 14
Parker, Cutland—D W Van Buskirk, Bayonne nom
Parker, Cutland, Jr—W S Bacot, Bayonne nom
Peterkin, John—W F Peterkin 2,000
Peterkin, W F—Jane Peterkin 2,000
Pittlit, Marie—H Fehler, Hoboken 2,850
Rusch, W F—Francis M McDonough, Hoboken 250
Schepeler, G F—J Doir nom
Schuetz, Chas—C Stuelzer, North Bergen 3,500
Sherman, B B by exrs—Magdalena Bishop 500
Siegfried, Adam—F A C Kaiser 750
Sinclair, Henrietta—G Casteen, West Hoboken 2,000
Sparks, H B—Mary A Page, West Hoboken 1,900
Spengler, Marie E—B N elker 1,750
Steenken, Arend—Katie Taylor 230
Symes, J H—F Hochart, Union 1,600
Van Buskirk, De Witt—C Parker, Jr nom
Vanderbeck, I I and F J—W G Muirhead nom
Van Horn, Jacob—C Martens nom
Weller, Julia—Margaret Haun, Hoboken 1,000
Welsh, Rachel—Elizabeth Welsh, Harrison 900
Wicht, Chris—C Hensing 4,000
Wood, Anna F and Florence Lembeck by special master—B Hohman, Bayonne 400
Wielfers, Anna and Martha by special guard to trustees of School District No 10, Union 310
Wulfers, Henry——same, Union nom
Zabriskie, Augustus—C Numbers, Jr 2,665

MORTGAGES.

Beck, Julia—C A Merzog, 3 years 1,000
Bergen, Mary—Bridget Leahey, Hoboken, 3 years 800
Broderick, Lawrence—Elizabeth S Noyes, 5 years 2,000
Casteen, Geo—Hoboken B and L Assoc, West Hoboken, installs 1,200
Coleman, J J—Exrs H Maass, 5 years 1,700
Couch, Laura A—D Felter, Bayonne, 3 years 1,750
Crevier, J C—Hoboken Bank for Savings, Hoboken, 3 years 6,000
Danmon, B D—S Burhans, Jr, 5 years 3,400
Dicks, Virginia F—J Duryea, Bayonne, 1 year 6,000
Driscoll, Maria C—W H Lewis, 1 year 750
Ehlkeck, H W—A J C Foye, installs 4,800
Ettling, David—A Campbell, 5 years 2,000
Frank, Magdalena—J S McMaster, Bayonne, 5 years 800
Frank, Philip—P M Griffith, Bayonne, 3 years 3,000
Hoffmann, Herman—S Langendorf, 1 year 1,016
Jewell, C C—Improved Land and Loan Assoc, installs 800
Kennedy, John—J H Curry, 3 years 250
Kenney, J F—The Jersey City B and L Assoc, installs 2,000
Kruse, Adele M—Jersey City Galvanizing Co, Kearney, 7 years 1,550
Lauterbach, Henry—Improved Land and Loan Assoc, installs 200
Leahey, Bridget—Catharine Murphy, Hoboken, 3 years 500
Lindsay, James—Rachel A Koff, 5 years 3,500
Lowe, T H—Virginia F Britten, 3 years 3,000
Magee, H D—Bayonne B Assoc No. 2, Bayonne, installs 1,400
Same——G Ford, Bayonne, 1 year 200
Martens, Christ—C G Grovenwoldt, 3 years 3,500
McCoy, Mary J—P T Callahan, Guttenberg, 1 year 1,000
Meineke, Paul—Anna M Ehrgoth, 3 years 500
Nist, Jacob—Agnes Van Horn, 3 years 225
Nolan, Catharine—D W Lawrence, 5 years 1,000
O'Connor, Margaret—Bayonne B Assoc, Bayonne, installs 1,800
Oesb, Helene M E—H Uber, Hoboken, 5 years 3,000
O'Reilly, Patrick—F C Hansen, West Hoboken, 3 years 300
Otto, F E—C Pape, 2 years 500
Otto, F E—Ottilie Grote, 5 years 2,500
Pfeiffer, William—Industrial M B and L Assoc, installs 3,000
Pollitz, Catharine—Bergen Land and Improvement Co, installs 1,920
Wood, James—J Trapp, 1 year 383
Reuter, John—C Kopf, 5 years 400
Scheeber, Conrad—G Vreeland, 5 years 1,200
Templeton, F C—P Boyle, Bayonne, 1 year 800
Thomas, Maria A—The Howard B and L Assoc, installs 3,400
Thomas, Mary L—The Centreville B and L Assoc, Bayonne, installs 2,000
Muhleg, C W—M Fries, Kearney, 3 years 1,500
Von Der Leith, Wilhelmina—E Wulff, Hoboken, 1 year 200
Wers, Ernest—Anna E Vreeland, Bayonne, 3 years 4,000

CHATTEL MORTGAGES.

Arnold, George—F G Smith, piano 165
Bartsch, Herman—R Bartsch, grocery store, &c 2,600
Berrian, John—C Birdsall, furniture 100
Bowler, Mary E—F G Smith, piano 240
Bremer, Harry—D Bermes, saloon 800
Brovedel, F A, Arlington—C I Cannon, furniture 200
Brodenick, Agnes—F G Smith, piano 280
Brown, James—National Cash Register Co, cash register 200
Brozolich, Anton, Hoboken—Favorite Clothing Co, furniture 23
Carroll, Mary F—F G Smith, piano 295
Carr, W H—C Birdsall, furniture 130
Faber, Louis, Hoboken—Wm Peter Brewing Co, saloon 784
Feinberg, Herman, Secaucus—I S Feinberg, 300 cows, &c 2,656
Foley, M F—The Bachman Brewing Co, saloon 1,130
Geisenheimer, George, Jr—F G Smith, piano 250
Goldschneider, Adolf, Bayonne—C Feigenspan, saloon 550
Greil, Ernest, Hoboken—C Birdsall, furniture 190
Griffith, H C—J H Lippe, undertakers wagon 230
Gruber, J P—E Gundrum, machinery 1,000
Hackett, R H—C Birdsall, furniture 100
Hanson, Jane—F G Smith, piano 165
Harms, Dietrich—H Betten, grocery store, &c 500
Harnett, Medora, Kearney—C Birdsall, furniture 130
Hopkins, Rosannah—J Mullins & Co, furniture 186
Horn, Adolf, Hoboken—Knickerbocker Brewing Co, saloon, &c 725
Hughes, J R—J Wallace & Son, saloon 385
Hurley, J H, Bayonne—F G Smith, piano 265
Inwright, J C—W J Limerich, piano, &c 160
Same——S Morgan, piano, &c 100
Jacoburtz, Barnett—F G Smith, piano 275
Klodt, William, Hoboken—Bernheimer & Schmid, saloon 800
Kolorik, John, Bayonne—F G Smith, organ 70
Kuch, Maria L—J Hecht & Co, cows and wagon 280
Linetan, John and Margaret—T C Lyman & Co, saloon fixtures 1,288
Luyster, W W—C Birdsall, furniture 130
Maher, P, Kearney—Nat Cash Reg Co, cash register 160
Mangels, Edward—Bavarian Brewing Co, saloon 500
Mansfield, Walter and Charles Senger, partners as Senger & Mansfield—Ada Mansfield, grocery store and cracker business 300
Same——Minnie Senger, grocery store and cracker business 600
Malitzki, Johanna—Wm Peter Brewing Co, ice box 120
McDonald, John—Bernheimer & Schmid, pool tables 450
Moeller, Theobald, Hoboken—E Gieche, horse, wagon, &c 150
Nolan, Jane, Hoboken—L Gordon, furniture 259
Nolan, Lizzie, Bayonne—L Baumann, furniture 116
O'Reilly, Bernard—T C Lyman & Co, saloon fixtures 466
Overbaugh, Annie L, Bayonne—F G Smith, piano 230
Peloubet, J R—G P Howell, jewelry business 1,320
Pennetts, M A—The Budweiser Brewing Co, saloon fixtures 425
Reich, Max and Emma his wife, Hoboken—L J Lesser, furniture 323
Saegren, Victor, Bayonne—J Gregg & Co, furniture 119
Sailer, R B—Wm Peter Brewing Co, saloon fixtures 850
Schmidt, J M—Bavarian Brewing Co, saloon 587
Schroeder, Henry, Hoboken—National Cash Register Co, cash register 175
Smith, F A—J Gregg & Co, furniture 57
Trapp, Mrs Edward—F G Smith, piano 330
Tyach, Mary V——same, piano 375
Vondy, T H, Bayonne—C Birdsall, furniture 120
Van Loan, Celina—F G Smith, piano 165
Walder, Jacob and Otto, West Hoboken—F Beuermann, butcher fixtures 250
Wallace, Mary E—C Birdsall, furniture 130
Wrede, Edward, Hoboken—C Stein, saloon 725
Young, J C—F G Smith, piano 290

BILLS OF SALE.

Balestriene, Michael—G Monaco, barber shop 100
Breusch, Jacob—Julia Miller, butcher shop fixtures, &c 250
Miller, William—J Breusch, butcher shop fixtures, horse, &c 250
Ziegenbalg, Alexander and John, Bayonne—P E Taylor, barber shop nom

JUDGMENTS.

Bloch, Frank—Snedecker & Boynton 142
Droyer, Edward—G Heinz 100
Geiger, F H—The Wm Peter Brewing Co 669
Hinchen, Rebecca M O—J H Wetjen 680
Kremer, Alois—N H Heyman 291
Leonard, F E—M Meyer 623
Meyer, G L—Austin, Nichols & Co 288
Murphy, James—J Emmons 442
O'Connor, J J—Annie Cordts 42
Taylor, William—Sherman, Tabor & Co 227
The Columbia Rolling Mill Company—The Beckett Foundry and Machine Co 3,137
The New York, Lake Erie & Western R R—Robert Henry admr of John Henry 2,000

BUILDING MATERIAL MARKET.

BRICKS.—We are informed that some reports were sent out from this market last week quoting prices 25c. per M higher. Of course, no such advance took place, but the effect was bad, as manufacturers were misled and correspondingly disappointed when they ascertained the facts. Nor has there been any gain this week that would warrant a making up of quotations. The payment of 12½ or even 25c. per M premium still has to be made where buyers insist upon having some pet make, and the delivery of which involves a special shipment, but the same stock offered on open market would have to go in with the general average, and there is nothing to indorse a quotation higher than $5.25 per M for a regularly established rate. The character of the business differs in no essential particular from that previously advised, buyers moving in a slow, indifferent manner, and appearing to feel as though there was little chance of any adverse turn to the market. Some cargoes are now and then taken to pile away where quality is peculiarly attractive, but most of the demand is said to be based solely upon early and positive consuming wants, with those somewhat curtailed during the week by the stormy unpropitious weather. Pales have found a trifle more attention, but would pay no higher prices and wanted the best of stock. From primary points no news comes to hand that appears fresh or pertinent. The season is being rapidly wound up and will in most cases leave the yards with an ample stock on hand from which some shipments are likely so long as the weather permits, and in other cases manufacturers will feel inclined to carry over until spring.

HARDWARE.—The distributive trade in all general lines of stock is very good and indeed broadening out somewhat, as dependent localities commence to hurry a little over getting in their fall and winter assortments, with a more or less cheerful feeling ruling accordingly. The local call is relatively the poorest, and especially so for builders' hardware, most of supplies for present consumption having been contracted for some time ago, and the prospect for additional wants proving quite slim. No announced changes of importance are given out on lists or discount sheets, but the tone on prices is easy and predictions of moderate declines are made.

LATH.—We do not discover much, if anything, really new upon the market this week. The immediate local demand is of limited proportions, owing to the comparatively liberal amounts laid in by dealers a short time ago and not over free consumption at the moment. Occasionally, however, a parcel is wanted, and that in conjunction with more or less call from dealers in neighboring cities creates an outlet balancing the limited offering and preserves the market upon a firm basis. Receivers claim they could raise the value line still higher if they so desired.

LIME.—Nothing really new comes into notice on this market. Demand has been fair enough to make a place for about all the cargoes coming to hand, and the tame tone of last week has not developed into an actual decline. Receivers, however, seem to be quite well satisfied with the quantity of stock they have to take care of and do not care to be called upon to handle any larger arrival. The actual consumption at the moment is only moderate.

LUMBER.—The distributive trade continues quite irregular, but evidently with less tendency toward an increase that had been hoped for. Some dealers appear to be doing very well, indeed a few may be found who are really quite busy, but as a rule the output of stock is moderate and confined to deliveries on the final end of contracts. In the meanwhile the yard accumulations are gradually filling up with supplies coming to hand from various directions in execution of engagements, and dealers are making some additional purchases as they discover where assortments will require filling out and rounding up. This makes the inquiry somewhat more difficult to satisfy as the selection is close with a disposition toward the better qualities, but as the grades most wanted are not particularly plenty, present or prospective, the influence is more or less stimulating to the line of valuation. There is a cheerful feeling in regard to chances for the export trade.

Eastern Spruce retains most of the former general features. Demand for random cargoes is of a somewhat indifferent character and when a number come in together receivers meet with the usual experience, though some claim to have driven rather better bargains of late, as locals find outside dealers affording more or less competing custom. On the other hand, however, buyers now experience considerable difficulty in securing attention to special bills, even though they may be willing to pay the full rates insisted upon. Manufacturers seem to think they have about all the orders on hand for which they are likely to obtain transportation, and naturally feel a hesitation about entering upon fresh engagements, especially as many of them propose shutting down at the earliest possible moment. Yard prices continue to be well sustained and dealers feel that they are entitled to considerable credit for the solid manner in which they have adhered to the spring compact in regard to retail rates.

Piling is a little disappointing to some of the trade. A few very good contracts have been perfected and a fair business done on small orders, but no real animation reached in the demand, and between fresh arrivals and the accumulation in the basins buyers promptly obtained accommodation without the necessity of increasing their bids.

Hemlock is more active than a month ago, yet it fails to move with quick, snappish trade, and most of the demand is of a character to indicate that it is for assortment rather than main stock, and considerable of what is ordinarily looked upon as regular custom is now missing. Prices are steady, possibly on some special calls a trifle firmer, but no quotable changes appear necessary in naming the general line of valuation.

White Pine may be called steady all along the line. Box boards have been called for somewhat more freely, not that there is any actual increase in the wants, but buyers who have been standing off for no particular reason, except that it was a fashion of the season, are now stirring themselves to obtain the supply likely to be necessary for usual winter wants. The effect is stiffening on values, aided somewhat by dealers who have on hand a pretty large accumulation collected at a lower line of cost. For uppers and select, demand is good and prices firm, buyers appearing to appreciate that the present scant offering is likely to continue, as primary points from which contributions to this market are ordinarily drawn have limited accumulations, with owners of the stocks assuming an indifferent attitude. On foreign orders a good trade is calculated upon this winter.

Yellow Pine by a portion of the trade seems to be considered as retaining quite an unsatisfactory position, but reports of an opposite character are less exceptional than heretofore, and there are dealers who indignantly deny that this division of the lumber trade is any worse than the rest. Prices are low, certainly, and there is no special vigor to the demand, but the stock retains favor for average consumption, and the cutting on rates is looked upon as about done with. Indeed, the movement for a combination among operators to which we were the first to call attention as progressing some weeks ago, is practically concluded, and the promise is for smoother sailing in the future.

Carolina Pine retains a firm market, with a good general demand, and the predictions that the cheapness of other woods would displace this class of stock have not been verified. Furthermore, the recent meetings of manufacturers and the agreement entered into in matters of supply and line of prices indicates that sellers feel every confidence in their advantages and are determined to stand out for them.

Hardwoods can at the best only be credited with a fairly active market for any description of stock, and in many instances we hear complaint of positive dull tone. The consumption of house trim for balance of the year it is thought can hardly extend beyond the completion of work now in hand, and for which provision has already been made. The furniture men may help somewhat, but it seems most likely they have about completed engagements for the supply of material most likely to be required. Dealers in consequence feel no great anxiety about adding materially to their accumulations, but there is some little trade to be found for first-class offerings of the staple grades, and on the prices reported few changes in line of quotations appear necessary.

GENERAL LUMBER NOTES.

GREAT BRITAIN.

The *Timber Trades Journal* as follows:

LIVERPOOL.

With reference to the Canadian imports, there has not been any further rise in the freight market. Owners of the regular liners from Montreal are still looking forward for a further rise in the quotations from Montreal for deals and similar goods. They are indicating 65s. per standard for the remainder of this month.

The principal importations now landing from Canada are of deals, by the regular liners.

GLASGOW.

Very few deals, it is still to be noted, are coming to hand per the regular weekly liners from Quebec and Montreal, though, as shown last week, this market has a good opening at present for additional supplies to a substantial amount, as stocks at present are exceptionally light. Everything points to rising prices as the season advances, freights being now higher, and stocks, both of log timber and deals, very moderate, while there is the prospect of a good demand continuing, as our wood-consuming industries are generally well employed. From the Clyde shipbuilding report for last month renewed inquiry was seen to have sprung up; the amount of new orders booked during the month being stated at 45,000 to 50,000 tons.

STATE.

The Albany *Argus* reports:

The market shows no change of importance as the result of the week, the general condition being practically the same as previously reported. As a whole, there is a fair trade doing, but the demand is rather irregular. The trade in pine continues pretty well spread out for all grades and sizes, but if there is anything doing especially well it is in the upper grades. Stocks on the market are quite full, with the exception of 1½-inch, while one or two other sizes are in moderate supply. Receipts during the week have been moderate. Trade in spruce has been scarcely up to the mark for the week, and not much lumber is coming forward. Hemlock continues quiet, while hardwoods are having a moderate trade. Shingles are doing fairly.

THE WEST.

The Northwestern *Lumberman* as follows:

Receipts during the week have been light. The winds have been adverse to incoming vessels, but that does not affect receipts as much as the disposition of the manufacturers to hold back their lumber for higher prices. It is said by some commission men that the yard dealers are now buying the larger portion of their lumber to be shaped up at the mills to suit special requirements. The dealers now want to even and fill up their stocks preparatory to going into winter quarters. The good demand that has prevailed for a month or more has broken up stocks and developed special calls for different sizes and lengths, so that dealers know what they want, and are trying to get such lumber as will satisfy it. So they negotiate with the commission men, the stuff is shaped up at the mills, and cargoes are forwarded directly to the yards without tying up at the market. Thus the commission men are really selling more lumber than appears at the sale docks.

Piece stuff has strengthened a little during the week. Cargoes that are shaped to suit the buyer have been sold at $10 a thousand within a few days. This is an indication that the weakest spot in the season has been passed. Now that trade has brightened up, and the yard men are seeking the market again, while freight rates have advanced, there is no further show this season for a decline. On the contrary the prospect is rather for an advance. It is probable that by next issue the bottom price of fair cargoes of piece stuff will be $10, with $10.25 for lots specially suited to the customer. Slim jims are quotable at $12 to $12.50 a thousand, and long wide joists at $14 for 22 and 24-foot lengths.

Coarse boards still drug a cargo where they predominate, but strips and boards running well to stock widths are in extra demand.

The following are from the Chicago *Timberman*:

Preparations are making which look as though lumbermen would make heavy demands upon the forests this winter. Throughout northern Michigan and Wisconsin camp equipments are going into the woods at a very rapid rate, supplies are being put in before the weather changes that lead to the belief that with plenty of men at command there will be an increased slaughter of pine trees in almost all sections of the northern woods.

The demand for labor for the woods work has already become very marked in certain localities and in some places it has even interfered with the mill work. With an eye to the main chance, workmen would prefer to accept berths for a winter in the woods rather than wait for about four or eight weeks, as the case may be, until the mills close down and then run their chance of getting as good jobs as are now offered them. Besides, it is a well-known fact that the farmers are employing more labor this fall by perhaps 20 per cent than last fall, and here is another rivalry for the loggers to contend with, and hence they are making drafts upon the mill employes to an unusual degree.

Here in the North the principal factor in the lumber trade is white pine, although large quantities of hardwoods, including yellow pine and cypress, are also handled. As was stated last week, the stock of lumber now on hand in Chicago is less than it has been at this season for the past ten years, with probabilities that the shortage will be greater on January 1st than it is now. And this state of affairs may be said to apply to all the great manufacturing and distributing centres of the North and Northwest. Marinette, Wis., and Menominee, Mich., are said to be the only points where the mills have not been seriously crippled for the past two or three months by the tardy arrival of logs, millions of which are to-day "hung up" on the various logging streams.

In ordinary years the mills, as a rule, carry over enough logs to enable them to start up and run for some weeks in the spring before the arrival of any new logs, but such is not the case this season. Logs have been cleaned up as they never were before, and the probabilities are that, with the exception of mills that are supplied by logging railroads, no considerable amount of sawing will be done until after the first of June, at least.

An Eastern buyer who was in the city this week and who has just returned from a trip through the hardwood belt of the South declares that this impression is a false one, particularly as applied to quarter-sawed oak. He says that the mills in the South have almost abandoned the practice of cutting quarter-sawed stock, and that there was not nearly as much of this class of lumber in pile as he had expected to find. It may be, therefore, that the Chicago yards will realize a good thing on quarter-sawed oak early the coming season. There is scarcely a dealer who did not stock up heavily in the spring, and as quarter-sawed oak has been moving slowly, they have abundant stocks now on hand.

With the number of mills that have stopped cutting quarter-sawed oak one would think that there would be a great deal more of plain-sawed lumber offered, but this is not the case. While plain-sawed oak is coming forward freely there is no particular surplus of dry stock, and in Wisconsin the price on red oak is as firm as ever. If the furniture trade should pick up this winter, as it ought to, there will be a ready market for all available stock, and it would be not at all surprising should a scarcity of oak develop before the end of the year.

In fact it is confidently predicted that there will be a marked scarcity of thick oak next spring. Very little thick oak has been cut this year, and as it requires some little time to dry this stock, with any demand at all it will not take long to exhaust the supply now in sight.

The Mississippi Valley *Lumberman* as follows:

Some of the saw mills favorably situated will be run this winter—more in all probability than have been operated in previous years. The owners will seize on the opportunity which has been created by the inability of the water mills to run during the past six weeks and pile up stock for the spring trade. If, however, the winter is as cold as some of the scientific as well as the unscientific weather prophets have promised it will be, there will not be a great amount of lumber manufactured at these winter mills. Inventive genius has been turned at different times in the direction of a process of thawing out logs—or overcoming the difficulties which present in sawing frozen logs—but not a great deal of success has thus far been achieved. The winter mills which have been able to command a good price for their timbers and bill stuff have generally proved profitable, but the weight of the evidence is against winter sawing in latitudes as far north as Minnesota and Wisconsin.

Stocks of lumber in Minneapolis are very complete—larger and fuller, probably, than at any point in the West. Lumber is being made at the rate of about 18,000,000 feet a week and being sold at the rate of about 10,000,000 a week. The sawing season is drawing to a close, however, but the dealers will go into the winter with exceptionally good stocks. This condition does not lessen their appreciation of the value of their holdings.

NAILS.—All hands are still grumbling and the market throughout is unsatisfactory. Even wire nails, notwithstanding a good export trade, in addition to the lion's share of home calls, do not secure a movement that is stimulating, and cut are considerably demoralized, with prices made to fit the negotiations immediately in hand. Threats of stopping production continue and that is all. We quote Cut at $1.50@1.60 per keg for car lots and $1.75@1.85 per keg for parcels from store, for iron, and add 5@10c. per keg for steel; Wire, $2.00@2.05 at mills, and 2.20@2.35 from store.

PAINTS, OILS, COLORS, ETC.—In pretty much every essential detail the market remains the same as last week. The volume of trade does not run full enough to create animation in any description of stock, and frequently operators may be heard expressing surprise over the moderation shown on part of buyers; yet it has been noticeable that some custom is duplicating orders of two or three weeks ago, and that is a fair indication of better consumption than jobbers and retailers had calculated upon. To meet the calls at present making there is a very good run of supplies, both in quantity and assortment available, and owners quite ready to negotiate. Indeed, in some instances a slight anxiety to realize is noticeable, which creates an unsettled tone on values and occasional quiet cutting. It is, however, claimed that on Leads the agreement line of valuation is closely adhered to for all pure pigment. Association Corroders' rates stand as follows: Lead in oil in kegs and dry lead in kegs, in lots of less than 500 lbs., 7½c. net; in lots of 500 lbs to 5 tons at one purchase, 7c.; 5 tons to 12 tons, one purchase, 5⅝c.; 12 tons and over, one purchase, 6¾c.; dry white lead in bbls. ½c. per lb. less than price in kegs. Lead in oil 12½ lb. in tin pails, add 1c.; in 25 and 50 lb. tin pails, add ½c.; and in 1 to 5 lb. tin cans, assorted (100 lbs. in case) add 2½c. per lb. to keg price. Terms on lots on 500 lbs. and over, note or acceptance at sixty days, or 2½ per cent. discount will be allowed for cash paid within fifteen days of invoice date. To make either of the above required quantities any assortment of packages of white lead, red lead and litharge may be counted. The above quotations are free on board cars or boat at corroding point. Linseed Oil has fair demand, with no further slashing rates of a serious character, but Western makers are eccentric and cannot resist the temptation to make an occasional cut. We quote at general range at 35@40c. for Western, and 40@56c. for City. Spirits Turpentine continues rater weak under the influence of a slow, indifferent demand. Holders, however, appear to have the supply very well under control, and they offer stocks with moderation in pretty much all cases. We quote at 37@38c. per gallon, according to quality, delivery, etc.

TAR AND PITCH.—For ordinary trade purposes there has been an average deal, but no large movement of stock, and the market without animation. Supplies are not abundant, but there is apparently enough of them to satisfy all present requirements. We quote Pitch at $1.70@1.75 per bbl.; Tar at $2.15@2.50, according to quantity, quality and delivery.

MISCELLANEOUS.

MISCELLANEOUS.

BUILDING MATERIAL PRICES

LUMBER.

Appended quotations are based almost wholly upon prices obtained for goods from first hands. Yard rates necessarily range much higher owing to the expenses attending sorting out and grading cargo and even car lots, besides which must be added the cost of handling and carrying until consumers are ready to invest. Terms of sale also prove important factors and, altogether, it is impossible to give a line of retail quotations thoroughly reliable in character.

SPRUCE—Eastern—special cargoes delivered N. Y.	$16 00 @	18 00
Random cargoes, narrow	12 00 @	13 00
Random cargoes, wide	13 50 @	15 00
PILING—Eastern—cargo rates:		
Ranging 30@40 per cent 12 inch butt, 35 to 40 ft average length	4 @	—
Ranging 45@50 per cent 12 inch butt, 35 to 40 ft average length	4¼ @	4½
Ranging 50@60 per cent One-half 12 inch butt, 38 to 40 ft average length	4¾ @	5
Two-thirds 12 inch butt, 38 to 42 ft average length	5½ @	6
Three-fourths 12 inch butt, 40 to 45 ft average length	5¾ @	6
All 12 inch butt and up, 40 to 45 ft average length	6 @	6¼
Piece stick, 40 feet each	4 00 @	—
do. 45	6 00 @	—
do. 50	8 00 @	—
do. 55	12 00 @	—
Inch spars, per inch	20 @	22
Scaffolding poles, each	60 @	1 00
Clothes poles, 45 to 65 feet, each	3 00 @	6 00
HEMLOCK:		
Penn. joist	12 00 @	12 50
do. boards	13 00 @	13 50
do. timber, 20 ft and under	12 50 @	13 00
do. do. 22 to 24 ft	13 00 @	13 50
do. do. 26 to 28 ft	13 50 @	14 00
do. do. 30 to 32 ft	14 00 @	15 50
do. do. 34 to 36 ft	15 50 @	16 00
do. do. 38 to 40 ft	16 50 @	17 50
WHITE PINE—Good uppers and select, 1 to 2 inch	40 00 @	48 00
Upper and select, 2½ to 4 inch	50 00 @	58 00
Shelving	26 00 @	31 00
Pickings, 1 inch	33 00 @	35 00
Cutting-up, 1 inch	25 00 @	28 00
Bracket plank	30 00 @	35 00
Dressing-boards	18 00 @	22 00
Box, inch	13 50 @	14 00
Box, thick	14 50 @	15 50
West India shippers	16 00 @	19 00
Rio Janeiro do.	20 00 @	21 00
River Plate do.	29 00 @	30 00
Australia do.	25 00 @	30 00
YELLOW PINE—Random cargoes delivered N. Y.	18 00 @	19 00
Ordered cargoes	19 50 @	21 00
Flooring	21 00 @	24 00
Step plank	26 00 @	28 00
Common siding	15 00 @	16 00
Heart face boards	24 00 @	28 00
Car orders	21 00 @	23 00
At Atlantic ports, f. o. b.	12 00 @	12 50
At Gulf ports, f. o. b.	11 50 @	12 50
North Caroline pine timber	13 50 @	15 00
do. flooring 1 inch	16 00 @	22 00
do. do. 1¼	16 50 @	22 50
do. do. 1½@2 inch	24 00 @	25 00
do Shipping culls or box	12 00 @	14 00
do Plain and mottled ½@1½ inch	18 50 @	25 50
Ash, white	36 00 @	43 00
Elm	20 00 @	22 50
Oak, plain	37 00 @	41 00
Oak, quarter sawed	52 00 @	55 00
Oak, quarter sawed, extra thick	56 00 @	60 00
Redwood	45 00 @	52 50
Maple, clear	28 00 @	33 00
Chestnut, clear	33 00 @	35 50
Cypress, clear	30 00 @	32 50
Black Walnut, good to choice	130 00 @	140 00
Black Walnut, ordinary to fair	100 00 @	120 00
Black Walnut, ⅝	78 00 @	83 00
Black Walnut, selected and seasoned	150 00 @	155 00
Black Walnut counters	110 00 @	150 00
Black Walnut, culls	35 00 @	40 00
Black Walnut, rejects	50 00 @	53 00
Cherry, wide	110 00 @	115 00
Cherry, good	85 00 @	100 00
Cherry, ordinary	65 00 @	80 00
Whitewood, inch	30 50 @	32 50
Whitewood, ⅝ inch	24 50 @	26 00
Whitewood, 1¼ to 2½ inch	32 00 @	34 00
Shingles, Pine, 16 inch, extra	2 75 @	3 10
do 18 inch, extra	4 10 @	4 80
do 18 inch, clear butt	2 90 @	3 10
do 16 inch, stocks	4 50 @	4 60
do 18 inch, stocks	5 30 @	5 40
Shingles, Cypress, 6x20	8 00 @	10 00
do larger sizes	11 00 @	16 00
do sawed	6 00 @	9 00
Cedar—Medium to large	6¼ @	7½
do. —Extra large	7¾ @	8
Mahogany—small	6½ @	7½
do —Medium	8 @	8½
do. —Large	9½ @	12
do. —Extra Large	12½ @	14

DEVOTED TO REAL ESTATE, BUILDING ARCHITECTURE, HOUSEHOLD DECORATION, BUSINESS AND THEMES OF GENERAL INTEREST

PRICE, PER YEAR IN ADVANCE, SIX DOLLARS.

Published every Saturday.

TELEPHONE - - - - CORTLANDT 1370.

Communications should be addressed to

C. W. SWEET, 14 & 16 Vesey St.

J. T. LINDSEY, Business Manager.

VOL. XLVIII OCTOBER 31, 1891. No. 1,233

Have you read the second number of THE ARCHITECTURAL RECORD *yet? Nobody interested in good building should be without it. Articles appear in this issue from the pens of such well-known writers on architecture as Prof. A. D. F. Hamlin, Barr Ferree and Montgomery Schuyler; the first of whom points out the "Difficulties of Modern Architecture;" the second discusses "What is Architecture?" and the third continues his critical account of the "Romanesque Revival in America." A paper by William J. Fryer, Jr., on "Skeleton Construction," others by Harry W. Desmond and Herbert D. Croly; a second part of Prof. Atchison's lecture on "Byzantine Architecture," and the regular departments complete a very interesting number. The magazine is, as usual, profusely illustrated, and in matter and appearance is fully equal to the first number. The publisher takes pleasure in announcing that the issue immediately following this one will be of unusual interest to architects and of great value to the general reader. Among the contributors will be Prof. E. A. Freeman, the English historian, G. Lindenthal, L. De Coppet Berg, Prof. Kerr and other authorities equally high.*

THE current number of the *North American Review* contains an article on the business prospects and business conditions of the United States that deserves the careful attention of everyone interested in their development. Mr. Charles S. Smith is a gentleman holding such intimate relations with several of our most important manufacturing industries, and his position keeps him so closely in touch with the business pulse that his opinions have a peculiar value. It is consequently more than usually interesting to note that he considers the trade of the country at the present time to be upon a sound conservative basis, without a trace of speculation. Some of the illustrations which he gives of the progress of our manufacturing industries are striking enough to take many of our readers by surprise. It seems that there is a larger aggregation of capital engaged in the production of textile fabrics than in any other manufacturing industry in the United States. The fifteen millions and a-half of cotton spindles represent a capital of $232,500,000, while the invested capital of the woolen, silk, and other mixed textile industries amount to $225,000,000 in addition. Of carpets we are the largest producers in the world, and in design, colors and quality our goods are quite equal to anything made in Europe of competing grades. In the manufacture of silk we are ahead both of England and Germany, and are second only to France. Lately we have been extending our foreign markets in many directions. For instance, American standard sheetings and drills have the preference in the Chinese market, being sold in competition with English and German-made goods, and always at better prices, because of their superior quality. Still more interesting is the fact that even in Great Britain's own dependencies American goods are finding favor, a prominent mill having 10,000 packages of standard sheetings and drills engaged for the African market. Furthermore it has been proved that America can successfully compete with Europe in the Oriental markets in the manufacture and sale of plain cotton goods, when the cost of labor of a piece of goods does not exceed 25 per cent of the total cost. The other facts mentioned by Mr. Smith respecting progress in the iron trade and allied industries have been more widely circulated, and it is unnecessary to repeat them here. The point, then, of Mr. Smith's illustration of the growing stability and diversity of our industries is that a country which is increasing its product and markets in the way that America is, and is doing so without running into feverish and inflated speculation will rapidly be possessed of so many and such varied resources that its commerce will stand on the amplest and surest basis possible. This fact of growth will tell on Wall Street in time, and while bonds and stocks may be dull for some months to come, the market will eventually be broadened and strengthened. With the business of the country prosperous, investment securities cannot long sell for cheap prices. The only possible source of trouble which Mr. Smith thinks that the future may bring forth is a depreciation of the standard of value due to the continued creation of silver money under the present law. On this complicated matter, however, Mr. Smith's opinion is no better than that of any other intelligent man. The law of last year provides for an increase of currency, just about sufficient to take the place of the national bank notes, which are being retired, and to meet the needs of our constantly increasing volume of business. While this is so the fear of any depreciation in the standard is an idle dream.

MESSRS. VERMILYE & CO. have allowed themselves to be interviewed on the subject of the second mortgage bonds which the Lake Erie & Western Railroad managers are attempting to issue; and state "that all the details in regard to the execution of the mortgage and the issue of the bonds have been examined and approved by their counsel, Stephen P. Nash." Is the investing public to understand that they and their counsel approve of the clear misuse of a proxy, and that, notwithstanding the indignation of stockholders, they will proceed with this business and offer the bonds to their clients at the risk of a litigation? We do not believe it. A reputation for care and conservatism must always be the indispensable capital of a recognized house of issue, and here is a case in which Wall Street is unanimous in condemnation of the directors, not only for their secret action, but for their artful suppression of it during nearly a year and a half. We append the opinion of legal counsel, upon which some of the opposing stockholders are acting, and we do not see that there can be any other side to the case. We give the opinion in full because we regard it as a lesson as to the legal duty of directors and their position before the law, as well as in morals, when soliciting proxies from their *cestuis qui* trust. Brokers and bankers who idly sign proxies for shares in their name, owned by clients, can read this opinion and take it to heart with great profit to themselves. This opinion will be found in the next two paragraphs.

"THE action at the stockholders' meeting at which a second mortgage of $5,000 per mile on all the property of the company was in form authorized was and is voidable; and the directors in carrying into effect the execution and delivery of said mortgage and the issuing of bonds secured thereby as provided at the meeting will commit a breach of legal duty to the stockholders, whose trustees they are. The facts, as we understand them, are these: The requisite vote authorizing in form the issuing of the new mortgage and mortgage bonds was given only by the aid of proxies held by directors of the company and solicited for the directors by the secretary of the company upon a notice stating the purpose of a meeting to be held in Bloomington, Ill., June 25th, 1890, but not stating in any mode which could convey to the person whose proxy was sought the slightest intimation that it was intended to impose an additional mortgage on the entire property, or that this was one of the purposes of the meeting. If such proxies had been requested by some third person, not a director or officer of the company, and not holding fiduciary relations to the persons whose proxies were asked for, then the persons who gave the proxies would have done so at their own risk as to the use to which they would be put; but in the present case the persons who, by an artfully veiled request, obtained the proxies, intending at the time to use them for the purpose of reorganizing the financial plan of the corporation, were directors who stood as the trustees of the very persons from whom they sought the proxies. Their position was a position of vantage and of fiduciary relations. They were bound not merely to tell no falsehood as an inducement to the stockholders to give their proxies, but they were bound affirmatively to disclose to the stockholders every material fact within their knowledge which could reasonably be expected, according to the judgment of ordinary minds, to influence the stockholders in determining whether they should send the proxies or not.

"THERE can be no question that the proposition to create an indebtedness by way of a specific lien ahead of the interest of the stockholders amounting to an addition of 50 per cent to the existing mortgage debt of the company was a subject quite material to be considered by every stockholder in determining whether he should or should not give his proxy at a meeting where that question was to come up. The directors took the proxies with the concealed intention of using them for this very purpose without in any way informing the stockholders that they were to be used for that purpose. The notice spoke only of issuing bonds. A bond is a mere evidence of debt, wholly different from a mortgage. Why did the notice make no mention of the proposed second mortgage? Not only did the notice and proxy make no reference to any mortgage, but even after the action had been taken at the meeting, the management suppressed the fact that it had been taken, and no report has ever yet been made which informs the stockholders that any new obligation or lien by way of a mortgage has been created ahead of their interest. The directors obtaining proxies by such concealment of facts are personally liable for breach of trust toward their beneficiaries and can be held for any loss which might result to the stockholders because of action taken in that manner. In addition, the action itself is voidable in the discretion of the stockholders who were imposed upon: and people negotiating or in any manner acquiring any interest in the securities thus issued, after learning in any way of these facts, acquire only a voidable security, subject to all the infirmities resulting from the constructive fraud, not to say actual fraud, of the proceedings from which the securities derived their existence. The fundamental distinction which lies at the basis of this matter is that a person holding fiduciary relations to another cannot deal with him at arms length or leave the *cestuis qui* trust to look out for himself and protect himself against the consequence of his own acts; but it is the duty of the trustees to protect the *cestuis qui* trust from the consequences of his own acts and to lay before him every circumstance known to the trustees which could reasonably influence him in the action which he would take. We desire to state that there is an additional circumstance which, unexplained, tends to cast suspicion upon the manipulation of the meeting, viz.: that although it was known to the directors holding the proxies that nearly all the stockholders resided at a distance in States other than that where the meeting was held, and that it must be very inconvenient for them to remain over an adjournment of three days and very unlikely that any not informed of the proposed mortgage would remain to oppose it, nevertheless the meeting was adjourned three days and action was only taken at the adjourned meeting."

Assessments on Riparian Property.

WE have already called attention to the light assessments on property along the water front. We have seen that in the 8th Ward, on the North River, at the point where the heaviest traffic of the port, and it may be said also of the continent, concentrates, $5,000 a lot, with such improvements as the owner finds it profitable to make, is a common assessment. On the East River, between Corlears Hook and the bridge, the situation is still worse. Along that section assessments commonly run as low as $3,500 a lot, and many lots with their buildings are assessed below $2,000. This seems incredible; but the records may be seen in the offices of the Commissioners of Assessment if any reader doubts the statement. Thirty years ago, before nearly all the traffic in heavy goods had gone to Brooklyn, the property along the East River had some value. But it is continually declining, and the time seems coming when the primeval swamps that once covered the neighborhood might be profitably restored.

We propose now beginning at the lower part of the city to give by wards the assessed value of all the riparian property that lies between Corlears street on the East River and the foot of 14th street on the North River. Those of our readers who are musical and understand thorough bass—we presume there are many—will have no difficulty in remembering the succession of wards on the North River. They are 1st, 3d, 5th and 8th, the perfect chords of octave, it will be seen. To these add the 9th, and we reach the foot of 14th street. On the East River the steps are not so musical; but as the numbers are composed mainly of the discords these too should be easily remembered. They are 1st, 2d, 4th, 5th and 7th.

Look first at the total assessment for the 1st Ward. This ward straddles the city and fronts upon both rivers, extending from the foot of Maiden lane on the East Side to the foot of Liberty street on the West Side. It has, therefore, a longer stretch of riparian lands than any other of the wards to be considered. But the total value of its magnificent distances, divided among nearly a hundred riparian land-holders, is only $2,724,500. Single building sites in other portions of the ward may not have sold for more money, but the site of the Equitable Building, supposing it to be vacant, could not be obtained for much less.

Turn now to the 2d Ward, also on the East River, and see a still more surprising exhibit. This ward extends from Maiden lane to Peck slip. Yet the total assessment on the entire riparian property of the ward is only $563,000, not nearly enough to build a first-class office building on Broadway, to say nothing of the purchase money for the site.

Perhaps the West Side can make a better showing. We will leave the East Side, then, for the moment, and find the 3d Ward on the North River. It extends from Liberty street to Reade street, and its riparian property lies just adjacent to the rich grocery district. It has several tributary ferries also, the Liberty street ferry, the Cortlandt street ferry, the Barclay street ferry, the Pavonia ferry, and the West Shore ferry. There may be other ferries that we wot not of; but these five should be sufficient to make the property valuable if it has any life either natural or galvanic. Do we find it valuable? It has a total assessed valuation of $1,813,500. This is hardly enough to encourage us to remain on the shores of the North River, and we will go over to the 4th Ward on the other side of the town.

This ward extends along the East River from Peck slip to Catharine street, not a very long stretch; and we shall not expect to find a mint of money invested along shore. We shall certainly be disappointed if we go with any such expectations. A total of $529,750 covers all the riparian property in the 4th Ward; and this makes us feel like taking another trip across town in search of some other philosopher's stone. Perhaps we shall find it in the 5th Ward.

But no, it is not here either. The 5th Ward has heaps of riparian property. It stretches all the way from Reade street to Canal street, and it is bisected by one of the much traveled ferries of the Pennsylvania Railroad. Yet all that the property is worth according to the assessors is $1,622,500, rather a slender showing for such a prolonged stretch of water front.

It is something of a pity that we undertook to follow the wards in their numerical order, for it compels us to alternate painfully across town without meeting with any adequate reward; but we will finish now with the East Side by going over to the 7th Ward. It extends from Catharine to Corlears street. This is a long ward along the water front, almost a mile long in the view of the pedestrian, but probably a little less as a matter of fact. Its assessment records are long, however. They cover seven pages in the commissioners' books, and when the figures are all footed up they amount to the enormous total of $1,450,500. Think of the amount. Nearly a mile of water front property in a long since improved section of the commercial metropolis of the new world for $1,450,500. Going, going, gone! But, then, this is the section where an improved lot is rated at less than $2,000. Let us go over to the West Side again, and finish up this whole wretched business.

But look out for another slap in the face directly. The 8th Ward extends from the foot of Canal street to the foot of Houston street and its riparian lands fronting on the improved section of West street lie just opposite some of the piers of the great ocean steamship lines. But that is of no consequence. It is all assessed at $801,000.

Follow the injunction of the police, then, and move on. The 9th Ward lies just above, and perhaps it will make a better showing. But the facts are even worse. The riparian lands extend from Houston street to 14th, more than a mile on West street and 13th avenue, and as nearly as the figures can be gleaned from the assessment records, somewhat confused on account of the prolongation of West street away from the river, the total is $991,500. It will not vary from those figures more than a few thousand either way.

These are the figures that represent the assessed value of the riparian property along nearly all the improved water front in the city. It would be too great a tax on patience to attempt to add together the different ward totals to find a general total. The reader may do that if he sees fit. It is total enough to know that all the riparian lands with their improvements between Houston street and 14th street are assessed at less than a million. The Erie Basin, in Brooklyn, is worth nearly half as much money as all the riparian property between Corlears Hook and 14th street.

IT is, doubtless, very unfortunate that New York will have only a $2,000,000 Tilden Library instead of one which would cost $5,000,000 or $6,000,000, but other consequences still less beneficial to the public will follow from the decision of the Court of Appeals in the matter of the Tilden will. Rich men who wish to leave their wealth so that the public will obtain the advantage thereof are a class distinctly to be encouraged, whereas the tendency of all the recent court decisions has been to make it about as difficult as possible for a millionaire to will his money to anybody but the heirs-at-law. Apparently the only way in which such fortunate people can distribute their accumulations in public benefactions is to make the grant while living, for although a part of the money may be used for the purpose intended by the testator, as in the Fayerweather and this Tilden case, still that this should be so seems to be due more to generosity on the part of the next of kin than to the courts or to the law. If we may judge merely by the number of examples of millionaires contributing to public benefactions during their lifetime, the conclusion might be drawn that the generous rich are taking this lesson to heart. It is not, however, enough to judge simply by the amount of these gratuities. More than likely the number of the rich are increasing just as fast or faster, and the proportion which the public benefactors bear to the total is no greater than it ever was. And of all of this class who are disposed to share their wealth with the public, it is not a very large percentage that are willing to make the division during their lifetime. After their death the next of kin and the courts, following Bacon, seem to believe that the deceased are giving away the property of somebody else. The present decision brings home forcibly the very arbitrary character that frequently attaches to opinions even of the highest courts. The validity of the trust created by Mr. Tilden was passed upon by the lower courts and a number of different decisions rendered. On the final appeal the trust was declared invalid by four judges, the three others in the division writing a minority opinion. With every disposition to admit the conscience and ability of the court, a layman cannot but feel that when a decision runs as "close" as this, the law is often as much a matter of chance as it is of wisdom. It would be difficult to suggest feasible improvements to our system of courts designed to reduce this arbitrariness to the lowest possible point; our system is already sufficient to this purpose. But in spite of the best system, it seems to be impossible to sift out the merely personal and hap-hazard element in judicial opinions. This last example is most striking and most unfortunate.

CHICAGO.

I spoke in my last letter of the dense, crass ignorance of the New Yorker about Chicago and its affairs. One of the largest owners of real estate here, who is not long back from Europe, said, when speaking of the subject: "Why, sir, though it might be an exaggeration to say that London knows more about Chicago than New York does, it wouldn't be to say it knows as much, and I found people in the British capital took a far more intelligent interest in our affairs than our Eastern countrymen do. The best article I ever read about Chicago appeared lately (October 5th) in the London *Times*." There is certainly no doubt of this fact: there is more bitterness, more of a feeling of estrangement so far as New York is concerned in this city than has ever existed in ordinary times in this country in the relationship of one city to another. Now, I speak of this matter not to touch upon the World's Fair squabble, but to suggest that probably the New Yorkers ignorance of Chicago may have something to do with the fact that relatively so little New York capital is invested here in real estate; although I don't think upon searching investigation it could be shown that outside of the metropolis there is another city where real estate is a better security or yields larger returns. Quite true, my dear sir, the future is always pretty extensively discounted in Chicago, and "present values" usually include a not illiberal draft upon future probabilities, but then there is no city in the country where the "future" is so near, if one may say so, and so certain as in Chicago. The destiny of this city is writ large and legibly and has a real *cash* value. At the same time the "outsider" needs to make investments here with caution. There is more real estate in and around Chicago the chief value of which lies in the possibility of selling it than in and around any other large city. The prairie is full of it. An intending investor should certainly protect and insure himself by transacting his business through some one of the many reputable and well-established brokers in this city. This class of men rank well with those in the metropolis. As a rule their offices are larger, in some particulars better equipped, and the staff employed is generally more numerous. The business they do, too, is more obvious, if it is not as large; but as the rate of commission here is 2½ per cent for city property and 5 per cent for country it should be profitable. At present, however, times are dull—decidedly so. Business during the past summer was particularly stagnant, and it is said not a few of the large offices were run at a considerable loss. Since the opening of fall there has been some increase in activity, but the complaint of dullness is still quite general, and a marked revival cannot be looked for this year. Little, very little is doing in high-priced property, the bulk of transactions apparently being for small priced lots—say from $500 to $1,000 a piece—for improvement and occupation.

For some time past the greatest activity has been in the direction of "sub-dividing"—as it is called here—converting acre property into lots. What has been done in this direction is simply marvelous. New York is "not in it" at this business. Some of the enterprises, of course, have been of an extremely cheap and flimsy character, but a number are of the most solid and substantial kind and are attempts at town-making beyond anything dreamed of in the East. Roswell P. Flower and W. F. Havemeyer are among the New Yorkers interested in these projects. The names of these "parks" and "sub-divisions," with statements about their advantages and other more mercenary information, meet the eye on colossal bill-boards all over the city and beyond it, as well as in the newspapers; though in the latter direction there has been a very marked decline lately, as is readily observable in going through a file of any representative "daily"—the *Tribune*, for instance. Kenilworth, Edgewater, Buena Park, Argyle Park, Rodger's Park, Birchwood Park, Riverside Park, Harvey, Grossdale, Humboldt Park Sub-division, Sheridan Drive Sub-division, University Sub-division—it's impossible to state a tenth of them—these are the names that meet one everywhere—good and bad. It is impossible for an outsider to appraise the value of each or make a selection. Take Kenilworth, for example—there are other places one might choose quite as well—its existence is due, I understand, to the enterprise of Joseph Sears, of the Fairbanks firm, the well-known lard manufacturers. It is located some forty-five minutes or so from the city on the Chicago & Northwestern R. R., northward on the lake side. They say over $800,000 has been expended in "laying out" the place, and I don't doubt it. The land there is well wooded, and the streets have been made on the right-angle plan—wide streets, well macadamized, with heavy granolithic pavements, flanked by trees and strips of lawn. The gutters, too, are of stone, and the place is sewered and provided with its own complete water and gas-works. The improvements so far made are few, though the houses built or building are of a very high class and of excellent design; and I mention this place to give you some hint of the big plan upon which some of these "sub-divisions" are carried out. The finest places of the kind in Long Island or in New Jersey are quite second-rate and "countryfied" compared with them.

But—we mustn't omit this "but"—how this sub-dividing, more particularly of the cheaper kind, has been overdone! One hesitates to use "can't" in reference to Chicago—so much has been accomplished here; the growth, the solid durable growth of the city has been so marvelous. But in the city itself, and these sub-divisions far and near, there is provision for a population of four or five millions, a metropolis as big as London.

This "sub-dividing" is no new thing. Over twenty years ago immense plans of the same nature were carried out, involving hundreds of thousands of dollars. The hard times of the early "seventies" came, and the few old heads here have still a decent respect for the experience. The grass to-day grows over not a few of the projects. All this doesn't go to say "hands off," but "caution." There is no doubt that in many of these "sub-divisions" much money will be legitimately made, the city is so rapidly reaching out in all directions. There are good and promising opportunities here for the New York investor—but, as said before, he will need the advice of the best and most solid brokers. This, of course, would be equally true of New York. The market is full of good things and bad, and it's easy enough to strike the latter.

An effort is making here just now to vitalize the Real Estate Board and convert it into an institution similar to the Liberty Street Exchange. So far auction sales of realty have not met with success in Chicago. The movement to alter this state of affairs has a good backing and the following circular may be of interest to the readers of THE RECORD AND GUIDE:

THE CHICAGO REAL ESTATE BOARD.

CHICAGO, October 21, 1891.

The committee appointed by the board met at the board rooms this afternoon "to take such action as is necessary to have stands placed in the board rooms to be rented to members of the board for the purpose of selling real estate at auction and to adopt necessary rules and regulations for the governing of those auction sales at the daily call."

The following communication was received:

To the Call Board Committee of the Chicago Real Estate Board:

GENTLEMEN—We, the undersigned members of the Chicago Real Estate Board, hereby agree to rent stands in the board rooms to hold auction sales of good real estate that must be sold at once. The rent of the stands not to exceed $ 00 per year for five years. The choice of stands to be settled by selling them at auction, the rules and regulations of the Call Board Committee to govern such sales. Respectfully,

CREMIN & BRENAN,	CHAS. A. SEYMOUR & CO.,
E. A. CUMMINGS & CO.,	DUNLAP, SMITH & CO.,
J. C. MAGILL & CO.,	SAMUEL E. GROSS,
BARNES & PARISH,	J. H. VAN VLISSINGEN & BRO.
W. A. MERIGOLD & CO.,	

Mr. John F. Cremin stated that this petition was obtained in about sixty minutes, and that he knew there were other members who would desire to sign it.

The general expression of the committee was that if auction sales were established they should be confined strictly to first-class property, and any property to be sold would have to first be approved by a committee of the board appointed for that purpose.

On motion it was *Resolved*,

1st. That the committee communicate with the "New York Exchange and Auction Room (Lim.)," and other similar bodies in this country, in order to more fully acquaint ourselves with their methods of procedure in sales of real estate by auction.

2d. That the lease of the present board rooms be examined and if the lease permits the removal of the board from its present quarters the cost of more suitable rooms on the first floor be ascertained and reported to the board.

3d. That the members of the board be communicated with to ascertain how many would desire to rent stands in addition to those already heard from.

The committee will at once ascertain as fully as may be all that can be learned from the different exchanges and boards and communicate it to the members of our board.

The "Call Board Committee," in procuring the signatures of the Bar to the petition for the holding of judicial sales at our board rooms, have met with but one objection, viz: That our board rooms should be on the first floor, and while this has not prevented the petition from being almost universally signed we are of the opinion that the time has come when our board rooms should be on the ground floor.

The names signed to the petition calling for auctioneer stalls at the board rooms, show that some of our strongest members are in favor of such a move, which would be one of the most important ever made by our board, and your committee earnestly desires that every member of the board having suggestions or advice should at once make the same in writing to your committee to the end that our report be of such a character as will meet your approval.

The lease of our present board rooms runs about 2½ years. The president of the board is of the opinion, however, that an equitable release can be obtained should the board desire to go elsewhere. Parties knowing of a central location near the Court House, first floor, room of proper size, would oblige by giving us any information they may have.

The president and secretary of the board attended this meeting.

We earnestly request every member of the board to give this matter his attention and to advise with or write to the committee his views on the subject.

C. L. HAMMOND,
Chairman.
JOHN F. CREMIN,
NELSON THOMASSON,
C. L. [illegible]ONNEY,
FRANK M. ELLIOT,
CHARLES E. RAND,
} Committee.

By the way, the framers of the new building law for New York City, to be presented to the Legislature early in the next session, should visit this city apropos of that part of the law which deals with skeleton construction. This new system of building is in a much higher state of development here than it is in New York. This method of construction is followed uncompromisingly here, and architects smile at the New Yorkers' timidity in adopting it, and particularly at the adherence in the East to cast-iron for the vertical support. Wrought iron or steel is used here exclusively. W. J. Fryer's article on "Skeleton Construction" in the *Architectural Record* has been read with great interest in Chicago and has been much commented upon. "But," the question is asked, "why the preference for cast-iron. It is not anything like so scientific a material as steel or wrought-iron. It is much more uncertain than these are, cannot be tested so perfectly, and as to the talk about deterioration through rust, we have taken up steel rails from the foundations of some of our buildings and find them after eight years in a condition as sound as the day they were put down." Architects here will not allow the validity of the suspicion that rust might attack the vertical columns inclosed in the brick-work, for the practice here is to encase the iron supports in water-tight fire-proof material and then in the brick-work. As the next building law is to come "to stay" the experience of Chicago architects and builders in a matter of the first importance should not be overlooked. H. W. D.

City Estimates for 1892.

The provisional estimates for expenditures for the city departments for 1892 are given below, the Board of Estimate and Apportionment having finished its work this week. One of the important items of increase is in the Street Cleaning Department, which is allowed $394,290 more than for the current year. The fund for street and park openings is more than doubled, while the sum under the head of "Miscellaneous" is nearly quadrupled. The Board of Education gets $179,289 more, and the Police Department $241,226. There is a large decrease for State taxes and smaller decreases in other departments. The allowances for 1892, compared with the final appropriations for 1891, are as follows:

	Finals for 1891.	Provisional for 1892.
The Mayoralty	$25,000 00	$25,000 00
The Common Council	76,800 00	76,800 00
The Finance Department	297,500 00	298,500 00
State taxes	3,050,630 47	2,898,304 91
Interest on the city debt	5,151,908 41	5,140,817 19
Redemption of the principal of the city debt	1,307,598 97	1,175,428 36
Armories and drill rooms—rents	42,050 00	39,050 00
Rents	178,729 00	184,559 50
Judgments	750,000 00	125,000 00
The Law Department	199,650 00	205,000 00
The Department of Public Works	3,124,470 00	3,101,176 00
The Department of Public Parks	931,500 00	963,150 00
The Department of Public Charities and Correction	2,166,287 00	2,255,525 00
The Health Department	419,400 00	437,388 00
The Police Department	4,777,575 38	5,018,801 65
The Department of Street Cleaning	1,584,250 00	1,978,540 00
The Fire Department	2,145,568 00	2,296,282 00
The Department of Taxes and Assessments	117,320 00	117,420 00
The Board of Education	4,267,367 00	4,446,656 64
College of the City of New York	147,000 00	147,000 00
The Normal College	125,000 00	125,000 00
Advertising, printing, stationery and blank books	247,300 00	254,200 00
Municipal service Examining Boards	25,000 00	25,000 00
Coroners—salaries and expenses	52,500 00	52,500 00
Commissioners of Accounts	27,500 00	32,500 00
The Sheriff	122,232 00	119,252 00
The Register	135,500 00	130,250 00
Bureau of Elections	439,300 00	411,300 00
Preservation of Public Records	45,030 00	45,930 00
Miscellaneous	183,816 10	703,726 68
Fund for street and park openings	215,508 16	451,508 00
Salaries, city courts	388,700 00	383,700 00
Salaries, Judiciary	1,083,406 91	1,020,058 00
Charitable institutions	1,246,225 87	1,261,216 10
Department of the 23d and 24th Wards	260,200 00	308,700 00
Total	$35,960,891 22	$35,905,212 03
Deduct general fund	2,800,000 00	2,750,000 00
Total	$33,160,891 22	$33,155,212 03

Organizing a Lumber Trust.

For some time past there have been rumors of the organization of a number of prominent yellow pine dealers into a single company. It is now given out that such a combination has been effected, under the name of "The Yellow Pine Company," with eight prominent firms comprised in its membership. These firms retain most of the stock, and offer, it is officially stated, but $500,000 of the preferred stock for subscription by the outside public, taking the remaining $2,000,000 themselves. THE RECORD AND GUIDE is enabled to publish the circular issued, which gives the particulars. This circular reads as follows:

THE YELLOW PINE COMPANY.

Capital stock, $2,500,000, divided as follows: $1,000,000. Preferred cumulative 8 per cent stock, 10,000 shares of $100 each, dividends payable semi-annually, May 1st and November 1st each year. $1,500,000. Common stock, 15,000 shares of $100 each.

The Yellow Pine Company has been formed to take over the entire wholesale and retail business in yellow pine timber and lumber, transacted heretofore in New York City, Brooklyn, Hoboken and Jersey City by the following firms: South Brooklyn Saw Mill Co., Chas. L. Bucki & Co., E. W. McClave & Co., A. T. Decker & Co., C. W. Wilson, Rapp & Johnson Lumber Co., A. B. Johnson & Co., W. A. Parke & Co. The aggregate business of the above-named vendors netted annual profits upon sales of 78 millions of feet of timber and lumber of $215,000; eight per cent dividend on $1,000,000 preferred stock, $80,000, leaving actual earnings applicable to common stock 9 per cent, $135,000.

To these earnings will be added a further amount available as income upon the common stock from the following sources: 1st. It is contemplated to close up at least two yards at an estimated annual saving of at least $30,000. 2d. The entire business territory now covered by the several parties will be divided into distributing districts, so that the expense of delivery will be materially lessened, saving yearly $30,000. 3d. By maintaining uniform prices, we eliminate the loss now caused each other by cutting prices, and as such uniformity will be based upon actual cost of manufacture and delivery, we estimate a saving of fully $50,000. 4th. Owing to their being no need of a duplication of stock by the different parties, a cost of carrying such needless stock can be saved, as well as the interest charged on same, amounting each year to fully $30,000. 5th. A general saving on the cost of managing the business as against our present expense for this purpose, such as unneeded clerk hire, salesmen, etc., $25,000. Total estimate of saving, $165,000

The preferred stock to the amount of $500,000 is offered to subscribers at par. The balance of the preferred stock, $500,000 and all of the $1,500,000 common stock of the company is taken by the vendors.

Management.—The business of the Yellow Pine Company will be managed by the vendors, all of whom have been actively engaged in the business for many years, and have agreed to give their services to the company for a period of five years. As they are the owners of one-half of the preferred stock, and the entire issue of the common stock, it is a guarantee that the affairs of the company will be managed judiciously and economically. Subscriptions for any part of $500,000 of preferred stock will be received in the Atlantic Trust Company up to and including November 1st, 1891, said subscription payable as follows: 25 per cent payable on November 1st; 25 per cent payable on November 15th; 50 per cent payable on January 2d, 1892.

The aggregate value of plants, including stock on hand, mills, stable equipment, office, machinery, tools, etc., amounts to $750,000; cash, $250,000; total, $1,000,000. This company has no mortgage or debts of any name or nature. Respectfully, C. L. Bucki, C. K. Buckley and E. W. McClave, committee.

The above circular is of considerable interest to the lumber trade, as showing the status of the business at the present time.

It is understood that the South Brooklyn Saw Mill Company is the only one in the organization about whose co-operation doubt exists. This is due to the fact that the company must obtain the consent of owners of two-thirds of the stock. Vice president C. K. Buckley stated that up to Thursday assents had been obtained from the majority of stockholders, but not two-thirds, and that it was possible that the company would not join the combination definitely unless the stockholders favored it unanimously.

REPORTED WHITE PINE LUMBER COMBINATION.

A report reached THE RECORD AND GUIDE that a combination was also on foot of dealers in export white pine lumber, the main object of which was to advance the prices of shipping grades of such lumber, and the members of which were to forfeit a considerable sum should they break faith with the combination. The names of the firms mentioned were: The Export Lumber Co.; Chas. E. Rogers & Co.; the Bullmer Lumber Co.; Z. Bergen, and the South Brooklyn Saw Mill Co.

A member of one of the above firms said: "There is no foundation for the report. Such a combine would be in violation of the law, and no forfeit could be legally enforced. Besides which there would be no chance of maintaining artificial prices. It is well known in the trade that the firms named have an agreement not to cut each other's prices below a reasonable mark, but no combine has been arranged upon.

Rapid Transit Commission.

At their meeting yesterday the Commission prepared its applications to the Park Department and to the Commissioner of Street Improvements of the 23d and 24th Wards for their consents respectively to the occupancy of the parks and streets that are by law under their control. This is required by the Rapid Transit Act, in addition to the consents of the Mayor and Board of Aldermen, to assure the consent of all the "municipal authorities."

William N. Amory, who has become familiar with the work through previous experiences of a similar character, has been put in charge of the task of securing the consents of abutting property-owners. He said yesterday that the books and blanks were nearly ready for the beginning of the canvassing, and he expected to get to work on the canvassing by next Wednesday.

Meeting of the Mechanics' and Traders' Exchange.

A special meeting of the Exchange was held at its rooms on Tuesday 27th inst.

Wm. C. Smith, the president, presided and Stephen M. Wright acted as secretary.

The meeting was held to provide for the holding of regular meetings whenever they would occur on a legal holiday, at some other date. The following amendment to the by-laws was adopted:

"But should the date of the annual or any quarterly meeting fall on a legal holiday, or a day set apart for public observances of any kind, then and in such case the meeting shall be held on the Tuesday following."

It has been evident for some time that the long hours on which the Exchange rooms were opened defeated the very purpose for which an Exchange is created—that of affording a convenient meeting place for those in a similar line of business, where they can usually be found—therefore the following resolution, which already had been approved by the Board of Managers, was unanimously adopted by the Exchange:

"*Whereas*, The Exchange rooms are now daily open to members from 9 o'clock, A. M., until 4 o'clock, P. M., a period too long to be advantageous to those who are accustomed to attend thereat for the purpose of business; and

"*Whereas*, It is believed that by shortening the hours the best interests of all will be served and the objects of the Exchange will be more nearly attained; therefore, be it

"*Resolved*, That it be recommended to the Exchange, for such action as a majority may deem advisable, that the Exchange rooms be opened each secular day (legal holidays excepted) from 12 o'clock, noon, until 3 o'clock, P. M."

The New Harlem Bridge.

At a special meeting held yesterday the Board of Street Opening and Improvement directed the Corporation Counsel to begin condemnation proceedings of land for approaches to the bridge of the New York & Northern Railroad across the Harlem River at 8th avenue and 155th street.

Obituary.

William Field, one of the oldest architects in New York City, died on Monday in the Seney Hospital, Brooklyn, of heart and kidney troubles. Mr. Field was born in Charlestown, Mass., in 1812, and was educated at Roxbury, removing later to Boston, where he became a builder. He removed to New York 54 years ago, and opened an office in 1846 in the Merchants' Exchange for the practice of architecture. Among the buildings which he designed are the Buckingham Hotel, the "Argyle" Hotel and cottages at Babylon, L. I., the Brooklyn Atheneum, the Orient Hotel, Manhattan Beach, and numerous other buildings. The funeral services took place at the Gates Avenue Unitarian Church, Brooklyn. Wm. Field, Jr., a son of the deceased, who was in partnership with his father, will continue the business.

New Incorporation.

The New York Land and Improvement Company filed a certificate of incorporation in the County Clerk's office on October 26th, for the purpose of purchasing and improving real estate in Westchester County, New York. The capital stock is $30,000, divided into 300 shares of $100 each. The names of the directors are Thomas C. O'Connor, George McH. Sandrock and seven others.

Real Estate Exchange Matters.

Considerable indignation has been aroused among members of the Real Estate Exchange by the circulation of a paper addressed to the "Taxpayers by the Real Estate Interests of New York," and advising the recipient to vote for the candidates of one of the principal political parties. The circular is signed by four members of the Real Estate Exchange, and its similarity in type and form to circulars previously issued by the Exchange led many of the members to believe that it emanated from that body, and, as it was addressed to all the members of the Exchange, as well as to others, it caused quite a flurry of excitement. The circular, of course, does not come from the Exchange, which is strictly a non-partisan body of business men, belonging to both of the great political parties. It carries with it only the influence of the gentlemen whose names are signed to it and represents in no way the Exchange or its Board of Directors.

At Tuesday's sale of stocks, forty shares of the Real Estate Exchange stock were sold at 102. This is the first Exchange stock that has been sold at auction for some time. Several attempts have been made to dispose of it at auction, but in every case it was bid in by the owners. The last quotation previous to that of Tuesday was 114, a price obtained several months ago.

James R. Booth has been proposed for membership by W. J. Van Pelt.

The new electric light plant which is now being placed in the Auction Room will be ready for use on Monday. The room is to be lighted by 150 Edison incandescent lamps. One hundred of these lamps will be arranged round the room just above the auctioneer's stands, while the remaining fifty will constitute one large light to be placed in the centre of the ceiling.

Personal

Charles E. Loud, a member of the Boston Real Estate Exchange, has been in New York during the past week examining into the workings of the Real Estate Exchange of this city. He expresses himself as much pleased with what he has seen and he goes back to Boston with a number of new ideas which he will endeavor to have his fellow-members incorporate into the local institution. Mr. Loud says that speculation in real estate in Boston is not near so general as it appears to be in this city, and that consequently the number of brokers and agents is comparatively not near so large as it is in New York. He says, too, that the revenue from auction sales held in the Exchange is very small, principally because the topography of Boston makes it an easy matter to hold sales on the premises.

Candidate Isaacs.

Myer S. Isaacs, the well-known lawyer, of the firm of M. S. & I. S. Isaacs, of the Boreel Building, has been nominated by the Republican and County Democratic organizations for Superior Court Judge. Mr. Isaacs is known in real estate circles as an able real estate lawyer, and has been a lecturer on real estate law subjects at the College of the City of New York. He has been for several years a director of the Real Estate Exchange, having also held the office of vice-president. His qualifications for the important office for which he is a candidate are conceded by friends and opponents alike.

Special Notice.

Fine Printing of All Kinds.

THE WEST SIDE INDEX.

Real Estate Department.

The real estate market has been even quieter this week than last, if the number of sales actually consummated represents to any extent the business that has been done. And unfortunately there are few indications that there is any great activity below the surface, any news being suppressed. The market is dull—very dull, and it will remain so until a remedy is applied. That this remedy lies in adopting the view so frequently advanced in this column of late, that owners must make concessions from present figures, real estate men are agreed. High prices is the main factor in the dullness at the present time, and if owners desire to dispose of their holdings they must recognize this fact, and it will be well for them to take the initiative and not be forced from their position by a market that has in it no elements of speculation or boom, and that is in the highest sense reasonable. The advantages of a section must be very apparent and its future prospects very bright, and very sure indeed for the present purchasers to take them into account at all. Unless they can see for themselves, and without any effort either, that all that is said of and promised for a property is true they will refuse to consider all the talk in the world. The present buying class does not expect to secure any very decided bargains, everything is too healthy for that. But they do not intend, on the other hand, to pay fancy prices such as are being asked in too many, in fact in nearly all, sections of New York to-day. As soon as owners recognize this, as soon as they see that the present real estate market is about as devoid of the speculative feeling as it is possible to be, they may come down in their present figures—figures that are suited only to a market and a season that are of the typical "boom" kind. And the discouraging part of this quiet market is that it is not entirely devoid of buyers. There are any number of men earnest in their intention to purchase when they can secure anything that is reasonable. These bona fide buyers commence negotiations in good faith and they offer sometimes prices that are really above the market value, but they nevertheless fail to close with holders, until now it is the rule and not the exception for brokers to get both parties very close together and then to have the sale fall through because of the obstinacy of both of them. Of course we are speaking now of buyers and sellers who are in earnest and not of that large floating class that is always going to invest and never does so. There are, of course, other factors in the present dullness, such as temporary tightness in the money market and the excitement incident to the coming election, but these are really small matters, for money is not so hard to borrow that when a good piece of property is to be had at reasonable figures the money cannot be had, and no one who knows the real estate operators of New York believes for an instant that their political preferences would interfere to any great extent with a successful business deal. And so when the matter is sifted down to the bottom and after all the facts have been taken into consideration we find that the trouble lies mainly with the owners who for a year or more have maintained prices at a level that buyers assert is not the true level. The market is generally very healthy, the buyers are quite numerous and fairly reasonable, and there are any number of present owners who are willing to sell out, but who, having no pressing necessity to do so, are holding on at high figures. The cure, then, for this stagnancy in the real estate market is for owners to make reasonable concessions from their present figures.

THE AUCTION MARKET.

A survey of the doings in the Auction Room during the past week does not encourage the hope that there will be any considerable activity during the time that remains of the present fall season. On nearly every day the Exchange floor was crowded; on Tuesday and Wednesday it was uncomfortably so, and there was quite an extensive list of offerings that included parcels in nearly every section of the city, and yet the actual number of sales consummated is small to a melancholy degree. This state of affairs was not brought about by lack of variety in the location and quality of the offerings, for the auctioneers' announcements included everything from suburban lots to business property on Canal street. Neither can the failure to sell be attributed to the excitement of the coming election, as the large daily attendance plainly shows. The coming election, of course, may have something to do with the present dullness, but it is a very small factor in it. The real reason has been told often enough in this column. It lies in the indifference of buyers and the unyielding firmness of present holders. The latter have had it in their power to increase the volume of business very largely by making only very small concessions, but they have steadily refused to do this, and unless the figures bid have reached their upset price they have either withdrawn the property from sale or bought it in themselves. The majority of the parcels voluntarily offered this week have in this way been taken off the market, and the sales actually consummated are scarcely interesting enough to mention. In the sale of lots at Yonkers only four or five lots were sold, the remainder being withdrawn. No. 259 Canal street was bid up to about $74,000, but this figure was evidently unsatisfactory to the owners for the property was bid in, as were also Nos. 459 and 461 3d avenue. Other properties of less interest situated in various parts of the city were either bid in or withdrawn. Auctioneer Wells, however, succeeded in selling two small parcels on 4th avenue. Nos. 246 and 248 4th avenue, 40x64, with the four-story buildings thereon, sold for $45,600, while No. 261, on the opposite side of the way, and north of 20th street, brought $36,200. It is a four-story building and store, on lot 23x90. The legal sales present nothing that is of interest to the genera market.

Next week will naturally be very dull in the Auction Room. Monday sandwiched in between Sunday and Election Day is practically counted out of the business days of the week quite as effectually as Tuesday, and the days which immediately follow will not see the transaction of much business in any line. Realizing this, owners and others have offered very little for the bidders who will attend next week's sales, and that little is of the most ordinary character.

On Thursday, November 5th, Richard V. Harnett & Co. will sell the four-story dwelling No. 131 East 45th street.

CONVEYANCES.

	1890. Oct. 24 to 30 inc.	1891. Oct. 23 to 29 inc.
Number	213	231
Amount involved	$3,661,361	$2,910,659
Number nominal	61	68
Number 23d and 24th Wards	43	58
Amount involved	$142,355	$155,502
Number nominal	15	12

MORTGAGES.

	1890.	1891.
Number	262	244
Amount involved	$2,805,691	$3,706,148
Number at 5 % or less	105	120
Amount involved	$1,599,580	$1,367,039
Number at less than 5 per cent	20	14
Amount involved	$273,500	$152,500
Number to Banks, Trust and Ins. Cos	35	19
Amount involved	$474,100	$611,000

PROJECTED BUILDINGS.

	1890. Oct. 25 to 31 inc.	1891. Oct. 24 to 30 inc.
Number of buildings	56	59
Estimated cost	$1,309,400	$1,001,115

Gossip of the Week.

SOUTH OF 59TH STREET.

It is reported that the two three-story dwellings, on plot 45x98.9, Nos. 12 and 14 West 54th street, have been sold for about $100,000. The owners were Edward W. Kearney and Thomas F. Barden. Brokers Rikers & Son.

C. A. Lutz & Co. have sold for Robert Ernst Nos. 229 and 231 West 16th street, two five-story double flats, each 30x90x102.2, for $72,000.

Fitzsimons & Smith have sold for Louis Pizer to Mrs. Alvina Haagen the four-story, high stoop, brown stone dwelling, 20x73, No. 664 Lexington avenue, for $19,500; and for Dr. William H. Fuller to a builder for immediate improvement, No. 36 West 35th street, on lot 20x98.9, with a three-story private dwelling thereon, on private terms.

Riker & Son have sold for Henry W. Putnam to H. L. Ferrell the three-story stable, on lot 25x100, No. 121 West 52d street, for $31,000.

Innes & Carter have sold for Mrs. John H. Bridge to Dr. G. V. Foster the five-story double apartment house known as "The Albion," No. 102 West 44th street, on private terms.

D. Kempner & Son have sold for a Mr. Vermilyea the five-story double brown stone apartment house, No. 406 West 36th street, 25x88x100, for $33,000.

Isaac T. Meyer was the broker who sold No. 233 West 14th street, not the purchaser, as previously reported. The price paid, Mr. Meyer says, was considerably more than $26,250. Mr. Meyer was also one of the brokers in the sale of No. 40 West 39th street, reported last week.

L. Napoleon Levy has sold to Wm. Reynolds Brown No. 103 East 39th street, a four-story brown stone dwelling, 16.8x60x98.9, on private terms. Brokers, E. H. Ludlow & Co.

Knox McAfee has sold for the estate of John F. Hinds to Henry Brady the three-story and basement high stoop dwelling, on lot 22x98.9, No. 330 West 27th street, for $14,550.

H. V. Mead & Co. have sold the four-story brick private house, 22x50x98.9, No. 337 West 29th street, for Thos. H. Hall for $14,500; also the four-story brick tenement with stores, 25x77x98.9, for D. Bonsharf for $18,000, and a five-story brick and brown stone tenement, 25x88x100, No. 322 East 35th street, for $20,750.

James Kyle & Sons have sold No. 207 East 39th street, a five-story brick tenement, for $18,000.

NORTH OF 59TH STREET.

Ames & Co. have sold for George Stone the eight lots on the south side of 98th street, 150 feet east of Amsterdam avenue, 200x100, to John Casey, for $72,000, for improvement; and for John Casey Nos. 172 and 174 West 81st street, two five-story single flats, 21x90x102.2 each, to George Stone, for $80,000.

James L. Libby & Son and C. K. Bill have sold for J. L. Brewster a four-story brown stone dwelling, 19.4x about 60x105.8, on Riverside Drive, 82.10 south of 82d street, to Mr. Phelps, of Phelps Bros. & Co., terms private. The same brokers have sold for Mr. Phelps two lots on the south side of 90th street, between Riverside Drive and West End avenue, to J. L. Brewster.

C. T. Barney has sold to A. G. Nason, of Breen & Nason, for improvement, the four lots on the north side of 76th street, 100 feet east of Columbus avenue, for $72,000. Broker, F. Zittel.

Albert S. Kalicke has sold for Ludwig Bros., the 14th street dry-goods men, to Sonn Bros., the wholesale grocers, the five-story brick aud stone flat, on lot 25.6x106, known as the "Amy," on the southwest corner of Columbus avenue and 86th street, for about $75,000. Ludwig Bros. took title to this property in February, 1890, at an expressed consideration of $75,000.

J. W. Stevens has sold for Bernard Cohen to John Curry and Joseph B. Gillie three lots on the north side of 91st street, between Central Park West and Columbus avenue, on private terms.

Jesse C. Bennett has sold for the James J. Winant's estate to Nicholas G. Geraty, plot 50x105, with frame building, south side of 71st street, 125 feet west of Lexington avenue, on private terms, for improvement.

T. E. D. Power states that the report that the "Brockholst" had been sold is premature. Negotiations are pending, but the contract has not been signed.

Woolley & Brinckerhoff, Jr., have sold the four-story high stoop brick and stone house No. 1 West 121st street, 22x54, and three-story extension x 76, to Wm. R. Beal, President of the Central Gas Light Company, for $33,000, and the three-story, high stoop, brown stone house No. 1323 Madison avenue, adjoining the northeast corner of 93d street, 20x55x74, to Walter G. Hennessy, the lawyer, for about $26,000.

Isaac T. Meyer has sold for Giblin & Taylor to Thomas G. Patten No. 147 West 80th street, 21x60x102.2, on private terms. Giblin & Taylor have now only one house left out of a row of five recently built by them on 80th street.

George F. Johnson has sold to Hawkes & Haaren two lots on the south side of 132d street, 460 feet west of Lenox avenue, on private terms, for improvement. Mr. Johnson has also sold to Ferdinand Yost four lots on the southwest corner of Brook avenue and 156th street, on private terms, for improvement.

Riker & Son have sold for David Christie the three-and-a-half-story dwelling, 21x65x80, on the northwest corner of West End avenue and 102d street, for $40,000; and for Wm. S. Lines to a Mrs. Purcell No. 70 West 94th street, a three-story dwelling, 18x55x100, for $26,000.

LEASES.

E. H. Ludlow & Co. have rented No. 13 West 48th street, a four-story furnished dwelling. They have also rented No. 30 West 19th street, a three-story furnished dwelling, to Bayard Clarke, on private terms.

During the month of October T. E. D. Power rented fourteen of the new 18-foot three-story houses built by J. G. Prague for D. Willis James on 85th and 87th streets, near Columbus avenue, at rents varying from $1,600 to $1,700 each per annum.

Brooklyn.

Corwith Bros. have sold the three-story frame dwelling and store, 22x40, on lot 25x100, No. 157 Eagle street, for George Grassick to Bridget O'Brien for $4,000.

CONVEYANCES.

	1890. Oct. 23 to 29 inc.	1891. Oct. 22 to 28 inc.
Number	273	313
Amount involved	$1,187,681	$1,002,850
Number nominal	64	88

MORTGAGES.

	1890.	1891.
Number	265	202
Amount involved	*$4,258,816	$1,070,739
Number at 5 per cent. or less	147	148
Amount involved	*$3,971,715	$600,614

PROJECTED BUILDINGS.

	1890. Oct. 24 to 30 inc.	1891. Oct. 23 to 29 inc.
Number of buildings	72	66
Estimated cost	$340,215	$227,325

*Includes mortgage given by the Edison Illuminating Co. to the Franklin Trust Co. for $2,500,000; also mortgage given by Citizens' Gas Light Co. to Central Trust Co. of New York for $750,000.

Ont Among the Builders.

John C. Burne has plans on the boards for six brown stone front private dwellings, 18.4x52, and extension, to be built on the south side of 120th street, 300 feet west of 5th avenue, by Thos. I. Robinson at a cost of $150,000; and for five five-story brown stone front flats which Wm. Broadbelt will build on the south side of 151st street, 100 east of 10th avenue, at a cost of $115,000. One house will be 19x86, and the remaining four houses 26x86 in size. The same architect has plans under way for a five-story brown stone and terra cotta flat, 25x92, which John W. French will erect on the south side of 85th street, 200 feet east of 3d avenue.

The Van Zandt estate will build on the south side of 12th street, 60 feet west of University place, a seven-story and basement brick, iron and granite warehouse, 71x96. The cost has not been fixed upon, but will not be far from $50,000. F. A. Minuth is the architect.

A seven-story addition is to be built by Mahon & Coyne on the avenue lot, 23x95, adjoining their building on the southeast corner of 4th avenue and 21st street. The structure was originally intended for an apartment house, and the plans filed so named it, but it is now to be turned into a hotel, which has been leased to Foster Bros. of the "Aberdeen," Broadway and 21st street, for twenty-one years from the date of occupation.

John Laimbeer intends to build a three-story brick and stone building, 25x100, at No. 339 West 50th street. He will use the first floor for his offices and the stories above as lofts. Architect, Geo. F. Pelham.

G. F. Pelham has plans on the boards for a three-story and basement stable, to occupy an area of about two-and-a-half city lots on the north side of 16th street, between 8th and 9th avenues, at an estimated cost of about $35,000. It will front 25 feet on the street, and have an interior lot about 40x100 in size, the building to cover the whole. Accommodation will be afforded for about 100 horses and numerous carriages. John Totten will be the owner.

John A. Hamilton will draw plans for a six-story brick, iron and stone factory, 60x90 and 75, to be built on the north side of Southern Boulevard, near Willis avenue. Thos. J. Rush is the owner and the cost is estimated at $40,000.

Charles Rentz will draw plans for a five-story and basement brick, stone and terra cotta flat, 25x88.6, to be built at No. 70 Forsyth street; and for another, same size and style, to be built at No 78 Norfolk street, for Loonie & Parker. These flats will be arranged for four families on each floor, and are to cost $22,000 each. The same architect has plans under way for another flat of like character, 25x63.6, to be built at a cost of $18,000 at No. 185 Allen street. The architect is agent for the owner of the last named.

John Casey is having plans drawn to improve the seven lots on the northwest corner of Columbus avenue and 88th street, 100 feet on the avenue and 175 feet on the street, by the erection of flats with stores on the avenue.

Hawkes & Haaren will build two five-story brick and stone flats on the south side of 132d street, 460 feet west of Lenox avenue.

Ferdinand Yost intends to erect four five-story brick and stone flats on the southwest corner of Brook avenue and 156th street.

Sheridan & Byrne will build two brick and brown stone dwellings, on plot 35x100, on the north side of 90th street, 240 feet west of West End avenue. They are to cost $12,000 each, and T. J. Sheridan is the architect.

Schneider & Herter are the architects for two five-story apartment houses to be built at Nos. 746 and 748 Columbus avenue. They will each be 25x88.6, and Weil and Mayer are the owners.

Out of Town.

New Rochelle, N. Y.—G. P. Putnam's Sons are having plans drawn by D. & J. Jardine for a large printing and publishing establishment for the "Knickerbocker Press," to be 50x150 feet in size, and three stories, basement and attic in height, to be erected opposite the junction of the main line of the New Haven Railroad with the Harlem River branch, the northerly side of the building to front on Webster avenue. It is to be of brick and stone, with an attractive facade, and will cost about $30,000. Putnam's have their printing works in New York at present, and this move is mainly for economical reasons.

Highlands, N. J.—C. L. Duvale will build from plans by J. A. Hamilton a two-story stone and frame stable, 60x40 in size, costing $3,500.

WANTS AND OFFERS.

WANTS.

WANTED.—A position as plan clerk in builder's office by a young man well versed in plans, specifications and taking off items, having had over seven (7) years' experience in architect's and builder's office. Address, SLOANE, 357 West 48th st.

WANTED.—Price-lists, catalogues and samples of building materials, &c., of all branches.
H. ALBAN REEVES, 426 Amsterdam av., City.

OPENING to learn real estate desired; experienced bookkeeper and office man; some outside experience; best references. JUSTICE, 355 West 17th st.

WANTED to lease, small farm for poultry, fruit and vegetables, near market and water.
WISE, Mt. Prospect av, Newark, N. J.

OFFERS.

Dwellings and Flats.

A MURRAY HILL PRIVATE RESIDENCE—Four-story; 20x60x80; exchange for tenement or lots.
JOHN M. KYLE, 120 Broadway.

A BARGAIN IF SOLD THIS WEEK.—Five-story flat, 25x80x100, near 57th st., Park av.; $35,000; mortgage $20,000.
JOHN M. KYLE, 120 Broadway.

A PERFECT HOUSE FOR SALE.—A bargain; need money; must sell; four-story; three-story extension; decorated, gas fixtures, electricity, gas logs; perfect order; foyer, built by Farley; no better house for the price in city; any one wanting to buy on speculation can rent to me at good price. Apply on premises, 56 West 92d st. Oct. 31-Nov. 7.

129TH ST., between Madison and 5th avs., six elegant new three-story, high stoop, brown stone dwellings, cabinet trim, parquet floors, decorated, and gas fixtures; terms easy; watchman on premises. JOHN W. PIRSSON, 149 Broadway.

WE HAVE TWO ENTIRE FRONTS on the best part of Riverside Drive for sale.
SCOTT BROS., Equitable Building, 120 Broadway.

FOR SALE.—2443 8th av and 210 and 212 West 105th st.; commission allowed brokers. Apply at
Aug. 29-uf. Room 19, 155 Broadway.

FOR SALE.—Five new first-class four-story and basement private dwellings, Nos. 109, 113 and 119 East 45th st., and Nos. 462 and 464 Lexington av.; all leased to desirable tenants or can arrange to give possession to some of them if desired. For further particulars apply to
THE C. GRAHAM & SONS CO., 309 East 43d st.
Sept. 19-1aw8w.

A—At reasonable prices and easy terms, three and four-story residences, with three-story extensions; all improvements. Call and examine or inquire of the owner and builder, on the premises.
S. O. WRIGHT, 128 West 121st st., open daily.
Oct. 3 uf.

OFFERS.

FOR SALE.—Six new cabinet-trimmed three-story and basement brown stone private dwellings, Nos. 142-152 West 1[illegible]d st.; prices reasonable and brokers commissions allowed. For further particulars apply at office of
FRED'K. M LITTLEFIELD, 156 Broadway.
Aug. 29-uf.

FOR SALE—2443 8th av.; 26.8½x100; easy terms; commission allowed brokers; apply at
Mar. 28-u-f. ROOM 19, 156 Broadway.

FOR SALE—210 and 212 West 105th st.; five-story apartments; each, 25x89x100; decorated and carpeted; apply at ROOM 19, 156 Broadway.
Mar. 28-u-f

Improved Property.

FOR SALE OR LONG LEASE.—Northwest corner of Greenwich and Canal sts. If immediately improved the entire price may remain on mortgage.
OWNER, 20 Nassau st., room 70.

FOR SALE.—Valuable business property in Liberty st., fully rented; selling price guarantees good present paying investment, and location insures increasing value. For terms and particulars apply to MURPHEY & METCALF, Attorneys, 15 Wall st.

OFFICE OF
FREDERICK SOUTHACK,
401 BROADWAY,
offers for sale some choice pieces
of property on
LEONARD ST., between Broadway and West B'way.
FRANKLIN ST., between B'way and West B'way.
WHITE ST., between B'way and West B'way.
BROADWAY, from Barclay to 14th st.
BLEECKER ST., from B'way to South 5th av.
GREENE ST., Canal to 8th st.
WASHINGTON PLACE, B'way to Wooster.
WAVERLEY PLACE, B'way to Wooster.
APPLY AS ABOVE.
FREDERICK SOUTHACK.
Oct. 3 uf.

Vacant Lots.

1ST AV., near 108th st; full lot, $5,700.
Oct. 31—1aw9w. EDWIN A. ELY, 103 Gold st.

DESIRABLE CITY LOTS, with liberal builders' loans; no brokers. Post-office box 3680.

24TH WARD.—For sale, lot in St. George's Crescent, Bedford Park; highest location, with southern frontage; price, $550. Apply,
SHIPLEY, 369 West 52d.

TO BUILDERS.—We have some very choice lots in different parts of the city, at reasonable prices, some of which we can sell with loan.
SCOTT BROS., Equitable Building, 120 Broadway.

40 CHERRY ST., between Roosevelt and Franklin sq., 32x64, vacant; $12,000; accommodating terms. EDWIN A. ELY, 103 Gold st.
Sept. 26-1aw8w.

OFFERS.

LEASEHOLD—FOR SALE.—23d st., between 10th and 11th avs., four city lots, 50 feet frontage on 23d st., running through to 22d st. Inquire at office, corner 11th av. and 22d st., or of
Oct17-1-aw-4w GEO. G. FARNHAM, 65 Broadway.

CORNER LOT, 75.5x95; excavated; location unsurpassed; light on all sides; will make a building loan of $30,000 for a first-class apartment, and a permanent loan of $80,000 on completion. Apply to
J. M. STRONG, Jr., 60 Liberty st.

100TH ST., between 2d and 3d avs.; ten lots cheap; all mortgage if improved.
Sept. 26-1aw8w. EDWIN A. ELY, 103 Gold st.

FOUR ATTRACTIVE LOTS, 149th st., adjoining southwest corner 7th av., $3,600 each; builders' terms. EDWIN A. ELY, 103 Gold st.
Sept 26-1aw8w.

Brooklyn Real Estate for Sale.

FOR SALE—Flats; 10 per cent net; price $9,000, rents, $1,086; price, $12,500, rents, $1,320; near 5th av. elevated, Brooklyn; good order; all improvements. H GILBERT, 37 Frankfort st.

FOR SALE IN BROOKLYN.—Three blocks from 39th st ferry, one full block of seventy lots for factory purposes; unsurpassed; terms easy; inquire of the owner. S. McDOUGALL,
Oct. 10-1aw4w. 242 and 243 Washington Market.

Country Property.

FOR SALE.—In plots to suit; eligible building sites (commanding view of sound for miles), on North st., Greenwich, Connecticut; price reasonable; terms easy; neighborhood aristocratic and fashionable. Apply to
FRED. J. STONE, owner, 60 Broadway, N. Y.
Sept. 12-uf.

Miscellaneous.

A SEAT IN REAL ESTATE EXCHANGE (Lim.) to rent; price, $40 per year, including all the privileges. Apply to H. RAWAK, 1 West 3d st.

THOMAS & ECKERSON, 33 West 30th st., have a large assortment of houses for sale, from 25th st. to 133d st., ranging in price from $13,000 to $125,000, and on easy terms.
Oct. 24-1aw4w.

A PARTY ABOUT TO BUILD A FIVE-STORY factory, 50x98, in Harlem, near water-front, will lease the three upper floors and build to suit tenant. Terms very moderate. Address
May 16 u. f. OWNER, 409 E. 107th St.

PRINTING.—Book, News and Job.
RECORD AND GUIDE PRESS,
14 Barclay, and 14, 16 Vesey sts.

SALES OF THE WEEK.

The following are the sales at the Real Estate Exchange and Auction Room for the week ending Oct. 30.

* *Indicates that the property described has been bid in for plaintiff's account:*

R. V. HARNETT & CO.

2d st, No. 320, s s, 288.7 e Av B, 21.9x105.11, three-story brk tenem't and four-story brk tenem't on rear. S. Jacobs $3,100

4th st, No. 216, s s, 348.9 e Av A, 24.9x96.2, four-story brk tenem't and four-story brk tenem't on rear. G. J. O'Connor 5,150

Canal st, No. 259, 25.4x84.6x27x86.5, six-story marble store and lot. (Bid in) .... —

27th st, No. 428, n s, 287.6 w 9th av, 25x83.9, five-story brk tenem't with stores. Geo. Adrain 16,100

57th st, s s, 175 w 6th av, 75x100, vacant. Simon Arendt 21,000

114th st, No. 147, n w cor Lexington av, 25x61, three-story brown stone dwell'g. John Kearns 13,100

123d st, No. 411 E., 18.9x100.10, three-story brk dwell'g. John Stone 5,700

Lexington av, No. 1848, w s, 61 n 114th st, 20x43, three-story brown stone dwell'g. Alexander Bros 6,150

Lexington av, No. 1850, adj similar dwell'g. E. J. Welling, Jr 6,000

7th av, Nos. 2146 and 2148, w s, 76.7 n 127th st, two five-story brown stone dwell'gs. William Berriam 48,150

133d st, Nos. 107-117, n s, 100 w Lenox av, 16.8x99.11, six three-story brown stone dwell'gs. (Bid in) .... —

A. H. MULLER & SON.

34th st, s s, 325 e 11th av, 75x98.9, 3 vacant lots. (Bid in) .... —

*124th st, No. 104, 30x100.11, five-story brk flat. H. L. Hoppin et al. trustees. (Amt due $36,387) 27,500

WM. KENNELLY.

Rider av, w s, 768 s 144th st, 75x125 to Mott Haven Canal, also all machinery, &c. E. Hyman 5,100

SMYTH & RYAN.

103d st, Nos. 155 and 157, n s, 120 e Lexington av, 30x100.11 each, two four-story brk and stone apartment houses, No. 155 $16,250, No. 157 $16,550. L. Z. Bach 32,800

Willis av, No. 463, s e cor 146th st, 25x100, five-story brk and stone apartment house. Ernest E. Meyer 32,385

JAMES L. WELLS.

4th av, No. 261, 23x90, four-story brk dwell'g. Platt & Bowers 36,200

4th av, Nos. 246 and 248, 20x64 each, two four-story brk dwell'gs. H. Iden 45,600

S. DE WALLTEARSS.

50th st, No. 204, s s, 75 e 3d av, 15x60, three-story brk dwell'g. John Mitchell 7,400

J. F. B. SMYTH.

8th av, w s, 24.11 n 154th st, 50x100, 2 vacant lots. (Bid in) .... —

29th st, No. 582, s s, 325 e 11th av, 25x98.9, five-story brk flat with five-story brk building on rear. (Bid in) .... —

63d st, s s, 150 e West End av, 100x100.5, 4 vacant lots. (Bid in) .... —

127th st, No. 148, s s, 350.9 w 3d av, 16.8x99.11, three-story stone front dwell'g. T. McGuire. (Amt due $3,736; prior morts, $8,000; sold Sept. 25, 1890, for $12,400) 11,215

130th st, No. 22, s s, 126.8 w Madison av, 16.8x99.11, three-story brk dwell'g. R. S. Church. (Amt due $2,712; prior morts, $11,000) 13,900

Sedgwick av, No. 1773, 50x100, two-story frame house. (Bid in) .... —

THOMAS C. SMITH.

3d av, Nos. 459 and 461, e s, 86.1 n 31st st, 18.4x85 each, two four-story brk buildings. (Bid in) —

J. C. LALOR.

20th st, No 20', 17.6x92, four-story brk tenem't. John Ederhardt. (Leasehold; amt due $3,300) 3,950

OTHER AUCTIONEERS.

Canal st, No. 119, 18.10x24.8, four-story stone front. Ernest Platt 15,650

Forsyth st, No. 158, w s, 125 s Rivington st, 25x100, five-story stone front store and tenem't. E. Jacobs. (Amt due $15,165) 32,700

Monroe st, No. 67, 25x100, four-story brk dwelling with five-story double tenem't on rear. Margaret Burns 26,500

49th st, No. 517, 25x100.4, five-story brk tenem't with two-story brk building on rear. H. C. Plass. (Amt due $9,971) 17,250

133d st, No. 220, 16.8x99.11, five-story brk flat. Wallace R. Eickhoff. (Amt due $2,498; prior morts $16,000) int and 16,500

103d st, No. 206, s s, 118 w 10th av, 99.6x72 to Clendenning lane, x99.7x77.2, five-story brk flat. Chas. Seidler 99,000

Total $347,315
Corresponding week, 1890 $1,083,986

BROOKLYN, N. Y.

For Week Ending October 29.

JOHN F. B. SMYTH.

56d st, No. 290, 13.4x100.2, two-story brk and frame dwell'g. P. Olwell $1,000

A. H. MULLER & SON.

Montague terrace, No. 6, w s, 68 s Montague st, 24x200, four-story brown stone mansion. (Bid in) —

JERE. JOHNSON, JR.

Clinton st, No. 264, four-story brown stone dwell'g, 15.2x43.4. Charles E. Torrey 6,500

Clinton st, No. 266, four-story brown stone dwell'g, 15x45.1. T. S. Terry 4,800

Clinton st, No 268, one-story brk building, 18.11½x44. Frank Andemars 8,850

Clinton st, No. 270, four-story brown stone dwell'g, 21x44. Charles E. Torrey 8,900

Lincoln pl, No. 126, 20.10x100, three-story brown stone dwell'g. John Glenhill 10,250

Remsen st, No. 28, 75x90, three-story brown stone dwell'g, 25x50. John Oscar Ball 38,500

Verandah pl, No. 8, three-story brk dwell'g, 21.5x32.3. T. H. Terry 2,450

Verandah pl, No. 36, three-story brk dwell'g, 24.6x50. John Fox 3,000

Verandah pl, No. 38, three-story brk dwell'g, 24.7x30. Same 3,000

Verandah pl, No. 40, three-story brk dwell'g, 14x30. Same 2,000

OTHER AUCTIONEERS.

Butler st, No. 697, 75x131, two-story frame dwell'g. Richard Iseman 5,700

*Decatur st, No. 49, n s, 229 w Throop av, 18x100, three-story brk dwell'g. Moses Sahlein 5,800

*Fulton st, n e cor Somers st, 127.4x27.11¾x124.9¾, gore. Eliz. W. Aldrich 10,000

*Garfield pl, No 174½, s s, 312.6½ w 7th av, 12.5½x100, three-story brk dwell'g. Lucius H. Beers 8,250

*McDonough st, No. 415, n s, 125 e Reid av, 16.8x100, two-story and basement brick dwell'g. Eliz. Tabor 4,100

*Monroe st, No. 320, s s, 405.8 w Tompkins av, 19.9x100, two-story and basement frame dwell'g. William B. Dill 3,800

*Raymond st, No. 122, w s, 25 s Bolivar st, 25x75, four-story brk tenem't. Lulu P. McGarry 10,100

*Raymond st, No. 124, w s, 50 s Bolivar st, 25x75, four-story brk tenem't. Same 10,000

*Raymond st, w s, 150 s Bolivar st, 25x75, four-story brk tenem't. Same 8,200

*Raymond st, w s, 175 s Bolivar st, runs west 75 x south — to Willoughby st, x east — to Raymond st, x north 26 to beginning, four-story brk tenem't and store. Same 13,150

*Union st, Nos. 221-229, n s, 227.6 w Clinton st, 140x100, five five-story double brk and stone flats. Spencer Aldrich 50,000

39th st, s s, 175 w 8th av, 25x100.2, two-story frame dwell'g. J. M. Snooks 1,250

*Albany av, s e cor Park pl, 20x80, three-story brk dwell'g and store. Richard Goodwin 4,000

*Albany av, n e cor Butler st, 235.7x80, thirteen three-story brk dwell'gs, corner with store. Same 30,000

Caton av, n s, 95.6½ w Ocean av, runs west 176.1½ x northeast 370.7 to Crooke av, x east 12.5½ x south 293.10 to beginning. Flatbush. John F. James 4,800

*Gates av, n s, 224 e Lewis av, 25x100, four-story double brk flat and store. John M. Quackenbos, Jr 8,100

*Glenmore av, Nos. 449 and 451, n s, 56 w Wyona av, 44x25, two-story frame dwell'g on plot. Richard M. Wyckoff 200

Lafayette av, No. 313, 16.8x100, three-story brown stone dwell'g. John Henderson 3,500

Myrtle av, No. 893, 20x100, three-story brk dwell'g and store. Robt. J. McMenamay 7,250

Myrtle av, No. 895, 20x100, three-story brk dwell'g and store. Same 6,050

Nostrand av, No. 666, 25x100, two-story frame dwell'g. Andrew Colvin 5,450

*Van Siclen av, e s, 125 s Blake av, 25x100, vacant. Chas. W. Osborne 2,000

Washington Park late Cumberland st, No. 204, e s, 114.0¾ n De Kalb av, 28x100, four-story brk dwell'g. A. Waldron 18,500

Total $197,930
Corresponding week 1890 $319,175

CONVEYANCES.

Wherever the letters Q. C., C. a. G. and B. & S occur, preceded by the name of the grantee they mean as follows:

1st—Q. C. is an abbreviation for Quit Claim deed, i. e., a deed in which all the right, title and interest of the grantor is conveyed, omitting all covenants or warranty.

2d—C. a. G. means a deed containing Covenant against Grantor only, in which he covenants that he hath not done any act whereby the estate conveyed may be impeached, charged or encumbered.

3d—B. & S. is an abbreviation for Bargain and Sale deed, wherein, although the seller makes no express covenants, he really grants or conveys the property for a valuable consideration, and thus impliedly claims to be the owner of it.

NEW YORK CITY.

October 23, 24, 26, 27, 28, 29.

Baxter st, No. 8, w s, abt 145 n Park row, 27.11x99.10x36x76.10, three-story brk store and tenem't with one-story frame buildings on rear. Fanny Silverstone to Hyman Epstein. B. & S. ½ part. *Mt.* $16,000. June 19. nom

Beekman st, No. 68, n s, 36.2 e Gold st, 27.8x44.9x25.2x45.8, five-story stone front store. Martha R. Pope, Rockville Centre, L. I., to Henry B. Pope. ½ part. May 14. nom

Canal st, No. 509, n s, 46.4 w Renwick st, runs northwest 18 x northeast 49 x east 15.1 x south 15.2 x south 43.5, three-story brk store and tenem't. Caroline Simonson, Northfield, N. Y., to Joseph Levi. Oct. 27. $9,000

Cannon st, Nos. 92-100, e s, 75 s Stanton st, 102.6x100.6; Nos. 92, 94, 98 and 100, four three-story brk tenem'ts, stores in No 98; No. 96, six-story brk factory with extension which covers the rear of whole plot. Amelia Robison to Morris Jacoby. ½ part. Sub. to morts. $62,000. Oct. 1. nom

Cannon st, No. 81, w s, 90 n Rivington st, 20x82, three-story brk tenem't. William Hausman to Ellen McBride. *Mt.* $7,500. Oct. 29. 10,800

Columbia st, No 56, e s, 120 n Delancey st, 20x100, three-story brk tenem't. Joseph Goldstein to Leon A. Liebeskind. *Mt.* $10,850. Oct. 28. 13,000

Cooper st, n s, 100 e Academy st, 100x100. Austin E. Woodman and Eliza A. his wife to Jessie J. Hunt. *Mt.* $3,000. Oct. 28. 6,000

Delancey st, No. 118, n s, 25 e Essex st, 25x50.11x25x51, five-story brk tenem't with stores. David Gerber to Kate Gerber. C. a. G. *Mt* $10,000. Oct. 29. nom

Division st, Nos. 188 and 190, n s, 66.6 e Norfolk st, 48.9x78x46x96, four-story brk tenement with stores. Charles Laue, Brooklyn, to Betsey wife of Harris Cohen. Oct. 27. 59,000

Essex st, No. 109, w s, 200 s Houston st, 25x87.6, with right to strip on rear 25x2.4, five-story brk tenem't with stores. Release mort. Joseph L Buttenwieser to John V. Campbell. Oct 23. nom

Same property. John V. Campbell to Henrietta Studinski. *Mt.* $24,000. Oct. 23 41,000

Greenwich st, No. 822, w s, 68.2 n Jane st, 21.7 x abt 93x21.7x92, three-story brk tenem't. De Witt Buckbee to A. L. and J. J. Reynolds Co. C. a. G. Sept. 30. 12,000

Same property. Release dower. Rachel L. wife of De Witt Buckbee to same. Sept. 30. nom

Greenwich st, No. 663, e s, 135 s Christopher st, 20x75, three-story brk tenem't. Rudolf Navaratt, Sr., Newark, N. J., to Rudolf Navaratt, Jr. Q. C. All title. Oct. 27. nom

Same property. Rudolf Navaratt, Jr., heir Susan Navaratt to Rudolf Navaratt, Sr., Newark, N. J. ¼ part. Q. C. Oct. 27. nom

Hamilton st, No. 24. Satisfaction of assignment of rents. John H. Dye to N. G. Kellogg. Oct. 28. nom

Henry st, No. 174, s w cor Jefferson st, 26.1x100, six-story brk tenem't with stores. John Fish to Jacob Kieser. *Mt.* $50,000. Oct. 29. 78,000

Henry st, No. 98, s s, abt 85 w Pike st, 25x100, three-story frame (brk front) tenem't with three-story brk building on rear. Eliza J. Perry widow to Michael Fay and William Stacom. Oct. 19. 21,750

Houston st, No. 331, s s, 15.6 w Washington st, 18.9x50, three-story brk tenem't.
Hester st, No. 211, n s, abt 25 w Baxter st, 24.11x103.6x21.8x102 in two courses, five-story brk tenem't with stores.
Foreclos. George F. Roesch to Louis M Jones. 1-5 part. Oct. 23 3,000

Leyden st, n e s, 100 s e Teunissen pl, runs northeast 100 x southeast 25 x south 36.6 x west 24.6 x southwest 56 to Leyden st, x northwest 25.
Terrace View av, w s, 156.9 n Leyden st, 125x101.6x125x100.
Joseph R. Brown to Fannie E. Lawrence. March 26. 4,018

Leonard st, No 22, s s, 149.7 w West Broadway, 25x100, six-story brk store. Henry Naylor to J. Edgar Leviness. Q. C. *Mt.* $23,000 Sept. 5, 1888. nom

Same property. J. Edgar Leviness to Frances S. wife of Henry Naylor. Q. C. *Mt.* $23,000. Sept. 5, 1888. nom

Lewis st, No. 30, e s, 125 n Broome st, 24.9x100, three-story brk tenem't with three-story brk tenem't on rear. Adolf Duckler to Samuel Juskovits. *Mt.* $13,300 and taxes 1891. Oct. 28. 15,000

Lewis st, No 102, e s, abt 75 n Stanton st, 21x100, three-story brk tenem't with six-story brk factory on rear. Contract to exchange for property in Brooklyn. Lewis Krulewitch to Jacob, Isidore and Moritz C. Alexander. Equality of exchange. Oct 14. 6,000

Madison st, No. 140, s s, abt 285 w Pike st, 25x100, five-story brk tenem't with stores. Bertie or Bertha wife of Philip Goldman to George Harris. *Mt.* $31,500. Oct. 26. 40,600

Minetta st, No. 23, s w s, abt 70 n w Minetta st, 25x75.10x29x65.10, two three-story brk tenem'ts.
Minetta st, No. 25, s w s, abt 45 s e Carmine st, 25x49.9x65.10, three-story brk tenem't with stores.
Joseph H. and John P. Freeman, Castle Meagher Co., Montana, to Sarah J. Freeman, Morristown, N. J. All title. *Mt.* $3,000. Sept. 22. 4,667

Mitchell pl (49th st), No. 9, n s, 144 e 1st av, 18x80.10, four-story stone front dwell'g. Foreclos. Tallmadge W. Foster to James V. McManus. *Mt* $6,000, with interest and taxes. Oct. 15. 2,650

Monroe st, No. 235, n s, 168 e Scammel st, 23.8x96x24x96, five-story brk tenem't with stores. Benedict A. Klein to Barnett Levy, Louis Gordon and Sophia Gruenstein. *Mt.* $17,500. Sept. 25. 24,000

Rutgers pl, No. 17 (Monroe st), n s, 130.6 w Clinton st, 26x110, four-story brk tenem't with stores. Hyman Schwartz to Benjamin Kaiser. *Mt.* $15,500. Oct. 28. 19,500

St. Marks pl, No. 101, n s, 200 e 1st av, 37.6x110, four-story brk store and tenem't. Paul Sonntag and Marie his wife, to George and Louise Hornberger. *Mt.* $15,000. Oct. 23. 35,000

Washington st, No. 479, e s, 182.6 s Spring st, 20.4 to alley, x80, with all title in alley, three-story frame (brk front) tenem't with two-story brk stable on rear. William J. Graham to Edward W. Youmans. Oct. 26. 14,250

Waverley pl, No 152, s s, 243 w 6th av, 22.3x97, four-story brk dwell'g. Foreclos. George P. Smith to George B. Howard. Oct. 24. 14,500

5th st, No. 740, s s, 168 w Av D, 22x96, three-story brk tenem't. Meyer and Solomon Goodmann to Adolph Newman. *Mt.* $7,000. Oct 27. 14,000

26th st, No. 317, n s, 250 e 2d av, 25x98.9, two-story brk tenem't with two-story brk stable on rear. Jennie A. wife of and John A. Potts to Patrick Gallagher. *Mt.* $4,000. Oct. 22. 12,500

27th st, Nos. 521 and 523, n s, 275 w 10th av, 50x98.9, two five-story brk tenem'ts with stores. Rachel A. Cartwright widow, Newark, N. J., to Rachel A. wife of Joseph Lynch, Newark, N. J. Jan. 13, 1891. nom

33d st, No. 324, s s, 275 e 2d av, 25x98.9, four-story brk tenem't with stores. Jane, Frederick G and E. Clifford Potter and Eliza J. Vaughan, New York, M. Ada Potter and Mire A. Bowie, Philadelphia, Pa., to Thomas R. Hughes, Weehawken, N. J. Oct. 16. 12,000

Same property. Thomas R. Hughes to Thomas R. Berkley. *Mt.* $4,000. Oct. 28. 12,000

34th st, No 316, s s, 228.9 e 2d av, 21.3x98.9, four-story brk tenem't. Foreclos. Wilbur Larremore to John Stewart. Oct. 27. 9,200

Same property. Sarah B. wife of Samuel B. W. McLeod to John Stewart. C. a. G. Oct. 24. nom

35th st, No. 250, s s, 250 e 8th av, 25x98.9, five-story brk tenem't with stores and two-story frame building on rear. Simon Bing, Jr., and Hyman Israel to Henry V. Mead. *Mt.* $10,000. Oct. 21. 26,000

38th st, No. 210, s s, 83.4 w 7th av, 16.8x98.9, four-story stone front dwell'g. William H. Van Wyck to Annie E. Van Wyck. *Mt.* $6,000. Oct 20. nom

39th st, No. 228, s s, 300 e 3d av, 20x98.9, three-story brk tenem't. Emma Castell to Thomas Edwards. In trust for use of grantor during her life and then to be conveyed to Isabella and Susan her sisters. Oct. 15. nom

39th st, No 207, n s, 100 e 3d av, runs north 70.9 x east 5 x north 28 x east 20 x south 98.9 to 39th st, x west 25, four-story brk tenem't. William Lippman to Aristides Martinez. Oct. 27. 18,000

41st st, No. 240, s s, 101 w 2d av, runs south 74.1 x west 4 x south 24.8 x west 23 x north 98.9 x east 28, five story brk tenem't with stores. Mary C. wife of Augustinus Trabert to Aiese d'Aquiar widow. Oct. 29. 22,500

41st st, No. 311, n s, 133.4 e 2d av, 16.8x98.9, four-story brk tenem't. Honoria Fox to Margaret I. Fox. *Mt.* $6,000. Aug. 27. 100

46th st, No. 208, s s, 138 w Broadway, 20x100.5, five-story stone front dwell'g. Magdalena C. wife of Robert Protheroe to Herman S. Phillips. Oct. 26. 19,750

49th st, No. 304, s s, 75 e 2d av, 25x50.3, four-story stone front tenem't with stores. Joseph Loeb to Marcus B. Bookstaver. *Mt* $6,500. Oct. 1. See 56th st. 15,000

49th st, No. 66, s s, 40.3 w 4th av, 19.10x25.5, four-story stone front dwell'g. Norman L. McElligott, Orange, N. J., to John H. Henshaw. *Mt.* $6,500. Oct. 28. nom

50th st, No. 405, n s, 100 w 9th av, 25x100.5, five-story stone front flat. Katharina Miller widow to Samuel L. Isaacs. *Mt.* $18,500. Oct. 28. 29,500

52d st, Nos. 156 and 158, s s, 256.6 e Lexington av, 48.6x100.5, two four-story stone front flats. Philip Bolender to Robert J. and Louis Maibach. *Mt.* $13,000. Oct. 29. 30,500

53d st, Nos 528-536 s s, 275 e 11th av, 125x100.5, five five-story brk tenem'ts, stores in No. 536. James O'Donelan to Alice Davies. B. & S. Correction deed. Oct. 26. nom

53d st, No. 325, n s, 295.8 e 2d av, 22.3x100.5, three-story frame dwell'g. Fanny Sussman to Henry Reese. *Mt.* $5,000. Oct. 23. 10,000

56th st, No. 76, s s, 100 w Park or 4th av, 18x100.5, four-story stone front dwell'g. Jane L Thomson to Greenleaf W. Crossman. Oct. 26. 30,000

56th st, Nos. 414 and 416, s s, 225 w 9th av, 50x100.5, two five-story brk flats. Maria B. Bookstaver to Joseph Loeb. *Mt.* $28,000. Oct. 1. See 49th st. 44,150

58th st, No. 234, s s, 390 e 3d av, 20x100.5, three-story stone front dwell'g. Garson J. Newwitter to Julius Newwitter. Sub. to mort. $3,000. Oct. 24. nom

59th st, No. 113, n s, 125 e Park av, 20x100.5, three-story stone front dwell'g. Josephine Del Risco, Brooklyn, to Myer Foster. Oct. 26. 17,800

63d st, No. 146, s s, 525 w Columbus av, 25x100.5, five-story brk flat. Charles Lowen, Edward F. Halliday and George Hessels to Michael Hayes. ¾ part. *Mt.* $18,000. Oct. 27. nom

62d st, No. 144, s s, 500 w Columbus av, 25x100.5, five-story brk flat. Michael Hayes to Charles Lowen, Edward F. Halliday and George Hessels. ¼ part. *Mt.* $18,000. Oct. 27. nom

66th st, No. 211, n s, 200 w 10th av, 25x100.5, five-story stone front flat. John S. Robinson to Margaret wife of Stephen Pendergast. *Mt.* $17,000 and tax 1891. Oct, 20. nom

68th st, No. 64, s s, 500 w 8th av, 18.9x100.5, four-story brk dwell'g. Ella B. wife of George Williams, Millerton, N. Y., to Sarepta M. Reid. *Mt.* $21,000. Oct. 23. 35,000

68th st, n s, 500 w 8th av, 75x100.5, vacant. John D. Crimmins to James R. Smith. Oct. 28. 39 000

68th st, n s, 325 w Central Park West, 150x100.5, vacant. David J. King et al. exrs. and trustees Edward J. King to Thomas E. Crimmins. Oct. 19. 78,000

68th st, bet Central Park West and 9th av. Agreement as to restrictions. Appleton D. Palmer et al. with James Rufus Smith et al., owners. Dec. 24, 1890.

69th st, Nos. 323–331, n s, 350 w West End av, 125x100.5, five five-story brk flats. Foreclos Ernest Hall to Margaretta Card. *Mt.* and int. $29,521. Aug. 24. 5,000

Same property. Margaretta Card to Pietro Indelli. C. a. G. *Mt.* $28,500. Oct. 26. 39,265

70th st, No. 324, s s, 279.4 w West End av, 25x100.5, three-story brk stable. Hubert Van Wagenen to Ida M. wife of Alphonse Loisette. Oct. 27. nom

73d st, No. 255, n s, 269 e West End av, 18x102.2, four-story brk dwell'g. Henry W. Le Roy to Simonds Mfg Co. B. & S. Dec. 4, 1889. nom

75th st, n s, 100 w 1st av, 25x97.2x25.4x93. Release mort. Charles Frazier to Emanuel Heilner and Moses J. Wolf. Oct. 26. 100

76th st, No. 504, s s, 123 e Av A, 25x102.2, two-story brk stable. Eva Muller widow to Lina Feltman. *Mt.* $5,000. Oct. 27. 10,500

78th st, No. 211, n s, 179 w Amsterdam av, 21x102.2, three-story stone front dwell'g. Jacob M. Newman to Lina R. wife of Leopold M. Whitehead. *Mt.* $15,000. Oct. 28. 26,750

79th st, No. 161, n s, 336 e 10th av, 14x102.2, five-story brk dwell'g. Barbara wife of and Henry Frohman to Daniel Frohman All liens. June 15. val. consid

79th st, No. 62, s s, 193 w Park av, 16.6x102.2, four-story stone front dwell'g. Rose wife of and David U. Herrmann to Ada wife of Harry Content. Oct. 27. 31,000

82d st, No. 345, n s, 175 w 1st av, 22.4x102.2, two-story frame dwell'g. Louis Plaut, Long Island City, to Carie Adler. *Mt.* $9,000. Sept. 30. 22,000

82d st, No. 554, s s, 85.4 w Av B, runs south 76.2 x west 12.8 x south 26 x west 13.4 x north 102.2 to 82d st, x east 26.
Interior strip, begins 85.4 w of Av A and 22 s 82d st, runs south 16.6 x east 2 x north 16.6 x west 2.
Five-story brk tenem't with stores.
Andreas Banzer to Emily Beckert. *Mt.* $13,000. Oct 29. 20,250

82d st, No. 315, n s, 186 e 2d av, 16x102.2, two-story frame dwell'g. Margaret G. wife of Edmund J. Tichenor to Joseph Heiman. Oct. 28. 6,800

83d st, No. 531, n s, 178 w Av B, 25x102.2, five-story brk tenem't. Rasmus Christensen to Katie Lasher. *Mt.* $14,000. Oct. 27. 22,500

83d st, No. 118, s s, 175 w 9th av, 25x102.2, five-story stone front flat. James Thomson and Mary A. his wife to John Chisholm. *Mt.* $27,055. Oct. 21. nom

Same property. John Chisholm and Annie his wife to James Thomson. *Mt.* $27,941. Oct. 22. nom

84th st, n s, 70 w Madison av, 75x102.2. Release mort. Washington Life Ins. Co. to Robert B. Lynd. Oct. 23. nom

84th st, n s, 175 w Central Park West, 50x102.2, vacant. Release dower. Abbie S. Thompson widow to Ferris S. Thompson. nom

Same property. Ferris S. Thompson to Augustus F. Holly. *Mt.* $15,000. Oct. 23. nom

84th st, n s, 175 w Central Park West, 50x102.2, vacant. Augustus F. Holly to David Richey. C. a. G. *Mt.* $15,000. Sub. to mort. $15,000 and encroachments. Oct. 29. nom

85th st, No. 310, s s, 144 e 2d av, 28x102.2, four-story stone front tenem't. Joseph Winter to Patrick Ducey. *Mt.* $10,000. Oct. 29. 21,000

85th st, No. 348, s s, 120 w 1st av, 26.8x102.2, four-story stone front tenem't. Anton Bayer to Karl Rosenbaum and Marie his wife. *Mt.* $12,000. Oct. 27. 19,000

86th st, No. 136, s s, 365 w Columbus av, 20x106.10, four-story stone front dwell'g. D. Willis James to Emil Carlebach. Oct. 12. 38,000

86th st, No. 76, s s, 70 w Park av, 17.10x102.2, four-story brk dwell'g. Frank E. Wise to Felix Levy and Johanna Voos. *Mt.* $20,000. Oct. 28. 23,750

86th st, No 310, s s, 140 e 2d av, 17.6x102.2, three-story stone front dwell'g. Helena wife of and Abraham Jones to Peter Zimmermann. *Mt.* $9,500. Oct. 29. 13,000

87th st, n s, 250 w Central Park West, 100x100.8, vacant. Charles Gahren to Patrick Farley. Sub to morts. Oct. 24. 60,000

89th st, n s, 100 w 8th av, 25x100.8, vacant. Bernard Cohen and Lewis Z. Bach to William S. Patton. Oct. 26 11,000

89th st, No. 316, s s, 270 w West End av, 21x100.8, four-story brk dwell'g. Francis M. Wilmurt, Pelham Manor, N. Y., to Henry Dale *Mt.* $22,000. Oct 26. nom

93d st, Nos. 114 and 116, s s, 119 e Park av, 32.6x100.8; No. 114, three-story stone front dwell'g; No. 116, five-story stone front flat. Mary E. wife of D. Brainerd Ray to John E. Stinson. ½ part. Oct. 26. 20,900

93d st, No. 140, s s, 375 w Columbus av, 20x100.8, three-story stone front dwell'g. Release mort. The Bradley & Currier Co. (Lim.) to Walden P. Anderson. Oct. 14. 2,000

Same property. Walden P. Anderson to Warren W. Brooks. *Mt.* $21,000. Oct. 27. nom

93d st, No. 160, s s, 224.6 e Amsterdam av, 17x100.8, three-story stone front dwell'g. Release mort The Bradley & Currier Co (Lim.) to Walden P Anderson. Oct. 22. nom

Same property. Walden P. Anderson to Catharine M. Esler. *Mt.* $17,500. Oct. 26. nom

94th st, n s, 100 w 9th av, 25x100.8. Release mort. Elizabeth Hillenbrand to Francis J. Hillenbrand. Oct. 23. nom

95th st, No. 126, s s, 199 e Park av, 18x100.8, three-story brk dwell'g. Sigmund Hirschberg to Sarah Harris. *Mt.* $12,000. Oct. 22. 14,750

96th st, s s, 125 w 8th av, 25x100.8, vacant. Charlotte A. Hamilton to Edward Kilpatrick Oct. 15. 11,625

96th st, s s, 175 w 8th av, 25x100.8, vacant Alice Hamilton to same Oct. 15. 11,625

96th st, s s, 225 w 8th av, 25x100.8, vacant. William G. Hamilton and Helen M. his wife, Ramapo, N. Y., to same. Oct. 15. 11,625

96th st, s s, 275 w 8th av, 25x100.8, vacant. Adelaide Hamilton to same. Oct. 15. 11,625

96th st, s s, 300 w Central Park West, 25x100.8, vacant. Henry C. Niedenstein and Louisa M. his wife to same. Oct. 12. 11,625

97th st, No. 155, n s, 154 w 3d av, 17x100.11, five-story brk flat. Thomas R. Hughes, Weehawken, N. J., to E. Clifford Potter. *Mt.* $14,000. Oct. 22. 21,000

98th st, Nos. 220–224, s s, 310 e 3d av, 75x100.11, three five-story brk tenem'ts. William Dempsey and John Smith to Joseph Newborg. *Mt.* $45,000. Oct. 29. nom

102d st, No. 204, s s, 100 e 3d av, 35x100.11, four-story brk livery stable. Contract. James Duffy to George J. Bernhard. July 15. 29,000

Same property. Assign. contract. Same to The Murray Hill Bank. July 17. nom

103d st, s s, 200 e 5th av, 75x100.11, vacant. Charles B. Moore to J. Allen Townsend. Oct. 28. 17,700

103d st, n s, 255 w Park av, 33.4x100.11, vacant. Martha A. Shirmer widow to J. Allen Townsend. Oct. 29. 8,666

103d st, n s, 288.4 w Park av, 16.8x100.11, vacant. Lavinia Cudlipp to same. Oct. 29. 4,333

103d st, n s, 255 w Park av, 33.4x100.11. George P. Shirmer to Martha A. Shirmer. Q. C. Oct. 2. nom

104th st, No. 243, n s, 116.8 w 2d av, 16.8x100.11, three-story stone front dwell'g. Wolf E. Rendsburg to Bertha Sternberg Oct. 26. nom

105th st, No. 3, n s, 100 e 5th av, 25x100.11, five-story stone front flat. Michael J. Bannon to F. Anthony and Louise F. Schmitter. *Mt.* $20,000. Oct. 26 30,000

106th st, No. 328, s s, 300 e 2d av, 25x100.11, five-story brk flat with stores. Robert L. Moores and Charles A. Le Quesne, Brooklyn, to Franz Franz. Sub. to mort Oct. 1. 28,000

109th st, No. 309, n s, 138 e 2d av, 19x100.11, two-story frame dwell'g with one-story frame building on rear. Elizabeth M. wife of James F. Dolan to Elizabeth wife of Michael Smith Oct. 27. See 131st st. 6,000

110th st, No. 52, s e cor Madison av, 20x100.11, five-story brk hotel with stores. William E. Callender to Myer Hellman. *Mt.* $25,000. Oct. 29. See 7th av. nom

111th st, No. 141, n s, abt 42.11 w Lexington av and being 537.11 w 3d av, 17.10x100.11, three-story stone front dwell'g. Lizzie R. wife of Frank Jarvis to Ida M. Jarvis. B. & S. Oct. 26. nom

111th st, No. 175, n s, 145 w 3d av, 24.6x100.11, four-story stone front flat. John Mitchell to Adelia K. O'Rorke. *Mt.* $8,000. Oct. 24. nom

112th st, No. 214, s s, 181.8 e 3d av, 13.10x100.11, two-story stone front dwell'g. Ann E. wife of Alfred E. Fountain to Marks Ziegler. *Mt.* $4,000. Oct. 24. 8,000

114th st, No. 322, s s, 162.6 e 2d av, 18.9x100.11, four-story brk dwell'g. Foreclos. Edward C. Perkins to James Lawlor. Oct. 28. 11,000

114th st, No. 418, s s, 240 e 1st av, 30x100.11, four-story stone front tenem't with frame shed on rear. Foreclos. S. H. L. Ward to Mary Myers. Oct. 29. 1,500

115th st, No 221, n s, 325 w 7th av, 18.9x100, five-story brk flat. Foreclos. David McClure to Richard Cummings. Oct. 23. 14,900

115th st, No. 223, n s, 343.9 w 7th av, runs west 18.9 x north abt 94.4 x northeast 14 x east 5.3 x south 100.11, five-story brk flat. Foreclos. Same to Gustav Boehm. Oct. 22. 14,900

115th st, No. 227, n s, 381.3 w 7th av, 18.9x100.11, five-story brk flat. Foreclos. Same to Matthias McDermott. Oct. 22. 14,900

115th st, No. 225, n s, 362.6 w 7th av, runs west 18.9 x north 100.11 x east 6.3 x south 10.7 x northeast 13.1 x south 94.4, five-story brk flat. Foreclos. Same to same. Oct. 22. 14,900

115th st, Nos. 225 and 227, n s, 400 w 7th av, runs north 100.11 x east 25 x south 10.7 x northeast 13.1 x south 94.4 to st, x west 37.6, two five-story brk flats. Matthias McDermott and Catherine his wife to Mary T. Kane. *Mt.* $31,000. Oct. 23. 20,000

117th st, No 441, n s, 394 e 1st av, 16.8x100.10, two-story brk dwell'g. Edward B. Fagan to Charles C. J. Fagan. *Mt.* $3,500. Oct. 27. 7,500

118th st, No. 131, n s, 315 e 4th av, 25x100.11, five-story brk flat. William A. Hynes to Henry Kohler. Oct. 23 21,000

119th st, s s, 135 w Lenox av, 200x100.11, vacant. Alida wife of John McAlan formerly Van Valkenburgh to Joseph I. West. May 23. 64,000

120th st, No. 345, n s, 150 w 1st av, 25x100.10, three-story frame dwell'g. Lucretia Silleck, Mary Pratt, William, Charles, Peter J. and Charles Cole heirs Lawrance Richards to William Richards. B. & S. May 4. nom

121st st, Nos. 207 and 209, n s, 66.9 e 3d av, 34.10x71.9x—x43.8, three-story frame tenem't with stores; also all title in real estate of which Simon Friedenberg died seized. Bertha wife of Bernhard Wolff to Isaac Meyer, Kingston, N. Y. ¼ part. *Mt.* $5,500. Oct. 26. 300

121st st, No 1, n s, 78 w Mount Morris av, 22x75.11, four-story brk dwell'g. James V. S. Woolley to William R. Beal. *Mt.* $15,000. Oct. 29. nom

Same property. Agreement as to easement for light and air. Same with same. Oct. 29. nom

122d st, No. 223, n s, 280 e 3d av, —x100.11x25x100.11, four-story brk tenem't. Jane Kirk widow to Julius H. Horwitz. *Mt.* $12,500. Oct. 27. 16,500

123d st, No. 151, n s, 515 e 4th av and being 35 e Lexington av, 17.6x100.11, two-story frame dwell'g. Edward C. Reinhardt to Lizzie Reinhardt. *Mt.* $3,500. Mar. 9, 1881. 6,000

126th st, s s, 168.6 e 4th av, 21.6x99.11. Release judgment. The Jewish Messenger Co. to William Bloodgood Oct. 19. 31

131st st, No. 28, n s, 285 w 5th av, 25x99.11, five-story brk flat. Henry Hawkes, Riverside, Conn., to Charles Bitz Q. C. and C. a. G. Confirmation deed. Oct. 20. nom

131st st, No. 58, s s, 212.6 w Park av, 17.6x99.11, three story stone front dwell'g. Michael Smith to Elizabeth M. wife of James F. Dolan. *Mt.* $6,500. Oct. 28. See 109th st. 11,000

133d st, s s, 110 e Lenox av, 75x99.11, vacant. James Brice to Mary E. Gault. *Mt.* $10,000 Oct. 27. 27,000

133d st, No. 220, s s, 400 w 7th av, 16.8x99.11, five-story brk flat Foreclos. George G. Fry to Wallace R. Eickhoff. Oct. 28. 500

133d st, s s, 110 e Lenox av, 75x99.11, vacant. Mary A. wife of William W. McLaughlin to James Brice. *Mt.* $10,000. Oct. 23. nom

138th st, s s, 500 e 6th av, 78.2x69.1x134.8x136.2, vacant James McClenahan to The Harrisonville Co-operative Building Assoc., New York. Oct. 26. 8,000

140th st, n s, 225 w Boulevard, 100x99.11, two-story frame stable and vacant. Oliver L. Shepherd to John Unger. Oct. 29. 12,500

Same property. Release mort. Richard M. Nichols to Oliver L. Shepherd. Oct. 23. 3,000

141st st, s s, 245 w Boulevard, 100x99.11, two-story frame dwell'g and vacant. Oliver L. Shepherd to Philippina Unger. *Mt.* $9,000. Oct. 29. 18,500

143d st, No. 304, s s, 100 w 8th av, 25x99.11, one-story frame building. George B. Robinson and Lilla B. his wife, of Bedford, N. Y., to Nicolaus Leibrock. Oct. 13. 4,000

143d st, Nos. 227–235, n s, 150 w 7th av, 125x99.11, five five-story brk flats.
144th st, Nos. 228–236, s s, 150 w 7th av, 125x99.11, five five-story brk flats.
Foreclos. Edmund T. Oldham to Francis M. Wilmurt, Pelham Manor, New York. *Mt.* $130,000. Oct. 22. 500

144th st, No. 465, n s, 121.2 e Amsterdam av, 16.6x99.11, three-story brk dwell'g. Foreclos. R. Duncan Harris to Robert J. Young. Oct. 28 13,300

144th st, No. 467, n s, 100 e Amsterdam av, 21.2x99.11, three-story brk dwell'g. Foreclos. Same to same. Oct. 28. 15,000

146th st, No. 415, n s, 175 w St. Nicholas av, 12.6x99.11, four-story brk dwell'g. Isabella N. wife of John P. Leo. to John P. Leo. *Mt.* $9,500. Oct. 28. 13,250

159th st, No. 526, s s, 300 w Amsterdam av, 50x99.11, three story frame dwell'g and vacant. William Drennan to William Seggie. *Mt.* $5,000. Oct. 28. 12,000

181st st, n w cor Audubon av, 75x100. Pauline Simon to Myles Tierney. June 12 15,500

185th st, n s, 200 e 11th av, 50x55.4x50x55.8. Charles Watkins to Jacob Gottgen, Oct. 28. 3,459

209th st, centre line, 108.7 w dividing line of block 7 on map Samuel Thomson and land Isaac Dyckman, runs west 125x147. Jens Petersen, Brooklyn, N. Y., to Christian Petersen. ½ part. B. & S. Oct. 27. 750

210th st, s s, 125 e Amsterdam av, 75x99.11. Annie E. Brown to Fannie E. Lawrence. June 1. 2,250

Amsterdam av, No. 185, e s, 50.5 n 68th st, 25x74.6, five-story brk store and flat. Friedrich H. Nagel and Elizabetha his wife to George Finck. B. & S. All liens. July 7. nom

Same property. George Finck to Friedrich H. Nagel. B. & S. All liens. July 7. nom

Amsterdam av, n w cor 184th st, 24.11x100. Louis Wendel, Jr., and Katie his wife to Mary A. Evans. Mt. $4,000. Oct. 22. 8,000

Amsterdam av, s w cor 130th st. Agreement as to easement for light and air. Mary Larkin individ. and trustee with Board of Health, New York. Oct. 27. nom

Amsterdam av, No. 792 } begins Amsterdam
99th st, No. 210 } av, w s, 40 s 99th st, 21.8x114.11 to centre Old Bloomingdale road, x north along same 58.4 to 99th st, x east 33.8 to e s said old road, x south 40 x east 80.2, two-story brk store and dwell'g on av and two-story frame dwell'g on st. Mary J. wife of George R. Clark to said George R. Clark and Mary J. his wife, joint tenants. B. & S. Oct. 29. nom

Av A, No. 1603, w s, 51.2 s 85th st, 26x75, five-story brk tenem't with stores. William Stern to Bella wife of Solomon Goldsmith. Mt. $10,000. Oct. 23. 23,500

Av A, s e cor 88th st, 25.2x100, vacant. Henry J. Mahr to Charles Stegmayer. Oct. 24, tax 1891 and assessm't. 15,000

Av A, No 1018, e s, 50.5 n 55th st, 25x79.8, five-story brk tenem't. Eugene Arnold to Ferdinand Greenebaum. Mt. $17,750. Oct. 27. nom

Av B, No. 101, e s, 60.8 n 6th st, 20.2x93, three story brk store and tenem't. John J. Aaron to Benjamin Blumenthal. Mt. $11,000. Oct. 28. 22,500

Av C, No. 99, w s, 61.4 s 7th st, 20x83, four-story brk tenem't with stores Philip Michaelson to Isaac Mayer and Jacob Levy. Oct. 28. 12,630

Columbus av, e s, 100.8 s 94th st, 6.1 to Apthorps lane, x251x16.1x250, with all title in lane. Elizabeth P. wife of Henry A. Robbins to John W. Rourke, Jr., Newport, R. I. C. a. G. Oct. 22. nom

Same property. John W. Rourke, Jr., Newport, R. I., to Henry A. Robbins. C. a. G. Oct. 23. nom

Columbus av, Nos. 881-869, n e cor 103d st. 160.11x100, five five-story brk flats with stores, excepting }
Columbus av, No. 883, e s, 40.11 n 103d st, runs south 30 x 100. }
Welcome R. Steinmetz to Susan Orcutt. All liens. Oct. 23. nom

Park (4th) av, n w cor 78th st, 20x75, vacant. Sarah E Cassidy et al. exrs. Hugh Cassidy to Gustav Gomprecht. Oct. 22. 15,000

Same property Louis G., Henry G. and Charles O'C., Mary L., Isabel M. and Margaret J. Cassidy, Sarah J. O'Shaughnessy, Alice d'Aguiar and Julia R. Kinkle late Cassidy heirs Hugh Cassidy to same. B. & S. Oct. 22. nom

Park av, No. 1201, n e cor 94th st, 17.8x66, three-story brk dwell'g. Henry Hachemeister to Annie Hachemeister. Mt. $17,000. Oct. 17. nom

Pleasant (Av A), No. 861, s w cor 119th st, 17.7 x75, four-story brk (stone front) store and tenem't. Moses Lehman to Rosetta Wolff. ½ part. All liens. Oct. 24. 8,500

Riverside av or Drive, s e cor 95th st, 25.6x89.9 x25.2x89.9, vacant. Adelaide E. wife of Alexander Johnston to Albert B. De Forest. Mt. $7,500. Oct. 21. 17,500

St Nicholas av, Nos. 200-206, n e cor 120th st, runs east 57 x north 100.11 x west 118.11 to av, x south 118.5, four five-story brk flats, store in No. 200. Isabella McCormack to Pheba C. Rapelye. B. & S. Oct. 13. 180,000

Same property. Pheba C. Rapelye to R. Clarence Dorsett. Mt. $120,000. Oct. 13. 135,000

Wadsworth av, s w cor 178th st, 25x100. Patrick Dolan to Peter J. Meehan. Oct. 22. nom

Wadsworth av, w s, 250 s 187th st, 20.3x150x 22.10x150. Release mort. James W. Smith trustee Jessie D. Bowne and remaindermen to Meyer Grayhead. Oct. 23. 485

1st av, w s, 50.5 n 108th st, runs west 100 x north 50 x east 83 x southeast 25.6 to av, x south 31, vacant. Bridget Hogan to James Keese. Sub. to taxes, &c. Oct. 12. 8,500

1st av, Nos. 2317 and 2319, w s, 50.5 s 119th st, 50.5x100, two five-story brk tenem'ts with stores. William H. Moore to Cornelius J. Mulvihill. Sept. 16. nom

2d av, No. 2308, e s, 80 n 118th st, 20.11x80, three-story brk dwell'g. Ella Kelly to Sophia A. Van De Mark. Mt. $8,000. Oct. 21. 12,000

2d av, n w cor 101st st, 100.11x100. Jessie C. McBride, Arverne, L. I., to Jessie Marks, Roselle, N. J. B. & S. Oct. 28. 43,000

2d av, n w cor. 101st st, 100.11x100, one-story frame buildings on corner, rest vacant. Arthur M. Mitchell to George A. Thomas. C. a. G. Oct. 5. other consid. and 30,000

2d av, n w cor 101st st, 100.11x100, one-story frame building and vacant. George A. Thomas to Jessie C. McBride, Arverne-by-the-Sea. Mt. $30,000. Oct. 23. other consid. and 33,000

2d av, No. 92, e s, 48.6 n 5th st, 24.3x100, four-story brk store and tenem't. John or Jean C. de Krom to Henry Stengel. Q. C. Oct. 24. nom

2d av, No. 472, e s, abt 50 s 27th st, 24.8x100, three-story brk store and tenem't with three-story brk building on rear. Charles Spoehrer to Hermann Spoehrer. Oct. 14. 23,500

5th av, No. 2144, w s, 130 s 132d st, 19.11x75, four-story stone front flat. Washington Life Ins. Co., New York, to Pauline Boettger. C. a. G. Oct. 26. 17,500

7th av, e s, 50.5 n 111th st, 50x100, vacant. Myer Hellman to William E. Callender. Mt. $8,000. Oct. 27. See 110th st. nom

8th av, No. 2140, e s, 51.4 s 116th st, 25.5x100, one-story brk stores. Foreclos. Francis B. Chedsey to Henry Von der Lieth. Mt. $11,000. Oct. 28. 7,300

8th av, No. 2456, e s, 25 n 131st st, 25x100, five-story brk store and flat. }
8th av, No. 2273, n w cor 120th st, 25.3x100, five-story brk flat with stores. }
James Riley and Margaret his wife to Richard Cummings. Mt. $60,966. Oct. 9. 75,500

8th av, w s, 25 n 126th st, 25x100. }
Fleetwood av, n s, 88.7 w Popham st, 30x100. }
Kate wife of William Power, Waterford, Ireland, to Mary Power. Q. C. June 6. nom

Same property. Lawrence Power, Waterford, Ireland, to same. Q. C. June 6. nom

11th av, w s, 24.11 s 184th st, 25x100. John C. Klett to Anna E. wife of Conrad Albeidt. Mt. $1,500 Oct. 26. 4,000

11th av, No. 898, e s, 50.5 s 62d st, 25x100, five-story brk tenem't with stores. James E. Hoctor to Bertha Smith. Mt. $15,000. Oct. 22. nom

Kingsbridge road, w s, 96 s w Dyckman st if extended, runs west 323.6 to point 134 s w of Dyckman st, x west 297 to point 158.7 s w of Dyckman st, x west 300.7 to point 176.3 s w of Dyckman st, x west 5 to point 181.3 s w of Dyckman st, x west 456 to point 216 s w Dyckman st, x northwest 92.6 to Hudson River R. R., x southwest along same 1,176 x southeast 587.6 x southeast 93.1 x east 301 x east 68.6 to w s Kingsbridge road, x north 134.6 x easterly still along road 285.10 x northeast still along road 429.9; also, }
All land bet e s of Hudson River R. R. and the Hudson River, bet the north and south lines of above, excepting land taken for railroad, the land lying bet the present w s and the former w s of Kingsbridge road. }
All title in land bet west line of Kingsbridge road, as it existed in 1863, and the west line of same as now established and to ½ of road adj. }
Mary J. Gordon to Walter S. Sheafer, Pottsville, Pa. Mt. $150,000. Oct. 21. 200,000

Interior lot, begins at point 80 w Amsterdam av and 50 s 130th st, runs east 6 x north — x southwest to point 43.9 s 130th st and 80 w av, x south 6.1½. John Lally and Mary his wife and Mary Whalen to Mary Larkin. B. & S. Oct. 21. nom

MISCELLANEOUS.

All part of mortgaged premises lying south of a line drawn parallel with 117th st and distant 97 n therefrom. Release mort. Morris Steinhardt to Elizabeth Johnston. Oct 20. nom

Same property. Release mort. Same to same. Oct. 20. 63,015

General release especialy as to claims under estate of Samuel Cohen. Clara Cohen to Michael Umstadter and Maurice S. Cohen exrs. Samuel Cohen. Oct. 23. 1,117

23d and 24th WARDS.

Ash st, n s, 150.9 w Morris av, 50x94.4x50x 94.7. Minnie F. Gouldrup, Auburn, N. Y., to William Hodgson. Oct 10. 2,000

Ash st, s s, 125.6 w Morris av, 50x100. Same to John A. Holden. Oct. 10. 2,400

Beech st, s s, 100 e Riverdale av, 50x100. John J. Bashford to Thomas C. Cornell. C. a G. Feb. 9, 1891. nom

Bender st (8th av), s e cor Jerome av, 30.6x100 x50x86 to Jerome av, x 23.11. Julius Kaesmeyer to Louisa Labro. Oct. 21. 7,000

Crotona pl, w s, 159.10 s 171st st, 100x100. Mary J. McGrath to Eugene D. McGrath. All liens. Sept. 16. nom

Crotona pl, w s, 134.10 s 171st st, 25x100. Same to same. All liens. Sept. 16. nom

Elmwood pl, n s, 100 w Clinton av, 25x95. }
Crotona av, w s, 100 s Lebanon st, 25x115.4x 26x122.9. }
John J. Brady to Jeremiah J O'Brien. Oct. 19. 1,740

Gambril st, n s, 321.8 e Marion av or Anthony st, 25x100. Emma wife of Louis W. Smith to James Allen. Oct. 28. nom

Suburban st, n s, 58.11 w Briggs av, 25x100. James M. Peebles and William J. McPherson to George Schmitt. Oct. 29. 1,050

Suburban st, n s, 83.11 w Briggs av, 25x100. Same to Louis Schmitt. Oct. 29. 1,050

Walnut st, n s, lot 27 map Mount Eden 50x100. John C. G. and Adolph G. Hupfel to Fredericka P. Conrad. B. & S. Jan. 20, 1883. 819

Willard st, s s, 400 e Kepler av, 50x100. Jane Potter individ. and extrx. of William H. Potter to Joel R. Warner, Boston, Mass. Oct. 16. 850

135th st, n s, 206.6 e Alexander av, 25x100. John Kelly to Catharine wife of James Kelly. April 6, 1891. nom

138th st, No. 632, s s, 106.6 w Willis av, 25x100. John M. Tracy to Sylvester E. Nolan. Mt. $13,500. Oct. 20. nom

142d st, s s, 100 w 3d av, 100x100. John and Nicholas Cotter to James T. Barry. Mt. $8,000. Oct. 5. 20,000

148th st, n s, 100 w Brook av, 50x100. William C. Loose, Jr., heir Maria Hilbert and Henrietta his wife to Frederic W. Meeske. Q. C. July 29, 1890. 250

Same property. Annie wife of George Ley heir Maria Hilbert to same. Q. C. Oct. 30, 1885. 500

152d st s s, 275 e Courtlandt av, 25x115. Peter Blauth, Jr., to Matthaus Mensch. Q. C. and correction deed. Oct. 19. nom

174th st, s s, now discontinued, 50 e Bender st formerly 8th av, 50x100. Julius Kaesmeyer to Emma Seitz. Oct. 24. 4,500

177th st, s s, 130 e Railroad av, 21.6x100.2x20.7 x103.6. Release mort. Adam Weiffenbach, Jr., to Kate Douglass. Oct. 7. nom

Same property. Release mort. Adam Weiffenbach to Kate Douglass. Oct. 29. nom

181st st, s s, at intersection with centre line of lot 208 map Prospect Hill estate, Fordham, runs west 25 x south 100 x 25 x 100. Charles Pitchie to Frances wife of John Wassner. Sept. 24. 3,000

Clinton av proposed, e s, 150 n from proposed n s Tremont av, 140x100x140.4x100. John J. Brady to Mary Seiferd. Sept. 26. nom

Clinton av, e s, 22 n Oakland pl, 44x100. }
Clinton av, n w cor Oakland pl, 114x100.5x 121.6x100. }
Crotona av, e s, 96 n Oakland pl, 24x100. }
Oakland pl, n e cor Cambreleng av, 19.7x98x 30.1x98.5. }
John J. Brady to Catharine and Julia Curran. Oct. 19. 5,185

Clinton av, w s, 125 n Tremont av as widened, 25x100. John J. Brady to George A. Castle. Oct. 19. 975

Crimmins av, w s, 562.4 n 141st st, 25x80. William R. Beal Land Improvement Co. to Alfred B. Hall. Oct. 22. 1,700

Crimmins av, w s, 462.4 n 141st st, 25x80. Same to William R. Beal. Oct. 22. 1,700

Forrest av, s e s, part lots 17 and 18 map Woodstock, runs southeast 300 x northeast 89.10 x northwest 200 x southwest 49.10 x northwest 100 to av x southwest 40. Joseph O. Downes to Sarah Jackson. Sept. 26. 5,000

Grove av, south cor John st, 150x133. Thomas H. Brown to Rufus R. Randall. Sub. to assessm'ts for widening John st or Franklin av and land taken for that purpose. Oct. 23. 2,500

Hull av, e s, 326.7 s Gun Hill road, 50x100. James Ferrier to Abraham Levy. Mt. $515. Oct. 26. 1,300

Jefferson av, s e s, lots 143-147 inclusive map of Samuel Ryer homestead, West Farms. }
Samuel st, s w s, lots 153, 154 and 155 same map. }
M. Teresa Murphy to Peter Farrell. Mt. $2,100. May 29, 1890. nom

Jefferson av, s e s, lot 147 map Samuel Ryer Homestead, 25x127x25x130. Peter Farrell to Pasquale Dauria. Oct. 28. 600

Lincoln av, e s, 50 n 135th st, 25x100. John Bode to Louise R. Pruher and Susannah Heffman. Mt. $7,000. Oct. 21. exch

Morris av, s w cor Ash st, 100x126.4x100x126.6. Minnie F. Gouldrup, Auburn, N. Y., to William J. Wiley. Oct. 10. 7,050

Old Fordham av, w s, 212.9 n 175th st and 1.8 w present 3d av, 27x102.6x27x103.7. The Mayor, &c., New York, to Theobald Mayer. Oct. 19. 4,000

Riverdale av, s e cor Beech st, 100x150x100x 100. Thomas C. Cornell to The Church of St. Margaret, City of New York. Feb. 18, 1891. gift

Stebbins av, e s, 258.9 w Freeman st, 25x114.10 x25.11x121.9. Edward E. Lumann to Franz Wilczewski. Oct. 26. 900

Stebbins av, e s, 283.9 n Freeman st, 25x107.11x 25.11x114.10. Same to Franz Frankowski. Oct. 26. 900

Teller av or Fleetwood av, w s, 116.6 s 164th st, 24x110. Ephraim C. Gates and Vashti R. his wife to James J. Fitzpatrick. B. & S. and C. a. G. June 15, 1891. 1,000

Tiebout av proposed, w s, 50 s Clark st, 25x100. William H. Duncan to Minna Bresler. Mt. $4,775. Oct. 26. nom

Tremont av proposed, n s, 46.1 e proposed Crotona av otherwise Franklin av, 25x 90.7. }
Cambreleng av, e s, 98.5 n Oakland pl, runs east 97.1 x north 73.2 x west 25 x west 81.6 to av, x south 82.9. }
John J. Brady to Margaret J. Howe. Oct. 19. 2,650

Tremont av, s s, 150 w Marmion av, 25x100. Lena Seiferd to Charles Munde and Franziska his wife. Oct. 27. 1,700

Union av, e s, 170 s 165th st, 5x165.7x5x165.4. Mary wife of William Haebnel, August and Frank Fechteler to Charles Schledorn. Oct. 15. 375

Valentine av, w s, 1,510.11 n of T. Bassfords land, being south ½ plot 16 map Peter Valentine property, Fordham, 50x250. Mary Pearson to Alice wife of Edward Burke, Jr. Oct. 29. 5,000

Vanderbilt av, e s, 150 n 173d st, 50x130. Sarah Spencer to William H. Leggett. Oct. 27. 3,000

Washington av, s e s, part lot 71 map Morrisania, 75.8x150.4x77.4x150.3. John F. Steeves and Imogene U. his wife to J. C. Julius Langbein. Mt. $5,000. Oct. 15. 11,500

Washington av, e s, part lot 63 map Morrisania, 75x122.7x75x117. Matilda Michaelis, Brooklyn, to Maria A. Wuytack. Mt. $3,000. Oct. 12. 7,000

Washington av, e s, 102 n Samuel st, 46x74x 62.2x80.6. Minnie F. Gouldrup, Auburn, N. Y., to Mary A. Hawkes. Mt. $1,000. Oct. 27. 2,400

Lot 412 map of building lots at Fordham, 24th Ward. The Industrial Co-operative Building and Loan Assoc. to Joseph H. Holland. Oct. 26. 3,250

New Drive as shown on map of M. E. Putnam at Spuyten Duyvil, w s, at intersection n s of lot 6, runs west 338.4 to N. Y. Central & Hudson River R. R., x south 50 x east 320 to drive, x north 50, except land under water Hudson River. Margaret E. wife of and Albert E. Putnam to Richard Pfeifer, Brooklyn. Oct. 14. 2,600

Road from Village of West Farms to Hunts Points, adj land of William Curser, runs northeast to Bronx River or West Farms Creek, 3 roods and 11 rods.
Road from Village of West Farms to Hunts Point at n w cor of land of Bronx Bleaching and Manufacturing Co., 3 roods and 12 rods.
Contract. Thomas, Jr., and Henry B. Bolton exrs. Ann Bolton to Jesse I. Eppinger. Sept. 26. 30,000

Interior lot, begins 125 n of Talmadge or 180th st, and 100 e of Railroad or Vanderbilt av, runs southeast 50 x northeast 125 x northwest 50 x southwest 125. Hester A. wife of and Robert H. Shannon to Peter N. Kotnowski. July 1. 1,000

Parcel begins 87.7 s of Hampden st formerly East 184th st and 104.3 w of Aqueduct av, runs west 125.9 x south 59.9 x east 139.3 to beginning, excepting any part included in Andrews av.
Parcel begins at intersection of west line of Helen L. Willis with n s of grantees lands, runs west 35.9 x north 22.6 x east 42.3.
Alfred J. Taylor and William D. Peck to The New York Skin and Cancer Hospital. June 19. 3,000

Strip adj e s of land conveyed by grantors to N. Y. & Hartford R. R. Co. and extdg. from 138th to 139th st, being 12 feet wide. Central Gas Light Co., New York, to The De La Vergne Refrigerating Machine Co. Grant of easement in consideration of the release of a former grant of easement over its property. Sept. 16.

Strip being west ½ of old Mill Brook, adj lots 51 and 50 map East Ward, Melrose, being 214 along brook, x— to centre brook. Henry L. Morris and ano. trustees Gouverneur Morris dec'd to Herman F. Kanenbley. Oct. 20. 50

General release, especially as to purchase of 6 lots on Washington av. Mary E. Sherwood individ. and extrx. Henry A. Sherwood to Simon Adler and Henry S. Herrman. Oct. 28. val. consid

LEASEHOLD CONVEYANCES.

Barclay st, Park pl — begins Barclay st, n e cor College pl, runs north 158.11 to Park pl, x east 28.6 x south 159 to Barclay st, x west 28.9.
Barclay st, Park pl — begins Barclay st, n s, 28.9 w College pl, 28.9x159.1 to Park pl, x 28.5x159.
Assign. lease. Joseph P. Knapp to Knapp Co., a corporation. Oct. 24. nom

Christopher st, No. 185. Assign. lease. Patrick D. O'Halloran to William Graham. nom

1st st, n s, 229 e 1st av, 42x105.11. William Astor to Alfred M. Sparks trustee John A. Gustin. 21 years, from May 1, 1886, per year, taxes and 650

14th st, No. 50, s s, 25 w Broadway, 24.9x118x26x108.11. Thomas Sanderson and Helen A. Elam, London, Eng., and Mary Furniss, Higham, Eng., Laura C. Camidge, Bathurst, New South Wales, and Samuel W. and William S. Johnson, Rye, N. Y., to The United Domestic Sewing Machine Co. 20 years, from Nov. 1, 1892, per year, taxes, &c., and 10,000

16th st, No. 57 W. Assign. lease. John Henry Sylvester and Christian Wahman to Haaren & Meinken. nom

Same property Assign. lease. Adelheit M. Holsten and ano. admrs. Richard Holsten to J. Henry Sylvester and Christian Wahmann. nom

23d st, No. 14 E. Assign. lease. Nathan Schwab to Leo Schlesinger. nom

28th st, No. 324 W., s s, 18.9x98.9. Nathalie E. Baylies to Isabella Van Dolsen. 21 years, from Sept. 1, 1891, per year, taxes, and 405

Av A, s w cor 3d st, 26.6x100. William Astor to Alfred M. Sparks trustee John A. Gustin. 20 years, from May 1, 1887, per year, taxes, and 1,100

Av B, No. 202. Assign. lease. Jacob Reinhard to Louise Heinrichs. nom

Same property. Assign. lease. Louise Heinrichs to David J. Bonoliel. nom

Willis av, No. 249. Assign. lease. John G. Baumgarth to Adolph Plangemann. nom

2d av, No. 1945. Assign. lease. Friedrich Huners and George Lebers to Thomas Graham. nom

3d av, n w cor 87th st, runs west 125 x north 100.8 x east 25 x south 49.3 x east 20 x south 25 x east 80 to av, x south 26.5. George W. Archer to Thomas B. Whiffen. 30 years, from Mar. 1, 1892, per year, 1,200, 1,500, 1,800, 2,000

3d av, No. 1118, w s, 80.5 n 65th st, 20x83.6. Consent to assign. lease. Louisa M. Gerry to Jonas Weil and Bernhard Mayer. nom

3d av, No. 449. Assign. lease. Bernard T. Kearns to William Matthies. nom

6th av, s w cor 39th st, 98.8x100. Assign. lease. Jules Charriere admr. and Marie J. C. Foglia admrx. Elizabeth Charriere to Bernard Heller. Mt. $20,000. 35,000

Same property Agreement to accept responsibility for rent and covenants under lease. Bernard Heller to Henry G., Jr., and Walter P. Silleck exrs., &c., Henry G. Silleck. Oct. 21. nom

7th av, No. 881. Assign. lease. Patrick Cashin to Henry Elias Brewing Co. nom

Same property. Assign. lease. Henry Elias Brewing Co. to Patrick Cashin. nom

10th av, No. 861, store building and premises. Assign. lease. Michael J. Lawlor to Maria E. Carley. nom

Same property. Assign. lease. Maria E. Carley to The Long Island Brewery. nom

KINGS COUNTY.

OCTOBER 22, 23, 24, 26, 27, 28.

Adelphi st, w s, 119.2 s Flushing av, 23x41.5x22x41.2. Charles L. Behlert to Anthony Vander Wulbeke. Mt. $1,200. $1,800

Bainbridge st, n s, 140 e Sumner av, 40x100. David F. Kimberly to Vina A. Sumner, of Syracuse. 5,200

Bainbridge st, n e cor Saratoga av, 23x100, h & l. Victor J. Dowling to Kate S. Good. B. & S. and C. a. G. All liens. nom

Baltic st, n e s, 300 s e Hoyt st, 25x100. Mary Mockler to David B. Mitchell. 2,700

Same property. David B. Mitchell to The Star Union Improvement Co. Mt. $1,400. 10

Barbey st, e s, 160 n Linnington av, 40x100. Edwin J. Koch, of Bayonne, N. J., to Alonzo E. De Baun. nom

Bergen st, n s, 270 e Ralph av, 50x107.2. Mary E. wife of Isaac D. Mason to George C. Hollister, Rochester, N. Y. Mt. $5,400. nom

Bergen st, s s, 222 e Schenectady av, 75x127.9. Sarah G. wife of Jonas H. Platt to Frederick Dhuy, Jr. 2,500

Bleecker st, s e s, 341.8 s w Central av, 16.8x100, h & l. William C. Van Duzer to George C. W. Ruck. 2,500

Bleecker st, n w s, 20.9 s w Evergreen av, 19.2x100. Hermann Fruwirth to William Waegerle. 4,000

Bradford st, w s, 175 n Glenmore av, 25x100. Julia Morrow, of South Nyack, N. Y., to Edward Fleming. 1,500

Broadway, n s, 100 e Schaeffer st, 20x100; also several parcels in Newtown. Marie wife of Frederick Schad, heirs, &c., Jacob Marquardt to Heinericke Marquardt widow. 14,250

Broadway, n s, 45 w Dodworth st, 45x94x45x94.10; also,
Dodworth st, n w s, 95.8 n e Broadway, 25x90.
Lewis Jacobs to Jacob Mayer. Sub. to morts. 20,500

Butler st, n s, 125 e Buffalo av, 50x127.9. Release dower. Mary E. wife of William H. Sherman to Thomas Jackson. nom

Same property. Thomas Jackson to Robert J. Griffith. 500

Carroll st, s s, 240 w Columbia st, 20x100, h & l. Jeremiah Mahoney to Antonio Gattavaro. 4,200

Cleveland st, w s, 225 s Hegeman av, 20x100.
Cleveland st, e s, 205 s Hegeman av, 60x100.
Eliza M. Stackhouse to Stephen W. Stoothoff. Mt. $500. exch

Congress st, s w s, 190 s e Columbia st, 25x91.9x25x91.8. Peter Mallon to Peter Connolly. nom

Cook st, n s, 200 e Ewen st, 25x100, h & l. Leopold Michel to Jacob Joseph and Mina his wife, joint tenants. Mt. $5,000. 10,500

Cooper st, s e s, 347.6 n e Evergreen av, 19.6x10. Robert Smith to George T. Moon trustee for George E. Moon. Mt. $2,200. 3,500

Dean st, n s, 120 e Albany av, 20x80. Catharine M. Manning to Charles Tannenbaum and Harry T. Dietz. Mt. $1,500. 5,000

Dean st, n s, 83.4 e Utica av, 116.8x107.2; also,
Bergen st, n s, 245 e Rochester av, 120x107.2.
Isaac Halstead to Henry Weil. Correction deed. nom

Dean st, n s, 271 w Nostrand av, 17.8x100, h & l. Grace M. Faulkner to Mary T. Faulkner. B. & S. and C. a. G. nom

Dean st, n s, 133.4 e Utica av, 33.4x100. Release mort. Lillie Cohen to Charles A. Martin. ——

Decatur st, n s, 132.6 e Reid av, 17.2x100. Esther Evans to Mary Skinner. Mt. $2,500. exch

Degraw st, n s, 200 w Clason av, runs west 50 x north 131 x east 75 x south 31 x west 25 x south 100. Jane O. Carpenter to Thomas Monohan. Mt. $400. 1,300

Diamond st, s s, 100 w Albany av, runs west to land of Messeberg, x south to lane, x — x —; also,
Lots 9 and 10 map J. Lang property, Flatbush.
Release mort. Frederick Middendorf to Frank C. Lang. 2,000

Douglass st, n s, 400 w Franklin av, 140x131. George Wilcox, of Summit, N. J., to Harrie Bulkley. 12,887

Same property. Foreclos. John Courtney, Sheriff, to George Wilcox. 5,000

Douglass st, s s, 161.8 e 4th av, 17.6x100. Eben W. Roby to John Fallon. nom

Same property. John Fallon to Maria C. Claesson. Mt. $3,050. 4,050

Dresden st, w s, 270.5 n Atlantic av, 75x108.11x75x104. Foreclos. Alonzo C. Farnham to Jane L. wife of Charles H. Smith. 1,150

Eastern Parkway, s w cor Powell st, 50x100. Feiga Kinjerska to Louis Rubenstein. nom

Eastern Parkway, s s, 20 e Montauk av, 20x90. Ernst Pauline to William H. Jackson. 375

Eckford st, e s, 200 n Nassau av, 25x100, h & l. Mary R. wife of William J. Lutz, John J., Annie L., Elizabeth C. and Teresa M. McCabe to Catharine McCabe widow. nom

Eldert st, n w s, 392 n e Evergreen av, 19x100. Release mort. Ann E. Cozine and ano. exrs. John G. Cozine and Jas. Gascoine individ. to Leopold J. Lippmann. 2,579

Same property. Leopold J. Lipmann to Ludwig Rotbaug. nom

Eldert st, n w s, 259 n e Evergreen av, 19x100, h & l. Leopold J. Lippmann to John G. Mitchell. nom

Same property Release mort. James Gascoine individ. and with ano. exrs. John G. Cozine to Leopold J. Lippman. 2,580

Eldert st, s e s, 287.6 n e Broadway, 18x100, h & l. Catharine M. Gregory to Charles A. Gregory. Mt. $1,800. 4,500

Elton st, w s, 175 n Liberty av, 25.2x90. Partition. Edward R. Vollmer ref. to Sarah Lipsky. Mt. $2,000 and int. 3,730

Elton st, e s, 125 s Arlington av, 25x100. James W. Crawford, of New York, to James F. Bidstrup. Mt. $600. 1,100

Essex st, w s, 120 n Arlington av, 20x100. Harmon A. Whitlock to Julia A. Terhune. Mt. $1,700. 3,650

Same property. Julia A. Terhune to Mary H. Magie, Kansas City. Mt. $1,700. 1,000

Freeman st, s s, 125 w Manhattan av, 25x100. Joseph M. Forbes to Eliza wife of Alexander Ray. 4,500

Fanchon pl, w s, 9.1 n Bushwick av, runs north 100 x west 100 x south to n e s Bushwick av, x southeast — x east 13.3. Eliza Happ to Christiana Haering. 5,000

Floyd st, No. 126, s s, 355 e Marcy av, 20x100. Hyman Schiwinski to The Board of Education of the City of Brooklyn. 5,250

Floyd st, s s, 350 w Tompkins av, 44.6x100. George M. Van Doren to The Board of Education of the City of Brooklyn. 9,800

Front st, n s, 107.6 e Jay st, runs north 100 x west 20 x south 51.6 x southwest 8.8 x south 41.6 to Front st, x east 25.9. James Devlin to George L. Pease and William B. Boorum. Mt. $2,500. 7,750

Gold st, e s, 20 n Front st, 20x54.3. Bridget A. Keyburn widow to Mary F. Darmody. 6,475

Grove st, n w s, 350 s w Central av, 20x100. Moses P. Prout to Eliza Nimmo. nom

Grove st, s e s, 585 s w Central av, 40x100. Charles E. Raynor to Frank Ibert. 3,200

Halsey st, s e s, 100 n e Bushwick av, 20x120. Louny Schroeder to John D. Helmken. Mt. $1,800. 2,000

Halsey st, s s, 350 e Reid av, 16.4x100. Release mort. Carrie Grove, of Amityville, to Frank C. Swimm. nom

Hancock st, s s, 36 w Patchen av, 16x75, h & l. Isabelle B. wife of John M. Booth to Joseph A. Cross. Mt. $4,000. nom

Hancock st, No. 311, n s, abt 95 e Tompkins av.
Hancock st, No. 339, n s, abt 347 e Tompkins av, 18x100.
Contract. William H. Reynolds to Mary A. Cornell widow. Exchange for following: Jefferson av, s s, No. 128, flat house; also Nos. 186–196 South 2d st, Plainfield, N. J.

Hancock st, s e s, 375 n e Bushwick av, 20x100. Eliza B. Burton to Eveline M. Kuster. Mt. $2,500. 4,800

Harman st, s e s, 275 n e Irving av, 25x95.8x25x96.11. Jacob Blank to Albert Markert. nom

Harman st, s e s, 225 n e Knickerbocker av, 25 x abt 134x25x134.7. Contract. Katharine Scheffel to William Renner. 1,500

Hart st, n w s, 200 n e Hamburg av, 25x100. Bernhard Goodstein to Mark Goodstein. nom

Hart st, n s, 278 e Nostrand av, 20x100. Thomas E. Greenland to Samuel Pickford. Mt. $3,000. 9,000

Hemlock st, e s, 228 s Fulton av, 25x100. Robert L. Woods and Robert L. Woods, Jr., to James Mulligan. 450

Hemlock st, e s, 253 s Fulton av, 81x100x75x100. Same to Patrick Mulligan. 1,350

Hemlock st, e s, 203 s Fulton av, 25x100. Same to Lawrence Mulligan. 450

Hendrix st, e s, 150 n Blake av, 25x100, h & l. Julia J. Whitlock to Julia A. Terhune. Mt. $1,450. 3,300

Same property. Julia A. Terhune to Mary H. Magie, Kansas City. Mt. $1,850. 1,000

Hendrix st, w s, 125 s Vienna av, 20x105.6. Thomas F. Watts to Anna Dedreux. 100

Herkimer st, s s, 150 e New York av, 20x100, h & l. William Shirden to Timothy Curran. Mt. $1,100. 4,125

Herkimer st, n s, 100 e Utica av, 25x100. Martin T. Sprague, of Brandon, Vt., to Elizabeth A. Hall. 2,000

Hicks st, w s, 76.2 n Orange st, 25x101. Daniel T. Leverich to Edward S. Atwood. 12,000

Hicks st, e s, 38 n West 9th st, 18x80. William R. Bartlett to Charles Thorsen. Sub. to all liens. 400

Hoyt st, w s, 74 s Carroll st, 22.10x47.10x22.10x45.9. David F. Manning to Louis Luckenbach. 3,000

Hubbard st, n w s, at intersection with Gravesend Bay, lots 1–5 inclusive map of C. G. Gunther property, Gravesend Beach, 99.8x129.2x144.5 to bay, x 137.6. Amelia A. Gunther and ano. exrs. and trustees to Edward C. M. Fitzgerald. 1,350

Same property. Release dower. Amelia A. Gunther widow to same. 650

Jefferson st, s w ½ of lot 505B map 4 Fort Hamilton Village, 25x110; also,
Southwest ½ of lot 216 map No. 3 South Greenfield, 50x100; also,
Lots 44 and 45 map T. H. Braisted property, Flatbush.
Orynthia wife of James A. Sargent to Wilfred Wiley. 700

Jerome st, e s, 100 n Dumont av, 40x100, hs & ls. Thomas G. Nottage, Jr., to Louise wife of Charles Spindler, Hoboken, N. J. Mt. $1,500. 2,900

Kosciusko st, n s, 146 e Lewis av, 18x100, h & l. Charles J. A. Goertz to Charles Rein. *Mt.* $6,085. 6,900

Kosciusko st, n s, 280.8 w Reid av, 18.11x100. Frederick Schilling to Joseph Petri. 2,850

Kosciusko st, s, 291.8 w Lewis av, 16.8x100. Partition. John H. Kemble to Robert H. Gibbs. 2,675

Linwood st, w s, 165 s Stanley av, 80x100. Peter Nehrbass to John Denninger. 575

Luquer st, n s, 116.9 e Columbia st, 16.9x100, excepting small gore off north end. Dennis Coakley to John McCarthy. Reverses life estate. nom

Lynch st, n s, 100 e Bedford av, 10x16.3x—x—. Ansel Jones, Deep River, Conn., to William P. Ryan. Q. C. nom

Main st, e s, 153.4 s Front st, 47.10x abt 105. Abraham Wolf et al. exrs. Samuel Bach to Deborah and Benjamin Bach. 16,000

Macon st, n s, 110 e Ralph av, 18x100, h & l. Andrew D. Baird to Annie Gilmour. *Mt.* $4,000. 6,700

Macon st, n s, 195.9 w Lewis av, 19.9x100, h & l. Daniel B. Norris to Sarah B. wife of Charles B. Holmes. *Mt.* $4,200. 9,000

Macon st, s s, 128 e Patchen av, 18x100. Frank McDonough to Carl J. Carlson. *Mt.* $4,000. 6,500

Macon st, s s, 272.6 w Stuyvesant av, 17.6x100, h & l. Mary E. Winters to J. Russell Taber. *Mt.* $6,500. 1,000

Macon st, s s, 346 w Ralph av, 18x100. William J. Anderson to Matilda Ballay. *Mt.* $4,000. 6,800

Macon st, s s, 272.6 w Stuyvesant av, 17.6x100, h & l. Arthur Taylor to Mary E. Winters. 7,500

Madison st, s e s, 370 n e Central av, 20x100, h & l. Emil F. Wildner to August Koch. *Mt.* $2,200. 5,500

Madison st, s s, 450 w Patchen av, 40x100. Joseph Irwin, of Huntington, N. Y., exr. John Clark to Charles B. Wheeler. 5,500

Same property. Joseph and Thomas E. and Daisy E. Irwin, of Huntington, N. Y., Cornelia A. wife of and Benjamin A. Duryea, Grace D. wife of and William H. Bishop, John C., Thomas S. and Alfred E. Irwin to same. nom

Same property. Robert N., Gertrude D., Daisy E., Frank, Henry E., Grace H., Alberta and George Irwin and William H., Mabel and George I. McFarland by guard to same. 5,500

Madison st, s s, 241 e Lewis av, 20x100. Release mort. Thomas S. Strong, of New York, to Phebe A Godfrey. 1,006

Same property. Phebe A. wife of and William Godfrey to Harvey Major. *Mt.* $6,000. 10,500

Madison st, n w s, 300 n e Hamburg av, 20x100. Release mort. James Gascoine individ. and with ano. exrs. Jno. G. Cozine to Adolphus Gload. 1,243

Madison st, n w s, 300 n e Hamburg av, 20x100. Adolphus Gload to Louis Feldheim. *Mt.* $2,500. 4,500

Marion st, st, 200 e Reid av, 25x100. Release mort. Henry Demarest exr. John Demarest, of Spring Valley, N. Y., to William J. G. Bearns. 1,219

Market st, e s, 1,666 s Brooklyn and Jamaica pike, 62.6x150. Aaron L. Roberts to Emily R. Roberts. Q. C. and correction deed. nom

Market st, e s, 1,666 s Brooklyn and Jamaica turnpike, 155x150; also,
Market st, e s, 1,541 s Brooklyn and Jamaica turnpike, 62.6x150.
Emily R. Roberts and Elizabeth A. Pinner to Marenus J. Goodenough. 5,625

Market st, e s, 1,603.6 s Brooklyn and Jamaica turnpike, 62.6x150. Louis P. Nostrand to same. 1,875

McDonough st, s s, 81 e Ralph av, 19x100, h & l. Thomas H. Radcliffe to Charles Fox, New York. *Mt.* $5,500. 9,000

Meserole st, s s, 25 w Humboldt st, 25x100. Christian Hack to Wilhelmine C. Haenlein. All title. nom

Same property. Wilhelmine C. Haenlein to August Haenlein. *Mt.* $1,200. nom

Monitor st, w s, 173.3 s Driggs av, 18x100. Charles Engert to Charles E. Lund. 4,000

Monroe pl, n w s, 161.6 n e Pierrepont st, 26.6x100. Alexander Studwell to George S. Studwell. Trust deed. nom

Monroe st, s s, 385.3 w Tompkins av, 20x100, h & l. Josephine Wyant to Samuel H. Newby. *Mt.* $2,000. 5,500

Monroe st, s s, 275 w Tompkins av, 17.7x100, h & l. Alfred B. Price to Lillian Price and Ida A. Connette. ½ part. nom

Monroe st, s w cor Lewis av, 22.6x81, h & l. Alfred B. Price to Lillian Price and Ida A. Connette. ½ part. Sub. to mort. $2,000. nom

Morrell st, n e cor Moore st, 25x81.7 to Bushwick av, x29.5x77.2. Patrick Hayes to Joseph Pender. 3,000

Nelson st, s w s, 181.4 s e Hamilton av, 25x64.9x27x54.6. Mary wife of Michael Anglim to Mary C. Anglim. Reserves life estate. gift

Nevins st, e s, 20 s Sackett st, 20x78, h & l. Amelia M. Behrens to William Campbell. 2,800

Ocean Parkway, w s, 524 s Sheepshead Bay and Coney Island road, 100x250 to roadway, excepting strip off rear for street, Gravesend. Peter Thomas to Ralphina Kirkman. *Mt.* $2,000. exch

Osborn st, w s, 150 n Glenmore av, 25x100, h & l. Louis Lebewohl, New York, to Abraham Ruth. ½ part. 2,600

Pacific st, n s, 125 e 4th av, 25x90, h & l. Israel Lebowitz, of New York, to Gustave Pius. *Mt.* $8,500. 13,500

Pacific st, s w s, 200 s e Hoyt st, 25x100. Mary A. Alder to William J. and Benjamin S. Alder. Sub. to mort. $6,000 and life estate grantor. nom

Pacific st, n s, 376 e Rochester av, 16x100. Frederick Dhuy, Jr., to John W. Deane. *Mt.* $1,800. 2,800

Pacific st, n s, 350 w Kingston av, 100x200 to Atlantic av. Charles L. Marsh to Charles H. Nichols. *Mt.* $10,000. 30,000

Parker st, lot begins 100 s Bennett st and 75 e Banzett st, runs southeast to centre of Parker st, x east to point 15 n e from centre of railroad, x northwest to land of C. H. Conklin—x south 19 x west 25.
Maspeth av, n w s, 15.8 w from centre of railroad, runs northwest to centre of Morgan av, x north to point 15 n e of centre of said railroad, x southeast to Maspeth av, x west —.
New York, Brooklyn & Manhattan Beach R. R. Co. and Austin Corbin individ. and trustees to Edward Cooper et al. exrs. Peter Cooper. Q. C. nom

Plymouth st, Nos. 321 and 323, n s, 28.3x100. Lizzie K. Reynolds to Henri L. Bates and Earl P. Lawrence, Portsmouth, N. H. B. & S. *Mt.* $11,000. nom

Powell st, e s, 125 s Liberty av, 45x100. Frank Seliger, Jr., to Elizabeth Seliger. *Mt.* $1,500. nom

Powell st, w s, 116 n Liberty av, 16x100, h & l. John F. Vrooman to Laura P. Gibbs. *Mt.* $1,800. 3,000

President st, s s, 177.6 e Hoyt st, 17.6x100, h & l. Brainerd Quarry Co to James H. Shaw. 2,800

President st, s s, 214.2 e 7th av, 20.4x100, h & l. Sarkis M. Minasian to Anna M. Minasian. *Mt.* $9,000. nom

President st, s s, 314.6 w 5th av, 17x100. N. Denison Morgan to Margaret E. and Celia A. Burnett. *Mt.* $5,000. 7,000

Prospect pl, n s, 97.7 e 5th av, 18.9x80.3. Robert A. Lindsay to Josephine wife of Herman Fruwirth. 6,250

Prospect st, s e cor Washington st, 21.9x80. Daniel T. Leverich to Edward S. Atwood. 13,000

Quincy st, n s, 60 e Bedford av, 20x100, h & l. Mary A. Platt to Matilda C. and Lydia L. Platt. Sub. to mort. and life estate. 1888. nom

Quincy st, No. 468, s s, 62 w Throop av, 19x80. William M. Gibson to Levi M. Scott, of Greensboro, N. C. *Mt.* $4,500. 7,800

Quincy st, n s, 85.6 w Ralph av, 20x100. Foreclos. John Courtney to Robert L. Moores and Charles A. Le Quesne. *Mt.* $6,500. 1,050

Quincy st, n s, 105.6 w Ralph av, 20x100. Foreclos. Same to same. *Mt.* $6,500. 1,050

Roebling st, e s, 50 s South 1st st, 50x83.4, reserving 6-foot alley. Mary A Spence, formerly Noonan an heir of Ellen Noonan to Alice McDonnell. ¼ part. 425

Ross st as continued, w s, 55.7 s Division av, runs west 28 x north 1.7 x west 22 x south 24.2 x southeast 22.2 to Ross st, x northeast 50. William Beck to Emma L. Dean. 1889. nom

Ryerson st, e s, 99.6 n Lafayette av, runs east 50 x north 0.6 x east 50 x north 15 x west 100 to st, x south 15.6, h & l. James Halliday to Sophia Halliday. B. & S. gift

Schenck st, e s, 323 s Willoughby av, 25x67.10x25x66.11. Release mort. Everett P. Wheeler et al. exrs. David Everett to Benjamin Andrews. nom

Scholes st, No. 135, n s, 130 e Ewen st, 25x100. George Wetzel to Franz C. Weber and Katherine his wife, joint tenants. *Mt.* $2,000. 5,100

Same property. Rosanna Bittner to George Wetzel and Eva his wife, joint tenants. *Mt.* 2,000. 4,800

Seigel st, s s, 565 e Bushwick av, 25x100. Charles W. Truslow admr. Wm. Wall to John Herling. 750

Seigel st, s s, 315 e Bushwick av, 25x100. Charles W. Truslow admr. Wm. Wall to John Herling. 1,025

Stanhope st, n w s, 375 n e Hamburg av, 25x100. Release mort. Theodore F. Jackson to Wilhelmina Schwenck. 1,225

Stockholm st, s s, 350 e Evergreen av, late Willow av, 25x100. Alois Dillmann to August Siefers. 6,700

Thames st, s s, 25 w Morgan av, 25x100. Conrad Sauer to Moritz Hausmann. 1,650

Tillary st, n s, 64.9 w Jackson st, 20x47.4x20.3x50.5, h & l. Herman Sacks to Sarah J. Sweet. *Mt.* $2,900. 5,000

Tulip st, n s, 229.1 w Troy av, 40x100, Flatbush. Contract Michael Sullivan to Catharine Sullivan. 700

Tulip st, n s, 169.1 w old Troy av, Flatbush. Contract. Same to Edward D. Cook. 700

Union st, s s, 77 w 6th av, runs south 90 x west 15 x south 5 x west 3 x north 95 to st, x east 18, h & l. Mary Seib to Henry J. Straukamp. *Mt.* $4,500. 7,000

Union st, s s, 225 w Ralph av, 146.5x140.2x121.7x103.3, Flatbush. William Bradshaw to George Ansell. *Mt.* $500. 1,100

Van Buren st, n s, 135.6 e Reid av, 17.9x100, h & l. Ellen E. Whittlesey to Susan M. Orr. *Mt.* $3,000. 5,900

Van Buren st, s s, 342.9 w Reid av, 14.3x100. Irwin Beasty to Henry Stewart, of New York. *Mt.* $1,400. 3,500

Van Buren st, s s, 328.6 w Reid av, 14.3x100. Same to Charles T. Lamb, of New York. *Mt.* $1,400. 3,500

Varet st, n s, 75 w Humboldt st, 25x100. Joseph Zirinsky to Joseph Levine. *Mt.* $2,300. 3,675

Varet st, s s, 150 w Humboldt st, 25x100. Leopold Michel and David Stern to Edward and Samuel D. Isaacson. *Mt.* $5,000. 11,000

Varet st, n s, 100 e Graham av, 25x100. Charles Maurer to The Broadway Bank of Brooklyn. 1,500

Varet st, n s, 125 e Graham av, 16.9x100. Theodore and Charles Maurer to same. 1,500

Warren st, n e s, 146.4 n w Court st, 20.9x62.6. Tecumseh Pierce, of New York, to Mary wife of Tecumseh Pierce. *Mt.* $1,500. nom

Warwick st, w s, 100 s Blake av, 20x100.
Warwick st, w s, 160 s Blake av, 20x100.
Emil A. Janssen to Annie McCartney. 450

Watkins st, e s, 250 s Union av, 50x100. Nikodem Tomassewski to Stanislau Pruss. *Mt.* $700. 4,000

Same property. Stanislaus Pruss to Anthony Plachecki. *Mt.* $700. 4,500

Weirfield st, n w s, 101.2 s w Central av, 20x100. Leopold J. Lippmann to Francis Stanton. *Mt.* $2,500. nom

Same property. Release mort. Oliver W. Coe to Leopold J. Lippmann. 2,486

Weirfield st, n w s, 161.2 s w Central av, 20x100. Leopold J. Lippmann to Henrietta Wilson. *Mt.* $2,500. nom

Same property. Release mort. Oliver W. Coe to Leopold J. Lippmann. 486

Weirfield st, n w s, 100 s w Bushwick av, 20x100. Daniel Muller to Mary wife of Daniel Muller. nom

Weirfield st, n w s, 321 s w Central av, 20x100. Release mort. Oliver W. Coe of New York, to Leopold J. Lippman. 2,486

Willoughby st, s s, 84.11 w Bridge st, 22.7x100.
Fleet st, n w s, 72.8 n e De Kalb av, runs northwest 21.5 x west 29.9 x north 20.7 x east 9 x north 2 x east 21.7 x southeast 31.10 to Fleet st, x southwest 20; also,
Lawrence st, w s, 125 s Myrtle av, 25x107.6.
Wyckoff st, s s, 36.8 e Bond st, 16.8x100; also,
Wyckoff st, s s, 53.4 e Bond st, 16.8x100; also,
Wyckoff st, s s, 103.4 e Bond st, 16.8x100.
Adolph Eichhorn to Sabina Eichhorn. Sub. to all liens nom

Woodbine st, n w s, 165 s w Knickerbocker av, 20x100. Release mort. James Gascoine individ and with Anna E. Cozine exrs. John G. Cozine to Albert Berckmeier. 2,559

Same property. Albert Berckmeier to John Schaeffer. nom

Woodbine st, s e s, 282 n e Hamburg av, 18x100. George W. and Charles H. Francisco to Daniel Obler. *Mt.* $2,500. 4,830

1st pl, s s, 25 w Court st, abt 25x½ block, h & l. Contract. J. C Metcalfe to Charles Feltman. Exchange for 70-acre farm at Chester, Mass. —

South 1st st, s s, 50 w Marcy av, 25x60. Mary E. wife of and Washington McLean to Elias L. Way, of New York. *Mt.* $3,000. 5,400

2d st, s w s, 197.10 n w 7th av, runs northwest 98.2 x southwest 95 x southeast 32 x southwest 5 x southeast 66.1 x northeast 100. Donald C. Ross to Henrietta Ross. nom

3d pl, n s, 40 e Henry st, 20x60. Foreclos. Tennis Williamson to Michael H. Hagerty. 3,500

4th st, s s, 271.10 w 7th av, 20x100. Release mort. Franklin Trust Co, to Mary L. Moses. 5,510

4th st, s s, 27.10 w 7th av, 20x100. Release mort. William L. Dowling to Mary L. Moses. nom

South 4th st, s e cor Havemeyer st, 19.2x81x19.2x81.1. William D. Koopmann to Anna Koopmann. B. & S. Correction deed. 6,000

7th st, n s, 97.6 w 5th av, 17.6x100. Samuel M. Hubbard to Bridget E. Tucker extrx. John T. Tucker. Q. C. 15

Same property. Release dower. Bridget E. Tucker to James Martin. nom

Same property. Bridget E. Tucker and John T. Moran exrs. John Tucker to same. *Mt.* $2,800. 4,500

8th st, s w s, 195.1 n w 6th av, 16.8x95, h & l. Kate Cohen to Patrick J. Kelly, Jersey City. *Mt.* $2,000. 4,500

9th st, s w s, 150 n w 2d av, 25x100. Joseph W. Little to Frederick H. Trowbridge. given as collateral security

South 9th st, s s, 171 e Bedford av, runs south 175 x northeast to point 196 from Bedford av, x north 170 to South 9th st, x west 25 to beginning. Edward E. Wells exr. John G. or L. Brown to Christian and Justus Doenecke. 6,200

South 9th st, n w cor Havemeyer st, 12x80.5x35x82. Benjamin C. Smith to Frederick Ulrich. Q. C. nom

10th st, n s, 194.11 w 5th av, 16.8x100. Catharine T. Fitzpatrick to Charlotte A. Bierds. exch

12th st, n s, 97.10 w 5th av, 20x100. William Corrigan to James V. L. Johnson. *Mt.* $4,500. 7,000

12th st, n s, 177.10 w 5th av, 20x100. William Corrigan to Hannah E. wife of Gilbert H. Brower. *Mt.* $4,500. 7,000

13th st, s s, 322.10 e 4th av, 20x100. Agnes Schleifer to Henry Burn. 6,000

14th st, s s, 122.10 e 5th av, 24x100. Sophia F. Shores to Leopold A. Basler. 3,800

East 18th st, e s, 400 n Av B, runs east to centre line bet East 18th and East 19th sts, x north to boundary line of parties hereto, x southwest to beginning; also,
Interior gore on centre line bet East 18th and East 19th sts, at point 425 n Av B, runs north to said boundary line above mentioned, x northeast and southeast to point 425 n Av B, x north to beginning, Flatbush.

William Matthews to Gertrude B. Lott and Maria B. Story. nom

East 21st st, e s, 129 s Voorhis av as narrowed, runs 27.6x127x24.3x126.6, Gravesend. Horace B. Allen to Harriet L. Allen. *Mt.* $4,961. nom

Bay 25th st, n w s, 380 s w Benson av, 60x96.8, New Utrecht. James D. Lynch to Annie L. Young. 1,650

46th st, s s, 180 e 4th av, 20x100.2. Release mort. James B. Murray, of New York, to James Tibball. 500

46th st, s s, 200 e 4th av, 0.2x100.2. Same to Mary J. Motram. nom

46th st, s s, 180 e 4th av, 20x100.2. James Tibball to Mary J. Motram, of New York. *Mt.* $2,500. 4,300

52d st, s s, 140 e 8th av, 40x100.2, New Utrecht. Jacob P. Hardt to John Toomey. 400

56th st, n e s, 150 s e 14th av, 50x100.2, New Utrecht. The West Brooklyn Land and Improvement Co. to Nellie R. Tangerman. 1,000

63d st, n s, 880 w 14th av, 20x100, New Utrecht. James V. S. Woolley to Miles O'Reilly. 225

64th st, s s, 760 e 14th av, 20x100, Lefferts Park. Effingham H. Nichols to Harry Egge. 225

66th st, e s, 175 s 6th av, 50x100.2, New Utrecht. Roger Taylor to Michael W. Kenney. nom

Same property. Michael W. Kenney to Roger Taylor. nom

72d st, s s, 450 w 15th av, 20x100, New Utrecht. James V. S. Woolley to Noel Bertrand, New York. 200

73d st, n s, 130 w 15th av, 40x100, Leffert's Park. Henry B. Lyons, of Flatbush, to Martha A. Dilliard. 550

76th st, s s, 250 w 15th av, 20x79 9x20x79.2, Lefferts Park. James V. S. Woolley to Harriet Cavaner and Bridget F. Rooney, New York. 125

77th st, centre line, n w of 11th av, begins on centre line between 76th and 77th sts at point 400 n w 11th av, runs northwest 102.7 x southwest 246.5 x east 126.10 x south to point 340 n w 11th av, x northeast to centre line 77th st, x northwest 60 x northeast 130, New Utrecht. Hoik D. Campbell to The Bay Ridge Park Improvement Co. nom

77th st, s s, 370 w 3d av, 50x109.4, New Utrecht. Charles A. Erickson to Henrietta W. wife of Floyd S. Sandford. *Mt.* $5,000. nom

79th st, s w s, adjoins land of Amelia Gubner on east, 243.1 to land late of J. F. Delaplaine, x 135.10 to Denyses lane, x 308.9 along same, x88.10.
74th st, s w s, gore bounded southeast by Amelia Gubner's land and southwest by Denyses lane, New Utrecht.
Hoik D. Campbell to Jane E. wife of Fred H. Johnson. nom

Same property; also,
79th st, n s, 340 w 11th av, runs north to land of J. F. Delaplaine, x southerly to 19th st, x west —.
Bay Ridge Park Improvement Co. to Hoik D. Campbell. nom

83d st, s w s, 280 s e 21st av, 60x100, New Utrecht. James D. Lynch to Stanton M. Child. 1,050

84th st, n e s, 240 n w 22d av, 60x100, New Utrecht. James D. Lynch to George P. and James S. Hall. 1,200

85th st, n e s, 260 n w 22d av, 60x100, New Utrecht. Annie L. Young to James D. Lynch. 1,050

Albany av, w s, 86.5 s Prospect pl, 16.7x80, h & l. Charles Robins to John Daly. *Mt.* $2,000. 4,500

Arlington av, s e cor Elton st, 50x100.
Elton av, e s, 100 s Arlington av, 50x100.
James F. Bidstrup to The Arlington Avenue Presbyterian Church. *Mt.* $2,700, paving assessm'ts, &c. 4,700

Atkins av, e s, 210 n Hegeman av, 20x100. William H. Jackson to Anton Ploharsky. 250

Atlantic av, n s, 80 w Russell pl, 17x20, h & l. Kate T. wife of Alfred Ogden to Vincenzo Bonelli. All liens. nom

Atlantic av, s e cor Warwick st, 35.3x113.10x34.6x109.2. Anna Schmidt widow to Anna K. Thau. 3,150

Atlantic av, s s, 283.4 e Rockaway av, 16 8x100, h & l. Andrew Van Opstal to Frederick Seefeldt. 2,400

Atlantic av, s w s, 810 s e Jefferson st, 50x159.6, New Utrecht. John E. McKeever, Catharine Huson and Mary E. Socias to Hannah Schlesinger. B. & S. nom

Atlantic av, s w s, 860 s e Jefferson st, 50x159.6, New Utrecht. Hannah Schlesinger, Catharine Huson and Mary E. Socias to John E. McKeever. B. & S. nom

Atlantic av, s w s, 910 s e Jefferson st, 25x159.6, New Utrecht. Mary E. Socias, Hannah Schlesinger and John E. McKeever to Catharine Huson, Jersey City. B. & S nom

Atlantic av, s w s, 935 s e Jefferson st, 25x159.6, New Utrecht. Catharine Huson, Hannah Schlesinger and John E. McKeever to Mary E. Socias. B. & S. nom

Atlantic or Railroad av, s s, 895.2 e Carlton av, 25x85. Mary E. Currie, Newark, N. J., to George Wald. Q. C. 1888. nom

Same property. Catharine Payne to same. Q. C. 1888. nom

Bay Ridge av, s s, 250 w 15th av, 40x100, Lefferts Park. James V. S. Woolley to Annie C. Maisak. 560

Bedford av, s w cor Rodney st, 138x100. Foreclos. Peter F. Lynan to John Hennessey, New York. 48,575

Same property. John Hennessey to Albert C. Henderson. *Mt.* $125,000. 50,000

Bedford av, n e cor Lynch st, runs north 71.8 x east to a line which at n s Lynch st is 100 e Bedford av, x south to n s Lynch st at point 100 e Bedford av, x west 100 to beginning. Ansel Jones, of Deep River, Conn., to William P. Ryan. 17,000

Belmont av, centre line, e s, extends from centre line Fountain av to centre line Logan st, x250, deed. Release mort. Peter Rapelje to Richard Geary. 3,375

Belmont av, s s, 40 e Atkins av, 20x90, h & l. Donald Laing to Henry G. Cullenburg. 2,950

Belmont av, n s, 25 w Watkins st, 25x100. Ralia Shapiro and Morris Gluckman to Jacob Levy. *Mt.* $2,000. 2,550

Carlton av, w s, 80 s Pacific st, 40x100.
Irving pl. n e cor Putnam av, 24x53.
Louise R. Trahar and Susannah Hoffman to John Bode. *Mt.* $13,000. exch

Cropsey av, north cor Bay 44th st, 65.2x110, South Bensonhurst. Thomas J. Cummins to James Molloy. 525

Cropsey av, east cor Bay 43d st, 128.2x110, South Bensonhurst. Same to William H. Heinsen. 1,050

De Kalb av, n s, 200 e Throop av, 25x100, h & l. Sarah J. wife of John F. Sweet to Herman Sacks. *Mt.* $5,700. 8,500

De Kalb av, s s, 60 w Marcy av, runs west 40 x south 75 x east 100 to Marcy av, x north 9.10 x northwest 61.1 x north 58.8, hs & ls. Clement Peters to Albert W. Lemcke and John Doscher, of Lemcke & Doscher. Sub. to morts., taxes, &c 8,115

Driggs av, north cor North 10th st, 100x200. James Brennan to John Colligan. B. & S. *Mt.* $8,000. nom

Driggs av, westerly cor North 11th st, 100x100. John Colligan to James Brennan. *Mt.* $3,900. nom

East New York av, n s, 340 e Albany av, 20x100. Benbow Ferguson to James Miller. *Mt.* $1,500. 2,400

Evergreen av, w s, 25 n Stanhope st, 25x100. Partition. William B. Hurd, Jr., to Joseph Ryan. 1,500

Flushing av, n s, 200 e Vandervoort pl, 25x103 x29.5x118 7. Joseph Maurer and John Heilman to Steingotter, Dietz & Co. *Mt.* $4,500. 6,900

Fort Hamilton av, easterly cor 73d st, runs southeast 160 x north 100 x northwest 60 x southwest 75 x northwest 95.6 to Fort Hamilton av, x southwest to beginning, New Utrecht. Lena I Mebt to The Bay Ridge Park Impt. Co. *Mt.* $3,900. nom

Fort Hamilton av, s w cor Ovington av, runs west 757 3 x south 200 x west 218.8 x south 275.10 x east 851.5 to Fort Hamilton av, x east 511.5, New Utrecht. Fred C. Cochen to The Bay Ridge Park Improvement Co. *Mt.* $2,510. 1890. nom

Georgia av, w s, 200 s Fulton av, 25x100. Partition deed. William H. Gale ref. to Charles G. Summers. 1,800

Georgia av, w s, 175 s Fulton av late Virginia av, 25x100. Partition deed. William H. Gale ref. to Rosanna McGee, of Canarsie. 1,350

Glenmore av, n s, 80 e Milford st, 20x90. Effingham H. Nichols to James Deery or Dury. 383

Glenmore av, n s, 60 e Milford st, 20x90. Same to Mary Smith. 383

Gravesend av, w s, 662 n 86th st, 58x223 to Lake st. Martin W. Joralemon, New Baltimore, N. Y., to Eben J. Beggs. *Mt.* $400. 750

Greene av, n w s, 250 n e Broadway, 50x100. Clarence M. Bumgrass to Michael Mulvihill. *Mt.* $3,500 and encroachments. 5,600

Greenwood av, s w cor Prospect av, 150x46.7x127.7x92.7, Flatbush. Anna M. Ferris to Windsor Terrace Methodist Episcopal Church. *Mt.* $1,700. 2,700

Harrison av, e s, 25 s Wallabout st, 25x84. Charles Rissler to Hilda wife of Julius Tishman. *Mt.* $5,000. 10,700

Howard av, e s, 167 s Herkimer st, 17x98.
Howard av, e s, 217.8 s Herkimer st, runs south 58.6 x northeast 50.11 x north 80.6 x east 48 x north 18.4 x west 98.
Foreclos. John Courtney to The German-American Real Estate Title Guarantee Co. 6,950

Howard av, e s, 98 s Herkimer st, 69x96. Eliza Reed to Frances G. Underhill. nom

Jamaica av, n s, 150 e Barbey st, 25x113.10x25 x113.8. Bernhard Long, of Anglesea, N. J., to Charles W. Hooper. 800

Jefferson av, n s, 117 6 w Howard av, 17.6x100. Samuel Ayers to Celia A. wife of William R. McNulty. nom

Jefferson av, s s, 280 w Nostrand av, 20x100. Foreclos. John Courtney to Thomas C. Van Hoesen exr. Catharine C. Culp. 5,500

Jefferson av, s s, 175 e Stuyvesant av, 40x80. Catharine Carey to Charles Isbill. 4,000

Jefferson av, s s, 300 w Nostrand av, 20x100. Foreclos. John Courtney to Elizabeth V. H. Nicholson. 5,500

Kent av, e s, 25 n Willoughby av, 17.4x100. William H. Heenan to Peter Fagan. 2,275

Kingsland av, w s, 153 s Meeker av, runs west 77 4 x southwest 84 x west 23.8 to the centre of an old road, x southeast 145.5 x east 23.6 to Kingsland av, x north 163.6 to beginning. Jeremiah V. Meserole to Peter Ruger. 3,500

Kingsland av, w s, 313 n Van Cott av, 20x100. Helen Crean to Patrick Comiskey. *Mt.* $200. 650

Kingsland av, w s, 333.9 n Van Cott av, 20x100. Sarah Crean to same. *Mt.* $200. 600

Lafayette av, s s, 300.6 e Reid av, 24.5x100. Mary Skinner to George Evans. *Mt.* $1,700. exch

Lafayette av, s w cor New Utrecht av, 318x abt 295x169x abt 414, Fort Hamilton. George G. and John H. Hornung to Frances E. Gordon. 2,875

Lexington av, n s, 356 e Stuyvesant av, 19x100, h & l. Annie B. Cannon to Joel H. Titus. *Mt.* $3,000. 4,500

Liberty av, s e cor Poplar st, 25x100. Lavinia A. T. Dearing to Henry Taylor. 400

Metropolitan av, s s, 27.2 e Olive st, 25x100. Sarah McCartin widow and William J. McCartin to Patrick McAnteer. 2,300

Miller av, e s, 175 s Glenmore av, 25x100. John T. McDermott to Michael Devitt. *Mt.* $1,000. 1,900

Montauk av, e s, 430 s Blake av, runs east 100 x south 9 to New Lots road, x southwest 105.1 to Montauk av, x north 41.4. Julia E. Browne to Courtland V. Anable, of Castleton, N. Y. 400

Morgan av, n e cor Ingraham st, runs north 30 x east 79.1 to Knickerbocker av as extended, x south 82 7 to st, x west 91.10. Release mort. Peter Wyckoff to Walter J. Klots. 10,000

Same property. Walter J. Klots to Lena wife of George Heericke. 14,000

Myrtle av, n s, 40 e Nostrand av, 50x86. Johanna Regan widow to Michael J and Daniel Regan. 8,000

New York av, s w cor Park pl. Covenants as to buildings. Mary B. wife of Joseph D. Huggins with Robert W. Gleason nom

Norman av, n e cor Guernsey st, 25x95. Catharine McCabe widow to Mary R. wife of William J. Lutz, John J., Annie L., Elizabeth C. and Teresa M. McCabe heirs James McCabe. nom

Ovington av, n e s, 1,126 s e Stewart av, 217.3x — to Bay Ridge av, x217x46.6, New Utrecht. Herman Schierloh to The Bay Ridge Park Improvement Co. 1,525

Ovington av, west cor Bay Ridge av, runs northwest along Bay Ridge av to land of H. Schierloh, x south along same to Ovington av, x east —, New Utrecht. David J. Darby, New Canaan, Conn., to Fred. C. Cochen. B. & S. and C. a. G. 75

Same property. Fred. C. Cochen to The Bay Ridge Park Improvement Co. B. & S. and C. a. G. nom

Ovington av, s w s, lots 70, 71 and half of 72 map of Ovington, 138x153.3x138x153.10. Michael J. Langan to George Kidney. 4,000

Putnam av, n s, 140 e Howard av, 80x100. Robert L. Moores and Charles A. Le Quesne to Lewis Leavens. *Mt.* $38,000. nom

Putnam av, n s, 231.7 e Patchen av, 18.9x100, h & l. Fannie J. Mugford to Gustave N. Oehmen. *Mt.* $3,500. 5,800

Putnam av, n s, 98 w Throop av, 18x100, h & l. W. A. Vail to Hattie D. M. Taylor. *Mt.* $4,500. 7,050

Putnam av, n s, 225 e Stuyvesant av, 18 9x100. Emma G. wife of Charles H. Corbett to Emma V. wife of Charles Isbill. *Mt.* $4,000. nom

Reid av, n w cor Halsey st, 50x100, h & l. George W. McCormick to Mary C. Booth, New York. *Mt.* $6,000. 12,500

Rogers av, n w cor Butler st, 100x95. William S. Jarvis to Louis K. Hansen. 8,000

Saratoga av, e s, 67 n St. Marks av, 63x100. Release mort. Emeline Parfitt to Walter E. Parfitt. 525

Schenectady av, e s, 16.6 n Atlantic av, 16.6x 80, h & l. Edward Johnson to Helen Post. *Mt.* $1,700. 3,550

Shepherd av, w s, 340 n Ridgewood av, 20x100. Edward F. Linton to Charles T. Testut. 800

Same property. Release mort. Williamsburgh Savings Bank to Edward F. Linton. 350

Shepherd av, e s, 331.5 n Ridgewood av, 17.2x 102.6. Sebastian T. Hollister to George G. Smith. *Mt.* $1,600. 3,150

Shepherd av, e s, 100 s Eastern Parkway, 25x 100. John L. Culver to George Raymond. Sub. to taxes from 1888. 1,350

Snediker av, w s, 255 n Liberty av, 20x100. William C. Powell, of Smithtown, N. Y., to Isabella G. Price. B. & S. and C. a. G. nom

Stanley av, n e cor Shepherd av, 120x95. William H. Jackson to Bernerd Bardon. 945

Stanley av, n s, 40 w Atkins av, 20x93. William H. Jackson to Esther wife of James Pearl. 140

Stone av, e s, 50 s Blake av, 50x100. Edward E. Stewart to Alfred P. Tostevin. 1,300

Stone av, e s, 50 s Blake av, 33.4x100. Alfred P. Tostevin to Anna wife of Joseph Matthews. nom

Stuyvesant av, w s, 158.2 n Madison st, 19.10x 100, h & l. Charles H. Heimburg to Claus J. Meyer. *Mt.* $5,200. 5,500

Stuyvesant av, w s, 158.2 n Madison st, 19.10x 100, h & l. Peter P. McLoughlin to Charles H. Heimburg, New York. *Mt.* $5,200. 7,800

Thatford av, e s, 150 n Livonia av, 25x100, error. Pauline Hartmann to Samuel Ellerstein. *Mt.* $1,500. 2,800

Thatford av, w s, 100 s Belmont av, 25x100. Morris Goldstein, of New York, to Suskind Alpert. ½ part. *Mt.* $1,360. 200

Thatford av, e s, 212 n Glenmore av, 88x100, hs & ls. Foroseagean J. wife of Paul W. Ledoux to Oscar W. Velsor, Hempstead, L. I. nom

Union av, n e cor Johnson av, runs north 50 x east 75 x north 50 x east 25 x south 100 to Johnson av, x west 100 to beginning. Henry Newman to Solomon Blumenstock. nom

Van Siclen av, n e cor Henry st, 101x104x91.5x 112.2, Gravesend. Henrietta W. wife of Floyd S. Sandford to Charles A. Erickson. *Mt.* $1,500. nom

Vernon av, n s, 165 e Lewis av, 20x100. Charles E. Ring to Simon Saenger. 8,500

Same property. Release mort. Paul W. Ledoux to Charles E. Ring. nom

Washington av, e s, 203 s Myrtle av, 14x100. Elizabeth A. Swift to Thomas A. O'Keefe. 1,200

Webster av, n s, 90 e 3d st, 90x112.4x90x112.7, Flatbush. James M. Richards, of Cornwall, N. Y., to Frederic J. Middlebrook. Q. C. 165

1st av, east cor 87th st, 18.8x225.1x26.5x225, New Utrecht. David D. Field to Charles F. Lutz. 850

3d av, south cor 27th st, 79.2x90, hs & ls. Martin V. Wood, Hempstead, to Ellen Cosgrove. 14,500

4th av, n w s, 43.2 s w 44th st. 19x80. William Maass, New York, to Bridget wife of William Maass. 4,400

6th av, east cor 44th st, 113.5x200x126.3x200. Matilda M. Strouse, New York, to Thomas F. Flynn, Flatbush. *Mt.* $2,980. nom

6th av, east cor 44th st, 113.5x200x126.3x200. Henry Franke to Matilda M. Strouse. *Mt.* $2,980. 6,000

6th av, s w cor 20th st, 100x100. John D. Murphy to John O'Connor. 20,000

8th av, w s, 20 s 13th st, 16x85, h & l. William J. Fitzpatrick to Charlotte A. Bierds. *Mt.* $3,200. exch

9th av, s w cor 50th st, 20.2x80.4.
50th st, s s, 80.4 w 9th av, 20x100.2, New Utrecht.
Adrian M. Suydam to Patrick Campbell. 500

10th av, s e cor 71st st, 100x100, hs & ls, New Utrecht. Fred. C. Cocheu to The Bay Ridge Park Improvement Co. nom

10th av, s e cor 67th st, runs east 372.8 x south 248 to n s 68th st, x west 167.8 x north 136.6 x west 100 x south 160.6 to 68th st, x west 102 to 10th av, x north 320.6.
Fort Hamilton av, s e cor 68th st, 176.8x488.11 x76.8x448 6.
Fort Hamilton av, s w cor 68th st, 203.4 to Bay Ridge av, x west 113.6, to 9th av, x north 200 to 68th st, x east 149.10.
9th av, s w cor 68th st, 200 to Bay Ridge av, 51.1x200x61.8.
Ovington av, n s, 102 e 10th av, 102.1x136.6x 100x166.6, New Utrecht.
Fred. C. Cocheu to The Bay Ridge Park Improvement Co. B. & S. and C. a. G. nom

12th av, westerly cor 57th st, 40.2x100, New Utrecht. William Nummey to Catherine D. Morgan, of New York. 1,200

21st av, n w s, 112.6 n e Cropsey av, 100x96.8, New Utrecht. Cornelius Furgusson, Jr., to Edward Kimpton. *Mt.* $3,000. 8,000

22d av, n w s, at line of Kate L. Hicks property if extended, 209.11x203.10x23.4, contains 52-1000 acre (?). New Utrecht. Sarah Rue, Amelia A. Stillwell, Jennie M. Read, Sarah G. Loud, Dora E. Rue and Catharine R. Ward to Kate L. Hicks. Correction deed. Q. C. nom

Same property. Kate L. Hicks wife of Alfred D. to James W. Murphy. 100

Lots 513 and 514 block 25 map 660 lots Cowenhoven farm, New Utrecht. Effingham H. Nichols to Onofrio Abruzzo, of New York. 330

Lots 26-39, 70-78, 89, 92-95, 123, 141-145, 147-150, 234-237, 252, 253 and 266 map property David D. Field, New Utrecht. David D. Field to Catharine A. Birdsall as trustee Guy H. Birdsall. 10,000

Lots 292-296 and 301, 302 block 12, and 390-397 block 14, and 461-470 block 15 Cath. L. Lott's 633 lots, Flatbush. Release mort. John Z. Lott admr. Cath. L. Lott to Effingham H. Nichols. 3,000

Lots 301 and 302 block 12 map of Cath. L. Lott's 633 lots, Flatbush. Effingham H. Nichols to Maddalena Camera. 605

Lot 419 block 10 map 618 lots Cowenhoven farm, New Utrecht. Effingham H. Nichols, of New York, to Marie A. MacKinney. 160

Lot 418 block 10 same map. Same to Constance A. MacKinney. 160

Lot 420 block 10 same map. Same to Francis B. MacKinney. 160

Lots 461-470 block 15 map of Cath. L. Lott's 633 lots, Flatbush and New Utrecht. Effingham H. Nichols, of New York, to Heinrich C. Beck. 3,500

Lots 2048 and 2049 block 3, and 2331-2334 and 2373-2375 block 12, and 2449-2454 block 13 map of 650 lots of E. H. Nichols, Lefferts Park. Release mort. Albert V. B. Voorhees to Effingham H. Nichols. 1,500

Lots 102, 103 and 104 block 18 and lots 332, 333 and 334 block 23 and lots 432-436 block 24 map Cowenhoven farm, New Utrecht. Release mort. Magdalena Cowenhoven admrx. Garret Cowenhoven to Effingham H. Nichols. 1,100

Lots 283-287, 296, 303-309, 313, 336, 341, 342, 347-349, 373, 374, 383-386, 389-393, 412, 416, 417, 429 and 430 map Worth & Strawson, Flatbush. Vincent A. Strawson to William M. Lynam and Adam Balzer, Jr. *Mt.* $3,800. 1,700

Lots 390 and 391 block 14 map of Cath. L. Lott's 633 lots in Flatbush and New Utrecht. Effingham H. Nichols to Oswald Schuessler. 610

Lots 263-260 block 11 map 1197 lots of W. Ziegler, Flatbush and New Utrecht. Release mort. William Ziegler to Franz Franz. 2,367

Lots 263-269 block 11 map W. Ziegler property, Flatbush. Franz Franz to Elizabeth Kramer. nom

Same property. Same to Lewis Leavens. *Mt.* $2,107. nom

Same property. Elizabeth Kramer to Franz Franz. *Mt.* $2,367 nom

Lots 394-397 block 14 map of Cath. L. Lott 633 lots, Flatbush and New Utrecht. Effingham H. Nichols to Joseph Park. 1,240

Lots 462-470 block 15 map 526 lots Thomas J. Cummins, South Bensonhurst. Erhardt Schmitt to Thomas J. Cummins. 1,350

Part lot 389 map D. D. Field, New Utrecht, begins on centre line of block 325 s e of 3d av, runs northeast 40.8 to land of May et al x northwest 5.1 x southwest 41.10 x southeast 5. Release mort. Francis T. Johnson to Giosne Gianini. 25

Same property. Giosne Gianini to Elizabeth Hamilton. 25

Indeft. right of way, adj H. W. Schmeelk's, 44 x100, Canarsie. Harry W. Schmeelk to Henry W. Schnaars. 100

Receipt and release of exr. Charles H. Gaus to Christian Pfeiff exr. Christian Saeler or Seiler. 1,258

Similar release, &c. Magdalena Pfeiff and Katie Kufahl to same. 101

WESTCHESTER COUNTY.

OCTOBER 21 TO 27—INCLUSIVE.

CORTLANDT.

Depew, Martha M. exr. of, to Cornelia R. Lancaster, s s Elm st, adj G. T. Taylor, abt 50x 200. $450

Driscoll, Michael to Helen C. Driscoll, n s John st, 55x150. 2,500

Fowler, Colie A. to Wm. Morton, tract on road to Odells Mills and Post road. 8,000

Frost, Leila S. to Minnie Brown, n s Lincoln terrace, 30x125, the Diamond House; s s same, the Maple House; n s same, the Orchard Lot, cor Compond road and Leila st; also s w cor Lincoln terrace and Leila st. nom

Snidaman, Jos. to Sarah Snidaman, s s Lincoln terrace, 25x125. nom

Same to Jennie Cohen and ano., s s same st, 25x125. nom

EASTCHESTER.

Andrews, John to Frank Paul, w s Howard st, 240 n Greenwich, 36.6x50. 301

Barkley, Deborah H. to Sophie M. Hebert, part lot 282 e s 4th av, Mt. Vernon, 25x105. 3,350

Carroll, Geo. K. et al., W. W. Penfield ref., to Wm. L. Thorne, lot 1026 and part 1027 s s Stevens av, Mt. Vernon, abt 199x80. 10,650

Foley, Edmund R. to Elizb. H. Sutton, lot 31 s w s Kossuth av, s Washingtonville, 36x 137. 725

Same to Wm. Ahmuty, lot 32 adj, 36x137. 750

Gundlach, Caroline to Geo. P. Castle, part lot 114 w s Railroad av, West Mt. Vernon, 50x 105. 800

Jennings, Clarkson to Frances L. Ferris, lot 515 w s 6th av, Mt. Vernon, 100x105. nom

Rheinfeldt, Adolph to Cath. L. Haag, s s 3d st, 609.5 e Fulton av, abt 115x240. 2,250

Ruth, Daniel J. to Charlotte E. Proe, n s "New" st, adj grantee, 29x85. 150

Slawter, Louisa W. to Harry V. Morgan, lot 579 e s 7th av, Mt. Vernon, 100x105. 1,280

Stearns, Jos. K. to Harriet S Hopkins, lot 938 s s 16th av, Mt. Vernon, 100x105. 1,075

Thompson, Mary V. to Fred. Knebel, e s Catharine st, 100 w Westchester av, 50x100. 700

Tier, Chas. A. to Jennie L. Tier, lots 52, 53, 128, 129 and parts 67 and 90, Chester Hill; also lot 466, Centre Mt. Vernon; also 643 and 645, Mt. Vernon. nom

Weitz, Geo. to Henry F. Rohde, lot 250 e s Railroad av, Northwest Mt. Vernon. 275

Wheeler, John to Patrick F. Byrne, lots 107-110 Vernon Park. 1,600

Walter, Ida L. to Fred. Mager, part lot 886 e s 11th av, Mt. Vernon, 33.4x105. 4,900

GREENBURGH.

Berry, Margt. to Welcome G. Hitchcock, ½ acre w s Harlem R. R., adj Rich. Barnes. 1,200

Brown, Wm. M. et al., Wilson Brown, Jr., ref., to The Metropolitan Savings Bank, s e cor Washington and Wildey sts, 53x103. 4,000

Elmsford Improvement Co. to Nellie Wilson, lots 35 and 37 block 19. nom

Earnshaw, Cornelia C. to Claude Wilson, lots 2-5 and 15-19 map Livingston Landing. 8,000

Erhardt, Joel B. trustee to Bessie Rodas, w s Stanley av, 275 s Lawrence st, 25x100. 350

Fields, And. C. to Mary E. Quigley, e s private road adj Thos. Moore, Dobbs Ferry, 40x144. 2,000

Jones, Cyrus P. and ano. to Chas. G. Storms, lots 28, 29 and 132, Ardsley. 455

Lefurgy, Mary L. to Jos. O. Dorland, s e cor Spring and Valley sts, Hastings, abt 47x126. 2,310

Mathews, Wm. exrs. of, to John Beggs, w s Lefurgy av, abt 114x107. 359

Sutton, Alfred A. exrs. of, to Crawford N. Smith, lot w s Washington av, Chatterton Hill, 50x158. 1,500

Smith, Martin exr. of, to Abram Bare, 0 acres adj J. Gould. 900

Stark, Jas. to Welcome G. Hitchcock, w s road from Hartsdale Depot to Harts Corners. 9,000

MAMARONECK.

Larchmont Manor Co. to Chas. H. Denison, n w cor Willow and Larchmont avs, 250x265. 7,952

Spencer, Jas. C. to Chas. Mitchell, lot 54. 650

Same to Wm. Corcoran, lot 53. 650

Same to Aug. Frund and ano., lot 13. 700

Same to And. W. Ekstrom, lots 20 and 21. 1,620

MOUNT PLEASANT.

Hall, Aaron to Louis Smadbeck, 28 acres, adj Sherman Park. nom

Smith, Wm. R. to Hugh Reilly and wife, lots 35-38 map Lake Kensico. 450

Same to W. O. Chrisman, lots 1-4. 600

Bliss, Albert E. and ano. to Eliz'h Cosgrove, lots 46 and 47 w s Amos st, and lot adj, 25x 50. 1,500

Rhinisch, Emma to Heyman Levy, s s Elm st, adj Thos. Quinn, 46x145. 3,615

Smadbeck, Louis to Jos. La Rosa, lot 1855 Sherman Park. 250

Same to Paul Hain, lot 1954. 250

Same to Wm. Moehring, lots 2208 and 2209. 250

Same to Jos. Simon and wife, lot 1540. 200

Same to Julius Sommerfeld, lots 1424 and 1425. 300

Same to Mary A. Hurley, lots 1595 and 1596. 450

Same to Edw. J. Riordan, lots 1628 and 1629. 300

Same to Mary Leehane, lots 1501 and 1502. 350

Same to John W. Kingston, lot 1884. 150

Same to Susan C. Dodge, lot 1554. 350

Same to Herman Georgi, lot 1655. 150

Same to Louis Hoyer, lots 1358, 1359 and 1572. 425

Same to Mary A. Kilroe and ano., lot 1637. 215

Same to Louis Lehms, lot 1657. 150

Same to John B. Schlesinger, lot 759. 150

Same to Alfred Koening, lot 1067. 250

Same to Henry Lebning, lots 1722 and 1725. 350

Same to Fredericka Miller, lot 2289. 200

Same to Emil Goetz, lot 573. 100

Same to Charlotte Borst, lots 1482 and 1483. 400

Same to Chas. Bothner, lots 1484-1487. 800

Same and ano. to Francesco Topaldi and ano., lots 738-744, Lakehurst. 1,600

Same to Albert Specht, lots 169 and 170. 400

NEW CASTLE.

Halstead, Wm. T. to Jas. S. Piersall, s w cor Smith av and Main st. 675

NEW ROCHELLE.

Baldwin, Abby S. to Henri J. Van Zehn, west ½ lot 131 s s Poplar pl, Residence Park, 25x 150. 700

Same to Lawrence E. Van Etten, east ½ same. 700

Early, Mary to Bridget Early, e s Locust av, 82 n Elm st, 39x100. nom

Lawton, Julia W. to Albert B. New, s e cor Grove and Av A, 50x150. 1,250

Tier, Chas. A. to Jennie L. Tier, lot 151, Residence Park. nom

OSSINING.

Hart, Jas. A. to Reuben H. Mapelsden, n w cor Edward and James sts, abt 100x50. 1,825

Mapelsden, Thos. exr. of, to Rose Mooney, w s Croton turnpike and "Swails" Bridge, 5 acres. 3,250

PELHAM.

Major, Geo. W. to Truman A. Jewell, n s Scofield av, 465 e Main st, 50x118. 700

Tier, Chas. A. to Jennie L. Tier, lot e s Main st, City Island. nom

RYE.

Bulkley, Mary E. and ano. to John D. Conaty, lot 46 s s Bulkley av map Poningo Dale, 50x 100. 500

Foster, Mary J. to Robt. L. Foster, e s Orchard av, 294 s Terrace av, 42x100. nom

Merritt, Jas. S. and ano. to Wm. Foster, e s Merritt st, 100 s Ellendale av, 50x100. 171

Same to Mary J. Foster, w s Merritt st, 100 n w William st, 100x100. 480

O'Malley, Patrick to Jos. C. Griffen, lot 29 w s Prospect st map Auser property, 50x210. 900

WESTCHESTER.

Camp, Hugh N. to John Buckley, lot 339 map McGraw estate. 225

Same to Jas. Clarke, lot 340. 225

Coles, Wm. T. to John Harrington, lot 28 s s Av A, Jerome, 25x100. 400

Dexter, Fred. C. to Elizb. T. Dunn, lots 54-57 and 153 and 154, Laconia Park. 1,500

Hughes, Miles to Jos. Diamond, w s Deane pl, 50 s Sackett av, 25x100. 225

Innis, Albert C. to Michael Burke, lot 220 s s 3d av, Wakefield, 100x114. 1,200

Sheridan, Margt. to John A. Singer and wife, lot 384 s s turnpike, Unionport, 67x312. 2,150

WHITE PLAINS.

Gahan, Jas. to Jas. McConville, 2 lots w s Bronx st, 100x—. 100

O'Rourke, John to De Witt C. Van Gaasbeek, n s Lake st, 100 e Warren, 50x92. 3,500

Purdy, Mary J. to Thos. H. Purdy, 6 acres w s North st. 1,000

YONKERS.

Bell, Jas. C. to Clementine Bay, e s North Broadway, adj grantee. 1,000

Cheguay, Henri to Jos. Armstrong and ano., lot 2 n s Park Hill av Herriot map, 25x95. 750

Duden, Herman to Wm. J. Light and ano., blocks 28, 29 and 30, Sunnyside Park. 40,875

East Side Land Co. to Jas. Nevins and ano., lots 62, 66 and 84, Shearwood Hill. 1,575

Edward, Adah and ano. to Geo. Fisher, lot 4 block 3 map property Lowerre Station. 550

Same to Mahlon B. Primrose, lot 7 block 3. 550

Same to Lewin Pennington, lot 8 block 3. 550

Same to Barth. T. Gibbons, lot 1 block 3. 250

Same to Robt. Lowrey, lots 12 and 13 block 3. 1,100

Same to Herbert W. Little, lots 19 and 20 block 4. 800

Freeman, Geo. A., Jr., to Henry G. Trevor, n s Ashburton av, 218 e Warburton, 50x100. nom

Gramatan Park Co. to And. Anderson, lots 132 and 133, Mohegan Park. 4 60

Lawrence, Fannie E. to Eliza Armstrong, No. 155 w s Park Hill av, 40x135x140. 550

Rothenbucher, Emil to Theo. Nordman, north ½ lot 151 map Hyatt farm. 187

Same to Rosa Malogick, south ½ same. 187

Thayer, Stephen H. exr. of. to Fannie E. Lawrence, e s road from Kingsbridge to Tuckahoe, 33 acres; also n s McLean av, 558x—. 65,000

Wilder, Marshal P. to Annie R. Buchanan. s s Randolph st, 255 e South Broadway, 50x100. 1,200

YORKTOWN.

Chevanney, Louis to Louis Berger, lot adj hotel, 50x100; also lots 21-26 map property Abby M. S. Paine. 12,000

MORTGAGES.

NOTE.—*The arrangement of this list is as follows. The first name is that of the mortgagor, the next that of the mortgagee. The description of the property then follows, then the date of the mortgage, the time for which it was given, and the amount. The general dates used as headings are the dates when the mortgage was handed into the Register's office to be recorded.*

Whenever the letters "P. M." occur, preceded by the name of a street, in these lists of mortgages, they mean that it is a Purchase Money Mortgage, and for fuller particulars see the list of transfers under the corresponding date. Whenever the rate is not given, read as 6 per cent.

NEW YORK CITY.

OCTOBER 23, 24, 26, 27, 28, 29.

Bell, Sallie R. wife of and Alexander P. to Jannette wife of A. Ramsay McCoy, Orange, N. J. Alexander av, e s, 15 s 137th st, 14.4x60. Oct. 22, 3 years, 5 %. gold, $5,000

Boehm, Gustav, Long Island City, to Edwin F. Raynor. 115th st. P. M. Oct. 22, 1 year. 13,000

Brosen, John to Andrew Wheeler. 56th st, s s, 150 w 9th av, 25x94.4x25.2x97.6. Oct. 21, due Oct. 22, 1896, 5 %. 10,000

Boettger, Pauline to THE WASHINGTON LIFE INS. CO. 5th av. P. M. Oct. 26, due Dec. 1, 1892, 5 %. 14,500

Brady, John R. to Catharine A. Kelly. Amsterdam av, No. 1408, w s, 74.11 s 130th st, 25 x100. Oct. 22, due Oct. 1, 1894, 5 %. 6,000

Brady, John T. to Robert Reitz. 118th st, No. 525, n s, 334.6 e Av A, 20.5x100.11. Oct. 28, 1 year or sooner. 1,000

Burwell, Charles D., Brooklyn, to Susan E. Le Roy. 23d st, s s, 325 e 4th av, 25x98.9. Oct. 21, due Nov. 1, 1896, 5 %. 35,000

Ballger, Catharine formerly Bosselmann to Henry Stemme. 28th st, n s, 40 e 6th av, 20x 74.1. Oct. 27, 1 year. 1,200

Brooks, Warren W. to Walden P. Anderson. 93d st, s s, 375 w Columbus av. P. M. 2d mort. Oct. 27, 3 years. 4,000

Same to same. Same property. P. M. 3d mort. Oct. 27, notes. 4,000

Berkley, Thomas R., Brooklyn, to Thomas R. Hughes, Weehawken, N. J. 33d st. P. M. Oct. 28, due Oct. 15, 1896, 5 %. gold, 8,000

Brennan, Bridget wife of and John H. to THE EMIGRANT INDUST. SAVINGS BANK 135th st, s s, 105.11 w North 3d av, 28x100. Oct. 13, 1 year, 4½ %. 4,000

Beal, William R. to William R. Beal Land Improvement Co. Crimmins av. P. M. Oct. 22, due July 8, 1894, or sooner, 5 %. 700

Bear, Amalie wife of Isaac to Mount Sinai Hospital. 3d st, s s, adj the s e cor Manhattan st and being 123 w of Lewis st, 23x70. Sub. to morts. $5,500. Oct. 29, 3 years, 5 %. 2,500

Beckert, Emily to Andreas Banzer. 82d st. P. M. Oct. 29, 1 year or sooner. 1,250

Binsse, Lewis J. to Benjamin T. Kissam, Bayonne City, N. J. 1st av, e s, 50.5 n 59th st, 25 x75. Oct. 29, 1 year, 5 %. 500

Castle, George A. to John J. Brady. Clinton av. P. M. Oct. 19, due Nov. 5, 1894, 5 %. 585

Cavinato, Augustine to Pierce, Butler & Pierce Mfg. Co. 85th st, s s, 144 e 5th av, 20.6x102.2. Collateral. Oct. 26, due Oct. 9, 1892, or sooner. 2,490

Cohen, Mores to Louis Benziger trustee Joseph N. A. Benziger dec'd. Hester st, No. 104, s s, 75.2 e Forsyth st, 25x100.8. Oct. 28, 5 years, 5 %. 25,500

Cohen, Betsey wife of Harris to Charles Laue, Brooklyn. Division st, Nos. 188 and 190. P. M. Oct. 27, installs. 9,000

Same to same. Same property. Oct. 27, notes. 5,975

Same to Henry N. De Forest, Oyster Bay, L. I. Same property. P. M. Oct. 27, due Nov. 1, 1896, 5 %. 35,000

Content, Ada wife of Harry to Rose wife of David U. Herrmann. 79th st. P. M. Oct. 27, 5 years or installs, 5 %. gold, 20,000

Campbell, John V. to The Baron de Hirsh Fund. Essex st, No. 169, w s, 200 s Houston st, 25x87.6, with all title to strip of land adj on the rear, 25x abt 2.4. Oct. 22, due Oct. 27, 1896, 5 %. See Conveys. 24,000

Cammann, Hermann H. mortgagee to John C. Klett mortgagor and present owner. Certificate that $1,000 has been paid on account of mort. made by John C. Klett and wife to Hermann H. Cammann April 28, 1890, and that there is now due on account thereof 1,500

Carlebach, Emil to D. Willis James. 86th st. P. M. Oct. 26, due Nov. 1, 1894, 4 %. 25,000

Cashman, Thomas to Bernheimer & Schmid. 102d st. No. 218 E. Saloon lease. Oct. 27, note, demand. 400

Carow, Emily T. to Caroline W. Astor extrx. and trustee Archibald B. Schermerhorn. Washington st, No. 88, w s, 65.6 s Rector st, 25x89.9x25x89.7. All title. Oct. 26, due Nov. 1, 1892, 5 %. 1,000

Crossman, Greenleaf W. to Jane L. Thomson. 56th st. P. M. Oct. 26, 5 years, 5 %. 5,000

Same to THE MUTUAL LIFE INS CO of New York. Same property. Secures bond of mortgagor and James W. Sands. Oct. 26, 1 year, 5 %. 20,000

Curry, John to THE GERMAN SAVINGS BANK, New York. 38th st, Nos. 359 and 361, n s, 125 e 9th av, 33.4x98.9. Oct. 24, due Oct. 26, 1892. 28,000

Carlos, Michael and Annie his wife to Eleanor J. Porter. Hoffman st, w s, 125 s Jacob st, 25x100. Oct. 22, 3 years. 1,200

Chisholm, John to Sarah Murray. 83d st, s s, 175 w Columbus av, 25x102.2. Oct. 22, due Nov. 1, 1896, 5 %. 22,000

Same to William Rankin. Same property. Sub. to last mort. Oct. 22, due Oct. 23, 1892, or sooner. 2,956

Same to The Bradley & Currier Co. (Lim.) Same property. Sub. to morts. $24,956. Oct. 22, 1 year. 2,986

Connolly, George to Bernheimer & Schmid. Amsterdam av, s w cor 184th st. Saloon lease. Oct. 22, note, demand. 500

Coyle, Francis H. and Ellen E. his wife to Sophia L. Cauldwell. 108th st, No. 162, s s, 150 e Lexington av, 17x100.11. Oct. 28, 1 year, 5 %. 1,000

Crimmins, Thomas E. to David J. King et al. exrs. and trustees Edward J. King. 68th st. P. M. Oct. 28, installs, 5 %. 66,000

Cummings, Richard to Edwin F. Raynor. 115th st. P. M. Oct. 23, 1 year, 5 %. 13,000

Callender, William E. to Alice G. Cobb. 7th av. P. M. Oct. 29, due Nov. 1, 1898. 3,000

Crosby, William H. to William B. Crosby exr. Ellen Roche. Cherry st, s s, 145 e Rutgers st, 25x abt 122.3 Jan. 8, demand, 5 %. 4,000

Curran, Catharine and Julia to John J. Brady. Clinton av, Crotona av and Oakland pl. P. M. Oct. 19, due Nov. 5, 1894, 5 %. 3,111

d'Aguiar, Alice widow to Mary C. Trabert. 41st st. P. M. Oct. 29, 3 years or installs, 4½ %. 17,000

Davies, Alice wife of David T. to Margaret O'Donelan. 53d st, s s, 275 e 11th av, 125x 100.5. Sub. to morts. Oct 28, demand, 5 %. 600

Same to William F. Fisher trustee, Sayreville, N. J. Same property. Sub. to morts. $87,-000. Oct. 1. See Conveys. 10,988

Dawson, John to The F. & M. Schaefer Brewing Co. 3d av, No. 1881. Lease. March 12, demand. 1,500

Dempsey, William and John Smith to Caroline L. Macy. 98th st, s s, 310 e 3d av, 25x100.11. Oct. 28, due Oct. 29, 1894, 5 %. gold, 15,000

Same to Emily S. wife of Glover C. Arnold. 98th st, s s, 335 e 3d av, 25x100.9. Oct. 28, due Oct. 29, 1894, 5 %. 15,000

Same to Salomon Marx. 98th st, s s, 360 e 3d av, 25x100.11. Oct. 28, due Oct. 29, 1894, 5 %. 15,000

Ducey, Patrick and Bridget his wife to Joseph Winter. 85th st. P. M. Oct. 19, due Nov. 1, 1894, or installs 5 %. 3,000

Douglass, Kate to Adam Weiffenbach. 177th st, No. 718, s s, 130 e Railroad av, 21.6x100.2x 20.7x103 6. Oct. 29, due Oct. 6, 1892. 4,000

Dobson, Henry C. to George Heussey, Seattle, Wash. Mott av, e s, 175 n 149th st, 25x101.5 x25x101.8. Oct. 21, 5 years or sooner, 5 %. 2,500

Duff, Mary widow to Adam Wetzler. 10th st, No 33, n s, 427.11 e 6th av, 24.11x94.9x25 6x 94.6. Oct. 26, due Dec. 30, 1894, 5 %. 5,000

Doak, George F. and Louis D. Beck mortgagors with Daniel J. O'Conor mortgagee. Extension of mort. Oct. 26. nom

Dunker, Herrmann to Bernheimer & Schmid. 1st av, No. 1697, s w cor 88th st. Saloon lease. Oct. 26, note, demand. 2,300

Eagleton, Thomas to Augustus T. Gillender committee of Alice F. M. Wood. South 5th av, Nos. 196, 198 and 200, w s, 120.11 n Grand st, 59.5x70; South 5th av, e s, 125 n Grand st, 25x100; Hudson st, No. 429, n e cor Leroy st, 23x60. Oct. 22, 3 years, 5 %. 26,000

Eschwei, George F. to The East River Mill and Lumber Co. Bradhurst av, s e cor 143d st, 100.6x79.4x99.11x68. Oct. 26, due Jan. 1, 1892, or sooner. 2,000

Eglise, St. Jean Baptiste, New York City, to Les Petits Freres de Marie (Freres Maristes) St. Genis Laval, Rhone, France. 76th st, n s, 225 w 3d av, 50x102.2; Lexington av, No. 1061, e s, 17.2 n 76th st, 17x70; 76th st, n s, 325 w 3d av, 25x102.2, except a strip on e s abt 0.2x62. Oct. 26, 5 years, 4½ %. 15,000

Eschwei, George F. to Enoch C. Bell. Bradhurst av, s e cor 143d st, 100.6x abt 79.4x99.11 x68. Oct. 26, demand. 2,000

Edwards, Agnes C. wife of and Thomas J. to Elizabeth Hayes. James st, No. 68, n e s, 51 n w James st, 23.1x100.6x22.6x100.3. Oct. 26, 3 months. 1,150

Farley, Mary V. wife of Philip H. to Benjamin Wright. 2d av, w s, 64.2 s 10th st, 15.1x 100. Oct. 27, due Nov. 1, 1892. 2,000

Farley, Thomas to Robert M. Dore. Chisholm st, w s, lots 10 and 11 map Wm. Birrell, 40x 119.7x40.5x113.7. Oct. 26, 1 year, 5 %. 2,000

Farley, Patrick to Charles Gahren. 87th st. P. M. Oct. 24, due Nov. 21, 1892, 5 %. 10,600

Fay, Michael and William Stacom to Eliza J. Perry widow. Henry st. P. M. Oct. 19, 1 year, 5 %. 14,750

Feldmann, John G. W. to Thomas L. Concklin. 93d st, n s, 103 w Park av, runs north 29.5 x northeast to point 42.7 n 93d st and 100 w Park av, x north 58.1 x west 39 x south 100.8 to st, x east 36 to beginning. Oct. 27, 1 year. 6,000

Feltman, Lina to Catharine Ernst. 76th st. P. M. Oct. 27, 3 years 3,000

Frommer, Robert to Eliza H. Neilson 185th st, s s, 100 w Amsterdam av, 25x79.11. Oct. 1, 3 years, 5 %. 3,000

Falconer, William H. to THE DRY DOCK SAVINGS INST. 62d st, s s, 179 e 5th av, 25x100.5. Oct. 27, due Nov. 1, 1892, 5 %. 10,000

Fitch, Benjamin to Louis Wilkens, New York, William Wilkens, Baltimore, Md., and Herman Schoenijahn, Brooklyn. 4th av, e s, 25 n 9th st, abt 25x— to point 175 w of 3d av, parcel begins 175 w of 3d av and 46 n 9th st, runs north 48 x east 75 x south 23.4 x west 37.6 to centre Lafayette court, x south 22.8 x west 37.6; Lafayette court or alley, centre line, e s, in vicinity of last above, 22.8 x37.6. Sub. to morts. Oct. 20, notes. 10,000

Foster, Myer to Mary M. Costello guard. of Julia L. and Richard R. Costello. 59th st. P. M. Oct. 26, 3 years or sooner, 4½ %. gold, 12,000

Gault, Mary E. to James Brice. 133d st. P. M. Oct. 27, due Jan. 1, 1892. 17,000

Gallagher, Patrick to Jennie A. Potts. 26th st. P. M. Oct. 23, 5 months or sooner, 5 %. 4,000

Graham, William to Beadleston & Woerz, a corporation. Christopher st, No. 185. Store lease. Oct. 28, demand. 2,500

Goldsmith, Bella wife of Solomon to William Stern. Av A or Eastern Boulevard. P. M. Oct. 26, due Feb. 1, 1895, 5 %. 4,000

Glass, John to Charles A. Peabody, Jr. 11th st, s w cor 6th av, runs west 56.10 x 140.6 x south 50.6 x east 166.7 to av, x north 9.6 to beginning Oct. 23, 6 months. 25,000

Gomprecht, Gustav to Sarah E. Cassidy et al. exrs. Hugh Cassidy. Park or 4th av, 78th st. P. M. Oct. 22, due Oct. 27, 5 %. 13,000

Green, George F. to Abraham B. Odell exr. Jacob D. Odell. 143d st, n s, 356.2 e Willis av, 18.10x100. Oct. 27, due Jan. 1, 1892, 5 %. 1,000

Goodman, Louis to Hyman Schnitzer. Henry st, No. 217, n s, 23.6x87.6. Oct. 26, installs, notes. 4,500

Grayhead, Meyer to Julia M. Bowerman et al. exrs. William D. Bowerman. Wadsworth av, w s, 250 s 187th st, 20x150. Oct. 1, 2 years 5 %. 1,200

Hall, Alfred B. to William R. Beal Land Improvement Co Crimmins av. P. M. Oct. 22, due July 8, 1894, or sooner, 5 %. 700

Heiman, Joseph to Frank M. Tichenor. 82d st, No. 315 E. P. M. Oct. 28, 1 year, 5 %. 800

Same to Frank C. J. Becker. Same property. P. M. Oct. 28, 5 years, 5 %. 4,000

Herter, Rossmond wife of and Frank W. to Barbara wife of Philip Leyendecker. 22d st, n s, 250 w 9th av, 25x98.9. Oct. 29, due Nov. 1. 1892. 5,000

Holden, John A. to Minnie F. Gouldrup, Auburn, N. Y. Ash st, 24th Ward. P. M. Oct. 10, due Oct. 29, 1894, or sooner, 5 % 1,200

Halloway, Ellen J., Brooklyn, to Mary G. Hoffman extrx. William B. Hoffman. 32d st, n s, 200 e 2d av, 20x98.9. Oct. 24, 3 years, 5 %. gold, 3,000

Harrigan, Thomas to Isaac P. Smith. 150th st, n s, 125 w Morris av, 25x118.6. Oct. 21, due Sept. 29, 1894. 100

Heller, Bernard to Jules Charriere and ano. admrs. Elizabeth Charriere. 6th av, s w cor 39th st, 98.8x100. Leasehold. Oct. 22, 5 years, 5 %. 20,000

Hershfeld, Levi N. with Benjamin G. Disbrow exr. and trustee Benjamin Disbrow, both mortgagees. Agreement as to priority of mortgages made by James G. Tyler. Oct. 21. nom

Hillenbrand, Francis J. to Joseph Schneider. 94th st, n s, 100 w 9th av, 25x100.8. Oct. 23, due Jan. 2, 1892, or sooner, 5 %. 9,000

Hornberger, George and Louise his wife to Paul Sonntag. St. Marks pl. P. M. Oct. 23, due July 1, 1892, 5 %. 9,000

Howard, George B. to THE TITLE GUARANTEE AND TRUST CO. Waverley pl. P. M. Oct. 24, due Oct. 26, 1894, 5 %. 12,000

Hagan, Susanna V. to The Murray Hill Bank. Amsterdam av, s w cor 79th st, 102.2x100. Oct. 26, 6 months. 2,000

Herter, Peter, Jersey City, N. J., to John J. Jones and ano. trustees David Jones dec'd. Rivington st, n w cor Suffolk st, runs west 34 x north 75 x west 44 x north 25 x east 78 to Suffolk st, x south 100 to beginning. Oct. 27, 5 years, 5 %. 75,000

Holland, Joseph H. to The Industrial Co-operative Building and Loan Assoc. Lot 412 map part of farm of Charles Berrian, Fordham, 24th Ward. Oct. 26, installs. 3,250

Howe, Margaret J. to John J. Brady. Tremont av; Cambreleng av. P. M. Oct. 19, due Nov. 5, 1894, or sooner, 5 %. 1,590

Hunt, Jessie J. wife of and William H. to Henry Keil. 123d st, n s, 200 w 7th av, 25x 100. Oct. 26, due Nov. 1, 1892. 2,000

Hynes, William A. mortgagor with Martha E. wife of Charles M. Ramsay, Brechin, Scotland, mortgagee. Extension of mort. Oct. 21. nom

Happel, Adam to Ann E. McCaddin, Brooklyn. 1st st, Nos. 22 and 24, n s, 70 w 2d av, 33.3x75. Oct. 28, 2 years, 4½ %. 10,000

Indelli, Pietro to Hubert Van Wagenen. 69th st. P. M. Sub. to mort. $28,500. Oct. 26. due March 1. 1892, 10,765

Same to same. Same property. P. M. Sub,

to morts. $39,265. Oct. 26, due March 1, 1892. 27,500

Isaacs, Samuel L. to Katharina Miller. 50th st. P. M. Oct. 28, 2 years, 5 %. 6,000

Jencks, Francis M. to Alexander McIntyre. 112th st, s s, 200 w 7th av, 50x100.11. Oct. 23, demand. 8,000

Journeay, Albert to THE FARMERS' LOAN AND TRUST CO. Lispenard st, Nos. 45 and 47, n s, 45.1x49.10x48x49.4; Lispenard st, Nos. 49 and 51, n s, 248 w Broadway, 40x42.2x40x40.4; Lispenard st, No. 43½, n s, 175 e Church st, — to No 45 Lispenard st, —x—x—x50. Oct. 27, 2 years, 5 %. gold, 47,500

Johnston, Elizabeth wife of and Richard E. to THE UNION DIME SAVINGS INST. 8th av, n w cor 117th st, 26.4x100. Oct. 23, due Nov. 1, 1894, 5 %. 32,500

Same to same. 8th av, w s, 26.4 n 117th st, 25.8 x100 Oct. 23, due Nov. 1, 1894, 5 %. 18,750

Same to same. 8th av, w s, 52 n 117th st, 19x 100. Oct. 23, due Nov. 1, 1894, 5 %. 15,000

Same to same. 8th av, w s, 71 n 117th st, 26x 100. Oct. 23, due Nov. 1, 1894, 5 %. 18,750

Same to Morris Steinhardt. 8th av, n w cor 117th st, 97x100. Sub. to morts. $85,000. Oct. 23, due Dec. 1, 1891, or sooner. 21,000

Kellard, Mary M. to Madeline Pierce. 63d st, s s, 250 w Columbus av, 25x100.5. Sub. to mort. $13,000. Oct. 23, due Oct. 24, 1892, or sooner. 2,500

Kenn, James to Joseph Murray. Creston av, e s, 118.7 s Donnybrook st, runs east 74.1 x south in three courses 40 x west 74.4 to av, x north 40. Oct. 23, 5 years. 1,500

Kilpatrick, Edward to Charlotte A. Hamilton. 96th st, s s, 125 w 8th av. P. M. Oct. 15, due Oct. 16, 1892, 5 %. 8,000

Same to Alice Hamilton. 96th st, s s, 175 w 8th av. P. M. Oct. 15, due Oct. 16, 1892, 5 %. 8,000

Same to William G. Hamilton, Ramapo, N. Y. 96th st, s s, 225 w 8th av. P. M. Oct. 15, due Oct 16, 1892, 5 %. 8,000

Same to Adelaide Hamilton. 96th st, s s, 275 w 8th av. P. M. Oct. 15, due Oct. 16, 1892, 5 %. 8,000

Same to Henry C. Niedenstein. 96th st, s s, 300 w 8th av. P. M. Oct. 12, due Oct. 29, 1892, 5 %. 10,000

Same to Harriet Overhiser. 96th st, s s, 125 w Central Park West, 200x100.8. Oct. 23, 6 months. 100,000

Kriete, John to Christian Ordemann. 80th st, n s, 100 e 2d av, 25x100. Oct. 26, installs. 1,000

Kip, Annie L. wife of and Clarence V. to William L. Vandervoort and ano. exrs. Lilla F. Jones. 95th st, n s, 364 w 8th av, 16x100.8. Oct. 28, due Dec. 1, 1894, 4½ %. 6,000

Same to William L. Vandervoort trustee for Helen Vandervoort. Same property Oct. 28, due Sept. 1, 1894, 4½ % 4,000

Kunzemann, Jacob to The John Eichler Brewing Co. 2d av, No. 176, e s, 25.9 n 11th st, 25.10x100; 2d av, No. 213, n w cor 13th st, 26 x92 6; 11th st, Nos. 327–331, n s, 225.4 w 1st av, runs north 40 x northeast 25.2 x north 3.8 x southeast 6 x northeast 39.6 x north 25 x 1 x west 43.8 x west 33.11 x southwest 69.10 x south 34.6 to st, x east 71.8. ½ part. Oct. 29, 1 year. 2,519

Levy, Bernard S. to Herman Long. 134th st, n s, 197.6 e 6th av before widening, 87.6x199.7 to 135th st, x87.6x199.10. Oct. 28, 5 months or sooner. 10,000

Loeb, Joseph to Marcus B. Bookstaver. 56th st P. M. Sub. to morts. $28,000. Oct. 1, installs, 5 %. 2,000

Levi, Joseph to Caroline Simonson, Northfield, S. I. Canal st. P. M. Oct. 27, 6 years, 5 %. 6,500

Lasher, Katie to Rasmus Christensen. 83d st. P. M. Oct. 27, due Nov. 1, 1895, or sooner. 4,000

Leggett, William H. to Sarah Spencer. Vanderbilt av E. P. M. Oct. 27, due Nov. 1, 1894, 5 %. 1,000

Loisette, Ida M. wife of Alphonse to James V. D. Card and ano. trustees for Mary E. Card. 7th st. P. M. Oct 27, due Nov. 1, 1897, 5 %. 14,000

Same to Hubert Van Wagenen. Same property. P. M. 2d mort. Oct. 27, due Nov. 1, 1894, installs., 5 %. 7,500

Langvelo, J. C. Julius to Ephraim C. Gates, Calais, Me. Washington av. P. M. Oct. 15, due Oct. 17, 1894, 5 %. 1,500

Lange, Frederick E. to Eduard Lange, Lonkorrek, Germany. Lexington av, e s, 20.5 s 57th st, 30x80. Oct. 20, due Jan. 1, 1891. marks, 50,000

Lawlor, James to Alice S. Constant. 114th st. P. M. Oct. 23, 3 years, 5 %. 9,000

Liebroek, Nicolaus to George B. Robinson. 143d st. P. M. Oct. 13, due Dec. 1, 1891. 3,000

Lyon, William and Nathan Hobart and ano. trustees James Lockett. West 10th st, No. 165, n s, 128 w Waverley pl, 22x95. Oct. 22, due Nov. 1, 1896, 5 %. 14,000

Lynd, Robert B. to Seth M. Milliken guard. of Emma L. and Sarah C. Gibbs. 84th st, n s, 70 w Madison av, 75x102.2. Oct. 23, 1 year or sooner. 10,000

Labro, Louisa to Julius Kaesemeyer. Bender st (8th av), s e cor Jerome av, runs south 30.7 x southeast 100 x northeast 50 x northwest 86 to Jerome av, x southwest 23.11. Oct 21, 3 years, 5 %. 4,000

Same to Bertha Doctor. Same property. Oct. 21, 1 year. 2,000

Lawrence, Fannie E. to Annie E. Brown. 210th st. June 1, 3 years, 5 %. See Conveys. 1,950

Same to J. Romaine Brown. Leyden st, n e s, 100 s e Tennison pl, runs northeast 100 x southeast 25 x south 36.7 x west 24.6 x southwest 56 to st, x northwest 25; Terrace View av, w s, 156.9 n Leyden st, 125x101.6x125x100. March 23, 3 years, 5 %. 2,278

Lawrence, Fannie E. to Frank Yoran. Anthony av, e s, 80.8 n 175th st prolonged, 50x 149.5x52x128. Oct. 24, 3 years, 5 %. 1,600

Marks, Jessie, Roselle, N. J., to Jessie C. McBride, Arverne-by-the-Sea, L. I. 2d av and 101st st. P. M. Oct. 23, 1 year or sooner. gold, 13,000

Same to Jessie Clark, Cornwall-on-the-Hudson. Same property. Oct. 23, 1 year or sooner. gold, 20,000

Same to same. Same property. Oct. 23, 1 year or sooner. gold, 20,000

Martin, Wilbur F. to Adam C. Martin exr. of Hannah S. Martin. 49th st, No. 223 W. Oct. 26, 1 year. 6,000

Mayer, Theobald to The Mayor, &c., of New York. Old Fordham av, w s, 212.9 n 175th st and 1.8 w of present w s 3d av, 27x102.5x27 x103.7. P. M. Oct. 19, 5 years. 2,400

Murphy, Lizzie to Bernheimer and Schmid. 1st av, No. 1601, n w cor 83d st. Saloon lease. Oct 27, note, demand. 2,500

Martin, William R. to THE MUTUAL LIFE INS. CO., New York. 138th st, n s, 175 e Lenox av, 125x199.11 to 139th st. Oct. 23, 1 year. 23,000

McDermott, Matthias to Edwin F. Raynor. 115th st, n s, 362.6 w 7th av. P. M. Oct. 22, 3 years, 5 %. 13,000

Same to same. 115th st, n s, 381.3 w 7th av. P. M. Oct. 22, 3 years, 5 %. 13,000

Same to Canda & Kane. Same property. Oct. 23, due Nov. 1, 1891. 2,500

Same to same. 115th st, n s, 362.6 w 7th av. Oct. 22, due Nov. 1, 1891. See Conveys. 2,500

Minor, Edna V. to Israel Minor, Jr., exr. Jane V. C. Cooper. 41st st, s s, 160.10 e 5th av, 20.10x102.6x20.10x103.1. Oct. 20, due Nov. 1, 1893, 4½ %. 5,000

Matthies, William to Bernard T. Kearns. 3d av, No. 449. Saloon lease. Oct 24, installs. 13,000

Mayer, Theobald P. to Andrew Wieser. Bronx River road, w s, lots 213, 215, 217 and 219 map part of Hyatt farm, near Woodlawn, 24th Ward. 100.4x117.5x100x125.8. Oct. 22, 3 years. 600

McCabe, Thomas F. to Eva Bechtel extrx. George Bechtel. 1st av, n w cor 21st st. Lease. Oct 26. 3,000

McCauley, John to James Flanagan. 10th av, n w cor 28th st, 24.8x100. Oct. 26, due July 7, 1893, 5 %. 8,000

McKnight, John F. to Terence Jacobson. 17th st, s s, 94 e 1st av, 25x92. Leasehold. Collateral to another mort. Oct. 24, due Nov. 1, 1893. gold, 550

Muhlker, Henry to Alice S. H. Davies, New Haven, Conn. 115th st, n s, 53 w Park av, 37x76.10. Oct. 24, due Oct. 26, 1896, 5 %. gold, 20,000

Mutual Reserve Fund Life Assoc. mortgagee with Henry M. Turk present owner. Extension of mort. Oct. 21. nom

McDonnell, Alexander and Mary his wife to Peter McDonnell. 25th st, n s, 177.6 w 9th av, 22.6x98.9. Oct. 27, 1 year, 5 %. 1,500

Mahon, Martin and Edward Coyne to George E. Hyatt, Brooklyn. 4th av, s e cor 21st st, 46x90. Oct. 27, due July 1, 1892, or sooner. 128,000

Martines, Aristides to William Lippman. 39th st. P. M. Oct. 29, 1 year, 5 %. 6,000

Masbach, Robert J. and Louis to Philip Bolender. 52d st. P. M. Oct. 29, due Nov. 1, 1893, or sooner, 5 %. 4,000

Mayer, Isaac and Jacob Levy to Philip Michaelson. Av C. P. M. Oct. 28, due Nov. 1, 1894, 5 %. 8,000

McKallen, Margaret to George Ehret. 10th av, No. 385. Store lease. Oct. 23, demand. 500

McManus, Mary, Brooklyn, to Hulbert Peck. 35th st, n s, 2.9 e 8th av, 23x98.9. Oct. 29, 1 year, 5 %. 1,000

Niemeier, Adelheit wife of and Frederick to Mary G. Hoffman extrx. William B. Hoffman 77th st, s s. 150 w Av A, 25x59.5x25.4 x68 6. Oct. 22, 3 years, 5 %. 4,000

Noble, William to Harriet Overhiser. 7th av, s w cor 57th st, runs west 115 x south 89 x east 15.2 x south 38.5 x east 22 x south 75.5 to 56th st, x east 78 to av, x north 200.10 to beginning. Sub. to morts. $895,000, taxes, &c. Oct. 26, 1½ years. gold, 75,000

Newman, Adolph to Myer and Solomon Goodman. 5th st. P. M. Oct. 27, due Oct. 8, 1894. 3,000

O'Brien, Jeremiah J. to John J. Brady. Elmwood pl and Crotona av. P. M. Oct. 19, due Nov. 5, 1894, 5 % 600

Ogden, Alfred B. to THE UNION TRUST CO., of New York, trustee for Cornelia L. Martin. 79th st, s e cor Madison av, 21x80. Oct. 27, due Nov. 1, 1893, 5 %. 4,000

Oppenheimer, Mina to John A. Stewart et al. trustees of THE LIVERPOOL AND LONDON AND GLOBE INS CO in New York. 95th st, No. 211, n s, 181 e 3d av, 25x100.8. Oct. 24, due Oct. 28, 1896, 5 %. gold, 15,400

Oppenheimer, Mina widow to Randolph Guggenheimer. 95th st, n s, 181 e 3d av, 25x 100.8. Oct. 15, due in Oct., 1894. 750

POUGHKEEPSIE SAVINGS BANK mortgagee with Wendelin Ruckert mortgagor and present owner. Extension of mort. at 4½ %. Sept. 1. nom

Parmly, Mary E. widow, Essex Co., N. J., and Susan J. M. Gregory widow to THE MUTUAL LIFE INS. CO. of New York. 23d st, s s, 75 e 4th av, 25x98.9. Oct. 28, 1 year, 5 %. 17,000

Poppite, Vincenzo to Beadleston & Woerz, a corporation. 13th st, No. 434 E. Store lease. Oct. 27, demand. 600

Platt, James N. exr. John G. Kane mortgagee with Ferris S. Thompson mortgagor. Extension of mort at 5 %. Sept. 24. nom

Platt, Richard G. to Sydney A. Smith. West End av, s w cor 85th st, 30.2x34. Oct. 14, due Oct. 15, 1892. 4,000

Same to same. West End av, w s, 30.2 s 85th st, 20x64x34.4x41. Oct. 14, due Oct. 15, 1892. 2,500

Same to same. West End av, w s, 50.2 s 85th st, 20x64 Oct. 14, due Oct. 15, 1892. 2,500

Same to same. West End av, w s, 70.2 s 85th st, 16x82. Oct. 14, due Oct. 15, 1892. 3,000

Same to same. West End av, w s, 86.2 s 85th st, 16x100. Oct. 14, due Oct. 15, 1892. 3,000

Same to same. 85th st, s s, 82 w West End av. 18x86.2. Oct. 14, due Oct. 15, 1892. 3,000

Same to same. 85th st, s s, 34 w West End av, 30x50.2x30.4x30.2. Oct. 14, due Oct. 15, '92. 4,000

Same to same. 85th st, s s, 64 w West End av. 18x70.2. Oct. 14, due Oct. 15, 1892. 3,000

Phillips, Herman S. to Thomas H. Messenger exr. Thomas Messenger. 46th st. P. M. Oct. 26, 5 years, 5 %. gold, 12,000

Same to Zillah Phillips. Same property. P. M. 2d mort. Oct. 26, 1 year or sooner. 3,000

Plangemann, Adolph to Bernheimer & Schmid. Willis av, No. 249. Saloon lease. Oct. 24, note, demand. 3,500

Pfeifer, Richard and Ottilde P. his wife to Margaret E. wife of Albert E. Putnam. New Drive, Spuyten Duyvil, 24th Ward. P. M. Oct. 14, due Oct. 15, 1894. 1,100

Rabill, James to Sophia wife of Carl G. A. Hoble. 169th st. n s, 150 e 11th av, 25x81.7. Sept. 30, due Oct. 1, 1894, 5 %. 250

Reid, Serepta M. to George Williams. 68th st. No. 64 W. P. M. Oct. 23, 3 years, 5 %. 4,000

Rockwell, John S. to George E. Kitching. Lexington av, n w cor 29th st, 24.8x39. Oct. 23, 1 year. 1,500

Ryan, Lawrence to Caroline L. Purdy. 152d st. n s, 125.5 e Morris av, 24.10x100. Oct. 24, 3 years, 5½ %. 1,000

Rohrs, Frederick to Reuben Ross. Madison av, s e cor 132d st, 99.11x150. Oct. 26, due March 1, 1892, or sooner. 50,000

Rosendorf, Hugo D. and Samuel M. to THE TITLE GUARANTEE AND TRUST CO. 24th st. No. 45, n s, 200 e 6th av, 20.10x98.9, except a strip of land on w s, abt 0.6x54.4. Oct. 28, due Nov. 1, 1892, 4½ %. 12,000

Randall, Rufus R. to Thomas H. Brown. Grove av. P. M. Oct, 23, 3 years or sooner, 5 %. 1,800

Rapelye, Pheba C. to David W. Bruce et al. trustees for George B. Brown. St. Nicholas av, e s, 89.1 n 120th st. P. M. Oct. 13, due Dec. 1, 1896, or sooner, 5 %. gold, 20,000

Same to Julia Wray. St. Nicholas av, e s, 59.9 n 120th st. P. M. Oct. 13, due Dec. 1, 1896, or sooner, 5 %. gold, 19,000

Same to James, Jeanette D., John A. and Katherine Chambers. St. Nicholas av, n e cor 120th st. P. M. Oct. 13, due Dec. 1, 1896, or sooner, 5 %. gold, 20,000

Same to George G. De Witt and ano. trustees Sarah Talman. St. Nicholas av, e s, 23.6 n 120th st. P. M. Oct. 13, due Dec. 1, 1896, 5 %. gold, 19,000

Same to Isabella McCormack. St. Nicholas av, n e cor 120th st, four houses. P. M. Sub. to morts. $78,000. Oct. 13, demand. gold, 41,000

Reese, Henry to Fanny Sussman. 53d st. P. M. Oct. 23, 8 years, 5 %. 4,000

Rhoden, Joseph F. to Ferdinand W. Geiler. 184th st, s s, 382 e 10th av, 11.6x108, being No. 8 Fullsin pl. Oct. 23, due Sept. 1, 1892. 653

Ripley, David to Augustus F. Holly. 84th st. P. M. Oct. 29, 1 year. 20,000

Robinson, Thomas J. to Abraham Steers. 8th av, e s, 24.7 s 112th st, 25.7x100. Sub. to morts. $22,000. Oct. 26, 6 months. 9,203

Same to same. 8th av, e s, 50.2 s 112th st, 25.2 x100. Sub. to morts. $20,000. Oct. 26, 6 months. 9,203

Same to same. 8th av, e s, 75.4 s 112th st, 25.7 x100. Sub. to morts. $21,000. Oct. 26, 6 months. 9,203

Same to same. 127th st, s s, 255 w 2d av, 25x 99.11. Sub. to morts. $21,000. Oct. 26, 6 months. 4,221

Same to same. 127th st, s s, 280 w 2d av, 25x 99.11. Sub. to morts. $21,000. Oct. 26, 6 months. 4,221

Same to same. 127th st, s s, 305 w 2d av, 25x 99.11. Sub. to morts. $21,000. Oct. 26, 6 months. 4,221

Rosenberg, Joseph to Adolph Pawel. 62d st, s s, 174.6 e 2d av, 25x100.5. Oct. 29, installs. 1,500

Schauwecker, Charles L. with Louise F. and Friederike Schauwecker. Agreement as to apportionment of morts. on lease. Dec. 30, 1889. nom

Smith, James R to John D. Crimmins. 68th st. P. M. Oct. 23, 1 year, 5 %. 13,500

Smith, Elizabeth wife of Michael to Elizabeth M. wife of James F. Dolan. 109th st. P. M. Oct. 27, due Oct. 28, 1896, 4 %. 1,500

Stinson, John E. to Mary E. Ray. 93d st. P. M. Oct. 26, due Oct. 27, 1892, 5 %. 2,500

Shortland, Stephen F. and Thomas S. to THE ALBANY SAVINGS BANK. Greene st, No. 98, e s, 175 n Spring st, 25x100. Oct. 22, 3 years, 4½ %. 20,000

Stewart, John to James B. Mix. 34th st. P. M. Oct. 27, 3 years, 5 %. 6,000

Striker, Elsworth L. and George B. Juckett to John J. Jones and ano. trustees David Jones, dec'd. 72d st, s s, 345 w 8th av, 22x102.2. Oct. 19, due March 1, 1892. 4,500

Stegmayer, Charles to Henry J. Mahr. Av A, s e cor 88th st. P. M. Oct. 24, due Oct. 15, 1892, 5 %. 14,900

Studinski, Henrietta to John V. Campbell. Essex st. P. M. Oct. 23, installs. 8,300

Tuozzo, Theresa to Alfonzo Guida. Mulberry st, w s, 75 6 n Park st, 25.4x103.4x25.3x103.9. Oct. 28, due Dec. 1, 1891. 4,000

Tyler, James G. to Benjamin G. Disbrow exr. and trustee Benjamin Disbrow. 156th st, No. 510, s s, 133.4 w Amsterdam av, 16.8x99.11. Oct. 22, due Oct. 20, 1896, 5 %. gold, 5,000

Traynor, Patrick to Bernheimer & Schmid. 1st av, No. 1100, n e cor 60th st. Saloon lease. Oct. 23, note, demand. 2,350

The Harrisonville Co operative Building Assoc., New York, to William Hatfield. 138th st, s s, 550 e 6th av, 73.?x69.1x134 8x136.2. Oct. 26, 3 years, 5 %. See Conveys. 5,000

Thomas, George A. to Arthur M. Mitchell. 101st st, n s, 510 e 3d av. P. M. Oct. 5, 1 year. 30,000

Tuke, Henry C. to Bradley & Currier Co. (Lim.) Lexington av, s w cor 121st st, 40x100.11. Sub. to mort. $52,500. Oct. 15, 6 months. 5,800

Thomas, Henrietta G. to Charles H. Murray, Jersey City, N. J. 119th st, No 15, n s, 151.5 w 5th av, 14x73x14.6x69.2. April 17, due Nov 13, 1900. 1,000

Townsend, J. Allen to Charles B. Moore. 103d st, s s, 200 e 5th av. P. M. Oct. 28, due Oct. 29, 1894, 5 %. 12,700

Same to Lavinia Cudlipp. 103d st, n s, 255 w Park av. P. M. Oct. 29, due June 1, 1892. 12,000

Towle, Stevenson to Frederick W. Joekel. 113th st, n s, 100 e 8th av, 124x100.11. Oct. 21, due Jan. 1, 1898. 500

Vogel, Heyman to The Mutual Life Ins Co., of New York Grand st, n s, 24.9 e Centre Market pl, runs east 50.6 x north 99.6 x west 6 x south 27.1 x west 38.6 x south 72.4 to beginning; Grand st, n s, 75.3 e Centre Market pl, runs north 99.6 x east 24.7 x south 59.5 x — 40.2 to Grand st, x west 24.9 to beginning (Nos. 176, 178 and 180 Grand st.) Oct. 24, due Oct. 27, 1892, 5 %. 80,000

Van Wyck, Annie E. to John R. Downey. 38th st, s s, 83.4 w 7th av, 16.8x98.9. Sub. to mort. $6,000. Oct. 23, due May 1, 1893, 5 %. 1,500

Von Eupen, Theodore to Wm. H. Edsall. Jones st, No. 23, n s, 150 e Bleecker st, 25x100. Oct. 21, demand. 3,500

Wendel, Louis, Jr., to Benjamin Altman. Amsterdam av, w s, 74.11 n 184th st, 25x100. Oct. 22, 3 years, 5 %. gold, 2,800

Same to same. Amsterdam av, w s, 24.11 n 184th st, 25x100. Oct. 22, 3 years, 5 %. gold, 2,900

Same to same. Amsterdam av, w s, 49.11 n 184th st, 25x100. Oct. 22, 3 years, 5 %. gold, 2,800

Same to same. Amsterdam av, n w cor 184th st, 24.11x100. Oct. 22, 3 years, 5 %. gold, 4,000

West, Joseph I. to Alida wife of John McAlan. 119th st, s s, 125 w Lenox av, 8 lots. 8 P. M. morts., each $6,750. Oct. 23, 5 years or sooner, 5 %. gold, 54,000

West, Joseph I. to Susan E. Le Roy. 27th st, n s, 325 w 6th av, 25x98.9. Oct. 20, due Nov. 1, 1891, 5 %. 10,000

Weiber, Lorenz F. J., Jr., to Mary L. Hall guard. of Edward L., Edith L and Maud L. Hall. 126th st, No. 223, n s, 237.6 e 3d av, 17x99.11. Oct. 28, due Nov. 1, 1896, 5 %. 13,000

Same to same. 126th st, No. 225, n s, 254 6 e 3d av, 17x99.11. Oct. 28, due Nov. 1, 1896, 5 %. 13,000

Same to Enoch C. Bell. 126th st, n s, 237.6 e 3d av, 34x99.11. Sub. to morts. $26,000. Oct. 28, 6 months. 3,000

Weiber, Lorenz to The Germania Life Ins. Co. 72d st, n s, 30 w Lexington av, 125x102.2. Oct. 27, due Aug. 1, 1892. 225,000

Weiler, Anna B. to Charles Regnault. 170th st, n s, 75 w Washington av, 51x72.3x51x74.6. Oct. 1, due April 1, 1894. 2,000

Weinberg, Charles to Margaret E. Zimmerman and ano. trustees of Sophia R. C. Furniss. Riverside Drive or av, s e cor 104th st, 100.11x100. Oct. 20, due Jan. 1, 1898, or sooner, 5 %. 45,000

Same to same. 104th st, s s, 100 e Riverside Drive or av, 100x100.11. Oct. 20, due Jan. 1, 1898, or sooner, 5 %. 25,000

Warner, Joel R., Boston, Mass., to Jane Potter trustee William H. Potter dec'd. Willard st P. M. Oct. 16, 3 years, 5 %. 550

Wassner, Frances wife of and John to The Daily News Building, Savings and Loan Assoc. 181st st. P. M. Sept. 24, installs. 3,000

Winter, Fredrike widow and George to Harriet Hebert. Av A, w s, 97.10 n 59th st, 27.8x106.6. Oct. 24, 3 years, 5 %. 8,500

Weismann, Kate M. G. to Adam Steinmann. Madison av, e s, 300 n Columbia av, 50x100. Oct. 26, 5 years. 2,500

Wilmurt, Francis M. to The Bradley & Currier Co. (Lim.) 89th st, s s, 220 w West End av, 21x100.8. Sub. to mort. $19,000. Oct. 26, 3 years, 5 %. 3,000

Welch, Edwin to Tarrant Putnam and ano. trustees for Geraldine W. Goddard. 59th st, No. 219, n s, 230 e 3d av, 22x100.4. Oct. 29, 3 years, 4¾ %. 7,500

Westerfield, Kate L to Jennie W. Francke, St. Louis, Mo. 46th st, s s, 98 w Broadway, 20x100.5. Oct. 29, due Nov. 1, 1896, 5 %. 13,000

Wiley, William J. to Minna F. Gouldrup, Auburn, N. Y. Ash st, s w cor Morris av. P. M. Oct. 10, due Oct. 29, 1894, 5 %. 3,500

Youmans, Edgar W. to William J. and Mary E. Graham. Washington st. P. M. Oct. 26, 3 years, 5 %. 9,000

Youell, Mary to The Emigrant Indust. Savings Bank. Bedford st, No. 107, w s, 83.4 s Christopher st, 12.3x62.7x13.5x—. Oct. 27, 1 year, 4½ %. 3,500

KINGS COUNTY.

October 22, 23, 24, 26, 27, 28.

Allers, Maria widow to The Title Guarantee and Trust Co. Clason av, w s, 25 n Van Buren st, 25x81. Oct. 21, 2 years, 5 %. $2,500

Anderton, Sarah widow to William Thompson. Dean st, s s, 209.4 w Underhill av, 25x105.8 to centre Debevoise st, x 28 8x91.8; interior gore, lot begins at point 200 w Underhill av and 105.7 n Bergen st, 27.11x57.4x50. Oct. 20, 1 year, 5 %. 200

Alt, Edward to Charles Greaessel. Atlantic av, s e cor Bradford st, 25x90. Oct. 26, due Oct. 1, 1894. 4,000

Boiles, Matilda, Bayport, Conn., to Frank E. Hart. Arlington av, s e cor Ashford st, 40x100. Oct. 22, 3 years. 1,600

Beasley, Alfred L. to Hetta M. Cameron. Van Buren st, n s, 119.6 w Lewis av, 19.6x100. Sub. to mort. $3,500. Oct. 23, 1 year, 5 %. 2,300

Same to The Home Life Ins. Co. Same property. Oct. 21, 1 year, 5 %. 3,500

Beasley, David S. to The Title Guarantee and Trust Co. Greene av, s s, 340 e Throop av, 2 lots, each 20x100. 2 morts., each $5,000. Oct. 26, 3 years, 5 %. 10,000

Same to same. Greene av, s s, 380 e Throop av, 4 lots, each 20x100. 4 morts., each $5,500. Oct. 26, 3 years, 5 %. 22,000

Same to same. Greene av, s s, 460 e Throop av, 2 lots, each 20x100. 2 morts., each $5,000. Oct. 26, 3 years, 5 %. 10,000

Bidstrup, James F. to James W. Crawford, New York. Elton st. P. M. Oct. 12, due Nov. 1, 1893. 600

Blixt, Andrew P. to Frank Jenks. Carroll st, n s, 339.11 e 4th av, runs north — x east 0.1¼ x north — x east 20 x south 100 to st, x west 20. Oct. 24, 3 years, 5 %. 3,000

Same to The Title Guarantee and Trust Co. Carroll st, n s, 360 e 4th av, 20x100. Oct. 24, 3 years, 5 %. 3,000

Brandt, Maria wife of and George W. to James Dean. 80th st, n s, 420 w 3d av, 100x109.4. Oct. 15, notes 6,000

Brandt, George W. to Mary G. Manning. 75th st, s s, 104 e 3d av, 21x100.2. Oct. 28, due Nov. 1, 1894. gold, 3,000

Brennan, James to John Colligan. Driggs av, west cor North 11th st, 100x100. Oct. 21, notes. 5,957

Buchenholz, Bernard to Minnie Goldstein. Gates av, n s, 217 w Stuyvesant av, 19.6x100. Oct. 16, 2 years. 2,500

Bulkley, Harrie to George Wilcox, Summit, N. J. Douglass st, n s, 400 w Franklin av. P. M. Oct. 12, demand. 3,000

Same to same. Same property. Oct. 12, demand. 12,887

Bardon, Bernard to William H. Jackson. Shepherd av, n e cor Stanley av. P. M. Oct. 1, 3 years. 700

Borrelli, Vincenzo and Vincenza his wife to Alfred Ogden. Atlantic av, n w cor Russell pl. P. M. Oct. 1, 4 years. 575

Brower, Hannah E. wife of Gilbert H. to William Corrigan 12th st. P. M. Oct. 24, installs, 5 %. 1,600

Barnum, Isaac W. to Lawrence L. Barnum. Halsey st, n s, 117.6 e Tompkins av, 17.6x100; Halsey st, n s, 205 e Tompkins av, 52.6x100. Oct. 19, due the third Monday in Oct., 1892. 2,000

Bannon, Anne widow to Mary E. Fox. North 7th st, s w s, 200 s e Wythe av, 25x100. Oct. 27, 2 years. 500

Bennett, Winant to Cornelius Cowenhoven. 73d st, s w s, 180 s e 3d av, 40x100, New Utrecht. Oct. 27, 3 years. 3,000

Burke, Edward to George W. Pearsall. 31st st, s s, 150 e 4th av, 25x100.2. Oct. 9, 3 years. 500

Curran, Timothy to William Shirden. Herkimer st. P. M. Oct. 26, 3 years, 5 %. 1,100

Clark, Bernard to Frank L. Schelpp. Skillman av, s s, 175 w Lorimer st, 25x100. Oct. 26, 2 years, 5 %. 794

Child, Stanton M. to James D. Lynch. 83d st, New Utrecht. P. M. Oct. 12, due Oct. 15, 1893, 5 %. 735

Clancy, John J. to Lowell M. Palmer. Berry st, east cor North 13th st, 93.1x373 to North 13th st, x361.2, gore. Sub. to mort. $5,200. Oct. 26. secures credits

Coates, Louise F. wife of and Henry J. to The Montauk Building and Loan Assoc. 67th st, s s, 380 e 14th av, 40x120, New Utrecht. Oct. 20, installs. 1,600

Carlson, Carl J. to Frank McDonough. Macon st. P. M. Oct. 22, installs. 2,000

Collenburg, Henry G. to Louisa W. Taylor, Boston, Mass. Belmont av, s s, 40 e Atkins av, 20x90. P. M. Oct. 20, due Oct. 1, 1894. 2,000

Same to Donald Laing. Same property. Oct 20, installs. 600

Collins, Joseph to George E. Kitching trustee for John H. Kitching et al. Hancock st, s e s, 185 n e Broadway, 20x100. Oct. 14, 3 years, 5 %. 2,000

Connelly, Edmond to The Brooklyn Hospital. Imlay st, s e s, 100 s w Summit st, 150x75. Oct. 22, due Nov. 1, 1894, 5 %. 8,000

Cornwell, Theodore I. W. and Jane his wife to Anna C. Palmer. Lexington av, s s, 200 e Nostrand av, 100x100. Oct. 23, 1 year. 6,000

Claesson, Maria C. to E. Willard Roby. Douglass st. P. M. Oct. 26, 1 year. 300

Campbell, William to The Equitable Co-operative Building and Loan Assoc. Nevins st. P. M. Oct. 23, installs, 5 %. 3,250

Cleary, Catharine widow to The Title Guarantee and Trust Co. Walworth st, e s, 450 s Park av, 25x100. Oct. 28, 3 years, 5 %. 1,000

Cosgrave, Ellen wife of and James to Martin V. Wood, Hempstead, L. I. 3d av, south cor 27th st. P. M. Oct. 26, 3 years, 5 %. 18,000

Dietz, Elise to Charles A. and William G. Hamilton trustee Alexander Hamilton. Fulton st, s e cor Schenck st, 24x84.8x40.7x77.8. Oct. 15, due Oct. 1, 1894. 3,000

Same to Crescentia Saile. Fulton st, s s, 24 e Schenck st, 24x89.3x24.6x84.8. Oct. 15, due Oct. 1, 1894. 2,000

Dougherty, Charles to The South Brooklyn Co-operative Building and Loan Assoc. 4th av, e s, 25.2 s 39th st, 18.9x100. Oct. 27, installs. 2,500

Desmond, Timothy to Lewis Walker. Huron st, s s, 225 w Oakland st, 25x100. Oct. 19, 2 years or installs, 5 %. 3,000

Donnelly, Mary to Sophie Iverson. 22d st, s w s, 250 s e 6th av, 50x100. Oct. 10, 7 years. 1,500

Douglas, William E. to Albro J. Newton. 2d st P. M. Oct 5, 3 years, 5 %. 3,000

Dowling, Victor to Francis H. Ross. Ralph av, n w cor Decatur st, 25x100. Oct. 22, 1 year. 3,000

Deane, John W. to Frederick Dhuy, Jr. Pacific st, n s, 376 e Rochester av. P. M. Oct. 24, 3 years, 5 %. 1,200

Same to same. Same property. P. M. Sub. to last mort. Oct. 24, 3 years, 5 %. 600

De Baun, Alonzo E to The Long Island Trust Co. guard. John T. Scanlon. Sackman st, w s, 300 s Dumont av, 100x200 to Christopher av. Oct. 26, due Dec. 1, 1892, 5 %. 1,500

Same to same. Sackman st, w s, 100 s Dumont av, 200x100. Oct. 26, due Dec. 1, 1892, 5 %. 2,200

Same to same as trustee Stephen Garretson. Livonia av, n s, extends from Christopher av to Sackman st, 200x100. Oct. 26, due Dec. 1, 1892, 5 %. 1,800

Same to same. Dumont av, s e cor Christopher av, 100x300. Oct. 26, due Dec. 1, 1892, 5 %. 3,000

Same to same as guard. Eugene W., Arthur H. and Mary A. Allen. Dumont av, s w cor Sackman st, 100x100. Oct. 26, due Dec. 1, 1892, 5 %. 1,200

Doenecke, Christian and Justus to Sarah A. Johnson widow. South 9th st. P. M. Oct. 23, due Dec. 1, 1894, 5 %. 5,000

Dilliard, Martha A. to The Flatbush Co-operative Savings and Loan Assoc 73d st, n s, 130 w 15th av, 40x100, New Utrecht. Oct. 15, installs. 450

Doran, Michael J. to Sarah H. Peppey and ano. trustees Robert A. Thiess dec'd. 7th av, n w cor 4th st, 21x88. Sub. to mort. $12,500. Oct. 23, 3 years. 2,500

Same to Catharine R. Vail. Same property. Sub. to morts. $15,000. Oct. 24, due Feb. 7, 1893, 5 %. 500

Eade, George to John L. Voorhies, Comm'r of Investment for Gravesend. 52d st, s s, 100 w 4th av, 20x100.2. Oct. 23, 3 years, 5 %. 2,500

Ellerstein, Samuel to Pauline Hartmann. Thatford av, e s, 150 n Linington av, 25x100. P. M. Aug 1, due Feb. 1, 1899. 900

Elflein, Frederick to Charles W. Truslow trustee William Wall. Moore st, n s, 329.5 w White st, 50x100. Oct. 23, 3 years or sooner, 5 %. 1,400

Emmons, Charles with Mathias Grossarth both mortgagees. Agreement as to priority of mort. made by George W. McCormack. Oct. 20. nom

Evans, George to Catharine Stuart. Lafayette av, s s, 300.6 e Reid av, 24.5x100. Oct. 22, due June 1, 1891 (?), 5 %. 200

Fagan, Peter to The Title Guarantee and Trust Co. Kent av. P. M. Oct. 23, 1 year. 600

Feeney, Michael to William P. Hillmann. Waverly pl, s e cor 4th av, 39.7x100x12.5x103.1. Oct. 15, 5 years. 850

Finckenauer, George B. to The Brooklyn City Co-operative Building and Loan Assoc. West 9th st, s s, 158.6 e Columbia st, 25x100. Oct. 22, installs. 1,250

Fink, Amalia wife of and Daniel to Peter Bertsch exr. William Broistedt. Harman st, s e s, 120.9 s w Wyckoff av, 25x87.3x25x86. Oct. 22, 3 years, 5 %. 2,500

Same to same. Harman st, s e s, 95.5 s w Wyckoff av, 25x86x25x84 9. Oct. 22, 3 years, 5 %. 2,500

Flood, Catharine to James P. Judge and Walter L. Durack. Tremont st, n s, 160 w Richards st, 40x100. Oct. 12, demand. 225

Foster, Esther J. wife of and William to The Colored Orphan Asylum and Assoc. for the Benefit of Colored Children, New York. Columbia st, w s, abt 50.8 n Pineapple st, 25.3x150. Oct. 23, 5 years, 5 %. 12,000

Francisco, George W. and Charles H. to Marie Wallach. Woodbine st, s e s, 120 n e Hamburg av, 18x100. Oct. 20, due Oct. 22, 1894, 5 %. 2,500

Same to same. Woodbine st, s e s, 174 n e Hamburg av, 18x100. Oct. 20, due Oct. 22, 1894, 5 %. 2,500

Same to same. Woodbine st, s e s, 192 n e Hamburg av, 18x100. Oct. 20, due Oct. 22, 1894, 5 %. 2,500

Same to same. Woodbine st, s e s, 282 n e Hamburg av, 18x100. Oct. 20, due Oct. 22, 1894, 5 %. 2,500

Friedel, John H. G. to Theodore Kiendl. Shepherd av, e s, 100 s Blake av, 100x200 to Berriman st. Oct. 22, due Jan. 1, 1892. 231

Fishman, Thilda to Charles Rissler. Harrison av. P. M. Oct. 23, 2 years. 3,200

Fruwirth, Josephine to Robert A. Lindsay. Prospect pl. P. M. Oct. 21, 3 years, 5 %. 1,700

Finch, Rachel A. to Charles S. Wood. Bergen st, s s, 350 e Brooklyn av, 2 lots, each 20x105.7. 2 morts., each $1,000. Oct. 26, 1 year. 2,000

Feldheim, Louis to Adolphus Gload. Madison st. P. M. Sub. to mort. $2,500. Oct. 26, 5 years. 1,500

Fitzgerald, Michael to The Title Guarantee and Trust Co. 4th av, w s, 80.2 n 33d st, 20x80. Oct. 27, 3 years, 5 %. 2,000

Fordiasky, Harris and Hannah to Mary A. L. Baker. Stone av, w s, 66 n Blake av, 23x100. July 20, installs, 5 %. 200

Frische, Christian to John M. Koenig. Stockholm st, s s, 100 e Central av, 25x100. Oct. 1, 5 years, 5 %. 1,500

Gibrson, Francis to Baldwin F. Strauss. Carroll st, s s, 22.3 w Bond st, 22.3x62.6x22.2x62.6. Oct. 28, 3 years. 700

Gordon, Frances E. to George G. and John H. Hornung. Lafayette av, s w cor New Utrecht av, New Utrecht. P. M. Oct. 27, 3 years, 5 %. 1,800

Grage, Henry to Henry Sandman and Frederick Borghard. Jamaica av, s w cor Logan st, 162x104x150x167. Oct. 22, due Jan. 2, 1893, 5 %. 2,500

Same to Henry Tamke. Same property. Oct. 22, due Jan. 2, 1893, 5 %. 2,500

Goodenough, Marenus J. to Lewis P. Nostrand. Market st. P. M. Oct. 28, 3 years, 5 %. 2,500

Gload, Adolphus to William J. Kerigan. Madison st, n w s, 300 n e Hamburg av, 20x100. Oct. 26, 3 years, 5 %. 2,500

Griffith, Robert J. to Thomas Jackson. Butler st. P. M. Oct. 22, 1 year. 450

Gill, Catharine to Philip Sullivan. Carroll st, n s, 240 w Bedford av, 25.3x114.5. Oct. 24, due Jan. 2, 1892. 740

Gill, Catharine to Alexander Davison, Rockville Centre, L. I. Carroll st, n s, 240 w Bedford av, 20x98.11x25.3x114.5. Oct. 24, due Nov. 1, 1894. 1,000

Geary, Richard to Thomas C. Balderston et al. Supreme trustees Order of Tonti. Belmont av, n s, extends from Logan st to Fountain av, 200x250. Oct. 17, due Oct. 22, 1894, 5 %. 25,000

Gentleman, Mary E. wife of and Moses H. to Virginia A. Kleine. Van Voorhis st, n s, 151 w Evergreen av, runs west 51 x north 100 x east 2 x north 100 to Schaeffer st, x east 50 x south 100 x west 1 x south 100. Sub. to mort. $8,000. Oct. 23, demand. 16,000

Same to The Title Guarantee and Trust Co. Same property. Oct. 23, demand. 8,000

Gibbs, Laura P. to John F. Vrooman. Powell st. P. M. Oct. 19, installs, 5 %. 900

Gibbs, Robert H. to George W. Eastman. Kosciusko st. P. M. Oct. 23, due Nov. 1, 1896, 5 %. 2,000

Gilmour, Annie to Andrew D. Baird. Macon st, n s, 110 e Ralph av, 18x100. Oct. 22, 5 years or installs. 2,300

Gillmore, Laura M. to The Mutual Life Ins. Co., New York. Remsen st, n s, 50 e Clinton st, 25x100. Already mortgaged to party of second part. Oct. 22, due Oct. 23, 1892, 5 %. 5,000

Gomer, August and Jacob Wollpert to Sarah H. Powell. Hopkins st, n s, 175 w Throop av, 25x100. Oct. 23, 3 years, 5 %. 6,000

Gregory, Charles A. and Catharine A. his wife to Catharine M. Gregory. Eldert st. P. M. Oct. 22, 5 years. 2,700

Giuli, Lorenzo to James Cruikshank and ano. trustees Eloise M. Bushnell. 50th st, s s, 100 w 3d av, 20x100.2. Oct. 23, due Oct. 24, 1894. 3,000

Same to same. 50th st, s s, 120 w 3d av, 20x100.2. Oct. 23, due Oct. 24, 1894. 3,000

Hansen, Louis K. to Welcome S. Jarvis. Rogers av, n w cor Butler st. P. M. Oct. 15, 5 years, 5 %. 5,000

Hall, Elizabeth A. to Nathan T. Sprague. Herkimer st. P. M. Oct. 22, 3 years. 1,700

Hall, George P. and James S. to James D. Lynch. 84th st, New Utrecht. P. M. Oct. 8, 2 years, 5 %. 750

Henderson, Albert C. to John Hennessey. Bedford av, s w cor Rodney st, 133x100. Sub. to morts. $137,500. Oct. 15, 3 months. 6,500

Same to same. Same property. Sub. to morts. $125,000. Oct. 15, 3 months. 12,500

Same to same. Same property. Sub. to morts. $131,500. Oct. 15, 3 months. 30,384

Same to Joseph M. De Veau. Same property. Sub. to morts. $100,000. Oct. 15, 1 year, 5 %. 25,000

Henricke, Lena wife of and George to Walter J. Klots. Knickerbocker av, cor Ingraham st. P. M. Oct. 20, 5 years, 5 %. 4,400

Holsten, John D. to John H. O'Roarke. 3d av, n e cor 49th st, 50.2x100. Oct. 23, 3 years, 5 %. 3,000

Hennessey, John to The Mutual Life Ins. Co., New York. Bedford av, s e cor Rodney st, 133x100. Oct. 20, 1 year. 100,000

Herling, John to Charles W. Truslow trustee William Wall. Seigel st, s s, 315 e Bushwick av, 25x100. Oct. 23, 3 years or sooner, 5 %. 500

Hess, Frank and Ernestine to Philip Alstadt. Warwick st, w s, 200 s Sutter av, 25x100. Oct. 17, 5 years. 1,100

Heuschel, William L. to Margaret Heuschel. Vesta av, e s, 150 n Eastern Parkway, 50x100. Oct. 10, 5 years. 1,000

Hollister, Sebastian T. to Rudolph and Otto E. Reimer. Shepherd av, e s, 348.7 n Ridgewood av, 17.2x102.7. Oct. 20, due Oct. 1, 1892. 800

Haff, Alvah C. to Alvah W. Haff. Chauncey st. P. M. Oct. 6, 5 years, 5 %. 2,100

Haenlein, Wilhelmine C. to Martha M. wife of John Butler. Meserole st, s s, 25 w Humboldt st, 25x100. Oct. 27, 3 years, 5 %. 1,200

Hendrickson, Skidmore to The Brooklyn Trust Co. St. Marks av, s e cor Rogers av, 16.6x95. Oct 27, 1 year, 5 %. 5,500

Hill, Alfred E. to John R. Anderson. Atlantic av. P. M. Oct. 15, 1 year. 1,100

Hohmeyer, Frederick and Mary his wife to Barbara Bauer. Liberty av, n e cor Alabama av, 50x100. Oct. 27, due Nov. 1, 1894, 5 %. 5,000

Haering, Christiane to The East New York Savings Bank. Fanchon pl. P. M. Oct. 27, 1 year. 1,500

Isbill, Charles to Caroline Carey. Jefferson av. P. M. Oct. 26, due Sept. 29, 1892, 5 %. 4,000

Isaacson, Edward and Samuel D. to Leopold Michel and David Stern. Varet st. P. M. Sept. 25, due Oct. 1, 1896, or installs, 5 %. 4,500

Joseph, Jacob to Leopold Michel. Cook st. P. M. Oct. 26, due Oct. 1, 1897, 5 %. 3,000

Johnson, James V. L. to William Corrigan. 12th st. P. M. Oct. 24, installs, 5 %. 1,200

Judson, Edward to Jennie W. Brown. 6th av, n w cor President st, 100x92. Sept. 28, demand. 2,210

Kirkman, Ralphina to Henry D. Lott. 16th st, s w s, 73.10 s e 7th av, 16x100; 16th st, s w s, 185.10 s e 7th av, 64x100; 16th st, s w s, 281.10 s e 7th av, 16x100. Oct. 15, 1 year. 1,750

Klots, Walter J. to Theodore F. Jackson et al. trustees Loftis Wood. Johnson av, s e cor Morgan av, runs south 140 x east 66.4 to Knickerbocker av, x northwest 152.1 to Johnston av, x west 7. Oct. 20, due Nov. 1, 1894, 5 %. 4,000

Kacerowsky, Wenzel to John Bauer. Flushing av, s s, 25 w Bremen st, 25x81.11. Oct. 20, due Nov. 1, 1893. 1,000

Kaplan, Nicholas to Frances Mueller. Scholes st, n s, 225 w Lorimer st, 25x100. Oct. 21, 2 years. 1,000

Keating, Patrick T. to Danold Laing. Montauk av, w s, 120 n Sutter av, 40x100. June 23, 1 year. 150

Kimpton, Edward to Harry A. Gubner. 21st av, n w s, 112.6 n e Cropsey av, 100x96.8, New Utrecht. Oct. 22, 1 year, 5 %. 1,000

Kremer, Herman to Stephen W. Stoothoff. Milford st, e s, 100 n Liberty av, 25x100. Oct. 8, installs. 400

Kidney, George to Michael J. Langan. Ovington av, s w s, lots 70 and 71 and ½ of lot 72 map Ovington, 136x153.3, New Utrecht. Oct. 26, due Nov. 12, 1891, 5 %. 1,500

Koch, George and Frederick Koerner to Louis Beer. Knickerbocker av, s w cor De Kalb av, 75x100. Oct. 23, 4 days. 5,000

Koetter, Sophie wife of and Gustave to Louis Hartung, Wyckoff, N. J. Union st, east cor Nevins st, 25x90. Sub. to mort. $1,900. Oct. 21, 1 year. 1,500

Koopmann, Anna wife of and Diederich W. to Anthony D. Kaufmann. South 4th st, s e cor Havemeyer st, 19.2x81.1. Sub. to mort. $3,500. Oct. 27, due Oct. 1, 1894. 2,500

Same to Mary C. Mooney. Same property. Oct. 27, due Nov. 1, 1896, 5 %. 3,500

Kramer, Elizabeth to Franz Franz. Lots 263-269 inclus. block 11 map William Ziegler, New Utrecht. P. M. Oct. 27, 1 year, 5 %. 2,307

Kratzer, Mary wife of and Adam to Charles W. Truslow trustee William Wall. Johnson av. P. M. Oct. 26, 3 years, 5 %. 750

Leverich, Charles R. to David N. Vanderveer, Greenport, L. I. Fulton st, s w s, 111.10 s e St. Felix pl, runs southeast 19.1 x southwest 48.5 to Lafayette av, x west 23.2 x northeast 62.2. Oct. 22, 1 year, 5 %. 5,000

Lamb, Charles T. to Irwin Heasty. Van Buren st. P. M. Oct. 22, 5 years. 1,150

Lebewohl, Louis and Abraham Ruth to Henry Demarest. Osborn st, w s, 150 n Glenmore av, 25x100. Oct. 22, 5 years. 2,719

Levine, Joseph to Joseph Zirinsky. Varet st. P. M. Oct. 20, due April 20, 1895, or installs, 5 %. 500

Leinfelder, Anna to Henry H. Adams, County Treasurer. New Lots road, s s, 20 e Hinsdale av, 40x107.6x40x93.6. Oct. 23, 1 year, 5 %. 450

Lindsly, Albert B. and Sarah A. his wife to Isaac E. Holbrook. Degraw st, s s, 97.10 e 3d av, 60x100. Oct. 22, 2 years. 1,500

Laing, Donald to Anna W. Walsh. Belmont av, s s, 60 e Montauk av, 20x90. Oct. 15, 3 years. 2,000

Lawless, Silas L. to Otto Gerdau. Hegeman av, s e cor Williams av, 10.2x100x48.7x—; Hinsdale av, e s, 90 s Hegeman av, 40x200 to Williams av; Vesta av, w s, 90 s Hegeman av, 100x95. Oct. 26, due Nov. 1, 1892, 5 %. 1,500

Leavens, Lewis to Robert L. Moores and Charles A. Le Quesne. Putnam av, n s, 180 e Howard av. P. M. Oct. 17, due Nov. 5, 1892. 1,000

Same to same. Putnam av, n s, 140 e Howard av. P. M. Oct. 17, due Nov. 5, 1892. 1,000

Lund, Charles E. to Charles Engert. Monitor st. P. M. Sub. to mort. $2,000. Oct. 1, installs, 5 %. 1,500

Same to The Kings County Savings Inst. Same property. Oct. 1, 1 year, 5 %. 2,000

Madden, Margaretta wife of and Luke to S. Liebmann's Sons Brewing Co. Park av, No. 516, s s, 50 e Spencer st, 25x100. Oct. 24, 1 year. 1,000

Mason, Mary E. to Paul W. Ledoux. Bergen st, n s, 151.4 e Ralph av, 3 lots, each 16.8x107.2. 3 morts., each $300. Sub. to 3 prior morts., each for $2,000. Oct. 1, 6 months. 900

Mason, Mary E. wife of Isaac D. to William J. Sickels. Bergen st, n s, 100 e Ralph av, 17.4x107.2. Sub. to mort. $2,000. Oct. 1, due March 1, 1892. 300

McCaffrey, Bridget to William L. Flanagan, managing director. 4th av, No. 257, e s, 25x100. Oct. 21, 2 years. 571

McDonnell, Alice to Theodore E. and George W. Green. Roebling st, e s, 50 s South 1st st, 50x83.4. Oct. 28, 1 year. 350

Michel, Leopold to John Knochel and Lena his wife. Humboldt st, w s, 75 n Maujer st, 25x100. Oct. 24, due Nov. 1, 1894, 5 %. 5,000

Morris, Amy to Theodore D Dimon. Clason av, w s, 375 n Myrtle av, 25x222.8x25x223.3. Oct. 28, 3 years, 5 %. 1,000

Mulligan, Patrick to Robert L. and Robert L., Jr., Woods. Hemlock st. P. M. Oct. 17, 2 years. 375

McCormick, George W. to Mary and Fannie McCormick. Reid av, w s, 50 n Halsey st, 50x100. Oct. 26, demand. 5,300

McLure, Emanuel D. to Albert V. B. Voorhies. 60th st, n e s, 300 s e 17th av, 60x100.2, New Utrecht. Oct. 1, due June 11, 1894. 500

Mayer, Jacob to Fanny Jacobs. Broadway, n s, 45 w Dodworth st. P. M. Oct. 26, 3 years, 5 %. 5,000

Same to same. Dodworth st, n w s, 95.8 n e Broadway. P. M. Oct. 26, 5 years, 5 %. 2,500

Mitchell, John G. and Mary A. to Leopold J. Lippmann. Eldert st. P. M. Sub. to mort. $3,000. Oct. 23, installs. 450

Same to Thomas C. Balderston et al. Supreme trustees of the Order of Tonti. Same property. Oct. 23, due Oct. 24, 1894, 5 %. 3,000

Mitchell, David B. to Mary Mockler. Baltic st, n e s, 300 s e Hoyt st, 25x100. Sub. to mort. $1,400. Oct. 22, installs. 671

Same to Telegraphers' Mutual Benefit Assoc. Same property. Oct. 22, installs. 1,400

Moses, Mary L. to Frank Leslie. 4th st, s s, 271.10 w 7th av, 20x100. Sept. 1, 3 years, 5 %. 9,000

Maitland, Alexander with The Flushing Co-operative Savings and Loan Assoc., Flushing, L. I., both mortgagees. Agreement as to priority of mortgages by George A. Knott. Oct. 21. nom

McBride, Edwin P., Boston, Mass., to William Coit, Brooklyn. Court st, No. 299. 1-6 part. Oct, 18, 1890. 175

McCormack, John H. to The Equitable Co-operative Building and Loan Assoc. 55th st, n e s, 300 n w 15th av, 50x100.2. Oct. 7, installs. 4,000

McCormack, John to Andrew D. Baird. St. Marks av, s s, 447.6 e Utica av, 20x127.9. Oct. 20, 3 years, 5 %. 2,400

McNeil, Donald and Lottie his wife to Frances C. Hill trustee John S. Hill. Hawthorne st, n s, 120.6 w Nostrand av, 80x166.3x80x166.2. Oct. 16, 3 years, 5 %. 3,000

McNulty, Celia A. wife of William B. to Samuel Ayres. Jefferson av. P. M. Oct. 21, 3 years, 5 %. 650

Same to same. Same property. P. M. Oct. 21, 5 years, 5 %. 3,500

Meyer, Emil G. to The Otto Huber Brewery. Greenpoint av, No. 31. Oct. 13, due Nov. 1, 1891, 5 %. 2,000

Miller, Jane to Rudolph and Otto E. Reimer. Macon st, n s, 290 e Patchen av, 56x100. Oct. 17, due Jan. 19, 1892. 3,000

Mohr, Alonzo D. and Ada his wife to Howard C. Conrady. Decatur st, s s, 145 w Lewis av, 20x100. Oct. 20, 1 year. 800

McKenna, Thomas to Julius Lehrenkrauss. Clinton st, s s, 75 e Centre st, 25x90. Oct. 26, due Jan. 1, 1893. 100

Moores, Robert L. and Charles A. Le Quesne to Sarah H. Powell. Quincy st. P. M. Oct. 26, 1 month. 1,550

Moores, Robert L. and Charles A. Le Quesne to The Union Stove Works. Putnam av, n s, 320 e Broadway, 20x100. Oct. 23, installs. 795

Murray, Kate and Lydia A. to Martha McCormick. Clermont av, e s, 446.11 n Myrtle av, 20x100. Oct. 23, 3 years. 500

Morgan, Catherine D. to William Murray and Mary his wife. 12th av and 57th st, New Utrecht. Oct. 26, 1 year. 800

Mullowney, Richard to Elizabeth S. Seymour. Halsey st, s s, 94 w Ralph av, 18x100. Sub. to mort. $4,000. Oct. 5, 1 year. 1,000

Mulvihill, Michael to Clarence M. Baumgras. Greene av. P. M. Oct. 26, 1 year, 5 %. 824

Neyland, Michael to Albert H. Van Siclen. Jerome st, w s, 180 s Dumont av, 20x100. Oct. 20, 2 years. 100

Nimmo, Eliza to Moses P. and Henry C. Bauer. Grove st. P. M. Oct. 20, 2 years, 5 %. 650

Newby, Samuel H. to Pauline Ruthardt. Monroe st. P. M. Oct. 24, 3 years. 1,500

Newman, Henry to Thomas F. Magner and ano. exrs. John G. Oldner. McKibbin st, s s, 150 e Graham av, 25x100. Oct. 26, due Nov. 1, 1892, 5 %. 7,000

Nichols, Charles H. to Charles M. Marsh, Morris Plains, N. J. Pacific st also Atlantic av. P. M. Oct. 27, demand. 30,000

Owen, S. Ferris to John S. Junior. Schenck av, e s, 225 s Blake av, 16.10x100. Oct. 27, 3 years. 1,000

Same to same. Schenck av, e s, 241.10 s Blake av, 16.5x100. Oct. 27, 3 years. 1,000

Oehmen, Gustave N. to Fannie J. Mugford. Putnam av, n s, 231.7 e Patchen av. P. M. Oct. 22, 3 years. 1,000

Ohler, Daniel and Katharina to George W. and Charles H. Francisco. Woodbine st. P. M. Oct. 22, installs. 1,200

Ogden, Ella G. to Perceis S. Pearsall. 50th st, s s, 300 w 3d av, 20x100.2. Oct. 24, 1 year. 300

O'Loughlin, Owen to John J. Bennett. Nelson st, s s, 189.4 e Hicks st, 22.6x100. Oct. 21, 1 year. 50

Parke, John to Charles C. Lowitz, San Francisco, Cal. Clermont av, e s, 75 n Gates av, 20x100. Oct. 22, due Feb. 15, 1892. 750

Same to Henry M. Kingman, Brockton, Mass. Same property. Oct. 21, 3 years, 5 %. 5,000

Pius, Gustav to Israel Lebowitz. Pacific st, n s, 125 e 4th av. P. M. Oct. 22, installs. 1,000

Pfeiff, Magdalena and Katie Kufahl devisees of Magdalena Sailer to Jacob H. Bernkopf. Thornton st, s s, 96.5 w Broadway, 25x72.11x29.5x88.5. Oct. 22, due Oct. 1, 1895. 1,500

Parsons, Hormer B. to The Equitable Life Assur Soc. of the United States. 7th av, s w cor Lincoln pl, 50x110. Oct. 26, due Jan. 1, 1898. 18,000

Pender, Joseph to Edmund D. Norris. Moore st, n e cor Morrell st. P. M. Oct. 26, 5 years, 5 %. 2,000

Pickering, Helen wife of Richard to John C. Schenck. Jerome st. P. M. May 12, 4 years, 5 %. 450

Price, Isabelle G. to William C. Powell, of St. James, L. I. Suediker av, w s, 255 n Liberty av, 20x100. Oct. 26, 3 years, 5 %. 1,800

Price, Lillian and Ida A. wife of Edward J. Connette to Adelia S. Price. Monroe st, s w cor Lewis av, 22.6x81. Oct. 21, due Jan. 1, 1895, 5 %. 6,500

Pilcher, Joseph M. to Charles S. Wood. Bergen st, s s, 310 e Brooklyn av, 2 lots, each 20x100. 2 morts., each $1,000. Oct. 26, 1 year. 2,000

Purnhagen, Barbara wife of and Mathias to The Title Guarantee and Trust Co. Franklin av, e s, 39 n St. Marks av, 24x87.11x60.6x80. Oct. 24, 1 year, 5 %. 1,000

Pearl, Esther wife of James to William H. Jackson. Stanley av. P. M. July 1, 3 years or installs. 70

Ploharsky, Antony to William H. Jackson. Atkins av. P. M. Oct. 6, 3 years or installs. 125

Pickford, Samuel to Thomas E. Greenland. Hart st. P. M. Oct. 27, 3 years, 5 %. 2,500

Post, Helen to Edward Johnson. Schenectady av. P. M. Oct. 13, installs. 5 %. 850

Prescott, Shubeal to Charles H. Hamberg. Rockaway av, w s, 20 n Sumpter st, 16x68.3. April 27, due Nov. 1, 1892. 500

Quehl, Adelheid to Hermann and Max Rosenthal. Thatford av, e s, 175 s Belmont av, 50x100. Oct. 1, 3 years. 400

Raymond, George to John L. Culver. Shepherd av. P. M. Sept. 26, 3 years. 800

Ruck, George C. W. to The East Brooklyn Co-operative Building Assoc. Bleecker st. P. M. Oct. 24, installs. 2,250

Reilly, Adeline wife of Hugh J. to The Title Guarantee and Trust Co. Meeker av, s w cor Humboldt st, 30x100x13.6x101.8. Oct. 22, 1 year, 5 %. 3,500

Rose, Hannah M. to Augustus S. Bedell. Cooper st, s e s, 386.6 e Evergreen av. 38.6x100. Oct. 1, due Jan. 1, 1892. 1,226

Rothaug, Ludwig and Margaretta his wife to Leopold J. Lippmann. Eldert st, n w s, 392 n e Evergreen av, 19x100. *Mt.* $2,500. Aug. 28, installs. 1,000

Same to William O. Moore et al. exrs. Abraham Underhill. Same property. P. M. Aug. 28, 3 years, 5 %. 2,500

Ruger, Peter to Jeremiah V. Meserole. Kingsland av. P. M. Oct. 20, 3 years. 3,000

Ryan, Joseph to Philip L. Balz, Jr. Evergreen av, w s, 25 n Conselyea st. P. M. Oct. 21, 3 years, 5 %. 1,500

Ryan, William P. to Ansel Jones, Deep River, Conn. Bedford av. P. M. Oct. 24, due Oct. 22, 1894. 12,000

Schaeffer, John to The Equitable Co-operative Building and Loan Assoc. Woodbine st. P. M. Oct. 22. installs. 3,750

Schmidt, Robert to Harvey Major. Grand av. P. M. Oct. 22, 3 years, 5 %. 2,500

Schnitzler, Hyman mortgagor with Israel Lebowitz mortgagee. Extension of mort. Oct, 21. nom

Seefeldt, Frederick to Andrew Van Opstal. Atlantic av, s s, 283.4 e Rockaway av. P. M. Oct. 24, 5 years, 5 %. 1,500

Same to same. Same property. Oct. 24, 3 years, 5 %. 300

Skinner, Mary wife of Robert to Charlotte L. Prout. Decatur st. P. M. Oct. 22, 1 year. 600

Sommers, George A. to John Sommers. Liberty av, s w cor Van Sielen av, 20x100. Oct. 21, 2 years. 2,000

Sparling, William H. C. to The East Brooklyn Co-operative Building Assoc. Covert st, s e s, 150 s w Evergreen av, 16x100. Oct. 22, installs. 2,500

Staats, William to The German Savings Bank, Brooklyn. Johnson av, n s, 50 w Lorimer st, 25x100. Oct. 20, due Dec. 1, 1892, 5 %. 3,000

Stewart, Henry to Irwin Heasty. Van Buren st. P. M. Oct. 22, 5 years or installs. 1,150

Sumner, Vina A. to David F. Kimberly. Bainbridge st, n s, 160 e Sumner av. P. M. Oct. 21, 4 years, 5 %. 1,000

Same to same. Bainbridge st, n s, 140 e Sumner av. P. M. Oct. 21, 4 years, 5 %. 3,500

Schoefer, Henry J. to L. H. Hurst. Gates av, n s, 80 w Vanderbilt av, 20x75. ½ part. Oct. 24, due Oct. 30, 1891, 5 %. 104

Smith, George G. to Sebastian T. Hollister. Shepherd av. P. M. Oct. 26, installs. 1,050

Sauer, Conrad and Annie C. to Jurgen Lins. Thames st, s s, 50 w Morgan av, 25x100. Oct. 26, 5 years or installs, 5 %. 600

Sayer, Richard S., Englewood, N. J., to George W. Everitt. Clinton av, w s, 20.2 s De Kalb av, 20x120.4x20.5x116.4. Oct. 21, 3 years, 5 %. 5,000

Schuster, Jenny C. to Edward A. Everit. Herkimer st, n s, 100 w Troy av, 20x100. Oct. 22, 2 years. 600

Schwenck, Wilhelmina to James Hall et al. exrs. Thomas C. Moore. Stanhope st, n w s, 375 n e Hamburg av, 25x100. Oct. 24, due Nov. 1, 1894, 5 %. 3,250

Shay, John M. to The Title Guarantee and Trust Co. Weirfield st. P. M. Sept. 8, due Oct. 26, 1892, 5 %. 2,500

Skelly, Mary C. wife of and William J. to Bernard McCaffrey. Pacific st, n s, 260 e New York av, runs east 20 x north 200 to Atlantic av, x west 40 x south 100 x east 20 x south 100. Oct. 26, 3 years, 5 %. 13,000

Spindler, Louisa wife of Charles, Hoboken, N. J., to Abram Rankin, Jersey City, N. J. Jerome st, e s, 100 n Dumont av, 40x100. Oct. 26, installs. 600

Sleight, James E. to Allen Gray. Clason av, w s, 75 s Gates av, 25x100. Oct. 28, 5 years, 5 %. 5,000

Stanton, Francis to Leopold J. Lippmann. Weirfield st. P. M. Oct. 26, due Jan. 1, 1895, 5 %. 2,500

Sayres, Phebe H. to Margaret Hendrickson, Jamaica, L. I. Lexington av, s s, 271 e Tompkins av, 18x100. Aug. 1, due Nov. 1, 1894, 5 %. 2,500

Siefers, August and Monika his wife to Charles Diebold and Katharina his wife. Stockholm st. P. M. Oct. 27, 5 years, 5 %. 2,000

The Bay Ridge Park Improvement Co. to The Title Guarantee and Trust Co. 71st st, n s, 100 w 10th av, runs north 200 to 70th st, x west 443 to Fort Hamilton av, x south 101.8 x east 401.2 x south 100 to 71st st, x east 60; 73d st, n s, 100 w 10th av, runs north 200 to 72d st, x west 537.7 to Fort Hamilton av, x south 203 4 to 73d st, x east 573.11; 72d st, s s, 100 e 10th av, runs east 550.1 x south 200.7 to 73d st, x west 536 3 x north 200; 74th st, n s, 100 w 10th av, runs north 200 to 73d st, x west 480 x south 100 x east 100 x south 100 to 74th st, x east 380; 10th av, 73d st, 74th st, land William Spence; 10th av, n w cor 75th st, runs north 100 x west 100 x north 100 to 74th st, x west 360 x south 100 x west 60 x south 100 to 75th st, x east 520; 76th st, n s, 163.1 e Fort Hamilton av, x east 588.4 x northeast 74.2 to 10th av, x north 184.1 to 75th st, x west 500 x south 100 x west 160 x south 100; 10th av, s e cor 75th st, runs east 220 x south 200 to 76th st, x west 164 9 x north 44.3 x west 59.6 to 10th av, x north 169.6; 77th st, n s, 400 w 11th av, x north 100 x west 80 x north 100 to 76th st, x west 167.3 x south 58.8 x west 51.2 to 10th av, x south 131.8 to 77th st, x east 300; 76th st, s s, 94 e Fort Hamilton av, runs east 384.5 x southwest 392.8 x north 80.1; 10th av, Denyses lane and 78th st, gore; 10th av, n e cor 79th st, runs east 160 x north 100 x east 80 x south 100 to 79th st, x east 120 x north 200 to 78th st, x west 360 to 10th av, x south 200; 10th av, 77th st and lands of heirs of Richard and Joost Stillwell, gore; 7th av, Fort Hamilton av, 78th st and land of Charles E. Delaplaine; Fort Hamilton av, s e s, adj land of mortgagor and land of Stillwell, runs northeast 115.10 x north 0.11 x west to Fort Hamilton av, x south —. Oct. 1, 3 years, 5 %. 58,500

The Bay Ridge Park Improvement Co. to The Title Guarantee and Trust Co. Ovington av, s w cor 11th av, runs west 45 x southwest 325.4 x north 110.1 to Ovington av, x west 362.4 to 10th av, x south 78.3 to Bay Ridge av, x east 700 to 11th av, x north 147.8; Ovington av, s e cor 11th av, runs east 700 to 12th av, x south 88.1 x southwest 153.10 to Bay Ridge av, x west 504.6 to 11th av, x north 146.7; 11th av, s e cor Bay Ridge av, runs east 350.8 x southwest 391.3 to 11th av, x north 131.2; Bay Ridge av, s s, 100 e 10th av, runs south 100 x east 20 x south 100 to 70th st, x east 570.6 x north 40.10 x east 6.4 to 11th av, x north 158.9 to Bay Ridge av, x west 600; 10th av, s e cor 70th st, runs east 160 x south 100 x east 140 x north 100 to 70th st, x east 386.4 x south 200.7 to 71st st, x west 572.6 x north 80 x west 100 to 10th av, x north 120; 71st st, s s, 100 e 10th av, runs east 60 x south 100 x east 180 x north 100 to 71st st, x east 328.3 x south 200.7 to 72d st, x west 554.5 to 72d st, x north 200; Fort Hamilton av, east cor 78th st, runs north — x northeast 98.10 to 77th st, x east 788.8 to 10th av, x south 200 to 78th st, x west —; 78th st, n s, 340 w 11th av, runs west 360 to 10th av, x north 200 to 77th st, x east 360 x south 200. Oct. 1, 3 years, 5 %. 51.000

The Bay Ridge Park Improvement Co. to The Title Guarantee and Trust Co. Ovington av, n s, at e line of Ellen or John Ward, runs north 46.6 to Bay Ridge av, x east 217 x south — x west 217.3; 70th st, n s, 86.3 w Fort Hamilton av, runs north 100 x east 20 x north 100 to Bay Ridge av, x west 80 x south to Ovington av, x west — x south 47 to 70th st, x east 607.6; 8th av, n e cor 71st st, runs north 73.2 x northeast 156.1 x north 96.5 to 70th st, x east to Fort Hamilton av, x southwest to 71st st, x west —; 8th av, s e cor 71st st, runs east 700 to Fort Hamilton av, x south 3.4 x southwest 714.5 to 8th av, x north 144.7; Bay Ridge av, n w cor 10th av, runs north 62.2 to Ovington av, x west 318.5 to Bay Ridge av, x east 311; Bay Ridge av, 10th av, 70th st and Fort Hamilton av, block; 71st st, s s, 160 w 10th av, runs west 490.4 to Fort Hamilton av, x south 101.8 x east 88.5 x south 100 to 72d st, x east 420 x north 200; 11th av, n w cor 75th st, runs north — x southwest — x north to 74th st, x west 614.1 to 10th av, x south 200 to 75th st, x east 700; Bay Ridge av, Ovington av and land of H. Schierloh, gore, New Utrecht. Oct. 1, 3 years, 5 %. 40,500

Tangeman, Nellie R. to South Brooklyn Co-operative Building and Loan Assoc. 56th st, n s, 150 e 14th av, 50x100.2, New Utrecht. Oct. 27, installs. 5,000

Titus, Joel H. to Phebe W. wife of Henry L. Nostrand, Jamaica, L. I. Dean st, n s, 100 e 3d av, 25x100. Oct. 26, due Nov. 1, 1896, 5 %. 1.000

Tannenbaum, Charles and Harry T. Dietz to Catharine M. Manning. Dean st. P. M. Oct. 26, installs. 1,900

Thorsen, Charles to The Hamilton Co-operative Building and Loan Assoc., Brooklyn. Hicks st, e s, 38 n West 9th st, 18x80. Oct. 26, installs. 2,160

Tibball, James to Mary J. Motram. 48th st, n s, 132 w 3d av, 16x100.2. Oct. 22, due Mar. 1, 1894, 5 %. 1,000

Thau, Anna K. to John Brommer et al. exrs. Frederick Ring. Atlantic av, s e cor Warwick st, 35.3x113.10x34.3x109.2. Oct. 22, 1 year, 5 %. 1,100

Testevin, Alfred P. to Andrew D. Baird. Saratoga av, e s, 144.5 s McDonough st, 17.9x80. Sept. 17, 1 year. 1,577

Same to Thomas C. Balderston et al. Supreme trustees of the Order of Tonti. Stone av, e s, 66.8 s Blake av, 16.8x100, Oct. 22, 3 years. 5 %. 1,800

Same to same. Stone av. e s, 50 s Blake av, 16 8x100. Oct. 22, 3 years, 5 %. 1,800

Same to same. Stone av, e s, 83.4 s Blake av, 16.8x100. Oct. 22, 3 years, 5 %. 1,800

Underhill, George B. to John McCormick. Halsey st, No. 784, s s, 102.11 e Ralph av, 19.5x100. Oct. 24, 3 years, 5 %. 5,000

Same to John T. Barnard. Same property. Oct. 24, due Dec. 10, 1892. 550

Van Deverg, John H. to John Kerswill. Sackett st. n s, 297.10 e 3d av, 60x100. Oct. 1, 1 year. 3,000

Van Veen, Jane L. wife of and Lewis to The Title Guarantee and Trust Co. Hopkins st, s s, 312.6 e Marcy av, 18.9x100. Oct. 22, 3 years. 1,000

Vreeland, George to Stephen C. Halstead. 4th st, n s, 114.11 w 6th av, 17.4x95. Oct. 21, 1 year. 100

Velsor, Oscar W. to Paul W. Ledoux. Thatford av, e s, 212 n Glenmore av, 88x100. Sept. 21, demand. 4,500

Same to same. Same property. Sept. 21, demand. 3.500

Wells, Benjamin G. to Abram B. Kolyer, Jr. Sumner av, w s, 20 s Quincy st, 20x80. Oct. 28, due Jan. 1, 1892, 5 %. 500

Wilson, Elizabeth M. to John M. Burt. Halsey st, s s, 262.2 e Reid av, 18.9x100. Oct. 22, 3 years, 5 %. 1.300

Wilson, Henrietta wife of George E. to Leopold J. Lippmann. Weirfield st. P. M. Sub. to mort. $2,500. Oct. 26, installs. 1,700

Same to same. Same property. Oct. 26, due Jan. 1, 1895, 5 %. 2,500

Weinreich, George A and John A., and Mary E. Lowe to Sophie G. Parker. Bergen st, n s, 525 e 3d av, 25x100. Oct. 22, 2 years. 250

Wells, James C. to Alvah W. Haff. Chauncey st. P. M. Oct. 6, 5 years, 5 %. 2,600

Werbelovsky, Jacob H. and Isaac Horowitz to Eliza M. wife of Robert B. Currier. Moore st, s s, 100 w Morrell st, 25x100. Oct. 22, 2 y a 15 %. 6,000

Werbelovsky, Jacob H. to Isaac Horowitz. Moore st, s s, 100 w Morrell st. 25x100. Oct. 22, 3 years or installs. 1,200

Wheeler, Charles B. to Mary J. McCormick. Coney Island, L. I. Madison st, s s, 470 w Patchen av. P. M. Oct. 22, due Jan. 1, 1895, 5 %. 2,500

Same to same. Madison st, s s, 450 w Patchen av. P. M. Oct. 22, due Jan. 1, 1895, 5 %. 2,500

Wagerle, William to Hermann Fruwirth. Bleecker st. P. M. Oct. 20, 5 years, 5 %. 1,500

Walsh, Hugh A. to Michael O'Keeffe. Cooper av, s s, 175 w Hamburg av, 25x100. Oct. 14, 3 years, 5 %. 750

Weber, Franz C. and Catherine his wife to George Wetzel. Scholes st. P. M. Oct. 24, due Nov. 1, 1894, 5 %. 600

Weed, Nellie S. to Aline Haines. Quincy st, s s, 22 e Marcy av, 35x80.6. Oct. 26, 1 year. 600

Winsor Terrace Methodist Episcopal Church to Anna M. Ferris. Greenwood av, s w cor Prospect av, Flatbush. P. M. July 10, 5 years, 5 %. 1,700

Winters, Mary E. to Arthur Taylor. Macon st, No. 446. P. M. Oct. 10, installs. 6,500

Young, Annie L. to James D. Lynch. Bay 25th st, n w s, 380 s w Benson av, 60x96.8. Oct. 16, due Oct. 19, 1898, 5 %. 1,150

MORTGAGES----ASSIGNMENTS.

NEW YORK CITY.

OCTOBER 23 TO 29—INCLUSIVE

Astor, William W. to Victor Bunzl. $37,500

Anderson, Walden P. to George De F. Lord. nom

Abrahams, Morris to Jacob New. nom
Brown, Almira J., Milburn, N. J., to James Floy, Elizabeth, N. J. 5,598
Bard, John, Annandale. N. Y., guard. of Rosalie De N. Bard to Rosalie de N. Bard. nom
Same to same. nom
Boyd, David to James Nevins, Hoboken, N. J. nom
Brewster, John L. to James M. Wentz, Newburg, N. Y. 23,000
Bach, Deborah and Benjamin, Brooklyn to Solomon Appel and Gustave Basch. 1,504
Colgate, Cornelius C. and William exrs. Edward Colgate to Elizabeth C. Maghee widow. nom
Cohen, Betsey to Charles Laue, Brooklyn 6,000
Campbell, John V. to Joseph L. Buttenwieser. 8,300
Crosby, William B. exr. Ellen Roche to Anna C. S. Mackenzie trustee Catharine C. Stevens dec'd. nom
Decker, Paul G. to Frederic G. Moore. 1,100
de Barril, Charles B. to Samuel Blackwell, Brooklyn. nom
Gantz, George F. to Daniel J. O'Connor. 3,5 5
Goldsmith, Solomon to William Stern. 7.000
Hagan, Thomas to Annie Gough. nom
Jones, Mary E. H wife of Townsend, Cold Spring Harbor, L. I., to John D. Jones. 4,500
Kassel, Jeanette to Ida wife of Abraham Kassel. 6,535
Kerwin, Andrew J. to Gerd H. Ahlers. 6,579
Knevals, Caleb B. guard. of Edwin F. Hicks to The Broadway Savings Inst. 5,000
Lowenstein, Fannie A. to James J Phelan. 3,600
McCreery, Anna C. to Joseph V. Pardow. 15,027
Murphy, Edward to Abraham Michelbecher. 1,537
McEachen, James C. to John Rankin. 5,000
Merriam, Henry E. et al. exrs. Benjamin W. Merriam to Henry E. Merriam. nom
Meyer, William H. G. to Elizabeth Black. 750
Same to Eliza C. Black. 545
Middlebrook, Frederic J., Brooklyn, to The Hudson River Bank. 11,775
Miller, George M. exr. Edward S. Hoffman to Mary Hitchcock, Morristown, N. J. 825
Meyer, Henry exr. Heloise M. Meyer, Bremen, Ger., and Eleanor L. Meyer to George A. and Theodore F. H. Meyer trustees. 20,644
Osterhoudt, Ellen S. wife of Julius formerly Baldwin, Kingston, N. Y., to Mary E. wife of Howard Osterhoudt. 4,800
Overington, Harry to Ernest McNeill. 400
Paige, Eugene W., Paterson, N. J., to James D. Wynkoop and ano. exrs. and trustees Henry H. Buckbee. 12,000
Parsons, John E. exr. Hugh Maxwell to Harriet O. and Annah P. Cruft. Confirmatory assign. nom
Pierce, Mary Le B and ano. exrs. Mary F. Pierce to Mary V. Jaques. 4,500
Pierce, Madeline to Charles E. Larned. 2,500
Punchard, George to William Rankin. 9,000
Ryer, Samuel and ano. admrs Mary J. Ryer to Abbie E. Wille. 3,122
Randell, Charles H. exr. Betsey A. Randell to Mary L Randell, Westchester. 2,379
Same to same. 5,000
Romer, William F. guard. of Ellen S., Julia and Jessie Baldwin to Ellen S. Baldwin. nom
Rieser, Jacob to John Fish. 6,000
Same to same. 4,000
Same to same. 6,000
Sands, Philip J. trustee to Marie A. Sherman, London, Eng. 13,000
Steinfeld, David to Goldchen Adler. 1,250
Sherman, Marie A., London, Eng., to Frederic De P. Foster. 13,000
Seiferd, Lena to M. Elizabeth Murphy. 400
Shaw, Emeline to Edwin F. Raynor. 6,066
Smith, Julia to George R. Smith. 1,500
Solomon, John to Charlotte Bastorf. 3,000
Sussman, Fanny to Simon Friedenstein. 4,000
Shultz, Charles to Fannie Metzger. 1,059
Sutorius, William to Elizabetha Neubauer. nom
The Simmonds Mfg. Co. to John E. Thacher. 8,000
Timpson, Henrietta F., Brooklyn, to Oscar T. Marshall. 7,500
Title Guarantee and Trust Co to Vassar Brothers Institute, of Poughkeepsie, N. Y. 12,000
Title Guarantee and Trust Co. to Frank E. Bliss and ano. trustees Lillie A. P. Bliss dec'd. 7,000
Title Guarantee and Trust Co. to Henrietta Swartz et al. exrs. Solomon M. Swartz. 10,000
Uhl, Louisa, Brooklyn, to Louise M. Fleischman. 3,500
Walbridge, Olin G., Brooklyn, to Louise L. Williams. nom
Wirth, Louis to Friedrich Graf and Marie his wife. 5,700
Wandell, Townsend exr. Jane E. Kelemen to Ann E. McCaddin, Brooklyn. 11,000
Wandell, Josephine to John Meller. 6,000
Woods, James to John H. Brennan. 1,000
Walkley, Annie J. to Mary Bostwick. 4,000
Weinman, Theresa to Homan Kohnstamm. 12,000
Winne, Maria N. to Henry C. Copeland. nom

KINGS COUNTY.

Oct. 23 to 28—Inclusive.

Andrews, John to Benjamin Andrews. $500
Betts, Charles A to Albro J, Newton. 1,541
Same to Whitman W, Kenyon. 800
Same to same. 1,332
Bryan, George J, to The People's Trust Co. 6,000
Brooklyn Trust Co. to Spencer Aldrich. 2,500
Brown, James E. to William F. Corwith. 300
Burrows, Mary A. to Agnes N. Lake. 700
Barnum, Lawrence L. to John Hamlin, Thompsonville, Conn. 2,000
Bailey, Matilda to Maria J. Thorne. 3,000
Bookman, Ralph to Marcus Bach. 350
Cole, Randolph H to The Title Guarantee and Trust Co. 13,000
Cole, Randolph H. to Phebe Stillwell. 4,000
Dodge, Clara E., Glen Cove, L. I., to George H. Smith 800
Dhuy, Frederick, Jr., to Sarah G. Platt. 1,200
Dunn, Susan A to John Leech. 3,000
Eichhorn, Adolph to Sabina Eichhorn. nom
Eubel, Elizabeth extrx. August Eubel to Philip Straus. 2,000
Frank, John and ano. exrs. Lewis S. Frank to Louisa Frank. 5,500
Gillespie, Earl A. to Edwin W. Ackerman. 1,000
Gomez, Catharine M. to Sarah A. Bergen. 3,500
Gibbon, Michael and Richard, of M. Gibbons and Sons, to Long Island Bank. 1,000
Gifford, Silas D. exr. Philip W. Verlander to Laura Verlander. nom
Gentleman, Mary E. to Cross, Austin & Co. 940
Hart, Frank E. to Emily A. Ring. 1,400
Same to same. 1,600
Same to same. 1,450
Same to same. 1,090
Henricke, Lena to Charles A. Klots. 4.618
Same to Julia E T. Matheson. 2,318
Hampton, Eliza G. and Mary and John C. Creveling, of Hampton & Creveland, to Frederick H. McCoun and ano. exrs. Hewlett T. McCoun. 500
Hennessey, John to Mary K. Ogden, Orange, N. J. nom
Same to Isaac C. Ogden, Jr. nom
Same to same. nom
Isbill, Charles to Michael Goodwin. nom
Isbill, Charles to Horace F. Burroughs. 2,400
Johnston, Jeannette wife of William to Anna C. Fellows. 900
James, Warren A. et al. exrs. Ira M. Lang to Clara F. Lang. nom
Same to same. nom
Klots, Walter J. to Richard M. Nichols. 4,400
Kimberly, David F. exr. Elizabeth Kimberly to Annie Kimberly. 5,000
Kimberly, David F. to same. 6,000
Lalor, Adaline to Clara E. wife of Agnes J. Lalor. 2,000
Levino, Bernard to Clinton D. Burdick. 2,500
Lippmann, Leopold J. to Peter Forrester et al. exrs. Lucinda Dougherty. 5,000
Mulligan, Patrick to Robert L. and Robert L., Jr., Woods. 1,900
Marsh, Charles M. to The Mutual Life Ins. Co., New York. 12,500
McDonough, Frank to Walter F. Clayton. 2.000
Miller, Samuel H. et al. exrs. Daniel R. T. Miller to Martha A. Millard. 1,000
Same to D. Spencer Millard. 1,500
Nielsen, Charles J. to William Schaefer. 1,500
Neely, Albert S. to Charles E. Pell. 877
Nostrand, George E. and J. Lott to Harmon W. Cropsey and Louis G. Mitchell of Cropsey & Mitchell. 195
Orthlieb, Odile to Leonard Eppig. 1,000
Osmann, Frederick to Freeman Clarkson and ano. trustees Eibe H. Steers. 1,000
Parker, Asa W. to Daniel Doody. nom
Roberts, George H. to Maria N. Anderson, Kingston, N. Y. nom
Rankin, James D. and James Ross to Lawrence Hurlburt. 1,500
Reynolds, William H. to James McLaren. 1,750
Same to same. 3,500
Rhodes, George R., Jr., to George R. Brown. 1,600
Schmidt, E Marie to John A. Schmidt. gift
Spitz, Louis to Otto Saalfeld and Addie his wife. 1,400
Sullivan, James to Bridget T. McClennen. 2,500
Skidmore, William A. to Edeliza R. Skidmore. 2,300
Siefers, August to Alois Dillmann and Caroline his wife. 1,000
Stearns, John M to Elias C. Pendleton. 2,000
Suydam, Isaac D. B. exr. Hendrick Suydam to Louis H. Dewey. 163
The Dime Savings Bank, Brooklyn, to Frederick Middendorf. 7,500
The Southold Savings Bank to George W. Brush. 3,038
Tapscott, Frank L. to The Richardson & Boynton Co nom
Title Guarantee and Trust Co. to Rebecca M. May. 3,000
Same to William M. Ingraham. 48,500
Same to People's Trust Co. 51,000
Same to John H. Smith. 8,000
Same to same. 8,000
Same to John Truslow et al. exrs. Thomas Truslow. 3,500
Same to same. 3,500
Same to same. 8,000
Same to same. 8,000
Same to Letitia M. and Josephine Wayland. 3,500
Same to Esther McElroy. 1,000
Same to Walter M. Aikman and ano. exrs. John Gilbert. 3,000
Same to Sarah Huggins. 2,000
Same to Bernard Cruse, Jr. 600
Same to South Brooklyn Savings Inst. 3,000
Same to John R. Platt et al. trustees Samuel R. Platt. 6,000
Same to same. 6,000
Same to Wesleyan University. 20,000
Same to Annie L. and Edmund Titus exrs. William W, Titus. 2,000
Same to Edmund Titus. 1,500
Same to same. 4,000
Same to James Robley. 4,000
Voorhies, John L., Comm'r for Investment, Gravesend, to Richard J. Berry trustee Annie E. Berry. 1,000
Same to Harmanus B. Hubbard. 1,000
Weed, Mary E. to Theodore F. Sauxay. nom
Whitney, Cordelia C. to Martha McCormick. 3,000
Welch, Huldah to Henry J. Zimmer, Far Rockaway, L. I. 3,036
Willis, William M. to Julia F. Willis. nom
Same to same. nom
Woods, Robert L. and Robert L., Jr., to Ida W. Woods. 375
Same to same. 1,900

JUDGMENTS.

In these lists of judgments the names alphabetically arranged, and which are first on each line, are those of the judgment debtor. The letter (D) means judgment for deficiency (*) means not summoned. (†) signifies that the first name is fictitious, real name being unknown. Judgments entered during the week, and satisfied before day of publication, do not appear in this column, but in list of Satisfied Judgments.

NEW YORK CITY.

Oct.
24 Alden, John B—Hubley Printing Co (Lim)........ $242 36
24 Asmus, Charles—Michael Schultz, Jr. 153 09
26 Ackerman, Edward P—Charles Sattler........ 284 99
26 Appelt, Samuel—F W Devoe & Co... 128 39
27 Allen, William S—Metropolitan Telephone and Telegraph Co........ 46 05
27*Albright, Charles H—Louis Rothstein. 504 20
27 Angell, Harold G—Southern Nat Bank........ 3,363 92
27 Ahearn, Margaret—Robert Hill...... 214 18
27 Amberg, Gustav—H R Jacobs........ 5,282 74
27 Alten, Meta H—Otto Heitz........ 489 73
27 Albright, Charles H—W H Hart, Jr.. 960 29
27 Akin, Richard W—Nicholas Henry... 736 03
27 Ainsworth, James—Katie MacColl... 561 57
29 Abrahams, Louis—Bernhard Levy.... 200 86
30*Albright, Charles H—Dwight Ashley. 941 18
30 the same—R J Hoguet........ 1,384 90
30 the same—Adolph Wimpfheimer 1,252 21
30 the same—Engelbert Hardt.... 1,354 86
30 Ayres, Charles H—S B Solomon...... 744 27
30 Adler, Samuel J K—M D Senior...... 4,383 32
30 Aronson, Alexander—A L Ashman.. 123 70
24 Blanchard, Charles W—S M Johnson. 219 37
24 Beard, Francis D—A L Washburn.... 201 45
24 Baumgarten, August—W A Cauldwell........ 145 51
24 Browning, Henry C / Browning William J / Browning, Jane } Andrew Beacom 296 64
26 Berus, Aaron—John Romain........ 266 97
26 Blumberg, William I—Joseph Rothschild........ costs 83 98
26 Bedell, William T—P W Helfst 106 61
27 Baas, Joachim—William Walsmann.. 168 27
27 Bigelow, Joseph H—John Berland.... 248 23
27 Bonnell, John Harper / Bonnell, Tammisin H } Nat Bank of Republic. 1,944 55
27 Broadbent, Robert S—J S MacCoy........ costs 123 15
27 Baldwin, Theron—Madison Square Bank........ 1,541 38
28 Beaver, Samuel—John Wilbur....... 55 08
28 Byrne, Peter J—Coleman Brewing Co 299 93
28 Boyle, Bernard—Jacob Ruppert...... 1,443 28
28 Bonnell, John Harper—Bank of N Y Nat Banking Assoc........ 9,289 03
28 Blondeau, Frederick—J H Tonyes.... 201 20
28 Brandt, Peter—Shepard & Morse Lumber Co........ 469 49
28 Bowers, Alfred—C W Russell........ 531 29
28 Boehm, John—W S Okie........ 1,127 69
28 Bennett, Francis C—W J Demorest... 237 03
28 Burroughs, Horace F—C G Saxe...... 2,695 34
28 Bobrick, Gabriel A—Mary M Travers 290 41
29 Black, Joseph R—Phoenix Iron Works Co........ 570 04
29 Baker, John A—A B Powell........ 941 82
29 Bell, William R—J M Graff........ 121 38
29 Bell, William R / Bell, Elizabeth } the same........ 76 07
29†Beyel, Elizabeth—F O Pierce........ 144 34
29 Ball, Max—S R Lesher........ 1,365 00
30 Blair, George—People's Bank of Buffalo........ 1,175 41
30 Blumenthal, Bertha—Eastmans Co... 526 20
30 Bonnell, John Harper—Market and Fulton Nat Bank........ 752 21
30 the same—Bank of N Y Nat Banking Assoc........ 6,893 04
30 Bacon, George H—Francis Pares..... 1,960 74
30*Baker, Ismar—John Baehr........ 578 00
30 Blanchard, Charles A—S B Solomon. 744 27
30 Barry, Michael H—Seventh Nat Bank........ 1,229 98
30 Beacham, John—W H Appleton...... 143 58
30 Backer, Abraham—S H Eckman.... 10,069 11
30†Baldwin, Jane L—Annie Steinhardt.. 47 50
30 Barriett, Samuel D—the same...... 75 15
24†Cusack, John H—Francis Higgins, recvr........ 152 26
24 Cook, Henry / Cook, John } A B Powell........ 122 58
24 Conner, William M—Mortlock Fetzt. 1,270 66
26 Cooke, Frank—Henry Klein........ 563 94
26†Chatterton, Maria C—Florida B McLellan........ 98 84

26 Chambers, Edwin J—Nason Mfg Co.. 149 07
26 Cooper, William S—A S Fordyce ....costs 110 49
27 Corneth, William N / Clark, David } Julius Harbers. 680 89
27 Cleary, John—Dederick Beckermann. 254 (0
28 Crossley, Charles A—W H Ayers ... 147 91
28 Cranston, Henry—Nat Bank of North America........ 533 74
28 Clapp, Henry D—J B Saalmann...... 438 75
29 Cranston, Henry—E W Ashley. 704 65
29 Clegg, Anthony M—Andrew Henderson........ 147 25
29 Camp, Fletcher W, admr Mary E Camp—J M Smith........ costs 270 48
29 Chaskel, James—Frederick Jacobi.(D) 1,831 95
29 Clark, Robert P—Jacob Grein........ 126 45
29 Cohn, Waller J / Cohn, William I } G W Toms....... 416 46
29 Combs, John W—Nat Bank of Republic........ 1,895 27
30 Curtis, Isabella M—Annie Martin.... 210 68
30 Core, Hannah—S R Olen........ 252 10
30 Catterson, Thomas—David Jones Co.. 313 01
30 Curtis, Wilkie M—Nat Cash Register Co........ 26 50
30 Cabot, B Frank—H G Hadden, Jr.... 34 50
30 Coschina, Frank—M B Edinger. 416 (0
24 Dahl, Peter J—Johanna Olsen 149 50
24 Dowd, William B—C J Milne........ 1,038 25
24 Davis, James R—Gilbert Oakley..... 494 07
24 Duff, Patrick F—Israel Lewis........ 363 67
26 Dunn, James—Edward McManus..... 222 06
27 Dreyfuss, Bernard—R N Perlee 222 00
27 Del Pino, Manuel Augustine / Del Pino, Gasper } Jackson Architectural Iron Works........ 2,029 96
27 Deltner, Henry—Mary Bullowa...... 302 78
28 Davis, George K—A W S Vankirk... 370 05
29 Duffy, James—Jacob Grein.......... 187 05
29 Dolan, Hugh——the same........ 120 45
29+Dederick, Edward H—Edmund Coffin, Jr 311 00
29 Drebos, Joseph—Jacob Hoffmann Brewing Co........ 252 50
29 Donovan, James T—Albert Gray.... 171 90
30 Divisitch, James—M B Edinger...... 416 00
24 Egan, Annie—A B Riker........ 269 44
24 Ellis, Edward S—Chatham Nat Bank. 852 98
24 the same——the same........ 925 46
26 Ellison, Thomas J—Nason Mfg Co.... 251 82
28 Euler, John H / Euler, Mary A } W N Foster......... 517 85
28 Ehlers, William—J S Foster........ 2,640 29
16 Edelmuth, Louis—Abraham Lichtenstein........ 647 43
30 Ellis, Edward S—Market and Fulton Nat Bank........ 752 21
30 the same——the same........ 785 72
30 the same——the same........ 1,899 43
30 Edelsohn, Louis—George Strauss..... 64 74
30 Ely, Harry A—W J Madden......... 559 18
24 Flynn, Peter H—J H Meyer.......... 161 00
26 Fisher, Frederick—Adolf Prince...... 173 08
26*Feibel, Nathan——the same........ 97 66
26 French, George B—J A Vega........ 4,050 00
26 Flataner, George—Adolf Prince...... 68 83
26 Friedrick, Frank—Pauline Friedrick. ....costs 99 28
28 Fowler, Warren / Fowler, J W } W A Dennis, exr... 648 83
29 Farley, Edwin E—W J Bryan........ 103 25
29 Frisbie, William M—Gormully & Jeffery Mfg Co........ 197 44
29 Frazer, John J—Edward Smith & Co. 76 44
29 Fogg, John C—M P Dunbar Co....... 291 64
29 Frascella, Dominico—F & M Schaefer Brewing Co........ 349 00
29 Frommelt, Alfred E—Nat Bank of Republic........ 1,895 27
30 Fitzgerald, Maurice—Colwell Lead Co 765 27
30 Fitch, Henry, Jr—Charles Kellogg... 805 25
30 Farrington, Jonas / Farrington, John } George Strans.... 204 60
30 Fox, Denis—John Baehr........ 1,065 00
30 Fischer, John E—Adam Boecher..... 190 61
24 Gill, George H—J H Ferguson....... 3,751 28
24 Gardner, Charles E—W W Heroy... 1,016 73
24 Gerstman, Simon—Rogers & Hamilton Co 76 77
24 Glore, John A P—E C Greene........ 232 05
24 Griswold, Margaret D—Madison Square Bank........ 1,610 72
26 Gorman, John J—Hay & Todd Mfg Co........costs 54 62
26 Gray, Charles Edward—P H Delahanty........ 902 77
26 Gallivan, Michael J—Asbury Park and Ocean Grove Bank........ 86 19
27 Goldthwaite, William M / Goldthwaite, James C } F A Ringler Co... 190 52
27 Grant, J Pierson—George Stewart.... 184 90
27 Goldthwaite, William M / Goldthwaite, James C } Jennie L Denig.... 113 39
27 the same——J E Linde........ 456 18
27 the same——Jennie L Denig........ 154 92
27 Gardner, Charles E—Harlem River Bank........ 953 51
29 Gertenbach, John—George Mand..... 490 41
29 Goerke, George S—C K Buchanan.... 74 45
29 Goldthwaite, William M / Goldthwaite, James C } T L De Vinne.. 111 55
29 Gaillard, Desire A—B C Nash........ 43 50
29 Genet, Louis F / *Genet, Jane S } Lulu Alexander.... 87 00
29 Grunbacher, Victor J—Stereo Relief Decorative Co........ 290 78
29 Gilligan, Hugh M—Ellen Hynes...... 411 95
30 Gallaudet, Peter W—Charles Kellogg. 805 25
30 Gersteinberg, Louis—Esther Moses... 185 40
30 Goodale, Howell P—B F Jayne........ 1,675 72
30 Gade, Ernest—E C Korner,........ 457 68
30 Gallinger, Joseph / *Gallinger, Samuel } William Vogelsang........ 18,745 67
30 Goldstein, Jeremiah—Samuel Firnski. 1,578 54
30 Gwillim, George—Abraham Schiller. 1,281 40
30 Goold, Michael—Mutual Brewing Co. 120 87
24 Hernstein, Albert L—Syracuse Heat and Power Co........ 410 61
24 Hauser, Gottfried Julius—W J de Rivera........ 514 74
24 Harper, William D—Market & Fulton Nat Bank........ 627 59
24 Hastorf, Herman—Thom Olsen..costs 68 61
24 Heinrich, Frederick—F H Levy...... 95 85
26 Hogan, Kate, admrx William Hogan—A C Smith........costs 22 70
26 Heitmanek, Frank J—Charles Grosse. 52 48
26 Hess, George / Hess, Henry } G L Wood........ 257 99
27 Healy, Julia—Jacob Gottschalk...... 139 21
27 Harper, William D—Market & Fulton Nat Bank........ 143 32
27 Havemeyer, William M—J H Smelpage........ 2,559 11
27 Heid, George—H L Rokobl........ 113 00
27 Howard, Roe H—D P Morse........ 98 79
27 Helmrich, Arthur E—F A Ringler Co 190 52
27 Harper, William D / Harper, Tacie McD } Nat Bank Republic........ 1,914 58
27 Horgan, Arthur O K—Christopher Nally........ 246 17
27 Horsfall, J H—Union Trust Co, trustee........ 111 45
27 Helmrich, Arthur E—J E Linde..... 158 18
27 the same——Jennie L Denig........ 154 92
28 Hess, George / Hess, Henry } H W Case........ 86 90
28 Harper, William Durbin—Bank of N Y Nat Banking Assoc........ 9,289 68
28 Heath, Marcellus C—Edward Ely Co. 223 68
28 Hofele, Jennie C / Hofele, Ferdinand W } Eloise I Chace, extrx........ 298 96
28 Hussey, Charles A—Edward Pannaci. 246 68
29 Hoey, John—David Lindenborn...... 790 11
29 Herman, Colvin—Conklin Smith ....costs 118 63
29 the same——P F Manning....costs 108 38
29 Helmrich, Arthur E—T L De Vinne. 111 55
29 Hoffman, Adolph A—Nat Bank of Republic........ 1,895 27
29 Haas, Joseph—Hastings Card Co (Lim)........ 140 00
29 Hannsen, Ole—Philip Semmer Glass Co (Lim)........ 140 00
29 Horner, Thomas—G W Post........ 119 39
29 Harper, William D—Western Nat Bank........ 876 35
30 Hussey, George W / Harriman, John N } B H Tuthill........ 267 45
30 Harper, William D—Market and Fulton Nat Bank........ 752 21
30 the same——the same........ 785 72
30 the same——the same........ 1,899 43
30 the same——the same........ 306 27
30 Harper, William Durbin—Bank of N Y Nat Banking Assoc........ 1,893 04
30 Hoyt, Adelbert E—F J Stone........ 468 82
30 Hurd, John—L B Bunnell........ 8,033 49
26 Indorsky, Isaac / Indorsky, William } Herman Meyer. 190 73
27 Isaac, Mayer—M M Manheim........ 273 59
24 Jourdan, Helen—Richard Geduldiger. 394 78
24 Jewell, William H—J A Hagy........ 821 31
26 Jenner, William J—J C Ogden, Jr... 5,714 08
26 Jacobs, Adolph / Jacobs, Max / Jacobs, William } Adolf Prince....... 173 08
26 the same——the same........ 97 66
26 the same——the same........ 68 83
28 Jempson, George F—Edward Gordon. 147 65
29+Jacobs, Adolph—John Kretzner........ 29 50
29 Jenkins, John T—D M Koebler....... 82 61
30 Judge, Anna M—W H Rogers........ 83 40
24 Kohn, Alois / Kohn, Arnold / Kohn, Edmund } Barnet Levy...costs 79 17
26 Keris, Hermann—Harry Held........ 99 94
26 Kingsberry, Carrie C—A L Meubenick 112 93
26 Knowlton, Willis—James Thomson.. 308 85
26 Kopelowich, Caroline—David Abrahams........ 477 13
27 Kiefer, John G—Michael Bernstein.. 370 02
27 Kelly, Lawrence / *Kelly, John } Sperry & Popham Coal Co (Lim)... 65 18
28 Kreuscher, John H—Danenberg & Coles........ 406 00
28 Kahn, Gus—F C Boehmer........ 40 00
29 Kelly, James—People State N Y..... 300 00
30 Kemper, William C—Israel Lewis.... 76 19
30 Klemann, Jacob—J A Michenfelder.. 143 84
30 Kolb, Louis—J L Jarvis 187 57
24 Loewenstein, Mayer—Adolph Edelmuth........ 36 03
24 Lauer, Peter—Enoch Morgan's Sons Co........ 143 45
24 the same——the same........ 88 16
26 Lowenstein, Joseph H—Ignatz Auer. 238 90
26 Livingston, James W—Frederick Hemming........ 633 47
26 Lishkofski, Samuel, by Lilly Lishkowfski, guard—John Duryea.costs 115 48
27 Lewis, John P—Communipaw Coal Co........ 324 49
27 Lake, Frederick C—C N Crittenton... 340 52
27 L'Hommedieu, Sylvester Y—Southern Nat Bank........ 3,863 93
27*Lowerre, William H—George Scott.. 140 39
27 Lascell, William T—Robert Hill..... 116 05
27 L'Hommedieu, Sylvester Y—Chemical Nat Bank........ 3,156 34
27 Lexton, John J—John Brown........ 119 97
27 Lesser, Joseph S—Pauline Kahn.costs 103 80
27 Lowenthal, Fred—A F Popham. 49 12
27 Lowe, William R—D H McDonnell... 251 24
27 Lyons, Bernard—G D Royston........ 78 45
27 Levitten, Michael—Elias Gans........ 79 05
27 Lowenstein, Joseph H—Louis Sachs.. 68 90
28*Lett, William F, Jr / Lett, Frederick R } Michael O'Brien 299 08
29 Leicher, Adolph—R S Lugneer........ 478 48
29 Le Compte, Sarah E—People State N Y........ 300 00
29 Lauer, Peter—Richard Sharpe, exr... 279 00
30 Lauer, Peter—F W Devoe & Co. 44 38
30 the same——J S Jacobs. 149 17
30 Lowe, William R—Abraham Schneider........ 203 87
24 Menker, Mortimer M—H G Burleigh. 935 26
24 Muller, Lewis M—I C Ogden, Jr.... 5,809 65
26 Mahalowitz, Hannah—B M Feldman ....costs 28 87
26 Mullen, John J—Campbell Printing Press and Mfg Co........ 79 74
26 the same——the same........ 80 17
26 Muller, Lewis M—I C Ogden, Jr..... 1,388 21
26 Matthews, Edward I—J F Waggoner 459 54
26 Mullady, Joseph R—Henry McShane Co (Lim)........ 242 32
26 Meyer, Esther—A M Woodruff....... 497 35
26 Morgan, Henry—Elizabeth Cooley.... 506 72
26 Miller, Elijah—F W Fink........ 1,256 96
26 Morinsky, Svobodin V—Billings, King & Co........ 281 31
26 Martin, Isaac P—Edward Gilon..costs 104 57
27 Muldoon, William H—Union Blue Stone Co........ 112 38
27 Maxfield, Charles W / Maxfield, John F } L M Lyon..... 7,218 00
27 Mabbett, Richard B—Nichols Henry. 736 08
27 Meyer, Siegmund T / Meyer, Arthur L / Moore, John } Lenox Nat Bank 2,734 20
27 Menut, Edward R—Catharine Garrick 385 20
28 Meyer, Samuel—Henry Herrmann. . 245 33
28 Michelson, David / Michelson, Abraham } Forest Delaney........ 331 38
28 Marks, Nathan—Joseph Hertzfield... 146 14
29 Mayers, Augustus—J R Smith 84 50
29 Maloney, Margaret—Eliza McB Sanderson 172 97
29*Muller, John—Lulu Alexander........ 87 00
29 Martin, Harvey—W E Dunn. 96 88
29 Mills, Anna W / Mills, Arthur E } Agnes K Murphy.. 612 73
29 Murphy, Agnes K—Anna W Mills et al........costs 108 55
29 the same——Albert L Mills..costs 109 43
29 Meyer, Philip L—Importers' and Traders' Nat Bank........ 3,458 59
29 Meyer, Siegmund / Meyer, Arthur L } the same........ 1,712 15
29 Mersereau, John—J C McEachen..... 70 80
30 Macri, Angelo—David Mayer........ 137 00
30 Mathison, Edward—W T Mersereau.. 138 00
30 Meyer, Esther—N A Merritt.......... 305 40
30 Moore, Hugh H—L J Callaman...... 114 08
30 Meinhart, Frank E—Abraham Schneider........ 203 87
30 Mansfield, Richard—A J Conuick.... 255 [illegible]
26 McRae, Virginia H—Anna M V Gildersleeve........ 185 01
26 McAloon, Barney—C P Tucker....... 127 17
27 McConologue, Charles V—Joseph Bierhopf........costs 106 79
29 McDermott, Thomas—Bernard Cahn. 571 02
30 McShayne, Samuel—Julius Stern. ... 102 48
30+McFarland, William—E J Norris.... 27 00
30 Mackenzie, William H—Margaret Gibney........ 2,722 34
30 the same——the same........ 2,722 34
26 Newton, Thomas—D A Vanhorne..... 128 11
28 Navaratt, Rudolf, Jr—Rudolf Navaratt, Sr........ 442 50
30 Nimmo, Sarah J / Nimmo, Charles W } W H Lee 447 50
26 Obendorfer, Nathaniel—Ignatz Auer. 238 90
26 Osborne, Mortimer—Seventh Regiment Veteran Club........ 119 76
26 Otto, August E—Louisa MaCanu..... 987 71
26 Oberhauser, Charles—Mary E Sherwood, extrx........ 1,930 10
27 Olmstead, George—Paul Treutler..... 116 40
27 Oberndorfer, Nathaniel—Louis Sachs 68 90
24 Pfeffner, George—V Loewer's Gambrinus Brewery Co........ 469 45
24 Price, Frank S—W J de Rivera...... 514 74
26 Perry, Benjamin L—C B Baker...... 991 88
27 Piering, Antonie—P G Decker....... 268 18
28 Pettit, James H—John McKesson, Jr. 1,776 19
28 Partheymuller, George B—John Hahn, Jr, recvr 363 22
28 Pollitzer, Emanuel—Coleman Brewing Co........ 84.87
28 Payne, George A—Asbury Park and Ocean Grove Bank........ 86 85
29 Pulfer, Bertha—Michael Muhler...... 176 12
29 Price, Jesse—N Y and Brooklyn Casket Co........ 143 08
29 Pfister, Frank J / Pfister, Louis F } Stereo-Relief Decorative Co........ 290 78
29 Pertsch, Frederick / Pertsch, William } C T Crocker..... 373 78
29 Pearson, Charles J—Jonas Stolts..... 224 73
29 Pennifill, James L—Peter Wolt........ 75 14
30 Pease, Frederick L—W F Lawrence.. 216 43
30 Prendergast, George F—H R Brown. 2,181 18
30+Preyer, John—H W Jordan........ 37 50
24 Ritterbusch, William—T T Lines 84 21
24 Rogers, Myron W—J S Steindler..... 123 82
26 Robinson, John—J W Thompson..... 3,684 81
26 Risley, Joseph H—C B Baker......... 991 88
26 Reinking, Ernst—G A Cassebeer. .. 2,805 62
26 Rosenblatt, William H—John Donnellon........costs 73 31
27 Richardson, Cass—Edwin Wallace.... 105 36
27 Ryerson, Wessels—Market and Fulton Nat Bank........ 148 38
27 Ralph, Henrietta A / Ralph, John M } Marshall Ayres, assignee........ 2,216 22
27 Russell, Mary A—Karnell Brook........ 143 55
28 Randell, David—G S Blunt........ 581 64

28 Root, James H—Nat Bank of North America.... 583 74
28 Rosenthal, Emma—James Talcott.... 337 45
29 Reyburn, Adaline E B—J J Taylor... 478 64
29 Reynolds, Ellsworth — Caroline M Fletcher.... 122 10
29 Ross, James Stewart—Bryant Building Co (Lim)... 53 54
30 Roosevelt, George W, Jr—Mechanics' and Traders' Bank.... 1,278 05
30 Rosenberg, Lohis—John Baehr.... 578 00
24 Sanger, Adolph L—J S Kaufman.costs 84 10
24 Schaefer, Robert—L H Viemeister.... 557 30
24 Sussman, Fanny — Mercantile Nat Bank.... 927 65
24 the same——the same.... 1,222 15
24 the same——the same.... 523 21
24 Simon, Benjamin—E M Angel.... 1,235 88
24 the same——Henry Solomon.... 1,158 67
24 the same——George Silva.... 1,331 35
26 the same——Virginie Picaut.... 625 91
26 the same——Rosa Simon.... 1,866 05
26 Skellen, Clarence M—J P Leo.... 98 21
26 Schroeder, Frederick—Samuel Colgate.... 90 48
26 Snedecker, John W—J G Hyatt.... 286 41
26 Schofield, Sevill / Schofield, William S / Somerset, William M } W W Justice. 5,486 53
26 Stampfer, William—Julius Somborn. 148 90
26 Silverman, Max—Adolf Prince.... 68 83
26 Semansky, Henry N—Joseph Rothschild....costs 83 98
26 Sexton, George H—Harmon Spruance 5,677 88
27 Sternberg, Jacob—Isaac Stern.... 88 30
27 Steindler, Joseph—Louis Rothstein... 504 20
27 See, Amos L / *See, E Garnier } George Scott.... 140 39
27 Shorter, James H—Nat Park Bank...2,356 38
27 Simon, Benjamin—Lewisohn Importing and Trading Co (Lim)....1,269 05
27 the same——the same....1,543 74
27 St George, Edward D—August Frenkmann.... 297 05
27 Steindler, Joseph—W H Hart, Jr.... 960 29
27 Simmons, James A—Lenox Nat Bank. 2,734 20
28 Street, George, Jr—Bernard Johnson. 82 15
28 Stevens, Frank A / Stevens, Adolphus E } C E Miller... 840 27
28 Stricker, Frederick / Stricker, Samuel } A B Powell.... 157 62
29 Solomon, Morris—Bernhard Levy.... 167 78
29 Schafers, William—Michael Lapp.... 244 88
29 Steiner, Jacob, Jr—Ann Brady.... 84 50
29 Scribner, Gilbert H, Jr / Scribner, Howard } M P Dunbar Co.... 290 64
29 Solomon, Ephraim—G W Toms.... 416 46
29 *Schaffner, George / Schaffner, Gustave F } Gansevoort Market Sheep Co.... 335 45
29 Schaefer, Theresa R—Herman Levy. 152 54
29 Stern, Simon / *Stern, Matthew } Alfred Greenbaum. 83 68
30 Simon, Benjamin—Cyrus Walser.... 1,892 09
30 Simonson, Michaelis—J F Degener..31,905 40
30 Steindler, Joseph—Dwight Ashley.... 941 18
30 the same——R J Hoguet.... 1,384 90
30 the same —— Adolph Wimpfheimer....1,252 21
30 the same——Engelbert Hardt.... 1,354 86
30 Simonson, Michaelis—G F Vietor....16,686 47
30 Simon, Jacob J—Max Marx.... 454 65
30 Stevenson, Vernon K—U S Illuminating Co.... 115 69
30 Stonestreet, George D—John Baehr.. 178 15
30 Stephens, Charles D—P F Morris.costs 49 88
30 Schaffner, George / Schaffner, Gustave F } Ferdinand Sulzberger. 609 33
30 Sackett, William E—M A Frisbie.... 135 16
30 Stoll, Joseph—Christ Protestant Episcopal Church.... 120 75
24 Smith, Edward—H G Burleigh.... 935 26
27 Smith, Waitstill A, individ / Smith, Frank F composing firm of W A Smith & Co } Marshall Herrick.. 228 24
27 Smith, Edward—Peter McIntyre.... 259 87
24 The American-Scotch Iron Co—J H McDowell.... 84 34
24 The Alden Publishing Co—Hubley Printing Co (Lim).... 242 36
24 Erie Transfer Co—O H Perry...costs 83 35
24 U S Grand Lodge of the Independent Order Sons of Benjamin—Meyer Bukofzer....costs 89 15
24 J H Bonnell & Co (Lim)—Market and Fulton Nat Bank.... 627 59
24 The Sixth Nat Bank—Lorillard Brick Works Co....costs 682 89
24 the same——the same.... 407 89
24 The C S Philips Patent Process Tobacco Growing and Curing Co—J H Porter.... 497 55
26 Germania Bank—William Stainton.. 469 07
26 The American Surety Co—Harry Wallerstein....costs 77 04
26 Thomas Murray Co—J A Roebling's Sons Co.... 308 42
27 United Electric Co—Metropolitan Telephone and Telegraph Co.... 73 99
27 The N Y Elevated R R Co / Manhattan Railway Co } C F Mattlage... 8,428 54
27 National Life Ins Co—Mary B De Frece, admrx....3,196 15
27 J H Bonnell & Co (Lim)—Market and Fulton Nat Bank.... 143 32
27 the same——Nat Bank of Republic.... 1,944 55
27 Chicago, Burlington & Quincy R R Co—L A Gould....costs 123 45
27 The Board of Assessors—Anna M Dean....costs 249 78
27 N Y Steamship Co—J M Constable... 236 11
27 Manhattan Railway Co / N Y Elevated R R Co } J F Malcolm....costs 84 17
27 The Mayor, Aldermen, &c—H S Mott 7,500 00
27 M Crane Electrotyping and Stereotyping Co—Thomas Wildes.... 95 29
28 Knickerbocker Steamboat Co—Edison General Electric Co.... 659 84
28 Beth Israel Hospital—Paul Kaplan.. 106 87
28 Supreme Council of the Catholic Mutual Benefit Assoc—Anna M Goldsmith, admrx.... 1,600 00
28 The Rendle Co (Lim)—William Nelson.... 403 80
28 The Mayor, Aldermen, &c—G L Green.... 103 74
28 J H Bonnell & Co (Lim)—Bank of N Y Nat Banking Assoc.... 9,289 68
28 the same——Western Nat Bank.. 468 19
28 the same——the same.... 1,978 02
28 the same——the same.... 1,120 34
28 Richensteen Lumber Co (Lim)—Shepard & Morse Lumber Co.... 469 49
29 The Backus Portable Steam Heater Co—Laura A Delano.... 933 81
29 Hazard, Hazard & Co—E G Freligh.. 799 73
29 J H Bonnell & Co (Lim)—Western Nat Bank.... 826 35
29 Pfister Book Binding Co—Stereo-Relief Decorative Co.... 290 78
30 The Metropolitan Elevated Railway Co / The Manhattan Railway Co } J M Young.. 116 98
30 Marcus Ward & Co—W H Ward.costs 91 63
30 J H Bonnell & Co (Lim)—Market and Fulton Nat Bank.... 752 21
30 the same——the same.... 785 72
30 the same——the same.... 1,899 43
30 the same——the same.... 306 27
30 Alabama and Georgia Mfg Co—C D Smith....4,244 78
30 Centennial Desk Mfg Co—J A Michenfelder.... 260 24
30 J H Bonnell & Co (Lim)—Bank of N Y Nat Banking Assoc.... 6,893 04
30 Mayor, Aldermen, &c—Isabel S Trippler....4,227 05
24 Thorne, Arthur—I S Steindler.... 123 82
26 Tureck, Lizzie—Henrietta Rice.... 40 63
26 Traitel, Bernard T / Traitel, Benjamin P } Christian Jourgensen.... 977 79
26 Tiffany, Burnett Y—Kate Malloy.... 701 47
26 Theobold, William H—Joseph Loth.. 678 89
27 Taft, Andrew B—D P Morse.... 98 79
27 Thompson, Walter—L A Lanthier.... 81 96
27 Taylor, George R—J J Sperry.... 33 60
27 Tompkins, William C — Strobridge Lithographing Co.... 269 93
28 Thebold, Henry—A B Powell.... 115 44
28 Tannehill, Frank A—Annie Yeamans....costs 89 64
28 Tilden, George H—W A Dennis, exr.. 648 82
28 Thempson, George, Jr—L A Lanther. 233 59
30 Timoney, Geraldine Josephine, extrx. Celia L Booth—J A Booth.... 240 82
30 Timony, Geraldine Josephine, extrx Cecelia L Booth—J A Booth.... 98 37
24 Valentine, Rober H C—Market and Fulton Nat Bank.... 627 59
27 Valentine, Robert H C—Market and Fulton Nat Bank.... 143 32
28 Von Eupen, Theodore—Paul Bechstein 180 88
29 Von Glahn, John—People State N Y. 300 00
29 Vaast, Amedee J—W & J Sloane.... 77 48
30 Vandevelde, Palmire — Hortense Schollart....costs 76 02
30 Van Horen, Theodore J—R L Coleman.... 102 48
26 Wickham, Etta—C H Cole.... 28 63
26 West, Frank M—I H Sanner.... 215 77
26 Walker, Edward B—Emil Dieckerhoff.... 707 61
26 Webber, Frederick—Henry Harrison. 123 78
26†Whitlock, Henry C—J G Hyatt.... 286 41
26 Woolfall, F Hartley—N Y Engraving and Printing Co.... 145 68
26 Winter, Otto—William Schultz.... 1,489 16
26 Walsh, Augustine—Christian F Paul. 566 87
26*Ward, Herbert—C P Tucker.... 127 17
27 Wilshusen, John—Christopher Pfluger....costs 77 35
27 Wheeler, Henry F / *Wheeler, Frank H } J A Doyle.... 102 00
27 Waefelaer, Louis—Louis Weiss..costs 102 62
28 Weinwurn, Isidor—Bernard Brod.... 72 50
28 Wellwood, John H—Gilbert & Baker Mfg Co.... 236 21
28 Ward, Edmund F—Manhattan Beef Co (Lim).... 89 58
28 Weiskopf, William—Jacob Cohen.... 631 40
29 Wheelock, Joseph B—P J Kelly.... 262 00
29 Wardrobe, Thomas—N Y Life Ins Co.... 108 58
29 White, Henry Kirk—Alexander Campbell.... 525 48
29 Walcott, Joseph C—Henry Dayton.. 2,514 06
29 Westcott, Robert, pres't Westcott Express Co—Florence Dudley....costs 85 22
29 Waldron, Robert H—People State N Y.... 300 00
29 Walker, John T / Walker, Joseph } Nat Bank of Republic.... 1,895 27
30 Weiss, Theodore—J F Degener....31,905 40
30 Weiss, Theodore—G F Vietor....16,686 47
30 Walker, Charles E—A J Connick.... 234 42
30 Wilson, John S—Market and Fulton Nat Bank.... 306 27
30 Yeandle William H / Yeandle, James / Yeandle, Thomas / Yeandle, John / Yeandle, George / Yeandle, Kate / Yeandle, Sarah } Celeste Yeandle. 59 43
24 Zapke, Adolph—Philip Helfrich.... 109 50
27 Zeh, Philip / Zeh, Philip, Jr } J A de Veer.... 131 11
29 Zimmermann, Ernest—C H Kranichfelt.... 240 84
30 Zauner, Robert H—John McKosson, Jr.... 104 49

KINGS COUNTY.

Oct.
26 Atwill, Edwin—Anna M V Gildersleeve.... $318 02
26 Appelt, Samuel—S C Prescott.... 100 93
26 Asche, J H—County of Kings.... 75 00
29 Appelt, Samuel—F W Devoe & Co... 128 30
22 Burroughs, Horace F, Jr—J C Carney....52,564 82
23 Banks, Thomas—C E Bliss.... 74 26
24 Britton, George F—C H Coggeshall.. 89 60
26 Butler, Charles T—Essex Co Nat Bank....1,227 64
29 Boehm, John—W S Okie....1,127 69
29 Burroughs, Horace F—C G Saxe.... 2,695 84
29 Bowers, Alfred—C W Russell.... 531 29
29 Bushfield, John C—M Sablein....(D) 2,119 53
24 Conway, John—J A & M Bross.... 248 94
26†Crawley, "William" K—W Johansen. 169 00
26 Colson, William H—J A Wyckoff.... 234 60
27 Cook, Henr / Cook, Johny } A B Powell.... 122 58
29 Cooke, Frank—H Klein.... 563 94
29 Creed, Sarah C—B Wasserman.... 83 89
27†Davis, "David"—J Busby.... 33 60
27 Davis, James R—G Oakley.... 494 07
26 Egan, Annie—A B Riker.... 269 44
22 Furey, Frank—Maria D Furey.... 99 87
23 Finn, Thomas—J Mendez.... 142 85
24 Fogarty, Katie L—Ellen Hynes.... 326 27
24 Fogebu, Alexander—R Bicket.... 81 35
28 Fischer, Frederick W—J Eppig.... 213 25
26 Gibbons, Thomas—J Amend.... 490 48
26 Gibby, George H—N Tebbetts.... (D) 3,009 54
27 Gibbons, Thomas—J Amend.... 202 80
23 Hale, William S—C E Pell....1,043 02
24 Hay, John / Hay, Robert } Henry McShane Mfg Co.... 32 50
26 Hahn, John—T Martin.... 164 89
27 Hill, Lester—J Busby.... 33 60
28 Hay, John / Hay, Robert } J Jamer.... 111 97
28 Hess, George / Hess, Henry } H W Case.... 36 90
24 Johnson, Peter—R Bicket.... 77 85
26 Jewell, William H—J A Hagy.... 521 38
27 Jaycox, Edward—Catharine Bohen.. 89 20
28 Irwin, George—H B Kirk.... 490 09
23 Klein, John—P J Ackerman.... 98 75
23 the same——S B Downes.... 84 39
23 the same——J Nix.... 114 68
23 the same——W M Hines.... 98 30
23 Kelley, George J—Fuller & Warren Co.... 121 94
24 Koerner, John—H F Gundrum.... 99 93
28 Kramer, Henry—A Grill.... 123 60
28 Klein, Charles J—Brooklyn City R R Co.... 57 57
27 Lyons, Bernard—G D Royston.... 78 45
23 Marsh, Frederick—N Kaplan.... 65 22
23 McAveeny, Owen—J Fitzpatrick.... 1,088 52
24 McConnell, Richard J / McLaughlin, Ann } Julia A McConnell.... 661 22
24 Meriam, Leo A—Benjamin Moore & Co.... 289 93
24 McLean, George—R Bicket.... 65 85
26 Malleson, Nellie H—E Gateson.... 151 86
26 Maurer, Ulrich—W Mogk.... 672 04
27 Merriam "Louis" A—H Williams... 69 97
27 Moeller, Henry—G T Lawrence.... 70 70
27 Malone, Joseph / McCabe, Margaret } D E Donovan.. 164 85
27 Meyer, Gesine—D Schmidt.... 255 34
28 Meyer, Siegmund T / Meyer, Arthur L } A Steers.... 735 12
29 McDermott, James O—D B Duncan.. 4,740 11
26 O'Donnell, J—County of Kings.... 50 00
23 Post, Sarah F—M Fishel.... 184 85
24 Plath, William—H M Bischoff.... 220 28
29 Price, Jesse—N Y and Brooklyn Casket Co.... 143 08
26 Quantin, Edward H—T Schloerb.... 632 75
26 Rose, Stephen B / Rose, George, Jr } E A Gillespie.... 1,025 67
27 Ryan, Marcus—J E Baker.... 178 73
27 Robinson, John—J W Thompson.... 3,684 81
28 Rooney, Frances J—H May.... 157 25
24 Sheehan, John—W H King.... 319 71
24 Schindler, Anthony—H F Gundrum.. 99 92
26 Sturdevant, James S—C D Prescott.. 183 79
26 Stohrs, John E—P D Armour.... 132 00
26 Schroeder, Frederick—S Colgate.... 90 48
27 Smith, Waitstill A / Smith, Frank F of W A Smith & Co / Smith, Waitstill A, individ } M Herrick.. 228 24
27 Sussman, Fanny—Mercantile Nat Bank, N Y....1,222 15
27 the same——the same.... 523 21
27 the same——the same.... 927 05
28 Schottman, Frederick—Gaus & Miller 45 55
29 Servis, Peter V—M Sablein....(D) 2,112 53
29 Sheldon, Cevedra B—E A Wildt.... 230 49
22 Thurston Robert H / Thurston, William C } Emma J Mason.... 87 49
23 The Fred Hower Brewing Co (Lim)—C Zoller.... 128 13
23 The trustees of the New York and Brooklyn Bridge—Clara J Curtis..46,318 71
24 The Metropolitan Elevated R R Co—T J Macvey.... 189 68

24 Traitel, Bernard D / Traitel, Benjamin P — C Jourgensen. 977 79

23 The City of Brooklyn—J W Gallivan. 164 27

26 The Knickerbocker Steamboat Co—Edison General Electric Co......... 659 84

29 Triotz, Annie—E Ridley & Sons..... 23 25

33 Wurshauer, Louis—A Dryfoos....... 104 86

23 Williams, William C—T C Lyman & Co.......... 321 50

24 Wilson, Francis W—M Harris....... 40 47

26 Wardrobe, Thomas—Buffalo Carriage Co.......... 121 81

27 Wells, William H—First Nat Bank, Brooklyn.......... 426 12

28 Washburn, Charles N / Washburn, Charles M — W S Washburn...... 309 89

28 Wilkes, George / Wilkes, Lizzie T — A Steers......... 685 57

29 Woodman, Nathaniel H—G W Kidd. 1,165 28

29 Wardrobe, Thomas—N Y Life Ins Co. 108 58

26 Yeaman, Mathew—County of Kings. 75 00

28 Zeh, Philip / Zeh, Jr, Philip — J A de Veer........ 131 11

SATISFIED JUDGMENTS.

NEW YORK.

October 24 to 30—Inclusive.

Armstrong, William A—George Everson, exr. (1891).......... $275 16

Adams, Robert L—Franz Eberlein. (1891).... 37 50

Alexander, Isidore and Jacob—A J Simpson. (1889).......... 71 44

Same——same. (1889).......... 71 28

Allen, Rudolph—Matthias Rock. (1891)....... 216 05

Same——same. (1891).......... 217 53

Bernheim, Charles L, Julius C and Abraham C / Bauer, Felix L — Simon Kierstein. (1891)......... 655 18

Same——same. (1891).......... 89 71

Boles, Scudder D—H R Ritch. (1891)......... 98 89

Coughlin, Mary A—H T Terry. (1891)......... 420 03

Church Publishing Co (Lim)—J R Angel. (1891). 84 48

Cane, Henry W, George W and Abraham—J L Bailey. (1885).......... 908 81

Same——Mayer Fruchtwanger. (1884)..... 691 71

Same——James Talcott. (1885).......... 822 05

Clark, Jacob E—James Phillips, Jr. (1891)....1,028 27

Cohen, Louis—Mary Margowitz. (1891)........1,153 63

Clearwater, Edward—J L Morgan. (1891).... 623 95

Cragin, William B—C S Day. (1891).......... 73_36

Dempsey, William — Lewis Schoonmaker. (1891).......... 70 12

Same——H F Gundrum. (1891).......... 173 72

Same——G H Flynn. (1891).......... 295 96

Same——Leopold Freisen. (1891).......... 302 48

Same——Patrick Cassidy. (1891).......... 352 48

*Dunphy, Martin J—People State N Y. (1889). 100 00

Guilfoyle, Dennis — George Everson, exr. (1891).......... 275 16

‡Gallagher, Patrick—D A Gaylord. (1891)....2,160 42

Gore, Calvin—J L Morgan. (1891).......... 449 60

Gobber, John—John Mangenheimer. (1891)... 69 57

Gaus, John—People State N Y. (1889)........ 100 00

*Hall, Thomas J—William Prodgers. (1891)...2,247 47

Haas, Frederick—R W Forbes. (1889)......... 807 20

Herrick, James F / Hollbrook, Francis W — Riverside Bank. (1889) 246 67

Holly, John I—James Phillips, Jr. (1891).....1,028 27

Heller, Emil—Aaron Furth. (1891).......... 222 27

Hooper, Rachel A—J L Morgan. (1891)....... 449 60

Hasselbach, Fritz—J G Heintze. (1879)....... 827 83

Keiser, Paul—John Buckley. (1884).......... 174 30

Lalor, William and James C—Jacob Marks. (1891).......... 381 06

Meagher, Timothy—R H L Townsend. (1890). 122 08

McCaffrey, William J—Mayer Fruchtwanger. (1884).......... 691 71

Same——J L Bailey. (1885).......... 908 81

Same——James Talcott. (1885).......... 822 05

McCue, Patrick—D M Koehler. (1891).......... 373 74

Same——same. (1891).......... 296 27

Monaghan, Margaret—H T Terry. (1891)...... 426 03

Metropolitan Elevated Railway Co / Manhattan Railway Co — Nancy L Sherwood (1890).......... 6,518 50

Muldoon, William H—Joseph Marren. (1891). 291 20

O'Donelan, James—Albert Taubert. (1891)... 259 50

Same——same. (1891).......... 109 50

Pennsylvania R R Co—Josephine Blakeslee. (1891).......... 225 00

Prodgers, Augustus D — William Prodgers. (1891)..........2,247 47

Smith, John—Lewis Schoonmaker. (1891)..... 70 12

Same——Leopold Freisen. (1891).......... 302 48

Same, and Schoemann, Abraham — Patrick Cassidy. (1891).......... 352 48

§Scheider, Joseph—Hymen Benedict. (1890).. 101 26

§Same——same. (1890).......... 374 61

Stewart, John—C S Lyon. (1890).......... 168 60

Stowell, Lillian E—Ella C Winslow. (1891).... 224 21

Suburban Rapid Transit Co—Mary Murphy. (1890)..........5,330 26

Same——same. (1891).......... 126 99

Vien, Henry A, exr Andrew Leonard—Elizabeth C Leonard. (1891)..........1,721 96

Wilsens, Christian—C W Wells. (1891)...... 106 41

Walcott, Joseph C—I E Hasbrouck. (1891)....14,703 13

§Wheeler & Wilson Mfg Co—G H W Curtis. (1891)..........6,972 41

White, Thomas F and Andrew J—Twelfth Ward Bank. (1890)..........2,773 37

Wolffe, Fred—S B Solomon. (1891).......... 272 66

*Vacated by order of Court. †Suspended on Appeal. ‡Released. §Reversal. ‖Satisfied by Execution.

KINGS COUNTY.

October 23 to 29—Inclusive.

Armstrong, William A—G Everson. (1891)... $275 16

Baumgras, C M—L Heldt. (1888).......... 213 19

Bliss, Archibald M—N L Archer. (1889)........ 382 87

Blossom, Joseph R / Blossom, Henry S — Village of Matteawan. (1891).......... 637 01

Clementson, James D—J T Murphy. (1890)... 384 90

Same——G Allen. (1889).......... 143 77

Conway, Agnes T / Conway, James J — C H Randell. (1891)....... 95 38

Same——same. (1891).......... 223 17

De Lano, George W—H W Grindal. (1891.) (Vacated).......... 840 08

Freuenthal, Joseph—E M Travis, exr. (1891).. 128 14

Gerald, Edmund—T E Green. (1891).......... 599 42

Guilfoyle, Dennis—G Everson. (1891)...... 275 16

Hamburg, Elkan—P Hart. (1888).......... 85 82

Same——same. (1888)..........5,422 79

Harris, George S—T E Green. (1891).......... 599 42

Honeyer, Christopher D—Claus Lipsius B Co exr. (1891).......... 116 41

Irwin, John C—A L Allaben. (1891).......... 300 84

Kiefer, Theresa—M Metzer. (1889)..........1,184 44

Kraus, William—P Hart. (1888).......... 85 82

Same——same. (1888)..........5,422 79

Lauer, Emanuel—P Hart. (1888).......... 85 82

Same——same. (1888)..........5,422 79

McGuinness, Jr, Joseph—T R Sheffield. (1890). 163 82

Mersereau, Charles E—N H Murray, exr. (1891) 98 18

Michel, Justin—D Hessberg. (1890).......... 118 67

Pilcher, Joseph M—T E Green. (1891)....... 599 42

Rosse, Louise and Auguste—W Ulmer. (1891). 264 12

Schwab, Jacob—T R Sheffield. (1890)......... 163 82

Taylor, J Monroe—Hugh Flynn. (1889)...... 73 42

Same——same. (1891).......... 95 72

Same——same. (1888).......... 161 78

The Metropolitan Life Ins Co — S Sterling. (1888).......... 88 62

Same——same. (1888)..........6,820 00

Turner, William C — International Tile and Trim Co. (1890).......... 219 62

White, Thomas F and Andrew J, of P White's Sons / White, Andrew J, individ — Twelfth Ward Bank, N Y. (1890).......2,773 37

MECHANICS' LIENS.

NEW YORK CITY.

Oct.

24 One Hundred and Twentieth st, No. 124, s s, 90 w Lexington av, 25x—. McCullough & Lindshoy agt W. E. Crandall and John W. Fisher, owners and contractors....... $426 35

26 Twenty-fourth st, n s, 271 e 9th av, 78x98.9. Moran Bros. agt Joseph McFarland, owner, and Thomas B. Snape and Frederick Wood, contractors.......... 460 65

26 Amsterdam av, Nos. 633-641, n e cor 91st st, 136x100. Joseph Grossman agt Edward Smith, owner and contractor.......... 35 00

26 Same property. Fritz Moser agt same owner, and John Reisinger, contractor... 67 50

26 Same property. William Woerner agt same owner, and same and Edward Smith, contractors.......... 108 25

26 Leroy st, Nos. 57-63, n s, 66.2x—. Ferdinand Gehiker agt John W. Stevens, Owen, Sr., and Owen McElroy, Jr., owners and contractors.......... 100 00

27 One Hundred and Thirty-fifth st, Nos. 5-17, n s, 110 w 5th av, 125x100. J. W. Binney agt William H. Verdon, owner and contractor.......... 159 25

27 Leroy st, Nos. 55 and 57. Steel, Van Rossum & Co. agt John W. Stevens and Owen, Sr., & Owen McElroy, Jr., owners and contractors.......... 810 00

27 One Hundred and Sixth st, No. 338, s s, 175 w 1st av, 25x100. William Weckwerth agt Patrick Dempsey, owner and contractor.......... 67 00

27 Ninety-sixth st, n s, 50 e Park av, 50x100. Harvey Forrest agt Frances J. Schnugg, owner, and George Meyers, contractor... 564 00

27 Anthony av, e s, 80 n 175th st, 50x125. Todd & Co. agt Hermann Masche, owner and contractor.......... 25 00

27 West End av, s w cor 103d st, 100.11x159.10. J. Q. Maynard agt Welcome R. Steinmetz, owner, and same and John H. Steinmetz, contractors.......... 315 00

28 Ninety-fourth st, Nos. 103 and 105, n s, 100 w Columbus av, 50x100.8. Frank Leimeister agt Francis J. Hillenbrand, owner and contractor.......... 168 00

28 Ninety-fifth st, Nos. 104 and 106, s s, 100 w Columbus av, 50x100.8. Same agt same.. 100 00

26 One Hundred and Seventy-sixth st, n s, 425 w Fleetwood av, 25x125. L. A. Soule agt Victor L. Veyroc, owner and contractor.. 450 00

28 One Hundred and Eighteenth st, s s, 240 w 4th av, 100x100.11. McElwee Mfg Co. agt Bernhard Ginsburg, owner, and same and Herman and Mary Masche, contractors.. 192 00

28 Fifty-sixth st, Nos. 405-409, n s, 100 w 9th av, 75x100. Nogara & Tmola agt Felice Adams, owner, and Antonio Gallo, contractor.......... 30 00

28 Sixty-fourth st, No. 231, n s, 180 w 2d av, 50 x100.5. John Stewart agt Louis H. Steinhardt, owner and contractor..........1,015 25

29 East Broadway, s e cor Jefferson st, 50x100. Robert Logan agt Hebrew Institute, owner, and L. A. Burke & Co., contractor 30 00

29 Fourteenth st, s s, 88 w Av C, 244x103.3. Lawrence Houlihan agt William H. Muldoon, owner and contractor..........1,164 90

29 Keppler av, n w cor Willard av, 75x100. J. B. Roberts agt Ida L. Senior, owner and contractor..........1,827 05

29 Pike st, No. 53, e s, 34.10 n Monroe st, 20x100. Mayor, Lane & Co. agt Nathan Ferber, owner, and Lazarus Black and A. Rochemowitz, contractor.......... 775 50

29 Ninety-sixth st, Nos. 159-167, n s, 70 e Lexington av, 125x100. Bernard Marrey agt Owen McElroy, Jr., and William McElroy, owners and contractors.......... 410 75

29 Platt st, No. 25, n w cor Gold st, 12.8x82x—x81.6. G. H. Hahn agt Gustav M. Herrenschmidt, owner, and James A. Daly, contractor.......... 20 06

29 Bleecker st, s e cor 8th av(?), runs northeast 44.11 x southeast 40 x east 17.2 x south 22.5 x west 76.9 to Bleecker st, x north 27.7 to beginning, known as Nos. 7 and 9 Abingdon sq. Moran Bros. agt Thomas J. Walsh and Louis M. Phelps, owner, and Thomas J. Walsh, contractor....... 643 80

30 Keppler av, n w cor Willard st, 75x100. Frederick Robinson agt Ida L. Senior, owner, and John B. Roberts, contractor.. 150 00

30 Kippler av, n w cor Willard av, 75x100. Samuel Price agt same.......... 330 00

30 Seventy-second st, s s, 213 e 1st av, 50x102.2. Manchester & Philbrick agt Joseph F. Gallagher, owner and contractor..........2,700 00

30 Seventh av, Nos. 2162 and 2164, w s. W. T. Mersereau & Co. agt Joel B. Smith, owner and contractor.......... 570 00

30 Water st, s e cor Market st, 26x76.4. Macknight Flintic Stone Co. agt Thomas Brennan, owner and contractor.......... 601 74

30 One Hundred and Nineteenth st, s s, 460 e Lenox av, 125x100.11. Reynolds & Quinn agt Tillie E. Smith and John J. MacDonald, owners, and John J. MacDonald, contractor.......... 675 00

KINGS COUNTY.

Oct.

23 Fourth st, s s, 160 w 7th av, 114x100. Patrick McGuigan agt Moses & Fanton, owners and contractors.......... $100 00

23 Flushing av, n e cor Vandervoort av, 25x100. Louis Bossert agt Peter Johnson, owner and contractor..........1,354 70

23 Livonia av, n e cor Osborn st, 25x100. Ollaf Larsen agt —— Monahan, owner and contractor.......... 10 62

23 Same property. Ludwig Solker agt same. 27 50

23 Same property. Joseph Solser agt same. 28 75

23 Same property. Hans Olsen agt same.... 10 62

23 Same property. Gabriel Olsen agt same.. 10 62

25 Same property. Robert Solker agt same.. 39 25

23 Same property. Peter Balcerek agt same. 27 50

23 Hamburg av, w s, — n Stockholm st, 25x100. See lien. John Hippler agt Jacob Klett, owner and contractor.......... 140 00

23 Porter av, s w cor Maspeth av, 400x400. North River Blue Stone Co. agt The Equity Gas Light Co., owner, and William C. Whyte, contractor.......... 333 20

23 East 95th st, e s, 150 s Av G, 28.5x105. Canarsie. John R. Hughes agt Pauline Hardy, owner, and Harry Hardy, contractor..... 148 57

24 Hart st, No. 990. George P. Jacobs & Co. agt Louis F. Broechart, contractor...... 560 74

24 Willoughby av, No. 765, s s, 179.6 w Lewis av, 20x100. Jacob Friedmann agt Jacob Bisson, owner, and Fred. J. Clough, contractor.......... 85 75

24 State st, s s, 100 e Henry st, 30x100. Jacob May agt John F. Robertson, owner, and Charles H. Collins, contractor.......... 68 02

24 Humboldt st, w s, bet Ten Eyck st and Stagg st, two frame houses. George P. Jacobs & Co. agt Lewis F. Broechart, contractor.......... 560 74

26 Livonia av, s e cor Osborn st, 20x100. Abraham Corn agt Abraham Seidenberg and R. Abramovitz, owner and contractor... 90 00

26 Ovington av, n s, 75 w Stewart av, 20x100. Francis Connelly agt John J. Page, owner, and Edwin Dennington, contractor..... 300 00

26 Boerum st, s s, 200 w Humboldt st, 25x100. Frank S. Haynes agt Samuel Cassel, owner, and Israel Jarashow and Samuel Cassel, contractors..........3,695 00

27 Watkins st, w s, 175 n Sutter av, 50x100. Henry McShane Mfg. Co. agt Elias Kaplan, owner, and Pasco & McCormick, contractors.......... 700 00

27 Eastern Parkway, s s, 50 w Christopher av, 50x100. Victor Isaakowitz agt Wolf Potashinsky, owner, and Davis Levi, contractor.......... 16 00

27 Thatford st, w s, 250 n Dumont av, 25x100. The Henry McShane Mfg. Co. agt Lewis Hurst, owner, and Pasco & McCormick, contractors.......... 250 00

27 Dumont av, n s, 25 w Thatford av, 25x100. Same agt Hyman Goldstein, owner, and same contractor.......... 150 00

27 Ninth st, n s, 200 e Hicks st, 25x100. David Morrissy agt Stephen Cosgrove, owner and contractor.......... 55 00

27 Patchen av, n e cor Putnam av, 20x100. Charles G. Soderholm agt Thomas Walling and Morris Hawkins, owners and contractors.......... 180 00

27 Dumont av, n s, 50 w Thatford av, 25x100. The Henry McShane Mfg Co. agt Hyman Goldstein, owner, and Pasco & McCormick, contractors.......... 150 00

27 Thatford av, w s, 125 n Dumont av, 25x100. Same agt Lewis Hurst, owner, and same contractor.......... 150 00

27 Gates av, s s, 250 w Knickerbocker av, 25x100. Watson & Pittinger agt John Lyons, owner, and Reilly & Lyons, contractors.. 434 50

27 Bergen st, s s, 100 w Hopkinson av, 25x100. George Schott agt Rosa Rosenfeld, owner, and Charles Becker, contractor.......... 70 00

27 Eastern Parkway, s s, 100.1 e Rockaway av, 25x100. Christopher Doyle agt Solomon Kringstin, owner, and Samuel Kaplansky and Samuel Samowitch, contractors..... 325 00

27 Rockaway av, e s, 100 s Eastern Parkway, 25x100. Same agt Charles Levy, owner, and B. Seerman, contractor.......... 232 50

27 Eastern Parkway, s s, 25 e Thatford av, 25x100. Same agt B. Seerman, owner and contractor.......... 232 50

27 Noble st, No. 117, n s, 418 e Franklin st, 25x100. George Call & Co. agt William P. Morrissy, owner, and Smith & Duffy, contractors.......... 486 50

28 Evergreen av, w s, 25 n Hancock st, 50x100. Henry McShane Mfg. Co. agt Carl and William Lehmann, of Lehmann Bros., owners, and Louis Broschart, contractor.. 75 00

28 Saratoga av, s e cor Bainbridge st, 100x115.6. Jacob May agt W. H. Good, owner and contractor.......... 108 98

29 Saratoga av, s e cor Decatur st, 115.6x100. Jacob May agt W. H. Good, owner and contractor.......... 108 98

29 Greene av, s w cor Vanderbilt av, 42x74. Thos. Read agt Chas. N. Washburn, exr., owner and contractor.......... 116 42

Editor RECORD AND GUIDE:

All liens filed by William J. Fitzpatrick are for labor and materials not furnished. All payments due are paid under his contract. MOSES & FANTON.

SATISFIED MECHANICS' LIENS.

NEW YORK CITY.

Oct.

24 Fiftieth st, No. 10 E. Samuel and Alexander Clark agt John Fox and William H. Ertell. (Lien filed Dec. 6, 1888)........ $940 00

24 Same property. Same agt same. (Dec. 10, 1888).......... 910 00

21 Same property. J. S., A. E. and W. E. Conover and Hugh Young agt same. (Dec. 11, 1888).......... 177 75

24 Same property. Same agt Mrs. Fox and William H. Ertell. (Dec. 6, 1888)........ 178_79

24 Same property. G. F. Babson and E. H. Harmon agt John Fox and William H. Ertell. (Dec. 6, 1888).......... 631_90

24 One Hundred and Sixth st, n s, 100 w Madison av, 125x100. Dimock, Fink & Co. agt J. J. & P. A. Fitzpatrick and Thompson & Leithauser. (Oct. 21, 1891)............. 128 09

26*Columbus av, w s, 75.5 n 97th st, 25.5x—. George Mungo agt John Doe and John Hatch. (Sept. 16, 1891)............ 39 50

26*Same property. Michael Tobin agt Harry Galway and Elias T. Hatch. (Sept. 9, '91) 100 00

27 Ninth av, w s, 100 s 94th st, 20x100. F. Koen agt Albert Flake and Percy Jacobs (Oct. 5, 1891).............................. 78 00

27 Same property. F. Brandt agt M. Schmeckenbecker. (Oct. 5, 1891).............. 136 00

27 Same property. Joseph Braun agt Albert Flake and M. Schmeckenbecker's Sons. (Oct. 6, 1891)........................ 150 00

27 Same property. East River Mill and Lumber Co. agt same and Percy Jacobs. (Oct. 6, 1891)............................ 372 60

27 Same property. G. Schmeckenbecker agt Albert Flake and Percy Jacobs. (Oct. 6, 1891)..1,000 00

27 Same property. George Pfister agt Albert Flake and M. Schmeckenbecker's Sons. (Oct. 6, 1891)........................ 100 00

27 Columbus av, No 688. Samuel Pollack agt same and Percy Jacobs. (Oct. 6, 1891)... 258 78

27 One Hundred and Thirty-fifth st, n s, 60 w 5th av, 100x100. J. W. Binney agt William H. Verdon. (Oct. 20, 1891)......... 159 25

28 Forty-eighth st, No. 57 W., 24.6x100. John Harper agt Fellowes Davis and Joseph B. Tiffany & Co. (April 1, 1891)............1,120 00

28 Same property. Wm. Hannam & Co. agt same. (June 9, 1891)...................... 565 12

28 Same property. John Mehrtens agt same. (April 6, 1891)........................ 338 00

28 Same property. Moody & Bracken agt same. (April 4, 1891)..................... 659 51

28 Same property. Robert Mayfield agt same. (April 3, 1891)........................ 235 00

28 Same property. Rudolph Walter agt Fellowes Davis and John Harper. (April 8, 1891).. 264 68

28 Same property. Anthony McQuade agt same. (March 25, 1891)..................... 33 00

28 Same property. Thomas McQuade agt same. (March 24, 1891)..................... 69 12

28 Same property. David Schuldiner agt Mrs. Fellows Davis and J. Harper. (April 17, 1891).. 51 76

28 Ogden av, e s, 100 s Union st. J. J. Lennon agt William Bisland and Maxwell J. Santnier. (Aug. 4, 1888)........................ 34 44

28 Same property. James Campbell agt same. (Sept. 4, 1888)............................ 27 00

28 Ogden av, e s, 114 s Union st, 21x36.5. J. W. Colwell agt same. (Aug. 2, 1888)...... 136 98

28 Lexington av, s e cor 87th st. Pierce, Butler & Pierce Mfg. Co. agt Cavinato Bros. (Oct. 12, 1891).................................2,453 00

28*Boulevard, s w cor 78th st. 28x96. Michael O'Rourke agt John Doe and James Livingston and Patrick Brennen. (Oct. 27, 1891).. 156 10

28*Seventy-fourth st, Nos. 132-138 W., 100x—. Michael O'Brien and 15 others agt James Carlew, Allston G. Culver and James H. Wells; 16 liens. (May 5, 1891)............ 462 13

28*Same property. Thomas O'Keeffe and 2 others agt same; 3 liens. (May 11, 1891).. 24 13

28*Same property. Patrick Murray agt same. (May 18, 1891)................................ 5 25

29 Fifty-third st, s s, 350 w 10th av, 125x100. Vermont Marble Co. agt James O'Donelan. (Aug. 22, 1891)......................... 686 80

29 Same property. Frank Graziadio agt same. (Aug 12, 1891)................................ 268 62

29 Same property. Albert Taubert agt same and James Volkening and David Davis. (Sept. 1, 1891)................................ 550 00

29 Fifty-third st, s s, 275 e 11th av, 125x100. Michael Tobin agt Henry Volkening, James O'Donelan and David Davis. (Sept. 9, 1891).. 161 65

29 Same property. Morton Bros. & Co. agt James O'Donelan. (Aug. 19, 1891)...... 1,750 00

29 Ninety-eighth st, Nos. 220-224 E., 75x100.11. P. Blumenthal agt Dempsey & Smith. (Oct. 1, 1891).. 383 00

29 Same property. Doretta Nie onner agt same. (Sept. 10, 1891)........................ 306 25

29 Same property. John O'Hare agt same. (Aug. 3, 1891).................................. 200 00

29 Same property. Canda & Mathews Mfg. Co. agt same. (Sept. 9, 1891)............5,418 00

29 Same property. Joseph Cobolevsky agt same and P. Blumenthal. (Aug. 12, 1891). 20 35

29 Same property. Samuel Oellagori agt same. (Aug. 11, 1891)........................ 22 75

29 Same property. T. G. Hojer agt same. (Aug. 6, 1891)................................ 114 38

30 Third av, s w cor 126th st, 25x90. William Haw agt William T. and James Purdy, and Arctander & Seabold. (Oct. 29, 1891)..1,400 00

30 Fifty-eighth st, n s, 350 w 8th av, 25x—. Charles Winters agt William M. Reynolds. (Dec 13, 1890).................................. 40 00

30 Third av, e s, 75 s 93d st, 50x100. Hugh Gallagher agt John B. Smith and Thomas Hickey. (Nov. 20, 1890)..................... 66 62

30 Same property. John Coleman agt same. (Sept. 26 (1890).................................. 55 12

30 Same property. Pasquale Magre et al. agt John B. Smith and John Appolony. (Feb. 17, 1891).. 67 00

30 Same property. John Coleman agt same. (Jan. 27, 1891)................................ 84 12

30 Same property. Rocco Uicone agt same. (Feb. 17, 1891)................................ 4 50

30 Third av, e s, 75 n 92d st. Michael O'Leary et al. agt J. B. Smith and Thomas Hickey. (Nov. 8, 1890)..................................... 177 86

30 Fourteenth st, s s, 88 w Av C, 244x100. Hughes & Scanlon agt William H. Muldoon. (Sept. 1, 1891).......................7,050 00

30 Same property. Murphy & Carroll agt same. (Oct. 16, 1890)........................2,100 00

*Discharged by depositing amount of lien and interest with County Clerk.

KINGS COUNTY.

Oct.

22 Bainbridge st, n s, 115.6 e Saratoga av, 188x100. Rudolph Reimer & Co. agt J. Mason Kirby, owner and contractor. (Lien filed Oct. 9, 1891)............................ $440 00

23 Eastern Parkway, n w cor Osborn st, 50x100. Hall Sash and Door Co. agt Elizabeth C. Powers, owner, and John Powers, contractor. (Sept. 30, 1891)................ 825 00

23 Bergen st, s s, 29" e Brooklyn av, 100x100. John J. Flynn agt Joseph M. Pilcher & Co., owners and contractors. (Oct. 23, 1891.) (Deposit)............................ 381 00

24 Kent av, n e cor Rutledge st, 40x80. John H. Bull agt R. M. Warren, Jr., owner, and F. W. Baldwin, contractor. (June 21, 1891).. 75 00

24 Third av, Nos. 1148 and 1150, w s, 56.2 n 48th st, 50x80. Morris Jacobson and Morris Margovitz agt Solomon Sonin, owner and contractor. (Sept. 8, 1891).............1,695 00

24 Reid av, w s, 50 n Halsey st, 50x100. Van Wagner & Co. agt George W. McCormick. (Oct. 22, 1891).................................. 480 50

24 Fourth av, w s, 54 s President st. John Walsh agt Domenico and Francisco Furo. (Oct. 13, 1891).................................. 192 50

26 Eighth av, s e cor 11th st, 100x120. O'Hara & Croak agt Allen V. B. Norris and William Turner, owners and contractors. (June 11, 1891).............................. 528 66

26 Same property. Paul Ayres & Co agt same owners and contractors. (June 26, 1891)..2,437 00

26 Same property. Thomas McCann agt same owners and contractors. (June 11, 1891).. 327 00

26 Same property. Nils Olsen agt same owners and contractors. (June 10, 1891)..... 252 00

26 Same property L. E. Mansfield agt same owners and contractors. (Aug. 18, 1891). 175 00

26 Same property. Fox & McCarthy agt same owners and contractors. (Aug. 26, 1891).. 136 00

26 Same property. Albert Goble agt same owners and contractors. (Aug. 28, 1891). 192 68

26 Same property. E. J. Hayes & Bros. agt same owners and contractors. (Sept. 5, 1891).. 84 00

26 Ewen st, No. 378, e s, 25x100. Joseph F. Hunt agt Margaret Coleman, owner, and McGarry & Moran, contractors. (Aug. 21, 1891).. 889 20

26 Seigel st, n s, 146.6 w Ewen st, 48x100.... } Seigel st, n s, 98.6 w Ewen st, 24x100..... } Charles Hofer & Son agt Henry Meyer, Jonas Feldberg and Sarah Barasch, owners and contractors. (Sept. 26, 1891)..... 341 37

26 Twenty-third st, s w cor 4th av, 20x50. Hobby & Doody agt Elizabeth Staebler, owner, and John Staebler, contractor. (Oct. 24, 1891).................................. 156 45

26 Cooper st, e s, 175 s Central av, 175x100. McGrath & Burns agt Thomas J. Allen, owner and contractor. (July 11, 1891) ... 178 00

26 Bergen st, s s, 250 w Kingston av, 60x100. F. G. Clarke Blue Stone Co. agt Joseph M. Pilcher, owner, and Edmund Gould, Joseph M. Pilcher and George S. Harris, contractors. (Oct. 16, 1891.) (Deposit)....2,647 17

28 Harrison av, e s, 25 n River st, 25x100. Alois Lazansky agt Sarah Taylor, owner, and Leopold J. Lippmann and Alexander Taylor, contractors. (Oct. 26, 1891)....... 121 00

28 Montague st, Nos. 159 and 161............. } Pierrepont st. Nos. 148 and 150............ } Brooklyn Real Estate Exchange (Lim.).. } South Brooklyn Saw Mill Co. agt The Brooklyn Real Estate Exchange (Lim.) and J. J. Garland Co. (July 7, 1891)......1,509 77

28 Same property. Watson & Pittinger agt same owners and contractors. (July 17, 1891).. 98 87

28 Montague st, n s, 175 w Court st, 50x200, Brooklyn Real Estate Exchange. C. B. Keogh Mfg. Co. agt The Real Estate Exchange (Lim.), Brooklyn, owner, and James J. Garland, contractor. (July 3, 1891)..6,751 00

28 Prospect av, n s, 250 w 8th av, 96x80. Adelbert S. Nichols agt Mrs. R. W. and R. W. Fielding, owners and contractors. (July 22, 1891).. 270 00

29 Van Sielen av, e s, 300 s Blake av, 50x100. Louis Bossert agt J. J. Quinn, owner and contractor. (April 7, 1891)................ 250 33

29 Eastern Parkway, n w cor Osborn st, 45x100. Richards & Taylor agt Elizabeth M. Power, owner, and John Power, contractor. (Oct. 26, 1891)............................ 61 68

29 Sixty-second st, s w cor 11th av. Bay Ridge Mfg. Co. agt Andrew Johnson, owner and contractor. (Aug. 7, 1891)... 264 15

BUILDINGS PROJECTED.

The first name is that of the owner; ar't stands for architect, m'n for mason, c'r for carpenter and b'r for builder.

NEW YORK CITY.

SOUTH OF 14TH STREET.

Downing st, No. 44, five-story brk flat, 28x84 3, tin roof; cost, $22,000; S. W. B. Smith, 1237 Franklin av; ar't, C. H. Israels. Plan 1363.

Mott st, No. 110, five-story brk factory, 16.7x23.7, tin roof; cost, $2,500 (?); W. H. Cooper, 25 Catharine st; ar't, T. S. Goodwin. Plan 1365. (Substituted for Alteration plan No. 1371 filed in July, 1891.)

West st, w s, bet Fulton and Vesey sts, Pier No. 14, one and two-story iron freight house, 69x700; tin roof; cost, $63,000; lessees, Baltimore & Ohio R. R. Co., foot Whitehall st. Plan 1371.

12th st, Nos. 307 and 309 E., four-story and basement brk and stone building, 40.6x53.3, tile and tin roof; cost, $47,000; Children's Aid Society, 24 St. Marks pl; ar'ts, Vaux & Radford; b'r, R. Deeves. Plan 1366.

BETWEEN 14TH AND 59TH STREETS.

34th st, Nos. 404-410 E., two-story brk building, 100x73, tin roof; cost, $12,000; F. X. Radley, 175 East 79th st; ar'ts, Radley & Greenough. Plan 1382.

55th st, Nos. 407 and 409 E., two-story brk building, 21.6x54, tin roof; cost $2,500; P. Doelger, 339 West 100th st; ar'ts, C. Stoll & Son. Plan 1378.

16th st, Nos. 331 and 333 W., two five-story brown stone flats, 25x80.4, tin roofs; cost, $18,000 each; T. Van Eupen, 307 Bowery; ar't, M. Muller. Plan 1391.

16th st, No. 530 W., one-story brk shop, 16.8x40, tar and gravel roof; cost, $500; B. Johnson, 430 West 16th st; m'n, T. Waters; c'r, J. Price. Plan 1393.

BETWEEN 59TH AND 125TH STREETS, EAST OF 5TH AVENUE.

103d st, n s, 180 w Park av, five five-story stone flats, 25x75, tin roofs; cost, $20,000 each; J. S. S , 4 West 113th st; ar't, J. C. Burne. Plan 1394.

116th st, No. 233 E., brk, stone and terra cotta church, 40x91, tin roof; cost, $14,000; W. Van Norden, treas., n w cor Nassau and Cedar sts; ar't, S. A. Warner; m'n, L. N. Crow; c'rs, McGuire & Sloan. Plan 1387.

122d st, s s, 100 e 1st av, one-story brk building, 88x95, tar and gravel roof; cost, $6,500; lessee, C. Tietjen, 335 East 119th st; ar't, A. Munch. Plan 1377.

Av A, s e cor 88th st, four five-story brk flats, one 25.2x75, three 25x60.2, tin roofs; total cost, $69,000; J. Schreiner, Jr., 104 West 123d st; ar't, J. Hauser. Plan 1389.

88th st, s s, 75 e Av A, two five-story brk and stone flats, 25x70, tin roofs; cost, $18,000 each; ow'r and ar't, same as last. Plan 1390.

BETWEEN 59TH AND 125TH STREETS, WEST OF CENTRAL PARK WEST AND 8TH AVENUE.

81st st, s s, 100 w Amsterdam av, two five-story brk and stone flats, 37.6x91.6, tin roofs; cost, $40,000 each; Rosina W. da Cunha, Montclair, N. J.; ar't, G. W. da Cunha, Jr. Plan 1383.

87th st, s s, 150 w 8th av, five four-story and basement stone dwell'gs, 20x58 with extensions, tin roofs; cost, $25,000 each; J. R. Breen, 152 East 60th st; ar't, J. H. Friend. Plan 1381.

West End av, s w cor 68th st, four five-story brk flats, one 25.5 and 96, three 25x89, tin roofs; total cost, $79,000; ow'rs and b'rs, Anwell & Cochlin, 327 East 117th st; ar't, J. W. Cole. Plan 1379.

Grand Boulevard, n w cor 122d st, three-story brk building, 15.2x60, tin roof; cost, $9,000; H. Boschen, 500 West 125th st; ar't, C. Sidney. Plan 1370.

90th st, s s, 240 w West End av, two three-story and basement stone dwell'gs, 18x55, tin roofs; cost, $12,000 each; Sheridan & Byrne, 145 East 67th st; ar't, T. J. Sheridan; m'n, E. Burns. Plan 1386.

106th st, s s, 200 w Amsterdam av, frame shed, 11x26, tar paper roof; cost, $40; agent, J. J. Semple, 446 West 47th st; c'r, Norcross Bros. Plan 1392.

NORTH OF 125TH STREET.

129th st, s s, 21.8 e 3d av, frame shed, 506x21.9, tin roof; cost, $1,250; Manhattan Railway Co., 71 Broadway Plan 1378.

136th st, Nos. 201-217 W., eighteen three-story and basement brk and stone dwell'gs, 16 and 17x50, tin roofs; cost, $10,000 each; ow'r and b'r, T. C. Van Brunt, 234 West 136th st. Plan 1384.

155th to 157th st, bet 8th and Edgecombe avs, three frame buildings, irreg. in size, roofs not mentioned; cost, $5,500 each; lessees, Manhattan Athletic Club, Madison av and 45th st; b'rs, Byrne & Perry. Plan 1385.

23D AND 24TH WARDS.

138th st, n s, 150 w Morris av, one-story frame shop, 30x18, tin roof; cost, $200; A. Burrows, 682 East 142d st; ar't, A. Pfeiffer. Plan 1372.

142d st, s s, 100 w 3d av, four five-story brk and stone flats, 25x68, tin roofs; cost, $18,000 each; J. T. Barry, 176 Willis av; ar't, A. Spence. Plan 1367.

144th st, n s, 200 e Morris av, two-story frame dwell'g, 20x35, asphalt and gravel roof; cost, $1,500; M. O'Neil, 482 Rider av; ar't, A. Gareiss. Plan 1375.

147th st, s s, 375 e Prospect av, two-story frame dwell'g, 25x20, tin roof; cost, $1,000; J. Henfling, Oak Point Lane, N. Y.; ar't, M. Dietsch. Plan 1369.

158th st, n s, 83 w Girard av, one-and-a-half-story frame shop, 12x20, gravel roof; cost, abt $175; W. J. Brennan, on premises; b'r, J. Richards. Plan 1380.

Bainbridge av, n w cor Garfield st, Fordham, two-story and attic frame dwell'g, 28.6x50, shingle roof; cost, $5,000; Mary L. Knox, 2771 Bainbridge av; ar't, S. B. Reed; c'r, J. B. Roberts. Plan 1376.

Cromwell av, w s, 169 s 161st st, two-story frame stable, 16x32 3, gravel roof; cost, $400; lessees, Miller & Robinson, 80 West 59th st; ar't, C. C. Churchill. Plan 1368.

KINGS COUNTY.

Plan 1961—Barbey st, w s, 125 s Sutter av, one two-story frame dwell'g, 20x30, tin roof; cost, $1,500; ow'r, ar't and c'r, Geo. Olsen, Ridgewood Heights.

1962—20th st, n s, 100 e 6th av, one two-story frame shop, 20x16, tin roof; cost, $150; ow'r, ar't and b'r, Nils Nelson, 347 20th st.

1963—24th st, s s, 320 e 3d av, one one-story frame storage for charcoal, 30x76, tin roof; cost, $400; James Devlin, on premises.

1964—McDonough st, s s, 150 e Reid av, three two-story and basement sand stone dwell'gs, 16.8x45, tin roofs and iron cornices; cost, $4,500 each; ow'r and ar't, Henry B. Hill, 243 Reid av.

1965—Montauk av, e s, 90 s Glenmore av, three two-story frame dwell'gs, 20x35, tin roofs; cost, $1,500 each; Jas. Ogilvie, Milford st.

1966—42d st, s s, 920 w 1st av, one one-story

frame stable, 30x50, peak roof; cost, $300; A. W. Humphreys, 71 Columbia st; c'r, J. Newham.

1967—Madison st, n s, 360 e Hamburg av, six two-story and basement frame (brk filled) dwellings, each 19 6x45, tin roofs; cost, $3,000 each; ow'r and b'r, Adolphus Gload; ar't, H. Vollweiler.

1968—45th st, s s, 340 e 3d av, three two-story and basement frame (brk filled) dwell'gs, each 20 x38, tin roofs; cost, $2,700 each; ow'r and b'r, Alexander Davidson, 3d av and 45th st; ar't, Thos. Bennett

1969—Willoughby av, n s, 375 w Wyckoff av, one one-story frame (brk filled) dwell'g, 25x25, tin roof; cost, $850; ow'rs and b'rs, Schenck & Schmidt, 1137 Willoughby av.

1970—Prospect pl, n s, 225 w Franklin av, one four-story brk and stone tenem't, 25x50, tin roof; cost, $7,000; ow'r and b'r, Wm. Morgan, 586 Prospect pl.

1971—Greenpoint av, No. 116, one four-story brk warehouse, 25x70, tin roof, galvanized iron cornice; cost, $4,000; Charles M. Englis, Clinton av; ar't, F. Jacobsen.

1972—Dupont st, No. 156, one four-story frame tenem't, 25x54, gravel roof; cost, $5,500; William Mangan, Clay st; c'rs, J. A. & W. H. Port; m'ns, J. & P. Reehil; ar't, Fred'k Weber.

1973—Seigel st, s s, 365 e Bushwick av, one two-story frame stable, 18x96, tin roof; cost, $700; ow'r and c'r, Michael Mayer, 20 Belvidere st; m'ns, Dornbach & Barutio.

1974—St. Marks av, n s, 400 e Brooklyn av, two one-story brk and stone dwell'gs, each 20x46, tin roofs, galvanized iron cornice; total cost, $20,000; John A. Bliss, 104 McDonough st; ar'ts, Langston & Dahlander.

1975—Greene st, No. 259, n s, 150 w Provost st, one two-story frame drug storage house, 25x100, gravel roof; cost, $600; ow'r and ar't, John C. Wiarda, 148 Kent st; b'r, E. Dreyer.

1976—Herkimer st, s w cor Kane pl, rear, one one-story frame stable, 12 and 10x12; cost, $60; Wilhelm Funch, 894 Herkimer st.

1977—Schenck av, e s, 250 n Arlington av, one two-story and attic frame dwell'g, 30x34, shingle roof; cost, $6,500; ow'r, ar't and b'r, S. T. Hollister, 106 Barbey st.

1978—Moore st, n s, 329.5 w White st, one three-story frame (brk filled) carpenter shop, 50x30, tin roof; cost, $2,000; Fred Elflein, 45 Gerry st; ar't, F. Holmberg.

1979—Willoughby av, n s, 225 e Irving av, one one-story frame tool house, 10x25, gravel roof; cost, $100; ow'rs, ar'ts and b'rs, Messrs. Spaeth & Sanger, on premises.

1980—Marcy av, w s, 170 s Macon st, one five-story stone flat, 32 and 37x90, tin roof, iron cornice; cost, $25,000; Betts Bros, 1292 Fulton st; ar'ts, Thayer & Wallace.

1981—Herkimer pl, n s, 200 w Nostrand av, two four-story brk tenem'ts, 25x50; gravel roofs, wooden cornices; cost $5,000 each; ow'r and ar't, G. R. Brown, 26 Court st; b'r, L. E. Brown.

1982—Morrell st, No. 63, one four-story frame (brk filled) tenem't, 25x50, tin roof; cost, $6,000; Saml. Cohan, on premises; ar't, H. Smith; b'r, not selected.

1983—Grand st, junction Metropolitan av, one three-story frame (brk filled) store and tenem't, 25x68.6 and 58 11, gravel roof; cost, $5,000; W. Meyenberg, on premises; ar't, F. J. Berlenbach, Jr.; b'r, not selected.

1984—Vermont av, s w cor Belmont av, rear, one one-story frame shop, 15x15.6, tin roof; cost, $185; Franz Kunz, on premises; c'r, K. F. Schmidt.

1985—Essex st, w s, 125 s Sutter av, one one-story frame carpenter shop, 15x20, gravel roof; cost, $100; ow'r and c'r, Robt. Forrest, on premises.

1986—47th st, s s, 125 w 3d av, one two-story frame stable, 20x16, tin roof; cost, $300; Walter Van Pelt, on premises; c'rs, Spence Bros.

1987—De Kalb av, No. 1461, one one-story frame shed, 20 and 24x12 and 18, tin roof; cost, abt $30; ow'rs, ar'ts and b'rs, W. B. Ostrander & Co., 1461½ De Kalb av.

1988—Stone av, e s, 100 n Sutter av, one two-story frame tailor shop, 20x30, tin roof; cost, $1,200; Jacob Axelrod, Thatford av.

1989—Humboldt st, e s, 50 s Varet st, two four-story frame (brk filled) tenem'ts, 25x57, tin roofs; cost, $10,000; Jacob Nagel, 18 Stagg st; ar't, H. Vollweiler; b'r, not selected.

1990—Ewen st, w s, 75 s Frost st, one one-story frame shop, 25x23, tin roof; cost, $100; Mr. Mausling, 66 North 3d st; ar't, H. Vollweiler; b'r, J. Schock.

1991—Eastern Parkway, n s, 81 w Elton st, one three-story frame store and dwell'g, 20.6x45, tin roof; cost, $3,000; Teresa Traverso, 2921 Atlantic av; ar'ts, Danmar & Fischer; b'r, not selected.

1992—24th st, s s, 250 e 3d av, one four-story brk storehouse for furniture, &c, 25x95, tin roof, wooden cornice; cost, $5,000; L. H. Schenck, on premises; ar't, J. L. Quesenberry; b'r, D. Ryan.

1993—Stanhope st, n s, 125 w Irving av, one one-and-a-half-story frame stable and shed, 11x15, tin roof; cost, $300; Pincus Seifters, 1403 Myrtle av; ar't, B. Finkensieper; b'r, not selected.

1994—Osborn st, e s, 200 n Sutter av, one three-story frame store and tenem't, 25x55, tin roof; cost, $4,000; ow'r and c'r, Joseph Morris, on premises; ar't, A. J. Warren.

1995—Elton st, w s, 300 n Arlington av, one two-story and attic frame dwell'g, 22x44, shingle roof; cost, $4,000; ow'r and b'r, Howard N. Acker, 179 Elton st; ar't, C. Conlon.

1996—Stone av, w s, 80 n Truxton st, one four-story frame (brk filled) tenem't, 20x55, tin roof; cost, $5,000; ow'r and c'r, Rob't B. Montgomery, 221 Chauncey st; ar't, M. F. Walsh.

1997—Rochester av, w s, 93 n St. Marks av, one two-story frame stable, 17x70, tin roof; cost, $400; Wm. Emken; 138 Rochester av; b'r, not selected.

1998—Sutter av, s w cor Essex st, one two-story frame stable and shed, 16x23, tin roof; cost, $600; Henry Rieker, 2022 3d av, New York.

1999—12th st, s s, 398.10 e 6th av, one three-story brk apartment house, 22x48, tin roof, wooden cornice; cost, $5,500; ow'r and b'r, Wm. Killey, 632 President st; ar't, W. M. Coots.

2000—Van Buren st, n s, 200 e Lewis av, ten two-story and basement brk dwell'gs, 17 6x42, gravel roofs, wooden cornices; total cost, $45,000; Albert Muir, 1086 Bedford av; ar't, J. L. Young.

2001—Commercial st, Nos. 93-99, n s, 100 from Manhattan av, one one-story brk storehouse for two oil tanks on dock, 28x20, gravel roof; cost, $350; E. P. Gleason, 181 Mercer st, New York; ar't, E. F. Gennert; m'n, G. Lydecker.

2002—Osborn st, e s, 175 n Sutter av, one three-story frame store and tenem't, 25x65, tin roof; cost, $4,000; ow'r and b'r, Joseph Morris, Osborn st; ar't, A. J. Warren.

ALTERATIONS NEW YORK CITY.

Plan 1852—Spring st, Nos. 109 and 111, interior alterations and new elevator and shaft; cost, $4,000; G. Legg, 25 West 81st st; ar't, F. A. Rooke; m'n, R. Deeves.

1853—10th st, Nos. 465 475 E., one-story extension, 19.6x34 8; cost, abt $200; W. E. Uptegrove, 1180 Dean st, Brooklyn; ar't, J. W. Moulton.

1854—1st av, No. 398, interior alterations, cellar walls altered and new store front; cost, $6,000; C. Siedler, 92 Liberty st; ar'ts, Jordan & Giller.

1855—45th st, No. 342 E., one-story extension, 30x25.5, interior alterations and front rebuilt; cost, $1,500; H. & P. Ziebiller, 411 East 84th st; ar't, C. Stegmayer.

1856—5th av, s w cor 139th st, moved to new foundation; cost, $200; lessee, J. Madden, 202 West 142d st; ar't, A. Spence.

1857—8th av, No. 216, one-story extension, 7.8x 25, doors and windows altered; cost, abt $2,500; agent, J. F. Bragg, 713 8th av; ar't, C. H. Richter, Jr.; b'rs, W. Wright's Sons.

1858—163d st, No. 752 E., one-story extension, 21x16.6, new store front; cost, $1,500; S. Cook, on premises; ar't, M. J. Garvin.

1859—Railroad av, e s, 175 n 168th st, raised to grade, two-story and basement extension, 15 and 8x15 and 12; cost, $1,300; Caroline Reuhl, 1244 Railroad av; ar't, A. Pfeiffer.

1860—Railroad av, e s, 188 n 168th st, raised to grade, two-story and basement extension, 18x15, and new front; cost, $1,500; ow'r and ar't, same as last.

1861—Elton av, w s, 125 s 157th st, one-story extension, 25x68.10, interior alterations and walls altered; cost, $3,000; J. M. Haffen, Courtlandt av and 152d st; ar't, A. Pfeiffer.

1862—Broome st, No. 573, roof altered; cost, $1,400; agent, J. Hopkins, 330 West 18th st; c'r, L. Sibley.

1863—11th st, Nos. 311-321 E., two tanks on roof; cost, $500; H. W. Erichs, 153 2d av; m'n, P. H. Murphy.

1864—Jerome av, n w cor St. James pl, four two-story extensions, 23x25, 13x9, 10.1x5 and 18x 26, and interior alterations; cost, $8,000; F. W. Devoe, 59 Park av; ar't, T. E. Thomson.

1865—Melrose av, s e cor 161st st, roof raised and alterations, three-story extension, 21x17, and walls altered; cost, $2,500; M. Hermelin, 652 East 161st st; ar't, C. F. Lohse.

1866—163d st, No. 783 E., one story extension, 12.6x15, and new windows; cost, $1,300; Christina Esch, on premises; ar't, M. J. Garvin.

1867—11th av, n e cor 36th st, new store front; cost, $900; F. McKenna, 211 Nassau st, Brooklyn; b'r, J. L. Lowry.

1868—170th st, n s, 234 e 3d av, rear, four-story extension, 88.7x29.4; cost, $18,000; H. Zeltner, on premises; ar'ts, Lederle & Co.

1869—75th st, No 432 E., two ovens under walk; cost, $1,500; agent, P. Tronsor, 439 5th av; ar't, F. Ebeling.

1870—1st st, No. 47½, new store front; cost, $500; R. Marten, on premises; ar't, F. Ebeling.

1871—8th av, Nos. 629 and 631, interior alterations, new elevator shaft; cost, $5,000; S. Loeb, 32 Nassau st; ar'ts, De Lemos & Cordes.

1872—36th st, No 8 E, one and three-story extension, 9x24, interior alterations, entrance changed, new plumbing and walls altered; cost, $40,000; J. P. Morgan, Jr., 64 West 35th st; ar'ts, Sturgis & Cabot; c'r, J. Y. Mainland.

1873—Broadway, s e cor 47th st, interior alterations and walls altered; cost, $1,200; lessee, P. Cuff, 2119 Madison av; ar't, J. M. Dunn; c'r, P. J. Ryan.

1874—Christopher st and North River, Pier 44, general repairs; cost, $4,000; Oceanic Steam Navigation Co., 29 Broadway; ar't, R. P. Staats.

1875—Hester st, No. 30, walls and roof altered; cost, $300; lessee, M. Bernstein, 39 Hester st; ar't, H. Horenburger.

1876—Cromwell av, w s, 169 s 161st st, rear, one-story extension, 50x16; cost, $150; lessees, Miller & Robinson, 80 West 89th st; ar't, C. C. Churchill.

1877—160th st, No. 509 E., bay window extended one story and new conservatory; cost, $800; J. L. Cavanagh, on premises; ar't, C. C. Churchill.

1878—87th st, No. 177 E., repair damage by fire; cost, $10,000; lessee, T. B. Whiffen, 46 North High st, Mt. Vernon, New York; ar't, F. Wennemer.

1879—Rector st, No. 7, interior alterations and repairs and front wall rebuilt; cost, $7,500; F. Nordsiek, 100 Broadway; ar't, W. B. Tuthill.

1880—Madison av, No. 80, raised two stories and interior alterations for hotel purposes; cost, $100,000; F. T. Robinson, president, on premises; ar'ts, Flag & Benson.

KINGS COUNTY.

Plan 1028—Myrtle av, Nos. 107-111, add one story; cost, $25,000; Mrs. A. E. Darling, New York City; ar'ts, Parfitt Bros.; b'rs, Anderson Bros. and L. W. Seaman, Jr., & Son.

1029—Berriman st, w s, 100 s Eastern Parkway, brick foundation; cost, $120; C. Woods, on premises; m'n, C. C. Baldwin.

1030—Rockaway av, e s, 200 s East New York av, new windows and slight interior alterations; cost, $200; R. Reader, Rockaway av; b'rs, W. Gormly and J. C. Flitche.

1031—Kent av, No 888, flat gravel roof, repair damage by fire; cost, $800; Edward Heston, on premises; ar't, M. J. Morrill; b'r, not selected.

1032—Cumberland st, Nos. 12, 14 and 16, one-story brk extension, 75x20, tin roof; cost, $3,500; C. T. Bainbridge, exr., on premises; ar't, M. Thomas; b'rs, T. Donlon and W. S. Wright.

1033—Moore st, No. 101, add one story of frame, flat tin roof; cost, $500; ow'r and b'r, David Stern, 86 Seigel st; ar't, H. Smith.

1034—Cooper st, s s, 180 w Evergreen av, two-story frame extension, 20x17, tin roof; cost, $300; —— Cordes, on premises; ar't and c'r, J. M. Fraser; m'n, not selected.

1035—Evergreen av, No. 503, one-story frame extension, 9x20, tin roof; cost, $250; Patrick Sarsfield, on premises; b'r, R. Wright.

1036—Evergreen av, No. 397, underpin foundation with stone wall; cost, $50; M. Kapeell, on premises; m'n, G. Walter.

1037—Humboldt st, No 506, one-story frame extension, 22x18, tin roof; cost, $250; Valetine Basel, 326 Maujer st; b'rs, J. King and R. Gallot.

1038—Ann st, n s, 200 w Commercial st, one-story brk extension, 91x46; cost, $3,000; ow'r, ar't and c'r, American Sugar Refining Co., Commercial st; m'ns, Carpenter & Woodruff.

1039—Blake av, s s, 100 w Linwood st, brk foundation under building; cost, $150; Jane Cook, on premises.

1040—Hopkins st, No. 181, raised 11 ft., brk walls, also one-story brk extension, 25x60, tin roof; cost, $1,500; Andrew Wohlgemuth, on premises; ar'ts, D. Acker & Son.

MISCELLANEOUS.

BUSINESS FAILURES.

N. Y. ASSIGNMENTS—BENEFIT CREDITORS.

Oct.

28 Martin, Wilbur F. (dealer in meats and general provisions, at No. 144 West st), to Elwood Donnelly; preferences $3,441.76.

28 Schlichting, Emil and Wolf E. Rendsburg (composing firm of Schlichting & Rendsburg, manufacturers of and dealers in walking canes and umbrellas, (at No. 12 Vesey st), to Abraham Sternberg; preferences $3,000.

PROCEEDINGS OF THE BOARD OF ALDERMEN AFFECTING REAL ESTATE.

APPROVED PAPERS.

Resolutions passed by the Board of Aldermen calling for the following improvements have been signed by the Mayor for the week ending October 24, 1891. *Indicates that the Mayor neither appoved nor objected thereto, therefore the same became adopted.

REGULATING, GRADING, ETC.

German pl, from Westchester av to 156th st.*

FLAGGING AND CURBING.

German pl, from Westchester av to 156th st, and crosswalks laid at intersecting and terminating sts and avs.*

BROOKLYN BOARD OF ALDERMEN.

* Under the different headings indicates that a resolution has been introduced and referred to the appropriate committee. † Indicates that the resolution has passed and has been sent to the Mayor for approval ‡ Passed over the Mayor's veto.

BROOKLYN, Oct. 19, 1891.

CULVERTS.

Hicks st, n e cor Bush st.
Jewell st, s w cor Nassau av.
Moffat st, s w cor Central av
Van Pelt st, n w cor Graham av.
Bedford av, n e cor North 15th st. †
Bedford av, s w cor North 15th st.
Central av, s w cor Harman st.
Flushing av, s w cor Steuben st.
Graham av, n w cor Van Pelt av.
Irving av, n e cor Harman st.

FENCING VACANT LOTS.

De Kalb av, n e cor Clinton av.†

FLAGGING.

Cooper st, s s, bet Broadway and Bushwick avs.
Stockton st, s s, bet Nostrand and Marcy avs. †
Buffalo av, bet Fulton and Herkimer sts.
Greene av, s s, bet Sumner and Lewis avs.

LAMP-POSTS ERECTED AND LIGHTED.

Grove st, bet Bushwick and Central avs.
Noll st, bet Central and Hamburg avs, at owners' expense. †
Schaeffer st, bet Broadway and Evergreen av.
Greene av, bet Bushwick and Evergreen avs.

ELECTRIC LIGHTING.

Powers st, s w cor Lorimer st.
Myrtle av, No. 684, opposite. †
St. Marks av, n e cor Grand av.

PAVING.

McDonough st, 100 feet w of Hopkinson av, at owners' expense.
Prospect pl, bet Schenectady and Utica avs. †
North 12th st, bet Berry st and Bedford av.
Saratoga av, bet Atlantic av and Herkimer st, one-half block at owners' expense.

REGULATING, GRADING, ETC.

McDonough st, 100 ft. w of Hopkinson av, at owners' expense.
Prospect pl, bet Schenectady and Utica avs.
North 12th st, bet Berry st and Bedford av. †
39th st, bet 4th and 5th avs.
Saratoga av, bet Atlantic av and Herkimer st, one-half block, at owners' expense.

STREET CLOSING.

Glen st, bet Railroad av and Enfield st †
Magenta st, bet Railroad av and Enfield st.

STREET OPENING.

Prospect pl, bet Schenectady and Utica avs.†

SEWERS.

Dean st, bet Utica and Rochester av, at owners' expense. †
Pacific st, bet Utica and Rochester avs, at owners' expense.

ADVERTISED LEGAL SALES.

REFEREES SALES TO BE HELD AT THE REAL ESTATE EXCHANGE AND AUCTION ROOM (LIMITED), 59 TO 65 LIBERTY STREET, EXCEPT WHERE OTHERWISE STATED.

Nov.

119th st, No. 7, n s, 95.5 w 5th av, 14x57.9x14.6x53.11, three-story brk dwell'g, by D. L. Kennelly. (Amt due $1,732) ... 2

123d st, Nos. 401 and 403, n w cor Columbus av, 57.10x94, two five-story brk and stone flats, stores in No. 401 ...
Columbus (9th) av, Nos. 1286 and 1288, s w cor 124th st, 53.10x100, two five-story brk and stone flats, store in No. 1288 ...
by William Kennelly. (Amt due $44,177; prior morts. $——) ... 4

Madison av, s w cor 118th st, 60x100, one-story frame shanties, by J. N. Golding. (Amt due $16,970) ... 4

Park av, Nos. 565, 567 and 569, e s, 75.3 s 63d st, 66.5x100.1x60x100, five-story brk flat, Lonsdale, by William Kennelly. (Amt due $10,967; prior morts. $90,000) ... 4

22d st, No. 157, n s, 165.7 e 7th av, 21.10x98.9, three-story brk tenem't, by P. A. Smyth. (Amt due $15,550) ... 4

131st st, No. 18, s s, 265 w 5th av, 15x84.11 ...
131st st, No. 22, s s, 295 w 5th av, 15x84.11 ...
Two three-story stone front dwell'gs ...
by R. V. Harnett & Co. (Amt due on No. 18 $1,978, $1,941 on No. 22; prior morts. $17,000) ... 4

100th st, Nos. 155-169, n s, 95 e Lexington av, 200x100.11, eight five-story brk flats ...
101st st, Nos. 154-168, s s, 95 e Lexington av, 200x100.11, eight five-story brk flats ...
by D. P. Ingraham & Co. (Amt due on each $26,808) ... 4

83d st, s s, 150 e 11th av, 100x100.5, vacant, by P. F. Meyer. (Amt due $12,658) ... 5

78th st, s s, 225 w 10th av, 50x100, vacant, by R. V. Harnett & Co. (Partition sale) ... 5

96th st, No. 54, s s, 240 e 9th av, 20x100.8 ...
96th st, No. 52, s s, 260 e 9th av, 20x100.8 ...
96th st, No. 50, s s, 280 e 9th av, 20x100.8 ...
Three four-story brk dwell'gs ...
by R. V. Harnett & Co. ... 5

103d st, No. 206, s s, 118 w Amsterdam av, 20x76 to Clendenning lane, x20x77.2, five-story brk flat ...
103d st, No. 208, s s, 138 w Amsterdam av, 20x75 to Clendenning lane, x20x76, five-story brk flat ...
103d st, No. 210, s s, 158 w Amsterdam av, 20x74 to Clendenning lane, x20x75, five-story brk flat
103d st, No. 212, s s, 178 w Amsterdam av, 20x73 to Clendenning lane, x20x74, five-story brk flat ...
by William Kennelly. (Amt due $17,686 on each) ... 5

152d st, n s, 850 w Courtlandt av, 50x100, by William Kennelly. (Amt due $2,520) ... 5

Av C, No. 80, e s, 48.6 s 6th st, 72.9x92.3, brk and stone church, by D. P. Ingraham & Co. (Amt due $20,579) ... 5

Amsterdam (10th) av / Hamilton pl — begins Amsterdam av, s w cor 142d st, 24.11x149.7 to Hamilton pl, 27.1 to 142d st, x139, vacant, by R. V. Harnett & Co. (Amt due $7,874) ... 5

7th av, No. 2271, e s, 49.11 s 134th st, runs east 75 x south 22.4 x southwest 4.5 x west 71.5 to 7th av, x north 25 to beginning, five-story brk store and flat, by P. F. Meyer. (Amt due $21,146) ... 5

7th av, No. 2273, e s, 24.11 s 134th st, 25x75, five-story brk flat with stores, by P. F. Meyer. (Amt due $21,146) ... 5

102d st, No. 155, s s, 325 w 3d av, 15x100.11, four-story stone front dwell'g, by R. V. Harnett & Co. (Amt due $8,569) ... 6

Boulevard, e s, 24.11 n 139th st, 75x100, vacant, by D. P. Ingraham & Co. (Amt due $31,451) ... 9

Private lane which would be 162d st if continued, n s, 122.3 n w 3d av, runs northeast 123.8 x southeast 27.9 x southwest 128.8 x to lane, x northwest 27.9 to beginning, by R. V. Harnett & Co. (Amt due $7.933) ... 9

KINGS COUNTY.

Nov.

Atlantic av, Nos. 870-874, s s, 340 w Underhill av, 60x100, two four-story double brk flats; assessed value, $14,000 ...
Willoughby av, n w cor Tompkins av, runs north 77.6 x west 80 x north 22.6 x west 45 x south 100 to Willoughby av, x east 125 to beginning, Reformed Presbyterian Church ...
by T. A. Kerrigan, at 13 Willoughby st ... 2

South 9th st, Nos. 167 and 169, n e cor Driggs st, 50x78x50x76, two three-story brk dwell'gs, corner with store; assessed value, $16,000; partition; by W. Cole, at 7 and 8 Court sq ... 2

Gold st, No. 334, w s, 100 n Myrtle av, 25x100.8, three-story brk dwell'g; assessed value, $3,900.
Montgomery st, No. 83, n s, 322.11 e 8th av, 20x88.5x20.0¼x81, three-story brk dwell'g; assessed value, $8,000; error ...
Montgomery st, No. 83, n s, 322 e 8th av, 20x88.5x20.0¼x81, three-story brk dwell'g; assessed value, $8,000 ...
Pacific st, s s, 363.10 e Rochester av, 16.9x107.2⅝, two-and-a-half-story frame dwell'g; assessed value, $1,400 ...
Pacific st, s s, 380.7 e Rochester av, 16.8x107.2⅝, two-and-a-half-story frame dwell'g; assessed value, $1,400 ...
Union st, Nos. 649 and 653, n s, 100 w 4th av, 50x95, two five-story brk tenem'ts; assessed value, $7,000 each ...
Evergreen av, Nos. 682 and 684, s w cor Eldert st, 36x75x39.11½x75, two three-story frame tenements and stores; assessed value, $6,300 ...
Lafayette av, No. 868, s s, 202.6 w Lewis av, 2 x 100, two-story and basement brk dwell'g; assessed value, $4,500 ...
by T. A. Kerrigan, at 13 Willoughby st ... 4

Plymouth st, No. 321, n s, 200.1 e Hudson av, 29.2½x100, four-story brk dwell'g; assessed value, $8,000 ...
South Oxford st, No. 62, w s, 123 n Lafayette av, 22x100, three-story brk dwell'g; assessed value, $11,000 ...
Lexington av, n s, 120 e Lewis av, 20x100 ...
by T. A. Kerrigan, at 13 Willoughby st ... 5

Dupont st, No. 146, s s, 275 e Manhattan av, 25x100, two-story frame (brk lined) dwell'g; assessed value, $1,200 ...
India st, No. 116, s s, 225 w Manhattan av, 25x100, two-story and extension frame dwell'g; assessed value, $1,800 ...
India st, No. 107, n s, 325 w Manhattan av, 25x100, two-story brk dwell'g; assessed value, $3,800; partition ...
by Jacob New, ref., at 142 Franklin st ... 5

Hicks st, No. 474, w s, 366.6 n Degraw st, 19.6x97.6, four-story brk tenem't and store; assessed value, $4,000; by W. Cole, at 7 and 8 Court sq ... 5

Dean st, No. 1598, s s, 100 e Utica av, 20x107.5, two-story frame dwell'g; assessed value, $1,200 ...
Dean st, No. 1600, s s, 120 e Utica av, 20x107.5, two-story frame dwell'g; assessed value, $1,200 ...
by T. A. Kerrigan, at 45 Broadway, E. D. ... 6

Halsey st, No. 41, n s, 410 e Bedford av, 20x100, three-story brk dwell'g; assessed value, $6,500.
Pacific st, s s, 380.7 e Rochester av, 16.8x107.2⅝, two-and-a-half-story frame dwell'g; assessed value, $1,400 ...
3d st, Nos. 160-166, s s, 372.9 e Bond st, 96.9x154.9 to Gowanus Canal, x 103.0¾x175.9, coal yard; assessed value, $14,000; re-sale ...
Putnam av, Nos. 824, s s, 236.6 e Reid av, 39x100, two-and-a-half-story brk dwell'g; assessed value, $5,000 ...
Putnam av, No. 632, s s, 314.0 e Reid av, 19.6x100, two-and-a-half-story brk dwell'g; assessed value, $5,000 ...
by T. A. Kerrigan, at 13 Willoughby st ... 9

LIS PENDENS, KINGS COUNTY.

Oct.

Baltic st, s s, 92.10 w 4th av, 15x100. Robert Shaw agt Brewster Conklin; att'y, Albert Smith ... 22

Saratoga av, s e cor Decatur st, 100x115.6. The Central Gas and Electric Fixture Co. agt William H. Good; action to set aside deed; att'ys, Birdseye, Cloyd & Bayliss ... 22

Bainbridge st, n s, 41.6 e Saratoga av, 18.6x100 ...
Bainbridge st, n s, 23 e Saratoga av, 18.6x100 ...
Bainbridge st, n e cor Saratoga av, 23x100 ...
Same agt Kate S. Good; action to set aside deeds; same att'ys ... 22

Lots 252 and 253 map Bellepiain, adj East New York. George H. Walker, Jr., agt Sarah Devoe; att'y, A. Burr Chalmers ... 23

Bergen st, s s, 520 e Franklin av, 30x128.6. Phebe M. Saxton agt Jennie E. S. Miller; att'ys, Strong & Spear ... 23

Carroll st, n s, 55 e Van Brunt st, 20x70. Fulton Co-operative Building and Loan Assoc. agt Conrad R. Pedersen; att'ys, Klein & Rendich ... 23

East New York av, n s, 483.6 e Washington av 60x205 to Lefferts av, Flatbush. Grace B. Berg agt Marie T. Hooper; att'y, John A. Taylor ... 23

6th av, south cor 7th st, 20x75.1. John R. Planten agt Lizzie L. Knapp; att'ys, Stitt & Phillips ... 23

Gates av, s s, 125 e Bedford av, 100x100. Thomas De Witt agt William A. De Witt; att'y, John T. Lockman ... 23

Lots 504 and 505 map Gilbert S. Thatford, East New York. Samuel Simonson agt Isaac Glaser; action for specific performance; att'y, H. J. Morris ... 23

Gunther pl, w s, 150.4 n Atlantic av, 17.8x95 ...
Gunther pl, w s, 133.1 n Atlantic av, 17.8x95 ...
Gunther pl, w s, 115.10 n Atlantic av, 17.8x95 ...
Gunther pl, w s, 98.7 n Atlantic av, 17.8x95 ...
John Petrie agt Oscar H. Doolittle; att'y, Adolph Vaurein ... 23

Ocean pl, e s, 98.7 n Atlantic av, 17.8x95. Same agt same; same att'y ... 23

Ocean pl, e s, 115.10 n Atlantic av, 17.8x95. Daniel B. Stearns agt Oscar H. Doolittle; att'y, Adolph Vanrein ... 23

Coney Island Bridge Co.'s Turnpike road, e s, adj land Maria Lott, 2 1-10 acres, Coney Island.
Lot at Guisbert's or Johnson's Island, near sea shore, adj Court Van Sicklen, Gravesend ...
John A. Planten agt Joseph Beno; att'y, Arthur Hurst ... 23

St. Marks av, s s, 60 w Carlton av, 20x81. John Donovan agt Mary A. Wheeler; att'y, James F. Swanton ... 24

Macon st, s s, 199 w Hopkinson av, 18.6x100. Edmund Blunt agt John G. Porter; action for accounting; att'ys, Amundson & Ward ... 26

North 2d st, n s, 100.10 e Union av, 49.4x68.6x49x62.8. Agnes E. Smith agt Albert R. Smith; action to recover dower; att'y, R. M. Johnston ... 26

Greene av, n s, extends from Clinton av to Waverly av, 200x118.8. Charles T. Willis agt Brooklyn Tabernacle and Russell Sage; foreclos. mechanic's lien; att'y, Abner C. Thomas ... 26

Atlantic av, n s, 281.10 w Utica av, 16.0x99.1. William L. Savage and ano. trustees for Henrietta C. Barclay agt Thomas S. Denike, atty's, S. F., F. H. & H. Cowdrey ... 26

16th st, n s, 211.9 w 8th av, 40x100. Hans S. Christian agt Matthew Ryan; foreclos. mechanic's lien; att'y, George V. Brower ... 26

Brooklyn and Jamaica turnpike, n w cor Barbey st, 44.5x112.9x45x112.7. Kate Foster agt Adiah W. Drake; att'y, J. B. Sabine ... 27

Spencer pl, s e cor Hancock st, 22x100. John H. Rhoades et al. exrs. Benjamin F. Wheelwright agt Charles M. Carpenter; att'ys, Owen, Gray & Sturges ... 27

McDonough st, n s, 22.6 w Ralph av, 18.8x100. Emeline E. Brower agt Kate S. Good; att'y, William T. Gilbert ... 27

All franchises, lines of road, properties, &c., of defendants. Henry D. Donnelly and John Englis agt The Brooklyn, Bushwick & Queens Co. R. R.; att'y, John A. Holzapfel ... 27

Jay st continued, w s, 291.10 s Concord st, runs south 25 x west 103.6 x 26.9 x 103.5 ...
Interior lot, 289.7 s Concord st and 82 e Pearl st, runs east 21.5 x south 22 x west 21.5 x north 22, with rights of way ...
Hannah M. Warbasse agt Susan C. Lee; partition; att'y, I. N. Stewright ... 27

Eastern Parkway, s s, 75 w Thatford av, 25x100. Abraham Roth agt Solomon Kreckenstein; action for specific performance; att'y, John T. Lindsay ... 27

Hendrix st, w s, 64 s Arlington av, 38x100. Ellen Kennedy agt Kate Kennedy; action to establish lien; att'y, Henry L. Brant ... 28

Alabama av, w s, 225 n Liberty av, 16.8x100. Edward Windel agt Rosa Windel; partition; att'y, August P. Wagner ... 28

95th st, lots 54-14 map Henry Lehmann, Canarsie, 275x90 to Brooklyn & Rockaway Beach Railroad. Jacob Nagel agt Frederick Finn; partition; att'y, John T. Barnard ... 28

2d st, n e s, 90.9 n w 7th av, 20x100 ...
Schermerhorn st, n s, 150 w 3d av, 150x100.9 ...
Bernard Berman agt Roderick Vongraff; notice of attachment; att'y, Geo. C. Comstock ... 29

4th st, s s, 171.10 e 6th av, 21⅞x100. Sarah H. Powell agt Charles H. Moses; att'y, Wilson M. Powell ... 29

6th av, e s, 39.8 s Carroll st, runs east 89.6 x south 5.2 x south 13.10 x west 90 to av, x north 19. John P. McDonald agt Frank C. Willcox; att'y, Albert G. McDonald ... 29

Atlantic av, n s, 275 e Bond st, 25x100. Catharine L. Gilfillan agt Teresa Ennis; att'y, Stephen Condit ... 29

East 21st st, w s, 129 s Voorhis av, 24.6x95, Gravesend. Horace B. Allen agt Henry Grauel; action for specific performance; att'ys, Treadwell & Catlin ... 29

Marion st, s s, 50 w Rockaway av, runs south 71.6 x southwest 71.6 to Old Jamaica plank road, x northwest 125 x northeast 35.5 x north 35.5 to st, x east 125. Spencer Aldrich agt Thomas H. Robbins; att'y, Spencer Aldrich, in person ... 29

RECORDED LEASES.

NEW YORK. Per Year

Broadway, No. 594 / Crosby st, No. 124 — first floor, basement and sub-basement. Sarah Beadel extrx. Henry Beadel to Martin and Joseph Freeman; 3 years, from Feb. 1, 1889. $5,750

Same property. Same to same; 3 years, from July 27, 1891 ... 5,750

Broadway, No. 240, store. George G. Block to David J. Benoliel; 4½ years, from Nov. 1, 1891 ... 600

Broad st, No. 59, store floor. Benjamin A., John B., William A., Jennie G. and Kate Aycrigg and Annie Fuller heirs Benjamin B. Aycrigg to John P. Friedhoff and Henry C. Meyer; 4 7-12 years, from Oct. 1, 1891 ... 2,500

Canal st, No. 40 / Division st, No. 148 — all. Samuel Rouse to Max Kobre; 3 years, from May 1, 1892 ... 2,100

Canal st, No. 26, store or ground floor. Elias Dubin to Adolph Falck individ and on behalf of Falck & Co; 4½ years, from Nov. 1, 1891. 1,560

Dey st, No. 20. Anna B. Dodd and Wm. L. Clark exrs. Elizabeth A. Blake to Charles L. Vath; 5 years, from May 1, 1892 ... 3,500

Maiden lane, Nos. 96 and 98, fifth and sixth floors rear building. Christian Jourgensen to Armeny and William C. Marion and Gyulo Armeny; 10 years, from Jan. 1, 1891 ... 960

Mott st, No. 17, two stores and basements. John P. White to Yee So; 9 years 8½ months, from Aug. 15, 1890 ... 2,750

Same property. Assign. lease. Yee So to Lee Yong Ling ... nom

Stanton st, No. 302, n w cor Lewis st, all. Daniel W. Gallagher individ. and The New York Life Ins. and Trust Co. guard. of children of Francis Gallagher to Caroline Duempelmann widow; 5 years, from May 1, 1889 ... 1,000, 1,100, 1,200

West st, No. 126, all. William Buck, Hoboken, N. J., to David Stevenson; 3½ years and 8 days, from Oct. 23, 1891 ... 3,000

13th st, No. 434 E., store and part cellar. Henry and Dorothea Von Haten to Vincenzo Poppiti; 3½ years, from Nov. 1, 1891 ... 1,280

26th st, No. 160 W., first floor, loft and cellar.
26th st, No. 158 W., cellar ...
Joseph I. West to William P. Ross; 4 10-12 years, from July 1, 1890 ... 1,200

27th st, No. 184, s w cor Broadway, all. George F. Gminder to Reinhard Busse; 6 years, from May 1, 1892 ... 8,000

28th st, No 50 W., bet Broadway and 6th av, all. Ascher Weinstein to Ernest and Sophie May; 10 years, from Oct. 1, 1891 3,500, 3,750, 4,000

37th st, No. 25 E., all. Margaret B. Crane extrx. Theodore Crane to Frederick B. Wendt; 7 years, from May 1, 1889 ... 3,250

49th st, No. 124 W., store and cellar and second floor. Thomas J. McLaughlin and Lewis Z. Bach to Dieterich Bruns; 5 years, from Nov. 1, 1891 ... 1,020

57th st, No. 163 W. William T. Lawrence and William A. Reise exrs. Peter Suydam to Josephine D. Taylor; 1 year, from Oct. 15, 1891 ... 2,000

73d st, No 428 E., west store floor. Caroline Larschen to Adolph Chervat; 3 years, with privilege of 2 years, from Oct. 8, 1891 ... 420

75th st, No. 324 E., all. Daniel Reynolds to Thomas Connors; 3 years, from Nov. 1, 1891. 360

102d st, No. 218 E., east store. Henry F. Bruntemann to Charles Evans; 5 years, from May 1, 1891 ... 240

Same property. Assign. lease. Charles Evans to The Burr Brewing Co ... 600

Same property. Assign. lease. Bavarian Brewing Co. formerly Burr Brewing Co. to Thomas Cashman ... nom

Vanderbilt av, n e cor 167th st, 54x69. Lorenz Gruneihoefer to Edward Frey; 5 years, from Oct 1, 1891 ... 1,200

West End av, No. 249. Mary E. Walker to F. H. Ryder; 3 years, from Oct. 15, 1891 ... 1,200

1st av, No. 1601, store floor and cellar. Joseph Seiferd to Lizzie Murphy; 5 years, from May 1, 1893 ... 1,300, 1,400

1st av, No. 1100, n e cor 60th st. store floor and cellar. Max Danziger and Newman Cowen to Patrick Frazier; 2 7-12 years, from Oct. 1, 1891 900

3d av, No. 2011. store cellar and backyard. Charles Heylman att'y for Harriet A. Heylman to Jennie Pachetean; 4 1-12 years, from April 1, 1891.......... 909

3d av, No. 571, store and first floor. Lewis G. Reed to David J. Turner and John P. McElroy; 4½ years, from Nov. 1. 1891.......... 1,080

3d av, No. 1881, store and part cellar. Richard H. L. Townsend to John Dawson; 5 1-12 years, from April 1, 1891.......... 1,200

5th av, No. 79. Bergmann Mfg. Co. to The Bergmann Gas and Electric Fixture Co.; 7 years 5 months and 29 days, from Nov. 1, 1891.......... 6,000

10th av, No. 385, store and basement. Honora Fox to Margaret McKallen; 5 years and 15 days, from Oct. 15, 1891.......... 540

CHATTELS.

NOTE.—*The first name, alphabetically arranged, is that of the Mortgagor, or party who gives the Mortgage. The "R" means Renewal Mortgage.*

NEW YORK CITY.

OCTOBER 23 TO 29.—INCLUSIVE.

SALOON AND RESTAURANT FIXTURES.

Adamko, S. 525 E 6th....Bernheimer & S. Saloon Pump. $113

Alexander, R. 63 E 4th....Wagner & S. Pool Table. (R) 35

Augenmeyer, G W. 220 St Nicholas av....Consumers' B Co. 1,500

Barns, Ida M. 3048 3d av....S Brumberg. Restaurant Fixtures. 125

Brotherton, G C. 2318 8th av....Rosenbaum Bros 4,000

Beckh, Gustav. 170th st and Vanderbilt av....L Grundhoefer. 700

Beisler, J T. 424 E 10th....Bavarian B Co. 600

Brettschneider, Robert. 2248 2d av....Wagner & S. Pool Table 140

Bock, George. 301 E 81st....Schmitt & S. 1,000

Costello, Timothy. 139½ W 25th....P Cassidy. 300

Cuzze, Joseph. 322 E 104th ...Bernheimer & S. Saloon Ice House. 170

Casbin, Patrick. 881 7th av ...H Elias B Co. 2,500

Cavagnaro & Sardella. 43 Baxter ....Bernheimer & S. 500

Connolly, Geo. 184th st and Amsterdam av....Bernheimer & S. 500

Cummusky, Patrick. 100 E 109th....J Everard. 1,025

Cashman, Thos. 218 E 102d....Bernheimer & S. 400

Conker, John 449 W 46th....T C Lyman & Co. (R) 862

Dunker, Hermann. 1697 1st av... Bernheimer & S. 2,300

Day, Nathaniel. 7 Greenwich av... Wagner & S. Pool Table. 185

Donleavy, Luke. 442 W 39th....D Stevenson. 600

Drescher, William. 107 Greenwich....D Stevenson 550

Same. 196 West....same. 1,800

Dunker, Henry. 270 W 129th....J Moore. 500

Same....J Kress B Co 1,000

Dieterlein, Fred. 1548 Av A....Schmitt & S. 740

Faussner, Jos. 217 Lewis....J Doelger's Son. (R) 300

Finnegan, John. 428 E 17th....F Munch. (R) 400

Flanagan, Michael. 127 W 33d .. D Mayer. (R) 732

Flynn, A J. 339 E 23d....Knickerbocker B Co. 1,000

Frey, Edward. 167th st and Vanderbilt av....L Grundhoefer. 3,000

Friedrich, John. 2003 2d av ...Bernheimer & S. Saloon Ice Box. 110

Same .. same. Saloon Ice Box. 95

Same .. same. Saloon Pump. 76

Glendon, Thos. 473 Willis av. ..Bernheimer & S. 800

Graham, William. 185 Christopher. ..Beadleston & W. 2,500

Same . P D O'Halloran. 1,500

Grucci, Felice. 383 Broome....W Craft. 115

Grassing, C H. 628 E 13th....P Weidmann. 500

Griebel, Julius. 683 E 17th ...F Ibert. 710

Grande, Nicola. 501 Broome... Bernheimer & S. Saloon Ice House. 75

Hochmeister, Julius. 102d st and 9th av . .Bernheimer & S. Saloon Pump. 65

Same....same. Saloon Ice House. 130

Hoynes, J H. 35 Madison... Beadleston & W. (R) 1,500

Hoecker, Frederick. 72 8th av. ..P & W Ebling B Co. (R) 1,200

Humphrey, R J. 1815 Park av....Wagner & S. Pool Table. 375

Junker, J C. 170 3d av....J Eichler B Co. 1,000

Karliner & Greenberg. 28 Clinton....Wagner & S. Pool Table. 210

Kelly, D J. 307 Spring .. C Stein. 1,400

Same J H Murphy. 300

Kramm, Henry. 832 E 53d....J Doelger's Sons. 800

Kaul, William. 101 Clinton pl....E Welte. Billiard Saloon 1,100

Keating & Syrnes. 507 3d av... J C G Hupfel B Co. 6,000

Lang, Lorenz. 401 East Houston....W Ulmer. 1,100

Lawler, J F. 2309 3d av....Restaurant Furn Co. Restaurant Fixtures. 117

Lamensdorf, Jacob. 170 Orchard....Williamsburgh B Co. (R) 1,000

Lawlor, M J. 861 10th av....M C Carley. 6,000

Ligon, Julius. 1236 2d av....B Cohn. 200

Matthies, William. 449 3d av....B T Kearns. 13,000

McCrorken, James. 326 1st av....Burr B Co. (R) 1,800

McCabe, T F. 361 1st av....G Bechtel exr of. 3,000

Morrissey, David. 1154 3d av ...G Ehret. (R) 500

Murray, T J. 112th st and 2d av ...H Vogel. 1,800

Murphy, Lizzie. 1601 1st av....Bernheimer & S. 2,500

McKenna, James. 52 Spring. J C G Hupfel B Co. 2,000

Mullen, John. 790 7th av....D P Grennon exr of. (R) 3,000

Nebel, Isidor. 430 W 40th....J Ahles B Co. 400

Nikensker, Konstantina. 197 2d....S Reitman. Restaurant Fixtures. 125

Novak, Imre. 233 2d ...Schmitt & S. 450

O'Halloran, P D. 185 Christopher....W Graham. 5,500

Ortlieb, Christian. 1093 1st av....H Elias B Co. (R) 400

Ozab, Joseph. 155th st and Courtlandt av....P & W Ebling B Co. (R) 284

Oberndorf, Gustave. 211 E 81st....G Ringler & Co. (R) 250

Poppite, Vincenzo. 434 E 13th....Beadleston & W. 600

Prince, Solomon. 119 Chrystie... H Steinhardt. 1,500

Proebsel, Phillip. 303 E 92d st and 1758 2d av....G Ehret. (R) 1,200

Plangermann, Adolph. 219 Willis av... Bernheimer & S. 3,500

Polak, Samuel. 686 Tremont av....Wagner & S. Pool Table. 165

Pearson, Sorelle. 26th st and 9th av....H Kochler & Co. 400

Rossuagol, A C H. 5 Water and 10 and 12 Moore. G Ringler Co. (R) 1,190

Reilly, Hugh. 1578 Broadway....B Hertzog. 500

Schneider, Friedrich. 1448 1st av... F Hower B Co. 500

Schueler, Casper. 183 Chrystie....J Hoffmann B Co. 550

Smith, J H. 34 Bond....Anchor B Co. (R) 1,000

Same....same. Beer Pump. 75

Spencer, William. 1792 3d av....D Stevenson. 740

Stiller, Jacob. 231 Broome....H B Scharmann & Son. 200

Skudma, August. 1121 1st av....H Steinhardt. 750

Stranczen, Stephen. 249 2d ...H Koehler & Co. 350

Sylvester & Wahmann. 250 6th av....Haaren & Meinken. 18,500

Shannon, James. 649 2d av....J Kress B Co. 500

Toman, Edward. 241 Av A....D Mayer. 2,000

Teichman & Jaeger. 527 5th av....J Ruppert. (R) 500

Traynor, Patrick. 1100 1st av....Bernheimer & S. 2,350

Von der Heider, Chas. 412 W 36th....F Oppermann, Jr. 500

Walsh & McKnight. 117 4th av....J Kress B Co. 120

Wezel, Magdalena. 9 1st....Anchor B Co. (R) 600

Wicbji, Fred. 414 Pearl ...M Eckstein B Co. (R) 1,500

Winter & Gloistein. 76 Grand....Beadleston & W (R) 5,000

Wessel, Louis. 23 Wooster. ..W Ulmer. 1,000

Wissmann, Jacob. 229 E 43d....P Doelger. 550

Wunderlich, Herman. 27 Hudson....G Ehret. 2,000

Same. 66 West Broadway ...same. 1,500

Zimmermann, Josephine. 190 E 3d....F Ibert. 500

HOUSEHOLD FURNITURE.

Allen, Katie. 241 E 104th....J J Coogan. 100

Anderson, H J. 219 E 19th... J R Keane & Co. 910

Abraham, Adelaide. 1477 Lexington av....S Baumann. 243

Adams, Hattie. 38 E 27th....Jordan & M. 500

Ahern, Theresa. 129 E 90th....S Baumann. 165

Althaus, Sadie. 223 E 74th....S Baumann. 300

Argyro, P C. 242 W 43d . T Kelly. 186

Arndistein, Moser. 336 E 86th....H Thoesen. 176

Ahern, H P. 248 E 119th ...H Thoesen. 229

Arnold, Maud. 114 3d av....S I Herschmann. (R) 295

Arras, William. 301 W 59th ...R M Walters. Piano. 335

Arteago, Jose. 228 E 75th....S I Herschmann. (R) 113

Bacon, G H. 2100 West Boulevard....J G Patton & Co. 189

Bennett, Mamie. 319 W 36th .. O'Farrell & Co. 218

Boyle, Julia. 219 E 32d ...Manges Bros. 138

Brown, E E. 346 W 36th....O'Farrell & Co. 188

Brown, J A. 1799 Lexington av....J G Patton & Co. 104

Buchanan, Geo. Hunters Point....McClain, S & Co. 116

Budict, Fred. 418 E 85th....O'Farrell & Co. 811

Bobrick, Mary E. 112 W 70th....G A Scott. 1,500

Baxter, Flora. 2038 7th av....W Ladew. secures rent

Becker, Carl. 404 E 82d....S Baumann. 145

Beck, Mary. 533 E 15th....Jordan & M. 104

Blackburn, Maude. 142 W 53d... D Schwarzkopf. 527

Blake, H P. 146 E 128th....Fennell & P. 127

Bond, Frederic. 100 W 73d ...S Baumann. 650

Buhler, Louise. 228 E 122d....Fennell & P. 108

Baker, Geraldine. 260 W 43d....L Baumann. 156

Bannister, Lillie. 2367 2d av....J Baumann. 194

Barnes, Frederick. 412 E 115th ....Fennell & P. 104

Bennett, Katie. 235 W 125th . L Baumann. 150

Beneley, Frederick. 252 W 128th. .L Baumann. 170

Beny, William. 225 W 43d....L Baumann. 125

Bewley, Thomas. 307 and 309 W 22d... O'Farrell & Co.. 216

Bierstadt, Helen. 133 W 64th....Fennell & P. 228

Blake, John. 507 Grand....D M Brown. 122

Bliss, Grace. 200 W 85th....L Baumann. 176

Boerum, Mary H. 147 W 41st....J Moriarty. 230

Boese, Chris. 510 Manhattan av....Dreisacker & Co. 200

Braun, Delia. 301 E 102d....S Baumann. 164

Brooks, Lillie. 229 W 40th....O'Farrell & Co. (R) 164

Brunner, Harry. 310 E 126th....J J Coogan. (R) 139

Butlers, Carrie G. 310 W 129th ....L Baumann. 173

Clark, Victoria. 267 W 40th....L Baumann. 133

Cohen, Bernard. 317 E 116th....D Schwarzkopf. 280

Cohn, B. 317 E 116th....Fennell & Co. 275

Cretien, Louisa. 106 Clinton pl....H S Eisler. 407

Crimmins, Mary. 1011 Park av....Fennell & Co. 119

Cutugno, Madaline. 110 W 16th....O'Farrell & Co. 115

Cestero, Julia. 5th av and 36th st .. J & J Dobson. Carpets. 202

Churchill, E S. 363 5th av ...F T Higgins. 317

Cormeier, J E. 324 West....H S Eisler. 166

Creed, G D, Mrs. 174 3d av....H S Eisler. 276

Campbell, Mary. 183 7th ...Jordan & M. 195

Carlton & Golden. 221 W 40th....J Baumann. (R) 542

Cherry, W A and L B. 175 Lexington av....L H Finlay. 200

Clarke, Lulu. 228 W 37th....T Kelly. 275

Clarke, Maud E. 101 E 123d....J Baumann. 221

Corbett, Mrs James. 226 W 37th ..T Kelly. 254

Crager, Annie. 440 E 118th ...Krakauer Bros. Piano. 295

Creagh, J A. 112 E 84th. ..S Baumann. 271

Cranston, Rose. 1968 7th av... Jordan & M. 242

Caldwell, A E. 140 W 16th....McClain, S & Co. 184

Campbell, E. 891 Caldwell av....J G Patton & Co. 128

Cantrell, Mrs L. 310 W 36th....O'Farrell & Co. 260

Carbonell, Emilie L. 400 W 57th. . E C Hinsdale. 250

Carpenter, Maggie. 759 Greenwich....H Thoesen. 214

Church, Alice. 152 E 98th....O'Farrell & Co. 172

Clark, Francis. 77 Bedford....Manges Bros. 146

Clark, Mary. 400 W 35th....O'Farrell & Co. 305

Oliver, Chas. 220 E 36th....L Baumann. 201

Cody, Thos. 547 E 16th ...L Baumann. 126

Conway, Bridget. 130 9th av....L Baumann. 118

Conyers, Mary A. 155 W 53d....S I Herschmann. (R) 334

Coote, C W. 68 W 93d....L Baumann. 314

Cortada, P M. 80 E 116th... J G Patton & Co. 104

Corington, T H. 1546 Broadway....O'Farrell & Co. 831

Croom, William. 600 E 143d....J G Patton & Co. 112

Cummings, Eva. 208 W 25th....O'Farrell & Co. 705

Davis, F E. 208 E 127th....J G Patton & Co. 119

Demers, Kate 238 E 6th....Manges Bros. 179

Dunham, Sarah. 153 W 44th....O'Farrell & Co. 131

Daubman, G J. 2285 1st av....Fennell & Pye. (R) 148

Dick, Francis. 1731 9th av....J Baumann. (R) 168

Driscoll, Annie. 256 W 38th....J Baumann. (R) 134

Drysdale, Effie C. 406 W 58th....S Baumann. 154

Daly, Margaret. 181 E 84th....J R Keane & Co. 594

De Freest, Mrs V. 262 Spring....D M Brown. 119

Dittmar, Louisa. 423 3d av....Carey & Sides. 126

Driscoll, Annie. 256 W 38th... J Baumann. (R) 134

Duffy, Jas. 653 Elton av....Dreisacker & Co. 165

Dunham, Sarah. 200 E 115th....L Baumann. 125

Dunstrup, Henry. 11 State .W Weed. 130

Enoch, John. 131 W 25th....F T Biggins. (R) 125

Ethel, Gertrude. 214 W 46th... J Gregg & Co. 258

Fauth, J J. 214 Willis av....Fennell & Co. 111

Feichman, Jennie. 527 5th av....J Baumann. (R) 127

Fitzgerald, Annie. 234 W 124th ...L Baumann. 106

Fitzgerald, Delia. 134 E 123d....Fennell & P. 193

Foster, Victorine. 61 and 63 W 92d....J Baumann. 140

Frankel, Samuel. 227 E 121st....Fennell & Co. 125

Frieary, Mary A. 227 E 47th....J Baumann. 254

Fried, Sam. 346 East Houston....L Wolf. 308

Fenn, A R. 227 W 19th....J Gregg & Co. 183

Friedlander, Theresa. 14 E 73d....J Baumann. (R) 287

Fricke, Fred. 54 1st av....J Moriarty. 139

Friedheim, Arthur. 852 Lexington av....J & J Dobson. Carpets. 308

Furey, Mary. 539 W 44th ...J Moriarty. 180

Faulkner, Mary. 164 E 68th....J Moriarty. 175

Farrell, Mary. 528 W 46th....O'Farrell & Co. 172

Feldman, B M. 170 E 79th . .I B Cassel. 1,000

Same....J Feldman. 2,000

Fennessy, Emma H. 438 W 57th....McClain, S & Co. 148

Fitch, Florence. 150 W 18th ...L Baumann. 266

Fitch, Mary L. 67 W 11th....Manges Bros. 282

Freeland, Anna. 71 E 123d. ..L Baumann. 120

Fresnoy, I. 227 W 15th....O'Farrell & Co. 146

Galwey, T F. 110 E 121st J Baumann. (R) 157

Garrison, M and F E. 34 Edgecombe av....E C Hinsdale. 500

Goodell, C M. 404 W 58th ...J Baumann. (R) 108

Green, Laura G. 420 W 19th ...O'Farrell & Co. 280

Gaffney, Annie. 419 W 39th .. L Baumann. 126

Galvin, Catherine. 157 Cherry....F G Smith. Piano. (R) 350

Garrison, Lizzie. 2021 Lexington av....Dreisacker & Co. 326

Gottschalk, F C. 35 Grove... R M Walters. Piano. 262

Hart, Lena. 219 W 40th....O'Farrell & Co. (R) 100

Heide, J F, Mrs. 305 W 14th... F T Higgins. 233

Halpin, Bernard. 519 W 50th....J Baumann. 127

Hanlon, Susan. 54 E 9th....J Baumann. (R) 225

Harris, Simon. 129 East Broadway....H S Eisler. 240

Hart, Lena. 217 W 40th....O'Farrell & Co. (R) 197

Haskell, W M. 229 W 23d... J Bauman. 306

Hausman, Belle E. 175 W 12th....J Baumann. (R) 102

Healy, Mrs Chas. 150 W 50th.. N Y F Co. 102

Hopkins, P H. 217 W 38th....J Baumann. (R) 314

Houston, Maria. 216 W 15th....S Knapp & Co. 677

Hunting, Russell. 101 2d av....J Baumann. 171

Hunt, J L. 332 W 59th....F Bolt. 100

Hammel, P C. 547 W 125th....Fennell & Pye. (R) 179

Hammond, Maggie. 218 E 73d....Jordan & M. 114

Harris, Frances. 19 Pell....Jordan & M. 113

Harmau, Elizabeth. 147 W 33d... H Thoesen. 103

Henderson, Jane. 695 Greenwich ...J Baumann. (R) 128

Hirsch, Rosa. 1655 1st av....Krakauer Bros. Piano. 200

Holmes, Mrs C E. 440 Lexington av....T Kelly. 164

Harwood, H W. 120 W 94th....L Baumann. 147

Hay, C C. 958 8th av....O'Farrell & Co. 180

Herbert, Cora. 321 W 21st O'Farrell & Co. 232

Herman, August. 420 W 29th....Manges Bros. 122

Bewett, Emma....J Williams. 312

Hexter, Phebe. 145 Waverley pl....J Moriarty. (R) 122

Herzog, A W. 322 W 23d ..L Baumann. 122

Hickie, Alice. 251 W 26th ... O'Farrell & Co. 276

Hoetzer, Selina. 42 E 3d....O'Farrell & Co. 671

Hope, Jennie... 205 W 21st....E Guernsey (R) 1,500

Hopkins, P H. 217 W 38th....J Baumann. (R) 460

Iruyyrst, P P. 327 E 111th....J G Patton & Co. 109

Immerman, Joseph. 1726 Madison av....R M Walters. Piano. 275

Ireland, Mary A. 217 Columbus av .. F T Higgins. 230

Jones, Clara H.. Storage....W P Burr. 2,000

Jordan, Mary. 411 W 24th....J Baumann. 160

Joseph, Abbie. 21 E 115th . Fennell & Pye. 184

Julius, Anna. 352 E 163d....L Baumann. 121

Jackson, Lizzie. 134 W 26th....J Moriarty. 152

Kean, Ellen. 167 W 23d....O'Farrell & Co. 260

Keelan, Kate. 1806 3d av....J G Patton & Co. 100

Kilroy, Katie. 209 W 21st ...J Baumann. (R) 166

Kopp, Betty. 126 W 83d....J Gregg & Co. 112

Kutner, H H. 422 E 52d... J Baumann. (R) 186

Kearney, John. 510 E 88d ...Fennell & Pye. 105

Kehoe, M L. 881 6th av....L Baumann. 128

Kelly, Ella. 86 E 3d....J Moriarty. 160

Kingsley, Kittie. 102 W 94th ...J Baumann. (R) 105

Kraus, Wenzel. 464 Brook av... W E Wheelock & Co. Piano. (R) 210

Krebs, Charles. 1278 Franklin av....S Baumann. 141

Keely, F B. 46 Clarkson....F T Higgins. 986

Le Roy, O S. 8 E 18th....American Guarantee Assoc. 100

Lasch, Adolph. 652 2d av....W Bjur. Piano. 225

Lodge, Mrs W B. 137 W 15th....T Kelly. 131

La Burt, Pauline. 421 E 86th ...S Baumann. 363

La Caveine, Elouise. Columbia and Grand sts ...D M Brown. 255

Largrader, Mrs Lewis. 344 E 42d....J Baumann. (R) 128

Lesser, Ettie. 10 E 86th....J Moriarty. 258

Lonie, Jacob. 562 E 139th....Dreisacker & Co. 133

Lusk, O L. 201½ W 24th....J Baumann. (R) 584

Lamont, Fannie J. 302 W 56th... H Thoesen. 228

Laufer, L. 410 W 36th....Manges Bros. 304

Litchfield, James. 252 W 88th ...L Baumann. 209
Maston, Fred. 230 W 95th....T Kelly. 152
Matthews, Mrs Arthur. 851 7th av....T Kelly. 282
Matthews, Mrs J F. 136 W 63d....T Kelly. 190
May, W H. 50 W 94th .. P P May. 1,000
McGivern, Ida T. 145 E 111th....Fennell & Pye. (R) 168
Meyer, John. 47 Lewis....J Baumann. (R) 146
McGonigal, Mamie. 306 Henry....Jordan & M 131
Miner, Matilda. 20 E 130th....J Gregg & Co. 187
Moore, Emily. 528 E 117th....Fennell & Pye. (R) 159
Mull, Minnie. 201 E 70th ....T Kelly. 190
Murray, Minnie. 1588 Madison av....Jordan & M. 140
Mather, Hattie. 53 W 44th....D Schwarzkopf. 1,395
McGowan, Mrs 59 North Moore....H S Eisler. 206
McKnight, Mary. 100 E 45th ...J Baumann. (R) 100
Mignot, Alexander. 207 E 22d....Garvey Bros. 112
Miller, Annie. 311 Columbus av ...J Baumann. 155
Mills, Francis. 311 W 21st... L Baumann. 110
Moon, Louise. 1813 3d av....Fennell & P. 108
Morse, Harry. 120 W 61st....J Baumann. 274
Mullins, Martin. 351 E 75th....L Baumann. 198
McKeeby, W C. 2194 7th av....E Mapes. 906
Mansfield, Emma A. 314 W 49th....O'Farrell & Co. 367
Mason, Louise M. 159 E 109th....J G Patton & Co. 190
McCarty, Ellie. 1440 4th av....J G Patton & Co. 119
McConnell, J J. 2137 7th av... J G Patton & Co. 172
McManus, Mary F. 316 E 57th....Manges Bros. 145
Mellin, P E. 26 E 116th....L Baumann. 446
Merrill, Florence L. 342 W 59th....O'Farrell & Co. 360
Modersolm, Ernst. 266 W 115th....J G Patton & Co. 239
Neary, John. 155 E 96th....J G Patton & Co. 119
Newton, Mrs Ray. 321 W 21st. ..O'Farrell & Co. 226
Northrup, C L. 158 W 84th... Fennell & Pye. (R) 161
Neville, Hattie 140 W 32d....A Wolff. (R) 172
Noyes, E J. 209 E 116th....Fennell & P. 117
Owry, Aceli. 285 7th av....O'Farrell & Co. 166
Paine, W E. 236 E 118th .. Manges Bros. 277
Patterson, James. 410 W 29th....O'Farrell & Co. 132
Peterson, Mrs W B. 230 W 38th....O'Farrell & Co. 161
Same....O'Farrell & Co. 127
Pomeroy, Mamie. 142 W 33d....O'Farrell & Co. 131
Paulson, Emma J....J Williams, 138
Preiss, Samuel. 42 Delancey....J Moriarty. (R) 120
Pratt, Mary. 120 W 13th....J Baumann. (R) 149
Pasco, Mary L. 247 W 126th....L Baumann. 110
Phillips, Eugenia. 7 St Marks pl... J Moriarty. 162
Pratt, Mary. 120 W 13th....J Baumann. (R) 245
Prime, Chas. 201 W 34th....H S Eisler. 190
Pepper, D L. 205 W 95th....Korner & Schwabeland. 686
Que, Ong. 19 Pell....H S Eisler. 187
Quinlan, Augusta. 524 E 142d....L Baumann. 214
Raberge, Henry. 403 Amsterdam av L Baumann. 151
Ranney, M L. 317 W 29th....J W Ranney. 2,800
Ramiriz, Jas. 102d st and Amsterdam av.... O'Farrell & Co. 233
Rebner, Cecilia. 231 E 10th....H Thoesen. 210
Reilly, Annie. 56 E 4th....Jordan & M. 637
Rendler, John. 2053 3d av....J G Patton & Co. 156
Rancour, Dusenbury. 352 E 41st....Fennell & Pye. (R) 120
Rees, Amelia. 346 E 119th....Fennell & Pye. (R) 149
Roche, Eliza McD. 84 Perry ...Jordan, M & Co. 667
Rayat, Chas. 503 E 116th....A Hecht. 100
Reinhard & Klein. 851 E 135th . Fennell & Pye. 111
Reiss, Bertha. 14 St Marks pl....J Baumann. (R) 348
Reynolds, Julia. 204 E 84th....L Baumann. 139
Rodman, Jane. 85 W 89th....J J Coogan. (R) 109
Ross, G D. 543 E 139th....Fennell & Pye. 199
Rozelle, Mrs Geo. 266 W 11th .. N Y F Co. 105
Ryan, J F. 1289 Park av... J J Coogan. 241
Ryan, John. 334 E 118th....Fennell & Pye. 174
Ryan, Kate. 723 Greenwich Manges Bros. 111
Schumar, J B. 326 W 33d....O'Farrell & Co. 536
Seixas, I. 684 E 139th....J G Patton & Co. 399
Seixas, R S. 224 and 226 W 24th....O'Farrell & Co. (R) 197
Sirasirow, Addie 255 W 32d....O'Farrell & Co. 180
Stormdofer, Debora. 234 E 104th....J G Patton & Co. 479
Strothers, Julia. 250 W 41st ..O'Farrell & Co. 168
Stuckey, W H. 130 11th av, Mt Vernon, N Y.... J G Patton. 255
Sager, Emma. 61 Morton....L Baumann. 121
Saumer, Essie. 173 W 64th....D Schwarzkopf. 166
Scott, G A. 174 W 97th... J Gregg & Co. 157
Scott, M K. 70 W 51st ...S Knapp. (R) 1,250
Schmidt, S and J. 227 E 53d....W H Griffin. 250
See, H G. 18 W 135th....T Kelly. 222
Sheridan, Katie. 758 2d av. T Kelly. 127
Simon, Wolf. 158 Broome....Krakauer Bros. Piano. 190
Singer, Samuel. 163 E 105th ...Krakauer Bros. Piano. 280
Smith, Julia A. 307 Pearl....Jordan, M & Co. 174
Storey, Jessie. 426 W 193d....T Kelly. 152
Strauss, August. 447 W 48d....J Baumann. 170
Schubert, Mrs John. 890 Boulevard....N Y F Co. 100
Sheridan, R B. 36 W 59th....McManus Bros. 142
Simms, John. 209 W 60th....L Baumann. 152
Simon, Jacob. 310 E 83d....L Wolf. 400
Stafford, S. 132 W 62d....D Schwarzkopf. 190
Sturm, Louis. 34 E 4th....H S Eisler. 248
Terrogrosse, A & R. 34 Oliver....I Zarnowsky. 135
Tobiau, Cassie. 401 E 72d....J Baumann. (R) 130
Tracy, W D. 1500 Park av....L Baumann. 126
Traynor, P F. West Farms ...W Reubel. 121
Tait, Alice. 260 8th av ...O'Farrell & Co. 122
Taper, Mamie. 248 W 33d....O'Farrell & Co. 145
Unsworth, G W. 8 Forsyth....Jordan & M. 127
Unger, William. 147 E 90th....Dreisacker & Co. 149
Van Gilder, Carrie A. 15 W 99th....J Baumann. 253
Volk, Fannie. 531 W 152d L Baumann. 193
Vans, J R. 1123 4th av....H Thoesen. 185
Vosco, James. 537 E 118th....J G Patton & Co. 110
Vaughn, Bessie. 220 E 36th....J Moriarty. (R) 161
Verdein, Emile. 134 W 90th....O'Farrell & Co. 180
Walker, Annie. 209 E 95th ...J Moriarty. 108
Walker, Henry. 201 W 28th....O'Farrell & Co. 162
Widmer, F A. 116 E 115th....J G Patton & Co. 113
Williams, Alfred. 134½ W 33d....O'Farrell & Co. (R) 109
Wilson, Delia. 1571 3d av....J G Patton & Co. 101
Wilson, Mabel. 151 W 16th ...O'Farrell & Co. 428
Walker, Annie. 417 W 53d....L Baumann. 103
Ward, Mary. 895 7th av....J Baumann. (R) 221
Williams, Elizabeth. 368 Willis av....L Baumann. 131
Wattel, Jules. 1586 Madison av....American Guarantee Assoc. 100
Wissmuck, A S. 453 Lenox av.. A Ballin. 759
Ward, Mary A. 346 E 42d....J Baumann. (R) 121
Webber, Mrs A E. 347 W 58th....G Fennell & Co. (R) 275
Weingart, Emil. 87 W 11th S Baumann. 320
Wheeler, G M. 174 St. Nicholas av... J Baumann. (R) 170
White, S B. 233 E 69th....S Baumann. 251
Wicks, Isabella. 219 W 15th ...L Baumann. 132
Wohltman, Dorethe. 220 Clinton....L Baumann. 187
Yung, Anna. 15 Bleecker....M Falkenberg. (R) 750

MISCELLANEOUS.

Arndt, Theodore. 854 Columbus av....J Matthews. Soda Fixtures. 400
Aronwitz, Aron. 2134 2d av .... C Dierking. Butcher Fixtures. 175
Abrams & Norton. 35 Frankfort.. Lincoln I and G Assoc. Photo Fixtures. 100
Adams, John. 1 Prince....L Lascassopolas. Oyster Stand. 10
Adler, S J K. 1938 3d av....Nat Cash Reg Co. Register. 200
Same....same. Register. 200
Awe, Chas. 102 Mulberry .... P Reidenbach. Wagon. 57
Abbott, C B and S A. 436 W 57th....J Rozell. Horses, Coaches, &c. 1,500
Baily, L E. 529 W 42d....J Cunningham Son & Co. Coach. (R) 421
Bianchi, G. 185 Park row... G Pecoraro. Barber Fixtures. (R) 300
Birmingham & Co. 9 Wall st and New Brighton, S I . W S Tobias. Printing Fixtures. 4,000
Bopp & Peters. 164 E 57th... R Leon. Costumes. 1,500
Barrett Electric Co. 10 Cedar....Prentiss Tool Co. Machinery. 90
Baker, George. 181 Broadway....C H Lyon. Office Fixtures. (R) 500
Basile, G. 202 E 59th....Archer Mfg Co. Barber Fixtures. 763
Benach, Wolf. 58 Orchard....H Machet. Barber Fixtures. 60
Benedix, Gus. 35 Park row.... Nat Cash Reg Co. Register. 200
Blees, Max. 575 2d av ...C Doescher. Confectionery Fixtures. 500
Blum, Nicolaus. Brook av and 167th and 168th sts....L Grundhoefer. Dyeing Fixtures. 1,100
Boeddiker, Otto. 954 6th av... E Molwitz. Drug Fixtures. (R) 2,000
Bowcock, Bartholomew. 850 Bowery ...L Fleet. Machinery. (R) 500
Breimer, Henry. 1123 Park av... Archer Mfg Co. Barber Fixtures. 450
Brickner, Samuel. 110 E 42d....A Schriesheim. Jewelry Box. 25
Byrne, Joseph. 33 Oliver....Nat Cash Reg Co. Register. 230
Barringer, J H & J E. 10 E 14th....E C Hinsdale. Office Fixtures. 160
Blumenthal, Pauline. 94th st, bet 1st and 2d avs ... P Brown. Horse, Wagon, &c. 300
Bushnell, Irving & Swartz. 105 and 107 E 13th ...Van Allens & B. Press. (R) 296
Bowles, Lillian. 83d st and Lexington av. ..Seligmann & Hahn. Horses. 875
Center, Granville. 1550 Broadway ...M Center. Coal Yard Fixtures. (R) 1,000
Central Oil Gas Stove Co....Boston Safe Deposit and Trust Co. Machinery, &c. 450,000
Clark Bros... P Barrett. Truck. (R) 350
Cohen, Daniel. 1 Bridge and 261 Division.... Lincoln I and G Assoc. Butcher Fixtures and Furniture. 100
Caliendo, Gaetano. 123 Baxter....H Brand. Butcher Fixtures. 32
Callagy, Thomas. 413 E 15th ...C Murry. Horse, Wagon, &c. 125
Canold, Haris. 13 Essex ...H Canold. Machines. 100
Carpenter, C R... S C Carpenter. Maps, &c. 3,450
Deutsch, Louis. 186 Cherry....F Loeser & Co. Machinery. 1,000
Duffy, Isaac. Myrtle av, Brooklyn .... F J Minck. Horse. 600
David, G G. 342 and 344 E 32d....P A Cassidy. Wagon. 180
D'Arena, Stanislao. 70 W 4th....G Lordi. Barber Fixtures. (R) 150
Daly, Cornelius. Park av and 116th st....Nat Cash Reg Co. Register. 175
Dawson, James. 22 Beekman....W H Gough. Machinery. 600
Delaney, W W. 117 Park row....A E Delaney. Press, &c. 250
Dolbeer, F K 294 W 116th....Nat Cash Reg Co. Register. 205
Dougherty, James. 430 E 72d....F P Perkins. Machinery, &c. (R) 1,000
Dreinis, Adoph 181 East Broadway....D Horwitz. Laundry Fixtures. 40
Ebnester, Jacob. 654 E 153d....J Drittenbars. Machines. 200
Eisler, Moritz. 301 and 303 W 14th ...L Heinsfurter. Butcher Fixtures. 400
Enderly, C E. 61 10th av....U E Wood. Horses, Trucks, &c. 150
Same....same. Horses, Trucks, &c. 150
Finnigan Bros. 536 W 29th .... Wolff Bros. Horses. 225
Fuchs & Wollenberg. 238 Canal....Lamson Consolidated S S Co. Register. 140
Feldman, S. 353 W 59th....Archer Mfg Co. Barber Fixtures. (R) 226
Fleming, C R. 75 Warren....E T Lee. Machinery. 100
Fritz, Frank. 144 W 19th and 204 W 18th.... Lembeck & Betz. Bottler Fixtures. 385
Fitzgerald, M J....P Barrett. Truck. (R) 400
Farrell, Frank. 318 Delancey....W Wieber. Truck. 200
Fontaine, Louise. 235 W 125th ...M T Farnham. Furniture and Store Fixtures. 500
Grimm, Jacob. 143 and 145 Elm ...Nicoll & Ohle. Machinery. 400
Germano, G. 328 8th av....P Andresh. Barber Fixtures. 55
Gundlach, John. 2011 Columbus av....Perrin P & Co. Wagon. 100
Goetting, E C. 100th st and Amsterdam av.... Nat Cash Reg Co. Register. 225
Goetz, Theodore. 323 West....Archer Mfg Co. Barber Fixtures. (R) 54
Golden, William. 565 3d av ...Golden Bros. Plumber Fixtures. 350
Griecco, F and A. 91 6th av....Archer Mfg Co. Barber Fixtures. 515
Griffin, Bernard....G Dessecker. Coach. (R) 318
Guglielaro & Carano. 171 Perry ...G Fimgia. Barber Fixtures. 100
Gunn, R A. 124 W 47th....Kate Smith. Furniture and Medical Fixtures. 3,300
Hammer, Edward. 185 East Houston....Nat Cash Reg Co. Register. 200
Hannefy, John. 520 10th av....E Ennis. Horse and Wagon. 40
Heffter, G O. 335 E 121st....G W Boskowitz. Horse, Wagon, &c. 500
Huebsch, S and D A. 322 Pearl....C B Cottrell & Son. Press. (R) 1,300
Hess, Charles. 356 W 40th....A Geiger. Barber Fixtures. (R) 75
Halik, Josef. 343 E 74th....J M Winterroth. Butcher Fixtures. 67
Hard, D H. 178 Broadway... McNeil & Anderson. Shoe Store Fixtures. 526
Hasenauer, Fritz. 218 Monroe....C Albrecht. Butcher Fixtures. 400
Heymann, Joseph. 710 9th av....J L Jarvis & Son. Bakery Fixtures. 200
Irons, J H. 3195 4th av....J M Harned. Machinery. 1,500
Iannelli, Antonio. 656 11th av....G Rainforth. Barber Fixtures. 75
Jackson, W M. Foot 23d st, Brooklyn.... H K Thurber. Engine. 5,000
Jones, F W. 135 W 18th....D B Dunham. Coach. 450
Jene, Peter. 2177 8th av....P Westphal. Barber Fixtures. 326
Jorden & Morrison. 680 8th av... J W Tufts. Soda Fixtures. 450
Kerr & Brown. 377 Bleecker....R J McClenehen. Grocery Fixtures. 1,000
Kipp, J H. 20 W 3d... J P Friedhoff. Machines. 180
Korff, H G and A L. 107 Liberty....C Freygang. Machinery. (R) 6,000
Keris, Hermann. 358 3d av....A & H Myers. Store Fixtures. 1,700
Kopel, George. 464 W 35th...J McLean. Butcher Fixtures. 63
Kaminsky, Moses. 1142 1st av....Archer Mfg Co. Barber Fixtures. (R) 132
Kiernan, James. 44th st and 3d av....Nat Cash Reg Co. Register. 200
La Grunen, Joe. 21 Monroe... Archer Mfg Co. Barber Fixtures. 87
Lennox, John. 233 E 80th....M L Lennox. Horses, Coaches, &c. 2,489
Levy, Morris. 12 Ludlow ...L Heinsfurter. Butcher Fixtures. 600
Ludwig, Robert. 130 E 32d. ..Archer Mfg Co. Barber Fixtures. (R) 89
Lawler, Jno F. 2309 3d av....Bramhall, Deane & Co. Range. 100
Lenz, A. 84th st and Amsterdam av....Nat Cash Reg Co. Register. 200
Langman, Jake. 1563 2d av....J Jaffin. Barber Fixtures. 125
McGloin, James. 417 W 32d....M. Rellenger. Horse and Grocery Fixtures. 850
Mariamson, M. 165th st and Cauldwell av....A D Puffer & Sons. Soda Fixtures. 200
Masterson, Chas. 29th st and 1st av... Nat Cash Reg Co. Register. 180
Matt, F N. 431 E 6th....Nat Cash Reg Co. Register 200
McDermott, John. 156 E 88th....A J Walker. Cab. (R) 125
Meyers & Knaeblein. 64 Nassau... M J Byrnes. Office Fixtures. 300
Morrissey, Michael. 98th st, bet 1st and 2d avs ....J E Connelly. Blacksmith Fixtures. 300
Mayer, Franz. 538 E 87th....Marvin Safe Co. Safe. 145
McElroy & Emmet. 36 Cortlandt....C B Cottrell & Son. Press. 1,250
Nonnenmacher, Felix. 826 2d av....A J Wengertar. Store Fixtures. 500
New York Sign and Letter Co. 307 Broadway ....M J Halsted. Tools, &c. 100
Newman, J H. 531 W 27th....J C Teepe. Horses, Trucks, &c. 500
Otto, Theo. 147 Baxter....Prentiss Tool Co. Machinery. 150
Ockley, John....G Dessecker. Coach. (R) 180
Paritz, Max. 296 Stanton....E Cohn. Machines. (R) 300
Peters, Ernst. 120 E 7th....C Haefele. Bakery Fixtures. 75
Plattner, Chas....G Dessecker. Coach. 725
Plump, Chas. 684 Columbus av....H Cordes. Machinery. 1,000
Peet, A J. 59 W 45th ...C Crete. Painting . 2,700
Quinn, J F. 419 Cherry....J Devlin. Horse, &c. 400
Rockwell, Mary E. 831 Amsterdam av .... I Dunn. Grocery Fixtures. 200
Roossin, A & L. 254 Delancey....L Cohen. Bottler Fixtures. 300
Rogers, W H H. 65 and 67 Crosby.. .G H Sanborn & Son. Cutting Machinery. 650
Ryan, Michael. 629 W 47th....W Kelly. Horses. 700
Radigan, Simon....A J Walker Coupe. 200
Shaljian, Peter. 9 Spruce....G H Sanborn & Sons. Cutting Machinery. 430
Sheridan, Bernard. 505 W 28th....J McLean. Butcher Fixtures. 150
Sherwood, A G & Co. 47 Lafayette pl....Van Allens & B. Press. (R) 2,250
Silver, Joseph. 160 Orchard... I A & H Kruienstch. Bakery Fixtures. 150
Snieder, Robt. 102 Fulton....Lincoln I & G Assoc. Press, &c. 150
Schappert, Joseph. 398 7th av....J Aufenanger. Grocery Fixtures. 1,000
Scheuer, Wm. 297 3d av....Archer Mfg Co. Barber Fixtures. 307
Schloeder, P. 10th av, 157th and 158th sts.... Archer Mfg Co. Barber Fixtures. (R) 421
Emith, R A. 257 E 127th....Archer Mfg Co. Barber Fixtures. (R) 34
Snyder, Frank .. G Dessecker. Coach. 675
Staaks, F H. 2328 2d av....D Ehlers. Plumber Fixtures. 450
Strauss, Edward. 60 Division....J H Rosenfeld. Bakery Fixtures. 185
Schirak, Samuel. 243 Delancey....L Siegman. Bakery Fixtures. 100
Terryn, Theophilus. 521 E 15th....B Lang. Milk Fixtures, &c. 200
Tienken, J C & Co. 969 3d av....Nat Cash Reg Co. Register. 175
Tomlinson, W T. 83d st, bet 1st av and Av A ....W G Raynor. Horse, Wagon, &c. 200
Taylor, J B. 100 Greene ...Marvin Safe Co. Safe. 120
Tams, A W. 416 W 28th....Damon & Peets. Cutter. 50
Tomlinson, W T. 171 E 86th....W G Raynor. Fish Market Fixtures. 200

Trautmann, D L. 24 New Chambers....Bramhall, D & Co. Ranges, &c. 118
Turck, John. 326 E 60th....J Nadeije. Bakery Fixtures. 400
Valiquet, L P. 226 Centre....Prentiss Tool Co. Machinery. 112
Weisgerber, William. 2396 3d av ...A Weisgerber. Barber Fixtures. (R) 350
Wiener, Lena. 167 Ridge....H Gampert. Bakery Fixtures. 100
Willner, Hannah. 152 Orchard....E Silberman. Cigar Fixtures. 300
Wagner, William. Oliver st and East Broadway ....Nat Cash Reg Co. Register. 150
Wallach, Wolf. 40 Columbia....H Gellert. Bottler Fixtures. 500
Wertheimer, Leopold. 270 East Houston.... Duparquet, H & M Co. Range. 92
West Coast Telephone Co....T N Vail et al trustees. Franchises, &c. (R) 250,000
Wieck, Emma C. 204 E 116th....I Obendorfer. Store Fixtures and Furniture. 125
Wennies, W & A. 105-113 Suffolk ...C Stevens. Machinery. 2,450
Werbeck, Aug & Co....A Werbeck, Sr. Machinery. 1,280
Wess, Hermann. 887 10th av....M F Lindhorn & Co. Bakery Fixtures. 500
Willis, Henry....Keeler & Jennings. Coaches. (R) 3,300
Same.. same. Coaches. (R) 1,200
Young, Louis. 287 and 289 Boulevard....W Delany. Butcher Fixtures. 450
Zeller, S and O 1846 2d av....Couper, Z & Co. Bakery Fixtures. 160
Zismar, Gustave. 432 E 77th ...G Zismar. Horses, Carts, &c. 500
Zinsser, H. 34th st and Lexington av....Archer Mfg Co. Barber Fixtures. 930
Zuccaro, C and F. 271 10th av... S Caffarelli. Barber Fixtures. 225

BILLS OF SALE.

Blaut, Simon. 86 Rivington....A Sieber. Bakery Fixtures. 400
Bavarian Brewing Co. 218 E 102d....T Casham. Saloon Fixtures. 300
Byrnes, J J. 434 E 13th....V Poppite. Saloon Fixtures. 1,000
Beniczky, Sarah. 2 New Chambers....G W Barnett. Photo Fixtures. 6,308
Blondeau, Fred. 99 Christopher....C S Ruegger. Restaurant Fixtures. 3,200
Cohen, Louis. 254 Delancey....A & L Roossin. Bottler Fixtures. 1,200
Donohue, John. 1090 10th av....E A Fraser. Saloon Fixtures. 3,000
Feldman & Kaplan. 7 Forsyth....M Friedberg. Barber Fixtures. 50
Frenna & Muli. 144 Varick....Pelosi & Nalbone. Barber Fixtures. 275
Germano, Giovanni. 328 8th av....F Buonainto. Barber Fixtures. 240
Jarvis, Lizzie B. 141 E 111th....G Busling. Furniture. —
Kennedy, John. 568 7th av....S Rosenweig. Saloon Fixtures. 4,000
Lauppe, Christian. Av D and 9th st....F Merkle. Saloon Fixtures. 1,000
Laurence, E C and S G....F C Murry. Horse, Wagon, &c. 177
Leon, Rebecca. 164 E 57th....Bopp & Peters. Costumes. 3,000
Muller, Peter. 2312 1st av....C F & F Williams. Grocery Fixtures. 525
Morbans, J H. 407 E 15th....G Strennecker. Grocery Fixtures. 540
O'Connell, John. 2d av and 74th st....D Stevenson. Saloon Fixtures. 800
Prince, L K. 729 and 731 1st av... Prince & Kinkel Iron Works. Machinery, &c. 5,284
Panaro, Michelangelo. 519 1st av....A Perone. Barber Fixtures. 205
Peeke, William. 205 W 95th....D L Pepper. Furniture. 1,100
Pepper, D and L K. 205 W 95th....W Peeke. Furniture. 500
Plaut, Louis. 1933 3d av....C Adler. Butcher Fixtures. 8,000
Rupp, Fred. 99 West Houston....C Frey. Machines, Furniture, &c. 550
Schroeder, William. 155 E 110th.....Katie Schroeder. Grocery Fixtures. 200
Scinto, Francesco. 119 Mulberry... Maria Mainieri. Saloon Fixtures. 1,500
Salmenovitz, Samuel, doing business under name of Samuel Solomon. 619 Madison av ....D Salmenovitz. Store Fixtures. 1,200
Sander, Sebastian. 167 E 105th....J & W Doemich. Bottler Fixtures. 4,400
Seyfarth, Julius. 733 Amsterdam av .... R Hine. Bakery Fixtures. 275
Voigt, C F. 452 E 78th....F W Voigt. Store Fixtures, &c. 700
Welch, Fracker Co....S H Kerins & Co. Electro Plates, &c. 1

ASSIGNMENTS OF CHATTEL MORTGAGES.

Bernheimer & Schmid to P Bohnet. (Mort given by Roetling & Beekmann, July 26, 1891). 1,225
Baumann, Ludwig to Emma Luster. 1,500
Berganini, Rachel to E M M Bridge et al. (C L F & M Bridge, Jan 15, 1891.) 500
Carley, Maria C to The Long Island Brewery. (M J Lawler, Oct 1, 1891.) 1
F Wesel Mfg Co to Julius Goldman. (A Rosenberg, Aug 3, 1891.) 75
Gellert, Harris to M Lazarus. (W Wallach, Oct 28, 1891.) 500
Grinnon, D P exr of to M C Grinnon. (J Mullen, Oct 30, 1889.) 1
Hinsdale, E C to M Armstrong. (H F A & C Pinckney, March 11, 1891.) 250
Lenton, J J to E M M Bridge et al. (C L F & M Bridge, April 15, 1891.) 300
Meyer & Lange to M Armstrong. (H F A & C Pinckney, Aug 14, 1891.) 1,000
Schecker, Fred to Alice Henry. (A Peter Henry, March 18, 1891.) 1
Steinhardt, Henry to Beadleston & W. (A Skudrna, Oct 26, 1891.) 750
Same to same. (S Prince, Oct 19, 1891.) 1,500

KINGS COUNTY.

OCTOBER 22 TO 28.—INCLUSIVE.

SALOON AND RESTAURANT FIXTURES.

Aylmar, J. 462 7th av... Claus Lipsius B Co. $700
Agnew, S. 244 Hoyt....W L Flanagan, managing director. (R) 2,250
Adamsky, P. 198 and 200 Court....A Wierl. 1,500
Bovie, O. 593 5th av....Danenberg & C. 696
Berger, F. 131 Kent av....Welz & Z. 1,000
Brockmann, H. 216 23d....S Liebmann's Sons B Co. 900
Butters, F. Georgia av, n e cor Glenmore av.... Obermeyer & L. 140
Capazucca, T. 11 Carroll....W H Griffith & Co. Billiard Table. 250
Cronin, T. Vernon av, Flatbush....D Ryan. Hotel Fixtures. 1,000
Cryan, T J. 205 Hudson av....J J Reid. 700
Dailey, D V. De Kalb av, cor Kent av....Wiggins & Co. Pool Table. 125
Deppe, L. 1243 Broadway....G Ringler & Co. 800
Duerkes, P. 1081 and 1083 Myrtle av....F Fedderke. Pool Table. 150
Eggert, G. 194 Conover....India Wharf B Co. (R) 500
Engel, J D. 70 Kent av ...Claus Lipsius B Co. 250
Erlenwer, C. 927 Flushing av ..S Liebmann's Sons B Co. 500
Fecke, F. 17 North Henry...E Ochs. 300
Fink, H. 5th av, s e cor 7th st....Claus Lipsius B Co. 750
Foley, J. Tremont st....Wagner & S. Pool Table. 215
Fromm, J F. 506 6th av....W Craft. 300
Hartstein, I H. 74 President....Wagner & S. Pool Table. 200
Johansen, E F. 231 Union...Wagner & Sandford. Pool Table. 150
Kaehnel, E. 117 Hopkins....Burger & Hower B Co. 450
Kahn, B. 249 Hopkins....W Ulmer. 600
Kenney, C E. 195 Franklin ...S Liebmann's Sons B Co. 1,000
Kirchner, A. 434 Glenmore av....L Eppig. 600
Kleinschmitz, A. 1273 and 1275 Broadway.... Franziska Kleinschmitz. 800
Kaiser, W and H Huldorf. 466 Manhattan av.... S Liebmann's B Co. 600
Kohn, A. 350 North 2d....L Eppig. 565
Konicky, G. 556 Driggs av....Burger & Hower B Co. 850
Lynan, Dela. 781 Atlantic av....Abbott B Co. 800
Lynch, B. Hudson av, s w cor Prospect st....P J Kelly. 3,450
Lemaire, H and F. 20 Brooklyn av....O Huber. (R) 2,500
Linton, H P. 128 Flatbush av... J H Bereuter. Billiard Table. 180
Matthews, Elisabeth. 216 Bedford av....S Liebmann's Sons B Co. 850
Marr, T H. 2549 Atlantic av....Mary M Kneip. 200
Martin, W. 32 Sands and 701 Fulton....M McElhinney. 5,000
Puniger, J. Williamson av....D G Yuengling, Jr, B Co. (R) 450
Pahls, F. 105 Montrose av....E Ochs. 2,000
Renner, J. 100 Raymond....Williamsburgh B Co. 700
Resch, C. 49 Montrose av....O Huber Brewery. (R) 635
Rube, H. 912 Madison....W Ulmer. 800
Ruble, J. 266 Floyd....J Eppig. 400
Schmidt, A P. 256 Court....G Ringler & Co. (R) 1,683
Stoss, F. 136 Boerum.. W Ulmer. (R) 400
Schmiederer, G. 426 Bushwick av ...S Liebmann's Sons B Co. 500
Schumaker, J. Jamaica av and Market st....W Ulmer. 800
Schwarzmuller, Barbara. 260 Johnson av....P Weidmann. 900
Silberstein, F. 2784 Atlantic av....Williamsburgh B Co. (R) 400
Stauch, J. 996 Flushing av....S Liebmann's Sons B Co. 300
Sutter, F. 557 Liberty av....L Eppig. 900
Vogel, H W. 1655 Broadway ...S Liebmann's Sons B Co. 1,100
Wayne, J. 104 Parkway av....T C Lyman & Co. (R) 182
Whitty, M. 75 Atlantic av ...P Ballantine & Sons. (R) 1,000
Same .. same. (R) 1,000
Weisenburger, G. 154 Johnson av....J Eppig. 500
Wolf, J. 162 Throop av ...Fred Hower B Co (Lim). 1,000

HOUSEHOLD FURNITURE.

Allen, Cath. 1135 Broadway ...R Silvermann. 105
Barber, Georgiana T. 490 9th ...S Baumann. 365
Briggs, Jennie. 34 South 5th av....L Baumann. 328
Bennett, Emma. 74 Wyona....T Kelly. 118
Davidson, Mary F. 210 11th....M M Webster. 100
De Costa, R. 22 Stockholm....J Baumann. 161
Dunn, J P. 200 7th av....S Baumann. 347
Frank, H W. 93 Roebling....A Schulz. 243
Hanson, E P. 518 6th av....M M Webster. 100
Henderson, I H. Greene av, cor Tompkins av ....S Baumann. 126
Harrison, J F. 675 Grand... J Baehr & Co. 120
Hock, J. 118 Calyer....S Baumann. 181
Hunt, J J. 395 Court....I Mason. 174
Jennings, Fidelia. 306 Clifton pl....J Wood. 209
Jones, T W. 654 Macon... S Baumann. 293
Kennedy, Ida. 127 South 2d ...L Baumann. 108
Langan, E A. 512 8th av....L Baumann. 262
Libbey, Cornelia H. 30 McDonough .. L Baumann. 122
Lundgren, E. 165 Lexington av....M Schulz & Bro. 331
Lisdell, T A. 844 Gates av....J McEnery & Co. 174
Makintosh, L A. 165 E 83d....N Y Commercial Credit Co 200
Masqueray, E L. 105 Clark....S Baumann. 202
Midgley, H S. 412 2d....M M Webster. 100
Morris, J C. 23 Linden....M M Webster. 100
Noe, Miss L P. 50 Hanson pl ...J McEnery & Co. 173
Petersen, Lizzie. 38 Willow pl....J McEnery & Co. 132
Person, P. 90 Baltic....T F Ryan. 184
Rowan, J. 59 Pilling....S Baumann. 100
Shaw, Emma. 62 South 3d....Jordan & M. 150
Saunders, A D. 273 Dean....M Schulz & Bro. 415
Stevenson, Lillian. 160 Cumberland .... C E Pierce. 100
Shuttelton, J. 1386 Greene av . H S Eisler. 102
Thym, L A J M 1283 Pacific....E C Hinsdale. 876
Turpin, R H. 409 Carlton av....J Baumann. 249
Thwaite, R A. 268 Gates av....F R Caulkins. 658
Van Cott, C. 507 Manhattan av....J Baumann. 171
Wargin, C. Palmetto st, cor Evergreen av....A Schulz. 196

MISCELLANEOUS.

Balfe, G W. 283 Van Brunt....Nat Cash Reg Co. Register. 175
Bartruff, C. 882 Bedford av....M Vosseler. Bakery Fixtures. 150
Blackford, C E and J B. 890 Stuyvesant av....D R Briggs. Fish Store. 500
Brown, W B. Ocean Parkway and Boulevard ....Nat Cash Reg Co. Register. 525
Beckh, H. 456 Bushwick av....M Schneider. Drug Fixtures. 2,500
Capbell, R. 166 Court....M Carroll. Store Fixtures, Furniture, &c. 300
Caprara, J. 903 Gates av....F Caprara. Store Fixtures. 200
Carlston, P H. 206 4th av .. J M Nelson. Grocery Fixtures. 100
Carpenter, C R....S C Carpenter. Maps of Queens County, Plates, Subscription Lists. 3,450
Cassano, E. 474 3d av... A Schwaab & Son. Barber Fixtures. 181
Christoffers & Gehrken. 290 Marcy av....H H Flathmann. Butcher Fixtures. (R) 402
Crofoot, Mary H. 124 Van Sielen av....F E Hart. Bakery Fixtures. 272
Devlin, W....P Barrett. Trucks. (R) 150
Deygan, T J...E K Winterbottom. Printing Office Fixtures. 125
Doescher J H. 784 Park av... Nat Cash Reg Co. Register. 225
Dohrmann, W H. 29 Conselyea....Wolff Bros. Horse. 175
Daudera, B. 209 Union av....R Rainforth. Barber Fixtures. 241
Fritz, V. 110 8th....J Bloch. Wagon. 125
Grange, J. 86 Duane, N.Y....T W & C B Sheridan. Bookbinder Machines. 2,500
Groge, Anna. Jamaica av, s w cor Logan st.... H Tamke. Grocery Fixtures. 1,500
Gates, M. Fort Hamilton....Nat Cash Reg Co. Register. 170
Grunewald & Son. 991 Fulton....Marvin Safe Co. Safe. 105
Guellich, F. 56 Knickerbocker av....A Dinkelucker. Grocery Fixtures. (R) 800
Hoyt, W G and H H. 302 Van Brunt....Nat Cash Reg Co. Register. 200
Hohmann & Maurer Mfg Co. 167 Plymouth.... Prentiss Tool and Supply Co. Tools. 480
Hopkins, C E. 22 and 24 Division....L Bradfisch. Machinery, &c, of Photographic Paper Factory. 20,000
Klemyer, H. 36 Milton....J Osselmann. Horse and Wagon. 600
Kopf, H. 11 Bedford av....W B A Jurgens. Grocery Fixtures. 600
Kornahrens, F. 69 Lafayette av....Nat Cash Reg Co. Register. 175
Kierst & Co. 81 New st, New York....W Long. Conveys contracts to build, &c. 600
Lipman, W. 142 Osborn....S and B Strauss. Cows. 70
Lowey Printing and Stationery Co. 6 Barclay, New York....Babcock P P Mfg Co. Press 2,600
Macy, W F. 502 Myrtle av....S Hanna. Bakery Fixtures. 800
Marten, A. 55 Harrison av....J N Puckhaber. Horse, Milk Wagon. 100
McCutcheon, F. 3 Willoughby...Nat Cash Reg Co. Register. 400
O'Connor Bros 224 Franklin av....Nat Cash Reg Co. Register. 170
Orazio, T A G. 99 Willoughby....Archer Mfg Co. Barber Fixtures. (R) 301
Pallaci, F. 725 Bergen....M Demby. Barber Fixtures. 200
Popp, J. 380 Keap....F Koop. Butcher Fixtures. 1,100
Pasco, H and G L McCormick. 445 Osborn....R Hill. Plumbers Tools, Horse, &c. 400
Ross, J S. 55 Liberty st, New York....Jennie Hyer. Law Library. 750
Rogers, W H H, agent. 65 Crosby st, New York ....G H Sanborn & Sons. Cutting Machine. 650
Rosenfelder, C A. Crescent st....O Loebner. Machinery. 150
Roy, S H. 437 5th av....Nat Cash Reg Co. Register. 200
Sabbatino, A. 321 Court....Archer Mfg Co. Barber Fixtures. (R) 434
Smith, Ellen L and Annie Seward. 15 Dutch st, New York....J S Smith admr. Machinery and Fixtures. 1,850
Smith, R... P Barrett. Truck (R) 450
Spitz, H. 619 Driggs av....L Spitz. Horses, Wagons and Stable Fixtures. 2,000
The Manhattan Beach Hotel and Land Co (Lim) ....Central Trust Co. Hotel Properties, Rights, Privileges and Franchises. (R) 1,500,000
The Novelty Foundry Machine Works. Driggs av and North 14th st . Prentiss Tool and Supply Co. Tools. 1,710
Tietzsch, R. 18 Bergen....Prentiss Tool and Supply Co. Tools 272
The Montauk Ice Co. Gowanus Canal and 3d av ....Sprague Nat Bank, Brooklyn. All Personal Property. (R) 15,000
Timms, R 468 9th... W B Davis. Coach. 297
Van Sickels, A. South Bay, L I....Addie V Tuthill. Schooner. 500
Von Glahn, W H. 1015 and 1017 Atlantic av.... S W & J A Haviland Bakery Fixtures. 1,200
Wynne, G F. 240 Flatbush av....Nat Cash Reg Co. Register. 225
Wagner, J. 400 Nostrand av ...G Wagner. Cigar Fixtures. 250
Wiehelns, H. 680 Bedford av....B Havecker. Confectionery Store. 516
Wetzel, Flora. Ambrys Stable....W S Travis Horses, &c. 1,060
Zeitlin & Greenberg. 364 Atlantic av... W H Butler. Safe. 100

BILLS OF SALE.

Gottschalk, C. 918 Bushwick av....E C Hinsdale. Furniture. 130
Grimm, P. 142 Leonard....J Kost. Bakery. 350
Groge, H. Jamaica av, s w cor Logan st....H Tamke. Grocery Fixtures. See Tamke. 1,500
Hanna, S. 502 Myrtle av ...W F Macy. Bakery. 800
Hildebrandt, C T. 9th av, s w cor 37th st....E Koch. Florist Business. 160
Koch, E. 9th av, s w cor 37th st ...G A D Nolte, Gardener and Florist. 1,000
Martin, H, Sr. 701 Fulton and 32 Sands....H Martin, Jr. Saloon Fixtures. 2,000
Sam ....same. Saloon Fixtures and Furniture. 2,000
McChesney, J T S. 594 Atlantic av....Elma J McChesney. Store Fixtures. 400
Nelson, Sven. 206 4th av....A Carlston. Grocery Fixtures. 650
Shannon, R M. 560 Vanderbilt av....Barbara E Shannon. Milk Business. 45
Tamke, H. Jamaica av, s w cor Logan st... Anna Groge. Grocery Fixtures. See Groge. 1,500
Weile, J. 889 Grand....C Daum. Saloon Fixtures. 400

NEW JERSEY.

ESSEX COUNTY.

CONVEYANCES.

Allen, A S et al—A E Johnson, Avon av $1,045
Allen, W L—E C Dimmick, Mt Prospect av 1
Alling, J C—J V Myers, East Orange 8,000
American Insurance Co—D Schenman, e s Wallace st 480 n South Orange av 28x95 3,700
Anderson, I S—M F Reilly, Montclair 2,145
Atkins, T B—M Hartley, West Orange 1
Same——same, West Orange 3,100
Same——same, West Orange 1,400
Baldwin, M A—H Jerolaman, Salt Meadow 2,200
Benjamin, M A—F T Hey, 2d av 1,500
Bock, F J—J A Dempsey, Littleton av 1
Bort, James—S P Gilbert, Bloomfield 4,150
Bramley, David—H Glorieux, w s Johnson av 625 s Clinton av 35x150 3,150
Brown, S D—E M Cornell, Milburn 355
Brown, Willard—H H Drahe, Milburn 1
Bullock, C M—J H Shofer, Bloomfield 1
Burke, John—Patrick Burke, Orange 400
Campbell, Aque—M Crawford, Montclair 1
Campbell, C G—G W Mason, w s North 5th st 125 n 5th av 100x100 .... —
Charlouis, J I—M R Reilly, Orange 1,100
Coe, Theodore—E Seikatz, South 7th st 750
Coeyman, Samuel—The Peabody Land and Loan Co, Parker st 375
Crawford, Margaret—A Campbell, Montclair 1
Culberson, H M—M N Shotwell, East Orange 9,500
Dempsey, J A—E W Bock, Littleton av 1
Devine, Arthur—E Schreiber, South Orange 165
Dodd, Eleanor—M W Bower, East Orange 1
Dodd, J F—E Dodd, East Orange 1
Dow, F E—H K Kistner, South 18th st 1
Drake, H H—S D Brown, Milburn 1
Eisele, J C—H Jelinek, Bergen st 800
Same——J Orthenberger, Bergen st 1,350
Farley, B M—C Trefz, Avon av 1
Fischer, Bertha—C Fischer, Belmont av 1
Fischer, Conrad—B Fischer, Bergen st 1
Same——C Kucher, Belmont av 1
Ford, F M—H C Edmiston, Orange 3,900
Fowler, Lewis—M W Hogan, South Orange 8,000
Trefz, Christina—B M Farley, Avon av 1
Fuller, L C—E B Wood, Orange 2,500
Same——same, Orange 27,000
Same——F Miller et al, Central av 2,000
Same——O Picard, Central av 1,500
Garber, Davis—A M Talbot, 5th av 2,000
Gedicke, M A—A W L Wirz, 1st tract e s Broad st 281 n e Kinney st 27x200, 2d tract an alley bet Broad and Orchard sts 280 n e Kinney st 29x84x27x55, 3d tract n s Ferry st w Oxford st 22x100, and other tracts and all int in estate of H W Gedicke dec'd 17,500
Gill, G H—Chas W Cox, Milburn 1
Gordon, H S—G C Collingwood, Bloomfield 1
Grant, Hannah—The trustees of the First Presbyterian Church in Newark, pew 100
Gweeney, Daniel—E Dempsey, w s Belleville av cor Crittenden st 41x100x83x100 5,500
Harrison, C J—C M Harrison, East Orange 1
Hassinger, Peter—W Beister, Badger av 800
Hine, C C et al—W L Rhoades, Summer av 2,000
Holmes, E M—J Steiegle, Milburn 750
Humphrey, Rosamond—J R Pitcher, Millburn 16,000
Isenburg, Joseph—C Kucher, Belmont av 1
Jensen, P H—M Christiansen, Orange st 1
Johnson, A E—A S Allen, South 20th st 1,245
Johnson, F T—W L Glorieux, Clinton 300
Kane, Mary—D Sweeny, South 13th st 4,200
Kreitter, Charles—R Trivett et al, Bond st 1
Kucher, Catharine—J Isenburg, Belmont av 1
Kussy, Meyer—M Liebstein, 15th av 1,500
Lee, A R—J Brady, n s Grant st 99 w Spring st 20x87 5,350
Lichtenfels, Fredk—R Lichtenfels, Clinton 1
Lindsley, M B—G Cimmiotti, Caldwell 9,800
Lindsley, O W—I Steenson, East Orange 185
Lister, J C et al—R Wyatt, e s Belleville av 554 s Harvey st 23x100 5,850
Lockwood, L G et al—M C Canfield, Caldwell 690
McCloud, Lydia—E Evertz, Gold st 675
Mitchell, A P—A E Burgess, East Orange 840
Monahan, S A—J Burns, Nichols st 900
O'Meara, E T—G H Saunders et al, Wright 2,250
Page, H A—Morris & Essex R R, South Orange 1
Paterson, Wm special master—T O'Grady, Bleecker st 2,900
Peshine, F S—P A Small, Hawthorn av 350
Peloubet, F W—J E Bingham, East Orange 4,100
Same—same, East Orange 400
Peloubet, F W—J E Bingham, e s North 14th st 201 s 6th av 85x100 4,500
Philip, Mary—P McGowan, West Monroe st 1,500
Phillips, Emma—G Wilkinson, recvr, Caroline st 1
Same——G Wilkinson, recvr, Caroline st 1
Pfizenmayer, Johanne—W J Pfizenmayer, Caldwell 1
Picard, Otto—L C Fuller, Central av 1,000
Righter, W A—A Bachmann, Morris Canal 250
Riker, William—B M Farley, South 11th st 1
Satterthwaite, J F—R S Cunningham, Franklin 700
Sayre, J R—E Evertz, Gold st 750
Same——I B Jolley, East Orange 2,600
Selfridge, A W—J Bort, Bloomfield 625
Stager, Margaret exr—C W Stager, Franklin 200
The Mayor, &c, of Newark—C Fischer et al, rear Belmont av 1
Thompson, T W—J D Thompson, Ogden st 1
The Peabody Land and Loan Co—E Develin, Parker st 420
The Underhill Mfg Co—The East Jersey Water Co, Franklin 1
Thistlethwaite, Jeremiah—E H Baker, East Orange 2,000
Same—L F Lord, East Orange 2,000
Thompson, F E—I F Thompson et al, Academy st 1,000
Tilford, F J—A P Dillon, East Orange 2,500
Trusdell, J G, Jr—E O Wheeler, Emmett st 1
Trippe, W R—G F Rudolph, East Orange 2,800
Wandless, L F—T J Griffin, 4th av 2,800
Ward, C W—C Pullin, North 6th st 1,200
Watts, Jane—G F Potter, Belleville 200
Weatherby, Harry et al—J Corb, Franklin 5
Weber, Nicholas—J Mueller, Clinton 425
Same——W Rumpage, Clinton 100
Williams, Caroline—W Parkinson, West Orange 3,595
Williams, E C—J Jordan, West Orange 500
Williams, S J—M J Best, Caldwell 1,000
Wrederspahn, Rosina—S Stockhammer, Prince st 2,000
Wyeth, W L et al—H K Benson et al, Bloomfield 4,500

MORTGAGES.

Andrews, George—The American Ins Co, Franklin 1,000
Bachmann, Adolph—W A Righter, Morris Canal 150
Ballard, H F—M Gounley, Orange 8,000
Beggan, J C—O E Hulse, Stone st 125
Benson, H K et al—J D Wyeth admr, Bloomfield 4,500
Blechschmidt, Rudolph—H E McElhose, Somerset st 2,300
Bonynge, H A—The Drexel Improvement Co, Montclair 359
Botiaux, Armand—M E von Gehrre, Clinton 2,500
Brady, John—Andrew R Lee, Grant st 3,000
Brundage, A D—J H Kase, Montclair 3,200
Buck, H L—The Roseville B and L Assoc, Mulberry st 3,000
Burns, Josephine—The N J B and L Assoc, Nichols st 350
Campbell, Agnes—The Bloomfield Savings Inst, Bloomfield 700
Canfield, M C—The Caldwell B and L Assoc, Caldwell 1,000
Carter, K B—E B M Wilkinson, Houston st 1,000
Christiansen, Matilda—E McCormick, Orange st 2,800
Cimiotti, Gustav—M B Lindsley et al, Caldwell 5,000
Coles, P J—The Aetna B and L Assoc, Morris av 1,500
Collingwood, G C—Mutual Life Ins Co of New York, Bloomfield 14,000
Condit, J S—Orange Savings Bank, West Orange 300
Cornell, R T—Produce Exchange B and L Assoc, Milburn 2,000
Cox, E W—G H Gill, Milburn 1,250
Crawford, Margaret—Bloomfield Savings Inst, Montclair 700
Daum, August—Orange B and L Assoc, Orange 600
Dorst, Margaret—C O Ripley, Livingston st 900
Drake, I S—J R Sayre, Jr, et al, Orchard st 1,811
Duffy, J T—E L Hallock, East Orange 5,000
Evertz, Edward—C R Wolters, Gold st 650
Same——H F Coffin, Gold st 750
Fanning, Mary—W Bonnet, East Orange 500
Finkbeiner, Christian—Firemen's Ins Co, South 6th st 1,900
Finter, W F—A Buermann, Congress st 5,000
Frank, Charles—Union B and L Assoc, Malvern st 3,300
Frey, Albert—E Radel, South Orange av 2,500
Frint, C H—E Meeker, East Orange 1,500
Hey, F T—M A Benjamin, 2d av 800
Higgins, C N—Fireman's Ins Co, Hecker st 8,000
Hogan, M W—L Fowler, South Orange 6,000
Horrigan, Thomas—H W Smith, Orange 1,300
Hotz, Lorenz—Teutonic B and L Assoc, Norfolk st 2,000
Ise, Johanna—M N Burner, West st 250
Jackson, T W—J L Keen, Summer av 880
Jamonneau, A M—Mutual B and L Assoc 4,000
Karr, George—Drexel Impt Co, Montclair 350
Kirschlechner, Ignatz, Passaic B and L Assoc, South 19th st 1,600
King, I W—J W Hall, Ogden st 5,000
Klink, J L—G Wilhelm, Lillie st 519
Kucher, Catharine—B Fischer, Belmont av 1,480
Lauer, Wilhelmina—L F Holzwarth, Bergen st 200
Lawrence, A A—F B Allen, East Orange 3,500
Lawson, C L—W F Jones, Jr, Montclair 166
Liebstein, Mary—M Kussy, 14th av 1,000
Lord, Frank et al—Drexel Impt Co, Montclair 405
Maher, Patrick—Standard B and L Assoc, Cortlandt st 3,200
Maltempo, Frank—Hill's Union Brewing Co, Orange 1,600
Matthews, C B—A Le Massena, Jr, N J R R av 4,500
McGee, E J—T J Regan, Bergen st 450
McGowan, Patrick—M Philip, Monroe st 700
Meyer, Herbert—W Goertz, Darcy st 900
Muller, Frederick—L C Fuller, Central av 500
Osborn, E J—The Mutual Benefit Life Ins Co, Marshall st 3,000
Parkinson, William—Caroline Williams, West Orange 2,400
Picard, Otto—L C Fuller, Central av 1,400
Pullin, Charles—Protection B and L Assoc, North 6th st 1,200
Saunders, G H—E T O'Meara, Wright st 450
Schmidt, Adam—F Frelinghuysen, Ferry st 500
Schmitt, H L—Roseville B and L Assoc, 16th av 2,000
Schenman, David—American Ins Co, Wallace st 1,350
Same——same, Wallace st 2,000
Scudder, B N—G F Tuttle exr, Winans av 1,500
Seekatz, Herman—E E Coe trustee, South 7th st 135
Seidler, Thomas—I H Munn, Springfield av 1,000
Smith, F H, Jr—F H Smith, e s old road from Bloomfield to Newark 15,000
Smith, Peter—The Security B and L Assoc, South st 600
Soden, H L—The Protestant Foster Home Society, Summer av 500
Speer, Richard—P S Pierson, Caldwell 800
Stockhammer, Solomon—Home B and L Assoc, Prince st 2,500
Sweeny, Daniel—E C Harris, South 13th st 1,200
Talbot, A M—D Garber, 5th av 1,500
Whitney, J A—S O Savage trustee, East Orange 6,000
Walsh, Catharine—J Buecher, Elm st 7,000
Ward, S M—Orange Savings Bank, West Orange 3,000
White, G M—Woodside B and L Assoc, North 6th st 1,000
Wirz, A W L—Fidelity Title and Deposit Co, Clinton 8,000
Wisner, Mary—J H Breakenridge et al, Montclair av 200

CHATTEL MORTGAGES.

Burtt, A F, Jr—M J Williams, furniture 1,000
Caeser, O R—J Hirschfield, safe 105
Craig, Thos—Hills Union Brewing Co, saloon 700
Dougherty, Mary—L Bloomer, furniture 42
Ellis, D C—N Richardson, store fixtures 600
Ernst, Alfred—C Fegenspan, saloon 350
Fish, W V—J F Kitchell, saloon 139
Forman, W E—Hill's Union Brewing Co, saloon 450
Geiger, Jacob——same, saloon 800
Kitchell, J M—F J Kastner, saloon 150
Loftus, S R—A L Dennis, horse 500
McCauley, B T—J M O'Connor, furniture 189
Same——W F Korb, piano 100
Meyer, Emil—Hill's Union Brewing Co, saloon 378
Muller, Herman—C Heintze, wagon 50
Rimback, Christian—E Baer, cows, &c 525
Thelm, C J—B L Rink, pool table, &c 810
Van Volkenburgh, Isaac H—P Hauck, saloon 500

JUDGMENTS.

Crane, E G et al—D A Bragaw 2,340
Coyne, F E—T E Jones 788
Kelly, F R et al—W H Bergfels et al 142
Oschwald, Joseph, Jr—J Bollard 251
Ross, B H—S E Ryerson 341
Sargeant, E K, Jr—C W Clayton 147

HUDSON COUNTY.

CONVEYANCES.

Allen, Robert and M M Forest—W Edwards, Kearney $1,100
Aralo, A J—P Arala, Hoboken .... nom
Backlund, Nils—J Hanson, Kearney 800
Bahlburg, Henry—C J Noeding, Hoboken 775
Benoit, Mary E—F J Mathews .... nom
Bidwell, M A—E F Emmons 335
Borrone, Antonio—Antonie Casazza, Hoboken 4,800
Braunstein, William—J Conway, Union 600
Budenbender, Margaret—M Ettinger, Hoboken 10,000
Bumsted, W G—N D Moody 4,150
Canfield, Miron—P Daveny, Hoboken 1,000
Chidester, Mary A and F B by sheriff—E Insley 3,000
Chidester, F B—Mary A Chidester .... nom
Close, J B—Sarah Plass, Bayonne .... nom
Condit, Fillmore—J Butterfield, Kearney 200
Same——T Lister, Kearney 250
Same——W Hanna, Kearney 150
Same——D McCaslin, Kearney 300
Connolly, John—Grace Smith, Harrison 400
Crossley, James—J W Crossley, Guttenberg 3,000
Dickenscheid, John—W Millenzwei .... nom
Dollfus, Jacques—Maria A Kuschinski 700
Donnelly, Margaret—Exr J Van Horn 25
Dougherty, J W—Margaret A English 4,000
Du Pont, Eugene and F G—H R Du Pont .... nom
Du Pont, H R—Eugene Du Pont de Nemours & Co .... nom
Embly, Meta R—Gesina Doscher .... nom
Emmons, E F—J Langan 500
Eilshemius, H G—E T Fanning, Kearney 650
Faley, Patrick—T Kurzius, Guttenberg 150
Fitzpatrick, Florence—Bridget McDonald, Harrison 1,000
Foley, Patrick—T Kurzias, Guttenberg 700
Frank, Edward—Magdalena Frank, Bayonne 1,000
Frank, Philip—E Frank, Bayonne 1,000
Frommel, Oscar—H Timford, Hoboken 500
Same——F Finck, Hoboken 475
Garbs, D H—J Laven, Bayonne 300
Gier, Lewis—Catharine M Quinn, Union 1,350
Gordon, H J—J D Rover, Union 1,400
Greenman, W B—H R Greenman, Bayonne .... nom
Haars, Otto—W Braunstein, Union 600
Hafemann, Wilhelm—Wilhelmine K Helmers .... nom
Hanson, John—Emma C Backlund, Kearney 300
Hanson, N F—Harriet Snell, Kearney 400
Harney, Herbert—Margarett Sloan 5,000
Haysen, F C—Georgina E Hofman, Union 2,000
Same——same, Union 400
Helmers, Ike—W Hafemann .... nom
Hiested, A N—Nicola Zozzord, Bayonne 350
Hille, F W—I Knobalsch, Union 5,000
Hoboken Land and Improvement Co—Marie Clausen, Hoboken 7,250
Hofman, Georgina E—J Eiler 6,000
Houdlett, Albert—L Lang, North Bergen 1,600
Insley, Earle—F B Chidester .... nom
Jersey City, Newark & Western R R Co—R H Sayre .... nom
Jones, J M—A Patike 450
Jordan, T D—S Gilbert 10,500
Kalanguin, Marguaret—F J Von Alzinger, West Hoboken 550
Kelly, Bryan—Julia Lincks, Hoboken 5,900
Knox, J H—G Boast, Bayonne 750
Lang, Marie E—Albert Houdlett, North Bergen .... nom
Lennon, Ed by sheriff—T P Lennon, North Bergen 286
Mackie, Isabella—Hannah A Donaldson .... nom
Mason, T L by exrs—F C Dames 1,350
Maver, William, Jr—F E Orrok 8,200
McCarren, James—J W Dougherty 4,000
McElmeel, Jno—C H Weller, Bayonne .... nom
Merchants' National Bank—F Junker, West Hoboken 1,500
Mitlenzwei, William—J Dickenscheid .... nom
Mount, F C—Henry J White 1,100
Nelson, Eliza J by collector—A Post 168
Neuscheler, Jacob—V Block, Union 1,800
Niely, D M and Jane Ann Baillard by sheriff—Susan J Wortendyke 100
Noonan, E J—O Sullivan .... nom
Paret, John by sheriff—O E Paret, Bayonne 5,500
Peoples, J J and Julia A by city collector—E S Cowles 302
Pfeffer, Lorenz—J Goldsmith 600
Plott, Frances—Catharine Caffrey 100
Porrett, Nora—H Puster 2,700
Rademan, Peter—J Plate 5,750
Reed, R L—J Pearson 4,500
Reichenbach, Jno—C Long, Guttenberg 450
Schaldeler, John—W Schaldeler, North Bergen .... nom
Scholl, Elizabeth—Dorothea Bermes, Union 8,450
Seitz, Arthur and T H Mickens—J Lamb, Hoboken 2,000
Smith, James—J P Smith 2,000
Sturgeon, Margaret—C H Schoch, North Bergen 5,500
The Pequanock Land and Building Co—J Tonnele .... nom
Thompson, Mary W—J Hunt 4,000
Tierney, Elizabeth L N—Mary I Dennin 8,800
Usher, James—J Crossley, North Bergen 15
Van Buskirk, J H—J W Bunn, Bayonne 3,200
Von Dreule, Herman by exrs—Matilda Lorentz, West Hoboken 1,000
Van Horn, Maria M—E Williams 550
Van Voist, Cornelius by trustee—Eliz E Coyle .... nom
Van Winkle, Edward by special guard—F Quinn 325
Vreeland, Marie A—J H Van Buskirk, Bayonne 200
Vreeland, Susan M—Sarah F Slavin 2,600
Walker, Herman—A Dielsche, Guttenberg 450
Weiss, Jos—A Endre, Union 925
Weller, C H—J McElmeel, Bayonne .... nom
Wescott, W P—J Henning, Bayonne 205
West Shore R R Co and New York Central & Hudson R R Co—Exr J Van Horne, Union 100
Wood, Anna F and Florence Lembeck by special guard—C Martin, Bayonne 200
Same——C Martin, Bayonne 550
Same——J Kemble, Bayonne 410
Same——C Gibbons, Bayonne 200
Same——A Jeskot, Bayonne 200
Yost, Peter—F Frambach, Jr 1,450
Zumstein, Jno—Bridget Jennings, Bayonne 550

MORTGAGES.

Aratre, Peter—W Hormann, Hoboken, 3 years 2,000
Bannon, George, Jr—G R McKenzie, 5 years 4,500
Bunn, J W—Bayonne B Assoc No 2, Bayonne, installs 2,400
Campbell, Neil—W G Bumsted, 3 years 7,500
Chidester, F B—S B Vreeland, 1 year 9,000
Same——same, 4 years 4,000
Cole, G B—Highland M B and L Assoc, installs 1,400
Cosine, Virginia J—A Stenken, 3 years 2,800
Crossley, J W—J Crossley, Guttenberg, 5 years 2,200
Dohm, Henry—J C Besson, North Bergen, 3 yrs 900
Daly, Catharine—Hudson City M B and L Assoc, installs 5,000

Dennin, Mary I—Elizabeth L N Tierney, 5 years 2,000
Same——same, installs 1,800
Deunter, Gottlieb—Hudson Trust Savings Inst, West Hoboken, 3 years 600
Dogherty, J W—M Hastings, 1 year 3,000
Doin, Henry—G Doin, 1 year 700
Eser, John—L F Hofman, 3 years 2,000
Edwards, J S—J A Gilbert, 1 year 2,000
Ewald, Henry—Washington B and L Assoc, installs 2,000
Gilbert, Maggie A—Star M B and L Assoc, installs 900
Gilbert, Simon—T D Jordan, 5 years 6,500
Gillen, Rosa—Hudson City M B and L Assoc, installs 2,400
Clancy, Owen—Ella Converse, 3 years 8,0
Golden, Jacob—Highland M B and L Assoc, installs 1,800
Hanrahan, James—Mary A Mainell, Hoboken, 1 year 400
Harned, H J—P G Van Zandt, 5 years 4,500
Heuschkel, Geo—Hoboken Bank for Savings, Hoboken, 4 years 9,000
Hogan, J J—Pavonia B and L Assoc, installs 3,000
Holstebroe, Edward—H Puster, 1 year 800
Hoppock, Margaret A—Provident Inst for Savings, 1 year 400
Housman, C W—Hoboken B and L Assoc, installs 200
Junge, Claus—H C Harms, 4 years 1,000
Junken, Frank—Merchants' National Bank, West Hoboken, 1 year 1,000
Kelly, William—The Mechanics' Trust Co, Bayonne, 1 year 7,000
Krobalsch, Ignatz—F W Hille, Union, 3 years 4,000
Kurzius, Theodore—P Faley, Guttenberg, 3 years 350
Lamb, James—H Iden, Hoboken, 5 years 5,000
Lane, John—R Pamly, West Hoboken, 3 years 300
Lang, Lorenz—A Houdlett, North Bergen, 3 years 800
Laux, Albert—North Hudson Co B and L Assoc, installs 800
Lehigh Valley Terminal Railway Co—Central Trust Co, 50 years 10,000,000
Lewis, Jos—Mary Becker, 5 years 8,000
Lusenhop, F O—New Jersey Title Guarantee and Trust Co, installs 8,000
McCormick, Thos—Agnes L Greig, 1 year 1,000
Mellert, Wendelin—Elizabeth Rengelmann, Bayonne, 4 years 600
Moody, N I—W G Bumsted, 5 years 2,500
Morton, William and Alice—F Lewis, 5 years 700
Norden, A B—Magdalena M Taylor, Union, 5 years 1,000
Paret, Anna E—Eliza G Reed, Bayonne, 3 years 4,000
Pearson, John—Elizabeth Elliott, 3 years 2,300
Plate, Johann—P Rademan, 3 years 2,000
Same——same, 3 years 2,250
Roberts, Harriet—J M Newkirk, 1 year 1,900
Rickett, A D—A M Layat, 4 years 500
Schillinger, Maria—Margaretha Sulfiusch, Union, 1 year 200
Schneider, Louisa—Union B and L Assoc, Guttenberg installs 1,900
Schock, C H—Margaret Sturegon, North Bergen, 1 year 900
Schunk, Margaretha—Jane D Newkirk, 5 years 1,500
Scully, John, Jr—S C Mount, Bayonne, 3 years 425
Siefhen Emma—Minnie H Linn, Bayonne, 5 years 1,900
Smith, J P—E A Wood, 1 year 1,200
Snell, Harriet—Harrison and Kearney B and L Assoc, Kearney, installs 1,600
Steele, G H—I I Vanderbeck et al, 1 year 300
Sullivan, Joseph—D B Baker, 3 years 500
Tumford, Henry—O Frommel, Hoboken, 1 year 200
Watson, W C—Columbia B and L Assoc, installs 494
Williams, Edwards—Marie M Van Horne, 3 years 350
Wills, Marcus D—Wilkinson, Gaddis & Co, Bayonne 1,500

CHATTEL MORTGAGES.

Beatty, John—H Thoesen, furniture 69
Blair, Mrs Julia——same, furniture 110
Bowles, Sarah—J Bauman, furniture 77
Brown, G T—Bernheimer & Schmid, saloon 1,500
Brown, James—C H Hangs, drug store fixtures 947
Corbeth, Charles—Bernheimer & Schmid, saloon 2,000
Correll, T J—E Sullivan, horses, wagons, harness 100
Etzkorn, William—The F & M Schaefer Brewing Co, saloon fixtures 450
Feely, Patrick—Woelff Bros, horses 425
Feely, Patrick—Wolff Bros, 2 horses 400
Fergratti, Melli, Hoboken—H Thoesen, furniture 79
Gerster, Joseph, West Hoboken—P Richterich, saloon fixtures 400
Griffin, J W and J C Struch—D G Hawthorn, one 4 horse-power Shipman engine No. 1203 and appurtenances 174
Grob, George, Secaucus—J H Mierdierch, saloon 300
Guest, H W—P Ballantine & Sons, saloon fixtures 797
Haas, Joseph, Union Hill—J E Linde, printing presses, &c 410
Harris, A P—C E Pierce, furniture 75
Keane, Andrew—Woelff Bros, horse 200
McCloskey, Patrick—P Reilly, horses, trucks, &c 200
McNulty, Mrs Annie T—Krakauer Bros, piano 335
Moje, John, Hoboken—Lembeck & Betz Eagle Brewing Co, saloon 2,500
Norton, Michael—Nat Cash Reg Co, one No 2 cash register 150
Pollak, Emil—C Ackerman, horses, wagons, &c 250
Rothenberg, Beckie, Bayonne—Mary Brown, bakery, horse, wagon, &c 825
Rucci, J G and Mancesco Trola, West Hoboken—Wm Peter Brewing Co, saloon 830
Ruttenberg, Rebecca and Meyer, her husband, Bayonne—H Lesser, grocery store 100
Sesta, Thomas—The Bavarian Brewing Co, saloon 400
Shaler, Frank, Hoboken—Wolff Bros, horses, coach, harness 850
Sturken, Albert, Hoboken—John Matthews Apparatus Co, soda water apparatus 125
Todd, C W—Reardon & Doremus, horses, wagon, grocery store 650
Voltz, J E—B E Ostrander, butcher shop fixtures 100
Wells, Catharine, Bayonne—Wilkinson, Gaddis & Co, grocery store 1,521

BILLS OF SALE.

Streng, Johanna, Hoboken—Jesse C Hansen, furniture 475
Stuhmer, Edward and Anna, Hoboken—J [illegible], horse, wagon, grocery store 2,150

JUDGMENTS.

Christ, Christopher—T C Kinkead 98
Hennessy, Bridget B—T C Kinkead 88
Lyons, Mary—G Russomanna 81
McDonald, Isabella—T C Kinkead 110
Meyer, Henry and Frederick—W Gunning et al. 88
O'Brien, W J—J D O'Neill 825
Taylor, N D, Jr—The William Peter Brewing Co 117
The Jersey City Electric Light Co—J H Foley 3,500
Timken, H L, Jr—H Cassidy 321
Weber, Charles—G Hauser 416
Witt, Albert—D A Haggerty 804

BUILDING MATERIAL MARKET.

BRICKS.—Pretty much the old strain is noticeable in the majority of reports, though if anything the pitch is toward a slight improvement. We find a number of receivers who are getting a shilling per M more now and then on immediate grades, and former extreme low figures are no longer quotable, the natural result of modified volume of supplies and lessened pressure to realize on surplus parcels. From no authoritative or reliable source, however, do we receive a suggestion that would warrant the advancing of top line of quotations, prices obtained in excess thereof being entirely upon exceptional deals and beyond the ordinary line of trading. Over quality there is very little complaint, stock running pretty good and well up to the average ordinarily expected from the different localities represented, and in matter of quantity there has been quite enough for the current requirements of the market, with always a trifle to spare, though the surplus was not great as the tides have been of a character to prevent loading and shipping from primary points. The nature of the demand has changed slightly, inasmuch as some dealers are now taking a little more stock for piling away consequent upon the fact that they have about completed deliveries to jobs in hand and no new work of importance is coming on at the moment. Some Pales are now and then called for, but buyers are particular in the selection of quality, and it is a difficult matter to induce them to pay extreme figures. We hear more about a reduction of shipments than heretofore, some manufacturers having about completed contracts, and they in common with others who are getting tired of ruling rates talking about pulling boats off on return trips.

LATH.—It has not been much of a market, probably owing as greatly to the absence of supplies as anything, the few arrivals having been previously disposed of. Notwithstanding the quietness, however, the undertone was pretty firm, gaining if anything, and while the latest sales of ordinary stock were at \$2.10, it would probably not be difficult to raise that figure, and some receivers feel very sure of their ability to make \$2.25 per M if they had good first-class stock to offer. Advices from the Eastward reiterate quite positively the stories of early closing of mills and the chances are thought to be against buyers getting any advantage during balance of the season.

LIME.—Some arrivals have been taking place from day to day, probably quite as many as the market really required, and cargoes were not in all cases promptly disposed of. The offering, however, was well managed, and, so far as known, no shading from the former line of cost developed on the popular brands at least. A little St. John stock came forward and was placed, but the offerings from the State are indifferent, and it is understood that Western manufacturers do not find the market very attactive.

LUMBER.—It is a far from animated market for any description of stock or upon any outlet. The dealers who are doing an active trade remain as the exception to the rule, and their good luck is due to some favored locality or other special influence, while agents who are succeeding in putting through negotiations for any considerable bulk parcels are not readily found. Values, however, are well sustained, but in some instances gaining a trifle, as with the now rapid drawing near of the end of the season the offerings are less plentiful, mills shutting down, freight charges advancing, and other features of a natural character developing calculated to enhance value of supplies. Yard stocks are filling up pretty well, but there is in many cases room for a little more, especially in the way of really choice goods of staple character.

Eastern Spruce has not been particularly active, because up to present writing the offering was limited, and buyers seem a little inclined to openly assume an indifferent attitude. Still receivers discover that they get a great many more quiet hints, that if there be any attractive random to offer certain dealers would like to have first chance to bid upon it, and that in conjunction with reduced tenders from primary sources, and most of the mills refusing to accept further bids for specials leads up to a stronger undertone, and the line of valuation is creeping upward. At one time and another considerable stock has crept in here this fall, and most of the goods are very well filled, though more is to come on orders.

Piling remains in a general way about as last noted, and there is not much of a market. Offerings cannot well be crowded upon sale in the absence of a natural outlet; but when demand does develop it is promptly met, and the general range of value stands as before.

Northern Spruce and Hemlock are offered moderately and command very good rates. Pennsylvania Hemlock can be reached readily enough when called for, and the call is not very general or loud, business as a rule proving unsatisfactory. At present rates, however, manufacturers are not urgent and are endeavoring to nurse their patience for next season.

White Pine retains a firm tone for all the better qualities of stock for which the demand is very fair and the offering comparatively limited with advances from the interior indicating that there is but little chance for an increase of seasoned stock this year. Box is about as before in value, but finding no special increase of demand. Shipping grades are more or less unsettled in tone and without satisfactory activity, with the acceptance of low prices still more or less a necessity in order to secure custom. In view of this disagreeable state of affairs and with a hope of recovering some of the value shrinkage of the past year five of the leading concerns handling export grades are said to have formed a combination for the purpose of advancing the price of white pine shippers 10@25 per cent, binding themselves under a heavy forfeit to adhere to the agreement. Some houses, however, are not in the pool and claim that the combination is illegal.

Yellow Pine is reported as doing better in both movement and general tone and some operators speak with really cheerful expression over the situation. The movement into consumption is said to equal in natural relative proportion that of any other leading wood, and the booking of specials is quite satisfactory, while on prices the tendency is to harden somewhat. Probably the most important development, however, is in the matter of the combination previously referred to, and the details of which can no longer be suppressed. Contrary to the calculations of some of the trade who have been cognizant of a consolidating movement among the yellow pine men, the manufacturing interest contributing to this locality are not included, nor has an ordinary price sustaining agreement been entered into, but the leading wholesale and retail dealers of this district have simply worked up and given publicity to a plan through which they agree to pool all their interests and form a regular trust. It is to be called the Yellow Pine Company, with a capital of \$2,500,000, of which \$1,000,000 is in preferred stock and \$1,500,000 in common stock. The perfection of the scheme is said to depend upon the decision of stockholders of one of the largest interested concerns at a meeting called for November 11th.

Carolina Pine has been selling along very well, and at steady rates, the market showing healthy elements as a rule with complaints from sellers few and far between. Offerings fair, but kept under control and not urged, the association of manufacturers preventing an over-supply.

Hardwoods present no really new feature. Consuming demand is moderate for pretty much all kinds, and with a good stock now together dealers furnish indifferent custom, but the offering appears limited and about former rates current. There is a better feeling over quarter-sawed oak, late advices from the interior indicating much less over-cut than had for some time been reported and a firmer feeling among manufacturers. Some export calls prevail, but only for carefully selected stock, the foreign market having a surplus of inferior stuff.

GENERAL LUMBER NOTES.

GREAT BRITAIN.

The London *Timber Trades Journal* reports:

Spruce has gone up materially, it is stated, quite 10s. a standard at the shipping ports. This, coupled with a rise in freights of quite that amount, will make a great difference in prices here. At Thursday's sale some Montreal 1st quality deals and planks made £10 1's. This for 9 to 18 ft. lengths was by no means bad; 2ds, however, were not so favorably received; 4ths at £6 10s., and 3ds at £7; but this was for remnant parcels. The advance in Canadian white will stimulate white stocks generally.

At public sale American walnut logs, without reserve, of which there were four parcels ex as many ships, were well competed for, and all sold at from 1s. 9d. to 3s. 3d. per foot cube, the auctioneer saying the day for low priced walnut was nearly over.

At Glasgow the arrivals of wood goods continue very light, the past week's list comprising only a few parcels per steam liners, and not any full cargoes. Parcels of deals per the regular weekly steamers from Quebec and Montreal are still coming forward in extremely limited quantities compared with former years, and at this advanced period of the season there is little time to make up for the paucity of supplies hitherto, and the probability is that the record of this season will show an unusually short supply. Some further shipments of United States whitewood logs are to be observed among the imports of the past week, though at present there is a full stock of this wood, and prices rather weak. Black walnut meets with good demand, and brings fair prices, except small and inferior logs, of which there are too large a stock on hand.

STATE.

The Albany *Argus* reports as follows:

It would be a pleasure to say and to read, if it were true, that the market is flourishing like the green bay tree, but unfortunately such is not the fact at present. The fact is on the contrary that matters are, as a whole, looking rather dull just now, and there is considerable speculation as to whether the colder weather and the approach of the closing of navigation is likely to stir up the demand in the near future. If business does not pick up materially the results of the year as far as the whole district is concerned are likely to be considerably below the average. Some few houses have unquestionably done more than usual this season, but they are decidedly the exceptions. About the only new feature in pine during the week has been an unusually good demand for 12-inch shippers, and some of the thicker grades are moving fairly. Otherwise the market is very quiet. While the demand for spruce, both good and culls, is much below the average and really slow, there is still the same difficulty in filling orders, by reason of the small receipts. Hemlock is dull and hardwoods are not doing much better, while shingles are just doing fairly, and that is all. Lath also are quiet.

THE WEST.

Reviewing the general situation the Northwestern *Lumberman* says:

Reports from along the Mississippi and throughout Wisconsin are unanimous that trade is active, while the supply is likely to run short of the demand for reason of a lack of logs. At Clinton the mills have been shut down; at Davenport and Rock Island the season is about closed. There is a shortage of logs all along the river from St. Louis to Winona, at the same time the manufacturers and dealers are looking forth to a season of unusually good demand. Naturally they are firm as to prices. Chicago men who have lately been through Wisconsin report that lumber is being held in that State relatively higher than it is in this city, except in cases wherein holders are overstocked with some particular sorts or sizes. In any case manufacturers do not manifest special anxiety to sell, unless they can get the prices they ask.

In this city the shipping movement out of the wholesale yards is large. The local requirement, aside from that for the World's Fair, is not proportionate to that for shipping, though, of course, it is by no means dull or inconsiderable.

In the Saginaw valley more lumber is changing hands than appears on the surface. There is a good deal of quiet trading going on, and the demand seems to be increasing. The prospect there is that by the year's end the result will be better than was feared earlier in the season. Still, this year's business has been a disappointment on account of the quiet condition of affairs in the east.

At Chicago receipts at the sales docks have not been heavy during the week and there has been a [illegible]

REGULAR

Democratic Nominations

FOR GOVERNOR,
Roswell P. Flower.

FOR LIEUTENANT-GOVERNOR,
William F. Sheehan.

FOR SECRETARY OF STATE,
Frank Rice.

FOR COMPTROLLER,
Frank Campbell.

FOR ATTORNEY GENERAL,
Simon W. Rosendale.

FOR STATE TREASURER,
Elliot F. Danforth.

FOR STATE ENGINEER,
Martin Schenck.

FOR SUPREME COURT JUDGE,
George L. Ingraham.

FOR SUPERIOR COURT JUDGE,
Henry A. Gildersleeve.

FOR JUDGE OF THE COURT OF COMMON PLEAS,
Roger A. Pryor.

FOR CITY COURT JUDGES,
Simon M. Ehrlich.
John Henry McCarthy.

FOR JUDGE OF THE TENTH DISTRICT COURT,
Christopher C. Clarke.

FOR CORONERS,
Louis W. Schultze.
John B. Shea.
Ferdinand Levy.

FOR CONGRESSMEN,
Dist
10 W. BOURKE COCKRAN
12 JOSEPH J. LITTLE

FOR SENATORS,
Dist
5 WILLIAM L. BROWN
6 JOHN F. AHEARN
7 GEORGE F. ROESCH
8 MARTIN T. McMAHON
9 EDWARD P. HAGAN
10 JACOB A. CANTOR
11 GEORGE W. PLUNKITT

FOR ASSEMBLYMEN,

Dist.
1. PATRICK H. DUFFY.
2. TIMOTHY D. SULLIVAN.
3. PERCIVAL FARQUHAR.
4. PATRICK H. ROCHE.
5. DOMINICK F. MULLANEY.
6. SAMUEL J. FOLEY.
7. JENKINS VAN SCHAICK.
8. PHILIP WISSIG.
9. WILLIAM H. WALKER.
10. WILLIAM SOHMER.
11. HENRY C. JUDSON.
12. MOSES DINKELSPIEL.
13. JAMES H. SOUTHWORTH.
14. WILLIAM SULZER.
15. LOUIS DRYPOLCHER.
16. WALTER G. BYRNE.
17. THOMAS McMAHON.
18. DANIEL F. MARTIN.
19. JOHN CONNELLY.
20. MYER J. STEIN.
21. LOUIS H. HAHLO.
22. JOSEPH BLUMENTHAL.
23. GEORGE P. WEBSTER.
24. THOMAS J. BYRNES.

FOR ALDERMEN,

Dist.
1. CORNELIUS FLYNN.
2. NICHOLAS T. BROWN.
3. PATRICK J. O'BEIRNE.
4. ANDREW A. NOONAN.
5. PATRICK J. RYDER.
6. WILLIAM CLANCY.
7. JOHN MORRIS.
8. CHARLES S. SMITH.
9. ABRAHAM MEAD.
10. JOSEPH MARTIN.
11. JAMES M. MOOREHEAD.
12. WILLIAM TAIT.
13. CHARLES W. FERRIS.
14. CHARLES J. SMITH.
15. FRANK ROGERS.
16. WILLIAM H. MURPHY.
17. PETER J. DOOLING.
18. JACOB C. WUND.
19. HORATIO S. HARRIS.
20. DAVID J. ROCHE.
21. ROLLIN M. MORGAN.
22. HENRY C. HART.
23. SAMUEL H. BAILEY.

Ward.
23. AUGUST MOEBUS.
24. THOMAS M. LYNCH

mand for offerings. The call is still for good schedules of piece stuff, stock width boards, and for strips. The dealers will buy what they are looking for if prices suit. They are willing to pay $10 for short piece stuff, and $12.50 for long. In respect to inch lumber that runs strong to promiscuous widths they are indifferent, and they are still quite particular as to tally. Still the market can be called considerably better all round. Buyers are not falling over one another for cargoes, and are inclined to defer purchasing when their docks are at all crowded. The season is apparently running along moderately, and it does not now look as if there would be much excitement before the close. Prices on piece stuff may advance a shilling or a quarter in November, especially if the present good demand in the yards shall hold out.

Commission men continue to say that the manufacturers are consigning to them stuff that has been robbed of the better grades and sizes. At the same time they expected to sell at full market prices—in fact, to make the cargo market for Lake Michigan product. The commission men think that this is rather hard lines, and that if the manufacturers would give them a chance at a fair average of lumber, they would be able to sell more stuff and at better prices.

Reviewing the Chicago hardwood market the *Timberman* says:

The first thing from which dealers will reap a substantial benefit is quartered oak. A local dealer takes exception to the statement made by the *Timberman* last week on the authority of an Eastern buyer, that there was very little quartered oak now in pile at the mill, but says it is undoubtedly true that nearly all the mills have quit manufacturing and sorting quartered stock. This being the case, it is evident that a few weeks of active demand would speedily make a change for the better in present prices. The Chicago yards have heavy stocks of this grade of lumber, and are waiting for just such a contingency as the above.

Nevertheless there is more money for the mill man just now in cutting plain stock. The market does not justify the additional expense of quarter sawing, and besides plain-sawed oak sells much more readily, there being no particular surplus of dry stock in sight.

Manufacturers who can afford to do so would probably find it to their advantage to cut thick oak while the market is dull. As has been stated thick oak is not plentiful and will be much scarcer next season.

There continues to be a fair movement in elm and basswood, but there are no new features to be noted. It is expected that there will be an increased call for elm early next year, but this depends greatly on the developments of the furniture trade.

It can hardly be said that there is any trade in walnut locally, although stock suitable for export is ready sale.

Cherry is comparatively quiet, but good stock brings fair prices, and no stock has accumulated in this market.

Wagon and implement stock, in both ash and hickory, continues to be scarce, with some little inquiry.

The Mississippi Valley *Lumberman* says:

There are two things that are conspicuously absent in the lumber trade of the Mississippi valley just at present—the usual suspicion that the other fellow is cutting the price list and the fall clamor that the cut of logs in the woods should be kept down. There is enough confidence in the situation at present to prevent both practices.

One of the striking things, connected with the unequal conditions prevailing in the lumber trade, taking the country over, is the escape of the white pine men from competition which might prove disastrous at the hands of the yellow pine dealers. Occasions have presented within recent times when the readiness of the Southern lumbermen to sell at almost any price, their eagerness to push their lumber into white pine territory and the inability of the Northern men to sell their lumber cut from expensive stumpage has demoralized values and taken the courage out of the white pine mill men. Apparently prices were never more demoralized in the South than at present. But yellow pine is not crowding into Iowa, Illinois, Nebraska and Kansas as it once was. This circumstance is due in part to the limitations placed upon shipments by the railroads, but more to a closer driving of the lines which determine the purpose for which the respective classes of lumber can be advantageously used. It is the white pine men's inning. It is believed that they have experienced far the worst features of competition with southern pine, for all time.

METALS.—Copper—Ingot has followed up the weakness noted in our last report by becoming somewhat demoralized, and at the present writing the general market is very much unsettled. At the considerable fractional reduction in cost actual consumers seem to be about as indifferent as ever, and the general movement is very slow. On an average range of valuations we quote at 11½@1[illegible]¾c. for Lake, and 11@11¼c. for casting brands. Manufactured Copper is finding no more than an ordinary call, and while about old rates are asked, there is some intimation of buyers getting small favors. We quote as follows: Sheet, not above 30x72 in., 16 oz. and over, 2[illegible]c.; do, 14 to 16 oz., 23c.; do, 12 to 14 oz., 24c.; do, 10 to 12 oz., 2[illegible]c.; do, 8 to 10 oz., 28c.; do under 8 oz, 30c. Sheets longer than 72 inches add 1c. for 12@14 oz., 2c. for 10@12 oz. and 3c. for 8@10 oz. Sheets, not above 36x96 in., 16 oz and over, 22c.; do, 14 to 16 oz, 24c.; do, 12 to 14 oz, 26c.; do, 10 to 12 oz, 30c.; do, 8 to 10 oz, 33c. Sheets longer than 96 inches 22c. for over 32 oz, and add 1c. for 16 to 32 oz.; 3c. 14 to 16 oz.; 5c. 12 to 14 oz. and 13c. for 8 to 10 oz. Sheets, not above 48x96 32 to 64 oz, 22c.; do, 16 to 32 oz, 25c.; do, 14 to 16 oz, 27c. do, 12 to 14 oz, 29c.; do, 10 to 12 oz. 33c. Sheets wider than 48x96 and longer, 22@25c. for 32 to 64 oz. and over, 27@[illegible]c. for 16 to 32 oz, [illegible] for 14 to 16 oz and 34c. for 12 to 14 oz. All bath tub sheets, per lb., 16 oz. [illegible] 14 oz, 29c.; 12 oz 3[illegible]; and 10 oz. [illegible]c. Bolt copper, ⅜ inch diameter and over, 2[illegible]c. Circles, 60 diameter and less, 3c. above price of sheets of same thickness; circles, 60 to 96 do do, 5c. do; circles, 96 do and over, 6c. do. Segment and pattern sheets, 3c. above price of sheets required to cut them from. Cold or hard rolled copper, 1@2c. per lb. above the foregoing prices. Copper bottoms, 26@32c. per lb. Iron—American Pig sells along very much in the same general form and volume as for some time past, and it is a practically unchanged market. Offerings of first-class brands are made with moderation, and some indifference, former rates being in all cases asked, but inferior stock is offered low, and there seems to be plenty of it. We quote at $17.00@18.00 per ton for No. 1 X foundry; $15.50@16.50 for No. 2 X do, and $14.0[illegible]

@15.00 for Gray Forge. Old material has been held with considerable firmness, and while demand shows some indifference small accumulations afford basis of confidence. We quote at about $22.00@22.50 for old rails; $19.00@20.00 for No. 1 wrought scrap; $17.00@18.00 for cast scrap and $17.00@17.50 for car wheels. Manufactured iron is without great change. From store not much stock is handled, and special orders are hardly up to expectation mark; but for most grades former values are supported. We quote Common Merchant Bar ordinary size, at 1.90@2c. from store, and refined at 2@2¼c; Rods, round and square, 2.10@2.30c.; Bands, 2.30@2.50c.; Norway Nail Rods 3¾@4c., and domestic sheet on the basis of 3.00@3.05c. for common Nos. 10@16. Other descriptions at corresponding prices, with 1-10c. less on large lots from cars. Steel rails have been more active, with quite a number of really good-sized orders gone to book of late. A great deal of the business, however, is looked upon as simply representing delayed demand, and more of it is hoped for at an early date. About everything has been taken at former basis of valuation and the tone is pretty firm throughout. We quote standard sections $30 per ton at mill, with usual advance for delivery at tide water. Pig Lead has continued steadily on the downward turn with full offerings of stock. Buyers, however, appeared to find no inducement to take hold beyond present natural wants, and it was a very light movement. The close is somewhat nominal. We quote at 4.20@4.25c. per lb. The manufactures of lead are quoted at 7c. for Pipe, 7¾c. for sheet, 15c. for Tin-lined Pipe, and 37½c. for Block Pin Pipe. Pig Tin has on the whole been very well held, the foreign advices affording little assistance and stocks standing rather full. Here and there, however, a holder appears nervous, and any attempt to realize would lead to a decline. We quote at about 20.05@20.10c. for round lots, and 20.15@20.20c. for jobbing parcels. Tin Plate in full invoices is not wanted, but quite a steady sale in small lots is reported and at prices showing a generally steady tone. We quote prices as follows: I. C. Charcoal, ½ cross assortment Melyn grade, $6.50@6.55, each additional X add $1.50; I. C. Charcoal, ½ cross assortment, Allaway grade, $5.85@5.90, each additional X add $1; Charcoal terne, M. F. grade, 14x20, $7.50@7.55; M. F. grade, 20x28, $15.50@15.55; Worcester, 14x20, $5.70@5.75; Worcester 20x28, $11.25@11.30; Dean grade, 14x20, $5.40@5.45; Dean grade, 20x28, $10.70@10.75; D. R. D. grade, 14x20, $5.25@5.30; D. R. D. grade, 20x28, $10.12½@10.15; I C. Coke. Penlan grade, $5.30@5.35; J. B. grade, 14x20, $5.45@5.50; I. C. Bessemer steel, squares, $5.75@5.80 basis; I. C. Siemens steel, squares, $5.85@6.00 basis. Spelter offered with some freedom, the demand moderate and prices ruling quite easy in most cases. We quote $4.95@5.05c. for Common Western, according to brand.

NAILS.—There is no doubt that consumption at all dependent points is curtailed, and as there does not appear to be compensation in corresponding shrinkage of production the market, as a whole, retains all the old unsettled disagreeable features. Nominally unchanged is a common way of referring to values, but frequent, and sometimes pretty deep cuts are believed to be made. We quote Cut at $1.50@1.60 per keg for car lots and $1.75@1.85 per keg for parcels from store, for iron, and add 5@10c. per keg for steel; Wire, $2.00@2.05 at mills, and 2.20@2.35 from store.

PAINTS, OILS, COLORS, ETC.—Standard runs of stock, such as dry colors, colors in oil, and ready mixed paints are finding very fair attention from regular sources, and this trade is likely to continue steadily, with occasional calls for other varieties, as assortments may happen to require filling out. There is, however, nothing in the action of buyers to inspire a hope that they are likely to become more anxious or liberal investors than at present, and both wholesale and jobbing operators have practically abandoned the idea of a quick, sharp trade this season. So far as the wants of the market require, there is an ample and well-assorted supply available of both domestic and foreign goods, and we hesitate about making an offering when the call develops, with buyers who are willing to pay former figures very quickly met, and some on a little effort managing to get moderate concessions. Leads of pure quality, however, are pretty well held and the combination basis adhered to in about all cases. Association Corroders' rates stand as follows: Lead in oil in kegs and dry lead in kegs, in lots of less than 500 lbs., 7½c. net; in lots of 500 lbs to 5 tons at one purchase, 7c.; 5 tons to 12 tons, one purchase, 6¾c.; 12 tons and over, one purchase, 6½c.; dry white lead in bbls. ½c. per lb. less than price in kegs. Lead in oil 12½ lb. in tin pails, add 1c.; in 25 and 50 lb. tin pails, add ½c.; and in 1 to 5 lb. tin cans, assorted (100 lbs. in case) add 2½c. per lb. to keg price. Terms on lots on 500 lbs. and over, note or acceptance at sixty days, or 2½ per cent. discount will be allowed for cash paid within fifteen days of invoice date. To make either of the above required quantities any assortment of packages of white lead, red lead and litharge may be counted. The above quotations are free on board cars or boat at corroding point. Linseed Oil remains more or less unsettled in tone, and now and then some pretty deep cuts on price are made. By way of average valuation, however, about former figures are named. We quote at general range at 35@40c. for Western, and 40@56c. for City. Spirits Turpentine show no change. Demand moves slowly and indifferently with a more or less weakening effect upon values, though holders manage to prevent a decided pressure to realize. We quote at 35½@37½c. per gallon, according to quality, delivery, etc.

TAR AND PITCH.—Business moves along fairly for the season of the year and without new features of a marked character. Stocks seem to be well managed, as they do not come upon sale under pressure, and former rates asked meet with response from buyers. We quote Pitch at $1.70@1.75 per bbl.; Tar at $2.15@2.50, according to quantity, quality and delivery.

MISCELLANEOUS.

MISCELLANEOUS.

MISCELLANEOUS.

ARCHITECTURAL WOOD WORKERS.

JARVIS B. SMITH,
DOORS, SASHES, BLINDS

Cabinet Trimmings, Mantels, Pier and Carved Frames a Specialty.

Nos. 174 to 180 East 116th Street, New York.

GEO. A. SCHASTEY, Pres. W. M. WILLIAMS, Treas. GEO. A. SCHASTEY, Jr., Sec'y.

GEO. A. SCHASTEY & CO.,

INCORPORATED,

CABINET MAKERS AND DECORATORS,

489 FIFTH AVENUE, NEW YORK.

Estimates furnished upon application.

GEORGE & CLIFFORD BROWN,
ARCHITECTURAL WOOD WORKERS
CABINET MAKERS
46 EAST 14th STREET, N. Y.
FACTORIES,
377 to 381 West 12th Street.
Proposals solicited. Estimates given

LOUIS BOSSERT,
LUMBER, MOULDING, SASHES,
Spruce Hemlock Timber. Blinds and Doors
CEILING, SIDING, PINE AND SPRUCE FLOORING, &c.
MOULDING AND PLANING MILL,
18, 20, 22, 24, 26, 28 and 30 Johnson Av.
Office, 6 and 8 Union Av., Brooklyn, E. D
Timber Yard, Newtown Creek and Grand Street.

MISCELLANEOUS.

PENRHYN SLATE CO.,
101 EAST 17th STREET, NEW YORK.
Treads and Platforms, Roofing, Sanitary Work, &c.
SLATE LINED LAUNDRY TUBS.

Mantels.
Slate Work.

BRAM & BIEG.
MANUFACTURERS OF
WHITE PORCELAIN WASH TUBS AND SINKS.
Each Tub made in one piece. No seams to open.
BEST SANITARY TUB ON THE MARKET.
Liberal Discount to the Trade. Send for Catalogue.
Office and Works: 46 to 56 Wallabout St. (near Clason Av.),
Telephone Call, 60 Williamsburgh. BROOKLYN, N. Y.

FRED. BRANDT,

No. 169 EAST 85th STREET, - - - NEW YORK.
Manufacturer of
BRANDT'S Patent Stationary Zinc Wash Tubs.
Warranted for 10 years. Price $8 50 per set.
Also a Bath and Wash Tub Combined.

Sheet Iron Sliding DUMB WAITER DOOR.
Price, put up, $5.50 Each.
These Doors are desirable because, moving vertically, they do not occupy valuable space, and can be used in narrow halls.
Send for Illustrated Catalogue and Price List.

WM. H. OLIVER,
(Late Hobbs & Oliver
PLAIN and DECORATIVE PAINTING
Paper Hangings and Interior Decorations.
62 and 64 UNIVERSITY PLACE - New York
Telephone 833—21st St. ESTABLISHED 1846.

Stone Wash Tubs.

ODORLESS, NON-ABSORBENT, DURABLE.
Material and Workmanship Fully Warranted.
MANUFACTURED BY
HUGH O'NEILL, Long Island City, N.Y.

RAPP SHEET METAL WORKS.
Man'f'rs of RAPP'S PAT. IRON Dumb Waiter DOORS AND FRAMES.
Send for illustrated catalogue and price list.
Indorsed by the leading architects and builders as being the best and cheapest Fire-Proof Door made.
Pat. May 6th, 1890.
J. W. RAPP, Sole Agent,
315-319 E. 94th St., N. Y. City.

JAMES MATHEWS & SON,

Sole agents and Manufacturers of
MAX KELLING'S Patent
FIRE-PROOF IRON
Dumb Waiter Doors and Casings. Sashes, Windows, Shutters and Wall Closets.
The most durable and cheapest articles in the market.
PRICES:
$3, $4, $6, $7, $8
and upward, according to size and style.
Illustrated catalogue, price list and references sent on application.
Over 5,000 in use in this city.
Main Office & Salesroom,
172 E. 110th St.
Branch & Factory,
510 & 512 E. 20th St.
Excelsior, Pat. Dec. 3, 1889.

PEERLESS COLORS FOR MORTAR.
RED, BLACK, BROWN and BUFF.
Guaranteed not to Fade if used according to directions. Send for circulars and full information to
ERSKINE W. FISHER, (Welles Building),
18 Broadway, N. Y.
Also Sole Agent for the Stettin ("Anchor" Brand) Portland Cement. Telephone No. 3078 Cortlandt.

THOMAS NUGENT,
Manufacturer of
Moist Warm Air Furnaces
AND VENTILATING APPARATUS.
214 EAST 80th STREET, NEW YORK.

MISCELLANEOUS.

IMPROVED RIDER HOT AIR ENGINE.
With recent valuable improvements, not on engines of other makes,
BUILT BY
Ourselves,
The Original Makers.
Reduced rates to Contractors, Architects and Plumbing Trade.
RIDER ENGINE CO.
37 Dey Street,
NEW YORK.

BUILDING MATERIAL PRICES

LUMBER.

Appended quotations are based almost wholly upon prices obtained for goods from first hands. Yard rates necessarily range much higher owing to the expenses attending sorting out and grading cargo and even car lots, besides which must be added the cost of handling and carrying until consumers are ready to invest. Terms of sale also prove important factors and, altogether, it is impossible to give a line of retail quotations thoroughly reliable in character.

SPRUCE—Eastern—special cargoes delivered N. Y.	$16 50	@	18 00
Random cargoes, narrow	13 50	@	14 50
Random cargoes, wide	12 50	@	15 00
PILING—Eastern—cargo rates:			
Ranging 30@40 per cent 12 inch butt, 35 to 40 ft average length	4	@	—
Ranging 45@50 per cent 12 inch butt, 35 to 40 ft average length	4¼	@	4½
Ranging 50@60 per cent One-half 12 inch butt, 38 to 40 ft average length	4¾	@	5
Two-thirds 12 inch butt, 38 to 42 ft average length	5½	@	6
Three-fourths 12 inch butt, 40 to 45 ft average length	5¾	@	6
All 12 inch butt and up, 40 to 45 ft average length	6	@	6¼
Piece stick, 40 feet each	4 00	@	—
do. 45	6 00	@	—
do. 50	8 00	@	—
do. 55	12 00	@	—
Inch spars, per inch	20	@	22
Scaffolding poles, each	80	@	1 00
Clothes poles, 45 to 65 feet, each	3 00	@	6 00
HEMLOCK:			
Penn. joist	12 00	@	12 50
do. boards	13 00	@	13 50
do. timber, 20 ft and under	12 50	@	13 00
do. do. 22 to 24 ft	13 00	@	13 50
do. do. 26 to 28 ft	13 50	@	14 00
do. do. 30 to 32 ft	14 50	@	15 50
do. do. 34 to 36 ft	15 50	@	16 00
do. do. 38 to 40 ft	16 50	@	17 50
WHITE PINE—Good uppers and select, 1 to 2 inch	40 00	@	48 00
Upper and select, 2½ to 4 inch	50 00	@	58 00
Shelving	26 00	@	31 00
Pickings, 1 inch	31 00	@	36 00
Cutting-up, 1 inch	25 00	@	28 00
Bracket plank	30 00	@	35 00
Dressing-boards	18 00	@	22 00
Box, inch	13 50	@	14 00
Box, thick	14 50	@	15 50
West India shippers	16 00	@	19 00
Rio Janeiro do.	2 00	@	21 00
River Plate do.	29 00	@	30 00
Australia do.	25 00	@	30 00
YELLOW PINE—Random cargoes delivered N. Y.	18 00	@	20 00
Ordered cargoes	20 00	@	21 00
Flooring	2. 00	@	24 00
Step plank	26 00	@	27 00
Common siding	15 00	@	16 00
Heart face boards	24 00	@	3 00
Car orders	21 00	@	28 00
At Atlantic ports, f. o. b.	12 00	@	12 50
At Gulf ports, f. o. b.	11 50	@	12 50
North Caroline pine timber	13 50	@	15 00
do. flooring 1 inch	16 00	@	22 00
do. do. 1¼	15 50	@	22 50
do. do. 1½@2 inch	24 00	@	25 00
do Shipping culls or box	12 00	@	14 00
do Plain and mottled ½@1¼ inch	18 50	@	45 50
Ash, white	38 00	@	43 00
Elm	20 00	@	22 50
Oak, plain	37 00	@	41 00
Oak, quarter sawed	52 00	@	55 00
Oak, quarter sawed, extra thick	56 00	@	60 00
Redwood	45 00	@	52 50
Maple, clear	28 00	@	33 00
Chestnut, clear	33 00	@	35 50
Cypress, clear	30 00	@	32 50
Black Walnut, good to choice	130 00	@	140 00
Black Walnut, ordinary to fair	100 00	@	120 00
Black Walnut, ⅝	78 00	@	88 00
Black Walnut, selected and seasoned	150 00	@	155 00
Black Walnut counters	110 00	@	150 00
Black Walnut, culls	35 00	@	40 00
Black Walnut, rejects	50 00	@	58 00
Cherry, wide	110 00	@	115 00
Cherry, good	85 00	@	100 00
Cherry, ordinary	65 00	@	80 00
Whitewood, inch	30 50	@	32 50
Whitewood, ⅝ inch	24 50	@	26 00
Whitewood, 1¼ to 2½ inch	32 00	@	34 00
Shingles, Pine, 16 inch, extra	2 75	@	3 10
do 18 inch, extra	4 10	@	4 30
do 18 inch, clear butt	2 90	@	3 10
do 16 inch, stocks	4 50	@	4 60
do 18 inch, stocks	5 30	@	5 40
Shingles, Cypress, 6x20	8 00	@	10 00
do larger sizes	11 00	@	14 00
do sawed	6 00	@	9 00
Cedar—Medium to large	6½	@	7½
do. —Extra large	7½	@	8
Mahogany—small	7½	@	8
do —Medium	8	@	8½
do. —Large	9½	@	12
do. —Extra Large	12½	@	14

Real Estate Record and Builders' Guide
Established March 21st 1868.
Devoted to Real Estate, Building Architecture, Household Decoration, Business and Themes of General Interest

PRICE, PER YEAR IN ADVANCE, SIX DOLLARS.

Published every Saturday.

TELEPHONE - - - - CORTLANDT 1370.

Communications should be addressed to

C. W. SWEET, 14 & 16 Vesey St.

J. T. LINDSEY, Business Manager.

VOL. XLVIII NOVEMBER 7, 1891. No. 1,234

CLOSE OF THE ARCHITECTURAL EXHIBIT.

The Exhibition of Architects' Drawings in the rooms of THE RECORD AND GUIDE, *Nos. 14 and 16 Vesey street must be closed on Saturday, November 21st. This exhibit is one of the finest and most extensive that has ever been displayed in New York City, and those who desire to study the 300 examples of the best architectural work of the day should visit the Exhibition without delay. Admission is free.*

Subscribers to THE RECORD AND GUIDE should see that they receive the Harlem Supplement with this issue of the paper.

AFTER something like six weeks of a waiting market, without any decided movement either one way or the other, the stock market has at length taken a downward turn. Bear attacks are successful in depressing values and bringing out long stock. The way in which prices yield shows that there is at present an utter absence of demand for good securities. It can hardly be said that stocks are cheap at present prices; they may be purchases on their prospects, but they are selling high enough considering the dividend or no-dividend that they pay. But a number of good bonds are still decidedly cheap, and the way in which they refuse to go up even in the face of gold imports which make easy money probable is one of the most discouraging features of the situation. It is a noticeable fact, however, that one of the principal bear arguments, the failure of the Maverick National Bank, was due to the fact that some Boston speculators had been shorting stocks this fall and consequently losing money. The incident served to unsettle confidence and thus helped to bring about the decline. Doubtless, also, the fact Congress will shortly meet has tended to make speculators cautious until the probable outcome of the present session is known. While, therefore, there are a number of not very satisfactory elements in the market just at present, it should be remembered that the permanent substantial conditions have seldom been better. Gold continues to come this way; our crops are selling at excellent prices; a veritable car famine exists out West, and the earnings of some of the railways are surprisingly large. One great system has already increased its rate of dividend distribution, and it is certain that others will ultimately follow suit. It is only speculation in Wall Street that is sick; and its malady is not likely to become serious, unless unexpected developments occur. Old speculators will recollect that anterior to the great rise of 1880, Gould and Cammack were short of stocks; and in face of most favorable conditions forced the market down from ten to twenty points. The same influences are conspiring against the present market, and may be equally successful. But in this case the slump will probably be followed by the same kind of a rise that occurred eleven years ago.

CONSIDERING that the Democrats have indubitably elected their candidate for Governor, there are strong reasons for wishing that they will also win in the present dispute over the Legislature. For years past we have annually been treated to partisan squabbles at Albany of so petty and contemptible a character that every true son of New York must have felt ashamed. Public business has been continually hampered by the bickering either between the Senate and the Assembly or between the Legislature and the Governor. Measures of great public importance, as for instance the Rapid Transit Bill, have failed to pass year after year because of these divisions. If the Republicans control during the present year either one or both of the legislative houses, we shall be compelled to bear another winter of partisan chattering and fighting, of "deals" and counter-deals, to be ended by the usual paucity of satisfactory legislation. As it happens, the local Democrats have a number of bills in hand of considerable importance to the real estate interests of this city. Many of them were introduced into the Legislature last winter, but failed of passage because of the deadlock in the Senate. Among these we may mention measures providing for needed new bridges over the Harlem, for a continuance of the present work of repaving our streets, and others of a like character. With the Democrats in complete control these bills for needed local improvements in New York City will have a far better chance of passage than they would in a Legislature divided against itself. In any case, however, the majorities will be so small that there will be considerable danger of miscarriages.

NOW that there is no longer any political necessity for claptrap about the World's Fair it may be possible for us to settle down to a clear apprehension of what our real position in the matter is. New York lost the Exposition, not primarily because of any political manœuvring, but because of the indifference of her citizens, their lack of public spirit and their dense stupidity regarding the power and position of their rival. That the prestige of the metropolis has suffered in the estimation of the country at large and of foreign nations there can be no doubt; the temper and opinion of the entire West evidence this, and the loss is likely to be greater when the Fair is opened and hundreds of thousands of people from all parts of the world visit the Western metropolis. Even worse, however, than the loss of the Fair has been the doubtful ambiguous and apparently "small" position which New York has occupied for some months past. We are rather inclined to think the position has been chiefly a newspaper one and represents the petty policy of our small-minded "journalists" a great deal more than it does the opinions and intentions of the majority of their readers. "Politics," too, probably had much to do with it, but that dirty thing has now reached its crisis and passed into other forms. New York should without further loss of time fall into line with the other States and extend a hearty co-operation to the great national enterprise which Chicago has on her hands. Though we have not the Fair, we should leave no doubt in the mind of visitors to the Exposition, many of whom will not come to Manhattan Island, that New York is the Empire City. Will we make a second mistake?

A RECENT report to the British Foreign Office shows very plainly the substantial similarity in the conditions and difficulties of the labor problem in Germany, Great Britain and the United States. It is stated positively that of late years the lot of the laboring man has been distinctly happier, for not only have his wages grown but their general purchasing power is greater than ever. The demand for a working day of eight hours is frequently heard, but it arises from the extreme Socialistic Party only. The movement for some sort of government intervention to regulate hours is stronger and has the general support of the Association of German Trades Unions, which embraces eighteen national and 14,000 local trades unions, with 63,000 members—not a very imposing number when it is remembered that the industrial population of Germany is estimated at 7,000,000. The difficulties in the way of such regulation are, however, very clearly understood, and even trades unions propose that any State intervention should adapt itself to the varying circumstances of the different trades—should, for instance, be in the hands of local bodies rather than the central government. As giving some idea of the hours of labor in Germany, the report quotes statistics collected in the district of Madgeburg for the year 1890. The figures embrace 35,986 workmen, employed in 1,002 factories, and of these it is shown that fourteen workmen were engaged fourteen hours a day, 5,236 for twelve hours, 25,748 for ten hours, 2,456 for nine hours and 42 for seven hours. A number of schemes have been proposed to ameliorate the lot of the laborer, but most of them have met with only a small share of success. Take, for instance, the case of profit sharing. The latest statistics collected on the subject are for 1888, and in that year only eighteen examples of successful profit sharing existed throughout the whole of Germany. Moreoveor, one or two of the large firms which are named as applying the system successfully adopted a scheme which seems to partake more or less of the ordinary bonus distribution rather than of any developed scheme of profit sharing.

SOME figures which have recently been published showing the large difference between the expense of operating a horse road and an electric road should be carefully studied by the municipal authorities all over the country. It seems from the figures (there is no reason to doubt their accuracy) that the cost of power is six times as much to a horse-car company as it is to an electric company; and that electric traction can haul the same number of passengers as animal power can at half the delay and twice the speed. When such an increase of efficiency is obtained at such a reduction of cost it is no wonder that horse-car companies are sweating all over the country to introduce an electric system. This comparatively new form of traction seems to be adequate not only to the dense traffic of a mid-city street, but to the lighter traffic of the suburbs. Its general introduction will, by increasing the urban area available at a given expenditure of time and money, make city life both cheaper and healthier than it now is, and will hence do a good deal to render still more emphatic the present decided tendency for population to concentrate in the cities. The railroads alone, however, should not benefit by this sudden and enormous cheapening of the service. The city corporations should obtain part of the saving to the railroads. The franchises operated by the latter have by means of the improvement become more valuable than formerly, and consequently they should be made to pay more for the privilege. The example of the authorities, here in New York, in forcing the Broadway Company to guarantee a considerably increased return to the city, as payment for permission to introduce a cable system, is worthy of widespread imitation. Unfortunately, according to a recent court decision, it is the State Railroad Commissioners that at present have jurisdiction in New York; and they are heedless of the claims of city treasuries for more compensation. This is a matter which requires the immediate attention of the Legislature; and while occupied with the subject, some intelligent revision of the Cantor Act would not be amiss.

THE removal of St. Luke's Hospital which must follow the sale of its property on 5th avenue will take away a pleasant bit of green from that thoroughfare; but is in other respects a matter for congratulation. Real estate on that avenue sells for very high prices, not because it is suited to be the site for hospitals, but because custom has made it desirable for the residences of the rich. Consequently it is a waste of money to have a hospital or any other similar institution occupy a block fro t, which is specifically adapted to a different purpose; the hospital can find other sites equally suitable for its purpose and far less expensive. The beneficiaries of the institution will obtain the advantage in better service. It would seem that the officials of St. Luke's ought to find a ready sale for the property at a fair price. Within the past three years two other block fronts on 5th avenue within a short distance from this one have been offered for sale, and have readily found purchasers: we refer, of course, to the Bonner property on the east side of the avenue, between 56th and 57th streets, and to the Hammersley property on the east side of the avenue, between 60th and 61st streets. The more expensive parcels into which these properties were distributed were all sold, either to rich men who propose to build or to a club of rich men. Apparently the same fortune will befall the block front now offered. The Union Club is negotiating for one of the corners, and will probably in the end secure it, for it is by far the most available site which has been placed at the disposal of that organization. As for the rest, no one but a millionaire seeking a residence will be liable to buy it, for no speculator would care to risk the large sum needed to purchase the other half of the 5th avenue frontage. Quite a fashion has set in of late for millionaires to build very expensive residences on upper 5th avenue; and there must be enough of them left to absorb this last remaining and very desirable property. When St. Luke's Hospital frontage has been placed in safe hands, the condition of upper 5th avenue may be considered as settled for an indefinite period. The stores will have no opportunity to locate above 50th street, and thence north to 80th street the avenue will be given over almost entirely to handsome dwellings. The only exceptions to this will be one or two club-houses, a couple of hotels and one large store. This last, we may be sure, will be the solitary one of its kind situated on that part of the avenue, because the wealthy men now lined along the thoroughfare will be able and willing to prevent the location of any other tradesmen in their midst. The hotels will doubtless to a certain extent introduce a heterogeneous element; but it will have no space to expand in. As for the clubs, they will help to consolidate the power of resistance to any outside or deteriorating influence. Here is one district in New York which is not in the process of change, but will remain permanent in condition for some time to come.

SOME of the decisions handed down by the Court of Appeals lately in suits for damages brought against the Manhattan Company serve to explain why that corporation is fighting these claims so bitterly. In one of these cases the plaintiff was the owner of four lots at 9th avenue and 27th street, and the lower court, in spite of the fact "that said premises would not be worth as much as they now are had the said railway and stations not been built," found that the fee of the plaintiff's real estate had been diminished to the extent of $8.0ს0. This finding was appealed to the General Term, the judgment being reversed, and the Court of Appeals affirmed the order. The first decision was based on the testimony of expert witnesses as to the value of the property if the road had not been built, and the opinion of the Court of Appeals held that such evidence was incompetent. Such also would be the judgment of common sense. Expert testimony as to the present value of real property has been often enough proved to be untrustworthy. How, then, can any one place the smallest confidence in the opinion of experts as to such value on the basis of some impossible supposition? It is no wonder that the Manhattan Company is obstructing the adjudication of the damage suits when they have to fight claims based on such testimony. If any property along the line of any of the roads is worth less money because of the presence of the structure let the company pay in full for such damages; but when the property is worth as much or more than ever, a suit for damages that have never existed is nothing better than a swindle.

A BOOK on the "Corporation Problem," by William W. Cook, of the New York Bar, forms an interesting indication of the drift of intelligent public opinion respecting the relations of the State to the forms and conditions of corporate wealth. Mr. Cook has already published a "Treatise on Stock and Stockholders and General Corporation Law;" but in this new volume he drops the legal aspects of the subject, and discusses it in its social, political and economic bearings. His book is a forcible presentation of the line of argument adopted in these columns, from which he quotes freely; and although he does not adduce any new facts or any original reasoning in support of his position, his discussion is marked throughout by a thorough acquaintance with the subject in all its ramifications and by considerable breadth of view. Briefly, his conclusions in respect to the railroad problem is frankly in favor of government regulation as the only means of protecting the interests of the public from the evils both of consolidation and competition. He also insists that natural monopolies, such as the lighting of cities, the water-works and the like, should be controlled by the municipalities. The volume should be in the hands of everyone interested in these matters.

A Severe Test for the Farmers' Alliance.

THE test of prosperous times is a most difficult one for trade organizations to bear. Men usually consent to work together and to sink their individual preferences and prejudices only "by the discipline of their virtues in the severe school of adversity." Trade-union membership is apt to increase most rapidly when some fight is on, and when there is immediate and pressing need for making a stand against unfair treatment. Yet the trade organization that does the most for its members is not a mere engine of industrial war, to be flung aside as soon as a particular crisis is past. In fact most of the abuses with which such bodies are justly charged, occur when those previously disunited come together for some pressing emergency, and wield their collective power, with the rashness of inexperience. On the other hand most of the benefits that such organizations confer at once upon their members and upon industrial society come from the steadying influence and spirit of conservatism which develops through long-continued co-operative effort, through much discussion of their "rights" and through some experience as to how far it is expedient to press these rights.

The phenomenon spoken of as "the embattled farmers" was possible only during a time of short crops and low prices following a time of undue eagerness to loan on Western real estate and railroad securities. Besides this, settlement and investment had been pushed into the semi-arid region and a temporary drawing back was inevitable. The owners of railroads, the holders of realty mortgages and the farmers made up the three parties in interest, and the latter were inclined to use their numerical superiority to settle all disputes in their own favor. In some sections they did unfair and foolish things and proposed to do many more.

Now comes a year of good crops and good prices; the railroads are said to be too busy handling and preparing to handle their own business even to spend much time in stealing the business of their rivals; and there are many instances where this year's crop will pay for all the expense of raising it, as well as an amount equal to the price of the land in fee. The partisan press has for some time been writing leaders on "politics and the crops," and a general feeling prevails that the farmers will settle back to the old order of things and leave organization and the power that comes from it to the other industrial classes. The leaders of the Alliance, of course, protest that the bounty of nature which has given good crops will make no difference in the temper of the membership, and that old scores are still remembered and will be settled.

It would be distinctly unfortunate were the predictions of either of these biased prophets to be fulfilled, but we do not think such a result at all likely. Heretofore farmers could dispense with the strength that organization gives, in that they were not necessarily dependent on any one else. Each farmer was independent because if worst came to worst he could isolate himself from the rest of industrial society and still secure almost as good a living as that to which he was accustomed. Others might depend on him, but he need to depend on no one but himself. This is no longer true, and is especially untrue at the West. A man who must secure from others and have brought to him by the railroads all his dry goods, clothing, groceries and fuel must raise crops not merely to consume, but to sell. But the staple farm products of the world's markets are now raised by agricultural specialists, and if the farmer is going to sell a large part of his product, he can raise for that purpose only the one or two things for which his section and his farm are best adapted. Other products he could produce only at a loss. Besides, this one thing or these few things which his location makes it most possible for him to raise can be raised only at a profit if he has the best modern appliances, and these require an amount of capital for which he must often resort to the money-lenders.

It will be seen that the prosperity of such a farmer is directly dependent on many fluctuating causes. Besides good or bad crops it depends on, first, the world's demand for what he produces; second, the supply of such products competing with his in the world's markets; third, fluctuations in the purchasing power of money which will lighten or decrease the weight of his debt; fourth, changes in agricultural method which may render many of his investments antiquated and useless; and fifth, rates of transportation both for what he consumes and what he produces. An industrial unit so placed is obviously in a situation that differs greatly from that of the American farmer of thirty years ago. Upon two of the five things named above as affecting his prosperity he can have a direct effect through political influence, and upon one or two of the others he can produce some effect by means of organized foresight.

Western railway journals urge that the interests of the farmers and the railroads are identical; but this is only the old cry of "peace" when there is no peace. Their interests are identical in developing the country; they are not identical, except remotely, in dividing the proceeds of the undertaking. Just as among railroads some organization or mutual understanding is necessary in order to enable them to treat each other fairly and to defend their common interests, so the interdependent classes in modern industry must each be organized in order that its members may co-operate with one another efficiently, and that the class, as a class, may command fair treatment. It is to be hoped that the organized farmers will undergo the test of prosperity.

Rapid Transit in Goods.

IT is curious that in a great commercial city like New York so many persons seem to think of nothing but rapid transit. It has been estimated after careful investigation that the truck service of the wholesale merchants of the city alone costs $25,000,000 a year. Yet this sum, large as it is, is only a small part of the total cost of handling merchandise in the streets. Ten years and more ago when permits were demanded for the right to run a truck, whether the owner was a merchant or truckman, the number of these vehicles had risen to 30,000. The number since then has certainly increased by several thousands, though the fact that merchants no longer take out permits makes any perfectly accurate computation impossible. But the number is very large, and these vehicles are engaged in the distribution of merchandise not merely between the piers, railway stations, and warehouses, but between wholesale and retail houses. They serve also the factories, and the expense of their operations is largely dependent on the length of their hauls. The number of market wagons and other freight vehicles, too, is legion. They are running to and fro at all hours of the day and night, making long and expensive trips. Following the method of computation used for the wholesale truck service it would not be too much to say that the local freight service of New York costs $100,000,000 a year.

Now, this should signify something. It ought to signify a great deal to those who are looking to rapid transit as a means of profit. It is four times as much money as the gross receipts for local passengers of all the railways, elevated and surface, in the city, or connecting with the city, and of the total amount it is almost certain that one-half could be secured by an underground freight railway with branches and sub-stations conveniently located.

Think of the volume of traffic passing between the lower part of New York, Harlem and the north end, a traffic that will be quite certain to much more than double within the next twenty years. Think, also, of the volume that passes between the wholesale district and the dry-goods district, the Yorktown district, and the large district that finds its main thoroughfare along 8th avenue, between 14th street and Central Park. The money wasted in truckage between those up-town districts and the district below Canal street would be enough to pay the running expenses of the heaviest trunk line railway in the country.

An underground freight railway penetrating over two lines the entire length of New York and having branches to the rivers and under the rivers to a connection with the trunk line railways that terminate in New Jersey has become the greatest need of the city, and the plans of the Rapid Transit Commissioners are good, because they can be so readily diverted to securing this object, the object to which the scheme must eventually be turned, no matter what the dreams of the original promoters. The truck service for prolonged hauls should be abandoned and rapid transit is already in the air. The true field for investment, therefore, will be found in the amendment of our freight transportation service.

An objection to tunnels for freight transportation between different sections of the city will be raised on the ground that they would necessitate the double handling of goods. Once loaded on a truck it will be thought cheaper to carry them directly to their destination than to meet the expense of reloading. But the chief cost of truckage is not due to the loading and unloading of goods. It is due to the loss of time while the goods are in transit, and an element of both economy and profit could be introduced by a tunnel company controlling its own delivery service. It should have its own vehicles, and the merchant or manufacturer should have no trouble when he wishes to dispatch a consignment of goods, except to give his order through telephone. This may sound like advocating a monopoly; but the most troublesome monopoly that is ever likely to afflict New York is the existing truck monopoly of the streets.

No investor need have any fear of the fate of investments made in the projected tunnels. There would be good grounds for fear were rapid transit the only service to which the enterprise could be turned. Our only danger from the undertaking comes from the lunatics who are using the scheme to cripple and delay the rapid transit service which is already at our doors.

CHICAGO.—III.

No reference to Chicago is complete without mention of the "high buildings" of the city. *Harper's Weekly* recently had an article on them, but Chicagoans are not pleased with it, for it is quite "complete" with errors and the illustrations are merely indications, indeed not even that, to readers who have not visited Chicago.

These "sky-scrapers" are concentrated in a very small section of the city, an area of ten to twelve blocks north and south by seven or eight east and west. This is "the city," the great commercial quarter wherein are situated all the large banks and financial institutions, all the big office buildings, the important stores, hotels, theatres, many of the clubs, the chief warehouses, and not a few of the doctors' offices. It can be easily understood that this section is somewhat "crowded," for practically everything but the residences and factories are there, and to a New Yorker it is a little curious to find such a jumble of businesses and purposes within so narrow a space. The Grand Pacific Hotel is, one may say, within touch of the largest office buildings in the city; the Board of Trade is "across the way;" the Post-office is opposite; a block off is the "dry-goods district;" big retail stores are around the corner, while five or six minutes smart walking brings a visitor to Michigan avenue and into one of the best residential parts of the city.

This fact suggests another, and both of these facts are due to a common cause.

The last thing a stranger expects to find in Chicago is "huddling." The general idea is that the city boundaries are moved out a mile or two further into the prairie in celebration of the birth of every child. Certainly, Chicago covers a great deal of ground, and (the Gothamite should not forget this) covers it quite as solidly with as few ranches, farms and wild waste places as are to be found in New York City south of the Yonkers line. But in a city supposed to have no geographical restrictions one does not look for great concentration, for very high buildings and for land values almost as high. We explain those things in New York by pointing to our insular position; but in Chicago——. Well, the explanation is very similar. The small "city" section is really the hub of Chicago, which may be likened to a wheel cut in half—the missing portion being represented by Lake Michigan. The reason for the existence of a centrifugal tendency that packs public buildings, hotels, stores theatres, clubs, office buildings, etc., into the hub is obvious—it is more accessible to *all* parts of the city than is any other part. A store there can easily draw its customers from north, south and west. It is the handiest spot for the greatest number of people. The further a store be moved northward the more distant does it become for western and southern trade. The same is true about the hotels and the theatres and so on. Besides, the centrifugal tendency is intensified considerably by the concentration within this small section of practically all the lines of transportation, surface and steam. All roads lead to it; and as barriers and impediments to enlargement there is the Chicago River to the north and to the west, while southward the way is blocked by several railroad stations. It has been calculated that the area of this business section is extended about 50 feet annually.

Herein, then, we see at once the reason for the high buildings, the high rents and high values and the concentration of population. Ten thousand people pass certain parts of State street hourly in certain parts of the day. This multitude, of course, stands for a vast "propensity to purchase," which is represented in store rents at $1,000 yearly for each foot of frontage. One store on State street, 30x40, rents for $30,000 per annum, and another, 16x74, brings to the owner $ 0,000 in the same time. About the latter of these—I think it is about the latter—a story is told which concerns a very prominent New York dealer in high-class furniture. He went to Chicago to establish a "branch." Upon making inquiries he was told that the proper place for him to be located was on State street, near to, if not right in the busiest part. "But the rents; Mon Dieu what rents! No Sir-r, I would not pay that rent in New Yor-rk." The furniture dealer opened his branch on Wabash avenue—and closed it within six months. Office rents, however, are not nearly so high as they are in New York. I judge that in first-class buildings in the Metropolis rents average about $3.00 (perhaps a little less) a square foot. Here $1.75 is the average. This, I believe, is the price in the "Rookery"—a very handsome building, by the way, from the boards of Burnham & Root. They say it contains a greater rentable floor-area than the Equitable Building—though the ground it occupies is not so large. There are 3,000 offices in it.

The real estate market is improving both in tone and activity. With the big harvests in the West and the Fair, it seems that Chicago is bound to "boom;" and there is every probability that considerable Eastern capital will flow into the city before the opening of the Exposition. H. W. D.

Rapid Transit Plans.

DESCRIPTION OF THE METHOD OF EXCAVATION AND CONSTRUCTION.

What the plans of the Commission are has been shown in THE RECORD AND GUIDE, so far as the published report would show them. How it is proposed to carry them out is shown in this issue. The accompanying illustrations show the method of excavation and construction designed for this great work by Chief Engineer Worthen and Consulting Engineer L. L. Buck. At the request of Mr. Worthen, Mr. Buck prepared the following description of the shield and its method of operation:

"The roof of the tunnel is to be composed of iron beams extending across the tunnel and covered by iron plates. The plates extend across the tunnel, and have such a width as to extend from the centre of one beam to the centre of the next one. The ends of the beams are to rest on the side walls, and they are to be supported at the centre by a longitudinal row of iron columns.

"*Description of apparatus.*—The pieces marked E, E, E, etc., are each composed of two parallel iron channels set on edge and covered by a 12 inch x ½ inch plate riveted to the upper flanges of the two channels. The upper side and each edge of the plates and the lower sides of the channels are to be planed (to overcome friction). These pieces, E, E, E, etc., are to be placed side by side, close together and lengthwise of the tunnel. The piece F is designed to support and guide the forward ends of E, E, E, etc. It consists of a broad steel or iron plate, lying nearly horizontal, extending in one or two pieces nearly across the tunnel and having riveted to it, at intervals of 13 inches, upright partitions made of 15-inch I beams or of plates and angles, so as to be in the planes of the channels of E. The rear end of the upper flange of each partition is provided with a set screw for the purpose of adjusting the inclination of F. The rear ends of the pieces E, E, E, etc., are supported by posts, G, which rest upon a sill, L, and are capped by a box girder, H, on which E rests. The pressure of the sill is distributed on the earth by horizontal longitudinal planks laid close together. The pieces H and L extend nearly across the tunnel.

"*Method of proceeding with excavation.*—The pieces E, E, E, etc., are each driven longitudinally forward into the earth, closely followed by the piece F. As they are forced forward the material included in their cells is dug out. The face of the heading below F is kept with a sufficient slope to form a support for F at all times. As often as all of the E pieces have been moved forward 13 inches, first K and H, G and L will be driven forward a like distance. Preceding each movement of the apparatus one roof beam and plate will be put in place under the projecting ends of the cover plates of E, these cover plates projecting to the rear beyond the channels sufficiently to always lap a few inches on to the next to the last roof plate in position. The apparatus will then be driven forward sufficiently to admit of the insertion of another roof beam and plate.

"The inclination of F will depend upon the nature of the material encountered. It should be just sufficient to compensate for the compression of the bank on which it rests, and thus keep the pieces E, E, E, etc., at the proper level. If the rear supports of E, E, E, etc., are found to be settling too much, it can be remedied by keeping the points of the planks driven farther forward of the sill L, when they will tend upward enough to compensate for the compression. The pieces E, F, H, G and L can be driven forward either by jacks or rams. The planks K can be driven by mauls.

"If the roofing beams were continuous over the middle supports, they would have points of contrary flexure at a certain distance each way from the middle supports. Hence, so far as the superincumbent dead load was concerned, they would be subject only to shearing force at such points, and could be cut in two at such points and the shear satisfied by web splices. If the abutting ends are squared and drawn closely together, a splice riveted to the lower flange will satisfy the requirement of any partial live load that may pass over any portion of the street above the tunnel. Hence, the beam could be taken into the tunnel in three pieces and riveted together in place. Temporary shores, I, will be placed so as not to obstruct the placing of roof beams and plates, and also to admit of sinking a trench along the middle of the tunnel in which to construct the foundations of the middle row of permanent columns."

As further explained by Mr. Worthen, it is proposed to work both ways from every station along the lines of the road. From the space to be occupied by the stations the wall supporting the curb on either side would be removed as far as to the roof of the proposed tunnel, which would be from 7 feet 9 inches to 9 feet below the grade of the street. The curb walls remaining would be supported on iron columns and plates or capitals extending to the foundations of the railway, about 19½ feet below the surface of the street. A heading would be driven across the street at each station, some 300 to 500 feet long, and then the apparatus would be started both ways, up and down the street, in the manner indicated.

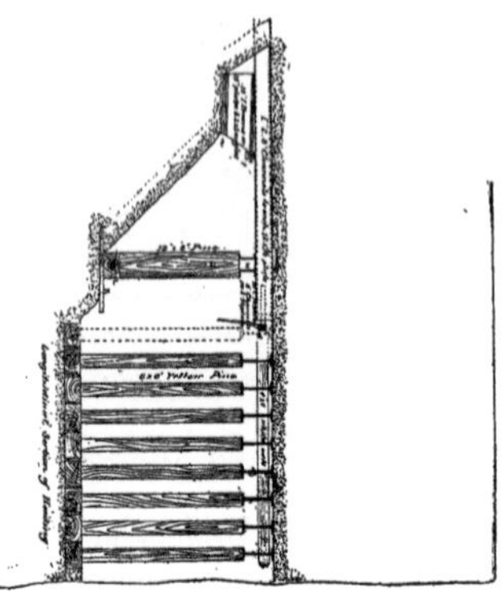

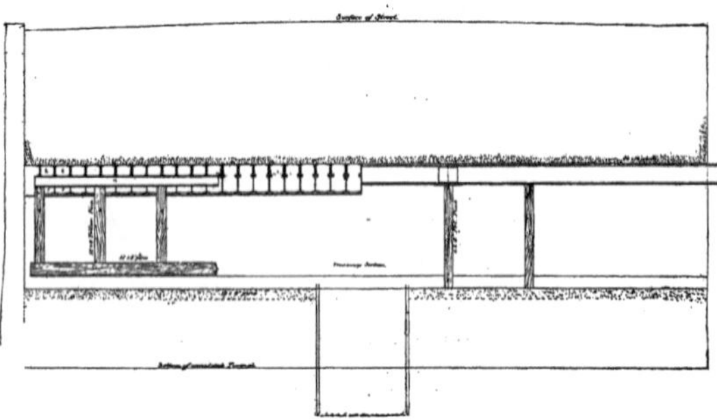

The roof beams will be placed 15 inches from centre to centre apart, leaving a space between their flanges of only 6 inches, which will be closed by the half-inch iron plates that are to compose the roof of the tunnel. The first heading will be only about 6 feet high. During the day the earth excavated will be run into the vaults at the stations, from whence it will be removed by carts at night. All the material to be excavated is valuable for building purposes and can be sold for enough to pay the cost of removal. The E pieces are to be at least 15 feet long and are to be kept driven far enough forward to find secure support in the earth and prevent any sagging or caving in of the superincumbent earth. They extend clear across the street, are close-jointed, but independent, and can be moved independent of each other, but they fit together so closely that not even the finest of sand can filter between them. They are hollow, and as they are driven forward the earth contained in them is dug out and removed.

As soon as a good start is made with the roof construction, the remaining 5 or 6 feet of excavation will be accomplished from several main stations by the aid of tramways, and the permanent supports will be put in. For the most part the walls supporting the curbs are from 12 to 30 feet deep. Generally they will be found deep enough on the sections between the stations to require no reinforcement, but where they are not deep enough they will be extended to the required depth, either by masonry or by iron columns, which will permit of the improved street construction described in last week's RECORD AND GUIDE.

With this method of construction the surface of the street will not be disturbed except where the level is so low that tide water will interfere with the construction, as at the Battery and at Canal street. At Canal street it is proposed to raise the grade some 5 or 6 feet, and to change the course of the sewer east of Broadway, so that it will run into the East River instead of the Hudson. This will be a valuable improvement to Broadway at this point, for it will overcome in large measure the steep grade which truckmen have found so difficult at all times, and which has caused more blockades of vehicles than any other defect in the roadway. It will also enable owners of adjacent property to use their basements for business purposes.

The Street Blockades.

IS THERE NO RELIEF FOR MERCHANTS?—TRUCKS THAT ARE DELAYED FOR HOURS BY OVERCROWDED STREETS—REMEDIES SUGGESTED.

The subject of our overcrowded streets is not a new one. Column after column has been written about it and the one great remedy proposed is the widening of streets. Other remedies appear to have received little attention. THE RECORD AND GUIDE has interviewed a few prominent merchants, truckmen and others and their views are given below.

The two important suggestions made are by F. B. Thurber, head of the Thurber, Whyland Company, and Michael Bradley, superintendent of trucks for that company. The former and latter, though seen separately, both suggested that more policemen should be placed at corners where traffic is thickest; while the superintendent proposes, and this is most important, that trucks and other vehicles south of, say, Washington square, shall only be allowed to move in one direction on the various streets, thus stopping the blockades which arise from vehicles going in opposite directions.

WHAT JOHN CLAFLIN SAYS.

John Claflin, head of the H. B. Claflin Company, said: "The problem is really difficult to solve. It could, indeed, be easily solved by tearing down the entire half of the sides of certain streets running parallel with Broadway and east and west from that thoroughfare; but this would involve such tremendous cost that it would be out of the question. I look forward with confidence to the utilization of the underground railway, such as is proposed by the Rapid Transit Commissioners, for the shipment of goods. This will take considerable freight traffic from Broadway and other streets. If the road is built, it will be possible for short branches to be run from Broadway, east and west, under side streets, thus connecting the basements of large wholesale and retail houses with the main line on Broadway. Such branches would not only be a considerable source of revenue to the company who built the road, but would be of great service to the business houses in enabling them to receive and ship goods from and to all parts of the city and country. In fact you may place me on record in your paper as saying that the H. B. Claflin Company would consider such a branch run from Broadway to their store as of great value, and that they would be willing to pay handsomely for it. It would save us considerable truckage and other expenses."

FRANCIS B. THURBER SEEN.

F. B. Thurber, head of the Thurber, Whyland Company, said: "Besides the widening of certain down-town streets, I do not think that any particularly valuable suggestions can be made. Still, I would place more policemen at various street corners with instructions to use diligent efforts to keep the vehicles continually moving and to use their authority in stopping blockades. This is imperatively needed at particular points down town, and the authority of a policeman, judiciously used, would often save delay to truckmen. would also suggest a regulation such as I saw in London—every driver when arriving at a crossing, slacks up very slightly to permit of a distance of about six or seven feet to be placed between his vehicle and the one in front, so as to allow pedestrians to pass. And the assage of pedestrians across crowded streets is an important item in the onsideration of this problem."

AN OPINION FROM ONE WHO KNOWS.

Michael Bradley, superintendent of trucks for Thurber, Whyland Co., said: "There is only one way out of the difficulty, and, if adopted, it would almost entirely solve the question. There ought to be a city ordinance making it necessary, under fine, for all vehicles to go in one direction through every street south of, say, Bleecker street or Washington square, west of Broadway. No truck should find another truck or vehicle coming the other way. Any man found coming in the opposite direction to any other team should at once be arrested."

"But how would you deliver or receive goods on a block when you were compelled to be at a certain store or warehouse, if you had to come in an opposite direction to do it," asked the reporter.

"That is easily answered," said Mr. Bradley. "Drivers should only be allowed to come in an opposite direction to receive or ship goods at the particular block where they may have to be. This is the only exception that should be allowed to the rule of 'all vehicles must go in the same direction.'"

"But how would you regulate this?"

"Well, it is very easy for the city authorities to lay out a plan. On streets with narrow roadways vehicles of any description should not, under any circumstances, be allowed to travel in different directions. How absurd it is for the city to let things run on in such a way that in a narrow carriageway of about 30 feet blockades occur delaying goods from five minutes to an hour or more, owing to the tide traveling both ways. It is owing to travel going in opposite directions that the blockades occur. If travel was all in one direction blockades would be rare. Suppose," he continued in illustration, "I was coming down Dey street and wanted to land goods on that street at a certain number; I would simply turn my horses to the right or left, according to the side of the street I was on, and stop my truck at that number. Suppose I had to stop at Thurber's and the tide of travel was up West Broadway, going north. If I was coming in the opposite direction I would be allowed to land at Thurber's. If I had to be on College place, however, south of Chambers street, I would not be allowed to come down West Broadway with my team going opposite to the current, but would have to come down another parallel street where the traffic was going in a southerly direction, not in a northerly direction. Then I would branch into College place at Chambers street to get to where I had to be on that block."

"How would drivers know which were 'up' and 'down' streets," asked the reporter.

"The city could have a sign put up on every street corner that would be a guide to drivers, either on the street lamps or on corner buildings."

"If streets are 100 feet in width and over, with carriageways 60 feet wide, would there not be enough room for vehicles to move both ways?"

"That would depend on whether the streets were free from surface road cars. If they were not, it would be a question for the city to decide. Experiments might be made to find out how it worked both ways. Placing more policemen at certain corners where blockades occur most frequently would also help matters, particularly between 2 and 5 P. M., when blockades are most frequent."

A "BOSS" TRUCKMAN INTERVIEWED.

Isaac Taylor, Jr., truckman and forwarder, who does a large business for merchants, said: "The greatest crush is at Chambers street and College place, and when the latter is opened it will be a great relief. There are also a great many blockades on West street, between Chambers and Cortlandt streets, especially at Murray street, where the Fall River Line pier is. Truckmen have to deliver great quantities of freight to the steamers and also take them from the steamers and boats to all parts of the city. If West street was widened it would save the blockades there. The blockades on Broadway were very bad while the roadway was torn up to lay the cable road. Now they are not so bad. The idea of putting more policemen on here and there is a good one. It would help some. When the cable cars run, so many horses will be taken off Broadway, and that will also help; but if they run two cars together, there will be no saving in room-space on Broadway, for you will be putting on a car in the place of a team of horses. Sometimes we have teams out for three or four hours through a blockade when they ought to get back in half-an-hour. Merchants lose a great deal by these blackades."

Several truckmen were seen and asked if the rates for hiring trucks are higher now than they were some time ago, owing to the delays on the streets. The invariable answer was: "No, the rates are about the same." Superintendent Bradley, Isaac Taylor, Jr., and Mr. Daniel Robinson, of the firm of Claflin's, all agree on this point. Where the greater cost comes in, however, is in the delay occasioned in recent years through the blockades on down-town thoroughfares. The prevailing general rate for a one-horse team seems to be from $5 to $6 per day, and for two-horse teams from $7 to $8 per day. Odd jobs are by contract.

THE CITY ENGINEER SEEN.

Engineer Webster, of the Public Works Department, when told of the suggestion to run traffic in one direction only, said: "It is very practicable. Indeed, after long considering the matter, I made a similar suggestion six years ago."

In reply to inquiries as to the present status of the widening of College place and the extension of Bethune street, both of them improvements which merchants complain are being delayed too long, Mr. Webster said: "Both improvements are being pushed forward as quickly as possible. There is a great deal of work to be done before condemnation proceedings can be completed. Many of the surveys on the College place property show that the building lines and the surveys differ, so that delays are thus occasioned. Property-owners have to be allowed to put in their evidence as to values. Then, in the area of assessment, the tax on every lot, and there are thousands, has to be minutely calculated, and maps, etc., have to be made. All this takes more time than the public who are on the outside imagine. In all my experience I have not seen any improvement pushed forward in its details so quickly as the College place matter."

It may interest many property-owners to learn that the area of assessment in the above matter, which originally took in all the property between Broadway and the North River, 14th street and the Battery, has been changed from Canal street to the Battery and the east side of Broadway to the North River. The estimated assessments are now being calculated. From what the writer could ascertain, this improvement, at the earliest, will only be completed to be of service to the public in about two years from date.

In the extending of Bethune street the present status is that the area of assessment is being arranged upon definitely. It will be about a mile square, Christopher street being the northerly boundary, the area being broken so as to cut out certain blocks and parts of blocks not benefited. This improvement, though not as extensive as the College place widening and extension, is hardly likely to be carried out so as to be of use to the public before 1894.

The Firm of A. H. Muller & Son.

The well-known firm of A. H. Muller & Son, consisting of Wm. F. Redmond, Louis Mesier and Peter F. Meyer, dissolved on Monday last, the day when their articles of co-partnership expired. Mr. Meyer, who was the auctioneer of the firm, retired from active participation in the business of the firm on account of ill health, it is said, but he still continues as the auctioneer of the house on a commission basis. It was reported in real estate circles that a younger man would do the minor auctioneering business of the concern, Mr. Meyer taking charge of only the more important sales, but this rumor was denied by Mr. Mesier when he was questioned in relation to the matter. Mr Meyer, he says, will as heretofore be the auctioneer of the firm, although he is no longer an active member in it.

Important to Property-Holders.

BOARD OF ASSESSORS.

OFFICE OF THE BOARD OF ASSESSORS,
NO. 27 CHAMBERS STREET,
NEW YORK, Oct. 28, 1891.

Notice is given to the owner or owners, of all houses and lots, improved or unimproved lands affected thereby, that the following assessments have been completed and are lodged in the office of the Board of Assessors for examination by all persons interested, viz.:

No. 1.—Paving 143d st, from 10th to 11th av, with trap block.
No. 2.—Receiving-basin on the s e cor of 115th st and 5th av.
No. 3.—Receiving-basin on the s w cor of 116th st and 5th av.
No. 4.—Fencing the vacant lots on both sides of 102d st, bet Columbus and Amsterdam avs.
No. 5.—Fencing the vacant lots on the block bounded by 85th and 86th sts, Boulevard and West End av.
No. 6.—Fencing the vacant lots on the block bounded by 121st and 122d sts, St. Nicholas and Manhattan avs.
No. 7.—Fencing the vacant lots on the s s of 119th st, from 5th to Lenox av.
No. 8.—Repaving Canal st, from West to Washington st, with granite blocks (so far as the same is within the limits of grants of land under water).

[The limits embraced by such assessments include all the several houses and lots of ground, vacant lots, pieces and parcels of land situated on—

No. 1.—Both sides of 142d st, from 10th to 11th av, and to the extent of half the block at the intersecting avs.
No. 2.—S s of 115th st, from 5th to Madison av.
No. 3.—S s of 116th st, from 5th to Lenox av.
No. 4.—N s of 102d st, bet Columbus and Amsterdam avs, on block 1029, Ward Nos. 23 to 28, inclusive.
No. 5.—Block bounded by 85th and 86th sts, Boulevard and West End av.
No. 6.—S s of 122d st, from St. Nicholas to Manhattan av, and w s St. Nicholas av, extending abt 120 ft. s of 122d st.
No. 7.—S s of 119th st, from 5th to Lenox av.
No. 8.—S s of Canal st, from West to Washington st, and to the extent of half the block at the intersecting sts.]

All persons whose interests are affected by the above-named assessments, and who are opposed to the same, or either of them, are requested to present their objections in writing to the Chairman of the Board of Assessors at their office, No. 27 Chambers street, within thirty days from the date of this notice.

The above-described lists will be transmitted, as provided by law, to the Board of Revision and Correction of Assessments for confirmation on the 28th day of November, 1891.

In the matter of the application of the Board of Street Opening and Improvement of the City of New York, for and on behalf of the Mayor, Aldermen and Commonalty of the City of New York, relative to acquiring title, wherever the same has not been heretofore acquired, for the use of the public, to the lands required for the opening and extension of 189th street, between Amsterdam and Wadsworth avenues, in the 12th Ward of the City of New York.

In the matter of the application of the Board of Street Opening and Improvement of the City of New York, for and on behalf of the Mayor, Aldermen and Commonalty of the City of New York, relative to acquiring title, wherever the same has not been heretofore acquired, for the use of the public, to the lands required for the opening and extension of 188th and 189th streets, between Amsterdam and Wadsworth avenues, in the 12th Ward of the City of New York. Pursuant to the statutes in such cases made and provided, notice is given that an application will be made to the Supreme Court of the State of New York, at a special term of said court, to be held at the chambers thereof in the County Court-house, in the City of New York, on Tuesday, the 8th day of December, 1891, at the opening of the court on that day, or as soon thereafter as counsel can be heard, for the appointment of Commissioners of Estimate and Assessment in the above-entitled matter. The nature and extent of the improvement hereby intended is the acquisition of title in the name and on behalf of the Mayor, etc., for the use of the public, to all the lands and premises, with the buildings thereon and the appurtenances thereto belonging, required for the opening and extension of 188th and 189th streets, between Amsterdam and Wadsworth avenues, in the 12th Ward of the City of New York.

OFFICE OF THE BOARD OF ASSESSORS,
NO. 27 CHAMBERS STREET,
NEW YORK, Oct. 31, 1891.

Notice is given to the owner or owners, occupant or occupants, of all houses and lots, improved or unimproved lands affected thereby, that the following assessments have been completed and are lodged in the office of the Board of Assessors for examination by all persons interested, viz.:

No. 1.—Regulating, grading, curbing and flagging 87th st, from West End av to Riverside Drive.
No. 2.—Paving Madison av, from 116th to 124th st, with granite blocks and laying crosswalks.
No. 3.—Paving 88th st, from Madison to 5th av, with granite blocks.
No. 4.—Laying crosswalks across 116th st, at the easterly and westerly sides of 1st av.
No. 5.—Flagging and reflagging, curbing and recurbing n s of 110th st, from 7th to 8th av.
No. 6.—Flagging and recurbing s s of 107th st, from Park to Madison av.
No. 7.—Flagging and reflagging, curbing and recurbing s s of 101st st, from 9th to 10th av.
No. 8.—Flagging and reflagging, curbing and recurbing both sides of 79th st, from Boulevard to Amsterdam av.
No. 9.—Flagging and reflagging, curbing and recurbing s s of 131st st, from Amsterdam av to Western Boulevard.

[The limits embraced by such assessments include all the several houses and lots of ground, vacant lots, pieces and parcels of land situated on—

No. 1.—Both sides of 87th st, from West End av to Riverside Drive.
No. 2.—Both sides of Madison av, from 116th to 124th st, and to the extent of half the block at the intersecting sts.
No. 3.—Both sides of 88th st, from Madison to 5th av, and to the extent of half the block at the intersecting avs.
No. 4.—To the extent of half the block, from the easterly and westerly intersections of 1st av and 116th st.
No. 5.—N s of 110th st, from 7th to 8th av.
No. 6.—S s of 107th st, from Madison to Park av.
No. 7.—S s of 101st st, from 9th to 10th av.
No. 8.—Both sides of 79th st, from Amsterdam av to the Boulevard.
No. 9.—S s of 131st st, from Amsterdam av to the Western Boulevard.

All persons whose interests are affected by the above-named assessments, and who are opposed to the same, or either of them, are requested to present their objections in writing to the Chairman of the Board of Assessors, at their office, No. 27 Chambers street, within thirty days from the date of this notice.

The above-described lists will be transmitted, as provided by law, to the Board of Revision and Correction of Assessments for confirmation on the 1st day of December, 1891.

In the matter of the application of the Board of Street Opening and Improvement of the City of New York, for and on behalf of the Mayor, Aldermen and Commonalty of the City of New York, relative to acquiring title, wherever the same has not been heretofore acquired, to East 171st street (although not yet named by proper authority), extending from Webster to Brook avenue, in the 24th Ward of the City of New York, as the same has been heretofore laid out and designated as a first-class street or road by the Department of Public Parks. Notice is given that the bill of costs, charges and expenses incurred by reason of the proceedings in the above-entitled matter will be presented for taxation to one of the Justices of the Supreme Court, at the Chambers thereof, in the County Court House at the City Hall, in the City of New York, on the 17th day of November, 1891, at 10.30 o'clock in the forenoon of that day, or as soon thereafter as counsel can be heard thereon; and that the said bill of costs, charges and expenses has been deposited in the office of the Department of Public Works, there to remain for and during the space of ten days.

Notice to Taxpayers.

FINANCE DEPARTMENT.

BUREAU FOR THE COLLECTION OF TAXES,
No. 57 CHAMBERS STREET (STEWART BUILDING),
NEW YORK, November 2, 1891.

Notice is given by the Receiver of Taxes of the City of New York to all persons whose taxes for the year 1891 remain unpaid on the 1st day of November of said year, that unless the same shall be paid to him, at his office, on or before the 1st day of December of said year, he will charge, receive and collect upon such taxes so remaining unpaid on that day, in addition to the amount of such taxes, one per centum on the amount thereof, and charge, receive and collect upon such taxes so remaining unpaid on the 1st day of January thereafter, interest upon the amount thereof at the rate of seven per centum per annum, to be calculated from October 5, 1891, the day on which the assessment rolls and warrants therefor were delivered to the said Receiver of Taxes, to the date of payment, as provided by sections 843, 844 and 845 of the New York City Consolidation Act of 1882.

About Assessments.

THE RIVERSIDE DRIVE ASSESSMENT.

The strongest opposition possible is to be made by citizens and property-owners against the assessment of $1,228,085.94 which it is proposed to levy for the above improvement. The area of assessment is bounded by the south side of 120th street on the north, the west side of West End avenue to the east, the north side of 72d street to the south, and the Riverside Drive to the west. The matter came before the Board of Assessors and was postponed till Thursday at the solicitation of a committee of property-owners within the area affected, who were headed by Jas. A. Deering, who resides on Riverside Drive and 103d street. They protested against the assessment as onerous and excessive, and asked for a postponement till Thursday, so as to be able to present to the Board, in printed form, an exhaustive history of the manner in which the assessment was made and the improvement carried out. This is one of the largest assessments ever made in New York.

A LENOX AVENUE ASSESSMENT.

The assessment for cross-walks on the north side of 130th street, across Lenox avenue, has been sent for confirmation to the Board of Revision and Correction of Assessments. The area of assessment takes in 400 feet on the north side of the street east and west of the avenue and 200 feet on each side of the avenue north of the street. The total assessment is $221.50, or $6.01 for every 25 feet of frontage.

ABOUT CONFIRMED ASSESSMENTS.

Property-owners should watch closely the proceedings of the Board of Revision and Correction of Assessments, which confirms all assessments made. At the very moment that this Board confirms an assessment it becomes a lien on the property assessed, and if not paid within sixty days from then, interest is charged at the rate of 6 per cent. per annum from the moment of confirmation.

DAMAGES CLAIMED THROUGH CHANGE OF GRADE.

Twelve petitions have been filed by property-owners claiming damages against the city due to the regulating and grading of 130th street, from 12th avenue to the 11th avenue Boulevard. The grade has been changed at one point as much as 10 feet to meet the rise in grade of West End (11th) avenue at 130th street. The properties affected include factories, tenements and houses.

The Organizers of the New York Tax Reform Association.

The New York Tax Reform Association has been busily at work since its organization in circulating literature in support of its principles, but it seems to have met with some opposition because of the suspicion cast on the motives of its organizers. The farmers have suspected that it is an emanation from Wall Street and is established in the interest of large owners of personal property. As a matter of fact, this is not true; neither is it true that the movement is allied with any projected reforms in the system of National taxation. That these statements are so may be gathered from the following list of the chief organizers of the association, most of whom are largely interested in real estate. Some of them are: David A. Wells, the celebrated statistician and writer on political economy; George H. Scott, of Scott & Myers, real estate brokers, and formerly president of the Real Estate Exchange; George R. Read, an extensive real estate operator and existing President of the Real Estate Exchange; Spencer Aldrich, a protectionist, owner of the Columbia Building, one of our largest office buildings, and representing the Aldrich estate, owners of the Aldrich Court; F. B. Thurber, of Thurber, Whyland & Co., who is as closely identified with the farming interests as any merchant in New York; Henry A. Hurlbut, a strong protectionist, director in the Equitable Life and holder of real estate; Wm. Gordon Fellows, owns farming land at Schagticoke, N. Y.; C. T. Christensen, President of the Brooklyn Trust Co.; Smith Ely, ex-Mayor of New York, and a large real estate investor; Amos R. Eno, a protectionist, who owns the Fifth Avenue Hotel and many other large properties in New York; Hall J. How, one of New York's oldest real estate brokers; James McCreery, the dry-goods merchant, whose interests in real estate are as large as those in his business, if not larger; Isaac M. Dyckman, of Dyckman estate, consisting largely of vacant property; Wm. Steinway, piano manufacturer, and owner of the town of Steinway, where the works are situated; John Sinclair, pork packer, and one of the founders of Cedar Rapids, Iowa, has large landed interest there, and has never had a strike among his workmen; August Richard, who invests in Tennessee timber and farm land, and has a magnificent house here; Thomas G. Shearman, a real estate lawyer and writer on taxation; Hugh N. Camp, dealer in suburban lands; R. R. Bowker, Secretary of the Edison Electric Lighting Co., and John Claflin, of H. B. Claflin Co.

Here and There.

The new Commissioner of Street Cleaning seems to be making an effort, in Harlem at least, to keep the streets clean, but the worst of it is the work is not intelligently directed. The present system is to have the streets first swept by the machines during the night. In the morning laborers sweep the dirt and rubbish into piles and leave it sometimes for hours. Now, of course, the streets cannot be kept clean in this way, especially in this blustering autumn weather, no matter how often the thoroughfares are swept. At this time of year, when much of the sweeping is made up of the dead leaves from the trees which line the streets, it takes the wind but a short time to blow the heaps of rubbish in all directions, making the streets look even dirtier than before. The only way to sweep the streets economically as well as satisfactorily is to have the sweepings gathered up immediately after the machines have passed. In this way the best results will be obtained for the least money.

One of the most discouraging things about the long travel to Harlem in the evening "rush" hours is the delay, sometimes of long duration, that occurs on the 6th avenue line, between 116th and 125th street stations, where most of the passengers leave the train. This delay is occasioned by the fact that at 125th street more people disembark than at any of the other up-town stations, and trains must therefore make a very much longer stop here than at any of the stations further down. In this way the trains behind get time to run up to 125th street before the cars then discharging their passengers are ready to proceed. And so it frequently comes about that five or six train loads of people are stored on the line south of 125th street waiting for their turn to disembark at this busy station. The Harlemites affected by this incapacity of the station to receive the train-loads of people who all want to use it at the same time, have thought of various plans to relieve the station, but all of them are open to more or less objection. The best one, however, appears to be that which looks to the building of a platform twice the length of that now in use at the present time. It seems to be perfectly practicable to build a platform long enough to allow the landing of ten cars instead of five as at the present time. This, of course, would double the capacity of the station, and the Harlemites would not object in the least to walking the long platform in preference to waiting ten or fifteen minutes when most of them are tired out with the day's work and all of them are anxious to get to their homes as speedily as possible.

Columbus avenue real estate men are again agitating the idea of a line of cable cars on that thoroughfare, but it is doubtful whether or not the present talk will amount to anything. It is pointed out that at present there is more necessity for a surface line of cars on Columbus avenue than there is on Central Park West or possibly on Amsterdam avenue. The elevated railway stations are at considerable distance from one another and there is no other means of transportation from one point on the avenue to another point not far distant. There is a great amount of local traffic on the avenue and there is not the slightest doubt that a line of cable cars would pay handsomely. Already there is a good deal of shopping done there, and the innumerable real estate brokers with their numerous customers would do much to support any line of surface cars that was started.

Our Letter Bag.

A CRITICISM ON THE COMMISSIONERS' PLANS.

Editor RECORD AND GUIDE:

It is undoubtedly a bold task to pass criticisms on a report that evinces such manifold indications of care, knowledge and ingenuity as that of our Rapid Transit Commission; but the magnitude of the interests at stake must be my justification. It is a sad fact, but true, that the decisions of the most competent are not always the most competent decisions; and I think that it can be shown that the plan of the Commission, nicely as it is adapted to a pre-conceived ideal, does not take into account certain very important conditions. The people and press of New York have also cherished an ideal of rapid transit very similar to that which has rendered useless and dangerous the work of the Commissioners. Our traveling public is bewitched with the idea of thundering through tunnels at the rate of forty miles an hour, one train following so swiftly on the heels of another that the smoke of their wheels would mingle. To the unfortunate people who have to lumber along on an elevated train, stuffed into a nauseating car, this picture is very enticing; but they should not indulge in it too freely. So long as bolts will break and railway employes nod, it is a ticklish business to ride very much at the rate of forty miles an hour over the open country in broad daylight, and it is entirely safe to say that we shall never pile one train after another through a tunnel under two or three minutes' headway at anything even approximating this rate of speed. But if we lengthen the intervals between trains we cut the head off of rapid transit and leave ourselves with very little substantial gain. This is one very palpable obstruction in the way of our dreamers.

This obstruction by no means stands alone. It has been proved over and over again that the property-owners of Broadway will not submit to the danger inseparable from running an underground tunnel so near to the foundations of their buildings. They are objecting just as strongly to this scheme as they have to all the others. Several agents have announced that they will get their clients to refuse consent to any plan of rapid transit which threatens the foundations—whether by the vibrations attendant upon the running of the trains or by any other cause. A number of large owners have also made declarations to the same effect. What this opposition will amount to, it is impossible as yet to estimate, but if it is as large as it has been in the past, even the skilled canvassers which are being sent out by the Rapid Transit Commission will fail to obtain a sufficient number of acquiescences. The recourse of an appeal to the Supreme Court remains; but it would be an outrage to force people with such immense interests at stake to submit, as the Broadway property-owners have to submit, against their will to a plan which they consider dangerous. I believe that any commission appointed by the Supreme Court would hesitate a long time before deciding against the wishes of so powerful a class of men.

I believe that it would be easier to get them to consent to an elevated structure on Broadway than an underground road near the surface. All the wiseacres will raise their hands at this and cry "preposterous;" but it is none the less true. Undoubtedly there is a prejudice against elevated roads in this city; and undoubtedly this prejudice has been justified in the past by the way in which our present elevated roads have disfigured the streets. But since the latter was built enormous strides have been made in iron and steel structural material; and I believe that it would be entirely possible to erect an elevated structure on Broadway which would be not only no disfigurement but an adornment to the street. This aspect of the matter will gradually become more popular. Broadway is undoubtedly the thoroughfare along the line of which the route ought to run. A surface tunnel will be found impracticable for the reasons already given; a deep tunnel would not command the traffic; a viaduct could not be made to pay. What New York needs is an elevated road on Broadway; and either the Rapid Transit Commissioners will be obliged finally to go to the Legislature for an amendment to the law making such a method of construction possible or we shall have no Broadway Rapid Transit route. At present everybody appears to be playing into the hands of the Manhattan Company.

A BROADWAY PROPERTY-OWNER.

Contractors' Notes.

Bids or estimates will be received at the Department of Public Works, No. 31 Chambers street, until 12 o'clock M. on Tuesday, November 10, 1891, for regulating and paving with asphalt pavement, on the present foundation, the carriageway of 12th street, from a line about 98 feet east of 7th avenue, and running easterly about 136 feet: for furnishing and delivering double nozzle case hydrants, and for furnishing cast-iron water pipes, branch pipes and special castings.

Estimates for dredging at sundry-named places on the North and East Rivers will be received by the Board of Commissioners, of the Department of Docks, at the office of said department, on Pier "A," foot of Battery place, North River, in the City of New York, until 1 o'clock P. M., of Thursday, November 12, 1891.

Sealed bids or estimates will be received by the Commissioner of Street Improvements of the 23d and 24th Wards, at his office, No. 2622 3d avenue, corner of 141st street, until 3 o'clock P. M., on Thursday, November 19, 1891, for regulating and grading, setting curb-stones, flagging the sidewalks and building culverts and inlets in 184th street, between Jerome avenue and Vanderbilt avenue West; for constructing sewer and appurtenances on both sides of the Southern Boulevard, from 137th to 138th street; for cleaning the sewer and appurtenances in Brook avenue, from its outlet in tidewater in the Bronx Kills, near the Harlem River to the centre of 165th street.

The Hall Residences.

[COMMUNICATED.]

The houses shown in the accompanying illustration comprise a row of five recently erected by James T. Hall, on the south side of 75th street, between Columbus avenue and Central Park West, within a few minutes' walk of the 72d street elevated road station. They are four stories and basement in height, with handsomely carved stone fronts in Indiana limestone. The box stoops and bay windows are the main features of the facade.

The interiors of the houses are trimmed in hardwoods, and the first floors contain suites of three fine rooms, capable of being thrown together for reception purposes, etc. These consist of a parlor, music-room and dining-room.

The bedroom floors on the second and third stories are arranged with dressing rooms, which divide the front and rear bedrooms in saloon style.

A State and City Supplement.

The *Commercial and Financial Chronicle* deserves the thanks of its patrons for the State and city supplement recently issued. This publication is designed to fill a field hitherto quite unoccupied. Investors have plenty of sources for information regarding railway companies and other corporations whose securities are widely distributed, but in spite of the large number of States, cities and counties whose bonds are held by investors, the only means that have hitherto existed whereby those interested could obtain the required information has been direct application to the municipal authorities, which took time, patience and trouble. This supplement of the *Chronicle* contains 184 pages and is as complete as it could be made under the circumstances. The work has been conducted under the greatest difficulties, because of the surprising and decided disinclination to give the required information which has been shown by the officers of so many municipalities.

Residences on Seventy-fifth street, between Columbus avenue and Central Park, West.

James T. Hall, Owner. Geo. H. Budlong, Architect.

There is a bath-room on each of these floors, containing porcelain tubs, nickel-plated plumbing, tiled floors, etc. The top floor and basement, in addition to the other floors, are in hardwood trim.

Among the general features which strike the visitor are the excellent workmanship, both in the front masonry work and the interior. The windows in the front and first story rear are of polished French plate-glass, the remainder being of French glass of double thickness. The plumbing is of a high sanitary order, and each house has a separate sewer connection. There is a complete system of speaking tubes, burglar alarms and electric bells throughout, and there is ample closet room on each floor. All the floors are double, as well as deafened. The mantels have open fire-places and tiled hearths and facings, and are piped for gas logs. The cellars have a 4-inch flooring of high grade Portland cement. Within a few minutes' walk of the houses are the Central and Riverside Parks, and within easy distance are the 8th, Boulevard and 10th avenue surface roads. The 72d street stages and 86th street cross-town cars give easy communication with the section east of 5th avenue.

In addition to the five houses which appear in the illustration, one of which has already been sold, Mr. Hall is building four handsome Belleville brown stone front houses on the same street directly opposite the houses above described.

WANDERER.

The Pennsylvania Railroad's Purchase.

John C. Wilson, of Philadelphia, has taken title for the Pennsylvania Railroad to Nos. 109-113 West street; Washington street, Nos. 164-166, and Cortlandt street, Nos. 81, 89, 91, 93, an irregular plot opposite the Cortlandt street ferry.

The City's Assessment Sale on Monday.

Property-owners who have not paid assessments due on certain lands and tenements in New York City, which were confirmed in 1886 and prior thereto, should see to it that the amounts charged against them are paid on or before Monday, November 9th, at 12 o'clock noon. Otherwise at that hour the city will sell their property "for the lowest term of years for which any person shall offer to take the same, in consideration of advancing the amount of the assessment so due and unpaid, and the interest and charges thereon," with costs and charges added. Owners of realty were first notified of this sale in January, 1891.

Property-owners can see the list in Rooms 31-35 Stewart Building. The sale was postponed from March 2, 1891, to June 1, 1891, and then again till November 9, 1891. Collector O. Macdaniel told a reporter of THE RECORD AND GUIDE that the sale will take place positively on Monday. The amount originally due, he said, in answer to a query, was about $1,300,000, and about four-fifths had been paid. A long line of property-owners were waiting to pay their assessments when the reporter called.

Obituary.

WILLIAM LALOR.

William Lalor, the veteran real estate broker, died suddenly of heart disease at his office, No. 69 Liberty street, at 1.50 P. M. on Thursday.

Mr. Lalor was one of the oldest habitues of the Real Estate Exchange and was universally respected for his honesty, his unvarying courtesy and his open, pleasant manner. Although sixty-nine years old he was as hale and active as a young man.

Mr. Lalor was born in this city, and at an early age entered the volunteer fire department, of which he was one of the veteran members. He commenced his business career as a butcher in Central Market, in which capacity he became known to many prominent citizens. This was in the days when every business man of importance was known to almost every-one in the community. By fair dealing and untiring effort he amassed a fortune, and early in the sixties began to operate in real estate. (In this he was successful, and his fortune increased until, on Black Friday, he met the fate of many of his contemporaries, being loaded up too heavily with mortgages. Since then he has endeavored to retrieve his fortunes, and it was the incessant hard work incidental to the accomplishment of this end that hastened his death.)

Mr. Lalor will be gratefully remembered by many who have been inmates of the Catholic Orphan Asylum, an institution which he started and of which he was treasurer for over a quarter of a century. He was also interested in other benevolent work.

The funeral service will take place at St. Lawrence's Church, Park avenue and 84th street, on Monday, at 10 A. M. The Real Estate Exchange, of which Mr. Lalor was a member, has appointed a committee to be present, consisting of Messrs. Benjamin P. Fairchild. John F. B. Smyth and Hall J. How.

Jackson Avenue to Be Opened.

The Board of Street Opening and Improvement yesterday directed that Jackson avenue, on the north side, be opened from Westchester avenue to the Boston road, a distance of 4,850 feet.

Real Estate Exchange Matters.

The Board of Directors held its regular monthly meeting on Wednesday last, seven members being present.

The president read a financial report which shows that there is cash on hand amounting to $12,413.69; bills delivered and as yet uncollected, $7,910.70, or a total of $20,324.39. Out of this amount during the next two weeks there must come $1,987.50 for interest and salaries, and it is proposed to pay a semi-annual dividend of 2½ per cent, which will amount to $12,-500, leaving a balance of $5,836.89 on hand. The president's report also showed that the knock-down fees this year amounted to $23,708.24 as against $16,410.50 last year, showing an increase of $7,297.74 in the fees received.

The Board also suspended three members under Rule 5A who are in arrears and whose names have been posted for some time in the Auction Room.

G. R. Katzenmayer and Thos. McGuire have been elected to stock membership, and Samuel Frothingham and Jas. R. Booth to annual membership.

The new electric light plant that is being placed in the Auction Room, consisting of 150 incandescent electric lamps, will cost $550.

Arthur L. Doremus has been proposed for membership by W. J. Van Pelt.

Real Estate Department.

There is some improvement to be noted this week in the character, if not in the number, of the sales consummated at private contract, and, so far as these sales represent the week's work, they are an indication that the talk about the disturbances prior and incident to the election had some foundation in fact. But the sales are not numerous, and the largest of those reported does not pass the quarter million mark, so that there is not very much cause to feel elated over the slight improvement in importance which this week's sales show over those of the past few weeks. Then, too, it must be remembered that although the sales that have just been made embrace a slightly better class of property they are comparatively few in number, and they are confined mainly to a few individuals. The majority of the brokers and dealers still complain of the dull times and general inactivity. Here and there there are real estate men who have had a very successful season of it, but the greatest number have had less business and have made smaller profits than they have to look back on for several years. It is a fact that many prominent and ordinarily prosperous brokers have made no sales since last spring, and unfortunately they are not the brokers and dealers in any one section of the city. The quiet real estate market is common to practically every district of New York, and it is ascribed nearly everywhere to high prices which prohibit ready and prudent buyers from purchasing and altogether discourages the general investor. In many of the offices this week matters have been as quiet as during midsummer, and it is not all explained by the fact that election day broke in upon the continuous work that was going on. Those very closely interested and related to the real estate market, and many of them are owners, very generally lay the blame of this state of affairs to the high prices that, as has been repeatedly pointed out in this column, have prevailed for about a year. It may be hard for owners to accept this fact and its consequences, but they must do so sooner or later if present indications are worth anything, and if they desire to dispose of their holdings. And yet, notwithstanding all that has been said about prices, notwithstanding the market almost of stagnation that we have had for over a year, owners, except in isolated cases, show no inclination to make concessions. On the other hand, many of them appear to be firmer than ever, and even talk of increasing their figures for the spring market now that the taxes have been paid. The country, they say, is so prosperous that merchants and others will have reaped large profits from their transactions by the spring, and much of this surplus they point out will find its way into real estate. This is largely true, but it must be remembered that in a time of healthy and legitimate business, even though large profits are being made, investors look very closely at incomes and other factors in values before placing their capital. Present holders should remember this, and they should ask only figures that are strongly and truly supported by income, location or other advantages. It is this showing of a fine income on paper only that has discredited real estate in times past, and it will not do just now when real estate is so favorably regarded by investors to repeat the offence.

THE AUCTION MARKET.

The auction business of a week that is broken up by a holiday is generally small and unimportant, and this week has been no exception to the rule. One case excepted, and that an $8,000 parcel, all the sales this week have been of a legal character, necessitated by orders of the courts. The properties included in the list of these legal sales do not offer much that is of general interest, and the only thing in connection with them to which attention should be called is the deficiencies that occurred in several foreclosure sales between the amount due and the selling price. As is generally the case when these deficiencies occur the plaintiffs were the purchasers. In the "Sales of the Week" column the details of the transactions referred to are given. Wherever it was possible to ascertain the mortgages and costs upon the foreclosed properties the amounts due are given, and a comparison of these with the selling price may be both interesting and instructive. In two cases where property was voluntarily offered the parcels were withdrawn, which is an indication that owners were right in not offering their holdings during the election week.

For next week the auctioneers present a very ordinary list of announcements, mainly of up-town property. Probably the only offering that will attract much attention is No. 139 Maiden lane, near Water street, running through to No. 17 Fletcher street. It is a five-story warehouse, on lot 17x about 81 feet, and was last sold in September, 1891, for $28,000.

On Tuesday, November 10th, Smyth & Ryan will sell the five-story and cellar brick store and warehouse, No. 139 Maiden lane, running through to No. 17 Fletcher street. This is a desirable piece of investment property located right in the tobacco district. On the same day the same auctioneers will sell the three-story brown stone dwelling, No. 244 West 23d street. It is suitable for altering into a business building.

On Tuesday, November 10th, Richard V. Harnett & Co. will sell the four-story brown stone dwelling No. 49 East 57th street.

On Tuesday, November 10th, Richard V. Harnett & Co. will sell the three-story brown stone dwelling, No. 1673 Madison avenue.

On Wednesday, Nov. 11th, Richard V. Harnett & Co. will sell the four-story brown stone dwelling, No. 132 East 44th street, and the three-story brick dwelling, No. 440 East 115th street.

On Wednesday, Nov. 11th, John F. B. Smyth will sell the five-story brown stone flat, No. 173 West 64th street, seven full lots on the south side of 96th street, 150 east of 2d avenue, and the brick tenements, Nos. 1842 to 1850 2d avenue.

On Tuesday, Nov. 17th, John F. B. Smyth will sell, to settle the estate of Benj. Bailey, deceased, the two four-story brick houses, Nos. 344 and 346 West 14th street.

On Tuesday, November 17th, James C. Lalor will sell for the executors a plot, 100x518.6, on the southwest corner of 3d avenue and 13th street, Brooklyn. The plot has on it a five-story brick factory, 200x40, and a one-story frame factory, 195x85.

On Wednesday, Nov. 18th, John F. B. Smyth will sell the two five-story brick tenements, Nos. 263 and 265 Avenue B.

On Thursday, November 19th, John F. B. Smyth will sell the five-story brick tenement No. 166 1st avenue.

On Tuesday, November 24th, John F. B. Smyth will sell Nos. 515 and 517 West 39th street, with one two-story building and one four-story tenement thereon; and the vacant lot at No. 535 West 39th street.

CONVEYANCES.

	1889. Nov. 1 to 7, inclus.	1890. Oct. 31 to Nov. 6, inclus.	1891. Oct. 30 to Nov. 5. inclus.
Number	374	336	306
Amount involved	$7,657,787	$6,360,876	$5,097,720
Number nominal	95	80	80
Number 23d and 24th Wards	57	30	64
Amount involved	$216,110	$246,166	$141,580
Number nominal	9	5	9

MORTGAGES.

	1889.	1890.	1891.
Number	361	338	289
Amount involved	$4,686,194	$5,233,664	$3,511,820
Number at 5 per cent	180	155	151
Amount involved	$2,173,720	$1,685,212	$2,018,029
Number at less than 5 per cent	68	49	28
Amount involved	$1,332,000	$1,079,500	$585,900
Number to Banks, Trust and Insurance Companies	71	60	47
Amount involved	$1,447,415	$3,519,100	$1,169,500

PROJECTED BUILDINGS.

	1889. Nov. 2 to 8.	1890. Nov. 1 to 7.	1891. Oct. 31 to Nov. 6, inc.
Number of buildings	45	38	30
Estimated cost	$717,275	$1,616,400	$903,200

Gossip of the Week.

SOUTH OF 59TH STREET.

The heirs of Harvey Kennedy have sold No. 675 5th avenue, a four-story brown stone front dwelling, 25x65 and extension x100, for a sum in the neighborhood of $200,000. The purchaser is reported as Samuel Untermyer, of the law firm of Guggenheimer & Untermyer. Broker, Chas. McRae.

It is reported that the Press Club has at last secured a site for their proposed new club-house. It is Nos. 17 and 19 Park place and Nos. 14 and 16 Murray street, running through a plot about 50x150. The property was owned by Chas. Renwick and Shortland Bros. and was sold, it is reported, for $265,000. It was decided to buy this site, it is said, at a meeting of the full building committee during the week, when six members of the committee voted to buy the Park place site, while five others favored the corner of Chambers and Centre street, which had been offered at the same price.

John N. Golding has sold for Samuel D. Babcock the vacant plot, 60x98.9 in size, on the south side of 40th street, commencing 500 feet east of 6th avenue, opposite the reservoir, to Dr. Herman Knapp, the oculist, conjointly with Dr. W. Gill Wylie, the surgeon, for $120,000. This plot was purchased by Mr. Babcock in 1873 for $43,000, and the price now paid is equivalent to $50,000 per city lot. A few weeks ago No. 8 West 40th street, in the same block, 19.6x98.9, with the four-story house thereon, sold for $50,000, Mr. Golding also being the broker.

Horgan & Slattery have sold to George B. Clark the seven-story brick and stone warehouse Nos. 91 and 93 Thompson street, for a sum in the neighborhood of $53,000. John R. Foley & Son have since resold the building to E. K. Hubbard for $90,000. This warehouse was the first structure of its kind to be erected on Thompson street.

It is reported that a syndicate is buying private houses at 31st street and Madison avenue, which they will tear down and erect on the site thus secured a large modern hotel.

F. R. Houghton has sold for Edward King, President of the Union Trust Company, to Wm. S. Patten, the six lots, with old buildings thereon, on the south side of 28th street, 235 feet west of 10th avenue, on private terms, and has since resold the two most westerly lots to E. R. Merrill for improvement.

Jacob Pizer has purchased from E. Ellery Anderson, No 516 2d avenue, a five-story double tenement, 25x80, on private terms.

W. B. Taylor & Sons have sold for R. J. Waddell the four-story brown stone house, No. 56 West 48th street, on lot 18.9x100.5 (Columbia College leasehold), for $17,000.

John R. Foley & Son have sold for I. S. & M. S. Korn the six-story double apartment house No. 252 West 36th street, 25.6x90x100, on private terms.

Hewitt & Co. have sold for Samuel Stewart the three-story brown stone private dwelling No. 237 West 49th street for $19,500 to Mary T. Carroll.

B. L. Kennelly has sold No. 41 West 35th street, a four-story English basement brick and brown stone dwelling, 18.9x55 extension x98.9, for Mrs. Janette Pirsson to Hyman M. Lazinsk, the 5th avenue ladies' tailor, for $30,030.

Harris Mandelbaum has purchased from J. Thorne, trustee for the Pearsall estate, No. 43 Essex street, a six-story brick tenement, 25x80x100, on private terms.

Sire Bros. have sold No. 110 Mott street, lot 23x70, with a three-story front building and store and a five-story new tenement on rear, for $32,000.

H. H. Cammann & Co. have sold the four-story brown stone dwelling No. 29 West 30th street, on private terms. The size of the lot is 21x half the block.

NORTH OF 59TH STREET.

Walter Lawrence has sold for Donald Mitchell to David Christie six lots on the northeast corner of West End avenue and 104th street for $79,000; and for the New York Orphan Asylum Society to W. Edgar Pruden seven lots on the north side of 74th street, 100 feet west of West End avenue, on private terms; and for Ellen M. Harlow to Charles L. Adrian, No. 248 West 104th street, a three-story and basement brown stone dwelling, 19x50x100, for $31,000.

Stabler & Smith and Albert L. David have sold for Thomas McGuire to Ex-Judge O'Gorman Nos. 120, 122 and 124 West 102d street, three five-story brown stone flats, each 26x87.6x102.2, on private terms. Mr. McGuire takes in exchange the northeast corner of Manhattan avenue and 118th street, a vacant plot, 100x125.

Frederick Aldhouse has sold No. 23 West 74th street, a four-story brown stone dwelling, 25x60 and extension x102.2, on private terms.

McDougal & Eckerson have sold for Increase M. Grinnell to Tony Pastor, the theatrical manager, No. 49 West 94th street, a four-story brown stone front dwelling, 20x55x102.2, for $27,500. This house is the second dwelling that Mr. Pastor has purchased on the West Side. The first house was for investment, while this last purchase will be used as the residence of its owner.

John R. Foley & Son have sold the four-story high stoop and basement private house, with three-story extension 20x70x100, No. 27 East 71th street, to Isidor S. Korn for $49,000.

Chas. F. White has sold No. 462 Columbus avenue, a five-story flat and store, on lot 25x100, for F. H. Walker to A. G. Ellison, on private terms.

G. D. Clark has sold for Mrs. Anna E. Valentine to Mrs. A. Cooper No. 213 West 131st street, a three-story brick dwelling, 16.8x50x100, for $15,325.

H. H. Cammann & Co. have sold for Catherine A. Cammann to J. C. Caldwell the six lots on the north side of 80th street, 100 feet west of Amsterdam avenue, on private terms.

D. B. Freedman has sold nine lots on the north side of Academy street, west of Kingsbridge road, on private terms.

J. B. Ketcham has sold for L. S. Samuels the four-story brown stone front house No. [illegible] West 126th street, 20x75x100, to a Mr. Howell for $30,000. This house has been vacant ever since it was built by Chas. Batchelder six years ago.

Goodman & Stern have sold for Isaac Hirsch to J. Keenan the three four-story brown stone double flats, Nos. 227, 229 and 231 East 83d street, [illegible]

Hellner & Wolf have sold to J. Steiner the five-story brick tenement, No. 339 East 75th street, for $21,000.

D. Willis James has sold No. 143 West 56th street, a four-story brick and stone dwelling, 22.6x60, and extension x102.2, on private terms.

LEASES.

John R. Foley & Son have leased for Charles Henry Butler to George Brotherton the six-story brick and stone flat and store, 50x100, on the southeast corner of 8th avenue and 126th street, for twenty years, at an average rental of $12,350 per annum. The same brokers have also leased for J. E. Hasler to John Murray the store southwest corner of 2d avenue and 112th street, for ten years at $2,500 per year.

Sire Bros. have leased to Alexander Stewart, the oyster-house man, the five-story building Nos. 1452-1456 Broadway, northeast corner 41st street, for 20 years, at from $20,000 to $25,000 a year. The size of the plot is 46.4 on Broadway, x113.4 on 41st street, x63x about 122. The building is being altered into a hotel. The rent for the first three years will be $20,000 per annum; for the second term of three years, $22,000 per year, and for the remainder of the term $25,000 per annum.

E. H. Ludlow & Co. have leased the four-story dwelling on full lot No. 139 Madison avenue. It is an unfurnished house.

Brooklyn.

Corwith Bros. have sold the two-story brick dwelling, on lot 25x100, No. 190 Dupont street, for Ellen Toomey to Mathilda Weinberger for $1,575; and the three-story frame dwelling, 16.8x40x100, No. 530 Leonard street, for Thos. J. Denman to Mary A. Shear for $3,400.

CONVEYANCES.

	1889. Oct. 31 to Nov. 6, inclus.	1890. Oct. 30 to Nov. 5, inclus.	1891. Oct. 29 to Nov. 3, inclus.
Number	330	376	337
Amount involved	$1,652,710	$2,047,476	$1,293,964
Number nominal	83	81	86

MORTGAGES.

Number	297	282	286
Amount involved	$1,400,520	$1,457,977	$1,806,845
Number at 5 per cent. or less	190	165	176
Amount involved	$906,489	$801,110	$988,005

PROJECTED BUILDINGS.

	1889. Nov. 1 to 7, inclus.	1890. Oct. 31 to Nov. 6, inclus.	1891. Oct. 30 to Nov. 5, inclus.
Number of buildings	32	78	60
Estimated cost	$172,400	$819,550	$830,560

Out of Town.

WOODLAWN HEIGHTS, N. Y.—Lewis & Holder have sold the Scott farm of thirty-four acres at this place to R. I. Lomas and E. J. O'Gorman, representing a syndicate, for the sum of $80,000.

Out Among the Builders.

Dr. H. Knapp, the oculist, and Dr. W. Gill Wylie, the surgeon, will each build a 30-foot four-story residence, on a plot of 60x98.9, on the south side of 40th street, 500 feet east of 6th avenue.

W. Edgar Pruden will improve the seven lots on the north side of 74th street, 100 feet west of West End avenue, by the erection of first-class private dwellings.

David Christie intends building a number of private dwellings on the six lots at the northeast corner of West End avenue and 104th street.

John C. Burne is the architect for two five-story brown stone front flats that John S. Scott will build on the north side of 111th street, 50 feet west of Madison avenue, at a cost of $40,000. Each house will be 25x60, with an extension 13.6 feet in the rear.

The Salvation Army intends to build a headquarters in the neighborhood of Union square. The secretary was seen yesterday at the present headquarters, No. 111 Reade street, and he stated that plans had been drawn by one of their members, assisted by a New York builder. They expected to secure 75x103.3, near Union square, and to build thereon a store and office building, with a hall in the rear, to seat 1,800 people.

Schneider & Herter have plans on the boards for an apartment house, 25.6x93.6, five stories, to be erected on the east side of 1st avenue, 25 feet south of 52d street, for Weil & Mayer.

Emil Gruwe is the architect for two five-story houses, 89.7x55.4, to be built at Nos. 167 and 169 Perry street. H. Schlobohm is the owner.

Richard R. Davis has plans on the boards for a five-story brown stone and brick front flat which Wm. Walsh will erect on the southeast corner of the Boulevard and 62th street, at a cost of $40,000. The size of the building will be 25.5x104.3x93.8x83.10.

H. Alban Reeves has plans on the boards for four brick and stone front flats and stores to be built by Thos. Webster on the northeast corner of Boston avenue and Teasdale place. The corner will be six stories high and 27x104 9¾ in size, and the others five stories high and 27x76.5, 27x63.11 and 19x56.11 in size. Their cost is estimated at upwards of $60,000.

James Stewart, builder, of 247 West 47th street, is about to erect at 213 West 55th street, a brick and stone private stable, 25x55, for Mrs. S. C. Twombly from plans of Jas. M. Farnsworth, architect, to cost about $12,000; also a two-story brick and stone extension to house at 212 West 59th street, same owner and architect, to cost about $3,000.

Andrew Spence has plans on the boards for two three-story and basement frame dwellings, 25x49 and 22x40, to be built on the southeast corner of Bathgate avenue and 174th street by Wm. F. Fernschild, at a cost of $12,000. The corner building will have stores on the ground floor.

John C. Burne will furnish plans for a five-story brick and stone flat, which Josiah S. Lindsay will erect on the south side of Morton street, 205.9 feet east of Hudson street. The size will be 25x85.8, and the cost $26,000.

E. R. Merrill will improve two lots on the south side of 28th street, 225 feet west of 10th avenue.

Special Notices.

The annual meeting of the stockholders of the Knickerbocker Trust Co. was held on Thursday, at its main office, No. 234 5th avenue, and the following directors elected: Joseph S. Auerbach, Harry B. Hollins, Jacob Hays, Charles T. Barney, A. Foster Higgins, Robert G. Remsen, Henry W. T. Mali, Andrew H. Sands, James H. Breslin, Gen. George J. Magee, I. Townsend Burden, John S. Tilney, E. V. Loew, Henry F. Dimock, John P. Townsend, Charles F. Watson, David H. King, Jr., Frederick G. Bourne, Robert Maclay, Walter Stanton, C. Lawrence Perkins, Edward Wood and William H. Beadleston. The following statement of the condition of the company at the close of its fiscal year, on the 31st of Oct., was submitted. Total resources, $4,812,493.61; liabilities, $325,782.59; which shows an increase in surplus of $50,832.41 net over the previous year. During the year the company also paid a semi-annual dividend of 3 per cent on its capital.

WANTS AND OFFERS.

WANTS.

SITUATION WANTED.—By a young man, 25 years of age, in a real estate or insurance office; has highest references; willing and obliging. Address, D. T. D., care of Walter Dewsnap, 157 Broadway, New York. Nov. 7-14

YOUNG MAN, 24, notary, extended business experience, desires situation in reliable real estate office at moderate salary. FREDERIC C. DIERKING, 228 East 10th st., N. Y.

OFFERS.

Dwellings and Flats.

A 72D ST. GEM, No. 308 West.—This superb house is beautifully decorated; has handsome gas fixtures; is in perfect order; ready for immediate occupancy; a prompt buyer can get a greater bargain than has been offered in months.
CONDIT, 1179 Broadway.

ONLY ONE LEFT, FOUR SOLD LAST MONTH—312 West 89th st., 20 feet, four stories; exceptionally well built; unexcelled location; am authorized to close this out at a bargain.
CONDIT, 1179 Broadway.

A PERFECT HOUSE FOR SALE.—A bargain; need money; must sell; four-story; three-story extension; decorated, gas fixtures, electricity, gas logs; perfect order; foyer, built by Farley; no better house for the price in city; any one wanting to buy on speculation can rent to me at good price. Apply on premises, 56 West 32d st. Oct. 31-Nov. 7.

FOR SALE.—On Madison av, two apartments; good rentals; can be sold cheap.
SCOTT BROS., 120 Broadway, Equitable Building.

FOR SALE.—2443 8th av and 210 and 214 West 105th st.; commission allowed brokers. Apply at
Aug. 29-uf. Room 19, 151 Broadway.

FOR SALE.—Five new first-class four-story and basement private dwellings, Nos. 109 113 and 119 East 45th st., and Nos. 462 and 464 Lexington av.; all leased to desirable tenants or can arrange to give possession to some of them if desired. For further particulars apply to
THE G. GRAHAM & SONS CO., 300 East 42d st.
Sept 19-1aw8w.

A—At reasonable prices and easy terms, three and four-story residences, with three-story extensions; all improvements. Call and examine or inquire of the owner and builder, on the premises.
S. O. WRIGHT, 128 West 121st st., open daily.
Oct. 3 uf.

FOR SALE.—Six new cabinet-trimmed three story and basement brown stone private dwellings, Nos. 142-152 West 122d st.; prices reasonable and brokers commissions allowed. For further particulars apply at office of
FRED'K. M. LITTLEFIELD, 156 Broadway.
Aug. 29-uf.

FOR SALE—2443 8th av.; 26.3½x100; easy terms; commission allowed brokers; apply at
Mar. 28-u-f. ROOM 19, 156 Broadway.

OFFERS.

FOR SALE—210 and 212 West 105th st.; five-story apartments; each, 25x89x100; decorated and carpeted; apply at ROOM 19, 156 Broadway.
Mar. 28-u-f

Improved Property.

PLANING MILL FOR SALE.—Is located at 24th st. and 11th av., on four or five city lots, leased ground, and consists of two and three-story brick buildings and adjoining sheds; also 80 horse-power engine and boiler, planers, moulders, saws, etc., all in good running order and now in operation; owner will leave a portion of value on bond and mortgage three years; this offers splendid opportunity to enlarge woodworking industry or to secure good mill business to add thereto. Advertiser intends to continue his lumber business now carried on at above address. For further particulars, etc., apply to
EBEN PECK, 24th st. and 11th av.

OFFICE OF
FREDERICK SOUTHACK,
471 BROADWAY,
offers for sale some choice pieces
of property on
LEONARD ST., between Broadway and West B'way.
FRANKLIN ST., between B'way and West B'way.
WHITE ST., between B'way and West B'way.
BROADWAY, from Barclay to 14th st.
BLEECKER ST., from B'way to South 5th av.
GREENE ST., Canal to 8th st.
WASHINGTON PLACE, B'way to Wooster.
WAVERLEY PLACE, B'way to Wooster.
APPLY AS ABOVE.
FREDERICK SOUTHACK.
Oct. 3 uf.

Vacant Lots.

EASTERLY FRONT BOULEVARD, with 200 ft. on 86th st. and 264 ft. on 87th st.; one or more plots.
Nov. 7-1aw6w. OTTO ERNST, South Amboy, N. J.

BEST LOCATED LOTS in the city; excavated; with or without building loan.
J. M. STRONG, Jr., 61 Liberty st.

CHOICE BUILDING LOTS, East and West Side; with liberal builder's loans; no brokers.
Nov. 7-14. P. O. Box 3,020.

RIVERSIDE DRIVE.—We have two entire fronts in the best location on the drive; for sale, cheap.
SCOTT BROS., 120 Broadway, Equitable Building.

WILL SELL LOTS or exchange two lots, 149th st., 10th and 11th avs; equity, $7,000, for small piece improved property.
SHELTON, 243 West 125th.

CAPITALISTS.—A piece of property on 125th st. at a great bargain.
SCOTT BROS., 120 Broadway.

TO BUILDERS.—We have some very desirable lots in best location which we can sell with builders' loans. SCOTT BROS., 120 Broadway.

1ST AV., near 108th st; full lot, $[illegible].
Oct. 31-1aw6w. EDWIN A. ELY, 103 Gold st.

OFFERS.

40 CHERRY ST., between Roosevelt and Franklin sq., 32x65, vacant; $12,000; accommodating terms. EDWIN A. ELY, 103 Gold st.
Sept. 26-1aw8w.

LEASEHOLD—FOR SALE.—23d st., between 10th and 11th avs., four city lots, 50 feet frontage on 23d st., running through to 22d st. Inquire at office, corner 11th av. and 22d st., or of
Oct 17-1-aw-4w GEO. G. FARNHAM, 65 Broadway.

100TH ST., between 2d and 3d avs.; ten lots cheap; all mortgage if improved.
Sept. 26-1aw8w. EDWIN A. ELY, 103 Gold st.

FOUR ATTRACTIVE LOTS, 149th st., adjoining southwest corner 7th av., $3,600 each; builders' terms. EDWIN A. ELY, 103 Gold st.
Sept 26-1aw8w.

Brooklyn Real Estate for Sale.

$2,000 CASH, $4,500 5 per cent mortgage, will purchase three-story bay front single flat, 192 13th st.; fully rented to good tenants.
CONDIT, 1179 Broadway.

SEVEN TWO-STORY AND BASEMENT HOUSES, renting for over $4,[illegible]50 per year; expenses low. Particulars from EXECUTRIX, RECORD AND GUIDE.

Country Property.

50 TO 200 ACRES, suitable for dividing into large or small plots; forty minutes from city; convenient to depot; can be sub-divided at small expense.
W. B. TIBBITS, agent, White Plains, N. Y.

FOR SALE.—In plots to suit; eligible building sites commanding view of sound for miles, on North st., Greenwich, Connecticut; price reasonable; terms easy; neighborhood aristocratic and fashionable. Apply to
FRED. J. STONE, owner, 60 Broadway, N. Y.
Sept. 12-uf.

Miscellaneous.

TO LET OR TO LEASE.—Two floors of a factory, 25x98, light on all sides, 1st av and 107th st; terms moderate. J. KLEBER'S SONS,
Nov. 7 uf. 409 East 107th.

THOMAS & ERICKSON, 31 West 30th st., have a large assortment of houses for sale, from 25th st. to 138d st., ranging in price from $13,000 to $125,000, and on easy terms.
Oct. 24-1aw4w.

A PARTY ABOUT TO BUILD A FIVE-STORY factory, 50x98, in Harlem, near water-front, will lease the three upper floors and build to suit tenant. Terms very moderate. Address
May 16 u. f. OWNER, 409 E. 107th St.

PRINTING.—Book, News and Job.
RECORD AND GUIDE PRESS,
14 Barclay, and 14, 16 Vesey sts.

SALES OF THE WEEK.

The following are the sales at the Real Estate Exchange and Auction Room for the week ending November 6.

** Indicates that the property described has been bid in for plaintiff's account.*

R. V. HARNETT & CO.

*78th st, s s, 225 w 10th av, 50x100, vacant. C. H. Williamson.......... $21,400
*96th st, Nos. 50-54, s s, 250 e 9th av, 6[illegible]x100.8, three four-story brk dwell'gs. F. P. Furnald.......... 67,000
102d st, No. 156, s s, 325 w 8d av, 15x100.11, four-story stone front dwell'g. T. H. Rauch. (Amt due $8,869).......... 7,000
131st st, No. 18, s s, 265 w 5th av, 15x84.11....
131st st, No. 22, s s, 295 w 5th av, 15x81.11...
Two three-story stone front dwell'gs ....
Thomas C. Van Brunt. (Amt due on No. 18 $1,973, and on No. 22 $1,911; prior morts. $17,000).......... 22,800

SMYTH & RYAN.

22d st, No. 157, n s, 165.7 e 7th av, 21.10x98.9, three-story brk tenem't. Louis Grunnut. (Amt due $15,550).......... 23,300

WM. KENNELLY.

103d st, No. 200, s s, 118 w Amsterdam av, 20x76 to Clendenning lane, x20x77.9, five-story brk flat. A. Walker. (Amt due $17,686).......... 19,500
103d st, No. 208, adj, similar dwell'g. David Dunbar. (Amt due $17,686).......... 19,400
103d st, No. 210, adj, similar dwell'g. Mary Fruch. (Amt due $17,686).......... 19,200
103d st, No. 212, adj, similar dwell'g. R. R. Pero. (Amt due $17,686).......... 19,250
*123d st, Nos. 401 and 403, n w cor Columbus av 57.10x94, two five-story brk and stone flats, store in No. 401. N. Y. Lumber and Wood Working Co. (Amt due on this and property below $14,177).......... 48,00[illegible]
132d st, n s, 330 w Courtlandt av, 50x100. W. Wills. (Amt due $[illegible]).......... 4,600
*Columbus (9th) av, Nos. 1286 and 1288, s w cor 124th st, 55 10x100, two five-story brk and stone flats, store in No. 1288. Same.......... 37,550
*Park av, Nos. 5[illegible]5-569, e s, 73 3 n 63d st, 60.5x100.1x60x100 five-story brk flat, the "Lonsdale." Randolph Guggenheimer et al. (Amt due $14,907; prior morts. $30,000).......... 32,350

B. L. KENNELLY.

*119th st, No. 7, n s, 95.5 w 5th av, 14x57.9x14.6x53.11, three-story brk dwell'g. Holland Trust Co., trustees. (Amt due $4,734).......... 5,425

A. H. MULLER & SON.

*22d st, s s, 150 e 11th av, 100x100.5, vacant. Annah E. Benedict. (Amt due $12,036).......... 12,400
*7th av, No. 2271, e s, 49.11 s 134th st, runs east 75 x south 22.4 x southwest 4.5 x west 71.5 to 7th av, x north 25 to beginning, five-story brk store and flat. Mary L. March. (Amt due $24 146).......... 20,600
*7th av, No. 2273, e s, 24 11 s 134th st, 25x75, five-story brk flat with stores. Mary L. Barbey. (Amt due $21,146).......... 21,000

OTHER AUCTIONEERS.

*100th st, n s, 95 e Lexington av, 200x100.11, vacant..........
101st st, s s, 95 e Lexington av, 200x100.11, vacant..........
Equitable Life Assurance Soc. (Amt due $[illegible]).......... 58,000
Renwick st, No 45, w s, 75 s Spring st, three-story and basement brk dwell'g. Caroline Etzel.......... 8,575
*Av C, No. 80, e s, 46.6 s 6th st, 72.0x92.8, brk and stone church. D. McGinnis et al. (Amt due $20,879).......... 4[illegible],000
Total.......... $[illegible]
Corresponding week, 1890.......... $[illegible]

BROOKLYN, N. Y.

** Indicates that the property described has been bid in for plaintiff's account.*

FOR WEEK ENDING NOVEMBER 5.

JERE. JOHNSON, JR.

Montague st, No. 55, n w cor Hicks st, 5[illegible]x1[illegible]0, two-and-a-half-story brk dwell'g. Sarah Crawford.......... $4[illegible],750
1st pl, No. 120, s s, 265 e Court st, 2[illegible]x123.6½, five-story brk flat. Lillian W. Leary.......... 6,400
4th st, No. 847, 18x100, two-story brown stone dwell'g. W. J. Pearson.......... 4,900

OTHER AUCTIONEERS.

*Hicks st, No. 474, w s, 366.0 n Degraw st, 19.6x97.6, four-story brk tenem't and store. Louise Cook.......... 5,500
*Montgomery st, No. 33, n s, 322 e 8th av, 20x88.5x20.[illegible]x81, three story brk dwell'g. Mallard M. Canda.......... 8,100
Oliver st, n s, 100 w Marine av, runs north 103.7 x northwest 25.8 to 1st av, x west — x south 200 to Oliver st, x east 50, New Utrecht..........
Oliver st, n s, 250 w Marine av, 150x200 to 1st av, New Utrecht..........
Oliver st, n s, 2[illegible]6 w Shore road, 25x200 to 1st av, New Utrecht; partition..........
Marine av, w s, 100 n Oliver st, 50x100, New Utrecht..........
3d av, s w cor 91st st, 50.2x[illegible]13.0x irreg., New Utrecht, except..........
D. R. Blanchard.......... [illegible],000
*Pacific st, s s, 363.10 e Rochester av, 18.9x107.1½, two-and-a-half-story frame dwell'g. Sarah C. Savage.......... 2,000
Plymouth st, No. 321, n s, 200.1 e Hudson av, 28 2½x100, four-story brk dwell'g. Julia W. Latimer.......... 9,000
*South Oxford st, No. 02, w s, 123 n Lafayette av, 12x100, three story brk dwell'g. E. F. Knowlton.......... 13,300
*Evergreen av, Nos. 629 and 631, s w cor Eldert st, 35x75x28.11½x76, two three-story frame tenem'ts and stores. Richard Goodwin.......... 9,002

Lexington av, n s, 120 e Lewis av, 20x100. Stephen W. Collins 5,600

Willoughby av, n w cor Tompkins av, runs north 77.6 x west 80 x north 22.6 x west 45 x south 100 to Willoughby av. x east 125 to beginning. Reformed Presbyterian Church. James N. Bell 20,100

South 9th st, No. 167, n e cor Driggs st, 25x 76, three-story brk dwell'g and store. Claus Doscher 15,000

South 9th st, No. 169, 25x74.6, three-story brk dwell'g. John McQuade 11,000

Total $157,850
Corresponding week 1890 ..... $191,780

CONVEYANCES

Wherever the letters Q. C., C. a. G. and B. & S occur, preceded by the name of the grantee they mean as follows:

1st—Q. C. is an abbreviation for Quit Claim deed, i. e., a deed in which all the right, title and interest of the grantor is conveyed, omitting all covenants or warranty.

2d—C. a. G. means a deed containing Covenant against Grantor Only, in which he covenants that he hath not done any act whereby the estate conveyed may be impeached, charged or encumbered.

3d—B. & S. is an abbreviation for Bargain and Sale deed, wherein, although the seller makes no express covenants, he really grants or conveys the property for a valuable consideration, and thus impliedly claims to be the owner of it.

NEW YORK CITY.

OCTOBER 30, 31, NOVEMBER 2, 3, 4, 5.

Allen st, No. 185, w s, 75 n Stanton st, 25x75, three-story brk tenem't. Lorenz Harbauer to Philip Kotlowsky. Taxes 1891. Nov. 2. $13,750

Barrow st, No. 54, n s, 65 e Bedford st, 25x98.4 x25x98.6, five-story brk flat. Albert E. Wesslau to Alphonse Hogenauer. ½ part. Oct. 28. nom

Barrow st, No. 52, n s, 90.5 e Bedford st, 25.5x 98.2x—x98.4, five-story brk flat. Alphonse Hogenauer to Albert E. Wesslau. ½ part. Oct. 28. nom

Bayard st, No. 61, s s, 272.2 w Bowery, 25x90, five-story brk tenem't with stores. Jane E. Cusack and Auguste L. Sevestre to William Burnstine and Jacob Rosenberg. *Mt.* $24,000. Oct. 30. 38,000

Broadway, No. 840, s e cor 13th st, 24.6x86.1x 91.1, gore, three-story brk store. Charles F. Waters, Norwich, Conn., heir Charles Waters, to Maria T. Sinnott, Mary J. De Bussy, Ann E., Matilda, Josephine and Frances C. Waters also heirs Charles Waters, ½ part. Oct. 26. 4,500

Broadway, Nos. 1691 and 1693, n w cor 53d st, 50.9x42.5x50.5x47.10.
Broadway, No. 1695, w s, 50.9 n 53d st, 25.2x 39.8x25x42.5.
Five-story brk flat, Irvington.
Etta wife of Bayard Woodruff to Georgia P. Williams and Georgia W. Warren. ½ part. *Mt.* on entire premises $50,000. Nov. 3. 47,000

Same property. Valentine Woodruff to same. ½ part. Nov. 2. nom

Same property. Henry D. Hotchkiss assignee of Valentine S. Woodruff to same. ½ part. Nov. 2. 47,000

Broome st, No. 103, s s, 50 e Willett st, 25x75, five-story brk tenem't with stores. Marks Chambers and Isidor V. Wittenberg to Max S. Korn. *Mt.* $16,000. Oct. 30. val. consid. and 100

Broome st, No. 448, n s, 50.1 e Mercer st, 25x 50, five-story brk store. Hobart E. Bernan to The American Society for the Prevention of Cruelty to Animals. Nov. 4. nom

Broome st, No. 141, s s, 20 e Ridge st, 20x60, two-story brk tenem't. Louis Aaron to Robert Berlinger. *Mt.* $5,000. Nov. 2. 9,000

Cannon st, No. 83, w s, 110 n Rivington st, 20x 80, three-story brk tenem't. Adolph Roth to Solomon and Simon Spandau. *Mt.* $8,500. Nov. 2. 11,000

Chrystie st, No. 90, e s, abt 175 s Grand st, 25x 100, four-story brk store and tenem't with three-story brk tenem't on rear. Partition. James P. Campbell to Martha M., Martha L., George and Archibald M. Shrady and Anna A. White. Nov. 2. 23,500

Cherry st, Nos. 258 and 260, n s, 26.3 e Rutgers st, 52.6x95.2x52.6x92.5, two five-story brk tenem'ts with stores.
Cherry st, Nos. 262 and 264, n s, 78.9 e Rutgers st, runs north 95.2 x east 26.3 x north 20.8 x east 26.1 x south 114.11 to st, x west 52.4, two five-story brk tenem'ts with stores.
Jonas Weil and Bernhard Mayer to Benedict A. Klein. Nov. 4. 138,500

Same property. Benedict A. Klein to Jonas Weil and Bernhard Mayer. *Mt.* $80,000. Nov. 4. 138,500

Columbia st, No. 116, e s, 24.10 n Stanton st, 21.8x75.4, three-story brk tenem't. Samuel Greenfeld to Abraham Schwarz. *Mt.* $10,000. Nov. 4. 13,750

Columbia st, No. 118, e s, 46.6 n Stanton st, 21.9 x75.4, three-story brk tenem't. Same to Philip Fried. Nov. 2. 16,000

Cornelia st, No. 22, s s, abt 195 e Bleecker st, 25x88.10x—x92.4, five-story brk tenem't. Mary A. wife of and Matthew M. Henry, Brooklyn, N. Y., to Michael Scanlon. *Mt.* $10,000. Oct. 31. 20,500

Delancey st, No. 239, s s, 100 w Willett st, 25x 87.6, five-story brk tenem't with stores. Edward Weinberger to Samuel Hoffman. *Mt.* $21,000. Oct. 30. 26,500

Delancey st, No. 53 } begins Delancey
Eldridge st, Nos. 145–151 } st, s w cor Eldridge st, 25x100, three-story frame (brk front) store and tenem't on Delancey st and two two and four-story brk and frame stores and tenem'ts on Eldridge st.
Delancey st, No. 51, s s, 25 w Eldridge st, 25x 100, three-story brk store and tenem't.
Partition. James P. Campbell to Benjamin F. Cohen. Nov. 2. 56,500

Same property. John, Jacob, William and George F. Shrady, New York, and Anna B. Van Kirk, New Brunswick, N. J., to same. All title. B. & S. Oct. 26. nom

Same property. John Shrady et al. exrs. and trustees Maria Shrady to same. Oct. 26. nom

Same property. Martha M., Martha L., George and Archibald M. Shrady and Anna A. White to same. All title. B. & S. Oct. 26. nom

Division st, No. 269, s s, 211.6 e Montgomery st, 21.10x42.5x22.2x42.6, three-story brk store and tenem't. Joseph Mentz to Samuel Slomon. *Mt.* $8,500. Nov. 2. 11,800

Duane st, No. 116, s w s, abt 100 s e Church st, five-story stone front store. John, Jacob and George Shrady exrs. and trustees Maria Shrady to John, Jacob, William and George F. Shrady and Anna B. Van Kirk. Oct. 26. nom

Same property. Martha M., Martha L., George Shrady and Anna A White to same. Q. C. Oct. 26. nom

Same property. Partition. James P. Campbell to same. Nov. 2. 83,000

Essex st, No. 101, w s, 77.6 n Delancey st, 22.6x 48.9, five-story brk store and tenem't. Louis Gordon to Lena Ladner. *Mt.* $14,250. Nov. 4. 18,000

Same property. Laemmlein Buttenwieser to Louis Gordon. *Mt.* $12,000. Nov. 4. 18,000

Forsyth st, No. 52, e s, 100.9 s Hester st, 25x100, five-story brk tenem't with stores. James J. Loonie and Eugene Parker to Ida Michalisky. Oct. 28. 46,000

Forsyth st, No. 70, e s, abt 100 n Hester st, 25x 100, three-story frame (brk front) tenem't with one-story brk building on rear. Emma Floring widow, formerly Messerschmidt to August Paffen. *Mt.* $19,850. Oct. 30. 22,000

Same property. August Paffen to James J. Loonie and Eugene Parker. *Mt.* $10,000. Nov. 4. 23,000

Forsyth st, No. 169, w s, 73 n Rivington st, 27x 50.2, five-story brk tenem't with stores. Balthasar Bosch to Henry A. Bade. *Mt.* $8,000. Feb. 16, 1891. 21,000

Franklin st, No. 51½, s s, abt 100 w Elm st, 22x 86, two and three-story brk and frame store. Contract. Malvina and Mary Heath, East Orange, N. J., Frederick and Frances M. Heath, Adeline Johnson and Emma Barnett and Eliza Simons to Solomon Loeb. Oct. 27. 20,000

Goerck st, No. 113, w s, 85.2 s Stanton st, 17.11 x50, three-story brk tenem't. John E. Wellenkamp to Anna wife of Ignatz Vogel. Oct. 31. 6,500

Goerck st, Nos. 75 and 77, w s, 64 s Rivington st, 36x59, two three-story brk tenem'ts. August Miller to Samuel Greenfeld. Sub. to any paving assessment. Nov. 2. 12,000

Henry st, No. 111, n s, abt 85 e Pike st, 25x108, three-story brk tenem't. Edward Knowlton to Harris Mandelbaum. Nov. 2. 21,000

Houston st, Nos. 196 and 198, n s, 163.6 w Bedford st, 25x119.8x25.11x126.7, three-story brk building with frame shed on rear. Ascher Weinstein and wife to Edward C. Heerwagen. *Mt.* $13,000. Nov. 2. 20,000

Hillside st, centre line, lot 135 map Isaac Dyckman, 50x226.4x50x226.2. Simeon Ford to John Stimmel. Q. C. All liens. Oct. 26. 5,000

Lewis st, No. 25, w s, 75 n Broome st, 25x100, three-story brk tenem't. Morris Franklin, Fanny M. Updike and Henry B. Weselman to James Cunningham. *Mt.* $6,000. May 1. 16,250

Ludlow st, No. 5, w s, 50 n Canal st, 25.5x87.6 x25.3x87.6, five-story brk tenem't with stores. Samuel Phillips to Jacob Postal. *Mt.* $29,000. Oct. 29. 36,000

Ludlow st, No. 115, e s, 175 n Delancey st, 25x 87.6, five-story brk tenem't with stores. Mary Fuhrken and Joseph Fuchs individ. and as exrs. of Barbara Schmidt and Lina wife of Franz Kohlsdorf to Israel Josefsohn. *Mt.* $18,000. Nov. 2. 26,500

Madison st, No. 348, s s, 192.11 e Scammel st, 23.6x95.1x23.6x95.3, five-story brk tenem't with stores. Barnet Solinger to Ida Solinger. Nov. 2. nom

Madison st, No. 336, s s, 56 e Scammel st, 19.5x 36x19.5x37, four-story brk tenem't. Nathan and Marks Rosenberg to Aaron Kaplan. *Mt.* $6,000. Oct. 29 10,000

Morton st, No. 56, s s, 205 e Hudson st, 25x100, three-story brk dwell'g. Carrie Bensel to Benjamin F. Cohen. *Mt.* $12,000. Nov. 4. 16,500

Same property. Benjamin F. Cohen to Josiah S. Lindsay. *Mt.* $12,000. Nov. 2. 18,900

Morton st, No. 31, n s, 50 s w Bedford st, 30x 20x30x20.2, three-story brk dwell'g. Henry M. Brush to Mary Carter. *Mt.* $2,000. Nov. 2. 7,250

Mott st, No. 193, w s, abt 190 s Spring st, 25x 100, three-story brk tenem't with four-story brk tenem't on rear. James and Maria A. Palumbo to Nicola Parente. Q. C. Oct. 30. nom

New Croton Aqueduct, n e cor 147th st. Party wall agreement. Diantha A., Rowena M. and Ellis B. Southworth to John G. Moore. July 8. nom

Park row, Nos. 142 and 144, n s, abt 90 w Pearl st, 25x96, three-story brk stores. Partition. James P. Campbell to Martha M., Martha L., George and Archibald M. Shrady and Anna A. White. Nov. 2. 39,600

Park row, Nos. 142 and 144, n s, abt 90 w Pearl st, 25x96.
Chrystie st, No. 90, e s, abt 175 s Grand st, 25 x100.
John, Jacob, William and George F. Shrady, New York, and Anna B. Van Kirk, New Brunswick, N. J., to same. Q. C. Oct. 26. nom

Same property. John Shrady et al. exrs. and trustees of Maria Shrady to same. Oct. 26. nom

Pitt st, No. 13[illegible], w s, 125 s Houston st, 25x100, five-story brk store and tenem't with four-story brk tenem't on rear. Charlotte Weimar, Solomon Mergler and Catherine Pfarrer to Elias Jacobs. Oct. 26. 25,000

Ridge st, No. 151, w s, 150 n Stanton st, 25x100, six-story brk tenem't with stores. Meyer Libman and Robert Wolff to Karl M. Wallach. *Mt.* $24,000. Nov. 2. 33,000

Stanton st, No. 191, s s, 16.8 e Attorney st, 16.8x 64, portion of three-story brk moulding mill, &c. Charles A. Bernhardt and Emma M. Meliert to Marie J. Bernhardt. B. & S. Oct. 30. nom

Stanton st, Nos. 223–227 } begins Stanton st, s e
Pitt st, Nos. 104 and 106 } cor Pitt st, 50x100, three four-story brk tenem'ts with stores on Stanton st and two five-story brk tenem'ts with stores on Pitt st. William Buhler exr. William Buhler dec'd to Caroline A. Buhler. Oct. 30. other consid and 45,000

Thompson st, Nos. 143 and 145, w s, 243.6 n Prince st, 49.4x100, two six-story brk tenements with stores and two-story brk tenem't on rear of No. 143. Elias Jacobs to Herman Cohen. *Mt.* $13,000. Oct. 30. 51,000

Washington st, No. 694, w s, 58.2 s Perry st, 19.4x61x21 to alley, x63.3, three-story brk tenem't with two-story brk stable on rear. Fannie J. Demarest formerly Moore, Woodbridge, N. Y., and William Moore to Bernhard Ziesig. C. a. G. *Mt.* $4,000. Jan. 21. nom

Washington st, No. 46[illegible], w s, 75 n Watts st, 25x 100, three-story brk store and tenem't and two-story brk building on rear. George H. Golden, Herbert O. and Kate C. Halsey, Eliza L. Norris exrs. John D. Norris to John Dickson trustee of Jane Gasten. *Mt.* $8,000. Oct. 29. nom

Same property. Kate C. Halsey and Eliza L. Norris, Elizabeth, N. J., to same. *Mt.* $6,000. Oct. 27. 17,250

Washington st, No. 765, e s, 20 s West 12th st, 15x78x75x76.3, five-story brk store and tenem't. Foreclos. Lorenzo Semple to Gertrude Jewell et al. exrs., &c., George W. Jewett. Sept. 25. 10,250

West st, Nos. 109–113 } begins
Washington st, Nos. 164 and 166 } West st,
Cortlandt st, Nos. 81, 89, 91 and 93 } s e cor Cortlandt st, runs south 106.4 x east 195.11 to Washington st, x north 52 x west 70 x north 58.7 to Courtlandt st, x west 23.5 x south 57.10 x west 63 x north 58 to Cortlandt st, x west 58.9, several two, three and four-story brk stores on West and Cortlandt sts and vacant lots on Washington st. William L. Hubbell, Bridgeport, Conn., to John C. Wilson, Philadelphia, Pa. *Mt.* $200,000. Oct. 21. 125,000

Waverley pl, No. 5, n s, 125 w Broadway, 25x 108, three-story brk store. Alois Gutwillig to Phebe Pearsall. *Mt.* $30,000 and taxes 1891. Oct. 30. 53,750

4th st, No. 275, n s, 288.2 w Av C, 24.9x96.3x 24.9x96.3, four-story brk tenem't with two-story brk building on rear. Mary Von Hatten extrx. Fabian Von Hatten to Abraham I. Bleistift. Nov. 2. 15,000

4th st, No. 273, n s, 313.11 w Av C, 24.9x96.3, four-story brk tenem't with two-story brk building on rear. Josephine Pietsch to same. Nov. 2. 15,000

4th st, No. 324, s s, 295.2 w Av D, 22.7x96, three-story brk tenem't. Henry E. Crampton exr. Dorcas M. Crampton to Rosa wife of Benjamin Friedman. Nov. 2. 12,500

5th st, Nos. 338 and 340, s s, 100 w 1st av, 50x 96.2, two and three-story brk buildings, mineral water factory, &c. Elias Jacobs to August Ruff. *Mt.* $20,000. Oct. 29. 44,000

6th st, Nos. 734 and 736, s s, 268 w Av D, runs south 70 x east 25 x south 49 x west 50 x north 119 to st, x east 25, five-story brk mineral water factory and two-story brk stable on rear of No. 738. Minnie Grau and Annie E. Renbel heirs Anna G. E. Lerch to George Grau. *Mt.* $12,000. Nov. 2. 34,100

7th st, No. 112, s s, 275 w Av A, 25x90.10, five-story brk tenem't. Frederick Huff and Jacob Gross to Solomon Stransky and Walter Zeimer. *Mt.* $21,000. Nov. 1. nom

7th st, No. 44, s s, 98 w 2d av, 22x90.10, three-story brk tenem't. Julius Langenbahn to John Schwoen. *Mt.* $7,000. Nov. 2. 18,000

9th st, No. 9 E., n s, abt 175 e 5th av, 25x92.3, four-story brk dwell'g. Hillah E. wife of John H. Foster, Tuxedo Park, N. Y., to Mary T. Livingston, Clermont, N. Y. Oct. 29. 40,000

12th st, No. 134, s w s, 100 n w 3d av, 15x106.6, four-story brk tenem't. Henry A. Cram and George H. Moore trustee George C. Cram to Augusta Boettcher. Q. C. and correction deed. Oct. 24. nom

12th st, No. 237, n s, 90 w 2d av, 20.6x103.3, five-story stone front tenem't. Frederick Jantzen to Henry Ruloff and Antonia his wife. *Mt.* $20,000. Nov. 2. 28,800

13th st, No. 189, n s, 125 w 6th av, 20x100, three-story brk dwell'g. John T. Hepburn, Sarah H. wife of and Henry Roberts, William H. Hepburn, Bell H. Edmonds, Julia A. Bell, Mary C. Hepburn, Annie E. and Kate S. Baker heirs Eliza Baker to Sheppard Knapp. B. & S. C. a. G. Oct. 26. 19,000

19th st, s s, 288.1 e 2d av, 20.11x92. Allotted in partition to Mary E. Betts.

19th st, s s, 309 e 2d av, 21x92. Allotted in partition to Emma S. Hover.

19th st, s s, 246.3 e 2d av, 20.11x92. Allotted in partition to Ida A. Swarts. Oct. 31. nom

20th st, No. 331, n s, 399.9 w 8th av, 24.9x92, four-story brk tenem't with two-story brk building on rear. Francis W. and Ellen J. Curran exrs. Ellen C. Curran to Ellen J., Francis W., John J. and Jennie E. Curran and Mary C. Anglim. Nov. 2. nom

23d st, No. 468, s s, 24 e 10th av, 22x98.9, five-story stone front dwell'g. Edward A. Smith, Hartford, Conn., devisee Isaac E. Smith to Jacob Appell. Nov. 2. 23,400

24th st, No. 411, n s, 125 w 9th av, 25x98.9, four-story brk tenem't with two-story brk stable on rear. Joseph R. Conklin and ano. exrs. Seth Conklin to Charles A. Robinson. Oct. 31. 15,350

Same property. Louisa L. Conklin widow to Charles A. Robinson. ⅛ part. Oct. 31. nom

25th st, No. 218, s s, 186.9 w 7th av, 15.6x98.9, four-story brk dwell'g. Joseph Strauss to Josephine H. Bissell. Oct. 31. 11,500

25th st, No. 336, s s, 150 w 1st av, 25x98.9, five-story brk tenem't. Partition. John H. Judge to Anna Kruse. Oct. 30. 21,200

26th st, No. 103, n s, 79 e 4th av, 21x49.4, three-story brk dwell'g. William R. Marsh to Leonard R. Kerr. Sept. 30. 14,000

26th st, No. 308, s s, 117.7 w 8th av, 18.9x98.9, three-story brk dwell'g. Joseph T. Farrington to Benjamin F. Cohen. *Mt.* $8,000. Oct. 13. 13,000

34th st, No. 302, s s, 80 e 2d av, 21.3x98.7, five-story brk store and tenem't. Anna Prabar to Frank S. Stueber. Oct. 31. 17,500

35th st, No. 440, s s, 475 w 9th av, 25x98.9, five-story stone front flat. Archibald Smith to Jane Smith. *Mt.* $24,800. Oct. 26. nom

35th st, No. 340, s s, 75 w 1st av, 25x98.9, three-story brk tenem't with one-story frame and two-story brk building on rear. Elizabeth wife of Robert Smith and John W. Carey devisees Charles P. Carey, Sr., to Charles P. Carey, Jr. 2-5 part.. B. & S. and C. a. G. Nov. 4. 4,000

36th st, Nos. 250 and 252, s s, 233.3 e 8th av, 51.9 x98.9, two five-story stone front flats. William H. Cornet and Jacob A. Zimmermann to Max S. Korn. *Mt.* $28,000. Nov. 5. See 5th av. val. consid. and 100

36th st, No. 250, s s, 258.11 e 8th av, 26.1x98.9. Max S. Korn to Pauline Greenwald. *Mt.* $28,000. Nov. 5. val. consid. and 100

36th st, No. 408, s s, 125 w 9th av, 25x98.9, five-story stone front flat. James I. Harper, Francis H. Vermilyea and John R. McKee to Simon A. Asch. *Mt.* $22,000. Oct. 30 33,000

36th st, No. 129, n s, 60 w Lexington av, 20x 74.7, four-story stone front dwell'g. Elias W. Van Voorhis to C. Grayson Martin and W. Clarence Martin. Nov. 2 nom

40th st, No 107, n s, 150 e Park av, original line, 21x98.8, four-story brk dwell'g. Release dower. Emma L. wife of Wheeler W. Edwards to John M. Knox and Maria L. his wife. Oct. 13. nom

Same property. John M. Knox to Gertrude L. wife of W. Brenton Welling. C. a. G. Oct. 22. 24,000

41st st, No. 55, n s, 105 w 4th av, 25x118.7x 25.5x113.8, three-story brk stable. Alfred Van Santvoord to Lincoln Safe Deposit Co. Oct. 31. 50,000

42d st, No. 334, s s, 358.4 e 2d av, 16.8x98.9, four-story stone front dwell'g. Eliza M. Merington to Thomas S. Harper. *Mt.* $6,000. Oct. 31. 9,250

43d st, No. 250, s s, 300 e 8th av, 20x100.5, five-story stone front flat. Alexander Moore to Thomas H. Smith. *Mt.* $24,000. Nov. 2. nom

43d st, No. 252, s s, 280 e 8th av, 20x100.5, five-story stone front flat. Same to same. *Mt.* $24,000. Nov. 2. nom

43d st, No. 250, s s, 300 e 8th av, 20x100.5, five-story stone front flat. Thomas H. Smith to Henry L. Clinton. *Mt.* $24,000. Nov. 4. nom

43d st, No. 252, s s, 280 e 8th av, 20x100.5, five-story stone front flat. Same to Elizabeth S. wife of Henry L. Clinton. *Mt.* $34,000. Nov. 4. nom

44th st, No. 26, s s, 400 w 5th av, 25x100.5, three-story brk stable. Charles Miller to A. Laufer Norrie, Ironwood, Mich. *Mt.* $18,000. Nov. 2. 33,000

44th st, No. 323, n s, 300 w 8th av, 24.11x100.4, four-story brk tenem't with three-story brk tenem't on rear. Auguste J. Paris to Frederick Grasmuck. *Mt.* $10,000. Oct. 31. See Edgecombe av. nom

46th st, No. 140, s s, 310 e 7th av, 15x100.4, four-story stone front dwell'g. Alfred B. Price to Adeline F. Detrick. *Mt.* $8,000. Oct. 31. 16,000

47th st, No. 126, s s, 475 e 7th av, 18.9x100.5, four-story stone front dwell'g. Charles S. Levy to Florence B. Ryan. B. & S. Oct. 31. nom

Same property. Charles T. Ryan to Charles S. Levy. Oct. 31. nom

49th st, No. 335, n s, 500 w 8th av, 25x100.5, three-story brk stable. Peter Scherrer to Leonhard Daub. Nov. 2. 24,000

49th st, No. 242, s s, 160 e 8th av, 20x100.5, three-story brk dwell'g. John H. McGinn to Arthur G. Leonard. *Mt.* $9,000. Nov. 2. 17,500

49th st, No. 244, s s, 140 e 8th av, 20x100.5, three-story brk dwell'g. Nelson Smith, Jr., to Emily L. Smith. Nov. 5. 18,000

50th st, No. 325, n s, 275 e 2d av, 19x100.5, four-story stone front dwell'g. William Knoepke to Meyer Stern. *Mt.* $7,000. Nov. 2. 15,000

51st st, No. 119, n s, 280 w 6th av, 20x100.5, two-story brk stable. Thomas Stokes and ano. exrs. Elizabeth C. Stokes to Lillian M. Stokes. Nov. 6. nom

52d st, No. 240, s s, 285 e 8th av, 20x100.5, four-story stone front dwell'g. William Buhler exr. William Buhler dec'd. to Caroline A. Buhler. Oct. 30. other consid and 15,000

53d st, No. 440, s s, 225 e 10th av, 25x100.5, four-story brk tenem't with stores and two-story frame building on rear. Jane Potter to Francis Mitchell and Charles Weis. Oct. 31. 16,000

53d st, No. 419, n s, 275 w 9th av, 25x100.5, five-story brk flat. Natale, Luigi, Guiseppe and Steffano Cavinato to Carrie T. Sage. Nov. 2. 32,000

54th st, No. 450, s s, 175 e 10th av, 25x100.5, five-story stone front tenem't.
53d st, No. 445, n s, 175 e 10th av, 25x100.5, five-story brk tenem't with two-story frame building on rear.
Jacob A. Zimmermann to Louis, Annie and Joseph J. Zimmermann. B. & S. C. a. G. ½ part. Oct. 24. 10,500

59th st, No. 337, n s, 225 e 9th av, 25x100.5, five-story stone front flat. Absalom W. Dieter, Brooklyn, to George Finck. *Mt.* $35,400. Nov. 4. nom

59th st, No. 339, n s, 200 e 9th av, 25x100.5, five-story stone front flat. Same to same. *Mt.* $36,300. Nov. 4. nom

63d st, No. 159, n s, 250 e Amsterdam av, 20x 100.5, five-story brk flat. Richard M. Raven, Bay Shore, L. I. to Mary A. Markey. *Mt.* $15,000. Oct. 29. 19,000

65th st, No. 146, s s, 220 e Lexington av, 20x 100.5, three-story stone front dwell'g. Nancy Aaron to Annie Jones. Nov. 2. 18,600

67th st, s s, 350 w Amsterdam av, 25x100.5, five-story brk tenem't. Foreclos. Gilbert M. Speir, Jr., to John W. Haaren. Oct. 30. 18,750

71st st, No. 312, s s, 200 e 2d av, 25x100.4, five-story brk flat. Louis Stern to James O'Gorman. *Mt.* $10,000. Oct. 30. 20,000

72d st, No. 302 W., s s, 27.6 w West End av, runs south 36 x east 13.6 x south 9 x west 13.6 x south 0.6 x west 18 x north 45.6 to st. x east 18, four-story stone front dwell'g. Hugh Lamb, East Orange, N. J., to Harvey S. Almy. *Mt.* $21,000. Oct. 29. 30,000

72d st, No. 308, s s, abt 81.6 w West End av, 18.6x58.4x18.6x58.11, four-story stone front dwell'g. Henry Dale to Francis M. Wilmurt, Pelham, New York *Mt.* $30,500. Nov. 2. See 89th st. exch

72d st, n s, 200 e Columbus av, 50x102.2, vacant. Julius A. Kohn to Alfred B. Scott. Nov. 4. 65,000

72d st, n s, 425 w Central Park West, 50x102.2, vacant.
73d st, s s, 425 w Central Park West, 50x102.2, vacant.
Rosina Hooley, Chicago, Ill., to Richard M. Hooley. *Mt.* $60,000. B. & S. Oct. 16. nom

73d st, No. 434, s s, 100 w Av A, 25x102.2, five-story brk tenem't. Wolf Bloom and Saville Levin to David Moses. *Mt.* $21,000. Nov. 2. 21,000

74th st, No. 124, s s, 242 w 9th av, 19x102.2, four-story stone front dwell'g. Henry R. Kunhardt, Jr., to Mabel F. Kunhardt. Nov. 5. nom

75th st, Nos. 328 and 330, s s, 175 w 1st av, 30 x42.5x—x47.5.
Interior lot, begins 178 w 1st av and 106.4 s 75th st, runs west 27 x north — x southeast to point 178 w 1st av, x south —.
Two four-story brk tenem'ts, stores in No. 328.
Mary Miltner to George F. Droste. *Mt.* $7,500. Oct. 31. 14,500

76th st, Nos 341 and 343, n s, 225 e 2d av, 50x 102.2, two five-story brk tenem'ts, stores in No. 341. Foreclos. Henry W. Sackett to John Mathews. Nov. 2. 2,000

76th st, No. 50, s s, 155 e Columbus av, 19x102.2, four-story stone front dwell'g. Edmund Guilbert to William C. Orr. *Mt.* $24,000. Nov. 2. nom

76th st, No. 100, s w cor Columbus or 9th av, 40x102.2, six-story brk flat with stores. Alexander Mc-Sorley to Joanna McSorley. *Mt.* $104,500. May 26. 130,750

76th st, n s, 100 e Columbus av, 100x100.2, vacant. Charles T. and Helen T. Barney heirs Ashbel H. Barney to Alfred G. Nason. B. & S. Oct. 26 72,000

77th st, No. 405, n s, 119 e 1st av, 25x102.2, five-story stone front tenem't. William Cohn to Rosa Neumann widow. *Mt.* $18,000. Oct. 22. 21,000

79th st, No. 442, s s, 75 w Av A, 19x79, five-story brk tenem't. Foreclos. Frederick G. Gedney to Cassie wife of William R. Muldoon. *Mt.* $11,500. Oct. 31. 14,600

79th st, No. 222, s s, 265 e 3d av, 20x102.2, three-story stone front dwell'g. Karl M Wallach to Huldah wife of Robert Wolff. *Mt.* $10,000. Nov. 2. 19,500

80th st, n s, 200 w 11th av, 100x102.2, vacant. John Heyzer, Brooklyn, to Edward Kelly. *Mt.* $32,000. Nov. 5. See 85th st. exch, and 5,000

81st st, Nos. 176, 178 and 180 } begins 81st st, s
Amsterdam av, Nos. 429–435 { e cor Amsterdam av, 116x102.2, three five-story brk flats, stores on av. John Casey to Mina Daiker. Oct. 23. See Edgecombe and St. Nicholas avs. 288,500

81st st, No. 169, n s, 93 w 3d av, runs north 67.2 x west 9.3 x north 16.9 x west 11.3 x south 83.11 x east 20.6, three-story brk dwell'g. Joseph Conrad to Henry Zimmermann. *Mt.* $4,000. Nov. 2. 13,000

Same property. Henry Zimmermann to Louis Alexander. *Mt.* $9,000. Nov. 2. 13,000

83d st, No. 333, n s, 250 w 1st av, 25x102.2, five-story stone front tenem't. Thomas Moore and John McLaughlin to Ida Krines. *Mt.* $15,000. Oct. 3. 25,500

83d st, No. 130, s s, 332.4 w Columbus av, 32.4x 102.2, four-story brk flat. Hugh Cheyne to Edgar W. Nye. *Mt.* $27,000. Oct. 30. exch

83d st, No. 436, s s, 80.6 w Av A, 26x102.2, five-story stone front tenem't. Henry Arnold to John Hess. *Mt.* $10,000. Oct. 31. 22,500

83d st, No. 534, s s, 148 w Av B, 25x102.2, five-story brk tenem't. Agnes Drescher to Jacob Werner. *Mt.* $11,500. Oct. 31. 22,500

84th st, No. 25, n s, 368 w Central Park West, 32x102.2, five-story stone front flat. David Richey to Daniel S. Slawson. *Mt.* $32,500. Nov. 2. val. consid. and 100

84th st, No. 23, n s, 350 w Central Park West, 18x102.2, five-story stone front flat. David Richey to Sarah B. McLeod. *Mt.* $17,500. Nov. 2. 30,000

84th st, No. 249, n s, 81.8 w 2d av, 20x82.3, four-story stone front flat. Mary E. McGarvey widow to John Manning. *Mt.* $7,000. Nov. 2. 15,750

85th st, No. 9, n s, 175 e 5th av, 25x102.2, four-story brk dwell'g with two-story brk stable on rear. Edward Kelly to John Heyzer, Brooklyn. *Mt.* $25,000. Nov. 5. See 80th st. exch

85th st, No. 46, s s, 425 w Central Park West, 25x102.2, four-story stone front dwell'g. William F. Havemeyer to Susan Orcutt. *Mt.* $32,500. Oct. 17. 32,000

Same property. Susan Orcutt widow to James B. Morrow. *Mt.* $45,817 Oct. 30. nom

86th st, No. 140, s s, 406.8 w Columbus av, 21.8x 106.10, four-story brk dwell'g. D. Willis James to George Shaw. Oct. 12. 40,000

88th st, Nos. 521–527, n s, 246 w Av B, 100x 100.8, four five-story brk tenem'ts in course of erection. Hyman and Henry Sonn to Joseph Schreiner. *Mt.* $14,730. Nov. 2. 27,000

89th st, n s, 184.5 w Park av, 25.7x100.8. Release mort. James Meehan to Sarah S. Runge. Oct. 28. nom

Same property. Release mort. Same to same. Oct. 28. nom

89th st, No. 67, n s, 184.5 w Park av, 25.7x100.8, one-story frame building. Sarah S. Runge widow to the rector, &c., of the Church of the Beloved Disciple, City New York. Oct. 29. 12,000

89th st, n s, 184.5 w 4th av, runs north to centre line bet 89th and 90th sts, x east 2.2 x south to 89th st, x west —. Sarah S. Runge widow to same. Oct. 29. nom

89th st, n s, 100 w Central Park West, 25x100.8, vacant. William S. Patten to Francis Crawford. *Mt.* $6,500. Oct. 27. 11,000

89th st, Nos. 318 and 320, s s, 241 w West End av, 41x100.8, two four-story brk dwell'gs. Francis M. Wilmurt to Henry Dale. *Mt.* $41,000. Nov. 2. See 72d st. nom

89th st, No. 317, n s, 230 w West End av, 20x 100, three-story stone front dwell'g. Release mort. Francis M. Jencks to William E. Lanchantin. Nov. 5. 1,000

Same property. William E. Lanchantin to George F. Langbein. *Mt.* $17,000. Nov. 5. nom

89th st, No. 314, s s, 200 w West End av, 20x 100.8, four-story brk dwell'g. Francis M. Wilmurt to Francis Skiddy Marden. *Mt.* $19,000. Oct. 28. 28,500

90th st, No. 321, n s, 300 e 2d av, 25x100.8, five-story stone front tenem't. Emil Roessert to Franz Chwatal. *Mt.* $15,000. Oct. 31. 22,500

90th st, No. 325, n s, 350 e 2d av, 25x100.11, five-story stone front tenem't. Frederick P. Hammel to Emil Roessert. *Mt.* $12,500. Nov. 2. nom

90th st, No. 323, n s, 325 e 2d av, 25x100.8, five-story stone front tenem't. Emil Roessert to Charles Weller. *Mt.* $15,000. Oct. 31. 22,500

92d st, No. 148, s s, 342 w 3d av, 33x100.8, three-story brk dwell'g. Foreclos. Thomas F. Gilroy, Jr., to Walter H. Stewart. Nov. 5. 19,550

93d st, Nos. 205–209, n s, 90 e 3d av, 60x100.8, three four-story brk tenem'ts. William J. Mathews to Robert H. Mathews. Oct. 1. nom

Same property. Robert H. Mathews to David McMahon. *Mt.* $26,000. Nov. 2. 33,000

94th st, No. 59, n s, 255 e Columbus av, 20x 100.8, three-story stone front dwell'g. Ida A. Emmel individ. and extrx. Ernest Emmel to George F. Mattlage. *Mt.* $16,000. Oct. 31. 27,000

96th st, No. 202, s s, 100 e 3d av, 27.3x100.8, five-story brk tenem't. Maria wife of and William Austin to George I. Cohen. Oct. 30. 25,000

100th st, n s, 100 w 2d av, 10x100.11. Irene B. and N. B. Roberts exrs. Edward Roberts to Thomas J. Oates. Nov. 2. 1,500

102d st, Nos. 208–214, s s, 160 e 3d av, 100x100.11, four five-story brk tenem'ts, stores in Nos. 212 and 214. Jonas Weil and Bernhard Mayer to Donato and Theresa Tuozzo. *Mt.* $54,000. Oct. 30. 86,000

103d st, No. 245, n s, 149 e West End av, 17x100.11, three-story stone front dwell'g. John T. Egan and Daniel Halley to Frank E. Wise. *Mt.* $13,500. Oct. 29. 19,000

104th st, s s, 100 e Riverside Drive, 200x100.11, vacant. Charles Weinberg to Egbert C. Simonson. *Mt.* $50,000 and assessm't $1,222. Oct. 21. nom

108th st, No. 61, n s, 175 e Madison av, 24.6x100.11. five-story brk flat. Charles W. Klebisch to Michael J. Beglen. B. & S. and C. a. G. Oct. 9. nom

111th st, n s, 50 w Madison av, 50x100.11, vacant. Morris and Jacob Steinhardt to John S. Scott. Nov. 2. other consid and 100

112th st, No. 217, n s, 216.8 e 2d av, 16.8x100.11, two-story frame dwell'g. Anne wife of Daniel Pratt to Mary A. Pratt. *Mt.* $4,000. Oct. 30. 6,250

112th st, No. 62, s s, 137.6 w 4th av, 16x100.11, three-story stone front dwell'g. Charles M. Foster to Michael E. Von Schoening. *Mt.* $5,000. Oct 28. 9,100

112th st. n s, 275 w 8th av, 125x100.11. }
113th st, s s, 225 w 8th av, 125x100.11. }
James R. Smith to William H. Lobmer and his grantees. Confirmation deed. July 24. nom

114th st, No. 215, n s, 235 e 3d av, 25x100.11, five-story stone front flat. John M. Conway to Hyman Israel and Simon Bing, Jr. *Mt.* $17,000. Oct. 30. 20,100

114th st, No. 136, s s, 73 10 w Lexington av, 26x100.11, four-story brk front dwelling. Betty wife of Abram Abrams to Johannah D. Favoret. *Mt.* $10,000. Nov. 2. 20,500

114th st, No. 437, n s, 113 w Av A, 25x100.10x25x100.10, two-story frame dwell'g with one-story frame building on rear. Barbara wife of George Hollerieth to Theodor Jost. *Mt.* $2,000. Nov. 4. 6,100

115th st, Nos. 319 and 321, n s, 250 e 2d av, 50x100,11, two four-story brk tenem'ts. John Falvella to Alessandro Delliparoli and Angelo Legniti. *Mt.* $19,500. Nov. 4. nom

116th st, No. 325, s s, 320 e 2d av, 15x100.10, three-story stone front dwell'g. Philip Kaiser to Charlotte M. Bullwinkel. *Mt.* $6,000. Oct. 31. See Lexington av. 18,000

116th st, Nos. 306-310, s s, 100 e 2d av, 90x100.11; Nos. 306 and 310, two four-story stone front flats; No. 308, two-story brk stable on rear of lot. Herman Beyer to Dina Muller. *Mt.* $42,500. Oct. 21. nom

Same property. Eva Muller widow to Herman Beyer, Newark, N. J. *Mt.* $42,500. Oct. 15. nom

116th st, Nos. 312 and 314, s s, 190 e 2d av, 42.6x100.11, two five-story stone front flats. Same to same. *Mt.* $12,500. Oct. 21. nom

Same property Herman Beyer, Newark, N. J., to Dina Muller. *Mt.* $12,500. Oct. 15. nom

116th st, No. 410, s s, 480.9 w Av A, 18 7x100.10, three-story stone front dwell'g. Mary wife of Thomas P. Walsh, Ansonia, Conn., heir Martin Quinlan to Mary J. Quinlan. B. & S. Oct. 29. nom

116th st, s s, 480.9 w Av A, 18.7x100.10. }
116th st, s s, 95 e 1st av, 18.7x100.10. }
43d st, s s. 100 e 10th av, 20x100.5. }
Margaret Williams sometimes called Ella Quinlan to Mary wife of Thomas P. Walsh, Ansonia, Conn. Q. C. Oct. 29. nom

118th st, No. 403, n s, 60 e 1st av, 28x53.5, four-story brk tenem't with stores. Avery T. Brown and Charles W. Cornell trustees Caroline I. Satchell to David Jarvis. C. a. G. Oct. 27. 6,000

119th st, No. 322, s s, 250 e 2d av, 25x100.10, five-story brk flat. Jacob Werner to Agnes Drescher. *Mt.* $10,875. Oct. 31. 28,000

119th st, No. 124, s s, 280 e 4th av, 22x100.11, three-story frame dwell'g with two-story frame dwell'g on rear. Mary E. Johnston to Abraham Laube. *Mt.* $5,500. Nov. 5. 6,750

120th st, No. 423, n s, 225.6 w Pleasant av, 24.6x100.11. five-story brk tenem't. Henry B. Zwinge to Susan M. Thall. *Mt.* $12,000. Oct. 31. 16,000

121st st, Nos. 202-207 (?), n s, 93 east from w s of 7th av, runs west 48x100.11, error, three three-story brk dwell'gs. Evelyn wife of and William B. Rendall to Seth Wheeler. *Mt.* $36,000. Feb. 14, 1890. 60,000

123d st, No. 268, s s, 100 e 8th av, 25x100.11, five-story stone front flat. Foreclos. Stephen B. Brague to Richard Cummings. Nov. 2. 20,000

123d st, No. 202, s s, 80 w 7th av, 16x100.11, three-story stone front dwell'g. William Cohn to Rosa Neumann widow. *Mt.* $12,000. Oct. 22. 16,500

127th st, No. 160, s s, 100 e 7th av, 25x99.11, four-story brk flat. Edward J. O'Gorman to Albert L. David. *Mt.* $17,500. June 18. nom

128th st, No. 33 and 35 on map Nos. 29 and 31, n s, 360 w 5th av, 25x99.11, two three-story stone front dwellings. Alfred E. and Alfred E., Jr., Fountain to Alfred E. Fountain. *Mt.* $14,000. Oct. 31. 26,000

133d st, No 256, s s, 183.4 e 8th av, 16.8x99.11, three-story stone front dwell'g. Foreclos. Edward Hassett to Cecile Rusch extrx. and trustee Adolph Rusch. Oct. 27. 6,000

134th st, No 236, s s, 225 e 8th av, 25x99.11, five-story brk flat. James C. McEachen to George Flinck. *Mt.* $28,500. Oct. 26. 30,750

141st st, n s, 302.1 e 11th av, original line, 12.2x99.11x12.10x99.11. John B. Carss and George B. Hewlett to Peter Lang. Nov. 4. 13,500

147th st, No. 604, s s. 147.2 w Boulevard, 16.8x99.11, three story brk dwell'g. William M. and Elizabeth M. Holmes to Martha McElroy. *Mt.* $5,000. Nov. 4. 11,000

Amsterdam av, No. 2689, w s, 60 n 147th st, 19.11x100, five-story brk store and tenem't. Anne E. Treacy to Peter Sackman. Oct. 30. 18,000

Audubon av proposed, w s, 50 s 187th st, 16.8x100. Oscar F. Blomstergren to Anna C. Blomstergren. *Mt.* $1,000. Oct. 30. nom

Av A, s e cor 88th st, 25.2x100, vacant. Charles Stegmayer to John Schreiner, Jr. *Mt.* $14,900, taxes 1891 and assessm'ts. Oct. 31. 17,000

Av B, No. 225, e s, 68.9 s 14th st, 22x68, five-story brk store and tenem't. John Schutz exr. Margarette Dreyer to Harriet Baer and Samuel Koch. Nov. 2. 17,250

Av B, No. 83, e s, 60.8 n 6th st, 20.2x93, four-story brk store and tenem't. Benjamin Blumenthal to Lucien Wolf. Sub to morts. Oct. 29. 22,500

Columbus av, No. 955, s e cor 107th st, 25x75, five-story brk flat with stores. Mary Bubler to William Bubler. B. & S. C. a. G. Sub. to mort. Oct. 29. nom

Columbus av. No. 883, e s, 40.11 n 102d st, 80x100, five-story brk store and flat. William H. Simonson to Susan Orcutt. Q. C. Oct. 30. nom

Columbus av, Nos. 881 to 889, n e cor 102d st, 160.11x100, five five-story brk flats with stores. Susan Orcutt widow to William Schneider. *Mt.* $201,000. Oct. 30. 325,000

Same property. Welcome R. Steinmetz to same. Q. C. Oct. 30. nom

Edgecombe av, e s, 99.11 n 145th st, 93.11x125, vacant. Mina wife of and George Daiker to John Casey. Oct. 23. See 81st st, also St. Nicholas av. 53 000

Edgecombe av, No. 209, w s, 275 s 145th st, 16.8x100, three-story brk dwell'g. Frederick Grasmuck to Auguste J. Paris. *Mt.* $5,000. Nov. 2. See 44th st. nom

Edgecombe av, e s, 749.6 n 145th st and at point intersection of centre line 148th st if extended, runs east 50 x north 129.11x50x128.11, vacant. Frank W. Blauvelt to Darius G. Crosby, Scarsdale, N. Y. Nov. 2. nom

Edgecombe av, w s, 275 s 145th st. Party wall agreement. Frederick Grasmuck to Charles E. Denhard. Nov. 9, 1889. nom

Same property. Party wall agreement. Same to Charles Lauer. Dec. 21, 1889. nom

Lenox av, n e cor 187th st, 24.11x75, vacant. William R. Fosdick exrs. Elizabeth J. Fosdick to Samuel Lynch. Nov. 2. 10,500

Same property. William R. Fosdick to same. Nov. 2. nom

Lexington av, No. 654, w s, 80.5 n 55th st, 20x75, four-story stone front dwell'g. Louis Pizer to Alvine Haagen. *Mt.* $14,000. Nov. 2. 19,500

Lexington av, No. 1763, n e cor 110th st, 20.11x70, four-story brk tenem't with stores. Charlotte M. Bullwinkel to Philip Kaiser. *Mt.* $15,000. Oct. 31. See 116th st. 22,500

Lexington av, No. 626, w s, 75.5 s 54th st, 20.8x70, four-story stone front dwell'g. Frederick Wood to Abram Slaight. Nov. 2. 5,000

Madison av, No. 2168, w s, 59.11 n 122d st, 20x80, three-story stone front dwell'g. Philip Bohnet to Lena Kahn and Adeline Meyers. *Mt.* $10,000. Nov. 2. nom

Madison av, No. 62, n e cor 27th st, 24.9x78, four and five-story brk flat with stores. John W. Haaren to Gevert Wendelken. B. & S. Oct. 19. 85,000

Madison av, No. 70, w s, 25 s 26th st, 24.7x95x24.5x95, four story stone front dwell'g. Dorothea W. Buttles to Marvin S. Buttles. Oct. 6. 80,000

Park (4th) av, No. 1680, n w cor 118th st, 25.11x90, five-story brk flat with stores. Elizabeth J. wife of and John H. Wellwood to Mary E. Higgins. *Mt.* $27,500. Oct. 31. 35,000

Park (4th) av, n w cor 75th st, 20x75. Release dower. Sarah E. Cassidy widow and devisee Hugh Cassidy and Marietta wife of Louis G. Cassidy and Anna F. wife of Henry G. Cassidy to Gustav Gomprecht. Oct. 24. nom

Park or 4th av, No. 1887 } begins Park av, s e
119th st, No. 102 } cor 129th st, 24.11x80, one-story frame stores on av and two-story brk stable on st. Margaret Dobbins to John H. Loos. *Mt.* $6,000. Oct. 31. 13,000

Same property. John Dobbins to John H. Loos. Oct. 31. nom

St. Nicholas av, Nos. 718 and 720, e s, 229.10 n 145th st, runs east 65.8 to centre old road, x north along same 33.2 x west 62 to av, x south 33.6, two four-story stone front dwell'gs. }
St Nicholas av, Nos. 728 and 730, e s, 355.10 n 145th st, 30.4x65 to centre old road, x31 5x67.3, two four-story stone front dwell'gs. }
Mina wife of and George Daiker to John Casey. *Mt.* $32,000. Oct. 30. See 81st st, also Edgecombe av. 56,500

Vermilyea av, n e cor Academy st, lots 14-148 map estate Isaac Dyckman. Cornelius J. Donovan to Joseph M. Fernandez, Havana, Cuba. *Mt.* $6,300. Nov. 2. nom

West End av, Nos. 331-339, s w cor 81st st, 102.2x100, five two-story frame dwell'gs and two-story frame chapel on corner. Benjamin M. Martin to Henry B. Wesselman. 1-3 part Sub. to morts. $37,500. Sept. 15. 100

West End av, e s, 19.11 s 98th st, 56x100. }
West End av, e s, 73.11 s 98th st, 18x100. }
Release mort. Harriet Overbiser to Edward Kilpatrick. Nov. 5. 35,000

1st av, No. 2254, e s, 40.11 s 121st st, 20x80, four-story brk store and tenem't. Henry G. Schiffel to George W. Kruger. *Mt.* $8,000. Nov. 2 11,000

1st av, No 1501, w s, 129.1 s 79th st, 29.1x94 6x20.9x93 9, four-story brk tenem't with stores. Margaretha Worth to Moses Lehmann. *Mt.* $7,500. Nov. 2. 20,500

1st av, No. 2274 } begins 1st av, s e cor 117th st,
117th st, No. 402 } 25.3x94, four-story brk tenem't with stores on av and three-story brk dwell'g on st. Max S. Korn to Isidor V. Wittenberg and Marks Chambers. *Mt.* $7,000. Nov. 2. val. consid. and 100

2d av, No. 2194, e s, 42.6 s 113th st, 16.8x100, three-story frame store and tenem't. Edward Cain to Samuel Kempner. Oct. 28. 8,500

2d av, No 92, e s, 48 6 n 5th st, 24.3x100, four-story brk store and tenem't. John or Jean C. de Krom to Henry Stengel. Q. C. Re-recorded Oct. 24. nom

2d av, No. 1405, w s, 25.6 n 73d st, 25.6x75, four-story brk tenem't with stores. Christian L. Oehler to Benjamin Oestreicher. *Mt.* $10,000. Oct. 31. 19,350

2d av, No. 929, w s, 129.8 s 50th st, 91.2x80, four-story stone front store and tenem't. Ernst Hopfensack to Emelie S. Lentz. *Mt.* $6,000. Oct. 29. 15,000

3d av, Nos. 705 and 707, e s, 20.1 n 44th st, 40.2x80, two three-story brk stores and tenements. David Cohen to Francis Scallion. *Mt.* $25,000. Oct. 30. 28,200

5th av, n w cor 114th st, 50.5x100, vacant. Max S. Korn to William H. Cornet and Jacob A. Zimmermann. *Mt.* $16,000. Nov. 5. See 36th st. val. consid and 100

7th av, s w cor 142d st. 74 11x75, vacant. Marx and Moses Ottinger to Patrick Hogan. Nov. 5. val. consid. and 100

7th av, w s, 74.11 s 142d st, 75x75, two and three-story frame and brk dwell'g and vacant. Catharine wife of and Charles F. Linde to George C. Currier. *Mt* $18,000. Feb 11, 1891. See below. 31,000

7th av, No. 2007, e s, 50.11 n 120th st, 16.11x77, three-story brk dwell'g. }
120th st, No 155, n s, 109 e 7th av, 16x100.11, three-story stone front dwell'g. }
George C. Currier to Catharine Linde. B. & S. *Mt.* $24,500 and int Nov. 1, 1890. Feb. 25. See above. 41,000

7th av, No. 1985, e s, 27 n 119th st, 27x98, five-story brk store and flat. George J. Cohen to Maria Austin. *Mt.* $26,000. Oct. 30. 40,000

7th av, Nos. 2166 and 2168, w s, 59.11 n 128th st, 40x75, five-story brk flat with stores. Contract Joel B. Smith to Caroline Uhlig. Sept. 11. 54,500

7th av, Nos. 283 and 285 } begins 7th av, s e cor
29th st, No. 160 W. } 29th st. 49.4x98.9, two four-story brk stores and tenem'ts on 7th av and four-story brk tenem't on 29th st. Margaret E. Morris formerly Butt, Central Valley, N. Y., to Helena S. Eckel. Nov. 2. 37,000

7th av, s e cor 3d st, 23.9x100. Release dower. Mary E. Hennegan to David Nugent in consideration of payment of $50 per month and party of 2d part charges his interest to secure same. Oct 23. nom

8th av, No 2171, n w cor 117th st, 26.4x100, five-story brk stores and flat. Release mort. Morris Steinhardt to Elizabeth Johnson. Nov. 2. 8,000

Same property. Elizabeth wife of and Richard E. Johnston to Abraham Meyer. *Mt.* $22,500. Nov. 2. nom

9th av, No. 746, e s, 50.5 n 50th st, 25x100, three-story frame store and tenem't with three-story brk tenem't on rear. Henry Thau and ano. exrs. and trustees Barbara Holtzman to Fisher Lewine. *Mt.* $5,700. Nov. 2. 18,000

Same property. Benedict Gesswein, Ernst, Andrew and Margaretha Holtzman and Gussie Ficken to same. Q. C. Oct. 31. nom

9th av, Nos. 746 and 748, e s, 50.5 n 50th st, 50x100, two three-story frame stores and tenements with two and three story frame and brk tenem'ts on rear. Fisher Lewine to Jonas Weil and Bernhard Mayer. Nov. 2. 40,000

Interior lot, begins at point 100 w 8th av and 25 n 17th st, runs north 67 x west 3 x south 67 x east 3. Charles W. and Harriet F. Howe exs. John W. Howe to Jane E. Miller. Sept. 10. 400

Same property. Jane E. Miller to Harriet F. Howe. Sept. 10. 400

Same property. Charles W., Benjamin F. and William B. Howe and Margaret J. Howe widow heirs John W. Howe to same. Q. C. Sept. 10. nom

MISCELLANEOUS.

General release. James Gibney and Martha Gibney or Brown to John McMillan and Robert McWilliam trustees John Gibney. Aug. 7, 1891. nom

General release. Julia E. Benjamin to Mary E. Case. March 2?, 1891. nom

23d and 24th WARDS.

Arcularius pl, n s, 549.6 e Gerard av, 50x100. Thomas W. Burridge to Hugo Wegener. Oct. 29. 2,200

Same property. Eliza Sutcliffe to Thomas W. Burridge. Oct. 28. 1,700

Cole st, n s, 37.6 w Prospect av, 25x69. Edward Burke, Jr., to Winifred wife of Edward Burke. Nov. 2. nom

Clinton st, w s, part lot 104 map Morrisania, 25.11x150. Henrietta C. Schwoppe extrx. Leonore Schwoppe to John F. Condon. Mar. 2. 1,250

Elmwood pl, n s, 100 e Clinton av, 21,4x95x21.6x95. John J. Brady to Charles Bjorkegren. Oct. 19. 700

Fox st, w s, 112.6 n 169th st, 20x85x23.6x69.7. Henry D. Tiffany to Gregorio Di Lorenzo. Nov. 19, 1890. nom

Kingsbridge road, e s, lots 70 and 71 map 16 villa sites and 80 lots, part of Anthony estate, Kingsbridge Heights, 24th Ward, 50x101x50.4 x95. Joseph A. Chambers to Arthur T. Berutiob. *Mt.* $474. Nov. 4. 800

Lebanon st, n s, 100 e Clinton av, 22x100x 22.2x100. John J. Brady to William J. Powers and Mary L. his wife, joint tenants. Oct. 19. 580

Lebanon st, s s, 100 w Crotona av, 52.10x 105.11x22.9x101.
Clinton av, e s, 75 n Lebanon st, 75x100.
John J. Brady to Martin J. Klug. Oct. 19. 2,980

Lebanon st, s s, 100 e Crotona av, 22.10x95x 22.3x95.
Lebanon st, n s, 124 n Prospect av, 24x100.
Same to John Armstrong. Oct. 19 1,315

Niles st, w s, 201.4 n Bainbridge av, 23.6x 188.6 to Mosholu Parkway, x156.6x124.5. Emanuel G. Bach and Ephraim B. Levy to Isabel W. Niles. *Mt.* $555. Nov. 5. 1,255

Oakland pl, n s, 124 w Prospect av, 24x108x24x 107.4. John J. Brady to William J. Kavanagh. Oct. 19. 540

Oakland pl, s e cor Cambreleng av, 31.3x100x 20.6x100.7. Same to Michael Katzbroski. Oct. 19. 540

Oakley st, s s, 100 w Kepler av, 50x100. Andrew Arvidson to Conrad Menzer. Oct. 27. 900

Pond pl, e s, lot 96 map part farm John Cromwell, 50x137x54x158. Catharine Moran widow, James J., Patrick and Martin Moran and Mary wife of Michael Reidy to James Wood. Nov. 2. 2,500

Southern Boulevard, w s, lots 101 and 102 map of 126 lots Geo. Faile property, 24th Ward, 50x130. Henry Strauss to Lemuel Strauss. ½ part. *Mt.* ½ of $1,470. Oct. 1. nom

132d st, n s, 125 e Cypress av, 75x110. Franklin A. Thurston to Pheba C. Rapelye. *Mt.* $3,000. Oct. 2. 5,400

141st st, n s, 100.3 w Beekman av, 25x111.4x25x 113.2. William R. Beal Land Improvement Co. to Henry B. Hall. Oct. 22. 2,500

141st st, n s, 150.4 w Beekman av, 25x107.10x25 x109.7. William R. Beal Land Improvement Co. to Franklin Lynch. Oct. 22. See Beekman av. 2,500

142d st, n s, 441.8 e Willis av, 16.8x100. Jennie Davis to John Stothers. March 19. 4,250

146th st, s s, 97 e 3d av, 25x100. Mary McCann, formerly Mackin, Patrick and Susan O'Hare, Alice and Minnie Mackin to Joseph Messerchmitt. Oct. 30. 8,250

146th st, s s, 122 e 3d av, 0.9x74. Mary McCann, formerly Mackin, to same. Oct. 30. nom

148th st, n s, west part lot 73 map Melrose South, 24x106.6. Lawrence Ryan to John Stothers. Sept. 29. 1,225

163d st, n s, 100 e Washington av, runs north 217.9 x east 100 x south 100 x west 75 x south 117.9 to 163d st, x west 25. Henry F. De Graaf to Samuel Garland. Nov. 5. 4,500

169th st, n e s, 122.4 n w Fox st, runs northeast 50.3 x northwest 33.6 x north 25 x northwest 50.6 x southwest 67.6 to 169th st, x southeast 91.10. Henry D. Tiffany to Gregorio Di Lorenzo. Oct. 28. 1,250

175th st, n s, 107.4 e Webster av, 50x109x50.6x 108.10. Charles O. Young to John Witt. Oct. 28. 500

177th st, No. 718, s s, 130 e Railroad av, 21.6x 108.6x20.7x100.2. Kate Douglass to Henry C. Meyer. *Mt.* $4,000. Oct. 29. 8,250

Beekman av, w s, 25 s Oak terrace, 25x100. Henry B. Hall to William R. Beal Land Impt. Co. C. a. G. Oct. 22. See Crimmins av. 2,000

Same property. Release mort. William R. Beal Land Impt. Co. to Henry B. Hall. Oct. 22. 1,050

Beekman av, w s, 50 s Beech terrace, 25x100. Franklin Lynch to William R. Beal Land Improvement Co. C. a. G. Oct. 22. See 141st st. 2,000

Clinton av, s w cor Elmwood pl, 25x100. Mary Seiferd to George Heuser. Nov. 4. 1,350

Crimmins av, w s, 387.4 n 141st st, 25x80. William R. Beal Land Improvement Co. to Francis B. Chedsey. Oct. 22. 1,700

Crimmins av, w s, 512.4 n 141st st, 25x80. Same to Wilbur L. Molyneaux. Oct 22. 1,700

Crimmins av, w s, 412.4 n 141st st, 25x80. William R. Beal Land Impt. Co. to John A. Norman. Oct. 22. 1,700

Crimmins av, w s, 487.4 n 141st st, 25x80. Same to Henry B. Hall. Oct. 22. See Beekman av. 1,700

Crimmins av, w s, 437.4 n 141st st, 25x80. Same to Franklin Lynch. Oct. 22. 1,700

Crotona av, e s, 49.4 s Elmwood pl, 25x96.1, error.
Clinton av, w s, 20 s Lebanon st, 75x100.
Crotona av, e s, 25 n Lebanon st, 50x100.
John J. Brady to Elizabeth F. Gallagher. Oct. 1, 1891. 5,680

Crotona av, s e cor Elmwood pl, 49.4x96.1x48.5 x96.1. John J. Brady to Michael Duffy. Oct. 19. 2,525

Crotona av, w s, 175 s Lebanon st, 50x85.7x52.2 x100.6. Same to Spencer Barrow. Oct. 19. 1,610

Crotona av, n e cor Lebanon st, 25x100x26x100. John J. Brady to James Mallon. Oct. 19. 1,325

Crotona av, w s, 125 s Lebanon st, 50x140.6x 52.2x115.4. Same to Joseph Balmford. Oct. 19. 1,800

Crotona av, w s, 225 s Lebanon st, 25x78.3x26x 85.7. Same to Patrick Foy. Oct. 19. 725

Crotona av, e s, 25 s Oakland pl, 25x100. Same to Gustav P. Bofinger. Oct. 19. 925

Crotona av, e s, 115.7 n Tremont av, runs east 96.1 x north 1 x east 74 x north 49.10 x west 170.6 to av, x south 50. Same to James Bracken. Oct. 19. 2,650

Crotona av, e s, 48 n Oakland pl, 24x100. Same to John Reinschmidt. Oct. 19. 700

Eagle av, e s, lot 55 map of Ursuline Convent, 25x115. Henry Strauss to Lemuel Strauss. ½ part. *Mt.* $500. Oct. 1. nom

Elton av, w s, lot 269 map South Melrose, 29x 100x35x100. Bernardina wife of and Joseph Wiener to Louisa Stein. *Mt.* $1,300. Oct. 31. 5,000

Forest av, w s, 100 s 156th st, 75x87.6. Henry P. De Graaf to John J. Brierly. Nov. 2. 2,700

Fulton av, s e s, part lot 107 map Morrisania, &c, 43.9x211, being 21-100 acres; with use of private sewer until after public sewer is completed in front of Nos. 1316 and 1328 Franklin av. Lucy R. wife of John E. Comfort to Carl Stehr. Nov. 4. 8,000

Jackson av, w s, 150.7 s 165th st, 18.3x75. Adolph G. Hegewald to Frank Sovak and Annie his wife. Sub. to mort. Oct. 31. 3,575

Jefferson av, s e s, lots 146 and 147 map Samuel Ryer homestead, 50x132x50x127. Release mort. Martha J. Sheridan to Peter Farrell. Nov. 2. 600

Jefferson av, s e s, part lot 144 map S. Ryer homestead, 25x127. Peter Farrell to Mary Campbell. *Mt.* $300. Oct. 28. 600

Jefferson av, s e s, part lot 146 map Samuel Ryer homestead, 25x127. Same to Patrick Lahey. Oct. 29. 600

Jerome av, south cor Southern Boulevard, 26.6 x120.11x25x134.7. Henry Strauss to Lemuel Strauss. ½ part. Oct. 1. nom

Morrisania av, e s, 81.6 s 162d st, 26.4x128.4 to Grant av, x25x136.2.
165th st, s s, 100.10 s Washington av, 25x100.
Contract. Margaret L. wife of John C. Fay to William L. Loftus. All title. Oct. 23. 450

Same property. Contract. Loretto L. wife of Richard J. Cogan to William L. Loftus. All title. Oct. 23. 450

Same property. Contract. Francis S. Loftus to same. All title. Oct. 23. 450

Prospect av, w s, 50 n Lebanon st, 50x100. John J. Brady to Henry Bescher, Jr. Oct. 19. 1,650

Prospect av, w s, 63 n Oakland pl, 21x100. John J. Brady to Martin Kelly. Oct. 19. 585

Prospect av, w s, 50 s Oakland pl, 25x100. John J. Brady to John Sheridan. Oct. 19. 800

Tinton av, e s, 51 s Denman pl, 17x95. John C. Fahl to Victor J. S. Baradel. *Mt.* $2,500. Oct. 30. 4,500

Tremont av, north cor Jefferson av, lot 11 map S. Ryer homestead. Leonard Lewisohn to John V. Lamarche. *Mt.* $1,200. Oct. 29. nom

Tremont av, n s, proposed, 100 e Clinton av, runs north 290 to Elmwood pl, x east 47.3 x south 145 x east 2 x south 145 to av, x west 48.6, with land bet said proposed n s and the present old n s of Tremont av, does not include any of the buildings. John J. Brady to John F. Boss. Oct. 19. 5,310

Union av, w s, 100 n Cedar st, 25x133.4x25x 133.1. Eugenie H. Stafford to Mary J. wife of Robert T. Clary. Nov. 4. 1,025

Vanderbilt av East, e s, 375 n 180th st, 125x 150.
Cauldwell av, e s, 100 s 163d st, 50x100.
Belmont av, s e s, lot 4 map East Tremont, 60.5x176x60x168.5.
Belmont av, s e s, 185.6 n e John st, 35.1x 168.5x35x168.11.
Belmont av, s e s, lot 6 map East Tremont, 70.3x159.5x70x151.8.
Jefferson av, e s, 175 n Tremont av, 75x100.
Edward J. O'Gorman to Albert L. David. All liens Oct. 31. nom

Walnut av, e s, lot 41 map Wilton, Port Morris and East Morrisania, 25x100. Katie Parker to Hugh Lennon. Nov. 5. 3,000

Westchester av, north cor 162d st, runs west 150.9 x north 123.7 x east 60.9 x easterly 53.9 x south 153 to av, x northwest 49. John W. Decker to R. Clarence Dorsett. *Mt.* $4,000. July 31. 10,000

Willis av, s w cor 135th st, 25x81.6. Release mort. Julius Weill, Titusville, Pa., to Charles P. Faber. Oct. 29. 500

3d av, s e s, 316 n e Grove st, 25x170. Elizabeth Campbell to Mary A. and Catherine T. Campbell. Oct. 29. nom

LEASEHOLD CONVEYANCES.

Greenwich st, No. 353. Agreement subordinating lease to mortgage. W. Lackmann to Hyman and Henry Sonn. Nov. 2, 1891. nom

Henry st, s s, 94 e Clinton st, 28.6x ½ block. Assign. lease. Tobias Krakower to Abram Kraner. 6,000

Ludlow st, No. 116, s e s, lot 8 map Henry Astor, 25x87.6. William B. Astor to Leopold Bohm. 20 years, from May 1, 1872, per year, taxes and 750

Same property. Surrender lease. Joseph Fuchs and Mary Fuhrken individ. and exrs. Barbara Schmidt to Max S. Korn. April 16. nom

Mercer st, No. 93, leasehold, and out-of-town property. Simon H. Stern as assignee Charles A. Herpich to Charles A. Herpich. Re assignment and re-conveyance. Oct. 15. nom

Rivington st, No. 251. Assign. lease. Siegfried S. Zarek to Henry F. Chavin. nom

13th st, No. 637 E., west store. Agreement modifying terms of lease. John L. Gillen and John Sauer to William Sturn. Sept. 1. nom

13th st, Nos. 614 and 616 E. Assign. lease. Floyd M. Horton to John Schlener. 750

22d st, n s, 79 w 8th av, 21x84.4. Katharine T. Moore to Thomas Ennis. 21 years, from Nov. 1, 1898, per year, taxes and 312

58th st, Nos. 225 and 227 W. Surrender lease. Clark H. McDonald to George E. Armstrong. nom

81st st, No. 435 E. Assign. lease. John Pospisil to H. Koehler & Co. nom

116th st, No. 408, s s, 95 e 1st av, 18.7x100.11. Mary wife of Thomas P. Walsh, Ansonia, Conn, heir of Martin Quinlan to Margaret Williams otherwise Ella Quinlan. Lease for life, from Nov. 4, 1891, per year, nom

Amsterdam (10th) av, w s, 25 s 157th st, store. Assign. lease. Elizabeth L. Merkent to Elizabeth G. Bussell. nom

Willis av, No. 390. Assign. lease. Henry C. Schrader to John Nurnberg. nom

1st av, s w cor 64th st, 50.5x100. Abraham B. Cox et al. exrs Abraham B. Cox to Denison P. Chesebro, Frank Larkin and Alfred E. Davidson, of Chesebro, Whitman & Co. 14½ years, from Aug. 1, 1891, per year, 600 to 800

2d av, No. 1512. Assign. lease. George W. Mitchell and John J. O'Connell to Dermott J. and Martin Potter. 3,500

3d av, No. 1482. Assign. lease. Louisa Grimm to Michael O'Brien. 28,000

7th av, No. 382. Assign lease. James McElhinney to Patrick and Charles Gallagher. nom

11th av, s w cor 22d st, 24.8x75. Consent to assign. lease. Maria T. B. Moore to Anton Schultze exr. Henry W. Hencke. nom

KINGS COUNTY.

OCTOBER 29, 30, 31, NOVEMBER 2, 3, 4.

Ainslie st, n s, 125 w Leonard st, 25x100. Bernhard Donop to J. Frederick Scheffer. $3,900

Ashford st, e s, 246.11 n Atlantic av, 16.8x100. Louis Ilsemann to John T. McDermott. *Mt.* $1,700. 2,700

Amity st, s s, 165 e Clinton st, 25x100. Release dower. Cornelia Mead widow to Arthur J. Heaney. nom

Same property. Cornelia Mead et al. exrs. George N. Mead to same. 9,600

Baltic st, n s, 75 w Nevins st, 25x100. Ignazy Pajuski to Samuel D. Kelley, of New York. *Mt.* $2,000. 3,600

Baltic st, s s, 488 e 3d av, 27x100, h & l. Edward Hartung to Sherman and Guy Loomis. *Mt.* $8,000. nom

Bainbridge st, n s, 115.6 e Saratoga av, 179.9x 100, h & l. J. Mason Kirby to Lina S. Blatt. 10

Same property. Lina S. wife of Isidor Blatt to Anna E. Kirby. 10

Bainbridge st, n s, 160 w Reid av, 28x100. Kate Acor to Julia Simon. *Mt.* $2,000. exch

Barbey st, w s, 100 n Arlington av, 50x95. Frederick Middendorf to Zipporah L. Hollister. nom

Same property. Zipporah L. Hollister to Greenleaf W. Crossman, of New York. *Mt.* $4,500. 8,910

Berkeley pl, n s, 254 e 7th av, 21x100. Amelia B. wife of and David S. Willard to Edith B. Blackwell. *Mt.* $8,000. 15,000

Berkeley pl, s w s, 342 n w 6th av, 18.9x95, h & l. Catharine J. McGirr formerly Tewell to Edward Hughes. *Mt.* $6,000. 8,000

Bogert st, s w cor Boerum st, 25x110.11x25x 111.10. Charles W. Truslow admr. Wm. Wall to Herman Gerdes. 1,825

Bogert st, e s, 25 n Ingraham st, 25x100. Charles W. Truslow admr. William Wall to Marx Wendstein. 1,203

Bogert st, e s, 50 n Ingraham st, 25x100. Charles W. Truslow as admr. William Wall to Sebastian Zentgraf. 1,150

Box st, s s, 325 w Manhattan av, 25x100. Release dower. Kate E. Immen to Joseph Lock. nom

Same property. Kate E. Immen et al. exrs. John H. Immen to same. 1-5 part. 1,300

Same property. Metta H. wife of Joseph Lock, Catharine M. wife of Charles F. Neidig, Christopher Immen and Annie L. W. wife of Joseph Paulsen to same. 4-5 parts. 5,200

Boerum st, s s, 111.10 w Bogert st, 100x100. Charles W. Truslow admr. Wm. Wall to Max Levy. 2,600

Broadway, s w s, 109.3 s e McDonough st, 20x 60x—x71. Partition. Samuel G. Adams to Henry C. Bauer. 2,725

Same property. Aaron Peck to same. Q. C. nom

Same property. Caroline Pierson, Mary J., George and Cyrus Peck to same. Q. C. nom

Broadway, s w s, 175 s e Lewis av, runs southwest 87.11 x south 41.6 x east 25 x north 31.2 x northeast 77.7 to Broadway, x northwest 25. William Schelp to Lizzie wife of Henry Monday, of New York. *Mt.* $10,000. 16,000

Broadway, e s, 37.6 s Madison st, 18.9x80, h & l. Henry Vollweiler to George Evans. *Mt.* $3,500. 6,500

Butler st, s w cor Smith st, 25x60. Ellen Murphy to Catharina Meissner. *Mt.* $4,000. 7,000

Butler st, s s, 25 w Smith st, 25x60. John Donohue to Catharina Meissner. *Mt.* $2,000. 3,750

Carroll st, n s, 112 w 5th av, 40x100. Lucinda Poulterer to George J. McFadden, of New York. *Mt.* $3,500. nom

Court st, w s, 200 n Degraw st, 25x112.6x75x 22.6x50x90. George W. Ford and Burton M. Perry to Hannah A. Silsbe. *Mt.* $13,000. 25,000

Centre st, n s, 175 w Smith st, 25x100. Thomas Croly to Michael Grady exr. Elizabeth Grady. *Mt.* $2,550. nom

Clay st, east cor Commercial st, 119.3x30.2x30.2 x119.3. Kate E. Immen et al. exrs. John H. Immen to Christopher Immen. 1-5 part. 1,645

Same property. Metta H. wife of Joseph Lock, Catherine M. wife of Charles F. Neidig and Anna L. W. wife of Joseph Paulsen to same. 3-5 parts. 4,935

Same property. Release dower. Kate E. Immen widow to same. nom

Cornelia st, s e s, 35 s w Evergreen av, 60x100. Richard Dreyer to Auguste Mehlen widow. *Mt.* $9,600. nom

Cornelia st, s e s, 75 s w Evergreen av, 20x100. Release mort. Eburn F. Haight to Richard Dreyer. 1,500

Court st, n w cor Degraw st, 16x83. John Bolger to Delia Fox. 11,600

Conselyea st, n s, 275 e Lorimer st, 25x100. John Darcey to Frank B. Sands. *Mt.* $2,000. nom

Cooper st, e s, 125 s Evergreen av, 18.4x100. Henry Kordes to Simon and Maria Reinhard. *Mt.* $2,000. 4,670

Cranberry st, s s, 100 e Hicks st, 25x100. Bruno E. Mayer, of Greenville, N. J., to Elinor M. Mayer. 600

Crescent st, e s, 100 n Liberty av, 25x100, h & l. Charlotte Cleveland to Ellen Gibbs. Taxes, &c., from 1889. 1,800

Crescent st, middle line, 826.4 n Brooklyn & Jamaica R. R., runs north 635.8 x east to middle line of Hemlock st, x south to middle Ridgewood av, x east to Railroad av, x south — x west 531.1 to beginning. Edward F. Linton to John M. Ward. Sub. to ½ of mort. $18,000, ½ part. 17,500

Dean st, n s, 130 e Nevins st, 20x100; also,
Vanderbilt av, w s, 215 n Gates av, 20x100.
John C. Murray devisee John Murray to Julia H. Murray. 2,000

Diamond st, n s, 1,202.1 e Main st, 50 x200, Flatbush. Henry Martin to Josephine N. Stafford. *Mt.* $5,500. 7,200

Diamond st, s s, 100 w Albany av, runs west to land of grantee herein, x — to lane —, Flatbush. Frank C. Lang to Gustave Wesseberg. 1,450

Dikeman st, s w s, 210 n w Conover st, 40x100. Abner Greenleaf to Henry C. Otten. 2,500

Dupont st, s s, 125 e Oakland st, 25x100, h & l. Ellen wife of Patrick Toomey to Mathilda Weinberger. *Mt.* $1,000. 1,575

East Broadway, n s, adj land J. F. Neefus, runs east along East Broadway 86.6 x north 268.5 x west 86.6 x south — to beginning, Flatbush. Henry Martin, Sr., to Elice Martin. *Mt.* $3,400. nom

Eastern Parkway, s s, 50 e Van Sielen av, 25x 100. Elizabeth C. wife of John Power to Herbert C. Smith. *Mt.* $3,100. nom

Eastern Parkway, n w cor Osborn st, 25x100. Release mort. Mary W. Smith to John Power. nom

Same property. Release covenant. Herbert C. Smith to John Power. nom

Same property. John Power to Moses Messinger and Meyer Chapkowksky. *Mt.* $3,500. 6,000

Eldert st, n w s, 180 s w Bushwick av, 18x100. Isadore E. Van Deverg to Mary L. Mason. *Mt.* $4,500. exch and 7,000

Ellery st, n s, 250 w Sumner av, 25x100, h & l. John Merkle to Rosalia Bechtold. 5,500

Fiske pl. Nos. 18 and 20, each 21.6x96.
10th st, No. 585, 20x100, apartment house.
Ida M. and James F. Ranson to Charles S. Kendall. Exchange for plot in North Hempstead on Jericho turnpike, 200x450.

Fulton st, n s, 25.6 e Elton st, 76.7x87.11x75x 103.4. James W. Crawford, New York, to Christian F. Nolte. 4,200

Fulton st, n s, 240.6 w Rockaway av, runs north 49.1 to Somers st, x west 19.6 x south 44.9 to Fulton st, x east 20. Nathaniel F. Jones to Nellie R. Shevlin. *Mt.* $4,500. 6,250

Fulton st, s w cor Ashford st, 51x85.5x50x95.9. Andrew J. and Albert Anderson to Mary J. Farrington. *Mt.* $1,200. 2,800

Garfield pl, s s, 312.6 w 7th av, 12.5x100. Foreclos. John Courtney to Daniel Lord, Jr. 3,250

Garnet st, n s, 100 w Smith st, 50x200 to 9th st, hs & ls. Margaret E Conlon to Francis J. Conlon. B. & S. nom

Glen st, s w cor Crescent st, 25x100. Foreclos. John Courtney to Charles W. Osborne and ano. exrs. Peter P. Schoonmaker. Sub. to all liens. 4,000

Gold st, s w cor Plymouth st, 45x99.6, hs & ls. Theresa and Donato Tuozzo to Benedict A. Klein. *Mt.* $15,100. 20,000

Greene st, s s, 270 e Franklin st, 25x100, h & l. Christian Mark to Charles L. Rowland. *Mt.* $2,000. nom

Halsey st, s s, 245 w Tompkins av, 20x100. Charles H. Tyson to Anna M. Perry. *Mt.* $3,000. 4,800

Halsey st, n s, 78.9 w Throop av, 32.6x100, p & l. George W. Almy to Hugh Lamb, New York. *Mt.* $10,000. exch

Halsey st, n s, 391 e Lewis av, 17x100, h & l. Hermon B. Homan trustee to Mary L. Langford. *Mt.* $5,860. 10,000

Halsey st, n s, 250 w Howard av, 16.8x100. James H. Loper to Almedia wife of Frank Lowe. 688

Halsey st, n s, 410 e Bedford av, 20x100. Sarah J. and Catherine T. Brooks to Mary wife of Dudley Kelly. *Mt.* $9,300, and taxes. exch

Halsey st, s s, 131.6 w Arlington pl, 17.6x100. Fidelia M. wife of Frank Stevens to Josephine E. Courtney. 8,700

Hancock st, s s, 217.6 w Reid av, 18.11x97.7 Mary Lambert individ. and extrx. Patrick Lambert and James H. Mason to Lucinda Teaz. 2,200

Hancock st, n s, 95 e Tompkins av, 18x100. F. Marion McAllister, of Elizabeth, N. J., to William H. Reynolds. *Mt.* $6,000. 8,500

Hancock st, s s, 300 w Howard av, 18.9x100, h & l. Henry Grasman to Katie B. Lockwood. *Mt.* $3,000, &c. 5,600

Hancock st, n s, 250 e Marcy av, 80x100. William Reynolds to William H. Reynolds. ½ part. Sub. to mort. $14,000. 1,125

Hancock st, n s, 310 e Marcy av, 20x100. Party wall agreement. William H. Reynolds with James A. Sharp. nom

Hancock st, n s, 412.6 e Reid av, 18.9x100. Mary E. wife of and Daniel H. Renton to Rebecca Burns. *Mt.* $3,000. 5,900

Hart st, s e s, 175 n e Hamburg av, 25x100. Lena Weis to Henry Kemmet. 1,400

Hart st, s s, 282 6 w Sumner av, 17.6x100. Marcus H. Hawkins to William H. Bath. B. & S. *Mt.* $3,700. other consid and 6,500

Hart st, s e s, 225 n e Hamburg av, 25x100. Jacob F. Schneider to John Steinert and Maria his wife. *Mt.* $2,500. 7,000

Harman st, s e s, 175 n e Central av, 25x100. Christian Hahn to Anna C. Cibulsky. *Mt.* $3,500. 7,500

Harrison st, s s, 112 e Hicks st, 22x77.7x22x78.7, h & l. Sarah wife of Gabriel Wolff to Renate Wolff. 100

Harrison pl, s s, 250 e Bogert st, 25x84.9x25x 85.8. Charles W. Truslow admr. Wm. Wall to Peter Fritz. 1,050

Harrison pl, s s, 175 e Bogert st, 25x87.6x25x 88.5. Charles W. Truslow admr. Wm. Wall to Michael Olikus. 1,100

Harrison pl, s s, 100 e Bogert st, 75x85.5x75.1x 91.8. Charles W. Truslow admr. William Wall to Henry Schlachter, Frank Spoeth and John Senger. 3,225

Hawthorne st, s s, 3,079.4 e Flatbush av, 50x 106, Flatbush. Ann Clark to Robert S. Walker. Sub. to mort. 75

Hewes st, n s, 167.8 w Harrison av, runs west 19.8 x north 100 x east 20 x south 57.5 x west 0.4 x south 42.6. Helen J. Smith, of Freehold, N. J., to August Kimmerle. 7,000

Hicks st, n w cor Garnet st, 50x106.6. Richard Kelly, New York, to Joseph Foley. Correction deed. Q. C. nom

Hill st, n s, 325 w Crescent st, 54.2x100. Charles D. King to James A. Bloomer. *Mt.* $2,225. 2,800

Himrod st, s e s, 570 s w Central av, 79x100. Katie wife of and Charles C. Kreppel to William Bayer, Alois Dillmann and Julius Dewald. nom

Himrod st, s s, 570 w Central av, 21x100, h & l. William Ruthmann to Adam Schmidt. exch

Hull st, s e cor Rockaway av, 20.8x100. John A. Schuessler to Gottfred Bock. *Mt.* $4,000. exch

Ingraham st, n s, 100 e Bogert st, 25x100. Charles W. Truslow admr. Wm. Wall to Helena wife of Joseph Abt. 1,175

Java st, s s, 75 w Franklin st, 20x50, h & l. Louise C. Hearson extrx. Wm. M. Lowry to Freiderich W. Wandmacher. 3,300

Kosciusko st, n s, 358.4 w Marcy av, 16.8x100. Mary L. Mason to Isadore E. Van Deverg. *Mt.* $4,000. exch and 4,500

Same property. Isadore E. Van Deverg to George L. Marinor. *Mt.* $8,000. 8,500

Lawrence st, w s, 173 s Willoughby st, 43x 100x42x100.
Lawrence st, w s, 152 s Willoughby st, 21x100.
Fulton st, No. 465, n s, 60 w Lawrence st, runs northeast 60 x southeast 14 6 x south 11 x southwest 50 to Fulton st, x20.
Lawrence st, w s, 113 n Fulton st, runs west 100 x south 0.4 x southeast 94.10 x east 14.5 to Lawrence st, x north 40.4.
Felix Campbell to James B. Healy. 115,000

Leonard st, e s, 330 s Nassau av, 16.8x100. Thomas J. Denman sole devisee Catherine E. Denman to Mary A. Shear. 3,400

Leonard st, w s, 75 n Withers st, 25x82.11x25x 82.4. Henry Schneider to Rosario Degruco and Fulumanna his wife, joint tenants. *Mt.* $2,050. 2,717

Lynch st, s e s, 108 s w Lee av, 22x100. Lincoln H. Hough to Henrietta and Henry M. Oster, of New York. 3,800

Macon st, n s, 235.3 w Lewis av, 19.9x100. Daniel B. Norris to J. Glen Allan. *Mt.* $4,200. 9,000

Macon st, n s, 94 w Ralph av, 18x100. Benjamin C. Raymond to Charles M. Miller. 7,000

Macon st, n s, 375 w Marcy av, 20x100. Frances L. Hubbard to Frances A. Pierson. *Mt.* $9,000. 1887. 9,000

Macon st, n s, 159.9 e Patchen av, 0.3x100. Jane Miller to George W. O'Berry. nom

Macon st, n s, 179.10 e Patchen av, 0.2x100. George W. O'Berry to James D. Rankin and James Ross. nom

Macon st, n s, 179.10 e Patchen av, 20.2x100. James D. Rankin and James Ross to Thomas Wood. *Mt.* $4,500. 6,900

Madison st, n s, 320 e Hamburg av, 20x100. Adolphus Gload to John J. Muller. 4,400

Magenta st, s s, 225 e Crescent st, 25x100. James W. King to Maurice Shannon. nom

Same property. Maurice Shannon to Jane wife of James W. King. nom

Malboue st, s s, 260 e Brooklyn av, 20x103x20x 98. Antonio Buonagura to Vincenzo La Greca. ½ part. 450

Marion st, n s, 150 w Patchen av, 25x100. Solomon wife of Philip Mergier and Charlotte wife of Nicholas Weimar to Catharine wife of William Pfarrer. 500

Marion st, n s, 175 w Patchen av, 25x100. Charlotte wife of Nicholas Weimar and Catharine wife of William Pfarrer to Salomea wife of Philip Mergler. 500

Marion st, s s, 325 w Patchen av, 25x100. Salomea wife of Philip Mergler and Catharine wife of William Pfarrer to Charlotte wife of Nicholas Weimar, Mt. Carmel, Ohio. 500

Marion st, n s, 150 w Patchen av, 50x100.
Marion st, s s, 325 w Patchen av, 25x100.
William Pfarrer exr. Jacob Dannemann to Charlotte wife of Nicholas Weimer, Salome wife of Philip Mergler and Catharine wife of William Pfarrer. 1,500

McDougal st, s s, 100 w Hopkinson av, 80.7x 100, hs & ls.
McDougal st, s s, 244.9 w Hopkinson av, 80.2 x100, hs & ls.
Susie D. wife of Peter L. Brokaw to Charles H. Reynolds. nom

McDougal st, s s, 212.8 w Hopkinson av, 16x100. Same to Adolph Kiendl. nom

McDonough st, s s, 156.8 e Ralph av, 18.8x100, h & l. Thomas H. Radcliffe to Lottie L. Farber. *Mt.* $4,500. 7,000

McKibbin st, n s 104.4 w Bogert st. 100x100. Charles W. Truslow admr. William Wall to Henry Schlachter, Frank Spoeth and John Senger. 2,800

McKibbin st, n s, 2?9.4 w Bogert st, runs west, 50 x north 153.6 to lands Schenck, thence along said land — x south, 185. Charles W. Truslow admr. William Wall to Christian A. Keppler. 1,800

McKibbin st, s s, lot 488 map made by Alex. Martin, 25x100. Joseph C. Von Urff to Philip Weis. 5,250

Same property. Amalia Zimmermann widow to Joseph C. Von Urff. 5,250

Meserole st, n s, 125 e Union av, 25x100. Minna Wich to Franz Wedeke. Q. C. 1890. 3,000

Same property. Carl F. Zenker to same. Q. C. 1890. 1,500

Melrose st, s s, 115.7 w Evergreen av, 18.1x100.1 x20.2x100, h & l. Emil F. Wildner to Charles Ernst. *Mt.* $2,000. 4,200

Milford st, w s, 350 s Blake av, 40x100. George A. Read to Cordelia Read, of New York. *Mt.* $1,450. nom

Monitor st, e s, 400 s Norman av, 20x100. Bernt Mathison to Iver Iversen. ½ part. nom

North Henry st, e s, 85 n Nassau av, 18.7x100. Otto W. Wolf to Louisa Wolf. nom

Oakland st, e s, 245 s Norman av, 25x100, h & l. Anna C. Cibulsky widow to Louis Hirsch and Abraham Michaels. 4,000

Same property. Louis Hirsch and Abraham Michaels to George H. Rowe. 4,500

Orange st, n s, 74.8 w Henry st, 50.4x100.9x50.8 x100.9. Edwin D. Phelps to Sarah L. Tingue. nom

Osborn st, w s, 150 n Glenmore av, 25x100. Louis Lebewohl and Abraham Ruth to Maggie Fischer and Katie Dougan. *Mt.* $2,710. 5,800

Pacific st, n e cor Bond st, 21.2x90. Julius B. Davenport to Emma J. Phillips. *Mt.* $5,000. 8,550

Pacific st, s s, 147 e Rochester av, 16x107.3. Kate I. Turner, of Elmira, N. Y., to James E. Baker. 3,200

Pacific st, n e s, 235 n w Hoyt st, 20x90. Herman Ziehler to William Zeller. *Mt.* $2,000. 4,500

Pacific st, n s, 25 e Grand av, 20x80. Gouverneur Tillotson exr. William Hawkins to Margaret T. Stoddart. *Mt.* $4,000. nom

Pacific st, n s, 147 e Hoyt st, 22.6x90, h & l. Mary A. Adler widow to Frank E. Adams. nom

Park pl, n s, 140 e Clason av, 60x131. Mary wife of Peter Cleary to Ella Free. *Mt.* $2,000. exch

Pine st, w s, 115.6 n Fulton st, 25x100. Marenus J. Goodenough to Frederick, Richard and Otto Kampfe. 600

Poplar st, n s, 77.4 e Hicks st, 22.8x25. Frank L. Tapscott to Frank Amoueailla and John Muzzio. 2,600

Prospect pl, s s, 205 e Grand av, 20x131. Mary wife of and Dudley Kelly to Catherine T. Brooks. *Mt.* $3,000. exch

Prospect st, s s, 50 w Green lane, 25x100. Patrick Quillan to James Ruggio and James Di Mearinio. 4,300

Pulaski st, n s, 203 e Nostrand av, 18x100, h & l. Anna M. wife of Peter Mangels to Andrew J. McCord. 5,500

Quincy st, s s, 213.4 e Lewis av, 17.4x100, h & l. Louis Bossert to Henry Roth. *Mt.* $3,800. 5,800

Quincy st, s s, 230.8 e Lewis av, 19x100, h & l. Same to same. *Mt.* $4,000. 6,000

Ralph st, n w s, 200 s w Central av, 50x100. William Schmidt to William Ruthmann. *Mt.* $1,700. exch

Richmond st, w s, 1,475 n 3d st, 50x150. Mary A. wife of Robert Thompson to Mary Turner. *Mt.* $1,500. 3,600

Radde pl, e s, 151.6 s Herkimer st, 15.6x97.6, h & l. Laura Munger to John B. C. Woodcock. *Mt.* $2,500. 4,500

Sackett st, s w s, 217 n w 5th av, 25x95. Joseph Keller to Mary A. Hilkey, New York. *Mt.* $7,000. 11,500

Sackett st, s s, 217.6 w 4th av, 160x95. Annie I. Mayher to Charles A. Brown. *Mt.* $5,325. nom

Sackett st, n s, 60 w Bond st, 40x100. John Broad to Harriet J. Radley. *Mt.* $3,000, taxes 1890 and 1891. nom

Sackett st, s s, 235 e Henry st, 28.6x100. John Murphy to Cecelia C. Lindsay. *Mt.* $10,000. nom

Sands st, s w cor Adams st, 24x80. Patrick Higgins to William A. A. Brown. *Mt.* $19,500. 20,000

Seigel st, s s, 690 e Bushwick av, 25x100.
Johnson av, s s, 75 e Bogert st, 25x100.
Charles W. Truslow as admr. William Wall to Mary Kratzer. 1,875

South Elliott pl, w s, 407 s De Kalb av, 20x100. Susan A. Crofut to Frank C. Joslin. *Mt.* $3,500. 5,500

Seigel st, s s, 240 e Bushwick av, 25x100. Chas. W. Truslow admr. Wm. Wall to Adam Christman. 1,075

Seigel st, s s, 715 e Bushwick av, 25x100. Charles W. Truslow admr. Wm. Wall to Lazarus Weil. 650

Seigel st, s s, abt 370 e Old Bushwick av, 25x100, on old map. Mary A. Colgan, Julia C. Hamer, Margaret C. Prout, William and Joseph Quigley and Sarah Kilbride heirs Edward Quigley to Henrietta Reinheimer. 1,450

Smith st, e s, 16.5 n 5th st, 5.8x87.5x5.9x88.6. Release mort. John J. Jones exr. David Jones to Patrick Larkin. nom

Same property. Release mort. The South Brooklyn Savings Inst. to same. 500

Smith st, s e s, 16.5 n e 5th st, 26.8x98.1x27.3x87.5. Patrick Larkin to Julia McKeon. 2,000

Spencer st, e s, 242.3 s Flushing av, 25x100. Anna M. wife of Claus Kopf to Sarah A. wife of William Moss. 2,500

Spencer st, w s, 78 n Willoughby av. 22x80. Partition. John R. Kuhn ref. to John Schlumann. 2,000

Spencer st, e s, 275 s Tillary st now Park av, 25x100. Partition. John H. Kemble to James D. Andrew. 1,325

Stanhope st, s s, 190 w St. Nicholas av, 40x100. Julia Beckroge to Anna Schumann. *Mt.* $500. 1,425

Steuben st, w s, 300 n Myrtle av, 25x100. Fanning J. Baldwin, Oyster Bay, L. I., to Christopher H. Peirce. nom

St. Marks pl, n s, 360 w 5th av, 20x100. Louise wife of Charles Kathe to Pelagia Crelinski. *Mt.* $3,000. 6,700

Sterling pl, No. 27, allotted to May Goldschmidt.
Sterling pl, No. 25, and McDonough st, No. 346 } allotted to heirs of John Goldschmidt.
Lewis av, Nos. 355 and 357, McDonough st, No. 348 } allotted to George B. Goldschmidt.
Clason av, Nos. 489 and 491, allotted to Edward G. Goldschmidt.
Prospect pl, No. 51, Decatur st, No. 253, Sterling pl, No. 31 } alotted to Phillipine E. Von Stade.
Partition of Samuel B. H. Judah's estate as above.

Stockton st, n s, 210 e Marcy av, 25x100, h & l. Margaretha Stephan widow to Tillie T. Emerson. 7,300

Stockholm st, n w s, 100 s w Irving av, 125x100. Henry Heins to Jacob Blank. *Mt.* $3,000. 6,250

Sumpter st, s s, 375 w Ralph av, 25x74.7x25x71.10, h & l. Mary K. Kerz widow to John Kraus and Anna his wife, joint tenants. *Mt.* $1,100. 2,000

Suydam st, n s, 372 e Evergreen av late Willow st, 28x95, h & l. Edward W. Morton to Mary L. Platt. 2,500

Sheepshead Bay to Coney Island Point road, n s, adj land of Coney Island Horse Car R. R., 1 acre, Coney Island. The Directors of the Kings Co. Gas Light Co. to The Coney Island Fuel, Gas and Light Co. nom

Tillary st, n s, 74 w Navy st, 22x58.3x22.2x61.6.
Tillary st, n s, 96 w Navy st, 22x79.9x22.3x76.
Tillary st, n s, 118 w Navy st, 22x76x22.3x72.6.
Peter and Joseph Young to James Howell and Daniel Y. Saxton. 6,000

Union st, s w s, 208.8 n w 5th av, 16.8x100. Annie E. Logue, of New York, to Annie M. Dunne. 3,800

Union st, n s, 227.6 w Clinton st, 140x100. Foreclos. John Courtney to Spencer Adrich. *Mt.* $40,000. 10,000

Van Buren st, s s, 414.4 e Lewis av, 17.10x100. Randolph H. Cole to William M. Norton. *Mt.* $4,400. nom

Vermont st, w s, 300 n Fulton av, runs west 100 x north 25 x east 25 x north 50 x east 75 to Vermont st, x south 75. Catharine wife of George Distler to John Gunther. 6,100

Warren st, No. 151, n s, 82 e Henry st, 20x85. Contract. Josephine Seymour widow to Kate Gallagher. 7,250

Warren st, s s, 298.4 w 5th av, 20x100. The Niagara Fire Ins. Co. to Frank Koseck. 4,400

Willoughby st, n s, 91.4 e Adams st, 22.10x100, h & l. Bridget Canavan, Susquehanna, Pa., to Thomas A. Kerrigan. *Mt.* $10,000. 18,000

Woodbine st, n s, 125 e Central av, 50x100. George Schwab to John Bosch. *Mt.* $7,000. nom

Woodbine st, n w s, 100 n e Central av, 25x100. Gottlob Haussmann to John Bosch. *Mt.* $3,500. nom

Weirfield st, s e s, 240 n e Bushwick av, 20x100, h & l. Joseph F. Shipsey to Emma H. Shipsey. B. & S. *Mt.* $2,000. nom

Willow pl, w s, 104.4 s Joralemon st, 22.10x80. Julia A. Smith to Edward Reilly. 6,300

1st st, n e s, 298.10 n w 8th av, 18x100. Frank W. Larom to Frances V. Cahill. Sub. to mort. 10,000

1st st, s w s, 386 n w 5th av, 53.11x100. Ezra D. Bushnell to William H. Adams. nom

South 1st st, n s, 24.10 w Roebling st, 28.3x44x22.6x43.6, h & l. Michael K. O'Neil to Honora Hogan, New York. *Mt.* $2,000. 3,800

1st pl, s s, 238 e Henry st, 26x133.5. John G. Saxe by Charles G. Saxe guard. to Seba M. Bogert. ½ part. 3,600

Samé p p ty. Charles G. Saxe to same. ½ part. ro·er 370 3,600

3d pl, n s, 40 e Henry st, 20x60. Michael H. Hagerty to Charles L. Bristoe. 6,x50

South 3d st, s w s, 125 n w Hooper st, 25x95. Emil Lehrian to Henry Metz. *Mt.* $6,500. 14,250

South 3d st, n s, 125 e 5th st, 25x100. Mary L. Fales to Robert T. Manjer. 7,900

North 3d st, s w s, lot 83 map of Williamsburgh by T. H. Poppleton, 25x ½ block. Charles A. Hubbard to Mabel H. wife of George P. Grant, Jr., and Maude H. wife of P. Francis Walker. Q. C. nom

South 4th st, No. 354, s w s, 145.6 n w 11th st, 25x95.10x25x95.7, h & l. Hugh Fehling to Lorenz Harbauer. *Mt.* $6,500. 14,500

5th st, s e s, 78 w 6th av, 19.10x100. George O. Van Orden to Harry Wiltshire. *Mt.* $7,500. 11,000

6th st, n e s, 229.10 n w 7th av, 20x100. Harriet E. Hartshorn to Max Whitehead. 8,000

7th st, n e s, 198.7 n w 4th av, 19.3x100. Release mort. Frank Bailey to Nicholas Ryan. nom

7th st, n e s, 197.9 n w 7th av, 18.8x100. William A. McLaughlin to Robert Buhsen. *Mt.* $4,000. 7,100

7th st, n e s, 235.1 n w 7th av, 18.8x100. Estella Christie to Adelaide E. Foulks. nom

East 9th st, e s, 200 n Av C, 100x136.2 to Coney Island av, x100.3x143.6, Flatbush. Mary E. Biggs widow to Frank A. Wollensack. 1,100

10th st, s s, 439.8 e 7th av, 20x100. Louis Bonert to Albert J. Bushong. *Mt.* $5,000. 9,250

12th st, n e s, 237.10 s e 4th av, 20x100. Alexander G. Calder to Angelica wife of Charles Delapierre. *Mt.* $3,000. 7,000

13th st, n e s, 82.10 n w 7th av, 15x50. George Stenger to Estelle M. Brown, Hudson, N. Y. All liens. nom

13th st, s s, 190.4 w 4th av, 17.6x100. Frank W. Belmont to Francis M. Wilmurt. *Mt.* $4,500. nom

North 13th st, n e s, 200 n w Wythe av, runs northeast 200 to North 14th st, x northwest 229.9 to Kent av, x southwest to point 125 n e North 13th st, x southeast 100 x southwest to point 100 n e North 13th st, x southeast 75 x southwest 100 to North 13th st, x southeast 52. James D. Leary to Henry, Charles and William Vogt. 13,500

14th st, n s, 197.6 e 8th av, 0.4x100. Release mort. Mary R. Wright to William Hawkins. nom

15th st, s s, 111 e 3d av, 18x66. Robert B. McIntyre to James Shannon. *Mt.* $3,000. 3,325

15th st, n s, 147.10 w 3d av, the one story and basement frame house only. James Fitzsimmons to Francis Gibrson. 325

17th st, n e s, 93.4 s e 9th av, runs northeast 80 x southeast 20 x northeast 20 x southeast 46.8 x southwest 100 x northwest 66.8. Thomas S. O'Reilly to Michael McCadden. 3,500

40th st, s s, 150 e 4th av, 25x100.2. Adolph Rheinfeldt, of New York, to Ellen E. Dunne. 650

42d st, n e s, 175 s e 12th av, 50x100. The West Brooklyn Land and Improvement Co. to Elsie E. Berry. 700

47th st, n s, 100 e 4th av, 20x100.2. Samuel T. Sherwood to George W. McKay. *Mt.* $3,000. 5,020

48th st, n e s, 200 s e 4th av, 20x100.2. Release mort. Emma A. Cantrell to Mark Hally. 600

48th st, n e s, 180 s e 4th av, 20x100.2. Release mort. Same to William R. Rogers. 600

Same property. John L. and George W. Craig to William R. Rogers. *Mt.* $600. 1,000

52d st, s w s, 180 s e 3d av, 20x100.2. William H. Shepard to Agnes B. Pool. *Mt.* $3,000. nom

55th st, s w s, 100 n w 3d av, 25x100. Charles W. Lansing to Francis J. Pierret. *Mt.* $1,500. 3,200

56th st, s s, 142 e 2d av, 18x100.2. John Downie to Elizabeth Driscoll. *Mt.* $2,300. nom

56th st, centre line, adj land of J. Koehler, runs west to Marg't Stillwells, x west 5 chains and 84 links x southeast 2 chains 50 links x east 12 chains 57 links x north to centre 56th st, x northwest —, New Utrecht. Leonard M. Kirby to Hoik D. Campbell. nom

60th st, s w s, 320 n w 17th av, 60x100, New Utrecht. Release mort. William A. Copp exr. Mary M. Warren to Hans C. Pfalzgraf. 300

66th st, n e s, 133 n w 18th av, 60x100.
67th st, n e s, 357.10 n w 18th av, 140.1x147.1x140x142.9.
67th st, n e s, 537.10 n w 18th av, 54.5x150x58.4x148.4.
66th st, s s, 140 e 13th av, 40x100, all New Utrecht.
Barbey st, e s, 205 s Hegeman av, 40x100.
Jerome st, w s, 140 n Hegeman av, 20x100.
Jerome st, w s, 100 s Repose pl, 40x100.
Repose pl, n s, 180 w John st, 20x108.10x20x108.7.
Repose pl, n s, 180 e Schenck av. 20x109.8x20x109.11.
Joseph T. Commoss to Daniel P. Darling. exch. and 900

70th st, n s, 230 w 15th av, 40x100, New Utrecht. James V. S. Woolley to Joseph B. Sears. 520

70th st, n s, 350 w 15th av, 40x100, Lefferts Park. James V. S. Woolley to David and Susan Sly. 520

75th st, n s, 470 w 15th av, 20x100, New Utrecht. Thomas Skimming to Joseph Wilson. 375

76th st, n s, 450 w 15th av, 20x100, Lefferts Park. James V. S. Woolley to William W. Harragan. 150

76th st, s s, 86.6 w 5th av, 40x100, hs & l, New Utrecht. Maria A. Hartung to Mary Hartung. B. & S. *Mt.* $3,000. nom

78th st, n e s, 400 n w 19th av, 60x100, New Utrecht. John L. Nostrand to Samuel J. Atwater. 900

81st st, n e s, 300 s e 12th av, 140x100.
80th st, s w s, 180 s e 12th av, 40x100.
80th st, n e s, 100 n w 12th av, 340x100.
80th st, n e s, 220 s e 12th av, 60x100.
79th st, s w s, 340 s e 12th av, 100x100.
75th st, s w s, 220 s e 12th av, 100x100, New Utrecht.
Release mort. George S. Ingraham to Hoik D. and Samuel I. Campbell. 2,500

81st st, s s, 110 w 3d av, 100x109.4. Release mort. Rulef J. Van Brunt to William W. and Robert M. Spence, Sylvester E. Coffin and Frank Forshew. 1,250

81st st, s s, 340 e 2d av, 60x109.4, New Utrecht. William W. and Robert M. Spence, Sylvester E. Coffin and Frank Forshew to Frank F. Koehl. 1,500

81st st, n e s, 340 n w 19th av, 100x100, New Utrecht. John L. Nostrand to Virginia L. Duphy. 1,500

Same property. Release mort. Townsend P. Van Pelt to John L. Nostrand. nom

East 94th st, n e s, 100 s e Flatlands av, 52.10x—x53x100, Canarsie. Hermann Lohmann to David I. Hughes. 400

Arlington av, s s, 25 e Wyona st, 25x100. John Deterling to Charles L. and Annie M. Schroeter. 1,200

Atlantic av, s s, 312.3 w Clason av, runs west 100 x south 100 x east 40 x south 100 to Pacific st, x east 60 x north 200. James L. Sayre to Thomas I. Dixon. 3,000

Bedford av, s e cor Degraw st, runs south 107.2 x southeast 30.10 x east 135 x north 127.9 x west 134.6.
Bedford av, e s, 22 n Degraw st, 108.4 x east 102.11 x127.9 to Degraw st, x40x21.6x84.
Rogers av, w s, 21.6 n Degraw st, 106.3x100.
Julia E. Carroll to Agnes J. wife of Charles J. Maguire. ⅝ part. nom

Belmont av, s w cor Watkins st, 16.8x100, h & l. Beckie Aronson, New York, to Morris Aronson. *Mt.* $1,800. 3,000

Belmont av, s s, 25 w Warwick st, 25x100.
Belmont av, s s, 150 w Warwick st, 25x100.
Sabra L. Duryea to George Schade. 900

Belmont av, n s, 50 w Jerome st, 50x100. Bridget Winters, of Port Jervis, heir Margaret McDermott to Thomas McDermott. nom

Same property. Elizabeth Faulkner, New York, and Mary E. Flynn, Stamford, Conn., heirs Margt. McDermott to same. nom

Blake av, s s, 25 w Barbey st, 50x100. Edw'd W. Lauer and Charles J. Kiesel to Charles E. Raynor. *Mt.* $1,500. 4,100

Blake av, n s, 125 e Schenck av, 25x100. Jared J. Chambers to Edward W. Lauer and Chas. J. Kiesel. 550

Bushwick av, s w s, 50 s e Gates av, runs southwest 100 x southeast 30.1 x southwest 25 x southeast 19.10 x northeast 125 to Bushwick av, x northwest 50. Thomas J. Betts to William Andrews, of New York. 6,375

Bushwick av, s w cor Woodbine st, 20x80. Edward Michaelis to Marie E. Kohlman. *Mt.* $2,000. 5,000

Christopher av, w s, 175 n Newport av, 100x100. William Oppenheim to Isaac Abrams and Isaac Gingold. ¼ part. Sub. to mort. $600. 500

Same property. Same to Abraham J. Dworsky. ¼ part. Sub. to mort. $600. 500

Same property. Same to Rosie Kram. ¼ part. Sub. to mort. $600. 500

Clason av, n w cor Quincy st, 20x80. Cornelius Sullivan to Frederick Mahnken, Jr. *Mt.* $6,000. 10,000

Clermont av, w s, 136.7 n Willoughby av, 16x76.2, h & l. George W. Tarbox to George H. K. White. *Mt.* $5,000. 8,000

Cropsey av, s w s, lot 37 map 28 Building Sections, Bath, 51x359.6 to New Utrecht Bay, x50.4x362.4.
Cropsey av, s w s, lot 38 same map, 50x362.4 to New Utrecht Bay, x97.11x373.7.
Cropsey av, s w s, 105 s e New Utrecht and Greenwood plank road, 50x373.7 to New Utrecht Bay, x10x370.
Cropsey av, s s, 256 s e New Utrecht to Bay road, 50x355.10 to Bay, x50.2x359.8, with land under water, &c.
Morgan J. O'Brien to Jeannette wife of Louis A. Lanthier. C. a. G. 6,500

De Kalb av, n w s, 100 s w Irving av, 150x100. John Von Glahn to Jacob Blank. *Mt.* $4,000. 7,500

De Kalb av, n w cor Adelphi st, runs north 106.3 x west 13.11 x south 26.2 x south 32 x south 45 to av, x east 27.1. Helen M. wife of and Spencer L. Hiller to Henry P. Read. *Mt.* $5,000. 10,000

Evergreen av, s w cor Melrose late Adams st, 54.9x90.1x50x72.6. William J. Haubert to Charles J. Haubert. 3,000

Flushing av, s s, 25.4 w Steuben st, 25x93.6x20x94.10. Benjamin Andrews to Alonzo E. De Baun. Q. C. nom

Franklin av, e s, 60 s Atlantic av, 20x81.1, h & l. Ella Free to Mary Cleary. *Mt.* $5,500. exch

Franklin av, s w s, adj Ellen Brown, 51x359.6 to New Utrecht Bay high water mark, 50.4x362.4.
Franklin av, s w s, adjoins above, 50x364 to high water mark New Utrecht Bay, x97.11x273.7.
Franklin av, s w s, abt 105 s e Bath, New

Utrecht and Greenwood plank road, 50x 373.7 to high water mark New Utrecht Bay, x10x370.5.
Franklin av, s w s, 256 s e Bath, New Utrecht and Greenwood plank road, 50x355.10 to New Utrecht Bay, x50,2x359.8, with all land under water.
Foreclos. Francis A. McCloskey to Morgan J. O'Brien. 20,000

Gates av, s s, 112.6 w Stuyvesant av, 18.9x100. James S. Bloomer to Charles L. Applegate, of New York. *Mt.* $3,000. 3,700

Gates av, n s, 50 w Vanderbilt av, 20x75, h & l. Henry J. Schaefer and Louise Ruhle to Maximillan Lang. *Mt.* $4,000. 7,750

Glenmore av, n s, 50 w Powell st, 14x84.4, with south ½ of alley across rear, h & l. Abram B. Morrell to Dean Sage, Albany. 6,000

Graham av, s w s, 50 n w Newton st, 25x93.5x 25.4x89.8. Leopold Michel to Malie wife of Hyman Harris. *Mt.* $2,700. 7,000

Greene av, w s, 410 n Knickerbocker av, 25x 76.8x25.1x75. George Feldman to Jacob Schock. *Mt.* $3,000. 6,500

Greene av, s s, 480 e Throop av, 20x100. David S. Beasley to Anna M. wife of Peter Mangels. *Mt.* $5,000. 8,700

Greene av, s s, 40.6 w Sumner av, 19.6x100. Thomas B. Bryant to Jennie Marshall. *Mt.* $5,000. 9,000

Harrison av, n e s, 23 s e Gwinnett st, 23x100. Frederick Weimann to Joel B. and Benson H. Goodman. *Mt.* $3000. 5,000

Irving av, n e s, 25 n w Greene av, 25x90. John Bosch to Margaretha Schwab. *Mt.* $3,000. nom

Irving av, northerly cor Grove st, 100x110. Janet and James Pirnie as exrs. John M. Pirnie to Charles Aichmann. 6,900

Same property. Release dower. Janet Pirnie widow to same. nom

Jamaica av, n s, abt 50 e New Jersey av, abt 50 x158.8. Robert Bieling to John H. Hilliker, Jamaica, and John W. Mehl. 2,200

Jefferson av, n w s, 329.8 n e Broadway, 20x100. Henry Fuehrer to Louisa Kwald. *Mt.* $3,250. 7,125

Johnson av, s s, 100 e Bogert st, 75x100. Charles W. Truslow as admr. William Wall to Charles Burzgy. 3,675

Johnson av, n s, 75 e Union av, 25x75, h & l. Solomon Blumenstock to Detlev Haase. 4,450

Johnson av, s s, 50.1 w Bogert st, 25.2x102.5x25 x99.5. Charles W. Truslow as admr. William Wall to Marx Wendstein. 1,375

Johnson av, s w cor Bogert st, 50.1x99.5x50x 98.8. Same to David Mayer. 3,550

Johnson av, s e cor Bogert st, 25x100. Same to Julia Levy. 2,100

Johnson av, n w cor Bogert st, 39.1x— to Bogert st, x 50.4, gore. Same to James Rodwell. 920

Knickerbocker av, n e s, 75 s e Himrod st, 25x 100. Ernst Augustin to Martin Guenther, *Mt.* $3,500. 6,750

Knickerbocker av, s w s, 40 n w Linden st, 40 x100. Daniel C. McEwen to Ignatz Martin. Q. C. nom

Same property. Ignatz Martin to Charles A. Cross. *Mt.* $700. 1,650

Knickerbocker av, s w s, 25 s e Stockholm st, 25x100. William Wolf to Charles C. Kreppel. *Mt.* $840. nom

Lafayette av, n s, 175 e Sumner av, 20x100, h & l. Margaret J. wife of William Reynolds to William Holland and Jacob G. W. Wurzler. 7,600

Lee av, e s, 60.4 n Penn st, 19.8x83.4. John F. Ryan to George N. Searle. B. & S. Correction deed. nom

Lexington av, s s, 458.4 e Sumner av, 16.8x100. Sarah L. wife of and William B. Lomas to Fanny J. Green, of New York. 4,550

Lexington av, s s, 259 w Nostrand av, 32x100. Edward Phillips to James C. McEachen. *Mt.* $7,000. nom

Lexington av, n s, 227 w Sumner av, 17x100.
Lexington av, n s, 295 w Sumner av, 34x100, h & l.
Daniel P. Darling to Joseph T. Commoss. nom

Lexington av, n s, 200 e Throop av, 15x100. David S. Beasley to Harry N. Kelley. *Mt.* $2,000. 4,600

Lexington av, n s, 215 e Throop av, 15x100. Same to Mary H. wife of Benjamin F. Kelley. *Mt.* $2,000. 4,600

Marcy av, w s, 50 n Park av, 25x75. George C. Dickman to Frederick Horn. 6,500

Montrose av, s s, 25 w Bushwick Boulevard, 25 x100, h & l. Louise Hob to Katrina Betz. 8,000

Montrose av, n s, 182.4 w old Bushwick av, 25 x100. John Bosch to Margaretha Schwab. *Mt.* $3,000. nom

Myrtle av, n s, 250 e Sumner av, 25x100. Henry Roth to Louis Bossert. *Mt.* $10,550. nom

Myrtle av, n s, 275 e Sumner av, 25x100. Same to same. *Mt.* $9,300. nom

Myrtle av, n s, 300 e Sumner av, 25x100. Same to same. *Mt.* $9,300. nom

Myrtle av, n s, 325 e Sumner av, 25x100. Same to same. *Mt.* $9,000. nom

New York av, n w cor Park pl, 65x121.6. Mary E. wife of Darwin R. James to William H. Lyon. 10,500

Ocean av, e s, 337 n Av A, 102 6x240, Flatbush. Jeremiah Lott to John Z. Lott. 800

Ovington av, n s, 166 w 14th av, 40x123.4x4' x 122.1, New Utrecht. Effingham H. Nichols to Claude Pojet. 400

Park av, n e cor Nostrand av, 50x67.9. Julia Simon to Kate Acor. nom

Park av, s s, 475 e Throop av, 25x100, h & l. Alphonse P. Rinck to Nelson Towne, Hudson, N. Y. 6,000

Patchen av, e s, 40 n Decatur st, 20x100, h & l. George Evans to Henry Vollweiler. *Mt.* $3,500. 6,500

Prospect av, n e s, 90.6 n w 6th av, runs northwest 25.10 x northeast 100 x southeast 11.9 x southwest 26.2 x southeast 14.2 x southwest 75.4. Sophronia M. Fickett to Michael N. Donovan. 6,500

Prospect av, s s, 140 w 8th av, 20x80. Frank M. Foye to Richard Chidwick. *Mt.* $500. 1,500

Putnam av, n w cor Lewis av, 22x100. Daniel B. Norris to Rebecca Lodge. nom

Putnam av, s e s, 160 n e Broadway, 20x100. George A. Craig to Morris Hart. *Mt.* $7,000. 7,000

Rockaway av, w s, 86 s Herkimer st, 27x97.6, h & l.
Rockaway av, w s, 140 s Herkimer st, 27x 97 6, h & l.
Catharine A. wife of Thomas Lawrence to Benjamin F. Briggs. *Mt.* $14,000. 20,000

Same property. Benjamin F. Briggs to Elizabeth W. Aldrich. *Mt.* $14,000. val. consid

Rockaway av, n e cor Glenmore av, 20x100.1. Charles J. Warren to Charles J. Warren, Jr. gift

Rockaway av, s w cor Hull st, 17x75; also,
Rockaway av, w s, 33.8 s Hull st, 16.8x75.
Gottfred Bock to John A. Schuessler. *Mt.* $6,500. exch

Rockaway av, w s, 400 n Eastern Parkway, 25 x100. Bernhard J. Pink to David Fertig, New York. 6,000

Schenck av, e s, 77.8 s Fulton av, runs east 65.1 x southeast 22.5 to point distant 69.7 e Schenck av, x west 69.7 to av, x north 22. Elise wife of and Albert Dietz to George U. Forbell. 1,050

Schenectady av, e s, 50 s Diamond st, 50x100, Flatbush; also,
Jefferson st, near Atlantic av, being part of lot 505 map 4 Fort Hamilton Village, New Utrecht, 25x110.
Wilfred Wiley to Henry P. Stevens. 400

Shepherd av, e s, 215 n Stanley av, 20x100. William H. Jackson to Mary H. King. 176

Shepherd av, e s, 235 n Stanley av, 80x100. Same to Walter H. King. 703

Snediker av, w s, 170 n Sutter av, 15x100, h & l. John P. Free to William L. Duc. *Mt.* $1,500. 2,600

South Portland av, e s, 137.6 s Lafayette av, 18.9x100. Augustus wife of Herman Liebmann to Flora E. or Nellie F. Manson. 6,600

Stuyvesant av, w s, 61.1 s Halsey st, 19.2x80.6. Andrew D. Baird to Francis A. Moore. *Mt.* $5,500. nom

St. Marks av, n s, 117.6 e Troy av, 46x127.9, h & l. Manhattan Savings Inst. to William Linson. 2,250

Same property. William Linson to The Keystone Nat. Savings Loan and Investment Assoc. *Mt.* $1,800. 2,250

St. Marks av, n s, 125 w Underhill av, 50x131. William Ruland, Keyport, N. J., to William J. Hart. Q. C. nom

Throop av, w s, 26 n Pulaski st, runs west 50 x north 1 x west 24.9 x north 73 x east 84.9 to av, x south 74, h & l. George B. Stoutenburg to Benjamin Armstrong. *Mt.* $22,000. 35,000

Vanderbilt av, w s, 215 n Gates av, 20x100, h & l. Julia H. Murray to Seraphine Matherson. 8,500

Vanderbilt av, w s, 594.2 n Myrtle av, 16.8x 100; also,
Vanderbilt av, w s, 610.10 n Myrtle av, 16.8x 100.
Peter and Joseph Young to Parmenus Jackson, of Westbury, L. I. *Mt.* $3,500. 7,000

Van Siclen av, e s, 125 s Blake av, 25x100. Henry Ingraham to Charles W. Osborne and ano. exrs. Peter P. Schoonmaker. Sub. to taxes, &c. 2,000

Vernon av, s s, 205.4 e Lewis av, 17.6x100, h & l. Alexander H. Mathesius to Henry Fuehrer. *Mt.* $4,500. 8,500

Vernon av, s s, 300 w Throop av, 80x100. Release mort. Thomas L. Atkins to Robert H. Anderson. 9,300

Vernon av, s s, 325 w Sumner av, 20x100, h & l. Charles F. Kueck to John E. Bullwinkel. *Mt.* $3,493. nom

Same property. John E. Bullwinkel to Charles F. Kneck and Catharine R. W. his wife, joint tenants. *Mt.* $3,493. nom

Washington av, w s, lots 81 and 82 map made by Isaac T. Ludlam in 1853, 25x231.4, h & ls. Clara H. wife of and Lewis H. Carhart to Thomas Sully, Buffalo, N. Y. *Mt.* $7,000. 7,000

Waverly av, e s, 575 n Myrtle av, 20x100. Joseph W. Myer to Margaret M. Hannan. *Mt.* $2,500. 4,000

Wyckoff av, n e cor Ralph st, 25x98.1x25x97.3, h & l. Jacob Blank to Edward E. Tucker. *Mt.* $4,500. 9,500

Wyckoff av, n e cor Himrod st, 25x93.11x25x 94.7, h & l. Jacob Blank to Henry Heins. *Mt.* $4,500. exch

2d av, s e s, 60.2 n e 56th st, 20x100. Mary A. wife of James White to Annie wife of Peter J. Rappel. *Mt.* $1,600. 2,700

3d av, w s, 83.4 n Wyckoff st, 16.8x78. Julius Hansel to Theodore Cordes. *Mt.* $2,000. 2,900

3d av, w s, 75.2 n 48th st, 25x80, h & l. Solomon Bonin to Morris Jacobson and Morris Margovits. *Mt.* $8,000, taxes, &c. 10,000

4th av, s e s, 60 s w 11th st, 20x97.10. Angelica wife of Charles Delapierre to Alexander G. Calder. *Mt.* $500. 1,900

4th av, s e s, 34.8 s w Degraw st, 16.4x75. Daniel J. Ramsdell to George R. Brown. *Mt.* $6,000. nom

4th av, n w cor 9th st, original line, runs north along av 120 x west 60 x south 33 x east 40 x south 87 to 9th st, x east 20. Frank Bailey to Frank A. Barnaby. nom

4th av, s e s, 34.8 s w Degraw st, 16.4x75. Foreclos. John Courtney, Sheriff, to David J Ramsdell. 5,800

5th av, s w cor 76th st, 107.2x125.1x100x56 6, New Utrecht.
52d st, s s, 353.4 w 3d av, 16.8x100.2.
77th st, n s, 123.7 w 5th av, 40x100, New Utrecht.
Gravesend av, w s, 180 s Av J, runs west 100 x south 160 x west 100 to West st, x south 280 x east 100 x north 20 x east 100 to w s Gravesend av, x north 420, New Utrecht.
76th st, s s, 86.6 w 5th av, 40x100.
19th av, east cor 54th st, ½ block x — to 20th av.
19th av, south cor 54th st, runs southwest to land of C. H. Criswell, x southeast to 20th av, x northeast along same to 54th st, x northwest —.
53d st, s w s, 200 s e 20th av, runs southwest 100.2 x southeast 60 x southwest 100.2 to 54th st, x southeast 221.6 x southeast 18.7 x northeast 198.1 to 53d st, x northwest 300, New Utrecht.
Edward Hartung to Maria A. Hartung. *Mt.* $21,750. 16,619

7th av, w s, 20.9 s 1st st, 110.10x90.9. Agreement to reconvey the premises upon payment of consid. in original deed with stipulation as to disposal of rents meanwhile. Joseph H. Swift with Lewis N. Muller. nom

10th av, s w cor 72d st, 60x100, New Utrecht. The Bay Ridge Park Improvement Co. to Joseph B. McQuillin and Wilkins K. Putnam. nom

Lots 103 and 104 map A. W. Parker property, Bath Beach. Edward Egolf to Anna M. Ghiele. 1,100

Lots 154, 155 and 164 and 165 map of John Emmons heirs, Gravesend. Clark T. Hamilton to Samuel S. and Maurice J. Sobel. 1,050

Interior lot, 108.10 w Bridge st and 183.4 n Fulton st, runs north 25 x west 6.2 x south 25 x east 6.2. Charles A. Loeser, of Sommerville, N. J., to Walter C. Gilson, of New York. B. & S. nom

Same property. Walter C. Gilson, of New York, to Frederick Loeser. nom

Interior lot, begins on centre line bet 10th and 11th sts at point 100 w 5th av, runs west 237.10 x south to land of Henry L. Clark, x east to point 100 w 8th av, x north —. Kate C. Henderson et al. exrs. and trustees Isaac Henderson to Charles E. Steck. 3,000

Interior strip, begins 115.4 n South 9th st on line which at n s South 9th st is 69 w Havemeyer st, runs north 4 x west 10x4x10. Isabella wife of John Frazer to Louis Zeobiel. 100

New Utrecht road, adj W. Cole, 35.3x148.7x 63.8x143.7, New Utrecht. Foreclos. William Hughes to Mary Tidd. 406

Plank road, e s, 100.6 n Grant st, 49.9x247.4x 49.2x231.7, Flatbush. Abby L. Wells and Maria J. Livingston to Jeremiah Lott. 2,800

Grantor's interest in estate of his mother and grandmother. Harrison W. Furnald to Margaret A. T. Lawrence. collateral for 500

One-half share of all real estate owned by Augusta Wirz in Kings Co. Augusta wife of William Wirz to Jacob Barth. In consideration of his services in pending litigation, &c.

General release estate of Charles Haubert. William J. Haubert to Charles J. Haubert individ. and exr. Chas. Haubert. 6,000

WESTCHESTER COUNTY.

OCTOBER 28 TO NOVEMBER 3—INCLUSIVE

CORTLANDT.

Billings, Stephen to Patrick King, lots 13-29 block 28, Verplancks. $600

EASTCHESTER.

Deady, Eliza to Marcus Walcher, part lot 35 n o s Highland av, Waverly, 50x100. 290

Ely, Smith and ano. to John H. Eden, s s Kingsbridge road, adj Certine, 70 acres. 100,000

Forster, Fred P. to Lewis Alexander, lots 184, 185 and 186, Chester Hill, 150x100. 2,250

Ford, Simeon to John Stimmel, lot 177, s e s West st, 100x100; also north ½ lot 180 w s Railroad av, 25x100, West Mt. Vernon; also part lot 1024 s s Stevens av, Mt. Vernon, 50x 80. 5,000

Held, Harry to Fred. C. Pinne, lot 182 n w s Bond st, West Mt. Vernon, 25x100. 1,900

Jaffray, Mary E. et al., Geo. W. Hunt ref., to Chas. C. Wright, part lot 1025 s s Stevens av, 50x—. 2,725

Moore, Alice to Wm. Schuster, n w cor Park and Prospect avs, 25x100. 4,500

McMurray, Jas. to Moses R. Crow, n w cor Fletcher av and Chester st, 100x100. 2,750

McKenzie, Sarah B. to Edmund J. Tichenor, s ½ lot 804 w s 10th av, Mt. Vernon, 50x105. 5,300

Owen, Daniel to Ulrich Schoch, lot 981 s s 17th av, Wakefield, 100x114. 1,800

Turner, Rich. W. to Edw. Martens, e s Park av, 343 e Sidney, 50x100. 2,500

Wheeler, John to Lewis Johnson, lots 165 and 166 Boulevard, Vernon Park. 950

Wright, Emily A. to Mary Kiessel, n ½ lot 162 w s 2d av, Mt. Vernon, 50x105. 2,500

GREENBURGH.

Boutelle, Fred. G. to Chas. W. Wheeler, 2 parcels w s Saw Mill River road. 900

Field, Laura B. to Jeanie L. Musgrave, w s Broadway at Hastings, abt 8 acres. nom

Harrison, Robt. L. to Fred. G. Boutelle, w s Saw Mill River road, 543x—. 775

Hilley, Johanna to Jos. H. Hugher, lots 20, 21 and 22 map lots at Ardsley. 775

Nolan, Jas. H. to Chas E. Storms, lots 162 and 163 e s Lefurgy av, map Purdy lots, 50x100. 1,400

Jones, Cyrus P. and ano. to Fred. Schade, lots 216, 217 and 218, Ardsley. 500

Lefurgy, Leonard T. to Jennie M. Judson, ½ acre s s Ashford av. nom

HARRISON.

Secor, Stephen exr. of, to David N. Haviland, n w s road from North st to Rye Neck, 2 acres. 2,450

MAMARONECK.

Boyd, Richard V. to Ellen S. White, s w cor Grove av and Florence st, 50x110. 400

Monense Mfg. Co. to Melaine Weill, lots 99 and 108, Grand Park. —

MOUNT PLEASANT.

Grady, Patrick to Michael Cashman, lot 12 e s Valley st, 25x—. 825

Lane, Ephraim to Chas. Boice, n e cor Rebecca av and Oak st, 40x102. 350

Soltz, Arcadius to Samuel Ashman, e s Lenox av, 125 n Broadway, 25x100. 100

Smith, Wm. R. to Henry Gonzales, lot 61 block 5 map Lake Kensico. 225

Same to Mansfield Hunt, lots 4 and 5 block 5. 350

Smedbeck, Louis to Patrick D. Shea, lot 892, Sherman Park. 100

Same to Geo. W. Allen, lots 1008 and 1,009. 350

Same to Aug. Schoenhen and ano., lot 1309. 175

Same to Caroline Schmit, lot 991. 150

Same to Mary C. O'Neil, lot 1942. 125

Same to Anna M. Jones, lots 1364 and 1365. 1,500

Same to Carrie M. Durgin, lots 977 and 978. 2,000

Same to same, lots 5018 and 5019. 20

Same to Huldah Staub, lots 1123, 1124 and 1125. 575

Same to Eugene Staub, lots 1071 and 1072. 400

Same to Julius Mahn, lots 986 and 987. 300

Same to Mary J. Lyons, lot 1577. 200

Same to Eugene Herrmann, lots 596 and 597. 200

Same to Aug. Castle, lot 490. 100

Same and ano. to John Brady and ano., lots 289 and 290, Lakehurst. 450

Same and ano. to Bernard Ashley and ano., lots 341 and 342, Lakehurst. 350

NEW ROCHELLE.

Carville, Cath J. C. to Genie H. Rosenfeld, w s Clinton av, 143x245. 2,000

Davids, Cortlandt I. to Grace A. Fornachon, lot E s s Mayflower av, Huguenot Park, 100 x300. 1,150

Disbrow, Susan W. exr. of, to John F. Lambden and ano., lot 198 s w s Meadow lane, Residence Park. 2,500

Reid, Mary E to Lizzie Ingalls, s w s Davis av, 1,133 s e Main st, 78x168. 5,500

NORTH CASTLE.

Blake, Robt. to John Koch, Ferguson's Four Corners, King st and Armonk road, abt 35 acres. 6,000

OSSINING.

Blandford, Emily T. to Chas. E. Cotton, e s Spring st, adj Michael Lent, 38x100. 2,600

Purdy, Hannah C. exr. of. to Minnie M. Miller, w s Highland av, adj Abr. Acker. 2,000

PELHAM.

Wild, Julia to Aug. Gerstle, lots 696, 697 and 698 w s Main st map King estate. 2,050

RYE.

Brooks, John to John A. Billington, lots 83 and 85 w s Davis av, map Hayward. 180

Same to Jas. Kirby, lot 16 s w cor Sylvan st and Davis av. 75x150. 175

Same to same, lot 17 s s Sylvan st, 75x150. 100

Fuchs, John to Marshall O. West, e s Orchard st, 210 s Terrace av, 42x100. 250

Griffin, Sydney B. to Emily Ackerman, w s Barry av, cor Depot road, 143x182. 8,000

McCarty, Richard T. to Fred M. Betts, e s Centre st, 351 s Westchester av, 50x199. 775

Merritt, Jas. S. and ano. to Louis Czerinak, lot 22 n s Ellendale av, Washington Park, 50x 150. 255

Same to same, lot 17 n s same, 50x150. 265

Same to Patrick McKay, lot 26 n s Ellendale av, 50x150. 103

Same to Mary McKay, lot 25 n s Ellendale av, 50x150. 175

Same to John W. O'Brien, lot 16 n s Ellendale av, 50x150. 255

Same to Frances Peters, lots 82, 83 and 84 n s Ellendale av, 150x150. 375

Same to Jas. Murphy, lot 69 s s Ellendale av, 50x150. 190

Same to Abr. L. Merritt, lots 47, 48 and 49 s s Ellendale av, 150x150. 153

Same to Anna Nolan, lot 88 w s Lyon st, 50x 100. 215

Same to John Currah, lot 123 s s West William st, 50x112. 200

Same to Jos. H. Gray, lot 87 n s West William st, 50x150. 110

Same to same, lot 114 n w cor West William and Regent sts, 63x153. 410

Same to Letitia Killeen, lot 24 n s Ellendale av, 50x150. 250

Same to Edw. Jones, lots 53 and 54 s e cor Ellendale av and Merritt st, 100x100. 405

Same to Mary J. Kelley, s s "New" road, 466 w Regent st, 77x—. nom

Theall, Margt S. to Samuel Benedict, e s Willet av, adj Thos. Wier, 50x100. 600

Todd, John, exr. of, to Hannah H. White, s s Mortimer st, 177 w Willett av, abt 50x120. 180

Walker, Geo. W., admr. of, to Wm. G. Slater, s w cor Irving av and Fountain st. 6,600

SCARSDALE.

White, Lydia M. to Chas. Butler and ano., tract opposite Hartsdale Depot, abt 50 acres. 25,825

WESTCHESTER.

Dexter, Fred. C. to Emanuel Burlando, lots 415, 416 and 1045, Wakefield. 5,500

Duncan, Wm. F. to Samuel E. Meyers, lots 75–95, 102–108, 119–124, 148–152, 157–160, Williamsbridge. 15,000

Mace, Levi H. and ano. to John M. Van Wagner et al., lots 188–195, Lacoma Park. 2,000

Mapes, John S. to Simon Garrigan, s s Cornell av, 250 w Mapes, 50x100. 460

Wilson, Wm. A. to Geo. W. Johnston, lot 274 n s 12th av, Wakefield, 100x114. 4,200

WHITE PLAINS.

Albro, Wm. H. to Benj. F. Haviland, w s Grand st, 416 s Quarropas st, 60x125. 1,050

Dykman, Henry T. to Hettie M. Young, w s Broadway, adj John W. Young, abt 100x300. 18,000

Genung, Merwin E. to Armenia Coventry, s s Post road, 60 e Davis av, abt 56x125. 600

Griffiths, Mary to Chas. Griffiths, lot 166 Battle Ridge. nom

Griffiths, Chas. to Sarah P. Griffiths, part lot 153 w s Kensico av, Battle Ridge, 90x218. 1,800

Young, Irving W. to Henry T. Dykman, w s Stewart pl, 250 n Lake st, 50x100. nom

Same to same, s e cor Railroad av and Rabbit st, abt 50x100. nom

YONKERS.

Armour Villa Park Assoc. to Ella W. Moore, lots 298 and 299. nom

Barnes, Ella L. to Johan D. Renz, part lot 94 map Hyatt farm, 50x—. 200

Blackwell, Jas. H. exr. of, to Franz Blatzheim, plots 2, 3 and 6 map of No. —, North Broadway. 7,850

Same to Cornelius J. Donovan, plot 1. 1,725

Same to Daniel E. Seybel, plots 4 and 5. 3,050

Butler, Wm. Allen to Nich. C. Kern, n w cor Van Cortlandt Park av and Wolffe st, 150x 101. 2,000

Brown, J. Romaine to Florence Frazer, n s Yonkers av, 645 w Walnut st, abt 50x110. 850

Crary, Jesse D. to T. Ashby Beall, lot 94 Armour Villa Park. nom

Cain, Jos. H. to J. Carrell Montanye, all grantors property at Lowerre Station. nom

Frazee, Florence to G. Hilton Scribner, n s Yonkers av, 595 w Walnut st, 50x100; also 695 w same, 50x110. 12,000

Fowler, Clarence M. to Mary H. Wright, lot 133 Shearwood Hill. 500

Lowerre, Warren H. to Herman Kramer, lot 84 Park Hill av, City map. 2,500

Lowerre, Seaman to same, n s Randolph st, 100 e South Broadway, 25x160. 1,000

Lockwood, Wm. A. to Fred. Doty and ano., No. 62 Post st, City map. 546

Ludlow, Thos. B et al to Robt. La M. Calkins, w s Fairfield road, 450 s Pier st, abt 43x153. 2,500

Monrovia Park Co. to W. A. Stokes, lots 155 and 156 s s Cambridge av, 50x100. nom

Montanye, J. Carrell to J. Romain Brown, s e cor South Broadway and Lawrence st, abt 100x110. nom

Rockwell, Phebe B. to Alice H. Schlesinger, No. 94, s s, Ashburton av, City map, 160x218. 10,000

MORTGAGES.

Note.—The arrangement of this list is as follows: The first name is that of the mortgagor, the next that of the mortgagee. The description of the property then follows, then the date of the mortgage, the time for which it was given, and the amount. The general dates used as headings are the dates when the mortgage was handed into the Register's office to be recorded.

Whenever the letters "P. M." occur, preceded by the name of a street, in these lists of mortgages, they mean that it is a Purchase Money Mortgage, and for fuller particulars see the list of transfers under the corresponding date. Whenever the rate is not given, read as 6 per cent.

NEW YORK CITY.

OCTOBER 30, 31, NOVEMBER 2, 3, 4, 5.

Armstrong, John to John J. Brady. Lebanon st. P. M. Oct. 19, due Nov. 5, 1891, 5 %. $789

Appell, Jacob to Edward A. Smith. 23d st. P. M. Nov. 2, due Jan. 1, 1897, or installs., 5 %. 15,000

Baer, Herriet widow to Emma Gutman et al. exrs. Mayer Gutman. Av B. P. M. Nov. 2, 4 years, 5 %. 10,000

Benedix, Oswald to Julius B. Denicke. Bainbridge av, n s, 122.8 e Southern Boulevard, 22.8x110.8. Nov. 2, 5 years. 1,000

Bissell, Josephine H. to THE TITLE GUARANTEE AND TRUST CO. 25th st. P. M. Oct. 31, due Nov. 4, 1893, 5 %. 7,000

Barrow, Spencer to John J. Brady. Crotona av. P. M. Oct. 19, due Nov. 5, 1894, 5 %. 906

Boss, John F. to John J. Brady. Tremont. av. P. M. Oct. 19, due Nov. 5, 1894, 5 %. 3,000

Bjorkegren, Charles to John J. Brady. Elmwood pl. P. M. Oct. 19, due Nov. 5, 1894, 5 %. 420

Bleistift, Abraham I. to Mary J. McWhorter and ano. exrs. and trustees John E. McWhorter. 4th st, No. 273 E. P. M. Nov. 2, due Nov. 1, 1893, 5 %. 10,000

Same to Nancy L. Sherwood and Mary E. Blodgett. 4th st, No. 275 E. P. M. Nov. 2, due Nov. 1, 1893, 5 %. 10,000

Bousquet, John to THE UNION TRUST CO. of New York as trustee. 24th st, No. 325, n s, 425 e 2d av, 25x98.9. Oct. 22, due Nov. 1, 1894, 5 %. 8,000

Bowes, Winifred wife of John to John McLaughlin. 77th st, n s, 285 9 w Av A, 62.2x 102.2. Oct. 30, due Nov. 5, 1891. 21,000

Bracken, James to John J. Brady. Crotona av. P. M. Oct. 19, due Nov. 5, 1894, 5 %. 1,590

Brierly, John J. to Henry P. De Graaf. Forest av. P. M. Nov. 2, 1 year, 5 %. 2,000

Bullwinkel, Charlotte M. to Philip Kaiser. 116th st, No. 308, s s, 300 e 2d av, 15x100.10. Oct. 31, due Nov. 1, 1893, 5 %. 500

Burnstine, William and Jacob Rosenberg to Jane E. Cusack, Brooklyn, and Auguste L. Sovestre. Bayard st. P. M. Sept. 30, installs. 5,000

Boettcher, Augusta to Ambrose K. Ely as trustee for Lena B. C. Evans. 12th st. s s, 100 w 3d av, 15x106.6. Oct. 26, 5 years, 5 %. 5,000

Boylston, Joseph to Elizabeth Barker. 37th st, No. 233, n s, 205 w 2d av, 25x66.11x25.3x63.3. Oct. 30, due April 1, 1896, 5 %. 1,000

Buhler, Caroline A. to THE UNITED STATES TRUST CO. of New York. Stanton st, s e cor Pitt st; runs south 100 x east 100 x north 25 x west 50 x north 75 to Stanton st, x west 50. Oct. 30, due Nov. 1, 1896, 5 %. 45,000

Same to same. 52d st, s s, 285 e 8th av, 20x 100.5. Oct. 30, due Nov. 1, 1886, 5 %. 15,000

Butler, Walter to Ernest McNeill. 151st st, n s, 275.3 e Morris av, 25x117.11x25x117. Oct. 30, 5 years. 1,000

Baker, John E. to Harriet J. and Julia Cruger. 134th st, n s, 175 e Lincoln av, 50x100. Nov. 4, due Nov. 1, 1892. 8,000

Bannon, John to THE METROPOLITAN LIFE INS. CO. of New York. 85th st, s s, 150 e Columbus av, 25x102.2. Nov. 5, due Oct. 1, 1894, 6 and 5 %. 28,000

Bannen, John to Stephen G. Bogert and ano. trustees Richard J. Morgan dec'd. 120th st, n s, 110 w 2d av, 3 lots, each 25x100.11. 3 morts., each $15,000. Nov. 5, 5 years, 5 %. gold, 45,000

Same to William Hall's Sons. 120th st, n s, 185 w 2d av, 50x100.11. Nov. 5, 1 year. 3,000

Becker, Jacob and Bernard Schopp to Leonard Scott. 16th st, s s, 195.6 e Av A, 25x103.3. Nov. 5, 10 years, 4½ and 5½ %. 10,000

Berlinger, Robert to Louis Aaron. Broome st. P. M. 2d mort. Nov. 2, due Nov. 1, 1894. 2,000

Beecher, Henry, Jr., to John J. Brady. Prospect av. P. M. Oct. 19, due Nov. 5, 1894, 5 %. 510

Bishop, Thomas to The Jacob Hoffmann Brewing Co. Hamilton st, No. 5, n s, 16.4x51.5x 16.4x50.8. Nov. 4, demand. 525

Brady, James W. to Mary wife of Patrick Garvin. 45th st, s s, 233 e 3d av, 27x100.4. Nov. 4, due Jan. 1, 1898, 5 %. 2,500

Britsch, William to Frank S. Stueber. 85th st, n s, 107.9 e 4th av, 25.7x102.2. Nov. 5, 1 year. 4,000

Brown, Jane R. A. to THE TITLE GUARANTEE AND TRUST CO. 72d st, No. 120, s s, 175 w Columbus av, 25x102.2. Nov. 2, due Nov. 5, 1896, 4½ %. 30,000

Carey, Charles P., Jr., to John W. Carey. 35th st, s s, 75 w 1st av, 25x98.9. Nov. 4, due April 1, 1897. 1,990

Same to Elizabeth Smith. Same property. Nov. 4, due April 1, 1897. 1,990

Charpentier, Rosalie to Ferdinand R. Minrath. 24th st, s s, 80 e 7th av, 20x90. Sub. to mort. $12,500. Oct 31, 1 year. 1,000

Cornet, William H. and Jacob A. Zimmermann to Max S. Korn. 5th av and 114th st. P. M. Nov. 5, due Sept. 4, 1893, 5 %. 4,000

Coyle, John to Thomas C. T. Crain as Chamberlain New York. 106th st, s s, 250 e Columbus av, 25x100.11. Nov. 5, 2 years, 4½ %. 10,000

Campbell, Mary to Peter Farrell. Jefferson av, s e s, part lot 144 map Samuel Ryer homestead, 24th Ward, 25x127. Sub. to mort. $800. Oct. 29, 6 months. See Conveys. 100

Cary, R. Anna wife of and Alanson to THE FRANKLIN SAVINGS BANK. 77th st, s s, 250 w Central Park West, 25x102.2. Oct. 30, 1 year, 5 %. 38,000

Chavin, Henry F. to Beadleston & Woerz, a corporation. Rivington st, No. 251. Store lease. Oct. 27, demand. 1,000

Chesebro, Denison P. Frank Larkin and Alfred E. Davidson, of Chesebro, Whitman & Co., to William S. Whitman. 1st av, s w cor 64th st, 50.5x100. Sub. to mort. $3,000. Oct. 30, due April 1, 1894. 3,500

Same to Elizabeth Shepherd. Same property Leasehold. Oct. 29, 3 years. 5,000

Clearwater, Edward to THE TWELFTH WARD SAVINGS BANK. 126th st, Nos. 109 and 111, n s, 140 e Park av, 50x99.11. Oct. 28, 1 year. 5,000

Creeden, James to THE EMIGRANT INDUST. SAVINGS BANK. 1st av, e s, 71 n 10th st, 23.8 x94. Oct. 31, 1 year, 4½ %. 15,000

Cronly, John E. mortgagor with Emma R. Riblet. Extension of mort. Oct. 28. nom

Cunningham, James to Morris Franklin, Fanny M. Updike and Henry B. Weselman. Lewis st. P. M. May 1, 6 months. 12,000

Chanler, William A. to THE NEW YORK LIFE INS. AND TRUST CO 3d av, e s, 22 s Westchester av, 51x79. Oct. 1, due Aug. 1, 1894, 5 %. 15,000

Clarke, Mabel mortgagor with Hannah Benrimo mortgagee. Extension of reduced mort. at 5 %. Oct. 29. nom

Cochran, Eva S. wife of William F., Yonkers, N. Y., mortgagee with Charles T. Ryan mortgagor. Extension of mort. Oct. 29. nom

Cohen, Benjamin F. to Frederic J. Middlebrook, Brooklyn. Delancey st, s w cor Eldridge st. P. M. Nov. 2, 1 year, 5 %. 16,000

Same to same. Delancey st, s s, 25 w Eldridge st. P. M. Nov. 2, 1 year, 5 %. 11,000

Same to same. Eldridge st, w s, 75.1 s Delancey st. P. M. Nov. 2, 1 year, 5 %. 9,000

Same to same. Delancey st, s w cor Eldridge st. P. M. Nov. 2, 1 year, 5 %. 6,000

Cohen, George J. to Leopold Katzenstein. 96th st. P. M. Oct. 30, due Nov. 2, 1894, 5 %. 15,000

Coleman, Sophia wife of Myer to THE CONNECTICUT MUTUAL LIFE INS. CO., Hartford, Conn. 29th st, No. 214, s s, 201 w 7th av, 24.10x98.9. Nov. 2, 5 years, 5 %. 10,000

Connolly, Dermott J. and Martin Potter to Peter Doelger. 2d av, No. 1512, s e cor 79th st Store lease. Oct. 31, demand. 2,500

Conover, Lawrence V. to Jennie C. Johnston guard. of Arthur H. Clincby. 162d st, s s, 388.11 w Elton av, 75x100. Oct. 30, 3 years, 5 %. 10,000

Cotter, John and Nicholas to The Bradley & Currier Co. (Lim.) 138th st, s s, 156.6 e Alexander av, 175x100. Sub. to morts. $107,500. Sept. 8, 8 months. 14,000

Crear, David to THE TITLE GUARANTEE AND TRUST CO. 105th st, No. 55, n s, 225 e Columbus av, 31x100.11. Oct. 31, due Nov. 2, 1894, 5 %. 20,000

Same to same. 105th st, No. 53, n s, 256 e Columbus av, 19x100.11. Oct. 31, due Nov. 2, 1894, 5 %. 15,000

Cummings, Richard to Frederic J. Middlebrook, Brooklyn. 123d st. P. M. Nov. 2, 3 years, 5 %. 13,000

Same to same. Same property. P. M. Sub. to last mort. Nov. 2, 1 year, 5 %. 2,000

Chedsey, Francis B. to William R. Beal Land Improvement Co., Crimmins av. P. M. Oct. 22, due July 8, 1894, 5 %. 700

Crosby, Darius G. Scarsdale, N. Y., to Frank W. Blauvelt. Edgecombe av. P. M. Nov. 2, 3 years, 5 %. 6,000

Curran, Ellen J., Francis W., John J. and Jennie E. and Mary C. Anglim to The Hebrew Benevolent and Orphan Asylum Society of the City of New York. 20th st, No. 331, n s, 399 9 w 8th av, 20.9x92x24.9x92. Nov. 2, due Nov. 4, 1894, 5 %. 10,000

Daly, Elizabeth T. individ. and trustee John H. and Mary A. Woodgate both dec'd to Joseph F. Daly. 31st st, No. 50, s s, 80 w 4th av, 17.6x98.9; 31st st, No. 48, s s, 97.6 w 4th av, 17.6x98.9. Oct. 31, due Nov. 1, 1896, 5 %. 4,800

Downey, Charles and George W. Curry to John L. Douglass as trustee. Park av, s w cor 93d st, 100.8x105. Sub. to morts Building agreement loan. Nov. 2, 3 months.

Dunkhorst, Louis to George Ehret. 8th av, No. 2716, s e cor 144th st. Store lease. Nov. 2, demand. See Conveys. 1,000

Dalker, Mina wife of and George to THE INSTITUTION FOR THE SAVINGS OF MERCHANTS' CLERKS. 81st st, s e cor Amsterdam av, 42x102.2. P. M. Oct. 23, 3 years, 4½ %. gold, 60,000

Same to same. 81st st, s s, 42 e Amsterdam av, 37x102.2. P. M. Oct. 23, 3 years, 4½ %. gold, 30,000

Same to same. 81st st, s s, 79 e Amsterdam av, 37x102.2. P. M. Oct. 23, 3 years, 4½ %. gold, 30,000

Same to John Casey. 81st st, Nos. 176, 178, 180, s e cor Amsterdam av, 116x102.2. Sub. to morts. $120,000. Oct. 23, due May 1, 1892, 5 %. 18,000

Dale, Anna T. wife of and James S. to Martha Kemp. 160th st, s s, 183.4 e St. Nicholas av, 18x100. Oct. 29, due April 3, 1893. 6,500

Same to Mary H. Sutton, North Andover, Mass. 160th st, s s, 201.4 e St. Nicholas av, 18x100. Oct. 29, due April 3, 1893. 6,500

Daub, Leonhard to Theresa Doerner. 5th st, n s, 307.8 e Av C, runs east 16 11 x north 53 x still north 30.5 x west 1 x north 13.8 x west 16.4 x south 96.11 to beginning. Oct. 30, due Dec. 30, 1894, 5 %. 5,000

Daub, Leonhard to THE UNITED STATES TRUST CO. of New York. 49th st. P. M. Nov. 2, due Nov. 1, 1896, 5 %. 12,000

Daly, Cornelius to James Millward and William P. Richardson, of Millward & Co. 34th st, s s, 63 e 11th av, 75x98.9. Lease. Oct. 30, note. 5,626

Detrick, Adeline F. wife of William W. to Lizzie S. Stocker, Cooperstown, N. Y. 46th st, No. 140, s s, 310 e 7th av, 15x100.4. Oct. 31, due Jan 1, 1895, 5 %. 2,000

D'Herblay, Emilie L. to Donald Mackay exr. Elizabeth R. B. King. 13th st, s s, 175 e 5th av, 23x92.9x—x94.6. Oct. 31, due March 14, 1893, 5 %. 900

Di Lorenzo, Gregorio to Susan B. Hutchison, Brooklyn. Fox st, w s, 112.6 n 169th st, runs west 69.8 x southwest 50.3 to n e s of st, x northwest 91.10 x northeast 67.6 x southeast 50.7 x south 25 x east 85 to Fox st, x south 30. Nov. 2, 3 years. See Conveys. 1,100

Duffy, Michael to John J. Brady. Crotona av and Elmwood pl. P. M. Oct. 19, due Nov. 5, 1894, 5 %. 1,515

Duggin, Charles to Josephine B. Meeks. 4th av, n w cor 41st st, runs west 80 x north — x east 45 x 35 6 to av, x south 92.9. Oct. 30, demand. 13,500

Dwyer, Denis J. and William Haigh to THE EQUITABLE LIFE ASSUR. Soc. of the U. S. 147th st, s s, 196 w Av St. Nicholas, 4 lots, each 20x99.11. 4 morts., each $15,000. Oct. 30, due Jan. 1, 1893, 5 %. gold, 60,000

Dolan, Timothy J. and Mary E. his wife to Mary Corsa. Mapes av, s e s, 265 n e Samuel st, 66x150. Aug. 21, 2 years. 800

Dooper, Auke mortgagee to L. Buttenwieser, present owner. Certificate of payment of $1,000 on account of mortgage made by Nathan Cohen to Auke Dooper, Nov. 1, 1890, and statement that amount due thereon is 4,000

Engster, Albert to Eva Bechtel extrx. George Bechtel. Elizabeth st, No. 125. Store lease. Nov. 5, note, 3 months. 350

Eckel, Helena S. wife of and August to THE FRANKLIN SAVINGS BANK. 7th av, Nos. 333 and 335, and No. 160 West 29th st, begins 7th av, s e cor 29th st, 49.4x98.5x49.4x97.6. Nov. 2, 1 year, 5 %. See Conveys. 27,000

Favorat, Johanna D. to THE TITLE GUARANTEE AND TRUST CO. 114th st P. M. Nov. 2, 3 years, 5 %. 12,000

Fernandez, Joseph M. to S. Sidney Smith and ano. exrs. Margaret E. de Fernandez. 130th st, s s, 200 w 7th av, 25x99.11. Bond $10,000 to secure annuity. Oct. 31, installs, per year. 600

Fernandez, Joseph M. devisee of Margaret E. de Fernandez to Frederic R. Coudert and ano. exrs Edward Stern. 5th av, No. 603, e s, 78 s 49th st, 22.5x100. Sub. to mort. $50,000. Oct. 30, 1 year. gold, 6,000

French, Ada L. to John J. Brady. Prospect av. P. M. Oct. 19, due Nov. 5, 1894, 5 %. 720

Fuller, J. Ensign, Chicago, Ill., to Clament A. White. 23d st, n s, 100 e 7th av, 22x112.6. Sept. 5, due Nov. 5, 1892. 6,000

Furlong, Martin to THE EMIGRANT INDUST. SAVINGS BANK. Columbus (9th) av, e s, 99.1 n 96th st, 26.8x100. Oct. 31, 1 year, 4½ %. 10,000

Fish, John, New York, and Jacob Miller, Astoria, L. I., to George Gerlach. 29th st, n s, 100 w 2d av, 25x98.9. Nov. 4, 1 year. 5,000

Friedman, Rosa wife of Benjamin to Henry E. Crampton exr. Dorcas M. Crampton. 4th st. P. M. Nov. 2, 5 years, 4½ %. 9,000

Same to Samson Wells. Same property. Nov. 2, demand. 1,500

Falconer, William W. and Lidie C. his wife to William H. Falconer. 131st st, No. 105, n s, 93.9 w 6th av, 18.9x99.11. Oct. 28, 3 years, 5 %. 5,000

Farley, John T. to William D. Manning. 70th st, s s, 125 e Columbus av, 225x100.5. Oct. 30, due July 1, 1892, or sooner. 50,000

Flannery, Simon P. to Patrick H., Agnes L. and Francis V. Tracy. 63d st, No. 409, n s, 156 e 1st av. 25x100.5. Oct. 30, due Nov. 1, 1894, 5 %. 10,000

Fried, Philip to Samuel Greenfeld. Columbia st. P. M. Nov. 2, due Nov. 5, 1895, or installs. 3,006

Same to Clara A. Feuchtwanger. Same property. P. M. Nov. 5, 5 years, 5 %. 10,000

Same to The Jacob Hoffman Brewing Co. Same property. Nov. 2, 2 years, without interest. 2,000

Garland, Samuel to Henry P. De Graaf. 163d st. P. M. Nov. 5, 5 years, 5 %. 4,000

Greenfeld, Samuel to GERMAN-AMERICAN REAL ESTATE TITLE GUARANTEE CO. Goerck st. P. M. Nov. 2, due May 5, 1892, 5 %. 7,000

Greenwald, Pauline to Max S. Korn. 36th st. P. M. Nov. 5, due Nov. 1, 1894, 5 %. 2,500

Gordon, Louis to Laemmlein Buttenweiser. Essex st, No. 101. P. M. Nov. 4, installs. 2,250

Gallagher, Kate wife of and Joseph F. to Juliet Douglas. 72d st, No 416, s s, 238 e 1st av, 25x102.2. Oct. 29, 3 years. 20,000

Same to Louis Roller individ and trustee for creditors. 72d st, Nos. 414 and 416, s s, 213 e 1st av, 50x102.2. Sub. to morts. $43,684. Secures bond of Joseph F. Gallagher. Oct. 29. 7,826

Same to The Bradley & Currier Co. (Lim.) 72d st, s s, 213 e 1st av, 25x102.2. Sub. to mort. $19,000. Oct. 28, 6 months. 2,684

Same to August Caille. 72d st, s s, 213 e 1st av, 25x102.2. Oct. 27, due Oct. 30, 1896, 5 %. 19,000

Same to William Caille, Jr. 72d st, s s, 238 e 1st av, 25x102.2. Oct. 27, due Oct. 30, 1892. 2,000

Gallagher, Patrick and Charles to J. Chr. G. Hupfel Brewing Co. 7th av, No. 382. Lease. Oct. 30, demand. 1,750

Gatfield, George to Edward. Wood et al exrs. and trustees Silas Wood. 127th st, s s, 360 e Lenox av, 25x99.11. Oct. 30, 3 years, 5 %. 8,000

Goldstein, Jacob to Isaac Levy. Ludlow st, No. 7, w s, 25x87.6. Oct. 28, due Nov. 1, 1894. See Conveys. 5,000

Gallagher, Elizabeth F. to John J. Brady. Lots 17, 89, 90, 91, 141, 142 map of Ryer homestead. P. M. Oct. 19, due Nov. 5, 1894, 5 %. 3,378

Greenfeld, Samuel to Norman S. Walker, Jr., trustee for Georgie G. and Bryce Stewart. Columbia st, No. 116, e s, 24.10 n Stanton st, 21.8x75.4. Nov. 2, due Dec. 1, 1894, 5 %. 19,000

Glass, Isabella wife of John to Mary L. Breese guard. of Eloise L. Breese. Washington st, s e cor Gansevoort st, 24.6x81.10x24.4x80. Oct. 27, 3 years, 5 %. gold, 35,000

Grau, George to Frank Kuhn. 6th st. P. M. Nov. 1, demand. 5,000

Gildersleeve, William H. to THE DRY DOCK SAVINGS INST. Av C, s e cor 6th av, 48 6x60. Nov. 4, due Nov. 1, 1892, 5 %. 5,000

Same to George V. Sloat. Same property. Nov. 4, 1 year. 8,000

Godwin, Sarah wife of William M. to THE EMIGRANT INDUST. SAVINGS BANK. 145th st, s s, 153.4 e 3d av or Boston road, 25x100. Nov. 4, 1 year, 4½ %. 3,000

Goldstein, Morris and Sarah his wife to Leopold Haas. Essex st, No. 85, w s, 25x87.6. Collateral to another mortgage. Nov. 2, due March 1, 1894. 10,000

Hasell, Mary M., formerly Jones, to Henry de F. Weekes. Warren st, n s, 125 e College pl, 25x175.10 to Chambers st, being 52 Warren st and 122 Chambers st. ½ part. Nov. 5, due Nov. 1, 1892 6,000

Hearn, John to Jane D. Cock, Locust Valley, L. I. 28th st, s s, 75 e 2d av, 25x74.1. Nov. 4, due Nov. 1, 1893, 5 %. 1,000

Hogan, Patrick to Marx and Moses Ottinger. 7th av and 142d st. P. M. Nov. 5, due July 1, 1892. 31,000

Same to same. Same property. P. M. Building loan. Nov. 5, 6 months. 30,000

Howe, Samuel to THE EMIGRANT INDUST. SAVINGS BANK. 2d av, No. 574, e s, 47.9 s 32d st, 25.6x72. Nov. 4, 1 year, 4½ %. 8,000

Haigh, William to THE EQUITABLE LIFE ASSUR. SOC. of the United States. 147th st, s s, 175 w Av St. Nicholas, 21x99.11. Oct. 31, due Jan. 1, 1893, 5 %. gold, 15,000

Herdtfelder, Elizabeth to Morris S. Thompson and ano. exrs. and trustees Charlotte A. Swords. Eldridge st, No. 196, e s, 80 n Rivington st, 24 x ½ the block. Nov. 2, 5 years, 5 %. 11,400

Hess, John and Anna to Henry Arnold. 83d st. P. M. Oct. 31, installs, 5 %. 7,500

Haaren, John W. to THE EQUITABLE LIFE ASSUR. SOC. of the United States. 67th st. P. M. Oct. 30, due Jan. 1, 1894, 5 %. gold, 13,000

Hall, Henry B. to William R. Beal Land Improvement Co. 141st st. P. M. Oct. 22, due July 8, 1894, 5 %. 1,550

Same to same. Crimmins av. P. M. Oct. 22, due July 8, 1894, 5 %. 700

Hendricks, Joshua and ano. exrs. and trustees Fanny Hendricks with Sophia Cohen individ. and extrx. and trustee Louis H. Cohen. Extension of mort. Oct. 11. nom

Hernstein, Esther wife of Albert L. to Lawrence Frazier & Co. College av, n w s, 150 n e 138th st, 55x125 to Mott Haven Canal, x18.8 x115, with rights, &c., in canal. Oct. 28, demand. 7,000

Herpich, Charles A. to Adolphe Haendler. Mercer st, No. 93. Lease. Oct. 15. 30,000

Herter, Peter, Jersey City, and Frank W. Herter, to Sender Jarmulowsky. Pike st, Nos. 33, 35 and 37 and Nos. 157, 159 and 161 Madison st, begins Pike st, n e cor Madison st, runs north 73 x east 89.7 x south 27.2 x west 8.6 x south 45.10 to Madison st, x west 81, with use of alley. Oct. 30, due May 19, 1893. 14,500

Same to John J. Jones and ano. trustees David Jones dec'd. Same property. Oct. 30, 6 months, 5 %. 65,000

Hohmann, Katherina widow to Andrew Stoeckel. 148th st, s s, 166.8 e Brook av, 16.8x100. Oct. 26, 1 year. 300

Herzog, Nina widow to THE MANHATTAN SAVINGS INST. Broadway, No. 686, e s, 41.2 n Great Jones st, 41.2x130 to Cross lane. Nov. 4, 5 years, 4½ %. 125,000

Hickey, John J. and Michael J. Jennings to George Ehret. 3d av, No. 1110. Lease. Nov. 2, demand. 5,000

Hoerle, Henry C. to Harmon W. Hendricks. 21st st, s s, 125 w 8th av, 25x91.11. Nov. 4, due May 15, 1892. 15,000

Same owner and mortgagor with same mortgagee. Agreement as to priority of mortgage, &c. Nov. 4. nom

Jacobs, Elias to The Baron de Hirsch Fund. Pitt st, No. 133. P. M. Oct. 26, due Oct. 30, 1896, 5 %. 15,000

Jarvis, David, Brooklyn, to Matilda Reynolds trustee for George Ross. 118th st. P. M. Oct. 27, 3 years, 5 %. 4,000

Jones, Annie to Nancy Aaron. 65th st. P. M. Nov. 2, 2 years, 4½ %. 8,500

Jencks, Francis M. to THE FRANKLIN TRUST CO. 77th st, n s, 210 w West End av, 90x102.2. Sub. to mort. $50,000. Nov. 2, due Dec. 15, 1891. 40,000

Kruse, Anna to THE GERMAN-AMERICAN REAL ESTATE TITLE GUARANTEE CO. 25th st, s s, 150 w 1st av. P. M. Oct. 30, due Nov. 5, 1894, 5 %. 7,500

Kavanagh, William J. to John J. Brady. Oakland pl. P. M. Oct. 19, due Nov. 5, 1894, 5 %. 324

Knapp, Sheppard to John T., William H. and Mary C. Hepburn, Sarah H. Roberts, Belle H. Edmonds, Julia A. Bell and Annie E. and Kate S. Baker. 13th st. P. M. Oct. 17, due Sept. 1, 1894, 5 %. gold, 16,000

Knolhoff, John F. W., East Orange, N. J., to John E. and Christian F. Glimm exrs. Christian Glimm. 24th st, No. 150, s s, 175 e 7th av, 25x98.9. Nov. 2, 5 years, 5 %. 17,000

Kotlowsky, Philip to Frederic J. Middlebrook, Brooklyn. Allen st. P. M. Nov. 2, 1 year, 5 %. 10,000

Kaufmann, Alexander to Frederic J. Middlebrook, Brooklyn. 58th st, s e cor Park av, 20x80; 58th st, s s, 38 e Park av, runs south 80 x east 36 x south 20.5 x east 36 x south 20.5 x east 36 x north 100.5 to 58th st, x west 72; 65th st, n s, 20 e Park av, 20x80; 65th st, n s, 60 e Park av, 20x80; 117th st, n s, 168.6 e Pleasant av, 36x100.10. ¼ part. Sub. to morts. $19,500. Nov. 5, 1 year. 10,000

Kempner, Samuel to Elbert Hegeman, Jr., Brooklyn. 2d av. P. M. Oct. 28, 5 years, 5 %. 5,000

Kennedy, Margaret J. and Letitia to Patrick Keating. 38th st, No. 548, s s, 600 w 10th av, 25x98.9. Oct. 29, due Nov. 1, 1892, 5 %. 3,000

Keating, James P. and Thomas W. Byrnes to The J. Chr. Hupfel G. Brewing Co. 3d av, No. 507, store; 34th st, No. 201 E., store and cellar. Lease. Oct. 27, demand. 6,000

Kilpatrick, Edward to The American Bible Soc. West End av, e s, 19.11 s 98th st, 18x100. Nov. 5, 3 years, 5 %. 15,000

Same to same. West End av, e s, 37.11 s 98th st, 18x100. Nov. 5, 3 years, 5 %. 15,000

Same to The Nursery and Childs Hospital. West End av, e s, 73.11 s 98th st, 18x100. Nov. 5, 3 years, 5 %. 15,000

Klein, Benedict A. to Robert S. Minturn trustee for Susan C. Baring. Cherry st, No. 258, n s, 26.3 e Rutgers st, 26.8x95.8x26.8x96.2. Nov. 4, 5 years, 5 %. gold, 20,000

Same to Robert S. Minturn and ano. trustees for Eliza T. Minturn. Cherry st, No. 260, n s, 52.11 e Rutgers st, 26x95.2x20x95.8. Nov. 4, 5 years, 5 %. gold, 20,000

Same to Robert S. Minturn and ano. trustees for Anna M. wife of Charles P. Quieke. Cherry st, No. 264, n s, 130.8 e Rutgers st, runs north 114.11 x west 25.8 x south 20.8 x east 0.7 x south 94.8 to st, x east 25. Nov. 4, 5 years, 5 %. gold, 21,000

Same to same. Cherry st, No. 262, n s, 78.11 e Rutgers st, 26.9x94.8x26.8x95.2. Nov. 4, 5 years, 5 %. gold, 19,000

Lehmann, Moses and Mina his wife to Margaretha Worth. 1st av. P. M. Nov. 2, due Aug. 1, 1892, 5 %. 7,000

Lenz, August to John F. Anthes. 2d av, No. 1540, e s, 25 n 80th st, 25x80. Nov. 2, due Dec. 20, 1894, 5 %. 8,000

Same to Margaretha Rauch. Same property. Nov. 2, 3 years, 5 %. 2,000

Leonard, Arthur G. to Albert M. Howell. 49th st. P. M. Sub. to mort. $9,000. Nov. 2, 1 year, 5 %. 3,000

Limbert, August trustee Frederick C. Gebhard dec'd to Edward H. Pirsson. Certificate of satisfaction of mort. Oct. 6. ——

Lindsey, Josiah S. to Benjamin F. Cohen. Morton st. P. M. Sub. to morts. $12,000. Nov. 2, due Oct. 1, 1892. 6,900

Same to same. Same property. Sub. to morts. $18,900. Nov. 2, due Oct. 1, 1892. 11,000

Loonie, James J. and Eugene Parker to August Paffen. Forsyth st, No. 70. P. M. Nov. 4, due Nov. 1, 1892. 5,000

Lamarche, John V., Brooklyn, to Leonard Lewisohn. Tremont and Jefferson avs. P. M. Oct. 29, 3 years, 5 %. 1,200

Livingston, Mary T. wife of and Robert R., Clermont, N. Y., to Susan M. C. Livingston. 9th st, No. 9 E. P. M. Oct. 29, due Nov. 1, 1894, 4½ %. 11,000

Same to Robert Winthrop. Same property. P. M. Oct. 29, due Oct. 30, 1894, 4½ %. 22,000

Lozier, Sarah J. wife of Abraham W. to William D. Warden, Burgess Hill, near Brighton, England. 136th st, n s, 168.4 w 8th av, 16.8x98.9. Oct. 30, 3 years, 5 %. 3,000

Lynch, Franklin to William R. Beal Land Improvement Co. Crimmins av. P. M. Oct. 22, due July 8, 1894, 5 %. 700

Lyon, Charles B. to New York and Suburban Co-operative Building and Loan Assoc. 184th st, n s, part lot 26 map heirs Rebecca Bassford, Fordham, 25x72.8. Oct. 29, installs, 5 %. 2,000

Linde, Catharine to George C. Currier. 7th av, e s, 50.11 n 120th st. P. M. Feb. 11, due Feb. 27, 1892, 5 %. 2,000

Same to same. 120th st, n s, 109 e 7th av. P. M. Feb. 11, due Feb. 27, 1892, 5 %. 1,500

Lumley, Alexander, Paris, France, to Cornelia U. Elliott, Baltimore, Md. 27th st, s s, 200 e 6th av, 23x98.9. Sept. 18, due Sept. 28, 1894, 5 %. 25,000

Lynch, Franklin to William R. Beal Land Improvement Co. 141st st. P. M. Oct. 22, due July 8, 1894, 5 %. 1,750

Lynch, Samuel to William R. Fosdick exr. Elizabeth J. Fosdick. Lenox av and 137th st. P. M. Nov. 2, 2 years, 5 %. 7,500

Lennon, Hugh to John McLoughlin. Walnut st, e s, lot 41 map Wilton, Port Morris and East Morrisania, 25x100. Nov. 5, 5 years or installs, 5 %. 1,700

Lindsley, Charles H. to Isaac L. Kip trustee for Adelaide B. Harris and Cornelia B. Kip. 83d st, n s, 210 w 8th av, 80x102.2. Nov. 5, 6 months, 5 %. 75,000

Martin, C. Grayson and W. Clarence to Charles E. Tracy and ano. trustees James Bogert dec'd. 36th st. P. M. Nov. 2, due Nov. 1, 1894, 5 %. gold, 22,500

Martin, William R. to Donald Mackay. 35th st, No. 159, n s, 123 w 3d av, 23x98.9. Oct. 30, due Nov. 1, 1894, 5 %. 20,000

McLeod, Sarah B. to David Richey. 84th st. P. M. Nov. 2, 2 years or installs. 7,850

Michalisky, Ida to James J. Loonie and Eugene Parker. Forsyth st. P. M. Oct. 29, 5 years, 5 %. 27,000

Same to same. Same property. P. M. 2d mort. Oct. 29, installs. 4,100

Maas, Lewis to Samuel Rice. Broome st, s e cor Clinton st, 40x47. Oct. 31, due Nov. 1, 1892, 5 %. 3,500

McElroy, Owen F. and William to John W. Stevens. 96th st, n s, 70 e Lexington av, 125x100.11. Sub. to morts. Oct. 24, demand. 7,000

Menzer, Conrad to Andrew Arvidson. Oakley st. P. M. Oct. 27, 3 years, 5 %. 450

Merklen, Michael to EMIGRANT INDUST. SAVINGS BANK. 17th st, s s, 168 w 1st av, 23x92. Oct. 29, 1 year, 4½ %. 4,200

Moore, James, Belleville, N. J., mortgagee with Sophia Cohen individ. and exr. and trustee Louis H. Cohen. Extension of mort. Oct. 11. nom

Moran, Theresa heir Peter and Ellen Saunier to Claudine M. Desaye. 65th st, s s, 100 e 11th av, 50x100.5. Oct. 22, 5 years, 5 %. 1,000

Mulholland, James to Maria D. Keyes. 44th st, s s, 175 e 11th av, 25x100.5. Oct. 30, due Nov. 1, 1892, or sooner. 3,000

Myers, Frederick S. to Henrietta F. Timpson widow, Brooklyn. 75th st, s s, 300 w 1st av, 49.4x102.2. Oct. 31, due Nov. 1, 1892, 5 %. 9,000

Miller, Eliza L. to THE UNITED STATES LIFE INS. CO., New York. Catharine st, Nos. 53 and 55, e s, 27x106.5x27x103.4. Oct. 31, due Oct. 1, 1896, 5 %. 27,000

Mitchell, Francis and Charles Weis to Jane Potter. 53d st. P. M. Oct. 31, 3 years, 5 %. gold, 13,000

Same to same. Same property. P. M. Sub. to last mort. Oct. 31, 1 year, 5 %. 1,000

Mogren, Nils to THE EMIGRANT INDUST. SAVINGS BANK. Henry st, No. 126, s s, 251.5 w Rutgers st, 27.4x99.11. Nov. 2, 1 year, 4½ %. 12,500

Muhlker, Henry to Alice S. H. Davies, New Haven, Conn. 115th st, n w cor Park av, 26x76.11. Oct. 31, due Nov. 2, 1896, 5 %. gold, 20,000

Same to same. 115th st, n s, 26 w Park av, 27x76.11. Oct. 31, due Nov. 2, 1896, 5 %. gold, 15,000

Mahan or Mabon, Elsie C. to Sarah A. Bourne. West st, s w s, lot 19 map Wardsville, 50x144x50.1x148. Nov. 2, 3 years. 500

Mandelbaum, Harris to Edward Knowlton. Henry st. P. M. Nov. 2, due Jan. 1, 1893, 5 %. 15,000

Martin, Eli to John R. Smith. 77th st, n s, 118.6 w Columbus av, 38.6x104.9x38.6x104. Sub. to morts. Oct. 28. Secures building materials to extent of 8,000

McPherson, Elizabeth to Ann R. Delnoce. 169th st, n s, 324.5 e Gerard av, 25x100. Oct. 29, 3 years or installs, 5 %. 2,200

Merritt, Mary M. to THE HARLEM SAVINGS BANK. 139th st, s s, 625 e Willis av, 25x100. Nov. 2, 1 year, 5 %. 4,000

Molyneaux, Wilbur L. to The William R. Beal Land Improvement Co. Crimmins av. P. M. Oct. 22, due July 8, 1894, 5 %. 700

Muhlfeld, Frank to Sophie Zeltner. Alexander av, No. 149, 25x72x100. Oct. 27, 1 year. 800

Muldoon, Cassie wife of Wm. H. to Henry Greenebaum. 79th st. Sub. to mort. $11,500. Nov. 4, 1 year. See Conveys. 5,384

Same to C. B. Keogh Mfg. Co. Same property. Sub. to morts. $16,884. Nov. 4, due April 1, 1892. 1,035

Murray, Susan to Bernheimer & Schmid. 2d av, No. 2177. Saloon lease. Nov. 2 note, demand. 3,000

Marden, Francis S. to Francis M. Wilmurt, Pelham Manor, N. Y. 89th st. P. M. Oct. 28, 3 years or installs, 5 %. 5,000

McKenna, James to The J. Chr. G. Hupfel Brewing Co. Spring st, No. 52. Store lease. Oct. 28, demand. 2,000

Mortimer, Thomas to The J. Chr. G. Hupfel Brewing Co. 1st av, No. 685, n w cor 39th st. Store lease. Oct. 19, demand. 2,500

Naegeli, Albert to THE NEW YORK LIFE INS. AND TRUST CO. 11th st, n s, 252.6 w 2d av, 25.6x100. Nov. 4, 5 years, 4½ %. 15,000

Nason, Alfred G. to Charles T. and Helen T. Barney. 76th st, n s, 100 e Columbus av, 100x102.2. Building loan. Oct. 26, demand. 60,000

Same to same. Same property. P. M. Oct. 26, demand. 72,000

Neis, Ferdinand to THE UNITED STATES TRUST CO., New York. 6th st, No. 405, n s, 70 e 1st av, 21.5x90.10. Nov. 4, due Nov. 1, 1892, 5 %. 12,000

Nesbitt, Hugh to Mount Morris Co-operative Building and Loan Assoc. 118th st, n s, 190 w 3d av, 20x100.11. Oct. 16, installs. 5,000

Norman, John A. to William R. Beal Land Improvement Co. Crimmins av. P. M. Oct. 22, due July 8, 1894, 5 %. 700

Orcutt, Susan widow to Valentine Moeslein. 85th st, s s, 425 w Central Park West. P. M. Sub. to morts. $42,500. Oct. 30, 1 year. 8,317

Same to William H. Simonson. Same property. Sub. to morts. $32,500. Oct. 30, 3 mos. 10,000

O'Brien, Michael to Louisa Grimm. 3d av, No. 1482, w s, 76.2 s 84th st, 26x93.6. Lease. Nov. 2, due Feb. 10, 1892. 7,800

Oates, Thomas J. to Irene B. Roberts and ano. exrs. Edward Roberts. 100th st. P. M. Nov. 2, 3 years, 4 %. 1,200

Oestreicher, Benjamin to Christian L. and Philipina Oehler. 2d av, w s, 25.6 n 73d st, 25.6x75. Oct. 31, installs. 4,300

O'Gorman, James and Ellen his wife to Louis Stern. 71st st. P. M. Nov. 2, 3 years or installs, 5 %. 4,000

Orr, William C. and Emma C. his wife to THE EMIGRANT INDUSTRIAL SAVINGS BANK. 76th st, s s, 155 e Columbus av, 19x102.2. Nov. 2, 1 year, 4½ %. 15,000

Poppe, Georgine E. E. wife of and Charles to THE GREENWICH SAVINGS BANK. West 4th st, No. 317, e s, 159.6 n Bank st, 20x75.3x20x75. Oct. 30, due Nov. 2, 1892, 5 %. 2,000

Postal, Jacob to Samuel Phillips. Ludlow st. P. M. Oct. 29, installs. 3,000

Quackenbush, Abraham and Daniel D. Lawson to THE GERMAN SAVINGS BANK. 25th st, s s, 155.9 w 7th av, 31x98.9. Oct. 31, due Nov. 2, 1892. 31,000

Rainsford, George D. to Rosa E. Rainsford. Broadway, w s, bet Liberty and Cortlandt sts, part of lots 155 and 157, being 39.6x110x40x110; Liberty st, e s, adj above, runs north 40 x west 4.6 x south 40 x east 4.6, being part 85 Liberty st. All title. Feb. 1, demand. gold, 6,375

Reim, Maggie heir Barbara Koetzner to August Freutel. 151st st, n s, 300 w Courtlandt av, 25x116.4x25x116.3. Nov. 2, due Nov. 1, 1894. 2,200

Robinson, Charles A. to Mary A. A. Woodcock, Bedford, N. Y. 24th st. P. M. Oct. 31, due Nov. 2, 1894, 5 %. 5,000

Reed, Charles H. to Hugh R. Hill trustee Edith A. Forwood. 29th st, No. 121, n s, 100 w Lexington av, 25x98.9. Nov. 2, 5 years, 5 %. gold, 30,000

Reilly, William to Patrick Mack. Grove av, n w s, 264 n e John st, 30x150. Oct. 29, 1 year. 100

Reinschmidt, John to John J. Brady. Crotona av. P. M. Oct. 19, due Nov. 5, 1894, 5 %. 420

Ramsey, Peter N. to Antonio Rasines. Madison av, Nos. 136 and 138, n w cor 31st st, 49.7x95. Oct. 24, 2 months. 13,000

Rapelye, Pheba C. to Franklin A. Thurston. 132d st, n s, 125 e Cypress av, 75x110. P. M. Oct. 2, demand. 2,400

Rohrs, Frederick to William I. Seaman, New Dorp, S. I. 102d st, n s, 52 e Park av, 50x100.11. Nov. 4, due Dec. 18, 1891. gold, 4,000

Romaine, Elizabeth A. wife of George E. to Jane Romaine. Bank st, n s, 100 e 4th st, 25x95. All title. Nov. 4, due Oct. 4, 1898, 5 %. 2,367

Ruland, Georgianna wife of and William to Mary Corsa. 175th st, n s, 31.1 e Webster av, 25x108. Nov. 4, 3 years. 3,600

Sackman, Peter to THE TITLE GUARANTEE AND TRUST CO. Amsterdam av. P. M. Oct. 30, 3 years, 5 %. 10,000

Schutt, John H. mortgagor with Leo G. Rosenblatt trustee for Sigmund G. Rosenblatt. Extension of mort. at 5 %. Nov. 4. nom

Scott, John S. to Morris Steinhardt. 111th st, n s, 50 w Madison av, 50x100.11. Building loan. Nov. 2, due June 1, 1892. 15,000

Sinnott, Catherine to Townsend & Mahan. 20th st, Nos. 414 and 416, s s, 199.6 e 1st av, 40x92. Nov. 4, due May 1, 1892, 5 %. 500

Stehr, Carl to Lucy R. Comfort. Fulton av, s e s, part lot 107 map Morrisania, 43.9x211. P. M. Nov. 4, 3 years, 4½ %. 4,000

Schafer, Simon to Charles Guidet. 113th st, n s, 220 w 3d av, 25x100.11. Oct. 29, 3 years, 5 %. gold, 17,500

Same to same. 113th st, n s, 245 w 3d av, 25x100.11. Oct. 29, 3 years, 5 %. gold, 17,500

Same to Peter Karsten. 113th st, No. 161, n s, 220 w 3d av, 25x100.11. Sub. to morts. $17,500. Oct. 30, 2 years, 5 %. gold, 2,500

Same to John Bell and Son. 113th st, n s, 245 w 3d av, 25x100.11. Sub. to mort. $17,500. Oct. 30, 6 months. 2,500

Smith, Catharine L. wife of Andrew J. to Phebe A. Henderson, Brooklyn. 112th st, No. 211, n s, 160 e 3d av, 20x100.5. Oct. 30, 3 years. 3,000

Shreiner, Joseph to Hyman and Henry Sonn. 88th st, n s, 246 w Av B, 100x100.8. Nov. 2, 1 year. See Conveys. 28,000

Same to same. Same property. P. M. Nov. 2, 1 year. 12,270

Scott, John S. to Morris Steinhardt. 111th st. P. M. Nov. 2, due June 1, 1892. 14,000

Shaw, George to D. Willis James. 86th st. P. M. Oct. 19, due Nov. 2, 1894, 4 %. 30,000

Shortemeier, Charles to Harriet Silliman, Brooklyn. 11th av, e s, 49.5 s 36th st, 24.8x100. Nov. 2, due Nov. 1, 1896, 5 %. 10,000

Smith, Thomas H. to Alexander Moore. 43d st. P. M. Nov. 2, due Nov. 1, 1893. 10,000

Sonn, Hyman and Henry to THE INSTITUTION FOR SAVINGS OF MERCHANTS' CLERKS. Greenwich st, s e cor Harrison st, 20.2x89.4x22.2x90.2. Nov. 2, 5 years, 4½ %. 35,000

Scott, Alfred B. to Julius A. Kohn. 72d st. P. M. Nov. 4, 1 year, 5 %. 5,000

Simonson, Egbert C. to Abraham Goldsmith. 104th st. P. M. Oct. 21, due April 30, 1892. 10,000

Same to Charles Weinberg. Same property. Oct. 21, due April 30, 1892. 10,000

Stewart, Walter H. to THE EMIGRANT INDUSTRIAL SAVINGS BANK. 92d st. P. M. Nov. 5, 1 year, 4½ %. 12,000

The Church of St. Charles Borromeo to THE EMIGRANT INDUST. SAVINGS BANK. 141st st, n s, 175 w 7th av, 125x199.10 to 142d st. Nov. 4, 1 year, 4½ %. 45,000

The Church of the Beloved Disciple, New York, to Sarah S. Runge. 89th st. P. M. Oct. 29, due Nov. 2, 1892, 5 %. 11,500

Telford, John to THE METROPOLITAN TRUST CO., New York, trustee William R. Garrison. 13th st, No. 148, s s, 200.6 e 7th av, 23.9x103.3. Oct. 30, due Nov. 1, 1894, 4½ %. 2,500

The Nassau Ferry Co. to Julia Waterbury, Brooklyn. All rights, privileges and franchises. Secures bonds. Nov. 1, 1882, 10 years, 5 %. 50,000

The John Eichler Brewing Co. to THE CENTRAL TRUST CO. trustee. 54th st, Nos. 207-221, n s, 94.11 e 3d av, runs east 190 x north 100.5 x west 150 x south 25.1 x west 40 x south 75.1 to beginning; 54th st, Nos. 218–224, s s, 210 e 3d av, 100x100.4, and all chattels, franchises, &c. Secures bonds. Oct. 1, 11 years, 5 %. gold. 250,000

Tuozzo, Theresa wife of and Donato to Jonas Weil and Bernhard Mayer. Mulberry st, No. 37, w s, 75.6 n Park st, 25.4x103.4x25.3x103.9. Collateral to above. Oct. 30. 23,000

Same to same. 102d st. P. M. Oct. 30, installs. 23,000

Vredenburgh, Harriet M. to THE HARLEM SAVINGS BANK. Monroe av, e s, 158.4 n Columbia av, 16.8x100. Nov. 2, 1 year, 5 %. 2,000

Same to same. Monroe av, e s, 141.8 n Columbia av, 16.8x100. Nov. 2, 1 year, 5 %. 2,000

Van der Emde Reinhold to THE MANHATTAN SAVINGS INST. 3d av, s e cor 113th st, 40.11x69. Nov. 3, 1 year, 4½ %. 20,000

Vaughan, Patrick to Clara and Jacob Cooper committee Jane Cooper. Columbine av, n e cor Cambreleng av, 50x100. Oct. 31, due Nov. 2, 1894, 5 %. 1,000

Victor, Amalie to Adolph Wallach. 63d st, No. 135, n s, 85 w Lexington av, 14x100.5. Oct. 29, due Oct. 31, 1894. 1,000

Vogel, Anna wife of Ignatz to Jacob Cohen. Goerek st. P. M. Oct. 31, due Nov. 1, 1896, 5 %. 4,500

Von Natzmer, Hermann, Dresden, Germany, to Rudolph Bohm. 36th st, No. 344, s s, 100 w 1st av, 25x98.9. Oct. 22, 3 years. 1,500

Welling, Gertrude L. wife of W. Brenton to trustees of the Lenox Library. 40th st. P. M. Oct. 23, 5 years, 5 %. 17,000

Weyl, Jettchen wife of and Henry to Peter A. H. Jackson. 1st av, No. 547, w s, 74.1 s 33d st, 20.7x100. Nov. 2, 5 years, 5 %. 7,000

Wilmurt, Francis M. to Bradley & Currier Co. (Lim.) 89th st, s s, 241 w West End av, 20x100.8. Sub. to mort. $19,000. Nov. 2, 3 years. 3,000

Same to same. 89th st, s s, 261 w West End av, 21x100.8. Sub. to mort. $19,000. Nov. 2, 3 years. 3,000

Wittenberg, Isidor V. and Marks Chambers to Max S. Korn. 1st av, s e cor 117th st. P. M. Nov. 2, 3 years, 5 %. 6,500

Waters, Maria T. widow, Maria T. wife of Thomas Sinnott, Mary J. wife of G. H. De Bussy, Ann E., Matilda, Josephine and Frances C. Waters heirs Charles Waters to Alexander Brown, Philadelphia, Pa. Broadway, s e cor 18th st, 24.6x86.1 to 18th st, x91.1. Oct. 31, due Nov. 31, 1892, 4½ %. See Conveys. 5,000

Wegener, Hugo and Carrie his wife to Edward B. Fellows. Arcularius pl, n s, 549.5 e Gerard av, 50x100. Oct. 29, 3 years. See Conveys. 800

Webb, Z. Swift to Hulbert Puck. 33d st, s s, 470 w 8th av. 20x98.9. Oct. 29, 1 year. 1,000

Wise, Charles to Henry Neustadter. Washington pl, n e s, 52 s e Mercer st, runs northeast 91.9 x northwest 52 to Mercer st, x southwest 91.7 to pl, x southeast —. Oct. 29, due Oct. 30, 1891, 5 %. 150,000

Wood, John W. to The New Home Sewing Machine Co. Grant av, n w cor 164th st, 35.3x88.4x35x83.11. Oct. 26, 6 months. 300

Woolsey, Theodorus B. to James A. Scrymser. Broad st, No. 107, e s, 55.7 s Water st, 25.8x47x25.5x46.10, with easement in yard and privy in rear of No. 25 Water st. Sub. to mort. $15,000. Oct. 30, 6 months. 3,000

Wendelken, Gevert to THE GREENWICH SAVINGS BANK. Madison av, n e cor 27th st, 24.9x71.1. Oct. 31, due Oct. 1, 1893, 5 %. 10,000

Same mortgagors with same mortgagee. Agreement for builder's loan of $15,000. Oct. 31. nom

Winthrop, Robert mortgagee with Francis Scallion mortgagor. Extension of mort. Nov. 4. nom

Wolff, Huldah wife of Robert to Meyer Lubman. 70th st, s s, 265 e 3d av, 20x102.2. Nov. 2, 1 year. 2,000

Wood, Frederick to William Hall's Sons, Morton & Bathe, Charles Winters, Thomas H. Snape, Ferd. Bock, John Hill (John being fictitious), Delphis Moisan and F. Oriofski & Son, all contractors on mortgaged premises. 88th st, n s, 175 w 8th av, 75x100.8. Nov. 2. 18,900

Wood, James to The Eureka Co-operative Savings and Loan Assoc., New York. Pond place 3d av. P. M. Nov. 2, installs, 5 %. 2,400

Zimmermann, Louis, Annie and Joseph J. to John E. and C. F. Glimm exrs. Christian Glimm. 54th st, No. 450, s s, 175 e 10th av, 25x100.5. Nov. 2, 5 years, 5 %. 15,000

Zimmermann, Henry to Joseph Conrad. 81st st. P. M. Nov. 2, due Jan. 1, 1897, 5 %. 5,000

Zimmermann, Jacob A. to Clarence Warden, Bath, Me. 51st st, s s, 484 w 8th av, 20x100.5. Nov. 5, 5 years, 5 %. 20,000

Same to Annie F. Dreyfus guard. 51st st, s s, 504 w 8th av, 20.8x100.5, with all title to strip adj on west, 0.4x100.5. Nov. 5, 5 years, 5 %. 20,000

Same to Philip Sammet. 51st st, s s, 504 w 8th av, 20.8x100.5, with all title to strip on west, 0.4x100.5. Sub. to above. Nov. 5, 1 year. 4,750

KINGS COUNTY.

OCTOBER 29, 30, 31, NOVEMBER 2, 3, 4.

Aichmann, Charles to Janet Pirnie and ano. exrs. John M. Pirnie. Irving av, north cor Grove st. P. M. June 9, due Oct. 29, 1891, 5 %. 30,033

Andrews, William to Thomas J. Betts. Bushwick av. P. M. Oct. 29, 3 years. 5 %. 3,000

Alikur, Michael to Charles W. Truslow trustee William Hall. Harrison pl, s s, 175 e Bogert st, 25x87.6x25x88.5. Oct. 29, 3 years, 5 %. 500

Acor, Kate to Julia Simon. Park av, n e cor Nostrand av. P. M. Nov. 2, 3 years. 5 %. 8,000

Adams, William H. to James H. Watson and James H. Pittinger. 1st st, s w s, 385 n w 5th av, 53.11x100. Sub. to mort. $10,340. Nov. 2, demand. 1,500

Same to Cornelius E. Donnellon. Same property. Oct. 12, demand. 10,240

Same to same. Same property. Oct. 12, demand. 3,650

Allan, J. Glen to Daniel B. Norris. Macon st, n s, 235.3 w Lewis av, 19.9x100. Nov. 2, 2 months, 5 %. 800

Allan, John T. and Nathaniel Proskey to Helvetia H. Dutcher. 6th st, n e s, 217.10 n w 5th av, 20x100. Sub. to mort. $4,500. Oct. 31, 1 month. 500

Anderson, Robert H. to Andrew D. Baird. Vernon av, s s, 340 w Throop av, 20x100. Nov. 2, 1 year. 2,000

Same to Thomas L. Atkins. Vernon av, s s, 300 w Throop av, 3 lots, each 20x100. 3 morts., each $4,525. Nov. 2, due Nov. 1, 1894, 5 %. 13,575

Same to same. Vernon av, s s, 360 w Throop av, 20x100. Nov. 2, due Nov. 1, 1894, 5 %. 5,000

Armstrong, Benjamin to George B. Stoutenburg. Throop av, w s, 26 n Pulaski st, runs west 50 x north 1 x west 34.9 x north 17.6 x east 84.9 to av, x south 18.6. Oct. 28, due Nov. 1, 1892. 1,000

Avis, William A. to Elizabeth C. Gassner. Lincoln pl, s s, 150 w 7th av, 20x100. Oct. 29, due Nov. 1, 1894, 5 %. 6,000

Atwater, Samuel J. to Stephen D. Pyle. 78th st, n e s, 400 n w 19th av, 60x100. Nov. 2, 1 year. 875

Betts, Charles A. to The Hamilton Trust Co. Fulton st, n s, 85.2 w Nostrand av, runs east 39.6 x north — x west to point 80 n Fulton st, x west — x south 80. Nov. 4, demand. 15,000

Bushong, Albert J. to Louis Bonert. 10th st. P. M. Nov. 2, 3 years, 5 %. 2,000

Bauer, Frederick to Charles Griffen and ano. exrs. Peter S. Titus. Halsey st, s s, 123.6 e Ralph av, 19.5x100. Oct. 29, 3 years, 5 %. 4,500

Bechtold, Rosalia to Frederick L. Dubois. Ellery st, n s, 250 w Sumner av, 25x100. Oct. 29, 5 years, 5 %. 3,000

Same to John Merkle. Same property. Oct. 29, 1 year, 5 %. 1,000

Becker, Herman and Patrick Maloney to The C. B. Keogh Mfg. Co. 6th st, s s, 180 w 4th av, 115x100. Oct. 30, demand. 2,700

Brooks, Catherine T. to Mary wife of Dudley Kelly. Prospect pl, s s, 205 e Grand av. P. M. Oct. 28, 2 years. 3,000

Bristol, Charles L. to Michael H. Hegerty. 3d pl. P. M. Oct. 28, due Oct. 29, 1894. 1,750

Same to The Title Guarantee and Trust Co. 3d pl. P. M. Oct. 28, 3 years, 5 %. 3,500

Brown, George R. to Stephen B. Sturges. Herkimer st. P. M. Oct. 15, demand. 1,000

Bryner, Adolph to Rudolph F. Emmerich. 77th st, New Utrecht. P. M. July 14, installs. 1,000

Byer, Anna and Etta to Charles B. Schellenberg. Smith st, s e s, 60 s w Baltic st, 20x100. Oct. 29, due Jan. 1, 1894. 1,500

Baylis, Louisa C. widow to John F. James. State st, n s, 149.9 w Court st, 20.1x109.8x20.1x109.11. Nov. 2, 1 year, 5 %. 220

Betz, Katrina wife of and Kasper to Louise wife of Sebastian Hob. Montrose av. P. M. Sub. to mort. $3,500. Oct. 31, 5 years, 5 %. 3,500

Same to The Kings County Savings Inst. Same property. Oct. 31, 1 year, 5 %. 3,500

Bloomer, James A. to Charles D. King. Hill st. P. M. Oct. 12, installs. 475

Boarer, Sarah wife of and James to Edward C. Underhill. Irving av, west cor Van Voorhis st, runs northwest 200 to Schaeffer st, x southwest 258.5 x southeast 100 x southeast 100 to Van Voorhis st, x northeast 264.8. Oct. 18, 1890, demand. 1,000

Boijer, George to Maria Forsterling. Degraw st, n s, 374 w Columbia st. 25x100. Nov. 2, 3 years, 5 %. 3,000

Brown, Lowell V. to Hope H. Colgate. Gates av, s s, 235 w Bedford av, 17x110. Oct. 31, due Jan. 1, 1892, 5 %. 4,500

Butterfield, Margaret E. wife of and Justin to The Riverhead Savings Bank. Myrtle av, n s, 102.9 w Pearl st, 20.6x74. Oct. 28, due Oct. 31, 1894, 5 %. 2,000

Chevallier, Clement E. to John T. Nelson. Halsey st, s s, 317.4 e Nostrand av, 17.6x100. Oct. 30, 6 months. 500

Clayton, Zebulon to Eliza J. Buskey, committee of Mary W. Wright lunatic. Fleet st, w s, 2.2 s Fleet pl, 25.9x17.2x20.9x38.11. Oct. 29, due Feb. 1, 1892, 5 %. 1,200

Coar, William to Obermeyer & Liebmann. Cedar st, No. 33. Saloon lease. Oct. 28, demand. 650

Cavanagh, James to The Kings Co. Savings Inst. Hope st, n e c r Roebling st, runs east 180.7 x north 87 x west 1.1.1 x north 23.3 to North 2d st, x west 85 to Roebling st, x south —. Oct. 31, 1 year, 5 %. 5,000

Collins, Henry to William B. Hartley. Halsey st, s s, 244.5 e Reid av, 18.9x100. Oct. 30, due April 3, 1893. 1,350

Commoss, Joseph T. to The Brooklyn Savings Bank. Classon av, e s, 40.9 n Lexington av, 19.10x80. Oct. 29, 1 year, 5 %. 3,000

Conway, James to The German Savings Bank, Brooklyn. Broadway, s w cor Hart st, 28x110x90.7x55.2. Oct. 26, due Dec. 1, 1892, 5 %. 13,000

Cahill, Frances V. to Frank W. Larom. 1st st. P. M. Nov. 4, installs. 4,500

Carney, John to The Title Guarantee and Trust Co. Dikeman st, n e s, 150 s e Conover st, 25x100. Nov. 2, 3 years, 5 %. 1,800

Chadwick, William H. and Elizabeth his wife to The Title Guarantee and Trust Co. Atlantic av, s s, 350 w Stone av, 16.8x100. Nov. 4, 3 years, 5 %. 800

Crossman, Greenleaf W. to Zipporah L. Hollister. Barbey st. P. M. Nov. 2, due Oct. 14, 1894. 2,813

Dunne, Annie M. to Annie E. Logue. Union st, s w s, 268.8 n w 5th av, 16.8x100. Oct. 28, due Nov. 1, 1895, 5 %. 3,300

Dunne, Ellen E. to Adolph Rheinfeldt. 40th st. P. M. Nov. 2, 1 year, 5 %. 350

Dannhauser, Max to The German Savings Bank, Brooklyn. Union av, e s, 50 s Meserole st, 25x100. Oct. 1, due Dec. 1, 1892, 5 %. 4,000

Davis, Maria L. wife of Allen M. to The Broadway Savings Inst. St. Marks av, s e cor New York av, runs east 150 x south 250.7 to Prospect pl, x west 40 x north 100 x west 110 to New York av, x north 150.7. Oct. 31, due Nov. 1, 1892, 4½ %. 22,500

Dickover, William M. to Cornelius Cowenhoven. 64th st, s w s, 200 n w 17th av, 50x102.2, New Utrecht. Oct. 29, 3 years. 3,000

Durphy, Virginia L. to John L. Nostrand. 81st st, New Utrecht. P. M. Oct. 31, due Nov. 1, 1892, 5 %. 1,000

Delapierre, Angelica to Alexander G. Calder. 12th st. P. M. Nov. 2, 2 years, 5 %. 2,000

De Witt, Mary E. with Catharine A. wife of John Cornell mortgagees. Agreement as to priority of morts made by Jacob J. Seelbach. Oct. 31. nom

Deran, William to Azariah W. Monfort. Atlantic av, s w cor Linwood st, 78.7x105.7x77.6x118.11. Oct. 1, 5 years, 5 %. 7,000

Drake, John J. to The Title Guarantee and Trust Co. Atlantic av, n s, 80 w Nostrand av, 80.1x64. Nov. 2, 3 years, 5 %. 6,000

Engel, Bertha to John A. Lott, Jr. Vernon av, n s, 375 e Prospect st, 25x200, Flatbush. Oct. 27, due Nov. 1, 1892. 125

Everding, Mary wife of and Henry to Ellen L. Wallace. Wyckoff st, s s, 99.2 e Court st, 19x71. Nov. 2, due Nov. 1, 1894. 2,000

Eagan, John to Minna Bruggemann. Union st, s s, 71.6 e Hicks st, 26.3x100. Oct. 28, 3 years, 5 %. 4,000

Eastment, Jennie to A. Stewart Walsh. Quincy st, s s, 30 e Patchen av, 25x100. Oct. 30, 1 year. 500

Same to Catharine Rodwell. Quincy st, s s, 30 e Patchen av, 25x100. Oct. 30, 5 years. 3,000

Ebert, Catharine to Edward C. Underhill. Wallabout st, n s, 250 w Harrison av, 25x100. Oct. 23, 5 years, 5 %. 600

Emerson, Tillie T. to Margaretha Stephan widow. Stockton st. P. M. Oct. 30, due Nov. 1, 1896, 5 %. 3,000

Erk, Mary wife of and Leonard to Charles W. Truslow trustee William Wall. Ingraham st. P. M. Oct. 6, 3 years. 700

Ernst, Charles to Joseph Esbeck. Melrose st. P. M. Oct. 28, due Nov. 1, 1894. 700

Evans, George to Henry Vollweiler. Broadway. P. M. Oct 31, 3 years, 5 %. 2,000

Fertig, David to Bernhard J. Pink. Rockaway av. P. M. Oct. 15, installs. 1,400

Finch, Rachel A. to Francis G. Clarke, Augustus Meyers and James J. and Frank P. Treanor, of F. G. Clark Blue Stone Co. Bergen st, s s, 270 e Brooklyn av, 20x105.7. Oct. 28, 1 year. 1,647

Fischer, Maggie wife of and George and Katie Dugan to Louis Lebewohl and Abraham Ruth. Osborn st. P. M. Oct. 30, installs 1,081

Fischer, Maria to William H. Huttenlocher. Fanchon pl, e s, 581.10 n Brooklyn and Jamaica turnpike road, 50x126.4x—x157.7. Aug. 12, due Oct. 1, 1896, 5 %. 2,000

Fleischmann, Rosina widow and devisee John A. Fleischmann, Barbara Bauer, Mary, Katie, Andreas and George Fleischmann heirs John A. Fleischman to Edward C. Reinhardt. Hopkins st, n s, 149.2 e Throop av, 25x100. Oct. 5, due Oct. 10, 1896, 5 %. 1,000

Forbell, George U. to Charlotte L. Kennedy. Hendrix st, e s, 174.11 n Arlington av, 16.7x100. Oct. 30, 3 years. 2,000

Same to same. Hendrix st, e s, 158.2 n Arlington av, 16.9x100. Oct. 30, 3 years. 2,000

Fraser, John to The Williamsburgh Savings Bank. McDonough st, n s, 300 e Tompkins av, 3 lots, each 20x120. 3 morts., each $10,000. Oct. 28, 1 year, 5 %. 30,000

Same to same. Macon st, s s, 358.6 e Tompkins av, 57.6x80. Oct. 28, 1 year, 5 %. 8,000

Same to same. McDonough st, n s, 400 e Tompkins av, 25x120. Oct. 28, 1 year, 5 %. 14,000

Same to same. McDonough st, n s, 781 e Tompkins av, 22x120. Oct. 28, 1 year, 5 %. 18,000

Same to same. McDonough st, n s, 260 e Tompkins av, 21x120. Oct. 28, 1 year, 5 %. 12,000

Farber, Lottie L. to Thomas H. Radcliffe. McDonough st. P. M. Oct. 30, due Oct. 31, 1898, 5 %. 1,400

Fey, Ann widow to Michael Goss. 9th st, n w cor 6th av, 20.2x90x20x90. Nov. 2, due Nov. 1, 1894, 5 %. 4,000

Finn, Maurice to John D. Prince, Jr., and ano. exrs. George R. Cutler. Bay 13th st, e s, 225 n Bath av, 100x118.4, New Utrecht. Oct. 31, due Aug. 18, 1896. 500

Foulks, Adelaide E. wife of and John W. to The Title Guarantee and Trust Co. 7th st. P. M. Nov. 2, 3 years, 5 %. 4,250

Fox, Delia wife of and James to The Title Guarantee and Trust Co. Court st, n w cor Degraw st. P. M. Nov. 2, 3 years, 5 %. 6,000

Furman, John C. to Charles W. Cooper. Maspeth av, s s, at intersection with centre line of Morgan av, runs south to centre Orient av, x east to centre Vandervoort av, x north to Maspeth av, x west —, also personal property. Oct. 26. 1 year, 5 %. 140,000

Gibbs, Ellen to Charlotte H. Cleveland. Crescent st. P. M. July 18, installs. 1,500

Gerdes, Herman to Charles W. Truslow trustee William Wall. Bogert st, s w cor Boerum st. P. M. Oct. 29, 3 years, 5 %. 1,000

Gunther, John to Catharine wife of George Distler. Vermont st. P. M. Oct. 30, 5 years, 5 %. 3,000

Hall, Mark to Mary E. Seaman. 48th st, n e s, 200 s e 4th av, 20x100.2. Oct. 30, 3 years, 6 %. 2,500

Hannan, Margaret M. to Joseph W. Myer. Waverly av. P. M. Oct. 29, 1 year, 5 %. 700

Hart, William to Thurber, Whyland & Co. Lots 78-234 and 235 map Jacob Worth and Vincent A. Strawson, Flatbush. Oct. 20, notes. 275

Hauck, Frederick to The German Savings Bank, Brooklyn. Ellery st, s s, 50 e Throop av, 25x—. Oct. 28, due Dec. 1, 1892, 5 %. 3,000

Hegeman, John M. to Jane C. Hall. Quincy st, s s, 265 w Nostrand av, 20x100. Oct. 30, due Oct. 29, 1898, 5 %. 500

Same to Alexander Wright. Same property. Oct. 30, due Nov. 1, 1894, 5 %. 2,800

Henderson, Albert C. to The Bradley & Currier Co. (Lim.) Bedford av, s w cor Rodney st, 138x100. Sub. to all morts. Oct. 28, 1 year. 29,376

Herrmann, Ida to Charles W. Truslow trustee William Wall. Seigel st. P. M. Oct. 28, 3 years, 5 %. 375

Same to same. Johnson av. P. M. Oct. 28, 3 years, 5 %. 1,500

Hilliker, John H. and John W. Mehl to Robert Bieling. Jamaica av. P. M. Oct. 29, 1 year. 1,000

Harris, Malie wife of and Hyman to Leopold Michel. Graham av. P. M. Oct. 31, due July 1, 1896, or installs, 5 %. 3,300

Healy, James B. to D. & M. Chauncey Real Estate Co. (Lim.) Lawrence and Fulton sts. Oct. 31, 2 years. See Conveys. 10,000

Same to Felix Campbell. Same property. Oct. 30, installs, 5 %. 95,000

Harvey, Hiland H. to Theodore D. Dimon exr. Hannah S. Dimon. Webster av, s e cor 3d st, 90x112.7x90x110.10, Flatbush. Oct. 31, 3 years. 1,000

Haase, Detlev to Solomon Blumenstock. Johnson av. P. M. Nov. 2, 5 years, 5 %. 3,000

Harden, William F. and Michael G. to Thomas C. Harden. North 2d st, n e s, lot 1521 assessment map No 2, New Williamsburgh, 25x75.6x25x75; North 2d st, n e cor Berry st, 8.5x78 7x5x78.8; North 2d st, n e s, abt 80 s e Berry st, 25x75x25x74.6. ½ part. Oct. 31, due Nov. 1, 1894, 5 %. 12,000

Hawkins, William to Sylvester Ross trustee Gulian Ross. 14th st, n s, 197.6 e 8th av, 20.8x100. Nov. 2, 3 years, 5 %. 4,000

Holland, William and Jacob G. W. Wurzler to Margaret J. Reynolds. Lafayette av. P. M. Oct. 31, 3 years, 5 %. 3,500

Hollister, Zipporah L. to Mary E. Hosier. Barbey st, w s, 100 n Arlington av, 50x95. Oct. 29, due Feb. 1, 1893. 4 500

Horn, Frederick to George C Diekman. Marcy av. P. M. Nov. 2. 5 years, 5 %. 4,000

Immen, Christopher to Kate E. Immen individ. and with others exrs. John H. Immen. Commercial st, east cor Clay st, runs northeast 119.3 x southeast 30.2 x south 30.2 to Clay st, x west 119.3. Oct. 20, 5 years, 5 %. 5,800

Jackson, Parmeanus, Westbury, L. I., to Peter and Joseph Young. Vanderbilt av, w s, 594.2 n Myrtle av, 16.8x100; Vanderbilt av, w s, 610.10 n Myrtle av, 16.8x100. Nov. 2, 3 years, 5 %. 1,000

Jenks, William A. to Sara H. Kent. Clason av, e s, 111 s Quincy st, 16x89.6. Oct. 29, 2 years, 5 %. 500

Johnson, Andrew to The Citizens' Co-operative Building and Loan Assoc. of Bath Beach, N. Y. 62d st, s w cor 11th av, 40x88x40x66.9. Oct. 28, installs. 500

Smith, Thomas to Constantia A. P. Duppen. 16th st, s w s, 377.10 n w 8th av, 20x100. Oct. 28, 3 years. 500

Johnson, Salome to Walter J. Klots. Eldert st, s e s, 300 n e Bushwick av, 20x100. Oct. 26, 1 year. 514

Keppler, Christian A. to Charles W. Truslow trustee William Wall. McKibbin st. P. M. Oct. 28, 3 years, 5 %. 1,100

Ketierle, John to Charles W. Truslow trustee William Wall. Seigel st. P. M. Oct. 29, 3 years, 5 %. 1,000

Same to same. Seigel st. P. M. Oct. 29, 3 years, 5 %. 1,000

Kay, George W. to Samuel T. Sherwood. 47th st. P. M. Oct. 29, due Oct. 31, 1892. 800

Kemmet, Henry to Lena Weis. Hart st, s e s, 175 n e Hamburg av, 25x100. Oct. 29, 1 year, 5 %. 500

Kirby, Joseph M. to Peter A. Embury, West Orange, N. J. Bainbridge st, No. 505, n s, 115.6 e Saratoga av, 17.6x100. Oct. 28, due Nov. 1, 1894, 6 %. 4,000

Same to Joseph P. Fowls. Same property. Sub. to mort. $4,000. Oct. 28, 1 year. 1,000

Knoip, Henry to Theresa Bill. Judge st, e s, 203.8 n Powers st, runs east 111.10 x south — x east 13 x south 176 x west 153 8 to st, x south 24.0; interior lot, begins 1??.7 e Judge st, runs north 120.1 x east 12.7 x south 2.10 x east 14.1 x south 112 3 x west 28; Powers st, n s, 100 e Judge st, 25x46.4x25x45.4; Devoe st, s s, 225 w Olive st, 25x125. Nov. 4, due July 1, 1892. 2,000

Konrath, Charles to Charles W. Truslow trustee William Wall. Seigel st, s s, 540 e Bushwick av. P. M. Oct. 29, 3 years, 5 %. 400

Same to same. Seigel st, s s, 515 e Bushwick av. P. M. Oct. 29, 3 years, 5 %. 400

Kerrigan, Thomas A. to The Peoples Trust Co. Willoughby st. P. M. Oct. 21, 1 year, 5 %. 10,000

Kiefer, John J. to Herald Employes Co-operative Building and Loan Assoc. Belmont av, s s, 25 w Hendrix st, 25x100. Oct. 28, installs. 3,250

Klaus, August to Charles Ullrich. New Jersey av, w s, 250 n Fulton av, 25x100. Oct. 31, due Jan. 1, 1895, 5 %. 2,000

Klein, Benedict A. to Jonas Weil and Bernhard Mayer. Gold st, s w cor Plymouth st, 45x99 6. Oct. 30, demand. 7,000

Koehler, Frank F. to Rulef J. Van Brunt. 81st st, New Utrecht. P. M. Oct. 26, 2 years, 5 %. 1,000

Keeler, Annie V. to Harriet L. Price. Madison st, s s, 79 e Sumner av, 19x100. Nov. 4, 5 years, 5 %. 5,800

Kimmerle, August to Helen J. Smith, Freehold, N. J. Hewes st. P. M. Nov. 2, 5 years, 5 %. 5,000

Klett, Jacob to Claus Doscher. Hamburg av, s w s, 50 n w Stockholm st, 25x100. Oct. 27, 5 years. 5,000

Leckey, Eliza to Maria D. Lott. Carroll st, s s, 137 w 6th av. 20x114x20x114.11. Oct. 30, due Nov. 1, 1894, 5 %. 1,000

Le Duc, William to John P. Free. Snediker av. P. M. Nov. 2, installs. 500

Lupo, Antonio to The Lafayette Fire Ins. Co. Carroll st, n s, 100 w 4th av, 25x100. Nov. 4, due Nov. 1, 1893. 3,500

Lyons, Henry B. to George H. Roberts. Berkeley pl, s s, 87.2 e 5th av, 54.3x95. All title. Nov. 4. 1,500

Lanthier, Jeannette wife of and Louis A. to Morgan J. O'Brien. Cropsey av, New Utrecht. P. M. Sub. to mort. $13,000. Oct. 31, due Nov. 2, 1896, 5 %. 7,000

Same to same. Same property. P. M. Oct. 31, due Nov. 2, 1896, 5 %. 13,000

Lock, Joseph and Metta H. his wife to Catharine M. Neidig. Box st, s s, 325 w Manhattan av, 25x100. Oct. 29, 1 year. 2,000

Loeser, Frederick to Home Life Ins. Co. De Kalb av, east cor Fleet st, 62.7x42.9x55.6x74.11. Oct. 29, due Nov. 2, 1892, 5 %. 15,000

Lefkowitz, Josephine to Henry Gottlieb. Thatford av, w s, 175 s Belmont av, 25x100.1. Oct. 9, 1 year. 500

Lehmann, Charles and William to Peter Bertsch exr. William Broistedt. Evergreen av, n e s, 75 n w Hancock st, 25x100. Oct. 30, 3 years, 5 %. 2,500

Leiufelder, Anna to Albert G. McDonald. Rockaway av, e s, 100 n Sutter av, 75x100. Oct. 28, demand. 1,500

Levy, Julia to Charles W. Truslow trustee William Wall. Johnson av, s e cor Bogert st. P. M. Oct. 29, 3 years, 5 %. 1,260

Lewis, Ellen J. to Title Guarantee and Trust Co. President st, s s, 98 e 7th av, 17.6x100. Oct. 31, 1 year, 5 %. 3,000

Linson, William to Manhattan Savings Inst. St. Marks av. P. M. Oct. 27, 10 years, 5 %. 1,800

Lockwood, Katie B. to Henry Grasman. Hancock st, s s, 30 w Howard av, 16.9x100, Oct. 29, 3 years, 5 %. 1,500

Lodge, Rebecca widow to Daniel B. Norris. Putnam av, n w cor Lewis av. 23x100. Oct. 30, 2 years, 5 %. 1,000

Same to South Brooklyn Savings Inst. Same property. P. M. Oct. 30, 1 year, 5 %. 7,500

Ludwig, Jacob to East Brooklyn Savings Bank. Floyd st, s s, 180 e Marcy av, 20x100, Oct. 30. 1 year. 5 %. 2,000

MacMartin, Isabella to Hetty B. Beatty, Morristown, N. J. McDonough st, s s, 375 e. Sumner av, 20x100. Oct. 31, 3 years, 5 %. 4,000

Mahen, Ann wife of Daniel to Flora A. Gordon. Chestnut st, n s, 125 e Evergreen av, runs north 84.5 x east to O. Gilmore's lands, x north 43.4 x east 25 x south 47.6 x west 8 x south 65.0 to st, x west 45. Oct. 29, 1 year. 1,200

Maher, Daniel to Sophia Holzhauser. Newell st, e s, 265.1 n Van Cott av, 25x100. Oct. 28, due Nov. 1, 1894. 5 %. 4 500

Mason, Mary L. to Isadore E. Van Deverg. Eldert st. P. M. Oct. 29, 1 year. 1,000

Matherson, Seraphine to Julia and Lillia F. Murray. Vanderbilt av. P. M. Oct. 28, installs. 6,000

Mayer, Michael to Charles W. Truslow trustee William Wall. Seigel st. P. M. Oct. 29, 3 years or sooner, 5 %. 2,220

McGuff, Patrick to Edward A. Everit. 45th st, s s, 200 e 4th av, 20x100.2. Oct. 29, 2 years. 300

McCormack, Mary A. wife of and Patrick to Walter J. Klois. Lexington av, n s, 229.2 w Broadway, 20x100. Oct. 26, due April 26, 1896, 5 %. 300

McCadden, Michael to Thomas S. O'Reilly. 17th st. P. M. Oct. 21, due Nov. 1, 1892, 5 %. 6,000

Meiley, Annie widow to The Title Guarantee and Trust Co. Ryerson st, e s, 162 s Myrtle av, 18.9x100. Oct. 30, 3 years, 5 %. 3,000

Messenger, Moses and Meyer Chapkowsky to John Power. Eastern Parkway, n w cor Os[illegible] st. P. M. Oct. 28, installs. 1,500

Michel, Leopold to Karl Hanse. Cook st, n s, 250 e Ewen st, 25x100. Oct. 29, 3 years, 5 %. 5,000

Miller, Charles M. and Nellie his wife to Benjamin C. Raymond. Macon st, n s, 94 w Ralph av, 18x100. Oct. 30, installs. 800

Morris, Solomon to The Serial Building Loan and Savings Inst. Watkins st, w s, 250 s Sutter av, 25x100. Oct. 20, installs. 3,000

Moss, Harris to The Serial Building Loan and Savings Inst. Duryea av, s w cor Thatford av, 50x100. Oct. 20, installs. 2,400

Muller, John D. to John Zipp. 5th av, s w cor Carroll st, 22 9x102.1x13.1x103.8. Oct. 29, due May 1, 1892, 5 %. 5,000

Maujer, Robert T. to Mary L. Fales. South 3d st. P. M. Nov. 2, 5 years, 5 %. 5,000

McEachen, James to George Finck. Lexington av, s s, 275 w Nostrand av. P. M. Oct. 26, 6 months. 500

Same to same. Lexington av, s s, 259 w Nostrand av. P. M. Oct. 26, 6 months. 500

McKeon, Julia to Equitable Co-operative Building and Loan Assoc. Smith st. P. M. Oct. 31, installs, 5 %. 1,500

McQuillin, Joseph B. and Wilkins K. Putnam to Cornelius Cowenhoven. 10th av, s w cor 72d st, 60x100, New Utrecht. Oct 1, 3 years. 3,500

Mehlen, Auguste to Richard Dreyer, Sea Cliff, N. Y. Cornelia st. P. M. Nov. 2, 1 year, 5 %. 5,500

Metz, Henry to Emil Lebrian. South 3d st. P. M. Oct. 31, 1 year, 5 %. 1,500

Montgomery, Lizzie to Clarence Tucker et al. trustees George W. Tucker. Pacific st. P. M. Oct. 31, due Nov. 1, 1892, 5 %. 7,500

Moore, John W. to The Bulmer Lumber Co. (Lim.) Kingsland av, w s, 95 s Norman av, 125x100. Oct. 29, installs. 1,100

Moss, Sarah A. to The Kings County Co-operative Building and Loan Assoc. Spencer st. P. M. Oct 9, installs, 5 %. 2,400

Maujer, Robert T. to Grace F. T. Harper. South 3d st, n e s, 125 s e 5th st, 25x120. Nov. 2, due Nov. 1, 1896. 1,500

McFadden, George J. to The Title Guarantee and Trust Co. Carroll st, n s, 112 w 5th av, 20x100. Nov. 4, 3 years, 5 %. 3,500

Melville, Alexander to Isabella Demorest. Atlantic av, n e s, 389.6 s e Grove av, 106.6x208x100.7x227, New Utrecht. Oct. 27, demand. 500

Moran, Jeremiah to Magdalene Cowenhoven. 5th av, w s, 50 s 22d st, 25x100. Oct. 23, due Nov. 1, 1896, 5 %. 3,000

Muller, Frances to John Dill, Jr. Warren st, n s, 400 e 3d av, 25x100. Nov. 2, due Nov. 1, 1893, 5 %. 500

Nilson, Gustaf, Hollis, L. I., to Mamie E. Cruse. Lot 2359 block 12 map 680 lots of Effingham H. Nichols, Lefferts Park, New Utrecht. Nov. 2, 1 year. 150

Nappier, Catharine, Ettie, Hugh, John, Thomas and Nellie by William H. Dill guard. and William Nappier to Harriet E. Dunn. Irving st, n s, 150 w Columbia st, 25x100. Oct. 20, 3 years. 1,500

Nappier, William to Henry H. Adams, County Treasurer of Kings County, trustee for Catharine, Ettie, Hugh, John, Thomas and Nellie Nappier. Irving st, n s, 150 w Columbia st, 25x100. Oct. 24, 19 years. 193

Notter, Maria A. wife of and Edouard to Robert Rhinow. Boerum st, n s, 150 w Graham av, 25x100. Oct 31, due Jan 1, 1897, 5 %. 1,800

Norton, William M. to Randolph H. Cole. Van Buren st. P. M. Oct. 30, due July 1, 1892. 600

Oster, Henrietta wife of and Henry M. to Lincoln H. Hough. Lynch st. P. M. Nov. 2, installs. 1,300

Same to Alice Senior. Same property. P. M. Nov. 2, 3 years, 5 %. 2,000

Ochs, Katherine to Jacob Kiendl. Vermont st, w s, 50 n Belmont av, 25x100. Oct. 29, due Nov. 1, 1893. 500

Perry, Anna M. to Charles H. Tyson. Halsey st. P. M. Oct. 29, due April 29, 1893, 5 %. 800

Phillips, Emma J. to Julius B. Davenport. Pacific st, n e cor Bond st. P. M. Oct. 30, due July 1, 1892, 5 %. 1,500

Pierret, Francis J. to Charles W. Lansing. 55th st. P. M. Oct. 28, due Nov. 1, 1894, 5 %. 1,100

Pilcher, Joseph M. to Charles S. Wood. Bergen st, s s, 290 e Brooklyn av, 20x100. Oct. 28, 1 year. 1,100

Platt, Lydia L. and Matilda C. wife of Percival W. Logan to Cornelius N. Hoagland. Quincy st, n s, 60 e Bedford av, 20x100. Oct. 20, due Nov. 1, 1892. gold, 2,000

Same to same. Same property. Oct. 20, due Nov. 1, 1894, 5 %. gold, 5,000

Parmer, Ada wife of and Lewis to Mary W. Smith. Watkins st, w s, 100 s Eastern Parkway, 26 8x100. Oct. 31, demand. 200

Peirce, Christopher H. to Stephen Baldwin, Hempstead, L. I. Steuben st, w s, 80.0 n Myrtle av, 25x100. Oct. 28, 5 years. 1,400

Pfalzgraf, Hans C. to Cornelius Cowenhoven. 60th st, s w s, 320 n w 17th av, 60x100, New Utrecht. Nov. 1, 3 years. 3,500

Ramsdell, David J. to Charles Griffou et al. trustees Samuel Willets. St. Marks av. P. M. Nov. 2, 3 years, 5 %. 6,100

Same to Robert F. Rhodes. 4th av, s e s, 24.8 s w Degraw st, 16.4x75. Nov. 2, 1 year. 1,000

Riechers, Louis to William Laytin et al. trustees William Laytin. Skillman av, n s, 225 e Lorimer st, 50x100. Nov. 4, 3 years, 5 %. 3,000

Riggio, James and James Di Mezzinio to Patrick Quillan. Prospect st. P. M. Nov. 2, installs. 1,800

Reilly, Edward to Julia A. Smith. Willow pl. P. M. Oct. 30, due Nov. 1, 1894, 5 %. 4,000

Rowe, George H. to The Title Guarantee and Trust Co Oakland st, n s, 245 e Norman av, 25x100. Nov. 2, 3 years, 5 %. 2,000

Ramsdell, David J. to Susan E. Blodgett Stockbridge, Mass. 4th av. P. M. Nov. 2, due Nov. 1, 1893. 5,000

Rappel, Annie wife of Peter J. to Mary A. wife of James White. 2d av. P. M. Oct. 15, due Oct. 1, 1894, 5 %. 350

Rath, Charles to Rosenthal Lodge 257, D. O. H. of Brooklyn. 23d st, w s, 110 n 4th av, 50x100. Oct. 29, due Jan. 1894, 5 %. 1,500

Raynor, Charles E. to Edward W. Lauer and Charles J. Kiesel. Blake av, s s, 25 w Barbey st, 50x100. Oct. 27, installs, 5 %. 1,100

Read, Henry P. to Helen M. Hillier. De Kalb av, n w cor Adelphi st. P. M. Oct. 27, due May 1, 1892, 4 %. 3,000

Reich, Abraham to Joseph H. Scanlan. Ewen st, e s, 50 n Varet st, 20x75. Oct. 29, due Nov. 1, 1896, 5 %. 2,500

Reinhard, Simon to Henry Kordes. Cooper st, e s, 125 s Evergreen av, 18.4x100. Oct. 20, installs, 5 %. 2,070

Richard, Mary E. wife of and James to Robert I. Miller, Philadelphia, Pa. Stuyvesant av, e s, 52 n Van Buren st, 16x79. Oct. 30, due . 1, 1894, 5 %. 2,800

Rogers, William R. to Mary E. Seaman. 48th st, n e s, 180 s e 4th av, 20x100.2. Oct. 29, 3 years, 5 %. 2,000

Rosenberg, Israel and Benjamin Ullman to Harris Max. Christopher av, e s, 150 s Blake av, 75x100. Oct 29, installs. 400

Rosh, Henry and Joseph E. Middle to Horace W. Walter guard. Hannah A. and Marie F. Walter. Macon st, s s, 16.8 e Marcy av, 16.8x100. Oct. 23, 3 years, 5 %. 4,000

Rowland, William A. to The Title Guarantee and Trust Co. Rutledge st, s s, 200 e Bedford av, 20.9x100. Oct. 31, 3 years, 5 %. 4,000

Samuelson, Samuel and Pincus Ronginsky to Sophie G. Parker, New Hamburgh, N. Y. Thatford av, w s, 125 s Eastern Parkway, 25x100.1. Oct. 29, demand. gold, 1,500

Schaffer, J Frederick to Bernhard Donop. Ainslie st. P. M. Oct. 30, 5 years, 5 %. 2,700

Schlachter, Henry and John Senger to Charles W. Truslow trustee William Wall. McKibbin st. P. M. Oct. 29, 3 years, 5 %. 1,680

Schlieske, Otto, Philadelphia, Pa., to John Bauer, Philadelphia, Pa. Greene av, s e s, 300 n e Knickerbocker av, 20x100. Oct. 16, 1 year, 5 %. 1,225

Schroder, Margaret extrx. Charles Schroder to John Gerald. 19th st, s w s, 175 n w 3d av, 25x142.1x25x141.8. July 1, 3 years, 5 %. 625

Schwicker, Christian to William A. Martin. Dean st, s w cor Sackman st, runs west 59.8 x south 32.8 x southwest 33.8 to East New York av, x northeast 50 to Sackman st, x north 31.10. Oct. 23, 3 years. 2,500

Searing, Andrew J. with The Brooklyn Door and Sash Co. mortgagees. Agreement as to priority of morts. made by Sylvester Searing. Oct. 29. nom

Searing, Sylvester to The Brooklyn Door and Sash Co 6th st, n s, 97.10 w 5th av, 100x100. Oct. 29, due Dec. 1, 1891. 727

Shelter, John B. to The Produce Exchange Building and Loan Assoc. Milford st, w s, 150 s Belmont av, 20x100. Oct. 16, installs. 1,200

Sheridan, Patrick to The Title Guarantee and Trust Co. President st, n s, 175 e 8th av, 2 lots, together 50.6x100. 2 morts., each $15,000. Oct. 30, 1 year, 5 %. 30,000

Sibley, Albert to Joseph P. Puels. Quincy st, s s, 100 w Throop av, 4 lots, each 18.9x100. Sub. to 4 morts. aggregating $20,000. 4 morts., each $750. Oct. 30, 1 year. 3,000

Same to The Title Guarantee and Trust Co. Quincy st, s s, 100 w Throop av, 10 lots, each 18.9x100. 10 morts., each $5,000. Oct. 30, 3 years, 5 %. 50,000

Schmidt, Adam to William Schmidt. Himrod st. P. M. Sub. to mort. $3,000. Nov. 2, 5 years, 5 %. 1,300

Same to Henry Ostermann. Same property. P. M. Nov. 2, 3 years, 5 %. 3,000

Seelbach, Jacob J. to Catharine A. wife of John Cornwell. Graham av, e s, 25 n Scholes st, 25x100. Nov. 2, 3 years. 8,000

Smith, John J., Thomas, Patrick, Henry and Peter heirs Henry Smith to James J. Roseman. Frost st, No. 225. Oct. 30. 60

Steinert, John and Maria his wife to Jacob F. Schneider and Magdalena his wife. Hart st. P. M. Oct. 31, due Nov. 1, 1896, 5 %. 2,450

Stoddart, Margaret T. wife of and William to The Methodist Book Concern Employes' Co-operative Building and Loan Assoc. Pacific st, No. 979, n s, 25 e Grand av, 20x80. Oct. 21, installs, 5 %. 2,500

Suydam, Catharine L. wife of and John B. to James McCormick. Madison st, s s, 98 e Sumner av, 19x100. Oct. 31, due Nov. 1, 1894, 5 %. 5,500

Smith, Emily O. to Morris Fosdick, Jamaica, L. I. Milford st, w s, 210 n Blake av, 60x100. Oct. 23, 1 year. 200

Smith, Julia wife of and Patrick to Michael Newman. Van Cott av, s s, 20 w Kingsland av, 20x95. Oct. 30, 2 years. 1,400

Stahl, Anton and Helena his wife to Michael Seitz. Bushwick av, n e cor McKibbin st, 28.1x98.9x26.7x100. Oct. 1, 5 years, 5 %. 1,000

Sutter, Peter to Henry H. Adams, County Treasurer, of Kings Co. Lot 197 map Whitehead Howard. Oct. 16, 1 year, 5 %. 3,500

Sacks, Pauline wife of and Herrman formerly Midas to The Title Guarantee and Trust Co. Fulton st, s e cor Sheffield av, 100x100. Nov. 4, 3 years, 5 %. 4,000

Schwab, Margaretha to John Bosch. Montrose av. P. M. Oct. 31, 1 year, 5 %. 800

Searle, George N. to Thomas Guille. Lee av, e s, 60.4 n Penn st, 19.8x83.4. Nov. 4, 3 years, 5 %. 6,000

Stinus, Lizzie to Maria L. Streeter. Barbey st, w s, 364.11 s Fulton av, 25x95. Nov. 4, 5 years 1,200

Stock, Charles E. to Kate C. Henderson et al. trustees Isaac Henderson. Lot begins at point in centre line bet 10th and 11th sts, 100 w 8th av. P. M. Oct. 19, 5 years, 5 %. 2,250

Taylor, Thomas to Nellie A. Hiers. Lexington av, s w s, 50 n w Forest pl, 50x100, New Utrecht. Nov. 4, due Jan. 2, 1892. 300

Thiele, Anna M. to John D. Prince and ano. exrs. George R. Cutter. Bay 11th st, s s, 131.5 w Cropsey av, 40x— to Bennetts lane, x40.5x—, New Utrecht. Oct. 27, 3 years. 2,000

Tappey, Eva to Citizens' Co-operative Building and Loan Assoc. of Bath Beach, N. Y. Bay 34th st, s e s, 680 s w Benson av. 91.2 to Bath av, x southeast 96.10 x northeast 97.5 x northwest 96.8, New Utrecht. Oct. 30, installs. 3,000

Teaz, Lucinda to James H. Mason. Hancock st. P. M. Nov. 2, 5 years, 5 %. 600

Same to Mary Lambert individ. and extrx. Patrick Lambert. Same property. Nov. 2, 5 years, 5 %. 600

Thompson, Edward to Bulmer Lumber Co. (Lim.) Myrtle av, s s, 60 e Bleecker st. 100x80. Sept. 19, demand. 5,000

Tingue, Sarah L., Portchester, N. Y., to Edwin D. Phelps. Orange st. P. M. Oct. 30, installs, 5 %. 25,000

Tomlinson, Charles and Charles W. to Mary W. Smith. Liberty av, s s, 50 e Osborn st, 100x100; Schenck av, w s, 100 n Blake av, 50x100. Oct. 30, demand. 500

Towne, Nelson, Hudson, N. Y., to Alphonse P. Rinck. Park av. P. M. Oct. 24, 2 years, 5 %. 3,000

Vogt, Henry, Charles and William to James D. Leary. North 13th st, n e s, 200 n w Wythe av. P. M. Oct. 12, 3 years. 5,000

Van Orden, George O. to James Williamson. 6th av, s e cor 11th st, runs east 93.4 x south 100 x east 48.7 x south 100 to 12th st, x west 129.11 x north 60 x east 0.6 x north 20 x east 55.6 x north 19.6 x west 77 to av, x north 100.6. Oct. 29, due Feb. 1, 1892. 15,000

Same to John Konvalinka. 12th st, n s, 21 e 6th av, runs north 60 x east 0.6 x north 20 x east 27.6 x south 80 to st, x west 28. Oct. 28, 3 years, 5 %. 9,500

Same to same. 12th st, n s, 49 e 6th av, 28x80. Oct. 28, 3 years, 5 %. 9,500

Same to same. 12th st, n s, 77 e 6th av, 28x100. Oct. 28, 3 years, 5 %. 9,500

Same to same. 12th st, n s, 105 e 6th av, 28x100. Oct. 28, 3 years, 5 %. 9,500

Vernon, Frederic R. and Francis J. to The Hoagland Laboratory. North 10th st, n e s, 100 s e Berry st, 125x200 to North 11th st. Oct. 19, due Nov. 1, 1896, 5 %. gold, 50,000

Same to Cornelius N. Hoagland. Same property. Sub. to above. Oct. 19, due Nov. 1, 1894. gold, 24,000

Van Orden, George O. to James Williamson. 6th av, e s, 81 s 11th st, 19.6x75.6. Oct. 29, 6 months. 7,500

Same to Indiana Giberson. 6th av, e s, 52 s 11th st, 29x75.6. Oct. 29, 6 months. 10,000

Same to Laura A. Griggs. 6th av, e s, 23 s 11th st, 29x75.6. Oct. 29, 6 months. 10,000

Same to John Williamson. 6th av, s e cor 11th st, runs east 78 x south 8 x west 1.8 x south 15 x west 76.4 to av, x north 23. Oct. 29, 1 year, 5 %. 14,000

Wood, Thomas to James D. Rankin and James Ross. Macon st. P. M. Oct. 26, due Oct. 31, 1892, 5 %. 750

Webb, Emma and Florence to Cornelius N. Hoagland. Bergen st, n s, 230 w Hoyt st, 20x100. Oct. 29, due Nov. 1, 1894, 5 %. gold, 4,200

White, George H. K. to George W. Tarbox. Clermont av, w s, 136.7 n Willoughby av, 16x76.2. Oct. 30, 1 year, 5 %. 1,000

Whitehead, Max, New York, to Title Guarantee and T Co. 6th st. P. M. Oct. 31, 3 years, 5 ¢ust 5,000

Wilkenfeld, Hirsch and Nathan Rittermann to Maria Linington. Watkins st, e s, 25 n Dumont av, 50x100. Oct. 30, due Nov. 1, 1892. 2,000

Wilm, Theodore to Charles W. Truslow trustee William Wall. Bogert st. P. M. Oct. 29, 3 years, 5 %. 690

Walther, Phillip and Johanna his wife to John C. Wirth. Central av, s w s, 50 n w Greene av, 25x90. Oct. 1, 3 years, 5 %. 3,500

Zeller, William to Herman Ziehler. Pacific st. P. M. Oct. 31, 5 years, 5 %. 1,500

Zentgraf, Sebastian to Charles W. Truslow trustee William Wall. Bogert st. P. M. Oct. 29, 3 years, 5 %. 690

Zion Church of the Evangelical Association of North America in East New York to Elizabeth O. Walter, New York. Liberty av, s s, 100 w Butler av, 50x100. Oct. 31, 5 years, 5 %. 3,500

MORTGAGES----ASSIGNMENTS.

NEW YORK CITY.

OCTOBER 30 TO NOVEMBER 5—INCLUSIVE

Antony, Betty to Peter Doelger and ano. exrs. and trustees Joseph Doelger. $5,000

Anderson, Robert S. and Cornelius E. trustees Cornelius V. Anderson to Mary E. Montgomery, Brooklyn. 600

Beckwith, Leonard F. to Louise L. Williams. 9,539

Same to same. 10,312

Chadwick, Emma L. formerly Davies to William P. Earle. 14,000

Same to same. 8,500

Same to same. 3,500

Cummings, Richard to The Bradley & Currier Co. (Lim.) 2,050

Cohen, Meyer to Clara J. Chase, Lacoma, N. H. 3,150

Cohen, Barnett to Meyer Cohen. 4,000

Christensen, Rasmus to George Muller. 1,000

Dorsett, R Clerence to Josiah F. Cadmus. 2,489

Ellis, John S. exr. Julia Waterbury to Gertrude C Winthrop. 24,000

Same to Antoinette L. Edwards. 56,000

Funke, Louis to John H. Doscher. 4,400

Franklin, Morris, Fanny M. Updike and Henry B. Weselman to George E. Hyatt. 12,000

Friedline, Louisa C. and Samuel A. to Frederick Zittel. other consid. and 100

Field, David Dudley to Jeanie L. Musgrave widow. 16,000

Ganzenmuller, August to Conrad Vorbach. 12,000

Goodman, Aaron, Brooklyn, to Sarah Lese. 2,000

Goldstein, Morris to Leopold Haas. 10,000

Hirsch, Clara to Elizabeth H. wife of Lucius C. Ashley. 1,236

Holmes, William M. to Elizabeth M. Holmes. nom

Hoffman, Burrall to Florence Geary, Brooklyn. 5,230

Hoffman, Susan O., Flushing, L. I., to same. 6,153

Hamlin, George A. and ano. exrs. Persis Hall to Ziba H. Kitchen. 3,739

Hughes, Thomas R., Weehawken, N. J., to Frederick G. and E. Clifford Potter trustees Samuel W. Potter dec'd. nom

Immen, Luer to Henry F. Quast, Brooklyn. 8,000

Johnston, Robert B., Yonkers, N. Y., to Jennie C. Johnston, Yonkers, N. Y. 6,300

Josephthal, Moritz and Louis to Lulu Mander, Brooklyn. 10,000

Klingenstein, Jacob to Joseph L. Buttenwieser. nom

Libman, Meyer to Karl M. Wallach. 2,000

Levy, Barnett, Louis Gordon and Sophia Mayer to Herman Fichter. nom

Lawrence, Frazier & Co. to Isaac Friedenheit. 8,240

Lyon, Anna E. to Whitfield Terriberry. nom

Levy, Isaac to William L. Jenkins, Mt. Vernon, N. Y. 5,000

Lawrence, Frazier & Co. to Charles Frazier. 7,000

Lawton, Newbury D., New Rochelle, N. Y., to John L. Daniels. 2,575

Loew, Sarah L. to Charles R. Parfitt, Stamford, Conn. 2,000

Loonie, James J. and Eugene Parker to Dennis Loonie. 27,000

McManus, Hugh J. to Ann McManus. nom

Milliken, Seth M. to Martha Kemp. 4,500

Same to Mary H. Sutton, North Andover, Mass. 4,500

Morgenthau, Henry to R. Clarence Dorsett. nom

Same to same. nom

Michelson, Samuel to Israel M. Cohen. 2,500

Marshall, Margaret and ano. exrs. Robert Marshall to Ann Miller. 20,333

Same to same. 10,167

Same to same. 12,200

Middlebrook, Frederic J., Brooklyn, to Lizzie S. Stocker, Cooperstown, N. Y. 2,000

Middlebrook, Frederic J., Brooklyn, to Bernhard Grunhut. 2,000

Same to same. 6,000

Same to Harriet E. Wilmerding extrx. Henry A. Wilmerding. 7,014

Same to same. 8,038

Niles, William W. to E. Burgess Warren, Philadelphia. nom

Ruff, August to Elias Jacobs. 6,688

Robert, Charles S., Mastic, L. I., to Simon R. Weil. 1,000

Rogers, Archibald, Hyde Park, N. Y., to Samuel S. Sands. 10,019

Reed, Mary N. to James N. Platt, South Haven, L. I. 1,000

Randell, Charles H. exr. Morris Randell to Charles H. Randell, Westchester, N. Y. nom

Same as exr. Betsey A. Randell to same. nom

Smadbeck, Louis, Isidore B. Brooks and Emanuel G. Bach, of Fidelity Indorsing and Guarantee Co., to John McCormick. 170

Stuyvesant, Amelia wife of Robert R. to Frederic J. Middlebrook. 10,080

Sage, Mary E. to Robert W. de Forest and ano. exrs. and trustees Burr Wakeman. 6,024

The Hudson River Bank to George Crawford. nom

The Manhattan Savings Inst. to Stephen V. R. Cruger. 10,767

Thurston, Franklin A. to Lincoln McCormack. 2,400

Tomlinson, John C. to Ezra T. Gilliland. 9,000

Same to same. 1,500

The F. & M. Schaefer Brewing Co. to Luer Immen. 5,000

The Lawyers' Title Ins. Co. of New York to Howard N. Martin. 17,347

Thorn, Emily A. et al exrs. William K. Thorn to William K. Thorn formerly Junior, Newport, R. I. 10,151

Title Guarantee and Trust Co. to Elizabeth Hanschild. 12,000

Same to Dwight S. Herrick trustee John Simpson dec'd. 20,000

Title Guarantee and Trust Co. to The National Savings Bank of the City of Albany. 50,000

Title Guarantee and Trust Co. to Phillips and Lloyd Phoenix exrs. Stephen W. Phoenix. 30,000
Travers, Maria L. extrx. William R. Travers to Ellen T. Duer. 4,611
Varker. Thomas individ. and guard. of Mary A. Varker and said Mary A. Varker to Mary G. Wood, Brooklyn. 10,069
Weinstein, Ascher to Bernhard Grunhut. 6,000
Wahlig, Babette to Babette Wahlig extrx. Charles F. Wahlig. 5,500
Wick, Jacob, Jr., to Peter A. H. Jackson. 13,000
Wilson, John T. trustee John Wilson dec'd to Orisen B. Smith trustee Anne Seguin. 7,000
Wright, Sarah K. to Elizabeth P. Runk. 3,000
Webb, Anna E. to Elizabeth Aymar. 12,000
Weiner, Jacob K. to Moses Goodman. 6,000

KINGS COUNTY.

Oct. 29 to Nov. 4—Inclusive.

Allen, Thomas J. to John Davies. $1,000
Barrett, Bridget to Louis Bossert. 1,150
Baumgrass, Clarence M. to Frederick W. Fielding. 500
Biehling, Robert to Christain Hunken. 1,000
Boslet, Jacob to Henry McShane Mfg. Co. nom
Baker, Mary A. L. to Hall Sash and Door Co. 430
Bossert. Louis to Henry Roth. 1,134
Same to same. 2,250
Same to same. 15,720
Brandt, John H. to Caroline Brandt. 3,500
Brennan, Thomas to Charles D. King. 380
Courtney, William J. to John Courtney. 1,000
Condict, Silas A. exr. Silas B. Condict to Warren P. Ackerman. 550
Condict, Silas A. individ. to same. 250
Ernst, Charles to Emil F. Wildner. 1,800
Ellis, John S. exr. Julia Waterbury to Antoinette L. Edwards. 9.000
Same to same. 2,000
Same to same. 8,000
Same to Gertrude C. Winthrop. 4,000
Same to same. 11,000
Same to same. 2,400
Same to same. 1,500
Same to same. 50,000
Same to same. 2,500
Frank. Herman to Emanuel New. 500
Francisco, George W. and Charles H. to George Covert. 1,300
Franke, Eunice R. and Henry to Anna C. Cary guard. Esther C. Cary. 5,500
Gay, Charles, Jr., to Josiah Foster committee Sophia J. Cooper. 2,500
Gay, William to Charles Gay, Jr. 2,500
Griffin, William C. to Henry Wills. 500
Hartmann, Conrad to Lazarus Weil. 3,100
Hassan, William S. to Sherman Loomis. 950
Hauck, Edward J. to Barbara Kraemer. 2,000
Hess, Ferdinand and Ludwig Harburger to George C. Clarke. nom
Ingraham, William M. to Maria A. Konwenhoven. 2,000
Jarvis, Welcome S. to James W. Smith trustee. 5,000
Krines, Joseph and Ida to Eugene R. Judge. 3,000
Kings Co. Trust Co to The German-American Real Estate Title Guarantee Co. 4,000
Same to same. 4,000
Kleinlein, Anna D. extrx. John Kleinlein to George Dittrich 2,000
Ledoux, Forosengean J. to Geneva C. Stopenhagen. 400
Lyons, George H. to Almira Jencks. nom
Lebewohl, Louis and Abraham Ruth to Minnie A. wife of James Demarest. nom
Linton, Edward F. to Susan Tompkins. 1,605
Loewenstein, Henry to Julia Lang. nom
Luyster, Phebe to Elizabeth S. wife of James Miller. 625
Long Island Bank to James Cropsey. 1,500
Parker, Asa W. to Mary E. Sweezey. 2,000
Peoples Trust Co. to Charles H. Roberts. nom
Phillips, Emma J. to Julius B. Davenport. 2,000
Power, John to Herman C. Smith. nom
Puels, Joseph P. to Bulmer Lumber Co. (Lim.) 1,500
Quirck, Susan R. to Bedford Co-operative Building and Loan Assoc. 1,000
Raynor, George C. to Margaret M. Rhodes. 4,500
Roberts, James G. to Albert W. Seaman. 970
Rose, Hannah M. to Thomas J. Allen. 700
Ross, James L. to Emile K. Ecks. 1,000
Schade, George to Sabra L. Duryea. 600
Schrott, Elizabeth wife of Amos to Phillip Bies. 1,004
Siedler, Charles recvr. Lorillard Brick Works, New Jersey, to Daniel Messmore, New York. nom
Statesir, William H. to Annie S. Wyckoff. 700
Stoutenburg, George B. to James D. Rankin and James Ross. 1,000
Schaeffer, John to Albert Berckmeier. 500
Smith, Mary W. to Patrick H. Warren, Long Island City. 750
Terrett, Sarah A., Harriet M. and Lillian R. and Sarah L. Holt to Rebecca F. Brooks. 1,400
Title Guarantee and Trust Co. to Brooklyn Young Women's Christian Assoc. 2,000
Same to same. 1,500
Same to Phebe E. Halsey et al. exrs. John A. Halsey. 1,000
Same to Julius Reiner. 3,500
Same to Cornelia M. Ten Eyck. 1,000
Same to Maria E. Davis and ano. exrs. Theodore R. Davis. 5,000
Same to John M. Dagnall. 3,500
Same to Frank Bailey. 3,600
Same to Peekskill Savings Bank. 2,500
Same to Nassau Trust Co. guard. Louis H. Emerson. 2,500
Same to Horatio G. Mirick exr. Edward A. Whaley. 6,000
Same to same. 6,000
Same to Blanche Alexander. 8,000
Van Wyck, Sarah E. extrx. of Anna L. Van Vechten to William Hyams. 1,900
Walsh, Anna W. to Julia Wood. 1,500
Weinrauch, Henry and Jacob Schaefer to Simon A. Weber. 1,000
Wyckoff, William F. to Annie S. Wyckoff. 300
Young, Margaret to Alice M. Dexter. 7,989

JUDGMENTS.

In these lists of judgments the names alphabetically arranged, and which are first on each line, are those of the judgment debtor. The letter (D) means judgment for deficiency (*) means not summoned. (†) signifies that the first name is fictitious, real name being unknown. Judgments entered during the week, and satisfied before day of publication, do not appear in this column, but in list of Satisfied Judgments.

NEW YORK CITY.

Oct. and Nov.

4 Abrahamson, Bernhard—G A Le Blanc $239 17
4 Aucker, Edwin—Metropolitan Telephone and Telegraph Co ... 11 56
5 Ahrens, David H—Henrietta Ahrens. 1,512 26
5 the same——the same ... 1,064 98
5 the same——the same ... 1,573 03
5 the same——the same ... 544 14
5 the same——the same ... 578 75
5 the same——the same ... 2,403 58
5 the same——H L Croll ... 1,210 95
5 Allard, Treffle H—Julius Heiderman. 34 87
5*Alyea, William—Bulmer Lumber Co (Lim) ... 74 48
6 Axtmann, Albert A—J J Jones ... 345 15
6 Adam, James A, or Adams, James A } Thomas Fell. 83 75
6 Anderson, Christian—Kirtland, Andrews & Co ... 816 30
6 Arnold, Joseph A—Franklin Tenny. 160 85
31 Black, Joseph R—John Spence ... 531 66
31 Bonnell, John Harper—Second Nat Bank of Red Bank, N J ... 3,739 01
2 Bloomson, Herman—Henry Terhune. 501 05
2 Briggs, William E—J J Donovan ... 40 78
2*Behrens, Peter—Bank of Harlem ... 229 47
2 Benedix, August—Pincus Pohalski ... 73 27
4 Blaise, Jules Joseph—Nineteenth Ward Bank ... 1,021 54
4 Bamberg, Isaac—Meyer Corn ... 73 65
4 Bloomfield, John J—Rosalia Muller, exr ... 683 87
4 Bruce, Madame K C—John Ames ... 182 46
4†Brosnan, John M—Oscar Taussig ... 852 00
4 Borrell, Jamie—E N Miner ... 172 08
4 Blake, Frederick D, Blake, Sarah F } Tradesmen's Nat Bank ... 3,943 69
4 Backer, Abraham—G F Baldwin ... 102,471 40
5 Blanchard, Charles A—Alexander, Barney & Chapin ... 282 85
5 Brumder, Charles F—Marie Holterbach ... 167 55
5 Blake, Adam—Robert Unger ... 82 74
5 Brick, Alexander—Rosa Green ... 32 50
5 Bulkley, Frank—Patrick Ryan ... 149 42
6 Bartlett, Abner, Jr—William Wilson 32 56
6 Brudi, Alexander L—Union Square Bank ... 161 37
6 Brennan, Jane—C H Van Buren ... 509 37
6 Bryere, Joseph O A—Charles Schlesinger ... 170 92
6 Brennan, Thomas—Isaac Rosenthal ... 495 54
6 Bach, Albert, Bach, Alice Hendricks } C F Laurence ... 942 41
6 Bennett, William—Beadleston & Woerz ... 73 00
6 Burmeister, Henry—G T Lawrence ... 429 34
31 Cowdrey, Jane H—A C Butts ... 2,980 04
31 Clifford, Edward—W H Berrian ... 123 75
2 Clifford, Henry B—Russell Sage ... 1,574 98
2 Cohen, Elias G—E B Bullock ... 105 15
2 Cramer, Mary C—Mary Schultz ... 391 02
2 Cumiskey, Owen—Joseph Glaser, costs 91 69
2 Clews, Henry, Clews, James B } Julia Scheiner, admrx ... 2,533 90
2 Clinton, James C—Singer Mfg Co ... 796 15
4 Cryder, William Wetmore—Guarantee Trust and Safe Deposit Co ... 9,269 61
4 Colleran, John—James Mack ... costs 82 58
4*Cobleigh, Gordis R—E S Jaffray ... 10,649 68
4 Connors, Thomas—Annie Healy ... 131 08
5 Croll, Samuel H—Henrietta Ahrens ... 616 09
5 the same——the same ... 1,512 26
5 the same——the same ... 1,064 98
5 the same——the same ... 1,573 03
5 the same——the same ... 544 14
5 the same——the same ... 598 75
5 Cross, William—T L C Gerry ... 132 37
5 Cryder, William Wetmore, Carmick, Edward H } Danbury Nat Bank 4,278 92
5 Coffin, Frederick R—Market and Fulton Nat Bank ... 208 36
5 Cure, U S Grant—Edgar Wright ... 246 75
5 Culver, Weeks W—M S Sire ... 84 00
5 Cranston, Henry—Bank of Harlem ... 565 93
5 Calame, August—Charles Carpy ... 315 97
6 Cranston, Henry—E W Ashley ... 416 88
6 Clews, Henry—W C Thompson ... 816 00
6 Case, Theodore B—Martin Armstrong 50 57
6 Crosby, Hiram B—Reed McIlvanie ... 84 11
6 Carroll, Michael, Jr—J M Karsch ... 254 09
2 De Barry, Mary—W C Pike ... 242 97
2 Dunnigan, Bernard—M P Meilby ... 1,108 40
4 Dimmock, Katherine C—J A Mitchell 182 46
4 *Day, Lucius, *Day, Herbert T } E S Jaffray ... 10,649 68
4 Draper, T W Morgan—O M Farrand 95 66
5 Daniels, Henry O—Goodyear Shoe Mfg Co ... 368 64
5 Duffy, Bernard—Moses Price ... 74 14
5 Donnell, Robert W—First Nat Bank of Carthage, Missouri ... 5,340 37
6 Dippel, Frederick—Henry McShane ... 813 92
31 Ellis, John—W M Sayer, Jr ... 751 03
2 Edelson, Louis, Edelson, Abraham } Abraham Kassel ... 734 50
4 Estang, Juan—E N Miner ... 172 08
5 Emken, Frederick—Christian Abele ... 1,356 31
5 Eaton, Orson—G W Venable ... 897 03
6 Edelson, Abraham—Daniel Rothstein. 781 08
6 Ellis, Edward S—Chatham Nat Bank. 885 18
6 Eisenberg, Frederick—Julius Wile ... 142 00
30 Frey, Daniel—Murray Hill Bank ... 4,059 01
31 Fuchs, Gustav—Frank McCoy ... costs 93 09
31 Frischke, Ernst—T R Sager ... 246 12
2 Forrest, Louise R—G R Brown ... 249 06
2 Fish, Ferdinand—William Hodsdon ... costs 91 62
2 Fitzgerald, Thomas—J J Donovan ... 37 08
2 Forster, Charles M—Julia Scheiner, admrx ... 2,533 90
2 Fullager, Kelsie—R C Van Wyck ... 17 01
4 Fanshawe, William S—C R Hickox. 1,048 84
4 Fredin, Olof H—H W Mitchell ... 40 37
4 Fisher, John H—A B Hart ... 303 00
5 Fitzgerald, Thomas—Ingersoll Sergeant Drill Co ... 199 71
5 Floyd, Theodore B—Edgar Wright ... 246 75
5 the same——G L Reynolds ... 1,317 22
6 Fanrot, Theodore W—J M Navarro ... 104 53
6 Fanton, Henry B—John Williams ... 108 32
6 Few, Edward W—Sanford Vroman ... 301 42
6*Freeman, Alfred A—Chemical Nat Bank ... 12,353 60
6 Falk, Isaac L, Falk, George W } Herman Hablo ... 612 55
6 Frank, John H—Henry Colgrove ... 97 90
30 Goldsmith, Jonas G—Holland Trust Co ... 377 68
30 Grenlich, Jacob—Elise King, extrx ... 168 08
30 Godwin, Parke—Jennie W Ashley. costs 87 72
30 the same—Jessie Woods ... costs 88 72
31 Glaser, Joseph—Israel Cohen ... costs 45 07
31 Gillis, Charles J, Geoghegan, Stephen J } Jacob Senn ... 2,068 59
31 Gottberg, Julius, exr Mendlich Gottberg—U S Nat Bank ... costs 87 23
31 Guth, Charles L—Benno Lask ... 102 47
2 Gifford, Charles H—E D Slater ... 3,087 55
2 Goldstein, Jeremiah—Meyer Chapkowsky ... 318 15
2 Grinspan, Abraham—Frederick Kaffeman ... 135 06
2 Grey, David S—A D Glueck ... 309 04
2*Gordon, Michael—Loeminster Shirt Co ... 205 31
2 Graff, Jacob G—E C Korner ... 624 60
2 Gault, James—W H Harrison, trustee ... (D) 223 84
2 the same——the same ... (D) 825 84
2 the same——the same ... (D) 427 84
4 Gru, Joseph—J G Worthley ... 910 74
4 Glaubrecht, Bernhardt—A L Phillips. 887 36
5 Gibbons, Austin P—Annie E Drummond, admrx ... 19 79
5 Grant, George—H M Fischer ... 76 49
5 Gillette, Emily D—Katie McElligot ... 206 17
6 Grodginsky, David—L T Powell ... 169 30
6 Gilmartin, James—J M Valentine ... 1,527 05
31 Hall, Robert H—E L Platow ... 259 50
31 Hubbell, Charles E—Emma Parter ... 330 17
31 Howell, Eugene N—Chemical Nat Bank ... 4,597 72
31 Hoffman, Michael A—Mayer Bickart. 460 97
31 Harper, William D—Second Nat Bank of Red Bank, N J ... 3,739 01
2 Hart, Alexander R—Western Nat Bank ... 468 13
2 the same——the same ... 1,273 48
2 the same——Chatham Nat Bank ... 376 35
2 Henriques, Alexander F—S E Gee ... 35 12
2 Hoover, Byron E—C H Hemmons ... 71 88
4 Hass, Frank—John Powers ... 121 41
4 Heeidt, Daniel—Henrietta Rice ... 128 76
4 Herz, Henry—Manhattan Electric Light Co ... 885 04
4 Hart, Alexander R—Chatham Nat Bank ... 822 64
5 Harper, William D—Market and Fulton Nat Bank ... 208 36
5 Hasbrouck, Frank—Philip Stein ... 73 48
5 Hammel, Leo—William Cohen ... 25 07
5 Hawkins, John T—M R Cook ... 146 75
6 Hogan, John—Pulsometer Steam Pump Co ... 796 93
6*Haight, Effingham C—Chemical Nat Bank ... 12,353 60
6 Hartung, Lorenzo R—J H Hervy ... 152 11
6 Hart, Julius—Trow's Printing and Book Binding Co ... 244 40
6 Harper, William D—Chatham Nat Bank ... 885 18
6 Hubbell, Charles J—Franklin Tenny. 160 85
6 Hall, Addie—Kate Williams ... 153 70
6 Hicks, William C—E C Hazard ... 365 00
31 Jacobs, Michael—Moritz Rosett ... 97 68
2 Johnes, Catharine—Eliza V H Ellis ... costs 168 52
5 Johnson, Nathaniel—A & W S Carr Co ... 816 22
5 Jones, Victoria A, Jones, William C } P H McCann ... 512 90
6 Jerkowski, Marcus—Samuel Marx ... 541 13
6 Johnson, Frank H—Martin Armstrong ... 50 57
6 Johnson, Christopher, Sr—C H Evans 44 76
6 Jackson, Jennie—George Seinel ... 157 45
31 Kraus, Joseph—Frank McCoy ... costs 93 09
31 Knowles, Frederick C—J F Parkes ... 54 28
31 Kurz, Jacob—T R Sager ... 246 12

2 Kline, Charles / Kreuder, Frank F } S J Nowell...... 190 92
2 Kraus, Joseph / Kraus, Julius C } Robert Froese...... 1,125 94
4 Klingenfeld, Nathan—S E Gee....... 21 85
4 Kohlhaas, Charles H—F G Weeks.... 177 68
4 Kaufmann, Emile—Manhattan Electric Light Co.................. .... 845 04
5 King, Harlan A—Alexander Worms. 65 01
5 Kirchner, Charles—Bulmer Lumber Co (Lim).......................... 74 48
5 Knoth, William—G W Venable...... 170 58
6 Keogh, Christopher B—Albany Venetian Blind Co...................... 774 81
6 Koper, Henry—Chemical Nat Bank..12,383 60
6 Kelly, John P—Jeremiah Geraty.... 176 27
6 Kronthal, Louis / Kronthal, Charles } James Talcott... 191 87
31 Lovejoy, Susan C—W D Peck, recvr. 26 93
31 the same——the same 26 93
2*Loweree, William H—Cornelius Desosway....... .... 95 52
2 Lyman, John B—S E Gee............ 16 75
2 Luce, Clarence S——the same........ 92 65
2 Link, Cornelius—Bank of Harlem.... 229 47
2 Lemon, Bridget A—T C Blake...... 325 75
2 Loewenthal, Adolph—George Freygang.. 322 38
2 Locke, Charles E—Georgini Neuendorff................................, 1,969 63
4 Lane, Charles H—C F Schmidt...... 819 64
5 Lindsey, Robert—Cecile Rusch, exr and trustee......................(D) 5,508 73
5 Levy, Louis—Charles Keilson.. ..... 169 37
5 Lawson, Leonidas M—First Nat Bank of Carthage, Missouri.... .... 5,340 37
5 Longworth, Thomas P—Davidge Fertilizer Co.............................. 705 01
6 Lockett, Charles H—Eliza J. Nicholson.. 109 21
2 Mosby, Julius A—Henry Herrmann.. 180 02
2 Maurer, Marco—Valentino Poletto.. ....costs 74 66
2 Main, John—Ruth O Delamater...... 301 08
4 Mahon, James F—Campbell Printing Press and Mfg Co................... 31 00
4 Myers, Lewis—Morris Brokman...... 47 22
4*Masters, William G—E S Jaffray....10,649 68
5 Muller, Richard W—E C O'Brien. .. 27 87
5 Munzinger, John C—Morris Schwerin 121 58
5 Maschi, Marie—John Merry.......... 175 62
5 Merritt, John A—Manhattan Beef Co (Lim).... .... 168 90
5†Moore, Henry J—L H Viemeister.... 121 13
5 Mack, Hugo S—P A Smyth.......... 562 23
5 Mitchell, John A—J A Frazee........ 299 34
6 Mayers, Isaac—S S Hatt, assignee... 272 00
6 Mann, Edward C / Mann, Barbara } Rosalie Cristadora............ 789 59
6 Moran, Owen—J C Hatzel........... 29 50
6*Magher, Patrick F—Thurber, Whyland & Co... .... 198 97
6 Meyer, Gustav H A—Charles Wilker. 174 02
6 Manner, Charles—Henry Colgrove... 97 90
31 McGlynn, Patrick—Eagle Brewery.. 892 49
4 McGluckin, Mary E — Nineteenth Ward Bank......:..................1,021 54
4*McMahon, James / McMahon, John } J J Phillips.. .... 167 60
4 McGann, John—Edward Tracy 656 00
5 McGirr, Peter—O'Reilly, Skelly & Fogarty Co........................ 429 78
6 McCullough, William J—I R Pereira. 220 86
6 McMahon, John / McMahon, James } S H Frost. 271 69
6 McGarrigal, William J—Charles Regnault.............................costs 23 64
6 McCaffrey, William — Benedickt Fischer.................................. 158 19
6 McCune, Addie—Kate Williams.... 153 70
6 McGowan, Daniel G—Otto Deuecke.. 880 32
6 McLaughlin, John—Michael Harrison 189 00
6 North, Charles F—Frank Eigabroadt. 687 13
6 Newitter, Nathan J. assignee D H Wickham & Co—Henry Fera..costs 76 00
6 Newton, Albert H—E A Behringer.... 162 42
2 Osborne, James L—Anna M Mackenzie, extrx...............................3,797 86
2 the same——T H Newman.........3,791 86
2 the same——C W Chase...........3,804 96
4 Ottman, William / Ottman, Louis } H C Briggs...... 667 43
5 Ogden, Anna B—L C Gray...........1,227 69
6 Overton, Charles C—W H Hendrickson.. 45 32
6 O'Neill, William F—Thurber, Whyland Co........................ . 198 97
6 Osterman, Abraham — German Exchange Bank.......................... 117 76
2 Price, Walter S—Fr Beck & Co......2,322 53
2 Prosnitz, William—Robert Froese....1,125 94
2†Preuss, Thomas—S E Gee. 18 23
4 Phelps, Louis N—Nineteenth Ward Bank......... ....1,021 54
4 Pfortner, Ignatz—Paul Goepel... ... 186 37
4 Phillips, Walter E / Phillips, Sidney A } Metropolitan Telephone and Telegraph Co....... 47 00
4 Pratt, James H—Chatham Nat Bank ....costs 93 32
6 Pfeiffer, Philip—Ephraim Bass....... 48 74
6 Pollard, John K, Jr—Mary E Terry. 407 02
6 Powers, Edward H—N Y Breweries Co (Lim)........................... 238 00
6 Pake, John H—C B Reilay.......... 140 21
6 Pierce, Tecumseh — Union Central Life Ins Co 374 00
6 Pool, Richard N—D F Wright... ... 606 99
6 Quantou, Edward H—Thurber, Whyland Co............ .... 99 98
6 Quinn, Luke C, as pres't Company I, 69th Regiment, Nat Guard—Robert Stoll... .... 118 00
31 Ross, William H—E P Carpenter.....3,156 70
31 Reiss, Henry—Moritz Rosett......... 97 68
2 Richmond, Louis—Sixth Nat Bank of Philadelphia....................... ... 879 79
2 Rosenthal, Louis—Loeminster Shirt Co................ .... 205 31
4 Romaine, George W—L W Ahrens... 132 65
4 Roll, George P—L A Wagner........ 239 03
4 Rossheim, Henrietta / Rossheim, Ella } M F McDermott....... 642 45
4 Rigney, Ella L—T G Rigney......... 218 53
5 Reglander, Jacob W—William Cohen 25 07
5*Richter, Herman / Richter, Albert G } W D Wines...... 124 04
5 Ross, Hattie—William Walsmann... 179 67
6 Reves, Ignatio T—Henry Hall........ 85 08
6*Rosenheim, Jacob / Reiff, Charles } German Exchange Bank.... ...... 117 76
31 Stevens, Agnes—William Walsmann. 449 07
31 Stafford, Miles A—J F Parkes........ 84 28
31 Sire, Henry B—William Engelsdorff. 898 80
31 Stevens, Frank A—Catharine Holtz.. 171 56
2 Stevens, Adolphus E / Stevens, Frank A } Edison Electric Illuminating Co, of Brooklyn.... 402 70
2*See, Amos L / See, E Garnier } Cornelius Discaway 95 52
2†Spitzer, Oscar L / Spitzer, Mary } B H De Boes........ 77 95
2 Simon, Wolf—George Freygang...... 322 38
2 Schondorff, Rudolph H A A—R D Hatch, American Surety Co by assign... .... 78 00
2 the same——Otto Seeler, same by assign................... .... 744 58
2 Spooner, William H—E B Dusenberry 127 54
2 Shwarts, Abraham / Shwarts, Abe } G J Hellemans. 1,232 93
4 Schmidt, Edmund P—C F Schmidt... 819 64
4 Snape, Thomas H—Nathaniel Wise.. 327 16
4 Slocovich, George—F H Parker...... 169 44
4*Serling, Jacob — Metropolitan Telephone and Telegraph Co 11 56
5 Sumner, Alice—Henry Smith....costs 368 22
5 Schultz, Louis—Charles Keilson...... 169 37
5 Stillgebauer, Henry—J J Folger..... 61 30
5 Siefke, Frederick—Henry Siefke..... 388 70
5 Schwarzler, Joseph—Peter Mathews. 2,105 65
5 Simpson, George E—First Nat Bank of Carthage, Missouri..............5,340 37
5 Sheehan, John—Samuel Coles........1,034 41
6 Schwartz, Meyer—Moses Cahan...... 108 82
6 Strong, William L—S B Sturges 4,712 63
6 Schiff, John—Samuel Marx.......... 541 13
6 Sommer, Moritz—J M Valentine..... 610 01
2 Smith, Philip—Louis Axt......costs 98 91
4*Smith, George C—Oscar Taussig. 852 00
6 Smith, Frank E—Calvin Frost.. ... 326 56
31 The Hudson River Boot and Shoe Mfg Co—Alfred Gilman, admr.........2,728 38
31 the same——T M Barnes.........2,080 24
31 the same——J L Bulkley.........5,191 48
31 the same——J J Lapham.........7,398 24
31 The N Y Ladies' Guide and Visitors' Bureau Co—Eliza M Mosher......1,304 47
31 U S Volta Electric Battery Co—Edward Vernon...................... ...3,620 32
31 The Hudson River Boot and Shoe Mfg Co—Chemical Nat Bank............4,890 72
31 J H Bonnell & Co (Lim)—Second Nat Bank of Red Bank, N J.............3,739 01
31 Hazard, Hazard & Co—Anna M V Gildersleeve.... .... 271 35
31 the same——J P Chrystal. 392 55
31 U S Trust Co, as trustee—U S Trust Co.........................costs 105 01
31 the same——Grace G Minton et al, by their guard.................costs 60 00
2 Hudson River Stone Supply Co—Empire Paving and Construction Co... 81 45
2 The Fred H Whipple Co—Eugene Kelly.................................... 577 33
2 The Homestead Bank—U S Nat Bank ....costs 120 56
2 C H Dunham Railway Equipment Co J M Constable.... .... 966 24
2 The Manhattan Railway Co—J M Cornell.................................. 98 35
2 The Excelsior Dynamite Co—Rosario Imperiale................................ 154 58
2 The N Y Elevated R R Co / The Manhattan Railway Co } Sarah A McGowan 1,395 08
2 the same——Philip Milligan 351 68
2 The N Y Elevated Railroad Co / The Metropolitan Elevated Railway Co / The Manhattan Railway Co } Valentine D Diefenthaler 1,764 68
2 The Mayor, Aldermen, &c — John O'Brien.......................... ......24,118 08
2 The Manhattan Railway Co—G W Willson.... .... 476 90
2 The Pfister Book Binding Co—E P Griffin....... .... 814 67
4 Lathrop Co—Grace F Miller..........1,140 37
4 the same——the same......... ..1,154 21
4 the same——the same............1,145 54
4 Willard Metal Co—G A Le Blanc.... 239 17
4 The National Accident Society—Mary A Younkes...............................6,049 21
4 The Scranton Steel Co—J A Nichols 125,181 18
4 The Manhattan Railway Co / N Y Elevated R R Co } W W Thompson........ 117 50
4 The McFear Flax Roofing Co—L H Allen 218 98
4 Empire Laundry Machinery Co—L S Bunnell...................................2,472 59
4 The Sheet Metal Machine Co—W N Vanderhoef.......................... 342 38
4 American Zylonite Co—G W McLean, recvr...............................3,395 64
4 Monense Mfg Co——the same......... 121 58
4 Higganum Mfg Corporation — F E Guy.............................. ..5,081 77
5 Lathrop Co—Richard Wood.......... 140 65
5 The Facer Refrigerating and Ice Machine Co—G B Wood.......... ..1,999 97
5 The American Electric Exercise Machine Co—W A Simmons.. ...costs 28 38
5 The Roxite Co—Christian Abele...... 42 34
5 J H Bonnell & Co (Lim)—Market and Fulton Nat Bank....................... 208 36
5 The Saugatuck Iron Works Co—Western Nat Bank................... 226 39
5 The Persian Rug and Carpet Co—Theodore Schumacher.............2,242 82
6 The N Y Cable Railway Co—J B Shaw 402,910 25
6 the same——the same...........99,733 13
6 The Homer Lee Bank Note Co—S B Sturges........ ....2,840 86
6 the same——the same............4,712 63
6 Lexington Improvement Co—Babcock & Wilcox Co........................ 655 79
6 The N Y Steamship Co—Boston Marine Ins Co.............. .... 561 18
6 Union Pavement Co—J M Fesk...... 485 86
6 The N Y Ladies' Guide and Visitors' Bureau—L'Artiste Publishing Co... 128 98
4 Tyrer, William E—R G Dun.......... 127 39
6 Taylor, Charles—People State N Y... 700 00
6 Thompson, Joseph R H—Tunis Lumber Co.................................. 674 89
2 Utley, William R—Melvin Stephens.. 529 78
4 Vernam, Remington—W C Demorest 634 85
5 Vehstedt, Henry—J M Lenahan...... 929 91
4 Van Sickler, Samuel H—E S Jaffray 10,649 68
31*White, Jonas—W M Sayer, Jr....... 751 03
31 Wells, William H—First Nat Bank of Brooklyn.................................. 426 12
2 Walker, Herbert H—William Albert. 99 19
2*Wiley, John W—Ruth O Delamater. 301 08
5 Wolf, Max—Charles Derlam......... 601 93
5 Winckler, Curt—H M Fischer....... 76 49
5 Wehenkel, George—Alexander Worms 133 46
5 Willershausen, George—G P Cron.... 181 46
5 Walker, Sarah F—Sarah McGrath... 424 44
5 Webster, John A—H F Wells........2,343 53
6 Welch, Henry—W H McGrory...... 141 45
6 Waggoner, Ralp H—A L Gardiner.. 149 79
6 Wolff, Oscar—Frederick Krutina ... 51 18
6 Wacker, John D—G T Lawrence 294 34
2 Yost, George W—L D Stapleton 97 52

KINGS COUNTY.

Oct. and Nov.
2 Andrews, Alfred J—C H Coggeshall.. $32 60
29 Brossard, Otto / Brossard, Theodore } H A Graet's Son.......... 235 12
30 Blair, George—People's Bank Buffalo................................1,175 41
31 Beach, Arthur—G F Parker......... 487 56
30 Conklin, Augustus, recvr of Samuel Self Wood Working Co—G B Ellis. 543 55
30 Collins, Charles H—G Halbert....... 874 26
30 Cook, George—M Gearon............. 278 61
31 Coschina, Frank—M B Edinger...... 416 00
31 Coschina, Francis—W C Dornin & Co.1,763 89
2 Cary, Sr, Hugh—L P Glover......... 119 56
2 Clark, Cordelia A—D R Terrett...... 279 45
29†Dederick, "Edward" H—E Coffin, Jr. 311 00
31 Divisitch, James—M B Edinger...... 416 00
2 Drummond, Robert W—J M Gibson.. 94 30
5 Dowling, Thomas—G W Venable. ... 57 48
5 Dickerson, Angeline L—G M Lupton. 46 67
29 Freel, Edward—People's District Telegraph Co............................ 57 89
30 Fuhrmann, Frank—J R Smith....... 84 11
5 Friedrick, Frank—Pauline Friedrick. 99 28
30 Greenop, Jr., Edward B—J A Eaton. 107 31
30 Greenwood, Charles M—M Gearon... 278 61
30 Graff, Victor—G Hagenbacher....... 158 17
31 Gilbert, Charles E—G F Parker 487 56
2 Gildersleeve, Moses R—First Nat Bank of Lebannon.............................. 883 02
5 Gibbs, David E—J P Dureimers...... 138 94
5 Gibbons, Thomas—Mary J. Williams 221 47
30 Hawkins, William M / Hawkins, Elias H } G B Ellis 615 30
30 Heffron, Thomas H—Margaret Kierst 59 86
30 Heid, George—H L Rokohl 113 00
4 Heckman, James A—G H Reeves.... 177 73
4 Haefelein, Francis J—S Streit....... 550 36
5 Hart, Alexander R—Chatham Nat Bank, New York.................... 822 64
5 the same——the same............ 868 23
5 the same——the same.... .... 376 35
5 Hodges, Ruth M / Hodges, Henry } E F Knowlton..(D) 1,801 86
2 Judson, Edward—L Schwartz... .,.. 36 25
30 Kreuscher, John H—Danenberg & Coles...................................... 406 00
31 Luca, Peter—H Sandman............ 445 54
31 Leicher, Adolph—R S Luqueer....... 423 48
2 Lewey, Charles W—J B Peck........ 174 53
2 Lindsay, W Wallace—R & O E Reimer............................ .... 293 80
5 Levy, Louis—C Keilson.............. 169 37
29 McDermott, Thomas—S Cahn........ 571 02
30 Mulligan, John J—Venable & Heyman........................... ... 512 75
30 McCaffery, John W—M Stiner....... 152 92
30 McDonald, Mathias—R Schriever.... 72 70
30 Macri, Angelo—D Mayer............ 137 00
2 Miele, Guiseppe—J Deperino 68 41
2 Morgan, John E—D R Terrett........ 279 45
4 Mead, George W—H C Schultz....... 98 22
4 Marsh, George L—A M Suydam.... . 136 80
5 Mosby, Julius A—H Herrmann 180 02
5 Merritt, Franklin—J J McCue 170 98
5 Ogden, Anna B—Landon C Gray.....1,227 69
29 Rocco, Domenico—Rosa Rocco....... 61 02

30 Ryan, Mark E—W L Wolfe... 272 82
30 Ross, J Stewart—W D Murray... 2:9 49
30 Ralph, Henrietta A } M Ayres, as-
Ralph, John A } signee... 2,206 22
31 Robbins, William H H } J E Keeler. 158 88
Robbins, Helena }
5 Reilly, William B—J McCormick... 393 68
30 Simonson, Michaelis—C A Auffmordt & Co... 31,905 40
30 Stevens, Frank A } C E Miller... 840 27
Stevens, Adolphus E }
31 Stevens, Frank A—Catherine Holtz.. 171 56
2 Stoll, Joseph—Christ Protestant Episcopal Church of N Y... 120 75
4 Sheldon, Cevedra B—E Cushman... 170 16
5 Stevens, Adolphus E } Edison Electric Illuminating
Stevens, Frank A } Co, Brooklyn 402 70
5 Scott, Jennie—W D Crowell... 27 43
5 Swenson, Peter—S Levy... 4?4 60
5 Schultz, Louis—C Keilson... 169 37
30 The recvr of Samuel Self Wood Working Co—G B Ellis... 543 55
Farr, Horace G H }
2 The American Diamond } F M Pierce. 1,113 19
Rock Boring Co }
2 Treacy, Richard—J Owser... 335 85
4 The Chadwick Two Wheeler Co—C Thayer... 1,171 49
4 the same——First Nat Bank of Orleans... 779 86
30 Van Slooten, Mary L—M Gearon... 278 61
4 Van Eugers, Abraham J—S Leavitt.. 89 66
30 Walling, Thomas—G B Ellis... 615 30
30 Weiss, Theodore—C A Auffmordt & Co... 31,905 40
2 Wicks, William E—R & O E Reimer. 298 80
5 Walker, Sarah F—Sarah McGrath... 424 44
2 Zaleski, A W—F Lozano... 88 86

SATISFIED JUDGMENTS.

NEW YORK.

October 31 to November 6—Inclusive.

Aldis, Charles Ambrose, an infant, by Edward S Savage his guard—J B Simpson. (1891). $108 98
Same——same. (1891)... 112 34
Bane, John—Annie E Ott. (1891)... 79 42
Bradley, Charles W—C F Doane. (1890)... 565 54
Bushnell, Nathan—F L Fisher. (1888)... 83 77
*Browning, Harry C, William J and Jane—Andrew Beacom. (1891)... 296 64
Bruce, Wallace—Louis Windmuller et al. (1891)... 555 08
Benjamin, Harry—Henry Iden. (1890)... 83 10
Beacham, John—John Gay. (1891)... 88 62
Baron, Max—Marks Lazarus. (1891)... 480 40
Cullen, John—S H Huxford. (1891)... 681 14
Same——Samuel Huxford. (1891)... 92 24
Charpentier, Rosalie—George Hollisker. ('91). 910 72
Clews, Henry C—Bank of N Y Nat Banking Assoc. (1883)... 816 40
Creagan, Michael J—W D Peck, recvr. (1891). 9,370 20
Same——Louis Windmuller et al. (1891)... 555 08
Same——Charles Lowenthal et al. (1891)... 157 02
Cavinato, Luigi, Gueseppo, Natale and Steffano—Thomas Rogers. (1891)... 89 59
Conover, Daniel D—American Exchange Nat Bank. (1891)... 10,071 05
Conover, James S, Alonzo E and William E—John Fox. (1891)... 10 00
Chace, Emily—J B Simpson. (1891)... 108 98
Same——same. (1891)... 112 34
Clews, Henry—Cornelius Reilly. (1887)... 683 03
Same——same. (1889)... 77 97
Same——F P Olcott, recvr. (1886)... 78 26
Chicago, Burlington & Quincy R R Co—L A Gould. (1890)... 5,171 61
Same——same. (1891)... 123 45
Foster, Charles M—Cornelius Reilly. (1887).. 683 03
Same——same. (1889)... 77 97
Same——F P Olcott, recvr. (1886)... 78 26
*Fielbig, George J—Richard Tangeman. (1891) 88 55
Felt, Albert T—Charles Lowenthal. (1891)... 215 77
Foster, Charles M—Bank of N Y Nat Banking Assoc. (1883)... 816 40
Ferguson, James H—W D Peck, recvr. (1891) 9,370 20
Same——Charles Lowenthal et al. (1891)... 157 02
Same, individ and exr——Louis Windmuller et al. (1891)... 555 08
Goldstein, Morris—Mendel Diamond, admr. (1891)... 2,064 58
Guenard, Lioule—Henry Witson. (1891)... 78 45
Giddings, Julia—J B Simpson. (1891)... 108 98
Giddings, Everitt, Edith and Emily C, by Edwin C Ward their guard——same. (1891).. 112 34
Gault, James—John Gleason. (1891)... 200 22
Holterbach, Xavier—J F Jacocks. (1891)... 119 19
Hausmann, Charles A—Mary J Hall. (1891)... 467 86
Hohmann, Mary—William Campioni. (1891). 94 37
Herpich, Charles A—J A Hewlett. (1887)... 4,580 38
Same——same. (1887)... 725 50
Same——R J Roquet. (1887)... 1,484 71
Same——L S Strovck. (1887)... 590 16
Hillman, Lucetta A—C F Taylor. (1891)... 218 42
Ingersoll, Lorin and James H—W H Inman. (1887)... 10,200 57
Keris, Hermann—John Isaacs. (1891)... 147 17
Kirby, Abram M—J P McGovern. (1890)... 96 91
Luckemeyer, Edward—Bernhard Metz. (1891). 79 00
Same——same. (1890)... 1,183 05
Lewy, Max—E A Gillespie. (1889)... 142 40
Lovejoy, Susan C—Louis Windmuller et al. (1891)... 555 08
Same——Charles Lowenthal et al. (1891)... 157 02
Lovejoy, Henry W, individ and exr—Louis Windmuller et al. (1891)... 555 08
Meister, Christian—Mills & Oates Co. (1888).. 218 38
Manhattan Railway Co—A D Shepard. ('91).. 675 14
Same——same. (1891)... 88 19
Same——Andrew Ewald. (1891)... 10,687 86
Metropolitan Elevated Railway Co } Christian Weber.
Manhattan Railway Co } (1891)... 153 78
Same——same. (1890)... 683 40
Same——W B Ross. (1889)... 6,498 94
Same——same. (1890)... 111 79
Same——Abraham Kalm. (1890)... 575 80
Same——same. (1891)... 147 28
Same——Lena Pappenheim. (1891)... 130 78
Same——same. (1890)... 1,959 70
Metropolitan Elevated Railway Co } T E Macy.
Manhattan Railway Co } (1890)... 1,608 15
Same——same. (1891)... 101 58
Same——same. (1891)... 196 46
Same——J M Knox. (1890)... 7,464 99
Same——same. (1891)... 141 18
Same——same. (1891)... 190 72
Nichthauser, Sigmund—Jacob Sternlanz. (1889)... 198 28
Same——Isaac Nebenzahl. (1887)... 149 40
Same——T M Spelman. (1888)... 110 22
Same——Abraham Weinberg. (1888)... 427 67
Same——Leopold Burger. (1889)... 485 10
N Y Elevated R R Co—A D Shepard. (1891).. 88 19
Same——same. (1891)... 675 14
Same——Andrew Ewald. (1891)... 10,687 86
Prince, Abraham C, exr—Louis Windmuller et al. (1891)... 555 08
Rauh, Samuel—C B Fillebrown. (1891)... 608 58
Reinhardt, Aaron and Henry—Matilda Berg. (1891)... 409 08
Schefer, Carl } Bernhard Metz. (1891).. 79 00
Schramm, William }
Same——same. (1890)... 1,183 05
Storminger, George—John Hanneman. (1877). 521 74
Same——same. (1890)... 755 52
Sherick, Mara—G A Richards, Jr. (1891)... 82 81
Shotter, Spencer P—F W Blossom. (1891)... 498 69
Suburban Rapid Transit Co—P W Germann. (1891)... 107 67
Same——same. (1891)... 70 19
Same——same. (1890)... 5,727 84
Steinmann, Seigmund B—Benno Lewinson. (1886)... 242 50
Same——Louis Doerzbacher. (1886)... 208 96
*Shotter, Spencer P—F W Blossom. (1890)... 937 12
Traders' and Travelers' Union—Franklin Bank Note Co. (1889)... 1 589 55
Thompson, Ambrose—J B Simpson. (1891)... 108 98
Same——same. (1891)... 112 34
Third Av R R Co—Jacob Shapierer. (1891)... 136 48
Same——same. (1890)... 455 43
Vix, Jacob and George—P J Dolan. (1891)... 661 98
Weisskopf, Sigmond—E A Gillespie. (1889)... 142 40
Wolf, Frank—Henry Iden. (1890)... 83 10
Wehrle, Joseph—C F Schmidt. (1886)... 1,136 71
Young, Hugh—John Fox. (1891)... 10 00
Zeisler, Ignatz—Louis Doerzbacher. (1886)... 208 26

*Vacated by order of Court. †Suspended on Appeal. ‡Released. §Reversal. ||Satisfied by Execution.

KINGS COUNTY.

October 30 to Nov. 5—Inclusive.

Baumgras, Clarence M—G F Chapman. (1891) $238 78
Chapman, George W—S Feltman. (1891)... 198 56
Denike, Thomas S—G W Melvin. (1891)... 298 47
Same——same. (1891)... 91 95
French, John—S McElroy. (1890)... 4,693 84
Same——same. (1891)... 4,781 57
Guerrard, Loonie—H Witson. (1891)... 78 45
Johnson, Andrew—C Furgueson, Jr. (1891).. 150 63
Kipp, Andrew—Mary Bellman. (1891)... 269 24
Krummel, Amanda—T Hand. (1890)... 66 72
Mumford, Henry—S McElroy. (1890)... 4,693 84
Same——same. (1891)... 4,781 57
McAveeney, Owen—J Fitzpatrick. (1891.) (Order of Court... 1,988 62
Newman, Emanuel—Levy & May. (1891)... 114 15
The Cewles Engineering Co—O R Whitney. (1891)... 172 86
The Brooklyn Underground R R Co—S McElroy. (1890)... 121 72
Same——same. (1887)... 122 97
Same——same. (1887)... 3,654 08
Tyrrell, Martin D—J P Cranford. (1891)... 88 77
Same——same. (1891)... 108 09
Same——same. (1891)... 505 75

MECHANICS' LIENS.

NEW YORK CITY.

Oct.
31 Walker st, No. 24. James Taylor agt John Doe, owner, and John B. Monot, contractor... $95 00
31 Water st, s e cor Market slip, 26x80. Joseph Marren agt Thomas Brennan, owner and contractor... 180 00
31 Kepler av, n w cor Willard st, 75x100. Thomas Johnston agt Ida L. Senior, owner, and John B. Roberts, contractor.. 296 00
31 Seventh av, Nos. 2162 and 2164. W. T. Mersereau & Co. agt Joel B. Smith, owner and contractor... 888 10
31 Fourteenth st, s s, 157 w Av C. J. D. & T. E. Crimmins agt William Muldoon, owner and contractor... 159 75

Nov.
2 One Hundred and Eighteenth st, s s, 240 w 4th av, 100x100.11. Bowes & Coombs agt Samuel Harris, Bernhard Ginsburg and Simon Sultan, owners, and James Nunan, contractor... 479 00
2 Greenwich av, Nos. 17 and 19, w s, 25.2 s 10th st, 50.5x90.6. Grissler & Son agt John Goerlitz, owner and contractor... 18,000 00
2 Fourteenth st, Nos. 624-630 E., s s. Gerni Angeletti et al. agt William H. Muldoon, owner and contractor... 210 00
2 Ninety-sixth st, Nos. 159-167, n s, 70 e Lexington av, 125x100.11. Windsor Lime Co. agt Owen McElroy, Jr., and William McElroy, owners and contractors... 968 05
2 One Hundred and Fourteenth st, n s, 495 w 5th av, 75x100. Emil Haenschen agt Peter Behrenger and Andrew Anderson, owners and contractors... 1,328 50
2 Goerck st, Nos. 104-108, e s, 246.7 n Rivington st, 75x100. C. B. Keogh Mfg. Co. agt William F. Lennon, owners and contractors... 184 00
2 Eighty-eighth st, n s, 175 w 8th av, 75x100.11. Manchester & Philbrick agt Frederick Wood, owner, and William Craig, contractor... 784 70
2*Tenth av, w s, extends from 182d to 183d st, 400x100. Antonio Altieri agt Daniel J. Sullivan, owner and contractor... 3,000 07
2 Varick st, No. 22, n e cor Beach st, 25x50. Patrick Sullivan agt Henry McArdle, owner, and Dennis O'Neil, contractor... 60 47
4 One Hundred and Tenth st, s s, 100 w Madison av, 50x100. Patrick Clavin agt John O'Connor, owner and contractor... 140 00
4 Jones st, No. 23, n s, 148 e Bleecker st, 25x100. Valentine Moeslein agt Theodore Von Euper, owner and contractor... 1,720 00
4 One Hundred and Thirty-fifth st, Nos. 13 and 15, n s, 176.8 w 6th av, 40x100. R. F. Sause agt William H. Verdon, owner, and Frederick R. Meres, contractor... 10 50
4 One Hundred and Thirty-fifth st, Nos. 5-17, n s, 110 w 5th av, 125x100. John Mitchell agt same... 28 75
4 Same property. J. A. Begley agt same... 27 25
4 Same property. John Heath agt same... 21 75
4 Same property. Andrew Davies agt same. 28 75
4 One Hundred and Thirty-fifth st, Nos. 11-17, n s, 160 w 5th av, 75x100. Burton Cable agt same... 24 25
4 Ninety-sixth st, Nos. 159-167, n s, 70 e Lexington av, 125x100. McDougall & Potter agt McElroy Bros. and T. Lowery, owners, and McElroy Bros., contractors... 600 00
4 Division st, No. 48, s s, 46 e Montgomery st, 22x47.6. Morris Jacobson agt Morris Weinstein and Morris Morgovitz, owners and contractors... 4,875 00
5 Fifty-first st, Nos. 244-248, s s, 126 e 8th av, 61x100.5. J. F. Gibbons agt Alexander Moore, owner, and David McMullin, contractor... 800 00
5 First av, No. 969, w s, 50.6 n 53d st, 25x78. Martin Muller agt Catharine Haight, owner and contractor... 50 00
5 Ninety-sixth st, Nos. 159-167, n s, 70 e Lexington av, 125x100.11. Mary A. Dolan agt Owen F. McElroy, Jr., and William McElroy, owners and contractors... 2,500 00
5 Ninety-sixth st, Nos. 157-165, n s, 70 e Lexington av, 115x—. O. D. Person agt McElroy Bros. and T. Lowery, owners, and McElroy Bros. contractors... 897 88
6 Eighty-first st, Nos. 426 and 428, s s, 336.6 e 1st av, 50x—. Mary Bermann agt John J. Macdonald, owner and contractor... 120 00
6 Franklin av, w s, 475 n 187th st, 25x—. Matthew McQuade agt John McSorley, owner and contractor... 298 00
6 Madison st, No. 314. Henry Israel agt S. Salomon, owner and contractor... 165 00
6 Convent av, n w cor 148d st, 100x100. W. G. Leeson agt Louise M. Hartwell, owner and contractor... 95 50

*Editor Record and Guide:

The lien filed against my houses on 10th avenue, 132d and 133d streets, by Antonio Alteria is unjust, as I have paid Mr. Alteria every dollar that his contract calls for and have got his receipts in full for the same, and do not owe him anything. I intend to bond the lien.

D. J. Sullivan.

KINGS COUNTY.

Oct.
30 Schenck av, w s, 100 n Blake av, 50x100. Samuel G. Richards agt C. W. Tomlinson, owner and contractor... $30 00
31 Seventh st, n s, 297.6 e 4th av, 50.4x100. Edward Nelson agt George Miller, owner and contractor... 80 00

Nov.
2 Sixth st, s s, 180 w 4th av, 115x100. Frank D. Creamer agt Baker & Maloney, owners and contractors... 298 75
2 Watkins st, w s, 125 n Sutter av, 25x100. James Moran agt Elias Kaplan, owner and contractor... 33 00
2 Sixth st, s s, 180 w 4th av, 115x100. Adaline A. Newman agt H. Becker, owner, and P. Maloney, contractor... 608 00
2 Sixth st, s s, 182 w 4th av, 118x100. Turnbull & Collis agt same owner and contractor... 400 00
2 Same property. Edward Nelson agt same owner and contractor... 300 00
2 Bergen st, s s, 100 e Clason av, 125x100. Edward H. Fuller agt George W. Brown, owner, and Noah W. Burtis, recvr., and Henry H. W. B. Parsons his agent, contractor... 156 50
2 Same property. John W. and Albert H. Summers agt same owner and contractor. 50 49
4 Eleventh st, s s, 232 w 8th av, 75x100. Commins & Evans agt Henry E. Murphy, owner and contractor... 150 00
4 Bergen st, s s, 310 w Kingston av, 40x105.7. }
Bergen st, s s, 350 w Kingston av, 60x100.0. } Brooklyn Door and Sash Co. agt Joseph M. Pilcher and Rachel A. Finch, owners, and Joseph M. Pilcher, contractor... 5,210 99
4 Herkimer st, n s, 20 w Saratoga av, runs west 80 x north 120 x east 100 to Saratoga av, x south 40 x west 20 x south 80 to beginning. Hall Sash and Door Co. agt Albert Johnson, owner and contractor... 893 00
4 Lewis av, s e cor Hancock st, 100x150. Albert J. Felty agt Thomas A. McWhinney and Jacob Aaronson, owners and contractors... 1,850 00
4 Eleventh av, n e cor 66th st, 60x100.2... }
Eleventh av, s w cor 66th st, 40x100.2, New Utrecht... } John H. Guthell agt O'Reilly Bros., owners and contractors... 450 00
4 Thirteenth av, n e cor 67th st, 40x100.2, New Utrecht. Michael Magarina agt Edward Peterson and Edward W. Stillwell, owners, and Ole Gunsten contractor... 197 95
5 Arlington av, n w cor Hale av, 25x100. John C. Creveling agt Fred. L. Grube and —— Grube, owners and contractors. (Redocket)... 161 10
5 Stone av, w s, 100 s Sutter av, 50x100. Henry McShane Mfg. Co. agt Mary E. Cook, owner, and Paseo & McCormick, contractors... 250 00
5 Dean st, n s, 280.7 w Buffalo av, 111.9x107. William H. Cable agt James W. Lane, owner and contractor... 800 00
5 Fourth av, s w s, 100 s e 32d st, 20x80. William Weingerath agt Michael Fitzgerald, owner and contractor... 524 26
5 Greene st, No. 259, n s, 25x100. Julius Heyer agt John C. Wiarda, owner and contractor... 15 00

SATISFIED MECHANICS' LIENS.

NEW YORK CITY.

Nov.
2‡Manhattan av, n w cor 114th st, 100.11x135 to Morningside av, x118.9x68.3. Bartholomew Donavan agt Hiram Morton Moore. (Aug. 20, 1891)... $622 00
2 Third av, Nos. 3608 and 3605, 50x100. Heroy & Marrenner agt Mrs. Casey and John J. Ryan. (June 30, 1891)... 109 [illegible]

2 Ninety-sixth st, n s, 70 e Lexington av, 125x—. Clark & Dolan agt Owen McElroy, Jr., and William McElroy. (Sept. 11, 1891)........ 2,100 00

6*Third av, w s, 55 n 153d st, 50x—. F. Pusemann agt Daniel Reynolds and Herrman & Blom. (Mar. 31, 1891)........ 210 00

6*Same property. Leopold Vath agt same. (Mar. 30, 1891)........ 89 14

6*Same property. E. M. Pritchard agt same. (Mar. 31, 1891)........ 897 77

6*Third av, w s, 38 n 153d st, 50x— to Elton av. George Watson agt same. (April 3, 1891)........ 207 50

6*One Hundred and Twenty-fourth st, s e cor Columbus av, runs east 186.7 to Manhattan st, x southeast 15.1 x south 93.11 x west 200 to 124th st, x north 100 to beginning. Vermont Marble Co. agt Henry M. Bendheim and Henry P. and William H. Niebuhr. (Nov. 2, 1891)........ 74 80

6 Seventy-second st, Nos. 414 and 416 E. Manchester and Philbrick agt Joseph F. Gallagher. (Oct. 30, 1891)........ 2,700 00

6‡One Hundred and Eighteenth st, s s, 240 w 4th av, 100x—. McElwee Mfg Co. agt Bernhard Ginsburg and Herman Masche. (Oct. 27, 1891)........ 192 00

6 Twenty-second st, No. 448 W. Allison & Smith agt Mrs. Ernestina Unger. (Sept. 26, 1891)........ 300 00

‡Discharged by order of Court on filing bond.
*Discharged by depositing amount of lien and interest with County Clerk.

KINGS COUNTY.

Oct.

26‡Fourth st, s s, 188 w 7th av, 114x100. William J. Fitzpatrick agt Charles H., S. F. and M. L. Moses, Henry B. and Eliza A. and Emma G. Fanton and Louis H. Myers, owners, and Moses & Fanton, contractors. (Lien filed Aug. 25, 1891.) (Order of Court)........ $1,621 44

26‡Fourth st, s s, 157.10 w 7th av, 40x100. Same agt Moses & Fanton, owners and contractors. (Aug. 26, 1891.) (Order of Court)........ 200 00

26‡Fourth st, s s, 197.10 w 7th av, 18x100. Same agt Louis H. Myers and Moses & Fanton, owners and contractors. (Aug. 26, 1891.) (Order of Court)........ 270 24

26‡Fourth st, s s, 215.10 w 7th av, 18x100. Same agt Moses & Fanton, owners and contractors. (Aug. 26, 1891.) (Order of Court) 270 24

26‡Fourth st, s s, 233.10 w 7th av, 19x100. Same agt Elizabeth A. Fanton, owner, and Moses & Fanton, contractors. (Aug. 26, 1891.) (Order of Court)........ 270 24

26‡Fourth st, s s, 253 w 7th av, 19x100. Same agt Emma G. Fanton, owner, and Moses & Fanton, contractors. (Aug. 26, 1891.) (Order of Court)........ 270 24

26‡Fourth st, s s, 271.10 w 7th av, 20x100. Same agt Moses & Fanton, owners and contractors (Aug. 26, 1891.) (Order of Court)... 270 24

26‡Fourth st, s s, 291.10 w 7th av, 20x100. Same agt A. J. Dynes, owner, and Moses & Fanton, contractors. (Aug. 26, 1891.) (Order of Court)........ 270 24

26‡Fourth st, s s, 97.10 e 6th av, 440x100. Thomas McCaun agt Moses & Fanton, owners and contractors. (Aug. 26, 1891.) (Order of Court)........ 1,000 00

26‡Same property. Thomas O'Hara agt Moses & Fanton, owners and contractors. (Aug. 27, 1891.) (Order of Court)........ 481 00

26 Fifth av, e s, 50 s 50th st, 25x100. John Lindner agt John Holt, owner and contractor. (July 29, 1891.) (Deposit)........ 25 00

28 Evergreen av, w s, 25 n Hancock st, 50x100. Henry McShane Mfg Co. agt Carl and William Lehmann, owners, and Louis Broschart, contractor. (Oct. 28, 1891.) (Deposit)........ 75 00

30 Bergen st, s s, 350 w Kingston av, 60x100. F. G. Clarke Blue Stone Co. agt Joseph M. Pilcher, owner, and J. M. Pilcher & Co., contractors. (Lien filed Oct. 16, '91) 2,647 17

31 Thatford av, e s, 100 s Glenmore av, 50x100. Creegan & Lyons agt Samuel Balsam and Morris Handler, owners and contractors. (Sept. 10, 1891)........ 140 00

31 Decatur st, n s, 100 e Howard av, 250x100. Martin Walsh agt J. Mason Kirby, owner and contractor. (Oct. 3, 1891)........ 150 00

31 Thatford av, e s, 100 s Glenmore av, 50x100. Charles E. Pell agt Samuel Balsam and Maurice Hendler, owner and contractor. (Sept. 12, 1891)........ 795 04

31 Watkins st, e s, 25 n Dumont av, 50x100. Schmidt & Esperstedt agt H. Wilkenfeld and N. Riterman, owners. (Aug. 28, 1891) 290 00

Nov.

2 Osborn st, s e cor Livonia av, 25x190. James O'Connor agt Abraham Seidenberg and Rochmiel Abromovitz, owners and contractors. (Sept. 28, 1891)........ 260 00

2 McDonough st, n s, 25 e Ralph av, 25x100. William C. Welton agt J. R. Pitt & Co., Robretto Goodenough, R. F. Clayton and J. R. Pitt, owners and contractors. (Oct. 31, 1891)........ 775 00

4 Barbey st, w s, 200 s Blake av, 50x100. Charles G. Schwartz agt Henry C. Heyser, owner and contractor. (Nov. 2, 1891.) (Deposit)........ 76 47

5 Herkimer st, No. 1061, n s, 200 e Howard av, 16.8x100. Jacob Steinbrecher agt William Wiedersum, owner, and James M. Fraser, contractor. (Sept. 29, 1891)........ 18 25

5 Bedford av, No. 136, w s, 80 n North 9th st, 20x80. Same agt W. H. Myers, owner, and James M. Frazer, contractor. (Sept. 30, 1891)........ 449 00

5 Hart st, No. 990. George P. Jacobs & Co. agt Lewis F. Broschart, owner and contractor. (Oct. 24, 1891)........ 560 74

5 Fifty-sixth st, n s, 150 w 14th av, 50x100. George J. Craigen agt Thomas Tangeman, owner, and Emel Keller, contractor. (Nov. 2, 1891)........ 93 00

5 Rockaway av, e s, 100 s Eastern Parkway, 25x100. Louis Bossert agt S. Levy, owner, and B. Seermann, contractor. (Sept. 9, 1891)........ 357 54

5 Same property. Same agt same. (Sept. 10, 1891)........ 381 34

5 Broadway, No. 1564, s w cor Halsey st. U. S. Mineral Wool Co. agt Henry Menken, owner, and T. D. Reilly & Sons, contractors. (Sept. 29, 1891)........ 188 68

5 Eastern Parkway, 50 e Christopher st, 50x100. Henry McShane & Co. agt Wolf Polashinsky, owner, and Pasco and McCormick, contractors. (Oct. 20, 1891)........ 164 31

‡Editor Record and Guide:

All liens filed by William J. Fitzpatrick are for labor and materials not furnished. All payments due are paid under his contract. Moses & Fanton.

BUILDINGS PROJECTED.

The first name is that of the owner; ar't stands for architect, m'n for mason, c'r for carpenter and b'r for builder.

NEW YORK CITY.

SOUTH OF 14TH STREET.

Hudson st, n e cor Duane st, seven-story brk warehouse, 52.11 and 40.11x74.2, tin roof; cost, $75,000; Wood & Selick, 49 Jay st; ar'ts, Babcock & Morgan; b'rs, L. N. & W. L. Crow. Plan 1415.

Lewis st, Nos. 57-61, three five-story brk and stone flats, 25x89, tin roofs; cost, $20,000 each; Weil & Mayer, 227 East 60th st; ar't, G. F. Pelham; m'n, J. Van Dolsen. Plan 1406.

Madison st, No. 289, rear, six-story brk shop, 24x60, tin roof; cost, $12,000; A. Sokolsky, 168 Monroe st; ar't, F. Ebeling. Plan 1411.

St. Marks pl, No. 101, five-story and basement brk flat, 37.6x95.6, tin roof; cost, $40,000; G. Hornberger, 95 7th st; ar'ts, Kurtzer & Rohl. Plan 1414.

BETWEEN 14TH AND 59TH STREETS.

2d av, No. 409 / 23d st, Nos. 241 and 243 E. } seven-story brk and stone factory, 48.10 and 24.4x98.8 and 94, tin roof; cost, $60,000; The Kranich and Bach Co., 235 East 23d st; ar'ts, Graul & Frohne. Plan 1395.

59th st, s s, 682.5 w 11th av, one and three-story brk building, 154x67, gravel roof; cost, abt $10,000; J. Eastman, treasurer, 1 East 72d st; ar't, J. E. Terhune. Plan 1402.

50th st, No. 239 W., three-story brk building, 25x100.5 and 80, tin roof; cost, $10,000; ow'r and m'n, J. Laimbeer, 416 West 20th st; ar't, G. F. Pelham. Plan 1407.

4th av, n e cor 22d st, two six and seven-story brk, stone and terra cotta buildings, 98.9x150, fire-proof roof; total cost, $400,000; J. S. Kennedy, 6 West 57th st; ar'ts, R. H. Robertson and Rowe & Baker. Plan 1405.

BETWEEN 59TH AND 125TH STREETS, EAST OF 5TH AVENUE.

80th st, No. 55 E., iron and glass conservatory, 22x9.2; cost, abt $1,000; J. C. De La Vergne, on premises; ar't, Weber & Drosser. Plan 1394.

116th st, No. 152 E., five-story stone flat, 25x88.10, tin roof; cost, $25,000; J. Fish, 330 East 9th st; ar'ts, Schneider & Herter. Plan 1401.

Lexington av, n w cor 90th st, five-story brk flat, 30x96.8, tin roof; cost, abt $25,000; J. Weber, 1121 Madison av; ar'ts, Weber & Drosser. Plan 1400.

Park av, n w cor 78th st, two-story brk building, 20x75, tin roof; cost, $14,000; G. Gomprecht, 210 East 61st st; ar'ts, Buchman & Deisler. Plan 1404.

BETWEEN 59TH AND 125TH STREETS, WEST OF CENTRAL PARK WEST AND 8TH AVENUE.

88th st, n s, 475 w Columbus av, two three-story and basement stone dwell'gs, 13x67, tin roofs; cost, $12,000 each; C. G. Judson et al., 74 West 54th st; ar't, C. True. Plan 1398.

75th st, s s, 85 w Central Park West, rear, one-story brk and iron building, 14x45, concrete roof; cost, $9,000; M. Brennan, 127 West 69th st; m'n, G. J. Harlow. Plan 1410.

110TH TO 125TH STREET, BETWEEN 5TH AND 8TH AVENUES.

117th st, n s, 225 e 8th av, seven-story brk warehouse, 50x96, tin and tile roof; cost, $40,000; J. J. Timmins, 170 West 133d st; ar't, J. A. Webster. Plan 1403.

NORTH OF 125TH STREET.

130th st, s s, 72 w Amsterdam av, four-story brk flat, 26x40, tin roof; cost, abt $7,000; agent and m'n, T. J. Larkin, 1418 Amsterdam av; ar't, R. Townsend. Plan 1399.

136th st, Nos. 237-253 W. and Nos. 201-217 W., eighteen three-story and basement brk and stone dwell'gs, 16 and 17x50, tin roofs; cost, $10,000 each; ow'r and b'r, T. C. Van Brunt, 234 West 136th st. Plan 1384. (Corrects omission in last issue.)

Bradhurst av, n e cor 142d st, four five-story brk and stone flats, irreg. in size, tin roofs; total cost, $54,000; K. Peters, Atlantic Casino, 8th av; ar't, A. Spence. Plan 1396. (Substituted for new building plan 502 filed during March, 1890.)

152d st, s s, 550 w Grand Boulevard, four-story and basement stone flat, 25x88.6, gravel roof; cost, $12,000; A. J. Fullam and ano, 685 West 151st st. Plan 1409.

23D AND 24TH WARDS.

Marion av, n w cor Kingsbridge road, brk, stone and terra cotta chapel, 44.4x76.8, tin and slate roof; cost, $13,000; N. Y. City Church E. and M. Society, 150 5th av; ar'ts, Cady & Co. Plan 1397.

Rockfield st, n s, 500 e Marion av, two-story frame stable, 16x16, gravel roof; cost, $300; H. Hoffstadt, on premises; ar't, A. Pfeiffer. Plan 1412.

Wolf st, n s, 257 e Sedgwick av, two-story frame dwell'g, 23x48, tin roof; cost, abt $3,500; ow'r and b'r, R. Ketcham, on premises. Plan 1416.

Daley av, w s, 200 n Samuel st, West Farms, one-and-a-half-story frame stable, 24x18, tin roof; cost, $400; S. Taylor, n e cor Hunniwell av and Samuel st; c'r, F. Lever. Plan 1408.

Jerome av, e s, 532 s Woodlawn av, three-story frame building, 40x65, tin roof; cost, $8,000; D. Heuer, 2308 8th av; ar't, J. J. Vreeland. Plan 1413.

KINGS COUNTY.

Plan 2003—Jefferson av, n s, 90 w Ralph av, one four-story brk tenem't, 20x55, tin roof, iron cornice; cost, $7,500; John T. Judge, 347 Warren st; ar't, M. F. Walsh.

2004—Conselyea st, No. 149, rear, one one-and-a-half-story frame stable, 24x17, tin roof; cost, $200; Ernst Heoppner, on premises.

2005—17th st, n s, 93 e 9th av, four two-story and basement brk dwell'gs, 16.8x40, tin roofs, wooden cornices; cost, $4,500 each; M. McCadden, 537 18th st.

2006—Guernsey st, w s, 25 s Norman av, one one-story frame spike shop, 25x30, gravel roof; cost, $400; J. J. Leibfried, 97 Guernsey st; b'rs, Randall & Miller.

2007—Arlington av, s s, 25 e Wyona st, one two-story frame dwell'g, 25x40, tin roof; cost, $2,000; Charles Schroeder, Jamaica av; ar't, C. Meins.

2008—Ralph st, s s, 350 w Central av, one two-story frame stable, 20x15, tin roof; cost, $100; E. A. Rudolf, 74 Ralph st.

2009—Blake av, n w cor Jerome st, one two-story frame store and tenem't, 25x40, tin roof; cost, $2,800; J. Haugh, Stone av and Pacific st.

2010—Chestnut st, e s, 474 s Jamaica av, one two-story frame dwell'g, 17.8x28, tin roof; cost, $2,500; Theo. M. Le Beau, 126 Van Siclen av; ar't, C. Infanger.

2011—Jefferson st, n s, 81 e Hamburg av, one one-and-a-half-story frame stable, 19x25, tin roof; cost, $675; J. Houighausen, Jefferson st, cor Hamburg av; b'r, H. Wolbeck.

2012—Wyona st, w s, 125 n Atlantic av, one two-story frame club-house, 22x26, tin roof; cost, $1,500; Fred Sackman, 2921 Atlantic av; ar't, Danmar & Fischer; b'r, not selected.

2013—Putnam av, n s, 220 e Howard av, one four-story brk flat 37x40x60, tin roof, iron cornice; cost, $10,000; ow'rs, ar'ts and b'rs, Moores & Le Quesne, 1440 Broadway.

2014—Bergen st, s s, 176.1 w Utica av, one two-story brk factory, 30x120, gravel roof, brk cornice; cost, $6,000; Francis Bannermann; ar't and b'r, H. J. Brown.

2015—4th av, n w cor 12th st, five four-story brk stores and dwell'gs, 20 and 27x65 and 60, tin roofs, wooden cornices; cost, total, $45,000; Scott & Carney, 993 Pacific st.

2016—Irving st, n s, 3.6 w Van Brunt st, one two-story brk engine house and stable, 36x26, gravel roof; cost, $4,000; Brooklyn Pier and Storage Co., 7 Bowling Green, New York; ar't, H. Gilvary; b'rs, M. Gibbons & Sons.

2017—12th st, s s, 322.10 e 6th av, three three-story brk apartment houses, 17.8x45, tin roofs, wooden cornices; cost, total, $15,000; ow'r and b'r, William Killey, 633 President st; ar't, W. M. Coots.

2018—Floyd st, No. 247, one one-story brk factory, 25x52, tin roof, brk cornice; cost, $1,800; L. Sior, 283 Ellery st; ar't, H. E. Funk.

2019—Decatur st, n s, 45 e Throop av, one four-story brk and limestone apartment house, 30x71, slate and tin mansard roof, iron cornice; cost, $30,000; Wm. W. Smith, 1 Bainbridge st; ar't, M. W. Morris; b'r, P. Cleary.

2020—Chestnut st, e s, 474 s Jamaica av, one two-story frame dwell'g, 17.8x28, tin roof; cost, $2,500; Theo M. Le Beau, 126 Van Siclen av; ar't, C. Infanger.

2021—Newport av, n s, 75 w Watkins st, one one-story frame dwell'g, 18x30, tin roof; cost, $1,000; Wm. Hartman, Newport av.

2022—Kingsland av, n w cor Frost st, one one-story frame shed, 25x25, gravel roof; cost, $75; Mr. Monzani, on premises.

2023—Pennsylvania av, e s, 125 s Glenmore av, one two-story frame dwell'g, 22.6x44, tin roof; cost, $2,800; Louis Liedtke, 219 Pennsylvania av; ar't, C. Meins; b'r, not selected.

2024—McDonough st, n s, 300 e Howard av, one three-story frame (brk filled) tenem't, 16.9x36, tin roof; cost, $4,000; Mary E. Geary, Worcester, Mass; ar't, M. F. Walsh.

2025—47th st, n s, 160 e 4th av, three two-story frame (brk filled) basement and cellar dwell'gs, 20x40, tin roofs; cost, each, $3,000; S. T. Sherwood, 3d av, cor 53d st; ar'ts, H. L. Spicer & Son.

2026—Vanderbilt av, w s, 50 s Atlantic av, rear, one three-story brk dwell'g, 25x27.6, tin roof, wooden cornice; cost, $2,500; A. W. S. Proctor, 24 Herkimer st; ar't, M. F. Walsh; b'rs, P. Sullivan and J. Powers.

2027—Fulton st, s s, 300 e Rockaway av, five four-story brk stores and dwell'gs, 20x60, tin roofs, iron cornices; cost, $10,000 each; Thos. McDonald, 1495 Bergen st; ar't, M. F. Walsh; b'rs, P. McMurray & Bro. and W. Uris.

2028—Nostrand av, w s, 125 s Flushing av, two four-story brk tenem'ts, 25x65, tin roofs, iron cornices; cost, $16,500; Mr. Jacoby, 145 Jackson st; ar't, F. Holmberg.

2029—Nostrand av, w s, 100 s Flushing av, two four-story brk stores and tenem'ts, 25x65, tin roofs, iron cornices; cost, $16,500; ow'r and ar't, same as last.

2030—Broadway, w s, 55 s Van Buren st, eight one-story brk stores, 20x45, gravel roofs, wooden cornices; cost, $600; ow'r, ar't and b'r, H. Grasman, 840 Hancock st.

2031—St. James pl, w s, 280 s Lafayette av, one four-story brown stone tenem't, 20x72, tin roof, wooden cornice; cost, $10,000; J. Gray, 323 Washington av; ar't, S. Peden.

2032—Harman st, n s, 100 w Hamburg av, six three-story frame (brk filled) tenem'ts, 25x60, tin roofs; cost, $5,000 each; Christian Hahn, 265 Central av.

2033—Humboldt st, e s, 32 n Van Cott av, one two-story frame lumber shed, 17x60, gravel roof; cost, abt $400; ow'r and b'r, Charles Engert, 182 Montrose av; ar't, F. J. Berlenbach, Jr.

ALTERATIONS NEW YORK CITY.

Plan 1881—Hester st, No. 86, new oven under walk and new piers; cost, $400; I. Block, 88 Hester st; ar't, H. Horenburger.

1882—Cooper st, s e cor Emerson st, to be moved and raised; cost, $1,000; ow'r and b'r, M. McQuade, on premises.

1883—Duane st, No. 176, interior alterations; cost, $600; agent, J. M. Jackson, 3 Mercer st; m'ns, Burns & Sons.

1884—39th st, No. 207 E., interior alterations and new front; cost, $1,500; A. Martinez, 207 Pearl st; ar't, A. V. O'Connor.

1885—34th st, No. 1 W., interior alterations, new elevator and shaft, walls altered, new piers and fronts; cost, abt $15,000; agents, W. A. White & Sons, 53 East 54th st; ar'ts, McKim, Mead & White.

1886—Ludlow st, No. 52, interior alterations; cost, $330; J. Kassel, 107 East 75th st; m'n, E. Gottlieb; c'r, M. Levy.

1887—10th av, s w cor Little 12th st, one-story portion raised one story, with mansard roof; cost, $6,000; J. Glass & Son, 426 West 23d st; c'r, L. A. Davis.

1888—27th st, No. 327 E., interior alterations, walls altered and new front; cost, $1,500; lessee, C. Edlich, 320 East 27th st; ar't, F. Ebeling; c'r, R. Martin.

1889—9th av, No. 581, new store window; cost, $300; Farley & McCaffery, 103 West 73d st; c'r, P. A. Ash.

1890—College av, w s, 142 s 164th st, one-story extension, 24x20; cost, $150; Ellen M. Harlow, College av and 164th st; ar't, M. V. B. Ferdon; b'r, G. J. Harlow.

1891—9th av, No. 861, walls altered; cost, $35; att'y, C. H. Diamond; 510 East 119th st; ar't, J. C. Brown.

1892—125th st, n s, 63.8 w 8th av, raised three stories, one-story extension, 36.4x16; cost, $15,000; lessee, W. H. Hunt, 217 West 123d st; ar't, J. A. Webster.

1893—Bergen av, No. 564, moved to new foundation and general repairs; cost, $1,200; Frances E. Du Bois, 700 Westchester av.

1894—35th st, No. 360 W., interior repairs; cost, $75; agent, J. Kydd, on premises; ar't, M. V. B. Ferdon; b'r, J. Curry.

1895—Hudson, Gansevoort and 13th sts, tank on roof; cost, abt $200; J. S. Kennedy et al., 6 West 57th st; ar'ts, Rowe & Baker; m'ns, Sheridan & Byrne.

1896—Broadway, No. 707, walls altered; cost, $250; lessee, I. Strauss, 329 East 58th st; ar't and b'r, W. S. Jennings.

1897—76th st, No. 504 E., one-story extension, 25.2x62; cost, $1,800; Lena Feltman, 520 West 44th st; ar't, R. Berger; b'r, G. Derr.

1898—Canal st, No. 61, new front; cost, $650; M. Rosenthal, 265 Henry st; ar't, W. Graul.

1899—145th st, No. 530 E., present building moved and raised 4 feet, two-story extension, 25x16; cost, $1,650; Ellen Newman and ano on premises; c'r, W. McEntyre.

1900—152d st, No. 476 E., moved and raised to grade, three-story extension, 25x9, front altered; cost, $1,750; T. Kraemer, on premises; c'r, W. McEntyre.

KINGS COUNTY.

Plan 1041—Bushwick av, n e cor Fanchon pl, one-story frame extension, 27x17, tin roof; cost, $200; Mrs. Hering, on premises; c'r, P. G. Kyow.

1042—27th st, No. 184, new stone foundation; cost, $200; P. Price, on premises.

1043—Williams av, e s, 125 s East New York av, two-story brk extension, 28.8x44.6, tin roof; cost, $2,400; Beadleston & Woerz, West 10th st, near West st, New York; ar'ts, Webber & Drosser; b'rs, D. Cook and H. Roecker.

1044—Bedford av, s w cor South 10th st, new store front; cost, $400; Stockes & Schoff, 462 Bedford av; ar't, B. Finkenseiper; m'n, S. Parker; c'r, not selected.

1045—Willoughby st, No. 55, one-story brk extension, 10.6x20, tin roof; cost, $1,000; Joseph Wechsler, 31 8th av; b'rs, D. Jones and H. Greenen.

1046—19th st, No. 320, two-story frame extension, 15x15, tin roof; cost, $200; Joseph Van Vouse, 320 19th st; b'r, A. Wallard.

1047—Liberty av, s w cor Van Siclen av, one-story brk extension, 20x20, tin roof; also one-story frame wagon shed, 20x22, tin roof; cost, $1,000; George A. Sommers, 28 Seigel st, ar't, H. Schmitz; b'rs, J. Fensch and A. Hughes.

1048—Willoughby av, No. 1120, one-story brk and frame extension, 25x40, tin roof; cost, $600; Alfred Huber, on premises; ar't, E. Schrempf; b'r, not selected.

1049—3d av, w s, 25 s 9th st, one-story brk and frame extension, 20x42, tin roof; cost, $500; Louis Betzold, 466 3d av; ar't, W. H. Wirth; b'r, S. Henchel.

1050—Washington st, No. 183, three and one-story brk extensions, 25x20 and 25x18, tin roofs, front and interior alterations; cost, $8,000; lessee, Frederick Kramer, 192 Washington st; ar'ts, Kurtzer & Rohl; b'r, not selected.

1051—Wyckoff st, No. 51, one-story brk extension, 24x18, gravel roof; cost, $400; F. D. Beard, 140 Amity st; ar't and b'r, C. M. Detlefsen.

1052—Boerum st, No. 54, one-and-a-half-story frame extension, 4x22, shingle roof; cost, $200; J. Dreyer, 104 Ewen st.

1053—4th av, No. 195, one-story brk extension, 8.9x6.2, tin roof; cost, $650; E. O. Tauchert, on premises; ar't, C. E. Muller; b'rs, G. H. O'Shea & Co. and H. D. Southard.

1054—Bradford st, w s, 200 s Liberty av, new foundation wall; cost, $200; W. Flemming, on premises; b'r, O. Nuber.

1055—Huntington st, s s, 100 w Henry st, new chimneys, interior alterations, cost, $400; P. J. Carlin, Franklin Building, Remsen st; ar't, C. F. Eisenach.

1056—Graham st, No. 95, flat tin roof, repair damage by fire; cost, $200; L. Friedman, Bushwick av, cor Troutman st; ar't, H. Vollweiler; b'r, J. Strong.

1057—Van Voorhis st, No. 72, one-story frame extension, 8x7, tin roof; cost, $75; C. H. Fink, on premises; ar't and b'r, C. Schneider.

MISCELLANEOUS.

BUSINESS FAILURES.

Schedule of assignments for the two weeks ending Nov. 6, 1891:

	Liabilities.	Nominal Assets.	Real Assets.
Chatfield, Thomas B. and Charles D......	$6,577 24	$1,941 11	$1,394 42
Hoag, Harry G.......	8,059 79	674 28	674 28
Kronthal, Louis and Charles.............	28,008 74	12,899 52	8,888 86
Simon, Benjamin....	25,918 09	24,857 09	7,577 53
Worthley, Peter A...	5,068 97	6,980 65	2,272 16

N. Y. ASSIGNMENTS—BENEFIT CREDITORS.

Oct.

31 Kohlhaas, Charles H. (manufacturer's agent and dealer in paper and twine, at No. 125 Elm st), to Theodore Peterson; preferences, $300.

Nov.

2 Stock, Herman J. (dealer in wines, liquors and cigars, at No. 252 5th av), to Edward J. Wilkins; without preferences.

KINGS COUNTY.

GENERAL ASSIGNMENTS.

Oct.

31 Backer, Jonathan to Charles H. Reilly.
31 Schneider, Charles to Charles H. Reilly.

PROCEEDINGS OF THE BOARD OF ALDERMEN AFFECTING REAL ESTATE.

APPROVED PAPERS.

Resolutions passed by the Board of Aldermen calling for the following improvements have been signed by the Mayor for the week ending November 2, 1891. *Indicates that the Mayor neither appoved nor objected thereto, therefore the same became adopted.

MAINS.

Bathgate av, from 188th st to 3d av; water.
Briggs av, from Garfield to Travers st; gas.
Madison av, from Kingsbridge road to Columbine av; water.
Villa av, from Potter pl to Southern Boulevard; gas.

LAMP-POSTS ERECTED AND LIGHTED.

Briggs av, from Garfield to Travers st.
Villa av, from Potter pl to Southern Boulevard.

CROSSWALKS.

155th st, from 3d to Elton av.
156th st, from 3d to Elton av.
158th st, from 3d to Elton av.

REGULATING, GRADING, ETC.

155th st, from 3d to Elton av.
156th st, from 3d to Elton av.
158th st, from 3d to Elton av

FENCING VACANT LOTS.

1st and 2d avs, 92d and 93d sts—the block.

PAVING.

156th st, from 3d to Elton av, trap block.
158th st, from 3d to Elton av, trap block.

BROOKLYN BOARD OF ALDERMEN.

* Under the different headings indicates that a resolution has been introduced and referred to the appropriate committee. † Indicates that the resolution has passed and has been sent to the Mayor for approval ‡ Passed over the Mayor's veto.

BROOKLYN, Oct. 26, 1891.

CULVERTS.

North 13th st, s e cor Kent av. †
North 13th st, s w cor Kent av. †
3d av, s e cor Degraw st. †
3d av, n e cor Degraw st. †
4th av, s w cor Bergen st. †

ELECTRIC LIGHTING.

Schaeffer st, n e cor Broadway.†

FENCING VACANT LOTS.

Sullivan st, s s, bet Richards and Van Brunt sts.*
Greene av, s s, bet Sumner and Lewis avs.†

FLAGGING.

Prospect pl, bet Bedford and Rogers av. †
13th st, s s, bet 7th and 8th avs. †
16th st, s s, bet 4th and 5th avs. †
Bedford av, e s, bet Park and Prospect pls. †
Georgia av, bet Fulton and Atlantic avs. †

LAMP POSTS ERECTED AND LIGHTED.

Eastern Parkway, bet Snediker and Stone avs. †
Harman st, bet Hamburg and Central avs. †
Herkimer st, bet Perry pl and Nostrand av. †
Schaeffer st, bet Bushwick and Central avs. †
55th st, bet 1st and 3d avs. †
Greene av, bet Knickerbocker and Central avs. †
Hamburg av, bet Stanhope and Bleecker sts. †

PAVING, GRADING, ETC.

Prospect pl, bet Troy and Schenectady avs.†
Newton st, bet Graham and Van Pelt avs. *
82d st, bet 4th and 5th avs.†
Van Pelt av, bet Graham av and Humboldt st.*

STREET OPENING.

Harman st, bet Irving and Wyckoff avs.†
Newton st, bet Graham and Van Pelt avs.*

ADVERTISED LEGAL SALES.

REFEREES SALES TO BE HELD AT THE REAL ESTATE EXCHANGE AND AUCTION ROOM (LIMITED), 59 to 65 LIBERTY STREET, EXCEPT WHERE OTHERWISE STATED.

Nov.

Boulevard, e s, 24.11 n 139th st, 75x100, vacant, by D. P. Ingraham & Co. (Amt due $31,451)........ 9

Private lane which would be 162d st if continued, n s, 122.3 n w 3d av, runs northeast 123.8 x southeast 27.9 x southwest 123.8 x to lane, x northwest 27.9 to beginning, by R. V. Harnett & Co. (Amt due $7,933)........ 9

Boulevard (11th av), s e cor 151st st, 24.11x100, four-story brk flat, by R. V. Harnett. (Amt due $1,201; prior morts. $12,000)........ 10

57th st, No. 49, n s, 19 w 4th av, 20x80.5, four-story stone front dwell'g, by R. V. Harnett. (Amt due $10,694)........ 10

Av C, e s, 100 n 5th st, 100x100, 24th Ward, by T. A. Kerrigan........ 10

98th st, Nos. 141-169, n s, 100 e 10th av, 325x113.2x—x129.6, fifteen five-story brk flats, by R. V. Harnett........ 11

187th st, n s, 275 e 6th av, 25x99.11, vacant, by William Kennelly. (Partition sale)........ 11

Madison av, s w cor 118th st, 60x100, one-story frame shanties, by J. N. Golding. (Amt due $16,970)........ 11

Broome st, No. 173, s s, 140 w Attorney st, 20x75, three-story frame (brk front) store and tenem't, by A. H. Muller & Son. (Partition sale)........ 12

Central Park West (8th av), Nos. 441-444, n w cor 104th st, 100.11x100, four five-story brk flats, by R. V. Harnett & Co. (Amt due $27,187; prior morts, ——)........ 12

96th st, No. 58, s s, 200 e 9th av, 20x100.8, four-story brk dwell'g, by R. V. Harnett & Co........ 12

136th st, s s, 294 e Alexander av, 37.6x100, by J. L. Wells. (Amt due $2,460)........ 12

Villa av, e s, 375 n Potter pl, 50x100, all right, title and int. which Edmond C. Allcott had on June 27, 1891, by Sheriff, at City Hall. (Sale under execution)........ 12

1st av, Nos. 650-662, s e cor 38th st, runs east 150 x south 98.9 x west 25 x south 49.4 x west 125 to 1st av, x north 148.1 to beginning, six-story brk malt house and two-story frame and brk stables, by R. V. Harnett. (Trustee's sale)........ 12

Amsterdam (10th) av / Hamilton pl } begins Amsterdam av, s w cor 142d st, 24.11x149.7 to Hamilton pl, 27.1 to 142d st, x139, vacant, by R. V. Harnett & Co. (Amt due $7,374)........ 12

Varick st, No. 228, e s, 48.7 s Carmine st, 20x58.5x21.5x48.2, three-story brk store and tenem't, all right, title and interest which David B. Richards had on Sept. 25, 1891, by Sheriff, at City Hall. (Sale under execution)........ 13

99th st, n s, 100 w 3d av, 75x100.11........ }
99th st, n s, 250 w 3d av, 75x100.11........ }
by D. P. Ingraham. (Trustee's sale)........ 13

8th av, Nos. 144 and 160 / 18th st, Nos. 248-262 / 18th st, Nos. 236-242 / 17th st, Nos. 243-273 } begins 8th av, s e cor 18th st, runs east 178 x south 92 x east 50 x north 92 to 18th st, x east 97.11 x south 145.8 x east 55 x south 88.5 to 17th st, x west 380 to 8th av, x north 26.4 x east 100 x north 131.4 x west 100 to 8th av, x north 26.4 to beginning, two, three, four, five and six-story brk stores and tenem'ts, stables, brewery, &c........
18th st, Nos. 239-243, n s, 249.4 e 8th av, 50.7x92, two, three and four-story brk buildings........
Together with personal property of Knickerbocker Brewery, plant, &c........
by B. L. Kennelly. (Amt due $104,437)........ 13

57th st, No. 102, s s, 100 w 6th av, 15x100, four-story stone front dwell'g, also all right, title and interest to strip of land 5 inches in depth and 15 feet wide, adj rear of above, by P. F. Meyer. (Amt due $21,147)........ 16

KINGS COUNTY.

Nov.

Halsey st, No. 41, n s, 410 e Bedford av, 20x100, three-story brk dwell'g; assessed value, $6,500.
Pacific st, s s, 387.7 e Rochester av, 16.9x107.2¾, two-and-a-half-story frame dwell'g; assessed value, $1,400........
Union st, Nos. 649 and 653, n s, 100 w 4th av, 50x95, two five-story brk tenem'ts; assessed value, $7,000 each........
3d st, Nos. 160-166, s s, 372.9 e Bond st, 96.9x154.9 to Gowanus Canal, x 103.0¾x175.0, coal yard; assessed value, $14,000; re-sale........
Putnam av, Nos. 844 and 846, s s, 236.6 e Reid av, 39x100, two two-and-a-half-story brk dwell'gs; assessed value, $5,000 each........
Putnam av, No. 832, s s, 314.6 e Reid av, 19.6x100, two-and-a-half-story brk dwell'g; assessed value, $5,000........
by T. A. Kerrigan, at 13 Willoughby st........ 9

26th st, No. 227, n s, 325 w 5th av, 25x70, two-story and basement frame dwell'g; assessed value, $700........

Atlantic av, Nos. 870-874, s s, 840 w Underhill av, 80x100, two four-story double brk flats; assessed value, $14,000

Hudson av, No. 77, e s, 175 s Evans st, 25x127x29.9x143.6, one-story frame stable and two-story frame dwell'g on rear; assessed value, $2,100

Lot at Gravesend, begins at Atlantic Ocean at division line bet old lots 22 and 23 on one side and old lots 20 and 21 on the other side, as shown on Kowolski's map of common lands of Gravesend, Coney Island, runs north — x west — x south to ocean, x east to beginning, except strip 40 ft. wide condemned for use of New York & Coney Island R. R. Co., and part lying south of centre of Surf av; partition

by T. A. Kerrigan, at 18 Willoughby st. 11

5th av, Nos. 10 and 12, w s, 130 n Pacific st, runs northwest 32.7 x southwest 14.2 x southeast 28.11 x northeast 1 x southeast 14.11 to 5th av, x north 32 to beginning, four-story dwell'g and store, by J. Cole, at 389 Fulton st. 11

Halsey st, s e cor Patchen av, 200x100, ten two-story and basement brk dwell'gs and four-story flat with store on corner

Macon st, n w cor Howard av, 185x100, five two-story and basement brk dwell'gs on plot; assessed value, $12,800

President st, No. 185 n s, 121 e Henry st, 14.6x100, three-story brk dwell'g; assessed value, $5,000

Union st, Nos. 901-909, n s, 100 w 8th av, 100x90, five five-story brk flats, unfinished; assessed value, $40,000

Graham av, No. 206, e s, 50 n Scholes st, 25x100, four-story brk dwell'g and store and three-story frame dwell'g in rear; assessed value, $6 000

by T. A. Kerrigan, at 18 Willoughby st. 12

President st, No. 185, n s, 120 e Henry st, runs north 55 x east 1 x north 45 x east 14.6 x south 100 x west 15.6 to beginning, three-story brk dwell'g; assessed value, $5,000; by W. Cole, at 7 and 8 Court sq 12

Atlantic av, Nos. 1648 and 1650, s s, 100 w Troy av, 40x100, three-story frame dwell'g; assessed value, $3,000; by T. A. Kerrigan, at County Court House 13

Smith av, w s, 100 s Broadway, 100x100, Flatbush, by T. A. Kerrigan, at 18 Willoughby st. 16

LIS PENDENS, KINGS COUNTY.

Oct.

St. Marks av, n s, 120 w Bedford av, 20x128.6. A. M. Sweet & Co. agt Nellie Townsend; att'y, Adolph Vanrein 29

Thatford av, w s, 100 s Sutter av, 25x100. Carrie Haydock guard. Charles E. Haydock agt Samuel Tankoos; att'y, George R. Haydock 29

Railroad av, w s, 199.2 s Danforth st, 20x100.2. Sarah E. Van Wyck agt William H. Baker; att'ys, Knox & Woodward 29

Railroad av, w s, 239.2 s Danforth st, 20x100.2. Matilda F. Pierson agt William H. Baker; same att'ys 29

Railroad av, w s, 219.2 s Danforth st, 20x100. Same agt same; same att'ys 29

9th st, s s, 218.1 w 8th av, 20.5x72.6x20.4x72.6
9th st, s s, 277.8 w 8th av, 18.10x72.6
9th st, s s, 335.4 w 8th av, 40.3x82.6
9th st, s s, 415.8 w 8th av, 40.6x82.6

Joseph H. McKenna agt John Moore; action for specific performance; att'y, Archibald C. Shenstone 29

Atlantic av, s s, 150 w Bond st, 25x200 to Pacific st. George T. Vingut guard. Augusta F. Vingut agt Sarah E. Duigan; att'ys, Roe & Macklin 30

Van Buren st, s s, 100 e Patchen av, 180x100. Henry Weil agt Francis Jezek; att'y, R. Murray 30

Nelson st, s s, 120 e Court st, 20x100. The Home Ins. Co. agt Thomas Foran; att'ys, Richards & Heald 31

Bay av, lots 126 and 127 map South Greenfield, 200x100, Gravesend. Timothy Fitzpatrick agt William Fitzpatrick; att'y, Edward F. Dooley 31

7th st, n s, 287.1 w 4th av, 57.10x100. Hall Sash and Door Co. agt Charles H. Collins; att'y, F. P. Bellamy 31

Nov.

Atlantic av, s e cor Vermont av, —x— to point 250 n North Carolina av, x106x—. Emilie Huber agt John D. Bennett; att'y, Frank Obermier 2

Greene av, n w cor Lewis av, 20x100. George W. Brush agt Hubert Giroux; att'ys, Estes, Barnard & Tiffany 2

Railroad av, w s, 259.2 s Danforth st, 20x100. Charles H. Knox agt William H. Baker; att'ys, Knox & Woodward 2

Nostrand av, w s, 80 s Lexington av, 20x100. Edmond Connelly exr. George Ford agt Franklin B. Purdy; att'y, James P. Campbell 2

Howard av, s w cor Macon st, 100x93.6. Theodore B. and Henry A. Willis agt Clarence Lincoln; foreclos. mechanic's lien; att'y, John F. Nelson 2

27th st, n s, 220 e 3d av, 20x101.2. James O'Neill agt John Nolan; att'y, John T. Barnard 2

Rockaway av, s w s, 87 n w land of Richard L. Baisley, runs northwest 200 x southwest — x southeast — x northeast 120
East 93d st, s w s, 100 n w Av K, —x100x80.8x100
Av K, s e s, 100 n e East 94th st, 95.10x121.4x106.7x124.6
Av K, n e s, 100 n w East 94th st, 87.5x181.7x86.4x180.5, Canarsie

Buffalo German Ins. Co. agt Samuel W. McDonald; action to set aside deeds; att'y, Wm. J. Gaynor 2

Alabama av, s w cor Fulton av, runs south 125 x west 100 x north 25 x east 25 x north 100 to Fulton av, x east 75
Brooklyn and Jamaica plank road, s s, 84.11 e Sheffield av, 21.8x86.2x20x79.1
Sheffield av, e s, 50.5 s Brooklyn and Jamaica plank road, 50x100
New Jersey av, w s, 100 n Evergreen pl, 100x100
Atlantic av, n e cor Vermont av, 21x91.8

Emilie Huber et al. exrs. Otto Huber agt William J. Bennett; att'y, Frank Obernier 2

Harrison st, s w cor Cheever pl, 21.4x76.4 in two courses, x25 to Cheever pl, x75. Sarah A. Bergen agt Herman Schulmerich; att'y, Benjamin Wright 2

St. Johns pl, n s, 204.7 e 7th av, 20x100, and property in adjoining counties. Henry R. Winant agt Mary J. Winant individ. and extrx. James J. Winant; partition; att'ys, Thornton, Earle & Kiendl 4

Rockaway av, e s, adj land of John C. Kaiser, 17,164-10,000 acres of swamp
Railroad av, s w s, lots 129 and 130 map Conklin et al., Canarsie

Frederick Kaiser agt Henry Mahland, Jr.; partition; att'y, Daniel R. Ames 4

Bainbridge st, n e cor Saratoga av, 28x100. Joseph P. Puels agt Kate S. Good; att'ys, Thornton, Earle & Kiendl 4

Wyckoff st, s s, 80 e 3d av, 20x100. Annie Fish agt Silas A. Underhill; att'y, Henry B. Johnson 4

Manhattan av, s w cor Noble st, 52.8x79.2x70.4 to Noble st, x54.6
10th st, s s, 245.9 e 8th av, 18.9x100

Louis R. Smith agt George A. Viemeister; action to set aside deed; att'y, George F. Bentley 4

Bushwick av, s w cor Woodbine st, 20x80. Edward Michelis agt Marie E. wife of John Kohlmann; foreclos. vendor's lien; att'y, C. R. Halsey 5

Myrtle av, Nos. 448-452, s s, 46 e Waverly av, 54x100
Myrtle av, Nos. 591-597, n w cor Graham st, 80x100

Brooklyn Elevated Railroad agt Eleanor and Eleanor R. Donnellon; action to condemn; att'ys, Hoadly, Lauterbach & Johnson 5

RECORDED LEASES.

NEW YORK. Per Year

Elizabeth st, No. 125, north basement, store and four rooms over same. Henry Siericks, Rockaway, L. I., to Albert Engster; 3 years, from Aug. 1, 1891 $540

John st, No. 15, part of second, third and fourth floors and basement. Emily Thorburn to James M. Thorburn and Frederick W. Bruggerhof, of James M. Thorburn & Co.; 2 years, from Sept. 30, 1894 4,800

Madison st, No. 201, corner store and cellar. Stephen Lovejoy to T. J. Backes; 5 years, from May 1, 1892 960

Mulberry st, Nos. 114 and 116. Assign. lease. Baratta Pietro to Felix Morelli 725

Same property. Assign. lease. Morino Rettagliata to same 1,800

Same property. Assign. lease. Same to same nom

Mulberry st, Nos. 114 and 116, front and rear. Felix Morelli to Vincenzo De Vito and Vito Gregorio; 5½ years, from Nov. 1, 1891 5,760

Spring st, No. 52, store and basement. Michael J. Quigley to James McKenna; 9¼ years, from Nov. 1, 1891 1,200, 1,500

Southern Boulevard, s w cor Lincoln av, 20x90. Moses G. and Gilbert A. Wright to Diedrich J. Wobse and Herman F. Selmers; 5 years, from May 1, 1891 1,200

Stanton st, No. 11, store and front floor. Henry Riffet to Alessio and Margherite Vallario; 4 years, from May 1, 1891 420

5th st, s s, 168 e Lewis st, 175x96. Betsey A. wife of Cyrus H. Fay to Meyer Ducker and Hoerig; 4½ years, from Nov. 1, 1890 2,400, 2,625

18th st, No. 637 E., west store floor, three rear rooms and part cellar. John L. Gillen and John Sauer to William Sturm; 4⅔ years, from Sept. 1, 1891 360

14th st, No. 444 W., all. Rose McDonnell to Robert J. Mills; 8⅓ years, from Nov. 1, 1891 1,600, 1,900

62d st, No. 45 E., all. Sarah F. Sanford to Eugene Higgins; 3 years, from Nov. 24, 1891 2,000

65th st, No. 349, n w cor 1st av, store floor and extension. Adolphine C. Thode to August J. Von Bohn; 5 years, from May 1, 1891 420

113th st, Nos. 478-488, s s, bet 1st av and Av A, all. Jonas Weil to Pietro Vallaro; 4 years, from Nov. 1, 1891 3,200

125th st. Hammerstein's Harlem Opera House Building, east store and basement and bowling alley. Oscar Hammerstein to Cecelia Baumann; 5 years, from Sept. 1, 1891 2,000, 2,300

150th st, No. 582 E., store, three rooms on second floor and front cellar. Joseph Nimphius to David Stevenson; 5 years, from Oct. 1, 1891 312

Amsterdam av, No. 821, cor store, one large room and basement. Robert Maywald to E. C. Goetting; 5 years, from May 1, 1891 780, 1,000

Amsterdam (10th) av, w s, 25 s 157th st, 25x100. Elizabeth G. Bussell to Elizabeth L. Merkent; 8¼ years, from Nov. 1, 1891 245

Columbus (9th) av, No. 1822, store. Jeannette Burchill to Charles Cuuz; 5 years, from Dec. 1, 1891 1,800

Greenwich av, No. 21, cor 10th st. Robert T. Marshall to William Schmidt; 6 years, from May 1, 1891 1,425

Park av, No. 1768, double store and cellar. William R. Bell, agent, to William Hook; 2 years, from Nov. 1, 1891, per year $360, with privilege of renewal for 3 years at 420

Vanderbilt av, No. 1184, all. Karl F. Mayer to Max Froehlich; 4 5-6 years, from July 1, 1890 420

1st av, No. 685, n w cor 39th st, store and front cellar. John Lynch to Thomas Mortimer; 5 years, from Nov. 1, 1891 1,200

1st av, No. 557, n w cor 32d st, 97x75. Patrick Looram to H. Koehler & Co., a corporation; 5 years, from May 1, 1892 1,700

1st av, No. 1340, corner store. John J. Cuskley to Samuel Cohn; 5 years, from May 1, 1891 1,200, 1,300

2d av, No. 2218. Marx Cohn to John Riordan and Charles D. Franigan; extension of lease for 8 years, from Oct. 30, 1891, on terms of original lease —

2d av, No. 1490, front basement. John O'Connell to Frank Rubina; 4 years, from Nov. 1, 1891 180

3d av, No. 507, store and basement
34th st, No. 201 E., store and part cellar

Dederick H. Bultmann to James P. Keating and Thomas W. Byrnes; 7½ years, from Nov. 1, 1891 3,800, 4,500

3d av, No. 1110, n w cor 65th st, 20x30. Mary A. wife of Hugh Newman to John J. Hickey and Michael J. Jennings; 10 years, from Oct. 1, 1891 3,600

3d av, No. 1997, ground floor. Frederick Binzen to Fritz Kohn; 5 years, from Nov. 1, 1891 960

8th av, No. 2393, store and basement. Henrietta Holzderber to Thomas F. Lyons; 4⅔ years, from Sept. 1, 1891 1,550

8th av, No. 2706, s e cor 144th st, store. Oliver H. P. Archer to Louis Demkhorst; 8¼ years, from Nov. 1, 1891 1,300, 1,500

8th av, No. 116, s e cor 16th st, store and basement. Jonas and Samuel Weil and Bernhard Mayer to George McKay; 5½ years, from Nov. 1, 1891 2,500

9th av, No. 58. George Kammer to Sigmund Guttfreund; 3 years, from Oct. 1, 1891 780

CHATTELS.

NEW YORK CITY.

OCTOBER 30 TO NOVEMBER 5.—INCLUSIVE.

SALOON AND RESTAURANT FIXTURES.

Arnold, Konrad. 175 Ludlow....J Kuntz B Co. $500
Boyle, J E. 557 1st av....H Koehler & Co. 700
Brown, D W. 72 East Broadway....J Everard. (R) 1,768
Burns, J J. 434 E 13th....Beadleston & W. Saloon Ice Box. (R) 50
Butler & Brown. 264 1st av ...Mutual B Co. 500
Berger & Wolken. 143 Broome....Beadleston & W. Saloon Ice Box. (R) 100
Berger & Wolkens. 143 Broome....Beadleston & W. Saloon Lamp. (R) 83
Same....same. Saloon Pump. (R) 75
Browne, Patrick. 1316 3d av....D Mayer. 2,700
Cansor, I & H. 57 Mott....G Geizog. Restaurant Fixtures. 100
Columbia Athletic Club. 12 E 15th ...J H Bereuter. Pool Table. 160
Connolly & Potter. 1512 2d av....P Doelger. 2,500
Chavin, H F. 251 Rivington....Beadleston & W. 1,000
Condit, G M. 49 Fulton....W E Gilbert. Restaurant Fixtures. 150
Cooney, M J & P J. 1644 3d av.. G Ringler & Co. (R) 1,500
Deeg, Elise. 333 E 47th... J Ahles B Co. 450
Devlin, John. 2591 8th av....Bernheimer & S. (R) 2,650
Dierking, Dora. 11th av and 41st st ...G Ehret. (R) 2,000
Donovan, T J. 2239 1st av....J Eichler B Co. 2,500
Dettinger, F S. 212 E 6th ...Auchor B Co. 400
Dermody, G H. 868 3d av ...A Weinstein. 1,500
Efinger, Bernhard. 535 3d av....Bernheimer & S. (R) 2,000
Eiser, Conrad. 185th st and Amsterdam av....C Schaeffer. 1,500
Egan, John. 63 Pearl .. D Stevenson. 300
Engster, Albert. 125 Elizabeth....G Bechtel exr of. 350
Eggeling, Herman. 457 Hudson....Bernheimer & S. (R) 1,150
Ehrmann, Leonhard. 3267 3d av...P & W Ebling B Co. 2,275
Feinberg, M A. 77 Bayard....J Eichler B Co. 600
Fitzpatrick, John. 217 E 101st....J J Reilly. (R) 225
Florio, Antonio. 332 E 115th... Bernheimer & S. Pool Table. (R) 140
Freund, G S & A. 1446 2d av....Schmitt & S. 800
Friedmann, Joseph. 247 E 77th....Lembeck & Betz. 584
Friedel, Reinhold. 313 E 83d....Schmitt & S. 450
Gallagher, P & C. 392 7th av....J McElbinney. 1,750
Gavin, Sam. Chambers and Centre sts....H Koehler & Co. Saloon Pump. (R) 64
Goldstein & Neuwirth....231 Rivington... Beadleston & W. Saloon Pump. (R) 83
Greve, Henry. 139 4th av....J Ruppert. 1,000
Gruber & Davidson. 134 Park row....J Kress B Co. (R) 800
Goodwin, P H 524 3d av....Bernheimer & S. 1,500
Guzzi, Vincenzo. 156 Mott. ..Ph Schaefer & Son. 500
Gallagher, P & C. 382 7th av....J C G Hupfel B Co. 1,750
Gans, Gertrude. 414 Washington....E Eising & Co. 450
Geigel, Chas. 19 Rector....Rubsam & H B Co. 500
Gloekner, Jacob. 142d st and Willis av... H Zeltner. (R) 1,000
Graziadio, Giacinto. 2186 1st av....Bernheimer & S. (R) 500
Hummelsheim, Joseph. 93 Chrystie....J Eichler B Co. (R) 850
Hickey & Jennings. 1110 3d av....G Ehret. 5,000
Hulert, Henry 794 2d av... F Oppermann, Jr. 1,000
Jaenicke, William. 165 E 72d....D Mayer. (R) 658
Jaeckle, Andrew. 612 6th av....G Ringler & Co. (R) 2,924
Kartjohn, I. C. 1063 1st av....Consumers' B Co. 5,000
Kiernan, Thos. 2049 2d av.. J Everard. 814
Killmer, Chas. 170 Essex....J Eppig. 1,200
King, Thos. 150 E 14th....M Cosgrove. Pool Table. 287
Same. 248 Bowery ...same. Pool Table. 287
Kohn, Fritz. 1997 3d av....G Ringler & Co. 1,000
Koster, Henry. 146 Forsyth....S Liebmann's Sons B Co. 600
Klages, J F L. 2401 2d av....H Steinhardt. (R) 1,400
Keeney, P J. 1765 1st av....Bernheimer & S. (R) 1,850
Klages, Fred 2401 2d av....Beadleston & W. Saloon Ice Box. (R) 100
Same ...same. Saloon Pump. (R) 120
Klussmann, Chas. 100 E 107th....W Kohring. 1,800
Koch, Valentine. 1074 1st av... Schmitt & S. (R) 625
Koppman, Ozias. 9 Essex....Feigenspan B Co. 500
Laugenstein, Joseph. 286 E 4th....Schmitt & S. (R) 400
Lutz, J S. 424 4th av ..Bernheimer & S. (R) 2,000
Loehr, Joseph. 619 Morris av ...J & M Haffen. 700
Lahn, Martin. 1637 Av A....J Ruppert. (R) 1,600
Leier, Anton. 158 E 2d....J Ruppert. 300
Lyons, T F. 2393 8th av ...H Koehler & Co. 400
Maggi, Guiseppe. 127 South 5th av....Bernheimer & S. 800
Maher, John. 411 10th av....Budweiser B Co. 2,000
Mahon, John. 42 Washington....J C G Hupfel B Co 1,500
McGoldrick & Carlin. 518 Canal....Beadleston & W. Saloon Ice Box. (R) 135
McGovern, Joseph. 362 7th av....Bernheimer & S. (R) 2,000
Minnough, Patrick. 2346 10th av....D G Yuengling, Jr, B Co. (R) 200
Musaoo, Frank. 339 E 109th....Bernheimer & S. Pool Table. (R) 175
McIntyre, Andrew. 1760 3d av....D Stevenson. 905
Michael, Dave. 121 Pitt ...Ph Schaefer & Son. 600
Murray, Susan. 2177 2d av....Bernheimer & S. 3,000
McCarthy, John. 265 E 122d....Bernheimer & S. (R) 1,200
McGrath, James. 48 Spring....Beadleston & W. Saloon Ice Box. (R) 125
Meyer & Speckerer. 129 Chrystie....G Bechtel, exr of. (R) 5,400
Moltzen, Andrew. 2534½ 8th av....Bernheimer & S. (R) 1,000
Oerter, Charles. 1524 Av A....Schmitt & S. (R) 1,000
Plunkett, John. 106 W 54th....P Doelger. (R) 800
Pospisil, John. 435 E 81st....H Koehler & Co. 800
Pfletschinger, Fred. 322 E 92d....F Ibert. 800
Pierson, T F. 172 Av C....F Ibert. 800
Poellot, Marie. 262 1st av....C Iba. 100

Pabdee, John. 202 E 109th....G Ringler & Co. (R) 256

Piper, F W. 57 Broadway and 59 New Church st ....J Hoffmann B Co. (R) 5,000

Ponds, F. 219 Hudson....Beadleston & W. Saloon Ice Box. (R) 65

Pulsifer, Joseph. 190 3d av....J L Lissner. Restaurant Fixtures. 500

Raimond, Domenico. 4 Roosevelt ...Budweiser B Co (R) 700

Riedl, Chas. 328 3d av....P & W Ebling B Co. (R) 1,454

Rockefeller, Elizabeth. 209 West....G Ringler & Co. 600

Rodges, Edward. 795 Washington....Bachmann B Co. (R) 1,200

Rosenbaum, H V. 344 Bowery....M Kirstein. 300

Roenne, Charles. 162 E 4th....S Liebmann's Sons B Co. 800

Ruehl, John. 620 St Anns av....J H Bereuter. Pool Table. 150

Rivoire, G. 105 Clinton pl....J H Bereuter. Pool Table. 160

Schmitt, Emile. 530 8th av....H Harburger. Restaurant Fixtures. 350

Schroeder, G H. 244 Cherry....Beadleston & W. Saloon Ice Box. (R) 80

Speekmann, Henry. 34 Goerck....P Doelger. 1,000

Stockert, M and M. 157 E 55th....J Kress B Co. 500

Sweeney, James. 301 Delancey....Howard & Childs. (R) 750

Sauer, A & R. 231 E 46th....D Stevenson. 800

Sheehan, Thomas. 649 1st av....J C G Hupfel B Co. 600

Steeg, F E. 2183 2d av....J Rupp rt. 2,719

Stein & Maley. 1599 Broadway e..E' Stenzig. Restaurant Fixtures. 200

Schuler, L and E. 228 E 74th....G Ringler & Co. 600

Sheridan, Thos. 56th st and 6th av....Bernheimer & S. Saloon Ice House. 95

Skehan, John. 2449 2d av ...J Eichler B Co. (R) 1,240

Spitz, Daniel. 70 2d av.. .S Reitman. Restaurant Fixtures. 2,000

Strubbs, William. 27 Frankfort....Beadleston & W. Saloon Ice Box. (R) 50

Taylor, G P. 34 and 36 Liberty....J Bohnet. Restaurant Fixtures. 800

Thather, James. 4215 3d av....Beadleston & W. Ice Box. (R) 99

Toebing, William. 216 E 126th ...P & W Ebling. 500

Tunstall, J T. 421 Canal....J Heidelburger. Restaurant. (R) 1,000

Wagner, Chas. 414 E 83d....J Hoffmann B Co. (R) 500

Weitierlle, A M. Bedloes Island....Brunswick-B-J Co. Pool. 200

Wilbars & Eggers. 146 Pearl....J Ruppert. (R) 1,000

Willis, Amelia P. 112 Grand.. .B Wasserman. (R) 1,200

Same....same. (R) 150

Wright, W W. 147 Fulton ...G W Venable et al. (R) 600

Williams, Deleram. 2089 7th av....Bernheimer & S. (R) 2,000

HOUSEHOLD FURNITURE.

Abbott, Lawrence. 143 W 62d ...S Heyman & Co. 165

Atwell, Mamie. 241 Madison....H Israel & Sons. (R) 175

Auerbach, Jennie. 133 E 84th....S Heyman & Co. 224

Alburtus, Ida A. 487 2d av....J Gregg & Co. 170

Acker, Mary. 338 W 28th....S I Herschmann. 551

Austin, Annie. 322 W 41th....L Baumann. 275

Bailey, George. 506 W 48th ...J Baumann. (R) 104

Barnwell, Mrs W. 346 W 45th ...A Ballin. 168

Betsch, Blanche. 147 Essex....J Moriarty. 101

Boyle, J L. 276 W 115th....J Baumann. 260

Brown, A S. 29 E 11th....J Baumann. 126

Bulkley, Mary E. 237 W 48th....A Ballin. 282

Butler, Isidor. 302 E 102d....L Baumann. 168

Butts, A E. 145 W 104th....J Baumann. 254

Bacon, Ellen M. 22 E 21st....J Gregg & Co. (R) 140

Barnard, Geo. 318 E 35th....H Israel & Son. 200

Berrien, Mary A. 62 W 35th ...M Thompson. 250

Same....same. 650

Black, Kate. 34 Columbia....H Israel & Son. 135

Blank, Michael. 835 E 104th....F J Brechtel. (R) 101

Burr, Ancrum. 263 W 37th....L Baumann. 137

Ball, Theresa. 161 E 48th.... L Baumann. 152

Bang, Julia A. 1662 2d av....W E Wheelock & Co. Piano. 300

Beigel, Lena. 43 Allen.. .Krakauer & Co. Piano. 240

Bergmann, Bertha. 345 W 30th....F E Miller. 800

Birney, Annie. 172 E 90th....W E Wheelock & Co. Piano. 325

Blanchard, Catherine. 7 Lafayette pl....A H Mangold. Piano. 300

Blakesle, Josephine E. 169 W 64th .. W E Wheelock & Co. Piano. 375

Bliss, Grace. 260 W 35th....L Baumann. 176

Brotherton, G C. 2348 8th av....J Gregg & Co. 339

Brewer, Homer. 2477 8th av ..Krakauer Bros. Piano. 275

Buckley, Mary J. 124 W 63d....W E Wheelock & Co. Piano. (R) 186

Bulkley, Mary. 237 W 48th....L Baumann. 262

Bundshub, Frank. 39 Ann....S Heyman & Co. 147

Cameron, Mary. 229 W 16th....H Israel & Sons. (R) 290

Capen, Henry....76 W 55th ...S Heyman & Co. 271

Carmen, Sylva. 134 W 32d....J Gregg & Co. 340

Case, Fannie A. 330 W 24th....L Baumann. (R) 145

Clancey, Mrs L B. 411 W 37th....W E Wheelock & Co. Piano. 300

Clark, Estelle. 168 E 107th....H Israel & Son. (R) 117

Clark, Mrs H. 682 E 138th....Brooklyn F Co. 119

Clifton, Mrs E. 314 W 70th....T Kelly. 187

Coleman, Julia. 63 W 9th....W E Wheelock & Co. Piano. (R) 140

Conolly, Mrs M. 27 Cannon ...W E Wheelock & Co. Piano. 175

Connors, Nora. 454 W 31st... W E Wheelock & Co. Piano 100

Covary, Eugenie. 192 Waverley pl....C R Ruegger. 113

Cornish, Effie. 109 W 62d....W E Wheelock & Co. Piano 300

Crane, Ellen M. 316 W 32d....L Baumann. (R) 100

Crawford, A F. 326 W 36th....L Baumann. (R) 202

Creamer, Lottie. 52 W 3d ...H Israel & Son. (R) 106

Cummings, Clara. Tremont st ...Krakauer Bros. Piano. 325

Cutler, G B 693 E 134th....S Heyman & Co. 100

Collins, Christopher. 631 9th av ...O'Farrell & Co. 205

Chittenden & Kester. 210 2d av ..R Spoerle. 700

Craft, Jennie V. 2210 7th av....D Schwarzkopf. 250

Cameron, Ann. 39 Cherry....F G Smith. Piano. (R) 110

Colyer, R H. 229 W 40th....Manges Bros. 198

Daly, Mary. 489 11th av....A Ballin. 121

Davies, Wm. 63 7th av... J Baumann. (R) 365

Downes, H S and M C. 138 W 63d....E C Hinsdale. 190

Dasiger, Julius. 306 E 125th....L Baumann. 183

De Leeuw, Sarah. 316 E 57th....L A Darnson. 135

Donohue, Michael. 11 Dunham pl, Brooklyn....J Wolf & Son. 161

Dunham, Sarah. 153 W 44th....O'Farrell & Co. 158

Daly, Dan'l. 257 W 39th... Brooklyn F Co. 328

Danielli, A. 107 Waverley pl....J S Rice. 126

de Montigny, Helen. 141 W 45th....H Israel & Son. (R) 209

Dorns, Minnie. 211 E 11th. . Fennell & Pye. 142

Donnely, B. 296 E 35th....L Baumann. 121

Donnelly, Nellie. 164 E 82d....S Heyman & Co. 118

Dorff, Mary. 818 Bedford av, Brooklyn....W E Wheelock & Co Piano. (R) 100

Douglass, Addie. 332 W 59th ...E C Hinsdale. 375

Dronia, Louisa. 26 Sutton pl ...S Heyman & Co. 205

Due, Chin Gin. 12 Pell.. .Jordan & M. 100

Dunham, I O. 344 W 51st....W E Wheelock & Co. Piano. 350

Eaton, Sadie M. 158 W 13th....Garvey Bros. 175

England, Sarah. 219 W 127th....F H England. 2,000

Furelle, Annie G. 153 Lexington av....T Kelly. 137

Emmons, Elizabeth. 420 W 52d....L Baumann. 122

Ellis, C L. 455 W 57th....A Ballin. 750

English, Sarah A. 5 E 12th and 20 and 22 W 12th....E Montgomery. 4,719

Fristeot, Mary C. 306 E 11th....Dreisacker & Co. 158

Feldman, Bernard. 208 E 114th....Simpson & P. Piano. 375

Fitzgerald, Lizzie. 375 Canal....Krakauer Bros. Piano. 270

Fallet, C and A. 110 E 27th....J F Manges. (R) 494

Farrell, M C. 502 W 32d ...L Baumann. 116

Flynn, May F F. 177 W 63d....W E Wheelock & Co. Piano. 250

Fowler, J L A. 31 Hancock pl....L Baumann. 288

Fullen, H A. 261 W 130th....J Stahl, Jr. 150

Galetzine, P A. 489 5th av....R M Walters. Piano. (R) 264

Gill, Catharine. 8 King. ..Manges Bros. 157

Gilmartin, Mary. 416 W 50th....L Baumann. 118

Greenfield, R A. 143 W 41st ...T Willis. (R) 158

Greenwood, Jane. 718 10th av....Fennell & Pye. 106

Gargen, Mary. 97 East Broadway....H S Eisler. 108

Gordon, Annie. 244 Broome....Krakauer Bros. Piano. 275

Gronfors, Sara L. 221 E 32d ..L Baumann. 189

Gaffney, Patrick. 179th st and Vanderbilt av ...J Baumann. 117

Goldstein, Bessie. 9 Stanton....Garvey Bros. 142

Hassig, G F. 1609 Park av....Dreisacker & Co. 148

Healy, Annie. 345 E 20th...S I Herschmann. 284

Huddleston, Rose. 120 W 96th....J Moriarty. 297

Hunter, A V. 653 Western Boulevard... R M Walters. Piano. (R) 120

Haulet, Honora. 216 W 40th....O'Farrell & Co. 351

Harmon, May. 282 W 14th....H Israel & Sons. 2,022

Hay, C E. 958 8th av... O'Farrell & Co. 186

Hannigan, Ellen. 64 E 128th....L Baumann. (R) 162

Hartman, Geo. 502 W 21st....L Baumann. (R) 118

Harvey, E E. 134 W 66th....W E Wheelock & Co. Piano. 300

Hatch, Annie L. 1673 2d av....W E Wheelock & Co. Piano. (R) 255

Hewlett, Julie. 438 W 34th ...H Israel & Sons. (R) 175

Hobbs, Maud. 332 E 77th ...T Willis. (R) 213

Hodges, James. 406 W 57th....L Baumann. 163

Howard, Sadie. 201 W 38th....H Israel & Son. (R) 225

Huebner, John. 132 W 63d....L Baumann. 118

Huntington, Mrs E F. 255 W 34d....W E Wheelock & Co. Piano. 175

Ireland, A A. 1045 Prospect av....S Baumann. 213

Jacobson, Chas. 1970 7th av....Dreisacker & Co. 200

Joel, Rosa. 309 E 50th. J Baumann. (R) 294

Johnson, Stella. 430 W 52d....A Ballin. 140

Jackson, J L. Storage....Emily Fox. 514

Jimmerson, Mrs. 9 Mangin....A H Mangold. Piano. 225

Jordan, E L....D Bentley. 300

Kelly, Dora. 238 W 126th....R M Walters. Piano. (R) 210

Kerner, Mary A. 211 W 35th....H Mannes & Son. 148

Kane, J J. 709 3d av ...L Baumann. 220

Keefer, Louis. 112 W 63d....J Baumann. 199

Kernan, Annie. 174 E 96th... J Baumann. 597

Kopeland, Jake. 2331 1st av....Dreisacker & Co. 221

Korner, Louise. 430 E 92d....S Baumann. 128

Kramer, Minnie. 988 6th av ...Garvey Bros. 103

Kahn, Bertha. 66 Monroe....Simpson & P. Piano. 200

Keupp, Josephine. 552 W 39th....H Israel & Sons. 117

Kueny, T D. 246 W 31st....O'Farrell & Co.. 134

King, Mrs C W. 240 W 14th....T Kelly. 121

Klinger, H and S. 181 Henry Amer Guar Assoc. 500

Krensky, M. 155 Ridge... A Grinspan. 87

Lemberger, S. 166 W 136th....W E Wheelock & Co. Piano. 285

Lichtenstein, A M. 370 W 29th....R M Walters. Piano. (R) 105

Lovett, Mary. 525 W 20th....W E Wheelock & Co. Piano. 167

Lester, R E & M J. 1048 5th av....A Frey. (R) 319

Long, Charlotte. 179 E 110th....F J Brechtel. (R) 121

Lord, Emma. 201 W 15th....Simpson & P. Piano. (R) 195

Lynch, Rosa. 15 James....O'Farrell & Co. 194

Laferre, T C. 136 W 63d....L Baumann. 145

Leitbner, Theresa. 349 E 15th....J Gregg & Co. 206

Lindbo, Mrs S E. 401 Lexington av... A Ballin. (R) 229

Mansfield, Emilia. 223 E 6th....J Moriarty. 173

Marvin, Helen. 145 W 61st .... Commercial Credit Co. 150

McBride, Mrs C E. 49 and 51 W 35th....Brooklyn F Co. (R) 9,855

McChesney, Mary A. 155 W 23d... A Ballin. 847

McCue, John. 436 W 35th ...L Baumann. 181

McShane, George. 323 E 85th... J J McGrorty. 140

Miller, Susan. 1841 3d av....J Baumann. (R) 132

Mohan, Ellen F. 425 E 14th....R M Walters. Piano. 294

Moncombie, Wm. 47 St Marks pl....S I Herschmann. (R) 195

McDermott, Ellie. 217 E 81st... Krakauer Bros. Piano. 200

Meason, Angelina. 315 W 36th....O'Farrell & Co. 201

Meehan, Bridget. 356 W 43d....O'Farrell & Co. 176

Metz, Joseph. 316 E 116th....American Guarantee Assoc. 400

Miller, J E. 247 W 15th .. H Israel & Sons 104

Murphey, Margaret. 609 Washington....H Israel & Sons. 233

Myers, Emmeline M. 268 W 136th....L Baumann. 128

Martine, W M. 63 Bank....L Baumann. 174

Marx, Barbara. 112 E 47th....S Heyman & Co. 200

Mathews, J J. 154 3d av....Manges Bros. 202

Mayer, John. 176 E 106th....T A Von Glahn. (R) 85

McCann, Katie. 341 W 16th....J Mullins & Co. 163

McCarthy T F. 555 W 48th....Jordan & M. 136

McGhee, Bertha. 227 W 40th.. .L Baumann. 126

McGiven, Katie. 245 Av B ...R M Walters. Piano. 110

McGuire, Margaret. 74 Monroe....R M Walters. Piano. (R) 108

Melchar, O E. 270 W 96th....S Heyman & Co. 160

Metzel, Katie. 221 E 100th ...Jordan & M. 175

Millard, W H. 262 W 122d ...H Thoesen. 410

Miller, O A. 32 E 14th....L Baumann. 165

Mlaker, Ferdinand. 216 2d....L Baumann. 121

Monday, Mary. 643 E 13th....Manges Bros 175

Noir, Charlotte. 198 6th av....G Fennell & Co. (R) 245

Nachtigal, Helen. 109 E 7th....Lieth & Schelling. (R) 91

O'Brien, Maggie T. 657 3d av....R M Walters. Piano. (R) 180

O'Neil, Emile. 411 E 116th....L Baumann. 125

O'Neill, John. 14 Amsterdam av....J Baumann. 265

O'Connor, Bartholomew. 293 Mott ... J S Michael. 100

O'Hara, W W. 268 W 130th ...I Mason. (R) 133

Ohler, P A. 129 E 119th ...H S Eisler. 103

O'Connor, Bridget. 32 Varick....H Israel & Sons (R) 200

Ohrdorf, Mrs L. 63 W 51st....H Thoesen. 104

Perrot, H. 7 Cornelia....Fennell & P. 138

Perlowitz, Mollie. 280 Division....Simpson & P. Piano. 400

Quigley, John. 120 Christopher ..Manges Bros. 125

Randel, S. 343 3d....H Israel & Sons. (R) 100

Richardson, W J. 140 W 11th ...W E Wheelock & Co. Piano. 450

Rich, Florence. 21 Pell ...Jordan & M. 200

Rice, Helen A. 21 E 46th....H Thoesen. 1,401

Richmond, T L. 449 W 40th....H Israel & Sons. (R) 150

Ritter, P R. 468 W 34th....L Baumann. 144

Rosenthal, J. 526 E 83d ..Brooklyn F Co. 255

Richon, Prudence C. 471 W 23d ..N Y F Co. (R) 150

Rust, Elise. 65 2d....L Baumann 298

Ryan, Sadie. 148 W 68th....L Baumann. 127

Rachford, Katie. 233 E 107th....Dreisacker & Co. 165

Romain, W G. 156 and 158 W 127th....G Meyer. Coaches. (R) 2,308

Schlessinger, A. 1051 Park av... S Heyman & Co. (R) 275

Schmoll, Theodore. 341 East Houston....G Ehret. Saloon Fixtures. 1,000

Schulz, Carl. 28 St Marks pl....H Thoesen. 311

Shea, Frances. 147 W 96th....T Kelly. 165

Sheridan, Mary. 210 E 30th....T Kelly. 260

Silverberg, F M. 631 E 140th ..W E Wheelock & Co. Piano. 135

Simon, Sarah. 213 E 78th ...S Heyman & Co. 566

Simpson, Mrs W. 314 W 46th....T Kelly. 304

Smith, S A. 414 E 58th ...S Heyman & Co. 112

Solomon, Annie. 1642 Lexington av....A Solomon. 1,300

Sprague, Eugene. 195 E 100th....W E Wheelock & Co. Piano. 275

St Clair, Georgia. 162 E 46th....Fennell & Pye. (R) 481

Stern, Minnie A. 9 E 59th....S Heyman & Co. 200

Streeter, F D. 438 Lexington av....Jordan, M & Co. 137

Sanches, George. 179 E 108th....J Baumann. 260

Schachner, Carl. 209 E 112th....Dreisacker & Co. 152

Schirmer, Kate. 193 Hudson....R M Walters. Piano. 142

Schnepel, Minnie. 307 E 76th ...S Baumann. 151

Schubeith, E & M. 402 E 51st....American Guarantee Assoc. 500

Schwarz, Ellen. 257 W 128th....J Baumann. 173

Shulz, Edward. Schenectady, N Y. ..Manges Bros. 193

Spengeman, Amelia. 59 W 98th....J Baumann. 181

Stoaxe, C W. 314 W 38th....J Baumann. 373

Swartz, S. 1710 Lexington av... L Baumann. 172

Spence, Mrs V. 736 7th av....H Israel & Sons. 116

Stampe, Carrie. 84 Greenwich... Simpson & P. Piano. 300

Syring, Wm. 525 E 83d . O'Farrell & Co. 151

Twiss, Agnes. 400 W 30th....L Baumann. 178

Telfair, Margaret M. 237 W 128th....T Kelly. 160

Thomson, Bernard. 845 Amsterdam av....T Willis. 380

Thorne, C T. 224 5th av....E C Hinsdale. 130

Tussner, Leonard. 411 W 36th....L Baumann. 127

Twiss, L S. 333 W 18th....T Kelly. 272

Urdang, Aron. 104 East Broadway....H Israel & Sons. (R) 182

Uhl, Sophia. 137 Av A....J Steinbugler, Jr. 170

Van Cott, Emily. 911 Park av....J Baumann. 179

Vause, J T. 90 E 111th....L Baumann. 358

Von Bussum, Dixon. 541 W 125th....W E Wheelock & Co. Piano. 150

Washburn, Mrs S A. 134 W 62d....W E Wheelock & Co. Piano. (R) 108

Weitheim, Leo. 223 E 70th ..H Thoesen. 119

Williams, Edward. 212 W 12th....L Baumann. (R) 120

Wilson, Lena. 226 W 4th....L Baumann. 240

Wolf, Dr. 97 Henry st and 129 East Broadway ...H S Eisler. 205

Wollerman, A H & C T. 354 W 14th....L Baumann. 122

Westfall, Alice. 219 W 42d .. M E Wallace. 2,500

Wagner, W. 409 E 17th....L Baumann. 116

Watts, Ira. 318 W 36th....A Ballin. 277

Weaver, Etta. 262 W 43d....F G Smith. Piano. (R) 245

Willet, Ernestine. 499 Lexington av....H Kremer. 115

Young, Watson. 99 Macdougal....L Baumann. 194

MISCELLANEOUS.

Alsdorf, John. 98 Columbus av....Nat Cash Reg Co. Register. 225

Aronson, Harris. 176 Monroe ....O Pierking. Butcher Fixtures. (R) 107

Agazzi, Antonio. 817 E 22d... J and F Cavagnaro. Machine. (R) 85

Blair, George. Morton st, near West st....Clinton Bank. Lumber, &c. 18,000

Bower, John, Jr. 586 Amsterdam av....P A Cassidy. Wagon. 89

Bricker & Siegel. 474 Grand....L Schaffer. Picture Fixtures, &c. 50

Bauer, George. 27 Cannon....J Weiss. Barber Fixtures. 26

Brenton, George. 460 W 17th....J Cunningham Son & Co. Coach. 21

Brereton & McIntosh. 149 11th av....M B Tidey, Jr. Machinery. 179

Boland, Michael. 68th st and East River... J Rothschild. Horse, &c. 500

Bourguignon, C L. 139 6th av....G Flatauer. Cigar Fixtures. 100

Bowen, H E....E A Bowen et al. Trade Mark, Fixtures, &c. 80,000

Bowles, Lillian. 83d st and Lexington av . G Meyer, Coupe, &c. 600

Boyman, Henry .. J Klee. Coal Fixtures. 100

Buellesbach, C & H. 364 and 366 E 3d....M A Birk. Horse and Wagon. 200

Byck, Gisele. 413 E 91st....J J Shillinger. Machinery. 850

Cargill, H H. 436 E 18th....J Leonard et al. Coal Yard Fixtures. (R) 1,374

Cleary, Chas. 51 Ridge....S Oestreich. Horse. 150

Daly, Cornelius. 562-568 W 34th....J Millward & Co. Machinery 5,625

Daley, Wm....G Meyer....Coupe. 400

Deisser, John....H D Mould. Horse, Truck, &c. 343

Dietz, Anna. 108 Spring....D Kerbs. Cigar Fixtures. 200

Eveleth & Marks. 155 Fulton....E Eveleth. Printing Fixtures. 1,500

Eyelet Button Hole Attachment Co. 1 Union sq ....A Mellin. Machines and Office Fixtures. (R) 4,030

Ehle, Otto. 1467 Av A....J Weiss. Barber Fixtures. 15

Emanuel, Benj....J W Tufts. Soda Fixtures. 200

Ehrman, Anton. 42d st, bet 9th and 10th avs.... J Helb. Horse, &c. 300

Freeman, Reuben. 14 Barclay....Babcock P P Co. Press. (R) 615

Frohwein, O T. 1620 3d av....C E Vetter. Drug Fixtures. (R) 3,250

Germania Pub Co .. G Staeber. Presses, &c. 10,000

Giacometto, Amabile. 124 W 25th....G Farina. Grocery Fixtures. 257

Graff & Smith. 56 Broad....Manhattan Type Co. Press. 369

Grambling, Elizabeth. 102 E 118th....N Schaumberger. Bakery Fixtures. 850

Gottlieb, Joseph. 49 Clinton....A Benedek. Barber Fixtures. 200

Gilbert, Heiland & Beitler. 1335-1339 Broadway ....Babcock P P Co. Press. (R) 1,305

Golen, Elias. 1 and 3 Pitt....C Dierking. Butcher Fixtures. 27

Herrmann, Armin. 8th av and 138th st. ..A D Puffer & Sons. Soda Fixtures. 600

Hochreutener, Heinrich. 620 Bergen av....C Fischer. Machine. 400

Haas, Frank. 30 Suffolk....S Richman. Soda Fixtures. 800

Haas, F X. 30 Suffolk....A Zipser. Selzer Bottles. 538

Henschel, Adolph. 33 Av D....J W Tufts. Soda Fixtures. 100

Hart, Daniel. 392 Bleecker....P A Cassidy. Wagon. 60

Haskin Wood Vulcanizing Co....Atlantic Trust Co. Patents, &c. (R) 200,000

Hescote, Henry. 130 W 23d ...E H Little. Hair Goods, &c. 250

Holt, Edward. 119th st and Pleasant av ...A D Puffer & Son. Soda Fixtures. (R) 10

Iuverlozzi, Annetta. 651 3d av....Aiello & Co. Grocery Fixtures. 206

J Kress B Co ...Central Trust Co. Brewery Fixtures. 250,000

Johnn, J A. 115 Hester ...G Franz. Machines. (R) 600

Klein & Hoffman. 145 Essex....E Marsheider. Butcher Fixtures. 96

Kniehase, Charles. 463 Willis av... J M Winterroth. Butcher Fixtures. 156

Komp, Albert. 496 Cherry....S Bailie & Son. Machinery. 390

Kaplan, Isaac. 16 Varick....Archer Mfg Co. Barber Fixtures. 310

Kelly, E and M. 136 W 4th....J H Lippe. Coach. 496

Klesius, Mathias. 52 New Bowery....A A Thomson & Co. Press, &c. (R) 4?1

Krause, O W. 5th av and 58th st, Barber Shop ....Edison General Electric Co. Electric Fixtures. 500

Krieger, S M. 102 Columbia....J Schmitt. Wagon. 100

Kunkel, Heyman. 64 Norfolk....C Dierking. Butcher Fixtures 180

Lehmann, Henry. 506 1st av....A M Rontey. Drug Fixtures. (R) 500

Liccione, Pittaro & Co. 189 Hester....Marvin Safe Co. Safe. 220

Lewensohn & Spector....J Stewart. Machines. 165

Lott, C H. 202 E 84th....A L Lott. Horses, Wagons, &c. (R) 300

Laub, Jacob. 23 Av C....Seligman Bros. Bakery Fixtures. 609

Leatham, W H. 60 W 22d... M A Joyce. Picture Store Fixtures. 190

Levinson, M. 115 Park row....J L Morrison & Co. Machinery. 175

Lynn, Lucy E. 136 4th....Mary E Higgins. Horses, Coaches, &c. 1,000

Lynch, Cornelius. 344 E 49th ... L Farley. Horses, Trucks, &c. (R) 1,400

Lorello, Giovanni. 202 E 101st....T Dragna. Barber Fixtures. 100

Manecke, Ph. 50 Centre... A D Puffer & Sons. Soda Fixtures. (R) 600

Marti, F R. 2442 8th av....A Lemlein. Store Fixtures. 125

Maycock, Henry. 219 W 26th....J Rudd. Milk Fixtures, Horse, &c. 600

McClellan & Patton. 121st st and Manhattan av ....J Matthews Co. Soda Fixtures. 310

Melzer, Florenz. 2495 3d av....Couper, Z & Co. Bakery Fixtures. 100

Menje, Charles. 782 10th av ...A Wick & Co. Bakery Fixtures. (R) 500

Minicucci, Beniamino. 1053 2d av....G D'Alnisa. Barber Fixtures. 117

Morehi, F A. 89th st and Columbus av....I S Clark. Horse, &c. 75

Merriam, E J....Teachers' Pub Co. "Teachers' World" Sub List. 1

McDonald, Thos....D P Nichols & Co. Cab. 325

Mullen, John....M Armstrong & Co. Coach. 650

McOnerty, Alexander ...J Gottsleben. Coach. 162

Meyer, Harry. 434 Broadway....A Vehon. Machinery. 250

Milekowsky & Krivelewitz. 169 Hester....S Shatz. Grocery Fixtures. 110

Minard, Lydia A. 271 and 273 W 87th....S W Allen. Horse, Wagon, &c. 100

Mueller, David. 177 Prince... D Shea. Machinery. (R) 330

Nadel, Leib. 92 Ridge....C Halier. Machine. 50

Nicolaus, A, Mrs. 446 W 19th....J McLean. Butcher Fixtures. 161

Neuman, Gustav. 130 2d av....J Koerber. Office Furniture. (R) 168

Niebard, Fanny. 246 Division ...S Altman. Bakery and Grocery Fixtures. 90

Nutter, J H. 2d av and 2d st....Nat Cash Reg Co. Register. 205

Panagrosso, Ferdinando. 801 E 110th....F Saltaformazzio. Barber Fixtures. 40

Paulus, Charlotte. 1174 E 142d....M & S Loeb. Horses, Cows, &c. 2,000

Perry, T F. 59 and 61 Liberty ..C Elliott. Cigar Fixtures. 80

Quencer, W J. 400 W 57th....H C Copeland. Drug Fixtures. 1,500

Roche & Russell. 110 6th av....M M Govan. Photo Fixtures. 117

Rosenthal, Israel. 222 and 224 Broome ...I Jacobs. Barber Fixtures. 215

Ragusa, Benedetto. 155 W 28th....S Pepe. Barber Fixtures. 275

Reiss, C F W ...G Meyer. Coupe. 500

Roberts, Thomas. 470 W 23d ...Nat Cash Reg Co. Register. 400

Rosenfeld, Jacob. 57 2d av....Duparquet, H & M Co. Range. 52

Sack, John. 591 10th av ...B Pesenecker. Bakery Fixtures. (R) 400

Saltaformazzio & Arcanjelo. 2357 3d av....G Napoli. Barber Fixtures. 270

Saugiorgio, Biagio. 1691 3d av....A Buonfiglio. Barber Fixtures. 50

Schmiedekamp, J F W. 230 W 4th ...Nat Cash Reg Co. Register. 175

Schrader, H....P Barrett. Truck. 500

Schuetzer, I S. 200 2d....F Wesel Mfg Co. Cutter. 135

Schumm, Mary A. 327 E 47th....M Bullova. Bakery Fixtures. (R) 350

Schlund, Charlotte. 444 W 48th....C Martin. Library. 85

Schwarz, Adolf. 336 E 57th....H Zeydel. Paintings, &c. (R) 35

Schulze, Gustave. 128 E 110th....M Schulze. Confectionery Fixtures. 500

Shalgian, Peter. 9 Spruce....J L Morrison & Co. Machinery. 325

Stratton, E. & Son. 61 Broadway....Manhattan Type Co. Press, &c. 700

Strohmeyer & Wyman. 2 New Chambers.... W Barnett. Photo Fixtures. 3,000

Scherff, William. 2114 3d av....J Luhrs. Confectionery Fixtures. 3,000

Schmidt, J C....G Dessecker. Coach. 225

Seward, D W. 2405 1st av....E Roberts. Drug Fixtures. (R) 2,000

Sullivan, T S. 337 E 14th....L Knapp. Laundry Fixtures. 200

Syska, W F. 5th av, bet 138th and 139th sts.... H Craimer. Horse and Truck. (R) 1,000

Schleuter & Bartholdi. 341 E 11th....J Stewart. Machines. 350

Trabold, Aquilia. 525-535 E 15th....P B Bracken. Horses, Trucks, &c. 200

Wallenstein & Heineman .... Rothschild Bro. Horse, Wagon, &c 274

Ward, John. 44 Barclay. ..J L Morrison & Co. Machinery. 325

Weidemann, William 125 Franklin st and 95 West Broadway. ..L W Hraba. Barber Fixtures. (R) 650

Ward, J B. 264 W 11th ....H Ward. Livery Stable. 5,000

Weitzer, Israel. 95 Sheriff....L Brand. Horse, Wagon, &c. 70

Weydig, Elizabeth....G Dessecker. Coach. (R) 74

Wallach & Co. 40 Columbia....Bennett & C. Soda Fixtures. 425

Weinkrantz, S. 151 East Broadway....J L Morrison & Co. Machinery. 80

Winch, C A....J C Winch. Horses, Ice Wagons. 5,000

White, C I....H Spies. Jewelry Fixtures. (R) 1,000

Zimmerman, Emil. 2112 8th av....Smith & Sills. Bakery Fixtures. 443

BILLS OF SALE.

Aillo, Raffaelo. 241 Mulberry.... F Forenzo. Grocery Fixtures. 265

Aaron, Charles. 274 8th av....J Rauth. Clothing Store Stock. 2,500

Catinelli, Ginseppo. 126 Baxter....P Scalera. Grocery Fixtures. 325

Chasanowitz, L S. 5 Orchard....L J Shelansky. Butcher Fixtures. 300

Edeler, Chas. 164 Av A and 1644 Columbia av ....O Noll. Store Fixtures, &c. 1,800

Grohusko, Isaac. 28 Grand....Annie Grohusko.. Stock, Fixtures, &c. 100

Hanifin, Jeremiah....A McOwen. Horses, Trucks, &c. 250

Hirsch, Jacob. 47 Wooster....J Koch. Machines. 25

Jaeger, Isaac. 442 8th av .. S R Postley. Cigar Fixtures. 350

Jacobs, A S. 32 Baxter....W F Clemmons. Clothing, Fixtures, &c. 1,500

Kerls, Herman. 358 3d av....H Damm, Jr. Store-Fixtures. 1,000

Klee, John. 559 1st av....H Boymann. Coal Fixtures. 340

Litzebower, William. 121 E 110th....A Hufner. Bakery Fixtures. 400

Longa, Salvatore. 4 Clarkson and 79 Bank.... Elizabeth Schwall. Barber Fixtures and Furniture. 375

Mandelblum, Henry. 112 Canal....M Schustak. Grocery Fixtures. 1,00)

Mitchell & O'Connell. 1519 2d av....Connolly & Potter. Saloon Fixtures. 3,500

Noll, Theobald. 164 Av A and 1644 Columbia av ....C Edeler. Store Fixtures, &c. 1,018

Pepia, Giovanni. 32 Bayard....G Pepia. Barber Fixtures. 300

Palumbo, Vincenzo. 408 Broome....Teodora Palumbo. Office Fixtures, &c. 1

Re, Gaetano. 233 Thompson....A Re. Grocery and Butcher Fixtures. 1,200

Simon, Fannie. 469 Broadway and 138 Madison st....S Stroock & Co. Machinery, &c. 278

Steinweg, Sam'l, auctioneer. 102 W 84th....C W Wells. Furniture. 567

Toppan, F W. 102 W 61st....F G Henry. Furniture. 500

Valente, Gabriel. 2105 3d av....V Sema. Barber Fixtures. 205

Vogel, Henry. 2177 2d av....Susan Murray. Saloon Fixtures. 1,600

Wacker & Burmeister. 300 E 70th....E Spatz. Grocery Fixtures. 2,000

Woods, Frederick....Smith, Bowman & Co. Leases. 3,000

Zelner, Charles. 24 Union sq....E Raphael. Machines, &c. 300

ASSIGNMENTS OF CHATTEL MORTGAGES.

Burpham, G H & Co to E A Bernis. (Mort given by Subscription List "Teachers' World.") 1

Frey, Augustus to G S Bracher. (R E & M J Lester, Nov 6, 1891.) 304

Redmond & Sheehy to Beadleston & W. (C Kingwell, Sept 3, 1891.) 2,000

Zeydel, H exr of to L Dinkelspiel. (A Schwarz, Nov 5, 1890.) —

KINGS COUNTY.

OCTOBER 29 TO NOVEMBER 4.—INCLUSIVE.

SALOON AND RESTAURANT FIXTURES.

Byrnes, H E. 965 Grand....Mary C Higgins. Restaurant Fixtures. $250

Bosch, J. 1925 Fulton....J H Thiemann. 1,975

Carlsen, S C. 214 Columbia....Bachmann B Co. 600

Churchill, A E. 320 Van Brunt... J Hoffmann B Co. 500

Coar, W. 33 Cedar....Obermeyer & L. 650

Endres, P. 326 Stockton....F Ibert. 400

Ferber, I. 33 Humboldt....L Eppig. 800

Gifford, J. 194 West....Leibinger & Oehm B Co. 100

Gink, P. 12 Sumner av....Claus Lipsius B Co. 700

Higgins, Annie P. 50 Sands....Budweiser B Co. 7,500

Same. 141 Front....same. 2,500

Haddon, E F. 358 Bainbridge... H Vogel. 500

Hollmann, J. 1522 Dean....Beadleston & W. Ice Box. 90

Same....same. Ice Box. 100

Isaacsen, M. 17 Hamilton av....Danenberg & C. (R) 325

Kennedy, T. 102 3d pl....Williamsburgh B Co (Lim). (R) 350

Lemmermann, H L. 1988 Broadway....P Frensen. 400

Lent, R. 18 Alabama av....Leibinger & Oehm B Co. 600

Markert, G. 677 4th av....H B Scharmann. (R) 1,000

McCourt, H E. 719 2d av....J Kress B Co. 755

Mascaro, A. 57 Front....Budweiser B Co. 450

McKillen, T. 163 2d av. ..Danenberg & Coles. 369

Nielson, W A. 264 Court... A Trabant. Billiards. 700

Orthlieb, L. 193 Graham av....Claus Lipsius B Co. 600

Riggs, W B. 2641 Atlantic av. ..Oppenheimer & Harby. 1,210

Rapporte, A. Cor Stone and Blake avs . Budweiser B Co. 275

Stephan P. 62 Scholes....Obermeyer & L. 300

Schineller, G. 60 George....M Saueracker. (R) 600

Stroeber, C. 172 Montrose av Claus Lipsius B Co. 600

Tormey Bros. 178 Greenpoint av....Beadleston & W. Saloon Ice Box (R) 1(5

Walsh, Johana. Kingsland av, cor Norman av ... J Wallace & Son. 415

Weiss, J. 16 Lewis av....Budweiser B Co. 1,100

HOUSEHOLD FURNITURE.

Anderson, A. 309 Van Brunt....H Johnson. 140

Bellows, C H. 323 Jefferson av....Brooklyn F Co. 260

Bittner, Maggie. 201 9th....L Z Murray. 112

Boorum, May. 224 Atlantic av .L Z Murray. 138

Broman, Bessie. 104 Concord....Manges Bros. 253

Brown, W. 18 3d ... Brooklyn F Co. 134

Cannon, M A. 300 De Kalb av....Brooklyn F Co. 229

Carlson, Mary A. 616 Macon....Brooklyn F Co. 100

Carlson, J. 618 Hicks....H Johnson. 140

Christian, Mary S. 1019 Putnam av....Cowperthwait & Co. 188

Connick, W H. 126 High ...Cowperthwait & Co. 127

Crowley, J. 38 North Portland av ...Brooklyn F Co. 152

Cowen, Jennie. 36 Fleet pl....A Pearson. 121

Dederich, E H. 14th av and 56th st ....M M Webster. 100

De Wilde, H M. 141 Jefferson av....Mullins & Sons. 116

Dolan, Jr, R. 98 Java ...Dreisacker & Co. 196

Drew, J. 124 Prospect....Cowperthwait & Co. 191

Durland, T C. 714 Quincy....L Baumann. 132

Ehrhart, Mary. 11 Willow pl....Cowperthwait & Co. 1,540

Ferares, Mary. 281 Bedford av....H Israel & Sons. 193

Fernandez, Louis. 1648 Pacific. ..Mullins & Sons. 146

Firmbach, Maria L. 1002 Myrtle av....W H Cummings. Piano. 120

Francis, Mrs L. 1707 Broadway....J A Schwarz. 210

Gould, J. 227 Woodbine....Cowperthwait & Co. 154

Hagne, K. 150 Hamilton av....Mullins & Sons. 126

Hall, J A. 33 Douglass....L Z Murray. 339

Hawkins, C. 342 St Marks pl....Brooklyn F Co. 117

Hanrahan, E A. 64 Middleton....A Schulz. 190

Hinchman, F. 284 Adelphi....R P Hinchman. (R) 3,796

Haithwaite, A. 401 8th ...L Baumann. 608

Jackson, H A. 1 Fleet pl ...L Baumann. 107

Jackson, J. 60 2d pl....H Johnson. 143

Kelling, M. 411 Carlton av....L Baumann. 206

Kane, Sarah M. 19 Grand av....F G Smith. Piano. (R) 200

Keefe, J J. 46 North Elliott pl... M M Webster 100

Kenny, M . 365 South 4th....Cowperthwait & Co. ary 120

Lander, Mrs T A. 129 Clifton pl....I Mason. 178

Laugerig, H. 856 Willoughby av....L Baumann. 115

Larraidy, J M. 218 Union....Brooklyn F Co. 948

Lillienthal, Katie. 53 Harman....A Schulz. 374

Lind, Minnie. 23 Suydam....A Schulz. 145

Lint off, Mrs J. 695 Macon....Cowperthwait & Co. 163

Levis, Ella T. 285 South 5th....L Baumann. 118

Merritt, G. 747 Macon....J A Rogers. 100

Miller, Elsie. 213 Pearl....Cowperthwait & Co. 154
Moore, H A. 80 Clifton pl....Cowperthwait & Co. 208
Morris, J T. 321A Jefferson av....Brooklyn F Co. 220
Morris, W. 377 Macon....Brooklyn F Co. 440
Mott, N. 220 Steuben... Cowperthwait & Co. 180
Nyman, S. 205 Middleton....H Johnson. 134
Norris, P J. 69 Clermont av....Jordan & M. 130
Overath, M. 1052 Broadway....J A Schwarz. 230
Olsen, J. 9 Beach pl....H Johnson. 126
Olsen, J. 231 Sackett....A Pearson. 100
Osterburg, O. 418A 6th av....Brooklyn F Co. 139
Ostrom, S E. 48 Williams av....I Mason. 282
Phillips, T M. 85 Sand....I Mason. 119
Price, Mary E. 429 Gates av ...L Baumann. 135
Purdy, H. 23 President ...O Shaun. 150
Purdy, Mary S. 80 Clifton pl....Brooklyn F Co. 217
Quinn, Margt. 81 Carroll....Cowperthwait & Co. 105
Richter, H. 418 Evergreen av....L Baumann. 208
Raymond, S. 225 Livingston....Cowperthwait & Co. 218
Read, J. Atlantic av, [cor Jerome] st....C S Lacey. 103
Roemer, Minnie. [340 Jay....Cowperthwait & Co. 308
Rougemont, Ade. 340 Lafayette av....Brooklyn F Co. 320
Ryland, C. 438 Gold... Brooklyn F Co. 172
Rand, M. 575 3d av....Whalen Bros. 216
Schuck, P. 35 Cooper ...J A Schwarz. 281
Smith, W H. 41 Prince....H S Eisler. 108
Sprague, Kate 124 57th....A Pearson. 262
Sartorius, F. 69 Penn. ..Mullins & Sons. 142
Schmitt, P. 128 Suydam....J Bauer. 206
Seabridge, C D. 150 Lafayette av... Cowperthwait & Co. 154
Showalter, W D. 156 South 5th....L Baumann. 318
Siebert, M. 866 Marcy av....I Mason. 107
Sinclair, Cath. 890 Van Buren....J Baumann. 113
Smith, M. 151 Ainslie ....J Baumann. 328
Stone, L. 325 Furman ...H Johnson. 130
Stout, W R. 52 Van Buren....Brooklyn F Co. 177
Thomas, E J. 11 St Marks av....H Israel & Son. 478
The American Society of Swedish Engineers. 250 Union....Mullins & Sons. 405
Tummon, F N. 15 Concord... A Dredge. 400
Warner, T B. 1724 Pacific....Cowperthwait & Co. 138
Webster, S. 195 Sands....Cowperthwait & Co. 140
Wells, Oda H. 435 Gold....Manges Bros. 308
Wendt, Mrs W. 71 Herman....Brooklyn F Co. 149
Wendt, Sadie. 1057 Fulton....Brooklyn F Co. 179
White, G W. 25 Stanhope ...Brooklyn F Co. 175
White, W. 721 Prospect pl....Brooklyn F Co. 132
Wicklund, Caroline. 582 3d av.. .H Johnson. 200
Williams, H. 1056 Jefferson av....Brooklyn F Co. 131

MISCELLANEOUS.

Anderson, W P. 925 Fulton....J W Tufts.... Soda Fountain. 100
Blanding & Co....J W Tufts. Soda Fountain. 8.0
Buckley, J. 653 Union ..J Fulton. Barber Fixtures. 330
Blaxlimsky, F A. 9 Varet....F & G Haag & Co. Barber Fixtures. 215
Bortel, F. 17 Fulton....E Rughesse. Horse. 300
Both, H. Metropolitan av . Nat Cash Reg Co. Register. 175
Brendecke, F. 335 Adams....C F Rohmann. Printer Fixtures. 1,200
Constantino, G. 78 Flatbush av....G Strangis. Fixtures. 100
Cussick, J. 676 Halsey....P B Bracken. Horses, Trucks, &c. 400
Clarkson, O G. 291 Bedford av....Nat Cash Register Co. Register. 400
Cooke, J T 123 Nostrand av....Steinwender & Co. Machinery. indebtedness
Donnelly, J H. . Weil Bros. Cows. 684
Donneley, T J. 274 Washington....National Cash Register Co. Register. 175
Ernest, Ochs, a corporation....M Weinman and J Steil trustees. Brewery. (R) 600,000
Febinger, Frederick. Cypress av, near De Kalb av ...S Jacobs. Hot Bed Sashes. 275
Furman, J C. Maspeth and Morgan avs....C W Cooper. Machinery, &c. 140,000
Graff & Smith 86 Broad....Manhattan Type Foundry. Press. 369
Henly, J. 205 Gates av ...J B Wright. Drug Fixtures. (R) 500
Holt, E S. [423 Clermont av....A L Wood. Fixtures. 350
Hunt, J F. Nassau av, s s, 75 e Newell st . J C Orr. Buildings and Leasehold. 1,100
Hill, T T. 31 Union sq, New York... L Houghton. Office Furniture. 1,400
Isaac & Son. 321 Rutledge....Arthur & Randel. Horses. 875
Israel, L. 172 Carlton....W B Davis. Coach. 1,444
Jenison, J. 1378 Fulton. ..J Stanton. Horses, &c. 2,000
Jennings, J G. 687 Myrtle av....N T Swezey's Sons & Co. Bakery. 750
Keating, J....P Barrett. Truck. 260
Kelleher, M J....P Barrett. Wagon. 280
Kings Co Elevated Railway Co....Central Trust Co, New York. Rights, Properties and Franchises. (R) 7,000,000
Kunz, G P. 74 Johnson av....Manhattan Type Foundry. Type. 156
Krieger, C. 475½ Myrtle av....Eliz Christman. Cigar Store. 2,000
Lewis, L F. Greene av....B E Valentine. Horses. 300
McIlvaine, C H. 164 Reade, New York ...Campbell P P & Mfg Co. Press. 200
Munchmeyer, H. 248A Reid av....United Confectioners Assoc. Candy Store. 325
Mayher, T C. Sackett st near 3d av....Brown & Fleming. Horses, Trucks, &c. 7,158
Peters, L. 281 Ainslie....National Cash Register Co. Register. 175
Ritterbusch, August. 369 17th....J Endemann. Bakery. 500
Reilly, J. 2 Richards....Nat Cash Reg Co. Register. 200
Roscher, L. De Kalb av, s e cor Graham st... Klemmer Bros. Grocery Fixtures. 500
Ruff, G. 188 Calyer....J Fleck. Butcher Fixtures. 600
Schwarzschild, A. 205 4th av ....Jennie Stern. Butcher Fixtures. 300
Schutt, J H. 51 Lincoln pl....J A Wheeler. Horse. 350
Sorek, H and J F Cameron. 81 Orange....Wallace & Kearney. Fish Store. (R) 275
Sandel, H. 594 6th av....Anna Ritterbusch. Bakery Fixtures. 208
Stegemann, H. 413 Myrtle av....J P Wierk. Store Fixtures. 600
Temme, J. 784 Bedford av ..Margaret Krug. Barber Fixtures. 100
Van Deverg, J H. Sackett st....J Kerswill. Machinery. 2,000
Willeburgher, G. 108 Bedford av....Nat Cash Reg Co. Register. 200

BILLS OF SALE.

Bargfrede, H. 111 Smith....Charlotte Cordes. Grocery. 1,300
Fleck, J. 188 Calyer... G Ruff. Butcher Fixtures 900
Stern, Jennie. 205 4th av ...A Schwarzschild. Butcher Fixtures. 800
Wiedman, Elise. 170 Hopkins....F Rothfuss. Bakery. 800

ASSIGNMENT OF CHATTLE MORTGAGE.

Meister, N to Annie R Meister. (Mort given by W Brunning, Candy Store Fixtures, 371 rand st.) 525

NEW JERSEY.

ESSEX COUNTY.

NOTE.—*The arrangement of the Conveyances, Mortgages and Judgments in these lists is as follows: the first name in the Conveyances is the Grantor; in Mortgages, the Mortgagor; in Judgments, the Judgment debtor.*

CONVEYANCES.

Allen, A S—G Thurbt, South 13th st.......... $150
Allen, F B exr—E P Ward, 13 tracts Avon av... 30,000
Allen, F B—J Hensler, Jr, s e cor N J R R av and Wright st 25x76x44x58, n e cor Miller and N J R R av 30x108x56x100.......... 5,100
Allsopp, E B—M L Schwartz, Alpine st.......... 625
Arnold, T L—F W Arnold, Montclair.......... 1
Bailey, C C—I O Wade, Garside st.......... 500
Baker, M T—Jos Hensler, Alyea st.......... 800
Beardsley, T R—The Health Bread Co, s s Drift st 100 e Clinton av 50x155.......... 30,000
Bedford, David—E M Bedford, Nevada st.......... nom
Berrian, E B—S M B Mitchell, Madison st 126
Boughner, D H—R S Gould, N Y av.......... 1,100
Bock, Michael—J W Brown, Bridge st.......... 500
Bornemann, George—B Bertsch, South Orange. 325
Brown, D G—The Newark Lumber Co, n w cor Parkhurst and N J R R av 44x100x68x102.... 10,000
Brown, J P—M Deliza, e s Adams st 215 n Downing st 80x95, n s Jackson st 200 e Downing st 50x70.......... 3,000
Brown, J J—M L Gasstrong, Frelinghuysen av.. 1
Buermann, August—L Schmidt, Madison av.... 2,160
Burnet, Timothy—The Hilton Union S S Assoc, South Orange.......... 1,000
Carter, S E—M T Barrett, w s Washington st 58 n Nesbit st 24x125..........17,006
Canting, A B—F C Canting, West Orange...... 1
Chapman, F A—S M Metcalf, Orange.......... 8,750
Condit, M S et al—M A Shaw, Belleville.......... 500
Crocker, Thomas—A Bake, Broad st.......... 1,000
Cullen, M R W—S J Cullen, 2d av.......... 1
Cullen, S J—W C Cullen, 2d av.......... 1
Dale, Henry—F M Wilmurt, West Orange...... 1
Daly, J J—S J Keefe, e s Mt Pleasant av, adj M L Ward 37x200.......... 4,020
Lauer, Albert—J Forster, Prince st.......... 1
Decker, Wilson—T Shadwell, South Orange.... 800
Dempsey, John—J M Rowe et al, Clinton.......18,000
Drake, I S—G W Tomkins et al, Orchard st 1
Duncan, H R trustee—P S Sondheim, Franklin.. 4,350
Same——P L Sondheim, Franklin.......... 4,350
Farrell, E E—A Faresh, Montclair.......... 1
Fettel, Henry—T J Wakefield, n s 6th av 150 e North 5th st 25x100.......... 4,300
Forster, John—M Schafer, w s Prince st 90 s Kinney st 49x1x50x30x100x32.......... 4,500
Fuder, Fritz—Carl F Seitz, Bergen st.......... 2,300
Fuller, L C—L A Vreeland, 3d st.......... 2,650
Gallagher, J D—G H Sedgwick, Bloomfield...... 1,500
Gibson, Wm—E B Muchmore, 7th av.......... 50
Gilmour, L D H—E C Robertson, Green st 14,400
Greason, E C—C Osborn, Washington av........ 700
Hagar, J F exr—M Wuesthoff, Ferry st.......... 1
Heyden, Edward—J F Schoener, Clinton........ 350
Hines, J H—J Maas et al, Somerset st.......... 1
Holloway, A E—Newark Lumber Co, Thomas st.......... 5,500
Holt, S H—H M Dunn, Hillside av.......... 2,000
Howard, G E P—A T Cahne, East Orange...... 6,000
Iselin, Adrian—O S Carter, West Orange....... 7,000
Jung, Daniel—H Pfeiffer, 18th av.......... 2,200
Lyle, L C—J Weber, Bruce st.......... 900
Maas, Joseph—M S Pippert, Somerset st........ 1,000
Masz, J—W Trautwein, Somerset st.......... 1,050
Mackin, Francis—S E Robirtson, Astor st 6,500
Maxfield, J F—H W Todd, Bloomfield.......... 3,000
Moessner, Gottlob—G E Heinkel, Ferry st....... 1
Moore, James—J Samuels, Fairmount av....... 950
Morrison, A E—L D Howard Gilmour, Green st.. 12,950
Pitney, Mahlon—F V Pitney, Clinton.......... 1
Rake, Annie—J Casale, Broad st.......... 800
Richardson, William—E J Reilly, East Orange. 2,600
Sallerthwaite, J F—A Blum, Franklin.......... 725
Satterthwait, J F—P F Guthrie, Franklin........ 1,378
Sargent, S S—A Del Guercio, 7th av 1,000
Sayre, S M—J R Sayre, Fulton st.......... 1
Schmidt, Louis—H M Dunn, Hillside av.......... 400
Southard, S M—C W Blake, Montclair.......... 4,200
Susstrong, Albert—J J Brown, Frelinghuysen av 1
Taylor, W A—S D Sheppard, n s Tichenor st 235 e Tichenor st 25x102.......... 3,000
Todd, H W—M C Maxfield, Bloomfield.......... 1
Trusdell, J G, Jr—E White, East Orange........ 200
Same——same, East Orange.......... 1
Trustees of Rutgers College, New Jersey—L B Heath, Hunterdon st.......... 750
Van Riper, P E—J Van Vleck, Montclair........ 30,000
Van Winkle, Ann—M J Cuckefair, Franklin. . 1
Ward, E P—A S Allen, 13 tracts Avon av 30,000
Ward, James—E D Sedille, 3d st.......... 600
White, Patrick—J O Heald, Orange.......... 1
Wilderatter, Xavier—M Harris, e s Boyd st, 225 n Kinney st 50x100.......... 6,700
Yatman, H J—J Hardman, Jr, Belleville........ 256

MORTGAGES.

Babcock, E C—M E Wilde, West Orange........ 500
Barrett, M T—S E Carter, Washington st........ 7,000
Blake, C W—H R Edmonston, Montclair.......... 3,000
Bruckner, Joseph—People's B and L Assoc, Mechanic st.......... 2,000
Cahill, John—C D B Crocker, East Orange...... 2,500
Cassidy, J H—T H Bliss, trustee, East Orange...12,500
Condit, E M—Orange Savings Bank, Orange.... 600
Conklin, E L—J W Hatt, trustee, M & E R R av.150,000
Conradi, Catharine—O Preterri, Springfield av.. 9,000
Corless, Michael—P C Williams, East Orange.... 1,000
Decker, Lyman—J Haines, Ferry st.......... 4,300
Decker, R M et al—Fourteenth Ward B and L Assoc, Miller st.......... 6,000
Deliza, Martha—I P Brown, Adams st.......... 1,500
Eisele, J C—Lincoln B and L Assoc, Orange av.. 2,000
Flynn, A M—A R Beach, Bloomfield av.......... 1,200
Guercio, Alphonso D et al—S S Sargeant, 7th av.......... 800
Hahne, August—G E P Howard, East Orange.. 5,000
Hart, J, Jr—W T Moore, Montclair 4,000
Harris, Max—Home B and L Assoc, Boyd st.... 5,500
Hart, H H—R C Browning, South Orange....... 1,500
Hilton Union Sunday School Assoc—T Burnet, South Orange.......... 750
Holzwarth, A E—C J Rademacher, High st...... 1,500
Jung, Daniel—Clark & Co, 18th av.......... 3,082
Same——Thirteenth Ward B and L Assoc, 18th av.......... 1,200
Kempf, E G—E C Diminick, Mt Prospect av..... 500
Kierstead, Jared—S H Foster, Montclair........ 1,600
Kussy, Meyer et al—R F Ballantine, 15th av.... 1,000
Ledgwick, G H—Jos D Gallagher, Bloomfield... 1,200
Lehigh Valley Terminal R R Co—Central Trust Company of New York, Essex and other counties..........10,000,000
Liehmstein, Amalia—S Doughty, Livingston st.. 1,000
Lone, Robert—B W Tucker, Aqueduct st 1,800
Maxwell, William—H Maxwell, Montclair....... 1,500
Millett, G S—Drexel Improvement Co, Montclair. 821
Mooney, M A—Enterprise B and L Assoc, Greenwich st.......... 500
Mueller, Arnold—Security B and L Assoc, Alyea st.......... 400
Pfeiffer, Henry—Thirteenth Ward B and L Assoc, 18th av.......... 1,600
Rake, Annie et al—G Krueger, Broad st........ 4,000
Reilly, E J—W Richardson, East Orange....... 1,000
Roe, J M et al—J Dempsey, Clinton..........10,000
Ross, C P—Eighth Ward B and L Assoc, Bloomfield av.......... 1,000
Schafer, Michael—Standard B and L Assoc, Prince st.......... 3,000
Schneider, Nicholas—C Akers trustee, Bloomfield.......... 1,500
Schoener, J F—E Heyden, Clinton.......... 150
Schoenfeld, Flora—F Borenstein, Belmont av... 212
Same — M A Wightman, Belmont av.......... 600
Same——J E Jackson, Belmont av.......... 4,500
Shadwell, Thomas—J M C Morrow trustee, South Orange.......... 200
Same——South Orange Free Public Circulating Library Assoc, South Orange 1,000
Sheppard, S D—Backus Water Motor Co, Tichenor st.......... 1,000
Smally, J S—S Doughty et al exrs, s s Market st. 3,000
Spinella, Nicola—Enterprise B and L Assoc, 14th av.......... 2,400
Susstrong, Albert—Mutual Life Ins Co, Frelinghuysen av.......... 1,000
Thurbt, George—A S Allen, South 13th st........ 275
Trautwein, George—Standard B and L Assoc, Somerset st.......... 2,200
Van Houten, M R—Tenth Ward B and L Assoc, Avon av.......... 4,000
Venino, Emilie—F Berg, Orange.......... 4,000
Vinorsky, Jacob—F J Kastner, Morton st........ 400
Vinorsky, Lena—M J Durham, Morton st.......... 2,200
Same——S B Jackson, Morton st.......... 300
Volz, Herman—F F Johnson, McWhorter st.... 500
Vreeland, L A—L C Fuller, Central av.......... 950
Wakefield, T J—Savings B and L Assoc, 6th av.. 400
White, Edward—J G Trusdell, Jr, East Orange. 1,500
Wilmurt, F M—Bradley & Currier Co, West Orange.......... 6,000
Woodruff, J T—Eighth Ward B and L Assoc, Montclair av.......... 600
Zahner, F S—L C Feldhusen, Lincoln av........ 800
Zarra, Vincenzo—A Del Guercio, Lock st.......... 550

CHATTEL MORTGAGES.

Becker, F C—G Krueger Brewing Co, saloon.... 175
Beldon, K B—I C Williams et al, horses and carriages.......... 1,700
Bidwell, Harry—W A Ripley, machinery.......... 1,000
Bock, A W—E S Wall trustee, coal business.... 1,200
Brady, Gilbert—The Nat Cash Reg Co, register. 250
Brutkopf, Jacob—Bennett & Gomper, siphon bottles.......... 80
Clancy, E A—J J Clancy, stock shoes.......... 800
Evers, Walters—H Thoessen, furniture.......... 42
Gross, Karl—Paterson Consolidated Brewing Co, saloon.......... 500
Jahn, Bernhart—G Krueger Brewing Co, saloon. 1,090
Leuthauser, Arthur — The Nat Cash Reg Co, register.......... 275
Lunny, J A—G Krueger Brewing Co, furniture. 107
MacKeon, M C—M E Gardiner, furniture....... 1,200
McGoldrick, James—P Ballantine & Sons, saloon.......... 120
Myers, Agnes—V H Field et al, stock drugs..... 2,000
O'Shea, J J—G Krueger Brewing Co, saloon.... 276
Pittman, George——same, saloon 590
Reilly, Thomas—J Sturm, horses and truck.... 100
Riker, E O—W W Muchmore, groceries.......... 271
Rizzolo, Felix—Lyon & Sons Brewing Co, saloon.......... 700
Sibbald, A G—The Nat Cash Reg Co, register... 200
Sibbald, Jennie—Fidelity and Casualty Co, furniture.......... 1,017
Spator, Max—C Diugolinsky, furniture.......... 200
Sporatio, Alfonso—F Lisiewski, saloon.......... 300
Stimer, Philip——same, saloon 725
Weber, Frank—G Krueger Brewing Co, saloon.. 213
Wolff, Henry——same, saloon.......... 220
Zimmerman, Charles—M Kane, horses.......... 46

HUDSON COUNTY.

CONVEYANCES.

Alt, Benedict—Ephraim De Groff, Union........ $3,500
Bene, Rehul T—L Favre, West Hoboken........ 750
Bettcher, L F—Bertha Badendick 3,500
Bentley, Peter, by exrs—Marg't Gaffney........ nom
Black, C C—A S Sim.......... 1,500
Brady, Henry—G M Severance, Kearney........ 300
Bush, Caleb, by exr—C W Parker, Bayonne..... nom
Same——same, Bayonne.......... nom
Butler, Susanna E—G W Conklin, Bayonne...... 1,200
Cleary, D E—Christian Hansen.......... 8,500
Cook, Avery, by exrs—J Guiton.......... 3,000
Combes, Mary E—Kate A Knapp, Bayonne..... 400
Condit, Fillimore—W Madoling, Kearney...... 150
Cosgrove, Pat—J Doran.......... 3,000
Coston, Pat—J McCarren.......... 700
Converse, Ella—O Glancy.......... 1,000
Cox, Geo—J Geddes, North Bergen.......... 200

Entry	Amount
Same——same, North Bergen	175
Cumming, Jas—G P Howell	900
De Clyne, Helena—T De Clyne, Union	nom
De Mott, Anna H, and Mary E Justin—The West Side Connecting R R Co	3,500
De Saulles, Catharine M—O Frommel, Hoboken	375
Doolittle, Jerry E—W Doolittle, Kearney	3,850
Dondero, Antonio and John, by sheriff—J B Peirano, Hoboken	3,100
Same, by sheriff——J B Peirano, Hoboken	5,050
Edelstein, John—D Lewis	4,000
Eilshemius, H G—Catharine B Lockwood, Kearney	1,300
Eisenlord, Lydia A exr J A Eisenlord, by sheriff—Exr G B English	500
Gaffney, Margaret—J Edelstein	nom
Gregory, Ed, and Robert McCarthy—Sarah Plaas, Bayonne	10
Hardy, G G—Delia Van Dyne, Kearney	1,800
Henson, H B—R Raschle, West Hoboken	467
Jacobs, Dina—F Eberhardt	5,600
Kearney Land Co—G Robertson, Kearney	200
Same——H S Conway, Kearney	200
Kelly, Ellen C—Mary E Russ	1,750
King, Eliza—J Cooper, Kearney	nom
Klumpp, J F and J S Bartleman—S W Gould	6,250
Lahey, Richard—P Kennedy	4,800
Lawless, Annie—Catharine Lawless	nom
Mason, J M—J Toobel	1,5 0
Matthews, Jas—M Aymone, West Hoboken	3,150
McDermott, W L—C Birdsall	500
Mogridge, Amelia S—Susan Luxton	19,925
Morris, Eleanor F—H M Brush, Bayonne	nom
Mount, S C—J Scully, Jr, Bayonne	525
Nichols, E H—Rose E Green	500
Merderlitz, William—J Geiger, West Hoboken	375
Nishivitz, Eliza—J B Temple, Kearney	700
Voe, Alb—A Scott, Kearney	1,600
North Jersey Land Co—H C Greene, Kearney	nom
Ogden, W B by exrs—J S Maguire	1,800
O'Rourke, Catharine—Carrie L Weser, Union	2,100
Parker, C W—Eleanor F Morris, Bayonne	nom
Same——same, Bayonne	nom
Same——J Hills, Bayonne	1,200
Pentermann, Henry—Annie Puck, Hoboken	12,000
Pope, James—W Lore, Union	4,500
Same——J Usher, Union	nom
Pullman, C G by sheriff—W P Wescott, Bayonne	400
Roeber, Henrietta—H Roeber, Union	250
Reakert, L G by sheriff—C W Parker, Bayonne	2,000
Scarry, Caroline by exr—D Sullivan	5,000
Schmidt, W B—H T Brandis, Union	2,500
Sewell, Sarah V V—T Hinds	2,000
Sillmen, C H—J Lewis, Kearney	800
Simonds, A B—R S Morpeth, Harrison	550
Syms, J H—H Richtold, Union	825
The Provident Inst for Savings—J J Regan	3,800
Thompson, John, Jr—Sarah Plaas, Bayonne	10
Tierney, Myles—C P Smith	3,025
Tivy, Peter—Josephine Gehlhaus, Hoboken	2,800
Tonsele, J P by exrs—J T Gedney	nom
Van Buskirk, Rebecca L—Leslie A Burrett, Bayonne	900
Van Dyke, C B—J Driscoll, Bayonne	1,450
Van Iderstine, Jno—G W Wright	1,700
Welsh, Matilda J—J C Bogart	2,500
White, J S by exrs—C Haag, Hoboken	3,850
Whitehead, Ira C—G Stripp, Harrison	1,175
Wiggers, Albert—Catharine P Solyom, West Hoboken	nom
Wogisch, Gustav—Emma H Wogisch	nom
Wogisch, Otto——same	nom
Wogisch, Herman——same	nom

MORTGAGES.

Entry	Amount
Anglesey, J J—Provident Inst for Savings, 1 year	12,000
Bacot, Mary—Minnie H Linn, 5 years	5,000
Birdsall, Chas—A L McDermott, 3 years	8,000
Blachouski, Stanislaus—Consumers' Coal and Ice Co, Bayonne, 1 year	285
Bohurst, Jos—William Peter Brewing Co, Weehawken, To secure payment of note, installs	900
Brandis, H F—W B Schmidt, Union, 5 years	2,000
Burriet, Leslie A—Rebecca L Van Buskirk, Bayonne, 3 years	400
Clayton, Annie C—J Blohm, 1 year	500
Connelly, P W—Mechanics' Trust Co, Bayonne, 1 year	2,618
Cook, J D—O W Van Campen	454
Coyle, John—Howard Savings Inst, Kearney, 1 year	5,000
Dietz, Frances—Improved Ld and L Assoc, installs	2,300
Doran, James—The Provident Inst for Savings, installs	2,500
Driscoll, John—The Union Co B and L Assoc, Bayonne, installs	160
Fisher, Jeannette F—J G Johnson, 2 years	400
Frank, J E—G G Vreeland, 2 years	3,000
Gould, S W—H C Roome, 3 years	5,000
Greene, H C—Jennie Winter, Kearney, 5 years	2,200
Same——The Howard Savings Inst, Kearney, 1 year	1,600
Same——same, Kearney, 1 year	800
Guiton, John—The Garfield B and L Assoc, installs	2,800
Haag, Chas—Exrs W White, Hoboken, 1 year	3,300
Haberstock, John—Rosalie Jahr, 5 years	1,000
Same——Emma Wogisch, 5 years	775
Hardy, W J—The Broadway Dry Goods Co-operative B and L Assoc, Bayonne, installs	3,750
Hills, Jno—H Roberson, Bayonne, 1 year	500
Holsten, J B—Beadleston & Woerz, Hoboken, demand	1,800
Jennings, W N—R A Henry, Kearney, 3 years	1,200
Same——same, Kearney, 3 years	1,250
Same——J M Barlow, Kearney, 3 years	1,800
Kaiser, Gottlieb—F Widner, Union, 1 year	800
Kelly, Ellen C—Catharine Baxter, 1 year	4,9 0
Same——same, 1 year	1,250
Kelly, Michael—Exr H G Vreeland, 3 years	350
Kelly, Patrick—Provident Inst for Savings, 1 year	12,000
Same——same, 1 year	7,000
Kelly, William—Industrial M B and L Assoc, installs	200
Kennedy, Pat—Hudson City Savings Bank, 1 year	2,400
Same——same, 1 year	2,000
Knoll, Mary—Jacob Hoffman Brewing Co, West Hoboken, 1 year	2,000
Koehler, Ludwig—C Schmidt, Union, 2 years	1,800
Lane, J H—Josephine Bourer, 3 years	1,50
Lewis, David—J Edelstein, 5 years	2,500
Lewis, James—A S Smith, Kearney, 4 years	1,500
Lockwood, Catharine B—Cecile E Eilshemius, Kearney, 3 years	650
Luxton, Susan—Amelia A Moyridge, 1 year	500
Maguire, J S—Hoboken Bank for Savings, 1 yr	2,000
Martens, E C—Anna M Forsthofer, 2 years	1,000
McCarren, Jas—P Coston, 2 years	900
McGovern, Mary—People's B and L Assoc, Harrison, installs	3,000
Miller, R C—Josephine Hughes, Union, 2 years	2,700
Miller, Adolph—Garfield B and L Assoc, installs	1,700
Obsahr, H W—W Gericke, 3 years	300
O'Connell, Michael—Katie A Bennett, Bayonne, 1 year	1,400
Post, Abraham—Provident Inst for Savings, 1 year	8,000
Puck, Anna—H Pentennann, Hoboken, 3 years	7,000
Same——same, Hoboken, 1 year	2,000
Rae, Walter—G R McKenzie, 1 year	6,000
Raschle, Rob—J Awers, West Hoboken, 1 year	450
Ratzel, Emil—C Fabeck, Union, 5 years	150
Regan, J J—Provident Inst for Savings, 1 year	2,800
Saint Joseph Catholic Church—Mutual Life Ins Co, 1 year	15,000
Schmidt, Augustus—W I Havens, 1 year	500
Schmidt, Elizabeth—The New Jersey Title Guarantee and Trust Co, installs	2,500
Scott, Alex—Hannah M Stanfield, Kearney, 1 yr	1,000
Slavin, Sarah F—Minna H Linn, 3 years	3,400
Smith, C P—The New Jersey Title Guarantee and Trust Co, installs	2,000
Smyth, Emma F—G G Hardy, Kearney, 1 year	220
Staats, Richard—C M Dalrymple, Bayonne, 1 year	100
Stephano, Dominick—Nicola Damein, Hoboken, 3 years	400
Steutzer, Chas—Helena Humphries, North Bergen, 5 years	4,500
Toobil, James—J M Mason, 5 years	500
Van Dyne, Delia—G G Hardy, Kearney, 1 year	984
Van Riper, Sarah J—G P Howell, 2 years	600
Verlihac, Oscar—Peoples B and L Assoc, Kearney, installs	400
Vom Atzinger, F J—Margaret Kalanguin, West Hoboken, 1 year	300
Weser, Carrie L—Catharine O'Rourke, Union, 1 year	1,000
Wilmer, Charlotte—H W Kuhl, 2 years	900

CHATTEL MORTGAGES.

Entry	Amount
Blockowski, Stanislaus, Bayonne—The Consumers' Coal and Ice Co, bakery, horse and wagon	285
Bohnert, Joseph, Weehawken—The Wm Peter Brewing Co, saloon fixtures	2,000
Royle, M H, Hoboken—C Iba, saloon fixtures	75
Burger, Cornelius, Hoboken—The Wm Peter Brewing Co saloon fixtures	715
Clark, J D, Kearney—G Krueger, saloon fixtures	150
Condon, Patrick—The Home Brewing Co, saloon fixtures	100
Cook, J D—O W Van Campen & Son, grocery store, horse, wagon, &c	454
Dischmann, C R, Secaucus—Adelbert Fleckenstein, hogs, &c	69
Goetz, Mrs A M, Hoboken—H Thoesen, furniture	83
Goll, Julius, Hoboken—C Goll, grocery store	1,200
Herbst, Charles—A Amman, horse, wagon and harness	100
Herder, Ernest et al—G Kurzel, saloon fixtures	3,250
Hill, William—Lembeck & Betz Eagle Brewing Co, saloon fixtures	590
Hixson, Sarah A, Hoboken—J Alley, furniture	475
Holsten, J B, Hoboken—Beadleston & Woerz, saloon and lodge fixtures, &c	1,500
Hormark, Peter, Kearney—F Hauck, saloon fixtures	600
Trushsess, W J—J Dilworth, wagon	45
Koller, Jacob—H E Nibblett, butcher shop	200
Long, John, Bayonne—Lembeck & Betz Eagle Brewing Co, saloon	450
McDonough, Julia—W F Elss, piano	167
Meyer, Frederick, Hoboken—The F & M Schaefer Brewing Co, saloon	750
Neuusinger, Charles, Hoboken—A D Puffer & Son, generator, &c	417
Noll, Giudo, West Hoboken—The Jacob Hoffman Brewing Co, saloon, &c	1,400
O'Dell, Samuel, Bayonne—Lembeck & Betz Eagle Brewing Co, saloon	485
Perley, D E—J Mullins & Co, furniture	124
Sheehan, J T, Hoboken—The D G Yuengling, Jr, Brewing Co, saloon fixtures	660
Storm, Inge, Bayonne—J Mullins & Co, furniture	181
The Germania Publishing Co—Geo Staber et al trustees, lease, presses, type, &c	10,000
Van Buskirk, Luther, Bayonne—O H Jadion, drug store	700
Wagner, Robert, Hoboken—J Huntz, saloon	400
Wangersheim, George, Hoboken—Lembeck & Betz Eagle Brewing Co, saloon	290
Wardell, Harry, Harrison—J Ketcham, furniture, bar room chairs, &c	130

BILLS OF SALE.

Entry	Amount
Bernitt, Eliza, Hoboken—J B Holsten, saloon and lodge room fixtures	800
The Henry Elias Brewing Co——same, saloon and lodge room fixtures	4,000
Kurzel, Gustav—E J White and Ernest Herder, saloon fixtures	6,500

JUDGMENTS.

Entry	Amount
Byers, J S—Helena Schultz et al	150
Casper, Jacob—C Sergawsky	90
Cook, R E—Julia Crane by her next friend Michael Crane	750
Donovan, Michael and William Barry—The State of New Jersey	900
Hausen, Anne C R and G C Tiencken—J M Klink	177
Mellin, Thomas—T L Tuxbury	61
Meyer, Henry and Frederick—Wm Gunning et al	88
Nevins, W D and J J Noonan, partners—D J Dannat	366
Sullivan, D F and D J Burke, partners as Sullivan & Burke—Venable & Heyman	119
Van Riper, Abraham—J J Carscallen	81
Van Riper, Sarah and Abraham——same	189

MECHANIC'S LIEN.

Entry	Amount
Herbert, James, builder and owner; J P Hall, claimant	172

BUILDING MATERIAL MARKET.

The regular season is gradually drawing to a close, and the markets for various kinds of structural material narrow down to the usual meagre proportions, with little o' pronounced interest developed from week to week. As a rule dealers are fairly stocked, which leads to rather indifferent interest toward first hand offering; but as a balance the arrivals of many leading articles are curtailed, and now and then to a sufficient extent to slightly stimulate values. The feeling seems to be that winter trade cannot run into very extensive proportions, and will as a rule consist of furnishing remaining supplies on finishing up work, but there are good expectations entertained for spring consumption.

BRICKS.—It is really somewhat disappointing to find the market still free from any positive change. There is a natural effort to infuse more strength into the position, and upon the few sales that are occasionally made above $5.25 per M a quotation is claimed, but according to views of majority of trade no fixed advance over recent figures has as yet become established. Demand during the week has been very good, indeed better than expected considering election day and its usual influences; but against the outlet came an increase of arrivals and the market was at all times plentifully supplied, with quite a surplus, including some cargoes of fine stock held here for a long while awaiting the rise in price, as yet failing to materialize. The increase in quantity of stock coming forward, we understand, was in part due to deliveries making on contracts concluded with dealers some week or two ago, and who are now ready to receive and pile away against the time when first hand offerings may become shut off. Of Pale there has been an unusually large number offering, and while they found very fair attention sellers were quite willing operators at about former rates. The current run of arrivals of hard brick came from pretty much all regular sources, and there has in consequence been a plentiful assortment from which to select almost any grade desired. The accounts from sources of supply do not appear to contain anything very important, except possibly that finding no benefit gained by holding back supplies, manufacturers are resuming shipments and may hurry them a little from upper section of the river in order to work forward as many as possible before the close of navigation.

LATH.—Conditions have remained very much the same as last week. No arrivals took place until within a day or two and then only to a very limited extent, leaving values practically without a test, except possibly that buyers were willing to bid $2.1 @2.15 and receivers asking up to $2.25 per M. On the whole, the selling side has retained advantage without much difficulty and might possibly have fully established a further gain with desirable stock to tender for negotiation, as the indications are that some dealers are becoming anxious for additions to stock.

LIME.—The market is no better and up to present writing apparently no worse than a week ago, about former rates being quoted all around. Arrivals from the Eastward, however, have of late been pretty full, with a considerable portion unsold, and the wind-up of the week looks a trifle slack, unless dealers show a little more vim and conclude to make a place for the cargoes at hand.

LUMBER.—Business has continued in much the previous general form with little or no increase of volume. The medium and common grades have been under most neglect and the falling off demand for that class of stock more than balances the special interest shown in the finer qualities for which there is a place to full extent of the offering. It looks as if some buyers had held off a little too long, and now, when seeking to obtain what they require for an assortment, discover that even in the face of present light consumption sellers really carry quite a little advantage. Desirable stock, however, is considered a good enough investment at present cost, and almost any operator who has the ability to carry a supply is willing to do so against the chances of spring trade, as confidence in an excellent market next year is unabated. There seems to be an idea that nothing but labor troubles will interfere to check a large amount of building, but the lumbermen feel quite able to cope with the walking delegate on their own domain and hope other trades will develop similar strength.

Eastern Spruce has a firm and even stronger market than a week ago, and the selling side appears to entertain justifiable confidence in its ability to hold advantage for balance of the season. Possibly the amount of stock actually wanted by dealers may not be very extensive, as they now claim, yet when there is little or nothing offering even a comparatively small demand makes a pretty good showing, especially as on successive bids fractional advances in prices are named. Some receivers report that they have no idea of getting another random cargo this season, and as soon as the mills they represent have finished the specials in hand they will shut down, making it quite probable the productive capacity will be brought down to the limit of manufacturers who use steam power at a much earlier date than ordinary. The yard dealers remain shoulder to shoulder in the agreement to sustain retail values.

Piling has not been arriving very freely and naturally the chances are against much stock coming forward until next spring. Buyers, however, can find a pretty good supply and assortment upon application to dealers, and at about former cost for ordinary stuff, but a firmer feeling is expressed over large sticks.

Hemlock shows about former general features, and there is practically nothing new for the week. Some custom may be found for the regular assortments of Pennsylvania stock where buyers have yard assortments to complete, but prompt accommodation is given and manufacturers would like to place considerable more of their supply, though they still abstain from anything in the way of direct pressure to realize.

White Pine has a market showing considerable general steadiness. For ordinary consumption the present movement is somewhat slow, and the chances are against much of an increase; but dealers make good customers and are especially attentive to any one having the better qualities to offer. Buyers, in fact, seem to have discovered that in addition to the shortage at Ottawa the Michigan operators have very little to offer, and that before new production can become available in desirable shape supplies are likely to enhance in value. Box is also firmly held, and shippers generally now appear upon a firmer basis, for while the combine of dealers, recently noted, does not include the entire export division of trade it is strong enough to carry a considerable measure of influence.

Yellow Pine remains pretty steady, and the position is one calculated to gain strength. The proposed trust among dealers is considered almost a sure thing as soon as certain necessary preliminary steps can be perfected, and will, of course, have a tendency to solidify the market. Dealers, however, desire to dissi ate any notion that may be entertained of the new organization as a price inflating affair. On the contrary the wave is intended solely as a measure to stop cut throat competition and afford a respectable living profit, and as the body of dealers working in harmony can do so upon a comparatively cheap basis, as well as command the respect of manufacturers, the chances are that consumers will not be placed at any serious disadvantage. Cargo rates are strengthening somewhat, as some of the mills feel more indifferent toward orders.

Carolina Pine remains firm in price, and while all that is wanted can be reached upon call, the offering is kept in such shape as to prevent even the semblance of effort to realize. There is a pretty good stock here of kiln dried, both rough and dressed, but no more than ordinary at this season of the year.

Hardwoods are well enough held, and rather sparingly offered, as it is not a good time to press supplies when dealers are pretty nearly stocked up for the season and making a more or less slow distribution. However desirable, hardwoods are never at a loss for some attention, and exceptionally there is stuff sure of a quick sale at extreme rates. Cherry, for instance, may be said to have a standing offer at $100.00 per M for anything up to standard, and choice lots of oak are in favor. Advices from Europe report the Scotch markets pretty well supplied with inferior American hardwoods, but wanting some choice stuff; London, Liverpool and Continental cities are customers for carefully selected walnut.

The exports of lumber, exclusive of hardwood, from the port of New York during the month of October were as follows:

	1890. Feet.	1891. Feet.
To West Indies	6,159,000	4,055,000
To South America	4,088,000	2,080,000
To East Indies	1,159,000	1,592,000
To Europe	264,000	54,000
Total feet	11,670,000	7,781,000
Previously reported	63,484,000	64 442,000
Total since Jan. 1	75,154,000	72,173,000

GENERAL LUMBER NOTES.

THE WEST.

The Chicago Northwestern *Lumberman*:

The only point at which there is an unusually large stock of white pine this fall is at Minneapolis, where it is reported that there will be 350,000,000 feet in pile at the season's close. This is because there was an unusually large input of logs last winter on streams tributary to that point, and more success has attended getting them into mill booms than in other districts of the upper Mississippi valley. The cut of the mills has consequently been large, exceeding that of last year by about 100,000,000 feet. But to counteract the influence of this large supply on the trans-river market, there is a serious shortage at the majority of mill points below Minneapolis, and, besides, there is an unusual demand on account of the good crops. Thus it appears that the Minneapolis oversupply will be more than offset by the condition named. Prices along the Mississippi are higher than they were in the summer, though it is intimated that at Minneapolis the October advanced list is not being fully maintained, since a good deal of lumber is still being shipped at September prices. Dealers say, however, that the lumber that is going out on the September list was bargained for during that month.

The state of trade in the Saginaw Valley is improving. It has been discovered that when the sawing season shall have closed there will not be much more unsold lumber on hand than there was at the close last year. The rail trade is good, and this will eat away a large portion of the unsold supply during the winter.

At the Chicago yards:

Mention is continually made of the scarcity of 10-inch and 12-inch boards. Those 18 and 20 feet long are about out of market, and they are selling at $18 a thousand, and higher than that price is sometimes being asked. All lengths of stock boards are also in good demand, with the prospect that before winter there will be an unusual shortage. Prices on all stock of this kind are stiffening.

In the p s condition of supply and demand, fencing should be good property, and it is. It is not only wanted for the local and western flooring, sheathing and roofing trade, but there is a constant demand in the east for common strips that can be worked into siding of the several forms used in that part of the country. Dealers who have good stocks of fencing in pile are sure to have a sale for it that will yield them some profit.

Piece stuff is in good demand, and prices are hardening. Short is selling on a basis of $12.50. Some dealers are inclined to concede on 2x8 and 2x10 long stuff, or slim jims, as it is called, but really there is no good reason for such concession. The farmers' demand will require a lot of such stuff for barn rafters, and the city building will absorb a good deal.

The recent sale of a World's Fair bill, amounting to between 8,000,000 and 9,000,000 feet, has again stirred up the dealers to a realizing sense of the importance of the great enterprise to the local and general lumber trade. It is considered a favorable incident that the contract was secured by a Chicago firm, since a large amount of the stuff required will have to be picked up in the yards here. The bill runs heavily to wide dimension, 40,000 pieces of 2x12-12 being required as one item. The collection of such a bill requires a great deal looking about for sorts, and that will be a benefit to the entire trade.

It is noticeable, in connection with the world's fair, that there is an increasing call for miscellaneous sorts to be employed in finishing up the great buildings that have been started. Besides, there is a large number of smaller structures that will be erected by the states, foreign governments and private enterprises. These will require large quantities of ordinary yard stock, and the local dealers will get the benefit of this business. They begin to see that a vast amount of trade is yet to result from the world's fair, and this consideration gives them a cheerful view of the situation. On the whole the dealers are feeling better than for several years.

The Mississippi Valley *Lumberman* as follows:

In the white pine district the season of production is drawing to a close rapidly. Not to exceed a couple of weeks more sawing remains even for the mills which are yet in motion. The St. Croix boom has been shut down and on the temporary rise in the stage of water in the Mississippi only a limited number of logs has been got out. The season is already practically ended at all Mississippi River points. At Minneapolis and at the mouth of the Menominie—the two large producing points, where operations have been uninterrupted the season through—the mills still have a full stock of logs and will run as long as the weather will permit. The large cut at these points will compensate somewhat for the lack of production at other points. But between the aggregate cut at all the mill points and increased sales the summing up at the end of the season is likely to show a large falling off in the visible supply.

On this condition preparation is being made for active logging operations during the winter. The forest fires which prevailed during the summer in many localities, will bring into next season's supply of logs considerable timber which would otherwise not have been cut.

The *Timberman* says:

Demand for oak is beginning to show some symptoms of a revival. The cabinet makers' strike has been settled, and although its effect on the lumber trade was at no time serious, the resumption of work by the several factories is bound to be of some benefit to the business. There is also a somewhat better demand for stock suitable for interior work.

The recent free offerings of oak have created the impression in many cases that this stock is in excessive supply, but buyers who have recently returned from trips through the oak producing sections say that this is not the case. There is of course considerable stock in pile throughout the country, but nothing like as much as some reports would indicate. The mills have nearly all stopped manufacturing quartered oak, and with a good demand, like that of a year ago, it would not be long until a shortage in this stock would be developed.

In plain-sawed oak there is a firmer feeling than the present demand and condition of stocks would seem to indicate. Wisconsin red oak is in fairly good request, and will easily bring from $1 to $2 more per thousand than the Southern product.

GREAT BRITAIN.

The London *Timber Trades Journal* says:

Pitch pine timber did not do badly at the sale on Wednesday, one buyer getting in at 52s., who was wise, perhaps, in securing all he could at the price. It was rumored last week that several cargoes were on their way, but we have heard nothing more of them. All the news we can learn is that a cargo of deals, battens and boards is destined for this market; but this of itself is insufficient to have any effect on prices.

At Glasgow there has been no material change to note in the position of this market, and as the season approaches a close and the present light stocks are seen to be receiving but slight additions in the way of fresh arrivals; the upward tendency of retail prices for Canadian goods is becoming more marked.

PAINTS, OILS, COLORS, ETC.—Demand has been fair to middling for the majority of goods, but rather inclined to increase somewhat now that the excitement of the election canvass has passed away, and the new month is fairly opened. Buyers evince no measure of anxiety, however, the run of orders being simply in old form of handling goods to extent of an average assortment and early necessity, and then withdrawing until new wants arise. The selection, too, is much the same as it has been for some time past, regular standard qualities and some favorite specialties getting the major portion of attention. Offerings of both imported and domestic goods have been made to a very fair general extent permitting of prompt selection and expeditions negotiation, though nothing comes upon sale under pressing efforts to realize, and cost is as a rule well sustained. Leads continue subject to rumor, but quotations are unchanged. Association Corroders' rates stand as follows: Lead in oil in kegs and dry lead in kegs, in lots of less than 500 lbs., 7¼c. net; in lots of 500 lbs to 5 tons at one purchase, 7c.; 5 tons to 12 tons, one purchase, 5⅞c.; 12 tons and over, one purchase, 6¾c.; dry white lead in bbls. ⅛c. per lb. less than price in kegs. Lead in oil 12½ lb. in tin pails, add 1c.; in 25 and 50 lb. tin pails, add ½c.; and in 1 to 5 lb. tin cans, assorted (100 lbs. in case) add 2¼c. per lb. to keg price. Terms on lots on 500 lbs. and over, note or acceptance at sixty days, or 2½ per cent. discount will be allowed for cash paid within fifteen days of invoice date. To make either of the above required quantities any assortment of packages of white lead, red lead and litharge may be counted. The above quotations are free on board cars or boat at corroding point. Linseed Oil probably shows no more than the ordinary irregularity on low grades, and for attractive makes is held pretty steadily, with an offering only about equal to the outlet. We quote at general range at 35@40c. for Western, and 40@56c. for City. Spirits Turpentine has been moderately at about former rates, closing with a more or less steady tone. We quote at 36½@37½c. per gallon, according to quality, delivery, etc.

NAILS.—General demand continues moderate and indifferent and there seems to be no improvement whatever in conditions of market. Cut nails sell at very irregular rates, and while a showing of steady feeling is made on wire nails, manufacturers are reported to be taking active measures to cut down production. We quote Cut at $1.50@1.60 per keg for car lots and $1.75@1.85 per keg for parcels from store, for iron, and add 5@10c. per keg for steel; Wire, $2.00@2.05 at mills, and 2.20@2.35 from store.

TAR AND PITCH.—Although somewhat irregular, business has on the whole been fuller. Demand came from regular sources, however, with no tendency to anticipate the future and was promptly met at about previous figures. We quote Pitch at $1.70@1.75 per bbl.; Tar at $2.15@2.50, according to quantity, quality and delivery.

"Entered at the Post-office at New York, N. Y., as second-class matter."

VOL. XLVIII. NEW YORK, NOVEMBER 7, 1891. SUPPLEMENT.

Harlem Supplement.

INTRODUCTION.

THE district between 125th street and the Harlem River, east of Washington Heights, has not been advertised so well as the West Side, and consequently a person who depends for information rather on general impression than special observation might well be surprised in passing through that section to see the extent to which improvements have been pushed. The first ten blocks north of 125th street are built over as solidly as most parts of the West Side proper, and although north of 135th street there have been as yet few buildings erected, the march of improvement will soon invade that region also. On the whole it may be confidently predicted that the flat lands to the east of the ride will be occupied with houses before the ridge will itself—much as the latter has been advertised and great as are its advantages. In the first place, its improvement will be less hampered by obstacles, such as rock, which is expensive to remove, and increases the time necessary to building. The flat lands are far more adapted to immediate improvement. It is true that no little rock will have to be blasted away on some of the streets in the northern part of the district, but the amount is strictly localized and does not compare in extent

Bank of Harlem Building, West 125th Street. J. B McElfatrick & Sons, Architects.

with similar rough spots on the Heights. The great and obvious advantage, however, which the flat lands have at the present time is the Manhattan west side track, which, by its curve to the east at 110th street, definitely forsakes the West Side proper and wends its airy way into a section, the improvement of which depends upon rather different conditions. A trip up and down town night and morning is practicable if not pleasant, and New Yorkers cannot afford to stick at a little discomfort. Consequently we may expect that the improvement of this Harlem district will proceed steadily and will not have to wait the convenience of a Rapid Transit Commission, which works none the less uncertainly because it works slowly.

No doubt the service on the Manhattan roads will to a certain extent be improved—even without a loop or additional switching facilities at the Battery. The third track is already completed over a large portion of the line north of 59th street; and before winter sets in the management of the road will probably be able to lay tracks over nearly all the rest. As soon as this is done, it will be increasingly easy to side-track local trains for the sake of expresses; and then more expresses will be put on. Col. Hain not long since assurred a reporter of this journal that very possibly the fast trains to 155th street would be increased next spring. At all events the better service will not be long delayed; and might be secured almost immediately if the public authorities would meet the Manhattan Company in anything like a fair spirit. These expresses are, of course, designed primarily for the use of the patrons of the New York & Northern road; but manifestly they can be made just as serviceable to the residents of 125th street North, for those people living near the 135th street or 145th street stations can take local trains to 125th street and the express trains south.

In considering the future of this district it must be remembered, also, that the plans of the Rapid Transit Commissioners do not leave the district entirely neglected. Their west side line, running as it does mainly up the Boulevard, will not be of any particular use to the plain below; but if the Madison avenue line of the commission is ever built it will be a powerful stimulus to this district—certainly as far west as Lenox avenue. Madison avenue crosses the river so soon that such a line will not do anywhere near as much good as it would if it curved to the west above 125th street somewhere and crossed the river at Lenox or 5th avenue; but its efficiency can be increased by a surface connection with other parts of the section. We should also point out in passing that a surface road on Lenox avenue is something which the district very much needs at present. The only means at present available for getting to 125th street are by the legs and the elevated roads—neither of which are agreeable or speedy.

The flat lands are not obliged to rely entirely for their future on transit facilities. They have another resource in the Harlem water front. When that little strip of water will be prepared finally for navigation by vessels of comparatively heavy draught no one may know. Republics are as slow as they are ungrateful. The Harlem River Improvement is, apparently, as far from completion as ever. If the work is finished in five years, New York City will be lucky. But, uncertain though the time of its completion may be, the fact of its completion is indubitable; neither is there any doubt about its enormous utility when completed. Manhattan Island has practically no water front except this to draw upon, for West-siders will not permit the authorities to spoil the river front on the West Side for commercial purposes, and this Harlem River frontage would be peculiarly valuable for a great many local trades—principally those connected with building. This fact will undoubtedly profoundly affect the district we are considering. Exactly how the district will be affected we do not pretend to know. Neither, apparently, does anyone else. Builders have left the property within ten blocks of the water front severely alone; and they are wise. A venture now would be attended by more risk than it is either necessary or desirable to undertake.

It is a curious and interesting fact not very frequently met with in the city that the speculative builders operating on some of the avenues of this district have not by any means been unanimous in their decisions as to the purpose to which these avenues are to be put. On Lenox and 7th avenues particularly one finds flats, dwellings and stores placed side by side—the owners evidently being in a state of complete doubt as to which class of improvement will finally prevail. The same fact may be observed to a certain, although to a far smaller extent on certain avenues on the East Side; but generally a sort of tacit understanding exists among the builders; and they combine to give a thoroughfare one dominant character. On the side streets, of course, flats are often erected next to dwellings; but dwellings are not built next to stores. If any street or avenue is adapted to retail trade, all the buildings are adjusted to stores. The reason for the doubt in this case is not, perhaps, so far to seek. Lenox and 7th avenues are broad pleasant thoroughfares; trees have been planted on the streets on either side, and they thus contain manifest advantages for residential purposes only. On the other hand, at least every other avenue north of 59th street is given over to retail trade, and the reason for this is that the population will be in time far denser in the northern part of the city, owing to the larger proportion of flats and tenements, and consequently they will need more stores per house. As the property-owners did not act in any concerted way in this Harlem section, the builders were at a loss whether to fix on one of the avenues or the other for retail trade. Furthermore, the large stores on 125th street enter into competition with all these local shops, and tend to decrease their number.

Interior Mount Morris Bank.

Taking all in all, however, by far the most interesting, singular and significant thoroughfare on the West Side is 125th street. Those who built there early did not appreciate its remarkable future. A number of rows of flats were erected without any provision for stores, and several rows of dwellings. It soon became apparent that this street was to be the leading business street of Harlem. The small stores that first established themselves there were so well patronized that they gradually became larger and larger. The trade that grew up began to attract long-established down-town houses; and one venturesome speculator felt so much confidence in the future of the district that he put up two large theatres and one large office building. All this did not take more than five or six years; and thus we find a street, itself new, already undergoing a metamorphosis. The dwellings originally put up are being changed into stores; and some of the flats are undergoing a similar transformation. Eventually they will all be changed; and we doubt not that before a decade is passed that both sides of the street, from 3d to 10th avenue, will be lined by imposing warehouses, stores, theatres and office buildings. Even at the present time the crowd which travel to and fro on its sidewalks are sometimes almost as great as those on 23d or 14th street. In the end they will be greater. If present indications are fulfilled trade, and consequently the value of property on 125th street, should reach a higher level than that of any other cross-town street in the city.

This may seem to be an extravagant statement; but a consideration of the various sources which will contribute to the streets trade and prosperity is sufficient to convince any one of its comparative moderation. There can be no doubt that the great length of New York City will force a duplication of its centre of retail trade. As population spreads over the rest of the island, and across the Harlem into the North Side, it will gradually be found that 14th street and 23d street are too far off to be used as the shopping district. It will be far more convenient for shoppers to come down to 125th street and make their purchases in that vicinity. The cable road will pour one flood of people into the street; the Manhattan road will bring down another swarm from along the line of the Northern road; and the New Haven and the Harlem, when their local service is perfected, will contribute as many more. If the stores become as reliable as those down town, if the stocks held become as varied and as large, 125th street will also be able to attract customers from as far south as perhaps 100th street. Notice, then, what an enormous area this is—all the city north of 100th street and a good deal of Westchester County. Surely this trade is worth making an effort to obtain, and we have no expectation that the retailers of 125th street will fail in the task. Of course, many years must still elapse before any considerable part of this enormous area will be built over, but meanwhile the trade will fully warrant stores and theatres of the best class, that will attract the trade as it comes. Under similar conditions an enormous retail trade has been built up in Brooklyn, and the conditions are equally favorable in Harlem and the North Side. Neither, of course, will the process stop with the retail trade. Other classes of business will inevitably follow. Harlem will some day have an autonomy as great as that of Brooklyn at present.

The Bank of Harlem.

The Bank of Harlem Building, on the north side of 125th street, about 175 feet west of 7th avenue, is one of the most notable structures of its kind up town. It adjoins to the west the Harlem Opera House, the building of which a couple of years ago first called the serious attention of capitalists to the possibilities of 125th street as a business thoroughfare. Together these two buildings present quite an imposing appearance. The Opera House is of light stone, with polished black granite columns, while the Bank building adjoining has a combination front of brown stone and mottled brick with columns of polished red granite that is very effective. The buildings mainly impress one with the idea of their substantialness. There is nothing cheap or shoddy about them. They are solid structures, well built and of the best material obtainable.

The Bank building which challenges the attention because it has perhaps the most attractive front elevation of the two is at present five stories in height. We say at present, for although there is no immediate intention of altering or adding to the building, it was originally built with the idea that as the demand for up-town offices became larger three more stories could be added to the structure, making an eight-story building. The walls, therefore, of this five-story building are as thick as the law requires for an eight-story structure, and within two or three years the Bank may conclude to take advantage of this fact.

The front elevation of the building, which is quite impressive, by the way, is in the Renaissance style of architecture, neither distinctly Italian nor French Renaissance, but partaking of the character of both. The architects, Messrs. J. B. McElfatrick & Sons, have divided the front into three sections vertically and the same number horizontally. The horizontal sections are defined by two entablatures placed immediately above the first and third floor windows respectively. In this way it will be seen that the building is horizontally divided up into two sections containing two stories each and a third section comprising the first floor, which is marked off from the rest of the building by the lowest entablature. The architects have used practically the same treatment in dividing the building vertically. Here again there are three sections, but with this difference that they are all of about equal width. Pilasters or columns running from top to bottom of the divisions are made the main features. In the first story the dividing pilasters are not particularly elaborate, but between the first and fourth stories they are made main features. Two round columns of polished red granite, with handsomely carved capitals, are made part of each of these pilasters and they support the carved stone piece upon which the second entablature rests. The main feature of this central portion is a large arch above the second story windows and connecting the two pilasters. Above, in the section comprising the fourth and fifth stories, there is not very much that is particularly striking. The central pilasters on these two floors differ from those below in that the columns of polished red granite which are so large a part of them are square instead of round, and not quite so elaborate in detail. The handsome pediment above the central portion of the building carries out what was evidently the architects' intention, viz., that of making this central division of the building very much more striking and imposing than the other sections. The topmost entablature is quite elaborate enough, and is in harmony with the rest of the building. Architecturally speaking, the building could not well be more advantageously situated. It is on a wide street which enables everyone to see it without the slightest inconvenience, and the queer policy that has hitherto dictated the erection of insignificant buildings on 125th street has, by furnishing comparisons, brought out all the architectural virtues of the Bank of Harlem building.

The size of the building is 75x110 feet, and in the rear is a court 10 feet wide running the length of the building, on which the Bank people hold an easement for light and air, so that, although they do not own the land, it can never be built upon. The building is absolutely fire-proof, the only inflammable material being the surface plank floors, that for comfort's sake are laid above the real brick floors. The first floor is about 20 feet high—that is, the ceiling is 20 feet from the floor. Already this first floor is fully occupied. The easterly store is occupied by Branch J of the Post-office, even now one of the largest of the branch offices; the central store and the rear space is occupied by the offices of the Bank of Harlem, and the third store is rented by the Twelfth Ward Savings Bank.

The interior is all that can be desired. The ceilings are high and every room is light and well ventilated, connecting as they all do with the outside air. The stairs and parts of the halls are of marble. The toilet rooms are the most elaborate and commodious that can be imagined. The builder has set apart on each floor a large room that contains everything that such a room should. The plumbing, which is of the very best, is all exposed to view. Every floor contains a seemingly endless number of offices, each room connecting with another so that starting at one end of the building it is possible to go through every office without encountering the hall before the other end is reached. This, of course, is a convenience where a tenant wishes more room than is contained in one office. The offices are occupied by the branch offices of life insurance companies, and by architects, lawyers, real estate brokers and others engaged in business of a similar character. The Conservatory of Music has also taken a row of offices that extend along the best part of the rear portion of the building.

The offices of the Bank of Harlem are very handsomely fitted up. Besides the usual accommodations this bank has provided a small space partitioned off for their lady customers. This space is neatly carpeted and contains a table and chairs, together with writing materials. The basement of the building is at present unoccupied, but within a few months now it will probably be rented to a safe deposit company. Already $100,000 has been raised and other subscriptions from some of the best residents of this section of the city are coming in. Besides a vault to contain about 1,000 safes, which the company will build, there is to be a large room set apart for the storage of valuable paintings and trunks containing valuables too large to be placed in the vault.

Practically the same men who are interested in the Bank are also interested in the safe deposit company, and that is a large point in favor of the success of the deposit company. The bank's officers and directors are not only residents of Harlem, their business is also located there, and this doubtless accounts for much of the success which this Bank has certainly achieved. The president of the Bank is Mr. David F. Porter, the best known real estate broker and agent in Harlem. Mr. Porter has been established on 125th street for years past and his large local business has given him a large acquaintance. Because of this, probably, the business of the institution over which he now presides has almost doubled since he assumed control, and it is still on the increase.

The other directors, with their businesses, are as follows: John J. Sperry, coal; William S. Gray, chemicals; Hanson C. Gibson, lawyer; D. M. Williams, dry goods; Frank Wanier, drugs; William H. Caldwell, real estate; Charles E. Trotter, cashier; James Rogers, building material; Rob't A. Hevenor, grocer; Geo. H. Sutton, woolens; Jared Lockwood, manufacturer of neckwear; J. E. McMichael, physician; John J. Fowler, grocer; E. B. Servoss, retired; Jno. B. Whiting, lawyer.

The following is an extract from the last quarterly statement issued September 12, 1891:

RESOURCES.	
Loans and discounts	$446,850
Stocks and bonds	2,100
Cash on hand and in banks	101,300
Furniture and fixtures	7,800
Real estate	29,250
	$587,300
LIABILITIES.	
Capital	$100,000
Undivided profits	15,700
Due to banks	29,700
Due to depositors	441,900
	$587,300

It is interesting to note that the statement made last December showed only $299,000 on deposit, while the statement above quoted shows $441,000, an increase of $143,000 in deposits in less than a year. This is a phenomenal growth for a local bank to show in about nine months' time.

Some Desirable Dwellings.

One of the very best private residence blocks in Harlem is 121st street, between Lenox and 7th avenues. This block is solidly built up on both sides of the street with private dwellings of a high order. Not only are there no vacant lots, but there are no houses of poor character on the block at all, so that an investor who purchases a dwelling here may live in peaceful security from the blackmailer as well as free from the dust and inconvenience which always accompanies improvements, no matter how desirable. In addition to these advantages there is a further attraction in the fact that the houses, nearly all of which are occupied, are owned by those who reside in them. The residents in the street count among themselves some of the best people, both socially and financially, in Harlem. As to the houses themselves, there is a pleasing variety of styles. While the majority of the houses agree in the fact that they have fronts of brown stone, they differ very widely in the style of architecture. There are of course rows of five or six houses together where the general style is the same, but notwithstanding this there is variety enough in the street to suit any one. The interiors of the houses are well-nigh perfect and some of them rival the best productions of the progressive West Side. Some of the builders in this best section of Harlem fully believe that no material is too good, no improvement too costly or no convenience too new to put into their houses and, as a consequence, the results obtained are highly satisfactory.

Such a builder is Mr. S. O. Wright, who has erected dwelling houses in many parts of Harlem, but nowhere with greater success than on 121st street, near Lenox avenue. These houses, Nos 128 to 134 West, are seven in number. Six of them are four stories in height, while the remaining house, not shown in the illustration, is only three stories. They have high stoops of brown stone, with handsome brown stone balustrades, and the fronts of the houses, too, are of brown stone handsomely and artistically carved. The detail of the carving is not fully shown in the accompanying illustration, and, indeed, it would be almost impossible to do the houses justice in any picture. They must be seen to be appreciated. Projecting from the second story is a stone bay window that will catch the eye of those who are tired of the plainness and severity of the front elevations of many of the best private houses.

Nos. 128 to 134 West 121st Street. S. O. Wright, Builder and Owner.

But if the exterior is pleasing and attractive the interior is more so. As outside so inside the houses everything is in the best of taste. It is only necessary to look around one at the exquisite quality and finish of the various hardwoods used in the trim, at the large plate-glass mirrors, the open tiled and gilt fire-places—so suggestive of comfort—and the many other features that strikes one's eye upon entering to see that the builder has been lavish in his expenditure. At the same time there is no suggestion of gaudiness or show. The houses not only would not offend the most refined and cultivated taste; they would please it. It can be truthfully said that these houses of Mr Wright's equal any similar houses of recent construction and they certainly have an advantage in location. And when it is said that the houses are the equals if not the superiors in material and finish of any other recently-built dwelling, everything has been said, for the modern builder spares neither pains nor expense to make his houses all that the most luxurious and exacting can desire.

The front parlor, hall and first floor staircase are finished in carved mahogany, beautifully polished, while the back parlor and the butler's pantry in the rear are in quartered oak. In both of the main rooms on this floor there are large open fire-places of the most attractive design and finish. In front and at the top and both sides of the fire-places there is tiling of prettily blending colors that in themselves alone give a certain warmth to the room. Around the fire-place is the most improved metal foot guard. It is gilt work that does not tarnish and that will never need to be cleaned as brass guards do. The back parlor has a parquet floor and also a large mirror over the mantel-piece. In the front room, too, there is a mirror over the mantel as well as one of nearly full length between the two windows.

The second floor is finished in quartered oak, much of it very handsomely carved. Nothing has been spared to make this floor attractive. There are two bedrooms and a bath-room. The bedrooms between them contain ten large plate-glass mirrors, several of them full length. There are large dressing-rooms containing decorated wash-basins, hot and cold water and an abundance of closet room. On this floor is located the burglar alarm as well as electric calls and speaking-tubes to the lower floors and an instrument for lighting and extinguishing the gas. The dumb-waiter also runs to this floor. The bath-room is a model of its kind. It has a quartered oak floor, porcelain bath-tub of the largest size made, decorated basins and the best plumbing, all of it exposed to view.

The floor above, the third, is finished in sycamore, and its main features are almost as attractive as those of the floor below. There are three rooms as well as a bath-room that is if possible an improvement on that of the floor below. Here, as below, there are numerous mirrors, an abundance of closet room, and the large tiled and open fire-places that form such an attractive feature throughout the house. The bath-room on this floor is divided into three compartments, a dressing-room with mirror, wash-basin and clothes closets, a smaller compartment for the bath-tub opening off the dressing-room, and still another sub-division co taining the water-closet. It will be seen that the water-closet and the bath-room proper are on this floor separated, an improvement that seems to be finding favor among first-class builders.

The fourth floor finished in ash contains four rooms and a storeroom. The trim here is of quite as good a finish as on the other floors, and altogether, although it is not as expensive a floor as the others, it is quite as substantial, which cannot be said of the fourth floors in many of even the best dwelling houses.

The basement contains a dining-room, kitchen and laundry. The dining-room, which is finished in ash, is very well lighted and contains all that such a room should. The kitchen, which is finished in quartered oak, is large and commodious. It contains a great large range of the most improved pattern, called the "Lenox," made by the J. L. Mott Iron Works. It also contains a large porcelain sink, the wall back of which is tiled. The laundry in the rear is of good size and contains porcelain tubs and a stove. Outside the kitchen door is situated the latest Larsen refrigerator. In the cellar is situated Mott's "No. 5" heater, the largest made.

These are the main features of some houses that equal anything that is now or has been put upon the market, and it will be strange indeed if Mr. Wright finds any difficulty in disposing of them. In passing, there are some material men and mechanics who deserve to be mentioned for the excellence of their work on this job. They are John Hutchinson & Sons, who did the stone work; Jarvis B. Smith, who furnished the trim, and George Wiggins, the polisher.

The Woolley-Brinckerhoff Houses in Harlem.

A CORNER RESIDENCE DESCRIBED WHICH, IN ITS INTERIOR AND EXTERIOR, IS ONE OF THE FINEST IN THE UPPER WARDS.

For a number of years past Dr. Jas. V. S. Woolley has erected a class of houses which, as time has shown, have met a public demand. That Dr. Woolley has been so successful in his building operations—that his houses sold where others were neglected—has been due to the thought bestowed on their design, as much as to the constant and careful supervision which he gave to all the details of construction.

What this thought, this supervision, means is only known to those who have invested their fortunes in building operations and who have watched with anxious care the construction of their houses, from the laying of the foundations to the completion of the roof and the plastering of the walls. It is not given to the many, it is given but to the few, to be successful. And in no business is there a greater element of uncertainty than in building; not only because each building locks up a small fortune in itself, but because the choice of a building, particularly if it be of a residential character, is determined just as frequently by the whim of the purchaser's wife as it is by the excellence of the interior and exterior plans.

But, the "successful" builder—he who sells his houses almost before completion—is above all these considerations. He starts out with an idea—with ideas. He has faith in the value of those ideas, and he forthwith proceeds to carry them into effect. He knows that certain features are desirable. The housewife must have an abundance of closet and store room, and he accordingly gives her all that her heart could desire. Every corner is utilized for this purpose and every vacuum is a ready prey to the inclosure. Hats, coats and dresses are to be preserved in hiding from the dust, just as china, plate and glassware is to be kept from sight where they may be easy of access. Bath-rooms must be wainscoted in marble, or tiled, so that the splash, splash, will not soil the walls. The hostess must press a small button, and presto!—the lights must blaze forth. There must be catches to apprise the household of burglars, and tubes set in the walls at the very bedsteads and couches in the bedrooms, so that the occupant may lazily turn over and summon breakfast or a cup of tea. New ideas must be introduced in various directions, any one of which may be sufficient to form the straw that may just turn the balance in favor of a sale. And the culinary department must not be neglected. Little conveniences must be introduced, particularly such as will please the prospective "help." And it is all but a truism to acknowledge that the housewife will sacrifice everything short of Paradise itself to produce conditions that will result in retaining and permanently mollifying that bane of housekeepers—the "help."

But we are digressing. It is from such considerations that we evolve the successful house. That Dr. Woolley has already succeeded in selling to advantage four of the five houses facing Mount Morris Park is due as much to the conditions named as to the delightful location of the houses themselves. In this and other recent enterprises Dr. Woolley had had as partner Mr. G. Grant Brinckerhoff, Jr., to whose able management and supervision, in conjunction with Dr. Woolley, the successful planning, completion and sale of the Mount Morris houses is due. The buildings are situated on the northwest corner of Mount Morris avenue and 121st street and comprise a quintet of the finest houses in the locality.

THE CORNER HOUSE DESCRIBED.

The house remaining unsold is that on the corner. It is a four-story, basement and attic structure. There is a circular tower on the uppermost story containing three windows, from which a bird's eye view is obtained of Mount Morrs Park to the east and southeast, the northern part of the Central Park to the south and Morningside Park to the west, with the Palisades in the distance beyond. The building is one of the costliest and best constructed in Harlem. The stoop, with the first and second story front, are in brown stone, while the facade above is in selected Philadelphia brick with brown stone trimmings. All the stone is laid on the natural bed. The basement is of rock-face finish and the stonework above is tooled.

THE INTERIOR.

Ascending the massive stoops we come upon the storm-doors, which are of hardwood, with ornamental hinges and handles. The upper panels contain large lights of beveled plate glass. Passing the vestibule doors we find the flooring in mosaic and the wainscoting of oak. The vestibule floors and side sash work are of an attractive design and are furnished with beveled plate glass.

The hall door is of oak and the hallway is handsomely wainscoted in panels of that wood, with a seat-rest in special design. The floor is parqueted.

THE PARLOR.

Entering the parlor we find a handsome salon in white and gold. The effect is both chaste and artistic. The first thing that strikes the visitor is the large number of windows in the room. These are six in number and afford views of the park opposite, the reflection of the trees being seen, also, in the mirror in the mantelpiece. This parlor offers a fine opportunity for decoration. The doors, window openings and chimney breasts are trimmed with paneled pilasters, with carved capitals supporting an architrave and a broad frieze, which extend around the room over the doors, the whole being surmounted with an ornamental architectural cornice. The frieze thus presents an excellent chance to the artist for a strong and effective decoration with cast or wrought plaster ornamentation, or with fresco or other suitable material, according to the taste of the occupant. There are fan-lights in the room in rich opalescent glass mosaics, which harmonize very well with the general finish of the room. There is a fine open fire-place, with a broad opening, surmounted by a beveled mirror in an ornamental frame.

THE DINING-ROOM.

Handsome folding doors lead from the parlor to the dining-room. This room is one of the finest in the upper part of the city. The floor is inlaid in quartered oak, with an ornamental border. The mantelpiece is the principal feature in the room. It runs from the floor almost to the ceiling. There is an immense mirror over the mantelshelf, set in an ornamental frame. The fire-place is broad and richly tiled, with shelves and cabinets on both sides. The fender and andirons are of brass, with box grates in iron metal work. There is a buffet fully equipped with shelves, drawers, cabinets and a mirror. A frieze extends around the room, under a cornice of oak, and the ceiling is timbered in panels of the same wood. The fan-lights, which are in colored glass, lend attraction to the room. The view from the windows takes in the park, as well as the street, a perspective of which shows it to be one of the neatest and cleanest in the city. The dining-room overlooks a small, but attractive yard, with a grass plot and ornamental railings.

THE BUTLER'S PANTRY.

Through the dining-room a door leads to the butler's pantry, which is trimmed in ash and has parqueted floors. It has numerous closets and drawers, and a dumb-waiter, which extends from the basement to the second story. The pantry also has an entrance leading to the hall.

THE BEDROOM FLOORS.

Leaving the parlor floor we pass up the stairway, with its trelliced lattice and supporting column of twisted carving, and its paneled wainscoting. Reaching the main bedroom floor, we find a handsome front bed-chamber overlooking the park. The trim is in cherry, and the mantel, fender and andirons are of attractive design. The room is arranged so that it can be used either as a bedchamber or sitting-room, and has an alcove which is capable of being partitioned off by a portiere from the remainder of the room. This alcove also has a door leading to the hallway.

THE DRESSING SALOON.

Adjoining the room just described, and separating it from the rear bed-room, is a saloon comprising what is practically a large dressing-room, with mirrors, drawers, closets, washstand, etc. The windows overlook the street, and give an unusually bright and cheerful aspect for a dressing saloon, besides giving direct light and ventilation. A separate closet is provided for the alcove, sitting-room and rear chambers, and large linen closets are found in the halls.

The rear bedroom adjoins the dressing saloon, and has a clock, annunciator, etc. A door leads to the hall as well as to the dressing-room.

THE BATH-ROOM.

The bath-room is judiciously planned to overlook the courtyard to the west. It thus has, like the dressing saloon, direct light and ventilation. It has a wainscoting in enamel tile and a porcelain bath-tub, etc., while the floors are inlaid in hardwood.

The Woolley-Brinckerhoff Houses, northwest corner Mt. Morris Avenue and 121st Street.

THE THIRD FLOOR.

The third floor is arranged on a somewhat similar plan to the floor below. It has front and rear bedrooms, with a dressing saloon and bath-room having direct light and ventilation. The trim is in ash.

THE FOURTH FLOOR.

The fourth floor has a very large front bedroom. It is in the southeast corner of this chamber that the tower appears which has already been referred to above. This tower is practically a cosy little observatory where the fortunate occupant of the room can snugly recline and read his (or her) morning newspaper or—the latest novel. The trim is in white wood, with a mahogany finish. Four smaller rooms, a sink-room, closets, etc., complete this floor. There is a good-sized attic above, reached by a flight of stairs. This attic is intended as a storeroom or children's play-room, or it can be used as a servants' bedroom.

THE BASEMENT.

Descending to the basement we find a large, light and airy room, with a grass plot in front inclosed in ornamental railings. This room can be used either as a breakfast-room, a billiard-room or a servants' sitting-room. The wainscoting is paneled in ash, and there are closets, a mantel, etc. Adjoining is a laundry, and leading through from the front room is a spacious kitchen, with a fine range, etc. Closets, refrigerators and other necessities for the culinary department complete the floor.

SOME IMPORTANT FEATURES.

Nothibg is more essential to the health of the occupants of every house than the plumbing. An examination shows that the plumbing in this house is of a very fine character, and in accordance with the laws of sanitation. The laundries are provided with porcelain wash-trays, and the kitchen and butler's pantry with porcelain sinks. The wall surfaces at the back of the sinks and boilers are protected with marble. The water-closets are of the most approved wash-out pattern, and stand on marble seats. A sensible arrangement on the fourth floor is the carrying up of the waste and supply pipes so that a bath-tub and water-closet for the use of servants may be set up at any time in a room arranged for that object.

The range has a separate ventilating flue to carry off the odors from cooking. The cellar is cemented and contains a large furnace.

All throughout the house the flooring is laid double. The finish of the hardwoods on the first and second stories is exceptionally fine, the woods being thoroughly rubbed and brought to a high degree of smoothness.

There are electric bells, annunciators and burglar alarms in the house, as well as wires for lighting the gas by electricity.

An important feature of this house (as well as the four adjoining houses sold) is the fact that it has been dried with artificial heat during the process of building and before the woodwork was put in place. The value of this precaution in avoiding cracks and rents in walls and plaster after completion is apparent.

The house, it may be added, was built under the daily personal supervision of the owners and under the care of Jas. E. Ware, the well-known architect.

The Mount Morris Bank Building.

ONE OF THE BEST EQUIPPED BANK BUILDINGS IN THE CITY.

Those who pass by the handsome structure erected by the Mount Morris Bank, on the northwest corner of 125th street and Park avenue, and who have never visited the different departments of that institution, have no conception of the complete and substantial character of the appointments.

To the exterior view the structure presents a handsome and attractive perspective in massive stone and brick, with a covered stoop leading to the bank by flights of stairs from approaches at the east and west. To those who have business transactions with the bank, and to depositors and visitors, the interior presents a view which for richness of effect is hardly surpassed by the great bank buildings erected in Wall street during recent years.

THE VESTIBULE.

The vestibule walls are adorned with a high wainscoting of Numidian African) marble, while the floors are tiled in stone of a like material. The Colonial windows are of a particularly excellent design, with the glass in colors effectively blended.

THE COUNTING-ROOM.

The main room, of which an illustration appears in this supplement, is a marvel of richness. It is surrounded by Numidian marble, the counters being all faced with that stone, and surmounted by bronze railings in a delicate and artistic design. Among the numerous openings noticed were special receiving and paying tellers' windows for ladies, so as to save the latter the inconvenience of waiting in line, which is so frequently seen on busy days at various banks. There is also a ladies' waiting-room, handsomely furnished in mahogany and richly carpeted, an attractive mantel and mirror being a feature of the room, with an open fire-place, mirror, fender, andirons, etc. The president's and cashier's rooms adjoining are also comfortably furnished. In the western wall of the counting-room are vaults for the safe-keeping of the money, books and securities of the institution, which are encased in a fire-proof safe that would defy the elements under any circumstances. On the same floor, and in the rear, is the directors' room, furnished in mahogany.

Mount Morris Bank Building, northwest corner 125th Street and Park Avenue.

THE SAFE DEPOSIT VAULTS.

The most interesting part of the building is the basement and sub-basement, where the Mount Morris Bank Safe Deposit Vaults are situated. Here Superintendent Martin is in charge, and he shows the visitor with a certain pride the massive doors weighing ten tons, which guard the treasure-vault from burglars and fire. "This vault, he says, "is built on its own foundation and is separate from the building, so that if the structure should catch fire and fall, the vaults and all they contained would still stand firm as a rock." The vaults are constructed of iron 2¼ feet in thickness, and this mass of metal is encased in mason work of a thickness impenetrable to fire. The doors contain thirty bolts, and the superintendent opened and closed them with a click to show how simply they work, notwithstanding their bewildering intricacy. It requires two people to open the safe, which is set to be unclosed at a certain hour by clockwork and cannot be opened before. In the vaults are hundreds of small shelves for the use of depositors, at a charge of from $5 to $150 each per annum, and no depositor can open his box without the insertion of the superintendent's special key as well as his own. Ladies' and gentlemen's private compartments, etc., are provided, so that depositors can count their money and other possessions in privacy.

In the sub-basement trunks, furs, silverware and other personal effects can be stored for long and short terms at a cost of 50 cents per month and upward, with an insurance for such payment of $500 and over. These are only a few features of the institution, hurriedly outlined. The bank and vaults are well worth a visit.

About thirty clerks and other employes constitute the working force. There are numerous offices above the bank floor, which are reached by an elevator from an entrance to the west of the bank.

NOTES.

The Mount Morris Bank was organized in 1880. It has a capital of $250,000, and has within a few years accumulated a surplus of $300,000. It has a large and important class of depositors, and is noted for its liberal yet conservative management. The president, Joseph M. De Veau, is widely known and respected in Harlem, and the bank has in Thomas W. Robinson an able manager and cashier.

Three Generations of Builders.

There are very few firms in New York City that can boast of a succession of three generations in the same business, and we know of no others, besides that of the Hopper family, who have for three generations been practicing builders.

The grandfather of Isaac A. Hopper, the present head of the firm of Isaac A. Hopper & Co., learned his craft in the first quarter of this century. He commenced business on his own behalf in the year 1833, over fifty-eight years ago. His son, father of the present builder, bearing the

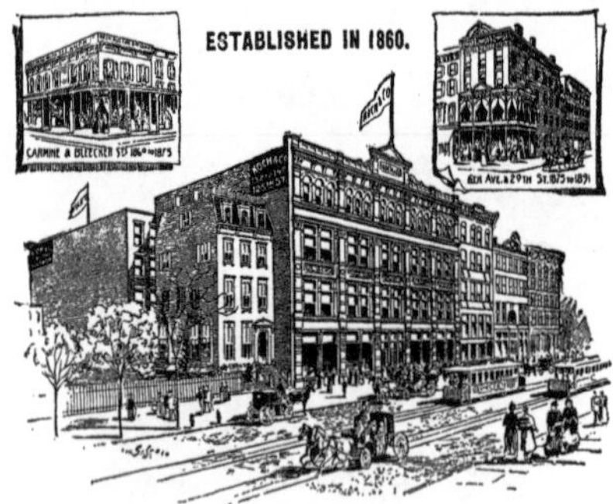

W. H. Hume, Architect. *The Koch Emporium on 125th Street.* Isaac A Hopper, Builder.

name, started out twenty years later, and the grandson of the founder of the firm began his career in 1875.

One of the first important contracts obtained by Mr. Hopper was that for the St. Barnabas Home on Mulberry street. This structure he built in 1878. Two years later he built the "Portsmouth" apartment house on West 9th street, and next year the "Hampshire," adjoining.

In 1884 Mr. Hopper secured the contract for the Hotel Normandie, of which W. H. Hume was the architect, by far the most prominent building secured by him up to that date. Later on he obtained the contracts for the Emigrant Industrial Savings Bank, on Chambers street, opposite City Hall Park; the Cable road depot, on 10th avenue, 128th and 129th streets; the Montefiore Home, on the Boulevard, 138th and 139th streets; the Academy of the Sacred Heart, on 9th and St. Nicholas avenues, 13?d and 133d streets; the emporium of Hy. C. F. Koch, on 125th street, near 7th avenue, which appears in an accompanying illustration; the Carnegie Music Hall; St. Michael's Episcopal Church, 99th street and Amsterdam avenue; and last, but not least, the New Netherlands Hotel, on the northeast corner of 5th avenue and 59th street, which is being erected for Wm. Waldorf Astor. Among the less important buildings erected by him were numerous flats, private houses and business structures, as well as three new station houses, etc. One of his most recent contracts is for the alteration of Andrew Carnegie's house, at No. 5 West 51st street, at a cost of $65,000.

Among the various organizations to which Mr. Hopper belongs is the Mechanics' and Traders' Exchange, which he has made his down-town headquarters for the last sixteen years. He is also a member of the Building Trades' Club and a vice-president of the Mason Builders' Association. Two fiduciary institutions in Harlem have secured his services as director, namely, the Hamilton Bank and the Twelfth Ward Savings Bank, of the latter of which he is vice-president. He is also a director of the Fort Lee Ferry Company.

The firm has for some time been designated as "Isaac A. Hopper & Co.," with offices at No. 200 West 124th street, Mr. Hopper's partner being James Kelly, Jr., who had for seven years been superintendent of the firm prior to becoming a party in interest.

The Farrell Building.

Nowhere is the advance in population and business in Harlem more exemplified than on 125th street. It is somewhat curious that, although 3d avenue was for many years the main shopping centre between 116th and 130th streets, the lead was eventually taken by 125th street. This has been markedly the case during the last two or three years. One has only to ride on the cable cars on 125th street, between 3d and 8th avenues, and glance to the right and left on both sides to note the vast changes that have taken place in the last few years, and to realize that this street is fast becoming—not alone the greatest business thoroughfare in Harlem, but the greatest in the city.

This proposition, at first sight, looks like an exaggeration. But, it may be asked, where is the crosstown street—be it 14th, 23d or 42d—that can show at this moment so many new and handsome business buildings under construction as may be seen on 125th street? Nay, it might be possible to add together every new business structure on all the crosstown streets in the city and they would not equal the number now being erected or completed on the great Harlem crosstown thoroughfare.

Again, the principal stopping streets, such as 14th and 23d, down town, are all confined mainly between Broadway and 6th avenue, with a recent tendency to extend east of Broadway and west of 6th avenue. On 125th street, however, there is almost a clean sweep of business between 3d and 8th avenues. True, every building is not a business structure, but such buildings as are of a private or residence character are one by one being converted into uses for business.

Again, 125th street is more of a business street, par excellence, than any other crosstown street in the city. It has more banks to begin with. It has theatres, dry-goods, grocery, real estate and other stores, besides several telegraph and messenger offices and other conveniences that go to make up the requirements of a large city. And Harlem is nothing if not a large city in itself, and 125th street is its centre. There is no crosstown street in New York that presents such a wide variety of business structures, nor is there any crosstown street which will compare with it in the course of ten years, unless all the signs fail. Those who have not recently been on 125th street will find as large and as well-dressed a crowd every fine afternoon, on the south side of the street particularly, as may be found on 14th or 23d street. Of course this crowd is not as compact as on the latter streets; for, instead of being compressed mainly between Broadway and 6th avenue, it is distributed over a distance of a mile, for it is nearly that distance between 3d and 8th avenues.

Among the recent new store buildings are those occupied by Hy. F. C. Koch, Corn, Kalisko & Co., and others. Then there are several new buildings under way, and among them is the structure now being completed for E. D. Farrell, the furniture dealer, on the south side of 125th street, just east of 7th avenue. The design was originally drawn for a six-story and basement building, as shown in the accompanying illustration. Only three stories and basement have been completed for the present, the walls and foundations having been constructed of sufficient strength to enable the three additional stories to be built whenever required.

The building covers a frontage of 100 feet on 125th street, with a depth of 100 feet over all, thus covering 10,000 square feet. It contains two stores, each 50x100 in size. These stores are divided by arches filled in by partitions, which can at any time be taken out should it be necessary to throw open the entire floor space of 100x100 into one large store. It can also be divided up to make three or four stores, if so leased.

The tendency for large stores on 125th street seems to be toward dry-goods. The Farrell building would seem to be of value for a large emporium of this character. Those who imagine that first-class trade in Harlem all goes to 23d street and vicinity will find themselves grossly deceived on visiting Koch's establishment on 125th street, near the Farrell building. They will there find an emporium equipped like Stern's on 23d street, and crowded just as much with a class of buyers—nearly all of the fair sex—who, to all appearances, are fully as well-to-do as the average buyers who do their shopping at the 23d street establishment. They may also see a second Macy's at D. M. Williams & Co.'s, on 3d avenue and 125th street. In other words, 125th street is the centre of a population which numbers close on 400,000 people, and it is from this vast population that the great Harlem stores draw their custom. Hence every store on that great business thoroughfare is destined to be of great value for business purposes.

This last statement will be made clearer when it is realized that a large number of towns on the New Haven Road and the New York & Northern Road in Westchester County and beyond pour their shoppers into 125th street. The Harlem branch of the New Haven Road brings passengers into 129th street and 3d avenue from Port Morris, Hunts Point, West Farms, Westchester, Baychester, Bartow, Pelham Manor, New Rochelle, etc. On the New Haven Road main line passengers come in from Larchmont Manor, Mamaroneck, Rye, Portchester, Greenwich, Stamford and beyond, while residents in Morrisania, Fordham, Tremont and other points in the 23d and 24th Wards, as well as from various towns along the Hudson on the line of the New York & Northern Road, are gradually coming in large numbers to 125th street to make their purchases. Within a very few years this thoroughfare will have tributary to it a population equal to half the present population of the City of New York. There is a continually advancing tide northward, and eventually the larger part of the city will be located beyond 125th street. During the last twelve months the progress of business on that street has been remarkable.

A feature of the Farrell building is the large plate-glass windows which appear in each store. These windows have created considerable talk. Jere. C. Lyons, who erected the building, is responsible for the statement that they are the largest windows in the city. An article recently appeared in a contemporary on plate-glass windows, in which it was stated that the largest ever set up are in a building on Vine street, Cincinnati, and are 101x186 inches in size. The windows in the Farrell building are 144x156 inches in size, and are, therefore, 3,678 square inches larger than those in Cincinnati.

The construction of the building is of a substantial character and has been under the supervision of Julius Munckwitz, who was for eighteen years supervising architect of the Department of Public Parks. The floors are constructed so that no obstacle interrupts the space, excepting six massive iron columns, which, with the walls, support the superstructure. These columns run to the top story. As originally designed the building will contain four elevators. There are two large boilers in the basement, and other machinery. Wide staircases lead to the upper floors, and steam heat and other improvements are supplied. A large skylight gives additional light in the rear, under which, on the ground floor, are patent lights that reflect into the basement below. There are also patent lights on the sidewalk that give extra light to the vaults underneath.

Various estimates are given as to the cost of the building. This is said to have been $175,000, while the ground is now valued at $350,000.

It is understood that Mr. Farrell has built the property for investment and that applications to lease the structure have been made to him from several quarters.

Mr. Farrell also owns the four lots covered with two-story and basement business buildings on the south side of 125th street, about 125 feet east of Koch's emporium. These buildings were originally erected with thick walls of sufficient strength to carry seven stories. It is in contemplation to add five stories to the present structure, so as to make the whole seven stories and basement in height. The property, as it now stands, is valued at $425,000.

E. D. Farrell, Owner. *The Farrell Building, south side 125th Street, east of 7th Avenue.* Julius Munckwitz, Architect.

A Large Dry-Goods Emporium.

The remarkable increase in the population of Harlem has naturally brought with it an increase in the number of stores and business buildings in the 12th Ward. Only a decade ago the people of Harlem made their important purchases down town. It was at that time believed that to buy goods at a reasonable figure and to obtain a large assortment from which to make a selection a journey to 14th street, 23d street, or Broadway, was necessary. There was, no doubt, very good reason for this, for only a very few houses existed then in Harlem where the public could purchase from a large and varied stock at reasonable figures.

Later on, however, dry-goods merchants began to realize that there was an immense population in Harlem that was worth catering for, not to speak of the tens of thousands north of the Harlem River. They saw that people would readily make their purchases within a few minutes' walk or ride of their homes in preference to journeying down town, paying car fares and spending half a day, or a day, in securing what goods they required.

Hence one or two, wiser than the others, said: "Why not bring a large stock and a great variety of goods right to their very doors, and make our prices just as low as Macy's or any other emporium down-town." And thus arose the large buildings, one by one, where dry-goods importers and retailers now attract their hundreds and thousands.

Among the earliest to perceive the advantage of large and varied stocks and low prices was the firm of D. M. Williams & Co. They started a small store on the northwest corner of 3d avenue and 125th street in 1880, the size of which was 17x75. By adopting the "small profit" system their business increased so rapidly that two years later they found it necessary to enlarge their building, and later on to extend it still further, until now they occupy a three-story and basement structure, with a frontage of 186 feet on 125th street and 50 feet on 3d avenue, the total surface area of the several floors being 37,200 square feet.

A GLANCE AT THE INTERIOR.

Inside the emporium scores of salesmen and saleswomen are employed attending to the wants of customers. The first floor contains the following departments: Gentlemen's furnishing, ladies' and misses' hosiery and underwear, notions, gloves, jewelry, perfumery, ribbons, dress trimmings, laces, velvets, shoes, silverware, dress goods, silks and domestics.

On the second floor are the following departments: Worsteds, art, cloaks, children's ware, ladies' and children's underwear and clothing, boys' clothing and millinery, and a well-equipped upholstery department.

The third floor is devoted to toys, etc., while in the basement an immense line of house furnishing goods is to be seen, as well as lamps and shades, glassware, china, etc. The machinery, including Worthington pumps, dynamos, four 65 horse-power boilers, etc., is also in the basement, as well as the receiving, marking, delivery and shipping departments, which are most elaborate and intricate, and display great thought and ability in the planning. From this part of the building goods are shipped not only to all parts of the city, but all over the country, purchases of $5 and over being forwarded free within a radius of 200 miles.

The building is equipped with two passenger elevators and one freight elevator. There are numerous electric lights spread over each floor, and other conveniences are provided. The employes of both sexes number about three hundred and an *entente cordiale* seems to exist between the members of the firm and those engaged in their service. "Courtesy to our employes and by our employes to our customers is one of our mottos," remarked one of the members of the firm to the reporter. Both members left important positions to commence business for themselves, and to-day they stand in the front rank among importers and retailers.

D. M. Williams & Co.'s Store, northwest corner 125th Street and 3d Avenue.

A Handsome Harlem Store.

The illustration presented herewith shows the building now occupied by Messrs. Corn, Kaliske & Co., the dry-goods retailers.

The structure is four stories high, with a fine basement. It has a frontage of 50 feet on 125th street, between Lenox and 7th avenues, and runs back 200 feet to 124th street. The building is owned by A. D. Russell, who leased the entire property to the present occupants for twenty years, from September, 1889. The building has an iron front on 125th street and a brick front on 124th street. The feature of the 125th street front is the immense window space, the entire facade, with the exception of the iron framework, being of glass.

The interior of the building is very handsome, the trim being largely of hardwood and the appointments of the most modern character. The floors are lighted by electricity throughout, and there is a passenger and freight elevator.

The building has numerous departments, fully equipped to meet the demands of Harlemites. Dress goods of every description, millinery, cloaks and suits, shoes, etc., are among the specialties noticed, as well as an upholstery department, with some attractive specimens in screens and portieres.

The members of the firm are well known in dry-goods circles both up town and down town. Mr. Corn was in the commission hat business for sixteen years, while Mr. Kaliske was in the shoe business for ten years, prior to the formation of the present partnership. The junior member of the firm, Mr. M. J. Platz, was for eight years a buyer for Ridley's. The firm employs between 150 and 200 people of both sexes.

Corn, Kaliske & Co.'s Store, Nos. 144 and 146 West 125th Street

DEVOTED TO REAL ESTATE, BUILDING ARCHITECTURE, HOUSEHOLD DECORATION, BUSINESS AND THEMES OF GENERAL INTEREST

PRICE, PER YEAR IN ADVANCE, SIX DOLLARS.

Published every Saturday.

TELEPHONE - - - - CORTLANDT 1370.

Communications should be addressed to

C. W. SWEET, 14 & 16 Vesey St.

J. T. LINDSEY, *Business Manager.*

VOL. XLVIII NOVEMBER 14, 1891. NO. 1,235

CLOSE OF THE ARCHITECTURAL EXHIBIT.

The Exhibition of Architects' Drawings in the rooms of THE RECORD AND GUIDE, *Nos. 14 and 16 Vesey street, must be closed on Saturday, November 21st. This exhibit is one of the finest and most extensive that has ever been displayed in New York City, and those who desire to study the 300 examples of the best architectural work of the day should visit the Exhibition without delay. Admission is free.*

A COMMUNICATION to the *Evening Post* last week states so clearly the complaints of stockholders as to the remarkable performances of the present management of the Lake Erie & Western R. R. Co., heretofore referred to in these columns, that we quote from it in part as follows:

If the management earnestly wishes to explain to the public what it has done, so that there may be no mistake about it, let it be understood that the stockholders complain:

(1) That the proxies given to certain directors at the request of the company's secretary, to be used at a special meeting of the stockholders, to be held at Bloomington, Ill., on June 25, 1890, to authorize the acquisition of the Fort Wayne, Cincinnati & Louisville Railroad, and the placing of a first mortgage thereon of the same amount per mile as on the rest of the line, were used at an adjournment held three days afterwards to put a second mortgage on the entire line, including the acquisition, thereby increasing the mortgage debt per mile by 50 per cent.

(2) Stockholders complain that after the wording of the proxy had been strained so as to give a colorable right to use it for a purpose which had been concealed from the stockholders when solicited, all news of the action was suppressed. Not only were the stockholders not informed of the intention, but they were not informed of the action until a fortnight ago. Nothing is said about a second mortgage in the president's report for the year ending December 31, 1890, nor in the company's statement appearing in Poor's Manual for 1891, issued only last June. The news only reached Wall street last month, and the shock was expressed by a decline of 25 per cent in the market value of the common shares and nearly 10 per cent in the preferred.

(3) Stockholders complain because the bonds have been privately disposed of to brokers on what they believe to be terms ruinous to the company.

(4) They complain that the mortgage does not protect them, inasmuch as the bonds are to be delivered by the trustee on demand of a majority of the Board of Directors, the trustee not being bound to know to what use the bonds or their proceeds have been or are to be put.

Calvin S. Brice, President of the Lake Erie & Western Railroad Company, makes an effort to answer these complaints in a circular letter to the stockholders this week, and we have the lawyer and politician combined in his attempt to do the best he can with a difficult case. So far as he quotes from the proceedings taken, he only confirms the facts stated by indignant stockholders. There were but two courses before him when he wrote this circular; one was to own up frankly, make the best excuse possible and announce that the question of ratifying the increase of 50 per cent in the mortgage debt would be regularly submitted at a meeting of stockholders to be called for that purpose, and that if the majority was opposed to the mortgage, why theirs was the sovereign will. This would have been the manly course, would have silenced all opposition and have placed the responsibility with the owners of the property and settled all question of validity of the bonds, but instead he attempts to throw dust in the eyes of the stockholders and befog the public by a production which evidences a low opinion of their intelligence, and will only tend to provoke the growing opposition to more determined action. The more the issue is forced between the deceived stockholders and the management, the worse it will be, not only for the management, but for the parties who have contracted to buy the new bonds.

ENGLISH investors have always preferred the colonies of their own country to all the available fields for placing their money; and consequently have enormous interests in Canada, India, Australia and South Africa. Of course, among the colonial investments those most sought after have been the issue of the colonial governments, and among the colonial governments none have stood higher than the Australian States. Recently a number of these colonies have been borrowing too largely in the English market, and cries of warning are being heard against lending so readily in the future. The prices of the issues of the various governments have declined and are declining. Nevertheless, the fever for borrowing still continues. Undeterred by an unfortunate experience only a few months since, Victoria has announced her intention of bringing out a Public Works loan aggregating $30,000,000. The new Premier of New South Wales, in a recent speech, also foreshadowed a largely increased outlay of money on public works. The finances of this second colony are in a far better shape than those of her neighbors; but the speech has, nevertheless, made the holders of her issues somewhat nervous. The smaller Australian colonies are pursuing a very similar policy; and at present it looks as if the result would be what it was in New Zealand. That is, the colonies will exhaust their credit in London, and then settle down to a period of depression, while the country grows up to its improvements. We mention these facts, because they may in the future affect the readiness of Englishmen to purchase American securities. Probably for the next couple of years the Australian demands on the English market will be met, but having been met, they will not therefore cease. On the contrary, the more that the Australians get the more they will want; they will come to crave the artificial stimulus added to trade by the spending of the borrowed money. Finally, of course, English investors will stop lending, and it will be increasingly easy to float American securities in that market. In this connection it is interesting to note that several of the Australian colonies are undergoing at present a period of reaction from a rather excited real estate speculation. The years of 1889 and 1890 were, the world over, years of a certain amount of inflation; but the recovery from it has been more rapid in America than in any other country.

IS it then true that Boss Croker is converted to ballot reform? In that case we can consider it to be assured that the voters of this State will have, in time for the next election, a blanket ballot as the sole legal medium of voting, the said ballot to be printed and distributed at the expense of the State. It is true that the elections have been won by a party whose record has not been favorable to ballot reform and whose recent declarations on the subject, through its candidate, have been, to say the least, equivocal. Nevertheless, no matter who controls the Legislature, there is no doubt that Boss Croker could, if so he chooses, have the ballot law brought to a pitch of Australian perfection, for the Republicans are committed to such a measure. But what does this mean? We have been told that the voters of this city were to such an extent the unwilling slaves of corruptionists that, if once we could get an absolutely secret ballot, which could in no way be tampered with, we should thereby put an end to any delivery of votes according to order. Furthermore, as "deals" and other dubious political technicalities are dependent for success on the ability of dealers successfully to deliver the votes, we were to expect that in the future there would be no more "deals" and that an era of honest politics would begin. So the secret ballot was loudly proclaimed to mean the downfall of the "practical" politician. Well! we obtained a ballot which is nearly secret; and in the fall of 1890 a candidate was placed in the field who was committed against "deals," and who, if he was elected, was to sit in the mayoralty chair as an embodiment of Virtue. Alas, however, Virtue seemed to have as little chance to enter the City Hall through the rather secret ballot boxes as through those which were open as the ambient air. This trial of the Australian system made its advocates still hotter for a blanket ballot, and during the campaign of this year the issue for and against this reform was vigorously pushed by the People's Municipal League. But what we should like to know is this: If the blanket ballot is going to be so effective as a squelcher of "deals," how is it that Boss Croker, whose political life, according to good authority, derives its sustenance from such fruity material, comes out in favor of so obnoxious an improvement? If Mr. Croker does bring about the passage of a blanket ballot act we may be sure that it is not going to harm Tammany. In truth, every election but provides additional confirmation of the contention so often advanced in these columns, that Tammany will never be dislodged by the employment of merely political methods.

ASININITY, at last, has had its day, and the newspapers of this city are now adopting the right tone about Chicago and the World's Fair. By and by, perhaps, even the *Herald* will recognize that it is both silly and in very bad taste to endeavor to belittle what, be it a success or a failure, is a great national enterprise involving the credit of the country. The petty spirit which the journals of New York have shown over this matter is a thing to be ashamed of, and, as we have pointed out before in these columns, has given this city a very bad name throughout the West. THE RECORD AND GUIDE has from the first been the only journal in the metropolis that has deprecated the "sneering policy" which the "dailies" adopted. The Fair buildings, however, are now well under way, the Western States and foreign countries have given evidence of intention to support the Exposition well, and Chicago has "something to show" which makes it quite clear that the Fair is not going to be a wayside exhibition of big pumpkins and farm produce. After our past ungraciousness we should see that New York has the finest State building on the Fair grounds.

THE proposition that New York City shall celebrate on October 12th next the four hundredth anniversary of Columbus' discovery of the New World is a good one, which the people of this city should accept. An occasion of such great and universal interest does not frequently present itself, and as Chicago will not be ready at that time with the World's Fair, New York might with advantage to herself seize the opportunity. The most suitable direction that the celebration could take would be to emphasize the position of the metropolis as the great seaport of the New World. The materials for a nautical festival on a vast scale are abundant, and all that is needed is proper preparation and organization to give it a national significance. This proposition is not new; but it has dropped out of the public mind amid the chagrin and "politics" which followed the selection of Chicago as the site for the World's Fair. The danger now is, that the great anniversary will fall into the desecrating hands of fakirs and showmen. The Kiralfy programme, of a spectacular street show of "supes" in armor, costumes, etc., "pertaining to the times of Columbus," but really pertaining to Manhattan Beach, should be suppressed at once as quietly as possible for the sake of the city's dignity.

How Private Property in Land Originates.

STUDENTS have made long journeys into the past to find out the historical origin of private property in land, and doctrinaires have made equally extensive journeys through the cloud-lands of their inner consciousness seeking a philosophical basis for the same institution. The former come back with a lot of information about the German Mark, the Russian Mir and the East Indian village community. They show that land was usually held by the community and not by persons, and intimate that it may have been a mistake to vary from the customs of the fathers. The doctrinaires reach widely divergent conclusions, but not infrequently assure us that private property in land originated in force and fraud, and that the persistence of the institution up to the present time is a huge wrong, begetting all the ills that present society is heir to.

The investigators of both these classes have gone far afield for an explanation that lies at their very door. If they will but come out from the twilight of primeval German forests and from the underbrush of their own theories and take a business-like view of the situation along the water front in New York City, or among the oyster beds of Chesapeake Bay, they will "learn something to their advantage" about the origin of private property in land. These fragments of submerged ground are not subject to private ownership and therefore give us a chance, not common in the United States, of comparing the advantages of communal with private holding. We have heretofore described the deplorable effect of this system of land tenure upon our water front, shown how it has placed us at a disadvantage in competing with neighboring rivals, and indicated that if the city would merely rid itself of the title to these lands it would be indefinitely richer through the enlarged basis of taxation that would result.

In Chesapeake Bay, the State of Maryland has a similar mischievous endowment in the oyster-bearing lands. To a student of primitive property it might seem fortunate that here exists an example of a large tract of land fertile in a curious but valuable way, which, because it lies under water, has been saved from becoming private property, and belongs to the community that governs itself as the State of Maryland. It might be said that here is a chance for the landless man to get a living from the "common" as in the "good old times;" everyone should be allowed to get oysters and so secure a living, scanty but certain, by applying to nature, without hindrance from a go-between known as a landowner. But if instead of philosophising we examine the actual situation, we find a state of things which goes far to explain the origin of private property in land.

Oysters are just as susceptible of cultivation as potatoes, and the natural oyster beds bear about the same relation in yield and quality of product to cultivated beds as do wild strawberry patches to the highly-developed beds of the market gardener. Unless cultivation is resorted to, the natural oyster beds are soon depleted and destroyed by the ever increasing demand. Under private ownership their productivity is almost unlimited. Upon a French farm of 50 acres 16,000,000 oysters were taken in six tides, although there were no oysters to be found there when the farm was established five years before. Maryland has 120,000 acres of natural oyster beds, but about 640,000 acres of land under water that might be made to yield oysters if properly cultivated. The only legislation for a long time enacted regarding the lands was restrictive in its nature—exactly analagous to game laws—it was forbidden to take oysters at certain seasons of the year, and to "dredge" upon certain grounds at any season of the year. Except for these restrictions any one could go and get oysters, and no one had any personal interest except in getting as many as possible with the least possible labor.

An expert who investigated the matter carefully reached the following conclusions as to the results of this method of getting oysters: "Under our present policy our beds have yielded about ten million bushels of oysters a year from grounds which are capable of yielding over five hundred million bushels annually. It has given employment to about fifty thousand of our people for part of the year, while our grounds should give profitable employment to five hundred thousand people for the whole year. It has paid our oystermen about two million dollars a year although our grounds should pay to their cultivators over sixty million dollars a year." The same investigator concluded that if the lands were handed over to private cultivators, under proper restrictions, the revenue derived from them by the State of Maryland might be increased a hundredfold.

After such a description of conditions the doctrinaire promptly suggests that the State ought to arrange for multiplying the oysters, but retain the title to the land, and so get the enormous unearned increment and the revenue it would yield. This option has always been open to the communities and governments of the world, and they have often resolved to try the policy indicated and have oftener drifted into trying it without deciding to do so. In fact the result of the publication of the report from which we have just quoted resulted in the attempt on the part of the State of Maryland to increase the yield of oysters. The result is suggestive. A bill was drawn for the better care and cultivation of the State oyster lands and introduced into the Legislature by the friends of the oyster industry. When it came out of committee it was metamorphosed into a bill giving a ward politician in Baltimore a contract to supply the State with oyster shells! The parents of the measure were obliged to kill their own child in order to prevent the consummation of a "job."

All of which indicates that the institution of private property in land has its origin in expediency. A corollary of this conclusion is that the same force that brought the institution into existence may, conceivably, hereafter modify or abolish it.

THE third track on the West Side elevated railroad may have been constructed in defiance of the spirit of the law, but as none of the property-owners along the line of the structure will be in any way injured by the intermediate girders, and as the third track will be of the greatest use to the company in increasing the efficiency of its service, no one but a few wise editors will feel afflicted at the news that it is practically completed. Col. Hain has been telling the reporters that its completion does not mean an increase of train service; it means only that hereafter the trains will be run more regularly and more nearly on time. This, however, means practically an increase of the service for Westsiders, and they will be devoutly thankful for such a small boon. Then, of course, the third track will be of great assistance to the company in developing its express service. Inadequate as that service is at present, it has been the cause of no little activity in real estate along the line of the Northern road. Next spring we presume that the company will further increase the number of these trains, and will perhaps run them so that they will be of use, not only to the commuters on the Northern road, but, more largely than they are at present, to the patrons of the company south of the Harlem. Of course the management will be so hampered by the lack of sufficient trackage south of 59th street, and the lack of switching room at the Battery, that the improvements which they can introduce will not touch the heart of the difficulty; but any alleviation will be better than none at all. It has been the policy of the company during the recent year to increase the number of trains just sufficiently to keep the overcrowding constant—evidently on the supposition that the present jamming, although most unpleasant, is not unendurable. Whereas, if any increase of the discomfort took place, the traveling public would rise in revolt. Apart from the fact that this policy, which is forced on the corporation by the stupidity of the local authorities and newspapers, is a terrible drag on the growth of the city, it is obviously not a policy which can be indefinitely continued. When the Manhattan Company will be obliged to stop putting on more trains is something that none of us know; but before long some such knowledge may be most important.

THAT Fonseca has practically destroyed constitutional government in Brazil and has set himself up as a Dictator will surprise no one who has followed the course of politics in that country since the fall of the Empire. The country is utterly unfit for self-government. The way in which Dom Pedro's overthrow was accomplished and acquiesced in by the people is sufficient to establish this statement. Their ruler was an old man who had for many years been their sovereign, and through the whole of that time he had governed temperately and constitutionally, if not with any great amount of political wisdom. He was just the kind of a ruler that would endear himself to a people who felt any pride in their institutions or any affection for their representatives. Yet in spite of his age and long service they allowed him to be deposed by a set of conspirators who could allege nothing more culpable in his government than a little extravagance on the part of a relative. It was not a revolution; it was simply a *coup d'etat* by a clique of bold soldiers who took advantage of the impotence of the government and the indifference of the people to seize control of the machinery of the State. If there had been any real wrongs to right, or any widespread popular desire for self-government arising out of adequacy to it, the revolution would have been a very different matter. It would have been spontaneous and concerted, instead of forced and local. Brazil is an enormous country where communication is slow and poor; the uprising was limited to one central city, and in a country peopled by an active aggressive race the interior districts would have protested against the usurpation, if for no other reason than that they failed to share in it. Instead they quietly submitted. What a group of men can do one man can also do. The revolution cloaked a defiance of constitutional methods by an appeal to Republican sentiment; this second usurpation is equally hypocritical and false, but will deceive fewer people. It is the natural sequence of the overthrow of Dom Pedro. Neither, in this connection, is the revolt of one of the provinces surprising. When the spirit of disorder, dissatisfaction with constituted authorities and self-aggrandisement on the part of the prominent men once possesses a country, the inhabitants of which are lazy and indifferent to public duties, it seldom ends in anything but a continual struggle between warring leaders and sections. The history of the South American Republics, so-called, has been little else, and there are no signs of improvement.

Building and Loan Associations.

BUILDING and Loan Associations are not an experiment. It has been fully sixty years since the first one was organized in the United States. During this time they have developed slowly and quietly—so quietly that not until very recently has their importance as an economic factor been recognized. And even now their real nature and the methods they employ are not generally known.

Building and Loan Associations are corporations, all the members of which are stockholders. The stockholder does not buy his stock outright, as in ordinary business corporations, but pays for it on the installment plan. He indicates the amount of stock he wishes to secure by his first payment, and agrees to pay at regular intervals an amount equal to this initial sum until his payments, plus the dividends based upon them, which he as a stockholder receives from the associations, reaches a certain value, or, in other words, until the shares which he has purchased mature. The money thus paid in by the members on stock held constitutes the working capital of the association. This fund may be loaned only to stockholders, and not to them in amounts exceeding the matured value of the share or shares which each holds, and unless good security is furnished.

The advantages afforded by these associations are at once apparent. They are more than savings banks; they stimulate as well as furnish a convenient depository for savings. They, in a word, aim to reduce saving to a system, for, as has been already said, one taking stock enters into an agreement to pay regularly a certain sum into the treasury of the association. But the real merit which may be claimed for this form of savings institutions lies in its application in an effectual way of the co-operative principle to the advantage of small investors. It introduces essentially the element of democracy, as opposed to that of plutocracy, in business. Each depositor is a part of the association, has a voice in the election of its officers and a say in the direction of its affairs. The confidence of depositors in a banking firm may properly be considered a part of its capital. Not only are the funds of the Building and Loan Association secured by reason of stringent regulations placed upon the issue of its loans, but also the depositor feels that they are secure because he is as well a director of the funds of the association.

There are now scattered throughout the United States six thousand Building and Loan Associations, representing, it is estimated, accumulated capital to the amount of over $450,000,000. It is safe to say, judging from the comparative rapid growth of these associations during the last few years, that in three years there will be double and in five years quadruple the present number throughout the country. Small and growing towns rather than large cities will be the field of their operations, and, naturally, the West rather than the East. Already the number of associations of this sort in the Western States exceeds that in the Eastern. A feeling of distrust, which had its origin in the collapse of the old state "wild-cat" banks, still lingers throughout a great part of the middle and northwest against banking institutions. The same feeling holds as regards the ordinary savings bank. It is only natural then that the people of that part of the country regards this new form of savings institution, of which they themselves may become directors, with favor. While Building and Loan Associations, for the reasons mentioned, will have the largest growth in the West, they will not cease to thrive in the East.

Real Estate During Ten Months.

THE filings representing real estate transactions during October possess about the same significance as the figures for the previous months. It is true that the falling off in October from the same month in 1890 is small; but it should be remembered that we are now reaching in our comparisons a period in 1890 which, if anything, was rather less favorable for real estate than was the same period in 1889. During the October of the present year 1,053 conveyances were recorded, involving $17,495,580; during the same month in 1890, 1,097 conveyances were recorded, involving $18,109,629. The number of transfers for the whole ten months was 11,742 in 1891 and 13,327 in 1890, the amount involved being $197,911,725 in the former case and $241,436,042 in the latter. The number of mortgages recorded during the same ten months in 1891 has been 12,030, involving $143,048,263, while 1890 can show for a like period 12,654, involving $215,168,677. The total for 1890 includes five mortgages aggregating $53,500,000 which were liens on both real and personal property. The building filings during the month of October show a considerable decrease from the same month in 1890 and, consequently, makes still worse the already meagre showing of the present year. During the first ten months of 1890 plans were filed for 3,151 buildings to be erected at an estimated cost of $66,238,959; during the same months of 1891 plans were filed for 2,382 buildings to be erected at an estimated cost of $47,772,474.

TEN MONTHS OF REAL ESTATE.

NEW YORK CONVEYANCES.

	No. Conveys.	Amount.	No. Nom.	No. 23d & 24th W.	Amount.	No. Nom.
1891.						
Jan.-Sep., inc..	10,689	$180,416,195	3,094	1,969	$8,397,522	513
October........	1,053	17,495,530	295	253	707,001	57
Total..........	11,742	$197,911,725	3,389	2,222	$9,104,523	570
1890.						
Jan.-Sep., inc..	12,230	$223,326,413	3,065	2,015	$10,242,724	513
October........	1,097	18,109,629	282	266	867,234	49
Total........	13,327	$241,436,042	3,347	2,281	$11,109,958	562
1889						
Jan.-Sep., inc..	11,401	$206,293,343	2,552	2,103	$9,090,138	516
October........	1,144	17,839,196	295	215	889,395	54
Total........	12,545	$224,132,539	2,847	2,318	$9,979,533	570

MORTGAGES.

	No. Morts.	Amount.	No. at 5 p. c.	Amount.	No. at less than 5 p. c.	Amount.	No. to B. T. & I. Cos.	Amount.
1891.								
Jan.-Sep., inc.	10,893	$130,437,021	5,502	$67,494,475	926	$20,746,439	1,574	$39,047,986
October.......	1,137	12,611,242	569	6,947,133	75	1,260,157	148	3,998,914
Total.......	12,030	$143,048,263	6,071	$74,441,608	1,001	$22,006,596	1,722	$43,046,900
1890.*								
Jan.-Sep., inc.	11,422	$200,078,699	5,503	$85,933,984	1,293	$67,002,336	1,694	$94,379,616
October.......	1,232	15,089,978	574	8,046,721	113	2,288,512	207	5,007,175
Total.......	12,654	$215,168,677	6,077	$93,980,705	1,406	$69,290,848	1,901	$99,386,791
1889.								
Jan.-Sep., inc.	10,626	$133,892,429	4,986	$61,470,014	1,327	$28,084,207	1,490	$35,686,518
October.......	1,167	14,466,422	512	7,769,874	147	2,574,750	149	5,130,595
Total.......	11,793	$148,358,851	5,498	$69,239,888	1,474	$30,658,952	1,639	$40,817,113

*Includes mortgage given in February, 1890, by the Manhattan and Metropolitan Elevated Railway Companies on real and personal property to The Central Trust Co. for $40,000,000; mort. given in March, 1890, by the Edison Illuminating Co. to The Central Trust Co. for $5,000,000; mort. given in August, 1890, by the Mount Morris Electric Light Co. to the Central Trust Co. for $4,000,000; morts. given in September by the United States Electric Light and Power Co. to the Union Trust Co. for $3,000,000, and the Standard Gas Light Co. to The Mercantile Trust Co. for $1,500,000.

NEW YORK BUILDINGS PROJECTED DURING TEN MONTHS, GIVEN BY DISTRICTS.

	1889. Jan. to Oct., inc.	1890. Jan. to Oct., inc.	1891. Jan. to Oct., inc.
Total No. of plans filed....	1,806	1,784	1,898
Total No. of buildings projected....	3,252	3,151	2,382
Estimated cost....	$61,975,481	$66,238,959	$47,772,474
No south of 14th st....	430	373	333
Cost....	$18,985,545	$15,604,875	$12,969,325
No. bet 14th and 59th sts....	275	354	247
Cost....	$8,599,706	$14,508,020	$8,072,920
No. bet 59th and 125th sts, east of 5th av	517	507	325
Cost....	$8,233,495	$9,766,680	$7,209,715
No bet 59th and 125th sts, west of 8th av	777	699	589
Cost....	$16,997,100	$15,844,350	$12,882,570
No. bet 110th and 125th sts, 5th and 8th avs	90	121	55
Cost....	$2,175,850	$2,268,025	$1,168,000
No. north of 125th st....	382	398	254
Cost....	$5,501,418	$4,562,008	$3,262,543
No. 23d and 24th Wards....	785	704	629
Cost....	$4,335,292	$3,705,001	$3,163,098

NEW YORK BUILDINGS PROJECTED DURING OCTOBER, GIVEN BY DISTRICTS.

	1889. October.	1890. October.	1891. October.
Total No. of buildings projected....	264	316	243
Estimated cost....	$5,331,269	$6,836,833	$3,505,905

No. south of 14th st	41	15	20
Cost	$1,172,700	$308,175	$710,500
No. bet 14th and 59th sts	20	23	12
Cost	$1,291,831	$926,550	$321,800
No. bet 59th and 125th sts, east of 5th av.	26	42	31
Cost	$415,595	$1,342,000	$413,800
No. bet 59th and 125th sts, west of 8th av.	51	48	45
Cost	$1,448,550	$1,224,000	$1,110,440
No. bet 110th and 125th sts, 5th and 8th avs	6	18	18
Cost	$228,000	$223,400	$260,000
No. north of 125th st	22	107	67
Cos	$345,518	$1,061,100	$762,850
No. 23d and 24th Wards	98	62	55
Cost	$454,575	$248,408	$227,015

	1889 No. b'ld'gs.	1889 Cost.	1890 No. b'ld'gs.	1890 Cost	1891 No. b'ld'gs.	1891 Cost.
Jan.-Sept., inc.	2,988	$56,644,212	2,835	$60,902,126	2,139	$43,966,569
October	264	5,331,269	316	5,336,833	243	3,805,905
Total	3,252	$61,975,481	3,151	$66,238,939	2,382	$47,772,474

FOR THE MONTH OF OCTOBER, 1891, CLASSIFIED.

	Flats and Tenem'ts No.	Flats and Tenem'ts Cost.	Private Dwell'gs No.	Private Dwell'gs Cost.	Hotels, Stores, Churches, Office Build'gs, &c. No.	Hotels, Stores, Churches, Office Build'gs, &c. Cost.	Miscellaneous, Stables, Shops, &c. No.	Miscellaneous, Stables, Shops, &c. Cost.
South of 14th st	13	$269,000	..	....	5	$376,000	2	$65,500
Bet 14th and 59th sts	4	74,000	..	....	2	$170,000	5	77,300
Bet 59th and 125th sts, east of 5th av.	16	269,000	9	$108,000	1	14,000	6	22,800
Bet 59th and 125th sts, west of 8th av	15	621,000	26	477,000	.	....	4	12,440
Bet 110th and 125th sts, 5th & 8th avs	12	240,000	..	....	..	....	1	20,000
North of 125th st	4	78,000	57	638,500	..	....	6	46,350
23d & 24th Wards	6	96,000	34	118,400	..	....	15	12,615
Total for Oct., 1891	69	$1,647,000	126	$1,341,900	8	$560,000	40	$257,005
Total for Oct., 1890	68	$1,6?2,500	190	$1,903,588	16	$1,710,500	49	$73,245

THE MOST IMPORTANT AND COSTLIEST BUILDINGS.

Location and Character.	Owners.	Cost.
Cortlandt st, Nos. 39 and 41, twelve-story building	M. Taylor	$200,000
21st st, foot of West on pier, one-story shed	R. Baldwin, agent	55,000
57th st, Nos. 211-215 W., four-story building	American Fine Arts Soc	150,000
Columbus av, s w cor 75th st, seven-story flat	S. Banner	200,000
Four buildings, to cost		$605,000

FLATS AND DWELLINGS IN ROWS.

Location and Character.	Owners.	Cost.
87th st, s s, 150 w 8th av, five four-story dwell'gs	J. R. Breen	$125,000
95th st, n s, 90 e Park av, nine three-story dwell'gs	F. J. Schnugg	108,000
96th st, s s, 205 w Central Park West, six four-story dwell'gs	E. Kilpatrick	108,000
102d st, n s, 180 w Park av, five five-story flats	J. S. Scott	100,000
136th st, Nos. 201-217 W. / 136th st, Nos. 237-253 W. } eighteen three-story dwell'gs	T. C. Van Brunt	160,000
Av A, s e cor 88th st / 88th st, s s, 75 e Av A } six five-story flats	J. Schreiner, Jr	105,000
Columbus av, n e cor 92d st / 92d st, n s, 40 e Columbus av } three five-story flats	C. Gahren	135,000
St. Nicholas av, n w cor 118th st, five five-story flats	P. Braender	100,000
St. Nicholas av, s w cor 119th st, five five-story flats	P. Braender	100,000
West End av, s e cor 103d st / 103d st, s s, 80 e West End av } six three and four-sty dwgs.	Carew & Drought	102,000
West End av, s e cor 77th st, seven three-story dwell'gs	F. M. Jencks	118,000
7th av, n w cor 139th st / 8th av, n e cor 139th st / 139th st, n s, 79 w 7th av } thirty-eight four-story dwell'gs	D. H. King, Jr	454,000
One hundred and thirteen buildings, to cost		$1,785,000

KINGS COUNTY CONVEYANCES.

	1890. Number.	1890. Am't involved.	1890. Nom.	1891. Number.	1891. Am't involved.	1891. Nom.
January	1,342	$5,816,826	341	1,429	*$7,878,196	419
February	1,293	5,137,587	344	1,219	4,704,985	390
March	1,685	7,608,870	423	1,602	6,245,195	475
April	2,176	11,587,708	490	1,998	9,042,227	490
May	1,882	9,317,275	437	1,802	7,290,963	482
June	1,515	5,920,270	357	1,751	6,233,014	405
July	1,738	7,729,816	351	1,680	6,020,359	402
August	1,274	4,696,970	322	1,238	4,251,552	327
September	1,224	4,519,766	305	1,324	5,004,584	345
October	1,603	6,253,287	377	1,629	5,622,563	446
Total	15,732	$68,588,371	3,747	15,654	$62,223,588	4,174

KINGS COUNTY MORTGAGES.

	1890. No.	1890. Am't involved.	1890. No. at 5 per cent. or less.	1890. Am't involved.	1891. No.	1891. Am't involved.	1891. No. at 5 per cent. or less.	1891. Am't involved.
Jan.	1,264	$4,994,740	792	$3,455,240	1,182	†$14,007,743	620	$2,417,480
Feb.	950	4,117,787	558	2,659,475	1,082	4,123,065	615	2,802,984
March	1,272	5,643,729	780	3,916,105	1,229	5,147,777	682	3,072,480
April	1,679	6,575,719	1,067	4,536,146	1,581	6,571,680	917	4,165,699
May	1,516	6,042,149	947	4,223,752	1,272	5,059,644	680	2,941,829
June	1,322	5,488,301	772	3,987,174	1,460	5,654,829	722	3,727,914
July	1,446	5,785,961	901	3,879,466	1,468	5,050,339	777	3,014,425
August	1,091	4,576,404	629	3,076,165	1,057	3,423,058	563	2,160,598
Sept.	1,067	4,091,155	611	2,639,688	1,090	3,622,546	538	1,972,690
October	1,408	‡9,245,283	898	‡7,313,205	1,451	5,354,551	779	3,166,455
Total	13,025	$56,561,218	7,854	$39,646,416	12,872	$55,326,223	6,963	$29,442,555

*Includes seven deeds at a total of $2,560,000 given by the various sugar companies in Brooklyn to The American Sugar Refining Co. of New Jersey.

†Includes mortgage given by The American Sugar Refining Co. of New Jersey to The Central Trust Co. of New York, for $10,000,000.

‡Includes mortgage given by the Edison Electric Illuminating Co. to the Franklin Trust Co. for $4,500,000; also mortgage given by Citizens' Gas Light Co. to Central Trust Co. of New York for $750,000.

KINGS COUNTY PROJECTED BUILDINGS.

	1890. Total No. b'gs.	1890. No. of brk, stone and iron b'gs.	1890. No. of frame b'gs.	1891. Total No. b'gs.	1891. No. of brk, stone and iron b'gs.	1891. No. of frame b'gs.	1890. Cost.	1891. Cost.
Jan.	344	108	236	268	61	207	$1,407,615	$1,108,235
Feb.	388	158	230	350	160	190	1,816,426	1,545,805
March	484	215	269	427	188	249	2,529,661	2,170,100
April	525	249	276	568	303	265	2,406,950	3,177,972
May	446	193	253	427	206	222	2,469,935	2,485,360
June	547	274	273	299	122	177	2,832,789	1,873,275
July	369	133	236	270	94	176	2,053,540	1,185,539
August	347	136	211	308	102	206	1,747,945	1,844,700
Sept.	323	106	217	408	145	263	1,558,255	2,324,112
Oct.	433	172	261	342	114	228	1,943,665	1,760,670
Total	4,186	1,744	2,442	3,661	1,498	2,169	$21,463,000	$19,44?,849

THE interview containing the opinions of merchants, truckmen, and public officials concerning the local handling of merchandise, published last week in these columns, was read with interest. It is very well known that the congested condition of the down-town streets in this city is becoming annually worse; and any suggestion that gives even a promise of relief should be considered thoughtfully. For the permanent commercial prosperity of New York, considered in the view of existing municipal boundaries, we cannot help regarding this as the most important subject now pressing on the attention of our citizens. Rapid transit will not serve us if the lower part of the city is to become an intolerable bedlam from which all mercantile and manufacturing transactions that can be conducted elsewhere will seek to depart. We see a possibility of great relief in the idea of underground railways. Men may have their own opinions about the practicability of such roads for the profitable transportation of passengers in competition with the about equally rapid and much pleasanter elevated railways; but there is not much room for a difference of opinion when it comes to a question of the transportation of freight. Not one-half the trucks and other street vehicles now in service would be needed had we a system of underground railways that could penetrate to every section of the city and carry to sub-stations conveniently located all the goods intended either for local consumption or for delivery to the railways. With such a system, supplemented by a sufficient number of tunnels under the rivers, the day would soon come when comparatively few trucks would be seen upon our streets, and these few would be engaged in the delivery of goods at only short distances. The fact that we live upon an island, and that the water ways are open for the transportation of merchandise, is about the chief thing that makes Harlem and the north end eligible places of residence. But it would be greatly better could those sections be reached from down town by an underground freight railway which could receive and deliver goods every few blocks at all hours of the day or night. Think of the benefits of such a road to marketmen, merchants, manufacturers, and indeed to all classes of citizens who have goods to handle. It would save the expenditure of more millions of dollars in five years than it would cost to build it, to say nothing of the relief that it would incidentally bring to the streets.

The Value of Trustworthy Management of Railways to Investors.

Messrs. John H. Davis & Co., the prominent bankers and dealers in investment securities, frequently make suggestions in their monthly circular which are well worth the attention of investors. In the one last issued some cautions are uttered to security-holders which are rendered peculiarly timely by the recent equivocal proceedings of the Lake Erie & Western R. R. Co. management. We give them herewith:

We said something last month of the value of a good name as illustrated in the leadership in the market of the Vanderbilt properties and the great strength of their stocks in the face of notable weakening of shares in other companies which, to say the least, had not been distinguished for equal open disclosures and conservative management. More and more, as opinions come to hand both from home investors and foreign capitalists, is the fact impressed that the personal and corporate character of railway officers and directors is being more closely looked at than ever before. The foreigner looks to the United States as the most promising field for the employment of his surplus funds, but he is going to make a sharp discrimination as to the men who administer upon his property. The Englishman has passed through the two contrasting periods of thinking everything American is bad on the one hand, and of blindly plunging into "Americans" on the other. He knows that neither country has a monopoly of railway scandals or corporate mismanagement. He has now enacted laws which hold directors to a very strict accountability in his own country. He hopes for similar legislation in America by which his investments may be encouraged and made more secure, but, meantime, he will, so far as he can, confine his dealings and his investments to men and boards of established character for honesty and conservatism. Both good fellowship and business shrewdness now incline him toward this country. To weaken or destroy this favorable tendency by upholding tricky and speculative officials would be an act of criminal folly for the people of this country. Such mismanagement should be made hazardous to the perpetrators by law; in the absence of such law it should be destroyed by stern public sentiment, and should be guarded against by every possible safeguard which our Stock Exchange can devise.

As for the home investor, he is waking up to the importance of this subject. His newspaper gives him daily lessons in finance through its disclosures of troubles with banks and other institutions as well as with railroads, through the mismanagement or dishonesty of trusted officials. The world is no worse than it once was; on the whole, it seems to be rather better than of old, but, all the same, there never was a time when careful scrutiny of the *morale* of persons in positions of trust or control was more needed or more useful than now.

Good Streets for Yonkers.

The indignant protests of residents and property owners in the fast-growing city of Yonkers against the bad condition of the roadways for some years past has at last borne fruit. Mayor Millward has recommended to the City Council the issue of $150,000 in city b d "to have the streets put in good order." It is understood that the council will authorize the issue at an early date and that the work will be prosecuted with vigor.

Men and Things.

When "Alabama," the "great American drama," was produced in New York last spring, the critics commended it and the public flocked to see it. Encouraged by this support Manager Palmer has put it on the stage of a larger theatre, to "run" the whole winter. This expectation will probably be fulfilled. "Alabama" is in many respects a delightful and wholesome play; it is furthermore the kind of play that is popular. The theatre is one of ample dimensions, but the audiences ought to try them. Although the spectacle of talent being thus generously rewarded is very gratifying, it is not specifically of this that I wish to write. That the talent is American talent, that it is American talent devoted to the writing of plays, and that it is Young American talent devoted to the writing of plays is the aspect of the matter which particularly claims attention. Good American dramatists are not found in the office of every manager; they are a rare species and need nourishment. Augustus Thomas has written a number of plays hitherto, of varying but no marked merit. "Alabama" is so great an advance and betrays such new, rare and valuable qualities that one's surprise and one's delight run hand in hand until one's sense of responsibility seizes them and bids them go slow. This moderation of the pace enables Criticus to catch up to the coterie; and that leisurely person immediately begins to ask questions. It is right, he says, that we should be grateful to Mr. Thomas for a pleasant time; but we should not let our gratitude bias our judgment: for, although it is doubtless very much in a play's favor that we do enjoy it, neither the fact nor the novelty of this enjoyment should prevent us from tracing our pleasure to its sources. "Alabama" is one thing; Augustus Thomas is another. The former will last a season or two; the latter, let us hope, has many years and many plays before him. It is really he that we are interested in. What qualities does "Alabama" indicate in its author? What are the limitations of his talent? These are the questions, the truthful answering of which may be of use to Mr. Thomas; and it is for his sake that they should be truthfully answered.

***

In "Alabama" Mr. Thomas succeeds in creating an atmospheric illusion which is certainly most enjoyable, and is, I believe, truthful. We are introduced to a little society in a small Southern town—a society in which there are a number of very good people and one very bad person. We can believe that this society existed. It has a plausible, if not an absolutely convincing, local atmosphere—an atmosphere that is made up of traits of character, methods of expression and ways of looking at things, in the inhabitants. Most of the conventional Southern types are included in the picture. We have the hasty, war-like, but good-hearted Colonel, who varies from the type in being rather less of a fire-eater than is usual, and, unfortunately, rather more of a caricature. We have several samples of Southern womanhood—impulsive, simple, diffident, confiding yet emotionally tenacious. Ex-Mayor Skaggs, of Talledega, says that these are the first Southern women that have ever been put on the stage. I leave those who are better acquainted both with the stage and with Southern women than I am to pass on the truth of this statement (Mr. Skaggs did not look accurate); but, even if they do not deserve such high praise as the gallant ex-Mayor gave to them, they are certainly living beings. In the same way we can pass old Mr. Preston as a man of flesh and blood, and the darkey servant. There is a Squire Tucker on the bills, who, while he does not destroy the illusion, does not himself add to it; for apparently he is more of a New Englander than a Southerner. These are the men and women in the play that breathe. True, Mr. Thomas' hand is not certain. Every once in a while some conventional trick or forced action reminds us very sharply that his invention is not always checked by observation and knowledge; but on the whole we have small reason for complaint. For the most part the talking is done in a quiet, natural, truthful way. The people speak to each other rather than to the audience. The humor is not dragged in forcibly or merely sandwiched between the serious passages; it arises organically out of the characters and situations. It is largely this that makes the play enjoyable just as it is largely the fact that some of the characters are real, which gives the play artistic worth.

***

Neither should commendation stop at this point. The excellences which I have enumerated are the result of Mr. Thomas' faculty for the intelligent understanding and veracious reproduction of certain delicate but strongly marked phases of character, as they appear under circumstances a little quaint but not abnormal. In various parts of the play he shows that he is capable of endowing his characters with intensity and sharpness of emotion that is equally real. He possesses both fineness and boldness of touch. Just here, however, commendation must end. All of Mr. Thomas' people are not as successful as those mentioned above. His strongest point appears to be local color. Such of the characters as were not all of Talledega had better never been born. Harry Preston lived long enough in the North to become a formless bit of fiction. He is too much of a hero to be a man. Some parts of him might have entered into a human being, but as a whole he is both mechanical and strained. Evidently there is a soft spot in Mr. Thomas' heart for didactic *deus-ex-machinas* and other banes of the play-house, which he would do well to harden while young. When he wrote "Alabama" this soft spot was still tender, and begat not only the hero on the one hand, but the hero's complement, viz., the dastardly villain. I forget the latter's name, but it does not make any difference. He is nothing but just a villain. His introduction into the play can be explained by the exigencies of plot; but no exigencies can excuse it. That Mr. Thomas should have shown such an utter lack of dramatic instinct as to interpolate this crude and arid puppet into society composed mainly of human beings is most disappointing. It indicates plainly that, although he is likely to do some excellent writing in the future, he is also liable to grave faults. His chief limitation appears to be a lack of dramatic imagination. He has the power to invent situations and reproduce plausible characters and stage pictures, but he is not able to fuse these elements into a strong, consistent play, with a really vital meaning. Mr. Thomas has had to impose his plot on his characters, and a wretched, foolish, exasperating imposition it is. Certain parts of the play as a composition grew naturally out of the characters and the local color. They are excellent. Certain other parts—the principal parts—grew out of Mr. Thomas' sense that he must have a "plot" which would hold his situations together, give climaxes to his acts and possess the interest of the audience, and this need of a "plot" coupled with the want of an ability to give dramatic significance to the relations among his characters, accounts for the total lack of any real plot in the play. It is sincerely to be hoped that in the future Mr. Thomas will be able to make his invention more completely fill the vacant space caused by this deficiency in imagination. Otherwise he will be nothing more than a writer of pleasant patch-work.

Secretary Ogden Optimistic.

E. H. Ogden, Secretary of the New York Lumber Trade Association, was called on by a reporter of THE RECORD AND GUIDE at his yards, foot of West 22d street, to ascertain whether the horizon in the lumber trade is clear of labor clouds. He replied:

"I am very certain that the labor troubles, as far as they affect the lumber trade, are over for some time to come. There is no evidence of any likely disturbance anywhere as far as I can see. The Truck Drivers' and Lumber Handlers' Association, which took the initiative in the recent unpleasantness, is now dissociated from the Board of Delegates of the Building Trades, and it is most improbable that they will cause any further trouble. I think you will be safe in telling such readers of THE RECORD AND GUIDE who have contracts on hand, or contemplate future contracts, that they can make their estimates with certainty, unless something very unexpected happens, without fear of further lumber troubles being ahead of us."

CHICAGO.—IV.

Several letters inquiring about Chicago real estate as an investment have been sent to the headquarters of this Journal. One of our correspondents asks, among other things: "Do you personally know of any real estate in Chicago which you can recommend as an investment for from $75,000 to $100,000?" Yes, and no. There is plenty of good, solid paying property in Chicago to be had at those figures, but we cannot undertake to recommend any particular piece. It is not our business. The proper persons to apply to are the reputable real estate brokers of this city. Whose names are? — legion. I fear it would be invidious to make a selection, and to name them all is impossible. Wm. D. Kerfoot & Co., 85 Washington street, is an old and wealthy firm here, so is Bogue & Co., Real Estate Board Building; Turner & Bond, 115 Dearborn street; Mead & Coe, 149 La Salle street (Mr. Mead, I believe, was some years ago in Horace S. Ely's office in New York); Baird & Bradley, 90 La Salle street; Norman T. Gassette & Co., 110 Dearborn street (the agents for the great Masonic Temple now building); Wm. A. Merigold & Co., 156 La Salle street; J. C. Magill & Co., Madison and La Salle streets; H. O. Stone & Co., La Salle street; Snow & Dickinson, corner of Dearborn and Washington streets (who carry on a very large business); Cremin & Brenan, 142 Dearborn street, (well-known in New York); Arthur C. Gehr & Co., 114 Dearborn street; E. A. Cummings & Co., corner of La Salle and Madison streets, do a large business in sub-divisions; so do Van Vlissengen & Ismond. These are a few names taken at random; the list might be greatly extended. Any of these firms could recommend plenty of sound property for investment.

About the future of realty in Chicago there can be no mistake, for the future of Chicago is a certainty. It is the only city in this country that will dispute the supremacy of New York. The entire West, Southwest and Northwest pay tribute to Chicago. It is the metropolis of those parts of the country. As indicating what this means the following figures may be of value: The State of Illinois alone has an area of 56,000 square miles; that is, it is about 4,000 square miles larger than the whole of New England. Now the spot value of all the pig iron made in the United States is about $125,000,000, but the market value of the wheat and corn crops in the State of Illinois is greater—the excess alone this year over last being $28,000,000. And in addition to Illinois there is Kansas still richer in agricultural wealth, and Iowa, the Dakotas, Nebraska, Minnesota, etc., for all of which Chicago is the great centre. The agricultural West is the foundation of Chicago's greatness. It isn't Eastern capital that has really built up Chicago, but the West, and as the West grows and prospers so will Chicago. Few cities in the world are built on a more solid foundation or one that better guarantees the future. Is there any wonder that real estate transaction increased from $43,682,900, in 1880, to $227,486,959, in 1890; that since 1876 56,240 buildings have been erected in the city, at a cost of $255,298,879, of which 11,608, costing $47,322,100, were built last year. The frontage of the new buildings erected since 1876 is about 256 miles. Chicago is now twenty-four miles long by ten miles at the widest point, and the area is 181.70 square miles. In 1835 the area was 2½ square miles.

There, that is one of the evils of Chicago — you have got to go into figures over the city. But what ringing figures they are, full of vitality, leaping at a bound from tens to hundreds and so on into the millions, where the mind is thrown into a sort of numerical vertigo. And then, every Chicagoan is, I believe, a professional statistician — about his own city. If your eyes are on Chicago there isn't a point within your mental horizon that he cannot cover with figures. No sensitive person can sit out an evening with an enthusiastic Chicagoan to whom he has thoughtlessly "given a chance" without having an arithmetical nightmare afterwards wherein he will find himself breathlessly dividing the number of houses built in ten years into

The Galleries of Fine Arts—World's Fair, Chicago.

C. B. Atwood, Architect.

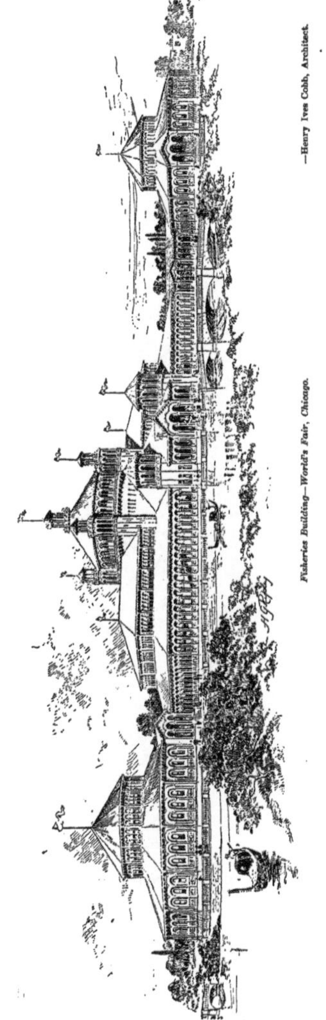

Fisheries Building—World's Fair, Chicago. —Henry Ives Cobb, Architect.

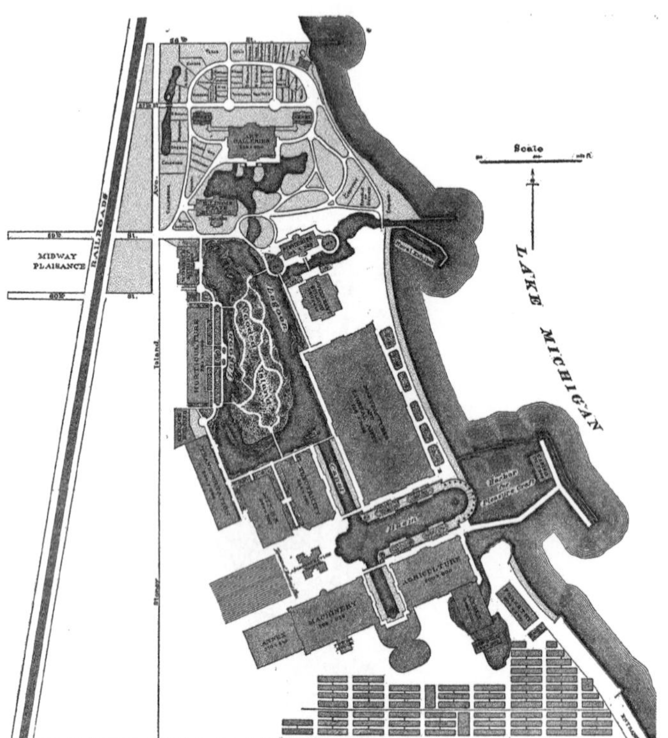

Site of the Fair Buildings, Chicago.

the population multiplied by the square miles, and at the end bounding along in frenzy into infinity over the backs of the hogs sent to the stock yards in the past twelve months.

Work is progressing rapidly at the World's Fair buildings. I send you some of the designs selected which may be of interest to your readers. The following gives the size and cost of the buildings:

STATEMENTS.

Buildings.	Dimensions in feet.	Area in acres.	Cost.
Mines and mining	350x700	5.6	$260,000
Manufactures and liberal arts	787x1687	30.5	1,000,000
Horticulture	250x1000	5.8	300,000
Electricity	345x700	5.5	375,000
Woman's	200x400	1.8	120,000
Transportation	250x960	5.5	80,000
Administration	260x260	1.6	450,000
Fish and fisheries	160x368	1.4	200,000
Annexes (2)	135 diameter	.8	
Agriculture	500x800	9.2	540,000
Annex	328x500	3.8	200,000
Assembly hall, etc	450x500	5.2	
Machinery	500x800	9.8	
Annex	400x551	6.2	1,200,000
Power house	80x600	1.1	
Fine arts	320x500	3.7	500,000
Annexes (2)	120x200	1.1	
Forestry	200x500	2.3	100,000
Saw mill	125x300	.9	35,000
Dairy	95x200	.5	30,000
Live stock (3)	53x330	1.8	150,000
Live stock sheds	....	40.0	
Casino	175x300	1.2	*150,000
		144.8	$5,890,000
U. S. Government	350x420	3.4	400,000
Battle ship	348x69.25	.2	100,000
Illinois State	160x450	1.7	250,000
		150.1	$6,640,000

*Including cost of pier.

In addition to these the States and Territories named below have made the following appropriations:

State	Amount	State	Amount
Arizona	$30,000	New Hampshire	$25,000
California	300,000	New Jersey	20,000
Colorado	100,000	New Mexico	25,000
Delaware	10,000	North Carolina	25,000
Idaho	20,000	North Dakota	25,000
Illinois	800,000	Ohio	100,000
Indiana	75,000	Pennsylvania	300,000
Iowa	50,000	Rhode Island	25,000
Maine	40,000	Vermont	15,000
Massachusetts	75,000	Washington	100,000
Michigan	100,000	West Virginia	40,000
Minnesota	50,000	Wisconsin	65,000
Missouri	150,000	Wyoming	30,000
Montana	50,000		
Nebraska	50,000	Total	$2,695,000

New York, it will be seen, doesn't figure here. As to foreign nations forty-five (including colonies) have so far made appropriations. Mexico heads the list with $750.000, Japan is next with $500,000, Brazil follows with $445,000 and then come France $400,000, Germany $250,000, Austria $168,000, Bolivia $150,000, Great Britain $125,000, Ecuador $125,000, Guatemala $120,000, Argentine Republic $100,000, Chili $100,000, Colombia $100,000, Peru $100,000, and so on. The total cost of the Exposition buildings proper will be about seven-and-a-quarter million dollars, and the expenses of preparation and maintenance over $10,000,000. That the Fair will be a great success there is now no reasonable doubt.

The Yellow Pine Company in Operation.

The eight firms of yellow pine dealers who have consolidated under the title of "The Yellow Pine Company," a prospectus of which was published in THE RECORD AND GUIDE on the 31st ult., commenced business under the new organization on Thursday. The firms consist of E. W McClave & Co., the South Brooklyn Saw Mill Co., C. W. Wilson, all with yards on Long Island; C. L. Bucki & Co., the A. T. Decker Co., Rapp & Johnson Lumber Co., W. A. Parke & Co. and A. B. Johnson & Co.

"The company has been organized under the laws of New Jersey," said E. W. McClave yesterday. "It is intended to carry on a general lumber business in the States of New Jersey, New York, Pennsylvania, Massachusetts, Virginia, North Carolina, Georgia, Florida, Alabama, Connecticut, Delaware, South Carolina, Rhode Island, Maine, Vermont, New Hampshire and West Virginia. The company is incorporated for forty-nine years. Our object is not to increase prices; our consolidation will rather result, if anything, in a decrease; for, instead of having each yard keep in stock various classes of goods, we will allot particular lines to different yards and so save labor, etc., and at the same time suit the convenience of our customers better."

The certificate of incorporation, which was filed at Jersey City on Tuesday, bears the names of Chas. K. Buckley, J. C. Woodhull, C. W. Wilson, Geo. D. Wilson, W. A. Parke, E. W. McClave, C. S. Hirsch, Chas. G. Rapp, B. P. Johnson, A. T. Decker, I. Hersey, A. B. Johnson, H. O. Sanders and H. P. Jones.

In reply to a report that two yards would be closed up out of the combination for the purpose of economizing, Mr. McClave said: "This is only under discussion; if done, it cannot be effected anyway before a year or two."

The Death of Mr. Lalor.

At a regular meeting of the Real Estate Auctioneers' Association, of the City of New York, held on Friday afternoon, November 6, 1891, the following was unanimously adopted:

"The members of this association have learned with heartfelt sorrow of the sudden death of our esteemed friend and fellow member, Mr. William Lalor, and by this record, duly entered upon the minutes of their proceedings, express their sense of the great loss sustained by his family and by his business associates in this sad event.

"In the death of Mr. Lalor each member of this association has sustained a severe personal bereavement in the loss of a friend and an associate who was universally respected for his rare tact, his untiring efforts, his open, pleasant manner, his unvarying courtesy, his honesty and fair dealing, and his generous, noble-hearted charities.

"The secretary is hereby directed to forward a copy of these proceedings to the sorrowing family of the deceased, tendering to them, in this hour of sad bereavement, the sincere condolence of every member of this association."

Real Estate Exchange Matters.

The Nomination Committee appointed by the Board of Directors some time ago to nominate directors for the ensuing year has submitted the following names: George R. Read, Richard V. Harnett, Charles A. Schermerhorn, William Cruikshank, Isaac Fromme, Ira D. Warren, Cornelius W. Luyster, Edward Oppenheimer, George De F. Barton, J. Romaine Brown, James E. Leviness, Charles S. Brown and Richard Deeves.

Members of the present board not named above are Messrs. H. H. Cammann, Philip A. Smyth and Jere. Johnson, Jr. The last two were purposely omitted by the Nominating Committee because, it is said, of their opposition to the new scale of knock-down fees which went into effect on January 1st, and because also of their adherence to the Auctioneers' Association, whose existence the Exchange authorities say is inimical to the best interests of the Real Estate Exchange. The omission of the names of Messrs. Smyth and Johnson was for these reasons expected, but the absence of Mr. Cammann's name came more in the nature of a surprise. It is best explained by the following letter :

"NOVEMBER 10, 1891.

"Messrs. JAMES RUFUS SMITH, FRANKLIN B. LORD and J. EDGAR LEAYCRAFT, *Nomination Committee*

"GENTLEMEN—I am in receipt of your favor of the 7th inst. offering me the nomination for director of the Real Estate Exchange and Auction Room (Lim.) Having served on the Board of Directors from the formation of the Exchange, and being well satisfied with the present management, I consider it time to give my place to some other member, and therefore request that my name be left off the ticket. Thanking you for your courtesy, I remain, very truly yours,

" (Signed) H. H. CAMMANN."

The places of the three former directors who will not serve this year are supplied by Charles S. Brown, Geo. De F. Barton and Wm. Cruikshank, all of them well-known real estate brokers.

The regular ticket named above will probably be elected without any opposition or even show of opposition, for the Legislature last year abolished the cumulative system of voting, and proxies enough are held by the nominees to elect them without any trouble. The composition of the next board will therefore be as follows: Six real estate brokers, two lawyers, two builders, one auctioneer, one insurance agent and one building-loan operator.

Organizing a State Board of Trade.

Geo. Moore Smith, of Candee & Smith, and Isaac A. Hopper, of I. A. Hopper & Co., were present, as official representatives of the Mechanics' and Traders' Exchange of New York, at the convention at the Rochester Chamber of Commerce on Thursday, held for the purpose of organizing the New York State Board of Trade. Delegates were present from boards of trade and other bodies organized for general commercial purposes from all parts of the State.

The State Board of Trade is a congress of representative commercial men and manufacturers of the whole State, who are selected by and from the separate or local affiliating organizations in the various cities and towns. Its objects are to unite the power and influence of all these organizations into one central representative body, who shall at stated times, and also when emergency demands, meet for the purpose of considering and acting on questions affecting the material interests of the State, and concentrating the whole influence of the local bodies on such measures as they may favor or oppose in the common interest. Legislation at Albany will be particularly watched with this purpose in view.

At Thursday's meeting the delegates present represented, it was said, about 20,000 members of different organizations, all of whom were employers. Two sessions were held, and committees and by-laws created.

The Corporation Sale.

The corporation sale of lands and tenements for unpaid assessments took place in the Court House, on Monday and Wednesday afternoons of this week, under the direction of O. Macdaniel, Collector of Assessments and Clerk of Arrears. Before the sale commenced over $1,000,000 in assessments had been paid to the Collector, and, of course, the parcels included in the paid up assessments were not offered. The withdrawal of so many of the catalogue numbers considerably reduced the work of Mr. Macdaniel, who also acted as auctioneer.

The assessments date back for twenty years from 1887, and while the catalogue contained only 4,820 numbers it included a very much larger number of parcels. Owners have two years after the day of sale in which to redeem their property by paying the taxes and 14 per cent interest per annum. At the end of that time a purchaser may serve notice on an owner, and if within six months' time the owner does not redeem his property he may get a lease from the city for the number of years which he bid at the sale, and take possession of the premises. The method of bidding is to start with a bid of 1,000 years' lease of the property, and where there is competition to lower the number of years at every bid down to five years, which is the lowest term for which a lease is given. The person bidding the lowest number of years secures the property. In this way 150 of the catalogue numbers were knocked down to interested parties, the remaining parcels being bought in by the city.

Villa in Nuremberg. —Th. Eyrich, Architect.

Building Notes.

The "Geraldine," the eight-story building which is being erected on, 16th street, east of 5th avenue, for Mary A. Lyddy, from plans by Alfred Zucker, is now up to the roof. The Guastavino arches are noticeable in the present unplastered condition of the building, which is already being offered to lease by Coudert Bros., who are the agents for the owner. The terra cotta work in the front of the building is very creditable. The "Geraldine" is to be ready for occupation in January.

Almost within a stone's throw is the seven-story building being erected at No. 114 5th avenue, for Wm. Ziegler, of Brooklyn. The front is classic, and no one interested in building stone can fail to admire the warm tint of the red sandstone used in the front, which is up to the third story. It forms a strong contrast to the light brick and stone in the *Judge* Building adjoining. Carlin & Co. are the masons, and J. Lee's Sons, the carpenters.

The "Tenney Company" is erecting a substantial structure to be used for a very different purpose at No. 915 Broadway, adjoining Park & Tilford's. This company has been successful in the manufacture of candies and confections, and to this purpose they propose to utilize the entire building. It is being erected from plans by E. H. Kendall for Margaret H. Schieffelin, who leases it to the company. It is six stories high, and the main feature of the front is the recessed balcony on the second story. The announcement on the building that it is to be ready "November 1st," like a similar announcement on the other buildings, anticipates too much. Contractors were considerably delayed by the summer strikes, and the Tenney Company will be fortunate if they are installed in their handsome quarters in time for the Xmas trade.

When R. H. Robertson received an order to draw plans for a ten-story office building on the northeast corner of Broadway and 18th street he had a knotty problem before him similar to that which Francis H. Kimball so successfully overcame with the Corbin Building on John street and Broadway. The former has a frontage of 24.1 on Broadway, and a rear width of about 47.8, the lot being less than full depth. The John street corner has a frontage of 20 feet on Broadway, with a rear width of 33.6, the average depth of the lot being just a trifle over 100 feet.

The string courses, medallions, festoons and other decorative work in the five upper floors of the building on the northwest corner of Broadway and 20th street, are much admired by passers by. They show to what perfection the manufacture of terra cotta is being carried, and the delicacy and finish of the designs and moulds from which it is made. It is in light brown color. The balconies on the fourth floor relieve the general design and a peculiar effect is produced by the old brick in the northerly extreme of the second floor on the Broadway side, which is worked in to blend with the stone. The building is eight stories high, with marble on the two first floors and polished columns at the several entrances on the first floor. It is owned by G. H. Warren, of No. 520 5th avenue, and has been erected from plans by McKim, Mead & White. T. J. Keveney & Co. announce that they will occupy the upper part of the building.

The Fifth Avenue Theatre is progressing very rapidly now. It is near the roof, and the 28th street front gives evidence of being attractive. The plastic-work in light terra cotta, which corresponds with the brick in color, is quite effective. The construction of this building was much delayed at the beginning owing to the character of part of the ground as well as to negotiations for adjoining property wanted by the Gilsey estate. When the first difficulty had been overcome and the second abandoned owing to the absurdly high price demanded by the adjoining property-owner, the work of construction was proceeded with and the Fifth Avenue will be opened to the public early in 1892.

The "Sevillia," the euphonious appellation given by Messrs. Hubert, Pirsson and Hoddick to their twelve-story apartment house on 58th street, near 6th avenue, is now up to the eighth floor. The most interesting feature noticed during its progress has been the iron construction, which is said to be of remarkable strength and somewhat on the principle of construction used in the Eiffel Tower. The columns are of wrought-iron and are concealed in the fire-proof partitions. A photograph of the skeleton iron-work, placed in position, which is now in the office of the architects, possesses considerable interest for engineers and others.

Here and There on the West Side.

A prominent down-town broker is authority for the statement that every lot between Central Park West and Columbus avenue, from 67th to 98th street, is restricted to private dwellings, with the exception of two lots upon a street that is already largely built up with flat houses. This is as it should be, and it is to be hoped that other owners on the West Side will take steps looking to the restriction of the lots on their own blocks. Only by this method can the designs of the blackmailing flat and stable builder be frustrated and perfect privacy secured. Death or some other accident may remove the present owners, whose intentions towards their neighbors are fair enough, and vacant lots may in this way pass into the hands of holders whose only object is to secure the highest price they can. Where property is intelligently restricted, nothing can take from adjoining owners the benefits which they derive from knowing that only dwelling houses can be built on their neighbors' lots. Beyond this nothing is secure no matter how plausible and apparently sincere. West siders should by this time have been educated to the knowledge that no promise of restriction amounts to anything until the papers have been signed and recorded. Numerous instances might be quoted where these promises have been made in good faith and then broken at the first temptation to sell at a high price. The owners between Central Park West and Columbus avenue have learnt a lesson from their exciting experience with blackmailers during the last couple of years, and they have taken pains to secure themselves against all further trouble in the same direction. Would it not be a good idea for other property-owners to learn from this experience and take active steps *now?* It is small satisfaction to expose the offender and attempt to ostracise him socially, especially if he has successfully mulcted you.

By the way they have a very elaborate and decided way of ostracizing a man on the West Side. It is related of one builder who several times gave adjoining property-owners trouble that he went into a barber's shop on the West Side to get shaved, and the proprietor refused to allow him to be served in the shop. When the builder remonstrated the barber replied that his other customers had given him warning that they would stop coming to the shop if they ascertained that the offending builder continued to be shaved there. The builder went to another shop. This way of boycotting a man may be very effective as a punishment; but it would be very much wiser and many times more profitable to prevent by restriction the evil that it is impossible to cure by persecution.

The West Side elevated structure about 125th street, and particularly just above that street, is particularly troublesome to residents of 8th avenue. In addition to the noise made by the passing of a train there is a rattle of the structure itself that is almost deafening, and persons in the stores and flats along the avenue generally find it necessary to cease conversation or to raise their voices to an uncomfortable pitch. It cannot be that the structure itself is defective for it is at one of the most elevated points of the road, and when it was built the railroad company were careful to select a bridge company who are noted for the solidity of their work. The fault probably lies in some of the numerous cross pieces which while serving their purpose of bracing the structure do not fit exactly in their places and so make considerable rattle when trains pass above them.

The new station on the elevated road at 66th street and Columbus avenue is rapidly nearing completion. There is a large force of workingmen employed, and already the plank floors for the station have been laid and the supports for the roof of the station-room have been erected. Property-owners in the vicinity view with more than ordinary pleasure the building of this station, for it was first promised them two or three years ago, and they had got to believe that it would never be built. Now that it is being actually constructed, they are awaiting with a good deal of anxiety the day when it will be opened for traffic. In this connection an officer of the company said: "We are pushing the work as fast as we can, and it is safe to say that you can stop off there on Thanksgiving Day if you choose." The success of the property-owners at 66th street has led other owners along the avenue to hope that further stations will be built. This is not likely. The section most in need of a station just now is at 87th or 88th street, but Col. Hain some time ago told a reporter of this paper that the grade at that point was so steep that it was out of the question to build a station there, and he said the management of the company had never seriously contemplated doing so.

Have you read the second number of THE ARCHITECTURAL RECORD *yet? Nobody interested in good building should be without it. Articles appear in this issue from the pens of such well-known writers on architecture as Prof. A. D. F. Hamlin, Barr Ferree and Montgomery Schuyler; the first of whom points out the "Difficulties of Modern Architecture;" the second discusses "What is Architecture?" and the third continues his critical account of the "Romanesque Revival in America." A paper by William J. Fryer, Jr., on "Skeleton Construction," others by Harry W. Desmond and Herbert D. Croly; a second part of Prof. Atchison's lecture on "Byzantine Architecture," and the regular departments complete a very interesting number. The magazine is, as usual, profusely illustrated, and in matter and appearance is fully equal to the first number. The publisher takes pleasure in announcing that the issues immediately following this one will be of unusual interest to architects and of great value to the general reader. Among the contributors will be Prof. E. A. Freeman, the English historian, G. Lindenthal, L. De Coppet Berg, Prof. Kerr and other authorities equally high.*

Port Morris Improvements.

Commissioner Heintz has been making praiseworthy efforts to improve the streets, lay sewers and otherwise advance the interests of property-owners and residents at Port Morris.

West of the Boulevard, between 134th and 135th streets, the section is already sewered, curbed, flagged and guttered, and the Commissioner is now endeavoring to push forward the work of sewering the section for three or four blocks further north. Surveys and sewerage plans have been made for the property south of 138th street and east of the Southern Boulevard, and the Board of Aldermen has passed resolutions to curb, flag and gutter a good part of this property. The largest holders of real estate in this vicinity are the Port Morris Land and Improvement Company, who own upwards of one thousand lots at Port Morris. They have made a large number of improvements, and have opened a number of streets on their own account, with city authority, instead of waiting for the usual long and tedious street-opening proceedings.

Port Morris is becoming a small centre for piano manufacturers. F. C. Decker has his factory on 135th street, while Newby & Evans have their place on 136th street, both being near the Southern Boulevard. Two other piano factories are to be built, one on the southeast corner of Cypress avenue and 134th street, and the other at the intersection of the Boulevard and 134th street.

The De La Vergne Refrigerating Machine Company have the largest place at Port Morris. It is situated at the foot of East 138th street, and the company has spent hundreds of thousands of dollars in improvements.

Port Morris connects with the South and West by the "Maryland," which conveys goods by water to the various railroad depots on the New Jersey shore. The New Haven Road gives it connections with New England, and the Port Morris branch of the Harlem Road gives it access to the New York Central Road, and thence to the West and North.

The principal thoroughfare at Port Morris is 138th street. It is destined to be the first great cross-town street of the 23d Ward. The Mott Haven depot has been the main cause of this. The street is gradually being covered with business and residence buildings.

The largest builders at Port Morris are the Cotter Bros., who have erected about fifty flats in the locality.

A Railway Route Little Known.

Editor RECORD AND GUIDE:

Will you please inform me and many North New Yorkers the Eastern route of the Suburban Rapid Transit Road north of the Bronx River—the City line.

AN OLD SUBSCRIBER.

The Suburban Rapid Transit Road does not go beyond the Bronx River. It stops there. That is to say, the eastern branch of the Road, which is not yet built, ends at the Bronx River, as now laid out on the plan-map of the company. At that point "The East Side & Mount Vernon Railway" is to join the proposed branch of the Suburban Road. The E. S. & M. V. R. R. has not yet been commenced. It was incorporated under the Rapid Transit Act of 1875, by Commissioners appointed by the Supervisors of Westchester County in 1880. Its route begins at the centre of the Bronx River, at the end of the contemplated easterly route of the Suburban Rapid Transit Company, runs northerly and parallel to the Harlem Railroad for about a mile, and then deflects to the east and runs parallel to the New York, New Haven & Hartford Railway about a mile south thereof, to and through Mount Vernon, and then connects with that railway. The delays caused by the passage of the New Parks Bill have prevented the construction of this line, and its rights have been extended by the Legislature until 1895. Under the recent decision of the Court of Appeals, the right to construct the road through Bronx Park is affirmed, and the projectors of the road anticipate early progress. At the office of the Manhattan Elevated Railway, which controls the Suburban Road, our reporter ascertained that the date of the construction of the eastern branch of the Suburban has not been decided upon. Without its completion, the E. S. & M. V. R. R. would be useless as a means of entrance into New York City, though it would be of local service.

Newark News.

The following are the latest plans filed with the Superintendent of Buildings: Anna E. Botticher, two 3-sty brk dwgs, 17½x39, 33 and 35 3d av; Julia Clark, 3-sty fr store and dwg, 24x59, cor Broad and Miller sts; D. J. Edwards, 2½-sty fr dwg, 21x28, 232 South 7th st; S. D. Lines, 3-sty fr dwg, 23x58, 13 Miller st; Newark Lumber Co., 3-sty fr storage of lumber, 50x97, 414 Thomas st; Oscar Milford, two 3-sty fr dwgs, 42x46½, 49 and 51 Barclay st; Elizabeth Ziehr, 2½-sty fr dwgs, 30x48, 217 Clifton av; E. Everetz, 1½-sty fr stable, 16x16, 22 and 24 North 11th st; W. L. Rhoads, 2-story brk dwg, 25x35, 570 Summer av; Caroline Dritze, 2 sty fr dwg extension 14x14, 35 Lilli st; August H. Linnemann, 2-sty fr dwg, extension 12x22, 14 Nevada st; Isbell-Porter Co., 3-sty brk machine shop, 65x102, 36 and 38 Bridge st; Crescent Watch Co., 2-sty fr dwg, 36x51, 13th st, near 5th st; John M. Williams, 2-sty fr dwg, 20x40, 244 Aqueduct st; Isabella Williams, 2-sty fr dwg, 20x28, 102 Milford av; A. Schaaf, factory, 30x84, 70 Jackson st; P. Bessman, 3-sty fr store and dwg, 25x45, 54 Jones st; Ellen Moneghan, 3-sty fr store and dwg, 25x54, n e cor Van Buren and Clover; O. H. Higgins, 3-sty fr store and dwg, 25x55, Orange and Hecker sts; Antonio Megaro, 3-sty fr store and dwg, 32x46, 7th av and Garside st; Weiss Albert, 3-sty fr store and dwg, 22x40, 219 Court st; F. H. Smith, Jr., two 2-sty fr dwgs, 14x26, extension 12x20, Wellburton pl; F. H. Smith, Jr., 3-sty fr dwg, 16x32, extension 12x16, 39 Wakeman av; F. H. Smith, Jr., 2½-sty fr dwg, 20x30, extension 16x16, 438 Summer av; Henry Lang, three 3-sty brk dwgs, 54x30, 14 and 16 Arch st; Mrs. Eliza Freund, 3-sty fr dwg, 26x38, extension 17x17, 69 Avon av; Patrick McGinty, 2-sty fr dwg, 20x40, 368 Walnut st; Teresa Kargl, 2-sty fr dwg, 20x34, 49 Grafton av; Kilian Baumgardner, 3 sty fr dwg, 22x40, 20 Brill st; H. T. Brumley, 2-sty brk dwg, extension 17x18, 172 Roseville av; J. M. Quinby, 4-sty brk carriage factory, 58x75, extension 50x75, 27 to 37 Division st; W. S. Brown, 2-sty fr dwg, extension 10x27, 123 Adams st; V. J. Hedden, 3-sty brk dwg, 25x60, 424 Ogden st; H. J. Schaedle, 2-sty fr stable, 18x16, rear, South Orange av and Fairmount av; Electric Cutlery Co., 1-sty brk forge house extension, 25x34, 4th and Dickerson sts; Electric Cutlery Co., 1-sty fr factory, 20x48, 4th and Dickerson sts; Jos. Mercy, 2-sty fr stable, 20x30, 128 3d st; Robt. S. Gould, 3-sty fr flats, 21x40, 65 New York av; Wm. H. Ford, 1-sty fr shop, 18x60, 378 Central av; F. S. Currier, 3-sty fr dwg, 24x35, cor Roseville av and Warren st; W. L. Rhoads, 2-sty brk dwg, 25x35, 570 Summer av; N. Spinnelli, 1-sty fr dwg, 22x22, extension 16x19.9 14th av; Julius Muller, 3-sty fr dwg, 25x32, 96 Barclay st; Schaefry & Farley, 2-sty fr office, 10x35, 18 Polk st; U. Eberhardt, 4-sty brk factory, 40x100, 97 N. J. R. R. av; Rocco Martoccio, 3-sty fr dwg, 25x50, 193 Broome st; P. B. Taylor, 2½-sty fr dwg, 17x14, 58 9th av; C. A. Jajard, 3-sty fr dwg, 20x30, 443 Summer av; T. J. Lintott, 2-sty fr dwg, 22x30, Washington av; Chas. Ullrich, 4-sty fr dwg and store, 25x65, extension 16x17, 73 Springfield av; D. J. Edwards, 2½-sty fr dwg, 21x28, extension 16x14, 232 South 7th st; J. R. Theberath, 2½-sty fr extension, 21x20, 262 South 7th st; R. M. Decker, 3-sty fr dwg, 25x58, 13 Miller st; R. P. Conlon, 3-sty fr dwg, 30x38, 35 James st; Mrs. Ashden, 2-sty fr extension, 12x11, 229 North 7th st; Killian Vogel, 2-sty fr shop, 30x45, 293 Bergen st; R. B. Sutphen, two 2½-sty fr dwgs, 32x30, 290 and 290½ South 9th st; John P. Wakeman, two 2½-sty fr dwgs, 21x30, 205 and 211 Mt. Prospect av; S. Beck, 3-sty fr dwg, 26x56, extension 15x17, 13 Rutgers st; R. J. Edwards, 2-sty fr dwg, 13x13, 443 South 17th st.; Mrs. H. A. Boylan, two 2-sty fr dwell'gs, 15x28, 128 and 130 Chester av; F. W. Helbig, four 3-sty brk dwell'gs, 50x60, 115-119 Roseville av; Reuben Abeles, 2-sty fr stable, 59x16, 186 and 188 Bruce st; Geo. Thornley, 2½-sty fr dwell'g, 22x40, 89 South 8th st; Christina Hilfer, 3-sty fr dwell'g, 22x52, 150 Littleton av; John Tittel, 1-sty fr shop, 16x30, 76 Delancy st; Wm. S. Righter, four 3-sty brk dwell'gs, 79x36, 1114-1118 Broad st; W. W. Collyer, 2-sty fr shop, 20x17, 97 9th av; Wm. Beisler, 3-sty fr store and dwg, 22x40, 146 Badger av; J. J. Henricks, 2-sty fr dwell'g, 22x36, 648 Bergen st; Chas. W. Menk, 2-sty brk storehouse, 18x20, rear 106 Market st; Margaret Wuesthoff, 2-sty fr extension, 20x19, 88 Ferry st; Leopold Lang, 2-sty brk store, 28x48, 226 Springfield av; Health Bread Co., 2-sty brk bakery, 38x75, 34 and 36 Drift st; Hellen Camm, two 2-sty fr dwgs, 37x53, 306 South 9th st; Christian Gillen, 2½-sty fr dwg, 21x32, 95 South 8th st; Henry Warner, 1-sty fr store, 26x50, 184 8th av; E. E. Bowdren, 2-sty brk dwell'g, 23x53, 98 Orange st; J. L. Pheiffer, 2½-sty fr dwg, 22x46, North 6th st; Peter Hasinger, 2-sty brk extension, 13x28, 152 Springfield av; Alice E. Patch, 2-sty fr dwg, 25x35, 84 South 10th st; M. J. Caffrey, 2-sty fr dwg, 21x45, South 9th st; trustees of the Tabernacle S. S., 1-sty fr church, 52x64, Lafayette st; H. Jelinck, 2½-sty fr dwg, 22x50, 444 Bergen st; C. M. Ryman, 2½-sty fr dwg, 19x31, 192 North 1st st; East Jersey Water Co., 1-sty brk South Orange Avenue Reservoir, 40x19, South Orange av; Michael Polito, 3-sty fr dwg, 25x25, O'Connell st.

Important to Property-Holders.

BOARD OF ASSESSORS.

OFFICE OF THE BOARD OF ASSESSORS,
NO. 27 CHAMBERS STREET,
NEW YORK, Nov. 9, 1891.

Notice is given to the owner or owners, of all houses and lots, improved or unimproved lands affected thereby, that the following assessments have been completed and are lodged in the office of the Board of Assessors for examination by all persons interested, viz.:

No 1.—Sewer in 52d st, bet Hudson River and 11th av.

No. 2.—Paving 147th st, from Amsterdam av to St. Nicholas av, with granite blocks and laying crosswalks.

No. 3.—Regulating, grading, curbing and flagging 99th st, from 3d to Park av.

No. 4.—Sewer in 91st st, bet 10th av and summit east.

No. 5.—Sewer in 101st st, bet Park and Madison avs.

No. 6.—Laying crosswalks across 117th st, at the easterly and westerly sides of Lexington av.

No. 7.—Paving 94th st, from 1st to 2d av, with granite blocks.

No. 8.—Paving 98th st, from 8th to 9th av, with granite blocks.

[The limits embraced by such assessments include all the several houses and lots of ground, vacant lots, pieces or parcels of land situated on—

No. 1.—Both sides of 52d st, from 11th av to Hudson River, and both sides of 12th av, from 52d to 53d st.

No. 2.—Both sides of 147th st, from Amsterdam av to Av St. Nicholas, and to the extent of half the block at the intersecting avs.

No. 3.—Both sides of 99th st, from 3d to Park av.

No. 4.—Both sides of 91st st, from Columbus to Amsterdam av.

No. 5.—Both sides of 101st st, from Park to Madison av, and block bounded by 100th and 101st sts, Park and Madison avs.

No. 6.—To the extent of half the block from the easterly and westerly sides of 117th st and Lexington av.

No. 7.—Both sides of 94th st, from 1st to 2d av, and to the extent of half the block at the intersecting avs.

No. 8.—Both sides of 98th st, from 8th to 9th av, and to the extent of half the block at the intersecting avs.]

All persons whose interests are affected by the above-named assessments, and who are opposed to the same, or either of them, are requested to present their objections in writing to the Chairman of the Board of Assessors at their office, No. 27 Chambers street, within thirty days from the date of this notice.

The above-described lists will be transmitted, as provided by law, to the Board of Revision and Correction of Assessments for confirmation on the 10th day of December, 1891.

In the matter of the application of the Board of Street Opening and Improvement of the City of New York, for and on behalf of the Mayor, Aldermen and Commonalty, relative to acquiring title, wherever the same has not been heretofore acquired, to East 144th street (although not yet named by proper authority), extending from River to St. Ann's avenue, in the 23d Ward, as the same has been heretofore laid out and designated as a first-class street or road by the Department of Public Parks. Pursuant to the statutes in such cases made and provided, notice is given that an application will be made to the Supreme Court of the State of New York, at a special term of said court, to be held at chambers thereof in the County Court-house, in the City of New York, on Friday, the 18th day of December, 1891, at the opening of court on that day, or as soon thereafter as counsel can be heard thereon, for the appointment of Commissioners of Estimate and Assessment in the above-entitled matter. The nature and extent of the improvement hereby intended is the acquisition of title in the name and on behalf of the Mayor, etc., for the use of the public, to all the lands and premises, with the buildings thereon and the appurtenances thereto belonging, required for the opening of said street.

Contractors' Notes.

Bids or estimates will be received at the Department of Public Works, No. 31 Chambers street, until 12 o'clock M., on Thursday, November 19, 1891: For alteration and improvement to sewers in 18th street, between

North River and 10th avenue, connecting with outlet sewer built by Department of Docks. For regulating and paving with asphalt pavement, on concrete foundation, the roadway of 114th street, between Manhattan and Columbus avenues. For regulating and paving with asphalt pavement, on concrete foundation, the roadway of 117th street, from 8th to Columbus avenue. For regulating and paving with asphalt pavement, on concrete foundation, the roadway of 122d street, between Manhattan and Columbus avenues. For regulating and paving with granite block pavement, with concrete foundation, the carriageway of 124th street, from Mount Morris to Lenox avenue. For alteration and improvement to sewer in 95th street, between 1st and 3d avenues, and in 2d avenue, east and west sides, between 95th and 96th streets, and curve in 2d avenue, south of 95th street.

THE WEST SIDE INDEX.

All persons interested in West Side real estate should possess an Index of Ten Years' Conveyances affecting property between the north side of 59th and south side of 125th streets, from west side 8th avenue to Hudson River. This Index is published by THE RECORD AND GUIDE, *and the period covered is the ten years prior to June 30th, 1884, to which has been added a list of the conveyances up to January 1st, 1885. Every transfer of real estate in that section, made between those years, is recorded in the Index, with a description of the property, the price paid for it, the liber and page in which the conveyances are recorded in the Register's Office, and the name of the seller and the purchaser. The volume is of the utmost value to conveyancers, lawyers, real estate brokers, agents and dealers in real estate generally, and we will supply the Index to our readers, if ordered before January 1st next, at the reduced price of $5.*

Real Estate Department.

A review of the market during the past week fails to disclose any marked improvement in either the number or character of the sales consummated. The conditions generally prevailing are about the same as those under which the market has been laboring for some time—high prices from which owners practically refuse to make any concessions and a spirit of indifference on the part of buyers. In some quarters it is true the criticism that has been leveled at prices has had an effect, and present holders are more reasonable in their demands. But the concessions already made are of the character that are forced by the extreme quiet prevailing, and they are not sufficiently large to induce a revival of activity. Where owners have shown an intention of receding from their former positions, they have done so with so much apparent reluctance that the concessions, such as they are, have done little good. The truth of the matter is that very few of the advantages desired and demanded by buyers have been granted, and these only in sections of the city where there was no other course open to owners who wished to dispose of their holdings. To those not in touch with the peculiar conditions governing the real estate world it must seem strange that owners refuse to learn anything from the oppressive stagnation that has prevailed now for a year or more. Seemingly it does little good to tell them the truth about the market, and one is almost discouraged in the task. This peculiar position is not very hard to explain. The real estate market has been on a rise for years now; prices have been going up with scarcely an interruption, and holders have believed, many of them still do believe, that they will still keep on going up, and there are men and newspapers enough who will tell them this for all time. They have become so used to this old song that they will not listen to or give credit to any other—naturally they do not care to do so, but they must recognize the truth in the end if they do not now. One very large factor in whatever activity there has been, and to which too little attention has been paid, is the large amount of trading that has been going on. Owners have been deceiving themselves and others into the belief that exchanges were straight out sales, and they have found only too many who have consented to believe them. They have frequently concealed from the public during the last year the fact that trades have been made giving out only one part of the sale and withholding the rest. When questioned as to whether certain transactions were trades, they have strenuously denied the fact, and they have succeeded in their deceptions until the deeds have been recorded and the exchange has become apparent to all. But although the fact becomes known eventually (provided both the properties are located in the city), it is not until the harm of falsely bolstering up the market has been done. Some of these contracts are made for ninety days and the sale of one of the parcels is concealed from the public for as much of that time as possible. It is not hard to see the harm that this practice does in deluding people into the belief that new buyers are taking up with real property as an investment and that there is really considerable activity. The fact that trading is going on to the extent it is now is in itself one of the most convincing signs that everything is not as it should be. It shows conclusively the desire of owners to dispose of their holdings, and it shows, too, that they can find no cash buyers, at least at their figures. And so they go to work and put high figures on their property, and they meet some other holder who has put high figures on his parcel, and they exchange the two, and each deceives himself into the belief that he has sold out at the high price that he has steadily demanded. Another fact that is not so apparent to outsiders is that these traders often accept in exchange property that they do not want and cannot handle, and they have then to commence other transactions looking to further trades.

THE AUCTION MARKET.

There is absolutely nothing new to record about the auction market during the past week. It has not differed materially from the auction market of the whole fall season. The offerings have been few and uninteresting and many of them, the majority in fact, have been of a legal character necessitated by orders of the courts. This state of affairs is due to the lack of "snap," and energy which has characterized the doings in the auction room during the whole season. There has hardly been a really active competition for Manhattan Island property since the season opened, which fact is due largely to the well-founded suspicions of bidders, that parcels in competition are often protected. In nearly every case where an important piece of property was offered there has been the most determined bidding on the part of the representatives of the owners, who, not satisfied with a fair price, tried to force buyers up to exorbitant figures. Seeing this, bona fida bidders have dropped out of the competition, and owners have bought their offerings in or withdrawn them from sale. This practice has been so open and so generally well known that nearly every one conversant with the market has been put upon guard, and it is only with the greatest caution that they will bid at these auction sales. And so this week the few voluntary offerings (they were not particularly inviting to be sure) met with a very indifferent reception, and many of them were either bought in or withdrawn, because no bids were offered. The two or three parcels voluntarily offered and which were sold are very low-priced properties and generally uninteresting. There have been no suburban or large lot sales, and the legal sales with one exception have been of very ordinary character, so that a review of the market is anything but cheerful. The remedy, of course, lies largely with the owners themselves. As soon as a sale advertised as "peremptory" is really so, as soon as bidders are assured that they are not competing against the owner or his representatives, just so soon will there be some improvement in the Auction Room transactions. As matters stand now a buyer is never sure that the statements on the bills as to "absolute sale without reserve" and all the rest of it means anything at all or not, and until this feeling is changed to one of greater confidence auctioneers can hope for but little better success in their public auction sales.

The notable sale of the week in the Auction Room was that effected by Auctioneer Bryan L. Kennelly, on Friday, of the buildings, lots and plant of the Knickerbocker Brewing Company. The sale was under foreclosure to satisfy mortgages of $700,000 with interest, and the bids were made above that figure. The action was brought by Henry W. Poor, and the sale was under direction of David McClure, by order of the Supreme Court. Naturally the sale attracted a large contingent of the brewing interest and in the crowd which faced the auctioneer, besides the regular attendants at the Exchange, were George Ehret, George Ringler, Jacob Ruppert, James Everard and Randolph Guggenheimer, the lawyer who has negotiated several sales of breweries to syndicates. The property included the southeast corner of 8th avenue and 18th street, besides property on 17th and 18th streets, just east of 8th avenue, and the buildings sold, including brewery, tenements, stables, etc., numbered twenty-three. These buildings, the land and the plant were sold together, practically prohibiting competition, and the property was knocked down to the plaintiff in the action, Mr. Poor, on his first bid of $10,000 over the mortgages of $700,000 and interest.

The reception accorded parcels previously offered has rather discouraged other owners from coming into the market, and, as a consequence, next week's list of announcements is a very poor one. There are very few sales of any kind and remarkably few at public auction, and even these are of a most ordinary character. At the same time if the parcels which are offered are only sold it will do much to invigorate the auction market, and just now it is sadly in need of some tonic. The most interesting parcel to be offered next week is probably the leasehold six-story building Nos. 37 to 43 Greene street, near Grand street, which is to be sold in foreclosure proceedings. The public auction announcements do not amount to anything.

On Tuesday, Nov. 17th, Adrian H. Muller & Son will sell in foreclosure, by order of Thomas F. Gilroy, Jr., Referee, an undivided one-half interest in the desirable leasehold property, Nos. 37, 39, 41 and 43 Greene street.

On Tuesday, Nov 17th, Richard V. Harnett & Co. will sell the four-story brown stone dwelling, No. 185 Lenox avenue; the five-story brick and brown stone flat on the southeast corner of Lexington avenue and 106th street; the five-story brick and brown stone flat, No. 1677 Lexington avenue; and the two-story brick dwelling, No. 696 East 144th street.

On Wednesday, Nov. 18th, Richard V. Harnett & Co. will sell the three-story brown stone dwelling, No. 327 East 57th street.

On Thursday, Nov. 19th, Richard V. Harnett & Co. will sell Nos. 240 and 242 Main street, Yonkers, with one two-story brick and one two-story frame dwellings thereon.

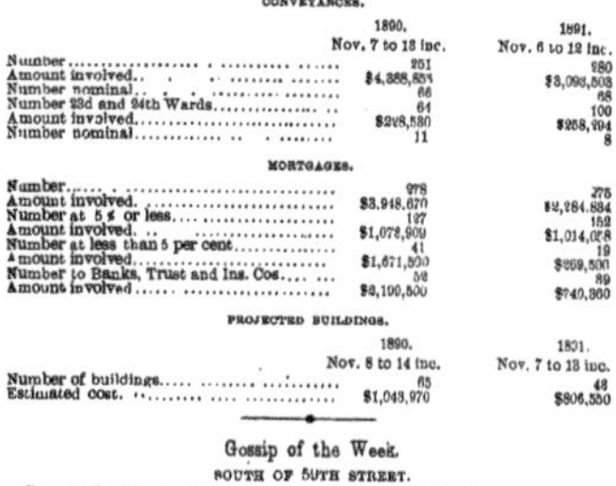

CONVEYANCES.

	1890. Nov. 7 to 13 inc.	1891. Nov. 6 to 12 inc.
Number	251	280
Amount involved	$4,388,853	$3,093,503
Number nominal	66	68
Number 23d and 24th Wards	64	100
Amount involved	$228,580	$258,294
Number nominal	11	8

MORTGAGES.

	1890.	1891.
Number	278	275
Amount involved	$3,948,670	$2,284,834
Number at 5 % or less	127	152
Amount involved	$1,078,909	$1,014,058
Number at less than 5 per cent	41	19
Amount involved	$1,671,500	$259,500
Number to Banks, Trust and Ins. Cos	52	89
Amount involved	$2,100,500	$740,360

PROJECTED BUILDINGS.

	1890. Nov. 8 to 14 inc.	1891. Nov. 7 to 13 inc.
Number of buildings	65	48
Estimated cost	$1,043,970	$806,550

Gossip of the Week.

SOUTH OF 59TH STREET.

Geo. R. Read has sold to a client, for investment, the two six-story and basement brick, iron and terra cotta stores and lofts, Nos. 128 and 130 Bleecker street, each 25x100, for $175,000.

J. R. Foley & Son have sold the six-story brick, iron and stone store and loft building, Nos. 152 to 158 Wooster street, 75x90x100, to S. K. Hubbard, president of a large manufacturing company in Chicago, for $140,000.

Julius Friend has sold for Hyman Sylvester to Mrs. Flora Mintzer No. 147 Wooster street, a four-story stone front building, 25x100, on private terms.

Ascher Weinstein has sold to Louis Stern, of Stern Bros., No. 50 West 28th street, a five-story brick store and hotel, 25x75x98.9, on private terms. Brokers, L J. Phillips & Co.

B. Flanagan & Son have sold for Ellen Eagen No. 121 West 27th street, a three-story brown stone dwelling, 16 8x50x100, for $11,500.

Robert Auld & Co. have sold for Sherwood Aldrich to Calvin S. Doig No. 409 West 53d street, a five-story apartment house, on private terms.

B. Flanagan & Son have sold for Elizabeth V. Farrel and Theresa J. Coughlan No. 225 West 29th street, a four-story brick building on front and three-story brick building on rear, lot 23.5x100, on private terms.

Goodmann & Stern have sold for A. Simon to J. Heilbrun No. 115 Avenue C for $13,000.

Lewis S. Samuel wishes the report that he has sold the southeast corner of 5th avenue and 35th street (old Christ Church), which found some circulation this week, denied.

E. H. Ludlow & Co. have sold for Wm. Salomon to John P. Emmet No. 108 East 40th street, a three-story brick dwelling, on lot 25x98.9, on private terms.

NORTH OF 59TH STREET.

Adler & Herrman have purchased the three five-story flats and stores at Nos. 848 to 852 Columbus avenue, near 102d street, 25x66x75 each, for a total of $78,000. The property purchased by them and Heilner & Wolf at auction recently, No. 1636 3d avenue, for $24,900, has been sold by them to J. Schwartz for $27,000. They were offered $26,000 for this parcel directly after the sale on 'Change.

Seton & Wissmann have sold for William Douglass to Jas, B. Dunnell the four-story, high stoop, brick dwelling, No. 56 West 82d street, on private terms.

F. Zittel has sold No. 27 East 61st street, a dwelling, 15x50x100, to a Mrs. Hunter for $22,125; for Jos. L. Meyers to Oppenheimer & Metzger the lot on the north side of 70th street, 200 feet east of Columbus avenue; and for A. F. Lascelles to the same buyers the lot adjoining the above on the east, on private terms.

Slawson & Hobbs have sold for J. C. Umberfield to A. H. Hatch No. 43 West 75th street, a four-story brownstone dwelling, 22x60, and dining-room extension x102.2, for about $51,000.

George Ruddell has sold his remaining four-story brown stone dwelling, 20x55 and extension x100.5, No. 67 West 70th street, to Dr. Simon Baruch for about $38,000. Brokers, L. J. Phillips & Co.

James Brown has sold to H. J. Potowsky, the cloak manufacturer, No. 23 West 90th street, a three-story brown stone dwelling, 18.6x55 and extension x102.2, for $26,500.

J. W. Stevens has sold for Walden P. Anderson to W. Prince Clagett, of the Produce Exchange, No. 144 West 93d street, a four-story brown stone dwelling, 20x55 and extension x102.2, on private terms.

No. 21 West 74th street, reported sold last week, was purchased by Oscar R. Meyer.

Max Simon has sold for Adler & Herman the northeast corner of Columbus avenue and 98th street, a five-story brick flat and store, 25x71x74, for $37,000. The purchaser is M. H. Levy.

G. D. Clark has sold No. 259 West 131st street, a three-story brown stone dwelling, 16.8x50x99.11, to Mrs. Annie E. Valentine for $14,000.

F. A. Condit has sold for Francis M. Wilmurt, of Pelham Manor, to Mrs Lilian Le Cato No. 512 West 89th street, a four-story 20-foot dwelling, for $32,000. Mr. Wilmurt takes in part exchange a place at Llewellyn Park, N. J.

L. J. Phillips & Co. have sold, through their 23d Ward office, the three-story brick dwelling, north side 135th street, about 125 feet east of St. Ann's avenue, for Hall & Entwistle to a Mrs Fox for $7,000; and the two-story frame dwelling on the north side of 159th street, 85 feet west of Elton avenue, for Edmund Coffin, executor, to Edw. Phelps for $3,000.

T. L. Reynolds & Co. have sold for Mrs. Adams to C. S. Crossman, No. 2009 7th avenue, a three-story limestone front 18-foot dwelling, for $22,500.

Ellen Barlow has sold one of the three-story dwellings on the south side of 104th street, between the Boulevard and West End avenue.

Edward Cabot Wilde has sold for Dr. Simon Baruch, who, this week, purchased a house on the West Side, to D. Sackett Moore No. 47 East 60th street, a four-story brown stone dwelling, for $28,000.

Smyth & Ryan have sold No. 553 Manhattan avenue, southwest corner of 123d street, to Mrs. Braham for $17,000. It is a three-story brown stone front dwelling, on lot 18.5x74. This house was announced to be sold at auction on Tuesday, but the auctioneers disposed of it previous to that day at private sale.

C. H. McLaughlin has sold No. 1321 Avenue A for $23,000.

Brooklyn.

Corwith Bros. have sold the two-story frame dwelling, 20x40x100, No. 186 Russell street, to John J. Sehutta for $3,600.

T. L. Reynolds & Co. have sold No. 23 Pennsylvania avenue for $8,500, and No. 77 Monroe street for $6,500.

CONVEYANCES.

	1890. Nov. 6 to 12 inc.	1891. Nov. 5 to 11 inc.
Number	357	305
Amount involved	*$1,476,777	$1,751,048
Number nominal	91	87

MORTGAGES.

Number	301	320
Amount involved	*$2,682,635	$1,068,446
Number at 5 per cent. or less	170	176
Amount involved	*$2,342,781	$795,878

PROJECTED BUILDINGS.

	1890. Nov. 7 to 13 inc.	1891. Nov. 6 to 12 inc.
Number of buildings	145	91
Estimated cost	$674,600	$810,825

*Includes mortgage given by Manhattan Beach Improvement Company (Lim.) to the Central Trust Company of New York for $1,500,000.

Out of Town.

LLEWELLYN PARK, West Orange, N. J.—F. A. Condit has sold for Mrs. Lilian Le Cato to Francis M. Wilmurt her residence and one and a-half acres at this place for $18,000. Mr. Wilmurt gives in exchange a house in New York City.

Out Among the Builders.

If the preliminary estimates are allowed by the Board of Estimate and Apportionment the Building Department hopes to largely augment its force of inspectors. At present the fifty inspectors in the employ of the Building Bureau have more work than they can attend to, and until the force is increased criticism of the department, such as occurred at the time of the Park place disaster, is hardly fair. Chief Clerk John R. Shields says that after the 1st of January, if the estimates are passed, fifteen new inspectors will be employed, a number of them experts who will give their whole time and attention to overloaded floors. These men, however, will work under difficulties, he says, for the law does not allow an inspector to remove any partitions to see whether post and supports are rotten or not, and under the circumstances an inspector can only surmise as to the exact condition of affairs. Then, too, as Mr. Shields points out, occupants will move heavy weights around as they choose between the visits of inspectors, and as accidents will oftentimes occur between such visits, he suggests that the best way of preventing the recurrence of disasters from overloaded floors is to make it very plain to both owners and occupants that they will be severely and promptly prosecuted in case of accident. The law at present provides that a negligent owner or occupant can be prosecuted for manslaughter in case of death, and for misdemeanor where no one is seriously hurt. It is because this law is not properly enforced that manufacturers and others continue to improperly overload their floors in defiance of the law.

Lewis Z. Bach will probably improve the six lots he purchased recently on Water street, northeast corner of Corlears street, by the erection of a warehouse.

F. A. Minuth is the architect for four three-story and basement private dwellings to be erected on the north side of 68th street, 150 east of Amsterdam avenue, at a cost of about $60,000. The houses will be 18, 19 and 20x55, with extensions of 10x13 feet in size, and they will have fronts of brown stone. The interior will have a cabinet finish of hardwood, and the houses will contain all the improvements.

E. L. Bradley is the architect for two five-story brick and stone apartment houses, each 37.6x70, which G. C. Currier will build on the west side of 7th avenue, 74.11 south of 142d street, at a cost of $60,000.

Charles S. Sidney has drawn plans for two five-story brown stone and brick front flats, 25x87.6, which George Austin Smith is about to erect on the south side of 125th street, 150 feet west of Amsterdam avenue, at a cost of $38,000.

Charles Rentz has drawn plans for a five-story apartment house, 25.2x99, at No. 29 Market street, for Fay & Stacom.

Two five-story apartment houses, 19x91 and 31x91 respectively, are to be erected on the north side of 84th street, 175 feet west of 8th avenue, for David Richey. G. A. Schellenger has the plans.

The Architectural League offers numerous first and second prizes, ranging from $15 to $50, by President Russell Sturgis, Tiffany & Co., Joseph Lamb and S. P. Avery. The subject of the president's prize is to be "A Design for a Certificate for the Prizes of the Architectural League of New York." The other prizes are to be for architectural, decorative or iron-work designs. Competitors are referred to E. T. Hapgood, the secretary. The Committee on Competition and Awards comprises Messrs. W. A. Coffin, E. H. Kendall, E. K. Rossiter, Thos. Hastings and Will A. Low. Designs are to be sent in, under cipher, by December 5, 1891.

Brooklyn.

H. E. Funk has plans for four four-story double flats in Renaissance style, to be built on the corner of Linden street and Wyckoff avenue for Mr. Riebling. They will each be 25x60 in size, and have stores throughout. Mr. Levy, of 763 Myrtle avenue, intends to erect a meeting-hall, lodge and club building, 28x55, at 1021 Myrtle avenue, from plans by the same architect. It will have bowling alleys in the basement, and room space for billiards, etc.

Out of Town.

THOUSAND ISLANDS.—J. H. Oliphant, of Latham, Smith & Oliphant, of New York, is about to build a two-and-a-half-story cottage at Neh-Mahbin Island. It will be 44x48 in size, with extensive verandahs, and will have an ornate exterior. Van Campen Taylor is the architect.

WHITE PLAINS, N. Y.—Mrs. Henry S. Moore is building on the south side of Railroad avenue, near Broadway, a two-and-a-half-story Queen Anne cottage, 40x50, with music hall and stage, 18x50, to be used for private entertainments for charitable purposes. Cost, $8,000.

F. H. Norvil has the foundation laid for a three-story brick and brown stone store and flats, on north side Railroad avenue, 100 eas Lexington avenue, 26x66. Cost, $10,000.

CLOSE OF THE ARCHITECTURAL EXHIBIT.

The Exhibition of Architects' Drawings in the rooms of THE RECORD AND GUIDE, *Nos. 14 and 16 Vesey street, must be closed on Saturday, November 21st. This exhibit is one of the finest and most extensive that has ever been displayed in New York City, and those who desire to study the 300 examples of the best architectural work of the day should visit the Exhibition without delay. Admission is free.*

Special Notices.

The Burlington Blind Company, of Burlington, Vermont, claim the following points of superiority for the Baldwin Patent Inside Sliding Blind: (1) That they can be operated more easily than any other blind on the market, for when raised the weight of the blind only is lifted. (2) Any section can be lowered without moving any other section by simply pressing a lever at the side of the casing. (3) This blind is held at the desired elevation by frictional contact of its entire length against the moving strips in right hand guides. They can easily be removed to clean the windows. The New York office is at No. 90 Nassau street, and Geo. E. Read is the manager thereof.

The firm of Ware & Odell has been dissolved, and the business will be continued by William R. Ware, formerly partner in the firm. Mr. Ware has had long experience in the real estate business, having been connected with L. J. Carpenter. Consequently he is well qualified to give satisfaction to customers. His office will be the same as before, No. 451 Columbus avenue.

A real estate and insurance firm new in the business is Livingston & Judson, who are established in the Arcade of 71 Broadway. Mr. Judson is a grandson of Cyrus W. Field, and Mr Livingston is a scion of the New York family of that name, so that in beginning business they have more than usual influence behind them. Besides a general brokerage business, they are paying especial attention to the sale of lots at Ardsley Park, Woodlands Station, on the New York and Northern Railway, fifteen miles from town. This is a locality which seems to be growing in popularity for residence purposes, and is an especially suitable neighborhood for the planting of manufacturing industries.

Fine Printing of All Kinds.

There has recently been added to THE RECORD AND GUIDE newspaper plant a complete Book and Job outfit, and we are now prepared to estimate for and execute all orders. Commercial, Real Estate and Architectural Printing of a high order, promptly delivered, will be a feature of this department. A postal card addressed to THE RECORD AND GUIDE Press, No. 14 Barclay street, or Nos. 14 to 16 Vesey street, will insure the attendance of a competent representative to give estimates, etc. Orders by mail will receive the same attention as if given personally.

Strong, neat binders, especially made for THE RECORD AND GUIDE, can be obtained at this office. Those of our subscribers who wish to keep a file of the numbers in a compact form and in regular sequence, can have the binder delivered at their office on receipt of order by postal card. Price at office, $1.00, by mail, $1.19.

WANTS AND OFFERS.

(Advertisements strictly in accordance with this title will be inserted at the practically nominal rate of 10 CENTS *per line agate). In figuring for themselves advertisers may count seven words for each line, the address to be taken as one line. The object of this department is to bring buyers and sellers into communication with customers. Advertisements must be marked "Wants and Offers Column," and sent to the office of publication, Nos. 14 and 16 Vesey Street, not later than 3 P. M. Friday.)*

WANTS.

SITUATION WANTED.—By a young man, 25 years of age, in a real estate or insurance office; has highest references; willing and obliging. Address, D. T. D., care of Walter Dewsnap, 187 Broadway, New York. Nov. 7-14

OFFERS.

Dwellings and Flats.

248 WEST 77TH, opposite Collegiate Reformed Church, handsome, modern, four-story, with gas fixtures and decorated. Premises or OWNER, 20 Nassau, Room 58.

NO. 18 GRAMERCY PARK.—Handsomely decorated; fine plumbing; lot 26.9x114; price, $[illegible]; easy terms. FRANK PETTIT, 2 Wall st, Room 60.

A 72D ST. GEM, No. 308 West.—This superb house is beautifully decorated; has handsome gas fixtures; is in perfect order; ready for immediate occupancy; $38,000; a greater bargain than has been offered in months.
Nov. 14-uf. CONDIT, 1179 Broadway.

ONLY ONE LEFT, FOUR SOLD LAST MONTH—312 West 89th st., 20 feet, four stories; exceptionally well built; unexcelled location; am authorized to close this out at a bargain.
Nov. 14-uf. CONDIT, 1179 Broadway.

$650,000 FOR ONE of the choicest pieces of investment properties on Manhattan Island; exceptionally well built and very desirably located; other good property (city or country) will be entertained in part payment.
Nov. 14—uf. CONDIT, 1179 Broadway.

WANTED—A first-class, energetic man, already acquainted with the cement trade, for the sale of imported Portland cement of superior quality. Very liberal conditions would be offered to the right man. Address, S. S., RECORD AND GUIDE.

A—At reasonable prices and easy terms, three and four-story residences, with three-story extensions; all improvements. Call and examine or inquire of the owner and builder, on the premises.
S. O. WRIGHT, 128 West 121st st., open daily.
Oct. 3 uf.

OFFERS.

FOR SALE.—2443 8th av and 210 and 212 West 105th st.; commission allowed brokers. Apply at
Aug. 29-uf. Room 19, 158 Broadway.

FOR SALE.—Six new cabinet-trimmed three-story and basement brown stone private dwellings, Nos. 142-152 West 123d st.; prices reasonable and brokers commissions allowed. For further particulars apply at office of
FRED'K. M. LITTLEFIELD, 156 Broadway.
Aug. 29-uf.

Improved Property.

OFFICE OF
FREDERICK SOUTHACK,
401 BROADWAY,
offers for sale some choice pieces
of property on
LEONARD ST., between Broadway and West B'way.
FRANKLIN ST., between B'way and West B'way.
WHITE ST., between B'way and West B'way.
BROADWAY, from Barclay to 14th st.
BLEECKER ST., from B'way to South 5th av.
GREENE ST., Canal to 8th st.
WASHINGTON PLACE, B'way to Wooster.
WAVERLEY PLACE, B'way to Wooster.
APPLY AS ABOVE.
FREDERICK SOUTHACK.
Oct. 3 uf.

Vacant Lots.

FOR SALE.—A desirable lot on 99th st., with $11,000 loan. J. M. STRONG, JR., 60 Liberty st.

EASTERLY FRONT BOULEVARD, with 200 ft. on 86th st. and 264 ft. on 87th st.; one or more plots.
Nov. 7-1aw6w. OTTO ERNST, South Amboy, N. J.

CHOICE BUILDING LOTS, East and West Side; with liberal builder's loans; no brokers.
Nov. 7-14. P. O. Box 3,680.

1ST AV., near 108th st; full lot, $[illegible]
Oct. 31—1aw9w. EDWIN A. ELY, 103 Gold st.

40 CHERRY ST., between Roosevelt and Franklin sq., 32x64, vacant; $12,000; accommodating terms. EDWIN A. ELY, 103 Gold st.
Sept. 26-1aw8w.

100TH ST., between 2d and 3d avs.; ten lots cheap; all mortgage if improved.
Sept. 26-1aw8w. EDWIN A. ELY, 103 Gold st.

OFFERS.

FOUR ATTRACTIVE LOTS, 149th st., adjoining southwest corner 7th av., $3,600 each; builders' terms. EDWIN A. ELY, 103 Gold st.
Sept 26-1aw8w.

Brooklyn Real Estate for Sale.

5-STORY BROWN STONE PRIVATE HOUSE IN Brooklyn to exchange for country property free and clear. C. H. McLAUGHLIN, 198 Broadway.

Country Property.

50 TO 200 ACRES, suitable for dividing into large or small plots; forty minutes from city; convenient to depot; can be sub-divided at small expense.
W. B. TIBBITS, agent, White Plains, N. Y.
Nov. 14—1aw3w.

AT MORRIS PARK, LONG ISLAND.—Elegant plot for sub-division, fifteen acres fronting on Liberty av., directly opposite Morris Park Improvement property. H. F. SCHELLHASS, 171 Broadway.

FOR SALE.—In plots to suit; eligible building sites (commanding view of sound for miles), on North st., Greenwich, Connecticut; price reasonable; terms easy; neighborhood aristocratic and fashionable. Apply to
FRED. J. STONE, owner, 60 Broadway, N. Y.
Sept. 12-uf.

Miscellaneous.

TO LET OR TO LEASE.—Two floors of a factory, 25x98, light on all sides, 1st av and 10[illegible]th st; terms moderate. J. REEBER'S SONS,
Nov. 7 uf. 409 East 107th.

THOMAS & ECKERSON, 35 West 30th st., have a large assortment of houses for sale, from 25th st. to 133d st., ranging in price from $13,000 to $125,000, and on easy terms.
Oct. 24-1aw4w.

A PARTY ABOUT TO BUILD A FIVE-STORY factory, 50x98, in Harlem, near water-front, will lease the three upper floors and build to suit tenant. Terms very moderate. Address
May 16 u. f. OWNER, 409 E. 107th St.

PRINTING.—Book, News and Job.

RECORD AND GUIDE PRESS,

14 Barclay, and 14, 16 Vesey sts.

SALES OF THE WEEK.

The following are the sales at the Real Estate Exchange and Auction Room for the week ending November 13.

** Indicates that the property described has been bid in for plaintiff's account:*

R. V. HARNETT & CO.

Canal st, No. 495, n s, 67.6 e Renwick st, 16.11x36.4x47.6x6.3x38.6x32.1 to beginning, three-story brk building with store. Estate Jane Menck $11,525

Central Park West, Nos. 441-444, n w cor 104th st, 100.11x100, four five-story brk flats. Steers & Menke. (Amt due $27,187) 126,170

*Private lane which would be 162d st if continued, n s, 122.8 n w 3d av, runs northeast 123.8 x southeast 27.9 x southwest 123.8 x to lane, x northwest 27.9 to beginning. Bowery Savings Bank. (Amt due $7,958) 7,000

44th st, No. 132 E., s s, 83.8 e Lexington av, four-story and basement brown stone dwell'g, 16.4x83. (Bid in) .... —

*57th st, No. 49, n s, 19 w 4th av, 20x80.5, four-story stone front dwell'g. Isidor Fellheimer. (Amt due $10,694) 34,500

98th st, Nos. 141-169, n s, 100 e 10th av, 325x113.2x—x129.6, fifteen five-story brk flats. Jacob Cohn. (Amt due ——) 161,100

Madison av, No. 1673, n e cor 111th st, three-story brown stone dwell'g, 15x50x70. S. Jacobs 12,800

A. H. MULLER & SON.

Broome st, No. 172, s s, 140 w Attorney st, 20x75, three-story frame store and tenem't. Rudolph Mash 12,000

22d st, No. 149, n s, 255 e 7th av, 22.6x98.9, four-story brk dwell'g. Jos. Hartley 26,100

2d av, s w cor 36th st, two four-story brk tenements and three three story brk houses. (Bid in) .... —

SMYTH & RYAN.

Maiden lane, No. 189 } abt 50 ft east of Water
Fletcher st, No. 17 } st, 17x81.1x17x80.9, five-story brk warehouse. Elias Bach & Co. 28,650

23d st, No. 244 W., 18.9x98.9, three-story brown stone dwell'g. Jacob Hirsh 23,200

64th st, No. 173, 25x100.5, five-story brown stone flat. (Bid in) .... —

B. L. KENNELLY.

*8th av, Nos. 144 and 160 } begins 8th av, s e
18th st, Nos. 248-262 } cor 18th st, runs
18th st, Nos. 236-242 } east 178 x south
17th st, Nos. 248-273 } 92 x east 50 x
north 92 to 18th st, x east 97.11 x south
145.8 x east 55 x south 38.5 to 17th st, x

west 880 to 8th av, x north 26.4 x east 100 x north 181.4 x west 100 to 8th av, x north 26.4 to beginning, two, three, four, five and six-story brk stores and tenem'ts, stables, brewery, &c ..
18th st, Nos. 239–243, n s, 249.4 e 8th av, 50.7x92, two, three and four-story brk buildings Together with personal property of Knickerbocker Brewery, plant, &c ....
Henry W. Poor. (Amt due $104,437)........ 717,258

WM. KENNELLY.

137th st, n s, 275 e 6th av, 25x99.11, vacant. E. Duffy........ 4,450

JAMES L. WELLS.

136th st, s s, 294 e Alexander av, 37.6x100. Thos. Overington. (Amt due $2,460)... 7,000

OTHER AUCTIONEERS.

Boulevard, e s, 24.11 n 139th st, 75x100, vacant. Chas. B. Barkley. (Amt due $31,451) 13,000

99th st, n s, 100 w 3d av, 75x100.11. Herbert W. See 63,097

99th st, n s, 250 w 3d av, 75x100.11. Same...... 64,117

19th st, No. 102 E., 24.6x92, three-story English basement brk dwell'g. (Bid in).... ... . —

Total........ $1,311,467
Corresponding week 1890.. .... $419,825

BROOKLYN, N. Y.

For Week Ending November 12.

TAYLOR & FOX.

*Dean st, No. 1598, s s, 100 e Utica av, 20x107.5, two-story frame dwell'g. Horace F. Burroughs $2,000

*Dean st, No. 1600, s s, 120 e Utica av, 20x107.5, two-story frame dwell'g. Horace F. Burroughs........ 2,000

Leonard st, No. 329, w s, 150 n Conselyea st, 25x86.6, two-story frame dwell'g and store. Thos. Sullivan........ 4,425

South 4th st, No. 45, n s, 140 w Wythe av, 20x106, three-story brk dwell'g. Margaret Smith........ 4,900

OTHER AUCTIONEERS.

*Halsey st, s e cor Patchen av, 200x100, ten two-story and basement brk dwell'gs and four-story flat with store on corner. Horatio S. Stewart........ 28,000

Jay st, n e cor York st, 25x90, three-story brk building. P. Denisco........ 5,000

*Macon st, n w cor Howard av, 185x100, five two-story and basement brk dwell'gs on plot. Bernard Levino........ 16,700

*Pacific st, s s, 387.7 e Rochester av, 16.9x107.2⅝, two-and-a-half-story frame dwell'g. Sarah C. Savage........ 2,000

*Union st, Nos. 649 and 653, n s, 100 w 4th av, 50x95, two five-story brk tenem'ts. Geo. R. Brown........ 18,500

Union st, Nos. 901–909, n s, 100 w 8th av, 100x90, five five-story brk flats, unfinished. John Tinsley........ 40,000

3d st, Nos. 160–166, s s, 372.9 e Bond st, 96.9x154.9 to Gowanus Canal, x 103.0¾x175.9, coal yard; resale. John D. Fish........ 21,500

*28th st, No. 227, n s, 325 w 5th av, 25x70, two-story and basement frame dwell'g. Virginia P. Kent........ 1,500

*Atlantic av, Nos. 870–874, s s, 340 w Underhill av, 60x100, two four-story double brk flats. Fred'k P. Bellamy........ 19,000

Hudson av, No. 77, e s, 175 s Evans st, 25x127x29.9x148.6, one-story frame stable and two-story frame dwell'g on rear. John F. Frost........ 8,510

Putnam av, Nos. 824 and 826, s s, 236.6 e Reid av, 39x100, two two-and-a-half-story brk dwell'gs Michael May........ 10,625

Putnam av, No. 832, s s, 314.6 e Reid av, 19.6x100, two-and-a- -story brk dwell'g. Michael May.....half........ 5,850

Total........ $185,010
Corresponding week, 1890........ $344,715

CONVEYANCES.

Wherever the letters Q. C., C. a. G. and B. & S occur, preceded by the name of the grantee they mean as follows:

1st—Q. C. is an abbreviation for Quit Claim deed, i. e., a deed in which all the right, title and interest of the grantor is conveyed, omitting all covenants or warranty.

2d—C. a. G. means a deed containing Covenant against Grantor only, in which he covenants that he hath not done any act whereby the estate conveyed may be impeached, charged or encumbered.

3d—B. & S. is an abbreviation for Bargain and Sale deed, wherein, although the seller makes no express covenants, he really grants or conveys the property for a valuable consideration, and thus impliedly claims to be the owner of it.

NEW YORK CITY.

November 6, 7, 9, 10, 11, 12.

Broadway, No. 840, s e cor 13th st, 24.6x86.1x—x—, three-story brk store. Maria T. Waters widow to Maria T. Sinnott, Mary J. De Bussy, Ann E., Matilda, Josephine and Frances C. Waters. ⅙ part. Sub. to mort. and dower right. Oct. 21. nom

Broadway, No. 390, e s, abt 85 s Walker st, five-story stone front store. Joseph B. Bruen to William L. Bruen. All title. June 8. gift

Broome st, No. 97, s s, abt 50 w Sheriff st, 25x75, four-story frame (brk front) store and tenement with three-story brk tenem't on rear. Baer Rosenberg to Karl M. and Samson Wallach. Mt. $13,750. Nov. 10. See 1st av. $22,000

Columbia st, No. 116, e s, 24.10 n Stanton st, 21.8x75.4, three-story brk tenem't. Abraham Schwartz or Schwarz to Samuel Greenfeld. Nov. 11. 13,750

Same property. Samuel Greenfeld to Bertha Harris. Nov. 11. 14,10

Delancey st, No. 127, s s, 40 w Norfolk st, runs south 56 x west 7 x south 12 x west 13 x north 68 to Delancey st, x east 20, four-story frame and brk store and tenem't. Rachel and Louis Weinberg to Semon Bache & Co. *Mt.* $12,500. Nov. 7. 15,500

Division st, No. 170, n s, abt 85 e Essex st, 28x75x25x88.7, five-story brk tenem't with stores. Nathan Cohen to Milia wife of Isaac Sidowsky. ½ part. Nov. 5. All liens. 2,000

Division st, No. 133, s s, 119 w Canal st, 25x63.1x25x62.4, five-story brk tenem't with stores. David Bloom and Isaac Ginsburg to Esther Hurovitz. *Mt.* $21,667. Nov. 9. 26,250

Fulton st, No. 202, s s, 253.10 e Greenwich st, 25x77.5x24.10x77.6, four-story brk store. Adam W. S. Cochrane to John W. Love. Nov. 9. 30,000

Fulton st, No. 19, n s, abt 55 w Front st, 29.11x27, five-story brk store. Lydia G. Lawrence widow, Palisades, N. Y., to Edith L. wife of George E. Chisolm. Dec. 16, 1890. nom

Greene st, No. 213, w s, 125 s West 3d st, 27.6x100, six-story brk store. John E. Parsons to Martin Schrenkeisen. Correction deed. June 4, 1891. 55,000

Grand st, No. 226, n s, bet Bowery and Elizabeth st, 25x100, two-story brk store and tenement. Joanna A. Davis, Elizabeth City, N. J., and Samuel K. Lyon to Alfred L. White. Nov. 10. 48,000

Grand st, No. 222 } begins Grand st.
Elizabeth st, Nos. 112 and 114 } n e cor Elizabeth st, 25x100, three-story frame (brk front) store and tenem't on Grand st and two two and three-story brk and frame tenem'ts on Elizabeth st. Susanna Deitering, Hoboken, N. J., individ. and extrx. Frederick W. Deitering to Alfred L. White, except portion conveyed to Marks Arnheim. All title. Nov. 12. 62,500

Lewis st, No. 102, e s, 75 n Stanton st, 21x100 three-story brk tenem't with six-story brk factory on rear. Jacob, Isidore and Morris C. Alexander to Lewis Krulewitch. *Mt.* $17,000. Oct. 27. 25,000

Madison st, No. 302, s s, 82 e Montgomery st, 23x108, three-story brk tenem't. Eveline A. Du Bois to John F. Coughlin. Nov. 9. 15,000

Market st, No. 29, w s, 75 s Henry st, 25x115, with use of 8 foot alley adj, three-story brk tenem't with two-story brk stable on rear. Joseph Geller to Michael Fay and William Stacom. *Mt.* $21,000. Nov. 2. 25,000

Monroe st, No. 11, n s, abt 175 e Catharine st, 25x100, five-story brk tenem't. Nathan Cohen to Louis Siegel. *Mt.* $32,500. Nov. 5. 38,500

Norfolk st, No. 154, e s, 50 s Stanton st, 25x100, five-story brk store and tenem't. Bernhard Silberstein to Max Kobre. ½ part. Sub. to mort. $32,000. Nov. 6. 21,000

Nassau st, Nos. 77 and 79. Agreement as to easement. Cornelius F. Kingsland to Daniel E. Sickels. Oct. 26. nom

Park row, Nos. 13 and 15, s e s, 85 n e Ann st, runs southeast 83.6 x northeast 4.6 x southeast 23.11 x north 29.5 x northwest 103.10 to Park row, x southwest 35, five-story stone front store and office building. August Belmont, formerly August Belmont, Jr., and Walter Luttgen, of August Belmont & Co., to John H. Cheever. *Mt.* $225,000. Q. C. July 20. nom

Same property. John H. Cheever to Henry B. Ker, Jr. *Mt* $225,000. Nov. 15. 475,000

Same property. Henry B. Ker, Jr., to The New York Belting and Packing Co. Annex. *Mt.* $225,000. Oct. 15. nom

Park st, Nos. 31 and 33, s s, abt 50 e Duane st, 48x92.5x45x90.10, two seven-story stone front stores and tenem'ts with two four-story brk tenem'ts on rear. Morris Franklin and Henry B. Weselman and Fannie M. Updike to Henry Lindenmeyr. *Mt.* $50,000. Nov. 5. nom

Rivington st, No. 161, s s, 25 w Clinton st, 25x100, five-story brk tenem't with stores. Foreclos. Henry F. Miller to George Rettinger, Passaic, N. J. Nov. 9. 28,000

Same property. George Rettinger to Jacob Pizer. Nov. 9. nom

Same property. Jacob Pizer to Herman Falkenberg. *Mt.* $18,000. Nov. 9. nom

Roosevelt st, No. 30 } begins Roosevelt st, e s,
New Bowery, No. 32 } abt 30 n New Bowery, 24.11x55 to New Bowery, x35 3x30.6, two-story brk store. Lorillard Spencer, Newport, R. I., to William P. Kirk. Nov. 6. 9,000

Spring st, No. 41, n s, 50.6 e Mulberry st, 25.3x119.3x25x118.6, four-story frame (brk front) store and tenem't. George Kraemer to Michael Lapp. Q. C. All title. Nov. 6. 248

Same property. Annie C. Kraemer widow, Jersey City, N. J., individ. and extrx. of Charles Kraemer to same. ½ part. *Mt.* $12,000. Nov. 2. 12,500

Thompson st, Nos. 29½, 31 and 33, w s, 177.5 s Broome st, runs south 47.7 x west 100 x north partly along an alley 7.7 x east along same alley 30 x north 58.5 to another branch of said alley known as Otter alley, x east along same 10 x south 18.5 x east 59, with all title in alleys, three three-story frame (brk front) tenem'ts, store in No. 29½, and three-story brk building on rear. Adelia A. Archer widow to Abraham Marks. Nov. 9. 15,000

Washington st, Nos. 750–754, s w cor Bethune st, 62.7x81, five-story brk paint factory. Archibald D. Russell to Thomas S. Williams. Oct. 31. nom

Water st, No. 738, n e cor Corlear st, 75x100, one-story brk office and frame sheds, spar yard, &c. Adrian G. and John A. Hegeman trustees of and Susan Jane Palmer to Lewis Z. Bach. Oct. 19. 11,300

Water st, n s, 75 e Corlear st, 75x100, frame sheds, spar yard, &c. Aletta M. wife of and Joseph Hegeman, Passaic, N. J., to same. Oct. 16. nom

Wooster st, Nos. 223–229, s w cor 3d st, 75x71.5, four two and three-story brk tenem'ts, stores in No. 229. Raphael Sturman to Adolph S. Kallscher. *Mt.* $74,000. May 19. nom

Wooster st, No. 53, w s, 18.1 s Broome st, 18x75, three-story brk store.
81st st, No. 151, n s, 275 w 3d av, 25x102.2, three-story frame dwell'g.
Ellen wife of Richard Ponds to James E. Campbell. Oct. 23. Q. C. and C. a. G. 3,000

5th st, No. 242, s s, 100 w 2d av, 20x80.10x20x80.8, three-story brk tenem't. Michael Springer to Michael A. Hoffmann. *Mt.* $4,500. Nov. 2. 16,000

7th st, No. 222, s s, 108 w Av C, 25x90.10, four-story brk store and tenem't with four-story brk tenem't on rear. Rosa Schlichter, Jennie Oppenheimer, Ida Lazarus, Levy and Samuel Frank devisees Kaufman Frank to John Harris. ⅙ part. *Mt.* $6,000. Oct. 26. 5,400

Same property. Hannah Pollack, formerly Davidsohn, an heir of Daniel Davidsohn to same. All title. *Mt.* $6,000. Oct. 26. 50

Same property. Jacob, Aaron, Philip, Tilly, Edgar, Jetta and Hannah Davidson, Jeannetta wife of Emanuel Cohn and Fanny Woog devisees of Daniel Davidsohn to same. ⅙ part. *Mt.* $6,000. Oct. 26. 5,400

Same property. Nannchen Davidsohn widow to same. ⅙ part. Oct. 26. 5,400

Same property. John Harris to Samuel Harris. ½ part. *Mt.* $10,000. Nov. 9. 8,125

12th st, No. 435, n s, 148.3 w Av A, 24.3x103.3. one-story frame building with four-story brk tenem't on rear. Peter Coyle and ano. exrs. Catherine McMahon to Elizabeth Coyle. Nov. 5. 11,300

13th st, No. 539, n s, 145 w Av B, 25x103.3, four-story brk store and tenem't with four-story brk tenem't on rear. James Dougherty to Philip Aichele. *Mt.* $8,000. Nov. 10. 18,500

18th st, Nos. 520 and 522, s s, 295.6 e Av A, 50x92, four-story brk contractors stables, &c. John Kehoe to Edward and Patrick Marrin. *Mt.* $10,000. Nov. 9. 25,000

22d st, No. 42, s s, 280 e 6th av, 23x98.9, three-story stone front dwell'g. Walker T. Miller to Robert T. Bellchambers. *Mt.* $20,000. Nov. 12. nom

22d st, No. 40, s s, 303 e 6th av, 23x98.9, three-story stone front dwell'g. Same to same. Nov. 12. nom

23d st, No. 104, s s, 50 e 4th av, 25x98.6, five-story stone front dwell'g. Alexander D. Duff and George McLeish to Oswald Oelschlaeger. *Mt.* $28,000. Oct. 3. 60,000

30th st, No. 324, s s, 307.2 e 2d av, 21x98.9, four-story brk tenem't. Aaron Wise to James Smith. *Mt.* $7,500. Oct. 27. 13,500

35th st, No. 142, s s, 125 e Lexington av, 14.9x97.6, four-story stone front dwell'g. Frederick F. Kieferdorf to Nellie Macdonald. *Mt.* $11,000. Nov. 9. 20,000

37th st, Nos. 102 and 104, s s, 62 w 6th av, 38x48.3, two four-story brk dwell'gs. Lucinda Y. Brown, East Livermore, Me., to William E. Kimball. *Mt.* $14,000. Nov. 5. nom

37th st, Nos. 530 and 532, s s, 400 w 10th av, 25x98.9, two four-story brk tenem'ts. Herman Wronkow to Judson G. Wells and Hosea Higgins. *Mt.* $9,500. Nov. 10. 15,000

40th st, No. 48, s s, 307.6 e 6th av, 17.6x98.9, four-story stone front dwell'g. Alfred H. Smith to Mary C. Knower. Nov. 5. 48,000

46th st, No. 244, s s, 100 w 2d av, 25x100.5, five-story brk tenem't. Anne M. wife of and Frederick Dannemann, Katie A. Heins, Lizzie wife of and Charles Lankeneu, formerly Heins, Frankfort, Ill, to Hinrich Heins. *Mt.* $19,000. Aug. 1. nom

Same property. Order of Court vacating conveyance made by Anne M. Dannemann to Frederick Dannemann.

52d st, No. 416, s s, 199 w 9th av, 26x100.5, five-story brk tenem't. Samuel Nelson to Albert I. Adams. *Mt.* $8,000. Nov. 10. 28,000

52d st, No. 121, n s, 215 w 6th av, 25x100.5, three-story brk stable. Henry W. Putnam to Herbert L. Terrell. Nov. 2. 31,000

53d st, No. 510, s s, 150 w 10th av, 25x100.5, five-story brk building. Elsworth L. Striker to George Bliss. B. & S. Aug. 28. nom

55th st, No. 213, n s, 170 e 3d av, 20x100.5, three-story brk store and tenem't. Elmira D. wife of Herman Rapp, Fairmount, N. J., to Hiram Slocum, of Beekman, N. Y. *Mt.* $10,000. Nov. 10. 16,000

58th st, No. 327, n s, 350 w 8th av, 25x100.5, four-story stone front dwell'g. Jane Downie to Anna J. Borie. *Mt.* $25,000. Nov. 19, 1890. 46,750

60th st, No. 229, n s, 400 w 10th av, 25x100.5, four-story brk tenem't. William H. Nafis to Diederick H. Tonjes. Q. C. C. a. G. *Mt.* $10,000. April 1. nom

61st st, No. 22, s s, 69 w Madison av, 26x73.5, four-story brk dwell'g. Charlotte wife of Solomon Turck to Solomon Turck. Nov. 6. 62,000

63d st, Nos. 161 and 163, n s, 200 e Amsterdam av, 50x100.5, two five-story stone front flats. William Rankin to John Rankin. Nov. 9. nom

Same property. John Rankin to William Rankin. Sub. to morts. Nov. 9. nom

63d st, n s, 200 e Amsterdam av, 25x100.5. William Rankin to Gumpert Seide. *Mt.* $18,500. Nov. 10. nom

64th st, No. 104, s s, 44 w 9th av, 19x100.5, four-story stone front dwell'g. Henry H. Cahn to Cora L. Cahn. Nov. 6. nom

65th st, No. 134, s s, 100 e Lexington av, 20x100.5, three-story stone front dwell'g. Bernhard Silberstein to Max Kobre. *Mt.* $17,000. Nov. 9. 20,000

66th st, No. 209, n s, 175 w Amsterdam av, 25x100.5, five-story stone front tenem't.
66th st, No. 223, n s, 350 w Amsterdam av, 25x100.5, five-story brk tenem't.
John S. Robinson to E. Clifford Potter. *Mt.* $35,000. Nov. 6. nom

66th st, No. 219, n s, 300 w 10th av, 25x100.5, five-story stone front tenem't. The Equitable Life Assur. Soc. of the United States to Thomas R. Hughes, Weehawken, N. J. Nov. 4. nom

66th st, No. 217, n s, 275 w 10th av, 25x100.5, five-story stone front tenem't. Same to same. Nov. 4. nom

66th st, No. 221, n s, 325 w 10th av, 25x100.5, five-story brk tenem't. Same to same. Nov. 4. nom

66th st, Nos. 217-221, n s, 275 w 10th av, 75x100.5. Thomas R. Hughes, Weehawken, N. J., to E. Clifford Potter. *Mt.* $51,000. Nov. 4. nom

66th st, No. 15, n s, 281 e 5th av, 19x100.5, four-story stone front dwell'g. George L. Ingraham to Charles Isham. Oct. 21. 40,000

67th st, s s, 100 e Columbus av, 50x100.5, six-story brk building. Edward Kilpatrick to Frederic de P. Foster. Nov. 2. 65,000

68th st, s s, 300 e West End av, 25x100.5, vacant. John E. Kaughran to Abraham A. Andruss. *Mt.* $4,000. Nov. 6. 6,000

68th st, s s, 275 e West End av, 25x100.5, vacant. Same to Charles Andruss. *Mt.* $4,000. Nov. 6. 6,000

70th st, Nos. 27-31, n s, 300 w 8th av, 75x100.5, one-story frame buildings. Peter J. McCoy to Edward Oppenheimer and Isaac Metzger. *Mt.* $17,000. Nov. 6. nom

70th st, n s, 275 w Amsterdam av, 75x100.5, vacant. J. Henrietta H. Rhoades to Nicholas Leibrock. Oct. 15. 27,000

70th st, n s, 350 w Amsterdam av, 50x100.5, vacant. John H. Rhoades to same. Oct. 15. 18,000

70th st, No. 25, n s, 275 w Central Park West, 25x100.5, one-story frame building. Russell Sage to John D. Taylor. Nov. 10. 16,000

70th st, Nos. 27-31, n s, 300 w Central Park West. 75x100.5, one-story frame shanties. Edward Oppenheimer and Isaac Metzger to John D. Taylor. *Mt.* $17,000. Nov. 6. nom

70th st, n s, 275 w Amsterdam av, 125x100.5, vacant. Nicholas Liebrock to August C. Hassey ½ part, and Carl F. and Julius Spiess ½ part. *Mt.* $37,800. Nov. 10. 50,000

72d st, No. 204, s s, 90 e 3d av, 20x102.2, four-story brk flat. Charles A. Singer to Sarah I. wife of Isaac A. Singer. Nov. 5. gift

72d st, No. 35, n s, 250 e 9th av, 25x102.2, four-story brk dwell'g. Release mort. The Mutual Life Ins. Co. of New York to John E. Huking. Oct. 30. 20,000

74th st, No. 243, n s, 210 e West End av, 20x102.2, three-story brk dwell'g. John W. Barrett to Henrietta G. Hallett. B. & S. Nov. 5. nom

Same property. Frederick G. Hallett to John W. Barrett. B. & S. Nov. 5. nom

79th st, No 328, s s, 306.3 w 1st av, 18.9x102.2, four-story stone front dwell'g. Charles Rosenberg to Samuel Milbauer. *Mt.* $9,000. Oct. 30. 15,000

80th st, No. 147, n s, 370.3 e Amsterdam av, 21x102.2, four-story brk dwell'g. Michael Giblin and James W. Taylor to Thomas G. Patten. Nov. 7. 32,250

81st st, No. 6 E. Agreement as to retaining wall. Samuel C. Boehm to exrs. of estate of Charles White. Nov. 6. nom

82d st, No. 7, n s, 150 w 8th av, 25x102.2, four-story brk and stone dwell'g. Amadee Spadone to Frank A. Seitz. Nov. 5. See 118th st. 45,000

82d st, Nos. 6-10, s s, 120 w 8th av, 55x100, three four-story stone front dwell'gs. Mary Gault to Mary E. Gault. *Mt.* $71,500. Nov. 10. nom

82d st, Nos. 224-228, s s, 250 w 10th av, 50x102.2, three three-story brk dwell'gs. William E. D. Vincent, New York, and Walter J. Weedon, Brooklyn, to Samuel D. Siler. *Mt.* $55,000. Nov. 10. 70,500

89th st, No. 262, s s, 82 e West End av, 18x100.8, four-story brk dwell'g. Armintha Merritt to Etta Loudertack. *Mt.* $16,000. Nov. 7. nom

90th st, No. 108, s s, 129.9 e 4th av, 29.2x100.8, four-story stone front flat. Margaret F. McIntyre to Ann Byrne. ½ part. *Mt.* $14,000. Nov. 1. 3,000

92d st, No. 148, s s, 342 w 3d av, 33x100.8, three-story brk dwell'g. Walter H. Stewart to George Ehret and Ashbel P. Fitch. *Mt.* $14,500. Nov. 5. 19,550

92d st, No. 58, s s, 275 e Columbus av, 17.6x100.8, four-story stone front dwell'g. Fannie M. Crowley, Sr. and Jr., exrs. Robert Crowley to Nancy Aaron. *Mt.* $17,500. Nov. 2. 24,500

Same property. Fanny M. Crowley, Sr., widow and Fannie M., Jr., Mary H., William E. and Charles H. Crowley to same. B. & S. Nov. 2. nom

93d st, n s, 326 w 4th av, 4x100 8. Release mort. Cecilia wife of Martin Keppler to James V. S. Woolley. Oct. 31. 2,000

96th st, n s, 175 e Amsterdam av, 25x100.11, five-story stone front flat. Alexander Cameron to Louisa M. wife of Alfred E. Stone. *Mt.* $20,000. Nov. 9. 35,000

96th st, n s, 150 e Amsterdam av, 25x100.11, five-story stone front flat. Same to Sarah F. wife of George R. Stone. *Mt.* $20,000. Nov. 9. 35,000

100th st, n s, 80 w 4th av, 20x100.11, five-story brk flat. Edward J. Kelly to John S. Robinson. *Mt.* $16,000. Oct. 24. 24,000

100th st, Nos. 155-169, n s, 95 e Lexington av, 200x100.11, eight five-story brk flats. Foreclos. Philip L. Wilson to The Equitable Life Assur. Soc. Sub. to morts. Nov. 4. 28,000

101st st, Nos. 154-168, s s, 95 e Lexington av, 200x100.11, eight five-story brk flats. Foreclos. Philip L. Wilson to The Equitable Life Assur. Soc., U. S. Sub. to morts. Nov. 4. 25,000

101st st, Nos. 67-71, n s, 175 e Columbus av, 75x100.11, three five-story brk flats. Frank Davis to Thomas Berkeley. Nov. 9. nom

101st st, Nos. 75 and 77, n s, 100 e Columbus av. 50x100.11, two five-story brk flats. Release mort. William D. Murphy to William M. Walsh. Nov. 5. 14,667

Same property. William M. Walsh, Williamsbridge, N. Y., to William H. Scott. *Mt.* $40,000. Nov. 12. nom

102d st, No. 204, s s, 100 e 3d av, 35x100.11, four-story brk livery stable. James Duffy to George and George J. Bernhard. Nov. 12. 34,000

Same property. General release especially as to contract. The Murray Hill Bank to George J. Bernard. Nov. 11. nom

102d st, No. 108, n s, 27 e Park av, 25x100.11, five-story brk store and tenem't. Frederick Rohrs to Frederick Hasselbach and Katharina his wife, joint tenants. *Mt.* $16,500. Nov. 11. 21,500

103d st, n s, 275 w 4th av, original line, 50x100.11. Release covenant. James F. Stansbury to J. Allen Townsend. Oct. 30. 60

103d st, n s, 255 w Park or 4th av, 50x100.11, vacant, new buildings projected. J. Allen Townsend to John S. Scott. *Mt.* $12,000. Oct. 30. 15,000

103d st, n s, 180 w Park av, 75x100.11, vacant, new b ild g projected. Same to same. Oct. 19. u in s 22,500

104th st, No. 202, s s, 70 e 3d av, 20x50.5, four-story brk store and tenem't. John Grebe to Samuel Altheimer. *Mt.* $5,500. Nov. 5. 9,750

107th st, No. 230, s s, 200 w 2d av, 25x100.11, four-story brk tenem't. August Wilks to Elise wife of Aaron Schonfeld. *Mt.* $7,500. Nov. 1. 13,500

111th st, Nos. 179 and 181, n s, 70 w 3d av, 50x100.11, two four-story stone front flats. Phillip Cramer to Ida Cramer. Sub. to mort. Nov. 11. nom

113th st, No. 408, s s, 120 e 1st av, 25x100.10, two-story frame dwell'g on rear of lot. Harry McNally to Biose Fucco. *Mt.* $4,000. Nov. 12. 5,900

114th st, No. 419, n s, 245 e 1st av, 25x100.11, four-story brk tenem't. Frederick C. Dexter, Brooklyn, to Margaret Young, Williamsbridge, N. Y. *Mt.* $10,000. Nov. 2. 14,500

114th st, No. 112, s s, 155 e 4th av, 18.9x100.11, three-story brk dwell'g. Henry Muller to Pauline C. B. wife of Henry Muller. Nov. 9. nom

116th st, No. 408, s s, 95 e 1st av, 18.7x100.10, three-story stone front dwell'g.
43d st, No. 470, s s, 100 e 10th av, 20x100.5, four-story brk tenem't.
Mary J. Quinlan widow to Mary wife of Thomas P. Walsh, Ansonia, Conn. B. & S. Oct. 29. nom

118th st, Nos. 272-278, s s, 100 e 8th av, 100x100.11, four five-story stone front flats. Release mort. Henry W. Ford trustee Augustus H. Ward to Thomas J. Jenkins and George Jenkins. Nov. 6. 5,000

Same property. Release mort. The Bradley & Currier Co. (Lim.) to same. Nov. 6. nom

Same property. Thomas J. and George Jenkins to Adolph M. Bendheim. *Mt.* $50,000. Nov. 6. See Columbus av. 100,000

118th st, n s, 210 w 5th av, 100x100.11, vacant. Frank A. Seitz to Amadee Spadone and Dorman T. Warren. *Mt.* $12,000. Oct. 22. See 82d st. 40,000

118th st, No. 427, n s, 305.4 w Pleasant av, 21.2x100.11, three-story brk dwell'g.
118th st, No. 431, n s, 263 w Pleasant av, 21.1x100.4, three-story brk dwell'g.
William G. Wood to Mary E. Wood. Nov. 10. nom

118th st, s s, 275 e 8th av, 25x100.11. Release mort. William N. Crane trustee to Thomas J. and George Jenkins. Nov. 11. 18,000

Same property. Release mort. The Bradley & Currier Co. (Lim.) to same. Nov. 6. nom

119th st
Claremont av
begins 119th st, s s, 9.4 w Claremont av, and which point is the w s of Old Bloomingdale road, runs south along said old w s to point 300 s 119th st, x east to Claremont av, x north along same to 119th st, x west — to beginning, vacant. Emily M. Petit to Charles C. and Henry M. Taber. Q. C. Sept. 30. nom

120th st, No. 124, s s, 90 w Lexington av, 25x100.10, five-story brk flat. William E. Crandall to Roderick P. Fisher. *Mt.* $17,000. Nov. 8. exch

Same property. Roderick P. Fisher to Maurice O'Brien. *Mt.* $17,000. Nov. 6. exch

Same property. Roger A. Pryor, Jr., to Roderick P. Fisher. Nov. 2. nom

122d st, No. 263, n s, 17.6 w 2d av, 14x71.8, three-story stone front dwell'g. Laemmlein Buttenwieser to Arthur Gorsch. B. & S. All liens. Nov. 5. 1,311

123d st, Nos. 401 and 403, n w cor Columbus (9th) av, 57.10x94, two five-story brk and stone flats, stores in No. 401.
Columbus (9th) av, Nos. 1286 and 1288, s w cor 124th st, 53.10x100, two five-story brk and stone flats, store in No. 1288
Foreclos. Bankson T. Morgan to Alan D. Kenyon. Nov. 11. 41,000

124th st, Nos. 110 and 112, s s, 90 e Park av, 50x100.11, two five-story stone front flats. Jane wife of William H. Browning to Frederick Zittel. Nov. 6. nom

125th st, s s, 150 w Amsterdam av, 50x100.11, vacant. Elizabeth J. wife of John H. Wellwood to George A. Smith. *Mt.* $11,000 and ass.ssm'ts $657. Nov. 9. 15,000

125th st, No. 307, n s, 130 w 8th av, 20x100, four-story brk store and flat. John Murray to Margaret Brady. Q. C. and B. & S. Oct. 24. 20,000

132d st, n s, 410 w 5th av, 25x99.11, vacant. Charles C. Noble to Luzon J. Adams. Q. C. *Mt.* $3,000. Nov. 10. nom

Same property. Mary B. D. wife of and Fordyce S. Caldwell to same. *Mt.* $3,000. Nov. 10. nom

133d st, No. 24, s s, 316.3 w 5th av, 18.9x99.11, three-story stone front dwell'g. Jacob Story to James Murphy. *Mt.* $6,000. Nov. 10. 10,500

142d st, s s, 75 e Lenox av, 100x99.11, vacant. Peter J. Brady, Brooklyn, to Edward J. Kelly. *Mt.* $9,000. Oct. 24. 16,000

143d st, No. 304, s s, 100 w 8th av, 25x99.11, one-story frame building. Nicolaus Leibrock to August C. Hassey and Jacob L. Kahn. *Mt.* $3,000. Oct. 26. 5,000

144th st, No. 465, n s, 121.2 e Amsterdam av, 16.8x99.11, three-story brk dwell'g. Robert J. Young, Brooklyn to Mary W. wife of John H. Morrison, Jr. Nov. 4. 16,000

147th st, No. 412, s s, 175 w St. Nicholas av, 21x99.11, three-story stone front dwell'g. Dennis J. Dwyer to William Heigh. Aug. 30. nom

147th st, No. 409, n s, 655.1 e Amsterdam av, 14.10x99.11, three-story stone front dwell'g. Charles S. Andrews to Joseph B. Roe. *Mt.* $5,600. Nov. 9. nom

148th st, s s, 350 w Amsterdam av, 50x99.11.
147th st, n s, 350 w Amsterdam av, 50x99.11, vacant.
John S. Bassett to Frank Koch. Nov. 6. 14,000

Av A, No. 1065, e s, 50.5 n 58th st, 16.8x75, three-story stone front dwell'g. Carrie B. Fielitz widow to John Koell. *Mt.* $2,500. Nov. 7. 7,350

Av A or Eastern Boulevard, No. 1321, w s, 70.4 s 71st st, 25x100, five-story brk tenem't. Susan McLaughlin to Fannie E. Metcalfe, Brooklyn. *Mt.* $18,000. Nov. 12. exch

Av B, Nos. 1608 and 1610. Agreement as to water. Louis Lochmann with August Herrlich and Elizabeth S. his wife. May 9. nom

Av C, No. 80, e s, 48.6 s 6th st, 72.9x94.8, brk church. Foreclos. Armour C. Anderson to Owen McGinnis. Arthur J. Horgan and Vincent J. Slattery. *Mt.* $30,000 Nov. 9. 10,000

Av C, Nos. 255 and 257
15th st, No. 645
begins Av C, n w cor 15th st, 45 9x88.2, four-story brk tenem'ts with stores on Av C with two-story brk stable on 15th st. Joseph F. Johnson to Eliza J. Johnson. *Mt.* $9,500. Oct. 23. gift

Av D, No. 54, e s, 23 s 5th st, 24.8x78, four-story frame (brk front) store and tenem't, Henry and Julius Bacharach to Adolph Gross and Samuel Harris. *Mt.* $5,000. Nov. 6. 13,750

Amsterdam av, No. 143, w s, 75.5 s 67th st, 25x100, five-story stone front flat with stores. Louis E. Oxee to George Roll. *Mt.* $22,250. Nov. 6. nom

Amsterdam av, s w cor 189th st, 24.11x100. Emily A. Smith to Isidor Haldenstein. Nov. 9. 7,500

Amsterdam av, w s, 99.11 s 189th st, 25x100. Same to Milton See. Nov. 9. 4,175

Amsterdam av, w s, 24.11 s 189th st, 75x100. Emily A. Smith to August Ritter. Nov. 9. 12,300

Amsterdam av, No. 861, n e cor 100th st, 25x75, five-story brk store and tenem't. Robert Maywald to William H and Seig Goldstein. *Mt.* $27,500. Nov. 10. 40,000

Amsterdam (10th) av, s w cor 131st st, 24.11x100, vacant. Samuel Nelson to Albert I. Adams. *Mt.* $3,000. Nov. 10. 13,000

Audubon av, e s, 74.11 s 189th st, 25x100. Emily A. Smith to Ellen M. Cremin. Nov. 9. 1,900

Audubon av, s e cor 189th st, 24.11x100. Same to Joseph W. Cremin. Nov. 9. 3,050

Audubon av, w s, 24.11 s 189th st, 25x100. Emily A. Smith to Rose Cawley. Nov. 9. 1,800

Audubon av, w s, 49.11 s 189th st, 50x100. Same to James H. Monheimer. Nov. 9. 3,560

Audubon av, w s, 99.11 s 189th st, 75x100. Same to Leonard Zeh. Nov. 9. 5,400

Audubon av, s w cor 189th st, 24.11x100. Same to Otto Geiss. Nov. 9. 3,000

Columbus av, Nos. 746 and 748, w s, 76.7 s 97th st, runs south 50 x west 80 x north 0.6 x west 20 x north 49.6 x east 100, two five-story brk stores and flats. Susanna Schmitt widow to John A., Isabella and Louisa Schmitt. *Mt.* $50,000. Nov. 9. nom

Columbus (9th) av, Nos. 1287-1293 Manhattan st or Hancock pl 124th st } begins Columbus av, s e cor 124th st, runs south 100.11 x east 200 x north 93.11 to s s Manhattan st, x northwest 15.1 to 124th st, x west 186 7, four five-story brk flats, store in No. 1293 on av and four five-story brk flats on 124th st and Manhattan st. Henry M. Bendheim to Thomas J. and George Jenkins. *Mt.* $84,550. Oct. 31. See 118th st. consid. omitted

Edgecombe av or road, e s, 1.226.10 along said road, s from south line of Highbridge Park, 49x130.8 to Aqueduct, x88.4x124.6. Annie E. Brown to Joseph Hamilton and Charles F. Johnson. Nov. 6. 4,000

Lenox (6th) av, s e cor 142d st, 99.11x75, vacant. Peter J. Brady, Brooklyn, to Henry P. Degraaf. *Mt.* $18,000. Nov. 10. exch

Lenox av, No. 259, s w cor 123d st, 24.8x80, four-story brk dwell'g. *Mt.* $25,000.
3d av, Nos. 2012-2018 } begins 3d av, s w cor 111th st, No. 186 } 111th st, 100.10x100, four four-story brk tenem'ts with stores on av and one four-story brk tenem't on st. *Mt.* $21,767.
William G. Wood to Virginia wife of William G. Wood. Nov. 10. nom

Madison av, Nos. 1321 and 1323, n e cor 93d st, 40.8x70, two three-story brk (stone front) dwell'gs. Release mort. Seth M. Milliken to James V. S. Woolley. Nov. 5. nom

Madison av, e s, 20.8 n 93d st, 20x74. James V. S. Woolley to Walter G. Hennessy. *Mt.* $16,000. Nov. 6. nom

Madison av, No. 2110, w s, 99.11 s 133d st, 20x80, three-story stone front dwell'g. Lena Kahn to Aaron Butler, Jamaica, L. I. *Mt.* $10,000. Nov. 4. 15,000

Same property. Aaron Butler, Jamaica, L. I., to John H. Henshaw. *Mt.* $12,500. Nov. 5. 15,000

Madison av, No. 1983, e s, 76 s 127th st, 23.8x110, three-story stone front dwell'g. Isaac E. Wright to Harry S. Wright. Q. C. Oct. 30. nom

Park (4th) av, No. 471, e s, 80.5 n 57th st, 20x70, three-story stone front dwell'g. James T. Quail et al. exrs. John W. Blanck to Eliza E. Blanck. Nov. 2. 15,500

Park (4th) av, No. 884, w s, 54.2 n 78th st, 15x75, four-story brk dwell'g. Foreclos. J. C. J. Langbein to Edith N. Wharton. Nov. 9. 19,675

West End av, s e cor 89th st, 100.8x100. Release judgment. Alfred B. Cruikshank to Joseph E. Weed, Brooklyn. Nov. 9. nom

West End av, No. 780, n e cor 103d st, 20.11x80, three-story brk (stone front) dwell'g. Alexander Walker and Martha A. Lawson to Margaret A. wife of Peter Duffy. Nov. 9. nom

1st av, No. 607, w s, 50.9 s 35th st, 24.1x75x23.4x75, four-story brk tenem't with stores. Samuel Kempner to Max Rawitzer. *Mt.* $7,250. Nov. 11. 12,100

1st av, w s, 50.9 s 35th st, 24.1x75x23.4x75. Samuel B. Hamburger to Max Rawitzer and Clementina his wife, joint tenants. B. & S. *Mt.* $7,250, taxes, &c. Nov. 12. nom

Same property. Max Rawitzer to Samuel B. Hamburger. B. & S. Nov. 12. nom

1st av, No. 1709, w s, 75.8 s 89th st, 25x77, five-story brk store and tenem't. August Witt to William L. Berles. *Mt.* $15,000. Aug. 25. nom

Same property. William L. Berles to August Witt and Bertha his wife, joint tenants. *Mt.* $15,000. Aug. 27. nom

1st av, No. 1604, e s, 27.2 n 83d st, 25x84, five-story brk tenem't with stores. Karl M. and Samson Wallach to Baer Rosenberg and Bertha his wife. *Mt.* $14,000. Nov. 10. See Broome st. 30,000

1st av, No. 1033, w s, 58.2 s 57th st, 28x75, five-story brk store and tenem't. William Cohen to Emma Cohen. *Mt.* $19,900. March 16. 28,000

3d av, No. 605, e s, 49.4 n 39th st, 21.4x75, two-story brk store and tenem't. The People's Bank of Haverstraw to Marion V. Butler, Brooklyn. C. a. G. Oct. 24. nom

3d av, No. 944, w s, 125.5 n 56th st, 25x95, five-story brk store and tenem't. Philip Gomprecht to Henry Lussmann. *Mt.* $20,000. Nov. 9. 40,500

3d av, e s, 75.6 n 92d st, 50.4x100, vacant. John B. Smith to Jacob Ruppert. *Mt.* $22,000. Nov. 10. 33,000

5th av, No. 675, e s, 25.5 n 53d st, 25x100, four-story stone front dwell'g. William L. Kennedy, New York, Lawren O. Kennedy, Galway, N. Y., Martin Kennedy, Johnstown, N. Y., Lucinda Stewart widow, Johnstown, N. Y., devisees, &c., Harvey Kennedy to Samuel Untermyer. Nov. 4. val. consid.

7th av, s e cor 32d st, 23.9x100. Agreement accepting provisions in lieu of dower and release. Mary E. Hannegan to David Nugent. Oct. 28. Annuity of $600 and 200

8th av, Nos. 2651 and 2653, w s, 49.11 s 142d st, 50x100, two five-story brk flats with stores. Mary P. Snow to Samuel Gussfield. *Mt.* $40,000. Nov. 2. 47,500

Same property. Samuel Gussfield to Minnie L. Simon. *Mt.* $22,500. Nov. 4. nom

8th av, w s, 74.11 s 142d st, 25x100. Same to Sallie Schuster. *Mt.* $23,500. Nov. 4. nom

8th av, No 2353, w s, 25 n 126th st, 25x100, five-story brk store and flat. James W. Power to Annie E. Frank. 1-12 part. Nov. 7. nom

Same property. Mary Power to Annie E. Frank. 11-12 parts. Nov. 7. 34,750

Same property. Teresa Power to Mary Power Q. C. June 6, 1891. nom

Same property; also,
Fleetwood av, n s, 33.7 w Popham st, 30x100. } Patrick Jones lunatic by Mary Power committee to James W. Power. 1-13 part. Nov. 5. 390

12th av, e s, 15.10 s 55th st, runs south to 54th st, x east to original high-water mark on Randels map, x along same to point 15.8 s 55th st, x west —.
12th av, e s, 15.10 s 55th st, runs west to w s bulkhead as now existing, x south 245 to 54th st, x east to av, x north —, with land under water, &c.
Mayor, &c., New York, to Hopper S. and Alexander H. Mott. Q. C. Oct. 27. 7,500

MISCELLANEOUS.

All title of grantor in estate of Felix Stoiber dec'd. Edward G. Stoiber to Gustavus H. Stoiber. Oct. 31. nom

23d and 24th WARDS.

Buchanan pl, n s, 275 w Jerome av, 25x100. Release mort. Francena B. Partridge to Oscar Norman. Oct. 5. 289

Elmwood pl, s s, 96.1 e Crotona av, 50.2x122.11 x49.4x123.5. John J. Brady to Catharine Fox. Oct. 19. 2,000

Elmwood pl, n s, 100 e Crotona av, 21x95x22.3 x95. John J. Brady to Michael P. Casey. Oct. 19. 725

Field st, e s, 100 n Rock st, 50x100. James F. and Patrick H. Sheridan and James S. Segrave to John Brocklehurst. Oct. 27. 1,200

Hill st, w s, 72.2 s Rock st, runs west 91.7 to s s Rock st, x southwest 10.5 x south 18.6 x east 100 to Hill st, x north 25. James F. and Patrick H. Sheridan and James S. Segrave to Benjamin G. Cropsey. Nov. 5. 500

Hill st, w s, 97.2 s Rock st, 25x100. Same to Ida L. Lockwood. Nov. 5. 475

Kingsbridge road, n e s, 399.6 n w of road to Williamsbridge, runs north 337.11 x east 279.3 to w s Williamsbridge road, x south along same 30.4 and 51.9 and 21.4 and 61 and 29.10x southwest 69 9 x south 207.2 to Kingsbridge road, x16 and 32 and 16 and 24.9 and 36. Arthur B. Claflin to Patrick Ryan and Thomas G. Patterson. Nov. 10. 20,000

Lebanon st, s s, 100 e Clinton av, 21x95x21.6x95. John J. Brady to Margaret Hoffman. Oct. 19. 630

Lebanon st, n s, 100 w Crotona av, runs north 100 x west 95.6 to Cambreleng av, x south 25.11 x south 77.7 to Lebanon st, x east 70.7. Same to John H. Maurer and Charles Kissenberth. Oct. 19. 1,530

Lebanon st, s s, 100 w Prospect av, 72x190 to Elmwood pl.
Elmwood pl, n s, 125 w Clinton av, 25x95. } Same to Minnie Knoch. Oct. 19. 5,180

Oak terrace, s s, 136 e Crimmins av, 50x100. William H. McCord, New York, and Andrew J. Post, Jersey City, to William R. Beal Land Improvement Co. C. a. G. Oct. 22. 4,000

Same property. Release mort. William R. Beal Land Improvement Co. to William H. McCord, New York, and Andrew J. Post, Jersey City. Oct. 22. 2,150

Oakland pl, s s, 100 w Crotona av, 75x100.
Lebanon st, n s, 100 e Crotona av, 73.3x200 to Oakland pl, x74.6x200.
Oakland pl, s s, 100 w Prospect av, runs south 100 x west 48 x south 100 to Lebanon st, x west 24 x north 100 x west 22.2 x north 100 to Oakland pl, x east 94.6.
Oakland pl, n s, 100 e Crotona av, runs north 121 x west 100 to Crotona av, x north 26.6 x east 177.9 x south 121.6 to Oakland pl, x west 74.10.
Oakland pl, n s, 100 w Crotona av, 92x98x92x98.11.
John J. Brady to C. Adelbert Becker. Oct. 19. 11,895

Oakland pl, n s, 100 w Prospect av, 24x107.4x24x106.7. Same to John J. Quigley. Oct. 19. 555

Oakland pl, n s, 100 e Clinton av, 22.6x108.7x22.10x109.4. Same to Mary A. Healy. Oct. 19. 500

Oakland pl, n s, 148 w Prospect av, 24x108.7x24x108. Same to Lizzie O'Brien. Oct. 19. 540

Rock st, n w cor Cornell pl, 50x100. James F. and Patrick H. Sheridan and James S. Segrave to Charles H. Meyer, Jr. Oct. 27. 1,000

Rogers pl, w s, 563.11 n Westchester av, 30x75.4 x35.8x71.9, hs & ls. Annie M. Metzeler to Genoefa Deis. Nov. 9. 4,000

Ryer st, w s, 100 s Irving st, 25x100. William H. May, Brooklyn, and Henrietta May heirs Henry May to Michael Doran. Oct. 22. 800

Summit st, s s, 673 e Marion av, 25x100. Martha A. De Witt to John J. Hyland. Nov. 12. 1,000

Travers st, n w cor Bainbridge av, 30.9x98x17.11x98.10. Fannie E. wife of William E. Brooker formerly Fawcett to Charles J. Coulter. *Mt.* $450. Nov. 7. 1,400

135th st, n s, 208.4 e St. Anns av, 16.8x100. John Entwistle to Augusta A. Brunjes. *Mt.* $3,500. Nov. 12. 6,800

139th st, s s, 625 e Willis av, 25x100. Agnes S. wife of Francis E. Graham, East Orange, N. J., heir John Shearer to Mary M. Merritt. Q. C. Oct. 16. nom

141st st, s s, lot 18 block 7 map of sections A and B North New York, 25x100. Henry Rothschild to Helene Maas. Nov. 12. 7,700

159th st, n s, 100 w Courtlandt av, 50x198.8 to 160th st. George Burkel, Hudson City, N. J., to Herman Lutz. Nov. 1. nom

167th st, n e s, 162 s e Railroad av, 27x100. Mary G. Ford to George Searle, Pearl River, N. Y. Q. C. Nov. 11. 200

173d st, n w cor former Brook st, 100x98x100x89. George H. Purser, Scarsdale, N. Y., to Ludger Chartrand. Nov. 6. 3,650

183d st, s s, 180.4 w Washington av, part lot 119 map heirs Thomas Bassford, Fordham, 16.8x100. John A. Knox to Henry Boak trustee William H. Boak. *Mt.* 2,000. Nov. 4. 3,250

Av A, n w s, lot 275 map building lots at Fordham, part farm Charles Berrian. 25x102x25x101.9. Edward F. Maguire to David Ryan. Nov. 9. 1,000

Same property. David Ryan to Jane Murphy. Nov. 9. nom

Cambreleng av, e s, lot 227 map Ryer homestead, Tremont, 32.6x126.5x28.1x122.6. Margaret J. Howe to Caroline McEvoy. Nov. 6. 350

Clinton av, s e s, lot 64 map East Tremont, 66x150, h & ls. Patrick Hogan to Margaret A. Wales. *Mt.* $3,000. Nov. 10. 5,750

Clinton av, w s, 25 n Lebanon st, 25x100. John J. Brady to Annie wife of Peter A. Engelson. Oct. 19. 810

Clinton av, w s, 50 n Lebanon st, 25x100. Same to Annie wife of Peter A. Engelson. October 19. 810

Clinton av, w s, 45 n Elmwood pl, 50x100. Same to William H. Birkmire. Oct. 19. 1,750

Clinton av, w s, 20 n Elmwood pl, 25x100. Same to Henry C. H. Rivett. Oct. 19. 900

Clinton av, n w cor Elmwood pl, 20x100x19.7x100. Same to Louis Koerner. Oct. 19. 1,175

Clinton av, s e cor Oakland pl, 25x100x24.7x100. Same to Elizabeth F. Gallagher. Oct. 19. 1,000

Clinton av, e s, 25 s Oakland pl, 25x100. Same to James O'Brien. Oct. 19. 695

Clinton av, n e cor Lebanon st, 25x100x25.4x100. Same to Rose Seiferd. Oct. 19. 1,050

Clinton av, w s, 100 n proposed Tremont av, 25x100x24.7x100. Same to Herman Ruf. Oct. 19. 900

Clinton av, e s, 125 n proposed Tremont av, 25x100. Same to Henry C. Wyand. Oct. 19. 975

Clinton av, w s, 75 n Lebanon st, 25x100.
Prospect av, w s, 100 n Lebanon st, 25x100. } Same to Louis Eickwort and Martin Walter. Oct. 19. 1,575

Clinton av, s e cor Elmwood pl, 25x100x24.7x100. Same to John Gribbin. Oct. 19. 1,425

Clinton av, w s, 25 s Oakland pl, 75x100.
Clinton av, e s, 25 n Lebanon st, 50x100.
Clinton av, e s, 66 n Oakland pl, 46.3x100x43x100.
Crotona av, n e cor Oakland pl, 48x100x49x100.
Crotona av, e s, 74.3 s Elmwood pl, 25x96.1.
John J. Brady to Lena Seiferd. Oct. 19. 7,425

Creston av, w s, 350 s 183d st, 50x125. Mary Haworth widow to Jane Riley. Nov. 9. 2,000

Crimmins av, e s, 100 n Beech terrace, 25x111. William H. McCord, New York, and Andrew J. Post, Jersey City, to Alfred B. Hall. C. a. G. *Mt.* $1,000. Nov. 9. 2,000

Crimmins av, w s, 537.4 n 141st st, 25x80. William R. Beal Land Improvement Co. to William H. McCord. Nov. 9. 1,700

Crimmins av, e s, 100 n Beech terrace, 25x111.
141st st, n s, 125 w Beekman av, 25x109.7x25x111.4.
Same to William H. McCord, New York and Andrew J. Post, Jersey City. Oct. 22. 4,500

Crimmins av, w s, 562.4 n 141st st, 25x80. Alfred B. Hall to Andrew J. Post, Jersey City. C. a. G. *Mt.* $700. Nov. 9. 1,700

Crotona av, s w cor Lebanon st, 25x100x26x100; also,
Crotona av, w s, 75 n Lebanon st, 50x100. } John J. Brady to Robert and Peter Chapman. Oct. 19. 2,675

Crotona av, w s, 275 s Lebanon st, 64.9x51.7x67.6x70.10. Same to Christian P. Roos. Oct. 19. 1,290

Crotona av, w s, 125 n Lebanon st, 25x100. Same to Cornelius Mullane. Oct. 19. 775

Crotona av, w s, 250 s Lebanon st, 25x70.10x26x78.3. Same to Katie A. Mullen. Oct. 19. 600

Crotona av, e s, 90.7 n Tremont av as intended, 25x96.1x26x96.1. Same to Mary and Rose V. Malone. Oct. 19. 1,000

Crotona av, w s, 75 n Oakland pl, runs west 100 x north 25 x west 23 x north 73.1 x east 126.6 to av, x south 81. Same to Mary E. Monaghan. Oct. 19. 1,905

Crotona av, w s, 25 n Oakland pl, 25x100. Same to Albert Schaefer. Oct. 19. 600

Crotona av, e s, 72 n Oakland pl, 24x100. Same to Edward J. Cronin. Oct. 19. 695

Crotona av, w s, 50 n Oakland pl, 25x100. Same to Annie S. McCormack. Oct. 19. 600

Crotona av, e s, 25 n Elmwood pl, 50x100. Same to Bernard Bray. Oct. 19. 2,080

Crotona av, e s, 99.4 s Elmwood pl, 25x96.1. Same to Mary A. and Kate Foley. Oct. 19. 1,075

Crotona av, n e cor Elmwood pl, 25x100. Same to Martin Paperczinsky. Oct. 19. 1,425

Crotona av, e s, 75 n Elmwood pl, 25x100.
Crotona av, w s, 25 s Lebanon st, 25x100. } Same to Karoline Weyand. Oct. 19. 1,955

Crotona av, n w cor Oakland pl, 25x100x24x100. John J. Brady to Kate Seiferd. October 19. 775

Forrest av, s b. s, parts of lots 17 and 18 map Woodstock, runs southeast 300 x northeast 89.10 x northwest 200 x southwest 49.10 x northwest 100 to av, x southwest 40, excepting land taken for Tinton and Concord or

Forrest avs. Sarah Jackson to Frank E. Wallace, East Orange, N. J. Oct. 16. 6,300

Grove av, w s. 400 n Cliff st, 50x125. Franklin B. Boudinot to August Sendelbeck. Nov. 7. nom

Intervale av, s w cor Tiffany st, 101.1x62.9x 27.4x115.10. Louise Harris widow to Ferdinand Hirsch. July 7. 500

Jefferson av, s e s, lots 126 and 127 Samuel Ryer homestead. Hannah M. Van Reed individ. and extrx. Jacob H. Van Reed to John L. Landis, Cape May, N. J. Q. C. Sept. 8. nom

Jefferson av, s e s, lots 126 and 127 map Samuel Ryer homestead, 50x175x50x170. John L. Landis and Florence N. his wife to Robert I. Lomas, Jr. Sept. 15. nom

Jerome av, w s, 200 n Wolf pl, 50.6x146x10.4x 140. Clara Fairchild to William C. Mead. Nov. 2. 2,200

Jerome av, w s, 175 n Wolf pl, 25x140. William B. Kaufman to Washington Mead. All title. Nov. 5. 1,600

Opdyke av, n s, 400 e 2d st, 50x151.4x50x151.10. William H. Newman to Michael J. Cohalan. Nov. 12. 900

Pelham av, s e cor Arthur av, 25.6x98.5x25x 98.6. Leonora C. Jones to Gaetano Del Bello and Angelo Di Ciocca. Oct. 31. 5,000

Prospect av, e s, 216.8 n from n w cor lot 67 map village of Woodstock, 16.8x100. Mary E. McCarthy to Margaret A. wife of Charles E. Fogerty. *Mt.* $2,500. Nov. 5. 5,250

Prospect av, s w cor Elmwood pl, 45x100.
Prospect av, n w cor Elmwood pl, 60x100.
Crotona av, n w cor Lebanon st, 25x100x24x 100.
Prospect av, n w cor Oakland pl, 21x100x 20.11x100.
Clinton av, n e cor Oakland pl, 22x100x22.4x 100.
Clinton av, proposed w s at intersection present n s Locust av, runs north to point 100 north from proposed n s Tremont av, x west 100 x south 109.3 to present or old n s Locust av, x east 100.
John J. Brady to Helen T. wife of Peter Coughlin. Oct. 19. 14,820

Prospect av, w s, 25 s Oakland pl, 25x100. Same to Thomas Graham. Oct. 19. 830

Prospect av, w s, 84 n Oakland pl, 19.9x100x22.9 x100. Same to Annie H. Farrell. Oct. 19. 525

Prospect av, s w cor Lebanon st, 20x100. Same to Libbie B. wife of R. E. Holder. Oct. 19. 1,000

Prospect av, w s, 95 n proposed Tremont av, runs north 75 x west 123 x south 25 x east 4 x south 49.10 x east 119.
Prospect av, w s, 20 s Lebanon st, 60x100.
Same to Margaret E. wife of Felix Amabile. Oct. 19. 5,070

Prospect av, n w cor Lebanon st, runs west 124 x north 100 x east 24 x south 50 x east 100 to av, x south 50. Same to Thomas J. Reilly. Oct. 19. 2,520

Railroad av, e s, 104 n 170th st, 25x150x30x150. Peter Handibode to Anna wife of Ferdinand Ruser. Oct. 29. 2,000

Railroad av, e s, 129 n 170th st, 25x150x30x150. Same to George P. Andrae. Nov. 5. 2,000

Stebbins av, w s, 145.4 n 167th st, runs north 30 x west 41.4 x west 41.4 to Prospect av, x south 30 x east 37.3 x east 37.3. John J. Brady to Henry Gugisperg. Nov. 10. 1,000

Tremont av proposed, n s, 44 w Prospect av, 25x95, with all land lying bet proposed n s aforesaid and present old n s Locust av. John J. Brady to William J. Reynolds. Oct. 19. 1,600

Tremont av proposed, n s, 119 w Prospect av, runs north 145 x west 4 x north 145 to Elmwood pl, x west 23 x south 145 x east 2 x south 145 to av, x east 25, with all land as above. Same to Frederick Boss. Oct. 19. 2,030

Tremont av proposed, n s, 100 w Clinton av, 23 x117.6x23 3x117.6, with all land as above. Same to Louis Frankenstein. Oct. 19. 1,675

Tremont av, n s, as proposed, 71.1 e Crotona av, 25x90.7. Same to Margaret J. Howe. Oct. 19. 1,600

Tremont av, s w cor Clinton av, proposed lines, 25x100. Same to Jacob Poulin. Oct. 19. 2,300

Tinton av, n w s, parts of lots 17 and 18 map Woodstock, runs northwest 150 x northeast 40 x northwest 19 x northeast 49.10 x southeast 169 to av, x southwest 89.10. Frank E. Wallace, East Orange, N. J., to Ellen Anderson. Nov. 5. 5,300

Tinton av, No. 914, e s, 181.4 s 163d st, 26.7x135, h & l. Friederich Breitenbach to Jacob Waller. *Mt.* $1,500. Nov. 2. 3,800

Valentine av, w s, north ½ of lot 17 map south part of Peter Valentine farm, Fordham, &c., 25x250. Mary Pearson to Alice Burke. Nov. 5. 2,500

Vanderbilt av, e s, 25 n Talmadge st or 180th st, sometimes Samuel st, 25x100. Auguste J. Paris to Jane Kelly. Nov. 4. 1,250

Washington av, w s, lot 91 partition map heirs T. Bassford, Fordham, 50.2x115x50x110.6. Henry A. Bassford trustee under trust deed to Otto Wagner. Nov. 6. 3,225

Webster av, s e s, 50 n e Scott av. 25x100. Anna wife of John McComb to John B. Armanino. *Mt.* $225. Nov. 14. 1,000

Webster av, e s, 172 n 171st st, not yet opened, 25x111.1 to Mill Brook, x25.6x107.6.
Webster av, e s, 247 n 171st st, not yet opened, 25x100.3 to Mill Brook, x26.1x107.10.
Fanny wife of Robert I. Lomas, Jr., to Nellie D. Traphagen, Brooklyn. Nov. 4. 3,200

Wetmore av, n w s, 125 s w Lafayette av, 100x 101 to Harlem River & Portchester R. R., x —x112. Foreclos. Robert L. Reade to A. Ward Brigham. June 1, 1891. 1,100

Willis av, s e cor 146th st, 25x100. Foreclos. Edmund D. Hennessy to Ernst E. Meyer. Sub. to judgment, foreclos. and sale $20,655, also $409. Nov. 5. 11,300

Lot 416 map part Chas. Berrian farm, Fordham. West End Co-operative Building and Loan Assoc. to Joseph Machevin. Oct. 30. 3,150

Lots 224–230 map of Edward T. Young, Springhurst. Contract of sale of ½ of proceeds of sale. Edward J. and Corinne Churchill with Lillie C. Nevil. Nov. 2. 200

Lots 219–222 inclus. amended map Central Mott Haven, with use of wharf in front of premises and right of way to river, &c. John H. Cheever to James and Olin J. Stephens. Aug. 12. 30,000

Lot of land under waters of Harlem River in front of and adj lands of Elizabeth M. Stephens, begins at east shore of River at common high water mark and line dividing lands of Jordan L. Mott from upland of said Stephens, runs northwest 581.2 to new bulkhead line established by Commissioners of Central Park, x northeast 123.3 x southeast 607.10 to common high water mark and centre of Grove st, x southwest 126, contains 1.682-1,000 acres. Letters patent. The people of the State of New York to Elizabeth M. Stevens. June 21, 1870. nom

Plot begins 5.8 n Kingsbridge road on line which at n s of same is 193.6 e of Marion av, runs north 51.6 x east 43.6 x southwest 15 to old n s of Kingsbridge road, x southwest 46.1 to beginning, with all title in land lying bet old and new lines of Kingsbridge road. Auguste J. Paris to William W. Edwards. Nov. 5. 2,500

LEASEHOLD CONVEYANCES.

Baxter st, No. 60, w s, 50 s Franklin st, 25x58.6 x25x60.10. Assign. lease. Nathan Cohen to Louis Siegel. Nov. 5. 5,000

Broadway, s w cor 9th st, 29.2x121.4x21.1x123.
Broadway, w s, 29.2 s 9th st, 26.6x119.7x26.7 x121.4.
Assign. leases. Clarence White and Henry M. Lewis trustees and James C. and Samuel S. White, Jr., exrs. Samuel S. White to Marks Arnheim. nom

Grand st, No. 381. Assign. lease. Morris Hodes to Pauline Hodes. 200

Same property. Consent that above assign. shall have priority over judgment and release. Sidney G. Hirschberg to Morris and Pauline Hodes. nom

Same property. Assign. lease. Pauline Hodes to Solomon Zirinsky. nom

Prince st, No. 145. Assign. lease. Frank Recher to Edward G. Schroeder. Nov. 5. nom

West Broadway, No. 74, w s. Assign. lease. Elmer M. Meyer to Henry Voege and Henry Wiegand. Nov. 9. nom

2d st, n s, 19.6 e Av A, 20.2x57.5. Assign. lease. Jacob Hinklein to Joseph Trefzger and Elise his wife. Oct. 27. 4,250

9th st, No. 191, s s, 307.6 w 2d av, 21x75. Hamilton Fish to The Singer Mfg Co. 21 years, from May 1, 1887, per year, taxes and 550

12th st, No. 728 E. Assign. lease. Shannon & Spellman to Mary Spellmann. nom

14th st, s s, 34 e 5th av, 33x103.3, all. Mary S. Van Beuren to Joseph L. Spofford and ano. exrs. Susan Spofford. 21 years, from Feb. 1, 1889, per year, taxes, &c., and 4,125

23d st, n s, 175 w 10th av, 25x98.8. Consent to assign. lease. Mary C. Ogden to Frederick Wood. Oct. 31. nom

28th st, No. 527 W. Assign. lease. Peter Fitzpatrick to M. Groh's Sons. Nov. 7. nom

36th st, n s, 375 e 9th av, 38x98.9. Consent to assign. lease. Asbury Methodist Episcopal Church to Anton Dobler. nom

Av A, w s, 22.10 n 6th st. Assign. lease. Barbara Ferdinand admrx. George Schwartz to Dinah Klein. 10,100

Av B, w s, 48.6 n 5th st, 24.3x100. Alonzo C. Monson guard. of Monson Morris to Isaak Schwarzkopf. 21 years, from Jan. 1, 1892, per year, taxes, &c., and 800

Av C, w s, 69.9 s 9th st, 23x83. Assign. lease. Phoebe A. Cheesman admrx. John L. Cheesman to James B. Scott. Oct. 27. nom

Amsterdam av, s e cor 83d st. Assign. lease. D. G. Yuengling, Jr., Brewing Co. to Catherine Aylward. Nov. 5. nom

Same property. Assign. lease. John W. Aylward to same. July 17. nom

Same property. Catherine Aylward to Roger W. Bligh. Nov. 5. nom

1st av, No. 1111. Assign. lease. Thomas Fleming to H. Koehler & Co. nom

8th av, w s, 28 n 22d st, 14x58. Katharine T. Moore, Ossining, N. Y., to John P. R. Wells. 21 years, from Nov. 1, 1893, per year, taxes, &c., and 312

11th av, 19th st, 18th st and exterior or 13th av. Assign lease. Darius C. Newell to D. C. Newell & Sons' Hudson River Mill and Lumber Co. Oct. 21. 200,000

11th av, exterior or 13th av, 19th st, 18th st. Consent to assign. lease. Adeline, William H., Annie H., Joseph and Charles Fischer, New Brunswick, N. J., to The D. C. Newell & Sons Hudson River Mill and Lumber Co. Sept. 11. nom

KINGS COUNTY.

NOVEMBER 5, 6, 7, 9, 10, 11.

Adams st, w s, 61.10 s York st, 21x88.4, h & l. Martin F. Conly to Catharine L. Gallagher. B. & S. *Mt.* $2,500. nom

Same property. Catharine L. Gallagher to Mary V. wife of Martin F. Conly. B. & S. *Mt.* $2,500. nom

Adelphi st, w s, 200 n Park av, runs north 20.4 x west 70 x north 40 x west 81.3 x south 116.1 x east 21 x south 15 x east to point 55.10 w Adelphi st, x north — x east 55.10. John Long and John Barnes to Patrick J. Carlin. Q. C. $1,200

Adelphi st, w s, 761.10 s Park av, 25.4x100. Ida M. Myers individ. and as extrx. Henry V. Myers and Charles P. Johnson, of Lopez Island, San Juan Co., State of Washington, to Allen Shryock, of Philadelphia, Pa. 3,000

Adelphi st, w s, 761.10 s Park av, 25x100. William K. and Allen Shryock, of Philadelphia, Pa., to James Beith. 4,000

Ashford st, e s, 150 n Eastern Parkway, 125x 90; also,
Ashford st, w s, 150 n Eastern Parkway, 100 x90.
George W. Hadfield to James H. Evans. nom

Ashland pl, No. 149, e s, 90 n Hanson pl, 15x 79.6x15x80.2. Foreclos. John Courtney to Charles and Sarah Dennis as exrs. Chas. Dennis. 4,000

Bergen st, n s, 197.10 w 4th av, 20x100. M. Edner wife of Oscar M. Lyon to Richard L. Davison. nom

Bergen st, n s, 197.10 w 4th av, 20x100. Richard L. Davison to John A. Palmer. 3,400

Bergen st, n s, 165 e Stone av, 10x107.2. Arthur H. Lowerre to Joseph La Fumee. Sub. to mort. nom

Bergen st, s s, 250 w Kingston av, 60x105. George K. Thomas to William H. Hoople. *Mt.* $3,000. nom

Bleecker st, easterly cor Knickerbocker av, runs northeast 107.8 to Myrtle av, x east 60 x south 80 x west 25 x southwest 74.2 to Knickerbocker av, x northwest 80 to beginning. Release mort. The Williamsburgh Savings Bank to John D. Fish. 6,000

Boerum st, n s, 28.1 e Broadway, 22x100, h & l. Johanna Nash to William Emich and Emma his wife, joint tenants. 7,600

Same property. Release mort. Peter Bertsch to Johanna Nash. 4,000

Boerum st, n s, 75 w Bogert st, runs west 85x — to Johnson av at point 78.3 w Bogert st, x east 5, x south 102.5.
Bogert st, n e cor McKibbin st, 175.2x110.11 x175x104.4.
Charles W. Trueslow admr. William Wall to Alois Lazansky and Henry Roth. 9,605

Boerum st, n s, 272.9 e Bushwick av, 25x73.5x 25x75. Frederick Reges to Andrew Hoffmann. *Mt.* $4,800. 6,700

Butler st, n s, 60 e Hoyt st, 20x100. J. Addie Byrnes heir Thomas Byrnes to Charles H. Lohr. Q. C. nom

Broadway, n e s, 21 n w Moffat st, 19x80. Release mort. Rudolph Reimer to Bernhard Davidsburg. 2,000

Same property. Bernhard Davidsburg to Henry Newman. *Mt.* $7,000. 10,000

Broadway, s w s, 109.3 s e McDonough st, 20x60 x—x71. Henry C. Bauer to Thomas Stone. 8,500

Broadway, s s, 540 w Brooklyn av, 40x100, Flatbush. Edward Egolf to Antonia Trezza. 500

Broadway, s w s, 94.9 s e McDougal st, runs southwest to w s of old road, x north to Broadway, x southeast —. City of Brooklyn to James T. Benedict. Q. C. nom

Chestnut st, w s, 1,375 n 4th st, 25x150. George Beach to John L. Hazard. 2,600

Clark st, s s, 175 e Hicks st, 25x185.6. Francis E. Dodge and William H. Boughton exrs. Richard J. Dodge to Henry L. Meyer. 13,500

Clark st, n s, 137.4 w Henry st, 22.5x100x22.8x 100. Joseph P. Wintringham to Sarah A. Wenzel. *Mt.* $8,000. 11,000

College pl, w s, 89.6 n Love lane, 19.8x82. Herbert D. Robbins exr. Matilda L. Robbins to Mortimer C. Ogden. 8,000

Cook st, s s, 187.3 e Humboldt st, 16.7x100. John P. McQuid to Louis Windstein. 2,000

Covert st, s s, 198 e Central av, 107.10x100. Release mort. Ida L. T. Ledoux to Isabelle B. Booth. nom

Dean st, n s, 300 w New York av, 20x100. John A. Bliss to Henry Elliott. *Mt.* $7,000. 14,500

Dean st, n s, 200 w Unionhill av, 50x117.5. James Shevlin to John Downie. 3,000

Decatur st, s s, 175 w Ralph av, 300x100. William C. Booth to Randolph H. Cole. 25,500

Dodworth st, s s, 178.2 e Broadway late Division av, 50x91.6. Withelmina Pfitzenmaier and Franciska wife of and Charles Seidel heirs George Brickner to George S. Wheeler. Q. C. 200

Same property. Wilhelmina Pfitzenmaier and Friedericka Seidel to same. Affirms deed made in 1881. nom

Dodworth st, s s, bet Broadway and Bushwick av, being on assessm't map 18th Ward, lot 10 block 1034. George S. Wheeler to William Herterick. nom

Dodworth st, s s, 160 e Broadway late Division av, 25x91.6. John Sinclair to Nicholas Will. 2,000

Dodworth st, e s, 206.7 n Broadway, 25x91.6. William Herterich to Nicholas Will. 2,300

Dodworth st, s s, 178.2 e Broadway late Division av, 25x91.6. George S. Wheeler to William M. Gibson. nom

Dunham pl, w s, 197 n South 7th st, old line, 18.7 x92.6. Elizabeth Sterling, Mary J. Hiller, Judith A. Lewis and William Vosburgh devisees William Vosburgh to William S. Liptrott. nom

Same property. Alexander F. Vosburgh, Dorcas E. Bortel, Evedna M. Weatherwax, George H. Vosburgh and Abbie E. Van Bramer devisees under will of William Vosburgh to same. nom

Same property. Francis P., Hiram, Jay and Edwd. H. Vosburgh and Charlotte Coon devisees under will of William Vosburgh to same. nom

Same property. Charles H. Vosburgh a devisee of William Vosburgh to same. nom

Same property. Jasper Van Wormer and Egbert W. Stone exrs. William Vosburgh to same. 4,000

Eastern Parkway, s e cor Jerome st, 25x100. Union Real Estate Co. of New York to Johanna H. wife of Peter H. Brandt. 1,500

Eastern Parkway, s e cor Milford st, 40x90. Julia E. Browne to William T. Goundie. 951

Eastern Parkway, s s, 25 w Bennett av, 25x100. John T. B. Pouch to John Bradley. 1,200

Eldert st, south cor Evergreen av, 75x— to W. Covert farm line. Foreclos. John Courtney to William F. Richards. 9,000

Elton st, e s, 345 s Stanley av, 80x100. Erastus D. Benedict to Kate wife of Charles Dahl. C. a. G. nom

Same property. Charles Dahl to Erastus D. Benedict. nom

Elton st, w s, 125 n Arlington av, 25x100. Benjamin S. Law to De Witt C. E. Baisley. 1,000

Ewen st, e s, 18 n Jackson st, 15.4x75. James Kelly to Bridget and Ann Kelly. nom

Fiske pl, w s, 182 n Garfield pl, 48x96. Ida M. wife of and James F. Ransom to Charles S. Kendall. *Mt.* $23,800. nom

Floyd st, n s, 125 w Throop av, 25x100. Andreas Mahr to Andreas Knapp. 7,100

Frost st, No. 179, n s, 175 w Humboldt st, 25x70x25.3x78.3. Erastus N. Root personally, Louisa E., Frank W., Elsie and Sarah Root by guard. to Peter Crean. All title. 700

Same property. Mary H. Clocher, Louisa E. Smith, Thos. S. and William J. Wells to same. 4-5 part. 2,800

Fulton st, n w cor Linwood st, 25.6x97.6x25x92.4. Frederick Newman, Middle Village, L. I., to Jacob H. Sturm. 3,250

Same property. Jacob H. Sturm to Mathilde Lehmann. 2,500

Glenada pl, w s, 100 s Decatur st, 49.9x100, hs & ls
Glenada pl, w s, 149.9 s Decatur st, runs west 100 x south 88.2 x east 24.11 x south 6.10 x east 77.2 to pl, x north 50 8, hs & ls.
Charles D. Rust to Herman T. Livingston, of Livingston, N. Y. *Mt.* $50,000. 85,000

Grand st, n s, 59 w Marcy av, 16x100. Herman Newman to James Black. 5,650

Grove st, n w s, 190 s w Central av, 40x100. Release mort. The Williamsburgh Savings Bank to John Rapp. nom

Halsey st, n w s, 120 n e Evergreen av, 40x100. Lucinda Mosdinger extrx. John Mosdinger to James A. Caufield or Canfield. 2,400

Halsey st, n s, 66.8 e Saratoga av, 16.8x100, h & l. Bernard Levino to Ellen McCarthy. *Mt.* $1,500. 3,000

Hancock st, n s, 475 e Reid av, 18.7x100. Edgar Logan, of Yonkers, N. Y., to Charles H. Schoch. *Mt.* $4,500. 8,000

Hancock st, n s, 475 e Reid av, 18.7x100. Charles H. Schoch to John S. Robinson. *Mt.* $4,500. 8,000

Hancock st, n s, 169 w Lewis av, 18x100, h & l. George W. Keiffen to Elizabeth Von Gersdorff. *Mt.* $6,000. 7,200

Harman st, s e s, 100 n e Hamburg av, 50x100. Release mort. Theodore F. Jackson and John G. Jenkins and Alexander Frazer trustees Loftus Wood dec'd to Abby E. Laytin. 3,500

Harman st, n w s, 100 s w Hamburg av, 100x100. Release mort. Same to Darwin R. James. 3,064

Same property. Darwin R. James to Christian and Andrew Hahn. 5,800

Harman st, s e s, 100 n e Hamburg av, 50x100. Abby E. Laytin, New York, to John J. Hennemann. 2,800

Harman st, n w s, 350 n e Central av, 50x100. Frederick Weisbrod to Andrew and Christian Hahn. 2,900

Hart st, s e s, 120 n e Broadway, 20x73.3x20x73.8, h & l. Henry Newman to Bertha Kaufmann. *Mt.* $5,800. 8,000

Hart st, n s, 338 e Nostrand av, 20x100. Thomas E. Greenland to Caroline wife of Jonathan Moore. *Mt.* $3,000. 9,100

Hart st, s e s, 120 n e Broadway, 20x73.3x20x73.8. Bertha Kaufmann to Leopold Weil. *Mt.* $5,800. 8,000

Hawthorne st, n s, 540.6 w Nostrand av, 80x166.8.
Winthrop st, n s, 100 e Rogers av, 50x106, Flatbush.
Stephen R. Sturges to John F. Hart. nom

Hawthorne st, n s, 540 6 w Nostrand av, 40x166.8; also,
Winthrop st, n s, 102 9 e Rogers av, 40x106, Flatbush.
Release mort. The Brooklyn Hospital to John F. Hart. 1,000

Hawthorne st, n s, 142 e Rogers av, 1.6x166.8, Flatbush. Release mort. Same to same. nom

Hawthorne st, n s, 540.6 w Nostrand av, 80x166.8, Flatbush. Release mort. Asa W. Parker to same. nom

Same property. Daniel Doody to John C. H. J. Kramer. *Mt.* $2,500. 5,500

Hendrix st, e s, 100 n Arlington av, 24.8x100. George U. Ferbell to Mary Skahan. *Mt.* $2,500. 3,750

Hemlock st, e s, 150 s Griffen pl, 50x100. Israel Y. Cochran to Anna M. Leinfelder. 4,600

Herkimer st, s s, 51 e Saratoga av, 15.6x87. Helena wife of and William H. H. Robbins to Charles D. King. *Mt.* $800. nom

Herkimer st, s s, 72 e Kingston av, 17.6x100. Henry W. Withrow to Carrie A. Withrow. *Mt.* $3,900. nom

Himrod st, s e s, 200 s w Irving av, 100x100. William L. Bowron and Mary E. Beattie to Richard T. Burke. *Mt.* $2,600. 4,500

Bull st, s s, 300 e Rockaway av, 30x100, hs & ls. William J. Howie to Ann C. Howie his wife. 10,000

Hull st, s s, 315 e Rockaway av, 15x100. Release mort. Albro J. Newton to William J. Howie. 900

Humboldt st, e s, 60 s Frost st, 20x80. Peter Mahon to James Wilson. *Mt.* $500. 1,500

Jefferson pl, n s, centre line, 475 e Nostrand av, 20x135, Flatbush. Margaret C. Shea to Mary Knoell. 275

Jerome st, e s, 175 n Belmont av, 25x100. Philip Altstadt to Louis H. Odler. 3,200

Johnson st, n s, 100 e Bowne st, 75x125.2x75x125.1. Thomas Watson to James Haley. 1,000

Johnson st, No. 184, and 95 Prince st, begins Johnson st, s e cor Prince st, 23x75. Nathaniel J. Stopenhagen to Emma and Mary Wilkinson. 300

Joralemon st, s s, 29 w Clinton st, runs south 65 x south 47.10 x west 18.7 x north 103.8 to Joralemon st, x east 25. Charles F. Schmidt to Mary E. wife of Frederick B. Richardson. 22,500

Kane pl, e s, 121.7 n Atlantic av, 46x105. Mary A. Taylor to John Fallon. nom

Kosciusko st, n s, 125 e Lewis av, 18x100. Oscar Stern and Hugo S. Mack, of New York, to Meta Salberg. 8,000

Lake st, e s, 138.2 n Av U, 40x75.
Gravesend av, w s, 280 n Av U, 40x75, Gravesend.
Mary E. C. Johnson to Michael Hayes. 470

Lincoln pl, s s, 237.6 w 6th av, 18.9x100. Henry V. Raymond to Edward P. Nichols. 7,200

Linden st, e s, 295.11 n Evergreen av, 20x100. Aaron Kaplan to Nathan and Marks Rosenberg. *Mt.* $2,500. 4,500

Macon st, s s, 411 e Reid av, 18x100. James G. Roberts to John F. Ross. *Mt.* $5,500. 9,000

Macon st, n s, 276.6 w Marcy av, 19.6x100, h & l. William H. Reynolds to Emma L. Freeman. *Mt.* $7,500. 14,000

Macon st. Party wall agreement. Mary A. Burrows with Frank C. Swimm. 125

Macon st, n s, 308.10 e Ralph av, 18x100. Grant L. Nichols, of New York, to Adelbert S. Nichols. *Mt.* $4,000. 6,500

Madison st, n w s, 320 n e Hamburg av, 20x100. Release mort. James Gascoine individ. and with ano. exrs. John G. Cozine to Adolphus Gload. 1,250

Madison st, No. 341. Elisha G. Selchow to John M. Baldwin. Contract to exchange for Fort Hamilton av, n e cor 65th st, 166.8x180.7x—x 188.6. —

Madison st, e s, 100 s Baltic av, 25x100. Frederick H. Lawrence exr. Geo. C. Tallman to Michael F. O'Connell. 325

Marion st, n s, 350 e Stuyvesant av, 100x100. Foreclos. John Courtney to Willis H. Young, George H. Gerard and Adolphus F. Quick. 32,225

McDonough st, n s, 158.6 e Reid av, 19.6x100. Ransom F. Clayton to Hattie L. Ehlers. *Mt.* $4,000. 6,500

McDonough st, n s, 302 e Reid av, 145.6x100. Release mort. Joseph C. Hoagland to John Peirce. 9,500

Same property. John Peirce to James G. Roberts. 13,095

McDonough st, n s, 366.8 w Reid av, 16 8x100. Mary M. Parsons to Caroline Wilkins, of Wakefield Heights, New York, and Mary E. Schilling. B. & S. gift

McDonough st, n s, 172 w Ralph av, 18.8x100. Albert Sibley to Howard M. Smith. *Mt.* $3,750. 1,522

McDonough st, n s, 265.4 w Ralph av, 18.8x100.
Bainbridge st, n s, 62.6 w Ralph av, 18.9x100.
Jefferson av, n s, 42 e Tompkins av, 19x80.3.
Chauncey st, s s, 205 e Howard av, 20x100.
Albert Sibley to Jacob G. Dettmer. *Mt.* $13,750. 6,000

McDonough st, n s, 190 8 w Ralph av, 18.8x100. Albert Sibley to William Ziegler. *Mt.* $3,750. 2,025

Meserole st, n s, 120 e Union av, 25x100. Louise Klamke an heir of Caroline Wedeke to Franz Wedeke. Q. C. 3,000

Meserole st, n s, 40 e Lorimer st, 40x100. Charles Renz exr. Raphael Renz to The Joseph Fallert Brewing Co. (Lim.) 11,000

Monitor st, w s, 83.8 s Driggs st, 18x100. Charles Engert to Oliver L. Judd, of New York. *Mt.* $1,900. 3,800

Monroe st, s s, 345.3 w Tompkins av, 20x100. Amanda T. Cole to Charlotte B. Cogswell. 5,050

Moore st, n s, 329.5 w White st, 50x100. Charles W. Truslow admr. William Wall to Frederick Elflein. 2,350

Osborn st, e s, 150 n Sutter av, 25x100. Salo Weinstein and Aaron Altmann to Joseph Morris. 900

Pacific st, s s, 50 w Kingston av, 50x107. Foreclos. John Courtney to Lizzie Montgomery. 9,500

Pacific st, n s, 45 e Grand av, 20x80. Gouverneur Tillotson exr. William Hawkins to Oscar A. See. nom

Pacific st, s s, 363.10 e Rochester av, 16.9x107.2. Foreclos. John Courtney to Henry A. Stone. 2,000

Pacific st, s s, 380.7 e Rochester av, 16.8x107.2. Foreclos. Same to same. 2,000

Pacific st, s s, 363.10 e Rochester av, 33.5x107.2. Henry A. Stone to Francis H. Cowdrey, of New Rochelle. *Mt.* $4,200. nom

Park pl, n s, 325 w Buffalo av, 40x127.9. George T. Van Doorn to Sophronia Taylor. 696

Partition st, n e s, 350 n w Conover st, 25x100, h & l. Jeremiah Batton to Caroline Rutlier. *Mt.* $600. 3,350

Pleasant pl, e s, 133.1 n Atlantic av, 34.10x95, h & l. Stephen B. Sturges to John D. Fish. nom

Plymouth st, n w cor Little st, 32.7x60x56 to Little st, x southwest 64.6. Lewis Krulewitch to Jacob, Isidor and Moritz C. Alexander. *Mt.* $8,000. 14,000

Plymouth st, n s, 200.1 e Hudson av, 28.2x100. Foreclos. John Courtney to Julia W. Latimer. 9,000

Powers st, s s, 136.2 w Graham av, 37 6x75. Eliza J. Westerfield, New York, to Jennie W. wife of Herman C. Francke, of St. Louis. *Mt.* $3,000. gift

Prescott pl, e s, 89.6 n Atlantic av, runs east 51 x north 0.6 x east 39 x north 15.6 x west 90 to pl, x south 16. Christopher P. Skelton to Mary wife of James Weir. 25

President st, No. 192, s s, 142 e Henry st, 25x100. Elizabeth W. Lewis, of Hempstead, to Nicolo Podesta. *Mt.* $3,500. 7,500

Prospect pl, n s, 105.5 w 6th av, 20x81. John E. Eustis assignee Wm. L. Burke to Harriet E. Burke. 100

Pulaski st, s s, 255 w Tompkins av, 57.6x100. Lizzie B. wife of and Niels Poulson to Matilde Eger. 16,000

Quincy st, s s, 84 w Lewis av, 41x100, h & l. Mary A. Cornell to Mary A. Bloom, New York. *Mt.* $8,000. exch

Quincy st, s s, 365 e Nostrand av, 20x100. Mary S. Everett to John E. Aldridge. *Mt.* $3,900. 5,500

Quincy st, s s, 100 w Throop av, 187.6x100.
Quincy st, s s, 306.3 w Throop av, 112.6x100.
Quincy st, s s, 437.6 w Throop av, 75x100.
Albert Sibley to David F. Manning. *Mt.* $99,161. other consid. and 12,000

Quincy st, s s, 287.6 w Throop av, 18.9x100. Albert Sibley to James White. *Mt.* $4,500. nom

Ralph st, n w s, 100 s w Knickerbocker av, 200x100. John D. Fish to Stephen P. Sturges. *Mt.* $1,700. exch and 5,000

Ralph st, n w s, 220 s w Knickerbocker av, 80x100. Release mort. Charles W. Truslow admr. Wm. Wall to John D. Fish. 1,000

Raymond st, s w cor Boliver st, 75x75. Lew E. Davis, of New York, to Augusta P. wife of Henry M. Johnson. *Mt.* $35,000. nom

Rodney st, s e s, 80 n e Wythe av, 20x100. Fannie A. Skeele to James C. McEachen. *Mt.* $4,500. nom

Russell st, e s, 115 s Norman av, 20x100, h & l. William F. Corwith to John J. Schutta. *Mt.* $1,800. 3,600

Sackman st, w s, 63.8 s Belmont av, 17.6x100. Simon C. Wilson, of Baldwins, N. Y., to James P. Clifford. *Mt.* $1,750. 3,250

Schaeffer st, n w s, 425 n e Broadway, 25x100. Henry Scherf to Adam Dietrich. 7,750

Same property. Adam Dietrich to Herman B. Scharmann. 7,761

South Oxford st, w s, 123 n Lafayette av, 22x100. Foreclos. John Courtney to Edwin F. Knowlton. 13,200

Starr st, n w s, 225 n e Hamburg av, 25x100, h & l. Barbara Spitzmiller to Anna M. Diehl. nom

Steuben st, w s, 121.2 s Flushing av, 25x100. Alonzo E. De Baun to Charles F. Bond. 1,850

Stockton st, s s, 200 e Throop av, 25x100. Catharine wife of and Thomas E. Talbett to Catharina Rothschenk. nom

Stockton st, s s, 428.6 e Nostrand av, 23.2x93.3. Henry Eich to Julius Hartmann. *Mt.* $2,500. 6,400

Stockton st, n s, 325 e Sumner av, 25x100. Henry Hoffmann to Lena Hoffmann. 7,000

Suydam st, s e s, 225 s w Knickerbocker av, 25x100. John Clement to John Koehler. *Mt.* $8,000. 6,375

Union st, s s, 450.2 e 4th av, 33.4x100. Hattie I. wife of Edwin C. Squance to Henry F. Newbury. *Mt.* $4,500. 7,200

Union st, n s, bet Schenectady and Utica avs, lot 55.
Eastern Parkway, s s, bet Schenectady and Utica avs, lot 16.
both being on assessm't map, 24th Ward, lots 55 and 16 block 141. John C. McGuire, Registrar of Arrears, to Henry B. White. 67

Van Buren st, n s, 199.8 e Lewis av, 50.4x100. Mary A. Burrows to Henry H. Cochran. 4,500

Van Buren st, n s, 250 e Lewis av, 75x100. E. Morris Stiger to same. 6,250

Van Buren st, n s, 325 e Lewis av, 50x100. Richard Ingraham to same. 4,000

Van Buren st, n s, 199.8 e Lewis av, 0.4x100. Release mort. Catherine Ditmis, of Jamaica, to Mary A. Burrows. nom

Vanderbilt st, s s, 491.8 e Short st, 16.8x108, Flatbush. Sophronia M. Fickett to Hugh R. Moffatt. 2,700

Van Voorhis st, s s, 100 e Evergreen av, 200x100. Gilbert Haynes to Noah Tebbets. nom

Walton st, n w s, 100 s w Harrison av, 25x100, h & l. Jacob Kappeler to Alois Barth. 8,000

Warren st, n s, 241.2 w 5th av, 20x100. John G. Stigler, South Bethlehem, Pa., to Mary Dowling. *Mt.* $3,500. 7,000

Warren st, n s, 407.2 e 4th av, 20x100. Same to same. *Mt.* $3,500. 7,000

Washington st, w s, 260.7 s Concord st, 23.5x

105.8x23.9x107. Dorothea and Fritz Weber to New York and Brooklyn Bridge. 21,500

Washington st, w s, 236.6 s Concord st, runs west 56 x south 0.2 x west 44 x south 23.9 x east 106.6 to Washington st, x north 23.7. Thomas W. Lowell and John S. Spencer to the trustees of the New York and Brooklyn Bridge. 23,500

Washington st, No. 214, w s, 184.4 s Concord st, 27.6x107.8x27.8x107. Abraham M. Stein to the trustees New York and Brooklyn Bridge. 20,000

Washington st, w s, bet Concord and Tillary sts and 29 s land of Francis Howard, 24x125. Samuel Firuski to same. *Mt.* $6,000. 30,000

Watkins st, e s, 175 n Belmont av, 23.6x100. David Blumberg to Herman Moretzky. *Mt.* $1,450. 2,500

Watkins st, No. 497. Party wall agreement. Elias Kaplan to Simon Schnapier. ——

Webster st, s s, 180 e Albany av, 160x100, Flatbush. Christopher C. Watson to Anna G. Williams. All title 880

Webster st, s s, 180 e Albany av. 20x100, Flatbush. Anna G. wife of Sidney Williams to John T. Cody. All title. Correction deed. 175

Weirfield st, n w s, 100 n e Evergreen av, 17.8x100. Annie wife of John Herzog to Michael D. Herzog. *Mt.* $2,250. nom

Wilson st, s s, 19.4 e Wythe av, 19.4x80. Frederick C. Jeandbeur to Theodore R. Lane. Q. C. nom

Winthrop st, n s, 108 9 e Rogers av, 40x106, Flatbush. Release mort. Asa W. Parker, of New Hamburgh, N. Y., to Daniel Doody. nom

Same property. Daniel Doody to Otto Rahnert. 800

Withers st, n s, 38.7 e North 9th st, runs north 50.3 x southwest 62.5 to North 9th st, x southeast 10 to Withers st, x east 38.7. Foreclos. John Courtney to Thomas P. Graham. 960

South 1st st, n w cor Hooper st, 25x77, h & l. Lur Wintjen to Dietrich W. Kaatze. 7,500

2d st, s s, 80 w 7th av, 38.3x100. Jennie L. Ross to Edward V. Slauson. Sub. to mort. 650

East 3d st, w s, 149.11 s Greenwood av, 20x100, Flatbush. Anna M. Ferris to Albert Jensen. 250

North 3d st, n s, 25 e 4th st, 25x85, h & l. James H. Bartley exr. Jane A. Burditt to Louis Morrow. 2,600

North 3d st, n s, 25 e 4th st, 25x85, h & l. Ira F., David W., Theodore H., Sr. and Jr., James B. and Jane A. Burditt to Louis Morrow. B. & S. nom

North 4th st, n e s, 288 s e Wythe av, 25x100. William S. Collins to William Brennan. nom

Same property. William Brennan to Sarah A. wife of William S. Collins. B. & S. nom

South 4th st, s s, 95 e 1st st, 65x140x65x137.7.
North 5th st, east cor 2d st, 300x100.
North 4th st, Kent av, East River and land of Decastro & Donner Sugar Refining Co.
Kent av, s e cor North 5th st, 50x100.
North 5th st and North 6th st, Kent av and East River—the block.
Austin Hulshizer, Jersey City, to Havemeyer & Elder. 1890. nom

Same property. Frederick C., Theodore A. and Henry O. Havemeyer and Charles H. Senff to Austin Hulshizer. 1890 nom

5th st, s w s, 97.10 n w 5th av, 100x100. Susan E. Fingarr, Charles D. Burwell and Frank A. Barnaby to George O. Van Orden. *Mt.* $4,170. 9,800

East 5th st, e s, 105 8 n Greenwood av, 90.10x100x56 9x105.8.
East 5th st, e s, 271.6 n Greenwood av, 125x100, Flatbush.
Samuel M. Whittelsey to Elihu B. Estes. 4,800

North 8th st, n e s, 175 s e Bedford av, 25x100. August C. Diestelhorst to Henry Schultheis. 5,000

East 9th st, e s, 53.4 n Ryer av, 40x100.
East 8th st, w s, 80 s Av M, 40x120.6, Gravesend.
Anna M. Leinfelder to Israel Y. Cochran. *Mt.* $260. nom

10th st, n s, 257.10 w 8th av, 20x100. Release mort. Charles E. Rogers to James F. and Ida M. Ransom. nom

Same property. James F. Ransom to Charles S. Kendall, of New York. *Mt.* $7,000. 9,000

South 10th st, s s, 28 e Berry st, 25x79. Angelica Stecker to Johanna Koch. *Mt.* $2,500. 6,850

11th st, n e s, 187.10 n w 8th av, 200x55.8x200x56.11. Phebe M. Clarke et al. exrs. and trustees Henry L. Clarke and Phebe M. Clarke individ. to Thomas Lahy. *Mt.* $9,000. 10,000

Same property. Thomas Lahy to Charles E. Steck. *Mt.* $9,000. 10,000

12th st, n e s, 187.10 s e 4th av, 20x100. Alexander G. Calder to Minnie S. P. Unwin. *Mt.* $8,000. 7,000

13th st, s s, 306.2 e 4th av, 16.8x100. Eliza A. Griffin to John H. Hall. 3,050

14th st, n s, 197.10 w 3d av, 20x100. Henry McLain, Alice Hempstead and Camilla McLain to Annie Beal. Confirmation deed. nom

Bay 17th st, w s, 125 s 86th st, 75x96.8, New Utrecht. Annie Graves to Adam Henrich. 1,500

East 18th st, e s, 200 s Av A, 50x100, h & l, Flatbush. Frank W. Gilbert to Emma L. Gilbert. *Mt.* $5,700. nom

19th st, s s, 256.6 w 8th av, 15.6x100.2. Henry C. Bull to Girard H. Wessell. *Mt.* $1,500. 2,750

20th st, s w s, 161 s e 5th av, 13x100. James S. McBride to George Hansen. *Mt.* $1,000. 1,600

21st st, n s, 253 e 6th av, 32x100. Release mort. Stephen B. Sturges to James R. Robb. nom

22d st, s s, 150 w 5th av, 25x100. Thomas Metchett to Fannie E. Metcalfe. *Mt.* $2,000. 100

Bay 25th st, n w s, 320 s w Benson av, 60x96.8, New Utrecht. James D. Lynch to Cornelius P. Rosemon. 1,650

26th st, centre line, 300 from 3d av, runs northwest to exterior line, x southwest to centre 27th st if extended, x southeast to point 300 n w of 3d av, x northeast —, with docks, land under water, &c William H. White to Brooklyn Warehouse and Dry Dock Co. 300,000

Same property. Brooklyn Water Front Warehouse and Dry Dock Co. to same. nom

Same property. Foreclos. William Hughes to William H White. 25,000

East 28th st, e s, 61.6 n Emmons av, runs northeast 87.6 x west 71.6 to East 28th st, x south 50.6 to beginning, Gravesend. Charles Naeher to George H. Fisher. nom

39th st, n s, 175 e 8th av, 25x100.2. Sarah Smith to John M. Snook, of Flatbush. 1,250

42d st, n s, 125 w 2d av, 25x100.2. Foreclos. Henry Ingraham to John P. Morris. 1,200

Same property. John P. Morris, New York, to Charlotte Schellenberger. 1,850

42d st, n s, 300 w 2d av, 25x100.2. Mary Riley to John Wickern. 800

42d st, n s, 190 w 2d av, 20x100.2. Mary wife of James Riley to Marie wife of Ferdinand Eysel. 1,900

47th st, n s, 120 e 4th av, 20x100.2. Samuel T. Sherwood to Francis J. Rotbo. *Mt.* $2,500. 4,600

47th st, s w s, 220 s e 4th av, 20x100.2. Release mort. Elizabeth H. Taylor to Alexander Waldron. nom

52d st, n e s, 160 s e 3d av, 60x100.2. Gertrude L. wife of William Martin to Charles A. Erickson. exch

52d st, n s, 280 w 6th av, 50x90. Contract. W. W. Crosby to James G. Carroll. 1,000

52d st, s w s, 320 n w 5th av, 20x100.2. Andrew Fitzpatrick to Mary A. wife of James A. White. 650

57th st, s s, 200 e 4th av, 40x100.2. Daniel Sloat to Charles B. Mount. *Mt.* $333. 1,100

57th st, s s, 240 e 4th av, 20x100.2. Release mort. Edward T. Hunt exr. Thomas Hunt to Daniel Sloat. 231

57th st, s s, 160 e of line bet Brooklyn and New Utrecht, 20x100.2, New Utrecht. Charles W. Lundquist to James J. Kane. 200

57th st, s s, 160 w 3d av, 20x100.2. William S. Hassen to William Croft. *Mt.* $2,700. 4,550

64th st, s s, 260 w 13th av, 40x100, Bath Junction. James V. S. Woolley to Nils Johnson. 350

68th st, s s, 100 e 14th av, 20x100, New Utrecht. Effingham H. Nichols, of New York, to Luigi Cicchette, of New York. 250

68th st, e s, 200 s 6th av, 25x100.2, New Utrecht. Roger Taylor to John J. Meehan. 250

74th st, centre line, n e s, 300 n w 13th av, —x 49.8x107.4x—, New Utrecht. Release mort. Long Island Loan and Trust Co. to The Bay Ridgewood Park Improvement Co. nom

77th st, n e s, 110 s e 3d av, 120x109.4, New Utrecht. James Ferguson to Mathew Dean. B. & S. nom

78th st, n s, 210 w 3d av, 75x109.4, New Utrecht. Charles A. Erickson to Gertrude L. wife of William Martin. *Mt.* $2,000. exch

78th st, centre line, n s, 197.6 e 4th av, 40x130, New Utrecht. Carolina M. Davison, of New York, to Syver Olsen and Peter O. Petersen. 750

80th st, s w s, 82.7 n w 7th av, 20x200, New Utrecht. William G. Fitzgerald to Charles Lawson. 450

Atlantic av, s s, 412.3 w Clason av, 20x100. James L. Sayre to William A. Mosscrop. 350

Atlantic av, s s, 266.8 e Rockaway av, 16 8x100, h & l. Contract. Andrew Van Opstal to James H. Hart. 2,400

Atlantic av, s s, 183.4 e Saratoga av, 16.8x100. Alfred Ogden to George Friedrich and Henry Kopp. *Mt.* $2,400. nom

Atlantic av, n e cor Clason av, 50x94x abt 92 x105.3.
Interior lot on centre line bet Atlantic av and Lefferts pl, at point 77.11 e Clason av, runs southeast 25 x southwest 25x25x25.
Robert Fernandez to Ida E. wife of George R. Lyons. *Mt.* $8,000. 11,500

Atlantic av, s s, 344 e Buffalo av, 17x45.5x17x48.6. Frank W. Carmon to Elizabeth Carmon widow. nom

Atlantic av, No. 2086, s s, 225 e Howard av, 25x100. Herman Wronkow to Mary C. O'Neil. *Mt.* $3,000. 5,250

Blake av, n e cor Madison st, 82x60x82x68. Francisco de Borroto to Jose Chacon, of New York. *Mt.* $1,000. 2,200

Bushwick av, southerly cor Aberdeen st, runs southwest 90 x southeast 200 to Hull st, x northeast 79.2 to Manhattan Beach R. R., x north 22.1 to av, x northwest 180.6. Louisa F. wife of John Reilly to Dennis Sheehan. val. consid. and 195

Bushwick av, n e s, 56.8 n w Schaeffer st, 18.4x75. Charles A. Wehr to Julius Schwarz. *Mt.* $3,500. nom

Bushwick av, n e s, 50.9 n w Cedar st, runs south 0.2½x69.8. Release mort. Julia Lang to Theresa Kiefer. nom

Clason av, No. 173. Agreement as to encroachment. Robert Reid with Daniel F. Dwyer. nom

Clason av, No. 173, e s, 363.3 n Myrtle av, 25x94.8x25x92.6. Daniel F. Dwyer to Frederick Niclas. 7,000

Conklin av, n w s, lots 11 and 12 map property Henry Conklin et al., Canarsie, 50x165.5, Flatlands. Charles McCrodden to Phebe wife of William H. Rogers. 1,750

De Kalb av, s s, 375 w Lewis av, 25x100. John Finken to Elizabeth wife of Henry Finken. 6,000

De Kalb av, n s, 80 e Waverly av, 20x82. Eliza J. Westerfield to Jennie wife of Herman C. Francke. gift

De Kalb av, n s, 171.8 e Stuyvesant av, 27.8x100, h & l. Mary J. wife of Edmond Tyler to Andre de Wilde. *Mt.* $5,040. exch

De Kalb av, s e s, 125 n e Irving av, 25x100. John Schaudel to Peter L. Schetting, New York. nom

Same property. Peter L. Schetting to John Schaudel and Eva his wife. C. a. G. nom

Evergreen av, south cor Himrod st, 16.8x80, h & l. Ellen C. Hommel to Caroline Dreyer. *Mt.* $2,000. 5,000

Franklin av, s e cor Crown st, 131x100. Alonzo E. De Baun to The Brooklyn Home for Aged Colored People. *Mt.* $2,000. 4,500

Gates av, No. 1217, n s, 185.6 e Evergreen av, 43.2x100. James Jenkinson to George J. Kay. *Mt.* $3,000. 4,700

Gates av, n s, 224 e Lewis av, 26x100. Foreclos. John Courtney, Sheriff, to John M. Quackenbos, Jr. *Mt.* $8,000. 100

Glenmore av, s s, 80 w Logan st, 20x90. Mary wife of and Donald Laing to Charles H. Fischer. *Mt.* $1,800. 2,700

Graham av, No. 206, e s, 50 n Scholes st, 25x100. Jacob J. Seelbach to Max A. Dassan. *Mt.* $7,000. 11,000

Grand av, e s, 237 n Willoughby av, 25x100. Annie Loftus to John T. Underwood. *Mt.* $1,200. 2,500

Greene av, s s, 27 w Sumner av. 19.6x100. Thomas B. Bryant to Arra S. Eastman. 9,000

Harway av, s w s, intersection n w line land Van Cleef Voorhies, runs northwest 35 to land Stillwell Voorhies, x west 470.8 to Gravesend Bay, x southeast 42.2 to land Van Cleef Voorhies, x east 455.4 to Harway av, Gravesend. Gertrude M. wife of and Charles M. Ryder to Marie Beraza, of New York. 2,900

Hopkinson av, n w cor Dean st, 107.2x225. James McMahon to the House of the Good Shepherd. 2,700

Hopkinson av, s w cor Pacific st, 107.2x140. Same to same. *Mt.* $4,000. 5,500

Howard av, e s, 98 s Herkimer st, 35x98. Foreclos. John Courtney to Samuel and John C. Burling. *Mt.* $2,750. 3,650

Jefferson av, n s, 100 w Howard av, 17.6x100, h & l. Samuel Ayres to Isabella N. wife of Sinclair W. James. nom

Johnson av, s s, 125 w Morgan av, 25x100. Theodore F. Jackson to Joseph Fuchs. 1,500

Johnson av, n e cor Bogert st, 50.4x145.6x—x108.9. Charles W. Truslow admr. William Wall to Alois Lazansky and Henry Roth. 3,425

Kent av, w s, 60 n North 8th st, 20x100.
North 10th st, centre line, 100 w Kent av, runs south 260 to centre North 9th st, x west 25 x south 130 x west 25 x south 130 to centre North 8th st, x west to exterior pier line, x — along same to centre North 10th st if extended, x east —, with docks, &c.
North 5th st, n s, 40 s e Berry st, 20x80.
Mechanics st, n e s, lots 15-16 inclus. on R. Carnley map, 125x90 to alley across rear.
North 4th st, s s, extends from Wythe av to Kent av, x— to alley.
North 3d st, n s, 81 w Wythe av, 50x90.
Wythe av, south cor North 4th st, 37.8x60x36.11x60.
Wythe av, s e s, 37.8 s w North 4th st, 22.4x60x23.1x60.
North 4th st, s s, abt 150 e 2d st, 25x60.
North 4th st, s s, 60 e 2d st, 25x60.
Theodore A. and Henry O. Havemeyer and Charles H. Senff to Austin Hulshizer. 1890. nom

Same property. Austin Hulshizer to Havemeyer & Elder. 1890. nom

Kent av, s w cor South 11th st, 133x— to permanent water line, x north to South 11th st if extended, x east —; also,
South ½ of South 11th st, extending from 1st st to permanent water line.
Division av, n w cor Kent av, runs west to low water mark East River, x north to line bet Brooklyn and Williamsburgh, x east along same to Kent av, x south —, with all title to land under water, docks, &c.
John Mollenhauer to Mollenhauer Sugar Refining Co. 242,000

Kingsland av, n e cor Meeker av, runs north 86 x east 43.5 x northeast abt 112 x east 24.10 x southeast 82.1 to Meeker av, x 139.5. George L. Kingsland and ano. exrs. Ambrose C. Kingsland and George L. Kingsland et al. exrs. Ambrose C. Kingsland, Jr., and Katharine Kingsland to Paul C. Greuing. 12,500

Kingsland av, w s, 232.6 n Van Cott av, 21.3x100. Emil Heger and Anton Kallina to Christian Kress. ⅓ part. *Mt.* $1,500. nom

Kingsland av, w s, 190 n Van Cott av, 21.3x100. Emil Heger to Anton Kallina. ⅓ part. *Mt.* $1,500. nom

Kingsland av, w s, 211.3 n Van Cott av, 21.3x100. Anton Kallina and Christian Kress to Emil Heger. ⅓ part. *Mt.* $1,500. nom

Knickerbocker av, n e s, extends from Himrod st to Stanhope st, 200x100. Theodore F. Jackson to Louis Beer and Michael Schaffner. nom

Lafayette av, s s, 350 e Bedford av, 25x100.
Stuyvesant av, No. 207, e s, 118 n Monroe st, 18x60.
Ann E. Billings widow to Charity S. Teeple. C. a. G. 1889. 200

Lefferts av, n s, 286 w Brooklyn av, 73-5x100, Flatbush. Release mort. Nat. Central Bank, Cherry Valley, Otsego County, N. Y., to Robert L. Woods. 500

Lefferts av, n s, 149 6 w Brooklyn av, 86.6x100. Release mort. Same to same. 500

Lexington av, s s, 259 w Nostrand av, 16x100. James C. McEachin to Fannie A. Skeeler. *Mt.* $4,000. exch

Liberty av, s e cor Milford st, 20x90. Effingham H. Nichols, of New York, to Nathan and Henry May and Michael Levy. 800

Liberty av, s s, 80 w Milford st, 20x90. Effingham H. Nichols to Mary E. Laing. 500

Liberty av, s s, 50 e Osborn st, 50x100, hs & ls. Israel Y. Cochran to Charles W. Tomlinson. 1,000

Liberty av, s s, 50 e Osborn st, 100x100, hs & ls. Charles and Charles W. Tolinson to Israel Y. Cochran. 2,000

Livonia av, s e cor Osborn st, 20x100, h & l. Abraham Seidenbergh to Sarah wife of Rochmiel Abrahamowitz. 300

Livonia av, s s, 50 e Watkins st, 25x75. Mary E. Cook, Newtown, to Moses Lushaver. *Mt.* $1,500. 2,200

Marcy av, w s, 170 s Macon st, 45x110. Charles W Betts to Charles A. Betts. nom

Marine av, w s, 100 n Oliver st, 50x100; also,
Oliver st, n s, 100 w Marine av, runs north 195.7 x northwest 25.3 to 1st av, x west — x south 200 to Oliver st, x east 50; also,
Oliver st, n s, 300 w Marine av, 150x200 to 1st av; also,
Plot bounded south by land of John Robinson, 112.9 x west — x north by land of Inebriates' Home, New Utrecht.
Foreclos. George W. Pearsall to Walter E. Blanchard, of Lynn, Mass. 5,000

Maspeth av, s s, intersection centre line Morgan av, runs south to centre Orient av, x east to centre Vandervoort av, x north to Maspeth av, x west —. John C. Furman to The Security Corporation. *Mt.* $140,000. nom

Same property. Charles W. Cooper to same. B. & S. nom

Myrtle av, s w cor North Portland av, 117.8x northeast 53.1 x northwest 18.9 x north 14.8 x east 100 x south 90.11. Henry C Tallman to Frederick H. Lawrence exr. George C. Tallman. 50,000

Myrtle av, n s, 100 w Tompkins av, 40x100. Joseph Wurzler to Robert J. McManamy. *Mt.* $7,500. 13,300

Nichols av, w s, 225 n Union av, 75x90. Alonzo Reed, of Quogue, N. Y., to Christina E. Lohrentz. 1,800

Nicholas av, w s, 300 n Union av, 50x90. Same to Stephen Mafera. 1,200

North Portland av, w s, 155.11 n Myrtle av, 75 x100. Michael O'Brien to Frank O'Brien. ½ part. B. & S. nom

North Portland av, w s, 70.7 s Auburn pl, 75x 100. Frank O'Brien to Michael O'Brien. ½ part. nom

Park av, n s, 57 w Adelphi st, 68.7x100x55.10x 75. Patrick J. Carlin to John Long and John Barnes. Q. C. nom

Putnam av, s e cor Lewis av, 25x100. Herman Lange to John F. Ryan. nom

Putnam av, n s, 340 e Reid av, 20x100, h & l. Mary Stoker to Belle Fisher. *Mt.* $6,500. nom

Putnam av, s s, 275 w Stuyvesant av, 20x100. Eli H. Bishop to Frederick Schmolze. *Mt.* $7,500. nom

Putnam av, s s, 100 w Ralph av, 200x100. Release dower. Jane E. Meeker widow to Francis T. Johnson. nom

Putnam av, n s, 206.9 e Stuyvesant av, 18.3x 100, h & l. John Mitchell and Charles Herr to Ellen C. wife of Christian F. Hommel. *Mt.* $4,500. nom

Putnam av, s s, 100 w Ralph av, 200x100. Jane E., Samuel M. and Anna L. Meeker exrs. Samuel M. Meeker to Francis T. Johnson. 12,000

Prospect av, n e cor Webster pl, 19.6x80. Mary A. wife of Thomas E. Wheeler to Matthew J. McCue. 3,700

Railroad av, w s, 100 s Griffin pl, 50x100, h & l. Frank C. Lang to Betsey Reichert. 1,000

Railroad av, w s, 75 s Weldon st, 25x100. Henry H. Pettit to John Schneider. 450

Saratoga av, n w cor Decatur st, 100x300. Peter Gardner to Ansel H. Van Buren. nom

Schenectady av, e s, 42.8 n Pacific st, runs east 10 x north 18.8 x west 70.10 to Schenectady av, x south 18.8. Ann A. wife of Henry A. Tilly, Rutherford, N. J., to Wharton W. Watson. *Mt.* $3,000. 3,002

Stanley av, s s, 40 e Jerome st, 20x85. Herbert J. Knapp to Estelle V. Knapp. 73

St. Marks av, n s, 125 w Underhill av, 25x131. David J. Ramsdell to Martin L. Rickerson. *Mt.* $6,100. nom

St. Marks av, n s, 175 w Vanderbilt av, 25x131, h & l. Margaret Hecker to Joseph Hackett. nom

St. Marks av, s s, 272.6 w Rochester av, 20x 255.7 to Prospect pl. Robert L. Woods, Jr., to Henry Ahrens. 1,000

St. Nicholas av, n e s, 50 s e Troutman st, 25 x90.
St. Nicholas av, s w s, 25 s e Troutman st, 25 x95.
St. Nicholas av, n e s, 25 s e Troutman st, 25 x94.
St. Nicholas av, east cor Madison st, 25x94.
Charles Miller to John Lapp. *Mt.* $1,600. 4,250

Stone av, w s, 125 s Sutter av, 25x100. Mary E. Cook widow to Louis Goldberg. *Mt.* $2,000. 3,800

Same property. Release mort. Lewis Hurst to Mary E. Cook. 500

Sunnyside av, n s, 200 w Miller av, 50x250, to Highland Boulevard. Abby J. Bills, of Newtown, New York, to Emma L. Johnston. nom

Sutter av, n s, 15 e Vesta st, 15x79.11, h & l. John P. Free to Sarah E. Wenz. 2,600

Thatford av, w s, 100 n Livonia av, 25x100. Pauline Hartman to Morris Silberstein and Jacob Goldstein. *Mt.* $1,200. 1,850

Throop av, s e cor Whipple st, 20x71.2. Henry Roth to Joseph E. Middle. *Mt.* $2,500. 5,500

Van Siclen av, e s, 303 n Fulton av, 22x100. John L. Carr to William J. Carr. gift

Vienna av, s s, 40 w Elton st, 60x85.
Vienna av, n s, 40 w Elton st, 60x85.
Anna E. Brewer to Charles T. Carnes. nom

Waverly av, e s, 272.3 n Atlantic av, 50x100. Phoebe A. Conn to Robert Reid and Walter R. Comfort. *Mt.* $1,500. 3,250

Willoughby av, s s, 125 w Tompkins av, 20x100, h & l. William G. Hotaling to Rose A. Mullan. *Mt.* $3,500. 6,750

Wyckoff av, n e s, 50 s e Stanhope st, 25x91.4x 25x90.8. Henry Eich to Joseph Riedmann. *Mt.* $3,000. 6,400

4th av, east cor 92d st, 130x118x124.10x82.7, h & l. New Utrecht. Clara Mang to August Krueger. 10,000

4th av, n w s, 60.2 s w 35th st, 60x82, h & l. Mary A. Kenny or Kenney, Spring Valley, N. Y., to Caroline E. Gainer. *Mt.* $9,000. nom

5th av, n w cor Bergen st, 20x73.4. Mary E. McGinley to William J. Danaher. nom

5th av, n w s, 18 6 n e Butler st, 26.6x90. John P. H. De Wint, of New York, to Ada C. Williams. *Mt.* $9,000. exch

6th av, s e s, 101.10 s w 14th st, 14.2x97.10x14x 97.10. Sarah E. Price to Claudius H. Dumahut. *Mt.* $2,000. 8,000

9th av, e s, 20.2 n 18th st, 20x100; also,
Lots 65–68 map 74 lots 8th Ward, belonging to The Inebriates Home.
Patrick Smith to Catharine Smith. *Mt.* $1,000. 5,500

12th av, southerly cor 56th st, 60.2x100, New Utrecht. The Blythebourne Improvement Co. to Pauline Cuno. 1,400

13th av, centre line at centre line 74th st, runs northeast 260 to centre line 73d st, x northwest 160 x northeast 115.4 x southwest 378.4 to centre line 74th st, x southeast —, New Utrecht. Release mort Long Island Loan and Trust Co. to Bay Ridge Park Improvement Co. nom

24th av, s e s, 240 n e Benson av, 120x96 8, Gravesend. James D. Lynch to George B. F. Randolph. 2,100

Old Mill road, w s, at n e cor land Van Cleaf Voorhies, runs west 279.6 x north 26.6 x east 279.6 x south 31.5, Gravesend, except portion as was conveyed to Allison G. Ames. Ellen Perkins to James Carter. 900

Lots 9, 10 and 11 block 2 map 597 lots W. Ziegler property, Gravesend. William Ziegler to Christopher J. Gelson. 390

Lots 12, 13, 14 and 39–44 block 2, and lots 92–94 block 3, and lots 271 and 272 block 5, and lots 371–373 and 385 and 386 block 7, and lot 483 block 9 same map. Same to James S. Packard. 3,090

Lots 387–390 inclus. block 7 map 597 lots W. Ziegler property, Gravesend. William Ziegler to Charles Barberie. 580

Lot 51 block 2, Adamsville, Kings Co. The People of the State of New York to Edward R. Vollmer. letters patent

Lots 100–150 inclusive block 3 map 618 lots Cowenhoven farm, New Utrecht. Effingham H. Nichols, of New York, to Charles L. Rickerson. 7,650

Lot 542 map land Reformed Dutch Church, Flatbush. Abby J. Bills, of Newtown, N. Y., to Ida W. Bragaw. nom

Lot 89 block 3 map 597 lots W. Zeigler property, Gravesend. William Zeigler to Louis Camera. 140

Lots 114, 115 and 116 map lots 1–487 at Van Pelt Manor, New Utrecht. Release mort. Townsend Van Pelt to John L. Nostrand. nom

Lot 118 Linden terrace and lot 92 Murphy property, Flatbush, section 5 map Oaklands.
Broadway, n w cor Monsell pl, 1⅛ acre, west part of section 154 map of 283 sections, opposite A. Vanderveers, 85.4x100, part of section 155 same property.
East New York & Canarsie R. R., 4 83–100 acres, Flatlands.
4th av, lot 234 map 5, Fort Hamilton, 87.11x 7.1x25x99.
4th av, lot 235 same map, 29.3x18.2x99x25x 119.6.
Edward Wemple, State Comptroller, to Willard Brown and Charles W. Wells. Tax deeds. 94

Lots 198, 526, 567, 569, 637 and 942 map A, East New York; lot 6 block L map C, East New York, and lot 3 block 19 map No. 2, East New York, and lot 57 block 30 same map; lot 62 map W. Alexander property; lot 165A map W. Howard property; lot 6 block 45 map of Sackman, Barbey and others property; lot 202 Wyckoff, Linning, &c., propert and 376 Williamson homestead, 26th Ward. Edward Wemple, State Comptroller, to Willard Brown and Charles W. Wells. Tax deed. 333

Interior lot, 62.8 n Seeley st and 420 e Middle st, runs north 14 x east 100x14x100, Flatbush, being on Temple court. Richard C. Layton to Waters B. Coats, Wellesevill, N. Y. nom

Interior lot, 75 s Stagg st and 100 e Leonard st, runs west 25 x north 0.7¼ x east 25 x south 0.7¼. Babette wife of Charles Mann to Max A. Dassau. 50

Highway in Gravesend, adj Jane H. Rumple, 73x135. Abram S. Emmons to Pheoe Ann Emmons. 1,000

Plot of meadow land in 18th Ward. Agreement as to several matters in connection with construction of gas works. John Devlin with The Equity Gas Works Construction Co. nom

Release from all claims agt estate of Geo. Cochrane dec'd. Sarah Jane Ross to Mary Cochrane Broome. val. consid.

General release, especially for damage by breach of promise. Mary Cleary to Michael J. Flood. 100

WESTCHESTER COUNTY.

NOVEMBER 4 TO 10—INCLUSIVE.

CORTLANDT.

Breining, Reinhold to Bertha Breining, e s road from Verplancks to Crugers Station, 50x 200. nom

Nelson, Cornelia M. to Jas. D. Adams, s s Constant av, 348 w Highland av, 40x194. $240

Same to same., adj above, 40x194. 240

EASTCHESTER.

Horn, Paul E. to Lizzie McNaier, part lot 2 e s Union av, East Mt. Vernon, 40x117. 3,900

Holler, Lawrence B. to W. H. Ireland Howe, south ½ lot, 555 e s 7th av, Mt. Vernon, 75x 105. nom

Howe, W. H. Ireland to Lawrence B. Holler, s s Boston road adj S. B Odell, 4 acres. nom

Koerner, E. Christian to Ann Havernick, part lot 250 n w s Terrace av, West. Mt. Vernon, 80x100. 250

Lohman, Ann M. to William L. Culbert, south ½ lot 772 e s 9th av, Mt. Vernon, 50x105. 5,500

Parker, Margt. M. to Peter Fury, lot 10 w s Fleetwood av map Farrington estate, 39.5x 100. 700

Treulich, Emma to Thos. Cunningham, s e cor 4th av and 3d st, 50x105. 15,250

Wood, Jos. S. to Wm. H. Treuer, lot 80 n s Urban st, Villa Park. nom

GREENBURGH.

Blackwell, Wilson H. to Louisa C. Leitch, lots 595 and 596, Ardsley. 250

Same to Charles G. Storms, lot 616. 235

Claggett, Eliz'h P. to Alf. J. Manning, s w cor Claggett and Harriman roads, 6 acres. 1,100

Erhardt, Joel B. trustee to Max J. Rochmis, s s Lawrence st, 75 w Western av, 25x100. 350

Jones, Cyrus P. and ano. to Henry Macnamara, lot 143, Ardsley. 350

Same to Henry J. Randolph, lots 65 and 66. 240

Milne, Alex. to Mary A. Swing, 4 acres e s Saw Mill River road. nom

MAMARONECK.

Rushmore, Everett to John T. Holt, lot 82 s s Stanley av, Grand Park, 50x150. 700

MOUNT PLEASANT.

Blackwell, Wilson H. to Chas. P. Burke, lots 66, 67, 70, 71, 72 and 119–148 map Mallory estate. 3,135

Fraissenet, Leonce to Louis Smadbeck, lot 1119 Sherman Park. 250

Fraissenet, Rose to same, lot 1118. 250

Smadbeck, Louis to Mary Sweeney, lot 580 Sherman Park. 100

Same to John J. Nagengast, Jr., lots 1780 and 1781. 300

Same to Samuel Jamison and ano., lots 16 and 17. 400

Same to Thos. Kelly, lots 1555 and 1556. 325

Same and ano. to Wm. Jamison and ano., lots 461–464 Lakehurst. 550

Smith, Wm. R. to John Hayhurst, lots 16 and 17 block 5 Lake Kensico. 300

NEW ROCHELLE.

Carville, Cornelia E. to Chas. F. Stagg, n s Winyah av, 1,294 w White Plains road, 210 x—. 9,500

Downey, Henry B. to Wm. McDonnell and ano., s w cor Lockwood's lane and North st., 27x100. 1,200

Dickerson, Estcourt to Emma A. Comstock, n e cor Clinton and Coligni avs, abt 125x300. 1,600

Hudson, Henry P. to Emma A. Van Saun, w s Woodland av, 188 s Main st, 80x180. 10,000

Hudson, Alex. B. to the Knickerbocker Press, s w s Webster av, 588 n w Main st, abt 246x 226. 3,200

Howe, Wm. H. Ireland to Eli A. Kellam, plot 25 lot 25 n s Guion st, grantor's map, 33.4x 161. 666

Same to Nellie C. Smith, part lot 26, 33.4x161. 666

Same to Sarah E. Legare, part lots 25 and 26, 33.4x161. 666

Lester, Henry M. to W. H. Ireland Howe, lot 32 n s Guion st, same map, 50x161. 650

Manhattan Life Ins. Co. to Hugh M. Harmer, lot 6 block E, Rochelle Park. 1,000

Same to Sarah H. Snow, lot 4 block F. 2,100

Same to Robert G. Pikes, Jr., lot 1 block B. 3,000

Porter, Sarah M. to Sarah F. Schmidt, w s North st, 128 s Morris st, 125x218. nom

POUNDRIDGE.

Mason, Jas. R. to Aaron Butler, 3 tracts on Stamford road, 180 acres. 12,000

RYE.

Cragin, Lydia B. to Abner B. Mills, lots 9, 37, 40, 21, 23, 29, 31, 34, 35, 39, 46 and 47, map West Rye. 2,700

Grigg, Harry K. to Thos. Fitzgerald and wife, w s Elm av, 291 n Cleveland st, abt 50x125. 295

McEntee, Rosanna et al. to John O'Brien, lots 10 and 11 w s Grove st, Mt. Jefferson, 100x125. 2,800

Senf, John et al., John H. Clapp ref., to Philip Wiegand, s s Fox Island road, w Byram River. 1,728

Tingue, Sarah L. to Edwin D. Phelps, n w cor Westchester av and Leicester st, 164x393, and gore adj nom

Woerner, Frederika to Matilda Crisfield, n e s Union av, adj Fred. Anthes, 50x255. —

WESTCHESTER.

Borel, Pierre to Frances Dunne, lot 1134 w s 2d st, Wakefield, 109.6x105. 6,000

Camp, Hugh N. to Jan. C. Velders, lot 370 map McGraw estate. 237

Same to Helena Bouwmiester, lot 369. 237

Clear, Maria A. to Frank Gass, lot 392 n s 14th st, Unionport, 108x190. 12,000

Gass, Frank to Sarah Orr, east ½ same lot. 700

Dexter, Fred. C. to Wm. H. Lamphear, west ½ lot 394 s s 6th av, Wakefield, 50x114. 1,025

Same to John Young, lots 1000 and 1046 n s 7th av, Wakefield, each 100x114. 4,000

Johnston, Geo. W. to Jos. M. Vanderpool, part lot 315 s s 10th av, Wakefield, 25x114. 500

Mace, Levi H. to Mary A. Lamb, lots 186, 187, 243 and 244, Laconia Park. nom

Miller, Wm. to Constantine Wagner, G 78 n s 7th av, Wakefield, 25x114. 350

Smadbeck, Louis to Haddon Steen, n s 7th av, 125 e Av D, 50x108. 330

Sanders, Joshua C. to Adrian Iselin, s s Elizabeth st, 125 e Newell av, 25x100. 400

Same to Mary C. Tarbox, s e cor Newell av and Elizabeth st, 100x100. 1,500

Snow, Alberto D. to Diederich Fincke, lot 180 n s 4th av, Wakefield, 105x114. 4,400

Young, John to Fred C. Dexter, lots 295 and 296 s s 1st av, Wakefield, ½ acre. —

WHITE PLAINS.

Albro, Wm. H. to F. Aug. C. Bogert, e s Court st, 100 n Post road, 50x100. 1,000

Ferris, Kath. C. to Geo. L. Miller, lot 9 w s Winchester st, Fisher map, 30x140. 204

Vandemark, Ida L. to John H. McArdle, s s Railroad av, abt 50 w Rabbitt st, 43x160. 8,400

Young, Albert J. and ano. to John H. McArdle, lot 163 Hillside st, Fisher map, 50x125. 1,825

YONKERS.

Bachus, Philo H. to Jas. C. Truman, w s Columbia av, 275 n Reade st, 25x100. 500

Berry, John to Clara M. Valentine, lots 90, 91 and 92, Alida st, Dunwoodie Heights, 75x100. 6,200

Bechstein, Aug. C. to Fred. Bechstein, s w cor Hawthorne av and Valentine's lane, 85x326x17x—. nom

Bechstein, Fred. to The Leake and Watts Orphan House, s w cor same, 4½ acres. 17,500

Cain, Jos. H. to Wm. J. Vincent, lot 28½ block 20 and 29-34 block 19½, Lowerre Station. 1,250

Caddoo, Thos. and ano. to Marvin R. Oakley, n s Maple st, 254.5 e Oak st, 30x100. 800

Coyle, Thos. to Jos. Carroll, No. 143 Woodland av, City map, 141x84x112. 400

East Side Land Co. to Jas. Nevins & Sons, lots 105 and 106, Shearwood Hill. 700

Frazee, Florence to G. Hilton Scribner, n s Yonkers av, 645 w Walnut st, abt 50x105. 850

Gordel, Geo. P. to John B. Sullivan, lot 35 Yonkers av, map Flagg estate, Nodine Hill. 400

Jones, John B. et al, J. F. Brennan ref., to Alex. F. Piltz, e s Cliff st, 282 s Elm st, 50x100. 1,530

Lowerre, Fannie M. to Isodore Burros, lots 19 and 20 block 2, w s Oak st, 50x100. 600

Same to Thos. Barry and ano., lots 23-26 block 2, w s Oak st, 100x100; also lots 21 and 22 block 3, w s Beech st. 1,800

Shonnard, Fred. to Thos. Graft, lot 154 Woodland av, City map. 255

Same to Thos. Coyle, 143 Woodland av, 141x84x112. 500

Shearwood Hill Land Co. to Clarence M. Fowler, lots 25, 26 and 27. 1,850

Short, Thomas to Mathew Cosgrove, s e cor Lake and Av F, 25x111.4. 1,000

Sullivan, John B. to Jessie H. Dunn, n s Glenwood av, 326 w North Broadway, 35x150. nom

White, Wm. R. to John Park, tract adj grantee w of Pipe Line road, 20 acres. 1,230

MORTGAGES.

NOTE.—*The arrangement of this list is as follows. The first name is that of the mortgagor, the next that of the mortgagee. The description of the property then follows, then the date of the mortgage, the time for which it was given, and the amount. The general dates used as headings are the dates when the mortgage was handed into the Register's office to be recorded.*

Whenever the letters "P. M." occur, preceded by the name of a street, in these lists of mortgages, they mean that it is a Purchase Money Mortgage, and for fuller particulars see the list of transfers under the corresponding date. Whenever the rate is not given, read as 6 per cent.

NEW YORK CITY.

NOVEMBER 6, 7, 9, 10, 11, 12.

Altheimar, Samuel to Harman Eekhoff. 104th st, No. 202 E. P. M. Sub. to mort. $4,500. Nov. 5, due Feb. 15, 1894, 5 %. $700

Andrae, George P. to Peter Handibode. Railroad av. P. M. Nov. 5, 3 years, 5 %. 1,000

Amabile, Margaret E. to John J. Brady. Prospect av. P. M. Oct. 19, due Nov. 5, 1894, 5 %. 3,042

Andruss, Abraham A. to John E. Kaughran. 68th st. P. M. Sub. to mort. $2,000. Nov. 6, 1 year, 5 %. 2,000

Aichele, Philip to James Dougherty. 13th st. P. M. Nov. 10, due May 10, 1893, 5 %. 5,000

Anderson, Ellen widow to Frank E. Wallace, East Orange, N. J. Tinton av, n w s, part lot 18. P. M. Nov. 5, due Nov. 9, 1893, 5 %. 1,200

Same to same. Tinton av, n w s, part lots 17 and 18. P. M. Nov. 5, due Nov. 9, 1893, 5 %. 1,300

Andruss, Charles to John E. Kaughran. 68th st. P. M. Sub. to mort. $2,000. Nov. 6, 1 year, 5 %. 2,000

Brennan, Thomas to David Jackson. Water st, s e cor Market st, 26.2x80. Oct. 20, due Dec. 20, 1891. 2,500

Bach, Lewis Z. to Miguel Garcia. Water and Corlears st. P. M. Oct. 16, due Nov. 1, 1893. 17,000

Bambach, Christian to Conrad Stein. 10th av, No. 749. Saloon lease. Nov. 9, demand. 3,500

Boetzkes, Helen wife of Edward, Dusseldorf, Germany, to Cornelia L. Marshall. 3d av, w s, 50.5 n 58th st, 50x100. Nov. 5, due Jan. 10, 1895, 5 %. gold, 5,000

Bormann, Conrad to George Breit, Brooklyn. 65th st, No. 302, s s, 64 e 2d av, 18x76.2x18.2x73.5. Nov. 10, 3 years, 5 %. 8,000

Bowman, Frank, Brooklyn, and Lucretia G. wife of Cornelius Corson mortgagors with Edward W. Southworth mortgagee. Extension of mort. Oct. 20. nom

Brown, Rose widow to An Association for the Relief of Respectable Aged Indigent Females in the City of New York. 112th st, s s, 315 e 3d av, 20x100.10. Sub. to morts. $5,600. Nov. 10, due May 1, 1893, 5 %. 900

Becker, C. Adelbert to John J. Brady. Oakland pl. s s, 100 w Prospect av. P. M. Oct. 19, due Nov. 5, 1894, 5 %. 1,686

Same to same. Oakland pl, s s, 100 w Crotona av. P. M. Oct. 19, due Nov. 5, 1894, 5 %. 758

Same to same. Oakland pl. n s, 100 w Crotona av. P. M. Oct. 19, due Nov. 5, 1894, 5 %. 900

Same to same. Oakland pl, s s, 100 e Crotona av, 74.6x100x73.10x100. P. M. Oct. 19, due Nov. 5, 1894, 5 %. 1,134

Same to same. Oakland pl, n s, 100 e Crotona av. P. M. Oct. 19, due Nov. 5, 1894, 5 %. 1,311

Same to same. Lebanon st. P. M. Oct. 19, due Nov. 5, 1894, 5 %. 1,350

Berges, Henry and Eliza heirs Henry Berges mortgagors with George Ruppel mortgagee. Extension of mort. Nov. 4. nom

Birkmire, William H. to John J. Brady. Clinton av. P. M. Oct. 19, due Nov. 5, 1894, 5 %. 1,050

Bligh, Roger W. to Bernheimer & Schmid. Amsterdam av, No. 477. Saloon lease. Nov. 5, note, demand. 4,000

Same to same. 3d av, No. 1551. Saloon lease. Nov. 5, note, demand. 2,000

Boak, Henry trustee William H. Boak to John A. Knox. 183d st. P. M. Nov. 4, installs. 1,000

Borie, Annie J. to Frederick A. Constable and ano. trustees for Georgianna E. Arnold, Jr. 58th st, No. 327, n s, 350 w 8th av, 25x100.5. Oct. 24, due Oct. 31, 1896, 4½ %. gold, 25,000

Same to Caroline Wandell. Same property. Oct. 24, due Oct. 31, 1892. 6,000

Bosch, Balthasar to THE EMIGRANT INDUST. SAVINGS BANK. 6th st, No. 223, n s, 264.3 w 2d av, 26.11x90.10. Nov. 6, 1 year, 4½ %. 16,000

Same to same. 6th st, No. 225, n s, 244.3 w 2d av, 20x90.10. Nov. 6, 1 year, 4½ %. 11,000

Bowe, Julia to Euphemia A. Nichols. 54th st, s s, 400 e 10th av, 22.6x55.2x22.7x58.6. Nov. 5, 3 years, 5 %. 300

Bray, Bernard to John J. Brady. Crotona av. P. M. Oct. 19, due Nov. 5, 1894, 5 %. 400

Budener, Harris to Morris Goldstein. Essex st, No. 84, e s, 25x100. Nov. 2, due April 6, 1892. 800

Butler, Aaron, Jamaica, to Lena Kahn. Madison av. P. M. Nov. 4, due Nov. 1, 1893, 5 %. 2,500

Balschun, Adolph to Charles E. O'Hara trustee Melancthon L. Seymour dec'd. 135th st, n s, 100 e Willis av, 32x100. Nov. 9, 3 years, 4½ %. 15,000

Brocklehurst, John to James F. and Patrick H. Sheridan and James S. Segrave. Field st. P. M. Oct. 27, 3 years, 5 %. 900

Baldwin, Mary L. and William A. to May G. Mellus, Worcester, Mass. 97th st. P. M. Sub. to mort. $11,000. Nov. 2, demand. 1,000

Butler, Marion V., Brooklyn, to Charles Coudert trustee Jean G. Torrilhon dec'd. 3d av, No. 605, e s, 49.4 n 39th st, 21.4x75. Nov. 9, 3 years, 5 %. gold, 16,000

Bailhe, Jean P. to August G. Strauch. Sedgwick av, e s, lots 15 and 16 map of K. B. Dalys 16 building lots, 23d Ward, 51.7x90x50.3x82.1. Nov. 9, 3 years, 5 %. 2,250

Beckmann, Peter to Frederick Roetting. 6th av, No. 427. Saloon lease. Nov. 11, notes. 3,275

Same to Bernheimer & Schmid. Same property. Saloon lease. Nov. 11, demand. 1,578

Bellchambers, Robert T. to THE TITLE GUARANTEE AND TRUST CO. 22d st, s s, 303 e 6th av. P. M. Nov. 12, 3 years, 5 %. 24,000

Same to Walter T. Miller. 22d st, s s, 280 e 6th av. P. M. Nov. 12, 3 years. 12,000

Same to same. 22d st, s s, 303 e 6th av. P. M. 2d mort. Nov. 12, 3 years. 9,000

Same to THE TITLE GUARANTEE AND TRUST CO. 101st st, n s, 250 w West End av, 50x100.11. Nov. 12, 3 years, 5 %. 13,000

Bernhard, George and George J. to The New York Orthopaedic Dispensary and Hospital. 102d st, s s, 700 e 3d av, 35x100.11. P. M. Nov. 12, due Nov. 1, 1896, 5 %. 17,000

Same to Bertha Volkening. Same property. Nov. 12, notes. 4,000

Bilovitz, Morris and Raphael Raphael to Lillie Van A. Graham. 63d st, n s, 106 e 1st av, 25x100.5. Nov. 16, 5 years, 5 %. 8,500

Same to Cassel Cohen. Same property 2d mort. Nov. 11, due Oct. 16, 1895. 2,000

Blinn, Alexander F. to Henriette Blinn. 8th av, w s, 25 s 137th st, 50x85; 8th av, w s, 50 n 136th st, 25x85. Nov. 2, demand. 2,000

Brazier, Thomas mortgagor with William H. Philips et al. exrs. and trustees Samuel Philips mortgagee. Extension of reduced mort. Nov. 2. nom

Brown, James to THE GERMANIA LIFE INS. CO. 91st st, n s, 100 e Amsterdam av, 100x100.8. Nov. 11, due May 1, 1892. 70,000

Same to Allen L. Mordecai. Same property. Nov. 11, 3 months. 1,600

Cobalan, Michael J. to William H. Newman. Opdyke av. P. M. Nov. 12, installs, 5 %. 800

Cordts, Emma to Bernheimer & Schmid. Av A, No. 1530. Saloon lease. Nov. 11, note. 2,500

Coyle, Elizabeth wife of Peter to Frances A. Ingraham. 12th st. P. M. Nov. 5, due Nov. 11, 1896, 5 %. gold, 7,000

Same to Gertrude Jordan. Same property. P. M. Sub. to last mort. Nov. 5, due Nov. 11, 1892. 3,667

Casey, John to THE GERMANIA LIFE INS. CO. Columbus av, s e cor 88th st, 100.8x125. Nov. 11, due Sept. 1, 1892. 130,000

Cohen, Herman to Morris and Henry Kahn. 85th st. P. M. Sub. to mort. $12,000. Nov. 9, due Dec. 10, 1895, or installs, 5 %. 2,500

Same to George R. Fearing and ano. trustees of Amey R. Sheldon. Same property. Oct. 30, 5 years, 5 %. 12,000

Coughlin, John F. to Eveline A. Du Bois. Madison st. P. M. Nov. 9, 5 years, 5 %. 10,000

Cropsey, Benjamin G. to James F. and Patrick H. Sheridan and James S. Segrave. Hill st. P. M. Nov. 5, 3 years, 5 %. 335

Chapman, Robert and Peter to John J. Brady. Crotona av and Lebanon st. P. M. Oct. 19, due Nov. 5, 1894, 5 %. 1,605

Chartrand, Ludger to Sarah Purser. 173d st. P. M. Nov. 6, due Nov. 7, 1894, 5 %. 2,000

Churchill, Edward J. to Lillie C. Nevil. Lots 224-230 map Edward T. Young, Springhurst. Sub. to morts. $2,200. Nov. 2, 2 years. 1,000

Coughlin, Helen P. to John J. Brady. Tremont and Locust avs. P. M. Oct. 19, due Nov. 5, 1894, 5 %. 8,892

Commisky, John to John Hardy. Summit av, w s, lot 3 map of 16 building lots of K. B. Daly, 23d Ward, 342 n e from north line of Renwick property, 25x90.2x25.2x87.6; Sedgwick av, e s, lot 9 same map, 486.4 n Renwick property, 25.6x103.9x25.2x101.9. Nov. 9, 3 years, 5 %. 1,000

Cremin, Ellen M. to Emily A. Smith. Audubon av, e s, 24.11 s 189th st, 25x100. Nov. 9, 5 years, 5 %. 1,330

Cremin, Joseph W. to Emily A. Smith. Audubon av, s e cor 189th st, 24.11x100. Nov. 9, 5 years, 5 %. 2,135

de Camprubi, Ysabel A., Barcelona, Spain, to Lillian L. Wiswall. 6th av, No. 687, w s, 104.11 s 40th st, 18.6x100. Nov. 2, 3 years, 4½ %. 4,500

Del Bello, Gaetano and Angelo Di Ciocca to Henry Zeltner. Pelham av and Arthur st. P. M. Oct. 31, 1 year or installs. 1,000

Detrick, Adeline F. wife of William W. to Adela S. Price. 46th st, No 144, s s, 280 e 7th av, 15x100.4. Oct. 31, due Jan. 1, 1894. 3,000

Doran, Michael to William H. May. Ryer av. P. M. Oct. 22, 3 years, 5 %. 300

Doyle, Michael, Montvale, N. J., to Elizabeth V. R. De Peyster. 166th st, n s, 150 e 10th av, 25x100. Nov. 2, due Nov. 1, 1892, 5 %. 500

Duffy, James to George J. Bernhard. 102d st, s s, 100 e 3d av, 35x100.11. Sub. to morts. Secures advances. Nov. 2, demand. (Discharged of record). 1,100

Dunne, Frances wife of and James J. to Henry C. Ely and ano. exrs. Nathan C. Ely. Manhattan st, n s, 186.11 w 10th av, 25x100. Nov. 7, due Nov. 1, 1894, 5 %. 6,000

Da Cunha, Rosina W. wife of and George W., Montclair, N. J., to George E. Hyatt, Brooklyn. 81st st, s s, 100 w Amsterdam av, 37.6x102.2. Nov. 9, due May 1, 1892. 5,000

Deis, Genoefa wife of and Fredoline to Lovisa S. Upson. Rogers pl, w s, 563.10 n Westchester av, 30x75.4x35.8x71.9. Nov. 9, 3 years, 5 %. 2,200

Dittenheimer, Louis and Peter Seaman, of Dittenheimer & Seaman, to William Dittenheimer. Centre st, No. 116. Lease. Sept. 30, notes. 14,000

Duffy, Margaret A. and Peter to THE TITLE GUARANTEE AND TRUST CO. 103d st. P. M. Nov. 9, 1 year, 4½ %. 12,000

de Bauduy, Leonor, Havre, France, mortgagee with Mary E. and Patrick Norton mortgagors. Extension of mort. Oct. 26. nom

Engelson, Annie wife of Peter A. to John J. Brady. Clinton av, w s, 25 n Lebanon st. P. M. Oct. 19, due Nov. 5, 1894, 5 %. 486

Same to same. Clinton av, w s, 50 n Lebanon st. P. M. Oct. 19, due Nov. 5, 1894, 5 %. 486

Edwards, William W. to Auguste J. Paris. Kingsbridge road. P. M. Nov. 5, 3 years, 5 %. 1,750

Eickwort, Louis and Martin Walter to John J. Brady. Clinton av; Prospect av. P. M. Oct. 19, due Nov. 5, 1894, 5 %. 945

Euler, Mary A. wife of and John H. to THE RIVERHEAD SAVINGS BANK, Riverhead, L. I. Prospect av, w s, 100 n 175th st, 69x100, with all title to strip of land lying bet s s above parcel and a line drawn parallel with and 100 n Fairmount av, 6x100; also all title to strip lying bet n s first parcel and a line drawn parallel with and 175 n 175th st, 6x100. Nov. 12, 3 years. 5,000

Farmer, Aaron D. to Frederic J. Middlebrook, Brooklyn. 53d st, s s, 68 w 7th av, 17x50.5; 53d st, s s, 85 w 7th av, 17x50.5; 53d st, s s, 119 w 7th av, 17x50.5. Sub. to morts. $21,000. Nov. 6, 1 year. 4,000

Farrell, Annie H. to John J. Brady. Prospect av. P. M. Nov. 19, due Nov. 5, 1894, 5 %. 315

Foley, Mary A. and Kate to John J. Brady. Crotona av. P. M. Oct. 19, due Nov. 5, 1894, 5 %. 645

Frame, John to THE GERMAN SAVINGS BANK, New York. 127th st, n s, 145 e Park av, 26x99.11. Nov. 5, due Nov. 6, 1892. 18,000

Same to same. 127th st, n s, 171 e Park av, 26x99.11. Nov. 5, due Nov. 6, 1892. 18,000

Same to same. 127th st, n s, 197 e Park av, 18x99.11. Nov. 5, due Nov. 6, 1892. 13,000

Frankenstein, Louis to John J. Brady. Tremont av. P. M. Oct. 19, due Nov. 5, 1894, 5 %. 1,005

Fox, Catharine to Catharine Maher. Washington av, e s, 519 n 180th st, 25x105.4x25.4x101. Nov. 9, 1 year. 500

Fox, Catharine to John J. Brady. Elmwood pl. P. M. Oct. 19, due Nov. 5, 1894, 5 %. 1,200

Flynn, Daniel to THE METROPOLITAN SAVINGS BANK. Vanderbilt av, e s, 135 s 178th st, 27x150. Nov. 6, 1 year, 5 %. 2,000

Same to William H. Craig, Jr. Vanderbilt av, e s, 162 s 178th st, 27x150. Nov. 6, 3 years, 5 %. 3,450

Franke, Edward to THE MUTUAL LIFE INS. CO. of New York. 117th st, s w cor 5th av, 45.6x100.11. Nov. 9, 1 year. 45,000

Same to same. 117th st, s s, 45.6 w 5th av, 79.6x100.11. Nov. 9, 1 year. 55,000

Frank, Annie E. to Mary Power. 8th av. P. M. Nov. 9, 1 year. 3,500

Fogerty, Margaret A. wife of Charles E. to Mary E. McCarthy. Prospect av, e s, 216.8 n lot 67 map of Woodstock, 16.8x100. Nov. 5, 3 years, 5 %. 1,100

Foster, Frederic de P. to William M. Kingsland trustee Daniel C. Kingsland dec'd. 67th st. P. M. Nov. 2, due Nov. 11, 1896, 4½ %. 50,000

Greenberg, Jacob to Franklin N. Billings, Windsor, Vt. Clinton st, No. 16, e s, 175 s Houston st, 25x100.2. Nov. 9, 5 years. gold, 19,000

Same to John and Israel L. Prager. Same property. Nov. 10, due Oct. 15, 1893, 5 %. 3,000

Same to Jonas Weil and Bernhard Mayer. Same property. Sub. to morts. $22,000. Nov. 10, installs. 5,000

Geiss, Otto to Emily A. Smith. Audubon av, s w cor 189th st, 24.11x100. Nov. 9, 3 years, 5 %. 1,800

Gross, Adolph and Samuel Harris to Jacques Bach. Av D. P. M. Nov. 6, due Nov. 9, 1894, 5 %. 9,500

Gussfield, Samuel to Mary P. Snow. 8th av, w s, 49.11 s 142d st, 25x100. Nov. 2, 2 years, 5 %. 3,500

Same to same. 8th av, w s, 74.11 s 142d st, 25x100. Nov. 2, 2 years, 5 %. 8,500

Goldstein, William H. and Seig. to Robert Maywald. Amsterdam av and 100th st. P. M. Nov. 10, installs, 5 %. 5,000

Greiff, Cecilia wife of Raphael to Apama I. Conde, Oswego, N. Y. Lexington av, e s, 79 s 25th st, 19.9x72. Oct. 15, due June 6, 1897. 5,000

Gallagher, Elizabeth F. to John J. Brady. Clinton av and Oakland pl. P. M. Oct. 19, due Nov. 5, 1894, 5 %. 600

Graham, Thomas to John J. Brady. Prospect av. P. M. Oct. 19, due Nov. 5, 1894, 5 %. 451

Gribbin, John to John J. Brady. Clinton av and Elmwood pl. P. M. Oct. 19, due Nov. 5, 1894, 5 %. 855

Grimley, Felix and Bridget his wife to Peter Doelger. 51st st, n s, 184 e Lexington av, 20.6x100.5. Nov. 4, due March 1, 1892. 5,000

Hagan, Susanna V. to The Zoller Lumber Co., Fort Plain, N. Y. Amsterdam av, s w cor 79th st, 102x100.2. Nov. 6, payable per agreement. 10,300

Hill, Joanna J. widow to Fred. E. Himrod, Brooklyn. 74th st, No. 129, n s, 119.6 w Lexington av, 17x102.2. Sub. to mort. $8,000. Nov. 7, 1 year. 2,000

Hoffman, Margaret to John J. Brady. Lebanon st. P. M. Oct. 19, due Nov. 5, 1894, 5 %. 200

Holder, Libbie B. wife of R. E. to John J. Brady. Prospect av and Lebanon st. P. M. Oct. 19, due Nov. 5, 1894, 5 %. 600

Hughes, Thomas R., Weehawken, N. J., to THE EQUITABLE LIFE ASSUR SOC of the United States. 66th st, n s, 275 w 10th av, 3 lots. 3 P. M. morts., each $17,000. Nov. 4, due Jan. 1, 1895, 5 %. gold, 51,000

Hull, Hannah E widow to THE TITLE GUARANTEE AND TRUST CO. 127th st, n s, abt 324.1 e Lenox av, 17.9x99.11. Nov. 10, 5 years, 4½ %. 5,000

Harris, Bertha to Samuel Greenfeld. Columbia st. P. M. Nov. 11, installs. 1,500

Henderson, Albert C. to The Bradley & Currier Co. (Lim.) 85th st, s s, 100 e West End av, 80x102.2. Sub. to morts. Nov. 7, 6 months. 12,000

Henderson, Albert C. to Homer J. Beaudet. 85th st, s s, 100 e West End av, 80x102.2. Sub. to morts. Oct. 22, due Feb. 6, 1892. 22,000

Hamilton, Joseph and Charles F. Johnson to Annie E. Brown. Edgecombe av. P. M. Nov. 6, 3 years, 5 %. 900

Herter, Henry to Mary L. Breese guard. of Anne P. Breese. Delancey st, s s, 44 e Sheriff st, 44x87.6. Nov. 12, 5 years, 5 %. gold, 45,000

Hoffmann, Michael A. to Michael Springer. 5th st. P. M. Nov. 2, 3 years or installs, 5 %. 5,500

Haldenstein, Isidor to Emily A. Smith. Amsterdam av, s w cor 189th st, 24.11x100. Nov. 9, 5 years, 5 %. 5,000

Harris, John to Alfred Steckler. 7th st. P. M. Nov. 9, 3 years, 5 %. 10,000

Howe, Margaret J. to John J. Brady. Tremont av. P. M. Oct. 19, due Nov. 5, 1894, 5 %. 960

Jacobs, Elias to Joseph Priest, Brooklyn. Orchard st, No. 189, w s, 226 n Stanton st, 25x87.6. Nov. 10, due May 12, 1893, 5 %. 13,000

Jenkins, Thomas J. and George to George E. Hyatt, Brooklyn. 118th st, s s, 100 e 8th av, 100x100.11. Nov. 6, due May 25, 1892. 10,000

Jenkins, Thomas J. and George to Harriet E. Anderson trustee James W. Anderson dec'd. 118th st, s s, 275 e 8th av, 25x100.11. Nov. 11, 3 years, 5 %. gold, 17,000

Same to The Bradley & Currier Co. (Lim.) Same property. Sub. to last mort. Nov. 6. 6 months. 1,500

Jewell, Margaret to William B. Boorum and ano. exrs. John O'Hara. West Washington pl, No. 83, n s, 102.8 e 6th av, 22x97. Nov. 12, due Nov. 5, 1893, 5 %. 1,000

Jung, Gottlieb to Bernheimer & Schmid. 1st av, No. 1144. Saloon lease. Nov. 11, demand. 3,000

Jordan, William G. to H. E. Stevens. 44th st, Nos. 437 and 439, n s, 300 e 10th av, 40x100.4. Sub. to morts. Oct. 31, demand. 1,800

Jessup, Henry W., South Orange, N. J., to Anna D. Bliss. 5th av, n w cor 8th st or Clinton pl, 28.6x100. Nov. 10, 3 years, 5 %. gold, 65,000

Knoch, Minnie to John J. Brady. Lebanon st, Elmwood pl. P. M. Oct. 19, due Nov. 5, 1894, 5 %. 3,108

Koch, Frank to John S. Bassett. 148th and 147th st. P. M. Nov. 6, installs, 5 %. 9,000

Koerner, Louis to John J. Brady. Clinton av and Elmwood pl. P. M. Oct. 19, due Nov. 5, 1894, 5 %. 400

Kaufman, Isidor to The New York Produce Exchange. 80th st, s s, 125 w Park av, 22x102.2. Nov. 9, 1 year, 5 %. 25,000

Kelly, Jane wife of Robert to Auguste J. Paris. Vanderbilt av. P. M. Nov. 4, due Nov. 5, 1894, 5 %. 875

Kerbs, Adolf mortgagee with Henry M. Bendheim mortgagor. Extension of mort. Nov. 2. nom

Kimball, William E. to Lucinda Y. Brown, East Livermore, Me. 37th st, s s, 62 w 6th av, 19x48.8. Sub. to mort. $6,000. Nov. 6, 2 years, 5 %. 6,000

Same to same. 37th st, s s, 81 w 6th av, 19x48.8. Sub. to mort. $8,000. Nov. 6, 2 years, 5 %. 6,000

Kaufmann, Ignatz to Ignatz Gluck. Cannon st, No. 113, w s, 95.9 n Stanton st, 20.9x100. Nov. 5, installs. 2,500

Lawton, Newbury D. to Elizabeth Burt. Lot begins 139.11 n 165th st and 25 w from line bet lots 29 and 30, being a part of said lots 29 and 30 map of Eltona, 18.9x90, with right of way. Nov. 7, due Nov. 10, 1894, 5 %. 3,750

Same to same. Part of lots 29 and 30 as above, begins 121 n 165th st and 25 w from line bet said lots, 18.11x90, with rights of way. Nov. 7, due Nov. 10, 1894, 5 %. 3,750

Lindo, Eliza wife of David formerly Solomon to THE TITLE GUARANTEE AND TRUST CO. 92d st, No. 61, n s, 184 w Park av, 17x100.8 Nov. 10, 5 years, 4½ %. 11,000

Lynch, Kate to Robert Courtright. The Drive, s s, 339 1 w Holt pl, 25x57.5 to lane, x54.4x79.4. Nov. 6. 5 years. 1,300

Leibrock, Nicholas to J. Henrietta H. Rhoades. 70th st. n s, 275 w Amsterdam av. P. M. Oct. 15, due Oct 19, 1893, 5 %. 22,800

Same to John H. Rhoades. 70th st, n s, 300 w Amsterdam av. P. M. Oct. 15, due Oct. 19, 1893, 5 %. 15,200

Louderback, Etta to Armintha Merritt. 89th st, s s, 82 e West End av, 18x100.8. Oct. 7, 3 years, 5 %. 1,000

Lange, Edward to Charles E. Silkworth, Brooklyn. 84th st, s s, 100 w 11th av, 100x102.2. Oct. 31, demand. 30,000

Lutz, Herman to George Burkel and Louisa his wife, Hudson City, N. J. 159th st, n s, 100 w Courtlandt av, 50x198.6 to 160th st. Sept. 1, 2 years, 5 %. 6,500

Lewy, Sigmund and Moritz Weiss, mortgagors with John Bohlken, mortgagee. Extension of mort. Nov. 7. nom

MacNevin, Joseph to The West End Co-operative Building and Loan Assoc. Lot 416 map part of Berrian farm, Fordham. P. M. Oct. 30, installs, 5 %. 3,000

McCormick, Michael and Henry Madden of McCormick & Madden to Margaret T. Nally and Ellen wife of Henry Madden. King st, n s, 84 w Bedford st, 66x75x66x75.2. Sub. to morts. Due March 15, 1892. 2,000

McIntosh, Martha to THE STATE TRUST CO. trustees for Annie Dressel. 85th st, s s, 67.3 w Lexington av, 13.10x102.2. Nov. 11, due Nov. 10, 1896, 4½ %. 5,000

Same to same. 85th st, s s, 81.1 w Lexington av, 13.5x102.2. Nov. 11, due Nov. 10, 1896, 4½ %. 5,000

Same to same. 85th st, s s, 94.6 w Lexington av, 13.7x102.2. Nov. 11, due Nov. 10, 1896, 4½ %. 5,000

McLaughlin, Susan, Brooklyn, N. Y., to Martha Carmichael, Brooklyn. Av A or Eastern Boulevard, w s, 70.4 s 71st st, 25x100. Sub. to mort. $12,000. Nov. 10, due Feb 15, 1892. See Conveys. 6,000

Maas, Helene widow to Henry Rothschild. 141st st. P. M. Nov. 12, 5 years or installs, 5 %. 5,700

Marks, Abraham to THE UNITED STATES TRUST CO., of New York. Thompson st. P. M. Nov. 9, due Nov. 1, 1894, 5 %. 15,000

Marks, Abraham and Mina his wife to Samuel J. Silberman. Thompson st, No. 29½, 31 and 33, w s, 177.5 s Broome st, runs south 47.7 x west 100 x north along an alley 7.7 x east 30 x north 58.5 to another alley, x east 10 x south 18.5 x east 59 to beginning, with all title to alley known as Otter alley. Nov. 11, demand. See Conveys. 7,500

Martin, Eli to New York Lumber and Wood Working Co. 77th st, n s, 157 w Columbus av, 39x105.7x39x104.9. Sub. to morts. ——, Sept. 25, notes. 8,000

Maurer, John H and Charles Kissenberth to John J. Brady. Lebanon st. P. M. Oct. 19, due Nov. 5, 1894, 5 %. 918

McCormack, Annie S. to John J. Brady. Crotona av. P. M. Oct. 19, due Nov. 5, 1894, 5 %. 360

Mead, William C. to Clara Fairchild. Jerome av. P. M. Nov. 2, due Nov. 5, 1894. 5 %. 1,330

Meades, Henry P. to THE STATE BANK. 23d st, No. 126, s s, 249 w 6th av, 26x98.9. Nov. 6, note. 4,000

Metzger, Christoph H. to THE GERMAN SAVINGS BANK, New York. Lewis st, No. 141, w s, 124.9 n Houston st, 21.2x100x21.4x100. Nov. 2, 1 year. 3,000

Monaghan, Mary E. to John J. Brady. Crotona av. P. M. Oct. 19, due Nov. 5, 1894, 5 %. 1,143

Mullane, Cornelius to John J. Brady. Crotona av. P. M. Oct. 19, due Nov. 5, 1894, 5 %. 465

Muller, Martin, otherwise John M., to Walter N. De Grauw et al. trustees for Frederick S. Aymer et al. 1st av, n e cor 11th st, 25.3x100. Nov. 6, due Nov. 1, 1893, 5 %. 17,250

Muller, Henry and Herman Oetjen to John M. Muller. 141st st, s s, 123.1 e 3d av or Boston road, runs east 100 to Alexander av, x south 75 x west 75 x south 25 to centre line of block, x west 25 x north 100 to beginning. Nov. 4, due Nov. 1, 1893, 5 %. 17,250

McBride, Peter to THE HARLEM SAVINGS BANK. Lorillard st, n w s, lot 132 map of Powell estate, Fordham, 24th Ward, 50x100. Nov. 9, 1 year, 5 %. 1,500

McCormick, Michael and Henry Madden to The Bradley & Currier Co. (Lim.) King st, n s, 84 w Congress st, 66x75x66x75.2. Sub. to morts. $59,000. Oct. 20, 5 months. 6,975

Meyer, Charles H., Jr., and Magdalena his wife to James F. and Patrick H. Sheridan and James S Segrave. Rock st and Cornell pl. P. M. Oct 27, 5 years, 5 %. 650

Milbauer, Samuel to Charles Rosenberg. 79th st. P. M. Oct. 30, due Nov. 1, 1894. 2,500

Monheimer, Jonas H. to Emily A. Smith. Audubon av, w s, 49.11 s 189th st, 50x100. Nov. 9, 5 years, 5 %. 2,492

Mattmuller, Annie to Adelbert S. Nichols. Prospect av, new e s, 69.6 s proposed new st, 15x100. Nov. 9, due Aug. 9, 1892. 324

McAnally, John to Howard & Childs. 9th av, No. 246, n e cor 25th st. Saloon lease. Nov. 9, demand. 1,866

McCord, William H., New York, and Andrew J. Post, Jersey City, to The William R. Beal Land Improvement Co. Crimmins av, e s, 100 n Beech terrace. P. M. Oct. 22, due July 8, 1894, 5 %. 1,000

Same to same. 141st st. P. M. Oct. 22, due July 8, 1894, 5 %. 1,000

Same to same. Crimmins av, w s, 537.4 n 141st st. P. M. Oct. 22, due July 8, 1894, 5 %. 700

Meyer, Ernst E. to THE DRY DOCK SAVINGS INST. Willis av, s e cor 146th st, 25x100. Nov. 10, 1 year, 5 %. 20,000

Morrison, Mary W. wife of John H., Jr., to Howard R. Martin. 144th st, n s, 121.2 e Amsterdam av, 16.6x99.11. Nov. 4, due Nov. 10, 1892, 5 %. 8,000

Murphy, Jane wife of and James D. to John Bussing, Jr. Washington av, w s, 100 s 7th st, 35x150. Nov. 9, 3 years. 1,000

Murphy, James to Jacob Story, Sr. 133d st. P. M. Nov. 10, 3 years, 5 %. 6,000

Myers, Frederick S. to Katharine T. Moore, Ossining, N. Y. 19th st, n s, 100 w 10th av, 25x91.11. Lease. Oct. 29. 786

Same to Mary C. Ogden, Newport, R. I. 19th st, n s, 125 w 10th av, 25x91.11. Lease. Oct. 29. 995

Naylor, Frances S. to George M. Githens. Water st, n w s, 24.2 n e Pine st, 25x84.11x27.8x82.4; Church st, No. 277, e s, 50.1 s White st, 25x75. Nov. 7, demand. 5,000

O'Connell, Agnes A. devisee, widow and extrx. of Daniel O'Connell to John B. Ryer. Frederick st, n e cor Bayard st, 50x87.6. Nov. 9, 3 years. 300

Oelschlaeger, Oswald to THE MANHATTAN SAVINGS INST. 23d st. P. M. Nov. 9, 1 year, 4½ %. 30,000

O'Rorke, Margaret A. wife of Thomas to Frank and Joseph Rauch. 165th st, s s, 200 w Trinity av, 25x100. Nov. 12, 5 years, 5 %. 1,200

Odell, Harriet S. wife of Henry C. to The East Side Co-operative Building and Loan Assoc. Railroad av, lot 29 map of Central Morrisania, part of Bathgate farm, 25x150. Oct. 9, installs, 5 %. 2,250

O'Brien, James and Fanny his wife to John J. Brady. Clinton av. P. M. Oct. 19, due Nov. 5, 1894, 5 %. 417

Overton, Caroline A. wife of and Charles B. to George A. Barker et al. exrs. and trustees George Bell. 22d st, No. 443, s s, 345 e 10th av, 15x78. Nov. 6, 3 years, 5 %. 8,000

Owens, Patrick J. to Sarah L Cooke 161st st, n s, 100 e Eagle av, 30x100. Nov. 10, 3 years, 5 %. 16,000

Peterson, Eugene to Henry S. Trenchard, Yonkers, N. Y. Grove st, s s, 300 w Anthony av, 59.11x100x58x100. Nov. 4, 3 years. 3,000

Paperczinsky, Martin to John J. Brady. Crotona av and Elmwood pl. P. M. Oct. 19, due Nov. 5, 1894, 5 %. 855

Pope, William R. to Theodore Sutro. Morton st, s s, 105 e Hudson st, 25x100. Nov. 6, 1 year. 2,500

Same to THE GERMAN SAVINGS BANK. Same property. Nov. 6, 1 year. 23,000

Pizer, Jacob to THE LAWYERS' TITLE INS. CO. of New York. Rivington st. P. M. Nov. 9, 5 years, 5 %. 18,000

Quehl, Max to George Ehret. 4th st, No. 185 E. Lease. Nov. 9, demand. 1,750

Riley, Jane to Mary Haworth. Creston av. P. M. Nov. 9, 3 years, 5 %. 1,000

Ritter, August to Emily A. Smith. Amsterdam av, w s, 24.11 s 169th st, 75x100. Nov. 9, 3 years, 5 %. 6,000

Roe, Joseph B. to Charles S. Andrews. 147th st. P. M. Sub. to mort. $5,600. Nov. 9, 2 years, 5 %. 3,800

Roth, Philip to Emilio Del Pino exr. Marcos Del Pino. 60th st, No. 215, n s, 195 e 3d av, 20x100.5. Nov. 5, due Nov. 12, 1894, 5 %. 12,000

Ruff, August to Eliza M. Sloane, Sands Point, L. I. 8th st, s s, 120 w 2d av, 26x120, being No. 34 St. Marks pl. Nov. 12, 5 years, 5 %. 35,000

Russell, John and Andrew M. and Sarah C. Abrams to Louis V. Boorsem, Montclair, N. J. 18th st, s s, 61.3 e 9th av, 38.9x52.7. Nov. 12, 1 year, 5 %. 8,000

Rankin, John to THE GERMAN SAVINGS BANK, New York. 63d st, n s, 225 e 10th av, 25x100.5. Nov. 9, due Nov. 11, 1892. 18,500

Same to same. 63d st, n s, 200 e 10th av, 25x100.5. Nov. 9, due Nov. 11, 1892. 18,500

Rawitzer, Max to Samuel Kempner. 1st av. P. M. Nov. 11, installs. 3,100

Rohrs, Frederick to Katharina Hasselbach. 102d st, n e cor 4th av, 27x100.11. Nov. 11, 1 year. 4,000

Ryan, Patrick and Thomas G. Patterson to Arthur B. Claflin. Kingsbridge road, e s, 339.4 n w road to Williamsbridge, runs northeast 337.10 x southeast 279.3 to w s of Williamsbridge road, x southwest 30.4 x southwest 51.9 x southeast 21.4 x southeast 61 x southeast 29.10 x southwest 69.9 x southwest 207 to e s Kingsbridge road, x northwest 16 x northwest 32 x northwest 16 x northwest 24.9 x northwest 38 to beginning. Nov. 10, 3 years, 5 %. 12,000

Reynolds, William J. to John J. Brady. Tremont av. P. M. Oct. 19, due Nov. 5, 1894, 5 %. 960

Rivara, John to Liugi Valente. Sullivan st, No. 64, w s, 17x40x—x47.6. Oct. 27, 2 years, 5 %. 2,200

Rivott, Henry C. H. to John J. Brady. Clinton av. P. M. Oct. 19, due Nov. 5, 1894, 5 %. 200

Roos, Christian P. to John J. Brady. Crotona av. P. M. Oct. 19, due Nov. 5, 1894, 5 %. 645

Rosenberg, Baer and Bertha his wife to Karl M. and Samson Wallach. 1st av. P. M. Nov. 10, due Nov. 1, 1894, or installs. 7,700

Ruck, Clara A. wife of and John M. and Esther E. wife of and Martin J. Barron to Sarah H. Powell. 131st st, n s, 300 w 10th av, 25x99.11. Nov. 10, 3 months. 8,000

Ruser, Anna wife of and Ferdinand to Peter Handibode. Railroad av. P. M. Oct. 29, 5 years, 5 %. 1,000

Ruser, Ferdinand to Martha A. Roby. Harlem R. R. land, lot 165 map Lower Morrisania. Oct. 31, 3 years. 1,000

Seiferd, Lena to John J. Brady. Lots 16, 158, 159, 160, 163, 164, 198, 199, 208, 209 map Ryer homestead, Tremont, 24th Ward. P. M. Oct. 19, due Nov. 5, 1894, 5 %. 4,476

Seide, Gumpert to William Rankin. 63d st. P. M. Sub. to mort. $18,500. Nov. 10, installs, 5 %. 8,500

Sanchez, Harriet A. wife of and Henry to Jessie R. Tremenheere, India. 92d st, n s, 355 w 9th av, 20x100.8. Nov. 4, 2 years, 5 %. 12,000

Shedlinsky, Harris and Julius and Isidore Shweitzer to Mary L. Breese guard. of William L. Breese. Sheriff st, w s, 125 s Rivington st, 25x100. Nov. 12, 5 years, 5 %. 19,000

Shulman, Yette wife of and Lazarus to Charles E. Tracy and ano. trustees James Bogert dec'd. East Broadway, n s, 104.7 w Jefferson st, 26x69.6. Nov. 12, due Nov. 1, 1896, 5 %. gold, 23,000

Spellmann, Mary to Bernheimer & Schmid. 12th st, No. 728 E. Saloon lease. Nov. 12, demand. 500

Stephens, James to William H. Payne. Walton av, s w cor Grove st, 100x248 to Gerard av, x 100.1 to Grove st, x248.2; Gerard av, s w cor Grove st, 100x— to high water mark, Harlem River, x— to Grove st, x— to beginning, with land under water of Harlem River. Secures bond of mortgagor and Olin J. Stephens. Nov. 11, 2 years. See Conveys. 15,000

Stephens, James and Olin J. to William H. Payne. Lots 219-222 amended map of Central Mott Haven of W. E. Rider et al. P. M. Aug 12, due Nov. 11, 1893. 15,000

Strauss, Henrietta widow to Max Zenn, Herman Flashner and Morris Levy trustees of Constellation Lodge No. 66, Independent Order Free Sons of Israel. 53d st, No. 822, s s, 236.4 e 2d av, 18x100.5. Nov. 12, 5 years, 4½ %. 5,000

Scott, John S. to Richard H. L. Townsend. 103d st, n s, 180 w Park av, 3 lots. 3 P. M. morts., each $15,500. Oct. 12, due June 1, 1892. 46,500

Same to same. 103d st, n s, 255 w Park av. P. M. Oct. 12, due June 1, 1892. 19,000

Sheridan, John to Julia M. Griebel. 143d st, s s, 175 w Brook av, 25x100. Nov. 7, 5 years. 700

Stone, Sarah F. wife of and George R. to Louisa M. wife of Alfred E. Stone. 96th st. P. M. Nov. 9, 5 years, 5 %. 9,000

Schaefer, Albert and Hannah his wife to John J. Brady. Crotona av. P. M. Oct. 19, due Nov. 5, 1894, 5 %. 360

Schmeckenbecker, Martin to Elizabeth Malone. Cypress av, w s, 188 s 149th st, 57x68x40, gore. Nov. 5, 3 years, 5½ %. 2,000

Scholle, Babette et al. exrs. Abraham Scholle mortgagees with George Ehret present owner. Extension of mort. Nov. 4 nom

Schonfeld, Elise to John Schreiber. 107th st, s s, 200 w 2d av, 25x100.11. Nov. 1, installs 2,000

Seiferd, Rose to John J. Brady. Clinton av and Lebanon st. P. M. Oct. 19, due Nov. 5, 1894, 5 %. 630

Smith, Eliza B wife of Spencer H. to John E. Parsons trustee. 99th st, n s, 350 w 8th av, 25x100.5, all; 99th st, n s, 100 w 8th av, 25x100.11, ½ part; 8th av, w s, 45.11 n 99th st, 53x100, ½ part. Sub. to mort. $14,000. Nov. 5, 1 year, 5 %. 10,000

Spadone, Amedee to THE EQUITABLE LIFE ASSUR. SOC. of the U. S. 82d st, n s, 150 w 8th av, 25x102.2. Nov. 5, due Jan. 1, 1893, 5 %. gold, 27,000

Same to same. 82d st, n s, 175 w 8th av, 23x102.2. Nov. 5, due Jan. 1, 1893, 5 %. gold, 24,000

Stern, Celia wife of and Emanuel to THE INSTITUTION FOR THE SAVINGS OF MERCHANTS' CLERKS. 6th av, e s, 61.5 n 123d st, 18x75. Nov. 6, 5 years, 4½ %. gold, 11,000

Stewart, Walter H. to Frank A. Ehret guard. Joseph, Jr., Ottilie M., Edwin and Julius Hauswirth. 92d st. P. M. Nov. 5, 3 years, 5 %. 2,500

Strang, Louisa, Pueblo, Col., to Sarah M. Shotts. Greenwich st, n e cor Charles st, 58.1x36 10x39.10x45.9. Oct. 26, 3 years. 4,000

Tallowitz, Franz to Henry Robert. 1st av, No. 117. Store lease. Nov. 5, demand. 250

Traphagen, Nellie D. to Fanny wife of Robert I. Lomas, Jr. Webster av. P. M. Nov. 4, due Nov. 6, 1892, 5 %. 1,500

Trefzger, Joseph and Elise his wife to Jacob Hinklein. 2d st, n s, 19 6 e Av A, 20.2x57.5. Lease. Oct. 27, installs, 5 %. 2,000

Taylor, Edwin to Frank Taylor. Barrow st, n s, 140.7 e Bedford st, 23.6x97.6x22x97.8. Nov. 6, 5 years or installs, 5 %. 4,000

Terrell, Herbert L. to Henry W. Putnam. 52d st. P. M. Nov. 2, due Nov. 9, 1892. 25,000

Taylor, John D to Edward Oppenheimer and Isaac Metzger. 70th st, n s, 275 w Central Park West, 100x100.9. Nov. 6, 1 year. 31,500

Same to same. Same property. Sub. to last mort. Nov. 6, 1 year. 32,000

Taylor, John D. to Russell Sage. 70th st. P. M. Nov. 10, 1 year, 5 %. 15,000

Tonjes, Diederick H. to William H. Nafis, Brooklyn. 60th st. P. M. April 1, installs. 3,400

Todd, Louis L. to Charlotte M. Goodridge. 36th st, No. 133, n s, 374.2 e 7th av, 19.11x98.9. Lease. Nov. 12, 1 year. 20,000

Trull, William C. to THE EMIGRANT INDUSTRIAL SAVINGS BANK. 134th st, s s, 250 e St. Anns av, 50x70. Nov. 11, 1 year, 4½ %. 1,500

Same to same. 134th st, s s, 300 e St. Anns av, 50x70. Nov. 11, 1 year, 4½ %. 1,500

Unger, Louis otherwise Luis and Regina his wife to Henry Gottgetreu. Attorney st, e s, 100 s Rivington st, 25x75. Nov. 7, 3 years, 5 %. 16,000

Underhill, Ann L. widow to Martha T. Sands. Bowery, No. 171, e s, 120 s Delancey st, runs east 125.4 x north 2.11 x east 3 x south 23.5 x west 126 x north 20.6 to beginning. Oct. 31, 3 years, 5 %. 5,000

Urban, Charles to Jennie Herrman. Mott st, No. 101, w s, 125 n Canal st, 25x100. Sub. to mort. $20,000. Nov. 10, 1 year. 3,500

Voege, Henry and Henry Wiegand to Beadleston & Woerz, a corporation. West Broadway, No. 74, w s. Lease. Nov. 9, demand. 2,700

Same to Elmer M. Meyer. Same property. Lease. Nov. 9, demand. 1,510

Van Cott, Jane wife of and Gabriel to THE EMIGRANT INDUST. SAVINGS BANK. 71st st, n s, 36 w 9th av, 16x74. Nov. 6, 1 year. 5,000

Voigt, Henry F. C. F. to George Ehret. 2d av, No. 1407. Lease. Nov. 6. 2,000

Wallace, Frank E., East Orange, N. J., to Sarah Jackson. Forrest av. P. M. Oct. 16, due Nov. 9, 1893, 5 %. 1,000

Westheimer, Isaac B. to THE DRY DOCK SAVINGS INST. 1st av, No. 121, w s, 57.6 n 7th st, 20x50. Nov. 10, 1 year, 5 %. 1,800

Weinstein, Ascher to THE UNITED STATES TRUST CO., New York. 18th st, n s, 100 e 2d av, 25x92, with all title to strip adj on east, 0.8¾x50. Nov. 5, due Nov. 6, 1891, 5 %. 22,500

Wood, Susan wife of Frederick and Abram Slaight to John Foster, Beloit, Wisconsin. Lexington av, w s, 75.5 s 54th st, 20.8x70. Nov. 5, 2 years. 8,000

Woolley, James V. S. to Frank T. Wall and ano. exrs. Michael W. Wall. Madison av, e s, 20.8 n 93d st, 20x74. Nov. 6, 3 years, 4½ %. 16,000

Same to same. Madison av, n e cor 93d st, 20.8x74. Nov. 6, 3 years, 4½ %. 20,000

Wright, Susan A. wife of and Stephen J. to Reuben Ross. 87th st, n s, 300 w 10th av, 50x98.9. Nov. 5, 6 months 3,500

Wyand, Henry C. to John J. Brady. Clinton av. P. M. Nov. 19, due Nov. 5, 1894, 5 %. 300

Waller, Jacob and Marie his wife to Leopoldine Breitenbach. Tinton av. P. M. Nov. 2, installs, 5 %. 1,500

Weimer, Henry, Philadelphia, mortgagee with Henri Strasbourger mortgagor. Extension of mort. Oct. 1. nom

Wright, Elizabeth formerly Grey widow to THE GERMAN SAVINGS BANK, N. Y. 36th st, s s, 250 e 6th av, 20x98.9. Nov. 11, 1 year. 1,500

Walsh, William M. to Henry A. Bogert, Flushing, L. I. 101st st, n s, 100 e Columbus av, 25x100.11. Nov. 1, 3 years, 5½ %. 20,000

Same to same. 101st st, n s, 125 e Columbus av, 25x100.6. Nov. 1, 3 years, 5½ %. 20,000

Ward, Catharine wife of James to Martha A. Roby. Creston av, e s, 200 s Irving st, 50x100. Nov. 2, 3 years. 1,000

White, Alfred L. to Susanna Deitering extrx. Frederick W. Deitering. Grand and Elizabeth sts. P. M. Nov. 12, 5 years, 5 %. gold, 30,000

White, Isaac and Matilda his wife to The Grand Lodge of the United States of the Independent Order Free Sons of Israel. 9th st, n s, 213 w Av A, 25x92.3. Nov. 9, 5 years, 4½ %. 20,000

Zeh, Leonard to Emily A. Smith. Audubon av, w s, 99.11 s 189th st, 75x100. Nov. 9, 1 year, 5 %. 3,780

KINGS COUNTY.

NOVEMBER 5, 6, 7, 9, 10, 11.

Addy, Richard C. to The Williamsburgh Savings Bank. Tompkins av, e s, 70.6 n Van Buren st, 29.6x80. Nov. 10, 1 year, 5 %. $11,000

Same to same. Tompkins av, e s, 41 n Van Buren st, 29.6x80. Nov. 10, 1 year, 5 %. 11,000

Adler, Louis and Mary J. his wife to Philip Alstadt. Jerome st. P. M. Oct. 1, 5 years. 2,500

Allan, John T. and Nathaniel Proskey to Fannie M. E. Ensell. 4th st, n e s, 197.10 n w 8th av, 20x95; 4th st, n e s, 235.10 n w 8th av, 62x95. Nov 6. 1,000

Alexander, Jacob, Isidor and Moritz C. to Lewis Krulewitch. Plymouth st, n w cor Little st. P. M. Sub. to mort. $6,000. Oct. 27, installs. 2,000

Amann, John and Anton to Catharine Bridge and ano. exrs. Samuels Williams. Jefferson st, s e s, 400 s w Irving av, 25x100. Nov. 7, 2 years, 5 %. 3,000

Same to William Laytin et al. trustees William Laytin. Jefferson st, s e s, 425 s w Irving av, 25x100. Nov. 7, 3 years, 5 %. 3,000

Anderson, Robert H. to Thomas I. Atkins. Vernon av, s s, 220 w Throop av, 80x100. Nov. 2, due April 1, 1892. 8,800

Anderson, Thorvald and Lewis to The Title Guarantee and Trust Co. Garfield pl, s s, 172.10 w 8th av, 100x100. Nov. 4, demand. 80,000

Axebrod, Jacob and Isaac Levingson to Anna Mangels. Stone av, e s, 125 n Sutter av, 25x100. Oct. 26, 5 years. 2,500

Baker, John G. and Charles L. Lincoln to The Title Guarantee and Trust Co. 9th st, n s, 232.10 e 7th av, 100x80, with title to courtyard in front. Nov. 10, demand. 30,000

Barkeloo, Harriet J. to Peter W. Williamson. 15th st, s w s, 294.8 n w 5th av, 25x175.5. Nov. 6, due Nov. 1, 1894. 1,000

Barnaby, Frank A. and Noah Tebbets with Albert Muir. Agreement as to priority of mortgages made by Albert Muir. Nov. 7. nom

Barnes, Julia R to Lillie B. Allien. All title in trust fund of $185,000 existing under will of Katharine A. Rockwell. Oct. 1. 1,000

Bauer, Simon and Appolonia his wife to William Schafer. Liberty av, n s, 50 w Christopher av, 25x100. Nov. 1, due in 1894, 5 %. 1,500

Beer, Louis and Michael Schaffner to Theodore F. Jackson. Knickerbocker av, n e s, extends from Himrod st, to Stanhope st, 200x100. Nov. 4, due June 1, 1897, 5 %. 13,500

Beith, James to Margaret Lawrence. Adelphi st. P. M. Oct. 31, due Nov. 6, 1896, 5 %. 2,000

Belcher, Charline W. widow to Charles F. W. Aukamp. Lafayette av, n s, 266.8 e Nostrand av, 16.8x100. Nov. 6, 6 months, 5 %. 1,500

Benson, Martha M. widow to Samuel Kraus, New York. Wilson st, s e s, 113 s w Bedford av, 22.6x100. Nov. 2, 3 years. 4,500

Betts, Charles A. to The Hamilton Trust Co. Marcy av, w s, 170 s Macon st, 45x110. Nov 11, demand. 3,500

Black, James to Herman Newman. Grand st, n s, 59 w Marcy av. P. M. Nov. 9, 5 years, 5 %. 3,100

Blanke, George C. trustee William C. Betts mortgagee to Juliette Holmes mortgagor. Extension of mort. Oct. 20. nom

Booth, Isabelle B. wife of and John N. to Paul W. Ledoux. Covert st, s s, 198 e Central av, 6 lots, together 107.10x100. 6 morts., each $3,000. Oct. 31, 1 year, 5 %. 18,000

Brandt, Johanna H. to Simon H. Stern. Jerome st, s e cor Eastern Parkway. P. M. Oct. 29, 2 years. 900

Brodsky, Joseph to Andrew Ginter. Myrtle st, s e s, 376.10 s w Wyckoff av, 25x100. Nov. 1, 5 years, 5 %. 1,700

Brownell, Asa C. to Frank A. Barnaby. State st, n s, 250 e Hoyt st, 100x100. Building loan. Nov. 7. 5,000

Burling, Samuel and John C. to George R. Haydock. Howard av. P. M. Oct. 19, due Nov. 1, 1893. 3,000

Burrows, Mary A. to Cornelius A. Stryker. Park av, s s, 231.8 e Nostrand av, 54.7x100. Oct. 7, due Nov. 1, 1894, 5 %. 4,000

Cannon, Annie E. to Sylvanus T. Cannon. Reid av, e s, 80 s Greene av, 20x80. Oct. 26, due May 1, 1892, 5 %. 700

Carr, William J. to Gilliam Schenck. Van Siclen av, e s, 303 n Fulton av, 22x100. Oct. 31, 3 years. 2,500

Carroll, James G. to Mary L. Granniss, Newark, N. J. 3d av, s e cor 53d st, 20.2x80. Nov. 2, due Nov. 1, 1894, 5 %. gold, 5,000

Caufield, James A. to Henry Schopps. Halsey st, n w s, 120 n e Evergreen av, 20x100. Nov. 2, due Dec. 15, 1894, 5 %. 2,500

Same to same. Halsey st, n w s, 140 n e Evergreen av, 20x100. Nov. 2, due Dec. 15, 1894, 5 %. 2,500

Chacon, Jose to Francisco de Borroto. Blake av, n w cor Madison st. P. M. Nov. 4, 1 year, 5 %. 200

Chinnock, Elizabeth L. wife of and George H. to Teachers' Building and Loan Assoc. 7th av, n w s, 19.3 s w 16th st, 18.4x75.1x18x75.1. Nov. 10, installs. 3,360

Clayton, Anna M. to The Title Guarantee and Trust Co. Gates av, n s, 236.6 w Stuyvesant av, 19x100. Nov. 5, installs, 5 %. 6,000

Clifford, James P. to Simon C. Wilson, Baldwins, L. I. Sackman st. P. M. Sept. 8, installs. 1,000

Cochran, Henry H. to Title Guarantee and Trust Co. Van Buren st, n s, 199.8 e Lewis av, 175.4x100. Nov. 9, demand. 9,000

Cochran, Israel Y. to The Teachers' Building and Loan Assoc., New York City. Liberty av, s s, 100 e Osborn st, 50x100. Nov. 10, installs, 5 %. 6,720

Coe, Elizabeth A. to Henry E. Burnett. South 6th st, s s, 120 e Wythe av, 25x99.2. Nov. 4, 3 years, 5 %. 2,000

Cogswell, Charlotte to Amanda S. Coles. Monroe st. P. M. Nov. 10, 5 years, 5 %. 2,800

Cole, Randolph H. to William C. Booth. Decatur st. P. M. Nov. 5, 2 years, 5 %. 8,500

Converse, Adelaide A. wife of and Charles E. to The Brooklyn Eye and Ear Hospital. Madison st, n s, 250 e Tompkins av, 20x100. Oct. 28, 3 years, 5 %. 5,000

Crean, Peter to The Bushwick Co-operative Building and Loan Assoc. Frost st. P. M. Nov. 11, installs. 3,500

Cuno, Pauline to The Blythebourne Improvement Co. 12th av and 56th st, New Utrecht. P. M. Nov. 5, 3 years. 900

Dahl, Kate wife of and Charles to Ann M. wife of Gilliam Schenck. Linwood st, w s, 85 n Wortman av, 100x100; Elton st, e s, 34.5 s Stanley st, 80x100. Nov. 9, 3 years. 1,000

Damen, George to Joseph Bihy. Fulton st, s s, 112.6 w Ralph av, 18.9x100. Oct. 13, due Nov. 1, 1894, 5 %. 2,500

Darling, Daniel P. to Caroline N. Francis, Roselle. Barbey st, e s, 205 s Hegeman av, 40x100; Jerome st, w s, 140 n Hegeman av, 20x100; Jerome st, w s, 100 s Repose pl, 40x100; Repose pl, n s, 180 w Jerome st, 20x108.10x20x108.7; Repose pl, n s, 180 e Schenck av, 20x109.8x20x110. Nov. 9, 1 year. 1,000

Dassan, Max A. and Christianna his wife to German Savings Bank of Brooklyn. Leonard st, e s, 74.5 s Stagg st, 25.7x100. Nov. 6, due Dec. 1, 1892, 5 %. 3,000

De Baum, Alonzo E. to Fredk V. Aldridge guard. of Magdalena E. Schmadeke. Franklin av, s e cor Crown st, 131x100. Nov. 5, due Nov. 1, 1892, 5 %. 2,000

Devine, Patrick to Josephine A. Thibaut. 7th st, e s, 150 s Nassau av, 25x100. Nov. 9, 3 years, 5 %. 500

De Wilde, Andre to Frederick Berenbroick. De Kalb av, n s, 171.8 e Stuyvesant av, 27.8x100. P. M. Nov. 4, 1 year. 800

Doherty, John to The South Brooklyn Co-operative Building and Loan Assoc. 74th st, s s, 550 w 15th av, 40x100, New Utrecht. Nov. 10, installs. 2,500

Domminey, George A. to Title Guarantee and Trust Co. Saratoga av, w s, 50 s Sumpter st, 25x75. Nov. 6, 1 year. 560

Dooling, Mary to Anna M. Allegist, Newark, N. J. Warren st. P. M. Nov. 4, 2 years. 600

Doughty, William H. to William W. Browning trustee William Browning dec'd. De Kalb av, s s, 275 w Lewis av, 25x100. Nov. 5, 5 years, 5 %. 3,500

Downie, John to James Shevlin. Dean st. P. M. Nov. 5, 1 year, 5 %. 2,000

Dryer, Caroline to Ellen C. Hommel. Evergreen av, south cor Himrod st. P. M. Sept. 31, 3 years. 1,000

Dumahert, Claudius H. to Charles Hart. 6th av. P. M. Nov. 9, 3 years, 5 %. 2,900

Erickson, Charles A. to Gertrude L. wife of William Martin. 52d st. P. M. Nov. 2, 3 years. 2,000

Same to Caroline R. Stephens. 52d st. P. M. Nov. 2, 3 years. 4,000

Eade, George to Anna M. Lott, New Utrecht, L. I. 52d st, s w s, 120 n w 4th av, 20x100.2. Nov. 5, 3 years, 5 %. 2,500

Eastman, Arra B. to Thomas B. Bryant. Greene av, No. 734. P. M. Oct. 21, 1 year. 2,900

Emich, William and Emma his wife to Elizabetha Meltzer. Boerum st, n s, 28.1 e Broadway, 22x100. Nov. 5, 1 year, 5 %. 5,000

Engert, Charles to The Kings Co. Savings Inst. Monitor st, w s, 83.3 s Driggs av, 18x100. Nov. 1, 1 year, 5 %. 1,900

Epworth, George W. to Mary E. and Belle Lawrence. Railroad av, e s, 383.2 n Atlantic av, 25x87.6. Nov. 4, due Nov. 1, 1894. 1,500

Erthal, Jr., John to Charles W. Truslow trustee William Wall. Harrison pl. P. M. Oct. 27, 3 years, 5 %. 645

Esola, John to Mary Gattavara. Union st, s s, 122 w Columbia st, 20.6x100. ½ part. Oct. 20, 3 years, 5 %. 1,200

Fallon, John to Stephen B. Sturges. Kane pl, e s, 152.3 n Atlantic av, 3 lots, each 15.4x105. 3 morts., each $3,450. Nov. 2, 1 year. 10,350

Falvey, Deborah widow to The Bedford Co-operative Building Loan Assoc. Park pl, s s, 200 e Rogers av, 25x45.4x25.6x43.3. Nov. 2, installs. 300

Feldberg, Johannes to Henry Schlachter. Osborn st, n e cor Glenmore av, 50x100. Nov. 5, 6 months. 2,400

Finken, Elizabeth to John Finken. De Kalb av. P. M. Nov. 11, 5 years, 5 %. 4,000

Fischer, Charles H. to Mary E. Laing. Glenmore av. P. M. Nov. 4, 2 years. 400

Fleck, Joseph to George Fleck, Jr. Calyer st, s w cor Leonard st, 25x75. Jan. 30, 1890, 3 years, 5 %. 2,000

Same to same. Same property. June 10, 1889, due July 1, 1894, 5 %. 4,000

Fleer, George and Henry to Mary R. Bennett. Liberty av, n w cor Elderts lane, 200.3x580.5x200x577.1. Nov. 2, 3 years. 12,000

Forrester, William O. to Margaret Hendrickson. Putnam av, n s, 280 e Reid av, 20x100. Nov. 7, due Nov. 1, 1894, 5 %. 5,500

Same to Elias J. Hendrickson. Putnam av, n s, 280 e Reid av, 20x100. Nov. 7, due Nov. 1, 1894, 5 %. 5,500

Same to Rudolph H. Cole. Putnam av, n s, 200 e Reid av, 20x100. Nov. 7, due Nov. 1, 1894, 5 %. 5,000

Same to same. Putnam av, n s, 220 e Reid av, 20x100. Nov. 7, due Nov. 1, 1894, 5 %. 5,000

Same to Edward Hincken. Putnam av, n s, 240 e Reid av, 20x100. Nov. 7, due Nov. 1, 1894, 5 %. 5,750

Fox, Charles to The Title Guarantee and Trust Co. McDonough st, s s, 81 e Ralph av, 19x100. Nov. 5, 2 years, 5 %. 3,000

Frank, Barnet and Simon Rose to Mary W. Smith. Eastern Parkway, s s, 50 e Osborn st, 25x100. Nov. 5, demand. 200

Freeman, Emma L. widow to William H. Reynolds. Macon st. P. M. Nov. 9, 2 years, 5 %. 3,500

Friedrich, George to Alfred Ogden. Atlantic av, s s, 183.4 e Saratoga av. P. M. Oct. 28, installs. 1,000

Gibson, John H. to Martin B. Vandusen, Patchogue, L. I. 19th st, s w s, 285 n w 7th av, 15x100. Nov. 10, due July 1, 1893. 350

Giese, Ewald F. to Elizabeth Wetzel, Utica, N. Y. 10th st, s s, 210 e 3d av, 20x100. Nov. 2, 3 years, 5 %. 1,000

Gilfillan, William exr. John Griffith mortgagee with Kate Mesritz and ano. Extension of 3 morts. Nov. 2.

Gleeson, Ann D. wife of and Joseph to John P. Morris. 39th st, n s, 200 w 6th av, 25x100. March 5, 1890, demand. 25

Goldberg, Louis to Mary E. Cook. Stone av. P. M. Oct. 26, installs. 1,275

Grant, John to The Title Guarantee and Trust Co. Lafayette av, n s, 200 w Stuyvesant av, 25x100. Nov. 9, 3 years, 5 %. 3,500

Groesbeck, Warren to Abraham N. Groesbeck. Hart st, s s, 265 w Sumner av, 17.6x100. Oct. 30, due Nov. 1, 1894, 5 %. 1,200

Grafing, Frederick to Leonhard Eppig. Ralph av, s e cor Halsey st, runs south 100 x east 44.8 x north 16 x west 19.5 x north 84 to st, x west 25.3. Nov. 11, 1 year, 5 %. 12,000

Grening, Paul C. to George L. and C. F. Kingsland exrs. Ambrose C. Kingsland. Kingsland and Meeker avs. P. M. Feb. 2, 1 year. 11,000

Guarniere, Felix to Carlo Guarniere. Columbia st, w s, 36.1 s Seabring st, 17.10x86x18x86; Columbia st, w s, 53.11 s Seabring st, 18.4x86. Oct. 31, 10 years or sooner, 4 %. 600

Gue, Martha J. to The Blythbourne Impt. Co. 12th av, north cor 58th st, 50.2x100, New Utrecht. Oct. 19, 2 years, 5 %. 1,175

Same to same. 12th av, n w s, 50.2 n e 58th st, 50x100, New Utrecht. Oct. 19, 2 years, 5 %. 1,175

Gutting, George to The Williamsburgh Savings Bank. Ewen st, s e cor McKibbin st, 25x75. Nov. 6, 1 year, 5 %. 5,500

Hall, John H. to The South Brooklyn Co-operative Building and Loan Assoc. 12th st. P. M. Nov. 10, installs. 3,250

Hannemann, John J. to Julia E. T. Mathison. Harman st, s e s, 100 n e Hamburg av, 25x100. Oct. 30, due Nov. 1, 1894, 5 %. 3,500

Same to Theodore F. Jackson et al. trustees Loftis Wood dec'd. Harman st, s e s, 125 n e Hamburg av, 25x100. Oct. 30, due Nov. 1, 1894, 5 %. 3,500

Harrington, Margaret A. wife of and John to Henry H. Adams, Treasurer Kings Co. Van Siclen av, w s, 150 n Fulton av, 25x100. Nov. 5, 1 year, 5 %. 3,500

Hartmann, Julius and Emilie to Henry Eich. Stockton st. P. M. Nov. 4, 5 years, 5 %. 2,400

Hazzard, John L. and Sarah M. his wife to Ditmars Eldert. Chestnut st. P. M. Oct. 31, due Nov. 1, 1894. 1,300

Hazard, John L. to George Beach. Chestnut st. P. M. Oct. 31, installs. 1,100

Hazzard, Stephen to William H. Hazzard. Pacific st, n s, 240 e Clinton st, 50x100. P. M. June 15, 1882. 8,000

Hoffman, Charles C. to Theodore Kiendl. Orient st, e s, 250 n Liberty av, 25x100. Nov. 2, 1 year. 325

Hoffmann, Andrew to Frederick Reges and Lena his wife. Boerum st. P. M. Nov. 1, due Nov 5, 1894, 5 %. 1,800

Hogan, Daniel to Frank W. Fuller. Imlay st, No. 149, s e s, 226 n e William st, 17x19. Sept. 21, 1 year. 500

Holland, George to Rudolph and Otto E. Reimer. Hancock st, n s, 91.8 w Ralph av, 19.11x85. Sub to mort. $4,000. Nov. 6, 1 year. 550

Hoppel, John K. to The City Savings Bank, Brooklyn. Elliott pl, e s, 254.2 s Hanson pl, 20.11x100. Nov. 9, due Nov. 1, 1893, 5 % 4,000

Horn, Anna to Otto Huber. Heyward st, No. 187, n , 80 w Marcy av, 19.6x100. Nov. 10, 1 year, 5 %. 3,500

Hornbostel, Johanna to Abraham Hegeman. Berdan av, east cor Hinsdale av, —x—, and all title in oyster pond so called and land under water, &c., Flatlands. Nov. 5, 3 years. 3,750

Howie, William J. to The Equitable Co-operative Building and Loan Assoc. Hull st, s s, 315 e Rockaway av, 15x100. Nov. 4, installs. 4,250

Irvine, William to South Brooklyn Savings Inst. Nostrand av, n w cor Monroe st, 30x85. Nov. 4, 1 year, 5 %. 17,000

Same to same. Nostrand av, w s, 30 n Monroe st, 30x85. Nov. 4, 1 year, 5 %. 9,000

James, Isabella N. wife of Sinclair W. to Samuel Ayres. Jefferson av. P. M. Nov. 6, due Nov. 7, 1896, 5 %. 3,500

Same to same. Same property. P. M. Nov. 6, installs, 5 %. 1,775

Jennerich, Dora to Philip L. Balz, Jr. Elton st, w s, 120.11 n Fulton av, 25x100. Nov. 3, due Nov. 1, 1892. 200

Jensen, Albert to South Brooklyn Co-operative Building and Loan Assoc. East 3d st, w s, 149.1 s Greenwood av, 20x100. Building loan. Oct. 27, installs. 1,575

Johnston, Albert to Alexander Underhill. Herkimer st, n s, 20 w Saratoga av, 80x80. Oct. 31. 500

Johnson, J. Christian to Virginia A. Kleine. Eldert st, n w s, 95 s w Evergreen av, 100x100; Eldert st, n w s, 215 s w Evergreen av, 20x100. Nov. 6, demand. 10,000

Same to Avery T. Brown and ano. trustees Caroline I. Satchell. Eldert st, n s, 115 w Evergreen av, 20x100. Nov. 1, 3 years, 5 %. 4,000

Same to Ruth Tompkins, Somers, N. Y. Eldert st, n s, 135 w Evergreen av, 20x100. Nov. 1, 3 years, 5 %. 3,500

Same to William E. Valentine. Eldert st, n s, 95 w Evergreen av, 20x100. Nov. 1, 3 years, 5 %. 3,500

Johnson, Salome wife of and Peter to Sarah H. Powell. Flushing av, n s, 270.6 e Morgan av, runs north 100 along Vandervoort pl, x north 1.2 x east 25.7 x south 94.5 to Flushing av, x west 25. Nov. 6, installs, 5 %. 6,500

Johnson, Francis T. to Jane E. Meeker et al. exrs. Samuel M. Meeker. Putnam av. P. M. Nov. 7, due Nov. 9, 1894, 5 %. 9,000

Jones, Annie to Giacanno Buronne. Dean st, No. 2106, s s, 28x108.4. Nov. 4, due May 4, 1893. 225

Kay, George J. to Joseph Lawson. Gates av. P. M. Nov. 7, 1 year. 1,000

Kelland, Philip to Ann Fry. Lafayette av, n s, 29.5 e Adelphi st, runs north 39 x west 0.2 x north — x east to point 51.1 e Adelphi st, x south 81 to av, x west —. Nov. 11, 5 years, 5 %. 5,000

Kaatze, Dietrich W. to Lur Wintjen. South 1st st, n w cor Hooper st. P. M. Nov. 5, 1 year, 5 %. 4,000

Kelly, Patrick to George H. Perry. Diamond st, w s, 384.10 n Driggs av, 25x100. Nov. 7, 1 year. 125

Kelsch, Agatha to William Tousey, New York. Macon st, s s, 338.8 e Reid av, 18.4x100. Nov. 4, 5 years, 5 %. 2,000

Kent, Artemicia wife of and Edward to Hamilton Trust Co. 68th st, s s, 86.9 w 2d av, 100x154.4. Nov. 6, due Nov. 1, 1892. 2,000

Kleinschnitz, August to Franziska Kleinschnitz. Broadway, No. 1273. Lease. Nov. 24, demand. 8,000

Knapp, Andrew to Leonhard Eppig. Floyd st, n s, 125 w Throop av, 25x100. Nov. 7, 1 year, 5 %. 4,500

Koch, Johanna to Angelica Stecker, South 4th st, s s, 23 e Berry st, 25x79. Nov. 4, 3 years, 5 %. 2,500

Koenemann, Meta widow to Benjamin P. Davis exr. and trustee Benjamin W. Davis. Liberty av, s e cor Crescent st, 50x100. Nov. 5, 3 years. 4,500

Koseck, Frank to The Niagara Fire Ins. Co. Warren st. P. M. Oct. 27, 5 years, 5 %. 3,900

Krueger, August to Clara Mang. 4th av and 9?d st. P. M. Nov. 7, due Nov. 1, 1908. 8,500

Lahy, Thomas to Phebe M. Clarke et al. exrs. and trustees Henry L. Clarke. 11th st, n e s, 137.10 n e 8th av. P. M. Oct. 31, due Nov. 2, 1893, 2 years, 5 %. 4,500

Same to same. 11th st, n e s, 237.10 n w 8th av. P. M. Oct. 31, due Nov. 2, 1892, 5 %. 4,500

Laing, Donald to William A. Cook trustee Charlotte E. Harris. Belmont av, s s, 40 e Montauk av, 20x90. Nov. 10, 3 years. 2,000

Same to Jonathan H. Crane trustee Anna Walsh Glenmore av, s s, 60 w Milford st, 20x90. Nov. 10, 3 years. 2,000

Lake, Mary V. widow to Mary L. Whiting. De Kalb av, n s, 306.3 w Stuyvesant av, 18x100. Nov. 6, 3 years, 5 %. 3,500

Lambert, Ellen wife of and John to Flora C. Fleisch. 42d st, s s, 125 e 2d av, 25x100.2. Nov. 1, 3 years. 150

Lazansky, Alois to Charles W. Truslow trustee William Wall. Boerum st. P. M. Oct. 29, 3 years, 5 %. 5,760

Lane, Theodore to Kate A. B. Darlington. Wilson st, s s, 19.4 e Wythe av, 19.4x80. Nov. 6, 1 year, 5 %. 2,500

Lang, Catharine wife of and Lewis to Phebe E. Sharp. Centre st, e s, lot 189 map Sarah A. Suydam property, 25x100, map destroyed. Nov. 4. 3 years. 500

Larsen, Peter to The Title Guarantee and Trust Co. 1st st, n s, 197.8 w 6th av, 4 lots, each 19.5x100. 4 morts., each $6,000. Nov. 9, 3 years, 5 %. 24,000

Lashaver, Moses to Mary E. Cook, Newtown, L. I. Livonia av. P. M. July 10, installs. 500

Leinfelder, Anna M. to Israel Y. Cochran. Hemlock st, e s, 150 s Griffen pl, 25x100. Nov. 5, 3 years. 400

Lewis, Jennie W. formerly Wyburn to The Kings Co. Trust Co. Washington av, e s, 67.3 s Myrtle av, 19.9x80. Nov. 6, 1 year, 5 %. 3,700

Liegeois, Constant to Lewis Hurst. Eastern Parkway, n e cor Christopher av, 100x100. Nov. 4, 1 year. 350

Lohr, Charles H. to The Title Guarantee and Trust Co. Butler st, n s, 60 e Hoyt st, 20x100. Nov. 9, 1 year, 5 %. 1,500

Lohrentz, Christina E. to Alonzo Reed, Quogue, L. I. Nichols av. P. M. and building loan. Sept. 5, due Sept. 15, 1891. 2,940

Lotz, Lorenz to John G. Reither. Pacific st, s s, 169 w Schenectady av, runs west 220 x south 107.2 x west to centre old Jefferson st, x southeast — x east to point 44.4 s Pacific st, x north 44.4. Nov. 5, 1 year, 4½ %. 4,250

Mafera, Stephen to Alonzo Reed, Quogue, L. I. Nichols av. P. M. and building loan. Sept. 5, due Sept. 15, 1891. 1,960

Magilligan, John to The Title Guarantee and Trust Co. 1st st, s w s. 393.10 s e 7th av, 20x100. Nov. 4, due Nov. 5, 1894, 5 %. 8,000

Same to same. 1st st, s w s, 372.10 s e 7th av, 20x100. Nov. 4, due Nov. 5, 1894, 5 %. 8,000

Martin, Elliot D. and Anna to Christian Nicklaus. Elton st, w s, 510 s. New Lots road, 40x100. Nov. 4, 3 years, 5 %. 1,870

Martinus, Gertraud wife of Thomas to Andreas Senger. Hopkins st, n s, 300 e Tompkins av, 25x100. Oct. 27, due Nov. 1, 1894, 5 %. 1,000

Mason, Mary E. wife of Isaac D. to Thomas Roberts Stevenson Co. Bergen st, n s, 134.4 e Ralph av, 17x107.2. Oct. 10, installs. 500

McCue, Matthew J. to Mary A. Wheeler. Prospect av, n e cor Webster av. P. M. Nov. 5, 1 year, 5 %. 1,600

McCready, Benjamin W. to Amelia T. Bieling. Milford st, e s, 175 n Liberty av, 37.6x100. Nov. 5, due Jan. 1, 1893. 2,000

McDermott, John T. to Louis Ilsemann. Ashford st. P. M. Oct. 26, installs, 5 %. 500

McDonald, Robert F., Flora M. and Grace heirs Charlotte M. McDonald to Martha H. Boiles, New York. Quincy st, s s, 141 w Franklin av, 23x100. Nov. 2, due Nov. 1, 1896, 5 %. 2,000

McEntee, Patrick to The Atlantic Co-operative Savings and Loan Assoc. Vanderveer st, No. 108, s s, 324.2 e Bushwick av, 17x100. Nov. 10, installs, 5 %. 2,600

McGinness, Charles to The East Brooklyn Savings Bank of Brooklyn. Bedford av, e s, 325 n Tillary st, 25x100. Nov. 6, 1 year, 5 %. 2,500

McKnight, Alexander to The Title Guarantee and Trust Co. Lafayette av, n s, 275 e Sumner av, 2 lots, each 18.9x100. 2 morts., each $5,000. Nov. 10, 3 years, 5 %. 10,000

McManamy, Robert J. to Joseph Wurzler. Myrtle av. P. M. Nov. 11, 1 year 5 %. 480

McGinley, Mary E. to Achille Fouquet. 5th av, n w cor Bergen st, 20x78.4. Nov. 9, 3 years, 5 %. 8,000

McLerney, Dorinda to Mary E. Fox. Grand st, n w cor Union av, runs north 100 x west 75 x south 25 x east 50 x south 75 to Grand st, x east 25; Union av, w s. 25.8 s North 1st st, 25x97.4x29.8x81.4. Nov. 9, 5 years. 1,000

Menzel, Sarah A. to Joseph P. Wintringham. Clark st, No. 63, n s, 137.4 w Henry st, 22.8x100. Nov. 9, due Nov. 1, 1896. 2,000

Meyer, Henry, Jonas Feldberg and Sarah Barasch to Edward A. Rawlings. Seigel st, Nos. 55 and 57, n s, 146.6 w Ewen st, 48x100; Seigel st, No. 61, n s, 98.6 w Ewen st, 24x100. Nov. 2, demand. 7,000

Meyer, Eibe to P. Ballantine & Sons. Grand st, No. 720. Lease. Nov. 6, note. 3,000

Meyer, Henry L. to Francis E. Dodge and ano. exrs. Richard I. Dodge. Clark st. P. M. Nov. 5, 3 years, 5 %. 5,000

Moffat, Hugh to The South Brooklyn Co-operative Building and Loan Assoc. Vanderbilt st, Flatbush. P. M. Nov. 10, installs. 2,750

Monahan, Thomas to The Title Guarantee and Trust Co. Park pl, s e cor Franklin av, 24x52.6. Nov. 6, 3 years, 5 %. 6,500

Same to same. Park pl, s s, 24 e Franklin av, 19x52.6. Nov. 6, 3 years, 5 %. 3,750

Same to same. Park pl, s s, 81 e Franklin av, 19x52.6. Nov. 6, 3 years, 5 %. 3,750

Same to same. Park pl, s s, 62 e Franklin av, 19x52.6. Nov. 6, 3 years, 5 %. 4,000

Same to same. Park pl, s s, 48 e Franklin av, 19x52.6. Nov. 6, 3 years, 5 %. 4,000

Moore, Caroline wife of and Jonathan to Thomas C. Greenland. Hart st. P. M. Nov. 9, 1 year, 5 %. 2,006

Moss, Christian to Beadleston & Woerz. Bedford av, No. 1096. Lease. Nov. 10, demand. 3,000

Mowbray, Edward H. with The Title Guarantee and Trust Co. both mortgagees. Agreement as to priority of morts. made by Thorwald and Lewis Anderson. Nov. 4. nom

Morrow, Louis to The New York and Wakefield Co-operative Building and Loan Assoc. North 3d st. P. M. Oct. 29, installs. 2,750

Moretzky, Herman to David Blumberg. Watkins st. P. M. Nov. 1, 4 years. 300

Mullan, Rose A. to William G. Hotaling. Willoughby av, s s, 125 w Tompkins av, 20x100. Nov. 10, installs, 5 %. 2,250

Muller, Dora wife of and Jacob to Joseph Furman. Ralph st, s s, 115.3 e Wyckoff av, 40x100. Nov. 5, due Nov. 1, 1892, or sooner. 5,000

Muller, John J. to Beers Frost. Madison st, n s, 320 e Hamburg av, 20x100. Nov. 2, 3 years, 5 %. 500

Muller, Robert B. to Peter Bertsch exr., &c., William Broistedt. Linden st, s e s, 325 s w Central av, 25x100. Nov. 6, 3 years, 5 % 3,000

Mullowney, Richard to Patrick and Luke Dunn. Halsey st, s s, 22 w Ralph av, 18x100. Sub. to mort. $4,000. Oct. 27, 1 year. 1,000

Murphy, Thomas J. to William J. Murnane. Union st, n s, 212 e 7th av, 21x95. Nov. 6, 1 year, 5 %. 3,000

Newman, Henry to Bernbard Davisburg. Broadway. P. M. Nov. 9, due July 16, 1892, 5 %. 2,000

Niclas, Frederick to Henry F. Rosenbrook. Clason av. P. M. Oct. 29, due Jan. 1, 1895, 5 %. 4,000

Niclas, Frederick to Daniel F. Dwyer. Clason av. P. M. Sub. to mort. $4,000. Oct. 29, due Nov. 1, 1892. 500

Nichols, Edward P. and Harriet his wife to Title Guarantee and Trust Co. Lincoln pl, s s, 237 w 6th av. P. M. Nov. 5, 3 years, 5 %. 4,000

Same to Henry V. Raymond. Same property. 2d mort. Nov. 5, 3 years, 5 %. 1,200

Oellrich, William to The Germania Savings Bank, Kings Co. Marcy av, n e cor Willoughby av, 21x85. Nov. 5, 1 year, 5 %. gold, 8,000

O'Connell, Michael F. to Frederick H. Lawrence exr. George C. Tallman. Elton st, w s, 129.5 s Atlantic av. P. M. Nov. 10, installs. 325

O'Neil, Patrick to The Title Guarantee and Trust Co. Greenpoint av, n s, 325 e Manhattan av, 25x100. Nov. 10, 3 years, 5 %. 4,000

Olsen, Syver and Peter O. Petersen to Carolina M. Davison. 78th st, New Utrecht. P. M. Nov. 10, due Nov. 1, 1892. 550

Palmer, John A. to The Fulton Co-operative Building and Loan Assoc. Bergen st. P. M. Nov. 7, installs. 4,500

Pariser, Philip to John Y. McKane. Part of old lot 19A map common lands Gravesend, Coney Island. Nov. 4, demand. 600

Parmer, Ada wife of Lewis to Mary W. Smith. Watkins st, w s, 100 s Eastern Parkway, 26.6x100. Nov. 5, demand. 400

Peter, Joseph to John L. Gaus and Charles Miller. Kosciusko st, n s, 280.8 w Reid av, 18.11x100. Oct. 23, 1 day, 5 %. 2,350

Peterson, Charles G. to The Title Guarantee and Trust Co. 7th st, s s, 184.10 w 7th av, 18x100. Nov. 4, due Nov. 5, 1895, 5 %. 5,000

Same to same. 7th st, s s, 166.2 w 7th av, 18.8x100. Nov. 4, due Nov. 5, 1895, 5 %. 5,000

Same to same. 7th st, s s, 147.6 w 7th av, 18.8x100. Nov. 4, due Nov. 5, 1892, 5 %. 2,500

Same to same. 7th st, s s, 202.10 w 7th av, 20x100. Nov. 4, due Nov. 5, 1894, 5 %. 4,000

Peterson, Caroline to Catharine Stoothoff. Liberty av, s w Hemlock st, 25x100. Nov. 9, due July 1, 1892. 100

Phythion, Thomas to Albert Berry. Warren st, n w s, 50 n e Lexington av, 50x125. Nov. 2, due July 1, 1896. 300

Parsons, Ellen wife of Edward to The Prospect Home Building and Loan Assoc. 51st st, n s, 180 e 7th av, 20x78.11x20.11x85.1. Nov. 5, installs. 750

Poulterer, Lucinda to Benjamin Larzelere, New Utrecht. 19th av, s e s, 525 s w 86th st, 50x96.8. Nov. 6, 2 years. 1,500

Poynter, Isabella to Janet McLure. Elliott pl, w s, 387 s De Kalb av, 20x100. June 8, 5 years, 5 %. 1,000

Prince, Carrie E., Peekskill, N. Y., to The Peekskill Savings Bank. Myrtle av, n e cor Duffield st, 20x80. Oct. 26, 1 year. 2,000

Rankin, James D. and James Ross to The Title Guarantee and Trust Co. Bond st, s e cor Carroll st, runs east 176 x south 100 x west 184.10 to Bond st, x north 100.4. Nov. 10, 1 year, 5 %. 5,000

Ransom, James F. to James White. 10th st, n e s, 277.10 n w 10th av, 20x100. Nov. 9, 1 month. 347

Reichert, Betsy to Mary E. and Belle Lawrence. Railroad av. P. M. Nov. 2, due Nov. 1, 1894. 1,750

Same to Frank C. Lang. Same property. P. M. Nov. 2, due Nov. 1, 1894. 500

Richard, William F. to Richard Goodwin. Evergreen av, s w cor Eldert st. P. M. Nov. 4, 1 year or sooner. 9,500

Richardson, Mary E. wife of and Frederick B. to Katherine Drexel. Joralemon st, s s, 29 w Clinton st, runs south 65 x south 47.10 x west 18.7 x north 103.8 x east 25. Nov. 9, 3 years, 5 %. 15,000

Rickerson, Charles L. to Effingham H. Nichols, New York. Lots 100-150 inclus. block 3 map No. 1 of 618 lots Cowenhoven farm, New Utrecht. Aug. 4, 3 years, 5 %. 6,120

Robb, James R. to J. Henry Anderson. 21st st, n s, 269 e 6th av, 16x100. Nov. 7, 3 years. 1,500

Same to same. 21st st, n s, 25.3 e 6th av, 18x100. Nov. 7, 3 years. 1,500

Same to Stephen B. Sturges. 21st st, n s, 253 e 6th av, runs east 31.5 x north 40.6 x east 0.3 x north 59.6 x west 32 x south 100. Nov. 7, demand. 1,500

Roberts, James G. to Anna J. Hamilton. McDonough st, n s, 320.9 e Reid av, 18.9x100. Nov. 5, due Nov. 4, 1896, 5 %. 4,500

Same to Fannie E. Spooner, North Plainfield, N. J. McDonough st, n s, 393.6 e Reid av, 18x100. Nov. 5, due Nov. 4, 1896. 5,500

Same to William Tousey. McDonough st, n s, 357.6 e Reid av, 18x100. Nov. 5, due Nov. 4, 1891, 5 %. 5,500

Same to Eleanor M. Bell. McDonough st, n s, 339.6 e Reid av, 18x100. Nov. 5, due Nov. 4, 1896, 5 %. 5,500

Same to Alice J. Eccles. McDonough st, n s, 302 e Reid av, 18.9x100. Nov. 5, due Nov. 4, 1896, 5 %. 3,500

Same to William Adams exr. David Adams. McDonough st, n s, 375.6 e Reid av, 18x100. Nov. 5, due Nov. 4, 1896, 5 %. 5,000

Rooney, Mary G. wife of Thomas E. to Oliver J. Wells. Pacific st, n s, 489.8 w Franklin av, 40x100. Oct. 17, due Dec. 1, 1891. 1,000

Rosemon, Cornelius P. to James D. Lynch. Bay 25th st. P. M. Nov. 5, due Nov. 7, 1894, 5 %. 1,155

Ryan, John F. to John McCormack. Putnam av, s w Lewis av. P. M. Oct. 5, due Nov. 6, 1892, 5 %. 3,500

Salberg, Meta to Hugo S. Mack and Oscar Stern. Kosciusko st, No. 469, n s, 128 e Lewis av, 18x100. Nov. 4, installs. 1,500

Sands, Frank B., West New Brighton, S. I., to Elizabeth M. Warner. Conselyea st, n s, 275 e Lorimer st, 25x100. Nov. 6, 3 years, 5 %. 2,000

Schellenberger, Charlotte to John P. Morris. 42d st. P. M. Nov. 6, installs. 1,350

Schenck, Alexandrina wife of and Charles W. mortgagors with Edwin A. Dodd mortgagee. Extension of mort. July 15. nom

Schlicher, John to Eunice R. wife of Jost Moller, Jr. Marcy av, e s, 125 s Flushing av, 25x100. Nov. 10, 3 years, 5 %. 1,000

Schluchtner, Carrie C. to George Borgfeldt. Shepherd av, e s, 100 s Baltic av now Glenmore av, 50x100. Nov. 2, 1 year. 2,000

Schmolze, Frederick to Clara wife of Julius Vom Hofe. Lewis av, e s, 110 s Lafayette av, 20x100. Nov. 7, due Nov. 1, 1894, 5 %. 3,500

Schnitzpahn, Louis F., East Orange, N. J., to Miriam H. C. Cannon, New York. Bergen st, s s, 218.9 e Hoyt st, 21.10x100; Bergen st, s s, 262.6 e Hoyt st, 43.9x100; Bergen st, s s, 328.3 e Hoyt st, 21.8x100; Court st, e s, 73.5 n Butler st, 25x57.6. All title. Nov. 2, 2 years. 3,000

Schoch, Charles H. to Louisa Koch. Hancock st. P. M. Nov. 9, 1 year, 5 %. gold, 4,500

Schultheis, Henry to August C. Diestelhorst. North 8th st. P. M. Sub. to mort. $3,000. Nov. 2, 4 years. 1,600

Same to The Co-operative Building Bank. Same property. Nov. 2, installs. 3,000

Sebutta, John J. and Maggie T. his wife to William F. Corwith. Russell st. P. M. Nov. 4, due Nov. 1, 1896, 5½ %. 1,400

Scott, Levi M. to William M. Gibson. Quincy st, No. 468, s s, 63 w Throop av, 19x80. Oct. 19, installs, 5 %. 2,218

Seaman, Ella E. wife of and Lewis W., Jr., to Phebe M. wife of Daniel G. Saxtan. Fort Greene pl, w s, 58.6 s De Kalb av, 32.3x38.9x32.10x34.1. Nov. 10, due Jan. 1, 1897, 5 %. 5,000

Same to same. De Kalb av, s w cor Fort Greene pl, 20x63.6x32.1x58.6. Nov. 10, due Jan. 1, 1897, 5 %. 10,000

Schwab, Margaretha to Gottlob Haussmann, Guttenberg, N. J. Irving av, n e s, 25 n w Greene av, 25x90. Oct. 31, 3 years, 5 %. 1,400

Schwab, Elizabeth to William H. Baker. Railroad av, e s, 619 s Jamaica av, runs east 200 x south 25 x east 100 x south 25 x west 300 to Railroad av, x north 50. Nov. 1, 3 years. 500

See, Oscar A. to The Methodist Book Concern Employes Co-operative Building and Loan Assoc. Pacific st, No. 981, n s, 45 e Grand av, 20x80. Oct. 21, installs. 2,500

Seifters, Pincus to Peter Blank. Stanhope st, n w s, 100 s w Irving av, 50x100. Nov. 7, 3 years. 4,000

Seiling, Josef to George Thum. Linwood st, w s, 275 n Liberty av, 25x90. Nov. 6, due April 1, 1895, 5 %. 550

Seyfried, Jacob to Henry Roth and Joseph E. Middle. Throop av, s e cor Whipple st, 20x71.2. Nov. 1, installs, 5 %. 2,000

Sheehan, Andrew to E. E. Pearsall. Surf av, n s, part old lot 39 map common lands of Gravesend, runs north 350.5 to land N. Y. & Coney Island Railroad Co., x east 70 x south 100 x east 50 to West 25th st, x160 x west 30 x south 104.2, Coney Island. Dec. 3, 1889, demand. 1,000

Sibley, Albert to Francis J. McBrien. Quincy st, s, 175 w Throop av, 18.9x100. Nov. 8, 2 years. 1,161

Skahan, Mary to George U. Forbell. Hendrix st. P. M. Sept. 2, installs. 250

Snook, John M. to Sarah Smith. 39th st. P. M. Nov. 5, 5 years. 1,000

Silberstein, Morris and Jacob Goldstein to Pauline Hartman. Thatford av. P. M. Nov. 4, installs. 375

Souter, Susan G. wife of John W. to Prospect Home Building and Loan Assoc. 52d st, s s, 220 w 4th av, 20x100.2. Nov. 11, installs. 2,500

Stanton, Francis to Leopold J. Lippmann. Weirfield st, n w s, 101.2 s w Central av, 20 x100. Nov. 4, installs. 1,500

Stearns, Caroline H. wife of George W. to John A. Latimer and ano. trustees for Anne M. Vought. Elton st, w s, 215.5 n Atlantic av, 25x100. Nov. 7, 3 years. 3,000

Steele, John A. to Edward B. L. Carter trustee Henry J. Sanford. Putnam av, n s, 151.3 w Tompkins av, 15x100. Nov. 1, 3 years, 5 %. 5,000

Stone, Henry A. to Sarah C. Savage, Philadelphia, Pa. Pacific st, s s, 380.7 e Rochester av. P. M. Nov. 11, 1 year. 2,100

Same to same. Pacific st, s s, 363.10 e Rochester av. P. M. Nov. 11, 1 year. 2,100

Stone, Thomas to Henry C. Bauer and Jacob Murr. Broadway, s w s, 109.3 s e McDonough st. P. M. Nov. 9, 2 years. 2,500

Sturges, Stephen P. to Mary A. Taylor. Ralph st, n s, 100 w Knickerbocker av, 200x100. Nov. 6, 1 year. 12,000

Summersgill, Carrie P. to Sarah J. Preston, Newtown, L. I. Waverly av, e s, 441.8 n Myrtle av, 16 8x100. Nov. 7, 5 years, 5 %. 3,000

Taylor, Sophronia wife of Noble A. to Mary B. Van Beuren. Park pl, n s, 325 w Buffalo av, 40x127.9. Nov. 11, due Jan. 1, 1895. 1,300

The Brooklyn Warehouse and Dry Dock Co. with consent of stockholders to The Dime Savings Bank Brooklyn. 26th st. P. M. Nov. 6, 1 year, 5 %. 50,000

The Metallic Relief Mfg. Co. to Helen A. Frost. Greene av, n s, 123.8 w Clason av, 23.8x100x 25.5x100; Greene av, n s, 577.4 w Grand av, runs north 100 x south 100 to Greene av at point 577.8 e Grand av, x west 0.4; Greene av, n s, 550 e Grand av, 27.4x100x24.1x100. Oct. 23, 3 years, 5 %. 5,000

The Lidgerwood Mfg. Co. to Amos F. Eno. Partition st, north cor Ferris st. P. M. Feb. 1, 1887, installs. 10,000

Same to same. Same property. Feb. 1, 1887, demand. 50,000

The Brooklyn Bath & West End R. R. Co. to The Title Guarantee and Trust Co. 5th av, west cor 27th st, 100.2x350; lot at New Utrecht, 167 n e Main st, runs northeast 182 x northwest 103 x northeast 99.8 x northwest 104 x south 32 to mortgagors lands, x south 327.9; also gore adj and land of James C. Church, runs northeast 95 x south 22 x northwest 78; also 5 25-100 acres of meadow land adj lands Sarah Benson, Gravesend; also 1 40-100 acres adj Garret W. Cropsey's land; also 5 acres adj New York & Coney Island R. R.; part lots 19A and 21 and all lot 18A map common lands of Gravesend, 6 8-10 acres, Gravesend; 5th av, n w cor 25th st, 100x350; also rights, privileges and franchises. Sub. to mort. $6,700. Secures issue of 2d mort. bonds. July 1, 5 %. 100,000

The Security Corporation to The Manhattan Trust Co. All lands, properties, rights, privileges and franchises. Nov. 2, bonds. gold, 6,000,000

Tomlinson, Charles W. to Teachers' Building and Loan Assoc., New York City. Liberty av, s s, 50 e Osborn st, 50x100. Nov. 10, installs, 5 %. 6,720

Trezzo, Antonia to Edward Egolf. Broadway, Flatbush. P. M. Aug. 19, 3 years. 450

Unwin, Minnie S. P. to Alexander G. Calder. 12th st. P. M. Nov. 10, installs, 5 %. 3,000

Van Buren, Ansel H. to Cornelius Macardell, Middletown, N. Y. Saratoga av, n w cor Decatur st, 100x300. Nov. 11, demand. 17,500

Same to Patrick Brown. Decatur st, n s, 43.4 w Saratoga av, 7 lots, each 18.4x100. 7 morts., each $4,000. Nov. 6, 3 years, 5 %. 28,000

Same to same. Decatur st, n s, 190 w Saratoga av, 4 lots, each 18.4x100. 4 morts., each $4,000. Nov. 6, 3 years, 5 %. 16,000

Same to Mary G. Wood. Decatur st, n s, 171.8 w Saratoga av, 18.4x100. Nov. 11, 3 years, 5 %. 4,000

Van Orden, George O. to Susan E. Fingarr, Charles D. Burwell and Frank A. Barnaby. 5th st. P. M. Sub. to mort. $20,000. Oct. 30, demand. 5,130

Same to The Title Guarantee and Trust Co. Same property. Oct. 30, demand. 20,000

Van Saun, Emma A., New Rochelle, to William J. Kerigan. Steuben st, e s, 108 s De Kalb av, 22.4x100. Nov. 7, 3 years, 5 %. 6,500

Vaughan, William to Henry B. Hudson, New Rochelle. De Kalb av, s s, 45.5 e Graham st, 23x90. Nov. 4, 3 years, 5 %. 3,000

Velsor, Oscar W., Hempstead, L. I., to Earl A. Gillespie, Woodhaven, L. I. Thatford av, e s, 212 n Glenmore av, 52.8x100. Sub. to morts. $8,000. Oct. 30, demand. 500

Vrooman, John F. to Angeline A. Davis, Huntington, L. I. Power st, w s, 250 n Liberty av, 25x100. Nov. 6, 3 years. 2,500

Waldron, Alexander to A. Gertrude Van Brunt and Eliza B. Monfort. 47th st, s w s, 220 s e 4th av, 20x100.2. Nov. 6, 3 years, 5 %. 3,500

Wardell, William H. to Daniel F. Kingsland and James C. Comstock. Highway leading from Yellow Hook to Brooklyn, s s, 179 5 e land Winant E. Bennet, 54.9x95, New Utrecht. May 1, 1891, 2 years or sooner, 5 %. 1,000

Weinstein, Sale and Aaron Altmann to Edward L. Snyder and ano. exrs. Samuel F. Engs. Osborn st, e s, 125 n Sutter av, 25x 100. Nov. 2, 3 years. 3,500

Weir, Mary wife of and James to Christopher P. Skelton. Prescott st. P. M. Nov. 2, installs. 1,050

Same to same. Same property. Nov. 2, due Nov. 5, 1894, 5 %. 1,250

Wend, Catharine E. widow to The Title Guarantee and Trust Co. Sumpter st, s s, 275 w Ralph av, 20x irreg. Nov. 9, 3 years, 5 %. 2,000

Wendt, Louisa S. widow to The Title Guarantee and Trust Co. Pacific st, s s, 85 w Albany av, 20x107.2. Nov. 6, 3 years, 5 %. 2,250

Wenz, Sarah E. to John P. Free. Sutter av, n s, 15 e Vesta av. P. M. Oct. 17, 3 years. 675

Wessel, Girard H. to Henry C. Bull. 19th st. P. M. Nov. 2, installs. 950

White, Mary A. to John B. Kennison. 52d st, s w s, 320 n w 5th av. P. M. Nov. 9, due Sept. 30, 1892. 350

Windstein, Louis to John P. McQuaid. Cook st. P. M. Nov. 10, 3 years, 5 %. 800

Williams, Ada C. to John P. H. De Wint. 5th av. P. M. Nov. 10, 2 years, 5 %. 9,000

Woodcock, John B. C. to Laura Munger. Radde pl, No. 15, e s, 151 6 s Herkimer st, 15.6x97.6. Oct. 23, 2 years. 500

Wyckoff, Annie M. to George D. Bangs. Quincy st, n s, 449.8 e Reid av, 18x100. Nov. 5, installs. 650

Wynne, Thomas to Patrick J. Carlin. Court st, s e cor 4th pl, 50x100. Nov. 5, demand, 5 %. 18,000

MORTGAGES----ASSIGNMENTS.

NEW YORK CITY.

November 6 to 12—Inclusive

Aston, William K. to Benjamin F. Constable. $5,404

Blanck, Eliza E. to James T. Quail et al. exrs. and trustees John W. Blanck. 15,056

Byrne, Ann to Margaret F. McIntyre. 3,000

Baldwin, George V. N. trustee for Mary C. de Terronerne to Mary C. de Terronenne. nom

Beaudet, Homer J. to Joseph M. De Veau. nom

Beekman, Henry R. to David B. Ogden. 1,772

Buck, Thomas C. to Walter S. Neilson. 10,000

Bergen, Mary F. to John Bussing, Jr. 800

Baldwin, William B. to Henry D. Winans and Albert Bellamy. 4,853

Booraem, Louis V., Montclair, N. J., to Russell Raymond and ano. trustees for Robert Russell. nom

Cary, Clarence trustee to Virginia Potter. nom

Cockran, Rhoda E. to Frederic J. Middlebrook, Brooklyn. 9,199

De Graaf, Henry P. to Ellen S. Griffith. 2,000

Donovan, Timothy and Alethea V. Harris to John B. Ryer. 400

Duffy, Peter E. to Samuel H. Stone. 2,000

Ellis, John S. exr. Julia Waterbury to Gertrude C. Winthrop. 24,000

Same to Antoinette L. Edwards. 44,000

Eickwort, Louis to Lillie Sanger. 750

dec'd to James Stokes. 20,000

Ford, Henry W. trustee Augustus H. Ward

Friedlander, Henrietta to Jacob Friedlander. 2,000

Feuchtwanger, Clara A. formerly August to Louis Bender. 6,537

German-American Real Estate Title Guarantee Co. to Edwin Sherman trustee for Clifford W. and John H. Day. 7,500

German-American Real Estate Title Guarantee Co. to Elizabeth Yuengling, Pottsville, Pa. 2,000

Goldstein, Jennie to William H. and Seig. Goldstein. 5,000

Goldstein, William H. and Seig. to Anna M. Maywald. 5,000

Gray, Martha G., Elizabeth, N. J., to Phebe A. Ring. 2,400

Same to Eliza C. Ring. 2,400

Horton, Floyd M. to Emile A. Hassey. 2,500

Haaren, John W. to Bessie Glass. 1,886

Hyatt, George E., Brooklyn, to Thomas S. Walker. nom

Hamel, James to Catherine A. Smart. 1,000

Jencks, Francis M., Newburgh, N. Y., to The Lawyers' Title Ins. Co., of New York. 13,000

Kurzman, Ferdinand to William and Jacob Scholle. nom

Kunzli, Joseph to Mary Kunzli. nom

Kunzli, Mary to Marianna Knecht, Brooklyn. 1,000

Lucas, George C. and Mary E. his wife trustees Noah T. Pike dec'd to Dwight H. Olmstead. 12,014

Lyon, Dore to Hosea R. Drew. nom

Middlebrook, Frederic J., Brooklyn, to Mary E. Robert. 6,626

Middlebrook, Frederic J. to Marie Robert. 12,674

Mott, Jordan L. to The Title Guarantee and Trust Co. 110,000

Marx, Salomon to Randolph Guggenheimer. 604

McGinnis, Owen to and with Arthur J. Horgan and Vincent J. Slattery. nom

Marshall, Margaret and ano. exrs. Robert Marshall to Ann Marshall. 12,200

Same to Margaret Marshall. 12,185

Same to same. 14,175

Same to same. 15,060

Morrow, James to Michael Caulfield. 1,500

Murphy, M. Elizabeth to John B. Ryer. 400

Mead, Arthur W. to David McClure. 2,250

Nesbitt, Thomas to Mary Gaines, Boonton, N. J. 1,200

Nathan, Benjamin to Abrahams & Grunauer. 6,000

Oettinger, Bernard J. and ano. exrs. Morris Altman to Benjamin Altman. 2,000

Postal, Jacob to Abraham Schulder. 1,300

Passman, Leonard B. exr. John G. Hick to The Citizens' Bank of Elizabeth, N. J. 3,000

Parsons, Mary M., Brooklyn, to Caroline Wilkins, Wakefield Heights, N. Y., and Mary E. Schilling, Brooklyn. gift

Powell, Sarah H. to Henry F. Daly. 10,000

Potter, Howard N. et al. exrs. Virginia M. Potter to Howard N. Potter et al. trustees of Caroline L. and Josephine Mitchell. nom

Same to Eleanor R. McEwen, London, England. nom

Same to same. nom

Ring, Eliza C., Elizabeth, N. J., to Phebe A. Ring and ano. trustees of Eliza C. R. Greene. 2,400

Radebold, William and Edward Wenz to Philip Bohnet. 1,000

Same to same. 6,000

Robert, Marie to Frederic J. Middlebrook. 5,621

Same to same. 4,599

Rieck, James G., Haverstraw, N. Y., guard. of Anna L. Rieck to Anna L. Rieck. 3 assigns. order of Court

Same to same. nom

Smith, Du Bois, Smithtown, L. I., to Minnie M. Mott, Smithtown, L. I. 2,500

Sauer, Joseph P., Jersey City, N. J., to George Roll. nom

Sheridan, James F. and Patrick H. and James S. Segrave to Thomas C. Cornell. nom

Sherlock, Richard and ano. trustees for Ellen Atkinson to John J. Monahan, Brooklyn. 6,000

Same to same. 7,000

Silberstein, Bernhard to Max Kobre. 3,500

Steers, Abraham to Edmund Trouton, West Orange, N. J. 3,000

The Bowery Savings Bank to Maria N. Anderson, Rondout, N. Y. 5,000

Title Guarantee and Trust Co. to Julia A. Chapman. 7,000

Title Guarantee and Trust Co. to Henry B. Barnes. 24,000

Same to Watson B. Dickerman and ano. trustees John Collins dec'd. 13,000

Title Guarantee and Trust Co. to Mary E. Andrews et al. trustees Thomas Andrews dec'd. 12,000

Title Guarantee and Trust Co. to The State Trust Co. as trustee for Annie Dressel. 5,000

Untermyer, Samuel to William H. and Alfred N. Beadleston trustees for Sarah N. Hallock, Helen M. Skidmore and Mary Maxwell. 4,000

United States Trust Co. of New York guard. of estates of John A., Winthrop A., Elizabeth W., William A., Marion W., Lewis S., Margaret L., Robert W., Alida B. and Egerton W. Chanler to The United States Trust Co. of New York as guard. of Margaret L Chanler. nom

United States Trust Co. of New York guard. of Margaret L. Chanler to The United States Trust Co. of New York. nom

Wilmurt, Francis M., Pelham Manor, N. Y., to The Bradley & Currier Co. (Lim.) 5,000

Watkins, John S., Fort Lee, N. Y., to Lawrence Lynch. 4,618

Wolff, Lee trustee to Samuel Blackwell, Brooklyn. 3 assigns. nom

Weinstein, Ascher to Simon Bing, Jr. 3,000

Woods, Henry to William H. Scott. 2,850

Young, Willis H., George H. Gerard and Adolphus F. Quick, of Young, Gerard & Co., to William Radebold and Edward Wenz. 1,757

Yuengling, Elizabeth, Pottsville, Pa., to German-American Real Estate Title Guarantee Co. 9,000

KINGS COUNTY.

November 5 to 11—Inclusive.

Ackerman, Edwin W. to Archibald C. Shenstone. nom

Betzel, George to Adam Kessel. $750

Bailey, Frank to John S. Lee. nom

Bennett, Michael and Edward Colgan to Mary A. C. Wheeler. nom

Bernstein, Nathan to Louis Bernstein. 1,500

Blanck, Eliza E to James T. Quail et al. trustees John W. Blanck. 8,642

Brown, Frank F., Buffalo, N. Y., to Mary H. Brown, Buffalo, N. Y. 10,500

Brown, Mary H., Buffalo, N. Y., to Katharine Vassar. nom

Condict, Silas A. to Warren P. Ackerman. 200

Conkling, F. Augustus to Charles H. Doremus. 2,400

Same to Thomas Everit. 2,000

Same to same as exr. Valentine Everit. consid. omitted

Connecticut Trust and Safe Deposit Co. trustee of Caleb Pratt to Rossiter W. Raymond. 2 assgns. nom

Cook, Mary E. to Lewis Hurst. consid omitted

Cook, Mary E. to John C. and Herbert C. Smith and Herman F. Koepke, of Smith & Koepke. nom

Cooper, Marvelle W. to Cornelius N. Bliss. nom

Craig, George A. to John and John F. Poppke, of Poppke & Son. nom

Cross, Austin & Co. to Thomas W. Holmes, Boston, Mass. 4,000

Dill, John, Jr., to Charles Kunz. 600

Dodge, Francis E. and ano. exrs. Richard J. Dodge to Elizabeth Brouwer. 500

Doody, Daniel to Sophie G. Parker. 1,500

Everit, Thomas exr. and trustee Valentine Everit to Edward A. Everit. 2,000

Everit, Thomas to Edward A. Everit. 2,000
Eldredge, Rebecca G. to The Title Guarantee and Trust Co. 2,000
Eliot, Robert to John W. Cornwell. nom
Field, David D. to Jeanie L. Musgrave, widow. gift
Frothingham, James H. guard. of Maria F., Albert L., Elizabeth F. and Francis Mason to Elizabeth F. Mason. nom
Greenwood, Joseph M. to Helen Embury. 4 assigns., each $2,000. 8,000
Gillespie, Earl A., Jamaica, to Albert H. Ackerman. nom
Hunt, Edward T. exr. Thomas Hunt to Charles W. Church. 431
Hentz, Nicholas to Jacob Hentz. 10,000
Hollister, Zipporah L. to Frederick Middendorf. 2,000
James, John F. to Russell Walden. 2,000
Kenny, Mary A. to Charity S. Teeple. nom
Kirschner, Bertha to Maria A. Schworm. 500
Kilduff, Bernard F., Newtown, L. I., to Annie A. Kilduff. 1,000
Krause, Sophia J. to The German Savings Bank, Brooklyn. 2,000
Kunennund, Ernest J. to Thomas Everit. 400
Lauer, Daniel to Albro J. Newton. 1,762
Lippmann, Leopold J. to John Haas. nom
Same to Joseph Ryan. nom
Same to Arp D. Wellbrock. nom
Linington, Maria L. to Anna M. Linington. gift
Same to Lucretia D. Linington. gift
Monaghan, Annie E. to James Stewart committee Henry A. Monaghan. 2,042
Same to same. 5,546
Same to same. 3,005
Max, Harris to Harris Gettinger. 1,700
Monroe, Eckstein Brewing Co., Richmond County, to Bernhard Schmidt. 2,000
Moss, Frank exr. Maltby G. Lane to Charles D. Smith, Huntington, L. I. 1,450
McCullagh, Jenkinson to Hugh Gaffney. 1,200
Newell, Mary G. to Margaret Lawrence. 3,500
Osborne, Carrie A. to Lydia Winant. 608
Offord, Robert M., Passaic, N. J., to Joseph E. Jewett. 900
Puels, Joseph P. to George H. Wheeler. 3,000
Power, John to Herbert C. Smith. 1,200
Peed, Charles N. to The People's Trust Co. 8,000
Quail, William to James F. Quail et al. trustees John W. Blanck. 4,017
Reilly, Bernard to Emilie Huber. 5,000
Rushmore, Stephen T. admr. Elizabeth R. Prior to James T. Hoile committee. 2,000
Reed, Albert G. to Katharine Bernheim. 1,225
Studwell, Elizabeth L. et al. exrs. John J. Studwell to Hannah K. Van Vranken. 10,000
Savage, Henry C. to Charles Griffen et al. trustees Peter S. Titus. 5,000
Sammis, Israel P. exr. Alexander Place to Addison Ford. 2,800
Stuckey, Lillie I. and William H. exrs. Alfred Stuckey to Lillie I. Stuckey. 1,500
Seney, Catharine W. to Salena Lublin. 1,080
Tebbetts, Noah to Charles Siedler. 15,000
The Brooklyn Trust Co. guards. Rosabelle, Marie L. and Minnie H. Brush to Minnie H. Brush. 3,500
The Bythebourne Improvement Co. to Charles E. Rogers. 1,175
Title Guarantee and Trust Co. to The Peekskill Savings Bank. 2,500
Same to The Wesleyan University, Middletown, Conn. 3 assigns., each $5,000. 15,000
Same to Estelle Christie. 3,500
Same to Harrison B. Moore. 7,500
Same to The Methodist Episcopal Hospital, Brooklyn. 5,500
Same to Joseph B. Elliott. 5,500
Same to Mary E. Parker. 2,000
Same to Julia E. Brick. 5,000
Same to Anna C. Cary. 3,500
Same to Hannah Cruttenden et al. exrs. Thomas Cruttenden. 3,000
Same to Eliza Ross. 6,000
Same to The Methodist Episcopal Hospital, Brooklyn. 4,000
Same to Sophia Loffler and ano. exrs. George Loffler. 3 assigns., each $2,000. 6,000
Same to Edward and James Whelan. 8,000
Same to William H. Chapman exr. Samuel Wanser. 4,000
Same to The Wesleyan University, Middletown, Conn. 5,000
Same to same. 5,000
Same to same. 2,500
Same to John Morton. 8,000
Same to Celestine Michel. 6,000
Valentine, William E., Jamaica, L. I., to Avery T. Brown and ano. trustees Caroline I. Satchell. 2,150
Wilder, Enos to The Title Guarantee and Trust Co. 5,000

JUDGMENTS.

In these lists of judgments the names alphabetically arranged, and which are first on each line, are those of the judgment debtor. The letter (D) means judgment for deficiency (*) means not summoned. (†) signifies that the first name is fictitious, real name being unknown. Judgments entered during the week, and satisfied before day of publication, do not appear in this column, but in list of Satisfied Judgments.

NEW YORK CITY.

Nov.

7 Alten, Moritz H—Adolph Friedman.. $182 95
9 †Allen, James E / Allen, John W } G D Sweetser...... 268 10
9 Appleton, William H / Appleton, William W / Appleton, Daniel / Appleton, Edward D } W S Yates.. 91 20
11 Ackerman, J Frederick—C P Huntington...costs 433 53
11 Alten, Moritz H—F P Osborn... 181 77
12 Angell, William D—W G Jones.... 15,171 01
6 Black, Joseph R—J G Robinson... 442 54
6 Brock, Louis M—Morris Arnold... 1,266 43
7 Blaney, Thomas—German Bulle... 117 73
7 Burke, William H—L D Hatton... 144 80
7 Bauman, Herman—John Nehb... 314 57
7 Beyer, Conrad—C H Evans... 80 09
7 Brice, John—Frederick Betz... 51 77
7 Bliss, Charles H—Metalithic Paving Co... 550 91
9 Boecher, Adam—G P Farmer... 78 05
9 Beers, Robert A—A J Rogers...costs 109 21
9 Beekman, John—H J Rosevelt... 95 25
9 Berlin, Simon N—G S Lings... 693 33
9 Beyer, Gustav E—D F Porter... 73 80
9 Beckhardt, Louis—I K Cohn, exr... 405 10
9 Blumson, Herman—Solom Bachrach.. 186 02
10 Brady, Thomas—Delia Brady... 259 50
10 Beacham, John—F L Boussod... 165 02
10 Butler, Ellsworth F—J N Darrah... 134 35
10 Blauth, Adam—C W Duncan, assignee 658 62
10 Burrows, John P / *Burrows, James C } Samuel Crooks.. 137 00
10 Bonnebeam, Louis G—Jacob Jamer.. 39 12
10 Bonnell, John Harper—Bank of N Y Nat Banking Assoc... 7,546 70
10 †Bloomson, Henry—New Haven Clock Co... 136 21
10 Boyan, Thomas—Jane Holland... 206 70
10 Bogardus, Alfred M—J W Hatch, assignee... 501 49
11 Bennett, William J—Charles Riederer 138 32
11 Betencourt, August—C H Vanwagner 312 20
11 Bonnell, John Harper / Bonnell, Tammisin H } Chatham Nat Bank... 5,043 24
12 †Byck, John—Celia Lipkowitz... 167 50
12 Buck, George—John Leffler... 565 58
12 Blumson, Herman—Farren Bros Co.. 314 99
12 Batty, Joseph H—George Towle... 70 90
12 Boyle, Andrew—Williamsburgh Brewing Co (Lim)... 643 00
12 Bennett, Francis C—A L Knevols... 126 16
13 Buckel, John—David Eilau... 94 86
13 *Brossard, Theodore / Brossard, Otto } Theodore Schmalholz... 608 60
13 Balcom, Arthur C—Robert Reis & Co 201 25
6 Callahan, Charles E—Benjamin Croner... 609 93
6 Chapman, Louisa W—J H Downes... 914 19
6 the same——the same... 332 91
7 Coady, Thomas J—N B Nickerson... 98 87
7 Coffin, Frederick R—Western Nat Bank... 1,025 17
9 Collins, Richard M—G H Walker... 194 34
9 Coley, Isaac N—G W Gibbons... 93 61
10 Conklin, Albert—Hathaway, Soule & Harrington... 515 72
10 Chabau, Joseph—Albert Edwards... 114 83
10 Cranston, Henry—Julia Blewitt... 239 95
10 Campbell, Lee W—G H Zinckert... 138 70
11 Chaffers, T—Charles Hofferberth... 292 28
11 Clyne, Patrick—T H Rohdenburg... 108 30
11 Campbell, Mary, admrx John Campbell—Bernard Campbell... 84 75
11 Cranston, Henry—O G Rafferty... 479 48
11 Curtis, Frank D—Strobridge Lithographing Co... 3,213 83
12 Cohn, Walter J / Cohn, William I } G M Miller... 639 79
12 Clancey, James—E H Kelly... 81 69
12 Culver, Alston G—C B Morris... 274 30
12 Cassidy, William J—T G Holland... 92 21
12 Capen, Walter N—Hiram Barber... 298 32
13 Cooke, Baldwin G—J T White... 37 87
13 Crosby, Lawrence H—William Mylius 254 93
14 Camp, John T—E W Converse... 5,574 47
13 Callahan, Charles E—Benjamin Croner... 503 96
6 *Davis, Charles J—Eugene Deteindre. 1,237 30
7 Diekman, Herman R—Metropolitan Telephone and Telegraph Co... 66 06
9 Demarest, Henry H—T D Mead... 625 00
9 Dempsey, William—E L Mooney... 2,772 34
9 Dreyfuss, Bernard—Henry Lieberknecht... 1,026 26
9 Darragh, John E—D F Porter... 73 80
9 Dempsey, William—John Eulyem ... 97 50
10 Dippel, Frederick—William McShane 341 48
10 Ducey, James—Mutual Brewing Co.. 396 63
10 Darling, Ehud N—G S Palmer... 489 90
10 Davis, John A—Mayor, &c... 7,000 50
10 Doyle, Thomas—Patterson Bros... 92 58
12 Deutsch, Amelia—Owen McGinnis...(D) 11,568 16
12 Devine, Thomas J—Thomas Kirkpatrick... 220 98
12 Douglass, Margaret K—Mary Monell...costs 91 37
12 †Doe, John—E J Ettlinger... 92 34
13 Durham, Fred F—F S Sanford... 219 92
13 Duffy, Michael / Duffy, Thomas L / Duffy, James } J T Shackelford... 169 56
13 Day, Charles—Joseph Sahwen... 231 80
6 Eustace, James A—J H Johnston... 1,220 43
10 Ernst, John H—S Liebmann's Sons Brewing Co... 167 00
10 Estes, Charles A—J R Kelly... 42 50
10 Everard, James—Mayor, &c... 108 47
11 Edwards, Ellis B—Kate M Doherty.. 10,383 79
12 Ernest, John S / Earnest, John S } E F Sanford... 426 00
12 Eaton, George S—I R Bruce... 562 65
7 Fox, Simon—A P Blake...costs 96 22
7 Fisher, John H—Gustav Amsinck... 320 53
9 Fink, Henry—W W Light... 123 12
9 Freund, Isidor—M H Eisner... 227 38
10 Farley, Edward E—J E Taylor... 301 59
10 Frankel, Paul—M V Frankel... 308 02
10 Frank, Bertha L—William Johnson.. 35 50
10 Franchi, Louis H—Brunswick-Balke-Collender Co... 109 21
10 Frantz, Jacob—Charles Schlesinger.. 136 73
10 Feinberg, Jacob—Abraham Alexander... 153 08
10 Fields, Samuel S—J W Hatch, assignee... 210 72
11 Flynn, Florence Cecil individ and extrx Maurice B Flynn—Kate G Brandon... 961 53
11 Flynn, Edward—N Y Mutual Gas Light Co... 202 75
11 Fink, Conrad—Martin Schrenkeisen.. 2,736 55
11 Frost, Leonard L—G H Morrill... 483 84
12 Fischer, John—Sigmund Rosenbluh.. 150 19
12 Farr, Emeline—Terence McGuire... 65 50
6 Gaffney, Joseph J—M R Cook... 103 70
7 Gault, James—John Gleeson... 200 22
9 Glaser, Adolph M—W S Anderson... 125 43
9 Grippentrog, Katie—Marie Geadwohl 80 00
10 *Gans, Conrad—S Liebmann's Sons Brewing Co... 167 00
10 Goodrich, Frank—Henry Kroger... 584 12
10 Gebhardt, Adam—Theresa Schoeman. 7 50
10 Greene, Harry W—R A Johnston...costs 279 98
10 Gundlach, John—Abraham Berliner. 224 00
10 Geisendorfer, Charles—David Mayer. 488 00
11 Goodwin, Edward—C P Huntington...costs 433 53
11 Gramliug, Julius—J K Meade... 819 32
11 Greenball, Abraham—J A Waddell.. 3,052 04
11 Gottschalk, Adolph—L S Friedberger. 27 18
12 Goodsell, James H—A G Smith... 1,645 95
12 Goldthwaite, William M—T B Johnston... 535 48
13 Gebhardt, Adolph—J A Nutter... 75 52
13 Gru, Joseph—Morris Schwerin... 96 27
13 Garrigan, Philip—Herman Rauscher. 298 66
6 Herts, Abraham H—Hermann Hablo. 2,724 87
7 Hoyt, Anson B—I P Smith... 308 88
7 Heine, Bernhard—J M Saulpaugh... 826 47
7 Hanlon, Thomas—Henry Herrmann.. 158 07
9 Hennesy, John—W D Starr... 102 15
9 Harriman, John N / *Harriman, Orlando } B H Tuthill... 1,330 82
10 †Hasse, Edward F—E C Hazard... 134 32
10 Hegarty, John—E S Alpaugh... 359 53
10 Hutchinson, Hiram—M L De Voursney... 267 91
10 Haughey, Edward—Mayor, Lane & Co 98 64
10 Hoefle, Fordinand—Charles Wall... 32 50
10 †Hall, Charles B—Edward Ledeliey... 125 00
10 Harper, William Durbin—Bank of N Y Nat Banking Assoc... 7,546 70
10 Hoag, Henry G—Jane Holland... 306 70
10 Hart, H Ellis—Bloomington Mining Co... 5,844 57
11 Halpin, Peter S—Mary L Halpin... 1,518 18
11 Heidelberg, Herman—Ignatz Gross... 227 20
11 Harper, William D / Harper, Tacie McD } Chatham Nat Bank... 5,043 24
11 *Hellberg, August—F W Devoe... 161 56
11 Hay, John / *Hay, Robert } J L Mott Iron Works.. 152 86
12 Hausser, Christian / Hausser, Charles } Adam Rathgeber... 240 63
12 Harrison, Clinton—W H Harrison, exr... 272 16
12 †Houghton, Charles H O—Henry Behning, Jr... 298 00
12 Heyer, William—Henry Ehler... 918 87
12 Hein, Heiman—E B Estes... 39 44
12 Hauser, G Julius—John Ott... 195 37
13 Hiergesell, William—N M Donahue...costs 70 88
13 Herzfeld, Jeannette—Samuel Steinfelder... 298 73
13 Hecht, Ansel—M A Ruland... 229 92
13 Heywood, George—J T White... 39 50
11 Irvine, Allen A—J J Joyce... 143 23
11 Jacobson, Charles—Neufeld Mfg Co.. 102 01
11 Jones, Edwin T—Nat Bank of Republic... 826 96
13 Jackson, Myer—J T White... 39 50
6 Kemble, John R—Rachel Goldstein.. 11,002 89
7 Keddie, Thomas—I P Smith... 263 78
9 Kearney, George—Richard Fitzpatrick...costs 116 62
9 King, William H—Robert Milbank... 137 25
10 Klaber, Augustus D / Klaber, Emil } Homer Lee Bank Note Co... 121 20
10 Kerrigan, John—J W Hatch, assignee 358 26
11 Kareski, Leo—E A Walter... 34 87
12 Kalmus, Philip—John Lutz... 285 56
12 Kissling, August—Edward Conway.. 273 98
12 Kennelly, Harry—J E Kelly...costs 112 30
13 Kennedy, Daniel R—Ambrose Ehrlich 370 10
13 Kelly, John—J J Kelly... 349 27
13 King, William M—Robert Milbank.. 227 16
6 Lieb, Thomas / *Lieb, Robert / *Lieb, Theodore } H D Brouer... 164 00
6 Lamb, James W / *Lamb, William J } Cook & Bernheimer Co... 234 49
7 Leeds, Henry, Jr—I P Smith... 263 78
7 Lawlor, James S—Henry McShane Co (Lim)... 170 80
9 Lum, Frederick C—A J Rogers..costs 109 21
9 Livingston, Lewis H—B H Tuthill... 1,330 82
10 Lockwood, William H—Catharine B Aitken... 85 08
10 Lindenmeyr, John—Lewis Maddux.. 4,236 08

11 Lichtenau, August—E I Hecht........ 140 94
11 Linscott, John A—W H Harrison, exr 251 26
11 Lowerre, George H—Kate M Doherty.............................10,383 79
11 Leeper, James—L B Lynch.......... 47 63
12 Lighthall, Almerin H—W R Stewart, exr.............................. 350 94
12 Lindenborn, David—Louis Spero..... 68 50
12 L'Hommedieu, Sylvester Y—First Nat Bank of Bennington, Vermont.....3,427 07
13 Loevin, Samuel—M D Stern.......... 92 74
13 Lavalle, Wallace—Robert Hill....... 89 87
13 Leach, Henry P—E W Converse.....5,574 47
6 Manning, James J—Christian Moerlein Brewing Co.................. 198 63
6 Morgan, George P—Martin Schrenkeisen.......................... 102 08
6 Myers, Lewis—M A Bockman........3,767 70
6 the same —the same........costs 86 78
7 Meyn, Nicholas—J V Jewell......... 310 40
9 Merwin, Samuel E—A J Rogers.costs 109 21
9 Macer, Daniel W—Forty-second St, Manhattanville & St Nicholas Av R R Co.........................costs 146 36
9 Mathus, Henry—C W Duncan, assignee.............................. 210 90
9 Maloney, Joseph—John Kelly........ 161 81
9 Mullaney, Ann—T E Greacen........ 874 31
9 Miner, Elizabeth F—Henry Hentz....3,095 44
10 Moog, Simon—John Baehr........... 390 50
10 Merritt, William J—Barber Asphalt Paving Co.......................6,258 75
10 Martin, Harry—Edge Hill Wine Co.. 472 64
10 the same—Christian Moerlein Brewing Co.................... 439 42
10 Meyer, Edwin O—Fulton Club 67 90
10 Murray, Catharine—H C Woolley.... 213 10
10 Mackusick, Elmer F — Girdhurtal Ratental Daphtary............... 1,550 32
10 Morse, G Livingston—Holmes & Griggs Mfg Co.........................3,081 32
10 Martin, Wilbur F—F H Stevens.....3,289 61
10 Mayer, Joseph—Adolph Haege....... 327 04
10 the same—the same............ 194 35
11 Marquard, Frank—J A Lynch........1,073 65
11 Mayer, Henry—Gustave Drachman.. 77 50
11 Matthews, James C—Beinecke & Co..8,052 00
11 the same—G B Weaver.......... 743 00
11 the same—William Ottmann & Co.............................7,977 00
11 Marquard, Frank—Julius Bien.......4,806 75
11 the same—Western Nat Bank.. 370 03
11 the same—the same............ 370 03
11 Muldoon, William H—J H Kilpatrick 250 74
11 Macfarlane, William S—John Patterson.............................. 276 97
11 Miller, Frederick—F W Devoe....... 161 56
11*Millikin, Samuel M—Hiram Pool....3,111 69
12 Martin, Wilbur F—F H Stevens.....2,995 03
12 Madden, Stephen K—Nathan Froman 117 87
12 MacEvoy, Charles—Mount Morris Bank.............................. 521 99
12 Mulqueen, Thomas F—Hartman Bartelmes............................ 382 58
12 Mayhew, Edward C—John Kroder.. 318 61
12*Marwede, Henry—John Leffler...... 565 58
12 Myers, Charles—John Lutz.......... 285 56
12 Maisner, Adolph—C F Gough........ 72 00
12 Morris, Melvin L—Washington Nat Bank.............................. 343 74
12 Miller, Nicholas C—J S Bache........4,310 80
12 Martin, Wilbur F—Henry Bauer..... 947 92
12 the same—William Ottmann & Co.............................. 297 70
13 Muller, Lewis M—Thomas Fitzgerald. 589 51
13 the same—the same............ 429 04
13 the same—the same............ 274 77
13 the same—the same............ 277 91
13 the same—the same............ 276 19
13 the same—the same............ 326 69
13 Martin, Lawrence—P A Riche....... 747 57
13 Meddleton, George C—Michael Beradini.............................. 117 50
13 Mayers, Isaac—D W Robinson....... 653 80
13 Maduro, Solomon—H M Hitchings... 116 30
6 McMahon, James / McMahon, John } R E Cochran..... 87 13
7 McKenna, Patrick / McKenna, Margaret } George Jaus... 326 47
9 McCarthy, Dennis J—John Kelly.... 161 81
10 McKenna, Patrick—C B Morris...... 496 42
11 Macfarlane, William S—John Patterson.............................. 276 97
12 MacEvoy, Charles — Mount Morris Bank.............................. 521 99
13 McAdams, John—J H Meyer......... 72 50
13 McLaughlin, Michael—Max Stiner... 125 07
10 Neff, Edward—Moses Neuberger...... 204 38
7 Obermeier, Frederick X—Beadleston & Woerz............................ 104 73
9 O'Rourke, Jeremiah W—Hester Bates, extrx and trustee................... 291 00
9 O'Neill, Dennis—G L Ely............ 117 16
9 Osborn, William—Cowperthwait Co 374 18
10 O'Brien, James—Henry Ullmen....... 191 87
12 O'Malley, Mary—James Gilmartin.... 282 00
13 O'Keefe, Jeremiah / *O'Keefe, Michael } W H Wood, Jr.. 97 79
6 Pollok, Jacques—Eugene Deteindre...1,237 30
6 Prince, John S—Robert Fullerton.... 259 74
9†Pearsall, William W—Cook & Bernheimer Co......................... 89 85
9 Perry, Charles L / Perry, Nellie T } Simon Hess........ 528 99
9 Platt, Spencer C / Platt, Nathan C } Bertha E Martin, admrx......costs 87 93
10 Pruzina, William J R—J C London.. 94 00
11 Perkins, George F—C P Huntington ....costs 433 53
11 Palmer, William A—C F Ketcham... 973 64
11 Prada, Charles—C W Vanwagner.... 312 20
11 Paulikoski, Emily H—Travelers' Ins Co of Hartford, Conn..........costs 366 00
11 Porterfield, Charles R—A H Selwyn.. 480 09

11 Pell, Ogden P—Nat Bank of Republic. 575 14
12 Payne, Robert—United Electric Light a d Power Co. 323 40
12 Pertsch, Frederick / Pertsch, William } C S Connor..... 149 70
13 Platt, John H—Bernard Meyer..costs 69 55
13 Perry, Charles L—G A Ostrander.... 118 30
10 Quandt, Paul—T B Frazer............ 89 32
7 Rosenberg, Moses—F P Earle........ 538 75
7 Ramer, John I—Thomas Strahan & Co.............................. 161 58
7 Rich, George E—Industrial Development Co........................ 533 41
9 Ryan, Michael—John Murray........2,252 59
9 Reynolds, Michael—Samuel McConnell 170 48
9 Riker, Carroll L—Brooklyn Union Elevated Railway Advertising Co.. 436 65
10 Rockwell, William—Caroline Z Stanton.............................. 96 52
10 Rosenfeld, Joshua, Jr—Frederick Bobiken.......................... 198 00
10 Rossheim, Henrietta / Rossheim, Ella } George Hahn 93 17
13 Reynolds, Patrick—Concord Co-operative Printing Co (Lim)............. 54 00
13 Ramme, Henry—Gustav Daniel...... 94 50
6 Seligman, Sigmund J / *Seligman, Philip } Hermann Hahlo..2,724 87
6 Stolpe, Hugo—J L Rowe............ 88 52
7 Steuerwald, Charles A—Philip Rudolph............................ 163 25
7 Schlansky, Sarah—David Simon..... 55 75
7 Striker, Elsworth L—Western Nat Bank.............................. 468 71
9 Stein, Gerson—M H Eisner.......... 227 38
9 Slattery, Edward F—John Kelly..... 161 81
9†Schmidt, Jack—John Eulyem........ 97 50
10 Scotto, Joseph—Michael Seitz........ 100 50
10 Schick, Frederick—F W Meeker...... 306 82
10 Schwack, Henry—Henry Kroger..... 524 12
10 Sieman, William F—Knickerbocker Brewing Co.......................... 201 00
*Stark, Isidor / 10*Stark, Edward J / Stark, Gustave } D W MacLeod... 578 00
10 Serensen, Fritz W—Louis Isenburger 282 13
12 Ryer, George W—Annie Haines.....1,038 87
12 Rousseau, Jules P / Rousseau, Jules E } A B Purdy........ 121 91
12 Robbins, Thomas H—G W Melvin.... 713 82
12 Riham, Abdow—E J Ettlinger....... 92 34
10 Shonnard, Frederick — Holmes & Griggs Mfg Co.....................3,081 32
10 Schmidt, Philip, or / Schmitt, Phillipp } Henry Herrmann...... 86 57
11 Simonson, Michaelis—J A Lane...... 233 51
11 Schwab, Gabriel / Schwab, Nathan / Schwab, Abraham / Schwab, Leo L } Thomas Forrest 1,973 01
11 Squier, Frank—C P Huntington..costs 433 53
11 Schaffmeyer, Martin J—C B Morris.. 178 02
11 Schick, George R—W P Wilder..... 262 53
11 Steinhart, Israel / Steinhart, William } Ignatz Gross.... 227 20
11 Schwartz, Charles—Adolph Rauch... 46 38
11 Stokes, Charles—Hiram Pool.........3,111 69
11 Sawyer, William M—Washington Nat Bank.............................2,628 65
12 Shearman, George—Nathan Froman. 117 87
12 Stix, Robert L—Samuel Corn 1,166 47
12 Solomon, Ephraim—G M Miller...... 639 79
12 Scofield, Lilian E—Bela B Roff....... 76 64
12 Secor, Theodosius F, Jr—Delamater Iron Works.......................... 76 64
12 Simpson, Edward / Simpson, Montague } C H Galliker... 153 26
12 Seedorf, Charles—Herman Rokobl... 80 00
12 Stone, Howard C—J H Wisner.......1,579 70
12 Stretch, Eliakim S—G F Carr........ 72 21
13 Stone, Howard C—W F Freeman..... 70 48
13 Sawyer, Lyman / Sawyer, Sarah J } Frank James ....costs 107 91
13 Stevenson, Vernon K—William Koch 27 50
13 Schroeder, William—Robert Hill.... 108 63
13 Stokes, William E D—Philip Biershenk ....costs 54 37
6 Smith, Waightstill A / *Smith, Frank F } Metropolitan Telephone and Telegraph Co........ 91 69
7 Smith, Morris H—Samuel Cole.......1,018 89
9 Smith, John—E L Mooney...........2,779 34
11 Smith, Waitstill A / *Smith, Frank F } Consolidated Stock and Petroleum Exchange Building Co..... 251 43
6 American Mfg Co—J M Emanuel..... ....costs 126 49
7 The Suffolk Mfg Co—Henry Martin.. 810 66
7 the same—the same............ 160 40
7 Lathrop Co—Roe Stephens Mfg Co.. 351 30
7 The Fred H Whipple Co—E W Lowe. 84 96
7 J H Bonnell & Co (Lim)—Western Nat Bank.........................1,025 17
7 The Empire Paving and Construction Co—Metropolitan Plate Glass Ins Co 483 68
7 The N Y Cable Railway Co—S R Elliott..............................1,024 45
9 The Snook Glove Mfg Co—B W Jones 1,379 02
9 Locey Mining and Mfg Co—Sigmund Hirschfelder 180 67
9 George H Kitchen & Co—Cassidy & Son Mfg Co...................... 241 85
9 The Third Avenue R R Co—Mary Lynch..........................costs 104 48
9 The W F Brown Co—T L Briggs..... 928 38
9 The Third Avenue R R Co—Mary Lynch 2,198 19
9 The Ellenville Gas Light Co—American Meter Co 142 06
9 The Sullivan Timber Co—Radcliffe Baldwin 2,454 91
10 J H Bonnell & Co (Lim)—Brooklyn Bank of Brooklyn.................. 529 42

10 Lathrop Co—D N Lathrop............ 692 58
10 The Manhattan Railway Co / The Metropolitan Elevated Railway Co } W T Geisse trustee... 4,002 53
10 The N Y Central & Hudson River R R Co / The West Shore and Ontario Terminal Co } Mayor, &c 7,000 50
10 J H Bonnell & Co (Lim)—Bank of N Y Banking Assoc..................7,546 70
10 The Hoboken Turtle Club—G R Wright.............................. 242 45
10 Lathrop Co—McNab & Harlin Mfg Co. 297 98
10 the same—Eaton, Cole & Burnham Co........................... 249 96
10 the same—Portchester Bolt and Nut Co............................. 453 54
10 The Holmes & Wessell Metal Co—Holmes & Griggs Mfg Co.........3,081 32
11 Lathrop Co—New Process Twist Drill Co.............................. 149 56
11 the same—Rhode Island Tool Co 152 72
11 The Sheet Metal Machine Co, of Newark, N J—I C Johnson............ 682 00
11 L F Genet Lumber Co—McGavin Murdock.......................... 343 22
11 Lathrop Co — Pennsylvania Brass Works............................1,552 76
11 North and South American Construction Co—Frederic Leach......3,114 70
11 J H Bonnell & Co (Lim)—Nat Bank of Republic.......................... 826 96
11 Danville Nail and Mfg Co—H M Warren..............................3,136 34
12 Hat Sweat Mfg Co—A N Wildman, trustee.......................(D)14,115 10
12 Lenox Hill Bank—Jacob Bockman... 272 30
13 Barr Electric Mfg Co—Aaron da Costa Gomez........................ 79 22
13 Lathrop Co—Union Drawn Steel Co.. 152 06
13 The European American Supply Co—T J Van Horen..................... 24 07
13 The Aluminium Product Co—Wellington Mfg Co....................18,219 88
13 Pure Ice Co—Yale & Towne Mfg Co.. 66 73
9 Trainor, James—T T Fortune........1,016 23
10 Turton, John / Turton, Edgar S } Brooklyn Bank of Brooklyn........ 529 42
12 Tegethoff, Charles—C E Murtagh.... 440 29
12 Todd, Charles J—W H Hussey.......2,040 68
12 Thompson, Denman—Annie Haines..1,038 87
12 Thompson, James—Sheppard Knapp. 400 09
1^ True, Charles L—James Gaunt.......1,086 96
12 Talmadge, Henry S—J G D Burnett.. 173 51
12 Tobey, Edward H—W & J Sloane... 421 41
13†Turkowsky, Otto F—John Muller..... 77 50
10 Urban, John—J C Hayt............. 293 35
10 Ueckerman, Frederick—F S Myers... 153 38
13*Uren, Thomas—Robert Reis & Co.... 201 25
12 Voorhis, Peter—W H Hussey........ 375 97
11 Van Leeuwen, Joseph—E J Eisenman 84 37
12†Vanderberg, John—Samuel Ehrich... 105 00
6 Wiener, Magnus—Morris Arnold....1,256 43
7 Waggoner, Ralph H—H L Bridgman 1,369 61
7 Wood, Frederick—Western Nat Bank 896 42
7 the same—the same............ 582 46
7 the same—Homestead Bank.... 891 76
7 the same—Western Nat Bank...1,806 24
7 the same—the same............1,460 62
9 Warner, Albert S—A B Purdy....... 169 33
9 Wischnewetzky, Lazare / Wischnewetzky, Florence K / Wakeman, Thaddeus B } J M Gove.. 158 98
10 Wunderlich, Herman—Henry Sylvester.............................. 362 18
10 Wolffe, Frederick—City Nat Bank of Birmingham........................2,396 68
10 Walsh, Johanna—Michael Seitz...... 207 00
10 Wertheimer, Leopold—Moses Zimmermann........................ 157 08
10 Weiss, Adolph—Isidore Herschfield.. 29 50
11 Weiss, Theodore—J A Lane........ 233 51
11 Werner, George—A P Vollmer....... 126 73
11 Weber, Roman W—N J Botsford ....costs 69 45
11 Warde, Frederick—M W Aveling.... 126 17
12 White, John—John Lynch........... 170 32
12 Waitzfelder, Solomon L—Herman Tieber.............................. 91 26
12 Walsh, Thomas J—N Y Lumber and Wood Working Co..................3,525 67
13 Wetherby, Henry—Osborn Oxnard.. 441 66
13 Wilson, Robert — Aaron da Costa Gomez.............................. 79 22
10 Young, William, Jr—John Simmons Co.............................. 750 99
7 *Zadofsky, Jacob / Zadofsky, Mary } Isaac Epstein.... 59 50
11 Zemansky, Aaron—J A Waddell....3,052 04
13 Zacharias, Aaron / *Zacharias, Zacharias } Johanna Steinberg........1,714 17

KINGS COUNTY.

Nov.
5*Alyea, William—Bulmer Lumber Co (Lim).............................. $74 48
6 Abrahams, Alfred—J Talcott........ 968 40
6 the same—G Aery.............. 512 11
6 Ackermann, Michael—J Gottschalk.. 452 14
6 Aldrich, William—J F Tilman....... 191 44
5 Bedell, Edward J—E Holmes........ 275 68
7 Blaney, Thomas—G Bulle............ 117 73
9 Beekman, John—H J Rosevelt....... 95 25
9 Brice, John—F Betz................. 51 77
9 Burke, Joseph F—J Lewy........... 43 80
10 Blydenburgh, Julius M—S B Kraus.. 109 31
11 Blaney, Thomas A—Fort Hamilton B Co (Lim).......................... 260 09
11 Boughan, James A—J R Bird........ 94 13
5 Clarke, Robert H / Clarke, Andrew J } F & M Schaefer.. 129 07

6 Cobb, George W—E W McClave...... 241 64
6 Cross, William—T L C Gerry......... 132 37
7 Case, Theodore B—M Armstrong.... 50 57
9 Carmiencke, John H—A Amend..... 78 80
9 Catterson, Thomas—David Jones Co.. 313 01
9 Chapman, Louisa W—J H Downes... 332 91
9 the same——the same............ 914 19
10 Collins, Charles H—J Jamer.......... 122 98
10 Case, Virgil R—S B Kraus...... .... 109 31
11 Carlin, John C—J M Canda.......... 254 79
6 Doscher, Henry D—O Gruhn........ 83 03
7 Denton, Frank—J Nix............... 167 35
9 Denison, Henry—E S Doubleday.....1,751 25
9 Donaldson, Joseph C—R T Booth..... 145 37
12 Dillon, James—J P Donnelly......... 277 69
9 England, George—J Lewy........... 74 35
12 Ernst, John A—S Liebmann's Sons Brewing Co.................. ...... 167 00
12†Edwards, "Mary" F—J G Johnson. 241 74
10 Foley, Peter B—G Venable.......... 92 88
10 Fehlbusch, Charles—P Weidmann.... 347 57
12 Frost, Leonard L—G H Morrill....... 483 84
6 Gallagher, John J—T Nailon.........1,088 96
9 Gregory, Thomas K—M H Carey, extrx.................................. 548 31
9 Grippentrog, Katie—Marie Gradwohl 80 00
10 Greson, John—L Kram............... 111 50
10 Griffiths, Thomas W / Griffiths, Margaret T } B S Donahue. 57 74
12*Gaus, Edward—S Liebmann's Sons Brewing Co.......... .... 167 00
12 Griebel, Henry—C D Rhinehart...... 196 36
6 Haight, Jennie—O Gruhn............ 83 03
7 Harrington, George—S T Valentine.. 314 39
7 Hawkins, Mary S / Hawkins, William M / Hawkins, Elias H } K Bergholz... 718 94
9 Hanlon, Thomas—H Herrmann...... 158 07
9 Hartman, Henry—F Young.......... 312 47
9 Hull, John H—Chicago Carriage and Cutter Co..............................2,126 08
10 Hoy, John / *Hoy, Robert } J Jamer............ .. 122 98
10 Hicks, William C—E C Hazard 365 00
11 Halliday, Hannah M—E F Linton ... 107 67
12 Hasse, Edward F—E C Hazard....... 134 32
12 Hennesy, John—W D Starr.......... 102 15
12 Hellberg, August—F W Devoe....... 161 56
7 Johnson, Frank H—M Armstrong... 50 57
9 Jones, Joseph R—C Opperman... ... 12 85
12 Jewell, James C—J Rauch......... .... 55 60
5 Kirchner, Charles—Bullmer Lumber Co (Lim)........................... 74 48
6 Kernan, Henry—Third Nat Bank of Buffalo.......................... 427 01
7 Kohlbaas, Charles H—Forest G Weeks 177 68
10 Knoth, William—G W Venable...... 150 58
11 Kissling, August—E Conway........ 273 98
11 King, Julius / King, Walter G / King, Burnam W / King, Clifford } W F Brainard. .. 114 54
6 Lutz, John—J G Jenkins.... .... 52 83
6 Lindholm, Victor W—C Gillespie.... 75 98
10 Lamb, James W—J Murphy......... 95 71
10 Lieb, Thomas / *Lieb, Robert / *Lieb, Theodore } H D Berner 164 00
12 Lott, Albert—G Boyce................ 123 91
12 the same——the same............ 93 28
12 the same——the same............ 98 50
5 Murtha, Carrie—Annie Raymond.... 144 15
6 Manning, Thomas J—T R Bird...... 71 06
6 Mueller, George J—G Deike.......... 115 85
7 Martin, Robert W—D Poelmann..... 39 19
9 Morrissey, John—B Reilly... .... 72 21
9 McDermott, Thomas—David Jones Co 369 76
9 Meyer, Louis / Meyer, Maurice / Meyer, Michael } Bessie Louchein.... 128 27
10 Mann, Edward C / Mann, Barbara } R Crisladoro..... 789 59
10 Martin, Harry—Christian Moerlein Brewing Co... .... 439 42
10 the same——Edge Hill Wine Co.. 472 64
12 Moog, Simon—J Baehr............... 390 50
12 Miller, Frederick—F W Devoe........ 161 56
12 Mulqueen, Thomas F—H Bartelmes.. 382 58
12 McCaffrey, William—B Fischer...... 758 19
6 North, Charles F—F Eigabroadt..... 687 13
7 Neuhaus, Alfred—D Ferry........... 54 28
11 Nickle, Louis C—Sarah A White..... 333 14
7 Overton, Charles C—W H Hendrickson............................ 45 32
9 O'Neill, Dennis—G L Ely........... . 117 16
9 Osborn, William—The Cowperthwait Co....... .... 374 18
11 Obermeier, Frederick—Beadleston & W................................ 104 73
12 Overton, David R / Overton, Wiley G } H J Rosevelt..... 66 98
6 Prendergast, George F—H R Brown.. 2,181 18
6 Pool, Richard N—D F Wright....... 606 99
7 Pierce, Tecumseh — Union Central Life Ins Co........................ 374 00
9 Pfeiffer, Martin—Mason, Au & Magenheimer Confectionery Mfg Co ... 51 20
9 Petersen, Gustavus A—A Feik........ 109 78
12 Perry, Charles L / Perry, Nellie T } S Hess 528 99
12 Pruzina, William J R—J C Loudon.. 94 60
9 Quibell, Sarah M—J W Quibell......3,908 09
11 Quanton, Edward H—Thurber, Whyland & Co.............................. 90 98
9 Raabe, Regina—H A Riebesehl...... 241 35
9 Ross, William H—E P Carpenter....3,156 70
10 Rockwell, William—Caroline Z Stanton.................................. 96 52
12 Robbins, Thomas H—G W Melvin.... 713 82
6 Staite, William—Cordelia Taggard(D) 150 12
6 Shields, J Van Pelt—J D Roberts.... 111 56
11 Schick, Frederick—F W Meeker...... 306 82
11 Simonson, Michaelis—G F Vietor.... 16,686 47
11 Springer, Annie M—Jennie Thall.... 425 22
12 Scott, Joseph—M Seitz................ 100 50
12 Schondelmeier, John J, admr of Alfred Schondelmeier, dec'd—J Geehan 108 07
6 The Suffolk Mfg Co—H Martin....... 810 86
6 the same——the same............ 160 40
7 The Brooklyn, Bushwick & Queens County R R—D D Mangam.........1,181 82
9 Tillotson, Charles N—L Hunter....... 268 47
11 The J H Bonnell Co (Lim) / Turton, John and Edgar S } Brooklyn Bank.. 529 42
12 The admr of Alfred Schondelmeier, dec'd—J Geehan.................... 108 07
12 The China Mutual Ins Co of Boston—W A Price.......................... 612 94
6 White, Henry K—A Campbell....... 525 48
6 Wichmann, Charles—W Grandeman. 201 43
7 Waggoner, Ralph H—A L Gardiner.. 149 79
7 Webster, John A—H F Wells. ....(D) 2,343 53
7 Waggoner, Ralph H—H L Bridgman 1,369 61
7 Wheeler, Henry F / *Wheeler, Frank H } J A Doyle........ 102 00
11 Wilson, Elbert C — Farmers' Loan and Trust Co...........................3,430 93
11 Weiss, Theodore—G F Vietor........16,686 47
12 Warde, Frederick—M W Aveling.... 126 17
12 Walsh, Johanna—M Seitz............ 207 00
12 Willets, F A—Commercal Bank....... 532 05

SATISFIED JUDGMENTS.

NEW YORK.

November 7 to 13—Inclusive.

Ayres, Charles H—Pierce Artesian and Oil Well Supply Co. (1891)................... $656 77
Blanchard, Charles A—Pierce Artesian and Oil Well Supply Co. (1891)............... 656 77
Bedell, George C and Edwin—A W Lindsay Type Foundry. (1891)........ .... 211 65
Blumberg, William I—Joseph Rothschild. (1891).. 83 98
Same— same. (1891).............................. 356 80
Baggot, Atmore L—W B Rice. (1888).........2,684 29
Bache, Semon—D H Lewis. (1889).............. 76 55
Same——same assignee. (1889)............1,257 68
Same and Siegmund I——same. (1889).....1,362 98
Same——D H Lewis. (1889) 76 54
Beran, Wilson Lloyd, admr Geo F Beran—T G Carroll (1891).................................. 158 33
Blair, George—People's Bank of Buffalo.(1891) 1,175 41
Barchay, Annie—James Hawthorne. (1891).. 32 50
Bernius, George—Ernest Eberle. (1884)....... 399 85
Baker, Carrie—William Simpson. (1890)...... 607 84
Block, Henry—Tradesmen's Nat Bank. (1889) 2,032 08
Clark, Samuel and Alexander—W H Ertell. (1891) 207 22
Civilie, Frank A—Alexander Hamilton, exr. (1884)...............................1,662 29
‡Cohn, Bernard—W R Potts. (1891)........... 276 16
Cramer, Mary C—Mary Schultz. (1891)....... 391 02
Cahn, Henry H—D H Lewis. (1889) 76 55
Same——same assignee. (1889)........... 1,257 68
Commercial Union Assurance Co (Lim) of London, England—M H Smith. (1890)... 119 19
Clark, Alexander and Samuel—W H Ertell. (1891).... .... 356 04
Cornet, William H—John Murray. (1891).....1,870 42
Cutting, Robert L—Mayor, &c. (1889)...... ... 100 00
Casey, Patrick—Thomas Sullivan. (1890)..... 934 44
Clewes, Henry and James B—Julia Scheiner, admrx. (1891)..........................2,533 90
*Donahue, Nathaniel M—William Hiergesell. (1891) 414 94
Dreyfuss, Bernard—Leopold Ullman. (1891).. 2,617 36
Duffy, James—Jacob Grein. (1891)........... 187 05
Egan, John—Thomas Sullivan. (1890)...... .... 934 44
Euler, Mary A and John H—W W Foster. (1891)................ .... 517 85
Forster, Charles M—Julia Scheiner, admrx. (1891). 2,533 90
Frank, Levi—Isaac Blumenthal. (1881) 156 07
Same——Lehman Samuels. (1884)........... 110 63
Finan, James—Esther Broadbent, extrx. ('91) 262 07
Fitzgerald, Thomas—Ingersoll Sergeant Drill Co. (1891).................................. 199 71
Flynn, Peter H—G W Venable. (1891) 269 51
Fleet, Edward W—G W Venable. (1889) 150 89
*Fanshawe, William S—C R Hickox. (1891).. 1,048 84
Freeman, H Alfred—M D Gardner. (1891).... 58 01
Grant, D Lewis—E A Gross. (1891) 172 19
Gondolfo, Joseph—Henry Habnenfeld. (1891) 237 76
Grant, Hugh J, as Sheriff—Emanuel Newman. (1891).. 655 65
Greenthal, Robert—Ernest Eberle. (1884) ... 399 85
Hartman, Ely—G W McLean, recvr. (1890)... 132 96
Henderson, John—Thomas Rafferty. (1882)... 1,352 80
*Hallecy, Daniel—Mayor, &c. (1889)...... ... 100 00
Homer Lee Bank Note Co—S B Sturges. ('91) 4,712 63
Same——same. (1891)...........................2,840 86
Jarvie, James N, admr—Geo F Beran and T G Carroll. (1891)........ .... 158 33
Kelly, Thomas—Joseph Kahn. (1891) 3,277 45
*Knoblock, Philip, Jr—Charles Reilly, comm'r. (1890) 100 00
Kelly, John E—Simon Morris. (1891).......... 164 06
Kieferdorf, Fred F—Florian Krug. (1891).... 267 25
Kayser, Julius—D H Lewis. (1889) 76 54
Same——same assignee. (1889).. . ... 1,362 98
Lehrburger, Henry—Gustav Schnaier. (1890). 985 76
Same——same. (1891)....... .... 90 80
Leyer, George H, Jr—Nat Broadway Bank. (1888)...4,005 86
Same——same. (1888).... .... .5,270 80
Maclaury, James—Rector, &c., Holy Trinity Church of Harlem. (1890).................. 111 30
Manhattan Railway Co / Metropolitan Elevated Railway Co } J M Young. (1891).. 116 98
Same——same. (1889)........................4,846 40
Same——same. (1889) 125 12
Manhattan Railway Co—B K Stevens. (1890). 183 20
Same——same. (1889) 18,051 59
Murphy, Agnes K—W W Mills. (1891)........ 108 55
Same——A L Mills. (1891)........ .... 109 43
Maritime Register Publishing Co (Lim)—H W Jones. (1891)............................ 103 40
Moore, William O—Henry Habenfeld. (1891). 237 76
Meister, Christian—Edward Brennan. (1884). 92 60
Nichthauser, Sigismund — William Purvin. (1880)... .... 46 42
Noel, August, Jr—D H Lewis. (1889).......... 76 55
Same——same assignee. (1889)............. 1,257 68
Newell Bros Mfg Co — Emanuel Newman. (1891)............. .... 955 65
N Y Elevated R R Co—B K Stevens. (1889)...18,051 59
Same——same. (1890)................ ..... 183 20
Osterman, Abraham—German Exchange Bank. (1891)................................ .... 117 76
O'Brien, Patrick J—First Nat Bank of Tampa, Florida. (1891) 585 80
Pierce, Tecumseh—Union Central Life Ins Co. (1891)......... .... 374 00
Pappenheim, Lena—Thomas Pettit. (1888)... 67 50
Pollock, William J and Louisa A—W P Tatham. (1890)..1,039 06
Roth, Ludwig—D H Lewis. (1889).... .... 76 54
Same——same, assignee. (1889)...... ......1,362 98
Rosenheim, Jacob / Reiff, Charles } German Exchange Bank. (1891)......... .... 117 76
‡Rogers, Asa L—E D Fogg. (1883)............ 120 03
‡Same——C P Easton. (1888)................ 394 95
Stewart, John M—Phœnix Furniture Co. (1891).3,530 91
Spies, Adam W—Mayor, &c. (1888)............ 62 57
Schmidt, Konrad—Gustav Schnaier. (1891)... 90 30
Same——same. (1890)........................ 985 76
Strong, William L—S B Sturges. (1891). 4,712 63
Sage, Russell—Mary C Hopper, extrx. (1887). 2,985 78
Semansky, Henry N—Joseph Rothschild.(1891) 356 80
Same——same (1891)............ ... . 83 98
Townsend, Maurice E — August Heckscher. (1890) 80 55
Ulman, Solomon and Joe E—D H Lewis. (1889) 76 54
Same——same, assignee. (1889).............1,362 98
Vernam, Florence G—David Wadsworth. ('91). 967 81
Same and Remington — Phœnix Furniture Co. (1891)............ ....3,530 91
Same——J W Clowes. (1891)... .... 578 61
Woods, Jane—Simon Katzenstein. (1891)..... 74 50
White, Andrew J—Emily Charles. (1889)..... 291 23
Wessels, Gerhard—First Nat Bank of Tampa, Florida. (1891)....................... .... 585 80
Zuber, Quinn—Frederick Buss. (1891).......... 112 52

*Vacated by order of Court. †Suspended on Appeal. ‡Released. §Reversal. ‖Satisfied by Execution.

KINGS COUNTY.

November 6 to 12—Inclusive.

Beyer, Jr, George H—Nat Broadway Bank. (1888)... $4,005 86
Same——same. (1888)...........................5,270 80
Conselyea, Wallace A—J E Baker. (1891)... . 335 11
Fernandez, Robert — Waterloo Wagon Co. (1888).. 86 47
Same——E E Homes. (1890).............. 45 25
Finken, John / Koster, Caspar / admrs Treno Yung } H Fleur. (1891)....3,051 34
Same——same. (1891)......................... 68 09
Fernandez, Robert / Hoffman, Charles } Mary B. Dorion. (1885)... 176 16
Same——same. (1885)........................ 176 16
Plath, William—H M Bischoff. (1891)......... 220 28
Stephens, Benjamin F—J B Wass. (1889)..... 843 57
Same——same. (1889)........................ 76 61
The Edison United Mfg Co—A H Rennie. (1891)...1,331 68

MECHANICS' LIENS.

NEW YORK CITY.

Nov.

7 Eighty-fourth st, No. 247, n s, 101.8 w 2d av, 20x100. Patrick Holohan agt ——, owner, and White & McGuire, contractors....... $39 75
7 Thirty-seventh st, Nos. 426 and 428, s s, 350 w 9th av, 50x100, McKelvey & Christie agt Mathew, Paul and Robert Micolini and Agatha Ottmann, owners, and Frederick Wood, contractor 575 00
7 Kingsbridge road, at north junction Nathalie av, 163.8x99.5x171.2, gore. S. L. Berrian agt Perry P. Williams and Hugh N. Camp and T. Judson Kilpatrick, owners, and Crockett & Weeks, contractors........... 862 14
7 Eighty-eighth st, n e cor Madison av, 36.7x100.8. Eberhard Fischer agt William Matthews, owner, and Sens, Scheubner & Frederick, contractors. 224 00
7 Macdougal st, No. 141, s e cor 4th st, 34.5x86. Bradley & Currier Co. (Lim.) agt Martin Diskin, owner and contractor. (Continued from Nov. 10, 1890).... ..... 4,808 90
9 One Hundred and Fifth st, n s, 280 w 4th av, 56x100.11. Saugatuck Iron Works Co. agt John O'Connor, owner and contractor. 280 00
9 Madison av, n w cor 115th st, 100.11x85. Same agt Wm. and Ann E. McEntee, owners, and Ann E. McEntee, contractor. 440 00
9 Amsterdam av, s w cor 99th st, 40x80.2x40x77.6. Henry Woods agt Lillian Rogers, owner and contractor..........................1,348 25
9 Ninety-fifth st, Nos. 145-165, n s, 150 e Amsterdam av, 200x100. Helena Mahler agt Bernard Cohn, owner and contractor..... 746 25
9 Morningside or Columbus av, s e cor 124th st, 100.11x201.9. W. G. Leeson agt Henry M. Bendheim, owner, and Henry and William H. Niebuhr, contractors........ 190 00
9 Bathgate av, No. 2279, w s, 67 s 183d st, 25x100. John Lanzer agt Daniel Kennelly, owner and contractor............ .... 555 75
10*Forty-first st, Nos. 530-534 W., 75x100. Clinton Iron Works agt Valentine Loewers Gambrinus Brewing Co., owners, and J. Coar & Co., contractors.....................1,068 76
10 One Hundred and Thirty-fifth st, Nos. 5-17, n s, 110 w 5th av, 125x100. John Simpkin agt William H. Verdon, owner and contractor..................................... 37 00
10 One Hundred and Thirty-fifth st, Nos. 15 and 17, n s, 198 w 5th av, 37x100. Frank Burgan agt same........ ... . 29 50
10 Amsterdam av, s w cor 99th st, 40x80.2x40x77.6. Ackert & Schroeder agt Lilian Rogers, owner and contractor.. .... 540 00
10 Prospect av, e s. 69.6 s 162d st, 80x100. J. A. & S. T. Woolf agt Annie Mattmuller, owner, and Robert Spreaton, contractor. 1,478 65
10 Ninety-fifth st, Nos. 145-165 W., 200x100.

*Editor RECORD AND GUIDE:

The lien filed against us by Henry C. Fisher is unjust as we have paid him according to contract and his work is not yet finished, and he has not yet paid his sub-contractor and will not allow us to do so. When his work is completed he will be paid whatever is found to become due to him on an equitable settlement.

J. COAR & CO.

Benedict, McIlroy & Fowler agt Bernard Cohn, owner and contractor.............. 119 30

10 Twenty-fourth st, Nos. 341-345, n s, 271.7 e 9th av, 78.4x100. Frank Orlofski agt Joseph McFarland, owner, and Frederick Wood, contractor.......................... 600 00

10 Eleventh st, No. 58, n s, 309 e 6th av, 24x103.3. Bradley & Currier Co. (Lim.) agt John J. Crawford, owner and contractor. 2,844 10

10 Fifty-second st, n s, 375 e 11th av, 75x100. J. B. McCoy & Co. agt John A. Linscott, owner and contractor..................... 183 40

10 Av A, No. 1629, w s, 25.6 s 86th st, 25x75.9. William Grote agt Dora Eden extrx, and William Myen exr. Henry E. Eden, owners and contractors........................ 220 00

10 Thirty-seventh st, Nos. 426 and 428, s s, 350 w 9th av, 50x98.9. Edward Becker agt Matthew, Paul and Robert Micolino and Agatha Ottmann, owners, and Frederick Wood, contractor........................ 186 24

11 Ninety-sixth st, Nos. 157-165, n s, 70 e Lexington av, 125x100. J. P. Duffy & Co. agt McElroy Bros. or T. Lowery, owners, and McElroy Bros., contractors............. 112 56

11 Av A, No. 1629, w s, 25 s 86th st, 25x66. G. C. Schmidt agt Dora Eden extrx, and William Meyer exr. Henry E. Eden, owners and contractors.......................... 62 00

11 Thirty-seventh st, s s, 650 w 9th av, 50.6x88. Murray & Hill agt Mrs. A. C. Nicolina, owner, and Frederick Wood, contractor.. 1,662 50

11 Same property. Herbert Hodgkins agt same.................................. 500 00

11 Eighty-eighth st, n s, 175 w 8th av, 75x110.11. William Craig agt Frederick Wood, owner and contractor 1,240 00

11 One Hundred and Fifth st, Nos. 221-225 W. G. W. Rader & Co. agt Louis Schepp and —— Schultheis, owners, and Mathesins & Vallosio, contractors............ 79 78

11 Prospect av, e s, 69 s 162d st, 80x100. P. G. Decker agt Anna Mattmuller, owner, and Robert Spreaton, contractor............. 478 45

11 Leroy st, Nos. 55 and 57, n s, 200 w Bedford st, 50x100. Cornelius Flynn agt McElroy, Stevens & Co., owners and contractors... 91 00

12 Seventy-ninth st, Nos. 200-206, s w cor Amsterdam av, 100x100.2. J. W. Russell agt Susanna Victoria Hogan, owner and contractor.................................. 102 84

12 Eighty-eighth st, n s, 175 w 8th av, 75x—. Michael Tobin agt Frederick Wood, w and contractor....................... 68 00

12 Kippers av, n w cor Willard av, 100x75. Ernst Weber agt Ida L. Senior, owner, and John B. Robert, contractor 187 00

12 West End av, w s, 100 n 67th st, 100x90. Martin Redmond agt Martin Barrin and John Ruck, owners, and Edward Anwell and Thomas Cochran, contractors....... 99 50

12 Bathgate av, e s, 60 n 172d st, 20x120. J. M. Wilson agt George Hurd, owner, and Theodore Rhein, contractor............. 100 00

12 Bathgate av, e s, 40 n 172d st, 20x120. Same agt Edward Gibb, owner, and Theodor Rhein, contractor........................ 100 00

12 Ninety-sixth st, n s, 70 e Lexington av, 125x100. Frank Graziadio agt Owen F. and William McElroy, owners and contractors 541 95

12 Thirty-seventh st, No. 51 W. Henry Guinard agt George S. Allan, owner, and Edward Van Orden & Co., contractors... 192 50

12 Ninety-second st, s s, 100 e 5th av, 150x100. H. G. Kelly agt Thomas Graham, debtor, and Thomas Graham, Randolph Guggenheimer and Isaac and Samuel Untermyer, owners.................................. 1,050 00

12 Ninety-eighth st, n s, 375 e Columbus av, 25x100.11. Andrew Byrne agt Gregory Leahy and Frank Reynolds, owner, and Frank Reynolds, contractor.............. 300 00

12 One Hundred and Forty-fourth st, No. 306, s s, 100 w 8th av, 25x102. Miller & Robinson agt Ernest Molwitz, owner, and C. Anderson................................ 918 18

13 Ogden av, e s, 220 n Devoe st, 18.6x42.8. Jas. W. Collwell's Sons agt John J. Byrne, owner and contractor...................... 187 48

13 Pearl st, No. 546, n s, 24.9x100. John McCallum & Co. agt Anna E. Leaycraft, owner, and Priebe & Co., contractor . 605 00

13 Madison st, No. 291, n s, 70 w Montgomery st, 23.6x80. J. C. Taylor agt John Dougherty, owner and contractor........ 280 00

13 Lexington av, s e cor 87th st, 90x50. Adam Happel agt Cavinato Bros., owners and contractors.............................. 420 00

13 East Broadway, No. 194, n s, 25 e Jefferson st, 25x70. Same agt John Isear, owner, and Lowen & Murray, contractors....... 420 64

13 Eighth av, n w cor 120th st, 25x100. Ann Reilly agt James Riley and Richard Cummings, owners, and James Riley, contractor................................ 425 00

13 Eleventh st, No. 58 W., 24x103. Adolph Shapiro agt John J. Crawford, owner and contractor.............................. 490 00

13 Manhattan av, e s, extends from 113th to 114th st—block, x100x block x125. James Rogers agt E. P. Briggs, A. Holmes, William H. Ross, J. B. Conckling and Homer Beaudet, owners and contractors. (Continued from Nov. 15, 1890)................ 1,731 70

KINGS COUNTY.

Nov.

6 Sixty-seventh st, s s, 380 e 14th av, 20x120, New Utrecht. William Silber agt Henry J. Coates, owner and contractor.......... $32 75

6 Boerum st, n s, 200 e Graham av, 25x100. Rosenberg & Feinberg agt Ose and Betty Strasunsky, owners and contractors...... 135 00

6 Thirty-ninth st, n s, 40 w 7th av, 40x100.2. Adaline A. Newman agt John Sheridan, owner and contractor..................... 182 70

9 Greene av, n s, extends from Clinton av to Waverly av, 200x118.3. Brooklyn Door and Sash Co. agt Brooklyn Tabernacle... 1,000

9 Seigel st, n s, 125 e Ewen st, 25x100. Michael Geier agt Pauline Garling, owner, and Bernard Goldstein, contractor........... 41 30

9 Bergen st, s s, 100 w Hopkinson av, 25x100. Michael Naumann agt Rosa Rosenfeld, owner, and Yonas Rosenfeld, contractor. 21 00

9 Jamaica av, n s, 132 e Miller av, 100x232 to Sunnyside av. William G. Osborn agt Charles G. Miller, owner and contractor.. 148 25

9 Seigel st, n s, 125 e Ewen st, 25x100. Leopold Michel agt Pauline Garling.......... 425 00

10 St. Marks av, s s, 150 e Howard av, 25x100. Hall Sash and Door Co. agt Mary A. Dawdel, owner, and Gustave Menzel, contractor.................................. 465 00

10 Thatford av, w s, 120 n Glenmore av, 75x100. John Sloan agt Stearns & Mizer, owners, and Joseph McGrath and Charles Nelson, contractors...................... 23 25

10 St. Marks av, s s, 250 e Howard av, runs east 50 x south 127.9 x west 75 x north 42.9 x east 25 x north 85. Earl A. Gillespie agt Mary A Dowdell, owner, and G. Menzel, contractor.......................... 234 28

10 Reid av, Nos. 254 and 256, w s, 25 n Halsey st, 75x100. Albermarle Soapstone Co. agt George W. McCormick, owner and contractor.................................. 131 00

10 Second st, s s, 100 w 7th av, 98.10x100. Malcolm McNeill agt Jennie L. and Donald C. Ross, owner and contractors.......... 700 00

10 Cook st, No. 21, n s, 150 w Graham av, 25x100. John Rueger agt John Kehl and Maria Kehl, owners and contractors.... 2,475 00

10 Seigel st, No. 83, n s, 125 e Ewen st, 25x100. Jacob Pomeranz agt Morris and Pauline Garling, owners and contractors........ 2,000 00

12 Seventh st, n s, 297.6 e 4th av, 50.4x100. George Dayton & Co. agt Mary E. Miller, owner and contractor................ 230 00

12 Bay 25th st, n w s, 100 s e Benson av, 60x96.8, New Utrecht. Cropsey & Mitchell agt Charles H. Simonson, owner, and Luc Rioux, contractor.......................... 366 78

12 Same property. Same agt same and R. J. Patterson, sub-contractor................ 79 68

12 Fourth av, s w cor 23d st. Benjamin Frankel agt John and Elizabeth Staebler, owners and contractors.................. 258 00

SATISFIED MECHANICS' LIENS.

NEW YORK CITY.

Nov.

7 Lenox av, No. 465, n w cor 133d st, 25x100. Christian Leyrer agt Mary J. and James Meagher. (Lien filed April 7, 1891)....... $529 35

9 Fifty-third st, s s, 350 w 10th av, 125x100. Bernard Marrey agt James O'Donelan. (Sept. 3, 1891).............................. 41 21

9 Eleventh and 13th avs, 27th and 28th sts, the block. Howard Howser agt William W. Rossiter and Coufrode & Saylor. (Oct. 13, 1891).............................. 7,430 48

10 One Hundred and Twenty-ninth st, Nos. 302 and 304 W., 50x—. George Palmer agt Christian Blin, Jr., and Alice Schwartz. (March 9, 1891)......................... 19 54

10 Lenox av, No. 465, n w cor 133d st, 25x100. Christian Leyrer agt Mary J. and James Meagher. (June 16, 1891).............. 529 35

10*One Hundred and Eighteenth st, s s, 240 w 4th av, 100x—. Bowes & Coombs agt Samuel Harris, Bernard Ginsburg, Simon Sultan and James Nunan. (Nov. 2, 1891). 472 00

11 Fort Independence st, w s, 500 s Bailey av, 25x—. Lawrence Bros. agt William J. Connell and John H. Klein. (April 15, 1891)................................ 485 38

11 Fort Independence st, w s, 401 n Montgomery av, 25x—. W. H. Hardie agt same. (March 27, 1891)......................... 55 00

11 One Hundred and Twentieth st, No. 124 E., 25x100. McCullough & Lindskog agt William E Crandall and John W. Fisher. (Oct. 24, 1891)........................... 426 35

11 Ninety-seventh st, No. 70 W. Cassidy & Son Mfg Co. agt George A. Hayunga and Squier & Whipple. (April 3, 1891)........ 117 25

11 Franklin st, No. 1, s w cor Baxter st. Isaac Hoffman agt Louis Levy and Samuel Chodicor. (Oct. 9, 1891).................. 41 50

12 One Hundred and Thirty-third st, s s, 250 w 7th av, 150x—. Buess & Co. agt F. R. Thurston and George and Frances L. Morrell. (Oct. 8, 1891).................. 124 00

12 One Hundred and First st, Nos. 75 and 77 W., 50x100.11. N. Y. Roofing Co. agt William M. Walsh. (Oct. 17, 1891)........... 400 00

12 Same property. Marcus Murray agt same. (Oct. 10, 1891)........................... 455 71

12 One Hundred and Second st, Nos. 202 and 204 E., 35x—. A. B. & W. T. Westervelt agt James Duffy. (Oct. 22, 1891).......... 133 00

12 One Hundred and Second st, No. 204 E., 35x—. M. F. Westergren and F. L. Anderson agt same. (Sept. 11, 1891).......... 268 00

12*Catharine st, Nos. 53 and 55. A. J. Delatour agt Eliza L. Miller and P. J. Whalen. (Nov. 24, 1890)............................ 71 29

12*One Hundred and First st, Nos. 75 and 77 W. A. R. Becker agt William M. Walsh. (Sept. 22, 1891)........................... 232 90

12*Same property. William and James Forbes agt same. (Oct. 12, 1891)................ 700 00

13 Eagle av, Nos. 58 and 59, e s, 262.8 n Westchester av, 50x—. Adam Gebhardt agt John Langermann, John and Carl Flachfort and Louis Treisner. (Oct. 22, 1891).. 2,087 89

*Discharged by depositing amount of lien and interest with County Clerk.

KINGS COUNTY.

Nov.

6 Hamburg av, No. 190. Martin Dernhardt agt Jacob Klett, owner and contractor. (Oct. 22, 1891)............................ $175 00

6 Same property. Gottfried Wolters agt same owner and contractor. (Oct. 22, 1891).................................. 663 50

6 West av, s s, 40 w West 2d st, 40x100, Coney Island. William Rubien agt Mary B. Rosenbaum, owner and contractor. (July 8, 1891)................................ 782 29

6 Lewis av, s e cor Hancock st, 150x100. A. J. Felty agt McWhinney & Aronson, owners and contractors. (Nov. 4, 1891)....... 1,850 00

6 Watkins st, w s, 125 n Sutter av, 25x100. James Moran agt Elias Kaplan, owner and contractor. (Nov. 2, 1891)............... 33 00

7 Eastern Parkway, Vesta av, Sutter av and Powell st—The Eastern Park Base Ball Grounds. Earl A Gillespie agt The Ridgewood Land and Improvement Co. and The Brooklyn Base Ball Club (Lim.), owners, and Charles B. Linton, contractor. (Sept. 8, 1890).............................. 1,061 55

7 Clymer st, n w cor Wythe av, 25x100. Washington Bulkley agt John E. Bullwinkle and John Kehoe, owners, and Williams & Collins, contractors. (Oct. 8, 1891.) (Deposit)................................ 98 60

9 Flushing av, n e cor Vandervoort av, 25x100. Louis Bossert agt Peter Johnson, owner and contractor. (Oct. 23, 1891)......... 1,354 79

9 Wyckoff av, No. 38, 25x95..................
Troutman st, e s, 147.2 n Wyckoff av, 25x100..............................
Boerum st, n s, 100 w Ewen st, 25x100....
Jacob Nasel agt Edmund Stein, owner, and Herman E. Funk. (Sept. 2, 1889).... 1,215 00

10 Glenmore av, s s, 50 e Vesta av. R. Cummings' Sons agt Charlotte Van Pelt, owner, and J. Caldwell, contractor. (Nov. 21, 1889).............................. 125 90

11 Humboldt st, w s, bet Ten Eyck and Stagg sts. George B. Jacobs & Co. agt Louis Broschart. (Oct. 24, 1891).............. 580 74

12 Navy st, e s, 100 n Myrtle av, 50x100. Peter Feeley agt Henrietta Fisk, owner, and William H. Glover, contractor. (Oct. 5, 1891)................................ 374 00

12 Howard av, s w cor Macon st, 93.6x100. Friedlander & Green agt Clarence Lincoln, owner and contractor. (July 9, 1891.) (Order of Court)................ 382 00

12 Same property. C. W. Williams & Son agt same. (July 23, 1891.) (Order of Court). 1,900 00

12 Same property. Graff & Co. agt same. (July 23, 1891.) (Order of Court)......... 845 00

12 Same property. Frederick W. Lawrence agt same. (July 28, 1891.) (Order of Court)................................ 901 14

12 Same property. Rudolph Reimer & Co. agt same owner and contractor. (July 18, 1891.) (Order of Court)............. 1,223 00

12 Schenck av, e s, 225 s Blake av, 50x100. Charles E. Cummings agt S. Ferris Owen. (June 25, 1891)......................... 400 00

12 Sixty-sixth st, s e cor 11th av, 22x100, New Utrecht. John Gall agt Magi Reichenback, owner and contractor. (Sept. 1, 1891) .. 222 00

12 Sixty-sixth st, s s, 260 w 11th av, 53.3x100.2x60.5x100. Abram C. Shelly agt Margaretha and Gustaf Reicenbach, owners and contractors. (Oct. 19, 1891).................. 54 49

13 Fort Hamilton av, n e cor 59th st, New Utrecht. Daniel and Hugh McNulty agt trustees of School District No. 2, of New Utrecht, owners, and Ole Gunston, contractor. (Order of Court).............. 105 00

BUILDINGS PROJECTED.

The first name is that of the owner; ar't stands for architect, m'n for mason, c'r for carpenter and b'r for builder.

NEW YORK CITY.

SOUTH OF 14TH STREET.

Allen st, No. 185, five-story flat and stores, 25x63.6, tin roof; cost, $20,000; Philip Kotlowsky, 235 Henry st; ar't, C. Rentz. Plan 1431.

Henry st, No. 111, five-story brk and stone flat, 25x88.6, tin roof; cost, $22,000; Fay & Stacom, 337 Pleasant av; ar't, Charles Rentz. Plan 1421.

Pitt st, No. 66, rear, five-story brk lodge room building, 25x60, tin roof; cost, $9,000; Herman Przeworsky, 59 Suffolk st; ar't, H. Horenburger. Plan 1420.

Washington st, s e cor Watts st, six-story brk and stone store, 50x100, slate roof; cost, $56,000; Fleming Smith, 11 East 35th st; ar't, S. D. Hatch; m'ns, R. L. Darragh & Co. Plan 1419.

Norfolk st, No. 78, five-story brk flat and stores, 25x88.6, tin roof; cost, $22,000; Loonie & Parker, 66 East 88th st; ar't, C. Rentz. Plan 1437.

Forsyth st, No. 70, five-story brk flat and stores, 25x88.6, tin roof; cost, $22,000; Loonie & Parker, 66 East 88th st; ar't, Chas. Rentz. Plan 1438.

Bayard st, n e cor Mulberry st, four-story brk and stone public school, 124.10x100.4, slate or tile roof; cost, $130,000; Mayor, &c., City Hall; ar't, C. B.J. Snyder. Plan 1440.

BETWEEN 14TH AND 59TH STREETS.

20th st, Nos. 535 and 537 W., four-story brk workshop, 55x92; cost, $12,000; Jas. R. Floyd, 42 West 88th st; ar't, J. M. Dunn. Plan 1430.

37th and 38th sts, foot of, North River, one-story frame shelter transfer bridges, 65x96.6, felt, tar and gravel roof; cost, $3,000; lessees, Pennsylvania R. R. Co.; agent, E. F. Brooks, Jersey City, N. J. Plan 1428.

BETWEEN 59TH AND 125TH STREETS, EAST OF 5TH AVENUE.

74th st, Nos. 5 and 7 E., two four-story and basement (stone front) dwell'gs, 25x91; cost, $50,000 each; J. V. S. Woolley & Co., 75 East 79th st; ar't, J. E. Ware. Plan 1424.

111th st, n s, 50 w Madison av, two five-story stone front flats, 25x75, tin roofs; cost, $20,000 each; John S. Scott, 4 West 113th st; ar't, J. C. Burne. Plan 1435.

BETWEEN 59TH AND 125TH STREETS, WEST OF CENTRAL PARK WEST AND 8TH AVENUE.

87th st, n s, 250 w 8th av, five four-story and basement (stone front) dwell'gs, 20x55, tin roofs; cost, $20,000 each; Patrick and John J. Farley, 1990 Madison av; ar'ts, Thom & Wilson. Plan 1418.

104th st, s s, 100 e Riverside Drive, ten three-story and basement brk and stone dwell'gs, 20x55, tin roofs; cost, $15,000 each; T. A. Squier, 308 East 90th st, and W. E. Lanchantin, 301 East 89th st; ar't, C. True. Plan 1433.

76th st, No. 108 W., four-story and basement stone front dwell'g, 25x76, tin roof; cost, $35,000; Fred'k Aldhous, 513 Lenox av; ar't, J. C. Burne. Plan 1436.

NORTH OF 125TH STREET.

155th st, s s, 125 e 8th av, one-story frame shed, 12.6x30, — roof; cost, $150; lessee, Geo. Greene, 2633 8th av; c'r, Chas. Ackerman. Plan 1432.

23D AND 24TH WARDS.

Dashwood pl, e s, 60 n Commerce av (proposed), one story frame shed, gravel roof; cost, $1,600; Gas Engine and Power Co., Morris Heights; ar't, Chas. McKinney. Plan 1425.

174th st, s s, 65.6 e Bathgate av, three-story frame dwell'g, 29x25, tin roof; cost, $2,500; Wm. Fernchild, 1777 Bathgate av; ar't, A. Spence. Plan 1427.

Bathgate av, s e cor 174th st, three-story frame dwell'g and store, 23x45, tin roof; cost, $4,000; ow'r and ar't, same as Plan 1427. Plan 1426.

Alexander av, s w cor 141st st, four five-story brk and stone flats with two stores, 25 and 25.6x 66, 71 and 87, tin roofs; total cost, $56,000; Henry Muller, 701 East 138th st; ar't, W. H. C. Hornum. Plan 1417.

Fulton av, e s, 162.3 n 169th st, rear, one-story frame stable, 16x20, tin roof; cost, $500; Carl Stehr, 347 Broome st; ar't, M. Schroff. Plan 1423.

Fulton av, e s, 162.3 n 169th st, two-story frame dwell'g, 23.3x60, tin roof; cost, $7,000; ow'r and ar't, same as Plan 1423. Plan 1422.

Inwood av, No. 22, e s, abt 100 s Wolf pl, three-story brk and frame dwell'g, 22.6x45, tin roof; cost, $2,500; ow'r, ar't and b'r, Henry Assmus, 165th st and Ridge road. Plan 1429.

Parsons st, s s, 150 e Broadway or Kingsbridge road, two-story frame dwell'g, 16x28, shingle roof; cost, $1,250; John Parsons, M. D., Kingsbridge; ar't and b'r, S. L. Berrian. Plan 1434.

Creston av, e s, abt 500 s Travers st, two-story frame dwell'g, 24x20, shingle roof; cost, $3,000; ow'r and ar't, K. M. Rosell, 155 Rockfield st. Plan 1441.

Nathalie av, e s, 854 n Kingsbridge road, three-story frame dwell'g, 29x50.6, shingle roof; cost, $5,000; A. T. Day, Fordham; ar'ts, Rossiter & Wright; b'r, R. G. Turner. Plan 1439.

KINGS COUNTY.

Plan 2034—Hemlock st, e s, 202 s Fulton st, two two-story frame dwell'gs, 20x46, tin roofs; cost $2,500 each; Lawrence J. Mulligan, 3019 Fulton st; ar't, J. W. Fletcher.

2035—Driggs av, n w cor North 10th st, one one-story frame cooper shop, 60x65, gravel roof; cost, $2,500; John Colligan, 202 Ainslie st; ar't and b'r, G. W. Schaedle.

2036—Hopkinson av, n e cor Marion st, one three-story brk store and tenem't, 20x56, tin roof, wooden cornice; cost, $6,000; Star Union Improvement Co., 195 Broadway, N.Y.; ar't, M. F. Walsh; b'r, P. Sullivan.

2037—49th st, s s, 80 w 3d av, six three-story brk tenem'ts, 20x60, tin roofs, iron cornices; cost $4,000 each; Thomas Nolan, 1178 3d av; ar't, T. Bennett; b'rs, S. Robinson and A. Klam.

2038—Marshall st, w s, 150 n Gold st, one one-story brk engine room, gravel roof; cost, $800; Atlantic White Lead Co., on premises; ar't and c'r, W. Rae; m'n, P. Castner.

2039—Bushwick av, s w cor Woodbine st, one three-story brk store and dwell'g, 20x63.6, tin roof, iron cornice; cost, $12,000; John Kohlman, Sumner and Lafayette avs; ar't, F. Holmberg.

2040—Herkimer st, s s, 200 w Nostrand av, two four-story brk tenem'ts, 25x68, gravel roof, iron cornice; cost, $8,000; G. R. Brown, 26 Court st; ar't, G. W. Brown; b'rs, L. E. Brown and E. Cozzins.

2041—57th st, s s, 260 e 3d av, seven two-story frame dwell'gs, 20x40, tin roofs; cost, $3,200 each; ow'r, ar't and b'r, Wm. E. Kay, Blythebourne, L. I.

2042—Devoe st, s s, 200 e Catharine st, one two-story frame (brk filled) tailor shop, 25x26, tin roof; cost, $1,500; F. H. Riefel, 346 Devoe st; b'r, M. Metzen.

2043—Eastern Parkway, n s, 100 e Christopher av, one two-story frame tailor shop, 16x24, tin roof; cost, $600; Constant Lieguers, Dumont av and Watkins st.

2044—Blake av, n s, 25 e Barbey st, one one-and-a-half-story frame stable and shop, 25x30, tin roof; cost, $100; Chas. E. Raynor, on premises.

2045—Ralph st, n s, 225 e Evergreen av, four three-story frame (brk filled) tenem'ts, 25x57, tin roofs; cost, $3,500 each; ow'r and ar't, Robert B. Muller, 37 Cornelia st; c'r, J. B. Hummel; m'n, not selected.

2046—Gardiner st, n e cor Johnson av, one three-story frame (brk filled) store and tenem't, 25x32 x60, tin roof; cost, $10,000; M. Schaefer, on premises; ar't, F. Holmberg.

2047—Ashford st, e s, 123.7 n Atlantic av, five two-story frame dwell'gs, 18x40, tin roofs; cost, $2,000 each; ow'r and c'r, Louis Ilsemann, Cleveland st, cor Fulton av; ar't, L. F. Schillinger.

2048—52d st, s s, 240 w 4th av, one three-story frame (brk filled) tenem't, 20x50, tin roof; cost, $4,500; Mrs. Susan Souter, 222 52d st.

2049—Morgan av, Nos. 72 and 74, 50 from s e cor Harrison pl, two three-story frame (brk filled) tenem'ts, 25x58, tin roofs; cost, $4,000 each; Cath. Steininger, 13 Gratton st; b'r, F. Steininger.

2050—Pacific st, s s, 168.4 e Utica av, five two-story frame dwell'gs, 17x38, tin roofs; cost, $2,000 each; ow'r, ar't and b'r, Chas. D. Terry, 1694 Dean st.

2051—Evergreen av, n e cor Halsey st, one three-story frame (brk filled) store and tenem't, 25x60, tin roof; cost, $4,000; ow'rs, ar'ts and b'rs, Cozine & Gascoine; 1223 Bushwick av.

2052—Driggs av, s e cor North 13th st, one two-story frame (brk filled) store and dwell'g, 23x50 and 29, tin roof; cost, $3,000; Fred. Westphal, 139 Driggs st; ar't, A. Herbert; b'r, J. Mitchell.

2053—Hamilton st, s e cor Etna st, fourteen two-story frame dwell'gs, 17x28, tin roofs; cost, $2,000 each; William H. Baker, Ridgewood av.

2054—Jamaica av, n s, 150 e Barbey st, one two-story and attic frame dwell'g, 20x30, tin roof; cost, $2,000; Chas. W. Hooper, 74 Van Siclen av.

2055—Lexington av, s s, 225 e Lewis av, four two-story brk flats, 20x45, tin roofs, wooden cornices; cost, each, $3,700; ow'r and b'r, D. S. Beasley, 187 Van Buren st; ar't, I. D. Reynolds & Son.

2056—Wythe av, n e cor North 13th st, one one-story frame blacksmith shop, 40x60, gravel roof; cost, $1,200; W. J. Logan, 100 Kent st; ar't, J. D. Logan; b'rs, Logan Iron Works.

2057—Hull st, s e cor Rockaway av, one two-story frame stable, 20x10, tin roof; cost, $200; George Bock, 126 Hull st; ar't, H. Ramsay; b'r, E. Prescott.

2058—Knickerbocker av, e s, 80 s Bleecker st, six three-story frame (brk filled) tenem'ts, 20x45, gravel roofs; cost, each, $3,300; ow'r and c'r, Edward Thompson; ar't, J. Thompson; m'n, R. Murphy.

2059—Barbey st, w s, 100 n Sutter av, one two-story frame dwell'g, 20x33, tin roof; cost, $2,000; J. R. Bergen, on premises; ar't, A. J. Warren; b'r, J. I. Neuman.

2060—Ashford st, e s, 123.7 n Atlantic av, one two-story frame carpenter shop and horse stable, 25x15, tin roof; cost, $250; ow'r and c'r, Louis Ilsemann, Fulton st, cor Cleveland st; ar't, L. F. Schillinger.

2061—Eastern Parkway, s e cor Christopher st, two three-story frame (brk filled) stores and tenem'ts, 25x55 and 72, tin roofs; cost, $11,500; Wolf Potashinski, Christopher st; ar'ts, D. Acker & Son.

2062—Moore st, No. 101, one four-story frame (brk filled) tailor shop, 25x30, tin roof; cost, $2,500; David Stern, 36 Seigel st; ar't, H. Smith.

2063—North 1st st, No. 121, one two-story brk stable, 25x18, gravel roof, brk cornice; cost, $500; Frank Joie, 121 North 1st st; b'r, H. Wild.

2064—Kingsland av, No. 64, e s, 75 s Bennett st, one one story brk stable, 17x18, tin roof, wooden cornice; cost, $100; Gustave Hesser, on premises; b'r, J. Hoppel.

2065—Lorimer st, w s, from Newtown to Bayard st, one one-story frame truck house, 200x275, gravel roof; cost, $55,000; Brooklyn Transportation Co., J. F. Bendernagle, treasurer; ar'ts, Thayer & Wallace.

2066—Morrell st, e s, 25 n Moore st, one three-story frame (brk filled) blacksmith shop, 25x45x 25x61.7, tin roof; cost, $4,000; ow'r and b'r, S. Hoh, 850 Bushwick av; ar't, W. B. Wills.

2067—Nichols av, w s, 225 s Etna st, four two-story frame dwell'gs, 18x28, shingle roofs; cost, $2,250 each; ow'r and c'r, Thos. E. Wills, 1847 Fulton st; ar't, C. M. Thompson; m'n, L. Dulcia.

2068—Troutman st, No. 389, one one-and-a-half-story frame stable, 13x19, tin roof; cost, $300; Nicholas Kerzner, on premises; ar'ts, D. Acker & Son.

2069—Lincoln av, e s, 200 s Adams st, two two-story frame dwell'gs, 21x26, shingle or tin roofs; cost, $2,200 each; ow'rs and c'rs, Wm. G. Osborn, Lincoln and Adams avs.

2070—Ainslie st, n s, 100 w Leonard st, one-story frame laundry, 25x43 and 46, gravel roof; cost, $475; John Lewis, 726A Quincy st; c'r, J. Brickhiner.

2071—Bushwick av, No. 267, one one-story frame (brk filled) tobacco storage and stable, 25x 60, tin roof; cost, $1,000; H. Berbert, Johnson av; ar'ts, D. Acker & Son.

2072—Bartlett st, No. 61, n s, 100 w Throop av, one two-story brk vinegar factory, 25x30, tin roof, wooden cornice; cost, $1,000; John Engeldrum, 61 Bartlett st; ar't, F. J. Berlenbach; b'r, not selected.

2073—South 9th st, No. 134, one two-story brk stable, 18x35, gravel roof, brk cornice; cost, $400; Doenecke & Bros., on premises.

ALTERATIONS NEW YORK CITY.

Plan 1901—14th st, No. 5 E., chimney to be built; cost, $150; J. B. Simpson, 12 West 129th st, b'rs, Jones & Co.

1902—161st st, No. 947 E., one-story frame extension, 11x14, tin roof; cost, $250; Herman Both, 947 East 161st st; ar't, John N. Decker.

1903—Gansevoort st, No. 6, interior alterations and walls altered; cost, $4,500; estate Erastus H. Muller, 21 West 126th st; ar'ts, French, Dixon & De Saldern.

1904—Beach, Varick, Hudson and Laight sts, St. Johns Park, walls altered; cost $150; N. Y. C. & H. R. R. R. Co., Grand Central Depot; ar't, W. Katte.

1905—Broadway, No. 749, interior alterations, &c.; cost, $1,500; S. Dessau, 4 and 6 John st; ar't, C. A. Donaban.

1906—Park st, No. 65, repair damage by fire; cost, $1,200; Daniel Sylvester, Flushing, L. I.; b'r, T. Ambrose.

1907—142d st, No. 545 E., walls altered; cost, $100; Edw. Gustaveson, 547 East 142d st.

1908—Goerck st, Nos. 75 and 77, walls altered; cost, $400; Sam'l Greenfeld, 105 Sheriff st; ar't, H. Horenburger.

1909—85th st, No. 518 E., two-story brk extension, 8x17, tin roof; cost, $100; Chas. J. G. Dressler; ar't and b'r, J. W. Smith.

1910—49th st, No. 447 W., repair verandah; cost, $20; Rose Leonard, on premises.

1911—Lenox av, No. 289, interior alterations; cost, $100; lessee, Charles Metzger; b'r, Chas. Hillert.

1912—26th st, No. 317 E., two-story brk extension, 25x34.8, tin roof, also interior alterations; cost, $500; Mrs. Jennie A. Potts, 317 East 26th st; ar't, Geo. Kerster.

1913—11th av, Nos. 202–208, walls altered; cost, $300; Behr Bros. & Co., 81 5th av; b'r, Automatic Sprinkler Co.

1914—1st av, No. 2329, one-story brk extension, 15.3x8, tin roof; cost, $600; Jas. P. Marren; ar't, A. Spence.

1915—Broadway, No. 1170, three new doors; cost, $30; John L. Malcher exr., 1160 Broadway; ar't, H. Simberlund; m'n, M. J. Harris.

1916—Greene st, Nos. 190 and 192, walls altered; cost, $300; agent, Edwin Oppenheim, 32 Thomas st; ar't, P. H. Murphy.

1917—Av C, No. 291, new show windows; cost, $700; John McWilliam exr., 219 West 33d st; c'rs, O'Connor & Sweeney.

1918—Beaver st, No. 37, one-story brk extension, 18.5x17.3, tin roof; cost, $500; Chas. Brown, agent, 59 Liberty st; ar't, M. Hutchinson.

1919—112th st, No. 130 E., repair damage by fire; cost, $600; A. S. de Jongh, 122 East 114th st; b'rs, Geaton & Glynn.

1920—Pond pl, e s, 200 n William st, Fordham, one-story frame extension, tin roof; cost $300; Jas. Wood, on premises; c'rs, Woodward & Jones.

1921—3d av, e s, 55 s 144th st, one-story frame extension, 12.9x12, tin roof; cost, $200; lessee, Adam Stein; ar't, E. Stichler.

1922—23d st, s w cor 7th av, interior alterations, walls altered; cost, $6,000; estate S. L. Bradley Stamford, Conn.; ar'ts, Brunner & Tryon.

1923—172d st, n s, 80 e Vanderbilt av, one-story frame extension, &c.; cost, $50; Henry F. Fischer, 1618 Vanderbilt av.

1924—Dover st, No. 10, interior alterations; cost, $100; lessee, Jas. H. Lavelle, 74 Market st; m'n, P. O'Keefe.

1925—59th st, No. 65 E., walls altered; cost, $530; Mary M. Stewart, 17 East 63d street; c'rs, Crokett & Weeks.

1926—Broadway, Nos. 1482 to 1490, s e cor 43d st, repair damage by fire; cost, $500; agents, Richards & Sause, 53 Liberty st; b'r, R. L. Walsh.

1927—26th st, No. 406 E., raise one story, &c.; cost, abt $800; C. H. Schultz, 440 1st av; ar't, L. T. Lourard; b'rs, R. L. Darragh & Co.

1928—13th st, No. 5 E., raise one story; also five-story brk extension, 19.9x8.9 and 4.5, tin roof; also interior alterations; cost $11,000; W. Jennings Demorest, 21 West 57th st; ar'ts, J. O. Bunce & Co.

1929—Pitt st, No. 7, new store front, &c.; cost, $380; agent, Minnie Bager, on premises; ar't, J. Wolf.

1930—Kingsbridge road, s w cor Boulevard, repair foundations; cost, $400; Bridget Nagle et al., 626 East 137th st; ar't, J. W. Davidson.

1931—170th st, n s, 274 e of 3d av, building to be moved; cost, $600; H. Zeltner, 1385 Fulton av; ar'ts, Lederle & Co.

1932—10th av, No. 23, interior alterations; cost, $50; lessees, Perrin Payson Co., on premises.

1933—South st, Nos. 63 and 64, raise one story, also interior alterations; cost, $7,500; Alfred C. King, 15 Wall st; ar't, J. Muuckwitz; b'r, J. C. Lyons.

1934—41st st, Nos. 506 and 508 W., one-story brk extension, 28x43, tin roof; cost, abt $800; Joe. Cabus, 343 West 30th st.

1935—93d st, s s, 100 w Av A, one-story brk extension, asphalt roof; cost, $8,000; Geo. Ehret, 92d st, bet 2d and 3d avs; ar't, J. Kastner; m'ns, J. & L. Weber.

1936—55th st, No. 8 E., one-story and basement iron extension, 7.6x10.7, tin roof; cost, $300; Sam'l Thorne, on premises; ar't, F. A. Rooke; m'n, R. Deeves.

1937—12th st, Nos. 349–353 W., raise one story, also three-story brk extension, 22x80, tin roof; cost, abt $30,000; estate Alfred L. Denis, 42 West 51st st; ar'ts, J. M. Macgregor & Son; contractor, J. D. Murphy.

1938—25th and 26th sts, 11th av North River—block, renew decayed posts, &c.; cost, $500; J. B. & J. M. Cornell, on premises; ar't, G. W. Debevoise.

1939—Henry st, No. 217, three-story and basement brk extension, 17.6x36.6 and 2; cost, $8,000, Louis Goodman, on premises; ar't, F. Ebeling.

1940—70th st, No. 163 E., walls altered, &c.; cost, $800; Regina Prosnitz, 1670 1st av; ar't, J. Hauser.

1941—11th st, Nos 206 and 208 E., walls altered, &c.; cost, $2,000; Mayor, &c., City Hall; ar't, C. B. J. Snyder.

1942—34th st, No. 363 W., raise one story, also five-story and basement brk extension, 13.1x20.6, tin roof; cost, $8,000; John J. Butler, on premises; ar't, M. V. B. Ferdon.

1943—43d st, No. 539 W., interior alterations, walls altered; cost, $1,500; Geo. Reichhard, on premises; ar'ts, J. Boekell & Sons.

KINGS COUNTY.

Plan 1058—Montague st, No. 130, three stories added to present extension, also a four-story brk extension, 8x5, alterations for stores and apartments; cost, $12,000; Henry Franke, Brooklyn av, cor St. Marks av; ar't, L. Cordes; b'r, not selected.

1059—Van Brunt st, No 302, one-story brk extension, 15.7x15, tin roof; cost, $250; Wm. G. Hoyt, 354 West 30th st, New York; ar't, H. Gilvary.

1060—Cook st, No. 187, raised 1.6 on brk foundation; cost, $800; Aaron Wishinsky, on premises; ar't, H. E. Funk.

1061—10th st, No. 252, one-story brk extension, 10x7.6, tin roof; cost, $200; ow'r and ar't, H. Hoffmann, on premises; m'ns, Burns & McCann; c'r, —— Howard.

1062—Palmetto st, No. 130, three-story frame extension, 25x17, tin roof; cost, $200; George Baker, on premises; ar't and b'r, T. Miller.

1063—Bartlett st, No. 27, brk wall under present foundation; cost, $300; H. Winter, Jr., 23 Bartlett st; m'n, W. Maske.

1064—Sackett st, No. 83, rebuld top story; cost, $300; Mary Burns, on premises; b'r, J. McGowan.

1065—Livingston st, No. 94, carried up to uniform height of three stories and one-story brk extension, 17 and 15x18, tin roof; cost, $6,000; Brooklyn Eye and Ear Hospital, on premises; ar't, J. Mumford; b'r, F. J. Ashfield.

1066—Hancock st, No. 476, raised 11 ft. on brk wall; cost, $250; J. N. O'Keefe, on premises.

1067—Withers st, No. 259, two-story frame extension, 9.9x16, tin roof; cost, $330; Mary Kelly, on premises; b'r, A. M. Utermark.

1068—Hoyt st, n e cor Dean st, one-story brk extension, 20x31, tin roof; cost, $400; Mrs. Schwarte, 319 Henry st; b'r, W. O'Donnell.

1069—Butler st, s s, 300 e Schenectady av, one-story frame extension, 13x24, tin roof; cost, $200; Michael O'Connell, on premises.

1070—Baltic st, No. 353, flat tin roof; cost, $400; Chris. Lee, on premises.

1071—South Elliott pl, No. 42, add one story, flat tin roof; cost, $500; F. C. Joslyn, 353 Myrtle av; b'rs, H. Konig and W. Mahler.

1072—Livingston st, No. 218, one-story and basement brk extension, 9x14, tin roof; cost, $500; Geo. Okley, on premises; b'r, J. De Mott.

1073—3d av, No. 474, raised 1.6 on brk wall; cost, $600; C. Lipari, 461 3d av; b'rs, T. Schoeneu and G. Wilders.

1074—Park av, n w cor Ryerson st, new store front; cost, $300; John Reis, Flatbush; ar't, A. J. Warren.

1075—Sandford st, No. 86, raised 2 feet on brk wall; cost, $215; Wm. P. McGrane, on premises; b'r, P. Moringstar.

1076—5th av, n w cor 2d st, one-story brk extension, 20x40, tin roof; cost, $300; Chas. Feltman, on premises; b'r, L. Bohlmann.

1077—Rockaway av, s w cor Herkimer st, one-story brk extension, 20x21, tin roof; cost, $250; H. Rourk, Nostrand, cor Putnam avs; ar't, R. Von Lehn.

1078—Bergen st, No. 1668, rebuild from foundation wall; cost, $35; Patrick Diamond, 1670 Bergen st.

MISCELLANEOUS.

BUSINESS FAILURES.

N. Y. ASSIGNMENTS—BENEFIT CREDITORS.

Nov.

6 Shantz, Mary C. (manufacturer of neckwear, at No. 831 Broadway), to William Angelo; preferences $5,281.12.

9 MacEvoy, Charles (manufacturer of glazed kid, at No. 14 Warren st), to E. B. Pond; without preferences.

10 Moskovitz, Ignatz (dealer in notions, hosiery and peddlers' supplies, at No. 257 2d st) to Jacob Vorhaus; preferences $860.

12 Bartlett, Thomas M. and Melbourn P. Smith (composing firm of F. H. Smith & Co., ship brokers and commission merchants, at Nos. 17 and 19 William st), to William W. Goodrich; without preferences.

12 Woolworth, James G. B. (dealer in milk, at No. 1667 Broadway), to Charles H. Daniels; without preferences.

KINGS COUNTY.

GENERAL ASSIGNMENTS.

Nov.

12 Bartlett, Thomas M—W W Goodrich.

12 Smith, Melbourne P—W W Goodrich.

PROCEEDINGS OF THE BOARD OF ALDERMEN AFFECTING REAL ESTATE.

* Under the different headings indicates that a resolution has been introduced and referred to the appropriate committee. † Indicates that the resolution has passed and has been sent to the Mayor for approval ‡ Passed over the Mayor's veto.

NEW YORK, Nov. 10, 1891.

LAMP-POSTS ERECTED AND LAMPS LIGHTED.

125th st, in front of No. 149 W., at expense of G. Stern.†

CROSSWALKS.

Greenwich st, in front of No. 198, at expense of Smith & McNell.†

28th st, in front of No. 32 W., at expense of John J. McGrath.†

MAINS.

d av, 12-in. iron pipe conducting steam from No. 1675, crossing av to 1676, at expense of Rhinelander estate.†

BROOKLYN BOARD OF ALDERMEN.

BROOKLYN, Nov. 9, 1891.

CULVERTS.

Cooper st, s e cor Central av.
Driggs st, s w cor Humboldt st.
Driggs st, n e cor North Henry st.
Driggs st, s w cor Russell st.
Schaeffer st, n w cor Evergreen av.
Schaeffer st, s w cor Evergreen av. †

FENCING VACANT LOTS.

Putnam av, n e cor Ralph av.†

FLAGGING.

Herkimer st, n s, bet Hopkinson and Rockaway avs.*
Kosciusko st, bet Stuyvesant and Lewis avs.
Putnam av, n e cor Ralph av. †

LAMP POSTS ERECTED AND LIGHTED.

Macon st, bet Ralph and Howard avs, at owners' expense.
Park pl, bet New York and Brooklyn avs.
43d st, bet 3d and 4th avs.
Evergreen av, bet Halsey and Eldert sts, at owners' expense. †

PAVING, GRADING, ETC.

Bergen st, bet Buffalo and Howard avs.
Guernsey st, bet Meserole and Driggs avs.
McDonough st, bet Saratoga av and Broadway. †
Pacific st, bet Ralph and Howard avs.*
Pacific st, bet Buffalo and Rochester avs, at owners' expense.
Richmond st, bet Fulton st and Jamaica av.
Suydam st, s s, 100 ft. e Hamburg av.
North 12th st, bet Bedford and Union avs.
Howard av, bet Atlantic and St. Marks avs.
New York av, bet Park pl and Parkway.
Ralph av, bet Atlantic and St. Marks avs.
6th av, bet 8th and 9th sts. †

STREET OPENING.

4th st, bet 7th and 8th avs.
Belmont av, bet Bradford st and Vermont av.
Miller av, bet Eastern Parkway and Atlantic av.
Ralph av, bet Fulton st and St. Marks av.
Vermont av, bet Belmont av and Eastern Parkway. †

ADVERTISED LEGAL SALES.

REFEREES SALES TO BE HELD AT THE REAL ESTATE EXCHANGE AND AUCTION ROOM (LIMITED), 59 TO 65 LIBERTY STREET, EXCEPT WHERE OTHERWISE STATED.

Nov.

57th st, No. 102, s s, 100 w 6th av, 15x100, four-story stone front dwell'g, also all right, title and interest to strip of land 5 inches in depth and 15 feet wide, adj rear of above, by P. F. Meyer. (Amt due $21,147) 16

Greene st, Nos. 37-43, w s, 65 n Grand st, 85x100, two six-story iron front stores, ½ part, by P. F. Meyer. (Amt due $63,343; leasehold) 17

96th st, No. 63, n s, 141 e 9th av, 21x100.11, four-story brk dwell'g, by R. V. Harnett & Co. 17

101st st / 102d st, begins 101st st, n s, 150 w West End av, runs west 100 x north 100.11 x east 75 x north 100.11 to 102d st, x east 25 x south 201.10 to beginning; No. 311 101st st, three-story brk dwell'g, rest vacant, by William Kennelly. (Amt due $7,977, sold Dec. 11, 1885, for $35,500) 17

136th st, s s, 256.6 e Alexander av, 37.6x100, by R. V. Harnett & Co. (Amt due $4,089) 17

Madison av s w cor 118th st, 100x60, one-story frame buildings, by B. L. Kennelly. (Amt due $17,189) 17

Av C, e s, 100 n 5th st, 100x100, 24th Ward, by T. A. Kerrigan 17

65th st, No. 332, s s, 331.3 e 2d av, 18.9x100, two-story brk dwell'g, by J. F. B. Smyth. (Partition sale) 18

82d st, No. 244, s s, 101.5 w 2d av, 19.3x102.2, three-story brk dwell'g, by D. P. Ingraham & Co. 18

Av D, Nos. 143 and 145, s w cor 10th st, 50x93, five-story brk cigarette factory
10th st, No. 444, s s, 93 w Av D, 25x92.3, four-story brk cigar factory
Interior lot, begins 72 s 10th st and 73 w Av D, runs west 20 x south 22 x east 20 x north 22
10th st, No. 442, s s, 118 w Av D, 21x92.3, four-story brk cigar factory with two-story brk building on rear
All right, title and interest to the following strips of land:
10th st, s s, 139 w Av D, 1.4x92.3
Interior strip, begins 92.3 s 10th st and 93 w Av D, runs south 1.9 x west 25 x north 1.9 x east 25,
by William Kennelly. (Amt due $33,282) 18

Columbus av, No. 934, s w cor 106th st, 25.11x75, five-story brk store and flat. Sub. to lease also to a mort. for $16,500
106th st, No. 68, s s, 100 e Columbus av, 25x100.11, four-story brk flat
106th st, No. 66, s s, 125 e Columbus av, 25x100.11, four-story brk flat; Nos. 66 and 68, sub. to mort. of $24,000
by D. P. Ingraham & Co. (Partition sale) 18

Stebbins av, s e s, 83.8 n e Freeman st, runs southeast 170 x north 169.2 x southwest 138.2 x northwest 125 to Stebbins av, x southwest 25 to beginning, all right, title and int which Wenzel Wavra has on April 8, 1891, by Sheriff, at City Hall. (Sale under execution) 18

8th av, No. 2609, s w cor 139th st, 19.11x75.4
8th av, Nos. 2605 and 2607, w s, 19.11 s 139th st, 40x75.4
8th av, Nos. 2601 and 2603, w s, 59.11 s 139th st, 40x75.4
8th av, Nos. 2597 and 2599, w s, 59.11 n 138th st, 40x75.4
8th av, Nos. 2593 and 2595, w s, 19.11 n 138th st, 40x75.4
8th av, No. 2591, n w cor 138th st, 19.11x75.4
Six five-story brk flats with stores
by P. F. Meyer. (Amt due on Nos. 2591 and 2609 $21,322 each, and $31,417 on each of others) 18

123d st, No. 447, n s, 138 w Av A, 17.1x100.11, three-story stone front dwell'g, by J. N. Golding. (Amt due $9,613) 19

41st st, No. 340, s s, 365 e 2d av, 16x98.9, four-story brk dwell'g, by J. F. B Smyth. (Amt due $6,892) 20

1st av, No. 2205, n w cor 113th st, 25x75, five-story brk store and tenem't with two-story brk stable on rear
1st av, No. 2207, w s, 25 n 113th st, 25x75, five-story brk store and tenem't
113th st, No. 355, n s, 75 w 1st av, 25x75, five-story brk tenem't
by A. H. Muller & Son. (Amt due on No. 2205 $17,596, $11,538 on No. 2207, and $9,504 on No. 355) 20

Broadway or Kingsbridge road, s e cor Macomb st, 48.6x100, by P. F. Meyer. (Amt due $6,969) 23

Cottage pl, e s, 258 n e 170th st, 57x127x56.3x127, by William Kennelly. (Amt due $3,515) 23

Oliver st, Nos. 100 and 102, e s, 55 n South st, 40x50, two two-story brk tenem'ts, store in No. 102, by R. V. Harnett. (Amt due $9,658) 23

KINGS COUNTY.

Nov.

Smith av, w s, 100 s Broadway, 100x100, Flatbush, by T. A. Kerrigan, at 13 Willoughby st 16

Schermerhorn st, n s, 150 w 3d av, 160x100.9x160x101.9, vacant; assessed value, $22,000; by T. A. Kerrigan, at 13 Willoughby st 17

Gold st, No. 334, w s, 100 n Myrtle av, 25x100.3, three-story brk dwell'g; assessed value, $3,900.
7th av, s e s, extends from 1st to 2d sts, 200x97.10½
Six four-story double brk flats and two five-story brk flats with stores on corners unfinished; assessed value, $25,000
Lot at Gravesend, begins at Atlantic Ocean at division line bet old lots 23 and 24 on one side and old lots 20 and 21 on the other side, as shown on Kowolski's map of common lands of Gravesend, Coney Island, runs north — x west — x south to ocean, x east to beginning, except strip 40 ft. wide condemned for use of New York & Coney Island R. R. Co., and part lying south of centre of Surf av; partition
by T. A. Kerrigan, at 13 Willoughby st. 18

President st, No. 185, n s, 121 e Henry st, 14.6x100, three-story brk dwell'g; assessed value, $5,000., by T. A. Kerrigan, at 13 Willoughby st. 19

Bergen st, n s, 200 w Kingston av, 100x114.5, five three-story brk dwell'gs; assessed value, $25,000; by T. A. Kerrigan, at 13 Willoughby st 20

Macon st, s s, 93.6 w Howard av, 107.6x100, six two-story brk dwell'gs, by Isaac Lublin, ref., at County Court House 20

Pulaski st, Nos. 274-280, s s, 530.2 e Throop av, 101.10x100
Van Voorhis st, n w s, 100 s w Evergreen av, 17x100
Van Voorhis st, n w s, 117 s w Evergreen av, 17x100
Van Voorhis st, n w s, 134 s w Evergreen av, runs northwest 100 x southwest 16 x southeast 51.9 x southwest 1 x southeast 48.1¾ to Van Voorhis st, x northwest 17 to beginning, unfinished frame dwell'gs; assessed value, $2,000 each
Van Voorhis st, n w s, 253 s w Evergreen av, 17x100, two-story frame (brk lined) dwell'g; assessed value, $3,000
by T. A. Kerrigan, at 13 Willoughby st. 23

Columbia st, No. 433, e s, 60 n West 9th st, 20x83.6, three-story frame dwell'g; assessed value, $1 00; by J. Cole, at 389 Fulton st 23

LIS PENDENS, KINGS COUNTY.

Nov.

Clinton st, centre line, n w s, 170 s w Bryant st, runs northwest 358 to centre Henry st slip, x southwest 1,241.3 to pier or bulkhead line Gowanus Bay Channel (if extended), x northeast 464.1 x northeast 945.10. Jeremiah P. Robinson et al exrs. Jeremiah P. Robinson agt Mary W. Poillon; amended notice; att'ys, Sullivan & Cromwell 6

5th av, n w s, 103.9 n e 32d st, 20.9x100. August Erey agt Samuel E. Thomas; att'y, E. T. Payne. 6

4th av, n w cor 7th st, 50x60
7th st, n e s, 160 n w 4th av, 38.7x100
7th st, n e s, 217.10 n w 4th av, 77.1x100
John S. Lee agt Charles H. Collins; att'y, Brewster Kissam 6

Lot 289 block 10 map 526 lots of Thomas J. Cummins, South Bensonhurst; att'ys, Richards & Brown 6

Gates av, n w s, 300 n e Central av, 25x108.9x25.1x107. Christopher W. Wilson agt William J. Cook; att'ys, Jackson & Burr 6

Gates av, s e s, 450 n e Central av, 25x115.6x24.9x121.7. Same agt same; same att'y 6

Degraw st, s s, 430 w Franklin av, 20x131x20x130. Agnes L. Yenni admrx. Edmund Yenni agt Henry F. Clark; notice of attachment; att'y, George B. Gough 7

McDonough st, s s, 175.5 e Sumner av, 99.7x100. Henry Wise agt Michael Rofrano; action to set aside deed; att'y, Jacob Manheim 7

Sumpter st, s s, 100 w Stone av, 90x100. Cordelia E. Macpherson extrx. Gardner G. Yvelin agt John Roesel; att'ys, Boardman & Boardman 7

Boerum st, No. 155, n s, 25x100. Elizabeth Fruh agt Samuel Pilcer; att'y, Fernando Solinger 9

Bergen st, s w s, 125 s e Nevins st, 25x100. James Wynne agt James Daken; partition; att'ys, Rolfe & Snedeker 9

Henry av, w s, 100 n Bay av, 50x100. Simon Rapalje and ano. exrs. Henry L. Rapalje agt William M. Miller; att'ys, Rolfe & Snedeker 9

York st, s s, 50 e Hudson av, 25x100. John Fitzpatrick agt Jane Fitzpatrick et al.; partition; att'y, Daniel B. Thompson 9

Moore st, No. 128, s s, 125 e Humboldt st, 25x100. Margaretha Ohlschlager agt Frank Ohlschlager; action for dower; att'y, Max Brill 9

Herkimer st, s s, 74 w Rochester av, 23x94. Dorothea Geier agt Louisa Sieboldt; action for dower; att'y, August P. Wagener 9

Nassau st, s s, 25 w Stanton st, 25x87. Sarah E. Stewart agt Horatio S. Stewart; partition; att'y, Wm. Sullivan 9

Warren st, n e s, 145.4 n w Court st, 20.9x62.6. Union Central Life Ins. Co. agt Tecumseh Pierce; action to set aside deed; att'y, E. De L. Smith 9

2d st, s s, 300 w Hoyt st, 20x90
2d st, s s, 340 w Hoyt st, 20x90
Alice M. Dexter agt Bertrand Clover; att'ys, Brown & Dexter 10

2d st, n s, 180.2 e Smith st, 15.6x90.6
Hoyt st, w s, 29.6 s Sackett st, 15x75
Hoyt st, w s, 74.6 s Sackett st, 15x75
Same agt same; same att'y 10

Sackett st, s s, 258.4 w Hoyt st, 16.8x90. Peter Donald agt Bertrand Clover; att'ys, Stitt & Phillips 10

Atlantic av, n s, 275 e Bond st, 25x100. Catharine L. Gilfillan agt Teresa Ennis; att'y, Stephen Condit 10

Dean st, s s, 200 e Nostrand av, 16.8x114.5. John W. Cornwell agt John C. Austin; att'y, Charles R. Halsey 10

Van Sicklen av, w s, 150 n Glenmore av, 25x100. Linda S. Roberts agt Michael Breen; att'ys, Thornton, Earle & Kiendl 10

Main road from Flatbush to New Lots, s s, adj land John H. Lott, 18 acres, Flatbush. George M. Williamson agt Elizabeth Binns; partition; att'ys, Thornton, Earle & Kiendl 10

Garfield pl, n s, 90 w 7th av, 30x100
Garfield pl, n s, 120 w 7th av, 30x100
Garfield pl, n s, 150 w 7th av, 30x100
Garfield pl, n s, 180 w 7th av, 30x100
Garfield pl, n s, 210 w 7th av, 30x100
Brooklyn Trust Co. agt John H. Styles; att'ys, Bergen & Dykman 10

7th av, w s, 50 s Lincoln pl, 100x110. William Post committee John Rogers agt Francis M. Faircloth; att'y, John J. Leary 10

Chapel st, s s, 250 e Jay st, 50x100. Stephen G. Parker agt Ann O'Connor; att'y, Asa W. Parker 11

5th av, e s, 20 s 13th st, 28x17.10. Jacob Steinert agt Joseph Thompson; att'y, Jacob Steinert in person 11

Snediker av. w s, 215 n Liberty av. 20x100. Joseph Seitz agt Peter Clark; att'y, John M. Stearns.... 11
Patchen av, n e cor Putnam av, 20x100. Canda & Kane agt Thomas Walling; att'y, J. Woolsey Shepard.... 12
9th st, s s, 150 w 8th av, 18.10x72.6....
9th st, s s, 218.1 w 8th av, 20.5x72.6x20.4x72.6....
9th st, s s, 277.6 w 8th av, 18.10x72.6....
9th st, s s, 335.4 w 8th av, 40.3x82.6....
9th st, s s, 415.8 w 8th av, 40.6x82.6x40.5x82.6....
Asa W. Parker agt John Moore; att'y, A. W. Parker in person.... 12

RECORDED LEASES.

NEW YORK. Per Year

Bloomfield st, No. 9, store and cellar. John Glass to Armour & Co., Chicago, Ill.; 10 yrs, from Nov. 1, 1891.... $2,500
Cherry st, Nos. 187 and 189 / Water st, Nos. 452 and 454, 50x120, all. Peter and Nicholas P. Young to Wm. H. H. Roberts, Orange, N. J.; 10½ years, from Jan. 1, 1889.... 5,000
Delancey st, Nos. 227 and 229, s w cor Willett st, all. Maria Halsey widow, Hanover, N. J., and Edmund D. Halsey and ano. exrs. Annie O. Hunter to Patrick Ruddy, Brooklyn; 5 years, from May 1, 1891.... 1,650
Hudson st, No. 50. Otto Frohlrott to Frederick Herrmann; 2¼ years, from Nov. 1, 1891. 540, 600
Lewis st, No. 233, all. Joseph McPhee to John Wilshaw; 3½ years, from Nov. 1, 1891.... 300
Mulberry st, No. 43, store. Nicola Laino to Giaccomo Pescherino; 3 years, from Jan. 10, 1891.... 288
Mulberry st, No. 78, all. Pompeo Mazzeo to Filomena Caracciolo; 1 year, from Dec. 1, 1891.... 1,440
Oliver st, No. 31. Hannah E. Keefe to Jeremiah Cronin; 5 5-12 years, from Dec. 1, 1891.. 1,000
Warren st, No. 108, n w cor Washington st. A. V. W. Van Vechten to George W. Seigfried; 5 years, from May 1, 1892.... 3,000
4th st, No. 165 E., store floor and rear part of basement. Marie Gunther to Max Quehl; 3 years, from Nov. 9, 1891.... 660
5th st, n s, lots 132 and 134 map Stephen Whitney. The United States Trust Co. trustee Stephen Whitney to George H. Miller; 5 years, from Nov. 1, 1891.... gold, 2,000
14th st, No. 113 E., store floor in basement. Jacob Balz to Fannie Warendorff; 2 years, from May 1, 1891.... 1,500
23d st, No. 470, s e cor 10th av, abt 24x abt 55. Jacob Appell to Thomas Roberts and Ann his wife; 7¾ years, from Aug. 1, 1891.... 3,400, 3,500, 4,000, 4,500
23d st, No. 449 W., all. Martha M. Smith to Amelia C. Tice; 3 years, from May 1, 1891... 1,100
98th st, n s, 375 w 8th av, 25x100.11, all. John Townshend to Valentine Wille; 10 years, from Nov. 1, 1891, taxes, &c., and.... 150
Av A, No. 1563, store floor and basement and second floor. Henry Ganzenmuller to John H. Ludemann; 5 years, from Sept. 1, 1891... 1,416
Columbus av, s e cor 75th st, corner store and basement. John P. Ryan to Fred. F. Kiefendorf; 10 years, from May 1, 1891.... 1,500, 1,600, 2,000, 2,200
Jerome av, w s, abt 600 s Gerard av, 26.8x100. Mary Scully to Andrew Schiffer; 7 years, from Dec. 1, 1891.... 450, 480
Lexington av, n e cor 109th st, store and part cellar. William Lyman to The J. Christian G. Hupfel Brewing Co.; 5 years, from Nov. 1, 1891.... 1,600
Lexington av, No. 730. Adrienne Pitzipio to Sarah B. and Mary C. Keegan; 3½ years, from Nov. 1, 1891.... 1,800
Madison av, s w cor 106th st, store and part cellar. Carsten H. Bohlen to Dora Ze Waltoff; 10½ years, from Jan. 1, 1892.... 900 to 2,000
St. Nicholas av, No. 220, cor 121st st, store. Martin A. Furchtenicht and Friedrick Ernst to George W. Augenmeyer; 7 years, from May 1, 1891.... 960, 1,080, 1,200
2d av, No. 1407, cellar, basement, store, hall and second floor. Katharine Becker to Henry Voigt; 5 years, from Nov. 1, 1891.... 1,800
3d av, No. 119, store and front basement. Ferdinand Ehrhart to George Feldhusen; 5 years, from Aug. 15, 1891.... 1,800
3d av, No. 282 / 25d st, Nos. 157 and 159, all. Eleanor C. Childs to Diedrich Plumb; 5 years, from May 1, 1892.... 3,240
3d av, No. 679, all. Harlan P. Smith to The J. Chr. G. Hupfel Brewing Co.; 4½ years, from Nov. 1, 1891.... 3,204, 3,600
6th av, No. 427. Jacob and William Scholle to Peter Beckmann; 2 years, from May 1, 1891.. 3,650
7th av, No. 2174, s w cor 129th st, store and part cellar. La Fora S. Baker to John J. Fay; 5 years, from May 1, 1891.... 1,000, 1,200
8th av, No. 878, all. Harlan P. Smith to John A. Woolson; 3 years, from May 1, 1890.... 1,900
8th av, No. 519, store and basement. Thomas F. Golding to Sallie Nichthauser; 7 years, from May 1, 1891.... 1,800
Same property. Assign. lease. Sallie Nichthauser to Sigmund Nichthauser. (Nov. 7).. nom
10th av, No. 749, store floor, second floor and part cellar. George Roschlau to Christian Bambach; 5 years, from May 1, 1892.... 1,800

CHATTELS.

NOTE.—The first name, alphabetically arranged, is that of the Mortgagor, or party who gives the Mortgage. The "R" means Renewal Mortgage.

NEW YORK CITY.

November 6 to 12.—Inclusive.

SALOON AND RESTAURANT FIXTURES.

Bligh, R W. 1551 3d av....Bernheimer & S. $2,000
Same. 477 Amsterdam av....same. 4,000
Brady, John. 2339 8th av....Bernheimer & S. (R) security
Bauer, Louis. South Beach....E Blaese. (R) 300
Bernstein, Morris. 226 Broome....D Mayer. 80
Beckmann, Peter. 427 6th av....F Rettig. 3,275
Beckmann, Peter. 427 6th av....Bernheimer & S. 1,578
Brecht, Felix. 197 E 4th....G Bechtel, exr of. (R) 700
Bambach, Christian. 749 10th av....C Steine 3,500
Boehmer, Rudolph. 120 and 122 Canal....Bernheimer & S. (R) 8,500
Coakley, Frank. 911 6th av....H H Heert & Co. 258
Coari, Louis. 359 and 361 W 59th....Acker, M & C. Restaurant Fixtures. (R) 4,610
Connor & McMahon. 724 2d av....J Kress B Co. (R) 3,713
Connor & Riffinburg. 755 3d av....H Clausen & Son B Co. (R) 1,000
Collington, Joe. 658 Washington ...Beadleston & W. Ice Box 100
Concannon, Thomas. 139th st and Morris av....D Stevenson. 1,000
Cordts, Emma. 1530 Av A Bernheimer & S. 2,500
Cahill, L M. 1635 3d av....J Doelger's Son. (R) 1,881
Carlo, Frank. 141 Mott....Bernheimer & S. Pool Table. 140
Coleman, John. 287 Av B....P Schaefer & Son. (R) 158
Cooney, Frank. 815 9th av....Bernheimer & S. 1,600
Duesing, L W. 98 Warren....Bernheimer & S. (R) 4,000
Dieterich, G M. 305 E 9th....Bernheimer & S. Ice House. 85
Same ...same. Ice House. 60
Dorsey, Mary A. 434 3d av... C Stein. 1,100
Diekmann, Frank. 2737 8th av....Bernheimer & S. 800
Di Palma & De Simone. 337 E 11th....Bernheimer & S. (R) 400
Dubin, Elias. 34 Canal....I Greenbaum, Restaurant Fixtures. 205
Dwyer, Michael. 29 Jones....W C Schewing. 150
Eames, G A. 2 White and 119 West Broadway ....H J Rottman. 6,000
Engenhoefer, Henry. 654 9th av....Bernheimer & S. Saloon Ice House. 100
Same....same. Saloon Pump. 94
Same....same. Saloon Ice House. 60
Ehler, H F. 322 Greenwich....P Doelger. (R) 1,000
Ehmann, Jacob. 113 Orchard....F Munch. (R) 300
Farrell, J H. 635 Hudson....P McQuade. (R) 1,189
Foley Bros. 115 Amsterdam av....D Stevenson. 2,750
Same. 74th st and 2d av....same. 4,000
Fox, Elizabeth. 99th st and 1st av....Mutual B Co. 800
Freund, Adolph. 178th st and 3d av....Brunswick-B-C Co. Pool Table. 200
Fidebogen & Jacobson. 48 Ludlow....E Ochs. Restaurant Fixtures. 150
Farrell, J J. 550 E 16th....V Loewers. (R) 389
Fitzpatrick, Peter. 527 W 28th....M Groh's Sons. 150
Grunniger, J. 73 E 4th .. Brunswick-B-C Co. Pool Table. 400
Gearon, Michael. 132d st and 7th av....G Ehret. (R) 7,500
Geier, Franz. 322 E 20th....M Seitz. 700
Goldstein, Jacob. 134 Eldridge....F Munch, exr of. (R) 400
Glas, Louis. 763 10th av....C Stein. (R) 3,000
Gottlieb, Fred. 383 E 4th....Budweiser B Co. (R) 1 400
Haas, Friedrich. 815 E 53d....W H Griffith & Co. Pool. 175
Haggerty, F F. 276 Grand....S Weil. Restaurant Fixtures. 400
Heller, Jacob. 63 Ridge....B Cohn. 170
Hochstetter, Rose. 118 Eldridge...P Schaefer & Son. (R) 150
Houghton, Nicholas. 3d av and 130th st... D G Yuengling, Jr, B Co. 8,600
Hagan, William. 134 W 19th....P Hagan. 300
Helmke, John. 969 3d av....D Stevenson. 272
Hermann, Frank. 152 W 28th....Bernheimer & S. Ice House. 40
Herdling, G P. Water, Pearl and Fulton sts....C Ottmann. Hotel Fixtures. (R) 14,000
Hofreiter & Ludwig. 1111 1st av....H Koehler & Co. 1,300
Helmke & Tienken. 969 3d av....A Finck & Son. 4,500
Johnson, Lena. 185 Chrystie....W Peter B Co. 686
Jaenicke, William. 159 E 72d....D Mayer. (R) 400
Jung, Gottlieb. 1144 1st av....Bernheimer & S. 3,000
Jones & Duffy. 22 8th av....N L North. 2,000
Jude, Frederick. 424 E 9th....J Eichler B Co. (R) 800
Kohn, Herman. 67 E 4th....C Kohn. Restaurant Fixtures. 600
King, William. 1861 3d av....D Stevenson. 1,700
Kleinschroth, Friedrich. 276 Delancey....J & M Haffen. 700
Klem, Adolph. 284 East Houston... J & F Toch. Restaurant Fixtures. 400
Klein, Joseph. 328 6th....G Ringler & Co. (R) 400
Kraemer, Adolph. 107 Sullivan....Bernheimer & S. (R) 400
Same....same. Pool. (R) 115
Kubasch, Alwin. 341 W 47th....G Ehret. (R) 3,000
Kurrus, Theodore. 122 Broome....P Schaefer & Son. (R) 200
Lawrence, J H. 769 10th av... Bernheimer & S. (R) 1,800
Levy, Jacob. 105 Division....D Stevenson. 450
Ludemann, J H. 1563 Av A. ..G Ringler & Co. (R) 800
Liebel, Nicholaus. 139 Rivington....F Oppermann, Jr. (R) 900
Lengemann & Schwaerzler. 323 W 41st....H Zeltner. 1,000
McAnally, John. 246 9th av... Howard & Childs. 1,866
Montagnon, Antonie. 123 W 26th....G Ringler & Co. 700
Moore, W J. 21 Ann .. T Bishop. 2,250
Maglio, Ginseppe. 102 Mott....J Wallace & Son. 300
Mariano, John. 84 Sullivan....Bavarian B Co. 300
Same. 62 Thompson....same. 500
Same. 160 W 4th....same. 1,000
Mauer, P C and G H. 2223 8th av....J Kress B Co. (R) 636
Mayers, Mark. 2400 3d av....Bernheimer & S. Saloon Pump. 119
Same....same. Saloon Ice House. 200
McGarry, Patrick. 570 1st av....V Loewers. 500
McDermott, Francis. 275 Av B....D Stevenson. 2,488
Meenan & McCarroll. 384 10th av....D Stevenson. (R) 2,000
Murphy, Jeremiah. 1741 Lexington av....J C G Hupfel B Co. 3,000
Maling, Philip. 1205 10th av....Bernheimer & S. (R) 3,000
Meperschmitt, Gustav. 246 1st av ...C Stein. (R) 700
Michels, N and T. 276 7th av....C Stein. 800
Moriarty, T M. 139 E 123d ...J Kress B Co. 2,700
Morosa, Amsel. 184 East Broadway ..Wagner & S. Pool. 175
Muger & Co. 630 8th av....Wagner & S. Pool. 160
Mullen, James. 242 W 33d....P Doelger. (R) 700
Murphy, Dennis. 329 W 17th... V Loewers. 600
Mutz, Eland R. 211 E 4th....J H Bereuter. Pool Table. 130
Nolan, William. 964 1st av....H Elias B Co. 1,500
Nickinig & Herrmann. 159 W 28th....Bernheimer & S. Ice House. 75
Same .. same. Pump. 75
Nolan, Michael. 532 W 43d....D Stevenson. 300
O'Brien, Robert. 161st st and Sedgwick av....G Schwenk. 899
O'Brien, William. 314 Front....D Stevenson. 900
O'Neill, Patrick. 612 6th av....Beadleston & W. (R) 6,000
Same. 200 W 42d... same. (R) 6,000
O'Brien, Lawrence. 1671 Av A....Bernheimer & S. (R) 1,500
Pfetzing, Kadie. 98th st and 10th av....Bernheimer & S. (R) 100
Poellet, Mary. 262 1st av....Ferger B & K Bavarian B Co. 300
Quehl, Max. 165 E 4th....G Ehret. 1,750
Riffs, Israel. 85 Rivington....F Melzer. Pool Fixtures. 190
Roberts, Thomas. 470 W 23d....G Ringler & Co. 6,000
Reilly, Lawrence. 1138 9th av....Bernheimer & S. (R) 2,500
Richter, Neurohr & Kasper. 5½ Pine ...W K Aston. (R) 5,000
Robertson, Alexander. 407 2d....F H Ross. Pool, &c. 100
Reeber, Frank, 145 Prince....E S Schroeder. 1,000
Reeh, William. 155 Alexander av....J Ruppert. 2,500
Richard, Jean. 668 8th av....Wagner & S. Pool Table. 380
Salzman, Israel. 146 Rivington....H B Scharman. 1,000
Schmidt, Ernst. 418 W 38th....J Kuntz B Co. (R) 300
Schmitz, Chas. 747 9th av ...C Stein. (R) 950
Schneider, John. 97 Orchard....P Schaefer & Son. (R) 129
Sheehan, James. 507 W 48d....F & M Schaefer B Co. 500
Smith & Nies. 177 Broome....Budweiser B Co. (R) 850
Stand, Adolph. 1978 3d av....Bernheimer & S. (R) 400
Schmidt, W J. 537 and 539 Hudson... W Kohring. 8,000
Schlagel, Mary. 1925 Main st, West Farms. .. J Eichler B Co. 417
Schroeder, William. 1855 Columbus av....C Stein. (R) 1,629
Schulte & Buell. 105 Broad....Bernheimer & S. (R) 1,400
Schroder, F E. 1618 3d av....J Ruppert. 3,000
Stahl, Louis. 55 Lispenard and 308 Canal....G Ringler & Co. (R) 900
Stanislaw, Dominick. 1901 Washington av... J Eichler B Co. 500
Steiner, Phil. 1618 Av B....G Ringler & Co. (R) 500
Sojnson & Johnson. 637 2d av....A Finck & Son. 175
Schambach, John, 136 East Houston . G Ringler & Co. (R) 500
Schwartz, Ignatz. 431 Broome....Restaurant Furniture Co. Restaurant Fixtures. 110
Spellman, Mary. 728 E 12th....Bernheimer & S. 500
Tallowitz, Franz. 117 1st av....H Roberts. Restaurant Fixtures. 100
Tobin & Featherston. 1285 1st av....J Everard. 4,075
Tennant, G H. 237 Sullivan... Consumers B Co. 940
Timm, William. 28 Cedar....G Ringler & Co. 715
Unger, Samuel. 164 Attorney....D Gross. (R) 200
Voege & Wiegand. 74 West Broadway....Beadleston & W. 2,700
Same... E M Meyer. 1,500
Voigt, H F C F. 1407 2d av....G Ehret. 2,000
Wendelken, J F. 872 11th av....Williamsburgh B Co. Ice Box. 60
Will, Peter. 56 Goerck ...P Schaefer & Son. (R) 200
Winant, G W. 2233 3d av....J R Winant. Restaurant Fixtures. 1,000
Van Bremen, D. 96 E 120th....A Hupfel's Son. 500
Werner, Herman. 27 Delancey....R Schuddekopf. 100
Weickert, Charles. 402 E 11th M Groh's Sons. 500
Welden, Lizzie V. 988 2d av....J Kress B Co. (R) 347
Xiques, Julian. 292 Bowery....Wagner & S. Pool Table. 465
Zemar, Louis. 1489 Broadway ...F Carrard. Restaurant Fixtures, &c. 475

HOUSEHOLD FURNITURE.

Adams, Ida. 227 W 40th....O'Farrall & Co. 259
Allen, Anna. 244 E 39th....O'Farrell & Co. 687
Anderson, Elsie. 6 W 136th....Jordan & M. 127
Anderson, R G. 167 E 77th. ..W Battermann. (R) 166
Ayers, Mary A. 225 W 40th....J Baumann. (R) 103
Barnes, Alberta. 166 W 125th....J Baumann. (R) 143
Blatchley, Lizzie. 118 Perry....Manges Bros. 116
Bradford, May. 181 W 63d... O'Farrell & Co. 114
Buddington, Marion F. 226 E 100th....H Thoesen. 185
Bradley, F H. 160 E 48th....Manges Bros. 346
Bidwell, C P. 285 W 76th....S Baumann. 168
Bordel, Germain. 107 W 25th....E F Manduit. (R) 1,000
Burke, Cora. 326 W 37th....O'Farrell & Co. 192
Bancker, Maria A. 129 E 62d....A Fowler. Paintings. (R) 1,888
Beck, H F. 533 E 15th....Jordan & M. 151
Brandon, Alex. 1271 Lexington av .... K I Brandon. (R) 1,000
Brennen, Theresa. 158 Park pl....Krakauer Bros. Piano. 300
Brock, Edwd. 439 W 28th ...Alexander Bros. 208
Bulkley, Mary. 237 W 48th....L Baumann. 215
Bush, S P. 14 Sylvan pl (W 161st st)....Lincoln I and G Assoc. 102
Caird, Mrs Alex. 304 Pleasant av....Krakauer Bros. Piano. (R) 180
Cohn, H. 2096 3d av....F G Smith. Piano. (R) 185
Coleman, C M. 155 W 84th....T Leonard. 346
Conlon, Mary. 324 W 25th....Alexander Bros. 106
Caldwell, Mrs. 231 Willis av ...J Moriarty. (R) 176
Canning, Fannie. 115 W 71st....Jordan & M. (R) 114
Carleton, Dollie. 49 E 106th....J Early. 173
Carr, Alice. 349 W 49th....J G egg. (R) 197
Carson, Kittie. 142 W 28th....J Moriarty. 231
Chaves, L M. 130 W 44th... J Gregg. (R) 268
Clark, Hattie M. 256 W 38th....S Baumann. 180
Clifford, Mamie. 265 W 34th....J Early. 295
Canfield, Hattie. 143 W 63d....Manges Bros. 180
Carberry, Mrs Pat. 84 Ridge....D M Brown. 122
Clark, E H. 147 Park row....H Israel & Sons. 249
Cosgrove, Daniel. 51 Leroy....H Israel & Sons. 162
Crimmons, T M. 425 E 7th ...D M Brown. 283
Cummings, Helen P. 206 W 23d....A Ballin. 218
Chester, Bessie. 988 6th av....Garvey Bros. 157
Coakley, Mary. 113 W 53d ...J Baumann. (R) 141

Conger, S D. 288 W 126th....J Moriarty. 198
Conkling, J F. 133 W 82d....J Baumann. (R) 114
Courtney, Estelle. 211 E 14th....Garvey Bros. 429
de Casso, Delores. 251 W 89th....J Baumann. (R) 221
do Kay, Mrs Chas. 103 E 15th....F G Smith. Piano. (R) 270
Delahy, Arthur. 1815 Lexington av ...A Heinzer. Piano. 100
Dunn, Winnie. 425 W 48th ...O'Farrell & Co. 155
Damaloville, L A. 51 W 26th. .E Natte. 600
Davis, Mrs L A. 361 W 36th....A Ballin. 180
Diehl, C. 642 E 13th....H Israel & Sons. 153
Diming, Mrs L. 260 W 122d....T Kelly. (R) 100
Donegan, Sarah. 1177 3d av....R M Walters. Piano. (R) 145
Deslauners, A E. 47 Greenwich av.... J Early. 270
Deves, Mary. 121 W 60th....Jordan & M. 172
Douglass, A & B. 158 W 53d....S Baumann. 4,628
Dannenberg, Emilie. 2490 2d av....L Baumann. 124
Dedeuck, C H. 2013 5th av .. L Baumann. 279
Delaney, Mrs S. 252 E 125th....Alexander Bros 160
De Lavalette, A E. 26 W 34th....Brooklyn F Co. 966
de Rougemont, A. 163 W 34th....F G Smith. Piano. (R) 285
Duke, Mary. 156 Perry....L Baumann. 120
Dunham, Ione A. 344 W 51st....A Gillies. 388
English, E H and M E. 171 E 33d....P S De Vries. 184
Etkin, Louis. 962 Cherry....L Baumann. 248
Epstein, P & J. 2549 8th av ...S Wohl. 240
Enderly, C E. 216 W 17th....C E Wood. 350
Earle, Mrs Wm. 159 W 23d....H Thoesen. 168
Ebeling, Henry. 4 Gouverneur....J Moriarty. 187
Estelle, G B. 237 W 38th....A Ballin. 224
Foster, Jennie. 101 W 101st.... T Kelly. (R) 188
Follard, Jno. 158 W 26th....F G Smith. Piano. (R) 150
Fowles, Lucy. 18 W 22d ...J P Delehanty. 120
Frazer, John. 1699 Madison av....J Baumann. (R) 138
Fanoni, Nicodemo. 173 West Houston ...C R Ruegger. 108
Ferguson, Mary. 343 W 24th....S Baumann. 190
Finkelmeier, Mary G. 110 W 44th....S Baumann. 175
Faulkner, Mary. 164 E 68th .. J Moriarty. 193
Fitzgerald, Mary. 542 10th av ...L Baumann. 215
Fitzsimoons, Mrs. 22 Watts....J S Rice. 117
Foley, Annie. 219 E 40th....L Baumann. 184
Friedman, Sadie. 234 W 51st....T Kelly. (R) 129
Gardner, F E. Gloucester, N J....O'Farrell & Co. 297
Goldstein, Gerson. 185 E 108th....H Stern. 150
Gray, C P. 310 W 134th....F G Smith. Piano. (R) 275
Gatjen, Dietrich. Storage....I C Northshield. 268
Gault, Mary. 14 W 94th....J Early. 1,661
Gavin, William. 21 W 3 th. . S Baumann. 218
Gee, Fong. 12 Pell....Jordan & M. 125
Galloway, Mrs J T. 28th st and 8th av....O'Farrell & Co. (R) 108
Garhart, R C and Lilla V. 265 W 85th....L Hinsdale. 1,000
Glover, Ida. 145 W 41st ...J Baumann. (R) 326
Grey, Belle. 241 W 40th....Manges Bros. 145
Grossman, V and C. 57 Mott....S I Herschmann. 152
Hardy, John. 223 E 32d....D M Brown. 177
Hannaford, Sarah. 157 E 57th....W J Gottlieb. 1,000
Herrick, Nellie K. 65 W 95th....T Kelly. (R) 230
Houston, Maria. 216 W 15th....J Gregg & Co. 132
Howard, Bertha J. 361 W 36th....A Ballin. 140
Hartwell, L F. 81 E 114th ...R M Walters. Piano. (R) 197
Hill, Anna. 158 W 120th....J Gregg. 217
Hipkins, Alice E. 134 E 28th... Krakauer Bros. Piano. (R) 113
Holmes, Mary. 941 6th av....J Moriarty. 1,497
Hopkins, P H. 217 W 38th J Baumann. (R) 934
Hart, Catharine. 236 W 42d....Jordan & M. (R) 340
Hill, Harriet ...J Moriarty. 252
Houlroyd, Jane E B. 2079 Washington av....J Roduy, exr of. 100
Haggin, Mrs J B. 7 E 3d....J Moriarty. 125
Halloran, Thomas. 191 1st av....J Moriarty. 131
Harris, Annie. 345 E 20th....L Baumann. 148
Harrison, Nellie. 18 W 24th.. .S Knapp & Co. 8,804
Hauerman, Marcus. 191 Madison....Alexander Bros. 144
Haughworst, J H. 306 W 113th... T Kelly. (R) 179
Hegarty, Mary. 309 W 21st....Alexander Bros. 108
Herbert, M L. 105 W 95th....L Baumann. 148
Hering, Lillie. 714 Washington....F G Smith. Piano. (R) 340
Heusel, Caroline. 321 W 33d....Brooklyn F Co. (R) 100
Hirchey, P J and M C. 1478 Lexington av....A V Smith. 140
Hunter, Josephine. 102 W 4th....Fennell & Pye. 101
Hyde, Nellie S. 29 W 38th....F G Smith. Piano. (R) 270
Jackson, Annie. 83 W 61st ...Brooklyn F Co. (R) 197
Jaffrey, V Z T. 220 E 38d....L Baumann. 233
Johnson, C W. 188 W 102d....T Kelly. (R) 119
Johnson, Lena. 185 Chrystie....L Baumann. 284
Jones, Sarah. 253 Columbus av....L Baumann. 168
Jory, H J. 276 W 119th....Alexander Bros. 258
Joslyn, Mary B. Park av ...Manges Bros. (R) 118
Jackson, Bessie. 254 W 38th....J Early. 215
Jackson, Florence. 81 W 10th....B Mannes & Son. 209
Kingsley, Kittie. 106 W 106th ...J Baumann. (R) 105
Kelly, Matthew. 250 W 10th.... J Moriarty. 215
Lennox, Nellie. 143 W 63d....S Baumann. 928
Lindheimer, Clara. 967 Fleetwood av....S Baumann. 505
Lombard, Mary E. 44 W 125th....W D Pennefeather. 300
Lambert, Richard. 163 E 74th....J F Manges. (R) 118
Longo, Salvador. 79 Bank....J Baumann. 149
Lusk, O L. 201½ W 24th....J Baumann. (R) 584
Lasker, Abraham. 985 Lexington av....S I Herschmann. 589
Levy, Mrs J D. 109 W 13th....T Kelly. (R) 125
Lamontegue, E. 206 W 41st....McClain, S & Co. 198
Lawe, James. 18 Perry.... J Moriarty. 380
Leahy, Kate. 208 E 46th....L Baumann. 112
Lord, James. 977 Washington av....J McCormack & Co. 141
Mann, Annie. 331 W 17th....L Baumann. 185
Martin, Margaret. 472 W 42d ....L Baumann. 149
McClaim, Della. 572 Broome....Jordan & M. 105
Miller, Max. 346 E 10th....L Baumann. 147
Mullin, Mrs M. 1906 10th av....Alexander Bros. 150
Manning, Ann. 708 E 12th....D M Brown. 100
McCallum, J G. 450 W 57th....A Ballin. 242
McLewell, F H. 144 E 125th....T Kelly. (R) 118
Murphy, Matthew. 1804 3d av....J Moriarty. 150

Medlow, Philip. 95 Macdougal....H Israel & Sons. 116
Mawson, Chas. 246 E 75th....O'Farrell & Co. 165
McKee, Emma. 117 E 24th.... J Baumann. (R) 126
McKnight, Mary. 100 E 45th....J Baumann. (R) 186
Murphy, D J. 943 3d av....J Gregg & Co. 129
Meehan, Thomas. 348 E 82d ...Jordan & M. 184
Morra, Hilda. 251 W 29th....O'Farrell & Co. 154
Mugnet, Jules. 902 8th av....O'Farrell & Co. 123
Neuberger, A M. 89 E 8th....R M Walters. Piano. 128
Newton, Annie. 16 Morton....Alexander Bros. 155
Nixon, Benjamin. 81 E 16th ...T Kelly. (R) 126
O'Keefe, Lucy. 418 E 114th....Alexander Bros. 183
O'Brien, Mattie. 231 E 21st....J Moriarty. 242
Page, Mary. 142 W 33d....O'Farrell & Co. 187
Pepin, Ogellone. 212 E 14th....H Thoesen. 240
Phillips, W L. 147 W 62d....J Early. 181
Planchenault, Gabriel. 64 South 5th av....O'Farrell & Co. 118
Pfrang, Pia. 84 St Marks pl....A Ballin. 147
Pike, M J. 218 W 40th....A Ballin. 129
Porter, Laura. 137 W 46th....T Kelly. (R) 100
Parento, G. 390 E 11th....Alexander Bros. 134
Petrie, Edith. 237 E 14th....J Gregg. 583
Reves, Fanny. 1738 Madison av....Spies Bros. (R) 186
Rhodes, Helen. 316 W 31st.... W Glenn. 900
Rivers, Frankie. 201 W 41st....T Kelly. (R) 153
Robbins, M and M. 82 W 97th....E C Hinsdale. 180
Robertson, Jessie. 347 W 40th....Krakauer Bros. Piano. 170
Robinson, M. C. 157 W 129d... Fennell & Pye. (R) 161
Rohland, Dora. 69 Ludlow....Alexander Bros. 194
Reilly, John J. 415 W 54th ...T Kelly. (R) 116
Richter, Mrs H. 190 Elm. ..D M Brown. 129
Rorty, M M. 49 E 106th....T Kelly. (R) 130
Ryan, Edmund. 79 W 109th....J Moriarty. 200
Reeves, F A. 115 W 62d....J Baumann. (R) 108
Riordan, Daniel. 113 E 87th....F G Smith. Piano. (R) 230
Rushworth, Clara. 159 W 23d....H Thoesen. 131
Robertson, Emma. 101 E 123d ...S Baumann. 194
Robinson, Elizabeth. 60 W 35th. ..M Barnett. 1,500
Rogers, Charlotte. 35 Bank....S Baumann. 225
Rolle, G. 2 Varick... C R Ruegger. 1..8
Rosenblad, J E. 211 E 38th ...Jordan & M. 121
Strauss, E and Y 243 E 78th....M Cohn. 560
Sammis, C S. 173 W 83d....L Baumann. (R) 135
Sanford, Anna M. 103 W 76th....F G Smith. Piano. (R) 375
Savage, T J. 33 W 63d....F G Smith. Piano. (R) 300
Simmons, W. A. 113 E 16th....F G Smith. Piano. (R) 315
Simonson, Henry. 161 Orchard ...Alexander Bros. 146
Smith, Jessie. 342 E 117th....L Baumann. 112
Smith, L F. 263 E 10th....Alexander Bros. 200
Steinberg, Jacques. 89 E 3d J Moriarty. 162
Stummer, Rachel. 24 Suffolk....H S Eisler. 105
Tauny, Mamie. 148 W 27th....A Ballin. (R) 113
Thomas, Robert. 137 W 26th....O'Farrell & Co. 250
Tonsing, H A. 376 2d av....J Mathis. 100
Traynor, H M and M J. 551 W 58th....H Mannes & Son. 148
Thomas, Robert. 392 7th av....O'Farrell & Co. 280
Tripault, Ludovic. 92 West Houston....E Sagnol. 1,060
Turner, Julia. 214 W 33d... O'Farrell & Co. 206
Unity League. 200 East Broadway....J Rubenstein. 1,765
Urquhart, W F. 301 W 19th....Manges Bros. 166
Valliant, L H. 57 W 45th....A B Kauffman. 500
Viano, A & N. 18th st, bet Broadway and 4th av....J & J Dobson. Carpets. (R) 1,000
Voss, Emma. 114 W 16th ...J Moriarty. 388
Van Aken, Ded. 247 W 54th....T Kelly. (R) 120
Van Behr, Paul. 329 E 43d....D M Brown. 207
Vanderberg, Mrs F....J Moriarty. 389
Van Hattie. 228 W 37th. . L Baumann. 176
Wadenpfuhl, John. 148 E 4th....W H Griffin. 100
Weinstock, L C. 547 W 125th . J Gregg. (R) 167
Werner, Annie. 620 E 150th....W Reubel. 114
Wood, Mrs M. 259 W 54th....I Mason. 287
Webb, Alice L. 328 W 55th....J Gregg & Co. 780
Weeks, Carrie. 613 E 142d....Manges Bros. 138
Weillert, William. 60 1st av....J Baumann. 118
Williamson, Sarah M. 304 W 14th....C O Bigelow. (R) 636
Wilson, Georgie. 138 E 48th....Garvey Bros. 576
Wylie, Laura. 1440 Lexington av ...J Baumann. 133
Walsh, Margaret. 266 W 123d....L Baumann. 183
Warren, Ella L. 256 W 84th....L Baumann. 250
Watson, Emily. 69 W 12th....American Guarantee Assoc. 500
Weeks, J W. 700 E 139th.... J Keeley. (R) 500
White, John. 63 E 128th....F G Smith. Piano. (R) 200
Wolfsheim, Belle K. 209 E 14th....S Gordon. 200
Woolis, F E. 316 W 36th....L Baumann. 178
Wissmach, Paul. 403 Lenox....A Ballin. 745
Zaulig, Mrs Fred. W 11th st....S I Herschmann. (R) 147
Zaulig, Mary. 64 W 11th....S I Herschmann. (R) 204
Zuckman, Emanuel. 117 East Broadway....Alexander Bros. 208
Zimmerman, Nettie. 121 E 20th.... J Moriarty. 560

MISCELLANEOUS.

Abbott, Sarah A. 225 E 40th....Hincks & J. Coach. (R) 100
Ametron, Nicholas. 180 Mulberry....A Schwaab & Son. Barber Fixtures. (R) 64
Avignone, Frank. 1874 3d av....A Schwaab & Son. Barber Fixtures. (R) 16
Avenarius, Otto. 693 Columbus av....G C Edgar. Store Fixtures. 192
Abbott, C & S A. 225 E 40th....H Killam Co. Coach. (R) 988
Adam, Albert. 572 Courtlandt av....E Higgins. Butcher Fixtures. 200
Adler, S J K. 1933 3d av....Lamson Consol S S Co. Register. 450
Antonie, F. 371 West....Marvin Safe Co. Safe. 120
Bender, Wendel. 339 9th av....O H Cook. Tools, &c. 300
Blankenberg, H and A. 11 State....M L Bernard. Machinery. 100
Baum, H M. City....E F Stewart. Photo Fixtures. 10,000
Brotherton, Geo C. 2348 8th av....Nat Cash Reg Co. Register. 225
Bryan, Hugh. 808 E 40th....A Bushy. Horse, Cab, &c. 75
Byrne, F J. 124 Henry ...Nat Cash Reg Co. Register. 120
Bowles, Lillian...W D Barnes. Horses, Coaches. 1,000
Baer, Max. 980 2d av....J McLean. Butcher Fixtures. 203

Bass, J C. 12th st, bet 10th and 11th aves....W Bass. Horses, Ice Wagon, &c. 750
Batholomew, C E. 22 College pl ...C Potter, Jr, & Co. Presses, &c. (R) 500
Bennach, Wolf. 58 Orchard....M Polonsky. Barber Fixtures. 80
Blanning, William. 439 W 27th....D Goodwin. Horse. 45
Blumenthal, A. 250 W 31st....E Winterbottom. Paper Cutter. 100
Bornstein, Morris. 24 Ann....M Gerrits. Store Fixtures, &c. 405
Carmon, F W. 223 Grand and 224 E 21st....E Carmon. Drug Fixtures and Furniture. 6,000
Chebra Atereth Israel Ausher Shakier. 18 Allen ....L Lealin et al. Church Fixtures. 240
Chesley, Ellen E. 416 W 31st....E Winterbottom. Press. 80
Collocchio & Maralusio. 7 Av B....A Schwaab & Son. Barber Fixtures. 205
Condon & Davenport. 2 Liberty....C Potter, Jr, & Co. Presses, &c. (R) 1,348
Corrao, Joseph. 101 E 88th....A Schwaab & Son. Barber Fixtures. 250
Coundouris, Spiros. Now at Tiffany & Co....J Adams. Statue. 8,000
Cranston, Henry. New York Hotel....J Jay. Hotel Fixtures. (R) security
Cummings, R J. 211 Snediker av, Brooklyn ...F Welsh. Machinery. 225
Cnocco, John. 549 and 583 3d av....A Schwaab & Son. Barber Fixtures. 583
Connolly, John. 611 and 613 E 19th....J H Lippe. Coach. (R) 2,700
Crowley, J and T. 181st st and 10th av....D B Dunham. Coach. 500
Cupodanno, Rocco. 463 6th av....J Souvay. Barber Fixtures. 263
Carr, B J. Claremont av and 102d st....B Mahon. Machinery. (R) 529
Cohen, Joe. 168 Clinton... S Levin. Butter Store Fixtures. 50
Davis, J T. 163 W 15th....O'Halloran Bros. Horses, Coach, &c. (R) 1,031
De Revere, G B. Union sq and 15th st....A J Dam. Hotel Fixtures. (R) 25,500
Davids Machine Works....T Keresey. Machine, Fixtures, &c. (R) 10,000
Dinkelman & Cohen. 88 Henry....C Haller. Machines. 95
Dippel, Frederick. 400 1st av....A C Slollenow. Fixtures, Tools, &c. 250
Duffy, James. 204 E 102d, Murray Hill Bank. Horses, Coaches, &c. 2,000
Daly, Wm. 461 W 52d....J Cunningham Son & Co. Coach. 100
D'Amico, Carlantonio. 6 Bleecker....M Spailone. Barber Fixtures. 235
Deanto, D & Co. 56 Pike....Bennett & G. Soda Fixtures. 100
Dimelon, Roland. 150th st and Cedar lane....J Cunningham Son & Co Coach. 75
Engesser, John. 715 E 11th....Manhattan Type Co. Press, &c. 160
Faris, H L. 36 New ...G Rogers....Office Fixtures. 2,756
Fisk, Sydney. 48 Beekman....C L Wright. Photo Fixtures. 4,000
Falck & Co. 26 Canal ...W H Butler. Safe. 800
Fern, G Ieppi. 333 E 11th....W H Butler. Safe. 145
Eastman, E O. 249 W 41st .... J H Sheean. Cab and Horse. 29
Fless & Ridge. 5th av and 16th st....C Potter, Jr, & Co. Presses, &c. (R) 6,000
Freeman, R & Bro. 69 Beekman ...G H Sanborn & Sons. Cutter. 775
Frick, Charles. 637 W 46th....F Foehrenbach & Co. Horse Fixtures, &c. 1,000
Goldstein, Samuel. 157 7th....A Krundieck. Confectionery Fixtures. 50
Goodwin, F H. 247 W 41st....J Cunningham Son & Co. Coach. 255
Goldfarb, Samuel....H H Oppenheim. Grocery Fixtures. 60
Grange, James. 66 Duane....T W & C B Sheridan. Machinery. 2,500
Gilbert, Helland & Beitler. 1335 Broadway....Liberty Machine Works. Press. 621
Galligan, Henry. 49th st and 11th av....A McCabe. Horses, Ice Wagon, &c. 700
Gault, Mary. 1833, 1835 and 1837 Madison av....G H Kitchen & Co. Gas Fixtures. 539
Gillies, John. 81 and 33 Broadway. . A J Murray. Pile Drivers. 1,500
Goldstein, Louis. 572 Grand....H Lehman. Cigar Fixtures. 550
Hartshorn, J W. 142 E 59th....Hincks & J. Coach. (R) 525
Hauck, Peter. 709 Greenwich....P Westphal. Barber Fixtures. (R) 180
Hehn, Frank. 526 E 16th....E Niebelein. Grocery Fixtures. 1,200
Hollborn, Carl....D P Nichols & Co. Cab. 800
Hunter, W W. 225 E 40th....Hincks & J. Coach. (R) 260
Hurley & Farwell. 1786 3d av....National Cash Register Co. Register. 175
Horton, T J. 785 3d av....D H Todd. Horses, Wagon, &c. 1,100
Hargous, P A. 261 Broadway and 147 W 83d st ....M Pareira. Office Fixtures, Horse, &c. 235
Hartog, J. 160 E 125th... Lamson Consol S S Co. Register. 250
Herzfeld, Joseph. 114 W 3d....C Dierking. Butcher Fixtures. 155
Haas, F X. 30 Suffolk....F L Haas. Bottling Fixtures. 3,000
Hessman, J H. 174-182 Bank....W V Simpson. Kindling Wood Fixtures, &c. 549
Jung, Heinrich. 27 8th av....J W Tufts. Soda Fixtures. (R) 150
Jack, Lizzie. 99th st and Western Boulevard....T Gross. Horse, Wagon, &c. 200
Jacoby, Henry. 130 W 4th....J Cunningham Son & Co. Coach. 450
Kalischer, W S....H Kantrowitz. Machinery. 500
Knapf, Max. 51 Ridge....W Cohn. Tailor Fixtures. 350
Kraft, Richard. 249 E 10th....H Dorzbacher. Barber Fixtures. 150
Kautor, A A. 391 Grand....Manhattan Type Co. Cutter. 100
Kavanagh, Thomas. 134 W 49th....Hincks & J. Coach. (R) 200
Kennedy, W J. 217 W 26th... M Dougherty. Horses, Coaches. 2,500
Kremer, John. 418 7th av....National Cash Register Co. Register. 225
Lucas, Philippine. 164 E 87th.... F Wieber, Jr. Horses, &c. 510
Lewin, Lewis. 1698 Lexington av....M Lydon. Horse, Wagon. 800
Loppert, D. 4 Walker....J Stewart. Machines. 441

Lustig, Max. 183 Rivington....Bramhall, Deane & Co. Range. 126
Lopez, Jose. 108 and 110 E 125th....Amer Guar Assoc. Photo Fixtures. 200
Lorie, Max. 2151 2d av ..E Freese. Machine. 70
Lieberman, S. 66 Delancey....S Berkovitz. Butcher Fixtures. 100
Lucas, August. 1294 3d av....C Rieger. Undertakers Fixtures. 3,000
Mahon & Martin. 66 Pine....W D Barkley. Machinery, &c. 800
Meryast, H. 11 Market ...L Meryast. Grocery Fixtures. 400
Munson, J H, J A Green and W O Merrill. 116 Lincoln av....A E Keim. Laundry Fixtures. 500
McGloin, J A. 707 Columbus av....H Oathers. Cigar Fixtures. 76
Melness, J & Co. 317 W 39th....J F Huner. Grocery Fixtures. 16
Miller, Catharine. 240 Columbus av....A Brakmann. Grocery Fixtures. 1,000
McQueen & Veritzan. 154 and 156 E 53d....Hincks & J. Coach. 7,775
Mendelowitz, Louis. 971 1st av....P Reidenbach. Wagon. 30
Metropolitan Ferry Co ...Central Trust Co. Boats, &c. (R) 1,250,000
Miller, C. 125 Mott... C B Rogers & Co. Machinery. 235
Moroso, Alexander. 61 South .... J Souvay. Barber Fixtures. 24
Murphy & Costello. W 15th....R Ellis. Machinery. (R) 1,300
Murphy & Costello....S A Wood's Machine Co. Machinery. (R) 2,622
Nappi, John. 459 W 46th....A Schwaab & Son. Barber Fixtures. 481
Neefus, A C. 2173 8th av....J T & J F Jackson. Butcher Fixtures. 70
Noble, C E... J Goold Co. Coach. 425
Nolan, James. 162 North 6th st, Brooklyn....Nat Cash Reg Co Register. 175
Otto, H B. 1096 9th av....J W Scheipert. Drug Fixtures. 1,400
Pape, Henry. 519 E 18th....H Koppermann. Grocery Fixtures. (R) 850
Price, Jesse. 63 Rutgers slip....J H Bonnell & Co Press, &c. (R) 3,750
Same....same. Press, &c. (R) 787
Pariser, M and A 56 East Broadway....Bennett & G. Bottling Fixtures. 850
Passantino, Philipo. 2070 2d av....A Schwaab & Son. Barber Fixtures. 122
Pope & Gottschalk. 653 and 655 1st av....P Pryibil. Machinery. 209
Quigley, Frank 194 Mulberry....J Cunningham Son & Co. Coach. 417
Rashkind, Abraham J Sternecker. Stationery Store Fixtures. 50
Rokeach, Israel. 470 Grand ...Baron de Hirsch Fund. Press. 200
Reich, David. 50 Willett....J Cunningham Son & Co. Coach. 75
Richardson, Carrie V....G P Elder, exr of. Newspaper Dramatic News. (R) 554
Rodgers, Edward. 795 Washington....Nat Cash Reg Co. Register. 200
Scacchette & Sagnor. 923 6th av....Columbia Wagon Co. Wagon. 130
Schmidt, Fred .... F McCormick. Horses, Truck, &c. 180
Schmitt, Adam. 203 E 36th... P Westphal. Barber Fixtures. 210
Scott, Nicholas. 617 and 619 W 37th. J Cunningham Son & Co. Coach. 45
Schwamm, Jacob. 638 E 5th....H Brand. Butcher Fixtures. 75
Schwarz, Ernest. 626 Hudson....Moore & Rogers. Boots, Shoes, &c. 525
Schweitzer, S. 207 Columbus av... T Farrell. Butcher Fixtures. 135
Siegelack, F J. 1st av, bet 61st and 62d sts. .. L Siegelack. Horse, Milk Wagon. 300
Stock, F J. 59 Macdougal....G B Bereton. Drug Fixtures. 900
Schick, Hyman. 81 Canal....Liberty Machine Works. Press. 90
Schonberger, Louis. 27 Centre....Liberty Machine Works. Press. 191
Sparnecht, August. 56 and 57 Tompkins Market....M Bendroth. Stands, &c. 250
Simon, Leon. 166 and 168 Spring....D W Bruce. Machines. (R) 439
Strauss, Joseph. 359 7th av .... A Strauss. Butcher Fixtures. 500
Sacristano, Ciro. 534 W 42d ...S Littman. Barber Fixtures. (R) 152
Salm, Toney. 512 7th av....Smith & Mills. Butcher Fixtures. 130
Schlanger, Isaac. 122 Ridge....I Reich. Machines. 150
Shaw & Frondle. 525 Brook av....S Littmann. Barber Fixtures. 181
Stark, Aaron. 87 Ridge....A Kurtz. Machines. 20
Stoll, Friederich. 84 Cortlandt,... M Stoll. Store Fixtures. 1,500
Towle, J R. 1124 3d av....D Marier. Cigar Fixtures. 1,000
Wendel, Joseph. 219 W 28th... Ernst Kaufman. Horse, Wagon, &c. 250
Weisbot & Ferteg. 58 Attorney ...D Senft. Machines. 65
Weitzen, I. 105 Sheriff....Bennett & G. Soda Fixtures. 20
Walker, J S. 401 Broadway....C H Fuller. Office Fixtures. 113
Wood, F E. 144 and 146 W 39th....J Rudd. Horse. 125
Weinberger & Marmorstein. 6 Av B....J Marmorstein. Press, &c. 300
Weinberger, Mary. 6 Av B....S Reitman. Press. 330
Wendell & Evans. 218 and 220 Pearl st, Brooklyn ...B Eastwood. Laundry Fixtures. 1,550
Wilson, Thomas. 304 W 10th....Nat Cash Reg Co. Register. 175
Winter, L F. 418 W 27th....Knapp Mfg Co. Machinery. 353
Ziniti, Frank. 1517 2d av....A Schwaab & Son. Barber Fixtures. 156
Zolin & Co. 128 East Broadway....Bennett & G. Soda Fixtures. 200
Zeller, J F. 236 E 59th....C F Gennerich. Horse. 500

BILLS OF SALE.

Barnett, Mary. 60 W 35th....E Robinson. Furniture. 2,000
Body & Zoller. 916 2d av....A H & H A Comfort. Butter Store Fixtures. 225
Comfort, A H and H A. 916 2d av....H Kinne. Butter Store. 150

Eberson, I and R. 46 Delancey....A Steinberg. Restaurant Fixtures. 200
Eckert, G M 8 Extra pl....M A Eckert. Horses, Trucks, &c. 1,800
Fitzsimons, Julia A. 592 Mott av....R K Dryer. Furniture. 500
Goodwin, Daniel. 489 W 27th....W Blannings. Horse. 75
Greenslade, Edward. 314 W 126th....S P Hoose. Horse, Trucks, &c. 300
Goldman, H J. 2 Chatham sq....M P Ansorge. Stock Clothing. security
Heyer, William. 2353 1st av....C N Bomeisler. Grocery Fixtures. 745
Hill, Robert. 2214 2d av....P Faber. Grocery Fixtures. 300
Hayward, Fredk. 2362 8th av and 61 E 125th st ...Mrs F Hayward. Store Fixtures, &c. 1,300
Ironside, C N... Free Masons Journal Co. Newspaper Journal Free Masons. 300
Loonie, Maurice. 964 1st av....W Nolan. Saloon Fixtures. 3,069
Ludwig, Bruno... J Gerlardt. Piano. 200
Melzer, Frank....I Riffa. Pool Table. 240
Meyer, E 74 West Broadway... Voege & Wiegand. Saloon Fixtures. 5,000
Marmorstein, G & Co. 6 Av B....A Stoffel. Printing Fixtures. 525
Moran, Samuel. 126 W 27th....H Nixon. Grocery Fixtures. 300
Neuschotz, Salomon. 399 Grand and 27 East Houston ...J Schnapmann. Millinery Fixtures. 650
Nevin, M W & Son. 66 Pine....Mahon & Martin. Machinery. 1,300
Oelting, Fred. 1956 3d av....H Busch. Grocery Fixtures. 1
Puvogel, John. 207 E 85th....A Kamna. Horse, Wagon, &c. 425
Pettit, C G. 7th av and 34th st....Lies & Seidenberg. Drug Fixtures. 1
Roubitsheck, Gabriel. 683 Broadway....Caroline Teller. Restaurant Fixtures. 750
Rhead, A D. 153 Western Boulevard....M Rhead. Horses, Wagons, &c. 25
Roche, Mary. 2214 2d av....R Hill. Grocery Fixtures. 300
Schmidt, C A. 620 E 9th....A E M Schmidt. Bakery Fixtures. 1
Sexton, Patrick. 1515 Broadway....J Sexton. Horses, Trucks, &c. 1,100
Silberstein, Heyman. 112 Broome....E Lubin. Cigar Fixtures. 250
Sherman, W P. 269 Pearl....A F Wainright & Co. Lease, Fixtures, &c. 3,000
Stuart, Belen....I Landman. Scenery, &c. 100
Teller, Julius. 683 Broadway....G Roubitsheck. Restaurant Fixtures. 750
Weisman, Adolph. 118 Bleecker....R Haurowitz. Gent's Furnishing Fixtures. 1,300
Wagner, John....J Wagner. Horse, &c. 100

ASSIGNMENT OF CHATTLE MORTGAGE.

Alsheimer, Anna to G Ehret. (Mort given by J M Hannon, Aug 28, 1891.) 775
Barnett, G W to V A Barnett. (Stroemeyer & Wyman, Oct 31, 1890.) 3,000
Bravton, F R to H R Laskamp. (June 1, 1888.) 1
Barnett, Mary to J C Devereaux. (E Robinson, Nov 9, 1890.) —
Gottlieb, W J to H Hahnenfeld. (Sarah Hannaford, Oct 8, 1891.) 1
Kurtz & Graham to 5th av Auction Rooms. (I Fountain—Bill of Sale—Oct 21, 1891.) 500
Lewis, Abraham to M Price. (A Edelson, Sept 21, 1891.) 1
Marcus, A to Knickerbocker B Co. (E and H Neuman, July 9, 1890.) 1
Mayer, David to D Mayer B Co. (M Bernstein, Nov. 3, 1891. 1
Saul, Emily M to 5th av Auction Rooms. I Fountain, Oct 16, 1891, 2-5 int.) 1,500
Van Rensselaer, M trustee to A Marcus. (E and H Neuman, July 9, 1890.) 1

KINGS COUNTY.

NOVEMBER 5 TO 11.—INCLUSIVE.

SALOON AND RESTAURANT FIXTURES.

Aronne, Carmine. 30 Maspeth av....Budweiser B Co. $450
Same....same. 130
Betzold, L. 466 3d av....Minck Bros & Co. 500
Bonner, P. 97 Flatbush av....Budweiser B Co. (R) 1,000
Burger, G. 439 Marcy av....Obermeyer & L. 125
Bast, C. 157 Woodbine....Claus Lipsius B Co. 550
Bracken, T. 228 Pearl... L I Brewery. 6 0
Brandenburg, P. 484 Marcy av....J Ruppert. 890
Brix, C. 99 Canton... Williamsburgh B Co. 300
Same. 210 Nassau....same. 500
Buckley, D. 9th av, cor 15th st....Obermeyer & L. (R) 1,500
Butzky, A. 1422 Broadway....S Liebmann's Sons B Co. (R) 100
Carlsen, L. 214 Columbia....Marg't Dobrawsky. 900
Connelly, J A. 138 Patchen av....C Lipsius B Co. 1,000
Dlauhy, Victoria. 2784 Atlantic av....Leibinger & O B Co. 300
Dugan, B F. 989 Fulton....S Munch and ano exrs H Munch. 746
Feeley, J & W. Wythe av and Rutledge st.... Budweiser B Co. 1,000
Fromm, J F. 506 6th av. . Fort Hamilton B Co. 900
Gratz, W F. Willow Grove, L I....O Huber Brewery. Saloon and Furniture. 3,500
Geyer, C. 22 Melrose....W Ulmer. 500
Griffith, J. 351 Park av....Budweiser B Co. (R) 600
Haimbach, L. 418 E 9th....J Fallert B Co. (R) 350
Haukap, J. 613 Kent av....J Fallert B Co. (R) 385
Hartman, M. 601 Pacific....Beadleston & W. (R) 2,000
Heins, J D. Driggs av and North 9th st....T Burke. 600
Same....same. 600
Hahn, T L. 21 Tompkins av....J Kress B Co. 250
Hanlon, J P. 124 North 6th....J Kress B Co. 450
Haring, Celestine. 22 Diamond....Burger & H B Co. 385
Heissenbuttel, H. 341 Nevins....J Kress B Co. 300
Hesterberg, H. Grant st, Flatbush... S Liebmann's Sons B Co. 927
Holtermann, H J. 2 Jefferson....S Liebmann's Sons B Co. (R) 900
Kline, J O. 34 and 36 Maujer....J Kress B Co. 7,500
Kelly, M. 262 Atlantic av....Budweiser B Co. (R) 1,600
Kirchhof, P J. 2072 Fulton....F Ibert. 580
Kopf, D W. 361 Hooper....M Worm & Sons. 650
Knorz, J. 395 Graham av....Burger & H B Co. 500

Lesser, J. 90 Moore. ..Burger & H B Co 800
McKaigney, P & Bro. 69 3d av....M F Garvey. 600
McMahon, J. 221 Union av....O Huber Brewery. 1,000
Moss, C. 1096 Bedford av.... Beadleston & W. 3,000
Markle, F. 359 Ewen....E Ochs. 100
Massa, C G. 237 Irving av....Eliz Meltzer. 475
Nallin, J J. 82 Hamilton av ...P Ballantine & Son. (R) 500
O'Neill, P. 178 Greenpoint av....Beadleston & W. (R) 4,000
Oechsner, J. 1271 Myrtle av... L Eppig. 547
Remmers, H .. J Fallert B Co. (R) 1,197
Faufi, J. 72 Diamond....J Kress B Co. (R) 1,189
Ratigan, M. 211½ Stockton... C Lipsius B Co. 805
Schmidt, C. 419 Kent av....S Liebmann's Sons B Co. (R) 1,110
Same. 595 Flushing av....F Munch B Co. 500
Schwarzmuller, Barbara. 260 Johnson av....P Weidmann. 1,100
Silber, E. 111 Varet....Abbott B Co. 100
Sistef, H. 939 De Kalb av... F Rower B Co. 600
Stokes, W B. 231 4th av ...Fort Hamilton B Co. 1,500
Schaefer, H. 19 Moore....W Ulmer. (R) 300
Schmitt, G. 122 Johnson av....J Fallert B Co. 525
Schneider, P. 63 Morgan av....J Eppig. 420
Steck, J. 577 Driggs av....E Ochs. 1,000
Tutty, J. Troy av, s w cor Bergen st,...E Ochs. 900
Weisenborn, J. 983 3d av....Fort Hamilton B Co. 1,200
Windstein, M. 256 Boerum. ..L Eppig. (R) 1,530

HOUSEHOLD FURNITURE.

Allen, W D E. 398 McDonough....Brooklyn F Co. 179
Boyle, A W. 263 12th... Brooklyn F Co. 118
Bratt, Cath. 149 Richards. . A Pearson. 123
Brooks, I. 585 Gates av....M Schulz & Bro. 221
Brooks, J. 35 Sands....I Mason. 170
Brunson, C. 106 Lawrence ...O'Connor & Treacy. 422
Runde, H. 43 Bergen....T F Ryan. 128
Burdick, A. 36 Pearl....McEnery & Co. 107
Baluka, A and Emma. 49 Middagh....J C Hegeman. 200
Bowles, C A. 407 Halsey... Mullin's Sons. 175
Brenack, T J and Emma T. 201 Marion....Sallie R Weinmell. 300
Cavaliere, J. 176 Atlantic av.... Alexander Bros. 110
Colgan, Mary. 263 Humboldt....L Baumann. 103
Christian, A H. 1236 Bedford av....Brooklyn F Co. 358
Cleland, J W. Fulton and Flatbush Storage Co....M M Webster. 130
Cunningham, J. Gravesend....M Schulz & Bro. 155
Diggs, Rosa. 351 Waverly av....M Schulz & Bro. 245
Dudenhausen, A. 86 Central av....O Wissner. Piano. 205
Denning, P G. 530 Herkimer....Mullin's Sons. 219
Evans, Maria. 591 Pacific... J McEnery & Co. 254
Foulks, J W. 451 7th....D Crowell. 110
Frazer, Isabella. 1067 Myrtle av... A Schulz. 175
Foley, Mrs. 432 Lewis av . Brooklyn F Co. 190
Freeman, H W. 239 Graham av....I Mason. 180
Gaffney, Mrs E. 110 North Elliott pl....I Mason. 122
Goerrig, C P. 170 Nevins....J McEnery & Co. 147
Griffin, Winifred. 228 Smith....T F Ryan. 174
Griffiths, T W. 103 Park pl ...F C Rogers. 3,500
Gibson, Mrs E. 66 Howard av....Alexander Bros. 122
Hill, Julia. 203 Bergen....Manges Bros. 165
Hoffman, A. 149 Greene . L Baumann. 202
Hawkins, W D and Ida C. Fulton st and Bedford av... J D Roberts. 200
Hayes, C K. 497 Franklin av. ..Brooklyn F Co. 170
Helmstadt, G. 22 Lewis av. ..McEnery & Co. 185
Hess, Mrs C. 428 St Marks pl....I Mason. 164
Hochheim, G. 1588 Gates av....Brooklyn F Co. 150
Jones, H. 982 Putnam av....T F Ryan. 134
Jeffrey, Kittie E. 48 Clifton pl....A Pearson. 119
Kirkegard, Anna. 172 President....Brooklyn F Co. 490
Laird, D. 356 State....A C Wahlfered. 100
Liddle, G. 432 7th av....W White. 483
Long, W D. 281 Warwick .... O'Connor & Treacy. 279
Mabie, R. 629 Bedford av....I Mason. 164
Macdonald, Mrs J. 307 Evergreen av....I Mason. 117
McGrorty, H E. 1238 Union....O'Connor & Treacy. 148
Monsees, M. 1660 Atlantic av....O'Connor & Treacy. 159
Mackey, Lizzie. 352 Bergen ...C S Lacey. 195
McCready, Rose. 138 19th . L Baumann. 101
Morton, Ida. 315 7th....Mullins & Sons. 178
Morton, W O and Cath A. 611 Madison....Augusta V Smith. 400
Neill, S. 112B Nassau av....A Schulz. 411
Niebuhr, M C. 341 Lafayette av... Brooklyn F Co. 120
Nostrand, Mary E. 163 Lefferts pl....Brooklyn F Co. 101
Payne, Irene L. 106 4th av....M Schulz & Bro. 401
Pfister, C. 297 Stockton....L Baumann. 110
Russ, W. 417 Franklin av....Simpson & P. Piano. 400
Riley, F. 364 Sumner av....R Silvermann. 140
Schutt, I F. 280 South 4th....A Schulz. 417
Scheible, J H. 19 Van Voorhis st ...L Baumann. 160
Schnitzler, P. 371 St Marks av....M Schulz & Bro. 507
Scott, J W. 1844A Atlantic av....Brooklyn F Co. 373
Schultze, A. 991 Halsey....Simpson & P. Piano. 310
Sheedy, Maria L. 375 Bergen....M Schulz & Bro. 142
Sheffer, J W. 264 Dean....I Mason. 207
Sloane, W. 632 Pacific....P B Bracken. 155
Stapleton, Mrs. M. 167 Cooper....I Mason. 139
Steever, J S. 463 Hancock....J C Aikio. 420
Stevenson, Mattie A. 52 Vanderbilt av....Alexander Bros. 216
Tugi, Y. 152 Hudson av....I Mason. 155
Tinker, C J. Shepherd av .. Manges Bros. 189
Underhill, J T. 182 Halsey....O Wissner. Piano. 205
Williams, Mrs. 846 Fulton .... O'Connor & Treacy. 127
Wargin, Addie. Palmetto st, cor Evergreen av ....A Schulz. 203

MISCELLANEOUS.

Brown, G. Duffield and Tillary sts....N Langler. Horses, Trucks, &c. (R) 650
Brueckmann, W. 665 Flushing av....G A Gardner. Horse, &c. 420
Baltz, P, Jr. 493 Gates av....Archer Mfg Co. Barber Fixtures. 137

Castello, M B. 489 Tompkins av....Brunswick-Balke-Collender Co. Pool Table. 210
Condon, J J. 2 Liberty st, N Y....C Potter, Jr, & Co. Presses, &c. (R) 1,309
Conklin, Emma R. 41 Clifton pl....W S Hurley. Bakery Fixtures. 400
Crofoot, Mary H. 122 Van Siclen av....J W Tufts. Soda Apparatus. 480
Cappelli, G. 413 Graham av....Carmella Cappelli. Barber Fixtures. 1,500
Chellborg, C. 402 Atlantic av....Lamson C S S Co. Register. 140
Christensen, N. Foot 25th st....J W Porter. Engin , &c. 200
Cordtsell W. 19 Broadway....Nat Cash Reg Co. Register. 175
Delei, L. 48 Sands....Archer Mfg Co. Barber Fixtures. 199
Dlanhy, V A K and Victoria. 1951 Bushwick av ....Isabella M Kelly. Bottling Business. 300
Eberhart, S. 59 Franklin. ..Theresea Eberhart. Saddlery Fixtures. 450
Fiess & Ridge. 5th av, n w cor 16th st....C Potter, Jr, & Co. Printing Office Fixtures. (R) 6,000
Freeman, R and W. 49 Rose st, New York.... Sanborn & Sons. Cutting Machine, &c. 775
Fisher, E. 485 Court....A D Puffer & Sons. Soda Apparatus. 163
Gillies, J. 31 and 33 Broadway....A J Murray. Four Pile Drivers, Scows, &c. 15,000
Gauch, J, Jr. 780 Park av....C Doerschuck. (R) 400
Gleason, M J. 56 Carlton av....Nat Cash Reg Co. Register. 175
Gurnee, O R. Bedford av, cor Gates av....J W Tufts. Soda Water Apparatus. (R) 282
Heckman, J A. 123 Nostrand av....B Illsfelder & Co. Chalk Crayon Business. 1,010
Hickey, P V. 18 Barclay st, New York....Babcock P P and Mfg Co. Press. (R) 308
Hayden, H. 692 Marcy av....E Hayden. Horse, &c. 800
Hunt Engineering Co....Manhattan Trust Co. Supplemental Mort. 800,000
Ireland, T B....G Dessecker. Coach. 925
Jennings, H N, and J J Burne. 378 Nostrand av ....W R Foster & Co. Engines, &c. 550
Johnson, P J. 46 Beekman st, New York....G H Walker. Machinery, &c. 480
Jones, E. 462 Putnam av....Lincoln Indorsement and Guarantee Co. Printing Office Fixtures. 100
Kaspar, L. 299 Marcy av....J Weiss. Barber Fixtures. 219
Kujawa, F. 39 Sumner av....Therese Muller. Grocery Fixtures. 600
Kane, J ...C Allen. Horses, &c. 800
Kern, V, and G Buegel. 107 Hamburg av....L Schoenherr. Butcher Fixtures. 150
Lauzaro, F. 44 Atlantic av....Felice De Rosa. Barber Fixtures. 300
Leggler, C. 246 Lynch....A Adler & Co. Bakery Fixtures. (R) 273
Lamoreau, J B. 671 Myrtle av ..T Rochford. Wagon. 148
Loeffler, R. 140 Throop av....National Cash Register Co. Register. 200
Mas, E and A. 14 Alice court....Lincoln Indorsement and Guarantee Assoc. 200
Murphy & Costello ...R Ellis. Planers, &c. 3,087
Manes, G. 256 Hoyt....A Schwaab & Son. Barber Fixtures. 318
Marolda, N. 47 Willoughby ...A Schwaab & Son. Barber Fixtures. 126
Mauff, A....I S Remson Mfg Co. Wagons, &c. 182
Patterson, Mary and J H .... C Hiltebrant. Boats, &c 1,950
Pearsall, A. 222-228 North 7th....E R Durkee & Co. Horses, &c. 1,050
Polchow, F. Berry and South 6th sts....H Wischhusen. Grocery Fixtures. (R) 290
Shelly, C C....Cath White. Presses, &c. (R) 1,329
Stillwell, C & F. 26 New .... W J Rumph. Horses, &c. 300
Santin, F. 541 Myrtle av .. Archer Mfg Co. Barber Fixtures. 111
Thonebe, A. 45 Central av....Weeks & Parr. Bakery Fixtures. 400
Thinney, L E. 111 Weirfield....Metropol Candy Co. Confectionery Fixtures. 140
Underhill, J H and Mary E Parr. 1199 and 1201 Atlantic av....F J Bennett. Horses, Wagons, &c. 500
Voigt, E. 350 Van Brunt....M Gompert. Bakery Fixtures. 300
Van Beuren, R A. Division st, cor Johnson st ... Singer Mfg Co Machines. 145
Vincent, J R. 343 Willoughby av ...Ellen L Vincent. Dairy Fixtures. 690
Vogel, S. 91 Moore....M Minden. Grocery Fixtures 200
Wendell, F C and F E Evans....B Eastwood. Laundry Machinery. 1,550
Weber, J. 697 Bergen....S Littman. Barber Fixtures. 261
Weiersbach, C P. 229 Greenpoint av ...J C Stead. Tanks, Boilers, &c. 300
Wenig, E O. 59 Court....Caroline McHench. Barber Fixtures. 250
Vasinolo, A. 64 Columbia....Archer Mfg Co. Barber Fixtures. 468

BILLS OF SALE.

Brady, Mary A extrx P H Brady. 110 Bridge.... Budweiser B Co. Saloon Fixtures. 650
Butt, H. 556 Marcy av....J H Cornebleen. Milk Business. 1,000
Cobb, B S. 131 Manhattan av....H W Wheeler. Machinery. 500
Crastataio, N. 82 Front....F Rago. Butcher Fixtures. 142
Durham, F F. 2d av, cor 54th st .. G L Ayres & Co. Grocery Fixtures. 571
Dewey, M D. 459 Fulton....H M Hollowell. Restaurant Fixtures. 2,000
Fottrell Patent Hygienic Concrete and Imperishable Asphalt Co. 6th st Basin....R D Sawyer et al. Machinery, Tools, &c. 17,500
Grossmann, Pauline. 1586 Broadway....W F Grossmann. Butcher Fixtures. 100
Mayer, C. 58 Humboldt... C Haug. Machine Shop. 550
Martin, H, Sr, and Jr. 701 Fulton st, 32 Sands st and Webster av, Parkville....M Seitz. Saloon Fixtures. 4,500
Matern, V. 40 Reid av....R Mucasle. Shoe Store. 150
Neumann, J. 295 Floyd ...A J Bess. Saloon Fixtures. 150
Schoenherr, L. 167 Hamburg av....Kern & B. Butcher Fixtures. 300
Smedley, H and H A Clear. 770 3d av ...T Rourke. Saloon Fixtures. 200

Worms, H. Canarsie....Ravenswood Art Glass Works. Machinery, &c. 2,018

ASSIGNMENTS OF CHATTEL MORTGAGES.

Schwencke, C to M M Ramsay. (Mort given by E Schwaner, Sept 22, 1891.) 100

NEW JERSEY.

ESSEX COUNTY.

NOTE.—*The arrangement of the Conveyances, Mortgages and Judgments in these lists is as follows: the first name in the Conveyances is the Grantor; in Mortgages, the Mortgagor; in Judgments, the Judgment debtor.*

CONVEYANCES.

Abbe, Walter—W Logan, Montclair............ $2,800
Ayers, I M—A E Johnson, n e cor Alpine st and Ridgewood av 25x91.... 5,500
Ball, Isaiah—J Illingworth, East Orange........ 24,000
Same——C B Matthews, East Orange.......... 300
Same——same, East Orange.................12,000
Baker, J W—S Ball, Milburn.......... 300
Barney, C T—C M Rutan, Franklin 1,800
Beam, M E—A F Bontecou, Bloomfield.......... 7,750
Bingham, J E—F W Peloubet, East Orange..... 6,500
Black, Foster—I Ball, East Orange.............. 1
Bonykamper, Frederick—C Honecker, Frankfort st 1
Bornemann, George—J J Dill, South Orange.... 300
Bray, J B—J Frankel, s s Montgomery st 80 e Broome st 31x123............ 5,100
Breakenridge, J H—H E Carman, Clinton...... 1
Brown, C. J—C Biermann, Adams st............
Brown, William—C J Brown, Adams st..........
Buermann, August—M Eisele, n e cor Belmont av and Madison av, 30x125........ [illegible]
Cadmus, A A—H P Gerbert, Orange.... 1
Casserly, Annie—E Y Nully, Orange.......... 1
Cheatle, A E—The [illegible] B and L L Assoc, 3d st 750
Coe, J A—J Merz, Spruce st............ 1,000
Coe, C A—T Coe, South 9th st............ 1
Coe, Abby dec'd by exr—C A Coe, South 9th st. 1,900
Same——M K Danzeisen, South 9th st......... 650
Collins, S L—Trustees of School Dist No 8, Montclair............ 9,000
Conduit, E W—A R Thompson, Franklin.... .. 1,600
Connolly, Thomas—J Martin, Belleville........ 160
Cook, E E—M L Lewis, s s Fulton st 60 n land of Van Rensellaer 35x100............12,000
Corey, S B—H Jerolamen, Salt Meadow........ 120
Courter, J L—J Denninger, Littleton.... 2,210
Crocker, C D B—J Cahill, East Orange........ 6,500
Day, H M—J Christiansen, Orange st.......... 1,000
Dess, A O—E Ufford, Cherry st.............. 1
Devine, Arthur—J C Wilson, Jabez st.......... 2,880
Dixon, D L—C E Watkins, Van Buren st......... 800
Edwards, F C—E Knorr, Wall st.............. 1
Eyrich, Emil—The American Ins Co, Camden st 500
Farley, E A—T S Kearns, New st............ 5
Fell, L T, assignee—F Berg, Orange 800
Ferreira, Joseph—W R Adams, Clinton.......... 275
Flohn, F L—A G Kirk, 2d av............ 225
Gardner, C A—The M & E R R Co, South Orange 100
Geach, E P—D P Cleary, Orange............ 700
Gorski, Catharina—J C Eisele, s s South Orange av 21 w Hayes st 25x100.......... 5,350
Graft, J C—A Lemassena, Jr, West Park st. ... 2,500
Hall, M J—L Lewis, Springfield av............ 1,000
Harrison, C J—J McInerney, West Orange...... 250
Same——J Lynch, West Orange............ 125
Havemeyer, W F—F M Wilmurt, South Orange. 25,000
Heyward, J H—T Connell, Bloomfield.......... 300
Headley, W C—M McDonough, Clinton 650
Henessey, M J—M Landry, South 9th st......... 1
Herman, Rosie—I Beekman, e s High st 50 s Court st 25x135............ 8,000
Heyden, Edward—C Schaeffer, Clinton 1,000
Hopkins, John—R Cross, East Orange........... 3,300
Jenle, Mary—J Harter, Hunterdon st........... 300
Johnson, A E—F B Allen, w s South 14th st 71 n Avon av............ 7,500
Kearney, Margaret—J Perry, East Orange...... 479
King, J R—E J Austin, n e cor Frelinghuysen av and Emmett st 25x100............ 3,500
Krug, I F—C W Menk, East Orange............ 5,500
Landy, Michael—M J Henessey, South 9th st.... 1
Le Massena, Andrew, Jr—J C Graft, s s West Park st 46 e Halsey st 22x84.......... 5,500
Leipert, Leopold—M Heller, Hamburgh pl...... 1
Lindsley, O W—A J Kotze, East Orange........ 200
Lyon, Aaron—R H Lyon et al, Orange.......... 1
McElhose, Wm—K Baumgartner, Brill st........ 650
McNally, Martin—A Casserly, Orange....... . 1
Mellen, Michael—A Guenther, s w cor Sussex av and Lock st 51x84...........10,000
Mitchell, S M B et al—J McKevitt et al, Madison st............ 1,100
Muchmore, E B—W F Wangner, 7th av.......... 425
Nichols, W S—F Newhauss, East Orange....... 450
Otis, H G—L W Doland, North 11th st.......... 1,400
Pain, A J—A E Cheatle, 3d st............ 725
Peterson, Samuel—P E Durst, Montclair........ 5,400
Pollard, D B—F L Meyer, s w s Elm st 300 w Prospect st 25x95............ 3,500
Pruden, C B—W H Trippe, n w s Myrtle av 180 s w Orange st 16x37............ 3,800
Rayner, J W—J E Weaver, Bloomfield.......... 1
Righter, W A—P Terluccio, O'Connell st 1
Same——P Carluccio, O'Connell st.... 500
Rossmann, Anton exr—K Friedrich, 12th av.... 2,800
Rowe, Michael—T W Dalton, Central av......... 1
Runyon, O E—C L Sesler, Poinier st............ 3,600
Schulz, John—B Schulz, South Orange av. 1
Schulz, Charles—J Schulz, South Orange av ... 1
Sheridan, Bernard—O McCabe, s s Market st 107 w Union st 31x22x18x16x80x25 4,300
Smith, F H, Jr—G W Stidfole, e s Summer av 125 s May st 25x116............ 4,400
Snyder, John—S M Aldridge, rear Plane st...... 1,361
Somerville, Alonzo—O E Runyon, Poinier st.... 1
Stubenazy, G H—Fidelity Title and Deposit Co, Elm st 2,500
Sullivan, M F—L Gottheimer, West Orange.... 375
The E G Faitoute Coal Co—B Strauss, Railroad av............ 1,400
The Prudential Ins Co—E Haines, s e cor Broad and Franklin sts 28x90............ 1
The Central N J Land Improvement Co—M A Craig, Market st............ 900
Thompson, A R—J L May, Franklin.... 800
Ticheuor, H H—J Henrich, Fairmount av....... 850
Tunison, Edward—J N Hesse, 1st tract s s 2d av 75 w North 6th st, 2d tract e s North 6th st, 3d tract n e cor 2d av and North 6th st...... 8,090
Trimble, J M—G Serratelli, Drift st............ 1,300
Ufford, Eleanor—C Reilly, s s Cherry st 135 n Canal st............ 3,500
Warren, D T—T C Wallace, Montclair......... .. 4,849
Ward, E G—W S Spalding, Bloomfield....... ... 4,250
Ward, F C—L B Nick, Bloomfield......... .. 4,000
Ward, P H—J S Bonnett, North 4th st........ .. 500
Weidenfeld, Camille—The Howard Savings Inst, West Orange 10,000
Whittingham, W C—W R Whittingham, Milburn 1
Weaver, E P—J W Rayner, Bloomfield.......... 1
Wichelhaus, Frederick — W E Wichelhaus, Academy st............ 1
Wichelhaus, W E—A Wichelhaus, Academy st.. 1
Wilmurt, F M—F W Belmont, Prospect av...... 1
Wilfruth, Emil—M Geckle, Littleton av.......... 1
Winchell, E E—A J Van Ness, East Orange...... 8,500

MORTGAGES.

Alruth, Ernst—C A Feick, Bank st............ 800
Atchason, E M—H Alling, 3d st..... 1,000
Attridge, Thomas—Ross C Browning, Orange. . 1,000
Ayres, C W—F D Baker, Montclair............ 4,000
Barnett, Thomas—C A Feick, 12th av.......... 150
Benedict, E E—The Newark Fire Ins Co, Fair st. 5,000
Berrien, M A—H S T Martin, East Orange 500
Boscaino, Lorenzo—10th Ward B & L Assoc, Factory st............ 1,400
Booth, J J, Jr—F Berg, Orange 2,100
Brady, John—B M Shanley, Bridge st 5,000
Same—— G W Tompkins, Bridge st.......... 3,000
Busse, J M—H Duerner, Sayres st............ 400
Caamano, Emanuel—A P C[illegible], West Orange. 2,000
Campfield, Alexander—B Me[illegible]inger, Penna av. 2,100
Chew, C P—F H Smith, Jr, Mt Pleasant av...... 1,000
Chittenden, H A—F D Baker, Montclair......... 2,300
Christiansen, John—H M Day, Orange st....... 750
Clark, M S—L H Trimmer, Wash[illegible] av 1,700
Clement [illegible] [illegible]00
Cog[illegible] [illegible]boom at the mouth of the Black River has shut down for the season. The output was the smallest in [illegible] story of the boom—smaller by nearly 100,000,000
Conn[illegible] [illegible] Belleville...... [illegible]
Connor, Peter—A Malloy, Aqueduct st.......... 1,600
Cowles, [illegible]—North Jersey Land Co, Montclair.. 1
Craig, M [illegible]—The Central N J Land Improvement Co, Market st............ 400
Crater, G B—Fidelity Title and Deposit Co, Johnson st............ 700
Cross, Richard—Orange Memorial Hospital, East Orange............ 3,000
Cummings, Frederick—G D Bernius, Orange.... 7,000
Same——J P McGovern, Orange....... 5,000
Demmick, E C—E G Kempf, Mt Prospect av.... 1,200
Dodd, Louisa—L E Cook, East Orange...... .. 2,500
Delano, L W—H G Otis, North 11th st.......... 700
Dougherty, Andrew—J Hague, East Orange.... 400
Douglass, E M—E G Everitt, Orange...... 6,000
Dietze, Caroline—J Busse, Fairview av.......... 1,800
Durst, P E—E M Sanford, Montclair............ 1,400
Same——same, Montclair 1,500
Edwards, Robert—The 14th Ward B and L Assoc, Clinton............ 1,200
Eichenlaub, Xaver—J E Jackson, Boyd st. 1,500
Eisele, Marie—A Buermann, Belmont av 3,700
Englert, Magdalena—13th Ward B and L Assoc, Court st............ 1,000
Everitt, E A—Half Dime Savings Bank, Orange. 2,000
Everitt, E G—E M Douglass, Orange............ 3,500
Fenner, Henry—B L Pierson, South Orange 6,486
Féra, Gaicomo—J M Trimble, Chestnut st...... 3,000
First National Bank—N P Vanderhoof, Broad st............ 2,775
Fischer, L A—L Klots, Caldwell.. 1,000
Flaherty, Ann—W S Williams, Orange 1,000
Frankel, Jacob—J B Bray, Montgomery st 2,000
Freeman, Grace—S Martin, Bloomfield......... 2,500
Friedrich, Kunigunda—G Toblemann, 12th av... 1,700
Fuller, E C—S A Edmonston, Montclair......... 9,500
George, M L—M Mellen, Central av............ 1,500
Gerbert, H P—Half Dime Savings Bank, Orange. 3,000
Gould, W H—B Klotz, Caldwell 1,000
Glassen, John—J C Smith, Fairview av 500
Guenther, Adam—Hill's Union Brewery Co, Sussex av............ 2,000
Same——M Mellen, Sussex av............ 7,500
Haines, Eleanor—Prudential Ins Co, Broad st... 8,000
Halsey, M E—W C Headley, 15th st.. 175
Hampson, William—Horace Dodd, Bloomfield.. 200
Henrich, John—C Treusch, Fairmount av...... 3,500
Herrmann, Gottlieb—F Bonykamper, Jr. Merchant st............ 1,000
Hesse, J N—E Tunnison, 2d av............ 4,700
Honacker, Christian—F Bonykamper, Jr, Frankfort st............ 1
Hovey, J B—Howard Savings Inst, Orleans st... 2,500
Howard, G E P—P E Penniman, South Orange. 4,240
Illingsworth, John—E Lister, East Orange......10,000
Ippolito, Vitale—J Romano, 8th av............ 150
Jenkins, F L—C Jenkins, Clinton........... ... 2,000
Jones, S M—J O Terhune, Caldwell.... 900
Kelly, Julia—J J Henry, Morris av.... 900
Kenny, John—J Grace, Mulberry st............ 5,000
Lewis, M L—L E Cook, s s Fulton st 60 n e land John Van Rensselaers 35x104.... 12,000
Lippincott, S N—Fraternal B & L Assoc, Franklin............ 2,000
Lock, Rosine—N Feick, Walnut st............ 300
Logan, William—W Abbe, Montclair............ 2,460
Lyon, H T—A D Hopping, Milford av... 500
Mackey, C E—Knights of Pythias B & L Assoc, Oriental st............ 100
Mallaby, Theodore—F R Dumont, Franklin 2,000
McCormick, Patrick—N Derostro, East Orange. 300
Memminger, Matthias—Orange Valley B & L Assoc, Orange............ 200
Mery, John—American Ins Co, Prince st........ 6,500
Meyer, F L—S B Pollard, Elm st.... 2,500
Meyer, Magdalena—Security B & L Assoc, Barclay st............ 500
Mortoccio, Rocco—J Frank, Broome st.......... 3,200
Murden, H L—Howard Savings Inst, East Orange............ 2,700
Neuhans, G O—M O'Brien, Clinton 800
Osborn, Thomas—The Newark B and L Assoc, Newark st............ 100
Parillio, Christoforo—J M Trimble, Sheffield st.. 200
Perkins, F W—F C Edwards, Bloomfield......... 565
Raab, W R—The Essex Co B & L Assoc, Bloomfield............ 1,800
Rathers, J J—The Essex Co B and L Assoc, Bloomfield 1,700
Reilly, Catharine—E Ufford, Cherry st.......... 1,000
Rogers, M A—Enterprise B and L Assoc, Summer av............ 2,500
Rossendale Belting Co—F Q Barston, Euclid av.30,000
Ross, C P—J J Henry, Bloomfield av.... 1,000
Rumpf, G E—The Woodside B and L Assoc, adj N Y & G L R R............ 1,000
Ryan, Michael—J V Diefenthaler, East Orange. 1,800
Scarpone, Donato—G Zanelli, Canal st.......... 1,500
Schaeffer, Carl—Edward Heyden, Clinton....... 500
Schanibacher, A K—S Steffens, Clinton. 4,000
Scheerer, G O—E Schickhaus et al exrs, Clinton 800

Schwankert, C W—C Tiff, 18th av.... 3,000
Shipman, Daisy—Fidelity Title and Deposit Co, Garside st.... 3,500
Smalley, M S—H Bidewell, Clinton.... 3,400
Smith, B E—A Campfield, South 13th st.... 1,500
Spatola, Gerardo—J M Trimble, Boyden st.... 100
Squier, F C—M E Camfield, East Orange.... 1,000
Stidfole, G W—F H Smith, Jr, Summer av.... 3,000
Stout, H P—Newark Fire Ins Co—East Orange.. 300
Strasburger, A C—M Lewis exr, Hayes st.... 400
Theberath, A R—C Poehlman, 7th st.... 1,000
Tompkins, G W—J Brady, cor Bridge st and Lombardy pl 24x48x30x4x25x40.... 8,500
Trustees of Cedar Grove Union Congregational Church—C F Wettyen, Caldwell.... 1,900
Valente, Giovanni—Tenth Ward B and L Assoc, 14th av.... 500
Van Ness, E A—J V Diefenthaler, Winthrop st.. 400
Villey, E A—J V Diefenthaler, East Orange.... 1,000
Vreeland, D J—E E Kierstead, Franklin.... 400
Same——same, Franklin.... 100
Vogel, Kilian—C F Rehmann, Bergen st.... 1,600
Wallace, T C—D T Wallen, Montclair.... 4,000
Ward, A S—F Frelinghuysen, Roseville av.... 4,000
Way, M J—The Howard Savings Inst, Plane st.. 300
White, C R—C O Ripley, Chestnut st.... 1,500
Wilson, S A—Knights of Pythias B and L Assoc, 4th av.... 2,200
Zarra, Nicola—A Del Guercio, 8th av.... 366

CHATTEL MORTGAGES.

Andrews, C K—E Walte, saloon.... 1,170
Berg, Charles—Standard Oil Co, horses and trucks.... 265
Bernhardt, G M—G Krueger Brewing Co, saloon 500
Blend, Frances—J Euckelshaus, furniture.... 134
Cooney, [illegible] which sold at about [illegible].... 400
[illegible]302,837 feet per Brederfolket, from Pasc[illegible] [illegible]
a dealer. The market is firm at 48$000 a 49$000 per dozen.
White Pine.—Receipts nil and the market is [illegible]
Farrelly, Matthew—P Ballantine & [illegible].... 175
Gaynor, T C—The Nat Cash Reg Co, register.... 175
Gernand, C A—C Feigenspan, saloon.... 500
Goette, Emil—J Ringeisen, machinery.... 200
Greenberg, K—Muller & Schmidt, furniture.... 120
Hafen, Jacob—Hirschfield & Co, safe.... 75
Helms, Ernst—L Fetter, greenhouses.... 2,000
Joachim, Benj—Hirschfield & Co, safe.... 80
Jung, Daniel—H Pfeifer, horse and wagon.... 150
Kinney, S O—T W R Rayner, furniture.... 100
Knight, H P—G Lewis, cows.... 50
Krauss, C W—A W Turten, machinery.... 95
Krauss, C W et al—A Hofft, machinery.... 100
Marks, Samuel—Hirschfield & Co, safe.... 120
Mitler, Pinkus—Hirschfield & Co, safe.... 55
McNally, Thomas—J M Hann, furniture.... 130
Murphy, T A—The Nat Cash Reg Co, register.... 175
Perkins, M V—E C Edwards, furniture.... 565
Pinelly, Thomas—Hirschfield & Co, safe.... 45
Ross, John—Essex Co Brewing Co, saloon.... 200
Sauerbier, Belle—J Ketcham, furniture.... 63
Steipe, Charles—C M Schmidt, horses and wagon 160
Temme, Ernst—A B Erdmann, printer fixtures. 1,800
Terbell, W D—E D Gardner, drugs.... 600
The Field Club of Short Hills—The Brunswick-Balke-Collender Co, pool table.... 290
Van Orden, Lyman—J Ketcham, furniture.... 100
Vincentz, T E—L Bloomer, machinery.... 50
Vogel, Kilian—C F Rehman, machinery.... 1,600
Walsh, J B—J Ketcham, furniture.... 100
Williams, W H—E J Woods, machinery.... 600
Wohlfarth, Emil—Hirschfield & Co, safe.... 60
Zeidler, F A—Essex Co Brewing Co, saloon.... 473

JUDGMENTS.

Adler, A S et al—V E Adler.... 9,924
Same——The Newark City Nat Bank.... 5,022
Same——H Mitchell.... 20,804
Heath, Charles et al—G W Robinson.... 483
Johnson, Richard—G R Gray et al.... 279
Krauss, C W et al—W L Glorieu.... 1,284
McDougall, J M—W Howarth et al.... 326
The Keystone Watch Club Co—I W Jaques.... 2,583

HUDSON COUNTY.

CONVEYANCES.

Alsberg, Zelina—F C Crevier, Hoboken.... nom
Ashdown, M M—Sarah J Purdy, West Hoboken. $1,000
Bancher, Ella A—Sallie Keely.... 6,450
Bonn, H J—O Schultz, West Hoboken.... nom
Borcher, August F—G Roman, Weehawken.... 000
Brown, Pauline C—A Ackerman, Hoboken.... 8,000
Bruno, Werner—G T Ebers.... 400
Bucklin, Arabella A—C A Bucklin.... nom
Burney, Josephine Y—A Scheubel, Harrison.... 600
Same——Gertrude Baierle, Harrison.... 600
Burns, Catharine—C D Ayres, Bayonne.... nom
Charlemaine, Eliza—J A Lane, West Hoboken. 2,800
Coles, Eliza C—S H Smith.... 3,500
Condit, Fillmore—E Sargeant, Kearney.... 450
Same——W Meiklejohn, Kearney.... 250
Connolly, John—T Smith, Kearney.... 1,450
Connolly, M T—Zelina Alsberg, Hoboken.... nom
Connolly, Jno—Grace Smith, Harrison.... 450
Condict, Sophia L—S A Condict.... nom
Cook, Mary—J E Carlock.... 100
Coster, E H—W H Leicht, Hoboken.... nom
Costello, Dennis—Julia Costello.... nom
Coyle, Anne—T Coyle.... nom
Coyle, Thomas——same.... nom
Daffeldecker, Elizabeth—C W Jacob.... 100
Drescher, Chas by exrs—P Schmidt, West Hoboken.... 400
Ebers, G T—E S McMurray.... 427
Eilshemius, H G—G W Uhlig, Kearney.... 1,500
Same——R A Wagner, Kearney.... 1,150
Emmons, E F—E P Young.... 8,050
Falkinburgh, Job—Ella J Kachler.... 900
Filker, Louis—W V Smith, Union.... 200
Fink, Fred—G Muller, Jr, North Bergen.... 3,000
Fishbourne, Robt—M Stalowisky.... 225
Fitch, Harriet—P Powderly.... 1,000
Frembley, Kate—Annie Muller, Bayonne.... 240
Gifford, Eleanor C—W H Speer.... 7,000
Gilchrist, Fredericka B—P Turley.... 8,230
Gils, Richard—H H Thurber, North Bergen.... 14,000
Gregory, Eliza M—C Handel.... 6,800
Hardy, G G—Emma F Smith, Kearney.... 600
Haver, E A—J B McNeill, Bayonne.... nom
Heinrich, F J by sheriff—W Smith, Union.... 1,300
Hoboken Land and Imp't Co—J C Crevier, Hoboken.... 5,040
Holzberger, Andreas—Catharine Holzberger.... nom
Jennings, W N—W Maloy, Kearney.... 2,500
Johnston, Caroline W—Caroline A Osborn, Kearney.... 400
Johnston, Caroline W—W M Kenworthy, Kearney.... 450
Keenan, Hugh—J Daly.... 1,950
Keller, J L—Julia Costello.... nom
Kendall, Amanda P—H Schulz, Kearney.... 4,250
Kneale, T A—W Cullen.... 1,500
Knighton, C L—T H Taylor, Bayonne.... 1,300
Lawless, Annie—H V Condict.... nom
Lembeck, Florence and Anna F Wood by special master—R Midgley, Bayonne.... 900
Lynes, Emily—W G Bumsted.... 100
McLoughlin, T J—Bridget E Byrnes.... 600
Meyer, W A—Eva Malkomesius, Hoboken.... 4,400
Mohne, Rosetta—W Hyka, Hoboken.... 1,800
Nolle, Albert—Mayor and Aldermen of J City.... 3,000
Moore, F H—F R Staats, Hoboken.... 4,500
Murphy, Michael by exrs—Elizabeth M Murphy. 4,000
Murphy, William—Bridget Mulvihill.... 400
O'Brien, Maurice—R P Fisher, Bayonne.... [illegible] exch of property and nom
Owen, Henry—P Brandt, Harrison.... 1,300
Pape, Gotthold—H B Rue, Hoboken.... 3,200
Parker, C W—T H Taylor, Bayonne.... 1,275
Same——J H Mahnken, Bayonne.... 3,900
Same——O Perry, Bayonne.... 1,8[illegible]0
Pflugsten, Conrad—Otellie Perrin.... 1,900
Poole, W T—Katharine Ewald.... 7,000
Richer, H A—C Spierling.... 3,500
Robbins, A S—Chas H Caulfield.... 1,200
Shafer, Frances L and Caroline L Bergen by sheriff—C E Annett, Bayonne.... 2,000
Sheridan, Pat—E J Foley.... 1,500
Shield, Emil—B Alt, Union.... 6,500
Siegfried, Adam—Dina Jacobs, West Hoboken. 1,400
Simonds, A B—J McWille, Harrison.... 800
Smith, Thomas—J Hendny, Kearney.... 1,700
Smyth, Warne—The William Peter Brewing Co, Union.... 1,800
Soria, Zipporah—Fidilia M Stevens.... 4,000
The American Ins Co—J J Scott.... 6,000
Thurber, H H—Board of Chosen Freeholders of Hudson County, North Bergen.... 36,500
[illegible] Mary S—H E Frue.... 500
To[illegible], Mary E—D Lewis.... 500
Tow[illegible] C S by special master—C T Van Dieren, Harrison.... 465
Same——same, Harrison.... 500
Van Buskirk, Rebecca L—W [illegible] O'Neill, Bayonne.... 1,800
Van Emburgh, J D—Mary Murray, Kearney.... 100
Van Wagenen, Jacob—Thos Kenney.... 600
Vom Fell, Auguste—E Freund.... 3,000
Wheeler, W R—J A Wikander.... 2,500
Whyte, W C—W G Bumsted.... 1,200
Winner, Jno—West Side Connecting R R Co.... 3,500
Wood, Ann F and Florence Lembeck by special master—M Ryan, Bayonne.... 325
Wood, Anna F and Florence Lembeck by special master—J H Mahnken, Bayonne.... 200
Same——same, Bayonne.... 200
Same——same, Bayonne.... 200
Woolsey, T B and H D Stucke by sheriff—Rosetta Mohn, J City and elsewhere.... 1,200
Wright, Naomi C E by exrs—M T Connolly.... 13,500

MORTGAGES.

Abbott, Ann—The Mount Morris Co-operative B and L Assoc, Bayonne, installs.... 1,230
Alsberg, Zerline—J Bruck, Hoboken, 3 years.... 9,000
Alt, Benedict—F Schimper, Union, 3 years.... 5,000
Banta, Louisa A—Julia A Pierson, 1 year.... 4,700
Same——same, 1 year.... 100
Bayer, Bernhard—Hoboken B and L Assoc, Hoboken, installs.... 600
Beck, Chas—Sarah Megonigil, Bayonne, 5 years 1,700
Brady, Peter, Jr—Greenville B and L Assoc, Bayonne, installs.... 5,840
Bucklen, C A—Garfield B and L Assoc, installs.. 1,900
Burch, Maria T—Hudson City M B and L Assoc, installs.... 600
Burke, Timothy and J H Jones—The New Jersey Title Guarantee and Trust Co, installs.... 4,500
Caulfield, C H—A S Robbins, 3 years.... 1,000
Carll, Carolina—Hudson Trust and Savings Inst, West Hoboken, 3 years.... 1,000
Crevier, J C—B Smith trustee, Hoboken, 1 year. 7,000
Same——same, Hoboken, 1 year.... 7,000
Cook, W H—W P Wescott, Bayonne, 1 year.... 150
Connolly, M T—Exrs Naomi C E Wright, 3 yrs. 9,000
Daly, John—H Keenan, 3 years.... 800
Ewald, Katharina—Mary M Miller, 1 year.... 3,500
Evans, Fannie—J E Andrus, Bayonne, 6 morts, each $2,500, 3 years.... 15,000
Felter, Lizzie R—Exrs H G Vreeland, 3 years.... 2,250
Fitzsimmons, Chas—Columbia B and L Assoc, installs.... 1,000
Freund, Emanuel—Auguste Vom Fell, 5 years.. 1,500
Same——same, 3 years.... 300
Fuss, Ludwig—Emily G Ridgely, Union, 5 years 3,000
Gill, William—Helen Cadmus, Bayonne, 1 year. 600
Gotthardt, Harriet—O Perry, 5 years.... 8,000
Haskard, Mary C—Greenville B and L Assoc, Bayonne, installs.... 3,650
Heinzelman, Jno—T King, Harrison, 1 year.... 1,000
Hermann, Sophie L—Emil Sohmann, 5 years.... 1,500
Hocke, Mary A—Jane O'Mara, 10 years.... 5,000
Houghlithin, Alfred—Lafayette M B and L Assoc, installs.... 2,400
Hyatt, Mary D—Kearney B and L Assoc, Kearney, installs.... 2,600
Hyka, William—J C Crevier, Hoboken, 3 years. 9,000
Jones, Julia T—Pamrapo B and L Assoc, Bayonne, installs.... 1,680
Kachler, August—F J Falkenburgh, 3 years.... 450
Keeley, Sallie—Exrs H G Vreeland, 3 years.... 3,000
Kenney, Thomas—J Van Wagenen, 1 year.... 800
Lincks, J F—H Puster exrs, 1 year.... 985
Livingston, William—Exrs N S Hibber, installs.. 2,500
Maebert, Alexander—C Poppen, installs.... 3,275
McCarthy, Mary F—G K Camp, 1 year.... 125
McMurray, E S—The Bergen Land and Imp't Co, installs.... 1,440
Miller, Gustav—C L G Lemhardt, West Hoboken, 5 years.... 250
Miller, J H—The Lafayette M B and L Assoc, installs.... 3,200
Petroins, J B—Exrs M Corsegier, Hoboken, 2 years.... 2,800
Rusterer, Anna—The Hudson Trust and Savings Inst, North Bergen, 5 years.... 500
Schmidt, Jno—S Fisher, Weehawken, 5 years.... 2,500
Schmidt, Phillip—Emily Schield, West Hoboken, 3 years.... 300
Schultz, Otto—J J McPhillips, West Hoboken, 1 year.... 6,000
Schuyler, C V—H K Schuyler, Kearney, 3 years. 3,000
Scott, J J—The American Ins Co, 1 year.... 4,500
Same——William Peter Brewing Co, 1 year.... 1,000
Sealey, J K—W G Nelson, 1 year.... 350
Smith, Grace—D Dunn, Harrison, 1 year.... 1,800
Staats, F R—F H Moore, Hoboken, 5 years.... 3,500
Strothmann, Henry—J Widmann, 1 year.... 550
The Norwegian Evangelical Congregational Church — The American Congregational Union, Hoboken, 1 year.... 1,500

CHATTEL MORTGAGES.

Brackner, G J—The Jas Cunningham Son & Co, Berlin coach.... 800
Budenbender, Louis, Hoboken—Bernheimer & Schmidt, saloon.... 1,000
Burt, G H, Newark—Brooklyn Furniture Co, furniture.... 151
Condon, Thomas F, Perth Amboy——same, furniture.... 141
De Barbiere & Lavazzi, West Hoboken—The William Peter Brewing Co, 1 beer apparatus and brass drip.... 108
Eckhoff, George—C J Durland, butcher shop.... 50
Fallon, M, Hoboken—Brooklyn Furniture Co, furniture.... 160
Farr, C J, Bayonne—J Baumann, furniture.... 301
Farrell, B—Nat Cash Reg Co, cash register.... 160
Feinberg, Harris, Secaucus—I Feinberg, cows, horses, trucks, &c.... 3,169
Frank, Alexander—H Thoesen, furniture.... 139
Garbs, D H—Bernheimer & Schmidt, saloon.... 600
Giesecke, Ehrich, Hoboken—The F & M Schaefer Brewing Co, saloon fixtures.... 275
Glass, Katie—J Mullins & Co, furniture.... 220
Griffin, W J and E C Struck, partners as Griffin & Struck—The Manhattan Type Foundry, printing press, &c.... 806
Guest, Richard, Bayonne—John Mullins & Co, furniture.... 301
Guyee, N Y——same, furniture.... 301
Hashagen, George—M & S Meyer, horses, trucks 350
Hauf, Vesta E—J S Beardsley, furniture.... 250
Hergert, Emert, Bayonne—C Feigenspan, saloon.... 75
Hill, L P—Brooklyn F Co, furniture.... 129
Lynch, J F—Nat Cash Reg Co, cash register.... 375
Neckham, Max, Hoboken—Philip Schaefer & Sons, saloon.... 650
Noll, Arthur—Beadleston & Woerz, saloon fixtures.... 750
O'Neill, Charles—J Mullins & Co, furniture.... 369
Paulsen, Herman and Johanna, Hoboken—E Clausen, furniture.... 70
Reining, Albert J C—J Baumann, furniture.... 129
Reppert, Frank—J Mullins & Co, furniture.... 170
Roeder, J H, Hoboken—A Cammezar, barber shop and furniture.... 150
Roppe, Diedrich, West Hoboken—H A Boschers, horse, wagon, grocery fixtures.... 400
Ryder, C B—D Steale, furniture.... 560
Schaefer, William, Hoboken—Lembeck & Betz Eagle Brewing Co, saloon.... 626
Schneider, Albert—L Heisterhagen, grocery store.... 300
Schmidt, William, West Hoboken—A W Theiler, barber fixtures.... 200
Stadler, Albert, Union—A M Peter, saloon fixtures.... 2,000
Stortenbecker, Charles, North Bergen—E Wulff, horses, wagon, harness, cows.... 150
Trers, Henrich, West Hoboken—H A Borcher, horses, wagons, feed business.... 500
Uarbach, Louis, Hoboken—H Kleit, sausage business.... 100
Van Bussum, G M—C Poppen, jewelry business 3,275

BILLS OF SALE.

Bailey, John and J M Gillespie, Arlington—Sarah M Gillespie, butcher business, horses, wagons and harness.... 2,400
Guaraglia, F M, Union—A Stadley, saloon.... 2,000
Krem, C G, Hoboken—J H Roder, barber shop, &c.... 150
Poppen, Charles—G M Van Bussum, jewelry business.... 3,275
Touchsers, W J—J Seals, horse, wagon, &c.... 100

JUDGMENTS.

Baher, Annie H—W S Emery.... 99
Lennon, Edward—C Tabeck.... 683
McCloskey, Patrick—H Simpson.... 42
Seals, P D—J Seals, admr of Harriet Sliber.... 40
Ward, Elizur—J L Gilbert.... 6,447
Ward, Mary V—J Seals, admr of Harriet Sliber. 40
Woltjen, Frederick and John—A Steenken et al. 95

MECHANIC'S LIEN.

Perrine, Mary H, builder and owner; C W Fisk, claimant.... 705

BUILDING MATERIAL MARKET.

BRICKS.—The general condition of the market for Common Hards is at least no worse than a week ago and in some respects there appears to be a slight gain On prices, for instance, a great many of the trade still think $5.25 a full enough quotation and sales above that level are certainly uncommon. Yet they seem to be a little more frequent than at the commencement of the month, and we feel justified in raising figures slightly. Supplies have been plenty enough right along and generally of good quality, but met by a fairly neutralizing demand, most of which receivers appear to think was for actual consumption and represented no important call from dealers to pile away, which is certainly one of the good features of the situation. There has been so full an offering of pale as to make the supply appear almost liberal, yet a pretty good run of custom was found for the stock, and prices well sustained at $2.00@2.25 per M for the best goods. The demand for them come in the main from sources indicating suburban trade, and where consumption can progress without much danger of interference. Fronts are reported as selling well for the season and commanding full former rates in pretty much all cases. Regarding the shipment of brick from along the river the accounts at hand reveal practically nothing new, some few manufacturers abstaining entirely from forwarding any stock, but the majority working off a greater or less amount as facilities may offer, and no doubt proposing to continue that method so long as navigation permits, and our market shows any exhaustive capacity whatever. Of course, all process of manufacture is now suspended, and the shipments are direct from the kilns.

LATH.—The market shows about former prevailing conditions, but in stronger force, and the line of value is creeping upward. Dealers as a rule are not in immediate want of stock, but a few are looking about all the time and it is believed would pay higher rates than any yet attained if they could find a desirable offering. Since our last business has been done at $2.25 and that seems to be now considered rather inside if anything, on first-class stock at all events.

LIME.—So far as the general line of valuation is concerned there is no change worthy of note except that some of the least popular makes of Eastern have sold somewhat less than regular quoted rates. The arrivals have been less liberal and the accumulation fairly well worked down, but receivers intimate pretty firmly that they would be quite well satisfied should no cargoes come to hand for some little time.

LUMBER.—The consuming demand for lumber shows no general increase, and even in the exceptional cases where a new line of orders has been booked, it was only against work planned some time ago and fully expected. There are, to be sure, some dealers who appear to be keeping up quite a liberal distribution, but, as has already been suggested, they represent an exceptional portion of the trade blessed with either special custom or with yards located in peculiarly favored localities, while the majority are compelled to submit to a sort of mere jobbing deal on catch business. The attention given wholesale or bulk parcels is free from any evidence of general spirit or anxiety. There are a great many buyers who have probably carried the display of indifference too far, and allowed themselves to get into a position where they must now hurry greatly if they obtain the odd parcels required to fill out assortments, and that form of demand against moderate offerings proves advantageous to sellers who have really desirable goods to dispose of. There is, however, nothing to show that our market requires or would readily exhaust any greater quantity of stock than has of late come within reach. We are given to understand that the by-laws and rules and regulations of the Lumber Dealers' Association are progressing rapidly toward completion and will soon be ready for publication and distribution among the members, and the local trade at last seems to have a fully equipped, working representative body likely to prove beneficial all around.

It is officially announced that the state canals will be closed at midnight, November 30, unless ice does the work at an earlier date.

Eastern Spruce continues in about the same line last noted, and all the evidences go to show a gradually hardening market. There is altogether a pretty good accumulation of stock now here, some dealers with ample storage room, good credit or ready cash showing really liberal amounts; but there are also a great many who want a cargo or two to complete assortment, and they furnish a demand against the limited arrivals that is becoming somewhat stimulating. There is a noticeable slight irregularity in the line of valuation made by some of the receivers, but of late the general talk has been in favor of about \$15@16.00 per M. as inside on 9, 10 and 12-inch stuff, and \$13.25@13.50 up to \$14.00 on narrow, while it would probably be difficult to place yard orders for less than \$17.00@17.50, with \$18.00@18.50 for difficult schedules, and not many mills ready to consider the latter. Many manufacturers are understood to have entirely ceased cutting random.

Piling secures some attention for small odd jobs coming out, but has no full or general demand as yet, and finds little foundation upon which to build up an improving tone. Occasional fresh arrivals are reported, but there is plenty of stock in the basins for all present needs.

Hemlock finds some demand on car lot orders from custom wanting to fill out yard assortments or to provide against a special necessity; but there is no open or free call, and the customary autumn upward spring of values is lacking. The tone, however, is stiffer, and offerings are so gauged as to prevent pressure.

White Pine retains a good general position, and reports are cheerful. Of the ordinary qualities there is a pretty good supply on hand, but not so much offering from primary sources as heretofore, and with local holders now naturally interested in giving the value line support expressions are noticeably confident and cheerful. For the better grades the firmness is quite pronounced, the natural proportion being quite small, and as many dealers are seeking to round out assortments they give an impression of probably greater demand than really exists, but nevertheless acting as a stimulant at this season of the year. The run of export business is fair, with a few very good contracts now going on board, and there is hope of getting more of this trade after navigation closes at the North and East.

Yellow Pine shows a fully steady market and it is easy to discover a more cheerful strain in the average run of reports at present making. As with every other description of stock the actual consumption at the moment is moderate, but there is work coming on that will influence this class of wood more directly than any other, and little hesitation is felt about making an accumulation even upon basis of what may be considered natural influences alone. The movement among dealers, however, is a good big supporting element and altogether the present condition of the market is reasonably cheerful and promising. There has of late been a fair sort of export trade worked up on f. o. b. orders at Southern ports, including a few cargoes for Europe, but in the main for shipment to West Indies and Brazil, with some lots sent to River Plate, but the latter are understood to be mainly in execution of old contracts.

Carolina Pine shows essentially the same features as of late advised. There is outlet sufficient to take care of a considerable quantity of stock of standard grade, and buyers make no objection to former rates, but demand narrows somewhat as a seasonable matter, and is a little more careful in the selection.

Hardwoods remain practically unchanged. Consumers' wants at the moment are small, and in part anticipated through purchases previously made, and dealers show no special anxiety to add to accumulation in yard. However, there is a little popular selling all the while, at full former rates, where quality is first-class and the attraction of desirable parcels of pretty much all the other descriptions is pretty sure to tempt custom and at reasonably full bids too. Advices from primary sources are considered strengthening inasmuch as they go to show a smaller production than had been expected.

GENERAL LUMBER NOTES.

THE EAST AND CANADA.

A St. John lumberman is authority for the statement that the lumber operations the coming winter on the waters of the upper St. John will equal those of last year.

The lumber cut on the Restigouche, in New Brunswick, this year, will be about 4,500,000 of Spruce, and about 50,000,000 of Cedar. The cut of Spruce, says the *Telegraph*, will, therefore, be much smaller than last year, and that of Cedar very much larger. The manufacturing of shingles has become quite an industry on the North shore.

The Guelph Lumber Company's limits are said to have changed hands, being twice in six months. The previous sale was for \$250,000, exclusive of mills, houses, offices and town property. The second sale is to a Michigan man, for \$345,000, exclusive of mills, houses, offices and town property, and this after some ten years' cutting, at an average of about 10,000,000 feet a year.

Only 80,000,000 feet of logs have been brought from Canada to Michigan points this season, and a large quantity of those went to Tawas. One raft of 800,000 feet went to Alpena, and 8,000,000 to Cheboygan. Last year there were not over 50,000,000 feet brought over. Operations in Canada by Michigan lumbermen the coming winter will be upon a larger scale than ever before, and it is quite within bounds to state that 150,000,000 feet will be cut.

Speaking in regard to the rumored re-imposition of the export duty on saw logs by the Dominion government, the Toronto *Mail* strongly advises the government to let well enough alone. It predicts retaliation, as follows: "The export duty having been removed, its re-imposition would attract a degree of attention that was never given to the subject before the repeal of the duty, and no doubt the result would be that, as retaliation in kind could not be resorted to in consequence of the constitutional prohibition of any export duty, the case would be promptly met upon the assembling of Congress by the passage of a joint resolution adding the export duty on logs to the import duty on lumber imported from countries imposing an export duty. Under this arrangement, if the export duty was the same as when repealed, the duty on pine lumber would be \$4 and upon spruce lumber \$3 per thousand. This course would force an ignominious back-down upon our government, and the export duty would again be removed under circumstances less pleasant than in October, 1890."

THE WEST.

The Northwestern *Lumberman* as follows:

The two markets in which the lumber trade is in a specially thriving condition are Chicago and Minneapolis. These are the two great centres west of Lake Michigan. The activity in each reflects the prosperous condition of the vast grain region in the midst of which they are situated. In this city the copious movement of stocks is augmented by the World's Fair requirement, which is beginning to assume a magnitude that was at first but meagerly estimated by the most sanguine operators. Not only is the Northern supply pouring into this great vortex of consumption, but large timber bills are being suppled from the yellow pine mills of the South. Besides this special and extraordinary World's Fair demand, this market is supplying a wide reach of territory with rather more than the ordinary amount of stock. The call from Mississippi river points and westward of that stream is greater than for several years past. This is because of a partial failure of the log supply on the great river, and coming so early indicates that there will be a further increase of this unwonted requirement before next spring.

At Chicago:

Receipts for the week were light, and inquiry was fairly brisk. The yard dealers want piece stuff and boards of stock width as well as strips, lath and shingles. Piece stuff has advanced a shilling on short lengths, and some commission men affirm that they are getting 50 cents a thousand advance on slim jim and long wide joists. The yard dealers are less averse to paying slight increases in price than they were earlier in the season, for they know that if the market shall close firm, with higher prices than a few weeks ago, it will have a good influence on their lumber in yard.

Some commission men are claiming \$10.25 as the price of short piece stuff, but inquiry does not show that much has been sold for that unless there was some long stuff or other desirable lumber in the tally. The prospect, however, is that the price will further rise, especially if lake freight rates again advance, as is probable.

It is said by commission men who sell Muskegon, Manistee, Ludington and White Lake lumber, that there is not much more to come to the cargo market from those points. What there is has been largely bought up at the mills by dealers here. There is considerable to come forward from Green Bay and Lake Superior ports, however.

The Mississippi Valley *Lumberman* as follows:

The sawing season in the white pine district is drawing rapidly to a close. Every week adds to the number of mills out of commission for the season. Not more than a week or two more of sawing can be expected under the most favorable conditions, although the stock of logs is such at Menominee and Minneapolis—the two large points of production this season—that most of the mills might be kept busy until the first of December. The logs held in storage booms or back on the streams are in such position that the spring floods are certain to insure an early start. The large cut at the points named will be more than offset by the reduced production along the Mississippi river, in the Wisconsin valley, at La Crosse and elsewhere.

The boom at the mouth of the Black River has shut down for the season. The output was the smallest in the history of the boom—smaller by nearly 100,000,000 than last year. Work has also ceased at West Newton where the output is about half what it was last year, amounting to only about 300,000,000 feet. These figures are eloquent of the reduced production along the Mississippi River. There is reduction quite as large relatively in the Wisconsin valley.

The reports from booms and rafting works at the principal Michigan producing points also show large reduction in the output, although the shipments by water from markets like Muskegan and the Saginaw Valley show a corresponding, even if not greater, reduction than is shown in production. The Michigan

---

manufacturers have enjoyed no such steady and large demand as has fallen to the lot of the lumbermen supplying the trans-Mississippi trade.

The *Timberman* says:

Log driving in Michigan, Wisconsin and Minnesota has, as a rule, been pretty expensive work this season. On another page the *Timberman* correspondent tells of the success that has crowned the efforts of the Menominee River Boom Company in getting the logs down that river with an inkling at the same time of the expense of the work. On some of the other rivers the trouble has been greater and on some less, and on quite a number of streams a considerable portion of the logs are hopelessly hung up—at least for the present. On the Au Gress River, in Michigan, for example, out of a total cut of 20,000,000 feet of logs not less than 7,000,000 feet are hung up on the east branch.

GREAT BRITAIN.

The London *Timber Trades Journal* says of the Glasgow market:

As to Canadian goods sellers have no disposition to press sales, as on various considerations they are sanguine about an increase in price. Goods from the lower ports (deals, etc.) have been sparingly supplied, and inquiries for spruce are frequent, but present stock is very moderate, and the advance in shippers' quotations and cost of importations enhance the value of what is now held here. Nearly all descriptions of Quebec pine and hardwoods at present rule high and exhibit no signs of any tendency to be lower in price.

SOUTH AMERICA.

The Rio *News* by last mail reports:

Pitch Pine.—Receipts are 548,478 feet per henriqueta from Savannah, which sold at about 49$000 per dozen, and 592,837 feet per Brederfolket, from Pascagoula, to a dealer. The market is firm at 48$000 a 49$000 per dozen.

White Pine.—Receipts nil, and the market is reported firm at 140-150 rs. per foot.

Swedish Pine.—Receipts have been 971 dozen red deals, per Annine, from Westerwick, sold at 51$000 per dozen; 1,410 dozen per Njerstein, red, from Gefle, sold at about 18$000; 1,032 dozen, white, per Najaden, from Hernosand, sold at about 46$000, and 657 dozen per Liv, from Frederikshald, on order. The market is reported steady.

Spruce Pine.—The only thing of interest is the advice that three cargoes are afloat or loading for this market.

METALS.—COPPER.—Ingot has been moving in the main on old contracts, the new demand proving very moderate and indifferent, and buyers generally refusing to allow themselves to be induced to depart from the hand-to-mouth policy. Prices are a little nominal, but lack strength. On an average range of valuations we quote at 11⅛@11⅝c. for Lake, and 10⅞@11⅛c. for casting brands. Manufactured Copper meets rather slow sale, with some irregularity of tone developing, though official figures are understood to be unchanged. We quote as follows: Sheet, not above 30x72 in., 16 oz. and over, 25c.; do. 14 to 16 oz., 23c.; do. 12 to 14 oz., 24c.; do. 10 to 12 oz., 25c.; do. 8 to 10 oz., 28c.; do under 8 oz. 30c. Sheets longer than 72 inches add 1c. for 12@14 oz., 2c. for 10@12 oz. and 3c. for 8@10 oz. Sheets, not above 30x96 in., 16 oz and over, 22c.; do, 14 to 16 oz. 24c.; do, 12 to 14 oz, 26c.; do, 10 to 12 oz. 30c.; do, 8 to 10 oz. 33c. Sheets longer than 96 inches 22c. for over 32 oz. and add 1c. for 16 to 32 oz.; 3c. 14 to 16 oz.; 5c. 12 to 14 oz. and 13c. for 8 to 10 oz. Sheets, not above 48x96 32 to 64 oz, 22c. do, 16 to 32 oz. 25c.; do, 14 to 16 oz. 27c. do 12 to 14 oz, 29c.; do, 10 to 12 oz. 33c. Sheets wider than 48x96 and longer, 22@25c. for 32 to 64 oz. and over. 27@ .c. for 16 to 32 oz, 2 .c. for 14 to 16 oz and 34c. for 12 to 14 oz. All bath tub sheets, per lb., 16 oz. 7 .c.; 14 oz. 20c.; 12 oz 3 .c.; and 10 oz. 35c. Bolt copper, ⅝ inch diameter and over, 22c. Circles, 60 diameter and less, 3c. above price of sheets of same thickness; circles, 60 to 96 do do, 5c. do; circles, 96 do and over, 6c. do. Segment and pattern sheets, 3c. above price of sheets required to cut them from. Cold or hard rolled copper, 1@2c. per lb. above the foregoing prices. Copper bottoms, 26@32c. per lb. IRON—American Pig has really been very quiet, so much so that for some brands values are little better than nominal in the absence of testing sales. Agents, however, quite generally claim the position to be about steady and will admit of no positive shading on cost. We quote at $17.00@18.00 per ton for No. 1 X foundry; 15.50@16.50 for No. 2 X do. and $14.00@15.00 for Gray Forge. Old material has secured only a moderate measure of attention and generally show a weak sort of tone on values, though supplies are not urged into notice. We quote at about $22.00@22.50 for old rails; $19.00@19.50 for No. 1 wrought scrap; $17.00@18.00 for cast scrap and $17.00@17.50 for car wheels. Manufactured iron is dull on business from store, and finds only an indifferent degree of attention from operators seeking to place special contracts. We quote Common Merchant Bar ordinary size, at 1.90@2c. from store, and refined at 2@2⅛c; Rods, round and square, 2.10@2.30c.; Bands, 2.30@2.50c.; Norway Nail Rods 3¾@4c., and domestic sheet on the basis of 3.00@3.05c. for common Nos. 10@16. Other descriptions at corresponding prices, with 1-10c. less on large lots from cars. Steel rails have shown an improvement, one leading road placing an order for 70,000 tons, and other corporations showing some revival of interest on the lead thus set. The contracts are understood to have been closed without deviation from the association rates. We quote standard sections $30 per ton at mill, with usual advance for delivery at tide water. Pig Lead sold to some extent in small lots, but in order to attract and secure custom it became necessary to slightly modify the line of cost. Supplies are ample at present. We quote at 4.05@4.10c. per lb. The manufactures of lead are quoted at 7c. for Pipe, 7¾c. for Sheet, 15c. for Tin-lined Pipe, and 8⅞c. for Block Tin Pipe. Pig Tin has been rather flat in tone, and while more or less fluctuation in value at times developed, it was simply responsive to the foreign position and not the result of any local influence. We quote at about 19.80@19.90c. for round lots, and 20@20⅛c. for jobbing parcels. Tin Plate as offered does not show a very extensive assortment, yet in the face of continued moderate and more or less indifferent demand there is quite enough to go around, and rates make no improvement. We quote prices as follows: I. C. Charcoal, ⅛ cross assortment Melyn grade, $6.50@6.55, each additional X add $1.50; I. C. Charcoal, ⅛ cross assortment, Allaway grade, $5.85@5.90, each additional X add $1; Charcoal terne, M. F. grade, 14x20, $7.45@7.50; M. F. grade, 20x28, $15.20@15.25; Worcester, 14x20, $5.70@5.75; Worcester 20x28, $11.25@11.30; Dean grade, 14x20, $5.40@5.45; Dean grade, 20x28, $10.70@10.75; D. R. D. grade, 14x20, $5.25@5.30; D. R. D. grade, 20x28, $10.10½@10.15; I. C. Coke, Penlan grade, $5.25@5.30; J. B. grade, 14x20, $5.40@5.45; I. C. Bessemer steel, squares, $5.75@5.80 basis; I. C. Siemens steel, squares, $5.85@6.00 basis. Spelter finds slow sale, only in small lots, and the general tone is quite easy throughout. We quote $4.95@5.05c for Common Western, according to brand.

NAILS.—Buyers have not hurried, nor do they seem to act as though they expected to do so at any time during balance of year, and the entire market is in a dull, stupid condition. Offerings as common for a long time past has been ample if not excessive, and until actual curtailment of make is felt it will be difficult to get an adjustment between supply and demand. We quote Cut at $1.50@1.60 per keg for car lots and $1.75@1.85 per keg for parcels from store, for iron, and add 5@10c. per keg for steel; Wire, $2.00@2.05 at mills, and 2.20@2.35 from store.

PAINTS, OILS, COLORS, ETC.—There has been little or no change in the average condition of the market during the week. Some operators report a very good trade, and others complain of positive quietness, orders coming to hand only as necessity may inspire custom to obtain something to renew depleted assortments and maintain an ordinary run of stock. Expectations of a more liberal and anxious call upon the approach of winter have not yet been realized, and about the only dependent custom taking in a supply of goods against the future is the run of operators situated at out-of-the-way places where transportation becomes difficult and costly at this season of the year. With quite a fair measure of success, there is an effort to keep the first-hand offerings from coming upon sale beyond the requirements of the outlet, yet there is no scarcity whatever and sellers could promptly respond to an increase of demand. Prices are as a rule a little ragged, the natural outcome of the situation, but where there are regular list rates they are retained. It is asserted that on White Lead only outside makes can be bought at an off price. Association Corroders' rates stand as follows: Lead in oil in kegs and dry lead in kegs, in lots of less than 500 lbs., 7¼c. net; in lots of 500 lbs to 5 tons at one purchase, 7c.; 5 tons to 12 tons, one purchase, 6¾c.; 12 tons and over, one purchase, 6⅝c.; dry white lead in bbls. ¼c per lb. less than price in kegs. Lead in oil 12½ lb. in tin pails, add 1c.; in 25 and 50 lb. tin pails, add ½c.; and in 1 to 5 lb. tin cans, assorted (100 lbs. in case) add 2¼c. per lb. to keg price. Terms on lots on 500 lbs. and over, note of acceptance at sixty days, or 2½ per cent. discount will be allowed for cash paid within fifteen days of invoice date. To make either of the above required quantities any assortment of packages of white lead, red lead and litharge may be counted. The above quotations are free on board cars or boat at corroding point. Linseed Oil has been meeting with ordinary proportionate demand, and while somewhat irregular at times it is claimed that no first-class city makes are shaded in value. We quote at general range at 35@40c. for Western, and 40@56c. for City. Spirits Turpentine has shaded somewhat in cost, but advices from primary sources are now firmer and the influence is felt here. We quote at 36@37c. per gallon, according to quality, delivery, etc.

TAR AND PITCH.—Demand has been fair for Tar with some purchases made to arrive, but no unusual or stimulating movement developed, and the market as a whole shows no specially significant feature. Offerings seem to be well enough controlled to maintain former rates. We quote Pitch at $1.70@1.75 per bbl.; Tar at $2.15@2.50, according to quantity, quality and delivery.

MISCELLANEOUS.

BLINDS.

BUILDING MATERIAL PRICES

LUMBER.

Appended quotations are based almost wholly upon prices obtained for goods from first hands. Yard rates necessarily range much higher owing to the expenses attending sorting out and grading cargo and even car lots, besides which must be added the cost of handling and carrying until consumers are ready to invest. Terms of sale also prove important factors and, altogether, it is impossible to give a line of retail quotations thoroughly reliable in character.

SPRUCE—Eastern—special cargoes delivered N. Y.	$16 50 @ 18 00
Random cargoes, narrow	13 50 @ 14 50
Random cargoes, wide	15 00 @ 16 00
PILING—Eastern—cargo rates:	
Ranging 30@40 per cent 12 inch butt, 35 to 40 ft average length	4 @ —
Ranging 45@50 per cent 12 inch butt, 35 to 40 ft average length	4¼@ 4½
Ranging 50@60 per cent One-half 12 inch butt, 38 to 40 ft average length	4¾@ 5
Two-thirds 12 inch butt, 38 to 42 ft average length	5¼@ 6
Three-fourths 12 inch butt, 40 to 45 ft average length	5¾@ 6
All 12 inch butt and up, 40 to 45 ft average length	6 @ 6¼
Piece stick, 40 feet each	4 00 @ —
do. 45	6 00 @ —
do. 50	8 00 @ —
do. 55	12 00 @ —
Inch spars, per inch	20 @ 22
Scaffolding poles, each	80 @ 1 00
Clothes poles, 45 to 65 feet, each	3 00 @ 5 00
HEMLOCK:	
Penn. joist	12 00 @ 12 50
do. boards	13 00 @ 13 50
do. timber, 20 ft and under	12 50 @ 13 00
do. do. 22 to 24 ft	13 00 @ 13 50
do. do. 26 to 28 ft	13 50 @ 14 00
do. do. 30 to 32 ft	14 00 @ 15 50
do. do. 34 to 36 ft	15 50 @ 16 00
do. do. 36 to 40 ft	16 50 @ 17 50
WHITE PINE—Good uppers and select, 1 to 2 inch	40 00 @ 48 00
Upper and select, 2½ to 4 inch	50 00 @ 58 00
Shelving	26 00 @ 31 00
Pickings, 1 inch	33 00 @ 35 00
Cutting-up, 1 inch	25 00 @ 28 00
Bracket plank	30 00 @ 35 00
Dressing-boards	18 00 @ 22 00
Box, inch	13 50 @ 14 00
Box, thick	14 50 @ 15 50
West India shippers	16 00 @ 19 00
Rio Janeiro do.	20 00 @ 21 00
River Plate do.	29 00 @ 30 00
Australia do.	25 00 @ 30 00
YELLOW PINE—Random cargoes delivered N. Y.	19 00 @ 20 00
Ordered cargoes	20 00 @ 22 00
Flooring	24 00 @ 24 00
Step plank	26 00 @ 28 00
Common siding	15 00 @ 16 00
Heart face boards	24 00 @ 28 00
Car orders	21 00 @ 28 00
At Atlantic ports, f. o. b.	12 00 @ 12 50
At Gulf ports, f. o. b.	11 50 @ 12 50
North Caroline pine timber	13 50 @ 15 00
do. flooring 1 inch	16 00 @ 22 00
do. do. 1¼	16 50 @ 22 50
do. do. 1½@2 inch.	24 00 @ 25 00
do Shipping culls or box	12 00 @ 14 00
do Plain and mottled ½@1½ inch.	16 50 @ 25 50
Ash, white	36 00 @ 43 00
Elm	20 00 @ 22 50
Oak, plain	37 00 @ 41 00
Oak, quarter sawed	52 00 @ 55 00
Oak, quarter sawed, extra thick	56 00 @ 60 00
Redwood	45 00 @ 52 50
Maple, clear	28 00 @ 33 00
Chestnut, clear	33 00 @ 35 50
Cypress, clear	30 00 @ 32 50
Black Walnut, good to choice	130 00 @ 140 00
Black Walnut, ordinary to fair	100 00 @ 120 00
Black Walnut, ⅝	78 00 @ 83 00
Black Walnut, selected and seasoned	150 00 @ 155 00
Black Walnut counters	110 00 @ 150 00
Black Walnut, culls	35 00 @ 40 00
Black Walnut, rejects	50 00 @ 53 00
Cherry, wide	110 00 @ 115 00
Cherry, good	85 00 @ 100 00
Cherry, ordinary	65 00 @ 80 00
Whitewood, inch	30 50 @ 32 50
Whitewood, ⅝ inch	24 50 @ 26 00
Whitewood, 1¼ to 2½ inch	32 00 @ 34 00
Shingles, Pine, 16 inch, extra	2 75 @ 3 10
do 18 inch, extra	4 10 @ 4 30
do 18 inch, clear butt	2 90 @ 3 10
do 16 inch, stocks	4 50 @ 4 60
do 18 inch, stocks	5 30 @ 5 40
Shingles, Cypress, 6x20	8 00 @ 10 00
do larger sizes	11 00 @ 16 00
do sawed	6 00 @ 9 00
Cedar—Medium to large	6¼ @ 7½
do. —Extra large	7¾ @ 8
Mahogany—Small	6¼ @ 7½
do —Medium	8 @ 8¾
do. —Large	9½ @ 12
do. —Extra Large	12½ @ 14

DEVOTED TO REAL ESTATE, BUILDING ARCHITECTURE, HOUSEHOLD DECORATION, BUSINESS AND THEMES OF GENERAL INTEREST

PRICE, PER YEAR IN ADVANCE, SIX DOLLARS.

Published every Saturday.

TELEPHONE - - - - CORTLANDT 1370.

Communications should be addressed to

C. W. SWEET, 14 & 16 Vesey St.

J. T. LINDSEY, Business Manager.

VOL. XLVIII NOVEMBER 21, 1891. No. 1,236

INDICATIONS have not been wanting during the past two days of a return of the bull feeling which a couple of months ago gave the stock market such a substantial rise. Operators, who since the collapse of the early autumn movement have been operating on the bear side, have now to all appearances turned around and are buying stocks. For a few days things appeared to be in the hands of the bears, when all of a sudden prices were whisked up in a way that shows that the bulls have the market well in hand. Northern Pacific, for instance, sells at 69¼ on Thursday; on Friday morning the news is not good, yet despite all news it advances sharply. This shows the result of manipulation; but it is manipulation backed by a powerful sentiment. Securities like the Richmond Terminal stocks and bonds, which are among the weakest in point of conditions and prospects, are sent up two points in sympathy with the general rise. Whether it will continue or not is doubtful. Experienced operators remember that for some cause or another the market always declines just before or after the meeting of Congress. But, at all events, the rise cannot long be delayed. About three years ago Mr. Depew made a statement in St. Louis to a reporter, predicting bankruptcy to a number of Western railroads, which statement caused a serious decline in the stock market. He was right then, and he is equally right now when he predicts prosperity, both to the railways and to the country throughout the coming year.

WE publish in another column the report of the Real Estate Exchange for the past fiscal year. The very satisfactory results set forth therein show that the institution is in a better condition to-day than it has even been. The gratifying increase in dividend is mainly due to the excellent management of the Exchange during the past twelve months and to the new policy which now is practically accepted with general satisfaction. The management and the stockholders are to be congratulated.

THE report of the Special Committee of the Board of Education appointed last spring to consider the important matter of reform in our public school system proposes to remedy some, at all events, of the worst defects of our present methods. In their organization and manner of instruction the schools of New York City are far inferior, not only to the European schools which have long had the benefit of the newer and better methods of teaching, but to the schools of this country. This the committee admits, and it suggests changes in the organization of our schools in their scope, in their manner of supervision and in their method of teaching. It is true that they do not touch upon the root of the difficulty, viz.: that public education in New York, like all other branches of our city administration is so much a matter of politics that professional educators of the best class, of which the colleges are turning out an increasing number, have practically nothing to say about the management of our schools, the machinery of which is most intricate and clumsy. Indeed, the reference to this matter by the committee is really very amusing. They believe that if any of the Commissioners were paid "educational experts" we should involve "our school interests with politics in such a way as to imperil the efficiency of our entire system." As if the efficiency of our entire system was not at present threatened by this very cause. Unfortunately, however, it is probably true that the liberal remuneration of some of the Commissioners with a view to obtaining educational experts would probably under prevalent methods of appointment only serve to deteriorate the character of the Board. But this does not abate one jot the necessity for such experts, and no great improvement can be expected until they are put in permanent possession. Some of the recommendations of the committee are, however, very much to the point. The addition of kindergartens would be in line with the best methods of initial instruction; physical training should be added to the exercises, and last, but not least, more attention should be paid to technical education. The report should receive careful and for the most part favorable consideration.

Facts, Law and Sense.

THE *Commercial and Financial Chronicle* is a paper which through able management and long experience has devised a complete and efficient machinery for the collection of financial news of importance to the investing public. It is safe to say that if any fact is known to any person or persons in a public sense, it will be known to the *Chronicle*, and, if important, will be published. Whatever there is of the affairs of a railroad corporation that the *Chronicle* cannot find out, it is safe to say the stockholders will be unable to ascertain. We are therefore somewhat surprised to see in its last issue (Nov. 14th), referring to the new second mortgage on the Lake Erie & Western Railroad, that the *Chronicle* refers to the call for the special meeting of June 25, 1890, and to the proxies used at that meeting, and says: "It would seem clear from these therefore, that any stockholder could have obtained information in regard to the matter." We have read the call for the special meeting, and have also read the proxy referred to, and we fail to find in either any statement, either expressly, or in substance and effect mentioning any purpose to impose a second mortgage on the property and assets of the road. We have also searched the files of the *Chronicle*, and we find no announcement prior to that made in the issue of November 14th in any way informing the public that the Lake Erie & Western Railroad Co. either expected to make such a mortgage or that it had done so. But not only has the *Chronicle* failed to give warning to the public of this new second mortgage, but it published April 26, 1890, in advance of said meeting of June 25, 1890, an account of the objects and purposes for which the meeting was called, which proceeds upon the clear understanding that the only issue of securities or obligations contemplated at that meeting related to the acquisition and equipment of the Fort Wayne, Cincinnati & Louisville Railroad Co., being 133 miles in length, and that the issue of bonds or securities for those purposes were to be at the rate of $10,000 of first mortgage bonds for each mile of the newly-acquired property. The entire article plainly implies that no further burden upon the property is intended to be imposed at that meeting.

No one has suggested, and certainly we shall not suggest, that the *Chronicle* intentionally misled any reader of its columns. The fact is that it laid before the public openly and honestly all the information which it possessed upon the subject of the meeting of June 25, 1890, and that when it did so it believed that it was not only telling the truth but the whole truth as to the objects and purposes of that meeting. Its understanding then was the same as the understanding of every stockholder and of Wall Street. We would like to republish entire the article of April 26, 1890, page 590, referred to, but space here forbids, and we call upon the *Chronicle* to set forth again in its own columns the article referred to. We shall also take the liberty to ask the *Chronicle*, in the same issue in which it makes such republication, to answer one or two simple questions, after refreshing its recollection by its own former publication.

First—Did the *Chronicle* in the article of April 26, 1890, or in any other article published by it prior to last month, ever state that the Lake Erie & Western Railroad proposed to make a second mortgage upon its property? If so, when and where did the *Chronicle* make such statement, and what was the precise language used to convey that intelligence to the public?

Second—Would not the *Chronicle* in its article of April 26, 1890, have stated plainly that it was proposed to make a second mortgage upon the entire property of the road, including the proposed acquisition, if the *Chronicle* had understood that fact?

Third—When did the *Chronicle* first understand or have knowledge that it was proposed to put a second mortgage on the property of the company?

We desire also to ask the *Chronicle* these further questions:

First—Did the words "second mortgage" occur anywhere either in the notice of the meeting of June 25th, or in the proxies which were solicited from the stockholders?

Second—Is there anywhere either in the notice or in the proxy a plain statement, even though not in express terms, that it was intended to put a second mortgage on the property?

Third—Does the *Chronicle* desire to be understood that it takes the word "bonds" as having the same meaning as "mortgage," or that the debentures of a company evidencing a debt are legally and in common acceptation one and the same thing as a mortgage, which operates as a specific transfer of the title to property? It is only upon some such theory as that the word "bond" means "mortgage," that the language of the *Chronicle* where it says, "It would seem clear from these (*i. e.* the notice and proxy) that any stockholder could have obtained information in regard to the matter," is intelligible at all. Does the *Chronicle* wish to be so understood?

In previous articles we have stated that there was an undue concealment of the action taken at the meeting of June 25, 1890, for nearly a year and a-half after the date of the meeting. The *Chronicle* says that long before the bonds were issued President Brice referred to them in his annual report and states that the abstract of the report is published in the *Chronicle* of March 28th, on page 407. In view of this very positive statement of the *Chronicle*, a statement to which its reputation would give the weight of authority if it were allowed to pass unquestioned, we take the liberty to ask the *Chronicle* one more question:

Where in the report of President Brice, or where in the abstract of that report published in the *Chronicle* of March 28th, is any statement made, either in express terms or in substance and effect, that any second mortgage had been imposed upon the property of the road? There is, it is true, a statement in that report, and also in the abstract of it given by the *Chronicle*, that certain obligations have been created which would enable the company to buy additional equipment; but to those persons who received the notice of the meeting of June 25th, and who also received another and fuller circular to which your article of April 26, 1890, refers, the natural understanding of the "*obligations*" referred to was, that they were the obligations contemplated in connection with the purchase of the Fort Wayne, Cincinnati & Louisville Railroad, viz.: First mortgage bonds at the rate of $10,000 a mile for each mile of newly-acquired track, or were such unsecured current obligations as they might deem advisable to negotiate for equipment. Obligations is a term of general and not of specific significance, and stockholders certainly would understand that term in Mr. Brice's report to refer to obligations of which they had had some previous intimation and not to transfers of title to property by way of mortgage of which they had had no intimation whatever. We are surprised that a paper so analytical in its methods and so exact in its statements should interpret the language of Mr. Brice's report, or of the abstract in its own pages, as setting forth the fact to the plain comprehension of the public that a second mortgage had been created.

If the article of last week had appeared in the *Morning Journal* or in the *World*, it might have been considered mere careless reportorial work; but here is a journal of the highest standing, with a position almost unique, whose utterances have an oracular importance, which takes language significantly plain in its omission and attempts to translate it to the public by adding matter which was not in any sense in the original text. We are unwilling to believe that the *Chronicle* has sought to wrest language from its proper meaning with no higher purpose than to aid an unscrupulous management of corporate property in maintaining its action against the efforts of stockholders to obtain justice; and the *Chronicle* owes it to itself to candidly explain away even the appearance of such an association. It is certain to our minds that however much the *Chronicle* may have seemed to be the willing instrument of Messrs. Brice & Thomas in this matter, it will be found that when the facts are brought home clearly it will refuse to lend countenance to any attempt to falsify a plain record.

IF the threatened water famine becomes actual the public will very much like to know where the responsibility lies. The taxpayers of this city have acquiesced to being taxed for the interest on a great many million dollars worth of aqueduct, the ostensible purpose for which the conduit was constructed being to pipe water into New York, so that our citizens may not be thirsty. Well, the aqueduct is all there, but it seems that there is no water stored to meet an emergency. The responsibility can hardly be placed with the weather, because, not only was the drought of moderate duration, but because one of our reasons for wanting an aqueduct built was to provide for droughts far more enduring than the one of this fall. The responsibility rests with some of the past or present officials of the city government. But with whom? The Aqueduct Commissioners flout the idea that they can be held in any way accountable for the threatened famine. The Public Works Department is equally explicit waiving aside any responsibility. Now we are not saying that either of these sets of officials are rightly chargeable with such an imprudent and possibly such a disastrous mistake. Few errors that are committed in the administration of the affairs of New York can, by any ingenuity, be traced to one indubitable source; the clumsy machinery seems designed to erect a number of conflicting jurisdictions, no one of which is completely inclusive of anything. The Mayor has a thin kind of general responsibility; but at present he is in Ireland and would not know anything even if he was in New York. And so it always is. In this particular instance if large numbers of industries are put to a heavy loss, and people from one end of the city to the other made to suffer exasperating inconvenience, there will be absolutely no one man or body of men who can be held accountable. The usual resource of editors, vituperation against Tammany, is of no avail, because the aqueduct matter has been carried to its present point without assistance from any representative of that society. This is bad government practically made irremediable. For it is wretchedly bad government that this water famine may take place; and when there is nobody who is responsible for bad government there is no way, that we can see, of stopping it.

EVIDENTLY nothing can be done to displace this diffusion of responsibility and substitute for it a harmoniously working system so long as the bulk of the intelligent people in the city have so little confidence in their rulers as they have at present. The fact that the Republicans at Albany and the majority of discriminating New Yorkers are always justly or unjustly reading "job" into any improvement proposed by the officials leads to the device of putting such improvements in the hands of commissions specially created. Instances of this are too numerous to require specification. These commissions come into conflict with the existing departments in a thousand ways, not only because the legislation is often so clumsily drawn that there is no accurate definition of jurisdiction, but because such conflicts are unavoidable in the nature of the things. It is these opposing sources of authority that frequently make it impossible to place one's hand on the agency that is chargeable for incompetence, carelessness or corruption. This is not as it should be: and if the time ever comes when the city is ruled by intelligent, disinterested and competent citizens, aided by a force of engineers, experts and administrative adepts, the necessity for all these commissions will have ceased. When we want a new bridge built we shall not have to appoint a body of immaculate merchants, send them abroad to study all the existing bridges in the world, hire special offices and secretaries for them, employ a brand new staff of engineers, and, in short, create an expensive machinery to do work that ought to be performed by the machinery already in existence. We will do as the New York Central Railroad Company does when it wishes to build a bridge. The engineering department of the corporation, which is supposed to keep well informed about all the new methods of bridge building and achievements therein, is instructed to prepare the surveys and draw the plans and make specifications. Then if the structure does not turn out all right the bridge engineer of the road is held accountable by his chief and can be discharged New York City is, however, apparently about as far away from a system of this kind as the North Pole is from the South.

Amending the Building Law.

THE Committee on Revising the Building Law have taken up the work that came to naught last winter, with the intention of bringing the amendments up to date and including the latest knowledge and experience that can be reached. The committee consist of the following gentlemen, arranged in their alphabetical order: Messrs. Conover, Dobbs, Fryer, Le Brun, Murray and O'Reilly, together with Superintendent Brady, Mr. Findley, the attorney to the Fire Department, and Chief Clerk Shields, who acts as clerk to the committee.

The committee held its first meeting yesterday (Friday) afternoon, in the rooms of the Board of Fire Underwriters, Mutual Life Building, 32 Nassau street, and will hereafter hold bi-weekly meetings in the same place on Wednesdays and Fridays, from 3 to 5.30 P. M., until the work of revision is completed. These meetings will be open to the public, and all persons interested in the matters to be treated are invited to attend and present their views orally or in writing. This practice pertained in the past and is to be followed this season by the committee. Any communication sent to the office of this paper will reach the committee, and we can give the assurance that the merits of any suggestion so offered will receive due consideration. No captious fault-finding should be indulged in but the efforts of everyone should be towards a fair and comprehensive law.

The amendments of last year received pretty general commendation. It will be recollected that the bill passed the Assembly without opposition, but was never acted upon in the Senate by reason of the political deadlock in that body over a proposed investigation of the canals that prevented the transaction of any business for some weeks immediately preceding final adjournment. The programme of the committee is to finish up the work of revision in time to present the bill to the Legislature when it convenes in January. The aid of Mayor Grant, who will by that time have returned from abroad, is then to be asked to secure the early passage of the bill. The Mayor will also be requested to take up the question of forming a separate Department of Buildings by uniting together various bureaus now scattered through several departments in one new department which will have the inspection and supervision over all building operations. Several building trade associations have recently taken action to this end. The Society of Architectural Iron Manufacturers led off by passing resolutions (1) favoring the passage by the Legislature of the building law bill of last year with such additional amendments thereto as may be found to be desirable; (2) expressing an intention to ask the Mayor to aid in securing the passage of such a measure, and (3) urging the creation of a Department of Buildings. The Mechanics' and Traders'

Exchange followed with resolutions to the same effect. The Master Masons' Association has similarly gone on record, and also the Real Estate Owners' and Builders' Association. It was deemed judicious not to hazard the chances of getting an amended building law through the Legislature by combining the separate department feature in the same bill. Therefore the technical amendments are to receive consideration first, as they are of the first importance to the building interests, and then go at the separate department feature, into which more or less politics will creep in its sinuous course at Albany, and perhaps compass its defeat.

The New Builders' Exchange.

WHEN the Builders' National Convention was held at the beginning of the current year, the builders of this city evinced in their otherwise free and hospital treatment of their guests a noticeable reticence (to speak of the matter gently) concerning their magnificent Exchange building on Vesey street. There were delegates and visitors here from Boston, Philadelphia, Chicago, Kansas City, and indeed from every other considerable municipality in the country, but though in all these places the building industry is nothing like so wealthy and important as it is here in the metropolis, the builders of New York acted in a sort of shame-faced way when any visitor looked or moved down town in the direction of their commercial headquarters.

To understand this shrinking timidity of ours concerning our great Exchange, so architecturally impressive, so thronged with busy traders (there are as many as a dozen there at times), we must look to other cities smaller than New York and to the Exchanges *their* builders possess. No! the supposition that we wished to spare the pride of our visitors from a rude blow is incorrect; for Philadelphia, Boston, Chicago, Kansas City have Exchanges which are not only impressive and important commercial institutions, real marts where traders meet to good purpose, but powerful social or guild organizations as well, wherein the interest and well-being of a vast industry are actively developed and protected. Our pride was in the right place after all when we shrank from too publicly exhibiting to the entire country our store on Vesey street. It was good in its day, but its day is long passed.

For a year past the project has been under consideration to erect a real Exchange building worthy of the builders of the metropolis. A committee of the Mechanics' and Traders' Exchange has been investigating the matter in its aspects, legal and financial, and it is now ready for final action. No one should know better than the builders of this city that with their resources of one kind and another any financial difficulties that may exist have scarcely more than to be faced to be overcome. The legal impediments in the way of action by the Exchange are more serious, and it is to deal with these, as well as to bring the entire project to the point of action that the following circular is issued this morning:

THE MECHANICS' AND TRADERS' EXCHANGE.
COMMITTEE ON PROPOSED NEW BUILDING,
NEW YORK, Nov. 17, 1891.

Mr............

DEAR SIR—The committee appointed by the Exchange to consider "the matter of an Exchange Building in all its phases, including the most feasible plan for creating the necessary fund," has given the subject very careful consideration, and during its deliberations the committee has sought and received the best legal advice, particularly in respect to that portion of the subject relating to the creation of the necessary fund.

This committee has had under consideration several schemes or plans for the creation or establishment of a fund by the Exchange, but after a thorough examination of their several merits, they were deemed to be impracticable, for the reason that the Exchange is by law debarred from capitalization and the issuance of stock; it possesses no powers except such as are contained in the special Act of the Legislature, known as chapter 370, Laws of 1863, or are incidentally necessary to be exercised in order to carry out the powers expressly granted.

It is, therefore, the opinion of this committee that the Exchange, as an organization, is without the power or means of raising a sum sufficient to purchase an eligible site and secure the erection thereon of a suitable building, estimated to cost, approximately, one million of dollars.

If a building is desirable, which in itself shall typify the vast interest of the building trades in this city—and it is generally admitted that such is the case—it is necessary for the individual members of the Exchange to contribute a sum equal, at least, to 25 per cent of this estimated cost, such contributions to remain as an investment in the form of equity in the property. It is believed that from such a building as has been suggested, centrally located, within the limit of 14th to 42d street, 4th and 6th avenues, and in all respects adapted to the needs of the Exchange and the requirements of a superior class of tenants, the net annual income will be from 8 to 10 per cent on the capital invested.

To enable this committee to make an intelligent and acceptable report to the Exchange, and one which will not be absolutely barren of results, it is desirous of learning whether you are disposed to favor the enterprise and make an investment therein; to that end you are requested to sign and return, at your convenience, not later than 10th December next, the attached slip.

Any additional suggestion as to the subject matter of this circular would be acceptable and appreciated by the committee.

Yours very respectfully.

JOHN J. TUCKER,
WILLIAM C. SMITH, GEO MOORE SMITH,
MARC EIDLITZ, ANDREW J. CAMPBELL,
JAMES B. MULRY, JOHN MCGLENSEY,
BENJAMIN A. WILLIAMS, JOHN BYRNS,
AUGUSTUS MEYERS, STEPHEN M. WRIGHT,
Committee.

Are you in favor of securing an Exchange Building at an approximate cost of $1,000,000? (Please answer Yes or No)

Are you willing to subscribe the sum of one thousand dollars towards the cost of such a building, said subscription to be paid in installments, and to remain as an investment in said building and the lots on which it is erected? (Please answer Yes or No)

What are the builders of this city going to do about it? They are surely capable of an enterprise which Boston and Philadelphia have carried through with marked success, financial and otherwise. That the project will pay there can be little doubt; the offices in a large building will surely rent well and easily to building material firms and others: the Building Material Exhibition should surpass that in any other city, and as to the social or guild aspect of the enterprise, the builders of this city (merely to look in a single direction) have suffered enough in legislative and labor troubles from the lack of adequate organization to be convinced that a stronger institution is now needed.

The Coming Legislature and New York City.

MEASURES HELD OVER FROM LAST SESSION THAT SHOULD BE PASSED—AN INTERVIEW WITH COMMISSIONER GILROY.

Ever since the election the municipal authorities of this city have been canvassing, with more or less anxiety, the question whether the Legislature is in the control of the Democrats or the Republicans, or, as it was last year, divided between the parties. There are many measures of importance to be presented to the Legislature this year, the fate of which is largely involved in this question. Unfortunately the Legislature cannot be relied upon to treat bills affecting New York City from the purely economic or business point of view, but it must make "politics" of them all, and make their enactment questions of partisan expediency.

In this view of the matter it is to be regretted that the election was not a little more emphatically Democratic than it appears to be from present indications. Most of the city bills that are to be presented in the Legislature during the coming session, are bills which passed the Assembly a year ago and were strangled in the Senate deadlock. Among them is the Mayor's bill to authorize the construction of a new municipal building in City Hall Park. The present law authorizes the construction of this much-needed building, on a site to be secured, outside of and contiguous to the City Hall Park.

Efforts that have been made from time to time to secure such a site have demonstrated that it would cost several millions more than it would to remove all the buildings now encumbering the park and in their places to erect a single modern structure that would serve the needs of the city for all time to come, and at the same time be a credit to the metropolis and the nation. The last effort made under the present law was to secure the blocks of irregular shape between Centre street, Park row, Tryon row and Reade street, but this brought down the *Staats Zeitung* and other property interests in such violent opposition that the effort seems to have been abandoned. Besides being an exceedingly expensive site (it would cost in the neighborhood of $4,000,000 to acquire it) it would be a positive disgrace to the city to build its chief administrative building, its chief architectural property, next to the elevated railroad and to a noisome thoroughfare such as Park row is above the bridge entrance.

Mayor Grant has all along been very strongly in favor of constructing this building on the site of the present City Hall, and all the opposition that has developed against this plan is of a sentimental character, too visionary and unreal to be given serious consideration. In the opinion of many influential property-owners, New York City can better afford to remove every one of the buildings now in the park and to spend five or six millions, if need be, for a municipal building commensurate with the greatness and wealth of the city, than it can to wait and hesitate much longer over the matter. The prestige of New York as first among the cities of the New World in population, in wealth and in architectural resources is seriously threatened by Chicago, and not only a new rapid transit system, but a decent display of civic pride in the character of her municipal structures is necessary to remove the danger.

Another important legislative movement which is of interest solely to New York City is that which provides for the extension of the block indexing system of real estate records to the preparation of new land maps and the identification of every parcel of land within the limits of the city by a block and lot number. It is proposed to extend this system not only to all the land records, but to the tax records and books as well, so that perfect uniformity shall be had in the descriptions of property and dealings with property-owners in all the departments of the city government. The lack of uniformity under the present system has been the source of many mistakes and much trouble and consequent expense to owners of real estate, and although there has never been any strenuous opposition in the city to the proposed remedial legislation, the passive, conservative spirit that rules in all such matters has been difficult to incite to the needed active effort to secure the reform. Mr. Dwight H. Olmstead, to whose persistent effort is due the credit for as much of the block system as we now have in operation, told THE RECORD AND GUIDE reporter that he would have some bills in Albany on this subject at the forthcoming session of the Legislature. He will endeavor with one of them to have a competent commission appointed to supervise the re indexing of all the records of real estate transfers in the county under the block system.

Commissioner of Public Works Thomas F. Gilroy was the most indignant sufferer from the effects of the Senate deadlock in the last Legislature,

Five important bills which he had prepared in the interest of public improvements in the city and a more efficient and satisfactory municipal service, and which were passed early in the year by the Assembly, were all strangled in the Senate. He said to THE RECORD AND GUIDE reporter: "I presume they will be tried again next year; but where is the use in my trying single-handed to secure these improvements? Every one of those bills passed the Assembly early in the session and not a single New York daily paper lifted its voice to help them through the Senate, although there wasn't a show of politics in any of them, but all of them were purely business measures.

"It is no more my business to be looking after these things than it is yours or that of any other newspaper man or public-spirited citizen. The specified duties of my office do not require me to originate legislation in the city's interest and to go to Albany to urge it upon the Legislature; but if from the vantage of my position I see where legislation is necessary to the welfare of the city and submit the proper bills and am not backed up by the local press, what show is there to get the bills enacted? Why should I trouble myself about them? Yes, there were five bills. There was the bill to authorize the construction of a high service pumping station and water tower on city property, near Washington Bridge, to supply the high ground on the West Side with water. There are several square miles of territory over there where the buildings stand so high above the present highest service that water has to be pumped above the second floor. A new water tower and pumping station to supply this section is badly wanted. Property-owners pay for the service, and they ought to have it. Another bill was to authorize the building of the bridge across the new Harlem ship canal, in the Kingsbridge road. This has got to be done and very soon, too. If the last winter's bill had become a law the foundations of the bridge would have been finished long ago. Now it will cost the city one hundred thousand dollars more to build it, because the water will be let into the cut before the Legislature will act on the bill, and the foundations that might have been constructed on the dry rock, as it was excavated, will now have to be laid in the water. Another bill that passed the House was to extend for two years the issue of one million dollars of city bonds in each year for repaving purposes. Nobody will deny the good work that has been done under that provision of the law, but there was much more to be done before even the streets in the business section were made what they should be.

"Then there were the two bills relating to street railways—one requiring the companies whenever the streets were repaved, and the Commissioner of Public Works should require it, to replace their abominable centre-bearing rails with wide flanged and grooved rails of the design adopted by the department. This is done or desired to be done not more in the interest of the pavements than in the interest of owners of wagons and carriages. The centre-bearing rail is terribly destructive to both, and it has been my policy to try to drive it entirely out of the streets of this city. It ought never to have been permitted to enter them. The other bill is to require street car companies to repave the street between their tracks whenever the rest of the street is being repaved. Most of these companies are in the enjoyment of very valuable and remunerative privileges of an exclusive character, for which they render little or no compensation, and since they use and destroy the pavements as much as anybody, it is only fair that they should be required to repave between their tracks. There may be other matters of which time shall disclose the necessity, but if we can get this much of a concession in the way of managing our own home affairs from the next Legislature I shall be thankful."

The Rapid Transit Scheme and Property-Owners.

Rapid Transit, in the hands of the Steinway Commission, made rapid progress during the week. Yesterday the Park Board, and on Wednesday Commissioner Heintz, gave their formal approvals to the construction of the road, and on Monday the canvassers of the commission will start out with their portfolios to solicit the formal consent of property-owners.

In the meantime circulars were mailed to all the property-owners, of whom the commission had the names and addresses, with blank forms of consent inclosed, soliciting the favorable action of the owners in question. Almost the first mail in response brought a number of the consents, and they have been coming in agreeable numbers ever since. The circulars brought down upon the individual members of the commission, furthermore, a large number of inquiries from their acquaintances among the property-owners, asking for detailed information regarding the general plan of construction.

As well as they could, the commissioners made off-hand answers to these inquiries, but for the purpose of more completely meeting the demand of the property-owners, the commission is having an edition of its report printed, with numerous illustrations showing all the details of the work of which it is necessary to know in order to form an idea of the extent to which the road will encroach upon vested privileges and rights in the occupancy of the street, or otherwise affect the interests of the abutting property-owner.

Some facts which have been learned during the week will be of interest to the readers of THE RECORD AND GUIDE; for instance, that it is not intended to come to the surface of the street in the construction either of the Broadway section from the Battery to 59th street, nor of the East Side section from Union square to 96th street. The tunnel will be excavated by blasting through the solid rock from 14th street to 96th street, through 4th and Madison avenues, at almost all points more than 10 feet below the surface of the street. Through Murray and Lenox Hills, and through the hill between 87th and 96th streets the tunnel will be deep down below the street grades, the stations coming in the lower levels between the hills. In Broadway, at Houston street, where the cable railroad company has constructed a masonry vault about 20 feet deep for a power station, the road will have to run beneath this vault. But the higher level at Houston street will permit this to be done without difficulty and particularly without materially changing the grade of the road, beyond the percentage that would be taken to give the road the advantage of the gravity principle in the starting and stopping of trains. An alleged interview with Wm. L. Elkins, of the Broadway cable railroad syndicate, published in the Philadelphia *Times* of Thursday, made him say that the cable company had built a vault 60 (*sic*) feet deep along the southerly side of Union square for its cable system, and that a person could walk through its cable trench from 32d street to Bowling Green. All of this is of course supremely ridiculous, but it is a fair example of the bug-a-boos which are being invoked in opposition to the project of the commissioners.

After December 1st, it is said, Mr. Wm. E. Worthen will retire from the position of Chief Engineer of the commission, but will continue his connection with the work as Consulting Engineer. His duties as a consulting engineer have been so pressing that he has not been able to find the time necessary for attention to the immense details of the work, and since the general plan has been settled the work can proceed better under the management of a younger man, who has no other engrossing engagements, but can give his whole time to the work. Such a man the commission believes it has in William Barclay Parsons, and after December 1st he will become the Chief Engineer of the enterprise.

The New York and New Jersey Bridge.

The project for the bridge proposed to be erected between 70th and 71st streets, New York, and the Jersey shore, as outlined at length in THE RECORD AND GUIDE of December 6 last and in other issues of this paper, seems about to take another phase. Chas. H. Swan, secretary of the company, yesterday said:

"The New York and New Jersey companies will consolidate next Friday. Directly thereafter we shall commence to build our land piers, either on the New Jersey or the New York side. Our total capital stock is $15,000,000, of which $1,300,000 has been subscribed, $300,000 in the New York company and $1,000,000 on behalf of the New Jersey company."

When asked to state definitely on which shore work would first be commenced, Mr. Swan declined to reply. He was also asked if the company had bought any property on the New York side, to which he replied: "Maybe it has," but he would not authorize the writer to say yea or nay in THE RECORD AND GUIDE. "We will pay for what we want," he said, "and if we cannot get it at a fair price we will have to take condemnation proceedings. We do not require the sanction of Congress. Our object in going to Congress last year was to head off any objection on the part of financiers to take our bonds from fear of possible future trouble. We really don't require the sanction of Congress. All we have to do is to build our bridge, so that it will not obstruct navigation. Congress and the Secretory of War have to see that such obstruction does not take place, and as we will build our bridge high enough for the largest vessels to pass through we will not obstruct navigation."

It may be remembered that the company proposes to land on the New York side, at about 70th street, North River, thence curving by a viaduct toward West End avenue, running southerly through the property fronting on that and 11th avenue down to 42d street; thence curving to 38th street and running through the north side of that street to 8th avenue, from which point, up to Broadway, a Union Depot would be built, to take in the ground bounded by 37th and 39th streets, 8th avenue and Broadway."

When the company appeared before Congress last year with a bill they were defeated by the efforts of West Side property-owners.

Massachusetts Legislators at the Register's Office.

In pursuance of a recommendation of Governor Russell, of Massachusetts, a special committee was appointed by the last Legislature of that State to investigate the various methods of land transfer reform and report thereon to that body. This committee have been actively pursuing their inquiries, and among other systems have devoted no little time to the scrutiny of the block indexing methods now employed in the Register's office of this city. Dwight H. Olmstead, the author of the plan of indexing papers affecting title according to local areas, was given a long hearing, in which he compared the system of block indexing to the Torrens' methods of land transfer. The Commission have been so much interested by the scheme that during the past week they came to New York personally to inquire into the details of its practical operation. On Friday morning the whole of this Commission, nine in number, were conducted through the Register's office by Mr. Fitzgerald and Mr. Olmstead. The following are the names of those present: The Chairman, Hon. Joseph Bennett; Senators Thayer and Fernald; and Representatives Warren and Clark, of Boston; Howard, of North Brookfield; Weir, of Lowell; Rice, of Worcester, and Butler. They spent a good part of the morning in listening to the explanations of Messrs. Olmstead and Fitzgerald. Naturally the points upon which most of the time was spent were the legal effects of block indexing, and the mistakes which have arisen in operation of the system. The Register showed that the latter were due to oversights of attorneys in entering the wrong block number in the paper; but added, that now even this element of error was eliminated by the system of checking, which had been established in the office. The Commission were evidently very well disposed towards the system, and it will doubtless enter into their report, when made.

Sites for New School Buildings.

The trustees of schools in their respective wards applied to the Board of Education on Wednesday for leave to purchase sites for new schools as follows:

Southwest corner of St. Nicholas avenue and 141st street.
No. 341 East 13th street.
Avenue A and 81st street.
First avenue and 9th street.
Madison avenue and 85th street.
Mosholu Parkway and Briggs avenue.

All the applications were referred to the Committee on Sites and New Schools.

The Annual Report of the Real Estate Exchange.

The Board of Directors of the Real Estate Exchange held a special meeting on Thursday afternoon.

A semi-annual dividend of 2½ per cent on the capital stock was declared, and it was ordered that the polls be open only from 1.30 to 3 P. M., on the day of the annual election, December 14th, instead of until 4 P. M., as was previously the custom. This action was taken because of the new law which forbids cumulative voting, and which thereby simplifies the election very much, as it practically eliminates all opposition.

In the report which the directors will issue to the stockholders at the annual meeting they say, among other things:

"The sales of real estate at auction during the past year have amounted to $37,115,661, which together with stocks and bonds, $22,000,000, make a total of $49,115,661. The receipts from rents have amounted to $31,322.48. Under the action of the new rules as to knock downs, which have now been in force for ten months, the receipts of the Auction Room have been considerably increased, amounting to the sum of $28,722.30. The total receipts of the Exchange have amounted to $63,714.43, being $8,435.91 in advance of last year, and the expenditure to $33,392.28, showing a decrease of $4,798.93.

"On the 1st of July a dividend at the rate of 2½ per cent for the half year was declared, and from the profits accrued up to the end of the fiscal year, November 15th. the directors have declared a further dividend at the same rate, making 5 per cent for the whole year, and carrying forward a balance of $5,339.46 to the next account.

"Since the last meeting of stockholders the mortgage has been reduced to $75,000.

"On the 1st of January last the new rules in regard to knock-downs went into effect, whereby the tariff on non-official sales was raised to one-tenth of 1 per cent, at the same time providing for a rebate in cases where the property is bid in by the owner and the fact reported to the Exchange. By the action of this rule in 397 instances the quotation of property so protected has been kept off the bulletin and the amounts of such sales are not included in the above totals.

"In the month of June last the General Term of the Supreme Court affirmed the decision of Judge Lawrence, whereby the contention of your directors as to the right of the Exchange to the auctioneer's stand was upheld.

"Although during the past year there has been no falling off on the part of those sellers and jobbers in realty who habitually attend our auction sales, there has been a much wider and more extensive attendance on the part of the general public, and a reference to the names of the buyers shows that this Exchange is becoming more widely popular every day among the investing classes. The increasing attendance plainly indicates that the present dimensions of the Salesroom will soon have to be extended. The Salesroom is now lighted by electricity.

"The labors of the Committee on Legislation have been exceptionally arduous during the past year. A number of bills favoring costly and mischievous legislation were introduced during the last session, all of which were carefully examined and successfully opposed by the committee. The bill proposing a tax on mortgages was opposed and failed to become a law. The bill enabled the representatives of deceased property-owners to vacate assessments improperly levied, was supported by your committee and passed.

"The most important bill to property-owners passed last session was the Rapid Transit Act, which placed the whole question in the hands of Commissioners fully possessing the confidence of the citizens of New York. Your committee have tendered to them the use of our records and Information Bureau. The Commissioners have availed themselves of the offered assistance.

"The committee have received the co-operation of the Board of Health in their endeavors to attach responsibility for injury to leased property by tenants, to the tenants themselves instead of the landlords, by compelling the process in the first instance, in the event of sanitary violations, to issue against the tenants committing the same."

The balance sheet which is issued with the report shows a balance on Nov. 15, 1890, of $17,087.31; income from rent of offices, $31,322.48; income from Exchange and Auction Room, $28,722.30, and other receipts of $3,669.65, or a total of $80,801.74. The expenditures: dividend 1890, $16,250; semi-annual dividend, $12,500, and other expenses of $34,212.28, leaving a balance on hand of $17,839.46, out of which the dividend of $12,500 just declared is to be paid, leaving a clear balance to go over to next year's account of $5,339.46.

Contractors' Notes.

Bids or estimates will be received at the Department of Public Works, No. 31 Chambers street, until 12 o'clock M. on Monday, November 30, 1891: For the necessary materials and labor for repairing sidewalks and curb around Clinton Market, on block bounded by Spring, Washington, Canal and West streets; for sewer in 100th street, between 3d and Park avenues, connecting with present sewer in 3d avenue, west side, north of 100th street; for sewer in 106th street, north side, between Central Park West and Manhattan avenue; for sewer in 162d street, between Amsterdam avenue and Jumel terrace, and in Jumel terrace, between 160th and 162d streets, and for repairs to sewer in Rivington street, between Goerck and Columbia streets.

Newark News.

The following plans have been filed with the Superintendent of Buildings: P. F. Adamy, 2½-sty fr dwg, 19x27, 171 Milford av; The Celluloid Company, 2-sty brk factory. 40x60, 7 and 9 Wescott st; John N. Hesse, 3-sty fr shop, 22x45, rear 471 North 6th st; John N. Hesse, twenty-five 3-sty fr dwgs, 21x45, 439–489 North 6th st; Louis Schmidt, 2½-sty fr dwg, 22x31, 7 Madison av; Martha F. Woodhull, 2½-sty fr dwg, 30x31, 16 and 18 South 9th st; Henry Brandley, 2-sty fr store, 18x36, 233 rear Bank st; U. Eberhardt, four 2-sty fr dwgs, 80x17, rear 61–65 Prospect st; Charles Pilippot, 3-sty brk dwg, 30x25, 296 Mulberry st; Jacob Weber, 2½-sty fr dwg, 22x38, 74 Bruce st; John McAbe, 2-sty brk dwg, 22x44, 193 South 9th st; John McKevitt, 3-sty fr dwg, 25x50, 119 Madison st; W. D. Traphagen, 3-sty fr dwg, 22x42, 280 South 9th st; Fred Pepits, 3-sty fr dwg, 22x40, 24 Somerset st; Matilda Christiansen, 3-sty fr dwg, 24x46, 420 Orange st; Compressed Barrel Co., 1-sty fr storage, 40x100, River road; A. M. Palmer, 2½-sty fr dwg, 32x35, 24 South 9th st; Julia Clark, 1½-sty fr stable, 22x22, cor Broad and Miller sts; D. Shipman, three 2-sty fr dwgs, 50x42, 272 and 274 Summer av; Lorenzo Boscoino, 3-sty fr tenem't, 25x27, rear 16 Factory st; F. S. Crane, 2-sty fr dwg, 33x41, cor Lincoln and Chester avs; Henry Spellmeyer, three 2-sty brk dwgs, 45x34, 114 and 116 Oraton st; Trustees Woodside Presbyterian Church, one fr church, 49x97, cor Fredonia av and Aqueduct st; Forest Hill Assoc., 2-sty fr dwg, 36x48, 871 De Graw av; Gabriel Valentino, 4-sty brk dwg, 50x50, 14 and 16 Drift st.

A Chicago Real Estate Firm.

[SPECIAL NOTICE.]

Within the next twelve months a large amount of outside capital is likely to be invested in Chicago—the Worlds' Fair city. The folly of strangers investing in real estate in a city, the local conditions of which they are ignorant of, will be readily admitted. The difficulty that puzzles non-residents is to find the name of some reliable and well-informed agent. In our advertisements, opposite the first editorial page, we print the card of J. C. Magill & Co., one of the largest and oldest real estate firms in Chicago. They do one of the largest businesses in the Western metropolis, and readers wishing to know what the Chicago market offers for investment, or information of any kind concerning Chicago realty, cannot go amiss in corresponding with this firm. Their address is corner of Madison and La Salle streets, Chicago, Ills.

Important to Property-Holders.

BOARD OF ASSESSORS.

OFFICE OF THE BOARD OF ASSESSORS,
No. 27 CHAMBERS STREET,
NEW YORK, Nov. 14, 1891.

Notice is given to the owner or owners, of all houses and lots, improved or unimproved lands affected thereby, that the following assessments have been completed and are lodged in the office of the Board of Assessors for examination by all persons interested, viz.:

No. 1.—Repaving Tompkins st, from Grand to Stanton st, with granite blocks and laying crosswalks (so far as the same is within the limits of grants of land under water).

No. 2.—Sewer in Park av, w s, bet 92d and 93d sts, with alteration and improvement to present sewer in 92d st, bet Park and Madison avs.

No. 3.—Flagging, reflagging, curbing, recurbing full width, s s 59th st, commencing at Grand Circle and extdg. 75 ft. westerly.

[The limits embraced by such assessments include all the several houses and lots of ground, vacant lots, pieces or parcels of land situated on—

No. 1.—Both sides of Tompkins st, from Grand to Stanton st, and to the extent of half the block at the intersecting sts.

No. 2.—W s of Park av, from 92d to 93d st, and both sides of 92d st, extdg. abt 135 ft. westerly from Park av.

No. 3.—S s of 59th st, extdg. westerly from the Grand Circle abt 40 ft.]

All persons whose interests are affected by the above-named assessments, and who are opposed to the same, or either of them, are requested to present their objections in writing to the Chairman of the Board of Assessors at their office, No. 27 Chambers street, within thirty days from the date of this notice.

The above-described lists will be transmitted, as provided by law, to the Board of Revision and Correction of Assessments for confirmation on the 15th day of December, 1891.

OFFICE OF THE BOARD OF ASSESSORS,
No. 27 CHAMBERS STREET.
NEW YORK. Nov. 17, 1891.

Notice is given to the owner or owners of all houses and lots, improved or unimproved lands affected thereby, that the following assessments have been completed and are lodged in the office of the Board of Assessors for examination by all persons interested, viz.:

No. 1.—Sewers in South st, bet Broad and Whitehall sts, connecting with present sewer in Whitehall st, and in Moore st, bet South and Water sts, connecting with sewer in South st.

No. 2.—Repaving 11th av, bet 27th and 30th sts, with granite blocks (so far as the same is within the limits of grants of lands under water.)

[The limits embraced by such assessments include all the several houses and lots of ground, vacant lots, pieces and parcels of land situated on—

No. 1.—Both sides of Moore st, from South to Water st; also n s of South st, from Whitehall to Broad st; also property bounded by South and Pearl sts, Moore and Whitehall sts; also e s of Whitehall st, extdg from South st to a point distant abt 181 ft. 1 in n of Stone st; also both sides of Pearl st, extdg easterly from Whitehall st, abt 92 ft.; also property bounded by State st, Battery pl and Whitehall st, and w s of Broadway, from Battery pl to Morris st and Battery Park.

No. 2.—Both sides of 11th av, from 27th to 30th st, and to the extent of half the block at the intersecting sts, including half the block from the intersection of n s of 30th st and 11th av.]

All persons whose interests are affected by the above-named assessments, and who are opposed to the same, or either of them, are requested to present their objections in writing to the Chairman of the Board of Assessors, at their office, No. 27 Chambers street, within thirty days from the date of this notice.

The above-described lists will be transmitted, as provided by law, to the

Board of Revision and Correction of Assessments for confirmation on the 18th day of December, 1891.

OFFICE OF THE BOARD OF ASSESSORS,
No. 27 CHAMBERS STREET,
NEW YORK, Nov. 18, 1891.

Notice is given to the owner or owners of all houses and lots, improved or unimproved lands affected thereby, that the following assessments have been completed and are lodged in the office of the Board of Assessors for examination by all persons interested, viz.:

No. 1.—Regulating, grading, setting curbstones and flagging 148th st, from 7th av to the Harlem River.

No. 2.—Paving West End av, from 96th to 104th st, with granite and asphalt pavements, and laying crosswalks (96th to 99th st with granite blocks and 99th to 104th st with asphalt).

[The limits embraced by such assessments include all the several houses and lots of ground, vacant lots, pieces and parcels of land situated on—

No. 1.—Both sides of 148th st, from 6th to 7th av.

No. 2.—Both sides of West End av, from 96th to 104th st, and to the extent of half the block at the intersecting sts.]

All persons whose interests are affected by the above-named assessments, and who are opposed to the same, or either of them, are requested to present their objections, in writing, to the Chairman of the Board of Assessors, at their office, No. 27 Chambers street, within thirty days from the date of this notice.

The above-described lists will be transmitted, as provided by law, to the Board of Revision and Correction of Assessments for confirmation on the 19th day of December, 1891.

OFFICE OF THE BOARD OF ASSESSORS,
No. 27 CHAMBERS STREET,
NEW YORK, Nov. 20, 1891.

Notice is given to the owner or owners, occupant or occupants of all houses and lots, improved or unimproved lands affected thereby, that the following assessments have been completed and are lodged in the office of the Board of Assessors for examination by all persons interested, viz.:

No. 1.—Alteration and improvement to sewer in Mercer st, bet Canal and Grand sts.

No. 2.—Receiving-basin on the n e cor of 55th st and Av A.

No. 3.—Sewer in 79th st, bet Boulevard and Amsterdam av.

[The limits embraced by such assessments include all the several houses and lots of grounds, vacant lots, pieces and parcels of land situated on—

No. 1.—Both sides of Mercer st, from Canal to Broome st; n s of Canal st, from Broadway to Mercer st; both sides of Howard and Grand sts, from Broadway to Mercer st; s s of Broome st, from Broadway to Mercer st, and w s of Broadway, from Howard to Broome st.

No. 2.—E s of Av A, from 55th to 56th st, and n s of 55th st, extdg abt 163 ft. easterly from Av A.

No. 3.—Both sides of 79th st, from Boulevard to Amsterdam av.]

All persons whose interests are affected by the above-named assessments, and who are opposed to the same, or either of them, are requested to present their objections in writing to the Chairman of the Board of Assessors, at their office, No. 27 Chambers street, within thirty days from the date of this notice.

The above-described lists will be transmitted, as provided by law, to the Board of Revision and Correction of Assessments, for confirmation, on the 21st day of December, 1891.

In the matter of the application of the Board of Education by the Counsel to the Corporation of the City of New York, relative to acquiring title by the Mayor, Aldermen and Commonalty of the City of New York, to certain lands on the northerly side of 104th street, between Amsterdam (formerly 10th) avenue and Columbus (formerly 9th) avenue, in the 12th Ward of said city, duly selected and approved by said Board as a site for school purposes, under and in pursuance of the provisions of chapter 191 of the Laws of 1888, as amended by chapter 35 of the Laws of 1890. Pursuant to the provisions of chapter 191 of the Laws of 1888, as amended by chapter 35 of the Laws of 1890, notice is given that an application will be made to the Supreme Court of the State of New York, at a special term of said court, to be held at chambers thereof in the County Court House, in the City of New York, on Saturday, the 12th day of December, 1891, at the opening of the court on that day, or as soon thereafter as counsel can be heard thereon, for the appointment of Commissioners of Estimate in the above-entitled matter.

In the matter of the application of the Mayor, Aldermen and Commonalty of the City of New York, acting by and through the Department of Docks, relative to acquiring right and title to and possession of the wharf property, rights, terms, easements, emoluments and privileges of, and to the lands under water, and land under water necessary to be taken for the improvement of the water front of the City of New York, on the North River, between 42d and 43d streets, between 12th and 13th avenues; also between 34th and 35th streets, 12th and 13th avenues; also between 41st and 42d streets, 12th and 13th avenues; also between 38th and 39th streets; also between 38th street and centre line of block northerly therefrom and 12th and 13th avenues; also between 39th and 41st streets, 12th and 13th avenues; also between 35th and 36th streets, 12th and 13th avenues; also the water front in the neighborhood of Albany street, on the North River, appurtenant to the southerly side and the westerly end of Pier, old No. 12, North River, and appurtenant to the bulkhead extending 58 feet 3 inches along the westerly side of West street, next southerly to Albany street; also between 36th and 37th streets, 12th and 13th avenues; also between 51st and 52d streets, 12th and 13th avenues, pursuant to the plans heretofore adopted by the said Department of Docks and approved by the Commissioners of the Sinking Fund. Pursuant to section 715, chapter 410 of the Laws of 1882, and the statutes in such case made and provided, notice is hereby given that an application will be made to the Supreme Court of the State of New York, at a special term of said court, to be held at chambers thereof, in the County Court House in the City of New York, on the 11th day of December, 1891, at the opening of the court on that day, or as soon thereafter as counsel can be heard thereon, for the appointment of Commissioners of Estimate and Assessment in the above-entitled matters.

In the matter of the application of the Board of Street Opening and Improvement of the City of New York, for and on behalf of the Mayor, Aldermen and Commonalty of the City of New York, relative to acquiring title, wherever the same has not been heretofore acquired, to East 168th street (although not yet named by proper authority), extending from Webster to Franklin avenue, in the 23d Ward, as the same has been heretofore laid out and designated as a first-class street or road by the Department of Public Parks. The Commissioners of Estimate and Assessment in the above-entitled matter, give notice to all persons interested in this proceeding, and to the owner or owners, occupant or occupants, of all houses and lots and improved or unimproved lands affected thereby, and to all others whom it may concern, to wit:

First—That they have completed their estimate and assessment, and that all persons interested in this proceeding or in any of the lands affected thereby, and having objections thereto, do present their said objections in writing, duly verified, at their office, No. 200 Broadway (fifth floor), in said city, on or before the 26th day of December, 1891, and that the said Commissioners will hear parties so objecting within the ten week days next after the said 26th day of December, 1891, and for that purpose will be in attendance at said office on each of said ten days at 4 o'clock P. M.

Second—That the abstract of said estimates and assessments, together with their damage and benefit maps, and also all the affidavits, estimates and other documents used by them in making their report, have been deposited with the Commissioner of Public Works of the City of New York, at his office, No. 31 Chambers street, in the said city, there to remain until the 28th day of December, 1891.

In the matter of the application of the Board of Street Opening and Improvement of the City of New York, for and on behalf of the Mayor, Aldermen and Commonalty of the City of New York, relative to acquiring title, wherever the same has not been heretofore acquired, to 136th street, from Amsterdam avenue to Convent avenue, 12th Ward; also to 111th street, from Amsterdam avenue to Riverside avenue, 12th Ward; also to 143d street, from Amsterdam avenue to Convent avenue, 12th Ward; also to 142d street, from Amsterdam avenue to Convent avenue, 12th Ward; also to East 144th street (although not yet named by proper authority), extending from River avenue to St. Ann's avenue in the 23d Ward of the City of New York, as the same has been heretofore laid out and designated as a first class street or road by the Department of Public Parks. Pursuant to the statutes in such cases made and provided, notice is given that an application will be made to the Supreme Court of the State of New York, at a Special Term of said Court, to be held at Chambers thereof in the County Court House, in the City of New York, on Friday, the 18th day of December, 1891, at the opening of Court on that day, or as soon thereafter as counsel can be heard thereon, for the appointment of Commissioners of Estimate and Assessment in the above-entitled matters. The nature and extent of the improvements hereby intended is the acquisition of title, in the name and on behalf of the Mayor, Aldermen and Commonality of the City of New York, for the use of the public, to all the lands and premises, with the buildings thereon and the appurtenances thereto belonging, required for the opening of certain streets or avenues mentioned above.

Real Estate Department.

The market this week has shown some improvement, as is evidenced by the sales, some of them very interesting in character, reported elsewhere. There has been a much better feeling abroad and though its effects may be only temporary the more life-like tone that has characterized real estate doings during the past few days is thoroughly welcome. That there will be any revival of immediate activity seems unlikely at this time. The Thanksgiving holiday will interfere with the business of next week and December is a notably dull month, due of course to the holiday preparations and the stock-taking and other business conditions. However, there is little use speculating as to the future, and real estate men, grasping the facts of the present, which show a better tone in an almost stagnant market will find much more comfort than in all the speculations or prophecies concerning the future. These present facts include a large sale on West 4th street for a warehouse, a sale on 14th street, sales of a 5th avenue corner and a large plot at 125th street and Lexington avenue. These sales include those of the greatest interest; and it will be seen that they are not confined to any one district of the city. This is a good sign, as is also the fact that trades do not appear to be as numerous as they have been. Let us hope that the improvement (it is not as great as it should be considering the time of year) is only the forerunner of a larger business consequent upon lower prices and more enthusiasm on the part of buyers.

THE SALES OF THE WEEK.

The doings in the Auction Room during the past week embrace very little that is of general interest. The announcements for the week contained few properties of more than ordinary importance, and not many of the inferior kind, and when all the sales had taken place it was found that even a number of the parcels advertised were still on their owners' hands, for one reason or another. Some of the properties when offered elicited not a single bid, while others, more successful in the matter of arousing some competition, were bought in when it was seen that no one would bid the upset prices. Still others, after trying the feeling of the bidders, were publicly withdrawn early in the competition. Through these means the already short list of proposed sales becomes even a shorter list of consummated transactions. It is unnecessary to recapitulate the reasons for thi stagnation in the auction market. As we said last week, much of it is attributable to the indifference manifested throughout the real estate world, both at auction and at private sale, but a telling cause for it is probably found in the suspicious of bidders that "peremptory" and "absolute" sales are nothing more than a name. When operators, investors and speculators really believe that property offered for public competition is in no way protected by the owner or his agents, there will be more successful auction sales. Until they become convinced of this fact it is not probable that there will be the active, unrestrained bidding by which alone the best results are to be obtained.

The sale exciting the largest amount of interest was that of the northwest corner of 3d avenue and 43d street, a five-story tenement and store, on lot 25.1x100. There was a considerable crowd in front of Auctioneer Meyer's stand during the sale, and the bidding started by Ascher Weinstein at $40,000 soon became general. It was sold to P. J. Kennedy for $58,900—a figure considered low by those competent to judge. The building at present rents for $5,300 per year, the mortgage being $40,000. Over in West 14th street, west of 8th avenue, John F. B. Smyth sold two four-story houses, on plot 49.6x103.3, on the south side of the street, for $45,200. In the way of foreclosure sales the leasehold six-story iron building, Nos. 37 to 43 Greene street, was sold for $40,000 to the plaintiff in the action. In another foreclosure sale the amount due exceeded the selling price by over $4,000. It was for a three-story dwelling on 123d street, west of Avenue A, which sold for $5,000 against mortgages and costs of $9,613.

THE ANNOUNCEMENTS.

Next week is broken by Thanksgiving Day, which fact, in part at least, accounts for the small list of offerings. In the city proper there are but few voluntary offerings, and these of very ordinary character, and the legal sales embrace but little that will attract the outside buyer. Suburban lot-owners, however, are still active, as is evidenced by the fact that two large lot sales are advertised to be held in the Exchange on Monday. Richard V. Harnett will offer about 100 lots in the 23d Ward, while James L. Wells, who has the other lot sale, will endeavor to dispose of the Hyatt estate of 173 lots at Woodlawn.

But if the announcements for next week are not an attraction those for the week immediately following will prove so. A. H. Muller & Son announce a sale in partition by order of the Supreme Court which will probably attract the biggest men in the market. It takes place on December 3d, and it includes No 145 Broadway, corner of Liberty street; Nos. 86 and 88 Liberty street, corner Temple; No 70 Cortlandt street and No. 219 Fulton street. This sale will probably give an added stimulus to the market and it may prove the means of reviving the auction business.

On Monday, November 23d, Richard V. Harnett & Co. will sell 100 lots in the 23d Ward, situated on Kelly (152d) street, Prospect avenue, Union avenue, Tinton avenue and Wales avenue, near Westchester avenue. The property is supplied with water, gas and sewerage, and the neighborhood is being rapidly improved. The sale is positive and the title is guaranteed by the Lawyers' Title Insurance Company.

On Tuesday, November 24th, Richard V. Harnett & Co. will sell the three-story brick dwelling, No. 70 7th street, and a three story frame dwelling on East 149th street (Gerard street), together with all right and title and interest in and to one-half of Gerard street.

On Tuesday, November 24th, Smyth & Ryan will sell by order of the Supreme Court, in partition, the valuable lot with frame buildings thereon on the southeast corner of East Broadway and Pike street, and the four-story brick building (leasehold) No. 103 Monroe street, near Pike street.

On Tuesday, November 24th, Smyth & Ryan will sell the four-story and basement factory building, lot 125x100.9, Nos. 227 to 235 East 102d street, and the property known as the Belmore Cottage, at Far Rockaway, on Central avenue. It adjoins the Ocean Hotel and Wave Crest and is within fifteen minutes' drive of Arverne by-the-Sea. The plot is 75x263x75x274.6.

On Thursday, December 3d, Adrian H. Muller & Son will conduct the most important sale of down-town business and investment properties offered this year. The list comprises an excellent variety of well-located parcels and constitutes an opportunity for obtaining real estate of the highest class seldom found even in New York. The most valuable of these parcels is No 145 Broadway, being the southwest corner of Liberty street. But in addition to this another corner, Nos. 86 and 88 Liberty street, the southwest corner of Temple place, will be sold; No. 70 Cortlandt street, between Greenwich and Church streets, and No. 219 Fulton street, between Greenwich and Church streets. The sale will be held under the direction of Wilbur Larremore, Referee, and 70 per cent of the purchase money may remain on bond and mortgage at 5 per cent.

CONVEYANCES.

	1890. Nov. 14 to 20 inc.	1891. Nov. 13 to 19 inc.
Number	256	269
Amount involved	$4,368,561	$3,908,609
Number nominal	77	67
Number 23d and 24th Wards	27	118
Amount involved	$102,320	$404,019
Number nominal	6	18

MORTGAGES.

	1890.	1891.
Number	348	312
Amount involved	$4,577,071	$4,748,455
Number at 5 %	174	186
Amount involved	$2,070,215	$1,480,852
Number at less than 5 per cent	42	18
Amount involved	$1,093,241	$519,000
Number to Banks, Trust and Ins. Cos	67	50
Amount involved	$1,940,750	$880,150

PROJECTED BUILDINGS.

	1890. Nov. 15 to 21 inc.	1891. Nov. 14 to 20 inc.
Number of buildings	65	60
Estimated cost	$939,300	$920,050

Gossip of the Week.

SOUTH OF 59TH STREET.

The Reeves estate has sold to L. Sachs & Bro., fur dealers, the Reeves residence and adjoining buildings on the lots Nos. 15, 17 and 19 West 4th street, comprising 71.6x93.3, on the northwest corner of Mercer street. The price is stated to have been $300,000, but Messrs. Sachs & Bro., when seen yesterday, would not verify the figure. John T. Doyle was the broker.

W. Jennings Demorest has purchased through S. E. Hebberd & Son from the Spofford estate, the Van Buren leasehold No. 4 East 14th street, a five story brown stone front building covering 23x103, with nineteen years to run and renewals, for $50,000. Mr. Demorest has also purchased from F. Schuler, the piano maker, the Van Buren leasehold property No. 19 East 14th street, a four-story building covering a lot 25x103, for $30,000.

James Bleecker & Son have sold Nos. 140 to 144 West 23d street, a five-story brick apartment house, 61.6x120x140, to W. D. Barnes, on private terms.

Wm. Buchanan has sold No. 61 Park avenue, a four-story brown stone front dwelling, for $80,000.

Walter H. Burns has sold the two 16-foot four-story brown stone dwellings, Nos. 249 and 251 Madison avenue, on private terms.

Morris B. Baer & Co. have sold for Miss Greenly the three-story, high stoop, Ohio stone house, 18.9x100.5, No. 59 West 45th street, for $47,250; and for a Mr. Chittenden the four-story brown stone house, No. 114 West 38th street, adjoining the Normandie Hotel, size 20x100, for $40,000

The three-story and basement high stoop dwelling, No. 327 East 57th street, 22x50x100.4, which was to have been offered by Richard V. Harnett & Co. at auction on Wednesday, was sold prior to the auction at about $13,000.

Emil Bachmann has sold No. 335 West 20th street, a four-story and basement brick dwelling, to Mrs. M. Schwab, for $18,500. The size of the lot is 25x92.

S. M. Blakely has sold for C. Vorbach No. 333 West 46th street, a three-story brown stone front dwelling, 16 8x53x100.5, for $16,000.

Otto Pullich has sold for Wm. Wuerz the two five-story and basement tenements, each 25x88x100, Nos. 423 and 425 West 52d street, for $60,000.

Philip Sammet has purchased from Mrs. Ball No. 14 Grove street, a three-story and basement dwelling, on lot 21x70, on private terms, and from Mrs. Thompson No. 203 West 35th street, four-story front and rear buildings, on lot 25x98 9, also on private terms.

NORTH OF 59TH STREET.

The Colwell estate have sold the block front on the east side of Lexington avenue, between 125th and 126th streets, for $150,000 The size of the plot is 200x60. The sellers, when questioned as to the name of the buyer, said that they were not at liberty to make it public just yet, but that they would probably do so next week.

John N. Golding this week sold what is said to be the last vacant north corner lot on 5th avenue, south of 72d street, that is for sale. The lot Mr. Golding sold is on the northeast corner of 5th avenue and 71st street, 29.3 x125, and the price is reported as more than $100,000. The seller is Chester W. Chapin and the purchaser Capt. Andrew C. Zabriskie, who will erect a residence on the lot.

Homer Lee, President of the Homer Lee Bank Note Company, yesterday purchased from the United States Life Insurance Company six lots on the northwest corner of the Boulevard and 86th street. The price paid was in the neighborhood of $100,000. Mr. Lee, with B. Gerson Oppenheim, represents a syndicate who will build a fourteen-story apartment hotel on the site of eleven lots, the other five being on the northeast corner of West End avenue and 86th street, and owned by Mr. Oppenheim.

Jas. L. Libby & Son have sold for Mrs Arminthia Merritt No. 264 West 89th street, a three-story brick and stone dwelling, to C A. Starbuck for $25,000; to E. G. Teel the four-story brown stone dwelling, 26x44.2x61.3, on the south side of 82d street, just east of Riverside Drive; for S. R. Donnellon to P. C. Ralli No. 165 West 88th street, a three-story stone front dwelling, on private terms; and two four-story dwellings on Riverside Drive, 44.2 south of 82d street, one of which was purchased by a Mr. Weisenfeldt.

Otto Pullich has sold for Adler & Herrmen the five-story flats and stores, on the northeast corner of 69th street and Columbus avenue, for $140,000; and for Michael Cashman the two lots on the north side of 151st street, 425 feet east of Amsterdam avenue, for $10,500.

Wm. H. Hollister has sold for Max Hirshkind to J. Sturk No. 219 East 83d street, a two-story brick and frame dwelling, on lot 25x102.2, for $12,-000. Mr. Sturk gives in exchange the five-story brown stone front double flat, No. 45 East 112th street, 25x84x100, for $18,750.

Dunn Bros. have sold No. 301 West 87th street, a three-story brown stone front dwelling, 19x55x100.8, for $25,500.

Wm. R. Ware has sold for Charles McDonald to A. W. Griswold No. 66 West 82d street, a four-story brown stone dwelling, 19x55 and extension x102.2, on private terms.

Giblin & Taylor have sold their remaining four-story dwelling on 80th street, north side, between Columbus and Amsterdam avenues, to James Flanagan, on private terms. The size of the house is 20.8x55x102.2.

Max Simon has sold for Mrs. H. Gordon to Charles N. Rossetti, No. 209 West 118th street, a five-story double flat, 25x72x100.11, on private terms.

F. Zittel, who last week sold to Oppenheimer & Metzger the two lots on the north side of 76th street, commencing 200 feet east of Columbus avenue, has resold them on private terms to Alfred G. Nason for immediate improvement. Mr. Zittel has also sold for Mr. John C. Umberfield, No. 39 West 75th street, a four-story brown stone dwelling, 20x60x102.2, for about $42,000. The purchaser is S. M. Styles.

LEASE.

Wm. R. Lloyd & Co. have rented for Dr. Eugene A. Hoffman the entire building, Nos. 168 and 170 Park row, from May 1, 1891, for five years at $9,500 per annum. This rent is said to be nearly 50 per cent advance on the figure now obtained.

Brooklyn.

Corwith Bros. have sold the three-story frame dwelling, 22x40, on lot 25 x100, No. 175 Huron street, for Annie M. Brady to Catharine Taylor, for $4,200; and the lot, 25x100, on the west side of Newell street, 200 feet north of Nassau avenue, for Elizabeth Schmitt, for $1,325.

Benjamin Sturges has sold for the estate of Mordica Johnson the house and lot, No. 377 Throop avenue, for $4,000; and for Richard B. Riker the two four-story flats, Nos. 483 and 485 Quincy street, for $24,000.

CONVEYANCES.

	1890. Nov. 13 to 19 inc.	1891. Nov. 12 to 18 inc.
Number	323	369
Amount involved	$1,436,072	$991,001
Number nominal	88	116

MORTGAGES.

	1890.	1891.
Number	292	333
Amount involved	$1,160,089	$1,345,584
Number at 5 per cent. or less	135	170
Amount involved	$631,516	$728,287

PROJECTED BUILDINGS.

	1890. Nov. 14 to 20 inc.	1891. Nov. 13 to 19 inc.
Number of buildings	88	95
Estimated cost	$398,885	$497,585

Out Among the Builders.

C. L. Holden is the architect of the large office building which the Delaware, Lackawanna & Western Railroad have decided to build on the site of the present old offices of the company on Exchange place. The new structure will front 56.9 feet on Exchange place and 79.6 on William street. It will be ten stories high, of Indiana limestone, with the vertical floor supports of steel. The design will be "Classic." The fittings and decoration of the building are to be of the finest character.

A syndicate of capitalists, represented by Homer Lee and B. Gerson Oppenheim, intend to build a fourteen-story fire-proof apartment hotel on the eleven lots on the Boulevard, West End avenue and 86th street, taking in the whole front on the north side of that street between those thoroughfares.

L. Sachs & Brother intend, in the spring, to erect three six-story brick, stone and iron front warehouses, on a plot 100x100, at Nos. 13 to 19 Washington place, from plans by Richard Berger. Messrs. Sachs & Bro. may also improve Nos. 15, 17 and 19 West 4th street, northwest corner of Mercer street.

Capt. Andrew C. Zabriskie will build a fine residence on the northeast corner of 5th avenue and 71st street, on the lot 29.3x125, which he has just purchased.

Lewis S. Wolff, the banker, of No. 30 Nassau street, has purchased Nos. 87-91 Fulton street for improvement, the exact character of which he informed a reporter of THE RECORD AND GUIDE has not yet been decided.

The Bowery Savings Bank, having recently purchased the property at Nos. 222 to 226 Grand street, beginning at the northeast corner of Elizabeth street, it is now the intention of the directors, so it is said, to commence the erection of a new bank building thereon. There will be a meeting of the full board in the early part of December, at which some definite action will be taken. President Edward Wood said to a RECORD AND GUIDE reporter that he was not quite certain that a new bank building would supersede the present one; no Building Committee had yet been appointed and no other steps taken by the directors. The bank was chartered in 1834. Under the terms of that charter it cannot move from the Bowery; it must at least have its entrance on that street. No one seems to know what will be done with the old building in case another building takes its stead.

Wallace C. Andrews, president of the New York Steam Company, is contemplating the erection of a combination of buildings on the block bounded by 86th and 87th streets, 12th and 13th avenues. The plans have been drawn, but nothing has been decided upon. According to them, the buildings will contain a market, storage room for light and heavy goods, a swimming school, a summer garden on the roof and a riding academy.

Richard G. Platt has had plans drawn for a four-story and basement dwelling, to be erected on the northeast corner of 85th street and West End avenue. The material will be red stone and Tiffany brick and the cost about $35,000. Clarence True is the architect.

Chas. L. Tiffany, the well-known jeweler, will shortly take title to about seven acres of ground at Forest Hill, in the suburbs of Newark, N. J., on which he contemplates erecting a large plate-ware factory. Forest Hill is on the New York & Greenwood Railway. Mr. Tiffany, when seen at his Union square office, said: "We have not yet had any plans drawn for the factory and do not expect to commence to build till the spring."

Andrew Judge will build a five-story flat, 25x69 and extension, on the north side of 131st street, 460 feet west of 5th avenue, from plans by J. C. Burne. The front will be of brick and stone and the cost $22,000.

D. & J. Jardine are the architects for a six-story building to be erected on the north side of 58th street, 200 feet west of 6th avenue, for Religio Lo Forte.

Walter H. C. Hornum has plans on the boards for two five-story houses, 25x68, for Harry L. Kidd. The location is the south side of 42d street.

John Fitzpatrick will erect a five-story apartment house at No. 365 3d avenue. Frederick Jouth is the architect.

Henry Wohlers will erect an apartment house, 27.4x62, with five stories, at No. 1624 2d avenue, from plans prepared by Charles Stegmayer.

John C. Burne is the architect for five five-story brick and brown stone front flats, which James F. Boyle and Michael J. Bannon will build on the southwest corner of 107th street and Park avenue, at a cost of $100,000. The corner house, containing stores, will be 25x71.11, an adjoining avenue house 25x61, while two street houses will be 25x61, and the 3d street house 25x64, with an extension 13x5.

John Hauser has plans on the boards for a five-story brown stone and brick front flat, which Louis Wirth will build on the south side of 90th street, 80 feet east of Madison avenue, at a cost of $32,000. The flat, which will be 30.4x90.6 in size, will contain all the improvements and will be finished in hardwood throughout.

J. C. Burne will furnish plans for two five-story brick and stone front flats, to be erected by Thos. J. Robinson on the east side of Amsterdam avenue, 25 feet south of 125th street, at a cost of $50,000. The sizes will be 25x90 each.

Brooklyn.

The Crescent Athletic Club, of Brooklyn, are contemplating the erection of a large club-house, to cost with land $450,000, on Pierrepont street.

F. Weenemer will furnish plans for a two-story brick stable and office, 171x40, which the Farmers' Feed Company intend to erect on Johnson avenue, at a cost of $17,000.

Langston & Dahlander have plans on the boards for a nine-story apartment house to have a frontage of 100 feet on St. John's place, 70 feet on Flatbush avenue and 50 feet on 8th avenue; cost, $300,000. The materials to be used are granite, sandstone, buff brick and terra cotta. V. F. Pelletrau represents the syndicate owning the building.

William H. Reynolds will erect an apartment house of brick, stone and terra cotta, 28x85, on the northwest corner of Halsey street and Nostrand avenue; and on Halsey street, adjoining, twenty dwellings, each three stories, 20x45; cost, $235,000.

James Mills will build three four-story apartment houses of stone and brick, 30x72, on the north side of 1st street, 250 feet west of 7th avenue; cost, $70,000.

Out of Town.

NEWARK, N. J.—Swinnerton & Poole have plans for a three-story brick flat for J. H. Shafer, to be built on the corner of Washington and Baldwin streets, to cost $8,000; also plans for a frame two-and-a-half-story dwelling for Christian Gillon, to be built at No. 95 South 8th street, to cost $2,500.

YONKERS, N. Y.—The two-story brick and two-story frame houses on a plot 70x81, at Nos. 240 and 242 Main street, which were to have been offered at the New York Real Estate Exchange by Richard V. Harnett & Co. this week were previously sold privately by the estate of John Harriman for $6,550.

Building Notes.

S. McClave, of 11th avenue and Bethune street, a relative of E. W. McClave, who has been prominent in organizing The Yellow Pine Company, said: "Oak has for some time been the predominating wood for interior trim. The reasons for its use are that it is a light wood and gives a cheerful effect to a room and that it costs less than mahogany."

"What is the difference in cost between a first floor and basement trimmed in oak or in mahogany?" asked the reporter.

"I should say, on a rough guess, about $300 per house," was the reply. "This applies to a house about 20x55 in size. It varies according to the amount of trim used. Of course mahogany has a particular value and will always be used more or less, but at present we are selling oak in very large quantities."

Traitel Bros. have some splendid examples of tiles and tile panels at their 5th avenue show-rooms, near 42d street. Two of these on the walls of their rooms are said to be the finest tiles ever imported into this country. They represent a huntsman of the 17th century and a lady of the same date. The colors and outlines are unusually good.

The McShane Plumbing Company, of 6th avenue, near 37th street, are fitting up several bath-rooms at their warerooms. These bath-rooms are models of richness and elegance and contain new ideas, the most striking of which is a porcelain tank. Mr. Murray, treasurer of the company, talking with the writer, said: "Five or ten years ago plumbers would have scoffed at the idea of such elaborate bath-rooms. At that time wooden baths lined with tin, and plumbing of ordinary lead, was the custom. Now we have nickel-plated plumbing, porcelain tubs, tiled walls and floors, etc., and while the cost of fitting up a bath-room then was a few hundred dollars, now it amounts to thousands. It is an ordinary thing for us to contract for one costing $3,000 and more. To have asked a lady to call on a plumber to select her own style of bath-room ten years ago would have been deemed an insult; whereas now it is quite usual for ladies, accompanied by their husbands, to call on us to discuss the style and appointments and to make their selections accordingly. The change is due —first to the higher taste of the public; second to the better regulations of the Board of Health, which have necessitated the use of fine plumbing and thus taught people the value of first-class plumbing work."

Personal.

Ex-President E. A. Cruikshank, of the Real Estate Exchange, has been elected a member of the Reform Club. He was proposed by Manager Benjamin Hardwick, of the Exchange, and seconded by Mr. Constant A. Andrews.

The West Side Democratic Club.

The West Side Democratic Club, the only incorporated Democratic organization from 54th street to 125th street, is an illustration of the energy of some of the prominent Westsiders. It was organized on October 7th last. On October 14th it had 122 members, a number which at the present time has increased to 520. It played an important part during the last campaign in bringing out the Flower vote in the 19th Assembly District, holding as much as two meetings a week, addressed by such speakers as Thomas C. T. Crain, Adolph Sanger, Bourke Cockran, Theodore W. Myers and others equally prominent. The club is composed of solid business men and is an independent Democratic club. The managers are Bryan L. Kenelly, Theodore N. Mellvin, Henry Lowenthal, James E. Kelly, William B. Ellison, Farrel F. O'Dowd, Clifford Boese, James F. McEntee, B. Oppenheim, James J. Harold, Louis B. Rolston, William J. Warburton, Charles F. Ohlstrom, George C. Coffin and Edward K. Murphy.

WANTS AND OFFERS.

WANTS.

YOUNG MAN, 24 years, college graduate, good family, desires to enter real estate office, learn business and be generally useful; can furnish capital in time, if desirable; small salary; best reference. Address, ENERGETIC, RECORD AND GUIDE Office.

WANTED.—Plot for theatre, 30th to 42d st., near Broadway; also have builders wanting lots with builder's loan; any good location.
H. T. SCHELLHASS, 171 Broadway.

OFFERS.

Dwellings and Flats.

THREE-STORY sub-cellar basement brown stone and brick house. 181 Thompson st., New York. Apply to
GEORGE M. RICE, 345 Franklin av., Brooklyn.

FOR SALE.—In Spring st., near Hudson, two houses, four-story, with store, 36x88.
WM. C. WALKER'S SONS, 299½ Broadway.

WE ARE REQUESTED to sell the following houses, without reserve, to close estate: 31st, adjoining Madison; 44th, corner Lexington; 49th, near Madison. Send for particulars.
LUDLOW, DAY & CO., 31st, near Broadway.

TWO FIRST-CLASS FOUR-STORY APARTMENT HOUSES; steam heat; all improvements; 93d st., near Lexington av.; size 30x90x100.8 each; price for both $52,000; mortgage $36,000 at 5 per cent; rent $5,780. FORD & WEISKER, 162 West 4th st.

A 72D ST. GEM, No. 308 West.—This superb house is beautifully decorated; has handsome gas fixtures; is in perfect order; ready for immediate occupancy; $38,000; a greater bargain than has been offered in months.
Nov. 14-uf. CONDIT, 1179 Broadway.

ONLY ONE LEFT, FOUR SOLD LAST MONTH.—812 West 89th st., 20 feet, four stories; exceptionally well built; unexcelled location; am authorized to close this out at a bargain.
Nov. 14-uf. CONDIT, 1179 Broadway.

$650,000 FOR ONE of the choicest pieces of investment properties on Manhattan Island; exceptionally well built and very desirably located; other good property (city or country) will be entertained in part payment.
Nov. 14—uf. CONDIT, 1179 Broadway.

A—At reasonable prices and easy terms, three and four-story residences, with three-story extensions; all improvements. Call and examine or inquire of the owner and builder, on the premises.
S. O. WRIGHT, 128 West 121st st., open daily.
Oct. 3 uf.

FOR SALE.—2443 8th av and 210 and 212 West 105th st.; commission allowed brokers. Apply at
Aug. 29-uf. Room 19, 156 Broadway.

OFFERS.

FOR SALE.—Six new cabinet-trimmed three-story and basement brown stone private dwellings, Nos. 142-162 West 123d st.; prices reasonable and brokers commissions allowed. For further particulars apply at office of
FRED'K. M. LITTLEFIELD, 156 Broadway.
Aug. 29-uf.

Vacant Lots.

$300 FOR LOT, 28x105, short walk north of Williamsbridge railroad station. Owner,
SPERLE, 309 East 118th st, City.

A CORNER PROPERTY on Water st., 50x50, suitable for factory; for sale; terms easy.
RULAND & WHITING, 5 Beekman st.

A PLOT, 40x98.9, on East 34th st., between 1st and 2d avs.; ready for immediate improvement; suitable for factory or tenement; will be sold cheap; terms to suit purchaser.
E. MICHAELIS & SON, 88 2d av.

EASTERLY FRONT BOULEVARD, with 200 ft. on 86th st. and 264 ft. on 85th st.; one or more plots.
Nov. 7-1aw6w. OTTO ERNST, South Amboy, N. J.

1ST AV., near 108th st; full lot, $5,700.
Oct. 31—1aw9w. EDWIN A. ELY, 103 Gold st.

Improved Property.

FOR SALE.—On 3d av., near 43d st., 20 or 60 feet, with buildings. For terms and particulars, apply to RULAND & WHITING, 5 Beekman st.

A FINE INVESTMENT PROPERTY on Fulton st.; for sale.
RULAND & WHITING, 5 Beekman st.

OFFICE OF
FREDERICK SOUTHACK,
401 BROADWAY,
offers for sale some choice pieces
of property on
LEONARD ST., between Broadway and West B'way.
FRANKLIN ST., between B'way and West B'way.
WHITE ST., between B'way and West B'way.
BROADWAY, from Barclay to 14th st.
BLEECKER ST., from B'way to South 5th av.
GREENE ST., Canal to 8th st.
WASHINGTON PLACE, B'way to Wooster.
WAVERLEY PLACE, B'way to Wooster.
APPLY AS ABOVE.
FREDERICK SOUTHACK.
Oct. 3 uf.

Brooklyn Real Estate for Sale.

FRONT AND REAR HOUSE in North 2d st., Brooklyn, E. D.; price, $4,150; mortgage, $3,500; leased for $540 a year.
CHAS. CONNERY, 92 South 2d st., Brooklyn.

192 13TH ST., BROOKLYN.—Three-story, bay front, single flat; $6,500; easy terms.
CONDIT, 1179 Broadway.

OFFERS.

FOR SALE.—New Queen Anne house, three blocks from city line; price, $2,600. Apply 1098 Lafayette av., cor Patchen av., Brooklyn; B. J. Dennis, Jr., builder.

Country Property.

TWO LOTS on 55th st., between 16th and 17th avs., just outside Brooklyn; will sell cheap.
T. J. IVANS, 7 Pitt st., New York.

TO SPECULATORS.—75 acres land, 7,000 feet street frontage, 400 yards from depot, 17 miles from city, $15,000, one-third cash; 90 acres, half mile from depot, 16 miles from city, adjoining R. R., for $8,500, one-third cash; 75 acres, 25 miles from city, fine frontage, for $7,500, one-third cash. Buildings worth $2,000 with each tract.
CHARLES L. WALLACE, Rockville Centre, L. I.

AN INVESTMENT OR SPECULATION.—Over 200 acres just north of Van Cortlandt Park, near two depots. Principals only.
PHILLIPS & WELLS, Tribune Building.
Nov. 21-1aw4w.

50 TO 200 ACRES, suitable for dividing into large or small plots; forty minutes from city; convenient to depot; can be sub-divided at small expense.
W. B. TIBBITS, agent, White Plains, N. Y.
Nov. 14—1aw3w.

FOR SALE.—In plots to suit; eligible building sites (commanding view of Sound for miles), on North st., Greenwich, Connecticut; price reasonable; terms easy; neighborhood aristocratic and fashionable. Apply to
FRED. J. STONE, owner, 60 Broadway, N. Y.
Sept. 12-uf.

FORTY ACRES, northern end and highest point on Manhattan Island, lying on Hudson River and Spuyten Duyvil, carrying all riparian rights; grand site for Hotel, Institution, &c; would exchange for improved city property.
LUDLOW, DAY & CO., 54 West 31st st.

Miscellaneous.

TO LET OR TO LEASE.—Two floors of a factory, 25x98, light on all sides, 1st av and 107th st; terms moderate. J. REEBER'S SONS,
Nov. 7 uf. 409 East 107th.

A PARTY ABOUT TO BUILD A FIVE-STORY factory, 50x98, in Harlem, near water-front, will lease the three upper floors and build to suit tenant. Terms very moderate. Address
May 16 u. f. OWNER, 409 E. 107th St.

PRINTING.—Book, News and Job.
RECORD AND GUIDE PRESS,
14 Barclay, and 14, 16 Vesey sts.

SALES OF THE WEEK.

The following are the sales at the Real Estate Exchange and Auction Room for the week ending November 20.

** Indicates that the property described has been bid in for plaintiff's account:*

R. V. HARNETT & CO.

*96th st, No. 63, n s, 141 e 9th av, 21x100.11, four-story brk dwell'g. Francis P. Furnald. $21,500
106th st, No. 150, s e cor Lexington av, 20x80.11, five-story brk and stone flat. Adler & Herrman 32,200
136th st, s s, 256.6 e Alexander av, 37.6x100. Wm. H. Taubert. (Amt due $4,089) 7,400
144th st, No. 596, s s, 375 e Willis av, 16.8x100, two-story and basement brk dwell'g. Chas. Van Riper and Jas. Lacoste........ 5,350
Lexington av, No. 1677, 80.11 s 106th st, 20x95, five-story and basement brk and stone flat. Adler & Herrman........ 15,200

A. H. MULLER & SON.

72d st, No. 124, s s, 159.11 w Lexington av, 20x102.2, four-story and basement stone front dwell'g. (Bid in)........ ——
3d av, No. 664, n w cor 43d st, five-story stone front building with stores. P. J. Kennedy 58,900
*Greene st, Nos. 37-43, w s, 65 n Grand st, 85x100, two six-story iron front stores, ½ part. Louis F. Dommerich trustee. (Amt due $63,343; leasehold)........ 40,900

J. F. B. SMYTH.

14th st, Nos. 344 and 346 W., 49.6x103.3, two four-story and basement brk houses. Thos. M. Mulry........ 45,200
64th st, No. 173 W., 25x100.5, five-story brk and stone flat. (Bid in)........ ——
Av B, Nos. 263 and 265, two five-story tenements and stores. (Bid in)........ ——
65th st, No. 332, s s, 331.3 e 2d av, 18.9x100, two-story brk dwell'g. Jonas Rosenthal.... 6,000
1st av, No. 166, e s, 23.8 n 10th st, 23.8x94, five-story brk tenem't and store. Carolina Baumert........ 26,500
*41st st, No. 340, s s, 365 e 2d av, 16x98.9, four-story brk dwell'g. Leonard Scott. (Amt due $6,892)........ 6,900

B. L. KENNELLY.

*Madison av, s w cor 118th , 100x60, one-story frame building. Jebiekt S. Raynor et al. (Amt due $17,189)........ 28,000

JOHN N. GOLDING.

*123d st, No. 447, n s, 138 w Av A, 17.1x100.11, three-story stone front dwell'g. Equitable Life Assur. Soc. (Amt due $9,513)........ 5,000

OTHER AUCTIONEERS.

13th st, No. 239 W., 20x81.8, three-story and basement brk dwell'g. (Bid in)........ ——
82d st, No. 244, s s, 101.5 W., 2d av, 19.3x102.2, three-story brk dwell'g. B. Richter.... 8,100
*Av C, e s, 100 n 5th st, 100x100, 24th Ward, Wm. M. Tebo........ 2,000

Total........ $270,750
Corresponding week 1890........ $870,068

BROOKLYN, N. Y.

FOR WEEK ENDING NOVEMBER 19.

Degraw st, Nos. 192 and 194, s w s, 110 n w Henry st, 40.10x100, two four-story brk dwell'gs and stores. John Egan........ $10,650
Dupont st, No. 146, s s, 275 e Manhattan av, 25x100, two-story frame (brk lined) dwell'g. John E. Kelly........ 2,000
Gold st, No. 334, w s, 100 n Myrtle av, 25x100.3, three-story brk dwell'g. L. Ahrensberg.... 7,010
India st, No. 107, n s, 325 w Manhattan av, 25x100, two-story brk dwell'g. J. P. Sloane. 4,600
India st, No. 116, s s, 225 w Manhattan av, 25x100, two-story and extension frame dwell'g. Susan Wheeler........ 3,800
President st, No. 185, n s, 121 e Henry st, 14.6x100, three-story brk dwell'g. F. J. Worcester 5,450
*Schermerhorn st, n s, 150 w 3d av, 160x100.9x160x101.9, vacant. Cornelius Donnellon ... 31,000
*Atlantic av, Nos. 1648 and 1650, s s, 100 w Troy av, 40x100, three-story frame dwell'g. Wm. J. Burnett........ 5,000
Hendrix st, w s, 100 s Broadway, 100x100, Hugo O. A. Dembke........ 4,650
*7th av, s e s, 1st to 2d st, 200x97.10½, six four-story double brk flats and two five-story brk flats with stores on corners unfinished. John Adamson........ 25,000
Lot at Gravesend, begins at Atlantic Ocean at division line bet old lots 22 and 24 on one side and old lots 20 and 21 on the other side, as shown on Kowolski's map of common lands of Gravesend, Coney Island, runs north — x west — x south to Ocean, x east to beginning, except strip 40 ft. wide condemned for use of New York & Coney Island R. R. Co., and part lying south of centre of Surf av; partition. A. D. Buschman........ 15,250

Total........ $114,410
Corresponding week, 1890........ $152,912

CONVEYANCES.

NEW YORK CITY.

NOVEMBER 13, 14, 16, 17, 18, 19.

Barrow st, No. 46, n s, 215 w Bleecker st, 22.6x97.6x22x97.4, three-story brk dwell'g. John Corse to Adolphine W. Thompson. *Mt.* $5,000. Nov. 16. $14,500
Bleecker st, South 5th av and Wooster st. Consent of creditors to new mortgage with power. James McMurray et al creditors to Alonzo T. Decker et al. trustees for creditors of Patrick H. McManus Aug. 5. nom
Broad st, Nos. 77 and 79 } begins Broad
South William st, Nos. 32 and 34 }
st, e s, 30.1 n South William st, runs north 40.6 x east 90.9 x southeast 38.2 to South William st, x southwest 38.5 x northwest 11.7 x west 68.1, four-story brk stores. Marian wife of Christian F. Schramme to Emily A. wife of Oscar F. Zollikoffer. Nov. 12. 105,000
Broome st, No. 86, n s, 25 w Columbia st, 25x85.10, four-story brk tenem't with stores and one-story brk building on rear. Mayer Lewin to Herman Maretzky. Nov. 14. *Mt.* $16,730. 18,315
Broome st, No. 527, s s, abt 73 e Sullivan st, 18x63x20x63, with use of alley to Thompson st, three-story frame (brk front) store and tenement. Julius J. Lyons to Cornelius J. Donovan. *Mt.* $9,000. Nov. 13. nom
Broome st, Nos. 77 and 77½, s s, 55 e Columbia st, 24.8x100, five-story brk tenem't with stores. Michael Fay and William Stacom to Joseph Geller. *Mt.* $22,500. Nov. 2. 26,500
Church st, old No. 8, on map No. 64, n w s, 75 n e Fulton st, 25x55, five-story brk store. James R. Marshall heir Benjamin M. Brown to Walter L., Delancey A., Samuel N., John I., Woodbury, Sybil K., and Louisa L. Kane and Emily A. K. Jay heirs Delancey Kane. Q. C. Sept. 10. nom
Same property. John J. Brown heir Benjamin M. Brown to same. Aug. 24. nom
Central Park West (8th av), Nos. 441-444, n w cor 104th st, 100.11x100, four five story brk flats. Foreclos. Gilbert M. Speir, Jr., to Henry Steers and John F. Menke. *Mt* $97,500. Nov. 16. 28,670
Cherry st, No. 258, n s, 26.3 e Rutgers st, 26.8x95.8, five-story brk tenem't with stores. Jonas Weil and Bernhard Mayer to Simon

Levy, Seabright, N. J. *Mt.* $20,000. Nov. 16. 34,750

Columbia st, No. 43, e s, 66.3 s Delancey st, runs east 50 x south 8 x east 50 x south 8.1 x west 100 to st. x north 16.10, three-story brk store and tenem't. Herman Friedmann to Max Landsman. *Mt.* $7,850. Nov. 4. 10,250

Delancey st, Nos. 186 and 188, n w, 43.6 e Attorney st, 43x86.5x43x86.6, two three-story brk tenem'ts. Louis Goodman to Charles Ruff. *Mt.* $19,500. Nov. 5. 29,500

Elizabeth st, No. 245, w s, 206.7 n Prince st, 22x89.1x21.4x90, five-story brk store and tenem't. Mary A. wife of Joseph I. Burke, Francis, James L. and Felix J. O'Neill heirs Francis O'Neill otherwise Francis O'Neil to John Early. Nov. 16. 19,000

Eldridge st, Nos. 218 and 220, e s, 25 s Stanton st, 49x87 6, two five-story brk tenem'ts. Lewis Adelson to Samuel Kempner. *Mt.* $38,500. Nov. 17. 60,000

Essex st, No. 35, w s, 150.9 n Hester st, 25x87, six-story brk tenem't with stores. Amalie Cohn to Louisa Kaufold. *Mt.* $29,750. Nov. 18. 41,000

Essex st, w s, 200 s Houston st, 25x87 6. Release covenant. Annie R. Scott, James W. and John J. Wilson individ. and exrs. Elizabeth M. Hazleton to James Morris Feb. 14. 250

Essex st, No. 102, e s, 89.3 n Delancey st, 18.11x75.1, three-story brk store and tenem't. Baruch Franck to Abraham I. Levy. *Mt.* $10,000. Nov. 19. 15,000

Goerck st, No. 41, w s, 75 s Delancey st, 25x100, five-story brk tenem't with stores and four-story brk tenem't on rear. Haris Kosinsky to Julius Israel. *Mt.* $20,500. Nov. 13. 23,500

Grand st, No. 224, n s, 25 e Elizabeth st, 25x110, three-story frame (brk front) tenem't with stores and four-story brk tenem't on rear. George Ubl to Alfred L. White. Nov. 13. 45,000

Same property. Alfred L. White to The Bowery Savings Bank. B. & S. C. a. G. Nov. 13. 45,000

Grand st, No. 222 } begins Grand st,
Elizabeth st, Nos. 112 and 114 } n e cor Elizabeth st, 25x100, three-story frame (brk front) store and tenem't on Grand st and two two and three-story brk and frame tenem'ts on Elizabeth st. Same to same. B. & S. C. a. G. Nov. 12. 62,500

Grand st, No. 226, n s, 50 e Elizabeth st, 25x100, two-story brk store and tenem't. Same to same. B. & S. C. a. G. Nov. 10. 48,000

Grand st, No. 34, n w cor Thompson st, 20.2x61 (19.1)x—, three-story frame and brk tenem't with stores. Contract. Ernst Franklin with William B. Davis. Sept. 21, 19,500

Same property. Assignment of contract. William B. Davis to Gotthardt A. Littbauer. Oct. 22. nom

Greenwich st, Nos. 662-666, w s, 66 4 n Barrow st, 56 8x107.5x56.4x105.10, three three-story brk dwell'gs. Patrick J. Roon to the United States of America. Nov. 4. 45,000

Madison st, No. 86, s s, 172.8 e Catharine st, 25x100.8, three-story brk store and tenem't. Anna V. Brunner and Rosetta P. L. B. Gengenbach individ. and extrxs. of Anna Wagner to Auguste L. Sevestre and Jane E. Cusack. *Mt.* $5,000. Nov. 16. See 36th st. exch

Madison st, No. 141, n s, 183 w Pike st, 25x83, four-story brk store and tenem't. Max Lipovitz to Louis Goodman. *Mt.* $15,700. Sept. 28. See Monroe st. 23,500

Madison st, No. 181, s s, 93 w Montgomery st, 23x108, two-story frame (brk front) tenem't with two-story brk building on rear. Eveline A. Du Bois to John F. Coughlin. Nov. 9. (Corrects error in last issue) 15,000

Monroe st, No. 168, s s, 163.4 w Montgomery st, 23.4x98.4x23.4x98.5, five-story brk store and tenem't. Louis Goodman to Max Lipovitz. *Mt.* $18,500. Sept. 28. See Madison st. 32,500

Morton st, No 25, n s, 87.8 e Bedford st. 18.8x81.3, three-story brk dwell'g with one-story frame shed on rear. Charles B. Stevens to Albert Etzel and Emanuel Kronacher. Nov. 16. 9,800

Morton st, No. 14, s s, abt 150 w Bleecker st, 25x90, three-story brk dwell'g with one-story brk building on rear. Euphemia wife of Gilbert B. Voorhis, David, Eva and William B. Huyler, Mary Stevens widow and Catharine Huyler heirs William Huyler to Bernard Cohen. Nov. 6. 14,000

Nassau st, Nos. 89 and 91 } begins Nassau st, s
Fulton st, Nos. 126-136 } w cor Fulton st, 32.9x112.2x25 7x113.9, vacant.
Nassau st, No. 87, w s, 82.7 s Fulton st, 25.1x110.9x24.8x112.3, vacant.
George W. Vultee to Lewis S. Wolff. *Mt.* $325,000. Nov. 11. nom

Same property. Moses S. Beach, Peekskill, to George W. Vultee. Nov. 11. 375,000

Rutgers st, No. 20, }
Henry st, No. 142. }
Release. David D. Toal to Frederick Schubardt. May 16, 1891. nom

Thompson st, No. 16, e s, 72.11 s Grand st, 21.9x93.6x24.6x93.6, two-story frame store and tenem't with three-story brk tenem't on rear. Lewis Z. Bach to Frederic D. Weekes. C. a. G. Nov. 17. 11,000

Thompson st, Nos. 91 and 93, w s, 125 n Spring st, 50x100, seven-story brk store and factory. Arthur J. Horgan, Sheepshead Bay, L. I., and Vincent J. Slattery to George B. Clark. *Mt.* $55,000. Nov. 16. 82,500

Same property. George B. Clark to Elijah K. Hubbard, Middleton, Conn. *Mt.* $55,000. Nov. 16. 89,750

Washington st, No. 637, e s, 50 n Barrow st, 26x106.2x—x105.5, four-story frame (brk front) store and tenem't with three-story frame tenement on rear. Ida L. wife of Thomas S. Prior, Roslyn, L. I., to the United States of America. B. & S. Nov. 16. 23,500

3d st, Nos. 91 and 93 W. Agreement that west line of west wall of building now in course of erection on No. 91 shall hereafter and in perpetuity be the division line. Amos R. Eno with Raymond P., William F. and Emil T. Palmenberg. Oct. 10. nom

7th st, No. 33, s s, 242.1 w 2d av, 24.5x90.10, three-story brk tenem't. David M. Morrison exr., &c., of James M. Morrison to Julius Laugenbahn. Nov. 19. 19,000

8th st, No. 109, n s, 531.5 w 5th av, 23x93.11, three-story brk dwell'g. Partition. Peter B. Olney to Mary F. Rudd. Nov. 16. 16,850

10th st, No. 163, n s, 103 w Waverly pl, 25x95, five-story brk flat. Frederick Finck exr. Alexander Stein to Charles Lindner. *Mt.* $18,000. Nov. 16. 37,000

Same property. C. Alexander Stein and Elizabeth Hoelger to same. *Mt.* $18,000. Nov. 16. 37,000

12th st, No. 134, s s, 300 w 6th av, 25x103.3, five-story stone front flat. Annie C. B. wife of George V. Foster to William Rhinelander. *Mt.* $35,000. Nov. 16. 49,500

17th st, Nos. 349 and 351, n s, 80 w 1st av, 42x92, two four-story brk stores and tenem'ts. Philip Sammel to Max Borger. *Mt.* $21,900. Nov. 14. 34,250

17th st, No. 138, s s, 500 w 6th av, 21.1x92, three-story brk tenem't. Elizabeth Altorfer to Isaac Dreyer. Nov. 10. nom

22d st, No. 44, s s, 257 e 6th av, 23x98.9, four-story stone front dwell'g. Foreclos. William N. Armstrong to Joseph H. Cain. Nov. 19. 38,700

23d st, No. 165, n s, 100 e 7th av, 22x112.6, five-story stone front store and flat. J. Ensign Fuller to Andrew L. Soulard. *Mt.* $30,000. Oct. 29. nom

24th st, No. 309, n s, 120 e 2d av, 20x98.9, four-story brk store and tenem't with four-story brk tenem't on rear. John B. Green to George J and William J. Kenny. *Mt.* $5,000 Nov. 16. 11,000

26th st, Nos. 308–312, s s, 117.7 w 8th av, 56.2x98.9, three three-story brk dwell'gs. Benjamin F. Cohen to William G. Jordan. *Mt.* $24,500. Oct. 30. 48,300

26th st, Nos. 311–315, n s, 122 w 8th av, 53x98.9, three three-story brk dwell'gs. Daniel D. Lawson to Abraham Quackenbush. ½ part. B. & S. Nov. 16. nom

28th st, No. 234, s s, 175 w 2d av, 25x98.9, two-story brk stable with three-story brk tenem't on rear. Thomas C. Smith to Mayor, &c., New York. Nov. 2. 16,000

29th st, No. 136, s s, 120.2 e Lexington av, 19.10x98 9, four-story stone front dwell'g. Charles McCready and ano. exrs. Henry C. Macdowell to St. Stephens Roman Catholic Church. *Mt.* $8,000. Nov. 13. 20,200

29th st, No. 228, n s, 253.3 w 7th av, 23.5x98.9, four-story brk tenem't with three-story brk tenem't on rear. Elizabeth V. Farrell and Theresa J. Coughlan to Iva Benjamin. Nov. 16. nom

30th st, No. 23, n s, 100 e Madison av. Corrects errors as to st in issue of March 4, 1882, page 194, where under conveyance of Madison av, n e cor 30th st, the former parcel erroneously appeared as No. 23 East 39th st.

30th st, No. 29, n s, 430 w 5th av, 20x98.9, four-story stone front dwell'g. Mary H. Curtis widow to Octavia A. Moss. Oct. 29. 45,000

32d st, No. 439, n s, 425 w 9th av, 25x98.9, four-story brk tenem't with stores. Damase Bouchard, Providence, L. I., to Aurelia S. Blauvelt, Nyack, N. Y. Nov. 14. nom

33d st, Nos. 140 and 142, s s, 187.6 e 7th av, 62.6x143.2x49x144, two five-story brk flats. Samuel S. Abbott, Brooklyn, to William D. Barnes. *Mt.* $90,000. Oct. 21. nom

35th st, No. 322, s s, 300 w 1st av, 25x100, five-story brk store and tenem't. Robert K. Downey to William A. C. Dougherty. *Mt.* $11,000. Nov. 12. 20,750

35th st, No. 335, n s, 410 e 9th av, 15x98.9, four-story brk dwell'g. Richard and Grace A. Hassard, Mary L. and James W. Van Keuren, Brooklyn, and Catherine J. Gilbertson heirs and legatees Cath. Hassard dec'd to Patrick W. Vallely. Q. C. Nov. 14. nom

Same property. Richard Hassard and ano. exrs. and trustees Catharine Hassard to same. *Mt.* $3,750. Nov. 14. 10,000

35th st, No. 309, n s, 111 w 8th av, 19.6x90x9.6x98 9, three-story brk tenem't. George W. Ludlum to James J. Thomson. Oct. 9. nom

36th st, No. 56, s s, 290 e 6th av, 20x98.9, four-story stone front dwell'g. George B. Salisbury to Henry E. Salisbury. ½ part. Nov. 16. 21,000

36th st, Nos. 220 and 222, s s, 295 e 3d av, 40x98.9, five-story brk flat. Auguste L. Sevestre and Jane E. Cusack to Anna V. Brunner and Rosetta P. L. B. Gengenbach. Sub. to mort. $36,000 and encroachment. Nov. 16. See Madison st. exch

37th st, n s, 400 w 10th av, 25x98.9. Agreement as to removal of westerly wall. James McClenahan to James Savage. Oct. 13. nom

39th st, No. 103, n s, 96.8 e 4th av, 16.8x98 9, five-story stone front dwell'g. L. Napoleon and Jefferson M. Levy to William R. Brown. Nov. 17. nom

39th st, No. 101, n s, 80 e Park av, 16.8x98.9, five-story stone front dwell'g. Daisy Florance to Agnes H. wife of Aaron Wolff, Jr. Nov. 14. nom

Same property. Aaron Wolff, Jr., to Daisy Florance. Nov. 14. nom

44th st, No. 354, s s, abt 175 e 9th av, 25x100.4, three-story brk store and tenem't with three-story brk and frame tenem't on rear. Adelbert Huber to Sylvester Eschbach. *Mt.* $4,000. Nov. 14. nom

Same property. Sylvester Eschbach to Adelbert Huber. *Mt.* $4,000. Nov. 14. nom

45th st, No. 536, s s, 275 e 11th av, 25x100.5, five-story brk tenem't. Magdalena Renner to Michael Renner. *Mt.* $12,000. Oct. 19. 18,000

45th st, No. 55, n s, 85 e 11th av, 15x75.4, four-story brk tenem't. Alexandrina Jordan an heir of Gertrude Jordan to Mary Jordan. Q. C. Nov. 16. 3,250

46th st, No. 525, n s, 400 e 11th av, 25x100.5, two-story frame dwell'g with two-story frame dwell'g on rear. John Stich to James Mulholland. *Mt.* $6,000 and tax 1891. Oct. 14. 7,475

46th st, No. 119, n s, 250 w 6th av, 25x100.5, four-story brk store and tenem't with one-story brk stable on rear. Benjemin Sire to Thomas Ogle. *Mt.* $11,000. Re-recorded. March 5, 1885. 16,050

Same property. Thomas Ogle to Flora I. Bradbury. Nov. 2. 24.000

46th st, No. 117, n s, 225 w 6th av, 25x100.5, four-story brk tenem't with stores. Richard Stacpoole to Flora I. wife of Charles Bradbury. *Mt.* $9,000. Re-recorded. Aug. 29. nom

46th st, No. 517, n s, 275 w 10th av, 25x100.4, five-story brk tenem't with two-story brk stable on rear. Foreclos. William Q. Titus to Herbert C. Plass. Nov. 2. 17,250

Same property. Herbert C. Plass to James P. Foster. *Mt.* $15,000. Nov. 10. 17,250

47th st, No. 606, s s, 125 w 11th av, 25x120.1x26x127.4, one-story frame building.
47th st, No. 608, s s, 150 w 11th av, 26x112.10x26x120.1, four-story brk store and tenem't with two-story brk tenem't on rear.
Mary Jordan an heir of Lewis C. Jordan to Alexandrina Jordan. Q. C. Nov. 16. 8,000

48th st, No. 244, s s, 144.8 w 2d av, 18.8x100.5, four-story stone front dwell'g. Isabella Schweizer widow to Jennie wife of Samuel Hershfield. *Mt.* $7,000. Nov. 16. 12,000

49th st, No. 64, s s, 60.1 w 4th av, 19.8x25.5, four-story stone front dwell'g. Reno R. Billington to Josephine E. Battersby. *Mt.* $8,300. Sept. 19, 1891. 15,000

50th st, Nos. 138 and 140, s s, 260 w 3d av, 40x100.5, two three-story brk dwell'gs. Bernard Metzger to Shaarai Berocho. Nov. 16. 80,000

52d st, No. 104, s s, 57.6 e 4th av, 19.2x79.5, four-story stone front dwell'g. Charles Meier to Nathan Kantrowitz. *Mt.* $14,000. Nov. 16. 17,000

52d st, No. 514, s s, 599 6 e 11th av, 24x½ block x16 11x100.5, four-story brk tenem't. Alexandrina Jordan an heir of Gertrude Jordan to Mary Jordan. Q. C. Nov. 16. 4,500

52d st, Nos. 409 and 411, n s, 156.6 e 1st av, 37.6x92.8x—x99.6, two four-story stone front dwell'gs. Ernest G. Stedman to Charles A. Gerlach. *Mt.* $10,000. May 6. nom

52d st, Nos. 432 and 434, s s, 400 w 9th av, 50x100.5, two five-story brk tenem'ts. Elsworth L. Striker to Meyer Auerbach. Q. C. Nov. 18. See 97th st. nom

52d st, s s, 425 w 9th av, 25x100.5. George B. Jucke to same. C. a. G. Nov. 18. nom

52d st, s s, 400 w 9th av, 25x100.5. Truman V. Tuttle to same. C. a. G. Nov. 17. nom

53d st, No. 153, n s, 212.6 e 7th av, 18.9x100.5, three-story stone front dwell'g. George Macintosh to Richard H. Smith trustee. *Mt.* $10,000. Nov. 16. 12,500

58th st, No. 328, s s, 278 w 1st av, 22x100.4x23.6x100.4, three-story stone front dwell'g. Frederick Krutina to Louis Levy. Nov. 17. 15,625

59th st, No. 239, n s, 130 w 2d av, 25x100.4, five-story stone front store and tenem't. Joseph B. Guttenberg to Ignatz M. Rottenberg. *Mt.* $9,500. Nov. 16. 17,500

60th st, No. 100 } begins 60th st, s e cor
Park (4th) av, No. 511 } 4th av, 20x100.5, four-story brk (stone front) dwell'g on 60th st and one-story brk store on av. Foreclos. John Vincent to George W. Vultee. Nov. 16. 29,000

Same property. George W. Vultee to Ferdinand R. Miorath. Nov. 18. 31,000

63d st, No. 34, s s, 142 e Madison av, 20x100.5, four-story stone front dwell'g. Annie Stone to Ellen J. Stone. ½ part. Feb. 11, 1891. nom

Same property. William Montgomery, Jr., to Annie and Ellen J. Stone. 1-3 part. Feb. 11, 1891. nom

Same property. Annie Stone to William Montgomery, Jr. 1-3 part. Feb. 11, 1891. nom

63d st, Nos. 415, 417 and 419, n s, 231.2 e 1st av, 75.5x100.5, three five-story brk tenem'ts. Ferdinand Sulzberger to Julius Dreyfus. *Mt.* $28,998. Nov. 17. 45,000

63d st, Nos 415–419, n s, 231.2 e 1st av, 75x100.5. Julius Dreyfus to Ferdinand Sulzberger. *Mt.* $24,000. Nov. 17. 45,000

69th st, No. 302, s s, 100 w 11th av, 25x100.5, five-story brk tenem't. Foreclos. Wilbur Larremore to Charles Noble. Nov. 16. 20,400

74th st No. 156, s s, 288.9 w 3d av, 18.9x102.2, three-story stone front dwell'g. Simon Adler to Henrietta wife of Herman Kaufman. Q. C. Correction deed. Nov. 11. nom

75th st, No. 43, n s, 241 e Columbus av, 22x102.2, four-story stone front dwell'g. John C. Umberfield to Mary E. wife of Albert H. Hatch. *Mt.* $29,100. Nov. 19. other consid. and 100

76th st, n s, 172 e 2d av, 28x102.2. Jacob Schlosser to Magdalena and Isabella Becker. *Mt.* $19,000. Nov. 16. 25,500

76th st, No. 305, n s, 116.8 e 2d av, runs north 18 x east 2.4 x north 84.2 x east 25.8 x south 102.2 to st, x west 28, five-story brk tenem't. Henry M. Bendheim to Charles J. Egler. *Mt.* $22,500. Nov. 16. 26,000

76th st, n s, 116 e 2d av, 0.8x18. Same to same. Q. C. Nov. 16. nom

76th st, No. 309, n s, 172 e 2d av, 28x102.2, five-story brk tenem't. Manuel Samuels to Jacob Schlosser. *Mt.* $19,000. Nov. 14. 25,500

76th st, No. 311, n s, 200 e 2d av, 25x102.2, five-story brk tenem't with stores. Foreclos. William J. Lardner to Caroline F. Sheehy. Nov. 8. 11,600

76th st. Nos. 311-317, n s, 151 w West End av, 78x102.2, four four-story brk dwell'gs. Mary F. wife of James R. Smith to Leonard Jacob, Jr. Q. C. July 25. nom

78th st, No. 135, n s, 375 e 4th av, 18x102.2, three-story stone front dwell'g. August Kohn to William J. Lippmann. *Mt.* $8,250. Jan. 5. 17,000

80th st, n s, 100 w Amsterdam av, 150x102.2, vacant. Catharine A. Cammann to Jennie Caldwell. Nov. 12. 63,000

80th st, Nos. 170-182, s s, 105 e 10th av, 145x102.2, seven four-story brk dwell'gs.
113d st, Nos. 124-128, s s, 240 e 4th av, 75x100.11, three five-story stone front flats.
Jacob B. Weinberg to Abraham Schneider. Sept. 22. nom

81st st, Nos. 172 and 174, s s, 116 e Amsterdam av, 42x102.2, two five-story brk flats. John Casey to George Stone. *Mt.* $40,000. Nov. 13. See 98th st. 80,000

81st st, No. 224, s s, 279.2 w 2d av, 25.10x102.2, five-story brk tenem't. Henry Menken to Julia J. de Bruin. *Mt.* $17,000. Nov. 16. 22,000

83d st, No. 214, s s, 125 w 10th av, 75x75.7x75.3 x81.6, two-story frame dwell'g, one-story frame stable on rear and vacant. Mary Jordan an heir of Gertrude Jordan to Alexandrina Jordan. Q. C. Nov. 16. 11,000

83d st, Nos. 133 and 135, n s, 300 w 9th av, 50x102.2, two five-story stone front flats. Nellie F. wife of and Mark P. Brennan to George Rauchfuss. *Mt.* $24,000. Nov. 19. See 7th av. 81,500

85th st, n s, 250 e 3d av, 0.10¾x102.1x1.4x102.1. Charles T. Cromwell, Manersing Island, N. Y., to Lizzie McGuiness. Q. C. Oct. 7. 100

87th st, n s, 119 w West End av, 106x100.8. Release mort. Edward Oppenheimer and Isaac Metzger to John and David Dunn. Nov. 18. 44,824

Same property. Release mort. Same to same. Nov. 18. 45,000

87th st, No. 56, s s, 164.5 e Madison av, 25.7x100.8, two-story frame dwell'g. James S., Sarah A., Mary E. and Emma L. Willet and Martha J. Wooster heirs James C. Willet to William J. Casey. Oct. 15. other consid. and 100

87th st, 86th st, 12th av, 13th av — the block, two-story brk building on cor 12th av and 87th st; frame yacht club-house on 86th st and rest vacant. Damon Dodge, Kootenm County, Idaho, to Wallace C. Andrews. Q. C. Oct. 30. nom

93d st, No. 150, s s, 291 e Amsterdam av, 17x100.8, three-story stone front dwell'g. Walden P. Anderson to Nicholas Brewer. *Mt.* $14,000. Nov. 16. nom

93d st, No. 156, s s, 333.2 w 3d av, 16.10x100.8, three-story brk dwell'g. William R. Potts, Nelson J. Gates, George S. Rockwell, Charles R. Oliver, George M. Weld and Edward Lawrence, individ., Sarah B. Potts et al. exrs. Frederick A. Potts, composing the firm of Frederick A. Potts & Co., to David C. Seltman. Oct. 31. 11,110

94th st, No. 61, n s, 236 e Columbus av, 19x100.8, three-story stone front dwell'g. Release mort. Edward Oppenheimer and Isaac Metzger to Increase M. Grenell. Oct. 30. 1,500

Same property. Increase M. Grenell to Thomas Dixon, Jr. *Mt.* $15,000. Nov. 14. 24,500

96th st, No. 66, s s, 120 e Columbus av, 20x100.8, four-story brk dwell'g. George H. Morris, Brooklyn, to Joseph Lewis. *Mt.* $22,000. Sept. 5. nom

97th st, No. 167, n s, 196 e 10th av, 17x100.11, three-story stone front dwell'g.
97th st, No. 173, n s, 154 e 10th av, 14x100.11, three-story brk dwell'g.
Meyer Auerbach to William H. Lee. *Mt.* $45,000. Nov. 16. 40,000

Same property. William H. Lee to Florence S. wife of Elsworth L. Striker. *Mt.* $26,500. Nov. 18. See 52d st. 40,000

98th st, s s, 150 e 10th av, 200x100.11, vacant. George Stone to John Casey. *Mt.* $31,500. Nov. 16. See 81st st. val. consid. and 100

98th st, s s, 475 w Central Park West, 150x100.11, six five-story brk flats. Thomas Webster to Charles T. and Helen T. Barney. Q. C. Oct. 26. nom

Same property. Elizabeth Schulze to same. Q. C. Oct. 26. nom

102d st, No. 247, n s, 130 e 3d av, 25x100.11, five-story brk tenem't. John Hammer to Anne Hammer. *Mt.* $14,000. Nov. 14. nom

102d st, No. 171, n s, 275 e Amsterdam av, 25.1x96.11x25.1x96.10, five-story brk flat. Jacob Young to Charles A. Muth. *Mt.* $16,500. Nov. 16. See 9th av. nom

103d st, s s, 101.6 e Lexington av, 108x100.11, two-story frame dwell'g and vacant. Lewis Z. Bach to Frederick Braender. *Mt.* $19,600. Nov. 11. 35,500

103d st, Nos. 206-214, s s, 118 w 10th av, 99.6x77 to Clendenning lane, x99.7x77.2, five five-story brk flats. Foreclos. Charles Wehle to Charles Siedler. Sub. to mechanics' liens $6,541, taxes, &c., also mort. on house $16,500. Nov. 4. 4,000

104th st, No 248, s s, 137 e West End av, 19x100.11, three-story stone front dwell'g. Ellen M. Harlow to Charles L. Adrian. *Mt.* $14,500. Nov. 13. 20,000

106th st, No. 21, n s, 175 w Madison av, 25x100. five-story stone front flat. Release mort. James McCreery to John J. and Philip A. Fitzpatrick. Nov. 16. 250

Same property. Philip A. and John J. Fitzpatrick to Mary Fitzpatrick. Nov. 14. 28,500

108th st, No. 222, s s, 311 e 3d av, 24.6x100.11, four-story brk tenem't John Hammer to Adolph Sigl. *Mt.* $10,500. Nov. 14. 13,000

112th st, No. 306, s s, 100 e 2d av, 25x100.11, two-story frame dwell'g with one-story brk stable on rear. Louis Z. Bach to Frederick D. Weekes. C. a. G. Nov. 17. 7,000

113th st, s s, 400 e Grand Boulevard, 50x91x55x114, vacant. Abraham Schneider to Mark M. Schlesinger. Aug. 29. nom

114th st, s s, 150 w 10th av, 50x100.11, vacant. Abraham Schneider to Mark M. Schlesinger. Aug. 29. nom

114th st, s s, 450 e Lenox av, 74.11x100.11, one and two-story frame buildings and vacant.
113th st, n s, 450 e Lenox av, 74.11x100,11, vacant.
Henry Franke, Brooklyn, to S. Liebmann's Sons Brewing Co. *Mt.* $25,000. Nov. 13. exch

118th st, No. 205, n s, 100 e 3d av, 18.9x100.10, two-story frame dwell'g. Henry Spicer to Ellen M. McCahill. Nov. 14. 7,000

118th st, No. 427, n s, 305.4 w Pleasant av, 21.2x100.11.
118th st, No. 431, n s, 263 w Pleasant av, 21.1 x100.11.
Two three-story brk dwell'gs.
William G. Wood to Mary E. Wood, Nov. 10. nom

119th st, No. 509, n s, 177.6 e Av A, 20.6x100.10, three-story stone front dwell'g. Silvestro Giglio to Mary E. Gueli. Q. C. Nov. 12. nom

121st st, Nos. 309-315, n s, 95 e Manhattan av, 100x100.11, four five-story brk flats.
121st st, No. 261, n s, 573 w 7th av, 17x100.11, three-story stone front dwell'g.
Jacob B. Weinberg to Abraham Schneider. Sept. 22. nom

122d st, No. 356, s s, 202 w Manhattan av, 16x100.11, three-story stone front dwell'g. A. Alonzo Teets to Mary A. Nicoll. Nov. 16. 17,000

126th st, Nos. 159 and 161, n s, 135 w 3d av, 50x99.11, five-story brk piano factory. Lesley wife of and Howard Hamm to Michael J. Adrian. *Mt.* $36,000. Nov. 16. 56,000

126th st, No. 160, s s, 130 e 7th av, 20x99.11, four-story brk dwell'g. John W. Hesse to Lewis S. Samuel. B. & S. *Mt.* $18,000. Nov. 13. nom

130th st, No. 65, n s, 196.3 w Park av, 18.9x99.11, four-story stone front flat. James F. Bishop to Michael Sternfels. *Mt.* $10,000. Nov. 16. 14,000

131st st, No. 213, n s, 191.8 w 7th av, 16.8x99.11, three-story stone front dwell'g Annie E Valentine to Lillie W. Cooper. *Mt.* $5,000. Nov. 13. 15,325

131st st, No. 259, n s, 183.4 e 8th av, 16.8x99.11, three-story stone front dwell'g. Isaac E. Wright to Annie E. Valentine. *Mt.* $9,000. Nov. 11. 14,000

131st st. Nos. 261-269, n s. 100 e 8th av, 83.4x99.11, five three-story stone front dwell'gs. Same to Samuel O. Wright, Rockville Centre, L. I. *Mt.* $78,000. Nov. 14. nom

131st st, No. 62, s s, 177.6 w Park av, 17.6x99.11, three-story stone front dwell'g. Richard L. Sweezy to Edward A. Rawlings. Nov. 12. See Convent av. 11,000

132d st, No. 54, s s, 526.8 w 5th av, 16.8x99.11, three-story frame dwell'g. Caroline A. wife of Edward A. Freystadt to Lulu M. Browne. *Mt.* $3,000. Nov. 14. 9,000

132d st, s s, 460 w 5th av, 50x99.11, vacant. George F. Johnson to Andrew T. Judge. Q. C. Nov. 17. nom

133d st, No. 220, s s, 400 w 7th av, 16.8x99.11, five-story brk flat. Wallace R. Eickhoff to Robinson Gill, Brooklyn. *Mt.* $16,000. Nov. 17. nom

135th st, No. 245, n s, 125 e 8th av, 25x99.11, five-story brk flat. Clinton W. Kellam, Islip, L. I., to Edwin D. Putney. *Mt.* $28,000. Oct. 30. 41,000

142d st, s s, 125 e Lenox av, 50x99.11, vacant. Edward J. Kelly to Harry L. Kidd. Nov. 16. 11,000

143d st, Bradhurst av — begins 143d st, n s, 361.10 w 8th av and at point where w s of Bradhurst av or a new av crosses, runs north along w s of said new av 100.6 x west 41.2 to centre of old road, x southwest 7 x south 124.6 to original centre line 143d st, x east 34.3 to said new av, x north 30.2, one-story frame building and vacant. Annie Dardis to Frederick Grasmuck. Nov. 11. 1,000

Same property. Catherine Dardis to same. Nov. 16. 1,250

144th st, No. 461, n s, 157.8 e Amsterdam av, 20x99.11, four-story brk dwell'g. Foreclos. R. Duncan Harris to James Sinclair. Nov. 18. 15,100

155th st, 156th st, 157th st — begins 155th st, n s, 100 e 12th av, runs northeast 453.8 to 157th st intended, x southeast 33 x southeast 295.3 along new proposed road to 156th st at a point 325 e 12th av, x southwest 60 to s s 156th st, x east 12.6 x southwest 199.10 to 155th st, x west 237.6 to beginning, vacant. George B. Grinnell to William M. Grinnell. *Mt.* $40,000. Nov. 13. 100

180th st, s s, 120 e Audubon av, 75x100.
179th st, n s, 95 e Audubon av, 125x100.
Joseph H. Cain to Robert T. Meeks. *Mt.* $12,600. June 15. nom

Amsterdam av, No. 791, e s, 50 s 99th st, 16.10x100.1x21.2x100, five-story brk store and flat. Rudolph Einbigler to Philipp A. Held. *Mt.* $14,000. Nov. 16. 16,500

Av D, Nos. 143 and 145, s w cor 10th st, 50x93, five-story brk cigarette factory.
10th st, No. 444, s s, 93 w Av D, 25x92.3, four-story brk cigar factory.
Interior lot, 72 s 10th st and 73 w Av D, runs west 20 x south 22x20x22.
10th st, No. 449, s s, 118 w Av D, 21x92.3, four-story brk cigar factory with two-story brk building on rear.
10th st, s s, 139 w Av D, 1.4x92.3.
Interior lot, 92.3 s 10th st and 93 w Av D, runs south 1.9 x west 25 x1.9x25.
Av D, No 139, w s, 72 s 10th st, 22x73, four-story brk tenem't with stores.
Alexander Lichtenstein to Benjamin Lichtenstein. *Mt.* $45,000. Nov. 18. nom

Av D. No 139, w s, 72 s 10th st, 22x73, four-story brk tenem't with stores. Benjamin Van Leeuwen to Alexander Lichtenstein. Nov. 16. 8,425

Columbus av, Nos. 848-852, w s, 25.11 s 102d st, 75x75, three five-story brk flats with stores. Jessie Julius Doernberg and Henry D Goodman to Simon Adler and Henry S. Herrman. *Mt.* $57,000. Nov. 14. 28,000

Columbus av, No. 781, n e cor 98th st, 25.11x74, five-story brk store and flats. Matilda Michaelis, Brooklyn, to David M. Levy. *Mt.* $26,000. Nov. 16. 37,000

Columbus av. No. 464, w s, 51.2 n 82d st, 25.6x100, five-story brk store and flat. George F. Ferris, Pomona, Cal., to Charles Fries. *Mt.* $24,000. Oct. 23. 33,500

Columbus (9th) av, e s, 76.8 n 83d st, 25x100x25.6x100, vacant. Release dower. Hannah H. Civill widow to Frank A. Civill. April 15, 1890. nom

Same property. Frank A. Civill, Los Angeles, Cal., to Lewis A. Civill, Colorado Springs, Col. Oct. 21. nom

Columbus av, s e cor 84th st, 127.8x100, vacant. Lewis A. Civill, Colorado Springs, Col., Acton C. Civill, Bovina Centre, N. Y., to Edward Oppenheimer. *Mt.* $55,000. Oct. 30. 85,000

Columbus (9th) av, s e cor 84th st, 25.8x100, vacant. Jacob W. Feeter to Lewis and Action T. Civill. Q.C. Oct. 20. nom

Convent av, No. 61, e s, 599.6 n 141st st, 20x100, three-story brk dwell'g. Edward A. Rawlings to Richard L. Sweezy. B. & S. Nov. 12. See 131st st. 22,750

Same property. Foreclos. Michael J. Scanlan to Edward A. Rawlings. Nov. 12. 19,600

Lexington av, No. 1449, n e cor 94th st, 19.8x95, three-story brk (stone front) dwell'g. Mary L. Fox, Stamford, Conn., to Raphael Ettinger. Oct. 28. nom

Lenox av, No. 181, 119th st — begins Lenox av, n w cor 119th st, runs north 25 x west 75 x north 75.11 x west 25 x south 100.11 to 119th st, x east 100, four-story brk (stone front) dwell'g on av and vacant lot on st. Urcilla wife of and Thomas Mackellar to Edwin B. Stanton. Nov. 9. 100,000

Same property. Edwin B. Stanton, Brooklyn, to William R. Martin. *Mt.* $55,000. Nov. 9. nom

Madison av, s w cor 118th st, 100x60, one-story frame buildings. Foreclos. Lorenzo Semple to Jehiel S. Raynor. *Mt.* $15,000. Nov. 18. 13,000

Madison av, No. 1847, e s, 67.4 n 120th st, 17.7x83, three-story stone front dwell'g. Olivia R. Blackman, East Orange, N. J., to John T. Meehan. *Mt.* $12,000. Nov. 10. 17,000

Madison av, s e cor 134th st, 99.11x60, four five-story brk flats with stores. Thomas Jetter to Regina Schmidt. *Mt.* $31,500. Nov. 7. 1,000

Madison av, No. 741, e s, 83.9 s 65th st, 16.8x60, four-story stone front dwell'g. Willett Bronson, Huntington, L. I., to Anna Jerzmanowski. Q. C. Re-recorded. Feb. 25, 1884. nom

Same property. Anna wife of Erazm J. Jerzmanowski to Eugene T. Connell. *Mt.* $23,000. Nov. 4. 30,000

Pleasant av, No. 335, w s, 20 s 118th st, 18.6x75, three-story stone front dwell'g. Ella L. Gault to Wilhelmine Broecker. *Mt.* $6,000. Nov. 11. nom

West End av, No. 220, n e cor 75th st, runs north 30 x east 48.6 x north 5 x east 26.6 x south 12.6 x west 10 x south 22.6 to st, x west 65, four-story brk dwell'g. Mary I. Myers, Chicago, Ill., to Elisha H. Talbott. C. a. G. *Mt.* $72,000. Oct. 3. nom

West End av, n e cor 85th st, 27.2x100, vacant. Robert and Joseph Gordon to Richard G. Platt. *Mt.* $11,000. Nov. 16. 26,250

Same property. Agreement restricting buildings in consideration of loan. Robert and Joseph Gordon and Richard G. Platt, with Edward Kilpatrick, William Carroll, Margaretta M. Smith, Thomas J. Colton, B. Gerson Oppenheim and Joseph P. Eager. Nov. 14. nom

West End av, e s, 25.8 n 92d st, 50x100, vacant. Edward Kilpatrick to Francis M. Jencks. *Mt.* $9,600 and any assessm'ts since Oct. 1890. Nov. 16. 19,885

1st av, No. 2206, e s, 56 n 113th st, 17.11x74.11, four-story brk store and tenem't. Celestino De Marco, to Faust D. Malzone and Giuseppe Asselta. *Mt.* $7,500. Nov. 17. 11,800

2d av, No. 2216, e s, 20.11 s 114th st, 20x80, four-story stone front stores and tenem't. Annie and Marks Meyers or Myers to Betsy Marks. *Mt.* $10,000. Nov. 16. 14,000

2d av, No. 1889, w s, 75.11 s 98th st, 25x96, five-story brk tenem't with stores. Christoph A. Schuber to Theodor Koch. *Mt.* $15,000. Nov. 13. 22,000

2d av, No. 614, e s, 49.7 s 34th st, 24.7x80, five-story brk tenem't with stores. E. Ellery Anderson to Leon Pizer. *Mt.* $22,000. Nov. 14. nom

3d av, No. 1922, s w cor 106th st, 25 2x100, five-story brk store. Isaac Friedenheit to Myer Hellman. ⅙ part. Sub. ⅙ liens. Nov. 13. 37,500

3d av, No. 1894, w s, 51.1 s 105th st, 25x100, three-story frame store and tenem't with two-story frame dwell'g on rear. Simon Dessau to Marcus Beckmann. Nov. 16. 17,500

5th av, No. 39, e s, 54.2 s 11th st, 54.9x100, four-story stone front dwell'g.
10th st, No. 1 on map No. 3, n s, 100 e 5th av, 24.6x94.9, two-story brk stable.
George N. Miller, Rhinebeck, N. Y., to William S. Miller. ⅙ part. Nov. 14. nom

6th av, No. 58, n e cor West Washington pl, 22x60x26x60, three-story brk store and tenem't.
19th st, No. 270, s s, 170 e 8th av, 20x93.8, three-story brk dwell'g.
Irene A. Leggat, Napa, Cal., to William A. Leggat. ⅙ part. Oct. 23. 21,000

Same property. Release dower. Anna Shakspear, Napa, Cal., to same. Oct. 23. nom

7th av, No. 824, n w cor 53d st, 25x100, five-story flat with stores. George Rauchfuss to Nellie F. wife of Mark P. Brennan. *Mt.* $45,000. Nov. 19. See 83d st. nom

7th av, w s, 25 n 53d st, 0.1½x100. John Curry and James B. Gillie to same. Q. C. Nov. 16. nom

7th av, Nos. 433 and 435 | 34th st, No. 168 } begins 7th av, e s, 24.9 s 34th st, runs east 42 x north 24.9 to 34th st, x east 29 x south 24.9 x east 29 x south 49.4 x west 100 to av. x north 49.4, five-story brk factory. John Thompson exr. Joseph Thompson to George H. B. Hill. Nov. 16. 100,000

9th av, No. 366, e s, 135.10 n 30th st, 18.6x100, four-story brk store and tenem't. Charles A. Muth to Catharine wife of Jacob Young. *Mt.* $7,000. Nov. 16. See 102d st. nom

9th av, No. 674, e s, 25.1 n 47th st, 30.11x70, five-story brk tenem't with stores. Alexandrina Jordan an heir Lewis C. Jordan to Mary Jordan. Q. C. Nov. 16. 12,750

11th av, No. 501, w s, 74.1 n 39th st, 24.8x100, one-story frame building with two-story brk building on rear. Abel J. Sharlow to William Sharlow. ⅙ part. Nov. 13. nom

Same property. Same to Thomas Sharlow. ⅙ part. Nov. 13. nom

MISCELLANEOUS.

All title in estate of Samuel D. Burchard dec'd. Mary J. Frenche, Waterloo, N. J., to William J. Leeds. Oct. 16. nom

General release. John M. Hogencamp and Lillie H. Rogers to John McWilliam exr. Daniel Hogencamp. Nov. 4. 94

23d and 24th WARDS.

Bristow st, e s, 125 n Jennings st, 50x100. Gregorio Di Lorenzo to George Baltzer. *Mt.* $800. Nov. 19. 2,000

Bush st, s s, 216.1 w Anthony av, 25x90. Release mort. James and Abram T. Buckhout to Mary E. Elder. Nov. 7. 600

Same property. Mary E. wife of and Robert D. Elder to Paul A. Harnett. Nov. 17. nom

Donnybrook st, s s, 153.2 w Creston av, runs east 13.1 x south 101.6 x east 40 x south 225 x west 80.11 to e s of a lane, x north 328.1.
Kingsbridge road proposed, n s, 191.10 w Creston av, runs west 18.5 to e s of a lane, x north 209.3 x east 95.7 x south 100 x west 91 x south 110.2.
Release mort. The Mutual Life Ins. Co. of New York to Hugh N. Camp. Nov. 17. 3,000

Elmwood pl, s s, 100 w Clinton av, 25x122.11x25x122.8. John J. Brady to William E. Brooker. Nov. 19. 1,000

Gouverneur pl, s e s, extends from 131st to 132d st, 200x300.
Cypress av, west cor 130th st, 152 to Harlem & Portchester R. R., x— to 130th st, x490.
Cypress av, n w s, bounded southeast by Cypress av abt 255, west by Bronx Kills, northwest by line 200 southeast Gouverneur pl abt 198 x east by curve on Harlem River & Portchester R. R.
Gouverneur and Anne C. Morris, Mary F. Davenport widow, Margaret R. wife of and Lewis E. V. Turner and Lewis S. Chanler to said Lewis S. Chanler. July 1. nom

Gouverneur pl, s w s, extends from 130th to 131st st, 275x350.
Cypress av, south cor 130th st, 143 to Harlem River & Portchester R. R., x— on curve to land of Patsey J. Morris, x36 to 130th st, x329.
Cypress av, s e s, bounded northwest by said av 255, south by Bronx Kills, southeast by line of P. J. Morris' estate 313, and north by curve in Harlem River & Portchester R. R., with all title in land under water Bronx Kills.
Gouverneur and Anne C. Morris, Mary F. Davenport widow, Margaret R. wife of Lewis E. V. Turner and Lewis S. Chanler to Clarence Cary and Henry L. Morris subtrustees for Margt. R. Turner. July 1. nom

Hawkstone st, e s, 350 n Walnut st, 100x100x125 x100. Daniel and James Fitzpatrick heirs Bridget Fitzpatrick to John F. Broderick. Nov. 7. 5,000

Park View terrace, e s, 375 n Wellesley st, runs east 130.6 x north 25 7 x east 134.5 x south 25, error. Ella M. Clymer to Edward M. Clymer. ½ part. Nov. 12. 525

Park View terrace, e s, 400.1 n Wellesley st, 104.7x128.9x102.7x134.5. The Twenty-fourth Ward Real Estate Assoc., New York, to Emma Ward and Mary A. Kronenbitter. Oct. 20. 4,100

Park View terrace, e s, 532.8 n Wellesley st, 28.8 x114.10 x 25.8 x 121.10. Same to Margaret Neerns. Oct. 20. 1,000

Park View terrace, e s, 210.4 s Kirkside av, 28.1 x107.11x25.8x100.11. Same to James D. Mahoney. Oct. 20. 1,000

Park View terrace, e s, 25 n Wellesley st, 75x100. Same to Mary R. Lincoln. Oct. 20. 3,825

Park View terrace, e s, 238.5 s Kirkside av, 28.1 x114.10x25.8x107.11. Same to Carrie V. Harlow. Oct. 20. 1,000

Park View terrace, e s, 275 n Wellesley st, 50x125. Same to Caroline A. Freystadt. Oct. 20. 2,000

Park View terrace, n e cor Kirkside av, 106.5x126.2x100.1x113.7. Same to Julius F. Toussaint and Albert Wiggers, West Hoboken, N. J. Oct. 20. 2,850

Park View terrace, n e cor Wellesley st, 25x100. Same to Eugenie Jauss. Oct. 20. 2,050

Park View terrace, e s, 126.2 s Kirkside av, 28.1 x87x25.8x80. Same to Edward Ehrlich. Oct. 20. 825

Park View terrace, e s, 375 n Wellesley st, 25.1 x134.5x25.8x130.7. Same to Ella M. Clymer. Oct. 20. 1,025

Park View terrace, e s, 325 n Wellesley st, 50x130.7x50.7 in two courses, x125. Same to Lillian M. Bradley. Oct. 20. 2,050

Park View terrace, e s, 154.3 s Kirkside av, 56 2 x100.11x51.4x87. Same to Henry J. Abels. Oct. 20. 1,900

Southern Boulevard, s s, 62.6 w Valentine av, runs south 120 x west 37.6 x north 20 x east 25 x north 100 to Boulevard, x east 12.6. Hattie L. Hayward to Charles H. Colman. Sept. 15. 1,500

Tower pl, s s, 125 e Webster av, 25x100. Release mort. John Claflin to Henry E. Murgatroyd. Nov. 14. 375

Travers st, s s, 200.3 w Creston av, 25x100.1. The Twenty-fourth Ward Real Estate Assoc., New York, to Ludwig J. Baumbach. Oct. 20. 580

Travers st, s w cor Creston av, 25x102.10x 25.1x99.8.
Jerome av, s e cor Travers st, 26.7x95.9x25x 85.7.
Creston av, e s, 586.3 n Wellesley st, 130.2x 10.5x131.3x22.4.
Creston av, e s, 816.6 n Wellesley st, 50.1x57.1 x52.5x38.10.
Same to Martin Simons. Oct. 20. 770

Wellesley st, s e cor Kirkside av, 24.7x102.9x 27.10x103.7. John McK. Camp to Charles W. Spooner. Oct. 20. 1,075

Wellesley st, s s, 44.7 e Kirkside av, 20x101 5 x20x102.1.
Kirkside av, e s, 128.7 s Wellesley st, 50x 110.4x50x108.8.
Same to David C. Tefft. Oct. 20. 2,325

Wellesley st, s s, 24.7 e Kirkside av, 20x102.1x 20x102.9. Same to John W. Newbury. Oct. 20. 725

Wellesley st, n e cor Kirkside av, 25.1x94.9. Twenty-fourth Ward Real Estate Assoc, New York, to William H. Kennagh. Oct. 20. 1,050

Wellesley st, n w cor Kirkside av, 47.11x100x .56x100.4. Same to Philip Toussaint. Oct. 20. 1,925

Wellesley st, n s, 25.1 e Kirkside av, 50.2x94.9. Same to Gesiene A. Schroeder widow. Oct. 20. 1,400

Wellesley st, n s, 75.3 e Kirkside av, 25x94.9. Same to Frederick and Sarah Allen. Oct. 20. 700

Wellesley st, n s, 25.1 e Creston av, 54.6x102x 44x105.11.
Wellesley st, n s, 25.1 w Creston av, 75.3x 94 9.
Kirkside av, w s, 602 n Wellesley st, 50.2x81.1 x51.3x88.7.
Same to Margaret Watt. Oct. 20. 4,390

Wellesley st, n w cor Creston av, 25.1x94.9. The Twenty-fourth Ward Real Estate Assoc New York, to John J. Mahedy. Oct. 20. 950

134th st, s s, 250 e St. Anns av, 50x70. William C. Trull to Frederick W. Ehrsam. *Mt.* $1,500. Nov. 11. 4,850

136th st, n s, 431.1 e Southern Boulevard, 15x 100. Rushanna Merritt to George Higgins. *Mt.* $1,700. Nov. 18. 1,950

136th st, n s, 416.1 e Southern Boulevard, 15x 100. Samuel H. Merritt to same. *Mt.* $1,700. Nov. 18. 1,950

149th st, s s, 226 w Courtlandt av. 50x106.6. Charles and Louis Zink to John Rehm. Nov. 16. 6,000

151st st, n s, 300 e Courtlandt av, 25x115. Helene Ahrensbeumer to Joseph Muhlebach. Nov. 14. 4,850

159th st, n s, 85 w Elton av, 15x50. Edmund Coffio, Jr., exr. Elizabeth Hogan to Jacob Becker. Nov. 16. 2,850

164th st, n s, 100 w Washington av, runs north 200 x west 67.8 x south 100 x east 50 x south 100 to st, x east 17.8. Eliza Lawall to William Roland. Nov. 16. 2,600

165th st, n s, 200 e Railroad av, 30x100. John J., Albert, Mary and Joseph Heckel to George E. and Reuben W. Carr all heirs John Heckel. Q. C. July 25, 1889. 2,000

Arthur av, w s, lot A. P. map 70 lots Cedar Hill plot, Powell farm, 25x122.6x25x124.3. Anastasia Lee widow, Fordham, N. Y., to Joseph C. Lee. Nov. 18. 500

Bathgate av, s e s, part lot 18 map Village Upper Morrisania, 36x88x36x86. John E. Connolly Co. to William and Andrew Gamble. Nov. 18. 6,400

Bainbridge av, n w cor Mosbolu Parkway, 62.10 x100x35.2x103.10. Emanuel G. Bach and Ephraim B. Levy to Fanny T. Taylor. *Mt.* $450. Nov. 5. 1,000

Brook av, n e cor Westchester av, 1,302.10 to 150th st, x east 39.6 to w s N. Y. & Harlem R. R., x south 1,241.10 to Westchester av, x west 301 9. John D. Crimmins to The New York Central & Hudson River R. R. Nov. 16. 170,000

Clay av, north cor Taylor av, 100x100. Daniel Murphy, Long Island City, Michael J. Murphy, Ellen M. Ficklin widow, Catharine and Phoebe Briggs to Catharine M. Ostin. Q. C. Nov. 9. nom

Clinton av, w s, being north ½ lot 11 map Mount Hope, 50x100. Henry Drescher to Frederick Reiss. *Mt.* $1,200. Nov. 12. 2,850

Clinton av, e s, 100 n proposed Tremont av, 25 x100x25.4x100.
Clinton av, s w cor Oakland pl, 25x100.
John J. Brady to Clara Fairchild. Oct. 19. 2,070

Creston av, w s, 494.9 n Wellesley st, 50x100.4. The Twenty-fourth Ward Real Estate Assoc. to George W. Moore. Oct. 20. 1,200

Creston av, e s, 107.11 n Wellesley st, 25x66.6x 25.2x69.1. Same to Eliza McCabe. Oct. 20. 430

Creston av, w s, 144.9 n Wellesley st, 50x100.4. Same to William Grune. Oct. 20. 1,450

Creston av, w s, 194.9 n Wellesley st, 25x100.4. Same to Walter S. Carey. Oct. 20. 725

Creston av, w s, 94.9 n Wellesley st, 25x100.4. Same to De Witt S. Wyckoff, Ghent, N. Y. Oct. 20. 775

Creston av, e s, 716.5 n Wellesley st, 100.1x 88.10x164.2 in two courses, x 10.5. Same to Hannah Silberstein. Oct. 20. 625

Creston av, w s, 119 9 n Wellesley st, 25x100.4. Same to Albin Spindler. Oct. 20. 750

Creston av, w s, 219.9 n Wellesley st, 25x100.4. Same to Joseph Mallan. Oct. 20. 675

Creston av, e s, 432.11 n Wellesley st, 25x33.10 x25.1x36.4
Creston av, e s, 511.2 n Wellesley st, 50.1x24.7 x50.6x29.2.
Same to Karl M. Rosell. Oct. 20. 585

Creston av, w s, 294.9 n Wellesley st, 100x 100.4.
Kirkside av, e s, 694.9 n Wellesley st, 100x 100.4.
Creston av, w s, 669.9 n Wellesley st, 125x 100.4.
Same to Edward W. Parsells. Oct. 20. 6,375

Creston av, w s, 444.9 n Wellesley st, 50x100.4. Same to Caroline R. Mosher. Oct. 20. 1,150

Creston av, e s, 357.11 n Wellesley st, 75x36.4x 75.4x43.10. Same to Mary L. Hartley. Oct. 20. 690

Creston av, w s, 394.9 n Wellesley st, 50x100.4. Same to James Finn and Jennie his wife. Oct. 20. 1,160

Cypress av, west cor 131st st, 275x340.
132d st, s e s, bounded northwest by said 132d st abt 278, southeast by Gouverneur pl 100, southwest by line 100 s w of 132d st 190, and west by mill brook, with land under water.
Gouverneur and Anne C. Morris, Mary F. Davenport widow, Margaret R. wife of Lewis E. V. Turner and Lewis S. Chanler to Clarence Cary and Henry L. Morris trustees for Mary F. Davenport. July 1. nom

Cypress av, s e s, extends from 131st to 132d st, 200x329.
Cypress av, s e s, extends from 130th to 131st st, 275x329.
Same to same as substituted trustees Gouverneur Morris dec'd. July 1. nom

Cypress av, n w s, extends from 131st st to 132d st, 200x390.
Gouverneur pl, n w s, 100 s w 132d st, bounded southeast by Gouverneur pl abt 442, west by e s Harlem River & Portchester R. R. abt 60, northwest by Mill Brook, and northeast 190, with all title in Mill Brook.
Gouverneur pl, n w s, parcel bounded southeast by said pl 185, east by Harlem River & Portchester R. R. abt 100, and northwest and west by shore line Mill Brook and Bronx Kills, with land under water, &c.
130th st, s w s, parcel bounded northeast by 130th st 180, southeast by line 200 s e of Gouverneur pl abt 87, and southwest by curve in Harlem River & Portchester R. R.
Gouverneur pl, s e s, bounded northwest by said pl abt 172, west and northwest by Bronx Kills, southeast by line 200 southeast of Gouverneur pl 198, and northeast by curve in Harlem River & Portchester R. R., with all title in Bronx Kills and land under water thereof.
Same to same substituted trustees for Anne C. Morris. July 1. nom

Elton av, e s, abt 50 s 157th st, lot 273 map Melrose, 50x127x50.1x127.3. Giacinto or George Russhon to Archangelo Rosciano. B. & S. Oct. 24. nom

Same property. Archangelo Rosciano to Mary wife of Giacinto Russhon or George Russhon. B. & S. Oct. 24. nom

Fulton av, w s, 343.3 s 171st st, 18 3x103.6x26.3 x101.1. James McCafferty to Francis Kelly. *Mt.* $612. Nov. 17. 1,400

Jerome av, e s, 26.6 s Travers st, 79.7x126.2x75 x95.9. Twenty-fourth Ward Real Estate Assoc, New York, to Susan M. Mallahan. Oct. 20. 2,175

Kirkside av, e s, 107 n Kingsbridge road, 50x 120.8x50x122.4. John McK. Camp to Blanche A. Holmes. Oct. 20. 2,300

Kirkside av, e s, 203.8 s Wellesley st, 25x111.10 x25x111.1. Same to Charles H. Babcock. Oct. 20. 925

Kirkside av, e s, 207.1 n Kingsbridge road, runs east 82.1 x north 75 x east 37 x north 50 x west 115.1 to av, x t 125.1. Same to Hugh N. Camp. Oct. 20sou h 4,500

Kirkside av, e s, 103.7 s Wellesley st, 25x108.8x 25x107.10. Same to Charles A. Cronin. Oct. 20. 825

Kirkside av, e s, 228.8 s Wellesley st, 100.1x115.1 x100x111.10. Same to George Dessoye. Oct. 20. 4,000

Kirkside av, e s, 178.8 s Wellesley st, runs east 110.3 x south 25 x west 111.1 to av, x25. Same to Gotthilf F. Wilhelm. Oct. 20. 900

Kirkside av, e s, 157.1 n Kingsbridge road, 50x 119.1x50x120.8. Same to Harriet A. Shepperd. Oct. 20. 2,050

Kirkside av, e s, 569.9 n Wellesley st, 50x 100.4.
Kirkside av, e s, 644.9 n Wellesley st, 50x 100.4.
Twenty-fourth Ward Real Estate Assoc., New York, to Frank B. Mesick. Oct. 20. 1,880

Kirkside av, w s, 401.4 n Wellesley st, 100.4x 103.8x102.7x118.9.
Kirkside av, e s, 244.9 n Wellesley st, 50x 100.4.
Same to Julius F. Toussaint. Oct. 20. 3,820

Kirkside av, w s, 551.9 n Wellesley st, 50.2x 88.7x51.4x96.2.
Kirkside av, w s, 301 n Wellesley st, 50.2x126.2 x50x122.3.
Kirkside av, e s, 144.9 n Wellesley st, 50x 100.4.
Same to Albert Wiggers. Oct. 20. 3,830

Kirkside av, n s, 113.7 e Park View av, 25x138.3 x125.1x100.1. Same to Fanny T. Taylor. Oct. 20. 630

Kirkside av, s e cor Park View terrace, 75.7x 102 9x132.4x126.1. Same to Columbus Stigeler. Oct. 20. 4,950

Kirkside av, w s, 200.7 n Wellesley st, 50.2x 118.2x50x114.1. Same to Mary F. Whitten. Oct. 20. 1,600

Kirkside av, e s, 619.9 n Wellesley st, 25x100.4. Same to Thomas M. Trainor. Oct. 20. 470

Kirkside av, e s, 194 9 n Wellesley st, 50x100.4. Same to Alfred P. Sharp. Oct. 20. 1,110

Kirkside av, w s, 100.4 n Wellesley st, 50.2x110 x50x106. Same to Louis C. Hahn. Oct. 20. 1,550

Kirkside av, e s, 794.9 n Wellesley st, 25x138.3x 112.4x100.4. Same to Michael L. Burke. Oct. 20. 630

Kirkside av, w s, 351.1 n Wellesley st, 50.2x 118.9x51.4x126.3. Same to William H. Birkmire. Oct. 20. 1,420

Kirkside av, e s, 294.9 n Wellesley st, 50x100.4. Same to Sarah E. Tuthill. Oct. 20. 1,110

Kirkside av, e s, 344 9 n Wellesley st, 50x100.4. Same to James G. Robertson. Oct. 20. 1,090

Kirkside av, w s, 250.10 n Wellesley st, 50.2x 124.3x50x118.2. Same to Frank E. Kohl. Oct. 20. 1,500

Kirkside st, w s, 150.6 n Wellesley st, 50.2x114.1x 50x110. Same to William De Mott. Oct. 20. 1,550

Kirkside av, e s, 444.9 n Wellesley st, 25x100.4. Same to Murdock F. Campbell. Oct. 20. 520

Kirkside av, e s, 94 9 n Wellesley st, 50x100.4.
Wellesley st, n s, 100 e Park View terrace, 75 x100.
Same to Alfred A. Crawford. Oct. 20. 3,600

Kirkside av, e s, 394.9 n Wellesley st, 50x100.4.
Kirkside av, w s, 501.7 n Wellesley st, 50.2x 96.2x51.4x103.9.
Same to Mary Campion. Oct. 20. 2,360

Kirkside av, w s, 652.1 n Wellesley st, runs west 81.1 x north 25.7 x east 52.4 x north 102.9 to s s Kirkside av, x east 33.3 to w s Kirkside av, x south 123.11.
Park View av, e s, 504.7 n Wellesley st, 28x 128.11x25 7x128.9.
The Twenty-fourth Ward Real Estate Assoc. to Thomas Hill. Oct. 20. 2,650

Lincoln av, w s, 50 n 135th st. Party wall agreement. James G. Riley to Joseph Spears. Sept. 22. nom

Mapes av late Johnson av, w s, southwest ½ lot 125 map East Tremont, 33x150. Patrick W. Kelly, Brooklyn to Mary E. Brady. B. & S. Nov. 12. nom

Morris av, e s, 30 n 151st st, 28.9x70.3. Sophia M. Riedemann to Anna D. Curley. *Mt.* $2,-500. Nov. 17. 6,500

Pelham av, s e cor Lorillard st, 25x117.6. Margaret Kipling to Agnes Yost. July 15. 2,000

Railroad av, e s, 190.5 n 169th st, 165.5x150, with right of way 10 ft. wide. Rosina Hurd formerly Hey to George Hey. Q. C. Nov. 16. nom

Railroad av, s e s, part lot 60 map of Morrisania, 100 s w from north cor said lot 60, 50x 150, with right of way over strip running from 169th st to land of Elizabeth A. Quick. Sub. to right of way of 10 ft. Same to George and Marianna Hey. All title. B. & S. C. a. G. *Mt.* $4,000. Nov. 16. nom

Taylor av, n w s, 25 n e Clay av, 25x100. Catharine M. wife of and Ernest Osten to Daniel Murphy, Long Island City. Q. C. Nov. 9. nom

Taylor av, n w s, 75 n e Clay av, 25x100. Same to Ellen M. Ficklin. Q. C. Nov. 9. nom

Union av, e s, 125 s 165th st, 36.3x165. Mary wife of William Haehnel and August and Frank Fechteler to Anselm and Margaretha Stollberg. Nov. 17. 2,949

Vyse av, n w s, adj District School lot now Baptist Ministers' Home, runs southwest 25x 145. Elizabeth Conway to James Livingston. Oct. 31. 800

Walton av, No. 611, w s, 216.8 n 150th st, 16.8 x92.
143d st, No. 690, s s, 336 e Willis av, 14x100.
Maggie U. Collins nee Martin to Mary A. Martin. Nov. 2. 9,500

Washington av, s w cor 166th st, 52x100 James I. Middleton to David Tetzlaff. *Mt.* $5,000. Nov. 16. 9,000

Webster av, e s, 100 n Mosholu Parkway, 50x 77.9x58.9x108.7. John E. and Helen E. Murgatroyd to Joseph Calamari. *Mt.* $675. Nov. 16. 2,500

Worth av, e s, part lot 140 map Mount Hope, Western Reserve. Upper Morrisania, 100x 250, except part taken for Webster av. Charles Coudert exr. and trustee Florine Pinchon to Mary Kramer and Margaret Hicks. Nov. 13. 6,000

Kingsbridge road, n s, 16 e Kirkside av, runs north 662.10 to Wellesley st, x east 12 9 x south 101.6 x east 40 x south 275 x west 37 x south 75 x east 37 x south 100 x west 91 x south 110.2 to road, x west 18.11. Hugh N. Camp to John McK. Camp. Oct. 20. nom

Kingsbridge road, n e cor Kirkside av, 34.10x 110.2x31.4x107. John McK. Camp to Mary E. Man. Oct. 20. 1,950

Kingsbridge road, n e cor Kirkside av, 16x 662.10 to Wellesley st, x51.10 to av, x 660.11. Twenty-fourth Ward Real Estate Assoc., New York, to John McK. Camp. Oct. 20. nom

MacCombs Dam or New road, e s, 150 n St. James st or Croton av, 665x230 to Aqueduct, x665x 225. George T. Davidson to Harriette S. D. Romeyn. All liens. May 23. nom

West Farms to Hunts Point road, e s, at n w cor of Wm. Curser's land, runs northeast 5 chains and 39 links to Bronx River or West Farms Creek, x south 2 chains and 65 links to Wm. Curser's, x horthwest 5 chains and 27 links to road, x north 44 links.
West Farms to Hunts Point road, e s, at n w cor of land of Bronx Bleaching and Manufacturing Co., runs east 2 chains x east 83 links x northeast 1 chain and 65 links x east 2 chains and 20 links to Bronx River or West Farms Creek, x south along same 1 chain and 42 links to W. Curser's land, x southwest 5 chains and 39 links.
Henry B., Thomas, John W. and Catharine E Bolton and William H. Birchall devisee Ann Bolton to Harlem Bridge, Morrisania & Fordham Railway Co. B. & S. Deed of assent. Nov. 14. nom

Same property. Thomas and Henry B. Bolton exrs. Ann Bolton to same. Oct. 23. 30,000

Lots 55 and 56 map 71 Beautiful Lots known as the Kingsland estate, Morris Heights. Hugh N. Camp to Charles G. Tousey, Clinton Corners, N. Y. Nov. 16. 2,000

Agreement releasing covenant not to sell land in parcels smaller than 100x300, contained in deed recorded in Liber 634 Cons., page 242, Westchester County Register's Office. Charles Bernhard and Sarah G. Hall to Minnie F. Gouldrup. Oct. 12. nom

LEASEHOLD CONVEYANCES.

Chrystie st, No. 2 / Division st, No. 46 } Surrender lease. Michael Wolbach to Michael F. Hoeffner. Oct. 22. nom

Grand st, No. 91. Assign lease. William Knoepke to Otto Schroeder and Henry Ernsberger. Nov. 10. nom

Monroe st, n s, 102,6 e Montgomery st, 20.5x 90.10x20.5x92.4. United States Trust Co. trustees Stephen Whitney to Henry Lemmerman. 21 years, from May 1, 1890, per year, taxes and 275

South st, No. 83. Assign. lease. Henry Puckhaber to Louis Schutt. nom

West st, No. 348. Assign. lease. Thomas Roberts to George H. J Neumann and Michael Kern, of Neumann & Kern. Nov. 18. 11,000

Same property. Assign. lease. George Ringler & Co. to Thomas Roberts. Nov. 12. 4,531

Willett st, No. 58. Assign. lease. Max Tanneubaum to Nathan Hyman and Benjamin Tannenbaum. nom

Willett st, No. 58, e s, 150 n Delancey st, 25x 100. Leasehold. Foreclos. Edward C. O'Brien to Max Tannenbaum. Sub. to mort. $3,000. Oct. 16. 3,000

3d st, s s, 313.4 e Av B, 24.9x105.11. Assign. lease. Robert B. Merritt to Edward Nause. Nov. 18. 6,750

11th st, No. 125 E., all. Ignace Goetz to Charles Goldstein. 14½ years, from May 1, 1892, per year, taxes, &c., and 1,200

14th st, n s, 42 e 5th av, 50x129. Assign. lease. Florence G. Vernam to The Central Safe Deposit Co. Oct. 31. 181,400

20th st, n s, lots F and 575 and 576 map Peter G. Stuyvesant (lost). Margaret P. Fenton to John Lawrence and ano. exrs. John R. Lawrence. 21 years, from Aug. 28, 1886, per year, taxes and 320

28th st, No. 326 W., s s, 18.9x98.9. Nathalie E. Baylies, Taunton, Mass., to Ebenezer Spooner. 21 years, from Sept. 1, 1891, per year, taxes and 405

28th st, n s, 300 w 10th av, 25x98.9. Assign. lease. William Smith exr. William W. Brown with consent of The New York Life Ins. and Trust Co. exrs. and trustees Robert Ray to James J. Garvey. Sept. 25. 312

45th st, n s, 143.9 w 8th av, 18.9x100.5. William Astor to David J. King. 20 years, from Nov. 1, 1891, per year, taxes and 375

46th st, n s, 220 e 5th av, 20x100.5. Hannah G. Gerry to Charles R. Leaycraft admr. Agnes J. Leaycraft. 20 years, from May 1, 1891, per year, taxes and 1,260

46th st, s s, 494 w 8th av, 15.6x100.5. Assign. lease. Jacob Pizer to Marcus Goodman. 8,500

Jerome av, lots 25 and 27 map Village of Mount Eden, 50x100. Release from lease. John M. Mayer to Louise Labro and Emma Seitz. Oct. 31. nom

Av A, w s, 45 6 n 6th st, 22.8x100. Assign. lease. Magdena Frey to Charles and Henrietta Koehler. 9,500

2d av, No. 1880. Assign. lease. James E. Gallagher and Thomas Curtin, as co-partners, to Ellen Gallagher. Nov 14. nom

3d av, No. 3101, n w cor 158th st, all. Caspar Hake to Henry C. Schrader. 15 7-12 years, from Oct. 1, 1891, per year, 1,200, 1,300, 1,400, 1,500

10th av, s e cor 29th st, 24.8x100, all. The New York Life Ins. and Trust Co. exrs. and trustees Richard Ray to Daniel E Seybel. 21 years, from Aug. 1, 1889, per year, taxes, &c., and 660

KINGS COUNTY.

NOVEMBER 12, 13, 14, 16, 17, 18.

Apollo st, e s, 125 n Nassau av, 25x100. Thomas Dempsey to George E. Carroll. $400

Adelphi st, e s, 157.9 s Willoughby av, 18.6x100, h & l. Louise Lagarde to Frank C. Mason and Medora E. his wife, joint tenants. *Mt.* $5,000. 9,000

Adelphi st, w s, 209.9 s De Kalb av, 21.5x100. William W. Henshaw, Jr., Laura O. wife of Warren C. Barber and Carrie B. wife of Sidney C. Guyon to Caroline Henshaw widow. *Mt.* $6,000. nom

Adelphi st, w s, 88.3 s De Kalb av, 16.8x100. Carrie M. wife of Frank Lyon, Jr., to Peter and Joseph Young. *Mt.* $3,500. 6,000

Ashford st, e s, 225 s Ridgewood av, 50x100. Edward F. Linton to Theodore M. Le Beau. 2,000

Ashford st, e s, 225 s Ridgewood av, 50x100. Release mort. The Williamsburgh Savings Bank to Edward F. Linton. 700

Ashland pl late Raymond st, e s, 270.2 n Fulton st, 19x75. Elizabeth B. Shedd, Boston, Mass., to Eva E. Shedd. ½ part. nom

Same property. Eva E. Shedd to John M. Shedd. ½ part. 3,250

Bainbridge st, n s, 339 w Reid av, 18x100. Louis R. Harsha to Edgar R. Hodgkinson. nom

Same property. Edgar R. Hodgkinson to Louis R. and Hannah E. Harsha. nom

Barbey st, w s, 250 n Blake av, 25x100. Mary A. Garrity to George Olsen. 500

Bergen st, n s, 117.4 e Ralph av, 17x107.2, h & l. Mary E. wife of Isaac D. Mason to Earl A. Gillespie. nom

Bergen st, n s, 151.4 e Ralph av, 50.8x107.2, hs & ls. Same to Isaac H. Curtis. *Mt.* $6,900. nom

Bergen st, n s, 219 e Ralph av, 34x107.2. Same to same. *Mt.* $4,600. nom

Bergen st, n s, 100 e Ralph av, 17.4x107.2, h & l. Same to Peter O. Bjorkner. *Mt.* $3,300. nom

Bergen st, n s, 235 w Ralph av, 120x107.2. Release mort. George G. Reynolds to Orson W. Sheldon, of Fort Ann, New York. nom

Bergen st, s s, 297 e Schenectady av, 61x127.9. Valentine Kerz to Frederick Dhuy, Jr. 2,500

Berry st, w s, 25 s North 9th st, 25x100. James Hughes to Margaret Hughes his wife. nom

Same property. Margaret wife of James Hughes to James J. Hughes. nom

Bleecker st, s e cor Knickerbocker av, 20x80. Release mort. Stephen B. Sturges to Harry F. C. Hopkins. nom

Bleecker st, s e s, 190 n e Irving av, 20x100. James F. Gillen to Elizabetha Isele. 1,000

Boerum st, n s, 422.9 e Bushwick av, 25.1x62.11 x25 1x64.8, h & l. Samuel Cohan to Israel and Jacob Cohen. *Mt.* $2,500. 4,000

Bond st, e s, 25 n State st, 50x50. Lodima Benedict extrx. and Wm. H. Roberson exr. Samuel R. Benedict to Edgar J. Taylor. *Mt.* $8,500. 8,800

Same property. Lodima Benedict widow to same *Mt.* $8,500. 8,800

Same property. Edgar J. Taylor to Lodima Benedict. *Mt.* $8,500. 8,800

Bradford st, e s, 50 s Arlington av, 25x100. William Diehl, Jr., to Charles Diehl. *Mt.* $2,000. nom

Bridge st, s e cor Front st, 25x77.9. Samuel M. Meeker exr. Frederick Herr to James Sharkey. 12,000

Broadway, west cor Willoughby av, runs northwest 65.2 x south 51 to Willoughby av, x east 67.4. Samuel M. Meeker exr. Frederick Herr to Simon Ash. 12,000

Broadway, n e s, 72 s e Willoughby av, runs southeast 23 x northeast 100 x northwest 21.5 x southwest 20 x northwest 1.2 x southwest 80. Samuel M. Meeker exr., &c., Frederick Herr to John Meller. 13,450

Broadway, s w s, 163.4 n w Willoughby av, 21x88.11x23.1x79.3. Samuel M. Meeker exr., &c., Frederick Herr to John Martin Otto. 9 525

Broadway, s w s, 123 n w Willoughby av, runs southwest 79.1 x north 17 9 x west 30.6x northeast 79.3 x southeast 40.4. Same to Henry Ruthmann 18,700

Broadway, s w s, 186.4 n w Hull st, runs northwest 7 x south 9.11 x northeast to beginning. Alfred J. Pouch to James T. Benedict. 300

Broadway, west cor Gerry st, 20.11x—x19.5x 78.11. William Andrews to Archibald Andrews. Q. C. nom

Broadway, s w s, 20.11 n w Gerry st, 22.3x69x 22.7x—. Archibald Andrews to William Andrews. nom

Broadway, southerly cor Hart st, runs southeast 20 x southwest 77.3 x north 68.7 to st, x east 40.6. Samuel M. Meeker exr. Frederick Herr to Charles Herr. 19,100

Butler st, n s, 200 w Smith st, 30x100. Mary A. Fehr to Emma E. Straub now known as Emma E. Fehr. B. & S. nom

Carroll st, s s, 346.8 e 8th av, 20x83.4, h & l. Anita E. wife of Edward E. Britton to Greenleaf W. Crossman. Mt $15,000. consid. omitted

Chauncey st, s s, 344 e Saratoga av, 19x100. Release mort. John W. Phelps to John C., Frank J. and Margaret Gallagher and Annie T. Anderson heirs Daniel Gallagher. 3,346

Clarkson st, s s, 440 e Bedford pl, 50x200, Flatbush. Jane J. Davenport to Jane G. Jones. Mt. $1,500. 2,600

Clifton pl, n s, 231.3 e Bedford av, 18.9x100, h & l. Edward W. Phillips to George W. Badger. 8,000

Clifton pl, n s. 212.6 e Bedford av, 18.9x100, h & l. Same to Reed Midmer. 8,200

Clinton st, w s, 284.6 n Degraw st, 20x106. Anna wife of and James Constable to Thomas A. Wilson. Mt. $4,000. 10,000

Collins st, n s, 346.1 e Canarsie av, 20x100, Flatbush. John E. Tousey to James McGloien. 190

Conover st, e s, 60 n Vandyke st, 20x80. Johanna wife of Herman Ostman to Dennis O'Brien. 2,000

Court st, w s, 60 s Church st, 20x80. Joseph A. Walsh to John F. Nelson. Mt. $2,500. nom

Covert st, s s, 198 e Central av, 36x100, h & l. Isabella B. Booth to George C. Cranford. Mt. $6,000. nom

Cranberry st, n s, 112.5 w Henry st, 20.8x100.10, h & l. John Crotty to Sarah A. Weeks. B. & S. nom

Cranberry st, s s, 100 e Hicks st, 25x100. Elinor M. Mayer to Eleonora Mayer widow, for life. nom

Dean st, n s, 83.4 e Utica av, 83.4x107.2. Charles A. Martin to Lillie Cohen. Mt. $10,600. nom

Debevoise st, s s, 100 e Humboldt st, 25x100. Christina Ochsenrether to Gustav Kaiser. Error, two courses omitted. B. & S. Mt. $900. nom

Same property. Gustav Kaiser to August Ochsenreither. B. & S. Mt. $900. nom

Decatur st, n s, 45 e Throop av, 40x80. New York and New Jersey Telephone Co. to William W. Smith. Mt. $4,000. 5,000

Decatur st, n s, 300 w Howard av, 150x100. Release mort. John S. Spencer to Thomas H. Radcliffe. 3,800

Decatur st, n s, 300 w Howard av, 150x100. Release mort. William Zeigler to Thomas H. Radcliffe. 10,000

Decatur st, n s, 149.8 e Reid av, 20.4x100. William H. Luyster to Susan A. wife of said William H. Luyster. Mt. $4,000. nom

Devoe st, n s, 67 w Ewen st, 33x50, h & l. Isaac C. Mills to Charles W. Voorhis. Mt. $1,360. 2,250

Diamond st, s s, part section 79 A. S. Robbins property, Flatbush, 45x157. Aaron S. Robbins to Emma F. wife of Oliver K. Buckley. 2,250

Dunham pl, w s, 197 n South 7th st, before widening, 16.7x92.6. John Vosburgh, Eliza Hart and Maria Mead devisee Wm. Vosburgh to William S. Liptrott. All title. nom

Eagle st, n s, 325 e Oakland st, 25x100, h & l. James A. Kenney to Sarah A. Kenney. nom

Eastern Parkway, s s, 50 w Berriman st, 25x 100. John H. Ives devisee Elizabeth H. Ives to Lois wife of William Jenkins. Mt. $500. 1,350

Eastern Parkway, n e cor Milford st, 100x90. Effingham H. Nichols to Julia E. Browne. 1,750

Eastern Parkway, n w cor Osborn st, 25x100. Moses Messinger to Annie Kronner. ½ part. Mt. ½ of $5,000. nom

Eastern Parkway, n s, extends from Osborn st to Watkins st, 200x100. Abraham Levine to Jacob Muller. ½ part. Sub. to morts. $7,-000. nom

Essex st, w s, 150 n Folsom pl, 17.5x64. Release mort. Agnes H. Davies to Daniel Laird. 1,450

Same property. Release mort. Eliza G. and Mary Hampton and John C. Creveling to Philip Mehl. 112

Same property. Daniel Laird to same. 2,000

Fenimore st, s s, 645.9 e Flatbush av, 100x125, Flatbush. Foreclos. Donald F. Ayres to Jacob V. Ackerman. 6,050

Floyd st, s s, 120 w Sumner av, 40x100. Susanna Helwig to Louis Beer and Michael Schaffuer. 5,500

Floyd st, s s, 100 w Sumner av, 20x100. Mary A. Riveire, Newark, N. J., to Louis Beer and Michael Schaffuer. 2,050

Fulton st, n s, 250 e Sumner av, 21.10x90.4x2x 87.4, h & l. David Harris to Fanny wife of Lewis Jacobs. Mt. $2,000. nom

Fulton st, n e cor Nostrand av, runs east 83.1 x 91.2 x 58.3 x 81.8. Charles W. Betts to Charles A. Betts. nom

Fulton st, n s, 575 e Tompkins av, 20x90, h & l. Edwin Sparks to Charles M. Marsh, Morris Plains, N. J. Mt. $8,500. nom

Fulton st, n s, 250 e Sumner av, 21.10x90.4x2x 87.4. Lewis Jacobs to David Harris. Mt $2,000. nom

Furmen st, e s, 101.2 s State st, runs east 86 x north 0.1½ x east 14 x north 91.1 x west 100 to st, x south 91.3, hs & ls. Albert H. Mehlhopt, New York, to Martin Nagengast. B. & S. nom

Furman st, e s, 101.2 n State st, runs east 86 x north .01½ x east 14 x north 91.1 x west 100 to Furman st, x south 91.5. Martin Nagengast, of Baltimore, Md., to Thomas Back. nom

Gallatin pl, e s, 135.5 s Fulton st, 22x93.9x22x 94. Louis and Hermann Liebmann to Joseph Wechsler and Abraham Abraham. exch

Garfield pl, n s. 175.9 w 5th av, 40x76.5x40x74.7. Thomas S. Doyle to Alexander G. Calder. Mt. $1,550. exch

Garfield pl, s w s, 172.10 n w 8th av. Party wall agreement. Thowald and Lewis Anderson with Henry Franke. nom

Garfield pl, s s, 92.10 w 8th av, 80x100. Henry Franke to Louis and Herman Liebmann. Mt. $6,000. exch

Garnet st, s s, 125 e Court st, 50x100. Alfred E. Hartington to William F. Wenisch. Mt. $5,000. exch

Gold st, e s, 310 s Willoughby st, 25x85. Michbel J. McLaughlin to J. Walter Thompson. Mt. $13,000. nom

Graham st, e s, 104.7 s Nassau st, on old map, 25x85; also,
Graham st, e s, 75 s Nassau st, 29.7x75.
John Gillen to Germario and Rose A. Fortsnato. Mt. $4,000. 5,000

Gunther pl, n e cor Atlantic av, 49x80, hs & ls. Eben W. Roby, Greenvale, L. I., to Otto Chils. Mt. $6,600. exch

Gunther pl, bet Atlantic av and Herkimer st, being the third house from Atlantic av of the row of six built by Cath. Hill. David M. Torrey to Catharine Hill. Q. C. nom

Halsey st, s s, 340 e Lewis av, 20x100. Henry V. Raymond to Jesse M. Sutton. Mt. $4,500. 6,800

Hancock st, s s, 42 e Lewis av, 108x100. Release mort. Charles M. Marsh, of Morris Plains, N. J., to Jacob Aronson. 24,000

Hancock st, s s, 337.6 w Howard av, 18.9x100. Henry Grasman to Sarah Rosenberg. Mt. $3,000. 5,500

Hancock st, s s, 20 w Patchen av, 16x75, h & l. Hyde & Gload Mfg. Co. to Adele Sandstrom. Mt. $3,800. exch

Herman st, n e s, 245 s e Irving av, 30x100. Babette F. wife of Francis H. Von Kayssers to Julius H. Franz Kayser. 500

Harrison pl, s s, 225 e Bogert st, 25x85.8x25x 86.7. Charles W. Truslow admr. William Wall to Frederick Stern. 1,075

Harrison pl, s s, 200 e Bogert st, 25x86.7x25x 87.6. Charles W. Truslow admr. Wm. Wall to John Erthal, Jr. 1,075

Hart st, s s, 282.6 w Sumner av, 17.6x100. William H. Bath to Robert Parkinson. Mt. $3,700. exch

Hart st, n s, 162.6 e Tompkins av, 18.9x100, h & l. Charles E. Wheeler to Robert J. Shadbolt. 5,000

Herkimer st, n s, 180 w Albany av, 20x100. Diana L. Edye, New York, to James Van Sielen. Q. C. nom

Herkimer st, n s, 150 e Schenectady av, 75x100. Adele Sandstrom to The Hyde & Gload Mfg. Co. Mt. $2,400. exch

Hicks st, n w s, 366.6 n e Degraw st, 19.6x97.6. Foreclos. Robert Merchant to Louise Cook, of New York. Mt. $5,000 and int., from Nov. 1, 1890. 800

Hicks st, s e s, 122.7 n e Love lane, 25x100, h & l. Anna B. wife of Edward W. Dodd to Henry L. Meyer. Mt. $6,000. 11,000

Himrod st, s s, 180 e Evergreen av, 21x100, h & l. William Ruthmann to Adam Schmidt. Correction deed. exch

Hooper st, s s, 258.1 e Bedford av, 19.2x100. John W. Theisz to Carlmi A. Schmonsees. Mt. $3,000. nom

Jay st, w s, 80 s Myrtle av, 20x69. Lewis Jacobs to David Harris. Mt. $4,000. nom

Jay st, w s, 80 s Myrtle av, 20x69. David Harris to Fanny wife of Lewis Jacobs. Mt. $4,-000. nom

Jerome st, w s, 225 s Eastern Parkway, 20x100. James E. Vincent to Ann Maxwell. Mt. $1,500. 2,750

Jerome st, w s, 200 s Eastern Parkway, 25x100. James E. Vincent to Jane L. Smith. Mt. $1,500. 2,750

Kosciusko st, n s, 200 w Reid av, 23.6x100. Franklin Beames to Sarah M. H. Beames. nom

Lafayette st, s s, 60 e Hudson av, 20x56.3. Mary A. Lockwood to Dewitt B. Wyckoff. ½ part. 3,375

Leonard st, w s, 100 n Couselyea st, runs west to land formerly John Skillman, x north to point 125 n Couselyea st, x east to Leonard st, x south 25. Agnes Meldowny widow to Ernst A. Sievers. 4,400

Leonard st, e s, 225 n Calyer st, 25x100. George B. Read to Paul Heilmann and Ellen his wife, joint tenants. 3,150

Leonard st, w s, 183.4 n Nassau av, 16.8x100. Sarah E. wife of and Cornelius Grinnell to Carrie K. Williams. 5,600

Livingston st, n e s, 575.10 s e Smith st, 25x74, h & l. Joseph Wechsler and Abraham Abraham to Louis and Hermann Liebmann. Mt. $4,000. exch

Locust st, e s, lots 360–364 map Rapalje property.
Nassau st, e s, lot 45 and north 5 feet of 46 map of 995 lots at East New York and lot 50 and north 5 feet of 49 same map.
Sheridan av, lots 17 and 18 map Adamsville.
Railroad av, w s, 50 n Willow st, lot 110 map Belleplaine.
Erastus D. Benedict to Michael J. Bourke. Correction deed. nom

Same property. Michael J. Bourke to Henry French. nom

Lorimer st, e s, 76.3 n Withers st, 23.9x100. Henry Braistedt to Hannah Weiser. Mt. $800. 2,500

Macon st, s s, 184 e Ralph av, 18x100. John R. Pitt to George P. Davis. Mt. $4,000. exch and 200

Macon st, Nos. 567, 569 and 571. Contract. J. C. Leahey to William H. Griffin. 15,000

Macon st, n s, 326.10 e Ralph av, 18x100. Andrew R. Baird to Mary A. Lupton. Mt. $4,000. 6,450

Madison st, s s, 221 e Lewis av, 20x100, h & l. Phebe A. wife of William Godfrey to George Covert. Mt. $6,000. nom

Same property. Release mort. Thomas S. Strong to Phebe A. Godfrey. 1,500

Madison st, w s, 91.10 s Evergreen av, 25x100. Abbie wife of Charles W. Aldom to Adrian M. Suydam. 3,320

Marion st, n s, 350 e Stuyvesant av, 100x100. Harriet S. wife of James A. Whalen to Samuel G. Holland. Q. C. Mt. $2,000. nom

Marion st, s s, 225 e Reid av, 25x100. Release mort. James S. Bearns to William J. G. Bearns. nom

Same property. Release judgment. Thomas B. Jackson to Mary C. Hill. 25

Same property. Mary C. Hill to Joseph Brand. Mt. $1,500. 2,600

McDougal st, n s, 325 e Saratoga av, 25x100. Lewis S. Davis to Benjamin F. Zindel. 2,000

McDonough st, n s, 225 w Tompkins av, 40x100. John H. Broach to Mortlock Pettit. Mt. $2,-500. 7,000

McDonough st, n s, 442 e Ralph av, 18x100. Wilfred Burr to Aline Kafer. Mt. $4,500. 7,000

Milford st, e s, 130 s Glenmore av, 20x100.
Belmont av, s s, 60 w Milford st, 20x90.
Susan H. Callahan, of New York, to Edward R. Jourdan. 600

Monroe st, n s, 185 e Bedford av, 13x100, h & l. Peter Wood to Henry J. Lankenau. Mt. $3,500. nom

Monroe st, s s, 405.3 w Tompkins av, 19.9x100. Foreclos. John Courtney to William H. Dill. Sub. to mort. $3,500 and int. Nov. 1, 1890. 300

Montgomery st, n s, 14.6 e Washington av, 78x 102.4. James W. Keveney to Amanda M. Drummond. exch

Moore st, n s, 379.5 w White st, 75x100; also,
Moore st, n s, 304.5 w White st, 25x100.
Charles W. Truslow admr. William Wall to Charles Diemer. 5,125

Moore st, n s, 279.5 w White st, 25x100. Charles W. Truslow admr. William Wall to Catharine Schwartz. 1,450

Moore st, s s, 446.5 e Bushwick av, 25x100. Harris Korsinsky to Eva Simon. Mt. $4,600. 6,500

Newell st, w s, 225 n Nassau av, 25x100. Elizabeth Schmitt or Schmidt individ. and extrx. of John Schmitt to John J. Robinson. 1,325

Ocean Parkway, n e cor Lotts lane, runs north 109.6 x east 250 to East 7th st, x south 4.3 to Lotts lane, x southwest 271.3, Flatbush. Release mort. Mary B. Ward et al. to Peter H. McNulty. 1,834

Olive pl, e s, 97.5 s Herkimer st, 17.5x97. Robert Parkinson to William H. Bath. exch and 300

Osborn st, e s, 50 s Sutter av, 25x100. Release mort. Melvin Brown to Harris Max. 650

Osborn st, e s, 125 n Sutter av, 50x100. Release mort. Gilbert S. Thatford to Sale Weinstein. nom

Osborn st, e s, 150 n Dumont av, 25x100. Catharine L. Babcock to Harris Lazarus. 350

Pacific st, s w s, 200 s e Hoyt st, 25.4x100. William G. and Benjamin S. Alder to Phoebe wife of Horace G. Hart. nom

Park pl, n s, 244 e Franklin av, 18x131. Edward P. Champerlin to Benjamin R. Kittredge. Mt. $5,300 7,000

Park pl, n s, 220.10 w Vanderbilt av, 20.10x 131. Telitha A. Stow to William McKnight. nom

Pierrepont st, s s, 175 e Henry st, 25x100. Silas A. Condict to Edward E. Bergen. Mt. $45,000. nom

Pineapple st, n s, 92.6 e Henry st, 50x137x51.6x 124.9. Louise A. and Emilie Burger to Edwin D. Phelps. nom

Same property. Edwin D. Phelps to Henry Franke. exch

President st, n s, 225 e 8th av, 0.6x100. William Flanagan to Patrick Sheridan. 350

Prospect pl, s s, 68 w Buffalo av, 16x52.9. William L. Beers to William H. Moore. Mt. $1,-250. 2,500

Prospect pl, n s, 201.6 e Utica av, 66x127.9. William Zang to Philip Goss. 755

Prospect pl, n s, 100 w Rockaway av, 25x 127.9.
Prospect pl, n s, 125 w Rockaway av, 25x 127.9.
Maria M. and Charles L. Friedel heirs Charles Friedel to Maria A. Friedel widow. All title. 700

Prospect pl, n s, 323.1 w Schenectady av, 30.3x 155.7. William H. Valentine to Mary L. Valentine. B. & S. nom

Quincy st, s s, 43 w Throop av, 19x80. William M. Gibson to Jane A. Smith. Mt. $4,500 and taxes 1891. nom

Quincy st, s s, 231.3 w Throop av, 18.9x100, h &

l. Harry A. Sibley to Charles E. Ring. *Mt.* $5,000. 8,800

Quincy st, s s, 474.8 w Throop av, 19.1x100, h & l.
Quincy st, s s, 437.6 w Throop av, 18.9x100, h & l.
David F. Manning to Charles E. Ring. *Mt.* $10,000. nom

Quincy st, s s, 100 w Throop av, 187.6x100.
Quincy st, s s, 343.9 w Throop av, 18.9x100.
David F. Manning to Harry A. Sibley. *Mt.* $58,661. nom

Quincy st, n s, 85.6 w Ralph av, 40x100. Robert L. Moores and Charles A. Le Quesne to Louisa L. Gibbins. *Mt.* $14,550. nom

Quincy st, s s, 280 w Patchen av, 20x100. Carrie L. wife of William H. Larkin, of New Rochelle, N. Y., to Catherine Nicholas. *Mt.* $5,000. 7,500

Quincy st, s s, 343.9 w Throop av, 18.9x100, h & l. Henry A. Sibley to Andrew A. Smith and John Quevedo. *Mt.* $4,500. 2,500

Rapelye st, e s, 173.4 s Van Brunt st, 41.8x65.2x42.6x73.6. John P. Cranford as assignee Morris H. Smith individ. and as partner F. B. Wallace & Co. to Helmin Johnson. *Mt.* $1,750. 2,400

Richmond st, e s, 1,000 n 4th st, 25x150. Mary wife of and John Martin to Pauline Blumenfeld. *Mt.* $2,300. 4,100

Sands st, s e cor Jay st, 25.10x103.3. Hermann A. Alsgood to John M. and Henry P. Alsgood and John W. Rasch. ¼ part. *Mt.* $10,000. 7,000

Schermerhorn st, s s, 145 e Hoyt st, 20x100. Mary E. Bates to Adolph I. Namm. 15,000

Seigel st, s s, 590 e Bushwick av, 75x100. Charles W. Truslow admr. William Wall to Charles Diemer. 1,975

Stagg st, s s, 175 w Waterbury st, 25x100. Edward Hughes to Francis E. Clark. *Mt.* $3,400. nom

Stagg st, n s, 75 w Waterbury st, 25x100, h & l. Joseph Maurer to Louisa K. Vetter. *Mt.* $2,500. 4,425

State st, s w s, 117.6 e Henry st, 25x100. James Murphy, New York, to Jane Gilfeather, New York. nom

Stockholm st, n w s, 100 s w Johnson av, 25x100. Charles C. Horning to John Horning. nom

Sumpter st, n s, bet Reid and Patchen avs, being lot 6 on block 82 assessm't map 25th Ward. John G. Gillig to Adam E. Schatz. 2,000

Tillary st, n w cor Raymond st, 28.3x100x18.2x101.3. Peter and Joseph Young to Carrie M. Lyons. 4,000

Truxton st, n s, 20 w Stone av, 80x80, hs & ls. Stephen Perry Sturges to Otto Chils. *Mt.* $21,000. exch

Truxton st, n s, 20 w Stone av, 40x80. Stephen B. Sturges to S. Perry Sturges. Sub. to liens. exch

Truxton st, Nos. 43 and 43A, n s, 200 e Stone av, 37.6x100, hs & ls. James Baker, Lawrence, L. I., to Alonzo E. De Baun. *Mt.* $7,000 8,000

Truxton st, n s, 200 e Stone av, 37.6x100, hs & ls. Alonzo E. De Baun to Peter Roeder. val. consid. and 1,250

Union st, n s, 331.3 w 8th av, 18.9x90. Henry F. Ogden, of Hoboken, N. J., to Frank F. Wood. 15,000

Union st, n s, 312.6 w 8th av, 18.9x90. Same to same. 15,000

Union st, n s, 200 w 8th av, 18.9x90. Same to same. 15,000

Union st, n s, 100 w 4th av, 50x95. Foreclos. John Courtney to George R. Brown. *Mt.* $17,500. 1,000

Union st, s s, 155 w Bond st, 20.4x100. Isabella Brown to The Hyde & Gload Mfg. Co. *Mt.* $4,000. 2,200

Van Buren st, n s, 199.8 e Lewis av, 175.4x100. Henry H. Cochran to Albert Muir. *Mt.* $9,000. 23,000

Van Buren st. Party wall agreement. Mary A. Burrows with Thomas P. Bryant. 135

Vanderveer st, n w s, 305 n e Bushwick av, 50x100. George Covert to Phebe A. Godfrey. *Mt.* $800. nom

Van Voorhis st, n w s, 202 w Evergreen av, 17x100. Annie F. Marrin to William H. Hawxhurst. Sub. to liens. 2,000

Verona st, easterly cor Imlay st, 25x75. John F. Nelson to James A. Walsh. *Mt.* $5,000, taxes 1891. 12,000

Walworth st, w s, 470 s Willoughby av, 20x100. Mary L. Carter widow to Eliza McAteer. *Mt.* 1,800. 3,800

Warren st, n e s, 146.4 w Court st, 20.9x62.6. Mary A. wife of Tecumseh Pierce to said Tecumseh Pierce. *Mt.* $1,500. nom

Warren st, n s, 82 e Henry st, 20x85. General release from contract, &c. Josephine Seymour to Kate Gallagher. 500

Watkins st, e s, 100 s Dumont av, 25x100.
Osborn st, e s, 225 s Dumont av, 25x100.
Frank C. Lang trustee, &c., to James O'Halloran. Confirmation deed. nom

Watkins st, e s, 100 s Dumont av, 25x100.
Osborn st, e s, 225 s Dumont av, 25x100.
Charles R. Lynde, of New Jersey, to James O'Halloran. nom

Weirfield st, n w s, 281 s w Central av, 20x100. Release mort. Oliver W. Coe to Leopold J. Lippmann. 2,486

Weirfield st, n w s, 301 s w Central av, 20x100, h & l. Leopold J. Lippmann to Sarah Taylor. nom

Same property. Release mort. Oliver W. Coe to Leopold J. Lippmann. 2,486

Weirfield st, s e s, 264.5 n e Evergreen av, runs east to point on Halsey st 297.8 from Evergreen av, x northeast 28.8 x west — to Weirfield st, x southwest 29.9. The City of Brooklyn to Lucinda Moadinger. Q C. nom

Weirfield st, s e s, 120 n e Evergreen av, runs northeast 169.6 x east to point on Halsey st 319.9 n e Evergreen av, x southwest 79.9 x northwest 100 x southwest 120 x northwest 100. Lucinda Moadinger individ. and as extrx. John Moadinger to Charles D. Hommel. 14,500

West st, e s, 340 s Av I, 60x100, New Utrecht. James Cropsey, of Gravesend, to Charlotte A. Erving. *Mt.* $1,600. 3,700

Wyckoff st, n s, 296.3 w Hoyt st, 43.6x100. William F. Wenisch to Alfred E. Hartington. exch

1st pl, s s, 25 w Court st, runs south to within 1 inch of centre line, bet 1st and 2d pls, x west 25 x north to 1st pl, x east 25. Fannie E Metcalfe to Susan McLaughlin. *Mt.* $10,000. nom

1st pl, s s, 225 e Court st, 25x133.5. Foreclos. Alonzo C. Farnham to Lillian W. wife of John J. Leary. 6,400

Same property. Lillian W. wife of and John J. Leary to Jeannette M. Finlay, of Bayonne, N. J. 10,000

2d st, s s, 243.4 e 6th av, 18.2x95. Amanda M. Drummond to James W. Keveny. *Mt.* $6,000. exch

South 3d st, s w s, 100 n w Hooper st, 25x95. Emil Lehrian to Katharina and George Fullbardt. *Mt.* $6,500. 14,250

4th st, n e s, 297.10 n w 8th av, 100x95, hs & ls. Henry B. Spencer to Alvan R. Johnson. *Mt.* $9,000. nom

Same property. Alvan R. Johnson to John T. Allan and Nathaniel Prosky. *Mt.* $9,000. nom

South 4th st, n s, 225 e 9th st, 25x95. Lewis P. Nostrand to Michael Jaeger. 4,250

6th st, n e s, 297.10 n w 5th av, 60x100. Release mort. The Title Guarantee and Trust Co. to Erwin G. Gollner. nom

6th st, s s, 75 w 4th av, 105x100. Foreclos. James F. McGee to Rachel A. Van Kirk. 3,000

6th st, n e s, 297.10 n w 5th av, 100x100. Catharine Knapp to Erven G. Gollner. nom

8th st, n s, 166.1 w 6th av, 18.3x100; also,
8th st, n s, 257.1 w 6th av, 54.5x100.
William Brown to William C. O'Keefe and James H. McKenna. 28,000

11th st, n s, 165.9 w 6th av, 16x90, h & l. Ellen wife of and James O'Reilly to Jeremiah Mahoney. *Mt.* $1,000. 3,300

11th st, n s, 111.10 w 9th av, 18.6x100. Charles G. Petersen to James S. McBride. *Mt.* $6,000. nom

12th st, n s, 117.10 w 5th av, 20x100. William Corrigan to Eliza A. wife of James Griffin. *Mt.* $4,500. 7,000

12th st, n e s, 197.10 s e 4th av, 20x100. Alexander G. Calder to Thomas S. Doyle. *Mt.* $3,000. exch

12th st, n e s, 257.10 s e 4th av, 20x100. Alexander G. Calder to Mary P. D. Waycott. *Mt.* $8,000. 7,000

14th st, n s, 297.10 e 8th av, 20x100, h & l. Catharine wife of and George F. Beatty to Richard Chidwick. 7,500

14th st, n s, 297.10 e 8th av, 20x100. Release mort. Emma R. Tappen to Catharine Beatty. nom

14th st, n s, 97.10 e 8th av, 26x100. Martha S. Hawkins to Isaac Spiero. *Mt.* $3,500. 6,600

15th st, s w s, 97.10 s e 7th av, 25x100. Flora A. Brown widow to Benjamin Warsanski. *Mt.* $300. 1890. 1,000

16th st, n s, 109.10 w 4th av, 27.10x103, h & l. Andrew Leslie to Sarah Jane Leslie his wife. nom

17th st, s w s, 100 s e 9th av, 100x100.2. Edward J. Connell to Cecelia A. Ballard. *Mt.* $7,287. 700

17th st, s w s, 339 s e 7th av, 16x100.2, h & l. Richard Chidwick to Catharine Beatty. 3,500

Same property. Catharine Beatty to Morton P. Christensen. 3,500

Bay 17th st, e s, 275 s 86th st, 25x96.8, New Utrecht. Sarah A. Haviland widow to John F. Haviland. 500

20th st, w s, 125 n Vanderbilt st, 50x100, Flatbush. Thomas Heffernan to Margaret Heffernan. nom

20th st, n s, 334.4 w 8th av, 15.7x100.2. Henry C. Bull to Charles Burgedahl. *Mt.* $1,500. 2,515

22d st, s w s, 82.9 n w 4th av, 16.8x100. Andrew Leslie to Sarah Jane Leslie his wife. nom

Bay 26th st, n s, 352.6 e Cropsey av, 40x96.8, Bath Beach. Edwina W. wife of William C. Brose to Octavia E. Swett, of New York. 1,100

27th st, s w s, 250 s e 4th av, 100x100.2. Walter L. Suydam and Helen S. wife of R. Fulton Cutting to William E. Kay. 3,000

40th st, n s, 366.8 e 3d av, 16.8x100, h & l. Ann McGregor widow to Alexander Ingram. 2,325

43d st, n e s, 100 s e 12th av, 25x100. George W. Skidmore to Gustaf F. Gustafson. 350

45th st, n e s, 225 n w 13th av, 50x100.2, New Utrecht. Brooklyn Land and Improvement Co. to Frederick Van Tine. 700

47th st, s s, 280 w 3d av, 80x100.2. David J. Tingley and ano. exrs. Marg't M. Van Pelt to William J. Morrison. 1,800

47th st, s s, 360 w 3d av, 20x100.2. David J. Tingley and Richard Slater exrs. Margaret M. Van Pelt to Charles Whitehead. 420

47th st, n s, 100 w 3d av, 20x100.2. Benjamin P. Applegate to Frederick M. Holfeld. 700

47th st, s w s, 220 s e 2d av, runs southwest 100.2 x southeast 20.8 to centre old Gowanus road, x northeast 100.6 to 47th st, x northwest 20.2. Mary Nappier to Patrick Slattery. 600

47th st, s s, 240 w 3d av, 40x100.2. David J. Tingley and ano. exrs. Margaret M. Van Pelt to Henry C. Wylie. 1,050

48th st, n s, 100 e 4th av, 20x100.2. Stephen Hazzard to Cassie A. Black. 4,000

48th st, n s, 80 w 3d av, 20x100.2. Frederick W. Starr to Mary J. Depp. 3,500

50th st, s s, 260 w 3d av, 20x100.2. Linda A. wife of and Dominick Adams to Jacob Schaefer. *Mt.* $3,575. 3,800

53d st, n s, 205 e 2d av, 18x100.2. Levi V. Martin to Mary C. Burt. *Mt.* $2,500. 4,200

56th st, s w s, 100 n w 14th av, 75x100.2, New Utrecht. The West Brooklyn Land and Improvement Co. to Amelia L. Bull. 1,500

56th st, s s, 220 e 3d av, 60x100.2, New Utrecht. Release mort. Edward T. Hunt exr. Thomas Hunt to Simon Stiner. consid. omitted

57th st, s w s, 180 s e 8th av, 40x100.2, New Utrecht. Carrie M. Hatten to Jennie Roberts. nom

57th st, n s, 320 e 3d av, 20x100.2. George H. Parshall to Mary H. Wood. 5,500

57th st, s s, 440 w 8th av, 20x100, New Utrecht. Charles W. Lundquist to Dorothea F. Gundberg. 200

59th st, s w s, 400 s e 13th av, runs southeast 20 x southwest 62.4 x east 0.10 x south — x northwest along same to centre of block, x northwest — x northeast 100.2, Bath Junction. James V. S. Woolley to Thomas H. Wilson. 300

66th st, e s, 225 s 6th av, 25x100.2, New Utrecht. William T. Scott to Anna R. wife of Ernst W. Altmann. *Mt.* $1,200. 1,400

66th st, s w s, 260 n w 11th av, 53.3x100.3x60.6x100, New Utrecht. Van Brunt Bergen individ. and as exr. Tennis G. Bergen to Margaretha Reichenbach. 375

Same property. Margaretha Reichenbach to Joseph H. Dowd, of Fanningdale, L. I. *Mt.* $2,000. 5,500

66th st, n e s, 180 s e 11th av, 20x100, New Utrecht. Van Brunt Bergen individ., exr. and trustee of Tennis Bergen to Jennie Evans. val. consid. and 100

72d st, s w s, 66.6 n w 7th av, 60x200 to 73d st, New Utrecht. Prospect Land and Improvement Co. to Louis Bradfish. 1,590

76th st, n e s, 340 s e 3d av, 50x107.2, hs & l, New Utrecht. Bay Ridge Mfg Co. to Johanna C. M. Prinzhorn. *Mt.* $3,000. 4,800

77th st, n e s, 140 n w 4th av, 100x109.4, New Utrecht. Frank M. Stephens, of Sayre, Pa., to Simon Stiner. *Mt.* $866. 2,000

77th st, n e s, 240 n w 4th av, 40x109.4, New Utrecht. Emma A. Tobias, of Sayre, Pa to Simon Stiner. 800

77th st, s w s, 100 n w 4th av, 40x109.4, New Utrecht. Frederick W. Davison, of New York, to Simon Stiner. 900

83d st, n e s, 100 s e 19th av, 60x100, New Utrecht. Release mort. Daniel Barre and Phebe M. wife of Charles E. Ammermann to John L. Nostrand. 1,000

89th st, s s, 160 e 3d av, 25x84.8x25.7x79.3, Fort Hamilton. Margaret Cornwell to Charles Doherty. 300

Atlantic av, s s, 100 w Troy av, 40x100. Foreclos. John Courtney to Helen D. Burnett, New York. 5,000

Atlantic av, s s, 75 w 3d av, 25x80. Aletha M. Drake to John J. Drake. *Mt.* $3,000. 5,000

Arlington av, n s, 34 e Elton st, 33x100. Anna M. Beach to Annie B. Dieterich widow and Barbara Bauer widow. *Mt.* $2,800 and assessments. 5,500

Atlantic av, No. 81, n s, 34 6 e Hicks st, 16.6x65. Anna F. Woodnutt to Hannah W. Emory, Mineola, Henry C. Woodnut, Jericho, Paul C. Woodnutt, New York, and Henrietta W. Woodnut, Nyack, N. Y. 4-6 part. B. & S. Reserves life estate. nom

Baltic av, n s, 56 w Wyckoff av, 44x25. Foreclos. John Courtney to Richard M. Wyckoff et al. exrs. John S. Andrews. 200

Bath av, n e s, 80 s e Bay 13th st, 28.4x95, New Utrecht. John Henni to William T. Paal. 2,000

Bedford av, e s, 20 s Wallabout st, 20x67. David M. Koehler to Annie M. Tonjes. Correction deed. *Mt.* $2,000. 4,590

Belmont av, n e cor Osborn st, 50x100. Samuel Rauer to Henry Meyer and Semche Simon. 1,475

Blake av, n w cor Montauk av, 25x90. John Doyle to Albert W. Sprott, New York. 400

Brooklyn av, e s, 87.10 s Carroll st, 20x100. Eliza wife of Alexander Ray and C. Olivia wife of John B. Sabine to James Ratigan. 300

Brooklyn av, e s, 107.10 s Carroll st, 20x100. Same to Andrew McCormick. 300

Brooklyn av, s e cor Carroll st, 127.10x100. Henrietta Frazier, of New York, to Eliza Ray and C. Olivia Sabine. 1,400

Brooklyn av, n w cor Lefferts av, 41.2x95.5x40x89.6, Flatbush. Robert L. Woods to Henry Groos. 550

Buffalo av, n w cor Atlantic av, 20x45. Christopher P. Skelton to Jacob Gunther. *Mt.* $3,000. 6,600

Bushwick av or Boulevard, s e cor Meserole st, 50x105, hs & ls. Louisa wife of Henry Loewenstein to Ernst Kreusler. 15,000

Bushwick av, e s, 138.3 s turnpike road, 54.4 x east 79.11 x south 25 to Devoe st, x east 10 x north 100 x west 25 x south 38.7 x west to beginning. Barbara wife of Anthony Klein to Anthony Klein. nom

Carlton av, w s, 137.3 s Park av, 25x100, h & l. The L. F. Genet Lumber Co., New York, to The Buffalo Hardwood Lumber Co. *Mt.* $15,500. nom

Central av, east cor Myrtle av, runs southeast 107.5 to Stockholm st, x northeast 105.4 to

Myrtle av, x west — to beginning. Samuel M. Meeker exr. and trustee Frederick Herr to Henry W. and John F. Dreyer and Henry C. Hunken. 6,800

Clinton av, e s, 233.3 n Greene av, 10x200 to Waverly av. John W. Hunter exr. Hester A. Hunter to William H. Hill. 8,000

Clinton av, e s, 168 2 n Greene av, 13x200 to Waverly av. John W. Hunter exr. Hester A. Hunter individ., &c., to Brooklyn Hotel Co. 12,000

De Kalb av, s s, 182 e Tompkins av, 18x100. Josephine wife of Frank M. Foot, of Tarrytown, N. Y., to Maggie C. Cashman, of New York. *Mt.* $3,600. exch and 600

De Kalb av, s e s, 225 n e Hamburg av, 25.3x100. George Ochs to Henry Roth and Alois Lazansky. *Mt.* $3,000. exch

East New York av, n w s, 190 s w Sackman st, 20x81 4x20 10x75.3. James Rodier to Christian T. Leffler. *Mt* $1,200. 1,600

Flatbush av, s e cor St. Marks av, 145.9x85.6x44.8x153.3. Joseph and Rudolph Liebmann to Louis and Herman Liebmann. nom

Same property. Louis and Herman Liebmann to Henry Franke. *Mt* $66,500. exch

Same property. Release mort. Joseph, Henry and Charles Liebmann to Joseph and Rudolph Liebmann. nom

Flatbush av, n e s, 149.10 n w Hanson pl, runs northeast 42.3 x east 21.9 to Raymond st, x north 19.3 x west 27.7 x southwest 54.3 to av, x southeast 20. John R. Du Bois and ano. exrs. William Spader, of Matawan, N. J., to Phebe Geran. 1-7 part. 1,000

Flushing av, s s, 25.4 w Schenck st, 21.10x83.8x22.11x85, h & l. Carrie M. wife of and Stephen Hatten to Joseph M. Rigney. *Mt.* $2,500. 2,750

Fountain av, w s, 110 s Eastern Parkway, 40x100. Nathan Kaplan to Sarah M. Bergen. 600

Fort Hamilton av, west cor Prospect Park & Coney Island R. R., 152.10 to 38th st, x92.10x154x120 3, Flatbush. Lewis Leavens to E. Willard Jones. *Mt.* $2,307. exch

Gates av, s e s, 125 s w Central av. 25x100, h & l. Louise wife of Michael Germuth to Moritz Friedman and Siegmund Newman. *Mt.* $3,200. 6,800

Gates av, n s, 302 e Nostrand av, 20x100. Eleanor Stevens et al. exrs. and trustees Barlow Stevens to Henry F. Megill. Taxes 1891. 4,500

Glenmore av, n e cor Osborn st, 100x100. }
Watkins st, w s, 100 n Glenmore av, 25x100. }
Release mort. Claus Luehrs to Herbert C. Smith. 2,500

Graham av, s w s, 75 s e Van Pelt av, 25x100. Alfred Bernheim to Samuel Rosenberg. *Mt.* $2,700. nom

Greenpoint av, s s, 345 e Franklin st, 25x95. William F. Englis to Charles M. Englis. nom

Greene av, n w s, 485 n e Knickerbocker av, 25x80 to Myrtle av park, x25x79.9, h & l. Catharina wife of John Loeffler to Francis E. Clark. *Mt.* $2,000. nom

Same property. Francis E. Clark to Charles E. Kreppel. *Mt.* $2,000. nom

Greene av, s s, 378 9 w Reid av, 71.3x100. }
Greene av, n s, 140 w Reid av, 239.8x100. }
Thomas Walsh to Elizabeth Walsh widow. nom

Same property. Elizabeth Walsh widow to Thomas Walsh and Elizabeth his wife. nom

Greene av, s s, 100 w Stuyvesant av, 20x100, h & l. Anna W. McCord to Katie Houghtlin. *Mt.* $5,500, taxes 1891. 8,250

Greene av, No. 643A, n s, 218.9 w Throop av, 18.9x100. Hattie M. Foster to Isaac L. Doughty. *Mt.* $4,500. 7,000

Greene av, s s, 200 e Lewis av, 125x100. Isabella Asche to Louis C Schliep. 14,000

Hamburg av, n e cor Hart st, 50x100. Max Brill to Henry Roth. ½ part. 2,250

Hudson av, No. 151, e s, 25x75; also, }
Hudson av, e s, 50 s Sands st, 25x75; also, }
Hudson av, e s, 46.11 s High st, 21.11x75 to Nassau pl; also, }
Conselyea st, n w s, 100 n e Central av, 25x100. }
Joseph K. Dains to William J. Dains. nom

Same property. Williams J. Dains to Eliza J. Dains. nom

Howard av, s w cor McDonough st, 100x350. William P. Rae to Ansel H. Van Buren. *Mt.* $29,000. exch

Jefferson av, s s, 224.3 e Throop av, 16.8x100. Maximilian Lang to Sarah J. Millet. *Mt.* $4,000. nom

Jefferson av, No. 359, n s, 137.6 e Tompkins av, 19.2x100, h & l. Robert B. Lynd to Niels Poulson. *Mt.* $7,000. 12,000

Johnson av, n s, 50.4 e Bogert st, runs north 145.6 x northeast to Montrose av, x east 86.11 x south 232.4 to av, x west 136.7. Charles W. Truslow admr. Wm. Wall to Farmers' Feed Co., New York and New Jersey. 8,325

Johnson av, n e cor Bogart st, 50.4x145.6x—x108.9. Alois Lazansky and Henry Roth to George Ochs. exch

Kent av, w s, 22.10 s North 9th st, runs west 80.4 x north 22.10 to North 9th st, x west 19.7 x south 50.4 x east 100 to Kent av, x north 27.5; also, }
Berry st, west cor North 9th st, 25x100; also, }
Madison st, n s, 320 e Lewis av, 20x100. }
James Hughes to James J. Hughes. B. & S. nom

Kingsland av, e s, 240 s Nassau av, 25x100. The Kings Co. Impt. Co. to Rudolph A. Frazer. 900

Knickerbocker av, south cor Linden st, 20x100. Samuel M. Meeker exr. and trustee Frederick Herr to Henry S. Nauls. 2,350

Lafayette av, s s, 197.1 w Lewis av, 19.5x100. David S. Beasley to Isaac C. Mills. *Mt.* $3,500. 7,000

Lefferts av, n s, 189.6 w Brooklyn av, 60x100, Flatbush. Robert L. Woods to Patrick McGovern. 675

Lexington av, s s, 83 e Marcy av, 17x50. George P. Davies to John R. Pitt. exch

Liberty av, s s, extends from Atkins to Montauk av, 200x100. George B. Stoutenburg and Charles F. Hunt to George H. Doughty. *Mt.* $3,000. exch

Lott av, s w cor Christopher av, runs west 200 to Stone av, x south 418.11 to New Lots road, x east 211.9 to Christopher av, x north 349.4. Otto Chils and Sophus Nielsen to Stephen P. Sturges. B. & S. *Mt.* $8,050. nom

Miller av, lot 888 block BB map A, East New York, 25x100, map worn out. George Farnsworth to George Weinstein. 1,000

Montrose av, s s, 155 e Bushwick av, 25x100. }
Bushwick av, w s, 55.4 s Varet st, 26.2x66x25x56.3 }
Release dower. Clara Scherer widow to Barbara Obmann. 237

Myrtle av, n s, 80.9 w Pearl st, 22.3x80.7. Brooklyn Trust Co. substituted trustees of Edward Harvey dec'd to Angeline E. Darling, Utica, N. Y. 14,000

Myrtle av, n s, 375 e Sumner av, 25x100. Henry Roth to Frederick W. Hoese, Jr. *Mt.* $9,500. nom

Myrtle av, south cor Bleecker st, runs east 20 x south 50 x southeast to point 80 from s s Myrtle av at point 46 e of Bleecker st, x west 10 x northwest 25.4 x northwest 55.4 to Bleecker st, x northeast 27.8. Harry F. C. Hopkins to Herman H. Schult. 7,000

Nassau av, n e cor North Henry st, 20x85. Release mort. James D. Lynch to George W. Palmer. 850

Newport av, n s, 100 e Stone av, 75x100. }
Christopher av, w s, 100 n Newport av, 25x100. }
Ascher Schiff to Samuel Stern, New York. 1,040

Nichols av, w s, 125 s Wood st, 100x200. Theo. H. and Raisey J. Fuller, Eloise F. Sexton and Emma F. Bodine and Elizabeth W. Peek to Charles M. Thompson. 2,200

Ocean av, e s, 103 n land Anna M. Ferris, 50x150, Flatbush. Susan C. Strain to John Parsons and Joseph D. Brown. 2,000

Ocean av, s w s, lot 204 map South Greenfield, town Flatlands and Gravesend, belonging to The United Freeman's Land Assoc. No. 3, 100x100. Alexander S. Gibson, of Norwalk, Conn., and Mary E. wife of George W. Street to Thomas Ferguson. 200

Same property. Thomas Ferguson to John Lahey. 265

Pardegat av, s s, 17.6 w East 37th st, runs southeast along av to land of Cath. G. De Baun, x south 50 to centre of Pardegat Basin, x northwest along same — x north 50 to n s of Pardegat Basin, x east —, also right of way through Av E and East 37th st, Flatbush. Gerrit Cortelyou, New Brunswick, N. J., to Town of Flatbush. 600

Park av, n s, 401 8 w Sumner av, 60x100. Frederick W. Hoese, Jr., to Henry Roth. *Mt.* $5,000. nom

Patchen av, w s, 20 n Putnam av, 80x80. Frances G. Underhill to Alexander Underhill, Jr. *Mt.* $3,000. nom

Prospect av, s w s, 275 s e 6th av, 50x90.2. Geo. A. Mack, Pleasantville, N. Y., to Josephine Fink. nom

Putnam av, n s, 85 e Sumner av, 20x100, h & l. Stewart A. Robinson to Emma G. wife of Stewart A. Robinson. B. & S. nom

Putnam av, n s, 42.6 w Sumner av, 17.6x100. E. Willard Jones to Louisa L. Gibbins. *Mt.* $5,250. exch

Putnam av, west cor Knickerbocker av, 80x100. Augustus S. Bedell to William M. Gibson. *Mt.* $2,500. nom

Putnam av, n s, 400 w Nostrand av, 25x100. Henry F. Megill to Arthur B. Dow. *Mt.* $1,500. 4,500

Reid av, No. 41, e s, 25 s Kosciusko st, 25x100. Franklin Beames to Sarah M. H. Beames. gift

Ridgewood av, n s, 60 e Essex st, 20x100. Release mort. The Williamsburgh Savings Bank to Edward F. Linton. 350

Ridgewood av, n s, 60 e Essex st, 20x100. Edward F. Linton to Adeline E. wife of William Smith. 800

Rockaway av, e s, 150 n Belmont av. 50x100.1. Israel M. and Isaac Cohen to Paulina Seerman. *Mt.* $1,000. 1,775

Ridgewood av, n e cor Cleveland st, 50x100. Owen Hagan to James W. Crawford. 2,200

Rockaway av, w s, 36 n Sumpter st, 16x68.3. Dennis Sheehan to Michael F. Walsh. *Mt.* $2,500. 2,500

Rockaway av, s e cor Glenmore av, 25x100.1, h & l. Rosie Jones to Rosie Cooper. *Mt.* $4,800. 6,500

Schenck av, e s, 175 n Dumont av, 100x100. S. Ferris Owen to John Baird. 4,500

Shepherd av, e s, 365.9 n Ridgewood av, 17.2x102.7. Sebastian T. Hollister to Cornelia E. Reed. *Mt.* $1,600. 3,200

Stewart av, south cor 81st st, runs southeast 351.6 x southwest 100 x northwest 260 x southwest 92.6 x west 33 4 to 82d st, x northwest 45.5 to av, x northeast 200.6. }
Fort Hamilton av, north cor 81st st, runs northeast 172.6 x west 93.8 x southwest 54.8 x northwest 189.4 x west 81.7 x southwest 32.4 x northwest 112 to 6th av, x southwest 64.4 to 81st st, x southeast 308.1–. }
6th av, south cor 81st st, 92.5x74.5x69.5x105.9, New Utrecht. }
Holk D. Campbell to Joseph H. Templin, of Reading, Pa. 9,600

Stone av, e s, 50 s McDougal st, 50x100. William Larder and Elbert J. Osborne to Margaret J. Herbert. 1,650

St. Marks av, n s, 50 w Underhill av, 25x131. Thomas H. Robbins to William J. Hart. Q. C. nom

St. Marks av, n s, 300 w Underhill av, 0.6x52. Release mort. Richard W. Rhoades to William Gane. nom

Same property. Release mort. Same to same. nom

St. Marks av, n s, 225 w Underhill av. Party wall agreement. Walter C. Lincoln with Erick Soderstrom. 200

St. Marks av, n s, 300 w Underhill av. Party wall agreement. William Gane with Erick Soderstrom. 175

St Marks av, s s, 140 w Carlton av, runs south 7 x east 0.6 x south 45 x west 0.6 x south 79 x west 18.6 x north 131 to s s St. Marks av, x east 18.6. Elizabeth M. Y. wife of and Patrick J. Kennedy to August Werner, of Summit, N. J. 11,000

St. Marks av, n s, 100 e Albany av, 25x165.4x25x156.9. John Hickey exr. Michael Callahan to Ellen Beatty. 1,600

St. Marks av, n s, 150 w Underhill av, 25x131. William J. Hart to David J. Ramsdell. 7,250

Sumner av, w s, 22 s Pulaski st, 38.8x93, h & l. James Hood to Annie Derundean. *Mt.* $13,000. nom

Surf av, N. Y. & Coney Island R. R., land of C. Steubenbrod and centre line proposed West 21st st, Coney Island. John Y. McKane to Kenneth F. Sutherland. 2,000

Van Pelt av, n s, 25 e Monitor st, 25x83.3. William J. G. Bearns to Regine Zierien, New York. 6,500

Vernon av, s s, 360 w Throop av, 20x100. Robert H. Anderson to Annie wife of Joseph Cohen. *Mt.* $5,000. 10,000

Vernon av, n s, 365 w Lewis av, 60x100. Alethea M. wife of John J. Drake to William Battermann. *Mt.* $2,000. 4,500

Vienna av, n s, 80 e Atkins av, 20x100. William H. Jackson to Henrietta wife of William Kalt. 175

Vienna av, n e cor Shepherd av, 160x100. William H. Jackson to James G. Horn. 1,420

Washington av, e s, 128.5 s Park av, 20x100. John K. Sibley heir Rebecca Berry to Albert R. Berry. ⅓ part. nom

3d av, e s, 87.4 n 8th st, 22x95 9. Lizzie T. Grace to Charlotte A. Bierds. nom

3d av w s, 100.2 s 47th st, runs west 100 x north 50.2 x east 5 x north 25 x east 95 to 3d av, x south 75.2. David J. Tingley and ano. exrs. Margt. M. Van Pelt to Stephen Martin. 6,000

3d av, w s, 70.6 s 55th st, 14.6x100. Release judgment. John Canty to Mary A. Canty. nom

6th av, e s, 28 n 15th st, 28x98x26x97.10. Blanche S. wife of Saurin Durell, Francoise M. Vienot and Marie A. de St. Vanne to George O. Van Orden. 2,800

7th av, w s, 60 s 2d st, 20x80. George H. Doughty to George B. Stoutenburg and Charles F. Hunt. *Mt.* $8,000. exch

7th av, w s, 70 s 4th st, 30x88. John T. Fox to Theodore B. and Henry A. Willis. *Mt.* $14,044. nom

7th av, w s, 22 s 11th st, 20x43.3x—x43. Release mort. James Williamson to Isabella Brown. 1,000

Same property. Isabella wife of and William Brown to William C. O'Keeffe and James H. McKenna, of O'Keeffe & McKenna. 7,300

8th av, n w cor 11th st, 54.10x37.10. Phebe M. Clark et al. exrs. and trustees Henry L. Clark and Phebe M. Clark individ. to George Keller. 8,300

8th av, w s, extends from 1st st to Garfield pl, 200x92.10. Henry Franke to Edwin D. Phelps. exch

8th av, w s, 20 s 13th st, 16x85. Charlotte A. wife of and William H. Bierds to Lizzie T. Grace. *Mt.* $3,200. exch

10th av, n e cor 71st st, runs north 60 x east 100 x north 40 x east 20 x south 100 to 71st st, x west 120, New Utrecht. Fred. C. Cocheu to The Bay Ridge Park Improvement Co. *Mt.* $3,500. nom

10th av, n e cor 71st st, 60x100, New Utrecht. Bay Ridge Park Imp't Co. to Mamie M. Reynolds. *Mt.* $3,500. 5,000

11th av, south cor 75th st, 100x100. }
75th st, s w s, 100 s e 11th av, 60x100, New Utrecht. }
Franklin Allen to John H. Hanley. 1,400

13th av, n w s, extends from 73d st to 74th st, 200x100. }
74th st, n e s, 100 n w 13th av, 40x100, New Utrecht. }
Franklin Allen to George W. Hanley. 3,250

18th av, n w cor 74th st, 40x101.9x40x102.4, New Utrecht. John H. Hanley to William H. Pierson. 950

18th av, n e cor 75th st, runs northeast along av to Jane Roberts land, x northeast along same to w s 20th av, x southwest along same to 76th st, x northwest to 19th av, x northeast to 75th st, x northwest —, New Utrecht. Samuel S. Abbott to William C. and Charles G. Martin. nom

Same property. William D. Barnes, of New York, to Samuel S. Abbott. *Mt.* $36,760. nom

Bath plank road, w s, 128 n 58th st, 60x110, Bath Junction. James V. S. Woolley to Philip Waldheim, Hoboken, N. J. 1,050

Lot 197 block 4 map 597 lots of William Ziegler, Gravesend. William Ziegler to Joseph Marshall. 13

Lots 205 map No. 1, Fort Hamilton village.
Lot 404 map No. 3, Fort Hamilton village.
Walter O. Lewis to John C. Sanders, New York. B. & S. 50

Lots 215 and 216 block 4 map 597 lots property Wm. Ziegler, Gravesend. William Ziegler to Helen Maixner, of New York. 400

Lots 424-426 block 13 map 1,197 lots, Flatbush and New Utrecht, of W. Ziegler. Contract. William P. Reed & Co. to Mary De Vito. 1,170

Plot at Canarsie, adj Jas. Campbell, 50x50. Amanda M. Hockneil to James J. Ryder. 125

Lots 61 and 62 block B map Zabriskie homestead, Flatbush. William J. Kaiser, John H. Vanderveer and George W. Dalton to Charles L. Lang. 485

Lots 63, 64 and 65 same map. Same to Henry T. Meyer. 705

Lots 96 and 97 block 3 map 597 lots of W. Ziegler, Gravesend. William Ziegler to John D. Anderson. 250

Lots 98-102 block B map Zabriskie homestead, Flatbush. William J. Kaiser et al. to George Kerler and Amelia Kline. nom

Lots 66-70 block B same map. Same to Valentin Popp. nom

Lots 130-134 block C map Zabriskie homestead, Flatbush. William J. Kaiser, John H. Vanderveer and George W. Dalton to Benjamin Olbricht. nom

Lots 260-264 block 21 map 660 lots Effingham H. Nichols, New Utrecht. Effingham H. Nichols to Thomas J. Churchill. 1,025

Lots 273 and 274 block 5 map of W. Zieglers 597 lots, Gravesend. William Ziegler to Kate Brennen. 260

Lots 477 and 478 block 9 map of 597 lots of W. Ziegler, Gravesend. William Ziegler to Charles F. Schleussner. 300

Lots 523-527 block 10 map 597 lots of William Ziegler, Gravesend. William Ziegler to Thomas O'Connor. 1,525

Lots 541-544 block 10 map 597 lots Wm. Ziegler, Gravesend. William Ziegler to William Wharton. 2,600

Lot 9 block A map Zabriskie property, Flatbush. William J. Kaiser et al. to Henry Kidd. 240

Lot 9 on block A, also lots 61-70, 76-80 and 98-102 block B, also lots 130-134 block C, map Zabriskie homestead, Flatbush. Release mort. Jeremiah L., John L. and Lansing Zabriskie to William J. Kaiser, John H. Vanderveer and George W. Dalton. 5,100

Lots 76-80 block B map Zabriskie homestead, Flatbush. William J. Kaiser et al. to Clara A. Woolley. 715

Lots 51 and 52 block 2 map 597 lots of William Ziegler, Gravesend, William Ziegler to Theodore F. Quackenbush. 250

Lots 190-196 and 215-218 and 283-286 and 297-300 plot 2 map G. Stryker's heirs, Gravesend, excepting from above as follows:
Van Siclen st, w s, 124.3 s Av T, 80x98x82.6x118.4.
Sarah A. Storm to Sarah V. Van Brunt. B. & S. nom

Interior lot, 75 e Reid av and 25 s McDonough st, runs south 25 x east 5 x north 25 x west 5. Peter Nehrbass to Peter G. Muller. 50

Indeft. right of way, e s, adj Herberts line and land of J. T. Voorhies, 75x70, Hog Point, Gravesend. Albert V. B. Voorhies to Peter Finegan, Sheepshead Bay. 150

Declaration of identity by David S. Stewart who has been erroneously called David S. Steward in three deeds.

WESTCHESTER COUNTY.

NOVEMBER 11 TO 17—INCLUSIVE.

CORTLANDT.

Bradley, Mary A exr of, to Peter Hickey, w s Hadden st, 60x60. $1,400
Lawlor, Julia G to same, same property. 1,400
Catlin, Austin H. and ano. to Helen M. Husted, e s Simpson pl, 280.6 s Lafayette pl, 40x140. nom
McCord, Robt. to J. Murray McCoy and ano., s s Bay st, adj grantee, 60x130. 480

EASTCHESTER.

Allerton, Charlotte A. to Jean R. Stebbins, 180 on road to New Rochelle. exch. and nom
Campbell, Arch. M. to Helen T. Adams, e s Fulton av, 500 n Sidney, 819x155.4. 250
Cudlipp, Chas. to Effie S. Bowman, lot 59 w s Summit av, Chester Hill, 50x140. 2,300
Darling, Alf. B. and ano. to Jacob Haag, w s Park av, 150 n Prospect, 100x150. 3,000
Owen, Daniel to Edw. L. E. Phipps, lot 86 s e s Railroad av, West Mt. Vernon, 68.3x159. 1,150
Rosebault, Sarah W. to Jos. S. Wood, lot 71 n s Urban st, Villa Park. nom
Rothenhausler, Chas. to Conrad Wessel, s w s Mt. Vernon av, 50 n w Short st, 25x100. 3,000
Seeber, Sarah to Mt. Vernon Suburban Land Co, 8 acres on East Chester Creek, adj And. Purdy. 500
Schuler, Augusta and ano. to Elizh. Devermann, lots 169, 397 and s w ¾ 180 map West Mt. Vernon. 4,000
Tuckahoe Real Estate Co. to Chas. Dusenberry, Jr., n s Park pl, 329 w Pondfield road, 25x78. 300
Dusenberry, Chas., Jr., to Geo. Lattimer, same property. 2,000
Van Santvoord, John to Jesse Lantz, lot 96½ n w s Union st, West Mt. Vernon, 24x100. 2,300
Wheeler, John to Burr Davis and ano., lots 34, 35 and 36, Vernon Park. 2,000
Wood, Jos. S. to Wm. H. Treuer, lot 81 Villa Park. nom

GREENBURGH.

Conover, Wm. to John McManus, s s Ashford av, adj O. S. Bradley, abt 85x200. 1,300
Dobbs Ferry Land and Improvement Co. to John Theofel, lot 48 e s Fields st. 650
Elmsford Improvement Co. to Peter Benz, lots 36 and 38 block 19 Elmsford Park. nom
Same to Geo. E. Carpenter, lots 1-8 block 52. nom
Jones, Cyrus P. and ano. to C. Henry Mead, lots 114 and 115 Ardsley. 242
Yerks, Isaac to Mary E. Goddard, s e s road from Centreville to Town Cross roads, 1¼ acres. 1,000

HARRISON.

Field, Rich'd, exr. of, to Jas. L. Reynolds, part Steph. C. Griffen farm, East Mamaroneck av, abt 5 acres, 1,000
Same to Chas. Warren Parker, part same farm, bet old W. P. road and Mamaroneck av (part in Mamaroneck), 98 acres. 9,000
Parker, Chas. Warren to Edw. Burns, same property. *Mt.* $5,000. 5,000

MAMARONECK.

Larchmont Manor Co. to Harry A. Van Liew, n e cor Larchmont and Willow avs, 168x250. 5,042

MOUNT PLEASANT.

Bliss, Albert E. and ano. to Eliz'h R. Endriss, lot 3 w s Bedford road, grantor's map, 25x100. 155
Briggs, Amos S. to Abr. Levy, lots 4, 5, 35 and 36 w s Sleepy Hollow road, Briggsville, 50x200. nom
Smadbeck, Louis to Thos. McCabe, lots 1770, 1771 and 1772, Sherman Park. 425
Same to Gustav Johnson, lot 695. 140
Same to Maurice Blanckensee, lots 401, 402, 1871 and 1872. 500
Same to John Cunniff, lot 2247. 100
Same to Mary McCarthy, lots 1869 and 1870. 300
Same to Charlotte M. Hayden, lots 1966, 1967 and 1968. 300
Soltz, Arcadius to Abr. Saltzman, e s Lenox av, 450 n Broadway, Pleasantville Park, 50x100. 800
Van Cott, Anna M. to Sylvester See, e s Wheeler av, Pleasantville, abt 72x90. 1,250

NEW ROCHELLE.

Disbrow, Susan W. exr. of, to Gus. Mohr, n s Horton av, 200 w Brook st, 100x180. 550
Gregg, Jas. A. S. to Edw. F. Cain, lots 7 and 30 Highland Park, each 100x200. 4,500
Moulton, Eliza to The Women's Christian Temperance Union, s e cor Union av and Division st, abt 37x130. nom
Porter, Sarah M. to Francis C. Bone, lot 20 n s Morris st, map Porter estate, 50x150. 800

NORTH CASTLE.

Aldrich, Eliz'h W. to Eugenia B. Robbins, the "Sam'l B. Ferris" farm, 130 acres. exch and nom

OSSINING.

Adcock, John T. to Jemima Fowler, n s William st, adj Barney Foshay, 40x112. 975
Westchester Town Site Co. to Henry Wendling, lots 11 and 12 n e cor Highland and Maple avs, 50x102. 750

PELHAM.

Delcambre, Gracie M. to Carrie L. Larkin, lot 123 w s 3d st, Pelhamville, 100x100. 10,000
Prevost, Geo. A. to Benj. Collins trustee, s w cor Collins av and Pelham road, 100x200. 1,000
Stilwell, Celia A. et al., David Switz, Jr., ref., to Eugenia A. Penfield, lots 262 and 265, Pelhamville. 1,50

RYE.

Cragin, Lydia B. to Chas. W. Landon, n w cor Maple av and High st, 100x126. 275
Fagan, Michael to Henry Peters, n w cor Washington st and Purdy av, abt 103x130. 810
Merritt, Jas. S. and ano. to Ellen Cole, lot 40 w s Regent st, Washington Park, 50x100. 450

WESTCHESTER.

Coleman, Arthur to The Seneca Land Co., lots 2 and 4-39 map part Givan homestead. 12,260
Headen, Henrietta to Sarah Jackson, lot 222 n s 9th st, Unionport, 100x108. 500
Kendrick, Samuel to Mary A. Murray, lot 159 and strip adj s s 8th st, Unionport. 350
Kelly, Thos. to Rosanna Kelly, w s Av A, 100 s Elliott av, Schuylerville, 50x100. 300
Lorillard, Louis L. to Martin J. Keogh, lots 1313-1327 and 1332-1346 map Lorillard estate. 6,000
Mapes, John S. to Wm. Mackey, w s road to Unionport, 130 s Westchester av, 25x125. 1,400
Palmer, John J., exr. of, to Arthur Coleman, lots 1-39 map part Givan homestead. nom
Prescott, Thos., exr. of, to Eliz'h A. Diller, lots 691 and 732 s s 3d av, also G 95, Wakefield. 1,250
Schambrue, Auth. to Jos. Gertz, lot 537 s s 4th av, Wakefield, 100x114. 1,350
Volz, Eliz'h to Mary L. Judge, part lot 340 n s 12th st, Unionport, 50x108. nom
Watkins, Cath. to Jas. Wilson, lot 589 s s 15th av, Wakefield, 100x114. 900

WHITE PLAINS.

Cypher, Sarah O. and ano., J. B. Lockwood ref., to Timothy Dick, n s Lake st, 150 w Kensico av, 50x200. 1,700
McArdle, John H. Ida L. to Vandemark, lot 163 Hillside st, Fisher map, 50x125. 2,200
Quimby, Henry R. to Minnie A. Hodgson, e s Davis av, 565 s Old Post road, 100x150. nom

YONKERS.

Fowler, Isaac V., exrs. of, to Thos. C. O'Connor, w s Mile Square road, 25 acres. 35,000
Hubbard, Murray to John F. McMahon, lot 254 w s Ashburton av, 25x100. 350
Hartshorne, Frank O. to John W. Hauser, lots 60 and 60½ Hawthorne av, map Bechstein property. nom
Hauser, John W. to Evangeline Hartshorne, same. nom
Jardine, John to Gert. V. Jardine, e s Warburton av, 400 n Lamartine, 100x300, also e s Croton aqueduct, 70x60. nom
Jones, Cyrus P. and ano. to Mary Darrigan, lot 14 block D 270
Lowerre, Seaman to Margt. C. Doran, w s Western av, 111 n Randolph st, abt 27x130. 500
Nathan, Marcus to Geo. E. Ronan, lot 75 Sherwood Park, 25x112. nom
Owen, Harvey H. to Wm. Post, Nos. 9 and 11 n s Archer st, 50x90, also 6 and 8 s s Ingram st, 50x90. nom
Oakley, Elizh. S. to Ezra B. Fancher, n w cor Glenwood av and North Broadway, abt 150x260. 21,500
Parsells, Edw. W. to Edmond Chastagner and wife, w s Palmer av, 127.6 n Fort Field av, 75x175. 1,200
Same to John Frizell, w s same, 152 s same, 25x100. 300
Pardoe, Wm. A. to Irene R. Morris, No. 158 w s Hawthorne av, 256 s Herriot st, 31x115. nom
Sherwood Land Co. to Francis C. Cohn, lots 71 and 72. 1,600
Sewall, Wm. B. to Michael J. Phelan, lots 757-793, Glen Park. 11,000
Truman, Jas. C., Jr., to Jas. C. Truman, s s Hearst st, adj Railroad, 326x—, also lots 1 and 9 block 1, Napera Park. nom
Valentine, Clara M. to Lander Finegold, w s Bennett av, 175 n Summerfield st, 25x100. 325
Same to John G. Strub, e s Cook av, 250 s Summerfield st, 50x100. 500
Valentine, Nath. B. and ano. to Walter B. Peet, lots 32-39 and 65-72 grantors map. 8,950
Wall, Isabel A. to Matilda Grinnell, lots 151 and 153 w s Park Hill av, abt 50x170. 1,400

YORKTOWN.

Moses, Mary to Elmer T. Butter, 52 acres adj Jas. Palmer. 3,750
Raymond, Mary E. and ano. to Evelyn P. Roberts, n s Crumpond road, cor Hog lane, 103 acres. 9,500

MORTGAGES.

NOTE.—*The arrangement of this list is as follows. The first name is that of the mortgagor, the next that of the mortgagee. The description of the property then follows, then the date of the mortgage, the time for which it was given, and the amount. The general dates used as headings are the dates when the mortgage was handed into the Register's office to be recorded.*

Whenever the letters "P. M." occur, preceded by the name of a street, in these lists of mortgages, they mean that it is a Purchase Money Mortgage, and for fuller particulars see the list of transfers under the corresponding date. Whenever the rate is not given, read as 6 per cent.

NEW YORK CITY.

NOVEMBER 13, 14, 16, 17, 18, 19.

Averill, Parmelia M. D., Little Falls, N. Y., to Frederick L. Hart, Brooklyn. 76th st, n s, 95 e Madison av, 12.6x102.2. Nov. 14, due July 1, 1893. $1,600
Auerbach, Meyer and Addie his wife to Magdalena Leidenthal. 52d st, No. 432, s s, 400 w 9th av, 25x100.5. Nov. 16, 3 years. 4,200
Abels, Henry J. to The Twenty-fourth Ward Real Estate Assoc. Park View terrace. P. M. Oct. 20, due Nov. 12, 1894, 5 %. 950
Babcock, Charles H. to John McK. Camp. Kirkside av. P. M. Oct. 20, due Nov. 12, 1894, 5 %. 500
Baumbach, Ludwig J. to The Twenty-fourth Ward Real Estate Assoc. Travers st. P. M. Oct. 20, due Nov. 12, 1894, 5 %. 900
Birkmire, William H. to The Twenty-fourth Ward Real Estate Assoc. Kirkside av. P. M. Oct. 20, due Nov. 12, 1894, 5 %. 700
Black, Joseph to John L. Hamilton. 45th st, n s, 220 w 8th av, 20x100.5. Lease. Sept. 2, due May 1, 1893, or installs. 4,500
Bowman, Julius to THE FRANKLIN SAVINGS BANK. 41st st, s s, 100 w 8th av, 25x98.9. Nov. 19, 3 years, 5 %. 11,000
Brennan, Nellie F. to Edward Brenen and Catharine his wife. 7th av and 53d st. P. M. Nov. 19, due Mar. 1, 1892. 13,200
Blauvelt, Aurelia S., Nyack, N. Y., to Damase Burchard, Providence, R. I. 82d st. P. M. Nov. 14, due Nov. 17, 1894, 5 %. 10,000
Blauvelt, Charles to Charles Weinberg. West End av, n w cor 101st st, 75.11x100. Nov. 12, 1 year. 5,500
Becker, Jacob to Euphemia S. Coffin. 159th st, n s, 85 w Elton av. P. M. Nov. 16, 3 years, 5 %. 1,900
Same to same trustee Elizabeth Hogan. Same property Nov. 16, 3 years, 5 %. 400
Benjamin, Iva to Frederic J. Middlebrook. 29th st. P. M. Nov. 16, 3 years, 5 %. 12,000

Same to same. Same property. P. M. Nov. 16, 1 year. 2,000

Brooker, William E. to John J. Brady. Elmwood pl. P. M. Oct. 19, due Nov. 5, 1894, 5 %. 600

Browne, Lulu M. to THE CITY SAVINGS BANK of Brooklyn. 132d st. s s, 526.8 w 5th av, 16.8 x99.11. Nov. 14, due Nov. 1, 1892, 5 %. 5,000

Barron, Esther E. wife of Martin J. to Henry Steeger. 8th av, w s, 49.11 n 154th st, 25x 100. Nov. 13, 1 year. 1,000

Boyden, Otis W. to The Home Mutual Building and Loan Assoc. Crotona av, n s, 128.6 e Broad st, 25x90.10x25x89.11. Nov. 14, installs. 3,000

Bradbury, Flora I. wife of Charles to THE FARMERS' LOAN AND TRUST CO. 46th st, n s, 250 w 6th av. P. M. Nov. 2, 1 year, 5 %. 15,000

Same to same. 46th st, n s, 225 w 6th av, 25x 100.5. Nov. 2, 1 year, 5 %. 15,000

Same to Thomas Ogle. 46th st, n s, 225 w 6th av. P. M. Sub. to mort. $15,000. Nov. 2, 3 years, 5 %. 1,500

Same to same. 46th st, n s, 250 w 6th av. P. M. 2d mort. Nov. 2, 3 years, 5 %. 1,500

Bradburn, Thomas to Clara Hopps. 175th st, s w cor 11th av, 25x65. Nov. 13, 3 years. 1,500

Bradley & Currier Co. (Lim.) with George Crawford both mortgagees and Duncan C. McKinlay mortgagor. Agreement as to priority of morts. made by said McKinlay. Oct. 14. nom

Braender, Frederick to Judson S. Todd. 108d st, s s, 101.6 e Lexington av, 4 lots, each 27x 100.11. 4 morts., each $13,900. Nov. 11, due May 1, 1892. 55,600

Same to Lewis Z. Bach. Same property. P. M. Sub. to morts. $55,600. Nov. 11, 1 year, 5 %. 15,900

Broderick, John F. to Daniel Fitzpatrick. Hawkstone st. P. M. Nov. 7, 1 year. 2,000

Brown, Robert I. to Marianna C. Cobb. 145th st, s s, 42 e Edgecombe av, 18x99.11. Nov. 9, 3 years. 3,000

Barnum, Robert D. to THE HARLEM SAVINGS BANK. 169th st. n s, 151 w Union av, runs northeast 70 x east 26 x northeast 45 x south 63 to av, x south 80 to st, x west 90 to beginning, except part taken for widening st. Nov. 18, 1 year, 5 %. 9,000

Blume, Frank A. to THE HARLEM SAVINGS BANK. 167th st, n s, 25 e Simpson st, 25x90. Nov. 18, 1 year, 5 %. 1,600

Bryson, Eliza T. widow to Cornelius N. Hoagland, Brooklyn. 82d st, n s, 538 e 10th av, 19 x102.2. Oct. 20, due Nov. 1, 1894, 5 % gold. 15,000

Brown, Henry H. to The American Surety Co. Fordham av, n w cor Monroe st, 108.2x64.6x 108.2x68; North 3d av, n w cor 167th st, 49.6 x87.7x49.6x68.6. Nov. 14. Secures surety to indemnity bond in penal sum of $20,000.

Campbell, John V. to Mary L. Barbey. Eldridge st, No. 55, w s, 25.2x101x25x101. Nov. 18, 5 years, 5 %. gold, 27,500

Clark, Patrick to Eugene and Ida Underhill exrs. Emily Underhill. Washington av, No. 833, n w s, 74.2 n e 159th st, 27.1x100. Nov. 17, 1 year, 5½ %. 500

Cohen, Meyer to Reuben Grunauer. Hester st, No. 51, n s, 21.10x46.8x21.10x46.6. ½ part. Nov. 16, 4 months. 500

Carr, George E., Reuben W. and Francis H. to Joseph F. Goble as guard., &c., Freehold, N. J. 165th st, n s, 200 e Railroad av, 80x100x 80x—. Nov. 11, 3 years, 5 %. 1,500

Cary, Mary to Thomas D. Mason and ano. trustees Sidney Mason. 117th st, n s, 152.4 w Av A, 16.8x100.11. Nov. 18, 3 years, 5 %. gold, 6,000

Casey, William J. to Sarah A., Mary E. and Emma L. Willet and Martha J. Wooster. 87th st. P. M. Oct. 15, 1 year, 5 %. 10,000

Coffin, Euphemia S. wife of and Edmund, Jr., to THE UNITED STATES TRUST CO. of New York. Amsterdam (10th) av, w s, 25.6 s 77th st, runs west 90 x north 25.6 to 77th st, x west 25 x south 102.2 x east 25 x north 51.1 x east 90 to av, x north 25.6; Amsterdam (10th) av, s w cor 77th st, 25.6x90. Nov. 13, due Nov. 1, 1894, 5 %. 30,000

Conlon, Margaret E., Brooklyn, to Francis J. Conlon, Brooklyn. 114th st, s s, 120 w 5th av, 125x100.11. Nov. 9, due Nov. 1, 1893, 5 %. 14,000

Conover, James S. to Alfred C. Cheney trustee. 25th st, s s, 400 e 11th av, 75x98.9. Sept. 26, 6 months 60,000

Cornet, William H to John Murray and Jeremiah Reid, Brooklyn. 54th st, n s, 150 w 10th av, 25x100.5. Nov. 13, installs. 1,512

Cornet, William H. and Mary A. his wife to Mark Goodwin. 54th st, n s, 150 w 10th av, 25x100.5. Nov. 13, note. 2,013

Cahen, James P. and Julius P. to THE NEW YORK LIFE INS. AND TRUST CO. 10th av, w s, 75.5 s 50th st, 25x75. Nov. 5, 3 years, 4½ %. 4,250

Same to same. 10th av, w s, 50.5 s 50th st, 25x 75. Nov. 5, 3 years, 4½ %. 4,250

Clark, Bernard S. mortgagor with Jonas B. Kissam, Fairfield, Conn., mortgagee. Extension of mort. Oct. 31. nom

Cohen, Bernard to Frederic J. Middlebrook. Morton st. P. M. Nov. 10, 1 year, 5 %. 10,000

Connell, Eugene T. to Anna Jerzmanowski. Madison av. P. M. Nov. 4, due Nov. 16, 1894, 5 %. 23,000

Cunningham, James to Morris Franklin, Fanny M. Updike and Henry B. Wesselman. Lewis st. P. M. May 1, 1891, 6 months. 4,350

Same to same. Same property. July 15. 10,000

Caldwell, Jennie to Catharine A. Cemmann. 90th st. P. M. Nov. 12, 9 months, 5 %. 62,000

Carroll, John to Rebecca wife of Jeremiah Lennon. Bethune st, s s, 55 e Washington st, 20x60x20x—. Nov. 16, due Jan. 1, 1898, 5 %. 3,000

Connolly, Dermott J. and Martin Bolter to Peter Doelger. 2d av, No. 1512. Store lease. Nov. 14, demand. 565

Cain, Joseph H. to THE TITLE GUARANTEE AND TRUST CO. 22d st. P. M. Nov. 19, 3 years, 5 %. 25,000

Campbell, Murdock F. to The Twenty-fourth Ward Real Estate Assoc. Kirkside av. P. M. Oct. 20, due Nov. 12, 1894, 5 %. 260

Crawford, Alfred A. to The Twenty-fourth Ward Real Estate Assoc. Kirkside av. P. M. Oct. 20, due Nov. 12, 1894, 5 %. 600

Same to same. Wellesley st. P. M. Oct. 20, due Nov. 12, 1894, 5 %. 1,200

Cronin, Charles H. to John McK. Camp. Kirkside av. P. M. Oct. 20, due Nov. 12, 1894, 5 %. 400

Curley, Anna D. to Sophia M. Riedemann. Morris av. P. M. Nov. 17, 3 years, 4 %. 2,000

Coughlin, John F. to Rose Sheridan. Madison st, s s, 92 w Montgomery st, 23x100. Nov. 9, 1 year. See Conveys. 6,000

Demarest, Augusta to Mary A. Gwyer and ano. exrs. and trustees Christopher Gwyer. 38th st, s s, 140 w 6th av, 20x98.9. Nov. 18, 1 year, 5 %. 20,000

Dailey, Frank C. to Morris S. Thompson. West st, s e cor Charles st, 44.9x70x43.1x 81.11, Nos. 403 and 404 West st. Nov. 11, due July 16, 1893, 5 %. 1,400

Dixon, Jr., Thomas to Increase M. Grenell. 94th st, No. 61 W. P. M. Nov. 14, due Aug. 15, 1894. 6,500

Drevet, Albertine wife of Ernest to Anna K. Adams. Sedgwick av, n w s, 416.7 n e Perot st, 49x84.4x43.4x92.10. Nov. 17, 3 years. 1,000

Dreyfus, Julius to Mary L. Hall guard. of Edward L., Edith L. and Maud L. Hall. 63d st, No. 415, n s, 231.2 e 1st av. P. M. Nov. 17, due Dec 1, 1896, 5 %. 8,000

Same to THE LAWYERS' TITLE INS. CO. of New York. 63d st, No. 417, n s, 256.2 e 1st av. P. M. Nov. 17, due Dec. 1, 1896, 5 %. 8,000

Same to The Society for the Relief of Poor Widows with Small Children. 63d st, No. 419, n s, 281.4 e 1st av. P. M. Nov. 17, due Dec. 1, 1896, 5 %. 8,000

Diller, William E. to THE METROPOLITAN LIFE INS. CO. of New York. 75th st, s s, 127 w Central Park West, 22x102.2. Nov. 17, due Oct. 1, 1894. 30,000

Same to same. 75th st, s s, 149 w Central Park West, 22x102.2. Nov. 17, due Oct. 1, 1894. 31,000

Same to same. 75th st, s s, 171 w Central Park West, 22x102.2. Nov. 17, due Oct. 1, 1894. 31,000

Same to same. 75th st, s s, 193 w Central Park West, 22x102.2. Nov. 17, due Oct. 1, 1894. 30,000

Same to same. 75th st, s s, 215 w Central Park West. 3 lots, each 20x102.2. 3 morts., each $28,000. Nov. 17, due Oct. 1, 1894. 84,000

Davis, Samuel to THE FARMERS' LOAN AND TRUST CO. Rivington st, n w cor Attorney st, 25x100. Nov. 16, due Nov. 18, 1894, 5 %. 35,000

De Marco, Celestino mortgagor with George M. Miller trustee for Sarah E. Lanier mortgagee. Extension of mort. Nov. 17. nom

Dougherty, William A. C. to THE EMIGRANT INDUST. SAVINGS BANK. 35th st, s s, 300 w 1st av, 25x100. Nov. 16, 1 year, 4½ %. 10,000

Dunn, John and David to James P. Kernochan and John J. Wysong as trustees. 87th st, n s, 154 w West End av, 18x100.8. Nov. 17, 3 years, 5 %. 16,000

Same to same. 87th st, n s, 172 w West End av, 18x100.8. Nov. 17, 3 years, 5 %. 16,000

Same to same. 87th st, n s, 207 w West End av, 18x100.8. Nov. 17, 3 years, 5 %. 16,000

Same to Howard and Maria H. Beck. 87th st, n s, 119 w West End av, 18x100.8. Nov. 17, 3 years, 5 %. 16,000

Same to Marie L. de Agreda. 87th st, n s, 187 w West End av, 17x100.8. Nov. 17, 5 years, 5 %. 15,000

Same to same. 87th st, n s, 190 w West End av, 17x100.8. Nov. 17, 5 years, 5 %. 15,000

De Mott, William to The Twenty-fourth Ward Real Estate Assoc. Kirkside av. P. M. Oct. 20, due Nov. 12, 1894, 5 %. 775

Desseye, George to The Twenty-fourth Ward Real Estate Assoc. Kirkside av, e s, 228.8 s Wellesley st. 4 lots. 4 P. M. morts., each $500. Oct. 20, due Nov. 12, 1894, 5 %. 2,000

Dreyer, Isaac to THE TITLE GUARANTEE AND TRUST CO. 17th st. P. M. Nov. 10, 3 years, 5 %. 8,500

Ettinger, Raphael to Maria Richard. Lexington av and 94th st. P. M. Oct. 28, 3 years, 5 %. 11,500

Etzel, Albert and Emanuel Kronacher to Mary Harrison. Morton st. P. M. Nov. 16, due Nov. 1, 1894, 5 %. 5,500

Eschwei, George F. to Henry J. Fischer. Bradhurst av, s e cor 143d st, 100.6x79.4x99.11x68. Nov. 16, 1 year. 3,000

Early, John to Thomas Plunkett. Elizabeth st. P. M. Nov. 16, 3 years, 5 %. 13,000

Farrington, Isabella D. to THE MUTUAL LIFE INS. CO. of New York. 20th st, n s, 290 e 2d av, 20x92. 2d mort. Nov. 14, 1 year, 5 %. 500

Fay, Michael and William Stacom to George B. Goldschmidt trustee Samuel B. H. Judah. Essex st, No. 62, e s, 100 n Grand st, 25x100. Nov. 14, 3 years, 5 %. 30,000

Fechtman, L. Foreman mortgagor with Pauline K. Schrenkeisen formerly Schneider mortgagee. Extension of mort. Nov. 11. nom

Fairchild, Clara to John J. Brady. Clinton av. P. M. Oct. 19, due Nov. 5, 1894, 5 %. 1,400

France, Edward E. to Mary J. Norman. Buchanan pl, n s, 150 e Grand av, 25x100. Nov. 14, 3 years. 1,000

Finn, James and Jennie his wife to The Twenty-fourth Ward Real Estate Assoc. Creston av. P. M. Oct. 20, due Nov. 12, 1894, 5 %. 580

Fitzpatrick, John J. and Philip A. to James McCreery. 106th st, n s, 175 w Madison av, 25x100. Nov. 16, 1 year, 5 %. See Conveys. 18,000

Fort, Alfred to Pierre Benoist. 19th st, No. 128 W., s s, 25x100. July 1, 5 years, 5 %. 7,000

Same to Henri Poujol. Same property. Equal lien with last mort. July 1, 3 years, 5 %. 3,000

Freystadt, Caroline A. to The Twenty-fourth Ward Real Estate Assoc. Park View terrace. P. M. Oct. 20, due Nov. 12, 1894, 5 %. 1,000

Ginsburg, Isaac to Camilla H. A. Keller, Port Richmond, S. I. Canal st, No. 47, n s, 66.10 e Orchard st, 24.4x50x24.3x50. Nov. 17, installs. 3,000

Gordon, Louis to Emily Cook. Madison st, No. 254, s s, 52.6 w Clinton st, 25x90. Nov. 19, due Sept. 3, 1893. 5,000

Goodman, Marcus to Lizzie W. Johnson, Yonkers, N. Y. 46th st. Leasehold. P. M. Nov. 17, due April 14, 1894. 4,250

Gerber, Kate widow to Sara M. Foster. Delancey st, No. 118, n s, 25 e Essex st, 25x50.11 x25x51. Nov. 17, 5 years, 5 %. 11,000

Griffiths, William to Matthew Farrell. 109th st, n s, 167.6 w 4th av, 43.9x100.11. Nov. 13, 1 year. 1,000

Gibbes, Adeline M., Marietta, Ga., to Charles J. Baker. Hudson st, w s, 126 n Hubert st, 25x100. Nov. 9, due Nov. 15, 1892. 1,500

Gent, Louis A. to Henry Schiffer. 94th st, n s, 180 e 3d av, 50x100.8. Nov. 17, 1 year. 6,000

Gueli, Mary E. to THE HARLEM SAVINGS BANK. 119th st, No. 509 E. Nov. 18, 1 year, 5 %. See Conveys. 2,500

Hartwell, Louise M. to John Barber, Philadelphia, Pa. Convent av, w s, 39.11 n 143d st, 20x100. Sub. to mort. $18,000. Nov. 17, due Feb., 1892. 5,000

Holden, Phoebe E. wife of Edward H. to Mary J. Radway. Cauldwell av, e s, at junction Boston av, runs northeast 14.6 x east 117.3 x south 30 x west 125 to Cauldwell av, x northeast 17.8, also land in front to centre of Cauldwell av; Trinity av, w s, adj above on rear, 20x100. Nov. 18, 3 years, 5 %. 6,500

Howell, Emma P. mortgagor with Louis Schneider exr. Anna Schwarz mortgagee. Extension of mort. Nov. 16. nom

Hicks, Margaret wife of and Thomas P. to Robert Courtright. Washington av, w s, 48 n 6th st, 24x150. Sept. 30, 2 years. 1,100

Hicks, Margaret wife of Thomas P. and Mary Kramer widow to Lucy R. Comfort. Worth av. P. M. Nov. 16, 3 years, 5½ %. 4,000

Hamilton, George J. to William Gillilan, London, Eng. 96th st, s s, 154.8 e 3d av, 27x 100.8. Nov. 1, 3 years, 5 %. 15,000

Same to William Gillilan exr. Edward H. Gillilan. 96th st, s s, 181.3 e 3d av, 27.8x100.8. Nov. 1, 3 years, 5 %. 15,000

Held, Philipp A. to THE GERMAN SAVINGS BANK, New York. 87th st, No. 339, n s, 300 e 9th av, 25.4x98.9. Nov. 12, due Nov. 13, 1892. 3,000

Hogenauer, Alphonse to THE GERMAN SAVINGS BANK, New York. Barrow st, No. 54, n s, 65 e Bedford st, 25.5x98.4x25x96.6. Nov. 12, due Nov. 13, 1892. 18,000

Hyman, Nathan and Benjamin Tannenbaum to Max Tannenbaum. Willett st, No. 58, e s, 150 n Delancey st. Lease. P. M. Nov. 1, 1 year. 3,000

Hey, George to Rosina Hurd. Railroad av. P. M. Nov. 16, 5 years, installs, 5 %. 20,000

Hill, George H. B. to THE WASHINGTON TRUST CO., New York, committee Martha Green. 7th av. P. M. Nov. 16, 1 year, 4½ %. 50,000

Hoffmann, Michael A. to Christina Hornung. 87th st, s s, 150 e West End av, 50x100.8. Nov. 14, due Jan. 1, 1897, 5 %. 10,000

Hohmann, Henry and Martha his wife to John Paul. Courtlandt av, w s, 75 n 15?th st, 25x 100.4. Oct. 1, 3 years, 5½ %. 5,000

Holmes, John F. to The Produce Exchange Building and Loan Assoc., New York. 165th st, No. 844, s s, 181.10 w Trinity av, 18.3x120.6. Nov. 7, installs. 6,000

Hart, Flora wife of Henry to Marcus Levison. Lexington av, w s, 51.2 s 102d st, 16.7x75. All title. Nov. 2, 1 year, 5 %. 300

Hershfield, Jennie wife of Samuel to Isabella Schweizer widow. 48th st. P. M. Nov. 16, due Nov. 15, 1894, 5 % and 6 %. 3,000

Hahn, Louis C. to The Twenty-fourth Wrad Real Estate Assoc. Kirkside av. P. M. Oct. 20, due Nov. 12, 1894, 5 %. 775

Harlow, Carrie V. to The Twenty-fourth Ward Real Estate Assoc. Park View terrace. P. M. Oct. 20, due Nov. 12, 1894, 5 %. 500

Hartley, Mary L. to The Twenty-fourth Ward Real Estate Assoc. Creston av. P. M. Oct. 20, due Nov. 12, 1894, 5 %. 345

Henderson, James to Henry B. Barnes. 122d st, s s, 202 w 3d av, 26.3x70.3x26.3x71.4. Nov. 19, 3 years, 5 %. gold, 15,000

Hill, Thomas to The Twenty-fourth Ward Real Estate Assoc. Kirkside av. P. M. Oct. 20, due Nov. 12, 1894, 5 %. 550

Hughes, Robert to THE TWELFTH WARD SAVINGS BANK. 126th st, No. 143, n s, 360 w 3d av, 25x99.11. Nov. 18, 1 year, 5 %. 6,000

Hughes, Theresa wife of and Robert to Adelia A. Bunnell. 125th st, No. 327, n s, 320 w 1st av, 20x99.11. Nov. 18, 3 years, 5 %. 4,000

Hyland, William H. to Conrad Stein. Park row, No. 156. Lease. Nov. 14, demand. 7,900

Jentes, Adolph and Henry mortgagors with Charles Rensch mortgagee. Extension of mort. Oct. 30. nom

Jones, Edward L. to Frances Emack, Baldwins, L. I. Greenwich av, No. 22, e s, 31.4 n West 10th st, runs north 15.4 x east 60.8 x south 5.9 x southwest 20.5 x west 41.2. All title. Nov. 12, 1 year. 600

Janeway, Hugh H. to Sarah R. N. wife of Willard P. Voorhees, New Brunswick, N. J. City Hall pl, No. 6, and No. 20 Centre st, begins Centre st, s e s, 12.8 s w Reade st, 41.7x85.3 to City Hall pl, x23.10x55.4. Nov. 18, due May 1, 1893. 1,000

Judge, Andrew T. to Henry Nobel. 132d st, s s, 460 w 5th av, 50x99.11. Sub. to morts. $35,900. ——, due May 17, 1892. 2,500

Same to Harold Brown, Newport, R. I. Same property. Nov. 17, due May 3, 1892, 5 %. See Conveys. 14,500

Same to The Bradley & Currier Co. (Lim.) Same property. Sub. to morts $32,500. Nov. 17, 6 months. 3,400

Same to George F. Johnson. Same property. Nov. 17, due May 3, 1892, 5 %. 18,000

Jordan, William G. to Benjamin F. Coben. 26th st. P. M. Sub. to morts. $24,500. Oct. 30, due July 1, 1892. 18,800

Same to same. Same property. Sub. to morts. $43,300. Oct. 30, due July 1, 1892. 22,000

Koebler, Charles H. and Henrietta his wife to Magdalena Frey. Av A, w s, 45.6 n 6th st. 22.8x100. Lease. Nov. 14, due Nov. 15, 1894, or installs, 5 %. 4,000

Krakower, Tobias to Morris Goldstein. Henry st, n s, 46.6 e Clinton st, 22.6x85. Nov. 10, due May 1, 1892. 5,000

Kenny, George J. and William J. to John B. Green. 24th st. P. M. Nov. 16, 3 years, 5 %. 2,000

Kidd, Harry L., Jamaica, L. I., to Lewis Morris. 142d st, s s. Nov. 16, demand. See Conveys. gold, 25,000

Same to same. Same property. Nov. 16, demand. gold, 3,000

Kuehnel, Adolf to Sophie M. Bach. Av C, e s, 175 s 161st st, 25x169.6. Nov. 16, 5 years, 5 %. 2,150

Same to same. Av C, e s, 200 s 161st st, 25x169.6. Nov. 16, 5 years, 5 %. 2,150

Keegan, Timothy mortgagor with Merritt Trimble trustee of George T. Trimble dec'd mortgagee. Extension of mort. Nov. 1. nom

Kantrowitz, Nathan to Samuel Kempner. 52d st, s s, 57.6 e 4th av, 19.2x79.5. P. M.; 113th st, No 353, n s, 100 w 1st av, 16.8x100.10. Nov. 16, installs. 500

Kaufman, Henrietta wife of and Herman to THE DRY DOCK SAVINGS INST. 74th st, No. 156, s s, 288.9 w 3d av, 18.9x102.2. Nov. 18, due Nov. 20, 1892, 5 %. 8,000

Keiser, Henry and Otilia his wife to Jacob Keiser. 3d st, No. 164, s s, 169.6 e Av A, 24.9x105.11. Aug. 19, due Jan. 1, 1895, 5 %. 4,000

Kenny, Arthur to Maurice Walsh. 112th st, n s, 175 e Lenox av, 75x100.11. Sub. to mort. $10,000. Nov. 17, 1 year. 2,500

Kervan, Matthew C. and Charles mortgagors with Charles Meyerhoff mortgagee. Extension of mort. Nov. 13. nom

Kennagh, William H. to The Twenty-fourth Ward Real Estate Assoc. Wellesley st and Kirkside av. P. M. Oct. 20, due Nov. 12, 1894, 5 %. 525

Klingenstein, Henry to THE UNITED STATES TRUST CO. of New York. Bowery, No. 109, e s, 20.7x105x20.10x103.8; Bowery, e s, abt 150 n Hester st, 20.10x100. Nov. 13, due Mar. 1, 1893, 5 %. 18,000

Kremer, W. P. to John H. Rhoades et al. trustees Benjamin F. Wheelwright. 25th st, s s, 225 e 8th av, 15x98.9. Nov. 19, due Dec. 1, 1894, 5 %. 7,500

Laugenbahn, Julius to THE GERMAN SAVINGS BANK, New York. 7th st. P. M. Nov. 19, 1 year. 10,000

Lee, William H. to Meyer Auerbach. 97th st. P. M. Nov. 16, due Nov. 1, 1892. 1,500

Leggat, William A. to John T. Lewis et al. trustees for Cornelia L. Fowler. 6th av, n e cor West Washington pl, 22x60x26x60. Nov. 19, 3 years, 5 %. See Conveys. 17,000

Same to Frederic J. Middlebrook, Brooklyn. 19th st, s s, 170 e 8th av, 20x93.8. Nov. 19, 1 year, 5 %. See Conveys. 7,000

Levy, Abraham I. to Baruch Franck. Essex st. P. M. Nov. 19, due Nov. 1, 1895. 2,000

Same to same. Same property. P. M. Nov. 19, due July 1, 1892. 1,000

Same mortgagor with William Ehlers mortgagee. Extension of mort. Nov. 19. nom

Same with same. Extension of mort. Nov. 19. nom

Lincoln, Mary R. to The Twenty-fourth Ward Real Estate Assoc. Park View terrace. P. M. Oct. 20, due Nov. 12, 1894, 5 %. 1,913

Lowen, Charles and Edward F. Halliday to George Young. 35th st, s s, 150 e 7th av, 25x98.9. Nov. 19, 3 years. gold, 30,000

Same to same. 35th st, s s, 175 e 7th av, 25x98.9. Nov. 19, 3 years. gold, 30,000

Levy, Louis to Frederick Krutina. 58th st. P. M. Nov. 17, due Oct. 26, 1894, 5 %. 10,000

Lipovitz, Max to Louis Goodman. Madison st. P. M. Sept. 28, installs. 6,200

Levy, David M. to Matilda Michaelis, Brooklyn. Columbus av and 98th st. P. M. Sub. to morts. Nov. 16, installs. 3,000

Leard, Thomas H. to Benjamin W. Wimans et al, exrs. and trustees William W. Wimaus. Park av, e s, 98 s 92d st, 18x89. Nov. 17, 3 years, 5 %. 12,000

Lewis, Edward to Lillie H. Duryee. Union av, e s, 108 n 165th st, 108x175. Nov. 17, 5 years. 6,500

Lynch, Lawrence with Rebecca Lennon both mortgagees. Agreement as to priority of mortgages made by Wilson Reid and John Carroll. Nov. 16. nom

Laufersweiler, Franz and Susannah his wife to Simon Haberman. 27th st, n s, 225 w 10th av, 50x98.9. Nov. 13, due Dec. 16, 1891. 500

Levy, Meyer to Henry Posinsky. Henry st, s s, 23.9 e Clinton st, 23.6x90, with use of alley in rear. Nov. 12, 3 months. 300

Licciardi, Antonio to Bernheimer & Schmid. 108th st, s s, 175 w 2d av, 25x100.11. Nov. 13, demand. 1,000

Laimbeer, John to Daniel K. De Beixedon, Brooklyn. 50th st, n s, 127.6 e 8th av, 33.9x100.5. Nov. 16, 3 years. gold, 7,000

Levy, Simon, Seabright, N. J., to Jonas Weil and Bernhard Mayer. Cherry st. P. M. Sub. to mort. $20,000. Nov. 16, installs. 9,500

Lichtenstein, Alexander to THE TITLE GUARANTEE AND TRUST CO Av D, s w cor 10th st, 50x93; 10th st, s s, 93 w Av D, 25x92.3; interior lot, 72 s 10th st and 73 w Av D, runs west 20 x south 22 x east 20 x north 22; 10th st, s s, 118 w Av D, 21x92.3; 10th st, s s, 139 w Av D, 1.4x92.3; interior lot, 92.3 s 10th st and 93 w Av D, runs south 1.9 x west 25 x north 1.9 x east 25; Av D, No. 139, w s, 72 s 10th st, 22x73. Nov. 16, 3 years, 5 %. See Conveys 45,000

Leaman, Alice P. wife of and Walter L. mortgagors with Nellie A. Crossman widow. Extension of mort. Oct. 23. nom

Marks, Hanna wife of Bennett to Sebastian Kerner and Mary his wife. 63d st, n s, 131 e 1st av, 25x100.5. Nov. 16, 5 years, 5 %. 8,000

Mars, Henrietta A., Brooklyn, to Charles Johnson. 152d st, n s, lots 2, 3 and 4 map of East Morrisania, contains 6 72-100 acres. Oct. 19, due Dec. 22, 1891. 2,050

Same to Mitchel Levy. Same property. Nov. 13, due Dec. 28, 1891. 1,000

McFarland, Joseph to George A. Stearns, Long Island City. 24th st, n s, 271.7 e 9th av, 26.1x98.9x25.11x98.9. Sub. to mort. $25,000. Nov. 2, 1 year. 2,000

Same to Thomas J. Short. 24th st, n s, 323.10 e 9th av, 26.1x98.9x26.3x98.9. Sub. to mort. $25,000. Nov. 2, 1 year. 8,296

McInnes, Archibald to Almira J. Brown, Milburn, N. J. Cortlandt st, No. 67, s s, 72.9 e Washington st, 23.8x77.3x19.4x77.1. Sub. to mort. $30,000. Nov. 16, due July 15, 1894, 5 %. gold 10,000

McInnes, Archibald mortgagor with Almira J. Brown, Milburn, N. J., mortgagee. Extension of mort. Nov. 16. nom

McCafferty, Mary E. wife of and Thomas F. and Joseph T. Mooney to Nathan L. Ely and ano. exrs. Nathan C. Ely. Lexington av, w s, 67.7 n 106th st, 16.8x75. Nov. 13, due Nov. 1, 1896, 5 %. 6,000

McDonald, Sarah to Eliza Dean. 31st st, s s, 420 w 8th av, 20x98.9. Nov. 17, due May 17, 1894, 5 %. 6,000

McCahill, Ellen M. to Thomas J. McCahill and ano. trustees Bryan McCahill. 118th st, n s, 100 e 3d av. P. M. Nov. 16, 3 years, 4 %. 2,500

McKenna, Charles F. to THE MUTUAL LIFE INS. CO., New York. 10th av, s w cor 141st st, 99.11x100. Nov. 17, 1 year. 12,000

Moss, Octavia A. to Mary H. Curtiss widow. 30th st. P. M. Oct. 29, due Nov. 2, 1894, 5 %. 20,000

Martin, Andrew to THE MUTUAL LIFE INS. CO. of New York. Monroe st, Nos. 51 and 53, n s, 137.2 e Market st, 50x100. Nov. 13, 1 year, 5 %. 17,000

Mermillod, Alphonse to THE HARLEM SAVINGS BANK. 166th st s s, 150 w Amsterdam av, 25x99.6x25.4x103.6. Nov. 9, 1 year, 5 %. 3,000

Moore, James to Joseph Hanlon. 2d av, e s, 47.2 s 20th st, 22.2x90. Nov. 14, 1 year. 800

Muhlebach, Joseph to Helene Ahrensbeumer. 151st st. P. M. Nov. 14, 2½ years, 5 %. 4,350

Mahoney, James D. to The Twenty-fourth Ward Real Estate Assoc. Park View terrace. P. M. Oct. 20, due Nov. 12, 1894, 5 %. 500

Mallahan, Susan M. to The Twenty-fourth Real Estate Assoc. Jerome av. P. M. Oct. 20, due Nov. 12, 1894, 5 %. 1,000

Mathews, William J., Yonkers, N. Y., to Newman Cowen. 88th st, n e cor Madison av, 36.8x100.8. Nov. 18, 6 months. 3,000

McCabe, Eliza to The Twenty-fourth Ward Real Estate Assoc. Creston av. P. M. Oct. 20, due Nov. 12, 1894, 5 %. 215

McClenahan, James, Harrison, N. Y., to Adelia Brown et al. exrs. Joseph T. Brown. 35th st, Nos. 526, 528 and 530, and 37th st, No. 529, begins 38th st, s s, 350 w 10th av, runs west 75 x south 197.6 to 37th st, x east 25 x north 98.9 to centre line of block, x east 50 x north 98.9 to beginning. Nov. 15, 3 years, 5 %. 20,000

McGirr, Robert J. to William Hall's Sons. 84th st, s s, 91 e Amsterdam av, 84x102.2. Nov. 18, due Feb. 19, 1892. 5,000

Mendes, Henry P. to Constance H. Lyons. 23d st, No. 126, s s, 249 w 6th av, 26x98.9. Nov. 19, note. 5,000

Mesick, Frank B. to The Twenty-fourth Ward Real Estate Assoc. Kirkside av. P. M. Oct. 20, due Nov. 12, 1894, 5 %. 940

Monks, William C. to The Twenty-fourth Ward Real Estate Assoc. Creston av and Wellesley st. P. M. Oct. 20, due Nov. 12, 1894, 5 %. 1,000

Moore, George W. to The Twenty-fourth Ward Real Estate Assoc. Creston av. P. M. Oct. 20, due Nov. 12, 1894, 5 %. 600

Moore, Lewis mortgagee with C. Adelbert Becker mortgagor. Extension of mort. at increased interest. Nov. 18. nom

Man, Mary E. to The Twenty-fourth Ward Real Estate Assoc. Kingsbridge road and Kirkside av. P. M. Oct. 20, due Nov. 12, 1894, 5 %. 1,000

Mosher, Caroline R. to The Twenty-fourth Ward Real Estate Assoc. Creston av. P. M. Oct. 20, due Nov. 12, 1894, 5 %. 575

Mount, Henry R. to THE BOWERY SAVINGS BANK 72d st, s s, 163 e 1st av, 25x102.2. Nov. 19, 1 year, 4½ %. 13,000

Nauss, Edward to Robert B. Merritt. 3d st. P. M. Nov. 18, 3 years. 1,250

Nobis, Agnes to Pauline M. Procter. Spencer pl, n w s, lots 246 and 247 amended map of Central Mott Haven, 50x60.6x50.2x65. Oct. 29, 1 year. 250

Nicoll, Mary A. to THE TITLE GUARANTEE AND TRUST CO. 122d st. P. M. Nov. 16, 2 years, 4½ %. 8,000

Noble, Charles to THE MURRAY HILL BANK. 69th st, s s, 100 w 11th av, 25x100.5. Nov. 16, note. 15,000

Neems, Margaret to The Twenty-fourth Ward Real Estate Assoc. Park View terrace. P. M. Oct. 20, due Nov. 12, 1894, 5 %. 500

Neumann, George H. J. and Michael Kern, of Neumann & Kern, to Thomas Roberts. West st, No. 348. Lease. P. M. Nov. 18, installs. 6,000

Same to George Ehret. Same property. Lease. P. M. 2d mort. Nov. 18, demand. 3,000

Neumann, Margaretha wife of and Philip to THE MUTUAL LIFE INS. CO. of New York. 19th st, s s, 258.8 w 6th av, 25x100. Nov. 19, 1 year, 5 %. 2,000

Newbury, John W. to The Twenty-fourth Ward Real Estate Assoc. Wellesley st. P. M. Oct. 20, due Nov. 12, 1894, 5 %. 363

Noonan, Edward to Charles Hartmann. 173d st, s s, 90 e Prospect av, 53x68x50x73, except part taken for opening 173d st. Nov. 16, 3 years. 400

Oppenheimer, Edward and Isaac Metzger to Lewis A. Civill, Colorado Springs, Col., and Acton T. Civill, Bovina Centre, N. Y. Columbus av and 84th st. P. M. Oct. 30, due June 9, 1893, 5 %. 55,000

Parsells, Edward W. to The Twenty-fourth Ward Real Estate Assoc. Creston av, w s, 294.6 n Wellesley st. P. M. Oct. 20, due Nov. 12, 1894, 5 %. 287

Same to same. Creston av, w s, 319.6 n Wellesley st, 3 lots. P. M. 3 morts., each $295, Oct. 20, due Nov. 12, 1894, 5 %. 885

Same to same. Creston av, w s, 669.6 n Wellesley st, 5 lots. 5 P. M. morts., each $215. Oct. 20, due Nov. 12, 1894, 5 %. 1,075

Same to same. Kirkside av, e s, 694.6 n Wellesley st, 4 lots. 4 P. M. morts., each $235. Oct. 20, due Nov. 12, 1894, 5 %. 940

Pettigrew, Agnes wife of David to THE EMIGRANT INDUST. SAVINGS BANK. Amsterdam (10th) av, w s, 23 s 184th st, 23x100x22.1x100. Nov. 19, 1 year, 4½ %. 3,500

Plump, Annie M. and Katie F. devisees John D. Plump to Henry Ziegler. Watts st, s w cor Sullivan st, runs west 31.2 x south 26.6 x 25.6 to point 16 w Sullivan st, x east 16 to Sullivan st, x north 61.2. 2-5 parts. Nov. 17, 3 years. 2,000

Pauritsch, Caroline wife of Joseph to Cyrille Carreau. Attorney st, Nos. 31 and 33, w s, 100 n Grand st, 50x100. Nov. 14, 1 year. 1,500

Pizer, Leon to E. Ellery Anderson. 2d av. P. M. Nov. 14, installs, 5 %. 12,000

Platt, Richard G. to Robert and Joseph Gordon. West End av and 85th st. P. M. Nov. 16, 1 year. 8,000

Potter, Orlando P. to THE HOME LIFE INS. CO. Astor pl, Nos. 10-18 and 57-61 Lafayette pl, begins Astor pl, s w cor Lafayette pl, 150.11x42x125.7x94. Nov. 16, 3 years, 4½ %. 150,000

Plass, Herbert C. to James P. Foster and ano. trustees William R. Foster. 46th st, n s, 275 w 10th av, 25x100.4. Nov. 10, due Nov. 14, 1892, 5 %. 15,000

Quin, Virginia J. also known as Virginia Janeway, Bayonne, N. J., to Francis B. Robert. 1st av, Nos. 659 and 661, w s, 25 s 38th st, runs west 75 x south 24.7 x southeast 28.10 x north along w s 1st av, 44—something omitted probably. Nov. 14, 1 year. 1,000

Quackenbush, Abraham and Daniel D. Lawson to THE GERMAN SAVINGS BANK. 26th st, n s, 148.6 w 8th av, 26.6x98.9. Nov. 16, 1 year. See Conveys. 24,000

Same to same. 26th st, n s, 123 w 8th av, 26.6x98.9. Nov. 16, 1 year. See Conveys. 24,000

Radley, William P. to Hyman and Henry Sonn. 27th st, No. 429, n s, 349.6 w 9th av, 18.6x88.9, with right of way through alley. Oct. 8, credits. 750

Rosenberg, Joseph to Adolph Pawel. 62d st, s s, 174.6 e 2d av, 25x100.5. Nov. 18, installs. 1,500

Same to Peter F. and H. J. Bruner exrs. Peter Bruner. 62d st, s s, 174.6 e 2d av, 25x100.5. Nov. 16, 5 years, 5 %. 15,000

Rawlings, Edward A. to Eleanor Wilmerding, Bay Shore, L. I. Findlay st, s s, lot 56 map Melrose, 50x100. Nov. 9, 1 year. 3,000

Same to Annie F. Dreyfus guard. 131st st. P. M. Nov. 13, 3 years, 5 %. 6,500

Reid, Walter, Madison, N. J., to Helenah Kouwenhoven, Long Island City. 93d st, s s, 74 e Madison av, 23x80.4. Nov. 16, 3 years, 5 %. 16,000

Same to Georgiana E. Arnold. 93d st, s s, 102 e Madison av, 18x100.8. Nov. 16, 3 years, 5 %. 12,000

Rehm, John to Charles and Louis Zink. 149th st. P. M. Nov. 16, 5 years, 5 %. 5,400

Rohrs, Frederick, Sr., to Caroline L. Macy. 126th st, s s, 125 e 2d av, 25x100.11. Nov. 12, 3 years, 5 %. gold, 13,000

Same to Eliza S. Bibby. Same property. Sub. to last mort. Nov. 12, 1 year. gold, 2,000

Rottenberg, Ignatz M. and Aaron Wise and Sabine his wife to Joseph B. Guttenberg. 59th st, n s, 130 w 2d av, 25x100.4. Sub. to mort. $7,500. Nov. 16, 1 year, 5 %. See Conveys. 2,000

Robertson, James G. to The Twenty-fourth Ward Real Estate Assoc. Kirkside av. P. M. Oct 20, due Nov. 12, 1894, 5 %. 500

Rockwood, George G. to J. Augustus Randel. 88th st, s s, 100 w Boulevard, 18x100.8. Nov. 16, 1 year. 1,500

Same to same. 88th st, s s, 118 w Boulevard, 18 x100.8. Nov. 16, 1 year. 1,500

Rosell, Karl M. to The Twenty-fourth Ward Real Estate Assoc. Creston av. P. M. Oct. 20, due Nov. 12, 1884, 5 %. 200

Schroeder, Gesiene A. to The Twenty-fourth Ward Real Estate Assoc., New York. Wellesley st. P. M Oct. 20, due Nov. 12, 1894, 5 %. 700

Sharp, Alfred P. to The Twenty-fourth Ward Real Estate Assoc. Kirkside av. P. M. Oct. 20, due Nov. 12, 1894, 5 %. 555

Shepperd, Harriet A. to The Twenty-fourth Ward Real Estate Assoc. Kirkside av. P. M. Oct. 20, due Nov. 12, 1894, 5 %. 1,025

Simons, Martin to The Twenty-fourth Ward Real Estate Assoc. Creston av, e s, 816.6 n Wellesley st. P. M. Oct. 20, due Nov. 12, 1894, 5 %. 725

Same to same. Jerome av, s e cor Travers st. Oct. 20, due Nov. 12, 1894, 5 %. 563

Same to same. Travers st, s w cor Creston av. Oct. 20, due Nov. 12, 1894, 5 %. 513

Spindler, Albin to The Twenty-fourth Ward Real Estate Assoc. Creston av. P. M. Oct. 20, due Nov. 12, 1894, 5 %. 200

Spooner, Charles W. to The Twenty-fourth Ward Real Estate Assoc., New York. Wellesley st, s e cor Kirkside av. P. M. Oct. 20, due Nov. 12, 1894, 5 %. 538

Stone, George to Henry C. Niedenstein. 98th st, s s, 150 e Amsterdam av, 200x100.11. Nov. 16, 3 years, 5 %. See Conveys. 8,500

Smith, Catharine I. heir Albert G. Smith to John E. Lockwood, Long Island City. Morris st, east cor Worth st, 88x139x126.6x195 to Worth st, x 309. 1-5 part. Nov. 13, 6 months. 500

Solomon, Joseph to Ann E. Mitchell et al. exrs. and trustees Samuel L. Mitchell. East Broadway, s s, 290.3 w Market st, 25x75. Nov. 17, 3 years, 4½ %. 15,000

Solomon, Fink to Bennett J. King. Suffolk st, No. 77, w s, 125.1 s Delancey st, 25x100. Nov. 17, 3 years. 3,000

Seiferth, Moses mortgagee to Isaac Clock present owner. Certificate of payment of $1,157 interest and $1,000 on account of mortgage and that amount due thereon is 4,250

Secor, Katharine G. to The Dry Dock Savings Inst. 70th st, n s, 175 w Columbus av, 20x100.5. Nov. 17, due Nov. 20, 1892, 5 %. 10,000

Schreiner, John, Jr., to Charles Dorn and Jacob Schmitzer. 84th st, No. 311, n s, 150 e 2d av, 25x102.2. Nov. 16, 3 years, 5 %. 12,000

Schroeder, Otto and Henry Ernsberger to P. Ballantine & Sons, a corporation. Grand st, No. 91. Lease. Nov. 16, note. 4,000

Sweezy, Richard L. to George R. Schieffelin and ano. exrs. Richard L. Schieffelin. Convent av. P. M. Nov. 12, due Nov. 1, 1893, 4½ %. 10,000

Same to Charles A. Peabedy, Jr. Same property. P. M. 2d mort. Nov. 12, due June 1, 1892, 5 %. 1,500

Sheehy, Caroline F. to Lewis Morris. 76th st. P. M. Oct. 12, due Oct. 1, 1896, 5 %. gold, 15,000

Simon, Minnie L. to Mary P. Snow. 107th st. s s, 75 w Lexington av, 16.8x100.11. Secures performance of agreement. Nov. 2. 1,000

Schmalholz, Laurent T. to The Emigrant Indust. Savings Bank. 2d av, No. 93, w s, 24.3x100. Nov. 17, due Nov. 18, 1892, 4½ %. 15,000

Scott, Mary A. wife of John to Isaac N. Hebberd. Bathgate av, e s, lot 4 map of Adamsville, 60x120. Nov. 16, 1 year. 1,000

Schreiner, George to The New York Savings Bank. Park av, e s, 75.8 n 115th st, 25.3x126. Nov. 17, due Dec. 1, 1894, 4½ %. 12,000

Same to same. 115th st, n s, 126 e Park av, 29 x100.11. Nov. 17, due Dec. 1, 1894, 4½ %. 13,000

Sinclair, James to The Metropolitan Life Ins. Co., of New York. 144th st. P. M. Nov. 18, due Oct. 1, 1894, 5 %. 11,000

Strauss, Sarah to Samuel Charig. 17th st, s s, 150 w 6th av, 25x92. Nov. 17, 1 year, 5 %. 10,000

Stanton, Edwin B., Brooklyn, to Urcilla Mackellar. Lenox av and 119th st. P. M. Nov. 9, 1 year, 5 %. 55,000

Stiegeler, Columbus to The Twenty-fourth Ward Real Estate Assoc. Kirkside av, s e cor Park View terrace. P. M. Oct. 20, due Nov. 12, 1894, 5 %. 1,362

Same to same. Park View terrace. P. M. Oct. 20, due Nov. 12, 1894, 5 %. 1,118

Taylor, Fanny T. to The Twenty-fourth Ward Real Estate Assoc. Kirkside av. P. M. Oct. 20, due Nov. 12, 1894, 5 %. 315

Tefft, David C. to John McK. Camp. Wellesley st, s s, 44.7 e Kirkside av. P. M. Oct. 20, due Nov. 12, 1894, 5 %. 337

Same to same. Kirkside av. P. M. Oct. 20, due Nov. 12, 1894, 5 %. 825

Toussaint, Julius F. to The Twenty-fourth Ward Real Estate Assoc. Kirkside av, e s, 244.9 n Wellesley st. P. M. Oct. 20, due Nov. 12, 1894, 5 %. 550

Same to same. Kirkside av, w s, 451.6 n Wellesley st. P. M. Oct. 20, due Nov. 12, 1894, 5 %. 680

Same to same. Kirkside av, w s, 401.4 n Wellesley st. P. M. Oct. 20, due Nov. 12, 1894, 5 %. 680

Same and Albert Wiggers to same. Park View terrace, n e cor Kirkside av. P. M. Oct. 20, due Nov. 12, 1894, 5 %. 1,425

Tousey, Charles G., Clinton Corners, N. Y., to Hugh N. Camp. Lots 55 and 56 map of 71 lots of Kingsland estate. P. M. Nov. 16, 3 years, 5 %. 1,200

Toussaint, Philip to The Twenty-fourth Ward Real Estate Assoc. Kirkside av, n w cor Wellesley st. P. M. Oct. 20, due Nov. 12, 1894, 5 %. 963

Tuffs, Hannah to Harriet L. Price. 69th st, n s, 195 e West End av, 20x100.5. Nov. 19, 3 years, 5 %. 5,500

Thomas, James F. to The Title Guarantee and Trust Co. 158th st, No. 686, s s, 125 w Elton av, 25x100. Nov. 16, 3 years. 2,500

Tannenbaum, Benjamin to Nathan Hyman. Willett st, No. 58, e s, 150 n Delancey st, 25x 100. ½ part. Lease. Nov. 1, 1 year, 5 %. 500

The Germania Life Ins. Co. mortgagee with Catherine H. Anderson mortgagor. Extension of mort. Nov. 7. nom

Thompson, Morris S. to Eliza Lockwood, Brooklyn. West st, Nos. 403 and 404, s e cor Charles st, 44.9x70x43.1x81.11. Nov. 13, 1 yr, 5 %. 3,200

Tynberg, Sigmund to Louis Isenburger et al. trustees Arnold Blum, Jr., dec'd. 62d st, s s, 149.6 e 2d av, 25x100.5. Nov. 14, 5 years, 5 %. 15,000

Tytler, Elizabeth E. to James M. C. and Ann M. Tytler. 126th st, n s, 168.1 w Lenox av, 17.10x99.11. Nov. 16, 3 years, 5 %. 12,000

The Central Safe Deposit Co. to George C. Waldo trustee. 14th st, n s, 42 e 5th av, 50x 129, also all rights, privileges and franchises. Oct. 31, bonds. See Leasehold Conveys. 175,000

Vallely, Patrick W. to Richard Hassard. 35th st, No. 335, n s, 410 e 9th av, 15x98.9. Nov. 14, due Nov. 16, 1893, 5 %. 1,000

Vultee, George W. to Moses S. Beach, Peekskill, N. Y. Nassau and Fulton sts. P. M. Nov. 11, 3 years, 4½ %. 225,000

Vultee, George W. to Therese Mack, Somerville, N. J. 60th st, s e cor Park av. P. M. Nov. 18, 2 years, 5 %. 18,000

Webster, Sarah W. mortgagor with Ida Sondheim and ano. exrs. and trustees Myer Sondheim mortgagees. Extension of mort. Oct. 15. nom

Wronkow, Herman to Lucia M. Cohen. 128th st. P. M. July 27, due Aug. 20, 1893, 4½ %. 25,000

Williams, Sophia wife of David to George G. De Witt et al. trustees Sarah A. Housman. Baxter st, No. 16, w s, 25x116. Nov. 17, 2 years. 3,000

Wyatt, Ida S. to Grace I. Brower. 93d st. n s, 268.9 w 9th av, 18.9x74.1x18.9x73.3, with all title to strip in rear, 18.9x18.4. Nov. 16, 4 years, 5 %. 16,867

Walthausen, Johan H. to Pauline Josephie. 41st st, s s, 150 e 10th av, 16.8x98.9. Nov. 16, 5 years, 5 %. 5,000

Weil, Simon R. with Francis B. Robert both mortgagees. Agreement as to priority of morts. made by Virginia J. Quin. Nov. 14. nom

Williamson, Mary F. wife of and D. D. mortgagors with Nellie A. Crossman widow mortgagee. Extension of mort. April 17. nom

Same with same. Extension of mort. April 17. nom

Wolff, Dorothea mortgagee with Louis A. Grass mortgagor. Extension of mort. Nov. 16. nom

Wynkoop, James D. mortgagor with Jonas B. Kissam, Fairfield, Conn., mortgagee. Extension of mort. Aug. 22. nom

Ward, Ellen E. mortgagee to Matilda Plahto mortgagor. Extension of mort. Nov. 11. nom

White, Anna M wife of and Sidney to The Fidelity and Casualty Co. of New York. Teller av, w s, 164.7 s 164th st, 24x110. Feb. 13, note. 1,550

Winterson, Maria L. to The Emigrant Industrial Savings Bank. 105th st, n s, 74.11 w 10th av, 25x75.11. Nov. 13, 1 year, 4½ %. 2,000

Watt, Margaret to The Twenty-fourth Ward Real Estate Assoc. Wellesley st, n s, 25.1 w Creston av. P. M. Oct. 20, due Nov. 12, 1894, 5 %. 1,050

Same to same. Kirkside av, w s, 602 n Wellesley st. P. M. Oct. 20, due Nov. 12, 1894, 5 %. 525

Same to same. Wellesley st, n s, 25.1 e Creston av. P. M. Oct. 20, due Nov. 12, 1894, 5 %. 620

West, Joseph I. to Susan E. Le Roy widow. 109th st, n s, 211.3 e 4th av, 18.9x100.11. Nov. 19, due Nov. 1, 1896, 5 %. gold, 6,500

Wiggers, Albert to The Twenty-fourth Ward Real Estate Assoc. Kirkside av, w s, 300.11 n Wellesley st. P. M. Oct. 20, due Nov. 12, 1894, 5 %. 725

Same to same. Kirkside av, e s, 144.9 n Wellesley st. P. M. Oct. 20, due Nov. 12, 1894, 5 %. 570

Same to same. Kirkside av, w s, 351.9 n Wellesley st. P. M. Oct. 20, due Nov. 12, 1894, 5 %. 620

Wilhelm, Gotthilf F. to John McK. Camp. Kirkside av. P. M. Oct. 20, due Nov. 12, 1894, 5 %. 300

Zollikoffer, Emily A. wife of Oscar F. to Edwin J. Witthaus exr. and trustee Gustav H. Witthaus. Broad st. P. M. Nov. 12, due Nov. 13, 1892, 5 %. 55,000

KINGS COUNTY.

November 12, 13, 14, 16, 17, 18.

Ackerman, Lillian wife of and Edwin W. to S. Church Welsh trustee for Ethel H. Tweddle. Waverly av, w s, 147.6 s Greene av, 20x75. Nov. 13, 3 years, 5 %. $4,000

Ackerman, Jacob V. to William J. Gaynor. Fenimore st, s s, 645.9 e Flatbush av, 100x125. Oct. 1, 1 year. 4,500

Abramovitz, Rochmiel to New York State Mortgage Bank and Savings Assoc. Livonia av, s e cor Osborn st, 25x100. Nov. 10, installs. 3,000

Ahlers, Adolph and John J. R. Paulsen to Beadleston & Woerz. Johnson st, No. 164. Saloon lease. Nov. 16, demand. 800

Allan, John T. and Nathaniel Prosky to Alvan R. Johnson. 4th st. P. M. Nov. 9, demand. 25,250

Allen, Franklin to George Cromwell. 73d st, centre line, 140 s e 12th av, runs northeast 130 x southeast 480 x southwest 130 to centre 73d st, x northwest 480; 12th av, centre line, at intersection with centre line 73d st, runs southwest 260 to centre 74th st, x northwest 500 x northeast 130 x southeast 360 x northeast 130 to centre 73d st, x southeast 140; 12th av, centre line, at intersection with centre line of 73d st, runs southeast 640 x southwest 130 x northwest 40 x southeast 130 to centre 74th st, x northwest 600 to centre 12th av, x northeast 260; 12th av, centre line, at intersection with centre line 74th st, runs southwest 280 to centre 75th st, x northwest 140 x northeast 150 x northwest 500 x southwest 150 to centre 75th st, x northwest 140 to centre 11th av, x northeast 280 to centre 74th st, x southeast 780; 12th av, centre line, at intersection with centre line of 74th st, runs southeast 220 x southwest 130 x northwest 220 to centre 12th av, x northeast 130; 11th av, centre line, at intersection with centre line 75th st, runs southwest 150 x northwest 200 x southwest 130 to centre 76th st, x northwest 320 x northeast 280 to centre 75th st, x southeast 520; 76th st, centre line, 360 n w 11th av, runs southwest 130 x northwest 160 x northeast 130 to av, x southeast 160. Nov. 13, 1 year. 21,000

Archer, Maria wife of and George E. to Ambrose S. Murray, Jr. Sullivan st, s s, 40 w Dwight st, 40x60. Nov. 9, 2 years. 1,000

Aronson, Jacob to Charles M. Marsh. Lewis av, s e cor Hancock st, 100x150. Nov. 16, demand. 27,875

Same to The Title Guarantee and Trust Co. Hancock st, s s, 42 e Lewis av, 108x100. Nov. 16, demand. 24,600

Ash, Simon to Samuel M. Meeker exr. Frederick Herr. Broadway. P. M. Nov. 13, 5 years, 5 %. 3,000

Asip, John and Timothy J. Buckley to Patrick G. Hughes. Strong pl, w s, 225 s Harrison st, 25x109.9. Aug. 31, due Sept. 1, 1892, 5 %. 6,000

Atwood, Alice E. to Charles N. Kingsland. President st, n s, 203.6 w Smith st, 20.3x100. Nov. 4, 2 years, 5 %. 5,000

Backman, Annie F. by John B. King guard. and Margaret M. Backman to William Vanderveer and ano. exrs. Aletta M. Vanderveer. 43d st, s s, 250 w 3d av, 16.8x100.2. All title. Nov. 14, 3 years. 1,300

Badger, George W. to Edward W. Phillips. Clifton pl. P. M. Nov. 14, 5 years, 5 %. 5,000

Baldwin, Linda to Eliza F. Seyers, Toronto, Can. Degraw st, No. 105, n s, 100 w Columbia st, 16.8x100. Sept. 3, 2 years, 5 %. 5,000

Barlow, Clinton W. and Edward M. Barlow to The Title Guarantee and Trust Co. Irving pl, w s, 150 s Gates av, 50x101. Nov. 18, 3 years, 5 %. 7,500

Barrett, Rosanna to Jane Chadwick. Eastern Parkway, n e cor Hendrix st, 75x100. Nov. 16, due May 1, 1894, 5 %. 500

Bartlett, Jessie E. to Allen Van Hagen. Quincy st, n s, 190 e Patchen av, 20x100. Nov. 16, 1 year. 700

Beatty, Ellen to John Hickey exr. Michael Callahan. St. Marks av. P. M. Nov. 17, due Dec. 1, 1894, 5 %. 1,000

Becker, Sina C. and Carl F. to Henry McShane Mfg. Co. Cowenhovens lane, s e cor 60th st, 40.4x100x84.3x100.2, New Utrecht. Nov. 6, 1 year, 5 %. 247

Bierds, Charlotte A. to Lizzie T. Grace. 3d av. P. M. Nov. 10, 1 year, 5 %. 250

Bell, William, Jr., to Town of New Utrecht Co-operative Building and Loan Assoc. 93d st, n s, 185 w 3d av, 25x100. Oct. 16, installs. 1,750

Benedict, Coleridge H. to Sarah M. Mygatt and ano. trustees Jacob A. Robertson. Sherman st, w s, 208.7 s Greenwood av, 40x100. Nov. 14, due Nov. 1, 1894, 5 %. 2,500

Betts, Charles A. to The Hamilton Trust Co. Fulton st, n e cor Nostrand av, 33.1x91.2x 52.3 to av, x81.8. Nov. 18, demand. 25,000

Bierds, John T. to George W. Pearsall. 24th st, s s, 175 e 3d av, 25x abt 97x26x100. Nov. 14, due Nov. 13, 1892. 500

Black, Cassie A. to South Brooklyn Co-operative Building and Loan Assoc. 48th st. P. M. Nov. 10, installs. 4,000

Blumenfeld, Pauline to Mary wife of John Martin. Richmond st. P. M. Nov. 14, 5 years. 1,000

Bieber, Gerson and William to Henry Wilson and ano. exrs. and trustees Mortimer C. Tunison. Vernon av, s s, 450 e Marcy av, 20x100. Nov. 16, due Nov. 1, 1894, 5 %. 3,500

Bloodgood, William H. to Mary A. Seaman, Manhasset, L. I. Fulton st, s s, 181.4 e New York av, 43.8x100. Nov. 16, due Nov. 1, 1893, 5 %. 500

Boetticher, Emma E. to The F. & M. Schaefer Brewing Co. Atlantic av, No. 286. Lease. Nov. 16, demand. 1,000

Boger, Gertrude K. wife of and Frederick to Catharine Boger. Alabama av, e s, 225 n Liberty av, 21.9x100. June 1, 5 years, 5 %. 1,000

Bonny, Frank S. to Eliza Lewis. Patchen av, n w cor Bainbridge st, 40x100. Nov. 16, 1 year 1,500

Brand, Joseph to Mary C. Hill. Marion st. P. M. Nov. 10, 2 years, 5 %. 450

Brown, Harvey H. to Henry J. Robinson Hicks st, w s, 25.4 n Pineapple st, 25.4x100.6. Nov. 16 2 years. 1,500

Brown, Isabella wife of and William to William C. O'Keeffe and James H. McKenna, of O'Keeffe & McKenna. New road from Brooklyn to Coney Island adj land Alfred Wiggins, 1 acre 1 rood 37-100 perches; New road from Brooklyn to Coney Island adj land John Tredwell, runs northwest 148.6 x southwest 337 x southeast 139.8 to Johnson av, x northeast 286.10, Flatbush. Nov. 16, 2 years, 5 %. 4,000

Brown, Isabella wife of and William to Hans S. Christian. 8th av, n e cor 11th st, 100x89.5. Oct. 13, 1 year. 3,500

Bulger, Jeremiah to The Brooklyn Savings Bank. Myrtle av, s s, 250 w Marcy av, 25x100. Nov. 14, 1 year, 5 %. 2,000

Buckley, Emma F. to Aaron S. Robbins. Diamond st, Flatbush. P. M. Nov. 16, 3 years, 5 %. 1,750

Bull, Henry C. to John H. Onderdonk. 56th st, s w s, 100 n w 14th av, 75x100.2. Nov. 10, due Nov. 1, 1896, 5 %. 3,200

Burland, John W. to John Miner. Chauncey st, s s, 325 w Patchen av, 25x100. Nov. 17, 3 years. 1,600

Burns, Agnes to Peter Donald. Halsey st, n s, 62.6 w Throop av, 16.3x100. Nov. 1, 3 years, 5 %. gold, 5,000

Same to same. Halsey st, n s, 30 w Throop av, runs north 42 x west 1 x north 58 x west 15.3 x south 100 to st, x east 16.3. Sept. 1, 3 years, 5 %. gold, 5,000

Burt, Mary C. to Levi V. Martin. 53d st, n s, 205 e 2d av, 18x100.2. Nov. 11, installs. 800

Butts, Caroline, New York City, to Emily A. Ring. Fulton st, s w cor Norwood av, runs south 110.10 x 50 x 102.2 x 50.8. Nov. 16, 3 years. 1,100

Campbell, Neil to Alexander Underhill, Jr. Bedford av, e s, 383.9 n Myrtle av, 25x100. Oct. 29, due Jan. 1, 1892. 350

Canty, Mary A. wife of and John to The Ninth Street Savings and Loan Assoc. 3d av, No. 1304, w s, 70.6 s 55th st, 14.6x100. Sept. 19, installs. 2,000

Cassidy, Deborah A. wife of and John H. to The Mutual Life Ins. Co., New York. State st, s s, 300 e Hoyt st, 25x100. Nov. 10, due Nov. 11, 1892. 5,000

Chidwick, Richard to George C. Gould exr. Conklin Gould. 14th st. P. M. Nov. 11, 3 years, 5 %. 4,000

Chils, Otto to Sophus A. Nielsen. Gunther pl, n e cor Atlantic av, 16.4x80. Nov. 11, 1 year. 500

Same to same. Gunther pl, e s, 16.4 n Atlantic av, 16.4x80. Nov. 11, 1 year. 600

Same to same. Gunther pl, e s, 32.8 n Atlantic av, 16.4x80. Nov. 11, 1 year. 700

Same to same. Truxton st, n s, 60 w Stone av, 20x80. Nov. 11, 3 years. 1,000

Same to same. Truxton st, n s, 20 w Stone av, 20x80. Nov. 11, 3 years. 500

Same to same. Truxton st, n s, 40 w Stone av, 20x80. Nov. 11, 3 years. 500

Same to Sophus A. Nielsen. Truxton st, n s, 80 w Stone av, 20x80. Nov. 11, 3 years. 1,000

Christensen, Morton P. to Catharine Beatty. 17th st. P. M. Nov. 14, 3 years, 5 %. 2,900

Clancy, Mary wife of and John to Richard R. Jordan. East New York av, n s, at s e cor of woodland of John Neefus, runs northeast 219.10 x northwest 474.2 to patent line, x southwest 215.4 x southeast 492.2, 2 272-1,000 acres; East New York av, n s, lots 75-89 map Roger Clancy, Flatbush, 110.6 to centre Clancy av, x north 442.8 to patent line, x 103.2x464.8, Flatbush. Nov. 17, 3 years. 2,000

Clark, Peter to The Coal Handling Machinery and Construction Co. (Lim.) Bedford av, cor Flushing av, lots 37-41 block 94 assessor's map. Lease. Collateral security. May 9. 8,400

Clayton, Frances A. to Helen R. Sumner. Cleveland st, w s, 100 n Arlington av, 37.6x100. March 10, note. 3,000

Cohen, Israel and Jacob to Samuel and Barnett Cohen. Boerum st, n s, 422.9 e Bushwick av, 25.1x62.11. Nov. 2, 4 years, 5 %. 900

Cohen, Annie wife of Joseph to Robert H. Anderson. Vernon av. P. M. Nov. 17, due Nov. 1, 1894, 5 %. 2,000

Conlon, Margaret E. to Francis J. Conlon. Carroll st, s s, 174.1 e 6th av, 38x—. Nov. 14, due Nov. 1, 1893, 5 %. 8,000

Same to same. Garfield pl, n e s, 252.9 s e 6th av, 22x150. Nov. 14, due Nov. 1, 1893, 5 %. 4,000

Costello, James J. and Elizabeth to Lawrence Hurlburt. Moffat st, s s, 232 e Central av, 18x100. Nov. 14, installs. 1,200

Crum, John R. to Cornelius N. Hoagland. Monroe st, s s, 130 w Sumner av, 20x100. Nov. 14, due Nov. 1, 1894, 5 %. gold, 4,000

Daniell, Elizabeth E. wife of and Joseph to Alexander Polglase, Jr. Sands st, s s, 149.9 e Gold st, 20.9x100. Nov. 18, 3 years. 1,000

Darling, Angeline E. to Brooklyn Trust Co. trustee Edward Harvey. Myrtle av. P. M. Nov. 7, 1 year, 5 %. 8,000

Decker, Joseph K. to Henry and Charles Lockwood, of H. & C. Lockwood, Huntington, N. Y. Powell st, e s, 170.3 s Liberty av, 45x100. Nov. 9, due Nov. 11, 1892. 600

De Mott, Alfred, Rockville Centre, L. I., to Amanda wife of Hamilton W. Pearsall, of Pearsalls, L. I. De Kalb av, n s, 407 w Reid av, 18x66.8x18x68.6. Nov. 7, due Nov. 1, 1894, 5 %. 2,000

De Zavala, Henry to Mutual Life Ins. Co., N. Y. Gold st, w s, 479.4 s Willoughby st, 16.2x115.6. Nov. 11, 1 year. 15,000

Same to Richard G. Phelps trustee for creditors. Same property. Nov. 12, notes. 2,410

Same to Peter Cleary. Same property. Nov. 12, 1 year. 4,071

Same to Rankin & Ross. Same property. Sub. to mort. $15,000. Nov. 10, 1 year. 1,050

Diemer, Charles to Charles W. Truslow trustee William Wall dec'd. Moore st, n s, 379.5 w White st, 75x100; Moore st, n s, 304.5 w White st, 25x100. Oct. 29, 3 years, 5 %. 3,000

Dow, Arthur B. to Henry F. Megill. Putnam av, n s, 400 w Nostrand av, 25x100. Nov. 12, installs, 5 %. 2,500

Dowley, Michael to Virginia A. Kleine. Cornelia st, s e s, 101.10 n e Central av, 144x100. Building loan. Nov. 12, demand. 18,000

Same to same. Cornelia st, s e s, extends from Central to Hamburg av, 60x100. Sub. to mort. $18,000. Nov. 12, demand. 20,000

Doyle, Thomas S. to Alexander G. Calder. 12th st. P. M. Nov. 14, 2 years, 5 %. 2,000

Dreyer, Henry W., John F. and Henry C. Hunken to Samuel M. Meeker exr. Frederick Herr. Central av, east cor Myrtle av. P. M. Nov. 12, 3 years, 5 %. 4,000

Durbrow, William to Peter Donald. Halsey st, n s, 46.3 w Throop av, 16.3x100. Sept. 1, 3 years, 5 %. gold, 5,000

Egan, John and Annie his wife to Abraham B. Ryker. Union st, s s, 71.6 e Hicks st, 23.3x100. Nov. 18, 6 months. 212

Ennis, John to Gertrude Prince. 57th st, s s, 240 e 2d av, 20x100.2. Nov. 13, 5 years, 5 %. 400

Erving, Charlotte A. to James Cropsey, Gravesend, L. I. West st, New Utrecht. P. M. Nov. 12, 2 years. 700

Farmers' Feed Co., New York and New Jersey, to Charles W. Truslow trustee William Wall. Johnston av. P. M. Oct. 29, 3 years, 5 %. 4,000

Finlay, Jeannette M. wife of and James, Bayonne, N. J., to William Post committee of John Rogers. 1st pl, s s, 225 e Court st, 25x133.5. Nov. 16, due Nov., 1894. 18,000

Fletcher, Margaret L. to Mary A. Seaman, Manhasset, L. I. Quincy st, n s, 193.9 w Throop av, 18.9x100. Nov. 16, due Nov. 1, 1892, 5 %. 500

Fordinsky, Harris to The Serial Building Loan and Savings Inst. Stone av, w s, 66 n Blake av, 23x100. Nov. 12, installs. 2,300

Forestel, Michael to Thomas McGrath. Bush st, s s, 126.6 w Hicks st, 20x100. Nov. 18, 1 year. 100

Fox, Alfred to The Williamsburgh Savings Bank. Bedford av, e s, 60 n North 7th st, 20x80. Nov. 17, 1 year, 5 %. 4,000

Fortenato, Germario and Rosa A. his wife to John Gillen. Graham st. P. M. Oct. 1, due Nov. 1, 1897, 5 %. 4,000

Frank, Barnet and Simon Rose to Franziska Witte. Eastern Parkway, s s, 50 e Osborn st, 25x100. Nov. 9, 5 years. 3,000

Frank, Henry to Edwin D. Phelps. Pineapple st, n s, 92.6 e Henry st. P. M. Nov. 12, 3 years, 5 %. 30,000

Same to The Title Guarantee and Trust Co. Garfield pl, s s, 92.10 w 8th av, 80x100. Nov. 12, 1 year, 5 %. 6,000

Frankel, Herman to Obermeyer & Liebmann. Gerry st, No. 102. Saloon lease. Nov. 13, demand. 300

Frenz, Hedrig to Daniel Doody. 15th st, s s, 75 e 3d av, 18x66. Nov. 7, 1 year. 400

Friedman, Moritz and Sigmund Newman to Louise Germuth. Gates av. P. M. Sub. to mort. $3,200. Nov. 16, installs, 5 %. 2,100

Gallagher, John C. and Margaret L. and Annie T. Anderson heirs Daniel Gallagher to Elizabeth M. Vanderbilt. Chauncey st, s s, 344 e Saratoga av, 19x100. Nov. 9, 3 years, 5 %. 3,500

Garrahan, Patrick to Thomas A. O'Keefe et al. exrs. Arthur McAvoy. Butler st, s s, 345 e Franklin av, 20x131. Nov. 16, 3 years, 5 %. 3,000

Garrahan, James to Thomas A. O'Keefe et al. exrs. Arthur McEvoy. Butler st, s s, 325 e Franklin av, 20x131. Nov. 16, 3 years, 5 %. 3,000

Geiersdorf, Jacob to Charles Emmons. Atlantic av. P. M. Nov. 1, installs, 5 %. 5,400

Gatechair, Samuel E. and Lucy W. Ralphs to Jane F. Ralphs. Putnam av, n w s, 230 n e Broadway. 20x100. Nov. 10, 1 year. 500

Gerken, John to Robert Martin trustee Daniel Marly. Union st, n s, 434.2 w 4th av, 26.8x95. Nov. 2, due April 1, 1893, 5 %. 6,500

Gibbins, Louisa L. to Maria H. Rider. Putnam av. P. M. Nov. 11, 10 months. 800

Same to Robert L. Moores and Charles A. Le Queene. Quincy st, n s, 105.6 w Ralph av. P. M. Oct. 30, due Nov. 1, 1892. 1,500

Same to same. Quincy st, n s, 85.6 w Ralph av. P. M. Oct. 30, due Nov. 1, 1892. 1,500

Giles, James F. to William T. Palmer. Guernsey st, s, 200 n Nassau av, 25x100. Nov. 1, 3 years. 1,000

Gilfeather, Jane to Title Guarantee and Trust Co. State st. P. M. Oct. 29, due Nov. 17, 1894, 5 %. 4,000

Gillies, John to Alfred J. Murray. Lots 632 and 633 map John A. Meserole. Nov. 13, demand. 8,000

Glasser, Frank and Sarah his wife to Rosa Levy and Annie Jackerson. Rockaway av, e s, 100 s Eastern Parkway, 25x100.1. Nov. 9, installs. 200

Gollner, Erwin G. to Frank A. Barnaby, Charles D. Burwell and Susan E. Fingarr. 6th st, n e s, 297.10 n w 5th av, 100x100. Nov. 17, demand. 1,800

Same to Hannah E. Miller trustee Hannah M. Lovett. 6th st, n e s, 381.2 n w 5th av, 16.8x100. Nov. 17, due Dec. 1, 1892, 5 %. 3,600

Same to same. 6th st, n e s, 364.6 n w 5th av, 16.8x100. Nov. 17, due Dec. 1, 1892, 5 %. 3,600

Same to Hannah E. Miller, Philadelphia, Pa. 6th st, n e s, 297.10 n w 5th av, 4 lots, each 16.8x100. 4 morts., each $3,600. Nov. 17, due Dec. 1, 1892, 5 %. 14,400

Gunther, Jacob to S. Liebmann's Sons Brewing Co. Buffalo and Atlantic avs. P. M. Nov. 14, due Dec. 1, 1895, 5 %. 1,500

Gunther, William to Christian C. Miller. South 5th st, s s, 125 e Hewes st, 60x100. Nov. 17, 1 year. 1,000

Hacklander, August to John Kress Brewing Co., New York. Wyckoff st, n s, 320.8 w Waterbury st, 24.8x95. Nov. 12, due Nov. 13, 1891. 700

Hallheimer, Esther wife of and Max to Robert I. Miller, Philadelphia, Pa. Myrtle av, n s, 200 w Lewis av, 25x100. Nov. 18, due Nov. 1, 1892. 800

Harman, James to Mary E. Fox. North 6th st, n e s, 150 s e Wythe av, 25x100. Nov. 13, 3 years, 5 %. 4,000

Harper, James D. E. and George W. Merritt to Lembeck & Betz Eagle Brewing Co., Jersey City. 5th av, No. 157. Lease. Nov. 11, 1 year. 750

Same to same. 4th av, No. 528. Lease. Nov. 11, due Nov. 12, 1892. 750

Hartington, Alfred E. to Adaline A. Hepworth. Garnet st, s s, 125 e Court st, 25x100. Nov. 12, 3 years, 5 %. 5,000

Same to Edmund Titus, New York. Garnet st, s s, 150 e Court st, 25x100. Nov. 12, 3 years, 5 %. 5,000

Same to William Hodge et al. exrs. Eliza Hodge. Garnet st, s s, 175 e Court st, 25x100. Nov. 12, 3 years, 5 %. 5,000

Hartman, William to Minnie Bennett. Newport av, n s, 75 w Watkins st, 25x100. Nov. 11, 3 years. 800

Haslam, Thomas to William M. Hull. Eckford st, e s, 361 n Van Cott av, 25x100. Nov. 12, due Jan. 1, 1895, 5 %. 3,000

Hastings, Patrick to Emigrant Industrial Savings Bank. 5th av, w s, 50.6 n 19th st, 24.3x80. Nov. 18, 1 year, 4½ %. 1,000

Haviland, Sarah A. widow to Anna M. Lott. Bay 17th st, e s, 250 s 86th st, 25x96.5. Nov. 2, 3 years. 1,500

Hawxhurst, William H. to Caroline Barry. Van Voorhis st. P. M. Nov. 10, 2 years. 2,000

Heilman, Paul to George B. Read. Leonard st. P. M. Nov. 16, 3 years, 5 %. 1,150

Helferich, Charles J. to Brooklyn Savings Bank. 14th st, n s, 172.11 e 7th av, 17.6x100. Nov. 11, 1 year, 5 %. 2,000

Hendrickson, Elizabeth to The Title Guarantee and Trust Co. Monroe st, n s, 197 e Throop av, 17.3x100. Nov. 16, 3 years, 5 %. 4,250

Same to same. Monroe st, n s, 250.8 e Throop av, 17x100. Nov. 16, 3 years, 5 %. 4,250

Herbert, Margaret J. wife of and John F. to William Larder. Stone av. P. M. Nov. 14, 1 year, 5 %. 1,400

Herr, Charles to Samuel M. Meeker exr. Frederick Herr. Broadway, south cor Hart st. Sept. 14, due Nov. 14, 1896, 5 %. 11,000

Hildebrand, Max to William Kolb. Knickerbocker av, e s, 25 s George st, 25x100. Nov. 14, 1 year, 5 %. 1,500

Hoffmann, Jacob to The German Savings Bank of Brooklyn. Lorimer st, e s, 60 s Conselyea st, 15x84. Nov. 16, due Dec. 1, 1892, 5 %. 1,500

Same to same. Lorimer st, e s, 75 s Conselyea st, runs east 84 x south 11 x west 90 x south 14 x west 75 to Lorimer st, x north 25. Nov. 16, due Dec. 1, 1893, 5 %. 3,000

Hogan, Thomas F. and Margaret his wife, L. I. City, to Christopher Hackett, L. I. City. Freeman st, s s, 115 e Oakland st, 25x100. Oct. 26, 1 year. 500

Hopkins, Henry F. C. to George Covert. Knickerbocker av, s e cor Bleecker st. P. M. Nov. 16, due Aug. 15, 1892. 1,323

Same to same. Same property. Nov. 16, 2 years. 4,500

Hommel, Charles D. to Lucinda Moadinger exr. John Moadinger. Weirfield st, s e s, 120 n e Evergreen av. P. M. Nov. 14, 1 year, 5 %. 13,600

Holsten, John D. to John F. Waldorf. 52d st, s w s, 260 s e 4th av, 40x100.2. Nov. 13, 3 years, 5 %. 2,500

Hunt, Sarah A. wife of George W. to The Brooklyn Life Ins. Co. Garfield pl, s s, 275 w 6th av, 150x100. Nov. 11, demand. 2,800

Ingram, Alexander to Ann McGregor widow. 40th st. P. M. Nov. 16, 5 years or installs, 5 %. 1,800

Jones, Jane G. to Jane J. Davenport. Clarkson st, Flatbush. P. M. Nov. 1, installs. 650

Jaeger, Michael to Emeline Bishop. South 4th st, n s, 225 e Rodney st, 25x95. Nov. 18, 3 years, 5 %. 2,000

Jahrsdoerfer, Theodore to Ira F. and Frank Brainard, of Brainerd Bros. Knickerbocker av, east cor Melrose st, 25x100. Nov. 11, 3 years., 5 %. 4,000

Jenkins, Lois wife of and William to Herman G. Kretschmer. Broadway, s s, 50 w Bennett av, 25x100. Nov. 5, 5 years. 800

Kalt, Henrietta wife of William to William H. Jackson. Vienna av. P. M. Nov. 5, 3 years. 75

Karrass, Oscar to The Serial Building Loan and Savings Inst. Gratton st, s s, 150 e Bogart st, 25x100. Nov. 16, installs. 200

Kay, William E. to Walter L. Suydam and Henry S. Cutting. 27th st, s w s, 250 s e 4th av. P. M. Nov. 7, due Jan. 19, 1892, 5 %. 2,500

Kearney, James to Maria N. Anderson. Hall st. P. M. Sept. 15, installs. 3,000

Kings Co. Improvement Co. to Daniel S. Arnold. Van Cott av, s e cor Sutton st, 25x113 x28.6x136.8. Nov. 5, due May 1, 1892. 7,000

Kleine, Virginia A. with Thomas T. Barr both mortgagees. Agreement as to priority of morts by Michael Dowley. Nov. 12. nom

Laing, Donald to Mary E. Glover, Detroit, Mich. Belmont av, s s, 20 e Montauk av, 20x 90. Nov. 12, 3 years. 2,000

Lake, Alfred to Cornelia D. Stevens, New York. Windsor pl, s w s, 197.10 s e 7th av, 13 8x100. Nov. 10, due Dec. 1, 1892. 500

Lang, Maximilian to The Title Guarantee and Trust Co. Jefferson av, s s, 223.4 e Throop av, 16.8x100. Nov. 12, 1 year, 5 %. 4,000

Lathers, Jr., William to Josephine A. Esler. Hart st, n s, 463 w Lewis av, 16x100. Nov. 14, 1 year. 1,000

Le Beau, Theodore M. to Cordelia C. Whitney. Ashford st, e s, 250 s Ridgewood av, 25x100. Nov. 16, 3 years. 3,000

Levy, Davis and Rosa his wife and Jacob Jackerson and Annie his wife and Frank Glasser and Sarah his wife to Louis Manheim. Rockaway av, e s, 100 s Eastern Parkway, 25x 100.1. Nov. 9, installs. 400

Liebmann, Louis and Hermann to Joseph Wechsler and Abraham Abraham. Livingston st. P. M. Nov. 11, due June 6, 1896, 5 %. 8,500

Lifschitz, Abraham to Mary Goldstein. Williamson av. P. M. Nov. 13, 1 year, 5 %. 300

Lippmann, Leopold J. to Thomas C. Balderston et. al. Supreme Trustees Order of Tonti. Weirfield st, n w s, 281.8 w Central av, 20x 100. Nov. 11, 3 years, 5 %. 3,250

Loughlin, John to Patrick Cassiday. Canton st, w s, 127 n Myrtle av, 130.4x49.5 to Division st, x124x105.3. Nov. 11, 1 year, 4½ %. 12,000

Lucas, Julian to Charles H. Willets, North Hempstead. Greene av, s s, 295 e Reid av, 18.3x100. Nov. 12, 3 years, 5 %. 3,000

Same to Hannah P. Underhill and ano. exrs. Alfred Underhill. Greene av, s s, 310.3 e Reid av, 16.11x100. Nov. 12, 3 years, 5 %. 4,000

Same to Richard M. Bowne, Oyster Bay, L. I. Greene av, s s, 327.2 e Reid av, 16.10x100. Nov. 12, 3 years, 5 %. 4,000

Same to Sarah H. Powell, New York. Greene av, s s, 344 e Reid av, 16.4x100. Nov. 12, 3 years, 5 %. 4,000

Same to Maria L. Moore. Greene av, s s, 274 e Reid av, 18x100. Nov. 12, 3 years, 5 %. 3,000

Lurzner, Edward to William C. Lowther. Lexington av, north cor Concord st, 125x100. Nov. 9, 3 years. 1,500

Lyons, Carrie M. wife of and Frank to Janet Pirnie and ano. exrs. add trustees John M. Pirnie. Tillary and Raymond sts. P. M. Nov. 14, 1 year, 5 %. 2,000

Lyons, Henry B. to George H. Roberts. Lincoln pl, n s, 100 e 5th av, 26x118 8. Nov. 13, 2 years. 8,000

Same to Ann R. Roberts. Lincoln pl, n s. 128 e 5th av, 18x118.8. Nov. 13, 2 years. 5,000

Maas, Henry to Philip L. Balz, Jr. Pacific st, n s, 180 e Rochester av, 16x100. Nov. 16, 3 years. 1,000

Mace, Frank to John F. Cory. South 2d st, s s, 50 w Roebling st, 24.3x96x24.5x96. Nov. 17, 3 years, 5 %. 3,000

Maher, Thomas J. to Jane Mylet. Greene av, n w s, 229.3 n e Broadway, 20 9x100. Nov. 12, 3 years or installs. 2,000

Mahr, Adam H. to Dorothea Mahr. Patchen av, e s, 60 s Monroe st, 20x80. Nov. 16, 5 years, 5 %. 400

Same to Magdalena Polhemus widow. Same property. Nov. 16, 5 years, 5 %. 700

Maixner, Helen wife of and Andrew T. to The Co-operative Building Bank. Lots 215 and 216 block 4 map William Ziegler, Gravesend. P. M. Nov. 2, installs. 200

Manneschmidt, Jacob to Sophia Loffler and ano. trustees George Loffler. Hamburg av, n e s, 25 n w Madison st, 18 9x80. Nov. 4, 5 years, 5 %. 2,000

Marcus, Meyer and Ida his wife and Baruch Seerman and Paulina his wife to Louis Manheim. Eastern Parkway, s s, 25 e Thatford av, 25x100. Nov. 12, installs. 1,250

Mahoney, Jeremiah to Ellen O'Reilly. 11th st. P. M. Nov. 14, installs, 5 %. 1,800

Martin, Charles A. to Henry Weil. Dean st, n s, 253.1 e Utica av, 101.10x ¼ block. Building loan. Nov. 2, 6 months. 7,200

Same to same. Same property. P. M. Nov. 2, 6 months. 4,800

Mason, Frank C. to Alonzo Brymer. Adelphi st, e s, 176.3 s Willoughby av, 18.6x100. Nov. 14, 1 year. 2,000

Masters, Jarvis and Jeremiah C. Murphy and Mary C. De Noyelles to William Bennett trustee Jacques J. and Maria E. Stillwell. 56th st, s w s, 260 s e 3d av, 20x100.2, New Utrecht. Nov. 12, 3 years, 5 %. 2,500

Same to A. Gertrude Van Bruut and Eliza B. Monfort. 56th st, s w s, 240 s e 3d av, 20x 100.2, New Utrecht. Nov. 12, 3 years, 5 %. 2,500

Same to same. 56th st, s w s, 220 s e 3d av, 20 x100.2, New Utrecht. Nov. 12, 3 years, 5 %. 2,500

Max, Harris to Franziska Witte. Watkins st, w s, 100 n Eastern Parkway, 25x100. Nov. 9, 5 years. 3,000

McBride, James S. to Charles G. Peterson. 11th st. P. M. Nov. 12, 1 year, 5 %. 1,000

Same to John H. Gamgee. 5th av, n w s, 19.10 n e 20th st, 16x50. Nov. 13, 3 years. 1,500

McCarty, Elizabeth to Budweiser Brewing Co. (Lim) Herbert st, n w cor William st, 25x 100. Nov. 16, 5 years, 5 %. 1,400

McCormick, Andrew to Bedford Co-operative Building and Loan Assoc. of Brooklyn. Brooklyn av, e s, 107.10 s Carroll st, 20x100. Nov. 7, installs. 600

McDonald, Ann wife of Patrick to Millie B. De Wint, New York. Troy av, n w cor Bergen st, 28 4x85.8. Sub. to morts. $1,600. Nov. 10, due Nov. 20, 1891. 800

McGovern, Patrick to Robert L. Wood. Lefferts av, n s, 189.6 w Brooklyn av. P. M. Nov. 9, 3 years, 5 %. 337

McKnight, William to Maria L. Travis. Park pl. P. M. Nov. 12, 3 years, 5 %. 2,500

McLean, Thomas to Helen S McLean. Furman st, w s, 213.8 n Pierrepont st if extended, runs west to bulkhead line x north — x east 274.11 to beginning, with land under water, wharfage rights, &c. June 10, demand. 35,000

Meyer, Henry and Semebe Simon to Samuel and Fanny Rauer. Belmont av and Osborn st. P. M. Nov. 6, demand, 5 % 875

Midmer, Reed to Edward W. Phillips. Clifton pl. P. M. Nov. 14, 5 years, 5 %. 5,000

Same to same. Same property. P. M. Nov. 14, 1 year, 5 %. 700

Millet, Sarah J. widow to Maximilian Lang. Jefferson av. P. M. Sub. to mort. $4,000. Nov. 14, 5 year. 1,250

Moore, Williams H. to William L. Beers. Prospect pl. P. M. Nov. 14, installs. 1,000

Morris, Stephen and Mamie his wife to William Van Cleefe. Harway av, e s, adj land M. Hanley, 35.1x115.11x35x109.9. Nov. 1, 5 years 800

Morrison, William J. to The Title Guarantee and Trust Co. 47th st. P. M. Nov. 14, due Nov. 16, 1892. 800

Muir, Albert and Frank A. Barnaby to The Title Guarantee and Trust Co. Van Buren st, n s, 199.8 e Lewis av, 175.4x100. Building loan. Nov. 11, demand. 23,500

Muir, Albert to Frank A. Barnaby. Same property. Sub. to above. Nov. 11, demand. 14,000

Mullowney, Richard to Horatio S. Stewart. Halsey st, s s, 22 w Ralph av, 178x100. Sub. to mort. $4,900. Oct. 27, demand. 6,000

Murphy, Sarah J. to Margaret J. Franklin. Greenwood av, s s, 45 w East 4th st, 30x100, Flatbush. Nov. 13, 3 years 1,200

Namm, Adolph I. to Mary E. Bates. Schermerhorn st. P. M. Nov. 16, installs. 14,000

Naul, Henry S. to Samuel M. Meeker exrs. Frederick Herr. Knickerbocker av and Linden st. Nov. 13, 5 years, 5 %. 1,200

Neubert, Dorothea widow to Emily Obernier. Varet st, s s, 362.8 w White st, 25x100. Nov. 16, 5 years, 5 %. 3,000

Noll, Barbara to Minnie Trautmann. Snediker av, e s, 250 s Baltic av, 50x100. Nov. 1, 1 year, 5 %. 250

Nugent, John R. to The Brooklyn Mutual Building and Loan Assoc. Van Buren st, n s, 375 e Lewis av, 19x100. Nov. 13, installs. 2,300

Olsen, George to Jane L. Smith. Barbey st, w s, 250 n Blake av, 25x100. Oct. 31, due Nov. 1, 1894. 1,600

O'Mara, Honora to George A. D. Bartmer. 18th av, n e cor Bath av, 150x108.4. Nov. 10, due Nov. 11, 1896, 5 %. 500

Otten, John C. to The Title Guarantee and Trust Co. De Kalb av, n e cor Lewis av, 20 x80. Nov. 17, 3 years, 5 %. 4,000

Oxfeld, Anna wife of and Lewis to Jonathan H. Crane trustee Anna Walsh. Stone av, w s, 200 s Sutter av, 25x100. Nov. 13, due Jan. 2, 1895. 2,000

Paal, William P. to John Henni. Bath av, New Utrecht. P. M. Nov. 16, 5 years or sooner, 5 %. 2,500

Parmer, Ada wife of and Lewis to Franziska Witte. Watkins st, w s, 100 s Eastern Parkway, 26.6x100. Nov. 10, 1 year. 3,200

Pettit, Mortlock to John H. Broach. McDonough st, s s, 225 w Tompkins av, 40x100. Nov. 17, 6 months, 5 %. 2,000

Phillips, Catharine M. to The South Brooklyn Savings Inst. State st, n s, 181 e Clinton st, 22x117.9. Nov. 14, 1 year, 5 %. 1,000

Pitt, John R. to The Title Guarantee and Trust Co. Lexington av, s s, 88 e Marcy av, 17x50. Nov. 13, 3 years, 5 %. 1,500

Plumpton, Jennie B. wife of Horace G. to William B. Kendall. 52d st, n s, 180 e 2d av, 80x 109.4, New Utrecht. Nov. 18, 1 year. 4,500

Prinzhorn, Johanna C. M. wife of William to The Bay Ridge Mfg. Co. 76th st. P. M. Nov. 11, installs. 800

Proctor, Albert W. S. with William C. Yeoman. Agreement as to priority of morts. made by Hannah Sullivan, Nov. 14. nom

Pearce, Hannah M. with The Mutual Life Ins. Co., New York, both mortgagees. Agreement as to priority of morts. made by Henry G. Pearce. Nov. 12. nom

Pearce, Henry G. to The Mutual Life Ins. Co., New York. 5th av, n w cor 11th st, 25x95.9. Nov. 12, 1 year, 5 %. 5,000

Radcliffe, Thomas H. to George Wilson. Decatur st, n s, 428 w Howard av, 18.4x100. Nov. 2, 3 years, 5 %. 4,500

Same to John C. Schenck. Decatur st, n s, 336.4 w Howard av, 5 lots, each 18.4x100. 5 morts., each $4,500. Nov. 12, 3 years, 5 %. 22,500

Same to Elizabeth H. Bowers. Decatur st, n s, 299.8 w Howard av, 2 lots, each 18 4x100. 2 morts., each $4,500. Nov. 6, 3 years, 5 %. 9,000

Ramsdell, David J. to Edmund Dwight and ano. trustees Ellen L. Macy. St. Marks av. P. M. Nov. 18, 3 years, 5½ %. gold. 6,000

Ransom, James F. to Frank W. and Arthur J. Robbins. 10th st, n s, 137.10 w 8th av, 20x 100. Nov. 10, 1 month. 180

Rattigan, James to Bedford Co-operative Building and Loan Assoc. of Brooklyn. Brooklyn av, e s, 87.10 s Carroll st, 87.10x100. Oct. 20, installs. 500

Ray, Eliza wife of and Alexander and C. Olivia Sabine wife of and John B. to Serial Building Loan and Savings Inst. Brooklyn av, s e cor Carroll st, 20x100. Nov. 16, installs. 800

Reichardt, Charles F. to Cross, Austin & Co. Lots 2370 and 2371 block 39 map Second Addition Bensonhurst-by-the-Sea, Gravesend. Nov. 14, due Nov. 15, 1893, 5 %. 1,200

Reichenbach, Margaretha to Maria C. Barnes. 66th st, s w s, 260 n w 11th av, 53.3x100.3x 60.6x100, New Utrecht. Nov. 11, 3 years. 2,000

Reynolds, Mamie M. to Bay Ridge Impt. Co. 10th av, n e cor 71st st. P. M. Nov. 14, installs. 1,000

Richards, Edward H. to The Nassau Co-operative Building and Loan Assoc. Miller av, e s, 150 n Liberty av, 50x100. Nov. 16, installs. 2,000

Richmond, William F. to The Equitable Co-operative Building and Loan Assoc. Herkimer st, n s, 116.8 e Stone av, 16x100. Oct. 19, installs, 5 %. 2,500

Ricketson, Catharine A. wife of and Joseph H. to Jane L. Smith. Osborn st, w s, 100 n Livonia st, 50x100. Nov. 6, due Oct. 1, 1893. 600

Rigney, Joseph M. to Francis Bauman. Flushing av. P. M. Nov. 18, 5 years, 5 %. 1,500

Robbins, Aaron S. to John S. Van Cleef and ano. exrs. and trustees Daniel A. Robbins dec'd. Fulton st, south cor Clermont av, 90.4 x83.5x23.9x119.11. Nov. 12, 3 years, 5 %. 30,000

Roberts, James G. to Cyrus and Fanny R. M. Hitchcock, Poughkeepsie. McDonough st, n s, 429.6 e Reid av, 18x100. Nov. 11, 3 years, 5 %. 5,500

Same to same. McDonough st, n s, 411.6 e Reid av, 18x100. Nov. 11, 3 years, 5 %. 5,500

Roberts, James G. to Eldred A. Carley. McDonough st, n s, 312 e Reid av, 18.9x100. Sub. to mort. $3,500. Nov. 5, due Nov. 4, 1896, 5 %. 1,000

Same to same. McDonough st, n s, 375.6 e Reid av, 18x100. Sub. to mort. $5,000. Nov. 5, due Nov. 4, 1896, 5 %. 500

Rosenberg, Samuel to Alfred Bernheim and Katharine his wife. Graham av. P. M. Nov. 2, due Nov. 1, 1896, 5 %. 3,200

Rosenberg, Sarah to Henry Grasman. Hancock st. P. M. Nov. 12, installs, 5 %. 2,000

Roth, Henry to John Lannig. Hamburg av, n e cor Hart st, 25x100. Nov. 14, due Nov. 1, 1894, 5 %. 4,500

Ryan, John F. to The Kings Co. Savings Inst. Lewis av, n e cor McDonough st, 20x90. Nov. 18, 1 year, 5 %. 10,000

Sands, Helen A. wife of and William P. to The Mutual Life Ins. Co., New York. Greene av, n s, 110 w Grand av, 20x100. Nov. 12, due Nov. 13, 1892, 5 %. 1,000

Sanford, Mary E. to Caroline M. Burcham. St. Marks av, n s, 98 e Rogers av, 18x80.7x 18.5x76.6. Nov. 18, 1 year. 5 %. 1,500

Schaeffler, Alfred to Hermann F. Scharmann. Kingsland av, e s, 200 s Nassau av, 20x100. Nov. 12, due Nov. 1, 1892, 5 %. 500

Scharen, Simon to Katinka Spohr. Snediker av, e s, 125 n Belmont av, 25x100. Nov. 14, 3 years, 5 %. 2,000

Schilling, Carrie E. wife of and John A. to The Title Guarantee and Trust Co. 9th st, s s, 158.6 w 8th av, 20.5x73.6. Nov. 14, 1 year. 1,800

Schlachter, Henry and Frank Spaeth and John Senger to Anna M. Muller. Harrison pl, s s, 150 e Bogart st, 25x88.5x25x89.4. Nov. 12, due Jan. 1, 1896, 5 %. 3,350

Schliep, Louis C. to Isabella Asché. Greene av. P. M. Nov. 14, 6 months. 13,900

Schmidt, Adam and Charlotte his wife to William Schmidt and Mary his wife. Himrod st. P. M. Nov. 2, 5 years, 5 %. 1,300

Same to Henry Ostermann. Same property. P. M. Nov. 2, 3 years, 5 %. 3,000

Schoch, Jacob to George Feldmann. Greene av. P. M. Oct. 29, due Nov. 1, 1892, 5 %. 1,000

Schatz, Adam E. to John G. Gillig. Lot 6 block 82 assessm't map 25th Ward. Oct. 19, 1 year, 5 %. 1,680

Schwarz, Catherine to Emilie Huber. Moore st, n s, 279.5 w White st, 25x100. Oct. 29, 1 year. 1,510

Shadboldt, Robert J. to Charles E. Wheeler and ano. exrs. William Wheeler. Hart st. P. M. Nov. 10, 3 years, 5 %. 3,000

Same to Charles E. Wheeler. Same property. Nov. 10, 3 years or installs, 5 %. 750

Searle, Cora F. wife of William F. to John R. McDonald. Henry st, w s, 269.4 s Clark st, 22.1x93.6. Nov. 12, due May 1, 1892. 500

Sharkey, James to Jeannette G. Brown. Bridge and Front sts. P. M. Nov. 12, 1 year, 5 %. 14,000

Sibbern, William H. to E. Christian Korner and Henry Schwabeland. Tillary st, s w cor Duffield st, 25x75. Nov. 9, 2 years. 1,000

Siedler, Charles, Morristown, N. J., to Alwina Liebler extrx. Theodore A. Liebler. Bushwick av, n w cor Eldert st, 30x81.6. Oct. 2, 1 year. 6,000

Sievers, Ernst A. to Agnes Meldonny. Leonard st. P. M. Nov. 12, 5 years, 5 %. 1,400

Sinnigen, Herman to Mary Sinnigen. Wyckoff av, south cor Grove st, 25x80.4x25x80. May 1, 3 years, 5 %. 5,500

Skelton, Christopher P. to James Gascoine et al. exrs. Benjamin Evans. Dean st. P. M. Oct. 31, due May 1, 1892. 10,000

Skidmore, George W. to Mary J. Conklin. 43d st. n e s, 150 s e 12th av, 25x100. Oct. 21, 5 years, 5 %. 1,300

Smith, Laurence to South Brooklyn Co-operative Building and Loan Assoc. Dean st. P. M. Nov. 10, installs. 1,500

Smith, Adeline E. to Edward F. Linton. Ridgewood av. P. M. Nov. 12, 3 years. 450

Smith, William W. to The New York and New Jersey Telephone Co Decatur st. P. M. Nov. 16, due May 15, 1893. 4,000

Soderstrom, Erick to Edward Hopper, Philadelphia, Pa. St. Marks av, n s, 250 w Underhill av, 25x131x—x—. Nov. 17, 5 years, 5 %. 5,500

Same to John Damon and Kate L. his wife. St. Marks av, n s, 275 w Underhill av, 25x131. Nov. 17, 5 years, 5 %. 5,500

Spaltboff, Adolph and Minnie his wife to Christian Mayer. Sutter av, n s, 25 e Van Sielen av, 25x100. Nov. 12, 5 years. 500

Stephens, Frank M. to Clarence A. Thompson guard. 77th st, n e s, 140 n w 4th av, 100x109.4. March 17, 3 years. 866

Sullivan, Hannah wife of and Philip to William C. Yeoman. Vanderbilt av, w s, 50 n Pacific st, 25x75. Nov. 14, installs. 1,000

Sullivan, Daniel to South Brooklyn Co operative Building and Loan Assoc. 40th st, s s, 125 e 4th av, 25x100.2. Nov. 10, installs. 3,000

Sutherland, Kenneth F. and Annie his wife to John Y. McKane. Lot 3 block 59 of School District No. 6, Coney Island, bounded north by land of New York & Coney Island R. R. Co., east by land of Conrad Sutherland, south by Surf av and west by centre line of proposed West 21st st. Nov. 17, 5 years or installs. 1,000

Sutton, Margaret E. wife of and Theodore W. to Olivia Reynolds. St. Marks av, s s, 16.6 e Rogers av, 16.6x95. Nov. 16, due Nov. 1, 1894, 5 %. 3,750

Taylor, Thomas to Nellie A. wife of Henry A. Hiers. Lexington av, s w s, 50 n w Forest pl, 50x100. Nov. 18, due Jan. 2, 1892. 400

Taylor, Sarah wife of and Alexander to Thomas C. Balderston et al. Supreme Trustees Order of Tonti. Weirfield st, n w s, 301 s w Central av, 20x100. Nov. 11, 3 years, 5 %. 3,250

Templin, Joseph H., Reading, Pa., to Hoik D. Campbell. Stewart av and 81st st, Fort Hamilton av and 81st st, 6th av and 81st st, New Utrecht. P. M. Nov. 10, 1 year, 5 %. 4,800

Same to same. Same property. 2d mort. Nov. 10, due Nov. 11, 1894, 5 %. 800

The Brooklyn Hotel Co. to John W. Hunter. Clinton st. P. M. Oct. 17, 1 year, 5 %. 11,000

The Church of Our Lady of Victory, Brooklyn, to Emigrant Indust. Savings Bank. Throop av, e s, extends from McDonough st to Macon st, 200x300. Additional mort. Nov. 7, 1 year, 4½ %. 70,000

The Kings County Improvement Co. to Daniel S. Arnold. Nassau av, n e cor Kingsland av, 200 to Sutton st, x100. Nov. 16, due June 1, 1893. 7,000

The Rector, Churchwardens and Vestrymen of the P. E. Church of the Holy Spirit, Bath Beach, L. I., to James H. Smith agent. Bay 17th st, e s, 50 s 86th st, 100x96.8, New Utrecht. Sept. 30, due Oct. 1, 1893, 5 %. 2,000

Thompson, Charles M. to Theodore H. and Rulsey J. Fuller, Eloise F. Sexton, Emma F. Bodine and Elizabeth W. Peck. Nichols av. P. M. Oct. 16, due Nov. 1, 1892. 1,500

Tonyes, Annie to David M. Koehler. Bedford av. P. M. Sept. 8, 1 year. 500

Urban, Frederick to Edward and Fernando Barbig. 17th st, south cor 10th av, 20x80. Sub. to mort. $3,000. Oct. 12, 1 year, 5 %. 1,628

Van Buren, Ansel H. to Henry J. Lankenau. Howard av, s w cor McDonough st, 100x350. Nov. 14, 2 years. 10,500

Van Kirk, Rachel A. to The Title Guarantee and Trust Co. 6th st. P. M. Nov. 11, 1 year. 4,000

Van Orden, George O. to The Title Guarantee and Trust Co. 6th av, n e cor 15th st, 56x98x54x97.10. Nov. 14, demand. 13,500

Same to Henrietta Griggs. 6th av, 15th st. P. M. This mort. was discharged Nov. 16, 1891. Sept. 9, due Dec. 1, 1891. 2,600

Van Tine, Frederick to The West Brooklyn Land and Improvement Co. 45th st. P. M. June 15, due Sept. 15, 1895, 5 %. 420

Vossler, Daniel, Jr., to Effie V. V. wife of Charles H. Knox. Rockaway av. w s, 36.4 s Marion st, 16x50. Nov. 16, 3 years. gold, 1,300

Same to Sarah E. Van Wyck, Johnsville, N. Y. same property. Nov. 16, 3 years. gold, 900

Same to Sarah E. Van Wyck extrx. Anna L. Van Vechten. Rockaway av, No. 60, w s, 20.1 s Marion st, 16.3x50. Nov. 16, 3 years. gold, 2,200

Vetter, Louisa K. to Joseph Maurer. Stagg st, n s, 75 w Waterbury st, 25x100. Sub. to morts. $2,500. Oct. 30, due Nov. 1, 1892. 500

Wagner, Antonie widow to Barbara Kraemer. Broadway, s w cor Park av, 36.5x81.4x33 3x31.8. Nov. 13, due Dec. 1, 1894, 5 %. 3,000

Waldron, John H. to Charles H. Smith. Jerome st. P. M. Sub. to mort. $2,500. July 15, installs. 125

Walsh, Michael F. to Watson & Pittinger. Rockaway av, w s, 36 n Sumpter st, 16x68.3. Oct. 7, demand. 500

Watrous, William L., Waverly, N. Y., to Clarence A. Thompson guard. 4th av, s w cor 75th st, 107.2x140, New Utrecht. March 13, 1890. 2,000

Weberlovsky, Jacob H. and Abraham Greenstone to Emily Obernier. Boerum st, s s, 200 w Graham av, 25x100. Nov. 10, 3 years, 5 %. 6,500

Weil, Frederick and Katie his wife to Mary W. Smith. Hinsdale st, w s, 275 s Dumont av, 20x100. Nov. 13, 3 years. 1,000

Weisenstein, George to Alexander Buderus. Miller av, w s, 125 n Broadway, 25x100; Miller av, w s, lot 882 block BB map A, East New York, 25x100. Oct. 2, due Dec. 1, 1893. 1,000

Welcher, Charles to Samuel M. Meeker exr. Frederick Herr. Central av, n e s, 50 n w Woodbine st, 25x100. Nov. 13, 3 years, 5 %. 3,500

Wheelan, Catharine A. wife of and George H. to Christian Mayer. Liberty av, n s, 75.7 w Schenck av, 25.5x100. Nov. 10, 3 years. 1,200

Wheeler, Mary A. wife of Thomas E. to The Home Life Ins. Co. St. Marks av, s s, 60 w Carlton av, 20x81. Nov. 11, 1 year, 5 %. 3,000

Wheeler, Charles B. to Sadie E. Rice. Madison st, s s, 470 w Patchen av, 20x100. Nov. 12, 1 year. 500

Same to same. Madison st, s s, 450 w Patchen av, 20x100. Nov. 12, 1 year. 500

Whitton, Alice F. to Cornelius N. Hoagland. Quincy st, n s, 80 e Bedford av, 20x100. Nov. 13, due Nov. 1, 1894, 5 %. gold, 2,000

Whitehead, Charles to William P. Hillmann. 47th st. P. M. Nov. 16, 2 years. 200

Wilhelms, Charles to The Title Guarantee and Trust Co. Eastern Parkway, s s, 63.3 w Utica av, 40x103.3. Nov. 14, 1 year, 5 %. 5,000

Willdridge, John S. to Raeburn, Latourette & Co. Reid av, e s, 60 n Hancock st, 19.2x100. Sub. to building loan not to exceed $9,000. Nov. 12, 4 months. 1,400

Williams, James M. to Esther Williams. 53d st, n e s, 300 s e 4th av, 20x100.2. Nov. 13, 5 years, 5 %. 1,000

Same to same. Same property. Nov. 13, 5 years, 5 %. 500

Williams, Carrie K. wife of William P. to Sarah A. Grinnell. Leonard st. P. M. Nov. 17, 3 years. 3,900

Williams, Percy G. and Thomas Adams, Jr., to The Home Life Ins. Co. 3d av, n w cor Schermerhorn st, runs west 75 x north 75 x west 0.7 x east 57.5 to Flatbush av, x south 52.11 to 3d av, x southwest 93.4. Oct. 29, due Nov. 18, 1892, 5 %. 25,000

Wilson, Thomas A. to Anna Constable. Clinton st, w s, 284.6 n Degraw st, 20x106. Nov. 14, demand, 5 %. 4,000

Wood, Frank F. to Henry F. Ogden, Hoboken, N. J. Union st, n s, 331.3 w 8th av. P. M. Sept. 11, 1 year, 5½ %. 12,000

Same to same. Union st, n s, 312.6 w 8th av. P. M. Sept. 11, 1 year, 5½ %. 12,000

Same to same. Union st, n s, 200 w 8th av. P. M. Sept. 11, 1 year, 5½ %. 12,000

Wood, Herman H. to James Cline. 8th st, n s, 185.4 w 7th av, 18.9x100. Nov. 2, 3 years, 5 %. 4,000

Wood, Angeline P. wife of Jefferson F. to Mary Wright. 14th st, s w s, 457.10 n w 4th av, 20x94 4x20x94.10. Nov. 18, 5 years, 5 %. 1,500

Young, Rosa A. wife of and Peter to The Title Guarantee and Trust Co. Berkeley pl, n s, 100 w 8th av, 22.6x100. Nov. 13, due Nov. 14, 1894, 5 %. 9,000

Same to same. Willoughby av, n s, 64.1 w Carlton av, 20x70.6x20.5x74.7. Nov. 14, 3 years, 5 %. 5,000

Zierleu, Regine to William J. G. Bearns. Van Pelt av. P. M. Sub. to mort. $3,000. Nov. 17, 5 years, 5 %. 2,000

Same to The Kings County Savings Inst. Same property. Nov. 17, 1 year, 5 %. 3,000

Zindel, Benjamin F. to Lewis S. Davis. McDougal st. P. M. Nov. 13, 3 years. 2,000

MORTGAGES----ASSIGNMENTS.

NEW YORK CITY.

NOVEMBER 13 TO 19—INCLUSIVE

Auerbach, Meyer to John N. Hayward. $1,500

Brenen, Edward and Catharine his wife to Nellie F. Brennan. consid. omitted

Barney, Charles T. to Alfred M. Hoyt. nom

Bazen, Mary A. to Bazena T. Downes. nom

Beemer, Elizabeth S. to Henrietta E. Shelton. 7,000

Beckmann, Marcus to William Fenn guard. of Ida Walli. 6,080

Cohen, Cassel to Joseph Winter. 6,000

Coleman, Meyer and Marx Manheimer, to Isabella Stewart. 4,008

Cook, George H. et al. exrs. and trustees Elisha Bloomer to Kate M. Spear, Brooklyn. 15,000

Cameron, Alexander to The Henry McShane Mfg. Co., Baltimore, Md. 3,000

Chambers, Sarah O., formerly Mitchell, wife of and Brinton H. Chambers to Abraham B. Odell exr. Jacob D. Odell. 2,370

Cheever, John H. to New York Belting and Packing Co. 250,000

Clarke, Sarah M. extrx. Corson W. Clarke to Robert B. Snowden, Brooklyn. nom

Corsa, Mary to William H. Palmer and ano. exrs. Mary A. Stead. 3,500

Daly, Margaret wife of and Patrick to Charles G. Deutch, New Haven, Conn. 2,005

De Bruin, Julia J. to Herman Levy. 4,000

Durant, William W., Saratoga Springs, N. Y., to Heloise H. Durant, Saratoga Springs, N. Y. 119,069

Durant, Janet L. wife of William W., Saratoga Springs, N. Y., to Heloise H. Durant. 17,000

Same to same. 17,000

Same to same. 27,500

Ellis, John S. exr. Julia Waterbury to Antoinette L. Edwards. 4,000

Same to same. 20,000

Same to Gertrude C. Winthrop. 24,000

Friedenheit, Isaac to Myer Hellman. nom

Same to same. nom

Ford, Henry W. trustee Augustus H. Ward to Frederick A. Snow. 52,000

Foster, Frederic de P. trustee George H. Carey to Philip J. Sands as trustee. 13,000

Gage, Eleanor P. to Wellesley W. Gage. 7,000

Gage, Wellesley W. to Orville D. Bennet. 7,000

Gordon, Katie to Helen Adams extrx. William Adams. 2,559

Same to same. 8,072

Goldberg, Lewis to Selda Goldberg. 150

Gordon, Robert and Joseph to Thomas R. A. and William H. Hall, of William Hall's Sons. nom

German-American Real Estate Title Guarantee Co. to Julius Goebel. 15,000

Hunter, Katharine R., Pelham Manor, N. Y., to Frederick Schuchardt, Newtown, L. I. nom

Hyatt, George E., Brooklyn, to Edward Winslow. nom

Hebberd, Isaac N. to William H. Palmer and ano. exrs. Mary A. Stead. 3,500

Hoffman, Daniel to Joseph Steiner. 4,500

Happel, Adam to Peter Schupp. 3,500

Hutchison, Susan B., Brooklyn, to Florence H. Cocks. nom

Jencks, Francis M. to Francis P. Furnald. nom

Lichtenstein, Benjamin to Alexander Lichtenstein. nom

Luyster, Peter exr. Sarah M. Luyster to Catharine L. Fairweather and Cornelia L. Luyster. 778

Le Count, John, New Rochelle, N. Y., to Charles A. Dean, Boston, Mass. 7,105

Landon, Charles G. trustee Peter S. Pillot to Peter S. Pillot, Orange, N. J. nom

Muller, Hugo R. to Bertha Krefft. 250

Middlebrook, Frederic J., Brooklyn, to Sarah V. Benson. 3,016

Same to same. 3,016

Middlebrook, Frederic J., Brooklyn, to Sarah E. Woodbury, Bayside, L. I. 6,076

Same to James N. Platt and ano. trustees for Lucy B. Seaver and Sarah R. Sheldon. 6,116

Same to same. 10,214

Middlebrook, Frederic J., Brooklyn, to Charles E. Rhinelander. nom

More, Elizabeth, Hoboken, N. J., to Lewis Moore. 2,000

Morris, Henry L. to Horace F. Pritchard. 3,500

Morgenthau, Henry to Alfred T. Leward. 5,201

Manheimer, Morris to Morris Mayer. 8,000

Mickle, George B., Flushing, L. I., to Lawrence E. Embree, Flushing, L. I. 1,000

McWilliam, John S. to Charles Meyerhoff. 2,000

Mahr, Henry J. to Jacob Schlosser. 14,900

Manning, William D. to William Hall's Sons. nom

New York Belting and Packing Co. to New York Belting and Packing Co. (Lim.) 250,000

Ogden, David B. to Mathilda Oppenheimer and Bertha Metzger. 28,000

Peabody, Charles A., Jr., to George L. Peabody. 5,000

Plunkett, Thomas to Patrick, John and Thomas Plunkett. 13,000

Platt, James N. trustee George A. Osgood dec'd to John A. Lewis et al. trustees for Cornelia L. Fowler. 7,244

Platt, James N. exr. and trustee Catharine A. Schuchardt to Frederick Schuchardt and Katharine R. Hunter. nom

Reid, Elizabeth to Herbert T. Lindsley. 2,502

Ranney, Harriet B. to Mary A. wife of Duane S. Everson. 5,112

Roosevelt, James A. trustee for Clarisse Ludwig to James A. and W. Emlen Roosevelt trustees for Clarisse Ludwig. Re-recorded. nom

Roosevelt, James A. trustee for Clarisse Ludwig to James A. and W. Emlen Roosevelt trustees for Clarisse Ludwig. nom

Rieser, Jacob to Jacob Schlosser exr. and trustee Christian L. Nunenkamp. 4,556

Robert, Francis B. to Lucia M. Cohen. 1,000

Ringler, Frederick A. to Florenz Hofmann. 5,000

Randel, J. Augustus to Albert R. Le Doux. 3,000

Schnitker, Justine to Henry Fulling. 4,000

Snowden, Robert B., Brooklyn, to Henrietta E. Shelton. 1,800

Parties	Amount
Sherman, Marie A., London, Eng., to Sarah A. Sands.	4,500
Spaes, Henry to Augustus H. Dieck.	8,000
Sherman, Marie A., London, Engd., to James A. Roosevelt and ano. trustees of Marcia R. Scovel.	5,000
Scott, William F. to Waldo Hutchins trustee of Martha Stewart dec'd.	2,000
Schwegler, Louise to Henry B. Auchincloss and ano. exrs. John Auchincloss.	18,000
Steers, Henry and John F. Menke to Lizzie A. wife of Henry Steers.	7,000
Snow, Mary P. to William N. Crane.	nom
Same to same.	nom
Schuck, Frederick to Katie Hoehn.	7,000
Snow, Frederick A. to James Stokes.	50,000
Schneider, Louis exr. Anna Schwarz to Louise Georgi.	2,500
Same to same.	3,500
Stevens, Howard A. to John Barber, Philadelphia.	2,500
The People's Trust Co. to The German-American Real Estate Title Guarantee Co.	15,000
Title Guarantee and Trust Co. to Henry B. Barnes.	25,000
Same to Maria L. Tillotson.	8,500
Same to James Sullivan.	2,500
Title Guarantee and Trust Co. to Ambrose K. Ely, Mary J. Walker and Emily A. Watson as exrs.	45,000
Walker, Thomas S. to Hall J. How.	nom
Wolff, Theresa to Hyman Schnitzer.	nom
Wolff, Dorothea to The Hebrew Benevolent and Orphan Asylum Society of the City of New York.	13,000
Witherell, Rebecca to Mathilda Oppenheimer and Bertha Metzger.	28,000
Winslow, Edward to William N. Crane.	nom
Same to same.	nom
Winslow, Edward to Charles Lanier trustee for Alexander C. Lanier.	16,000
Walsh, Maurice to Catharine Nunan.	2,500
Ziegler, Louis to William Knoepke.	5,000

KINGS COUNTY.

NOVEMBER 12 TO 18—INCLUSIVE.

Parties	Amount
Balz, Jr., Philip L. to John E. Greany.	$1,200
Benedict, Sarah S. et al. trustees George and Henry B. Cromwell to George Cromwell.	10,000
Beames, Franklin to Leni L. Dietz extrx. Charles H. Dietz.	1,800
Brown, Mary L. to Pierre M. Brown.	2,500
Brown, Pierre M. to The Title Guarantee and Trust Co.	2,000
Brown, George R. to George H. Grannis.	12,000
Brown, Adam admr. Hannah Goodman to Lizzie and Margaret H. Dunn extrxs. Patrick Dunn.	1,130
Burger, Clarence L. trustee Elenezer H. Burger to Mary E. Moffat.	6,000
Barnard, George G. to John Webber and ano. trustees for George G. Barnard.	3,000
Cortelyou, Lawrence V. et al. exrs. Jacques Cortelyou to Lawrence V. Cortelyou.	4,000
Covert, George to Phebe A. Godfrey.	3,355
Campbell, Holk D. to George S. Ingraham.	2,800
Chamberlin, Theodore G. to Noah Tebbetts.	500
Cozine, John H. to William H. McKee.	400
Culver, John L. to Jacob W. Erregger.	1,200
Chamberlin, Theodore G., Orange Co., Vt., to Paul W. Ledoux.	500
Crane, Laura C. to Elizabeth Low.	11,069
Dexter, Henrietta D. to S. K. Dexter.	nom
Fullhardt, George to Emil Lehrian.	3,000
Gay, Jr., Charles, to Huldah Smith.	1,200
Geary, H. Seymour trustee Malvina W. Appleton to Daniel S. and Malvina Appleton.	3,000
Geertz, Charles J. A. to William H. Friday.	nom
German-American Real Estate Title Guarantee Co. to The People's Trust Co.	4,000
Same to same.	4,000
Goodwin, Richard to Theodore F. Jackson et al. trustees Loftis Wood dec'd.	6,729
Hinrichs, C. F. A. to Edwin Packard trustee for Elizabeth L. Hutchinson.	6,000
Hubburt, Lawrence to Mary J. Edwards and ano. exrs. Jonathan Edwards.	3,250
Hay, Margaret E. to Frederick C. Schmidt.	500
Hawley, Richard to A. C. Bournonville, Philadelphia, Pa.	2,400
Hollister, Sebastian T. to Albert G. McDonald.	1,050
Jackson, Theodore F. et al. trustees Loftis Wood to Susan P. Du Bois trustee Susan P. Du Bois.	3,042
Jackson. William H. to Catharine E. Rowland, Woodhaven Junction, L. I.	1,500
Kleine. Virginia A. to Thomas T. Barr.	15,000
Koch, Frank W. & Co. to Jacob Manneschmidt.	nom
Klots, Charles A. to Gayton Ballard.	2,100
Lowell, Sidney V. to David J. Deane.	1,500
Lehrian, Emil to Charles J. Rauck, Sr.	3,000
Manning, Catharine M. to Clarence B. Smith.	1,900
Martin, Levi V. to Leffert L. Bergen.	750
Magaw, Matilda W. to Jennie Botsford, New York.	3,000
Munch, Sophie and ano. exrs. Ferdinand Munch to The Ferdinand Munch Brewery.	nom
Neely, Robert S. to Peter Anderson.	800
Nostrand, J. Lott to Mary A. Young.	2,000
Nulty, Francis to Anne wife of Maurice Daly.	500
Ochs, George to Henry Roth and Alois Lazansky.	2,227
Remsen, George A. to Edmund A. Gearon.	500
Rice, Sadie E. to Frederick W. Rebhann.	1,000
Rauer, Samuel and Fanny to Eva Siegel.	875
Rheinfeldt, Adolph to Augustus C. Fischer.	350
Rosenfeld, Lena to C. Olivia Sabine.	225
Stockman, Elizabeth to William H. Chapman admr. Adaline Wanser.	900
Serini, Frederica to Frederick Seibel.	1,000
Story, Francis, Jr., exr. Margaret M. Brown to Ira, Theodore H., David, James B. and Theodore H. Burditt, Washington, D. C.	nom
Swan, Ellen L., extrx. Ozias McCarty to John A. Melven.	1,800
Tapscott, Frank L. to Charles Schaper.	1,500
The Coal Handling Machinery and Construction Co. (Lim.) to Charles M. Bellows.	consid. omitted
Taylor, Peter exr. Barbara Robertson to John McCourt.	1,200
Title Guarantee and Trust Co. Mortimer J. Lyons.	5,000
Same to Michael J. Garvey.	3,500
Same to George S. Ingraham.	15,000
Same to Edwin Packard trustee Elizabeth H. Callender.	6,000
Same to Mary A. Knight et al. trustees Henry Knight dec'd.	5,000
Same to same.	5,000
Same to George H. Wheeler.	5,000
Same to same.	5,000
Same to Lewis D. Mason and ano. exrs. and trustees Theodore L. Mason.	5,000
Same to Malcolm Graham and George L. Nichols as trustees.	9,000
Same to Frank Jenks.	4,000
Same to Josephine Parcels guard. of Lester G. Parcels.	3,500
Same to The Young Women's Christian Assoc. of Brooklyn.	3,000
Same to The Brooklyn Trust Co.	4,000
Same to same.	4,000
Same to The Franklin Trust Co. trustee for Alice O. Low Sand.	4,950
Same to Nellie E. Tousey guard. Ralph, Elizabeth and Louise Tousey.	800
Wheeler, Mary A. to The Title Guarantee and Trust Co.	1,600
Woodhull, Ann M. wife of Jesse C. to Olivia Reynolds.	1,100
Wade, William J. to Rebecca Kissam.	gift
Wyckoff, William F., Jamaica, L. I., to Ditmars Eldert.	1,200

JUDGMENTS.

NEW YORK CITY.

Nov.	Parties	Amount
14	Auspitz, Julius—G W Venable	$446 00
14	Appleton, William H; Appleton, William W—G T Newhall	6,420 15
16	Ambrose, Thomas—Marcus Murray	42 50
16	Abrams, Annie—Harris Goldstein	544 44
17†	Appel, Alexander—M L Simon	155 45
17	Adams, William—B G Coles	107 60
17	Aronson, Alexander—David Block	225 58
17	the same—the same	325 78
17	Arthur, Frank D—L M Castner	730 77
17	Adler, Phil—N Y Bottlers' Supply Mfg Co	182 33
17	Abrams, Abraham R—G M Miller	534 47
18	Appel, Emanuel—James Talcott	376 76
18	Aquiar, Fiburcio—Sigmund Ashner	175 60
18	Allen, John—Julia Crowley	92 18
19	Allen, John C—T S Croly	3,418 44
19*	Albright, Charles H—F S Passavant	1,554 20
19	the same—the same	758 70
19	Abeles, Emil—T F Johnson	414 73
19	Anderson, Lawrence—People State N Y	100 00
20†	Ambuhl, John—Albert Goettmann	287 92
20	Anderson, George W—J A Hyland ...costs	90 02
20	Acker, William J—David Meyer	301 55
14	Blass, Charles; Blass, Theresa—Valentine Kirsch	452 63
14	Beacham, John—W J Weedon	349 70
14	Brush, Louis M—Bay State Shoe and Leather Co	190 51
14	Brennan, Mark P—W D Lent	400 11
14	Barth, Adam—Charles Kramer	204 27
14	Buhre, Daniel—John Glackner..costs	81 14
14	Browne, Jacob—Jacob Heilbronn	900 91
14	Bach, Albert—Thomas Houston	756 89
16	Burue, William C—Peter Otto	146 08
16	Bernard, Joseph; Bernard, John—S W Ebrich	280 00
16	Byrnes, Matthew—Union Boat Club	38 50
16	Barnum, Stephen—Henry Zahn	190 03
16	Burmeister, Henry—C F Gennerich	388 94
16	Bridge, Charles L F—Madison Square Bank	284 81
16	Brinkerhoff, Cornelius M; Brinkerhoff, Mary E—C E Wilmot	813 06
16	Brennan, Thomas—F W Meeker	544 84
17	Behr, Lewis—Leopold Jacobson	200 17
17	Brennen, Matthew—A F Brugman	304 95
17	Bennett, Andrew S—Merchants' and Farmers' Nat Bank	282 53
17	Barringer, Harvey C—L G Quinlan	109 50
17	Bridge, Charles L T—H P Carlson	171 37
17	Bonnell, J Harper—Nat Shoe and Leather Bank	1,065 88
17	Bonnell, John Harper—Bank of N Y Nat Banking Assoc	5,529 22
17	Buckley, John—Hancke Hencken	129 34
17	Bendix, August—Myer Foster	80 13
17	Bischoff, Franklin J—Mary J Gleason	578 52
18	Batcheller, William H; *Beal, Royal A—E A Moir	606 77
18†	Brower, John D—H M Rogers	120 10
18	Brennan, Michael—Henry Brunhild	165 95
19	Beacham, John—F A Ringler Co	255 76
19	Becker, Louis—L W Duesing....costs	121 72
19	Bonfield, Peter; Bournakis, Nicholas—People State N Y	100 00
19	Blackburn, Robert S—Alexander McSorley	95 62
19	Bournakis, Nicholas—People State N Y	100 00
19	Busch, Henry—the same	100 00
19	Bournakis, Nicholas—the same	100 00
20	Best, William J, recvr—Davis Sewing Machine Co of Watertown, N Y, et al....costs	155 34
20	the same—H M Stevens....costs	105 40
20	the same—Williard Ives...costs	105 40
14	Collins, Charles H—The J L Mott Iron Works	128 51
14	Cohen, David—German Exchange Bank	122 41
14	Cranston, Henry—Carlo Maspero	326 46
14*	Conrath, Charles W—A A Thomson	587 19
14	Carr, Walter T; Carr, Delwin B—Herman Reel	541 08
16	Cramer, Frederick—Donatus Rieger	262 07
16	Cox, W L—Alfred Walton......costs	28 72
16	Conway, James—Herrmann Weiller	512 41
16	Cummings, William A—Diederich Abbes	776 98
17	Corrigan, William; Carroll, John—People State N Y	300 00
18*	Cabot, William S—H M Rogers	120 10
18	Clark, Francis A—East River Electric Light Co.....costs	87 47
18	Cohn, Albert—John Eichler Brewing Co	203 68
18	Chasseau, Alfred—C E Mather	138 08
18	Chace, Earl B—D L Bartlett....costs	95 86
19	Crowe, Eugene F—Cora C Rusbby	159 70
19	Cranston, Henry—Ferdinand Neumer	325 59
19	the same—Elise Dittmar	488 50
19	Cohen, Henry—People State N Y	300 00
19	Comisky, Louis; Comisky, Solomon—the same	100 00
19	Callum, Charles—Isaac Boehm	124 00
20	Chapman, Charles J—N Y Cooperage Co	692 69
20	Cavinato, Luigi; *Cavinato, Guiseppi; *Cavinato, Stefano; *Cavinato, Natale—John Donnellon	217 41
20	Cochrane, John Wilson, admr William Smith—Mayor, &c	336 82
20	Celeio, Vincenzo; Celeio, Marie—Angelo Ghiglione	157 85
20	Carling, John—William Purcell..costs	90 63
20	Chieffo, Frederigo—George De Mets	67 80
20	Cobb, Frederick W—Dunbar Box and Lumber Co	1,157 05
20	Cassidy, George H—James Whitall	42 56
20	Crawford, Robert J—Hollister Mfg Co	366 02
14	Durham, Frederick F—D F Cunningham	395 58
16§	Dyckoff, John C—Importers' and Traders' Nat Bank	779 87
16	Davis, Wolff—Dry Dock, East Broadway & Battery R R Co.......costs	116 39
16*	David, Albert A—J B Case	2,201 15
16	the same—F W Otheman	2,047 08
17	Davis, Ralph—M E Dailey	764 91
17	Demarest, William E—H C Pell, exr and trustee	120 79
17	Derbyshire, William H—Gabriel Fensterer	149 40
17	Dempsey, William—Arlando Marine	1,086 78
17	Dougherty, William J—Barriett Electric Co	202 18
17*	David, Albert A—H J Hinch	2,156 81
18	Davids, Charles H—Metropolitan Telegraph and Telephone Co	43 49
18	Dudenhausen, Frank—John McKesson, Jr	241 53
19	Dilks, Mary D—W J Ruddell	148 52
19	the same—the same........costs	17 50
19	Donohue, Philip—M P Breslin	492 51
19	Dolan, John—People State N Y	100 00
19	Dean, William M—E F Ely	176 32
19	Downey, Charles—F W Robbins.costs	88 93
19	Dolan, Nora—People State N Y	100 00
20	Delahanty, James J—W H Schmohl	844 09
20	Delafield, Richard—Downie Boiler Incrustation Preventive Co	365 13
20*	Doe, John—Dunbar Box and Lumber Co	1,157 05
20	Dunlop, George I—Georgiana P Hotchkiss	222 16
14	Ewing, Justus E—Lenox Hill Bank	5,430 75
16	Eisenberg, Henrietta—Jacob Feuchtwanger	84 56
16	Ehlers, William—J S Foster, exr	1,551 08
16§	Eising, Emanuel—Importers' and Traders' Nat Bank	779 87
16	Erslev, Victor P P—Abraham Steers	3,653 48
17*	Esberg, Isaac B—Emanuel Frey	100 82
18	*Ellis, Delia; Ellis, John—Elizabeth Schwarzwalder	127 87
18	Ensmenger, Philip—Isaac Sugarman	277 00
19	Ellis, Edward S—Market and Fulton Nat Bank	1,012 96
19	Earl, John W—People State N Y	100 00
20	Egan, Ann—Max Wolff	78 41
20	Evans, Frederick—Adolph Bondy	107 07
14	Fitzpatrick, Louis J—H M Hitchings, recvr	464 23
14†	Fortony, Elizabeth C—Metropolitan Life Ins Co	98 50

§Editor RECORD AND GUIDE:

A stay has been granted of thirty days in which to make a case on appeal. Appeal is now being perfected, and security will be given before stay expires.

EMANUEL EISING,
JOHN C. DYCKHOFF.

14¶Fallon, Thomas F—De Lamater Iron Works.......... 275 18
17 Friedland, Abraham S—David Block. 225 58
17 the same——the same.......... 325 78
16 Fink, Marcus—Harris Goldstein...... 544 44
17 Fitzgerald, James—G W Venable.... 418 21
18 Fuld, Samuel / Fuld, Seligman } Burr Brewing Co.. 101 04
18 Fieseler, John C—G H Stege.........1,464 45
18 Friedman, Alfred—G R Brown...... 73 74
18 Franz, John—Leopold Schwarzkopf.. 32 63
18 Foster, Julius—Russell & Erwin Mfg Co.......... 87 19
19 Feiner, Solomon—John Coyne..costs 91 75
19 Fuhlrott, Otto—John Isenman 422 69
19 Faulkner, James A—Alexander McSorley.......... 95 62
19 Flynn, Thomas—People State N Y... 300 00
19 Farrell, James H—Mayor, &c.........1,644 47
20 Fechteler, Henry—J H Merritt....... 81 46
16 Goodwin, William H—N F Vought... 287 85
17 Geschwind,, Samuel — Abraham Schlein.......... 618 85
17 Green, William B—M R Cooke....... 281 80
17 Garrison, Ferdinand C / Garrison, Emma } Richard Johnson.... 79 60
18 Goldberger, Marlin—H N Camp...... 19 50
18 Gillie, Daniel R, Jr — Elizabeth Schwarzwalder.......... 89 27
18 Griffith, John F—G F Bassett........ 106 21
19 Gillen, Patrick H—William Peter Brewing Co 865 71
19 Gould, David B—A S Hunter......... 558 61
19 Gilday, Michael—People State N Y.. 100 00
19 Grimes, Stephen——the same....... 300 00
19 Gembs, George—Louis Funk.......... 210 49
19 Grant, Joseph F / Grant, Edward G } T E Greacen....1,211 75
20 Goldsmith, Pauline—Health Dept.... 209 87
20 Gray, David S—Hamblin & Russell Mfg Co.......... 83 67
20 Graham, John C—Morris Schwabie... 29 80
20 Griffin, La Roy F—S T Dauchy...... 583 71
20 Grossman, Emanuel—Rosa Rubovitz. 455 00
20 Gottshalk, Charles—C V Fornes...... 120 57
14 Hay, John / *Hay, Robert } J L Mott Iron Works.. 128 51
14 Hungerford, Egbert H—R T Pierce..1,018 95
14 Hazard, Rowland N / *Hazard, John C / *Hazard, Herbert } J W Loveland.1,330 25
14 Harris, Azariah B — Southern Nat Bank..........5,619 22
16 Horan, Kerren—M A Cunningham... 334 53
16 Halpine, William D—John Baehr.... 326 00
16 Horn, Jacob M—H S Eisler.......... 48 08
17 Holmes, Edward—J V Black.......... 328 91
17 Hagan, Bernard—People State N Y.. 300 00
17 Harper, William D—Nat Shoe and Leather Bank..........1,065 88
17 Harper, William Durbin—Bank of N Y Nat Banking Assoc..........5,529 22
17 Hoy, Nicholas—C H Rose.......... 159 57
17 Howell, Eugene N—Fourth Nat Bank 4,832 56
17 Howard, Hary T—E S Greeley & Co. 314 18
17 Hassell, Henry—G S Hamlin, assignee 296 15
18 Hess, Edward—Isaac Boehm.......... 97 40
18 Hoyt, Russell P—G T McCormick.... 632 27
18 Hammond, Catharine R—J D Townsend.......... 838 18
19 Harper, William D—Market and Fulton Nat Bank 1,012 96
19 Hartley, Sarah E—E J Denning.....1,095 60
19 Hearn, Francis D V / Hearn, Mary I } L K Smith..... 108 72
19 Hurwitz, David / Hurwitz, Rebecca } People State N Y 300 00
19 Heinrich, Joseph——the same......... 300 00
19 Hull, Lewis—Gertrude E Clark...... 64 50
19 Heinzer, John—Mary S Wood......... 447 08
20 Hamilton, John—R B Gray.......... 467 69
20 Hart, Lizzie H—Samuel Haas........ 73 58
20 Holcomb, Wright — Nat Shoe and Leather Bank.......... 409 46
20 Isaacs, Isaac A—Campbell Printing Press and Mfg Co.......... 234 99
14*Jarvis, Frank—Phœnix Furniture Co. 39 60
16 Jerkowski, Marcus—F W Otheman...2,047 08
16 the same——J B Case..........2,201 15
17 Jones, Lyman N—E C Tracy.......... 163 08
17 Jerkowski, Marcus—H J Hinck......2,156 31
19 Jennings, Patrick, Jr — Herman Schweider.......... 89 96
19 Jurratus, James—People State N Y.. 100 00
20 Jacobi, Theodore—Royer Wheel Co .. 154 84
14 Kneeland, Sylvester H—J E Simmons, recvr..........27,367 02
16 Kellogg, A Bigelow—W W Astor..... 660 47
16 Kobbe, Herman——the same 730 08
16 Kosiusky, Harris—Chambers St & Grand St Ferry R R Co.......... 113 18
16 Kyle, Peter—W V Burcher.......... 578 63
16 Kiwent, Philip / Kiwent, Rebecca } F & M Schaefer Brewing Co..... 223 72
17 Kingsland, Albert A—Daniel Brubacher..........3,418 96
18 Kienart, Jacob—Elizabeth Schwarzwalder.......... 139 33
19 Klaber, Edith—Annie Steinhardt.... 49 50
19 the same——the same.......... 49 50
19 Kiernan, Patrick—People State N Y. 100 00
20 Kohlmann, Lewis—Health Dept...... 209 87

¶*Editor* RECORD AND GUIDE:

The judgment obtained against me by Delamater Iron Works has been obtained by endorsement on note of John F. Behlmer, builder, given for pump purchased by me and set up in Behlmer's building. The pump is not satisfactory and is perfectly useless. The Delamater Iron Works refused to accept for repair same, so other courses will be taken immediately.

THOS. F. FALLON.

20 Kennedy, Patrick J—James Murphy. 365 89
20 Kissel, Rudolph—Downie Boiler Incrustation Preventive Co.......... 365 13
20 Kalischer, William S—Joseph Schor. 219 40
20 Kiefer, Christian—Alexander Blum.. 319 87
14 Leeds, William J—Maria A Wilson... 70 12
14 Lieb, George, Jr—Cook & Bernheimer Co.......... 216 47
16*Levy, Abraham—Martin Enders..... 155 00
16 Lippmann, Albert—Adolph Kessler.. 357 82
16 Le Fevre, Rome G—E J Kerr........ 27 35
16 Loening, Albert—W A Hume. 154 51
16 Lawrence, George W—H J Grant.... 281 54
17 Lauppe, Christoper—Emanuel Frey... 100 82
17 Lasber, George B—Colwell Lead Co.. 89 56
18 Linscott, John A—W M May.. ...... 117 74
18 Lenahan, Emily—G R Brown........ 172 96
18 Levey, Emanuel M—J W Howie...... 165 08
18 Lester, Julius—C H Eldridge......... 167 90
18 L'Hommedieu, Sylvester Y—Western Nat Bank..........2,474 24
18 the same——the same..........2,544 44
19 Lightball, Almarin H—N Y Life Ins Co..........1,212 27
19 Leslie, Harry S—People State N Y... 100 00
19 Long, John——the same. 100 00
20 Layden, John—Thomas Johnson..... 69 45
14 Mainville, Laura—Hippolyte Nicolas. 161 12
14 Matthews, James C—Thurber, Whyland & Co..........1,620 28
16 Minnis, William H—R G Thomas.... 140 00
16 Meyer, Nathan—James Stephens..... 192 87
16 Martin, Harry — American Champagne Co (Lim).......... 141 89
16 Moonelis, Adolph—Alexander Lichtenstein.......... 15,841 37
16 Morgan, Mary L—Charles Koleman.. 941 42
16 Masterson, Frank J—John Townsend ....costs 270 00
16 the same——Mary N Townsend et al, exrs..........costs 283 75
17 Meyer, Fred—J Y Duryea...... ...... 271 61
17 Mansell, Tilly—Mary A Weir......... 65 50
17 Mullaney, Ann—W M Ketcham, recvr.......... 214 64
17 Munzinger, John C / Mierisch, Charles } J H Knoop...... 559 24
17†Meyer, Mary—Mary J Harris......... 95 28
17 Matushewich, Mary—George Matulewich..........costs 71 47
17 Myers, Frederick S—Thomas Dougherty.......... 65 90
18 Maliett, Edwin A—J M Gove......... 42 78
18 Morris, Abraham—L M Ernst........ 697 68
18 Myers, Lewis—A S Friedland........1,546 28
18 Miller, John—A S Lascelles.......... 106 61
18*Mulle, Ida—H A Thomas. 116 20
19 Madden, William—Julia Gross..costs 116 54
19 Mentz, Lena—N J Newwitter...costs 522 44
19†Mars, Henrietta A—J W Butler...... 107 00
20 Murphy, Edward—Health Dep't...... 209 87
20 Moore, William O—Henry Habenfeld 228 23
20 the same——the same........costs 85 24
20 Murphy, John—T K Foster........... 759 03
20 Meyer, Catharine H—William Seouller.......... 223 89
20 Morgan, D Percy—Downie Boiler Incrustation Preventive Co.......... 365 13
20 Morell, George P / Morell, Frances } C S Locke........ 869 10
20 Moore, W Oliver—Martin Armstrong 318 01
16 McPherson, Duncan / McKenzie, John } H C Anderson.. 48 97
16 McVeaty, William—John Scott....... 203 84
16 McGuire, Bernard A—O K Dimock... 152 45
17 McGonigle, Daniel—People State N Y 300 00
18 McGrath, Mary J—William McShane 651 60
18 McKeon, Bartholomew — Elizabeth Schwarzwalder.......... 79 73
18†McComb, J J, Jr—Benjamin Rich... 75 90
19 McGuire, John J—F & M Schaefer Brewing Co.......... 626 81
19 McPyke, Charles H — People State N Y.......... 100 00
19 McKenna, James—Edward Gordon.. 201 48
19 McPyke, James—People State N Y... 100 00
20 McGovern, Thomas B—Downie Boiler Incrustation Preventive Co.......... 365 13
20 McKenna, James—G E Curtis........ 44 07
18 Niewohuer, August—Charles Pasewark.......... 519 75
20 Navaratt, Rudolf—Rudolf Navaratt, Jr.......... 17 50
14 O'Brien, William—Edison Electric Illuminating Co.......... 109 64
16 O'Sullivan, Dennis—L S Hamson..... 174 13
18 O'Hara, Michael — M L Biggane, assignee.......... 382 11
19 Oppenheimer, Joseph — Manhattan Railway Co.......... 113 13
14 Pinkham, Charles H, Jr—J B Tompkins.......... 723 74
17*Phraner, Wilson S—L M Castner ... 730 77
17 Pericss, Leon—Bavarian Brewing Co. 70 91
19 Plumb, Ben M—E V Ciergue.... .... 772 40
19 Park, Will F—B W Buxton.......... 544 76
19 Plummer, George D—Caleb Elliott... 200 79
19 Pearlstein, Hyman—People State N Y 100 00
14 Richter, Louis H—W D Wines....... 261 71
14 Rammer, Johannes — H A Hurlbut ....costs 38 48
16 Reinheimer, John F—J E Wells...... 175 65
16 Ryer, Andrew B—G W Post......... 91 75
16 Rofrano, Michael—W V Burcher 578 63
17 Ramhorst, William—Thomas Patten. 39 50
17 Reed, Augusta B—Lydia A Strong.. 85 50
18 Rosche, Daniel R / *Reed, William K } J H Fink......... 173 87
18 Rosencrans, Michael—Sender Jarmulowsky..........costs 27 90
18 Rice, Henry A, assignee—D L Bartlett..........costs 96 86
19 Ross, Mary B—Annie Steinhardt..... 67 50
19 Rennie, Arthur H—M R Muckle, Jr.. 84 18

19 Rafferty, Timothy—People State N Y 100 00
19 Raymond, Lester——the same........ 100 00
20 Remington, Tony—Nathaniel Wise... 220 52
20*Roe, Richard—Dunbar Box and Lumber Co. 1,157 65
20 Ross, J Stewart—Edward Settle.....1,395 24
14 Simonson, Michaelis—J S Leavitt.... 588 05
14 Styles, Frederick W—Thomas Hagan 762 74
14 Stevens, Mary E—Eaton, Cole & Burnham Co.......... 414 24
14 Sonin, Solomon—Lucien Wolf........ 121 81
14 Sneckner, William H—Herman Reel. 541 08
14 Swick, John J—I J Cole............ 424 32
16 Sonand, Annie—Emil Berger........ 100 62
16†Salomon, Isaac—Martin Enders...... 155 00
16 Speers, Alexander—R G Thomas..... 154 00
16 Stewart, John—Real Estate Record Assoc.......... 28 41
16 Sheehan, John—F W Meeker.... ....2,019 43
16 the same——the same..........1,557 77
16 Scudder, J Evans—Campbell Printing Press and Mfg Co.......... 99 71
16 Seilliere, Raymond Marie Nicolas—C E Miller..........11,162 16
16 Switzer, Walter E — Highland Nat Bank, Newburgh..........1,364 46
16 Schiff, John—F W Otheman 2,047 08
16 the same——J B Case..........2,201 15
17 Saunders, Simon M—George Whitaker 107 08
17 Schwartz, Bertha—T E Frazer....... 122 08
17 Silberstein, Max—Meyer Berliner....1,525 54
17 the same——the same..........1,022 84
17 Steinreich, George W / Steinreich, Benjamin } G M Miller... 534 47
17*Schiff, John—H J Hinck..........2,156 31
18 Stark, Isidor / Stark, Edward J / Stark, Gustave } Brainerd Armstrong Co....... 316 99
18 Schirmer, Gustav—F S Myers...costs 88 32
18 Stimson, Henry C—F L Requa, assignee..........2,552 10
18 Simon, Thomas M—W H Shieffelin... 44 12
18 Strong, J Montgomery, Jr—Alexander Johnston.......... 156 48
19 Shaw, Benjamin — Broadway & Seventh Avenue Railway Co..costs 82 18
19 Shinkman, Samuel—People State N Y 100 00
19 Steindler, Joseph—F S Passavant....1,554 20
19 the same——the same.......... 758 70
19 Strom, Nathan—People State N Y ... 100 00
19 Sturges, Lewis B——the same........ 100 00
20 Sattenstein, Reuben—Health Dep't... 209 87
20 Steinrich, Benjamin F / Steinrich, George W } John Kerr.. 293 66
20 Salpeter, Jacob—Jacob Macher. 310 61
20 Sloat, Henry E—J I Goodrich........ 223 41
20 Schwarze, John—Joshua Hendricks.. 440 85
20 Spiegel, Morris—Importers' and Traders' Nat Bank.......... 923 65
20 Sattenstein, Reuben—Gabriel Galef.. 910 64
20 Stewart, John—C G Colpe........... 224 96
20 Siefert, Henry, admr Jacob Siefert—W G Nicoll, guard 121 30
20 Sablidowsky, Joseph—Fannie Bershfield.......... 194 25
20 Scott, Warren L—A H Stebbins..... 101 99
17 Smith, John—Arlando Marine.......1,086 78
17 Smith, Theophilus G—Metropolitan Telephone and Telegraph Co....... 16 75
17 Smith, James B—Seaboard Lumber Co 851 28
14 The Sheet Metal Machine Co—Edward Hine. 990 04
14 the same——Waldon Ferguson...2,176 11
16 The Blandon Iron and Steel Co—S G Winternitz.......... 441 27
16 Richenstein Lumber Co—E C Gates.. 224 78
16 Goshen Car and Railway Equipment Co—W A Perry.......... 299 97
16 Lathrop Co—P A Moss... .... 101 77
16 The Mayor, Aldermen, &c — C L Bucki & Co..........7,373 96
16 the same——A J Murray.........3,243 30
16 the same——Beard & Kingsland.. 950 00
16 the same——H B Newall Co...... 800 00
16 the same——H A Rogers......... 700 00
16 the same——Louis Jurgens....... 55 80
16 the same——Bendix Johanson.... 14 40
16 the same——Otto Danielson....... 28 83
16 the same——W W Hegeman...... 300 00
17 the same——J S Barry.......... 136 60
17 the same——Alexander Berley.... 304 00
17 Richenstein Lumber Co (Lim)—Lemon Thomson.......... 323 64
17 the same——Shepard & Morse Lumber Co.......... 953 75
17 Court Murray Hill Ancient Order of Foresters of America — Edward Strasberg.......... 36 00
17 The Banker & Campbell Co (Lim)—Bedford Bank..........5,159 46
17 The South Brooklyn Dock and Warehouse Co—Jacob Dubois.......... 670 10
17¶J H Bonnell & Co (Lim)—Nat Shoe and Leather Bank..........1,065 88
17 the same——Bank of N Y Nat Banking Assoc..........5,529 22
17 The Mayor, Aldermen, &c—C A Morrison.......... 95 00
17 The Manhattan Railway Co—Christian Anderson..........5,401 82
18 The Fred H Whipple Co—L W Pratt. 174 91
18 The Mayor, Aldermen, &c—James Quinn, Jr..........1,129 00
18 J H Bonnell & Co (Lim)—Nat Bank of Republic..........1,455 38
18 Lathrop Co—Dame & Townsend Co.. 195 08
19 Passaic Quarry Co — Ingersoll Sergeant Rock Drill Co. 1,250 31
19 J H Bonnell & Co (Lim)—Market and Fulton Nat Bank..........1,012 96
19 The Bardillo Marble Mfg Co—C E Thompson 1,484 20

19 M Crane Electrotyping and Stereotyping Co—Thomas Wildes............ 130 59
19 The Stereo Relief Decorative Co—G W Millar........................ 425 02
19 the same——the same............ 271 84
20 The Cunard Steamship Co (Lim)—Mayor, &c............ 145 75
20 J H Bonnell & Co (Lim)—Market and Fulton Nat Bank 1,872 85
20 Banker & Campbell Co (Lim)—Rouse, Hazard & Co.................. 2,910 04
20 M Crane Electrotyping and Stereotyping Co—J C Cook.............. 49 51
20 The Twenty-third St Railway Co—Mary A. Somers.................. 667 57
20 Pfister Bookbinding Co—C B Baeder. 106 62
20 The Postal Telegraph Co—Charles McCrosson.................. 17 27
20 The Mayor, Aldermen, &c—James Hughes.................. 201 00
17†Thornton, Arthur R—M L Simon.... 238 99
17 Tonner, Nicholas J—Christopher Swezey.................. 200 25
17 Thompson, William H—E T Battey... 105 36
17 Tyson, Nettie—Landers, Frary & Clark.................. 73 57
18 Thompson, James—Bradley & Currier Co (Lim).................. 125 62
18 Thompson, Mary E—William Albrecht.................. 318 76
18 Tompkins, William—Abraham Vanderbeck 299 66
18 Tuthill, Ben—H A Thomas............ 116 20
19 Travis, Edward L—Edwin Scott.... 90 51
20 Taylor, John / *Terhune, Peter S } J B Clark........ 235 00
20 Tyrer, William E—G H Rosenblatt.. 1,094 23
20 Uffuer, Francis M—Charles Gillespie. 122 38
14 Vigus, Thomas—Thomas Seeley...... 108 50
17 Vermilye, William R—Richards Latters.................. 168 46
17*Varona, Lucy C—E S Greeley & Co.. 314 18
18 Vernon, Edward—E B Hawkins...... 252 25
18 Valentine, Robert H C—Nat Bank of Republic.................. 1,435 38
19 Vorder, James—People State N Y.... 100 00
19 Van Cleve, Garret—I C Hendrickson 125 29
14 Van Cleve, Garret—William McShane, admr.................. 1,050 14
14 Weiss, Theodore—J S Leavitt 388 65
14 Wilmurt, Jefferson—Phœnix Furniture Co.................. 39 60
14 Waterbury, Frederick L—A A Thomson.................. 587 19
14 Whitmore, Benjamin C, exr Hopeton Drake—Rufus Foster, exr.......... 1,569 44
14 Weier, George W—I J Cole.......... 424 32
16 Watson, Richard M—Margaret F Ward 5,876 85
16 the same——Blanche K Dougherty.................. 1,800 35
16 Waeker, John—C F Gennerich....... 388 94
16 Weil, David—Joseph Beck........... 566 58
16 Wilkinson, Joseph—R H Morrison..... 78 69
16 Williams, Leighton, recvr Blair Iron and Steel Co—H A Taylor.......... 901 57
16 Walsh, William M—William McShane, admr.................. 67 34
16 Wood, Frederick—N F Vought...... 267 85
17 Warsawski, Abraham / Weissman, Adolph } Isaac Alexander......... 10 00
17 Weydig, Charles / *Weydig, Julius } Nat Casket Co... 132 38
17 Wynne, Elizabeth L, admrx Hannah Wynne—Cornelius Callahan......... 61 92
17 Walker, Abraham—D A Vanhorne.. 544 89
18 Whipple, Fred H—L W Pratt......... 174 91
18 Webster, Thomas—C T Barney..costs 90 81
18 Walker, Herbert H—Dennis Regan.. 321 47
18 Wood, Edward F—Louis Leakey..... 97 22
18 Wallach, Julius / Wallach, Joseph G } Rosa Kind ....costs 95 05
18 Woolworth, James G B—J H Thorp.. 205 06
19 Winslow, Margaret—Utica City Nat Bank 230 98
19 Wollowitz, Abraham—Samuel Fleck. 487 15
19 the same——Solomon Frankel.... 156 40
19 Webster, John A—August Wille..... 1,899 36
20 Woolworth, James G B—Real Estate Investment Co, of Philadelphia..... 625 94
20 Whyard, William W—Marvin Safe Co.................. 152 11
16 Yale, Bradford / Yale, George / Yale, Carrie D / Yale, Ida } C E Wilmot 813 06
19 Youngling, George S—People State N Y.................. 100 00

KINGS COUNTY.

Nov.
16 Allen, Stephen H—G Levy..........$1,066 83
17 Alhouse, Simeon J—A L Crandall... 234 00
18 Avery, Charles R—E J Price......... 4,333 73
13 Boyle, Andrew—Williamsburgh Brewing Co 643 00
13 *Brossard, Theodore / Brossard, Otto } T Schmalhols .. 608 60
16 Beale, Joseph H—Mary C Fox, admrx Sidney A Fox.................. 363 26
17 Blake, John—C H Eggert & Bro..... 26 35
17 Baldwin, George P—Mary Boyle, admrx Ambrose Geohegan......... 217 64
17 Bayan, Thomas—Jane Holland. 206 70
17 Bedell, Edwin J—J W McLaren..... 773 24
18 Brook, Julius—L H Hambro......... 236 11
19 Bennett, Philo S / Blendermann, Albert } Chas E Burke, assignee.... 459 29
19 Berglund, Peter W—F A Straus. 1,642 81
14 Cole, Sarah E—W S Pendleton...... 81 16
16 Collins, Chas H—J L Mott Iron Works 128 51
17 Clement, Elizabeth E—Albert B Van Orden.................. 1,212 71
18 Cock, Mary—J Andrews............ 78 35
19 Closius, Eva / Closius, Henry T } H Reiners......... 1,583 93
19 Conradi, William—J G Grauer....... 550 05
12 Droste, Adolph M—Mary H Barrett.. 94 04
13 Durham, Fred F—F S Sanford....... 219 93
14 Durham, Frederick F—D F Cunningham.................. 395 53
16 Dixon, James—M Kelly............ 36 30
16 Dunbar, Clara A—W H B Childs ... 320 25
17 Douglass, Henrietta—Mary Coyle, as admrx. Ambrose Geohegan....... 217 64
17 Dutcher, Isaac—A B Van Orden..... 1,212 74
17 Dunn, James F—H E Williams....... 42 34
18 Dreschler, August—T Lieb........... 155 75
14 Fischman, Joseph—L Rosen.......... 121 79
16 Ferguson, John S—C B Hall.......... 37 00
17 Fiesler, John C—G H Steger.... ... 1,464 45
17 Few, Edward W—S & P Vroman.... 201 43
19 Forman, Alexander A—L Chevanney 86 29
13 Glickoff, Isaac—J Connell........... 298 86
18 Good, Samuel R—I Horowitz......... 254 25
14*Gould, Edmund—J Geehan......... 814 89
16 Gildersleeve, Moses R—W F Shotwell 939 66
17 Gallagher, John J—P G Hughes..... 1,936 12
18 Gibby, George H—N Y Architectural Terra Cotta Co.................. 682 57
18 Grage, Henry—E E Ryerson, Jr...... 200 05
19 Gould, Edmund—J White............ 253 78
19 Goodeve, James W—H R Elliot..... 23 90
19 Garret, Charles T—W L McCorkle... 117 58
13 Hough, John—Bulmer Lumber Co.... 381 37
13 Huber, August—W E and J P Uptegrove.................. 759 00
11 *Hay, Robert / Hay, John } J L Mott Iron Works . 152 86
14 Harris, George S—J Geehan.......... 314 39
14 Halfelio, Frank J—The Cook & Bernheimer Co. 37 10
10 Henry, Amanda—J M Rider....... 52 85
16 Huntington, Austin—T D Olena...... 67 42
10 *Hay, Robert / Hay, John } J L Mott Iron Works.. 126 51
17 Horgan, Arthur O K—C Wally...... 246 17
17 Hill, Dr J O—B F Maury 177 42
17 Hoag, Henry G—J Holland 206 70
17 Hackett, William C—C T Austin. ... 537 91
17 Hursch, Rosalia—C H Bruel.......... 504 43
19 Higgins, Patrick H—M Sinnott 58 77
14 Julien, Francis—L White............ 263 58
13 Koerner, Fritz W—J A Koerner..... 69 44
14 Koelle, William G—E Koelle......... 5,117 75
16 Kyle, Peter—W V Burcher........... 573 68
17 Krauss, Martin—D M & M D Koehler 162 23
17 Kane, Henry E—Mary Coyle, as admrx Ambrose Geohegan......... 217 64
17 Kingman, Richard S—C A Dorney... 932 56
17 Kingman, Richard S—P Derley...... 1,419 01
18 Kehler, Emil—H McShane Mfg Co... 201 93
18 Kingman, Richard S—J E Haberer.. 163 69
18 Kane, Andrew—J Andrews 210 00
18 Kingman, Richard S—J E Haberer.. 163 69
18 Keith, Royal—G N Hard... .... 126 43
18 Kane, Andrew—J Andrews............ 210 35
16 Lanphire, George F—H M & A M Rogers.................. 403 46
16 Lehman, James F—J McArthur...... 27 85
16 Levy, Benjamin—G Levy............ 1,066 83
16 Lawrence, Cath A—C B Hall......... 87 00
18 Leix, Jacob M—S Ruppel............. 280 33
18 Lambert, Rufus C—E F Lambert.... 76 45
18 Leix, Jacob M—S Ruppel............. 280 82
19 Lindsay, Helen—Olena & Craig...... 783 89
12 Muller, Lewis M—T Fitzgerald....... 274 77
12 the same——the same............ 449 04
12 the same——the same............ 326 69
12 the same——the same....... .... 276 19
12 the same——the same............ 277 91
12 the same——the same............ 589 51
13 Manning, James J—C Moerlein Brewing Co.................. 198 63
13 Martin, Samuel C—H Kastner... .... 250 89
13 the same——the same............ 149 06
13 Meguire, Charles E—L Axfeld......... 115 10
13 Mars, Henrietta A—E Fromme..... .. 88 02
13 Metcalf, Mary M—J Smidt........... 31 10
16 Morris, Armenicus T—C G Soderholm.................. 136 75
17 Mechnich, Jacob—Armour & Co..... 194 35
17 Minnis, William H—R G Thomas.... 140 00
17 Martin, Charles E—C H Bruel 504 48
17 McCauley, Catharine—E Sweeny 287 50
18 McGowan, Hugh—S Strauss.......... 226 00
18 Maloney, Mary—W K Murray...... 128 17
19 Newman, Emma—O F Eichberg 204 24
13 O'Malley, Mary—J Gilmartin......... 284 00
12 Palmer, Wm H—M H Barrett......... 94 04
13 Pell, Ogden P—National Bank of Republic.................. 575 14
13 Pfohlmann, Sophie and Michael—B Hof.................. 133 35
14 Pilcher, Joseph M—J Geehan......... 314 39
14†Pearsall, William W—Cook & Bernheimer Co.................. 89 85
14 Pinkham, Jr, Charles H—J B Tompkins.................. 723 74
16 Pearson, Eugene—The Queen City Furniture Co.................. 344 13
19 Pilcher, Joseph—J White 253 78
12 Ryan, Mark—J Staals............... 50 25
13 Reily, John J—H Lins............... 24 95
13 Reitz, John—C D Rhinehart......... 490 07
13 Roch, Ernest—C H Attwater 599 29
16 Ransom, James F—L Schwartz...... 95 87
16 Rofrano, Michael—W V Burcher..... 573 68
16 Roth, Ferdinand—C B Jennings...... 83 39
16 Riley, Bridget—E Sweeney........... 287 50
18 Richter, Emil—F Roth............... 99 22
18 Ross, John S—L Samuel.............. 254 97
19 Robinson, Frank—F P Osborn....... 493 20
19 Ross, Theodore H—M Lang........... 72 41
13 Sawyer, William M—The Washington Nat Bank.................. 2,628 65
13 Seedorf, Charles—H Rohohl.......... 80 00
16 Scott, Charles R—The Queens City Furniture Co.................. 344 13
16 Smith, George M—W F Shotwell. ... 939 66
17 Switzer, Walter E—The Highland Nat Bank of N Y.................. 1,304 46
17 Sanford, Leda V—T L Stuart........ 157 04
17 Sweeney, Elizabeth A / Sweeney, Charles L / Sweeney, John L } O T Bennett.. 64 74
17 Speers, Alexander—R G Thomas..... 154 00
18 Smith, Sophia C—C D Willetts...... 74 47
13 Tobey, Edward H—W & J Sloan..... 421 41
13 The Greenpoint Turn Verein—J Gottschalk.................. 249 30
14 The Brooklyn City R R Co—H Ehrman, Jr.................. 3,523 34
16 The Banker & Campbell Co (Lim)—Redford Bank.................. 5,159 46
16 The Covered Tube Cable Railway Co—H E Pierrepont.................. 243 72
16 the same——The Brooklyn Heights R R Co 334 77
16 the same——The Montague Construction Co.................. 235 93
17 Tillman, John—T McCabe............ 172 87
17 Thrush, Minnie—M Coyle............ 217 64
17 Thrush, Henry—A B Van Orden..... 1,212 74
17 The admr of Bridget Riley—E Sweeney 287 50
13 Wolff, Augusta—G Hyman.......... 34 50
13 Weisenstein, George—J W Gastriger. 19 51
13 Wetherby, Henry—O Oxnard........ 441 66
17 Warsawski, Abraham / Weissman, Adolph } I Alexander.. 10 00
18 Waring, William—O Stevens........ 168 90
14 Yarwood, Frederick J—J V Jewell.. 126 72
14 Young, Emma A—G A Simon....... 1,348 80
17 Yale, Carrie D—S Lichtenstein...... 583 35

SATISFIED JUDGMENTS.

NEW YORK.

November 14 to 20—Inclusive.

American Surety Co—Harry Wallerstein. (1891).................. $77 04
American Diamond Rock Boring Co—F M Pierce. (1891) 1,113 10
Associated Lace Maker Co—Engelbert Hardt. (1891) 230 22
Beard, Francis D—A L Washburn. (1891).... 201 45
Bowers Henry C—J C Weinpahl. (1887)...... 539 92
*Brooks, Edwin J—George Coggill. (1891).... 974 54
Boyle, Mary—Joseph Walsh. (1891)........... 481 80
Bates, Hester / Bingham, Mary } W H Johnston. (1891)...... 104 43
Cornell, John M—Manhattan Railway Co. (1889).................. 68 50
Same——same. (1891) 96 35
Cameron, Roderick W—J S Cameron. (1889). 110 88
Cohen, William—Leo Hammel. (1891) 35 07
Cavinato, Luigi, Guisseppi, Steffano and Natale—F G Moore. (1891) 585 00
Davis, Fannie—John Wanamaker. (1891).... 112 97
Defendorf, Allen D M and Winifred I, by Joshua Kantrowitz, guard. (1891) ... 729 80
*De Raismes, John A—William Rankin. ('91). 481 84
†Dessau, Simon—Richard Hirbton. (1891).... 1,968 12
Fauret, Theodore W—J M Navarro. (1891).... 104 58
*Glick, Adolph—H B Claflin Co. (1891)........ 934 02
Greene, Harry W—R A Johnston. (1891)...... 279 98
German Bank—William Stainton. (1891)...... 469 07
Goodsell, Edward S—Enrico Cassbranca. (1891) 73 06
Globe Fire Ins Co—John Wanamaker. (1891). 112 97
Grove, Gustave—L E Neuman. (1886)......... 1,069 87
Hogue, Camille—M B Eulinger. (1891) 165 70
Hasenpflug, George—Thomas Crane. (1891).. 170 51
Holly, John I—German Nat Bank of Newark. (1890).................. 1,588 88
Haagen, Franz—William McShane. ('888).. 184 70
Same——A J Campbell. (1886).............. 40 50
Same——Louis Kaufman. (1884)........ .... 141 55
Same——E H Schwatz. (1886)............. 88 55
Same——Leander Blinck. (1885)............ 623 46
Same——Enoch Ketcham. (1885)........ ...... 93 58
§Hay, Amelia—Walter Scott. (1891)........... 466 39
Herrmann, Morris—Leo Hammel. (1891)..... 35 07
Hayes, William B—W M Watson. (1891)...... 45 50
Hoyt, Janet R C—J E Kelly. (1889).......... 2,441 39
Hatch, Oramil C and Harriet—Eugene Smith. (1891).................. 84 11
Innis, William J—C P McCartny. (1891)....... 606 79
Knowles, Frederick C—J F Parkes. (1891). .. 84 28
Same——same. (1891)........ .... 597 86
Same——same. (1890).................. 533 04
Keyser, Isaiah—W H Johnston. (1891) 104 43
Lenten, John J—John Brown. (1891)......... 109 97
Lowe, William R—Abraham Schneider. (1891) 203 87
Lancashire Ins Co—John Wanamaker. (1891) 112 97
Mainhart, Frank E—Abraham Schneider. (1891).................. 203 87
Metropolitan Elevated Railway Co / Manhattan Railway Co } J H Watson. ('90) 119 84
Same——same. (1889).................. 5,698 50
Same——Mary E Hughes. (1889).............. 4,147 90
Same——W W Thompson. (1889) 3,745 77
Manhattan Railway Co——same. (1891)....... 117 50
*Morehead, Franklin C—W F Daniel. (1891).. 649 76
Martin, Leon—Jacob Wicks, Jr. (1891)........ 1,579 96
New York Elevated Railway Co—W W Thompson. (1891).................. 117 50
Same——same. (1889).................. 3,745 77
Nealis, Thomas J—Henry Wilson. (1891)..... 200 39
*Ogden, John R—W F Daniel. (1891).......... 649 76
Payne, George A—Asbury Park and Ocean Grove Bank. (1891).................. 86 86
Pierson, Edgar L—German Nat Bank of Newark. (1890).................. 1,588 88
*Rosenberg, Jacob—H B Claflin Co. (1891)... 964 02
Rose, Charles J—Peter Kauth. (1878).......... 379 26
Stockton, Mary J—T M Isted. (1891).......... 110 95
Scott, John—Charles Reilly, Comm'r. (1890). 110 00
Stretch, Eliakim S—G F Carr. (1891) 72 21
Surbrug, John W—L E Neuman. (1886)....... 1,069 87
Same—Abraham Cohn. (1886)................ 584 97
Stafford, Miles A—J F Parkes. (1890).......... 533 04
Same——same. (1890).................. 597 86
Same——same. (1891).................. 84 28
Smith, James H / Street, William A } J S Cameron. (1891)...... 170 88
Surburg, John W—Leonard Friedman. (1886). 5,820 62
Schmid, Althea—W H Johnston. (1891)....... 104 43
Third Av R R Co—Mary Lynch. (1891)....... 104 48

Same——same. (1891)........ 69 95

Townsend, Maurice, Edward and Solomon—Tunis Lumber Co. (1891)........ 223 85

Tarr, Horace G H—F M Pierce. (1891)........ 1,118 19

Von Eupen, Theodore—Paul Bechstein. ('91). 189 88

Same——C W—Elisbisch. (1888)........ 41 50

Van Leeuwen, Joseph—E J Eisenman. (1891) 84 57

Werner, Louis P—Abraham Cohn. (1886)........ 584 97

Ward, Edmund F—Manhattan Beef Co (Lim.) (1891)........ 89 58

White, Andrew J—N Y Cab Co (Lim.) (1891).. 162 80

*Vacated by order of Court. †Suspended on Appeal. ‡Released. §Reversal. ||Satisfied by Execution.

KINGS COUNTY.

November 13 to 19—Inclusive.

Allison, Charles—G W Burt. (1885)........ $630 94

Brown, Harvey H—C A Holcomb. (1891)........ 60 56

Block, Henry—P Glashoff. (1890)........ 127 15

Same——Tradesmen's Nat Bank. (1889)........ 2,042 08

Same——C F Koehn. (1889)........ 1,574 80

Same——Beadleston & Woerz. (1889)........ 1,238 54

Same——C A Fach. (1889)........ 405 18

Blair, George—People's Bank of Buffalo. ('91) 1,175 41

Casey, Patrick—T Sullivan. (1890)........ 934 44

Davenport, William B, admr—M McElroy. (1891)........ 582 47

De Baum, Housman, estate of—J D Fessenden. (1890)........ 270 00

Fernandez, Robert—H P Jones. (1890)........ 52 60

Jezek, Francis—G S Harris. (1890)........ 160 98

Pierce, Tecumseh—Union Central Life Ins Co. (1891)........ 374 00

Selleck, Noah—D Decker, Jr. (1889)........ 3,112 51

Same——C Sweet. (1889)........ 2,420 89

Same——J Burkhead. (1889)........ 2,075 04

Same——C Housman. (1889)........ 2,420 89

Same——D Decker. (1889)........ 1,037 55

Same——C Miner. (1889)........ 1,037 55

Same——M Roof. (1889)........ 518 79

Same——W Deyo. (1889)........ 1,210 46

Same——M Cohen. (1889)........ 518 79

Same——S J Byers. (1889)........ 1,210 46

Same——A Deyo. (1889)........ 2,420 89

Same——C Wright. (1889)........ 2,075 04

Same——J Decker. (1889)........ 2,075 04

The Williamsburgh Gas Light Co—John J Hennessey. (1891)........ 2,202 97

The Brooklyns (Lim)—C L Ward. (1891)........ 810 45

Zeiss, Katharine W—Myers Excursion and Navigation Co. (1887)........ 2,052 92

MECHANICS' LIENS.

NEW YORK CITY.

Nov.

14 One Hundred and Fourteenth st, s s, 140.0 w 5th av, 140.6x99.8. A. S. Nichols agt Margaret E. Conlon, owner and contractor........ $817 50

14 Fifty-second st. Nos. 527-531, n s, 350 w 10th av, 75x100. Thomas Roberts Stevenson Co. agt J. A. Linscott, owner and contractor........ 1,247 00

10*Waverley pl, No. 12, s s, 25 w Mercer st, 25x 82.6. K. N. Smith & Co. agt Samuel and Henry Corn, owners and contractors........ 28,200 00

16 Bathgate av, No. 1618, e s, 40 n 172d st, 20x 100. Joseph Hlawatsch agt Edward Gibb, owner, and Theodore Rhein, contractor. 173 00

16 Bathgate av, No. 1620, e s, 60 w 172d st, 20x 100. Same agt George Hurd, owner, and Theodore Rhein, contractor........ 173 00

16 One Hundred and Thirty-fifth st, n s, 110 w 5th av, 125x100. Abraham Steers agt Warren B. Smith, owner, and William Verdon, contractor........ 438 77

16 One Hundred and Thirty-fifth st, Nos. 5-17, n s, 110 w 5th av, 125x100. C. M. O'Connor agt William Verdon, Frederick R. Meres and William Smith, owners, and William Verdon and Frederick R. Meres, contractors........ 120 00

16 Eleventh st. No. 53, n s, 309 e 6th av, 24x 103.3. Mary A. McEvoy agt John J. Crawford, owner and contractor........ 1,978 00

16 Eighty-seventh st, No. 123, n s, 191 w Columbus av, 17x100.8. J. W. Kruger agt Harry S. or Henry S. Knapp, owner, and Fuchs. Wilkinson & Co., contractors........ 99 00

16 Ninety-third st, Nos. 11-17, n s, 220 e 5th av, 78.8x55. Kruger & Albert agt Philip Braender, owner, and same and Fritz Uckermann, contractors........ 1,260 00

16 One Hundred and Twenty-fifth st, Nos. 148 and 150, s s, 125 e 7th av, 50x100. D. A. Fitzpatrick agt William Hargrave, debtor, and Edgar Ketchum, owner........ 190 00

17 Fifty-second st. Nos. 527-531, n s, 375 e 11th av, 75x100. Snyder & Rode agt John A. Linscott, owner and contractor........ 357 00

17 Kingsbridge road, e s, 50 s Nindham pl, 40x 95. Elmer Schoonmaker agt James Hodge, owner and contractor........ 1,166 35

17 Hamilton pl, e s, 38 s 142d st, 72x85. Ingelbright Mikkelson agt Mary E. and Mark A. Stevens, owners and contractors. 170 00

17 Fifty-third st, s s, 275 e 11th av, 125x100. John Green agt Alice E. Davies, owner, and David Davies, contractor........ 51 40

17 Eleventh st, s s, 125 e 2d av, 60x94. W. N. Sternkopf agt Henry Riffel, owner and contractor........ 2,570 68

17 Sixty-fifth st, Nos. 29 and 31, n s, 200 w 8th av, 50x100.5. G. A. Hunter agt James O'Brien, owner and contractor........ 460 02

18 Columbine av, s w cor Jackson av, 30x50. Jesse Reynolds agt Mrs. A. Donohue, owner, and Andrew Donohue, contractor. 80 04

18 Eleventh av, No. 754, e s, 75 n 53d st, 25.5x 125. James Corbett and Eugene Ring agt Annie Murphy, owner, and Christopher Murphy, contractor........ 350 00

18 Sixteenth st, Nos. 331 and 333, n s, 400 e 9th av, 50x100. Canda & Kane agt Theodore Van Eupen, owner and contractor........ 1,810 61

18 Eighty-eighth st, n s, 175 w 8th av, 75x110.11. Frank Orlofski agt Frederick Wood, owner and contractor........ 50 00

*Editor RECORD AND GUIDE:

The lien of K. N. Smith & Co. against Messrs. S. & H. Corn is unjust and is now being defended.

ALFRED ZUCKER, Architect,

18 One Hundred and Forty-fourth st, No. 304, s s, 100 w 8th av, 25x100. Pelham Hod Elevating Co. agt Ernest Molwitz, owner, and Christian Andersen and Henry Schaefer, contractors........ 80 00

18 Ninety-sixth st, n s, 70 e Lexington av, 125x 100.11. Same agt Owen F., Jr., and William McIlroy, owners and contractors........ 100 00

18 Bathgate av, No. 2279, w s, 67 s 183d st, 25x 100. William Clarke agt Daniel Kenuelly, owner and contractor........ 75 09

18 Fifty-second st, n s, 375 e 11th av, 75x100.5. Morton Bros. & Co. agt John A. Linscott, owner and contractor........ 1,575 00

18 Eleventh st, No. 53, n s, 309 e 6th av, 24x 103.3. Same agt John J. Crawford, owner and contractor........ 1,100 00

19 West End av, n w cor 102d st, 100x100. Van Note & Daly agt David Christie, owner and contractor........ 850 00

19 Sheriff st, Nos. 91 and 93, w s, 100 s Stanton st, 50x100. Jacob Hecker agt R. Mapelsden, owner and contractor........ 87 60

19 Park av, n w cor 133d st, 100x100. Gime Attam agt Addison Brown, owner, and William R. Bell, contractor........ 453 07

19 One Hundred and Thirty-third st, n s, 100 w Park av, 50x100. Same agt same........ 47 00

19 Ninty-sixth st, Nos. 159-167, n s, 70 e Lexington av, 125x100. D. H. Toby agt Owen F., Jr., and William McElroy, owner and contractor........ 550 00

19 One Hundred and Fifth st, n s, 200 w Madison av, 100x100 J. T Johnson agt William and Hugh Thornton, owner, and James Attams, contractor........ 96 80

19 Fifty-third st, s s, 275 e 11th av, 125x100. D. R. De Wolf & Co. agt Henry Volkening, David Davies and wife and James O. Donald, owners, and David Davies, contractor........ 112 00

19 Greenwich st, No. 185. Peter Kreiner agt Charles Lenz, owner and contractor........ 1,185 01

19 One Hundred and Forty-fourth st, No. 304, s s, 100 w 8th av, 25x100. Michael Conforti agt Ernest Molwitz, owner, and Christian Andersen, contractor........ 500 00

20 Twenty-fourth st Nos. 333-339 W. n s, 77x 100. Burton Gliddon agt Joseph McFarland, owner, and Frederick Wood, contractor........ 230 00

20 Sixty-sixth st, s s, 400 w 8th av, 100x100. Ben Danielson agt Edward Lapierre, debtor, and Henry Raabe & Sons, owners 36 75

20 Same property. Patrick McDonald agt same........ 38 50

20 Same property. Harris Berman agt same. 91 00

20 Same property. Thomas Lee agt same... 33 75

20 Same property. Christ Jespersen agt same 38 50

20 Eleventh st, No. 53, n s, 309 e 6th av, 24x100. Benedict, McIlroy & Fowler agt John J. Crawford, owner and contractor........ 435 08

20 Forty-third st, Nos. 151-153, n w cor 3d av, 100x25. H. S. Helm agt John Philips, owner and contractor........ 77 00

20 Ryer av, e s, 200 s 183d st, 25x—. Willson, Adams & Co. agt Theodore Rhein, owner and contractor. (Continued from Nov. 21, 1890)........ 122 05

20 One Hundred and Forty-fourth st, s s, 100 w 8th av, 25x—. W. G. Leeson agt Ernest Molwitz, owner, and Christian Anderson, contractor........ 154 00

KINGS COUNTY.

Nov.

13 Fulton st, s s, 100 e Stone av, 100x100. Wyandance Brick and Terra Cotta Co. agt Jennie L. Ross, owner and contractor........ $147 70

13 Decatur st, n s, 100 e Howard av, 260x100. John Dowd agt J. Mason Kirby, owner, and Edward Speare, contractor........ 47 50

13 Marcy av, se cor Hooper st, 89x175. H. F. Burroughs & Co. agt John Loughlin, owner, and The Stereo Relief Decorative Co., contractor........ 636 70

13 Eighth av, e s, extends from 15th st to 16th st, 200x160. Richard Calrow agt Edwin J. Bedell, William J. Fitzpatrick, Thomas McCann and William Martin, owners, and Edwin J. Bedell, contractor........ 20 40

14 Bay 22d st, n w s, 370 s w 86th st, 40x96.8, New Utrecht. Louis E. Quick agt Agnes M. Binns, owner, and Louis Larsen, contractor........ 284 00

14 Same property. Cropsey & Mitchell agt same owner and contractor........ 433 00

14 Eighth st, Nos. 225-731, n s, 110.10 e 4th av, 100.8x100. William H. Burrill agt Paul Gantert, owner, and John H. Flock, contractor........ 62 98

16 Bay 26th st, n w s, 100 s e Benson av, 60x 96.8. New Utrecht. Walter T. Hudson agt Charles H. Simonson, owner, and Luc Rioux, contractor........ 258 00

16 Twentieth st, s s, 150 w Vanderbilt av, 25x 100. John Campbell agt Thomas Heffernan, owner and contractor........ 9 70

16 Saratoga av, w s, 45 n Marion st, 25x100.. } Saratoga av, w s, 95 n Marion st, 50x100.. } The Thomas Roberts Stevenson Co. agt Jacob Aronson, owner and contractor........ 219 00

16 Reid av, Nos. 254 and 256, w s, 25 n Halsey st, 75x100. Adelbert S. Nichols agt George W. McCormack, owner and contractor........ 132 00

16 Bay 26th st, n s, 100 e Benson av, 60x96.8, New Utrecht. Brooklyn Door and Sash Co agt Charles H. Simonson, owner, and Luc Rioux, contractor........ 300 00

16 Fulton st, s s, bet Stone and Rockaway avs, 100x100. Guenthaler & Halpin agt Jennie L. Ross, owner, and D. C. Ross, contractor........ 525 00

16 Fort Hamilton av, n e cor 50th st, 10x100, New Utrecht. John Cook agt Trustees for School No. 2, New Utrecht, owners, and Ole Gunsten, contractor........ 100 26

17 State st, s s, 100 e Henry st, 25x 00. Frank H. Collins agt John F. Robertson, owner, and Charles H. Collins, contractor........ 73 00

17 Stillwell av, n e cor 86th st, 29x40. Gravesend. Joseph Romano agt John Morrisey, owner, and Christian Brown, contractor. 35 00

17 Eastern Parkway, s s, 75 w Thatford av, 25 x100. Meyer Kuriandzik agt Solomon Krenkenstein, owner, and Samuel Kaplanski and Samuel Samowicz, contractors 140 00

17 Watkins st, w s, 250 s Sutter av, 25x100. H. S. Christian agt Solomon Morris, owner, and Gormley & Lynch, contractors........ 127 07

17 President st, No. 568. Watson & Pittinger agt Frank Williams and Frank Luce, owners and contractors........ 165 99

17 St. Marks av, s s, 250 e Howard av, 50x127.9. Jacob Schneider agt Mary A. Dowdel, owner, and G. Menzel, contractor........ 110 00

17 Fulton st, s s, 200 w Stone av, 100x100. J. Mock & Co. agt Jennie L. Ross, owner, and Donald C. Ross, contractor........ 600 00

17 Decatur st, n s, 340 w Saratoga av, 260x100. Patrick Kenny agt J. Mason Kirby, owner and contractor........ 423 50

17 Fourth st, s s, 197.10 w 7th av, 114x100. Wallbridge Bros. agt Moses & Fanton, owners and contractors........ 2,659 29

17 Bainbridge st, n s, 115.6 e Saratoga av, 179.9 x100. Patrick Kenny agt J. Mason Kirby, owner and contractor........ 105 00

17 Second st, s s, 80 w 7th av, 117.10x100. J. Mock & Co. agt Jennie L. Ross, owner, and Donald C. Ross, contractor........ 160 00

18 Patchen av, n e cor Putnam av, 20x100. Builders' Wood Working Co. agt Thomas Walling, owner and contractor........ 809 40

18 Roebling st, w s, 80 n North 6th st, 20x75. Morris Barfiel agt Helena Danziger and Frommet Simensky, owner and contractor 90 00

18 Fulton st, s s, 400 w Rockaway av, 5 houses. N. R. Shevlin agt Jennie L. Ross, owner and contractor........ 700 00

18 Reid av, e s, 60 n Hancock st, 87.6x100. Dugan Mfg. Co. agt J. S. Willdridge, owner and contractor........ 1,163 38

18 Same property. Hall Sash and Door Co. agt same owner and contractor........ 984 50

18 Seventh st, n s, 297.6 e 4th av, 50.4x100. Dennis Murray agt Mary E. Miller, owner and contractor........ 68 00

18 Garfield pl, n s, 90 w 7th av, 150x100. Charles Williams agt Edward L. Beekman, owner and contractor........ 532 00

18 Seventh st, n s, 297.6 e 4th av, 50.4x100. Gage & Wallace agt Mary E. and George M. Miller, owners and contractors........ 84 28

19 Fulton st, Nos. 2184-2192. Snethen & Stoney agt Jennie Ross, owner and contractor... 75 00

19 Stone av, e s, 200 n Blake av, 50x100. Louis Bossert agt Richard Roe, owner, and Louis Regenbogen, Samuel Davis, Bernard Schechtel and William Schechtel, contractors........ 792 87

19 Second st, s s, 80 w 7th av, 117.10x100. McMurray Bros. agt Jennie L. Ross, owner, and Donald C. Ross, contractor........ 125 00

19 Same property. Snethen & Stoney agt Jennie Ross, owner and contractor........ 100 00

19 Hancock st, s e cor Lewis av, 150x100. Jacob Willman agt Jacob Aronson, owner, and Thomas A. McWhinney, contractor........ 370 09

SATISFIED MECHANICS' LIENS.

NEW YORK CITY.

Nov.

14 Thirtieth st, No. 7, n s, 145 w 5th av. G. F. Taussig & Co. agt Isaac Walker. (Lien filed June 18, 1891)........ $957 07

16 Thirty-fifth st, n s, 331 e 8th av, 69x100. Pelham Hod Elevating Co. agt William H. Ramsey, George Beebe and Thomas Sanderson. (Sept. 17, 1891)........ 260 00

17‡One Hundred and Ninth st, n s, 150 w 1st av, 25x100. K. N. Smith & Co. agt Francesco Ruggiero. (Aug. 31, 1891)........ 5,000 00

17 Thirty-first st, No. 215 W. John Sheridan agt Mary Wilson. (Oct. 10, 1891)........ 4,000 00

17 Forty-first st, Nos. 580-584 W., 75x100. Clinton Iron Works agt Valentine Loewers Gambrinus Brewing Co. and J. Coar & Co. (Nov. 10, 1891)........ 1,058 76

17*Fifty-first st, Nos. 244-248 W., 60x—. J. F. Gibbons agt Alexander Moore and David McMullin. (Nov. 5, 1891)........ 300 00

17*West End av, e s, 25 n 92d st, 50x—. Kaufman Simon agt Jacob B. Tallman and Thomas McLaughlin. (Sept. 25, 1891)... 250 00

18 Mulberry st, No. 284, e s, 183 s Prince st, 25 x100. John Roth agt Jonas Weil, Bernard Meyer, Hermann Fichter and Charles Frank. (May 13, 1890)........ 569 00

18 Pleasant av, No. 361, w s. William Barrow agt Mary and John Young. (April 11, 1891)........ 4 00

18 One Hundred and Fifteenth st, n s, 200 w 5th av, 45.2x—. Coons & Bradbury agt Adam Gebhardt and Peter Halpin. (Aug. 29, 1891)........ 110 00

18 Morton st, Nos 47 and 49, n s. Ferdinand Gehlker agt Victoria F. Dauphinais and H. MacLaughlin. (Sept. 17, 1891)........ 110 00

18‡Fifty-eighth st, s s, 100 w 6th av, 40x100. Abraham Steers agt Charles T. Barney and Garret Van Cleve. (May 18, 1891)... 273 88

18‡Same property. Thomas Hagan agt same. (May 21, 1891)........ 312 00

18‡Same property. Edward Tipping agt same. (Aug. 27, 1891)........ 1,100 00

18‡Same property. W. S. Williams, Jr., agt same. (May 12, 1891)........ 250 00

18‡Same property. Graff & Co. agt same. (May 13, 1891)........ 260 00

18‡Same property. P. and F. Corbin agt same. (Aug. 25, 1891)........ 406 79

19 One Hundred and Thirty-sixth st, s s, 100 e 8th av, 60.0x99.11. Thomas Osborne agt Thomas C. Van Brunt. (Jan. 24, 1891)... 6,642 12

19‡Kingsbridge road, e s, 50 s Nindham pl, 40 x95. William McMahon agt James Hodge and Elmer C. Schoonmaker. (Oct. 10, 1891)........ 100 00

19 Sixty-sixth st, Nos. 132-136 W., 75x—. Schnatz & Massoth agt Thomas and Margaret Shannon. (Sept. 2, 1891)........ 630 00

20‡Fifty-first st, Nos. 450-456 W., 100x—. Cornelius Beecher, Jr., agt Church of the Sacred Heart and James McWalter. (Nov. 17, 1891)........ 410 40

20 Eighty-third st, n s, 300 w 9th av, 100x—. J. B. McCoy & Co. agt Mark P. Brennan. (May 5, 1891)........ 481 14

20*Third av, e s, 98.11 n 125th st, 25x—. A. B. Johnson & Co. agt Louis J. Kahn or New York Beef Co., R. J. McDonald and Percy Jacobs. (Aug. 28, 1891)........ 477 55

20*Same property. W. H. Simonson agt Louis J. Kahn, Roderick J. McDonald and Percy Jacobs. (Sept. 9, 1891)........ 169 93

20 Walker st, No. 24. James Taylor agt John Doe and J. B. Monot. (Oct. 31, 1891)........ 95 00

20*Ninety-second st, n s, 200 w Columbus av, 75x—. Michael Kenney agt Mary and John W. Smith. (Nov. 14, 1891)........ 341 8

20 Pike st, No. 28 } begins Pike st, Henry st, Nos. 108 and 110 } s e cor Henry st, 25x80. Kotlowsky & Levy agt Louis Goodman. (May 5, 1891) 4,030 00

*Discharged by depositing amount of lien and interest with County Clerk.
‡Discharged by order of Court on filing bond.

KINGS COUNTY.

Nov.

12 Thirteenth av, n e cor 57th st, 40x100.2, New Utrecht. Michael Magorino agt Peterson & Stillwell, owners, and Ole Gunsten, contractor (Lien filed Nov. 4, 1891.) (Deposit) $197 95

14 Third st, n s, 431.9 e 6th av, 44x100. Thomas McCann agt Moses & Fanton, owners and contractors. (Aug. 25, 1891.) (Order of Court).......... 465 00

15 Navy st, e s, 61.8 n Myrtle av, 50x100. The Wilson & Baillee Mfg Co. agt William H. H. Glover. (June 5, 1891.) (Deposit). ... 142 45

16 Liberty av, s s, 100 w Watkins st, 6 houses. Salvatore Bove agt George Treville and Charles W. Tomlonson, owners and contractors. (Sept. 28, 1891.) (Order of Court).......... 340 40

16 Howard av, s w cor Macon st, 93.6x100. W. H. and J. T. Bierds agt Morris Isaacs, Emily Gilfoy, Thomas Purcell, Grove M. Horwood, Mary Leonhardt and Clarence Lincoln, owners and contractors. (July 25, 1891.) (Order of Court).......... 1,826 45

16 Same property. W. H. & J. T. Bierds agt same owner and contractor. (July 25, 1891.) (Order of Court).......... 1,826 45

16 Same property. W. H. & J. T. Bierds agt same. (July 29, 1891.) (Order of Court). 1,826 45

18 Same property. Adelbert S. Nichols agt Clarence Lincoln, owner and contractor. (July 17, 1891.) (Order of Court).......... 900 00

18 Same property. Bulmer Lumber Co. (Lim.) agt same owner and contractor. (Aug. 3, 1891.) (Order of Court).......... 1,598 88

17 Fort Hamilton av, n e cor 59th st, 100x100. John Cook agt trustees for School No. 2, New Utrecht, owners, and Ole Gunsten, contractor. (Nov. 16, 1891.) (Deposit)... 190 26

17 Eighth st, s s, 135 w 4th av, 50x100. James O'Hara agt Mr. McGuire, owner, and Edward Stinson, contractor. (June 23, 1891). 79 25

17 Ovington av, n s, 75 w Stewart av, 25x100, New Utrecht. Frank D. Creamer agt Mr. Pade, owner, and M. Dennington and Connolly & Smith, contractors. (Oct. 19, 1891).......... 138 74

18 Patchen av, w s, 90 n Putnam av, 100x90. Edward F. Spear agt Messrs. Underhill & Yarber, owners, and Mr. A. White, contractor. (June 26, 1891.) (Order of Court) 17 50

18 Ovington av, n s, 75 w Stewart av, 20x100, New Utrecht. Francis Connelly agt John J. Page, owner, and Edwin Dennington, contractor. (Oct. 26, 1891.) (Deposit)... 300 00

18 Stillwell av, cor 86th st, Gravesend. Joseph Romano agt John Morrisey, owner, and Christian Brown, contractor. (Nov. 17, 1891).......... 35 00

18 Bay 22d st, n w s, 370 s w 86th st, 40x96.8, New Utrecht. Cropsey & Mitchell agt Agnes M. Bruns, owner, and Louis Larsen, contractor. (Nov. 14, 1891).......... 435 00

18 Same property. Louis E. Quick agt same owner and contractor. (Nov. 14, 1891)... 284 00

18 Same property. Isaacson & Pearson agt same owner and contractor. (Oct. 5, 1891).......... 40 00

18 Same property. Halstead Bros. agt same owner and contractor. (Sept. 30, 1891)... 300 00

18 McDougal st, n s, 325 e Saratoga av, 25x100. Charles Ratner agt D. Davison, owner, and Joseph Davison, contractor. (Sept. 29, 1891).......... 605 00

18 Bushwick av, w s, 83 s Kossuth pl, 20x84. Philip Dugro agt Ludwig Levy, owner, and Martin and George Kuhn, contractors. (Oct. 20, 1891).......... 189 00

18 Same property. Hyde & Gload Mfg. Co. agt same. (Oct. 20, 1891).......... 136 00

18 Same property. George Kuhn agt Ludwig Levy, owner and contractor. (Oct. 19, 1891).......... 536 50

BUILDINGS PROJECTED.

The first name is that of the owner; ar't stands for architect, m'n for mason, c'r for carpenter and b'r for builder.

NEW YORK CITY.

SOUTH OF 14TH STREET.

West st, w s, 50 n Harrison st (Pier No. 23, N. R.), one-story galvanized iron shed, 66x672, gravel roof; cost, $60,000; N. Y. C. & H. R. R. R. Co., Grand Central Depot; ar't, W. Katte. Plan 1443.

13th av, w s, bet Little West 12th and 13th sts, bulkhead line, one-story galvanized iron ferry house, 120x90, tin roof; cost, $20,000; Pennsylvania Railroad, Exchange pl, Jersey City, N. J.; c'rs, Benner & Opdyke. Plan 1468.

BETWEEN 14TH AND 59TH STREETS.

18th st, No 7 E., five-story brk and iron store, 25x82, tin roof; cost, $30,000; Robert and Ogden Goelet, 9 West 17th st; ar't, J. Murphy; m'ns, M. Reid & Co.; c'r, Peter McCormick. Plan 1442.

24th st, s s, 50 e 1st av, three-story brk and stone workshop, 100x73, tin roof; cost, $30,000; Frank X. Radley, 175 East 79th st; ar'ts, Radley & Greenough. Plan 1444.

47th st, s s, 50 e Broadway, one-story glass and wood store, 25x20, tin roof; cost, $850; lessee, Patrick H. Cuff, 2119 Madison av; ar't, J. M. Dunn; c'r, P. J. Ryan. Plan 1449.

41st st, No. 55 E., eight-story brk warehouse, 24.6x100, asphalt roof; cost, abt $135,000; Lincoln Safe Deposit Co.; ar'ts, G. E. Harney and W. S. Purdy; m'ns, McCabe Bros. Plan 1467.

9th av, Nos. 746 and 748, two five-story brk flats and stores, 25x88.6, tin roofs; cost, $23,000 each; Weil & Mayer, 227 East 60th st; ar'ts, Schneider & Herter. Plan 1463.

BETWEEN 59TH AND 125TH STREETS, EAST OF 5TH AVENUE.

60th st, Nos. 235 and 237 E., two four-story and basement stone front dwell'gs, 18.6x50 and 55, tin roofs; total cost, $38,000; Jacob Klingenstein, 72 St. Marks pl; ar't, G. F. Pelham. Plan 1469.

103d st, s s, 209.6 e Lexington av, four five-story stone front flats, 27x75 and 84, tin roofs; cost, $16,000 and $19,000 each; Jas. H. Swan, 1114 3d av; ar't, F. Wennemer. Plan 1461.

Av B, n w cor 88th st, four five-story brk and stone flats, 25 and 25.4x9, tin roofs; total cost, $64,000; Geo G. Banzer, 339 East 22d st; ar't, O. Wirz. Plan 1472.

87th st, No. 177 E., four-story brk factory, 25x90, tin or gravel roof; cost, $10,000; lessee, Thos. B. Whiffen; ar't, F. Wennemer. Plan 1473.

BETWEEN 59TH AND 125TH STREETS, WEST OF CENTRAL PARK WEST AND 8TH AVENUE.

68th st, n s, 150 e Amsterdam av, four three-story stone front dwell'gs, 18, 19 and 20x55 and extension, tin roofs; cost, $18,000 each; Peter Wagner, 844 Amsterdam av; ar't, F. A. Minuth. Plan 1446.

NORTH OF 125TH STREET.

151st st, s s, 150 e Amsterdam av, four five-story brk and stone flats, 26x78, tin roofs; cost, $23,000 each; Wm. Broadbelt, Main and Beechwood avs, New Rochelle; ar't, John C. Burne. Plan 1454.

151st st, s s, 254 e Amsterdam av, five-story brk and stone flat, 21x89.11, tin roof; cost, $23,000; ow'r and ar't, same as last. Plan 1455.

181st st, n s, 25 e Wadsworth av, five three-story frame dwell'gs, 20x37, tin roofs; cost, each, $4,500; Charles Weinberg, 109 East 60th st; ar't, G. H. Budlong. Plan 1450.

11th av, n e cor 173d st, two-story frame dwelling, 18x25, tin roof; cost, abt $1,500; John A. Lachner, 11 West Broadway; ar't, C. H. Richter, Jr. Plan 1451.

168th st, n s, 225 w Amsterdam av, three-story frame dwell'g, 22x45, tin roof; cost, abt $4,000; Andrew Friede, 512 West 168th st; ar't, F. S. Schlesinger. Plan 1466.

7th av, s w cor 142d st, three five-story brk and stone flats, 34.5x71 and 20 and 20.6x65, tin roofs; total cost, $64,000; Patrick Hogan, 1614 Lexington av; ar't, G. Robinson, Jr. Plan 1465.

23D AND 24TH WARDS.

Suburban st, s s, 94 w Hull av, one-story frame stable, shingle roof; cost, $1,000; Drake V. Smith, Bedford Park; ar't, E. K. Bourne; b'rs, McElroy & Son. Plan 1447.

Travers st, s s, abt 150 e Bainbridge av, five two-and-a-half-story frame dwell'gs, 20x30, and extensions, slate roofs; cost, each, $3,000; Walter J. Lee. Plan 1453.

134th st, s e cor Cypress av, five-story brk piano factory, 50x92, tin roof; cost, $26,000; Francis Connor, 4 East 42d st; ar'ts, A. B. Ogden & Son. Plan 1457.

Boston av, n e cor Teasdale pl, four five and six-story brk and stone flats and stores, —x65.11 and 104.9, tin roofs; cost, $40,000 each; Mrs. G. F. Webster, 232 East 134th st; ar't, H. A. Reeves. Plan 1445.

Crotona av, w s, 125 s Lebanon st, three two-story frame dwell'gs, 16.8x44, tin roofs; cost, $3,000 each; ow'r and ar't, Jos. Balmford, Webster av, near 170th st. Plan 1459.

Fulton av, w s, 212 n 168th st, rear, one-story brk and stone shed, 60x30, tin roof; cost, $1,000; ow'r and ar't, Daniel Mayer, 1043 Fulton av. Plan 1452.

Lafontaine av, e s, abt 100 n 178th st, two-story frame dwell'g, 20x30, tin roof; cost, $2,800; Margaret Thomas, Kingsbridge road and Adams av; ar't, T. J. Blair. Plan 1456.

Sedgwick av, e s, abt 796 n Jerome av, two two-story frame dwell'gs, 15x50, tin roofs, cost, $3,000 each; Geo. and Wm. Reeber, 243 East 113th st; ar't, J. H. Valentine; br's, Behrens & King. Plan 1448.

Trinity av, e s, 300 n 161st st, three two-story and basement frame dwell'gs, 16.8x38, tin roofs; cost, $3,000 each; Edward Robitzek, 944 East 165th st; ar't, A. Pfeiffer. Plan 1458.

3d av, s w cor 163d st, rear, one-story frame billiard hall, 32.8x25, tin roof; cost, $2,200; lessee, Henry C. Schrade, on premises; ar't, A. Pfeifer. Plan 1460.

1st av, n s, 100 e 3d st, Woodlawn, two-story frame dwell'g, 18x26, tin roof; cost, $1,000; Alex. Forsyth, Woodlawn; ar't and c'r, S. L. Berrian. Plan 1462.

Vanderbilt av, e s, 104 n 170th st, two-story frame workshop, 21x40, tin roof; cost, $1,000; Anna Rusor, Brook av, near 170th st; ar't, Louis Kaysser. Plan 1464.

Forest av, s e cor 163d st } two three-story Tinton av, s w cor 163d st } frame dwell'gs, 17.5x44, tin roofs; cost, $4,000 each; ow'r and ar't, John W. Decker, 841 Forest av. Plan 1470.

Forest av, e s, 17.5 s 163d st } four three-story Tinton av, w s, 17.5 s 163d st } frame dwell'gs, 18.5x44, tin roofs; cost, $3,800 each; ow'r and ar't, same as last. Plan 1471.

KINGS COUNTY.

Plan 2074—Palmetto st, No. 317, one three-story frame (brk filled) flat, 25x50, tin roof; cost, $4,900; James Dawson & Co., 860 Quincy st; ar't, E. Dennis.

2075—St. Marks av, s s, 147.2 w Schenectady av, one three-story frame tenem't, 25x50, tin roof; cost, $4,000; W. H. Caufield, 1028 St. Marks av; ar't, H. R. Asserson.

2076—Liberty av, n s, 28 e Warwick st, one two-story frame shed, 16x42, tin roof; cost, $100; Henry Gans, Liberty av, cor Warwick st; ar't, C. Infanger.

2077—Jefferson st, s s, 161.4 w Bushwick av, one two-story frame silk braid factory, 19x65, tin roof; cost, $1,500; Geo. Wetzel, 17 Locust st; ar't, T. Engelhardt; b'r, C. Schneider.

2078—14th st, s s, 222.10 e 8th av, three two-story and basement brk dwell'gs, 18.6x45, tin roof, wooden cornice; cost, $4,000 each; ow'r and c'r, Wm. Hawkins, 449 14th st; ar't, H. B. Hawkins.

2079—South 11th st, — —, 76.6 w Kent av, one nine-story brk sugar refinery, 64.7x90.4, gravel roof, brk cornice; cost, $48,000; Mollenhauer Sugar Refining Co., on premises; ar't, C. C. H. Schmadt.

2080—Pacific st, No. 358, one two-story brk chapel, 24.5 and 25x92, and one-story extension 8x25, slate roof, terra cotta and iron cornice; cost, $8,000; Cuyler Chapel, trustees, Brooklyn; ar't, C. A. Sargent; b'rs, J. B. Woodruff and L. W. Seaman, Jr., & Son.

2081—4th av, e s, 20 n 53d st, one three-story brk tenem't, 30x50 and extension 7x14, tin roof, wooden cornice; cost, $6,000; James Cosgrove, 3d av and 27th st; ar'ts, H. L. Spicer & Son.

2082—57th st, n s, 100 e 3d av, three two-story basement and cellar brk dwell'gs, 20x40, tin roofs, wooden cornices; cost $3,000 each; H. S. Hassan, 3d av, cor 58d st; ar'ts, H. L. Spicer & Son.

2083—56th st, s s, 380 w 3d av, five two-story and basement frame (brk filled) dwell'gs, 20x38, tin roofs and party walls; cost, $2,300 each; A. E. Bigelow, 3d av and 52d st; ar'ts, Spence Bros.

2084—Java st, n e cor Oakland st, one three-story frame (brk filled) store and tenem't, 20x62.6, gravel roof; cost, $4,500; ow'r and b'r, W. H. Sturgis, 158 Noble st; ar't, F. Weber.

2085—Herkimer st, s s, 375 w Utica av, one two-story frame carpenter shop, 22x40, tin roof; cost, $550; Wm. H. Reynolds, 273 Hancock st; b'r, R. S. Timper.

2086—Empire Stores adj Dock, one one-story frame shed, 110 and 100x270, gravel roof; cost, abt $12,000; Henry E. Nesmith, trustee, 117 Remsen st; b'r, J. H. Euler.

2087—Sutter av, s s, 25 e Snediker av, one one-story frame stable, 13x16, pa roof; cost, $85; J. Perline, Sutter av; b'r, O. Perfotten.

2088—2d av, e s, 34 s 7th st, one two-story and attic frame saw and planing mill, 120x168, gravel roof; cost, $7,000; C. E. Valentine; b'r, S. W. Howard and J. P. Whittier.

2089—Knickerbocker av, e s, 50 n Himrod st, four four-story frame (brk filled) stores and tenem'ts, 25x60, tin roofs; total cost, $28,000; Baer & Shaffner, Flushing av, near Broadway; ar't, F. Holmburg.

2090—Knickerbocker av, s e cor Stanhope st, two four-story frame (brk filled) stores and tenements, 25x60, tin roofs; total cost, $15,000; ow'rs and ar't, same as last.

2091—Knickerbocker av, e s, 25 s Stanhope st, and Knickerbocker av, e s, 25 n Himrod st, two four-story frame (brk filled) stores and tenem'ts, 25x60; tin roofs; total cost, $14,000; ow'rs and ar't, same as last.

2092—Belmont av, n w cor Osborn st, two three-story frame tenem'ts, 25x55, tin roofs; cost, each, $4,500; Sol. Wolff, Watkins st; b'r, L. Rattner.

2093—Eastern Parkway, s s, 40 e Watkins st, one two-story frame (brk filled) engine house, 25x55, tin roof; cost, $4,500; Ada Farmer, Watkins st.

2094—Leonard st, n w cor Boerum st, one four-story frame (brk filled) store and tenem't, 45x21.5, tin roof; cost, $2,800; S. Bellar and N. Lenber, 36 Seigel st; ar't, H. Vollweiler; b'r, not selected.

2095—Ralph av, s e cor McDonough st, one four-story brk and Lake Superior stone double flat, 24.6x90, gravel roof, iron cornice; cost, $20,000; Thos. H. Radcliffe, 826 Fulton st; ar't, J. A. Sinclair; b'r, not selected.

2096—Logan st, e s, 90 s Belmont av, eight two-story frame dwell'gs, 20x44, tin roofs; cost, each, $2,000; Richard Geary, 576 Madison st; ar't and c'r, W. Godfrey; m'n, J. Tauder.

2097—Sutter st, n s, 60 e Logan st, and Belmont av, s s, 60 e Logan st, eight two-story frame dwell'gs, 20x44, tin roofs; cost, $2,000 each; ow'r, ar't and b'r, same as last.

2098—Osborn st, e s, 125 n Eastern Parkway, one three-story frame store and dwell'g, 20x30, tin roof; cost, $3,800; Solomon Goldburg, Atlantic av and Williams pl.

2099—37th st, s s, 250 e 4th av, six two-story frame (partly brk filled) dwell'gs, 16.8x42, tin roofs; cost, $1,800 each; ow'r, ar't and b'r, Wm. E. Kay.

2100—Halsey st, s s, 125 e Bushwick av, one one-story frame shed, 13.6x28, tin roof; cost, $200; Helkem & Bros., 1267 Halsey st; ar't and c'r, A. D. Vreeland.

2101—Fanchon pl, e s, 125 n Bushwick av, one one-story frame silver beater's shop, 21x32, tin roof; cost, $500; Wm. Acker, 18 Fanchon pl; ar't and c'r, H. Rocker; m'n, D. Cook.

2102—Eastern Parkway, s e cor Barbey st, one three-story frame (brk filled) store and tenem't, 25x60, tin roof; cost, $6,200; Theo. M. Le Beau, 726 Van Siclen av; ar't, C. Infanger.

2103—Warwick st, e s, 50 n Liberty av, one three-story frame moulding mill, 42x27, tin roof; cost, $7,000; Henry Gans, on premises; ar't, C. Infanger.

2104—Johnson av, n s, 150 e Varick av, one one-story frame shed, 20x40, tar paper roof; cost, $25; C. Erthal. 288 Bushwick av.

2105—Grove st, e s, 200 from Evergreen av, one four-story brk brewery storage house, 50x70, tin roof, brk cornice; cost, $23,000; Frank Ibert, on premises; ar't, F. Wunder.

2106—11th st, s s, 21.6 e 4th av, four three-story brk tenem'ts, 19x45, tin roofs, wooden cornices; cost, $4,500 each; ow'r and c'r, A. G. Calder, 420 8th st; ar't, W. M. Calder; m'n, not selected.

2107—Floyd st, s s, 125 w Sumner av, two four-story brk tenem'ts, 30x65.4, tin roofs, iron cornices; total cost, $19,000; Beer & Schaffer, Flushing av and Broadway; ar't, F. Holmberg.

2108—Irving pl, w s, 300 n Putnam av, one four-story brk flat, 25x69, tin roof, iron cornice; cost, $9,000; C. W. and E. M. Barlow, 16 and 18 Irving pl; ar't, I. D. Reynolds & Son; b'r, —— Winter.

2109—McDougal st, s s, 250 w Stone av, one one-story frame carpenter shop, 14x20, gravel roof; cost, $75; A. F. Cox, 191 McDougal st; ar't and b'r, W. R. Case.

2110—Elton st, w s, 125 n Arlington av, one two-and-a-half-story frame dwell'g, 20x33, tin roof; cost, $2,000; De Witt C. E. Baisley, 1550 Pacific st; b'r, W. D. Losee.

2111—4th av, n e cor 48th st, one one-story frame stable, 20x20, tin roof; cost, $350; Frank Roenbeck, on premises; ar't and b'r, J. H. Frenet.

2112—Marion st, s s, 27 w Howard av, one three-story brk store and tenem't, 26.9x53, tin roof, wooden cornice; cost, $4,000; ow'r and m'n, Ernst Sutterlin, 11 Russell pl; ar't, C. Infanger.

2113—Pacific st, n s, 450 w Kingston av, five three-story and basement brk and brown stone dwell'gs, 20x45, gravel roofs, iron cornices; cost, $8,000; Charles H. Nichols, 28 New York av; ar'ts, Langston & Dahlander.

2114—Ewen st, No. 383, one one-story brk cook house, 17x23, tin roof; cost, $400; Chas. Mausling, 63 North 3d st.

2115—Hamburg av, w s, 25 s Harman st, one three-story frame (brk filled) store and tenem't, 25x65, tin roof; cost, $7,500; J. Bohnert, 621 Willoughby av; ar't, F. Holmberg.

2116—52d st, n s, 320 w 5th av, one three-story frame tenem't, 20x40, tin roof; cost, $2,500; M. A. White, 3d av, cor 53d st; ar'ts, H. L. Spicer & Son.

2117—Hamburg av, w s, 50 s Harman st, four three-story frame (brk filled) tenem'ts, 25x65, tin roofs; cost, $24,000; J. Bohnert, 621 Willoughby av; ar't, F. Holmberg.

2118—Essex st, w s, 23 s Blake av, one one-and-a-half-story frame stable, 24x20, shingle roof; cost, $150; ow'r and c'r, Wm. Laird, Linwood and Blake avs.

2119—5th st, s s, 300 w 5th av, five three-story brk tenem'ts, 20x45, tin roofs, wooden cornices; cost, $5,000 each; Raffalo Rivillo, 51 Oliver st, New York; ar't, M. F. Walsh; b'r, not selected.

2120—Tompkins av, e s, 150 n Pulaski st, one four-story brk store and flat, 28x77.6, tin roof, metal cornice; cost, $11,000; Mrs. M. F. Batalora, 74 Sumner av; ar'ts, I. D. Reynolds & Son; b'r, not selected.

ALTERATIONS NEW YORK CITY.

Plan 1944—14th st, No. 32 E., interior alterations; cost, $1,000; W. Jennings Demorest, 21 East 57th st; ar'ts, J. O. Bunce & Co.; c'r, W. Watts.

1945—Union sq, No. 21, extend show window; cost, $450; lessee, Chas. Lembke, 655 Lafayette av, Brooklyn; ar't, E. M. Greene.

1946—152d st, No. 651 E., raise one story, also move building; cost, $1,500; Henry Pfeiffer, on premises; ar't, F. J. Miller.

1947—153d st, s s, 100 w Melrose av, building to be moved; cost, $200; Francis Stolz, 686 East 153d st; ar't, F. J. Miller; m'ns, Lofink & Ledoger.

1948—153d st, s s, 100 w Melrose av, rear building to be moved; cost, $200; ow'r, ar't and m'ns, same as last.

1949—Creston av, w s, bet Highbridge road and St. James st, two-story frame extension, 16.6x21, tin roof; cost, $1,000; John B. Haskin, Fordham; ar't, A. B. Marshall.

1950—4th av, s e cor 21st st, seven-story brk and stone extension, 23x89 and 90, tin roof; cost, $55,000; Mahon & Coyne, 119 East 47th st; ar't, G. F. Pelham.

1951—Madison st, No. 289, interior alterations, walls altered; cost, $4,500; Albert Sokolsky, 168 Monroe st; ar't, F. Ebeling.

1952—Pelham av, s e cor Arthur st, interior alterations; cost, $75; G. De Bello, on premises; c'r, C. B. Jones.

1953—Boston av, e s, 115 s 166th st, one-story frame extension, 20x9, tin roof; cost, $200; John G. Williams, 1074 Boston av; ar't, J. J. Vreeland.

1954—3d av, Nos. 789 and 791, raise one story, also five-story brk extension, 36.3x54.6, tin roof; cost, $20,000; agent, E. H. Nordlinger, 8 Harrison st; ar't, H. Kafka.

1955—115th st, No. 346 E., walls altered; cost, $300; John Cohen, 43 Attorney st; ar't, A. Spence.

1956—Broadway, No. 1286, repair damage by fire; cost, $1,685; D. H. McAlpine, 673 5th av; c'r, G. Culgin.

1957—Bond st, Nos. 7 and 9, walls altered, &c.; cost, $500; Dr. Wm. Detmold et al., 7 Bond st; ar't, G. Vassar, Jr.; m'ns, G. Vassar & Son.

1958—40th st, Nos 636 and 638 W, walls altered; cost, $500; Jos. Stern, 50 West 55th st; ar't and m'ns, same as last.

1959—Melrose av, n e cor 153d st, raise one story, also interior alterations; cost, $900; A. Lebder, 655 East 153d st; ar't, C. F. Lohse; c'r, F. Bremer.

1960—Broadway, No. 853, walls altered, &c.; cost, $1,800; lessee, Domestic Sewing Machine Co., on premises; ar't and b'r, L. Adams.

1961—156th st, n s, 325 w Courtlandt av, move building; cost, $750; Jos. Hoetzel, 549 East 156th st; ar't, C. F. Lohse.

1962—Melrose av, s e cor 155th st, move building; cost, $800; Regina Nieland et al., 654 East 155th st; ar't, F. Lohse; m'n F. Zimmerman.

1963—Hudson st, No. 265, new store front; cost, $125; Henry Wolf, on premises.

1964—8th av, s w cor 143d st, walls altered; cost, abt $800; lessee, Fred. Frey, on premises; ar't, W. A. O'Hea; c'r, P. Casserly.

1965—161st st, n s, 54 w Melrose av, raise one story; also three-story frame extension, 20x16, tin roof; cost, $3,000; John Abelbor, 649 East 161st st; ar't, C. F. Lohse; m'n, H. Hoffstadt.

1966—Monroe st, No. 56, interior alterations, walls altered; cost, $1,500; Eagle Distillery Co., on premises; ar't, H. Horenburger.

1967—Clinton st, No. 171, new store front; cost, $200; Louise Wiebolt, 451 Kouwenhoven st, Astoria; ar't, H. Horenburger.

1968—Pitt st, No. 130, four-story and basement brk extension, 22.6x25, tin roof; cost, $4,500; S. Fischer et al., 315 East Houston st; ar't, H. Horenburger.

1969—Morris av, s e cor 152d st, new store front; cost, $625; Julia McIntyre, on premises.

1970—Broadway, n w cor 38th st, interior alterations, walls altered; cost, $2,000; Max Schroff, 23 Union sq.

1971—Av A, n w cor 68th st, three-story brk extension, 24.10x38, tin roof; cost, $1,200; lessee, Thos. E. Crimmins, 725 Park av; ar't, J. H. Friend.

1972—Boston road, s w cor Vyse st, two-story frame extension, 25x20, shingle roof; cost, $300; Frank Becker, 1861 Boston road; ar't and c'r, C. Biller; m'n, C. McDonald.

1973—22d st, Nos 40 and 42 W., two story brk extension, 23x6 and 38 9, tin roof; cost, $12,000; Robert T. Bellchamber, 317 6th av; ar't, M. C. Merritt.

1974—8th av, n e cor 12th st, two-story brk extension, 11x4 6, tin roof; cost, $1,500; lessee, Sylvester S. Jones, 38 Perry st; ar't, W. H. Boylan.

KINGS COUNTY.

Plan 1079—Driggs st, n s, 75 w Lorimer st, raised 6 feet on brk piers; cost, $175; John Tucker, 322 Driggs st; b'rs, Randall & Miller.

1080—Humboldt st, No. 619, stone foundation; cost, $300; John Teajeien, 619 Humboldt st; b'r, J. Sheppard.

1081—Graham av, No. 227, rebuild part foundation; cost, $75; Mr. Ebert, on premises.

1082—Union st, No. 96, iron beams on front; cost, $800; Giovani Isola, 92 Baxter st, New York; ar't, H. Dudley.

1083—Henry st, No. 493, two-story brk extension, 12x20, tin roof; cost, $700; Fred'k Wrede, 493 Henry st; ar't, W. H. Wirth; b'r, Mr. Downie.

1084—Walton st, No. 90, raised 4 feet on ork wall; cost, $250; George Kahn, on premises; ar't, H. Vollweiler; b'r, not selected.

1085—Broadway, No. 1260, one-story brk extension, 25x37, tin roof; cost, $1,333; E. F. Jenkins, Park av; ar't, F. Holmberg.

1086—Sackett st, No. 26, front and interior alterations; cost, $800; J. Munroe Taylor, 113 Water st, New York; b'rs, M. Gibbons & Sons.

1087—President st, No. 34, one-story brk extension, 20x3, tin roof, iron cornice, front and interior alterations; cost, $1,200; Antonio Gottavario, 14 Mott st, New York; ar't, H. Dudley.

1088—Norman av, No. 150, new store front; cost, $250; ow'r and c'r, M. L. Antonius, 108 Newell st.

1089—Joralemon st, No. 146, bay window and interior alterations; cost, $3,000; F. B. Richardson, on premises; ar't, M. W. Morris.

1090—Chester st, e s, 250 s East New York av, raised 4 ft. on stone foundation; cost, $200; G. Koch, 2 Bristol st.

1091—Pacific st, n e cor Bond st, one-story brk extension, 21x8, tin roof, new store front and interior alterations; cost, $4,000; Frank Phillip, 239 Skillman st; ar't, I. D. Reynolds; b'r, not selected.

1092—Atlantic av, No. 1515, front alterations; cost, $350; Waters estate, 25 South Oxford st; b'r, W. H. Tunison.

1093—Seigel st, No. 145, one-story frame extension, 16x14, tin roof; cost, $25; O. Reich.

1094—Bushwick av, n e cor Meserole st, flat tin roof, new walls; cost, $2,800; Warren G. Abbott, on premises; ar't, F. Wunder.

1095—Broadway, No. 1670, new store front; cost, $300; Thomas Stone, 159 Hall st; ar't, M. F. Walsh; b'rs, P. McMurray & Bro.

1096—Washington st, No. 251, one-story brk extension, 25x10, tin roof, front and interior alterations; cost, $4,000; Witmore estate, 42 Wall st; b'r, T. K. Schermerhorn.

1097—Eastern Parkway, s s, 50 w Berriman st, two-story frame extension, 12x15, tin roof; cost, $150; Wm. Jenkins, on premises; b'r, W. Winter.

1098—Eagle st, No. 163, dig cellar, build foundation; cost, $350; Thomas Cowly, on premises.

1099—Myrtle av, No. 872, one story brk extension, 10 and 14x30, gravel roof; cost, $600; J. Shumacker, 135 Joralemon st; b'r, S. Rippingale.

1100—Fulton st, No. 2051, one-story brk extension, 20.6x38, tin roof; cost, $1,500; Mrs. C. M. Gomez, 920 President st; ar'ts and c'rs, H. Ramsay & Son; m'n, P. Husmann.

1101—15th st, No. 289, one-story and basement brk extension, 8x12, tin roof; cost, $150; Church of St. Stanislaus

1102—6th av, Nos. 463–467, one-story and basement brk extension, 8x18, tin roof; cost, $350; same as last.

MISCELLANEOUS.

BUSINESS FAILURES.

N. Y. ASSIGNMENTS—BENEFIT CREDITORS.

Nov.

17 Done, Henre (commission merchant and dealer in foreign and domestic fruits, at No. 50 Gansevoort st), to Le Roy M. Lyon; without preferences.

17 Brunclik, Joseph (furrier, at No. 270 Mercer st), to Vincent W. Woytisek; preferences $368.68.

20 Rypinski, Herman (jobber in jewelry, at No. 51 Maiden lane), to Henry M. Tech; preferences $6,420.14.

KINGS COUNTY.

GENERAL ASSIGNMENTS.

Nov.

13 Baehr, Jacob to George H. Billings.

17 Blanchard, Russell W. S. to Noah Tebbetts.

16 Durham, Fred. F. to George W. Wastee.

PROCEEDINGS OF THE BOARD OF ALDERMEN AFFECTING REAL ESTATE.

APPROVED PAPERS.

Resolutions passed by the Board of Aldermen calling for the following improvements have been signed by the Mayor for the week ending November 14, 1891. *Indicates that the Mayor neither appoved nor objected thereto, therefore the same became adopted.

LAMP POSTS ERECTED AND LIGHTED.

29th st, in front of No. 30 W., at expense of Samuel T. Young.

Park av, from 96th to 105th st.

147th st, from Boulevard to a point 500 feet west therefrom.

MAINS.

75th st, bet West End and Riverside avs; water.

147th st, from Boulevard to a point 500 feet west therefrom; gas.

Park av, from 96th to 105th st; gas.

FENCING VACANT LOTS.

77th st, s s, abt 150 e Columbus av, runs east abt 100 feet.

1st av, n e cor 90th st, 50 on av and 100 on st.

ADVERTISED LEGAL SALES.

REFEREES SALES TO BE HELD AT THE REAL ESTATE EXCHANGE AND AUCTION ROOM (LIMITED), 59 to 65 LIBERTY STREET, EXCEPT WHERE OTHERWISE STATED.

Nov.

Broadway or Kingsbridge road, s e cor Macomb st, 48.6x100, by P. F. Meyer. (Amt due $6,969)... 23

Cottage pl, e s, 288 n e 170th st, 57x127x56.3x197, by William Kennelly. (Amt due $3,515)... 23

Oliver st, Nos. 100 and 102, e s, 55 n South st, 40x50, two two-story brk tenem'ts, store in No. 102, by R. V. Harnett. (Amt due $9,658)... 23

57th st, No. 104, s s, 100 w 6th av, 15x100, four-story stone front dwell'g, also all right, title and interest to strip of land 5 inches in depth and 15 feet wide, adj rear of above, by P. F. Meyer. (Amt due $21,147)... 23

102d st, Nos. 227–237, n s, 105 w 2d av, 126x100.9, four-story brk silk mills, by Smyth & Ryan. (Assignee's sale)... 24

Gerard st, n e s, 154 s e Bergen av, 25x100, by R. V. Harnett & Co. (Partition sale)... 24

Pike st, No. 9 } begins Pike st,
East Broadway, Nos. 123 and 125 } s e cor East Broadway, 24x85, three-story frame store and tenem't on Pike st and one and two-story brk and frame stores on East Broadway, by Smyth & Ryan. (Partition sale)... 24

39th st, No. 517, n s, 250 w 10th av, 25x38.9, four-story brk store and tenem't with one-story frame buildings on rear, by J. F. B. Smyth. (Partition sale)... 24

119th st, No. 63, n s, 526.8 w 5th av, 16.8x100.11, three-story stone front dwell'g, by R. V. Harnett & Co. (Amt due $12,2[illegible])... 24

Columbus av, s e cor 118th st, 50.5x100, vacant, by Richard V. Harnett. (Amt due $18,065)... 24

Lexington av, No. 443, e s, 40 n 45th st, 20x70.6, four-story brk dwell'g, by A. H. Muller & Son. (Amt due $17,400)... 24

1st av, Nos. 2035–2041, n w cor 105th st, 100.9x100, four five-story brk tenem'ts with stores... }
105th n s, 125 w 1st av, 75x100 9, vacant... }
by D. P. Ingraham & Co. (Amt due $68,187)... 25

Broome st, Nos. 2–14, n w cor Tompkins st, 125x75, five five-story stone front tenem'ts, store in No. 2, by D. P. Ingraham & Co. (Amt due $40,149)... 27

Houston st, No. 448, n s, 131 e Av D, 21x105.10, three-story brk store and tenem't, by William Kennelly. (Amt due $2,861)... 27

93d st, Nos. 153 and 155, n s, 249 e Amsterdam av, 34x84 to Apthorpes lane, x34.6x85.4, two three-story stone front dwell'gs, by C. S. Brown... 27

93d st, No. 156, n s 219 e 10th av, 15x86 to Apthorpes lane, x15x86.8, three-story stone front dwell'g, by C. S. Brown... 27

120th st, No. 304, s s, 100 e 2d av, 19.5x100.11, three-story stone front dwell'g, by William Kennelly. (Amt due $6,540)... 27

132d st, Nos 26–30, s s, 285 w 5th av, 100x100.11, three five-story brk flats, by William Kennelly. (Amt due $8,274; prior morts. $——)... 27

Edgecombe av, No. 40, e s, 51.10 s 137th st, 17.6x90, three-story brk dwell'g, by A. H. Muller & Son. (Am't due $12,879)... 27

Willis av, n w cor 146th st, 25x106, by Horatio Henriques. (Amt due $12,937)... 27

42d st, No. 250, s s, 280 w 2d av, 25x79.6x27.11x92.1, four-story brk tenem't with stores, by Smyth & Ryan. (Amt due $16,416)... 30

Riverside av or Drive, No. 100 / 82d st, Nos. 318-324 — begins Riverside av, s e cor 82d st, runs east 161.1 x south 102.2 x west 16.8 x north 19.4 x west 32 x north 18 8 x west 14.4 x north 15.6 x west 8 4 x north 26.6 x west 79.9 to Riverside Drive, x north 24.9 to beginning, four-story stone front dwell'g on av and four four-story stone front dwell'gs on st, by R. V. Harnett & Co..... 30

Willis av, n w cor 145th st, 25x106..........
Willis av, n w cor 146th st, 25x106..........
Willis av, w s, 25 n 146th st, 25x106..........
Three five-story brk and stone flats..........
by William Kennelly. (Amt due on each corner house $21,055, and $14,858 on other).......... 30

3d av, Nos. 2197 and 2199 / 120th st, Nos. 202 and 204 — begins 3d av, s e cor 120th st, runs east 100 x south 75 x west 20 x north 25 x west 80 to 3d av, x north 50.6 to beginning, two two and three-story frame stores and tenem'ts on av and one-story and three-story brk stores and tenem'ts on st, by A. H. Muller & Son. (Partition sale)... 30

7th av, Nos. 2166 and 2168, w s, 99.11 s 129th st, 40x75, two five-story brk flats with stores, by William Kennelly. (Amt due $4,486; prior mort, $40,000).......... 30

KINGS COUNTY.

Nov.

Pulaski st, Nos. 274-280, s s, 880.9 e Throop av, 101.10x100, four four-story double brk flats.....
Van Voorhis st, n w s, 100 s w Evergreen av, 17x100..........
Van Voorhis st, n w s, 117 s w Evergreen av, 17x100..........
Van Voorhis st, n w s, 134 s w Evergreen av, runs northwest 100 x southwest 16 x southeast 51.9 x southwest 1 x southeast 48.1¾ to Van Voorhis st, x northwest 17 to beginning, unfinished frame dwell'gs; assessed value, $4,000 each....
Van Voorhis st, n w s, 258 s w Evergreen av, 17x100, two-story frame (brk lined) dwell'g; assessed value, $3,000..........
Johnson av, Nos. 45 and 47, n s, 150 w Lorimer st, 35x100, two three-story frame dwell'gs and stores; all right, title and int.; assessed value, $4,500..........
by T. A. Kerrigan, at 13 Willoughby st.......... 23

Columbia st, No. 473, e s, 60 n West 9th st, 20x83.6, three-story frame dwell'g; assessed value, $1,000; by J. Cole, at 389 Fulton st.......... 23

Pacific st, Nos. 1505-1511 / Kingston av, No. 69 — n e cor Kingston av, 80x90, three four-story double brk flats; assessed value, $13,500.
7th av, w s, 150 s Lincoln pl, 33.6x110..........
7th av, No. 7?, w s, 83 6 s Lincoln pl, 33.6x110....
7th av, No. 72, w s 116.6 s Lincoln pl, 33.6x110, three four-story double brk flats; assessed value, $36,000..........
by T. A. Kerrigan, at 13 Willoughby st 24

Henry st, No. 561, e s, 75 n Carroll st, 25x117, three-story brk dwell'g; assessed value, $3,000; by W. Cole, at 7 and 8 Court sq 24

Madison st, No. 789, n s, 278 w Ralph av, 18x100, two-story frame dwell'g; assessed value, $1,400; by T. A. Kerrigan, at 13 Willoughby st.......... 25

5th av, No. 10, w s, 180 n Pacific st, runs northwest 82.7 x southwest 14.9 x southeast 28 11 x northeast 1 x southeast 14.11 to 5th av, x north 32 to beginning, four-story brk dwell'g and store, by J. Cole, at 389 Fulton st.......... 25

Dean st, No. 1297, s s, 140 w Kingston av, 20x100, two-story frame dwell'g; assessed value, $3,000..........
Warren st, No. 419, n s, 75 n w Bond st, 25x100, two-story frame dwell'g and store; assessed value, $1,500; partition..........
St. Marks av, n s, 175 w Grand av, 25x182.7x26.6x173.08, three frame dwell'gs on plot; assessed value, $2,500..........
by T. A. Kerrigan, at 13 Willoughby st.......... 27

President st, No. 185, n s, 130 e Henry st, runs north 55 x east 1 x north 45 x east 14.6 x south 100 to President st, x west 15.6 to beginning, three-story brk dwell'g; assessed value, $3,000; by W. Cole, at 7 and 8 Court sq 27

Ashland pl, No. 139, e s, 167.07 n Hanson pl, 17.6x94.4½x17.0x94.1¼, three-story brk dwell'g; assessed value, $4,500; partition; by J. Cole, at 389 Fulton st.......... 30

Greene av, Nos. 1212-1216, s s, 125 w Central av, 61.10x100, four two-story frame (brk lined) dwellings; assessed value, $2,100 each..........
Greene av, No. 1236, s s, 232.10 w Central av, 16.2x100, two story frame (brk lined) dwell'g; assessed value, $2,100..........
Throop av, No. 565, s e cor Hancock st, 23x81, four-story brk flat; assessed value, $18,000....
Throop av, No. 547½ e s, 42.1 s Hancock st, 19.6x81, four-story brk flat; assessed value, $9,000.
by T. A. Kerrigan, at 13 Willoughby st.......... 30

Jefferson av, No. 964, s s, 420 e Howard av, 20x100..........
Jefferson av, No. 968, s s, 440 e Howard av, 20x100..........
Two two-story and basement brk dwell'gs; assessed value, $3,500 each..........
by Jere. Johnson, Jr., at Real Estate Exchange, 189 and 191 Montague st.......... 30

LIS PENDENS, KINGS COUNTY.

Nov.

Willoughby st, s s, 17.6 e Lawrence st, 36.4x60. The General Synod of the Reformed Church in America agt James O'Connor; att'ys, Sutphen & Lefferts.......... 12

5th av, north cor 19th st, 17.6x80..........
13th st, s e s, 372.10 s w 5th av, 25x100..........
George Weightman agt Mary Foore; partition; att'ys, Dillaway, Davenport & Leeds.......... 12

Arlington av, n w cor Hale av, 25x100. Katharine Bernheim agt Elizabeth Goetz; att'y, Fernando Sollinger.......... 13

Hancock st, n s, 100 e Stuyvesant av, 55x100. Adelbert S. Nichols agt Charles L. Pashley; foreclos. mechanic's lien; att'y, Ernest Hall.... 13

Willoughby av, s s, 179.6 w Lewis av, 20x100. Jacob Friedmann agt Mary E. Bisson; foreclos. mechanic's lien; att'ys, Fuhrer & Laug.......... 13

Liberty av, s s, 102 e Railroad av, 25x100. Isaac Embree agt Carl Gotthelf; att'y, A. J. Spencer. 13

Columbia Heights w s, 110.7 s Pineapple st, 25x117. Aminta de Samper agt Asa C. Brownell; att'ys, Arnold, Greene & Patterson.......... 13

Irving av, n e s, 75 n w Stanhope st, 25x100. John Rueger agt Mary Feigenbaum; att'ys, Moffet & Kramer.......... 13

Glenada pl, s w cor Decatur st, 50x85. Metropolitan Life Ins. Co. agt William W. Reynolds; att'ys, Arnoux, Ritch & Woodford.......... 13

Glenada pl, w s, 50 s Decatur st, 50x80. Same agt same; same att'y.......... 13

Greene av, s e s, 157 s w Central av, 15.10x100. Sarah C. Savage agt Virgil R. Case; att'ys, S. F., F. H. and R. Cowdrey.......... 14

Greene av, s e s, 203.10 s w Central av, 15x100. Same agt same; same att'ys.......... 14

Greene av, s e s, 172.10 s w Central av, 15x100. Same agt same; same att'ys.......... 14

Watkins st, w s, 100 n Sutter st, 25x100. Isaac Marx agt Elias Kaplan; action for ejectment; att'y, Jacob Rieger.......... 14

6th st, s s, 190 w 4th av, 115x100. Frank Bailey agt Emil Lindburg; att'y, Charles R. Halsey... 14

North Portland av, w s, 70.7 w Auburn pl, 75x100. Michael O'Brien agt Frank O'Brien; partition; att'y, John B. Meyenborg.......... 14

Lewis av, n e cor McDonough st, 20x90. Gustav A. Meyn agt Sarah C. Strause; att'y, George W. Delano.......... 14

Chauncey st, s s, 75 e Saratoga av, 200x100. George P. Jacobs & Co. agt James Smith; foreclos. mechanic's lien; att'ys, Jacobs & Butcher.......... 16

Carroll st, s s, 76.11 w Hoyt st, 19.1x96.6..........
2d st, n s, 270 w Hoyt st, 15.6x96.6..........
Edmond A. Gearon agt Bertrand Clover; att'y, M. Gearon.......... 16

Patchen av, s e cor Van Buren st, 25x100. Clementine S. Patchen agt Francis Jezek; att'y, Rufus T. Griggs.......... 16

Hoyt st, w s, 29.6 s Sackett st, 15x75. Joseph C. Hendrix agt Bertrand Clover; att'y, George V. Brower.......... 17

Dikeman st, s s, 90 e Van Brunt st, 25x100..........
Elizabeth st, s w s, 140 s e Conover st, 25x100..........
Margaret Gacquin agt Mary Gacquin; partition; att'y's, James & Thomas H. Troy.......... 17

Clinton av, n e cor Fulton st, 18x52. John L. Lansdell agt Peter Roeder; action for specific performance; att'y, Alfred R. Page.......... 17

Christopher av, e s, 100 s Sutter av, 25x200 to Hackman st. John Bergman agt Bernard Wilson; action for specific performance; att'y, Alex. S. Rosenthal.......... 17

Jamaica av, n s, 132 e Miller av, 100x232 to Sunnyside av. William G. Osborn agt Charles G. Miller; foreclos. mechanic's lien; att'y, Charles S. Taber.......... 17

Brighton pl, n e cor Coney Island road, 50x134.7x50x133.7, Gravesend. Dorothy H. Edmonds extrx. agt Margaret Snedeker; att'ys, Coudert Bros.......... 17

Carlton av, s w cor Pacific st, 20x80. William H. Doremus agt Cora Waldron; att'y, Lawton B. Garside.......... 17

Linden st, n w s, 525 s w Central av, 55x100. Benjamin F. Spruill agt Frank Ibert; att's, Foley & Powell.......... 18

Saratoga av, s e cor Decatur st, 100x115.6. The Title Guarantee and Trust Co. agt H. Good; att'y, Edwin Kempton.......... 18

Hancock st, s s, 168.9 w Reid av, 48.9x98.11. Otto E. Reimer agt Samuel J. Stilson; atty's, Sackett, Lang, Reed & McKewan.......... 19

RECORDED LEASES.

NEW YORK.

Per Year

Broome st, No. 519, all. George Solomon to Max Loewenstein; 10 years, from Feb. 1, 1892 $1,400

Bowery, No. 212, store and basement. Eliza J. wife of Alfred M. Sparks to David Augusta and Leopold Yesky; 8 years, from May 1, 1892.......... 2,400

Cannon st, No. 12, all. Abraham I. Bleistift to Benjamin Boley; 5½ years, from Jan. 1, 1892.......... 1,90

Cherry st, No. 32, store floor. Demetrio Laprete to Agostino Trorano and Guiseppe Gentillesco; 1½ years, from Dec. 1, 1891..... 240

Cherry st, No. 256, n e cor Rutgers st, all....
Rutgers st, No. 59, second floor of extension.
Jacob Kortlang to George A. D. Bartmer; 4 5-12 years, from Dec. 1, 1891.......... 2,160

Delancey st, No. 12. Ernest Plath to Martha Meincke; 4 years, from May 1, 1895 1,800

Hester st, No. 57, store and back rooms. Joseph Kassel to Louis Swetneik; 3 years, from May 1, 1892.......... 336

Jones st, No. 17. Eliza Hunter widow and Eliza J Hunter and Julia A. Pettengill devisees Willet C. Hunter to Michael Gleason; 7½ years, from Nov. 1, 1891.......... 1,800

Park row, No. 156. Francis X., Joseph P., Stephen A. and Mary Hyland infants, by Clifford Boese special guard., to William H. Hyland; 8 years, 1 month, 9 days, from Nov. 16, 1891.......... 8,250

12th st, Nos. 611 and 613 E. Louis Kircher to Friedrich Ebling; 5 5-12 years, from Dec. 1, 1891.......... 1,500

38th st, No. 432 W., all. Frederick Haffner agent to Josephine Tremer; 5 years, from Oct. 1, 1891 480

41st st, No. 448 W., store, basement and second floor. Louisa Wasmuth to George Bonhag; 3 years, from Feb. 1, 1891.......... 720

43d st, No. 153 E., store floor and basement. John E. Stillwell to Willard H. Jones; 5 years, from May 1, 1890.......... 2,000

59th st, No. 63 E., all. Reuben Ross to William F. Crockett and William W. Weeks, of Crockett & Weeks; 5 years, from Oct. 1, 1890 1,800

60th st, No. 100 E. Ferdinand R. Minrath to Sophia Schwab; from Nov. 16, 1891, to April 30, 1892.......... 1,400

62d st, No. 26 E., all. New York Life Ins. Co. to Herman Goldenberg; 8 years, from May 1, 1891.......... 2,500

74th st, No. 223 E. Esther D. Stensby to Lawrence Schuler; 3 years, from Nov. 1, 1891.... 540

115th st, No. 305 E. Jacob J. Mattern to William Haelzig; 5 years, due Oct 15, 1891...... $3.0, 360

Same property. Assign. lease. William Haelzig to George Ringler & Co.......... nom

Courtlandt av, No. 763. Bertha Harrison to Mina Pertsch; 1 year, from April 1, 1891.... 300

2d av, cor 104th st, store and rooms. Isaac Bitterman to Jacob Rosenberg; 2 years, from May 1, 1891.......... 1,200

2d av, No. 2025. Assign. lease. Felix Hagan to Karl J. Sommer. Nov. 14.......... nom

2d av, No. 2025, store and front basement. Peter A. Cassidy to Michael Dwyer; 5 years, from Nov. 15, 1890..........1,300, 1,400

3d av, No. 1964, s w cor 108th st, store and basement. Margaret King to James F. Michels; 5 years, and renewal of 5 years more, from Dec. 1, 1891.......... 2,050

8th av, Nos. 59, 61 and 63, all. Martha A. H. Cordes and Caroline Otten to Thomas Moore; 5 years, from May 1, 1890.......... 1,500

8th av, s w cor 140th st, store and part cellar. Francis J. Schnugg to Morris Spiegel; 3 years, from Nov. 1, 1891.......... 1,140

CHATTELS.

NOTE.—The first name, alphabetically arranged, is that of the Mortgagor, or party who gives the Mortgage. The "R" means Renewal Mortgage.

NEW YORK CITY.

NOVEMBER 13 TO 19.—INCLUSIVE.

SALOON AND RESTAURANT FIXTURES.

Assalone & Sforge. 317 E 111th....G Teyyr. $375
Behnken & Lussen. 4th av and 121st st....H Zeltner. 1,000
Biedermann, Eberhardt. 68 Spring....V Loewers. 440
Brokman, Victor. 222 East Houston....Wagner & S. Pool Table. 150
Barmbold, Frederick. 1828 2d av....V Loewers. 4.0
Bauer, Charles. 511 6th av....G Ehret. (R) 1,500
Bauer, Louis, Jr. 490 W 4?d....G Ringler & Co. 1,199
Bertie, Annie. 80 and 82 Oak....A Kremer B Co. 750
Brady, Mary E. 115th st and Lexington av....H Rochschild's Sons Co. 1,030
Brenner, Jacob. 101 Hester....Burger & H B Co. 803
Burns, Michael. 4 Spring....D G Yuengling, Jr. 500
Beck, Moris. 31 Willett....Feigenspan B Co. 700
Bertie, Annie. 82 and 84 Oak....J Arnstein. 800
Beuermann, L F. 454 8th av....G Ehret. (R) 2,500
Boerum, A J E. 16 Roosevelt....Weiz & Z. 300
Byone, T J. 2451 3d av....A Hupfel's Sons. (R) 1,000
Bell, W E. 541 Canal....J Ahles B Co. 400
Blackburn, A J. 344 W 11th....P Ballentine & Sons. (R) 1,500
Bleier, Henry. 423 E 5th....Burger & H B Co 350
Bode, Christian. 210 Eldridge....J C G Hupfel B Co. (R) 400
Braun, Rudolph. 348 E 11th....P Schaefer & Son. 150
Bruns, Diedrich. 124 W 49th....F & M Schaefer B Co. 500
Chapman & Wright. 147 Fulton....Brunswick-B-C Co. Pool Table. (R) 163
Caggiano & Tadisernio. 39 Mulberry....D Mayer B Co. 900
Callahan, Michael 105 Park row....I Roth. 3,000
Connelly, Bernard. 241 Av A....D Mayer B Co. 1,500
Crucci, F and M. 533 Broome....H B Scharmann & Sons. 900
Caputo, Vincenzo. 192 Worth....Bernheimer & S. Saloon Pump. 105
Same. 8 Mulberry....same. Ice House. 110
Cavallatti & Busta. 23 University pl ..Wagner & S. Pool Table. (R) 70
Connolly & Potter. 1512 2d av....P Doelger. 565
Callahan, W F. 1807 Park av....J Ruppert. (R) 1,000
Delecker, C F. 178 Prospect av, Brooklyn....India Wharf B Co. 1,200
Enders, J A. 463 E 46th....G Ringler & Co. (R) 515
Faulhaber, J and M. 1551 2d av ...V Loewers. 2,000
Fiala, Frank. 1362 Av A....H Vogel. 249
Frank, Solomon. 107 Delancey....Burger & H B Co. 800
Friberg & Schwarz. 711 E 5th....J & M Haffen. 450
Fabish, M S. 49 Bowery....O Von Borries. Billiard Saloon. (R) 1,450
Flubs, Philip. 1800 1st av....A Fischl. 1,000
Fierth, Casper. 160 2d....G Retchel exr of. (R) 500
Fischer, George. 1417 Amsterdam av ...P & W Ebling B Co. 500
Frank, Martin. 283 Broome....Rubsam & H B Co. 600
Gallagher & Curtin. 1860 2d av....H Koehler & Co. (R) 3,000
Glazier, Chas. 68½ Carmine....Beadleston & W. Ice Box. (R) 75
Goetzinger, Chas. 130 Prince....G Ringler & Co. (R) 1,500
Goldberg, Jacob. 31 Pitt....E Walker. Pool Table. 45
Grote, W F. 429 East Houston....V Loewers. (R) 1,500
Groveur, Charles. 7 Baxter....J Kress B Co. 100
Greenberg, S A. 151 Essex....C A Bereuter. Pool Table. 140
Gruner, J D. 1061 Lexington av....G Ehret. (R) 830
Gillespie, J J. 234 Clinton....M Eckstein B Co. 1,800
Haelzig, William. 305 E 115th....G Ringler & Co. 700
Halpin, Peter. 520 Broome....J Ruppert. 1,030
Heuser, Wilhelm. 2789 8th av.... M Spiegel. 2,612
Herrmann, Frank. 152 W 28th....Bernheimer & S. 1,175
Higgins, Michael. 103 E 118th....P Doelger. 2,530
Hundgeburth, Henry. 2557 8th av....P & W Ebling B Co. (R) 900
Hutchinson, Richard. 176 8th av....Burr B Co. (R) 2,000
Hyland, W H. 156 Park av....C Stein. 7,900
Jaenicke, C R. 507 E 5th....Abbott B Co. (R) 600
Kessler, Josephine. 306 E 6th....K Hahn. Restaurant Fixtures. 75
Krause, H F, Jr. Irving pl and 14th st....J Kuntz. (R) 8,150
Krieger, Joseph. 302 E 11th....M Groh's Sons. 570
Kaskell, Jacob. 1584 3d av....G Ringler & Co. 2,000
Kohner & Herman. 61 Sheriff....H B Scharmann & Sons. 1,200
Kurnisky & Levy. 412 Grand....H B Scharmann & Sons. 800
Kinney, J F. 582 7th av....J J Reilly. (R) 2,500
Kellam, D L. 284 Greenwich ...Lincoln I and G Assoc. Hotel Fixtures. 420
Klein, Freiderick. 532 6th ...M Groh's Sons. (R) 400
Kupfer, Edward. 1400 3d av....Knickerbocker B Co. 1,200
Kennedy, George. 187 West....Beadleston & W. 2,000
Kerle, Augusta. 398 3d av....Beadleston & W. 586
Kerwick, P and J E. 8d av and 50th st....Beadleston & W. (R) 4,000
Kessler, Josephine. 306 E 6th... K Hahn. Restaurant Fixtures. 75
Kleindienst, Louis. 413 W 50th...Bachmann B Co. 1,100
Kraemer, George. 124th st and 7th av....Brunswick-B-C Co. Billiard Saloon. 7,600
Krisch, J C. 29 and 31 E 20th ...G Ehret. (R) 4,000
Liebmann, P & K. 57 Clinton....J H Meierdierck. 300
Lippert, Joseph. 175 Chrystie....J C G Hupfel B Co. (R) 700
Loewinger, Joseph. 319 E 74th....Bavarian B Co. 870
Liebtran, Frederick. 121 Washington ... J Kamps. 900

Lullevan, John. 1341 1st av....J H Bereuter. Pool Fixtures. 150
Langenstein, Conrad. 341 E 117th....G Ehret. (R) 6,000
Lind, Isaac. 44 Attorney....H B Scharmann & Sons. 1,000
Lorenzo, G. 2214 1st av....Bernheimer & S. Ice House. 75
Same....same. Ice House. 75
Same....same. Saloon Pump. 65
Lyons, C J. 2271 8th av....F & M Schaefer B Co. (R) 2,000
Lynch, James. 87 Mulberry ...W Peter B Co. Ice Box. 187
Martini, W A and L A. 672 11th av....G Ringler & Co. 1,798
Moore, A L. 80 Varick....L C Kuybendale. Restaurant Fixtures. 150
Mach, Frank. 117 Pitt ...J Doelger's Sons. (R) 225
Masucci, Alfonso. 711 Mulberry....Welz & Z 450
Matheus, Martin. 17th st and 8th av... J Roth. 2,350
McGuire, J and J F. 521 Canal....C W McAuliff. (R) 550
Muller, William. 220 E 90th....H Koehler & Co. Saloon Pump. (R) 56
Murphy, J J. 286 W 32d....J Kuntz B Co. (R) 192
Mack, James. 108 Cherry....F Klentz. (R) 510
Mallender, Christian. 188 Forsyth ...F Oppermann, Jr. (R) 600
Mars Henrietta A. 284 President st, Brooklyn, and 9 Thames, New York....M Levy Furniture, Restaurant Fixtures. 1,000
McCarthy, Con. 55 Cherry....Williamsburgh B Co. (R) 250
Murphy, Jeremiah. 1741 Lexington av....J C G Hupfel B Co. 110
Neumann & Kern. 848 West ..T Roberts. 6,000
Same ...G Ehret. 8,000
Niclas, J F. 444 Washington....P Doelger. 1,000
Nutter, J H. 476 2d av....C E Nutter. 5,000
O'Brien, Robert. Sedgwick av, Highbridge....J Wallace & Son. 75
O'Connor, Joseph. 241 E 57th....Brunswick-B-C Co. Pool Table. 150
Olmstead, Charles. 954 3d av....F Oppermann, Jr. (R) 9,000
O'Connor & Wilson. 304 Bowery....M Gombossy. 2,000
Parker & Singer. 69 Forsyth....Wagner & S. Pool Table. (R) 60
Quick, William. 401 E 34th....Consumers' B Co. 7,885
Quinn, J F and P E. 131 W 23d ...T E Quin. Restaurant Fixtures. 180
Rabler, Henry. 434 6th....J Doelger's Sons. 358
Rathgeber, F and M. 211 Chrystie and 24 Stanton ...G Ehret. (R) 2,400
Reynolds, M J. 364 10th av....J H Bereuter. Pool Table. 150
Ryan, Frank. 633 Washington....Beadleston & W. 625
Scharmann, Julius 112 3d av....H B Scharmann. Restaurant Fixtures. 3,502
Schmidt, Andreas. 518 10th av....V Loewers. 600
Schroeder & Emsberger. 91 Grand....Sonn Bros 500
Schumann, Hermann. 1341 3d av ...J Ruppert. 700
Sebasch & Brigist. 236 2d....H B Scharmann & Sons. 700
Silverstein, Ross. 93 Ludlow....Feigenspan B Co. 450
Simon & Russack. 94 Essex....Burger & H B Co. 400
Schambacher, John. 91 and 91½ Bowery....C Stein. (R) 1,561
Seyfert, Arthur. 595 2d av....G Ehret. (R) 1,000
Schleiermacher, August. 76 Allen....G Bechtel, exr of. (R) 1,000
Schumann, Hermann. 1341 3d av....India Wharf B Co. 700
Stange, Henry. 430 E 92d....J Ruppert. (R) 508
Steeg, F E. 329 E 105th....Bernheimer & S. Ice House. 75
Stuerhof, J G. 77 Pike....P Doelger. (R) 1,500
Sassmann, August. 121 E 110th... J C G Hupfel B Co. 748
Schroeder & Ernsberger. 91 Grand....P Ballantine & Sons. 4,000
Texter, William. 203-207 E 56th....N Y Maennechor. Saloon; Restaurant Fixtures. (R) 8,000
Tighe, J C. 861 Amsterdam av....C Stein. 8,188
Van Clief, Jacob. 883 Park av....H Vogel. 3,000
Wagner, Albrecht. 1465 3d av ...G Ehret. (R) 2,506
Wasser & Benjamin. 146 Suffolk....Wagner & S. Pool. (R) 40
Weygandt, Adolph. 164 E 88th....G Ehret. 1,500
Walsh, J J. 415 2d av....J Wallace & Son. (R) 600
Wermuth, Hermann. 410 Pearl....M Seitz. 300
Xiques, Julian. 294 Bowery....Wagner & S. Pool Table. 155

HOUSEHOLD FURNITURE.

Adams, Ida. 227 W 40th ...O'Farrell & Co. 283
Adolphus, Louise. [illegible] W 44th....L & Lumley. 1,000
Alexander, Geo. 439 E 53d....Fennell & P. (R) 186
Algeo, Mrs [illegible]....T Kelly. 117
Arnheimer, Louis. 2256 2d av....Estey Piano Co. Piano. 375
Arnold, Mrs F. 219 W 40th....T Kelly. 558
Agresta, P A. 185 E 49th....J Baumann. 154
Ahreus, Chas. 226 E 6th ...B M Cowperthwait & Co. 285
Anderson, L, Mrs., 216 E 85th....Brooklyn F Co. 273
Augustin, Ferraud. 39 Monroe....B M Cowperthwait & Co. 128
Austie, Paul. 61 Park row....B M Cowperthwait & Co. 116
Allison, Theo. 729 Amsterdam av....J H Little. 185
Bade, C H. 232 E 26th....G Reubel. 186
Barrow, W & M 247 W 50th... E C Hinsdale. 110
Benson, Nettie. 206 Forsyth....Jordan & M. 189
Bossenaux, Alphonse. 83 Macdougal....J Moriarty. (R) 102
Brombacker, Ellen. 81 E 108th....J Moriarty. 207
Brooks, Emma. 121 W 78th....J H Little. 1,111
Barnes, Alburta. 166 W 125th....S Baumann. (R) 1,249
Bennett, C D. 216 W 29th....J Moriarty. (R) 116
Bennett, Fannie. 140 W 36th....F T Biggins. 861
Bennett, Maggie. 9 W 116th....American Guar Assoc. 100
Bibler, G F. 488 W 35th....F T Biggins. 134
Bissell, Maria H. 134 W 23d....J O'Byrne. 1,864
Boenhardt, Albin. 413 8th .. D Schmitt. 150
Brathwaite, A E 140 W 63d....W J Ruddell. 189
Breuning, Mary. 235 E 114th S Baumann. 124
Burns, Mrs E. Bank and Washington sts ...McClain, S & Co. 121
Bartel, Adolph 3 1107 Park av....L Baumann. 137
Baird, W A. 158 E 116th....L Baumann. 132
Barringer, G H. 346 W 105th....Brooklyn F Co. 862
Bodn, L J. 414 W 83d....J Baumann. 121
Bornitz, E S. 109 W 60th....B M Cowperthwait & Co. 137
Boylan, Maggie. 131 W 31st....L Baumann. 141
Brady, F B. 251 W 124th... L Baumann. 165
Bridgewater, Martha. 824 3d av....H Thoesen. 148
Brodbeck, Katie. 82 Av D....B M Cowperthwait & Co. 135
Brown, A S. 59 E 11th....J Baumann. 170
Buchan, T R. 163 W 130th....B M Cowperthwait & Co 144
Buckner, Jessie. 309 W 43d....J Baumann. (R) 1,0
Busfield, Martha. 949 8th av....B M Cowperthwait & Co. 180
Same. ..same. 122
Bancker, Mary E. 47 W 63d....F D Clark. 110
Banks, nEuna P. 21 and 23 W 129th....S Baumann. 145
Bewley, Thos. 162 Lexington av....O'Farrell & Co. 322
Blake, Mabel. 145 W 52d....Alexander Bros. 600
Boerum, Mary H. 147 W 41st... J Moriarty. 258
Bohen, A S. 127 E 109th....Jordan & M. 180
Bollerman, Arthur. 285 E 120th....Spies Bros. (R) 130
Bonner, Eliza. 1463 2d av....L Baumann. 124
Botifur, Anna. 780 Greenwich....Alexander Bros. 116
Breckerk, Lizzie. Waverley pl and 6th av....O'Farrell & Co. 1,119
Burke, Joseph. 497 7th av....O'Farrell Co. 110
Chamberlain, K P. 53 W 12th....W E Wheelock & Co. Piano. 400
Clark, Edwin, Mrs. 519 E 85th....T Kelly. 125
Crane, Wm, Mrs. 34 and 36 Carmine... T Kelly. 173
Cades, Louis. 1813 3d av....B M Cowperthwait & Co. 138
Calkins, J H. 110 E 41st....L Baumann. 190
Calderwood, Agnes. 355 W 47th....J Baumann. 111
Chapperon, May. 1050 Park av....B M Cowperthwait & Co. 159
Clark, Nica. 141 W 45th .. L Baumann. 209
Clifford, May. 309 E 88th....B M Cowperthwait & Co. 214
Colerick, Mary. 313 E 60th....L Baumann. 153
Cornelis, E C. 120 Pearl....B M Cowperthwait & Co. 311
Coventry, Eva. 56 W 48th....S Knapp & Co. 100
Cahill, M D. 403 W 22d....J H Sexton. (R) 2,000
Cammon, H A. 32 Jay....Mathushek & Son Piano Co. Piano. 340
Cettelain, Bertha. 229 E 14th ...T Willis. 315
Clarke, Rosie. 414 E 72d....J J McGrorty. 142
Chichester, W R. 214 W 25th....Manges Bros. 196
Civelleito, Stephero. 350 3d av....Krakauer Bros. Piano. 165
Cummings, Eva. 208 W 25th... O'Farrell & Co. 599
Diehl, J, Mrs. 247 E 106th....Bollermann & Son. Piano. 140
Dixie, H F. 480 Columbus av....Brooklyn F Co. 134
Dessar, L A. 58 W 49th ..J Baumann. (R) 102
Donaldson, Chester. 115 W 71st....American Guar Assoc. 500
Davis, Emma. 58 E 4th....B M Cowperthwait & Co. 103
De Costa, Elizabeth. 430 E 80th... B M Cowperthwait & Co. 116
Da Miguel, Virginia. 101 W 98th... J Baumann. (R) 196
Devlin, William. 579 Greenwich....B M Cowperthwait & Co. 212
Donohue Thomas. Boulevard and 104th st....B M Cowperthwait & Co 176
Dunlop, A P. 1102 Broadway....B M Cowperthwait & Co. 205
Dawson, F F. 122 Clinton pl....W E Wheelock & Co. Piano. (R) 106
Deutschberger, S & L. 108 W 42d....W J Wolfe. 600
Dient, Anna R. 75 W 55th....L Baumann. 184
Donohue, Owen. 166 E 73d....T Kelly. 161
Drescher, Otto. 309 E 72d....R M Walters. Piano. (R) 205
Everall, G H, Mrs. 113 E 31st....T Kelly. 152
Eberle, F H. 1469 Columbus av....B M Cowperthwait & Co 226
Edgar, Mrs F. 363 W 57th....B M Cowperthwait & Co. 535
Edwards, J and D. 455 W 24th....American Surety Co. 500
Emerson, Elizabeth. 835 9th av....L Baumann. 118
Ekholu, Axel. 229 W 66th....Jordan & M. 110
Eshner, F, Mrs. 252 W 43d... J H Little. 116
Esposito, F S. 178 E 77th....J H Little. 342
Evans, Annie. 142 W 33d....O'Farrell & Co. (R) 281
Ferry, Rose T. 301 W 143d ...W J Ruddell. 273
Flunegan, Edward. 227 E 127th....Dreisacker & Co. (R) 110
Fairbanks, Adelaide. 105 W 129th....Krakauer Bros. Piano. 300
Fay, Mary. 140 W 83d....L Baumann. (R) 112
Feifer, Heinrich. 248 Rivington... Krakauer Bros. Piano. (R) 140
Feist, L. 67 E 105th....S Heyman & Co. 181
Fierz, Washington. 517 E 83d....B M Cowperthwait & Co. 142
Fay, Edith. 2495 2d av. ..W E Wheelock & Co. Piano. 290
Fitzpatrick, M E. 724 Amsterdam av....S Baumann. 297
Fournier, Leo. 268 W 46th....D Schwarzkopf. 1,365
Foley, H C. 224 W 131st....S Baumann. 185
Fox, G J. 210 E 45th....O'Farrell & Co. 221
Flynn, Anna L. 433 W 19th ...W E Wheelock & Co. Piano. 225
Francis, Jane. 12 E 47th... Lord & Taylor. 528
Gauntt, Mary S. 156 E 82d....Spies Bros. 143
Gottschalk, Hermann. 1577 Madison av....Jordan, M & Co. 131
Gurry, John. 967 2d av....S Baumann. 128
Galway, Cecelia. 311 W 47th....J Baumann. 158
Gifford, Josie. 320 W 35th .. H Israel & Sons. 513
Giles, Sarah. 426 W 52th... B M Cowperthwait & Co. 283
Gollery, Mary. 48 Gouverneur....J Baumann. 134
Gee, Jane E, Mrs. 410 St Nicholas av....J H Little. 121
Georgi, W, Mrs. 361 W 55th....J H Little. 301
Gilman, Lillias M. 243 W 46th....H Mannes & Son. 115
Glynn, Mrs G W. 165 W 102d....J H Little. 180
Groot, Frederica. 156 W 85th....J H Little. 188
Gusser, Toney. 213 E 74th... G Reubel. 136
Gilman, Winona. 100 W 94th... J Baumann. (R) 1,175
Goodwin, E J. 130 E 118th....J Baumann. (R) 191
Gorton, G W. 8th av....J S Rice. 195
Greenwood, Edna. 120 W 49th....J Baumann. (R) 1,464
Halfpenny, Emma. 117 E 53d....S Baumann. 147
Hausman, J H. 175 W 12th....J Baumann. (R) 102
Hart, Lawrence. 171 E 105th... Jordan & M. 155
Hazel, Jennie. 161 Hudson ..H Israel & Sons. 103
Hennersdorf, Richard. 537 E 17th....Manges Bros. 158
Herrmann, Lottie. 103 W 17th....J Moriarty. 471
Higginbotham, Mary. 168 Lexington av....J H Little. 201
Howard, Michael. 209 E 100th....H S Eisler. 114
Huddelston, Rose D. 190 W 96th....J Moriarty. 356
Hughes, Mrs M A. 12 W 60th... H Mannes & Son. 144
Hughes, Ellen. 221 W 16th....H Israel & Sons. 142
Hyland, J F. 130 W 124th ...Jordan & M. 100
Heckler, Josephine. 33 W 68d... B M Cowperthwait & Co. 313
Helfgatt, Sarah. 380 Grand....B M Cowperthwait & Co. 120
Hirschfeld, L A. 408 E 79th....Krakauer Bros. Piano. (R) 287
Hodge, Charlotte. 255 W 20th....J Baumann. 150
Holly, Annie. 229 W 4th....B M Cowperthwait & Co. 153
Horth, Chester. 407 E 16th....B M Cowperthwait & Co. 178
Hanley, W H. 1482 3d av....J Rubenstein. 300
Hartford, William. 246 1st av ..L Baumann. 135
Harting, F W. 162 E 84th....Dreisacker & Co. 176
Harwood, Eugenia C. 35 E 122d ...Fennell & P. (R) 254
Heath, M H. 60 W 93d, 9 E 41st and 117 and 119 E 44th....O'Reilly Bros. 132
Hoffman, O C and M D. 471 W 145th....E C Hinsdale 130
Hyatt, Mrs J L. 68 W 100th....Brooklyn F Co. 231
Hynes, Mrs R. 208 E 41st... W E Wheelock & Co. Piano. 100
Hutchings, Mary J. 110th st and Manhattan av ....C A Hutchings. (R) 700
Isaacs, Annie. 216 6th av....S Baumann. 143
Imans, H M. 149 E 48th....S Baumann. 174
Inerney, Mrs S E. 60 W 22th ..J H Little. 157
Johnson, E K. 36 W 24th....J H Little. 185
Jacobson, Fanny. 244 W 41st... W E Wheelock & Co. Piano. (R) 163
Johnson, S M. 151 W 81st....L Baumann. 175
Jones, A A. 17 Bethune ..J Moriarty 312
Jessup, Emily. 217 W 28th....Brooklyn F Co. 1,081
Jordan, Aletta. 328 W 47th ...J Baumann. 114
Keegan, Mary. 780 Lexington av....L Baumann. 592
Keeley, H J. 423 E 83d ...L Baumann. 108
Kerr, Helen. 150 W 34th....R Devlin. 2,550
Kirtland, Fannie. 219 E 23d .. B M Cowperthwait & Co. 136
Kolle, Pauline. 207 E 78th....F W, Jr. and R E Mertens. (R) 1,256
Kahn, Bertha. 66 Monroe....Simpson & P. Piano. 200
Kimmey, W W. 203 W 141st... Amer Guar Assoc. 100
Klaber, Mrs Herman. 170 W 83d....T Kelly. 175
Kiernan, Maggie T. 301 E 69th....W E Wheelock & Co. Piano. 200
Kolb, Mrs L A. 149 W 16th....J Moriarty. 156
Kortz, Joseph. 60 Ridge....J Rubenstein. 140
Krauss, Amelia. 105 E 56th....W E Wheelock & Co. Piano. (R) 155
Kelton, Catharine. 183 Lexington av....J Moriarty. 568
Knoepfel, Chas. 5 St Marks pl... T Willis. 102
Koenigsberg, Theresa. 161 E 63d ...T F McLaughlin. 156
Kellogg, Mary F. 350 W 56th....M Cashin. 100
Kellogg, Mrs M T. 350 W 60th .. J H Little. 677
Kidder, Mrs I. 20 W 61st....J H Little. 318
Littlefield, Alice. 235 W 13th....Estey Piano Co. Piano. 207
Lynde, Franko 320 W 117th....J H Little. 348
Lait, Leon. 222 Henry ...A Greenberg. 500
Larsmen, Rachel. 94½ Essex....H S Eisler. 150
La Vielle, Dora. 18 W 22d....Jordan, M & Co. 210
Lodge, Mrs W B. 187 W 15th... L Baumann. 184
Loughran, J C. 1746 Madison av....Dreisacker & Co. 171
Leo, Cellia. 225 W 40th....B M Cowperthwait & Co. 325
Limpson, Lizzie E. 224 W 33d ...L Baumann. (R) 154
La Veille, Mrs D. 18 W 22d ...T Willis. 146
Leonard, Mrs L. 170 W 65th....McClain, S & Co. 150
Leslie, Henry. 234 E 85th .. S Baumann. 270
Lewis, Grace....J Williams. 200
Lloyd, William. 216 E 115th....D Schwarzkopf. 146
Mackey, Joseph. Fordham....B M Cowperthwait & Co. 200
Macklin, Margaret. 55 Leroy....B M Cowperthwait & Co. 160
Maher, J M. 457 W 35th....L Baumann. (R) 111
Maicher, Emma. 332 W 31st....L Baumann. 157
Martin, Anna. 329 E 13th....B M Cowperthwait & Co. 141
Masterson, S A. 132 W 82d....B M Cowperthwait & Co. 284
Mason, Grace. 151 W 85th....J Baumann. 716
Mathews, Ella. 275 W 88th....L Baumann. (R) 138
McDermott, Mrs T. 25 Leroy....B M Cowperthwait & Co. 290
McMurray, A C. 433 Wythe av, Brooklyn....J Baumann. 271
Mee, C F. 541 E 131th....B M Cowperthwait & Co. 250
Meroth, Jacob. 127 E 110th....B M Cowperthwait & Co. 219
Miller, J R. 311 W 128th... E Swager. (R) 100
Mitchell, Ellen. 411 W 27th.. B M Cowperthwait & Co. 110
Moog, Lizzie. 67 Broadway....B M Cowperthwait & Co. 119
Moore, William. 349 E 37th....B M Cowperthwait & Co. 167
Macdonald, J S. 107 E 86th ...S Heyman & Co. 124
Mcardle, Mathilda. 958 Washington av...Dreisacker & Co. 189
McDermott, John. 159 W 81th....L Baumann. 345
McKenna, Bridget. 442 W 19th....L Baumann. 145
Melhado, Kate. 104 W 94th....S Baumann. 478
Murray, Annie. 137 Washington....Jordan & M. 121
Murphy, M C. 113 E 75th....W E Wheelock & Co. Piano. 250
Martin, Mary K. 174 W 58th ...I H Tifft. (R) 562
McCleery, Mary J. 157 W 81th....J H Little. 558
McDevitte, Mrs M. 204 E 47th....J H Little. 286
Morgenstern, Nettie. 352 E 3d .. H Israel & Sons. 110
Murray, Michael. 888 2d av....G Reubel. 204
Marooney, H. 497 Greenwich....W J Ruddell. 214
Middlebrook, Laura. 800 W 41st....McClain, S & Co. 108
Milton, Mabel 144 W 28th....J Baumann. 209
Moore, Matilda. 40 W 2-th....T Willis. 279
Nagle, Mamie. 248 E 80th....O'Farrell & Co. 150
Naughton, Frank. 216 E 28th... O'Farrell & Co. 147
Newcomb, Lizzie E. 209 10th av... J H Little. 544
New, Katie. 327 W 2-d....M Cashin. 617
Niland, John. 1959 3d av....J Gregg. (R) 156
Nolan, Lillian. 251 E 105th....B M Cowperthwait & Co. 372
Oakes, Maria L. 357 W 23d....L Baumann. 130
Oliver, Margaret A. 1 E 55th....Sypher & Co. (R) 818
Olsen, Clara. 824 W 4th....S Baumann. 118

Olson, J R. 7th av and 123d st....B M Cowperthwait & Co. 382
Ormsby, Susan E. Highbridge.... L Baumann. 117
O'Connor, E A. 158 E 107th....Jordan & M. (R) 118
Osborne, Pearl. 228 E 76th....J Moriarty. 164
Orrin, M M. 109 W 83d.. L Baumann. 251
Page, Annie. 400 E 23d.. J S Rice. 132
Parsons, Hy. 269 W 17th....L Baumann. 158
Post, W C. 334 E 17th....J Moriarty. (R) 274
Priess, Anna. 248 E 3d....J S Rice. 137
Priess, Anna. 238 E 3d....O'Farrell & Co. 161
Page, Sarah E. 146 W 16th....J Baumann. 568
Peck, Carrie. 229 W 16th... Brooklyn F Co. 150
Pena, M de la. 116 W 61st....B M Cowperthwait & Co. 144
Perkins, W B. 227 W 135th....B M Cowperthwait & Co. 927
Parker, Mrs D H. 254 W 58th....T Kelly. 219
Peacock, Marie. 268 W 25th....W E Wheelock & Co. Piano. 281
Peaulejenne, Henry. 12 Charles....Dreisacker & Co. 181
Pink, Amanda. 511 E 81st....H S Eisler. (R) 150
Porter, Kate. 124 W 31st....S Woods. 1,500
Patterson, John. 34 St Marks pl....J P Delehanty. 174
Petrie, Edith. 255 W 39th ...H Mannes & Son. 868
Pitman, Carrie I. 246 W 51st....J H Little. 792
Raymann, Geo. H. 450 E 89th....J H Little. 119
Randall, Annie. 356 W 56th....W E Wheelock & Co. Piano. 250
Reed, M C. 18 W 22d... Jordan, Moriarty & Co. 117
Roche, Kate H. 165 E 69th....W E Wheelock & Co. Piano. 240
Rountree, Joseph 137 W 60th....Jordan & M. 170
Russell, E de F. 81 W 65th....L Baumann. 200
Ryan, Sadie. 148 W 68th....L Baumann 121
Rause, J F. 97 Charles....B M Cowperthwait & Co. 137
Raymond, Bertrice. 266 W 39th....L Baumann. 248
Renwee, G C. 268 W 136th....B M Cowperthwait & Co. 145
Reynolds, Chas. 1758 3d av....B M Cowperthwait & Co. 158
Rosenbaum, Samuel. 208 E 85th....J Baumann. 146
Rupp, J J. 17 E 7th....B M Cowperthwait & Co. 813
Reddy, Annie S. 540 W 47th....J S Rice. 118
Rohde, R W. 211 E 11th ...J Baumann. 113
Russell, Nellie. 99 W 3d....F T Higgins. 342
Sangster, Minnie H. 40 W 25th .. Strong Bros. 630
Schneider, Joseph. 105 E 10th....L Baumann. 115
Schwarz, Helen. 257 E 128th... J Baumann. 296
Sargent, W H. 226 W 16th .. L Baumann. 102
Sexsmith, Sadie. 218 W 21st ...S Baumann. 158
Smith, Annie. 170 Bleecker....W J Ruddell. 167
Smith, Mary E. 264 W 22d... McClain, S & Co. 278
Smith, Maggie. 121 W 27th....L Baumann. (R) 102
Stafford, J L. 100 W 64th....N Y F Co. (R) 100
Sullivan, Ellen. 116 E 53d ...L Baumann. 177
Sullivan, Edward. 61 W 99th....L Baumann. (R) 101
Scheinberg, Roschen. 163 Norfolk....Krakauer Bros. Piano. 370
Selleck, Kay. 208 E 118th....Dreisacker & Co. 240
Shapiro, Philip. 244 Clinton....J Rubenstein. 107
Skae, John. 279 W 128th....W E Wheelock & Co. Piano. 400
Sohm, Alice. 25 E 21st....Jordan, M & Co. 487
Sprong, E A. 206 W 96th....L Baumann. 357
Starke, L H. 294 W 116th....W E Wheelock & Co. Piano. 320
Sternberger, Lena. 319 E 6th... W E Wheelock & Co. Piano. 350
Sutherland, Mrs C. 74 W 102d....J H Little. 141
Spengeman, Amelia. 59 W 98th ...J Baumann. 211
Stearns, Minnie A. 31 W 65th....R Brooks. 255
Stewart, Ida. 128 W 31st....O'Farrell & Co. 176
Taylor, Ada F. 270 W 43d... S Baumann. 1,240
Thompson, G J. 117 Sullivan....Alexander Bros. 104
Thompson, Mrs J. 527 W 125th... T Kelly. 159
Trancy, Maggie. 523 Grand....Alexander Bros. 158
Thorp, Marcella. 155 E 54th....W E Wheelock & Co. Piano. (R) 218
Trummer, Henrietta. 105 E 75th....N Compton. 105
Taft, C S. 155 E 54th....B M Cowperthwait & Co. 278
Tansill, J F. 2 Grove....L Baumann. 128
Taylor, R B. 316 W 44th....B M Cowperthwait & Co. 204
Thompson, R H. 242 W 35th ...L Baumann. 159
Thornley, J J. 674 E 133th....B M Cowperthwait & Co. 184
Topping, Mrs Chas. 191 E 115th ...B M Cowperthwait & Co. 150
Tunison, Mrs G B. 48 W 97th....J H Little. 294
Unger, William. 147 E 90th....Dreisacker & Co. 202
Viles, F M. 951 Broadway....T Kelly. 181
Verdier, Emil. 134 W 20th....O'Farrell & Co. 225
Vollano, Jacob. 74 E 115th....L Baumann. 270
Von Eitzen, Nicholas. 323 E 78d....B M Cowperthwait & Co. 128
Van Bouten, Mrs K. 336 W 59th....J H Little. 299
Wackermann, P E. 325 W 37th ...Manges Bros. 121
Warner, L C. 177 Bleecker ...G Reubel. 140
Winteroth, Louise M. 71 W 94th....J H Little. 338
Wolf, Gustav. 109 Essex ...H S Eisler. 128
Wood, Jennie. 42 Perry ...Jordan & M. 155
Walker, Nellie. 314 E 23d....B M Cowperthwait & Co. 158
Watkins, Annie. 315 E 121st....B M Cowperthwait & Co. 357
West, Jesse. 109 W 60th....A Baumann. 163
Wetergren, George. 329 W 43d....L Baumann. 188
Wright, Mrs Geo. 296 St Nicholas av....B M Cowperthwait & Co. 163
Warwick, J M. 501 Manhattan av....Brooklyn F Co. 545
Watson, John. 303 W 11th....L Baumann. 272
Weiss, Alexander....J Williams. 576
Wheeler, Maria B. 222 E 68th....A Fowler. (R) 1,546
Wilkinson, Dora. 221 E 21st....Jordan & M. 112
Willoughby, D C. 93 Lexington av....J Gregg. (R) 415
Williams, Maude L. 115 W 63d....S Heyman & Co. 211
Wilson, Jennie. 217 E 60th....Lincoln I and G Assoc. 100
Winter, Jennie. 444 W 58th....O'Farrell & Co. 195
Wolf, G. 97 Henry ..H S Eisler. 215
Wright, F H. 007 E 11th....J Moriarty. 119
Ward, J F. 305 E 117th .. J Baumann. 265
Yuille, Geo E. 155 E 96th....J Baumann. (R) 161

MISCELLANEOUS.

Angevine, W H. 234 E 59th....J Sheran. Tools, Horse, &c. 050
Aubut, Marie J....M A Jungers. Sloop. 75
Appleton, W S....W A Beach. Letters Patent, &c. (R) 39,306
Atkinson, M B. 19 Platt....W Fisk. Press, &c. (R) 1,150
Anderson, H J. 35 E 19th....R E Anderson. Store Fixtures. 255
Aetna Soap Machine and Mfg Co. 32 Washington. S A Swenson. Machinery. security
Beninoasp, Pietro. 128 E 120th....A Grimaldi. Barber Fixtures. 100
Berger & Stern. 99 Spring....J Stewart. Machinery. 214
Bronson, Harry. 201st st and Harlem River ... C M Riddle. Boat House. 133
Barnard, G H. 9 Clinton pl....E Wileck. Machinery. 1,500
Bodine, J. 74 Maiden lane....M Renshaw. Safes. 600
Bahr, John F. 38 Dey....W S Corwin. Machinery, &c. (R) 3,000
Boesenberg, Fred. 115th st and Lexington av Nat Cash Reg Co. Register. 200
Bradley, W J. 620 W 52d .. L S Keller. Horses, Trucks, &c. (R) 550
Brosemer, E. 2188 2d av....Lamson Consol S S Co. Registe. (R) 210
Brown, Charles. r 304 W 11th....J P Rathbun & Co. Press. 80
Chaban, William. 535 Broome... M Gleason. Horses, Trucks, &c. 250
Chalmers, James. 23 Spring....Eardley & W. Machinery. 75
Canary, Timothy....M Armstrong & Co. Coach. (R) 200
Combs, Thomas....J Gottsleben. Coach. (R) 283
Coenen & Roos. 352 E 76th....B Fischer & Co. Wagon. 140
Connolly, Patrick. 401 W 27th....P A Cassidy. Wagon. 75
Curtis, G W....Wheeler & W Machine Co. Machines. 148
Cohn, Sam. 319 Rivington....B Koenig. Machines. 50
Davis, F M....G Wirving. Type Writer. 65
Drewes, Meta. 172 E 106th....C Mangels. Grocery Fixtures. 500
Davis, G A. 859 and 861 10th av. ..E Smith Machinery. (R) 400
Diehl, P A. 840 7th av ...H Harper. Butcher Fixtures. 600
Dow, C La, Jr. 283 W 30th . C Diehl. Truck. 150
Dihrberg, A. 128 7th ...Gennerich & Von B. Grocery Fixtures. 238
D G Yuengling, Jr, B Co....Farmers' Loan and T Co. Fixtures, &c. (R) 1,300,500
Drummond, Robert. 444 Pearl ...I C Ogden, Jr. Press, &c. (R) 2,029
Eggling, Herrmann. 457 Hudson....Nat Cash Reg Co. Register. 175
Eastman, E O ...M Armstrong & Co. Coach. (R) 339
Finkenstein, W. 212 E 80th....C C Frost. Barber Fixtures. 37
Friesline, C W, S A and L C. 54-60 W 33d.... Gorton & Lidgerwood. Machinery. 629
Faist, Andrew. 37 2d av....G Faist. Grocery Fixtures. 500
Goldberger, J and S. 31 Pitt....G Grinspan. Pool and Cigar Fixtures. 143
Green, Terence. 172 Lincoln av ...J Reilly. Horses, Trucks, &c. 500
Gebhardt, E. 1048 1st av....Nat Cash Reg Co. Register. 200
Gibbs Bros & Moran 45 Rose....F S Wait. Press, &c. 2,500
Graeser, H A R. 40 Stanton....E Glokner. Drug Fixtures. (R) 3,000
Gorjewsky, Jacob. 74 East Broadway.. R Hoffman. Butcher Fixtures. 245
Guerrieri, Salvatore. 58 Nassau....I Donenberg. Barber Fixtures. 150
Gundlach, F A. 654 10th av....F Simon. Drug Fixtures. (R) 2,100
Henrici, William. 59 Grand .. Flanders Mfg Co. Coffee Urn. 60
Hocito, Giuseppe. 193 Elizabeth....I Di Giovanni. Grocery Fixtures. 272
Hoffmann, Philip. 61 Columbia....P B Bracken. Horses, Trucks, &c. 385
Howell, D B & Co. 389 Broome....S T Willcox. Machinery. (R) 394
Hall, Samuel....Campbell P P Co. Press. (R) 50
Haug, J B. 414 E 59th....C G Keator. Horses, Trucks, &c. 3,000
Hayward, T S. 2236 7th av... Rothschild Bros. Wagon. 60
Horth, C & Co. 255 Greene....Campbell P P Co. Press. (R) 430
Haas, F X 30 Suffolk....J H Bates. Horse, Truck, &c. 150
Hall, W E. 44 Beekman and 25 E 14th ...Damon & P. Press, &c. 66
Haw, William. 90 Amsterdam av....B H Meyer. Butcher Fixtures. 250
Junghsbuel, G C M. 1379 Av A....H Stuebing. Drug Fixtures. (R) 280
Jacoby, Henry. 186 W 4th....J Cunningham Son & Co. Coach. 450
Jenkins & McCowan....Campbell P P Co. Press. (R) 1,400
Same....same. Press. (R) 25
Jotz, Simon. 120 E 4th ...J Weiss. Barber Fixtures. 40
Jackson, W H 323 8th av....S Littmann. Barber Fixtures. 109
Jersavitz, B. 189 East Houston F Deitz. Soda Water, Bottling Fixtures, &c. 250
Koenig, W C. 132 E 83d ...J & C Jud. Grocery Fixtures. 300
Kruger & Lipshitz. 173 East Broadway....F Wesel Mfg Co. Press, &c. 310
Kaufmann, M. 1808 Lexington av....J W Tufts. Soda Fixtures 150
Koopman, Chas. 167 Amsterdam av....H Held. Grocery Fixtures. 600
Lockwood, F H. 900 6th av ...D C Ward. Jewelry Fixtures. 500
Lait, Leon & Co. 378 Grand....A Greenberg. Office Fixtures. 700
Linscott, J A. 527-531 W 52d....Albany Venetian Blind Co. Blinds. 290
Lyons, William....Wolff Bros. Horse. 100
Lewis & Romm. 35 Rutgers... H Solotaroff. Press, &c. 1,500
Loeb, Ester. 505 E 79th....L Roos. Horse, Truck, &c. 800
Machet, Becky. 207 Broome....I Parker. Barber Fixtures. 40
McDonough, John. 584 11th av....J McLean. Butcher Fixtures. 142
McGowan, John. ..M Armstrong & Co. Coach. (R) 75
McGuire, John. 12 Frankfort....Whitlock Machine Co. Machinery. 1,300
Meyer, E D. 178 E 89th....H F Bohlen. Grocery Fixtures. 366
Michels, J F. 1964 3d av....Thos Johnson. Store Fixtures. 500
Muller, Catharine. 240 Columbus av....J H Mohlman Co. Grocery Fixtures. 600
Moran & Green. 69 3d av....C P Ketterer. Wagon 245
Murphy, Jeremiah. 109th st and Lexington av ....Nat Cash Reg Co. Register. 200
McCormick, Francis....M Armstrong & Co. Coach. 650
McEathron, J E. Tremont....C H Childs & Co. Horses, &c. 499
Margoniusky, Moses. 87 E 8th . J T Robinson & Co. Machinery. 275
Merrill & Bartold. 41 Bedford av, Brooklyn... L Conrad. Drug Fixtures. 3,500
Murray, J T. 2177 and 2179 2d av .. Lamson Consol S S Co. Register. 140
Nickermann, Fred. 310 and 312 E 75th....Kilpatrick & Roviance. Machinery. 579
N Y Portrait Supply and Frame Co 4 and 6 W 14th....V Steiner. Machinery, &c. 300
Naughton, J J, J H, L C and Joseph. 33-37 Mott....J Naughton. Horses, Coaches, &c. (R) 17,826
N Y Purified Milk and Cream Co. 44 8th av.... N P Freeberg. Milk Wagon. 200
O'Loughlin, Mary. 13 Astor pl....J Fitzgerald. Electro Plates, &c. 3,250
Ormsby, D L ...J W Tufts. Soda Fixtures. 761
Petricek, Frank. 336 E 73d....Society Spolek Ceskych Mistru rezmickych a uzemarskych v New York. Butcher Fixtures. 150
Piciocchi, A and Mrs. 81 Mulberry....P Brannan. Grocery Fixtures. 180
Powers, C R. 386 3d av ...Nat Cash Reg Co. Register. 200
Phelps, F C. 185 Hudson....Berlin Machine Works. Machinery. 1,098
Same....C H O'Neill & Co. Machinery. 3,500
Pingpank, G F. 193 Washington....C N Boschen. Barber Fixtures. 150
Rockey, W S. 501 8th av....A B Baltzly. Drug Fixtures. 3,744
Reuttinger, Samson. 317 E 77th....G Clemens et al. Wagon. 200
Reynolds, Agnes. 121st st and 7th av....Wilson & Lewis. Horses, Trucks, &c. 2,800
Rohdenburg, Henry. 192 Hester....R B Klussmann. Grocery Fixtures. 101
Rosenberg & Liskowsky. 238 Delancey ...C Dierking. Butcher Fixtures. 205
Roux, C W. 736 11th av....A Schlehemied. Drug Fixtures. 1,000
Russell, R C. —— W 46th....F J Brennen. Horse, Wagon, &c. 160
Rowland, R & Co....J Goold Co. Coach. 1,000
Scachetti & Raynor. 923 5th av...E Marscheider. Butcher Fixtures. 242
Scherrer, George. 214 and 216 W 65th....M Scherrer. Horses, Coaches, &c. 800
Smith, G C. 500 3d av ...Lamson Consol S S Co. Register. (R) 185
Stein, F C. 10th av, 181st and 182d sts....G W Zahn. Milk Fixtures, Horse, &c. 1,000
Scharf, Adolf. 87 Essex....J L Gottlieb. Barber Fixtures. 220
Simonson, M H. 1637 Lexington av....Nat Cash Reg Co. Register. 175
Sanders, J E . R T Sanders. Jewelry. 750
Schloeder, W P. 1532 3d av....G F Leise. Photo Fixtures. 300
Settgrast, William. 125 Cannon....J Germeroth. Cigar Fixtures. 130
Sherwood, Geo....M Armstrong & Co. Coach. (R) 145
Shields, James. 557 W 52d....D B Dunham. Coach. 385
Siemer, J H. 544 W 15th....W T Ockendon. Horses, Trucks, &c. 1,200
Stewart, A M. 167 and 201 E 34th... A H Bultman. Furniture and Dental Fixtures. 1,000
Stone, A L. 60 Broadway....American Writing Machine Co. Type Writer. 115
Strodl, Edward. 190 Grand....J H Strodl. Music Store Fixtures. 2,800
Sackett, J W. 128 W 40th ...O'Reilly Bros. Store Fixtures. 100
Schwartz, Pinkus. 179 Eldridge....C Dierking. Butcher Fixtures. 133
Snyder, Frederick ...J Gottsleben. Coach. 700
Toman, Edward. 15th st and Av A. ..Nat Cash Reg Co. Register. 175
Tugnot, Geo E. 137 W 125th....J W Tufts. Soda Fixtures. 2,800
Teitelbaum, A & H. 152 Attorney....I A & H Krulenvith. Bakery Fixtures. 250
Virgil, Smith & Sloane. Saratoga Springs....W H McElroy. Machinery. (R) 8,500
Walsh, Robert. 19 9th av....C S Stowell. Horses, Ice Wagon. 525
Willis, Henry....Keeler & Jennings. Coaches. (R) 2,900
Wilheim, S and A. 1193 3d av ...American Guarantee Assoc. Furniture and Cigar Fixtures. 200
Wilkins, E B & Co. 303 5th av....A Goodwin. Shoe Store Fixtures. 2,000
Same....same. Shoe Store Fixtures. 2,000
Warunac, Vaclav. 1405 Av A....J A Raale. Butcher Fixtures. 100
Willard, J Le H 47 Leonard....Chadwick Bros. Office Fixtures. 234
Wahl, Louis. 144 E 129th....G Schroedter. Machinery. (R) 850
Webster, J A....E C Webster. Bicycle. 100
Westbay, H E. 57 W 42d....L Eieke. Dental Fixtures. 450
Wyburn, J H. 502 2d av....Lamson Consol S S Co. Register. 165
Zeller, William. 203 E 53d....J Weiss. Barber Fixtures. 120

BILLS OF SALE.

Alexander, Joseph. 316 E 12th....J H Otten. Grocery Fixtures. 500
Annato, D. 829 3d av....C Cortese. Barber Fixtures. 128
Brennan, J C and D F....W J Brennan. Milk Fixtures, Horse, &c. 800
Bornengo, Battista. 218 Mulberry....Rocco & Terza. Grocery Fixtures. 315
Caputer, Joseph. 2431 8th av....Sarah S Caputer. Boot and Shoe Store. 1
Chappell, Harry. 175 3d av....Phoebe Chappell. Butcher Fixtures. 500
Durham, F F. Bay Ridge, N Y ...Hart Bros. Horse, Wagon, &c. 1
Erlbeck, H A. 195 10th av....F Schneider. Furniture.

Faracca, Vincenzo. 202 E 85th....P Michele. Barber Fixtures. 160
Freund, Fredrick. 90 Amsterdam av....W Haw. Butcher Fixtures. 500
Garritson, C B....R E Brand. Steam Launch. 1
Gregory, Minnie. 30 and 32 Oak... Annie Bertie. Saloon Fixtures. 1
Glemby, Saul. 789 6th av....A Damsky. Hair Fixtures, &c. 350
Kalischer, W S. 211 Hudson....A S Kalischer. Office Fixtures, &c. 400
Kimball, C C. 9 Baxter...Mary E Kimball. Carpenter Fixtures. 250
Kotil, A and J. 1544 2d av....J Harris. Jewelry Fixtures. 1,600
McCormack, Frank....M Gleason. Horses, Trucks. 939
Merz, Catharine F. 637 9th av....R Blake. Confectionery. 275
Mangels, Claus. 172 E 100th....M Drewes. Grocery Fixtures. 1,000
O'Connell, John...M O'Connell. Piano. 10
Poulson, Euna J. 335 W 20th....G H Blanchard. Furniture. 150
Pouessel, Jules. 142 W 4th....E Sindie. Furniture, &c. 700
Spramer, Henry. 95 E 4th ...W Gerwert et al. Butcher Fixtures. 150
Schneider, Fritz. 10th av....F 198 Erlbeck. Furniture. 1
Schultz, John. 316 E 12th....J Alexander. Grocery Fixtures. 600
Strebel, Charles. 2727 3d av....C Wenzel. Restaurant Fixtures. 350
Wallace, J C. 1231 2d av....Margaret Wallace. Horses, &c. 2,500
Zuckerman, Fannie. 18 Norfolk....B Zuckerman. Saloon Fixtures. 1,050

ASSIGNMENTS OF CHATTEL MORTGAGES.

Breslin, M P to M Groh's Sons. (Mort given by D J Grinnon, Feb 12, 1891.) 1
Breslin, M P to M Groh's Sons. (D J Grinnon, Feb 12, 1891.) 1
Blant, Simon to Livingston & Matthews. (R Trauoman, May 7, 1891.) 1
Buckel, Peter to L Anguer. (J J Horan, July 9, 1890.) ——
Devlin, Robert to M B Bookstaver. (Helen Kerr, Oct 23, 1891.) 1
Flammer, J G to W G Schwarz et al. (A Dobler, July 23, 1891.) 975
Lappin, James to G Ehret. (J McDonough, May 11, 1891.) 300
Mitchill, J G to J Maclay. (J A & G C Anderson, Aug. 5, 1891.) 30
Richman, Samuel to M Levy. (F Haas, Nov. 2, 1891.) 1
Toch, J and F to S Reitman. (A Klein, Oct. 26, 1891.) 580

KINGS COUNTY.

NOVEMBER 12 TO 18.—INCLUSIVE.

SALOON AND RESTAURANT FIXTURES.

Becker, A. 681 De Kalb av....H Elias, Jr. $500
Belcher, C. 221 Devoe....F Ibert. 300
Boetticher, Emma E. 286 Atlantic av....F & M Schaefer B Co. 1,000
Bradley, J H. 186 Richards....M Seitz. 347
Brockmann, W. 500 Grand ...Claus Lipsius B Co. (R) 1,150
Bayer, H. 257 Johnson av....C Frese. 500
Blaum, P A. 157 Division av....J A Hilcken. 3,000
Boyle, P. 8th av and 12th st... C Frese. (R) 625
Braudtjen, C. 169 Norman av....C Frese. 700
Burck, Cath L and E. 730 Dean ...Budweiser B Co. 254
Coar, W. 33 Cedar ..Obermeyer & L. 245
Costello, J. 261 Conover....H Koehler & Co. (R) 528
Campbell, T. 562 Atlantic av ...India Wharf B Co. 700
Casey, W. 574 Manhattan av... J Ruppert. 225
Clifford, J. 194 West....W Ulmer. 400
Clifford, J. 540 Manhattan av....W Ulmer. 2,000
Connolly, P. 118 Raymond....J Murtaugh. 2,800
Collins, M G. 209 Hoyt....Claus Lipsius B Co. (R) 400
Delecker, C F. 178 Prospect av....India Wharf B Co. 1,200
Doerfler, J. 437 Bushwick av....Claus Lipsius B Co. (R) 600
Doyle, P. 205 Hudson av....Claus Lipsius B Co. 575
Duffy, A. 112 Court....M Seitz. 1,600
Dunne, R J. 206 Columbia....M O'Keefe. 2,510
Farro, V. 30 Maspeth av.. .Budweiser B Co. 130
Falvello, M and A Topo. 30 Main....Burr & Son. (R) 125
Fetten, F. 31 McKibbin....O Huber Brewery. 1,200
Frankel, H. 102 Gerry....Obermeyer & L. 300
Fuchs, C. 805 Marion....Claus Lipsius B Co. (R) 400
Gosswein, M. 113 Withers....M Seitz. 300
Guderian, G. 186 Varet....Leibinger & O B Co. 550
Henichen, A. 393 Central av. ..Leibinger & O B Co. 350
Hill, E F. 318 Grand....J W Shields. 1,000
Hoppe, H. Fulton av, s w cor William pl.... Budweiser B Co. 300
Hacklaender, A. 117 Seigel... J Kress B Co. 700
Hare, W and H O'Neill. 17 Van Cott av....W Ulmer. 350
Harper, J D E and G W Merritt. 528 4th av.... Lembeck & B Eagle B Co. 750
Same. 157 5th av....same. 750
Himbeler, A. 97 Varet....Claus Lipsius B Co. (R) 300
Holmes, J A. 223 Conover....M Seitz. 1,302
Johnston, A. 110 Van Cott av .. Claus Lipsius B Co. (R) 250
Kehres, E. 216 Norman av....P Doelger. 620
Kaine, J P. 197 Greenpoint av....India Wharf B Co. 600
Kettner, G J. 58 Floyd....Williamsburgh B Co. 850
Kleiss, Anna D. 156 Myrtle av... Claus Lipsius B Co. 300
Knubel, J and W F. 551 Gates av....J C Meyer. 1,000
Kopf, D W. 364 Hooper. C Froeb. 1,057
Liebow, Anna. 414 Liberty av....V Brahm. 225
Linecke, E. 181 Montrose av....Leibinger & O B Co. 375
Loos, O. 201 Throop av....Claus Lipsius B Co. (R) 600
Markez, Mr. 1,08 3d av....W Ulmer. (R) 600
Maus, J. 155 Boerum....Claus Lipsius B Co. (R) 500
Mueller, A and F. 121 Graham av....O Huber Brewery. 700
Malone, Jane E. 604 Vanderbilt av... J Wallace & Son. (R) 75
McAllister, P. 195 Greene....P Doelger. (R) 600
Muller, A. 18 Lewis av....Williamsburgh B Co. 800
Puckhaber, N. 1109 Bedford av....P Ballantine & Sons. 4,000
Reddy, J. 599 1st av....M Seitz. (R) 290
Reilly, M. 189 Hoyt....J Murtaugh. (R) 3,750
Riecken, H. 11 President....M Seitz. (R) 806
Rupp, G. 219 Johnson av....Leibinger & O B Co. 529
Ruddy, E J. 281 Flatbush av....W L Ronntree. (R) 400
Schmitt, K. 233 Ellery....L Eppig. (R) 800
Smith, P J. 228 Driggs av....P Doelger. 505
Schindler, A. 245 Johnson av ...M Seitz. (R) 809
Schmidt, P. 48 Walton....Claus Lipsius B Co. (R) 150
Schmitt, P. 227 Montrose av....L Eppig. 450
Schollerer, G. 216 Stagg....Eliz Meltzer. (R) 725
Seekamp, J H. 973 Bedford av....F Munch B Co. 1,000
Same. 616 De Kalb av....F Munch. (R) 1,500
Serrian, J. 350 Hamilton av....D Stevenson. (R) 150
Shields, J W. 318 Grand....Williamsburgh B Co. 1,000
Wynne, P. 76 Taylor....Williamsburgh B Co. 1,075

HOUSEHOLD FURNITURE.

Allan, Mrs J T. 285 Jefferson av....J H Little. 160
Bernard, D E. 239 12th....I Mason. 151
Berthon, W. 513 Hart....J H Little. 160
Brown, Mrs L E. 126 Adelphi....I Mason. 165
Brown, W. 300 Court....Cowperthwait & Co. 121
Bullard, J H. 203 Pulaski . Cowperthwait & Co. 166
Beatty, J W. 205 Lee av....C T Kendrick & Co. 237
Bennett, Nellie. 229 North 7th....Jacob Bros. 255
Booth, Kate. 243 Withers....Jacob Bros. 220
Boyle, Mary A. 89 Douglass....Brooklyn F Co. 121
Bryant, Mrs L. 114 Gates av....Cowperthwait & Co. 598
Burke, T. 46 Nostrand av....C T Kendrick & Co. 127
Carberry, Kate. 92 Marion....Jordan & M. 118
Cassel, S. 59 Ewen ...Jacob Bros. 180
Cassidy, Mary. 783 3d av....A Pearson. 178
Charrun, J M. 51 Schermerhorn....C T Kendrick & Co. 240
Cleveland, G W. 1368 Gates av....C T Kendrick & Co. 154
Clune, E. 63 Bleecker....Jordan & M. 203
Colrey, Addie. 155 Franklin....A Schulz. 224
Corzilius, O H. 28 Suydam....L Zinsheimer. 275
Crotty, Margt. 225 South 1st....A Schulz. 180
Cary, T. 63d st and 14th av....Manges Bros. 139
Cinnamond, C H. 259 Carlton av ...L Z Murray. 197
Coyle, A B. 304 Quincy....Brooklyn F Co. 146
Davis, E. 448 McDonough....L Z Murray. 556
Dieter, G M. 249 and 251 4th av....G Ehret. Bottling Fixtures. 800
Ernst, A. 128 Central av....C T Kendrick & Co. 108
Ernst, Marie. 248 Stockton....C T Kendrick & Co. 315
Everett, Lizzie. 857 2d av....A Pearson. 218
Ford, Mrs A. 1089 Pacific....H Israel & Sons. 140
Fischer, Ellen. 319 Central av....Mullin's Sons. 149
Grady, T H. 73 Henry....Brooklyn F Co. 331
Grunendahl, C. 32A Pulaski....Lincoln Ind and G Assoc. 200
Gracy, Elizabeth. 360 Greene av....J Wood. 1,158
Grimes, E M. Flatbush....Brooklyn F Co. 179
Harkins, W J. 116 Clermont av....O'Connor & T. 212
Hall, Mary E. 52 2d pl....Lincoln Ind and G Assoc. 200
Hedden, C. 217 Monroe .. J Foulkes, Jr. 195
Hennesey, E. 729 Myrtle av....C T Kendrick & Co. 160
Hocktor, Cath. 675 Myrtle av....C T Kendrick & Co. 102
Hogan, D F. 189 Sandford....C T Kendrick & Co. 130
Hollis, Mrs S E. 100 Driggs....Jacob Bros. 170
Holt, Martha. 464 Jefferson av . Brooklyn F Co. 319
Horner, J. 142 Frost....C T Kendrick & Co. 152
Howell, H R. 523 6th av....J Coyne & Co. 210
Jones, E. 462 Putnam av ...E C Hinsdale. 750
Jones, C W. 369 Keap....Jacob Bros. 255
Kahn, Rosa. 18 Whipple....Jacob Bros. 186
Kelly, J C. 397 7th....J Coyne & Co. 196
Kennedy, Mary. 60 South 8th....A Schulz. 143
King, C W. 379 16th....M Nason. 227
Kingsley, Mrs K. 101 Ten Eyck....Mullin's Sons. 162
Kenny, Alice. 124 Lynch....Manges Bros. 117
Larsen, E. 411 20th... O'Connor & T. 197
Lawson, T. 155 Lawrence....M M Webster. 100
Maire, Maria P. 234 Washington....T E Stillman. (R) 750
Mayo, Agnes. 86 Gwinnett....Jacob Bros. 265
McConnell, J J. 151 South 9th....T Kelly. 136
McElwee, H. 100 Waverly av....C T Kendrick & Co. 264
Mead, Eliza A. 325 Berry....Jacob Bros. 220
Moore, Fannie. 132 Cooper....F Eckhardt. 132
Moore, Mrs F. 340 Hart....T Kelly. 320
Murray, S R. 928 Gates av....Mullin's Sons. 116
McManus, Theresa. 18 Hamilton av....Cowperthwait & Co. 106
Michaeles, C M. 438 Gold....Brooklyn F Co. 224
Morris, Margt H. 377 Macon....J H Little. 167
Murphy, Emma. 283 Grand....Cowperthwait & Co. 147
Nallin, J J. 58 2d pl....L Z Murray. 162
Renaud, Anna. 106 De Kalb av....M M Webster. 150
Roles, Emma R. 17A Stewart .. D M Brown. 152
Ray, G W. 349 Adelphi....J H Little. 471
Rizzel, S. 414 7th....J H Little. 118
Rogers, J Z. 769 Monroe....Cowperthwait & Co. 150
Sanford, E L. 625 Bedford av....A Gillette. (R) 500
Strait, Josie. 176 Hopkins....Manges Bros. 185
Stern, Charlotte. 336 St Marks pl....L Z Murray. 189
Schneicy, J. 588A 3d av....M Nason. 155
Schwartz, J. 79 Gwinnett....F Eckhart. 138
Sims, H. 619 Carlton av ...M Nason. 510
Smith, P. 330 Stockton....C F Kendrick & Co. 141
Soubenheimer, Mrs A. 175 North 3d....Jacob Bros. 220
Stellwagon, W. 365 South 4th....Jacob Bros. 265
Stern, Mrs Y. 236 Floyd....C T Kendrick & Co. 125
Ulmer, Mrs R. Hamburg av....C T Kendrick & Co. 168
Walker, Carrie. 37 Broome....A Schulz. 118
Wall, Eliz. 242 Leonard....A Schulz. 149
Weycott, L. 250 19th.... M Nason. 257
Whelan, P. 667 Union....J Coyne & Co. 154
Williamson, J H. 442 Pulaski ...Jacob Bros. 255
Wittmann, R C. Vienna Flats....A H Salmon. 800
Waterbury, J. 373 Bainbridge....C P Peterman. 150
Wolfe, L P. 481 Lorimer....Manges Bros. 113

MISCELLANEOUS.

Adams, P. 198 and 200 Court....Nat Cash Reg Co. Register. 175
Buffett, J. Sackman st and Sutter av..J Strauss. Cows, &c. 622
Brooklyn Elevated R R....Central Trust Co. All Property, &c 2d mort. (R) 1,250,000
Booth, W. 108 Broadway....J Wright. Paint Store. 500
Boyle, Bridget. 168 Dupont....B Weill. Horses, Carts, &c 125
Bramble, D K. 353 Kosciusko....D B Dunham. Brougham. (R) 101
Brehm, H, J and J. 307 and 309 Kent av....P M Dingee & Son. Presses, &c. (R) 3,116
Brown, G....McDougal & P. Steam Hammer. 750
Cohen, H. 190 19th....L Adler. Horse, &c. 275
Cohen, S. 57 Seigel.. M Zimmermann. Fixtures. 200
Crawford Mfg Co. Hagerstown, Md....E W Bliss Co. Presses. 1,422
Doyle Bros. 689 5th av....Lamson Consol S S Co. Register. 140
Drummond, R. 444 Pearl....I C Ogden, Jr. Printers Fixtures. (R) 2,029
Dudenhausen, F. 86 Central av....W A Rettberg. Drug Fixtures. 2,000
Eggers, W. 79 and 81 Washington....Prentiss Tool and S Co. Lathe, Drill, &c. 1,100
Fox, P. 184 5th av....N Langler. Horses and Business. 200
Gurrier, S. 53 Nassau....I Danenberg. Barber Fixtures. 150
Harloe, Mary C. 594 5th av....Boehmcke & Co. Butcher Fixtures. 200
Hatch, H W. 1069 Bedford av....Mary L Swift. Laundry Fixtures. 750
Heitmann, D. 334 South 4th, cor Keap....H C Ruether. Grocery Fixtures. 500
Hillyard, Sarah E. 1727 Fulton...Emma E Williams. Fancy Goods Store. 287
Holofcener, I J. 628 and 630 4th av....Oshinsky, L & Co. Sewing Machines, &c. 1,000
Hohmann, J. 3101 Atlantic av... S W & J A Haviland. Bakery Fixtures. 75
Horth, C & Co....Campbell Press and Mfg Co. Machine. (R) 430
Jenkins & McCowan. 224-228 Centre st, New York. Campbell Press and Mfg Co. Press. (R) 25
Same ...same. Press. (R) 1,400
Kenney, J. 280 Smith....R Cronin. Coach. 350
Kopke, J. 959 Gates av....Nat Cash Reg Co. Register. 175
Matthews, M. 242 Harrison....National Casket Co. Undertaker Fixtures. 1,531
Merrill, M L and H Bartold. 441 Bedford av.... L Conrad. Drugs. 3,500
McGuire, H....J Gottsleben. Coupe. (R) 127
McKenna, J. Park pl and Albany av....B Weill. Horse. 500
Meyer, H... A J Visel. Truck, Mules, &c. 250
Murphy, H. Foot of Columbia st... J Stover. Engine, &c. 200
Norris, B & Son. 905 Myrtle av ...New York and Brooklyn Casket Co. Coaches, Horses. 910
Ottmann, M S and C Nielsen. 242 and 244 Smith ....J, Nielsen. Grocery. 1,000
Pierce, D J. 518 Halsey....J W Tufts. Soda Apparatus. (R) 250
Ridley, R A. 328 Smith ...J M Maurer. Candy Factory, &c. 700
Reilly, J. Degraw st and Bond st....Nat Cash Reg Co. Register. 175
Schultes, J J. 826 Myrtle av....T F Russell. Register. 180
Schumacher, D. 242 Ralph av....Wilhelmine Schmacher. Horses, &c. 2,000
Schlitz, J. 60 Moore....J Cunningham Son & Co....Hearse, &c. 600
Turner & McDonald. 106 Livingston....Mary H Semple. Book Trimming Machine. 175
Wilhjelm, S & Co. 118 Union....Mosler Safe Co, New York. Safe. 100
Willmeier, J H and C W Bremer. 121 and 123 Humboldt....W B A Jurgens. Horses, &c. 10,471

BILLS OF SALE.

Bergemann, O C. 403 Sumpter....W G Ahrens. Grocery Fixtures. 550
Ehle, Martha. 592 Baltic....Myra Hiscox. Furniture. gift
Hilcken, J A. 157 Division av....P A Plaum. Saloon Fixtures. 3,000
Kenney, P....J Kenney. Coach and Horses. nom
McElroy, H K. 451 Manhattan av....A Forbes. Coffee and Tea Fixtures. nom
Ruether, H C. 334 South 4th....D Heitmann. ½ of Grocery Fixtures. 1,500
Shields, J W. 318 Grand....E F Hill. Saloon Fixtures. other consid and 500
Vogt & Reichert. 504 Hamilton av....G Hansen. Harness Store and Shop Fixtures. nom
Volk, J C. 28 State... G A Phelps. Newspaper known as "Nordlyset." 1,000
Winter, G. 497 Atlantic av....G F Winter. Saloon Fixtures. 1,000

ASSIGNMENT OF CHATTEL MORTGAGE.

Brehm, V to Margt Brehm. (Mort given by Anna Liebow, Oct 14, 1891.) 225

NEW JERSEY.

ESSEX COUNTY.

NOTE.—*The arrangement of the Conveyances, Mortgages and Judgments in these lists is as follows: the first name in the Conveyances is the Grantor; in Mortgages, the Mortgagor; in Judgments, the Judgment debtor.*

CONVEYANCES.

Allwood, J R—P Hassinger, Belmont av......... $600
Ball, Isaiah—A S Robbins, East Orange......... 1
Bassini, Charles—T E Heyden, Clinton......... 2 0
Beach, J W—G R A Meyer, South Orange....... 2,6 0
Berg, Frederick—F Densinger, Orange.......... 8
Bingham, David—W J Faith, East Orange...... 1,1
Same—E L Huff, East Orange.............. 1,1
Booth, Edward—F N Fisk, North 13th st...... 1,0
Breakenridge, J H—F M Witte, Clinton........ 1
Brown, Herman—S M Vreeland, Belleville.......
Brown, S D—H K Lyon, Milburn.............. 4
Brown, W B—A L Dennis, East Orange........ 1
Bunough, Charles—E F Ayers, n w cor Penna av and Wright st 25x100................... 3,000

Burkhardt, J A—A Horn, Orange ... 1
Campbell, R C—S Miller, Caldwell ... 125
Carter, T R—F D Dowley, Montclair ... 16,630
Cassidy, J H—J A Frink, East Orange ... 250
Same——H H Groshong, East Orange ... 2,500
Cavanagh, E T—G Krueger, 18th av ... 700
Chaplin, C F—M Dyer, Belleville ... 1,800
Clapp, A B—I Ball, South Orange ... 15,000
Cochran, Sarah—A J Hunt, Clinton ... 2,450
Condit, E M—W H Fleming, West Orange ... 500
Connelly, Arthur exr—Hugh Connelly, Bergen st ... 1,800
Coyne, Richard—F L Fieger, East Orange ... 1,927
Crane, G D—M N Crane, Caldwell ... 1,900
Crescent Watch Case Co—J G Jenkins, North 19th st ... 1
Crommelin, A M—J G Jenkins, 4th av ... 1
Davis, Catherine—C Gartland, Clayton st ... 25
Dennis, A L—C E Brown, East Orange ... 1
Dime Savings Inst—J Baier, Pacific st ... 2,900
Dobbins, R L—M L Dobbin, Caldwell ... 1
Draper, A C—F B Draper, Montclair ... 1
Draper, F B—A C Draper, Montclair ... 1
Eastwood, John—M Dean, Bloomfield ... 1,400
Edwards, S R—I Honsel, Gray st ... 1,150
Ely, G C—S M Jones, Caldwell ... 1
Fudder, J P—D G Baird, Stanton st ... 1
Farley, B M—M E Hickok, Clinton av ... 1,200
Fearey, F F—J Woodhouse, Washington av ... 800
Fiedler, J H—R P Lehlbach, Holland st ... 1
Fister, W F—G T Hatt, w s Bruen st cor Hamilton st 68x85 ... 8,500
Flohn, F L—J K Lemond, 2d av ... 225
Forest Hill Assoc—H B Crane, Elwood av ... 2,850
Fort, J F—R F Greacen, East Kinney st ... 1
Fredericks, Ida—M M Markey, New st ... 500
Fulton, E M—National Paper Mfg Co, Bloomfield ... 1
Gartland, Catharine—I Jatkowsky, Clayton st ... 500
Geach, E P—S s Colt, Orange ... 900
Same——M S Colt, Orange ... 945
Same——same, Orange ... 850
Gebhart, Nicholas—C Gebhart, 16th av ... 1,100
Gegenheimer, J P—J Kellner, e s Prince st 525 s Montgomery st 25x100 ... 6,100
Greacen, Orlando—J F Fort, East Kinney st ... 1
Hall, J W—N Sutman, Oliver st ... 450
Same——same, Oliver st ... 1
Haug, Herman—J C Haug, Somerset ... 1,000
Hassinger, Peter—A H Hassinger, Alpine st ... 1
Hesse, J N—J D Sharp, e s 1st st 150 n 7th av 120 x150x165x46 ... 32,550
Hockinjos, Anna—J H Jagle, Fair st ... 1
Same——same, s s Fair st adj land J F Dunker 49 links x 2 chains 43 links ... 20,000
Horn, Mary—J A Burkhardt, Orange ... 1
Howard Savings Inst—A Piari, Barbara st ... 1,100
Jacobus, P E—J N Stonaker, Caldwell ... 1,250
Kearns, T S—M Markey, New st ... 1
Keasbey, A Q—C Parker, several tracts ... 1
Keen, J L—T W Jackson, s w cor Summer av and Washington st 28x100 ... 1,250
Kingman, A H—G W Bramhall, South Orange ... 375
Kitchell, J T—L M Randolph, North End terrace ... 1,100
Larwill, Alfred—J H Shafer, Baldwin st ... 6,500
Lehlbach, R P—W Fiedler, Holland st ... 1
Lillie, C M—T W Jackson, Mt Prospect av ... 1,600
Lindsley, O W—P Beck, East Orange ... 150
Same——H F Smith, East Orange ... 245
Same——T H Miles, East Orange ... 362
Lister, J C—T Rose, e s Belleville av 366 s Harvey st 25x100 ... 4,900
Lockward, L G—J J Van Order, Caldwell ... 250
Mackin, Francis—E W Ward, s s Brenner st 89 e South 10th st 75x127x86x135; n s Brenner st 225 w Kent st 50x105 ... 3,000
Markey, James—E A McGovern, New st ... 650
Martin, Hugh—P Brady, Bridge st ... 100
McGrath, C A—I A Person, 2d av ... 700
Mead, E L admrx—I H Ormsby, Broad st ... 1
Mellen, Michael—J Eitenberger, Central av ... 1
Miller, Henry—J Burns, West Orange ... 510
Mitchell, Marcus—E T Terhune, West Orange ... 3,000
North Jersey Land Co—G S Porter, Montclair ... 1,881
Parkhurst, S E—J P Gegenheimer, Broome st ... 2,000
Parker, Cortlandt—A Q Keasbey, n s Chestnut st 390 w Adams st 144x137x161x105 ... 8,000
Same——same, 6 tracts ... 1
Pennington, A J F—W P Field, South Orange av ... 1
Peterson, Samuel—J S Carlson, Montclair ... 450
Pierson, Harriet—Wm P Field, Coes pl ... 1
Same——E H Baldwin, Coes pl ... 1
Same——J O Kiesele, Prince st ... 2,000
Same——A F Pennington, Court st ... 1
Poecker, John—W S Doyle, Montclair ... 150
Pollard, G S—A Wiley, Warwick st ... 1
Protestant Foster Home—J Walters, Summer av ... 1,000
Randolph, L M—J T Kitchel, North End terrace ... 1,100
Reilly, T M—H R Trivett, Norfolk st ... 800
Robbins, A S—I Ball, East Orange ... 1
Same——L D Morrison, East Orange ... 10,800
Roe, J M—N E Willets, Clinton ... 600
Same——W H White, Clinton ... 500
Root, A H—G Spottiswoode, Orange ... 2,750
Sargeant, S S—J S Stockton, 7th av ... 1
Schmidt, C M—J F Hoops, Fairmount av ... 2,400
Same——L Rommel, South 10th st ... 2,300
Sena, Giuseppe—F Zarra, Lock st ... 1
Shipman, C F—W Schnatterer, North 7th st ... 275
Smith, James, Jr—L A Mitchell, w s McWhorter st, 100 s e Kinney st 95x100x155x61x3x229x4x 117 ... 43,000
Spottiswoode, George—T M Cusack, Orange ... 1,375
St Lukes Methodist Episcopal Church—W F Bell, Clinton av ... 1
St Patricks Church—M D Burnett, South st ... 2,500
Tomkins, S A—W W Anderson, Caldwell ... 1,350
Trimpi, H F—A H Trimpi, w s North 6th st, 100 s 7th av 41x100x38x100 ... 6,000
Tunison, Edward—C E Glentworth, w s Pacific st, 45 s Walnut st 27x94 ... 6,500
Same——same, Sherman av ... 500
Tynan, J J—M Heitzman, South Orange ... 250
Vernet, G W—B Astley, High st ... 2,000
Wallace, J P—J Grintz, Belleville ... 100
Ward, J, Jr—G F Reeve, Plane st ... 750
Ward, S R—S M Strobell, n s Court st 230 w Broad st 19x74 ... 8,950
Whitlock, M A—E M Fulton, Bloomfield ... 30,000
Wiley, Addison—G S Pollard, Warwick st ... 1
Williams, E C—S A Tomkins, West Orange ... 2,500
Wilson, J C—New York Bay R R, Murray st ... 94
Zarra, Filomena—G Sena, Lock st ... 1

MORTGAGES.

Arnold, Christoph—E Barnes, Rutgers st ... 2,000
Baldwin, B M—A G Plume, Garside st ... 650
Burnett, M D—St Patricks Church, South st ... 1,500
Cadmus, G W—American Ins Co, Bloomfield ... 2,900
Cassidy, J C—Trustees of Rutgers College of N J, East Orange ... 9,000
Clark, Julia—A De Lemans, Jacob st ... 1,600
Same——J Gemeinert, Broad st ... 8,000
Cooke, J A—Bloomfield B and L Assoc, Bloomfield ... 200
Connell, Hugh—C E V C Mershon, Bergen st ... 800
Crane, Ella F—Jacob Valentine et al trustees, Montclair ... 3,800
Crane, H B—Firemen's Ins Co, Elwood av ... 3,000
Danber, Chas—C Wirth, 16th av ... 800
Dean, Matilda—J Eastwood, Bloomfield ... 1,000
Del Guercio, Alfonso—W S Brown, 7th av ... 2,900
Densinger, Frederick—F Berg, Orange ... 775
Develin, Elizabeth—Howard B and L Assoc, Parker st ... 2,000
Dobbins, C W—Caldwell B and L Assoc, Caldwell ... 600
Dyer, Michael—Chas F Chaplin, Belleville ... 1,400
Eiterberger, J E—C M Woodruff, Central av ... 1,200
Faith, W J—D Bingham, East Orange ... 500
Faitoute, E C—A R Lee, Broad st ... 4,000
Fleming, W H—W Pierson, West Orange ... 1,500
Frederick, August—F Sipple, West Orange ... 600
Gegenheimer, J P—Mechanic's B and L Assoc, Prince st ... 4,000
Same——same, Prince st ... 4,000
Same——S E Parkhurst, Broom st ... 1,400
Goble, L S—J A McGown, Astor st ... 2,400
Hozack, Robert—Belleville B and L Assoc, Belleville ... 1,200
Huff, E L—D Bingham, East Orange ... 600
Hunt, A M—S Cochran, Clinton ... 1,800
Hunt, R E—M T Pack, 3d st ... 1,000
Same——same, 3d st ... 1,000
Ives, H F—Peabody Land and Loan Co, Clifton av ... 500
Jagle, J H—G W Jagle, Fair st ... 1,000
Same——same, Fair st ... 9,000
Janes, J E—J F McLogan, Clifton av ... 458
Same——Peabody Land and Loan Co, Clifton av ... 650
Jerolaman, Theodore—Belleville B and L Assoc, Belleville ... 5,000
Kane, Mary—Half Dime Savings Bank, Orange ... 800
Kelley, Bridget—S Doughty et al exrs, Kinney st ... 200
Kellner, Joseph—J E Jackson, Prince st ... 3,000
Kocher, Catharine—G Denman, West Orange ... 500
Krumwiede, H F—Mutual Ben Life Ins Co, West Kinney st ... 6,000
Lyon & Sons Brewing Co—American Ins Co, Montclair ... 1,100
McKinley, John—J Tormey, East Orange ... 700
McKevitt, John—Owen McCabe, Madison st ... 3,500
Meyer, G H A—J W Beach, South Orange ... 1,000
Michel, Isidor et al—S E Carter, Prince st ... 3,500
Miller, Sarah—J W Young, Caldwell ... 250
Moeller, Emil—P Byrne, West Orange ... 150
Morningstern, L A—The Mut Ben Life Ins Co, East Orange ... 2,000
National Paper Mfg Co—E M Fulton, Bloomfield ... 30,000
Piarr, Adelaide—Howard Savings Inst, Barbara st ... 900
Porter, G S—North Jersey Land Co, Montclair ... 2,000
Rummel, Louis—C M Schmidt, South 10th st ... 2,000
Sauer, Chas—Orange Valley B and L Assoc, Orange ... 1,500
Scaine, James—Belleville B and L Assoc, Belleville ... 600
Scheiner, Leonhard—C Hock, 5th av ... 3,000
Scheps, Nathan—Newark German B and L Assoc, Sayre st ... 600
Shepard, Benjamin—M E Wilde, East Orange ... 10,000
Spottiswoode, George—A H Root, Orange ... 2,000
Stone, Mary—Reliable B and L Assoc, Mt Prospect av ... 200
Sutman, Nicholas—I Georges, Jelliff av ... 300
Same——J W Hall, Oliver st ... 200
Suydam, J P—Woodside B and L Assoc, Seabury st ... 800
Taylor, William—M Stumpff, 8th av ... 400
Trivett, H R—Norfolk B and L Assoc, Norfolk st ... 700
Vermilye, S G—R R Pinch, East Orange ... 7,500
Vreeland, W J—A Manners, Franklin ... 2,800
Wallace, John—M E Munn, East Orange ... 3,500
Walker, John—J S Higbie, Belleville ... 1,500
Ward, E C—L S Ward, South 10th st ... 4,000
Williams, C P—M Grover, Bloomfield av ... 1,500
Woman's Christian Temperance Union, of Newark, N J—T Runyon, Mulberry st ... 3,000
Zarra, Filomena—Fourteenth Ward B and L Assoc, Lock st ... 12,000

CHATTEL MORTGAGES.

Bader, William—H Schneider, horses ... 150
Ball, Joseph—J Ketcham, furniture ... 130
Bassini, L C—J Ketcham, furniture ... 130
Blood, C H—C Biermann, furniture ... 100
Bogardus, Frederick—L E Schneider, furniture ... 100
Boscanio, Lorenzo—F Lisiewski, saloon ... 650
Bowers, M A—H W Watson, machinery ... 498
Bradford, Louise—M Kane, carpet, &c ... 52
Burtt, A F, Jr—J M Quinby & Co, wagons, &c ... 1,300
Corby, Maggie—M Kane, furniture ... 40
Corr, M J—Muller & Schmidt, furniture ... 60
Douglas, W D—M Kane, furniture ... 32
Eagles, A M—F G Smith, piano ... 390
East Orange Riding Co—M E Schnitzspahan, horses, &c ... 1,200
Fletcher, George—I M Williams, horses ... 170
Gaertner, A, Jr—A Gaertner, store fixtures ... 400
Gilson, C C—C Bierman, furniture ... 180
Greinbalch, J C—C Trefz, saloon ... 400
Fenderton, James—J Ketcham, furniture ... 100
Hertler, William—R Richter, store fixtures ... 800
Hirshfield & Co—G W Aber, safe ... 70
Same——L Lessel, safe ... 75
Jung, Daniel—H Pfeiffer, horse, &c ... 150
Kenny, Thomas—A Finger, factory fixtures ... 2,500
King, Nelson—C Bierman, horses ... 65
Kirstein, Joseph—F Lisiewski, saloon ... 600
Kolb, George—F Lisiewski, saloon ... 600
Lee, J J—E E Spencer & Co, machinery ... 270
Mailer, Sophie—C A Feick, furniture ... 100
McCall, Arthur—J Ketcham, furniture ... 65
Meixner, Joseph—G Lewis, wagons, &c ... 193
Meyer, Ernest G—J L Bollin, machinery ... 500
Napoliello, Felix—P Ballantine & Sons, saloon ... 150
Opp, E A—F G Smith, piano ... 325
Passer, John—Muller & Schmidt, carpet ... 14
Puffer, A D & Sons—C J Lipp, soda apparatus ... 35
Puffer, A D & Sons—F E Clough, soda apparatus ... 1,300
Rozanuiro, Vincenzo—F Lisiewski, saloon ... 650
Ruther, Max—Muller & Schmidt, furniture ... 159
Schadow, Frederick—C Trefz, saloon ... 400
Schaefer, Philip—L Schaefer, machinery ... 1,100
Splitt, W N—J G Patton Co, furniture ... 485
Steck, F C—Muller & Schmidt, carpet ... 33
Townley, G H—W C Garrison, horses, &c ... 960
Tucker, O F—C Bedford, horses, &c ... 225
Turner, H F—E R Ogden, horses, &c ... 3,500
Winterhalt, George—P J Hoeler, store fixtures ... 1,100

JUDGMENTS.

Baker, J E et al—The North Ward Nat Bank ... 1,193
Heath, Charles et al—G W Robinson ... 475
La Mancha Lodge K of P—S Granger ... 516
McGrath, Thomas—M Happaugh ... 2,418
Osborne, J K—T Devlin ... 4,000
Riker, E O—W W Muchmore ... 276
Serbe, A F et al—Thurber Whyland Co ... 402

HUDSON COUNTY.

CONVEYANCES.

Allen, Robert and M M Forrest—J B Dupey, Kearney ... $1,500
Beich, Mary J—C Judge ... 150
Blauvelt, I H—J J Cadmus, Kearney ... nom
Same——same, Kearney ... nom
Bogert, Garrett—Sarah J Mupsell, Hoboken ... 800
Browne, C E—J Hamilton, Jr ... 8,500
Cadmus, J J and D H Blauvelt trading as the Arlington Coal and Lumber Co—North Jersey Land Co, Kearney ... nom
Cannon, M J—J Dawson ... nom
Condict, Fillmore—Sophia Wurste, Kearney ... 825
Connolly, M T—H J Bonn ... 13,500
Cox, Terence—M McAvay ... 2,850
Crevier, J C—H Weinbayer, Hoboken ... 17,000
Crossett, Samuel—B F Schmeckpeper, Hoboken ... nom
Dawson, James—M J Cannon ... nom
Dolan, Mary—T Braniff, Union ... 650
Donn, Henry—B F Hurd ... nom
Embury, Augustus by exr—Caroline M Haskin, Bayonne ... 12,000
Embury, P A—Caroline M Haskin, Bayonne ... 12,000
Emmons, E F—T M Murphy ... 1,010
Fene, Helen M—T L Crawford ... 4,100
Timken, Betty L—G H Hilge, Hoboken ... 6,500
Fishbouene, Robert—F Stalowisky ... 225
Frew, G H—Margaret Maher ... nom
Fuller, Ferdinand—W Peter ... 12,000
Gies, J M—H Fuster ... 1,000
Godfrey, Harriet E by exr—H H Godfrey, Bayonne ... 1
Gorman, Jas—Margaret Gorman ... 1,000
Gorman, Catharine E—Margaret Gorman ... 1,600
Grace, Mary—E J Grace, Harrison ... nom
Greene, H C—Ellen Wynn, Kearney ... 2,000
Guaraglia, Frank—C Guaraglia, Hoboken ... nom
Guaraglia, Rosa—F Guaraglia, Hoboken ... nom
Haggerty, Maria A—D Donegan, Hoboken ... 3,000
Hall, Jacob—L Dieliam, Jr, West Hoboken ... 1,650
Hebert, Clara P A—W T Cauliffe, Kearney ... 1,250
Heney, Jennette—Elizabeth MacKennon ... nom
Hoboken Land and Impt Co—J C Crevier, Hoboken ... nom
Hurd, B F—Barbara Dorn ... nom
Klaus, Theresa—J Thomson ... 4,700
Knapp, Kate A—Annie Andrews, Bayonne ... 2,700
Knighton, E B—J H Mahnken, Bayonne ... 4,000
Kniebuhler, Maggie—Rosa Heider ... 400
Same——Maggie Kniebuhler ... 400
Kreienkamp, Anna—F Markwardt ... —
Kruse, John—Justina Kruse, Union ... 500
Lawless, Michael—T F Lawless ... 500
Lehmann, Christine—August Vom Fell ... 7,500
Limonze, Gustav—W Goedecke, North Bergen ... 1,900
Mahon, W V V and Jno Van Vorst—The Board of Chosen Freeholders, North Bergen ... 36,000
Mackennon, A T—Jennett Henry ... nom
Mahew, Patrick—G H Frew ... nom
McKenna, Bridget—Mary McMahon, North Bergen ... 215
Meehan, F C by sheriff—J H Mullins ... 820
Muller, Louis—H Peters, Bayonne ... nom
Nichols, E H—T Ellinghouis ... 2.0
North Jersey Land Co—G W Cooper, Kearney ... 2,750
North Jersey Land Co—J J Cadmus, Kearney ... nom
Niesen, Michael—W Gross, North Bergen ... 450
Pisenecker, Christopher—West Side Connecting Railroad ... 1,700
Pierce, C A—R W McCaul, Kearney ... 3,600
Post, Catharine A—A Heritage ... nom
Pruser, Anna G—H B Pruser, Hoboken ... 5,500
Regan, James—L Taglıabue, West Hoboken ... 1,450
Rockett, A D—Kate Foster ... 600
Rural Homestead Co—The Board of Township Committee, Kearney ... nom
Schmeckpeper, B F—Adele J Crossett, Hoboken ... nom
Seide, G A—C M Depew, Hoboken ... 5,500
Sheehan, Dennis—J Manning ... 10
Siegfried, Adam—Emil Tietjen ... 1,500
Simonds, A B—C Weisenborn, Harrison ... 800
Same——C S Goldberg, Harrison ... 500
Steele, Catharine M—D S Steele ... nom
Stearns, J O—J Newman, Bayonne ... 1,190
Tierney, Myles—Sophie Lincks, Hoboken ... 7,000
Toffey, Adeline S—Marg W Lowe ... 1,100
Van Wart, C A—C O Van Wart ... nom
Van Wart, C O—C A Van Wart ... nom
Weille, Margaret B—Maggie A Gilbert ... 8,000
Werther, Anna—G Nelson ... 800
Whyte, D C—O Stoss, Secaucus ... 500
Winkle, Katharine—Caroline Haster, Harrison ... 500
Wolff, Laura—F C Hansen, Union ... 2,300

MORTGAGES.

Barnes, F C—The Provident Inst for Savings, 1 year ... 2,000
Bastan, Chas—The Jersey City B and L Assoc, installs ... 2,000
Behrens, Henry—The Hudson Trust Savings Inst, Union, 1 year ... 3,800
Block, Valentine—N H Chesebrough, Union, 3 years ... 3,000
Cadmus, J J—The Provident Inst for Savings, Kearney, 1 year ... 2,000
Same——Hannah C Cadmus, Kearney, 2 years ... 5,100
Carlock, J E—J Matthews, 5 years ... 900
Champallier, Frances—Pauline Ecker, West Hoboken, 4 years ... 800
Cunliffe, W T—The Harrison and Kearney B and L Assoc, Kearney, installs ... 2,000
Davenport, Miles—J Benson, Hoboken, 2 years ... 500
Donnelly, Gertrude A—The Provident Inst for Savings, Bayonne, 1 year ... 2,500
Doolittle, William—D Dunn, Kearney, 1 year ... 2,400
Feste, Alphonse—The Hudson Trust and Savings Inst, West Hoboken, 2 years ... 2,100
Foster, Kate—J F Gibbins, 3 years ... 4,000
Foye, F M—The Montgomery M B and L Assoc, installs ... 1,800
Gilbert, Maggie A—Susan M Vreeland, 3 years ... 205
Grace, E J—Nellie Ford, Harrison, 1 year ... 1,200
Gross, Wilhelm—M Nilsen, North Bergen, 1 year ... 250
Harkeness, W J—Minnie Magee, 3 years ... 500
Hartnett, Eugene—The Mutual Life Ins Co, 1 year ... 60,000
Hilge, G H—Betty L Timken, Hoboken, 5 years ... 4,000
Hofman, Georgina E—J Crossley, Union, 4 years ... 3,500
Kellers, F N—J Rohmeier, 3 years ... 10,000
Kramer, Louis—Martha L Deraismus, Union, 5 years ... 1,200
Lawless, Catharine—H V Condict, 3 years ... 1,000
Lewis, Josephine—C Schweinler, Hoboken, 3 years ... 2,500

Links, Sophia—M Tierney, Hoboken, 3 years	3,400
Markwardt, Fred—Anna Kleienkamp, 3 years	950
McCaul, B W—C A Pierce, Kearney, 2 years	400
McCourt, Henry—W G Harper, 3 years	400
McKensey, Bernhard—Elizabeth Furrer, Union, 2 years	2,500
Morris, Eleanor F—Mary Demarest, Bayonne, 3 years	2,000
Moriarty, Margaret—New Jersey Title Guarantee and Trust Co, installs	4,000
Murphy, T M—H Van Buskirk, 3 years	500
Nelson, Geo—O Crouse, 3 years	1,100
O'Neill, T B—Crescent M B and L Assoc, installs	8,000
Orteig, Jos—Hudson Trust and Savings Inst, West Hoboken, 3 years	900
Phillips, Mary—H Von Glahn, 3 years	200
Pitcher, W L—Juliet L Dewey, 3 years	250
Ready, Thos—The New Jersey Title Guarantee and Trust Co, installs	3,500
Richter, Arthur—Louise Aitken, 3 years	1,600
Rooney, Patrick—J Mullins, 1 year	800
Scott, John—A A Lutkins, 5 years	8,500
Smith, Emma G—Electric B and L Assoc, Kearney, installs	300
Stalowisky, Mike—Crescent M B and L Assoc, installs	1,400
Van Riper, Mary F—Excelsior M B and L Assoc, series 2, issue 4, installs	6,400
Voehl, Jacob—Minnie H Linn, Bayonne, 3 years	6,000
Vreeland, R A—D Van Winkle, 1 year	1,000
Weiner, Mary—Emma Schmidt, North Bergen, 3 years	400
Same—F H Cordts, North Bergen, 5 years	308
Wynn, Ellen—H C Greene, Kearney, 1 year	500

CHATTEL MORTGAGES.

Bacon, G H—J G Patton & Co, furniture	465
Barning, Maggie—Bernheimer & Schmid, pool table	160
Beyer, Nora, Harrison—P Hauck, saloon fixtures	500
Bothwell, Sarah—F G Smith, piano	175
Compton, J L—J Metz, printing press	391
Condon, Patrick and Thomas—The Burton Brewing Co, saloon fixtures	250
Crown, J H, Bayonne—I Mason, furniture	375
Cuthbert, Caroline—C Birdsall, furniture	130
Degnan, Elizabeth—Brooklyn F Co, furniture	166
Devine, Annie—L Baumann, furniture	290
Doty, Emma L—F G Smith, piano	208
Espositi, Antonio, Hoboken—M Jaccarino et al, confectionery store	200
Fallon, Peter—A Finck & Son, saloon	300
Fendtner, Jacob—Dorothea Fahr, ornamental iron works	345
Finlay, Jeanette M, Bayonne—F G Smith, piano	192
Foster, Sarah J—C Birdsall, furniture	100
Fuchs, Joseph—The Burton Brewing Co, saloon	808
Gardner, T H, Bayonne—F G Smith, piano	200
Garrigan, Julia—L Baumann, furniture	100
Gee, E C—H Thoesen, carpet	47
Gesner, Clarence—J Mullins & Co, furniture	175
Good, A F—Brooklyn F Co, furniture	139
Garjen, Dietrich, Hoboken—J Bauman, furniture	123
Hamm, Lorenzo, Bayonne—F G Smith, piano	287
Hart, J D—C Birdsall, furniture	100
Hennessy, Almeda—L Baumann, furniture	179
Hitchcock, W O—F G Smith, piano	190
Hubb, Martin J—C Birdsall, furniture	100
Kappe, Albert and Maggie—C Smith, bakery and restaurant	130
Kolkman, J H, Hoboken—P Weigele, grocery store, horse, wagon, &c	425
La Fryette, Agnes—C Birdsall, furniture	100
Lehne, C F—L Bauman, furniture	94
McEntee, John—The Lembeck & Betz Eagle Brewing Co, saloon	500
McGillovay, Phoebe M, Bayonne—F G Smith, piano	250
Merscheimer, John—C Birdsall, furniture	180
Miltner, John and John, Jr, partners as John Miltner & Son, saloon	424
Mitchell, Arthur—F G Smith, piano	216
Monenschein, Julius and Franz Wolk—Bernheimer & Schmid, saloon	900
Same, Hoboken—Bernheimer & Schmid, saloon	1,000
Monenschein, Julius and E G Kriele, Hoboken—Bernheimer & Schmid, saloon	800
Nabers, E C, Bayonne—A Dallas, carriage	70
Poole, Ernest—L Baumann, furniture	86
Prime, J H—C Birdsall, furniture	190
Reilly, Jane, Hoboken—L Bauman, furniture	101
Schepflin, Henrietta—C Birdsall, furniture	98
Seymour, Louise—F G Smith, piano	178
Shafto, Florina, Bayonne—F G Smith, piano	185
Sherman, H C—C Birdsall, furniture	180
Smith, Maude, Elizabeth—Brooklyn F Co, furniture	229
Smith, Thomas, Bayonne—Lembeck & Betz Brewing Co, saloon	1,135
Spohr, G H, Hoboken—C Birdsall, furniture	125
Struch, Ernest, Hoboken—L Bauman, furniture	391
Stryker, M F—The Canton Surgical and Dental Chair Co, Yale chair	65
Travis, Anna E, Bayonne—F G Smith, piano	250
Van Bambach, Gussie—L Bauman, furniture	105
Van Bloem, P H, Bayonne—F G Smith, piano	375
Wagner, B R, Hoboken—The J Chr G Hupfel Brewing Co, saloon fixtures	400
Yates, J J—Lembeck & Betz Eagle Brewing Co, saloon	500

BILLS OF SALE.

Midlege, W F recvr of The American Concave Spring Co—Elizabeth W Spencer, machinery	3,040
Ray, James—Jeannette Clark, horse, wagon and harness	200
Warus, Rudolph, Hoboken—M Rosenstein, saloon	925

JUDGMENTS.

Giroux, Arthur, Rudolph and Theodore Oesman—F Hall	159
Same—same	33
Kelly, E R—A Crossman	455
Mohn, Rosetta and Wm A—H L Timken et al, partners	98
Porrett, Frederick—J Mullins	362
The Hoboken Supply Co—Brook, Oliphant & Co	218

MECHANICS' LIENS.

Morris, John, builder and owner; Frank A Mackie, claimant	484
Otto, Ernest, builder; H R Civel, owner; E D Vanderbilt et al, partners	787
Sheldon & Simon, builders; William Brinkerhoff, owner; Aaron B Woodruff et al, claimant	2,409

BUILDING MATERIAL MARKET.

BRICKS.—Upon the general line of cost for Common Hards we find just about former rates mentioned, with the tone pretty steady, though top figures are only on decidedly exceptional stock. The character of the deal since our last report has, on the whole, revealed a pretty solid condition of the market and an apparent insurance against any further decline this season. On Monday morning the arrivals were very liberal, larger in fact than for any corresponding time for many weeks past and showing quite variable quality from ordinary to prime. A fairly compensating demand, however, was found, at times opening out rather freely, and the accumulation was gradually reduced until of late proportions have been looked upon as comparatively moderate. This result, however, was in part obtained through the influence of low tides along the river, which prevented loading and shipment. Of Pales, however, the offering has not been so readily managed, the amount available proving exceptionally large and the quality irregular, ranging from very poor to very good. On the latter the named rates were $2@2.25 per M, with occasional sales, but on the less desirable stock it was a sort of go-as-you-please deal, with sellers compelled to fit a rate according to the chance they had for securing custom, and in some cases it was thought advisable to accept $1.50 per M rather than lose a customer. From primal points there is not much news obtainable. It is understood that manufacturers from far up river calculate upon risking about two more shipments and then hauling off unless the weather puts on an embargo beforehand, but from Fishkill down the forwarding will no doubt continue until navigation is positively closed.

CEMENT.—For some time the movement of supplies has been liberal, owing in a measure to large quantities available and the determination of sellers to find a market. For domestic, quotations were named at 80c.@$1, according to brand, and dealers piled away stock freely on the natural assumption that they could lose nothing, many now having quite as full an accumulation as they can take care of, and that curtails custom somewhat. Manufacturers, however, are pushing supplies forward, and it looks as though they were determined the market should not suffer for want of stock. On foreign it seems to be the stereotyped story of the season, simply a constantly arriving supply with steady pressure to realize, and easy rates a necessity for securing custom, especially as every source of demand has been so well met that natural outlets are about full. Rates have for a long time been very irregular, with some business done as low as $2 per bbl. from wharf, and while there is now an effort to brace up a little we have report of sales within a couple of days at $2.25 delivered for one of the best English brands.

GLASS.—The market for Window Glass remains very dull, some operators think unusually so for this time of the year. Contrary to custom, there is no demand now for future delivery and an evident disinclination to worry much about the future, an indication that buyers have no idea of any addition to cost taking place, a theory obtaining considerable support from the fact that at the manufacturers' meeting recently held in the West it was concluded unadvisable to work up prices, and consequently the general line of quotations remains unchanged. Offerings of stock are plentiful enough, indeed a little excessive if anything, and that in the face of quite a number of factories shut down and some refusing to tender their surplus. Imported glass is firm and selling in satisfactory manner. Plate holds a steady position and has a fairly satisfactory run of trade.

LATH.—It remains a very strong market, fully supporting former rates, and receivers apparently carrying advantage enough to raise the value line even higher if so inclined. During the week there has been business at $2.20, but followed by sales at $2.25, and a fraction more asked and claimed in one instance. As a matter of fact, the actual natural demand is not of extensive proportions, but in comparison with the limited arrivals and absent offerings of afloats is sufficient to afford receivers encouragement and confidence.

LIME.—A change of wind brought in some pretty full arrivals coastwise for a couple of days and the market really had considerable more stock than it needed. As against the offering, therefore, the selling was rather slow and receivers found no great amount of satisfaction in the condition of trade, but so far as known they have managed to preserve a fairly steady tone and up to the present writing old rates are quoted.

LUMBER.—The story of the local lumber market differs in no essential particular from that of the preceding two or three weeks. At some yards business appears to be really good, but that is by long odds the exception, and many of the largest and most important dealers are complaining of quiet conditions, and a trip of observation through the district bears ample testimony to the small amount of stock moving. The really new business of late appears to be mainly confined to cabinet-makers and other manufacturing supplies, the deliveries for building purposes being almost entirely upon old orders. From dealers there really seems to be very little natural demand at the moment and while agents can by hard work occasionally place some odd lots of stuff the evidences go to show that accumulations are pretty nearly completed and this locality is getting to be quite a difficult market to place any considerable amount of lumber of any kind. Values, however, are sustained, because the pressure of supplies from primal points has almost entirely ceased, and the local holder of lumber is naturally well disposed to give all the support possible to his stock on the assumption that carrying expenses will more than come back, through the advantages obtained when spring trade commences to develop. Exporters are not feeling very brilliant at the moment. The River Plate trade shows no signs of improvement, the condition of affairs in Brazil, it is feared, will reduce or cut off an outlet that was taking considerable stuff, and it looks very much as if the West Indian wants were temporarily supplied. We have noticed, this week, considerable grumbling among the trade over the poor dock accommodations to which they are still compelled to submit, and hope at no distant period to investigate the matter more thoroughly.

Eastern spruce has been quiet for the two reasons that there was very little stock offering, and a really indifferent sort of demand. Some of the yards are crammed full of stuff, others have only a moderate supply, and while to the large accumulations more would readily be added if there was storage room to pile it, the small amounts are the results in many cases of inability to meet the settling terms of sellers, and for which no immediate relief is promised. Advices from the Eastward reiterate in strong terms the determination of manufacturers to shut down mills just as soon as they complete the work now in hand. A rumor has been floating to the effect that some of the dealers were cutting prices, but we have it from authority that upon investigating, charges to that effect were found to be without foundation and all dealers may be considered as standing up to the agreement to maintain the rates settled upon early in the season.

Piling has remained about as before in matter of value and fairly steady, but found no special demand, and the supply has been ample for all wants, including one or two cargoes arriving. The Board of Trade and Transportation has been considering the danger to shipping through the transportation of lumber rafts along the coast, and after referring the matter to a committee, the latter reports that there was nothing to be apprehended.

Hemlock is meeting with the ordinary slow inquiry and reveals a market of small and unimportant character, with values nominally unchanged. A communication from Ridgway, Pa., referring to the recent meeting there of Hemlock Association and the attempt to raise price, names the following suggestions as reported by the secretary of the association: "First, the curtailment of product; second, to make the association the selling agent and to dictate the amount each mill was to cut; third, to issue certificates, after the plan of the oil trade, on the amount of lumber in yards; fourth, incorporate the association and take all the stock from the producers at a certain price and sell it for the gain of the association." No positive plan was agreed upon.

White Pine does not show a generally active market, and indeed has lost character if anything of late. The demand for the finer qualities has already commenced to show signs of indifference as an evidence that dealers have obtained the not over large quantities desired to fill out assortments, and beyond that will not invest. For 10 inch boards, however, the call continues pretty good owing to scarcity at the primal points, though about all handled are for stock against future contingencies with some haste where the movement forward is dependent upon the canals. The export business is light and unimportant so far as fresh deals are concerned, but quite a fair quantity of stuff is loading on old contracts.

Yellow Pine has not an active market at the moment, but on the whole a very good one, as the new order of things will adjust and equalize prices and generally keep the market in order. It is found that most of the trade are rather inclined to approve the recent action of yellow pine dealers upon a basis of the plan published, but it is in some cases suggested that a powerful combine is apt to become dangerous unless managed with the utmost skill both as to the purchase and sale of supplies.

Carolina Pine has a fairly steady demand and from regular sources, with no special feature to the market, except that the effort to lift values is not successful. Buyers, however, can obtain no concessions on standard stock at the moment.

Hardwoods have been very dull all around, and we cannot find operators who have anything new to suggest at the moment. Stock in yard is firmly held and added to occasionally, but in the latter case it is only because some desirable lot is poked at the customer, with something in the way of a price allowance to make it attractive. From points of supply advices are coming to hand to indicate more or less scant cut of all kinds of stock, and there is certainly a somewhat firmer tone on interior markets, though possibly that is simply the natural seasonable change. Exporters are picking up a little stock, but, as usual, want it very fine.

GENERAL LUMBER NOTES.

STATE.

The Albany *Argus* reports:

Ice forming in the slips in the lumber district gives warning that the season of shipping by water is nearly at an end, and that before long the lumbermen will be seeking winter quarters down town. From present indications there is no appearance of any very great rush of business to wind up the season; in fact it looks as if it would be an off-year to the extreme end. Business has, however, increased to a slight extent during the past week, and the fact is indisputable that more buyers have been in the market than for some time past. As a rule, however, they are not placing any very large orders, for they are here generally to see what they may be able to pick up in the way of bargains, and are purchasing a little of this and some more of that in order to fill up broken stocks in their yards for the winter trade. Still, with a considerable looking about, this trade eventually takes quite a quantity of lumber out of the market to be shipped before navigation closes. The stock of thick pine lumber here is moderate, while the demand is fairly good. Prices are very firmly held, as the stock cannot readily be replaced. Low grade shippers for the South American trade are in good request, while the stocks on hand are not large. Box lumber is in good supply and selling well. Receipts of pine for the week have been very light and not much more is expected. In spruce the three popular sizes, 1¼ inch, 1½ and 2 inch, good and culls, are wanted and the stocks are very light. The statement is made, and is doubtless, true, that less spruce will be wintered here this season than at any time in the past ten years. Ten-inch hemlock boards are still wanted and are getting scare, otherwise hemlock is dull. Quartered oak and basswood are leading in demand among the hardwoods, and the latter is having quite an active trade. Stocks are dry and well assorted. Shingles and lath show no special features, having a fair demand and selling at recently quoted prices.

THE WEST.

The Northwestern *Lumberman* as follows:

As winter approaches, and the season of navigation on the lakes draws near the close, it becomes evident that less lumber will be left unsold at the mills than was calculated on in midsummer. Even in the Saginaw valley, where the lake shipping business has been considered slow, the amount to be left unsold will be considerably less than last year. The tendency of fall business has been to clear off stocks so that few burdensome blocks remain on the hands of producers.

It is evident that the winter demand is to be unusually heavy, for the reason that the large fall trade has depleted wholesale stocks, and supplies to balance them up will have to be brought forward during the winter.

Doubtless there will be a good deal of winter sawing, especially if the weather is mild. This will set all the railroad mills in Michigan and Wisconsin going full capacity. This should be taken into account in estimating the probable supply next winter and spring as compared to the demand.

The hardwood trade is still rubbing along on a rough bottom. In some markets, and in respect to some woods and lines of demand, there is a fair condition of things; but as a whole the hardwood trade is less prosperous than that in soft. Poplar shares to some degree in the rising prosperity of the white pine trade, especially in the better grades that compete with pine in house material. There is also a fair demand for ash and oak that enter into wagon and agricultural machine and implement manufacture.

When we sum up the situation in the country at large, we find that the present condition is that there is activity in white pine, and Norway dimension, in the northwest, with some shortage of stocks and a good outlook, while in respect to trade in other sections of the union no striking features are presented.

At Chicago:

It is evident that the season is near its close. Receipts are light, and the boats are stripping and tying up for the winter. There is not an overwhelming amount to come forward, it being remarked by manufacturers, commission men and yard dealers that there is less surplus product left over than usual. Inquiry from the yards is strong, and prices of piece stuff, good strips and shingles tend to a further advance. The price of short dimension is now solid at $10.25 as the bottom, and the commission men confidently expect to score another advance of 25 cents a thousand before the close of navigation. In respect to slim-jims, though we do not this week raise the quotation, it can be said that in case the cargo, or part of a cargo, runs a good p ag to 22 and 24-feet stuff, it might make a difference in favor of the seller of 25 to 50 cents a thousand. The same would be true in case a lot contained a good percentage of long 2x12. The buyer is now more willing to pay an advance for desirable sorts than he was earlier in the season.

The call for strips of all grades is good, as it has been all the season. Thick selects and uppers are, however, in less urgent request. The trouble with a good deal of upper grade thick stuff, this year, is that it is apt to be crowded in the grading at the mill. This results from the natural tendency of manufacturers to get all they possibly can out of their logs, which average poorer as the seasons pass. Some lots of thick selects have been disappointing on account of shakes, so that dealers are inclined to scan lots offered them with close discrimination.

Promiscuous width common and cull inch is not in sharp demand, though possibly the demand is a little better than it was, and prices are a little stiffer on account of the advance in lake rates.

The Mississippi Valley *Lumberman* as follows:

The sawing season in the white pine States is practically at an end. Very few mills will be running after the current week, and if the weather continues increasingly cold all sawing will be stopped except in the distinctively winter mills. The down river mills have for the most part been out of commission for some time past.

While the lumber market in the West and Northwest has shown healthy conditions, and Minneapolis and Chicago, the great centres of the Western trade, have fairly reflected the activity which has prevailed in the agricultural West, it is evident that the complaint from other quarters has not been without foundation. Failures in the trade south and east and on the Pacific coast have een numerous. These can be traced to the financial stringency from which the country has not yet recovered. Even the big crops have not been sufficient yet to restore the financial equilibrium in certain localities.

A good deal of yellow pine is finding its way into Iowa, Nebraska, Illinois and Ohio, in distinctively white pine territory, but the stocks of white pine are so limited and the demand so great that there is but little complaint heard of competition from the South. But yellow pine is being sold in the more northerly districts, it is claimed, at much less than it might bring, and still command purchasers. Trade in the South even with the call from Northern fields of consumption is by no means vigorous.

NAILS.—The market does not secure any solid improvement, and in some cases operators indulge in a loud wail over the conditions of trade. It seems to be generally conceded that demand must run light and indifferent for balance of year, and the only hope for strengthening is in curtailment of production; but it is doubtful if latter course can be immediately effective in restoring a margin. We quote Cut at $1.50@1.60 per keg for car lots and $1.75@1.85 per keg for parcels from store, for iron, and add 5@10c. per keg for steel; Wire, $2.00@2.05 at mills, and 2.20@2.35 from store.

PAINTS, OILS, COLORS, ETC.—A measure of irregularity may be found in the volume of trade from time to time and dealers say that is due to the shifting custom as one dependent locality fills up with stock and another commences to develop wants. Except for certain very staple articles in the way of house-painters' supplies, etc., the outlet is now tending to shrink away somewhat, but in common with all other trades operators are calculating upon a much better condition of affairs with the advent of spring. Supplies are kept down by manufacturers as much as possible and will taper off in still more decided manner at the end of the year. No quotable changes in values can be learned of and the position may be considered steady for all leading goods, including leads. Association Corroders' rates stand as follows: Lead in oil in kegs and dry lead in kegs, in lots of less than 500 lbs., 7⅛c. net; in lots of 500 lbs to 5 tons at one purchase, 7c.; 5 tons to 12 tons, one purchase, 6⅞c.; 12 tons and over, one purchase, 6¾c.; dry white lead in bbls. ⅛c. per lb. less than price in kegs. Lead in oil 12½ lb. in tin pails, add 1c.; in 25 and 50 lb. tin pails, add ½c.; and in 1 to 5 lb. tin cans, assorted (100 lbs. in case) add 2½c. per lb. to keg price. Terms on lots on 500 lbs. and over, note or acceptance at sixty days, or 2½ per cent. discount will be allowed for cash paid within fifteen days of invoice date. To make either of the above required quantities any assortment of packages of white lead, red lead and litharge may be counted. The above quotations are free on board cars or boat at corroding point. Linseed Oil remains about steady for prime stock and finds a seasonable amount of trade, but common sorts continue more or less unsettled. We quote at general range at 35@40c. for Western, and 40@56c. for City. Spirits Turpentine moves along slowly and without new feature of a pronounced character. On the whole the tone is easy in sympathy, with advices at hand from Southern markets. We quote at 36@37c. per gallon, according to quality, delivery, etc.

TAR AND PITCH.—The movement of supplies continues fairish, but probably on the whole not quite so full as heretofore, and confined in the main to actual immediate wants of buyers. Prices, however, seem to be kept about steady. We quote Pitch at $1.70@1.75 per bbl.; Tar at $2.15@2.50, according to quantity, quality and delivery.

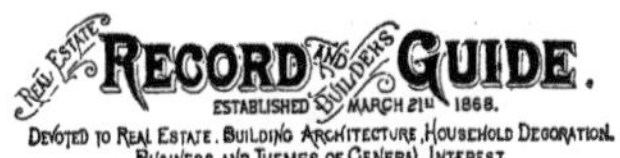

DEVOTED TO REAL ESTATE. BUILDING ARCHITECTURE, HOUSEHOLD DECORATION. BUSINESS AND THEMES OF GENERAL INTEREST

PRICE, PER YEAR IN ADVANCE, SIX DOLLARS.

Published every Saturday.

TELEPHONE - - - - CORTLANDT 1370.

Communications should be addressed to

C. W. SWEET, 14 & 16 Vesey St.

J. T. LINDSEY, Business Manager.

VOL. XLVIII NOVEMBER 28, 1891. NO. 1,237

THE conditions determining the movement of prices in Wall Street have not varied to any extent during the past week; consequently values have remained about constant. There has, indeed, been a perceptible easing up in the money market; for currency is beginning to return from the West. With a continuation of the present very heavy exports of wheat and other products we may expect during the early months of the coming year an exceptionally low rate for money—a state of things which ought to give to the bond market its long-expected rise. Then, too, the foreign situation is far less threatening than it was. Financiers in all the large European cities seem to be gaining confidence; and while they are not likely to buy our stocks largely, while so many of their own good investment securities are selling cheaply, still their troubles will for the present cease to menace our market. These better conditions have not, however, had any very material effect on prices. The probable reason that the excellent prospects are not immediately discounted to a larger extent is that an indisposition to advance prices is always felt just around the beginning of a Congressional session; and this year is not liable to prove an exception to the general rule. Furthermore there are some undeniably weak spots in the situation. The South is still to such a large extent dependent on cotton for prosperity that the prevailing low price which that product brings will keep that large section of the country depressed for some time to come. This fact, however, is not of any general significance. It remains true that the year 1891 closes with the financial outlook far brighter than were the prospects at the end of 1889 or 1890. A little earlier than this last year the Baring crisis tried men's pockets, while the December of 1889 was troubled by rumors of rate wars and like financial disasters. Now, however, our troubles are either local or rather impalpable. For the last ten years eminent financiers have been nervous about Congress' action respecting silver. All these fears have proved groundless hitherto, and this year also they are not likely continuously to affect prices adversely.

A HOPEFUL sign which may be fairly claimed as the first result of the protest against the secret use of the Lake Erie & Western Railroad stockholders' proxies is the statement in the *Sun* of Thursday that "a resolution was passed (by the Board of Directors of the Richmond Terminal Company) stating definitely to what purpose the proxies should be put, which Mr. Inman is authorized to solicit and vote at the annual meeting on December 8th." This is precisely as it should be. Trustees ought never to ask for a proxy, which is but a power of attorney from their *cestuis qui* trust, without stating explicitly for what purpose the proxies are to be used. If THE RECORD AND GUIDE has in any measure contributed to the alteration of these loose methods it will consider itself amply repaid for all the space given to this matter. A collateral result of this neglect to do this is as follows: If the stockholders of the Lake Erie & Western Railroad had been clearly informed in advance that it was proposed to use their proxies in June, 1890, to put a second mortgage on the property, they would have been able to see to it that the resolutions authorizing such action embodied in their terms every condition and restriction which was necessary as a safeguard for the proper marketing of the securities and the expenditure of the money realized. As it is no stockholder has any means of knowing what the securities are going to bring, nor precisely what the company is going to get back in the way of assets in exchange for them. All the stockholders do know is that if the extraordinary and outrageous action of their trustees can stand unquestioned, they will be left only to the tender mercies of Mr. Brice for such return as they may eventually get. What the mercies of Mr. Brice are likely to be stockholders can perhaps infer from general repute and from such knowledge as they may possess of the fate of other properties which have fallen into his hands. It might not be amiss just at this juncture to point with warning finger to the fate of the Richmond Terminal property as illustrative of what stockholders in the Lake Erie & Western Company may expect if at this juncture they fail to assert their rights and protect themselves against this way of doing business.

Rapid Transit Possibilities.

PENDING the result of the canvass of Broadway property-owners, which is now being vigorously undertaken, discussion respecting the prospects, merits and dangers of the Commission's plan has almost entirely ceased. The Commonwealth Club have indeed been considering their old oft-pondered problem, but the discussion was edifying, not so much because of the light which it threw upon the plan of the Commission as because of the effectual manner in which it refuted the claim of the enemies of the Manhattan Company that the intelligent public opinion of the city is opposed to granting to that corporation any extension or enlargement of its present system. But the opinions of the speakers at the Commonwealth Club have not brought forth any comment by the newspapers, which are waiting for the Commission to go on with its work—if it can.

Very possibly this silence will be succeeded by a storm. The Commission's plan was received with ill-concealed hostility by certain of the papers and we may be sure that this hostility was exhausted in the trivial criticisms which constituted the whole of its ostensible justification. Apart, however, from the more or less powerful enmity of this character which the plan has encountered and will encounter, there are several obstacles of a more serious character, the existence of which is known, but the resistance of which still remains dubious. In the first place, delays may take place in satisfying legal requirements. Probably a number of Broadway property-owners will give their consent to the plan sufficient to make an appeal to the Supreme Court unnecessary; but this is by no means certain, several of the largest owners having expressed themselves as opposed to any tunnel near the surface. Consequently no one can tell when the Commissioners will be in a position to offer the franchise for sale. Equally uncertain is the prospect of selling the franchise to advantage. It is necessary that any company operating should put on a service of unusual speed and convenience, for it will be an indispensable element in the work to be performed by the new system that t should be efficient enough to overcome the advantage which Brooklyn possesses over the upper wards of this city in respect to contiguity to the business districts. The Rapid Transit Commissioners will then have to insist on a service of this character, and yet at the same time will scarcely wish to sell a franchise of such great ultimate value upon very unfavorable terms.

The difficulties attending such a sale have been repeatedly pointed out by THE RECORD AND GUIDE. The system will be especially designed to meet the needs of the least remunerative class of traffic; it will have to give its patrons unusual comforts and conveniences, and even if capital sees money in the project, in spite of these mitigating circumstances it will have to be constructed at a time when the best classes of bonds are difficult of sale. We are not trying to estimate the resistance of these obstacles, neither are we trying to predict the outcome; but one important question arising from the possibility that these obstacles will prove insuperable needs asking and answering. If the Commissioners find it impossible to satisfy legal requirements with their plan, they will have no alternative but to relieve the almost intolerable inadequacy of the present service by giving to the Manhattan Company, so far as lies within their power, authority to improve its service. But what if the Commission finds that the franchise cannot be sold, or that it can be sold only on such terms as will make the contract a very bad bargain for the city? This question may have to be faced, and it is well to search for an alternative. Doubtless, any corporation that bids will believe that it has the municipality in a tight place, and if possible it will squeeze concessions out of the commissioners, which would place our authorities at a great disadvantage in all its subsequent dealings with the corporation, and would fasten on the transit service of New York another railroad as insatiate and unmanageable as the Manhattan Company.

That this is scarcely a desirable consummation every one will admit; but what are we going to do about it? The plan might be altered, but it could be altered only by decreasing the efficiency of the system, and that is, from the necessity of the case, excluded. The logic of events seems to be drawing our authorities to consider seriously whether the city should not be placed, by legislation, in a position to build the system for itself. New York can issue bonds for more than $45,000,000 before its borrowing power under the constitutional limitation will be exhausted, so that there are no obstacles in that direction. The system could be built far more cheaply by the municipality than by a private corporation; for New York could borrow at 3 per cent, while a private corporation would have to pay at least 8 per cent. If the system should cost

$60,000,000 the fixed charges would be $1,800,000 less in one case than in another. This is nearly one-fifth of the gross income of the Manhattan Company at the present time; it is 5 cents a head from 36,000,000 passengers every year—more than the number of passengers at present carried by the Broadway & Seventh Avenue Railroad Company. The saving of such a sum every year might mean all the difference between the failure of the system to accomplish its purpose and its success; for, in order to succeed completely, in order to place Westchester County and the upper wards of New York on equal terms with Long Island and New Jersey in the competition for our increase of our population, the system will have to give a service unequalled the world over for speed, for convenience, and for cheapness.

"But," some will cry, "admitting the force of these arrangements, we do not dare to place the spending of all this money into the hands of Tammany. It would provide an unlimited opportunity for jobbery, and the work would employ a number of laborers sufficient to turn the scale in any closely-contested election meanwhile." But surely the Legislature can provide that the money need not be spent by Tammany; any more than that the money spent in the present Aqueduct was distributed through the agency of that organization. The work could be done under the supervision of the present Rapid Transit Commission, the integrity of whose members and their ability to take care of the interests of the city are beyond question. The Tammany contractors would have just as much show as any other set of contractors.

The final solution of this rapid transit question will have an effect on the city's future more vital than any other condition within the present perspective. New York's topography renders it dependent upon rapid transit service in a unique degree; more than any other city of which we know, it has more to gain by an excellent service and more to lose by a mediocre one. With the commercial and property interests of the city thus largely dependent on a supremely excellent transit system, it would not be unnatural for New York to own it. Foreign municipalities with much less at stake have built and leased the local transit systems, so that there are plenty of precedents. Furthermore the solution of the tenement house problem hinges precisely on the same point. We do not say that New York should undertake this stupendous task, but we do say that under the circumstances it is worth the carefullest consideration.

THE Park Commissioners have finally decided not to revoke the permit, whereby the Manhattan Company retains its structure in Battery Park. How ridiculous would have been a decision to the contrary effect! If at the very moment when the rapid transit facilities of New York were cryingly deficient, its public officials had seriously hampered the only corporation that can pretend to give the public anything like a sufficient service, it would, indeed, have been bad government raised to a very high power. This ought to be the end of that childish "Citizens'" movement—a movement which, from its inception, and in spite of its enormous pretensions, has been representative of nothing save a pitiful minority of well-intentioned citizens, backed by newspaper demagogy. Its career has served to show what a small influence is exercised editorially by our daily journals. Nearly all of them for years have been condemning the Manhattan Company and calling its occupation of Battery Park a "steal," yet when some few reputable men endeavored to crystallize the sentiment against the company, which, as one might have supposed, had been thus created, they failed signally to give the slightest vitality to their campaign. If they endeavor to keep it up in the Legislature during the coming year they will meet with another rebuff equally decisive. When political or personal interests are not concerned legislators frequently permit themselves to be bull-dozed into compliance with demands that are made in the name of the "people," even though their judgment is opposed to such an action; but in this case the false nature of such a claim has been so clearly shown that they can afford to ignore it. But even if by any chance a bill dispossessing the company should slip through, Governor-elect Flower could hardly go so far back on his well-known partiality to "home rule" as to help revoke the action of our municipal officials on a purely local matter.

THE circular published last week in these columns and issued to members of the Mechanics' and Traders' Exchange by the committee who have charge of the matter has drawn attention pointedly to the much-delayed project to erect a handsome exchange in this city in keeping with the wealth and importance of the building interests of the metropolis, even if it has not created instantaneously great financial enthusiasm. But this latter will follow. The circular has at least done this good office; it has brought the project to the point of action. There is a centre now to the scheme which has hitherto been nothing more than a vague and undefined intention. It is yet too early to estimate the probability of the 250 subscribers with $1,000 each coming forward; but this is certain, the first step towards the establishment of a great exchange on the lines of those in Boston and Philadelphia has been taken. There are many people, we believe, who would subscribe much more than a thousand dollars to a well-planned and organized enterprise of the kind, and we are sure there are a much larger number who, possessing smaller means, would yet subscribe enough to bring the aggregate far above the $250,000 which the committee require for a "starter." Of the ultimate success of the project there is no doubt. A building of the kind proposed is needed; it will pay,—and that is the guarantee of success.

WE print in another column a series of interviews with prominent merchants, which is of the nature of a protest against the bad faith of the Dock Department and their gross disregard of the general public interests in their management of the city's water front. The piers on the East and West Sides, particularly down town, are now practically completely in the hands of private individuals and corporations. The shipping accommodations provided for the general public use are miserably inadequate and inconvenient. The building trades particularly are sufferers, and through them, of course, the entire city. The vast lumber interest, for instance, located on the North River, between Houston and 30th streets, are compelled to a large extent to load and unload their supplies above 42d street, though no inconsiderable portion is used in the southern part of the island. Indeed, as one of the gentlemen interviewed points out, the thousands of tons of material used in the reconstruction of the Equitable Life Assurance Society's building had to be carted from, it may be said, up-town, because there was no pier south of 11th street for public use. The policy or certainly the practice of the Dock Department in this matter does not accord with public interests, and the rental which the city receives from the piers needed doesn't pay or begin to pay for the damage done.

IT is very well known that in London and the English cities generally, local taxation is assessed not upon the saleable value of the property, but on the rent per annum. The system has certain advantages over our own, but above all it has this advantage: it interests the occupiers in the spending of public moneys far more than they are interested under our own method. In New York only the few thousand owners come into any immediate contact with the tax collector; under the English system the million and more of occupiers would pay money directly into the municipal treasury. Nevertheless, the Local Government and Taxation Committee of the London County Council have become dissatisfied with the action of this method of levying taxes, and have submitted a report, in which they plead strongly for a division of the taxes between occupiers and owners. The argument is that the present method of levying local taxation is unjust to the owner. It is true no one denies that the occupier gets his house at a lower rent than he would have to give if a portion of the taxes were charged to the owner; but despite this fact it is held that the incidence of local taxation falls with unfair severity on the lessee, and that this injustice would be removed by the proposed division. The argument used is as follows: In London, most of the ground property is leased on long terms, and it is complained that the lessees have of late years had to bear the burden of a much heavier rate of taxation than formerly. Furthermore, this growth of London taxes has to a large extent been on account of expenditure that has enhanced the value of house property. The committee call attention to the fact that in 1855 the first combination of London into a whole for purposes of improvement took place. "The immediate purpose was arterial drainage, but this proved to be only the first step in a course of general improvement which has been pursued ever since with increasing rapidity. In 1870 the School Board began to act. Other demands have since been made for improvements of a more local character, such as open spaces, baths, wash-houses and libraries. Under our leasehold system the bulk of all this new and very heavy expenditure has been borne by tenants and occupiers. The landlords have contracted themselves out of the payment of rates and the other parties to the covenants have been saddled with burdens which they could not possibly have anticipated or taken into account when they entered into the contract. It is impossible that those who in 1855 covenanted to pay all rates for a number of years contemplated such a complete change of policy, or that for many years afterwards those who made like covenants thought that the stream of expenditure was to increase in volume as it has done." This argument, it will be seen, rests entirely upon the fact that covenants respecting the leasing of London realty are made for a long term of years; in these covenants taxes enter as a variable element, and they have been varying altogether on the side of the property-owners. As it has been the action of the Legislature which has rendered these contracts inequitable, so the Legislature may justly vary the term so as to restore their fairness.

THIS argument, although it carries some weight, ought to be qualified far more than the committee of the County Council thought necessary to qualify it. For it must be remembered that the lessees, if they bear the whole burden of the increase in taxes, also reap the whole of the benefit so long as their lease lasts, and it is only so long as the lease lasts that any injustice can take place. Undoubtedly, however, their increased expenditures for taxation would add something to the permanent value of the property, and consequently in equity some small share of any increase in taxation might with equity be transferred to the shoulders of the owners. If by any possibility, however, the system of making the occupiers of real property pay the taxes immediately, as they now do immediately, there would be no need of complicating the system. The practice of leasing ground property for long terms is, fortunately, not very common in New York, and it is only large buildings that are sometimes let for an exteusive period of years. The aggregate would not be sufficient to justify any distribution of the incidence of taxation. The fact, however, that the proposal of taxing owners is being seriously considered in London is an interesting indication of the extent to which the administration of that city are studying American examples in this matter. Lately the County Council were discussing a proposition to widen the Strand, which at present is choked with traffic. Under the present English system the expense of such improvements would be met entirely out of a general fund instead, as is the prevalent practice through the whole of this country, of assessing a certain part of it on the property directly benefited. A strong effort was made by some of the reformers to introduce American methods in the matter of this widening of the Strand. They were beaten in the attempt; but the opinion is that eventually they will be able to transplant the system to English soil. The London County Council contains, unfortunately, so many cranks that almost every innovation proposed in that body is met with distrust by conservative people.

More Public Piers Required.

For some years past business men, particularly on the East and West Sides, have been complaining of the inadequate facilities which the Dock Department has provided for merchants and business men for the receipt and shipment of goods and material on the city's water front. The policy of that department appears to have been to lease nearly all the piers to steamship and railroad companies and to let the great business interests of New York, outside of the sphere of those companies, take care of themselves.

The greatest sufferers from this policy have been the building material interests. As building is one of the largest local interests of the metropolis it would seem that the authorities would give it due consideration in their plans for pier accommodations. So far from receiving considerable attention, it appears to have received very little whatever. Not only that, but the Dock Department, which had set aside certain piers for public use, has now leased such piers for private use, and so broken faith with the business men of New York. An instance of this is to be seen in the pier at the foot of 21st street, North River. In 1880 the Dock Commissioners agreed, in writing, with a committee representing the lumber and other interests, to set aside that pier for the public use. Some time ago, however, they leased it to the State Line, thus cutting it off from public use. The business men sent a remonstrance to the department, and the Commissioners' reply was that the agreement had been "forgotten." The counsel for the business men referred them to the books of the department and showed them the record of the agreement. However, the lease had been effected, and it was felt that to go into court would only involve long and costly proceedings, in which the business men stood a fair chance of being worsted. Sufficient pressure was brought to bear on the department to secure a promise that another pier would be substituted for that taken away. It was agreed that the pier at the foot of 20th street, North River, should be the one, and on Wednesday of last week work was commenced on that pier, which is contracted for to be completed in March, 1892. In the meantime, lumber merchants—who are most affected by the breach of faith of the Dock Department—will be compelled to do the best they can with the present dock facilities.

Another pier which was set aside for public use was that at 27th street and North River. It has since been leased by the Dock Department to the Terminal Warehouse Company, and the general public is deprived of its use. The pier at 19th street and North River was also set aside, but half of it is used for dumping purposes.

Chas. A. Meigs, of the old-established lumber firm of Ogden & Co., No. 411 Washington street, said: "There is a vast lumber interest on the North River, between Houston and 30th streets. We are to a large extent compelled to load and unload above 42d street. This is unjust to us and to the building material trade. Hundreds of thousands of tons of material have to be hauled long distances every year to buildings between the Battery and 42d street, and a vast expense is caused to consignors, contractors and others because there are no piers down town where goods can be landed near the buildings into which they are to be put. There is another side to this. THE RECORD AND GUIDE has recently been writing about our blocked streets, and suggesting remedies. It has been estimated that 35,000 tons of building material had to be carted through the streets for the Equitable Life Assurance Society's building alone because of the non-existence of public piers south of 11th street. In 1886 the New York Lumber Trade Association, the Board of Trade and Transportation and the Mercantile and Maritime Exchanges obtained the passage of a measure through the Assembly and Senate providing for a public pier at every quarter of a mile along the city's water front. This bill, when it got to Governor Hill, was vetoed by him on technical grounds, but it was generally believed that the railroad and steamship companies who would have been affected by its passage brought their influence to bear on the Governor. It was also opposed by the Dock Department through the President of the Metropolitan Steamship Company, an ex-Commissioner of that department. Besides the New York organizations I have mentioned, the lumber associations and exchanges of Rochester, Buffalo, Tonawanda and Albany supported the bill, and it was only by the combined efforts of the country and city members that we were able to get the bill to the Governor."

Geo. W. Wanamaker, of Geo. W. Karr & Co., lumber merchants, who was for seventeen years in the Dock Department and for nearly four years Dock Master along the North River, said: "I have come to the conclusion, after several years of hard work in this matter, that it is useless to try and fight the railroad and steamship companies who want the piers. You cannot get up enough enthusiasm of the right sort among the business men in New York, affected, to get them to enforce the passage of a bill which will set aside a sufficient number of piers to accommodate the vessels that bring building material to this city. At this moment there are only three or four bulkheads south of 11th street for public use; the rest are leased to private parties."

"How many piers, in your opinion, would be sufficient for the building material interests south of 14th street?" asked the reporter.

"Two piers would be enough, in addition to the present bulkheads," was the reply.

E. H. Ogden, Secretary of the Lumber Trades Association, was seen. He said: "Our nearest pier was at 21st street. They have leased that and we now have to go to 28th street. Such indignation was expressed at the lease of the 21st street pier to a private corporation that the Dock Department was compelled to give us the pier at 20th street; but we shall lose the advantage of it at a time when we stand in need of it. We ought to have a great many more piers on the city water front for public use. The city leases most of its piers to private corporations."

S. McClave, son of John McClave, 11th avenue and 22d street, said: "Now that the Dock Department is going to substitute the 20th street pier for the 21st street pier, I think we had better dismiss the subject as far as the merchants in our immediate vicinity are concerned." John McClave is Police Commissioner, and one of the large lumbermen on the West Side.

W. R. Wilder, of No 33 Pine street, lawyer for the merchants who obtained an injunction against the use of Pier 27, East River, by the Baltimore & Ohio Company, said: "Our injunction has been removed by the Superior Court, and I have had no instructions as yet to carry the matter to a higher court. This pier was reserved, under statute, for deep water vessels for the general public, and was used by boats in the China and Eastern trade. Its lease by the Dock Department to the B. & O. people is illegal, in the opinion of my clients." The B. & O. R. R. Co. have commenced to construct a shed on the pier.

A West Side merchant who was seen yesterday said that vessels had to wait for days sometimes to get into dock and obtain a berth to unload, in the meantime paying demurrage. The other day he learned of a case where $50 demurrage was paid on a small cargo owing to the boat being unable to get a berth on arrival. "Does any one suppose," he said, "that these things are not hurting the business of New York."

Questions for the Dock and Public Works Departments.

1. A bill was passed in the session of 1890 making it obligatory that an upper deck for the use of the people should be built on all sheds constructed on piers thereafter. A number of sheds have since been built, but no upper decks have appeared. How is it that the Dock Department has permitted the violation of this law?

2. For miles along the water front, particularly on the West Side, the public streets are being used by various corporations and individuals for storage purposes. In some places about 130 to 140 feet of the street is taken up. By what right does the city allow this? The corporations make no payment therefor and are trespassers. Why are they not compelled to store their goods? "That stuff ought to go into storage warehouses," said a prominent business man to a RECORD AND GUIDE reporter. Another business man pointed to several hundred barrels of poisonous chemical matter. These barrels often get broken and become a source of danger to horses and pedestrians. In December last a boy was nearly burned to death at the dock of the Inman Steamship Company by lye which had rolled out of some barrels and formed into a puddle of water into which he had slipped. The other day a team of horses had their legs badly burned by some chemicals under similar circumstances and they had to be killed.

For Failure to Supply Water.

A somewhat unusual case was decided against the Trinity Church Corporation on Wednesday. The Health Department entered suit against that corporation for failure to supply Croton water on the first, second and third floors of Nos. 77 and 84 Charlton street, after being requested to do so by the department. These buildings are occupied for living purposes, and their only sources of supply are in the basement and back yard. The action was first brought in the Third District Court and then removed to the Court of Common Pleas. Judge Giegerich rendered a verdict against the Corporation for $200. The latter took exceptions to the ruling, and these exceptions will be heard at the Common Pleas General Term. W. S. Prentice appeared for the Health Department, and S. P. Nash for Trinity Church Corporation.

New Up-Town Streets.

In Supreme Court Chambers, on Wednesday, commissioners were appointed in the matter of acquiring title by the city to the necessary property for opening 131st street, from 10th to Convent avenue; 187th street, from 10th avenue to Kingsbridge road; Fort Independence street, from its junction with Boston avenue to Broadway; Welch street, from the New York & Harlem Railroad to Webster avenue, and Pelham avenue westward to Webster avenue.

Echoes of a Better Market.

Geo. R. Read, President of the Real Estate Exchange, states that there is a greatly improved tone to the market compared with a few weeks ago. There is a plethora of money in the banks and he anticipates a good real estate market in the immediate future.

John R. Foley states that buyers are much more numerous than they have been. There is a decided disposition to invest in real estate. A little concession by both buyer and seller in many cases would result in a number of sales.

F. R. Houghton says that the market is in a healthier state. He did not anticipate the improvement till after the new year, but it has already shown itself.

Secretary Jas. E. Leviness was seen on 'Change. "Money," he said, "is much easier, and I look toward a good market for real estate in the spring. I made some loans this week on a valuation of 70 per cent of the property, and I would have found it difficult last month to obtain the money."

To Annul Assessments.

Several petitions were handed into Comptroller Myers, on Wednesday, by property-owners who desire the assessments annulled for filling in vacant lots on 143d and 145th streets.

Contractors' Notes.

Bids or proposals for building two brick engine houses for the portable hoisting plants, one of which to be located at the Dunwoodie Gate House, Yonkers, N. Y., and the other at the Pocantico Gate House, North Tarrytown, N. Y., of the New Croton Aqueduct, as called for in the approved forms of contract and specicfiations on file in the office of the Aqueduct Commissioners, will be received at their office No. 280 Broadway, Room No. 209, until 3 o'clock P. M. on Wednesday, December 9th.

Sealed bids or estimates for furnishing materials and work required for steam heating pavilion for New York City Asylum for Insane, Blackwell's Island; also materials and work required for repairs to Randall's Island stables, will be received at the office of the Department of Public Charities and Correction, No. 66 3d avenue, in the City of New York, until Wednesday, December 9, 1891, until 10 A. M.

Real Estate Department.

The improved feeling in the realestate market, of which we spoke last week, continues, and is, if anything, more pronounced than it has been. Men are talking brighter and acting quicker, and parties to transactions under way are apparently less obstinate in the matter of concessions than they have been for some time past. Altogether, while real estate is still rather quiet, it is less so than it has been, and that is matter for congratulation. December is always a dull month, and this year will probably prove no exception to the rule, but compared with the preceding eleven months of the year it may in a measure retrieve the record for the whole year. The week's business was interrupted by a holiday, and the number of consummated transactions reported is, therefore, not quite so large as it would otherwise have been. But this week has not been nearly as dull as many of recent date, when there has been no holiday. Our reports include a $650,000 sale of the northeast corner of Broadway and 32d street, a five-story building, a plot 98.9 on Broadway by 123 on 32d street, with irregular depths. It was bought by a member of the firm who occupy the ground floor, which is in itself an interesting fact, emphasizing as it does the movement on the part of large business concerns to acquire the buildings in which their establishments are located. This sale will probably do much to revive the confidence that has been lacking for some time in transactions where the property concerned was even so safe an investment as New York City business buildings. Besides this Broadway sale the lot market has shown a more active disposition. On the West Side this week there have been numerous large lot sales and re-sales to builders who will immediately improve their purchases. When these sales have become more generally known a great many other transactions that have been hanging fire, some of them for months, may be closed, and then, perhaps, with a successful December we may have some warrant in expecting the prosperous spring season that has been talked about quite confidently, notwithstanding the dull fall market. Brokers seem more cheerful over the situation than they have for months past, and the enthusiasm almost encourages one to believe that the long sleep is over. It is surely time.

NORTH SIDE AND WOODLAWN LOTS SOLD.

Evidently the cheap lot business has not been overdone, at least that is what Monday's sales of lots in the 23d Ward and the City of Yonkers would seem to indicate. Notwithstanding the unpleasant weather the Auction Room was comfortably filled with a well-to-do looking crowd, whose bidding was ready, though not anxious. An incident to these sales, and an incident that is thought to have had a very good effect on prices, was the use, for the first time, of the 150 electric lights which have been placed in the Exchange. The room was dark and gloomy, as it always is on rainy days before the lights were turned on, and the auctioneers doubtless would have had a hard time in arousing any amount of enthusiasm as matters then stood. The lights were turned on, and both the room and the buyers became more cheerful on the instant. As has been said, this cheerfulness in their surroundings doubtless influenced the bidding; but the attendance and the general attitude of those present seems to indicate that there is still a fair chance to sell suburban property at reasonable figures.

Auctioneer Richard V. Harnett sold about ninety lots in the 23d Ward, on Prospect, Union, Tinton and Wales avenues, near and on 152d street. The prices obtained ranged from $510 to $1,150 for inside lots and from $1,025 to $1,600 for corners. These figures are considered very good by those competent to judge of neighboring values. On Prospect avenue inside lots sold at from $650 to $800, and the corner of 152d street for $1,500. Union avenue inside lots ranged from $535 to $650, and $1,025 and $1,075 for corners, while immediately in the rear, on Tinton avenue, corner lots sold at $1,300 and $1,600, and inside lots from $510 to $900 each. The most interesting feature of the sale was the purchase by St. Anselm's Roman Catholic Church of a block of sixteen lots at Tinton avenue, corner of Dawson street, upon which they propose to erect a church, parish house, school, etc; $800 apiece was paid for these lots. The other buyers included B. P. Fairchild, Wm. R. Bloodgood, J. F. Vosatka, Charlotte Ohle, Jas. B. Baxter, Jas. Beggs and Leonora Bell.

The other lot sale was held under the direction of James L. Wells, and it consisted of 173 lots belonging to the Hyatt farm, at Woodlawn. About fifteen of these lots are in this city, while the remainder are located across the city line in Yonkers. These were, as advertised, cheap lots, and the low figures at which they were sold were, all things considered, very good prices. The lots being less expensive than those offered at the other sale attracted a larger crowd which bought up every lot that was offered. The lots in the 24th Ward, on the Bronx road, sold for $275 and $450, according to their depth, while those on the same road, but in Yonkers, and a little further from the railway station, brought $220 and $250 each. On Oakley avenue the prices ran from $60 to $130 for inside and from $100 to $235 for corner lots. The remaining lots on the intersecting places sold from $50 to $85 each.

THE OTHER SALES.

The city and the one or two out-of-town offerings during the week do not suggest much that is of interest to the general market. The week, broken as it was by Thanksgiving Day, had only a short list of offerings to start with and when the withdrawals and fictitious sales had been subtracted there remained but a small list of completed transactions. As during last week, and in fact throughout the season, owners put their holdings up at auction seemingly with the single intention of testing it, and finding that the buyers had more modest ideas than themselves in the matter of prices they withdrew what they had offered in one way or another. Many of the voluntary offerings, therefore, did not meet with a successful sale and those that did were neither interesting nor important. The legal sales of the week were little better. The properties offered were insignificant and the competition far from exciting. In two cases parcels sold under foreclosure failed to realize the amount due. The first of these was the northwest corner of 1st avenue and 105th street, which sold for $60,000 as against $68,187, the amount due, and the second was the southeast corner of Columbus avenue and 118th street, upon which there were mortgages and costs of over $18,000 due and the selling price of which was only $10,000.

THE ANNOUNCEMENTS.

Next week the offerings will not be particularly numerous, but they will include the most interesting property that has been put up for sale at auction this year. It includes a partition sale of the Dash estate properties, which comprise No. 145 Broadway, and Nos. 86 and 88 Liberty street—taking up the entire front on Liberty street, from Broadway to Temple street; No. 70 Cortlandt street and No. 219 Fulton street. This sale, to take place on Thursday, will be under the direction of A. H. Muller & Son, who will also offer, on the same day, No. 697 6th avenue, southwest corner of 40th street. This property has not been transferred since 1857, when it was sold for $3,000. In addition to the above sales, which in themselves are enough to attract the widest attention, Wm. Kennelly will offer in partition No. 753 Madison avenue, near 65th street. This house was last transferred in 1886 for $40,000. Richard V. Harnett & Co. also have a sale that will doubtless attract attention. It is of Nos. 20 and 22 New Bowery, running through to New Chambers street, and immediately adjoining the junction of those streets.

On Monday, November 30th, Smyth & Ryan will sell the four-story brick tenement, No. 604 West 45th street.

On Wednesday, December 2d, Richard V. Harnett & Co. will sell the four-story brick dwelling, No. 76 Horatio street; the two three-story brick buildings, Nos. 20 and 22 New Bowery, and the four-story brown stone dwelling (leasehold) No. 13 West 50th street.

On Thursday, December 3d, Richard V. Harnett & Co. will sell the three-story brown stone dwelling, No. 211 East 34th street.

One of the most important sales of the year will be held on Thursday, December 3d, by Adrian H. Muller & Son. This sale is by order of the Supreme Court, in partition, and the property offered is the choicest kind of business and investment parcels. The following is a list of them: No. 145 Broadway, on the southwest corner of Liberty street; Nos. 86 and 88 Liberty street, on the southeast corner of Temple place; No. 70 Cortlandt street, between Greenwich and Washington streets, and No. 219 Fulton street, between Greenwich and Church streets. The sale is held under the direction of Wilbur Larremore, Esq., and 70 per cent of the purchase money may remain on bond and mortgage for three or five years at 5 per cent. It is seldom that such a valuable class of property is offered on the Exchange on such favorable terms.

CONVEYANCES.

	1890. Nov. 21 to 27 inc.	1891. Nov. 20 to 26 inc.
Number	257	205
Amount involved	$3,454,208	$2,759,290
Number nominal	72	67
Number 23d and 24th Wards	81	51
Amount involved	$257,045	$101,235
Number nominal	11	14

MORTGAGES.

	1890.	1891.
Number	267	262
Amount involved	$3,630,169	$3,109,103
Number at 5 $	127	122
Amount involved	$1,460,311	$1,776,158
Number at less than 5 per cent	31	21
Amount involved	$554,600	$248,000
Number to Banks, Trust and Ins. Cos	43	49
Amount involved	$935,808	$1,005,684

PROJECTED BUILDINGS.

	1890. Nov. 22 to 28 inc.	1891. Nov. 21 to 27 inc.
Number of buildings	80	45
Estimated cost	$1,037,229	$528,015

Gossip of the Week.

SOUTH OF 59TH STREET.

J. Romaine Brown & Co. have consummated one of the most important sales of the season. They have sold for the estate of George Sloane the property on the northeast corner of Broadway and 32d street to Wm. R. H. Martin, of the firm of Rogers, Peet & Co., for $650,000. The parcel comprises an irregular plot of about three and three-fifth lots, with the five-story store, office and apartment building thereon, the first floor of which is occupied by Rogers, Peet & Co., and the second floor by D. & J. Jardine, the architects, the upper floors being mainly leased for private residence purposes. The property has a frontage of 53.10 feet on Broadway and 123 feet on 32d street, with a depth on the northerly side of 147.2 feet irregular and a depth on the easterly side of 98.9 feet. It was purchased in 1872 by George Sloane for $265,000, the corner, 17x10x74.2x—x50, and the lot adjoining, 36x74.2, being transferred to Mr. Sloane by Pierpont Morgan, the banker, on July 15, 1872, for $225,000, and the street lot adjoining, 23x98.9, on August 31, 1872, by Edgar Williams, of Woodstock, to the same purchaser for $40,000. This shows an advance of $385,000 in the nineteen years. Mr. Martin does not propose to make any alterations to the property at present.

Morris B. Baer & Co. have sold for the Burns estate the two four-story French basement brick and stone front houses, Nos. 249 and 251 Madison avenue, 16x60x80, adjoining the northeast corner of 38th street, on private terms.

Fred. A. Carll has sold for Mark P. Brennan the northwest corner of 53d street and 7th avenue, a five-story store and flat, 25x100, for $78,250.

Louis Lese has purchased from Mrs. Charlotte Harris No. 79 Columbia street, 25x100, with four-story front and rear buildings thereon, on private terms, and from H. Mandelbaum No. 42 Essex street, a six-story brick tenement, 25x80x100, also on private terms.

The United Grocers' Association has purchased from Chas. Lang and J. H. Berge the two 18-foot dwellings on the south side of 57th street, 100 feet east of Lexington avenue, on private terms.

B. Taylor has sold for Sarah Taylor to Herman Michaels No. 436 West 23d street, a four-story brick dwelling, 24.10x55x98.9, for $24,000.

Wm. R. Mason has sold for the estate of M. E. Hassard the three-story brick dwelling, No. 335 West 35th street, 15x50x98.9, for $10,000, and for T. B. Thompson the four-story front and rear buildings, on a lot 25x98.9, No. 365 West 35th street, on private terms.

W. B. Taylor & Sons have sold the four-story high stoop house No. 52 West 49th street (Columbia College leasehold), 20.10x55x100.5, running for eighteen years and two renewals, for $17,500.

E. A. Cruikshank & Co. have sold for the Horatio Schermerhorn estate the four-story dwelling and lot, northeast corner Lexington avenue and 46th street, 20x100, for $29,000.

Plunkitt & McKenna have sold No. 553 West 44th street, for Mrs. Mary Carey to F. M. Horton, on private terms.

Sire Bros. have purchased the five-story tenement, 26x70, at the corner of Hester and Mott streets, for $36,500.

C. Wolinski has sold to Philip Kotlowsky No. 187 Allen street for $16,500 for improvement.

Ascher Weinstein has purchased from Mary L. Conners No. 34 West 27th street, a four-story and basement brown stone dwelling, 23x65x98.9, on private terms. Mr. Weinstein has sold to Benedict A. Klein No. 28 Henry street on private terms for improvement.

NORTH OF 59TH STREET.

John W. Stevens has sold to Guttwillig Bros. and Hirsh Bros. the following lots: For a Mr. Patton one lot on the south side of 90th street, 325 feet west of Central Park West, on private terms; for Thomas Hitchcock the four lots south side of 90th street, 350 feet west of Central Park West, and for Mary A. Vandewater and Mrs. Douglass the three lots adjoining, also on private terms. Mr. Stevens has resold the above lots, together with five additional lots on the south side of 90th street, 200 feet west of Central Park West, for Gutwillig Bros. and Hirsch Bros. to Walden P. Anderson, with a building loan, on private terms, for improvement. Mr. Stevens has also sold for W. P. Anderson to a Mrs. Ransom No. 158 West 93d street, a three-story brown stone front dwelling, 15.6x50 and extension x102.2, on private terms.

F. Zittel has sold for John P. Huggins to Walker & Lawson, two lots on the north side of 95th street, 300 feet east of Columbus avenue, on private terms, for improvement; for Charles T. Barney to John C. Umberfield about seven lots on the north side of 75th street, 388 feet east of Columbus avenue, for about $130,000; also for improvement and for John Conley to John C. Umberfield a 20-foot lot adjoining the above for $16,600.

Alfred E. Beach, of the *Scientific American*, has sold to F. M. Jeucks, the lawyer, the block front on the west side of West End avenue, between and on 98th and 99th streets, 201.10x100, on private terms. Lawyer John H. Deane is understood to have been the broker.

Charles T. Barney has sold four lots on the north side of 76th street, 100 feet east of Columbus avenue, for $72,000, and a plot 35 feet front on the north side of 90th street, between West End avenue and Riverside Drive, for $20,000.

Edw. P. Hamilton & Co. have sold two four-story brown stone dwellings on Riverside Drive south of 82d street, to C. Weidenfeld for $74,000.

Walden P. Anderson has sold to J. D. Hall No. 142 West 93d street, a four-story brown stone dwelling, 20x52 and extension x102.2, on private terms. This leaves only three houses unsold out of a row of eighteen built by Mr. Anderson on this street.

B. Taylor has sold for Giblin & Taylor to Sarah Taylor No. 136 West 75th street, an uncompleted four-story brown stone dwelling, 21x58x102.2, for $40,000.

J. M. Flanagan has sold for Samuel Soul No. 39 West 60th street, a five-story flat, for $47,000, and for G. T. Dechert a plot of about eighteen lots on McCombs Dam road, north of 184th street, for $25,000.

Henry Waters has sold to Isaac Wyman the five-story single steam heated flat, 21x88x100 feet, No. 72 East 93d street, near Madison avenue, for $30,000.

M. Barnett has sold to Senator Jacob A. Cantor No. 137 West 120th street, a three-story and basement brown stone, 20x60x100, for $22,500.

Bryan L. Kennelly has sold No. 7 West 119th street, a three-story high stoop brick dwelling, size 14x37x54 (renting for $600 a year), for $7,000 for Morris P. Ferris to Colonel Oliver L. Shepherd.

Jas. L. Libby & Son have sold for J. L. Brewster a three-story brown stone dwelling, 16.8x about 60x102.2, on the south side of 82d street, 143.5 east of Riverside Drive, on private terms.

Brooklyn.

Corwith Bros. have sold the three-story and basement frame dwelling, 16.8x45x100, No. 581½ Lorimer street, for Charles A. Berton to Carman A. Robinson for $6,000.

CONVEYANCES.

	1890. Nov. 20 to 25 inc.	1891. Nov. 19 to 24 inc.
Number	327	238
Amount involved	$1,036,494	$590,570
Number nominal	83	13

MORTGAGES.

	1890.	1891.
Number	258	205
Amount involved	$277,104	$813,710
Number at 5 per cent. or less	148	104
Amount involved	$625,363	$436,615

PROJECTED BUILDINGS.

	1890. Nov. 21 to 26 inc.	1891. Nov. 20 to 25 inc.
Number of buildings	53	49
Estimated cost	$206,050	$299,575

Out Among the Builders.

St. Anselm's Roman Catholic Church, Rev. Alexius Edelbrock, O. S. B., pastor, has acquired sixteen lots corner of Tinton avenue and Dawson street, upon which they will erect a church, parish house and school, etc. A convent, in addition to the above buildings, may be erected on the site, and this convent will be under the auspices of St. Anselm's Church.

John C. Umberfield will improve a plot containing over seven lots on the north side of 75th street, 388 feet east of Columbus avenue, by the erection of eight first-class dwellings, between 20 and 23 feet front each. The houses, which adjoin those recently built by Mr. Umberfield, will contain every improvement, and will embrace many novel features.

Walden P. Anderson, who has just purchased thirteen lots on the south side of 90th street, 200 feet west of Central Park West, will improve the same by the erection of three and four-story private dwellings, 20 and 21 feet front.

F. A. Minuth is the architect for nine private dwellings to be erected on the northeast corner of West End avenue and 104th street. Five will face on the avenue and four on the street. Four will be 20x54 each, one 22x50, three 18x58 and the corner 21x73, all to have butler's pantry extensions. They will be trimmed in hardwood and provided with the best sanitary plumbing and fixtures. All the fronts will be of different design, in stone, brick and terra cotta combination. The total cost is estimated at $150,000.

Fred. Ebeling is drawing plans for a five-story tenement, 25.4x65, to be built at No. 96 East Broadway for Harry D. Haber, to cost $18,000, and for extensive alterations to No. 211 East Broadway for the same owner.

James W. Cole has plans on the board for three five-story apartment houses, 25x88.9, to be built on the south side of 135th street, 285 feet east of 6th avenue, for Joseph Turner.

Herrmann Horenburger has plans on the boards for a five-story brick and stone flat, with bowling alleys in basement and meeting rooms on first floor, to be built for Xávier Schafer on the northwest corner of Melrose avenue and 152d street. The building will be 25x96 feet in size.

Benedict A. Klein will build a six-story brick and stone flat at No. 28 Henry street.

Walker & Lawson will improve two lots on the north side of 95th street, 300 feet east of Columbus avenue, probably by the erection of private dwellings.

Philip Kotlowsky will improve the lot No. 187 Allen street, by the erection of a five-story tenement.

Fine Cabinet Work and Interior Wood Work.

[SPECIAL NOTICE.]

The attention of architects, builders and owners is directed to the card of Wood, Jenks & Co. which appears on another page. This firm manufactures fine cabinet work and interior wood work for public and private buildings, and are able to execute orders with dispatch in a satisfactory manner. Among the work recently executed the Brooklyn Post-office and the Pittsburgh Post-office may be mentioned. For the former Wood, Jenks & Co. supplied all the wood work. They are now doing the cabinet work in Banker G. B. Schley's house at No 812 Madison avenue. Mr. Henry C. Adams, well and favorably known, is the New York manager for the firm, with offices at No. 3 Union square, Lincoln Building.

Trap-Siphonage.

We are in receipt of a pamphlet by Prof. J. E. Denton, presented at the eighteenth annual meeting of the American Public Health Association, Charleston, containing experiments and researches on trap-siphonage, showing the comparative merits of the principal appliances used for trap-seal protection. These experiments have been in progress over a year and a-half, at the Stevens' Institute of Technology, and are a contribution to the subject of a scientific character. The experiments are illustrated. We shall make more extended comments on this publication next week.

WANTS AND OFFERS.

WANTS.

WANTED.—As clerk in Real Estate Office, young man about 25 years of age; must be a good penman, quick at figures, and capable of using typewriter. Address stating salary expected.
"A," office of REAL ESTATE RECORD.

WANTED—For cash customers, desirable investment property, flats, stores and tenements; entire charge taken of estates; personal attention given to renting and collecting.
JOHN G. BORGSTEDE, 207 East 54th st.

OFFERS.

Dwellings and Flats

A DESIRABLE CORNER PROPERTY.—1st av.; three stores and apartments; income $1,700; price $27,500; easy terms.
PECK, 4 West 28th st.

104TH ST., NEAR MADISON AV.—Five-story flat; price $23,500; all rented; bargain.
JOHN G. BORGSTEDE, 207 East 54th st.

105TH ST., NEAR MADISON AV.—Five-story flats; all improvements; price $23,000; mortgage $18,000—$20,000. Apply to
JOHN G. BORGSTEDE, 207 East 54th st.

NEAR 79TH ST. AND LEXINGTON AV.—Four-story private stable and flats; must be sold; any reasonable offer entertained. Apply to
JOHN G. BORGSTEDE, 207 East 54th st.

BARGAIN.—Three-story private dwelling, 52d st., near Lexington av.; will sell at a sacrifice; must be sold. TORREY & SCHRAG, 124 West 23d st.

A 72D ST. GEM, No. 308 West.—This superb house is beautifully decorated; has handsome gas fixtures; is in perfect order; ready for immediate occupancy; $38,000; a greater bargain than has been offered in months.
Nov. 14-uf. CONDIT, 1179 Broadway.

$650,000 FOR ONE of the choicest pieces of investment properties on Manhattan Island; exceptionally well built and very desirably located; other good property (city or country) will be entertained in part payment.
Nov. 14—uf. CONDIT, 1179 Broadway.

A—At reasonable prices and easy terms, three and four-story residences, with three-story extensions; all improvements. Call and examine or inquire of the owner and builder, on the premises.
S. O. WRIGHT, 128 West 121st st., open daily.
Oct. 3 uf.

OFFERS.

248 WEST SEVENTY-SEVENTH ST., opposite Collegiate Reformed Church; handsome, modern gas fixtures; decorated. Apply on premises, or to Owner, 20 Nassau st., Room 58.

FOR SALE.—2443 8th av and 210 and 212 West 105th st.; commission allowed brokers. Apply at
Aug. 29-uf. Room 19, 153 Broadway.

FOR SALE.—Six new cabinet-trimmed three-story and basement brown stone private dwellings, Nos. 142-152 West 123d st.; prices reasonable and brokers commissions allowed. For further particulars apply at office of
FRED'K. M. LITTLEFIELD, 156 Broadway.
Aug. 29-uf.

TO LET, FURNISHED.—680 Lexington av.; to strictly private family; 3-story and basement house; new plumbing; thorough ventilation; painted walls; perfect order; rent, $1,500. Apply at house.

Vacant Lots.

FORTY ACRES, northern end and highest point on Manhattan Island, lying on Hudson River and Spuyten Duyvil, carrying all riparian rights; grand site for hotel, institution, &c.; would exchange for improved city property.
LUDLOW, DAY & CO., 54 West 31st.

FOR SALE—On 99th st, one lot with $11,000 building loan. J. M. STRONG, JR., 60 Liberty st.

A DESIRABLE LOT FOR SALE, with a frontage of 106 ft. on Brooklyn Bridge.
RULAND & WHITING, 5 Beekman st.

AN INVESTMENT OR SPECULATION.—Over 200 acres just north of Van Cortlandt Park, near two depots. Principals only.
PHILLIPS & WELLS, Tribune Building.
Nov. 21-1aw4w.

EASTERLY FRONT BOULEVARD, with 200 ft. on 86th st. and 284 ft. on 85th st.; one or more plots.
Nov. 7-1aw6w. OTTO ERNST, South Amboy, N. J.

1ST AV., near 108th st; full lot, $5,700.
Oct. 31—1aw9w. EDWIN A. ELY, 108 Gold st.

Improved Property.

A VALUABLE PROPERTY on Fulton st. for sale.
RULAND & WHITING, 5 Beekman st.

FOR SALE.—On 3d av., near 48d st. 20 or 60 ft., with buildings. For terms and particulars apply to RULAND & WHITING, 5 Beekman st.

OFFERS.

AN INVESTMENT PROPERTY adjoining 5th av. corner; also one adjoining Broadway; both below 34th st. PECK, 4 West 28th st.

A STORE PROPERTY on Canal st., near South 5th av.; short block; grand investment.
CHAS. S. PECK, 4 West 28th st.

OFFICE OF
FREDERICK SOUTHACK,
401 BROADWAY,
offers for sale some choice pieces
of property on
LEONARD ST., between Broadway and West B'way.
FRANKLIN ST., between B'way and West B'way.
WHITE ST., between B'way and West B'way.
BROADWAY, from Barclay to 14th st.
BLEECKER ST., from B'way to South 5th av.
GREENE ST., Canal to 8th st.
WASHINGTON PLACE, B'way to Wooster.
WAVERLEY PLACE, B'way to Wooster.
APPLY AS ABOVE.
FREDERICK SOUTHACK.
Oct. 3 uf.

TO LET OR TO LEASE.—Two floors of a factory, 25x98, light on all sides, 1st av and 107th st; terms moderate. J. REEBER'S SONS,
Nov. 7 uf. 409 East 107th.

Country Property.

50 TO 200 ACRES, suitable for dividing into large or small plots; forty minutes from city; convenient to depot; can be sub-divided at small expense.
W. B. TIBBITS, agent, White Plains, N. Y.
Nov. 14—1aw8w.

FOR SALE.—In plots to suit; eligible building sites (commanding view of Sound for miles), on North st., Greenwich, Connecticut; price reasonable; terms easy; neighborhood aristocratic and fashionable. Apply to
FRED. J. STONE, owner, 60 Broadway, N. Y.
Sept. 12-uf.

Miscellaneous.

A PARTY ABOUT TO BUILD A FIVE-STORY factory, 50x98, in Harlem, near water-front, will lease the three upper floors and build to suit tenant. Terms very moderate. Address
May 16 u. f. OWNER, 409 E. 107th St.

PRINTING.—Book, News and Job.
RECORD AND GUIDE PRESS,
14 Barclay, and 14, 16 Vesey sts.

SALES OF THE WEEK.

The following are the sales at the Real Estate Exchange and Auction Room for the week ending November 27.

* *Indicates that the property described has been bid in for plaintiff's account.*

R. V. HARNETT & CO.

Dawson st, s s, 59.8 w Tinton av, 4 lots. Fred. McCarthy $3,900
Gerard st, n e s. 154 s e Bergen av, 25x100, vacant. John Cools 4,675
Kelly (152d) st, n e cor Wales av, 2 lots. J. F. Vosatka 2,350
Oliver st, Nos. 100 and 102, e s, 55 n South st, 40x50, two two-story brk tenem'ts, store in No. 102. S. Gemans. (Amt due $9,658) 11,000
Columbus av, s e cor 118th st, 50.5x100, vacant. Wm. Cohen. (Amt due $18,085) 10,000
Prospect av, n w cor Kelly st, 1 lot. Jas. B. Baxter 1,500
Prospect av, w s, adj. 4 lots. Same 3,200
Prospect av, adj. 2 lots. Anna Wrorer 1,370
Prospect av, adj. 2 lots. Michael Connor 1,450
Prospect av, adj. 2 lots. —— Pistolet 1,480
Prospect av, adj. 5 lots. Charlotte Ohle 3,250
Tinton av, n e cor Kelly st, 1 lot. D. Knabe 1,300
Tinton av, e s, adj. 2 lots. E. Nass 1,550
Tinton av, adj. 2 lots. M. J. Biehan 1,365
Tinton av, adj. 3 lots. C. Smith 1,680
Tinton av, adj. 8 lots. B. P. Fairchild 4,480
Tinton av, adj. 2 lots. T. Higgins 1,020
Tinton av, n w cor Kelly st, 1 lot. J. F. Vosatka 1,600
Tinton av, w s, adj. 2 lots. Same 1,800
Tinton av, adj. 2 lots. John O'Connor 1,000
Tinton av, adj. 12 lots. Fred. McCarthy 9,000
Union av, n e cor Kelly st. 1 lot. Jas. Heggs 1,075
Union av, e s, adj. 1 lot. Same 605
Union av, adj. 2 lots. Charlotte Ohle 1,210
Union av, adj. 2 lots. E. J. Flood 1,190
Union av, adj. 1 lot. Frank Guth 585
Union av, adj. 4 lots. —— Pistolet 2,300
Union av, adj. 5 lots. Charlotte Ohle 2,675
Union av, n w cor Kelly st, 1 lot. Leonora Bell 1,025
Union av, w s, adj. 1 lot. Same 630
Union av, adj. 4 lots. Charlotte Ohle 2,620
Wales av, e s, 36.6 n Kelly st, 2 lots. Wm. Dalton 900
Wales av, e s. 86.6 n Kelly st, gore. W. E. Bloodgood 2,500

JAMES L. WELLS.

Bronx River road, e s, at intersection of city line, 3 lots. M. J. Klug 825
Bronx River road, adj. 2 lots. E. Van Tassel 550
Bronx River road, w s, 410.3 s McLean av, 4 lots. L. Z. Bach 1,800
128th st, No. 214, s s, 100 e 3d av, 18.9x99.11, three-story English basement brown stone dwell'g. L. A. Rogers 7,400
Oakley av, n s w cor city line, 2 lots. O. Burpaur 200
Oakley av, w s, adj, 3 lots. A. Gorsch 200
Oakley av, s e cor city line, 4 lots. M. J. Klug 400
Oakley av, e s, adj. 1 lot. Elizabeth Schilling 115

A. H. MULLER & SON.

Broadway or Kingsbridge road, s e cor Macomb st. 48.6x100. Ludwig Kinstler. (Amt due $6,969) 8,500
57th st, No. 102, s s, 100 w 6th av, 15x100, four-story stone front dwell'g, also all right, title and interest to strip of land 5 inches in depth and 15 feet wide, adj rear of above. D. M. Kellogg. (Amt due $21,147) 30,000
159th st, n s } 375 w Amsterdam av, 6 lots.
150th st, s s } (Bid in) .... ——
Edgecombe av, No. 40, e s, 54.10 s 137th st, 17.6x90, three-story brk dwell'g. Henry Schmitt. (Amt due $12,879) 13,800

WM. KENNELLY.

Cottage pl, e s, 283 n e 170th st, 57x127x56.8x127. Sarah Jackson. (Amt due $3,515) 6,825
120th st, No. 304, s s, 100 w 2d av, 19.5x100.11, three-story stone front dwell'g. S. V. Constans. (Amt due $6,300) 8,400
13?d st, Nos. 26-30, s s, 235 w 5th av, 100x100.11, three five-story brk flats. Margaret T. Nally. (Amt due $3,274) 81,506

J. F. B. SMYTH.

Public Drive, near 158th st, plot containing abt 4½ city lots. (Bid in) .... ——
30th st, No. 517, n s, 250 w 10th av, 25x98.9, four-story brk store and tenem't with one-story frame buildings on rear. W. G. McCray 9,300
39th st, No. 515 W., 25x98.9, two-story building. Same 8,300
39th st, No. 535 W., 25x98.9, vacant. Same 5,600

SMYTH & RYAN.

East Broadway, Nos. 123 and 125, s e cor Pike st, 25x85, three-story frame store on Pike st and one and two-story brk and frame stores on East Broadway. A. Cohen 33,600
Monroe st, No. 103, 25x100, four-story brk dwell'g. Timothy Roche. (Leasehold) 5,700
102d st, Nos. 227-237, n s, 105 w 2d av, 123x100.9, four-story brk silk mills. A. E. Schatz. Interest and taxes and 70,025

OTHER AUCTIONEERS.

*93d st, Nos. 153 and 155, n s, 249 e Amsterdam av, 34x84 to Apthorpes lane, x34.6x85.4, two three-story stone front dwell'gs. John Bartford 34,000
*93d st, No. 159, n s, 219 e 10th av, 15x86 to Apthorpes lane, x15x86.8, three-story stone front dwell'g. Adelia F. Philp 16,500
*1st av, Nos. 2035-2041, n w cor 105th st, 100.9x100, four five-story brk tenem'ts and stores .... }
105th st, n s, 125 w 1st av, 75x100.9, vacant .... }
Ira Shafer. (Amt due $63,197) 60,000
*Willis av, n w cor 140th st, 25x100. Gustavus L. Lawrence. (Amt due $12,977) 31,065

Total $519,946
Corresponding week, 1890 .... $404,013

BROOKLYN, N. Y.

FOR WEEK ENDING NOVEMBER 26.

*Bergen st, n s, 200 w Kingston av, 100x114.5, five three-story brk dwell'gs. Jennie C. B. Reynolds $40,145
Columbia st, No. 433, e s, 60 n West 9th st, 20x83.6, three-story frame dwell'g. Ellen Sullivan 1,800
*Henry st, No. 561, e s, 75 n Carroll st, 25x117, three-story brk dwell'g. Gwendoline Burgess 8,000
Madison st, No. 789, n s, 278 w Ralph av, 18x100, two-story frame dwell'g. Jacob Spettel 1,750
Pacific st, Nos. 1505-1511 } n e cor Kingston av,
Kingston av, No. 69 } 80x96, three four-story double brk flats. Daniel Doody 34,100
*Pulaski st, Nos. 274-280, s s, 330.2 e Throop av, 101.10x100, four four-story double brk flats. Charles D. King 28,700
Van Voorhis st, n w s, 100 s w Evergreen av, 17x100 .... }
Van Voorhis st, n w s, 117 s w Evergreen av, 17x100 .... }
Van Voorhis st, n w s, 134 w Evergreen av, runs northwest 100 x southwest 16 x southeast 51.9 x southwest 1 x southeast 48.1¾ to Van Voorhis st, x northwest 17 to beginning, unfinished frame dwell'gs .... }
W. H. E. Jay 8,400
*Van Voorhis st, n w s, 253 s w Evergreen av, 17x100, two-story frame (brk lined) dwell'g. Julian Lucas 3,000
5th av, No. 10, w s, 130 n Pacific st, runs northwest 32.7 x southwest 14.2 x southeast 28.11 x northeast 1 x southeast 14.11 to 5th av, x north 32 to beginning, four-story building and store. Arthur Hurst 6,875
*7th av, No. 66, w s, 50 s Lincoln pl, 33.6x110. }
7th av, No. 70, w s, 83.6 s Lincoln pl, 33.6x110. }
7th av, No. 72, w s, 116.6 s Lincoln pl, 33.6x110, three four-story double brk flats .... }
William Post 61,000

Total $193,770
Corresponding week 1890 .... $125,181

CONVEYANCES.

NEW YORK CITY.

NOVEMBER 20, 21, 23, 24, 25, 26.

Bank st, No. 121, n s, 252.8 w Greenwich st, runs west 16.5 x north 95 x east 8.11 x north 21.10 x east 7.8 x south 114.2, five-story brk tenem't. John Schreyer to Morris Goldstein. *Mt.* $10,000. Nov. 20. $14,900
Boulevard, Nos 296 and 298, e s, 56.10 n 74th st, 26.1x73.8x25x66.1, one-story frame buildings. Edward A. Morrison to Daniel Katz. *Mt.* $10,000. Nov. 2. 14,500
Cherry st, No. 354, n s, 151.9 e Montgomery st, runs east 22.10 x north 40.9 x north 56.5 x west 18.8 x south 7.5 x west 2.4 x south 89.9, three-story frame (brk front) store and tenement. Adolph Cohen and Harry Fischel to Rosanna Rosenfeld. Nov. 20. 13,500
Delancey st, No. 127, s s, 40 w Norfolk st, runs south 56 x west 7 x south 12 x west 13 x north 8 to st, x east 20, four-story frame and brk tenem't with stores. Solomon B. and Joe S. Ulmann, Siegmund J. Bach and Leopold S. Bache, of Semon, Bache & Co., to Rachel wife of Louis Weinberg. C. a. G. Nov. 24. 15,500

Elizabeth st, No. 244, e s, 283.11 s Houston st, 24.3x81.7, five-story brk tenem't with stores.
Elizabeth st, No. 246, e s, 307.2 s Houston st, 24.5x91.4x20.3x92, five-story brk tenem't with stores.
Daniel Rothstein to Vito Cimino. *Mt.* $40,-750. Nov. 21. See Mulberry st. 55,750

Grand st, No. 34 } begins Grand st, n w cor
Thompson st, No. 21 } Thompson st, 20x60.10, three-story frame and brk tenem't with stores. Gotthardt A. Litthauer to Ernest Franklin. Q. C. Nov. 25. nom

Hudson st, w s, 184 s Christopher st, 75x125.
Hudson st, w s, lots 124 and 125 map Church farm, 50x125
Hudson st, w s, 280 s Christopher st, 30x125. Nos. 477-485, three-story brk dwell'g, church, school offices, &c.
The rector, &c., St. Lukes Church to the rector, &c., Trinity Church. Oct. 17. 150,000

Hester st, Nos. 67 and 69.
Forsyth st, No. 129.
Delancey st, No. 31.
Amsterdam av, s e cor 103d st, 4½ lots.
Edwin Welch individ. and exr. Jacob Leon to Tarrant Putnam and Lemuel Skidmore. Consent to mortgage. Nov. 20. nom

Same property. Authorization to satisfy above. Albert Welch to Edwin Welch exr. Jacob Leon and individ. Nov. 19. See Morts. nom

Jane st, No. 73, n s, 111 7 w Greenwich st, 20.8 x87.5, three-story brk tenem't. Mark M. Nicholls to Richard H. Mitchell. Nov. 23. nom

Same property. Richard H. Mitchell to Elizabeth J. Nicholls. Nov. 28. nom

Leroy st or St. Lukes pl, No. 6, n s, 123.9 e Hudson st, 21.8x100, three-story brk dwell'g. John G. Ackerson exr. Elizabeth Stagg, The St. Lawrence University, Canton, N. Y., and The New York Universalist Relief Fund and Ann Osborn widow to William H. Walker. Nov. 20. 14,000

Same property. John G. Ackerson exr. David I. Stagg and John G. Ackerson and Elizabeth S. Pangburn devisees Elizabeth Stagg to same. Q. C. Nov. 20. nom

Morton st, No. 34, s s, 75 w Bedford st, 25 x91.
Morton st, No. 36, s s, 100 w Bedford st, 25 x91.
Two five-story brk flats.
Guiseppe, Steffano, Natale and Luigi Cavinato to James P. Foster. *Mt.* $60,107. Nov. 24. 73,750

Mott st, No. 110 e s, 43.2 s Hester st, runs east 45.11 x south 6.10 x east 22 x south 16 x west 68.5 to Mott st, x north 22.10, three-story frame (brk front) store and tenem't. Benjemen Sire to James W. Ketcham. Nov. 21. 20,000

Mulberry st, No. 58, e s, 125 s Bayard st, 25x 94.9x25x93.11, three-story frame and brk tenem't with stores and four-story brk tenement on rear. Vito Cimino to Daniel Rothstein. *Mt.* $10,000. Nov. 21. See Elizabeth st. 27,750

Suffolk st, No. 57, w s, abt 50 s Broome st, 25x75, five-story brk tenem't with stores. Frederick Muller, Jr., to Philipp Fabel. *Mt.* $15,000. Oct. 15. 25,000

Vandewater st, s e s, 131.3 n e Frankfort st, runs southeast along bridge lands 106.5 x east 13.9 x northwest 110 to st, x southwest 35.1, vacant. Andrew Little to John Pettit, Orange, N. J. Nov. 19. nom

William st, Nos. 88 and 90. Agreement as to use of 5-foot gangway adj above, Benjamin L. Swan, Jr., individ., William L. Swan, Emily E. and Pauline Post, Adeline E. wife of and Jean J. Reubel, Benjamin L. and Edward H. Swan, Jr., trustee Caroline E. wife of Thomas S. Young, Jr., Benjamin L. Swan, Jr., trustee Allison Post, Benjamin L., Jr., and Edward H. Swan trustees for Julia S. Post to Charles Le Ray de C. de St. Paul, Paris, France. Sept. 1. nom

5th st, No. 740. Release mort. and confirmation. Henry A. de Meli individ. and trustee Antoinette L. de Meli to Meyer and Solomon Goodman. Nov. 7. nom

10th st, No. 222, s s, 325 e 2d av, 25x92.4, four-story brk tenem't. C. Alexander Stein to Elizabeth Hoelger. B. & S. Nov. 19. 27,000

11th st, No. 519, n s, 245.8 e Av A, —x103.3x25x 103 3, five-story brk tenem't with stores. Charles W. Meyer, Brooklyn, to Thomas J. Johnston. *Mt.* $24,000. Nov. 23. 5,500

12th st, No. 348, s s, 99.9 w 1st av, 19.7x68.4, four-story brk store and tenem't. Jeannette Markus widow to Henry Markus. *Mt.* $5,000. Jan. 4, 1888. nom

13th st, Nos. 47, 49, 51 and 53 W. Party wall agreement. Benjamin O. Chisolm with William Rhinelander et al. exrs. and trustees Julia Rhinelander. July 15. nom

16th st, Nos. 229 and 231, n s, 337.1 w 7th av, 59.10x100, two five-story stone front flats. Robert Ernst to Henry Gucker. *Mt.* $55,000. Nov. 16. nom

17th st, No. 327, n s, 290 e 2d av, 22x92, three-story brk tenem't. Caroline W. Drew to Henry P. Drew. Sept. 18. nom

19th st, No. 131, n s, 185 e Irving pl, 24x79, five-story brk flat. *Mt.* $37,200.
53d st, No. 417, n s, 250 w 9th av, 25x100.5, five-story brk flat. *Mt.* $25,500.
Willis av, w s, 25 n 134th st, 25x81.6.
Willis av, w s, 150 n 134th st, 25x81.6.
134th st, n s, 81.6 w Willis av, 25x100.
135th st, s s, 81.6 w Willis av, 25x100. Last four parcels sub. to morts. $66,000.
Luigi, Guiseppe, Steffano and Natale Cavinato to Agostino Cavinato. Nov. 24. 152,000

20th st, No. 153, n s, 169 e 7th av, 22x92, two-story brk stable. Robert L. and Walter Cutting to Ferdinand Neumer. Nov. 3. 19,000

22d st, No. 157, n s, 165.7 e 7th av, 21.10x98.9, three-story brk dwell'g. Foreclos. Michael J. Langan to Louis Grunhut. Nov. 20. 23,800

22d st, No. 159, n s, 143.9 e 7th av, 21.10x98.9, three-story brk dwell'g. Frederick F. Kieferdorf to Cecelia V. Kieferdorf. *Mt.* $14,000. Nov. 18. nom

28th st, Nos. 516-528, s s, 225 w 10th av, 150x 98.9, seven two, three and four-story brk tenem'ts, stores in Nos. 320 and 324, and seven two-story brk and frame buildings on rear. Partition. Charles D. Burrill to William S. Patten. Nov. 20. 42,000

28th st, s s, 325 w 10th av, 50x98.9. William S. Patten to Edward R. Merrill. Nov. 20. 16,000

29th st, No. 40 W., s s, abt 184 e 6th av, 20.6x 98.9, six-story brk store and flat with five-story brk building on rear. Contract. John Friedrich with William Sperb, Jr. Oct. 32. 36,000

29th st, No. 333, n s, 388.7 e 2d av, 24.5x98.9, five-story brk tenem't. Mary L. wife of Walter A. Reilly to Thomas C. Smith. *Mt.* $8,-000. Nov. 23. 100

32d st, No. 141, n s, 441.8 w 6th av, 16.8x77.7x 17.3x82.1, four-story brk store and tenem't. Rosa Mendelson widow to Herman S. Mendelson. Nov. 18. nom

32d st, No. 350, s s, 412.6 w 8th av, 19x98.9, four-story stone front dwell'g. Henry Allen and William G. McCrea to Ascher Weinstein. *Mt.* $9,000. Nov. 19. 14,000

35th st, Nos. 154 and 156, s s, 150 e 7th av, 50x 98 9, two five-story stone front flats. Charles Lowen and Edward F. Halliday to Daniel V. Galvan. *Mt.* $60,000. Nov. 19. 88,500

35th st, Nos. 241-245, n s, 331 e 8th av, 69x98.9, three four story brk dwell'gs. Asa R. Davison to William H. Ramsey. *Mt.* $75,000. Sept. 11. 115,000

36th st, No. 253, s s, 233.3 e 8th av, 25.8x98.9, five-story stone front flat. Max S Korn to Matilda wife of Jacob W. Riglander. *Mt.* $28,000. Nov. 20. See 74th st. other consid. and 100

36th st, No. 117, n s, 160.4 w Lexington av, 16.2x98.9, four-story stone front dwell'g. Daisy Florance to Agnes H. wife of Aaron Wolff, Jr. Nov. 14. nom

Same property. Aaron Wolff, Jr., to Daisy Florance. Nov. 14. nom

38th st, Nos. 526-530, s s, 850 w 10th av, 75x 98 9, one and two-story frame and brk mineral water factory, &c.
37th st, No. 579, n s, 400 w 10th av, 25x98.9, three-story brk stable.
James McClenahan to William H. Callanan and Francis McDermott. *Mt.* $20,000. Nov. 20. 35,000

42d st, Nos. 157 and 159 E. Assign. of contract. Frederick Robinson to Roland McNichols. Nov. 20. ——

44th st, No. 102, s s, 75 w 6th av, 25x100 5, five-story brk flat. Frances S. wife of and James H. Bridge to Annie C. B. wife of George V. Foster. *Mt.* $35,000. Nov. 24. 52,000

47th st, No. 30, s s, 390 w 5th av, 20x100.5, four-story stone front dwell'g. Harriet S. wife of Theodore M. Burton to Samuel A. Drew, Burlington, Vt. Nov. 5. nom

Same property. Samuel A. Drew, Boston, Mass., to Theodore M. Burton. Nov. 5. nom

49th st, No. 345, n s, 168.9 w 1st av, 18.9x100.5, four-story brk dwell'g. John Goerlitz to Louis Miller. *Mt.* $7,000. Nov. 23. nom

50th st, No. 204, s s, 75 e 3d av, 15x60, three-story brk dwell'g. Peter B. Olney to John Mitchell. *Mt.* $4,000. Nov. 24. 3,400

51st st, No. 248, s s, 127 e 8th av, 20x100.5, five-story brk flat. Alexander Moore to Frank Tilford. *Mt.* $25,000. Nov. 25. 40,000

53d st, Nos. 546-550, s s, 100 e 11th av, 75x100.5, three five-story brk tenem'ts. Foreclos. Joseph I. McKeon to Spencer Aldrich. Oct. 27. 12,000

53d st, Nos. 540-544, s s, 175 e 11th av, 75x100.5, three five-story brk tenem'ts. Foreclos. Charles J. Breck to same. July 10. 12,300

53d st, Nos. 540-550, s s, 100 e 11th av, 150x100.5. Spencer Aldrich to Harrie Bulkley. Brooklyn, N. Y. Oct. 27. 60,000

58th st, No. 110, s s, 120.6 w 6th av, 20x100.5, four-story brk dwell'g. Charles T. and Helen T. Barney to Emily L. Browne. Oct. 15. 37,500

62d st, No. 138, s s, 435 w Columbus av, 25x 100.5, five-story brk flat. Mary J. Doyle to Peter Doyle. *Mt.* $20,000. Nov. 24. nom

65th st, No. 144, s s, 378 e 10th av, 20x100.5, four-story stone front dwell'g. Bernard and Amy E. Cohn to The Amsterdam Improvement Co. *Mt.* $25,000. Nov. 17. 29,358

65th st, Nos. 162 and 164, s s, 192 e 10th av, 36 x100.5, two four-story stone front dwell'gs. Bernard Cohn to John Heyman. *Mt.* $46,-000. March 26, 1890. 56,500

69th st, n s, 175 e 11th av, 20x100.5, vacant. Hannah Tuffs widow to Ellen M. Harlow. Nov. 20. See 104th st. nom

71st st, n s, 305 e 5th av, 20x102.2. Release mort. Alexander Maitland et al exrs. Henrietta A. Lenox to Edward H. Van Ingen. Nov. 23. 20,000

71st st, No. 13, n s, 305 e 5th av, 20x102.2, four-story brk dwell'g. Edward H. Van Ingen to Eric P. Swenson. April 10. nom

72d st, No. 159, n s, 150 w 3d av, 29.7x102.2, four-story stone front dwell'g. Daniel V. Galvan to Mary P. Galvan heirs Ellen McGuiness, &c. ½ part. Nov. 17. 19,000

74th st, Nos. 152 and 154, s s, 522 w 9th av, 40x 102.2, two four-story stone front dwell'gs. Thomas H. Knox to Matthew Clark. All liens. Nov. 20. nom

74th st, No. 87, n s, 125 e Madison av, 20x102.2, four-story stone front dwell'g. Matilda wife of Jacob W. Riglander to Max S. Korn. *Mt.* $12,000. Nov. 20. See 36th st. other consid. and 100

75th st, No. 39, n s, 283 e Columbus av, 20x102.2, four-story stone front dwell'g. John C. Umberfield to Samuel D. Styles. *Mt.* $26,900. Nov. 19. other consid. and 100

77th st, No. 115, n s, 250 e Park av, 25x102.2, three-story brk stable. Frank P. Perkins to Simon Goldenberg. *Mt.* $16,000. Nov. 24. other consid. and 33

80th st, No. 338, s s, 125 w 1st av, 25x102 2, four-story stone front dwell'g. Simon Weinberger to John Ott. *Mt.* $7,000. Nov. 23. 15,000

81st st, No. 156, s s, 230.6 w 3d av, 19.9x104.4, three-story stone front dwell'g. Kate M. wife of Charles M. Williams, Hartford, Conn., to Babette Wahlig. *Mt.* $7,000. Nov. 24. 18,000

82d st, No. 66, s s, 166 e Columbus av, 19x102.2, four-story stone front dwell'g. Charles McDonald to Maud A. Griswold. *Mt.* $13,000 Nov. 23. nom

82d st, No. 173, s s, 116 8 e Amsterdam av, 18.8 x102.2, three-story stone front dwell'g. John H. Wessel to James Murphy. *Mt.* $15,000. Nov. 25. 21,000

83d st, n s, 249 w Columbus av, 17x102 2, four-story stone front dwell'g. Thomas H. Knox to Matthew Clark. All liens. Nov. 20. nom

86th st, No. 143, n s, 334 6 e Amsterdam av, 22.6 x100.5, four-story stone front dwell'g. D. Willis James to John Duer, New Brighton, S. I. Nov. 20. nom

86th st, No. 130, s s, 305 w 9th av, 20x106.10, four-story stone front dwell'g. D. Willis James to J. Rhinelander Dillon. Nov. 20. 35,000

87th st, No. 136, s s, 350 w 9th av, 20x100.8, four-story stone front dwell'g. Foreclos. Edward T. Bartlett to William Brennan. Nov. 23 25,500

87th st, No. 172, n s, 125 e Amsterdam av, 18x 100.8, three-story stone front dwell'g. William C. G. Wilson and James Tichborne to Ella Sugden. Nov. 16. other consid. and 100

88th st, No. 412, s s, 181 e 1st av, 25x100.8, five-story brk tenem't. Charles and Charles J. Muller to Margaretha Worth. Nov. 25. 20,250

89th st, Nos. 15 and 17, n s, 113.4 w Madison av, 51.1x100.8, two five-story brk flats in course of construction. Thomas Graham to Charles Graham. *Mt.* $29,500. Sept. 17. nom

Same property. Charles Graham to Jennie Graham. *Mt.* $49,500. Nov 23. nom

Same property. Jennie wife of Thomas Graham to Allen N. Conover. Sub. to mort. Nov. 24. nom

89th st, No. 16, s s, 113 4 w Madison av, 25.7x 100.8, seven-story brk flat in course of erection. Isaac Untermyer to Charles Graham. C. a. G. *Mt.* $9,500. Aug. 1. 15,000

90th st, s s, 200 w West End av, 50x100.8, vacant. Jane J. wife of Howard Phelps to Egbert C. Simonson. C. a. G. *Mt.* $10,500. Nov. 16. nom

90th st, No. 23, n s, 220 w Central Park West, 18.6x100.8, three-story stone front dwell'g. Release mort. Edward and Henry Hirsch to James Brown. Nov. 13. nom

Same property. Release mort. Same to same. Nov. 13. nom

Same property. Release mort. Morris B. Baer to same. Nov. 17. nom

90th st, No. 23, n s, 220 w 8th av, 18.6x100.8, three-story stone front dwell'g. James Brown to Cecilia Potosky. *Mt.* $17,000. Nov. 24. 26,500

91st st, No. 169, n s, 125 w 3d av, 25x100.8, four-story stone front flat. Joseph Koch to Johanna Cohen. *Mt.* $13,450. Nov. 25. 18,700

91st st, No. 171, n s, 100 w 3d av, 25x100.8, five-story stone front flat. Partition. Meyer Butzel to Thomas A. Campbell. Nov. 25. 24,000

91st st, No. 173, n s, 75 w 3d av, 25x100.8, five-story stone front flat. Partition. Meyer Butzel to Romanus Eusner and Helene his wife. Nov. 25. 18,000

91st st, No. 173, n s, 100 w 3d av. Party wall agreement. Romanus Eusner and Helene his wife with Thomas A. Campbell. Nov. 25. nom

92d st, No. 13, n s, 204.5 e 5th av, 25x100.8, four-story brk dwell'g. Samuel Untermeyer to Isaac Untermeyer. ½ part. Nov. 11. 35,000

93d st, n s, 225 e Columbus av, 25x46.6 to Apthorps lane, x25x47.7, vacant. Francis M. Jencks to Henry A. Robbins. Q. C. Oct. 23. nom

93d st, No. 144, s s, 364.10 e Amsterdam av, 20x 100.8, three-story stone front dwell'g. Release mort. Adelia F. Philp to Walden P. Anderson. Nov. 20. nom

Same property. Release mort. Robinson Gill to same. Nov. 19. nom

Same property. Release mort. The Bradley & Currier Co. (Lim.) to same. Nov. 16. 2,000

Same property. Walden P. Anderson to W. Prince Clagett, Baltimore, Md. *Mt.* $21,000. Nov. 18. nom

95th st, n s, 350 e Columbus av, 39x100.8, vacant. Julian B. Hart, Boston, Mass., David B. and John I. Hart to Alexander Walker and Judson Lawson. C. a. G. Nov. 16. nom

Same property. Julian B. Hart et al. exrs. Benjamin J. Hart to same. C. a. G. Nov. 16. 4,000

95th st, n s, 410.9 w Central Park West, abt 0.2¾x100.8. Henry J. Anderson, Scranton, Pa., to same. B. & S. Nov. 17. nom

95th st, n s, 350 e Columbus av, 39x100.8.
95th st, n s, 410.9 w Central Park West, 0.2¾ x100.8.

Alexander Walker and Judson Lawson to Ellen M. Harlow. *Mt.* $12,000. Nov. 20. nom

98th st, s s, 475 w Central Park West, 150x100.11, six five-story brk flats in course of construction. Charles T. Barney and Helen T. Barney to John O. Baker, Newark, N. J. B. & S. Oct. 26. other consid. and 82,000

Same property. John O. Baker, Newark, N. J., to William A. de Auquinos. B. & S. *Mt.* $82,000. Nov. 6. other consid. and 82,000

102d st, No. 219, n s, 280 e 3d av, 25x100.11, five-story brk flat. Philip Goldmann to Charles Weisberger. *Mt.* $12,000. Nov. 20. 15,900

102d st, No. 156, s s, 325 w 3d av, 15x100.11, four-story stone front dwell'g. Foreclos. John B. Pine to Thomas H. Bauchle. Nov. 25. 7,000

103d st, No. 212, s s, 178 w Amsterdam av, 20x73x20x74, five-story brk flat. Foreclos. Sylvester L. H. Ward to Robert R. Pero. Nov. 25. 19,250

103d st, No. 210, s s, 158 w Amsterdam av, 20x74x20x75, five-story brk flat. Foreclos. Same to Mary Finch. Nov. 25. 19,200

104th st, No. 246, s s, 156 e West End av, 19x100.11, three-story stone front dwell'g. Ellen M. Harlow to Hannah Tuffs. *Mt.* $14,000. Nov. 20. See 98th st. nom

110th st, Nos. 162-168, s s, 170 w 3d av, 100x100.11, four five-story brk flats with stores. Anna W. Townsend, Thomas S., Eliza L. and S. Clinton Willetts and Louis and Charlotte Schermerhorn to Joseph Carreau. Q. C. May 16. nom

114th st, No. 436, s s, 193 w Av A, 25x100.10, four-story stone front tenem't with two-story brk building on rear. Emma wife of Louis Krug, Brooklyn, to Moritz Pinner, Elizabeth, N. J. Nov. 23. exch

115th st, No. 69, n s, 165 w 4th av, 25x100.5, five-story brk flat. Lamont McLoughlin to Annie McLoughlin. *Mt.* $12,000. Nov. 18. nom

115th st, No. 409, n s, 75 e 1st av, 20x75.10, four-story brk tenem't. Max Bernstein to Bernhard Galewski. *Mt.* $7,000. Nov. 16. 9,550

115th st, s s, 205 w 4th av, 25x100.10, one-story frame building on rear of lot. Mary H. McGlynn to Theresa wife of Robert Hughes. *Mt.* $3,500. Nov. 20. 5,000

116th st, No. 314, s s, 211.6 e 2d av, 21x100.11, five-story stone front flat. Dina Muller to Babeth Doctor, Albany, N. Y. *Mt.* $12,500 23,000

116th st, s s, 82.11 e Madison av, 27.1x101, vacant. Foreclos. George B. Newell to Tillie E. Smith. Oct. 22. 4,700

116th st, No. 58, s s, 130 e Madison av, 20x100.11, five-story brk flat. Henry L. Rutherfurd to Anna L. Gardner. B. & S. *Mt.* $20,000. Nov. 16. 26,500

116th st, No. 58, s s, 130 e Madison av, 20x100.11, five-story brk flat. Anna L. Gardner to William W. Howland. B. & S. *Mt.* $20,000. Nov. 25. 27,000

117th st, n s, 225 e 8th av, 50x100.11, vacant. William A. Martin to John J. Timmins. Nov. 18. 19,000

118th st, No. 422, s s, 244 e 1st av, 25x100.10, three-story brk dwell'g. George W., Adelaide M. and C. Corinne Rice and Cecilia A. Dougherty, Brooklyn, to George Hollerith. Nov. 17. 7,068

119th st, No. 7, n s, 93.5 w 5th av, 14x57.9x14.6x53.11, three-story stone front dwell'g. Foreclos. Edward Clark to Oliver L. Shepherd. Nov. 11. 5,245

120th st, Nos. 239-243, n s, 375 w 7th av, 50x100.11, three three-story brk dwell'gs. Foreclos. William J. Lardner to Stephen H. Martling, Ridgefield, N. J. Nov. 23. 46,500

125th st, s s, 140.10 e 6th av, 0.5x100.11x0.5x100.11. Release mort. Jacob L. Williams exr. Emeline B. Perry to James L. Perry. Oct. 1. nom

Same property. Release mort. Harriet E. Perry, Mansfield, Mass., to same. Nov. 13. nom

Same property. James L. Perry to John J. Sperry. Q. C. Nov. 11. 600

126th st, No. 150, s s, 180 e 7th av, 20x99.11, four-story brk dwell'g. Lewis S. Samuel to Phillip Howell. *Mt.* $18,000. Nov. 24. nom

Same property. Mary R. Samuel to Philip Howell. Q. C. Nov. 24. nom

127th st, No. 148, s s, 350.9 w 3d av, 16.8x99.11, three-story stone front dwell'g. Foreclos. William R. Syme to Terence McGuire. *Mt.* $7,000. Oct. 30. 4,100

130th st, No. 59, n s, 252.6 w 4th av, 18.9x99.11, four-story stone front flat. William A. Martin to George Cordner and Annie his wife, joint tenants. Nov. 24. 14,500

131st st, n s, 83.4 e 8th av, 16.8x99.11. Release mort. Reuben Ross to Isaac E. Wright. Nov. 14. nom

137th st, s s, 430 w Lenox av, runs south 99.11 x west 20 x north 48 x west 22 x north 51.11 to 137th st, x east 42, three-story brk dwell'g and vacant. Patrick Farley to Ida wife of John J. Farley. C. a. G. *Mt.* $12,750. Nov. 14. nom

144th st, No. 313, n s, 199.6 w 8th av, 26x99.11, five-story brk flat. Collin H. Woodward to Charles H. Woodward. Oct. 1. nom

147th st, Nos. 303 and 305, n s, 75 w 8th av, 50x99.11, two five-story brk flats. Mary J. wife of Henry J. Burchell to George W. Vultee. *Mt.* $24,000. Nov. 16. 32,000

147th st, n s, 75 w 8th av, —x—. Q. C. and release party wall. John W. Haaren and James King to George W. Vultee. November 18. nom

8th st if extended, centre line, n s, 50 e Edgecombe av, 50x129.11, vacant. William C. Trapbagan to Darius G. Crosby, Scarsdale, N. Y. Nov. 6. other consid. and 100

Amsterdam av, Nos. 794 and 796, s w cor 99th st, 40x80.2x40x77.6, five-story brk flat with stores. Lilian wife of and George W. Rogers to Henry C. Acker. Nov. 18. 80,000

Amsterdam av, Nos. 720-734
96th st, Nos. 202-206
95th st, Nos. 203-207
begins Amsterdam (10th) av, s w cor 96th st, 201.5 to 95th st, x168x201.6 to 96th st, x175.6, eight five-story brk flats with stores on av, and three five-story brk flats on each st.

4th av, n s, bounded north and east by line bet Yonkers and New York and west by lot 192 map of partition part of Hyatt farm, near Woodlawn, being lot 193 said map.

Vermilyea av, s s, 200 w Emerson st, 50x150. Andrew T. Doyle to Annie C. Doyle. *Mt.* $441,000. Dec. 4, 1890. nom

Amsterdam (10th) av, n e cor 116th st, centre lines, 112x—x133.10x—, three two-story frame buildings and vacant. Contract. Charles Reckling to George O. Curtiss. July 8. 33,000

Amsterdam (10th) av, n e cor 116th st, centre lines, 112x—x133.10x—. Joseph Orthaus to Charles Reckling. Aug. 5. 26,500

Same property. Charles Reckling, Brooklyn, to Margaret I. Makewen. *Mt.* $22,500. Nov. 25. 37,500

Av A, No. 97, w s, 22.10 n 6th st, 22.8x100, four-story brk store and tenem't. Dinah Klein to Julius and Edward Klein. 10,200

Av D, No. 54, e s, 22 s 5th st, 24.8x78, four-story frame (brk front) store and tenem't. Adolph Gross and Samuel Harris to David and Israel Schiff. *Mt.* $9,500. Nov. 20. 15,200

Columbus (9th) av, w s, 50.5 n 124th st, runs west 100 x north 50.6 x east 76.6 to Manhattan st, x southeast 26.5 to 9th av, x south 38.4, one-story frame storehouse with one-story frame building on rear.

Manhattan st, s w s, 26.2 n w 9th av, runs west 76.9 x north 39.11 to Manhattan st, x southeast 86.5, gore, two-story frame dwelling.

George R. Schieffelin to Margaret L. Chanler, Barrytown, N. Y. B. & S. Nov. 18. 26,000

Greenwich av, Nos. 17 and 19, w s, 26.2 s 10th st, 50x90.6x50.4x81.8, two five-story brk stores and flats. John Goerlitz to Adam Happel. *Mt.* $25,000. Nov. 23. nom

Lexington av, s w cor 103d st, 56x100, vacant. Frederick Willenbrock and Egbert Winkler to Blinn Memorial Methodist Episcopal Church. Nov. 20. 17,000

Lexington av, No. 666, w s, 75.11 s 56th st, 24.6x90, four-story stone front dwell'g. Poline wife of Morris Byk to Joseph Byk. *Mt.* $27,000. Nov. 19. 2,000

Lexington av, No. 1731, e s, 84.3 n 108th st, 16.8x75, four-story stone front flat. Edward J. a a to Amelia E. Hummel. *Mt.* $11,000. Nottig. n nom

Lexington av, No. 2115, e s, 100.11 s 128th st, abt 18x30, three story brk dwell'g. John P. Jones to Ella C. J. Tappen. *Mt.* $4,000. Jan. 16. 2,000

Madison av, Nos. 136 and 138, n w cor 31st st, 49.7x95, seven-story brk flat. Peter N. Ramsey to Samuel G. Revans. B. & S. Nov. 24. 100

Madison av, No. 150
32d st, Nos. 22 and 24
begins Madison av, s w cor 32d st, 24.9x94.8, four-story brk and stone dwell'gs. Mary Monell widow to Julia M. wife of William Habirshaw. Sub. to mort. $78,250. Nov. 2. 25,000

Madison av, No. 1236, s w cor 89th st, 25.8x75.
89th st, No. 18, s s, 75 w Madison av, 38.4x100.8.
Seven-story brk flat in course of erection.
Thomas Graham to Charles Graham. All liens. Oct. 13. nom

Madison av, No. 1701, e s, 75.5 n 112th st, runs north 25 x east 20 x north 0.6 x east 55 x south 25.6 x west 75, five-story brk flat. Philip Kaiser to Edward Weinburger. *Mt.* $15,000. Nov. 24. 22,000

Madison av, No. 1673, n e cor 111th st, 15x70, three-story brk (stone front) dwell'g. J. George Flammer to Solomon Jacobs. *Mt.* $7,000. Nov. 14. 12,300

Manhattan av, e s, extends from 100th st to 101st st, 201.10x95, vacant.
Manhattan av, w s, extends from 100th st to 101st st, 201.10x100, vacant.
Girard otherwise Leonce G. Romaine and Julia A. Romaine devisees Benjamin F. Romaine to Benjamin F. Romaine formerly B. F., Jr., Louis T. and Washington T. Romaine. 2-5 part. Aug. 13. nom

Manhattan av
102d st
103d st
begins Manhattan av, w s, extends from 102d st to 103d st, 201.10x150, vacant. Same to same. 2-5 part. Aug. 13. nom

Same property. Release dower. Julia A. Romaine widow to Benjamin F. formerly B. F., Jr., Romaine, Louis T., Girard otherwise Leonce G., Julia A. and Washington T. Romaine devisees Benjamin F. Romaine. June 16. nom

Manhattan av, e s, extends from 100th st to 101st st, 201.10x95.
Manhattan av, w s, extends from 100th st to 101st st, 201.10x100
Release dower. Same to same. June 16. nom

Manhattan av, s e cor 105th st, 17.3x70. Release mort. Ann Miller to Henrietta M. Bostwick. Nov. 21. 5,000

Manhattan av, No. 553, s w cor 123d st, 18.5x74, three-story brk (stone front) dwell'g. Sarah E. wife of Justus Cooke to Annie T. Braham. Nov. 21. 18,500

Morningside av, s w cor 119th st, 100.11x100, vacant.
119th st, s s, 100 w Morningside av, 50x100.11, vacant.
Joseph W. Spencer, East Orange, N. J., to John Pettit, East Orange, N. J. Aug. 13. nom

Park (4th) av, No. 890, w s, 102.2 s 79th st, runs west 58 x north 10 x east 17 x north 17.2 x east 41 to 4th av, x south 27.2, four-story brk dwell'g. Harry A. Groesbeck to Walton Storm. *Mt.* $20,000 and taxes 1891. Nov. 25. nom

Park av, No. 74, w s, 74.1 n 38th st, 24.8x80, four-story stone front dwell'g. Francis E. Ogden, Chicago, Ill., to Frances O. Jones. Oct. 24. 70,000

Riverside av or Drive, e s, 82.10 s 82d st, 19.4x105.8x—x110.9, four-story brk and stone dwell'g. The Squier & Whipple Co. to Jane J. wife of Howard Phelps. Nov. 14. nom

Same property. Release judgment. Frank L. Smith to The Squier & Whipple Co. Nov. 20. nom

Same property. Release mort. John L. Brewster to same. Nov. 13 nom

Same property. Release mort. The New York Lumber and Wood Working Co. to same. Nov. 13. 2,600

Same property. Release mort. Francis M. Jencks and William N. Crane guards. of William M. Crane and trustees for Annie L. Merriam to same. Nov. 13. nom

1st av, No. 549, w s, 49.4 s 32d st, 24.8x100, four-story brk tenem't with stores. The Amsterdam Improvement Co. to Patrick Campbell. *Mt.* $10,500. Nov. 23. 12,250

1st av, No. 2208, e s, 73.11 n 113th st, 18x75, four-story brk tenem't. Louisa Garofalo to Rocco D'Onofrio. *Mt.* $8,500. Nov. 21. 10,900

1st av, No. 1454, e s, 122.2 n 75th st, 20x78, four-story brk store and tenem't. Morris Heyman to Fanny Sichel. Confirmation deed. *Mt.* $5,000. Sept. 25. 13,250

1st av, Nos. 1294-1300, s e cor 70th st, 100.5x113; Nos. 1294 and 1296, two five-story brk tenem'ts with stores; Nos. 1298 and 1300, five-story brk cigar factory.
70th st, s s, 113 e 1st av, 50x100.5, two five-story brk tenem'ts.
Ignatz Lederer, Prague, Austria-Hungary, to Charles Bondy. 1-9 part. Dec. 23, 1889. 9,000

2d av, No. 677, w s, 49.4 s 37th st, 24.8x105, four-story brk store and tenem't. Thomas Hume heir William Hume or Humes to James A. Hume. Q. C. May 13. 5,000

2d av, No. 891, w s, 80.10 s 48th st, 19.7x69.6, four-story brk store and tenem't. John Baum to Leah Weinberg. Nov. 25. 13,500

3d av, No. 1622, n w cor 91st st, 25.2x75, five-story brk (stone front) store and flat. Partition. Meyer Butzel to Jacob Ruppert. Nov. 25. 41,500

4th av, No. 261, e s, 46 s 21st st, 23x90, portion of four-story brk hotel. Foreclos. Waldo Hutchins, Jr., to Martin Mahon and Edward Coyne. Sub. to mort. $15,000 and int. at 5%, from May 2, 1891. Nov. 24. 20,779

4th av, Nos. 246 and 248, w s, 20 s 20th st, 40x64, two four-story brk tenem'ts with stores. Foreclos. Waldo Hutchins, Jr., to Henry Iden. *Mt.* $40,000. Nov. 24. 25,075

5th av, No. 2074, w s, 23.5 s 128th st, 19x75, four-story brk dwell'g. Absalom W. Dieter to Amelia E. Hummel. *Mt.* $25,000. Nov. 20. nom

5th av, No. 141, e s, 90 n 20th st, 25x90, four-story stone front dwell'g. Walter Cutting, Pittsfield, Mass., to Robert L. Cutting. ½ part. C. a. G. Oct. 31. 47,500

7th av, No. 2271, e s, 49.11 s 134th st, 25x71.6x+5x22.4x75, five-story brk store and flat. Foreclos. John S. Cram to Matthew Coogan. Nov. 5. 20,600

10th av, No. 546, e s, 78.9 s 41st st, 20x64, four-story brk store and tenem't. Dirk C. F. Janssen to Henry Langer. *Mt.* $6,000. Nov. 24. 14,000

Same property. Henry Langer to Joseph Greff. *Mt.* $6,000. Nov. 24. 14,500

All title of grantor in all alleyways in block bet Grand and Canal sts and Sullivan and Thompson sts and which lie north of line commencing on e s Sullivan st, 67 s of Grand st, runs east 62 x south 3 x east 28, with consent to close same. John T. Williams to William H. Johnston, Greenport, L. I. B. & S. Nov. 25. nom

23d and 24th WARDS.

Arcularius pl, s s, 309.3 e Gerard av, 100x157.3x102x177.3. George M. Miller and Wheeler H. Peckham to Thomas W. Surridge. Nov. 19. 3,500

Arcularius pl, s s, 359.3 e Gerard av, 50x100. Thomas W. Surridge to George and Lena Wilkins. Nov. 24. 2,200

Berry st, n s, 100 w Anthony av, 50x96. William J. Gilmore to Sophia A. Van Demark. *Mt.* $4,500. Nov. 7. exch

Bristow st, w s, 297.6 n Jennings st, 20x52.4x20x53.4
Bristow st, w s, 272.6 n Jennings st, 25x53.4x25x54.6.
Stebbins av, e s, 911.4 n Freeman st, 39.9x12.10x106.4x43.6x116.10.
Charles A. Sproessig to Christiana A. Sproessig. Oct. 17. gift

Lillian pl, east cor Rodman pl, 30x100x33x100.6. Michael J. Breidenbach to Charles M. Breidenbach. Nov. 21. 1,000

Rock st, n e cor Cornell pl, 50x100. James F. and Patrick H. Sheridan and James S. Segrave to James O'Shea. Nov. 16. 1,100

Suburban st, n w cor Briggs av, 33.11x100x91.4 x115.4. James M. Peebles and William J. McPherson to Agnes wife of James M. Peebles. Nov. 23. nom

Tiffany st, e s, 79.3 s 167th st, runs east 200 to Fox st, x north 25 x west 100 x northwest 85.10 to 167th st, x southwest 74.8 to Tiffany st, x south 79.3. Joseph L. O'Brien to Roderick P. Fisher, Brooklyn. Nov. 18. exch

Willard st, n s, 400 e Kepler av, 25x100. Jane Potter individ. and extrx. William H. Potter to Mary E. Monaghan. Nov. 24. 425

136th st, n s, 296 e Southern Boulevard, 25x100. Charles H. Doremus to John Whitaker and Herbert Richmond. Nov. 21. 2,550

143d st, new, n s, 542.6 e from old e s Willis av, 16.9x94.6x16.9x96, h & l. Matilda Haggerty to Edward C. Betzig. *Mt.* $2,500. Nov. 23. 5,500

159th st, s s, lot 112 map Melrose, 50x100. Francis Meyer to Margaretha Meyer his wife. B. & S. Oct. 8. gift

169th st, lot 97 map Morrisania, 39x98.9. Henry Weiss, Brooklyn, grandson and an heir of John Weiss to Henry Weiss. B. & S. Nov. 23. 500

Bathgate av, n w s, 32.6 s w from line bet lots 35 and 36 and being part of lot 36 map Upper Morrisania, 32.6x100, near 176th st, h & l. Francis B. Hagen to Francis A. Brown. Nov. 20. 3,900

Bathgate av, e s, 60 s 182d st, 20x90. William J. Pragnell to Margaret L. Moses. Nov. 20. 4,250

Central av, north cor Talmadge st, 65x100; also ½ of Talmadge st. adj premises. 25x100. William Cauldwell to Philip Stacom. Nov. 16. 1,850

Clinton av, e s, 25 s Elmwood pl, 115x100. John J. Brady to Lena Seiferd. Nov. 19. 6,000

Courtlandt av, s e cor 160th st, 98.6x92. Charles Eckel, Brooklyn, to Barbara Heorr. Nov. 18. 8,000

Cypress av, s e cor 149th st, 50x64. John Haffen to Philip Karcher. Nov. 21. 7,000

Intervale av, n w s, 483.5 n e 169th st, 25x71.3x 36.10x104.4. Luigi Pepe to Theresa Sofia. Aug. 14. nom

Same property. Theresa Sofia to Diodoro Sofia. Sept. 5. nom

Intervale av, e s, 194.3 n 165th st, 75x100.
Kelly st, s w cor 167th st, 30x75.
Kelly st, w s, 90 s 167th st, 75x100.
Fox st, w s, 20.7 s 169th st, 25x131.10x25.4x136.
Tiffany st, n e cor 167th st, 135.2x113.2x irreg.
168th st, south cor Tiffany st, 176.2x irreg.
Jacob B. Weinberg to Abraham Schneider. Sept. 22. nom

Jackson av, s e s, part lot 93 map of Belmont, runs southeast 6 x west to av, x northeast 3.5. Darius Lyon to Robert Welsh. Q. C. Nov. 20. nom

Jerome av, w s, 70.7 s Fordham pl, 141.5x19.7x 136.9x43.9. Nathan Wise to Elias Spingarn. Nov. 23. 2,500

Mall av, n w cor Perot st, runs north to s s Knowlton st, x west to Elwood av, x south to Perot st, x east to beginning.
Elwood av, n w cor Perot st, runs north to Oakley pl, x west to Sedgwick av, x south to Perot st, x east to beginning.
Elwood av, Oakley pl, Sedgwick av and Oakley pl—block.
Release mort. New York Life Ins. Co. to Samuel W. Fairchild. Nov. 17. 74,183

Morris av, e s, 25 n 149th st, 25x70.3. Kate De Vall to Adam Uhl. Nov. 6. 7,800

Perry av, w s, 150 s Scott av, 25x100. Robert N. Quinn to Henry Lucy. *Mt.* $215. Nov. 19. 800

Prospect av, s w cor Lebanon st, 20x100. Libbie B. wife of Robert E. Holder to Henry W. Stratton, of Seymour, N. Y. *Mt.* $800. Nov. 28. nom

Prospect av, w s, 45 s Elmwood pl, 75x100.
Clinton av, n e cor Elmwood pl, 20x100x20.4 x100.
Crotona av, s w cor Oakland pl, 50x100x51x 100.
Crotona av, e s, 75 n Lebanon st, 75x100.
John J. Brady to Nelson Smith, Jr. Oct. 19. 8,080

Stebbins av, s w cor Jennings st, 75.7x38.6x48.8 x69.6. Release mort. Sarah H. Crane and Zilla K. Napier, Brooklyn, to Charlotte F. Trowbridge, Brooklyn. Nov. 20. nom

Same property. Charlotte F. wife of and Miner Trowbridge to Simon M. Sheldon. Nov. 24. 1,400

Tinton av, e s, 225.10 s 166th st, 16.8x100. William H. Whittle to Mary A. Whittle. Nov. 18. nom

Tinton av, e s, 269 n 165th st, 12.1x100. William Bloodgood to Albert J. Gaiser. Nov. 24. 450

Tremont av, n s, 96.1 e Crotona av, 50.3x117.6x 50.10x117.6, with all land bet old and new lines of sts. Lena Seiferd to Michael F. Shelley and Margaret his wife, joint tenants. Nov. 28. 3,800

Washington av, e s, 300 n Schuyler st, 50x 121.6 to w s old Boston road, x51.3x109.6.
Elton late Washington av, e s, 275 n Schuyler st, 25x109.6x25x108.6.
Lavenia J. Palmer, Philadelphia, Pa., to Franklin G. Palmer. Jan. 13, 1890. nom

Willard av, n s, 425 e 3d st, 50x100.
Willard av, n s, 350 e 3d st, 50x100.
Thomas otherwise Thomas L. White, Toronto, Canada, to Mary E. Monaghan. Nov. 9. 1,600

3d av, e s, 229.11 s 163d st, 25.2x133.4x25x130.4. Jacob B. Weinberg to Abraham Schneider. Sept. 22. nom

3d av, e s, 171.2 s 163d st, 33.6x127.5x33.4x123.6. Patrick J. Casey exr. Michael Casey to Mary A. Casey widow. Oct. 29. 8,000

Lots 12, 13 and 14 block 442 map 919; also all estate of Michael Haley dec'd. Release dower. Ellen Mullarkey widow to James Haley and Mary Coyne. Nov. 13, 1891. 200

Lot 5 map 153 select lots, &c., Kingsbridge Heights, 24th Ward. Samuel W. Fairchild to Frank G. Bronson, Mt. Vernon. Nov. 16. 1,080

Lot 30 same map. Same to Charles Blyth. Nov. 16. 1,000

Lot 14 same map. Same to William J. Chestnut. Nov. 16. 1,175

Lot 54 same map. Same to Peter Engelmann. Nov. 16. 850

Lot 13 same map. Same to Andrew Galbraith. Nov. 16. 850

Lot 31 same map. Same to Frederick Koster. Nov. 16. 1,000

Lot 51 same map. Same to Robert D. McGarrah. Nov. 16. 825

Lots 15 and 16 same map. Same to James McGinty. Nov. 16. 1,750

Lot 35 same map. Same to Edward McFadden. Nov. 16. 1,375

Lots 11 and 12 same map. Same to Mary E. A. Ryan. Nov. 16. 1,700

Lot 29 same map. Same to William Strachan and Janet his wife, joint tenants. Nov. 16. 1,025

Lots 32, 33 and 34 same map. Same to John M. Brown. Nov. 16. 3,000

Lots 6-10 inclus. same map. Same to Adelaide V. Anness. Nov. 16. 5,325

Lot 32 map Ash property, West Farms, 24th Ward. Partition. James W. Hawes to Caroline Diehl. All title in tax lease. May 18, 1886. 80

Lot 34 map 153 select lots, &c., Kingsbridge Heights, 24th Ward. John M. Brown to Edward McFadden. Nov. 21. nom

LEASEHOLD CONVEYANCES.

Elizabeth st, No. 258. Assign. lease. Joseph Gorman to The Budweiser Brewing Co. (Lim.) Nov. 18. nom

Mott st, No. 141. Assign. lease. Frank Carlo to Biagio Tremmaglio and Gaetano Scalzi, of Scalzi & Tremmaglio. Nov. 25. nom

4th st, s s, 175 w Av A, 25x96.2, all. Franklin H. Delano et al. trustees for John J. Astor to Anton Nussbaum. 20 years, from May 1, 1879, per year, taxes, &c., and 350

12th st, Nos. 630 and 632 E. Assign. leases. Louis C. Muller and Mary C. his wife to Aaron Rosenblum. Nov. 11. 6,150

Same property. Assign. leases. Aaron Rosenblum to Morris Franklin. ½ part Nov. 25. 3,075

24th st, n s, 258 w 8th av, 17x86.8x17x87.9. Assign. lease. John Charlton exr. and trustee John Charlton dec'd with consent of Katharine T. Moore to Rebecca Smith widow. May 13. nom

46th st, s s, 332 e 8th av, 18x100.5. Assign. lease. Thomas C. Smith to Ascher Weinstein. Nov. 28. nom

74th st, No. 228 E. Assign. lease. Lawrence and Elise Schuler to George Ringler & Co. nom

West End av, No. 487, w s, 66.8 n 88th st, 18x 100. Alonzo Kimball to Arthur G. Thompson. 25 years, from Nov. 24, 1891, per year, taxes, &c., and 1,250

1st av, No. 489. Assign. lease. Henry Martin to David Stevenson. Nov. 21. nom

1st av, No. 2036, n e cor 105th st. Assign. lease. Annie Callaghan to Margaret McDonough. Sept. 26. nom

Same property. Assign. lease. Margaret McDonough to Joseph McGovern. Nov. 23. nom

3d av, s e cor 111th st. Assign. lease. Peter Coleman to H. Koehler & Co., a corporation. Nov. 24. nom

8th av, w s, 14 n 22d st, 14x58. Katharine T. Moore to Mary L. Clements. 21 years, from Nov. 1, 1893, per year, taxes and 312

8th av, No. 600, cor 39th st. Assign. lease. Patrick J. Gray to John D. Haffner. Nov. 24. nom

8th av, w s, 56.6 n 22d st, 28.4x58. Mary E. Moore to Josephine Wells, East Orange, N. J. 21 years, from Nov. 1, 1893, per year, taxes and 624

9th av, No. 790. Assign. lease. Henry Goltze to John Krug. Nov. 24. nom

Mill Brook, at intersection of Westchester road or turnpike, runs east 390 to land of Port Morris Branch of N. Y. & Harlem R. R., x north to point 100 n of Westchester road, x west to centre of Mill Brook, x south to beginning, 100x390. Town of Morrisania by Board of Trustees to Hugh Kelly. 1,000 years, from Feb. 21, 1870, for 1,729

Same property. Assign. lease. Virginia P. Kelly extrx. Hugh Kelly to The House of the Good Shepherd. April 6, 1887. 1,729

KINGS COUNTY.

NOVEMBER 19, 20, 21, 23, 24, 25.

Adelphi st, w s, 761.10 s Park av, 25x100; also strip south of above, 0.4x100. Edwin De Baun to Ida M. Myers. nom

Adelphi st, No. 18, w s, 161.2 s Flushing av, 20x 42. Peter McCoy to Annie Loftus. $2,850

Barbey st, e s, 140 s Blake av, 20x100. Joseph Tibball to Charles F. Mourlot. 415

Bergen st, s s, 117.6 e Troy av, 48x127.9. The Manhattan Savings Inst. to John B. Marquand. C. a. G. 1,400

Bergen st, n s, 253 w Ralph av, 102x107.2. Orson W. Sheldon, of Fort Ann, N. Y., to Eliza Reed. nom

Bergen st, n s, 134.4 e Ralph av, 17x107.2.
Bergen st, n s, 253 e Ralph av, 17x107.2.
Mary E. wife of Isaac D. Mason to Esther B. wife of Orson W. Sheldon, of Fort Ann, N. Y. *Mt.* $4,800. nom

Bergen st, s s, 100 w Hopkinson av, 25x127.9, h & l. Rosa and James Rosenfeld to Leo Moretzki, New York. *Mt.* $3,200. 3,600

Berriman st late Bennett av, w s, 175 n Liberty av, 205x½ block x180x100.
Broadway late Eastern Parkway, n w cor Shepherd av, 150x95.
Broadway, n s, 25 e Shepherd av, 50x100.
Shepherd av, w s, 100 n Bay av now Belmont av, 100x100.
Laura H. Curtis widow to Alonzo E. De Baun. 7,000

Berriman st, e s, 130 s Bennett av, 40x100. Richard Long to William and Katharina Schultze, New York. 525

Bleecker st, n w s, 59 s w Evergreen av, 19 100. Mathilda Crist to Matthew Robb. nom

Boerum st, s s, 211.10 w Bogert st, runs south 100 x west 85 x north 25 x northeast to st, x east 10. Charles W. Truslow admr. William Wall to Ernst Oehner. 350

Bridge st, n e cor Tallman st, 17x50. Samuel M. Meeker exr. Frederick Herr to Catharine T. wife of Michael Faulkner. 5,250

Broadway, easterly cor Willoughby av, 72x80. Samuel M. Meeker exr. Frederick Herr to Fanny Jacobs. 24,500

Canton st, e s, 67.6 n Myrtle av, runs east 73.8 x northwest 68.4 x southwest 61.9 x west 23.7 to st, x south 20. George W. Heatley to Kate Dowling. 3,500

Carroll st, n s, 160 e Nevins st, 21x100. Amalia Seuferling widow to Christopher Stockmann. *Mt.* $700. 1,100

Carroll st, n s, 320 e 4th av, 60x100, h & l. Andrew P. Blixt to Gustava Anderson. *Mt.* $6,000. 1,400

Cedar st, s s, 400.7 e Evergreen av, 20x79.3x20.1 x81.6, h & l. Mary A. Lyon to Newman C. Lyon. 3,000

Cooper pl, e s, 190 s Herkimer st, 46x100. Charles F. Bunt to James D. Rankin and James Ross. *Mt.* $1,250. nom

Court st, s e cor 4th pl. Party wall agreement. Thomas Wynne with Patrick J. Carlin.

Court st, e s, 71 s Huntingdon st, 20.8x97. Mary Lennon to John Lennon. ½ part. 4,950

Chauncey st, s s, 275 w Stuyvesant av, 25x60.3 x25.1x57.6. Catharine M. Hewison, of New York, to Michael N. Donovan. *Mt.* $1,200. 2,400

Covert st, s e s, 326 n e Evergreen av, 18x100. John Herzog to Joseph Gschwind. *Mt.* $1,600. 3,500

Degraw st, s s, 230.6 e Van Brunt st, 19.6x100, h & l. Martin Devitt and ano. exrs. Julia Peterson to Anthony Sessa. *Mt.* $1,500. 4,275

Dresden st, w s, 270.5 n Atlantic av, 75x108.11x 75x104. Hiram Westbrook, of Ridgewood, N. J., to Jane L. Smith. nom

Same property. Jane L. wife of and Charles H. Smith to John H. Kerrigan. 1,300

Dupont st, s s, 375 e Oakland st, 25x100. The trustees of Union College, Schenectady, N. Y., to John McGrath. 1,000

Earl st, n s, 640 w Brooklyn av, 20x100, Flatbush. Edward Egolf to John A. Behr. 250

Eastern Parkway, n s, 184.3 e Schenectady av, runs north 220.7 to Degraw st, x south and east 225.10 to Eastern Parkway, x west 44.9. Release mort. William M. Evarts, of New York, to Charles Fahr. 2,000

Same property. Charles Fahr to Charles Wilhelms. 2,000

Eastern Parkway, n s, 25 e Thatford av, 25x 100, h & l. Harris Newblatt to Rebecca Newblatt. *Mt.* $5,000. 6,000

Eldert st, s e s, 100 s w Knickerbocker av, 60x 100. Augusta wife of William Schoenborn to Michael Moran. exch

Essex st, e s, 100 n Ridgewood av, 20x100, h & l. Minnie Josiah to Andrew E. Owens. *Mt.* $1,500. 3,000

Essex st, w s, 797.4 n New Lots road, 24x189.5 to Linwood st. William Lucas to William Laird. 850

Fulton st, s w cor Wyona st, 100x100.
Fulton st, s e cor Vermont av, 106x100.
Louis Haeberle to Charles P. Engelbrecht. ½ part. Sub. to ½ part of morts. $6,000. 1,470

Frost st, s s, 275 e Lorimer st, 25x100, h & l. Peter and Michael Pierri to Antonio Ciorciari and Giusseppe Cobiccio. *Mt.* $500. 2,400

Frost st, s s, 225 e Leonard st, 25x100. Peter Mahon to Marshall G. Dodds. 900

Same property. Release mort. Claus H. Bogel to Peter Mahon. 450

Grove st, n s, 190 w Central av, 20x100. Frank Ibert to Lueder Schulenburg. exch and 100

Grove st, n s, 190 w Central av, 40x100. John Rapp to Frank Ibert. 2,100

Grove st, n w s, 190 s e Central av, 140x100. Josephine Bowron extrx. Watson Bowron to John Rapp. Q. C. Correction deed. 35

Hall st, e s, 304 n Myrtle av, 20x100, h & l. George A. Caldwell to Kate wife of Thomas S. Edgar. 4,650

Halsey st, n s, 550 e Bedford av, 25x376.10 to Nostrand av, x north 4.0 x west 100 x north 60 x west 300 x south 100. Thomas B. Jackson to William H. Reynolds. 29,000

Halsey st, n s, 100 w Nostrand av, runs north 26 x southwest to n s Halsey st, at point 375 west of Nostrand av, x east 275. Mary A. Lynch, New York, to William H. Reynolds. nom

Halsey st, s s, 22 w Ralph av, 178x100. Richard Mullowney to Bernard Levino. Sub. to mort. nom

Halsey st, s w cor Ralph av, 22x100. Same to Horatio S. Stewart. *Mt.* $18,000. nom

Hancock st, n s, 335 6 w Tompkins av, 19.6x100. William H. Reynolds to Margaret J. wife of William Reynolds. *Mt.* $6,000. nom

Hancock st, n s, 80 w Lewis av, 18x100, h & l. Poline wife of Morris Byk to Joseph Byk. nom

Hart st, n w s, 200 n e Broadway, 20x75. David Williams to Charles H. Ohler. 5,050

Hart st, s s, 109.2 e Wyckoff av, 20x100. Jacob Staehler to William L. Murphy, of New York. 800

Hemlock st, w s, 175 s Liberty av, runs west 100 x south 71.5 to Conduit av, x southeast 118 to Hemlock st, x north 134.11. John H. Ives to Chas. M. Julian and Theodore Sanger, Jr. 800

Henry st, e s, 27 n Degraw st, runs east 125.2 x north 31.7 x west 27.2 x south 9.10 x west 98 to st, x south 22, h & l. Ellen Constant to John J. Roche exr. Ellen Roche. Q. C. nom

Same property. John J. Roche exr. Ellen Roche to Frances M. Keefe, New York. *Mt.* $4,500. 7,750

Same property. John J. Roche to James M. Keefe, New York. *Mt.* $4,500. 7,750

Henry st, e s, 43.10 s Congress st, 22 8x80x27.8x 89.2. Thomas H., William T., Samuel H. and James H. Liddle to Ruth H. Liddle. nom

Herkimer st, n s, 20 w Saratoga av, 80x80.
Saratoga av, w s, 80 n Herkimer st, 40x100.
Albert Johnston to Harriet Johnston. nom

Herkimer st, n s, 60 w Nostrand av, 40x97. James O. Carpenter to Marvin T. Lyon. nom

Herkimer st, n s, 75 w Sackman st, 73x100. Robert E. Topping to William H. Bath. *Mt.* $3,300. nom

Hicks st, s e s, 122.7 n e Love lane, 25x100, h & l. Henry L. Meyer to Ida H, wife of Henry L. Meyer. *Mt.* $6,000. nom

Himrod st, n w s, 250 s w Irving av, 75x100. Charles H. Stoetzer to George Paulding. *Mt.* $2,175. 3,525

Hewes st, s e s, 208.4 s w Marcy av, 20.10x100, h & l. Eva wife of Joseph L. Ross to Andrew R. Baird. *Mt.* $5,500. nom

Jackson st, n s, 175 w Graham av, 25x100. Julius Jacoby to Valentine & Co. 1,450

Jacob st, s e s, 100 n e Central av, runs southeast 40.8 x southwest — x southeast to centre block bet Jacob and Cornelia sts, x northeast 70 x northwest 100 to Jacob st, x southwest 60. Release mort. Alfred J. Pouch to Margarett Purgold. 2,000

Jefferson st, n w s, 125 n e Central av, 25x100. John Klein to Mary Klein. *Mt.* $2,100. nom

Jerome st, e s, 580 n Hegeman av, 20x100. William B. Nichols to John C. Elliott. 100

Same property. John C Elliott to Robert S. Neely. 200

Java st, n s, 300 e Oakland st, 25x100. Lewis Boulger to Charles McCauley. 1,375

Kane pl, e s, 121.7 n Atlantic av, 46x105. John Fallon to John D. Fish. *Mt.* $10,350. nom

Kosciusko st, s s, 450 w Reid av, 100x100. Elizabeth E. Hutchins widow, New York, to James Cumiskey. 6,800

Kosciusko st, s s, 100 w Stuyvesant av, 25x100. Frank Roessle to Jacob Leib. All liens. nom

Kosciusko st, s s, 76.8 w Lewis av, 18 6x100, h & l. Catharine E. wife of Joseph W. Sharp to Rose Guntzberger. *Mt.* $4,000. 4,600

Same property. Rose wife of Isidor Guntzberger to Mary C. wife of Herman H. Schorling. *Mt.* $4,000. 4,800

Kosciusko st, s s, 100 e Lewis av, 38.3x100, hs & ls.
Kosciusko st, s s, 204.3 e Lewis av, 34.6x100, hs & ls.
Samuel P. Potter to Asa A. Spear. Sub. to all liens. 500

Linwood st, e s, 100 n Arlington av, 40x107.2x 40x106 11. Release mort. The Williamsburgh Savings Bank to Edward F. Linton. 700

Macon st, No 509, n s, 200 e Stuyvesant av, 18.9 x100. Arthur Taylor to Harriet B. Salisbury. *Mt.* $4,500. 8,500

Macon st, s s, 260 w Sumner av, 20x100. Patrick O'Reilly to James H. Sherwood. 6,600

Madison st, n s, bet Ralph and Patchen avs, being on assessm't map 25th Ward lot 28 block 47. John J. White to William H. White. nom

Madison st, n w s, 280 n e Hamburg av, 20x100. Release mort. James Gascoine individ and with ano. exrs. Jno. G. Cozine to Adolphus Gload. 1,248

Same property. Adolphus Gload to Hannah Michaelis. nom

Madison st, s e s, 480 n e Central av, 20x100. Emil F. Wildner to Mathilda Crist. nom

Madison st, No. 590, s s, 281 e Lewis av, 19x100. Contract. Phebe A. Godfrey and Joseph E. Paisley. 9,750

McDonough st, s s, 181.8 w Ralph av, 18.4x100. Miles Murphy to Eva Murphy. nom

Meserole st, n s, 80 e Lorimer st, 20x100. Michael J. Kneff to Joseph Fallert Brewing Co. (Lim.) exch

Meserole st, n s, 40 e Lorimer st, 20x70. Joseph Fallert Brewing Co. (Lim.) to Michael J. Kneff and Anna his wife. exch

Marion st, s s, 387.7 e Howard av, 18 8x100. Release mort. James McLaren to Elizabeth P. McNab. 875

McKibbin st, n s, 204.4 w Bogert st, 25x100. Charles W. Truslow admr. Wm. Wall to Ernst Oehner. 900

Monroe st, s s, 405.3 w Tompkins av, 19.9x100. William H. Dill to Maggie L. Peet. *Mt.* $3,500 and tax 1891. 4,250

Monteith st, n s, 100 w Bremen st, 20x100, h & l. Renata Herget to Eugene Herget. B. & S. nom

North Elliott pl, w s, 86 n Auburn pl, 20x100. William M. Dickover to John J. Moran. 5,400

North Henry st, w s, 95 s Norman av, 120x100 James D. Lynch to Joseph Hunt. 6,000

Ocean Parkway, w s, 150 s Coney Island Elevated R. R., runs west 160 x northwest 283 7 to Coney Island Elevated R. R., x west 52.10 x southeast 239 x east 160 to Parkway, x north 50; also,
Coney Island Elevated R. R., s s, 371.6 w Ocean Parkway, runs southeast — x110 to s s Coney Island Elevated R. R., x west 80, Gravesend.
John Y. McKane to The Sea Beach & Brighton R. R. Co. Dated 1886. nom

Oak st, s s, 367 e Franklin st, runs east 22 x south 65.3 x west 16.9 x west 5.11 x north 70. Carman A. Robinson to Max Berliner. 4,050

Osborn st, s w cor Livonia av, 50x100. Margaret A. Tostevin to Annie wife of Joseph Mathews. 1,800

Pacific st, s s, 166.8 e Rockaway av, 33.4x107.2, hs & ls. Robert S. Neely to William A. Hancock. nom

President st, s e cor 7th av, 38x100, h & l. Hans N. Christian to Amelia E. Hummel. *Mt.* $45,000. exch

President st, s s, 365.6 w 5th av, 34x100, hs & ls. Isabella, Mary H., and John L. Conklin and Fanny S. wife of George D. Stevens to Robert F. Rhodes. *Mt.* $12,500. 125

Prospect pl, s s, 283 4 e Rogers av, 16.8x100. Minor M. Mayward to William H. Preston, Riverhead, L. I. 1,200

Same property. John N. Wirth to Caspar Mengel. B. & S. nom

Ross st, s s, 325 w Marcy av, 25x200 to Rodney st. Mary E. Blohm to Edward E. Blohm. 7,500

Sandford st, e s, 232.8 s Park av, 25x100. Mary Messinger, of Newark, N. J., to Catharine Geyer. *Mt.* $4,000. nom

Seigel st, s s, 665 e Bushwick av, 25x100. Charles W. Truslow admr. Wm. Wall to Ida Herrmann. 625

Stanhope st, n w s, 150 n e Central av, runs northwest 89.5 x east 27.1 x southeast 78.11 to st, x southwest 25. Emma wife of and Charles Isbill to Ernestine Ulschmid. *Mt.* $2,000. 4,200

Skillman st, n s, 175 e Ewen st, 25x100. Conrad A. Schuman exr. and trustee Catharina A. Schuman to Valentine & Company. 2,200

Skillman st, w s, 133 4 s Park av, 16.8x100. Hjalmer Holm to William M. Rider, of Dunellen, N. J. *Mt.* $1,800. exch

Skillman st, w s, 200 n Park av, 25x100. Peter J. Brett to The Gutta Percha and Rubber Mfg. Co., of New York. 2,750

State st, n s, 125 e 3d av, 60x73.5x65.8x100. James W. Martens, of Mohegan, N. Y., to Percy G. Williams. 18,000

Steuben st, e s, 197.4 s De Kalb av, 22.4x100. Moritz Pinner to Emma Krug. *Mt.* $11,000. nom

Stockton st, s s, 200 e Throop av, 25x100. Catharina Rothschenk widow to Christian Huber. *Mt.* $4,700. 7,400

Taylor st, n s, 173.6 e Kent av, 19.11x80. Partition. Robert Merchant to Jacob Honig and Esak Klein. 3,575

Union st, n s, 363.4 e Hoyt st, 16.8x75. James B. Watson to Frederick W. Schneider. *Mt.* $1,400. 2,400

Van Buren st, n s, 22 w Lewis av, 19.6x100. Lena Rosenzweig to Alfred L. Beasley. *Mt.* $5,000. exch

Wallabout late River st, n s, 200 e Harrison av, 25x100, h & l. Caspar Mengel to John N. Wirth. nom

Watkins st, e s, 175 n Belmont av, 23.6x100, h & l. Herman Moretzky, of New York, to Meyer Lewin. *Mt.* $1,800. exch and 2,500

Windsor pl, s w s, 334.9 s e 7th av, 18.3x100. Jeannie F. Crane, of San Antonio, Texas, to Frederic Ryan. 2,000

Withers st, n s, 50 w Lorimer st, 25x100. Sabbato Rosso and Arsenic Corio to Sabino Sondoriello and Pietro Corio. 1,650

1st st, n s, 275 w 6th av, 0.4x100. Peter Kelly to Peter Larsen. nom

1st st, n s, 275 w 6th av, 0.4x100. Release mort. Brooklyn Life Ins. Co. to Peter Larsen. nom

1st st, s s, 70 e Hoyt st, 20x77.11x20x77.5. Maurice Brown to George W. Eastman. Q. C. nom

South 1st st, n s, 25 e Roebling st. 25x77. Release dower. Sarah J. Parmenter widow, of Summit, N. J., to John Middleton. nom

Same property. Samuel O. Parmenter, of South Sudbury, Mass. and Appleton D. Parmenter, of Berlin, Mass. to same. 2,300

South 2d st, s w s, 125 s e 2d st, 25x75. Charlotte B. McCullough to James Strachan. exch. and 100

6th st, s s, 180 w 4th av, 115x100. Patrick Maloney and Herman Becker to Albert Johnston. nom

7th st, No. 496, sub. to morts $6,500 and taxes, &c., $283. Contract to exchange for Herkimer st, s s, 156 8 w Rochester av, runs south 43 6 x south 40.7 x west 16 x north 40.9 x north 43 6 to st, x east 18, sub. to mort. $4,000. Mary J. Harvey to Holk D. Campbell.

8th st, n s, 260.4 w 7th av, 18.9x100, h & l. Louise Plowman to Mary R. Balken, New York. *Mt.* $3,500. nom

South 9th st, s s, 121 w Driggs av, runs west 25 x south 145 x northeast to point 121 w Driggs av, x north 140. Mary E. Blohm to Edward E. Blohm. 6,600

11th st, s s, 264.6 e 4th av, 16.8x100. Kate Cohen to Sophie and Maria Cohen, joint tenants. All title. 1,697

11th st, s s, 30 e 8th av, 18x81.10, h & l. Allison V. B. Morris to William J. Fowler. *Mt.* $5,500. 6,600

11th st, s s, 48 e 8th av, runs south 81.10 x east 36 x south 18.9 x east 18 x north 100 to 11th st, x west 54. William H. Hudson to James W. Wagstaff. *Mt.* $16,500. 20,700

11th st, s s, 30 e 8th av, runs south 81.10 x east 54 x south 18.2x east 36 x north 100 to st, x west 90. Release mechanic's lien. Thomas McCann to Allison V. B. Norris. nom

Same property. Release mort Raeburn, Latourette & Co. to same. 200

Same property. Release mort. Ira O. Miller to same. 25,500

Same property. Release judgment. Michael Rofrano to same. 100

Same property Release judgment. Napoleon Schneider to Allison Norris and William Turner. 150

11th st, s s, 102 e 8th av, 18x100, h & l. Allison V. B. Norris to Ella H. Robbins. *Mt.* $5,500. 6,900

11th st, s s, 48 e 8th av, runs south 81.10 x east 36 x south 18.2 x east 18 x north 100 to 11th st, x west 54, hs & ls. Allison V. B. Norris to William H. Hudson. *Mt.* $16,500. 20,700

12th st, s s, 222.10 w 7th av, runs south 100.3 x west 15.1 x north 0.3½ x west 7.5 x north 100 to 12th st, x east 22.6. Daniel W. Talcott to Charlotte E. McMurray. *Mt.* $5,750. nom

12th st, n e s, 217.10 s e 4th av, 20x100. Alexander G. Calder to Walter Mottram. 7,000

14th st, n s, 172.11 e 7th av, 17.6x100, h & l. Charles J Helfrich, New Brunswick, N. J., to Louisa Helfrich, same place. nom

15th st, s s. 97.10 e 7th av, 25x100. Catharine G. Ferry to The Fulton Bank, Brooklyn. *Mt.* $6,000. 2,500

17th st, n e s, 340 n w 6th av, 20x100.2, h & l. Release mort. Benjamin and William A. Andrews to Ellen F. Hermans. nom

Same property. Ellen F. Hermans to Fabie Berkeley. *Mt.* $3,000. nom

17th st, s s, 300 e 6th av, 22x100, h & l. George W. Conselyea and Anna M. Irwin to Katharine A. Low. 3,800

Bay 17th st, n w s, 450 s w 86th st, 50x193.4, New Utrecht. John Parke to Oliver H. Kingsland trustee. 2,000

Same property. Oliver H. Kingsland to Frederick Voss, New York. 1.000

19th st, n e s, 225 n w 7th av, 25x43x—x45. John Andrews to James Conway. 690

21st st, n s, 220.9 e 6th av, 32x100. Release mort. Stephen B. Sturges to James R. Robb. nom

27th st, s w s, 175 s e 4th av, 75x100.2. Walter L. Suydam and Helen S. wife of R. Fulton Cutting to The Norwegian Lutheran Trinity Church. 2,400

45th st, n e s, 300 s e 3d av, 120x100.2. Release mort. Stewart McDougall to James F. O'Rourke. 6,000

47th st, s s, 420 w 3d av, 39.10 to centre Old Gowanus road, x—x39.4x100.2. David J. Tingley and ano. to Annie M. Gibson. 490

50th st, s s. 100 e 6th av, 25x100.2. Celia F. wife of Charles H. Golding to Maria wife of Albert Erickson. 1,900

53d st, n s, 181.3 e 3d av, 18x100.2. Lawrence Maier to John H. Maier. nom

54th st, s w s, 235 n w 4th av, 20x100.2. Harry L. Bradley to John J. Gsanger. *Mt.* $2,500. See 79th st. 4,350

54th st, n s, 200 w 4th av, 20x100.2, h & l. Peder A. Larsen to Peder Andersen. *Mt.* $2,200. 4,200

55th st, n e s, 390 n w 3d av, 40x100. Samuel S. Coles to Samuel Roebuch or Roebuck. *Mt.* $3,100. 500

57th st, n e s, 100 s e 3d av, 60x100.2. Alexander Davidson to William S. Haman. *Mt.* $1,500. 3,000

58th st, n s, 100 e 13th av, 60x100.2, New Utrecht. James V. S. Woolley, of New York, to E. Ivan Hammarberg. 600

67th st, n s, 220 e 13th av, 40x100. Effingham H. Nichols to Robert Yates, Jr., and Henry V. Lane. 370

73d st, n s, 410 w 15th av, 40x100, Lefferts Park. James V. S. Woolley to Edward F. Krantz. 350

78th st, centre line, n s, 397.6 e 4th av, 40x130, New Utrecht. Abbie Q. Renwick to Carrie A. wife of Charles Gildersleeve. 750

79th st, s w s, 496.6 n w 18th av, runs southwest 100 x northwest 20 x southwest 100 to 80th st, x northwest 49.7 x northeast 200 to 79th st, x southeast 74, New Utrecht. James A. Townsend to Emma A. Tobias, of Sayre, Pa. 1,500

79th st, s s, 100.6 w 1st av, 120.8x124.8x120.4x 118.6. John J. Gsanger to Harry L. Bradley. *Mt.* $1,500. See 54th st. 3,000

83d st, n e s, 220 s e 24th av, 100x100, Gravesend Patrick Dempsey to Thomas F. May. *Mt.* $3,357. 4,200

East 93d st, e s, 125 s Av G, 50.5x100x50.11x 100, Canarsie. John H. Ireland to Erastus W. Seaman. 400

Atlantic av, n s, 250 e Bond st, 25x100. Foreclos. Duncan Edwards to Jacob Gerersdorf. 4,800

Belmont av late Bay av, n s, 50 e Schenck av, 50x100. John Quinn to John J. Hogan. *Mt.* $1,500. nom

Clinton av, n e cor Fulton st, runs north along av 18 x east 63.10 x south 42.5 to Fulton st, x west 52, hs & ls. Peter Roeder to Alonzo E. De Baun. *Mt.* $13,000. nom

Central av, n e s, 25 s e Eldert st, 25x80. Michael Moran to Augusta wife of William Schoenborn. *Mt.* $3,250. exch and 1,000

Central av, n e s, 45 n w Gates av, 20x80. Magdalena wife of and George Welsch to Henry Ranch. *Mt.* $2,800. See Knickerbocker av. 5,000

Clason av, w s, 36 n Putnam av, 16x76.6. Arthur L. Tomes to George W. Godward. *Mt.* $3,000. nom

Clason av, e s, 124.2 s Pacific st, 24.4x88. Margaret Connor to Edward D. Dwyer. *Mt.* $3,000. nom

Coney Island av, w s, 80.3 s Av D, 60.2x119.4x60x114.11, Flatbush. Joseph Wechsler to Carrie L. Jones. 3,200

De Kalb av, s s, 280 w Stuyvesant av, 20x100. Emma A. Hamel to Mary A. Lyon. *Mt.* $2,500. exch and 3,500

De Kalb av, n w s, 175 n e Hamburg av, 25x100. Theodore H. Werner to Louis Krause. *Mt.* $3,500. 6,500

Evergreen av, w s, 125 n Covert st, 39x95x34.10x95. Abby J. Bills to Emma L. Johnston. *Mt.* $2,400. nom

Elmwood av, s w cor East 4th st, 50x100, New Utrecht. John A. Bennet to Albert F. Johnson. other consid. and 600

Gates av, s s, 135 e Sumner av, 20x100. Alfred L. Beasley to Lena Rosenzweig. *Mt.* $4,500. exch

Georgia av, e s, 50 s Glenmore av, 25x100. Charles Ernst to Lawrence J. Frank. 800

Glenmore av, n s, 50 e Shepherd av, 50x85. Agnes S. Clayton to Ursula Klatt 2,100

Graham av, s w cor Powers st, 50x75. Rudolph J. Goerke to Pauline Goerke. ½ part. 5,250

Greene av, s s, 460 e Throop av, 20x100. David S. Beasley to Mary E. Steves. *Mt.* $5,000. 8,700

Hamilton av, n e s, 98.10 n w Carroll st, 20x—x25x76 4, h & l. Abraham Solomon exr. Sarah Solomon to John Anson. 8,000

Johnson av, s s, 25 e Bogert st, 50x100. Charles W. Truslow admr. Wm. Wall to Ida Herrmann. 2,500

Knickerbocker av, n s, 150 w Putnam av, 20x88. Henry Ranch to Magdalena wife of George Welsch. See Central av. 500

Lexington av, s s, 125 w Tompkins av, 100x60.8x101x46.9. David S. Brush to Gilbert P. Brush. 2,443

Lexington av, n s, 189.7 w Bedford av, 25x100. Joseph P. Puels to Samuel Garre. *Mt.* $500. nom

Lexington av, s s, bet Marcy and Tompkins avs, being on assessm't map 23d Ward, lots 62, 63, 64 and 65 block 39. The City of Brooklyn to D. S. Brush. 4 Q. C. deeds 2,443

Lexington av, north cor Concord st, 125x100, New Utrecht. Edward Lunzner to Louise Kropf. B. & S. Sub. to mort. nom

Same property. Louise Kropf to Maria Lunzner. B. & S. nom

Lexington av, n s, 107.2 w Broadway, runs north 18.5 x northeast 63.4 to Broadway, x northwest 20 x southwest 71.8 x south 26 9 to Lexington av, x east 20. Christian and Justus Doenecke to Bernard T. Biffar. *Mt.* $1,550. 3,500

Liberty av, n s, 25 w Bradford st, 25x100. Emilie F. Ernst to Frank F. Ernst. ½ part. Sub. to mort. $400. 1,400

Linwood av, e s, 100 n Arlington av, 40x107.2x40x106.11. Edward F. Linton to Christian Rupp. 1,500

Martense av, north cor Clementine st, 109.3x145x100x abt 100, Flatbush, error. Joseph Heckel to Francis H. Carr. 200

Myrtle av, n s, 54.7 w Carlton av, 24.6x88.6x25x93.2. Nisan Hess to Henry W. Healy. *Mt.* $4,000. 10,250

Norman av, s s, 80 e Humboldt st, 40x95. William Riebenstein to John Macdonald. 1,000

Nostrand av, w s, 40 n Halsey st, 60x100. James D. Lynch to Mary A. Lynch. nom

Nostrand av, n w cor Halsey st, 35.6x376.10 to n s Halsey st, x375. Emily F. Lynch to Mary A. Lynch. Q. C. nom

Same property. James D. Lynch and ano. exrs and trustees Jas. Lynch to same. 10,000

Same property. Release dower. Catharine Lynch widow to same. nom

Nostrand av, w s, 35.6 n Halsey st, 4.6x100x—x—. William H. Reynolds to Mary A. Lynch. nom

Ovington av, n s, 480 e 12th av, 40.5x140.5x34.5x141.1, New Utrecht. James V. S. Woolley, of New York, to Charles H. Silvia. 450

Park av, s s, 30 w Throop av, 25x75. Charles Doerschuck to Robert Kuttig. *Mt.* $5,000. 7,300

Putnam av, s s, 90 e Central av, 70x100. Release mort. Virginia A. Kleine to Margaret Purgold. 1,000

Putnam av, s e s, 90 n e Central av, 140x100. John T. Barnard to Sarah wife of Walter Hopkins. *Mt.* $5,500. 7,500

Same property. Sarah Hopkins to Margaret Purgold. Sub. to morts., &c. 4,000

Putnam av, n s, 340 e Reid av, 20x100. Belle Fisher to Sadie E. Rice. *Mt.* $6,500. nom

Putnam av, s s, 395 e Tompkins av, 20x100, h & l. Absalom W. Dieter to Amelia E. Hummel. *Mt.* $6,500. nom

Putnam av, s e s, 220 n e Broadway, 20x100, h & l. Michael Mulvihill to Frederick W. Hoese, Jr. *Mt.* $5,000. 6,500

Ridgewood av, s s, and Linden Boulevard, n s, section 26 amended map Linden terrace, Flatbush. Eliza A., Adrian V. and Helen Martense and Mary M. Prince to Jamas Cosgrove. 200

Rogers av, s w cor Douglass st, 127.6x175. William Eldridge. Julia A. Stevens, Eliza A. Bullis and Phebe A. Copeland heirs of Phebe Valentine to Morris J. Jackson. Q. C. 4,000

Ralph av, e s, 50 n Sumpter st, 25x100. William Eckert to George Gross. 2,500

Schenck av, w s, 200 n Liberty av, 25x100, h & l. Rosina Huttenlocber to Bertha Combe. 3,000

Sheffield av, e s, 25 n Eastern Parkway, 25x100. Sophie wife of and William Kolkhorst to Herman Endlich. *Mt.* $1,350. 1.925

Shepherd av, e s, 75 s Union av, 25x100. Charles E. Davis to Mary Davis his wife. nom

Snediker av, e s, 160 n Vienna av, 120x100. }
Hinsdale av, w s, 100 n Vienna av, 200x100. }
Kate Pickering to Annie L. Lamson. nom

South Portland av, w s, 301.6 n Atlantic av, 45x100. Solomon S. Jackson, of Jericho, N. Y., to George F. Corlis. 8,600

South Portland av, w s, 350 s Hanson pl, 20x100, h & l. James Gillen to Walter B. Merlin. 3,800

Stanley av, n w cor Atkins av, 40x95. William H. Jackson, of New York, to Margaret E. wife of Patrick F. O'Toole. 365

St. Marks av, n s, 316.6 w Underhill av, 38.6x131. Release mort. Richard W. Rhoades to William Gane. nom

St. Marks av, n s, 150 w Underhill av, 25x131. David J. Ramsdell to Martin L. Richardson. *Mt.* $6,000. nom

St. Nicholas av, s w s, 25 s e Troutman st, 25x95. John Lapp to John Loeffler. 700

Stone av, e s, 100 s Sutter av, 75x100. Louisa wife of Nicholas Kaufold to Amale Cohn. *Mt.* $1,650. 14,000

Stone av, e s, 100 n Sutter av, 25x100. Herbert C. Smith to Jacob Axelrod and Isaac Levingson. 600

Stuyvesant av, w s, 41.10 s Halsey st, 19.3x80.6, h & l. Andrew D. Baird to Sidney Bloodgood. *Mt.* $5,500. 7,500

Thatford av, s w cor Belmont av, 25x100.1. Daniel J. Sheeby to Meyer Wolinsky and Isaac Bernstein, New York. 1,100

Tompkins av, w s, 33.4 s Hart st, 16.8x75. Ann Taylor to Lemuel S. Clark. Q. C. nom

Same property. Ann, Frank K. and Joseph C. Taylor exrs. William Taylor to same. 4,800

Throop av, w s, 20 s Stockton st, 20x100. Sarah H. Tuttle, of North Hempstead, N. Y., to William Hoffman. 4,260

Van Cott av, s s, 25 e Sutton st, 25x109.5x28 6x123. Jeremiah V. Meserole to John G. Distler, Jr. 1,100

Washington av, e s, 150 n Willoughby av, 37.6x100. Jean N. wife of Charles Caldwell to Katharine C. wife of Frank Freeman. *Mt.* $5,000. nom

Willoughby av, n w cor Tompkins av, runs north 77.6 x west 80 x north 22.6 x west 45 x south 100 to Willoughby av, x east 125. Foreclos. John Courtney to James A. Bell. 20,100

4th av, w s, 88 s 14th st, runs west 54.10 x south 16 x west 0.2 x south 0.7 x east 55 to 4th av, x north 18.8. Mary wife of and James Ford to George Duncan. *Mt.* $3,000. 4,000

4th av, n w cor 40th st, 25 2x100. Elizabeth, Michael and Catharine Gilligan heirs Ellen Oakle to Margaret A. Oakley, of New York. 225

5th av, e s, 75.2 n 53d st, 25x100. Hans S. Christian to Ellie Toye. *Mt.* $227. 800

6th av, n w cor President st, 100x92. Edward Judson to Catherine Judson. nom

6th av, e s, 78.8 s 6th st, 15.8x78.10. Kate G. wife of Allison J. Van Brunt, Delawanna, N. J., to Cora V. Achor. *Mt.* $3,000. nom

6th av, s e cor 5th st, 99.5x87.10x99.1x87.10. William J. Gelston to Louis Bonert. 11,750

7th av, west cor 72d st, 21.5x74.3x20x66.6, New Utrecht. Prospect Land and Improvement Co. to John P. Stein. 375

7th av, southerly cor 61st st, 100x80, New Utrecht. Alfred Mettler to John H. and Charles A. Hornung. 775

7th av, w s, 60 s 2d st, 20x80. George B. Stoutenberg and Charles F. Hunt to Benjamin Armstrong. *Mt.* $8,000. nom

10th av, n w cor 67th st, 100x200, New Utrecht. James A. Townsend to Frank M. Stephens, of Sayre, Pa. *Mt.* $900. 2,500

15th av, w s, 60 n Bay Ridge av, 20x90, New Utrecht. James V. S. Woolley to Julius Kaplan. 325

Lots 520, 521, 522, 538, 539 and 540 block 10 map 597 lots of W. Ziegler. Gravesend. William Ziegler to William Wharton. 2,400

Lot 414 block 8 same map. Same to Robert H. Nesbitt. nom

Lots 204, 205 block 4, and lots 299 and 300 block 6 map 597 lots of W. Ziegler, Gravesend. William Ziegler to Mary T. Gallagher. 550

Lots 516, 517, 534 and 535 block 10 same map. Same to Mary T. Gallagher. 1,820

Lots 411, 412, 413, 415 and 416 block 8 same map. Same to Robert H. Nesbitt. 840

Lot 440 block 8 same map. Same to John Corr. 160

Interior lot, 55 n w 4th av and 95.5 n e 15th st, 0.7x0.2; also, }
Interior lot, 55 n w 4th av and 95.5 n e 15th st, runs southwest 0.5 x northwest 25.9 x southeast 25.9. }
John Weisenborn to Mary wife of James Ford. nom

Brooklyn and Jamaica turnpike road, s s, 200 e Patchen av, runs east 37.6 x north 33x37.6x33, being part of said road. Jane Stow to Belle S. Sutton. Q. C. nom

Coney Island road, n e cor Van Sielen pl, 49x100x49x107.4, h & ls, Coney Island. John Y. McKane to Agnes T. Conway. 3,800

Land under water New York Bay, adj premises of grantee, 1 5-100 acres. People State New York to Charles M. Bull. letters patent

New Lots road, s e cor Atkins av, 40x100. William H. Jackson, of New York, to Joseph Niederegger. 850

New Lots road, s s, lot 3 map made by J. Rapalje in 1841. Johannes Eldert and Jacob Rapalje to Henry Eldert, Flatbush. 1841. 20

Parcel in New Utrecht adj R. A. Van Brunt, ¼ acre and 38 perches. Andrew Miller to Fred. C. Cocheu. Q. C. nom

Same property. Fred. C. Cochen to Bay Ridge Park Improvement Co. Q. C. nom

Shore road, w s, upland and land under water bounded east by Shore road, west by high water line New York Bay, north by line 95 s of 83d st, and south by land of grantee herein; also land under water in front of premises. Charles M. Bull and John H. Van Brunt to The Crescent Athletic Club. 4,202

Old Newtown and Bushwick pike, n s, 75 e Bushwick av, 25x100, h & l. Hans C. Pfalzgraf to Alfred Stoffregen. 4,600

WESTCHESTER COUNTY.

NOVEMBER 18 TO 24—INCLUSIVE.

BEDFORD.

Babbitt, Benj. T. exr. of, to L. Bryan Robinson, 80 acres on road to Lewis Browns, adj school house. $2,000

CORTLANDT.

Brown, H. Lionel to Robt. McCord, s e cor Grand and Lincoln terraces, 66.6x100. nom

McCord, Robt. to Minnie Brown, same property. nom

Horton, Emily C. to Anna M. Cox, w s Simpson pl, 100x140. nom

Hubbell, Geo. to Chas. E. Curry and ano., s e cor Highland and Constant avs, abt 50x120. 1,900

Roe, Cornelius to The Mohegan Granite Co, s s Five Mile turnpike, 27 acres; also n s lane from Locust av, 37 acres. 6,411

Roe, Fred. F. to same, n s same lane, 7 acres. 711

EASTCHESTER.

Ashley, Marion T. to Mary I. Brennan, south ½ lot 297 e s 4th av, Mt. Vernon, 25x105. nom

Bard, Geo. W. to Wm. H. Bard, lot 581 s s 19th av, Wakefield, 100x114. nom

Bard, Wm. H. to Edmund R. Foley, part same lot, 66.8x114. 1,066

Brennan, Cath E. to Jas. R. Haney, lot 46 w s Union av, Mt. Vernon, 100x105. 1,900

Bundy, Emily C. et al. to Geo. W. Bard, lot 581 s s 19th av, Wakefield, 100x114. 800

Birkenstock, John to Leo Sielke, part lot 34 West Mt. Vernon and part 22 Northwest Mt. Vernon. nom

Boyd, Susie E. to Issac Anderson, lots 5, 6, 21, 22 and 23 map Penfield property. 6,000

Duke, Margt to Jane Tufts and ano., lots 756 and 804, 3d st and 17th av, Wakefield, 114x205, ½ int. 650

Earle, Charlotte M. to Isaac B. Lent and ano., lot 10 map Gould lots, Tuckahoe. 2,600

Forster, Fred. P. to Jas. N. Webb, lot 167, Chester Hill, 50x100. 1,000

Flohr, Anna E. and ano. to John Birkenstock, G lot 34 map West Mt. Vernon. 100

Glover, Hattie P. to Frank N. Glover, south ½ lot 684 e s 8th av, Mt. Vernon, 50x105. 3,500

Hoyt, Adelbert E. to John S. Lane, lot 119 Villa Park. nom

Hustace, Wm. A. to Edw. Caterson, Jr., lot 661 s s 18th av, Wakefield, 100x114. 1,625

Ostrander, Chas. H. to Fred. Abel, north ½ lot 613 w s 7th av, Mt Vernon, 50x105. 975

Penfield, Geo. J. to Sophie M. Hebert, lot 177 s w s Huguenot st, Penfield property. 980

Same to Emily V. Gaillard, lot 178. 790

Sielke, Leo to John Birkenstock, part lot 34, West Mt. Vernon. nom

Wheeler, John to Maxwell P. Johnston, lots 81-84 Boulevard, Vernon Park. 1,800

GREENBURGH.

Jones, Cyrus P. and wife to Johanna Hilley, lots 102 and 103, Ardsley. 245

Reilly, Malvina R. to Caroline R. Gibon, e s Broadway, adj Caroline Le Roy, 81x192. 7,000

LEWISBORO.

Hoyt, Wilbur H. to Jas. H. Clark, 37 acres on road from Vista to Wilton. 1,000

MAMARONECK.

Larchmont Manor Co. to Oswald Sanderson, n w cor Chestnut and Larchmont avs, 170x265. 5,431

Lyon, Harriet to Chas. H. Young, w s Mt. Pleasant av, 2 acres. 3,900

Van Arsdale, Wm. E. to Sarah M. Downs, lots 123 and 124, Grand Park. 400

MOUNT PLEASANT.

Minnerly, Wm. F. to Henry Wood, e s Bedford road, Tarrytown Heights, 50x120. 2,500

Smadbeck, Louis to John Hamilton and ano., lots 1567 and 1568, Sherman Park. 400

Same to Christian Lutz and ano., lots 1130-1133. 1,150

Same to Eugene Stone, lot 1386. 3,000

Same to John Clear, lot 1204. 250

Same to Jane McCulloch, lot 1889. 150

Same to Mary McCarthy, lot 182. 200

Same to Flora Marks, lot 1093 B, C and D and 1093-1097 A. 5,000

NEW ROCHELLE.

Barton, Susan A. to Annie H. Portman, e s Pelham road, adj Mill Pond, 152x280. 7,000

Deveau, Geo. H. to Mary A. Deveau, w s Woodland av, 655 s Elm st, 80x175. nom

Same to John Deveau, n w s Birch st, 388 n e Boston Post road, 50x102. nom

Disbrow, Susan W. exr. of, to Edwin G. Osborne, n e s White Oak st, 265 n w Mayflower av, abt 50x170. 3,000

Kershan, Lawrence to Anna McCormick, n s William st, 275 e Webster av, 50x115. 800

Lathers, Rich'd to Rich'd Lathers, Jr., s s Winyah av, 715 e Webster, 2½ acres. nom

Mulligan, John to Michael Sheilds, n s Elm st, 120 e Locust av, 40x120. 2,500

Parker, Horace J. to Helen D. Parker, lot 5 block D, Rochelle Park. nom

Porter, Sarah M. to John Erickson, lot 7 s s Winyah av. 250

Real Estate Trust Co. of Philadelphia to Henry L. Wolff, lot 81½, Residence Park. 3,250

RYE.

Bush, And. L. et al. to Wm. E. Ward, abt 3 acres on King st, cor Regent. 4,500

Mead, John L. to Chas. P. Schupp, w s Orchard st, 167 s Terrace av, 72.6x—. 500

Newcombe, Asbury to Eliz'h P. Delanoy, w s Melbourne av, 680 n Tompkins, 120x195. 6,200

Van Amringe, Theo. to Patrick Clooney. Lot w s Barry av. 1,000

SCARSDALE.

Butler, Chas. to Welcome G. Hitchcock, lots 16, 18 and 19 map property John S. Coles at Hartsdale, 16 acres. ½ interest. 4,055

WESTCHESTER.

Baker, Wm. P. to Sarah E. Kidder and ano., lot 214 s s 6th av, Wakefield, 100x114. 1,600

Brown, Mary L. to Robt. J. McCracken et al, w s Elm st, 175 n Maple st, 25x100. nom

Burlando, Emanuel to Adolph G. Crane, part lot 692 n s 2d av, Wakefield, 33.4x100. 3,050

Clarke, Jacob P. to Jas. F. Clarke, n s Elizabeth st, 125 w Barker av, 25x100. 1,000

Camp, Hugh N. to Jan C. Velders, lots 367 and 368 map McGraw estate. 500

Cooper, Margt. et al. J. B. Lockwood, ref., to Wm. E. Ferris, lots 60-67 s s Grant st. 440

Same to same, lots 9, 10 and 11 w s Franklyn av. 630

Gass, Frank to The German Odd Fellows Home Assoc, lots 214 and part 215 s s 10th st, Unionport. 1,400

Same to Annie M. Newbold, west ½ lot 392 n s 14th st, Unionport. 700

McCaffrey, Jas. to Patrick Mullin, lot 11 s e s Lyvere pl map lots Westchester, 50x100. 500

Miller, Oliver J. to And. J. Wightman, lots 454 and 488 s s 11th av, Wakefield, each 102x114. 1,000

O'Connor, Jeremiah to Michael P. Murphy, part lots 784 and 832, Wakefield, 20x100. 550

Perriel, Adele to Fred. C. Dexter, lot 93 w s Maple st, Jerome, 25x100. 850

Reilly, Jas. to Jas. H. Riley, lots 92 and 93 map McGraw estate. 700

Smadbeck, Louis to Edw. C. Eustace, n s 7th st, 125 e Av D, Unionport, 50x108. 350

Same to Fred. W. Ehrsam, n e cor same, 100x108. 720

White, John to Margt. E. Golden, e s Deane pl, 100 s Pierce av, 25x100. nom

WHITE PLAINS.

Read, John to Ann Powers, w s Grove st, adj Emma Underhill, abt 44x150. 500

Sniffen, Elijah C. to Eliz'h M. Burling, e s Stewart pl, 100 s Clinton st, 48x—. 500

YONKERS.

Barnes, Jerome D. to Irene Brenchand, lots 35 and 36 block 19½ map lots Lowerre Station. 950

Vincent, Wm. J. to same, part lot 34, adj above. 550

Beery, Angie to Carey W. Moore, lots 296 and 297, Armour Villa Park. nom

Brownell, And. S. to Geo. J. Ord and wife, w s Alta av, 113.9 n Parkway, abt 105.8x250. nom

Flagg, Howard W. to Harry E. Hankinson, e s Riverdale av, 50 s Hudson st. 50x50. 6,500

Fockes, John V. to Geo. A. Ackerman, s s Post st, 230 e Riverdale av, 50x190. 500

Gramatan Park Co. to Peter Jansen, lots 134 and 135. 400

Jones, Cyrus P. and wife to Wm. D. Basley, lot 11 block A. 250

Same to Kate M. Brown, lot 14 block A. 250

Same to Chas. J. Dando, lots 3 and 4 block A. 650

Lawrence, Jas. V. to Ellis B. Edwards, part block 2 n s McLain av, Lowerre Station nom

Ludlow, Thos. W. and wife to Paul S. Bolger, lots 16 and 17 Sunnyside Drive and Fairfield road map Cottage Lawn. 9,500

Monrovia Park Co to Thos. J. Molloy, lot 194. 135

North End Land Co. to Kinoyonder Haag, lot 45 n e s Vernon pl, Sherwood Park, 25x100. 425

Parrott, Henry R. to Kate E. James, n w cor Columbia av and Reade st, 100x100. 1,500

Ware, Enoch R. trustee of, to Jas. Shipman, 8 acres n w s Kimball av. 10,200

MORTGAGES.

NEW YORK CITY.

NOVEMBER 20, 21, 23, 24, 25, 26.

Annees, Adelaide V. to Arthur B. Claflin. Lots 6-10 map 153 lots at Kingsbridge, &c. P. M. Nov. 16, due Nov. 19, 1894, 5 %. $3,195

Acker, Henry C. and Emma L. his wife to George H. Byrd. Amsterdam av, s w cor 99th st, 40x80.2 to e s of late Bloomingdale road, x40x77.6. P. M. Nov. 23, 3 years, 5 %. gold, 42,500

Acker, Henry C. to Julius Lipman and William Cohen. Same property. Sub. to last mort. Nov. 23, 6 months. 15,821

Same to same. Same property. Sub. to mort. $42,500. Nov. 23, 6 months. 2,500

Same to The McElwee Mfg. Co. Same property. Sub. to morts. $60,821. Nov. 23, due May 1, 1892. 3,398

Same to Henry Woods. Same property. Sub. to morts. $66,717. Secures mechanic's lien. Nov. 23. 1,348

Same to Ackert & Schroeder. Same property. Sub. to morts. $67,566. Secures mechanic's lien. Nov. 23. 450

Same to Benedict, McIlroy & Fowler. Same property. Sub. to morts. Nov. 23, 6 months. 899

Same to William McShane admr. James Philp. Same property. Sub. to morts. Nov. 23, due May 1, 1892. 1,599

Adler, Leopold to August L. Peters. 2d av, e s, 75.11 s 104th st, 25.6x75. Nov. 23, due Dec. 1, 1894, 5 %. 12,000

Breen, James R. and D. Allison Breen to Edward Oppenheimer and Isaac Metzger. 87th st, s s, 150 w Central Park West, 100x100.8. Oct. 2, 1 year. 50,000

Brennan, William to THE TITLE GUARANTEE AND TRUST CO. 87th st. P. M. Nov. 23, 1 year, 4½ %. 10,000

Brown, James to Frances E. Holt. 90th st, n s, 220 w Central Park West, 18.6x100.8. Nov. 23, 3 years, 5 %. gold, 17,000

Bulkley, Harrie, Brooklyn, to Spencer Aldrich. 53d st. P. M. Oct. 27, demand. 60,006

Same to same. Same property. Building loan. Sub. to last mort. Oct. 27, demand. 44,000

Same to Edward L. Spencer, Brooklyn. Same property. Sub. to morts. $104,000. Nov. 20, demand. 10,000

Babls, J. M. Gustave to William H. Gardiner. 83d st, s s, 255.7 w 3d av, 25.7x102.2. Nov. 19, 1 year. 500

Bennett, Fannie to Jacob Freystadt. Manhattan av, No. 509, w s, 20.11 n 121st st, 16x90. Sub. to mort. $7,500. Nov. 19, due March 24, 1895. 4,000

Same to THE TITLE GUARANTEE AND TRUST CO. Same property. Nov. 19, 3 years, 4½ %. 7,500

Bogan, Annie E. wife of Thomas to THE EMIGRANT INDUST. SAVINGS BANK. Houston st, s e cor Washington st, 23.11x50. Nov. 21, 1 year, 4½ %. 2,000

Braham, Annie T. to Frederic J. Middlebrook, Brooklyn. Manhattan av and 123d st. P. M. Nov. 21, 3 years, 5 %. 10,000

Brodhead, Jessie W., Detroit, Mich., to Frederick D. Tappen. 29th st, s s, 192 w Madison av, 27.6x98.9. ½ part. Nov. 6, 3 years. 6,000

Bronson, Frank G., Mt. Vernon, to Arthur B. Claflin. Lot 5 map 153 select lots, &c. P. M. Nov. 16, due Nov. 19, 1894, 5 %. 648

Bruen, Charlotte A. to James G. Swords, Newark, N. J., exr. Robert S. Seward. 126th st, s s, 100 w 8th av, 16.8x99.10. Nov. 19, 2 years, 5 %. 4,000

Bucker, Frederick to A. Hupfel's Sons. Courtlandt av, No. 916, s e cor 162d st. Store lease. Nov. 17, note, demand. 3,500

Baker, John O., Newark, N. J., to Charles T. and Helen T. Barney. 98th st, s s, 475 w Central Park West, 5 lots. 5 P. M. morts., each $13,700. Oct. 26, due Aug. 1, 1892. 68,500

Same to same. 98th st, s s, 600 w Central Park West. P. M. Oct. 26, due Aug. 1, 1892. 13,500

Block, Ferdinand to August Horrmann et al. exrs. and trustees Joseph Rubsam. 102d st, n s, 155 e 3d av, 25x100.11. Nov. 24, due Nov. 13, 1896, 5 %. 12,000

Brandes, Diedrich to August Horrmann et al. exrs. and trustees Joseph Rubsam. 121st st, s s, 180 e Lenox av, 20x100.11. Nov. 20, due Nov. 30, 1896, 4½ %. 10,000

Brown, James to THE NEW YORK LIFE INS AND TRUST CO. 92d st, s s, 400 w Columbus av, 20x100.8. Nov. 25, 1 year, 5 %. 18,000

Same to same. 92d st, s s, 420 w Columbus av, 4 lots, each 20x100.8. 4 morts., each $16,500. Nov. 25, 1 year, 5 %. 66,000

Same to the trustees of St. Stephen's College, of Annandale, N. Y. 92d st, s s, 400 w Columbus av, 20x100.8. Sub. to mort. $18,000. Nov. 25, 3 years, 5 %. 3,000

Same to same. 92d st, s s, 420 w Columbus av. 20x100.8. Sub. to mort. $16,500. Nov. 25, 3 years, 5 %. 2,000

Brown, Robert I. to William S. Opdyke and ano. trustees Alfred C. Post dec'd. Greenwich st, No. 486, w s, 89.3 n Canal st, 20x60 to alley, x20x53, with all title to alley. Nov. 25, due Dec. 1, 1894. 5,000

Berman, Mary wife of and Alois A. to THE MUTUAL LIFE INS. CO., New York. 42d st, No. 225, n s, 345 e 3d av, 20x100.5. Nov. 24, 1 year, 5 %. 2,500

Browne, Emily L. to THE SEAMEN'S BANK FOR SAVINGS, City of New York. 58th st. P. M. Oct. 15, due Nov. 24, 1892, 5 %. 18,000

Cavinato, Luigi, Steffano, Natale and Guiseppe, of Cavinato Bros., to Abraham Steers. 87th st, s e cor Lexington av, 62.3x100.8x62.3x—. Nov. 24, 6 months. 4,268

Church Society for Promoting Christianity Amongst the Jews to THE CITIZENS' SAVINGS BANK. 7th st, s s, 275 w 1st av, 25x91. Nov. 24, 1 year, 5 %. gold, 10,000

Cordner, George and Annie his wife to William A. Martin. 130th st. P. M. Nov. 24, 3 years, 5 %. 9,500

Cutting, Robert L. to THE MUTUAL LIFE INS. CO. of New York. 5th av, e s, 90 n 90th st, 25x90. Oct. 31, 1 year, 5 %. See Conveys. 60,000

Cullen, Elizabeth to The John Kress Brewing Co. Canal st, No. 107, n w cor Forsyth st, 25.3x25. Nov. 24, due Nov. 1, 1896. 7,000

Campbell, Thomas A. to Mary A. and Andrew W. Smith exrs. and trustees Samuel Smith. 91st st. P. M. Nov. 25, 5 years, 5 %. gold, 15,000

Same to Hugh Brien. Same property. Nov. 24, 5 years. 5,000

Clark, George to James F. Caldwell. 30th st, No. 34 W. Leasehold. Nov. 24, 90 days. 2,500

Cohen, Adolph and Harry Fischel to Hyman Israel and Simon Bing, Jr. Rivington st, Nos. 269 and 271, s e cor Columbia st, 45.8x55.10x45.8x55.8. Nov. 25, due Feb. 18, 1892. 3,000

Cohen, Hattie wife of Barney to Stephen H. Olin trustee for Alice Macalester. Willett st, No. 49, w s, abt 44.8 n Delancey st, 25.1x88. Nov. 25, due Dec. 1, 1896, 5 %. gold, 8,000

Same to Stephen H. Olin committee of Benjamin Page. Same property. Equal lien with last mort. Nov. 25, due Dec. 1, 1896, 5 %. gold, 4,500

Same to Jonas Weil and Bernhard Mayer. Same property. Nov. 25, installs. 2,800

Conlon, Thomas to The Stuyvesant Co-operative Building and Loan Assoc. Decatur av, n s, 150 e Mosholu Parkway, 50x110. Nov. 16, installs, 5 %. 3,000

Coogan, Matthew to THE MURRAY HILL BANK. 7th av, e s, 49.11 s 134th st, runs east 75 x south 22.4 x southwest 4.5 x west 71.6 to av, x north 25. Sub. to mort. $18,500. Nov. 23, 1 year. 4,000

Coogan, Matthew to Mary L. March, Staatsburgh, N. Y. 7th av. P. M. Nov. 5, due Nov. 24, 1896, 5 %. gold, 18,500

Coster, Edward H. committee of John H. Coster mortgagee with Jacob and Rebecca Larchan mortgagors. Extension of mort. at 4½ %. Nov. 18. nom

Callahan, Michael J. to James Everard. Webster av, proposed, w s, 225 n Southern Boulevard, 50x121; Decatur av, s w cor Mosholu Parkway, runs south 50 x west 159.6 to an angle, x west again 65.5 to Hull av, x north 122.7 to Mosholu Parkway, x southeast 246.10. Nov. 20, demand. 5,000

Carew, Charles J. and William Drought to Amelia Haines guard. Florence B. and Edward J. Haines. 21st st, No. 211, n s, 150 w 7th av, 25x98.9. Nov. 7, due Nov. 20, 1894, 5 %. gold, 30,000

Chestnut, William J. to Arthur B. Claflin. Lot 14 map 153 select lots, &c. Nov. 16, due Nov. 19, 1894, 5 %. 705

Campbell, John V. and Elizabeth M. C. his wife to Joseph L. Buttenwieser. Eldridge st, No. 55, w s, 25.2x101x25x101. Nov. 18, 5 years, 5 %. See Morts. in last issue. 14,112

Duer, John, New Brighton, S. I., to D. Willis James. 86th st. P. M. Nov. 24, 5 years or installs, 4½ %. 30,000

Doyle, Peter to THE FRANKLIN SAVINGS BANK, New York. 62d st, s s, 445 w Columbus av, 25x100.5. Nov. 24, 1 year, 5 %. 15,000

Same to Sarah H. Powell. Same property. Sub. to last mort. Nov. 24, 3 years, 5 %. 3,000

Doctor, Sabeth to Dina Muller. 116th st. P. M. Nov. 14, due Nov. 18, 1896. 4,500

De Walltears, Frances wife of Solomon to Theodore De Witt. 131st st, No. 64, s s, abt 185.4 e Lenox av, 16.8x99.11. Nov. 25, 3 years, 5 %. 7,000

Dowdall, Thomas to THE EMIGRANT INDUST. SAVINGS BANK. 51st st, n s, 100 e 11th av, 25x100.5. Nov. 25, 1 year, 4½ %. 6,000

Duffy, Hugh to Bernheimer & Schmid. Willis av, No. 441. Saloon lease. Nov. 23, note, demand. 2,500

Devenport, William J. and Stephen H. to George H. Coutts. Manhattan av, w s, 17.7 n 103d st, 5 lots, each 16.8x75. 5 morts., each $9,000. Nov. 23, 5 years, 5 %. 45,000

Same to Elizabeth F. R. Laing. Manhattan av, n w cor 103d st, 17.7x75. Nov. 23, 1 year, 5 %. 10,000

Dillon, J. Rhinelander to D. Willis James. 86th st. P. M. Nov. 23, 3 years, 4 %. 25,000

D'Onofrio, Rocco to Frank Garcfola. 1st av, No. 2208. P. M. Nov. 21, 6 months. 2,000

Eder, August to Edward Higgins. Washington av, n w s, 100 n e Clay av, 25x100. Nov. 20, 1 year. 600

Ehrhart, Ferdinand and Mary his wife to Mary A. P. Gordon. 5th st, s s, 386 e 3d av, 26x120. Nov. 20, 3 years, 5 %. gold, 13,000

Elliott, John H. to Julia M. Griebel. 154th st, n s, 220 w Elton av, 25x100. Nov. 21, 4 years. 1,000

Eisenberg, William to James G. Bennett and ano. trustees for Isaac Bell, Jr. 116th st, No. 270 W., s s, 425 e 8th av, runs south 103.7 x northeast 8.10 x east 16.10 x north 100.11 to 116th st, x west 25. Nov. 25, 3 years, 5 %. 26,000

Same to same. 116th st, No. 272 W., s s, 400 e 8th av, 25x103.7x26x111.6. Nov. 25, 3 years, 5 %. 26,000

Eisenstein, Julius D. to Agnes M. Strebeigh. East Broadway, No. 57, s s, 190 w Market st, 25x75. Nov. 25, due May 1, 1893. 5,000

Essner, Romanus and Helene his wife to Louisa Ungrich. 91st st, n s, 75 w 3d av. P. M. Nov. 25, 3 years, 5 %. 10,000

Same to Hugo Maier. Washington av, e s, 92.10 n 163d st, 25x100. Nov. 16, due Sept. 15, 1893, 5 %. 1,000

Engelmann, Peter to Arthur B. Claflin. Lot 54 map 153 select lots, &c. P. M. Nov. 16, due Nov. 19, 1894, 5 %. 35

Ebeling, Henrietta mortgagee with Annie B. Lippold formerly Denhert mortgagor and present owner. Extension of mort. at 6 %. Nov. 13. nom

Fisher, Roderick P., Brooklyn, to Joseph L. O'Brien. Tiffany st, e s. 79.3 s 167th st, runs east 200 to Fox st, x north 25 x west 100 x northwest 85.10 to 167th st, x southwest 74.8 to Tiffany st, x south 79.3 to beginning. Nov. 18, 3 years, 5 %. 4,000

Fullam, A. Judson and Margaret D. his wife to THE TITLE GUARANTEE AND TRUST CO. 151st st, n s, 525 w 11th av Boulevard, runs north 99.11 x west 25 x north 99.11 to 152d st, x west 25 x south 99.11 to middle of block, x east 16.8 x south 99.11 to 151st st, x east 33.4 to beginning. Nov. 19, due May 1, 1893, 5 %. 7,000

Fabel, Philipp to Frederick Muller. Suffolk st, No. 57, w s, 25x75. P. M. Sub. to mort. $10,000. Oct. 15, 5 years or installs, 5½ %. 5,000

Foster, James P. to Agostino Cavinato. Morton st, No. 34, s s, 75 w Bedford st. P. M. Nov. 24, due Dec. 1, 1892. 3,885

Same to Abraham Steers. Morton st, No. 36, s s, 100 w Bedford st, 25x91. Nov. 24, due Dec. 1, 1892. See Conveys. 4,268

Fischer, Ernest H. to Catharine E. Fischer widow. Baxter st. Nos. 23 and 24. All title. Nov. 21, due before Jan. 2, 1898, or sooner, 5 %. 2,000

Finch, Mary to Cassidy & Adler. 103d st. P. M. Sub. to mort. $16,500. Nov. 25, 1 year. 2,850

Same to Robert C. Watson et al. exrs., &c., William Watson. Same property. P. M. Nov. 25, 3 years, 5 %. 16,500

Foster, Annie C. B. wife of George V. to Frances S. Bridge. 41st st, No. 102 W., s s, 75 w 6th av, 25x100.5. Nov. 24, due Nov. 25, 1893, 5 %. 5,000

Graham, Thomas to George See, Bayonne, N. J. 89th st, n s, 113.4 w Madison av, 51.1x100.8. Sub. to mort. Sept. 14, 1 year. 5,500

Graham, Jennie wife of and Thomas to Allen W. Adams trustee for creditors. Same property. Sub. to morts. Nov. 23, due April 29, 1893. 12,000

Gehr, Magdalena widow and devisee of George Gehr to Conrad Gehr and Mathilda his wife. Elton av, e s, 125 s 158th st, 25x136.10x25x138.6. Nov. 23, due Nov., 1895, 5 %. 800

Gillespie, Michael H. to THE UNITED STATES LIFE INS. CO. 21st st, No. 224, s s, 300.6 w 7th av, 28x106. Nov. 23, due Nov. 1, 1896, 5 %. 33,000

Same to same. 21st st, No. 222, s s, 281.10 w 7th av, 18.8x106. Nov. 23, due Nov. 1, 1896, 5 %. 23,000

Gledhill, Henry, William H. and James E. and George H. Keim, of Henry Gledhill & Co., to Edward M. Cameron trustee Marie L. Cameron. 34th st, n s, 225 e 11th av, runs north 98.9 x east 25 x north 98.9 to 35th st, x east 50 x south 197.6 to 34th st, x west 75. Nov. 6, due Nov. 1, 1894, 5 %. gold, 90,000

Gaiser, Albert J. to Howard Coghill, Morristown, N. J. Tinton av. P. M. Nov. 24, due April 30, 1893. 450

Gentzlinger, Henry to Conrad Stein. 1st av, e s, 47.4 n 10th st, 23.8x94. Nov. 24, 5 years, 5 %. 13,000

Goerlitz, John to Louis M. Jones. Spring st, Nos. 131–137, n s, 48.2 w Greene st, runs north 95.6 x west 17.10 x southwest 8 x north 7 x west 27.3 x north 3.6 x west 46.2 x south 100 to Spring st, x east 98.2 to beginning, with use of alley in rear. Nov. 23, 2 months. 20,000

Goerlitz, John to Emily A. Thorn, Newport, R. I. Greenwich av, No. 17, w s, 51.5 s West 10th st, 24.9x90.6x25.2x86.2. Nov. 23, 5 years, 5 %. 25,000

Same to same. Greenwich av, No. 19, w s, 26.2 s West 10th st, 25.3x86.3x25.2x81.8. Nov. 23, 5 years, 5 %. 25,000

Galbraith, Andrew to Arthur B. Claflin. Lot 13 map 153 select lots, &c. P. M. Nov. 16, due Nov. 19, 1894, 5 %. 510

Galvan, Daniel V. to Charles Lowen and Edward F. Halliday. 35th st, s s, 150 e 7th av. P. M. Nov. 20, due Feb. 10, 1894. 2,750

Same to same. 35th st, s s, 175 e 7th av. P. M. Nov. 20, due Feb. 10, 1894. 2,750

Galvan, Mary P. to Alfred C. Clark, Cooperstown, N. Y., guard. Frederick A. Clark. 73d st, n s, 150 w 3d av, 29.6x102.2. Nov. 20, 5 years, 4½ %. 19,000

Gault, Mary E. wife of and John H. to William B. Baldwin. 82d st, s s, 157 w Central Park West, 18x100. Sub. to mort. Nov. 17, 1 year. 5,000

Graham, Charles to William Archer trustee. Madison av, s w cor 89th st, runs south 25.8 x west 75 x south 75 x west 63.11 x north 100.8 to st, x east 138.11 to beginning. Secures loans for work and materials. Sub. to morts. Nov. 19. See Conveys. 50,276

Same to THE MURRAY HILL BANK. Same property. Sub. to morts. $60,000. Nov. 5, 1 year. 6,500

Same to Isaac Untermyer. Same property. Nov. 5, 1 year. 34,500

Same to same. 89th st, s s, 113.4 w Madison av, 25.7x100.8. P. M. Aug. 1, due Nov. 5, 1892. 5,500

Grunbut, Louis to Frederic J. Middlebrook, Brooklyn. 22d st, n s, 165.7 e 7th av. P. M. Nov. 20, 3 years, 5 %. 14,000

Same to same. Same property. 2d mort. Nov. 20, due Nov. 30, 1891. 7,000

Hand, Eugene S. to Elizabeth L. Whiting, Saugerties, N. Y. 121st st, n s, 260 e Park av, 17x100.11. Nov. 17, due Nov. 21, 1894, 5 %. 8,000

Hayward, Hattie L. to Isabella G. Francis, Bridgehampton, L. I. Southern Boulevard, n w cor Valentine av, 62.6x120. Nov. 19, due Nov. 21, 1894, 5 %. 7,000

Harlow, Ellen M. to Alexander Walker and Judson Lawson. 95th st. P. M. Sub. to mort. $12,000. Nov. 20, 6 months. 8,000

Harlow, Ellen M. to THE TITLE GUARANTEE AND TRUST CO. 69th st. P. M. Nov. 20, 6 months. 4,000

Hart, Emma S. to THE TITLE GUARANTEE AND TRUST CO. 125th st, s s, 225 e 5th av, 20 x100.11. Nov. 23, due Nov. 24, 1894, 5 %. 15,000

Hollerieth, George to THE TITLE GUARANTEE AND TRUST CO. 118th st. P. M. Nov. 17, due Nov. 23, 1896, 5 %. 4,000

Hartmann, Kasper and Mary his wife to Philipp Hill and Katie his wife. Vanderbilt av, east cor 169th st, 40x100. Nov. 21, 5 years, 5 %. 4,000

Henderson, Robert to J. Romaine Brown. 7th av, w s, 49.4 n 23d st, 19.9x80. Nov. 12, 1 year. 1,000

Haffner, John D. to Patrick J. Gray. 8th av, No. 600. Saloon lease. Nov. 24, note, demand. 2,000

Same to Bernheimer & Schmid. Same property. Nov. 24, note, demand. 2,000

Humphreys, Henry to THE EMIGRANT INDUST. SAVINGS BANK. Anthony av, e s, 5.9 n 175th st, prolonged, 25x113.5x26x106.2. Nov. 25, 1 year, 4½ %. 1,000

Jenkins, Thomas J. and George to Henry B. Barnes. 118th st, s s, 200 e 8th av, 3 lots, each 25x100.11. 3 morts., each $17,000. Nov. 24, 3 years, 5 %. gold, 51,000

Same to Bradley & Currier Co. (Lim.) 118th st, s s, 200 e 8th av, 100x100.11. Sub. to mort. $68,000. Nov. 11, 6 months. 6,000

Jameson, Margaret, Sarah H. Whitlock and Mary and Martha Hill heirs John H. Hill to Hugo Maier. 44th st, s s, 231.3 e 10th av, 18.9 x100.5. Nov. 18, due Oct. 28, 1894, 5 %. 1,000

Judge, Andrew T. to John W. Haaren. 133d st, s s, 460 w 5th av, 50x99.11. Sub. to morts. $38,400. Nov. 17, 6 months. 2,500

Jones, Frances O. to Frances E. Ogden, Chicago, Ill. Park av. P. M. Nov. 24, due Aug. 24, 1894, or installs. 60,000

Jones, Isabella B. wife of Edward W. to Artlissa V. wife of Miles Gearon, Brooklyn. 3d av, No. 15, e s, 50.5 s St. Marks pl, 16.11x74. Nov. 25, 1 year. 850

Kruse, Henry to Lisette Heller. Elton or 152d st, s s, lot 366 map Melrose South, 20x114.3x20x114.4. Sept. 15, 1 year, 5 %. 2,000

Kelly, Rose and Ellen Ulrich, both Hoboken, N. J., heirs Rose Gillen to Josiah A. Hyland. Lot begins at west line of land now or late of John Seeler at points 150 w Church st and 113 s proposed new st, runs south 50 x west 100 to Water st as extended, x north 50 x east 100. Nov. 20, 2 years. 350

Koch, Joseph to John P. Chatillon and ano. exrs Harman Wagner. 91st st, n s, 270 e Lexington av, 25x100.8. Nov. 24, 5 years, 5 %. 13,450

Krug, John to Conrad Stein. 9th av, No. 790. Saloon lease. Nov. 24, demand. 1,600

Kaufman, Ferdinand and Babette his wife to Hyman Schnitzer. 28th st, n s, 325 e 10th av, 25x98.9; 28th st, n s, 300 e 10th av, 25x98.9. Nov. 17, due Dec. 18, 1893. 3,200

Keiler, Gustave to A. Hupfel's Sons. 3d av, No. 3192, n e cor 161st st. Store lease. Nov. 17, note, demand. 1,500

Kerwin, Andrew J. to THE NEW YORK LIFE INS. CO. 92d st, s w cor Park av, 21x67.7. Nov. 19, 3 years, 5 %. 18,000

Same to same. 92d st, s s, 21 w Park av, 16.8x67.7. Nov. 17, 3 years, 5 %. 13,000

Same to same. 92d st, s s, 37.8 w Park av, 16.8x67.7. Nov. 19, 3 years, 5 %. 13,000

Same to same. 92d st, s s, 88 w Park av, 17x100.8. Nov. 19, 3 years, 5 %. 16,000

Ketcham, James W. to Abram E. Bamberger guard. of Alice C. J. and Lewis E. Bamberger. Mott st, No. 110, e s, 43 s Hester st, runs east 45.8 x south 6.7 x east 22.1 x south 16.8 x west 68.3 to Mott st, x north 22.11 to beginning. Nov. 21, 5 years, 5 %. 12,000

Klein, Julius and Edward to Dinah Klein. Av A, w s, 22.10 n 6th st, 22.8x100. Lease. Nov. 18, due Nov. 12, 1896, or installs, 5 %. 8,000

Kolloge, Ludwig W. to Henry F. C. Rahe. 109th st, No. 311, n s, 157 e 2d av, 14.8x100.10. Nov. 20, installs. 1,200

Koster, Frederick to Arthur B. Claflin. Lot 31 map of 153 select lots, &c. P. M. Nov. 16, due Nov. 19, 1894, 5 %. 500

Karcher, Philipp to J. & M. Haffen. 149th st, s s, part lot 184 map East Morrisania, 50x84. P. M. Nov. 21, 3 years. 4,500

Katz, Daniel to Edward A. Morrison. Boulevard. P. M. Nov. 2, due Nov. 23, 1893, 5 %. 10,000

Kelly, Ella mortgagee with Levenia H. Montross mortgagee. Extension of mort. Oct. 6. nom

Same mortgagor with Henry G. Peters mortgagee. Agreement apportioning mortgage. Oct. 7. nom

Same with same. Extension of mort. Oct. 7. nom

Kelly, John mortgagor with the trustees of the New York Cotton Exchange Gratuity Fund mortgagee. Extension of mort. at 5 %. Nov. 23. nom

Lange, Edward and Margaret J. his wife to Horace K. Thurber. 84th st, s s, 100 w 11th av, 100x102.2. Secures advances and guarantees present and future. Nov. 5. ——

Larkin, Michael and James J. to THE UNITED STATES TRUST CO., New York. Eldridge st, No. 136, e s, abt 125 n Broome st, 25x87.6. Nov. 19, due Dec. 1, 1896, 5 %. 20,000

Lange, Frederick to Isabel W. Niles. Marion av, e s, 75.3 s Rockfield st, 25.1x108.2x25x110. Nov. 20, 1 year. 300

Lewis, Josephine to Charles Schweinler, Orange, N. J. Beach st, No. 7, 18.6x79.4. All title. Nov. 14, 3 years. 2,500

Lewkowitz, Isidor to THE EMIGRANT INDUST. SAVINGS BANK. 125th st, s s, 325 e 5th av, 37.6x100.11. Nov. 24, 1 year, 4½ %. 20,000

Lockwood, Louise A. wife of and Henry F. to Frederic J. Middlebrook. Catharine st, n e cor Henry st, 23x102x23x100. ½ part. Nov. 24, due June 1, 1892. 550

Loew, Louis A. to Charlotte E. Odell widow. 12th st, n s, 60 w Av B, 17.6x91.9. Nov. 2, due Nov. 1, 1892, 5 %. 5,000

Lang, Charles to Matilda Weil et al. exrs. Max Weil. 91st st, s s, 75 e Madison av, 18.4 x100.8. Nov. 17, due Nov. 19, 1896, 4½ %. gold, 10,000

Levy, Henrietta wife and Bernard S. to THE FARMER'S LOAN AND TRUST CO. 78th st, n s, 250 w Columbus av, 17.11x102.2. Oct. 20, due Nov. 20, 1894, 5 %. 19,000

McDonald, Alexander L., James Pott and Charles R. Contoit to Rector, &c., Trinity Church. Convent av, n e cor 141st st, 100x125; 141st st, n s, 525 e 10th av, 100x75; Hamilton terrace, w s, 75 n 141st st, 50x100. Nov. 20, due Dec. 1, 1892, 5 %. 16,400

McGovern, Joseph to Bernheimer & Schmid. 1st av, No. 2036. Saloon lease. Nov. 24, note, demand. 2,300

Miller, Charles A. to Frederick G. Bourne. 72d st, n s, 215 w Columbus av, 20x102.2. Nov. 2, 3 years or installs, 4½ %. 25,000

Monaghan, Mary E. to Thomas or Thomas L. White, Toronto, N. Y. Willard av. P. M. Nov. 9, due Nov. 25, 1894, 5 %. 800

Moore, Alexander to Clara A. M. wife of Charles Greer, Rye, N. Y. 51st st, s s, 147 e 8th av, 20x100.5. Nov. 25, 3 years, 5 %. 25,000

Same to same. 51st st, s s, 127 e 8th av, 20x100.5. Nov. 25, 3 years, 5 %. 25,000

Same to same. 51st st, s s, 167 e 8th av, 20x100.5. Nov. 25, 3 years, 5 %. 25,000

Morette, Joseph mortgagor with Ann Bussing mortgagee. Extension of mort. at 5 %. Aug. 10. nom

Musgrave, Edward G. to Edward B. Foote, Sr. Madison av, w s, 203 n Kingsbridge road, 25x100. Sept. 28, 10 years, 5 %. 500

McGarrah, Robert D. to Arthur B. Claflin. Lot 51 map 153 select lots at Kingsbridge Heights. P. M. Nov. 16, due Nov. 19, 1894, 5 %. 450

Moses, Margaret L. to William J. Pragnell. Bathgate av, e s, 60 s 182d st, 20x90. Nov. 20, 5 years. 750

McCormack, Mary A. wife of and Michael to THE BOWERY SAVINGS BANK. 127th st, s s, 310 e Lenox av, 50x99.11. Nov. 23, 1 year, 5 %. 15,000

McCoy, Daniel W. F. to Lydia M. White. 1st av, s w cor 53d st, 25.5x100. Nov. 23, 2 years, 5 %. 7,500

McReynolds, Anthony to Emilie J. Murray. 131st st, s s, 208.4 w 7th av, 16.8x99.11. Nov. 23, 2 years, 5 %. gold, 7,000

Muller, Maria C. wife of and Frederick A. to THE HARLEM SAVINGS BANK. 157th st, s w s, west ½ lot 258 map of Melrose, 25x191.7x25 x abt 190. Nov. 20, 1 year, 5 %. 3,500

Mans, Marcus F. and Jacob Barbey, of Mans & Barbey, to Bernheimer & Schmid. Lion Park Hotel; also The Belvidere, except upper part and lower floor. Lease. Nov. 20, note, demand. 6,500

Neumer, Ferdinand to Julia F. Henes. 20th st. P. M. Nov. 3, 3 years, 5 %. 10,000

Nestell, John J. to THE TITLE GUARANTEE AND TRUST CO. 125th st, No. 76, s s, 85 e Lenox av, 18.9x100.11. Nov. 23, due Nov. 24, 1894, 5 %. 15,000

Ord, George J., Yonkers, N. Y., to Francis B. Chedsey. 145th st, n s, 173.1 e 3d av, old line, 17.7x100. Nov. 10, 1 year. 2,000

Ott, John to Simon Weinberger and Emma his wife. 80th st. P. M. Sub. to mort. $7,000. Nov. 23, 3 years or installs, 5 %. 3,500

Platt, Richard G. to Sydney A. Smith. West End av, w s, 86.2 s 85th st, 16x100. Sub. to mort. $15,000. Oct. 14, due Oct. 15, 1892. 3,000

Same to same. West End av, w s, 30.2 s 85th st, 20x54x34.4x41. Sub. to mort. $14,500. Oct. 14, due Oct. 15, 1892. 2,500

Same to same. 85th st, s s, 34 w West End av, runs south 30.2 x west 7 x southwest 30.4 x north 50.2 to st, x east 30. Sub. to mort. $17,000. Oct. 14, due Oct. 15, 1892. 4,000

Same to same. 85th st, s s, 64 w West End av, 18x70.2. Sub. to mort. $14,500. Oct. 14, due Oct. 15, 1892. 3,000

Same to same. West End av, w s, 70.2 s 85th st, 16x82. Sub. to mort. $14,500. Oct. 14, due Oct. 15, 1892. 3,000

Same to same. West End av, w s, 50.2 s 85th st, 20x64. Sub. to mort. $15,500. Oct. 14, due Oct. 15, 1892. 2,500

Same to same. 85th st, s s, 82 w West End av, 18x85.2. Sub. to mort. $15,000. Oct. 14, due Oct. 15, 1892. 3,000

Same to same. West End av, s w cor 85th st, 30.2x34. Sub. to mort. $19,000. Oct. 14, due Oct. 15, 1892. 4,000

Patten, William S. to Isabella C. King. 28th st, s s, 225 w 10th av, 4 lots. 4 P. M. morts., each $3,500. Nov. 20, due Dec. 1, 1892, 5 %. 14,000

Peebles, Agnes wife of J. M. to William J. McPherson. Suburban st, n w cor Briggs av, 34x80x—x90. Nov. 23, 4 years, 5 %. 400

Pero, Robert R. to Robert C. Watson et al. exrs. William Watson. 103d st. P. M. Nov. 25, 3 years, 5 %. 16,500

Pentz, Enoch C. to THE MUTUAL LIFE INS. CO. Gouverneur lane, w s, 72.8 s Water st, 37.10x25.1x38.5x25.1. Nov. 24, due Nov. 25, 1892. 5,000

Pettit, John, East Orange, N. J., to THE MUTUAL LIFE INS. CO., New York. Morningside av, s w cor 119th st, 100.11x150. Nov. 23, due Nov. 25, 1892. 35,000

Pettit, John to Charles E. Tracy and ano. trustees James Bogert. Vandewater st. P. M. Nov. 19, due Nov. 1, 1894, 5 %. gold, 35,000

Revans, Samuel G. to THE METROPOLITAN LIFE INS. CO. of New York. Madison av, Nos. 136 and 138, n w cor 31st st, 49.7x95. Nov. 24, due Oct. 1, 1896, 5 %. See Conveys. 300,000

Same to Joseph F. Stier. Same property. Nov. 24, demand. 90,000

Ruggiero, Francisco to Abial M. Hawkins and ano. exrs. and trustees Peter Asten. 109th st, n s, 150 w 1st av, 25x100.11. Aug. 12, 3 years, 5 %. 7,000

Rankin, John to William Rankin. Leroy st, n s, 67 e Bedford st, runs north 22.6 x east 8 x north 67.6 x east 25 x south 90 to Leroy st, x west 33. Nov. 25, due Nov. 20, 1892. 3,527

Same to George H. Byrd. Leroy st, n s, 67.3 e Bedford st, runs north 22.6 x east 7.9 x north 67.6 x east 25 x south 90 to st, x west 32.9. Nov. 24, 3 years, 5 %. gold, 25,000

Reckling, Charles to THE MUTUAL LIFE INS. CO., New York, 10th av, n e cor 116th st. P. M. Nov. 25, 1 year. 24,500

Reinhardt, Henry and Theresa his wife to Sender Jarmulowsky. Av B, No. 105, e s, 40.5 s 7th st, 20.3x98. Nov. 25, notes. 2,000

Rosenblum, Aaron to Louis C. Muller, Brooklyn. 12th st. Lease. P. M. Nov. 11, installs. 5,150

Ramsey, William H. to George Crawford. 35th st, n s, 331 e 8th av, 69x98.9. Nov. 20, 3 months. 5,000

Riker, Ella C., Woodside, L. I., to James J. Phelan. 2d av, w s, 74.1 n 28th st, runs northwest 53.11 x southwest 18.8 x southeast 16.6 x north — x southwest to av, x 18.10. Nov. 20, 2 years. 1,200

Rogers, Archibald to THE HUDSON RIVER BANK. Central av, e s, adj lands known as Inwood, contains 30 234-1,000 acres, except lots 1-4, 36, 37, 38, 39, 44-47, 67 70, 98-111 and 123-125 on map Morris Stebbins' property; also lots 44-47 and 108-111 on same map; also lots 124-127 and 167-170 on a map of Inwood, town of Morrisania and West Farms. Nov. 16, due Nov. 18, 1892. 100,000

Rosenfeld, Rosanna wife of and Moses to Charles Lanier trustee for Elizabeth G. Bacon. Cherry st. P. M. Nov. 20, due Dec. 1, 1896, 5 %. gold, 8,000

Rothstein, Daniel to Vito Cimino. Mulberry st. P. M. Nov. 21, due Jan. 1, 1892. 4,000

Russell, Dane D. and Annie B. his wife to Adeline C. Arnold. Willis av, w s, 19 s 140th st, 20x66. Nov. 17, 3 years, 5 %. 1,500

Sampter, Michael to THE NEW YORK SAVINGS BANK. 131st st, s s, 127 w 5th av, 6 lots, together in size abt 108x99.11. 6 morts, each $7,500. Nov. 2, due Dec. 1, 1896, 4½ %. 45,000

Schiff, David and Israel to Adolph Gross and Samuel Harris. Av D. P. M. Nov. 20, installs. 4,200

Schulz, Christian mortgagor with Johanna Strauss, Frankfort, Germany, mortgagee. Extension of mort at reduced interest. Oct. 21. nom

Schwartz, Max to John and Henry Stemme. Houston st, s s, 25 w Suffolk st, 25x80. Nov. 20, installs, 5 %. 25,000

Smith, Emma H. to Daniel Buhler, Brooklyn. Spring st, No. 149, n s, 75 w Wooster st, 25x100. ½ part. Nov. 19, due May 19, 1894. 3,500

Smith, Tillie E. widow to Sarah H. Powell. 119th st, s s, 460 e Lenox av, 125x100.11; also 116th st. P. M. Nov. 19, demand. 3,000

Southworth, Diantha A., Rowena M. and Ellis B. to George R. Williams trustee John Southworth. 147th st, n e cor New Croton Aqueduct, 50x99.11. Oct. 24, 1 year, 5 %. 9,000

Steiner, David to District No. 1 of the Independent Order Benai Berith. 58th st, n s, 279 8 e 2d av, 23.6x100.5. Sub. to morts. Nov. 20, 1 year, 4½ %. 12,500

Schmitt, Margaret to William Austin. 121st st, n s, 130 e 1st av, 75x100.11; 121st st, n s, 205 e 1st av, 58x100.11. Leasehold. Nov. 20. 3,000

Scully, John J. to Julius Kaesemeyer. Jerome av, w s, adj Edwin Frazers land, 25x200. Leasehold. Nov. 25, due Dec. 1, 1894. 1,500

Spero, Julius M. and Minna his wife to Louis D. Levy. In trust for estate of Abraham D. Levy and for Silia Wolf and Rosa Levy. Lexington av, No. 1622, s w cor 102d st, 18x75. Sub. to mort. $8,500. Nov. 20, 5 years. 3,000

Sheldon, Simon M. to Charlotte F. Trowbridge, Brooklyn. Stebbins av and Jennings st. P. M. Nov. 24, 5 years or installs. 840

Schmidt, Charles G. to Joseph Rupprecht. Amsterdam av, No. 295. Saloon lease. Nov. 23, note, demand. 2,000

Schramm, John N. to Jennie Reeves, Bay Shore, L. I. 146th st, s s, 99.8 e Willis av, 25x100. Sept. 30, 2 years. 1,700

Seiferd, Lena to John J. Brady. Clinton st, e s, 25 s Elmwood pl, 115x100. P. M. Oct. 19, due Nov. 5, 1894. 8,000

Shelley, Michael F. and Margaret his wife to John J. Brady. Tremont av. P. M. Nov. 23, 3 years. 1,900

Stahl, Elizabeth to THE HARLEM SAVINGS BANK. 160th st, s s, 550 e Courtlandt av, 50x100. Nov. 23, 1 year, 5 %. 700

Straiton, John to Thomas Stokes and ano. exrs. and trustees Elizabeth C. Stokes. 150th st, s s, 80 e 10th av, 102x99.11. Nov. 23, 3 years, 5 %. 24,000

Same to Augustus D. Juilliard et al. trustees Frederick H. Cossitt. 150th st, s s, 182 e 10th av, 68x99.11. Nov. 23, 3 years, 5 %. 16,000

Straub, Elizabeth widow and Frank and Frederick Straub and Clara wife of Louis F. Bischof heirs Franz Straub to Peter Schupp. 2d av, No. 99, w s, 24.3 s 6th st, 24.3x105. Nov. 23, 3 years. 5,000

Sugden, Ella widow to THE TITLE GUARANTEE AND TRUST CO. 87th st. P. M. Nov. 16, due Nov. 23, 1892, 4½ %. 10,500

Swenson, Eric P. to Henry A. C. Taylor, Newport, R. I. 71st st, n s, 305 e 5th av, 20x102.2. April 10, due Nov. 25, 1892, 5 %. 40,000

Tilden, Anna P. wife of and Marmaduke, Madison, N. J., to Louisa Coddington. Lexington av, No. 285, e s, 25 s 37th st, 22.9x80. Nov. 25, due Jan. 1, 1893, 5 %. 5,000

Timmins, John J. to William A. Martin. 117th st. P. M. Nov. 18, 1 year. 38,000

Tremmaglia, Biagio and Gaetana Scalzi, of Scalzi & Tremmaglia, to Bernheimer & Schmid. Mott st, No. 141. Saloon lease. Nov. 25, note, demand. 800

The Congregational Shearith Bnai Israel of Avenue C to Mary S. Oppenheimer. 6th st, s s, 215.11 w Av C, 21x97. Nov. 23, 3 years. 3,500

Tynan, Anastasia to John Murphy. 149th st, n s, 150 w Courtlandt av, 25x100. Nov. 20, due Jan. 1, 1893, 5 %. 1,200

The Church of St. Margaret to THE EMIGRANT INDUSTRIAL SAVINGS BANK. Riverdale av, s e cor Beech st, 100x150. Nov. 16, 1 year. 4½ %. 15,000

Tremere, Eleanor B. wife of and William T. to James C. Foley, Brooklyn. 99th st, s s, 275 e 9th av, 25x100.11. Nov. 9, 1 year. 242

Uhl, Adam to THE METROPOLITAN SAVINGS BANK. Morris av. P. M. Nov. 7, 1 year. 5 %. 3,000

Same to Katie Devall. Morris av, e s, 25 n 149th st. P. M. Nov. 20, 3 years, 5 %. 2,300

Van Demark, Sophia A. to James C. de La Mare. Berry st, n s, 100 w Anthony av, 50x90. Nov. 23, 6 months. 500

Veyrac, Victor L. to Frederic R. and Chas. Coudert exrs. Antoine E. Welche. 16th st, No. 251, n s, 209 e 8th av, 17x80. Nov. 25, 2 years, 5 %. gold, 1,000

Van Clief, Clorinda to Bernheimer & Schmid. Park av, No. 883, n e cor 78th st. Saloon lease. Nov. 23, note, demand. 3,000

Vultee, George W. to Mary J. Burchell. 147th st, n s, 75 w 8th av. P. M. Nov. 16, 5 years. 5 %. 12,000

Same to same. 147th st, n s, 100 w 8th av. P. M. Nov. 16, 5 years, 5 %. 12,000

Same to Ferdinand R. Miurath. 147th st, n s, 75 w 8th av, 50x99.11. Sub. to morts. $24,000. Nov. 16, 1 year. 5,000

Weinberg, Leah to John Baum. 2d av. P. M. Nov. 25, due Dec. 1, 1901, or installs, 5 %. 11,000

Same to Isaac Cohen. Same property. P. M. Sub. to last mort. Nov. 25, 1 year. 500

Weinberger, Edward to Philip Kaiser. Madison av. P. M. Sub. to mort. $15,000. Nov. 24, due Dec. 1, 1894, 5 %. 3,000

Worth, Margaretha to Charles and Charles J. Miller. 88th st. P. M. Nov. 25, due Aug. 1, 1892, 5 %. 4,250

Wurz, Charles, Catharine and Lizzie to Louisa Wagener. 154th st, n s, 170 w Elton av, 25x100. Sept. 12, 4 months. 1,800

Wales, Margaret A. to Patrick Hogan. Rustic av. P. M. Nov. 10, 5 years, 5 %. 1,500

Welch, Albert an heir, &c., Jacob Leon to Tarrant Putnam and ano. trustees for Geraldine W. Goddard. Hester st, No. 69, n s, 21.10x100; Hester st, No. 67, n s, 21.10x100; Forsyth st, No. 129, w s, 25x100; Delancey st, No. 31, s s, 20x75; Amsterdam av, s e cor 103d st, runs south 88.10 x east 94 x south to point 100.11 from 103d st, x east to point 128.6 e Amsterdam av, x north 100.11 to 103d st, x west 128.6, excepting a gore thereout. ⅙ part. Nov. 23, due Dec. 1, 1892. See Conveys. 2,000

White, Richard to Ethelbert Wilson. 135th st, s s, 200 e 7th av, 50x99.11. Nov. 17, due Oct. 12, 1892. 14,000

Williams, Nathaniel D. to Anne E. Brice. 90th st, n s, 337.6 w 3d av, 12.6x100.8. Nov. 23, due Dec. 1, 1894, 5 %. 5,000

Woodward, Collin H. to THE FIRST NATIONAL BANK, Yonkers. 144th st, n s, 225.6 w 5th av, 32.4x100.6x21.5 to Bradhurst av, x 99.11. Nov. 19, installs., notes. 484

Wallace, John to George J. Troll, Jersey City, N. J. 153d st, s s, 150 w Morris av, 25x100. Nov. 14, due Nov. 18, 1894. 1,200

Walker, Alexander and Judson Lawson to Julian B., David B. and John I. Hart. 95th st. P. M. Nov. 16, due Nov. 24, 1892, 5 %. 12,000

Whitaker, John and Herbert Richmond to Model Building and Loan Assoc. of Mott Haven. 138th st, n s, 296.1 e Southern Boulevard. Nov. 21, installs, 5 %. 2,500

Wright, Louisa L. widow to Thomas H. Rodman, Brooklyn. 36th st, s s, 380 w 5th av, 15x98.9. Nov. 10, 3 years, 5 %. 10,000

KINGS COUNTY.

NOVEMBER 19, 20, 21, 23, 24, 25.

Abramowitz, Sarah to Jennie Seidenberg. Livonia av, s e cor Osborn st. P. M. Nov. 2, due Feb. 2, 1892. 675

Abramovitz, Rochmiel to Earl A. Gillespie, Jamaica, L. I. Livonia av, s e cor Osborn st, 20x100. Sub. to mort. $3,000. Nov. 23, installs. 1,000

Aichele, Philip to Philip Aichele guard. Minnie and Elizabeth Zentgraf. Rutledge st, s e s, 100 s w Harrison av, 20x100. Nov. 1, 5 years, 5 %. 3,500

Aldom, Abbie wife of Charles W. to Anna C. Fleischmann. Madison st, w s, 116.10 s Evergreen av, 25x100. Nov. 20, 3 years. 400

Allen, Maurice P. to The Greenpoint Savings Bank. Oakland st, w s, 75 s Clay st, 25x100. Nov. 19, 1 year. 5 %. 1,600

Armstrong, Benjamin to James D. Rankin and James Ross. 7th av, w s, 60 s 2d st, 20x80. Nov 20, 1 year. 1,000

Aronson, Julino and Pauline to August R. Hartmann. Walton st, n s, 325 e Marcy av, 25x100. Nov. 20, due Jan. 1, 1893. 1,000

Battle, Martin to Ellen Burns. Monroe st, n s, 200 w Tompkins av, 20x100. Sub. to mort. $3,000. Nov. 14, 5 years, 5 %. 3,000

Behr, John A. to Edward Egolf. Earl st. P. M. Nov. 18, 3 years. 200

Bell, Martha to The Title Guarantee and Trust Co. South 5th st, s s, 228.6 w Bedford av, 25x100. Nov. 20, 1 year, 5 %. 8,000

Berkeley, Fabie to Frances S. Thomson. 17th st, n e s, 340 n w 6th av, 20x100.2. Nov. 19. 616

Berliner, Max and Minnie his wife to Theobald L. Reichel. Oak st. P. M. Nov. 23, 5 years, 5 %. 2,000

Blackwell, Emily to Hannah Dunham. Macon st, s s, 170 e Ralph av, 18x100. Nov. 19, 4 years, 5 %. 2,500

Blinn, Ernest H. to John S. Junior. Stewart st, n w s, 75 n e Broadway, 28.1x50x27.7x50. Nov. 19, 3 years. 2,500

Bonert, Louis to William J. Gelston. 6th av and 5th st. P. M. Nov. 19, due Nov. 20, 1892, 5 %. 9,750

Breivogel, John to The City Savings Bank, Brooklyn. 5th av, w s, 50 s Warren st, 25x93.4. Nov. 20, due Nov. 1, 1894, 5 %. 3,000

Brown, Henry J. to Walter and George Luke exrs. Andrew Luke. Herkimer st, n s, 202 e Kingston av, runs north 85 x west 18 x north 15 x east 16.1 x southeast 104.6 to st, x west 28.7. Nov. 20, 5 years, 5 %. 4,000

Same to same. Sumner av, w s, 125 s Decatur st, 100x81.11x101.7x99.8. Nov. 20, 5 years. 5 %. 11,000

Brunck, Charles J. to Leander W. Stockwell. Hancock st, s e s, 339 n e Broadway, 18x100. Nov. 23, due Dec. 21, 1894, 5½ %. 3,300

Brundage, James H. to Peter Rapelje. Jerome av, e s, 160 s Dumont av, 20x100. Nov. 20, due Jan. 1, 1895. 1,800

Burgedahl, Charles to Henry C. Bull. 20th st. P. M. Nov. 14, installs. 500

Carpenter, James O. to The Title Guarantee and Trust Co. Nostrand av, n w cor Herkimer st, 97x60. Nov. 20, 1 year. 6,000

Churchill, Edward J. to C. C. Abel & Co. Jefferson av, Nos 104 and 106. Sub. to morts. $18,000. July 21, due Jan. 1, 1892. 300

Ciorciori, Antonio, Guisseppe to Angelo Ciorciori. 1st st. Nov. 18, 3 years, 5 %. See Conveys. 500

Clark, Lemuel S. to Ann Taylor. Tompkins av, w s, 33 4 s Hart st. P. M. Sub. to mort. $1,500. Nov. 19, installs, 5 %. 1,000

Same to Ann Taylor et al. exrs. Joseph C. Taylor. Same property. P. M. Nov. 19, due Nov. 1, 1894, 5 %. 2,500

Cohen, Sophie and Marian F. to The Title Guarantee and Trust Co. 11th st, s s, 264.6 e 4th av, 16.8x100. Nov. 20, 3 years, 5 %. 2,500

Colne, Harriet S. wife of and Charles to The Title Guarantee. Bleecker st, s e s, 310 n e Irving av, 60x100. Nov. 19, 1 year. 600

Combe, Bertha to Rosina Huttenlocher. Schenck av. P. M. Nov. 23, 3 years, 5 %. 1,500

Conway, Agnes T. wife of and James J. to John Y. McKane, both of Gravesend, L. I. Coney Island road, n e Van Siclen pl, 49x108x49x107.4; Van Siclen pl, e s, 107.4 n Coney Island road, 40x100, Gravesend. Nov. 18, 3 years. 3,800

Conway, Bridget wife of Patrick to The Bedford Co-operative Building Loan Assoc. Park pl, n s, 135 e Schenectady av, 20x155.7. Nov. 2, installs. 100

Conway, James to John Andrews. 19th st. P. M. Nov. 2, due Nov. 1, 1896. 300

Cooper, Florence M. wife of Frank A. to The Title Guarantee and Trust Co. Prince st, w s, 150 s Myrtle av, 22.10x85. Nov. 19, 3 years, 5 %. 1,000

Corlis, George F. to Solomon S. Jackson, Jericho, L. I. Portland av. P. M. Nov. 18, due Nov. 1, 1894, 5 %. 5,000

Crawford, Sarah with The German-American Title Guarantee Co. both mortgagees. Agreement as to priorty of morts. made by Henry B. Fanton, Jr. Aug. 25. nom

Cumiskey, James to Elizabeth E. Hutchins. Kosciusko st, s s, 450 w Reid av. P. M. Nov. 24, 3 years or installs, 5 %. 3,780

Dlauby, Vincens to The Williamsburgh Brewing Co (Lim.) Bushwick av, n e s, 79.8 s e Vandeveer st, 20x79.6. Nov. 19, demand. 500

Doherty, Charles to James O'Connell. 89th st, New Utrecht. P. M. Nov. 13, 2 years, 4 %. 136

Doyle, Peter to Underhill, Jackson & Co. 5th av, No. 248. Saloon lease. Nov. 17, note. 300

Ernst, Frank F. to Emilie F. Ernst. Liberty av. P. M. Nov. 16, 5 years, 5 %. 1,000

Edgar, Kate to The South Brooklyn Co-operative Building and Loan Assoc. Hall st. P. M. Nov. 17, installs. 4,750

Eich, John to James L. Kortright. Hamburg av, n e s, 75 s e Suydam st, 25x100. Nov. 2, due Nov. 1, 1894, 5 %. 3,500

Eiermann, Frederick to Adolph Kiendl guard. Charles Kalb Belmont av, 50 w Schenck av, 25x100. Nov. 17, 3 years. 2,000

Emich, William and Emma his wife to Henry Burnett. Boerum st, n s, 28 1 e Broadway, 22x100. Nov. 21, due Nov. 1, 1894, 5 %. 5,000

Fabr. Charles to Charles Nagel and George Werner. Eastern Parkway, s s, 103.3 w Utica av, 60x225.3 to Union st. Nov. 23, 3 years, 5 %. 2,500

Faulkner, Catharine T. wife of Michael to Samuel M. Meeker trustee Frederick Herr. Bridge st, n e cor Tallman st. P. M. Nov. 19, 3 years, 5 %. 3,000

Fegan, Isabella T. to Edward R. Fegan, Flatbush. 10th st, n w cor Hope st, 21x55.8. Nov. 21, due Feb. 1, 1892. 1,700

Fischer, Ernest H. to Catharine E. Fischer. All title in estate of Ernest W. Fischer. Nov. 21. 2,000

Foley, James C. to Susan A. Bacon, Hempstead, L. I. 52d st, s w s, 160 n w 4th av, 20x100.2. Nov. 20, due Nov. 1, 1894, 5 %. 2,500

Same to Jaques Bennett. 52d st, s w s, 140 n w 4th av, 20x100.2. Nov. 20, due Nov. 1, 1894, 5 %. 2,500

Fowler, Bernard to James D. Rankin and James Ross. Washington av, w s, abt 75 n Gates av, 25x100. Nov. 2. 2,500

Francis, George S. to William C. Lowther. 86th st. n e s, plot 5 map Rutgert A. Van Brunt, 25x100, New Utrecht. Nov. 20, 3 years. 800

Free, John P. and Whitman M. to Thomas G. Ritch trustee for Sadie M. Sturges. Sutter av, s s, 20 e Snediker av, 20x92.6. Nov. 23, 3 years. 2,000

Same to Julia W. Douglas, Middleton, Conn. Snediker av, e s, 167.6 s Sutter av, 15x100. Nov. 23, 3 years. 1,500

Same to same. Snediker av, e s, 182.6 s Sutter av, 15x100. Nov. 23, 3 years. 1,500

Gane, William to The Brooklyn Home for Consumptives. St. Marks av, n s, 350 w Underhill av, 33.6x131. Nov. 18, 5 years. 5,000

Gerken, John to Ira Pettit, Queens, L. I. Union st, n s, 510.10 w 4th av, 16.8x95. Nov. 17, due Nov. 1, 1894, 5 %. 5,500

Giblin, Michael to Henry Weil. Pacific st. P. M. Nov. 6, due May 1, 1892. 4,000

Same to same. Same property. Nov. 6, due May 1, 1892. 6,000

Gildersleeve, Carrie A. to Jane A. Bergen, Port Jefferson, L. I. 78th st, New Utrecht. P. M. Nov. 23, 3 years. 1,500

Gill, Adelaide F. wife of Harry D. to William Gill. Bedford av, w s, 186.10 s Myrtle av, 25x100. Aug. 18, due Jan. 1, 1893, 5 %. 4,000

Goodkind, Theresa to James W. McDermott et al. exrs. Ellen M. Murray. Seigel st, n s, 176 e Graham av, 25x100. Nov. 23, due Dec. 1, 1894, 5 %. 7,000

Graper, Laura B. wife of and Henry A., Paterson, N. J., to The Title Guarantee and Trust Co. Madison st, s s, 180 w Ralph av, 20x100. Nov. 23, 3 years. 450

Grassman, Henry to Mary J. Cory. Monroe st, n s, 110 e Stuyvesant av, 20x100. Nov. 19, 3 years, 5 %. 3,500

Same to Ella Cory. Monroe st, n s, 130 e Stuyvesant av, 20x100. Nov. 19, 3 years, 5 %. 3,500

Gsanger, John J. to Harry L. Bradley. 54th st. P. M. Nov. 18, due Dec. 1, 1892. 350

Gschwind, Joseph to John Herzog. Covert st. P. M. Nov 23, installs, 5 %. 1,700

Gyles, Katherine B. to John Caufield. Hicks st, w s, 288.6 n Degraw st, 19.6x97.6. Oct. 16, 4 years, 5 %. 3,800

Hackradt, Maria wife of Otto to Emeline E. Brower. Harrison av, e s, 25 s Walton st, 25x100 Nov. 20, 3 years. 4,500

Hancock, William A. to Robert S. Neely. Pacific st, s s, 166.8 e Rockaway av, 2 lots, each 16.8x107.2. 2 morts., each $325. Nov. 14, 1 year. 650

Hanna, Robert M. to A. C. Bournonville. 42d st, s w s, 130 8 n w Fort Hamilton av, 50x100, New Utrecht. Nov. 2, 5 years. 2,200

Healy, Henry W. to Nisan Hess. Myrtle av. P. M. Nov. 23, 5 years, 5 %. 3,000

Herget, Eugene to East Brooklyn Co-operative Building Assoc. Monteith st, n s, 100 w Bremen st, 20x100. Nov. 13, installs. 1,250

Hockemeyer, Eliza wife of and Frederick C. to Charles C. H. Schmardt. De Kalb av, n w cor Marcy av, 25x80. Nov. 20, 3 years, 5 %. 2,500

Hoffman, William to Sarah H. Tuttle. Throop av. P. M. Nov. 23, 3 years, 5 %. 3,000

Holm, Charles F. to John Vanderbilt. 7th st, s s, 317.10 w 7th av, 20x100. Nov. 23, 3 years, 5 %. gold, 4,800

Huber, Joseph M. to William D. Appleget. 40th st, s s, 170 e 2d av, 180x100.2. Nov. 19, 3 years, 5 %. 8,000

Hunt, Joseph to James D. Lynch. North Henry st. P. M. Nov. 12, due Nov. 16, 1893, 5 %. 5,400

Innes, Joseph to Home Life Ins. Co. Putnam av, n e cor Sumner av, 25x100. Nov. 19, 1 year, 5 %. 4,000

Iverson, Iver to Bushwick Co-operative Building and Loan Assoc. Monitor st, e s, 400 s Norman av, 20x100. Nov. 23, installs. 3,500

Jacobs, Fanny to Samuel M. Meeker exr. Frederick Herr. Broadway and Willoughby av. P. M. Nov. 14, 5 years, 5 %. 14,500

Johnson, Albert F. to Harriet B. Ranney. Elmwood av, s s, 62.6 e 3d st, 87.6x125, New Utrecht. Nov. 24, 3 years. 5,000

Same to Sarah M. Striker. Same property; also, Elmwood av, s w cor East 4th st, 50x125, New Utrecht. Nov. 24, 3 years. 1,000

Jones, Carrie L. to Joseph Wechsler. Coney Island av. P. M. Nov. 17, due Nov. 16, 1896. 2,450

Kern, John to Michael and George Kern. Varet st, n s, 305.6 e Bushwick av, 25x100. Sept. 17, due Oct. 1, 1893, 5 %. 500

Kidd, Adelaide L. widow to Matilda Hobby. Clifton pl, s s, 338.8 w Nostrand av, 18.8x100. Nov. 18, due Nov. 1, 1894, 5 %. 500

Kiernan, Joseph to John F. Doyle. Court st, e s, 104 s Livingston st, runs north 26 x east 99 x south 14 x east 2 x south 13 x west 101.4. Sub. to mort. $15,000. Nov. 23, due Dec. 1, 1892. gold, 2,500

Kirk, John H. to Asa W. Parker, Hamburg, N. Y. Monroe st, s s, 294 w Throop av, 19.3x100. Nov. 24, 1 year. 400

Klein, Isak and Jacob Honig to Elizabeth Baylis, Jamaica, L. I. Taylor st, n s, 173.8 e Kent av, 19.11x80. Nov. 20, 3 years, 5 %. 2,30

Katt, Carl A to William B. A. Jurgens. Ocean Parkway, e s, adj land John L. Roberts, Jr., 130.1x620.6x175x617.8, Gravesend. Nov. 20, 1 year, 5 %. 750

Klein, John to Joseph Knoblauch. Jefferson st, n w s, 125 n e Central av, 25x100. Nov. 23, 3 years, 5 %. 1,160

Korte, Charles H. to Leonhard Eppig. Liberty av, n e cor Bradford st, 25x100. Nov. 19, 1 year or installs. 5 %. 2,500

Kraus, Louis to Theodore H. Werner. De Kalb av. P. M. Nov. 19, 3 years, 5 %. 1,000

Krug, Emma to Moritz Pinner. Steuben st. P. M. Nov. 23, due March 1, 1892. 600

Kunz, Franz to Charles Dexheimer. Bay av, s w cor Vermont av, 50x—. Nov. 14, due Nov. 15, 1892. 200

Lamkay, Amelia wife of Aaron to Maria wife of Henry E. Kantorwiz. P st, s s, 302.4 e Lee av, 20.2x100. Nov. 18, due March 30, 1894. 1,500

Leinfelder, Anna to Henry H. Adams, Treasurer Kings Co. Lots 188 and 189 block 6 map Jacob Snediker. Nov. 21, 1 year. 2,000

Leslie, Fannie wife of and Alexander F. W. to John W. Sullivan. Ocean Parkway, w s, 160 s Av E, 60x250 to East 5th st. June 2, 1 year. 2,500

Levy, Morris to Julia Hyer. Christopher av, s e cor Glenmore av. P. M. Aug. 4, 5 years or installs. 2,200

Lockwood, Harold S. to Phebe A. Henderson. Garden st, n w cor State st, 38.10x95.9. P. M. July 1, 1890, 1 year. 8,000

Loftus, Annie to Peter McCoy and Margaret his wife. Adelphi st. P. M. Nov. 18, 5 years, 5 %. 1,800

Lowe, Katharine A. to George W. Conselyea and Anna M. Irwin. 17th st. P. M. Nov. 23, installs. 2,800

Luck, John to Maria D. Lott, Flatbush, L. I. White st or Newkirk av, s s, 1,147.6 e Brooklyn and Coney Island plank road, 195x137.9x139.6x125.2, Flatbush. Nov. 10, 3 years, 5 %. 3,500

Lyon, Newman to The Bushwick Co-operative Building and Loan Assoc. Cedar st. P. M. Nov. 20, installs. 2,500

Macri, Thomas to Robert P. Johnson. Myrtle av, s s, 142.2 e Stockholm st, 25x47.6x27.1x58. Nov. 20, 4 years, 5 %. 600

Madio, Domenico to Watson & Pittinger. 61st st, n s, 200 w 14th av, 20x100. Nov. 21, demand. 700

Maier, John H. to Lawrence Maier. 53d st, n s, 181.3 e 3d av, 18x100.2. Nov. 9, 3 years, 5 %. 2,000

Manning, Denis to Henry M. and Chester S. Kingman exrs. Martin E. Kingman. Bedford av, w s, 68.3 s Park av, 14x78. Nov. 17, due Nov. 18, 1894, 5 %. 1,500

Marquand, John B. to The Manhattan Savings Inst. Bergen st. P. M. Nov. 20. 1 year, 5 %. 1,000

Mason, Emma W. wife of and William to The Title Guarantee and Trust Co. Halsey st, s s, 290.6 e Ralph av, 18.2x100. Nov. 19, 3 years, 5 %. 3,000

Same to John T. Barnard. Same property. P. M. Nov. 1, installs. 440

Mathews, Annie wife of and Joseph to Thomas C. Balderston et al. Supreme trustees of the Order of Tonti. Osborn st, s w cor Livonia av, 25x100. Nov. 23, 3 years, 5 %. gold, 6,000

Same to same. Osborn st, w s, 25 s Livonia av, 25x100. Nov. 23, 3 years, 5 %. gold, 5,000

McNab, Elizabeth P. to William Geyer. Marion st, s s, 387.7 e Howard av, 18.8x100. Nov. 18, 3 years, 5 %. 3,000

Michaelis, Hannah wife of and Bertrand to The Title Guarantee and Trust Co. Madison st. P. M. Nov. 20, 1 year, 5 %. 2,500

Middleton, John to Eliza J. Bogart. Newtown, L. I. South 1st st. P. M. Sept. 22, due Nov. 1, 1894. 5 %. 1,300

Mills, Mary A. to Ida A. Ryerson, Gravesend, L. I. Spencer st, e s, 225 s Park av, 25x100. Nov. 16, 3 years, 5 %. 1,000

Morris, Joseph to Virginia L. Dunham and Mary E. Lowe. Osborn st, e s, 150 n Sutter av, 25x100. Nov. 18, 3 years. 3,500

Moses, Charles and Henry B. Fanton, Jr., to The German-American Real Estate Title Guarantee Co. 3d st, n s, 220 w 7th av, 44x90. Aug. 25, demand. 35,000

Mundell, Jeremiah mortgagor with William A. Hinchmann and ano, exrs. George W. Hinchmann mortgagees. Extension of mort. Oct. 1. nom

Mowbray, Edward H. to The Title Guarantee and Trust Co. 3d st, n s, 297.4 e 7th av, 100.6x95. Nov. 20, demand. 4,000

Murphy, John W. to William A. Kissam, Little Neck, L. I. Oakland st, w s, 120 n Norman av, 25x100. Nov. 17, due Nov. 1, 1894, 5 %. 3,500

Niederegger, Joseph to William H. Jackson. Atkins av and New Lots road. P. M. Aug. 15, 3 years. 480

Nelson, Charles to Julia P. and Isabelle B. Underhill, Locust Valley, L. I. Essex st, e s, 350 s Gay st, 125x200 to Shepherd av; Essex st, e s, 525 s Gay st, 25x100; Shepherd av, s e cor Glenmore av, 75x100. Nov. 16, due Nov. 1, 1896. 5,000

Norris, Allison V. B. to Ira O. Miller. 11th st, s s, 102 e 8th av, 18x100. Oct. 31, due Nov. 2, 1896, 5 %. 5,500

Same to same. 11th st, s s, 84 e 8th av, 18x100. Oct. 31, due Nov. 2, 1896, 5 %. 5,500

Same to same. 11th st, s s, 30 e 8th av, 3 lots, each 18x81.10. 3 morts., each $5,500. Oct. 31, due Nov. 2, 1896, 5 %. 16,500

O'Toole, Margaret to William H. Jackson. Atkins av. P. M. Nov. 10, 3 years or installs. 192

Ohler, Charles H. and Eliza his wife to Emilie Huber. Hart st, n w s, 200 n e Broadway, 20x75. Nov. 20, 1 year, 5 %. 2,500

O'Rourke, James F. to William O. Moore et al. exrs. Abraham Underhill. 45th st, n s, 340 e 3d av, 4 lots, each 20x100.2. 4 morts., each $2,800. Nov. 24, 3 years, 5 %. 11,200

Same to Edward C. Underhill. 45th st, n s, 300 e 3d av, 2 lots, each 20x100.2. 2 morts., each $2,800. Nov. 24, 3 years, 5 %. 5,600

Owens, Andrew E. to Minnie Josiah. Essex st, e s, 160 n Ridgewood av, 20x100. Nov. 21. 800

Pabst, Elizabeth to Emeline E. Brower. Fulton st, n s, 4.3 w Somers st, runs north 52.1 x west 6.10 x north 4.8 x west — x south 4.8 x again south 52.1 to Fulton st, x east 19.6. Nov. 20, 5 years. 4,500

Parks, William C. to Edward F. Cain. Cropsey av, east cor Bay 11th st, runs northeast 261.5 x southeast 169.2 to Bennetts lane, x southwest 255.7 to av, x northwest 131.11. Nov. 13, 5 years, 5 %. 4,000

Phelan, Gussie L. to Carrie Blyn. Pilling st, n s, 87.4 w Bushwick av, 17x100. Nov. 23, 4 months. 575

Phillips, Theckla to Herman Hartman. Sumpter st, s s, 140 w Rockaway av, 20x100. Nov. 21, 5 years, 5 %. 1,500

Prendergast, Mary A. to Caroline P. Latimer. Atlantic av, s w cor Hicks st, 19.10x60. Nov. 24, 2 years, 5 %. 4,500

Purgold, Margrett to Virginia A. Kleine. Putnam av, s s, 90 e Central av, 70x100. Sub. to mort. $5,000. Nov. 21, demand. 1,200

Same to The Title Guarantee and Trust Co. Same property. Nov. 21, demand. 5,000

Quackenbush, Harriet widow to Charles Griffen et al. trustees Samuel Willets dec'd. Gates av, n s, 205 e Marcy av, 20x105. Nov. 20, 5 years, 5 %. 5,000

Ratner, Louis to Levi N. Fuller. Belmont av, s e cor Osborn st, 25x100. Nov. 17, 3 years. 5,500

Reid, Eliza to Paul W. Ledoux. Bergen st, n s, 253 w Ralph av, 102x107. Nov. 16, demand. 5,400

Same to same. Same property. Nov. 16, demand. 6,000

Reynolds, William H. to The Title Guarantee and Trust Co. Halsey st, n s, 200 w Nostrand av, 200x100. Nov. 23, 1 year. 20,000

Same to William M. Ingraham. Halsey st, n s, 100 w Nostrand av, 100x100. Nov. 23, 1 year. 9,000

Same to Mary A. Lynch. Halsey st, n s, 100 w Nostrand av, 300x100. Sub. to mort. $20,000. Nov. 23. 2 years, 5 %. 24,000

Reynolds, Charles G. to Clementine S. Patchen. McDonough st, s s, 267.8 e Reid av, 17x100. Nov. 20, 3 years, 5 %. 4,500

Same to Edward F. Patchen admr. Martha W. Patchen. McDonough st, s s, 338.4 e Reid av, 18x100. Nov. 20, 3 years, 5 %. 4,500

Same to Clementine S. Patchen. McDonough st, s s, 320.8 e Reid av, 17.8x100. Nov. 20, 3 years, 5 %. 4,500

Same to Eliza A. Gregory extrx. Justus E. Gregory. McDonough st, s s, 285.4 e Reid av, 17.8x100. Nov. 20, 3 years, 5 %. 4,500

Same to same. McDonough st, s s, 250 e Reid av, 17.8x100. Nov. 20, 3 years, 5 %. 4,500

Ritting, Henry to The Germania Savings Bank. Floyd st, n s, 300 e Throop av, 25x100. Nov. 20, 1 year. gold, 5,500

Ritting, Henry to Joseph C. Hacker. Floyd st, n s, 275 e Throop av, 25x100. Nov. 20, due Nov. 1, 1892, 5 %. 600

Robb, James R. to General Synod of the Reformed Church in America. 21st st, n s, 236.8 e 6th av, 16.1x100. Nov. 23, 2 years. 1,500

Same to same. 21st st, n s, 220.9 e 6th av, 15.11x100. Nov. 23, 2 years. 1,500

Robinson, Margaret L. to The Brooklyn Trust Co Henry st, s e s, 167 s w Joralemon st, 25x100. Nov 20, 1 year, 5 %. 10,000

Rosbotham, Robert to The Brooklyn City Co-operative Building and Loan Assoc. 5th av, w s, 50.2 n 48th st, 25x100. Nov. 19, installs. 500

Rosenzweig, Lena to Alfred L. Beasley. Gates av. P. M Nov. 23, 1 year. 500

Rupp, Christian to William H. Gill. Linwood st, e s, 100 n Arlington av, 40x107.2x40x106.11. Nov. 19, due Dec. 1, 1892, 5 %. 1,000

Ryan, Frederic to Jeannie F. Crane, San Antonio, Texas. Windsor pl. P. M. Sub. to mort. $1,000. Nov. 2, installs, 5 %. 600

Same to same. Same property. P. M. Nov. 2, 3 years, 5 %. 1,000

Sackmann, Washington to Charles J. Hobe. Baltic st, s s, 100 w Hopkinson av, 125x127.9. Sept. 1, demand. 250

Salisbury, Harriet B. to Arthur Taylor. Macon st. P. M. Nov. 16, installs. 3,255

Schneider, Frederick W. to James H. Watson. Union st. P. M. Sub. to mort. $1,400. Nov. 14, 3 years. 200

Schoenborn, Augusta to Michael Moran. Central av. P. M. Nov. 13, due Nov. 12, 1892, 5 %. 700

Seermann, Baruch and Meyer to Charles F. Hitzelberger. Eastern Parkway, s s, 25 e Thatford av, 25x100. Oct. 26, 5 years. 3,000

Sherwood, James H. to Elizabeth T. Gardiner. Macon st. P. M. Nov. 21, 3 years, 5 %. 3,500

Smith, Phebe M. to Charles D. Rust. Nostrand av, w s, 60 s Lexington av, 20x100. Nov. 21, 1 year. 500

Sprenger, Charles A. to The Safety Co-operative Building Loan and Savings Assoc. Weirfield st, s e s, 280 n e Bushwick av, 20x100. Nov. 21, installs. 5,000

Snow, Henry B. to Benjamin C. Raymond. Macon st. P. M. Oct. 1, installs. 727

Striepecke, Friedrich to George H. Perry. Eckford st, w s, 275 n Calyer st, 25x100. Nov. 18, 1 year. 200

Stein, John P. to The Prospect Land and Improvement Co. 7th av, west cor 72d st. P. M. Nov. 13, due Nov. 19, 1894, 5 %. 225

Stemmler, William and Lena his wife to Philip L. Balz, Jr. Liberty av, s s, 50 e Crescent st, 25x100. Nov. 21, due Nov. 1, 1893. 500

Stephen, Frederick to Lydia Winant, Roseville, N. Y. Warwick st, w s, 150 n Glenmore av, 25x100. Nov. 20, 2 years. 500

Sterling, Susie F. to Robert A. Davison, Rockville Centre, L. I. Duffield st, w s, 235 n Willoughby st, 25x100. Nov. 20, due Nov. 1, 1892, 5 %. 500

Steves, Mary E. to David S. Beasley. Greene av, s s, 460 e Throop av. P. M. Nov. 20, 2 years, 5 %. 2,000

Strawson, Vincent A. to William J. Kaiser, John Vanderveer and George W. Dalton. Lots 12-16 block 1 map Worth & Strawson, Flatbush. Sub. to mort. Nov. 20, due Dec. 1, 1891, 5 %. 877

The West Brooklyn Land and Improvement Co. to Louis Bergdoll; New Utrecht av, e s, at intersection with centre line of 40th st, 737-1,000 acre; Fort Hamilton av, s e s, at intersection with centre 40th st, 1 7-100 acres; Lot bet lands Garrett G. Bergen dec'd and John G. Bergen, 7 acres; also 7 acres adj above and land of Adrian Martense; also 5 acres adj above and land of George Mertense and Anna M. Ferris; also 5 acres adj above and land of Lucy Barron; Wood lot, No. 2, as described in will of Adrian Martense, Jr., contains 9 acres; Woodland devised to Elizabeth Martense under same will, 10 acres; Cowenhoven lane, n s, adj land John Cowenhoven, 66 acres 17 perches and 1 859-1,000 acre; New Utrecht av, adj land of Mrs. L. V. Magaw, 19 4,210-10,000 acres, except portions taken for streets; Cowenhoven lane, adj lands Lucy E. Barron, 44 358-1,000 acres, excepting the following parcels: 41st st, n e s, 76.4 s e 10th av, 500x100.2; 12th av, north cor 41st st, runs northeast 50.2 x northwest 100 x northeast 50 x northwest 75 x southwest 100.2 to 41st st, x southeast 575; 41st st, n e s, 100 s e 12th av, 75x100; Fort Hamilton av, north cor 42d st, runs northwest 394.4 x northeast 100.2 x northwest 175 x northeast 100.2 to 41st st, x southeast 605 8 to Fort Hamilton av, x southwest 51 x northwest 121.7 x southwest 75 x southeast 107.11 to Fort Hamilton av, x southwest 76.5; 12th av, north cor 43d st, runs northwest 225 x northeast 100.2 x northwest 75 x northeast 100.2 to 42d st, x southeast 200 x southwest 150.2 x southeast 100 to av, x southwest 50.2; 42d st, s w s, 625 n w 12th av, 50x100.2; 42d st, s w s, 450 n w 12th av, 100x64.11x111.9x15.1; 12th av, south cor 42d st, runs southeast 450 x southwest 100.2 x southeast 50 x southwest 100.2 to 43d st, x west 400 x northeast 100.2 x northwest 100 to av, x northeast 100.2; 12th av, west cor 43d st, 50.2x100; 12th av, north cor 44th st, 50.2x100; 12th av, east cor 44th st, 100x100.2; 43d st, s w s, 100 s e 12th av, runs southwest 100.2 x southeast 50 x southwest 100.2 to 44th st, x southeast 50 x northeast 100.2 x southeast 50 x northeast 100.2 to 43d st, x northwest 150; 44th st, n e s, 250 s e 12th av, runs northeast 100.2 x southeast 50 x northeast 100.2 to s w 43d st, x southeast 50 x southwest 100.2 x southeast 50 x southwest 100.2 to 44th st, x northwest 150; 43d st, s w s, 400 s e 12th av, 50x100.2; 43d st, s w s, 500 s e 12th av, 50x100.2; 44th st, n e s, 450 s e 12th av, 50x100.2; 44th st, n e s, 550 s e 12th av, 50x100.2; 12th av, north cor 45th st, runs northwest 375 x northeast 100.2 x southeast 25 x northeast 100.2 to 44th st, x southeast 350 to av, x southwest 200.4; 45th st, n e s, 100 s e 12th av, runs northeast 150.2 x northwest 100 to 12th av, x northeast 50.2 to 44th st, x southeast 525 x southwest 200.4 to 45th st, x northwest 425; 46th st, n e s, 100 n w 12th av, runs northeast 200.4 to 45th st, x northwest 150 x southwest 100.2 x southeast 75 x southwest 100.2 to 46th st, x southeast 75; 46th st, n e s, 200 s e 12th av, runs northeast 100.2 x northwest 100 x northeast 100.2 to 45th st, x southeast 350 x southwest 200.4 to 46th st, x northwest 250; 47th st, n e s, 200 s e 12th av, 225x100.2; 48th st, n e s, 300 s e 12th av, runs northeast 100.2 x northwest 150 x northeast 100.2 to 47th st, x southeast 250 x southwest 200.4 to 48th st, x northwest 100; 14th av, east cor 49th st, 130 x—x—x100; 14th av, east cor 50th st, 200.4 to 49th st, x125x—x250; 17th av, north cor 50th st, 90x— to 16th av, x40 to st, x790; 52d st, n e s, 150 s e 13th av, 100x100.2; 53d st, n e s, 100 n w 14th av, 75x100.2; 52d st, s w s, 100 s e 14th av, 150x100.2; 14th av, e s, extends from 53d st to 54th st, 200.4x100; 54th st, n e s, 225 s e 14th av, runs northeast 200.4 to 53d st, x southeast 375 x southwest 200.4 to 54th st, x northeast 375; 57th st, n e s, 150 n w 15th av, runs northwest 375 x northeast 100.2 x southeast 200 x northeast 100.2 to 56th st, x southeast 175 x southwest 200.4; 58th st, n e s, 150 n w 15th av, runs northwest 150 x northeast 100.2 x northwest 300 x northeast 100.2 to 57th st, x southeast 450 x southwest 200.4; 12th av, n w s, extends from 41st to 42d st, 200.4x625; 13th av, east cor 42d st, runs northeast 150.2 x southeast 100 x northeast 50.2 to 41st st, x southeast 175 x southwest 100.2 x southeast 50 x southwest 100.2 to 42d st, x northwest 325; Fort Hamilton av, west cor 42d st, runs northwest 305 8 x southwest 100.2 x southeast 287.6 to av, x northeast 100; Fort Hamilton av, north cor 43d st, 51x103.5x50.2x94.4, all in New Utrecht. Nov. 17, 5 years, 5½ %. 115,000

The Crescent Athletic Club of Brooklyn to The Hamilton Trust Co. Narrows av, s e cor 83d st, extends to New York Bay, with letters patent, rights and privileges. Nov. 2, 10 years, 5 %. 65,000

Thompson, Charles M. and Catharine Molloy to Edward A. Ackerly, Rochester, N. Y. Enfield st, w s, 400 n Union av, 75x314x75x315; Nichols av, e s, lots 341-348 inclus. parcel 28 map 2 of Union Race Course property, 100x200 to Richards lane. Nov. 10, 3 years. 1,000

Tobias, Emma A. to James A. Townsend. 79th st, New Utrecht. P. M. Nov. 16, 3 years, 5 %. 900

Tonyes, Annie widow to Mary and Theresa White. Bedford av, s e cor Wallabout st, 20x67. Nov. 21, 3 years, 5 %. 4,000

Turner, Joseph to The Safety Co-operative Building Loan and Savings Assoc. Warren st, s s, 200.10 w 4th av, 20x100. Nov. 20, installs. 3,500

Tyler, Frank H. and Frederick B. Langston to The Title Guarantee and Trust Co. Hancock st, n s, 380 e Nostrand av, 21x100. Building loan. Nov. 20, demand. 13,000

Tyler, Frank H. and Frederick B. Langston to The J. F. Pease Furnace Co. Hancock st, n s, 380 e Nostrand av, 21x100. Nov. 21, due July 1, 1892. 800

Ulschmid, Ernestine to Emma V. Isbill. Stanhope st. P. M. Nov. 24, 1 year. 1,000

Van Note, Peter J. to Garret P. Cowenhoven. Bay 35th st, n w s, 312.10 s w Bath av, 50x96.8, Gravesend. Nov. 20, 3 years. 2,000

Vrieland, George to Stephen C. Halstead. 4th st, n s, 114.11 w 6th av, 17.4x95. ⅛ part. Nov. 19, due Dec. 1, 1892. 200

Walker, Maria to Walter N. Walker. Linden Boulevard, s s, lots 41 and 42 map Linden terrace, &c., —x— to Martense av. Nov. 19, 1 year. 2,000

Walter, Sarah B. to Elias J. Hendrickson, Jamaica, L. I. Putnam av, s s, 110 e Marcy av, 20x100. Nov. 17, due Nov. 1, 1892, 5 %. 500

Waltman, Sophia to Margaret Muir. 22d st, s w s, 425 s e 6th av, 25x100.2. Nov. 19, 2 years. 350

Wardell, Margaret A. to Frank P. Roper. St. Marks av, s s, 280 w Saratoga av, 40x127.9. Nov. 7, 5 years, 5 %. 320

Warner, Benjamin J. to The Title Guarantee and Trust Co. Rogers av, s e cor Degraw st, 185.7x100; Eastern Parkway, s s, 200 w Bedford av, 100x192 to Union st; Eastern Parkway, n s, 340 w Bedford av, 100x192 to Degraw st. Nov. 28, 1 year, 5 %. 10,000

Werner, August to The Title Guarantee and Trust Co. St. Marks av. P. M. Nov. 12, due Nov. 21, 1892, 5 %. 4,000

Wilhelms, Charles to Charles Fahr. Eastern Parkway. P. M. Nov. 23, due July 10, 1896, 5 %. 1,000

Wildridge, John S. to The Bulmer Lumber Co. Reid av, e s, 79.2 n Hancock st, 19.2x100. Sub. to mort. $9,000. Nov. 18, 4 months. 400

Williams, Edgar D. to Catharina Lipsius. Court st, s e cor Warren st, runs east 110.1 x south 100 x west 22 x north 79.6 x west 86.2 to Court st, x20.8. Nov. 23, 1 year, 5 %. 4,000

Williams, Mary T. wife of Samuel I. to Ann E. Williams. Jefferson av, s s, 150 e Putnam av, 43x100. Nov. 20, 10 years, 4 %. 1,900

Williams, Percy G. to The Title Guarantee and Trust Co. State st. P. M. Nov. 13, due Nov. 19, 1892, 5 %. 10,000

Wright, Mary L. to Benjamin C. Leech. Putnam av, s s, 130 e Marcy av, 20x100. Nov. 18, due Nov. 1, 1894, 5 %. 4,000

Zindle, Benjamin to Isaac H. Curtis. McDougal st, n s, 325 e Saratoga av, 25x100. Sub. to mort. $2,000. Nov. 18, 1 year. 375

MORTGAGES----ASSIGNMENTS.

NEW YORK CITY.

NOVEMBER 20 TO 26—INCLUSIVE

Byk, Poline, Brooklyn, to Joseph Byk, Brooklyn. nom

Cram, Henry A. and ano. exrs. and trustees George C. Cram to Jacob Cram. nom

Churchill, Lily W. formerly Hamersley et al. exrs. Louis C. Hamersley to Lily W. Churchill et al. trustees Louis C Hamersley dec'd. nom

Cutting, Robert L. admr. Gertrude Cutting to Frederic J. Middlebrook, Brooklyn. 3 assigns., each $5,000. $15,000

Crain, Thomas C. T. as Chamberlain of City New York to Blanche A. Petit. nom

Dillaway, George W. to The Mutual Life Ins. Co. consid. omitted

d'Aguiar, Alice to Julia R. Kinkele. 3,833

De Witt, George G. et al. exrs. George G. De Witt to Theodore De Witt, Nyack, N. Y. nom

Edmonds, Belle H., White Plains, N. Y., to Julia A. Bell. 1,600

Ely, Nathan L. and ano. exrs. Nathan C. Ely to Amelia E. Scranton. 4,000

Frank, Marcus A. to The Murray Hill Bank. 4,000

Same to same. 4,000

Ford, Henry W. trustee Augustus H. Ward to William N. Crane trustee. Re-recorded. 12,500

Same to same. Re-recorded. 12,500

Gucker, Henry to Robert Ernst. 15,000

Gescheidt, Henry M. to Aaron Cohn. 5,924

Gifford, Silas D. exr. Philip W. Verlander to Harriet Balcom. 1,500

Guggenheimer, Randolph to Emily P. Woolsey. 10,000

Gordon, Katie widow to The Metropolitan Trust Co., New York, trustee of William R. Garrison dec'd. 20,000

Gordon, Katie to Kittie G. Wiley, Brooklyn. 4,016

Same to Mary Fitzgerald widow. 6,021

Same to August Mehler. 17,342

German-American Real Estate Title Guarantee Co. to James Fellows and ano. exrs. Catharine Williams. 10,000

Same to same. 15,000

Same to same. 15,000

Same to same. 12,000

Horgan, Denis to Myrick Plummer. 12,000

Halley, Mary E. to Edwin S. Updike, Sr. nom

Heilner, Emanuel and Moses J. Wolf to Adelheid Brill. 4,449

Same to The Murray Hill Bank, New York. 4,000

Same to same. 4,000

Bogan, Patrick to P. McDowell & Co. consid. omitted

Haft, Alexander to Max Cohen. 2,875

Hand, Clifford A. exr. Charles G. Havens to The Havens Relief Fund Society. 9,000

Happel, Adam to Louis M. Jones. 5,134

Haydock, Robert and ano. exrs. Joseph D. Thurston to Joseph Wharton exr. Joseph D. Thurston. order of Court

Hall, Albert C. to The Brooklyn Trust Co. 30,000

Holt, Robert S. exr. G. M. C. Klingler to The Orphan Asylum Society of City of New York. 20,000

Isenburger, Louis et al. exrs. Arnold Blum, Jr., to Louis Isenburger et al. trustees for Rosina Blum. consid. omitted

Kane, John P. to Enoch C. Bell. 4,600

Kissam, Mary J. wife of Grenville A. to Marie F. Georgen. 8,000

Kimberly, David F. exr. Elizabeth Kimberly to Annie Kimberly, Brooklyn. 4,000

Kimberly, Mary individ. and David F. Kimberly exr. Elizabeth Kimberly to Louisa Kimberly. nom

Kaufmann, Abraham to Samson Wallach. 3,096

Kaufmann, Abraham to Adolph Schalk. 2,000

Lugar, Frank to Anna L. Rutherfurd. nom

Lyons, Constance H. to Lucius N. Littauer. 5,000

Levy, Pauline guard. of Florence N. Levy to Florence N. Levy. nom

Lyon, Dore to Sarah H. Wentworth. 1,006

Levi, Joseph C. as trustee to Bellina Froehlich. 12,500

Martin, Florence E. wife of Horace H., Chicago, Ill., to Bessie Collamore. 2,000

Minrath, Ferdinand R. to Mary Ryan. 6,000

Murray, Charles A., England, to American Employers' Liability Ins. Co. 12,500

McGinnis, Owen to Abraham Stein. 8,000

Myers, Lewis to Simon Bing, Jr. Re-recorded. 1,100

Miller, Ann to Alexander Miller. nom

Same to Annie Miller. nom

Miller, J. Bleecker to Ellis G. Welch, Bergen County, N. J. 400

Michaelis, Matilda, Brooklyn, to Simon Herman and Hyman Israel. 3,000

Pettit, John to William Duryea, Nyack, N. Y. 50,000

Powell, Sarah H. to George E. I. Glasson. 10,000

Powell, Wilson M. guard. of George E. I. Glasson to Sarah H. Powell. 7,444

Same to same. 2,733

Prime, William C. and R. E. exrs. Edward D. G. Prime to Kate Prime, White Plains. 600

Raichle, Barbara admrx. Christian Raichle to William H. Newschafer. 6,800

Rhoades, John H. et al. exrs. Julia C. Coleman to John R. Rhoades et al. trustees of Lucinda Smith. nom

Riemann, Frederick to Conrad Stein. 2,000

Roe, Joseph B. exr. Frances A. Howell to Jane Whitson, Jamaica, L. I. 9,000

Schweinler, Charles, Orange, N. J., to Herbert L. Bridgeman, Brooklyn. 2,500

Shuttleworth, Edwin to George Campbell. nom

Schaefer, Henry to George Campbell. nom
Schermerhorn, William C. exr. Edmund H. Schermerhorn to The New York Life Ins. and Trust Co. 37,500
Smith, H. Allen to The Western National Bank, New York. nom
Smith, Percival C. to Edward P. Lyon. 1,755
Schlesinger, Leo to Alexander List and Thomas Lennon. 3,500
Seaman, Samuel J. admr. Mary Underhill to James H. Seaman, Oyster Bay, L. I. 6,000.
Todd, Judson S. to Edward Winslow. nom
The People's Trust Co. to German-American Real Estate Title Guarantee Co. 30,000
Title Guarantee and Trust Co. to The National Savings Bank of Albany. 12,000
Title Guarantee and Trust Co. to The Poughkeepsie Savings Bank. 8,000
Same to same. 11,000
Same to Margaret P. Schwab. 4,000
Title Guarantee and Trust Co. to The Home Life Ins. Co. 10,500
Weeks, Francis H. exr. John J. A. Bristed to Mary A. S. Seabury. 7,000
Wielandt, Michael and Johanna Pfenning to Henry Sturz. 4,500
Weinstein, Ascher to The Corn Exchange Bank. 11,000
Welch, Ellis G., Bergen County, N. J., to James R. Ely. 500
Winslow, Edward to Henry W. Ford trustee Augustus H. Ward dec'd. nom
Same to same. nom

KINGS COUNTY.

NOVEMBER 19 TO 25—INCLUSIVE.

Anderson, Robert H. to Thomas I. Atkins. $1,900
Aschenfarb, Samuel to Bernhard Weinberg. 200
Axelrod, Jacob and Isaac Levingston to Caroline Witte. 1,050
Bancus, Mary to Maria C. Bogert. 824
Becker, Julia to The John Kress Brewing Co. 468
Browning, Ross C., West Orange, N. J., to Catherine E. Lyman widow. nom
Baird, Andrew D. to George H. Wheeler. 3,500
Beesley, Alfred L. to Anna Wilson. 500
Brush, George W. to Mary L. Bowers. nom
Byk, Poline to Joseph Byk. nom
Cozine, George R. to Peter Rapelje. 900
De Wint, John P. H. to Maria E. Whitehead. 9,000
Ellis, John S. exr. Julia Waterbury to James M. Waterbury and ano. exrs. Lawrence Waterbury. 100,000
Engelhardt, Charles W. to John S. Loomis. 330
Fithian, David A. to Lemmy A. Halstead. 500
Fitzgerald, Maurice to David A. Fithian. 100
Fuhr, Charles to William M. Evarts. 1,000
Huttenlocher, Rosina to Christian Huttenlocher. nom
Herrman, Moses to Mary F. Carroll. 1,964
Hill, Frederick T. exr. Caroline L. C. Amos to Brewster Kissam. 181
Hall, Eliza to Sarah H. Tuttle. 1,000
Hoagland, Cornelius to N. Annie wife of Joshua Cromwell. consid. omitted
Huggins, Mary B. wife of Joseph D. to Mary B. Huggins guard. Mary A. Bowne 1,300
Hyatt, Elizabeth A. L. to Cornelia B. Remsen. 2,570
Jewett, James C. to Samuel Blackwell. nom
Klein, Karoline to Josephine Klein. 3,000
Keck, Karoline to Minnie A. Dellith. 2,500
Kimberly, David F. exr. Elizabeth Kimberly to Louisa Kimberly. 1,272
Same to same. 2,500
Linton, Edward F. to Friedericke Newman, Middle Village, L. I. 2,100
Lott, Maria D. to Ellen Williamson. 3,500
Maurer, Joseph to Charles J. Patterson. 500
McLean, George to David S. Beasley. nom
Moody, Leonard to James C. Jewett. 450
Mowbray, Edward H. to Whitman W. Kenyon. nom
Same to Albro J. Newton. nom
Murray, J. Archibald to Bronson Murray. 700
Same to same. 500
Newman, Michael to W. F. Corwith. 1,400
Nickols, A. S. to Clark T. Hamilton. 1,000
Nelson, Alfred N. to John Auson. 2,000
Newton, Margaret A. to Annie wife of Joshua Cromwell. 1,200
Parker, Sophie G., New Hamburgh, N. Y., to Peter Brady. 4,000
Parker, Asa W. to same. 2,805
Raymond, Benjamin C. to George C. Crawford. 800
Same to same. 728
Ruth, Abraham to Warren B. Sammis, Edgewater, N. J. 750
Reimer, Rudolph and Otto E. to George B. Lane. 1,000
Riggs, Herman C., Rochester, N. Y., to The Ninth St Savings and Loan Assoc. 2,000
Roessle, Christina to Hermann Hoppe. 500
Ryan, Joseph to John G. Price. nom
Seaman, Samuel J. admr. Mary Underhill to Sarah H. Powell. 3,500
Same to James H. Seaman. 900
Schneider, Henry to Cardera Collin. 1,200
Saunders, Leslie M. admr. James Saunders to Ervin Saunders, Yonkers, N. Y. 3,000
Stearns, John M. to Katie Stearns. 1,400
Snediker, Isaac to Isaac R. Snediker. nom
Snelling, Alonzo F. to Benjamin F. Lownsbery. 5,000
The Williamsburgh Brewing Co. to Moses Herrman. 1,964
Townsend, James A. to Hiram P. Wyant. 900
Troy, James to William J. Gaynor. 1,065
Taylor, Arthur to John H. Looff. 3,500

Title Guarantee and Trust Co. to Michael Hagerty et al. trustees John McConvill. 6,000
Same to Mary A. Goodsell. 1,800
Same to Charles T. Geyer guard. May L. Engs. 5,000
Same to George Rome guard. Lifford and Sara Rome. 5,000
Same to The Brooklyn Trust Co. 5,500
Same to same. 5,500
Same to Board of Education of the Reformed Church in America. 4,250
Same to same. 4,000
Same to Adelia K. Broome. 5,000
Same to The South Brooklyn Savings Inst. 5,000
Same to same. 6,000
Same to The Atlantic Trust Co. trustee. 4,500
Underwood, Mary A. to John H. Doscher. 7,012
Witschen, Annie J. to Leopold Jonas. 5,000

JUDGMENTS.

NEW YORK CITY.

Nov.
20 Arnheimer, David—M J Hazelton.... $101 05
21 Appleman, Asbury G—G A Goldsmith 308 86
23 Ancker, Edwin—Metropolitan Telephone and Telegraph Co............ 68 83
23 Allcott, Edmund C—A D Knapp..... 632 65
24 Arnheimer, Levi—A H Tridenberg... 26 47
24 Allen, Albert V—C J Fagan.......... 51 50
24 Adam, Angelo—Louis Roller..........2,680 76
25 Anderson, William C — Christian Moerlein Brewing Co.............. 87 13
25 Armstrong, George K—C D Mayer... 174 09
27*Albright, Chas H—C J Davis........ 1,086 86
27 Andarson, Solomon—Robert Reis & Co................................ 301 30
27*Ayres, Charles H—Julius Engel...... 259 50
27*Aguilerd, Manuel L—W S Middleton. 583 07
20 Breidenbach, Rudolph A — Leopold and Max Rosenberger.............. 242 10
20 the same——Importers' and Traders' Nat Bank...................... 241 03
20 the same——Chemical Nat Bank.. 240 25
21 Bauer, Moritz—W G L King.......... 358 51
21 Barneman, Edward—T C Lyman..... 351 95
23 Bacon, George H—I C Ogden, Jr..... 1,159 18
23 Baumgarth, George—J W Murphy... 572 18
23 Barker, Charles E—W E Cougdon.... 112 12
23 Baier, Henry—Solomon Stein......... 303 07
23 Bach, Albert—J M Gove............... 89 23
23 Bernheim, Katie—M L Rhein.......... 29 50
23 Boyan, Thomas—H P Kremer......... 380 70
23 Brahm, John—R A Stevenson......... 83 01
24 Bell, William—J W Dunican.......... 28 50
24 Brown, James A—C H Kelly.......... 259 55
24 Brown, Ezra—Indianapolis Wagon Co.................................. 388 14
24 Bardague, Louise Anna — Camille Warrennier........................ 195 97
24 Birdsall, Samuel E—J R Cavlleer.... 1,070 86
24 the same——the same............ 546 36
24 Beacham, John—C F Lawrence...... 204 61
24 the same——the same............ 324 45
24 Behlmer, John F—Henry Rauch...... 471 83
24 Bruen, Charlotte A—Phebe T Lewis.. ....costs 428 47
24 Barry, James / Barry, Ellen } Jenny Nelson....... 745 42
24 Brada, John E—W and J Sloane..... 81 51
25 Baker, Albert / Baker, Robert } W A Hyde........... 614 76
25 Bodine, Thomas C—Pierce, Butler & Pierce Mfg Co.................. 369 73
25 Barns, Charles Edward—Georgiana I Hotchkiss........................ 174 15
25 Buchan, Thomas R—J L Reynolds.... 82 19
25 Burmeister, Henry—W A Scarborowgh 219 00
25 Boehmer, Arthur—J D McEntee..... 34 50
25 Brennan, James — Marshall Van Hoesen.............................. 128 94
25 Baker, John O—H S Hawk......costs 108 25
25 Brinkerhoff, Cornelius M—W P Baker 415 79
27 Brennan, John—Ferdinand Loewenthal.............................. 103 38
27 Burke, James A—H J Grant.......... 174 05
27 Babcock, Charles B—Maria L Ferres. 372 28
27 Bonnell, John Harper—Brooklyn Bank of Brooklyn.................. 687 73
27 Braender, Philip—Frank Wennemer. 3,583 43
27 Blanchard, Charles A—Julius Engel. 259 50
27 Bonnell, John Harper / Bonnell, Tammisiu H } Chatham Nat Bank...... 5,048 39
21 Cole, Charles R—W H Holmes........ 290 25
21 Crocker, Ralph W—Kate M Crocker. 8,161 92
21 Crooks, Thomas—Second Avenue R R Co.............................costs 110 51
21 Conner, William M—C H Hyams....11,891 39
21 Cusack, John H—William Labahan.. 163 84
21 Connor, John O—Vermont Marble Co 262 21
23 Crosher, James—Bernard Kaskell.... 31 24
23 Cramer, Philipp—Charles Vogt, Jr... 307 04
23 Clark, Heman—First Nat Bank of Canton, N Y........................7,116 21
23 Camp, John T—J P Lee...............1,265 58
23 the same——the same............1,274 29
24 Cornish, Nehemiah N—G J Russell... 97 05
24 Clifford, Henry B—W and J Sloane.. 103 60
25 Clancey, Patrick E—Dennis Harrington................................ 272 37
25 Carter, Charles H—M J Couch....... 135 90
27 Cranston, Henry—Daniel Tamagno... 382 82
27 Crans, Henry S—Mary F. Sallade....1,435 09
27 Chaffer, Jacob—J J Donovan....... 27 13
27 Orego, Russell—Oscar Smith.........1,248 64
27 Chancellor, Mary A—John Merry.... 424 45
27 Crumb, George R / Crumb, George A / Cavanagh, Philip B } Louis Weiss.... 535 62
27 Cavinato, Luigi / Cavinato, Steffano / Cavinato, Guiseppe / Cavinato, Natale } Northern Nat Bank ....1,554 76.
27 the same——the same.............1,554 76
27 the same——the same.............1,554 76
27†Coleskey, John—Herman Broady..... 15 35
27 Cook, Valentine—Lena Schmidt......1,168 05
27 Callahan, Thomas F—J J Kittel......2,450 35
20 Douglas, Adam—M J Hazelton....... 79 68
21*Davidson, William—Cook & Bernheimer Co.......................... 628 16
21 Derbyshire, William H—L T Schmalholz................................. 521 87
21 de Castro, Edward—H A Vonneidshutz.............................costs 23 80
23 Dempsey, William—Patrick Reynolds 946 02
23 Delapenha, Uriah—Northrop & Lyman Co............................. 241 61
23 Duff, Patrick—C H Childs............ 167 62
23 Dettinger, Frank—George Ringler... 367 25
24 de Zielinski, Jorawslo—A H Littleton. 190 23
24 Dempsey, William—George Spaeth... 326 68
25 Dyott, Charles G—R G Dun.......... 177 80
25 Delahunty, John, as committee of Felicia L Denison—David Rosenbaum...............................2,170 65
25 Dempsey, William—Leopold Friesen.. 145 21
25 Doremus, Charles G—Joseph Marren. 176 08
25*†Doe, John—E D Maun............... 149 57
25 Donnelly, James, as guard Josephine Donnelly—W J Riordan........costs 20 72
27 Deutschberger, Frederick — David O'Shaughnessy....................... 268 51
27 Downing, Joseph M—Israel Lewis... 300 58
21*Ettinger, Isaac J—D J Phelan....... 318 59
21 Eisenberg, William—Sims Lumber Co 1,182 89
23 Ehrhardt, Henry—R J Chapman Co. 172 75
24 Eichhorn, Albertina A—Frank Moss, exr.................................... 104 45
24 Esler, William T—E F Collins........ 72 88
24 Ellison, Thomas J—O K Dimock..... 182 13
24 Eccles, John L—Margaret Wells..... 74 87
24 Eisenberg, Joseph—F J Preston & Co. 84 39
25 Eckstein, Monroe—German Nat Bank.1,865 93
27 Ellis, Edward S—Brooklyn Bank of Brooklyn 687 73
21 Fettretch, Mary L—Diedrich Heitshusen.................................. 111 33
21 Fechtler, Henry—T G Hojer......... 117 50
23 Fohs, Benjamin—East Side Bank..... 425 78
23 Fuller, Eugene F—Catherine F Ryerson 144 75
24 Falk, Isaac L / Falk, George W } C H Kelly..........1,050 00
24 the same——the same............ 84 00
24 Fraser, John M—Annie Steinhardt... 47 50
24 the same——the same............ 47 50
24 Franklin, Benjamin—J A Grenzebach 141 24
24 Fleming, Robert—Frank Moss, exr... 222 55
24 Fogarty, Katie L—Herrmann Guggenheim.............................. 110 63
24 Fusco, Guiseppe—Louis Roller........2,630 76
25 Friedman, Abraham—Abraham Westheimer.............................. 141 65
25 Frink, Edwin S—J B Lawrence...... 89 65
25 Fessenden, Samuel—Lena Wright.... 366 72
25 Fitts, John W—Pierce, Butler & Pierce Mfg Co........................ 369 73
27 Foreit, Vojtich—Peter Buel.......... 32 25
27 Flynn, Cornelius—Peter Buckel......1,820 12
27 Fountain, Inez—Mary A George..... 380 23
20 Gaillard, Desire A, M.D—J W Farmer 77 00
20*Grossman, Morris—Perry Store Co... 113 11
20 Gould, Thomas E—H W Haas........ 372 76
20 Gibbins, Austin P—John Helmsky... 176 43
21 Grose, Joseph—W M Alford.......... 214 42
21 Greenfield, Mark—Michael Glassman ....costs 39 39
21*Gordon, Michael—Gardner Hall, Jr.. 185 04
23 Goldthwaite, William M / Goldthwaite, James C } J C Ogden, Jr....... 324 39
23 Gottscho, Herrman / Gottscho, Isaac } Bernard Kaskell 41 89
23 Griesmeyer, Carl L—Samuel Titus.... 246 45
23 Gedney, Morris—G V Hann........... 267 50
23 Goodwin, Henry J—Carl Voigt......13,009 20
23 Gross, Louis N—N S Ackerly, guard. 221 41
23 Gay, John—Helen M S Sweeney.....1,915 98
23 Gilfillan, James—W S Chamberlain ....costs 146 42
23 Gerdes, William H—Nat Cash Register Co.................................. 211 87
24 Goerlitz, Philip—Mavor, Lane & Co.. 276 44
24 Gademan, Louise—M D Stern........ 391 30
24 Graeve, Henry W—Gramercy Co.... 95 24
27 Giesler, Catherine E—Moses Hertz... 540 79
27 Gillie, Daniel R—Henry McShane Co (Lim)................................. 268 62
27 Goldstein, Isaac—S J Weaver.........2,002 04
27 Goldstein, Sarah — Samuel Jacobs ....costs 131 01
27 Gartlan, James H—J J Kittel.........2,450 35
21 Hawkshaw, Richard—East River Beef Co (Lim)............................. 428 52
21 Hirsch, Aaron—Kate M Crocker.....8,161 92
21 Hecht, Ansel—Louis Demuth......... 181 54
23 Haas, Frank X—Gabriel Goldsmith.. 259 50
23 Husted, Sabina E / Husted, Peter V } Hyman Schnitzer............1,215 43
23 Higgins, Cecil Campbell—H G Dunstan..................................1,214 82
23 Hudson, Romulus F—Carl Voigt....13,009 20
23 Hoag, Henry G—H P Kremer......... 380 70
23 Herman, Henry—G W Travers....... 91 38
24 Hawley, Oscar F—J D Spicer......... 770 81
24 Howell, Eugene M — Western Nat Bank...............................8,530 47
24*Hooper, Nicholas B—Henri Schorestone.................................1,151 64
24 Havey, Thomas—E F Collins......... 72 88
24 Hume, Charles E—O K Dimock..... 182 13
24 Hahn, Henry / Hahn, Joseph } T J Preston & Co.... 424 07
24 Henriques, Joseph C——the same..... 262 05
24 Haran, Michael — W J Anderson ....costs 74 37

Day	Entry	Amount
25	Herold, Emil—Isaac Stern	109 60
25	Heumann, Mary—D J Murphy	203 02
25	Haynes, John M—G R Brown	79 22
25	Herzfeld, Jeanette—J G Johnson	217 98
25	Haas, Christian—M R Cook	302 49
25	Hart, Lizzie H—B H Herts	392 35
25	Hein, Hyman—Mary Thomas	301 57
25	Hawkes, Quayle W—H A Forbes	138 83
25	Hennessy, William P—James Everard	171 15
25	Hazard, Rowland N—James Rozell	316 34
25	Hyland, Margaret; *Hyland, James P—H Koehler & Co	855 65
27	Hyams, Joel E—Ferdinand Bock	310 15
27	Harper, William D—Brooklyn Bank of Brooklyn	687 73
27	Harper, William D; Harper, Tacie McD—Chatham Nat Bank	5,048 39
27	Reagen, Peter J—H C West	280 14
27	Hillman, Uno H—W S Middleton	583 67
27	Hattle, Elizabeth—Max Blumberg	35 50
27	+Hassenger, William; Haas, Christian—M R Cook	215 00
27	Hawley, George W—Louis Steiner	810 23
21	Jetter, Thomas—S J Taylor	136 21
21	Jones, Herbert A—E T Dickinson	221 35
24	Johnson, Mary—John Layden	536 37
24	Jones, John E—J R Cavaneer	1,070 86
27	Jantz, John—Jacob Flettner	264 46
27	James, Edward F—Theodore Fitch	418 24
27	Jenkins, John T—Abraham Silverstone	44 90
27	Johnson, Jacob—S S Brown	199 96
27	Jones, Edwin T—Nat Bank of Republic	429 68
21	Karsten, Peter—S A Anderson	107 80
21	King, William H—William Grunow, Jr	1,526 68
21	Kropp, Joseph; Kropp, William—J G Kropp	801 72
23	Kosowsky, Julius—Louis Finestone	523 37
23	Kramer, Leopold—Nelson Morris	369 03
24	Kleinfeld, Morris—Benjamin Sel	289 77
24	Keyes, Frank R—J G Holland	699 08
24	Kraus, George J—G K Smith Hay and Grain Co	112 00
24	Keller, Conrad—Mayor, Lane & Co	276 44
24	+Kleinfeld, Morris—Louis Hoopes	117 97
24	Keon, Hugh—J J Staren	603 80
25	Kenyon, Enoch—J H Lippincott	47 60
25	Kujawa, Franz—Ermenegildo Paladina ... costs	112 78
25	Kolben, Nettie—Benno Seidler	197 50
25	Kelly, Martin H K—John Copcutt	300 55
27	Keith, Henry C—J L King	485 17
27	the same——the same	124 71
27	the same——W J Fegan	142 12
21	Lucas, Philippine—John Aichele, admr	1,198 11
23	Le Barbier, Charles—Steinway & Sons	135 08
23	Levenson, Thomas—Harris Ackerman	35 50
23	Lyon, Charles; *Lyon, David—H A Caeser	933 76
23	*Leach, Henry P—J P Leo	1,265 53
23	the same——the same	1,274 29
24	Laurowitz, Louis; Landau, Bernard—Louis Hoopes	117 97
24	Linder, Ernest—Albert Acken	109 18
24	Linscott John A—J H Havens	1,128 09
24	Langerman, Walter L S—Charles Du Vivier	236 72
24	*Laurowitz, Louis; Landau, Bernard—Benjamin Sel	289 77
25	Levi, Jacob—Abraham Schneider	33 50
25	Lennon, Edward—Joseph Meeks	192 16
25	the same——George Seeman	369 35
25	Luthy, Adolph—James Regan ... costs	81 19
27	Lockwood, Albert F—B J Falk	1,501 74
27	Liebowitz, Hyman—Mary A Dorbie	219 57
27	Ledwith, Charles—James Smith	98 60
21	Mellen, Letitia A—A B Ryker	258 86
21	Martin, Wilbur F—F H Stevens	670 58
23	Moore, William—Ferdinand Lowenthal	71 00
23	Mooney, John H—First Nat Bank of Canton, N Y	7,116 21
24	Moore, William J—J E Austin	118 87
24	Muller, Valentine—John Brosen	828 13
24	the same——the same	138 24
24	Meyers, Max; Myers, George—People State N Y	500 00
24	Mayers, Isaac—J F Skelly	937 29
24	Molner, Herman; Mnozer, Henry—W E Tefft	175 58
24	Morrissey, James W—Edward Gordon	153 25
24	Morell, Francis L; Morell, George—O K Dimock	484 91
24	Matthews, James C—W & J Sloane	521 17
25	Mulcahey, Michael J—Dennis Harrington	272 37
25	Miller, Robert H—Chatham Nat Bank	656 17
25	the same——the same	460 97
25	Mordaunt, Clementine J—Mary A George	364 11
25	Mascher, John—Adolph Edelmuth	228 03
25	Moog, Simon—T W Osborne	447 41
27	Molner, Samuel—E C Smith	436 41
27	Myers, Sinclair—R S Moore	167 50
27	Marsh, Gideon W—Louis Weiss	535 62
27	Mars, Henriette A—Milton Robbins	265 78
27	Middleton, George C—Cook & Bernheimer Co	34 14
21	McCarthy, Charles—Nick Loritz	206 38
21	McManus, Patrick H—Samuel Lord	618 41
25	McGrath, Mary J—John Kips	173 07
27	McAleer, John—Max Stiner	359 91
27	McNabb, George R—A B Crocker	253 60
27	McAlear, John J—Oscar Abraham	37 00
27	McClure, Elisha P P—Rosalie Muller, extrx	281 91
27	McCarthy, Denis P—P K Lantry	1,084 60
20	Nesbit, John—New England Brown Stone Co	341 60
21	Neill, William A—Cook & Bernheimer Co	100 74
23	Neumark, Julius—N S Ackerly, guard	221 41
23	Nesbit, William F—Sharon Dairy	218 22
25	Norris, George—Equitable Life Assurance Society	275 90
27	Needles, Caleb H—Louis Weiss	535 62
21	O'Connor, Nicholas R—George Johnson	41 77
23	O'Brien, John—First Nat Bank of Canton, N Y	7,116 21
24	O'Donoghue, Dennis—H N Twombley	130 97
25	O'Connell, John D—G W Venable	43 60
25	Ottenberg, Nathan—W P Fessler	259 92
25	O'Callahan, David—C F MacLean ... costs	57 96
27	Ochse, Frederick—G W Mantel	127 80
21	Pincott, Francis—M J Drucker	189 44
23	Pitt, William—Mayor, &c ... costs	91 28
23	Petersen, Christian; Petersen, James H—J B Morrell	107 84
24	Pulsifer, Joseph—T D O'Connor	220 30
24	Percy, Townsend—G D Overin	66 09
24	Pratt, Charles W—Adaline H Taylor	783 85
24	Pryor, James—Henri Schorestene	1,151 64
25	Patterson, Charles G—G F Blandy, exr	5,055 99
25	Paige, Edward W—Continental Ins Co	1,785 11
27	Prior, Robert J; Prior, George B—Elizabeth Wright	261 13
24	Quinn, Sarah G—D M Koehler	137 21
20	Roeth, Louis—John Helmsky	176 43
21	Rosenthal, Joseph—Paul Weinberg	14 50
21	Robineau, Adele—Michael White	259 50
21	Roth, Victoria—Israel Speizer ... costs	69 32
23	Rodding, Max—Solomon Bauman	41 50
23	Rihan, Abdow; Rihan, Fares—Catharine Thompson	160 12
23	Roth, Peter—George Ringler & Co	640 28
23	Ross, John S—Lewis Samuel	354 97
23	Reynolds, William W—E H Reynolds	194 80
23	*Rosenheim, Louis—H A Caeser	933 79
24	Reilly, Albert J—Jackson Architectural Iron Works ... costs	80 72
24	Radford, Henry Carlton—George Whitaker	160 61
24	Remig, Philip W—Albert Acken	109 18
24	Reed, Clarence E—Thomas Wildes	175 84
24	Rollins, George M—John O'Connell	97 66
24	Russell, James; Russell, Bridget—Jenny Nelson	745 42
25	Rockwood, George G—C A Terry	90 89
25	Reed, Ellen F—B J Foshay, admrx	158 17
25	Rousseau, Jules P—Cook & Bernheimer Co	9 98
25	Roch, Ernest—C H Attwater	599 29
27	Roudillon, George—American Exch Nat Bank	2,735 43
27	Rodegerdts, John P—John Haas	628 92
27	Roberts, William H H—St John Cylinder Packing Co	109 37
27	Reynolds, Jessie—Marie Schutz	189 81
27	Rosevelt, George W, Jr—J S Rice	1,917 06
27	Rosenthal, Louis—Gardiner Hall, Jr	185 04
27	Rigg, William—J T Kennedy	40 43
27	Roberts, Mortimer O—Baxter Barku	694 19
27	Radley, John J—Lena Schmidt	1,168 05
20	Syska, William F—H M Fostevin ... costs	79 35
20	Scott, George H—New England Brown Stone Co	341 60
20	Stern, Samuel—Perry Stove Co	113 11
21	*Stanton, George I—W H Holmes	290 25
21	Stone, Elkan—D J Phelan	313 59
21	Shanks, James—Cook & Bernheimer Co	628 16
21	Snape, Thomas H—Vermont Marble Co	166 43
21	Sinclair, William—Diedrich Heitshusen	111 33
23	Scott, Walter; Scott, Albert E—N J Haines ... costs	69 67
23	Stark, Isidor; Stark, Edward J; Stark, Gustave—North Adams Mfg Co	501 15
23	Schoemann, Abraham—Joseph Marren	245 00
23	Sandiforth, Mollie—Charles Otten	36 20
23	Stern, Herman—Nelson Morris	369 03
23	Sutherland, James—T H Thorn ... costs	87 00
23	Satterlee, John—B K Jamison	1,469 65
23	the same——the same	1,369 14
23	Sargent, Francis T—J L Mott Iron Works	1,738 38
23	+Stetson, John B—M G Palmer	33 24
23	Schnitz, Charles—H E Williams	59 91
24	Shaw, Joshua B—T E Stewart ... costs	22 97
24	the same——Lizzie R G Shaw ... costs	22 97
24	Scott, Horace—G H Cannon	1,925 84
24	+Squance, Henry I—M R Cook	176 64
24	Scofield, Charles W—Frank Moss, exr	182 98
24	Starlight, Marcus; Starlight, Emanuel—Catharine Poynter	66 25
24	Stubenrack, August—T J Preston & Co	262 05
24	Striefler, Jacob—W and J Sloane	98 63
24	Schlusser, George J—C W Nason	175 83
25	Secor, William H—John Dobson	400 66
25	Sproessig, Henry—Julius Kentel ... costs	68 12
25	Secor, William Holt—R E Thibaut	99 44
25	Stevenson, Vernon K—E D Mann	149 57
25	Schweitzer, Samuel—Susan L Wells	78 74
25	Steuerwald, Charles A—Henry Gledhill	175 75
27	Steindler, Joseph—C J Davis	1,086 86
27	Stafford, Edwin F—Marcus Benjamin	261 50
27	Striker, Elsworth L—C E Talbott	274 27
27	*Shields, Dennis; Shields, Henry F—E W Youmans	481 47
27	Schwartz, Wolf—S J Weaver	2,002 04
27	Scully, John—S M Smith	133 98
27	Sheehan, John—James Robertson	374 90
27	Sesse, Michael—John Bell	140 41
27	Steinway, Charles, recvr—Moses Strauss ... costs	59 63
27	Swift, George F—J W Oliver	85 70
27	Stark, Isidor; Stark, Edward J; Stark, Gustave—Amory Leland	1,533 66
27	Sheldon, Hazard J—Louis Steiner	810 23
21	Smith, Charles F—Antony Reisert	340 82
24	Smith, Justus J—J W Dunican	59 50
24	Smith, John—George Spaeth	326 68
20	Gibson Electric Co—H L McDowell	1,003 83
20	the same——the same	1,167 84
21	The Consolidated Printing and Publishing Co—H C De Witt	209 78
21	The Mayor, Aldermen, &c—Frank Phelps	80 53
21	The Fred H Whipple Co—James Kempster	755 79
23	The Niagara Fire Ins Co—Mary Fisher	107 64
23	the same——the same	118 89
23	the same——the same	918 86
23	The Underground Railway Construction Co—Metropolitan Telephone and Telegraph Co	70 71
23	The Mayor, Aldermen, &c—E A Lynde	2,467 16
23	London Toilet Bazaar Co—Joseph Movuis	86 63
23	Sheet Metal Machine Co—J S Dickerson	3,487 91
23	The Mayor, Aldermen, &c—John Mullen	586 50
23	The United Life and Accident Ins Assoc—Charlotte E Patten ... costs	79 34
24	Blum & Stein Co—Aaron Rice	1,021 34
24	the same——the same	1,521 84
24	the same——the same	1,021 34
25	the same——Leopold Friesen	145 21
24	Hurley Stone Co—G N Robinson	404 30
24	The Mayor, Aldermen, &c—G L Green	103 75
24	Unity League—Minnie E Feinberg	200 48
24	Welch Fracker Co—Thomas Wildes	175 84
24	The N Y Daily Bulletin Assoc—H H Rose ... costs	126 47
24	The Metropolitan Elevated Railway Co; The Manhattan Railway Co—Agnes G Golden, extrx ... costs	1,065 17
24	the same——the same	10,591 40
24	The Columbian Publishing and Purchasing Co—B M Whitlock	747 38
24	The Mayor, Aldermen, &c—W L Brangan	426 14
24	the same——P J Loughlin	175 36
24	the same——J F Sweeny	162 00
24	the same——O C Flynn	154 20
24	the same——C J Reilly	188 00
24	the same——W F Guerin	109 58
24	the same——E H Best	223 56
24	the same——T J Fallon	109 82
24	the same——Michael Brady	123 28
24	the same——John Montague	849 32
24	the same——Sarsfield Kennedy	126 26
24	the same——W A McAllister	49 30
24	Knickerbocker Printing and Publishing Co—Campbell Printing Press and Mfg Co	231 22
24	The Washburn Machine Co—William Whitlock	1,530 38
25	N Y Refrigerating Construction Co—Frederick Berg	492 89
25	Welch Fracker Co—Georgiana I Hotchkiss	174 15
25	The Metropolitan Elevated Railway Co; Manhattan Railway Co—A R Eno	388 55
25	the same——the same	398 00
25	Manhattan Railway Co—Frederick Brunner	410 08
25	The Mayor, Aldermen, &c—E H Judson	100 64
25	the same——J H Ackerman	134 20
25	the same——John Gorman	121 87
25	N Y Elevated R R Co; Manhattan Railway Co—Richard Vandenhenden	1,714 29
25	the same——James Saxton	1,775 29
25	the same——John Slater	1,064 79
25	the same——J J McHugh	532 87
25	the same——G A Heinig	952 21
27	Barr Electric Mfg Co—Textile Publishing Co	102 03
27	Spring & Stafford Mfg Co—Marcus Benjamin	261 50
27	The Philadelphia Bond and Investment Co—Louis Weiss	535 62
27	Pfister Book Binding Co—Henry Lindenmeyer	194 00
27	J H Donnell & Co (Lim)—Brooklyn Bank of Brooklyn	687 73
27	the same——Nat Bank of Republic	429 68
21	Tenner, Bertha—Morris Spiegel	674 96
23	Turner, Philip T—Michele Pascocelli	208 42
23	Thissen, Jacob; Terheggen, Henry—Adolf Kirchoff	558 46
24	Tangemann, Richard—Herman Behrmann	120 05
24	Taylor, Theodore F—D F Wright	95 41
25	Thalheimer, Albert—Charles Stahl	634 36
27	Turton, John; Turton, Edgar S—Brooklyn Bank of Brooklyn	687 73
27	Thorne, Edwin—Strobridge Lithographing Co	3,412 43
24	Van Ness, John K—J M Stevens	920 15
20	Wogan, John J—H W Haas	372 76
21	Wendt, Charles M—Eppens, Smith & Wiemann Co	224 04
21	Wolf, George—Sims Lumber Co	1,182 89
23	Wilbur, Philip C—Henry Eggers	156 62
23	Winter, Herman T—T H Thorn ... costs	87 00

23 Worsnop, Alfred—J B M Duche.. ... 424 92
24 Wetzel, John—John Brosen.......... 828 13
24 the same——the same... .... 188 24
24 Webster, H B—J C Mix.............. 171 87
24 Walker, James E—T G Palmer....... 196 16
25*Williams, Edward B—R G Dunn..... 177 80
25*Wacker, John—W A Scarborowgh.. 219 00
25 Wadsworth, Edwin M—H S Hawk... 471 88
25 Wertheimer, Leopold—German Nat Bank... ....1,865 93
27 Weil, David—E H Smith............ 45 02
27 Wiechers, Harry—W L Wolfe.. .... 404 90
21 Young, Emma B—P J Loughlin...... 231 81
25 Yale, Ida—W P Baker.............. 415 79
27 Yesky, Charles—Emanuel Denzer.... 128 90

KINGS COUNTY.

Nov.
20 Altenbrand, Albert—H Mueller..... $1,022 58
20 Bader, Charles—Gerard & Conklin... 139 52
20 Beard, William H—M E Gage... .... 267 96
21 Bauer, Caroline, extrx of—F Obernier 100 00
21 the same——J Bauer.......... ... 281 21
21 Bostelmann, William H—P Weinel... 238 46
24 Barry, Rosalie C / Barry, Henry A } G T Riley........ 420 39
20 Crowther, Charles / Crowther, Martha } G Greyson 76 68
20 Clark, Henry F—Agnes L Yenni.....1,063 71
21 Crawfort, Robert J—Hollister Mfg Co. 866 03
21 Cole, Charles R—W H Holmes....... 200 25
21 Cobh, Frederick W—Dunbar Box and Lumber Co......................1,187 05
23 Cameron, John—W B Lemmon 86 92
23 Chadwick, William—Richardson & Morgan Co....................... 27 60
24 Carpenter, Charles H—E A Price.... 23 85
24 Collins, Charles H—P A Johnson.... 515 93
24 Craigen, George—Smith & Inskup.. . 499 21
25 Carter, Charles H—M J Couch....... 135 90
21 Dudenhausen, Frank—J McKesson, Jr 241 53
21 Davidson, William—The Cook & Bernheimer Co.......... .... 628 16
24 Denton, Frank—B F Heard.......... 116 93
24 Devermann, William—R J Stokes.... 275 00
20 Ersted, Victor P P—W Eckert....... 808 09
23 Eusmenger, Philip—I Sugannan...... 277 00
25 Egerton, Jasper C—J V Egerton..... 90 00
21 Fielder, David P / Fielder, Melissa } R Reimer......... 350 01
21 Fowler, David H—Fuller & Warren Co.................................. 720 83
24 Flynn, Thomas D—Hudson River Line 133 05
24 Foye, Frank M—Obermeyer & Liebmann.............................. 273 88
24 Fogarty, Katie L—H Guggenheim ... 110 68
25 Ficken, Henry — Thurber, Whyland Co.... .... 85 31
19 Gaff, Thomas C—H McShane Mfg Co. 1,186 41
20 Gunston, Ole—Hyde & Gload Mfg Co. 70 82
21 Grimes, James—E Munsell 1,682 25
23 Gould, Edmund—Wyoming Co Nat Bank of Warsaw..................... 756 83
28 Green, Cassius A—J Loader.......... 140 13
24 Glover, William H H—J White...... 103 05
25 Gay, John—Helen M Sweeney.......1,915 98
25 Gabbett, Mary—P Wyckoff.......... 110 31
18 Holland, Sol—M Isaac............... 175 41
18 Halstead, Stephen C—E S Rosenbluth 144 89
20 Hewsey, Mary S—Title Guarantee and Trust Co.......................... 227 73
21 Henno, Ferdinand—A Meier......... 144 29
23 Harris, George S—Wyoming Co Nat Bank of Warsaw..................... 786 83
23 Hartman, Louis—J R Berbling....... 39 88
24 Heckman, James A—T G Patterson.. 39 35
25 Horton, Oliver J—Thurber, Whyland Co.................................. 74 22
21 Isaacs, Isaac A—Campbell F P and Mfg Co.............................. 234 99
21 Jackson, Daniel—N W Schottler..... 152 59
24 Johnson, Charles A—Obermeyer & L. 273 88
24 Judson, Edward—E R Shipman...... 283 17
20 Kriete, John—E D Gerard 129 52
23 Katz, Margaretha—J Levy.. ..... 132 95
25†Kennedy, "David"—National Cash Register Co........................ 27 60
20 Levy, Robert—P H Samilson......... 144 60
23 Lorck, Herman C—W B Lemmon.... 86 92
23 Loeser, David—J Brielmann......... 110 03
23 Lowther, Sarah E—Wechsler & Abraham.............................. 168 55
24 Lewis, Sidney H—T Tynant.......... 176 60
24 Lucas, August—M B Euler........... 271 01
19 McKee, Osborn H—J Haviland....... 40 75
20 Mallon, Thomas, admr of / Mallon, Joseph A, dec'd } J McLean 109 04
20 Middlebrook, Frank S—Del, Lackawanna & W R R Co.............. 23 18
21 Muller, Lewis M—I C Ogden, Jr.....5,809 65
23 Merschaff, Adam—J Kramer......... 13 25
24 McLean, Alexander — Long Island Bank...................................4,943 18
24 Matthews, Edward I—J F Waggoner. 459 84
24 McGinn, Daniel—Brooklyn City R R Co................................... 85 54
19 Noonan, Peter J—J Wallace.......... 623 21
23 Neill, William A—Cook & Bernheimer Co 100 74
23 O'Neil, John—P Ragona............. 63 85
24 O'Connor, James—W M Evans....... 126 15
20 Pfeiffer, William—J Goodheart 106 98
23 Pilcher, Joseph M—Wyoming Co Nat Bank of Warsaw..................... 786 83
20 Reese, Louis—P Duff................. 88 90
21 Reinheimer, John F—J E Wells...... 175 65
21 Rommeuney, Frederick—A Meier.... 144 29
21 Ross, J Stewart—E Settle............1,305 24
23 Rodegerdts, William A—A J Nutting 27 85
23 Rohedee, Charles P—W H Bierds 418 44
24 Reynolds, William W—E H Reynolds 194 84
20 Schwarze, Elizabeth / Schwarze, John } F M Pierce.... 317 29
21 Spannagel, Barbara, extrx Caroline Bauer, dec'd—F Obernier........... 100 00
21 the same——the same 281 21
21 Sitterberg, Bernard—F & M Schaefer B Co................................ 278 80
21 Stanton, George I—W H Holmes..... 290 25
21 Shanks, James—Cook & Bernheimer Co......... .... 628 16
23 Schneider, Karl F—J Brielmann 110 03
23 Schwarze, John—J Hendricks 440 85
23 Smith, Richard D—W H Bierds...... 418 44
24 Spoehr, Sr, Charles—Cross, Austin & Co.................................. 280 57
24 Schaefer, Louisa G—P T McGuinness. 415 51
24 Serensen, Fritz W—L Isenburger.... 282 13
24 Stone, James S, otherwise / Schoonmaker, George H and / Stone, Jennie A } Helen M Robinson... 150 17
25†Squance, "Henry I"—M R Cook.... 176 64
24 Sargent, Francis F—J L Mott Iron Works..............................1,738 38
20 The admr Joseph A Mallon, dec'd—J McLean........................... 109 04
20 Tepe, Henry—W Van Alstyne..... .. 237 58
20 The South Brooklyn Dock and Warehouse Co—J Dubois................ 670 10
21 The extrx Caroline Bauer, dec'd—F Obernier.............................. 100 00
21 the same——J Bauer............ 281 21
21 Thwaites, George—W Thwaites ..1,419 56
21 the same——the same............ 95 02
24 The Brooklyn City R R Co—J Alexander.. .... 500 00
19 Whitehouse, James—G Brandies..... 700 21
20 White, C L—Hyde & Gload Mfg Co (Lim)................................ 84 18
20 Winter, Catharine R—S P Sturges... 115 89
23 Waring, Anthony—M Schwarz...... 35 85
24 Wyburn, Joseph—T Tynant.......... 176 60
24 Walsh, William and Margaret J—B J Dennis............................ 92 06
24 Way, Daniel—H Christoffers......... 122 97

SATISFIED JUDGMENTS.

NEW YORK.

November 21 to 27—Inclusive.

Anderson, Mary—J A Metcalfe. (1887) $78 87
†Astor, William W—J W Holloway. (1891).... 216 64
†Same——same. (1891) 216 64
Andrews, William S—N Y Insulated Wire Co. (1891) 849 86
Alton, Henry—H W Benedict. (1891) 1,358 06
Bedford, George W—G H Kellogg. (1883)..... 637 54
Churchill, Alfred D—J G Murphy. (1887)..... 399 44
Dimmock, Katherine C—J A Mitchell. (1891). 182 46
Dickson Mfg Co—Safety Steam Generator Co. (1891)...2,344 87
Devine, John—James O'Shea. (1882).......... 288 83
Devine, John C and Michael J—Charles Watrous. (1879)..................................... 109 71
Same——J D Trimble. (1879).................. 374 39
Same——Hugh Murray. (1879).............. 259 56
Same——F C Lawrence. (1879)............ 196 68
Same——same. (1879)........................ 111 66
Delafield, Richard—Downie Boiler Incrustation Preventive Co. (1891).................... 365 13
†Day, Henry, trustee William Astor—J W Holloway. (1891)............................. 216 64
†Same——same. (1891)........................ 216 64
†Delano, Franklin H, trustee Wm B Astor——same. (1891)................................ 216 64
†Same——same. (1891)......................... 216 64
Daly, Patrick—Michael McConville. (1886).. . 184 50
Dreyfuss, Bernard—E C Philbrick. (1891)....1,622 62
Decker Adolphus M—A J Hood. (1891) 181 05
Gardiner, Harriet—Sarah McCool. (1891).....1,228 74
Gould, Frederick H—Lucius Moses (1891)....3,691 09
Same——same. (1891)......................... 251 45
Same——Giles Everson et al. (1891).........5,351 42
Same——E C Wright. (1891) 1,747 96
Glinn, John E and Christian F, exrs John M Otten—H G Otten. (1891)....................2,489 88
Hodges, Amory G—Lucius Moses. (1891).....3,691 09
Same——same. (1891).......................... 251 46
Same——Giles Everson et al. (1891)..........5,351 42
Same——E C Wright. (1891)..................1,747 96
Holmes, Edward—J V Black. (1891)........... 323 91
Same——W R Raynor. (1891) 78 81
Same——I C Kiggins, as pres't. (1891)...... 341 38
Same——same, as treas. (1891)............... 79 52
Hosnedel, Frank—Charles Machoosky. (1891) 104 56
Izard, Benjamin M—N Y Insulated Wire Co. (1891)... 849 86
Jewett, Hugh J, recvr Erie Railway Co—Charles Robinson. (1886)........................2,730 91
Same——same. (1888)........................ 178 82
Jacobs, Asher, by J. Allen Townsend guard—Central Stamping Co. (1891).................. 128 88
*Klaber, Augustus D and Emil—Homer Lee Bank Note Co. (1891) 121 20
Kissel, Rudolph—Downie Boiler Incrustation Preventive Co. (1891)......................... 365 13
†Kissam, Philip, trustee William Astor—J W Holloway. (1891)............................. 216 64
†Same——same. (1891)........................ 216 64
Kursheedt Mfg Co—Leopold Staudecker. ('91) 7,200 88
Leonard, Henry Ward—N Y Insulated Wire Co. (1891)....................................... 849 86
Luce, Alfred J—T A Knowlton. (1891)......... 86 83
Same——same. (1891)........................ 221 65
McOwen, Anthony—Agnes Nobis. (1891)...... 118 44
Metropolitan Elevated Railway Co / Manhattan Railway Co } Mary E Hughes. ('90) 161 49
Morgan, D Percy / McGovern, Thomas B } Downie Boiler Incrustation Preventive Co. (1891) 365 13
Miller, John—A S Lascelles. (1888)............3,967 07
Same——same. (1889).......................... 85 03
Ottman, William and Louis exrs. Jacob Ottman—H C Briggs. (1891).......................... 667 43
Postal Telegraph Co—Charles McCrosson. (1891)... 17 27
Read, William G, Jr—Lucius Moses. (1891)...3,691 09
Same——same. (1891).......................... 251 46
Same——Giles Everson et al. (1891).........5,351 42
Same——E C Wright. (1891)..................1,747 96
Rosenbloom, Philip—Samuel Stern. (1885)... 559 67
Rogers, Lilian—H W Benedict. (1891).........1,358 96
Squier, Alfred O—Francis Becker. (1891)...... 150 44
Same——E W Hazazer. (1891).................. 253 84
Same——W R Creed. (1891)...................1,078 01
Shaver, George F—J A Hyland. (1888).......... 73 41
Slater, William G, Howard P and Seymour D—H C Graves. (1891).......................... 384 08
†Southmayd, Charles F, trustee William Astor—J W Holloway. (1891)....................... 216 64
†Same——same. (1891)........................ 216 64
†Same, trustee Wm B Astor——same. ('91). 216 64
†Same——same................................. 216 64
Shapiro, Samuel—Solomon Isaacs. (1887) 1,852 00
‡Skinner, Samuel P — Frances A Skinner. (1889)...2,555 59
‡Same——same. (1889).........................51,899 92
White, Andrew J—Nat Bank of West Troy. (1887)...3,898 71
Willard, Edward K—Lucius Moses. (1891)....3,691 09
Same——same. (1891)........................... 251 46
Same——Giles Everson, et al. (1891).........5,351 42
Same——E C Wright. (1891)..................1,747 96
Welch, Henry—W H McGrory. (1891).......... 141 45
Welch, Henry—W H McGrory. (1891).......... 141 45
Wyatt, Irving—A J Hood. (1891)............... 182 18
Wetmore, Benjamin C—Exr Mary H Drake. (1891)...1,559 44
Whipple, Nelson M—Francis Becker. (1891)... 150 44
Same——E W Hazazer. (1891) 253 84
Same——W R Creed. (1891)...................1,078 01

*Vacated by order of Court. †Suspended on Appeal. ‡Released. §Reversal. ‖Satisfied by Execution.

KINGS COUNTY.

November 20 to 26—Inclusive.

Brunnemer, John / Reunett, Willard H } W E Northup. (1891) ... $288 56
Buchanan, George N—Sturges & Roby. (1890) 141 11
Bailey, William T—J W Powell. (1891)........ 3?0 58
Baumgrass, Chas W—R A Sibley. (1891)...... 170 82
Broach, John H—G Stryker (1891)........... 58 50
Halliday, Hannah M—E F Linton (1891)..... 107 67
Hill, George W—A J Provost. (1891).......... 941 78
Same——same. (1891)...........................1,633 94
Kleuber, Leopoldine—E B Estes. (1890)...... 653 75
Langston, Frederick and K Pau Lee—D Bacon, exr. (1888).................................. 69 48
McLaughlin, Michael J—W R Grant. (1891).. 300 60
Nelson, Charles—E B Estes. (1890)........... 653 75
Ostman, Johanna—M Flanigan. (1887)....... 50 00
Pfohlmann, Michael / Pfohlmann, Sophie } B Hof. (1891).......... 138 35
Petterson, John—W E Northup. (1891)....... 288 56
Phelps, Richard G / Platt, George P } Old Nat Bank of Whitehall. (1887)........... 1,119 46
Riley, Patrick J—Sturges & Roby. (1890)..... 141 11
Selleck, Noah—J Burkhead. (1889)............2,475 04
Same——J Decker. (1889).......................2,075 04
Same——D Decker 2d. (1889)..................1,087 55
Same——Catharine Miner. (1889)............1,087 55
Same——Caroline Sweet. (1889)..............2,420 89
Same——W Deyo. (1889)........................1,210 46
Same——Cornelia Housman. (1889)......2,420 89
Same——A Deyo. (1889)........................2,420 89
Same——Catharine Wright. (1889)..........2,075 04
Same——Matilda Roof. (1889) 518 79
Same——Sarah J Byers. (1889)...............1,210 46
Same——Mary Cohen. (1891)................ 518 79
Same——D Decker, Jr. (1891)..............3,112 51
Stephens, Benjamin F—J B Wass. (1891)..... 124 15
Same——Nason Mfg Co. (1888).............. 94 07
Same——same. (1891)...........................2,485 28
Stokes, William H / Turner, William C } L Hooper. (1891)....... 200 27
Tarr, Horace G H, and / The American Rock Boring Co } F M Pierce. (1891) 1,118 19
Zeiss, Katharine W—Adam Bossung & Co. (1884).. 74 30

MECHANICS' LIENS.

NEW YORK CITY.

Nov.
21 Eleventh st, n s, 309 e 6th av, 24x103.3. W. E. Pruden agt John J. Crawford, owner, and William H. Crawford, contractor $186 95
21 One Hundred and Forty-fourth st, s s, 100 w 8th av, 25x100. Henry McDermott agt Ernest Molwitz, owner, and Christian Anderson, contractor 85 00
21 Pike st, No. 67, e s, 94 s Monroe st, 25x104. Morris Jacobson and Morris Margovitz agt Coleman M. Faherty, owner and contractor...2,600 00
23 Third av, No. 2813, e s, 99.11 n 125th st, 25x80. Percy Jacobs agt Louis J. Kahn, owner and contractor. 8,500 00
23 Church st, e s, extends from Cortlandt to Dey st, 220x51x—x62. J. B. Smith agt Theodore A. Havemeyer, owner, and John M. Hughes, contractor....... .... 393 19
23 Union av, w s, 175 s 166th st, 50x100. John Layden agt Jane Macarthur, owner and contractor 304 75
23 East Broadway, Nos. 121-125, s e cor Pike st, 85.6x24. Kelly & Daly agt Anna M., Timothy J. and Annie Roche an infant, owners, and Anna M. and Timothy J. Roche, contractors............................ 29 02
23 One Hundred and Forty-fourth st, s s, 100 w 8th av, 25x100. C. F. Pichtel agt Ernest Molwitz, owner, and Christian Anderson and Henry Schaefer, contractors......... 142 52
23 Seventy-eighth st, No. 168, s s, 200 w 3d av, 25x100. Henrietta Bretzfelder agt William C. Burne, owner and contractor ... 118 00
23 Seventy-eighth st, No. 170, s s, 175 w 3d av, 25x100. Same agt same.................... 118 00
25 Monroe st, No. 103, n s, 230 w Rutgers st, 25.9x100. Kelly & Daly agt Anna M. Roche admrx. Patrick Roche and Timothy J. Roche, owner and contractor... .... 94 13
24 Thirty-first st, No. 215, n s, 175 w 7th av, 25x98.9. Morton Bros. & Co. agt Mary Wilson, owner, and John Sheridan, contractor... 416 00
24 Garfield st, n s, 100 w Valentine av, 50x100. James Johnston agt John Kline, owner, and Frederick Robinson, contractor...... 42 60
24 One Hundred and Thirty-fifth st, No. 17, n s, 285 w 5th av, 16.4x99.11. Thomas Turton agt David E Fisher, owner, and Frederick R. Meres, contractor....... .... 98 00
24 One Hundred and Thirty-fifth st, Nos. 5-15, n s, 110 w 5th av, 106.8x99.11. Same agt

William Verdon, owner, and Frederick R. Mares, contractor.......... 587 00
24 Third av, No. 2813, e s, 93.11 n 125th st, 25x80. Percy Jacobs agt Louis J. Kahn, owner and contractor.......... 8,538 50
24 Eighty-eighth st, n s, 175 w 8th av, 75x100.8 Charles Winters agt Frederick Wood, owner and contractor.......... 673 00
24 Ninety-third st, No. 178, n s, 120 e Lexington av, 19.8x—. Harris Beerman agt Charles A. Fox, owner and contractor.......... 30 00
25 Forty-seventh st, Nos. 119 and 121, n e cor 47th st, 50.5x80.......... } Lexington av, No. 497, e s, 80 n 47th st, 20x100.......... } Christopher McRae agt Charles Wise, owner and contractor.......... 289 01
25 Eighty-fourth st, No. 247, n s, 75 w 2d av, 25x100. Franceso Cersosimo agt John Doe, owner, and John McGuire, contractor.......... 112 00
25 One Hundred and Twenty-fifth st, n s, 200 w 7th av, 75x110. Benno Erichson agt Oscar Hammerstein and John Doe, owners, and Oscar Hammerstein, contractor. (Continued from Nov. 26, 1891).......... 407 00
25 Ninety-eighth st, Nos. 11-17, n s, 78½ e 5th av, 76.8x55. Rudolph Mathesheimer agt Philip Braender, owner, and Fritz Uckermann, contractor.......... 144 20
25 Bradhurst av, s e cor 143d st, 100x53. Thomas Riggs agt Fernando Yost, owner, and Lafayette Elwell, contractor.......... 42 00
25 Same properey. Lafayette Elwell agt Fernando Yost, owner and contractor.......... 480 00
26 Bleecker st, No. 58, s e cor Crosby st, 29.11x101.6x irreg. x 134. H. C. Anderson & Co. agt Herman B. Michaelson and Henry A. Rieker, owners, and Julius Bernhardt, contractor.......... 18 85
27 Broome st, No. 209, s e cor Norfolk st, 25x50. Henry Arlt agt Eva Myers, owner and contractor.......... 2,750 00
27 Fourteenth st, s s, 88 w Av C, 250x103.3. Bowes & Combs agt William H. Muldoon, owner and contractor.......... 937 00
27 Fifty-third st, s s, 250 w 10th av, 150x100. G. T. Noe agt John Crawley, owner and contractor.......... 225 00
27 Bowery, No. 46, w s, known as the Thalia Theatre. P. E. Hall agt Carl and Theodore Rosenfeld, owners, and Ernest Otte, contractor.......... 165 00
27 Boston av, s e cor 164th st, 53x75. Edward McLaughlin agt Thomas Webster, debtor, and Georgiana F. Webster, owner.......... 250 00
27 Sixty-sixth st, s s, 400 w 8th av, 100x—. Hugh Shanks agt Edward Lapierre, debtor, and Henry Raabe & Sons, owners. 35 00
27 Ninety-fifth st, No. 171, n s, 100 e 10th av, 50x—.......... } Ninety-sixth st, No. 168, s s, 100 e 10th av, 50x—.......... } Davis, Reid & Alexander agt Clara Styles, owner and contractor.......... 821 78

Editor Record and Guide:

The lien filed last week against my property at northwest corner of West End av and 102d st, by Van Norte & Daily, is without foundation. There is no money due them, but, on the contrary, they have received more money than I should have paid them. Natural enough for their kind they abandoned the job, and the Plasterers' Union is finishing the job (by the day), and when done I will seek a settlement from them. The lien will be bonded. David Christie.

Editor Record and Guide:

Regarding the lien filed against my houses in 87th street by J. W. Dunican, I beg to say that I only owe him $31 according to the surveyor's measurements, which I hold. I have bonded the lien as I am not a victim for blackmail. I will contest it (See Satisfied Liens). John C. Heney.

KINGS COUNTY.

Nov.
23 Osborn st, e s, 50 n Glenmore av, 50x100. David E. Fox agt David Stern, owner, and Pasco & McCormack, contractors.......... $27 03
23 Schenck av, w s, 175 n Blake av, 50x100... } Schenck av, w s, 200 s Blake av, 25x100... } Richard Julian agt Charles Tomlinson, Jr., owner and contractor.......... 77 00
24 Fourth av, s w cor 23d st, 25x50. Frank D. Creamer agt John and Elizabeth Staebler, owners and contractors.......... 45 38
24*Walton st, n w cor Marcy av, 88x75. Raeburn, Latourette & Co. agt North American Iron Works, owner, and K. N. Smith
25 Fulton st, s s, 200 w Stone av, 100x100. John Morrissey agt D. C. Ross, owner and contractor.......... 525 00
25 Navy st, e s, 61.7 n Myrtle av, 50x100. Berkmeier Bros. agt Henrietta Fisk, owner, and William H. H. Glover, contractor ... 165 00
25 Sutter av, s s, 50 w Watkins st, 50x100. Ginsberg & Cohen agt Sarah Krupitzky, owner and contractor.......... 88 00
25 Jerome st, e s, 105.3 n Atlantic av, 50x95. Schluchtner Bros. agt Bridget Sinot, owner, and John Hogan, contractor. (Redocket).......... 220 88
25 Tenth st, Nos. 593-601. Heroy & Marrenner agt James F. Ransom, owner and contractor.......... 60 00

Editor Record and Guide:

The lien filed against us by Raeburn Latourrelle & Co. for which we have deposited amount yesterday. Payment has never been demanded of us.

K. N. Smith & Co.

SATISFIED MECHANICS' LIENS.

NEW YORK CITY.

Nov.
21 Convent av, n e cor 147th st, 25x61. James Slavin agt Ellis B. Southworth and John and Thomas Donellon. (Lien filed Oct. 9, 1891).......... $157 72
21 Riverside Drive, s e cor 82d st, 109.8x126.4x102.2x161.1. Philip Bierschenk agt Squier & Whipple. (July 30, 1891).......... 1,550 00
21 Same property. G. F. Werner agt same. (July 6, 1891).......... 1,311 00
21 Same property. Dunn Bros. agt same. (Aug. 30, 1891).......... 4,950 00
21 Madison av, s w cor 89th st, 25.8x139.4. W. E. Lyon agt Thomas Graham. (Aug. 22, 1891).......... 2,332 21
21 Same property. Willson, Adams & Co. agt same. (Aug. 24, 1891).......... 4,243 48
21 Same property. Dawson & Archer agt same and Randolph Guggenheimer and Isaac and Samuel Untermeyer. (Aug. 21, 1891).......... 25,500 00
21 Madison av, s w cor 89th st, 100x138.10. Frederick Haas agt same. (Aug. 24, 1891.) (Released).......... —
21 Madison av, s w cor 89th st. Josephine Collins agt same. (Aug. 22, 1891).......... 6,000 00
21 Same property. Patrick Fogarty agt same. (Aug. 27, 1891).......... 2,101 70
21 Same property. T. J. Dunn agt same. (Aug. 29, 1891).......... 1,050 00
21 Same property. W. E. D. Vincent agt same. (Aug. 25, 1891).......... 2,050 00
21 Eighty-ninth st, s s, 113 w Madison av, 25x—. W. E. D. Vincent agt same. (Aug. 26, 1891).......... 350 00
23‡Madison av, n e cor 88th st, 36.7x100.8. Eberhard Fischer agt William Matthews and Scheubner & Fredrich. (Nov. 7, 1891) 244 00
23 Amsterdam av, s w cor 79th st. J. W. Russell agt Susanna Victoria Hagan and Thomas Osborne. (Sept. 10, 1891).......... 963 60
23 Amsterdam av, s w cor 99th st, 40x100. Benedict, McIlroy & Fowler agt L. Rogers. (June 9, 1891).......... 1,187 63
23 Same property. T. F. Hoctor agt same. (Aug. 20, 1891).......... 258 16
23*Riverside Drive, s e cor 82d st, 109.8x161.1. Cream City Furniture Co. agt Squier & Whipple. (Aug. 6, 1891).......... 2,080 00
24 Greenwich st, Nos. 17 and 19. 56.6x—. Grissler & Son agt John Goerlitz. (Nov. 2, 1891).......... 13,000 00
24 Seventy-eighth st, Nos. 158-167 W., 180x100. John Swenson agt William Hall's Sons and Walter Hanley. (Dec. 2, 1890).......... 156 00
24 First av, No. 969, 25x78. Martin Mueller agt Catharine Haight. (Nov. 5, 1891).......... 50 00
24 Amsterdam av, s w cor 99th st. Henry Woods agt Lillian Rogers. (Nov. 9, 1891) 1,348 25
24 Same property. August Ackert agt same. (Nov. 10, 1891).......... 540 00
24 Kippler av, n w cor Willard av, 75x100. J. B. Roberts agt Ida L. Senior. (Oct. 29, 1891).......... 1,827 05
24 Same property. Thomas Johnston agt same and John B. Roberts. (Oct. 31, '91) 296 00
24 Same property. Ernest Weber agt same. (Nov. 12, 1891).......... 137 00
24*Kippler av, n w cor Willard st, 75x100. Frederick Robinson agt Ida L. Senior and John B. Roberts. (Oct. 30, 1891).......... 150 00
24*Kippler av, n w cor Willard av, 75x100. Samuel Price agt same. (Oct. 30, 1891)... 230 00
25*Madison av, n w cor 31st st, 49.7x87.6. Valentine Moeslein agt Peter N. Ramsey. (Oct. 12, 1891).......... 5,602 00
25 Greenwich st, Nos. 387-391, 75x100. Gaetano Mangioletti agt Frederick Dalber and W. Livingston and P. Herman's Sons. (April 24, 1891).......... 45 20
25 Tenth av, n e cor 91st st, 136.4x100. James Mathews & Son agt Edward Smith or Smith & Menken. (Sept. 15, 1891).......... 400 00
25 Eighty-ninth st, n s, 113.4 w Madison av, 51.1x—. Tully & O'Connell agt Thomas Graham. (Sept. 17, 1891).......... 730 00
25 Same property. G. B. Robbins & Co. agt same. (Sept. 3, 1891).......... 72 52
25 Same property. See & Conover agt same. (Aug. 25, 1891).......... 6,113 04
25 Same property. W. E. Lyon agt same. (Aug. 22, 1891).......... 1,475 00
25 Same property. Willson, Adams & Co. agt same. (Aug. 24, 1891).......... 1,059 04
25 Same property. W. E. D. Vincent agt same and Guggenheimer & Untermeyer. (Aug. 26, 1891).......... 450 00
25 Same property. Frederick Haas agt same. (Aug. 24, 1891).......... 4,836 15
25 Same property. T. J. Dunn agt same. (Aug. 29, 1891).......... 732 00
25 Same property. Josephine Collins agt same. (Aug. 22, 1891).......... 1,500 00
27 Twenty-first st, Nos. 222 and 224 W. Thomas Cutler agt Thomas Kenney, Michael Gillespie and John McCluther. (Aug. 25, 1891).......... 12 00
27‡Eighty-seventh st, s s, 100 w West End av, 100x100. J. W. Dunican agt John C. Heney. (Nov. 23, 1891).......... 1,221 00
27 Spring st, Nos. 131-137, n s. John Kehoe agt John and Philip Goerlitz. (July 31, 1891).......... 4,000 00

*Discharged by depositing amount of lien and interest with County Clerk.
‡Discharged by order of Court on filing bond.

KINGS COUNTY.

Nov.
17 Troy av, n w cor Bergen st, 28.4x— to st, x 85.8. Ross & Snyder agt Ann McDonald, owner and contractor. (Lien filed May 8, 1891.) (Order of Court).......... $783 42
20 Seigel st, No. 83. Jacob Pomeranz agt Morris and Pauline Garling, owner and contractor. (Nov. 10, 1891).......... 3,250 00
20 Bay 26th st, n s, 100 e Benson av, 60x96.8, New Utrecht. Brooklyn Door and Sash Co. agt Charles H. Simonson, owner, and Luc Rioux, contractor. (Nov. 16, 1891) ... 300 00
20 Fourth st, s s, 160 w 7th av, 114x100. Patrick McGuigan agt Moses & Fanton, owners, and — Ferris, contractor. (Oct. 23, 1891.) (Deposit).......... 100 00
20 Atlantic av, s w cor Bedford av, runs southeast 218.11 to Pacific st, x west 501.2 x north 200 to Atlantic av, x east 412.2, Twenty-third Regiment Armory. William King agt The People of the State of New York, owners, and Bernard McAveney, contractor. (Oct. 21, 1891.) (Deposit)... 36 72
21 Thatford av, w s, 250 n Dumont av, 25x100. Henry McShane Mfg. Co. agt Lewis Hurst, owner, and Pasco & McCormack, contractors. (Oct. 26, 1891).......... 250 00
21 Thatford av, w s, 125 n Dumont av, 25x100. Same agt same owner and contractors. (Oct. 27, 1891).......... 150 00
21 Dumont av, n s, 25 w Thatford av, 25x100. Same agt same owner and contractors. (Oct. 27, 1891).......... 150 00
21 Dumont av, n s, 50 w Thatford av, 25x100. Same agt same owner and contractors. (Oct. 27, 1891).......... 150 00
21 Lewis av, s e cor Hancock st, 150x100. Jacob Willman agt Jacob Aaronson and Thomas A. McWhinney, owners and contractors. (Nov. 19, 1891).......... 870 09
21 Thatford av, w s, 120 n Glenmore av, 75x100. John Sloan agt Stearns & Nizer, owners, and James McGrath and Charles Nelson, contractors. (Nov. 10, 1891).......... 28 25
23 Watkins st, w s, 250 s Sutter av, 20x100. James O'Connor agt Solomon Morris, owner, and Abraham Stone, contractor. (Sept. 21, 1891).......... 200 00
23 Third st, n s, 431.9 e 6th av, 40x100. Hobby & Doody agt Moses & Fanton, owners and contractors. (Aug. 29, 1891).......... 488 84
23 Schenck av, e s, 225 s Blake av, 50x100. August Hensinger agt S. Ferris Owen, owner and contractor. (June 13, 1891)... 188 00
23 Reid av, e s, 60 n Hancock st, 57.6x100. Tilly & Van Hagen Co. agt J. S. Willdridge, owner and contractor. (Nov. 23, 1891).......... 270 00
23 Same property. Hall Sash and Door Co. agt same owner and contractor. (Nov. 18, 1891).......... 934 50
23 Same property. Dugan Mfg. Co. agt same owner and contractor. (Nov. 16, 1891).. 1,168 38
23 Watkins st, w s, 200 s Sutter av. Schmidt & Esperstedt agt Solomon Morris, owner, and Abraham Stone, contractor. (Aug. 26, 1891).......... 53 00
& Co., contractors. (By deposit.) (Nov. 27, 1891).......... 1,836 06
24 Bedford av, n e cor Hancock st, 20x92. Robert W. Starr agt W. L. Baker, owner and contractor. (July 16, 1891).......... 6 25
24 Eleventh st, s s, 30 e 8th av, runs south 81.10 x east 54 x south 18.9 x east 36 x north 100 to st, x west 90. O'Hare & Croak agt Allison V. B. Norris. (Release from lien dated June 23, 1891).......... 528 66
24 Eighth av, s e cor 11th st, 100x120. Adelbert V. Nichols agt Allison V. B. Norris and William Turner, owners and contractors. (July 17, 1891).......... 168 00
25 Eckford st, e s, 86 n Van Cott av, 75x100. Meserole & Walker agt George D. Hamlin, David E. Morris and Andrew Nisbet, owner, and William Lynch, contractor. (June 23, 1891).......... 247 13

BUILDINGS PROJECTED.

The first name is that of the owner; ar't stands for architect, m'n for mason, c'r for carpenter and b'r for builder.

NEW YORK CITY.

SOUTH OF 14TH STREET.

Forsyth st, No. 20, five-story and basement brk workshop, 22.2x45, tin roof; cost, $10,000; Louis Goodman, 217 Henry st; ar't, F. Ebeling. Plan 1496.

Morton st, s s, 205.2 e Hudson st, five-story brk and stone flat, 25x85.3, tin roof; cost, $25,000; Josiah S. Lindsay, 67 West 12th st; ar't, J. C. Burne. Plan 1492.

5th st, Nos. 338 and 340, two five-story brk flats, 25x85.8, tin roofs; cost, $18,000 each; August Ruff, 78 East 4th st; ar'ts, Kurtzer & Rohl.

BETWEEN 14TH AND 59TH STREETS.

16th st, n s, 325 w 9th av, two-story brk and stone stable, 25x82, gravel roof; cost, $20,000; John Totten, 240 West 49th st; ar't, G. F. Pelham. Plan 1493.

44th st, No. 63 W., one-story brk workshop, 21x62, tin roof; cost, $1,200; Robt. Sewell, 68 West 45th st; ar't, H. A. Reeves. Plan 1477.

BETWEEN 59TH AND 125TH STREETS, EAST OF 5TH AVENUE.

87th st, No. 177 E., four-story brk factory, 25x90, tin roof; cost, $10,000; lessee. Thos. B. Whiffin; ar't, F. Wennemer. Plan 1473

96th st, s s, 90 e Park av, five five-story brk and stone tenem'ts, 22, 20 and 19.4x86, tin roofs; cost, $14,000 each; L. C. & A. C. Quackenbush, 342 East 87th st; ar't, G. Robinson, Jr. Plan 1474.

85th st, s s, 304.9 e 3d av, five-story brk flat, 24.9x92.2, tin roof; cost, $22,000; John W. French, 114 East 125th st; ar't, J. C. Burne. Plan 1491.

90th st, s s, 80 e Madison av, five-story brk and stone flat, 33.4x90.6, tin roof; cost, $32,000; Louis Wirth, 166 East 81st st; ar't, J. Hauser. Plan 1494.

118th st, No. 422 E., rear, one-story brk workshop, 25x30, tin roof; cost, $900; Geo. Hollerieth, 437 East 114th st; ar't, A. Spence. Plan 1499.

Lexington av, s w cor 103d st, brk church, 45.6x69.4, and three-story brk parsonage, 17.10x41.8, tin and slate roof; total cost, $30,000; Winkler & Willenbrock, 165 East 95th st; ar't, F. Baylies. Plan 1489.

1st av, e s, 25 s 82d st, five-story brk flat, 25.6x93.6, tin roof; cost, $23,000; Weil & Mayer, 227 East 60th st; ar'ts, Schneider & Herter. Plan 1486.

BETWEEN 59TH AND 125TH STREETS, WEST OF CENTRAL PARK WEST AND 8TH AVENUE.

68th st, s s, 300 e Columbus av, nine three-story and basement brk and stone dwell'gs, 19.3, 19.6 and 26x50 and extension; cost, $7,500 each; John D. Crimmins, 40 East 68th st; ar'ts, W. Schickel & Co. Plan 1484.

70th st, n s, 275 w Central Park West, five four-story and basement stone front dwell'gs, 20x60 and extension, tin roofs; cost, $20,000 each; John D. Taylor, 111 West 122d st; ar't, G. A. Schellenger. Plan 1483.

120th st, s s, 100 w 8th av, one-story brk shed, 13x100, tin roof; cost, $300; lessee, Chas. Weisbecker, 330 West 125th st. Plan 1475.

69th st, No. 257 W., five-story brk and stone flat, 20x87, tin roof; cost, $21,000; Ellen M. Harlow, 164th st, near Morris av; ar't, M. V. B. Ferdon; b'r, G. J. Harlow. Plan 1497.

NORTH OF 125TH STREET.

Boulevard, e s, 75 n 159th st, one-story frame stable, 11x17, felt and tar roof; cost, $15; Geo. Smith, on premises. Plan 1485.

131st st, n s, 460 w 5th av, five-story brk flat, 25x76, tin roof; cost, $20,000; Andrew Judge, 164 St. Nicholas av; ar't, J. C. Burne. Plan 1490.

142d st, s s, 125 e 6th av, two five-story brk and stone tenem'ts, 25x68, tin roofs; cost, $10,000 each; Harry L. Kidd, Brooklyn Hill, Queens County, L. I.; ar't, W. H. C. Hornum. Plan 1495.

23D AND 24TH WARDS.

Elmwood pl, n s, 100 e Clinton av, two-story frame dwell'g, 21x38, tin roof; cost, $1,800; Chas. Bjor Kegreu, 548 East 134th st; ar't, C. Arenander. Plan 1478.

Jerome av, e s, 300 s Travis st, two-story frame dwell'g, 18.6x36, and one-story frame stable, 25x16.6, tin roofs; total cost, $3,500; Carrie V. Harlow, 480 West 24th st; ar't, E. J. Harlow; c'r, E. S. Polk. Plan 1481.

Taylor av, s w cor Columbine st, one-story frame dwell'g, 23x28, shingle roof; cost, $1,500; C. Rubsam, 580 East 157th st; ar't, G Schwarz. Plan 1480.

Union av, s w cor 161st st, two-story frame dwell'g and store, 25x45, tin roof; cost, $300; Mr. Annette Strasser, 161st st and Union av; ar'ts, Leicht & Havell. Plan 1476.

Valentine av, w s, 225 s 184th st, two-and-a-half-story frame dwell'g, 31x45, shingle roof; cost, $6,000; Mrs. Alice Burke, care of C. A. Berrian, Fordham; ar't, J. A. Hamilton. Plan 1482.

Willard av, s s, 275 w 2d st, Woodlawn, two-and-a-half-story frame dwell'g, 16x26, shingle roof; cost, $1,250; A. G. More, Woodlawn Heights; ar't and b'r, A. Campbell. Plan 1479.

Travers st, s w cor Bainbridge av, three-story frame dwell'g, 20x42, slate roof; cost, $4,500; ow'r and ar't, Walter J. Lee, Fordham. Plan 1488.

1st av, s w cor Devoe st, Highbridge, one-story frame stable, 20x30, shingle roof; cost, $250; Mrs. B. Lennon, 21 Lynn av; ar't, J. C. Kerby. Plan 1487.

KINGS COUNTY.

Plan 2121—Myrtle av, n s, 86 6 e Harman st, four three-story frame (brk filled) stores and tenem'ts, 25x55, iron roof; cost, each, $4,500; N. A. Stemmermann, 874 Broadway; ar't, F. J. Lessing.

2122—Box st, n s, 240 w Oakland st, one one-story frame shed, 110x50, gravel roof; cost, $400; ow'rs and c'rs, Church & Co., 36 Ash st

2123—Stockholm st, s s, 325 w Knickerbocker av, two three story frame (brk filled) tenem'ts, 55x60, tin roofs; cost, each, $4,200; ow'rs and c'rs, Wm. Hillenbrand, 167 Harman st, and A. Treunel, 196 Knickerbocker av; ar't, G. Hillenbrand; m'n, not selected.

2124—Essex st, w s, 55 s Blake av, two two-story frame dwell'gs, 20x32, tin roofs; cost, each, $2,200; Anna Laird, Linwood st and Blake av; b'r, W. Laird.

2125—Wyckoff av, No. 57, one two-story frame (brk filled) store and tenem't, 25x48, tin roof; cost, $3,200; Joseph Fuhrmann, 37 Wyckoff av; ar't, H. E. Funk.

2126—26th st, pier at foot of st, two one-story frame smith shop and machine shop, 22 and 40x70.9 and 52x76, corrugated iron roofs; cost, $3,000; ow'r and ar't, E. P. Morse, 325 4th st; b'rs, Douglass & Bernard.

2127—Eagle st, No. 120, one one-story frame stable, 25x12; cost, $50; William Atkinson, on premises.

2128—Livingston st, n e cor Nevins st, one four-story brk store, halls and lodge rooms, 58.4 and 25x50 and 119.4, tin and tile roof, iron cornice; cost, $110,000; Johnston Bros., Flatbush av and Nevins st; ar't, M. J. Morrill; b'r, not selected.

2129—Decatur st, s s, 76 w Sumner av, one two-and-a-half story and basement brown stone dwell'g, 20x42, tin roof, wooden cornice; cost, $6,000; ow'r and c'r, R. Sweet, 511 Macon st; ar'ts, S. W. & C. J. Dodge.

2130—Vermont av, w s, 175 n Jamaica av, one one-and-a-half-story frame stable, 18x26, shingle roof; cost, $300; F. Hopp, 21 Vermont av; ar't, A. J. Warren.

2131—Palmetto st, No. 317, n s, 200 w Irving av, one two-story frame workshop, 25x25, tin roof; cost, $1,000; James Dawson & Co., 860 Quincy st; ar't, E. Dennis.

2132—Osborn st, e s, 100 n Eastern Parkway, one three-story frame store and dwell'g, 20x38, tin roof; cost, $3,000; Abraham Ruth, Osborn st.

2133—Floyd st, No. 245, one one-story brk storage for old lumber, 12x12, tin roof, brk cornice; cost $250; George Luttringshauser, on premises; ar't, H. E. Funk.

2134—Johnson av, s e cor Bogart st, one two-story brk planing and moulding mill, 40x60, gravel roof, brk cornice; cost, $10,000; George Ochs, 785 Bushwick av; ar't, G. Hillenbrand; b'r, not selected.

2135—Johnson av, n s, 147.6 e Bogart st, one two-story brk stable and office, 40 and 28 6x171, gravel roofs and brk cornices; cost, $15,000; Farmer's Feed Co.; C. Steblin, pres't, 154 East 93d st, New York; ar't, F. Wennemer; b'r, J. Auer.

2136—Linwood st, w s, 162 s Eastern Parkway, one two-story frame dwell'g, 20x28, tin roof; cost, $2,000; Mr. Seidler, Linwood st, cor Sutter av; ar't, M. L. Page; b'r, R. Forrest.

2137—Osborn st, s s, 175 e Dumont av, two three-story frame (brk filled) stores and tenem'ts, 25x67, tin roofs; total cost, $15,000; Ann Mathews; ar'ts, D. Acker & Son; b'r, P. Monahan.

2138—Osborn st, e s, 100 n Eastern Parkway, one two-story frame tailor shop, 20x30, tin roof; cost, $800; Abraham Ruth, Osborn st.

2139—Willoughby av, n s, 50 w Evergreen av, two four-story frame (brk filled) stores and tenem'ts, 25x62, tin roofs; total cost, $13,000; ow'r and b'r, M. Bossert; ar'ts, D. Acker & Son.

2140—Starr st, No. 106, one two-story frame (brk filled) dwell'g, 16x14, tin roof; cost, $1,800; Hinrich Moehrhoff, on premises; ar't, H. E. Funk; b'r, A. Schmidt.

2141—Jefferson st, s s, 100 e Knickerbocker av, one one-story frame (brk filled) stable, 25x18, tin roof: cost, $150; ow'r and b'r, A. Amann & Son; ar'ts, D. Acker & Son.

2142—Woodbine st, s s, 180 w Knickerbocker av, six two-story and basement frame dwell'gs, 18.9x45, tin roofs; total cost, $24,000; Ann Mathews; ar'ts, D. Acker & Son; b'r, P. Monahan.

2143—Jefferson st, s s, 100 e Knickerbocker av, one two-story frame (brk filled) dwell'g, 25x50, tin roofs; cost, $4,000; ow'rs and b'rs, A. Amanns & Sons; ar'ts, D. Acker & Son.

2144—5th st, s s, 97 10 w 5th av, five three-story brk tenem'ts, 20x45, tin roofs, wooden cornices; cost, $4,000 each; ow'r and c'r, Geo. O. Van Orden, 495 6th av; ar't, W. O. Tait; m'ns, Kelly & Buchanan.

2145—Monroe st, No. 189, one one-story brk carpenter shop, 24x18, gravel roof; cost, $250; Henry Major, 250A Clifton pl; c'r, D. Hinds.

2146—4th av, s e cor 11th st, one four-story brk store and tenem't, 21.6x80, tin roof, wooden cornice; cost, $10,000; ow'r and c'r, A. G. Calder, 420 8th st; ar't, W. M. Calder.

2147—Adelphi st, w s, 200 n Park av, one four-story brk tenem't, 20.4x45, tin roof, iron cornice: cost, $6 000: P. J. Carlin, Franklin Building; ar't, C. F. Eisenach.

2348—Blake av, s e cor Snediker av, one two-story and attic frame dwell'g, 17.6x42, tin roof; cost, $2,000; ow'r, ar't and b'r, John P. Free.

2149—Adelphi st, w s, 200 n Park av. one two-story brk carriage house, 25.6x38, tin roof, iron cornice; cost, $2,500; P. J. Carlin, Franklin Building; ar't, C. F. Eisenach.

2150—Adelphi st, w s, 220 n Park av, rear, two two-story brk stables, 17.6x38, tin roofs, iron cornices; cost, day's work; ow'r and ar't, same as last.

2151—Starr st, No. 106, s s, bet Knickerbocker and Hamburg avs, one one-and-a-half-story frame stable, 16x14, tin roof; cost, $75; Mr. Meyerhoff, on premises.

ALTERATIONS NEW YORK CITY.

Plan 1975—3d av, No. 507, interior alterations, walls altered; cost, $4,000; lessee, Jas. P. Keating, 19 Prospect pl; ar't, J. E. Ware.

1976—Catharine st, No. 15, three-story brk extension, 27.1x63, tin roof; cost, $5,000; Frank D. White, 140 South Portland av, Brooklyn; ar't, J. E. Ware; b'rs, T. Joyce & Son.

1977—10th av, s w cor 30th st, walls altered; cost, $350; lessee, John McGarry, 9th av and 26th st; ar't, J. W. Cole.

1978—132d st, s s, 110 e 12th av, repair damage by fire; cost, $250; Jas. Lyons, 134th st and Boulevard; b'r, J. Renville.

1979—Maiden lane, No. 60, and Liberty st, No. 21, running through, raise one story, also interior alterations, walls altered; cost, abt $7,000; E. A. Nichols, 620 5th av; ar'ts, J. M. Macgregor & Son.

1980—110th st, No. 334 E., repair damage by fire; cost, $160; John O'Brien, on premises.

1981—Nassau st, No. 144, raise two stories; cost, $2,500; David Banks, 14 West 48th st; ar't, M. Muller

1982—53d st, No. 153 W., interior alterations; cost, abt $800; Society of Sons of New York, on premises; ar't, E. F. Ely; b'r, H. H. Vought.

1983—Boston av, No. 1314, two-story frame extension, 5x8, tin roof; cost, $300; Mrs. Henrietta Barnum, on premises; c'r, S. F. Frisbie.

1984—Melrose av, w s, 80 n 156th st, raise one story, also interior alterations and walls altered; cost, $1,500; Fred. Welty, Melrose av, cor 156th st; ar't, A. Pfeiffer.

1985—Grand st, No. 16, walls altered; cost, $200; lessee, Chas. Burkelman, 195 Elm st; ar't, P. Roberts; b'rs, Petteton Bros.

1986—5th av, n e cor 94th st, interior alterations, walls altered; cost, $2,000; Henry Siefke, 307 West 26th st; ar't, J. Stroud.

1987—10th st, No. 42 E., walls altered; cost, $75; att'ys, Coudert Bros., 68 and 70 William st; m'n, T. Wall.

1988—Canal st, No. 303, walls altered; cost, $1,200; Sam'l Inslee, 410 Broadway; ar't, S. A. Warner.

1989—1st av, e s, 40 s 121st st, one-story brk extension, 20x30, tin roof; cost, $1,700; Geo. W. Kruger, 253 East 10th st; ar't, A. Munch.

1990—130th st, No. 147 E., walls altered; cost, $65; lessee, W. C. Mason, 41 West 125th st; c'r, John A. Baines.

1991—26th st, s s, 200 e 11th av, walls altered; cost, $150; lessees, J. B. & J. M. Cornell, on premises; ar't, G. W. Debevoise.

1992—8th av, No. 222, interior alterations; cost, $150; agent, Jas. F. Bragg, 218 8th av; c'r, A. Henderson.

1993—2d av, No. 1624, one-story brk extension, 15x27.4, tin roof; cost, $1,200; Henry Wohlers, on premises; ar't, C. Stegmayer; b'r, J. Stegmayer.

1994—10th st, Nos. 293 and 295 W., interior alterations, walls altered; cost, $7,500; Beadleston & Woerz, 291 West 10th st; ar't, O. C. Wolf; m'ns, J. & L. Weber; c'r, J. F. Moore.

1995—173d st, s s, 50 e Morris av, two-story frame extension, 16x20.6, slate roof; cost, $2,000; Max Schmittberger, on premises; ar't, J. J. Vreeland.

1996—159th st, s s, 46 e Melrose av, interior alterations, walls altered; cost, $1,500; Dan'l J. Conway, 17 East 11th st; ar't, M. J. Garvin.

1997—Melrose av, e s, 85 n 151st st, raise one story, also interior alterations, walls altered; cost, $1,600; Pauline Erb, 151st st and Melrose av; ar't, A. Pfeiffer.

1998—Melrose av, s e cor 152d st, raise one story, also interior alterations, walls altered; cost, $1,500; Henry Kruse, 652 East 152d st; ar't, A. Pfeiffer.

1999—Melrose av, s e cor 152d st, and s s 152d st, 410 e Courtlandt av, raise one story, also interior alterations, walls altered; cost, $2,200; ow'r and ar't, same as last.

2000—Melrose av, s e cor 152d st, interior alterations, walls altered; cost, $1,200; ow'r and ar't, same as last.

2001—Courtlandt av, e s, 28 n 161st st, two-story frame extension, 28x26, tin roof, also interior alterations, walls altered; cost, $2,000; Charles Moritz, 679 East 155th st; ar't, C. F. Lohse.

2002—150th st, n s, 200 w Morris av, interior alterations, walls altered; cost, $800; Sam'l Cohen, 447 East 150th st; ar't, C. F. Lohse.

2003—161st st, s s, abt 50 w Melrose st, raise one story; cost, $800; John Kaiser, 636 East 161st st; ar't, C. F. Lohse.

2004—157th st, s s, 75 w Courtlandt av, interior alterations, walls altered; cost, $1,500; Henry Wilker, 938 East 150th st; ar't, C. F. Lohse.

2005—Park pl, Nos. 9 and 11, interior alterations; cost, abt $1,500; Mrs. Julia Billings, 279 Madison av; ar't, W. W. Harrington; c'r, J. Fulton.

2006—Jerome Park Race Course, one-and-a-half-story frame extension, 30x17, tin roof; cost, $400; lessee, Monmouth Park Assoc., Fordham; c'r, M. Schuyler.

2007—Forsyth st, No. 20, interior alterations, walls altered, &c.; cost, $5,000; Louis Goodman; 217 Henry st; ar't, F. Ebeling.

2008—Chrystie st, Nos. 23 and 25, repair damage by fire; Isaac Marx, 538 5th st; ar't, H. Horenburger.

2009—163d st, No. 764 E., walls altered, &c.; cost, $400; John F. Vosatka, 764 East 163d st; ar't, F. J. Miller.

2010—151st st, s s, 145 e Railroad av, walls altered; cost, $200; Katharina Lohr, 458 East 151st st; ar't, F. J. Miller.

2011—Broadway, Nos. 1242-1248, new elevator; E. A. and R. Hurry, 58 William st; ar'ts, Otis, Bros. & Co.

2012—160th st, n s, 100 w Melrose av, building to be moved; cost, $600; Valentine Gleason, 243 West 48th st; ar't, M. J. Garvin.

2013—Franklin av, No. 1185, one-story frame extension, 11x10.6, tin roof; cost, $500; Patk. E. Walsh, 485 Franklin av; ar't, M. J. Garvin.

2014—13th av, s e cor Jane st, repair damage by fire; cost, $10,000; Worthen & Aldrich, 25 North Moore st; ar't, S. B. Reed.

2015—8th av, No. 668, interior alterations; cost, $25; J. Richard, on premises.

2016—Ryer av, n e cor Kirk pl, interior alterations, walls altered; cost, $5,000; Wm. Nelson, 7 Chambers st; ar't, J. S. O'Meara.

2017—Greenwich st, Nos. 245 and 247, and Park pl, Nos. 76 and 78, interior alterations, walls altered; cost, $10,500; lessee, Mrs. Hannah A. Crain, 54 East 53d st; ar't, George B. Post; b'rs, McGuire & Sloan.

2018—Park pl, s e cor College pl, interior alterations, walls altered; cost, abt $16,000; Jos. F. Knapp, on premises; ar't, N. Le Brun; m'n, J. T. Smith.

KINGS COUNTY.

Plan 1103—Flushing av, cor Bremen st, one-story frame extension, 25x31.6, tin roof; cost, $2,000; H. Hausen; ar't, H. E. Funk.

1104—York st, No. 100, flat tin roof, interior alterations; cost, $600; Mary Green, on premises; ar't and c'r, B. W. Blazier; m'n, J. Wiles.

1105—26th st, foot of, repair damage by fire; cost, $1,000; Dry Dock Co., on premises; b'r, J. Byrne.

1106—Gates av, No. 1217, two-story frame and brk extension, 34.8x16, tin roof, front altered; cost, $880; Chas. W. Metcalf, 1048 Madison st.

1107—Fulton st, No. 125, interior alterations; cost, $2,500; J. D. Godwin, 65 Wall st, New York; ar't, G. Niblo; b'rs, Parry & Niblo.

1108—Vesta av, w s, 100 s Herkimer st, flat tin roof; cost, $100; ow'r, ar't and b'r, John Amend, on premises.

1109—Seigel st, No. 121, flat tin roof; cost, $200; S. B. Goodkind, 60 East 108th st, New York; ar't, H. E. Funk.

1110—Stockholm st, No. 183, one-story frame extension, 20x25, tin roof; cost, $25; Wm. Edwards, 180 Stockholm st.

1111—Vandyke st, No. 161, raised 1 ft on brk piers; cost, $300; Mrs. Horton, on premises.

1112—Graham av, n e cor Jackson st, one-story frame extension, 20x16, tin roof; cost, $375; S. Liebmann's Sons Brewing Co., on premises; c'r, A. M. Utermark.

1113—Atlantic av, No. 288, lower store floor on yellow pine supports, &c; cost, $1,000; Herman Thimig, 435 Atlantic av; ar't, C. Werner; b'r, not selected.

1114—Fulton st, n e cor Carlton av, add one story on rear of building; cost, $2,000; Samuel B. Duryea, 46 Remsen st; ar't, M. J. Morrill; b'rs, C. Cameron and J. H. Vandeverge.

MISCELLANEOUS.

BUSINESS FAILURES.

N. Y. ASSIGNMENTS—BENEFIT CREDITORS.

Nov.

21 Birdsall, Samuel E. and John E. Jones (composing firm of Jones & Birdsall, ship chandlery and groceries, at No. 203 West st), to Andrew J. Newberry; preferences, $10,218 34.

21 Birdsall, Samuel E. (ship chandlery and groceries, at same address), to same; without preferences.

21 Jones, John E. (same business and same address), to same; without preferences.

23 Sametz, Adolph (stationery and plush and satin novelties, at No. 28 Reade st), to Herman G. Loew; preferences, $4,100.

25 Gangel, Max and Gustave Nelson (Gangel & Nelson, manufacturing and selling neckwear), to William B Filer; preferences, $700.

25 Lockwood, Henry F. (wholesale liquor business, at No. 44 West Broadway), to Gilbert P. Sherwood; without preferences.

27 Bird, William H. and William L. Lansing (William H. Bird & Co., cigar merchants and agents, at No. 47 Broadway), to Benjamin F. Jackson; prefcrenees, $1,061 49.

PROCEEDINGS OF THE BOARD OF ALDERMEN AFFECTING REAL ESTATE.

* Under the different headings indicates that a resolution has been introduced and referred to the appropriate committee. † Indicates that the resolution has passed and has been sent to the Mayor for approval ‡ Passed over the Mayor's veto.

NEW YORK, Nov. 24, 1891

CHANGE OF GRADE.

183d st, from Boulevard to 12th av.*

MAINS.

Allen st, three 6-inch iron pipes for conducting steam from No. 56, crossing st to No. 59, at expense of E. Riuley & Sons.†

Greenwich st, a 4-inch iron pipe for conducting steam from No. 607, crossing st to No. 610, at expense of R. J. Dean & Co.*

CROSSWALKS.

6th av, in front of No. 357, at expense of Ehrich Bros.†

APPROVED PAPERS.

Resolutions passed by the Board of Aldermen calling for the following improvements have been signed by the Mayor for the week ending November 21, 1891. *Indicates that the Mayor neither appoved nor objected thereto, therefore the same became adopted.

CROSSWALKS.

28th st, in front of No. 22 W., at expense of John J. McGrath.

LAMP-POSTS ERECTED AND LIGHTED.

125th st, in front of No. 149 W., at expense of G. Stern.

BROOKLYN BOARD OF ALDERMEN.

BROOKLYN, Nov. 16, 1891.

CULVERTS.

North 11th st, cor Roebling st (all corners). }
Washington av, s w cor Bergen st. } †

ELECTRIC LIGHTING.

Hudson av, e s, bet Fulton st and De Kalb av, opposite No. 479. }
Kent av, w s, bet Myrtle and Willoughby avs. } †
9th st, No. 166, opposite. }

FLAGGING.

Pacific st, s s, bet 3d and 4th avs. }
3d av, s e cor Pacific st. } †

LAMP POSTS ERECTED AND LIGHTED.

Chestnut st, bet Fulton st and Jamaica av. }
Eldert st, bet Bushwick and Central avs. } †

PAVING, GRADING, ETC.

Essex st, bet Arlington and Atlantic avs. }
Humboldt st, bet Driggs and Van Pelt avs. } †
Hopkinson av, bet Atlantic av and Bergen st.*

ADVERTISED LEGAL SALES.

REFEREES SALES TO BE HELD AT THE REAL ESTATE EXCHANGE AND AUCTION ROOM (LIMITED), 59 TO 65 LIBERTY STREET, EXCEPT WHERE OTHERWISE STATED.

Nov.

Riverside av or Drive, No. 100 } begins Riverside av, s e cor 82d st,
82d st, Nos. 318-324 }
runs east 161.1 x south 102.2 x west 16.8 x north 19.4 x west 32 x north 18 8 x west 14.4 x north 15.6 x west 8.4 x north 26.6 x west 79.9 to Riverside Drive, x north 24.9 to beginning, four-story stone front dwell'g on av and four four-story stone front dwell'gs on st, by R. V. Harnett & Co.... 30

Willis av, n w cor 145th st, 25x106 }
Willis av, n w cor 146th st, 25x106 }
Willis av, w s, 25 n 146th st, 25x106 }
Three five-story brk and stone flats }
by William Kennelly. (Amt due on each corner house $21,065, and $14,868 on other)... 30

3d av, Nos. 2197 and 2199 } begins 3d av, s e cor
120th st, Nos. 202 and 204 } 120th st, runs east 100 x south 75 x west 20 x north 25 x west 80 to 3d av, x north 50.6 to beginning, two two and three-story frame stores and tenem'ts on av and one-story and three-story brk stores and tenem'ts on st, by A. H. Muller & Son. (Partition sale)... 30

7th av, Nos. 2166 and 2168, w s, 99.11 s 129th st, 40x75, two five-story brk flats with stores, by William Kennelly. (Amt due $4,485; prior morts. $40,000)... 30

Dec.

Abingdon sq, Nos. 7 and 9 } begins 8th av, s e cor
Bleecker st, No. 425 } Bleecker st, runs
8th av, No. 2 } northeast 44.11 x
southeast 40 x east 17.2 x south 22.5 x west 76.9 to Bleecker st, x north 27.7 to beginning, seven-story brk flat with stores, by R. V. Harnett. (Amt due $88,267; prior morts. $——)... 1

Beekman pl, No. 2, n w cor Mitchell pl, 19x80, five-story brk (stone front) dwell'g, by William Kennelly. (Amt due $8,197)... 1

56th st, No. 426, s s, 400 e 10th av, 25x100.5, five-story brk flat, by William Kennelly. (Amt due $2,258; prior morts. $18,000)... 1

69th st, n s, 275 w 11th av, 25x100.5, vacant, by William Kennelly. (Amt due $13,802)... 1

107th st, No. 77, n s, 81 w 4th av, 16x100.11, three-story brk dwell'g }
107th st, No. 75, s s, 97 w 4th av, 16x100.11, three-story stone front dwell'g }
by R. V. Harnett & Co. (Amt due on each abt $10,772)... 1

144th st, No. 464, s s, 191 e 10th av, 20x99.11, four-story brk dwell'g, by D. P. Ingraham & Co. (Amt due $3,991)... 1

Madison av, No. 754, e s, 27 n 65th st, 23x63, four-story stone front dwell'g, by William Kennelly. (Partition sale... 1

Av A, No. 1549, w s, 76.6 s 82d st, 25.6x106.6, four-story brk (stone front) tenem't, by R. V. Harnett & Co... 1

Lexington av, No. 463, e s, 40 n 45th st, 20x70.6, four-story brk dwell'g, by A. H. Muller & Son. (Amt due $17,300)... 1

Centre st, No. 14 } begins Centre st, e s, abt 5 n
City Hall pl, No. 2 } junction of City Hall pl, x44.10x21 to City Hall pl, x44.10x6 to beginning, three-story brk store, by William Kennelly. (Partition sale)... 2

27th st, Nos. 154 and 156 W., seven-story brk factory, lease, all right, title and int., presses, &c., by J. F. B. Smyth. (Receiver's sale)... 2

56th st, No. 308 E., 25x100, two-story brk and frame building, all right, title and int., leasehold, by B. L. Kennelly... 2

58th st, No. 315, n s, 220.6 w 8th av, 34.10x100.5, five-story stone front flat, by J. F. B. Smyth. (Amt du $17,478)... 2

142d st, No. 208, s s, 1251 w 7th av, 16.5x99.11, three-story stone front dwell'g, all right, title and int. which John E. Braca had on Aug. 19, 1891, by Sheriff, at City Hall. (Sale under execution) 2

8th av, No. 2609, s w cor 139th st, 19.11x75.4 }
8th av, Nos. 2605 and 2607, w s, 19.11 s 139th st, 40x75.4 }
8th av, Nos. 2601 and 2603, w s, 59.11 s 139th st, 40x75.4 }
8th av, Nos. 2597 and 2599, w s, 59.11 n 138th st, 40x75.4 }
8th av, Nos. 2593 and 2595, w s, 19.11 n 138th st, 40x75.4 }
8th av, No. 2591, n w cor 138th st, 19.11x75.4 }
six five-story brk flats with stores }
by P. F. Meyer. (Amt due on Nos. 2591 and 2609 $21,322 each, and $31,417 on each of others). 2

Fulton st, No. 219, n s, 25x82, three-story brk store }
Cortlandt st, No. 70, n s, 28.5x60.3, four-story brk store }
Broadway, Nos. 145 and 147 } begins Broadway, }
Liberty st, Nos. 61-68 } s w cor Liberty }
st, runs west 157.10 to Temple st, x south 84.2 x east 58.7 x north 8.7 x west 9 x north 35.10 x west 0 8 x north 9.6 x east 109.10 to Broadway, x north 29.5 to beginning, five-story stone front office buildings }
by A. H. Muller & Son. (Partition sale)... 3

5th av, No. 2162, w s, 24.11 n 132d st, 27x100 }
5th av, No. 2164, w s, 51.11 n 132d st, 27x100 }
5th av, No. 2166, w s, 78.11 n 132d st, 27x100 }
5th av, No. 2168, w s, 105.11 n 132d st, 19x100 }
Four five-story brk flats }
by T. S. Clarkson & Co. (Amt due each on Nos. 2162-2166 $27,416 and $19 976 on No. 2168)... 3

Leroy st, No. 4, n s, 80 e Hudson st, 22.1x100, three-story stone front dwell'g, by R. V. Harnett & Co. (Amt due $18,092)... 4

48th st, Nos. 638 and 642, s s, 525 w 11th av, 150x100.5, four-story brk planing and moulding mill, one-story frame shed, &c., by A. H. Muller & Son. (Amt due $10,381)... 4

Amsterdam (10th) av, Nos. 870-876, s w cor 103d st, runs west 118 x south 77.2 to Clendenning lane, x east 18 x north 10.6 x east 100.1 to 10th av, x north 72.8 to beginning, seven-story brk flat with stores, by P. A. Smyth... 4

96th st, No. 57, n s, 204 e 9th av, 21x100.11, four-story brk dwell'g, by R. V. Harnett & Co... 4

64th st, No. 208, s s, 100 w 10th av, 25x100.5, five-story brk flat, by J. T. Boyd... 7

92d st, Nos. 139-149, n s, 245 e Amsterdam av, 105 x100.8, six three-story stone front dwell'gs, by C. S. Brown. (Amt due $4,356; prior morts. $——)... 7

103d st, No. 208, s s, 128 w Amsterdam av, 20x75 to Clendenning lane, x20x76, five-story brk flat, by William Kennelly. (Amt due $17,686)... 7

Madison av, Nos. 1742-1748, n w cor 115th st, 100.11x85, four five-story brk flats, store in No. 1742, by J. C. Lalor. (Amt due $59,134)... 7

Manhattan av, No. 507, n w cor 121st st, 20.11x90, three-story brk (stone front) dwell'g, by J. N. Golding. (Amt due $5,074; prior morts. $12,500) 7

KINGS COUNTY.

Nov.

Ashland pl, No. 189, e s, 157.07 n Hanson pl, 17.6x94.4½x17.6x95.1¼, three-story brk dwell'g; assessed value, $4,500; partition; by J. Cole, at 389 Fulton st... 30

Greene av, Nos. 1212-1216, s s, 125 w Central av, 63.10x100, four two-story frame (brk lined) dwellings; assessed value, $2,100 each }
Greene av, No. 1206, s s, 233.10 w Central av, 16.2 x100, two-story frame (brk lined) dwell'g; assessed value, $2,100 }
Throop av, No. 545, s e cor Hancock st, 23x81, four-story brk flat; assessed value, $18,000 }
Throop av, No. 547½, e s, 42.1 s Hancock st, 19.6 x81, four-story brk flat; assessed value, $9,000 }
by T. A. Kerrigan, at 13 Willoughby st... 30

Jefferson av, No. 964, s s, 420 e Howard av, 20x100 }
Jefferson av, No. 968, s s, 440 e Howard av, 20x100 }
Two two-story and basement brk dwell'gs; assessed value, $3,500 each }
by Jere. Johnson, Jr., at Real Estate Exchange, 189 and 191 Montague st... 30

Dec.

South 2d st, No. 374, s w s, 75 n w Hooper st, 25x120, three-story frame dwell'g; assessed value, $2,600; by J. Cole, at 389 Fulton st... 1

Powell st, w s, 150 s Blake av, 100x100, two-and-a-half-story frame dwell'g and one-and-a-half-story frame stable on plot; assessed value, $2,800 }
North 2d st, No. 182, s s, 220.6 w Bedford av, 25x116.6 to North 1st st, x25.03½x114.9, three two-story frame dwell'gs; assessed value, $1,700 }
by T. A. Kerrigan, at 13 Willoughby st... 2

Broadway, n s, 100 e Monroe st, 50x100, by Jose E. Pidgeon, ref., at County Court House... 2

Bushwick av, n w cor Willoughby av, 22x80x18; assessed value, $500, all right, title and int.; by Myron E. Tanner, assignee, at County Court House... 4

Front st, No. 281, n s, 192 e Gold st, 18.9x100, three-story brk dwell'g; assessed value, $2,300; partition }
Herkimer st, No. 1320, s e cor Pleasant av, 19x90, three-story brk dwell'g; assessed value, $3,700 }
Macon st, No. 70, s s, 355 e Nostrand av, 20x100, three-story brk dwell'g; assessed value, $7,500 }
Schermerhorn st, No. 355, n s, 100 w 3d av, 25x100, three-story frame dwell'g; assessed value, $3,500; partition }
Throop av, No. 547½, e s, 42.1 s Hancock st, 19.6½x81, four-story brk flat; assessed value, $9,000 }
6th av, s w cor Pacific st, runs south along 6th av 142.6 x west 125 x north 32.6 x east 25 x north 110 to Pacific st, x east 100 to beginning, three-story brk factory; assessed value, $28,000 }
by T. A. Kerrigan, at 13 Willoughby st... 4

Prospect av, No. 313, n s, 110 6 w Webster pl, 18.5x80, two-story frame dwell'g; assessed value, $1,500; by John R. Kuhn, ref., at County Court House... 4

Columbia st, e s, 49.6 s Warren st, 25.6x67.5x25.5½x65.11 }
Warren st, No. 96, s s, 70.3 e Columbia st, 27.9x74.10½, five-story brk tenem't and stores; assessed value, $6,500 }
Warren st, No. 98, s s, 98 e Columbia st, runs south 74.10½ x east 3.9 x south 24.1½ x east 25 x north 99 10 to Warren st, x west 27.9 to beginning, five-story brk tenem't and store; assessed value, $6,500 }
St. Marks av, No. 289, n s, 100 w Underhill av, 25 x131, four-story brk dwell'g; assessed value, $7,000 }
Vanderbilt st, s s, 437.5 e Short st, 12 6x108, Flatbush }
by T. A. Kerrigan, at 13 Willoughby st... 7

LIS PENDENS.

NEW YORK.

Nov.

49th st, s s, 300 w 6th av, 25x138.10x25x145.6. Henry F. Siebold agt Theo. Priebe et al.; foreclose mechanic's lien; att'y, Chas. B. Mason. 21

118th st, n s, 125 n 7th av, runs north 201.10 to 119th st, x west 259.5 to St. Nicholas av, x south 236.10 to 118th st, x east 135.6 to beginning. Bradley & Currier Co. (Lim.) agt Andrew T. Judge et al.; att'y, Wm. Stone... 21

114th st, No. 432, s s, 235.6 w Pleasant av, 12.6x100.10. Caroline E. Perkins agt Chas. F. Schultz; att'y, Theo. R. Shear... 21

112th st, s s, 627.1 w 3d av, 17.11x100.11 }
110th st, n s, 94.6 e Madison av, 25x100.10 }
114th st, s s, 255 e 4th av, 25x100.11 }
107th st, s s, 130 e 4th av, 25x101.1 }
Julio Julia agt Abraham D. de Jongh et al.; att'a, Daly, Hoyt & Mason... 21

Summit st, s s, 403 e Marion av, 50x100. Rosetta H. Bronson agt Thos. Butler; att'y, Wm. Clarke Roe... 21

83d st, No. 127, n s, 249 w Columbus av, 17x102.2. Mutual Reserve Fund Life Assoc. agt Mary J. Coar; att'y, F. A. Burnham... 21

Lexington av, No. 144, w s, 36.11 n 29th st, 12.5x100. Wm. Knight agt Albert D Newlin; att'ys, Cudlipp & Glover... 23

48th st, No. 324, s s, 300 e 2d av, 25x100. Jacob Hansen agt Henry Holck; foreclose mechanics' lien; att'y, F. P. Trautmann... 23

Hamilton pl, e s, 22.10 s 142d st, 15.9x48.9x14.6x48.3. Chas. Brock et al. agt Mary E. Stevens; att'y, Murray Corrington... 23

Amsterdam av, s w cor 131st st, 24.11x100 }
52d st, No. 416 W., s s, bet 9th and 10th avs }
Dennis Moloney agt Samuel Nelson; att'ys, Kellogg, Rose & Smith... 23

Columbus av, e s, 51.2 s 75th st, 51x100. Newman Cowen agt John J. Hughes; att'y, Simon M. Roeder... 23

89th st, n s, 175 w 8th av, 75x100.8. Spencer Aldrich agt Fredrick Wood et al.; att'y in person, Spencer Aldrich... 23

Amsterdam av, n w s, plot 8 map of 128 acres of land in 12th Ward part of estate Isaac Dyckman, 100x485.7x100.1x489.7 }
Amsterdam av, n w s, plot 9 same map, 100.1x439.7; also out-of-town property }
Mary E. Stewart individ. and extrx. of David Stewart and ano. agt Thos. Paton et al.; partition; att'y, James N. Platt... 23

5th av, s e cor 76th st, 102.2x150. Ferdinand Mayer agt Temple Beth El; action for establishment of a lien; att'y, Wm. G. McCrea... 24

12th st, n s, 325.1 e 5th av, 25x104.3. Atlantic Trust Co. agt Michael Curley and ano.; att'ys, Peet, Smith & Murray... 24

65th st, s s, 248 e 10th av, 18x100.5. Ambrose Snow et al. agt Bernard Cohn et al.; att'y, W. Tazewell Fox... 24

3d st, n e s, 230.4 s e Av C, 20.8x—. Thomas F. O'Connor agt Charles A. King exr. and trustee, et al.; partition; att'y, Jos. G. Mathews... 24

3d av, No. 2313, e s, 99.11 n 125th st, 25x80. Percy Jacobs agt Louis J. Kahn; foreclos. mechanic's lien; att'ys, Simpson & Werner... 25

120th st, n s, 175 e 3d av, 40x100.10. John T. Hunt agt John Ammon et al; amended; att'y, James R. Marvin... 25

Amsterdam av, w s, extends from 95th to 96th st, 201.5x175.4, except 95th st, n s, 116 w Amsterdam av, 27.6x100.9x81.3x100.8. John M. Canda and ano. agt Andrew T. Doyle et al.; foreclos. mechanic's lien; att'y, J. Woolsey Shepard...... 25

5th av, w s, 25 s 136th st, 24.11x85. John W. Haaren agt Elias B. Nicholas et al.; att'y, H. H. Glass.. 25

15th st, s s, 142 e Irving pl, 13.6x84. Alexander Lust and ano. agt Morris Bimberg et al.; att'ys, Durpin & Hendrick...... 25

39th st. n s, bet 8th and 9th avs, 75x98.9, known as lots Nos. 258, 259 and 260 map of the Glass House farm of George Rapelyea. Elise Segelken agt Babette A. Dobler extrx. et al.; leasehold; att'y, J. Geo. Flammer...... 25

85th st, s s, 141 w 8th av, 20x102.2. James H. Hume as trustee of Robert H. Hume agt Mary G. Utley et al.; att'y, Henry B. Weselman...... 25

Amsterdam av, s w cor 79th st, 102.2x100. John W. Russell agt Susanna Victoria Hagan et al.; foreclos. mechanic's lien; att'ys, Mapes & Kelly. 25

1st st, No. 36, n s, 132.8 e 2d av, 24.5x51.2x24.11x56.1. Barbara Kaufmann agt Charles Joseph Edward Kaufman; action to recover ½ part; att'y, August P. Wagener...... 25

Grand st, No. 34 / Thompson st, No. 21 } begins Grand st, n w cor Thompson st, 20x60.10. Lambert Hahn agt Ernest Franklin; foreclos. mechanic's lien; att'y, Christian G. Moritz...... 25

Columbus (9th) av, n w cor 102d st, 25.11x75. New York Institution for the Instruction of the Deaf and Dumb agt Albert E. Smith et al.; att'ys, Adams & Comstock...... 25

133d st, s s, 195 w 4th av, 20x99.11. Trustees of the Astor Library agt Charles A. Stein et al.; att'ys, Lord, Day & Lord...... 25

133d st, s s, 135 w 4th av, 20x99.11. Same agt same; same att'y...... 25

Lewis st, w s, 150 s Houston st, 25.1x100.2. Henrietta Cohen agt Louis Wolf et al.; att'ys, Goldfogle & Cohn...... 25

Montgomery st, No. 7, n e s, 14.9 s East Broadway, 24x75. Charles Ranhofer agt Simon Hershkovich Malzak et al.; att'ys, Coudert Bros...... 27

1st av, n e cor 69th st, 25.1x118. Solomon Jacobs agt Mary Monell and ano.; att'ys, Taylor & Parker...... 27

Same property. Same agt Mary Monell et al.; att'ys, same as last...... 27

Allen st, No. 169, w s, 175 Stanton st, 25x87.6. Same agt Mary Monell and ano.; att'ys, same as last...... 27

24th st, n e s, known as lot No. 214 map of Bellevue lots in 16th Ward, 25x98. John J. Greehy agt Mary Greehy et al.; partition; att'ys, J. W. & C. W. Ridgeway...... 27

Madison av, n w cor 127th st, 99.11x35. Mutual Life Ins Co. agt Sarah F. Mead et al.; amended; att'y, Robert Sewell...... 27

KINGS COUNTY.

Nov.

Walton st, n s, 402 e Harrison av, 22x--. Frank Dietz agt John Dietz; partition; att'ys, Richards & Brown...... 19

Willow pl, n w s, 100.7 n e State st, runs northwest 150 to Columbia pl, x northeast 25.3 x southeast 70 x northeast 22.11 x southeast 80 to Willow pl, x southwest 47.5. Morris Piatigorsky agt David Finelite; att'ys, A. & L. Levy...... 19

Hewes st, s e s, 208.4 s w Marcy av, 20.10x100. Eliza M. Sloane agt Eva Ross; att'y, Richard O'Gorman, Jr...... 20

Herkimer st, n s, 20 w Saratoga av, 80x80...... }
Saratoga av, w s, 80 n Herkimer st, 40x100...... }
Noah Tebbetts agt Albert Johnston; att'y, Noah Tebbetts in person...... 20

Liberty av, s s, 77 e Railroad av, 25x100. Isaac Embree agt Louis Rosse; att'y, Joseph M. Greenwood...... 20

Hoyt st, w s, 29.6 s Sackett st, 15x75...... }
Hoyt st, w s, 74.6 s Sackett st, 15x75...... }
Joseph C. Hendrix agt Bertrand Clover; att'y, George V. Brower...... 20

North 7th st, s w s, 528.10 s e 7th st, runs southwest 53.8 x southeast 53.8 to North 2d st, x east 22 x north 45.10 x northeast 45.10 to North 7th st, x southwest 22. Nellie C. Van Keypen agt James Mahon; att'ys, Wells & Waldo...... 20

Ocean pl, w s, 89.6 s Herkimer st, 19.6x97.6. Mungo Nairne agt William A. Montignani; att'y, R. A. Morrison...... 20

Kent av, lot 34 map J. Moser and J. Thursby, 25x100. Annie H. Donovan agt Bridget Breen; partition; att'y, J. A. Lott, Jr...... 21

Butler st, s s, 300 w Clason av, 25x131. Edmund A. Gearon agt Charles Winterwerb; att'y, M. Gearon...... 21

Pearl st, n e cor Water st, 50x90.8. Louis Wendel, Jr., agt William Sherwood; att'y, Louis Wendel, Jr., in person...... 21

7th st, n s, 297.10 e 4th av, 50x100. Title Guarantee and Trust Co. agt Mary E. Miller; att'y, Leonard Paige...... 23

Parcel at Gravesend on Johnsons lane, adj land Voorhies et al., 35 acres, 3 roods, 224-1000 perches. William Lott agt Brooklyn Jockey Club; action for ejectment; att'y, Edward D. Childs...... 23

Lexington av, n s, 140 e Lewis av, 20x100. Elizabeth Storm agt Thomas H. Robbins; att'y, Oliver S. Ackley...... 23

Howard av, e s, 133 s Herkimer st, 34x98. Alexander Underhill, Jr., agt Ernest D. Yarber; att'y, S. A. Underhill...... 23

4th av, w s, 120 n 9th st, 3?x80. Watson & Pittinger agt Charles H. Collins; att'y, J. Herbert Watson...... 23

Stuyvesant av, n e cor Macon st, 22x82. Mary Schmalstiah agt Matilda M. Farrington; att'y, Andrew Lemon...... 24

York st, No. 211, n w cor Green lane, 25x100. Brooklyn Elevated R. R. Co. agt Sophia Chargell; action to acquire real estate; att'ys, Hoadly, Lauterbach & Johnson...... 24

Vanderveer pl, s e cor Cortland st, runs east 288.5 x southwest 186.9 x northwest 183.9 x northeast 78.9 x northwest 100 to Cortland st, x northeast 75, Coney Island. Isaac Hirsch agt Nathan L. Hahn; att'y, A. Czaki...... 24

45th st, s s, 100 e 4th av, 20x100.2. Joseph D. Cunningham agt Catherine McGowan; action to set aside deed; att'y, Milton S. Guiterman...... 24

1st pl, n s, 200 w Court st, 25x183.5. Julia G. Lockwood et al. trustees Roe Lockwood agt William V. Studdiford; att'ys, Bristow, Peet & Opdyke. 24

94th st, centre line, at intersection with centre line Shore road, runs east 688 to Marine av, x south 130 x west 688 to Shore road, x north 130...... }
Marine av, south cor 94th st, 108.1x80x73.2...... }
2d av, west cor 93d st, runs northwest 140 x southwest 100 x southeast 40 x northeast 80 x southeast 100 to 2d av, x northwest 20...... }
Marine av, e s, 218.8 n 94th st, 34.9x17.4x58.8x56.9...... }
3d av, north cor 91st st, runs northwest 110 x northeast 32.6 x southeast 112.6 to 3d av, x southwest 9.1, New Utrecht...... }
Fifth Nat. Bank of Pittsburgh agt John Robinson; action to set aside deed; att'y, Frederic de P. Foster...... 25

Shore road, centre line, at intersection with centre line bet 2d av and 95th st, 13 acres, with land under water, New Utrecht. Same agt same; action to set aside deed; same att'y...... 25

Stuyvesant av, e s, 20 n Chauncey st, 20x100. Frank Jencks agt Kate L. Fogarty; att'y, William H. Ford...... 25

Nassau st, s s, 284.3 e Jay st, 25x100. George R. Brown agt Henry Dundas; att'y, George R. Brown in person...... 25

Nassau st, s s, 309.3 e Jay st, 24x100. Same agt same...... 25

RECORDED LEASES.

NEW YORK. — Per Year

Canal st, No. 348, store and basement. John J. Clark to Charles N. Martin; 5 years, from Feb. 1, 1891...... $1,500

Duane st, No. 201, n w cor Washington st, 22.11x49.6. James D. Hall to Albert Wagner; 6 years, 5 months and 14 days, from Nov. 16, 1891...... 3,000, 3,500

East Broadway, No. 201, parlor and basement floors. Calman Apple to David N. Feigensohn; 5 years 8½ months, from Aug. 15, 1891. 660, 720

Greenwich st, No. 330 / Greenwich st, No. 332 } part of cellar. Herman H. Hingslage to Gennerick & Von Bremen; 3 years, from May 1, 1891, with privilege of renewal for 5 years. 3,500

Hudson st, No. 101 / Christopher st, No. 131 } stores. Manning F. Lawson to A. Franklin Lanson; 5 5-12 years, from Dec. 1, 1890... 2,000

Hudson st, No. 298, s e cor Spring st, store and part cellar. Abial M. Hawkins, Brooklyn, to Frank J. McCarty; 4 5-12 years, from Dec. 1, 1890...... 1,800

Same property. Consent to assign. lease. Abial M. Hawkins to Frank J McCarty...... —

Same property. Consent to assign lease. De Forest Fox to same...... —

Same property. Assign. lease. Frank J. McCarty to Patrick W. Divers...... nom

Same property. Assign. lease. Patrick W. Divers to Beadleston & Woerz...... nom

Mulberry st, Nos. 43 and 45, eight rooms, store, stable, &c., not including store and basement of No. 45. Agostino Sbarbaro, Carmine Cava, and Guiseppe Ciccarelli to Nicola Laino; 3 years, from May 1, 1891...... 1,800

Mulberry st, No. 37, basement. Donato Tuozzo and Therese his wife to Carmine Caggiano and Giacinto Tadisernia; 3 years, from Nov. 1, 1891...... 432

Mulberry st, No. 118, store floor and part cellar. John G. Burns and ano. exrs. Mary J. Burns and Ellen T. Clancy to The John Kress Brewing Co.; 4 5-12 years, from Dec. 1, 1891...... 540, 600

Pearl st, No. 419. W. & R. Evans to John Ring; 4 years, from May 1, 1892...... 750

South st, Nos. 34 and 35 all. Bernard Cohen to De Grauw, Aymar & Co.; 3 years, from May 1, 1892...... 3,750

White st, No. 2 / West Broadway, No. 119 } being White st, n e cor West Broadway. Christian F. Miller to Henry J. Rottman; 5 years, from May 1, 1893...... 3,000

12th st, No. 229 W., all. F. S. Howard exr. James Webster to Lawrence Feuerbach; 5 years, from May 1, 1891...... 1,400

Same property. Consent to assign. lease. F. S. Howard exr. to Lawrence Feuerbach...... —

Same property. Assign. lease. Lawrence Feuerbach to Mary Fisher...... 4,000

26th st, s s, 575 e 6th av, runs southwest 98.9 x southeast 50 x northeast 10.4 x southeast 92.11 to Broadway, x north 94.8 to 26th st, x northwest 109.1 to beginning. "St. James' Hotel." Thomas W. Pearsall and ano. trustees Paul Spofford to Gustav Dorval; 10 years, 5 months and 17 days, from Nov. 14, 1891, taxes, &c., and...... 55,000

53d st, No 441 E., store floor and basement. Maria Schultz to David Stevenson; 5 years, from Nov. 1, 1891...... 264

63d st, No. 344 E., all. Frederick Meyer to Giseppo Soccodno; 5 5-12 years, from Dec. 1, 1891...... 1,104

103d st, No. 247 W., all. William C. Flanagan to William H. Crolius; 5 years, from Sept. 1, 1891...... 1,100

115th st, No. 328 E., all. Mary Spitz and Julia Henschel to Guiseppe Milano; 5 years, from Sept. 1, 1891...... 600

Av A, s e cor 84th st, cor store and cellar. George, John, Jr., and Joseph Schreiner trustees for John Schreiner, sr., to John H. Vahjen; 5 years, from Oct. 1, 1891...... 1,020, 1,140

Av A, No. 1313, n w cor 70th st, store floor and basement. Martin Schmeckenbecker to Thomas Reilly; 5 5-12 years, from Dec. 1, 1891...... 1,020

Amsterdam av, No. 72, south half store floor and cellar. Christina Schweitzer to David Stevenson; 1 year, 5 months and 15 days, from Nov. 16, 1891...... 660

Amsterdam (10th) av, s e cor 74th st, storeroom in basement and part of sub-cellar. Jacob A. Chamberlain to Charles H. Schmidt; 4 11-12 years, from Feb. 1, 1889...... 1,200, 1,300, 1,400, 1,500

Courtlandt av, n e cor 149th st, store floor. William Luhr to Charles Strattner; 3 years, from May 1, 1889...... 500

Same property. Assign. lease. Mary Strattner extrx. Charles Strattner to John Zoller.. nom

Same property. Consent to assign. lease. William Luhr to same...... nom

Courtlandt av, No. 906, store and two rear rooms, also four rooms on second floor. J. D. Blume to Frederick Bucker; 5 years, from Dec. 1, 1891...... 1,200

Jerome av, w s, adj Aitkens estate, —x—200x—x200. John A. and Jesse De C. Fraser to John Scully; 10 years, from July 1, 1888, taxes, &c., and...... 50, 75, 100

Jerome av, adj Edwin Fraser's land, 25x200. Charles Fraser to John Scully; 10 years, from July 1, 1888, taxes, &c., and...... 50, 75, 100

Lexington av, Nos. 3?3 and 351, all. Martha S. D. Heitmann, New Brighton, S. I., to Rudolph Mattlage; 5 years, from May 1, 1892.. 3,000

Morris av, n w cor 148th st, except three rooms in front part of building. C. H. Otten to Henry and Otto Rickmann; 5 years, from May 1, 1891...... 720

Park av, No. 888, store and basement. August Schwarzler to Jacob Van Clief; 5 years, from Nov. 1, 1891...... 1,800, 1,900, 2,000

Park av, No. 888. Assign. lease. Jacob Van Clief to Clorinda Van Clief...... nom

1st av, No. 1496½, store, basement and floor over store. Herman Cohen to G. Sichel; 2 years from May 1, 1891...... 624

2d av, No. 660, s e cor 36th st. Extension of lease. Catharine Devlin to Thomas J. Boylan; 3 years, from expiration, on original terms...... —

2d av, No. 1052, first floor. William H. Young and ano. exrs. John S. Young to Frederick Baumann; 3 5-12 years, from Dec. 1, 1891.... 276

3d av, No. 206, n w cor 18th st, all. George F. Carey to Henry and Charles Dahnke; 5 years, from May 1, 1892...... 5,000

3d av, No. 2102, store and basement. Simon Fox to Christopher Nooney; 5 5-12 years, from Dec. 1, 1891...... 2,040, 2,100, 2,160

3d av, No. 3192, store floor, floor above and basement. Paul G. Decker to Gustav Keller; 5 5-12 years, from Dec 1, 1891...... 1,800, 2,000

8th av, No. 640, store and basement. Albert J. Adams to H. Clausen & Son Brewing Co.; 5 years 6 months and 15 days, from Oct. 15, 1891...... 3,500

9th av, No. 790, store floor and basement. Samuel A. Cutner to John Krug; 3 years, from May 1, 1893...... 780

9th av, No. 502, all. Sarah A. McGowan to Michael J. Quinn; 5 years, from May 1, 1894 3,000

CHATTELS.

Note.—The first name, alphabetically arranged, is that of the Mortgagor, or party who gives the Mortgage. The "R" means Renewal Mortgage.

NEW YORK CITY.

November 20 to 26.—Inclusive.

SALOON AND RESTAURANT FIXTURES.

Altmann, Joseph. 52 Av D....W Peter B Co. $750

Assalone, Antonio. 317 E 111th....Bernheimer & S. Ice Box. 135

Bardague, Louise A. 109 Clinton pl....C Warrennier. 198

Browne, P. 1816 3d av....David Mayer B Co. 4,700

Baumgarten & Mechaine. 101 Hester....Restaurant Furn Co. Restaurant Fixtures. 32

Bingay, S F. Christopher and Greenwich... H Vogel. 1,000

Bloch & Kraus. 239-245 E 56th....J Doelger's Sons. (R) 2,800

Boekle, A and M. 177 Essex....W Hill. (R) 150

Brown & Garvey. 18 and 20 Carmine....Wagner & S. Pool. 885

Beisler, J F. 424 E 10th....Schmitt & S. $800

Birnbaum, Samuel. 145 Attorney ...A Prince. 1,200

Brignole, Paul. 136 5th av....H Freund. Restaurant Furniture. 417

Same... H Schlosser. Restaurant Furniture. 1,000

Brinckmann, E and R. 980 1st av ...J Kress B Co. 1,000

Bucker, Frederick. 906 Courtlandt av....A Hupfel's Sons. 3,800

Clark, Patrick. 314 E 36th....D Stevenson. [illegible]

Coffey, J J. 640 8th av....W L Flanagan. 8,000

Cornel or Counel or Coonie & Ihrig. 13 Elm....McParland Bros. Restaurant Fixtures. 100

Coyle & Lennon. 231 W 19th....Bernheimer & S. Pool Table. 150

Coleman, P. 2027 3d av.. H Koehler & Co. 800

Conway, M. 11 Chrystie....W A Miles & Co. 600

Daly, Ellen. 391 Av A....J Wallace. (R) 800

Degraw, James. 203 E 15th ...Bavarian B Co. 1,200

Deery, Michael. 120 Leonard....J Wallace & Son. (R) 600

De Vito, Vincenzo. 116 Mulberry....W H Griffith & Co. Pool Table, &c. 210

Duffy, T F. 750 Greenwich....F Oppermann, Jr. (R) 500

Duffy, Hugh. 441 Willis av....Bernheimer & S. 2,500

Edwards & Malone. 282 7th av ...J Everard. 3,045

Eder, August. 336 E 31st.. T C Lyman & Co. 500

Erleeck, H A. 198 10th av....J Ruppert. 1,000

Ernst, Leopold. 1105 1st av. . H Elias B Co. (R) 600

Fondl, Frank. 1091 1st av....Welz & Zerwick. 500

Fraenkle, Karl. 383 Bowery Wagner & S. Pool. 600

Farr, Therese. 322 E 22d....F Ibert. 600

Gallagher, Ellen. 1080 2d av....H Koehler & Co. 400

Giegentash, Stephan. 2609 8th av ... Bernheimer & S. Pump. 180

Gabriel, Barbara. 35 W 43d....A Finck & Son. 650

Grande, Nicola. 66 South 5th av....T K Lane. 151

Geschke, Otto. 149 Essex ...C Iba. 185

Greer, William. 246 Henry....D Stevenson. 1,800

Grimes, J P. 641 W 47th....D Stevenson. (R) 100

Grogan, W H. 47 University pl ...H Clausen & Son B Co. (R) 2,000

Gormann, Joseph. 258 Elizabeth... Budweiser B Co. 550

Hagerty, James. 156 and 158 E 105th....Albany B Co. 3,000

Harris, Sarah A. 354½ Greenwich....D & I A Demarest. Hotel Fixtures. (R) 4,000

Heinle, Mathess. 155th st and 8th av....J Kress B Co. 2,407

Hertel & Nitschke. 413 Broadway....J P Kinney. Restaurant Fixtures. 500

Haffner, J D. 600 8th av....Bernheimer & S. 2,000

Heilshorn, Henry. 20 11th av....Consumers' B Co. 1,000

Haffner, J D. 600 8th av....P J Gray. 2,000

Irving, Hannah, 441 3d av....Clausen & Flanagan. (R) 1,200

Kaiser, Dionis. 177 E 96th....Bernheimer & S. Ice Box. 160

Same....same. Ice Box. 75

Same....same. Beer Pump. 70

Keller, Gustave. 3192 3d av....A Hupfel's Sons. 1,800

Kilpatrick, Robert. 117th st and 1st av....D Stevenson. (R) 575

Killer, George. 1621 1st av....J Hoffman B Co. (R) 600

Klein, T and E. 345 E 78th .. India Wharf B Co. 800

Krimholz, A. 112 Suffolk....P Rubel. 500

Krug, J. 790 9th av....C Stein. 1,690

Llenan, Emil. 104 E 14th....W L Flanagan. 1,500
Lippert, Joseph. 175 Chrystie....J C G Hupfel B Co. 800
Lauppe, Christ. 126 Av D ...J Doelger's Sons. 600
Lenz, Charles. 812 W 27th....J Kress B Co. 1,000
Lynam, M J. 504 1st av. ..G Ehret. 500
Mangels, William. 351 E 10th....P Doelger. (R) 1,200
Mans & Barbey. 109th st and 9th av....Bernheimer & S. Saloon and Garden Fixtures. 6,500
Marcus, Abraham. 11 1st....H Fichter. 400
Martin & Hughes. 489 1st av... D Stevenson. 400
Mattenfeld, Henry. 548 3d av....A Elser. Restaurant. 800
Mauschler, Ernst. 804 E 5th....D Stevenson. 450
McCarthy, William. 1616 Broadway....J H Bereuter. Pool Table. 150
McCarthy, William. 1616 Broadway. Lembeck & Betz. 500
McDonald, J J. 11th av and 23d st....D G Yuengling, Jr, B Co. (R) 525
McGuire, John. 519½ Canal....P & W Ebling B Co. (R) 373
Meyer, Henry. 929 2d av... P Buckel. 1,500
Michaelis, Henry. 1605 Park av....F Oppermann, Jr. (R) 800
McGovern, Joseph. 2086 1st av....Bernheimer & S. 2,800
Murphy, D J. 329 W 17th ...Bavarian B Co. 600
Nixon, G H. 800 Washington....W Peter B Co. (R) 400
O'Connell, M. 1st av and 48th st....J H Bereuter. Pool Table. 135
Petry, Anton. 497 W 41st ...P Buckel. 500
Pick, Morris. 218 E 89th....H Vogel. 100
Ravera & Kaufmann. 49 W 24th....Restaurant Furn Co. Restaurant Fixtures 68
Rooney, Andrew. 617 3d av....J C G Hupfel B Co. 6,000
Reilly, J J. 1121 2d av....Langdon & Granger B Co. 2,000
Reissmann, Oswald. 1438 1st av....J Kuntz B Co. 700
Reiss, Wilhelmina. 87 Greenwich....F Brodsky. 250
Reynolds, T. 364 10th av....M Seitz. 1,100
Smith, Elizabeth. 6 Roosevelt ...T Mahoney. (R) 800
Schutte, Caroline A. 76 Spring....J Kuntz B Co. 300
Seltzer, H and P. 45 Henry....E Ochs. 800
Singhi, C J. 2039 3d av....Brunswick-B-C Co. Pool Table. 133
Spencer, William. 1792 3d av ...Bavarian B Co. 800
Stoliom, Alex. 65 Cortlandt....Bernheimer & S. 500
Schaake, C F. 350 E 76th....Danenberg & Coles. 364
Schuler, John. 1751 1st av....G Hildebrandt. 1,450
Schutt, Hermann. 164 South....Consumers' B Co. 2,000
Seidl, Annie. 340 E 71st .. H Vogel. 185
Teller, Caroline. 683 Broadway....Bernheimer & S. 275
Trommaglio, B. and G Scalzi. 141 Mott....Bernheimer & S. 800
Van Clief, Clorinda. 883 Park av....Bernheimer & S. 8,000
Van Clief, Jacob. 883 Park av. ..W H Griffith & Co. Pool Table, &c. 600
Wagner, Albert. 201 Duane....G Ehret. 4,500
Wallasch, Geo. 811 3d av....G Ringler & Co. 9.0
Warner, Moses. 83 Av C....L Cohen. Restaurant Fixtures. 250
Weber, Charles. 143 Mulberry....J Kress B Co. 1,500
Wolfe & Courtney. 59 E 12th....Restaurant Furn Co. Restaurant Fixtures. 68

HOUSEHOLD FURNITURE.

Allen, W D. 246 W 31st....O'Farrell & Co. 195
Ashley, Joseph. 158 E 106th....Jordan & M. 181
Ashton, W J. 115 W 60th....S Heyman & Co. 114
Ansorge, Martha. 526 E 87th....Fennell & Pye. (R) 180
Same....same. (R) 450
Anderson, J H and Sarah A. 139 W 104th....E C Hinsdale. 130
Assent, Fanette. 101 W 48th....L Baumann. (R) 207
Adams, H B. 322 E 118th....D M Brown. 201
Baldwin, B P. 599 6th av....Alice Croker. 500
Barnes, P J. 235 W 18th....Manges Bros. 130
Barnes, Alberta. 166 W 125th....J Baumann. (R) 404
Bay, Frederick. 216 E 128th....E Quetzsch. (R) 850
Behr, Tina. 875 2d av....H Thoesen. 141
Behrman, A. 230 E 116th .. H S Eisler. 824
Bolend, Mrs John. 344 1st av....H Thoesen. 162
Booth, Maria W. 147 E 30th....J Baumann. (R) 101
Bord, C J. 884 Forest av....Fennell & Pye. 110
Buckingham, Hellen. 250 W 43d ...J Baumann. 1,736
Bassett, F N. 2301 7th av....F G Smith. Piano. (R) 350
Bates, William. 240 W 35th....L Baumann. 117
Berger, Bernard. 260 Division....F G Smith. Piano. (R) 175
Branze, Herman. 71 2d av....S I Herschmann. 389
Barry, Kathleen E. 114 W 63d... H Thoesen. 183
Becker, Josepbine. 665 Forsyth....F J Brechtel. 101
Bernard, William. 257 W 128th....Mathushek & Son Piano Co. Piano. 275
Bewley, Thos. 1628 Lexington av....O'Farrell & Co. 347
Blakeney, W E. 148 E 45th....E Chaffee. 1,879
Camban, Justin. 146 W 4th... O'Farrell & Co. 256
Collins, Margaret. 233 E 30th ....Fennell & Pye. (R) 146
Cornwell, Mrs C M. 200 W 69th....O'Farrell & Co. 152
Creighton, Frederica. 227 E 14th....G Reubel. 189
Croxton, Mary P. 1 E 19th....J Gregg & Co. 107
Clark, N E. 101 W 93d . L Baumann. (R) 350
Conrad, Herman. 801 W 30th....L Baumann. (R) 109
Cox, Sarah L....F G Smith. Piano. (R) 260
Creelman, Martha. 447 W 23d....W D Barclay. 600
Callahan, John. 228 E 26th....S Baumann. 138
Carson, R. 1797 3d av....Jordan & M. 114
Clark, G 84 W 30th....J F Caldwell. 2,500
Colling, Amelia. 1005 Washington av....Fennell & Pye. (R) 163
Cooper, J R. 469 Pacific st, Brooklyn....O'Connor & Treacy. (R) 120
Corey, Margaret. 1200 10th av....J Baumann. (R) 158
Delgado, J. 454 E 81st....Fennell & P. (R) 110
Doyle, Lizzie. 342 W 11th....O'Farrell & Co. 166
Dunham, Sarah H. 153 W 44th....O'Farrell & Co. 200
Davis, E B. 745 Amsterdam av....L Baumann. 425
Day, Elizabeth. 357 W 37th.. .L Baumann. (R) 130
d'Elseaux, F C. 215 W 100th....O'Farrell & Co. 138
Drifendorf, Jennie E. 238 6th av....H Israel & Son. 185
Driscoll, C V. 319 W 134th....F Scallion. 216
Edmonson, Carrie A. 158 W 56th....Jordan & M. 111

Edwards, Florence. 6 E 113th....I Mason. 175
Ernest, J S. 55 W 83d ..A Frey. 125
Flannery, J J. 408 W 48th....J F Doherty. 170
Fuller, Sarah L. 156 W 35th....O'Farrell & Co. 267
Fahrenholz, Amelia. 113 W 45th....L Baumann. 143
Frantzen, Charles. 303 E 21st....S Heyman & Co. 264
Faas, Tessie. 79 W 124th....Fennell & P. 110
Files, L. 688 E 135th .. Fennell & P. 158
Foley, James. 251 E 43d....J Grege & Co. 128
Geldern, Joseph, Mrs. 301 E 11th....H Thoesen. 108
Gilson, Lottie. 148 E 54th....Jordan & M. 197
Griffin, R H. 155 E 54th....Fennell & P. (R) 256
Gunoa, G. 253 W 15th....J H Little. 181
Gleitz, Stephonie. 535 W 46th... L Baumann. 181
Gotthold, Ida. 664 Lexington av E Greenberger. 182
Gretsch, B J. 65 2d....F J Brechtel. 287
Guinan, Annie. 81 Henry....Jordan & M. 107
Haig, Elizabeth. 446 W 47th....O'Farrell & Co. 325
Haigh, F V and J L. 114 W 124th....G W Stephens. 1,200
Harris, J and M A. 172 Willis av....E C Hinsdale. 100
Hart, Mabel. 251 W 39th ...R W Inman. 400
Hart, Bertha. 252 E 110th .. R M Walters. Piano. (R) 166
Hastings, S L and C A. 16 W 24th....Commercial Credit Co. 120
Hicks, Mary. 89 10th av....O'Farrell & Co. 148
Howes, Sarah J. 124 E 102d....W P Chase. 255
Hart, H S. 280 W 19th....L Baumann. 119
Herrmann, Rosa. 149 W 53d....J Moriarty. (R) 141
Hodges, A J. 73 W 96th....F G Smith. Piano. (R) 215
Hammond, Katherine. 215 W 40th....J Baumann. (R) 536
Hennessy, Mary J. 258 W 129th ...Manges Bros. 127
Heymann, Caroline M. 246 W 23d....F Kurzman. (R) 1,271
Higgins, Mary. 205 W 60th....N Y F Co. 141
Hinchey, P J. 180 E 114th....Fennell & P. (R) 141
Holland, T A. 354 10th av....Manges Bros. 100
Huggins, G. 162 E 106th....Manges Bros. 307
Jones, Edward. 342 E 12th... H Thoesen. 147
Jones, Sarah. 145 W 27th....Jordan & M. 114
Jones, Cambell. 247 W 50th....Manges Bro. 188
Jones, Mrs Wm. 317 W 44th....J F Doherty & Co. 180
Johnson, Thomas. 173d st and 10th av....L Baumann. 126
Koch, Charles. 472 8th av ...L Baumann. 141
Kattner, F. 22 E 114th....L Heyman & Co. (R) 217
Kellogg, Norman. 109 W 105th . .Brooklyn F Co. 200
Kallensee, Rudolph. 318 E 48th.... J Baumann. (R) 136
Lahey, J. 312 E 126th....J H Little. 185
Lee, Mamie. 18 Doyer... H S Eisler. 112
Lehmann, C W. 112 E 128th....Fennell & P. 198
Lucas, E S. 1756 3d av....Jordan & M. 104
Lyon, A M. 309 E 14th....J H Little. 128
Lambrecht, J F. 131 E 84th....M Daley. 500
La Forge, Isabella. 223 W 45th....D Laughlin. 233
Same .. same. 327
La Vielle, I B, Mrs. 13 W 22d....S Knapp & Co. 170
Lee, W B. 60 Broad... Mullins & Sons. 231
Lawrence, Alice. 129 W 58d ...S I Herschmann. 243
Layton, Sarah E. 226 E 39th....F G Smith. Piano. (R) 331
Levey, J B. 325 W 35th....L Baumann. (R) 148
Lyons, Nathan. 206 W 31st....L Baumann. (R) 111
McCarthy, Nora. 47 Catharine....F G Smith. Piano. (R) 191
Meissner, Race. 333 E 88th....L Baumann. (R) 121
Morrill, Charlotte E. 348 W 24th ...L Z Murray. 179
Mortimer, Louise. 1964 7th av....L Z Murray. 399
Mahlein, Martin. 400 E 54th....F J Brechtel. 124
McBride, Corrine E. 51 W 35th....R P Whitfield. 1,000
McGeachy, Chas. 253 5th av....J Gregg & Co. 208
McIntyre, J F. 978 Trinity av ...J F Doherty. 206
Meerslmann, Julian. 319 W 38th....F J Brechtel. 117
Meyers, Hannah. 235 E 39th....S Heyman & Co. 204
Miltitemark & Stern. 55 Forsyth....J Kurtz. 156
Mallon, W H. 216 Madison....J H Little. 260
Mansion, M. 118 W 31st....E Regnier. 3,000
McCashin, R C. 307 E 18th ...J H Little. 160
McGuire, Mary T. 684 E 137th... Jordan & M. 255
McLane, S B. 159 W 83d ...J H Little. 138
Melville, Mary. 548 W 45th....O'Farrell & Co 177
Metz, Jacob. 1099 1st av....H Thoesen. 129
Millerleile, J C. 118 Christopher....H S Eisler. 125
Molar, E S. 282 W 132d....Fennell & Pye. (R) 134
Monteverde, Adenia. 130 W 36th....J Baumann. (R) 200
Morse, Carrie E. 10 W 125th....Fennell & Pye. (R) 108
Same....Fennell & Pye. (R) 225
Munde, Bertha. 162 W 103d....Krakauer Bros. Piano. 285
Mulbauer, Felesia. 174 2d av....Fennell & Pye. 337
Noonan, Mary. Pelham av, cor Arthur av....Fennell & Pye. (R) 112
Nagle, Mamie. 228 E 89th....O'Farrell & Co. 180
O'Bisco, Joseph. 563 W 30th....J J Coogan. (R) 108
Ohrdorf, L. 63 W 51st....H Thoesen. 1,785
Opfinger, Adolph. 699 10th av....F J Brechtel. 133
O'Rourke, Mary Ann. 1929 3d av.. J Baumann. (R) 145
Parker, Agnes. 989 6th av....J Baumann. 120
Paul, C W. 159 Delancey . .J H Little. 279
Pennock, Zolmon. 250 W 36th....J F Doherty. 176
Toussaint & Harmon. 215 E 97th....Fennell & P. (R) 201
Prader, Tillie. 18 Doyer....Jordan & M. 120
Preiss, Caroline. 323 E 80th ...H Thoesen. 288
Pitman, Carrie J. 244 W 5th....F G Smith. Piano. (R) 410
Rauscher, Edward. S e cor 55th st and 6th av ....L Baumann. (R) 172
Rente, W T. 456 9th av....L Baumann. (R) 134
Riordan, Jas ...F G Smith. Piano. (R) 175
Ross, Fannie. 142 W 33d....L Baumann. (R) 283
Ryan, Frank. 51 Broome....J Moriarty. 121
Riddick, Helen. 32 W 24th ...D Laughlin. 125
Rodman, Mrs J. 209 E 14th....J J Coogan. (R) 131
Rodman, Theresa. 312 E 8th. . J J Coogan. 212
Roche, Katie. 285 1st av....Jordan & M. 111
Roegener, Mrs A. 102 E 2d ...H Thoesen. 107
Ritschy, F W. 47 E 18th....J H Little. 242
Savin, T L. 46 W 55th....J H Little. 318
Scozzan, G. 403 W 49th....J Rubenstein. 375
Schuh, Amelia. 308 E 10th....Jordan & M. 189
Schottmann, Fred. 330 E 90th....Jordan & M. 262
Stevens, W F. 140 E 48th....J Gregg & Co. 222
Smith, Sarah. 190 E 75th....Amer Guar Assoc. 100
Swanzie, Hugh. 448 W 33d....L Baumann. 130
Ten Eyck, S J. 109 W 96th....J H Little. 178
Vogel, Mina. 95 E 7th....S Baumann. 134

Van Vlint, Barnard. 327 E 89d....Philips & Berliner. 326
Walsh, M J. 208 5th....Manges Bros. 132
Washauer, Gracie. 109 1st . J Moriarty. 139
Watson, C J. 414 Lexington av....W H Sage. 635
Webb, Harry. 1108 Park av....J J Coogan. (R) 109
Webster, A S. 341 W 32d....J Moriarty. 154
Week, August. 221 E 45th O'Farrell & Co. 698
White, Mrs Chas. 228 W 17th....H Thoesen. 157
Webster, A S. 341 W 23d....J Moriarty. 169
Welters, Annie. 218 E 34th... L Baumann. 111
Williams, Elnora. 235 W 32d....L Baumann. 198
Williams, F D. 162 E 46th....H Thoesen. 127
Walsh, J. 307 E 69th....Jordan & M. 368
Waterbury, Emma A. 427 E 122d....Fennell & Pye. 129
Watson, Euphemia. 164 W 129th... Fennell & Pye. 112
Wilson, Hattie. 262 W 43d....J Baumann. (R) 172
Wright, R A. 142 E 111th....R M Walters. Piano. (R) 260
Wylie, Laura. 1440 Lexington av....S Baumann. 161
Young, Henry. 356 E 3d.. .F J Brechtel. 177
Zurhelem, August. 509 W 48th....L Baumann. 155
Zutte, Leon. 107 Hester....S I Herschmann. 208

MISCELLANEOUS.

Ackerman, N P. 199 W 10th....A M Prigger. Horses, Trucks, &c. 900
Anderson & Co. 459 6th av....Whitlock Machine Co. Machinery. 585
Atwood, C C. 2154 7th av....L B Stillman. Fish Market, &c. 500
American Automatic Spray Perfume Co....Leaycraft & Mayrhofer. Machinery. 1,510
Appel, D. 194 South....W L Loew. Furnishing Goods. (R) 420
Balmuth, J. 63 Clinton....M Rosner. Machines. 250
Bedell, D M. Broadway, cor 26th st....H A Parr. Jewelry. 145
Bosel, Albert. 412 Lenox av....A Amberg. Bakery Fixtures. 200
Buney, Peter. 488 and 490 Water....M Buney. Horses, Trucks. (R) 1,500
Baehser, Fred 457 W 58th....K Baehser. Painter Fixtures. 500
Bell, C H. 351 Bleecker....M E Bell. Drug Fixtures. 1,100
Bush, J L. 525 W 40th....Banner B Co. Bottling Fixtures. (R) 1,352
Bushnell, Irving & Swartz ...Campbell P P Co. Press. (R) 720
Bay, Frederick. 166 E 125th ...E Queitzsch. Barber Fixtures. 350
Behrens, H L. 220 Columbus av ..J Matthews Co. Soda Fixtures. 600
Behrens, S and J. 235 W 125th....J Rudinger. Barber Fixtures. 1,000
Bergen, B A. 3495 3d av....F & G Haag & Co. Barber Fixtures. 30
Callahan, M J. 105 Park row....Lamson Con S S Co. Register. 495
Carter, R J. 216 W 42d....J Cunningham Son & Co. Coach. 1,900
Christ, Geo. 206 6th ...W Fritz. Barber Fixtures. (R) 400
Crans, H S. 54 and 56 Park ..Aluminum Brass & B Co. Machinery. 1,763
Crawford, J W. 834 Broadway....G S Walworth. Office Fixtures. (R) 361
Crowley, J and T....J Cunningham Son & Co. Coach. 150
Caro, S A. 125 Grand. ..B Caro. Machinery. 2,000
Celiano & Ovato. 43 Mott and 145 Sullivan....S M Jour. Butcher Fixtures. 1
Calafato, C. 401 E 15th....G Mento. Barber Fixtures. 220
Cappucci, G. 459 3d av ..A Schwaab & Son. Barber Fixtures. 53
Cardiano, D. 42 Water ...D Bua. Barber Fixtures. 60
Castella, S. 314 W 145th....A Schwaab & Son. Barber Fixtures. (R) 172
Cotrone, G. Pelham av and Lorillard pl....A Schwaab & Son. Barber Fixtures. 184
De Rosa, R. 8 Delancey....A Schwaab & Son. Barber Fixtures. (R) 52
De Somma & De Sapio. 30 Thompson....N Ercolino. Grocery Fixtures. 240
Doran, J J. 267-278 W 17th....G Ringler & Co. Bottling Fixtures. 1,000
Dunn, L J. 1231 2d av....J Livingston. Horses, Wagon, &c. (R) 1,000
Egbert, James. 15 William....A D Puffer & Sons. Soda Fixtures. (R) 10
Ernsberger, A M. 3 Burling slip....W B Sheddon. Tools, Fixtures, &c. 173
Edgar, Charles. 161 W 29th....G H Sanborn & Sons Cutter. (R) 105
Esper, F W. 156th st and 10th av....L Sanger. Livery Stable Fixtures. (R) 5,000
Edwards, M. 363 W 31st....T Leonard. Fixtures. (R) 239
Eisert, Alwin. 874 8th av....E Eisert. Locksmith's Business. 1,500
Fallon, T F. 854 7th av....A O'Gara. Plumber Fixtures. 300
Farash, T W. 247 W 41st....J Cunningham Son & Co. Coach. 50
Fink, A & Sons. 78 Suffolk....J Kramer & Son. Cart. 470
Garofalo, Louisa. 2190 1st av....R D'Onofrio. Jewelry Fixtures. 500
Geraty, John. 449 E 123d....I Smith. Horses, Carts, &c. 300
Goldfinger, J and S. 783 E 5th ...D Deutsch. Butcher Fixtures. 85
Granger, Gideon. 153-159 11th av....Lincoln I and G Assoc. Fixtures, &c. 150
Grinspan, E. 399 Grand....W H Butler. Safe. (R) 312
Gever & Dettleff. 1-5 Broome....L Ullricht. Machinery, &c. nom
Goldfinger & Lannensdorf. 783 E 5th....D Deutsch. Butcher Fixtures. 35
Harrison, G R. 1281 Lexington av... H L Niver. Horses, Wagons, &c. 400
Henry, F H. 87 Nassau .. F P Forster. Printing Office Fixtures. 12,000
Hoag, Kate. 128 South 5th av.. Emma F Hoag. Machinery. 2,000
Hanson & Hogan. 194 Duane....Whitlock Machine Co. Machinery. 900
Heinzer, Barbara. 171 Suffolk ... F Miller. Machinery. 2,200
Hopfer, Bernard. 810 E 63d....C Schmidt. Horse and Ice Wagon 500
Hall, H A. 99 4th av....H Hurtzig. Band Uniforms. 400
Hillebrand, Gustave. 15 Howard....J Nieder. Machinery, &c. 500

Hopfer, Bernard. 310 E 68d... C Schmidt. Horse, Ice Wagon, &c. 500
Jannetta, Vincenzo. 147 Elizabeth....V Prota. Grocery Fixtures. 142
Jachman, T. 216 Canal....M Hoym. Cigar Fixtures. 50
Jennings, L H. 117 Christopher....G C Stegmann. Truck, Horse, &c. 300
Johnson, P J, & Co. 46 Beekman....John Royle & Sons. Machinery. 125
Kalmusk, Leo. 25½ Sheriff....J Cunningham Son & Co. Coach. 100
Kreienberg, Henry.. 425 2d av... R M Lush. Fish Market Fixtures. 300
Kahrs, W. 507 Boulevard....J Matthews Co. Soda Fixtures. 1,000
Kargl, A. 26 E 28d....J Matthews Co. Soda Fixtures. 665
Kay Pamphlet and Book Mfg Co. 141 Leonard ....C Beck Paper Co. Machine. 224
Lester, J. 39 Essex....S Littenberg. Horses, Wagons. 500
Loeber, John. 64 Broome....Roberts & Collin. Bakery Fixtures. (R) 500
Leichtman & Herz. 392 E 10th....A Silady. Butcher Fixtures. 65
Lohman, J and G. 212 Clinton and 274 Cherry ... Commercial Credit Co. Furniture and Milk Fixtures. 125
Lovell, F F, & Co. 142 and 144 Worth....First National Bank of Champlain. Presses, &c. 26,700
Lawler, J F. 2309 3d av....Bramhall, Deane & Co. Range, &c. 134
Meyer, H U. 653 E 16th....J C Muller. Horse, Wagon and Fixtures. 100
Meyer, Marx. 56 Hester ...N Levy. Horses, Trucks, &c. 1,000
Mutual Real Estate Co. 610-618 Broadway ... Farmers' L and T Co. Leasehold. (R) 225,000
Malzone & Asselta. 2206 1st av....W H Butler. Safe. 275
Manheimer, Minnie. 306 W 145th....E Marscheider. Butcher Fixtures. (R) 310
Mason & Nichall. 444 8th av and 261-263 W 33d st ..National Casket Co. Undertaker Fixtures. 1,119
Mathews, W O. 122 W 100th....M J Mathews. Express Fixtures. 750
Maynard, Florence....I M Finkelstein. Seal Jacket. 250
McWhood, Ed, Jr. 75 John....Whitlock Machine Co. Machinery. 750
Muller, Conrad. 321 5th....A Ruff. Livery Stable Fixtures. (R) 3,600
Muhl, J L. 329 E 33d....C E Ring. Machinery. 800
Muller & Co. 510 West 56th ...Nuffer & Lippe. Coach. 718
Nitti, Victor. 246 Delancey....S Pius. Barber Fixtures. 210
Newton, C W. 231 and 233 E 43d....J Carrall. Horse and Cab. 50
O'Donnell, Nora....G Dessecker. Coach. 250
Olney, Geo. 19 Broadway....Lincoln I and G Assoc. Office Fixtures. 100
O'Connell, T J. 529 W 131st ...Nuffer & Lippe. Coach. (R) 126
Orgera, V. 403 E 84th... A Schwaab & Son. Barber Fixtures. 550
Parrish, M. 62 East Broadway... P Reidenbach. Wagon. 100
Petraglia, J. 12 Chatham sq....A Schwaab & Son. Barber Fixtures. 140
Pillsbury & Co. 59 W 39th....Jane Buchanan. Machinery. 250
Pine, Elias G. 128 E 84th....E R Pierson. Horse, Milk Wagon, &c. (R) 429
Payne, G A. 32-36 W 43d....S G Payne. Horses, Coaches, &c. 3,000
Phelps, F C. Beach and Hudson sts....S A Woods Machine Co. Machinery. (R) 1,565
Quinto, T. 219 Forsyth....A Schwaab & Son. Barber Fixtures. (R) 197
Riemer, E and A. Voeliker. 103 West Broadway ....A Schwaab & Son. Barber Fixtures. (R) 130
Rosiello, M. 95 3d av....A Schwaab & Son. Barber Fixtures. 84
Rubin, S. 58 Ludlow ...Bramhall, Deane & Co. Ranges. 120
Reu, Ludwig. 144 E 88th . J J Carroll, Jr. Horses, Trucks, &c. 400
Rennie, J L. 264 W 28th ...H S Chano. Barber Fixtures. 25
Ring, H P. 241 E 115th ...F G Horn. Express Fixtures. 150
Romano, Gaetano. 65 Madison....A Schwaab. Barber Fixtures. 381
Schlobohm, Caroline. 495 Pearl....H Kuhle. Grocery Fixtures. 150
Sontheimer, Benjamin. 61 Crosby....M Stern. Fixtures, &c. 1,500
Scheyer, Carl....J Souvay. Barber Fixtures. 110
Schmidt, C H. 295 Amsterdam av....J Ruprecht. Drug Fixtures. 2,000
Schneider, George. 29 Mangin....S Sandowich. Horses, &c. 220
Schroeder, C F. 1641 Broadway....H M F Botjer. Horse, Wagon, &c. 350
Schuss, M. 114 Willett....A Zweifach. Horse and Wagon. 100
Shapiro, Morris. 1902 4th av....N Harris. Cigar Fixtures. 191
Schmidt, A and C H. 33 1st av. .A S Bischof. Drug Fixtures. 2,250
Schendlinger, M. 44 Essex ...Bramhall, Deane & Co. Ranges. 189
Sheeby, Bridget. 161 E 85th... Nuffer & Lippe. Coach. (R) 447
Spanga, C. 453 9th av....A Schwaab & Son. Barber Fixtures. (R) 215
Syracuse, F E. 160 E 49th....A Schwaab & Son. Barber Fixtures. 111
Thomson, E and C A. 160 8th av....Duparquet, H & M Co. Range, &c. 238
Vysipal, Alois. 331 E 71st....J Olajek. Butcher Fixtures. 165
Vonhaus, Louisa. 12 W 28th....A Vonhaus. Tailor Fixtures. 500
Weiler, E G. 488 6th av....A Schwaab & Son Barber Fixtures. 300
Willis, H....Kerber & Jennings. Brougham. (R) 900
Wissmach, Paul, and U S Bonded Warehouse. 102 E 12th....L Heidt. Stores, Office Fixtures, &c. 6,000
Wilson, Charles. Bowery and 5th st....J & J Dippel. Wagon. 253
Waite, W A. 1377 Vanderbilt av. .."J C Watson Co." Horses, Trucks, &c. 750
Whelan, J F. 164 Monroe....J Cunningham Son & Co. Coach. 200
Whilldin, E P. 382 3d av....E E Cox. Store Fixtures. 150

BILLS OF SALE.

Armster, Bertha. 152 Allen....B Krause. Grocery Fixtures. 500
Brodsky, Solomon. 7 Baxter... S Jacobs. Clothing, Stock, &c. 5,302
Bocker, Annie. 1291 1st av....b Cohn. Grocery Fixtures. 500
Burmeister, C H. 2358 1st av....Muller Bros. Grocery Fixtures. 2,150
Bergman, Louis. 1867 Lexington av....F Soosen. Grocery Fixtures. 500
Celio, K and V. 319 and 321 E 115th....C Arona. Saloon and Butcher Fixtures. 650
Dieckman, J H. 167 E 121st....Henrietta Dieckman. Undertaker Fixtures. 1,000
Ennis, J. 741 2d av... Ellen Fagan....Butcher Fixtures. 200
Ehler, Henry. 2358 1st av....Muller Bros. Grocery Fixtures. 1
Grabedunkel, E F. 20 11th av....H Heilshorn. Saloon Fixtures. 5,700
Grossberg, John. 148 Ridge....A Pentzman. Grocery Fixtures. 90
Goodrich, C E. 498 8th av....A Fitzpatrick. Hardware Store. 8,000
Gottschalk, A. 113 Av A....Fannie Gottschalk. Dry Goods. 2,500
Heyer, W. 2358 1st av....H Ehler. Grocery Fixtures. 1
Jack, Lizzie. 823 Amsterdam av....J Backer. Bakery Fixtures. 300
Jackman, John. 513 W 55th....M Jackman. Horses, Trucks, &c. 1,000
Kirk, Edward. 351 E 32d....Sarah Kirk. Grocery Fixtures. 183
Levine, Morris. 201 Delancey....E Cohn. Cigar Fixtures. 375
Levin, W....Ellen Levin. ¼ Interest in Patent. 2,000
McEathron, Mary A....W A Waite. Horses, Trucks, &c. 1
Roessler, Frank... J Roessler. Stock and Book Accounts. 687
Sexton, John. 1615 Broadway....P Sexton. Horses, Trucks, &c. 100
Vogel, Henry. 883 Park av....Clorinda Van Clief. Saloon Fixtures. 2,500
Wilson & Richdale. 89 Murray....J P Richdale. Furniture. 600
Waite, W A ..M A McEathron. Horses, Trucks, &c. 1
Zuckerman & Blumenfeld and "Assigne" Bergmann....P J Grinberg. Goods, Fixtures, &c. 1,728

ASSIGNMENT OF CHATTEL MORTGAGES.

Glackner, John to J Kress B Co. (Mort given by B Boyle, May 1, 1891.) 652
Hildebrandt, Gertrude to Haaren & Meinken. (J Schuler. Nov 29, 1889.) 1,500
Hoag, Emma F to M Stifter. (Kate Hoag, Oct. 29, 1891.) 1,600
Krieger, M and R to S Ashner. (S Fraenke, Aug 17, 1891.) 175
Scotch Presbyterian Church to A Steele. (D S Wilson, Feb 3, 1891.) 300
Weisz, C E to F Baar. (S Simon, Oct 30, 1890.) 200

GENERAL ASSIGNMENT.

Hennion & Vanderker to J T Scott & Co. Watches, Pawn Tickets, &c. 1

KINGS COUNTY.

NOVEMBER 19 TO 25.—INCLUSIVE.

SALOON AND RESTAURANT FIXTURES.

Berlin, W. 100 Cooper ...Williamsburgh B Co (Lim.) $300
Bess, A. 295 Floyd....Claus Lipsius B Co. 600
Buckheit, A. 945 Grand ...J Eppig. (R) 600
Borchert, F. 825 Myrtle av... W Ulmer. 500
Clark, J. B. 1300 3d av....M Seitz. 589?
Cole, L B. 48 Flushing av....M Seitz. 3,500
Duncan, P. 735 Myrtle av ...Danenberg & C. 736
Dooley, T. 136 Sands ...J Carr. 2,000
Doyle, P. 248 5th av....Underhill, Jackson & Co. 300
Egan, T and W Keough. 500 Smith....Danenberg & C. (R) 350
Farro, V. 30 Maspeth av....Budweiser B Co. 450
Goetz, M. 531 Graham av....Weiz & Z. (R) 1,200
Goodman, P. 178 Greenpoint av....Beadleston & W. (R) 4,000
Hadden, E G. 358 Bainbridge....H Vogel. 150
Hadden, E G. Ralph av and Bainbridge st.... Standard Pump Mfg Co. Reer Pump, &c. 181
Harrison, Ann. 8 Utica av....Budweiser B Co. 1,200
Harrison, Ann. 1800 Atlantic av....Budweiser B Co. 1,400
Haubert, W J. 33 Rock....L Eppig. 725
Hertrich, J. 804 Broadway....J Doelger's Sons. 673
Hilpert, J G. 141 Montrose av....Fort Hamilton Brewing Co. 550
Hoffmann, H. 23 Fulton....J Moeller. Restaurant. 250
Hinchman, E R. 641 Wythe av ...A E Townsend Oyster Saloon. 130
Janke, A. 28 Thornton ...Burger & H B Co. 400
Johrsdrerfer, C. 145 Throop av....L Eppig. 1,100
Karkilla, P. 138 Cook....E Ochs. 1,000
Keller, L. 46 Graham av....Burger & H B Co. (R) 300
Kiesel, J. 225 Franklin....F Krombholz. 3,000
Same. 146 Franklin....same. 1,500
Klatthaar, Maria A. 1438 Myrtle av....G Grauer. 1,065
Krebs, G. 394 South 3d....Burger & H B Co. (R) 400
Krieg, J A. 18 Montrose av....J Eppig. (R) 550
Leilig, J. 82 Throop av... Leibinger & O B Co. 530
Lake, A. 472 6th av....S Liebmann's Sons B Co. 1,200
Leibbacher, G. 812 Grand. .Weiz & Z. 700
McCarthy, P. 595 Kent av....S Liebmann's Sons B Co. 1,200
Michel, C. 81 Harrison . .Wagner & S. Pool Table. 150
Moller, W. 7 Cook....W Ulmer. (R) 600
Miller, G W. 222 Myrtle av ...W C Scheuing. Bar and Bar Fixtures, Ice House, &c 753
O'Brien, J H. 915 De Kalb av....S Liebmann's Sons B Co. 1,500
Orchard, Jennie. 746 3d av....J Klein. Oyster Saloon. (R) 300
Pfleiderer, Johanna. 290 Powers....Weiz & Z. 400
Pitz, G. 1067 Grand....Weiz & Z. 1,800
Rourke, T. 770 3d av....W Craft. 240
Rafferty, M. 1073 3d av....M Seitz. 600
Reilly, J. 479 Humboldt....E Ochs. 200
Rebenklan, R H & Co. 380 De Kalb av ... Beadleston & W. Ice Box. 100
Schoor, H. 420 Graham av....Eva Bechtel, extrx George Bechtel. 2,500
Schoeller, J. 273 Sumner av....M Seitz. 400
Spen, C J. 68 Kent av....P Weidmann. 350
Stolting, A. 879 Broadway....W Ulmer. (R) 1,500
Taylor, E. 51 Wolcott....S Liebmann's Sons B Co. 300
Tully, T. 1065 Fulton....W Ulmer. 1,000
Weber, W H. 690 5th av....Claus Lipsius B Co. 550
Wohlfarth, Christine. 179 Richards .... Fort Hamilton B Co. 450
Wright, J. 140 Harrison av....Burger & H B Co. 650
White, J C. 276 Van Brunt....G Ringler & Co. 479

HOUSEHOLD FURNITURE.

Anderson, Mary L. 1116 Putnam av....A Schulz. 240
Ball, Mary A. 467 Adelphi....Brooklyn F Co. 147
Bell, H K. 547 and 541 Henry....S A Firth. 1,800
Denson, G S. 1338 Gates av....L Z Murray. 207
Bryant, Lucie. 114 Gates av....M M Webster. 150
Brown, Jane. 389 Herkimer....M M Webster. 100
Brown, R T and Julia M. 46 Tompkins pl... Mary L Francis. Piano. 250
Coates, M D. 237 9th....Fennell & P. 299
Cawl, R O. 58 Clifton pl....L Z Murray. 149
Clark, Maggie. 942 Myrtle av....C T Kendrick & Co. 172
Cooney, P. 213 13th....M M Webster. 100
Day, Margt. 318 Columbia....J Moriarty. 150
Dodge, J E. 1257 De Kalb av... Mullins & Sons. 189
Durbem, Mrs F F. 2d av and 54th st....M Nason. 255
Dunn, Susie. 269 Bedford av ...A Schulz. 246
Fitzpatrick, Maggie. 21 Filmore pl....A Schulz. 194
Folsom, Mrs M. 564 Monroe....Brooklyn F Co. 180
Flanagan, J P. 287 5th av....Financial and Credit Co. 100
Gasson, A. 99 Monitor....C T Kendrick & Co. 134
Hartman, C. 63 South 5th....J Moriarty. 121
Hawkes, W A. 173 Front....Mullins' Sons. 173
Daynes, Abbie C. 921 Greene av....L Z Murray. 256
Heckler, Mrs M B. 561 Monroe....Brooklyn F Co. 295
Heneman, Sarah. 858 Lafayette av....L Z Murray. 161
Jacob, A. 199 Jackson....C T Kendrick & Co. 102
Kaufmann, G G. 544 Marcy av....C T Kendrick & Co. 335
Kune, F G. 786A Union....J Gregg. 559
Lawrence, Louise H. 254 W 15th st, New York. D O'Farrell & Co. 123
Moon, J S and Isabelle T. 487 State....E C Hinsdale. 160
Madden, T A. 136 Halsey....A H King & Co. (R) 408
McLaney, L J. 685 Hancock....L Z Murray. 219
Mersert, Jeannette L. 159 Bushwick av....A Schulz. 150
Monroe, Dora. 181 Gold ..L Z Murray. 418
Macrery, Mrs M E. 96 State....O Wissner. Piano. 235
Martin, Mrs W. 78th st, Bay Ridge... Brooklyn F Co. 226
Monroe, S L. 199 7th av....Brooklyn F Co. 142
Murray, A L. 188 Sumner av....M M Webster. 100
Nilsson, F B 258-262 6th av....L Baumann. 224
Palmer, S R. 37 Lafayette av....L Z Murray. 485
Pool, J F. 50 Smith....L Z Murray. 32
Provoost, Mrs J S. 12 Macon....J McEnery & Co. 274
Pfister, A. 108 Throop av.. J C Hegemann. 200
Robinson, Mary 127 Stockton....L Z Murray. 121
Tobler, J. Bushwick av, cor Jefferson st....F J Brechtel. 229
Walker, I D. 61 Henry....F R Caulkins. 160
Wolff, Mens L. 79 Cooper .. Brooklyn F Co. 151

MISCELLANEOUS.

American Diamond Rock Boring Co. 41 Van Brunt ...F Semken. Drills, &c. 2,500
Bernhard, V....G Dessecker. Coach. (R) 300
Blauvelt, W A. 193 St Marks av....H Mahnken. Wagons, &c. 1,000
Brandecke, F. 335 Adams....Van Allens & B. Press. 200
Davis, W W. 6 and 8 Front ...M Erlanger. Presses, &c. (R) 4,250
Dewald, C. 987 Flushing av .... J Dewald. Butcher Fixtures. 300
Dlauhy & Schmitt. 1591 Bushwick av....Puffer & Son Mfg Co. Soda Apparatus. (R) 445
Eckenroth, F & Son . S A Woods Machine Co. Planer, &c. (R) 300
Forbes, A. 451 Manhattan av... Seeman Bros. Grocery Fixtures. 1,200
Grieco, A. 112 Lexington av....A Schwaab. Barber Fixtures. 129
Hamilton, W H. 1098 Bedford av... W P Mathews. Bakery Fixtures. 500
Hartmann, H K. 132 Forrest ...Marie Schneider. Drug Fixtures. 2,400
Hoffman, M. 106 5th av....W C Blades. Bakery, Contract to Sell. 1,800
Holden, H. 82 Raymond....A M Stein & Co. Horses. 2,000
Bolufcener, I J....P Barrett. Wagon. 179
Bahn, W. 52 Ten Eyck....N Y & Brooklyn Casket Co. Undertaker Fixtures. 781
Ives, E M ...A Man. Watch and Chain. 175
Johnson, P J & Co. 46 Beekman st, New York ....J Royle & Sons. Engraver's Lathe. &c. (s) 125
Kane, J A. 222 5th av....J W Tufts. Soda Fountain. 900
Kuhl, L P. 819 Broadway... E J Merriam. Motor, Lathe, &c. 250
Karge, P. 293 Ralph av....Meyer & Lange. Grocery Fixtures. 100
Lambert, Mary E. 25 Quincy....W H Lambert. Milk Business, Horses, &c. 500
La Senire Art Co. 886 Leonard....P Broden. Lathes, Engines, &c. 5,600
Lewis, L F. 30 Clifton pl ...Sarah A Casanova. Library Fixtures, &c. 300
Lightell, M A. Patchen av, cor Monroe st....W F Simmons. Milk Business. 1,000
Lombardo, F. 47 Main ...P Porzia. Barber Fixtures. 100
Morrissey, J. 735 Myrtle av... J Wurzler. Fixtures. (R) 700
Newmark, S. 184 Boerum....M Gewirtsmann. Sewing Machines, &c. 250
Osborne, W. 48 5th av....Wallace & K. Fish Business. 313
Pierson, E F. 1422 Fulton.. .W B Pierson. Drug Fixtures. 700
Fouch, A B. 247 Willoughby....Mosler Safe Co. Safe. 180
Reynolds, D M. 46 Troy av....B Fowler. Horses. 700
Rooney, J. 646 Pacific....N Langler. Tools, &c. 27
Schwenker, F A. 52 Main....Roberts & Collin. Bakery Fixtures. (R) 500
Schablowsky, A....Barrett & B. Grocery Fixtures. 214

Schwarz, H. 67 Grand....F Koehler. Knitting Machines. 1,500
Stanwood Mfg Co....E W Bliss & Co (Lim.) Press. 1,385
Taylor, R H 588 President....Eliza Taylor. Milk Business. 1,200
Thissen, J. 184 North 8th....Cope & Co. Machinery. 1,500

BILLS OF SALE.

Bayer, W. 109 Hamburg av....M Loesch. Butcher Fixtures. 800
Bluemke, Caroline. 298 Johnson av...R Bluemke, Jr. House Mover's Tools, &c., All Title. 200
Byk, Poline. 501 Hancock....Francis Byk. Furniture. nom
Dunn, F A. 136 Lawrence....H C Wilson. Furniture. 430
Durham, F F....Hart & Bro. Horses, Wagons. nom
Eckel, F & Co. 288 Eckford....E Nemann. Delicatessen Business. 500
Fischbeck, C L. 106 Reid av....Fischbeck & Glitjen. Grocery Fixtures. 2,900
Kohn, I....H Levine. Oil Business. All title. 50
Lambert, Mary E. 168 Gates av....Annie M Lambert. Piano and Sewing Machine. nom
Loesch, W. 109 Hamburg av ...W Bayer. Butcher Fixtures. 800
Moeller, J. 23 Fulton ...H Hoffmann. Restaurant Fixtures. 950
Pickford, H....Harriet Pickford. Furniture. nom
Porzia, P. 47 Main ...F Lombardo. Barber Fixtures. 150
Ross, D C. 237 Tompkins av....F L Tapscott. Building Material, Tools, &c. 100
Ruoff, M. 59 Stockton .... W Helmerick. Butcher Fixtures. 105
Schwarz, H. 67 Grand .. J Klent. Knitting Machines. 1,500
Spreen, L. 209 Lewis av .... Wm Spreen. Butcher Fixtures. 300

NEW JERSEY.

ESSEX COUNTY.

NOTE.—The arrangement of the Conveyances, Mortgages and Judgments in these lists is as follows: the first name in the Conveyances is the Grantor; in Mortgages, the Mortgagor; in Judgments, the Judgment debtor.

CONVEYANCES.

Agmar, E B—I Irwin, East Orange............ $1
Alling, Horace—E M Atchason, 3d st 1,500
Armstrong, William—J Parker, Monmouth st.. 1,000
Ball, Isaiah—F Chandler, East Orange.......... —
Benjamin, M A—M O Parish, 2d av.......... 2,100
Bocher, W L R et al—S C Ball, Kinney st 1
Booth, Edward—M A Boylan, North 13th st..... 748
Same——E Carlin, North 13th st............... 500
Bornemann, George—P Kurtz, Clinton........... 410
Breakenridge, J H et al—F Callen, Jr, Clinton.. 250
Brisn, David—C H Roll, Milburn.............. 4,500
Brumley, J D—The Home for the Aged of the Little Sisters of the Poor, South 8th st....... 900
Burke, John—H Berg, West Orange............. 1,850
Burnet, Timothy—T Cooper, Clinton 100
Cadmus, S V C—F L Salmon, Clinton av 1
Ciulotti, Gustav—S I Corby, Montclair 6,500
Condit, E M—D Banister, West Orange 1,000
Conger, Theodore—F W Hilbig, e s Roseville av 80 s M & E R R av 60x100..................... 8,750
Connolly, T W—H McEnery, Belleville 800
Cook, William—P Bessman, e s Prince st 149 s Court st 40x100.............................. 10,600
Coolbaugh, F W—M A Marsh, East Orange..... 2,000
Corb, John—R Weatherly, Franklin............ 5
Cravens, F L—The Roseland Railway Co, Caldwell.. 1
Culberson, A M—H M Culberson, East Orange . 1
Culberson, N M—A M Culberson, East Orange.. 1
Same——K C Kirwan, East Orange............ 1
Dain, Frederick—C Lutz, w s Church st adj S A Congars land 25x99.......................... 4,000
Davis, C D—S Holmes, Bloomfield............ 850
Dodd, S H—J Finan, Bloomfield.............. 4,440
Drexel Improvement Co—S C G Watkins, Montclair.. 205
Dunn, Elizabeth—Wm H Emerson, Boyden st... 1
Emmerson, W H, Jr—E Dunn, Boyden st....... 1
Feich, C A—M Engelleiter et al, South Prospect st... 2,500
Same——L Helm, s w cor Pacific and Garden sts 26x52.................................... 3,000
Forest Hill Assoc—G B Crater, De Graw av..... 700
Freeman, Grace—L Dowkins, Bloomfield........ 2,500
Geckle, Margaretha—C Wilfruth, Littleton av... 1
German, Scott—M C Peto, McKenzie st.......... 1
Gerbert, Bonifatzius—F E Danzlisen, South 9th st... 1
Gillispie, David—C A Maius, e s Summer av 112 n 4th av 25x100............................. 3,600
Goldstein, Max—I Rosen, Charlton st.......... 1
Greacen, Walter—A G Conant, East Orange.... 1
Hauffer, G F—C A Koelsch, North 5th st.... 700
Hauley, Patrick—J Stamviski, Bloomfield...... 1,150
Harthopf, C F—J Denninger, Littleton av....... 2,100
Hice, E W—J M Smith, Mt Prospect st......... 1
Inness, George, Jr—The Children's Home Assoc of Montclair, N J, Montclair................ 1
Juale, Michael—M Tulley, Orange.............. 600
Lister, J C—H Dickson, Broad st.............. 2,500
Same——J Curran, s e cor Summer av and Crane st 57x100............................ 3,400
Same——T Smith, s e cor Clay and Spring sts 81x82x52x25x85........................ 15,900
Maltwood, William—F M Cantine, Orange...... 1
McGuire, Theresa—C A Feich, s e cor Broome st and South Orange av 25x100. 6,000
Miller, H C—H Werpupp, South 17th st......... 330
Miller, M E—M Miller, Nelson pl............... 1
Mitchell, A P—J A Mornit, East Orange 840
Morton, L P et al trustees—P Leonard, Belleville av.. 2,500
Mayers, J T et al—M J Way, e s Atlantic st 104 n Lombardy st 20x65........................ 4,000
Neigel, Magdalena—H E Bedford, e s Beacon st 94 n Springfield av 24x96................. 5,500
Newell, W C B—E J Gillen, s s Commerce st 70 e Lawrence st 21x90......................... 5,250
O'Brien, T J—H Hinrichs, South Orange 1
O'Rourke, John—J L Hartford, West Orange... 1
People's Mutual Benefit B and L Assoc—C Winckelhoffer, Chester av.................. 300
Paefferle, J F—L Fox, 1st tract n s Bank st cor E J Thompson 20x110, 2d tract n s Bank st 20x110, 3d tract adj Bank st 20x110......... 24,000
Peto, Joseph—S German, McKenzie st 1
Prieth, L J—A Devine, Clinton.................. 100
Range, C J—J F Fort, East Orange 50
Redden, Jane—J Connolly, Wakeman av........ 735
Righter, W S—W A Righter, Garrison st........ 1
Roeland, J M—J Logel, Clinton................ 825
Rudden, Thomas—G Anderson, South 7th st.... 1
Salmon, F L—E J Cadmus, Clinton av.......... 1
Satterthwaite, J F—J A Frobose, Franklin..... 900
Schaubacher, J G—M M Eisele, w s Quitman st 280 n Spruce st 38x104................... 5,900
Schickhaus, Edward—G W Wiedenmayer, Hamburgh pl.. 1
Shearer, W H—M Van Keuren, South Orange... 400
Smith, J M—E Smith, e s Mt Prospect av 598 s Bloomfield av 25x100....................... 4,000
Spencer, A G—N R Fletcher, Montclair........ 700
Spinning, Annie—Elizth Teusch, s s Centre st 45 x23x61x45x22.............................. 7,000
Straub, Henry—Essex and Hudson Land Imp Co, St Charles st.............................. 500
The Newark Fire Ins Co—M W Schenk, Delancey st....................................... 900
The Sherman Av Baptist Church—J H Wood, Elizabeth av................................. 1,600
Tilton, J L—A G Barron, Franklin............. 2,800
Trotter, T V A—Roseland Railway Co, Caldwell. 1
Van Gieson, H O—C Stringer, Montclair....... 250
Van Order, J I—The Roseland Railway Co, Caldwell.. 1
Viscidi, Filippo—R Orlando, s s Drift 205 w Factory st 28x150........................... 5,400
Same——G Serratelli, Drift st............... 600
Wallace, J P—E N Schrand, Belleville. 150
Same——T Montgomery, Belleville........... 100
Same——H Lynch, Belleville 100
Warman, T E—N L Tuch, rear Lombardy pl.... 1
Weatherby, Harry et al—G H Patston, Franklin.. 500
Weber, Nicholas—C A Schweers, Clinton........ 1,700
White, Ann—J F Freeman, East Orange........ 1,100
Weatherby, Harry et al—C B Ford, Franklin... 275
Wiedenmayer, M M—E Schickhaus, Stockton st 1
Wilkinson, Geo recvr—A S Hewitt, Belleville.... 7,500
Williams, H R—P K Osborn, n s Orange st 25 w Thompson st.................................. 3,500
Yauch, Engelbert—F Schreck, Bremen st 1
Young, David—R M Shanley, Rose st.......... 750
Young, T E—A A Wolff, Orange............... 4,000

MORTGAGES.

Amodio, Francesco—W S Brown, South Orange av.. 500
Anderson, Mary—W C Bunn, Walnut st....... 1,000
Anderson, W W—R S Francisco, Caldwell..... 550
Arnold, Christoph—G Krueger, Rutgers st...... 559
Arnold, Christian—G Krueger, Rutgers st...... 559
Aspden, M A—D Lawrence, North 7th st........ 400
Banister, De Witt—E M Condit, West Orange... 500
Barnes, F H—W A Smith et al, South 7th st 70
Barron, A Y—Franklin B and L Assoc, Franklin 2,500
Beach, E W—P Pierson, Caldwell.............. 400
Beck, Peter—F Berg, East Orange 500
Same——J S Chance, East Orange.......... 500
Berg, Henry—J Burke, West Orange.............. 850
Berger, Rachel—J Schloss, Prince st.......... 2,100
Bessman, Pinkus—W Cook, Prince st.......... 7,000
Blackwell, A M—A M Woodruff, South 19th st.. 240
Brady, M E—M S Richards, Adams st.......... 2,100
Brown, C E—The Newark B and L Assoc, Bleecker st...................................... 300
Browe, T L—J Spear, Belleville.............. 900
Bruchner, Joseph—Peoples' B and L Assoc, Mechanic st..................................... 400
Cadden, James—G F Reeve, Bleecker st.... .. 500
Cifrodello, Sabbato—Security B and L Assoc, North 3d st 2,500
Cody, David—Newark B and L Assoc, East Kinney st 600
Colombo, Philip—S Froelich, Orange.... 671
Cook, G H—American Ins Co, East Orange..... 300
Delaney, George—Newark Orphan Asylum Assoc, High st.................................. 8,000
Eisele, M M—A M Field, Quitman st.......... 3,000
Farrington, G E—M Harrison, Caldwell......... 700
Finan, John—S H Dodd, Bloomfield........... 900
Same —T P Lindsley, East Orange......... 1,000
Finger, F L—R Coyne, East Orange........... 1,000
Fischer, Catharine—J A Hay, Clinton.......... 100
Fletcher, Israilla—M F Chase, Caldwell 400
Fletcher, N R—M F Chase, Montclair 1,000
Fleming, W A—Orange Memorial Hospital, West Orange....................................... 3,000
Fox, Leopold—J F Pfefferle, Bank st.... 15,000
Galente, Vito—Security B and L Assoc, Van Buren st.................................... 1,600
Gardner, A K—Mutual Life Ins Co, Bloomfield.. 2,500
Gillen, E J—Mutual B and L Assoc, Commerce st... 4,500
Gyzewski, Marion—Essex Co B and L Assoc, Bloomfield................................... 600
Hadley, W C—Roseville B and L Assoc, North 11th st...................................... 2,800
Hagen, John—J Hughes, Belleville............. 600
Hartig, Emanuel—Fidelity Title and Deposit Co, Baldwin st.................................... 1,900
Hasselman, F C—The Orange Memorial Hospital, Orange .... —
Hawes, G R—J J Burtan, Orange.............. 400
Helen, Leonard—Tenth Ward B and L Assoc, Pacific st. 2,500
Hinrichs, H J—The Security B and L Assoc, Bergen st 2,100
Holmes, Sarah—The Essex Co B and L Assoc, Bloomfield.................................... 3,000
Huber, Jacob—The Newark German B and L Assoc, Bruce st............................... 200
Hutman, Susan—M F G Hutman, East Linney st... 300
Jansen, Otto—The Standard B and L Assoc, South Orange av............................... 1,900
Kingsland, J H—The Franklin B and L Assoc, Bloomfield................................... 1,800
King, K B—M S Munn, East Orange 4,500
Mallia, John—J W Condit, Orange............. 1,400
Marley, H C—S A Durning, South 7th st....... 1,000
Same——J H H Breintnall et al trustees—South 7th st 7,300
Marsh, M A—G W Blackwell, East Orange...... 4,000
McCabe, John—L F Crowell, South 9th st....... 1,300
McKirgan, A M—W C Garrison, Garside st 1,600
McNally, Ellen—Rose Murphy, Orange.......... 1,500
Metzger, Chas, Jr—Reliable B and L Assoc, Houston st.................................... 1,500
Milford, Oscar—Firemen's Ins Co, Barclay st.... 5,500
Miller, Jacob—Security Savings Bank, Orange.. 100
Moon, David—M M Walsh, Summer av..... 2,450
Newman, Hugh—E Wertlaup, adj Morris Canal. 400
Orlando, Rosaria—First Italian B and L Assoc, Drift st.. 4,400
Oschwald, Gertrude—The German Savings Bank, Walnut st.................................. 5,000
Parker, John—W Armstrong, Monmouth st.,... 500
Same——same, Monmouth st.................. 500
Reinhard, Anna—C A Feich, 18th av............ 100
Richardson, W S—Howard B and L Assoc, South 10th st 5,000
Robinson, F A—G W Blackwell, East Orange... 1,750
Rob, Robert—Theodore Coe et al, South 7th st.. 500
Schenk, M W—Newark Fire Ins Co, Delancey st. 600
Schwarz, E J—G A Ortmann, Columbia st.... . 300
Schweickert, Barbara—C Mans, South 7th st.... 500
Serratilli, Guisseppe—F Viscidi, Drift st......... 400
Sisum, W H B—J E Terhune, Belleville......... 18,000
Smith, Edwin—M Strauss trustee, Mt Prospect av... 2,500
Solomon, Cecelia—The Newark B and L Assoc, Springfield av............................... 5,000
Spurr, I J—Protestant Foster Home Soc, Mt Pleasant av................................... 8,000
Staberoth, Frederick—J W Hatt, South Orange. 600
Sianwiski, John—Essex Co B and L Assoc, Bloomfield 900
Steenson, Isaac—Orange Valley B and L Assoc, Bedford st.................................... 1,200
Taylor, S W—Orange Memorial Hospital, East Orange.. 4,000
Tenlon, F W—H A Headley, Milburn 300
Teusb, Elizabeth—A E Spinning, Centre st...... 5,000
Tompkins, S A—E C Williams, West Orange.... 1,500
Wagner, Edward—Firemen's Ins Co, 15th st.... 4,000
Way, M J—R H Van Cleaf, Atlantic st........... 600
Whitney, Eliza—W G Ward trustee, East Orange. 6,000
Wolff, A A—T E Young, Orange.. 2,900
Wood, J H—P Wood, Elizabeth av............. 800

CHATTEL MORTGAGES.

Ames, Catherine—W J Knight, furniture....... 510
Archer, S B—C Bierman, furniture............. 44
Bader, Gottleb—G Blum, horse and wagons..... 110
Benjamin, H—I Stern, furniture............... 50
Cronin, E M—Hill's Union Brewery Co (Lim), saloon... 498
Doolittle, J E—F W Truman, lumber........ ...10,000
Dylla, Gustav—W Schmitt, horses and wagons.. 175
Edwards, William—C Feigenspan, saloon....... 450
FitzGerald, J C—A J Simpson, furniture........ 406
Frost, H—F Lisiewski, saloon....... 1,900
Greenhalgh, J C—National Cash Reg Co, register.. 175
Hill, Elmer—C Bierman, furniture.... 110
Holzwarth, Fred—G Blum, wagon.... 170
Hummel, M D—P H Hanley, furniture......... 65
Jansen, Otto—J Reiber, saloon.. 1,000
Keating, Thomas—C Feigenspan, saloon........ 220
Kerpel, David—L Q White, Jr, stock shoes...... 323
Kruger, Nathan et al—Essex County Brewing Co, saloon.. 1,500
Lachner, Albert—Hill's Union Brewing Co, saloon.. 400
Maltiene, Frank—Hill's Union Brewing Co, saloon.. 450
McCloud, J P—C Bierman, piano............... 100
Menagh, H P—C Bierman, furniture.... 130
Moore, S S—A H Van Horn, furniture........... 240
Orleansky, Charles—M Star, machinery 300
Riedee, Robert—F J Kasner, saloon.... 500
Sandford, F E—J Ketcham, furniture 86
Scheper, Clemens—C Bierman, furniture........ 169
Silverthorn, E A—C Bierman, furniture......... 88
Slate, Eli—E Walker, machinery............. ... 150
Smith, A A—I M Williams, horses 205
Strack, Philip—C Bierman, furniture........... 100
Vander Roest, Henry—W Vander Roest, horses and carriages...... 1,000

JUDGMENTS.

Heath, Charles et al—G W Robinson.... 475
Stone, Alexander—H Seelig et al............... 136
Sherman, L I—C W Clayton.................... 999

HUDSON COUNTY.

CONVEYANCES.

Adams, William—Carrie R Smith............... $440
Ashcroft, H E—E F Randolph, Kearney......... 10
Benz, Elizabeth—J Benz........other consid and nom
Bettcher, L F—J Sharrock..................... 600
Birney, Josephine Y—R Lennox, Harrison... .. 500
Bounell, Alexander by exrs—S H Low 201
Bramhall, Nettie J—T McK Taylor. 350
Broughton, Catharine—J A Reed............... 1,550
Brown, E G by exrs—G W Rogers .... nom
Brown, T C—A McKay......................... 2,500
Buchanan, Florence S—C Treptow, Bayonne.... 400
Same——H Boirmann, Bayonne............ 400
Close, Ellen M—W Sloat, Bayonne 350
De Groff, Florida W—J G Gerber, Weehawken.. 50,000
Devoe, E M—Sarah Hall, Kearney.............. nom
Donovan, Peter—J J Reilly, Bayonne....... ... 2,100
Durken, Christina R—B Pesani................. nom
Durken, E J by admrs—B Pesani.... 965
Ehrhardt, Geo and C C F by masters—H W Fischer, West Hoboken.................... 1,005
Elandrine, Mary by sheriff—Ezra J Rudderow.. 500
Farrell, Margaret—Rosina Gilligan, West Hoboken... 1,000
Feytel, Adele—Eugenia Oesmann, West Hoboken.......................exch and nom
Fisher, R P—J L O'Brien, Bayonne.. ..exch and nom
Foye, A J C—Ida Prasser.... 1,000
Fuller, D B—The Swedish Evangelical Lutheran Church of Gustavus Vasa of Arlington, &c, Kearney.. 500
Goggens, Mary—W Disch, Hoboken.......... .. 2,000
Goston, Della—F Whelhan..................... 1,000
Hoboken Land and Improvement Co—A Burley, Weehawken............................... 1,000
Same——Catharine Murray, Weehawken..... 1,500
Same——R W Dewey, Hoboken.............. 10
Hogan, Mary and Rosanna Hines by master—M McDermott................................. 3,000
Kern, W F—Catharine Broughton............ .. 120
Killen, Pat—Margaret Killen................... 800
Lee, Maria—Anna Goeger, Union 950
Lennon, Edward—T P Lennon, North Bergen... 2,500
Same——same, North Bergen............... 500
Same——W G Robinson, North Bergen.... ... 800
Mainzer, William—Julia Broderick, Hoboken... 7,500
Maxwell, S R—C Hoyt, Hoboken.......... .. nom
McGonigil, Sarah—C Beck, Bayonne............ 4,500
Mershon, Carrie J V C—Mary Forrest, Kearney. 2,000
Mockridge, A W—H S Parmalie........... .. 4,500
Morgan, Agnes E by special master—D W Diamond... 1,400
Mount, S C—J H Van Buskirk, Bayonne,........ 150
Newbold, H A—Rebecca L Van Buskirk, Bayonne.. 250
Newkirk, Jane D—Margaretha Schunk... 2,500
Newkirk, Jacob—M Kuntz 450
Oesman, Eugenia—Adele Feytel, West Hoboken ....mutual partition and nom
Oesuer, August—G Stoehr, Guttenberg... 375

Pope, T P and W C by master—J Usher, Union	290
Rademann, Peter—W Van Lith	3,900
Rauschnabel, P M—H F Duhart	250
Reichenbach, John—J Harfinger, Guttenberg	450
Reilly, Geo—D J Nixon	nom
Reilly, J J—Catharine Donovan, Bayonne	3,000
Robinson, Mary C—W C Stuart, Bayonne	nom
Rub, C F—F Webbing, Union	1,696
Schmitt, Elizabeth by sheriff—C F Rub, Union	1,004
Seymour, Harriet A—T C Brown	nom
Sherwood, Charlotte—J G Gerber, Weehawken. other consid and	nom
Smith, T M—Emma A Rackett	3,500
Steele, L A—D Steele	nom
Sullivan, Owen—Mary A Noonan	nom
Symes, J H—A Meblig, Union	600
Symes, J H—J P Kaclen, Union	300
The Central N J Land and Impt Co—A L McDermott, J City and elsewhere	22,000
The Central N J Land and Impt Co—Julia Burke, Bayonne	450
The Mayor and Aldermen of Jersey City—U Allen	2,900
Van Horne, Cornelius—E Cobert	500
Vecken, Henry, by the Inhabitants of Township of North Bergen—E Lennon, North Bergen.	4
Walker, Herman—Christiana Lacroix, Guttenberg	750
Warnken, Frederick—C T Polhemus, North Bergen	10
Warnken, Henry—Sophia Warnken, North Bergen	nom
Webbing, Adaline by sheriff—C Frub, Union	1,000
Whitney, J H—O H Lohsen	2,750
Whittlock, Samuel—Ida E Kennard	nom
Winchester, A S—J Morris, Kearney	400
Winchester, E C—same, Kearney	400

MORTGAGES.

Allen, Wemor—North Hudson Co B and L Assoc, Issue B, installs	200
Allen, William—North Hudson Co B and L Assoc, Issue B, installs	2,800
Beier, Florian—M W Bode, Union, 1 year	300
Berg, Daniel—Catharine Von der Leith, Hoboken, 3 years	2,500
Black, Daniel—Lafayette M B and L Assoc, installs	800
Brennan, Ann—T Hinds, 3 years	8,000
Burley, Alpheus—D Bennes, Weekawken, 5 years	9,000
Corell, H R—W Hackett, 2 years	1,800
Damm, Henry—Hoboken Bank for Savings, Hoboken, 2 years	1,000
Darmer, Frederick—J H Gansburgen, 5 years	800
Diamond, D W—The Chancellor of the State of New Jersey, Bayonne, 3 years	600
Dieck, H W E—C Bishoff, West Hoboken, 3 years	1,500
Forrest, Mary—Carrie E V Mershon, Kearney, 1 year	1,800
Fruman, Ellen—Howard Savings Inst, Kearney, 1 year	6,000
Garrabrant, Jacob—H Richards, Bayonne, 3 yrs	2,000
Gerber, J G—Florida Degroff, Weehawken, installs	35,000
Hand, C M—Delia A Bumsted, 3 years	2,500
Hansen, F C—Lina Wolff, Union, 1 year	2,000
Heitshusen, Fred—R Funger, 3 years	3,000
Hillard, Henry—Trustees of First Presbyterian Church of Mendhause, Harrison, installs	2,200
Hermance, W I—Kearney B and L Assoc, Kearney, installs	1,400
Jennings, Mary A—Mutual Life Ins Co, Bayonne, 1 year	1,500
Killeen, Margaret—Star Mutual B and L Assoc, installs	800
Klein, Peter—P Klein, Union, 5 years	4,000
Kohlmann, F H—C F Ruh, North Bergen, 5 yrs	1,800
Kull, John—Annie M Kilmeade, 5 years	2,000
Lacroix, Christian—Hudson Co Cal B and L Assoc, Guttenberg, installs	1,115
Lohsen, O H—The Security B and L Assoc, installs	3,000
Lyons, Mary J—M Lancton, 1 year	400
Macnab, G R—R A Keasbey, 1 year	141
McAvay, Michael—T Cox, 3 years	2,000
McDermott, A L—The Central N J Land and Imp't Co, 4 years	16,000
McDermott, Michael—J Herbert, 5 years	1,500
McInytre, J S—Trustee of E H Payton	200
McKay, Archibald—The Lincoln B and L Assoc, installs	6,000
Miller, W A—L Linn, 4 years	800
Morris, Cumings Dredging Co—Mary L Leary, 5 years	100,000
Morris, Jno—P S McKenney, Kearney, 2 years	800
Mullone, Michael—H H Farrier. to secure promissory notes.	6,000
Murray, Catharine—The Hudson Trust and Savings Inst, Weehawken, 3 years	5,500
Olmstead, Virginia—Alice F Lewis, 1 year	5,000
Perrin, Ottillie—Marie Bornemann, 3 years	3,000
Pohley, Geo—J Kiefer, Guttenberg, 3 years	1,000
Pollitz, Catharine—F J Kastner, 1 year	600
Rowland, Mary L—Fairmount M B and L Assoc, installs	600
Schmidt, Elizabeth—C M Vreeland, 1 year	400
Schurr, Joseph—L Emmerick, Guttenberg, 1 year	100
The Swedish Evangelical Lutheran Church of Gustavus Vase of Arlington—Kearney B and L Assoc, Kearney, installs	2,000
Thomson, Sarah J—Centreville B and L Assoc, Bayonne, installs	4,000
Tietje, Emil—A Siegfried, 1 year	750
Timoney, Bryan—Martha J Foster, Bayonne, 1 year	500
Trenton, Carl—I Cadmus, Bayonne, 3 years	1,000
Van Lith, William—P Rademann, 3 years	2,000
Same—same, 3 years	1,200
Ward, Eliza—The Provident Inst for Savings, 1 year	5,000
Whelan, Thomas—Columbia B and L Assoc, installs	800
Wilkinson, W F—Mary A Hay, Kearney, 1 year	700
Wittenschein, Jacob—The Provident Inst for Savings, 1 year	3,000
Same—Hannah C Cadmus, 1 year	2,125

CHATTEL MORTGAGES.

Abel, F M, and Valentine Steinmetz, Bayonne—C Feigenspan, saloon fixtures	550
Crowley, Jeremiah—C Birdsall, furniture	180
Cummings, D F—C Birdsall, furniture	180
Duffy, Albertina—C Birdsall, furniture	35
Fagan, Margaret—J Mullins & Co, furniture	146
Finger, William—D Bermes, bottling business, horse, wagon, &c	100
Foley, J H—C Birdsall, furniture	130
Heymann, W B, Kearney—M A Stafford, florist business	1,728
Hobbs, F H—G Hobbs, boot and shoe store	982
Hohnadel, Henry—The W R Wheeler & Davis Co, butcher shop fixtures	100
Johnson, Isabella, Bayonne—C Birdsall, furniture	130
Keele, Annie—C Birdsall, furniture	180
Kreuger, William, Hoboken—L Bauman, furniture	144
Lampert, F J—Bernheimer & Schmidt, saloon	2,000
Lea, C E—Potter, Linsly & Co, crockery and glassware business	975
Leist, Albertine—L Baumann, furniture	74
Links, A F, Weehawken—T N Bowles, barber fixtures	250
Lischke, Joseph, Hoboken—B Reinhardt, oyster saloon fixtures	85
Newmann, A A and Lissetta—Denton & Shaw, horse, wagon, cart, &c	219
Schulz, Emma, Hoboken—L Baumann, furniture	402
Vasel, Theodore, Hoboken—L Vasel, horse, buggy, harness	100
Wagner, Albert, Hoboken—Eva Bechtel, saloon	600
Wiedman, John, Harrison—Carolina Haster, lager beer brewery	600
Wolf, Henry and Mary, Harrison—J S Mohr, barber shop furniture	187
Zeiger, E and R, firm Zeiger Bros—G Dessecker, hearses	950

BILLS OF SALE.

Loesch, C A—Fanny Loesch, coal yard, &c	3,000
Lepore, Giuseppe—Rosario Mueci, barber shop.	40

JUDGMENTS.

Fuller, E F—F J Matthews	880
Steinmann, Matthias—Chas Goodmann's Son	448
The Mayor and Council of the City of Hoboken—S Helfer	2,434

BUILDING MATERIAL MARKET.

BRICKS.—It is hardly expected that any great change can take place on the general market for Common Hards during balance of the year. An unusual cold spell and entire closing of navigation would, of course, make some difference, giving all stock this side of the freeze an advantage, but the weather to produce that result could hardly fail to act as a check to out-door work, and would, in consequence, just so much curtail the consumption, and operators are not inclined to be over hopeful of any special buoyancy for the present. However, it seems safe to assume that the market has at least passed its worse stage, and between now and the time for commencing preparations for next crop may take sufficiently improved form to bring considerable gratification to the selling side. The current week has been broken by a storm at the outset and a holiday later, bringing demand down to rather narrow proportions, but not otherwise altering the conditions on Common Hards, the line of value standing about as before, with quite a showing of steadiness, the general range showing \$4.50@5 50c. per M as to quality. Supplies have throughout been ample, with good average of quality, and shipments are still coming forward. Manufacturers in the "Bay" show no particular haste to make shipments, but from more distant points there is a tendency to push forward the last cargoes, in order to insure them against a shut-off by the ice. Not many Jersey bricks come to hand at the moment, as manufacturers find a better market nearer the point of production. Pales have been less plentiful, the low rates of last week proving successful in working down the accumulation, and although only best lots now exceed \$4 per M the tone is somewhat firmer.

LATH.—Receivers as a rule now come upon 'Change through force of habit, as they rarely have any stock to offer either on spot or to arrive, and with about the same conditions prevailing for timber their occupation is more or less gone. The market, however, is really a good one, as without making a special open demonstration a number of dealers are known to be ready to negotiate the moment there is anything to offer and might possibly be brought to a competing and stimulating position. Out-of-town as well as local custom is represented in the demand. Since our last the few arrivals were readily disposed of with \$2.25 inside, and \$2.30 obtained with apparent sufficient freedom to make it a quotation.

LIME.—About previously current features continue to characterize the market, the dominant tone being more or less nervous. Some of the trade deny this and claim that the selling side is unlikely to surrender any advantage, but competition among receivers is becoming keener, and unless the outlet for arrivals is prompt and effective it may make some difference in the line of cost, especially for the least popular product. For the present no change in quotations is announced, but trade rules slow compared with the amount of stock offering or likely to become available and the tone cannot be called better than barely steady.

LUMBER.—It is getting to be a very small and unimportant market for lumber of all kinds, with general tendency toward further shrinkage. Among the yards there may be found the usual experience of here and there a dealer turning out quite a bunch of stock, but the great majority reporting from quiet down to absolutely dull, and finding nothing to encourage them in the hope for any improvement during the next two months. On market for bulk parcels there is still a little demand for certain special descriptions of stock such as might be expected toward the close of the season, but hardly a grade of stock toward which buyers feel any positive anxiety, and of everything within the line of standard quality there will probably be enough in accumulation to make average proportions. There is little or nothing new regarding the position of exporters, most of whom seem a little dissatisfied with present conditions and general prospects both as regards local and f. o. b. deals.

Eastern Spruce has undergone little or no change in general characteristics. The advantage of the situation is upon the selling side and likely to remain there for balance of this year, through the meagreness of the offerings. Nature is evidently about ready to extend a helping hand by closing the streams and aiding manufacturers in bringing production down to the limit of the steam mills, and as these will run only in executing special orders the supply of random is expected to keep down to the limit of such stock as may happen to be piled where navigation is open. The local demand is moderate and from some of the largest customers entirely suspended, but with the small arrivals they have to take care of receivers can generally manage to skirmish around and find custom ready to take anything of standard quality at full rates. At the moment the impression seems to be that work in the woods this winter will show cautious methods and possibly a comparatively moderate cut.

Piling is being delivered in some cases to a fair extent on contract and also gets an occasional fresh demand, but the business is not evenly distributed and many operators are grumbling. In common with all other kinds of stock, however, it is expected that piling will secure increased attention after the turn of the year and holders are endeavoring to carry with becoming faith.

Hemlock is called steady, and no holder would probably be willing to offer any inducements in the way of cost, but there is nothing of a stimulating character and very little really new demand on this market. From Pennsylvania there are some arrivals in fulfillment of contracts and dealers are bringing forward some 10-inch boards obtained North, most of which are going to round out and complete assortments to commence next season's work upon, as very few of the goods are wanted for immediate consumption.

White Pine has a steady market, and is no doubt past the time when any ordinary chance of a turn in buyers' favor could be expected. It is not the support of active or anxious demand, however, but simply the relief from pressing supplies, with a slight actual scarcity of some grades, such as uppers of extra thick cut, 10-inch boards, etc. It is claimed also that desirable parcels of shippers are not over plenty and while the immediate demand for them is rather limited the propriety of putting in some stock against immediate contingencies is evident.

Yellow Pine is quiet at the moment, but otherwise the market seems to be in very good shape and in a fair way toward recovery of healthy tone. The state of demoralization on this class of wood has been of such long duration, it is hardly reasonable to expect the position to at once recuperate, but if the trust accomplishes all it has laid out to do and places the retail trade upon a sound, healthy basis, with an increase of consumption, it is natural to expect that receivers, and through them manufacturers, will secure proper proportion of the benefits.

Carolina Pine changes very little, if any, in its average features, and we find practically nothing new to report since our last. There does not appear to be any excess of stock offering, yet always enough for the demand, and the talk of advancing prices has got no further, as the general range remains as last advised.

Hardwoods are without improvement as to demand, and the average run of value remains much the same as for some time past, because there is very little stock offering and an absence of pressure to realize. Those conditions will apply with equal force to all standard kinds of wood and little, if any, change seems to be anticipated during balance of the year. Dealers, however, commence to talk about the promising outlook, as a class of buildings now just getting above ground in many cases are of a kind to require a great deal of trim, and by spring hardwoods are expected to be fully in the swim again.

GENERAL LUMBER NOTES.

THE WEST.

The Northwestern *Lumberman* as follows:

Winter has taken an early start and the loggers of the Northwest are encouraged by the prospect. They picture to themselves frozen swamps, hard bottoms generally and plenty of snow when it is wanted, and the contemplation is usually very satisfactory. The hopes may not be realized, but appearances indicate a different sort of winter this time from the two or three preceding. If everything is favorable lumber men will be unable to resist the temptation to get out a good many logs, even though they be in a conservative mood.

At Chicago:

It is evident that the season is drawing toward the close. The late gale and cold weather has accelerated the finish. The steam barges will continue to run for probably a couple of weeks longer; but the schooners will tie up about as fast as they come in and discharge their loads. Several schooners, however, have gone out since the gale, the high freight rates being a strong temptation to take extraordinary risks. Most of the schooners are going to Green Bay for loads, as they can hug the lee shore in the passage. Vessels that went through the gale had a tug to get in, and a majority lost a part of their deck loads, and a few all that was on deck. The bows, lumber forward and lower rigging were coated with ice.

Yard dealers are ready to buy such cargoes as they need to fill up their assortments, and pay outside prices for the lumber. Several cargoes of piece stuff have been sold at \$10.50. Slim jims are quick sale at \$13, and long 2x12 at \$15, with especially long selling at \$16. These are much stronger prices than earlier in the season, and evidence the upward tendency of values. Of course, the high lake rates prevailing are in a measure accountable for this. There is a good demand for strips, and for boards of stock width of any grade. Course promiscuous widths, if dry, sell better than earlier; if green they are not so well thought of. Short lumber from Manistee or other east shore ports is selling from \$10 to \$10.25 a thousand.

The *Timberman* has the following on the logging season:

All signs point to activity in logging in the Northwest more so than last year and also to an increased cut. The season of 1890-91 was a peculiarly trying one to the loggers of that section and to quite a number of operators, more especially to those in a small way of business, proved to be disastrous. The fall was mild, with no cold weather nor snow until after the first of January and not very much thereafter, and the making of ice roads proved so expensive that the small loggers were unable to get out the quantity of logs they had anticipated. Then came the tribulations of the drivers, which caused many of the booming companies largely enhanced expenditures over ordinary seasons and proving the last straw to break the back of many a small logger.

This season the outlook is different. Northern Michigan, Wisconsin and Minnesota are already in many places covered with blankets of snow, and the advent of a genuine cold wave this week has stirred the entire logging fraternity to activity. On the upper Mississippi many, if not most, of the camps are already established and in operation, and a materially increased cut may be looked for in that section. The capacity of the mills throughout that region has been materially increased during the summer by alterations and repairs, and to give them sufficient stock will require a very considerable increase in the cut.

The preparations also being made in Northern Michigan and Wisconsin are, as a rule, on an enlarged scale and point to an increased cut, and the small logger may be counted on with confidence as endeavoring to retrieve the misfortunes of last winter by an input of logs this season which shall be as large as he can possibly make it. Another indication of an increased cut is the fact that the note of curtailment which is usually sounded very loudly about this time is not heard at all this fall, many operators, in fact, boldly proclaiming that they are going to cut more logs this winter than ever before. In view of the fact that next year promises to be of more than ordinary activity in all departments of trade, it can be predicted, however, with some degree of confidence, that be the cut what it may it will all be absorbed in the ordinary channels of trade without depression of prices.

And also the following:

Notwithstanding the slackness of demand for yellow pine, there has been quite a little contest for the trade between white and yellow pine in Iowa during the past few months. One Kansas City car shipper who had out a great many contracts at fairly full prices, pushed many cars of lumber into Iowa this season in order to realize for himself and his mills at the south, and sold finishing stock so low as to outrival his rivals. He placed many cars of inch finishing in central and southern Iowa on a 23½ cent rate, at $:0. This lumber was snapped up promptly, as it was considerably below the regular price.

But the low price of yellow pine timbers in 24, 26 and 28 feet lengths, 8x14's, cut considerable white pine out of the markets in that State, even where the freight rate was as high as 29½ cents, $24.50 being the price on 28's. White pine men have been advancing prices right along and when it came to long timbers, which required some very substantial butt ends, they were not disposed to meet this kind of competition, and are not now.

When it came to straight grained flooring white pine had to take a back seat, and that class of Southern lumber has a good sale throughout Iowa at the present time. It sold at $23 per thousand on a 23½ cent rate, in carload lots. It is still in very good demand, and the firms who cater particularly to that trade in that territory have about all they can attend to when cars are obtainable to ship the lumber.

Following is a table showing the lumber cut of Minneapolis each season for the years named:

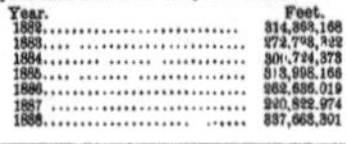

Year.	Feet.
1882	314,363,168
1883	272,798,322
1884	301,724,373
1885	313,998,166
1886	262,636,019
1887	290,822,974
1888	337,663,301
1889	375,855,648
1890	344,574,362
1891	447,713,259

—*Mississippi Valley Lumberman.*

A dispatch to Detroit *Free Press* from Saginaw, Michigan, says:

The sale of lumber for lake shipments is over for the season. Those who ought to be informed on the subject estimate that there is not to exceed 200,000,000 feet of lumber that is unsold on the mill docks on this river. Last year at this date the quantity unsold was 279,000,000 feet. Lumber stocks are reported short at Eastern distributing points, and generally at manufacturing points in the northwest, owing to the large quantity of logs hung up during the summer, hence it is believed there will be an active trade during the ensuing winter and spring, and holders of lumber here expect that stocks will be sold up closely and moved off by rail during the winter.

An unusually large quantity of hemlock logs will be put in during the winter in this section of the State. Five years ago a proposition to put in hemlock would have subjected the person making it to the suspicion of lunacy, but now hemlock is not only sought after, but large quantities are cut and shipped. Hemlock bill stuff sells here at $8.50 per M and boards at $10.

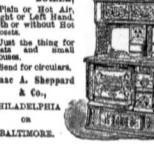

METALS.—COPPER—Ingot has continued in a very dull condition, and the market evidently in the highest degree unsatisfactory to sellers. Exporters do not appear to receive encouragement from abroad, speculation is passive, and the low ruling rates fail to encourage the home demand in any shape. On an average range of valuations we quote at 11@11½c. for Lake, and 10¼@10¾c. for casting brands. Manufactured Copper remains quiet with cost standing as before. We quote as follows: Sheet, not above 30x72 in., 16 oz. and over, 25c.; do, 14 to 16 oz., 23c.; do, 12 to 14 oz., 24c.; do, 10 to 12 oz., 26c.; do, 8 to 10 oz., 28c.; do under 8 oz., 30c. Sheets longer than 72 inches add 1c. for 12@14 oz., 2c. for 10@12 oz. and 3c. for 8@10 oz. Sheets, not above 36x96 in., 16 oz and over, 22c.; do, 14 to 16 oz, 24c.; do, 12 to 14 oz, 26c.; do, 10 to 12 oz, 30c.; do, 8 to 10 oz, 33c. Sheets longer than 96 inches 22c. for over 32 oz, and add 1c. for 16 to 32 oz.; 3c. 14 to 16 oz.; 5c. 12 to 14 oz, and 13c. for 8 to 10 oz. Sheets, not above 48x96 32 to 64 oz, 22c.; do, 16 to 32 oz, 25c.; do, 14 to 16 oz, 27c. do, 12 to 14 oz, 29c.; do, 10 to 12 oz, 33c. Sheets wider than 48x96 and longer, 22@25c. for 32 to 64 oz. and over, 27@[illegible]c. for 16 to 32 oz, 29c. for 14 to 16 oz and 34c. for 12 to 14 oz. All bath tub sheets, per lb., 16 oz. [illegible]; 14 oz, 29c.; 12 oz 3[illegible]; and 10 oz, 35c. Bolt copper, ⅝ inch diameter and over, 29c. Circles, 60 diameter and less, 3c. above price of sheets of same thickness; circles, 60 to 96 do do, 5c. do; circles, 96 do and over, 6c. do. Segment and pattern sheets, 3c. above price of sheets required to cut them from. Cold or hard rolled copper, 1@2c. per lb. above the foregoing prices. Copper bottoms, 26@32c. per lb. IRON—American Pig fails to obtain much recognition from buyers beyond the limits of the necessities of the hour, and as actual consumption is moderate just now the outlet proves narrow. That excites competition among sellers and produces some weakness on value without lowering the general range. We quote at $17.00@18.00 per ton for No. 1 X foundry; [illegible]@16.50 for No. 2 X do. and $14.00@15.00 for Gray Forge. Old material has not been recognized by any line of custom wanting liberal amounts of stock, and while the quantity offering is not enough to be obtrusive it serves to keep values down. We quote at about $22.00@22.50 for old rails; $19.00@19.50 for No. 1 wrought scrap; $17.00@18.00 for cast scrap and $17.00@17.50 for car wheels. Manufactured Iron is quiet all around, and neither from store or on contracts can much stock be placed. Valuations are made from about former basis, however, and the market as a whole rules steady. We quote Common Merchant Bar ordinary size, at 1.90@2c. from store, and refined at 2@2⅛c; Rods, round and square, 2.10@2.30c.; Bands, 2.30@2.50c.; Norway Nail Rods 3¾@4c., and domestic sheet on the basis of 3.00@3.05c. for common Nos. 10@16. Other descriptions at corresponding prices, with 1-10c. less on large lots from cars. Steel rails continue to meet with some demand, but not as heavy as had been calculated upon, and manufacturers express disappointment. The cost, however, is generally understood to be well preserved and no indications of weakness among any of the companies. We quote standard sections $30 per ton at mill, with usual advance for delivery at tide water. Pig Lead has taken a turn for the better on a demand in part speculative and in part for actual and natural consumption. The amount of available stock was also moderate, which aided the position of sellers and led to an advance in price, but at the close there is some slight irregularity. We quote at 4.30@4⅜c. per lb. The manufactures of lead are quoted at 7c. for Pipe, 7¾c. for Sheet, 15c. for Tin-lined Pipe, and 37½c. for Block Tin Pipe. Pig Tin responds to the manipulation of speculators on both sides of the ocean and fluctuates in price accordingly. Consumers, however, are apparently supremely indifferent to any influence except their natural wants and trade for distribution is slow. We quote at about 20@20.05c. for round lots, and 20¼@20⅝c. for jobbing parcels. Tin Plate moves into the channels of consumption quite slowly and there seems no likelihood of any immediate change. Prices have a weak undertone, though holders of the supply of standard plate do not urge their goods to any extent. We quote prices as follows: I. C. Charcoal, ½ cross assortment Melyn grade, $6.50@6.55, each additional X add $1.50; I. C. Charcoal, ½ cross assortment, Allaway grade, $5.85@5.90, each additional X add $1; Charcoal terne, M. F. grade, 14x20, $7.45@7.50;

M. F. grade, 20x28, $15.00@15.05; Worcester, 14x20, $5.70@5.75; Worcester 20x28, $11.50@11.55; Dean grade, 14x20, $5.40@5.45; Dean grade, 20x28, $10.70@10.75; D. R. D. grade, 14x20, $5.25@5.30; D. R. D. grade, 20x28, $10.10@10.15; I C. Coke, Penlan grade, $5.25@5.30; J. B. grade, 14x20, $5.35@5.40; I. C. Bessemer steel, squares, $5.75@5.80 basis; I. C. Siemens steel, squares, $5.85@6.00 basis. Spelter has again been only moderately active and the market at times exceedingly narrow, with prices lower, but a little more steadiness shown at the close. We quote $4¾@4.80c. for Common Western, according to brand

NAILS.—Buyers do not become any more plenty and there is very universal complaint over the condition of the market. For cut nails we hear of no remedy attempted or suggested, but on wire manufacturers are moving to bring the production into narrower compass in hopes of gaining a foundation for some improvement of tone. We quote Cut at $1.50@1.60 per keg for car lots and $1.75@1.85 per keg for parcels from store for iron, and add 5@10c. per keg for steel; Wire, $2.00@2.05 at mills, and 2.20@2.35 from store.

PAINTS, OILS, COLORS, ETC.—A good measure of conservatism characterises the movements of operators all along the line and it makes business a trifle irregular. Buyers do not come into the market until they are exactly sure as to their wants; they confine investment to just the amounts indicated as likely to be required within a fixed period, and the moment they have checked off memorandums as completed, it is simply a waste of time to attempt selling them any more goods. That course leads to more or less erratic volume of business, but manufacturers, importers and jobbers are fairly accustomed to the conditions and accept them philosophically. A good supply of both domestic and foreign descriptions can be found available, and upon fairly easy terms, so long as no radical breaking down of the value line is expected, but in some cases small shadings are admitted. Block Chalk has been working lower for some time, and the manufacturers of putty are giving customers the benefit of the lower cost of oil. Pure lead remains steady, but doubtful product rules easy. Association Corroders' rates stand as follows: Lead in oil in kegs and dry lead in kegs, in lots of less than 500 lbs., 7¼c. net; in lots of 500 lbs to 5 tons at one purchase, 7c.; 5 tons to 12 tons, one purchase, 6⅞c.; 12 tons and over, one purchase, 6¾c.; dry white lead in bbls. ⅛c. per lb. less than price in kegs. Lead in oil 12½ lb. in tin pails, add 1c.; in 25 and 50 lb. tin pails, add ½c.; and in 1 to 5 lb. tin cans, assorted (100 lbs. in case) add 2½c. per lb. to keg price. Terms on lots on 500 lbs. and over, note or acceptance at sixty days, or 2½ per cent. discount will be allowed for cash paid within fifteen days of invoice date. To make either of the above required quantities any assortment of packages of white lead, red lead and litharge may be counted. The above quotations are free on board cars or boat at corroding point. Linseed Oil has the usual irregularities on ordinary grades, but when it comes to prime stock holders are pretty firm and inclined to offer with moderation. We quote at general range at 35@40c. for Western, and 40@56c. for City. Spirits Turpentine has sold only in a jobbing way, and while the offering was not excessive it proved more than sufficient for the outlet, with the effect upon values somewhat depressing. We quote at 35@36c. per gallon, according to quality, delivery, etc.

TAR AND PITCH.—Business has been moderately active and somewhat uncertain with not much of a market existing at the moment. The supply seems to be quite as well controlled as could be expected, but owners willing to negotiate upon all full bids. We quote Pitch at $1.70@1.75 per bbl.; Tar at $2.15@2.50, according to quantity, quality and delivery.

MISCELLANEOUS

MISCELLANEOUS.

BUILDING MATERIAL PRICES

LUMBER.

Appended quotations are based almost wholly upon prices obtained for goods from first hands. Yard rates necessarily range much higher owing to the expenses attending sorting out and grading cargo and even car lots, besides which must be added the cost of handling and carrying until consumers are ready to invest. Terms of sale also prove important factors and, altogether, it is impossible to give a line of retail quotations thoroughly reliable in character.

SPRUCE—Eastern—special cargoes delivered N. Y.	$16 50	@ 18 00
Random cargoes, narrow	14 00	@ 15 00
Random cargoes, wide	15 50	@ 16 50
PILING—Eastern—cargo rates:		
Ranging 30@40 per cent 12 inch butt, 35 to 40 ft average length	4	@ —
Ranging 45@50 per cent 12 inch butt, 35 to 40 ft average length	4¼	@ 4½
Ranging 50@60 per cent One-half 12 inch butt, 38 to 40 ft average length	4¾	@ 5
Two-thirds 12 inch butt, 38 to 42 ft average length	5½	@ 6
Three-fourths 12 inch butt, 40 to 45 ft average length	5¾	@ 6
All 12 inch butt and up, 40 to 45 ft average length	6	@ 6¼
Piece stick, 40 feet each	4 00	@ —
do. 45	6 00	@ —
do. 50	8 00	@ —
do. 55	12 00	@ —
Inch spars, per inch	20	@ 22
Scaffolding poles, each	60	@ 1 00
Clothes poles, 45 to 65 feet, each	3 00	@ 6 00
HEMLOCK:		
Penn. joist	12 00	@ 12 50
do. boards	13 00	@ 13 50
do. timber, 20 ft and under	12 50	@ 13 00
do. do. 22 to 24 ft	13 00	@ 13 50
do. do. 26 to 28 ft	13 50	@ 14 00
do. do. 30 to 32 ft	14 00	@ 15 50
do. do. 34 to 36 ft	15 50	@ 16 00
do. do. 38 to 40 ft	16 50	@ 17 50
WHITE PINE—Good uppers and select, 1 to 2 inch	40 00	@ 48 00
Upper and select, 2½ to 4 inch	50 00	@ 58 00
Shelving	26 00	@ 31 00
Pickings, 1 inch	33 00	@ 36 00
Cutting-up, 1 inch	25 00	@ 28 00
Bracket plank	30 00	@ 35 00
Dressing-boards	18 00	@ 22 00
Box, inch	13 50	@ 14 00
Box, thick	14 50	@ 15 50
West India shippers	16 00	@ 19 00
Rio Janeiro do.	20 00	@ 21 00
River Plate do.	29 00	@ 30 00
Australia do.	25 00	@ 30 00
YELLOW PINE—Random cargoes delivered N. Y.	19 00	@ 20 00
Ordered cargoes	20 00	@ 22 00
Flooring	24 00	@ 24 00
Step plank	26 00	@ 28 00
Common siding	15 00	@ 16 00
Heart face boards	24 00	@ 28 00
Car orders	21 00	@ 23 00
At Atlantic ports, f. o. b.	12 00	@ 12 50
At Gulf ports, f. o. b.	11 50	@ 12 50
North Caroline pine timber	13 50	@ 15 00
do. flooring 1 inch	16 00	@ 22 00
do. do. 1¼	16 50	@ 22 50
do. do. 1½@2 inch	24 00	@ 25 00
do Shipping culls or box	12 00	@ 14 00
do Plain and mottled ½@1½ inch	18 50	@ 25 50
Ash, white	36 00	@ 48 00
Elm	20 00	@ 22 50
Oak, plain	37 00	@ 41 00
Oak, quarter sawed	52 00	@ 55 00
Oak, quarter sawed, extra thick	56 00	@ 60 00
Redwood	45 00	@ 52 50
Maple, clear	28 00	@ 33 00
Chestnut, clear	33 00	@ 35 50
Cypress, clear	30 00	@ 32 50
Black Walnut, good to choice	130 00	@ 140 00
Black Walnut, ordinary to fair	100 00	@ 120 00
Black Walnut, ⅝	78 00	@ 83 00
Black Walnut, selected and seasoned	150 00	@ 155 00
Black Walnut counters	110 00	@ 150 00
Black Walnut, culls	35 00	@ 40 00
Black Walnut, rejects	50 00	@ 58 00
Cherry, wide	110 00	@ 115 00
Cherry, good	85 00	@ 100 00
Cherry, ordinary	65 00	@ 80 00
Whitewood, inch	30 50	@ 32 50
Whitewood, ⅝ inch	24 50	@ 26 00
Whitewood, 1¼ to 2½ inch	32 00	@ 34 00
Shingles, Pine, 16 inch, extra	2 75	@ 3 10
do 18 inch, extra	4 10	@ 4 30
do 18 inch, clear butt	2 90	@ 3 10
do 16 inch, stocks	4 50	@ 4 60
do 18 inch, stocks	5 30	@ 5 40
Shingles, Cypress, 6x20	8 00	@ 10 00
do larger sizes	11 00	@ 15 00
do sawed	6 00	@ 9 00
Cedar—Medium to large	6¼	@ 7½
do. —Extra large	7¾	@ 8
Mahogany—Small	6½	@ 7¼
do —Medium	8	@ 8½
do. —Large	9½	@ 12
do. —Extra Large	[illegible]	@ 14

REAL ESTATE RECORD AND BUILDERS' GUIDE.
ESTABLISHED MARCH 21st 1868.
DEVOTED TO REAL ESTATE, BUILDING ARCHITECTURE, HOUSEHOLD DECORATION, BUSINESS AND THEMES OF GENERAL INTEREST

PRICE, PER YEAR IN ADVANCE, SIX DOLLARS.

Published every Saturday.

TELEPHONE - - - - CORTLANDT 1370.

Communications should be addressed to

C. W. SWEET, 14 & 16 Vesey St.

J. T. LINDSEY, Business Manager.

"Entered at the Post-office at New York, N. Y., as second-class matter."

VOL. XLVIII DECEMBER 5, 1891. NO. 1,238

THREE startling and telling failures, disturbing and menacing the standing and security of the largest three money centres of the country, give imperative emphasis to the demand for the more adequate protection of the credit system. Within the short period of a year the reputation of Philadelphia as the most conservative and safe of the seaboard cities, in its financial dealings, has been shattered; the most astonishing rascality and official indifference disclosed. Boston, hardly less conspicuous in its conservatism, has been rudely shaken by the failure of one of its heaviest banking houses. While, close following, a leading New York house has gone down in disaster and dishonor; its balance represented in $5,000 of assets and liabilities of three millions. Financial centres are but just recovering breath at the narrow escape from a serious panic. Yet neither the wreckage of the Keystone, at Philadelphia; the Maverick, at Boston, nor the house of Field, Lindley, Welchers & Co., in New York, are the result of the late stringency nor related especially to it. In yet another light, if we consider how slight a percentage of the immense business interchange of the country is upon an actual money basis, and how large a proportion rests upon the credit system alone, the need, the necessity of a better, surer and sounder basis for the credit system than at present exists becomes manifest. Whatever be the objection to government interference, whatever the cry against growing socialistic tendencies, it is evident that the State, represented either in its natural or local functions, must assume a more direct responsibility, with the entail of stricter and sharper supervision, and complete the work which it has so imperfectly begun. In the three prominent instances the year has presented, the fact of inadequate protection of the public against speculators and thieves has been unequivocally stated. It has been demonstrated that government examiners do not examine, and that clearing house associations are no alternative for relief. For the immediate protection of public credit a reserve fund collected by taxation or assessment pro rata upon the amount of deposits appears the most effective and feasible. Whether this fund be lodged with the government or with the clearing house associations it matters little. The one or the other then becomes a responsible guarantor to every depositor in the land. The direct responsibility thus entailed insures the most searching scrutiny of bank affairs possible, while each bank made liable for the conduct of every other in return for the absolute protection of its own customers would become not the shield, but the agent for the detection of corrupt institutions.

THIS is the only way the *Commercial and Financial Chronicle*, in its supplement of November 28th, page 67, answers our questions of November 21st. It says, "In June, 1890, it was voted to authorize $3,625,000 of second mortgage bonds ($5,000 per mile), and $1,500,000 was afterwards sold, dated June 30, 1891, but the issue was not known to the public till October, 1891." The sentence is a little clumsy, but we are glad that at last the *Chronicle* states things as they are; but it should have added, as it is the fact, that the stockholders of the Lake Erie & Western R. R. Co. also knew nothing about the issue until October, 1891, and this is the meat of their complaint, and of this they will ever complain.

THAT expert corporation accountant and writer, Mr. Chas. Barrett, has in a recent article furnished a strong illustration of our point in criticism of the financial management of the Lake Erie & Western Railroad Company. "In 1873, 1874 and 1875 the dividends on the preferred stock of the Chicago, Milwaukee & St. Paul, aggregating $2,476,232, were fully earned, but in lieu of the cash which was in the company's hands the amount was paid in newly-created consolidated 7 per cent bonds of 1875-1905 at par, and a great outcry was raised because the St. Paul was paying dividends in bonds instead of cash. The situation was then—in 1876—very much as it is now. Bonds and stocks were depressed. Investors were scared and would not buy. These bonds commanded only 85 per cent in the market, and the effect of using them in lieu of cash for the payment of the dividends was nothing more than the selling of $2,476,232 thereof to the stockholders at par instead of to the public at 15 per cent discount. They are now quoted at above 120. Interest has been regularly paid. They have yet fifteen years to run, and there is no better secured bond in the market. Certainly the preferred stockholders have had no reason for complaint. It is singular that roads that are in want of cash for the payment of floating liabilities, additions to their properties, new construction or new equipments do not adopt the same policy."

A NERVOUS inaction characterizes all the exchanges of Europe at the present time. The panic which took place in Vienna on November 14th was traceable directly to the apprehensive feeling with which the Austrian bankers and speculators regarded the present political situation. It is known that the German people are becoming very belligerent about Russia; and it is feared that, despite the pacific intentions of the Emperor, he may be forced into beginning the inevitable conflict. This in itself would be sufficient to keep the markets of Europe quiet; and when, in addition to this, general business is depressed and credit shaken, the prevailing depression is scarcely a matter for surprise. Neither can any revival of business be looked for until the present situation has worked itself out. The strain under which the commercial fabric of Europe is suffering acutely must be removed; and the many weak issues on the Stock Exchange lists must be either gotten rid of or else find their proper level. Even, however, if nothing occurs violently to disturb the current of events, no very great activity can be expected abroad during the immediate future. In Germany, it is not only the stocks of foreign countries which are declining, but the values of domestic industrial securities are adjusting themselves to what is apparently to be a season of small business, narrow profits and declining prices. France will during the next year be adapting itself to a tariff, the schedules of which have undergone considerable alteration, which in itself will be a task difficult and of uncertain outcome. England's manufacturing industries are far from being in a prosperous condition. The exports of that country show a heavy falling from the figures of last year, and the cotton, woolen and iron manufacturers are particularly depressed. It is, however, some political shock only which would be likely to produce a panic. The depression has come on very gradually and will not culminate for some time yet.

THE consents of the property-owners along the route laid down by the Rapid Transit Commission are not coming in as fast as they ought to. The refusal of some large owners and the hesitation of many more mean that these gentlemen do not appreciate all that the proposed system will do for their property. In the absence of any reliable expert testimony to the contrary effect, THE RECORD AND GUIDE takes it to be settled that existing foundations will not be endangered by the tunnel. The guarantee of such skilled engineers as those who have passed on the plan ought to be sufficient for the most cautious owner of the biggest building along Broadway. If all possibility of danger from this source is excluded, there can be no shadow of doubt whether the interest of a property-owner lies on the side of acquiescence or refusal. A rapid transit system such as the Commissioners propose for Broadway would make that thoroughfare to a greater extent even than at present the very heart and core of New York City. The fact that the street runs diagonally across the city at a very long angle has been sufficient in the past to secure its supremacy over every other thoroughfare in the metropolis; but, nevertheless, there has always been something of a straining to get away from Broadway. Down town, during the past five years, the capitalists and corporations who could afford to erect office buildings many stories high, have built off that thoroughfare just as much as they could—mainly because the present rapid transit lines never get nearer to that street than a block away. Thus property on other streets was to some extent more convenient than Broadway property; and hence it is that, although the value of real estate on that thoroughfare has been strong, there no longer exists the same difference as formerly between the price which it brings and the price paid for land on contiguous streets. A process of leveling up has been going on whereby Broadway has been gradually losing its marked pre-eminence. Neither is this true only of the district south of Chambers street. The last two or three years have seen the transferral of much business formerly transacted on Broadway, between Broome and 14th streets, to the new mercantile district on the streets to the immediate west; and concomitant with this, there has been a rise of values on those side and parallel streets to a level much more nearly approaching the Broadway standard. A similar process is noticeable in the retail district. The Sixth Avenue Elevated road concentrated on 6th avenue many of the best retail stores; and those not on 6th avenue are as a rule found on either 14th or 23d streets. The surface railroad has done something to retain for Broadway its supremacy, and when cable traction is introduced it will do still more; but unless a system such as the Commission propose is built and operated, this equalizing of values will continue for an indefinite period and to an indefinite extent.

IF the Commissioners' plan is carried out, the pre-eminence of Broadway will be restored and maintained. Nothing is more certain than that the value of property along that thoroughfare will be materially increased. The majority of business men or employes who travel up and down town during the rush hours will be dependent on the new system for their daily journeys; and the fact that it will run under Broadway will largely increase the desirability of offices situated thereon. The same cause will produce the same effect throughout the mercantile district; while above 14th street, in the region of the theatres and the retail stores, the tunnel will be particularly beneficial to the value of property. All of this will not take place at once; but it must be remembered that nearly all of New York's increase in population will settle along one of the northern routes planned by the Commission, and that immense throngs of people will be poured down into that narrow thoroughfare. It should also be remembered that the loop in the City Hall Park will bring many Brooklyn people to our offices, stores and theatres—more than frequent them at present. Consequently Broadway will become not only increasingly accessible to many of the present residents of New York, but in direct communication with much of the future growth. No physical force acts more certainly than a rapid transit system. When it makes a limited area more accessible than formerly it concentrates within that area an enormous increase of aggregate value; just as when it makes an enlarged area more readily accessible it distributes a like increase of value throughout all the land affected. The new rapid transit system, by making many square miles in North New York about twice as near as they are at present to a few square miles in South New York, will materially enlarge values at both ends, and it will do so particularly on the thoroughfare along which it will land most of its passengers. Just here we are insisting on only the most obvious advantage of such a tunnel to Broadway property-owners. As we pointed out, when the details of the plan were first announced, it is perfectly possible that the relations of the tunnel to the property along the street may lead to what will practically be a subterranean street lined with stores and of considerable rental value. But whether this proves to be so or not, the enormous benefit of such a system to Broadway property is indubitable.

IS it not about time for the New York and New Jersey Bridge Company to put its enterprise on a rather more business-like footing? This corporation obtained from a careless and incompetent Legislature a charter, carrying with it enormous power and providing for only a ridiculously insufficient protection of the public interests. Over a year ago it announced the details of a scheme to throw a bridge across the Hudson, a scheme that included most elaborate and expensive approaches on the New York side. From Broadway and 39th street, across the city to about 70th street and the North River, a black line was drawn; and that black line has materially affected the saleability of the property thus threatened. Furthermore, it has brought improvements to a standstill along the route of the proposed approach. A bridge across the Hudson would doubtless be a good thing for New York; and any corporation that can seriously undertake its construction should, of course, be allowed to draw its plans even if the announcement of such a plan would render large areas of real estate for the time stagnant; but when such a plan is announced, the public should have some guarantee of the corporation's seriousness of purpose and competence to the work. In the present case there is no such guarantee. The officials of the company are always declaring that they are just about to begin construction, but no intelligent man can believe the statement. When work on the tunnel costing only a few million dollars has been stopped for lack of funds, is it likely that work on the bridge costing $50,000,000 is going to proceed very rapidly? Renting offices and drawing plans are interesting and remunerative occupations for officials, but rather unsatisfactory to the public. Yet, if all these officials say is true, it ought to be a comparatively easy matter to confound any one skeptical of the success of the enterprise or the seriousness of the intentions of its projectors. They claim that the railroads, with their termini in New Jersey, will be eager to send their express, local and freight trains over the bridge. Although one might suppose that if this were the case these rich companies would have themselves long since combined to build the bridge; still, the plausibility of this contention may, for the sake of argument, be admitted. But, if the railroads are so eager to use the bridge, it ought surely to be an easy matter to get their managers to sign an agreement to that effect. Let the New York & New Jersey Bridge Company show contracts with the Pennsylvania, the Jersey Central, the Baltimore & Ohio, the Erie, the Lehigh Valley, the Lackawanna and the Reading, whereby those companies bind themselves to use the bridge, and all objectors to the project would forthwith take back their objections and capitalists would jump at the prospect of investing money in a structure that could command such a traffic. If the New York & New Jersey Bridge Company is in earnest and is capable, here is the one way to prove it.

On the Propriety of Emasculating Legislatures.

AMERICAN municipal legislatures are almost a thing of the past. The powers of the town councils or boards of Aldermen have been reduced by "reform" after "reform," till nearly all the important functions of city government are discharged by boards or commissions acting with a great degree of independence. Many who have favored this development so far as it affects cities have failed to notice that something of the same sort is taking place in the State governments. Just as it is thought to be wise to govern cities by long charters or State enactments which operate through administrative boards and commissions, so the States are coming to govern themselves by means of long constitutions which bind the Legislature and provide for a great variety of administrative boards. Things that were formerly left to the Legislature are now either settled by constitutional enactment, or else are left for decision to a commission having semi-judicial power.

So great has the distrust of legislative bodies become that the States in which the Legislature meets for a strictly limited session and but once in two years, are thought to be peculiarly fortunate. All the newer State constitutions are long enough to answer in a rough way for volumes of compiled statutes. These elaborate documents circumscribe the powers of the legislatures with great particularity, even in some cases forbidding the creation of any new State office without an amendment to the constitution. But where there is no such provision as this the State legislatures are frequently willing to give away voluntarily many of the powers remaining to them. Instead of fixing railroad rates or trying to regulate corporation affairs themselves, they provide for the appointment or election of railway commissioners, banking commissioners, insurance commissioners and so on. Instead of appointing legislative committees to investigate industrial conditions, permanent bureaus of labor are established in twenty-three States. Instead of passing elaborate laws for the protection of the public health and leaving them to be enforced by the ordinary courts of justice thirty States at present have State Boards of Health. Instead of trusting their own committees to report on State institutions for charitable purposes fifteen States now have boards of charities. The demand for prison reform has been met by the appointment of prison commissioners. Inspectors of factories in the leading manufacturing States have very positive powers of supervision and control, and mining inspectors enforce mining laws, prevent the employment of children below the legal age, see that mines are properly ventilated and that precautions are taken against accidents. Hardly one of these important administrative bodies existed before the war, and most of them have been called into existence within the last two decades.

In so far as this development merely indicates a tendency to shift the emphasis from the legislative to the administrative branch of government it is healthful and proper. When the Legislature retains its control over the subordinate bodies that it has created it is a wise delegation of power and will result in better service. But when these boards and commissions are begotten of the constitution and when their influence is used to circumscribe and diminish the prerogatives of the Legislature the beneficence of their influence may be questioned. In so far as the development has its origin in the widespread distrust of Legislatures—that is, in the same feeling that has led to the progressive paralysis of State and municipal Legislatures, through constitutional limitations, we doubt its wisdom. We have yet to hear of a town council or a State Legislature that has been improved by being rendered insignificant.

Possibly there is no need of a municipal legislature, or rather, perhaps, it is possible to get along without one; but we submit that the States must have such bodies. This being true it seems likely that blood-letting is not the only treatment desirable in attempting to cure legislative evils. If all the ingenuity that has been devoted to the emasculating of legislative assemblies had been turned in the direction of devising for them better methods of procedure the results would be more creditable and more indicative of that "genius for self-government" on which we pride ourselves. The formal rules for the passing of bills that have been adopted are inadequate to the work of securing publicity for proposed legislation; the multiplicity of committees and their general irresponsibility and secretiveness, together with the great mass of bills dumped on the tables of all legislative assemblies, prevents even the press from following the course of proposed legislation, and makes it easier to pass laws without discussion than with it. Towards the close of a session when the final bewildering crush has begun some of the State Legislatures appoint "sifting committees" to decide what shall be considered. A wiser way would be to appoint a sifting committee at the start to separate general from special and local acts, and to throw out the worthless bills, "introduced by request," before any of the regular committees had been bothered with them. This, together with rules for committee work that would insure publicity and regularity of procedure, would let the light into the dark places of legislation, and at least show us what further is necessary. The many investigations into the methods of the lobby, bad as are some of the things they bring to light, seem to show that the things for which we fear and blame our legislators result less from corruption than from awkwardness on the part of the members. The legislator cannot give satisfaction, partly because he has not time enough to learn his business; but also because he is put to work under a set of rules which thwart and perplex him at every turn, which make honorable distinction difficult or impossible of attainment, and give every facility for underhand and dishonest practices. The great moral disinfectant is publicity, and if we can devise some way of using this agent in our legislative halls, lobbies and committee rooms, perhaps we can make our Legislatures comparatively safe, without the need of rendering them impotent.

The Obstructed District.

THE sudden impulse given to building in the district bounded by Broadway on the east, Houston street on the south, Wooster street and Washington square on the west, and the Sailors' Snug Harbor property on the north, does not yet show any very pronounced signs of abatement. There has been less building in the district during the current year than was seen last year; but operators give encouraging reports on the prospects for the coming year. All or nearly all the buildings finished or under construction have been rented on terms highly satisfactory to the owners; and with this demonstration in view it does not require a very sanguine spirit to anticipate a profit in the construction of more buildings of a corresponding kind.

Still, we do not observe any movement on the part of the people living in the immediate neighborhood to go north. The students of the University of the City of New York, meeting for their mental gymnastics in the immediate district, are still noisy enough to drown the hammers of neighboring house carpenters, and the residents along North Washington Square are beginning to open their habitations for another winter campaign. The neighborhood, indeed, is becoming more instead of less attractive for residences. The Washington Centennial Arch is approaching completion, and the new Memorial Church, considered by artists to be one of the most perfect church structures in the country in proportion and color, is adding to the architectural attractions of a neighborhood that never had any original architecture of its own.

But, notwithstanding the tenacity with which the old families cling to North Washington Square and lower 5th avenue, there are many persons who believe that they are struggling against the tide, and that the currents will be strong enough to sweep them away in a very brief period. It is exceedingly hard, however, to make a forecast on this subject. The allies of those who wish to remain are found in the Trustees of the Sailors' Snug Harbor. These gentlemen maintain a very formidable breakwater against the encroachments of the mere speculator in lands and houses, and so long as it is maintained it will be hard to conjecture the probable extent of any building movement in the neighborhood. Of one thing only can we be reasonably certain. The mercantile movement must continue strong enough to prevent the construction of any new private dwellings on this ground, and it is only a question of time when those now tenanted will tumble down about the ears of the occupants. Hence, it is reasonable to presume that the neighborhood of Washington Square, outside the Snug Harbor property, must finally become either an exclusively mercantile and manufacturing district, or a combined mercantile, manufacturing, tenement house and apartment house district. The private dwelling we think must inevitably vanish.

But what is to be the fate of the Snug Harbor property? Here, again, prophecy becomes as difficult as it is for American players to win a game at cricket. It would be easy to say what we would like to see happen or what ought to happen. The Snug Harbor property should be dispersed throughout the city and not be permitted to remain an incubus on any single neighborhood, especially on a neighborhood that offers the first opportunity for an extension of the overflowing mercantile, manufacturing, and financial district that lies below Canal street. The property lies in the very neighborhood that builders would have selected for their operations any time within the last thirty years had they been free to make the selection, and it should go without saying that it has been a mistaken policy that permitted it to remain a public obstruction. If thirty years ago the managers of the property had obtained an act of the Legislature permitting them to move on, Broadway between Canal street and 14th street would present a very different picture from the spectacle now witnessed.

There are men who believe that the influence of the residents on Washington square and lower 5th avenue is exerted in favor of maintaining the Snug Harbor property in its present location. It furnished the breakwater that they need to prevent the overflow of traffic, and helps to keep them in the undisturbed possession of their dwellings. But if there be any foundation for this idea it only furnishes additional proof that very astute men may sometimes mistake their own best interests. It is not to be presumed that Washington square is of so much importance to New York socially that the 400 would dissolve or be multiplied by 10,000 were they to cease making their headquarters in the neighborhood. They could go north without losing their primacy. Many have already gone north without suffering reduction to the ranks. There the remainder may go with no feeling of insecurity. There is certainly nothing in their dwellings that should invite them to remain. Their houses are not generally built of marble with bronze doors. They are among the most common dwellings in the city, such as only a recognized aristocrat can afford to inhabit, and nothing but the ground upon which they stand and the recollections of infancy are worth preserving. But the ground would be best preserved by covering it with new apartment houses, and, to the misery of many men and a few women, recollections can never be left behind.

There are two exceedingly sore spots in New York. One is along the water front where the city is muddling franchises to which it has no right, and the other is this Snug Harbor excrescence. Of the two, the first of course is the worst, because it strikes vitally at our commercial supremacy in the port. But either one of the two is bad enough to call for heroic remedies.

THE projectors of the Standard Gaslight Company must have had a large idea of the profits to be made in the manufacture of gas for the citizens of New York at the rate of $1.25 per thousand feet. It has been charged and not denied that the passage of the bill by the Legislature granting the charter was obtained strangely, and that as soon as the bill was passed and the charter secured these gentlemen, or one of them, began to issue large quantities of stock to himself and his political friends. This stock did not represent a dollar in cash paid into the treasury of the company; it was water, pure and simple, based on whatever value the Legislature had corruptly created by the granting of the charter. Verily, the exploitation of public franchises is a profitable business! Because a corporation has the right to lay pipes and sell gas its manager thought that enough value has been thereby charmed into existence to justify the creation of an indefinite amount of obligations. And he was right. No matter what the real estate, the plant or the pipes of a gas company are worth, the franchise is as a rule worth a good deal more, and these franchises are for the most part given away by our authorities all over the country to these corporations, just as this charter of the Standard Gaslight Company was given away by the Legislature. In this particular case the stockholders may have been subjected to some sharp practices, but in every case the consuming public is defrauded. It is made to pay far more than the article costs to produce in order that the projectors of these enterprises, who nine times out of ten run no risk in investing their money in this way, may reap enormous profits. The difference between what the consumers do pay and what they ought to pay is divided between the "shrewd business men" and the "rascally politicians." There are a great many ways of stealing, and politicians are not the only class that do it deftly.

The Historical American Exhibition at Madrid.

Editor RECORD AND GUIDE:

Among the celebrations next year of the quatra-centennial of the discovery of America, that of the Historical American Exhibition at Madrid, calls for special mention. This celebration was authorized by Royal Decree of February 9th, 1891, and is to comprise every kind of object that will give an idea of the civilization of the New World both previous to the time of European discovery and conquest and coeval with it. In a certain sense the exhibition might be termed ethnographic as well as historical, and is thus not an international exhibition such as we will have at Chicago, but a distinct exhibition that cannot but prove of the greatest interest and benefit to students of primitive American races and peoples. The exhibition is, therefore, intended not only as a contribution to art and science but to serve as a tribute paid by modern Spain to the genius of the great navigator.

The committee having the exhibition in charge desire especially from Americans the loan of objects of all kinds that illustrate the special subject at hand, and which refer to American civilization and the conquest prior to the seventeenth century. The exhibition will open on September 12, 1892, in the new palace built for the Library and National Museum, in the park of Madrid, which will be inaugurated on this occasion and will close on December 31st following. Goods properly packed for transportation abroad will be conveyed to Madrid by the committee free of all cost to the exhibitor. No charge is made for space and every effort will be made to properly care for the exhibits while in the hands of the committee and at Madrid. Everything is required to be in readiness on or before August 31st. Articles intended for this exhibition will be admitted to Spain free of duty if they are returned abroad at the conclusion of the celebration, two months being allowed after the close of the exhibition for their with drawal from Spain. While the committee assumes care of the exhibits arrangements may be made by exhibitors or associations of exhibitors for the care and display of their own articles. An international jury will be appointed, proportionate to the foreign exhibitors, to examine and judge the displays made. The prizes will consist of a first prize of honor, a gold medal, a silver medal, a bronze medal and honorable mention, each accompanied with a diploma.

There is every reason why this exhibition should prove of sufficient interest to Americans to induce them to loan some of the many objects in their collections illustrative of the time and the civilization it is proposed to represent. The exhibition stands quite distinct from any other celebration of the year 1892. It is natural and right that the Spanish people should wish to emphasize the important part they have taken in the development of the New World, and in proposing a Historical American Exhibition, they have not only selected a distinct method of celebration themselves, but have devised a unique way of expressing their interest in the Western world. As a nation we are not yet old enough, perhaps, to fully appreciate the interest the Spaniards feel towards a people separated from them by so many circumstances and customs as ourselves; yet, while this exhibition is intended to interest all Americans, the people of South as well as of North America, it is from our own country that many of the objects that will render it complete must come. It is eminently fitting that Americans should aid in the success of an enterprise in which the Spanish people so graciously ask their assistance. BARR FERREE.

NEW YORK, Nov. 25th, 1891.

The West Side Real Estate Market.

The real estate market has been undeniably dull during the past year. The volume of business transacted has been comparatively very small and that it continues so from one cause or another is very plainly shown by the statistics published in these columns from week to week. But the situation is not altogether without its bright side. If there has not been a great many sales there has probably been even less building, and in this fact there is cause for much congratulation.

At this time last year it was admitted on all hands that the city wa overstocked with new houses. The over-production had been confined to no one class of houses nor to any one section of the city. It was found everywhere and was common to almost every class of structure. So long as business was good and the builders and building material men fairly prosperous it was of little or no use to warn them that building was being overdone. Some sort of trouble was needed to force them into recognition of the facts, and it was well that the warning came in such a mild form. The Baring difficulties followed by the financial stringency and the two or three failures in this country finally aroused builders, building-loan and material men to the facts of the situation, and since then there has been much more discrimination in undertaking new work.

The rows of vacant and unsold dwelling-houses and the innumerable half-occupied flats which it was impossible to dispose of were at last recognized as signs of an over-supply. It was seen that unless a halt was called there would be trouble of a serious nature. Fortunately those concerned were far-sighted enough to see and act on the necessity of a cessation of building activity. The building material men led off by refusing credit to a class of builders whom they had readily trusted before. This move increased the caution of the loan men who had been rather uneasy for some time, and, with the exception of men of the very front rank, builders found it impossible to secure lots with a loan. Added to all this the builders who operate with cash commenced to restrict their undertakings to a very few houses, and until these were sold they commenced no new work.

The result of all this caution has been, of course, to greatly lessen both the number and cost of the buildings erected, but to an extent that probably is scarcely realized. The statistics for the last ten months show that there have been 769 less buildings representing an estimated expenditure of $18,466,485 projected this year than during the corresponding period last year. In other words, while last year from January 1st to November 1st 3,151 buildings estimated to cost $66,238,959 were projected, this year during the same period only 2,382 buildings were planned at an estimated cost of $47,772,474. The figures for the month of November, and in fact for the present month up to date show the same general tendency.

Now, of course, while the sales business has been dull this year, and while the transfers have been considerably less than during the same period last year the difference in the conveyances is comparatively not so great as in the buildings projected. The inference from this, of course, is that there has been a steady absorption by investors of the houses already erected, but up to last November still unsold by their builders. But this statement it will be seen immediately can very properly be questioned. While the fact stated above may be fairly inferred from a study of the statistics it is in no way determined by them. Fortunately, however, the facts are as they appear. The selling has included a large number of houses that were held by builders last year and in this way the market has been eased up considerably for there has not been sufficient building to balance the number of houses sold.

On the West Side these facts appear more plainly probably than in any other section of the city. Here building has been most active and here, too, sales for several years have been very numerous. At the end of last year there were a great many unsold new houses on the West Side and the indications were that if building continued its accustomed pace many of those operating on the West Side would be involved in financial difficulty. Fortunately there has been a very large falling off in the number of houses erected, and to-day probably real estate on the West Side is in better condition than it has been for some time. It is to be hoped that this improvement will not induce any "boom" in building. The West Side has passed the period for "booming," and its best friends will do well to leave those methods to the undeveloped sections of the city and suburbs. It now occupies an enviable position among the recognized residence districts of New York and its affairs should be directed by a conservatism that allows the supply to only just exceed the demand. By this course its real estate values will be best maintained and its prosperity most successfully insured.

It is not an easy task to ascertain the exact relations between the selling and building on the West Side, but careful estimates by those who are most closely identified with its interests will do much to give a fair idea of the work of the past year in that section.

Between 72d and 81st streets, from the park to the river, there has been a fair but not an active business done, probably because the trade has been largely in expensive private dwellings. While, of course, there have been some cheap houses sold, the major portion of those that have changed hands have been of the costlier kind. Several houses have been sold for sums in the neighborhood of $80,000, a number of others have brought more than $50,000, and most of the remainder have sold for between $35,000 and $50,000. It is estimated that there are seventy-five less houses for sale in this district than at this time last year, notwithstanding the building. Most of these are dwelling houses.

In the next division, between 81st and 93d streets, there has been some selling of flats and a number of trades taking in apartment houses of the very high-priced class, but the largest business has been made up of dwelling houses which have averaged about $25,000 to $30,000 apiece. Some of the dwellings sold in this district have, of course, sold for more than $30,000 just as a number of them have sold for less than $25,000; but the average price has been in the neighborhood of these figures. Most of the selling in this district has been on West End avenue and near and in the nineties. It is estimated that this has been a slightly busier section than the one just below, and the number of houses taken out of the market is placed at between 100 and 125.

In the next and last section of the West Side residence district proper, between 93d and 104th streets, the largest business seems to have been done. Here, although the sales of dwellings have been fewer than in either of the other districts considered, there have been a great many flats sold. More flats probably than in both the other sections combined, and this has helped to swell the total number of houses sold. It is not so easy to name figures in this district as it was in either of the others, for flat speculation enters so largely into them that they are more or less deceiving. A conservative broker, however, who has done more business in this section than any other, says that there are 150 less houses for sale this year than there were last, and his figures are confirmed by those of other active real estate men.

It must not be inferred from what has been said that the surplus of houses has been entirely wiped out by the falling off in the number of houses being erected, but it has been considerably decreased. There are still too many houses for sale for the entire good of the market, and it behooves the operators, both on the West Side and elsewhere, to be careful that they do not build too fast for the demand, which, it must be admitted, is none too large at the present time.

Sales on West Seventy-fifth Street.

Seventy-fifth street, between Columbus and Amsterdam avenues, has been enjoying a mild sort of "boom" during the last few days, and the hearts of builders on the spot are rejoiced accordingly. During the last week or so four houses have been sold, two of which have been built by John Selfridge, though hardly completed, and two by Giblin & Taylor. Other sales are under negotiation.

Between Central Park West and Columbus avenue three houses have been sold within the last few weeks. John C. Umberfield et al. disposed of these, their numbers being 28, 39 and 41. Other houses have been sold by Jas. T. Hall, the well-known decorator and builder, and by F. Thurston, though these were disposed of somewhat earlier in the season.

The Proposed New Exchange.

The number of subscribers to the fund to build a Mechanics' and Traders' Exchange until yesterday afternoon was about fifty. Each one pledges himself to invest $1,000, and it is said that at least $100,000 will be obtained in this manner. The balance required will, it is said, be forthcoming, though no definite promises have been made to that effect. In some directions it is said that $1,000,000 is too much to spend on an exchange building, but the prevailing desire is that a structure worthy of the great building interests shall be erected, even though the cost be considerable. The concensus of opinion favors an up-town site.

John J. Tucker, ex-president of the National Builder's Association, said: "I am a thorough believer in the proposed exchange, and I shall give my best energies toward the accomplishment of so desirable a plan. The exchange should be up town."

Isaac E. Hoagland, Canda & Kane's representative on 'Change, said: "Our people believe in the new Exchange. It is necessary to have a structure which shall worthily represent the great building interests. There is no doubt that the offices would be filled by builders, architects, contractors and others. There is no trouble to do this in Philadelphia, Chicago and other cities, and many firms connected with these different interests would only be too glad to be together in the same building."

John Byrnes, ex-President of the National Plumber's Association, said: "It is a brilliant idea and ought to be carried out as soon as possible."

E. D. Garnsey said: "I do not think an Exchange is required. My belief is that we can get along very well without one."

Isaac A. Hopper: "Any attempt to throw cold water on the plan will be both short-sighted and futile. The building interests are of vast importance in this city, and they ought to be adequately represented. One hundred million dollars is now spent annually in building in this city. It is absurd that while Boston, Philadelphia and other cities should have their building exchanges, New York is without one."

Col. James Moore Smith: "Every member of the Exchange ought to work thoroughly for the success of the plan. Not only that, but builders like Charles Buek, C. F. Luyster and many others who might be named, should join our organization and work with us. There are also a great number of contractors for all sorts of building work who are not members of the Exchange, and who ought to be with us. There is not the slightest difficulty in my mind about the necessary money. It will certainly be forthcoming."

Frank E. Conover: "I favor the plan most heartily; we ought to have a fine exchange of our own. I thought a few years ago that the neighborhood of Wall street would be a suitable one, but I have since come to the conclusion that somewhere between 14th and 42d streets would be a proper site. The architects are to a large extent moving up town, and a very large part of them are above 14th street, while most of the building is done north of that street."

E. Dobbs: "It is an excellent idea, and should long since have been carried out."

J. C. Doremus: "I think very well of the idea."

J. H. Drew: "I strongly favor it. If we all pull together we will make it a success."

Wm. E. Munroe: "I am strongly in favor of the plan."

E. S. Vaughan, Jr.: "I am in favor of it if we can raise the money."

J. B. Mulry: "It is a grand plan."

Gustavus Isaacs: "It is a splendid proposition, and should be carried out as soon as possible."

Two prominent members of the Mechanics' and Traders' Exchange said they were willing to invest considerably more than $1,000 in the new exchange, and they knew of others who would do likewise. They would be heard from later on.

Chas. Buek said: "I think the proposed Exchange would be very valuable to contractors and others engaged in the building material business. Whether it will be useful to owners who employ and pay contractors, or whether an effort will be made to bring them in as members so as to strengthen the general building interests, I do not know. I should not think we would join such an Exchange unless we could see where we, as owners, would be welcome."

John Selfridge, the builder who has just sold two newly-completed houses on 75th street, said: "I am heartily in favor of the Exchange, and will be glad to join it when it is built. I think every builder will wish to belong to such an institution."

Richard Deeves did not look upon the plan to build a new Exchange with such enthusiasm as some of his fellow-members. "When there were no telephones," he said, "we required the Exchange more than we do now. I would only favor the building if it were erected under some law."

Public Pier Roofs and Wharf Privileges.

A Record and Guide reporter called at the Dock Department to ascertain the facts in relation to the questions put in last week's issue of this paper as to the use, by the public, of the tops of sheds built on new piers, according to a law passed a few years ago, and to the violation of the law by corporations and others who use part of the public thoroughfares on West and South streets, along the water front, without authority or payment therefor.

The Commissioners were in session, and President Post referred the reporter to the secretary, Augustus T. Docharty, who said: "There have been only two piers built on the East River since the passing of the law making it obligatory to build sheds for the public use. These are at Pier (new) 36 and Pier (old) 45, at the foot of Jefferson street, and they are now occupied by the New England Terminal Company. I believe the roofs of the sheds are constructed for public uses. As to using the streets without warrant, that is frequently done, and our dockmasters are continually reporting such occurrences to us. I may add, however, that the right to use the wharves, which the courts have decided are part of the street, is possessed by all citizens. These wharves can be used for loading and unloading goods, and I have no doubt that the privilege is abused by many who use more space, and who occupy that space longer, than they have any right to do. The wharf space in some cases is as narrow as 25 feet; in others it is as wide as 140 feet and over. The business of this city is very great, and our dockmasters do their best to keep people from overstepping their privileges."

Chief Engineer Greene was then seen. He stated that as far as he knew plans for new piers had only been sanctioned when so constructed that the roofs of sheds could be used by the people. He doubted, however, whether it was a wise measure, for a spark from a lighted pipe or cigar might easily set on fire cotton and other inflammable merchandise. Besides which the roofs would be liable to be used by thieves and others. He suggested that the reporter call on one of the police captains and see what he would have to say on this subject.

The reporter did so. He dropped in to see Captain Max F. Schmittberger, of the Twenty-eighth Police Precinct, who has had exceptional experience along the water front: "I don't think the points raised about smoking, thieves and disreputable characters ought to kill any general plan for giving recreation to the people on the roofs of piers. As to smoking, there is some danger from a burning spark, but smoking should be strictly prohibited and its enforcement made a matter of heavy fine or imprisonment. As to thieves, what would there be to steal? Now and then a thief might attempt to go through the pockets of a sleeping man; but the watchmen would look out for that. The hours for using the pier roofs could be limited. As for the rest, the watchmen and police would be sufficient. Every dock has from six to ten watchmen. The Pennsylvania, Baltimore & Ohio and Hudson River railroads have each ten men. It would be a good thing if the city would set aside a few piers, where the people could come in summer with their weak and sickly children to get a whiff of sea air. We often see them come out of their stuffy tenements and sit down with their children on the slips and wharves."

Chap. 509 of the Laws of 1889, relating to pier-roofs for breathing spaces for the people, reads: "It shall not be lawful to permit the use as a dumping ground of any wharf, pier or slip, or bulkhead adjacent thereto, in the navigable waters of the East River, in the City of New York, which has heretofore been used for the loading or discharging of sailing vessels regularly employed in free commerce and having a draft of more than 18 feet of water, nor shall any plan for covering or inclosing any such wharf, pier or bulkhead be approved by the Department of Docks unless the said plan shall provide that the roof of the said shed proposed to be erected shall be so constructed as to admit of the free public use of said roof for purposes of resort and recreation."

What Men Talk About.

H. Alban Reeves, an architect, who has practiced in England, said: "Although I have been established in this country for two years, and notwithstanding the repeated efforts which I have made to secure material men's catalogues, I am as yet but poorly supplied with them. While in England I took a great deal of interest in wrought-iron work, and I must say that they can now execute the most delicate designs in wrought-iron. The large makers, too, have nearly every conceivable design in stock, and it is possible for persons of widely differing tastes to select what they want from the catalogue. Now, in this country I have made designs for execution in wrought-iron, and I have been told that large makers had nothing of the kind in stock, and the designs were what would be considered simple and ordinary enough in England. To have my design executed to order was, of course, too expensive a proceeding, so I was forced to adopt a more ordinary design. Now, I can't believe that American iron workers or other material men are behind their English brethren, but the difficulty of the matter is to get material men's catalogues. Now, can you tell me where I can get not only the ornamental iron-work catalogues, but those of all other building materials? I find great need of them in my business."

"I saw an advertisement in the daily paper, the other day, of a cheap flat, desirably located and well rented," said an up-town broker, "and hoping that it was really as represented, I answered the 'ad.' I found that the flat was poorly located and that it rented for only $2,100 a year. The owner's price, bottom price I believe, was $30,000. For curiosity's sake I went over the files of The Record and Guide, and found two transfers of the property; within a year. The first consideration was $31,500 and the second $24,000. Now, if anything, the neighborhood and with it the flat have deteriorated since the last transfers, and yet the owner will sell *cheap* at $30,000."

The Opinions of Others.

Thos. W. Robinson, cashier of the Mount Morris Bank, was met pushing through a crowd in the Equitable Building the other day. In a hurried talk with the writer he stated that the outlook for real estate in the near future was better than it had been for some time past. "The money market," he said, "is now very easy, while a few weeks ago it was tight enough to cause embarrassment in very many quarters. The change has been almost sudden, and we are going to have the easiest money market we have had for a long time. This is going to help real estate, and I look for a more active movement in that class of investment after the new year."

"It is an error to suppose," said Wm. B. Taylor, of W. B. Taylor & Sons, "that the purchase of leasehold houses is looked upon with disfavor by shrewd buyers. Walter S. Gurnee, the banker, bought the northwest corner of 5th avenue and 50th street and No. 36 West 49th street; Le Grand B. Cannon bought Nos. 19 and 21 West 47th street; Chas. F. Southmayd, one of the most level-headed of our New York lawyers, bought No. 13 West 47th street, while others equally shrewd have made similar purchases. All these are Columbia College leaseholds."

The changes on 34th street, between Broadway and 7th avenue, denote that this block will in a very short time become transposed from a private residence to a business thoroughfore. On both sides of the street, near Broadway and 7th avenue, business has crept in little by little, while in the centre of the block, on the north side, Hammerstein's theatre, and on the south side George Keister's alterations to No. 146 are making noticeable encroachments on the privacy of the neighborhood. The latter house has been turned into a five-story store and office building, with three floors of bachelors' apartments above.

The efforts of tenants to get into new offices in desired localities is illustrated in the case of the Germania Fire Insurance Company's building, now being erected on the southeast corner of Cedar and William streets. Although the building is only up to the third story, the agent, Ferdinand Fish, states that he has already had application for offices in the new structure. It is not unusual for an entire building to be rented before completion, the lessees taking the floor plans for their guide as to dimensions, etc. This was the case with the Bank of America's Building on Wall street and other structures of recent date.

The Building Trades' Club.

The House Committee of the Building Trades' Club evidently intends to make it pleasant for the members of that rising organization. They have arranged for Charles Erickson, the champion pool player, to exhibit his skill at the club house on Monday evening, the 7th inst. He will play several friendly games with members, after which refreshments will be served in the grill room.

Westsiders are awaiting with interest the result of the injunction placed by neighboring property-owners on Andrew J. Kerwin, who has nearly completed five flats at Nos. 151 to 167 West 82d street, notwithstanding that the property is restricted.

The efforts made by Wm. S. Patten and others to restrict the block on 90th street, between Central Park West and Columbus avenue, have resulted in confining the section to private houses.

High-Priced Real Estate.

The following list of high-priced real estate located in the lower part of the city may prove of interest in view of the sale on Thursday of the southwest corner of Broadway and Liberty streets:

Location.	Date sold.	Purchaser.	No. of sq. feet.	Cost.	Price per sq. foot
S w cor Wall and Broad sts..........	April, 1882..	M. Wilks	508	$168,000	$330.70
No. 149 Broadway and No. 83 Liberty st, n w cor.....	Mar. 14, 1890	Singer Mfg. Co.....	3,006.6	544,500	181.12
No. 7 Wall st, s w cor Wall and New sts.	May 1, 1882.	W. W. Smith.......	1,525	240,000	157.37
N e cor Broadway and Pine st........	Jan. 2, 1885.	Eq. Life............	4,896	762,500	155.75
No. 137 Broadway...	Mar. 15, 1887	Niagara Fire Ins Co.	2,525	356,200	141.10
No. 145 Broadway, s w cor Liberty st, Nos. 86 and 88 Liberty st, s e cor Temple st.........	Dec. 3, 1891.	Mrs John Wolfe et al	6,587	770,000	118.47
N e cor Liberty and Broadway....	May 31, 1882	W'msbg. Fire In. Co	3,070	356,000	115.96
Nos. 8 and 10 Pine st.	Mar. 8, 1884.	Eq. Life		400,000	115.00
No. 12 Wall st..... ..	Nov. 1, 1882.	J. J. Astor...........	2,695	300,000	111.81
No. 133 Broadway, n w cor Cedar st, extending to Temple st.......	Mar. 15, 1887	Horace Waldo......	3,283	351,000	106.94
Nos. 4 and 6 Pine st.	Mar. 8, 1884.	Eq. Life..	2,505	267,500	106.74
Nos. 8 and 10 Wall st	Jan. 22, 1881	J. J. Astor	5,709	500,000	87.58
S e cor Cedar and Nassau sts........	July 31, 1882	Ger. Life Ins. Co....	5,494	462,000	84.18
No. 19 Nassau st....	May 10, 1882	Julia F. Ludlow.....	2,050	170,000	82.92
No. 11 Broad st.....	Mar. 11, 1881	D. O. Mills	2,486	200,000	80.44
Nos. 17 and 19 Broad st, and 55 Exch. pl.	April 27, 1881	D. O. Mills..........	8,655	637,500	73.65
Nos. 35 Wall and 13 and 15 Broad sts..	May 2, 1882.	D. O. Mills..........	8,622	625,000	72.48
No. 9 Pine st........	Mar. 17, 1881	J. J. Astor..........	1,752	100,000	57.07
S e cor Broadway and Exchange pl.	Jan., 1883....	J. J. Astor..........	19,115	1,000,000	52.31

A Builder on Rapid Transit.

Richard Deeves was seen down town a few days ago by a reporter of THE RECORD AND GUIDE. In a talk on the rapid transit problem he was very outspoken. "The underground road proposed by the Rapid Transit Commissioners will," he said, "in my opinion, never be built. The majority of the property-owners will not agree to it, as it will tear up Broadway and drive away business. The talk of building the road without tearing up Broadway is all nonsense. Besides, there is enough influence among the Broadway cable people alone to kill the road. They have built conduits twenty feet deep at Houston street, and how is the underground road going to pass these without being torn up. There are vested rights in the cable road which cannot easily be overcome. My belief is that the present plan was doomed beforehand to defeat, the object being to so disgust the public that they will hail with gladness a plan that will give early rapid transit. Such a plan would be found in a two-story elevated road on Broadway, corner buildings to be purchased and utilized for stations, so that the platforms should not project into the street, darken windows and take up room. The two-story road would be necessary so as not to take up too much space in the middle of the street. The one-story could be used for way trains and the other for express. This is the cheapest, simplest and quickest solution of the problem. The cost of the present scheme will probably kill it, without anything else."

Architects and the Health Board in Dispute.

An up-town architect, who draws the plans for a great number of tenement and flat houses, is very indignant at a decision of the acting Chief Inspector of the Bureau of Light and Ventilation of the Health Department made in connection with an application filed by him this week. The architect referred to filed a set of plans for a corner flat house with a store on the ground floor, locating the janitor's apartments in the basement. The whole trouble hinges onthe janitor's apartments. The architect interprets the law to mean that the ceiling of the janitor's apartments, located in the basement, shall be at least one foot above the sidewalk, and that it is not necessary for the ceiling of other parts of the basement to be above the sidewalk at all. The acting Chief Inspector of the Bureau of Light and Ventilation insists that the law requires the ceiling of all parts of the basement wherein janitor's apartments are located to be at least two feet above the level of the sidewalk, which would necessitate at least five steps to be built for entrance to the first floor. As the architect points out, if this new regulation is allowed to stand it will practically prohibit the location of janitor's apartments in the basement of any building where there is a store, for it has been shown that stores not on a level with the street are generally unsuccessful. An appeal has been taken to the Board of Health for an interpretation of the law on this point, and the decision is awaited with considerable anxiety.

Another requirement that is exciting a good deal of opposition and criticism is an alleged new rule which requires transom windows to be placed in pantries and clothes closets. The architects insist that these windows can serve no useful purpose and that they entail unnecessary expense on the builder.

The Proposed Hudson River Bridge.

On the 20th inst. Chas. H. Swan, Secretary of the New York and New Jersey Bridge Company, stated to a reporter of this paper that the consolidation of the companies in the two States would take place on the following Friday, and that work on the land piers for the Hudson River Bridge, which they propose to build, would commence directly after. Mr. Swan was seen yesterday, but said the work had not yet been commenced.

The company has written to Postmaster-General Wanamaker in reference to the latter's report recommending the removal of the New York Post-office up town, stating that the "work of the Bridge Company has advanced to a stage where it has become necessary to consider the details of the plans for the great Union Depot proposed to be constructed "on Broadway, between 37th and 39th streets," and that "the company is prepared to enter into an arrangement with the United States authorities to furnish them with all the space required for a great distributing postal centre."

Readers of THE RECORD AND GUIDE *may subscribe to the new illustrated quarterly magazine,* THE ARCHITECTURAL RECORD, *by sending their names and addresses to the office of publication, Nos. 14-16 Vesey street. The annual subscription is $1.*

The General Society of Mechanics and Tradesmen.

The 106th annual election of the General Society of Mechanics and Tradesmen was held on Wednesday last at the Mechanic's Hall, which resulted in the election of the following officers for the ensuing year: For President, Joseph J. Little; for Vice-President, Guy Culgin; for Second Vice-President, John L. Hamilton; for Treasurer, Richard T. Davies; for Secretary, Stephen M. Wright.

Strong, neat binders, especially made for THE RECORD AND GUIDE, can be obtained at this office. Those of our subscribers who wish to keep a file of the numbers in a compact form and in regular sequence, can have the binder delivered at their office on receipt of order by postal card. Price at office, $1.00, by mail, $1.19.

Important to Property-Holders.

BOARD OF ASSESSORS.

OFFICE OF THE BOARD OF ASSESSORS,
NO. 27 CHAMBERS STREET,
NEW YORK, Nov. 21, 1891.

Notice is given to the owner or owners, of all houses and lots, improved or unimproved lands affected thereby, that the following assessments have been completed and are lodged in the office of the Board of Assessors for examination by all persons interested, viz. :

No. 1.—Alteration and improvement to sewers in 8th av, w s, bet 124th and 137th sts, and connections with present sewers in 126th, 127th, 128th, 133d, 134th, 135th and 136th sts.

No. 2.—Sewers in West st, bet Jay and Desbrosses sts, connecting with sewer to be constructed by the Department of Docks through Pier No. 39, also bet Canal and Desbrosses sts, with alteration and improvement to existing sewers in Watts, Desbrosses, Vestry, Hubert, Beach, North Moore, Franklin and Harrison sts.

No. 3.—Sewer in 10th av, w s, bet a point abt 316 feet n of 178th st, and a point abt 10 feet n of 190th st.

[The limits embraced by such assessments include all the several houses and lots of ground, vacant lots, pieces and parcels of land situated on—

No. 1.—Blocks bounded by 124th and 137th sts, 8th av and Av St. Nicholas, and w s of Av St. Nicholas, from 131st to 137th st.

No. 2.—Blocks bounded by Jay and Canal sts, Hudson and West sts; also e s of Hudson st, from Franklin to Beach st.

No. 3.—Blocks bounded by 178th and 185th sts. 10th and 11th avs; both sides of 11th av, from 178th to 185th st; both sides of 183d st, from 11th to Wadsworth av; blocks bounded by 185th and 187th sts, 10th and Audubon avs; w s of Audubon av, from 185th to 187th st; w s of 10th av, from 187th to 193d st; both sides of Audubon av, from 190th to 193d st; both sides of 190th st, from 10th to 11th av.]

All persons whose interests are affected by the above-named assessments, and who are opposed to the same, or either of them, are requested to present their objections in writing to the Chairman of the Board of Assessors, at their office, No. 27 Chambers street, within thirty days from the date of this notice.

The above-described lists will be transmitted, as provided by law, to the Board of Revision and Correction of Assessments for confirmation on the 22d day of December, 1891.

OFFICE OF THE BOARD OF ASSESSORS.
NO. 27 CHAMBERS STREET,
NEW YORK, Nov. 25, 1891.

Notice is given to the owner or owners of all houses and lots, improved or unimproved lands affected thereby, that the following assessments have been completed and are lodged in the office of the Board of Assessors for examination by all persons interested, viz.:

No. 1. Sewer in 90th st, bet Av A and 2d av.

No. 2. Paving Reade st, from West to Washington st, with granite blocks and laying crosswalks, under chapter 449, Laws of 1889.

No. 3. Paving Spring st, from West to Washington sts, with granite blocks, under chapter 449, Laws of 1889.

No. 4. Paving Chambers st, from West to Greenwich st, with granite blocks and laying crosswalks, under chapter 449, Laws of 1889.

No. 5. Paving Jay st, from West to Washington sts, with granite blocks and laying crosswalks, under chapter 449, Laws of 1889.

No. 6.—Paving Franklin st, from West to Washington st, with granite blocks, and laying crosswalks, under chapter 449, Laws of 1889.

No. 7.—Paving Harrison st, from West to Washington st, with granite blocks, and laying crosswalks, under chapter 449, Laws of 1889.

No. 8.—Paving 110th st, from 1st av to the bulkhead line on the East River, with granite blocks, under chapter 449, Laws of 1889.

No. 9.—Receiving basins on the n e and s e cors of 52d st and 12th av.

No. 10.—Flagging, reflagging, curbing and recurbing w s of Amsterdam av, from 101st to 102d st.

No. 11.—Flagging, reflagging, curbing and recurbing both sides of 117th st, from 7th av to Av St. Nicholas.

No. 12.—Flagging, reflagging, curbing and recurbing w s of Church st, bet Vesey and Fulton sts.

[The limits embraced by such assessments include all the several houses and lots of ground, vacant lots, pieces and parcels of land situated on—

No. 1.—Both sides of 90th st, from Av A to 2d av; also blocks bounded by 2d av and Av A, 89th and 90th sts.

No. 2.—Both sides of Reade st, from West to Washington st, and to the extent of half the block at the intersecting sts.

No. 3.—Both sides of Spring st, from West to Washington st, and to the extent of half the block at the intersecting sts.

No. 4.—Both sides of Chambers st, from West to Greenwich st, and to the extent of half the block at the intersecting sts.

No. 5.—Both sides of Jay st, from West to Washington st, and to the extent of half the block at the intersecting sts.

No. 6.—Both sides of Franklin st, from West to Washington st, and to the extent of half the block at the intersecting sts.

No. 7.—Both sides of Harrison st, from West to Washington st. and to the extent of half the block at the intersecting sts.

No. 8.—Both sides of 110th st, from 1st av to the Harlem River, and to the extent of half the block at the intersecting avs.

No. 9.—Both sides of 52d st, from 11th to 12th av, and east side of 12th av and west side of 11th av, extending half way between 51st and 52d sts and 52d and 53d sts.

No. 10.—West side of Amsterdam av, extending northerly from 101st st about 125 feet 11 inches.

No. 11.—Both sides of 117th st, from from 7th av to Av St. Nicholas.

No. 12.—West side of Church st, from Fulton to Vesey st.]

All persons whose interests are affected by the above-named assessments, and who are opposed to the same, or either of them, are requested to present their objections in writing to the Chairman of the Board of Assessors, at their office, No. 27 Chambers street, within thirty days from the date of this notice.

The above-described lists will be transmitted, as provided by law, to the Board of Revision and Correction of Assessments, for confirmation, on the 26th day of December, 1891.

In the matter of the application of the Board of Street Opening and Improvement of the City of New York, for and on behalf of the Mayor, Aldermen and Commonalty of the City of New York, relative to acquiring title, wherever the same has not been heretofore acquired, to Robbins avenue (although not yet named by proper authority), from the Southern Boulevard to Westchester avenue, in the 23d Ward, etc.; also to Willow avenue (although not yet named by proper authority), from Bronx Kills to East 138th st, in the 23d Ward, etc. Notice is given that the bill of costs, charges and expenses, incurred by reason of the proceedngs in the above-entitled matters, will be presented for taxation to one of the Justices of the Supreme Court, at the Chambers thereof, in the County Court House, at the City Hall, in the City of New York, on the 8th and 10th day of December, 1891, at 10.30 o'clock in the forenoon of those days, or as soon thereafter, as counsel can be heard thereon; and that the said bill of costs, charges and expenses has been deposited in the office of the Department of Public Works, there to remain for and during the space of ten days.

In the matter of the application of the Board of Street Opening and Improvement of the City of New York, for and on behalf of the Mayor, Aldermen and Commonalty of the City of New York, relative to acquiring title, wherever the same has not been heretofore acquired, to 144th street, from Amsterdam avenue to Convent avenue, in the 12th Ward of the City of New York; also relative to the opening of 105th street, between Riverside avenue and the Boulevard, in the 12th Ward of the City of New York. Pursuant to the statutes in such cases made and provided, notice is hereby given that an application will be made to the Supreme Court of the State of New York, at a Special Term of said Court, to be held at the Chambers thereof, in the County Court House, in the City of New York, on the 6th day of January, 1892, at the opening of the Court on that day, or as soon thereafter as counsel can be heard, for the appointment of Commissioners of Estimate and Assessment in the above entitled matters. The nature and extent of the improvements hereby intended is the acquisition of title, in the name and on behalf of the Mayor, Aldermen and Commonalty of the City of New York, for the use of tha public, to all the lands and premises, with the buildings thereon and the appurtenances thereto belonging, required for the opening and extension of the above streets.

OFFICE OF THE BOARD OF ASSESSORS,
NO. 27 CHAMBERS STREET.
NEW YORK, Dec. 3, 1891.

Notice is given to the owner or owners of all houses and lots, improved or unimproved lands affected thereby, that the following assessments have been completed and are lodged in the office of the Board of Assessors for examination by all persons interested, viz.:

No. 1.—Paving Greenwich st, from the s s of Vesey st to the n s of Barclay st, with granite blocks and laying crosswalks (so far as the same is within the limits of grants of land under water).

No. 2.—Paving North Moore st, from West to Washington sts, with granite blocks and laying crosswalks (so far as the same is within the limits of grants of land under water).

No. 3.—Paving 1st av, from the southerly to the northerly intersection of 126th st, with granite blocks and laying crosswalks.

No. 4.—Paving 64th st, from Central Park West to the Boulevard, with granite blocks.

No. 5.—Paving 115th st, from Park to 5th av, with granite blocks.

No. 6.—Regulating, grading, curbing and flagging 103d st, from 1st av to the East River.

No. 7.—Sewer in 102d st, bet Park and Madison avs.

No. 8.—Fencing the vacant lots on the block bounded by 103d and 104th sts, Central Park West and Manhattan av.

No. 9.—Fencing the vacant lots on the s s of 77th st and e s Columbus av, being 100 ft. on the av and 150 ft on the st.

No. 10.—Fencing the vacant lots at the n w cor of Av B and 81st st.

No. 11.—Laying crosswalk across 124th st at the westerly side of Lenox av.

No. 12.—Laying crosswalk across 7th av at the northerly side of 130th st.

No. 13.—Curbing and flagging n s of 73d st, from 1st to 2d av.

No. 14.—Flagging, reflagging, curbing and recurbing s s of 66th st, bet Columbus and Amsterdam avs.

No. 15.—Flagging, reflagging, curbing and recurbing e s of 5th av, from 116th to 117th st.

No. 16.—Flagging and reflagging, curbing and recurbing s s 131st st, from 5th to Lenox av.

No. 17.—Flagging, reflagging, curbing and recurbing n s 8th st, commencing at Broadway and extdg abt 80 ft. easterly.

No. 18.—Flagging, reflagging, curbing and recurbing n w cor 120th st and 7th av, extdg abt 100 ft. on av and st.

No. 19.—Fencing the vacant lots situated on 104th and 105th sts, bet 5th and Madison avs.

No. 20.—Constructing an iron fence on the easterly side of Edgecombe av, from 145th st to St. Nicholas pl.

No. 21.—Laying crosswalk across Av A at the northerly side of 70th st.

[The limits embraced by such assessments include all the several houses and lots of ground, vacant lots, pieces and parcels of land situated on—

No. 1.—Both sides of Greenwich st, from Vesey to Barclay st, and to the extent of half the block at the intersecting sts.

No. 2.—Both sides of North Moore st, from West to Washington st, and to the extent of half the block at the intersecting sts.

No. 3.—To the extent of half the block from the northerly and southerly intersection of 126th st and 1st av.

No. 4.—Both sides of 64th st, from Central Park West to the Boulevard, and to the extent of half the block at the intersecting avs.

No. 5.—Both sides of 115th st, from Park to 5th av, and to the extent of half the block at the intersecting avs.

No. 6.—Both sides of 103d st, from 1st av to the East River.

No. 7.—Both sides of 102d st, from Park to Madison av, also block bounded by 101st st and 102d st, Park and Madison avs.

No. 8.—Block bounded by 103d and 104th sts, Central Park West, and Manhattan av.

No. 9.—South side of 77th st, extending easterly from Columbus av 175 feet and extending southerly on Columbus av 102 feet 2 inches.

No. 10.—Northwest corner of Av B and 81st st, on block No. 44, Ward Nos. 22, 23 and 24.

No. 11.—To the extent of half the block from the westerly side of Lenox av and 124th st.

No. 12.—To the extent of half the block from the northerly side of 130th st and 7th av.

No. 13.—N s of 73d st, from 1st to 2d av, on block 189, on Ward Nos. 14, 15 and 16.

No. 14.—S s of 66th st, bet Boulevard and Amsterdam av, on block No. 154, Ward Nos. 46, 53, 54, 55, 56 and 57.

No. 15.—E s of 5th av, from 116th to 117th st.

No. 16.—S s of 131st st, from 5th to Lenox av, on block No. 615, Ward Nos. 49 to 63 inclusive, and Ward No. 65.

No. 17.—N s of 8th st, commencing at Broadway and extending abt 106 ft. easterly.

No. 18.—N w cor of 120th st and 7th av, on block No. 821, Ward Nos. 27 to 32 inclusive.

No. 19.—N s of 104th and s s of 105th sts, from Madison to 5th av.

No. 20.—E s of Edgecombe av, from 145th to 155th st.

No. 21.—To the extent of half the block from the northerly side of 70th st and Av A.]

All persons whose interests are affected by the above-named assessments, and who are opposed to the same, or either of them, are requested to present their objections, in writing, to the Chairman of the Board of Assessors, at their office, No. 27 Chambers street, within thirty days from the date of this notice.

The above-described lists will be transmitted, as provided by law, to the Board of Revision and Correction of Assessments for confirmation, on the 4th day of January, 1892.

In the matter of the application of the Board of Street Opening and Improvement of the City of New York, for and on behalf of the Mayor, Aldermen and Commonalty of the City of New York, relative to acquiring title, wherever the same has not been heretofore acquired, to Convent avenue (although not yet named by proper authority), from 135th street to 145th street, in the 12th Ward of the City of New York; 119th street, between Boulevard and Riverside avenue, 12th Ward; 121st street, between Boulevard and Amsterdam avenue, 12th Ward; 117th street, between Amsterdam and Morningside avenues, 12th Ward. Pursuant to the statutes in such cases made and provided, notice is hereby given that application will be made to the Supreme Court of the State of New York, at a Special Term of said court, to be held at the Chambers thereof, in the County Court House, in the City of New York, on the 12th and 13th days of January, 1892, at the opening of the court on that day, or as soon thereafter as counsel can be heard thereon, for the appointment of Commissioners of Estimate and Assessment in the above-entitled matters. The nature and extent of the improvement hereby intended is the acquisition of title, in the name and on behalf of the Mayor, Aldermen and Commonalty of the City of New York, for the use of the public, to all the lands and premises, with the buildings thereon and the appurtenances thereto belonging, required for the opening of above streets.

In the matter of the application of the Board of Street Opening and Improvement of the City of New York, for and on behalf of the Mayor,

Aldermen and Commonalty of the City of New York, relative to acquiring title to Decatur avenue (although not yet named by proper authority), from Brookline street to Mosholu Parkway, in the 24th Ward, etc ; 175th street, from Carter avenue to 3d avenue, 24th Ward; Harlem River terrace, from Ceder avenue to Fordham road, 24th Ward; Woodruff street, from Southern Boulevard to the Bronx River, 24th Ward; and relative to the opening of Avenue B, from 86th street to the marginal street bulkhead line, Harlem River, in 12th Ward. Notice is hereby given that the bill of costs, charges and expenses incurred by reason of the proceedings in the above-entitled matters will be presented for taxation to one of the Justices of the Supreme Court, at the Chambers thereof, in the County Court House, at the City Hall in the City of New York, on the 10th and 14th days of December, 1891, at 10:30 o'clock in the forenoon of that day, or as soon thereafter as counsel can be heard thereon, and that the said bills of costs, charges and expenses have been deposited in the office of the Department of Public Works, there to remain for and during the space of ten days.

In the matter of the application of the Board of Street Opening and Improvement of the City of New York, for and on behalf of the Mayor, Aldermen and Commonalty of the City of New York, relative to acquiring title, wherever the same has not been heretofore acquired, to Lind avenue (although not yet named by proper authority), extending from Devoe street to Sedgwick avenue, in the 23d Ward of the City of New York, as the same has been heretofore laid out and designated as a first-class street or road by the Department of Public Parks. The Commissioners of Estimate and Assessment in the above-entitled matter, give notice to all persons interested in this proceeding and to the owner or owners of all houses and lots and improved and unimproved lands affected thereby, and to all others whom it may concern, that they have completed their estimate and assessment, and that all persons interested in this proceeding, or in any of the lands affected thereby, and having objections thereto, do present their said objections in writing duly verified, at No. 51 Chambers street (Room 4), in said city, on or before the second day of January, 1892, and that the said Commissioners will hear parties so objecting within ten week days next after the said second day of January, 1892, and for that purpose will be in attendance at said office on each of said ten days at 3 o'clock P. M. Their report herein will be presented to the Supreme Court of the State of New York, at a special term thereof, to be held at the Chambers thereof, in the County Court House, in the City of New York, on the 27th day of January, 1892, at the opening of the Court on that day, and that then and there, or as soon thereafter as counsel can be heard thereon, a motion will be made that the said report be confirmed.

Notice to Property-Owners.

CITY OF NEW YORK, FINANCE DEPARTMENT,
COMPTROLLER'S OFFICE, December 1, 1891.

In pursuance of Section 997 of the "New York City Consolidation Act of 1882," the Comptroller of the City of New York hereby gives notice to all persons, owners of property affected by the assessment list in the matter of acquiring title to Manhattan street, from 12th avenue westerly to the established bulkhead line, Hudson River, which was confirmed by the Supreme Court, October 22, 1891, and entered on the 27th day of November, 1891, in the Record of Titles of Assessments kept in the "Bureau for the Collection of Assessments and Arrears of Taxes and Assessments and of Water Rents," that unless the amount assessed for benefit on any person or property shall be paid within sixty days after the date of said entry of the assessment, interest will be collected thereon, as provided in section 998 of said "New York City Consolidated Act of 1882."

The above assessment is payable to the Collector of Assessments and Clerk of Arrears, at the "Bureau for the Collection of Assessments and Arrears of Taxes and Assessments and of Water Rents," Room 31, Stewart Building, between the hours of 9 A. M. and 2 P. M., and all payments made thereon on or before January 26, 1892, will be exempt from interest as above provided and after that date will be subject to a charge of interest at the rate of 7 per cent per annum from the date of entry in the Record of Title of Assessments in said Bureau to the date of payment.

Notice to Taxpayers.

FINANCE DEPARTMENT.

BUREAU FOR THE COLLECTION OF TAXES,
NO. 57 CHAMBERS STREET (STEWART BUILDING),
NEW YORK, December 2, 1891.

The Receiver of Taxes of the City of New York gives notice to all persons who have omitted to pay their taxes for the year 1891, to pay the same to him at his office on or before the first day of January, 1892, as provided by section 846 of the New York City Consolidation Act of 1882.

Upon any such tax remaining unpaid on the first day of December, 1891, 1 per centum will be charged, received and collected in addition to the amount thereof; and upon such tax remaining unpaid on the first day of January, 1892, interest will be charged, received and collected upon the amount thereof at the rate of 7 per centum per annum, to be calculated from the fifth day of October, 1891, on which day the assessment rolls and warrants for the taxes of 1891 were delivered to the said Receiver of Taxes, to the date of payment, pursuant to section 843 of said act.

Fine Printing of All Kinds.

Contractors' Notes.

Sealed bids or estimates for furnishing the materials and work required for a cow stable on Ward's Island will be received at the office of the Department of Public Charities and Correction, No. 66 3d avenue, in the City of New York, until Wednesday, December 9, 1891, until 10 A. M.

Bids or estimates will be received at the office of the Department of Public Works, No. 31 Chambers street, until 12 o'clock M., on Tuesday, December 15, 1891: For furnishing and delivering double-nozzle case hydrants; for laying water mains in Bristow, 72d, 75th, 91st, 101st, 138th, 139th, 142d and 161st streets, and in Tinton avenue; for flagging 8 feet wide and reflagging, curbing and recurbing the sidewalks on 34th street, from 10th avenue to North or Hudson River; for flagging and reflagging, curbing and recurbing the sidewalks on both sides of 64th street, from Central Park West to the Boulevard, and on the east side of Boulevard, from 63d to 65th street; for flagging full width and reflagging, curbing and recurbing the sidewalks on north side of 115th street, from 3d to Lexington avenue; for flagging full width and reflagging, curbing and recurbing the sidewalks on northwest corner of Mount Morris avenue and 120th street; for flagging full width and reflagging, curbing and recurbing the sidewalks on Madison avenue, from 131st to 132d street: for flagging and reflagging, curbing and recurbing the sidewalks on the south side of 132d street, from Lenox to 7th avenue; for regulating and grading 148th street, from Boulevard west to 12th avenue, and setting curbstones and flagging sidewalks and laying crosswalks at intersecting avenues, and for regulating and grading 149th street, from Boulevard west to 12th avenue, and setting curbstones and flagging sidewalks therein and laying crosswalks at intersecting avenues.

Sealed bids will be received by the Department of Public Parks, at its offices, Nos. 49 and 51 Chambers street, until 11 o'clock A. M., on Wednesday, December 16, 1891, for the erection of an iron railing around one park in Park avenue, between 66th and 67th streets.

Sealed bids or estimates will be received by the Commissioner of Street Improvements of the 23d and 24th Wards at his office, No. 2622 3d avenue, corner of 141st street, until 3 o'clock P. M., on Thursday, December 17, 1891: For constructing sewer and appurtenances in John street, from the existing sewer in Brook avenue to Eagle avenue, with branches in St. Ann's avenue, from 156th street to Clifton street; also for constructing sewer and appurtenances in 142d street, from Brook avenue to St. Ann's avenue.

The attention of readers is directed to the "Wants and Offers" at the end of the Real Estate Department.

New Incorporation.

The Century Savings and Loan Co. filed a certificate of incorporation on December 1st for the purpose of buying and improving real estate. The number of shares shall not exceed 1,000,000 at $100 a share. The names of the officers and trustees are John A. Tonner, C. W. Kobisaat and seven others.

The New West Side Station.

The opening of the new elevated road station at Columbus avenue and 66th street is giving an improved tone to neighboring property. It will be remembered that the cost of this station was defrayed by West Side property-owners and brokers, and among the subscribers were James Rufus Smith, F. Crawford, John T. Farley, E. Livingston, Walton Storm, J. H. Godwin, B. Cohen, A Van Buren, W. C. Lesster, I. M. Grenell, Wm. Rankin, Chas. E. Schuyler & Co. and P. S. Treacy, the two latter brokers having been particularly active in obtaining subscriptions. The owners of the four abutting corners at 66th street have given the Manhattan Road a perpetual release from damages for loss of light, etc.

Back Numbers Wanted.

Fifteen cents each will be paid for copies of this paper, No. 1087, dated Jan. 12, 1889, and No. 1147, dated March 8, 1890. Twenty-five cents will be paid for index of volume 43, Jan. to June, 1889.

Special Notices.

The Union Iron Works, of 29 Broadway, who are prominently known as contractors for the iron work of the Columbia Building, Arbuckle Building, New York Academy of Medicine and other large structures, have recently secured the services of Mr. Henry W. Hodge as chief-engineer of the company. Mr. Hodge is eminently fitted for the position, as he is a graduate of the Rensselaer Polytechnic Institute, and for a number of years past has been prominently connected with one of the largest bridge and construction companies of the country, where he has acquired a valuable and practical experience in designing structural iron work of all descriptions. He has resigned his former connection to take charge of the engineering department of the Union Iron Works, so that this company is fully prepared to make designs for any variety of structural iron work as well as estimates thereon. They are now engaged in the preliminary studies for the constructional iron work of a fifteen-story building under contemplation in this city.

The attention of readers is directed to the "Wants and Offers" at the end of the Real Estate Department.

THE WEST SIDE INDEX.

All persons interested in West Side real estate should possess an Index of Ten Years' Conveyances affecting property between the north side of 59th and south side of 125th streets, from west side 8th avenue to Hudson River. This Index is published by THE RECORD AND GUIDE, *and the period covered is the ten years prior to June 30th, 1884, to which has been added a list of the conveyances up to January 1st, 1885. Every transfer of real estate in that section, made between those years, is recorded in the Index, with a description of the property, the price paid for it, the liber and page in which the conveyances are recorded in the Register's Office, and the name of the seller and the purchaser. The volume is of the utmost value to conveyancers, lawyers, real estate brokers, agents and dealers n real estate generally, and we will supply the Index to our readers, if ordered before January 1st next, at the reduced price of $5.*

Readers of THE RECORD AND GUIDE *may subscribe to the new illustrated quarterly magazine,* THE ARCHITECTURAL RECORD, *by sending their names and addresses to the office of publication; Nos. 14-16 Vesey street. The annual subscription is $1.*

Real Estate Department.

It seems evident from the events of the past weeks that the real estate market, so long dormant, has at last awakened. The transactions closed are more important and interesting, the negotiations more spontaneous and cheerful, and the whole feeling dominating the market very much better than has been the case for some time past. There is no reason why this improved condition of affairs should not continue, if sellers will keep themselves within bounds in the matter of prices. The purchasers, for such a long time few in number and very indifferent in their feelings, are becoming more numerous and willing every day. With this more or less anxious attitude on the part of buyers and with present holders on a reasonable basis as to prices, with the country prosperous and with money easy, there is no good reason why we should not have an active real estate market from now until the midsummer months of next year, with the unavoidable holiday interruptions. But everything must be conducted on common-sense principles. Owners must realize that there is no room for a "boom," and buyers that there is not the slightest sign of a collapse of, or a break in, prices. The position of both parties to transactions must change from what they have been if there is to be any sort of a spring business. It is true that owners have held property at figures unwarranted by facts, but they are now willing to make reasonable concessions, thanks to the criticism that has been levelled at prices. On the other hand the market now contains a goodly number of straight out buyers who have cash to pay for what they purchase. These buyers are not half so obstinate or indifferent as they were a few months ago. They, too, are willing to advance a little and meet sellers half way. This is as it should be, and now the main thing is to see that there is no back-sliding from the present attitude of either buyer or seller.

The sales and leases this week include some very interesting items of importance to all those engaged in the real estate business. They include transactions in property in the down-town business district, in the retail dry-goods district and further up town where private dwellings, flats and lots have been sold. The activity has extended to Yonkers, where J. Romaine Brown & Co., have sold 400 lots on Mile Square road and resold the same for the purchaser. The down-town transactions referred to are of peculiar interest. In the retail dry-goods district Alden & Sterne have sold Nos. 40 and 42 West 14th street and running through to 13th street, a plot 50x200, part of it leasehold, for Jacob Rothschild to Ludwig Bros., who now occupy adjoining quarters. This news item becomes of particular importance when the talk about Ludwig Bros. selling their buildings on 14th street is recalled. This firm now owns the larger part of the stores which they occupy and it is just possible that they have purchased Nos. 40 and 42 adjoining for the purpose of selling their entire holdings to some capitalist or syndicate of capitalists who have been anxious to invest in 14th street real estate. This conjecture, based on the rumor and talk of the market, is offered for what it is worth. It is unconfirmed. Another transaction worthy of notice is the lease by Geo. Hillen, of the northwest corner of Broadway and Chambers street, for twenty-one years, at an annual rental of $40,000, or for a total of $840,000 for the whole term. Mr. Hillen, it may be remembered, was the man who more than any other started 125th street values on an up grade by his speculations at the southeast corner of that street and 7th avenue. The other sales given in detail in our "Gossip" column are more ordinary in their character.

In passing it is worthy of note that the remarks made in this column a month ago as to the number and extent of the trades is fully borne out by the filings of conveyances printed in another part of this paper. At the time it was said that, although there were a number of trades, the condition of affairs was not so bad as it was here painted. That the statements made in regard to trades, as in regard to many other unpleasant facts, were true is plainly shown by the official records, which now confirm the position which we took a month ago. It is about time that real estate men consented to recognize the truth when it is put before them. Their vain denials of patent facts will neither help their own private business or the general condition of the real estate market. Real estate has nothing to fear from the truth plainly and honestly spoken, but great discredit is cast upon it as an investment by the policy of secretiveness and misrepresentation, seemingly so popular in some quarters.

THE AUCTION SALES OF THE WEEK.

A review of the doings in the Auction Room during the past week is very generally satisfactory. The offerings have been more interesting and important than those of any other week of the year, and the character of the audiences has been correspondingly higher. The auctioneers announcements, of course, included parcels that were not desirable, and these go to make up the list of withdrawals and fictitious sales to which the real estate world has become accustomed lately. It is, however, pleasant to be able to record the fact that this list of failures is much smaller than it has been for months past—smaller and less important in its effect on the general market. The numerous voluntary auction sales given in detail elsewhere met with a fair degree of success, and the foreclosure sales show only one case, and that a very insignificant one, where the selling price failed to realize the amount due. The features of the week were, of course, the Broadway corner, two down-town parcels and two notable up-town corner sales.

A BROADWAY CORNER AND OTHER DOWN-TOWN PROPERTY SOLD.

As we predicted in these columns last week, the sale of the Dash estate properties attracted a large and representative crowd to the Auction Room. It is only very occasionally that a down-town Broadway corner is offered, either at auction or at private sale, under any circumstances, and when it is offered by order of the Supreme Court, and must therefore be sold, the event is one not to be missed by those closely identified with real estate interests. The crowd, therefore, which attended Thursday's sale, was an exceptional one and it included not only large capitalists but well-known brokers, who are only now and then seen on the Exchange. Among them were such men as Byam K. Stevens, Wm. R. Martin, Sire Bros., Hugh N. Camp, F. K. Kellar, W. W. Goodrich, John Morgan, Francis O'Neill, L. S. Wolff, P. J. Kennedy, Mayer Kahn, Jefferson M. Levy, Daniel S. McElroy, Jacob Kohn, Ottinger Bros., Gutwillig Bros., Heilner & Wolf, Jacob Bockman, L. N. Levy, Hoffman Bros., who represent the Weld estate, of Boston; L. S. Samuel, Sonn Bros., Josiah Belden, S. Bernheimer, Timothy Donovan, Geo. R. Read, F. R. Houghton, J. Romaine Brown, S. De Walltearss, A. M. Arneberg, E. M. Wilkins, N. T. Lawrence, E. J. Sause, Jr., Wm. M. Ryan, Jere. Johnson, Jr., B. Cohen, John R. Foley, D. B. Freedman, W. H. Blackwell, A. Weinstein, B. P. Fairchild, A. L. Mordecai, J. C. Lalor, I. T. Meyer, J. J. Plummer and J. Jay Smith. This list, of course, is a very incomplete one, but it will give some idea of the interest that the sale excited.

The parcel that attracted the greatest attention naturally was No. 145 Broadway, southwest corner of Liberty street, and Nos. 86 and 88 Liberty street, southwest corner of Temple street, all of which was sold in one parcel. The plot contains about 6,587 square feet and it is covered by three five-story brick office buildings which together rent for $45,735 per annum. Some of the leases on the building run until 1894. The terms of sale were 5 per cent cash to be paid at the time of sale with an option to allow 70 per cent to remain on mortgage for three or five years at 5 per cent. Before the sale commenced speculation was rife as to what the Broadway corner would bring. The estimates were based on the sale of the northwest corner of Broadway and Liberty street, sold over a year ago for $181.12 per square foot, and vague rumors as to what had been offered at private sale. Nearly all the estimates were in excess of the price obtained and several of them exceeded it by several hundreds of thousands of dollars. In fact the whole sale of this Broadway corner was a surprise. As it turned out, instead of the price being over $180 per square foot it was only about $118, and if the prices said to have been offered for it were really offered the question is, why did not the would-be purchaser step up and bid?

A group of brokers, who stood to the right of Mr. Meyer when the sale began, were asked to name the figure the corner would bring and al agreed on sums ranging from $900,000 to $1,100,000, while Mr. Alfred L. White's estimate was $750,000, or within $20,000 of the price realized. A gentleman present at the sale told the writer that Mr. Bowie Dash was born on the corner of Broadway and Liberty street and that the plot has been owned by the Dash family ever since. One of the stories circulated was that the National Express Co. had offered $900,000 for the property eight years ago, their intention being to erect a fourteen-story building on the site. This offer was declined.

The bidding was started by S. De Walltearss, the auctioneer, at $700,000, and for some time that figure remained the bid. Then $10,000 was added, and slowly and regretfully further bids of $10,000 were made until $770,000 was reached, and Mr. De Walltearss became the purchaser. He represented Mrs. John Wolfe and two other heirs. The great crowd of rich real estate men offered no bids on the property, and this attitude is not explained by the fact that Mr. De Walltearss represented the heirs. Very few of those present were aware of the fact until long after the sale, and even if they had known it, the property was offered under partition, and every one had an equal chance with all the others. On all sides the opinion was expressed that the property had sold below what it was expected to bring, and every one was trying to account for it. It is impossible to explain it. The only profitable comparison that is possible is with the northwest corner of Liberty street and Broadway which was sold in March, 1890, to the Singer Manufacturing Co. for $540,500. It contained 3,006 square feet. The difference in price is hardly explained by the fact that much of 6,587 square feet sold on Thursday was on a side street. It was all in one parcel, and it has a wide frontage on Broadway, which would permit the erection of a large office building. Under these circumstances it would seem that the southwest corner of Broadway and Liberty street was a cheap property.

The other two parcels belonging to the Dash estate were quickly disposed of; the first was No. 70 Cortlandt street, near Washington, about 23.7x67, which is rented for $2,420 per annum, until 1894. The bidding on this parcel started at $25,000 and ran up to $37,100, when Bernard Cohen became the purchaser. The adjoining parcel, No. 72, of about the same size, was transferred in 1888 for $35,000. The first bid on No. 219 Fulton street, a three-story building, 24.10x

82.10, was also $25,000. It is rented for $2,000 a year until 1894. After some competition, it was sold to S. Niewenhouse for $28,800.

TWO NOTABLE SALES OF CORNER LOTS.

The two most interesting competitions of the week were for corner properties on 3d and 6th avenues respectively. The first of these sales took place on Monday under a Supreme Court decree in a partition suit. It was of Nos. 2195½, 2197 and 2199 3d avenue, southeast corner of 120th street, a plot a little over 50.6x100, with one, two and three-story brick and frame buildings thereon. The first bid of $50,000 was followed by a very general competition in which many well-known speculators took part. After the $75,000 mark was passed the bidding settled down to a competition between S. Niewenhouse and Edw. Rafter. The latter finally succeeded in purchasing the property on a bid of $96,250. Mr. Rafter said he had purchased the property for Henderson Wilson. The increase in values which this corner shows is clearly indicated in a transfer of one-fifth part of it, which was recorded last year. The consideration stated was $13,000, which would bring the price for the whole property up to $65,000.

The second sale referred to was of the southwest corner of 6th avenue and 40th street, a four-story brick building and store, on lot 24.8x78, which was sold by order of the executors after the Dash estate sale on Thursday. This sale excited more interest than the great down-town corner that had been sold just before, and the work of the auctioneer, Peter F. Meyer, in advancing the bids was admirable. Morris Littman made the first bid of $55,000, but he soon dropped out of the race and Walter C. Woolley and Frederick Alfcat had the field to themselves. First by bids of $500 and $250, then by $100, $50 and $25 the figure was forced up, notwithstanding the temporary objections raised by the bidders until $79,200, when Mr. Alfcat became the purchaser. The large crowd who had watched the hard-fought competition almost as though they had a persona interest in it then indulged in a demonstration not usual on the business-like floor of the Real Estate Exchange—they spontaneously and quite enthusiastically applauded the successful bidder. These two sales of avenue corners show more clearly and distinctly than any other sales of the week the improved tone and generally better feeling of the market.

On Monday, December 7th, John N. Golding will sell the dwelling on the northwest corner of Manhattan avenue and 121st street.

On Wednesday, December 9th, Richard V. Harnett & Co. will sell the four-story brown stone flat, No. 229 East 80th street, and the six-story double tenement, No. 350 East 33d street.

On Thursday, December 10th, Richard V. Harnett & Co. will sell the six-story brick malt house on the southeast corner of 38th street and 1st avenue.

CONVEYANCES.

	1890. Nov. 28 to Dec. 4 inc.	1891. Nov. 27 to Dec. 3 inc.
Number	334	339
Amount involved	$6,302,860	$5,920,498
Number nominal	72	92
Number 23d and 24th Wards	61	37
Amount involved	$324,618	$176,065
Number nominal	14	10

MORTGAGES.

	1890.	1891.
Number	371	328
Amount involved	$4,680,598	$5,498,989
Number at 5 per cent	175	157
Amount involved	$1,709,386	$1,954,270
Number at less than 5 per cent	60	20
Amount involved	$947,740	$344,600
Number to Banks, Trust and Ins. Cos	58	71
Amount involved	$1,877,000	$3,026,512

PROJECTED BUILDINGS.

	1890. Nov. 29 to Dec. 5 inc.	1891. Nov. 28 to Dec. inc.
Number of buildings	84	50
Estimated cost	$569,400	$1,183,000

Gossip of the Week.

SOUTH OF 59TH STREET.

Alden & Sterne have sold for Jacob Rothschild, head of the well-known millinery house, the five-story brick and iron front building, Nos. 40 and 42 West 14th street, running through to and including Nos. 39 and 41 West 13th street, between 5th and 6th avenues, to Ludwig Bros., the dry-goods firm, for a sum stated variously at $337,500 and $350,000. The building is one of the most substantially constructed on 14th street, and is noted for its handsome arched entrance, running up to about the third tier of beams. It is now occupied by J. & J. Dobson, the Pennsylvania carpet manufacturers and dealers, who will probably vacate the property in May, when it will be occupied by Messrs. Ludwig Bros., who occupy the adjoining building. The 14th street property is Van Buren leasehold; the 13th street lots are in fee. The plot covered is 50x200 in size, and the purchasers will make alterations, as announced elsewhere.

L. J. Phillips & Co. have sold for the Steam Heating Co. their plot on the west side of Thompson street, between Broome and Spring streets, 114.6x100, to David L. Einstein, the price being stated at about $80,000. The plot will be improved. The same brokers have sold a parcel of property on Greene street.

Morris B. Baer & Co. have sold for G. Ramsberger the five-story brown stone front store and flat building on the southeast corner of 6th avenue (No. 672) and 39th street, lot 24x60, all covered, for $70,000, the name of the purchaser not having transpired. The store is leased and occupied by Hazard, Hazard & Co. It may be interesting to note that this week on 'Change the southwest corner of 6th avenue and 40th street, 24.8x78, with a four-story building, sold for $79,200.

A. Quackenbush and D. D. Lawson have sold No. 214 West 25th street, a five-story brown stone apartment house, 31x88.9 and lot 98.9, for $55,000 to A. M. Hawkins.

F. R. Houghton has sold for the Bergmann Manufacturing Co. the three lots on the north side of 34th street, commencing 300 feet east of 11th avenue, to Ferd. Schaettler, manufacturer of cabinet work, on private terms.

Henry Wise and another have sold to John Maggi for Francis C. Reed the five-story tenement, No. 489 Pearl street, 30.8x86, for $32,000.

Harris Mandelbaum has sold to Louis Lese, No. 42 Essex street, a six-story tenement.

Henry Waters has sold to Jacob Jacoby the five-story and basement apartment house, No. 32 Attorney street, 25.9x90x100, for $42,500.

James Kyle & Sons have sold on private terms the three-story and basement private dwelling No. 147 East 38th street.

Henry Wise and another have traded Daniel Rothstein's two houses, Nos. 244 and 246 Elizabeth street, for $55,750, for Vito Cimino's house, No. 58 Mulberry sttreet, for $25,750, and have resold No. 58 Mulberry street for $28,000 cash to a Mr. Goody.

Philip Sammet has purchased No. 287 Madison street, a three-story and basement brown stone dwelling, 23.6x100, on private terms.

NORTH OF 59TH STREET.

J. D. Butler has purchased from Richard M. Hooley, of Chicago, four vacant lots, two of which front on the north side of 72d street and two on the south side of 73d street, running through, commencing 425 feet west of Central Park West, size 50x204.4, for about $100,000. The property will be improved as announced elsewhere. The lots adjoin the lawn of the "Dakota."

B. S. Levy has purchased from John Townshend the eight lots on the south side of 81st street, running through to the north side of 80th street, and commencing 100 feet east of Riverside Drive, four lots on each street. The lots will be improved, as reported in another column.

L. J. Phillips & Co. have sold for John Selfridge two of his five houses on 75th street, Nos. 148 and 150 West, between Columbus and Amsterdam avenues, to Geo. Rosenfeldt, one for his own occupancy and one for that of a near relative. The buildings are not yet completed, and the price paid is understood to have been about $75,000. They are each 20x56x102.2 in size, and have three-story extensions.

J. D. Butler has sold two of his houses on the south side of 145th street, near Edgecombe avenue, to Richard M. Hooley, of Chicago, in part exchange for his four lots on 72d and 73d streets, between Central Park West and Columbus avenue, referred to above.

Arthur Gorsch has sold for Sidney Guggenheimer to D. Schlechtmann, No. 209 East 95th street, a five-story brick tenement, on lot 27x100, for $22,000; and for Mrs. T. Roesner to Rachel L. Epstein, No. 318 East 114th street, a four-story single flat, 18.9x100, for $9,500.

J. Romaine Brown & Co. have sold for D. H. Sheppard eight lots on the north side of Clark place, west of Jerome avenue, running through to Findlay place, four lots fronting on each place, on private terms.

Ames & Co. have sold for Mr. Mitchell, the coffee merchant, the three-story high stoop brown stone No. 46 West 84th street, 18.4x52x102.2, to Samuel J. Storrs, on private terms.

Paul Halpin has sold to Peter McCoy, the plot 100x100, on the north side of 142d street, between Hamilton place and the Boulevard, with the dwelling thereon, for $38,000.

Wm. Rankin has sold to Joseph Turner three lots on the south side of 135th street, between 5th and Lenox avenues, for $25,500. Broker, J. Montgomery Strong, Jr.

Samuel McMillan has sold to Chas. G. Judson the northwest corner of Central Park West and 97th street, a lot 25.11x100, for $21,000.

Dr. Robert H. M. Danbaru has purchased from Charles Mayne, No. 105 West 74th street, a 20-foot four-story private dwelling, for $31,000.

Gibbin & Taylor have sold another of their four-story houses on West 75th street, No. 124, size 21x58 and three-story extension x102.2, to Geo. Stanton for $40,000.

Dr. F. E. Robinson has sold the four-story English basement house, No. 307 West 72d street, overlooking the Hudson River, 17x60x102.2, with three-story extension, on private terms, to a Mr. Thompson, who will occupy it after his marriage. Bellamy & Winans are understood to have been the brokers.

Slawson & Hobbs have sold for Daniel Slawson No. 25 West 84th street, a five-story brown stone flat, 32x90x102.2, for about $52,000.

Harris Mandelbaum has bought of the Whiting estate five lots, each 25x100, on south side of 137th street, between Lenox and 7th avenues.

LEASES.

Potter & Brother, representing the Andrews estate, of Boston, in conjunction with Alden & Sterne, have leased the five-story stone front building on the northwest corner of Broadway and Chambers street, to Geo. Hillen, of restaurant fame, for a period of twenty-one years, from May 1, 1892, at a total of $840,000 net, an average of $40,000 per annum. The building, exclusive of the basement, is now occupied by Tredwell & Slote, the clothiers, who will vacate the property on May 1 next. The structure will be remembered as the old Delmonico building. It faces the Stewart Building and overlooks the City Hall Park, and has a frontage of 50.6 feet on Broadway (No. 273), and 93.7 on Chambers street) No. 73). The ground on which it stands has been in the Andrews family since the beginning of the present century. Mr. Hillen contemplates improving the property, as announced in another column.

E. G. Gilmore has leased Niblo's Theatre on Broadway to Elmer E. Vance, the electrician, from January 1, 1892, for a term of years.

Brooklyn.

Corwith Bros. have sold the lot, 20x85, on the northeast corner of Nassau avenue and Russell street, for Geo. W. Palmer to John Wittschen for $2,050.

J. P. Sloane has sold for Patrick Meehan the three-story frame dwelling, 28x38, with lot 25x100, No. 103 Dupont street, to Robert Hufnagel for $2,900.

C. H. McLaughlin has traded No. 96 1st place, a four-story brown stone building, at $18,000, for a seventy-acre farm in Chester, Mass.

CONVEYANCES.

	1890. Nov. 27 to Dec. 3 inc	1891. Nov. 26 to Dec. 2 inc.
Number	442	383
Amount involved	$1,928,406	$1,779,679
Number nominal	111	109

MORTGAGES.

	1890.	1891.
Number	394	322
Amount involved	$1,290,817	$1,875,131
Number at 5 per cent. or less	234	169
Amount involved	$893,834	$812,405

PROJECTED BUILDINGS.

	1890. Nov. 28 to Dec. 4 inc.	1891. Nov. 27 to Dec. 3 inc.
Number of buildings	67	60
Estimated cost	$394,370	$153,055

Out of Town.

YONKERS, N. Y.—The estate of Stephen H. Thayer has sold, through J. Romaine Brown & Co., about 400 lots on Mile Square road and McLean avenue. The price and the name of the purchaser has not transpired. It is said that the latter has resold the property to parties who will develop and improve it.

Out Among the Builders.

Albert Wagner has finished plans for the down-town power-house cable station for the Third Avenue Railroad Company, Albert J. Elias, president, to be built on the northwest corner of the Bowery and Bayard street, extending to and including the northeast corner of Bayard and Elizabeth streets. The building will be 100x200 in size, nine stories in height, and the cost about $650,000. The basement, sub-basement and first story will be used for power purposes, and the upper stories for manufacturing, the main engine and other power plant, machinery, tension runs, etc., to be placed below the first floor level, the foundation floor to be 36 feet below curb level. The front will be of dark buff brick and iron, with granite trimmings.

B. S. Levy intends to build ten three-story 20-foot private houses on eight lots on the south side of 81st street, running through to the north side of 80th street, and commencing 100 feet east of Riverside Drive, four lots on each street.

Geo. Hillen contemplates the erection of a twelve-story fire-proof building on the plot, 50.6x93 7x50x94.5, on the northwest corner of Broadway and Chambers street. He takes possession on May 1, 1892, when he will probably tear down the present building on the site to make way for the improvement.

J. D. Butler intends to erect a ten-story fire-proof apartment hotel on four lots, covering a plot of 50x204.4, on the north side of 72d street, running through to 73d street and adjoining the open grounds of the "Dakota."

Cleverdon & Putzel have plans on the boards for a six-story and basement store and loft building, which F. H. Mela intends to erect at Nos. 25 and 27 West Houston street, at a cost of $110,000. The building will have all the modern improvements, including steam heat, elevator, etc., as well as several novel features. It will be of fire-proof construction. The same architects are engaged on plans for a six-story and basement business building, 25x100, to be built by L. Freeman at No. 79 Mercer street. This building will contain steam heat, elevator and other improvements. Cleverdon & Putzel will also furnish plans for a cottage which Mrs. F. Ulrich will build on Mount Hope place.

Ferd. Schaettler, manufacturer of cabinet-work, will build at once a six-story factory on three lots on the north side of 34th street, beginning 300 feet east of 11th avenue. It will contain elevators, steam heat, machinery, etc.

Frank Wennemer is drawing plans for a five-story stone front flat, 25x84, to be built by John Sturck on the south side of 83d street, between 2d and 3d avenues, at a cost of $18,000.

John C. Burne has plans on the boards for two five-story brick and stone flats, 25x69, with extension, 13x7, to be built by Andrew Judge on the north side of 132d street, 110 feet west of 5th avenue, at a cost of $20,000 each.

Graul & Frohne are the architects for a six-story brick, stone and iron front office and warehouse building to be built at No. 48 Great Jones street, at a cost of $35,000.

Ludwig Bros. intend to alter the five-story building at Nos. 40 and 42 West 14th street, running through to Nos. 39 and 41 West 13th street, and to add two elevators to the building. The changes will be made directly they obtain possession, which they expect will be in May next.

Mary E. Gault will erect three five-story apartment houses, 75x86, on 133d street, 100 feet east of 6th avenue. Bungart & Fox have the plans.

Schneider & Herter, the architects, are to build on their own account a six-story apartment house, 49x74.4, at Nos. 232 and 234 Delancey street.

David L. Einstein will improve a plot on the west side of Thompson street, between Broome and Spring streets, size 114.6x100, probably by the erection of business buildings.

Out of Town.

PASSAIC, N. J.—Math. Kakoly intends to have a four-story and basement frame apartment house built here with stone and brick foundations, 25x80 in size, with baker's oven under the yard and stores in the basement, to cost $10,000, from plans by Fred. Ebeling.

ARVERNE-BY-THE-SEA.—Cleverdon & Putzel will draw plans for two cottages to be erected at this place by A. Sampter and A. B. Anspacher, at a respective cost of $7,000 and $6,000; and for a Union Church structure, also to be erected here.

WANTS AND OFFERS.

(Advertisements strictly in accordance with this title will be inserted at the practically nominal rate of 10 CENTS *per line agate). In figuring for themselves advertisers may count seven words for each line, the address to be taken as one line. The object of this department is to bring buyers and sellers into communication with customers. Advertisements must be marked "Wants and Offers Column," and sent to the office of publication, Nos. 14 and 16 Vesey Street, not later than 3 P. M. Friday.)*

OFFERS.

A 70-ACRE FARM.—Good buildings; 30 acres timber. $4,000; exchange for drygoods; good second mortgage or real estate.
C. H. McLAUGHLIN, 198 Broadway.

FOR SALE.—In plots to suit; eligible building sites (commanding view of sound for miles), on North st., Greenwich, Connecticut; price reasonable; terms easy; neighborhood aristocratic and fashionable. Apply to
FRED. J. STONE, owner, 60 Broadway, N. Y.
Sept. 12-uf.

OFFERS.

Miscellaneous.

A NICE FITTED UP REAL ESTATE OFFICE FOR SALE in the dry-goods district; rent very low, also price. Address, "H," RECORD AND GUIDE

BUILDERS, ATTENTION!—$265,000 to loan on 1st mortgages; easiest terms; no brokers, savings bank. 135 Herald Office.

$2,000 STOCK JEWELRY to exchange for good second mortgage or anything useful. C. H. McLAUGHLIN, 198 Broadway.

OFFERS.

A PARTY ABOUT TO BUILD A FIVE-STORY factory. 50x98, in Harlem, near water-front, will lease the three upper floors and build to suit tenant. Terms very moderate. Address
May 16 u. f. OWNER, 409 E. 107th St.

PRINTING.—Book, News and Job.
RECORD AND GUIDE PRESS,
14 Barclay, and 14, 16 Vesey sts.

SALES OF THE WEEK.

The following are the sales at the Real Estate Exchange and Auction Room for the week ending December 4.

** Indicates that the property described has been bid in for plaintiff's account:*

R. V. HARNETT & CO.

Horatio st, No. 76, 25x67.8, four-story brk dwell'g. Wm. H. Gray $13,900
New Bowery, Nos. 20 and 22, running through to New Chambers and Chestnut st, 35.2x45.1 x20x7x15.1 to beginning, two three-story brk buildings. S. B. Rogers 10,400
50th st, No. 13, n s, 285 w 5th av, 15x100.5, leasehold, four-story brown stone dwell'g. S. Berrian 14,000
34th st, No. 211, n s, 137.6 e 3d av, 12.6x98.9, three-story and basement brown stone dwell'g. S. B. Rogers 9,500
*96th st, No. 57, n s, 204 e 9th av, 21x100.11, four-story brk dwell'g. F. P. Furnald et al 21,400
*107th st, No. 77, n s, 81 w 4th av, 16x100.11, three-story brk dwell'g. New York Life Ins. Co 11,000
*107th st, No. 75, n s, adj. 16x100.11, three-story stone front dwell'g. Same 7,500
Av A, No. 1549, w s, 25.8 s 82d st, 25.6x106.6, four-story stone front dwell'g. F. A. Libby. 13,000

A. H. MULLER & SON.

Broadway, No. 145 / Liberty st, Nos. 86-88 { begins Broadway, s w cor Liberty st, runs south along Broadway 29.9 x west 110.5 x south 46 x east 8 x south 8.8 x west 53.5 to Temple st, x north 82.4 to Liberty st, x east along Liberty st 159.2 to beginning, three five-story brk buildings (total rent per annum, $45,785). N. De Waltears, for Mrs. John Wolfe and two other heirs 770,000
Cortlandt st, No. 70, n s, 61.3 e Washington st, 23.7x67.3x23.4x66.11, four-story brk building. Bernard Cohen 37,100
Fulton st, No 219, n s, 92.2 e Greenwich st, 24.1x82.10x24.6x82.4, three-story brk building on front and two-story brk building on rear. S. Niewenhous 28,800
48th st, Nos. 538-542, s s, 525 w 11th av, 150x100.5, one-story brk planing and moulding mill, one-story frame shed, &c. H. Stevens. (Amt. due $10,341) 19,500
3d av, Nos. 2197 and 2199 / 120th st, Nos. 202 and 204 { begins 3d av, s e cor 120th st, runs east 100 x south 75 x west 20 x north 25 x west 80 to 3d av, x north 50.6 to beginning, two two and three-story frame stores and tenem'ts on av and one-story and three-story brk stores and tenem'ts. Henderson Wilson 96,250
6th av, No. 697, s w cor 40th st, 24.8x78, four-story brk building with store. Frederick Alfcat 79,200

WM. KENNELLY.

Beekman pl, No. 2, n w cor Mitchell pl, 19x80, five-story brk tenem't. Wm. P. Byrne. (Amt due $8,197) 12,000
Centre st, No. 14 / City Hall pl, No. 2 { begins Centre st, e s, abt 5 n junction of City Hall pl, 24.1x21 to City Hall pl, x 24.10x6 to beginning, three-story brk store. Adler & Herrman 13,400
*Houston st, No. 436, n s, 131 e Av D, 21x105.10, three-story brk store and tenem't. Chas. Lewis et al. (Amt. due $2,861) 14,080
56th st, No. 426, s s, 400 e 10th av, 25x100.5, five story brk flat. A. Hirschfield. (Amt due $2,258; prior morts. $18,000) 22,588
*69th st, n s, 275 w 11th av, 25x100.5, vacant. Charles H. Noyes et al. (Amt due $13,802) 12,000
Madison av, No. 754, e s, 27 n 65th st, 23x63, four-story stone front dwell'g. Gertrude del Ludlam 41,000
7th av, Nos. 2166 and 2168, w s, 99.11 s 129th st, 40x75, two five-story brk flats with stores. (Amt due $4,486; prior morts. $40,000) .... —

SMYTH & RYAN.

45th st, No. 634, s s, 100 w 11th av, 25x100.5, four-story brk tenem't. Peter McCollough 10,500
Amsterdam (10th) av, Nos. 870-876, s w cor 103d st, runs west 118 x south 77.2 to Bloomingdale lane, x east 18 x north 10.6 x east 100.1 to 10th av, x north 78.8 to beginning, seven-story brk flat and stores. P. & D. Mitchell. 190,250

JOHN F. B. SMYTH.

Broome st, No. 348, 22.9x93.6x23x93.6, four-story brk tenem't and store. (Bid in) .... —
47th st, No. 340, 25x100.4, five-story brk tenem't on front and four-story brk tenem't on rear. Andrew Brice 18,150
58th st, No. 315, n s, 220.6 w 8th av, 34.10x100.5, five-story stone front flat. J. A. Ellis. (Amt due $17,418) 68,000
11th av, No. 714, 25.1x60, two-story frame store. (Bid in) .... —

B. L. KENNELLY.

*57th st, No. 308 E., 25x100, two-story brk and frame building, all right, title and int., leasehold. Edw. P. Steers 100

OTHER AUCTIONEERS.

31st st, Nos. 413-427, s s, 200 w 9th av, 200x98.9, six-story brk factory. (Bid in) .... —
Willis av, n w cor 140th st, 25x106. Jacob Schlosser. (Amt due $12,947.) (Correction) 31,065
5th av, No. 2162, w s, 24.11 n 132d st, 27x100, five-story brk flat. J. C. Overhiser. (Amt due $27,410) 28,450
*5th av, No. 2164, w s, adj, 27x100, similar flat. Mutual Life Ins. Co. (Amt due $27,416) 28,000
5th av, No. 2166, adj, 27x100, similar flat. John C. Overbiser. (Amt due $27,416) 28,250
*5th av, No. 2168, adj, 19x100, five-story brk flat. Mutual Life Ins. Co 20,000

Total $1,558,968
Corresponding week, 1890 .... $426,087

BROOKLYN, N. Y.

FOR WEEK ENDING DECEMBER 3.

JERE. JOHNSON, JR.

Jefferson av, No. 964, s s, 420 e Howard av, 20x100, two-story and basement brk dwell'g. James Cropsey $4,643
Jefferson av, No. 968, s s, 440 e Howard av, 20x100, two-story and basement brk dwell'g. M. B. Adams 4,635

OTHER AUCTIONEERS.

Ashland pl, No. 139, e s, 167.07 n Hanson pl, 17.6x94.4½x17.6x94.1¼, three-story brk dwelling. Clarence M. Nelson 5,500
Eastern Parkway, n s, 150 e Linwood st, 50x100, vacant. Lazansky & Roth 450
President st, No. 185, n s, 130 e Henry st, runs north 55 x east 1 x north 45 x east 14.6 x south 100 to President st, x west 15.6 to beginning, three-story brk dwell'g. Henry B. Corey 4,527
Warren st, No. 419, n s, 75 n w Bond st, 25x100, two-story frame dwell'g and store. Patrick Byrne 2,300
*North 2d st, No. 132, s s, 240.6 w Bedford av, 25x57.4½x25x58.3, two two-story frame dwell'gs. Gottlieb W. H. Harigel 900
South 2d st, No. 374, s w s, 75 n w Hooper st, 25x120, three-story frame dwell'g. Emma Teiber 3,900
*Greene av, No. 1206, s s, 283.10 w Central av, 16.2x100, two story frame (brk lined) dwell'g. Virginia A. Kleine 2,000
*Greene av, Nos. 1212-1216, s s, 125 w Central av, 63.10x100, four two-story frame (brk lined) dwell'gs. Same 10,400
Throop av, No. 545, s e cor Hancock st, 23x81, four-story brk flat. John R. Planten 17,500

Total $57,365
Corresponding week 1890 .... $115,891

CONVEYANCES.

Wherever the letters Q. C., C. a. G. and B. & S occur, preceded by the name of the grantee they mean as follows:

1st—Q. C. is an abbreviation for Quit Claim deed, i. e., a deed in which all the right, title and interest of the grantor is conveyed, omitting all covenants or warranty.

2d—C. a. G. means a deed containing Covenant against Grantor only, in which he covenants that he hath not done any act whereby the estate conveyed may be impeached, charged or encumbered.

3d—B. & S. is an abbreviation for Bargain and Sale deed, wherein, although the seller makes no express covenants, he really grants or conveys the property for a valuable consideration, and thus impliedly claims to be the owner of it.

NEW YORK CITY.

NOVEMBER 27, 28, 30, DECEMBER 1, 2, 3.

Bleecker st, No. 130, s s, 100 e South 5th av, 25x100, six-story brk store. *Mt.* $50,000.
Bleecker st, No 128, s s, 125 e South 5th av, 25x100, six-story brk store. *Mt.* $50,000.
George R. Read, Rye, N. Y., to Margaret L. de Stuers, Sioux Falls, South Dakota. Nov. 30. $175,000
Bedford st, No. 68, e s, abt 73 s Commerce st, 18.9x125, three story frame (brk front) dwelling. Mary J. McNiece widow to Albert Etzel and Emanuel Kronacher. Dec 1. 10,150
Boulevard, e s, 24.11 n 139th st, 75x100, vacant. Foreclos. William H. Willis to Charles B Barkley. Dec. 1. 13,000
Broome st, No. 97, s s, abt 50 w Sheriff st, 25x75, four-story frame (brk front) store and tenem't with three-story brk tenem't on rear. Karl M. and Samson Wallach to Ernst Schmidt and Max Bechter. *Mt.* $12,000. Dec. 1. 17,250
Broome st, No. 141, s s, 20 e Ridge st, 20x80, two-story brk dwell'g. Louis Aaron to Robert Berlinger. *Mt.* $5,000. Sept. 21. 9,000
Broome st, No. 423, s s, abt 50 e Crosby st, 25x100x25x108, with strip in rear extdg from above to a 12-foot alley, 25x13, with use of said alley, seven-story brk store. Austen G. Fox and Rebecca F. Riggs widow to Anna Schell widow. 17-96 parts. May 20, 1891. 11,833
Catharine slip, No. 7, e s, 40 n Water st, 20x65.1x20x63, with use of alley to Water st, two story frame store and tenem't. Annie Solomon to John W. Artmann. Taxes 1891 and 1892. Dec. 3. 6,230
Central Park West, No. 246, w s, 113.3 n 84th st, 24x100, four-story brk dwell'g. Elizabeth Coates widow, Albany, N. Y., to William Noble. *Mt.* $37,000. Nov. 30. nom
Cherry st, No 324, n s, 186 e Clinton st, 24.3x98.9, four-story brk factory. Joseph H. Barker and Charles F. Chamberlaine to J. H. Barker & Co. Dec. 1. nom
Columbia st, Nos 105 and 107, w s, 60 n Stanton st, 40x25, four story brk tenem't with stores. Simon Baruch to Morris Levy. *Mt.* $14,125. Nov. 30. 18,000
Columbia st, No. 79, w s, 100 n Rivington st, 25x100, three-story brk store and tenem't with four-story brk tenem't on rear. Charlotte Harris extrx. of Philip Harris to Louis Lese and Morris Goldstein. *Mt.* $11,500. Nov. 30. 16,750
Delancey st, No. 192½, n s, 41.10 w Ridge st, 25x51.10, five-story brk tenem't with stores. Simon Bolit to Abraham Bolit. ½ part. All liens. Oct 26. 1,000
Elizabeth st, No 87, w s, 177.6 s Grand st, 26x93.9x26x93.11, four-story brk store and tenement. Isaac C. Johnson to August Mietz. *Mt.* $17,000. Dec 1. 32,500
Essex st, No 14, e s, 125 s Hester st, 19.3x100x19.8x100, five-story brk store and tenem't with five-story brk tenem't on rear. Nathan Levy to Sarah Levy. ½ part. Nov. 30. nom
Same property. Marx Meyer to Nathan Levy. ½ part. *Mt.* $9,000. Nov. 30. nom
Forsyth st, No. 153, w s, 125 s Rivington st, 25x100, five-story stone front tenem't with store. Foreclos. Sidney Harris to Elias Jacobs. Nov 30. 32,700
Same property. Release mort. Jessie Clark, Cornwall-on-Hudson, to same. Nov. 30. nom
Franklin st, Nos. 51 and 51½, s s, 274.9 e Broadway, 22x55.2x22x55.11, two three and five-story brk and frame stores. Malvina Heath widow and Mary Heath, East Orange, N. J., Edward Heath, Rockville Centre, L. I., Frederick, Frances W. widow and Henry M. Heath, Brooklyn, Eliza wife of Julius F. Simons, Roselle, N. J., Adeline Johnson widow and Emma wife of and William Barnett to Solomon Loeb. *Mt.* $8,500. Dec 1. 20,000
Front st, n w s, 89.7 n e Wall st, 0.8x75. Sarah A. Spicer to William B., John N. and James H. Beekman exrs., &c., William F. Beekman. March 31, 1881. 525
Gansevoort st, Nos. 100 and 102, s s, 75 e West st, 50x83.5x50x84.9, five-story brk building. Archibald D. Russell to Thomas S. Williams. *Mt.* $35,000. Nov. 27. nom
Gansevoort st, s s, 75 e West st, 50x83.5x50x84.9. Thomas S. Williams to Archibald D. Russell. *Mt.* $30,000. Dec. 2. nom
Greenwich st, No. 317, e s, abt 60 s Harrison st, 25x100, four-story brk store and tenem't with two-story brk stable on rear. Charles Von Eiff, Brooklyn, N. Y., to Joseph Bacharach. *Mt.* $6,000. Dec. 1. 35,000
Greenwich st, No 663, e s, 135 s Christopher st, 20x77, three-story brk dwell'g. John Barber to Mary Navaratt. Q. C. All title. Nov. 24. 100
Same property. Rudolph Navaratt, Jr., to John Barber. Q. C. All title. Nov. 24. 100
Grove st, No 67 on map No. 69 / Christopher st, No. 70 { begins Grove st, n s, 56 w 4th st, 27x84.2 to Christopher st, x 26x77.6, five-story brk flat with stores. Release mort. Mary Hartwig to Anthony J. Dittmar and John Goerlitz trustees. Nov. 20. 5,137
Same property. Anthony J. Dittmar and John Goerlitz trustees for creditors of Philip Goerlitz to Peter V. Stocky. C. a. G. *Mt.* $27,000. Nov. 24. 36,750
Henry st, No. 117, n s, 135 e Pike st, 25x87.6, five-story brk tenem't. Julia Feldman to Harry Baron. *Mt.* $26,200. Nov. 30. 37,500
Henry st, No. 306, s s, 259.3 e Scammel st, 24x¼ block, five story brk tenem't. Abraham Schlesinger to Hyman Claman. *Mt.* $16,500. Nov. 28. 23,000
Houston st, No. 265, s s, 78 w Suffolk st, 25x80, five-story brk store and tenem't. Henry Stemme and Rudolph Trost to Elias Jacobs. *Mt.* $10,000. Nov. 30. 30,000
Jones st, No 11, n s, 119.8 w 4th st, 25x100, five-story brk flat. Raphael Kuschewsky to Kaufman Henschel. *Mt.* $49,633. Nov. 30. See 124th st. nom
Lewis st, No 219 / 7th st, No. 201 { begins Lewis st, w s, 24.4 n 7th st, runs south 24.4 to 7th st, x west 80 x north — x east 25 x south 48.10 x east — to beginning, two-story brk office and frame sheds on Lewis st and three-story brk building on 7th st.
Lewis st, Nos. 221 and 223, w s, 73.2 n 7th st, runs southeast 48.10 x west — x north — x east to beginning, frame shed.
Kate M. Reilly and Daniel W. and John B. Kahl to George H. Kahl all heirs of Cath. Kahl. ¾ part. *Mt.* $12,000. Nov. 24. 11,250
Lewis st, Nos. 91-97, w s, 50 s Stanton st, 72.4x100, three five story brk tenem'ts. Jonas Weil and Bernhard Mayer to Benedict A. Klein. Nov. 27. 110,000
Same property. Benedict A. Klein to Jonas Weil and Bernhard Mayer. *Mt.* $60,000. Nov. 27. 110,000

Lewis st, No. 66, e s, 80 s Rivington st, 20x50, three-story brk store and tenem't. Samuel Schoen to Louis Schoen. *Mt.* $7,450. Dec. 1. 9,000

Lewis st, No. 87, w s, 140.5 s Stanton st, 18.1x100.
Lewis st, No. 89, w s, 122.4 s Stanton st, 18.1x100.
Four-story brk store and tenem't with six-story brk factory on rear.
Jonas Weil and Bernhard Mayer to Moritz Itzkovitz and Abram Berkovitz. *Mt.* $19,000. Nov. 30. 18,650

Madison st, No. 348, s s, 192.11 e Scammel st, 23.6x95.1x23.6x95.3, five-story brk tenem't with stores. Ida wife of and Barnet Solinger to Charles Leibring. *Mt.* $16,700. Nov. 30. 22,700

Madison st, No. 238, s s, abt 125 e Jefferson st, 20x90, three-story brk tenem't. Edward Pennefether to Alexander Rittmaster. *Mt.* $11,000. Dec. 1. 15,350

Madison st, No. 132, s s, abt 135 e Market st, 25x100, five-story brk tenem't. Israel M. Cohen to Barnett Levy, Louis Gordon and Sophia Gruenstein. *Mt.* $34,000. Nov. 30. See Stanton st. 45,000

Market slip or st, No. 87, w s, 40.6 s Cherry st, 20x51, three-story brk tenem't. Harry D. Haber to Isaac Levene. *Mt.* $4,000. Nov. 24. 7.000

Market slip or st, No. 85, w s, 20.6 s Cherry st, 20x51, five-story brk store and tenem't. Same to same. *Mt.* $7,000. Nov. 24. 9,500

Mercer st, w s, bet Bleecker st and 3d st. Receipt in payment for party wall. Samuel and Henry Corn to Joseph Solomon. Sept. 11. 1,300

Monroe st, No. 56, s s, 20.7 e of junction of Hamilton st, 25.1x92.8, three-story brk building. Davis Marx to The Eagle Distillery Co. *Mt.* $14,000. Dec. 1. 26,000

Mott st, No. 110, e s, 43.2 s Hester st, runs east 45.11 x south 6.10 x east 22 x south 16 x west 68.5 to Mott st, x north 22.10, three-story frame (brk front) store and tenem't. James W. Ketcham to Joseph Felino. *Mt.* $12,000. Nov. 27. 22,000

Mott st, Nos. 42 and 44, e s, 57.3 n Pell st, 59.8x25x59.7x25, five-story brk factory. George Lane to Victor A. Harder. ½ part. *Mt.* $6 000. Nov 30. 9,500

Mott st, No. 181, w s, abt 124 n Broome st, 25x100, five-story brk tenem't with stores. Simon Fine and Harris Boskey to Isidore Abrahams. *Mt.* $23,000. Dec. 1. 38,000

Mulberry st, No. 58, e s, 125 s Bayard st, 25x93.9x25x93.11, three-story frame and brk store and tenem't with four-story brk tenem't on rear. Daniel Rothstein to Giovanni Lordi. *Mt.* $10,000. Nov. 30. 28,000

Norfolk st, No. 78, e s, abt 125 n Broome st, 25x100, three-story frame (brk front) store and tenem't with two-story brk stable on rear. Foreclos. Jacob A. Cantor to James J. Loonie and Eugene Parker. Dec. 2. 21,400

Park st, No. 29, e s, abt 24.4 n Duane st, 23.7x89.6x24.3x88.9, three-story brk store with two-story brk building on rear. Charles W. Torrey to Henry Lindenmeyr. *Mt.* $4,500. Nov. 24. nom

Pitt st, No. 90, e s, 175 s Stanton st, 25x100, five-story brk tenem't with stores. Maria Hillenbrand widow and Francis Hillenbrand individ. and exrs. Francis Hillenbrand to Theodore Keller. Dec. 1. 28 500

Renwick st, No. 45, w s, 75 s Spring st, 20x75, three-story frame (brk front) tenem't. Mary L. and Margaret McClary widow to Karoline wife of Philipp Etzel. Dec. 1. 8,575

Same property. Mary L. McClary to Margaret McClary. *Mt.* $4,500. Oct. 18, 1890. 9,500

Ridge st, No. 35, w s, 21.6 s Broome st, 20x55, two-story brk dwell'g. Robert Gerson to Morris K. Lustig. *Mt.* $5,500. Dec. 1. 12,000

Rivington st, Nos. 101 and 103 } begins Rivington st, s e
Ludlow st, Nos. 126-130 } cor Ludlow st, 43.9x100, several two and three-story frame and brk stores and tenements. James G. Wallace to Harris Mandelbaum. Nov. 30. nom

Sniffin court, No. 5, w s, 39.6 s 36th st, 19.9x41, two-story brk stable. Edward F. Brown assignee Jacob F. Wyckoff to Hugh L. Cole. C. a G. *Mt.* $8,000. Nov. 19. 25

Same property. Elizabeth H. wife of Abram B. Wyckoff, Hightstown, N. J., to same. Nov. 19. 5,500

Stanton st, No. 318, n s, 25 w Goerck st, 24.5x75, five-story brk tenem't with stores. Barnett Levy, Louis Gordon and Sophia Gruenstein to Israel M. Cohen. *Mt.* $12,750. Nov. 30. See Madison st. 21,200

St. Marks pl, No. 67, n s, abt 195 w 1st av, four-story brk tenem't. Peter Lyding to August Ruff. *Mt.* $15,000. Nov. 28. See 5th st. 32,000

Same property. Conveys all title in the courtyard only. Same to same. B. & S. Nov. 28. nom

Sullivan st, e s, 67 s Grand st. Party wall agreement. John T. Williams to William H. Johnson. Nov. 25. nom

Thompson st, No 57-63, w s, 100 n Broome st, 114.10x100x113.9x100, several two and three-story brk and frame stables, tenem'ts, &c. New York Steam Co. to David L. Einstein. Nov. 30. 75,000

Same property. Release mort. Union Trust Co. to The New York Steam Co. Dec. 2. nom

Water st, No. 228, north cor Beekman st, 25x33.4x25.1x33.4, five-story brk store. Charlotte M. Townsend widow, Caroline B., James M. and Frederick R. Townsend and Annie his wife, Isabella wife of Lomax Littlejohn, children of James B. Townsend to The Barstow Stove Co. Re-recorded. June 24, 1875. 2 ,000

Same property. The Barstow Stove Co., Providence, R. I., to George W. Bond. Nov. 25. 35,000

Waverley pl, No. 174, w s, 75 n Christopher st, 21.4x85, three-story brk dwell'g. Lewis Cohen and Raphael Lewis to James W. Ketcham. *Mt.* $9,000. Nov. 16. See 21st st. 12,000

Waverley pl, s s, 50 e Greene st. Release of contract as to party wall. Simon Goldenberg to Samuel and Henry Corn. Nov. 20. 3,716

Willett st, No. 62, e s, 175 s Rivington st, 25x100, four-story brk store and tenem't with three-story brk tenem't on rear. Klennan Hirsch to Reuben and Ida Robinson. *Mt.* $17,000. Nov. 30. 22,000

Willett st, No. 59, w s, abt 175 n Delancey st, 25x100, four-story brk tenem't with four-story brk tenem't on rear. Harris Siegel to Jacob Dauman, Brooklyn. *Mt.* $16,200. Nov. 25. 20,100

Wooster st, No. 147, w s, abt 219.4 s Houston st, 25x100, four-story stone front store. Hyman Sylvester to Flora Mintzer. *Mt.* $25,000. Nov. 28. 38,400

Wooster st, Nos. 137 and 139, w s, abt 118 n Prince st, 50x100, one, two and three-story brk and frame stores. William T. Lee to Henry Levy. Nov 27. 55,750

Wooster st, Nos. 137 and 139, w s, 50x100. Henry Levy to Daniel Rosenbaum and Nathan Metzger. *Mt.* $45,750. Dec. 1. 58,000

2d st, No. 253, s s, 76.6 w Av C, 20.6x64x20.6x63, three-story brk store and tenem't. Emma Keller and Flora M. Lindner to Sigmund Friedman. Dec. 1. 11,500

4th st, No. 345, n s, 168 w Av D, 24x96, three-story brk tenem't. Albert Klauber to Thomas C. Smith. *Mt.* $7,000. Nov. 11. 17,500

4th st, n e s, 193.9 s e Av C, 21.5x96. Release dower. Lizzie T. wife of George J. Harley to Louis Cohen. Nov. 25. nom

4th st, No. 317, n s, 193.9 e Av C, 21.5x96, three-story brk tenem't. Louis Cohen to Louis Quenzer. Dec. 1. 13,750

5th st, No. 325, n s, 300 e 2d av, 25x97, six-story brk tenem't with stores. August Ruff to Peter Lyding. Nov. 28. See St. Marks pl. 5 ,000

5th st, No. 725, n s, 307.8 e Av C, runs east 16 11 x north 53 x north 30.5 x west 1 x north 13.8 x west 16.4 x south 96 11, three-story brk tenem't. Leonhard Daub to Adolph Galewski. *Mt.* $5,000. Nov. 30. 10,000

8th st, No. 406, s s, 51 w Lewis st, 21.11x22.2, four-story brk store and tenem't. George Neun to Bernhard Reinach. *Mt.* $6,000. Nov. 30. nom

10th st, Nos. 138 and 140, s s, 150 e Waverley pl, 51.6x95x48.9x95, two five-story brk flats, stores in No. 138. Peter Lyding to Charles Lindner. *Mt.* $56,500. Nov. 30. See Av B. 80,000

11th st, No. 519, n s, 245.6 e Av A, 25x103.3, five-story brk tenem't with stores. Thomas J. Johnston, Brooklyn, to Morris Berkowitz. *Mt.* $24,000. Nov. 27. 37,000

12th st, No. 348, s s, 99.9 w 1st av, 19.7x68.4, four-story brk store and tenem't. Henry Markus to Charles Frey. *Mt.* $5,000. Nov. 23. 10,000

12th st, No. 38, s s, 232.3 w Broadway, 25x103.3.
12th st, No. 36, s s, 257.2 w Broadway, 25x103.3.
Two four-story stone front stores and dwell'gs.
Samuel and Henry Corn to Theodore Weble. *Mt.* $55,000. Nov. 27. other consid. and 100

12th st, No. 109, n s, 350 w 3d av, 25x103.3, four-story brk tenem't. Mary F. wife of Patrick F. McGowan to Justus J. Spreng exr. Catharine Lenihan. Q. C. Sept. 26. nom

13th st, No. 415, n s, 194 e 1st av, 25x103.3, four-story brk tenem't with stores. Katharine J. Haddock widow, Thomas T. Read, Josephine A. and Adelaide Habirshaw, Mary A. Skidmore and Mary R. Haddock heirs Catherine M. McCoskry to John Wynne. Q. C. Nov. 12. nom

Same property. George G. Williams and William J. Quinlan, Jr., exrs. Catherine M. McCoskry to same. Nov. 12. 10,000

Same property. Katherine Van Wyck Haddock, by J. Edward Swanstrom guard., to same. All title. B. & S. Nov. 30. val. consid

14th st, No. 504, s s, 96 e Av A, 25x103.3, five-story brk store and tenem't with four-story brk tenem't on rear. Frederick R. Koezel to Wilhelm Soll and Mary his wife. *Mt.* $13,000. Dec. 1. 20,500

16th st, Nos. 514 and 516, s s, 220.6 e Av A, 50x103.5, two five-story brk tenem'ts with stores with two-story brk building on rear of No. 514, and three-story brk building on rear of No. 516. Mitchell A. C. Levy to David Liou. Dec. 3. 14,000

21st st, No. 109, n s, 282.6 e 4th av, 27 6x88.9, four-story brk dwell'g. James A. Scrymser to Susanna S. Minturn. *Mt.* $40.000. Dec. 1. 68,000

21st st, No 246, s s, 517.6 w 7th av, runs west 28.4 x south 92 x west 2.4 x south 17 x east 25 x north 109, three-story brk dwell'g. James W. Ketcham to Raphael Lewis and Lewis Cohen. *Mt.* $16,000. Nov. 27. See Waverley pl. 21,350

21st st, No. 123, n e cor Lexington av, 35x98.9, four-story stone front dwell'g.
Lexington av, No. 3, e s, 98.9 n 21st st, 24.8x105, two-story brk stable.
Cyrus W. Field, Irvington, N. Y., to Isabella F. Judson, Irvington, N. Y. Nov 30. 120,000

22d st, No. 149, n s, 255 e 7th av, 22.6x98 9, four-story brk tenem't. Charles E. Silber to Joseph Hartley. Nov. 30. 26,100

23d st, No. 244, s s, 462.6 w 7th av, 18 9x98.9, four-story stone front dwell'g. James W. McCaffrey to Jacob Hirsh. Nov. 30. 23,200

24th st, No. 133, n s, 400 w 6th av, 25x114 6, three-story brk tenem't with two-story brk stable on rear. William H. Sanford, Hauppauge, L. I., and ano. trustees of Mary Beadleston to Mary Beadleston. C. a. G. Nov. 30. nom

27th st, No. 107, n s, 100 e 4th av, 16.8x98.9, three-story brk dwell'g. James S Huyler to Edward Cooper et al. exrs., &c., Peter Cooper. Dec. 1. 15,000

27th st, No. 152, s s, 232.4 e 7th av, 22.2x98.9, three-story brk dwell'g on rear of lot. Harris Mandelbaum to Clara N. Baldwin. *Mt.* $7,000. Nov. 25. 12.000

27th st, No. 121, n s, 266.8 w 6th av, 16.8x98.9, three-story stone front dwell'g. Susan A. Baldwin widow to Ellen Eagen, Flushing, L. I. Confirmation deed and Q C. Dec. 1. nom

Same property. Release judgment. Oliver F. Berry to Ellen Eagen, Flushing, L. I. Nov. 30. nom

Same property. Ellen Eagen to Joseph I. West. *Mt.* $9,000. Dec. 2. 11,500

29th st, No. 352, s s, 550 w 8th av, 16.8x98.9, four-story stone front dwell'g. Charles Roos to Mathilda Roos. *Mt.* $9,000. Nov. 27. nom

29th st, No. 335, n s, 466 w 8th av, 22x98 9, four-story brk dwell'g. James D. Hall to Anna Hartwig. *Mt.* $9,000. Nov. 30. 14,500

30th st, No. 47, n s, 86.6 w 4th av, runs north 53 x west 2.6 x north 45.9 x west 16.6 x south 98.9 to st, x east 19, four-story brk dwell'g. Huntington Richards to Joseph S. Richards. B. & S. Sub. to mort. and legacy. December 1. nom

Same property. Foreclos. Charles A. Jackson to Huntington Richards. *Mt.* $13,000 and legacy $3,000. Aug. 3. 18,600

35th st, No 41, n s, 375 e 6th av, 18.9x98.9, four-story brk dwell'g. Janette Pirsson widow to Hyman M. Lazinsk Dec. 2. 29,300

35th st, No. 267, n s, 94 e 8th av, runs north 47 6 x east abt 0.6 x north 51.3 x east 18 9 x south 98.9 to st, x west 19, four-story brk store and tenem't. Elmore D. Alvord, Fairfield, Conn., to Rudolph Federroll. *Mt.* $12.000. Nov. 27. 18,500

35th st, No. 267, n s, 94 e 8th av, runs north 47.6 x east 0.6 x north 51.3 x east 18 9 x south 98 9 to st, x west 19, four-story brk store and tenement. Lewis H. Hyde, East Orange, N. J., to Elmore D. Alvord, Bridgeport, Conn. July 30, 1891. nom

Same property. Elmore D. Alvord, William C. Haight, Bridgeport, Conn., to Lewis H. Hyde. *Mt.* $12,000. May 25, 1891. nom

38th st, No. 114, s s, 180 w 6th av, runs west 20 x south 74.1 x east 8 x south 24.8 x east 12 x north 98.9, four-story stone front dwell'g. Henry T. Chittenden, Columbus, O., to Walter S. Hobart, San Francisco, Cal. *Mt.* $15,000. Nov. 21. 40,000

39th st, No. 336, s s, 175 w 1st av, 25x98.9, five-story brk tenem't. Benjamin Holmes to Patrick McCauley, West Burlington, N. Y., and Thomas McCauley, City New York. *Mt.* $12,000. Dec. 1. 18,000

39th st, No. 321, n s, 300 w 8th av, 24.1x98 9, four-story brk store and tenem't with three-story brk tenem't on rear. Louisa wife of Philip Hofmann and heir of Andrew Boucsein to Philip Hofmann. Q. C. Dec. 1. nom

40th st, s s, 530 e 6th av, 30x98.9, vacant. Samuel D. Babcock to Jacob H. Knapp. Dec. 1. 60,000

40th st, No. 8, s s, 165.6 w 5th av, 19.6x98.9, four-story brk dwell'g. Theodore Stanton, Paris, France, Harriot S. wife of William H. Blatch, Jr., to Joseph J. Henna. All title. Nov 4. nom

Same property. Henry Stanton exr. Tryphena Bayard to same. *Mt.* $5,000. Nov. 4. 50,000

Same property. Harriet E. Eaton, Baltimore, Md., widow, Elizabeth C. Stanton widow, Margaret C. wife of Duncan McMartin, Beaman, Ia., Catharine C. Wilkeson, Norristown, Pa., widow, Henry and Robert L. Stanton, Margaret S. Lawrence widow and Gerrit S. Stanton, Allegheny City, Pa., to same. All title. Nov. 4. nom

40th st, s s, 500 e 6th av, 30x98 9, vacant. Samuel D. Babcock to Fannie D. wife of Walker G. Wylie. Dec. 1. 60,000

41st st, No. 340, s s, 365 e 2d av, 16x98.9, four-story brk dwell'g. Foreclos. Robert E. Deyo to Leonard Scott. Nov. 27. 6,900

45th st, No. 59, n s, 251.5 e 6th av, 18.9x100.5, three-story stone front dwell'g. Cornelia M. Greenly, East Orange, N. J., to Elias Le R. M. Bristol. *Mt.* $11,500. Nov. 30. 27,250

45th st, No. 454, s s, 75 e 10th av, 25x75.3, five-story brk tenem't. Jacob F. Seeger to Henry G. Cassidy. *Mt.* $14,000. Dec. 1. 18,275

45th st, No. 528, s s, 375 e 11th av, 25x100.5, five-story brk tenem't. Helen wife of R. V. Bonnell, Metuchen, N. J., to Dora wife of Frederick Grasmuck. *Mt.* $12,250. Dec. 1. 18,000

45th st, No. 75, n s, 100 e 6th av, 20x100.5, four-story stone front dwell'g. A. Gertrude wife of Henry T. Cutter to Ascher Weinstein. Nov. 30. 23,000

47th st, No. 455, n s, 205 e 10th av, 20x100.5, four-story stone front dwell'g. Bartholomew

F. Kenney to George Reichbhard. Dec. 2. 13,250

48th st, No. 330, s s, 375 e 2d av, 25x100.5, five-story brk tenem't. Mary B. Hughes and Annie J. Buillon to Joseph Noethen. *Mt.* $15,000. Nov. 20. 24,500

49th st, No. 232, s s, 249 w 2d av, 19x100.5, four-story stone front dwell'g. George Reid to Robert Niemann. *Mt.* $8,000. Nov. 27. 12,250

49th st, No. 334, s s, 250 w 1st av, 25x100.5, five-story stone front store and tenem't. Michael Keiser to Anna Prabar. *Mt.* $7,000. Dec. 1. 18,250

49th st, No. 228, s s, 287 w 2d av, 19x100.5, four-story stone front dwell'g. Clara wife of and Abraham Rosenthal to Regina Kassler. Nov. 30. 13,700

52d st, No. 326, s s, 318 e 2d av, 19x100.5, four-story stone front dwell'g. Anne Kasner to Alexander Haft. *Mt.* $10,500. Nov. 30. 12,200

52d st, No 519, n s, 250 w 10th av, 25x100.5, five-story brk tenem't. Elsworth L. Striker to William H. Lee. Nov. 30. 30,000

52d st, No. 315, n s, 204.6 e 2d av, 20x100.5, four-story stone front dwell'g. Foreclos. Isidor Grayhead to George Hall. Nov. 30. 12,200

53d st, No. 41, n s, 145 e Madison av, 20x100 5, four-story stone front dwell'g. D. Sackett Moore to Laura B. wife of Francis W. Otheman. *Mt.* $30,000. Nov. 27. 50,750

53d st, No. 424, s s, 350 w 9th av, 25x100 5, five-story brk tenem't. Herman Lambert to Hannah wife of Henry Adler. *Mt.* $15,000. Nov. 28. nom

53d st, No. 417, n s, 250 w 9th av, 25x100.5, five-story brk tenem't. Agostino Cavinato to Cornelius R. Blauvelt, Nyack, N. Y. *Mt.* $20,000. Dec. 3. 32,000

58th st, No. 158, s s, 306 w 6th av, 20x100.5, four-story stone front dwell'g. George B. Page, Newark, N. J., to Fannie wife of John Le Boutillier. *Mt.* $37,000. Dec. 1. nom

58th st, n s, 200 w 6th av, 25x100.5, vacant. Clifford Coddington et al. exrs. Matilda Coddington to Remigio Loforte. Rerecorded. Aug. 2, 1890. 28,500

58th st, No. 440, s s, 375 w 9th av, 25x100.5, five-story stone front flat. William H. Doty, Yonkers, N. Y., to John S. Robinson. *Mt.* $18,000. Nov. 30. exch and 300

58th st, s s, 140 w 6th av, 0.6x100.5. Release mort. Francis J. Gasquet and John Duer trustee for Marie Marshall to Charles T. and Helen T. Barney. Nov. 10. nom

60th st, No. 47, n s, 136 w Park av, 15x100.5, four-story stone front dwell'g. Belle wife of Simon Baruch to Margaret L. wife of D. Sackett Moore. *Mt.* $14,000. Nov. 27. 28,000

60th st, No. 332, s s, 266 w 1st av, 20x100.5, frame and brk shed with two-story brk stable on rear. John Goerlitz or Georlitz to Henry Lingelbach. *Mt.* $8,000. Nov. 30. nom

61st st, No. 43, n s, 85 e Madison av, 15x100.5, four-story stone front dwell'g. A. Gertrude wife of Henry T. Cutter to Elizabeth M. Hunter. *Mt.* $11,000. Nov. 1. 22,175

62d st, n s, 100 e 11th av, 75x100.5, one and two-story frame buildings and vacant. John B. Smith to William E. D. Vincent. *Mt.* $18,000. Dec. 1. nom

62d st, No. 326, s s, 175 w 1st av, 25x100.5, five-story brk tenem't with stores. Esther Lewis and Lena Rinaldo to Bartolomeo Fulgoni. *Mt.* $10,000. Dec. 1. 14,000

63d st, s s, 150 e 11th av, 100x100.5, vacant. Foreclos. Louis B. Hasbrouck to Annah E. Benedict. Nov. 12. 12,400

66th st, No. 217–221, n s, 275 w Amsterdam av, 75x100.5, three five-story brk and stone front tenem'ts. E. Clifford Potter to R. Irene Thompson, Millerton, N. Y. *Mt.* $17,000. Nov. 18. See 97th st, also 119th st. nom

70th st, No. 67, n s, 225 e Columbus av, 20x100 5, four-story stone front dwell'g. George W. Ruddell to Simon Baruch, Camden, S. C. *Mt.* $22,500. Nov. 27. 37,000

72d st, No. 111, n s, 127 w Columbus av, 23x102.2, four-story brk dwell'g. Joseph L. Spofford exr. Paul Spofford to Amelia N. wife of Robert Dunlap. Ratification deed. Nov. 30. nom

73d st, No. 55, n s, 122.6 w 4th av, 17.6x102.2, four-story brk dwell'g. Emma V. Monheimer to Agnes C. Lyon. *Mt.* $19,500. Nov. 27. nom

73d st, No. 408, n s, 87 e 1st av, 26x77.2, five-story brk tenem't with stores. Sigmund Katz and Ludwig Polacek to Theodore E. Heidenfeld. *Mt.* $14,000. Nov. 28. 29,000

74th st, No. 21, n s, 494 e Columbus av, 25x102.2, four-story brk dwell'g. Frederick Aldhous to Oscar R. Meyer. *Mt.* $35,000. Nov. 28. nom

75th st, s s, 175 e Amsterdam av, 100x102.2.
75th st, n s, 500 w Columbus av, 100x102.2
Release dower. Eliza J. Arkenburgh widow. Nyack, N. Y., to Edward Hirsh. Feb. 12. nom

75th st, No. 203, n s, 100 w 10th av, 25x107.5, two-story brk stable. John A. Kelly to Thomas P. Kelly. *Mt.* $15,000. June 4. nom

76th st, n s, 151 w West End av. Party wall agreement, receipt and conveyance. Elizabeth S. Miller to Leonard Jacob, Jr. Nov. 25. 611

76th st, No. 156, s s, 262 4 e 10th av, 20.10x102.2, four-story brk dwell'g. Henry F. Morewood, Englewood, N. J., to George B. Morewood, Jr. *Mt.* $24,500. Nov. 23. 10,500

76th st, No. 305, n s, 86 w West End av, 21x76.1, four-story brk dwell'g. Release mort. William B. Isham to Hugh Lamb, East Orange, N. J. Nov. 25. nom

Same property. Release mort. James R. Smith to same. Nov. 28. 22,000

Same property. Release mort. Same to same. Nov. 28. nom

Same property. Hugh Lamb to Robert P. Martin, Summit, N. J. *Mt.* $22,000. Nov. 28. nom

76th st, n s, 200 e Columbus av, 5x102.2. Release mort. James McMahon, Washington, D. C., to Joseph L. Myers. Nov. 21. 2,000

76th st, n s, 200 e Columbus av, 25x102.2, vacant. Joseph L. Myers to Isaac Meizger and Edward Oppenheimer. *Mt.* $9,000. Nov. 27. 16,000

76th st, n s, 225 e Columbus av, 25x102.2, vacant. Alfred S. Lascelles to same. *Mt.* $11,000. Nov. 27. 16,000

76th st, No. 307, n s, 144.8 e 2d av, 27.4x102.2, five-story brk tenem't. Charles Wellner to Jacob Schlosser. *Mt.* $19,000. Nov. 30. 25,600

78th st, No. 135, n s, 375 e 4th av, 18x102.2, three-story stone front dwell'g. William J. Lippmann to Flora W. Kohn. *Mt.* $8,250. Nov. 30. 17,500

81st st, Nos. 306–316, s s, 100 e 2d av, runs east 90 x south 84 x west 42.2 x north 0.10 x west 47.3 x north 72.11, six three-story stone front dwell'gs. Mary S. Douglas to W. Jennings Demorest. *Mt.* $30,000. Nov. 30. 45,000

81st st, No. 117, n s, 133.11 w Columbus av, 17x102.2, four-story stone front dwell'g. Rowena H. wife of Albert L. Cohn to Beatrice H. Phillips. Dec. 1. nom

81st st, No. 435, n s, 80 w Av A, runs north 26 x west 5 x north 25 6 x west 21.6 x south 51.6 to 81st st, x east 26.6, five-story brk tenem't with stores. Elizabeth Loeffler widow to Catharine Gerhards. *Mt.* $7,000. Nov. 28. 13,000

81st st, No. 331, n s, 350 w 1st av, 25x102.2, five-story brk tenem't with stores. Ida C. Lilienthal to Emilie Salberg. ⅜ part. Dec. 1. nom

82d st, s s, 76 5 e Riverside Drive, runs south 22.2 x east 13.4 x south 26.6 x east 8.4 x south 15.6 x east 14.4 x north 64.2 to st, x west 36.
82d st, s s, 144.5 e Riverside Drive, 16.8x102.2.
Release judgments. Frank L. Smith to The Squier & Whipple Co. Nov. 24. nom

82d st, s s, 76.5 e Riverside Drive, runs south 22.2 x east 13.4 x south 26 6 x east 8.4 x south 15.6 x east 14.4 x north 64.2 to st, x west 36. Release mort. John L. Brewster to same. Nov. 24. nom

Same property. Release mort. Same to same. Nov. 24. nom

Same property. Release mort. The Holland Trust Co. to same. Dec. 1. nom

82d st, No. 318, s s, 144.5 e Riverside Drive, 16.8x102.2, four-story stone front dwell'g. The Squier & Whipple Co. to Egbert C. Simonson. Dec. 2. nom

82d st, No. 422, s s, 231.6 w Av A, 25x102.2, four-story stone front tenem't. Charles Hlavac to Ida Siseh. *Mt.* $18,600. Nov. 30. 17,000

82d st, s s, 144.5 e Riverside Drive, 16 8x102.2. Release mort. John L Brewster to The Squier & Whipple Co. Dec. 2. nom

Same property. Release mort. Holland Trust Co. to same. Dec. 2. nom

Same property. Release mort. John L. Brewster to same. Dec. 2. nom

82d st, No. 153, n s, 106.11 e Lexington av, 19 2x102.2, three-story stone front dwell'g. Thomas Brennan to Mary E. Kelly. *Mt.* $14,000. June 10. 21,000

82d st, No. 324, s s, 76 5 e Riverside Drive, runs south 22.2 x east 13.4 x south 26.6 x east 8.4 x south 15.6 x east 14.4 x north 64.2 to 82d st. x west 36, four-story stone front dwell'g. Squier & Whipple Co. to Everard G. Tocl. Nov. 24. nom

82d st, Nos. 227–231, n s, 203.4 w 2d av, 76 8x102.2, three four-story stone front tenem'ts. Isaac Hirsch to John Keenan. *Mt.* $39,000. Nov. 30. 58,000

83d st, No. 219, n s, abt 250 e 3d av, 25x100, two-story frame dwell'g. Lilly Hirshkind to John H. Sturk. Nov. 30. See 112th st. 12,000

83d st, No 449, n s, 70,6 w Av A, 20x102.2, five-story stone front tenem't. George Berbener to Christian Turck. *Mt* $12,000. Nov. 30. 18,000

84th st, No. 519, n s, 234.2 e Av A, 19.5x102.2, three-story stone front dwell'g. Babetta Buess to Carl Boeber. *Mt.* $6,000. Nov. 28. 11,750

86th st, No. 100, s w cor Columbus av, 25x106.9, with easement, light and air over strip adjoining on west, 5 6x50, five-story brk flat with stores. Bernhard J. Ludwig to Hyman and Henry Sonn. *Mt.* $40,000. Dec. 1. 75,000

88th st, No. 208, s s, 160 e 3d av, 25x100.8, five-story brk tenem't. George Pries to Jacob Hinklein. *Mt.* $15,000. Nov. 30. 20,200

88th st, Nos. 171–177, n s, 133 4 e Amsterdam av, 66.4x100.8, four three-story stone front dwell'gs. Samuel R. Donnellon, Brooklyn, to Leo Dinkelspiel. *Mt.* $57,000. Nov. 25. nom

89th st, No. 312, s s, 180 w West End av, 20x100.8, four-story brk dwell'g. Francis M. Wilmurt, Pelham Manor, N. Y., to Lilian wife of W. N. Le Cato, West Orange, N. J. *Mt.* $19,000. Nov. 24. nom

90th st, s s, 250 w West End av, 50x101.5, three-story brk dwell'g with two-story brk stable on rear. Charles T. Barney and Francis M. Jencks to Jane J. wife of Howard Phelps. Release of personal liability. Nov. 17. nom

91st st, n s, 275 e Columbus av, 75x100.8, vacant. Bernard Cohen to John Curry and James B. Gillie. Nov. 30. 44,500

93d st, No. 19, n s, 268 w 8th av, 20x100.8, four-story brk dwell'g. Mary F. Weil, Brooklyn, to Thomas C. Ennever. B. & S. and C. a. G. June 8. nom

93d st, No. 72, s s, 105 w Park av, 21x100.8, five-story stone front flat. Henry Waters to Isaac Wyman. *Mt.* $19,000. Dec. 2. 30,000

94th st, No. 70, s s, 150 e Columbus av, 18x100.8, three-story stone front dwell'g. William S. Lines to Mary Purcell. *Mt.* $16,000. Nov. 30. 26,000

94th st, No. 49, n s, 355 e Columbus av, 20x100.8, four-story stone front dwell'g. Increase M. Grenell to Antonio Pastor. *Mt.* $17,000. Nov. 30. 27,000

96th st, No. 19 on map No. 29, n s, 280 w Central Park West, 20x100.11, four-story stone front dwell'g. Edward Kilpatrick to Nicholas Schloeder. *Mt.* $22,500. Nov. 30. 35,500

96th st, No. 50, s s, 280 e 9th av, 20x100.8, four-story brk dwell'g. Foreclos. Ernest Hall, to Francis M. Jencks. Nov. 25. 24,600

96th st, No. 52, s s, 260 e 9th av, 20x100.8, four-story brk dwell'g. Foreclos. Same to same. Nov. 25. 22,500

96th st, No. 63, n s, 141 e 9th av, 21x100.11, four-story brk dwell'g. Foreclos. Same to same. Nov. 25. 21,500

96th st, No. 54, s s, 240 e 9th av, 20x100.8, four-story brk dwell'g. Foreclos. Same to same. Nov. 25. 22,500

97th st, No. 64, s s, 182 e Columbus av, 19x100.11, four-story brk dwell'g.
89th st, No. 321, n s, 270 w West End av, 20x100 8, three-story stone front dwell'g.
R. Irene wife of and Edward H. Thompson, Millerton, N. Y., to E. Clifford Potter. *Mt.* $41,000. Nov. 20. See 66th st, also 119th st. exch

97th st, Nos. 61–67, n s, 135.6 e Columbus av, 64.6x100.11, four four-story brk dwell'gs. Benjamin F. Romaine to Charles Buek, Westport, Conn. *Mt.* $59,000. Nov. 30. See Columbus and Manhattan avs. nom

101st st, No. 131, n s, 75 w Lexington av, 25x100.11, five-story brk flat. Don A. Gaylord to Sarah J. Howes. *Mt.* $13,000. Nov. 28. 22,000

102d st, Nos. 120–124, s s, 299.7 w Columbus av, 78x100.11, three five-story brk flats. Thomas J. McGuire to Richard O. Gorman. *Mt.* $60,000. Nov. 30. See Manhattan av. 93,000

102d st, No. 285 on map No. 239, n s, 78.10 w 2d av, 25.2x100.6, five-story stone front tenement. Jules Weill to Harry Lehr. *Mt.* $14,000. Dec. 1. 23,500

102d st, No. 285, on map No. 239, n s, 78.10 w 2d av, 25.2x100.6, five-story stone front tenement. Emma Hayman to Jules Weill. *Mt.* $14,000. Aug. 10. 22,500

103d st, No. 206, s s, 118 w Amsterdam av, 20x76 to centre Old Clendening lane, x20x abt 77.2, five-story brk flat. Foreclos. Sylvester L. H. Ward to Madeline Pierce. Dec. 2. 19,500

103d st, s s, 102.6 w 3d av, 108x100.11, two-story frame building and vacant. Lewis Z. Bach to Thomas J. McLaughlin. *Mt.* $22,000. Nov. 27. 36,000

105th st, No. 245, n s, 152.6 w 2d av, 16.8x100.9, three-story frame dwell'g. Henry G. Autenrieth to Eliza C. Klim. *Mt.* $2,500. Dec. 1. nom

106th st, No. 323, n s, 275 w 1st av, 25x100.11, four-story brk tenem't. Joseph Steiner to Libe Stern. *Mt.* $12,500. Nov. 24. nom

106th st, No. 21, n s, 175 w Madison av, 25x100.11, five-story stone front flat. Philip A. and John J. Fitzpatrick to Mary A. wife of John J. Fitzpatrick. Q. C. Nov. 30. nom

107th st, No. 179, n s, 236 e Lexington av, 17x100.11, four-story stone front flat. Eliza McAdam widow to Morton H. C. Foster. *Mt.* $7,500. Nov. 27. 11,250

108th st, No. 71, n s, 136 w 4th av, 17x100.11, four-story stone front dwell'g. Ehrick Parmly and Charles H. Ward trustees of Anna R. Adams and Ehrick K. Rossiter to Jacob Levy. Nov. 23. 11,750

109th st. n s, 225 e 11th av, 50x100, vacant. Roby A. wife of J. Henry Smith to James J. Ryan. *Mt.* $8,500. Nov. 28. See Lexington av. nom

112th st, No. 45, n s, 75 e Madison av, 20x100.11, five-story brk flat. John H. Sturk to Lilly Hirshkind. *Mt.* $10,000. Nov. 23. See 83d st. 18,825

113th st, No. 183, n s, 270 e Park av, 20x100.11, two-story frame dwell'g. Mary A. wife of Michael F. O'Neill to Michael F. O'Neill. *Mt.* $8,000. Nov. 27. nom

114th st, No. 352, s s, 100 w 1st av, 25x100.10, five-story brk flat. Simon Schafer to Anna Hindenlang. *Mt.* $11,000. Nov. 25. 16,700

114th st, No. 421, n s, 270 e 1st av, 25x100.11, four-story brk tenem't. Frederick C. Dexter, Brooklyn, to Minnie T. Shelton. *Mt.* $10,000. Nov. 30. See 149th st. 14,500

114th st, No. 433, n s, 420 e 1st av, 25x100.10, four-story brk tenem't. Daniel Heim and Jacob Strauss to William Wach, Brooklyn. *Mt.* $10,000. Nov. 24. 14,500

115th st, No. 341, s s, 150 w 1st av, 25x100.10, four-story brk tenem't with stores. Max Bernstein to Domenico and Francesco Tipaldi. *Mt.* $8,650. Nov. 27. nom

115th st, No. 17 on map No. 13, n s, 160 w Madison av, 25x100.11, five-story brk flat. Louis Stern to Louisa Grimm. *Mt.* $18,000. Nov. 30. 25,000

115th st, No. 414, s s, 132.6 e 1st av, 18.9x100.10, four-story brk tenem't. Alexander G. Johnson to John J. Sullivan. *Mt.* $5,500. Dec. 1. 8,350

115th st, s s, 100 e 3d av, 50x100.11, vacant.

The rector, &c., St. Bartholomews Church, New York, to The Second Universalist Soc., New York. B. & S. Sub to any encroachment on east side. Dec. 2. See 127th st. 16,000

116th st, s s, 270 w 5th av, 225x100 11, vacant. Marx and Moses Ottinger to Simon Bittner. *Mt.* $56,000. Nov. 30. other consid. and 100

117th st, No. 211, n s, 150 e 3d av, 25x100.10, three-story brk dwell'g. Catharine Murphy to Frederick Frank. Dec. 1. 13,000

119th st, No. 305, n s, 125 w 8th av, 25x100.11, five-story brk flat. James H. Merchant to E. Clifford Potter. *Mt.* $18,000. Dec. 3. See 66th st, also 97th st. exch

119th st, No 327, n s, 285 e 2d av, 20x100.10, four-story brk tenem't. Adolph Plisser to Adolph Hochstein. *Mt.* $9,500. Dec. 1. 15,000

120th st, No. 102, s s, 85 w Lenox av, 18x100.11, three-story stone front dwell'g. Margaret A. wife of Llewellyn T. Griffiths to Henrietta Fletcher. Sub. to mort. Sept. 8. nom

121st st, s s, 100 w 8th av, 175x100.11, vacant.
65th st, No. 53, n s, 100 w 4th av, 17x100.5, four-story stone front dwell'g.
Jacob B. Weinberg to Abraham Schneider. Sept. 22. nom

122d st, No. 161, n s, 109.4 e 7th av, 15.8x100, three-story brk dwell'g. Isaac A. Hopper to Michael C. O'Brien. *Mt.* $10,000. July 20. 19,250

123d st, No. 137, n s, 365 e 4th av, 25x100.11, three-story frame dwell'g. Elizabeth McKeon widow to Annie and Elizabeth McKeon. B. & S. Nov. 27. gift

123d st, No. 34, s s, 74 e Lenox av, 13x90.10, four-story brk dwell'g. John Thompson exr. Joseph Thompson to Josephine Van Loan. Nov. 30. 17,000

123d st, No. 28, s s, 87 e Lenox av, 13x90.10, four-story brk dwell'g. Same to Sarah L. Mellor. Nov. 30. 17,000

123d st, No. 447, n s, 138 w Av A, 17.1x100.11, three-story stone front dwell'g. Foreclos. Frederick P. Foster to The Equitable Life Assur. Society U. S. Nov. 19. 5,000

124th st, No. 326, s s, 370.6 w 1st av, 18x100.11, three-story stone front dwell'g. William R. Potts to Chessie E. Zeller. B. & S. *Mt.* $6,000. Nov. 27. 10,000

124th st, No. 104, s s, 60 e 4th av, 30x100.11, five-story brk flat. Foreclos. Jacob P. Solomon to Hamilton L. and Samuel H. Hoppin trustees for Louisa H. Hoppin. Nov. 24. 27,500

124th st, No. 205, n s, 100 e 3d av, 40x100.11, five-story brk flat. Kaufman Henschel to Raphael Kuschewsky. *Mt.* $38,000. Nov. 30. See Jones st. nom

124th st, No. 430, s s, 225 e 8th av, 25x100.11, four-story stone front flat. Benjamin W. Hitchcock, Lawrence, L. I., to Walter L. Bogert, Flushing, L. I. Nov. 30. 30,000

125th st, No. 327, n s, 320 w 1st av, 20x99 11, three-story brk dwell'g. Mary H. Ingraham widow, Daniel P. Jr., George L. and Arthur Ingraham heirs Daniel P. Ingraham to Theresa wife of Robert Hughes. Correction deed. Q. C. Nov. 18. nom

127th st, No. 121, n s, 290 e 4th av, 50x99.11, brk and stone church. The Second Universalist Society, New York, to the rector, &c., St. Bartholomews Church, New York. B. & S. Dec. 3. See 115th st. 29,300

127th st, s s, 275 w 6th av, 25x99 11, vacant. Oscar E. Bartels to Sarah E. Le Compte. Nov. 5. 9,500

128th st, Nos. 257-261, n s, 150 e 8th av, 108x99.11, three four-story stone front flats. Herman Wronkow to John Broad, Brooklyn. *Mt.* $75,000. Nov. 30. 125,000

129th st, n s, 481.3 w 7th av, 18.9x99.11. Release dower. Mary Oakley widow to Minnie T. Shelton. Dec. 1. 100

131st st, n s, 460 w 5th av, 25x99.11, vacant. Harry S. Wright to Andrew T. Judge. *Mt.* $7,000. Nov. 28. 7,500

136th st, No. 303, n s, 85 w 8th av, 16 8x99.11, three-story brk dwell'g. *Mt.* $14,389.
137th st, No. 302, s s, 85 w 8th av, 16.8x99.11, three-story brk dwell'g. *Mt.* $14,500.
William E. D. Vincent to Amalia Stepper. Nov. 1. val. consid.

137th st, s s, 125 e 7th av, 50x99.11, one-story frame buildings. Mary G. Pinckney to John Beatley, Brooklyn. Nov. 30. 13,000

144th st, No. 313, n s, 199.6 w 8th av, 26x99.11, five-story brk flat. Charles H. Woodward to Herman H. A. Wagner. *Mt.* $15,000. Nov. 27. 20,000

144th st, No. 455, n s, 214.2 e Amsterdam av, 20x99.11, three-story brk dwell'g. Foreclos. R. Duncan Harris to Charles W. Rounds. Dec. 2. 12,200

144th st, No. 459, n s, 177.8 e Amsterdam av, 20x99.11, four-story brk dwell'g. Foreclos. Same to same. Dec. 2. 15,100

144th st, No. 463, n s, 137.8 e Amsterdam av, 20x99 11, three-story brk dwell'g. Foreclos. Same to same. Dec. 2. 14,025

Same property. Charles W. Rounds to Thomas Nevins, Orange, N. J. *Mt.* $12,000. Dec. 2. nom

145th st, Nos. 300-314, s w cor 8th av, 208x99.11, eight five story brk flats with stores. Horace Ingersoll to Jacob D. Butler. C. a. G. Morts., taxes, &c. Oct. 20. nom

145th st, No. 314, s s, 181.2 w 8th av, 26 10x99.11, five-story brk store and flat. Jacob D. Butler to William C. Keller. *Mt.* $18,000. Dec. 1. See 149th st. exch

Same property. Release mort. Joseph F. Cullinan to Jacob D. Butler. Nov. 30. nom

Same property. Release mort. Julius G. Miller to same. Nov. 30. nom

Same property. Release mort. Otto L. Stix to same. Nov. 30. nom

Same property. Release mort. Nathan Wise to same. Nov. 30. nom

Same property. Release mort. Samuel W. Weiss to same. Nov. 30. nom

149th st, s s, 475 e Amsterdam av, 75x99.11, vacant. *Mt.* $7,750.
149th st, s s, 225 e Amsterdam av, 50x99.11, vacant. *Mt.* $6,375.
William C. Keller to Jacob D. Butler. Dec. 1. See 145th st. exch and 2,500

149th st, n s, 350 w 10th av, 50x99.11, vacant. Minnie T. Shelton to Frederick C. Dexter, Brooklyn. *Mt.* $4,000 and taxes 1891. Nov. 30. See 114th st. 9,000

167th st, s s, 158.5 e Amsterdam av, 20.7x97.4x17.3x109.3, three-story brk dwell'g. Foreclos. Andrew S. Hamersley, Jr., to John E. Cronly. Nov. 27. 5,200

171st st, s s, 100 e 11th av, 25x95. *Mt.* $7,500.
Edgecombe av or road, s w s, lots 425 and 426 map Jumel estate, runs east 50 x north 105.6 to Edgecombe road, x northwest 65.2 x147.4. *Mt.* $6,400.
David C. Kee to Nancy Kee. Dec. 1. nom

178th st, n s, 125 w 11th av, 25x100. Catharine E. wife of William Haggerty to Charles G. Haggerty. ⅚ part. Nov. 23. nom

Av A, Nos. 211 and 213 } begins Av A, n w
13th st, Nos. 447 and 449 } cor 13th st, 51.8x100, two four-story brk tenem'ts with stores on av and two four-story brk tenem'ts with stores on st. Mayer Gottlieb to Sophia Robert. *Mt.* $15,000. Nov. 27. 63,000

Av A, Nos. 1354 and 1356, n e cor 72d st, 51.2x98, two five-story stone front tenem'ts with stores. John J. Reilly to Adam Moran. *Mt.* $50,500. Nov. 30. nom

Av B, No. 196, n w cor 12th st, 18.4x60, five-story brk tenem't with stores. Charles Lindner to Peter Lyding. *Mt.* $9,000. Nov. 30. See 10th st. 32,500

Av D, No. 98, e s, 48.8 n 7th st, 24.4x85, four-story brk store and tenem't. Sarah Metzler widow and Emma wife of Abraham Weinberg to Henry Strauss. Nov. 30. 13,000

Amsterdam av, No. 649, e s, 109.11 n 91st st, 26.6x100, five-story brk flat with stores. Foreclos. Jerome Buck to Simon Arendt. Sub. to morts $112,500 and judgment of foreclos. on which is due $8,316 and costs $373. Aug. 31. 29,000

Amsterdam av, No. 641, n e cor 91st st, 27.11x100, five-story brk store and flat. Foreclos. Same to same. Sub. as above. Aug. 31. 29,000

Same property. Release mort. Julius Lipman and Moses Kind to Simon Arendt. Nov. 30. nom

Same property. Release judgment. Same to same. Nov. 25. nom

Amsterdam av, e s, 109.11 n 91st st, 26.6x100. Release mort. Same to same. Nov. 30. nom

Same property. Release judgment. Same to same. Nov. 25. nom

Amsterdam av, n e cor 91st st, 27.11x100.
Amsterdam av, e s, 109.11 n 91st st, 26.6x100.
Release mort. Heloise H. Durant to same. Nov. 30. 54,000

Amsterdam (10th) av, e s, 49.11 s 159th st, 50x100, vacant. Mary C. Pentz, Brooklyn, to Henry P. De Graaf. Correction deed. Oct. 28. See 7th av, also Teasdale pl, 23d Ward. nom

Amsterdam av, e s, 109.11 n 91st st, 26.6x100. Simon Arendt to Ellen Tracey, Fall River, Mass. *Mt.* $24,000. Dec. 1. nom

Same property. Ellen Tracey, Fall River, Mass., to Margaret T. Nally. *Mt.* $24,000. Dec. 1. 37,500

Columbus av, No. 462, w s, 25.8 n 82d st, 25.6x100, one-story brk store. Frederick H. Walker to Adolph S. Ellison. *Mt.* $8,000. Dec. 2. nom

Columbus (9th) av, s e cor 73d st. Party of first part reserves right to damages, and parties of second part to become parties to suit agt N. Y. Elevated R. R. Co. if necessary. Charles Buck to Benjamin F., Louis T. and Washington T. Romaine. Oct 15. nom

Columbus av, Nos. 269 to 275 } begins Columbus av, s e
73d st, Nos. 46 and 48 } 73d st, 103.2x100, three six-story brk flats with stores. Charles Buck, Westport, Conn., to Benjamin F., Louis T. and Washington T. Romaine. *Mt.* $325,000. Nov. 30. See Manhattan av, also 97th st. nom

Same property. Benjamin F., Louis T. and Washington T. Romaine to Girard and Julia A. Romaine. 2-5 parts. Nov. 30. nom

Convent av, n w cor 144th st, 24.11x94.5, three-story brk dwell'g. Foreclos. R. Duncan Harris to Charles W. Rounds. Dec. 2. 20,000

Convent av, w s, 24 11 n 144th st, 25x94.5, three-story brk dwell'g. Foreclos. Same to same. Dec. 2. 15,850

Convent av, w s, 49.11 n 144th st, 25x94.5, three-story brk dwell'g. Foreclos. Same to same. Dec. 2. 15,850

Convent av, w s, 74.11 n 144th st, 25x94.5, three-story brk dwell'g. Foreclos. Same to same. Dec. 2. 15,850

Edgecombe av or road, s w s, lots 425, 426 map of Jumel estate north of 159th st, 65.2x147.4x50x105.6. Charles Kee to David C. Kee. *Mt.* $6,400. Nov. 28. nom

Lenox av, w s, 75.11 n 121st st, 25x100, vacant. Stephen R. Pinckney to William S. Hollingsworth. *Mt.* $10,000. Nov. 30. 19,500

Lenox av, w s, 75.11 n 121st st. Receipt in part payment for party wall and ratification. William H. Hall to Stephen R. Pinckney. Dec. 1. 740

Lenox av, No. 451, w s, 88.3 n 132d st, 16.8x74, three-story stone front dwell'g. John F. Pupke to Edward J. Hamilton. *Mt.* $8,500. Dec. 1. 14,000

Lenox av, Nos. 202-206, e s, 21 n 120th st, 60x80, three four-story brk dwell'gs. Jacob Morgenthaler, Brooklyn, to Zimri West, of Orange, N. J. *Mt.* $54,000. Nov. 30. See Lincoln road, Kings County Conveys. exch

Lexington av, Nos 1639-1643, e s, 25 n 104th st, 50x70, three five-story stone front flats. James J. Ryan to Ruby Ann Smith. *Mt.* $37,500. Nov. 30. See 109th st. 49,000

Manhattan av } begins Manhattan av, n e cor
118th st } 118th st, 100.11x120, vacant. Release mort. The Emigrant Industrial Savings Bank to Richard O'Gorman. Nov. 30. nom

Same property. Release mort. Same to same. Nov. 28. nom

Same property. Richard O'Gorman to Thomas J. McGuire. Nov. 30. See 102d st. 43,000

Manhattan av } begins Manhattan av, w s, ex-
102d st } tends from 102d to 103d st,
103d st } 201.10x150, vacant. Benj. F. and L. T. Romaine exrs. Benj. F. Romaine to Charles Buek, Westport, Conn. Oct. 16. nom

Same property. Benjamin F., Louis T. and Washington T. Romaine to same. Oct. 16. See Columbus av, also 97th st. nom

Park av, Nos. 189-1893, s w cor 129th st, runs west 45.6 x south 68.11 x west 4.1 x south 31 x east 52 7 to av, x north 99.11, four-story frame building with stores. Henry Brash to Gustave R. Fries, Cincinnati, O. *Mt.* $18,000. Nov. 28. nom

Park av, No. 61, e s, 49.7 s 38th st, 24.7x80, four-story stone front dwell'g. Mary J. wife of William Buchanan to Hannah E. wife of Douglass W. Burnham. *Mt.* $20,000. Dec. 2. 87,000

Park av, No. 926, w s, 82.2 n 80th st, 20x80 6, four-story brk dwell'g. William P. Lynch to Frank E. Randall. *Mt.* $25,000. Dec 1. 15,000

Riverside av or Drive, No. 92, e s, 82.10 s 84d st, 19.4x110.9x19 4x105.8, four-story stone front dwell'g. Albert C. Squier to Jane J. Phelps. Warranty of title. Nov. 20. nom

Riverside av, Nos. 60-64 } begins Riverside av
78th st } or Drive, n e cor
79th st } 78th st, 207.2 to 79th st, x 86.4x204.4 to 78th st, x120.4, five four-story brk dwell'gs on av, cor 78th st, the 79th st corner is vacant, and two three-story brk dwell'gs on 78th st. Christopher R. Robert to Arthur R. Robert. Oct. 30. nom

St. Nicholas av, n w cor 151st st, 102.2x85.5x99.11x106.11, vacant. Margaret wife of Luke O'Brien to Michael H. Cashman. B. & S. and C. a. G. Nov. 12. nom

West End av, No. 513, w s, 64 s 90th st, 18x90, four-story brk dwell'g. Emma V. Monheimer to Agnes C. Lyon. *Mt.* $19,500. Nov. 27. nom

West End av, n e cor 92d st, 25.8x100.
West End av, e s, 75.8 n 92d st, 104.4x100x101.7x100.
One-story frame building and vacant.
Matilda Weil et al. exrs Max Weil and Ida Meyer et al. exrs. Isaias Meyer to Frank L. Smith. *Mt.* $34,000. Oct. 22. 48,000

Same property. Frank L. Smith to Francis M. Jencks. *Mt.* $34,000. Dec. 3. nom

1st av, No. 2800, e s, 50.5 n 118th st, 25.8x94, four-story brk store and tenem't. Ida C. Lilienthal to Mary wife of Joseph Efinger. *Mt.* $10,000. Dec. 1. 17,000

1st av, No. 506, e s, 74 1 n 29th st, 24.8x100, five-story brk tenem't with stores. Katie wife of Henry Lehmann to Amalia Hopper. *Mt.* $8,750. April 10, 1891. nom

2d av, Nos 939 and 941 } begins 2d av, s w cor
50th st, No. 250 } 50th st, 44.5x80, two five-story stone front stores and tenem'ts on av and four-story brk tenem't on st. Charles Wolfenstein to William Knoepke. *Mt.* $30,000. Dec. 1. 52,750

2d av, No. 802, e s, 20.5 s 43d st, 20x81, four-story stone front store and tenem't. Alexis Michailoff to Hyman Greenstone. *Mt.* $9,000. Dec. 1. 14,100

2d av, No. 1591, w s, 102.2 n 82d st, 25.6x101.8, four-story brk store and tenem't. Charles Messerschmidt to Christopher H. Steinkamp. *Mt.* $15,000. Dec. 1. 26,650

2d av, No. 2405, w s, 50 7 n 123d st, 25.2x90, five-story brk tenem't with stores. Simon M. and Jennie Roeder to Christian W. Wembacher. *Mt.* $13,000. Nov. 30. 25,000

2d av, No. 2118, s e cor 109th st, 17x66, three-story frame and brk store and tenem't. Rose M. and Michael L. Coyle to Philip J. and Rose M. Coyle. Trust deed. Nov. 30. nom

2d av, No. 1917, n w cor 99th st, 26x79, five-story brk tenem't with stores. William C. Martin to John Von Oesen. *Mt.* $15,500. Nov. 30. 29,000

3d av, No. 1414½, e s, 40 s 74th st, 11.2x60, four-story brk store and tenem't. Jacob Lederer to Martin Wurzner. *Mt.* $5,000. Dec. 1. 10 800

3d av, No. 1646, w s, 50.4 n 91st st, 25.2x75, five-story stone front store and tenem't. Matilda Michaelis, Brooklyn, to Marie Schwartz *Mt.* $18,000. Dec. 1. 27,000

3d av, No. 1628, w s, 75.6 n 91st st, 25.2x75, five-story stone front tenem't with stores. Partition. Meyer Butzel to Theodore Hessberg. Dec. 1. 27,000

3d av, No 794, w s, 20.5 s 49th st, 20x60, four-story brk store and tenem't. Yette Stern widow to David L. Durra. Sub. to claim against Elevated R. R. *Mt.* $10,000. Dec. 1. 20,500

3d av, Nos. 1624 and 1626, w s, 25.2 n 91st st, 50.4x75, two five-story stone front tenem'ts with stores. Partition. Meyer Butzel to Matilda Michaelis. Dec. 1. 49,800

5th av, No. 1041, e s, 25 n 85th st, 21.10x100, four-story stone front dwell'g. William K. Aston to W. Livingston Hamersley. *Mt.* $30,000. Oct 5. 70,000

6th av, No. 476, e s, 43.5 s 29th st, 20x75, four-story brk store and tenem't. Isabella Stewart to Jane C. wife of William Britton. Nov. 10, 1888. 20,000

7th av, s w cor 138th st, 99.11x100, vacant.
138th st, s s, 100 w 7th av, 575x99.11, vacant.
139th st, n s, extends from 7th to 8th av, 775x99.11. Two two story frame, brk and stone buildings, rest vacant.
Frank G. Hallett, New Brighton, S. I., to David H. King, Jr., Mamaroneck, N. Y. C. a. G. June 1. 482,500

7th av, Nos. 1968-1974, s w cor 119th st, 100.11x100, four five-story brk flats, store in No. 1974. Fannie M., Sr., and Fannie M., Jr., Crowley and William E., Mary H. and Henry Crowley to Benjamin F. Beekman, West Hoboken, N. J. *Mt.* $16,000. Oct. 26 exch

Same property. Fannie M. Crowley and ano. exrs Robert Crowley to same. *Mt.* $16,000. Oct. 26. See Amsterdam av, also Teasdale pl, 23d Ward. nom

7th av, No 2273, e s, 24.11 s 134th st, 25x75, five-story brk flat with stores. Foreclos. John S. Cram to Matthew Coogan. Dec. 5. 21,000

8th av, No. 2173, w s, 26.4 n 117th st, 25.8x100, five-story brk flat with stores. Elizabeth wife of Richard E. Johnston to John J. Benzing. *Mt.* $18,750. Nov. 27. 30,000

11th av, No. 838, n e cor 57th st, 25.5x50, five story brk store and tenem't. Bernard Schopp and Jacob Becker to Max Ullmann. *Mt.* $13,000. Dec. 1. 20,000

All title in alleys, &c., south of line on e s of Sullivan st, 67 s of Grand st, runs east 62 x south 8 x east 28, with consent to close all such alleys. William H. Johnston, Greenport, L. I., to John T. Williams. B. & S. Nov. 25. nom

Part of mortgaged premises lying south of a line drawn parallel with 117th st and distant 54 north therefrom. Release mort. Morris Steinhardt to Elizabeth Johnston. Nov. 27. 5,000

MISCELLANEOUS.

Appointment of new trustee under deed of trust by Marcia O. Roosevelt. James Roosevelt trustee to W. Emlen A. Roosevelt. July 10. nom

All dower in estate of Woodbury Langdon dec'd. Release. Helen Langdon widow to Woodbury G. Langdon. Nov. 21. nom

General release, especially as to estate of Peter M. Suydam and his exrs. Catharine A. Humphrey widow to William T. Laurence et al. exrs. Peter M. Suydam. Nov. 16, 1891. nom

23d and 24th WARDS.

Arcularius pl, s s, 209.3 e Gerard av, runs east 50 x south 100 x east 50 x south 77.3 x west 102 x north 197.3. Patrick F. Ferrigan et al. exrs. Hugh Ferrigan to Alexander A. Jordan. Nov. 23. See Inwood av. 4,025

Chisholm st, e s, 28 s Freeman st, runs south 22 x east 37 x southeast 26.10 to Stebbins av, x northeast 25 x northwest 31.5 x west 55.6. Denison P. Chesebro to Frank Zdenovec. *Mt.* $300. Nov. 21. 600

Delancey pl or Washington av, w s, 138 n Bayard st or 188th st, 25x110. Thomas Houghlahan to Harris Pierce. Q. C. Nov. 23, 1888. nom

Same property. Harris Pierce to Thomas Houghlahan and Elizabeth his wife. Q C. Nov. 24. nom

Elsmere pl, s s, 262.4 e Prospect av, 20x200 to Fairmount pl. John H. Metzler to Annie M. Metzler. *Mt.* $3,500. Dec. 1. 8,000

Findlay pl, s s, 409.6 e Central av. 100x200 to Clark pl. Henry Sheppard to Florence Frazee. Nov. 24. 6,400

Morton pl, n s, lots 21, 22 map 71 lots Kingsland estate, Morris Heights, 24th Ward. Hugh N. Camp to Frank M. Hodges. Nov. 27. 1,100

Niles st, s s, 150 w Bainbridge av, 25x122.3 to Mosholu Parkway, x25.3x125 10. Emanuel G. Bach and Ephraim B. Levy to Anzi L. Barber, Washington, D. C. *Mt.* $490. Dec. 2. 575

Niles st, s s, 175 w Bainbridge av, runs south 124.3 to Mosholu Parkway, x west 25.2 x north 124.5 to Niles st, x east 10.3 x still east 15.11 to beginning. Same to Edmund Hayes, Buffalo, N. Y. *Mt.* $490. Dec. 2. 575

Park View terrace, e s, 200 n Wellesley st, 75x125.
Travers st, s s, 25 w Creston av, 25x106.1x25.1x102.10.
The Twenty-Fourth Ward Real Estate Assoc., New York, to George V. Krauss. Oct. 20. 4,200

Ritter pl, s s, 100 e Union av, 60x90. Elizabeth wife of Thomas Farley formerly McCarthy to John G. Hohmann. *Mt.* $3,500. Dec. 1. 5,500

Riverview terrace, w s, 225 n Stone monument set in w s Sedgwick av at n e cor of lot of grantee, 25x81.7x25x82.7. Lewis G. Morris to Wells Sponable. Nov. 28. 1,500

Riverview terrace, w s, 250 n Stone monument set in w s Sedgwick av at n e cor of lot of Wells Sponable, 25x80.9x25x81.7. Lewis G. Morris to John P. Sponable, Fort Plain, N. Y. Nov. 28. 1,500

Rock st, s e cor Forest st, runs south 65 x east 100 x north 143.6 to Rock st, x southwest 127. James F and Patrick H. Sheridan and James S. Segrave to William and Gustave Breithaupt. Nov. 25. 2,400

Rogers pl, e s, 300.1 n Westchester av, 25x90, h & l. Matthew Farrell to Margaret A. wife of Thomas O'Rorke. *Mt.* $1,600. Nov. 27 500

Rogers pl, e s, 325 n Westchester av, 25x90. Margaret wife of James Farrell to Thomas O'Rorke. Nov. 27. 3,500

Teasdale pl, s s, 425 w Grove av, 100x100.
3d av, e s, 325 n St. Anns av, 25x125.
Amsterdam (10th) av, e s, 49.11 s 139th st, 50x100. *Mt.* $4,000.
Boulevard, s e cor 114th st, 100.11x100. *Mt.* $20,370.
148th st, n s, 125 e 8th av, 225x99.11.
148th st, n s, 225 w 7th av, 100x99.11. *Mt.* $39,000.
Henry P. De Graaf to Fannie M. Crowley widow, ½ part, and Fannie M., Jr., William E., Mary H. and Henry Crowley, each 1-6 part. Oct. 30. See Amsterdam av, also 7th av. exch

Walnut st, s s, lot 59 map Mt. Eden, &c., 50x100. Gertrude Moble widow to Mary T. Gallagher. Nov. 16. 2,000

134th st, s s, 125 w Alexander av, 25x100. Frederick Rohrs to David Quigley. *Mt.* $13,000. Nov. 30. 19,000

134th st, No. 972, s s, 266.8 e Cypress av late Trinity av, 16.8x103.8x16.8x107.8, h & l. Charles Hohl to James H. Riley. *Mt.* $2,500. Nov. 30. 4,300

134th st, No. 485, n s, old line, 84.3 e of old line 3d av, 20x75x—x75. Cornelius H. Carling to James Ferrier. Dec 2. 4,500

138th st, s s, 75 e Southern Boulevard, 25x100. Release morts. James Welsh, Westfield, N. J., to Delia Gibson. B. & S. Nov. 7. nom

Same property. Foreclos. Michael T. Sharkey to Delia Gibson. Nov. 27. 6,125

151st st, s s, 100 w Courtlandt av, 25x118.5. John and John G. Guendling heirs Catharine Guendling, Brooklyn, to Carl Hulster. Dec. 1. 4,050

151st st, s s, 155 e Wales av, 25x175. Patrick Grady to James Thompson. Nov. 27. 3,600

154th st, n s, 233.4 w Courtlandt av, 16.8x100. George Stolz to Helena Freudenmacher. *Mt.* $2,000. Dec. 1. 4,300

154th st, n s, 300 w Courtlandt av, 24x100. William T. Brewer to Joseph Henning. Nov. 30. 2,000

154th st, No. 677 E., n s, 170 w Elton av, 25x100, error. Contract. Lizzie and Catharine Wurz to Louisa Wagener. Sub., besides consideration, mort. $1,300 and taxes for 3 years. Nov. 5. 1,900

157th st, n w cor Lorillard st or pl, 58x88.9. Charles H. Jenkins, Brooklyn, to Beth Eden Baptist Church. *Mt.* $8,800. March 1. 8,800

Andrews av, w s, 250.10 n Hampden st, runs west 100 x north 50 x east 130 x south 50 x west 30. William D. Peck to Stephen C. Hunter. Nov. 25. 3,000

Bathgate av, e s, 20 n 172d st, 20x100. Cornelius Donovan to Margaret V. Gallagher. Nov. 18. 1,500

Clinton av, n s, 250 e 3d st, 50x100. Edward Moran to The Mayor, &c. Nov. 14. 1,050

Concord av, w s, part lot 138 map of Wilton, Port Morris and East Morrisania, 50x100. John Clear to William Maher. Nov. 19. 3,300

Decatur av, n w s, 378.11 n e Southern Boulevard, 37.8x110. Release mort. The Mount Morris Co-operative Building and Loan Assoc. to Henry Wiechmann. Dec. 1. 700

Same property. Henry Wiechmann to John Falvey. Dec. 2. 2,300

Fulton av, e s, 308 n 7th st, 24x211. Hugo Maul to Peter Asmussen. Nov. 28. 8,000

Fulton av, e s, 308 n 169th st. Agreement to close windows on 30 days' notice. Peter Asmussen to Hugo Maul. Nov. 28. nom

Inwood av, n e cor Gerard av, 29.11x87.6x—x100. Patrick F. Ferrigan et al. exrs. Hugh Ferrigan to Alexander A. Jordan. Nov. 23. See Arcularius pl. 2,550

Jefferson av, w s, adj lot 11 map S. Ryer homestead, 44x—x38.6x100. Isaac Anderson to Susie E. Boyd, Tea Neck, N. J. *Mt.* $900. Nov. 21. 3,500

Opdyke av, n s, 350 e 3d st, 50x100. James H. Dodd to Caroline Schwarz. Nov. 18. 800

Tinton av, e s, 61 n Denman pl, 20.8x92. John W. Decker to Theodore and Charles E. Demmerle. *Mt.* $3,500. Dec. 1. 5,800

Washington av, w s, 200 s 165th st, 50x100. Susan E. Cooper to Sarah A., Anna S. and H. Louise Cooper. Dec. 2, 1885. nom

Washington av, e s, 67.8 n 163d st, 25x100. Hans Pohlmann to Anna Jung. *Mt.* $4,000. Nov. 19. 6,000

Washington av, e s, 100 s 163d st, runs east 125 x south 50 x west 53.8 to Brook av, x northwest 92.3 to Washington av, x north 1.9. Same to same. *Mt* $9,500. Nov. 19. 20,000

Washington av, w s, 75 n 170th st, 25x150x25.1x150. Maria L. Dike, Port Jervis, N. Y., heir Anderson Bloomer to Isabella Jenkins. Q. C. and C. a. G. Nov. 10. nom

Same property. Isabella Jenkins to Anna B. Weiler. Taxes, &c., 1891. Oct. 28. 3,500

Same property. George P. Bloomer, Bellmore, L. I., heir Anderson Bloomer to Isabella Jenkins. Q. C. C. a. G. Nov. 10. nom

Same property. Mary E. Jones, Bridgeport, Conn., to same. Q. C. C. a. G. Nov. 10. nom

Willard av, s s, 200 e 3d st, runs east 100 x south 100 x west 50 x south 100 to Clinton av, x west 50 x north 200. Myron C. Burton to The Mayor, &c. Nov. 14. 3,150

Woodruff av, n s, 326.2 w Prospect st, 25x98.6. Owen Toher to John H. Metzler. Oct. 30. nom

Yonkers av proposed, w s, 100 s Van Courtlandt av, 50x100, Hudson Park. Albert E. Putnam to Thomas B Hallanan. Nov. 21. 800

Lot 28 map 158 select lots at Kingsbridge Heights, 24th Ward. Samuel W. Fairchild to Henry Reimer, Somerville, N. J. Nov. 16. 1,030

Lot 32 map of Ash property, West Farms. Caroline Diehl to John Esch. B. & S. All title under tax lease. Oct. 29. 285

Lot 235 map of 339 lots at Riverdale and Mosholu, 24th Ward, of F. P. & H. A Forster, 25x100. Frederick P. Forster exr. George H. Foster to Charles Pape. Nov. 30. 600

Lot 234 same map, 25x100. Same to Edward J. Janikula. Nov. 30. 600

Lots 192, 193 and 194 map of E. K. Willard property. Woodlawn Heights, and being in block bounded Knox st, Katonah av, Kemble st and Kepler av, 75x100. James Munn, Deadwood, S. D., to Adelbert J. Howe. *Mt.* $400. Nov. 9. 1,200

Interior lots 90 s of Ritter pl and 100 e Union av. runs east 60 x south 90x60x90. Thomas Farley to John G. Hohmann. Dec. 1. See Ritter pl. 2,500

Fordham Landing road, n e s, 50 s e New York & Northern R. R., runs southeast along road 60.9 x northeast 107.4 x north 97.9 x west 62 to said railroad, x south and away from the railroad 96.5 x southwest 100 to beginning. Charles E. Sentell, Brooklyn, to the Mayor, &c., New York, for street. April 23, 1890. grant

West Farms to Hunts Point road, lots 13 and 14 map Hedges Farm, 24th Ward formerly West Farms, 100x197 to burying ground, x 82.6x193; as to a strip of above, 1x22.5x0.8x225, all title only is conveyed. Amanda Bussing widow to Emma M. wife of F. Denninger. Dec. 1. 2,850

Private lane which would be 162d st if extended, the parcel begins on division line bet acres 2 and 3 on map of Morrisania, abt 1¼ miles from Harlem River, &c., at point 124.3 n w 3d av, runs southeast on said line 27.10 x northeast 123.9x27.10x123.9. Foreclos. Michael J. A. McCaffery to The Bowery Bank, New York. Nov. 18. Sub. to mort. $4,000. 3,000

LEASEHOLD CONVEYANCES.

Barclay st, No. 27. Assign. lease. Christina Dress formerly Gross to Henry Gross. gift

Clinton pl, n s, 64.5 e University pl, 26.6x93.11. Ass'gn. lease. Amalie wife of Nathan Mayer to Barbara Hoffman. Nov. 20. 11,500

Henry st, s s, abt 80 e Catharine st, 20x50. Clarence R. Conger individ. and trustee to Rese Fisher. 21 years, from May 1, 1892, per year, taxes and 350

Thompson st, Nos. 57-63. Cancellation of lease. The Standard Gas Light Co. to The New York Steam Co. Dec. 2. nom

Same property. Certificate that party of first part has no interest in above lease. The Mercantile Trust Co. trustee to same. Dec. 2. nom

Thompson st, Nos. 57 and 59. Modification of lease. Baker Transfer Co. to same. Nov. 30. nom

4th st, s s, 318 e Av A, 24.9x96.2. Assign. lease. Isaiah H. Hanna referee to Kilian Weigand. Dec. 1. 5,750

4th st, s s, 175 w Av A, 25x96.2. Assign. lease. Caroline Nussbaum extrx. Anthony Nussbaum to Henry Diefenthaler. 9,250

11th st, Nos. 310 and 312 E. Consent to assign. lease. Rector, &c., of the P. E. Church of St. Marks in the Bowery to Sophie and Samuel Weil admrs. Moses Weil to Katie Weil. nom

11th st, s s, 188 e 2d av, 48.4x94.10. Assign. lease. Sophie and Samuel Weil admrs. Moses Weil to Katie Weil. 25,000

12th st, n s, 350 w 3d av, 25x103.3. Assign. lease. Justus J. Spreng exr. Catherine Lenihan to William Hamilton. Nov. 28. 6,750

14th st, No. 104 E. Assign. lease. Emil Lienau to William H. Rethwisch. Nov. 30. nom

Same property. Assign. lease. Same to William L. Flanagan, managing director. Nov. 20. nom

28th st, No. 115 E. General release and cancellation of lease. Charles H. Traitteur admr. Eugenie C. Traitteur to Talmadge Parsons individ. and admr. Levi Parsons. Dec. 3. 700

45th st, n s, 100 e 8th av, 16.8x100.5. Assign. lease. Joseph T. Wortendyke to A. M. Carter. nom

45th st, s s, 170 e 8th av, 20x100.5. William W. Astor to Thomas McK. Brown, James P. Paulding and James Burt trustees. 20 years, from May 1, 1891, per year, 500

48th st, No. 56 W., s s, 654.3 w 5th av, 18.9x100.5. The trustees of Columbia College to Robert J. Waddell. 21 years, from Nov. 1, 1891, per year, taxes and 608

48th st, No. 56 W. Assign. lease. Robert J. Waddell to Estelle Richards. *Mt.* $15,000. 17,000

123d st, No. 137, n s, 305 e 4th av, 25x100.11. Elizabeth and Annie McKeon to Elizabeth McKeon widow. Lease for life.

Amsterdam (10th) av, No. 1780. Assign. lease. H. Koehler & Co. to Conrad Stein. nom

Columbus av, No 466, s w cor 81st st. Assign. lease. Herman C. Borger to Henry Hyman. 8,000

Same property. Assign. lease. Henry Hyman to John McCormack. 8,000

River av, n w cor 150th st, runs north 494.6 x west 200.3 to Cromwell av, x south 492.2 to 150th st, x east 200.4.
150th st, n s, 418.5 w Cromwell av, runs north 126.8 to slip, x west 25 to pier line on Harlem River, x south 88 to 150th st, x east 84, with land under water.
Henry L. Morris to Levi H. Mace, Frederick S. and John L. Gwyer and Arthur J. Mace, of L. H. Mace & Co. 21 years, from Nov. 1, 1891, per year. 2,000

River av, n w cor 150th st, runs north 493.1 x west 200.3 to Cromwell av, x south 49?.3 to 150th st, x east 200.5. Agreement to cancel lease. Henry L. Morris to L. H. Mace & Co. nom

3d av, e s, 133.5 n 47th st, 22x73. Assign. lease. Jonas Weil and Bernhard Mayer to Fisher Lewine. 12,250

8th av, s e cor 19th st. Assign. lease. Bavarian Brewing Co. to James Everard. nom

10th av, s e cor 24th st, 24.8x100. Consent to assign. lease. The New York Life Ins. and Trust Co. exr. Richard Ray to Daniel E. Seybel. nom

10th av, e s, 24.8 s 29th st, 24.8x100. Consent to assign. lease. Same to same. nom

10th av, e s, 24.8 s 29th st, 24.8x100. Assign. lease. Daniel E. Seybel to Mary A. Walton, East Orange, N. J. 51,500

KINGS COUNTY.

NOVEMBER 25, 26, 27, 28, 30, DECEMBER 1, 2.

Ainslie st, n s, 93.4 w Bushwick av, 20x100, very bad error. Arthur F. Merklein to Hylande MacGrath. ½ part. $1,000

Bainbridge st, n s, 187 e Saratoga av, 26x100. Anna E. Kirby to Katharina wife of Philip Geyer. *Mt.* $10,000. nom

Bainbridge st, s s, 205 e Ralph av, 345x100. Charles M. Marsh to Robert F. Minto. 36,225

Baltic st, n s, 80 e Clinton st, 20x60. Rose E. wife of Richard S. Hegeman to William Greene. 5,300

Barbey st, w s, 180 s Repose pl, 40x100. William B. Nichols to Isdor Stern, New York. 1889. 350

Barbey st, w s, 225 s Blake av, 16.8x100. Henry C. Heyser to Daniel P. Nowlan, of New York. 2,200

Barbey st, w s, 175 n Blake av, 25x100. Albert H. Van Sielen to Pauline Tuerk. 365

Barbey st, w s, 180 s Repose pl, 40x100. Isidor Stern to Charles S. Hicks. 700

Bartlett st, s s, 150 w Throop av, 25x100, h & l. Annie wife of Louis Haidt to John G. Ruge. 3,000

Bergen st, s s, 175 w Hopkinson av, 25x127.9. Rose Rosenfeld to John P. Shea. *Mt.* $400. 142

Bergen st, n e s, 175 s e Smith st, 100x100. Elizabeth Harper to Lewis Josephs. *Mt.* $28,000. 89,000

Berriman st, w s, 175 n Liberty av, 175x100
Eastern Parkway, n w cor Shepherd av, 150x95; also,
Eastern Parkway, n s, 25 e Shepherd av, 150x100; also,
Shepherd av, w s, 100 n Belmont av, 100x100.
Alonzo E. De Baun to Israel F. Fischer. Error. 9,000

Bleecker st, w s, 290 s Hamburg av, 100x100. Jacob Miller to Meinrad Keck. Q. C. 836

Same property. Simon Kitt to Meinrad Keck and Jacob Miller. Q. C. 809

Boerum st, n s, 50 e Humboldt st, 25x100, h & l. Adolph T. Glunz to Sigmund Bleyer. 6,000

Boerum st, n s, 150 w Morrell st now Bushwick av, 25x100. George Hagenmuller to Leonhard Martin. 4,100

Boerum pl, n w s, 73.2 s w Livingston st, 27.4x—x24.3x86.4. Morris Berkowitz to Thomas J. Johnston. *Mt.* $15,000. 28,000

Broadway, e s, 56.8 s Madison st, 18.9x80. Conrad Hecker, of New York, to George Evans. *Mt.* $6,100. 8,800

Broadway, s w s, 19.9 s e McDougal st, runs southwest 74.1 x south 35.1 x east 54.2 x northeast 77.11 to Broadway, x northwest 75. James T. Benedict to Stephen P. Sturges. *Mt.* $5,500. 1,550

Broadway, n e s, 62 s e Fairfax st, 19x95. Release mort. Henry Weil to Henry, William and Joseph Schwall. nom

Broadway, s s, 8.2 e Division av, runs south 77.7 x southeast 7.11 x northeast 20 x north 61.10 to Broadway, x west 23. John H. McCoy to Robert Liptrott. 7,800

Broadway, s w s, 125 s e Lewis av, 25x91.10. David Ernstthal to William Schelp. *Mt.* $4,000. 15,000

Broadway, n e s, 154.6 s e De Kalb av, 20x100, h & l. Louis Schaffner to Jacob Willman. *Mt.* $6,500. 18,750

Carroll st, n e s, 175 s e 3d av, 25x100. Fredericka C. wife of William Vohs to John Bishop. *Mt.* $2,000. 3,700

Carroll st, n e s, 150 s e 3d av, 25x100. Raphael, Antione and Francisco Ramato to John Bishop, New York. 3,700

Carroll st, n s, 180 w Columbia st, 20x100, h & l. Jane Potter widow, New York, to Giovanni B. Castagnino. 3,950

Carroll st, s w s, 70 s e 3d av, 20x81.3x20.1x—. William J. Conway to Sigfrid Cederstrom. 4,000

Chauncey st, s s, 249 e Saratoga av, 19x100. Release mort. Charles D. King and George W. Adams to Henry Smith. nom

Same property. Release mort. John W. Phelps to same. nom

Chestnut st, e s, 474 s Jamaica av, 50x150. Caroline Bick to Theodore M. Le Beau. 2,000

Cleveland st, e s, 330 s New Lots road, 80x100. Adolph Sussman to Mary Smith. 1,200

Clinton st, n e cor Pierrepont st, runs north along Clinton st, 88.4 x east 75.1 x south 88.7 x west 75; also,
Clinton st, e s, adj above on the north, 24.11x100; also,
Pierrepont st, n s, 75 e Clinton st, 50x80.5x50.1x88.7.
The First Baptist Church in Pierrepont st to The Brooklyn Savings Bank. 200,000

Clinton st, s e cor Carroll st, 20x90. Mary E. Hall to Ella A. Duy. 8,225

Clinton st, n w s, 30.2 s w Verandah pl, 18.1x55.6x18.1x54.9. James M. Varnum and ano. exrs. and trustees Charles A. Eckert to Hortense wife of Frank Audemars. Taxes 1891. 8,850

Cook st, n s, 250 e Ewen st, 25x100. Leopold Michel to Morris Minden. *Mt.* $5,000. 11,100

Cooper st, s e s, 134.9 s w Bushwick av, 34x100. Ernest F. Sutterlin to Frederick Strobsall. *Mt.* $8,500. 13,500

Cooper st, s e s, 100 s w Bushwick av, 34.2x100. Same to Claus Schlichting. *Mt.* $8,500. 13,500

Covert st, s e s, 200 n e Central av, 120x100. Release mort. Alfred J. Pouch to Isabelle B. Booth. 2,250

Covert st, s s, 269.11 e Central av, 85.11x100, hs & ls. Isabelle B. wife of John N. Booth to Joseph A. Cross. *Mt.* $6,000. nom

Cumberland st, w s, 31.10 n Atlantic av, runs west 40 x northwest 51.6 x northeast 14 x southeast 43.6 x east 40 to st, x south 20. Carlton S. an heir of Lambert S. Reynolds to Cora A. and Florence Reynolds. nom

Same property. Cora and Florence Reynolds heirs of L. S. Reynolds to Joel W. Sherwood. 5,500

Dean st, s s, 100 e Utica av, 20x107.5. Foreclos. John Courtney to Horace F Burroughs. 2,000

Dean st, s s, 120 e Utica av, 20x107.5. Foreclos Same to same. 2,000

Dean st, s s, 100 e Utica av, 40x107.5. Horace F. Burroughs to Julia B. F. wife of John D. Fish. 4,200

Dean st, s s, 50 e Brooklyn av, 45.6x100. George H. Stone to Edward R. Chapel. *Mt.* $12,000. 24,000

Dean st, s s, 200 e Rochester av, 100x107.2. Henry Weil to John T. Birch. 4,800

Dean st, n s, 253.1 e Utica av, 101.10x½ block. Same to Charles A Martin. 4,800

Dean st, n s, 167.2 w Buffalo av, 16.8x107.2. James McGuigan to John W. Gasteiger. *Mt.* $2,200 and tax 1890 and 1891. 2,300

Dean st, n s, 150.4 w Buffalo av, 16.10x107.2. Same to George H. Crawford. *Mt.* $2,200 and tax 1890 and 1891. 2,300

Dean st, n s, 117 w Buffalo av, 16.8x107.2, h & l. Same to same. *Mt.* $2,200 and tax 1890 and 1891. 2,300

Decatur st, s s, 262 e Ralph av, 18x100, h & l. Charles M. Marsh to Joseph P. Fuels. 900

Same property. William J. Northridge to James R. Stracham. *Mt.* $4,500. exch and 750

Decatur st, n s, 135 w Saratoga av, 18.4x100. Ansel H. Van Buren to William G. Dillingham. *Mt.* $4,000. 6,500

Degraw st, n s, 170 w 5th av, 20x98.6. Peter Kelly to Mary E. Collins. *Mt.* $4,000. 7,200

Degraw st, n s, 290 w 5th av, 80x95.6. Release mort. The Bedford Bank to Robert L. Woods. 1,000

Same property. Robert L. Woods to Richard D. Robbins. exch

Dodworth st, s s, bet Broadway and Bushwick av, being assessm't map 18th Ward lot 9 block 1034. William M. Gibson to Margaret Bossart. 2,600

Devoe st, n s, 75 w Graham av, 25x75, h & l. Daniel L. Jones to Charles Harms, Jr. 3,550

Douglass st, n s, 110 w 5th av, 20x100. Mary J. wife of James Gowdey to Christiana Gebhardt. 1,600

Douglass st, n s, 291.1 e Albany av, 133.10x130. Peter Y. Kyle to Harris J. Latta. ½ part. nom

Dupont st, s s, 275 e Union av, 25x100. Partition. Jacob Neu to John E. Kelly. 2,000

Enfield st, w s, 100 n Havens formerly Union av, 25x103x25x104, h & l. Nicholas T. and Elizabeth A. Andrew, Stony Creek, Conn., to Jonas M. Anderson. 1,050

Eagle st, s s, 250 w Manhattan av, 25x100. Mary A. wife of and William H. Lupton to William Atkinson. *Mt.* $1,850. 3,500

Eastern Parkway, n e cor Milford st, 100x90. Julia E. Brownne to William T. Goundie. 2,150

Eckford st, w s, 3.5 s Meserole av, 25x100. Frederick A. Meyer to Benjamin E. Lowe. *Mt.* $2,500. 5,500

Eldert st, Nos. 31, 33 and 35.
Van Buren st, No. 512.
Frank Hyde to Charlotte McTighe. Contract to exchange Gates av, north cor Bushwick av, 120x100.

Eldert st, s e s, 75 s w Evergreen av, 20x89.11x20x89.1. Edward H. Deming, of Farmington, Conn, to Herman Griebert. *Mt.* $2,600. 50

Eldert st, n w s, 100 n e Evergreen av, 40x100. Release mort. The Title Guarantee and Trust Co. to Ernestine Gastmeyer. 4,000

Essex st, w s, 200.11 n Atlantic av, 100x100. Gilliam Schenck to John P. Free. Correction deed nom

Essex st, n w cor Folsom pl, 20x70, h & l. John P. Free to Daniel Lauer. Sub. to mort. exch

Essex st, w s, 80 n Folsom pl, 20x100. Release mort. Samuel S Free to John P. Free. nom

Same property. John P. Free to Francis Merritt. *Mt.* $2,400. 3,000

Ewen st, s w cor Stagg st, 25x72. Elek Sundel to Fanny Goldberg. ¼ part. *Mt.* $10,500. 7,000

Fort Greene pl, w s, 340.6 s Lafayette av, 21x100, h & l. Maria W. Schroeder to Georgine wife of F. Lasette. 16,000

Same property. Georgine Lasette to Anna B. wife of F. N. or H. Collins. 16,000

Fulton st, n e cor Adelphi st, runs southeast 20 x northeast 55 x north 16.3 x west 48.9 to Adelphi st, x south 48.8. Herman Posbergh to Emma C. wife of Philip J. Korinder. 30,000

Garfield pl, s w s, 172.10 n w 8th av. Assignment party wall agreement. Thorvald and Lewis Anderson to Edward H. Mowbray. nom

Garfield pl, s s, 272.10 w 8th av, 18.9x100. Jeremiah J. Gilligan to Anna S. wife of Thomas H. Bennis. *Mt.* $8,000. 14,000

Garden st, s w s, abt 30 s e Locust st if extended, 20x83.
Garden st, s w s, abt 50 s e Locust st, 20x75x20x80.
Garden st, s w s, abt 70 s e Locust st, 20.7x75.1x17.8x75.
John W. Weber to William Ulmer. 3,000

Grand st, s s, 150 e 3d st now Berry st, 25x100. Joseph Mentz and B. Rubenstein to Rose Mintz. 9,000

Gunther pl, e s, 49 n Atlantic av, 49x80. Eben W. Roby to James T. Benedict. *Mt.* $8,750. exch

Halsey st, s s, 400 e Reid av. Party wall agreement. Margaret J. Kennedy to Frank C. Swimm. 100

Halsey st, s e s, 160 n e Evergreen av, 40x100. Josephine wife of D. J. Holland, of New York, to Charles F. Gastmeyer. *Mt.* $1,500. 2,300

Halsey st, n s, 56 w Patchen av, runs north 80 x west 44 x north 20 x west 10 x south 100 to Halsey st, x east 54. Mary A. Cantrell to Rosa Levy. *Mt.* $12,250. 14,700

Halsey st, n s, 56 w Patchen av, 36x80. Rosa Levy to John Gough. nom

Halsey st, s e s, 231.8 n e Broadway, 18x100. Louisa Acton of New B[illegible]dg, N. J., to Clement Moore. *Mt.* $2,200. r[illegible]e 2,400

Harman st, s s, 125 e Central av, 25x100. Andrew and Christian Hahn to Charles Jaeger. *Mt.* $3,500. 7,500

Havemeyer st, west cor North 8th st, 25x75. Patrick Shea to William S. Collins and Nathan Stein. 2,500

Havemeyer st, n w s, 50 s w North 8th st, 25x75. Same to same. 1,200

Hancock st, n s, 111.7 w Ralph av, 16.8x85. George Holland to Barbara Bolz and Louisa Roegel. *Mt.* $2,000. 3,500

Henry st, e s, 75 n Carroll st, 25x117, h & l. Foreclos. Robert Merchant to Gwendoline Burgass. 8,000

Hendrix st, w s, 150 n Bay av now Belmont av, 25x100. Charles W. Engelhardt to Alfred Reinhauer, New York. 4,500

Henry st, s w cor President st, 20x75. Andrew Koch to Margaret McNamara. *Mt.* $7,000. 14,100

Hicks st, No. 24, n w s, 25x76 to McKenney st, x25x74.
Hicks st, w s, 50 n Poplar st, 0.6x42.
J Graham Glover to John I. Glover. ½ part. 3,000

Highland Boulevard, s w cor Pellington pl, 20x96.11x20.10x91.1. John D. Bennett to Peter Seauret. *Mt.* $1,750. nom

Same property. Peter Seauret to Sophie Hafner. *Mt.* $1,750. 2,137

Hinsdale st, w s, 90 n Hegeman av, 60x100. Charles J. Curtin to Albert J. Lawles. Q. C. Correction deed. nom

Hubbard st, n w s, intersection west line land of John L. Williamson, contains 486-1,000 acres, Flatlands. Rebecca S. wife of John L. Williamson, Joanna and Sarah D. Kouwenhoven to Teunis Williamson. nom

Same property. Teunis Williamson to Rebecca S. Williamson, Joanna and Sarah D. Kouwenhoven. nom

Huron st, n s, 100 e Manhattan av, 25x100, h & l. Annie M. wife of and Patrick Brady to Catherine Taylor. 4,200

Hooper st, w s, 95 s South 3d st, runs west 75 x north 20 x east 25 x north 3.6 x east 50 to Hooper st, x south 23.6, h & l. Frank G. Clark to John T. Matthews. *Mt.* $1,000. nom

Hooper st, n w s, 95 n e South 2d st, 25x97.10; also,
Hooper st, n w s, 45 s w South 1st st, 25x78.
Hannah M. widow, Charles W. Eldridge, of Hartford, Conn, to Henry C. Hearm. nom

Hooper st late 11th st, n w s, 95 n e South 2d st, 25x—x25x97.3.
Hooper st late 11th st, n w s, 45 s w South 1st st, 25x78.
Release mort. The Dime Savings Bank, Hartford, releases mort. made by James W. Eldridge. nom

Same property. James W. Eldridge heirs of Chas. W. Eldridge to same. Tax 1891. 5,550

Hooper st, s e s, 20 n e Harrison av, 20x70, h & l. Samuel Wells to Frank H. Evans. 5,200

India st, n s, 325 w Manhattan av, 25x100. Partition. Jacob Neu to James P. Sloane. 4,600

Jackson st, n s, 150 e Ewen st, 50x100. Mary M. Atwater, of Callecoon, N. Y., to Valentine & Co. 4,000

Jerome st, w s, 60 n Blake av, 20x100. Frank Dedreux to Charles Kreutzer. 350

Kosciusko st, s s, 100 w Stuyvesant av, 25x100. Jacob Leib to Lottie wife of Otto F. Suhr. other consid. and 200

Lafayette pl, e s, 198 7 n Atlantic av, 28.100. Charles M. Marsh to William H. H. Robbins. 2,500

Lincoln pl, s s, 329.2 e 6th av, 20.10x100. The Brooklyn Trust Co. exrs. Samuel T. Spear to John Gledhill. 10,250

Lincoln road, n s, 104.3 w Rogers av, 585.9x 205 to Lefferts av.
Lincoln road, n s, 680 w Rogers av, 40x205 to Lefferts av.
Lincoln road, n s, 760 w Rogers av, 90 to Bedford av, x 205 to Lefferts av, Flatbush.
Zimri West, Orange, N. J., to Jacob Morgenthaler. S'e Lenox av, N. Y. Conveys. exch

Linwood st, w s, 170 s e Eastern Parkway, 25x 90. John Lynch to John A. Seidler. 400

Livingston st, n s, 93 e Gallatin pl, 22.4x99.7. Sarah L. Bloomfield, of New York, to Robert Mannheimer, of New York. 14,250

Logan st, w s, 130 s Eastern Parkway, 20x 100. Mary wife of Joseph Hofmeister, of New York, to Sarah F. wife of Alsop V. Green. 815

Logan st, w s, 190 n Belmont av, 20x200 to Milford st. Charles Mitchel to Mary Hofmeister. 500

Logan st, w s, 100 n Liberty av, 50x100. Elizabeth S. Lowerre to Joseph C. Butler. *Mt.* $1,750. 2,850

Lorimer st, w s, 25 s Richardson st, 25x100. William A. Leaver to Domenico Fornino. 2,200

Lorimer st, w s, 75 s Richardson st, 25x100. Ann Treacy widow and Thomas F., Michael J. and John Treacy and Mary A. wife of Thomas B. Hobby heirs Thomas Treacy to Giuseppe Cioricari and Venanzia Citera. *Mt.* $1,000. 2,500

Lorimer st, w s, 316.8 s Meserole av, 16.8x100. Charles A. Berton, of Richmond Hill, N. Y., to Carman A. Robinson. 6,000

Lynch st, n w s, 164 n e Harrison av, 20x100. Magdalena E. Pflug widow and George F. Pflug one of the heirs of George Pflug to William F. Hanse. 1,202

Same property. Louis H., Charles J., Magdalena, Henry E. and Eugene A. Pflug by Magdalena E. Pflug guard. to same. 2,497

Macon st, s s, 249 w Patchen av, 18x100, h & l. James G. Roberts to Joseph D. Hildreth. *Mt.* $4,500 and tax $52. 7,275

Same property. Release judgment. William Ziegler to same. nom

Macon st, s s, 16.8 e Marcy av, 16.8x100. Henry Roth and Joseph E. Middle to Mary A. Lee. *Mt.* $4,000. 6,500

Macon st, n w cor Ralph av, 58x100, hs & ls. Benjamin C. Raymond to Frederick W. Starr, James D. Rankin and James Ross. *Mt.* $15,589. nom

Madison st, n w s, 360 n e Hamburg av, 117x 100. Anna E. Cozine widow individ. and with ano. exrs. of John G. Cozine to Adolphus Gload. ½ part. 3,051

Same property. James Gascoine to same. ½ part. nom

Malbone st, n s, 150.10 e Brooklyn av, 238.7x 131.9x237.2x131.6. Melvin Brown to Rose M. wife of William A. Watson. nom

Marion st, s s, 50 e Hopkinson av, 50x75. Edward A. Carley, New York, to William P. Hill, Paris, France. Q. C. nom

McDougal st, n w cor Stone av, runs west along st 100, x north to land Brooklyn and Jamaica Turnpike Co, x northeast to point 100 north from McDougal st, x east to northeast line of land of above company, x southeast to Stone av, x 9.7 to beginning. Robert O'Brien to Elihu J. Granger. 3,500

McDonough st, n s, 300 e Howard av, 20x100. Charles A. Haviland to Ulysses A. Cannon. nom

McDonough st, n w cor Reid av, 25.6x100. Foreclos. Randolph H. Cole to Charles G. Reynolds. *Mt.* $8,000. 1,600

McDonough st, n s, 125 w Howard av, 18x100. Thomas McDonald to Norma V. D. Griffith. *Mt.* $4,800. 5,200

Milford st, e s, 170 n Sutter av, 20x100. Effingham H. Nichols to Charles H. Machin. 300

Milford st, w s, 170 s Blake av, 20x100. Margaret C. wife of Frederick P. Greaves, of Hot Springs, Ark., to John A. Orr. 175

Milford st, w s, 190 n Blake av, 20x100. Sarah M. Hulin to Edward R. Jourdan. 285

Monroe st, n s, 133.4 e Patchen av, 16 8x100, h & l. Absalom W. Dieter to Amelia E. Hummel. *Mt.* $4,000. nom

Monroe st, n s, 530 w Ralph av, 60x100. Richard D. Robbins to William W. Relyea, of New Hurley, N. Y. *Mt.* $9,000. exch

Monroe st, s s, 364.9 e Reid av, 19.11x100. Emma F. Starrett and Naomi E. Coy to Christopher J. Watson Taxes 1891. 3,350

Montague st, n w cor Hicks st, 50x100. Fanny E. Gilkison to Sarah Crawford. *Mt.* $30,000. 42,750

Moore st, s s, 50 e Ewen st, 25x100, h & l. Jacob H. Werbelovsky to Simon Rosenblum and Joseph L. Werbelovsky. *Mt.* $5,000. 11,500

Moore st, s s, 50 w Humboldt st, 25x100. Gerson Krakower and Nathan Goldberg to Elek Sundel. All title. *Mt.* $4,000. 5,000

Moore st, n s, 50 e Leonard st, 25x100. Leopold Michel to Samuel Gallin. *Mt.* $5,000. 13,500

Morrell st, w s, 25 s Moore st, 25x100. Abraham Wisbinsky and Harris Rosenberg to Anna Jaraschow. *Mt.* $1,600. 3,600

Myrtle st, s e s, 175 s w Evergreen av, 25x78 5 to Myrtle av, x29x93.2, h & l. John Gerlich to Thomas Derbyshire and Margaretha his wife, joint tenants. *Mt.* $3,500. exch

Pacific st, s s, 168.3 e Utica av, 34.11x107.2. Henry Well to Michael Giblin. 4,000

Park pl, n s, 440 e Clason av, 50x131. Daniel Lauer to John P. Free. exch

Same property. Mary wife of and Peter Cleary to Daniel Lauer. nom

Park pl, s s, 420 e Vanderbilt av, 25x131. Edwin A. O'Brien to George F. Cooper. *Mt.* $718. 3,000

Pearl st, w s, 50 n High st, 27.6x97.6, with all title to strip on rear, 27.6x6.6. David W. Jordan to Eliza A. Macauliff, Catherine P. McMahon and Anna A. Jordan. 2,350

Pearl st, w s, 177 n Tillary st, 20.8x102.11x20.8x 102.11. Mary E. Murtha widow, George W., Adelaide, Minnie L. and Cordelia C Rice, Minnie L. Jones and Cecelia Dougherty children of Peter Rice to Herrmann Sacks. Q. C. nom

Same property. Herrmann Sacks to Catharine Rowan. *Mt.* $3,000. exch

Pierrepont st, n s, 26.3 w Hicks st, 25x87.5x25x 85.10. John Adamson to Ezra D. Bushnell. *Mt.* $15,000. nom

Pierrepont st, n s, 26.3 w Hicks st, 25x85.10x25 x87.5. Edwin D. Phelps to John Adamson. exch

Pierrepont st, s s, 175 e Henry st, 25x100. Edward S. Bergen to Sidney S. Darling, of New York. *Mt.* $40,000. exch

Pineapple st, s s, 85 e Hicks st, runs south 29.9 x east 15 x south 5.3 x east 3 x north 35 to st, x west 18, h & l. George F. Rogers to Louise E. Winton. *Mt.* $5,000. 6,500

Powell st, w s, 250 n Liberty av, 25x100. John F. Vroonan to James E. Seaman, New York. *Mt.* $2,500. 3,500

President st, s s, 100 w 4th av, 25x100. George S. Wheeler exr. Nancy B. Wheeler to Mary Kane. Taxes 1891. 1,500

Pulaski st, n s, 140 w Tompkins av, 20x100, h & l. Annie M. Mahen, Kingston, N. Y., to William A. Driver. 4,800

Quincy st, s s, 493.9 w Throop av, 18.9x100, h & l. David F. Manning to Charles D. Mackay, New York. *Mt.* $4,500. 7,800

Quincy st, s s, 165 w Marcy av, 20x100. William Wach to Daniel Heim and Jacob Strauss, of New York. *Mt.* $3,000. 6,000

Ross st, n s, 275 e Lee av, 25x100. Ferdinand R. Hein to Robert Kerr, of Newport, R. I. *Mt.* $8,000. nom

Rush st, No. 18, s s, 150 w Wythe av, 20x100. Jacob Damman or Dauman to Harris Siegel, N. Y. *Mt.* $8,450. 11,000

Sandford st, e s, 232.3 s Park av, 25x100. Catharina Geyer to Lena S. wife of Isidor Blatt. *Mt.* $3,650. nom

Same property. Lena S. wife of Isidor Blatt to Anna E. wife of J. Mason Kirby. *Mt.* $5,-150. nom

Sackett st, s w s, 241.8 n w Smith st, 16.8x100. Martha S. Clarke to Jacob D. H. Bergen. *Mt.* $2,500. 3,450

Schaeffer st, n w s, 100 n e Knickerbocker av, runs northeast 294.6 x northwest 165.9 x northwest 34.4 to Covert st, x southwest 80 x southeast 100 x southwest 224 x southeast 100. Charles Gundlich, of New York, to Minna wife of Gustav Feigenspan, of Newtown, N. Y. *Mt.* $5,000. 9,500

Schermerhorn st, n e s, 93.1 n w Boerum pl, runs northeast 78.5 x southeast 3.5 x northeast 26.10 x northwest 23.1 x southwest 104.3 to st, x southeast 19.7, h & l. Henry Werner to Thomas B. Sidebotham, Jr. *Mt.* $6,500. 7,500

Seigel st, No. 61, n s, 98.6 w Ewen st, 24x100, h & l. Henry Meyer to Sarah Barasch. ½ part. nom

Seigel st, Nos. 55 and 57, n s, 146.6 w Ewen st, 48x100, hs & ls. Jonas Feldberg and Sarah Barasch to Henry Meyer. All title. nom

Seigel st, s s, 415 e Bushwick av, 100x100. Charles W. Truslow admr. William Wall to Michael Mayer. 3,700

Seigel st, s s, 50 e Ewen st, 25x100. Jacob H. Werbelovsky to Isaac Cohen. *Mt.* $5,500. 14,000

Spencer st, w s, 450 n Park av, 25x80. Mary F. Meyers devisee John Sheridan to John Nooney. 1,375

Stanhope st, n w s, 175 n e Irving av, 25x100. Charles G. Curtin to Charles A. Cross. *Mt.* $500. nom

Stanhope st, n w s, 275 n e Hamburg av, 25x 100. Louis Jaeck to Jacob Kirchherr. *Mt.* $3,000. 5,742

Stanhope late Conselyea st, n s, 725 e Evergreen late Willow av, 39.9x100x36.6x100. Michael Proestler to Leonhard M. Fessler. 2,750

State st, n s, 185 e 3d av, 20x64.6x20x78.4, h & l. Mary A. Reynolds, Orange, N. J., individ. and extrx. Clinton G. Reynolds to Percy G. Williams. 6,250

Starr st, s e s, 88.5 s w Wyckoff av, 25x100. Jeremiah M. Smith to Samuel N. Garrison. 325

St. Felix st, w s, 518.2 n Fulton st, 18.4x64.1x 18.4x64.10. Daniel Van Nostrand to Denton H. Hopkins. *Mt.* $3,500. 5,450

St. Marks pl, No. 414, s s, 201.1 w 5th av, 20x 100, h & l. Adelaide L. Painter to Louise Kathe. *Mt.* $4,500. nom

St. Marks pl, No. 410, s s, 241.2 w 5th av, 20x 100, h & l. Adelaide L. Painter to same. *Mt.* $5,000. nom

St. Marks pl, No. 406, s s, 281.2 w 5th av, 20x 100, h & l. Same to same. *Mt.* $5,000. nom

Stockholm st, s e s, 100 n e Irving av, 25x100. Jeremiah M. Smith to Samuel N. Garrison. 425

Stockholm st, n w s, 225 n e Hamburg av, 25x 100. Henry Schlachter to Frank Winterrath. *Mt.* $2,000. nom

Suydam pl, w s, 135.7 n Atlantic av, 21x97. Preston K. Webster to Margaret wife of and Jacob Glockner. Tax 1891. 3,000

Union st, n s, 191.10 e 4th av, 50x95; also,
Union st, n s, 366.10 e 4th av, 25x95.
Henry A. McCarthy, of New York, to Rebecca F. Forman and Thomas J. Ford. *Mt.* $23,000. exch

Van Buren st, s s, 503 e Sumner av, —x100x19x 100. Frank R. Moore to William H. Reynolds. *Mt.* $6,500. exch

Van Buren st, s w cor Patchen av, 22x80. Absalom W. Dieter to Amelia E. Hummel. *Mt.* $12,000. nom

Van Buren st, n s, 125 e Tompkins av, 19.5x100. William H. Whiting to Jane A. Franklin. *Mt.* $4,000. 6,100

Van Voorhis st, n w s, 202 s w Evergreen av, 17 x100. Release mort. Edward Macdonald to William H. Hawxhurst. 100

Varet st, n s, 280.6 e Bushwick av, 25x100. Frederick Gaertner to Josef Biedenbach. *Mt.* $2,000. 2,600

Verandah pl, No. 36, 38 and 40, s s, 53 w Clinton st, runs south 48.7 x west 14.1 x south 21.2 x west 48.2 x north 70.3 to pl, x east 63.1. James M. Varnum and ano. exrs. and trustees Charles A. Eckert to Patrick Fox. Tax 1891. 8,000

Verandah pl, Nos. 36, 38 and 40.
Clinton st, Nos. 268 and 270.
Release dower. Claudine Eckert widow to James M. Varnum and ano. exrs. and trustees Chas. A. Eckert. nom

Walton st, s s, 175 e Harrison av, 25x100. Morris Silverman, of New York, to Rosie Silverman. ½ part. nom

Weirfield st, n w s, 117.8 n e Evergreen av, 141.4x100. Richard Goodwin to Harris J. Latta. 22,064

Same property. Harris J. Latta to Joseph D. Jennings, of New York. 22,064

Weirfield st, n w s, 241 s w Central av, 20x100. Theodore L. Schultze to Isidor Wellerson and Philip Rhein, of New York. nom

Same property. Release mort. Owen W. Coe, of New York, to Leopold J. Lippman. 2,498

Weirfield st, n w s, 121.2 s w Central av, 20x 100. Leopold J. Lippmann to Mary Madden New York. nom

Same property. Release mort. Oliver W. Coe to Leopold J. Lippmann. 2,481

Winthrop st, n s, 305.7 e Flatbush av, 50x100, Flatbush. Annie wife of and Francis J. Werneck to Anna E. Perpall. 5,300

1st st, n e s, 125.6 w 9th av, runs north west 174.9 x northeast 99.6 x southeast 175.8 x southwest — x southwest 47.6. John Adamson to Edwin D. Phelps. *Mt.* $25,000. exch

North 2d st, n s, 146.1 w 6th st, 25x54.7x82x48.8. Henry Houser to Mary G. Werstein. 5,000

South 2d st, s s, 25 e Marcy av, 50x100. Catharina Offerman to Matthaus Beck. 6,300

3d st, s s, 28.6 e Smith st, runs south 53.5 x south 27.4 x east 32.2 x north 80 to 3d st, x west 37.6. William O. Sumner to Michael D. Ryan. *Mt.* $6,500. nom

3d st, s s, 372 9 e Bond st, runs south 175.9 to Gowanus Canal, x east 103.1 x north 154.9 to 3d st, x west 96.9, with all title in canal, &c. John D Fish to Nick Davids. *Mt.* $10,000 and tax 1891. nom

South 3d st, s s, 100 w Havemeyer st, 25x95. Caspar Spiess to Ferdinand R. Hein. nom

4th st, n e s, 197.10 n w 8th av, 20x95. Release mort. Fannie M. E. Ensell to John T. Allan and Nathaniel Proskey. nom

4th st, No. 503, n e s, 197.11 n w 8th av, 20x95. John T. Allan and Nathaniel Proskey to Helen F. wife of Theodore L. Cuyler, Jr. *Mt.* $7,000. nom

South 4th st, n s, 210 e Roebling st, 20x95, h & l. Bernhard Muench to Pauline E. Hayes. 7,800

5th st, s s, 217.10 w 5th av, 20x100. Release mort. Title Guarantee and Trust Co. to Charles D. Burwell and Frank A. Barnaby. nom

Same property. Charles H. Denison to Anders Johnsen. *Mt.* $4,500. nom

Same property. Charles D. Burwell and Frank A. Barnaby to Charles H. Denison. nom

North 5th st, s s, 144 3 e Wythe av, 18.9x100. James Flaherty to John Kovasc. 4,000

North 6th st, n s, 100 e 6th st, 25x100. Charles Leibring, New York to Ida wife of Barnet Solinger. *Mt.* $3,600. 8,000

North 6th st, n s, 23.8 e Roebling st, 18.11x50. Jane M. Tilt to William J. Dodds. 3 000

7th st, s s, 317.10 w 7th av, 20x100. Charles F. Holm to Thomas H. Decker. *Mt.* $4,800. 7,300

7th st, s s, 166.2 w 7th av, 18.8x100. Charles G. Peterson to Mary J. McLaughlin. *Mt.* $5,000. nom

7th st, s s, 147.6 w 7th av, 18 8x100. Same to Nellie M. wife of Frederick O. Ernesty. *Mt.* $2,500. nom

North 7th st, s w s, 150 n w Wythe av, 25x 100. Isaac L. Doughty and James Jones. exrs. Thomas Bartley to Mary Adams. 4,650

8th st, s s, 220.9 e 4th av, 25x100. George Gough, Bay Shore, L. I., to Horace Gough. nom

East 8th st, w s, 300 n Av M, 40x120.6, Gravesend. Robert H. Nesbitt to James McGill. 280

9th st, n e s, 372 n w 2d av, 25x100. Hamlet E. Forest to Mary A. Poole. *Mt.* $4,500. 9,000

North 9th st, s s, 100 w Driggs av, 50x100. Patrick Booden to William J. Brennan. *Mt.* $5,600. nom

Same property. William J. Brennan to Elizabeth Booden. *Mt.* $5,600. nom

North 10th st, s w s, 200 s e Kent av, 75x100, h & l.
North 9th st, n e s, 225 s e Kent av, 75x100, hs & ls.
Henry Bohnson to Joseph A. Burr, Jr. *Mt.* $10,000. 18,000

North 10th st, s w s, 75 s e Roebling st, 100x100. Thomas P. Graham to John Pirkl. *Mt.* $1,500. nom

10th st, s s, 166.8 w 8th av, 16.8x100. Ida M. wife of and James F. Ransome to George R. Pearson. *Mt.* $5,550. 6,200

10th st, s s, 216.3 w 5th av, 18.6x100. Minford S. Clark to Martin Reynolds. *Mt.* $4,500. 500

11th st, s e cor 8th av, runs east 30 x south 81.10 x east 54 x south 18.2 x west 84 to 8th av, x north 100, h & l. Allison V. B. Morris to William H. Morris. nom

North 11th st, s w s, 50 s e Roebling st, 50x123.6 to centre Bushwick Creek, x50x130.
Union av, w s, 50.5 n Roebling st, 25x102.1x26.11x92.
Mary Conway to Thomas Conway. 5,500

12th st, n e s, 157.10 s e 4th av, 20x100. Alexander G. Calder to Frederick Gloat. *Mt.* $3,000. 7,000

12th st, n e s, 177.10 s e 4th av, 20x100; also,
12th st, n e s, 277.10 s e 4th av, 20x100.
Alexander G. Calder to Henry F. Smith. *Mt.* $6,000. 13,700

12th st, n s, 177.10 e 4th av, 20x100. Henry F. Smith to Henry Dohrmann. *Mt.* $5,850. 7,500

Bay 13th st, n w s, 315 s w 86th st, 100x108.4, New Utrecht. Edward I. Horsman to John Henne. 1,625

14th st, n s, 237.10 e 8th av, 20x100. Catherine wife of and George F. Beatty to Mark Carroll. 7,250

14th st, s s, 222.10 e 8th av, 100x100. The Nassau Land and Improvement Co. to William Hawkins. 9,000

20th st, n s, 200 w 6th av, 37x100. James P. Philip to Rachel A. Van Kirk. *Mt.* $1,970. nom

20th st, e s, 125 n Vanderbilt st, 50x100, Flatbush. William E. Murphy exr. Thomas Murphy to Lottie L. Dailey. 500

22d st, s e s, 200 n e Benson av, 100x96.8, Bensonhurst. James D. Lynch to Tom A. Kitson. 5,000

26th st, n s, 325 w 5th av, 25x70. Foreclos. John Courtney to Virginia P. Kent. 1,500

34th st, n s, 288.4 w 5th av, 16.8x100.2. Harry Armstrong to Harry Thorning. 3,400

36th st, n s, 100 w 4th av, 25x100.2. Patrick Maloney to Frances Maloney. nom

45th st, n e s, 300 n w 12th av, 50x100.2, New Utrecht. The West Brooklyn Land and Improvement Co. to Sarah M. Roberts. 700

47th st, s s, 120 w 3d av, 20x100.2. David J. Tingley and ano. exrs. Margaret M. Van Pelt to Walter Van Pelt. 550

48th st, s s, 140 e 5th av, 60x100.2. Edward T. Hunt to John Murphy. 570

48th st, s s, 216 w 4th av, 16x100.2. William McMonegal to Henry S. Taylor. *Mt.* $1,500. 3,000

50th st, s s, 260 w 3d av, 20x100.2. Jacob Schaefer to James Costello. *Mt.* $2,500. 3,700

53d st, n s, 160 w 5th av, 60x100.2.
52d st, s s, 160 w 5th av, 40x100.2.
Louis Bradfisch to Clarence E. Hopkins. ½ part. 2,000

55th st, n s, 95 w 4th av, 60x100.2. Christina Gilman to Robert W. Firth. 2,200

57th st, n s, 300 e 4th av, 20x100.2. Christina Gilman to Robert W. Firth. 650

57th st, n s, 160 w 5th av, 50x100.2. John Egan to James F. Murphy. 2,700

57th st, s s, 100 e 4th av, 100x100.2. Sarah A. Robertson to Edward Goodheart. *Mt.* 1,000. 3,500

59th st, s w s, 160 n w 17th av, 60x100.2, New Utrecht. Hans C. Pfalzgraf to Mathilda C. Stahlberg. 4,850

61st st, n s, 260 w 12th av, 40x100, New Utrecht. Elias Johnson to John L. Lawson. 500

61st st, s s, 20 w 12th av, 40x—, New Utrecht. Catharine wife of John McAuliffe to Hugh B. Christy. 150

73d st, s s, 390 w 15th av, 40x100, New Utrecht. James V. S. Woolley, of New York, to Jost H. Schmidt. 350

73d st, n s, 450 w 15th av, 40x100, New Utrecht. James V. S. Woolley to Henry Dadson. 350

74th st, s w s, 300 s e 12th av, 100x100, New Utrecht. Hoik D. Campbell to Albert W. Jackson. nom

Same property. Albert W. Jackson to Jane E. wife of Fred. H. Johnson. nom

75th st, s s, 330 w 15th av, 20x100, New Utrecht. James V. S. Woolley, of New York, to Frank K. Scott. 175

75th st, n s, 410 w 15th av, 40x100; also,
14th av, n e cor Bay Ridge av, 80x90, New Utrecht.
James V. S. Woolley to Ralph Delmore, of New York. 1,650

75th st, n s, 90 w 15th av, 40x100, Lefferts Park. James V. S. Woolley to Teresa Fallon. 350

83d st, n e s, 300 n w 23d av, 60x100, New Utrecht. James D. Lynch, of New York, to Frances V. Egerton. 1,050

Same property. Frances V. Eg t to Frederick A. Egerton. *Mt.* $735. er on 1,050

84th st, s s, 350 e 2d av, 50x103.10, New Utrecht. Reuben Riley to Amanda wife of Reuben Riley. gift

East 94th st, s w s, 50 s e Flatlands av, 50x100, Flatlands. Gustaf Nystrom to Isaac H. Curtis. *Mt.* $1,000. nom

Albany av, n e cor East New York av, 20x100. Georgianna Richters, of Bayside, N. Y., to Valentine Kerz. 750

Atlantic av, s s, 69.11 w Sackman st, 19.3x100. John Ryley committee Richard Tucker lunatic to John F. Chappell, Orange, N. J., Florence F. Griglieth and Gideon T. Chappell, Jersey City, Estelle C. Tucker, Upper Nyack, heirs Richard Tucker. nom

Atlantic av, n s, 268 e Schenectady av, 26.10x99.1. Mary C. Nostrand widow to Edward S. Hand, Milburn, N. J. Q. C. nom

Atlantic av, n w cor Perry pl, being assessm't map 23d Ward lot 93 block 83. John C. McGuire, Registrar of Arrears, to Joanna E. wife of Hugh McCrossin. 285

Atlantic av, s s, 75 w Sheffield av, —x—x75x—. Ann E. Wemmell to Sallie R. Wemmell. 1885. nom

Atlantic av, n s, 660.1 w Nostrand av, runs east 12 x north 149.1 to Herkimer pl, x east 8.1 x north 92.9 x west 22.1 x south 241.10. Release judgment. The Mutual Life Ins. Co., New York, to Joanna E. wife of Hugh McCrossin. nom

Same property. Release judgment. T. J. Oakley Rhinelander, of New York, to same. nom

Av B, n s, 551.7 w Ocean av, 150x100, Flatbush. Release mort. Emeline Gallup to John McElvery and Robert Getty. 1,200

Av B, n w cor East 18th st, 100x100, Flatbush. John McElvery and Robert Getty to James Geery. 2,800

Belmont av, s s, 40 w Atkins av, 20x90. Thomas Dalton to Mary E. Laing. 400

Baltic av, n s, 75 e Henry av, 25x100. Henrietta Baird to Martial G. Jouffret. *Mt.* $500. exch

Blake av, n w cor Linwood st, 46x78x46x80. William Wheeler to Luis Weiner. *Mt.* $1,000. 3,500

Carlton av, w s, 200.11 s Fulton st, 19.5x100. Julia A., Benjamin S. and John C. Taylor, of Jersey City, N. J., and Julia L. Wessels, of Roselle, N. J., to George D. Aldridge. 4,250

Carlton av, s w cor Pacific st, 20x80. Maria Roberts to Greenleaf W. Crossman. *Mt.* $7,100. nom

Carlton av, e s, 362.11 s Fulton st, 20x100. Julius and Julius B. Davenport exrs. Ann Wilson to Charles J. Rippingale. 4,900

Carlton av, s w cor Pacific st, 20x80. Cora Waldron to Greenleaf W. Crossman, New York. *Mt.* $7,100, taxes, &c. nom

Central av, s w s, 20 n w Harman st, 40x80, h & l. Charles C. Kreppel to Henry A. Beiler. Q. C. nom

Central av, s w s, 40 n w Harman st, 20x80. Henry A. Beiler to Theodore Gubring, of New York. 5,700

Central av, west cor Halsey st, runs west 200 x south 250 x south 100 x east 200 x south 100 to Halsey st, x northeast 80. Leopold J. Lippmann to Joseph F. Ellery. *Mt.* $12,500. nom

Central av, north cor Palmetto st, 25x75. Charles Gundlich, of New York, to Minna wife of Gustave Feigenspan, of Newtown, N. Y. *Mt.* $4,000. 10,500

Division av, s s, 60.5 w Harrison av, 20x84. Andrew P. Gilloon to Susanna Helwig. *Mt.* $2,000. 4,200

Evergreen av, east cor Madison st, 25x100. Christian Hunken to Anson W. Turner. 3,200

Flatbush av, w s, bet John A. Lott and heirs of Margt. Van Nuyse and in depth to Flatbush plank road, Flatlands. Nicholas W. Brown to Rose B. wife of Richard S. Hegeman. 6,000

Flushing av, n s, 90.7 w Knickerbocker av, 25x71.10x27.10x84.1. Sigmund Bleyer to Adolph T. Glunz. 9,300

Fort Hamilton av, n w cor 70th st, 61x97.2x60x86.3.
Fort Hamilton av, s e cor 72d st, 61x108.5x60x97.7, New Utrecht.
Bay Ridge Park Improvement Co. to Fred. C. Cocheu. 12,000

Franklin av, e s, 90 s Fulton st, runs south 108.1 x east 130.8 x northeast 28 x west 0.3 x north 20 x west 153.2, hs & ls. Edward Rowe exr. and trustee Maria Rowe to Curtis W. Conn. 25,000

Gates av, n s, 125 w Reid av, 20x100. A. Stewart Walsh to Matthew Dignan. *Mt.* $6,000. exch

Gates av, s s, 510 w Ralph av, 56x100. Richard D. Robbins to Robert L. Woods. *Mt.* $22,000. exch

Grand av, e s, 422.6 s Gates av, 22.6x101.6. Crowell Hadden exr. Fannie L. Earle to Mary J. Carter. 12,000

Greene av, n w s, 210 n e Broadway, 19.3x100. Henry W. Winter to Pauline and Lothar Bauch. *Mt.* $3,000. 6,600

Greene av, s e s, 200 n e Knickerbocker av, 20x100. Matthew Dignan to A. Stewart Walsh. *Mt.* $2,300. exch

Greene av, s s, 120 w Marcy av, 20x100. Anna E. wife of and William H. Ash to Jennie Hopkins. *Mt.* $8,000. 4,200

Greene av, s s, 125 w Central av, 63.10x100.
Greene av, s s, 233.10 w Central av, 16.2x100.
Foreclos. John Courtney to Virginia A. Kleine. *Mt.* $10,000. 2,500

Hamilton av, s e s, 150 n e Atlantic av, 50x116.3, New Utrecht. John C. Brinck and ano. exrs. and trustees Augustus H. Ely to George W. Silber. 700

Hegeman av, n s, 40 w Cleveland st, 20x100. Adolph Sussman to Joseph Pietchman. 300

Hopkinson av, w s, 150 s Baltic st, runs west 100 x north to centre block bet Baltic st and Butler st, x west 25 x south 127.9 to Butler st, x east to East New York av, x northeast to Hopkinson av, x north to beginning. Rebecca F. Forman to Silas A. Condict. 8,000

Hamburg av, easterly cor Harman st, 100x100. Abby E. Laytin, of New York, to John Bohnet. *Mt.* $4,000. 7,000

Irving av, n e s, 75 s e De Kalb av, 50x100. Daniel Bradley to Charles C. Kreppel. nom

Jefferson av, n s, 156.8 e Tompkins av, 19.2x100. Nellie G. wife of and George H. Russell to Emma A. wife of Horace B. Rawson. nom

Jefferson av, n s, 295 e Tompkins av, 16.8x100. Mary E. wife of and Oscar E. Boyd to Catherine J. Gilbertson. *Mt.* $3,600. 7,700

Jefferson av, s s, 120 w Nostrand av, 20x100. Edwin A. Beck, of New York, to Peter Clancy. 8,250

Jefferson av, s s, 100.3 w Nostrand av, 19.9x100. Same to Agnes Keyburn. 8,100

Johnson av, n s, 150 w Lorimer st, 35x100. Charles Sefferien to Louis and William Stumpf. 9,250

Johnson av, s s, 100 e Bogert st, 75x100. Charles Butzgy to George W. and Brewster Conklin. nom

Johnson av, n e cor Humboldt st, 26.2x100x25x100, h & l. Peter Stromberger to Margaretha Stromberger. nom

Knickerbocker av, w s, 25 s De Kalb av, 25x80. Release mort. Louis Beer to George Koch and Frederick Koerner. 2,000

Same property. George Koch and Frederick Koerner to John Schneider. *Mt.* $3,500. 7,400

Knickerbocker av, westerly cor Jefferson st, 25x100. Franz Millon to Andrew Mahr. 11,500

Lafayette av, s s, 300 6 e Reid av, 24.5x100. George Evans to Conrad Hecker, New York. *Mt.* $1,900. 4,000

Lafayette av, n s, 200 e Stuyvesant av, 100x100. Charles E. Larned, of New York, to William J. Kaiser. 9,000

Lafayette av, s s, 246 e Grand av, 54x100. Edward Driscoll to Charles N. Wheelwright. 65,000

Lee av, s w cor Taylor st, 20.10x75. Hutchings Bath Co. to William Smyer. *Mt.* $6,500. 15,000

Lefferts av, s s, 125 e Grove st, 125x100 on old map, lots are now gore lots on s s Warren st, abt 110 w Schenectady av. Cora wife of Henry Bock to Isaac Halstead. 1,900

Lefferts av, n e cor Albany av, 101.2x280.4 to city line, x104.8x214.6, Flatbush. David C. Reid to John W. Hussey. Correction deed. nom

Lewis av, e s, 110 s Lafayette av, 20x100, h & l. Frederick Schmoize to Albert Rudischhauser. *Mt.* $3,500. 6,750

Lexington av, s s, 225 e Throop av, 100x200 to Quincy st, h & l. Anna wife of Charles McDonald to David S. Beasley. Taxes 1891. 14,500

Liberty av, s s, 50 e Osborn st, 100x100. Release mort. Claus Luehrs to Herbert C. Smith. 2,000

Maspeth av, s s, 200 e Bushwick av, runs south 89.4 x east 16.6 x northeast 38.7 x north 54.5 to av, x west 25, h & l. Gaetano Manganaro, New York, to Donato and Maria Pucillo and Giambattista and Margherita Maurella. 3,000

Meeker av, n w s, 70 s w North Henry st, 25x123. Mary A. wife of John Reydel to Owen McCullough. nom

Montrose av, n s, 125 e Union av, 25x100. Sarah A. and Martha R. World to Alwin Donop. Taxes 1891. 3,200

Myrtle av, s s, 25 e Kent av, 44.8x111.9. John Gray to Frank X. Kuphler. *Mt.* $10,000. 19,600

Myrtle av, n s, 29.5 w Stockholm st, 20x80. Stewart L. Woodford trustee of Mary Beadleston to Mary Beadleston, of Hauppauge, N. Y. nom

Myrtle av, s s, 625 e Nostrand av, 50x100. George Covert to Jacob Bossert. 5,800

Myrtle av, s s, 23 e Clason av, 28x71.2. Johanna F. Ficke individ. and with ano. exrs. William F. Ficke to David Barry. *Mt.* $2,300. 7,500

Nassau av, n e cor Russell st, 20x85. George W. Palmer to John Wittschen. 2,050

Same property. Release mort. James D. Lynch to George W. Palmer. 1,025

Nassau av, n e cor North Henry st, 20x85. George W. Palmer to Patrick F. Fitzgerald. 2,050

Nostrand av, n w cor Jefferson av, 40x100. William H. Reynolds to Joseph P. Puels. *Mt.* $7,500. exch

Ovington av, n s, 100 e 13th av, 60x133.6x60x135.3, New Utrecht. Effingham H. Nichols, of New York, to William H. Tait, of New York. 825

Park av, n s, 20.6 w Sandford st, runs east 0.6½x97.9x0.6x97.9. Lewis & Fowler Mfg. Co. to Honora Purcell. Correction deed. nom

Park av, n w cor Sandford st, 20.6x97.9. Honora Purcell to Andrew J. Dower. nom

Putnam av, n s, 120 w Nostrand av, 20x100, h & l. Hannah E. Miller to Greenleaf W. Crossman, New York. *Mt.* $3,500. nom

Putnam av, s e s, 240 n e Broadway, 20x100, h & l. Michael Mulvihill to David Williams. *Mt.* $3,000. 6,500

Railroad av, n w cor Ridgewood av, runs north 91.1 x west 100 x south 20 x west 100 to Hemlock st, x south 99 to Ridgewood av, x east 201.11. Ida Gordon to William L. Large. ½ part. 500

Reid av, e s, 98.4 n Hancock st, 19.2x100. John S. Willdridge to Thomas Berkeley. exch

Rockaway av, e s, 200 n Livonia av, 25x100. Joshua Fletcher to Charlotte Radford. *Mt.* $1,500. 2,200

Rockaway av, w s, 100 s Marion st, runs west 88.10 x southwest 19.2 x east 90.2 x north 16. John O. Whitenack to Wyatt B. and Archie B. Roberts. *Mt.* $2,950. 3,550

Ralph av, n e cor McDonough st, runs north 100 x east 44 x south 15 x west 17.11 x south 26.5 x west 0.½ inch x south 58.7 to st, x west 26. John R. Pitt to Catharine C., Winifred and Helena Connolly. *Mt.* $16,5 0. 25,750

Saratoga av, w s, 50 s Sumpter st, 25x75. George A. Domminey to Emma Klauberg. 1,400

Schenck av, w s, 185 s Van Brunt av, 20x100. William McIlroy to Mary E. Peacock. 200

Schenck av, w s, 100 s Glenmore av, 100x100, hs & ls. Ernest Henken to Hiram Nododilman. 5,000

Shepherd av, e s, 100 s Blake av, 100x200 to Berriman st. John H. G. Friedel to William Fintzel. 2,800

Shepherd av, e s, 240 n Ridgewood av, 20x102.5, h & l. James Graham to Emma L. wife of William Reeveland. *Mt.* $1,800. 3,800

Shepherd av, e s, 3,9,10 s Ridgewood av, 16.7x101.10, h & l. Zipp L. Hollister to Mary A. Cummings. *Mt.* $2,755 and taxes 1891. 2,950

Sheridan av, e s, 425 n Adams av, 25x100. Rudolph Reimer to George Holland. *Mt.* $150. nom

Skillman av, s s, 50.8 w Kingsland av, runs east 50.8 to Kingsland av, x south 150.7 to Maspeth av, x west 3.4 x north 157. Thomas Derbyshire to John Gerlich and Sophia his wife, joint tenants. exch

Skillman av, n s, 150 w Humboldt st, 25x100. Hellen P. Marran to John J. Penny and Louisa U. his wife, joint tenants. Sub. to morts. nom

St. Marks av, n s, 166.6 w Albany av, 16.6x145.7. Alfred Tilly to De Roy E. Bunker. *Mt.* $5,500. 9,000

St. Marks av, s s, 245 5 w 6th av, 20x81.7x20x81 8. James M. Brady to The Keystone National Savings Loan and Investment Co. 9,000

Stone av, w s, 150 s Belmont av, 25x100. Bernard Landau to Sarah Landau. ½ part. *Mt.* $1,950. 1,425

Same property. Peter Kleinfeld to Carry Kleinfeld. *Mt.* $1,950. 1,425

Stone av, w s, 100 n McDougal st, runs west to n e s of land Brooklyn and Jamaica Turnpike Co., x southeast to Stone av, x north — to beginning; also,
McDougal st, n s, 100 e Stone av, runs north 100 x west 100 x north 75 x east — x southeast to McDougal st, x west to beginning.
Robert O'Brien to Elihu J. Granger. 3,500

Stone av, e s, 100 n McDougal st, runs east 100 x north 50.8 x northwest 32.8 x west 77.10 to av, x south 75. Elihu J. Granger to Sidney V. Lowell. nom

Same property. William Larder to same. Q. C. nom

Stone av, w s, 42 n Pacific st, 58x80, hs & ls. Foreclos. John Courtney to John M. Stearns. *Mt.* $7,500 and int. April 15, 1891. 1,000

Stone av, w s, 42 n Pacific st, 19 4x80. John M. Stearns to Jessie Greenberg, Corona, L. I. *Mt.* $2,500, taxes 1890 and 1891. exch

Stone av, e s, 183.4 s Blake av, 25x100. Lewis Hurst to Annie Steinberg. 725

Stone av, w s, 9.7 n McDougal st, runs north 65.4 x west 49.8 x southeast 77 to Stone av. Partition deed Peter W. Ostrander ref. to William Larder. 225

Stuyvesant av, w s, 22.8 s Halsey st, 19.2x80.6. Andrew D. Baird to Anna W. McCord. *Mt.* $5,500. consid. omitted

Stuyvesant av, e s, 61 n Macon st, 19.6x84. George A. Domminey to Ella K. Jelliff, New York. *Mt.* $4,000. 6,500

Tompkins av, s w cor Madison st, 20x85. Release mort. Caleb S. Woodhull to Ulysses A. Cannon, of New York. nom

Same property. Ulysses A. Cannon to Charles A. Haviland. other consid. and 6,700

Utica av, n e cor Broadway, centre lines, 7 234-1,000 acres, Flatbush. Elizabeth M. wife of Charles Rushton to Charles M. Marsh, Morris Plains, N. J. *Mt.* $8,000. 12 500

Van Pelt av, n s, 150 w Humboldt st, 150x100. Henry Traphagen, of Jersey City, N. J., to Charles Eugert. 5,100

Van Sicien av, e s, 158 s Atlantic av, 25x100. William A. Ball to The Brooklyn City Co-operative Building and Loan Assoc. nom

Vernon av, n s, 225 e Nostrand av, 19x100, h & l. John Parkin to Daniel F. Dwyer. *Mt.* $4,000. 7,800

Waverly av, e s, 150.10 n Gates av, 13.4x100. Joseph I. Kirby to Mary P. Kirby. *Mt.* $4,500. 8,950

Washington av, e s, 189 1 s Greene av, 18.1x120. Edward M. Shepard to George B. Bretz. 5,000

Williams av, e s, 99.5 s Atlantic av, 20.3x100. John McGeehan to J. Henry Heckle. 5,500

Same property. Release mort. The Williamsburgh Savings Bank to John McGeehan. 2,750

Same property. Release mort. Frederick Middendorf to same. nom

Willoughby av, s s, 36 w Walworth st, 10x90. Israel Loewenthal et al. children and heirs of Jetta Loewenthal to Maria wife of Otto Hackradt. nom

Same property. Release judgment. Henry Loewenthal, of New York, to Israel Loewenthal. nom

Wyckoff av, n w cor Ralph st, 25x100. Charles Gundlich, of New York, to Minna wife of Gustav Feigenspan, of Newtown, N. Y. *Mt.* $4,000. 9,500

Wyckoff av, north cor Troutman st, 25x94.11x25x95.7. Ignatz Martin to Charles A. Cross. 1,700

3d av, w s, 60 s Wyckoff st, 40x80, hs & ls. Julia H. Billings and ano. exrs. James M. Billings to John J. Dillon. 9,000

3d av, e s, 36.6 n 11th st, 18.3x70. Edward Keogh to Michael Leyden. *Mt.* $2,600. 5,000

4th av, east cor 12th st, 120x80. John Adamson to John R. Scott and George J. Carney. *Mt.* $6,000. 16,000

5th av, e s, 191 s 16th st, 17.2x97.4. William M. and Charles P. Burr and Burr Wendell exrs. Calvin Burr to John A. Schilling. 1890. 5,000

Same property. John A. Schilling to Edwin A. Willcox. *Mt.* $4,000. 6,500

5th av, w s, No. 450. Contract of sale. Eliza J. Thyler and Anna E. La Pierre, of Clarksville, Ga., to John W. Kimball. other consid. and 9,335

6th av, n w cor President st, 100x92. Catherine Judson to Stephen M. Hoye. nom

7th av, westerly cor 19th st, 25x72. Alexander G. Calder to Andrew Oltmans, of New York. 12,000

7th av, w s, 60 s 2d st, 20x80. Benjamin Armstrong to Charles F. Hunt. *Mt.* $9,000. nom

8th av, n e cor Garfield pl, 100x112. Annie L. wife of and Charles E. Rogers to Asa L. Rogers. nom

15th av, n w cor 75th st, 20x90, Lefferts Park. James V. S. Woolley to Mary A. Riley. 375

Lots 2-5 and 68-75 and so much of lots 6 as lies n w centre line bet Bay 10th and Bay 11th sts map property Asa W. Parker, New Utrecht. Charles Gundlich, of New York, to Minna wife of Gustav Feigenspan, of Newtown, N. Y. 13,000

Lot 193 block F map Vandeveer homestead, 26th Ward. Release mort. John H. Vanderveer to Emil Reineking. 180

Lots 206 and 207 block 4 map 597 lots of Wm. Ziegler, Gravesend. William Ziegler to Emma Smith. 280

Lots 208 and 209 block 4 same map. Same to Daniel E. Sutliff. 280

Lots 143, 144 and 145 map property Hans C. Pfalzgraf, New Utrecht. Release mort. William A. Copp exr. Mary M. Warner to Hans C. Pfalzgraf. nom

Flatlands Neck to Canarsie road, s e s, 194 n e Varkens Hook road, runs southeast 100 x northeast 100 x southeast 25 x southwest 125 x northwest 125 to road, x northeast 25, Canarsie. Heinrich A. Schlichting to Meter Helmken, New York. 337

Same property. Hermann Lohmann to Heinrich A. Schlichting. nom

Land under waters Gravesend Bay in front of and adj upland of Gerd. H. Heujes, New Utrecht. The People of the State of New York to Gerd H. Henjes. letters patent

Gravesend Beach to Gravesend road, s s, 461.8 from 86th st, 3 acres extending to centre of creek, Gravesend. Marion, George B. and Frederick C. Murphy by M. Rennie Bateman guard. to Margaretta Z. Pedersen. 2,250

Gravesend Beach to Gravesend road, s s, 461.8 from 86th st, 3 acres, extending to centre of creek. Susan Moynehan, Claudia Murphy and Annie Hartt to Margaretta Z. Pedersen. Q C. 2,250

Cypress Hills plank road, s s, 44.8 e Bushwick av, 24.7x100. Peter Stromberger to Margaretha Stromberger. nom

Coney Island Snell road, n w cor Coney Island Creek, 1 acre, Gravesend. George A. Thompson to Helen D wife of George A. Thompson. ½ part. B. & S. nom

Assignment of interest in estate of Cath. S. Cooper. Frederick M. Cooper as devisee under will Catherine S. Cooper to Robert Thorne. val. consid

Release legacy, &c. Annie Banks, Margaret Brandt, Caroline Scheibel and Willie Slater to John Christman and ano. exrs. Jacob Schlotterer. nom

WESTCHESTER COUNTY.

NOVEMBER 25 TO DECEMBER 1—INCLUSIVE.

CORTLANDT.

Ansorge, Lena J. to Benj. Welcher, s s Station road, Montrose, ½ acre. $725

EASTCHESTER.

Burtis, Alb. S. to Niels P. Nielson, part lot 331 s w s Cortlandt st, West Mt. Vernon, 25x125. 550

Boyle, John et al. to Anna J. Newman, lot 296, West Mt. Vernon, abt 37x320. nom

Caldwell, Eliz'h to Jas. Caldwell, part lot 56 s e s Greenwich st, West Mt. Vernon, 33.4x100. 3,600

Campbell, Annie A. to Alb. C. Ayer, part lot 133 w s Bond st, West Mt. Vernon, 50x100. 1,200

Dietz, Helena to Gustav A. Schindler, lot 374 w s 5th av, Central Mt. Vernon, 50x100. nom

Jackson, Julia H. to Aug. Lenz, part lot 201 s e s Bond st, West Mt. Vernon, 40x100. 3,000

Liebler, Michael to Cath. Eltz, part lot 115 n w s Railroad av, West Mt. Vernon, 50x—. 2,000

Penfield, Geo. J. to Adolph Brieger, lot 267 n w s Catharine st, Washingtonville, 50x100. nom

Same to Gideon Fountain, lots 190 and 191 s e s Fulton st, grantors map, South Mt. Vernon. 1,585

Same to Timothy Meagher, lots 214, 215 and 216 s e s Marion st, 100x100; also lot 189, cor Demilt av and Fulton st, 25x—. 2,900

Troman, Jos. to Patrick Treacy, lot 984 n s 15th av, Wakefield, 100x114. 1,300

GREENBURGH.

Lander, Geo. A. to Tim. C. Eastman, lot 85 s s Paulding st, map Irving, 50x140. 1,500

MAMARONECK.

Palmer, Wm. D. to Cath. Grady, lot 59 e s Grand av, Grand Park. 1,800

MOUNT PLEASANT.

Smadbeck, Louis to John Tieman, lots 1664-1665 and 1674, Sherman Park. 750
Same to Flora Marks, lots 427 and 428. 500
Same to Kate Clancey, lot 1578. 250
Same to Nellie M. Chase, lot 206. 150
Smith, Wm. R. to Annie J. Chrisman, lots 57-60 block 6, Lake Kensico. 600

NEW CASTLE.

Ryder, Willett to Martin Greenwalt, w s Croton turnpike, adj Jane M. Vail, 13 acres. 1,500

NEW ROCHELLE.

Porter, Sarah M. to Julia M. Woodbury, Morris st cor North st, 193x125x219x127. nom

Cole, Chas. A. to Lillie G. Stivers, n s 5th av, 552 e North st, 75x305. 5,500

OSSINING.

Greenwalt, Martin to Walter W. Law, n s road from Buckhout's Corners to Briarcliff, 200x110. 1,500

Sherwood, Steph. M. to Samuel Watson, s s Everett av, 320.9 w old Post road, 50x175. 1,200

POUNDRIDGE.

Olmstead, Belinda to Axell Bergh, 100 acres on road to Bostonville. 1,500

Reynolds, Titus to Wm. Q. Reynolds, w s road from Bedford to Longridge on Mianus River, 40 acres. 2,000

RYE.

Rynner, Margt to Abbie L. Mellor, s e s Grace Church st, adj Samuel Bailie, abt 36x528. 2,400

Bounty, Chas. E et al. to Jas. D. Kelley, e s Pearl st, adj Lydia Rasco, 50x—. 1.810

Clapp, John H. to Howard S. Hall, s e cor Main and Adee sts, 16x28x25x29.6. 12,000

Hall, Howard J to Julia F. Cheevers, same property. 12,000

McCarty, Richard to Levere Clark, lot 80 n s Seymour road, Poningo Dale, 50x100. 490

WESTCHESTER.

Camp, Hugh N. to Ellen M. Fallon, lots 50 and 51, map McGraw estate. 540

Fitz, Henry G. et al., to Levi H. Mace, lots 1032 and 1077 n s 14th av, Wakefield, 205x114. 1,500

Hamm, And. J. to Wm. Fitzek and wife, east ½ lot 247 s s 9th av, Wakefield, 50x114. 650

Same to Jos. Hoyenski and wife, west ½ same lot. 650

Heilman, Elizh. to Christine Knoeppell, s s Kings st, 175 White Plains road, 33x100x72.6x100. 700

Levy, Ephraim B. to David S. Gluck, n w cor Blondel av and Halpern st, 25x100; also s w cor same and Mary st, 75x100. 2,400

Martin, Edw. to Jos. F. Dalbec, w s Elliott av, 200 n Julianna st, 100x250. 4,000

Murphy, Michael P. to Levi H. Mace, part lot 146 w s White Plains road, Olinville, 2 x—. 1,400

Owen, Daniel to Filomena Cipolla, lot 532 n s 6th av, Wakefield, 100x114. 1,800

Strachan, Jas. R. to Jos. P. Puels, east ½ lot 394 s s 6th av, Wakefield, 50x114. 6,000

Sullivan, Maurice J. to Fred. Eder, part lot 1040 n s 10th av, Wakefield, 50x114. 6,000

Williams, Mary C. et al. to Florence S. Crosby, s s 4th st, 305 e Av C, Unionport, 100x216. nom

WHITE PLAINS.

Albro, Wm. H. to John T. Rehill, w s Grove st, 154 n Post road, 50x175. 350

Same to Frank W. Pierce, w s Grand st, 356 s Quarroppas st, 60x10, Grove st. 1,600

Briggs, Chas. A. to Henry T. Dykman, s s Railroad av, e of Brook, 33.1x150. 6,500

Dowdall, Richard to Daniel W. Maloney, lot 24 e s Bronx st, Hart Purdy map, 48x150. 300

Thiers, Margt. A. to Stephen W. Smith, e s Lexington av, abt 100 n Fisher av, 65x300. 1,700

YONKERS.

Edwards, Ellis B. and ano. to Jos. H. Cain, s e cor South Broadway and Lawrence st, 51x112. nom

East Side Land Co. to Daniel Murray, lots 17-20, Shearwood Hill. 2,700

Jones, Cyrus P. and ano. to Chas. Sullivan, lot 344 block B and 24 block C. 855

Lowerre, Fannie M. and ano. to Emma F. Dunn, lot 11 block 1 e s Cornell av, Lowerre Station. 475
Same to Ida M. Dunn, lot 12 adj. 475
Same to Amos P. Dunn, lot 13 adj. 450
Same to Cora H. Dunn, lot 14 adj. 450

Nathan, Marcus to Mary Fleming and ano, lot 109 Bronx River road map Sherwood Land and Imp. Co., 25x80. 400

New York and Yonkers Land and Imp. Co. to Henry Amar, lot 31 Bryn Maur Park. 350

Same to Michael Quinn, lots 123 and 124, 142 and 147. 1,045

O'Connor, Thos. C. to New York and Yonkers Land and Imp. Co., plot of The I. V. Fowler farm, w s Mile Square road, s of Pipe Line, 25 acres. nom

People's Savings Bank to Jas. J. Sullivan, lot

12 n s Suydam pl map Archer property, abt 27x58. 1.100

Raynor, Geo. to Jas. G. Beemer, w s Thomas terrace adj grantee, abt 50x180. 4,000

Schickel, Wm. to Rosanna Welsch, lots 34 and 36 Lewis av, grantors map, 50x100. 700

Washburn, Isaac T. to Harrison B. Washburn, w s Broadway, 215 s Ludlow st, 43x245. 15,000

MORTGAGES.

NOTE.—*The arrangement of this list is as follows. The first name is that of the mortgagor, the next that of the mortgagee. The description of the property then follows, then the date of the mortgage, the time for which it was given, and the amount. The general dates used as headings are the dates when the mortgage was handed into the Register's office to be recorded.*

Whenever the letters "P. M." occur, preceded by the name of a street, in these lists of mortgages, they mean that it is a Purchase Money Mortgage, and for fuller particulars see the list of transfers under the corresponding date. Whenever the rate is not given, read as 6 per cent.

NEW YORK CITY.

NOVEMBER 27, 28, 30, DECEMBER 1, 2 3.

Asmussen, Peter to Hugo Maul. Fulton av. P. M. Nov. 28, 3 years, 5 %. $3,000

Arendt, Simon to Marion M. Swinyard, Gilbertsville, N. Y. Amsterdam av, n e cor 91st st. P. M. Dec. 1, 2 years. 40,000

Same to John Mathews and ano. trustees Thomas E. Davis, dec'd. Amsterdam av, e s, 100.11 n 91st st. P. M. Nov. 20, 3 years, 5 %. gold, 24,000

Arendt, Simon to Julius Lipman and Moses Kind. Amsterdam av, n e cor 91st st, 27.11x100. Sub to mort. $40,000. Dec. 1, 6 months. 17,500

Same to same. Same property. Sub. to mort. $40,000. Dec. 1, 1 month. 2,500

Arnoux, George T. to Amy C. Phyfe. South 5th av. P. M. Jan. 20, due June 1, 1892. 4,000

Same to same. Same property. P. M. Jan. 20, due June 1, 1892. 2,000

Bernstein, Isaac and Abraham Jacobs to THE NEW YORK SAVINGS BANK. 17th st, s s, 250 w 8th av, 75x127.5x75.4x120.5. Dec. 3, due Dec. 1, 1896, 4½ %. 60,000

Baron, Harry to Julia Feldman. Henry st. P. M. Nov. 30, installs. 4,000

Bernheimer, Lehman, Munich, Bavaria, mortgagee with Jacob Bookman mortgagor. Extension of mort. at 4½ %, in gold. Nov. 24. nom

Bleistift, Jeannette wife of and Abraham I. to Greenwood Cemetery, Brooklyn. Norfolk st, No. 17, w s, 50 n Hester st, 25x50. Nov. 30, due Dec. 1, 1896, 5 %. 18,000

Bogert, Henry K., Cisco, Utah, to Laura H. Curtis. 61st st, n s, 100 e 11th av, 25x100.5. Dec. 1, 1 year, 5 %. 8,000

Breithaupt, William and Gustave to James F. and Patrick H. Sheridan and James S. Segrave. Forest and Rock sts. P. M. Nov. 25, 5 years, 5 %. 1,500

Buckmann, John to P. Ballantine & Sons, a corporation. Chrystie st, No. 2; Division st, No. 46. Saloon lease. Dec. 1, note, demand. 3,650

Butler, Jacob D. to Richard M. Harison, Astoria, L. I. 145th st, s s, 181.2 w 8th av, 26.10 x99.11. Dec. 1, 3 years, 5 %. See Conveys. 18,000

Bittner, Simon to Marx and Moses Ottinger. 116th st. P. M. Nov. 30, due Sept. 1, 1892. 52,000

Same to same. Same property. Building loan. Nov. 30, due Sept. 1, 1892. 90,000

Boeber, Carl and Marie to Babetta Buess. 84th st. P. M. Nov. 28, due Jan. 1, 1895, or installs. 1,750

Boggs, William mortgagor with Henry A. Barling, Englewood, N. J., and Edward D. Mandell, New Bedford, Mass., trustees Edward M. Robinson mortgagees. Extension of mort. at increased interest. Nov. 25. nom

Broad, John, Brooklyn, to Herman Wronkow. 128th st. P. M. Nov. 30, 1 year, 5 %. 5,000

Buek, Charles, Westport, Conn., to THE MUTUAL LIFE INS. CO., of New York. Manhattan av, w s, extends from 102d to 103d st. P. M. Nov. 30, due Dec. 1, 1892. 75,000

Baldwin, Clara W. wife of John to Harris Mandelbaum. 27th st, s s, 232.4 e 7th av, 24.2x98.9. Nov. 27, 1 year, 5 %. 3,000

Benedict, Annah E. to Ludwig A. Freund, Frankfort-on-Main, Germany. 63d st. P. M. Nov. 12, due Nov. 25, 1894, 5½ %. gold, 7,500

Blankenburg, William to Andreas Wrede. 154th st, s s, 250 w Elton av, 50x100. Nov. 24, 3 years. 600

Bosworth, Juliet A. to Elizabeth S. Brice. 22d st, No. 454 W., s s, 28.9x98.9. Nov. 27, due Dec. 1, 1892. 1,000

Burkhard, Thomas to William H. Oakley exr. Dennis Valentine. White st, No. 125, s s, 21 x99x20.9x99.8. Nov. 27, 5 years, 5 %. 8,000

Blair, George to THE CLINTON BANK. Canal st, No. 392, s s, 63.2 w West Broadway, 21x82x26x65.7. Recorded Nov. 19, 1891. Nov. 31, demand. 18,000

Same to same. Eldridge st, No. 55, w s, 25.2x100.1. Recorded Nov. 19, 1891. Nov. 17, demand. 14,112

Barnum, Amelia A. to Frederic J. Middlebrook, Brooklyn. Chatham sq, No. 194, n w s, 26x129.8x26.7x133; Chatham sq, No. 196, n s, 105.11 w Doyer st, runs north 154 x west 5.8 x south 8.10 x south 18.3 x west 5.11 x south 77 x west 1.6 x south 54.1 to Chatham sq, x east 25.8 to beginning. Nov. 10, 4 months. 9,000

Barthel, Gertrude wife of and Henry to Frederick Brewer. Washington av, w s, 127.4 s Union st, 31.10x116.6x25x136. Nov. 24, 2 years, 5 %. 1,000

Cadwell, Laura A. wife of and Warren W. to Alfred J. Taylor. Hampden st, s s, adj land of Malvina P. Angar. 52x145.3x51.4x170.1. Nov. 27, due Dec. 1, 1892. 2,000

Carroll, Mary E. wife of and John J. to THE MUTUAL LIFE INS. CO. of New York. 10th av, s e cor 43d st, 20x80. Nov. 27, 1 year, 5 %. See Conveys. 6,000

Cavinato, Natale, Luigi Guiseppe and Steffano, of Cavinato Bros., to Dale Tile Mfg. Co. (Lim.) 87th st, s e cor Lexington av, 62.3x100.8. Nov. 24. 1 year. 1,121

Same to R. W. Kane & Co. Same property. Nov. 25, 1 year or sooner. 3,051

Cheever, John H. to THE MERCANTILE TRUST CO. Mott av, w s, extends from 138th st to Cheever pl and runs to bulkhead or channel line on e s Harlem River, with land under water, &c.; Lot bounded on west by Railroad av and land of John B. Haskin, south by the new bulkhead or channel line aforesaid, east by w s of Canal, and north by land of John B Haskin, with land under water. Secures debt of New York Belting and Packing Co. Nov. 25, 6 months. 350,000

Clark, Martha E. to Catharine R. Dunscomb. 46th st, n s, 304 e 6th av, 22x100.5. Nov. 25, 1 year, 5 %. 15,000

Cox, Louis M., Santa Cruz, Cal., to Clara Cox widow. University pl, s e s, abt 375 s w Broadway, 44x83.3x150x100x107.10; Dey st, No. 15, s s, 25x85; Broome st, Nos. 382 and 384, n s, abt 48 e Mulberry st, 35.2x90.10x26.6 x97.2. All title. Sept. 25, due Oct. 15, 1892. 6,750

Corcoran, Jeremiah to Adam C. Rintelen. Intervale av, n w s, 258.5 n e 169th st, 25x184.10. Nov. 27, 3 years. 1,500

Cronly, John E. to THE TITLE GUARANTEE AND TRUST CO. 167th st. P. M. Nov. 27, 1 year, 5 %. 3,500

Same to Celine Rheinhold. Same property. P. M. Sub. to last mort. Nov. 27, 1 year. 1,200

Curry, John and James B. Gillie to Bernard Cohen. 91st st. P. M. Nov. 30, 1 year, 5 %. 40,000

Carroll, Lucy A. to S. Emilie Woodbury. 8th av, n e cor 14th st, runs north 68.11 x east 68.6 x north 34.4 x east 25 x south 103.3 to st, x west 93.6; 8th av, s e cor 28th st, runs east 100.4 x south 98.9 x west 36.2 x south 45.9 x west 64.1 to av, x north 144.6; 6th av, s e cor 21st st, 20x73.9, error; 8th av, e s, 54 s 17th st, 34x60; 5th av, w s, 103.1 n 12th st, runs west 125 x north 25.8 x east 25 x north 0.1¼ x east 100 to av, x south 25.9; Broadway, n w cor 21st st, runs west 195.3 to 5th av, x north 63.4 x east 80.11 x south 28.9 x east 68.2 x northeast 32 to Broadway, x south 44.1. 1-9 part. Dec. 1, 5 years. 10,000

Cuskley, Patrick J. mortgagor with Henry A. Barling et al. trustees Edward M. Robinson mortgagee. Extension of mort. at increased interest. Nov. 13. nom

Campbell, Ellen widow, Rahway, N. J., to Helen L. wife of John W. Martin, Rahway, N. J. Mercer st, w s, 100 n Grand st, 25x100. ⅙ part. Nov. 24, 1 year. 500

Cochran, Eva S. wife of William F., Yonkers, N. Y., mortgagee with Mariette P. Cooke mortgagor. Extension of mort. Nov. 20. nom

Cohen, Harris and Abraham to Leopold Haas & Co. Worth st, Nos. 170 and 174, and 19, 21 and 23 Baxter st, begins Worth st, s e cor Baxter st, 125x4.9x west 101.5x77.3. Secures credits. Oct 21. ——

Coogan, Matthew to Mary L. Barbey, Geneva, Switzerland. 7th av. P. M. Nov. 5, due Nov. 30, 1896, 5 %. gold, 18,500

Same to THE MURRAY HILL BANK. Same property. Sub. to last mort. Nov. 28, 1 year. 4,000

Coon, Louisa T. to Mary E. Birrell formerly Sarles guard. of Susan A. Sarles. 132d st, No. 146, s s, 469 w Lenox av, 14.8x99.11. Dec. 3, due Dec. 1, 1896, 5 %. 7,000

Daly, Daniel to THE WEST SIDE SAVINGS BANK. 3d av, s e cor 30th st, 24.8x110. Dec. 3, due May 3, 1893, 5 %. 3,000

Dunlap, Amelia N. wife of and Robert to THE MUTUAL RESERVE FUND LIFE ASSOC. 72d st, No. 111, n s, 127 w Columbus av, 23x102.2. Dec. 2, due Dec. 1, 1893, 5 %. 40,000

Darling, Louise A. wife of William L. to Charles S. Ward. 123d st, s s, 150.6 e Lenox av, 16.3x100.11. Dec. 1, 2 years, 5 %. 13,000

Demmerle, Theodore and Charles E. to John W. Decker. Tinton av. P. M. Dec. 1, installs. 2,100

Denninger, Emma M. wife of F. to Amanda Bussing widow. West Farms to Hunts Point road. P. M. Dec. 1, 1 year, 5 %. 2,000

Durra, David L. to Yette Stern. 3d av. P. M. Sub. to mort. $10,000. Dec. 1, installs. 5,500

Da Cunha, Rosina W. wife of and George W. to George E. Hyatt, Brooklyn. 81st st, s s, 137.6 w Amsterdam av, 37.6x102.2. Nov. 30, due July 1, 1892. 25,000

Decker, George to The John Eichler Brewing Co. Clifton st, n e cor Tinton av, 35.8x100. Nov. 28, 1 year, 5 %. 1,000

Demorest, W. Jennings to Mary S. Douglas widow. 81st st, s s, 100 e 2d av. P. M. Nov. 30, installs, 5 %. 5,000

Same to same. 81st st, s s, 145 e 2d av. P. M. Nov. 30, installs, 5 %. 5,000

Diefenthaler, Henry to Caroline Nussbaum extrx. Anthony Nussbaum. 4th st. Lease. P. M. Nov. 30, installs, 5 %. 4,000

Dursie, Frank P. and Terisina his wife to Robert Courtright. Van Courtlandt av, s w cor Villa av, 29.7x122.6x25x138.4. Nov. 30, due Sept. 10, 1896. 500

Dyckman, Susan mortgagee with Daniel E. Seybel mortgagor. Extension of reduced mort. Nov. 27. nom

Dauman, Jacob to Harris Siegel. Willett st, No. 59. P. M. Nov. 25, due Dec. 1, 1894, installs. 1,000

Davidson, James to THE WASHINGTON LIFE INS CO. Commerce st, No. 10, s s, 125 w Bleecker st, 25x70. Nov. 27, due Dec. 1, 1892, 5 %. 7,000

De Arquinos, William A. to Elizabeth Schulz, Holbrook, L. I. 98th st, s s, 500 w 8th av, 25x100.11. Nov. 20, due July 1, 1892. 2,000

Same to Sarah W. Rosebault, Brooklyn. 98th st, s s, 475 w 8th av, 25x100.11. Nov. 20, due July 1, 1892. 1,500

Same to same. 98th st, s s, 600 w 8th av, 25x100.11. Nov. 20, due July 1, 1892. 1,500

Deane, Arthur H to Dennis Horgan. 40th st, n s, 105 w Lexington av, 20x98.9. Nov. 27, 1 year. 6,000

Deane, Henry W. to same. 16th st, n s, 250 e 9th av, 25x91.9. Nov. 27, 1 year. 6.000

Same to Caroline L. Macy. Same property. Nov. 25, 3 years, 5 %. 20,000

Eagle Distilling Co. to Davis Marx. Monroe st, s s, 20.7 e Hamilton st, 25.1x92.8. Dec. 1, due June 1, 1893. See Conveys. 6,000

Same to same. Same property. Dec. 1, due June 1, 1893. 3,000

Edelmeyer, John H. and William C. Morgan to THE TITLE GUARANTEE AND TRUST CO. 71st st, s s, 175 w Amsterdam av, 18x100.5. Dec. 1, 3 years, 5 %. 14,000

Same to same. 71st st, s s, 193 w Amsterdam av, 18x100.5. Dec. 1, 3 years, 5 %. 14,500

Same to same. 71st st, s s, 211 w Amsterdam av, 18x100.5. Dec. 1, 3 years, 5 %. 14,500

Same to same. 71st st, s s, 229 w Amsterdam av, 17x100.5. Dec. 1, 3 years, 5 %. 14,000

Same to same. 71st st, s s, 246 w Amsterdam av, 18x100.5. Dec. 1, 3 years, 5 %. 14,500

Same to same. 71st st, s s, 264 w Amsterdam av, 18x100.5. Dec. 1, 3 years, 5 %. 14 500

Same to same. 71st st, s s, 281 w Amsterdam av, 18x100.5. Dec. 1, 3 years, 5 %. 14,000

Etzel, Karoline and Philipp to Henry Kohlhoff. Renwick st. w s, 75 s Spring st, 20x75. Dec. 1, due Jan. 1, 1897, 5 %. 5,000

Ettinger, Rachel mortgagor with Marie Gruner mortgagee. Extension of mort. at 5 %. Nov. 2. nom

Etzel, Albert and Emanuel Kronacher to Robert B. Nooney. Bedford st. P. M. Dec. 1, 1 year, 5 %. 7,000

Eglinger, Louis F. formerly Louis to THE GREENWICH SAVINGS BANK. 6th av, No. 31, w s, 17.6x100. Nov. 30, due Dec. 1, 1892, 5 %. 3,000

Eschwei, George F. to James J. Owens. Bradhurst av, s e cor 148d st, 100.6x abt 79.4x99.11x68. Dec. 2, 6 months. 1,000

Falvey, John to Henry Wiechmann. Decatur av. P. M. Dec. 2, 1 year, 5 %. 1,000

Ferrier, James to Cornelius H. Carling. 134th st. P. M. Dec. 2, 3 years, 5 %. 4,000

Freudenmacher, Helena to George Stolz. 154th st. P. M. Dec. 1, 1 year. 1,000

Felino, Joseph to James W. Ketcham. Mott st. P. M. Nov. 27, installs. 6,000

Frazee, Florence to Henry Sheppard. Findlay pl. P. M. Nov. 24, due Nov. 27, 1896. 4,400

Freund, Edward to Beadleston & Woerz. 1st av, No. 1121. Stores, &c. Lease. Nov. 27, demand. 1,000

Fitzpatrick, John J. and Philip A. to the trustees of the Lenox Library. 106th st, n s, 100 w Madison av, 25x100.11. Nov. 30, due Dec. 1, 1894, 5 %. gold, 20,000

Same to William H. Beadleston. 106th st, n s, 125 w Madison av, 25x100.11. Nov. 30, due Dec. 1, 1894, 5 %. gold, 20,000

Same to same. 106th st, n s, 150 w Madison av, 25x100.11. Nov. 30, due Dec. 1, 1894, 5 %. gold, 20,000

Fitzpatrick, Mary A. wife of John J. to The Presbyterian Home for Aged Women in the City of New York. 106th st, n s, 175 w Madison av, 25x100.11. Secures debt of John J. and Philip A. Fitzpatrick. Nov. 30, due Dec. 1, 1894, 5 %. gold, 20,000

Frank, Frederick to Catharine Murphy. 117th st. P. M. Dec. 1, 5 years, 5 %. 8,000

Friedman, Sigmund to John Schneider. 2d st. P. M. Dec. 1, 3 years, 5 %. 7,500

Same to Emma Keller and Flora M. Lindner. Same property. P. M. Sub. to last mort. Dec. 1, 2 years or installs. 2,000

Geitz, George W. to Cortlandt de P. Field. Lawrence st, s w s, 106 s e Bloomingdale road, 51.4x100x50.4x100. Sub. to morts. $15,500. Nov. 12, 5 years. 2,500

Green, Edward H. trustee Edward M. Robinson dec'd mortgagee with Patrick J. Cuskley mortgagor. Extension of mort. at 4½ %. Nov 25. nom

Same with Margaret McCormick mortgagee. Extension of mort. at 4½ %. Nov. 25. nom

Galvan, Mary P. to Roger Donegan. East Broadway, s s, 43.2 e Gouverneur st, 21.7x110.10 to alley, x21.4x110.8. Nov. 27, 3 years, 5 %. 2,000

Galewski, Adolph to Leonbard Daub. 5th st. P. M. Nov. 30, due June 1, 1894, or installs. 2,250

Gluck, Hannah and Ignatz to Mayer Katzenberg. Stanton st, n s, 25.6 e Attorney st, 24.6 x70. Nov. 30, due July 1, 1892. 1,500

Grimm, Louisa widow to Louis Stern. 115th st. P. M. Nov. 30, 6 months. 8,000

Gebhardt, Adam to Jacob Muhlfelder. Brook av, n w cor 148th st, runs west 90 x north 50 x east 20 x south 25 x east 70 to av, x south 25; 115th st, n s, 200 w 5th av, 45x100.11 Sub. to morts. Nov. 30, 1 year. 4,000

Gibson, Delia wife of and John to THE TITLE GUARANTEE AND TRUST CO. 138th st, P. M. Nov. 27, 1 year, 5 %. 1,500

Gies, Valentine to George Gebhardt. Park or 4th av, w s, 75.8 n 109th st, 25.3x80. Lease. Nov. 27, 1 year. 1,000

Goerlitz, John to Frank Schaeffler. Spring st. Nos. 131, 133, 135, 137, n s, 48.2 w Greene st, runs north 95.6 x west 17.10 x southwest 8 x north 7 x west 27.8 x north 3.6 x west 46.2 x south 100 to Spring st, x east 98.2 to beginning, with use of alley in rear. Dec. 1, 2 months. 4,114

Goerlitz, John to Jacob Stockinger. Spring st, Nos. 131-137, n s, 48.2 w Greene st, runs north 95.6 x west 17.10 x southwest 8 x north 7 x west 27.8 x north 3.6 x west 46.2 x south 100 to Spring st, x east 98.2. Dec. 2, due Feb. 1, 1892. 5,000

Geer, Mary wife of Walter to Augusta D. wife of A. C. Geer, Hoosick Falls, N. Y. 72d st, No. 246, s s, 250 e West End av, 20x102.2. Dec. 1, 3 years, 5 %. 15,000

Same to Caroline E. Benedict, Hoosick Falls, N. Y. Same property. Equal lien with last mort. Dec. 1, 3 years, 5 %. 15,000

Goodnow, Lucy C, widow to THE MUTUAL LIFE INS. CO. of New York. 15th st, No. 222, s s, 298.1 w 7th av, 24.9x86.6. Dec. 1, 1 year, 5 %. 5,000

Henna, Joseph J. to Elizabeth C. Stanton. 46th st, s s, 165 6 w 5th av, 19.6x98.9. Sub. to mort. $5,000. Dec. 1, 5 years, 5 %. 30,000

Hodges, Frank M. to Hugh N. Camp. Morton pl, lots 21 and 22 map of 71 lots of Kingsland estate, 24th Ward. Nov. 27, due Dec. 3, 1894, 5 %. 800

Horton, Charlotte A. to Edward D. Hicks et al. exrs. Hanford Horton. 129th st, n s, 350 w Boulevard, runs north 199.10 to 130th st, x west 50 x south 195.3 to Manhattan st, x southeast 11.2 to 129th st, x east 39.11 to beginning. Sub. to mort. $8,000. Declaration of accounting and mortgage. Nov. 2. 8,000

Hessberg, Theodore to THE DRY DOCK SAVINGS INST. 3d av, w s, 75.6 n 91st st, 25.2x75. Dec. 2, due Dec. 15, 1892, 5 %. 14,500

Hirsh, Jacob to THE TITLE GUARANTEE AND TRUST CO. 23d st. P. M. Nov. 30, due Dec. 1, 1894, 5 %. 16,000

Houghlahen, Thomas and Elizabeth his wife to Robert Courtright. Delancey pl or Washington av. w s, 158 n 188th st, 25x110. Dec. 1, 3 years. See Conveys. 200

Hansson, Christine wife of and Ola to Jessie Alexander, New York, Isabella Craig and Rebecca E. Mackenzie, Jersey City. 165th st, s s, 250 e Amsterdam av, 50x70.4x50.6x 68.4. Nov. 11, 3 years. 4,000

Hoppin, Hamilton L. and ano. trustees for Louisa H. Hoppin to D. Sackett Moore. Certificate of receipt of $5,000 on account of mortgage made by Charles Noble. May 1.

Hurley, Katie E. wife of Frank E. to Susan Dyckman. Cherry st, s s, 350 e Jackson st, 25x ½ block. Nov. 17, 3 years, 5 %. 2,000

Hall, George to Henry A. Loth exr. Leopold Lehmann. 52d st. P. M. Nov. 30, due Jan. 1, 1892, 4½ %. 7,500

Hamilton, George J. to THE MUTUAL LIFE INS. CO., New York. 89th st, n s, 575 w 8th av, 75x100.8. Nov. 30, due Dec. 1, 1891. 24,000

Hartley, Joseph to Johannah S. Seymour. 22d st. P. M. Nov. 30, 3 years, 5 %. 16,000

Hartwig, Anna to James D. Hall. 29th st. P. M. Nov. 30, due Feb. 1, 1892, 5 %. 1,000

Howes, Sarah J. to Charles W. Klebisch. 101st st, n s, 75 w Lexington av, 25x100.11. Nov. 28, due July 1, 1892, 5 %. 500

Same to Don A. Gaylord. Same property. P. M. Nov. 28, 2 years. 5,500

Hurwitz, Esther wife of and Raphael to The Greenwood Cemetery, Brooklyn. Monroe st, No. 60, s s, 25x98. Nov. 27, due Dec. 1, 1896, 5 %. 13,000

Haberman, Simon to Maurice S. Bondy. 7th av, s e cor 116th st, runs east 150 x south 100.11 x west to e s St. Nicholas av, x northwest along same to 7th av, x north —. Dec. 1, due April 15, 1893. 10,000

Hamersley, W. Livingston to William K. Aston. 5th av. P. M. Oct. 5, 2 years. 12,500

Hinklein, Jacob to George Pries and Katharina his wife. 88th st. P. M. Nov. 30, due Dec. 1, 1893, 5 %. 1,000

Hirsch, Julius to THE TITLE GUARANTEE AND TRUST CO. Water st, No. 239, s e s, 125 n e Beekman st, 25x73.4. Nov. 30, due Dec. 1, 1894, 4½ %. 11,000

Same to same. Water st, No. 237, s e s, 100 n e Beekman st, 25x73.9x25x73.4. Nov. 30, due Dec. 1, 1894, 4½ %. 12,000

Hohmann, John G. and Fransiska B. his wife mortgagors with Thomas Farley guard. of Irene Lailis mortgagee. Extension of mort. Dec. 1. nom

Hulster, Carl to Moses G. Wright. 151st st. P. M. Dec. 1, 2 years, 5 %. 2,000

Hunter, Stephen C. to William D. Peck. Andrews av. P. M. Nov. 25, due Dec. 1, 1892. 2,500

Hunter, Elizabeth M. to A. Gertrude Cutter. 61st st. P. M. Dec. 1, 3 years, 5 %. 8,000

Hynes, Peter to THE EXCELSIOR SAVINGS BANK, City New York. 7th av, s e cor 26th st, 20.9x70. Dec. 1, due April 1, 1893, 5 %. 24,000

Itzkovitz, Moritz and Abram Berkovitz to Jonas Weil and Bernhard Mayer. Lewis st, Nos. 87 and 89. P. M. Nov. 30, installs. 6,650

Isabeau, Louise to Catharine A. De Peyster. 163d st, n s, 125 e 10th av, 50x112.6. Already mortgaged to mortgagee for $3,000. Nov. 30, due Oct. 1, 1893, 5 %. 1,000

Jacobs, Elias to THE UNITED STATES TRUST CO., New York. Forsyth st. P. M. Nov. 30, due Dec. 1, 1894, 5 %. 18,000

Same to Henry Stemme and Rudolph Troest. Houston st. P. M. Sub. to mort. $10,000. Nov. 30, installs, 5½ %. 10,000

Jordan, Alexander A. to Patrick F. Ferrigan et al. exrs. Hugh Perrigan. Arcularius pl, s s, 209.3 e Gerard av, P. M. Nov. 23, 3 years, 5 %. 2,012

Same to same. Inwood av and Gerard av. P. M. Nov. 23, 3 years, 5 %. 1,275

Janikula, Edward J. to Frederick P. Forster. Lot 234 map of F. P. and H. A. Forster's 399 lots, Riverdale, &c., 24th Ward, 25x100. P. M. Nov. 30, 2 years 400

Johnson, Edward H. to Elizabeth L. wife of William J. Morton. 56th st, s s, 500 w 5th av, 25x100. Sub. to mort. $55,000. Nov. 4, due Nov. 1, 1892, 5 %. gold, 15,000

Judgment of Supreme Court vesting mortgages in James T., Annie L., Sarah L. and Mary T. Horn and authorizing satisfaction. Nov. 28. nom

Judge, Andrew T. to John W. Haaren. 131st st, n s, 460 w 5th av, 25x99.11. Dec. 1, 6 months. See Conveys. 4,000

Same to same. 131st st, n s, 460 w 5th av, 25x 99.11. Dec. 1, 6 months. 6,000

July, Elizabeth to Isabell Hasbrouck. 21st st, No. 340, s s, 160 w 1st av, 20x92. Dec. 1, 5 years, 5 %. gold, 7,500

Jacobson, Morris and Morris Margovitz to Morris Berger. Hester st, s s, 75 w Suffolk st, 25 x69.11x25x70.2. Nov. 27, demand. 3,000

Jones, John L. exr. and trustee to Charles Falkenberg. Certificate of receipt of $2,000 on account of mortgage made by Justus H. Zimmermann. Nov. 23.

Jones, Frederic R. to Albert E. Foster. Broadway, No. 58, and New st, Nos. 25-29, begins Broadway, n e cor Exchange pl, runs southeast 132.7 to New st, x northeast 42.8 x northwest 8.11 x south 1.5 x northwest 18.4 x southwest 8.4 x northwest 101.8 to Broadway, x southwest 32.5: Broadway, s e s, 32.5 n e Exchange pl, runs southeast 101.8 x northeast 8.4 x southeast 18.4 x northeast 1.5 x southeast 8.11 to New st, x northeast 24.2 x northwest 66.7 x southwest 0.8 x northwest 60.6 to Broadway, x southwest 35. ½ part. Recorded Nov. 19, 1891. Nov. 19, 3 years. gold, 100,000

Jung, Jacob and Charles Stegmayer to James P. Kernochan and John J. Wysong trustees. 83d st, s s, 254.2 w 2d av, 23.5x102.2. Nov. 25, 5 years, 5 %. 17,000

Jencks, Francis M. to Francis P. Furnald. 96th st, s s, 240 e 9th av, 3 lots, each 20x100.8. 3 morts., each $15,000. Nov. 25, demand. 45,000

Same to same. 95th st, n s, 141 e 9th av, 21x 100.11. Nov. 25, demand. 16,000

Jacobs, Abraham and Isaac Bernstein to William Rankin. 17th st, s s, 250 w 8th av, 75x 127.5x75.4x120.5. Dec. 3, installs. 5,000

Kelly, Catherine wife of and James to THE EMIGRANT INDUST. SAVINGS BANK. 135th st, n s, 206.6 e Alexander av, 25x100. Sub. to mort. Dec. 3, 1 year, 4½ %. 1,000

Karcher, Philipp and Louisa his wife to Jakobina Bindernagel. Cypress av, s e cor 149th st, 50x84. Nov. 28, due Nov. 1, 1892. 1,000

Kassler, Regina to Clara Rosenthal. 49th st. P. M. Nov. 30, due Dec. 1, 1896, or installs, 5 %. 10,000

Kennedy, Thomas F. to Hosea B. Perkins. Ogden av, n e cor Union st, 59x100. Dec. 2, 3 years. 4,500

Ketcham, James W. to Lewis Cohen and Augustus L. Hayes. Waverley pl. P. M. Nov. 16, due June 1, 1892. 1,000

Kilpatrick, Thomas to Gideon Fountain. 92d st, s s, 125 e 9th av, 99.8x100.8. Sub. to mort. $40,000. Nov. 27, 4 months. 20,000

Klein, Benedict A. to David McClure. Lewis st, No. 93. P. M. Nov. 27, 3 years, 5 %. 20,000

Same to THE FARMER'S LOAN AND TRUST CO. Lewis st, No. 91. P. M. Nov. 27, 3 years, 5 %. 20,000

Same to same. Lewis st, No. 93. P. M. Nov. 27, 3 years, 5 %. 20,000

Klein, Luise to Philip Bolender. 88th st, s s, 131 e 1st av, 25x100.8. Nov. 27, due Jan. 1, 1897, 5 %. 12,000

Klemt, Adolf to THE GERMAN SAVINGS BANK, New York. Av B, old line, s w cor 72d st, 76.8x98. Nov. 25, 1 year. 35,000

Same to Hyman and Henry Sonn. Same property. Nov. 25, demand. 20,000

Klinger, Moses A. to Selig Gross. Henry st, No. 132, s s, 23.10x100. Nov. 27, due April 18, 1893. 4,000

Kuhnemann, Henry to Walter N. De Grauw, Jr., and ano., exrs. and trustees Samuel Aymar. 123d st, n s, 275 e 4th av, 15x100.11. Nov. 23, due Nov. 25, 1896, 5 %. 6,000

Kahl, George H. to Kate M. Bailly. Lewis st, n w cor 7th st, 24 4x—x25x80; Lewis st, w s, 24.4 n 7th st, 48.10x—x—x—. The intent is to mortgage three lots facing on Lewis st and the one adj in the rear facing on 7th st. Nov. 24, 3 years, 5 %. See Conveys. 7,500

King, David H., Jr., to THE EQUITABLE LIFE ASSUR. SOC., of the United States. 7th av, s w cor 138th st, 99.11x675; 139th st, n s, extends from 7th av to 8th av, 775x99.11. June 1, due Jan. 1, 1893. See Conveys 925,000

Same to same. Same property. P. M. June 1, due Jan. 1, 1893. 389,500

King, Mary to Kate Keefe. 162d st, s w s, 186 s e Courtlandt av, 54x100. Nov. 6, 5 years, 4 %. 1,500

Kotnowski, Peter N. to Robert H. and Hester A. Shannon. Lots 11 and 12, lying bet Vanderbilt and Washington avs, map of Hester A. Shannon property, 24th Ward, 50x125. June 1, due July 1, 1896, 5 %. 1,000

Kimball, Alonzo, mortgagee with Julia J. De Bruin, mortgagor. Extension of mort. at reduced interest. Nov. 30. nom

Koopmann, John C. to West End Co-operative Building and Loan Assoc. 171st st, s s, 150 e 11th av, 25x95. Nov. 30, installs, 5 %. 4,500

Krause, George V. to The Twenty-fourth Ward Real Estate Assoc., New York. Park View terrace, e s, 200 n Wellesley st, 3 lots, each 25x125. 3 P. M. morts., each $600. Oct. 20, due Nov. 12, 1894, 5 %. 1,800

Same to same. Travers st, s s, 25 w Creston av, 25x106x25x102.11. Oct. 20, due Nov. 12, 1894, 5 %. 300

Keller, Theodore to Maria Hillenbrand. Pitt st. P. M. Dec. 1, 5 years, 5 %. 15 000

Lambert, Henry to Stephen Merrihew and ano. trustees for Edwin T. Putnam. 61st st, n s, 175 e Columbus av, 25x100.5. Dec. 1, due Nov. 1, 1894, 5 %. 10,000

Lane, Isabella A. wife of and Jonas H. to Augustus C. Brown trustee Augustus Cleveland. 21st st, n s, 278.8 w 3d av, runs north 73.3 x east 6.6 x north 9.3 x west 6.4 x north 16.3 x west 33.4 x south 98.9 to 21st st, x east 33.4. Dec. 1, 5 years, 4½ %. 60,000

Le Cato, Lillian wife of W. N., West Orange, N. J., to Francis M. Wilmurt, Pelham Manor. 89th st. P. M. Sub. to mort. $19,000. Nov. 24, installs. 5,500

Levy, Emil to THE TITLE GUARANTEE AND TRUST CO. 8th av, No. 699 and Nos 302 and 304 West 44th st, begins 8th av, s w cor 44th st, 25.2x100x25.2x100.1. Dec. 1, 5 years, 4½ %. 21,000

Levy, Henry to William T. Lee. Wooster st, Nos. 137 and 139. P. M. Nov. 30, 3 years, 4½ %. 43,750

Levy, Jacob to Ebrick Parmly and ano. trustees Anna R. Adams and Ehrick K. Rossiter. 108th st. P. M. Nov. 28, due Dec. 1, 1898, 5 %. 8,750

Levy, Barnett, Louis Gordon and Sophia Gruenstein to Israel M. Cohen. Madison st. P. M. Nov. 30, due Sept. 1, 1892. 2,500

Lockwood, John B. mortgagee with Daniel E. Seybel mortgagor. Extension of reduced mortgage. Nov. 27. nom

Lyding, Peter to August Ruff. 5th st. P. M. Sub. to mort. $26,000. Nov. 28, due Jan. 1, 1895. Installs. 8,000

Same to THE GERMAN SAVINGS BANK, New York. Same property. Nov. 28, due Nov. 30, 1893. 26,000

Loos, John H. to THE EMIGRANT INDUST. SAVINGS BANK. Park av, s e cor 129th st, 24.11x 80. Dec. 1, 1 year, 4½ %. 6,000

Levene, Isaac to Barry D. Haber. Market st, No. 85. P. M. Nov. 30, installs. 750

Same to same. Market st, No. 87. P. M. Nov. 30, installs. 750

Lamb, Hugh, East Orange, N. J., to James R. Smith. 76th st, n s, 86 w West End av, 21x 76.1. Nov. 28, 3 years, 5 %. 21,000

Larkin, Mary wife of Stephen to THE HARLEM SAVINGS BANK, New York. Amsterdam av, s w cor 130th st, runs west 100 x south 51 x east 62 x east 43 to av, x north 24.11, except gore, begins 43 w Amsterdam av, and 25 s 130th st, runs west 4 x southwest — x northeast —; also gore 60 w av and 50.1 south 130th st, runs west 12 x northeast 13.5 x south 6. Nov. 27, 1 year, 5 %. 7,000

Lee, John C. to Sarah Murray. 127th st, No. 248, s s, 383.4 e 8th av, 16.2x99.11. Nov. 24, due June 13, 1895, or installs, 5 %. 5,500

Lyon, Dora wife of Charles to THE CENTRAL NATIONAL BANK, City of New York. 87th st, s s, 145 w 9th av, 17.6x100.8. Nov. 27, note. 7,000

Lange, Alida wife of and Gustav to THE NEW YORK SAVINGS BANK. 78th st, s s, 263.9 w 3d av, 18.9x102.2. Dec. 2, due Dec. 1, 1896, 4½ %. 7,500

Lawrence, Charles W. to John R. Suydam trustee John R. Suydam dec'd. 15th st, s s, 253.7 e 7th av, 21.5x100. Nov. 24, 1 year, 4½ %. 1,600

Lustig, Morris K. to Robert Gerson. Ridge st. P. M. Dec. 1, installs. 2,500

Lazinsk, Hyman M. to John Bohnet, Jr., and ano. exrs. Mary Braun. Suffolk st, No. 14, e s, 100 n Hester st, 25.1x100.5x25.3x100.5. June 25, 3 years, 5 %. 18,000

Same to Clara R. Bacon. 35th st. P. M. Dec. 2, 3 years, 5 %. 20,000

Lo Forte, Remigio to THE MUTUAL LIFE INS. CO. of New York. 58th st, n s, 200 w 6th av, runs west 100 x north 90 x east 75 x north 10.5 x east 25 x south 100.5. Dec. 3, 1 year. 60,000

Lehr, Harry to Scenora Mandle. 102d st. P. M. Dec 1, 1 year. 2,800

Loonie, James J. and Eugene Parker to Therese Weinman. Norfolk st. P. M. Dec. 3, due Dec. —, 1892, 5½ %. 12,000

Madden, Stephen to THE DRY DOCK SAVINGS INST. Market st, e s, 75 n Monroe st, 25x87.5. Dec. 1, 1 year, 5 %. 6,000

Martin, Eli to John R. Smith. 77th st, n s, 118.6 w Columbus av, 38.6x104.9x38.6x104. Sub. to morts. $47,500. Secures building materials. Nov. 30, notes. 8,000

Same to New York Lumber and Wood Working Co. 77th st, n s, 157 w Columbus av, 39x105.7x39x104.9. Sub. to morts. $45,000. Secures building materials. Nov. 30, notes. 8,351

Martin, Eli to THE NEW YORK LIFE INS. CO. 77th st, n s, 138.6 w Columbus av, 18.6x104.9.x18.6x104.5. Nov. 30, 1 year, 5 %. 22,000

Same to same. 77th st, n s, 177 w Columbus av, 19x105.7x19x105.2. Nov. 30, 1 year, 5 %. 22,000

Same to same. 77th st, n s, 157 w Columbus av, 20x105.2x20x104 9. Nov. 30, 1 year, 5 %. 23,000

Same to same. 77th st, n s, 216 w Columbus av, 19x106.4x19x106. Nov. 30, 1 year, 5 %. 23,000

Same to same. 77th st, n s, 255 w Columbus av, 20x107.2x20x106.9. Nov. 30, 1 year, 5 %. 26,000

Same to same. 77th st, n s, 235 w Columbus av. 20x106.9x20x106 4. Nov. 30, 1 year, 5 %. 26,000

Same to same. 77th st, n s, 196 w Columbus av. 20x106x20x105.7. Nov. 30, 1 year, 5 %. 25,000

Same to same. 77th st, n s, 118.6 w Columbus av, 20x104.5x20x104. Nov. 30, 1 year, 5 %. 25,500

Same to same. 77th st, n s, 100 w Columbus av, runs north 100.8 x west 3.2 x north 3.? x west 15 4 x south 104 to st, x east 18.6. Nov. 30, 1 year, 5 %. 22,500

Mayer, Hugo to James A. Bailey, of Barnum & Bailey's Greatest Show on Earth. Walnut st, n w cor Fleetwood av. 50x100. Dec. 3. Secures agreement of, per week, 200

Mayer, John M. to George Ehret. 124th st, No. 152 W., s s. Lease. Nov. 25, demand. 4,300

Moloney, Thomas to L. Bayard Smith et al. trustees Charlotte T. Smith. 181st st, s w cor Amsterdam av, 24.11x100. Dec. 2, 3 years, 4½ %. 25,000

McEntyre, George B. to George G. De Witt and Jacob Lockman trustees Sarah Talman dec'd. 25th st, No. 319, n s, 275 e 2d av, 25x98.9. Dec 3, 5 years, 5 %. gold, 20,000

Same to Philip Sammet and Abraham Alexander. Same property. Sub. to last mort. Dec. 1, 6 months. 2,000

Mace, Levi H. and Arthur J. and Frederick S. and John L. Gwyer to Henry L. Morris. River av, n w cor 150th st, 494 6x200.3 to Cromwell av, x492.2 to st, x200.4; 150th st, n s, 418.5 w Cromwell av, 84x83 to pier line of Harlem River, x125x126.8. Lease. Nov. 1, 5 years. 8,000

Mardorf, Mina wife of and Henry to Betty Bader. 88th st, s s, 106 e 1st av, 25x100.8. Nov. 27, 5 years, 4½ %. 10,000

Same to Frederick W. and Conrad Gross. 88th st, s s, 106 e 1st av, 25x100.8. Sub. to last mort. Nov. 27, due Nov. 15, 1893, 5 %. 2,500

Martin, Ann widow to THE GREENWICH SAVINGS BANK. 4th st, Nos. 165-169, n s, 189.10 w 6th av, runs northeast 70.2 x east 55.5 x southwest 22.2 x west 71.4 to st, x northwest 63 to beginning. Nov. 27, due Dec. 1, 1892, 5 %. 900

Moore, William T. to THE GREENWICH SAVINGS BANK. 42d st, n s, 40 w 6th av, 20x75.4. Nov. 17, due Dec. 1, 1893, 5 %. 15,000

Mack, Hugo S. to Susan Dyckman. 10th av, w s, 50.5 s 55th st, 2 lots, each 25x100. 2 morts., each $16,000. Nov. 28, 3 years, 5 %. 32,000

Same to James Connoly, New Orleans, La. Same property. Nov. 30, 3 years. 3,000

Maher, William to The Eureka Co-operative Savings and Loan Assoc. Concord av. P. M. Nov. 19, installs, 5 %. 2,600

Michaelis, Matilda to Fannie Folk. 3d av, No. 1626. P. M. Nov. 19, 3 years, 5 %. gold, 18,000

Same to Gustav Folk. 3d av, No. 1624. P. M. Nov. 19, 3 years, 5 %. gold, 18,000

Mills, William W., Albert L., Arthur E. and Ann W. widow and heirs of Abiel B. Mills to THE MUTUAL LIFE INS. CO., New York. Amsterdam (10th) av, e s, 25 s 156th st, 25x100. Nov. 7, due Nov. 30, 1892, 5 %. 3,000

Morgenthau, Henry to Rebecca Ehrich. 125th st, s s, 175 w 7th av, runs south 201.10 to 124th st, x west 40 x north 65 x east 1 x north 136.10 to 125th st, x east 39. Lease. Nov. 27, due Jan. 1, 1895. 40,000

Morrison, Anna R., wife of and James J. to THE UNITED STATES TRUST CO., New York. 7th av, s w cor 37th st, 24.9x60. Nov. 30, due Dec. 1, 1894, 5 %. 25,000

Mull, De Witt and Gotlieb Promer to Bradley & Currier Co. (Lim.) Park av, n w cor 103d st, 100.11x80. Sub. to mort. Nov. 13, 3 months. 7,319

Muller, Fred. and Elizabeth C. his wife to Rebecca Lennon. Bailey av, lot 82 map W. O. Giles, Kingsbridge, 50x113.6x57.9x130.10. Nov. 24, due Jan., 1893. 500

Murphy, John T., Michael H. and Charles P. heirs Joseph Murphy to Ann E. McCaddin. 78th st, No. 307, n s, 125 e 2d av, 25x102.2. Nov. 25, due Nov. 27, 1894, 4½ %. 13,000

Same to same. 78th st, No. 309, n s, 150 e 2d av, 25x102.2. Nov. 25, due Nov. 27, 1894, 4½ %. 13,000

McGuire, Thomas J. to John N. Brown, Newport, R. I. Manhattan av and 118th st. P. M. Nov. 30, 1 year. 25,000

McCormick, Margaret mortgagor with Henry A. Barling et al. trustees Edward M. Robinson dec'd mortgagees. Extension of mort at increased interest. Nov. 13. nom

McLaughlin, Thomas J. to George E. Hyatt, Brooklyn. 103d st, s s, 102.6 w 3d av, 4 lots, each 27x100.11. 4 morts., each $14,500. Nov. 27, due June 1, 1892. 58,000

Same to Lewis Z. Bach. 103d st. P. M. Sub. to mort. $14,500. Nov. 27, due Nov. 12, 1892. 14,000

Neilley, John H., Stony Point, N. Y., to John A. Weekes. 22d st, s s, 243.9 w 6th av, 18.9x98 9. Nov. 27, due Nov. 1, 1894, 5 %. gold, 1,500

Same to Alice D. Weekes. 22d st, s s, 262.6 w 6th av, 18.9x98.9. Nov. 27, due Nov. 1, 1894, 5 %. gold, 1,500

Noethen, Joseph to Mary B. Hughes and Annie J. Bouillon. 48th st. P. M. Nov. 20, installs. 3,500

Nolan, Patrick to Margaret Hurley, Brooklyn. Forest av, w s, 125 n 156th st, 25x87.6. Nov. 24, 2 years. 500

Nally, Margaret T. wife of and Christopher to Ellen Tracy. Amsterdam av. P. M. Sub. to mort. $24,000. Dec. 1, notes. 1,500

Newman, Ellen wife of and William H. to THE TITLE GUARANTEE AND TRUST CO. Audubon av, s e cor 171st st, 20x95. Dec. 3, 2 years, 5 %. 2,000

O'Donoghue, Denis to THE EMIGRANT INDUST. SAVINGS BANK. 22d st, n s, 350 w 9th av. 20x98.9. Dec. 3, 1 year, 4½ %. 1,000

Pirsson, Janette to Bryan L. Kennelly. Greenwich st, n e cor Charles st, 58.1x36.10x39.10 to Charles st, x45.9. 1-5 part. Dec. 2, due March 1, 1892, 5 %. 303

Pierce, Madeline to Robert C. Watson et al. exrs. and trustees William Watson. 103d st. P. M. Dec. 2, 3 years, 5 %. 15,500

Prabar, Anna to Michael Keiser. 49th st. P. M. Dec. 1, installs, 5 %. 6,000

Purcell, Mary widow to THE EMIGRANT INDUST. SAVINGS BANK. West Broadway, s w cor Worth st, 55x51x55x51.3. Nov. 27, 1 year, 4½ %. 15,000

Pape, Charles to Frederick P. Forster. Lot 235 map of F. P. and H. A. Forster, 399 lots, Riverdale, &c. P. M. Nov 30, 2 years. 400

Phelps, Louis N. to Henry W. Benedict, William McElroy and Robert A. Fowler. Bleecker st, s c cor 8th av, runs northeast 44.11 x southeast 40 x east 17.2 x south 23.5 x west 76.9 to Bleecker st, x north 27.7. Dec. 1, 6 months. 4,000

Pupke, John F. mortgagor with John L. Miller mortgagee. Extension of mort. at 5 %. Nov. 2. nom

Quenzer, Louis and Margaret to Louis Cohen. 4th st. P. M. Dec. 1, 5 years or installs, 5½ %. 10,000

Rafter, Edward mortgagor with Robert C. Watson et al. exrs. and trustees William Watson mortgagees. 4 extension of morts. Nov. 23. nom

Reid, Walter, Madison, N. J., to Amelia B. Lazarus. 93d st, n s, 146.9 e 5th av, 21.6x100.8. Dec. 3, 3 years, 5 %. 25,000

Same to Caroline M. Sewell. 93d st, n s, 189.3 e 5th av, 20.6x100.8. Dec. 3, 3 years, 5 %. 22,000

Same to Julia E. Cameron. 93d st, n s, 168.3 e 5th av, 21x100.8. Dec. 3, 3 years, 5 %. 23,000

Same to Samuel Riker. 93d st, n s, 124.9 e 5th av, 22x100.8. Dec. 3, 3 years, 5 %. 26,000

Same to The Good Samaritan Dispensary. 93d st, n s, 102.3 e 5th av, 22.6x100.8. Dec. 3, 3 years, 5 %. 28,000

Same to Catharine L. Fairweather and Cornelia L. Luyster, Flushing, L. I., Peter and Caroline J. Luyster, Newtown, L. I., and Sarah F. and Margaret C. Luyster, Brooklyn. 93d st, n s, 209.9 e 5th av, 19.6x100.8. Dec. 3, 3 years, 5 %. 21,000

Same to, Isaac and Samuel Untermyer. 93d st, n s, 102.2 e 5th av, 127x100.8. Sub. to morts. $145,000. Dec. 3, 1 year. 20,000

Rittmaster, Alexander to Edward Pennefather. Madison st. P. M. Dec. 1, installs, 5 %. 11,000

Robert, Sophia to THE CONNECTICUT MUTUAL LIFE INS. CO., Hartford, Conn. Av A and 13th st. P. M. Dec. 1, 5 years, 5 %. 30,000

Same to Mayer Gottlieb. Same property. P. M. Dec. 1, 1 year, 5 %. 10,000

Rosenfeld, Rosanna to Adolph Cohen and Harry Fischel. Cherry st. P. M. Sub. to mort. $8,000. Nov. 20, 3 years, installs. 2,000

Ratkowsky, Harris to Mary Thomas. Ludlow st, No. 121, w s, 19x87.6. Nov. 30, due Dec. 1, 1896, 5 %. gold, 10,000

Reimer, Henry, Somerville, N. J., to Arthur B. Claflin. Lot 28 map of 153 select lots on Kingsbridge Heights. P. M. Nov. 16, due Nov. 19, 1894, 5 %. 810

A. L. and J. J. Reynolds Co., a corporation, to THE TITLE GUARANTEE AND TRUST CO. Greenwich st, No. 822, w s, 68.2 n Jane st, 21.7x abt 93x21.7x abt 92. Nov. 28, due Nov. 30, 1892, 5 %. 10,000

Rothenberg, Lena wife of and Theodor to William Cowen. 85th st, s s, 80 w 2d av, 20x88.2. Nov. 25, due Nov. 30, 1892. 500

Rourke, Bernard to The John Kress Brewing Co. Forsyth st, No. 35. Saloon lease. Nov. 24, demand. 7,000

Rabold, Daniel to Alice S. H. Davies, New Haven, Conn. 133d st, No. 157, n s, 250 e 7th av, 25x99.11. Nov. 25, due Nov. 27, 1894, 5 %. 13,000

Same to Enoch C. Bell. Same property. Sub. to last mort. Nov. 28, 3 years, 5 %. 2,000

Regan, John to William H. Greene, Sing Sing, N. Y. Franklin st, No. 153, s s, 173.10 e Hudson st, 26.10x71.2x25.7x60.4. Sub. to mort. $16,000. Nov. 30, due April 18, 1894. 5,000

Richards, Estelle to Robert J. Waddell. 48th st. Leasehold. P. M. Nov. 27, due Nov. 30, 1896, 5 %. 10,000

Same to same. Same property. Leasehold. P. M. Nov. 27, due Nov. 30, 1894, or installs. 5,000

Riddell, Henry W. to John R. Planten. Brooklyn. 43d st, s s, 500 w 6th av, 25x100.5. Nov. 30, due Dec. 2, 1894. 1,000

Robinson, Reuben and Ida his wife to Kleiman Hirsch. Willett st. P. M. Nov. 30, installs. 1,500

Same to Abraham Stern. Same property. P. M. Nov. 30, 6 months. 500

Rounds, Charles W. to THE METROPOLITAN LIFE INS. CO. Convent av, w s, 24.11 n 144th st, 3 lots. 3 P. M. morts., each $16,000. Dec. 2, due Oct. 1, 1894. 48,000

Same to same. Convent av, n w cor 144th st. P. M. Dec. 2, due Oct. 1, 1894. 22,000

Same to same. 144th st, n s, 214.2 e Amsterdam av. P. M. Dec. 2, due Oct. 1, 1894. 12,000

Same to same. 144th st, n s, 177.8 e Amsterdam av. P. M. Dec. 2, due Oct. 1, 1894. 14,000

Same to same. 142th st, n s, 137.8 e Amsterdam av. P. M. Dec. 2, due Oct. 1, 1894. 12,000

Schiff, Herman J. to Lottie Schlussel et al., exrs. of Alexander Schlussel. 82d st, No. 420, s s, 256.6 w Av A, 25x102.2. Dec. 2, 10 years, 4½ %. 8,500

Schmidt, Ernst and Max Bechter to Karl M. and Samson Wallach. Broome st. P. M. Dec. 1, installs. 1,750

Schwartz, Marie to Therese Steindler. 2d av. P. M. Dec. 1, 3 years. 5,000

Simonson, Egbert C. to THE TITLE GUARANTEE AND TRUST CO. 82d st. P. M. Dec. 2, 3 years, 5 %. 14,000

Scinto, Frank to The India Wharf Brewing Co. Mulberry st, No. 119. Saloon lease. Feb. 8, note. 600

Smith, Frank L. to Matilda Weil et al. exrs. Max Weil. West End av, 92d st. P. M. Oct. 22, due Nov. 30, 1893, or sooner, 5 %. 15,000

Same to Ida Meyer et al. exrs. Isaias Meyer. West End av. P. M. Oct. 22, due Nov. 30, 1893, 5 %. 19,000

Schloeder, Nicholas to Edward Kilpatrick. 96th st. P. M. Nov. 30, due Dec. 1, 1892. 4,000

Schlagel, Mary wife of and Bernhard to The John Eichler Brewing Co. West Farms road, n w s, 25 n e Cross st, 50x100. Nov. 6, 1 year, 5 %. 900

Strauss, Henry to Sarah Metzler and Emma Weinberg. Av D. P. M. Nov. 30, due Dec. 1, 1896, 5 %. 10,000

Smith, Roby A. wife of and J. Henry to Max Just. 109th st, n s, 225 e 11th av, widened, 50x100. Nov. 27, 1 year. 1,500

Smith, John B. to Isaac L. Smith. 62d st, n s, 100 e 11th av, 3 lots, each 25x100.5. 3 morts., each $2,000. Nov. 30, due Dec. 1, 1892, 5 %. 6,000

Smith, Thomas C. to Albert Klauber. 4th st. P. M. Nov. 11, due Dec. 1, 1892, 5 %. 6,500

Stadler, Charles A. et al., stockholders of The Sebastian Mfg. Co., to Ambrose K. Ely exr. Consent to mortgage. Nov. 30. nom

Steinkamp, Christopher H. to John W. Bolton. 2d av, n w cor 46th st, 25x73. Dec. 1, 3 years or installs., 5 %. 10,000

Sturk, John H. to Lilly Hirshkind. 83d st. Dec. 1, 1 year, 5 %. See Conveys. 3,174

Stewart, Mary M. with Gideon Fountain both mortgagees. Agreement as to priority of morts. made by Thomas Kilpatrick. Nov. 27. nom

Striker, James A. to John M. Scribner exr. and trustee Edward Quinn. Strikers lane, s s, 202.6 w 11th av, 18.5x63x—x—. Nov. 25, 3 years. 6,000

Same to same. 55th st, s s, 545 w 8th av, 20x40.5. Lease. Nov. 25, 3 years. 6,000

Sutton, Simon with Louis D. Levy both mortgagees. Agreement as to priority of morts. made by Julius M. Spero. Nov. 20. nom

Tallman, Jacob B. to THE UNITED STATES TRUST CO. of New York. 53d st, n s, 460 w 5th av, 50x100.5. Nov. 30, due Dec. 1, 1894, 5 %. 82,000

Thompson, James to Patrick Grady. 151st st. P. M. Nov. 27, 3 years, 5 %. 2,000

The Sebastian Mfg. Co. to Ambrose K. Ely et al. exrs. 43d st, n s, 255 e 3d av, 100x100.5; 44th st, s s, 305 e 3d av, 25x100.5. Nov. 28, due Nov. 30, 1896, 5 %. 50,000

The Bradley and Currier Co. (Lim.) to Frederick Rohrs. Certificate of receipt of $1,500 on account of mort. Nov. 23.

Thiel, Anna C. mortgagor with Simon Dresel. Extension mort. Nov. 21. nom

Van Tine, John H. to James Suydam. 125th st, n s, 263.9 w 6th av, 20x99.11. Nov. 30, due Dec. 1, 1896, 5 %. 10,000

Van Brunt, Thomas C. to THE EQUITABLE LIFE ASSUR. SOC. 136th st, n s, 100 w 7th av, 151x99.11. Nov. 28, due Jan. 1, 1893. 54,180

Same to same. 136th st, n s, 401 w 7th av, 151x99.11. Nov. 28, due Jan. 1, 1893. 54,180

Same to same. 136th st, n s, 251 w 7th av, 150x99.11. Nov. 28, due Jan. 1, 1893. 54,000

Same to same. 136th st, n s, 552 w 7th av, 98x99.11. Nov. 28, due Jan. 1, 1893. 35,640

Vogel, William to Charles E. Butler trustee John Ward dec'd. 3d av, n e cor 26th st, 24.8x110. Dec. 2, 3 years, 4½ %. 25,000

Weed, Henrietta W., Norwalk, Conn., to Emma J. and Matilda H. Douglas. 58th st, s s, 206.4 e 2d av, 21.10x100.5. Dec. 1, 3 years, 5 %. 9,000

Weller, Anna B. to Isabella Jenkins. Washington av. P. M. Oct. 28, 3 years. 2,500

Weinstein, Ascher to A. Gertrude Cutter. 45th st. P. M. Nov. 30, 5 years, 5 %. 17,000

Williams, Richard and Edward Jones to Andrew Brose. Lexington av, n e cor 54th st, 25.5x100. Nov. 2, 6 months, 5 %. 13,000

Wurzner, Martin and Babette his wife to Jacob Lederer. 2d av. P. M. Dec. 1, installs. 5½ %. 4,000

Wittkowski, Henry and Jacob Vorhaus to Eve Wolfenstein. Hester st, No. 115, n s, 21.9x75. Dec. 3, 3 years, 5 %. 14,000

Wylie, Fannie D. wife of and Walker G. to Henry B. Barnes. 40th st, No. 40, s s, 388 e 6th av, 18x98.9. Dec. 1, 1 year, 5 %. 30,000

Same to The Central Trust Co., New York. 40th st, s s, 500 e 6th av. P. M. Dec. 1, 1 year, 5 %. 35,000

Wembacher, Christian W. to Simon M. Roeder. 2d av, No. 2405. P. M. Nov. 30, due Dec. 1, 1892. 4,000

Williams, Thomas S. to Anna Woerishoffer. Gansevoort st, s s, 75 e West st, 50x83.5x50x84.9. Dec. 1, 5 years, 5 %. 50,000

Wynne, John to Mary A. wife of Manley A. Raymond. 13th st, n s, 194 e 1st av, 25x103.3. Nov. 30, due Dec. 1, 1896, 5 %. 5,000

Weber, John S. and Hellmuth W. Jarchow to Annie Weber. Sheriff st, n w cor Stanton st, being No. 206 Stanton st and 101 Sheriff st, 18.9x60. Nov. 24, due Dec. 1, 1894, 5 %. 1,000

Wissmann, Jacob to Peter Doelger. 48d st, No. 229 E. Store lease. Nov. 13, demand. 550

Weil, Katie to George Steinbrecher. 11th st. Lease. P. M. Nov. 30, installs. 12,000

Williams, William H. and Thomas K. Egbert trustees mortgagees to Adam Gebhardt mortgagor. Certificate that mortgage made by said Gebhardt is held as security for 35,000

Woolsey, Edward J. mortgagor with The State Trust Co. as trustee of Florence and Edith Bates mortgagee. Agreement to collect rents and apply same to payment of mortgage, &c. Nov. 25. nom

Zeller, Chessie E. to William R. Potts. 124th st. P. M. Nov. 27, 1 year, 5 %. 1,500

KINGS COUNTY.

November 25, 26, 27, 28, 30, December 1, 2.

Anderson, Carman E. to Mary Bennett. Clinton st, n w s, adj Second Presbyterian Church of Brooklyn, 17.5x121x17.4x121. Lease. Nov. 11, 1 year. $618

Anderson, John and Andrew Sundell to Ellen M. Suydam, Parkville, L. I. 21st st, s s, 225 w 5th av, 25x100.2. Nov. 25, due Nov. 1, 1894. 3,000

Anderson, Jonas M. to Nicholas T. and Elizabeth A. Andrew, Stony Creek, Conn. Enfield st. P. M. Nov. 27, due Dec. 1, 1896. 700

Adams, Mary to Herman Sauer. North 7th st. P. M. Nov. 28, 3 years, 5 %. 2,100

Adamson, John to Edwin D. Phelps. Pierrepont st. P. M. Nov. 25, due Dec. 1, 1892, 5 %. 15,000

Aldridge, George D. to William Harkness. Carlton av. P. M. Nov. 18, due Dec. 1, 1894, 5 %. 1,000

Allan, James N. to William G. Low. Herkimer st, No 636, s s, 154.3 e Schenectady av, 20.2x92.9. Nov. 30, due Dec. 1, 1896, 5 %. 2,000

Atkinson, William to Mary A. Lupton. Eagle st, s s, 250 w Manhattan av, 25x100. Dec. 1, 3 years, 5 %. 1,350

Barnes, Mary R., Preston, Conn., to Henry Rauschenberg Devoe st, n s, 241 e Graham av, 19x100. Nov. 20, due Dec. 20, 1896, 5 %. 1,500

Beasly, David S. to Anna McDonald. Lexington av. P. M Nov. 28, 1 year, 5 %. 12,000

Belz, Barbara and Louisa Boegel to George Holland. Hancock st. P. M. Oct. 31, installs. 900

Benedict, James T. to Eben W. Roby. Gunther pl, e s, 49 n Atlantic av. P. M. Nov. 16, 1 year. 817

Same to same. Gunther pl, e s, 65.4 n Atlantic av. P. M. Nov. 16, 1 year. 817

Same to same. Gunther pl, e s, 81.8 n Atlantic av. P. M. Nov 16, 1 year. 917

Same to Lillian Berry. Confirmation of former mort. especially in its effect upon an old road forming a portion of mortgaged premises. Nov 27. nom

Bennet, Charles C. to The Dime Savings Bank, Brooklyn. Parcel at New Utrecht, begins 740 w 1st av, contains 3 76-100 acres. Nov. 24, 1 year, 5 %. 10,000

Bennett, Sarah E., Flatbush, L. I., to Ellen Williamson. Diamond st, s s, 2,193.4 e Main st, 40x117.9x40x117.4, Flatbush. Nov. 10, 3 3 years, 5 %. 2,600

Blatt, Lena S. wife of and Isidor to Katharina Geyer. Sandford st P. M. Sub. to mort. $4,000. Nov. 30, 3 years, 5 %. 2,500

Birch, John T. to Henry Weil Dean st. P. M. Nov. 27, due May 1, 1893. 4,800

Same to same. Same property. Nov. 27, due May 1, 1893. 7,200

Bliss, Eliphalet W. to The Dime Savings Bank of Brooklyn. Adams st, s e cor John st, runs east 103.4 x south 100 x west 12.6 x south 50 x west 90.9 to Adams st, x north 150. Nov. 24, 1 year, 5 %. 65,000

Bohnet, John to Abby E. Laytin. Hamburg av, east cor Harman st. P. M. Dec. 1, 3 years, 5 %. 4,000

Bossert, Jacob to George Covert. Myrtle av. P. M. Nov. 28, due Dec. 1, 1892, 5 %. 4,800

Brennan, James to Sarah D. Allen, Manhasset, L. I. Court st, w s, 40 s Church st, 20x80. Nov. 5, due Nov. 1, 1894, 5 %. 2,000

Brennan, Martin to The East Brooklyn Savings Bank. Clermont av, w s, 125 s Flushing av, 25x100.6x25x100.9. Nov. 30, 1 year, 5 %. 3,000

Brett, Maria L. widow to The Title Guarantee and Trust Co. Keap st, n s, 162.4 w Bedford av, 20x100. Dec. 1, 3 years, 5 %. 5,500

Bretz, George B. to Edward M. Shepard. Washington av. P. M. Dec. 1, 3 years, 4½ %. 3,500

Brokaw, Susie D. to Annie A. Lovell. McDougal st, s s, 180.7 w Hopkinson av, 32.1x100. Nov. 19, 6 months. 750

Brown, Thomas to Mary C. M. Ingraham and ano. exrs. Hiram Kirk. 5th av, e s, 67.6 s Berkeley pl, 27.6x87.2. Nov. 27, due Dec. 1, 1892, 5 %. 11,000

Brush, Matilda E. wife of and George S. to The Co-operative Building Bank. 21st av, n w s, 300 n e Benson av, 100x96.8, New Utrecht. Nov. 24, installs. 2,300

Burns, Margaret A. A. widow to Benjamin Andrews. Gates av, s s, 200 w Tompkins av, 20x100. Dec. 2, 3 years, 5 %. 5,000

Bush, Wesley C. to Title Guarantee and Trust Co. Hancock st, n s, 250 e Lewis av, 200x100. Dec. 2, demand, 5 %. 51,000

Butler, Joseph C. to Elizabeth S. Lowerre. Logan st. P. M. Dec. 1, installs. 400

Byrant, Thomas B. to The Title Guarantee and Trust Co. Van Buren st, s s, 269.6 e Lewis av, 55.6x100. Nov. 28, demand. 11,000

Same to same. Greene av, n s, 160 w Lewis av, 2 lots, each 20x100. 2 morts., each $5,500. Nov. 28, 3 years, 5 %. 11,000

Same to same. Greene av, n s, 100 w Lewis av, 3 lots, each 20x100. 3 morts., each $5,000. Nov. 28, 3 years, 5 %. 15,000

Byrne, William to Edward Lavin. 18th st, west cor 10th av, 20x80. Dec. 1, 5 years or installs. 2,000

Carter, Mary J. to Crowell Hadden exr. Fannie L. Earle. Grand av. P. M. Nov. 25, 3 years, 5 %. 9,000

Castagniao, Giovanni B. to Jane Potter. Carroll st. P. M. Sub. to mort. $2,500. Nov. 29, installs. 500

Same to The Assured Building Loan Assoc. same property. Nov. 27, installs. 2,500

Cederstrom, Sigfrid to Sophie Shilbock. Carroll st. P. M. Dec. 2, 3 years. 2,250

Chappell, John, Jersey City, N. J., to John T. Bailey, Jr., Tenafly, N. J. Atlantic av, s s, 69.11 w Sackman st, 19.3x100. Nov. 28, due Dec. 1, 1892. 250

Ciorciari, Guiseppe and Venanzia Citera to Ann Treacy. Lorimer st, w s, 75 s Richardson st, 25x100. Nov. 28, 5 years. 550

Chapel, Edward R. to George H. Stone. Dean st. P. M. Nov. 30, 2 years, 5 %. 7,000

Clancy, Peter to The Title Guarantee and Trust Co. Jefferson av. P. M. Dec. 1, 1 year, 5 %. 4,000

Clancy, John M. to The Emigrant Indust. Savings Bank. Sands st, n e cor Bridge st, 50x100 Dec. 2, 1 year, 4½ %. 14,000

Clarke, Thomas to The Title Guarantee and Trust Co. 6th av, s e cor 20th st, 25x80. Nov. 30, 3 years, 5 %. 3,000

Clark, David H. to Adolph Vanrein. Park av, n s, 31 e Portland av, 22x78.8x22.5x83.1. Nov. 28, due July 1, 1892. 550

Cochen, Fred. C. to Mary F. Stoughton extrx. Edwin W. Stoughton. Fort Hamilton av, n w cor 70th st, 61x97.2x60x86.3, New Utrecht. Nov. 18, 1 year. 3,500

Coffin, Abbie E. wife of and Edward H. to Salena Lublin. Sutter av, n w cor Logan st, 100x90. Nov. 24, 2 years. 800

Cohen, Isaac to Jacob H. Werbelovsky. Seigel st. P. M. Nov. 27, 4 years or installs. 2,250

Collins, Mary E. to Peter Kelly. Degraw st. P. M. Dec. 1, installs. 2,400

Condict, Silas A. to Elihu J. Granger. Hopkinson av. P. M. Nov. 19, 2 years, 5 %. 1,200

Conklin, George W. and Brewster to Charles Butzgy. Johnson av. P. M. Nov. 24, 3 years, 5 %. 4,000

Conn, Curtis W. to The People's Trust Co. and Sarah E. Weller trustee Sidney V. Lowell. Franklin av. P. M. Discharged of record. Nov. 24, 1 year, 5 %. 10,000

Conn, Curtis W. to The People's Trust Co. and ano. trustees Alfred T. Weller and Sidney V. Lowell individ Fulton st, s e cor Franklin av. P. M. Nov. 28, 1 year, 5 %. 10,000

Connolly, Catharine C., Winifred and Helena to John R. Pitt. Ralph av, n e cor McDonough st. P. M. 2d mort. Dec. 1, due June 1, 1893. 2,250

Costello, James to James F. O'Rourke. 50th st. P. M. Nov. 30, due Nov. 5, 1898, installs, 5 %. 700

Courtney, Robert P. to S. Charles Welsh trustee for Ethel H. Tweddle. Union st, n s, 140 e 7th av, 21x95. Dec. 2, due Jan. 1, 1895, 5 %. 1,500

Coyle, Catharine to Henry J. Robinson. Waverley av, e s, 153.6 s Fulton st, 6x90. Nov. 25, 3 years, 5 %. 7,000

Crane, Frederick and Sarah F. to Anna M. Ferris. Flatbush. East 7th st, w s, 105.8 s Greenwood av, 49.3x100x20x104.10, Flatbush. Nov 25, due Oct. 5, 1894, 5 %. 300

Cross, Charles A. to Ignatz Martin. Wyckoff av, north cor Troutman st, 25x94.11x25x93.7. Nov. 21, 2 years, 5 %. 1,000

Cummings, Mary A. to Zipporah L. Hollister. Shepherd av. P. M. Nov. 25, 1 year. 257

De Groff, Abraham A. to William S. Moore. Ovington av, n s, 103.6 w Stewart av, 30x170.2, New Utrecht. Oct. 1, 3 years, 5½ %. 3,000

Davids, Nick to John D. Fish, Hempstead, L. I. 3d st. P. M. Nov. 21, 1 year, 5 %. 5,000

Denison, Charles H. to Frederick H. Wiggin and ano. trustees Catherine Lawrence et al. 5th st. P. M. Dec 2, 3 years, 5 %. 4,500

Dillingham, William G. to Peter Gardner. Decatur st. P. M. Dec 1, 2 years. 1,100

Dillon, John J. to James A. and Julia H. Billings trustees Henry M. Billings. 3d av, w s, 60 s Wyckoff st, 2 lots. 2 P. M. morts., each $3,250. Dec. 1, 3 years, 5 %. 6,500

Dodds, William J. to Mary E. Fox. North 6th st. P. M. Nov. 30, 5 years, 5 %. 1,500

Dolan, Mary to James Ward. Metropolitan av, Scott av and Ten Eyck st. ½ of upland shown on map E property of Abraham Vandervoort, 18th Ward, with land under water, &c. P. M. May 8, 1891, 3 years, 5 %. 1,000

Donop, Alwin to Mary H. and William C Kennedy exrs. Thomas Kennedy. Main st, e s, 100 s Plymouth st, 20x104x20.6x96.10. Dec. 1, 1 year, 5 %. 3,000

Driver, William A. and Mary J. his wife to The Title Guarantee and Trust Co. Pulaski st. P. M. Nov. 23, due Nov. 25, 1892, 5 %. 1,000

Drummond, Mary E. to Elizabeth Mackinney, Philadelphia, Pa. Carlton av, e s, 382.11 s Fulton st, 20x100. Nov. 28, due Dec. 1, 1894, 5 %. 2,600

Duy, Ella A. to Mary E. Hall. Clinton st, s e cor Carroll st. P. M. Dec. 1, 5 years or installs, 5 %. 5,700

Eckelkamp, John W. to The Title Guarantee and Trust Co. Sumpter st, s s, 100 w Ralph av, 25x100. Nov. 30, 1 year. 1,200

Egerton, Frances V. to James D. Lynch. 83d st, n e s, 300 n w 23d av, 60x100. Nov. 17, due Nov. 23, 1898, 5 %. 735

Egolf, Edward to Eliza A. Martense, Flatbush. Bay 11th st, n s, 129.3 w Cropsey av, 20x193.4 to Bay 10th st, x200x193.4, New Utrecht. Dec. 2, 3 years, 5 %. 5,000

Engeman, George H., William A. and John J. to Michael F. Dwyer. Plumb Island. Gravesend, that part being w of and adj part now owned by the United States and bounded east thereby, south by Sheepshead Bay, west by Hog Creek and north by Broad Creek. Nov. 20, due Nov. 23, 1893. 20,000

Engert, Charles to Henry Traphagen, Jersey City. Van Pelt st. P. M. Nov. 23, 2 years. 5 %. 2,600

Evans, George to Patrick Farrell. Patchen av, e s, 60 n Decatur st, 20x100. Nov. 19, due March 1, 1892. 500

Evans, Frank H. to Samuel Wells. Hooper st. P. M. Nov. 25, 10 years, 5 %. 4,000

Fairservis, Robert to Cornelius N. Hoagland. Clifton pl, s s, 120.8 e Grand av, 18x100. Nov. 30, due Nov. 1, 1894. 5 %. gold, 4,500

Same to Thomas M. Barr. Same property. Nov. 30, due Dec. 1, 1893. 1,000

Feldberg, Jonas and Sarah Barasch to Edward A. Rawlings. Seigel st, No. 61, n s, 98.6 w Ewen st, 24x100. Nov. 25, demand. 2,833

Fintzel, William, New York, to John H. G. Friedel. Shepherd av. P. M. Nov. 24, 1 year. 1,400

Fish, Julia B. F. wife of and John D. to Horace F. Burroughs. Dean st. P. M. Nov. 21, 1 year. 3,000

Fowler, Mary E. wife of and Levi to Adolph Vanrein. St. Marks av, n s, 280 e Franklin av, 80x128.6. Dec. 1, 1 year or installs. 4,000

Frank, Adam H. to The Title Guarantee and Trust Co. Van Brunt st, w s, 125 s Verona st, 18.9x90. Nov. 27, 2 years, 5 %. 1,000

Franklin, Jane A. to William H. Whiting, Bound Brook, N. J. Van Buren st. P. M. Nov. 28, installs. 1,500

French, Albert L. to Hans S. Christian. 57th st, s s, 200 w 2d av, 20x100.2. Nov. 28, 3 years, 5 %. 2,500

Frost, Mary C. to Georgianna H. Bishop, Philadelphia, Pa. Sumner av, w s, 60 s Quincy st, 20x80. Nov. 30, due Dec. 1, 1894, 5 %. 1,000

Gallin, Samuel to Leopold Michel. Moore st. P. M. Nov. 30, due Oct. 1, 1896, 5 %. 6,500

Garvey, Bernard to John A. Deraismes. Pacific st. P. M. Nov. 23, due Dec. 2, 1896, or sooner, 5 %. 4,000

Gastmeyer, Robert to The Title Guarantee and Trust Co. Evergreen av, s e cor Bimrod st, 20x80. Nov. 30, 3 years, 5 %. 4,000

Gastmeyer, Ernestine wife of and Charles F. to Edmund D. Norris. Eldert st, n w s, 120 n e Evergreen av, 20x100. Nov. 30, 3 years, 5 %. 2,500

Same to same. Eldert st, n w s, 100 n e Evergreen av, 20x100. Nov. 30, 3 years, 5 %. 2,500

Geery, James to John Reis. Av B, n w cor 18th st, 100x100, Flatbush. Dec. 1, 7 months. 200

Same to John McElvery and Robert Getty. Same property. P. M. Nov. 25, 2 years. 1,800

Gload, Adolphus and Lizzie his wife to James Gascoine individ. and with Anna E. Cozine exrs. John G. Cozine. Madison st. P. M. Nov. 2, 6 months. 6,102

Goldsmith, Herman to The East Brooklyn Co-operative Building Assoc. Stockholm st, s s, 125 e Evergreen av, 13.9x100. Nov. 30, installs. 2,500

Granger, Elihu J. to Robert O'Brien. McDougal st, n s, 100 e Stone av, 5 lots. Nov. 23, 2 years, 5 %. 2,000

Same to same. McDougal st, n w cor Stone av, 100x— to Brooklyn and Jamaica pike. P. M. Nov. 23, 2 years, 5 %. 3,000

Green, William to Rose B. wife of Richard S. Hegeman. Baltic st, n s, 80 e Clinton st. P. M. 2d mort. Nov. 25, 3 years, 5 %. 300

Same to The Title Guarantee and Trust Co. Same property. P. M. Nov. 25, 3 years, 5 %. 3,500

Goat, Frederick to Alexander G. Calder. 12th st. P. M. Nov. 24, 3 years, 5 %. 2,000

Gubring, Theodore to Henry A. Beiler and Mary his wife. Central av. P. M. Nov. 30, due Dec. 1, 1898, 5 %. 3,000

Same to same. Same property. P. M. Nov. 30, due Dec. 1, 1895, 5 %. 1,700

Hackradt, Maria wife of Otto to Emeline E. Brower. Harrison av, e s, 25 s Walton st, 25x100. Sub. to mort. $4,500. Nov. 13, due Nov. 30, 1892. 250

Same to same. Willoughby av, s s, 36 w Walworth st. 16x90. Sub. to mort. $2,000. Nov. 13, due Nov. 30, 1892. 250

Hall, Julia wife of and John J. to Frank Hall, Hudson, N. J. Pacific st, n s, 83.4 w Utica av, 16.8x100. Nov. 27, 5 years. 500

Hanse, William F. to The Kings Co-operative Building and Loan Assoc. Lynch st. P. M. Nov. 25, installs. 5,200

Harms, Charles, Jr., to Daniel L. Jones. Devoe st. P. M. Dec. 1, 5 years, 5 %. 3,500

Haug, William to Johann G. and Wilhelmina Haug. Jerome st, n w cor Blake av, 40x100. Nov. 23, due Jan. 1, 1897, 4 %. 2,000

Haviland, Charles A. to The Title Guarantee and Trust Co. Tompkins av; Madison st. P. M. Nov. 24, due Nov. 25, 1894, 5 %. 5,000

Hawkins, William to The Nassau Land and Imp't Co. 14th st. P. M. Nov. 30, 1 year, 5 %. 8,000

Hayes, Pauline E. to Bernhard Munch. South 4th st. P. M. Nov. 25, 5 years, 5 %. 5,300

Hearms, Henry C. to John Brown. South 1st and Hooper sts. P. M. Nov. 21, 3 years. 3,000

Same to Helena Schneider. Hooper st, n w s, 95 n e South 2d st; Hooper st, n w s, 45 s w South 1st st. P. M. Nov. 21, due Dec. 31, 1896, 5 %. 2,000

Heckle, J. Henry to The Williamsburgh Savings Bank. Williams av, e s, 99.5 s Atlantic av, 20.3x100. Dec. 1, 1 year, 5 %. 2,750

Hegeman, Rose B., Flatbush, to Aletta B. Brown, Flatlands, L. I. Flatbush av, Flatlands. P. M. Oct. 1, 5 years, 5 %. 8,000

Hein, Ferdinand R. to Caspar Spiess. South 3d st. P. M. Nov. 30, 1 year, 5 %. 3,000

Hicks, Charles S. to Isidor Stern. Barbey st. P. M. Nov 25, installs. 500

Hildreth, Joseph to James G. Roberts. Macon st. P. M. Nov. 23, installs. 2,185

Hill, Henry B. to John Peirer. McDonough st, s s, 249 s w Patchen av, 4 lots, each 18x100. 4 morts., each $500. Nov. 27, 1 year. 2,000

Holland, George to Rudolph and Otto E. Reimer. Hancock st, n s, 91.8 w Ralph av, 19.11x85. 2d mort. Nov. 21, 1 year. 550

Holland, George to Martha K. Chaffee. Hancock st, n s, 91.8 w Ralph av, 19.11x85. Oct. 31, 3 years, 5 %. 2,750

Same to same. Hancock st, n s, 111.7 w Ralph av, 16.8x85. Oct. 31, 3 years, 5 %. 2,000

Hover, Lorinda to George W. Forsyth. Penn st, n s, 243.1 e Wythe av, 20x100. Oct. 2, 3 years, 5½ %. 3,000

Ingham, William A. and John M. Butler to The Title Guarantee and Trust Co. 5th av, n w cor 28th st, 100x350. Secures bonds of Brooklyn, Bath & West End R. R. Nov. 13. ——

Same to same. 5th av, west cor 27th st, 100.2x350; Lot at New Utrecht, 167 n e Main st, runs northeast 182 x northwest 103 x northeast 99.8 x northwest 104 x southwest 33 x south 327.9; also, gore lot adj lands Jacques Barre, runs northeast 95 to line of way of Brooklyn, Bath & West End R. R., x south 123 x northwest 78; Tract of meadow land at Gravesend, adj lands of Sarah Benson, 5 25-100 acres; Tract of meadow land abutting on road from Gravesend to Gravesend Beach and old Mill road, 3½ acres; also 1 acre adj lands of Garret W. Cropsey and part lots 20 and 21 map common lands, Gravesend, contains 5 acres; also part lots 19A and 21 and all lot 18A same map, 6 8-10 acres. Secures bonds of same Co. Nov. 13. ——

Jaeger, Charles to Andrew and Christian Hahn. Harman st, s s, 125 e Central av, 25x100. Nov. 24, due Nov. 30, 1896, 5 % 1,700

Jaraschow, Anna to Abraham Wischinsky and Harris Rosenberg. Morell st, w s, 25 s Moore st, 25x100. Nov. 19, installs, 5 %. 1,500

Jaquet, Rachel and Emma heirs Auguste Jaquet to Patrick H. Howlin. Willoughby av, s s, 25 e Sandford st, 25x70. Dec. 1, 3 years, 5 %. 2,000

Jennings, Joseph D. to Harris J. Latta. Weirfield st, n w s, 117.8 n e Evergreen av. P. M. Sub. to mort. $22,064. Nov. 2, 6 months. 5,200

Same to same. Same property. Nov. 2, 6 months. 22,064

Johnson, David W. to New York Produce Exchange Bank. 20th st, s s, 100 w 4th av, 25x80. Sub. to mort. $2,000. Nov. 28, note. 1,600

Johnsen, Anders to Frank A. Barnaby, Charles D. Burwell and Susan E. Fingarr. 5th st. P. M. Dec. 2, installs, 5 %. 1,100

Joppert, Margaret to John Zipp. Ocean Parkway, n e cor Webster av, —x100 to point 523.3 w 1st st, Flatbush. Nov. 24, due Jan. 2, 1892. 1,138

Kaiser, William J. to Charles E. Larned. Lafayette av, n s, 200 e Stuyvesant av. P. M. Nov. 30, 1 year, 5 %. 6,000

Kaplan, Elias to Isaac Marx. Watkins st, w s, 225 s Belmont av, 49.9x100. Nov. 25, 1 year. 1,600

Kaplan, Nathan to Carrie L. Winne. Bay 28th st and 86th st, New Utrecht. P. M. Nov. 25, due Dec. 1, 1894, 5 %. 1,400

Kane, Mary to George S. Wheeler exr. Nancy B. Wheeler. President st. P. M. Nov. 24, 5 years. 1,200

Kelly, Annie heir John Dunn to Streeter & Denison. Walworth st, No 68, n e cor Park av, 25x100. Nov. 25, 1 year. 675

Keogh, Thomas to Edward M. Townsend exr. Belinda R. Townsend. Smith st. P. M. Nov. 30, due Dec 1, 1893. 1,000

Keyburn, Agnes widow to The Title Guarantee and Trust Co. Jefferson av. P. M. Dec. 1, 3 years, 5 %. 4,000

Keystone National Savings, Loan and Investment Assoc. to James M. Brady. St. Marks av. P. M. Nov. 2, installs, 5 %. 7,500

Kirby, Joseph M. to Bulmer Lumber Co. (Lim.) Decatur st, n s, 100 e Howard av, 86.8x100. 2d mort. Nov. 25, demand. 800

Kornder, Emma C. wife of and Philip J. to Herman Posbergh. Fulton st, n e cor Adelphi st. P. M. Sub. to mort. $12,000. Dec. 1, 5 years, 5 %. 6,000

Same to Henry P. Hendrickson. Same property. P. M. Dec. 1, 3 years, 5 %. gold. 12,000

Kreppel, Charles C. to Daniel Bradley. Irving av. P. M. Dec. 2, 2 years, 5 %. 1,200

Langston, Isabella wife of and Frederick B. to Annetta C. Bergen. Lafayette av, No. 552, s s, 574.9 e Bedford av, 25.3x100. Dec. 1, 2 years. 3,000

Le Beau, Theodore M. to Albert V. B. Voorhies. Chestnut st, e s, 474 s Jamaica av, 50x150. Nov. 30, 3 years. 2,000

Le Beau, Theodore M. to Annetta C. wife of Teunis H. Bergen. Ashford st, e s, 225 s Ridgewood av, 25x100. Nov. 28, 3 years. 8,000

Lee, Mary A. to Henry Roth and Joseph E. Middle. Macon st. P. M. Nov. 30, 3 years, 5 %. 1,000

Levine, Benjamin E. to Frederick A. Meyer and Annie C. his wife. Eckford st. P. M. Nov. 30, 3 years, 5 %. 2,000

Lippmann, Leopold J. to Thomas C. Balderston et al. Supreme trustees of the Order of Tonti. Halsey st, n w s, 80 s w Central av, 10 lots, each 20x100. 10 morts., each $3,000. Dec. 1, 3 years, 5 4-10 %. 30,000

Same to William Laytin et al. trustees William Laytin. Central av, south cor Weirfield st. runs southeast 200 to Halsey st, x southwest 80 x northwest 100 x southwest 200 x northwest 100 to Weirfield st, x northeast 280. Dec. 1, 1 year. 12,500

Love, Mary J. wife of John, Jr., Germantown, Pa., to The Title Guarantee and Trust Co. Clason av, e s, 60.8 n Lexington av, 19.1x80. Nov. 27, due Nov. 30, 1894, 5 %. 3,500

Lynch, Mary E. to Jonathan Ogden exr. and trustee Margt. H. Senford dec'd. Fulton st, e s, 40.9 n York st, 38.9x107.6 to James st, x 38.9x106.8 in four courses, excepting part taken for bridge purposes. Nov. 21, due Dec. 1, 1893, 5 %. 10,000

Liptrott, Robert to John H. McCoy. Broadway. P. M. Dec. 1, 3 years, 5 %. 5,500

Mackay, Charles D. to David F. Manning. Quincy st. P. M. Nov. 21, installs. 2,800

Mannheimer, Robert to Susan A. Elliott, Flushing, L. I. Livingston st. P. M. Nov. 28, 3 years, 5 %. 8,500

Martin, Robert S. and Mary H. his wife to Robert Onderdonk. Skillman av, n s, 125 e Lorimer st, 16.8x100. Nov. 16, 1887, 5 years. 1,600

Martin, Leonhard to George Hagenmuller and Barbara his wife. Boerum st. P. M. Dec. 1, 3 years or installs, 5 %. 3,100

Matthews, John T. to Francis E. Clark. Hooper st. P. M. Dec. 1, 1 year. 900

Maurer, Ulrich, Adolf J. Jacobsen and Christian H. Meller to Charles J. Patterson. 3d av, n e cor 96th st, if continued, 104x167.2x100x138.8, New Utrecht. Nov. 27, 1 year. 2,000

McCarthy, Henry A. to Charles M. Marsh, Morris Plains, N. J. Union st, n s, 191.10 e 4th av, 2 lots, each 25x95. 2 morts., each $2,000. Nov. 25, 2 years. 4,000

Same to same. Union st, n s, 366.10 e 4th av, 25x95. Nov. 25, 2 years. 500

McCord, Anna W. to Andrew D. Baird. Stuyvesant av, w s, 22.8 s Halsey st, 19.2x80.6. Nov. 30, 1 year. 400

McNamara, John to The Title Guarantee and Trust Co. Dean st, s s, 120 e Smith st, 20x100. Dec. 2, 3 years, 5 %. 6,500

McCormick, George W. to Hall, Sash and Door Co. Reid av, w s, 50 n Halsey st, 50x100. Nov. 30, demand. 1,200

McKiernan, Catharine wife of and Peter and Margaret wife of Perico A. Canavello to Charles A. Canavello, Englewood, N. J. President st, s w s, 121.6 n w Columbia st, 21.5x100; 1st pl, s s, 250 e Court st, 25x100, with all title to court yard in front. Nov. 23, 3 years. 2,000

Meehan, Michael to Mary J. Kamp, New York. 56th st, n s, 85 w 4th av, 125x100.2. Nov. 25, 3 years, 5 %. 3,500

Mehrmann, Maria M. to John Buick. Magnolia st, s e s, 100 s w Central av, 25x100. Nov. 20, due Jan. 1, 1893, 5 % 900

Merlin, Walter B. to James Gillen. South Portland av. P. M. Nov. 24, installs. 5 %. 2,800

Merritt, Jr., Francis to John P. Free. Essex st. P. M. Nov. 1, installs 1,100

Metcalfe, Fannie E. to The Bank Clerks' Co-operative Building and Loan Assoc. 22d st, s s, 150 w 5th av, 25x100. Nov. 23, installs. 3,000

Meyer, Henry and Jonas Feldberg to Sarah H. Powell, New York. Seigel st, n s, 146 6 w Ewen st, 25x100. Nov. 25, 3 years, 5 %. 7,500

Same to same. Seigel st, n s, 170.6 w Ewen st, 24x100. Nov. 25, 3 years, 5 %. 7,500

Same to Mary Ett Colyer, North Hempstead, L. I. Seigel st, n s, 98.6 w Ewen st, 24x100. Nov. 25, 3 years, 5 %. 7,500

Meyer, Henry to Edward A. Rawling. Seigel st, Nos. 55 and 57, n s, 146 6 w Ewen st, 48x100. Nov. 25, demand. 4,667

Miller, William J. C. to Samuel M. Meeker exr. Frederick Herr. De Kalb av, n s, 150 w Tompkins av, 50x100. Nov. 30, 1 year, 5 %. 2,000

Mills, Mary F. wife of Robert J. to William R. Bennett. 1st av, w s, at intersection with centre line bet 77th and 78th sts, runs west 35 x north — x east to av, x south 109.5, New Utrecht. Nov. 27, 2 years. 1,500

Minden, Morris to Leopold Michel. Cook st. P. M. Nov. 24, 5 years. 3,600

Minto, Robert F. to Charles M. Marsh, Morris Plains, N. J. Bainbridge st. P. M. Nov. 30, demand. 86,225

Mintz, Rose to Joseph Mentz and Barnard Rubenstein. Grand st. P. M. Nov. 24, 2 years, 5 %. 5,000

Morgenthaler, Jacob to Zimri West, Orange, N. J. Lincoln road, Flatbush. P. M. Nov. 30, 5 years, 5 %. 9,000

Muir, Mary J to Samuel T. Stewart. Atlantic av, n s, 75 e Bradford st, 25x109.9x25x109.10. Nov. 24, 5 years. 500

Munson, Louis to John Cowenhoven. 11th av, w s, 120 s 67th st, 20x100. Nov. 28, 5 years. 1,400

Murphy, Eva to Margaret Cudmore. McDonough st, s s, 181.8 w Ralph av, 18.4x100. Nov. 28, due Dec. 1, 1894. 2,000

Murphy, James F. to John Egan. 57th st. P. M. Dec. 1, 5 years, 5 %. 1,700

Nodoolman, Hyman to Ernst and Christina Henken. Schenck av. P. M. Nov. 24, 5 years, 5 %. 4,000

Nolan, Thomas to John Williamson. 3d av, s w cor 49th st, 100x200. Nov. 25, due Feb. 1, 1892, 5 %. 12,000

Nowlan, Daniel P. to Henry C. Heyser. Barbey st. P. M. Nov. 28, installs, 5 %. 750

O'Connor, John to The City Savings Bank, Brooklyn. 6th av, s w cor 20th st, 24x62. Nov. 25, due Nov. 1, 1893, 5 %. 2,000

Same to same 6th av, w s, 24 s 20th st, 4 lots, each 19x62 4 morts., each $1,000. Nov. 25, due Nov. 1, 1893, 5 %. 4,000

Oltmanns, Andrew to Alexander G. Calder. 7th av, west cor 19th st. P. M. Sub. to mort. $6,000. Dec. 1, installs. 5 % 2,750

Same to Charles Cory. Same property. Dec. 1, 3 years, 5 %. 6,000

Osborn, Mary C. widow to The Title Guarantee and Trust Co. Willoughby av, s e cor Clinton av, 200 to Waverly av, x171. Nov. 9, demand. 100,000

Owen, Samuel F. to Joseph R. Clark. Broadway, n e s, 25 s e Ditmars st, —x100x23.4x100. Nov. 24, 1 year. 6,000

O'Neill, Anne to Henry Wagner. 20th st, s s, 160 w 4th av, 25x100. Nov. 5, 5 years, 5 %. 1,000

Parmer, Ada wife of and Lewis to Mary W. Smith. Watkins st, w s, 100 s Eastern Parkway, 28.6x100. Nov. 28, demand. 400

Peiser or Piser, Jacob and Harris Wolf to John Damon. Seigel st, n s, 122.6 w Ewen st, 24x100. Nov. 25, 3 years, 5 %. 7,500

Pedersen, Margarethe Z. to Susan Moynehan, Annie E. Hartt and Claudia Murphy. Gravesend Beach to Gravesend village road, Gravesend. P. M. Nov. 27, due Dec. 1, 1896, 5 %. 1,000

Same to Henry H. Adams, Treasurer Kings County. Same property. P. M. Nov. 27, due Dec. 1, 1896, 5 %. 1,000

Perpall, Anna E., Flatbush, to Daniel S Miller. Winthrop st, Flatbush. P. M. 2d mort. Nov. 1, due Dec. 1, 1894, 5 %. 2,000

Same to Isaac E Holbrook. Same property. P. M. Nov. 1, due Dec. 1, 1894, 5 %. 2,000

Pfalzgraf, Hanz C. to Magdalene Cowenhoven. 59th st, n e s, 420 n w 17th av, 60x100.2, New Utrecht. Nov. 6, 3 years. 3,000

Phillips, George to Anna A. and Adeline Garrison. Hancock st, n s, 280 e Nostrand av, 20x100. Nov. 27, due Nov. 1, 1896, 5 %. 2,000

Pietchman, Joseph to Adolph Sussman. Hegeman av. P. M. Aug. 15, 3 years. 190

Pinckney, Jane A. wife of Charles C. to The Brooklyn Savings Bank. New York av, e s, 208.8 s Herkimer st, runs east 100 x south 1.10 x east 100 x south 25 x west 200 to av, x north 26.10. Nov. 30, 1 year, 5 %. 5,000

Perkl, John to Thomas P. Graham. North 10th st. P. M. Dec. 2, due Dec. 1, 1892. 1,500

Prince, Herman and Emma his wife mortgagors with Henry Waterman mortgagee. Extension of mort. Nov. 21. nom

Pucillo, Donato and Maria, Giambattista and Margherita Maurella to Gaetano Manganaro. Maspeth av. P. M. Nov. 25, due Nov. 30, 1896, 5 %. 2,000

Quinn, Patrick E. to The South Brooklyn Savings Inst. Wyckoff st, s s, 235 w Bond st, 20x100 Nov. 28, 1 year, 5 %. 500

Radcliffe, Thomas H. to Jacob C. Bergen. Decatur st, n s, 333.4 w Howard av, 18.4x100. Sub. to mort. $4,500. Nov. 16, 1 year. 800

Ransom, James F. to Robert Miller. 10th st, n s, 157 10 w 8th av, 40x100. Nov. 11, note. 505

Ratigan, John to Michael Kamp. St. Marks av, n s, 150 w Grand av, 25x164.6x26.6x173. Nov. 24, due Nov. 1, 1894. 500

Rawson, Emma A. wife of Horace B. to Nellie wife of George H. Russell. Jefferson av. P. M. Nov. 30, due Dec. 1, 1894, 5 %. 5,000

Reineking, Emil to John H. Vanderveer. Lot 198 block F map Vanderveer homestead. Dec. 1, 3 years. 500

Reineking, Emil to Albert H. W. Van Siclen. Bristol st, w s, 90 n Eastern Parkway, 20x123 Nov. 30, 3 years, 1,800

Raymond, Benjamin C. and Annie E. his wife to Horatio S. Stewart and Bernard Levino. Macon st, n w cor Ralph av, 22x100. Dec. 2, demand. 800

Raymond, Benjamin C. to Horatio S. Stewart. Macon st, n w cor Ralph av, 22x100. Nov. 10, demand. 1,234

Remson, Isaac S. to Charles E. Harris. Maujer st, n s, 175 e Humboldt st, 23x100. Nov. 28, 5 years, 5 %. 2,000

Reuter, Conrad to John G. Jenkins et al. trustees William Laytin. Jefferson st, s e s, 150 n e Knickerbocker av, 25x100. Nov. 25, due Nov. 1, 1894, 5 %. 3,000

Reynolds, Charles G. to Elizabeth M. wife of Williamson Rapalye. McDonough st, s s, 303 e Reid av, 17.8x100. Nov. 25, 3 years, 5 %. 4,500

Riley, Mary T. wife of and George T. to Coleman Benedict. Flatbush av. w s, 22.8 s Prospect pl, runs west 26.8 x southwest 65.3 x east 16 x northeast 53.8 x east 27.9 to av, x north 20. Nov. 23, due Dec. 1, 1894, 5 %. 6,000

Rippingale, Charles J. to William Harkness. Carlton av. P. M. Nov. 30, due Dec. 1, 1894, 5 %. 3,000

Ritson, Tom A. to James D. Lynch. 22d av, New Utrecht. P. M. Nov. 28, due Nov. 30, 1892, 5 %. 2,000

Robb, James R. to Stephen B. Sturges. 21st st, n s, 220.9 e 6th av, 32x100. Nov. 17, demand. 1,500

Robbins, William H. H. to Charles M. Marsh, Morris Plains, N. J. Lafayette pl, e s, 198.7 n Atlantic av, 38x100. Nov. 30, demand. 2,500

Roberts, Sarah M. to The West Brooklyn Land and Impt. Co. 45th st, New Utrecht. P. M. Nov. 18, due Aug. 29, 1894, 5 %. 420

Roberts, Wyatt B. and Archie B to John O. Whitenack. Rockaway av. P. M. Nov. 27, 1½ years, 5 %. 450

Robinson, Carman A. to Charles A. Berton, Richmond Hill, L. I. Lorimer st. P. M. Nov. 24, 4 years, 5 %. 2,000

Rose, Hannah M. to Clarence E. Homan. Cooper st. s e s, 250 n e Evergreen av, 19x100. Nov. 28, due May 1, 1893. 550

Same to Augustus S. Bedell. Cooper st, s e s, 269 n e Evergreen av, 58.6x100. Nov. 28, due May 1, 1892. 1,084

Rosenblum, Simon and Joseph L. Werbelovsky to Jacob H. Werbelovsky. Moore st. P. M. Nov. 24, 2 years. 1,500

Royle, Robert J. to James Fallon. High st, s s, 225 e Bridge st, 25x95 to alley with use of same. Nov. 25, due Jan. 4, 1892. 350

Ruddermann, Elias to Jacob W. Erreger. Osborn st. P. M. Sept. 15, 3 years. 2,000

Ruge, John G. and Charlotta W. his wife to Annie Heidt. Bartlett st. P. M. Nov. ^, 5 years, 5 %. 2,500

Scheep, William to The Title Guarantee and Trust Co. Broadway. P. M. Dec. 1, 3 years, 5 %. 8,000

Schilling, John A. to William M. Burr et al. exrs. Calvin Burr. 5th av. P. M. Feb. 5, 1890, due Nov. 1, 1894, 5 %. 4,000

Schlitz, John to Mary R. Bennett, New York. Moore st, s s, 150 w Graham av, 50x100. Nov. 25, 3 years. 7,000

Schliviuski, Hyman and Hyman Schwartz to Peter Mayer. Varet st. P. M. Dec. 1, 5 years, 5 %. 16,000

Schneider, John to George D. Koch and Frederick Koerner. Knickerbocker av. P. M. Nov. 25, 5 years. 1,400

Scholey, Thomas J. to William Grandy. Herkimer st, s s, 145 e Utica av, 30x185.6. Nov. 27, due Dec. 1, 1896. 3,000

Schweikert, Friederke to Charles J. Jonas. Bushwick av, s w s, 60 n w Weirfeld st, 20x75. Nov. 30, due Dec. 1, 1892, 5 %. 4,000

Scott, John R. and George J. Carney to D. & M. Chauncey Real Estate Co. (Lim.) 4th av, east cor 12th st, 19x80. Oct. 23, demand. 25,000

Same to John Adamson. Same property. Sub. to last mort. Oct. 23, demand. 10,000

Scott, Mary A. wife of and Edward S. to John Robertson. Bedford av, n w s, 40 s w North 7th st, 20x80. Dec. 1, 3 years, 5 %. 7,000

Seaman, James E. to John F. Vrooman. Powell st. P. M. Nov. 30, installs. 750

Seymour, Alice C. wife of and Charles W. to The Title Guarantee and Trust Co. President st, n e s, 260.5 s e 5th av, 17.9x95. Nov. 16, 3 years, 5 %. 3,500

Sibley, Harry A. to Theodore and William Kilian. Quincy st, s s, 193.9 w Throop av, 18.9 x100. Nov. 27, due Dec. 1, 1892. 2,000

Siedler, Charles, Morristown, N. J., to Charles G. Spencer. Raymond st, w s, 75 s Bolivar st, 25x75. Dec. 1, 3 years or installs. 6,000

Siller, George W. to The New Utrecht Co-operative Building and Loan Assoc. Hamilton av, s e s, 150 n e Atlantic av, 50x116.3. New Utrecht. Oct. 13, installs, 5 %. 2,500

Simis, Adolph, Jr., to Kings Co. Trust Co. Brooklyn av, s e cor Park pl, 255 to Butler st, x150. Nov. 27, due Dec. 1, 1892. 14,000

Skiff, Emma McG. wife of Paul C. to Alexander H. Ritchie. Release and satisfaction of mort. Nov. 27. nom

Smith, Henry to Charles D. King. Chauncey st, s s, 249 e Saratoga av, 19x100. Sub. to mort. $4,000. Nov. 16, 1 year. 850

Same to Fannie McDonald Mead. Same property. Nov. 16, 3 years. 4,000

Smith, Mary to Matilda Sussman. Cleveland st, e s, 330 s New Lots road, 8x100. Sept. 1, 6 months. 1,500

Same to Adolph Sussman. Same property. P. M. Sept. 1, 6 months. 1,200

Smith, Henry T. to Alexander G. Calder. 12th st. P. M. Dec. 1, installs, 5 %. 2,350

Same to same. 12th st. P. M. Dec. 1, 2 years or installs, 5 %. 2,350

Sloane, James P. to The Title Guarantee and Trust Co. India st. P. M. Dec. 2, 3 years, 5 %. 3,000

Snyder, William to Hutchings Bath Co. Lee av, s w cor Taylor st. P. M. Dec. 1, 2 years, 5 %. 3,500

Soloweitzik, Jacob to Abraham Libowitz. Eastern Parkway, n s, 125 e Thatford av, 28.7x100x28.9x100. Nov. 17, 3 years. 900

Speck, Frank G., Emma L. Terwilliger widow and Frances M. Henry widow to Alexander S. Clarke trustee Sarah E. Carter. Fort Greene pl, e s, 416.6 s Hanson pl, 20.6x100. Nov. 19, 1 year. 3,500

Stahlberg, Mathilda to Hans S. Pfalzgraf, New Utrecht. 59th st, New Utrecht. P. M. Nov. 27, due Nov. 30, 1892, 5 %. 800

Steinberg, Annie to Lewis Hurst. Stone av. P. M. Nov. 24, 3 years. 500

Steves, Richard S. to John Leech, Jamaica, L. I. Van Buren st, s s, 237.9 w Throop av, 18x100. Nov. 19, due Nov. 1, 1894, 5 %. 3,000

Stokes, Thomas to Matilda S. Taylor. St. Johns pl, s s, 140.2 w 6th av, 20x119.3x20x118.1. Nov. 1, 1 year, 5 %. 5,000

Stone, Harriet F. to Jennie A. Rhodes. Monroe st, n s, 350 e Lewis av, 15x100. July 6, 1 year. 400

Storch, Reinold and Bertha his wife to Henry Reuschenberg. Gwinnett st, n w s, 122 n e Harrison av, 22x100. Oct. 31, due Dec. 20, 1894, 5 %. 2,500

Stumpf, Louis and William to Minnie Trautmann. Johnson av. P. M. Nov. 30, 1 year, 5 %. 1,000

Sundel, Elek, Gerson Krakower and Nathan Goldberg to Harris Levy. Moore st. Oct. 15, 3 months. See Conveys. 4,000

Swain, Spencer to Eunice M. Rawson. Lewis av, e s, 130 s Lafayette av, 20x100. Nov. 19, 1 year, 5 %. 500

Swayze, Caroline widow to Mary Kinahan. Herkimer st, s s, 165 w Buffalo av, 15x89.9. Nov. 25, due Nov. 1, 1893. 1,000

Swimm, Theodore W. to The Title Guarantee and Trust Co. Jefferson av, s s, 80 e Lewis av, 3 lots, each 21x100. 3 morts., each $7,500. Dec. 2, 1 year, 5 %. 22,500

Taylor, George E. and Sophia his wife to Henry H. Adams, Treasurer of Kings Co. Dresden st, e s, 250 n Ridgewood av, 50x100. Dec. 1, 1 year. 1,500

Taylor, Catherine to Luther G. Corwith. Huron st. P. M. Nov. 28, due Dec. 1, 1893. 500

Same to Annie M. Brady. Same property. P. M. Nov. 28, due Dec. 1, 1893, 5½ %. 2,500

The Sea Beach and Brighton R. R. Co. to Alrick H. Man and George W. Wingate trustees. All railroad lines, rights, properties and franchises. March 30, 1888, bonds. gold, 30,000

The New York Outing Club to Henry Offerman. Cropsey av, n e s, part lots 35 and 36 map 28 building sections at Bath Beach, 100.8 x412x100.8x415; Cropsey av, n e s, lot 24 same map, 65x295. Dec. 2, 5 years or installs. 15,000

Thorning, Harry to The South Brooklyn Co-operative Building and Loan Assoc. 34th st. P. M. Dec. 1, installs. 3,400

Thorne, Robert to Nellie C. Van Reypen. Stuyvesant av, s w cor McDonough st, 100x120; Macon st, n s, 219 w Stuyvesant av, 18x100; McDonough st, s s, 180 w Stuyvesant av, 20x100; also all title in estate of Frederick M. Cooper dec'd. All title. Nov. 28, due Nov. 1, 1893, or sooner. gold, 600

Turner, Anson W. to Christian Hunken. Evergreen av and Madison st. P. M. Nov. 24, 3 years, 5 %. 2,500

Ungerland, Henry to Henry Uihlein. Howard av, w s, 85.1 n St. Marks av, 64.3x101.9. Nov. 25, 2 years, 5 %. 600

Walmsley, Joseph H. to The Henry McShane Mfg. Co., Baltimore City. Provost st, w s, 25 s Freeman st, 75x100. Nov. 18, notes. 2,433

Warner, James to Charles R. Miller, Newtown, L. I. East 98th st, e s, 150 s Av G, 30.8x100 x30.7x100. Nov. 11, installs. 950

Watson, Rose Mary wife of William A. to Melvin Brown. Montgomery st. P. M. Dec. 1, 5 years. 1,000

Weiner, Louis and Lena his wife to William Wheeler. Blake av, n w cor Linwood st, 46x78x46x80. Nov. 27, due Dec. 1, 1894. 2,200

Wellerson, Isidor and Philip Rhein to Jacob Manneschmidt. Weirfield st. P. M. 2d mort. Nov. 27, installs. 1,600

Same to William Laytin et al. trustees William Laytin dec'd. Same property. Nov. 27, 3 years, 5 %. 2,300

Werstein, Mary G. to Hellen M. Phillips. North 2d st, n s, near 8th st, lot 283 and part lot 282 map of Edward Frost et al., 25x53x30 x59.8. Nov. 23, 3 years. 2,500

Wheelwright, Charles W. to Asa W. Parker, New Hamburgh, N. Y. Lafayette av, s s, 273 e Grand av. P. M. Dec. 1, 3 years, 5 %. 18,000

Same to same. Lafayette av, s e, 146 e Grand av. P. M. Dec. 1, 3 years, 5 % 18,000

Winterrath, Frank to Henry Schlachter. Stockholm st. P. M. Dec. 1, 3 years, 5 %. 360

Williams, Carrie K. to Seventeenth Ward Bank, Brooklyn. Leonard st, w s, 190 n Nassau av, 16x100. Nov. 21, 4 months. 850

Williams, Percy G. to Title Guarantee and Trust Co. State st, n s, 125 e 3d av, 80x64.6x 87.5x100. Nov. 23, due Nov. 25, 1892, 5 %. 14,000

Winchester, William H. to Elbert Hegeman, Jr. Prospect av, n e s, 185.3 s e 4th av, 25x 80. Nov. 27, due Dec. 1, 1894, 5 %. 4,000

Windhorst, Ferdinand E. to Mary L. Windhorst. Erasmus st, s e cor Johnson pl if extended, 25x150, Flatbush. Sub. to morts. $2,500. Nov. 19, 3 years. 2,500

Winton, Louisa E. to George F. Rogers. Pineapple st. P. M. Dec. 1, 3 years, 5 %. 5,000

Same to Elizabeth Krapp. Same property. Sub. to last mort. Dec. 1, due Jan. 1, 1894. 800

Wolf, Harris and Jacob Peiser to Henry Meyer. Seigel st. P. M. Nov. 25, installs. 5,000

Yungk, Anna wife of and John to "Ernest Ochs." Meserole st, n s, 275 w Waterbury st, 25x100. Nov. 25, 1 year, 5 %. 1,500

MORTGAGES---ASSIGNMENTS.

NEW YORK CITY.

November 27 to December 3—Inclusive.

Bader, Betty to Minnie Junemann. $1,000

Baldwin, Sarah J. Y. to Joseph W. Dugliss. 10,300

Buttenwieser, Joseph L to Bernhard Klingenstein. 16,000

Blackwell, Robert W. former exr. and trustee James M. Mills to Franklin Trust Co. as trustee for Ellen M. Blackwell. order of Court

Bittiner, Simon to Arthur Bittiner. nom

Campbell, James P. to Mary A. Hanigan extrx. Phillips Weeks. nom

Chappell, Bartholomew B. to Theresa Faron, Woodhaven, L. I. 375

Cornell, Margaret C. to Maria W. Gifford. nom

Coleman, Robert H. trustee for Anne C. Rogers to Frederic J. Middlebrook. 6 assigns. consid. omitted

Same to same. 30,750

Same to Thomas C. T. Crain. consid. omitted

Carnes, Harriet to John A. Weekes. 3,526

Clark, Jessie, Cornwall-on-Hudson, to Jessie C. McBride. 2,000

Civill, Lewis A., Colorado Springs, Col., to Acton T. Civill, Bovina Centre, N. Y. 15,500

Cordts, Eibe D. to Roger V. Bonnell. 766

Cruger, James P., Newburgh, N. Y., to the trustees of St. Stephens College, of Annandale, N. Y. 8,500

Decker, John W. to R. Clarence Dorsett. nom

Dress, Christina formerly Gross individ. and extrx. Jacob Gross to Henry Gross. gift

Elias, Cecilia, Buffalo, to Emily Beaver. 5,000

Freeman, Frank J. to Alice I. Connoly. 4,000

Ford, Henry W. trustee Augustus H. Ward dec'd to William N. Crane trustee. 3 assigns., each $12,000. 36,000

French, William A. and ano. admrs. Isaac S. Cruft to Charles E. Strong. 12,000

Froehlich, Bellina to Joseph C Levi trustee. 9,000

Goldstein, Dora to Moses Valentine and Jacob Rabinowitz. 1,590

Gaylord, Don A. to John F. Eustis. nom

Germania Life Ins. Co. of New York to James F. Pierce, sup't of the Insurance Department of New York. 2 assigns. nom

German-American Real Estate Title Guarantee Co. to The People's Trust Co. 17,000

German-American Real Estate Title Guarantee Co. to James A. and Edwin D. Trowbridge trustees for Mary A. Davis. 12,500

Glass, Henry H. to Alfred L. White. 5,000

Ginger, Franzisca extrx. Wilhelmina Lust to Ellen H. Cotheal. 3,500

Hyatt, George E., Brooklyn to Frederick A. Snow. nom

Hyatt, George E., Brooklyn, to Frederick A. Snow. nom

Henschel, Kaufman to Raphael Kuschewsky. 2,000

Same to same. 2,000

Hill, Frank, Llewellyn Park, N. J., to Frederick T. Hill. 2 assigns. nom

Hinklein, Jacob to George Pries. 2,008

Isham, William B. to James R. Smith. nom

Jennings, John W. trustee to Grenville M. Dodge. 2 assigns. nom

Keck, Karoline, Brooklyn, to Georgeanna Fricke. 1,000

Knoeppel, Christine, Williamsbridge, N. Y., to Elizabeth Heilman, Williamsbridge, N. Y. 450

Kahn, German to Irving S. Charig. 1,500

Ketcham, James W. to Meyer L. Sire. 6,000

Katte, Walter and Walter J. to William E. Haws trustee. nom

Levin, Marks to John Ahrens exr. Gesche Meyer. 4,350

Larocque, Joseph to Henry C. Tinker, Warren N. Goddard and Henry B. Anderson. 3 assigns. nom

Lydecker, Charles E., Public Administrator, as admr. will annexed of Hermann Beine to Bernandine Edel admrx. of Mary Beine. 2 assigns. nom

Marshall, Margaret and ano. exrs. Robert Marshall to Charles R. Stilwell. 10,000

Martin, Lydia F., Woodbridge, N. J., to The Union County Bank, Rahway, N. J. 1,500

Mayer, Bernhard to Jacob Klingerstein. 1,500

McCabe, James J. to Charles Dexheimer. 2,350

Meyer, Henry to Henry Waters. consid. omitted

Middlebrook, Frederic J., Brooklyn, to George A. Treadwell trustee. val. consid

Same to Clara R. Gerken. 10,035

Middlebrook, Frederic J., Brooklyn, to James N. Platt and ano. trustees of Eliza B. Garrett. 10,003

Middlebrook, Frederic J., Brooklyn, to The Hudson River Bank. 30,000

Meyer, Oscar R. to Frederick Aldhous. 5,012

Marx, Davis to Thomas Barnett. 6,000

Morgenthau, Henry to Oscar R. Meyer. nom

Norz, Martin to James Haggerty. 2,500

Opdyke, William S. and George F. to William S. and Charles W. Opdyke trustees. 6,000

Peck, Lois A. and ano. exrs Albert L. Peck to Annie L. Peck, Patterson, N. Y. nom

Philp, James to John Hartford. 3,300

Phyfe, Amy C. to Eliza S. Bibby, Baltimore, Md. 4,000

Same to William E. Callender. 2,000

Place, George W. to Lewis Krewlewitch. 500

Rosenberg, Barbara to Charles Rosenberg. 3,000

Rothmann, George exr. Ebregott P. Wichum to Ida Wichum trustee Ehregott P. Wichum. nom

Reichbard, George to Mary E. Kennedy and Bridget Millmore. nom

Rudd, Frank, Brooklyn, to Catharine F. Street, Brooklyn. Re-recorded. 511

Randell, Charles H. exr. Morris Randell to Charles H. Randell, Westchester, N. Y. 1,500

Same to same. 500

Same to same. 1,500

Stokes, James, West Orange, N. J., to The Title Guarantee and Trust Co. 35,000

Stern, Abraham to Betsey Davis. 8,000

Seuss, Rudolph, Joseph Scheubner and Edward Fredrich, of Seuss, Scheubner & Fredrich, to William B. Baldwin. 2,500

Short, Thomas J. to Garfield National Bank. nom

Seybel, Daniel E. to John E. Lockwood trustee Charles A. Lockwood dec'd. 1,395

Sire, Meyer L. to Edward F. Browning. 6,000

Spriggs, Jennie wife of and Robert H. to Charles D. Rush. 1,660

Snow, Frederick A. to James Stokes. 20,000

Stallknecht, Barry S., Brooklyn, to Edwin Shuttleworth. 537

Satterlee, Francis Le Roy and ano. exrs. Henry Suydam to Mary E. wife of Faneuil D. Weisse, Wappinger, N. Y., and Laura S. wife of Francis Le Roy, Satterlee. nom

Troest, Rudolph to Henry Stemme. 5,000

Trautmann, Franklin P. to Caroline Flattich. 1,000

The Hudson River Bank to Robert H. Coleman trustee for Anne C. Rogers. 30,000

The McElwee Mfg. Co. to John E. Eustis. nom

The People's Trust Co., of Brooklyn, to German-American Real Estate Title Guarantee Co. 16,000

The Bradley & Currier Co. (Lim.) to Simon Adler and Henry S. Herrman. 1,450

The McElwee Mfg. Co. to The Northern National Bank. 2,500

The Wallis Iron Works Co, Jersey City, to The First National Bank, Jersey City. nom

Title Guarantee and Trust Co. to Amy Eldredge, Caroline E. Benedict and Rebeca Burrell. 15,000

Same to James P. Hall trustee for Anna G. and Henry H. Hall. 10,000

Same to Poughkeepsie Savings Bank. 10,000

Title Guarantee and Trust Co. to James M. Wentz. 4,000

Title Guarantee & Trust Co to Lizzie Olivella. 11,000

Same to Denis Horgan. 16,000

Same to George W. Adams. 15,000

Same to E. Walter Snyder, Bayonne, N. J. 1,500

Title Guarantee and Trust Co. to Gustav H. Schwab and ano. exrs. and trustees Gustav Schwab. 14,500

Same to Louisa P. Bronk. 2,000

Same to The Poughkeepsie Savings Bank. 21,000

Thain, Mary T. to Edwin Shuttleworth. 2,000

Tracey, Ellen, Fall River, Mass., to Julius Lipman and Moses Kind. 1,500

Underhill, Zoe D. to Annie E. Underhill. 11,000

Underhill, Annie E. to Zoe D. Underhill extrx. Walter M. Underhill. 10,000

Updyke, Edwin S., Sr., to Samuel Aronson. 1,900

Updike, Edwin S., Sr., to Mary A. Ford. nom

Weyand, Karoline to Simon Duesel. 1,750

Wood, Kate G. wife of and Harry H. to The Dobbs Ferry Bank. 500

Wohlleben, Dorothea and Wilhelmina Dritschel both formerly Kaiser extrxs. Dorothea Kuchen to Wilhelmina Dritschel. 4,500

Wallace, Robert to Addie A. La Coste. 650

Wilde, Edward C. trustee for Julia C. Wilde to John W. Jennings trustee. 8,000

Wilde, Julia C. to John W. Jennings trustee. 7,000

Weisse, Mary E. wife of Faneuil D., Wappinger, N. Y., and Laura S. wife of Francis Le Roy Satterlee to The Equitable Life Assurance Soc. 49,800

Wilmurt, Francis M., Pelham Manor, N. Y., to The Bradley & Currier Co. (Lim.) 5,500

Woolverton, Samuel to Andrew J. Kerwin. nom

Wallach, Samson to Karl M. Wallach. nom

Winslow, Edward to Henry W. Ford trustee Augustus H. Ward dec'd. 3 assigns. nom

KINGS COUNTY.

Nov. 25 to Dec. 2—Inclusive.

Adams, Jeannie S. to Patrick McGowan. $3,500

Andrews, John to Irving Fish. 1,543

Burr, Charles P. and ano. exrs. Calvin Burr to Henry F. Risch. 930

Bailey, James S. and Charles H. exrs. Solomon Freeman to Charles H. Parsons admr. Harriot Freeman. 7,000

Bodkin, Dominick G. to George H. Wunschel. nom

Bearrs, James S. to Minnie A. Demarest. 750

Beer, Louis and Michael Schaffner to Emma Krieger. 1,000

Brady, John J. to Thomas Kitts. 1,200

Clayton, Ransom F. to Charles E. Rogers. 1,200

Carroll, James G. to Whitman W. Kenyon. 1,200

Constable, Anna to Martha M. Binns. 4,000

Dean, Isaac M. to Ophelia M. Dean. 3,750

Dietz, George H. to Solomon Cohen. 850

Doody, Daniel to Asa W. Parker. 664

Dowdell, Mary A. to Clinton R. James. 800

Dugro, Philip to Rosa Roth. 8,000

Denike, Thomas S. to Charles B. Wheeler. 1,000

Dwyer, Michael F. to Orlando A. Jones. 20,000

Doody, Daniel and Benjamin F. Hobby, of Hobby & Doody, to Asa W. Parker. 400

Doody, Daniel to same. 200

Same to same. 600

Draper, Daniel to George W. Pearsall. 1,800

Dailey, John and Bridget to William F. Corwith. 1,700

Demarest, Minnie A. to Frederick P. Bellamy. 805

Embree, Isaac to Anna E. Richardson. nom

Eastman, George W. trustee William B. Sands to Edward S. Hand. nom

Everit, Thomas exr. Valentine Everit to Edward A. Everit. 1,900

Same to same. 600

Elliott, Susan A. formerly Hendrickson to Sarah H. Powell. 1,200

Fielder, David P. to Emma J. Byrt. 200

Feinberg, Jacob and Joseph Rosenberg to Louis Bossert. 500

Geertz, Charles J. A. to Rose B. H. Geertz. nom

Hewlett, Phoebe to George W. Pearsall. 600

Hand, Edward S. to The Reformed Church, Oyster Bay, L. I. 1,000

Hessberg, Felix to Jacob Feinberg and Joseph Rosenberg. 525

Hutchinson, Henry to Charles Hart. 1,000

Hutchings Bath Co. to John C. Hutchings. 3,500

Hahn, Henry to John Hahn. 1,000

Jacobson, Marie E. to Anna M. E. Watkins. 1,500

Jonas, Leopold to Mina Jonas. 5,000

Katte, Walter and Walter J. to William E. Haws trustee. 3 assigns. nom

Kirby, Joseph I. to Daniel S. Arnold. 1,750

Knight, Henry W. and Joshua L. Barton to Charles E. Teale trustee. 1,800

Laing, William V. H. to Ellen J. Williamson and William W. Phraner. 1,000

Lott, Cynthia to Harmanus B. Hubbard exr. Peter Wyckoff. 2,875

Lang, Henry to Frederick H. Kastens. 1,500

Ledoux, Paul W. to C. D. Hammel. 500

Mann, Albon and William trustee to Asa T. Hascall. 2,500

Minden, Morris to Leopold Michel. nom

Mutual Life Ins. Co. to Albon and William Man trustees for Asa Hascall. 1,000

Marsh, Charles M., Morris Plains, N. J., to Annie M. Hughes. 750

Max, Harris to Earl A. Gillespie, Woodhaven, L. I. 400

Melven, John A. to Ellen L. Swan. 1,800

McCord, Anna W. to Andrew D. Baird. 700

Neely, Robert S. to The Hyde & Gload Mfg. Co. 650

Nicholson, John to Michael Hanrahan. 250

Perry, Chauncey to John Dailey. 200

Raeburn, Latourette & Co. to Warren P. Ackerman. 500

Ratner, Louis to Alois Lazansky. 1,800

Rein, Charles to Charles J. A. Geerty. nom

Roth, Henry to John Frank. 2,000

Stroetzel, Ida to The Title Guarantee and Trust Co. 3,000

Smith, Blanche E. wife of Russell D., East Marion, L. I., to Charlotte A. Allen. 500

Smith, Mary W. to Maria H. Elwell. 1,000

Strong, Thomas S. trustee for Lucy Derby to Charles H. Burtis exr. Martha L. D. Burtis. 4,000

Sumner, Helen R., Newark, N. J., to William M. Polk. nom

The United States Life Ins. Co. to Benjamin L. Coffin and ano. exrs. Pierre A. Mayor. 1879. 2,500

The Henry McShane Mfg. Co., Baltimore, Md., to John C. Rogers. nom

Title Guarantee and Trust Co. to Edson W. Burr. 1,500

Same to Pauline May. 3,000

Same to Brooklyn Trust Co. 14,000

Same to Mary S. Ford. 1,000

Same to Charles and William H. Wiley and Edward P. Hamilton trustee. 1,000

Same to Marietta Coffin. 3,500

Same to Alice M. Osborne. 6,000

Same to William M. Ingraham. 20,000

Same to The Brooklyn Female Employment Society. 4,000

Same to Chauncey J. Hastings. 6,000

Same to Charles Emmons. 4,000

Same to same. 4,000

Same to Kate E. Nevin trustee. 1,000

Same to Kings County Trust Co. 20,000

Same to Alice M. Osborne. 5,000

Same to Charles Emmons. 3,000

Taber, David S. and Silas A. Underhill trustees of the Missionary Fund of the New York Yearly Meeting of Friends to David S. Taber and Robert W. Lawrence trustees of said Fund. nom

Thomas Roberts Stevenson Co., a corporation, to Orson W. Sheldon, Fort Ann, N. Y. 500

Wheeler, George S. exr. Nancy B. Wheeler to Ella G. Hotchkiss. 1,200

Williamson, Ellen to James H. Williamson. 2,600

Woodford, Stewart L. and ano. trustees Mary Beadleston to Mary Beadleston. nom

Wolf, Ignatz to Peter Doelger. 4,000

Weis, Lena to Julius Dewald. 1,400

Widmann, Frederick to Bernard Cruse, Jr. 650

Williamson, Ellen J. guard. William W. and Merwin R. Phraner to William V. H. Laing. 1,000

JUDGMENTS.

In these lists of judgments the names alphabetically arranged, and which are first on each line, are those of the judgment debtor. The letter (D) means judgment for deficiency (*) means not summoned. (†) signifies that the first name is fictitious, real name being unknown. Judgments entered during the week, and satisfied before day of publication, do not appear in this column, but in list of Satisfied Judgments

NEW YORK CITY.

Nov. and Dec.

28 Abrahams, Abraham—Lazarus Levy. $259 48

30 Alfke, William—Broadway & Seventh Av R R Co....costs 150 97

30 Anthony, Meyer—Solomon Simonson. 393 41

1 Anderson, Alexander—F B Whitney. 284 58

1 Ashenfarb, Samuel—Dora Sobel..... 126 07

1 Aguilera, Manuel L—W S Middeton.. 687 34

2 Anderson, Henry J—W J Smith..... 119 26

2 the same——John Moore.......... 178 50

3 Adams, William—R G Mitchell...... 311 71

3†Abrahams, John—Henry Bauer...... 67 94

4 Albright, Charles H—Canal Street Bank.......... 1,843 07

4 the same——Leopold Gusthal..... 1,913 75

4 the same——the same........... 1,701 53

28 Bates, Erskine S—Metropolitan Telephone and Telegraph Co........ 15 61

28 Burr, William H—Otis Corbett....... 379 85

28 Blom, Franz L—E M Pritchard...... 354 65

28 Bach, Albert—S A Brooker......... 43 46

28 Buel, Oliver P—Selig Steinhardt..... 256 90

28*Busse, Michael H—W F Clemmons... 435 81

28* Brossard, Theodore; Brossard, Otto } Crocker-Wheeler Motor Co.... 78 77

30 Bosworth, Jane M—J K Cullin....... 2,158 14

30* Baumann, Leopold; Baumann, Max } Isaac Moskovitz 115 88

30†Brummer, Florence—C F Scott...... 33 69

30 Brodsky, Harris—William Solomon.. 515 50

30 Baker, Daniel K—B F Einstein, assignee........ 4,732 87

1 Bentley, George H—Julius Lehman, recvr........ 681 47

1 Beardsley, Charles—W J Eaton...... 238 75

1 Brinkerhoff, Cornelius M—Isidor Mitchell........ 119 04

1 Bonnell, Tammissin H—Merchants' Exchange Nat Bank........ 10,087 85

1 Booth, William E—Mabbett Travis... 197 62

1 Bonnell, John Harper; Bonnell, Tammissin H } Merchants' Exchange Nat Bank 1,552 35

1 Burger, Lewis—Joseph Sawyer....... 396 26

1 Bacigalupo, Charles—East Side Fireproof Stabling and Storage Co...... 151 58

1 Ball, Max—J L Baily............... 397 08

2 Borrmann, William—J F Heinbockel. 238 00

2 Barrett, Clarence T—G L Squier Mfg Co........ 91 00

2 Bendall, Robert A—William Martin.. 324 00

2 Brant, Henry B; Brant, Ella L } H A Sperry........ 287 11

2 Bloch, Arthur; Bloch, Isidor } Thomas Bradford.... 77 50

2 Bush, Hildreth—A F Winkle......... 42 01

2 Blackinton, William H; Blackinton, Summer; Blackinton, Louis A; Braun, John; Barrows, Henry, Jr; Barrows, Ira } A J G Hodenpyl.. .costs 111 07

2 Bateman, Arthur E—C W Al Burtis.. 2,187 58

2 Bressant, Andrew—Brunswick-Balke-Collender Co........ 356 17

2 Barnes, Charles A—D C Dake .. costs 23 62

3 Burns, James—Lena Kopetzky....... 605 65

3 Bausch, Frederick E—Henry Bauer.. 13 21

3 Brown, Gussie—People State N Y.... 300 00

3 Bernet, Ernst O, Jr—August Schaefer........ 95 93

3 Bixby, Francis M, Jr—Louis Losi.... 301 07

*4 Baldwin, Theodore F—W H Baldwin. 2,180 98

4 Bock, George—D M Koehler......... 147 08

4 Birnbaum, Morris—Joseph Goldberg. 863 27

4 Beaudrias, Alphonse J—Edward Smith........ 782 73

4 Bini, Titto; Bessi, Pietro } C R Ruegger.......... 79 15

4 Bini, Titto——the same.............. 99 73

4 Brunclik, Joseph—N F Monjo........ 573 14

4 Bauer, Moritz—W G L King....costs 117 67

4 the same——the same............ 2,299 54

4 Busch, Charles—Joachim Stein....... 60 85

4 Brandt, Frederick, admr John Huber—J A Roth........ 113 14

4 Bixby, Francis M, Jr—E O Thompson. 134 21

4 Barns, Charles Edward—De Witt C Gardner........ 129 11

28 Childs, Nathan—State Nat Bank of Denver, Colorado........ 377 10

28 Cohen, Samuel—Isaac Marx.......... 215 72

28 Cornell, John M—W J Logan........ 480 59

28 Coady, Thomas J—R L Griffith...... 96 81

28 the same——E J Ettlinger........ 117 35

28 the same——W A Read.......... 122 61

30*Crain, W E S—C L Thompson..... 76 99

30 Couture, Anthony P—J W Thompson 3,224 62

30 Carrick, Robert A—D D Reeve....... 160 67

30 Carmick, Edward H—East River Nat Bank........ 3,036 69

30 Campbell, William—Crawford Maxwell........ 689 87

30 Clark, Charles A—B F Einstein, assignee........ 4,732 87

Crook, Andrew—Amalie Crook....... 55 01
1 Cragin, William B—C L Fleming 349 89
1 Chapman, Charles J—E A Saunders.. 588 93
1 Crosman, James Heron—J M Brown .... costs 97 16
1 Coelho, A H de Paula—Frank Adams 130 15
1†Crawford, Abraham J—First Nat Bank of Chattanooga............... 373 58
1 Cohnfeld, Rachel—C F Thompson.... 471 12
1 Clark, William H—Susan F Walter.. 84 42
1 Chapman, Charles J—E A Saunders. 1,758 89
1 Casey, Robert E—J A Robinson.... 15,037 19
1 Cook, Charles W—A E Pressinger.... 687 60
2 Clark, John Delos—Charles Schlesinger.......... 276 46
2 Cranston, Henry—William Wright, exr........ 815 00
2 the same——J J Carter, recvr.... 106 58
2 Cameron, William L—J H Sweetser. 1,202 15
2 Corbin, Edwin—O P Hazard......... 274 72
2 Corbin, Donald R—A J Hodenpyl .... costs 111 07
2 Clarke, John—J F Flomer........... 193 56
2 Celia, Carlon—Brunswick-Balke-Collender Co........ 356 17
3 Cavinato, Luigi; Cavinato, Guiseppi; Cavinato, Steffano; Cavinato, Natale } F G Moore..... 645 47
3 the same——the same............ 815 86
3 the same——the same............ 461 32
3 Cannold, Samuel—People State N Y. 300 00
4 Carter, John M—Henry Hahenfeld.. 203 29
4 Clarkin, Peter—D M Koehler........ 240 84
4 Cummings, William A—Canal Street Bank........ 1,343 07
4 Copin, August A—A W Atwater.... 264 74
4 the same——the same.... 267 17
4 Cochrane, John Wilson, admr William Smith — Michael Coleman, comm'r........ 336 82
28†Dowling, Mary M—J G Johnson..... 415 12
28 Davis, Edward M—J P Tuttle........ 112 43
28 Deane, John H—Caroline C Bishop...70,019 58
28 Donaldson, Joseph C—R T Booth, exr 145 37
30 Dudley, Frederick R—Richardson & Morgan Co........ 192 91
30 Dickinson, George F—Angelo Morello 208 66
30 Deringer, Walter H—G F Swift...... 253 58
2 Deemer, John M—O D Munn....costs 372 50
2 Dinkelspiel, Maggie; Dinkelspiel, Simon L } J A Mahony. 6,725 38
2 De Forrest, Othinel—T H Robins.... 183 90
3 Deyerberg, Henry—People State N Y 300 00
3 Dunn, Thomas—Henry Sommermeyer 73 87
3 Ditchen, Edward H—American Hosiery Co........ 877 90
4 Daidson, Marshall T—Merchants' Nat Bank of Albany........1,138 17
4 Dueker, Otto D — Frederick Tiedemann, assignee........ 109 50
4 Donahue, Nathaniel M—C E Byerne. 28 13
4*Doe, John—Mary Zucca............ 611 85
4 Devitt, John J—Edward Smith...... 782 78
4*Dietsche, Joseph—Joachim Stein..... 60 85
4†Dayton, Alice—J H Johnston........ 85 76
4 Davis, J Charles—Joseph Clare....... 522 18
28 Ettleson, Henry—W F Clemmons.... 435 81
28 Ehrlich, Abraham; Ehrlich, Hyman } Julius Engel.... 401 12
2 Edelson, Louis—German Bank....... 724 52
2 Engelfried, John—A J G Hodenpyl .... costs 111 07
2 Eichler, John Frederick — Jacob Raichle........ 212 14
3 Emerson, Frank H—R H Burrows... 419 15
3 Engel, Leopold—Arnold Kohn....... 209 50
3 the same——the same.......... 209 50
3 Emery, Alfred D—William Rhinelander, trustee........ 30 00
3 Edelson, Louis; Edelson, Joel } East Side Bank..... 605 16
4 Edderkin, John—J R Steers, Jr...... 1,267 35
28 Fountain, Inez—J J McMelvey....... 456 58
28 Florence, Mary—Flora Gross......... 218 55
28 Flanagan, Michael—J F Emanuel.... 844 05
30 Flieg, John—Julius Auerbach........ 275 80
30 Farrell, Frank—James Carstairs...... 323 93
30*Falkenstein, Martin—David Auerbach 89 37
30 Farrington, John A; Farrington, Jonas S } J J Harrington........ 1,233 09
30 Freund, Theodore F—D M Koehler... 231 10
1*Friedman, Solomon; Friedman, David } S J Nowell..... 89 24
1 Fechteler, Henry—P C Langdon..... 124 67
1 Frost, L Wesley—R W Vanderhoff... 110 74
1 Fowler, George—F L C Martin....... 168 09
2 F e , Peter—M R Cook............ 85 23
2 Falk, Isaac L; Falk, George W } John Baehr. 913 00
2 Francesconi, Guido—R J Dean....... 275 00
2 Freeman, Frank C—L J Behringer... 624 03
2 Frink, Edward S—Seaboard Nat Bank 225 75
Frothingham, Thomas G—A J G Hodenpyl........costs 74 72
2 Fuchs, Christian W—John Moore.... 178 50
2 Freeman, Frank C—A B Powell...... 486 63
2 Fox, Edwin M—J R Bartlett......... 1,076 08
3 Fisher, Conrad J—Merchants' Nat Bank of Syracuse........ 6,337 62
3*Fuchs, Christian—Leissner, Midlen & Hughes Co........ 176 83
4 Flynn, Peter H—D M Koehler....... 45 25
4 Flatow, Richard — Theodore Von Bremsen........ 264 60
4 Florence, Mary—William Drucker... 236 48
4 Finley, Thomas B—F A Baier...... 132 17
28 Gent, Louis A — Dundee Chemical Works........ 136 56
28 Goldberg, Nathan—Christoph Horn.. 145 19
30 Gundling, David; Gundling, Harry } Louis Kahn...... 3,399 84
30 the same——Allen Lounsbury.... 255 10
30 Graff, Charles H—J R Igelstrom..... 279 20
30 Godfrey, James W—C J Godfrey.... 345 21
30 Gunn, John G — Knickerbocker Ice Co........ 69 17
30 Gelb, Abraham—David Simon 41 05
30 Griesel, Henry—Thomas Cunningham 275 97
1†Granniss, C K—F M Croisett......... 172 20
1 Goodman, Burkhard—R A Springs, recvr........ 1,677 72
1 Gurney, Frederick B—Grand Trunk Railway Co of Canada........costs 125 55
1 Gumpel, David—Sam Deutsch........ 117 40
1 Gaines, Hiram F—J A Robinson.... 15,037 19
1 Garson, Moses H—Julius Hammerslough........ 2,547 92
2 Geisenheimer, Jacob—Pauline Frank, admrx........ 182 50
2 Gans, David—John Baehr............ 147 00
2 Gent, Louis A—T M Armstrong...... 481 00
2 Gembs, George—Henrich Krauss.... 5,881 67
2 Grunwald, Max—Christopher & Tenth Street R R Co........costs 121 69
2 the same——Forty-second Street & Grand Street Ferry R R Co..costs 122 67
2*Green, Douglas—C W Al Burtis..... 2,187 58
2 Gillespie, Frederick—Jacob Shaver... 116 25
2 Grunwald, Julius by Louis J Baum, guard—Christopher & Tenth Street R R Co........costs 88 59
2 the same——Forty-second Street & Grand Street R R Co......costs 88 59
3 Garner, William H—People State N Y........ 300 00
4 Goldberg, Isaac—Joseph Goldberg.. 803 27
4 Geiger, Samuel; Geiger, Joseph R } Jonas Bunzel..... 115 19
4†Gordian, Harry—W F Clemmons.... 198 98
28 Herrmann, Louis—E M Pritchard... 354 65
28 Hartfield, William—People State N Y 500 00
28 Harrison, William H; Harrison, Eliza, exrs and trustees Henry Harrison } W H Harrison, trustee 108,146 99
30 Hess, George; Hess, Henry } Isaac Lewis.......... 216 86
30 Hewitt, Henry S—K V Oebler........ 47 56
1 Hulshof, John L—Francis Bauermann........ 22 70
1 Harper, William D—Merchants' Exchange Nat Bank........10,087 85
1 Hall, Robert H—Frank Curtiss...... 255 73
1 Hauser, Gotlieb J—W J Eaton...... 238 75
1 Huuerbein, Julius—W B Dubois...... 224 47
1 Howe, Benjamin—A E Pressinger.... 687 60
2 Hall, Robert H—Frank Curtiss 254 71
2 Heiselman, John A—Valentine & Co. 108 50
2 Halloran, Daniel J—E W Durkee ....costs 129 10
2 Hoetzel, Max—S S Utter............ 124 86
2 Holt, Frederick L—Herman Sulzer... 104 14
2*Haase, Benjamin—Benie Friedman... 40 80
3 Haggerty, Frederick F — Patrick Mogaahan........ 898 01
4 Harvey, Michael—Empire State Brewing Co........ 111 55
4 Hoppock, Moses A—R S Crane...... 198 68
4 Huber, Louisa, admrx John Huber—J A Roth........ 113 14
1 Jones, Winston, assignee Bank of Mobile—Merchants' Nat Bank........1,218 36
2 Johanson, Johan A — Henry Herrmann........ 123 97
3 Jones, George O—N D Whipple...... 434 09
4 Jones, Royal P Floyd—Sterling Wallace........ 225 42
4 Jetter, Thomas—Joseph Stern........ 1,432 99
4 Johnston, Taylor; Johnston, John Humphreys; Johnston, Mary H, exrs James B Johnston } Eugene O'Sullivan 4,594 83
28 King, Emma; Klinger, Jacob } People State N Y.... 100 00
28 the same——the same............ 300 00
28 Kelly, John J; Kelly, Daniel } W F Quick.......... 1,593 00
28 Koper, Henry—First Nat Bank of Hazleton, Pa........ 6,265 49
30†Krugler, John—Jacob Jamer........ 15 89
30 Klaus, William J—G F Swift........ 374 63
30 Kneeland, Sylvester H—R S Bacon.. 152 51
1 Kopschai, Michael—Vincent Jirasek. 797 70
1 Klemann, Jacob; Keller, Adam } John Keller....... 468 01
1 Kronthal, Louis; Kronthal, Charles } Max Feist....... 656 17
1 Kenny, Frances H—John Polhemus.. 329 50
4 Kirk, William—Municipal Brewing Co........ 675 79
4 Knauss, William H—Gottfried Krueger Brewing Co........costs 77 52
4 Kelly, John W—Louis Goldstein..... 212 38
4 King, William H—Robert Milbank... 135 72
30 Ladd, Alfred W—Robert Stoll....... 95 65
30 Leigh, Louis—Jacob Jamer......... 15 89
30 Leigh, Oliver H J—W P Robinson... 30 58
1 Lowther, Sarah E—Joseph Wechsler. 168 55
1 Luce, Clarence—Herman Jacobi...... 25 00
1 Lynch, George M—H P Toler........ 383 02
1 Litchfield, George H—L S Streit..... 2,049 55
1 Lawlor, James S—William Buess.... 40 69
1 Libby, James L—A H Goelet......... 88 01
1 Leyrer, Christian—T A Shaw........ 117 19
1 Lescow, Albert—G W Smith......... 259 13
1 Loeb, Adolph—E J Denning......... 109 73
2 Lemmermann, Henry L—M R Cook.. 241 44
2 Low, Joseph M—J C Cook........... 585 87
2 Lyman, John B—W F Weber........ 129 49
2 Lewis, Sidney H—J R Smith........ 427 06
2 Ladd, Joseph T—Chatham Nat Bank. 322 54
2 Lazare, Mathilde—Samuel Katz..... 104 19
3 Landan, Samuel—Solomon Fischer... 28 50
3 Lloyd, Alfred—Talbot Root......... 145 25
4 Levy, Marcus—Henry Bach.......... 322 55
4 Locke, Charles E—Joseph Clare...... 522 18
28 Morris, Henry N—Indiana Paint and Roofing Co........ 469 25
28 Miller, Thomas — F W Hunnewell, trustee 2,089 83
28 Madden, James F—People State N Y 500 00
28 Miller, Bernard—Christopher Horn.. 145 19
30 Montgomery, Henry—J S Connolly.. 472 18
30 Mooney, Henrietta R—Ludwig Rothschild........ 4,745 84
30 Mahony, Daniel P—J E Linde........ 225 74
30 Morris, Aaron—Giuseppe Abaruo.... 87 50
30 Magrath, Henry—T J Preston & Co.. 83 46
1 Meger, Louis—John Keller........... 468 01
1 Minard, Lydia A—Robert Hill....... 122 14
1 Mayer, Mark—W A Miles & Co...... 387 16
1 Matthews, James C—R C Brown..... 494 10
1 Mooney, Jane—Sarah Brooks........ 226 04
1 the same——Joseph Moorhead.... 146 36
1 Maynard, Edwin B—A E Pressinger.. 687 60
1 Martin, Wilbur F—Eastmans Co..... 1,028 27
2 Meyer, Maurice—W O Wyckoff...... 153 23
2 Maguire, Daniel F—Mayor, &c....... 47 60
2 Marks, Alfred—J J MacKeown...... 133 99
2 Magnus, Emma—J G Johnson....... 217 22
2 Morton, Marcus W—A J G Hodenpyl ....costs 111 07
2 Miller, Thomas—First Nat Bank of Hazelton, Pa........ 6,800 36
2 the same——First Nat Bank of Shenandoah, Pa........ 5,944 90
3 Muhlbauer, Felicia—Henry Robert... 144 00
3 Murphy, George C—Henry Bauer.... 93 09
3 Mytnik, Myer—Henry Bauer......... 17 78
3 Monne, Peter—Martin Senger........ 304 44
3 Manus, David—People State N Y..... 300 00
3 Matthews, James C—H G Hilton..... 121 30
3 the same——the same............ 121 91
3 Mastuson, Sarah—E C Conrad........ 93 60
3*Mason, John—H W Steinhauser, assignee........ 14,136 77
3 Mendell, Charles N—A F Blinn..costs 29 51
4 Marsh, Samuel—Benjamin Altman... 126 99
4 Matthews, James C—Consolidated Gas Co........ 898 38
28 McDonald, James A—F B Whitney.. 213 09
28 McLean, Alexander — Long Island Bank........ 4,942 18
28 McKenna, Margaret; McKenna, Patrick } Flora Gross.... 218 55
30 McGuckin, Henry J—J E Linde.... 225 74
1 McSwyny, Bryan G—C A Coffin 475 95
1 McQuoid, William H—C H Wilcox.. 683 98
2 McCalister, John F—Taylor Co...... 230 00
2 McLean, John J—Third Nat Bank of Syracuse........ 11,377 55
2 McKenna, Joseph E; McKenna, Elizabeth } Charles Connor 92 88
2 McNamara, John J—E R Lewis...... 433 22
3 McNally, Thomas; McNally, Henry } People State N Y........ 500 00
3 McBride, Charles E—Leissner, Midlen & Hughes Co........ 176 83
3 McCabe, Edward D—Harriet A Sheppard........ 230 20
3 McNab, John A—McNab & Harlin Mfg Co........costs 94 62
4 McEvoy, Charles—Mount Morris Bank........ 875 42
4 McKenna, Patrick; McKenna, Margaret } William Drucker 236 48
4 McKay, Stewart—H M Rogers....... 230 39
28 Noll, Theobold—Philip Rudolph...... 177 54
2 Newton, Richard W—W J Wheeler, exr........ 406 98
28 O'Brien, John—David Jones Co...... 155 41
28 Ouderkirk, Isaac Y—F A Hall....... 157 07
30 Osborne, Thomas W—G E Jones, treasurer........ 426 98
1 O'Brien, Michael—G W Hart 317 32
1 Oldham, Edmund T, assignee Pearce & Co—Myer Foster........ 117 50
2 O'Leary, James—A G Black......costs 174 43
2 Overin, George D—J H Veil........ 88 54
3 O'Gorman, Mary—Harry Held 222 32
4 Orr, Alexander E—George St Amant ....costs 112 42
28 Pacheteau, Jaques—N F Degoury. 3,890 17
30 Patterson, Charles G — Henry de Forest, exr........ 6,466
30 Phillips, Walter E; Phillips, Sidney A } Charles Parrish. 255
30 Phillips, Waldorff H—G E Jones, treasurer........ 42
30 Potter, Jeremiah N—Jed Frye....... 200
1 Pratt, Mary—A S Brown............ 296 59
1 Price, Frank S—W J Eaton......... 208 75
1 Page, William E—John Duryea...... 140 92
1 Pryor, S Morris—Western Nat Bank.. 504 45
3 Phelps, Ford C—Bulmer Lumber Co (Lim)........ 278 21
4 Philbrook, Stella—Julia L Rowland.. 271 50
4 Power, Watterman D — Edward Smith........ 782 73
4 Perlman, Louis—Max Studinski...... 29 10
4 Price, Jesse—Thomas Crosley 142 93
4 Payne, George A—William Ahlborn. 80 40
4 Pfluger, Jacques; Pfluger, Mary } John Koster 69 73
28 Quinn, Peter—Timothy Riordan..... 50 50
28†Robinson, Moses; Richman, Samuel } Isaac Marx...... 215 72
28 Ryan, Michael—John Brown 144 67
30 Redington, W D—C L Thompson..... 76 99
30 Raubitschek, Max H—S G B Gourlay, Jr........ 37 15
30†Reichert, Barnett—Isaac Moskovitz.. 110 00
30 Ryer, William W—Albro Howell..... 293 31
1 Read, Cassius H—A S Brown........ 296 59
1 Reudel, Henry—Sam Deutsch........ 117 40
1 Ritz, Nicholas—Richard Vom Hofe... 105 99
1 Roberts, Austin G; Roberts, Walter J } R G Hoyt........ 8,012 44
1 Richardson, Jay C—George France... 48 33
2 Rhoades, Lyman—L J Behringer..... 624 03

2 Rosenblum, August H—Philip Rudolph.... 153 84
2 Rockwell, Stephen L—Third Nat Bank of Syracuse.... 11,377 55
2 Riley, William—A G Black....costs 174 43
2 Royce, Stephen W—E E Eames.... 16,067 84
2 Rhodes, A S—A B Powell.... 486 63
2 Ruppell, George — Beadleston & Woerz.... 250 00
2 Robinson, John—Youghwgheny Bank of Connellsville, Pa.... 4,644 12
2 the same—First Nat Bank of Rochester, Pa.... 5,134 70
3 Raluziner, Adolph—Arnold Kohn.... 209 50
3 the same—the same.... 209 50
4 Read, Cassius H—Moses Esberg.... 524 57
4 Rossiter, Ehrick K—J R Steers, Jr, trustee.... 1,267 35
28*Sawyer, Samuel A—F W Hunnewell. 2,089 83
28 Spencer, Harvey, Jr—Reginald Hanson.... 1,815 18
28 Sussman, Fanny — Mercantile Nat Bank.... 1,020 84
28 Schwartz, Joseph—J H Miller.... 85 47
28 Stein, Lewis—G B Gurley.... 2,914 47
30 Smythe, Andrew E—George Olney.... 375 88
30 Schaefer, John E—C L Thompson.... 75 99
30 Stevenson, Vernon K—P E Ranford. 623 01
30 Squire, Rollin M—Benjamin Wright. 122 97
30 Snook, William W—C B Fosdick.... 2,906 81
30 Sondheim, William—N Y Life Ins Co 142 68
30 Schrott, Henry — Thomas Cunningham.... 275 97
30 Shepard Thomas G—Gustave Gunkel 234 61
1 Swift, George—J F Delury.... 110 75
1 Sinclair, James—the same.... 49 30
1 Strauss, Joseph—German Exchange Bank.... 500 67
1 Schickle, Bernhard—Francis Bauner-mann.... 22 70
1 Sause, Richard E—W R Comfort.... 83 62
1 Schoenberg, Rosalie—Leopold Zimmermann.... 85 34
1 Simonson, Michaelis—W A Hardt.... 898 03
1 Steiner, Emma R—W H Daniels.... 1,017 00
1 Stewart, Albert P—W P Walton.... 67 31
1 Strawson, Vincent A—H J Leach.... 496 42
2 Schidlower, Ludwig—Frank R Walker individ and assignee....costs 343 72
2 the same—Fernando R Walker ....costs 86 00
2 the same—J H Walker....costs 336 00
2 Strauss, Ferdinand—John Baehr.... 95 00
2 Stein, Lewis—Osborne & Cheeseman Co.... 1,806 06
2 Saucier, Samuel A—F J Berman.... 79 60
2 Schenkin, Hyman—A J G Hodenpyl ....costs 111 07
2 Souberg, Josef—Pauline Ryshpan.... 322 09
2*Sawyer, Samuel A—First Nat Bank of Hazelton, Pa.... 6,800 36
2 the same—First Nat Bank of Shenandoah, Pa.... 5,944 90
3 Snook, William W—Merchants' Nat Bank of Syracuse.... 6,337 62
3 Silberg, Joseph; Silberg, Lena } J A Arnold.... 127 00
3 Steinhardt, Lesser—Peter Murray.... 73 09
3 Sanger, Abraham—First Nat Bank of Hazelton, Pa.... 5,603 49
3 Stern, Rachael—Arnold Kohn.... 209 50
3 the same—the same.... 209 50
3 Sperling, William—People State N Y 300 00
3 Seklar, Abraham; Seklar, Lewis } Solomon Fischer.. 143 78
3†Shearcraft, Frank A—Richard Vom Hofe.... 111 49
4 Schlutzky, Hyman—Henry Bach.... 322 55
4 Salamoni, Paul—Mary Zucca.... 611 35
4 Steindler, Joseph—Canal Street Bank 1,343 07
4 Senninger, John P, Sr—Carl Beck.... 121 50
4 Stein, William—A J Seligsberg.... 167 18
4 Steckler, Louis—Evalina Ball De Land 2,038 91
4 Steindler, Joseph—Leopold Gusthal.. 1,913 75
4 the same—the same.... 1,701 53
30 Smith, James C—J H Mann.... 30 67
30 Smith, James M—J S Manning.... 31 46
1 Smith, Joel B—Williamsburgh City Fire Ins Co.... 436 96
2 Smith, William E—A J G Hodenpyl. ....costs 74 72
2 Smith, Matthew—M P Breslin.... 201 75
2 Smith, Robert E—Frank Vitor.... 27 50
3 Smith, Franklin H—Knickerbocker Printing and Publishing Co.... 599 69
4 Smith, Edward—C M Hoffman.... 22 50
28 Welch, Fracker & Co—W E Golden.. 147 61
28 The Pelham Hod Elevating Co—Mary Devies, admrx.... 2,290 39
28 First Hungarian Slavonian Society—August Petz....costs 251 83
28 U S Volta Electric Battery Co—James Thomson.... 356 36
30 Adams & Sons Co—Henry Worms.... 232 87
30 Belford Co—Photo Electrotype Engraving Co.... 231 49
30 the same—the same.... 352 06
1 E G B Cakslees Sons Iron Works Co—Robert Robertson.... 421 45
1 United Ice Lines—First Nat Bank.... 8,047 01
1 The Mayor, Aldermen, &c—E S Coe. 122 28
1 the same—James Hayes.... 155 98
1 Bowery Nat Bank—R A Springs, recvr.... 1,370 10
1 Richensteen Lumber Co (Lim)—W B Dubois.... 224 47
1 Mercantile Building and Loan Assoc—D L Cardoza.... 48 35
2 The Stereo Relief Decorative Co—Iron Nat Bank, Plattsburgh, N Y.... 3,040 81
2 Willard Metal Co — Bissell Carpet Sweeper Co.... 184 80
2 The Stereo Relief Decorative Co—F E Smith.... 1,021 11
2 The Fenton Metallic Mfg Co—J W Nicholson.... 110 04
2 The Hygeia Water Ice Co—N Y Hygeia Ice Co (Lim)....costs 131 70
2 The American Electric Moter Co—G H Fitzwilson.... 667 08
2 Columbus Watch Co—A J G Hodenpyl ....costs 111 07
2 The Stereo Relief Decorative Co—F H Lindner.... 357 28
2 Fonda Lake and Port Leyden Paper Co—Nicholas Lennig.... 17,055 41
2 the same—the same.... 45,435 44
2 The Stereo Relief Decorative Co—John Anderson.... 354 00
2 The Hudson River Boot and Shoe Mfg Co—Bank of America.... 4,624 20
3 The McElwee Mfg Co—W E Pruden.. 359 89
3 The Snook Glove Mfg Co—Merchants' Nat Bank of Syracuse.... 6,337 62
3 The Mayor, Aldermen, &c—C J Thorburn.... 1,817 09
3 the same—John Byrne.... 187 20
3 Gies & Co—Peter Adams Co.... 18,474 06
3 The Manhattan Railway Co; The N Y Elevated R R Co } G E Sterry ....costs 118 60
3 New York Elevated R R Co—C S Hine....costs 110 30
4 Andrus & Conklin Tobacco Co—E F Ferdinand.... 637 98
4 American Automatic Spray Perfume Co—William Bryan.... 2,219 70
4 The Mechanics' Nat Bank; The National City Bank } George St Amant ....costs 112 42
4 Stereo Relief Decorative Co—Charles Scribner.... 243 12
4 the same—G N Manchester.... 234 17
4 the same—G D Curtiss.... 117 60
4 Welch-Fracker Co—De W C Gardner 129 11
28 Thom, John C—W E Dodge.... 168 02
30 Thompson, Walter; Thompson, George } Agawam Nat Bank.... 324 93
1 Thompson, Robert A—Vincent Pisek. 89 99
1†Trimm, George L—A H Goelet.... 91 44
1 Thompson, James—American Stoneware Co.... 279 20
1 Tate, John M—A E Pressinger.... 687 90
1 Thorman, Philip — Frank Foehrenbach.... 246 95
2 Thompson, John—Flora Barnett.... 2,115 45
2 Tallman, Clarence E—Z O Nelson.... 378 09
2 Turner, Samuel E—A J G Hodenpyl. ....costs 111 07
4 The Rembrandt House—J R Steers, Jr, trustee.... 1,267 35
4 Thwaites, George — Winnifrad Thwaites.... 1,419 56
2 Vallentine, Benjamin B—W A Attenborough.... 229 61
3 Valentine, Francis H—E M Tisdale.. 132 75
2 Vandervoort, Edward M—J F Delury 92 00
28*Wallace, David L—F W Hunnewell, trustee.... 2,089 83
28 Wermuth, Herman—L C King.... 193 62
30 Westbay, John F—Abraham Linde.... 44 06
30†Warshauer, Bertha—C F Scott.... 64 25
30†Weill, Albert L—David Auerbach.... 126 17
30† the same—the same.... 89 37
30 Wisan, Samuel D—Louis Goodman ....costs 69 87
30 Werner, Jacob—John Eichler Brewing Co.... 695 74
1 Weiss, Theodore—W A Hardt.... 898 03
1 Whyard, Grace E—H W Knapp.... 236 99
1 Wyckoff, Annie M — Agnes O'Neil, admrx.... 329 08
2*Weed, Smith M—Iron Nat Bank of Plattsburgh, N Y.... 3,040 81
2 Weiss, Adolf—H B Scharman & Sons 131 00
2 Wendel, Louis—J W Hatch, assignee. 154 86
2 Willmann, John—E A Behringer.... 349 90
2 Wolff, Oscar—Herman Sulzer.... 124 24
2 Weltfisch, Leon—Germania Bank.... 724 52
2 Wyburn, Joseph N—J R Smith.... 427 06
2 Wickham, Daniel H; Wickham, George S; Weidmann, Robert } A J G Hodenpyl....costs 111 07
2*Wright, Helen F—W J Smith.... 119 26
2 Wilkinson, Joseph—John Moore.... 178 50
2 Weizner, Jacob—Cornelius La Forge 32 50
2 Weisz, Jonas—Benie Friedman.... 40 80
2 Wallace, David L—First Nat Bank of Hazelton, Pa.... 6,800 36
2 the same—First Nat Bank of Shenandoah, Pa.... 5,944 91
3 Wells, William E—People State N Y. 155 42
3 Weiss, Adam—Henry Bauer.... 60 58
3 Weiss, Joseph—the same.... 47 96
3 Wells, Charles W—First Nat Bank of Hazelton, Pa.... 5,603 49
3 Wintermeyer, Bernard—C A Stock.. 264 74
3 Weisser, Michael; Weisser, Joseph } People State N Y. 100 00
3 Wilkinson, Joseph—Leissner Midlen & Hughes Co.... 176 83
3 West, J Garner—Sigmund Cohn.... 183 33
3 Witte, Henry—John Eichler Brewing Co.... 745 00
3 Weeks, Noah L—William Rhinelander, trustee.... 118 49
4 Weil, Louis—Richard Uhlmann.... 387 64
4 Wogan, John J—J C Hatzel.... 40 36
4 Wermuth, Herman—Jacob Kleinhans 230 52
4 Wolffe, Fred—S B Solomon.... 325 05
4 Wag , Albert W—Keuffel & Esser Co nes.... 71 15
30 Young, Charles—Gustav Gunkel.... 253 32
30 the same—the same.... 183 01
30 the same—the same.... 234 61
1 Yale, Ida—Isidore Mitchell.... 119 04
30 Zimmermann, Ernest—Knickerbocker Brewing Co.... 73 87
1 Zeiler, Isaac—Abraham Kornbluth.... 64 12

KINGS COUNTY.

Nov. and Dec.

28 Abrahams, Abraham—L Levy.... $259 45
30 Austin, George W—H B Mixer.... 208 39
2 Adamski, Paul—M Schulz.... 81 65
3 Albers, Henry — Eppens Smith & Wiemann Co.... 136 00
25 Baker, Herman—M J McManus.... 241 50
27 Barnum, Stephen C—American Rubber Co.... 287 68
27 Brown, James A—C H Kelly.... 259 55
27 Baker, Wells—G Wald.... 49 25
27 Burke, James A—H J Grant.... 174 05
27 Brommond, Adolph—E Zerweck.... 568 23
27 Baur, Christian—D J Dannat.... 88 43
28 Blauvelt, William A—J W Couser.... 297 03
28 Bonnell, John H—Brooklyn Bank.... 687 73
30 Babcock, Charles B—M L Ferres.... 372 28
30 Burke, John J; Burke, John E } Thomson Meter Co.... 58 79
1 Brown, William J—F H Tyler.... 207 20
1 Barneman, Edward—T C Lyman & Co.... 851 95
2 Birch, Thomas B—M B Euler.... 110 85
2 Baker, Frank S—W H Rogers.... 80 04
2 Bonnell, John H; Bonnell, Tammassin H } Merchants' Ex-Nat Bank, N Y.... 1,652 85
2 Bonnell, Tammissin H—the same.. 10,087 85
3 Brennan, Daniel—Maria Kiernan.... 64 49
25 Crandall, Harlan—Calvary Baptist Church.... 121 01
27 Crosby, George—American Rubber Co.... 287 68
27 Crego, Russell—O Smith.... 1,248 64
30 Clark, John J—F Betz.... 61 86
30 Caruthers, Robert L—J F Mahnken.. 146 51
30 Cooper, Marvelle W—City of Brooklyn.... 57 65
1 Campbell, William—C Maxwell.... 639 87
1 Conklin, F Augustus—G W Brown.. 216 85
2 Cockshaw, Albert—W F Gardiner.... 28 35
2 Coffin, Margaret A—D L McDonald.. 98 78
2 Charlick, Gardener—V Willis.... 261 22
3 Cohen, Henry—A Meurer.... 198 16
3 Canavello, Benjamin J—J W Lockwood.... 41 83
3 Canders, Hugh J—A Stark.... 36 39
25 De Moline, Charles—N Mehrof.... 52 50
27 Delaney, Patrick—E B Smith.... 45 40
27 Davis, Joseph—H F Koepke.... 1,144 82
27 Davis, Milton B—H Chapel.... 414 32
28 Del Negro Nicola—N D'Angela.... 154 83
30 De Wolffe, Charles H—T J Preston & Co, a corporation.... 33 86
1 Douglass, John H; Douglass, Richard H; Douglass, Mary } P H Flynn.. 94 57
1 Dudley, Frederick R—Richardson & Morgan Co.... 192 91
1 Dunleavy, Dennis—C B Smith.... 36 60
2 Davidow, Samuel, Henry and Annie—C V Formes.... 80 25
2 Davis, Harrie and Rosita—E P Ide.... 273 29
28 Ellis, Edward S—Brooklyn Bank.... 687 73
30 Eckert Henry—C D Lippold.... 631 82
3 Erster, Victor P P—J S Jacobs.... 231 75
25 Freygang, Hugo W — Ferdinand Munch Brewery.... 537 81
1 Ferris, Lillian—J Pullman.... 13 98
1 Fox, Robert—B Levison.... 85 20
2 Felty, Albert J—T F Mannex.... 197 87
2 Foley, Peter—Cook & Bernheimer.... 85 23
27 Grau, Alexander—E B Smith.... 45 40
30 Gibbins, Austin P—J Helmsky.... 176 43
30 Grieb, George—H Sior.... 95 74
1*Granwald, Frederick—A H Rosenberg.... 42 85
2 Gelb, Abraham—D Simon.... 41 05
27 Hummel, Henry H—S L Treadwell, trustee.... 181 52
27 Hines, Herman—H Sacks.... 516 59
28 Harper, William D—Brooklyn Bank 687 73
30 Hendrickson, Charles—I Jacobs.... 97 64
30 Huestwohl, Frank—R R La Bau.... 515 00
30 Hamilton, Samuel—the same.... 293 21
1 Hemmer, Peter—Weeks & Parr.... 128 30
2 Harper, William D—Merchants' Exchange Nat Bank.... 10,087 85
2 Heiselman, John A—Valentine & Co. 108 50
3 Hornung, Edward—J Harrington.... 29 76
3 Haight, John D—E Johnson.... 1,051 78
25 Joyce, Thomas; Joyce, Maurice J } A J Campbell.... 1,337 87
30 Joyce, Andrew A—M Partridge.... 984 83
1 Judson, Edward—H Miles.... 249 48
1 Jonson, Peter—J M Wreidon.... 238 03
2 Joyce, Edward; Joyce, Catharine } L Bossert.... 135 00
27 Kramer, Emma—C Horstman.... 1,165 13
27 Klump, Frederick J—S Liebmann's Sons B Co.... 173 23
27 Kleinfeld, Morris—B Sel.... 289 77
28 Klein, Joseph—J R Berbling.... 201 20
28 Klee, Henry W—B G Coles.... 130 45
1 Keer, Joseph T—K C Herne.... 67 57
27*Laurowitz, Louis; Landau, Bernard } B Sel.... 289 77
28 Lauro, Rosaria—N D'Angela.... 154 83
2 Litchfield, George H—L H Street.... 2,049 55
2 Lemmermann, Henry L — Cook & Bernheimer.... 221 44
2 Lees, Samuel—R R Cornell.... 168 26
2 Lewis, Sidney H—J R Smith.... 427 06
25 Martin, Henry—Cook & Bernheimer. 19 10
25 Maloney, Patrick—M J McManus.... 241 50
27 Matt, Albert; Matt, Minnie } R J Shadbolt.... 148 00
27 Molner, Samuel—E C Smith.... 436 41

27 Maue, Philip / Maue, Barbara } L Michel.......... 209 25
28 Moog, Simon—T W Osborne........ 447 41
30 Merritt, Charles H—H B Mixer...... 203 39
30 Merriam, Leo A—E B Smith......... 137 68
30 the same—the same.... .... 123 13
30 Mulqueen, Thomas F—Wakefield Rattan Co.................... 216 64
30 McDermott, Thomas—Nat Cash Register Co....................... 104 64
30 Meagher, James—R R Lao Bau. 293 21
1 McFarland, Michael—T Keogh...... 58 66
1 Murray, Robert—Rochester Distilling Co.................... 258 90
2 McAleer, John—M Steiner.......... 359 91
2 Monaghan, Patrick—M F McGoldrick, trustee....................... 341 67
3 Martin, Henry — American Champagne Co (Lim).................... 141 89
2 O'Reilly, William V—M Steiner...... 33 60
3 O'Connor, James—J H Lee........... 208 08
25 Perkins, Josephine E—F B Wheeler.. 1,215 00
25 Pearson, Ely F—W B Pierson........ 949 26
25 Potter, Luther H—Calvary Baptist Church 121 01
27 Poole, Sidney G / Poole, Mary A } Mary Runde....... 41 78
1 Paul, Edward A—K R Wolcott, trustee............................ 270 07
28 Randall, Andrew—P L Eastman..(D) 973 04
30 Roeth, Louis—J Helmsky........... 176 43
30 Rotnenburg, John W—H B Mixer... 203 39
30 Roche, Edward—M Hall............. 39 55
1 Ratbkamp, August—A H Rosenberg. 42 85
2 Rodden, Michael—N Y Mutual Gas Light Co......................... 109 81
2 Rosenbaum, August H—P Rudolph... 153 84
27 Schlusser, George J—C W Nason..... 178 83
27 Sims, Edward H—Samuel Winslow Skate Mfg Co. 788 71
27 Schneider, Charles—Municipal Electric Light Co...................... 130 75
27 Scott, James R—Edison Electric Illuminating Co....................... 194 43
28 Sloat, Henry V—J I Goodrich. 223 41
30 Schmidt, Rosina—D L McDonald..... 114 94
30 Slater, William / Slater, Seymour } S C Talbot......... 328 27
30 Stout, Joseph H—J Vollkommer..... 119 22
30 Scholl, John / Scholl, Louisa } W H Bierds......... 75 73
1 Strawson, Vincent A—H J Leach..... 496 42
1 Sterns, Herman—B Levison.......... 85 20
2 Scholl, John—J F Truslow........... 47 85
2 Schwerdtfeger, Emil—T J Preston & Co, a corporation.................. 86 05
27 The N Y Soap and Chemical Co—C Pflieging.............................. 145 81
27 Townsend, Edward N / Townsend, Maurice E } W T Klots & Bros' Sons.. 164 74
28 The J H Bonnell & Co (Lim) / Turton, John / Turton, Edgar S } Brooklyn Bank... 687 73
30 The guard John E Burke—Thomson Meter Co.......................... 58 79
30 The Adams & Sons Co—H Worms... 234 87
30 Thom, John C—W E Dodge......... 168 02
1 The Coney Island & Brooklyn R R Co—F V Gillespie.................. 81 47
1 Thissen, Jacob / Thissen, Henry } A Kirchoff......... 558 46
1 The Italo-American Co-operative Savings and Loan Assoc—T F Larkin.. 100 92
30 Upson, Uriah L—H B Mixer.......... 203 39
1 Van Vorhis, Cornelius W—W M Woods.............................. 785 11
25 Wood, William H S—J B Horton.... 1,435 09
27 Wines, Charles H—W W Hulse.. ... 642 89
27 the same—W L Young...... ... 118 49
28 Walling, Edward P—W H Sawyer Lumber Co.......................... 1,453 63
28†Walworth, "Robert" B—G E Jeffery 78 22
28 Winter, George—National Cash Register Co 94 56
30 Wyckoff, Charles B—C J Reed....... 220 96
1 Weed, Vitruvius E—K R Wolcott, trustee............................ 270 67
2 Windbladh, Victor—P C Stendrup... 180 34
2 Wyckoff, Annie M—A O'Neil, admrx 329 08
2 Wyburn, Joseph N—J R Smith...... 427 06

SATISFIED JUDGMENTS.

NEW YORK.

November 28 to December 4—Inclusive.

Andrews, Charles B—Nora A Rook. (1886).. $6,151 67
Butler, Jacob D—John Birkenstock. (1891)... 222 81
Bulk, Gustave H and Charles—P R Weller. (1891) 843 13
Brendon, Edwin V—W E Forest. (1889)....... 352 71
Same—same. (1890)...................... 90 59
Same—same. (1890)...................... 97 94
Bendheim, Henry M—Fannie Fruhauf. (1887) 1,543 11
Same—same. (1889)...................... 77 40
Brown, John—H W Riddell. (1888)........... 51 27
Clews, Henry—W C Thompson. (1891)....... 810 10
Capen, Walter N—Hiram Barber. (1891)...... 296 32
Cavinato, Luigi, Guiseppe Stefano and Natale—John Donnellon. (1891)................... 217 41
Callahan, Cornelius—Nason Mfg Co. (1891)... 1,742 57
Davis, Wolff—Dry Dock, East Broadway & Battery R R Co. (1891)................... 116 39
Darling, Ruel D—P D Searles. (1890)........ 142 84
Ernst, John H—S Liebmann's Sons Brewing Co. (1891)................................ 167 00
French, Helen A—Abel Crook. (1890).......... 2,551 50
Fox, Levi—Herrmann Koehler. (1881)........ 549 06
‖Fox, Levi—Isaac Maguire. (1881)............ 195 06
Fleet, Edward W—S R and J C Mott. (1886).. 140 51
Fere, Fernand—Marie Babin, admr. (1887). 624 03
Gilhooly, Patrick H—J F Arnold. (1891)...... 720 22
Gans, Conrad—S Liebmann's Sons Brewing Co. (1890)............................. 167 00
Gilmour, John—Annie E Brown. (1890)...... 1,258 45
Same—Saugertus Bank. (1891)............ 597 21
Same—Third Nat Bank of Buffalo. (1891). 645 30
Gill, Edith—Rapid Printing Co. (1891)....... 821 87
Hall, Henry J—A A Grant. (1891) 160 93
Kennedy, James / Kemp, John } H A Curiel. (1891)....... 112 20
Kelly, Thomas P—C T Barney. (1891)........ 808 75
Kelly, Thomas P and John A—P D Searles. (1890).. 149 84
Kelly, Thomas P—Murray Hill Bank. (1891).. 179 84
Same and Michael J—J T Nevin. (1891) 45 34
Same—J W Fiske. (1891) 90 50
Kelly, Michael J—Murray Hill Bank. (1891).. 208 58
Kelly, Thomas P—William Koch. (1891)...... 85 69
Same—same. (1891).... .... 96 01
Kempenard, Gerard—Beadleston & Woerz. (1883).. 31 75
L'Allemand, Marcus James—Philip Goetcher. (1890) 89 45
Lotty, William H—H W Riddell. (1888)...... 61 97
Lyon, Charles and David—H A Caesar. (1891). 938 76
Levy, Abraham and Louis—Nat Park Bank. (1891).. 33,868 52
Same—Adolph Rawitser. (1891)................ 1,864 30
Same—Charles Sternbach. (1891).......... 10,799 18
Manhattan Railway Co—E R. Scott (1891)... 1,701 44
Same—same (1891)............ .... 92 64
McDermott, Patrick J—M R Cook. (1891)..... 344 00
Morris, Adolph M / Mark, Nathan } I. B. Cassell. (1889)......... 998 47
Moss, Frank, exr—S B Brague. (1891)......... 1,192 14
†Mack, Hugo S—P A Smyth. (1891)........... 562 23
Morriss, Adolph / Marks, Nathan } Jacob Jacoby. (1889)....... 116 47
Same—Herman Falkenstein. (1889)....... 216 47
Same—C V Fornes. (1889)..................... 1,961 08
Same—same. (1889)............................ 516 47
Mills, Ann W and Arthur E—A K Murphy. (1891).. 612 72
Miller, John—A S Lascelles. (1891) 106 61
N Y Steam Co—Mercantile Buffet Co. (1891). 2,061 75
North American Phonograph Co—K K Jenkins. (1891)...................................... 1,915 73
Same—George Smallwood. (1891) 1,916 73
Pratt, James H—Chatham Nat Bank. (1891). 94 32
Same—same. (1889)................................ 11,485 00
Preble, John Q and Walter E—Garfield Nat Bank. (1890).................................. 10,118 00
Same—same. (1890)............................ 5,039 47
Same—American Exch Nat Bank. ('90). 20,268 72
Same—Hartford Nat Bank of Hartford, Conn. (1890)............................... 4,855 20
Same—O H Grunleaf. (1890)................ 50,485 38
Same—N Y Life Ins and Trust Co. ('90). 50,047 00
Same—Bank of America. (1890)............ 5,096 38
Same—Rockville Nat Bank. (1890)......... 5,078 71
Same—Elijah Nichols. (1890).................. 3,579 38
Same—William Skinner. (1890)............... 2,498 41
Same—Cambridgeport Diary Co. (1890)... 2,507 47
Same—same. (1890)............................ 2,407 47
Same—Hartford Nat Bank of Hartford, Conn. (1890)................................ 5,082 82
Same—Nat Park Bank. (1890)................ 5,089 40
Same—George Leask. (1890)................. 12,451 67
Same—W F Russell (1890).................... 15,276 79
Same—Nat Park Bank. (1890)............... 5,046 32
Same—N Y Life Ins Co. (1890).............. 5,041 16
Same—O H Greenleaf. (1890)................ 50,581 22
Same—Nat Park Bank. (1890)................ 5,044 46
Same—Ninth Nat Bank. (1890).............. 20,028 03
Same—same. (1890)............................ 15,609 03
Same—Fourth Nat Bank. (1890)............. 20,366 04
Same—Holyoke Nat Bank of Holyoke, Mass. (1890)................................. 5,043 23
Same—Importer and Traders' Nat Bank. (1890).. 10,096 72
Same—Mercantile Nat Bank. (1890)...... 10,203 57
Same—First Nat Bank of Rockville. ('90).. 5,095 72
Rankin, William H—J F Arnold. (1891)....... 1,720 21
Rosenheim, Louis—H A Caesar. (1891)........ 931 76
Rosenbloom, Phillip—Jacob Gladke. (1887)... 1,033 90
Same—Charles Werner. (1890)............... 974 31
Sixth Nat Bank—Lorillard Brick Works Co. (1891)... 682 89
Schirmer, Gustav—F S Myers. (1891).......... 88 32
Same—same. (1891) 242 44
Simpson, Ernest L / Spence, Lewis H } David McG Means, recvr. (1891)........ 1,597 18
Streeseman, John F—G F Swift. (1891) 394 41
Snook Glove Mfg Co / Snook, William W } C B Fosdick............. 2,906 81
Singhi, Henry U—Mary E Singhi. (1888).... 1,516 29
Same—W F Redlich. (1888)..................... 342 94
Stanton, Robert L—Frederick Sonnenburg. (1890).. 147 55
Shapiro, Samuel—Henry Newman. (1884).... 170 23
Same—M L Manheim. (1885)................ 419 12
Same—R I Cowen. (1883)..................... 161 04
Same—Bernard Schleestein. (1884) 560 40
Same—Emanuel Rosenberg. (1884)...... 2,541 47
Same—Louis Jacobson. (1884) 994 24
Same—Julius Schattman. (1884).......... 1,891 08
Same—Joseph Segall. (1885).................. 1,215 74
Townshend, Mary N and John—C G Landon. (1891) 132 70
Taylor, Jacob E—George Smith. (1890) 336 28
Wolf, William—C V Fornes. (1889)............. 516 47
Same—same. (1889)............................ 1,961 08
Same—Herman Falkenstein. (1889)....... 216 47
Same—Jacob Jacoby. (1889)................. 116 47
Wolf, William—I B Cassell. (1889).......... 998 47
Wieck, Francis G—C G Landon. (1891)....... 132 70
Westerberg, Charles—C E Bruce. (1891)..... 300 98
Young, William M—David McG Means, recvr. (1891).. 1,597 18

*Vacated by order of Court. †Suspended on Appeal ‡Released. §Reversal. ‖Satisfied by Execution.

KINGS COUNTY.

November 27 to December 3—Inclusive.

Bennett, William J—B H Brow. (1891)....... $243 35
Cory, Nathaniel T—Merchants' Nat Bank, New Bedford. (1890)..................................... 546 81
Evarts, Charles M—Merchants' Nat Bank, New Bedford. (1890).......................... 546 81
Ernst, John H—S Liebmann's Sons B Co. (91) 167 00
Felty, Albert J—F Emmerich. (1891). (Execution).. 111 20
Fleet, Edward W—G W Venable. (1889)....... 150 89
Same—S R & J C Mott. (1886).............. 140 51
Fallon, John—C C F Otto. (1891)............... 250 69
Grolle, Charles—H Sandman. (1888)........... 295 45
Gross, Henry A and Margaret—F D Bailey. (1891.) (Execution)...... realized 42.62 on 72 79
Green, Henry—Edison Electric Illuminating Co. (1891.) (Execution)........................ 81 59
Gans, Conrad—S Liebmann's Sons B Co. (1891) 167 00
Hall, Henry J—A A Grant. (1891)............. 160 93
Kleuber, Leopoldine—E C Smith. (1890)...... 1,293 76
Levy, Robert—P H Samilson. (1891.) (Execution).. 144 60
Mars, Henrietta A—Eliz Fromme. (1891.) (Execution).. 88 02
Muller, George J—G Deike. (1891)............. 115 85
Nelson, Charles—E C Smith. (1890)............ 1,293 76
Rogers, Asa L—E D Fogg. (1888)............... 130 03
Same—C E Easton. (1883)..................... 394 25
Smith, Henry—S M Meeker. (1888)........... 470 38
Tietje, Henry—H M Bischoff. (1891.) (Execution) 88 90
The Brooklyn City R R Co—J Alexander. (1891).. 500 00

MECHANICS' LIENS.

NEW YORK CITY.

Nov.
28 Jones st, No. 23, s s, 150 e Bleecker st, 25x100. Dempsey & Smith agt Theodore Van Eupen, owner and contractor........ $880 00
30*Seventy-seventh st, s s, 104 w West End av, 62x102.2. C. T. Mott agt Edward Purcell, owner and contractor 800 00
30 Ninety-fifth st, s s, 100 w Columbus av, 50x84.2. Albany Venetian Blind Co. agt F. J. Hillenbrandt, owner, and McElwee Mfg Co., contractors.......................... 95 00
30 Ninety-sixth st, n s, 150 e Amsterdam av, 125x87.6. Same agt Alexander Cameron, owner, and McElwee Mfg Co., contractors 195 00
30 Ninety-fourth st, n s, 100 w Columbus av, 50x81.2. Same agt F. J. Hillenbrandt, owner, and McElwee Mfg. Co., contractors 95 00
30 Ninety-seventh st, No. 64, s s, 182 e 9th av, 19x100. M. L. English agt R. Irene Thompson, owner, and I. Halstead Dunn, contractor.................................... 245 00
30 Twentieth st, No. 450, s s, 175 e 4th av, 18.8x92. B. B. Pew agt Richard McCaul, owner and contractor.............................. 196 56
30 Bradhurst av, s e cor 143d st, 100x53. Royal Elwell agt Fernando Yost, owner, and Lafayette Elwell, contractor............ 75 00
30 Same property. John Riggs, Jr., agt same. 75 00
30 Third av, No. 2313, e s, 99.11 n 125th st, 25x80. Burrows & Smith agt Louis J. Kahn, owner, and Percy Jacobs, contractor..... 350 00

Dec.
1 Ninety-eighth st, n s, 265.6 e Amsterdam av, 159.6x100. Daniel Tooher agt John W. Hutton, Julius Lipman, Moses Kind and Jacob Cohen, owners, and John W. Hutton and Robert Wheeler, contractors..... 710 00
1 One Hundred and Fifteenth st, s s, 275 e 8th av, 175x100. Fort Plain Furniture Co. agt Muller & Hauff, owners and contractors.. 2,520 00
1 One Hundred and Twenty-fifth st, Nos. 209 and 211, n s, 107 e 3d av, 52x100. Rapp & Johnson Lumber Co. agt J. Cooks, owner, and K. N. Smith & Co., contractors...... 3,348 86
1 One Hundred and Thirty-seventh st, n s, 60 e Rider av, 50x100. Same agt J. L. Mott Iron Works, owners, and K. N. Smith & Co., contractors................ 2,746 28
1 Amsterdam av, No. 1882, e s, 50 s 83d st, 25x80. Mitchell Vance Co. agt John E. Hodges or Mina Daiker and Thomas Hagan, owners, and Burchell & Hodges, contractors. (Continued from Dec. 3, 1890).. 109 10
1 Amsterdam av, No. 1881, e s, 25 s 83d st, 25x80. Same agt same. (Continued from Dec. 3, 1890)................................ 109 09
1 Amsterdam av, No. 1880, e s, 75 s 83d st, 24.4x80.3x30.8x80. Same agt same. (Continued from Dec. 3, 1890). 109 10
1 One Hundred and Thirty-second st, s s, 125 e 5th av, 85x100.11. Thomas Tracy & Son agt Lizzie T. Wilks, owner, and Geo S. Wilks, contractor.............................. 1,195 00
1 Amsterdam av, s w cor 81st st, 100x90. Frank Falell agt Patrick Dempsey, owner and contractor. (Continued from Dec. 1, 1890) 570 00
1 Forty-fourth st, Nos. 437 and 439, n s, 320 e 10th av, 40x100. N. Y. Anderson Pressed Brick Co. agt William G. Jordan, owner and contractor 410 35
1 Broadway, No. 1570, s e cor 47th st, 20x75. P. J. Ryan agt Patrick H. Cuff, owner and contractor 1,113 15
2 One Hundred and Twenty-fifth st, n s, 105 e 3d av, 51x90. A. D. Knapp agt J. Cook, owner, and K. N. Smith & Co., contractors 328 28
2 Interior chimney, abt 144 s 134th st and 228 w 3d av, 10.2x10.2. Same agt J. L. Mott Iron Works, owners, and K. N. Smith & Co., contractors 248 53
2 One Hundred and Thirty-seventh st, n s, abt 60 e Rider av, 50x75. Same agt J. L. Mott Iron Works, owners, and K. N. Smith & Co., contractors................ 447 88
2 Seventy-second st, No. 130, n w cor Lexington av, 30x102.2. Flemer & Koehler agt Sarah Levenson, owner and contractor.. 1,800 00
2 Same property. C. H. Bunn agt same.... 4,790 63
2 One Hundred and Twenty-fifth st, n s, 105 e 3d av, 50x100. Thomas Hagan agt Justin Cooke, owner, and K. N. Smith & Co., contractors.. 1,000 00
2 One Hundred and Fifth st, s s, 175 e Columbus av, 21.6x100. Same agt John Duke, owner, and John Nesbitt, contractor..... 483 42
2 Bowery, e s, 15.7 n 1st st, 15.8x71.5. G. B. Christman agt Theodore Von Eupen, owner, lessee and contractor 67 73
2 One Hundred and Eighteenth st, s s, 60 e Madison av, 100x100.11. J. A. Attieri agt Samuel Harris, owner, and Bernhard Ginsberg, contractor 158 12
2 One Hundred and Forty-fourth st, s s, abt 100 e 8th av, 25x100. J. W. Binney agt Ernest Molwitz, owner, and Christian Anderson, contractor.......................... 45 00
2 Eighty-fourth st, s s, abt 350 w Columbus av, 50x100. F. Hydoon agt George J. Cohen, owner, and McElwee Mfg. Co., contractor.. 887 90
2 Interior chimney, abt 228 w 3d av and 145.2 s 134th st, 10.2x10.2. John Gibson agt J. L. Mott Iron Works, owner, and K. N. Smith & Co., contractors.................. 56 00
2 One Hundred and Thirty-seventh st, n s, 60 e Riker av, 50x100. Same agt same 197 25
2 One Hundred and Twenty-fifth st, Nos. 209 and 211, n s, 150 e 3d av, 50x90. Same agt

Justus Cooke, owner, and K. N. Smith & Co., contractors 250 25
3 Amsterdam av, s w cor 99th st, 80.2x40. W. J. Law agt Lilian Rogers and Henry C. Acker, owners, and Lilian Rogers, contractor 80 00
3 Columbus av, No. 766, w s, 75 n 97th st, 25x100. T. E. McLoughlin agt Harry Galway, owner, and Elias T. Hatch and Michael Tobin, contractors 145 00
3 Eighth av, No. 2348, e s, 50 s 126th st, 25x100. T. F. Hines agt —— Fitzpatrick and George E. Brotherton, owners, and George E. Brotherton, contractor 516 27
3 Waverley pl, s s, 25 w Mercer st, 25x82. A. D. Knapp agt H. & S. Corn, owners, and K. N. Smith & Co., contractors 186 36
3 Broome st, No. 209, s e cor Norfolk st, 24x51.8. Louis Aronowitz agt Eva Myers, owner and contractor 600 00
3 Eighty-eighth st, n s, 175 w 5th av, 75x100.8. Burton Gliddon agt Frederick Wood, owner and contractor 75 00
3 One Hundred and Fourteenth st, s s, 149.6 w 5th av, 140.6x99.6. Same agt Margaret E. Conlon, owner and contractor 50 00
3 Boston av, s e cor 164th st, 25.10x83x25x81. Thomas Lyons agt Georgianna Webster, owner, and Thomas Webster, contractor. 332 75
3 Madison av, Nos. 136 and 138, n w cor 31st st, 50x95. L. K. Dusenberry agt Peter N. Ramsey and Samuel G. Revens, owners, and Peter N. Ramsey, contractor 990 00
4 One Hundred and Twenty-fourth st, Nos. 106 and 108, s s, 135 e Park av. J. H. Merritt agt W. J. and H. C. Browning, owners and contractors 55 70
4 Leroy st, Nos. 55 and 57, n s. Jenkins Co. agt John W. Stevens and Owen McElroy, Sr., and Owen McElroy, Jr., owners, and George A. Baker, contractor 83 87
4 Ninety-third st, Nos. 11-17, n s, 250 e 5th av, 76.8x100.8. Bonneau Wightman & Co. agt Philip Braender, owner, and Fritz Uckermann, contractor 300 00
4 Seventh av, n w cor 27th st, 88.8x irreg x 98.9x143.2. Friendship Mfg. Co. agt William F. Rohrig, owner, and McElwee Mfg. Co., contractor 1,500 00
4 Same property. H. W. Foote agt same .. 1,000 00
4 Fifty-fourth st, No. 448, s s, 250 e 10th st, 25x—. Jame Rose agt Nicholas McCool, owner and contractor 286 00
4 Third Av. Railroad Company's road bed from Ann to 130th st, bridges, &c. John McQuade agt Third Av. R. R. Co., owner, and William Wharton, Jr., & Co., contractors 79,000 00
4 One Hundred and First st, No. 73, n s, 156 e Columbus av, 25x100.11. David Malcolm agt Sophia Oppenheimer, owner and contractor 111 64
4 Third av, No. 2313, e s, 99.11 n 125th st, 25x80. Alex. Weigand agt Louis J. Kann, owner, and R. J. McDonald, contractor. 70 00

Editor RECORD AND GUIDE:

The lien filed last week against property southeast corner Bradhurst avenue and 143d street by Lafayette Elwell is very unjust, he having been overpaid $240, according to contract. Said lien will be bonded and contested.

FERNANDO YOST.

* *Editor* RECORD AND GUIDE:

The lien filed November 30th by Charles T. Mott against my property in West 77th street is unjust. Proceedings have been taken to bond the lien.

EDWARD PURCELL.

KINGS COUNTY.

Nov.
25 Reid av, w s, 50 n Halsey st, 50x100. Bulmer Lumber Co. (Lim.) agt George W. McCormick, owner and contractor $386 58
27 Patchen av, n e cor Putnam av, 20x100. Evans Brothers agt Thomas Walling and Morris Hawkins, owners, and Thomas Walling, contractor 785 00
27 Ellery st, No. 255, n s, 175 w Sumner av, 25x100. Louis Bossert agt Adolph Schlesinger, owner, and F. H. Waldron, contractor 40 72
28 Ralph av, n w cor Macon st, 100x125. William P. Barker agt N. H. & B. C. Raymond, owners and contractors 529 54
28 Reid av, s s, 50 w Halsey st, 50x100. Van Wagner & Co. agt George W. McCormick, owner and contractor 348 24
30 De Kalb av, Nos. 676-680½. Frank H. Collins agt Elizabeth A. Maitland, owner, and Charles H. Collins, contractor 400 00
30 Patchen av, n e cor Putnam av, 20x108. Thomas Sheffield agt Thomas Walling, owner, and Thomas Walling and E. H. & W. M. Hawkins, contractors 885 00
30 Fourth av, s w cor 34th st, 100x100. Frank D. Creamer agt Alger & McCool, owners and conorators 901 05
30 Reid av, w s, 51 n Halsey st, 50x100. Thomas Sheffield agt George W. McCormack, owner and contractor 80 00
30 Second st, s s, bet 6th av and 7th av, 117.10x100. See lien. Eric Erickson agt Jennie L. Ross, owner, and Donald C. Ross, contractor 460 00
30 Fulton st, s s, 200 w Stone av, 100x100. Same agt same owner and contractor 876 00

Dec.
1 De Kalb av, s s, 150 w Marcy av, 100x100. Francis H. Collins agt Elizabeth Maitland, owner, and Chas. H. Collins, contractor .. 400 00
1 Sixth st, s s, 180 w 4th av, 115x100. Brooklyn Slate Mantel Co. agt H. Becker and M. Maloney, owners and contractors 340 00
1 Rockaway av, e s, 100 s Eastern Parkway, 25x100. Same agt B. Seerman, owner and contractor 48 00
1 Tenth st, Nos. 593-601. Same agt James Ransom, owner and contractor 70 00
1 Eastern Parkway, s s, 25 e Thatford av, 25x100. Same agt B. Seerman, owner and contractor 36 00
1 Lewis av, n w cor Hancock st, 100x150. Jacob May agt Joseph Aronson and Thomas A. McWhinney, owners and contractors 93 07

1 Fourth av, s w cor 34th st, 100x100. Adaline A. Newman agt Algie & McCool, owners and contractors 1,208 71
2 Fourth av, s w cor 44th st, 80x100. Vermont Marble Co. agt Peter Algie and Nicholas McCool, owners and contractors 20 00
2 Herkimer st, n s, 20 w Saratoga av, runs west 80 x north 100 x east 100 to Saratoga av, x south 40 x west 20 x south 60. George Iles agt Harriet Johnston, owner, and Albert Johnston, contractor 64 00
2 Garfield pl, Nos. 191-199, n s, 100 w 7th av, 155x100. The Thomas Roberts Stevenson Co. agt E. L. Bukman, owner and contractor 980 00
2 Fifty-seventh st, n s, 300 e 11th av, 40x100, New Utrecht. James Lindsay agt —— Umbach, owner, and Emil Kehler, contractor 28 83
2 Pennsylvania av, w s, 50 n Belmont av, 100x100. Jacob May agt Mrs. Boyle, owner, and A. F. Hill, contractor 158 00
2 Bushwick av, cor Beaver st, irreg. and indeft. (see Lien). Joseph A. Heim agt Henry Huther, owner, and Schultz & Auffinger, contractors 142 13
2†Woodbine st, n w s, 25 s w Knickerbocker av, 200x100. Bulmer Lumber Co agt Albert Berckmeier, owner and contractor .. 1,639 90
2 Ridgewood av, s s, 20 w Linwood st, 40x100. John C. Creveling agt Philip M. Knight, owner, and Newton & Donaldson, contractors 87 16
2 Same property. Adam Donaldson agt same owner, and Isaac Newton, contractor 247 00
2 Smith st, s s, 180 w 4th st, 115x100. John Monahan agt H. Becker, owner, and P. Maloney, contractor 53 52
2 Lewis av, s e cor Hancock st, 100x150. Bulmer Lumber Co. agt Thomas A. McWhinney and Jacob Aaronson, owners and contractors 67 29

Herkimer st, n s, 20 w Saratoga av, 80x80,
2 Saratoga av, w s, 80 n Herkimer st, 40x100 ....
Aaron Almstrom agt Albert Johnson, owner and contractor 350 00
3 Same property. James J. Higgins agt Harriet Johnson, owner, and Albert Johnson, contractor 60 00
3 Grand st, Nos. 636-640, s s, 100 e Leonard st, 75x80. William Schaefer agt Joseph Carney, owner, and James A. Terhune, contractor 63 28
3 Bergen st, s s, 145 e 6th av, 50x107. Cross, Austin & Co. agt The Olivet Chapel, owner, and Charles G. Lloyd and William J. Wilson, contractors 862 69
3 Eastern Parkway, s s, 75 w Thatford st, 25x100. Schmid & Esperstadt agt Soloman Kreuckstein, owner, and Solomon Koplansky and Samuel Samowitz, contractors. 170 75
3 Noble st, No. 117, n s, 418 e Franklin st, 22x100. Patrick McHugh agt William P. Morrissy, owner, and Smith & Duffy, contractors 250 00
3 Howard av, w s, extending from Hancock to Jefferson st, 100 deep. George S. Harris agt Thomas H. Robbins, owner, and Thomas Robbins, contractor. (Redocket) 135 00

† *Editor* RECORD AND GUIDE:

The lien filed by us on Dec. 2d against Albert Berckmeier has been satisfied to-day and will be discharged of record to-morrow morning.

December 4, 1891. BULMER LUMBER CO. (Limited).

SATISFIED MECHANICS' LIENS.

NEW YORK CITY.

Nov.
28 South st, No. 8, n w cor Moore st. Nicholas Ryan agt Edward Landers and William C. Turner. (Lien filed June 30, 1891). $108 80

Broadway, Nos. 610-616 ....
30 Crosby st, Nos. 30-36 ....
Broadway, No. 472 ....
W. H. Coot agt The Mutual Real Estate Co. (May 19, 1891) 610 08
30 Eleventh st, Nos. 310 and 312 E. C. W. Klappert Sons agt Moses Weil. (July 3, 1890) 2,000 00
30 Same property. Muhn & Strobaecker agt same. (June 28, 1890) 890 00
30 Same property. Peter Schaeffler agt same. (June 28, 1890) 3,000 00
30†Waverley pl, No. 175. Goss & Edsall agt William C. Burniston and Julian Ehrig. (July 23, 1991) 75 00
30†Same property. W. F. Campbell agt same. (July 21, 1891) 394 00
30†Same property. Jane Garvey agt same. (July 21, 1891) 276 00
30†Same property. Louis Jeans and three others agt same. (July 31, 1891.) (4 liens) 45 50

Dec.
1 One Hundred and Twenty-fifth st, Nos. 148 and 150 W. D. A. Fitzpatrick agt William Hargrave and Edgar Ketchum. (Nov. 16, 1891) 190 00
1 Hall pl, e s, 468 s 167th st. C. W. Yasenski and three others agt John J. Rentz and Edmond C. Allcot. (Nov. 3, 1891.) (4 liens) 385 10
1 Same property. W. T. Allcot agt same. (Nov. 10, 1891) 162 00
1 Same property. Gilbert Morrison agt same. (Nov. 7, 1891) 155 00
2 Sixteenth st, No. 345 W., 25x100. C. J. Everett agt Henry W. Deane. (Aug. 12, 1891). 68 34
2 Seventeenth st, No. 28 W., 25x—. James Blackhurst agt Mrs. Samuel Borrowe. (June 6, 1891) 1,625 00
2 Suburban st, n s, 346.8 e Anthony av, 25x—. John McCabe agt John Kinney, William Rose and William Hoff. (Oct. 19, 1891) ... 7 75
2 Same property. Edward McCabe agt same. (Oct. 19, 1891) 22 50
3 Waverley pl, No. 18, 33.5x82. A. D. Knapp agt H. & S. Corn and K. N. Smith & Co. (Dec. 2, 1891) 186 36
3 Thirty-fifth st, No. 41 W., 25x—. Philip Smith agt Janette Pirsson. (Aug. 11, 1891) 508 50
3 Same property. R. A. Patterson agt same. (Sept. 23, 1891) 96 20
3 Ninety-fourth st, n s, 150 w Columbus av, 100x100. Edward Barry agt James Brady and McLoughlin, Clegg & Co. (July 30, 1891) 14 62
3 Same property. James Dempsey agt same. (July 30, 1891) 14 62
3 Seventy-eighth st, s s, 100 w Amsterdam av, 75x100. Bernard McHugh agt Arthur Boehmer and McLoughlin, Clegg & Co. (July 28, 1891) 7 88
3 Same property. Matthew Lynch agt same. (Sept. 21, 1891) 11 20
3 Ninety-fourth st, n s, 150 w Columbus av, 100x100. H. S. Deshon treasurer agt James Brady and Clegg, Richards & Co. (July 22, 1891) 108 85
3 Same property. Samuel Hanna agt same. (June 30, 1891) 21 37
3 Same property. Pasquale Carmeto agt same. (June 30, 1891) 6 87
3 Same property. Thomas Heaney agt same. (July 30, 1891) 11 87
3 Same property. John Heerling agt same. (July 30, 1891) 16 00
3 Same property. Patrick Sampson agt James Brady and McLaughlin, Clegg & Co. (July 30, 1891) 29 25

3‡Seventh av, Nos. 300-306 ....
Twenty-seventh st, Nos. 205 and 207 W ...
Sutphen & Meyer agt William F. Rohrig and McElwee Mfg. Co. (Nov. 28, 1891) 600 00
3 One Hundred and Thirty-third st, n s, 240 w 7th av. Meyen & Stock agt Gilbert Robinson, Jr. (April 28, 1891) 403 80
3*Sheriff st, Nos. 91 and 93, w s, 100 s Stanton st, 50x—. Jacob Becker agt R. Mapelsden. (Nov. 12, 1891) 87 60
4 Home st, Nos. 1070-1076, s s, 154 e Stebbins av, 18x—. Brady & Anderson agt Treffle H. Allard. (Aug. 15, 1891) 150 00
4 Same property. J. J. Coyne agt same. (Aug. 15, 1891) 490 00
4 Same property. Richard Zobelt agt same. (Aug. 14, 1891) 707 50

*Discharged by depositing amount of lien and interest with County Clerk.
†Cancelled by order of Court.
‡Discharged by order of Court on filing bond.

KINGS COUNTY.

Nov.
27 Marcy av, n w cor Walton st, 38x75. Raeburn Latourette & Co. agt The North American Iron Works, owners, and K. N. Smith Co., contractors. (Nov. 24, 1891.) (Deposit) 1,836 08
28 Livonia av, s e cor Osborn st, 25x100. Potts Bros. agt Abraham Seidenbergh and Rochmiel Abramowitz, owners and contractors. (Lien filed Oct. 9, 1891) $146 58
30 Bainbridge st, n s, 115.6 e Saratoga av, 179.9x100. Patrick Kenny agt J. Mason Kirby, owner and contractor. (Nov. 17, 1891) ... 105 00
30 Thirteenth av, n e cor 67th st, 40x100.2, New Utrecht. Michael Magorino agt Edward Petersen and Edmund W. Stillwell, owners, and Ole Gunsten, contractor. (Nov. 4, 1891) 197 96
30 Chauncey st, s s, 249 e Saratoga av, 19x100. George P. Jacobs & Co. agt Adriana Smith, owner and contractor. (Release lien filed Dec. 6, 1890) 81 78
30 Same property. George B. Blydenburgh agt same owner and contractor. (Release lien filed March 10, 1891) 20 00

Dec.
2 Cropsey av, n s, 160 w Bay 19th st, 165.9x415 x irreg., New Utrecht. John Regan agt The New York Outing Club, owner and contractor. (Sept. 24, 1891) 1,238 80
2 Eastern Parkway, n s, 50 w Sackman st, 50x100. Henry McShane Mfg Co. agt Solomon & Goldberg, owners, and Pasco & McCormack, contractors. (Oct. 20, 1891). 164 81
2 Fourth st, s s, 160 w 7th av, 114x100. Patrick McGuigan agt Moses & Fanton, owners, and John Ferris, contractor. (Oct. 28, 1891) 100 00
2 St. James pl, w s, 75 s Fulton st, 50x70. Hugh J. Barron agt George R. Brown, owner and contractor. (Sept. 21, 1891.) (Order of Court) 800 00
3 Cropsey av, n e cor Bay 20th st, 100.5x415. Joel Aronson agt New York Outing Club, owner and contractor. (July 2, 1891) 848 00

BUILDINGS PROJECTED.

The first name is that of the owner; ar't stands for architect, m'n for mason, c'r for carpenter and b'r for builder.

NEW YORK CITY.

SOUTH OF 14TH STREET.

Allen st, No. 187, five-story brk flat, 25x77.10, tin roof; cost, $20,000; Philip Kotlowsky, 235 Henry st; ar'ts, Graul & Frohne. Plan 1510.

Bowery, n w cor Bayard st.
Bayard st, n e cor Elizabeth st.
nine-story brick and granite cable power station and factory, 100x200, asphalt and cement roof; cost, $650,000; Third Av R. R. Co., 3d av and 65th st; ar't, A. Wagner. Plan 1516.

Delancey st, Nos. 186 and 188, six-story brk flat and stores, 43x74.6, tin roof; cost $45,000; Chas. Ruff, 228 East 10th st; ar'ts, Schneider & Herter. Plan 1514.

5th st, Nos. 338 and 340, two five story brk flats, 25x85.8, tin roofs; cost, $18,000 each; August Ruff, 78 East 4th st; ar'ts, Kurtzer & Rohl. Plan 1498.

BETWEEN 14TH AND 59TH STREETS.

26th st, s s, 200 e 11th av, rear, one story frame shed, 26x26, gravel roof; cost, $150; J. B. & J. M. Cornell, foot of W. 26th st, North River; ar't, G. W. Debevoise. Plan 1507.

29th st, s s, 316 e 6th av, one-story brk workshop, 5x98.9, tin roof; cost, $1,000; lessee, H. C. Miner, 115 East 34th st; ar't, W. H. C. Hornum. Plan 1505.

3d av, No. 365, five-story brk flat and store, 24.8x96.6, tin roof; cost, $17,000; John Fitzpatrick, 363 3d av; ar't, F. Jenth. Plan 1501.

BETWEEN 59TH AND 125TH STREETS, EAST OF 5TH AVENUE.

107th st, s s, 200 w 1st av, four five-story brk flats, 25x88, tin roofs; cost, $20,000 each; Mathew Coogan, 423 East 115th st; ar'ts, Cleverdon & Putzel. Plan 1508.

118th st, No. 423 E., one-story brk workshop, 25x30, tin roof; cost, $900; Geo. Hollerieth, 437 East 114th st; ar't, A. Spence. Plan 1499.

BETWEEN 59TH AND 125TH STREETS, WEST OF CENTRAL PARK WEST AND 8TH AVENUE.

84th st, n s, 175 w 8th av, two five-story stone front flats, 19 and 31x91, tin roofs; total cost, $53,000; David Richey, 74 West 84th st; ar't, G. A. Schellenger. Plan 1517.

Columbus av, s w cor Manhattan st, three-story brk dwell'g and store, 44.6x38.1 and 58.10, tin roof; cost, $15,000; John E. Baker, 529 East 134th st; ar't, T. E. Thomson. Plan 1518.

Manhattan st, s s, 55.6 w Columbus av, two-story brk flat, 57x39.10x66.13, gravel roof; cost, $10,000; John E. Baker, 529 East 134th st; ar't, T. E. Thomson. Plan 1519.

Manhattan st, s s, 55.6 w Columbus av, rear, one-story brk stable, 24x30, gravel roof; cost, $800; ow'r and ar't, same as last. Plan 1520.

NORTH OF 125TH STREET.

136th st, Nos. 219–235 and 235–265 W., fifteen three-story and basement brk and stone dwell'gs, 16 and 17x50, tin roofs; cost, $10,000 each; ow'r, ar't and b'r, Thos. C. Van Brunt, 232 West 136th st. Plan 1504.

12th av, w s, 45 n 129th st, two-story brk and stone storehouse, 53x66 and 76, composition roof; cost, $16,000; Mary G. Pinkney, 19 Manhattan Market; ar't, P. J. O'Brien; m'n, W. J. Moran; c'r, A. W. Black. Plan 1511.

23D AND 24TH WARDS.

Woodruff st, n s, 351 w Prospect st, two-and-a-half-story frame dwell'g, 21x26, and extension, shingle roof; cost, $2,500; John H. Metzler, 18 Elsmere pl; ar't, C. S. Clark. Plan 1502.

Vanderbilt pl, n s, proposed, 86 e Railroad av, four two-story frame dwell'gs, 16x48, tin roofs; cost, each, $2,000; Chas. Van Riper and Jas. M. La Coste, 378 Mott av; ar't, H. S. Baker. Plan 1509.

150th st, s s, 75 w Morris av, three-story frame dwell'g, 22x40, tin roof; cost, $5,000; Jacob H. Westheimer, 242 West 130th st; ar't, P. Pfeiffer.

133d st, n s, 200 e Trinity or Cypress av, three two-story frame dwell'gs, 16.8x48, tin roofs; cost, $2,300 each; Chas. Hohl, 970 East 134th st; ar't, A. Gareiss. Plan 1580.

Bathgate av, e s, 20 n 172d st, two-story frame dwell'g, 18x28, tin roof; cost, $3,000; Mrs. Margaret V. Gallagher, 158 East 47th st; ar't, A. E. Davis; c'r, T. J. Blair. Plan 1508.

Creston av, w s, 525 n Kingsbridge road, one-and-a-half-story frame stable, 24x20, shingle roof; cost, $500; Wm. Wicke, 34 East 68th st; c'r, G. Armstrong. Plan 1512.

Forest av, w s, 100 s 156th st, four two-story frame dwell'gs, 18.9x32, tin roofs; cost, $3,300 each; John J. Brierly, 777 East 148th st; ar't, M. J. Garvin. Plan 1500.

3d av, No. 3605, one-story frame greenhouse, 10x30, glass roof; cost, abt $50; Henry Krull, on premises. Plan 1506.

KINGS COUNTY.

Plan 2152—Atlantic av, n s, 195 w Buffalo av, one two-story frame (brk filled) dwell'g, 11.8x34, tin roof; cost, $600; ow'r, ar't and b'r, Christopher P. Skelton, 296 6th av.

2153—Sackman st, e s, 150 n Liberty av, one two-story frame tenem't, 25x54, tin roof; cost, $2,400; ow'r and m'n, Charles Harles, Sackman st, near Liberty av; ar't, C. Infanger.

2154—Stone av, e s, 100 n Sutter av, one three-story frame store and dwell'g, 20x48, tin roof; cost, $4,500; Jacob Axelrod, Thatford av.

2155—Cornelia st, s s, 352 e Central av, nine two-story and basement frame (brk filled) dwellings, 18x42, tin roofs; cost, $2,500 each; ow'rs and c'rs, Raymond & Donly; ar't, C. N. Raymond.

2156—Ridgewood av, n w cor Elton st, three two-story and attic frame tenem'ts, 16.4x39, tin roofs; cost, $2,500 each; Daniel Fanshaw, 28 Elton st; ar't, C. Infanger; b'r, not selected.

2157—Dean st, s s, 300 e Rochester av, six two-story frame dwell'gs, 16.8x40, tin roofs, cost, each, $2,000; J. T. Birch, 95 Rochester av.

2158—Putnan av, s s, 290 e Throop av, five three-story and basement brown stone, Lake Superior and Dorchester stone dwell'gs, 20x45, tin roofs, iron cornices; cost, each, $7,000; R. Mullowney, 770 Halsey st; ar't, G. H. Madigan.

2159—Flushing av, s s, 50 w Sanford st, one two-story brk coppersmith shop, 20x80, tin roof, brk cornice; cost, $3,000; Thomas Burkhardt, 145 Monroe st; ar't, Th. Engelhardt; b'r, not selected.

2160—Schenck av, w s, 150 s Liberty av, one three-story frame (brk filled) tenem't, 25x58, tin roof; cost, $3,500; Wm. Max, 196 Schenck av.

2161—Glenmore av, n s, 60 e Milford st, one two-story frame dwell'g, 20x30, tin roof; cost, $1,600; James Smith, Jerome st, near New Lots road; ar't and c'r, W. D. Losee.

2162—Stone av, e s, 125 n Sutter av, one two-story frame tailor shop, 20x30, tin roof; cost, $750; Jacob Axelrod, Thatford av.

2163—Greene av, n s, 250 e Broadway, three three-story frame tenem'ts, 19x55, tin roofs; cost, total, $8,000; Michael Mulvihill, 1069 Greene av,

2164—Evergreen av, w s, 125 n Willoughby av, one three-story frame (brk filled) tenem't, 30.9 and 40.6x56, tin roof; cost, $5,600; Jane Pfeffers, 190 Evergreen av; ar't, E. Dennis.

2165—Hancock st, s s, 217 w Reid av, one two-story and basement brown stone dwell'g, 18.11x44, tin roof, wooden cornice; cost, $5,000; William Teaz, 52 Truxton st; ar't and c'r, G. Thomson; m'n, J. Lambert.

2166—Frost st, s s, 150 w Ewen st, one one-story frame carpenter shop, 25x60, gravel roof; cost, $600; ow'r and c'r, M. G. Dodds, 107 Amity st; ar't, F. Weber.

2167—Hamburg av, n w cor Stanhope st, rear, one two-story frame grocery storage building, 15x25, tin roof; cost, $300; ow'rs and b'rs, Frank Eller and J. Klein, 312 Melrose st; ar't, E. Schrempf.

2168—Stockholm st, s s, 325 w Knickerbocker av, one one-story frame carpenter shop, 22x20, tin roof; cost, $80; Wm. Hillenbrand, 167 Harman st.

2169—Glenmore av, s s, 25 w Essex st, one two-story and attic frame dwell'g, 20x36, tin roof; cost, $2,000; Joseph Trubauf, Essex st, near Glenmore av; ar't, L. F. Schillinger.

2170—Bleecker st, s s, 180 e Irving av, one three-story frame (brk filled) tenem't, 20x50, tin roof; cost, $3,000; Mrs. Isele, 346 Bleecker st; ar't, F. Holmberg; b'r, not selected.

2171—Osborn st, s s, 175 e Dumont av, one one-story frame carpenter shop, 50x20, gravel roof; cost, $100; Ann Matthews, 1466 Broadway.

2172—Hamburg av, s w cor Harman st, one three-story frame store and tenem't, 25x65x65, tin roof and brk cornice; cost, $8,000; J. Bohnert, 621 Willoughby av; ar't, F. Holmberg.

2173—Berry st, s e cor North 12th st, one two-story frame stable and dwell'g, 50x21.6, gravel roof; cost, $800; ow'r and ar't, T. L. Johnson, 194 Vernon av; b'r, not selected.

2174—Coles st, n s, 132.10 e Columbia st, one three-story frame tenem't, 20x45, tin roof; cost, $3,000; Patrick McGovern, on premises; ar't and m'n, J. F. Nelson; c'r, D. J. Lynch.

2175—Wyona st, w s, 125 s Eastern Parkway, one two-story frame dwell'g, 20x40, tin roof; cost, $2,500; Henry C. Heyser, 2732 Fulton st; ar't, J. C. Heyser.

2176—Knickerbocker av, w s, 25 n Stockholm st, one one-story frame tailor shop, 20x20, tin roof; cost, $500; ow'r, ar't and b'r, A. Fleischmann, on premises.

2177—Hendrix st, e s, 154.6 n New Lots av, one one-story and loft frame stable, &c., 20 and 26x34, shingle roof; cost, $575; Jacob T. Vansiclen, Hendrix st, cor New Lots av; ar't and b'r, W. A. Sloan.

2178—Buffalo av, w s, 47.11 s Bergen st, five two-story frame (brk filled) dwell'gs, 16x40, tin roofs; cost, $2,500 each; ow'r, ar't and c'r, N. A. Taylor, 126 Buffalo av.

2179—Kingsland av, w s, 25 n 1st st, one one-and-a-half-story frame carpenter shop, 25x30, gravel roof; cost, $100; Adolph Leppert, on premises.

2180—Van Voorhis st, s s, 100 w Bushwick av, one one-story frame stable, 25x16, tin roof; cost, $100; Frank Bennett, on premises.

2181—Miller av, w s, 125 n Eastern Parkway, one two-story frame barn and shed, 16x37.1, tin roof; cost, $250; George Weinstein, 111 Bradford st; ar't, C. Infanger; b'r, not selected.

2182—Rockaway av, w s, 150 n Belmont av; two three-story frame stores and tenem'ts, 25x55, tin roofs; cost, each, $3,500; ow'r and b'r, B. Seerman, on premises; ar't, H. Smith.

2183—Johnson av, s s, 125 w Morgan av, one two-story frame (brk filled) blacksmith shop and dwell'g, 25x60, tin roof; cost, $2,000; Joseph Fuchs, 361 Bushwick av; ar't, Th. Engelhardt; b'r, not selected.

2184—Stanhope st, s s, 653 e Evergreen av, one two-story frame (brk filled) dwell'g 22x42, tin roof; cost, $2,500; Thomas McPhearson, 99 Cornelia st; ar't, F. J. Lessing.

2185—46th st, s s, 100 e 3d av, one one-and-a-half-story frame tin shop, 20x20, tin roof; cost, $200; Henry Buegeman, 1106 3d av; ar'ts, H. L. Spicer & Son.

ALTERATIONS NEW YORK CITY.

Plan 2019—156th st, s w cor St. Nicholas av, interior alterations; cost, $1,200; Mayor, Aldermen, &c., City Hall; ar't, C. B. J. Snyder.

2020—Broad st, No. 59, and Beaver st, No. 35, walls altered, &c.; cost, $500; lessee, John P. Friedhoff, 400 5th st; ar't, B. W. Berger.

2021—12th st, Nos. 708 and 710 E., interior alterations; cost, $800; lessee, Sam'l Sloss, 635 6th st; ar't, B. W. Berger.

2022—Chambers st, No. 75, interior alterations, &c; cost, $1,000; lessees, Koster & Bial, 6th av and 24th st; ar't, J. Kastner.

2023—165th st, n s, 100 w Washington av, rear, one-story frame extension, 14x19, tin roof; cost, $325; Mrs. C. La Comey, 721 East 165th st; ar't, B. F. Frisbie.

2024—125th st, Nos. 116 and 118 W., interior alterations, walls altered; cost, $1,100; Edward D. Farrell, 329 West 57th st; ar't, J. Munskwitz.

2025—42d st, Nos. 568 and 570 W., one-story brk extension, 20x39.9, tin roof; cost, $2,000; Wm. Von Twistern, West Shore Hotel, 42d st and 11th av; ar'ts, Thom & Wilson.

2026—Forest av, No. 864, raise one story; cost, $1,500; Catherine Wilson, on premises; ar't, M. J. Garvin.

2027—3d av, No. 2327, one-story brk extension, 19.6x21, tin roof; cost, $1,000; John C. Frey, 220 Hewes st; ar't, C. A. Millner, Jr.

2028—Henry st, No. 94, seven-story brk extension, 25x68, tar and gravel roof; cost, $15,000; lessee, Margarethe Munch, 305 East 115th st; ar't, A. Munch.

2029—Lexington av, No. 179, interior alterations, walls altered; cost, $600; Peter A. H. Jackson, 53 East 67th st; ar'ts and c'rs, Williams & Jones.

2030—Cambrelling av, e s, 350 s Pelham av, raise one story, also one-story frame extension, 17x20, tin roof; cost, $400; Andrew Ostenburg, Fordham; ar't, H. C. Ryars; m'n, T. Wilkinson; c'r, R. Hoze.

2031—Varick st, No. 206, walls altered; cost, $400; agent, H. S. Ely, 19 East 55th st; c'r, L. Sibley.

2032—78th st, No. 110 W., one-story brk extension, 96x24, tin roof; cost, $2,000; Henry F. Marbrunn, on premises; ar't, G. A. Schellinger; m'ns, A. E. Bogert & Bro

2033—90th st, No. 12 E., repair damage by fire; cost, $25; Mrs. L. Bennett, on premises.

2034—Amsterdam av, n e cor 185th st, one-story frame extension, 19x46.8, tin roof; cost, $3,000; Conrad Eiser, on premises; ar't, E. Wenz.

2035—45th st, Nos. 328–332 E., raise four stories; cost, $30,000; Frederick Offermann, Jr., 154 East 46th st; ar'ts, Chas. Stoll & Sons.

2036—12th st, Nos. 408–438 W., interior alterations, walls altered; cost, $5,150; John Taylor Johnston, 8 5th av; m'n, C. T. Wills; c'rs, Steele & Costigan.

2037—Broadway, Nos. 427 and 429, walls altered; cost, $300; John N. Hayward, 243 East 17th st; ar't, P. H. Murphy.

2038—110th st, No. 330 E., repair damage by fire; cost, $90; Michael Churchill, 343 East 28th st; c'r, W. Nostrock.

2039—Woodruff st, n w cor Lillian pl, three-story frame extension, 23x12, tin roof; cost, $500; Mrs. C. Andrews, s w cor Woodruff st and Lillian pl; ar't, C. S. Clark; c'r, C. W. Brown.

2040—3d av, No. 2399, s e cor 130th st, repair damage by fire; cost, $900; Marietta H. Hull, 159 East 127th st; c'r, J. E. Poole.

2041—7th av, No. 185, walls altered; cost, $300; John Post, 341 West 57th st.

2042—32d st, No. 125 W., interior alterations; cost, $530; Sarah Amada Colt, s e cor 8th av and 125th st; b'r, J. D. Ferguson.

2043—3d av, No. 2620, s e cor 141st st, interior alterations; cost, $400; Thos. Foy, 1054 Franklin av; ar't, A. E. Davis.

2044—Washington st, No. 789, repair damage by fire; cost, $530; estate Edmund McLoughlin, 154 Henry st, Brooklyn; ar'ts and b'rs, Yeaton & Glynn.

2045—54th st, No. 415 E., interior alterations; cost, $350; John Bolen, 792 Lexington av; ar't, C. H. Dresser.

2046—South st, No. 42, raise one story, also walls altered; cost, $2,300; Wm. Hill, 243 Hewes st, Brooklyn; m'n, Geo. Quinn; c'r, C. L. Johnson's Son.

2047—Fulton st, No. 92, interior alterations; cost, $250; lessees, Smith & Seward, 140 Clinton av, Brooklyn; ar't and b'r, R. L. Walsh.

2048—169th st, No. 506 W., walls altered; cost, $425; Jas. C. Brady, on premises; m'n, E. C. Lynch.

2049—5th av, No. 640, n w cor 51st st, one-story brk extension, 20x8, tin roof, also interior alterations, walls altered; cost, $10,000; agent, Geo. W. Vanderbilt, on premises; ar't, R. M. Hunt.

2050—Greenwich st, No. 822, three-story brk extension, 21.2x38; tin roof; cost, $4,000; A. L. & J. J. Reynolds, 246 West 12th st; ar't, C. Rentz.

2051—Melrose av, e s, 75 n 158th st, interior alterations; cost, $400; Sylvester Kromer, 651 East 158th st.

2052—8th av, No. 2150, raise one story; also one-story and basement brk extension, 25x48, tin roof; cost, $3,000; E. Modersohn, 266 West 115th st; ar't, W. D. Hunter.

2053—3d av, No. 1894, one-story brk extension, 25x28, tin roof; cost, $2,500; Marcus Beckmann, 1574 3d av; ar't, E. W. Greiss.

2054—Wooster st, Nos. 35 and 37, interior alterations; cost, $1,200; Theo. Tiedemann, on premises; ar'ts, Graul & Frohne.

2055—Rivington st, No. 160, new store front, &c.; cost, $600; Louis Goldberg, 6 Allen st; ar't, H. Horenburger.

2056—Sheriff st, Nos. 91 and 93, new store fronts; cost, $600; Elias Jacobs, 57 East 80th st; ar'ts, Kurtzer & Kohl.

2057—54th st, Nos. 403–413 E., walls altered, cost, $700; Henry Elias Brewing Co., on premises; b'r, J. Muller.

2058—Broadway, No. 1170, new show windows; cost, $500; Francis O'Neill, 86 Madison av; c'r, P. J. Walsh.

2059—4th st, No. 345 E., one-story brk extension, 24.9x49, tin roof; cost, $10,000; St. Elizabeth Church, Rev. Francis Jaunscheck, pastor, 301 East 8th st. ar't, E. Wenz.

2060—Astor pl, s s, bet 4th av and Lafayette pl, six-story brk extension, 52.6x14.6, tin roof, also interior alterations, walls altered; cost, $75,000; lessees, Brokaw Bros., on premises; ar'ts, Rose & Stone.

2061—143d st, No. 624 and 626 E., one and two-story frame extension, 17.8x12.6 and 15.4x49.10, tin roofs; total cost, $1,300; Franklin A. Wilcox, 938 Madison av; ar't, C. A. Millner, Jr.

2062—Broadway, Nos. 377 and 379, walls altered; cost, $325; Estate W. B. Lawrence, 54 William st; ar'ts, Levinson & Just; b'rs, Harkness Fire Extinguisher Co.

2063—Morris av, e s, 75 s 154th st, raise one story, also interior alterations; cost, $1,800; Helena Freudenmacher, Morris av and 153d st; ar't, A. Pfeiffer.

2064—149th st, s s, 175 w Courtlandt av, rear, alter roof, also interior alterations, walls altered;

cost, $2,400; Fritz A. Selje, 3d av and 149th st; ar't, A. Pfeffer.

2065—Houston st, No. 374 E., walls altered, &c; cost, $500; Heman Rushin, 402 East 87th st; ar't, A. Huttira.

2066—Allen st, Nos. 122-126, walls altered; cost, $100; Congregation Tiefereth Israel, on premises; ar't, H. Horenburger.

2067—Division st, No. 133, interior alterations, walls altered; cost, $1,000; R. Harwitz, 44 Pike st; ar't, G. W. Kenny.

KINGS COUNTY.

Plan 1115—Bond st, No. 7, add one story to extension, put in large skylight; cost, $1,200; E. H. Dana, 827 Broadway, N. Y.; b'rs, F. Hullet and R. McGregor.

1116—Carlton av, No. 417, add one story on rear of building; cost, $2,000; Samuel B. Duryea, 46 Remsen st; ar't, M. J. Morrill; b'rs, C. Cameron and J. H. Vandevorge.

1117—Marcy av, s e cor Rutledge st, one-story brk extension, 10.2x16, tin roof; cost, $150; H. Bishoff, 313 Marcy av; ar't, b. Finkensieper; m'n, L. Parks.

1118—7th av, n w cor 19th st, one-story frame extension, 25x27, tin roof; cost, $600; Hermann Witte, 554 7th av; ar't, C. Dieckmann.

1119—29th st, n s, 300 e 3d av, cellar, foundation, &c.; cost, $300; ow'r and m'n, Antonio Colosino, 137 29th st; ar't and c'r, J. Stanley.

1120—Bainbridge st, No. 197, add two stories; cost, $700; J. Simons, 167 Bainbridge st; ar't, J. S. Stevens; b'r, L. Acor.

1121—Atlantic av, No. 2610, one-story frame extension, 16x25; cost, $100; Chas. A. Beckert, Atlantic av, cor Sheffield av; ar't, C. Infanger.

1122—Morrell st, No. 73, add one-story frame store; cost, $400; Swallberg & Aron, 73 Morrell st.

1123—Leonard st, No. 38, new store front; cost, $300; Chas. Goldstein, on premises.

1124—Carroll st, No. 287, repair damage by fire; cost, $3,000; Edward Downing, 160 Carroll st; b'r, S. Hazzard.

1125—Bergen st, No. 1412, new store front and interior alterations; cost, $500; ow'r and b'r, John Turner, on premises; ar't, J. Irish.

1126—Cumberland st, No. 134, one-story brk extension, 16x24, tin roof; cost, $100; Spencer & Wallace, 111 South Portland av.

1127—Garrison st, No. 17, new sill and repair corner post; cost, $100; Mr. Hinman, 87 Hanson pl; b'rs, E. F. Smith and R. V. Wicks.

1128—McKibbin st, No. 27, add one frame story; cost, $75; George Doering, on premises.

1129—53d st, n s, 220 e 4th av, two-story frame extension, 8x24, tin roof; cost, $150; Mary C. Black, 269 53d st; ar't and c'r, J. Black.

1130—Van Sielen av, w s, 100 n Atlantic av, one-story frame extension, 20x4, interior alterations; cost, $250; Chas. Christ, 74 Van Sielen av; ar't, C. Infanger; b'r, not selected.

1131—Grove st, No. 139, raised 10 ft. on brk wall; cost, $500; Linder Schulenburg, 112 Grove st; ar't, C. F. Eisenach.

1132—4th av, No. 440, new store front; cost, $400; ow'r, ar't and b'r, Frank A. Barnaby, 201 Montague st.

1133—Gates av, No. 290, covered piazza in front; cost, $250; C. A. Dubois, on premises; b'r, J. Williamson.

1134—Meserole st, s s, 50 e Bushwick av, add one story; cost, $1,600; Otto Huber, Meserole st and Bushwick av; ar'ts, C. Stoll & Son.

MISCELLANEOUS.

BUSINESS FAILURES.

Schedule of assignments for the four weeks ending Dec. 4, 1891:

	Liabilities.	Nominal Assets.	Real Assets.
Alexander, Robert...	$4,609 25	$3,396 62	$2,959 25
Moskovitz, Ignatz	9,197 40	5,883 68	3,618 46
Martin, Wilbur F....	41,124 48	46,150 22	21,527 77
MacEvoy, Charles....	52,975 82	68,020 62	48,431 30
Pfister Book Binding Co	29,511 92	29,163 52	750 00
Sametz, Adolph......	8,042 16	8,513 82	6,691 86
Stock, Herman T.....	4,023 82	836 80	836 80
Stern, Isaac.........	17,077 02	24,295 39	11,116 48

N. Y. ASSIGNMENTS—BENEFIT CREDITORS.

Nov.

27 Field, Edward M., Daniel A. Lindley, John Frederick Wiechers and Herman C. Hilmers (composing firm of Field, Lindley, Wiechers & Co., bankers and brokers, at No. 1 Broadway), to Charles W. Gould; without preferences.

30 Otto, Anna E. (produce dealer, at No. 24 Little 12th st), to James Rowland; preferences, $8,758.27.

30 McCue, Edward to Alfred J. Casse and William J. Lackey; re-assignment.

Dec.

1 Tremper, Clarence S. (men's furnishing goods, at No. 18 Fulton st), to Albert E. Coon; preferences, $366.68.

1 Ladd, Joseph T. (jeweler and dealer in jewelry, at No. 3 Wall st), to William H. Wiley; preferences, $2,064.30.

3 Angelo, William to Mary C. Shantz; re-assignment.

KINGS COUNTY.

GENERAL ASSIGNMENTS.

Dec.

1 Mulqueen, Thomas F. to Paul E. De Fere.
1 Self, Samuel to George Sherwood.
3 Bullwinkel, Martin A. to John F. Bullwinkel.

PROCEEDINGS OF THE BOARD OF ALDERMEN AFFECTING REAL ESTATE.

* Under the different headings indicates that a resolution has been introduced and referred to the appropriate committee. † Indicates that the resolution has passed and has been sent to the Mayor for approval ‡ Passed over the Mayor's veto.

NEW YORK, Tuesday, Dec. 1, 1891.

FENCING VACANT LOTS.

103d st, from Nos. 108 to 140. (?)
Park av, e s, from 95th to 96th st. †

REGULATING, GRADING, ETC.

Manhattan st, from 12th av to bulkhead line, North River.
41st st, from 1st av to bulkhead line, East River.
64th st, from 11th av to bulkhead line, North River.
111th st, from Amsterdam to Riverside av.
189th st, from Amsterdam to Wadsworth av. †

PAVING.

9th st, from Av D to East River, and crosswalks laid at intersecting avs.
41st st, from 1st av to bulkhead line, East River.
73d st, from Av A to bulkhead line, East River.
91st st, from w s 1st av to e s 2d av, and crosswalks laid at intersecting avs.
102d st, from West End to Riverside av.
118th st, from Madison to Park av.
181st st, from 12th av to Boulevard, and crosswalks laid at intersecting avs.
granite block. †

CROSSWALKS.

14th st, at w s 7th av.
Greenwich av, s of 11th st. †

FLAGGING, CURBING, ETC.

Broadway, w s, from 31st to 32d sts.
Dominick st, in front of No. 7.
Dominick st, n w cor Clarke st, 50 ft. on Dominick st and 75 ft. on Clarke st.
Hudson st, in front of Nos. 252, 254, 312 and 314.
Manhattan st, from 12th av to bulkhead line, North River.
31st st, 32d st, 33d st, both sides, from 1st av to East River.
41st st, from 1st av to bulkhead line, East River.
64th st, from 11th av to bulkhead line, North River.
88th st, from Central Park West to Riverside av.
89th st, from West End av to Riverside av.
111th st, from Amsterdam to Riverside av.
189th st, from Amsterdam to Wadsworth av.
7th av, from 36th to 37th sts. †

MAINS.

Albany Post road, from Riverdale av to Broadway; gas.
Clark pl, bet Jerome and Sheridan avs; water.
Pond pl, from William st to Bainbridge av; gas.
Sherwood st, from Bainbridge av to Briggs av; gas.
Sherwood st, from Bainbridge av to Briggs av; water.
Southern Boulevard, from Kingsbridge road to Pelham av; gas.
Woodruff st (176th st), from Prospect av to Southern Boulevard; water.
27th st, 28th st, 29th st, bet 11th and 12th avs; water.
88th st, from Av B to a point 225 w therefrom; water.
189th st, from Amsterdam av to Boulevard; gas.
183d st, bet Morris, Creston and Ryer avs; gas.
Briggs av, from Sherwood st to a point 400 n therefrom; gas.
Briggs av, from Sherwood st to a point 400 n therefrom; water. †
Edenwood av, from St. James st to Kingsbridge road; gas.
Edenwood av, from St. James st to Kingsbridge road; water.
Fulton av (Pyne st), bet 187th st and Pelham av; gas.
Hull av, from Scott av to Jerome Park Railway; water.
Jerome av, bet Gerard av and Clark pl; water.
Kirkside av, from Kingsbridge road to Donnybrook st; water.
Mt. Vernon av, from 3d st to 5th av; water.
Vanderbilt av E., from 180th st to a point 500 n therefrom; gas.
Vanderbilt av E., from 180th st to a point 500 n therefrom; water.
Willard av, to a point 400 e from 3d st; water.
1st av, from Grand av to city line; water.
3d av, to a point 600 e from 3d st; water.
4th av, from Mt. Vernon av to 2d st; water.
5th av, from Mt. Vernon av to 2d st; water.
12th av, bet 23d and 38th sts; water.
13th av, bet 16th and 23d sts; water.

LAMP POSTS ERECTED AND LIGHTED.

Albany Post road, from Riverdale av to Broadway.
Pond pl, from William st to Bainbridge av.
Sherwood st, from Bainbridge to Briggs av.
Southern Boulevard, from Kingsbridge road to Pelham av.
21st st, in front of No. 142 W.
30th st, in front of No. 305 W.
139th st, from Amsterdam av to Boulevard.
183d st, bet Morris, Creston and Ryer avs.
Briggs av, from Sherwood st to a point 400 n therefrom. †
Edenwood av, from St. James st to Kingsbridge road.
Fulton av (Pyne st), bet 187th st and Pelham av.
Vanderbilt av E., from 180th st to a point 500 n therefrom.
Willard av, Woodlawn, from Bronx River to 3d st; naptha lamps.
5th av, cor 76th st, in front of Temple Beth El; 2 lights.

BROOKLYN BOARD OF ALDERMEN.

BROOKLYN, Nov. 23, 1891.

CULVERTS.

Bedford av, n w cor North 11th st.
Railroad av, n e cor Liberty av.
Railroad av, n w cor Liberty av. †

ELECTRIC LIGHTING.

Bergen st, bet Bedford and Kingston avs.
Graham st, bet Myrtle and Willoughby avs.
Tiffany pl, bet Harrison and Degraw sts. †

FENCING VACANT LOTS.

Gold st, w s, bet High and Sands sts. †

FLAGGING.

Hicks st, n e cor Congress st. †

PAVING, GRADING, ETC.

Dean st, bet Buffalo and Ralph avs.
President st, bet Franklin av and B. B. Railroad.
Scholes st, bet Waterbury st and Morgan av.
Van Voorhis st, bet Central and Hamburg avs.
Vermont st, bet Atlantic av and Evergreen Cemetery. *
St. Marks av, bet Buffalo and Saratoga avs. †

SEWER BASIN.

Reid av, n e cor Lexington av. †

STREET OPENING.

Varick st, bet Flushing and Metropolitan avs. †

ADVERTISED LEGAL SALES.

REFEREES SALES TO BE HELD AT THE REAL ESTATE EXCHANGE AND AUCTION ROOM (LIMITED), 59 to 65 LIBERTY STREET, EXCEPT WHERE OTHERWISE STATED.

Dec.

64th st, No. 208, s s, 100 w 10th av, 25x100.5, five-story brk flat, by J. T. Boyd 7

92d st, Nos. 139-149, n s, 245 e Amsterdam av, 105x100.8, six three-story stone front dwell'gs, by C. S. Brown. (Amt due $4,356; prior morts. $——) 7

103d st, No. 208, s s, 128 w Amsterdam av, 20x75 to Clendenning lane, x20x76, five-story brk flat, by William Kennelly. (Amt due $17,686) 7

Madison av, Nos. 1742-1748, n w cor 115th st, 100.11x85, four five-story brk flats, store in No. 1742, by J. C. Lalor. (Amt due $59,134) 7

Manhattan av, No. 507, n w cor 121st st, 20.11x90, three-story brk (stone front) dwell'g, by J. N. Golding. (Amt due $5,074; prior morts. $12,500) 7

Riverside av or Drive, No. 100; 82d st, Nos. 318-324; begins Riverside av, s e cor 82d st, runs east 161.1 x south 102.2 x west 16.8 x north 19.4 x west 32 x north 18 8 x west 14.4 x north 15.6 x west 8 4 x north 26.6 x west 79.9 to Riverside Drive, x north 24.2 to beginning, four-story stone front dwell'g on av and four four-story stone front dwell'gs on st, by R. V. Harnett & Co 7

Willis av, n w cor 145th st, 25x106 ....
Willis av, n w cor 146th st, 25x106 ....
Willis av, w s, 25 n 146th st, 25x106 ....
Three five-story brk and stone flats ....
by William Kennelly. (Amt due on each corner house $21,065, and $14,868 on other) 7

Abingdon sq, Nos. 7 and 9; Bleecker st, No. 425; 8th av, No. 2; begins 8th av, s e cor Bleecker st, runs northeast 44.11 x southeast 40 x east 17.2 x south 22.5 x west 76.9 to Bleecker st, x north 27.7 to beginning, seven-story brk flat with stores, by R. V. Harnett. (Amt due $38,267; prior morts. $——) 7

119th st, No. 63, n s, 526.8 w 5th av, 16.8x100.11, three-story stone front dwell'g, by R. V. Harnett & Co. (Amt due $12,285) 8

144th st, No. 454, s s, 214 e 10th av, 20x99.11, four-story brk dwell'g, by J. C. Lalor. (Amt due $3,742) 8

144th st, No. 458, s s, 178 e 10th av, 17x99.11 ....
144th st, No. 452, s s, 234 e 10th av, 21x99.11 ....
Two three-story brk dwell'gs, by J. C. Lalor. (Amt due on No. 458, $2,819, and $3,736 on No. 452) 8

Av C, No. 112, s e s, 67 n e 7th st, 18.3x82.5 ....
Av C, No. 110, s e s, 48.9 n e 7th st, 18.3x82.5 ....
Two three-story brk tenem'ts, by William Kennelly. (Partition sale) 8

Lexington av, No. 463, e s, 40 n 45th st, 20x70.6, four-story brk dwell'g, by A. H. Muller & Son. (Amt due $17,300) 8

West End av, No. 408, e s, 62.2 s 85th st, 20x80, four-story brk dwell'g, by J. F. B. Smyth. (Amt due $6,537; prior morts. $——) 8

20th st, No. 212, s s, 434 w 2d av, 22x92, three-story brk tenem't, by D. P. Ingraham & Co. (Amt due $15,936) 9

92d st, No. 81, n s, 418 e 9th av, 19x100.8, four-story brk dwell'g, by McKean & Katzenmeyer. (Amt due $1,929; prior morts. $18,075) 9

96th st, No. 56, s s, 220 e 9th av, 20x100.8, four-story brk dwell'g, by R. V. Harnett & Co 9

120th st, Nos. 304-308, s s, 125 w 8th av, 75x100.11, three five-story brk flats, by William Kennelly. (Amt due $28,489; prior morts. $——) 9

2d av, Nos. 1808-1814, s e cor 94th st, 100.8x100, four five-story brk tenem'ts with stores, by William Kennelly 9

1st av, Nos. 650-662, s e cor 38th st, runs east 150 x south 98.9 x west 25 x south 49.4 x west 125 to 1st av, x north 148.1 to beginning, six-story brk malt house and two-story frame and brk stables, by R. V. Harnett. (Trustee's sale) 10

8th av, No. 2609, s w cor 139th st, 19.11x75.4 ....
8th av, Nos. 2605 and 2607, w s, 19.11 s 139th st, 40x75.4 ....
8th av, Nos. 2601 and 2603, w s, 59.11 s 139th st, 40x75.4 ....
8th av, Nos. 2597 and 2599, w s, 59.11 n 138th st, 40x75.4 ....
8th av, Nos. 2593 and 2595, w s, 19.11 n 138th st, 40x75.4 ....
8th av, No. 2591, n w cor 138th st, 19.11x75.4 ....
Six five-story brk flats with stores ....
by P. F. Meyer. (Amt due on Nos. 2591 and 2609 $21,322 each, and $31,417 on each of others). 10

Broome st, Nos. 2-14, n w cor Tompkins st, 125x75, five five-story stone front tenem'ts, store in No. 2, by D. P. Ingraham & Co. (Amt due $47,149). 11

76th st, s s, 300 w West End av, 44x102.2, vacant, by J. F. B. Smyth. (Amt due $7,750) 11

105th st, Nos. 210 and 212, s s, 100 w 10th av, 50x100.11, two five-story brk flats, by William Kennelly. (Amt due $6,649; prior morts $43,200) 11

130th st, No. 14, s s, 193.7 w Madison av, 16.4x99.11, three-story brk dwell'g, by A. H. Muller & Son. (Amt due $11,868) 11

42d st, No. 220, s s, 280 w 2d av, 25x79.6x27.11x92.1, four-story brk tenem't with stores, by Smyth & Ryan. (Amt due $16,416) 14

83d st, No. 83, n s, 448.9 e 9th av, 26.9x60, three-story brk dwell'g, by William Kennelly 14

Av A, Nos. 389 and 391, w s, 49.5 s 24th st, 49.4x81.5; No. 389, one-story brk building with two-story brk building on rear; No. 391, four-story brk store and tenem't, by Smyth & Ryan. (Amt due $21,841)........ 14

Av A, s w cor 24th st, 49.5x81.5, vacant, by Smyth & Ryan. (Amt due $26,500)........ 14

KINGS COUNTY.

Dec.

Columbia st, No. 85, e s, 49.6 s Warren st, 25.6x65.11x25.5½x67.5, four-story brk tenem't and store; assessed value, $4,500........
Warren st, No. 96, s s, 70.3 e Columbia st, 27.9x74.10½, five-story brk tenem't and stores; assessed value, $6,500........
Warren st, No. 98, s s, 98 e Columbia st, runs south 74.10½ x east 2.9 x south 24.11½ x east 25 x north 99 10 to Warren st, x west 27.9 to beginning, five-story brk tenem't and store; assessed value, $6,500........
St. Marks av, No. 288, n s, 100 w Underhill av, 25x131, four-story brk dwell'g; assessed value, $7,000........
Vanderbilt st, s s, 487.5 e Short st, 19.6x108, Flatbush........
by T. A. Kerrigan, at 13 Willoughby st........ 7

Degraw st, No. 682, s s, 431.5 1-5 w 5th av, 19.2x100, three-story brk flat; assessed value, $4,200.
2d st, No. 483, n s, 90 9 w 7th av, 20x100........
2d st, No. 481, n s, 110.9 w 7th av, 20x100........
2d st, No. 477, n s, 150.9 w 7th av, 20x100, three two-story brk dwell'gs; assessed value, $2,000 each........
by T. A. Kerrigan, at 13 Willoughby st........ 8

Roebling st, No. 118, e s, 75 n North 5th st, 25x100, two three-story frame tenem'ts on plot; assessed value, $4,000........
Wythe av, n w cor North 11th st, runs northeast along Wythe av 200 to North 12th st, x northwest 100 x southwest 100 x northwest 75 x southwest 100 to North 11th st, x southeast 175 to beginning, glass works; assessed value, $25,000........
by T. A. Kerrigan, at 45 Broadway, E. D ... 9

Powell st, w s, 150 s Blake av, 100x100, two-and-a-half-story frame dwell'g and one-and-a-half-story frame stable on plot; assessed value, $2,500, by T. A. Kerrigan, at 13 Willoughby st.. 9

3d st, No. 500, s s, 44 w 7th av, 22x90, four-story brk dwell'g; assessed value, $6,300........
3d st, No. 504, s w cor 7th av, 22x90, four-story brk dwell'g; assessed value, $7,000........
by W. Cole, at 7 and 8 Court sq........ 9

Madison st, No. 1266, s s, 188 w Knickerbocker av, 18x100, two-story frame dwell'g; assessed value, $2,000........
Pierrepont st, No. 61, n s, 129 e Hicks st, runs north 183.6½ to Love lane, x east 27.0½ x south 184.0½ to Pierrepont st, x west 27 to beginning, three-story brk dwell'g; assessed value, $21,000........
Prospect pl, Nos. 748 and 750, s s, 250 e Rogers av, 38.4x100, two three-story brk dwell'gs; assessed value, $8,500........
1st st, Nos. 272–278, s w s, 305 n w 5th av, 81x100, three four-story double brk flats........
Willoughby av, No. 220, s s, 20 w Steuben st, 20x80, three-story brk flat; assessed value, $5,500..
by T. A. Kerrigan, at 13 Willoughby st........ 10

50th st, Nos. 175–179, n s, 120 w 4th av, 60x100.2, three two-story and basement frame dwell'gs; assessed value, $1,000 each; by J. Cole, at 389 Fulton st........ 10

Sackett st, No 490, s s, 75 w Bond st, runs south 100 x west 70 x south 25 x west 33.4 x north 50 x east 73.4 x north 75 to Sackett st, x east 30 to beginning, three-story brk tenem't on plot; assessed value, $4,600........
Jefferson av, No. 164, s s, 200 w Nostrand av, 20x100........
Jefferson av, No. 162, s s, 220 w Nostrand av, 20x100........
Jefferson av, No. 160, s s, 240 w Nostrand av, 20x100........
Jefferson av, No. 158, s s, 260 w Nostrand av, 20x100........
Jefferson av, No. 156, s s, 280 w Nostrand av, 20x100........
Five four-story brk flats; assessed value, $6,500 each........
by J. Cole, at 389 Fulton st........ 14

Dean st, n s, 419.5 e Rochester av, 16x107.9¾........
Dean st, n s, 435.5 e Rochester av, 16x107.9¾........
Dean st, n s, 451.5 e Rochester av, 16x107.9¾........
Dean st, n s, 467.5 e Rochester av, 16x107.9¾........
Four two-story frame dwell'gs; assessed value, $1,600 each........
Hudson av, No. 285, e s, 24 s Tillary st, 21x50x15x50, three-story frame dwell'g; assessed value, $1,000........
by T. A. Kerrigan, at 13 Willoughby st........ 14

LIS PENDENS.

NEW YORK.

Nov.

46th st, n s, 304 e 6th av, 22x100.5. Frederick K. Clark agt Martha E. Clark; action to enjoin defendant from selling or encumbering, &c.; att'y, F. K. Clark........ 28

184th st, n s, 300 w Courtlandt av, 100x168. Robert J. McCracken and ano. agt Joseph Hoerzel et al.; action for mechanic's lien; att'y, Ernest Hall........ 28

21st st, Nos. 157 and 159, n s, 160 e 7th av, 40x—.
7th av, Nos. 256 and 258, w s, 25 s 25th st, 50x100
45th st, No. 109, n s, 100 w 6th av, 20x100........
18th st, No. 150, s s, 125 e 7th av, 25x100........
Theresa C. Graham agt John Graham; action to set aside ante-nuptial agreement; att'ys, Bliss & Schley........ 28

St. Marks pl, Nos. 19–23, n s. Leopold Freund agt Charlotte Gottheimer extrx.; foreclos. mechanic's lien; att'y, Benno Loewy........ 30

24th st, n s, 250 w 7th av, 25x100. Theresa C. Graham agt John Graham; action to set aside ante-nuptial agreement; amended notice; att'ys, Bliss & Schley........ 30

123d st, s s, 100 w Manhattan av, 16x100.11........
127th st, n s, 335 w 3d av, 15x99.11........
Lexington av, e s, 68.11 n 127th st, 36x20........
William T. Jones agt Cyrena L. Jones and ano.; partition; att'y, G. H. Brewster........ 30

Willett st, No. 99, w s, 105 s Stanton st, 25x88.6. Fire Dept. City New York agt Isaac Goodstein; action to enforce building laws; att'y, William L. Findley........ 30

95th st, Nos. 201–205, n s, 86 w Amsterdam av, 3 lots, each 27x87. Same agt Andrew T. Doyle; 3 similar actions; same att'y........ 30

96th st, Nos. 202–206, s s, 89.9 w Amsterdam av, 3 lots, together in size 83.6x87. Same agt same; 3 similar actions; same att'y........ 30

Dec.

114th st, Nos. 420 and 422, s s, 270 e 1st av, 55.2x100.11. Daniel Rabold agt Lydia Friedberg; specific performance; att'y, Morse & Wensley.. 1

5th av, n w cor 116th st, 100.11x143........
133d st, n s, 385 e Lenox av, 33.4x99.11........
133d st, n s, 435 e Lenox av, 33.4x99.11........
132d st, n s, 75 w Park av, 20x99.11........
N. Y. Gas Fixture Co. agt John Walker et al.; action to set aside conveyances; att'ys, Phillips & Avery........ 1

118th st, s s, 240 w 4th av, 100x100.11. Arthur Boehmer agt Samuel Harris and ano.; action for purpose of procuring judgment; att'y, James Kearney........ 2

7th av, n w cor 53d st, 25x100. William D. Lent agt Mark P. Brennan and ano.; action to set aside conveyances; att'y, Thomas C. Ennever.. 2

Morris av, e s, 175 n 164th st, runs east 104.10 x north 25 x east 80 10 x north 35 x west 185.9 to Morris av, x south 60 to beginning........
Teller av, w s, 140.6 s 164th st, 24x110........
J. L. Mott Iron Works agt Arthur Parrett and ano.; action to have conveyance adjudged fraudulent; att'y, John J. Gleason........ 2

39th st, Nos. 609 and 611, n s, 175 w 11th av, 50x98.9. Rufus Darrow agt Katharine N. Smith et al.; foreclos. mechanic's lien; att'y, W. W. Westervelt........ 2

Broadway, No. 219, n e cor Fulton st, 29x77.2x29x76.2. G. L. Ronalds agt Catharine Ann Cammann et al.; partition; amended notice; att'ys, A. P. & W. Man........ 3

14th st, s s, 88 w Av C, 250x103.3. Bowes & Coombs agt William H. Muldoon et al.; foreclos. mechanic's lien; att'y, James Kearney........ 3

80th st, s s, 105 e 10th av, 145x102.2. Cassidy & Adler agt Morris Schneider et al.; foreclos. mechanic's lien; att'y, Thomas C. Ennever........ 3

121st st, No. 280, s s, 304 w 7th av, 17x100.11. Ann Maria Jenny agt George Lane; action for specific performance; att'ys, Davis & Kaufmann. ... 3

Washington av, w s, 25.1 s 184th st, 25.1x119.6x25x121.9. Owen Toher agt Cecelia T. Lappine; foreclos. mechanic's lien; att'y, Samuel E. Duffy........ 3

Morris av, e s, 100 s 184th st, 25x100. William Huck assignee agt Thomas T. Peterson et al.; foreclos. mechanic's lien; att'y Ernest Hall........ 4

Wooster st, No. 156, e s, 120 s Houston st, 25x100.1. William W. Borton agt Patrick H. McManus and ano.; action to abate a nuisance; att'y, James C. Murray........ 4

7th av, s e cor 32d st, 23.9x100. David Nugent agt Mary Elizabeth Hannegan et al.; partition; att'y, Samuel E. Duffey........ 4

Willis av, w s, 25 n 134th st, runs west 81.6 x south 25 to 134th st, x west 25 x north 200 to 135th st, x east 25 x south 25 x east 81.6 to Willis av, x south 25 x west 81.6 x south 100 x east 81.6 x south 25........
19th st, n s, 135 e Irving pl, 24x79........
Frederic G. Moore agt Luigi Cavinato et al.; action to set aside conveyance; att'ys, Phillips & Avery........ 4

86th st, s s, 200 e Riverside av, 20x102.2. William Bayard Cutting and ano. agt William E. D. Stokes et al.; action to restrain deft. from maintaining openings, &c., in westerly party wall; att'ys, Burrill, Zabriskie & Burrill........ 4

FORECLOSURE SUITS.

Nov.

23d st, No. 359, n s, 200 e 9th av, 25x98 9. Amelia Spiess formerly Amelia Einstein and ano. as guard. of Claribel, Arthur and Viola Spiess agt Constantino de Vivo Hess; att'ys, Townsend & McClelland........ 28

73d st, n s, 285 e 3d av, 25x102.2. Roseua W. Smith extrx Henry A. Smith agt Charles Goldstein et al.; amended notice; att'y, Coleridge A. Hart.. 28

33d st, s s, 200 e 1st av, 25x98.9. William Mackenzie agt Colson B. Hamilton et al.; amended notice; att'ys, Greene & Welch........ 28

22d st, No. 146, s s, 190 w 3d av, 20x98.9........
22d st, No. 14, s s, 256.8 w 5th av, 27x98.9........
First Nat. Bank of Plainfield, N. J., agt Ellen Jane Harper Haight et al.; amended notice; att'y, Eugene H. Hatch........ 30

West End av, e s, 22.2 n 74th st, 20x70. Home for Incurables of City New York agt Ella V. A. Dayton and ano.; att'ys, Butler, Stillman & Hubbard........ 30

9th av, e s, 100 n 57th st, runs east 20 x south 10 x east 80 x north 35.5 x west 100 to 9th av, x south 25.5 to beginning. Farmer's Loan and Trust Co. agt Stephanie B. Sparks et al.; att'ys, Turner, McClure & Rolston........ 30

93d st, n s, 100 e 9th av, 17x71.5x17x72.1. Charles F. Lawrence et al. agt Joseph Turner et al.; att'ys, R. & D. Mitchell........ 30

St. Nicholas av, n w cor 117th st, 29.7x92.5x25.2x107.11. Philip M. Lydig agt Jennie Mitchell et al.; att'ys, Weekes Bros........ 30

Monroe st, n s, bet Market and Pike sts, known as lot No. 524 on map estate of late Hendrick Rutgers made by Bridges & Poppleton, 25x100. German-American Real Estate Title Guarantee Co. agt Catharine T. Reilly et al.; att'y, Chas. Unangst........ 30

Dec.

Greenwich st, w s, 58.2 n Cortlandt st, runs west 96 x north 4.6 x west 13.9 x south 4.6 x west 10.8 x north 18 x west 6 x north 40.4 x east 106 7 to Greenwich st, x south 58 to beginning.
Greenwich st, w s, 133.10 n Cortlandt st, 24.8x71x24x64........
Washington st, Nos. 173 and 175, e s, 45.11x86.6x40.5x98.6........
Dey st, No. 59, s s, 48 w Greenwich st, 21.11x76.5x22x76.5........
Dey st, No. 61, s s, 23x75.5........
Ellen E. Ward widow agt N. Y. Steam Co. et al.; att'ys, Strong & Cadwalader........ 1

Mulberry st, No. 137, e s, 25x100. Samuel Aronson agt Luigi Mega et al.; att'y, Henry B. Wesselman........ 1

Convent av, n w cor 143d st, 99.11x100. Stephen Buckingham Sturges agt L. M. Hartwell et al.; att'ys, Sturges & Roby........ 1

33d st, s s, 150 e 1st av, 50x98.9. Williamsburgh Savings Bank agt Thirty-fourth Street Ferry and Eleventh Avenue R. R. Co. et al.; att'ys, S. M. & D. E. Meeker........ 2

Av C, n e cor 11th st, 26x83. N. Y. Free Circulating Library agt William C. Burne et al.; att'y, J. Frederic Kernochan........ 2

58th st, w s, 189.9 e 1st av, 16.8x100.4. U. S. Trust Co. trustee agt Henry Kroger et al.; att'ys, Stewart & Sheldon........ 2

Prince st, n s, 100 e Sullivan st, 25x95.6. Thomas F. Cock and ano. trustees agt Eugene T. Westerfield et al. exrs. and trustees; att'ys, De Forest & Weeks........ 3

135th st, s s, 260 e Lenox av, 25x99.11. Eliza A. Clark agt John F. Flanagan and ano.; att'y, Thomas Hooker........ 3

82d st, s s, 250 w Amsterdam av, 16.8x102.2. Frank Hill agt Walter J. Weeden et al.; att'ys, Train & Hill........ 4

82d st, s s, 266.8 w Amsterdam av, 2 lots, each 16.8x102.2. Frederick T. Hill agt Walter J. Weeden et al.; same att'ys........ 4

3d av, n e cor 134th st, 25.11x30. John Kress Brewing Co. agt Lizzie Fitzpatrick; att'ys, Forster, Hotaling & Klenke........ 4

47th st, s s, 437.6 e 7th av, 18.9x100.5. James L. Lowry exr. agt Burk G. Carleton et al.; att'y, James P. Campbell........ 4

129th st, s s, 110 e Lenox av, 25x99.11. Mary L. Walton agt William C. Boyd et al.; att'y, John E. Ellison........ 4

59th st, s s, 156.5 e 1st av, 25x100.4. Frederick H. Allen agt John McGann et al; att'y, Henry B. Weselman........ 4

LIS PENDENS, KINGS COUNTY.

Nov.

Road from Flatbush and Flatlands to Canarsie Landing, contains 25 acres, Flatlands. Stephen L. Vanderveer agt Albert Lott; att'y, Henry D. Lott........ 25

Greene st, n s, 275 w Provost st, 25x100. Mary E. Smith agt Daniel R. Davis; action to establish title; att'y, I. Newton Williams........ 25

10th st, n s, 197.10 w 8th av, 20x100........
10th st, n s, 217.10 w 8th av, 20x100........
10th st, n s, 237.10 w 8th av, 20x100........
10th st, n s, 277.10 w 8th av, 20x100........
Henry A. Moore agt James T. Ransom; 4 actions; att'y, John F. Nelson........ 27

Henry st, No. 301, n e cor State st, runs east 117.1 x north 82.4 x west 24.7 x south 56.8 x west 92.6 to Henry st, x south 25. James H. Lee agt Charles H. Collins; foreclos. mechanic's lien; att'y, Tallmadge W. Foster........ 27

New York av, w s, 25.9 s Union st, 25.6x100. Townsend Dickinson admr. Alfred Dickinson agt Mary C Elkins; att'y, John H. Betts........ 27

Fenimore st, s s, 645.9 e Flatbush av, 10.2x125, Flatbush. Isabella G. Price agt Edward Roche; att'y, Augustus M. Price........ 27

Clinton av, n w cor Lafayette av, 23x110. The People's Trust Co. agt Henry T. Chapman, Jr.; att'ys, Wingate & Cullen........ 28

Herkimer st, n s, 20 w Saratoga av, 60x80........
Saratoga av, w s, 80 n Herkimer st, 40x100........
Noah Tebbetts agt Harriet Johnston; att'y, Noah Tebbetts, in person........ 28

Lots of salt meadow bet 2d and 3d creeks in 26th Ward adj land of Cozine, 14 acres; also 5 acres on s s of New Lots adj meadow of John Blake. John H. Ireland agt Francis J. Farley; partition; att'ys, Fischer & Voltz........ 28

Thatford av, w s, 225 s Belmont av, 25x100 1. Andrew R. Culver agt Tobie Eimann; att'y, Herbert C. Smith........ 28

South 3d st, s e cor 8th st, 50x55. Phoebe M. Adams agt Milton Woolley; att'ys, Smith & Perkins........ 28

Jay st, e s, 50 n Water st, 25x90. George J. Anderson agt Robert Kent; att'ys, Hess, Townsend & McClelland........ 28

Jay st, e s, lot 110 map Thomas H. Smith, 25x100. Same agt same; same att'ys........ 28

84th st, s w s, 100 s e 22d av, 60x100, New Utrecht. Citizens' Co-operative Building and Loan Assoc. agt John J. Ryan; att'y, C. Furgueson, Jr. ... 30

Alabama av, w s, 225 n Liberty av, 16 8x100. Abraham W. Martin agt Albin Leonhardt; att'y, Philip L. Balz, Jr........ 30

12th av, n w cor 58th st, 60x100, New Utrecht. Francis Mayott agt Jane Seavel; att'y, John Cooney........ 30

4th av, w s, 50 s 8th st, 50x60. James Thompson agt Charles H. Collins; foreclos. mechanic's lien; att'y, Charles S. Taber........ 30

Dec.

Plymouth st, n s, 244.11 w Gold st, 21.8x100. George H. Wunschel agt Ann Lynch; att'y, John R. Kuhn........ 1

Quincy st, s s, 200 w Patchen av, 20x100. Abram M. Swett agt William H. H. Glover et al; att'y, A. Vanrein........ 1

Av B, s s, extends from Coney Island av to East 9th st, 5 lots........
Av B, s e cor East 3d st, runs east 60 x south 100 x east 40 x south 200 x west 100 to East 3d st, x north 300, Flatbush........
The H. B. Claflin Co. agt Solomon and Leopold Lyons; attachment; att'ys, Kneeland, Stewart & Epstein........ 1

Hancock st, s s, 140 w Lewis av, 20x100. Henry Roth agt Mary Lenhart formerly Wahl et al.; att'y, M. Hallheimer........ 1

Temple court, No. 16, centre line, e s, 104.8 n Seeley st, 14x100. William J. La Roche agt Sarah P. Darby et al.; att'ys, Phillips & Avery........ 1

Temple court, No. 14, centre line, e s, 90.8 n Seeley st, 14x100. Same agt same; same att'ys........ 1

Temple court, No. 18, centre line, e s, 118.8 n Seeley st, 14x100. Same agt same; same att'ys........ 1

Myrtle av, No. 1116........
Spencer st, e s, 257.9 n Myrtle av, 50x100........
Stephen M. Hoye agt Frances Jezek; action for pay for services; att'y, S. M. Hoye........ 1

4th av, w s, 100 s 8th st, runs west 160 x south 100 to 7th st, x east 100 x north 50 x east 60 to av, x north 50. The Mutual Life Ins. Co., New York, agt Charles S. Kendall et al.; att'y, R. Sewell... 2

Putnam av, n s, 20 e Howard av, 40x100. Same agt Robert L. Moores et al.; same att'y........ 2

Halsey st, No 479, n s, 408 e Lewis av, 17x100. Same agt William Andrews and Annie L. Murtagh; same att'y........ 2

La Grange st, w s, 150 n Manjer st, 25x91.6. Peter J. Brahm agt Ursula Stolbieger formerly Schmeizer and John Schmeizer; att'y, J. N. Ross 2

2d st, s w s, 117.10 n w 7th av, 80x100. Thos. C. Higgins and C. E. Donnellon agt Jennie L. Ross et al.; att'y, Chas. R. Halsey........ 2

2d st, s w s, 80 n w 7th av 37 1-x100. Cornelius E. Donnellon agt Jennie L. Ross et al.; same att'y. 2

Essex st, e s, 420 n Ridgewood av, 20x100. John Thomas agt Califf F. Smith; att'y, A. P. Hinman........ 2

Blake av, n w cor Powell st, 10.2x100. Moses Kinzler agt Abraham Rabbi; notice of attachment; att'y, Adolph Cohen........ 2

Sumpter st, s s, 325 e Ralph av, 25x100. William Kammann agt William J. Hartmann; att'y, Geo. T. Gertum........ 2

North 2d st, n s, 159.10 w North 6th st, 40x70.11x42.4x56.9. Jost Moller agt Sophia C. C. Kretzmer; att'ys, S. M. and D. E. Meeker........ 2

South 4th st, n s, 100 e Havemeyer st, 25x90. Caroline E. Prentiss extrx. William Coit agt Arthur B. Gretman; att'y, John Winslow 2
Hudson av, e s, 23.4 s Plymouth st, 23.4x75. Susan E. Blodgett agt Thomas Wood; att'y, Joseph M. Greenwood 3
State st, n s, 145 e Nevins st, 20x100. Libbie S. Russell agt Jacob S. Moore; att'y, Jos. M. Greenwood 3
North 2d st, n s, 100 w Lorimer st, —x—x25x—.. }
North 2d st, n s, 125 w Lorimer st, 0.6x—x0.6x73. }
Abraham Rosenson agt Kusche Idelsohn; att'ys, Hirsh & Rasquin 3
Kent av, w s, 214 s De Kalb av, 20x91.5. John J. Loftus agt Patrick L. Loftus; partition; att'ys, Goodrich, Deady & Goodrich 3
Macon st, s s, 64 w Ralph av, 18x100. Walter F. Clayton agt George F. Turner; att'y, James P. Philp 3

RECORDED LEASES.

NEW YORK. — Per Year

Bowery, No. 340, store floor and basement. Ignazio Mercadante to Joseph M. Burnes; 4 5-6 years, from July 1, 1891 .... $2,875
Canal st, No. 162, all. Jacob Davidson to John Mulrooney and Joseph Carpenter, of Mulrooney & Carpenter; 4 5-12 years, from Dec. 1, 1891 2,500
Chrystie st, No. 10, cor store and basement. Mayer Baum and Yetta Friedman to John E. Coonan; 5 5-12 years, from Dec. 1, 1891 .... 840, 900
Same property. Assign. lease. John E. Coonan to H. Koehler & Co., a corporation; Nov. 30 900
Columbia st, No. 109, south store floor. David Grunberg to Louis L. Trinkel; 3 years, from May 1, 1892 300
Gansevoort st, No. 6, and No. 17 Horatio st. Jane A. Miller and ano. exrs. Erastus H. Miller to Jacob H., John C. and Stephen T. Van Houten; 10 years, from Dec. 1, 1891 4,000
Hester st, No. 77, stoop floor and first floor. B. Berkowitz to H. Block; 3⅝ years, from Sept. 2, 1891 780
Hester st, No. 82, top floor. Aaron Goodman to Chewrah Anshie Chesed Bialystock; 10 5-12 years, from Dec. 1, 1891 360
Hudson st, No. 685. William E., Henry A. and Julia F. Gahn and Carmel, New York, and Blanche A. Frost to Patrick Farrell; 5 years, from May 1, 1891 1,560
Houston st, No. 22 W., first floor and basement. Paul Sonntag to Leopold Philippi; 1 year, from Feb. 1, 1892 2,000
Same property. Same to same; 4 years, from Feb. 1, 1893 3,500
Park row, Nos. 168 and 170. Eugene A. Hoffman to Leopold Haas, Jacob K. and Leopold S. Weiner, of Leopold Haas & Co.; 5 years, from May 1, 1892 9,500
Spring st, No. 10. Peter Massoth to Frederick Matthusen; 3 years, from May 1, 1893 1,500
Spring st, Nos. 131-137. John Goerlitz to A. Wimpfheimer & Bro.; 5 years, from Feb. 1, 1892 6,200
Water st, No. 223, all. George W. Bond to The Barstow Stove Co., Providence, R. I.; 9 5-12 years, from Dec. 1, 1891 2,600
4th st, No. 312 E., store and front cellar. Herman Weil to Jacob Hartwein; 5 years, from Dec. 1, 1891 396
13th st, No. 505 E., all. Jane Lambrecht to Robert Rosenthal; 3 years, from May 1, 1891 660
34th st, No. 36 W. Louise Herzog extrx. Max Herzog to Teresa M. and Julia M. Fox; 6 years, from May 1, 1889 3,750
43d st, No. 229 E. E. Ellery Anderson to Jacob Wissmann; 3 7-12 years, from Oct. 1, 1891 420
46th st, No. 444 W., store, basement or cellar and two rooms on store floor. Anna C. wife of Otto Wessell to Dennis Martin; 5 years, from Nov. 1, 1891 600
50th st, No. 233, n s, 270 e 8th av, 25x100.5. John Pettigrew et al. exrs. Robert Pettigrew to Keran J. Guilfoyle; 7 years, from Nov. 1, 1891 600
100th st, Nos. 9 and 11 W. George W. Eggers to Benjamin Pfifferling; 5 years, from May 1, 1890 13,800
114th st, No. 349 E., store floor and four rooms. Emilie Bruns to Fredrich Hettinger; 3 years, from June 1, 1891 420
124th st, No. 152 W., store and five rooms in rear with part of cellar. Oscar D. Dike to Andrew Spietaler; 5 years, from May 1, 1891 .... 1,050, 1,200
Same property. Assign. lease. Andrew Spietaler to John M. Mayer .... nom
Av A, No. 220, store and back room. Anna Hashagen to George Heckmann; 10 years, from Jan. 1, 1892 900
Av D, No. 28, store floor and bakery. Schuyler E. and Willard S. Brumley, of S. S. Brumley's Son & Co., to Henry Knaupp; 2 5-12 years, from Dec. 1, 1891 540
Columbus (9th) av, s w cor 103d st, store and front cellar. Charles Connor to John J. Smith; 3 11-12 years, from June 1, 1891 ... 1,600, 1,800
Madison av, No. 2120, s w cor 133d st, 19.11x80. Samuel A. Thompson to Patrick H. Daly; 10 years, from Dec. 1, 1891 1,500
1st av, No. 1121, store and rear rooms. Emanuel Pisko to August Skudrna; 5 years, from May 1, 1891 840
Same property. Assign. lease. August Skudrna to Edward Freund .... nom
1st av, No. 2246, store and front cellar. Henry Ficken to Timothy Growley; 3 years, from May 1, 1891 660
1st av, No. 178, all. Margaret Murphy to Herman Reugel; 3 5-12 years, from Dec 1, 1891 1,020
2d av, No. 2321, n w cor 119th st. Henrietta Neuhaus to Herman H. Holter; 5 years, 9 months and 15 days, from July 15, 1891 ... 1,500, 1,700
2d av, No. 1121, s w cor 59th st, store and basement. Josephine Schmid to James J. Nolan; 10 1-6 years, from March 1, 1891 ... 1,500, 1,800
Same property. Assign. lease. James J. Nolan to John J. Reilly .... nom
3d av, No. 1815, store. Mary E. Lithauer to Patrick Browne; 5 years, from May 1, 1892 .... 1,600, 1,800
6th av, n e cor 42d st, 20.5x62. Amanda M. De Graaf to James Wakely; 10 years, from May 1, 1891 10,000
10th av, No. 734, store floor and basement. Rosina Schreifer to Peter McDermott; 5 years, from May 1 1891 1,500

CHATTELS.

NOTE.—The first name, alphabetically arranged, is that of the Mortgagor, or party who gives the Mortgage. The "R" means Renewal Mortgage.

NEW YORK CITY.

NOVEMBER 27 TO DECEMBER 3—INCLUSIVE.

SALOON AND RESTAURANT FIXTURES.

Ackrons, C E. 136 Liberty and 141 Cedar .. Beadleston & W. Pump, &c. $265
Allport, J G. High Bridge....J H Bereuter. Pool Table. 150
Arnstein, George. 90 John. .Bernheimer & S. (R) 1,500
Bernhard, Valerian. 74 South 5th av....G Ringler & Co. (R) 311
Blasius, Michael. 2089 3d av....H U Singhi. 1,850
Brinckman, Emil. 980 1st av....Wagner & S. Pool Table. 175
Beyer, Elizabeth. 1165 Broadway....Brunswick-B-C Co. Pool Table. (R) 225
Barron, Robert. 130 W 52d....D M Koehler. 800
Blackburn, A J. 344 W 11th....P Ballentine & Sons. 1,000
Brennen, Thomas. 84 West.. .J A Allers, supt. (R) 2,000
Brodbeck, Jacob. 25 Broome....Langdon & G B Co. Pump. 54
Bush, J L. 525 W 40th. ..Consumers' B Co. 400
Barlow, J F. 200 W 42d....H Wilkins, Jr. (R) 7,000
Blasius, Michael. 2039 3d av....G Ringler & Co. 2,000
Buckmann, John. 2 Chrystie and 46 Division ....P Ballentine & Sons. 3,650
Buechler, Carl. 105 Stanton. ..Schmitt & S. (R) 750
Cole, C H. 48 W 35th....J Leviberg. Restaurant Fixtures. 225
Coonan, J E. 10 Chrystie....H Koehler & Co. 900
Cunningham, E F. 323 Av A....P J Muphy. 1,500
Craig, Patrick. 2259 10th av....Bernheimer & S. (R) 1,700
Dalesia, Fabia. 338 E 109th....H Zeltner. 700
Del Gindice, Michael. 524 E 149th....F & M Schaefer B Co. (R) 200
Doerr, C A. 188 Av B....G Ringler & Co. (R) 500
Dwyer, Michael. 29 Jones... Bavarian B Co. 500
Daly, P H. Madison av and 133d st....S A Thompson. 1,500
Delany, Daniel. 418 W 32d....Bernheimer & S. (R) 225
Emmrich, Henry. 204 E 104th....G Ehret. (R) 450
Engel, Chas. 175 Chrystie....J C G Hupfel B Co. 300
Friedman, Fritz. 86 2d av ...Friedman Bros. Restaurant Fixtures. 1,000
Friedhoff, August. 994 2d av .. J Ahlers B Co. (R) 400
Fisher, Mary. 229 W 12th....Bachmann B Co. 1,500
Fitzsimons, J H. 746 6th....Wagner & S. Pool Table. 160
Ford, Margaret. 72 Amsterdam av D Stevenson. 710
Freund, Edward. 1121 1st av....Beadleston & W. Pump. 125
Same....same. Ice Box. 110
Same....same. 1,000
Same....same. Pump. 125
Same....same. Box. 110
Frohlesen, John. 136 East Houston. . S Liebmann's Sons B Co. 800
Fuchs, Julia. 615 E 9th....C Iba. 225
Foth, A H. 121 2d av....W Losha. 2,000
Gallagher, James. 651 10th av....O'Reilly, Skelly & F. (R) 2,000
Gillen, J E. 638 Southern Boulevard ...J & M Haffen. 600
Greenberg & Fishlowitz. 151 Essex....F Ibert. (R) 300
Greinert, Alex. 4 St Marks pl....J C G Hupfel B Co. (R) 700
Grose, L, & Co. 112 3d av ...R Rothschilds' Sons Co. 1,543
Glasser, C & B. 1010 Av A... J Kress B Co. 1,100
Goodwin, P H. 133 Hudson....Bernheimer & S. (R) 1,000
Gormond, Michael. 533 W 46th... A Finck & Son. 700
Grambart, F W. 2305½ 3d av....Bennett & Co. Restaurant Fixtures. 150
Griffiths, William. 1665 Madison av....Bernheimer & S. (R) 3,000
Gloster, Maurice. 734 10th av....J Everard. 2,080
Guinan, Thomas. 84 Centre....Consumers' B Co. 500
Heyer, P W. 1556 9th av....Bernheimer & S. (R) 2,000
Humphrey, H J. 1815 Park av....Wagner & S. Pool Table. 340
Haase, Herman. 415 10th av....V Loewers. (R) 450
Haffey, John. 318 Spring....J Everard. 304
Haffner, J D. 600 8th av ...Bernheimer & S. Ice House. 110
Same....same. Pump. 109
Hall, Samuel. 606 43d....J Ahlers B Co. (R) 250
Houlihan, D. 180th st and Old Broadway.... Bernheimer & S. Ice House. 85
Same....same. Ice House. 20
Same....same. Ice House. 140
Huber, L and A. 148 Spring... A Schneider. Restaurant Fixtures. 200
Hawkins, H M. 2140 8th av....Beadleston & W. 3,000
Hughes, Edward. 860 1st av....Pat Cunningham. 3,250
Kennelly, Daniel. 3341 Bathgate av .... H Zeltner. 700
Koehne, J H. 530 W 50th....C Stein. 1,342
Kukoly, Matyas. 147 Attorney. . J Eppig. (R) 500
Krug, John. 790 9th av... Schmitt & S. 1,600
Korel, John. 161 E 4th....P Weidmann. 400
Kurz, Anna. 32 Rivington....J A Jaeckel. Restaurant Fixtures. 50
Kearns & Cassidy. 1687 3d av... H Elias B Co. (R) 300
Keegan, Bernard. 1389 3d av... J Ruppert. 1,500
Kelly, Patrick, exr of Margaret Brady. 575 10th av....J Ruppert. 1,500
Lesser, Henry. 40 Carmine....J Rieser. 400
Lolle & Paulino. 149 Elizabeth....Bernheimer & S. Pool Table. (R) 140
Lotterhas, Wm. 199 E 58th. P Buckel. (R) 700
Laderer & Hogan. 176 8th av....J Everard. 2,550
Lebenheim, Ludwig. 180 E 112th.... Wagner & S. Pool Table. (R) 60
Ligon, Julius. 1736 2d av....A Kremer B Co. 400
Maguire, Stephen. 528 W 34th....Bavarian B Co. 800
Mayer, J M. W 124th st....G Ehret. 4,300
Meyer, Frederick. 36 Desbrosses....J Hoffmann. (R) 200
Masterson, F J. 291 Av C....Beadleston & W. Ice Box. (R) 85
Morrisey & Collins. 1959 2d av....F & M Schaefer B Co. 945
Muller, Ernst. 190 3d av....J L Lissner. Restaurant Fixtures. 925
Mulrooney & Carpenter. 162 Canal....W Craft. 1,800
Murray, S. 112th st and 2d av....Bernheimer & S. Ice House. 135
Murray, S and T J. 112th st and 2d av.. Bernheimer & S. Pump. 110
Many, John. 2062 8th av... Bernheimer & S. 550
McCabe, Charles. 333 2d av....T McMahon. (R) 400
Same....J Whyte. (R) 480
McKabaray & Mowbray 2025 2d av....J Ruppert. 1,390
Moloney, Daniel. 250 W 41st....J & M Haffen. (R) 130
Mueller, E E. 47 E 105th ...J Ruppert. 1,500
Murray, T J. 1600 9th av....Bernheimer & S. (R) 4,500
Neuner, George. 399 E 26th....H Elias B Co. (R) 500
Neiheiser, William. 546 11th av....C Braum. (R) 1,500
Nugent, Patrick. 1316 2d av....India Wharf B Co. 600
O'Connell, Michael. 49th st and 2d av....Bernheimer & S. Ice House. 185
Pfeiffer, Fred. 713 2d av....H Elias. (R) 250
Popitto, Vincenzo. 195 Mulberry .... Bernheimer & S. Ice House. 60
Same....same. Ice House. 75
Quigley, M J. 2 and 4 Church....C Spiess. 2,500
Ranke, Henry. 7 Jackson....V Loewers. (R) 1,340
Reich, Bernard. 50 Essex....Sekosky Bros. 185
Rohl, Hermann. 230 Eldridge....Rubsam & H B Co. 475
Rourke, Bernard. 85 Forsyth....J Kress B Co. 7,000
Ruzalski, Frank. 72 Rivington....Wagner & S. Pool Table. 160
Raupach, William. 273 Elizabeth....G Ehret. (R) 900
Rowan, Michael. 540 W 55th....Bernheimer & S. Ice House. 103
Renfer, Chas. 140 W 17th....G Ringler & Co. (R) 300
Rose, Leonard. 69 Leonard....W T Knapp. Restaurant Fixtures. (R) 1,200
Samson, Elias. 70 Division....Budweiser B Co. (R) 800
Schiffer, Frank. 73 Allen....C Frese. 320
Smith, J J. 34 Jackson....V Loewers. (R) 389
Schneider, Geo. 1541 1st av....Schmitt & S. (R) 600
Specht, William. 1734 Madison av....W Tuite. (R) 700
Sweeney, S E. 2072 2d av... J King. 900
Schulz, Julian. 855 2d av... Lembeck & Betz. 900
Scherf, Henry. 504 E 14th....P Schaefer & Son. 800
Seventh Co Club. 113 W 38th....Brunswick-B-C Co. Pool Table. 500
Sachs, S. 92 Division....J H Bereuter. Pool Table. 145
Scherney, William. 589 E 144th ...J Ruppert. 500
Schulhof, Sigmund. 431 E 73d... P Buckel. (R) 1,600
Siemers, Herman. 506 E 133d....H Elias B Co. 1,300
Sranski, W. 185 Chrystie....W Peter B Co. 696
Thatcher, James. 177th st and 3d av....H Zeltner. 266
Ubben, Otto. 885 2d av... F Oppermann, Jr. 600
Wollesen, Theodore. 874 1st av... H Elias B Co. 800
Wermer, George. 305 E 9th... Bernheimer & S. 500
Wicht, Christopher. 1407 Av A....J Mulhearn. 1,200
Wendel, Chas. 360 W 47th....Bernheimer & S. (R) 250
Wendel, Fritz. 620 9th av....J Ruppert. (R) 3,500
Weldrick, J D. 20 Chatham sq....Bernheimer & S. Ice House. 145
Same....same. Ice House. 95
Same....same. Pump. 115
White, B & T. 213 E 102d....D Mayer B Co. 700

HOUSEHOLD FURNITURE.

Adams, Mrs. 19 Minetta pl....H S Eisler. 128
Aris, W T. 341 E 124th....D Schwarzkopf. 155
Adelson, Philip. 150 E 88th... J Berlinsky. 500
Anderson, H J. 219 E 19th....A C Carpenter. 500
Anstey, Phebe A. 101 W 19th....Mary E Busselle. 500
Aldrich, John. 117 E 105th....D M Brown. 125
Baldwin, C K. 427 E 78th....L Baumann. 188
Bellamy, Alice. 355 E 89th .... A Hafelin. Piano. 182
Berger, John. 216 E 7th ...A Hafelin. Piano. 275
Breman, J T. 268 W 118th....L Baumann. 145
Brown, J J. 112 E 110th....A Hafelin. Piano. 240
Bauberger, Philip. 75 Vandam....L Baumann. 124
Benton, Addie. 212 E 45th....F G Smith. Piano. (R) 115
Boucher, T J. 157 E 76th....A Hafelin. Piano. 175
Bridge, Margaret. 1364 3d av....A Hafelin. Piano. 177
Buckbee, Minnie I. 231 W 23d....M B Taylor. 2,000
Burke, Maggie. 833 11th av....L Baumann. 175
Bates, Lizzie. 101 W 81st....Lincoln I and G Assoc. 300
Bates, Lizzie. 14 Av A... G Fennell & Co. 120
Beinard, Leo. 259 W 39th....O'Farrell & Co. 344
Brownell, Mrs E. 297 W 116th... L Baumann. 201
Brown, Mary. 158 W 36th....J J Halloran. 250
Bruno, Adelaide. 21 Eldridge....Fennell & P. (R) 182
Bodenkoop, August. 215 W 13th....J Baumann. 173
Bourguignon, C L. 245 W 46th....J Baumann. 153
Briody, Margaret. 928 2d av....S Baumann. 361
Bunnett, Jennie. 14 W 65th....S Heyman & Co. 380
Carew, Sadie. 448 W 27th....J Baumann. 200
Chambers, W J. 398 3d av....J Baumann. 242
Charbonneau, Napoleon. 226 E 81st....J Baumann. 111
Charlesworth, C A and M F. 68 Macdougal....L L Wright. 1,850
Cohen, L E. 508 E 85th ...R M Walters. Piano. (R) 157
Connor, Mrs Wm. 212 E 44th....T Kelly. 140
Caffrey, Thomas. 63 Watts....M Donohue. 160
Campbell, Bridget. 135 E 65th .. E D Farrell. 148
Castellanos, M. 142 W 127th... L Baumann. 260
Clark, Nina. 141 W 116th... J Guinevan. 227
Clinch, Mrs John. 145 E 126th. .E D Farrell. 282
Clute, Florence W. 324 E 48th....Manges Bros. 106
Connelly, M S. 208 W 103d....L Baumann. 117
Connor, J F. 30 Columbia... W E Wheelock & Co. Piano. 400
Cordon, Caroline. 28 Greenwich av....O'Farrell & Co. (R) 101
Coyne, J F. 2477 8th av....L Baumann. 194
Cummings, P J. 527 W 36th....L Baumann. 110
Cunningham, Mary. 549 10th av....W E Wheelock & Co. Piano. 275
Cashin, Matilda F. 108 W 31st....M Kenholts. 2,000
Chessman, Amelia. 51 E 87th ...A Hafelin. Piano. 224
Cole, Dollie. 307 E 76th ..H Israel & Sons. 159

Connolly, P F. 253 W 18th... L Baumann. 148
Corday, J and L. 132 W 15th....H Israel & Son. (R) 106
Cushing, W A. 632 E 139th....W T Cushing. 175
Cahill, Hettie A. 23d st and 5th av, Brooklyn ....R M Walters. Piano. 225
Diekman, H R. 70 W 38th st and 661 6th av... Amer Guar Assoc. 400
Dooley, Katherine. 1129 Park av....A Hafelin. Piano. 150
Dougherty, G S. 334 E 26th....L Baumann. 135
Donnelly, J J. 110 E 128th....Dreisacker & Co. 261
Dueth, Rosa. 106 E 90th....A Hafelin. Piano. 218
De Gorge, C. 116 E 115th ..L Baumann. 173
de Mesa, Mrs M M. 234 W 14th.... W E Wheelock & Co. Piano. (R) 105
Denison, Bessie. 1327 Broadway....O'Farrell & Co. (R) 137
Denzan, George. 2226 North 3d av....G Zirnstein. 115
Diekmann, Henry. 337 E 16th....L Baumann. 182
Dodge, Mary M. 1 Parnel pl....L Baumann. 192
Doran, Elizabeth. 503 E 15th....W E Wheelock & Co. Piano. 175
Dunn, Sarah A. 274 W 4th....E D Farrell. 325
Delafield, Mrs H N. 1699 Madison av....T Kelly. 133
Donnelly, Anthony. 417 W 53d....J Baumann. 147
Donovan, Mary. 911 6th av....J Baumann. 134
Eastman, Nellie. 312 W 42d....J Baumann. 174
Edwards, F M. 319 W 58th ...E D Farrell. 468
Ehrich, Elise. 704 8th av....J F Manges. (R) 130
Eicke, Josephine. 112 E 81st ...L Wertz. 193
Einstein, Rudolph. 304 E 28th....L Baumann. 182
Esguerea, N. 25 E 21st....W E Wheelock & Co. Piano. (R) 145
Esler, M H and P C. 1927 Madison av....A L Esler. 1,000
Elze, Ida. 124 India st, Brooklyn....A Hafelin. Piano. 220
English, Mrs G W. 310 W 116th ...D M Brown. 379
Frankenstein, Jacob. 178 E 90th....A Hafelin. Piano. 205
Furphy, Annie. 9 College pl....L Baumann. 116
Feericks, Peter. 251 W 31st ...L Baumann. 196
Fielding, Sarah. 101 W 93d ...J & J Dobson. 156
Fitzpatrick, Lizzie. 139 E 48th....Fennell & P. 119
Flanagan, Mrs B. 134 Av D....Fennell & Pye. 196
Fountain, P T. 374 W 116th....Spies Bros. (R) 135
Farrill, Joseph. 754 7th av....J Baumann. 122
Flaherty, Mary. 374 2d av....Jordan & M. 143
Gilbert, Amelia S. 206 and 218 E 9th....E Horton. (R) 140
Gunther, George. 292 Willis av....L Baumann. 110
Gentle, Lillie M. 2138 8th av....J Gregg & Co. 210
Gilson, Frank. 517 3d av....H S Eisler. 109
Glover, Ella. 208 5th av....W E Wheelock & Co. Piano. (R) 145
Grant, Mrs Thomas. 418 W 57th ...Krakauer Bros. Piano. 288
Grindle, Mattie E. 171 W 12th....R M Walters. Piano. (R) 162
Gross, Herman. 429 E 52d....Fennell & P. (R) 275
Gude, Emma. 435 W 56th....W E Wheelock & Co. Piano. 225
Gunther, William. 164 E 38th....L Baumann. 208
Gormley, J W. 120 E 121st....J McCormack. 192
Grant, Marietta....J Williams. 200
Grumbstrum, Amy. 212 W 42d... J Baumann. 248
Goodstein, Johanna. 204 E 65th....Krakauer Bros. Piano. 150
Grout, Kittie W. 667 E 136th ...A Hafelin. Piano. 275
Gumplowitz, L E. 859 9th av....J J McGrorty. 114
Hart, Patrick. 444 W 39th ...D M Brown. (R) 104
Hindle, A S. 410 W 42d... H Thoesen. 131
Hackett, Amos. 473 Columbus av....J Baumann. 125
Hecker, Carl. 60 W 22d....J P and J P Caben. Paintings. 3,856
Henderson, Mrs Wm. 693 Greenwich....T Kelly. 130
Holian, Jane. 310 W 128d .. J Baumann. 148
Hubbard, J C. 81 W 101st....F W Russell. 110
Hasse, Harry. 502 E 119th. ..H Israel & Son. 135
Hausheer, Mrs H. 73 2d av....H Israel & Son. 182
Heine, Emma. 161 E 114th....H F Kasschau & Co. 214
Hunderpfund, Amelia. 546 W 50th . .L Baumann. 109
Hunting, Russell. 2190 8th av....L Baumann. 128
Hager, Mary. 834 Eagle av....W E Wheelock & Co. Piano. 350
Hallock, Mrs J E. 25 W 45th....O'Farrell & Co. (R) 154
Hall, W F. 174 W 94th....Fennell & P. 540
Hart, Thos J. 779 10th av....O'Farrell & Co. 148
Hart, Henry. 2071 2d av....W E Wheelock & Co. Piano. (R) 147
Haskell, T R. 29 Broadway....Brooklyn F Co. 148
Hearle, E J. 252 W 16th....L Baumann. 204
Hecker, Antonia J. 188 E 70th....L Baumann. 148
Horwitz, A W. 160 E 107th....H Thoesen. 379
Huling, H P. 21 Grove....L Baumann. 170
Ide, F W. 609 E 151st.. J Gregg & Co. 135
Ince, Emma. 111 E 27th....R N Blackhall. 500
Judah, Margaret. 531 E 82d....A Hafelin. Piano. 255
Jones, F L. 109 E 127th....L Baumann. 128
Johnson, J W. 1762 3d av....H Mannes & Son. 130
Jordan, Jennie. 445 W 48th ...J Baumann. 128
Judge, J J. 225 E 43d... J Baumann. 174
Jones, Ida. 239 W 124th....Manges Bros. 125
Kaufman, L. 1925 2d av. ..S I Herschmann. 181
Knoepfle, Julia A. 237 Greenpoint av, Brooklyn. A Hafelin. Piano. 210
Kuder, August. 577 9th av....H Thoesen. 119
Kearn, Julia. 1964 7th av ...J Baumann. 258
Kerr, John. 505 E 118th ...J McCormack & Co. 143
King, Margaret. 56 Scammel ...Jordan & M. 110
Kueny, J D. 246 W 31st....O'Farrell & Co. 183
Kuestner, John. 238 E 108th... J Baumann. 183
Lahn, Gertie. 417 W 4th....L Baumann. 152
Kastor, Francis. 109 E 93d ...L Baumann. 614
Kelly, Daniel. 347 E 87th....L Baumann. 428
Kennedy, Lizzie. 509 E 83d....L Baumann. 208
Koehler, John. 87 Stanton.. G & W Bieber. 145
Kendall, Lillian. 189 Lexington av....H Israel & Son. 1,150
Keyes, Mary H. 283 Av C....H F Kasschau & Co. 308
Kolb, Rose. 149 W 53d... Bruner & Moore. 836
Liebert, Magdelene. 204 E 39th....L Baumann. 134
Lowry, S W. 85th st and Western Boulevard.... L Baumann. 361
Lahn, Henry. 408 W 48th....L Baumann. 156
Laverty, William. 1510 10th av... O'Farrell & Co. (R) 114
Lennon, Mary. 171 E 108th....E D Farrell. 130
Leslie, Rachel. 101 9th av. . L Baumann. 115
Law, Marion G. 230 W 42d....E M Cauda. 600
Landry, Ludwig. 923 Park av....S Heyman & Co. 220
Lewis, Christina. 574 3d av....Jordan & M. 191
Lange, Johanna. 71 W 44th ...J Baumann. 125
Lecomte, R J. 145 East 30th....O Dupre. 400
Lewin, Rosa. 325 E 5th....S I Herschmann. 259
Lillenstern, Carrie. 440 E 85th.. Krakauer Bros. Piano. (R) 115
Lloyd, W J. 312 W 42d....J Baumann. 266
Lowther, J B and S E. 298 Manhattan av.... Financial Credit Co. 250
Meyer, Freda. 215 E 25th....D M Brown. 381
Maple, Matthias. 322 Columbus av....J Baumann. 169
McGinn, Mrs Jas. 42 Charlton. T Kelly. 180
Mennis, James. 46 Manhattan. J Baumann. 124
Meyer, John....J Williams. 219
Miller, Nettie. 34 St Marks pl ...Jordan & M. 197
Mitchell, Georgie. 786 6th av....O'Farrell & Co. 1,137
Moroney, R K. 426 W 52d ...J Baumann. 178
Markes, Mrs E E. 523 E 83d....H S Eisler. 174
May, Agnes. 505 E 15th....E D Farrell. 150
McEwen, John. 319 W 21st....D Schwarzkopf. 407
McGuire, Mary. 504 W 21st... W E Wheelock & Co. Piano. 225
McHugh, J J. 407 W 26th....L Baumann. 111
McIntyre, E L. 316 E 79th....Fennell & P. (R) 155
McNamee, Rose. 440 W 28th....J P Delehanty. 138
Miller, Grace V. 332 W 18th ...W E Wheelock & Co. Piano. 275
Minton, Augusta L. 101 E 89th....W E Wheelock & Co. Piano. 275
Musgrave, Mrs M L. 29 E 36th....W E Wheelock & Co. Piano. 300
Maher, Henry. 246 E 120th....L Baumann. 159
Mannix, Lizzie. 447 E 80th ... A Hafelin. Piano. 179
McLoughlin, Minnie. 402 W 59th....F J Brechtel. (R) 162
McNaughton, C A. 822 Columbus av....C H McNaughton. 100
Muller, Peter. 61 Oliver....F G Smith. Piano. (R) 180
Nagengast, Theo. 552 W 49th....L Baumann. 128
Neaman, Mary. 44 Beach....L Baumann. 176
Nicholsburg, Sarah. 223 E 84th....Manges Bros. (R) 111
Nee, Mary. 407 W 53d....J Baumann. 121
Nixon, A C. 317 W 54th....J Baumann. 190
O'Brien, Annie. 191 Forsyth....E D Farrell. 162
Ochlhey, Emma. 148 Columbus av....J Gregg & Co. 179
Oeikers, Amelia. 1084 Park av....A Hafelin. Piano. 105
O'Hara, Mollie. 206 E 36th....R M Walters. Piano. 250
Osborne, Pearle. 223 E 76th....J Moriarty. 322
O'Neill, Bessie. 315 E 46th....J Rubenstein. 194
Pierce, Nina. 231 W 41st.... J Baumann. 121
Pierson, Mrs F S. 520 E 84th....D M Brown. 240
Patten, Harriett C. 42 W 34th....L B List. 3,400
Pool, R N. 9 W 29th....H Reddick. 388
Same....same. 7,516
Patterson, John. 34 St Marks pl....J P Delehanty. 163
Paurche, Theise. 149 E 27th....O'Farrell & Co. 366
Pearson, Gertrude. 126 E 25th....A A Lawrence. 500
Peters, C J. 241 W 35th....Manges Bros. 200
Plain, Hazel. 258 W 33d....L Baumann. 138
Polo, John. 319 E 72d....E D Farrell. 184
Pettinato, Michelangelo. 181 W 53d....E Bent. 2,000
Quinn, Edward. 56 Horatio....H Mannes & Son. 191
Queen, Annie. 80 W 3d....L Baumann. 253
Ratty, Albert. 1717 Madison av....E D Farrell. 160
Raymond, Carrie. 55 E 122d....Fennell & P. 136
Reichert, Wm. 357 W 38th....L Baumann. 213
Reilly, Mary. 110 E 41st.... E D Farrell. 143
Reinold, A E, Mrs. 889 E 161st....E D Farrell. 156
Rennison, Bella. 696 Water....L Baumann. 136
Robinson, Anne. 256 E 89th ...L Baumann. 123
Robinson, M C. 2001 7th av....Fennell & P. (R) 161
Robison, Adelina. 324 W 49th....R M Walters. Piano. 120
Rodgers, Annie. 365 W 50th....L Baumann. 110
Rohrs, Mary. 523 E 83d....H S Eisler. 174
Rapp, Marie. 18 Crosby....J A Most. 450
Rousch, Richard. 2693 3d av....R M Walters. Piano. 115
Rice, Henry. 520 E 83d....American Guarantee Assoc. 150
Richie, Florence. 241 W 35th ...J Baumann. 221
Rooe, R J. 520 W 41st....T Kelly. 169
Rolph, N C.... J Williams. 200
Ruland, L E. 1840 3d av....J Baumann. 224
Roberts, Rosalie. 249 W 21st....J Baumann. 300
Sanchez, Catherine. 179 E 108th....J Baumann. 302
Sarbin, Joseph. 226 E 102d....T Kelly. 130
Scherr, Henry. 258 E 62d....J Baumann. 148
Scoffin, F F. 216 W 25th ...J Baumann. 469
Shepard, Kate. 199 W 134th....J Baumann. 245
Silber, Catherine. 242 E 12th .. J Baumann. 313
Sinclair, Addie E. 950 Lexington av....J Baumann. 294
Smith, C W. 78 Ege av, Jersey City, N J.... O'Farrell & Co. 131
Smyth, Lillie. 934 6th av....J Baumann. 130
Solomon, Jennie. 27 Rutger....Jordan & M. 129
Steet, Frances. 631 Amsterdam av....J Baumann. 126
Stoaxe, C W. 314 W 32d... J Baumann. 427
Stubel, Camille. 489 W 28th....H Mannes & Son. 181
Scheffmeyer, C J. 536 Greenwich....F J Brechtel. (R) 123
Silverstone, Jacob. 542 W 126th ...L Baumann. 230
Smith, May P. 570 7th av....H Israel & Son. (R) 317
Soich, Mrs R. 113 E 121st....F G Smith. Piano (R) 180
Strittmatter, Lina. 34 2d ....F A Reymann. 100
Sullivan, Lizzie. 329 E 80th....A Hafelin. Piano. 121
Schonhard, August. 246 E 94th ... H Thoesen. 168
Shea, Sarah L. Fordham ...W E Wheelock & Co. Piano. 575
Sincox, Mary. 41 1st av....E D Farrell. 172
Simmons, Jennie. 218 E 82d .. L Baumann. 115
Smith, E K and A E. 222 W 104th....J E Crow. (R) 223
Smith, Fenton. 10 W 104th....D Schwarzkopf. 219
Speer, Minnie. 2055 Western Boulevard....Krakauer Bros. Piano. 165
Spengler, Philip. 34 Amsterdam av....Estey Piano Co. Piano. 400
Stephenson, Octavia. 264 W 24th....J P Delehanty. 267
Stephens, Annie M. 136 E 49th....Fennell & P. (R) 264
Stoecker, A J. 436 E 122d... W E Wheelock & Co. Piano. 350
Storms, Mrs John. 616 E 135th....Fennell & P. 144
Swain, O F. 2 King.. J J Coogan. (R) 112
Sweeney, Martin. 257 W 32d....L Baumann. 274
Shepard, Alice T. 354 W 56th....Krakauer Bros. Piano. 237
Shields, Mary T. 111 W 31st....R M Walters. Piano. 275
Simon, Louis, Jr. 1988 Lexington av....J G Patton & Co. 178
Skill, Mrs. 210 W 123d....J G Patton & Co. 153
Sonneborn, Leah. 117 E 69th... J N Hayward. (R) 8,500
Speicy, Annie L. 24 Rutgers....J Gregg. 114
Stiller, Agnes. 645 Columbus av... J G Patton & C. 267
Tilford, Ellen. 336 W 42d....J Baumann. 209
True, A C. 8 W 99th....J Baumann. 233
Topp, R. 189 Henry ...H Israel & Sons. 112
Tice, A E. 363 W 36th....H Mannes & Son. 237
Tilley, William. 103 E 108th....J Baumann. 211
Todd, R H. 1497 Lexington....J Baumann. 220
Vogel, Alfred. 316 E 77th....Jordan & M. 100
Verhas, Wm. 1049 Park av....A Hafelin. Piano. 215
Waters, Emma. 9 W 133d....J Baumann. 194
Wisne, Arthur. 43 E 59th....J Baumann. 275
Wood, Mrs L A. 1262 Lexington av....E Apple. 585
Walsh, Mary E. 315 E 118th....Dreisacker & Co. 180
Walter, A W. 212 E 115th....L Baumann. 298
Watt, Mrs. 449 W 48th....Bollermann & Son. Piano. 225
Weinberger, Ed. 433 E 9th....E D Farrell. 161
Whaley, Minnie. 155 Av A....L Baumann. 133
Same....same. 140
Williams, Bertha. 328 W 37th....L Baumann. 197
Woodman, Mary M. 75 W 95th....H E Stoutenborough. 1,186
Woychinski, Frank. 414 E 83d....L Baumann. 327
Walker, Mary P. 92th st and Amsterdam av.... L Baumann. 540
Whitmore, Graham. 262 W 122d....L Baumann. 160
Wright, Maggie. 206 Madison....R M Walters. Piano. 250
Yuill, J G. 429 W 24th ...L Baumann. 165
Zirnstein, G and C. 2751 Webster av....L Weitz. 151

MISCELLANEOUS.

Adams & Duane....J Cunningham Son & Co. Coach. (R) 361
Allman, I F. 394 Greenwich....A Thompson. Machinery. 1,000
Abramowitz, J. 23 Hester ...Archer Mfg Co. Barber Fixtures. 172
Aschmann, John. 414 E 11th....Archer Mfg Co. Barber Fixtures. 24
Arnstein, Henry. 658 Broadway and 109 E 60th ....Amer Guar Assoc. Jewelry Fixtures. 100
Baltzly, A B. 2278 7th av....Nat Cash Reg Co. Register. 225
Bollmann, Elise. 33½ Stanton....E Wolf. Cigar Fixtures. 500
Bowles, Lillian. 33d st and Lexington av.... Seligman & H. Horses. 600
Burmeister, Bernard. 300 E 70th....C Droge. Grocery Fixtures. 496
Bahr & Campbell. 192 E 121st....Fifth Av Storage Co. Van. 340
Bennett, J W. 589 Columbus av....E V Skinner. Laundry Fixtures. 497
Burt, William. 350 E 125th....L Burt. Horse, Wagon, &c. 250
Bader, William. 173 Av B....J Weiss. Barber Fixtures. 130
Battilla, D. 411 W 42d....F Tecoraro. Barber Fixtures. 100
Berkovitz, Jake. 263 Bowery....H Berkovitz. Machines. 300
Berkfeld, B L. 154th st and Amsterdam av.... F Wilcox. Horse, Milk Fixtures, &c. 500
Campbell, Henry....D P Nichols & Co. Coach. (R) 430
Christopher, M S. 307 and 309 E 115th....J Krooss. Horses, Milk Wagons, &c. 975
Corneth & Clark. 151 W 18th....A W Ahrens. Bottling Fixtures. (R) 1,286
Cuppers, Barbara. 996 10th av....J Liesenberg. Confectionery Fixtures. 200
Cook, Mrs W H. Hudson, Mich... Mieble P Press Co. Press. 800
Capodanno, Rocco. 61 South 5th av ...J Souvay. Barber Fixtures. 468
Cuomo & Pagano. 31st st and Broadway ... Archer Mfg Co. Barber Fixtures. 118
Cava, Carmine. Barnegat, N J ...K Simon. Horses, Trucks, &c. 2,600
Cohen, Davis. 183 Norfolk....H Tulman. Grocery Fixtures. 65
Connor, Dominick. 56 Pike....Nat Cash Reg Co. Register. 200
Dittenheimer & Seaman. 116 Centre ...Nat Cash Reg Co. Register. 200
Dietzmann, Richard. 187 10th av....G Ridler. Bakery Fixtures. 200
Dougherty, Joseph. 580 10th av....Beadleston & W. Office Fixtures. 55
Demorest, E H.... C Meinhofer. Horse, Wagon. 100
Dodman, Robert. 160 E 45th ...P Westphal.... Barber Fixtures. 200
Duryea, W B. 104 W 64th st, Central Market, Broadway and 38th st....O Duryea. Furniture, stand and butcher Fixtures. 6,000
Dietrich, Chas. 270 4th av....J Leiong. Butcher Fixtures 1,000
Dunning, A J. 1405 2d av....A D Roe. Butter store Fixtures. 500
Ernst & Woestendick. 840 St Nicholas av ...F A Pfitzner. Grocery Fixtures. 600
Fried, Amy. 164 E 110th....Seligman Bros. Grocery Fixtures. 700
Fifth Av Transportation Co....E F Shepard. Horses, &c. (R) 47,594
Fagley, W C. 345 W 12th....A Fagley. Horse, &c. (R) 560
Fleischhauer, G & E. 1805 3d av....J Fetzer. Butcher Fixtures. 85
Foster, A E. 165 and 166 W 133d....J O'Connell. Horse, Wagon, &c. 300
Friday, W H. 25th st and Broadway....Archer Mfg Co. Barber Fixtures. (R) 389
Galligan, Henry. 49th st and 11th av....A McCabe, Horses, Ice Wagon, &c. 700
Gibbs Bros., Moran & Co....Campbell P P Co. Press. (R) 2,555
Glaeser, Emanuel ...Mieble P Press Co. Press. 800
Guarino, Giuseppi. 647 1st av....V De Girolano. Barber Fixtures. 127
Globe Mutual Benefit Society. 697 Broadway.... T Harding. Office Fixtures. (R) 195
Goodlette & Pratt. 155 W 23d....E M Pratt. Store Fixtures. 125
Hayden, C O. 627 and 629 Washington....C Eckhard. Horses, Trucks, &c. (R) 1,500
Herman, L. 83 Sheriff .. J Mathews. Soda Fixtures. (R) 35
Hess, G A. 1021 6th av....R E Hess. Barber Fixtures. 700
Hagopian Photo Engraving Co. 8 Great Jones ....H S Favshanjian. Machinery, &c. 1,500
Hartmann, F J. 1448 2d av....C P Goerrig. Drug Fixtures. 2,250
Hamill & Van Ness....Keen & Lines. Coach. 909

Hitchcock, C A. 325 W 58th....J W Cross. Horse. 1,000
Hodecker, Anton. 645 9th av....W Smith. Butcher Fixtures. 140
Hughes, Henry. 24 New Bowery....D M Koehler. Horses, Trucks, &c. 350
Hendler, Hyman. 88 Monroe C Haller. Machine. 50
Humphrey, Lee. 261 W 61st....Archer Mfg Co. Barber Fixtures. 180
Haan, R M. 1284 Broadway....S B Wortmann. Store Fixtures. (R) 560
Haise, Henry. 599 1st av ...G Haise. Horses, Ice Wagon, &c. 650
Hartshorn, J W. 142 E 59th.... Hincks & J. Cab. (R) 60
Immen, H K. 57 Beach....H Immen. Grocery Fixtures. 600
Industrial Development Co. 186 Liberty....F A Codey. Office Fixtures. 1,200
Kellerman, Adolph. 261 2d....L Stern. Horse, Wagon. 190
Kalumk, Leo. 25 Sheriff .... D Stamper. Horses, Coaches, &c. 2,000
Kaufmann, Henry. 548 E 13th.... Bohm & Pfeiffer. Truck. 175
Kent, John. 69 Varick....L Hurst. Machines. (R) 507
Kramer, Alois. 111 Canal....M Kramer. Store Fixtures, &c. 1,000
Kleinberg, Samuel. 258 Delancey....Archer Mfg Co. Barber Fixtures. (R) 389
Knowles, William. 104 E 13th....A Erskine. Machinery, Presses, &c. 2,000
Kruppenbacher, Andrew. 1675 Av A....K Kruppenbacher. Barber Fixtures. 250
Keilin, S. 184 Division....G Gerzog. Store Fixtures. 30
Keith, James. 317 W 15th....Hincks & J. Cab. (R) 175
Klorun, Abraham. 95 Canal....F & G Haag & Co. Barber Fixtures. 295
Kronengold, Adolph. 25 Broadway....B Buchenholz. Barber Fixtures. 550
Laskan, -....P Barrett. Truck. 618
Little, G R .. Campbell P P Co. Press. 13,200
Loning, W K. 1316 3d av....A Goldsmith. Jewelry Fixtures. 328
Lynch, Patrick. 2294 1st av....Nat Cash Reg Co. Register. 170
Laurence & Malton. 41st st and Broadway.... J Mathews. Soda Fixtures. (R) 557
Lefkowitz, Sem. 152 Monroe....W B Davis. Coupe. 550
Lichenstein & Hertz. 18 Suffolk....Bennett & G. Soda Fixtures. 50
Loeffler, J & M. 148 Norfolk....S Feusterheim. Horse, Wagon. 195
Lisner, Sigmund. 228 E 102d....H Gumpert. Bakery Fixtures. 400
Livellara, Lugi. 183 Sullivan....G Toscano. Butcher Fixtures. 130
McCormick, J H. 149 Sullivan....A F Tolard. Horse, Coach. 150
McIntyre, Peter. 812 10th av ...National Cash Register Co. Register. 200
McKay, B J. Clinton Market....T Cusack. Stands 121 and 124. Horses. 400
Minard Bros. 271 W 87th. ..Hincks & J. Cab. (R) 275
McKenney, Thos. 517 W 55th....A C Bull. Horse and Milk Fixtures. 100
Moerder, Harris. 185 Suffolk. .B Fleck. Butcher Fixtures. 50
Muller, W A. 246 W 18th...C M Stein. Grocery Fixtures. 400
Mainer, Andrew....Kean & Lines. Coach. 115
Mars, L C. 649 E 9th....J Metz. Presses, &c. 164
McCullagh, James. 37 Sheriff....J McNamee. Horse, Wagon, &c. 500
McGarl, G W. 45 Jackson....Nat Cash Reg Co. Register. 200
McGinnes, Daniel. 150th st and 7th av.... Wright, Gillies Bro. Horse, &c. 65
Metz, Charles. 218 6th .. A Meyer. Butcher Fixtures. 400
Moeckel & Kersting. 788 Amsterdam av.... John Dern. Cigar Fixtures. 200
Moser, H and W. 472 Lenox av....F T Ippich. Bakery Fixtures. 300
Morbard, F L and A. 291 3d av....K E Rugg. Dental Fixtures. (R) 3,520
Moore, J J... J Cunningham Son & Co. Coach. (R) 669
Morse, George. 149th st and 3d av .. C M Morse. Printing Fixtures. 700
Newman, J H. 531 W 27th....M Shea. Horses, Trucks, &c. 2,000
Oigel, Simon. 386 E 10th....M Auchisiger. Machines. 150
Oppenheim, Jacob. 197 Greenwich....E P Shields. Barber Fixtures. 150
Ormsby, J D. 6th av and 36th st... M J Manly. Stand. 325
Pasquale, Corrado. 587 Canal....L Ruggero. Barber Fixtures. 230
Perless, Dora. 84 Eldridge....M Rosenthal. Butcher Fixtures. 300
Pillsbury & Campbell. 57 W 29th....Whitlock Machine Co. Machinery. 1,800
Pascale, Pasquale. 402 E 113th....A Schwaab. Barber Fixtures. 42
Pintener, Max. 70 Forsyth....C Haller. Machine. 60
Quarles, J. 48 Broadway....Archer Mfg Co. Barber Fixtures. 600
Rae, Robert. 442 and 444 Water....W H Phillips. Machinery. 4,730
Rehfield, C F. 136th st and Madison av....Varbey & Farley. Horse and Milk Wagon. 300
Rehm, A S. 511 E 154th ...F Meng. Blacksmith Fixtures. 30
Reinheimer, Carrie. 2674 8th av....A Gerleit. Wagon. 90
Raeber, August. 1690 Park av....L Heinsfurter. Butcher Fixtures 300
Reid, David. 132 W 31st....B Fischer & Co. Horse, Wagon, &c. 185
Reinheimer, Adolf. 1489 Av A....C Reinheimer. Milk Fixtures, Horse, &c. 120
Rogers, W H H, agent. 65 and 67 Crosby ... Jeffers & K. Machinery. 725
Ryan, David. 168th st and Vanderbilt av....P J Owens. Horses, Machinery. 1,500
Seligman, Louis. 258 7th av....J J E Maher. Horse, Wagon. 150
Shea, H C. 11 Morton....A Strauss. Horses, Trucks, &c. 80
Sprengel, Louis. 822 Columbus av....J Dolgner. Store Fixtures. 467
Schonholzer, A. 446 W 40th....J Brandle. Bakery Fixtures. 75
Shaut & Bennett. 2298 3d av....J E Shant. Printing Fixtures. 100
Spiegel, Morris. 1618 1st av....M Gluck. Machines. 300
Schaelling, Martin. 717 6th....G Kraeter. Milk Fixtures, Horse, &c. 800
Schilling, Henry. 26 Albany....J & J Stahl. Lodging House. 1,800
Schmidt, John. 844 Columbus av....P Biege. Milk Fixtures. 300
Schwartz, Moritz. 40 Clinton....P Westphal. Barber Fixtures. (R) 111
Schwartz, Simon. 93 Ridge....A Adler & Co. Bakery Fixtures. 50
Scott, Ephriam. 134 W 23d....H R Hamersley. Presses, &c. 1,500
Smith, Samuel. 208 St Nicholas av....S E Lynch. Laundry. 50
Standard Fashion Co. 342 W 14th....E P Donnell Mfg Co. Machinery. 242
Stengelier, John. 81 Elm....C E Stengelier. Machinery. 375
Struthers, Servoss & Co. 24-34 New Chambers ....Ivison B T Co. Presses, &c. (R) 3,000
Swezey & Gawger. 280 Front....N T Swezey's Son & Co. Horses, Trucks. (R) 3,900
Sosnoski, Isaac. 104 W 25th....T De Sieghardt. Store Fixtures. 400
Specht, Geo. 44 1st....W J Meyers. Horses, Trucks, &c. 200
Syracuse, F M. 207 Broadway....Archer Mfg Co. Barber Fixtures. (R) 584
Tiedeman, Peter. 2296 3d av....J W Tufts. Soda Fixtures. 110
Tolk, Moritz. 89 Canal....Nat Cash Reg Co. Register. 175
Tondorf, J C. 1481 2d av....P A Cassidy. Wagon. 101
Timmermans, Baptiste. 130 West Houston ... A Jegnin Fixtures, &c 125
Trumbull, C R. 292 Bowery.. Whitlock Machine Co. Machinery. 2,200
Tidcomb, George. 219 W 26th....Hincks & J. Cab. (R) 60
Tully & O'Connell. 92d st and 1st and 2d avs... D Murray. Horses, Carts, &c. (R) 750
Urnstein, Otto. 54 Rivington... Lamson C S Co. Register. (R) 210
U S Illuminating Co....Mercantile Trust Co. Machinery, &c. (R) 400,000
Van Clief, Jacob. 888 Park av....Lamson C S S Co. Register. 210
Veinans, Alex. 1800 Lexington av.. Archer Mfg Co. Barber Fixtures. 260
Walsh, E J. 17 Vandewater....F Wesel Mfg Co. Printing Fixtures, &c. 543
Westervelt & Co. 18th st and 7th av....Nat Cash Reg Co. Register. --
White, C T. 508 Southern Boulevard....Lamson C S & Co. Register. 210
Wiebel, Julius. 160th st and Amsterdam av.... R A Greacen. Leases, Buildings, &c. 250
Willis, Henry....Kean & Lines. Coach. 425
Wira, Maria. 634 Courtlandt av....G Burk. Bakery Fixtures. 100
Wood, Whitney. 142 W 39th....J Cunningham Son & Co. Coaches. 900
Zolin & Co. 128 East Broadway....Bennett & G. Soda Fixtures. 175

BILLS OF SALE.

Altman, Max. 157 Ridge .... A Goldstein. Butcher Fixtures. 400
Bloomer & Palmer. 344 Columbus av....J Schmidt. Milk Fixtures. 650
Becker, Louis. 385 Broome....American Straw Board Co. Machinery. 1
Brody, Rachel. 92 Divison ...S Sachs. Restaurant Fixtures. 300
Brumley, S E and W S. 28 Av D....H J Knapp. Store Fixtures. 275
Cornetto, Pasquale. 175 Mulberry . M Attiers. Grocery Fixtures. 55
Cranston, Henry. 721 Broadway....W N Adams. Office Fixtures. 1
Cranston, Henry. 721 Broadway....Mary D Cranston. Wines, Groceries, &c. 2,720
Coughlan, Patrick, estate of....323 Av A. P J Murphy. Saloon Fixtures. 500
Dickheiser, Kalman. 7 E 125th....Z DeKeyser. Cigar Fixtures. 110
Dunn, Patrick....B McCarroll. Horses, Trucks, &c. 285
Fried & Furst. 164 W 110th. ..A Fried. Grocery Fixtures. 1
Goldberg, Nathan. 56-64 Clinton ...A Schlessinger. Machinery, &c. 200
Heckman & Bro. 277 Av C....Langdon & G B Co. Saloon Fixtures. 100
Hillebrandt, Christopher. 246 8th av....D Hillebrandt. Grocery Fixtures. ½ int. 2,400
Junge, William. 1255 3d av....H and F Markfeld. Grocery Fixtures. 1,900
Kile, C U. 2321 7th av....W Weil. Drug Fixtures. 700
Lescow, Albert. 822 Columbus av....L Sprengel. Store Fixtures. 1
Lowy, Moritz. 228 E 74th....A Levy. Grocery Fixtures. 500
Lescom, Albert. 822 Columbus av....Korner & S. Grocery Fixtures. 557
Lienan, Emil. 164 E 14th....Wm H Rethwick. Saloon Fixtures. 8,000
Miller, Eiben. 845 1st av ...J Miller. Grocery Fixtures. 1,000
Murphy, P J. 323 Av A....E F Cunningham. Saloon Fixtures. 2,000
McKay, Stewart. Clinton Market....B J McKay. Stands 121 and 124. 406
Oathers, Henry. 707 Columbus av....J A McGloin. Cigar Fixtures. 270
Pusateri, G. 858 10th av....Selvaggio & Bondi. Barber Fixtures. 125
Reddick, Helen. 9 W 29th....R N Pool. Furniture. 2,000
Rohrs, Mary. 1445 2d av....A J Dunning. Butter Store Fixtures. 450
Rohrs, Mary. 1833 3d av....J D Tietjen. Grocery Fixtures. 600
Rosenfeld, W W. 110 Reade... A Stern. Cigar Fixtures. 1
Soosen, Frederick. 1867 Lexington av....E Bergman. Grocery Fixtures. 554
Spuhler, Lizzie. 754 8th av... D Steizle. Grocery Fixtures. 305
Steidler, B. 124 Prince....A Aromanto. Barber Fixtures. 200
Susstrong, Albert. 14 Maiden lane....C M Susstrong. Machinery. 1,060
Wanner, John. 188 E 104th....C Wanner. Barber Fixtures. 550
Wersebe, Louis. 8 Manhattan ..K Ahlers. Grocery Fixtures. 600
Wobse, Diedrich. 506 E 133d.. H Siemers. Saloon Fixtures. 1,800

ASSIGNMENT OF CHATTEL MORTGAGES.

Berkovitz, I to S Reitman. (Mort given by J Schoenberger, Sept 28, 1891.) 250
Henry Elias B Co to J Kress B Co. (R Brinkman, April 8, 1891.) 400
Newman, J H to Ellen Newman. (C E Newman, Feb 17, 1891.) 1
Simon, K to Rexford Bros. (C Cava, April 14, 1891.) 1,350

KINGS COUNTY.

NOVEMBER 26 TO DECEMBER 2—INCLUSIVE.

SALOON AND RESTAURANT FIXTURES.

Anderson, C E. 6 Clinton....Mary Bennett. Restaurant Fixtures. $618
Berger, J. 16 Grand... P Doelger. 900
Coyle, O. 51 Spencer....Budweiser B Co. (R) 250
Cassidy, J A. 113 Fulton....S Liebmann's Sons B Co. (R) 1,450
Clark, E. 857 Myrtle av....J H Bereuter. Pool Table. 140
Cooke, P. 68 Sedgwick....C Frese. (R) 591
Collins, M G. Hoyt st, s e cor Baltic st....H Koehler & Co. (R) 1,000
Courtney, J H. 267 Driggs....W Ulmer. (R) 500
Denzler, B. 188 Columbia ...G Bechtel. (R) 1,000
Dranen, B. Thatford av, near Dumont st....L Eppig. 375
Engel, B. 287 Broadway... Danenberg & C. (R) 1,200
Fahlbusch, C. 240 Flushing av....F Ibert. 700
Finley, W. 117 Hamilton av.. E Ochs. 1,600
Fleischmann, O. 131 Montrose av....Feigenspan B Co. 800
Franklin, M H. 640 Broadway....M Seitz. 900
Geller, G. 569 Grand....J Eppig. (R) 600
Hattenlocher, L B. 673 6th av. ..M Seitz. 1,000
Heek, K. 78 Varet....Tillie Welz. 400
Hanser, J. 688 Broadway....Leibinger & Oehm B Co. 620
Hoffmann, F. 980 St Marks av....J Eppig. 250
Huschle, F. 184 Harrison av....S Liebmann's Sons B Co. 700
Kleiner, J. 182 Stagg. ..Abbott B Co. 800
Koncher, W. 774 Grand....S Liebmann's Sons B Co. 1,000
Kunkel, C. 76 Monteith....Elizabetha Meltzer. 350
Keeley, W. 151 3d av....Cath Keeley. 1,300
Leaver, T. 579 Court....M Seitz. 600
Lyness, B J. Eastern Parkway....C Frese. 620
Mansert, G 624 Grand....E Ochs. (R) 300
McLaughlin, W. 407 Central av....L Eppig. 740
Mueller, A E. 602 Evergreen av....S Liebmann's Sons B Co. (R) 800
Mulroy, M W. 2130 Fulton....F Ibert. 356
Morrisey, Thomas. 203 W 9th....M Seitz. 600
McDermott, T and Cath. 157 Myrtle av....Bavarian B Co. 1,500
McKeever, C. 132 Clason av....H Koehler & Co. (R) 2,000
Miller, G W. 222 Myrtle av.. Otto Huber Brewery. 600
Same .. W C Scheuing. (R) 753
O'Hagan, J. 213 Greenpoint av. . H Koehler & Co. (R) 86
Obermaier, C. 25 Bushwick av....Otto Huber Brewery. 600
Paetzig, G. 1042 Flushing av....Fiegenspan B Co. (R) 1,098
Riedel, G. 554 Flushing av....P Weidmann. 550
Robb, S G. 52 Underhill av....Williamsburgh B Co. 400
Ring, M. Nassau av and Monitor st...Budweiser B Co. 975
Ryan, P. 148 West....Joseph Fallert B Co. 400
Shea, J T. 270 5th av... M O Keefe. 3,000
Shea, J T. 270 5th av....Schmitt & S. 1,210
Spies, E J. East New York av....Budweiser B Co. (R) 400
Schneider, P. 97-101 Bradford ...Leimbeck & B Eagle B Co. 1,000
Schneider, S. Osborn st, s e cor Eastern Parkway....W Ulmer. 500
Schoendorf, M. 139 Union av....F Ibert. 600
Smith, T A. Putnam av... Wagner & S. Billiard Table, &c. 305
Temme, F A. 76 Morrell....O Huber Brewery. 400
Von Bohen, A J. 659 Franklin av....Budweiser B Co. 1,000
Van Dyke, C H. 368 Bedford av ..Joseph Fallert B Co. 400
White, R. 577 Court....Joseph Fallert B Co. 700
Werner, C. 365 Central av....J Eppig. (R) 600
Wagner, J. 1057 Flushing av....C Frese. 568
Walsh, J. 121 Harrison....M Seitz. 650
Wright, C. 16 Alabama av....Feigenspan B Co. (R) 280

HOUSEHOLD FURNITURE.

Alexander, J. 349 Waverly av .. L Z Murray. 136
Allison, A. 236 7th av... J McEnery & Co. 284
Appel, J. 1077 Flushing av... J A Schwarz. 127
Arend, F. 222 Ellery... J A Schwarz. 194
Bell, Mary J. 324 Smith....Emily Aisthorpe. 500
Brooks, Mary C. 64 Schaeffer....J A Schwarz. 103
Baehr, G. 497 6th av....O'Connor & Treacy. 248
Bailey, T W. 660 Clason av ...L Baumann. 140
Baird, L. 63 Fulton .. E D Farrell. 190
Bastiansan, H. 44 Rush . N F Smith. 240
Berry, Mrs J. 98 Waverly av... Manges Bros. 146
Bloom, H. 415 Evergreen av....L Z Murray. 190
Burke, J J. 500 1st....L Z Murray. 651
Caffrey, Mary A. 34 India....J Moriarty. 268
Callan, G F and Mary. 236 Prince ...E C Hinsdale. 130
Chapter, Catherine. Liberty av and Junius st ....J Baumann. 116
Cardwell, J A. 114 Court ..T Kelly. 205
Crofts, Mrs M. 7 Lafayette av... Brooklyn F Co. 581
Curry, S A. 15 Patchen av....Mullins & Sons. 131
Cohen, C. 20 Leonard....H Silverstine. 250
Corun, Mattie A. 88 Stone av....S Baumann. 192
Dailey, Jane M. 74 Kosciusko....M Bottstein. 150
Dempsey, E C. 258 Hewes....M M Webster. 100
Daly, Charlotte. 193 Lorimer....J Baumann. 129
Debus, Louisa. 85 Clay....L Baumann. 147
Downie, Annie. 179 Vandyke....L Z Murray. 190
Esposito, V. 13 Hamilton av J Rubenstein. 194
Ford, Mrs. 1089 Pacific....H Israel & Sons. 290
Fox, Maggie. 458 Madison ...L Z Murray. 242
Frazier, Eliz. 100 Vanderveer....O'Connor & T. 122
Garwood, H A. 264 Woodbine ...L Z Murray. 122
Gahagan, H. 399 Sackett....B F Watson. 1,063
Heyer, R. 66 Harman....J A Schwarz. 210
Harris, Margt A. 40 Powers....Mullins & Sons. 187
Hartman, C. 68 South 5th....J Moriarty. 194
Hintze, J E. 306 Sumpter....E Bauch. 172
Holmberg, G. 67 Floyd....O'Connor & T. 226
Hurley, T A. 52 Rogers av ...S Knapp & Co. 558

Holler, Annie. 19 Kosciusco pl....I Mason. 198
Jacobson, B. 629 Myrtle av....Mullins & Sons. 191
Justus, D. Washington av, near 3d st, Parkville....H S Eisler. 107
Kesses, C. 250 Rutledge....L Baumann. 242
Langerfeld, G. 103 Melrose....A Schulz. 149
Lord, W R. 144 Stuyvesant av... S W Woolsey & Son. 212
Lesslie, B. 1060 De Kalb av....C A Barnett. 198
Metzler, G D. 94 Harman....Brooklyn F Co. 361
Meurer, A. 153 Evergreen av....I Mason. 179
Mortimer, W. 290 Jay ...Brooklyn F Co. 127
Mathews, J M. 377 Lexington av....I Mason. 141
Melville, Maggie. 332 Sackett....W E Wheelock & Co. Piano. 250
Mercurio, A. 79 Degraw....J Rubinstein. 338
Milan, Margaret. 84 Hendrix....M M Webster. 100
Murnane, Mrs. 270 Degraw.. Brooklyn F Co. 184
Murphy, Annie E. 186 Duffield....H Israel & Sons. 630
Murphy, W R. 148 Nelson....Manges Bros. 287
Meyer, Lizzie. 247 Central av....J A Schwarz. 139
Nelson, Charlotte. 165 Ashford....L Baumann. 137
Nolan, Lillie E. 24 Warren pl....J Baumann. 184
O'Manny, Ellen. 219 Duffield....L Z Murray. 154
Ostrander, C. 20 Newell. ..L Baumann. 156
Parr, Mary E. 1277 Atlantic av....E C Hinsdale. 190
Parr, R A. 1277 Atlantic av....Mary E Parr. 500
Rothennel, P C. New Jersey av, cor Fulton av ....C A Barnett. 135
Radecke, Lucy. 147 North 8th....L Baumann. 270
Robinson, Annie. 262 Waverly av....J Baumann. 115
Schneider, Louise O. 251 Putnam av....M M Webster. 100
Scovil, W T. 400 5th....Brooklyn F Co. 163
Sedgwick, C. 711 President....L Z Murray. 111
Siegrist, J. 26 Filmore pl....L Baumann. 112
Squires, C J. 1115 Fulton. ..M M Webster. 100
Stearns, M A. 128 Hewes ...Brooklyn F Co. 242
Stagg, A L. Pearl st, cor Concord st ...O'Connor & T. 218
Swann, Hannah M. 1495 Broadway... L Z Murray. 417
Swann, Hannah. 179 Marion....L Z Murray. 198
Smyley, C. 159 Livingston....M Bottstein. 140
Snow, B F. 53 Maiden lane, Brooklyn... M Bottstein. 185
Tierney, D J. 168 Carroll....T Cassin. 598
Trommer, Anna. 14 Park....S Baumann. 100
Wiggins, Mary. 760 Marcy av....L Z Murray. 185
Williams, A E. 585 Warren....J Baumann. 300
Wood, Sarah. 80 Skillman av A Schulz. 173
Yaeger, G S. Flatbush av and Clarkson st....J A Schwarz. 289

MISCELLANEOUS.

Allen, G F. 713 Fulton....M B Erskine. Bakery Fixtures. 1,000
Bennett, R R....W B Davis. Coach. (R) 400
Bottjer, D. 513 5th av....N C Seedorf. Bottling Business. 350
Burke, Catherine .. W B Davis. Coach. (R) 575
Buttner, T. 356 Evergreen av....C F Schlosstein. Bakery Fixtures. (R) 150
Cameron, D L. 281 Reid av....A D Puffer & Sons. Soda Fountain. 30
Campbell, T. 238 McDougal.. .Minnie Kromer. Wagon. 110
Carlsen, F. 236 Atlantic av....Archer Mfg Co. Barber Fixtures. (R) 135
Churbuch, R T. 457 Atlantic av....Van Allens & B. Press. 89
Cowino, L. 75 Smith....Archer Mfg Co. Barber Fixtures. (R) 157
Coots, W M. 26 Court....M Bottstein. Office Furniture. 210
Dieckmann, F. 1373 Herkimer....C Houschelmann. Butcher Fixtures. 200
Drewes, J. 289 Conover....J Fehlhaber. Grocery Fixtures, Horse and Wagon. 500
Dunn, T. 797 Driggs....L H Dickerson. Horse and Wagon. 100
Eaguey, W L. 276 Nostrand av....Nat Cash Reg Co. Register. 175
Engelhardt, C W. Pennsylvania av, n w cor Liberty av....A Beinhauer. Carpenter's Tools and Fixtures. 500
Earll, L T. 458 Myrtle av....P Young. Cigar Fixtures. 100
Faron, Mary E. Park and 21st avs, Bath Beach ....M Moloughney. Grocery Fixtures. 91
Falke, Maria E. 167 Ewen . J Frisse. Hat Store Fixtures. 500
Falke, Maria E. 167 Ewen....A Marx Hat Store Fixtures 500
Gugelimino, G 91 Greenpoint av ...Archer Mfg Co. Barber Fixtures. 345
Geis, P J. 20 Thornton and 42 Hopkins E Glock. Undertaker's Fixtures. 2,000
Gottmann, H. 187 Scholes....W S Hurley. Bakery Fixtures. (R) 300
Gallagher, M....W B Davis. Coach. (R) 200
Geyer, H. and G Dettleff. 1-5 Broome....L Ullricht. Machinery. 1,000
Grobe, W. 413 Broadway ...Puffer & Sons. Soda Apparatus. 32
Henry, W. 490 Throop av....W B Davis. Coupe. (R) 650
Herzog, A C. 150 Throop av.. .H Duhamel & Co. Coffin Wagon. 350
Hesterberg, H. Grant st, Flatbush Nat Cash Reg Co. Register. 175
Hemma, J. Coney Island road....Nat Casket Co. Caskets, &c. 127
Heerdt, C B .. C Pfeifer. Milk Wagon, Horses. 600
Kinnier, W. 1032 Gates av....M Finley. Paper Hangers' Fixtures. 1,000
Loehr, H. 267 Central av . M F Lindhorn. Store Fixtures. (R) 800
Little, G R....Campbell P P and Mfg Co. Presses. 13,200
Lynch, T. 334 8th av ...Nat Cash Reg Co. Register. 200
Leopaldi, G. 757 Bergen....A Barretta. Barber Fixtures. 65
Lyons, S. 162 Carlton av....J Cunningham Son & Co. Carriage. 900
Mann, E G. 377 Hancock....W Hoops. Drug Fixtures. 6,300
Martens, H. 760 Clason av....J Freeman. Grocery. 800
McClain, J. 2 1 York....W B Davis Coach. (R) 200
Meyer, H C. Lewis av, n w cor Kosciusko st.... R H Bunney & Co. Grocery Fixtures. 525
Mollo, V. 54 Broadway....Archer Mfg Co. Barber Fixtures. (R) 272
Moran, J. Av A, cor 12th st....Nat Cash Reg Co. Register. 205
Muller, Emma. 18 Lewis av....Mosler Safe Co. Safe. 100

McNally, T. 52 Stockton....F Lyons. Buggy. 100
Oppelt, J. Liberty and Van Sielen avs....Gaus & M. Grocery Fixtures. 48
Ottens, J H. 643 Grand....D F S Forshay. Confectionery Store. (R) 1,000
Pease, E K....Campbell Printing Press and Mfg Co. Press, &c. (R) 1,150
Rathjen, J. 175 Stuyvesant av....H Rathjen. Grocery Fixtures. 900
Reeves, M L. 107 South 5th....J Cunningham Son & Co. Wagon. (R) 78
Rae, R. 442 Water st, N Y....W H Phillips. Machinery. (R) 4,730
Reilly, J....Barrett & Brush. Wagons. 350
Sessa, F ...G Dessecker. Coach. 700
Schmidt, J G. 683 6th av....D Rohling. Bakery Fixtures. (R) 300
Simonson, H J. De Kalb av, cor Waverly av ....J Cunningham Son & Co. Carriage. (R) 260
Simmons, Rachel C. 31 South 5th ...J Martin. Machinery. 1,500
Storm, F. 63 North 11th... Emilie M Storm. Glassware Factory. 5,331
Schmittmeyer, W. 82 Leonard....W Bachert. Bakery Fixtures. 475
Thompson, S A. 2120 Madison av....Nat Cash Reg Co. Register. 170
Wardell, J B. 398 5th av....J P Rathbun & Co. Press. (R) 312
Wadsworth, A W. 1269 Gates av ..Archer Mfg Co. Barber Fixtures. (R) 247
Washington, S. 431 5th av....M Wisdom. Paper Hangers' Fixtures 450
Wowereit, C H. Gates av....Archer Mfg Co. Barber Fixtures. 440
Williams & Co....Mary H Semple. Trimming Machine. 250
Zur & Asthausen....R Jones. Wagon. 290

BILLS OF SALE.

Bergin & Hildebrand. 148 Sackett....J & C Johnson. Saloon Fixtures. 125
Berschatsky, J. 72 Seigel....N Berschatsky. Bathing Establishment. 217
Beusmann, H and F. 654 6th av....H Ploeger. Grocery Fixtures. nom
Brahm, V. 414 Liberty av ...Anna Liebow. Saloon Fixtures. 225
Boehncke, E. 109 Varet st....H Horwitz. Grocery Fixtures. 120
Choate, G A. 1157 Fulton ...Hannah J. Choate. Paper Hanging Fixtures. nom
Green, W. 17 Red Hook lane . .J H Wardell. Livery Stable. nom
Hauser, J. 633 Broadway....Leibinger & Oehm B Co. Saloon Fixtures. 620
Hauser, J. 633 Broadway....J M Schaefer & O Kidhardt. Saloon Fixtures. 325
Janke, A. 28 Thornton....J Wenzler. Saloon Fixtures. 185
Liebow, Anna. Liberty av, s e cor Vermont av ....Leibinger & Oehm B Co. Saloon Fixtures. 275
Martin, T F. 5th av, s w cor Garfield pl. ..J T Shea. Saloon Fixtures. 5,100
McLean, J. 74 Tompkins av ...Ann McLean. Undertaker's Fixtures, &c. nom
Neumann, R. 794 Grand....E O Hauser. Saloon Fixtures. 900
Schoenemann, C. 244 Wyckoff....B May. Saloon Fixtures. 1,300
Wardell, J H. 17 Red Hook lane....Mary A Green. Livery Stable. nom
Willeburgher, G. 81 North 6th....T Wienborg. Saloon Fixtures. 2,000

ASSIGNMENT OF CHATTEL MORTGAGES.

Blinp, E H to Lena Durchholz. (Mort. given by J Durchholz, Dec. 22, 1890.) 2,000
Hinsdale, E C to M Armstrong. (H M Hintze, Nov. 7, 1890.) 48

NEW JERSEY.

ESSEX COUNTY.

NOTE.—*The arrangement of the Conveyances, Mortgages and Judgments in these lists is as follows: the first name in the Conveyances is the Grantor; in Mortgages, the Mortgagor; in Judgments, the Judgment debtor.*

CONVEYANCES.

Allen, W L—C F Seitz, Avon av.......... $150
Atchison, J I—M A Atchison, Orange.......... 1
Ball, D W—W C Smith, East Orange.......... 1
Ball, Isaiah—F Chandler, East Orange.......... 8,000
Bassett, A L—H J Bloemecki, South Orange.... 1
Becker, Charles—T R Guild, William st.......... 1
Bell, R P—A A Bell, 4th av.......... 1
Berryman, John—A C Force, Orange.......... 600
Black, W H—E S Black, Pennington st.......... 900
Blake, Daniel—The Domestic Sewing Machine Co of Ohio.......... —
Blesch, John—A Schuldt, w s Pac fic st 57 n Garden st 25x93.......... 4,200
Boepple, John—L S Samuel, Jones st.......... 2,450
Bonnett, M I—C B Pruden, North 7th st.......... 1,325
Bruen, J C—P Fox, 11th av.......... 1,400
Canfield, John—J Copeland, Caldwell.......... 15
Chew, C P—H F Cook, w s Mt Pleasant av 226 s Harvey st 25x100.......... 6,400
Cleary, Bridget—D Stern, Bowery st.......... 1,550
Condit, Samuel—A L Matthews, Orange.......... 1,650
Condit, Fillmore—L Dietsch, Belleville.......... 1
Cook, H B—G W Riee, Caldwell.......... 6,000
Cornwell, James—W Elser, Winthrop st.......... 650
Cummings, Frederick—M T Trimmons, West Orange.......... 5,250
De Witt, M J—M J Kumerle, Taylor st.......... 1,200
Duran, James—J Skipp, South 8th st.......... 800
Duryee, J R—A Trandt, Sussex av.......... 1,000
Eichelberg, Peter—H Berger, w s Prince st 124 s Montgomery st 32x67x20x100x25.......... 8,550
Fortmeyer, G W—G D Scriba, East Orange.......... 1
Gallagher, George—W H Townsend, East Orange 1,600
Guild, T R—H A Becker, William st.......... 1
Haffert, A J—M Kraidt, Monmouth st.......... 1
Haggerty, Thomas—A H Van Buren, Bridge st. 1
Haight, C M—O Miller, Franklin.......... 1
Hampston, F S—E A Hampton, East Orange.... 900
Havemeyer, W F et al—H P Finlay, South Orange.......... 2,500
Hays, J L—Finley Rubber Varnish and Enamel Co, n s Thomas st 25 w rear line lots on Dawson st 72x107.......... 7,500
Heath, C C—F Pfankratz, Wall st.......... 500
Henry, James—M T Dwyer, East Orange.......... 600
Hopper, C M—J Schoch, Clinton.......... 2,000
Howell, M G—J T Kitchell, s s North End terrace.......... 3,500
Jacob, Frederick—X Wilterotter, Morris av.......... 1,900
Jatkowski, Aaron—P Rothschild, e s Prince st, 80 n Morton st, 25x100.......... 7,800
Jones, S H—A Scharff, Woodside av.......... 200
Keasbey, E Q—W C Bailey, East Orange.......... 700
Kelly, Eugene—L L Howe, Caldwell.......... 5,500
Kies, Barbara—S Mihlon, s s Academy st, 93 w Wickliffe st.......... 4,350
Kling, Anthony—M Muller, s w s New st 25 s Essex st, 25x83.......... 7,000
Kraidt, Magdalena—E M Haffert, Monmouth st. 1
Kumerle, J U—M J De Witt, Taylor st.......... 1,200
Lightbipe, C A—M A Stockton, Orange.......... 2,400
Lister, J C—H Becker, Komorn st.......... 985
Same——same, Komorn st.......... 1,000
Same——J B Dusenberry, w s Broad st, 315 s Harvey st, 20x100.......... 4,000
Same——P Callen, Komorn st.......... 1,000
Same——J S Wingett, n s Komorn st 281 e Niagara st 80x100.......... 3,600
Same——S M Cogan, w s Broad st 435 s Harvey st 20x100.......... 4,000
Lloyd, H M—H B Mason, Montclair.......... 1
Lyon, M J—W F Havemeyer et al, South Orange.......... 1,750
Mandeville, Anson—E Irene McKirgan, s s Academy st adj Job Mieker's land 40x100.... 3,600
Marr, A C—E G Ward, Bloomfield.......... 81
Mason, C H—H M Lloyd, Montclair.......... 1
Miller, Charles—C Miller, Caldwell.......... 1
Mums, R W—B W Jacob s, Montclair.......... 1,950
Mussen, J C—L A Yale, e s Johnson av 623 s Bigelow st 50x164.......... 5,250
Nesler, Charles L—J C Pierson, Chadwick av.... 1,500
Nisch, Margaret—R F Hellriegel, Hunterdon st. 2,725
New York Co-operative Building Lot Assoc—C Kamlah, Belleville.......... 1
Norwood, M S—E D Roff, Orange st.......... 2,800
Orange Heights Land Co—H H Truman, West Orange.......... 1
Same——same, West Orange.......... 1
Same——same, West Orange.......... 1
Orange Mountain Cable Co—H H Truman, West Orange.......... 1
Ostrander, W A L—A H Swift et al, Clinton.... 12,000
Pallitta, Gregorio—O Gesumaria, Van Buren st. 530
Reebar, John—M Bleier, Sayre st.......... 750
Rice, G W—C P Chew, Caldwell.......... 1
Rice, J D—C C Lienan, Fairmount av.......... 1,200
Rich, W S—C M Leonard, Clinton.......... 150
Robbins, A S—A B Clapp, East Orange.......... 15,000
Robertson, E C—L D H Gilmour, first tract n e s Sussex av 335 n Sheffield st 23x100, second tract n e s Sussex av 305 n Sheffield st 30x100, third tract Sussex av, cor Jonas Agees.......... 10,000
Robinson, F A—M R Reilly, East Orange.......... 7,000
Rust, Fredricka—H Cohen, w s Prince st 125 n Montgomery st 25x100.......... 4,500
Schreiber, Edward—A Devine, South Orange.... 130
Seitz, C F—W L Allen, rear Avon av.......... 1
Scriba, G D—P A Fortmeyer, East Orange.......... 1
Smith, J A—A Devine, South Orange.......... 100
Stager, Jesse—M McKeon, Jefferson st 507 s Ferry st 28x117.......... 3,300
Stevenson, Louisa—G Cutter, e s Ogden st 410 n 3d av 25x100.......... 3,500
Suffen, H W—Real Estate and Improvement Co, Bloomfield.......... 2,800
Sullivan, D J—R Guggenheimer, West Orange.. 1
Sullivan, M F—J Morrisroe, West Orange.......... 300
Tebbetts, Noah—G Wilcox, South Orange.......... 6,000
The Domestic Sewing Machine Co of Ohio—G W Goepke, s w s Orange st 58 s e High st 27 x101.......... 3,500
The Mountain Water Co—The Commonwealth Water Co, Milburn and South Orange.......... 1
Townley, Emily—L F Francisco, Montclair.......... 8,000
Wade, W S—W C Headley, South 15th st.......... 1
Warren, H C—L C Kloman, Montclair.......... 4,350
Williams, C E—D Shipman, e s Belleville av 154 n Gouverneur st 25x100.......... 8,000
Wilmurt, F M—A P Horn, South Orange.......... 11,750
Woodruff, H O—W Koch, e s Johnson av 30x278. 4,300
Woodruff, J W—L E Horton, 4th st.......... 600

MORTGAGES.

Amodio, Francesco—J M Trimble, South Orange av.......... 500
Arnold, T L—M E Arnold, Bloomfield.......... 2,000
Bailey, W C—E Q Keasbey, East Orange.......... 540
Bacon, H S—T Sully, East Orange.......... 3,000
Ball, J P—S C Ball, East Orange.......... 7,200
Blake, Christopher—J M Johnson, Clinton.......... 1,500
Bleier, Mary—F Ochs, Sayrs st.......... 1,800
Bonnert, John—Ætna B and L Assoc. Newton st 2,000
Bond, E E—Mt Pleasant Cemetery Co, Washington st.......... 8,000
Brandley, A B—J A Schmidt, South Orange.... 1,700
Caffrey, M J—People's B and L Assoc, South 9th st.......... 2,200
Cara, Pasquale—P Puglia, Lillie st.......... 4,000
Cohen, Harris—Newark B and L Assoc, Prince st.......... 3,600
Colt, S S—C J Shaw, Orange.......... 2,000
Commonwealth Water Co—C G Rockwood et al trustees, to secure bonds to amount on all their water rights and property.......... 135,000
Conklin, W T—E A W Williams, Montclair.......... 1,000
Coolbaugh, F W—S E Carter, East Orange.......... 4,500
Coppersmith, John—Newark B and L Assoc, Wallace st.......... 800
Curtis, G D—F M King, East Orange.......... 1,000
Dally, M L—G H Willis, Fullerton av.......... 500
Dauber, C W—C Wirth, 16th av.......... 800
Eichenberg, William—W G Eichenberg, Garden st.......... 300
Elser, Wm—J Cornwell, Winthrop st.......... 3,000
Engelhardt, Margaretta—C Barkhorn, Belmont av.......... 500
Fox, Peter—Mutual B and L Assoc, 11th av.... 1,600
Frank, Christian—Enterprise B and L Assoc, Barclay st.......... 500
Frederickson, C J—Fidelity Title and Deposit Co, Clinton av.......... 8,000
Fricke, John—Roseville B and L Assoc, Aqueduct st.......... 1,800
Garrigan, John—J H Kase, Orange.......... 2,500
Geopke, G W—Domestic Sewing Machine Co, Orange st.......... 2,000
Gilmore, L D H—Firemen's Ins Co, Sussex av.... 4,000
Glen, C T—A E Spinning, Ogden st.......... 750
Same——same, Passaic st.......... 750
Gordon, Elizabeth—J M Courter, Maiden lane... 1,150
Grimm, Joseph—A J Heller, South 7th st.......... 9,500
Haufler, G F—S Atwater, South 10th st.......... 1,000
Harrison, G R—W Pierson, West Orange.......... 1,400
Health Bread Co—Fraternal B and L Assoc, Drift st.......... 5,000
Same——same, Drift st.......... 1,490

Hill, G A—M Ketcham, Roseville av ... 5,500
Howe, L L—E Kelly, Caldwell ... 4,500
Jacobus, S V—C M Blain, Parker st ... 2,500
Joachim, Benjamin—Standard B and L Assoc, Boyd st ... 600
Keasbey, E O—St Barnabas Hospital, Clinton av ... 5,000
Keoman, L C—H C Warren, Montclair ... 10,850
Kirk, A C—E C Fewsmith, 2d av ... 1,200
Kroebl, Anthony—E J Osborne, Livingston st ... 400
Leith, Margaret—Howard B & L Assoc, Parker st ... 1,600
Littell, R S—W T Rae, Mt Prospect av ... 4,000
Looker, H H—S E Parkhurst, Brunswick st ... 1,000
Lyons, Patrick—G A Richards, Ferguson st ... 500
Madison, C H—F Whiteley, Roseville av ... 6,500
Maria, O G—A Fortorielo, Van Buren st ... 250
Mason, H B—F M Henshaw, Montclair ... 2,000
Matthews, C B—Prudential Ins Co—Washington av ... 6,000
McEntee, Charles—Newark Fire Ins Co, Norfolk st ... 150
McKeon, Miles—J Stager, Jefferson st ... 2,000
McKirgan, E J—R W McKeon, Academy st ... 2,000
Mihlon, Sophie—B Ries, Academy st ... 1,000
Murray, Ann—A Areson, Montclair ... 500
Nessler, F W—G Kuhnle, Bloomfield av ... 2,000
Osborne, Henry—S S Thompson, Halleck st ... 1,200
Pankratz, Fritz—C C Heath exr, Wall st ... 400
Parillo, Vito—J M Trimble, Adam st ... 200
Perry, J H—A Loehnberg, Colden st ... 6,000
Pilito, Michele—Enterprise B and L Assoc, O'Connell st ... 2,000
Plummer, M E—W Pierson, Orange ... 800
Pruden, C B—J S Bonnett, North 7th st ... 1,000
Reinbold, Bertha—Phoenix B and L Assoc, South 11th st ... 2,500
Rice, G W—H F Cook, Caldwell ... 3,000
Roadline, John—J Ward, Jr, Chapel st ... 100
Roff, E D—C Stoutenburgh, Orange st ... 1,500
Rothchild, Philippeana—Newark B and L Assoc, Prince st ... 3,600
Samuel, L S—Excelsior B and L Assoc, Jones st ... 2,400
Sayles, E S P—Mutual Benefit Life Ins Co, Bloomfield av ... 10,000
Schaeffer, John S—E James, Littleton av ... 1,500
Schliep, L C—J McMorrow, South Orange ... 500
Scully, Samuel—Mutual B and L Assoc, Morris av ... 200
Schuldt, Auguste—J Blesch, Pacific st ... 3,200
Searing, A A—P Zihlbauer, Academy st ... 1,300
Slingerl, Wm R—H N Parkhurst, Broad st ... 200
Smith, A B—W S Quinby, Mercer st ... 2,000
Spalding, W S—S C Ward, Bloomfield ... 3,750
Stanley, Jacob—J C Lister, Komora st ... 650
Taylor, P B—Roseville B & L Assoc, 9th av ... 3,400
Timmons, M T—Orange Savings Bank, Orange ... 1,050
Same——Orange Savings Bank, West Orange ... 600
Thornley, George—J W Bancroft, South 8th st ... 2,500
Tichenor, M E—H J Graut, Orange ... 1,500
Wahl, Charles—M Mellen, Newark st ... 1,000
Wallace, J P—C Barkborn, Belleville ... 1,000
Walker, John—J S Higbie, Belleville ... 1,500
White, Eeward—Knights of Pythias B and L Assoc, Academy st ... 3,400
Whiting, N I—S A Frost, Montclair ... 2,000
Williams, M M—C D Hayes, Bloomfield ... 1,200
Yale, L A—J C Mussen, Johnson av ... 250
Zellers, E J—C M Linabury, Clinton av ... 2,000

CHATTEL MORTGAGES

Addison, James—J Ketcham, furniture ... 125
Acocella, Ginlio—V Salemme, barber fixtures ... 192
Ammann, William—M Burne & Co, bakery ... 1,522
Archer, J B—The Prentiss Tool and Supply Co, machinery ... 600
Cara, Pasquale—P Puglia, horses and trucks ... 1,500
Doyle, William—W G White, horse ... 100
Emerson, Irving—L Baumann, furniture ... 174
Harrington, J M—J Ketcham, furniture ... 80
Hassler, Karl—L Bloomer, furniture ... 80
Heppe, Louis—J Walsn, furniture ... 170
Kessler, Louis—J Hofer, saloon ... 200
Lee, J J—Hirschfield & Co, safe ... 60
Livingston, Frank—B Livingston, barber fixtures ... 350
Maynard, Ada—C I Camm, furniture ... 175
Moesic, Jacob—C Moesle, horses ... 78
Morg, Christian—G Krueger Brewing Co, saloon ... 815
Pierson, Addie—C I Camm, furniture ... 182
Reinhardt, Augusta—G Krueger Brewing Co, saloon ... 200
Rizzolo, Felix—Herschfield & Co, safe ... 70
Schaumburg, Lena—J Gregg & Co, furniture ... 120
Schill, Wilhelm—G Krueger Brewing Co, saloon ... 185
Schmitt, Wilhelm—J Wassermann, machinery and tools ... 1,000
Thompson, I N—C Smith, piano ... 231
Walmsley, Fannie—A H Van Horn, furniture ... 195
Wenzel, Charles et al—I Hertz, hides, &c ... 775
Same——same, tools and fixtures ... 850
Zellars, I S—C M Linabury, horses and trucks ... 1,000

JUDGMENTS.

Angstman, Wilhelmina et al—M Sayre et al ... 125
Hanseling, Jacob—H Poole ... 81
Kearsing, J G—A & W S Carr & Co ... 843
McMahon, M F—C G Dennis ... 448
Van Ness, A E et al—J G Vermilye ... 389

HUDSON COUNTY.

CONVEYANCES.

Boker, J G—J F Rechters, Kearney ... exchange of property and nom
Birdsall, Jane E—Mary C Vanderbeek ... nom
Bohn, Gertrude—J Wielougoski, Bayonne ... $409
Caffray, Catharine—J H Prillwitz ... 805
Carle, Martin—Amelia Nicoll ... 50
Coster, Mary L—J Nicholls ... 1,200
Currie, James by exr—Mary F Plott, Bayonne ... 40
Currie, William—Mary F Plott, Bayonne ... 60
Denielson, W J—trustee J Henderson, Jr, North Bergen ... 400
Decker, Abraham—C B Jordan ... nom
Dornacher, Christina—F Tieger ... 550
Doubleday, W C—F J Mallory ... 300
Edelstein, John—D E Cleary ... 6,250
Same——same ... 6,250
Ettinger, Louis—J C Burso, Hoboken ... 5,150
Fitch, Harriet—T F Culla ... 450
Fleming, James—H F Meyers ... 16,250
Haine, Christian—H Kattenborn ... nom
Hoboken Land and Improvement Co—Augusta Hasbrouck, Weehawken ... 990
Holman, Perrin by City Collector—Jno H Scott ... 169
Same——same ... 111
Hudson, J H and Maria Mangels—J Fecher ... 2,500
Jordan, C B—Eliza J Sip ... nom
Jarvis, Nathaniel, Jr, by trustee—Trustees T Wynns ... nom
Kattenhorn, John—H Kattenhorn ... nom
Leonard, Catharine—H Stappenbek, Hoboken ... 2,000
Lynch, Bridget—J J Lynch ... 500
Mallory, F J—W C Doubleday ... 400
Malloy, John by exrs—H Niederlitz, West Hoboken ... 1,800
McGavisck, James—J H Gidney, Hoboken ... 500
Minnock, Margaret—W Kelly, Bayonne ... 1,500
Moran, Michael—R E Galbraith, West Hoboken ... 1,650
Morris, G W—The Mayor and Aldermen of J City ... 5,000
Niles, W W—J Scherp, Weehawken ... 550
Page, Thomas by exrs—C Bartz, Union ... 200
Pape, Gotthold—Eva E Selvage, Hoboken ... 970
Paulsen, J O—W Meyer ... 2,300
Raimer, Catharina—J A Ross, Union ... 4,000
Robbins, G T, by City Collector—J H Scott ... 52
Robson, William—E C Taylor, Harrison ... 1,950
Roes, Elizabeth—Elizabeth Buhn ... 125
Rudiger, J H—H Niederlitz, Hoboken ... 500
Salter, D B—D Salter, Bayonne ... 600
Schenck, Sophia L—V R Schenck ... nom
Schmidt, W H—A Wurm, Union ... 400
Schultz, Otto—J Dedrick, West Hoboken ... 200
Seide, G A—F N Eberhard, Hoboken ... 600
Smith, Mary W—G Goller ... 2,850
The Provident Inst for Savings—Mary McDermott ... 3,500
Tierney, Myles—B Kelly ... 5,700
Same——Susan Thorne, Hoboken ... 5,700
Same——W J Kennedy ... 3,100
Tognatte, Antonio—N Hoffmann, West Hoboken ... 6,400
Tolen, William—W L Henderson, Kearney ... 2,100
Tuxbury, T L—Trustees Society of First Congregational Church of J City, Rahway ... nom
Van Wagenen, H N—Ruetta Ward ... 1,050
Weskamp, Nellie—C Martens ... 850
Wettlaufer, Ludwig—J A Ross, Union ... nom
Wiggins, William—Emily Wiggins, Union ... nom
Wilson, Sarah L—Janet L Brower, North Bergen ... 6,000
Wiskamp, Nellie—J Fecher ... 500
Wood, Anna F and Florence Lembeck by special master—J McCarthy, Bayonne ... 150
Same by same——J Colwell, Bayonne ... 200
Zabriskie, C W—N Leitmer ... 545

MORTGAGES.

Ackerman, A G—Eliza Ackermann, Hoboken, 7 years ... 800
Barso, Margaret—J C Bisson, Hoboken, 1 year ... 2,000
Barso, John—L Ettinger, Hoboken, 2 years ... 2,500
Bertschy, G A—Augusta Rauff, Union, 3 years ... 750
Blum, L E—The People's B and L Assoc, Kearney, installs ... 300
Brady, Peter, Jr—Greenville B and L Assoc, Bayonne, installs ... 5,840
Burke, Mary E—W Dixon, 1 year ... 191
Butler, Ernestine—Hoboken Bank for Savings, Hoboken, 4 years ... 5,000
Carmody, Thos—H H Hankins, Hoboken, 2 years ... 3,500
Clarkson, Catharine—W H Jerolemon, Kearney, 3 years ... 1,850
Cleary, D E—J Edelstein, 3 years ... 10,000
Cubberly, J H—H E Niese, 3 years ... 18,258
Culla, T F—Hudson City Savings Bank, 1 year ... 500
Daiber, Chas, Jr—The North Hudson County B and L Assoc, Issue B, installs ... 1,000
Daly, Catharine—The New Jersey Title Guarantee and Trust, installs ... 800
Davidson, J B—M Younger, Harrison, 2 years ... 3,000
Doolittle, William—W B Lewis, Kearney, 1 year ... 2,000
Dusanek, Joseph—The New Jersey Title Guarantee and Trust Co, West Hoboken, installs ... 3,600
Fecher, John—Hannah Hudson, 1 year ... 2,000
Feldman, Emma—Industrial Co-operative B and L Assoc, Bayonne, installs ... 3,750
Flynn, Chas—The People's B and L Assoc, Kearney, installs ... 400
Gillespie, James—A Engelbrecht, 1 year ... 1,500
Goller, Geo—M Kalaugneu, Jr, 3 years ... 800
Hall, P E—Hoboken B and L Assoc, Hoboken, installs ... 3,000
Hartpence, Emma—Susan J Wortendyke, Bayonne, 3 years ... 1,400
Hasbrouck, Augusta—The Mutual Life Ins Co, Weehawken, 1 year ... 5,000
Heidt, H A—The Provident Inst for Savings, 1 year ... 20,000
Henderson, W L—The People's B and L Assoc, Kearney, installs ... 2,000
Hildner, Joseph—A Asselmeyer, Hoboken, 4 years ... 2,000
Homey, J F—Clara I Sleicher, Union, 3 years ... 750
Keaveu, Cornelius—Beadleston & Woerz, Bayonne, demand ... 400
Kelly, Bryan—M Tierney, 3 years ... 3,100
Kennedy, W J—The Columbia B & L Assoc, installs ... 2,000
Same——same, installs ... 1,100
Kuhn, C L—Hoboken B and L Assoc, Guttenberg, installs ... 4,000
Lamb, John—Exr Rebecca Von Dreble, West Hoboken, 3 years ... 600
Lynch, J J—J A Franklin, 2 years ... 1,300
McAvoy, Jas—Trustee L Appleby, 5 years ... 3,000
McDermott, Mary—The Provident Inst for Savings, 1 year ... 1,500
Meyers, H R—J Fleming, 1 year ... 12,500
Miller, Frank—Guard A Schroeder, Jr, 3 years ... 1,000
Mills, S R—W E Hutchings, Bayonne, 3 years ... 5,500
Nicholls, James—Mary L Coster, 5 years ... 1,000
Nierderlitz, Henry—Sarah Havens, West Hoboken, 1 year ... 700
Nolte, Amondus C A—Beadleston & Woerz, West Hoboken, demand ... 3,000
Ohning, Oscar—Mary E Van Winkle, Bayonne, 6 years ... 2,800
Paoli, Jno—Hoboken B and L Assoc, Hoboken, installs ... 5,000
Sansloiri, Antonio—P Romano, Hoboken, 3 years ... 600
Schreiber, Ed—Matthias Collet, 5 years ... 2,500
Selvage, Eva E—G Pape, Hoboken, 1 year ... 485
Symes, J H—J Kissinger, Union, 1 year ... 1,500
Thorne, Susan—M Tierney, Hoboken, 5 years ... 1,200
Same——same, Hoboken, 5 years ... 2,500
Wielougoski, Jos—Centreville B and L Assoc, Bayonne, installs ... 1,400
Wurm, Alexius—W H Schmidt, Union, installs ... 350

CHATTEL MORTGAGES.

Avery, Augusta B, Bayonne—F C Smith, piano ... 210
Baans, C P, Hoboken—The Lembeck & Betz Eagle Brewing Co, saloon and furniture ... 3,000
Basch, Frederick, Hoboken—L Bauman, furniture ... 166
Bays, G M—P Van Nostrand, horse, wagon, &c ... 275
Connelly, James—The Wm Peter Brewing Co, saloon fixtures ... 450
Cronin, M F—The Wm Peter Brewing Co, pool table ... 150
Curtis, George, Hoboken—The Lembeck & Betz Eagle Brewing Co, saloon ... 750
English, M W—A Finck & Son, saloon ... 500
Falk, John, Union—The Wm Peter Brewing Co, pool table ... 155
Fischer, Gustav—The Lembeck & Betz Eagle Brewing Co, saloon ... 350
Fitzsimmons, Joseph—Sarah J Boucher admr of James Boucher, saloon ... 400
Frauser, Alfred—R Simpson, horse and wagon ... 250
Glock, I H—National Cash Register Co, grocery and market ... 200
Gormley, Janie—J Gregg & Co, furniture ... 50
Heyman, W B, Hackettstown—M A Stafford, furniture ... 1,500
Same, Kearney—I W Weathereds Sons, heating apparatus ... 500
Same——M A Stafford, horse, wagon and harness ... 210
Holte, H A—A Netz, furniture ... 95
Kohl, R C—Marvin Safe Co, safe ... 145
Lisk, Frida, Hoboken—J Bauman, furniture ... 188
McLean, Edward—L Bauman, furniture ... 6,127
Meehan, F C—Julia E Meehan, furniture, masons scaffolding, &c ... 330
Mueller, Henry—H Schumacher, saloon ... 300
Narty, F L and Louis Neygret, West Hoboken—O Schultz, saloon and furniture ... 1,500
Nolte, A C A, West Hoboken—Beadleston & Woerz, saloon, &c ... 3,000
Ross, J F, Bayonne—C Birdsall, furniture ... 250
Reyser, Peter—The Wm Peter Brewing Co, saloon fixtures ... 300
Rusch, W F, Hoboken—M Sanders, furniture ... 240
Serviss, Deborah and W H—J A Hyland, canal boat Deborah ... 2,149
Sickingen, Frederick and Joseph Joerg—X Dellinger, saloon ... 800
Smith, Henry—J Mullins & Co, furniture ... 184
Sturken, W A, Hoboken—A H Sturken, furniture ... 241
Tillier, Jennie—L Bauman, furniture ... 253
Trois, Francesco, West Hoboken—V Allistata, saloon ... 400
Vogler Bros—P Barrett, wagon ... 215
Winkler, Charles, Hoboken—The F & M Schaefer Brewing Co, saloon ... 450
Zibelin, August—The Lembeck & Betz Eagle Brewing Co, saloon ... 400

BILLS OF SALE.

Fenn, T L—E W Fenn, coal and wood business ... other consid and 500
Ludwig, Bruno, Union—H Ludwig, grocery store, horse, &c ... 1,500
Schultz, Otto, West Hoboken—F L Narty et al, saloon and furniture ... 3,000

JUDGMENTS.

Blachovski, Stanislaus—D E Cleary ... 118
Fitzgerald, E F and J F—J A White ... 29
Henry, Mary—Catharine Fallaher ... 275
Kraft, Wilhelm—C Kraft ... 1,449
Langan, J F—J A Logan ... 131
Lewin, S L—A J Delatour ... 316
Mattsen, John and Clara—G C Perry ... 115
Same——New Jersey Title Guarantee and Trust Co ... 82
Mulry, Martin—Steinhardt Bros ... 412
Seitz, Charles—H L Timken ... 188
The Mayor and Aldermen of J City—C H Milliken ... 500
Van Ness, J K—I Ingraham ... 42
Xavier, Mary L—W J Davis ... 54

MECHANICS' LIENS.

Bruns, Werner, owner; F Meyer, builder; Dodge & Co, claimants ... 182
McMurray, E S, owner; F Meyer, builder; Dodge & Co, claimants ... 182

BUILDING MATERIAL MARKET.

BRICKS.—The market for Common Hards is running along in much the former channel, and the new features developed since our last are of a minor and unimportant character. The actual consumption, some of the trade think, has not been quite so liberal, with no very definite cause for the shrinkage, except possibly the effect of the little cold snap, but general demand was just about as full, as there has been a larger quantity taken for the purpose of piling out in stack against possible winter wants. For such purpose the natural desire was to make a careful selection, and buyers in consequence manifested greater discrimination over the parcels handled, giving really good and attractive brick the quickest call, and keeping the best cargoes closely sold up. The general supply, however, was full enough, and sellers gained no advantage in the matter of price, nothing being shown to warrant a quotation above the limit of last week. Pales have on the whole been somewhat steadier, owing to the absence of pressing supply, but so special demand came into notice beyond ordinary trade lines, and there was quite enough stock to go around. Some manufacturers have shut up shop and ceased shipments for the season, but the milder weather of the past day or two will tempt some to try just one more cargo before hauling off their boats.

GLASS.—For imported window glass there is a fair seasonable demand and the market in a general way retains a pretty steady position. It is, however, intimated that competition over large orders at times becomes a little sharp and results in moderate price cutting to hasten the movement of customers. Over domestic glass the showings are a little irregular, some of the tenders of supplies leading to impressions that manufacturers have a surplus upon which they are anxious to realize, while against that comes reports claiming a really active trade, with factories booking orders to full extent of capacity. The general line of quotations stands about as for some time past. Plate is steadily held and selling fairly well.

LATH.—The indications of last week that dealers were in want of stock have been fully verified and anxiety to obtain the small quantity available acted as a pronounced stimulus to values. The latest business we hear of was at $2.40 for a cargo of pine lath from Ottawa, said to be the last boat through for the season, and at the close buyers are bidding $2.50 for spruce, with none offering as receivers who may have anything on the way do not care to negotiate, knowing that the entire amount expected would not half satisfy the demand now existing. Unless there is some serious mistake as to the expected supply, it looks very much as though sellers must carry advantage for balance of year.

LIME.—We hear of no pronounced change in the general condition of market. Arrivals have been smaller, but the odd cargoes coming to hand, with held over lots, made a supply quite sufficient for the outlet and values gained no strength. The closing of the canals will make some difference in movement of State stock, though shipments can be made by rail if the market requires it.

LUMBER.—All conditions go to show the narrowing down of the market to the stagnation ordinarily to be found at mid-winter even in the best of seasons. Distribution is limited to counteract deliveries on small parcels wanted for odd specific purposes of pressing character, and bulk lots are not openly sought after, but as not many of the latter are offering, it is possible to find a place for anything really standard and useful at full figures. Indeed, so far as the support of values is concerned, that appears to be all right, as the condition of navigation and the cost of transportation would prevent fresh offerings except at extreme figures even with stuff coming forward beyond the small amounts here and there indicated. Furthermore on all local stocks the grip of holders is very firm and confident, and there is a general determination to carry cheerfully until an opportunity is afforded for testing the prediction of a good trade to come upon the approach of spring.

Eastern Spruce retains a firm enough market and receivers calculate upon selling without difficulty everything that may come to hand. Their confidence, however, is based principally upon information regarding the small amounts of stock expected forward and not upon any force to the demand, as the yards now waiting for additions to assortment are really quite few. There seems to be no doubt of the practical suspension of production to the limit of specials booked, and a falling away of random shipments to a few desultory cargoes now and then loaded from the very limited supplies on hand. Advices come of intentions to make a careful and probably reduced cut in the woods this winter, and the only comment is that such advices always come at this season.

Piling undergoes little or no change in general characteristics, the supply keeping quite as full as the wants of the market call for, and holders ready to negotiate, though some of them incline to the feeling that they are entitled to a firmer position owing to reduced run of arrivals and certain indications of a good trade ahead.

Hemlock continues to arrive by car lot to some extent but principally in perfection of orders, as no one would risk bringing anything here to sell at the moment. Indeed the market is reported quite dull and with little hope of a revival of demand until after the turn into the New Year. According to some of the trade papers, the Western lumbermen will cut a considerable amount of hemlock this winter. This State cut is also likely to be made as large as possible, but the Pennsylvanians are apparently in a mood to curtail.

White Pine has been rather quiet all around, so far as the out-turn of stock for consuming purposes is concerned, and there does not appear to have shown up any very broad or anxious demand for round lots of stuff. We hear, however, of a few pretty good contracts placed for desirable box and shippers, principally the latter, of cheaper grades, and at steady rates. Altogether there seems to be a growing sort of faith in white pine, based not alone upon prospects of good consumption but also upon the indications that both Western and Canadian producers will be more circumspect with the cut and inclined to a great deal of firmness on price. Exporters are doing a little business, but nothing of an unusual character and close figuring is required to secure custom.

Yellow Pine has no special demand outside of what is ordinarily expected at this season, nor are there any really new features upon the wholesale market. Receivers seem to have a very hopeful idea of the general prospect ahead and are predicting a good season, both with the local trade and with the various points ordinarily coming to this market for negotiation. There is also a pretty good idea entertained of the English trade in cargoes for direct shipment, besides a fair chance of perfecting f. o. b. deals for South America and the West India Islands.

Carolina pine is meeting with some little demand, but buyers neither anxious or likely to increase during the present month. Offerings seem to be carefully made and that helps support values, with a good chance that sellers can retain present advantages without much difficulty.

Hardwoods have a more or less stupid position at the moment in view of indifferent consumption and the absence of special anxiety on part of dealers to add to supplies. The feeling, however, is cheerful enough regarding general prospects ahead, and there is little in the shape of a standard grade of stock that owners are not willing to carry against expected wants. Poplar and quartered oak remain in the lead so far as popularity is concerned, but ash, elm, cypress and birch as a substitute for cherry are all in favor on home account, and walnut continues to receive attention from exporters.

The exports of lumber, exclusive of hardwood, from the port of New York during the month of November were as follows:

	1890. Feet.	1891. Feet.
To West Indies	[illegible]	4,828,000
To South America	4,863,000	1,751,000
To East Indies	1,491,000	1,105,000
To Europe	885,000	116,000
Total feet	10,621,000	7,895,000
Previously reported	75,154,000	72,173,000
Total since Jan. 1	85,775,000	79,468,000

GENERAL LUMBER NOTES.

STATE.

The Albany *Argus* as follows:

The ending of the present week will about wind up business for this season, as far as shipping by water is concerned, and there is scarcely any doubt that by that time all late orders will be largely gotten out of the way. Last week the shipping was very active and a large hole was made, but thus far this week the activity in that line has been much less pronounced. Already many dealers are [illegible]

established themselves for the winter. While some shipping is going on still there are not many new orders being received, the rush at the latter end of the season being practically over. Stocks wintered here will be light, particularly of spruce and hemlock, while of pine the same statement holds true regarding many grades and sizes. The last few days have brought nothing new in values.

THE WEST.

The Northwestern *Lumberman* as follows:

The condition of values is satisfactory so far as white pine is concerned. That is, while they are not as high as the greed of operators might dictate, they are high enough to yield a fair profit in judicious manufacture and handling, while they are firm all along the line. There is nowhere a burdensome surplus that causes fear that it will have a depressing effect on next spring's market, except possibly at Minneapolis, where there is a full stock, and one in excess of last year. But even there the prospects for next spring's demand are so good that no fear is entertained that sales will not be equal to the emergency. So many logs were hung up in the several districts of northern Wisconsin and upper Michigan that a considerable curtailment of the intended cut was the result. This has prevented an overload of the market that might have otherwise been experienced.

While there is no reason to suppose that there will not be enough white pine and Norway lumber to meet next spring's demand, except perhaps in some special instances, conditions indicate a healthy demand, with prices that will be well maintained until the present stock has been well sold out.

The cargo business on the great lakes is being wound up for the season. Nearly all stocks destined for the markets have been moved to destination. Freight rates on the lakes are high and sailors' wages have been advanced to an unprecedented figure. At Saginaw Valley points there will be little more shipment by water this year. Sales on dock for the yards at Saginaw and rail shipment will, it is thought, clear off the lumber that is left over, so that there will be less than usual to be shipped by water in the spring.

There is early and active work going on in the logging camps of Michigan, Wisconsin and Minnesota, indicating that there will be a heavy input of logs if the season shall be favorable.

At Chicago the demand is still good for all desirable lots of lumber. The commission men are urging out all the boats they can charter, even at the high rates now charged, for the yard men are anxious to get forward all the lumber they can before the close of navigation. The skippers are independent, because there are few boats in commission, and they know that they can get about what rates they choose to ask. Sailors' wages were declared to be $5 a day on Wednesday, so that is another incentive to charging high freight rates. It is not likely that many more charters will be made this year, though should the weather continue favorable receipts will be considerable hereafter. Steam barges will ply between the east shore and Green bay ports, and this point for some time to come.

The market season closes with prices firm at quotations. Short piece stuff is selling at the same figure that was paid a year ago. Slim jims are 50 cents higher than last year at a like time. The average price of long wide joists is $15 a thousand, with the range covering particular instances from $14 to $16, which is slightly higher than last year. Hemlock piece stuff is in demand at $8 for good cargoes.

There is a scarcity of dimension 18 feet long, and cargoes of short containing a large percentage of such lumber would sell for a strong price.

The inquiry for 10 and 12-inch boards is urgent—especially for the last-named width. Strips are also in demand. The market for No. 2 inch is better than it was earlier, and prices are somewhat stronger.

Reviewing the hardwood situation the Chicago *Timberman* says:

All things considered the market has held remarkably firm, hardly any more complaint of price cutting being heard than during more prosperous seasons. Latterly it has been necessary to offer concessions in order to move any quantity of stock, but this has only been done by dealers whose necessities have required them to turn lumber into cash. Others are still willing to hold off for a few months, confident that they can then market their entire stocks at advanced prices.

Dealers continue to disagree in their opinions on the oak situation. There is no doubt but present stocks are ample, but it is hardly possible that there is the surplus some appear to imagine. In view of the present dullness there exists no inducements for manufacturers to make an effort to get out a large quantity of logs this winter. Neither is it likely that the farmers, who have timber and log more or less on their own account, will get out as many logs as they usually do. This season's good crops have left them better fixed financially than for several years past, which relieves them of the necessity of selling their timber in order to carry them through the winter. But be this all as it may, should the coming season bring with it an active demand for oak, prices would not be long in recovering all the ground they have lost the past few months.

The Mississippi Valley *Lumberman* says:

The figures showing the cut at the principal producing points begin to become available. They substantiate the statements made during all the season. There has been a large increase in the cut at Minneapolis, only a slight increase at the mouth of the Menominee, a decrease in the St. Croix Valley, and a much smaller one in the Chippewa Valley than it was expected would be the case. Down-river centres are not yet available, but the falling off at these points and in the Wisconsin Valley will be very marked. The railroad mills which have nearly all shut down have all made big cuts. But, taking the Mississippi Valley and be Northwest as a whole a large reduction in production will be shown.

The various cargo markets around the great lakes have practically closed and the movement of lumber by water ceased. Stocks have been sold much closer than it was anticipated would be the case.

Preparations for work in the woods is being made upon an extensive scale and it is evident that if the conditions are favorable there will be a large increase in production—at least the loggers are so building their expectations. The exception to this statement may be found in the Chippewa Valley where the large number of logs carried over from last winter's cuts makes curtailment obligatory.

FOREIGN.

The *Timber Trades Journal* as follows on the Glasgow market:

The stock of U. S. whitewood logs, although considerably reduced since last stocktaking, is still an ample present supply; prices of this wood, which had become weakened owing to a too heavy import for some time, are now decidedly improving.

Few parcels either of walnut or whitewood have been landed here for a good many weeks past. Walnut logs of good dimensions are in demand, and bring fair prices, but of small wood the stock is still ample.

The ss. Bellagio, from Baltimore, is presently expected and brings several parcels of oak planks, logs, etc.

The Allan liner from Montreal that arrived this week had no deals on board, and the Donaldson liner had only two consignments of deals, about 4,000 pieces, and some oak planks.

There is certainly plenty of opening for the large steamer cargo, the Byjorven, from Quebec, now due here with deals, our market standing much in need of this import.

CANADA.

Lumber is accumulating very rapidly on the government pier at St. John, N. B., says the *Sun*. There are now about 140 cars loaded with deals on the pier awaiting shipment to Europe. These cars contain somewhere in the vicinity of one and one-half millions of lumber.

NAILS.—Demand fluctuates and never really reaches any liberal proportions, as buyers continue positively non-speculative and refuse to invest against the future. This policy is naturally becoming more marked just now, as there is a desire to carry as small stocks as possible in taking yearly inventories. There is said to be a better chance for diminished production. We quote Cut at $1.50@1.60 per keg for car lots and $1.75@1.85 per keg for parcels from store for iron, and add 5@10c. per keg for steel; Wire, $2.00@2.05 at mills, and 2.20@2.35 from store.

A dispatch from Pittsburg says the works of the Bellefonte Nail Co., at Bellefonte, Pa., of which ex-Gov. James A. Beaver is President, closed down nearly two weeks ago. There is an air of mystery about the place, and numerous rumors are circulated of disruption in the management of the concern. One of these reports is to the effect that Gen. D. H. Hastings will succeed the ex-Governor in the Presidency of the concern.

A private telegram from Harrisburg says that the sender has been quietly informed that the Nail company is embarrassed, and that the financial ruin of ex-Gov. Beaver will follow. He is said to be on the paper of the company for $150,000.

Another dispatch from Bellefonte says that the reason given for the shutting down of the Nail Works is a dull market and the holding or the product for better prices. This was not verified by a visit to the warehouse, because it was found to be empty. There is a renewal of the report that the mill has changed hands. Hastings succeeding Beaver.

PAINTS, OILS, COLORS, ETC.—Trade is dwindling and will probably continue to do so for balance of this month in accord with precedent. No one, therefore, will be either surprised or disappointed over conditions, and the market is in a measure prepared for a dull period. With very few exceptions the accumulation of imported goods is at least manageable and the home production seems to have a check upon it that prevents a surplus seeking sale. With the conditions mentioned control of values is very fair, and while here and there some minor irregularities are at times shown, there is no tendency to place pronounced advantage in the hands of buyers. There are the usual rumors about changes in cost of lead, but apparently unfounded. Association Corroders' rates stand as follows: Lead in oil in kegs and dry lead in kegs, in lots of less than 500 lbs., 7¼c. net; in lots of 500 lbs to 5 tons at one purchase, 7c.; 5 tons to 12 tons, one purchase, 5⅞c.; 12 tons and over, one purchase, 6¾c.; dry white lead in bbls. ¼c. per lb. less than price in kegs. Lead in oil 12½ lb. in tin pails, add 1c.; in 25 and 50 lb. tin pails, add ½c.; and in 1 to 5 lb. tin cans, assorted (100 lbs. in case) add 2½c. per lb. to keg price. Terms on lots on 500 lbs. and over, note or acceptance at sixty days, or 2½ per cent. discount will be allowed for cash paid within fifteen days of invoice date. To make either of the above required quantities any assortment of packages of white lead, red lead and litharge may be counted. The above quotations are free on board cars or boat at corroding point. Linseed Oil shows no important change. Productions from imported seed is generally firmly held, but the domestic make is variable with no great degree of strength shown. We quote at general range at 35@40c. for Western, and 40@58c. for City. Spirits Turpentine continues under more or less neglect, and the market as a whole has a tame sort of tone with further reduction made in line of valuation. We quote at 34@35c. per gallon, according to quality, delivery, etc.

TAR AND PITCH.—A slow sort of deal with most outlets, and nothing particularly new to suggest. Without becoming excessive the offerings are ample and in all cases appear to be available at former rates. We quote Pitch at $1.70@1.75 per bbl.; Tar at $2.15@4.50, according to quantity, quality and delivery.

MISCELLANEOUS.

PENRHYN SLATE CO.,
101 EAST 17th STREET, NEW YORK.
Treads and Platforms, Roofing, Sanitary Work, &c.
SLATE LINED LAUNDRY TUBS.

Mantels.
Slate Work.

BRAM & BIEG.
MANUFACTURERS OF
WHITE PORCELAIN WASH-TUBS AND SINKS.
Each Tub made in one piece. No Seams to open.
B ST SANITARY TUB ON THE MARKET.
Liberal Discount to the Trade. Send for Catalogue.
Office and Works: 46 to 56 Wallabout St. (near Clason Av.),
Telephone Call, 600 Williamsburgh, BROOKLYN, N. Y.

FRED. BRANDT,
No. 169 EAST 85th STREET, - - - NEW YORK.
Manufacturer of
BRANDT'S Patent Stationary Zinc Wash Tubs.
Warranted for 10 years. Price $8 50 per set.
Also a Bath and Wash Tub Combined.
Sheet Iron Sl'ding DUMB WAITER DOOR.
Price, put up, $5.50 Each
These Doors are desirable because, moving vertically, they do not occupy valuable space, and can be used in narrow halls.
Send for Illustrated Catalogue and Price List.

THOMAS NUGENT,
Manufacturer of
Moist Warm Air Furnaces
AND VENTILATING APPARATUS.
214 EAST 80th STREET, NEW YORK.

WM. H. OLIVER,
(Late Hobbs & Oliver
PLAIN and DECORATIVE PAINTING
Paper Hangings and Interior Decorations.
62 and 64 UNIVERSITY PLACE, - - - NEW YORK
Telephone 833—21st St. ESTABLISHED 1846.

PEERLESS COLORS FOR MORTAR.
RED, BLACK, BROWN and BUFF.
Guaranteed not to FADE if used according to directions. Send for circulars and full information to
ERSKINE W. FISHER, (Welles Building),
18 Broadway, N. Y.
Also Sole Agent for the Stettin ("Anchor" Brand Portland Cement ... 2978 Cortlandt.

BOSTWICK PATENT

A GREAT SAVING OF MATERIAL AND LABOR.
Recommended by architects and extensively used by builders.
ILLUSTRATED PAMPHLET & SAMPLES FREE,
BOSTWICK METAL LATH CO.,
38 Park Row, N. Y., and Niles, Ohio.

HAYES N.Y. 71 8TH AV. METALLIC LATHING

WILLIAM HILGERS,
Artificial Stone and Asphalt Works
163 WEST 104th ST., N. Y.
Concrete and Asphalting for sidewalks, yards, and areas, paving for stables and warehouses.
ARCHES IN CEMENT.

Stone Wash Tubs.
ODORLESS, NON-ABSORBENT, DURABLE.
Material and Workmanship Fully Warranted.
MANUFACTURED BY
HUGH O'NEILL, Long Island City, N.Y.

JAMES MATHEWS & SON,
Sole agents and Manufacturers of
MAX KELLING'S
Patent
FIRE-PROOF
IRON
Dumb Waiter Doors and Casings, Sashes, Windows, Shutters and Wall Closets.
The most durable and cheapest articles in the market.
PRICES:
$3, $4, $6, $7, $8
and upward, according to size and style.
Illustrated catalogue, price list and references sent on application.
Over 5,000 in use in this city.
Main Office & Salesroom,
172 E. 110th St.
Branch & Factory,
510 & 512 E. 20th St.

Excelsior, Pat. Dec. 3, 1889.

RAPP SHEET METAL WORKS.
Man'f'rs of
RAPP'S PAT.
IRON
Dumb Waiter
DOORS
AND
FRAMES.
Send for illustrated catalogue and price list.
Indorsed by the leading architects and builders as being the best and cheapest Fire-Proof Door made.

Pat. May 6th, 1890'

J. W. RAPP, Sole Agent,
315-319 E. 94th St., N. Y. City.

ESTIMATES TO BUILDERS
FOR
CARPETS, OIL CLOTHS, SHADES
MATTING, MATS, ZINC PLATES, Etc.,
CHEERFULLY FURNISHED.
H. RAUCH & SON,
3d AVENUE B., bet. 2d and 3d Sts.

BUILDING MATERIAL PRICES

LUMBER.

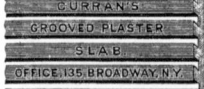

Appended quotations are based almost wholly upon prices obtained for goods from first hands. Yard rates necessarily range much higher owing to the expenses attending sorting out and grading cargo and even car lots, besides which must be added the cost of handling and carrying until consumers are ready to invest. Terms of sale also prove important factors and, altogether, it is impossible to give a line of retail quotations thoroughly reliable n character.

SPRUCE—Eastern—special cargoes delivered N. Y.	$16 50 @	18 00
Random cargoes, narrow	14 00 @	15 00
Random cargoes, wide	15 50 @	16 50
PILING—Eastern—cargo rates:		
Ranging 30@40 per cent 12 inch butt, 35 to 40 ft average length	4 @	—
Ranging 45@50 per cent 12 inch butt, 35 to 40 ft average length	4¼@	4½
Ranging 50@60 per cent One-half 12 inch butt, 38 to 40 ft average length	4¾@	5
Two-thirds 12 inch butt, 38 to 42 ft average length	5¼@	6
Three-fourths 12 inch butt, 40 to 45 ft average length	5¾@	6
All 12 inch butt and up, 40 to 45 ft average length	6 @	6¼
Piece stick, 40 feet each	4 00 @	—
do. 45	6 00 @	—
do. 50	8 00 @	—
do. 55	12 00 @	—
Inch spars, per inch	20 @	22
Scaffolding poles, each	60 @	1 00
Clothes poles, 45 to 65 feet, each	3 00 @	6 00
HEMLOCK:		
Penn. joist	12 00 @	12 50
do. boards	13 00 @	13 50
do. timber, 20 ft and under	12 50 @	13 00
do. do. 22 to 24 ft	13 00 @	13 50
do. do. 26 to 28 ft	13 50 @	14 00
do. do. 30 to 32 ft	14 00 @	15 50
do. do. 34 to 36 ft	15 50 @	16 00
do. do. 38 to 40 ft	16 50 @	17 50
WHITE PINE—Good uppers and select, 1 to 2 inch	40 00 @	48 00
Upper and select, 2½ to 4 inch	50 00 @	58 00
Shelving	26 00 @	31 00
Pickings, 1 inch	33 00 @	35 00
Cutting-up, 1 inch	25 00 @	28 00
Bracket plank	30 00 @	35 00
Dressing-boards	18 00 @	22 00
Box, inch	13 50 @	14 00
Box, thick	14 50 @	15 50
West India shippers	16 00 @	19 00
Rio Janeiro do.	20 00 @	21 00
River Plate do.	29 00 @	30 00
Australia do.	25 00 @	30 00
YELLOW PINE—Random cargoes delivered N. Y.	19 00 @	20 00
Ordered cargoes	20 00 @	22 00
Flooring	24 00 @	24 00
Step plank	26 00 @	28 00
Common siding	15 00 @	16 00
Heart face boards	24 00 @	28 00
Car orders	21 00 @	23 00
At Atlantic ports, f. o. b.	12 00 @	12 50
At Gulf ports, f. o. b.	11 50 @	12 50
North Caroline pine timber	13 50 @	15 00
do. flooring 1 inch	16 00 @	22 00
do. do. 1¼	16 50 @	22 50
do. do. 1½@2 inch.	24 00 @	25 00
do Shipping culls or box	12 00 @	14 00
do Plain and mottled ½@1½ inch.	18 50 @	25 50
Ash, white	36 00 @	43 00
Elm	20 00 @	22 50
Oak, plain	37 00 @	41 00
Oak, quarter sawed	52 00 @	55 00
Oak, quarter sawed, extra thick	56 00 @	60 00
Redwood	45 00 @	52 50
Maple, clear	28 00 @	33 00
Chestnut, clear	33 00 @	35 50
Cypress, clear	30 00 @	32 50
Black Walnut, good to choice	130 00 @	140 00
Black Walnut, ordinary to fair	100 00 @	120 00
Black Walnut, ⅝	78 00 @	83 00
Black Walnut, selected and seasoned	150 00 @	155 00
Black Walnut counters	110 00 @	150 00
Black Walnut, culls	35 00 @	40 00
Black Walnut, rejects	50 00 @	53 00
Cherry, wide	110 00 @	115 00
Cherry, good	85 00 @	100 00
Cherry, ordinary	65 00 @	80 00
Whitewood, inch	30 50 @	32 50
Whitewood, ⅝ inch	24 50 @	26 00
Whitewood, 1¼ to 2½ inch	32 00 @	34 00
Shingles, Pine, 16 inch, extra	2 75 @	3 10
do 18 inch, extra	4 10 @	4 30
do 18 inch, clear butt	2 90 @	3 10
do 16 inch, stocks	4 50 @	4 60
do 18 inch, stocks	5 30 @	5 40
Shingles, Cypress, 6x20	8 00 @	10 00
do larger sizes	11 00 @	16 00
do sawed	6 00 @	9 00
Cedar—Medium to large	6¼@	7½
do. —Extra large	7½@	8
Mahogany—Small	6½@	7½
do —Medium	8 @	8½
do. —Large	9½@	12
do. —Extra Large	10½@	14

VERMONT MARBLE CO
35 HANCOCK PLACE, N. Y.
Near 125th St. and 9th Av.
C. T. HULBURT, Agent.
Rear Sills, Lintels, Steps, Roof Coping, Pier Stones, Etc., a Specialty.
Telephone Call—522 Harlem.

ALWAYS KEEP A COPY OF WHAT YOU WRITE.
In writing your Estimates, Letters, Orders, etc., use **A Gold Medal Copying Book.** Letter and copy at one writing, without press, etc. Always ready for use. Used by all prominent Builders and Stone Dealers.
Send for circular.
G. E. PAPE, 169 William St., N. Y.

DEVOTED TO REAL ESTATE BUILDING ARCHITECTURE, HOUSEHOLD DECORATION. BUSINESS AND THEMES OF GENERAL INTEREST

PRICE, PER YEAR IN ADVANCE, SIX DOLLARS.

Published every Saturday.

TELEPHONE - - - - CORTLANDT 1370.

Communications should be addressed to

C. W. SWEET, 14 & 16 Vesey St

J. T. LINDSEY, Business Manager.

"Entered at the Post-office at New York, N. Y., as second-class matter."

VOL. XLVIII DECEMBER 12, 1891. No. 1,239

SPECULATION in Wall Street is still confined within very narrow limits. In many cases prices are too high for the present rate of dividends, having been bid up in anticipation of an increase in distribution. This anticipation is sure to be realized, but with prices so high speculators are naturally cautious. On the other hand the bears have no arguments except the disappointingly small increases in earnings on some large systems in face of the heavy crop movement, and the small decreases in others. These decreases are due to the comparatively light freighting of general merchandise, which is a feature of the business situation, but obviously only a temporary feature. The prospects for the spring trade are considered excellent. Although there has been some discriminating buying of bonds, it still remains true that a fair margin of profit exists in many good issues. Furthermore their position is much more secure than that of the best stocks, which might be very much hurt by an unforeseen calamity, whereas the bonds are safe under any circumstances. Money is rapidly becoming cheaper the world over, and it is bound to become cheaper still. The prices of investment securities will, of course, adapt themselves to the lower rate of money, and just as during the period when bonds were falling the process of readjustment took a long time, so now that they are rising the adaptation will consume many months. But it is certain to come, and in all probability foreign buying will do much to help the rise.

WHAT the depression in Germany has amounted to may be judged from the following facts, taken from a Berlin newspaper. At the end of the year 1889 there appeared on the official list of the Berlin Stock Exchange industrial securities, with a nominal value of 1,458,000,000 marks, and a market value of over 2,244,000,000 marks. In the July of this year their nominal value figured 1,506,000,000 and their market value 1.844.000,000, new values to the amount of 40,000,000 marks having been added. The difference between the market price of the two periods was in round figures 400,000,000. Since July the quotations have fallen in the average at least 25 per cent. The loss, therefore, is increased by about 450,000,000 marks, and the shrinkage in value can be estimated at 900,000,000 marks for the last two years. In bank stocks the contraction has been equally severe, being estimated at between 600,000,000 or 700,000,000 marks. Accompanying this it should be remembered that the issues of foreign governments, some of which are largely held in Berlin, have undergone a similar, though rather less severe, trial. Lately the statement being made that both the German Empire and the Kingdom of Prussia would soon make another appeal to the money market, has led to the depression of these funds. The rumor was subsequently contradicted, the truth appearing to be, however, that both the kingdom and the empire are in want of money, and will not be able to put off their requirements very long. The indebtedness of the German Empire has grown rapidly. In 1874 it was only about $1.000,000; now it is $800,000,090, for which the Budget has to provide $12,000,000 interest. Of course this is a trivial debt compared with that of France, Russia or England, but the heavy expenditures which caused it are naturally leading to some critisism in the present hard times.

EVERY shareholder in the Consolidation Coal Company, of Maryland, must wish the stockholders of the Ohio & Mississippi R. R. Co. God-speed in their efforts to prevent the Ohio & Mississippi property from falling under the control of the Baltimore & Ohio Railroad Co. In almost every case such a consolidation means disaster to the interests of the shareholders of the smaller corporation, which is operated solely in the interests of the operating company. The history of the Consolidation Coal Company exemplifies this truth admirably. In the old days, fifteen years ago, when it was managed solely for the benefit of its stockholders its shares were actively dealt in on the Stock Exchange and ranked with those of other companies paying 4 and 5 per cent annually, the range of market quotation being from 50 to 70. At the same period and contending with the same market conditions for its product the Maryland Coal Company was unable to pay dividends and its shares generally ranged at about one-third the price of the Consolidation Coal Company. In other words, before the Consolidation Co. fell under the withering control of the B. & O. one hundred of its shares would sell for enough to buy three hundred shares of the Maryland Coal Co. Now the Maryland Co., under a fostering management working solely for the stockholders, has gone on steadily appreciating until with the depreciation of the Consolidation Co. the prices nearly approximate, while as to dividends, the Maryland Co. will this year pay its shareholders a large amount. It has just declared what is called a semi-annual dividend of 1¼ per cent, having already paid 1 per cent before this year, making 2¼ per cent in all. There has been some talk of 3 per cent on the Consolidation Co., but it is not likely the B. & O. management will allow more than 2.

IT may not be generally known that the Speaker of the Assembly is, by virtue of his office, a member of the State Board of Equalization of Assessments. In addition to the three State Assessors, the board consists of the Lieutenant-Governor, the Speaker, the Secretary of State, the Comptroller, the Treasurer, the Attorney-General, and the State Engineer and Surveyor. For the coming year New York City will not have a single representative on this board of ten persons unless the Speaker is selected from this city. New York has long complained of the unjust proportion of State taxes levied upon her. Is this city to be totally deprived of a representative to look after her interests in that board? In the contest now going on for the Speakership it is said that the Tammany leader hesitates to demand that place for fear that the country Democratic members of Assembly will resent the city's getting the much-prized office when the chief credit for the party victory in the late election belongs to the country districts. But in view of the importance to New York of equitable taxation a member from this city should be selected for Speaker, and the country members will doubtless see the propriety of acceding to the only way in which this city can be given a representative on the Board of Equalization of Assessments. Tammany will neither be true to the best interests of this city nor to her own organization, both interests being identical according to Democratic premises, unless an earnest effort is made to have one of the members from this city elected as Speaker of the Assembly.

THE petty, senseless opposition on the part of the press of this city towards the coming Exposition in Chicago which THE RECORD AND GUIDE has combatted for more than a year past, has at last given way to an intelligent, and in places even a sympathetic appreciation of the vast enterprise in progress in Jackson Park. Quite naturally, following this editorial change of heart, there is to be noticed now a greater popular interest in the World's Fair, and this is certain to increase as the Exposition approaches completion. It would be ungracious to criticise the tardiness of the arrival of this better feeling towards a great national enterprise, and we are sure that Chicagoans and the people of the West generally, who have hitherto been inclined to resent the apathy of the metropolis, will recognize this and welcome the support of New York without looking backward. All said, New York can contribute more to the success of the Fair than any other two cities. The coming dinner which the Secretary of the Union League Club is to give to the directors of the Exposition is both judicious and timely, and will serve not only to direct public attention to the Fair, but will give a cordial tone to the new attitude of the metropolis.

SINCE the Democrats have been protesting so loudly against the appropriations of the "Billion Dollar Congress," it is hardly to be expected that they will be particularly liberal in their disbursements; but the representatives of New York should see that ample funds are provided for the new post-office so very much needed in this city. Ignorant Congressmen from the country districts cannot be made readily to understand the enormous price which land is worth in New York, and consequently the appropriations made for the purchase of property for government buildings tend rather to be too small for the purpose. More important, however, than the size of the appropriation, is the necessity that it should be made during the session just begun. The delay of every year will tend not only to increase the cost of the improvement to the government, but to add considerably to the inconveniences of the present situation. Already the post-office is overcrowded, and the service to the public is hampered by the lack of sufficient room. At best the acquisition of a site and the construction of the new building is a matter, at the rate in which government officials do the work, of five years. It is evident that whatever the lack of space is now, it will be far more serious five years from now, and though some alleviation may be obtained by alterations to the present building it is probable that before the expiration of so long a period the mail service of New York would be very much hampered. Consequently the necessity for early action is obvious. As to the location of the new post-office, the arguments of the Postmaster-General in favor of selecting an up-town site are conclusive—on one condition. The service to the business districts of the city must not suffer through the change. In the southern wards of the city is transacted the major part of the city's business, and this condition is not likely essentially to change as time goes on. It is true that the northward growth has been very pronounced, particularly during the past few years, but it has not taken place at the expense of the southern wards. On the contrary, building held its own very well in that part of the city. If the post-office is moved up to 42d street the change should be made, not because of any shifting of the business centre, for the new rapid transit system will secure to property south of Chambers street all its present value, but because by this change the enormous residence area will be better served. It will be everlasting a pity that the Stock Exchange did not move up town before the present elevated roads were built, for the other exchanges, the banks, etc., would have been obliged to follow, and New Yorkers would have been forever saved a great deal of unnecessary traveling; but such a step could never be taken now. Too much money has been invested south of Chambers street under the stimulus of present conditions.

A Possible Case.

ALTHOUGH THE RECORD AND GUIDE has felt it to be only just to defend the Manhattan Company from the many ignorant and prejudiced attacks that have been made upon it, and although we have persistently urged the expediency of granting to that corporation every reasonable concession needed in order that the requirements of its service may be adequately met, we by no means consider the Manhattan Company to be an unmixed blessing to the City of New York. The elevated roads have been an indispensable element in its growth, and their serviceability is not yet exhausted; but useful to the public as they have been and will be their history is an instructive illustration of the grafting of a railroad corporation on a municipality so that the former will reap the benefit of the latter's growth in population without surrendering one penny of the increase. Nearly everybody in the city is obliged to use the elevated roads; the number of people paying tribute to the corporation operating them is growing constantly and will continue to grow; yet the payments made by the company into the City Treasury do not vary materially, and will not so vary, no matter how enormously its earnings may expand, unless at the same time there be an increase in the trackage operated. Such a state of things could never have existed in a city, the public interests of which were carefully and intelligently protected. In a well-governed municipality, either the road would have been built by the authorities and leased to a company on such terms that the return to the city would increase as the traffic increased, or else the authorities would have sold the franchise in such a way that in case the gross earnings reached a certain amount, the city would obtain a share or a larger share thereof. But all the Manhattan Company does is to pay a tax on its structure and its real estate, which vary with the tax rate of New York, instead of the traffic earnings of the company.

From the way in which they objected to surrendering the tax which is now collected on the structure, doubtless the owners of the elevated roads consider that it is a gross imposition to be obliged to pay the $600,000 a year or so, which is the amount of their present contribution, to our Municipal Treasury; but in equity that sum is pitiably insufficient to stand for the total contributions of a company so circumstanced to the body of people from which it derives its franchises. When capital is invested in a railroad running through some comparatively fresh country, the risk is so great that this capital deserves a return larger than that which it would bring when loaned at the prevalent rates of interest; but in a city like New York, with hordes of people waiting to jump on board the trains, no risk attends the investment of capital in elevated railroads, and anything over the current rate of interest on capital so invested ought for the most part to be employed for the benefit of the people who give to the franchise its value. When the Elevated railroads were built, this principal was unfortunately not at all recognized; and the result is nothing less than the loss annually to the public of New York of several million dollars.

Such an estimate may seem to be excessive, but the consideration of a few figures will show that the case is not overstated. Let us suppose that all of our elevated roads had been originally built by the city, and for the moment we will suppose also that they have been operated by the municipality just as economically as the Manhattan Company operates them. What would the city make during the period covered by the last report of the corporation? This is not an easy calculation to make because a number of the elements of the estimate would be certain to vary under the two different ownerships. The results can only be approximate, but they will be but little less edifying because of their lack of exactitude.

There are 32.40 miles of elevated roads in this city. The capitalization of the Manhattan Company will not help us at all in an endeavor to reach the actual cost of this structure, for, as everyone knows, there is a very large measure of water mixed with the cash sunk in construction. We may, however, take the corporation's own figures for the cost per mile of elevated roads. When Jay Gould presented to the Rapid Transit Commission the company's plan for extending and perfecting its system, the estimate was made at the rate of $600,000 per mile of double track. Doubtless this estimate did not include car shops and a number of expenses necessary to the creation of a plant; doubtless, structural iron is cheaper now than it was then; and doubtless out of all the money that would pass through the hands of the politicians some would remain therein. Consequently we must add a good deal to this $600,000 per mile. Probably $1,000,000 a mile would cover all such auxiliary expenses, or, in round numbers, $32,000,000 for the whole system. If this money had been borrowed at 3½ per cent it would represent an annual charge on the City Treasury amounting to $1,120,000. The gross earnings for 1890–91 were $9,959,710, and the operating expenses about $5,460,000, which makes the net earnings somewhere near $4,500,000. But as the operating expenses include the $600,000 at present paid to the city in taxes that sum must be added to the net under municipal management. Against this $5,100,000 there would be charges aggregating $1,120,000 per annum, leaving a surplus every year of something like $4,000,000, or $3,400,000 more than the municipality obtains under the present circumstances. This is 38 per cent of the gross earnings, which is probably a fair general average of the margin of stealing in such enterprises.

Naturally it will be objected that the system could not be operated as cheaply by the municipality as it could by a private company. Admitting the probability that such would be the case, we will assume that the elevated roads were leased by the city to a corporation. It is, of course, impossible to tell how much this corporation would charge for its services and for the capital invested in rolling stock, but $500,000 per annum would seem to be liberal recompense for all that such a company would do. Very certainly the city would make a bad bargain if it paid any more. This would leave a sum $2,900,000 per annum larger than we are getting at the present time, which would more than meet our street cleaning bill and reduce our tax levy by something like a twelfth. Furthermore, if the city owned the roads, none of that stupid prejudice against their extension which is hampering the growth of the city would exist, and the traveling public would consequently be far better served than it is at present. Indeed, the city could afford to spend the whole of the surplus in perfecting the service. Whatever would be done with the money, it would undoubtedly form a valuable and increasingly valuable margin to work upon, and could be spent to the great advantage of our whole population.

ATTENTION has frequently been called in these columns to the national pension system which some years ago was put into operation in the German Empire, and reference has also been made to the system which has been proposed in France to accomplish a similar purpose. Equally interesting is the discussion called forth by a suggestion from Joseph Chamberlain towards a restricted application of the same plan to the British workingmen. The German and French systems provided for insurance not only against old age, but against accidents, death and all the casualties to which a laborer is exposed. Mr. Chamberlain advocates his scheme as a means whereby some portions of the millions now spent each year in Poor Law relief may "be expended more economically in promoting thrift from the outset rather than in dealing with the worst, the most fatal results of improvidence." If Mr. Chamberlain's plan should prove to effect such a purpose, it would have an obvious application to our own conditions. The pension scheme which Mr. Chamberlain seeks to establish is based upon the German model in so far as he wishes to supplement the payments of the workmen by contributions from the employers and the state. He calculates that a compulsory deduction of a farthing in the shilling off the wages of a man earning twenty shillings a week, supplemented by another farthing from the employer and another farthing from the state, would give that man £20 a year from the age of sixty, and, in addition, would enable him to withdraw his subscription for the benefit of his family if he died before the age at which his pension became due. Mr. Chamberlain does not propose, however, to make his scheme compulsory. He would like to do so, but such a proposal would only incur the opposition of the friendly and trade societies whose assistance he wishes to obtain. Various objections are made to the plan as outlined. One journal considers that such a scheme would "involve the taxation of what we may designate the lower strata of the working classes for the benefit of those above them." But why not? It is surely wiser to tax improvidence for the benefit of thrift than to tax thrift for the benefit of improvidence. Mr. Chamberlain's plan is avowedly designed to tempt men to save. Again, it is said that under such a scheme there would be no perceptible reduction of the Poor Law expenditure, for the section of the working men who would be benefited are at the present time but very little dependent on relief. To this it might be answered, that although in the beginning this would undoubtedly be so, it would be less and less true as time went on, and the improvident were induced to save more than they do at present. Joseph Chamberlain is sufficiently in earnest over the matter to develop his plan, and present it to the country in the specific shape of a Bill.

Eleven Months of Real Estate.

FROM the announcements already made in our news columns, and from the reports which are circulating among property-owners and brokers, it is probable that a revival in building may be expected during the spring of the coming year. It is true that there are no signs of such a revival in the totals of the plans filed at the Building Department; and perhaps these will not begin to increase until the winter months are passed: but indications, as we have said, of such prospective increases are not wanting. This is what might have been expected, from a consideration of the more general conditions affecting the activity of real estate. During 1891, financiers have been hampered by a protracted financial uncertainty. Money has loaned at very high rates, on time; and consequently comparatively little of it has been locked up in real estate. These conditions have been gradually relaxing their restrictive effect; and by the end of February at any rate loanable funds will be abundant in New York, and the lenders will not be averse to putting them out on time. This means that the local conditions of our market will be left to assert themselves; and they will be favorable to an increase in activity. Last week we showed that throughout the West Side there were far fewer houses left unsold than at about this time in 1890. The moderate number erected during the past summer brought the supply into a healthier relation with the demand, and a somewhat increased rate of improvement will be now justifiable. So far as the West Side is concerned, however, the most noticeable circumstance of its prospects for 1892 is the large number of plans which have been announced for erecting large apartment hotels. Some six or seven of these projects are on foot and will probably be pushed to completion. In view of the success achieved by the buildings of this class already erected west of the Central Park, it is no wonder that the example is being followed. The other part of the city in which rather more activity in building may be expected is south of 14th street. This section, also, has been somewhat depressed during 1891; and the prospects are that there will be a return of activity. A few years of the plentiful erection of more than sixteen-story buildings is due in this city. It is very much on the cards that such a movement should set in immediately.

Below will be found the totals for the month of November and for the first eleven months of the year. The records do not present any characteristics which we have not already placed before our readers. The year 1891 will be remembered as one in which real estate was dull, and in weak spots a shade lower in prices; but while this dullness has existed and these concessions have been made, it can hardly be called a year of depression. The troubles from which the market has been suffering were trying enough to check activity without being so trying that widespread weakness or any heavy selling was developed.

ELEVEN MONTHS OF REAL ESTATE.

NEW YORK CONVEYANCES.

1891.	No. Conveys.	Amount.	No. Nom.	No. 23d & 24th W.	Amount.	No. Nom.
Jan.-Oct., inc..	11,742	$197,911,725	3,389	2,222	$9,104,524	570
November.....	1,111	15,590,765	297	327	927,988	41
Total.........	12,853	$213,502,490	3,686	2,549	$10,032,511	611
1890.						
Jan.-Oct., inc..	13,327	$241,436,042	3,347	2,281	$11,109,968	562
November.....	1,127	18,716,900	299	226	956,024	41
Total.........	14,454	$260,152,942	3,646	2,507	$12,065,992	608
1889						
Jan.-Oct., inc..	12,545	$224,132,559	2,847	2,318	$9,979,533	570
November.....	1,296	22,019,193	294	273	910,831	43
Total.........	13,841	$246,151,752	3,141	2,591	$10,890,364	613

MORTGAGES.

1891.	No Morts.	Amount.	No. at 5 p. c.	Amount.	No. at less than 5 p. c.	Amount.	No. to B. T. & I. Cos.	Amount.
Jan.-Oct., inc.	12,030	$143,048,263	6,071	$74,441.0 8	1,001	$22,(06,596	1,722	$43,046,900
November....	1,185	12,273,107	630	5,901,576	84	1,5 4.7 0	194	4,356,394
Total......	13,215	$155,321,370	6,701	$80,343,484	1,085	$23,511,296	1,916	$47,402,794
1890.*								
Jan.-Oct., inc.	12,654	$215,168,677	6,077	$93,980,706	1,406	$69,290,843	1,901	$99,386,791
November....	1,265	18,064,640	608	6,351,298	171	4,186,841	246	8 102,158
Total........	13,919	$233,233,323	6,685	$100,331,095	1,577	$73,477,689	2,147	$107,488,949
1889.								
Jan.-Oct., inc.	11,793	$148,358,851	5,493	$69,279,888	1,474	$30,658,952	1,649	$40,817,113
November....	1,287	17,243,656	618	8,193,831	177	$3,402,612	205	5,670,771
Total........	13,080	$165,607,507	6,111	$77,473,719	1,651	$34,061,564	1,844	$46,487,884

*Includes mortgage given in February, 1890, by the Manhattan and Metropolitan Elevated Railway Companies on real and personal property to The Central Trust Co. for $40,000,000; mort. given in March, 1890, by the Edison Illuminating Co. to The Central Trust Co. for $3,000,000; mort. given in August 1890, by the Mount Morris Electric Light Co. to the Central Trust Co. for $4,000,000; mortg. given in September by the United States Electric Light and Power Co. to the Union Trust Co. for $3,000,000, and the Standard Gas Light Co. to The Mercantile Trust Co. for $1,500,000.

NEW YORK BUILDINGS PROJECTED DURING ELEVEN MONTHS, GIVEN BY DISTRICTS.

	1889. Jan. to Nov., inc.	1890. Jan. to Nov., inc.	1891. Jan. to Nov., inc.
Total No. of plans filed.....	1,987	1,894	1,501
Total No. of buildings projected....	3,455	3,341	2,577
Estimated cost.....	$68,469,886	$70,997,898	$51,033,389
No south of 14th st.....	462	391	354
Cost.....	$14,823,595	$16,202,175	$12,724,335
No. bet 14th and 59th sts.....	298	368	263
Cost.....	$9,541,108	$15,702,739	$8,947,270
No. bet 59th and 125th sts, east of 5th av	554	535	356
Cost.....	$8,247,475	$10,991,490	$7,785,518
No bet 59th and 125th sts, west of 8th av	811	754	578
Cost.....	$20,545,700	$16,881,850	$13,411,870
No. bet 110th and 125th sts, 5th and 8th avs	92	137	56
Cost.....	$2,073,850	$2,360,025	$1,208,000
No. north of 125th st.....	410	407	280
Cost.....	$6,156,318	$4,787,008	$5,582,708
No. 23d and 24th Wards.....	838	756	690
Cost.....	$4,481,867	$3,978,611	$3,481,148

NEW YORK BUILDINGS PROJECTED DURING NOVEMBER, GIVEN BY DISTRICTS.

	1889. November.	1890. November.	1891. November.
Total No. of buildings projected.....	217	190	193
Estimated cost.....	$4,001,905	$4,638,939	$3,262,865
No. south of 14th st.....	27	18	21
Cost.....	$592,000	$597,800	$865,000
No. bet 14th and 59th sts.....	17	14	16
Cost.....	$1,056,300	$1,194,219	$775,050
No. bet 59th and 125th sts, east of 5th av.	34	28	31
Cost.....	$522,837	$1,294,810	$375,800
No. bet 59th and 125th sts, west of 8th av.	46	65	39
Cost.....	$1,285,000	$1,057,000	$576,800
No. bet 110th and 125th sts, 5th and 8th avs	2	9	1
Cost.....	$50,000	$92,000	$40,000
No. north of 125th st.....	34	14	26
Cost.....	$231,100	$225,000	$320,165
No. 23d and 24th Wards.....	57	59	61
Cost.....	$261,675	$268,610	$718,050

	1889 No. b'ld'gs.	1889 Cost.	1890 No. b'ld'gs.	1890 Cost.	1891 No. b'ld'gs.	1891 Cost.
Jan.-Oct., inc.	3,248	$62,467,431	3,151	$66,348,959	2,389	$47,774,474
November......	217	4,001 9 5	190	4,638,939	193	3,262,865
Total.	3,455	$66,469,336	3,341	$70,997,898	2,577	$51,033,339

FOR THE MONTH OF NOVEMBER, 1891, CLASSIFIED.

	Flats and Tenem'ts. No.	Flats and Tenem'ts. Cost.	Private Dwell'gs. No.	Private Dwell'gs. Cost.	Hotels, Stores, Churches, Office Build'gs, &c. No.	Hotels, Stores, Churches, Office Build'gs, &c. Cost.	Miscellaneous, Stables, Shops, &c. No.	Miscellaneous, Stables, Shops, &c. Cost.
South of 14th st.....	13	$283,000	..	....	8	$281,000	5	$111,000
Bet 14th and 59th sts	8	63,000	..	....	4	$555,000	9	147,050
Bet 59th and 125th sts, east of 5th av.	20	371,000	4	$138,000	1	80,000	6	86,800
Bet 59th and 125th sts, west of 8th av	1	21,000	30	543,500	.	....	2	9,300
Bet 110th and 125th sts, 5th & 8th avs..	..	....	..	....	1	40,000	..	....
North of 125th st..	17	291,000	7	28,000	..		2	165
23d & 24th Wards..	8	135,000	49	122,810	1	13,000	10	41,250
Total for Nov., 1891.	61	$1,166,000	89	$312,300	10	$959,000	34	$345,565
Total for Nov., 1890.	52	$1,148,500	88	$378,000	10	$1,990,500	40	$341,939

THE MOST IMPORTANT AND COSTLIEST BUILDINGS FILED DURING NOVEMBER, 1891.

Location and Character.	Owners.	Cost.
Bayard st, n e cor Mulberry st, four-story school.....	Mayor, etc......	$180,000
41st st, No. 55 E., eight-story warehouse.....	Lincoln Safe Deposit Co	185,000
4th av, n e cor 22d st, two six and seven-story office buildings.....	J. S. Kennedy......	400,000
Four buildings, to cost.....		$765,000

FLATS, TENEMENTS AND DWELLINGS IN ROWS.

70th st, n s, 275 West Central Park West, five four-story dwell'gs.....	John D. Taylor.....	$100,000
74th st, Nos. 5 and 7 E., two four-story dwellings.....	J. V. S. Woolley & Co.	100,000
87th st, n s, 250 w 8th av, five four-story dwell'gs.....	P. & J. J. Farley......	100,000
104th st, s s, 100 e Riverside av, ten three-story dwell'gs.....	T. A. Squier and ano...	150,000
151st st, s s, 150 e Amsterdam av, five five-story flats.....	Wm. Broadbelt	113,000
Twenty-seven buildings, to cost.....		$563,000

KINGS COUNTY CONVEYANCES.

	1890. Number.	1890. Am't involved.	1890. Nom.	1891. Number.	1891. Am't involved.	1891. Nom.
January	1,349	$5,216,898	341	1,429	*$7,878,196	419
February......	1,293	5,137,587	341	1,219	4,704,985	390
March......	1,63?	7,678,870	428	1,604	6,245,195	475
April......	2,176	11,587,708	491	1,998	9,042,227	490
May......	1,882	9,317,276	437	1,804	7,580,908	482
June......	1,515	5,930,273	357	1,781	6,233,014	405
July......	1,738	7,729 316	351	1,680	6,920,839	402
August......	1,274	4,098,970	312	1,238	4,251,552	327
September......	1,221	4,510,763	305	1,324	5,004,534	345
October......	1,609	6,953,467	377	1,649	5,952,663	446
November......	1,403	6,070,653	341	1,318	4,847,703	398
Total	17,135	$74,659,039	4,089	16,965	$67,031,398	4,572

KINGS COUNTY MORTGAGES.

	1890. No.	1890. Am't involved.	1890. No. at 5 per cent. or less.	1890. Am't involved.	1891. No.	1891. Am't involved.	1891. No. at 5 per cent. or less.	1891. Am't involved.
Jan......	1,264	$4,994,740	798	$3,455,940	1,182	*$14,007,748	690	$2,417,480
Feb......	960	4,117,787	558	2,659,475	1,082	4,128,056	615	2,802,064
March .	1,272	5,648,729	780	3,916,105	1,229	5,147,777	682	3,072,420
April ...	1,679	6,575,719	1,067	4,586,146	1,561	6,871,680	917	4,165,699
May......	1,516	6,042,149	947	4,288,754	1,772	5,059,644	680	2,941,820
June......	1,322	5,488,301	772	3,987,174	1,460	5,654,829	791	3,727,914
July......	1,446	5,785,961	901	3,879,486	1,468	5,050,839	777	3,014,425
August...	1,091	4,576,404	622	3,076,165	1,057	3,438,058	563	2,160,599
Sept......	1,067	4,091,155	611	2,639,698	1,090	3,678,546	588	1,972,690
October..	1,409	†9,245,288	828	†7,313,205	1,451	5,354,551	779	3,166,455
Nov......	1,141	§6,371,104	618	§4,530,629	1,186	4,981,801	612	2,915,575
Total..	14,166	$64,934,342	8,467	$44,177,045	14,008	$68,258,094	7,576	$32,858,130

*Includes seven deeds at a total of $2,560,000 given by the various sugar companies in Brooklyn to The American Sugar Refining Co. of New Jersey.

†Includes mortgage given by The American Sugar Refining Co. of New Jersey to The Central Trust Co. of New York, for $10,000,000.

‡Includes mortgage given by the Edison Electric Illuminating Co. to the Franklin Trust Co. for $2,500,000; also mortgage given by Citizens' Gas Light Co. to Central Trust Co. of New York for $750,000.

§Includes mortgage given by Manhattan Beach Improvement Company (Lim.) to the Central Trust Company of New York for $1,500,000.

KINGS COUNTY PROJECTED BUILDINGS.

	1890. Total No. b'gs.	1890. No. of brk, stone and iron b'gs.	1890. No. of frame b'gs.	1891. Total No. b'gs.	1891. No. of brk, stone and iron b'gs.	1891. No. of frame b'gs.	1890. Cost.	1891. Cost.
Jan......	344	108	236	268	61	207	$1,407,615	$1,108,235
Feb......	288	158	230	350	160	190	1,816,425	1,548,895
March...	484	215	269	417	175	242	2,829,661	2,170,100
April..	525	249	276	563	305	258	2,409,930	3,177,972
May....	478	193	284	477	205	272	2,469,098	2,485,350
June....	547	274	273	299	122	177	2,632,739	1,873,275
July....	369	133	236	270	94	176	2,653,540	1,185,530
August.	347	136	211	308	102	206	1,747,245	1,844,700
Sept ...	323	106	217	408	145	263	1,758,265	2,324,112
Oct.....	433	172	261	341	114	228	1,943,625	1,769,670
Nov....	382	167	215	322	105	217	1,766,460	1,424,915
Total.	4,568	1,911	2,657	3,984	1,598	2,386	$23,229,260	$20,870,764

Consents to the Plan.

The Rapid Transit Commission has now been a little over two weeks engaged in the effort to secure the consents of owners along the line, to the construction of the underground electric railroad, and the record of its doings and accomplishments in this direction is presented herewith. This particular branch of the work has been put in charge of Mr. William Newland Amory, a gentleman of larger acquaintance with Broadway owners, perhaps, than any other man in the city, from the fact that he had canvassed them thoroughly once or twice before, in opposition to the Arcade Railroad and in other matters. A small corps of canvassers was sent out by Mr. Amory, to visit the owners and lay the plans of the Commission before them and to solicit their consents to the proposed construction.

It would be foolish to deny that the canvassers have had but scant success thus far. The scheme has encountered the opposition of a considerable number of the larger property-owners and the passive hostility of some who apparently propose to wring as much out of it in the way of damages as they can without regard to the question as to whether it will be of benefit to their property or not. But a good many of the larger owners along the line have already consented and the canvassers report assurances from many more that they will probably sign the formal consents as soon as they shall have completed their investigations of the plans of construction. That a great deal of misinformation has reached the property-owners as to the intentions of the Commissioners is evident from the extraordinary grounds of the opposition of most of those who oppose the scheme.

If, for instance, O. B. Potter was not an extensive owner on Broadway, his sayings on the rapid transit question would not be given any weight whatever; but because he is the owner of considerable property he gets a hearing, and in all of his utterances on the question he has managed to spread more misinformation than can be overcome by any other means than the slow process of personal visits to the infected owners. A meeting of Madison avenue owners has been called for Monday evening at Jaeger's Hall, at 53d street and Madison avenue, to protest against the construction of the road through Madison avenue, from 43d to 96th street. The committee which has called this meeting has based its call upon an entirely mistaken conception of the manner in which the road is to be built. It presumed that the road was to run close to the surface of the street and that it would be necessary to excavate the street for the full depth of the road from the surface. This is denied by the engineer of the Commission, Mr. William Barclay Parsons, who says that it will not be attempted to come to the surface of the street anywhere along the east side line below 98th street, the tunnel running so far below the surface of the street that it can be excavated through rock the entire way without in any manner disturbing the pipes or other sub-surface works now in the street.

The consents thus far received number 190, and amount in the aggregate to $48,861,448. In detail they are as follows:

BROADWAY.

Owner.	Number.	Assessed Valuation.
Cyrus Clark	1614-1626	$48,000
Mrs. Mary M. Ward	165 and 167	245,000
Mrs. Eleanor Dyan	599	120,000
R. G. Dun	292 and 294	190,000
L. Hepburn	489	62,000
C. F. Kuhn	1439	20,000
Mrs. Helen McGaw Smith	1540 and 1541	54,000
George Livermore	1686 and 1688	12,000
Estate Wm. Rhinelander	477, 180	260,000
Thomas F. Murtha	1574-1576 and 1697	70,000
Mrs. Sarah M. Starr	328	121,000
R. J. Ford	1514-1520	200,000
Estate Wm. Beach Lawrence	377, 379, 441, 498 and 500	535,000
Charles Broadway Rouss	549 and 551	500,000
Estate James E. Cooley	173	158,000
East River Bank	680	73,120
Edward A. Morrison	1279-1291	137,000
Union Dime Savings Bank	1271 and 1273	850,000
Otto Ernst	1512	45,000
A. Cleveland Estate	203	139,000
John Brower	1412-1416	200,000
Edward Rothschild	428	95,000
Estate of George Ross	1539 and 1541	396,000
Clark Bros	603	50,000
Louis Shoolberr	494	62,000
E. Grafton	1179, 1214	110,000
James McCreery	801, 803 and 805	440,000
Charles Payen	786 and 788	150,000
Emily V. Jackson	1570	17,000
Powers Estate	1628 and 1630	20,000
John Haffey	1270	60,000
Helen Wismann	732	48,000
Henry B. Livingston and Margaret L. Lee	912	35,000
Cammann Estate	872	65,000
Appleby Estate	1164	58,000
Louis L. Todd	1365 and 1367	515,000
Louis L. Todd	1448 and 1450	215,000
Chas. W. Dayton	5, 7, 9 and 11	418,000
Estate of James Russell	1587	9,000
James McFarlane	1560	16,000
Jas. A. Brody	1554	18,000
John S. Sutphen	1571, 1585	250,000
Hyacinth A. Sutphen	1545	20,000
Isabella Jex	1231, 1235, 1618, 1621	2[illegible]8,000
Elizabeth P. Floyd Estate	1451, 1455	41,000
C. H. Doherty	1563	24,000
P. H. McCann	1671, 1677	123,000
Wm. M. Haight	Gladstone Hotel	100,000
Austin G. Fox and Rebecca P. Riggs	31 Union square	120,000
N. Y. Produce Exchange		1,500,000
Levi P. Morton	462 and 464	230,000
J. Charles Appleby	1162	55,000
The Mayor, Aldermen and Commonalty of the City of New York	Parks and Triangles	$4,660,000

WHITEHALL AND STATE STREETS.

Owner.	Assessed valuation.
John Taylor Johnson	$55,000
August Struck	28,500
Franc H. Seckel	13,500
John McIntire	34,500
John Gatzan	36,000
Wm. Wilkening	26,500
Frederick Knief	33,000
David H. Decker	39,500
Alfred Roe	11,000

PARK ROW, CENTRE AND CHAMBERS STREETS.

Owner.	Assessed valuation.
New York *Times*	$775,000
J. Searle Barclay	22,500
Emigrant Savings Bank	375,000
Alfred Storm	15,000
The *Sun* Publishing Co.	153,628
Patrick Cunningham	40,000
Russell & Erwin Mfg. Co.	279,000
American News Co.	280,000

BOULEVARD.

Owner.	Description of Property.	Assessed Valuation.
Edward A. Morrison	North of 74th st	$4,500
Adolph Urban	N w cor and 115th st	7,000
J. J. Campion	N e cor and 60th st	16,5[illegible]0
Ruth A. Stevenson	1028-1034	25,000
John Claflin	Boulevard	25,500
Bernard Smith	98th st	16,810
Estate Harriet L. Stilwell	7 lots, cor 125th st	20,000
Edward Connelly	Near 142d st	5,000
George Crawford	N e cor 84th st	20,000
A. H. Wellington	Bet 151st and 152d st	3,500
George Achenbach	1020-1026	14,300
Andrew J. Connick		35,400
Daniel Channey	N w cor 130th st	3,500
Wm. B. Dick	S w cor 142d st	8,000
Francis Crawford	N e cor 65th st	13,500
Conrad Albeidt	S w cor 11th av and 134th st	13,000
Anna E. Alberdt	11th av, south of 134th st	1,100
J. A. H. Stevens	Bet 131st and 132d sts	34,000
G. K. Sheridan	S w cor and 100th st	9,500
Alfred Corning Clark	S e cor and 75th st	95,500
Frederick P. Foster	Bet 83d and 84th sts	3,500
Moritz Walter	N w cor and 96th st	8,000
Estate of Bernard Mayer and estate of Solomon L. Mayer		7,500
Julia P. French	Bet 139th and 140th sts	14,000
B. & G. Siegel	N e and n w cor 174th st and 11th av	10,200
Thomas Dimond	398-405	23,000
Geo. N. Lawrence	4 lots, s w cor 67th st	34,000
Elizabeth F. Sawaus	N w cor 100th st	9,500
Louis Stix	Cor 159th st	4,000
John G. Prague	Bet 121st and 122d sts	21,000
Nathan Wise	N e cor Boulevard and 145th st	14,000
Jno. W. Haaren	S e cor Boulevard and 142d st	11,000
Fr. Beck, Chas. E. Runk	Bet 104th and 105th sts	12,000
Austin Hall	73d, 74th and 108th sts	24,500
John Brower	Bet 108th and 109th sts	35,500
Benj. F. Romaine	76th st	85,000
Jos M. Varnum	10 lots, 152d to 158d st	19,500
Estate of George Jones		24,500
Isidor Straus		45,000
Timothy Donovan		3,100
Jno. N. Odell		11,000
Jos. A. Booth		1,600
Jos. H. Lichtenauer	172d and 173d sts and 11th av	6,600
John A. Loebner	East 173d and 174th sts	3,400
L. H. Marsteller	Bet 92d and 93d sts	5,000
D. Mitchell	N e cor Boulevard and 105th st	5,000
Otto Ernst	E s, bet 85th and 86th sts	38,000

John K. Oats	11th av, cor 187th st	3,100
H. Maibruun	4 lots, cor 97th st	8,000
Hugh Stevenson	S w cor 147th st	9,300
Geo. W. Walker	890, 892 and 894	26,000
Thomas Loughran	S e cor 146th st	3,500
Chas S. Kendall	702	18,000
Susan Brute	11th av, near 173d st	4,400
Alfred Roe	S e cor 160th st	3,900
Augusta C. Perry	Cor 75th st	40,000
Thos. H. O'Connor	Cor 11th, 12th and 141st sts	23,600
Thaddeus Moriarty	Boulevard	6,100
John T. Rooney		1,500
Edward Uhl		7,500
John L. Cadwalader		8,500
Mathias Rook	Cor 130th st	12,900
Daniel S. Slawson	Cor 112th st	7,000
Jeremiah Devlin	Cor 145th st	13,500
Samuel L. Lederer	Near 172d st	5,900
Chas. T. Wills	Cor 84th st	6,000
Theodore W. Myers	Cor 75th st	17,000
John H. Conway		6,500
R. T. Auchmuty	Near 94th st	11,000
Philip Fearing		3,300
Martha A. Leavitt	183d st and 11th av	16,000
Henrietta Blinn	Cor 82d st	62,000
Ottendorfer, Anna, Estate of		17,700
Mary E. Miles	Bet 170th and 171st sts	1,000
Estate D. C. Wilcox	Bet 107th and 108th sts	3,500
Richard O'Gorman, Jr	113th and 114th sts	10,509
David J. Stein	163d–165th	4,500
Louis A. Sheen	148th and 149th sts	5,000
Jos. S. Wood	94th and 95th sts	18,000
Shepuard Knapp		8,000
Wm. Devlin		1,400
New York City		125,000
Estate of Chester A. Arthur		13,000
A. Liebmann's Sons		11,000
Edward J. Woolsey		3,500
Gertrude Boescher		2,000
Bowie Dash		2,500
Louisa Dash		34,000
Geo. F. Gantz		5,000

EAST SIDE LINES.

Owner.	Assessed valuation.
Leonard Jacobs	$35,000
Randolph Guggenheimer	1,800
Randolph Guggenheimer	6,300
Charles W. Kiebisch	12,500
Leo Schlesinger	25,000
Eleanor Jonasson	20,000
P. K. Dickenson	12,000
Francis Blessing	5,500
Troosa Hughes	2,500
Robert Hughes	3,500
Baptist Moran	5,600
Eliz. A. Raisbeck	23,000
Frank Lugar	14,000
Sigmund Adler	5,500
Oliver P. C. Billings	20,000
Geo. W. Walgrove	13,000
Charles Graham & Co	6,500
Ellen H. McCabe	12,000
Edward Rafter	16,000
M. J. Biglan	12,500
A. L. Myers	4,500
David Boyd	7,500
B. Goldstein	14,000
Johannes Brinke	16,000
James C. Fargo	32,000
Fannie L. Field	16,000
John Livingston	50,000
John Townshend	2,700
Simon Adler	7,000
Wm. F. Boller	3,200
Julius Schaul	7,500
F. Bayendorfer	11,000
Andrew H. Decker	3,700
Isaac V. Brokaw	20,000
Lizzie J. Lawlor	4,000
G. W. Walgrove	29,000
New York City	1,180,000
George Cantrell	12,000
John C. Lyons	8,000
J. F. Dolan	5,500
Anna Lehman	7,500
M. A. McGrath	7,500
Levi P. Morton	19,000

The Opinions of Others.

Henry W. Donald, of the firm of Richard V. Harnett & Co., was seen the other day. He said: "The real estate market undoubtedly shows signs of improvement. I think we shall see a larger number of sales in the near future than we have had during the earlier months of the year. Good down-town investment property is in demand, and it is often difficult to supply what is asked for. Sellers hold their property at good prices because they feel that it would not be easy to duplicate it. A feature of the market is the large amount of money that is now offered on bond and mortgage. I think that during the early part of this year there was too much talk about the tightness of money and the high rates demanded. As far as our firm is concerned I can say that there was not at any period this year a time when we had not an abundance to loan, and at low rates. In fact, we have all along had money at 4 per cent, and we have been placing mortgages at that low rate on first-class property."

L. J. Phillips, of L. J. Phillips & Co., speaks in very definite terms of the future condition of the market. "I not only believe, but I am positive," he said, a few days ago, "that we are on the threshold of a good market. Buyers and sellers are now more easily brought into accord, and I am confident that the winter, and probably the spring, will be prosperous seasons for real estate men. I have just made two sales aggregating $400,000, and am on the eve of consummating others. There is a strong tone to the market, and there are more buyers in the field than for many months past."

Secretary Wright on the Proposed Exchange.

The interviews on the proposed Exchange to be erected for the Mechanics' and Traders' Exchange and kindred interests, which appeared in last week's issue of THE RECORD AND GUIDE, have been read extensively. Stephen M. Wright, Secretary of the Exchange, was called upon by a reporter of this paper to ascertain his views on the matter. In answer to various questions, he said:

"Yes, it is a big undertaking, but I sincerely believe in its ultimate triumph. If I understand the spirit of the committee who have the matter in charge, they intend to make the movement a success. We have to overcome the feeling that, like former efforts, this is only talk. That may account for the comparatively small number of responses which have been made to the committee's circulars. I am afraid New Yorkers sometimes lack the civic pride which is to be found in Chicago, Boston and other cities in the erection of fine buildings representing great interests. Still, instances are not wanting where, when they are thoroughly aroused, our citizens carry things through and succeed beyond anticipation. As an illustration of this I would refer to the recent entertainment of the National Convention of Builders. At the beginning it was doubted if it could be made a success; but when the Exchange members became aroused, subscriptions flowed in, even beyond requirement, and the Convention was so great a success that its echoes still remain with us. The object of the committee is, I believe, to expand the Exchange beyond what it now signifies—merely meeting together for merchandising. They propose that it shall be so extended as to include all the trades identified with the construction of a building, many of which are not connected with the Exchange, and by mutual intercourse enable them all to understand each other's needs, so that in times of financial or other trouble, particularly in the face of strikes, they may be able to render each other a united, intelligent and effective assistance. To encourage the union into their own separate organizations of the employers in each trade should be one of the objects of the Exchange. To provide for this it is proposed that the new building shall contain a properly equipped suite of rooms for the meeting of such organizations."

"How is the building to be erected?" asked the reporter. "It will require considerable money."

"It can be erected by demonstrating, as it can be beyond doubt, that it will be a paying investment. And what body of men understand this better than the builders of New York City? They are constantly engaged in the erection of commercial buildings for capitalists for investment. There is no great hurry about the Exchange. The committee will, I presume, act without undue haste. They will take proper legal advice in every step in future as they have in the past, and this will naturally inspire confidence as they proceed to develop the plans which they have been considering and maturing for nearly a year."

Readers of THE RECORD AND GUIDE *may subscribe to the new illustrated quarterly magazine,* THE ARCHITECTURAL RECORD, *by sending their names and addresses to the office of publication, Nos.* 14-16 *Vesey street. The annual subscription is* $1.

About Paving Assessments on Water Grant Property.

Editor RECORD AND GUIDE:

I have been assessed on my property on Lewis street, between Stanton and Houston streets, for the repaving of streets fronting land once under water granted by the city to purchasers who agreed to keep the streets adjoining in repair. (1) Is my property located in the area of such water grants? (2) Is the assessment levied on my property under the law of 1889 freeing owners of such property from further repaving such streets if paved by the city and assessed after the passing of such law? (3) If I pay such assessment will I and my heirs and assigns be forever free from the obligation of keeping such streets paved and in repair as covenanted under the original water grant?

[In reply to our correspondent we would say. 1. His property is located in the area of lands formerly under water and granted by the city on condition that the grantee should keep the streets in front of the property paved and in repair. 2. Yes. 3. Yes. It may be added that when the above law was passed Commissioner Gilroy gave notice to owners of lands formerly under water and granted by the city that nearly all the grants of such lands contained covenants on the part of the grantees, their successors and assigns, to maintain and keep in repair the adjacent streets. The condition of many of such streets, which had been neglected by such grantees, was so bad as to make it necessary that they should be repaired and repaved, and that the obligations resting on owners of lots fronting on such streets to do the work should be enforced. At the time many owners took advantage of the new law which quashed the covenant made by them under the original grant from the city to keep the streets in repair, by paying the city once and for all for a repavement, and since then many others have followed suit. The result has been that the city has paved and placed in good condition miles of streets along the water front and within the lines of the lands formerly under water, and assessed the owners accordingly. Our correspondent's assessment, it appears, is $146.62 on each of his lots, and his assessment was levied for repaving Lewis street, between Delancey and Houston streets, the total cost of which was $12,410.68. The assessment was confirmed August 7, 1891.]

The Ninth Avenue Surface Road.

NEW YORK, December 9, 1891.

Editor RECORD AND GUIDE:

Consents are being asked of the property-owners for the construction of a surface railroad up 9th avenue to 105th or 110th street, to connect with the present 9th avenue horse railroad system.

While I think it is desirable that there should be a surface railroad on the avenue, it seems to me essential that this railroad should connect with a system running much further to the east below the Park than the 9th avenue horse railroad does.

This road when built will be largely used by women and children, women for shopping, etc., and children on their way to and from school. In nearly every case anyone going below 59th street, east of 9th avenue, would have to change to another system and pay an additional fare, so that it seems to me very desirable, if not essential, that the extension up 9th avenue, if made at all, should be made by one of the roads running as far east as 6th avenue or Broadway, below the Park.

As consents are often granted without all sides of the question being considered, it might be wise to bring this particular aspect of the case before the owners of property on 9th avenue.

NINTH AVENUE PROPERTY-OWNER.

Readers of THE RECORD AND GUIDE *may subscribe to the new illustrated quarterly magazine,* THE ARCHITECTURAL RECORD, *by sending their names and addresses to the office of publication, Nos. 14-16 Vesey street. The annual subscription is $1.*

Grand Street Looking Up.

A visit to Grand street recently, after an absence from New York of two years, was quite a surprise to a young New Yorker. He found much more had been done in the way of putting up new buildings during that period than had been done in the decade before. The improvements were most numerous as well as most valuable, between Broadway and the Bowery, as the following table shows:

	Cost.
Nos. 10, 12 and 14, six-story brick, 74.6x83	$60,000
Northeast corner Elm street, six-story brick factory, 68.5x110.11x111.5	75,000
Nos. 176-180, six-story brick building, 75.4x84.10 and 91.7	75,000
Nos. 182 and 184, six-story brick and iron 51.6x85	50,000
Northwest corner Orchard street, five-story brick and stone store, 87.6x100	95,000
Northwest corner Attorney street, six-story brick flat, 25x95	40,000
Northwest corner Pitt street, six-story brick and stone flat, 25x96	40,000
Total	$435,000

From the foregoing it will be seen that close to half a million dollars has been spent on seven improvements, and furthermore that the section between Broadway and the Bowery has been improved for business and light manufacturing. One of the first improvements of those tabulated is the work of Mr. O. G. Bennett. He drew the plans and superintended the construction of the handsome and well-ventilated factory on the northeast corner of Elm street.

Recent sales show clearly enough that other first-class improvements will soon be made on the same street. For instance, the excellent purchase by the Bowery Savings Bank, through Wm. A. White & Sons, of three lots on the northeast corner of Elizabeth street at $155,500. These lots adjoin others owned by the bank, and it is on the cards that a handsome bank building will be erected as soon as existing leases expire.

The attention of readers is directed to the "Wants and Offers" at the end of the Real Estate Department.

Real Estate Exchange Notes.

The Board of Directors held their regular monthly meeting on Tuesday afternoon, President Geo. R. Read in the chair.

A letter from the Rapid Transit Commission, accepting the offer of the Exchange to call a meeting of Broadway property-owners and others in the Real Estate Exchange for the purpose of having the effect which the proposed tunneling would have on adjoining buildings explained, was read. The idea is to invite all members of the Exchange, together with a number of other influential citizens and property-owners to a meeting at which an engineer of the Rapid Transit Commission will demonstrate that the proposed system will in no way injure the foundations, the cellars or sub-cellars of the buildings along Broadway. It is believed that most of the opposition of property-owners to the proposed system finds its origin in this fear, and the Directors of the Exchange think that at a meeting like the one to be called probably next month, these objections can be overcome by an explanation of the effect of the tunneling by a competent engineer. The meeting will probably be called some time in January, after the inauguration of the new Board of Directors, and the Exchange authorities will use every means to secure the attendance of a representative body of Broadway property-owners and other real estate men.

Isaac Fromme moved a resolution expressing the thanks and appreciation of the "Officers, Directors and members of the Real Estate Exchange," of the services rendered the Exchange by Mr. Herman H. Cammann during the past ten years, and expressing regret that Mr. Cammann had declined a renomination for the office of Director of the Exchange. The resolution, which was seconded by Vice-President Schermerhorn, was unanimously carried. Mr. Cammann replied briefly.

Mr. Cammann then moved a resolution of thanks to the President, Mr. Geo. R. Read, for his services to the Board and to the Exchange during the past year. This resolution was seconded and also carried unanimously.

The Manager's office and the Bureau of Information will be closed, by order of the Board of Directors, on December 26th and January 2d, the Saturdays following the holidays.

Thomas H. Terry has been elected a stock member, and A. L. Doremus and J. A. Roberts annual members of the Exchange.

The annual meeting of the Real Estate Exchange will take place on Monday at 1 P. M., when a Board of Directors for the ensuing year will be elected and the annual report, a synopsis of which was printed in these columns some time ago, read.

The regular ticket, as announced a month ago, is as follows: George R. Read, Richard V. Harnett, Charles A. Schermerhorn, William Cruikshank, Isaac Fromme, Ira D. Warren, Cornelius W. Luyster, Edward Oppenheimer, George De F. Barton, J. Romaine Brown, James E. Leviness, Charles S. Brown and Richard Deeves.

No opposition ticket has been announced, and it is probable that there will be none, for under the new system of non-cumulative voting it would be impossible to elect it, or any of it, there being more than a majority of the proxies now in the hands of the "regulars." Notwithstanding the fact that the ticket named above can be elected without the slightest difficulty, the Directors hope that every member will either attend the meeting and vote or send in his proxy, so that a large vote will be polled. They are anxious for this large vote as they think it will be an indorsement by the stockholders of the policy they have pursued during the past year, and the best answer possible to the criticisms of the Exchange management.

Judge Dugro and Frederick Wagner have borrowed from the Title Guarantee and Trust Company $650,000 on temporary mortgage on the Hotel Savoy, which they are just completing at 5th avenue and 59th street.

The attention of readers is directed to the "Wants and Offers" at the end of the Real Estate Department.

THE WEST SIDE INDEX.

All persons interested in West Side real estate should possess an Index of Ten Years' Conveyances affecting property between the north side of 59th and south side of 125th streets, from west side 8th avenue to Hudson River. This Index is published by THE RECORD AND GUIDE, *and the period covered is the ten years prior to June 30th, 1884, to which has been added a list of the conveyances up to January 1st, 1885. Every transfer of real estate in that section, made between those years, is recorded in the Index, with a description of the property, the price paid for it, the liber and page in which the conveyances are recorded in the Register's Office, and the name of the seller and the purchaser. The volume is of the utmost value to conveyancers, lawyers, real estate brokers, agents and dealers in real estate generally, and we will supply the Index to our readers, if ordered before January 1st next, at the reduced price of $5.*

Real Estate Department.

The market this week has fully justified the hopeful predictions made for it in this column last Saturday. As our interesting reports elsewhere clearly indicate real estate is again bright and active and nearly everyone standing in close relations to the market is more cheerful than they have been for some time past. There is a vitality and snap to the market, a desire on the part of both buyers and sellers to close transactions that was almost entirely lacking a month ago. On every hand an improved feeling and a decidedly better condition of affairs generally is manifest. Money is comparatively very easy, buyers are fairly numerous for this time of year, sellers are more reasonable in their demands than they have been and the brokers themselves regard the prospect with a degree of cheerfulness that would not have been believed if it had been predicted a month or more ago. Everything is on the mend and the pleasant part of it is that unless the unforeseen happens, the present satisfactory state of affairs will continue. Considering that this is December, business in real estate circles may be said to be very active, for as has been pointed out in this column the last month of the year is generally a dull time for more than one reason. Arguing in this way, from the present fairly prosperous condition of affairs, the real estate men are predicting a larger activity in the spring than the market has seen for a long time past. That they are justified in drawing the conclusions they do from present facts there is no doubt. The large investments in real estate are largely the investments of profits made in general trade, and it seems very likely that next spring, and in fact next year, will be a prosperous year for trade in the United States. A very large slice of these profits will come to New York for investment, and they will seek it in the safest of securities—real estate—provided, of course, that real estate is as healthy and desirable as it is at the present time.

Again this week several large and important transactions have been closed at private sale. Down town we have a report of a remarkable price paid for less than half a city lot—$182,000. The property is No. 75 Park row, and it was sold by Seton & Wissmann for a family who have held it since 1830, when it was purchased for $400. In connection with this high figure the brokers tell us that they have since been offered an advance of

$20,000 on the selling price. This interesting sale is, however, not the only transaction south of 59th street that demands the attention of the market. Hoffmann Bros. have closed one larger in amount and of quite as much importance to the real estate world. It is of the two dwellings, Nos. 524 and 526 5th avenue, 52x125, and the stable in the rear, No. 2 West 44th street, 25x98.9, which they have sold to Isaac V. Brokaw for $875,100. Mr. Brokaw at present owns the southwest corner of 5th avenue and 44th street and this week's purchase gives him a plot 94x175. Rumor says that Mr. Brokaw may sell or lease the property to a club—the Union, perhaps—but this story is as yet unconfirmed. Further up town quite as remarkable a sale has been consummated. Four 125th street lots east of the Koch store, with one lot on 124th street, sold for a figure that is variously reported as $251,000 and $260,000. This is a considerable increase in price over the sale of the adjoining Koch lots last year, when $250,000 was paid for eight lots, four on 125th and four on 124th street. In addition to these sales there have been numerous lot transactions on the West Side and elsewhere, all of considerable interest. It may not be out of place, in connection with these lot sales, to remind builders that it is possible to very quickly overstock even the present market with houses that will be a heavy burden to carry if dull times should make their appearance.

THE AUCTION MARKET.

The doings in the Auction Room this week have been quite as uninteresting as those of the week previous were interesting. So far as the sales affect the general market practically nothing has been done. A small list of legal sales, embracing very ordinary property, a few parcels, all of them under $80,000, voluntarily offered, a combined executor's sale of about a dozen parcels, widely scattered over North New York, and some offerings in Brooklyn, which were unsuccessful, comprises the auctioneers' offerings during the past week. The city sales were not entirely a success, few in number though they were. Some parcels were bid in, one was withdrawn, and none of the others were interesting enough to attract the attention of the general market. The legal sales were very commonplace, and were heeded by very few persons outside of those connected with them, either directly or indirectly. In some of the foreclosure sales the amounts due for mortgages and costs exceeded the selling price, as is shown in another column, but in no case was the discrepancy large or important enough to call for special comment.

Next week's announcements show no improvement over those of the week just closed. The offerings, consisting of legal sales, one or two executor's sales and some voluntary offerings, are few in number and generally unimportant in character. The most attractive sales are those by Richard V. Harnett and B. L. Kennelly. Mr. Harnett will offer a large plot on Mangin street, near Stanton, while B. L. Kennelly advertises an executor's sale that includes two parcels on lower 8th avenue as well as other down-town and up-town property. The other auctioneers have nothing quite as attractive as the above, so that it will be seen the coming week will be anything but a conspicuous one in auction circles.

On Tuesday, December 15th, Richard V. Harnett & Co. will sell the two-story frame dwelling No. 237 East 109th street, and a plot, 80x100, at Nos. 89, 91 and 93 Mangin street, with three-story brick factory buildings thereon.

On Tuesday, December 15th, Smyth & Ryan will sell a lot, about 23x100, on the northeast corner of Henry and Catharine streets. The plot is improved with three-story brick and frame buildings containing four stores.

On Wednesday, December 16th, Richard V. Harnett & Co. will sell, by order of the executors of the estate of Margaret M. Leverich, deceased, the three-story and basement brick and brown stone dwelling, 26x65x100, No. 48 Pierrepont street, Brooklyn, and about three acres of upland, with many improvements thereon, at Greenport, Long Island, fronting the hotel and cottages of Shelter Island.

On Thursday, December 17th, Richard V. Harnett & Co. will sell the two-story brick stable No. 163 West 29th street.

On Thursday, December 17th, Bryan L. Kennelly will sell by order of executors the four-story business building No. 429 8th avenue, the three-story brick dwelling No. 315 West 32d street, the four-story business building No. 348 8th avenue, the four-story brown stone dwelling No. 471 West 22d street, the five-story double tenement No. 693 1st avenue, the four-story single flat No. 52 West 123d street, the lot with improvements at No. 438 East Houston street, the five-story double tenement No. 426 West 46th street, and the three-story brick dwelling No. 228 Baltic street, Brooklyn. A portion of this property belongs to the estate of Abraham Lewis, the old-time 8th avenue dry-goods merchant. This is the most important sale that will take place during the present year.

CONVEYANCES.

	1889. Dec. 6 to 12, inclus.	1890. Dec. 5 to 11, inclus.	1891. Dec. 4 to 10, inclus.
Number	[illegible]	260	246
Amount involved	$5,066,554	$2,778,450	$3,618,896
Number nominal	77	107	77
Number 23d and 24th Wards	47	66	81
Amount involved	$286,873	$192,645	$457,994
Number nominal	14	20	24

MORTGAGES.

	1889.	1890.	1891.
Number	253	276	217
Amount involved	$4,158,984	$3,492,804	$2,720,706
Number at 5 per cent	116	98	86
Amount involved	$2,288,478	$1,577,814	$878,683
Number at less than 5 per cent	26	19	9
Amount involved	$791,000	$773,500	$872,155
Number to Banks, Trust and Insurance Companies	52	31	29
Amount involved	$1,607,790	$910,500	$1,178,750

PROJECTED BUILDINGS.

	1889. Dec. 7 to 13, inclus.	1890. Dec. 6 to 12, inclus.	1891. Dec. 5 to 11, inclus.
Number of buildings	54	55	49
Estimated cost	$751,896	$897,800	$708,770

Gossip of the Week.

SOUTH OF 59TH STREET.

[illegible] wood wainscoting should be prohibited by requiring that the plastering be carried down to the floor line; A. R. Whitney, representing Carnegie & Co., and Mr. Bedell, of Cooper, Hewitt & Co., on the strength of different metals and their comparative merits. The committee hope to finish their task before the present month expires, and be able to present their amendments early in the session of the approaching Legislature.

What Men Talk About.

"There has been some talk about a boom in real estate lately," said Francis Crawford, "but it is by the young men who have never seen a real boom. The men are living to-day who remember the speculation in real estate when vacant lots in the sixties, near Madison avenue, brought $31,000 and $32,000 apiece, and not a house within thirty blocks of them. That was a real boom. This talk about a boom on the West Side, where already there are millions of dollars invested, is all nonsense. Long ago, I said

Seton & Wissmann this week consummated one of the most interesting sales of the year. They sold for Princess Cenci (nee Miss Lorillard Spencer) to Ogden & Clark No. 75 Park row, a two-story frame building, on lot 20.6x16x76, for $122,000. The plot contains less than half a full city lot, so that the price was over $100 a square foot. Messrs. Seton & Wissmann say that since the sale they have been offered $20,000 advance on the selling price. It is interesting to note that old Peter Lorillard, who purchased this ground, it is said, in 1830, paid only $400 for it. The property has never been transferred since then.

Fay & Stacom have sold to a Mr. Reeser the southwest corner of Henry and Market streets, a six-story flat, 25x114, for $80,000, and the northwest corner of Grand and Pitt streets, a similar building, on lot 25x100, also for $80,000 to the same buyer. Fay & Stacom have also sold to a Mr. Hilderbrandt the six-story tenement No. 62 Essex street for $52,000.

The estate of John T. Agnew has sold to Mrs. M. A. Ogden the four-story brick dwelling, 24.9x100, on the northwest corner of Madison avenue and 89th street, on private terms. The house is at present occupied by a college fraternity.

Geo. R. Read has sold No. 107 East 35th street, a four-story English basement brown stone dwelling, on lot 18.9x98.9, for James J. K. Hackett to W. E. Dodge for $33,000.

John H. Dye has sold for D. Meagher Nos. 282 and 284 Spring street, two four-story buildings, on private terms, to a Mr. Wilmart who will alter the same into a stable.

J. P. and E J. Murray have sold No. 118 West Broadway and No. 6 North Moore street, with the old buildings thereon, on private terms.

Samuel McMillan has sold the five-story brick and stone flat, on lot 26x100, No. 208 West 54th street, on private terms. Broker, I. T. Meyer.

Wm. Sperb, Jr., who recently purchased No. 233 West 14th street, a four-story brown stone dwelling, on lot 25x120, has resold the same through Broker Isaac T. Meyer.

Joseph Rutz & Son have sold for Mrs. Katherine G. Secor the two five-story tenements Nos. 43 and 45 Allen street to Weil & Mayer for $36,500, and for Joseph Rutz the three-story and basement house No. 281 Delancey street to John Barning for $6,500.

Ascher Weinstein has sold to Alexander Muir No. 341 West 13th street, a four-story old building, 25x60x92, on private terms, for improvement.

Morris B. Baer & Co. have sold for Ascher Weinstein to Miss Mary A. Buchan No. 34 West 27th street, a four-story brown stone dwelling, 23x65x98.9, on private terms.

Emil Bachman has sold to Christian Gerhardt No. 437 West 48th street, a five-story double flat, 25x85.5, for $28,500.

Fitzsimons & Smith have sold for John C. Wirtz No. 38 West 35th street, a three-story, high stoop, brown stone private dwelling, lot 20x98.9, to a firm of builders on private terms. This parcel adjoins No. 36 West 35th street, which Fitzsimons & Smith sold recently to the same parties.

H. K. Thurber has sold No. 40 West 38th street, a four-story brown stone dwelling, on lot 21x98.9, on private terms. The purchaser is reported as Colonel Daniel S. Appleton, of the Seventh Regiment.

Lewis Z. Bach has sold to Sire Bros. the southeast corner of Lexington avenue and 29th street, a four-story dwelling, 22.4x85, for $33,500. The purchasers will alter and improve the property at a cost of $12,000.

Adler & Herrman have sold No. 14 Centre street and No. 2 City Hall place to a Mr. Kennedy at an advance over the price, $13,400, which they paid at auction last week. There is a three-story building on the plot which is very irregular. Beginning at Centre street the size is 24.10x31 to City Hall place x24.10x6.

C. A. Lutz & Co. have sold for John Balken the southeast corner of Norfolk and Stanton streets, 50x57, for $33,500.

R. C. Winters has sold to Casper Engler No. 714 11th avenue, 25.1x60, with the two-story frame store thereon, for $7,200.

NORTH OF 59TH STREET.

The estate of Joseph B. Hart has sold to George Ehret, the brewer, the four lots on the south side of 125th street, 325 feet west of Lenox avenue, adjoining Koch & Co.'s large store, together with one lot in the rear on 124th street, for a sum that is variously stated at $251,000 and $260,000. The 125th street lots are at present covered by a residence now occupied by Mrs. Hart and the 124th street lot by a small brick building. The price was a surprise to Harlem people, who thought that Koch & Co. had paid high figures when in June, 1890, they bought eight lots, adjoining, four on 125th street and four on 124th street, for $250,000. A rumor stated that George

Ehret would improve the plot by the erection of a concert garden, but the story is not generally believed up town. L. J. Phillips & Co. are said to be the brokers.

Editor RECORD AND GUIDE:

Consents are being asked of the property-owners for the construction of a surface railroad up 9th avenue to 105th or 110th street, to connect with the present 9th avenue horse railroad system.

While I think it is desirable that there should be a surface railroad on the avenue, it seems to me essential that this railroad should connect with a system running much further to the east below the Park than the 9th avenue horse railroad does.

This road when built will be largely used by women and children: women for shopping, etc., and children on their way to and from school. In nearly every case anyone going below 59th street, east of 9th avenue would have to change to another system and pay an additional fare, so that it seems to me very desirable, if not essential, that the extension up 9th avenue, if made at all, should be made by one of the roads running as far east as 6th avenue or Broadway, below the Park.

three-story dwellings, each 20x50x100, on the north side of 102d street, 100 feet west of West End avenue, for $75,000.

Chas. Macdonald has sold the four-story high stoop house, No. 68 West 82d street, 18x55, and three-story extension, x102.2, to H. Tobias on private terms; broker, E. B. H. Myers.

Joseph Bierhoff has sold for C. D. Degenhard to a Harlem builder two rock lots, 50x100, on the east side of Amsterdam avenue, 75 feet south of 133d street, on private terms. These two lots will be improved at once.

Caroline W. Astor, as executrix, has sold to Ascher Weinstein No. 29 West 81st street, a four-story English basement brown stone dwelling, 16.8 x60x98.9, on private terms. Broker, Wm. Cruikshank.

Henry H. Dreyer has sold for R. E. Johnson to Adam Wesp No. 2151 8th avenue, a five-story brick flat, 25.8x78x100, on private terms; and No. 206 West 103d street, a five-story single buff brick flat, on lot 20x80, for $21,200, to Catherine Meagher.

Joseph Bierhoff has sold for M. C. & C. Kervan to Cort Degenhard, a five-story brick and brown stone apartment house, 25x88x100, on the east side of Amsterdam avenue, about 150 feet north of 131st street, for $35,000.

Hunt & Wendell have sold No. 158 West 72d street, a four-story brown stone dwelling, 20x60x102.2, for about $50,000.

J. P. & E. J. Murray have sold for Heilner & Wolf the five-story improved flat on the southeast corner of Amsterdam avenue and 151st street for $55,000.

Stabler & Smith have sold for Thomas J. McGuire to S. Battenberg No. 163½ West 102d street, a five-story brick single flat, on lot 16.3x100, on private terms; and for Merriam R. Benjamin to L. Huerman No. 151 West 94th street, a three-story dwelling, on lot 17x100, for $18,000.

It is reported that J. Bently Squier has sold four lots on the north side of 82d street, just east of Riverside Drive.

Adler & Hermann have sold No. 1677 Lexington avenue, a five-story flat, to a Mr. Steinreich at an advance over the price, $15,200, which they paid when they purchased the flat at auction three weeks ago.

H. H. Bliss, who negotiated the trade between Richard M. Hooley, of Chicago, and J. D. Butler, informs us that the price of the four lots on 72d and 73d streets, 425 west of Central Park West, was nearer $130,000 than $100,000, the figure reported last week. The two flats given in exchange by Mr. Butler were on the south side of 145th street, 28 feet west of 8th avenue. They are five stories in height, 26x75x100, and they were sold for $70,000.

T. L. Reynolds & Co. have sold for M. Simonson No. 12 West 133d street, a five-story flat, for $28,000.

LEASES.

Mainbart & Lowe have leased for E. D. Farrell one of his stores on West 125th street, south side, east of 7th avenue, No. 154, 50x100 in size, to Saita, Sons & Co., fruiterers, for five years, at $3,500 per annum.

E. H. Ludlow & Co. have rented, furnished, No. 4 Washington square North and No. 15 East 53d street, both four-story dwellings.

Brooklyn.

Benjamin Sturges has sold for Thos. Brown the four-story brick flat building with store, 20x55x100, No. 669A Gates avenue, for $10,500, and resold the same property for Frank D. Smith for $11,000. Mr. Sturges has also sold for Arnold Sanford, M. D., his gore lot, beginning at a point on the south side of Madison street, 195 feet west of Sumner avenue, for $6,000.

J. P. Sloane has sold for Edward Reehil the four-story and cellar brick double flat house, 25x53x100, No. 216 Huron street, to Patrick Meehan for $10,000.

Corwith Bros. have sold the three-story brick store and dwelling, 25x40x66.7, on the northwest corner of Oakland and Eagle streets, for the estate of Claus Plath to Ernest Ochs for $6,500.

CONVEYANCES.

	1889. Dec. 5 to 11, inclus.	1890. Dec. 4 to 10, inclus.	1891. Dec. 3 to 9, inclus.
Number	269	285	320
Amount involved	$955,947	$1,875,726	$1,216,736
Number nominal	82	77	108

MORTGAGES.

	1889.	1890.	1891.
Number	229	272	270
Amount involved	$871,718	$892,311	$968,918
Number at 5 per cent. or less	146	130	112
Amount involved	$554,064	$442,340	$451,700

PROJECTED BUILDINGS.

	1889. Dec. 6 to 12, inclus.	1890. Dec. 5 to 11, inclus.	1891. Dec. 4 to 10, inclus.
Number of buildings	116	80	79
Estimated cost	$563,295	$322,610	$331,025

Out of Town.

GREENWICH, CONN.—Chas. Field, Griffin & Co. have sold for F. J. Stone ten acres of pasture ground to Warren E. Smith, of Best & Co., for $4,500. Mr. Stone still retains a number of acres of high ground, with improvements.

MARION, N. J.—Geo. F. Gantz, of New York, has bought from H. N. Van Wagenen ninety-seven lots on Broadway, Pavonia, West Side and Romaine avenues, for about $29,000, an average of nearly $300 per lot. J. W. Smith & Sons were the brokers.

Out Among the Builders.

John Hauser has drawn plans for a five-story brick and stone front flat, 25x86.6, to be erected by John Schreiner, Jr., on the south side of 127th street, 156 east of Park avenue, at a cost of $24,000. Mr. Hauser will also furnish plans for extensive alterations to the buildings Nos. 309 and 311 East 65th street, to be made by Peter Hassinger. An extension 30 feet deep will be added to the buildings, and they will be remodeled for flat purposes. Cost, $9,500.

Professor Henry F. Osborn has prepared plans for the new Biological Laboratory to be erected for Columbia College, at 59th street and 9th avenue.

George J. Kraus, the owner of the Volks' Garden, will build a concert hall, modeled after the famous Kroll's Garden in Berlin, on 29th street, between Broadway and 6th avenue. Cost, $50,000. The site which the building will occupy is that upon which the old Hoffman House stable is at present.

A. D. Pickering and Vaulx Carter are the associated architects for the four-story and basement trades school building to be built at Nos. 225 and 227 East 9th street by the Hebrew Technical Institute. The building will be 50x80 in size and will be constructed of brick and stone.

King & Symonds have drawn plans for a two-story brick stable, 50x198, with asphalt and gravel roof, to be built for J. E. Connolly, between 19th and 20th streets, 10th and 11th avenues. The stable is for boarding, livery and express purposes, and is to have accommodations for 120 or more horses.

The two four-story buildings, Nos. 282 and 284 Spring street, will be altered into a stable by the owner, a Mr. Wilmart.

Two five-story flats and stores will be erected on the east side of Amsterdam avenue, 75 feet south of 133d street.

Alexander Muir will build a six-story tenement at No. 341 West 18th street.

Richard R. Davis has plans on the boards for a four-story brick flat, 25x66, which Mrs. E. E. Barron will build on the west side of Bradhurst avenue, between 153d and 154th streets, at a cost of $ .6,000.

The West Side Democratic Club, of which Edward H. Murphy is financial secretary, met at the Hotel Endicott on Tuesday and opened subscriptions for the new club-house they intend to erect.

John A. Hamilton has plans under way for an eight-story brick, iron and stone apartment house, 50x50, to be built on the West Side, up town, at a cost of $85,000. The building will be finished with a dome 35 feet in diameter and 35 feet high, in which will be a stage and hall for receptions, musical entertainments and the like. The four corners of the building will be carried up in towers capped with smaller domes similar in character to the central feature of the building. Above the roof line of adjoining houses this building will be circular in form, and surrounding the entire building at the eighth story will be an iron colonnade of skeleton construction. The interior finish is to be in hard woods and all the appointments will be first-class, embracing fire-proof stairs, elevators, steam heat, electric light, etc. Each floor will contain but one apartment, which will be complete with every convenience of a modern dwelling.

The ten-story apartment house which J. D. Butler intends erecting on the four lots on 72d and 73d street, 425 feet west of Central Park West, will have a front of Belleville gray stone, with light red Baltimore brick and terra cotta trimmings. The apartment house will embrace many novel features, among which will be a conservatory filled with tropical plants, to be located on the roof proper of the structure, and which will be inclosed by a sliding roof. Work will begin March 1, 1892. R. H. Robertson, architect.

F. Grasmuck reports that he has had plans drawn for twelve three-story and basement brick and stone front houses, 17 to 22 feet front x 32 to 38 deep, which he contemplates building in the spring on the north side of 143d street, between Bradhurst and Edgecombe avenues, at a cost of $7,500 to $8,000 each.

F. Ebeling will draw plans for a $3,000 alteration to be made for Mrs. L. Rinalds in the building at No. 28 Scammel street. One story will be added, a new store front put in, the walls altered and the interior changed and remodeled.

H. Horenburger has plans under way for sixteen private dwellings to be built for Walden P. Anderson on the south side of 90th street, 200 feet west of Central Park West. Five of these will be four stories, and eleven three stories in height. They will be trimmed in hardwoods and provided with the best sanitary plumbing and fixtures. The front of each house will differ from its neighbor in design, making a row of handsome houses and a marked improvement in this section. This improvement was mentioned in a recent issue.

John Casey will improve the southeast corner of Columbus avenue and 84th street, 127.8x100, probably by the erection of a six or seven-story improved apartment house.

Geo. Johnson will improve four lots on the south side of 88th street, 62 feet east of Madison avenue by the erection of five-story flats.

Wm. Hall's Sons will improve the eight lots on the north side of 69th street, 125 feet east of Columbus avenue, by the erection of first-class dwellings.

Geo. C. Edgar's Sons will build five four-story first-class brown stone dwellings on the four lots on the north side of 69th street, 450 feet east of Columbus avenue.

John Hauser is the architect for a five-story brick and stone flat and store which John Schreiner, Jr., will build on the west side of 1st avenue, 102.2 south of 84th street, at a cost of $24,000. Size, 25x86.6.

Andrew Spence is engaged on plans for the following houses: Eight two-story and basement brick and stone dwellings, 18.6 and 18x46, to be built on the south side of 185th street, 80 feet east of St. Ann's avenue: one five-story brick and stone flat, 25x65, to be built on the north side of 147th street, 75 feet east of Bradhurst avenue, at a cost of $15,000, and one two-story and basement brick and stone dwelling to be erected at Arcularius place and Central avenue by Wm. Hargrave, at a cost of $7,000. Size, 21x42.

Brooklyn.

John Hauser is drawing plans for a three-story and basement brown stone private dwelling to be built by Patrick Fitzpatrick at 925 Kent avenue. The size is 25x50, and the cost $12,000.

Out of Town.

FLUSHING, L. I.—Stephenson & Greene will draw plans for a $5,000 frame dwelling, two stories and attic high and 35x32 in size. Miss A. L. Drake is the owner.

HIGHLANDS, N. J.—Some weeks ago we made mention of the fact that C. L. Duvale would build a stable here from plans by John A. Hamilton. The scheme then under consideration was abandoned and the architect commissioned to work up new plans for a two-story frame and stone stable, 40x50 in size, with a water tower 60 feet high. $5,000 will be spent on the improvement as at present developed.

HERKIMER, N. Y.—The Adirondack & St. Lawrence Railroad Co. and The New York Central & Hudson River Railroad Co. will build a union station at this place. It is to be a two-story stone building 30x100, with extension sheds. The second story will be arranged for offices. The structure will have a slate roof and is to be similar in style to that ordered for Malone, N. Y. King & Symonds will draw the plans.

MIDDLEVILLE, N. Y.—King & Symonds have plans under way for a two-story brick boiler and pump house, 40x60, of fire-proof construction, with asphalt and gravel roof, and for a two story frame office building, 42x48, with shingle exterior, to be built here for G. H. Thomas & Co. They are also the architects for the two-story frame depot, 25x125, which is to be built for the Adirondack & St. Lawrence Railway Company.

MINEVILLE, N. Y.—Stephenson & Greene have completed plans for the Witherbee Memorial building.—A club-house for the iron miners, which is to be a four-story stone and frame structure, 94x111 in size. It will contain a library, with reading rooms, a gymnasium and baths, bowling-alleys, kitchen, restaurant, billiard and sleeping rooms, and a hall for entertainments, which will seat about 400. The estimated cost is about $30,000.

MALONE, N. Y.—The Adirondack & St. Lawrence Railroad Company and The Ogdensburg & Lake Champlain Railroad Company will build a union station at the junction of their two roads. The building is to be but one story high, with a frontage on each road of about 300 feet. It will be finished with a slate roof and is to be in the chalet style. King & Symonds are the architects. This same firm have drawn plans for a two-story and attic frame dwelling, 45x80 in size, to be built here for F. G. Paddock. The house will be cabinet trimmed throughout, have all modern improvements and shingle-finished exterior.

NEWARK, N. J.—A. D. Pickering has drawn plans for a two-story and attic frame dwelling, 30x35, to be built on the east side of Gold street, near Orange street, for Dr. Anna T. Nivison.

NORFOLK, CONN.—Dr. E. H. Peaslee will build a two-and-a-half-story frame dwelling, 42x64, from plans by Stephenson & Greene. This house will cost about $7,500.

RIDGEWOOD, N. J.—Paul Waton will build a $6,100 dwelling from plans by Stephenson & Greene. The house will be a two-and-a-half-story frame, 46x43 in size.

SHORT HILLS, N. J.—Stephenson & Greene are the architects for the one-story brick extension to the Casino. This extension will be 22x90 in size, and is to contain the bowling-alley. It will be finished with a slate roof and is to cost $2,500.

UTICA, N. Y.—Jules Doux has commissioned King & Symonds to furnish sketches for a two-story and attic frame dwelling, 40x60 in size. The house is to be shingle finished and trimmed with hardwoods throughout.

WESTCHESTER, N. Y.—The residence of F. de R. Wissman is to be remodeled and enlarged by a two-story frame extension, from plans drawn by Heins & La Farge.

WOODBINE, N. J.—Fifty two-story frame cottages, 18x20, will be built here, costing in the neighborhood of $21,000, by the Baron De Hirsch Fund, intended as the nucleus of an agricultural settlement for the Russian Jews. A three-story frame building, 40x60, arranged for the manufacturing of shoes and clothing, is also included in the scheme. Pickering & Carter are the architects.

Amending the Building Law.

The Committee on Revision of the Building Law will conclude its open public sessions on Friday next, the 18th instant, in the Board room of the Fire Underwriters. The bill prepared last year has been gone over, section by section, and the various suggestions received by the committee have been noted down in orderly arrangement for the final action that will be taken later on. Among the experts in building construction who have appeared in person before the committee and made valuable suggestions are Engineer Charles H. Haswell, on the subject of piles and foundations; Architect F. H. Kimball, on theatre construction; John McGlensey, Chairman of the Employing Plasterers' Society, who urged a requirement for more extended use of wire cloth for plastering, and that hollow spaces behind wood wainscoting should be prohibited by requiring that the plastering be carried down to the floor line; A. R. Whitney, representing Carnegie & Co., and Mr. Bedell, of Cooper, Hewitt & Co., on the strength of different metals and their comparative merits. The committee hope to finish their task before the present month expires, and be able to present their amendments early in the session of the approaching Legislature.

What Men Talk About.

"There has been some talk about a boom in real estate lately," said Francis Crawford, "but it is by the young men who have never seen a real boom. The men are living to-day who remember the speculation in real estate when vacant lots in the sixties, near Madison avenue, brought $31,000 and $32,000 apiece, and not a house within thirty blocks of them. That was a real boom. This talk about a boom on the West Side, where already there are millions of dollars invested, is all nonsense. Long ago, I said that lots on side streets, between Central Park West and Columbus avenue, in the West Side residence district proper, would be worth $25,000 apiece. Now I will make a further prediction. In five years you will not be able to buy a lot on a restricted street, between those avenues, for $25,000. There is no boom over here; there's no room for any. The growth in values has been steady and reasonable and it is warranted by the facts."

Important to Property-Holders.

BOARD OF ASSESSORS.

OFFICE OF THE BOARD OF ASSESSORS,
No. 27 CHAMBERS STREET,
NEW YORK, Dec. 11, 1891.

Notice is given to the owner or owners, of all houses and lots, improved or unimproved lands affected thereby, that the following assessments have been completed and are lodged in the office of the Board of Assessors for examination by all persons interested, viz.:

No. 1.—Regulating, grading, curbing and flagging 109th st, from 9th av to the Riverside Drive.

No. 2.—Regulating, grading, curbing and flagging 130th st, from the Boulevard to 12th av.

[The limits embraced by such assessments include all the several houses and lots of ground, vacant lots, pieces or parcels of land situated on—

No. 1.—Both sides of 109th st, from 9th av to the Riverside Drive.

No. 2.—Both sides of 130th st, from the Boulevard to 12th av.]

All persons whose interests are affected by the above-named assessments and who are opposed to the same, or either of them, are requested to present their objections in writing to the Chairman of the Board of Assessors, at their office, No. 27 Chambers street, within thirty days from the date of this notice.

The above-described lists will be transmitted, as provided by law, to the Board of Revision and Correction of Assessments for confirmation on the 12th day of January, 1892.

In the matter of the application of the Board of Street Opening and Improvement of the City of New York, for and on behalf of the Mayor, Aldermen and Commonalty of the City of New York, relative to acquiring title, wherever the same has not been heretofore acquired, to Forest avenue, extending from the southerly side of Home street to the northerly side of East 168th street, in the 23d Ward, as the same has been heretofore laid out and designated as a first-class street or road by the Department of Public Parks; also relative to the opening of Cauldwell avenue (although not yet named by proper authority), from Boston road to East 163d street, and from Clifton street to Westchester avenue, in the 23d Ward, etc.: Notice is given that the bill of costs, charges and expenses incurred by reason of the proceedings in the above-entitled matters, will be presented for taxation to one of the Justices of the Supreme Court, at the Chambers thereof, in the County Court House, at the City Hall, in the City of New York, on the 17th and 21st days of December, 1891, at 10:30 o'clock in the forenoon of those days, or as soon thereafter as counsel can be heard thereon; and that the said bill of costs, charges and expenses has been deposited in the office of the Department of Public Works, there to remain for and during the space of ten days.

Contractors' Notes.

Bids or estimates will be received at the Department of Public Works, No. 31 Chambers street, until 12 o'clock M. on Monday, December 21, 1891, for furnishing materials and performing work in the repairs of the buildings known as Nos. 8, 10, 12 and 14 Chambers street.

Estimates for preparing for and building a new wooden pier, with its appurtenances, near the foot of Vesey street, North River, and depositing rip-rap stone in connection therewith, will be received by the Board of Commissioners at the head of the Department of Docks, at the office of said Department, on Pier "A," foot of Battery place, North River, in the City of New York, until 1 o'clock P. M. of Wednesday, December 23, 1891.

Sealed proposals will be received by the Board of School Trustees for the 12th Ward, at the hall of the Board of Education, No. 146 Grand street, until 10 o'clock A. M., on Thursday, December 24th, 1891, for sanitary work, etc., at Grammar School No. 46, corner of 156th street and St. Nicholas avenue; also by the Board of School Trustees for the 17th Ward, at the hall of the Board of Education, No. 146 Grand street, until 3 o'clock P. M., on Wednesday December 23, 1891, for fitting up premises Nos. 206 and 208 East 11th street for Primary School No. 22.

The Southwest Corner of Broadway and Liberty Street.

Editor RECORD AND GUIDE:

In your criticism of the price which the Liberty street corner brought you speak of it as being, perhaps, small. Was it? The Broadway piece is, say, 28x107—2,996. The back piece is, say, 45x80—3,600. Allowing $200,000 as the price for the back piece the price for it is $55.555 per square foot. Is not that enough? There is left the sum of $570,000 for the Broadway part which, divided by 2,996, yields $190+ as the price for that per square foot. H.

Building Trades' Club Entertainment.

The first of a series of monthly entertainments to be given at the Building Trades' Club, took place on Monday evening, when Prof. Erickson, a champion poolist, for two hours entertained a large number of members by an exhibition of intricate combination shots, after which a collation was served. The January entertainment, for which arrangements are in progress, will be of an entirely different character.

Contracts Awarded.

The Dale Tile Manufacturing Co. have the contract to furnish all the vault lights required for the new Potter buildings on Lafayette and Astor place.

Wood, Jenks & Co., of Cleveland (Henry C. Adams, New York manager), will furnish all the woodwork for the new Equitable Life building at Des Moines, Iowa. B. D. Whitcomb & Co., of Boston, are the contracting builders, and Shipley, Rutan & Coolidge the architects.

Back Numbers Wanted.

Fifteen cents will paid for copies of this paper, No. 1090, dated April 6, 1889; No. 1166, July 19, 1890; No. 1142, February 1, 1890; and No. 1087, January 12, 1889. Fifty cents will be paid for index volume 43, January to June, 1889.

New Incorporations.

The Suburban Realty Company filed a certificate of incorporation in the County Clerk's office on December 7th for the purpose of buying and improving real estate in New York, New Jersey and Connecticut. The capital stock is $25,000, divided into 500 shares at $50 a share. The names of the directors are Albert Bell, Ferris W. Henry, and ten others.

Readers of THE RECORD AND GUIDE *may subscribe to the new illustrated quarterly magazine*, THE ARCHITECTURAL RECORD, *by sending their names and addresses to the office of publication, Nos. 14-16 Vesey street. The annual subscription is $1.*

Fine Printing of All Kinds.

There has recently been added to THE RECORD AND GUIDE newspaper plant a complete Book and Job outfit, and we are now prepared to estimate for and execute all orders. Commercial, Real Estate and Architectural Printing of a high order, promptly delivered, will be a feature of this department. A postal card addressed to THE RECORD AND GUIDE Press, No. 14 Barclay street, or Nos. 14 to 16 Vesey street, will insure the attendance of a competent representative to give estimates, etc. Orders by mail will receive the same attention as if given personally.

WANTS AND OFFERS.

(Advertisements strictly in accordance with this title will be inserted at the practically nominal rate of 10 CENTS *per line, agate). In figuring for themselves advertisers may count seven words for each line, the address to be taken as one line. The object of this department is to bring buyers and sellers into communication with customers. Advertisements must be marked "Wants and Offers Column," and sent to the office of publication, Nos. 14 and 16 Vesey Street, not later than 3 P. M. Friday.)*

WANTS.

GOOD law copyist desires situation in law office.
LEX, RECORD AND GUIDE office.

BUILDERS having property to exchange. Send full particulars to
H. J. DOUGLAS, 171 Broadway.

WANTED to purchase for investment, two five-story double tenements, bet Grand and 23d sts., east of Av A. Address R., RECORD AND GUIDE.

ATTENTION, BUILDERS!—Wanted, a dwelling $15,000 to $20,000; located convenient to 125th st. station, 8th av., or south of 104th st., west side. Send full particulars to
H. J. DOUGLAS, 171 Broadway.

OFFERS.

Dwellings and Flats

A 72D ST. GEM, No. 306 West.—This superb house is beautifully decorated; has handsome gas fixtures; is in perfect order; ready for immediate occupancy; $18,000; a greater bargain than has been offered in months.
Nov. 14-uf. CONDIT, 1179 Broadway.

A—At reasonable prices and easy terms, three and four-story residences, with three-story extensions; all improvements. Call and examine or inquire of the owner and builder, on the premises.
S. O. WRIGHT, 128 West 121st st., open daily.
Oct. 3 uf.

FOR SALE.—Six new cabinet-trimmed three-story and basement brown stone private dwellings, Nos. 142-162 West 122d st.; prices reasonable and brokers commissions allowed. For further particulars apply at office of
FRED'K. H. LITTLEFIELD, 156 Broadway.
Aug. 29-uf.

Vacant Lots.

EASTERLY FRONT BOULEVARD, with 200 ft. on 86th st, and 204 ft. on 87th st; one or more plots.
Nov. 7-1aw6w. OTTO ERNST, South Amboy, N. J.

OFFERS.

TO BUILDERS.—Five choice lots for sale in first-class neighborhood; ripe for improvement; no finer plot in the market. For particulars apply to
H. JENKINSON & CO., 1470 Madison av.

ADJOINING WEST 66TH "L" STATION (now operating). Choicest lots, single or plots, for manifold uses; private stables, flats, factories, &c., real bargains. P. S. TREACY,
101 West Boulevard (near 66th st "L").

AN INVESTMENT OR SPECULATION.—Over 20 acres just north of Van Cortlandt Park, near two depots. Principals only.
PHILLIPS & WELLS, Tribune Building.
Nov. 21-1aw4w.

1ST AV., near 108th st; full lot, $5,750
Oct. 31—1aw9w. EDWIN A. ELY, 103 Gold st.

Improved Property.

FOR SALE.—Business property below 14th st., near Broadway; price $31,000; rental $5,000; mortgage $15,000; 20 per cent. net on investment.
W. VANDER ROEST, 1477 Lexington av., City.

$650,000 FOR ONE of the choicest pieces of investment properties on Manhattan Island; exceptionally well built and very desirably located; other good property (city or country) will be entertained in part payment.
Nov. 14—uf. CONDIT, 1179 Broadway.

OFFICE OF
FREDERICK SOUTHACK,
401 BROADWAY,
offers for sale some choice pieces
of property on
LEONARD ST., between Broadway and West B'way.
FRANKLIN ST., between B'way and West B'way.
WHITE ST., between B'way and West B'way.
BROADWAY, from Barclay to 14th st.
BLEECKER ST., from B'way to South 5th av.
GREENE ST., Canal to 8th st.
WASHINGTON PLACE, B'way to Wooster.
WAVERLEY PLACE, B'way to Wooster.
APPLY AS ABOVE.
FREDERICK SOUTHACK.
Oct. 3 uf.

OFFERS.

FULTON STREET PROPERTY for sale. Particulars of RULAND & WHITING, 5 Beekman st.

3D AVENUE PROPERTY, near 44th st.; very cheap; must be sold.
RULAND & WHITING, 5 Beekman st.

TO LET OR TO LEASE.—Two floors of a factory, 25x98, light on all sides, 1st av and 107th st; terms moderate. J. REEBER'S SONS,
Nov. 7 uf. 409 East 107th.

Country Property.

FOR SALE.—Lake Hopatcong, N. J.; lots and plots at Minnisink Park, near Railway Station and Lake Shore; for sale or lease, valuable mill property; constant water supply; railway siding and canal on property. Apply to J. WARD SMITH, Sec'y M. P. Co., 800 Broad st., Room 9, Newark, N. J.
Dec 5-1aw7w.

BEAUTIFUL SUBURBAN HOUSE.—Eight rooms; all improvements; house new; a perfect gem; driveway and barn; all for $8,500.
Dec. 5-1aw4w D. MULL, 1888 Washington av.

FOR SALE.—In plots to suit; eligible building sites (commanding view of Sound for miles), on North st., Greenwich, Connecticut; price reasonable; terms easy; neighborhood aristocratic and fashionable. Apply to
FRED. J. STONE, owner, 60 Broadway, N. Y.
Sept. 12-uf.

Miscellaneous.

A PARTY ABOUT TO BUILD A FIVE-STORY factory, 50x98, in Harlem, near water-front, will lease the three upper floors and build to suit tenant. Terms very moderate. Address
May 16 u. f OWNER, 409 E. 107th St.

PRINTING.—Book, News and Job.
RECORD AND GUIDE PRESS,
14 Barclay, and 14, 16 Vesey sts.

SALES OF THE WEEK.

The following are the sales at the Real Estate Exchange and Auction Room for the week ending December 11.

* *Indicates that the property described has been bid in for plaintiff's account:*

JAMES L. WELLS.

Brook av, e s, 125 s 144d st, 25x100, vacant. Nelson Smith, Jr. $3,700
Brook av, w s, 75 n 144th st, 25x90, vacant. Geo. Maud 3,200
Brook av, e s, 43 n 161st st, 28.10x33x20.2x90.6x50.5x155.8 to beginning, vacant. N. Smith, Jr. 3,550
162d st, No. 759, n s, 175 e Washington av, 25x117, two frame dwell'gs. Mrs. Hann 3,200
159th st, s s, 99.5 w 3d av, 61.2x98x29.10x96.3, two-story frame dwell'g. Josephine L. Peyton 7,360
Clinton av, w s, 200.4 s Jefferson st, 18.8x150, vacant. T. B. Fogg 2,450
Bristow st, w s, 215 s Jennings st, 20x100, vacant. Maria L. Emra 580
Chisholm st, junction Stebbins av, triangular plot, vacant. J. Emra 850
Chisholm st, s e cor Freeman st, 28x55.6. Same 700
Samuel st, s e cor Mapes av, 75x188, vacant. Geo. Lockyer 2,580
Weeks st, u e cor 173d st, 45x100, vacant, Wm. Elliott 3,100
Road from Spuyten Duyvil to Kingsbridge, 50x60 to N., D. & P. M. R. R., x51x71 to beginning, two one and two-story frame buildings. David Stevenson 6,000

R. V. HARNETT & CO.

8th st, No. 219, n s, 254.2 w 2d av, 25.1x102.2, four-story brown stone flat. Mrs. John Kelly 17,000
*90th st, No. 58, s s, 200 e 5th av, 25x100.8, four-story brk dwell'g. Francis P. Furnald et al. Wm. Kennelly 20,000
*120th st, Nos. 314-308, s s, 125 w 8th av, 75x100.11, three five-story brk flats. John C. Overhiser. (Amt due $28,469) 17,680
1st av, Nos. 620-652 s e cor 36th st, runs east 150 x south 98.9 x west 25 x south 49.4 x west 125 to 1st av, x north 148.1 to beginning, six-story brk malt house and two-story frame and brk stables. Ambrose K. Ely 86,000

A. H. MULLER & SON.

130th st, No. 14, s s, 193.7 w Madison av, 16.4x99.11, three-story brk dwell'g. Simpson Tolan. (Amt due $11,368) 12,800
Lexington av, No. 463, e s, 40 n 45th st, 20x70.6, four-story brk dwell'g. G. B. Ashley. (Amt due $17,900) 18,000
8th av, No. 2609, s w cor 139th st, 19.11x75.4, five-story brk flat and store. C. A. Buhler. (Amt due $21,322) 29,750
8th av, Nos. 2605 and 2607, w s, 19.11 s 139th st, 40x75.4, five-story brk flat and store. E. A. Fiske. (Amt due $31,417) 33,000
8th av, Nos. 2601 and 2603, adj, 40x75.4, five-story brk flat and store. Same. (Amt due $31,417) 33,550
8th av, Nos. 2597 and 2599, adj, 40x75.4, five-story brk flat and store. C. A. Buhler. (Amt due $31,417) 34,050
8th av, Nos. 2593 and 2595, adj, 40x75.4, five-story brk flat and store. Same. (Amt due $31,417) 34,000
8th av, No. 2591, n w cor 138th st, 19.11x75.4, five-story brk flat with store. Same. (Amt due $21,322) .... 33,9[illegible]

WM. KENNELLY.

*108d st, No. 208, s s, 118 w Amsterdam av, 20x75 to Clendenning lane, x20x76, five-story brk flat. Robt. C. Watson et al., exrs. (Amt due $17,483) 17,000
105th st, Nos. 210 and 212, s s, 100 w 10th av, 50x100.11, two five-story brk flats. V. A. Harper. (Amt due $6,649; prior morts $43,200) 48,700
Av C, No. 112, e s, 67 n 7th st, 18.3x82.5, three-story brk tenem't. H Osterweis 8,150
Av C, No. 110, e s, 43 9 n 7th st, 18.3x82.5, similar tenem't. M. Franklin 8,175

JOHN N. GOLDING.

Manhattan av, No. 507, n w cor 121st st, 20.11x90, three-story stone front dwell'g. D. A. Gaylord. (Amt due $5,074; prior morts, $12,500) 18,450

JOHN F. B. SMYTH.

Amsterdam av, e s, 50.5 s 115th st, 50.5x100, vacant. F. P. Forster 11,500
*West End av, No. 408, e s, 82.2 s 85th st, 20x80, four-story brk dwell'g. Wm. Morton et al. (Amt due $3,531) 25,900

SMYTH & RYAN.

Delancey st, No. 294, 25x100, five-story brown stone tenem't and stores. T. H. Wilcox 28,025

OTHER AUCTIONEERS.

Broome st, Nos. 2-14, n w cor Tompkins st, 125x75, five five-story stone front tenem'ts, store in No. 2. (Amt due $40,149.) Sold for $108,835 and re-sold the same day to R. B. Douglass Mfg. Co. for 87,835
23d st, No. 359, n s, 199 7 e 9th av, 25x98 9, four-story and basement brown stone dwell'g. (Bid in) .... —
64th st, No. 208, s s, 100 w 10th av, 25x100.5, five-story brk flat. Spencer Aldrich 18,887
*92d st, Nos. 139-149, n s, 245 e Amsterdam av, 105x100.8, six three-story stone front dwell'gs. H. Kertscher et al. (Amt due $4,306) 146,257
Madison av, Nos. 1742-1748, n w cor 115th st, 100.11x85, four five-story brk flats, store in No. 1742. John J. Bell. (Amt due $59,134) 88,858

Total $981,687
Corresponding week, 1890 .... $381,072

BROOKLYN, N. Y.

FOR WEEK ENDING DECEMBER 10.

*Columbia st, No. 85, e s, 40.6 s Warren st, 25.6x65.11x75.5½x67.5, four-story brk tenem't and store. Henry F. L. Hollrock $8,000
*Degraw st, No. 682, s s, 431.5 1-3 w 5th av, 19 2x100, three-story brk flat. Lyman D. Calkins 5,750
*Front st, No. 281, n s, 192 e Gold st, 18.9x100, three-story brk dwell'g. James Cornyn 2,000
*Berkimer st, No. 1320, s w cor Pleasant pl, 19x90, three-story brk dwell'g. Eliz. W. Aldrich 5,500
King st, Nos. 127-141, s s, 100 e Conover st, 200x100, two-story brk factory. W T. Ames 18,000
Kosciusko st, n s, 250 e Marcy Av, 150x100, vacant. (Bid in) .... —
*Macon st, No. 70, s s, 355 e Nostrand av, 20x100, three-story brk dwell'g. Jemima Thallon 11,825
Madison st, No. 1286, s s, 198 w Knickerbocker av, 18x100, two-story frame dwell'g. Charles V. Tily 8,100
*Pierrepont st, No. 61, n s, 129 e Hicks st, runs north 133.8½ to Love lane, x east 27 0½ x south 133.0½ to Pierrepont st, x west 27 to beginning three-story brk dwell'g. The Equitable Life Assurance Soc 20,000
Powell st, w s, 150 s Blake av, 100x100, two-and-a-half-story frame dwell'g and one-and-a-half-story frame stable on plot. C. W. O. Dreher 4,800
*Prospect pl, Nos. 748 and 750, s s, 250 e Rogers av, 33 4x100, three-story double brk flat. James H. Watson 7,334
*Roebling st, No. 113, e s, 75 n North 5th st, 25x100, two three-story frame tenem'ts on plot. William Journeay 8,000
Schermerhorn st, No. 355, n s, 100 w 3d av, 25x100, three-story frame dwell'g. Frank Audemars 8,000
*Vanderbilt st, s s, 437.5 e Short st, 12 6x108, Flatbush. Hannah C. McCracken 1,650
*Warren st, No. 96, s s, 70.3 e Columbia st, 27.9x71.10½, five-story brk tenem't and stores. Henry F. L. Hollrock 7,500
*Warren st, No. 98, s s, 98 e Columbia st, runs south 74.10½ x east 2.0 x south 24.11½ x east 25 x north 99 10 to Warren st, x west 27.9 to beginning, five-story brk tenem't and store. Same 7,500
*1st st, Nos. 272-278, s w s 305 n w 5th av, 81x100, three four-story double brk flats. C. E. Donnellon 13,360
*2d st, No. 477, n s, 150.9 w 7th av, 20x100, two-story brk dwell'g. Lyman D. Calkins 6,500
*2d st, No. 481, n s, 110.9 w 7th av, 20x100, two-story brk dwell'g. Wm L. Dowling 6,500
*2d st, No. 483, n s, 90 9 w 7th av, 20x100, two-story brk dwell'g. Same 6,500
50th st, No. 179, n s, 120 w 4th av, 20x100.2, two-story and basement frame dwell'g, unfinished. W. J. Conway 2,225
50th st, No. 177, n s, 140 w 4th av, 20x100.2, two-story and basement frame dwell'g, unfinished. Same 2,320
50th st, No. 179, n s, 160 w 4th av, 20x100.2, two story and basement frame dwell'g, unfinished. Lawrence McGrath 2,530
*Bushwick av, n w cor Willoughby av, 22x3 x 15, vacant, all right, title and int. Louis Totans 5
De Kalb av, s s, 250 e Marcy av, 150x100, two three-story frame dwellings. (Bid in) .... —
Marcy av, n w cor Kosciusko st, 50x100, vacant. (Bid in) .... —
*Prospect av, No. 313, n s, 110 5 w Webster pl, 18.5x80, two-story frame dwell'g. John S. Griffith 1,050
*St. Marks av, No. 283, n s, 100 w Underhill av, 25x131, four-story brk dwell'g. William L. Culbert 7,500
*Throop av, No. 547½, e s, 42.1 s Hancock st, 19 6½x81, four-story brk flat. The American Baptist Home Mission Society 9,000
*Willoughby av, No. 220, s s, 25 w Steuben st, 20x80, three-story brk flat. John Mitchell 7,250
Willoughby av, No. 687, n s, 125 e Throop av, 50x120, four-story brk dwell'g. (Bid in) .... —
6th av, s w cor Pacific st, runs south along 6th av 142.6 x west 125 x north 32.6 x east 25 x north 110 to Pacific st, x east 100 to beginning, three-story brk factory. Joseph B. Colyer 46,000

Total $221,699
Corresponding week 1890 .... $98,010

CONVEYANCES

Wherever the letters Q. C., C. a. G. and B. & S occur, preceded by the name of the grantee they mean as follows:

1st—Q. C. is an abbreviation for Quit Claim deed, i. e., a deed in which all the right, title and interest of the grantor is conveyed, omitting all covenants or warranty.

2d—C. a. G. means a deed containing Covenant against Grantor only, in which he covenants that he hath not done any act whereby the estate conveyed may be impeached, charged or encumbered.

3d—B. & S. is an abbreviation for Bargain and Sale deed, wherein, although the seller makes no express covenants, he really grants or conveys the property for a valuable consideration, and thus impliedly claims to be the owner of it.

NEW YORK CITY.

DECEMBER 4, 5, 7, 8, 9, 10.

Allen st, No. 187, w s, 100 n Stanton st, 25x87.6, three-story frame (brk front) tenem't. John Koell to Philip Kotlowsky and Barnet Levy. Dec. 7. $16,070

Allen st, No. 185, w s, 75 n Stanton st, 25x75, three-story brk tenem't. Philip Kotlowsky to Barnet Levy. B. & S. ½ part. Mt. ½ of $10,000. Dec. 8. 6,875

Bayard st, No. 35, s s, 94.6 e Bowery, 20x49.9, three-story brk tenem't. Barney Isaacs to George Blume. Mt. $9,500. Dec. 4 15,000

Baxter st, No. 38, w s, 87.11 s Leonard st, 17.6x90.
Baxter st, No. 40, w s, 70.3 s Leonard st, 17.6x90.
Two six-story brk stores and tenem'ts with two six-story brk tenem'ts on rear.
Joseph Kassel to Abraham Kassel. Mt. $36,000. Dec. 9. 48,000

Boulevard, 122d st, 121st st — begins Boulevard, s e cor 122d st, runs east 325 x south 90.11 to former centre line of block, x west 200 x south 100 11 to 121st st, x west 125 to Boulevard, x north 191.10, vacant. Randolph Guggenheimer and Henry Clausen, Jr., to John G. Prague. Mt. $45,000. Dec 1. See Columbus av. 180,000

Bleecker st, Nos. 98 and 100. Agreement as to easement. Erastus E Marcy to Leo Schlesinger, Joseph F. and Jacob F. Cullman. July 10. nom

Central Park W. (8th av). Nos. 426-430, s w cor 103d st, 100 11x100, three five-story brk flats. James Stevenson, Boston, Mass., to Joseph O'Connor. Mt. $132,000. Oct. 17 nom

Delancey st, No. 315, s s, 50 w Goerck st, 25x75, five-story brk tenem't with stores. Benjamin Holmes to Frank V. McAllister. Mt. $15 000. Dec. 1 24,000

Division st, No. 243, s s, 46 w Montgomery st, 23x48.6, six-story brk store and tenem't. Morris Weinstein and Morris Margovitz to Morris Jacobson. Mt. $16,000. Dec 1 11,'00

Downing st, Nos. 63-67, n s, 91.3 e Varick st, runs north 39.3 x north 51.6 x east 49.7 x south 90 to st, x west 64.7, two five-story brk tenements with stores. Frank B Treiber to William W. Flannagan. Mt. $50,000. Feb. 25. 110,000

Eldridge st, No. 55, w s, abt 100 s Hester st, 25.2x101x25x101, five-story brk tenem't with stores. John V. Campbell to Therese Wolf. Mt. $27,500. Dec. 8. 45,500

Front st, No. 202, n w s, abt 25 n e Fulton st, 23.8x73.11x24.2x73.11, five-story brk store. Eliza L. and James L. Arcularius exrs. Andrew M. Arcularius to George E. Chisolm. Nov. 24. 24,000

Henry st, No. 28, s s, abt 150 e Catharine st, 25x100, three-story brk tenem't. William Hodge et al exrs Eliza Hodge to Ascher Weinstein. Dec. 2 21,000

Same property. Ascher Weinstein to Joseph L. Buttenwieser. Mt. $12,000. Dec. 3. 22,000

Lewis st, Nos. 91-95, w s, 50 s Stanton st, 72.4x100, three five-story brk tenem'ts. Jonas Weil and Bernhard Mayer to Aaron and Barnett Levy and Sophia Gruenstein. Mt. $60,000. Dec. 4. 99,650

Lewis st, No. 93, w s, 74.1 s Stanton st, 24.1x100, five-story brk tenem't. Aaron and Barnett Levy and Sophia Gruenstein to Solomon Feinberg. ½ part. Mt. $26,250. Dec. 4. nom

Lewis st, No. 95, w s, 50 s Stanton st, 24.1x100, five-story brk tenem't. Same to same. ½ part. Mt. $24,000. Dec. 4. nom

Lewis st, No. 107, w s, 140 n Stanton st, 20x100, five-story brk store and tenem't with three-story brk tenem't on rear. Henry Schoen to Adolph Gross and Samuel Harris. Mt. $10,000. Dec. 1. 17,200

Lewis st, No. 111, w s, 180 n Stanton st, 20x100, five-story brk store and tenem't with three-story brk tenem't on rear. Pinkus Gaus to Joseph Newburg. Mt. $13,400. Dec. 1. See 98th st. 20,500

Market st, No. 28, Henry st, Nos. 62-66 — begins Market st, s w cor Henry st, 25x abt 115, six-story brk tenem't with stores. Michael Fay and William Stacom to Jacob Rieser. Mt. $47,000. Nov. 30. 80,000

Monroe st, No. 258, s s, 200 w Jackson st, 25x half the block, three-story brk tenem't. Mary E. Quick to William, George W. and Henry Dusenbury. Q. C. Nov. 12, 1887. nom

Same property. Elizabeth Dusenbury, Emma D. Frederick and Pauline D. Walker to same. Q. C. Oct 31, 1887. nom

Monroe st, No. 73, n s, abt 110 w Pike st, 25x100, three-story brk school. Daniel E. Sickles late Sheriff to Adolph Koppel. Deed on execution. Oct. 12. 200

Park row formerly Chatham st, s s, lot 113 map Mayor, &c., New York, 35.6x64 6. Assign. lease. Mary T. Morss et al. exrs. and trustees John Morss to Mary W. Woodruff and Julia R. Southack formerly Woodruff extrx. and trustees Marcus P. Woodruff. Dec. 2. 7,000

Park st, No. 87, s s, abt 100 w Pearl st, 25x93 1x25x93, six-story brk store and tenem't with six-story brk tenem't on rear.
Park st, No. 89, s s, abt 75 w Pearl st, 25x95, six-story brk tenem't with six-story brk tenem't on rear.
Aaron Levy to Herman Fichter and Louis Gordon. 1-6 part. Mt. on whole premises $40,000. Nov. 30. 3,100

Pearl st, No. 379, n w s, 106.6 n e Hague st, 20.11x65.3x39.8x97.6, five-story brk store. Joel W. Mason to James Sullivan. Dec. 1. 25,000

Renwick st, Nos. 32-39, w s, 131.4 s Spring st, runs west 36.2 x south 8.3 x northwest 28.4 x west 1, x northwest — x south 69 x east 5 x south 25.4 x east 70 to st, x north 72 8, four-story brk stable. Horace K. Thurber to Annie A., George R., Edward C. and John T. Smith. Mt. $30,000. Dec. 2 60,000

Sheriff st, Nos. 91 and 93, w s abt 100 s Stanton st, 50x100, two six-story brk tenem'ts with stores. Elijah C. Keys exr. Charles C. Keys to Elias Jacobs. Nov. 30. 50,000

Sheriff st, No. 87, w s, abt 175 s Stanton st. 25x100, five-story brk tenem't Louis W. Prager and Sarah wife of Oscar Dobroczynski to Morris and Joseph Glass. Mt. $27,750. Dec. 10. 36,500

St. Nicholas pl or New av, e s (first east of 9th av), 464 8 s 155th st, 25x100, vacant. William Gully to Anne Gully. Dec. 10. nom

Water st, No. 180, Burling slip, Nos. 4-10 — begins Water st, west cor Burling slip, 26x88.6x31x88.8, with ½ of strip adj on rear or northwest side 1x31, four-story brk stores. Marcus Oppenheimer to Mathias Rosenshine. ½ part. Mt. $30,000. Dec. 5. 20,000

Waverley pl, No. 174, w s, abt 75 n Christopher st, 21.4x85, three-story brk tenem't. James W. Ketcham to Dora D. Kesner. Mt. $10,000. Dec. 7. nom

West st, No. 120, s e s, 3d lot, being abt 55 s w Dey st, 20x72x20x75, five-story brk store. William Buck, Hoboken, N. J., to John W. Love. Dec. 7. nom

Worth st, No 104, s s, 225 3 e Broadway, 25x80.2, five-story iron front store. Lorillard Spencer, Newport, R. I., to Marshall Field, Chicago, Ill. Mt. $40,000. Dec. 4. 80,200

4th st, No. 345, n s, 168 w Av D, 24x96, three-story brk tenem't. Thomas C. Smith to the Church of St. Elizabeth of Hungary. B. & S. Dec. 8. 7,500

10th st, No 261, n s, 344 w Av A, 25x94.8, five-story brk tenem't with stores. Annie wife of Samuel Rosenthal to Jacob Wiebe and Magdalena Kndholz. ½ part. Sub. to ½ of morts $28,000. Dec 10. 17,500

Same property. David Leventritt to same. ½ part. Mt. ½ of $23,000. Dec 10. 17,500

13th st, No. 506, s s, 100 w Av A, 24.8x103.3, four-story brk tenem't with stores and four-story brk tenem't on rear. Julius, William and Margaretha Schmidt to Mary Bier. Mt $8,500. Dec. 1. See 69th st. 14,000

13th st, No. 623, s s, 293 e Av B, 25x103.3, five-story brk tenem't with four-story brk tenem't on rear. Anna C. Storner to Henry Oberscheimer. Mt. $14.500. Dec. 7. 18,750

16th st, Nos. 514 and 516, s s, 220.6 e Av A, 50x103 3, two five-story brk stores and tenem'ts with two-story brk building on rear of No 514 and three-story brk building on rear of No. 516. David Lion to Max Lion. ½ part. Mt. ½ of $34.000. Dec. 4. 22,000

16th st, Nos. 331 and 333, n s 350 w 8th av, 50x92, two and three-story brk and frame dwellings. Theodore Van Eupen to William H. Schaefer. Mt. $25,000 and encroachments. Dec. 4. 100

18th st, No. 404, s s, 94 e 1st av, 25x93, four-story brk tenem't. Mt. $7,000.
18th st, No. 414, s s, 219 e 1st av, 25x92, five-story brk tenem't with stores Mt $8,000.
Mary F. wife of Joseph S. Judge to Samuel Kempner. Nov. 24. 34,200

20th st, No. 212, s s, 179 4 w 7th av, 25x83.11x25x83.8, three-story brk store and tenem't with three-story brk tenem't on rear. William Lederer to Lizzie and Millie Lederer and Annie Klee. ½ part. Dec. 3. 3,000

20th st, No. 114, Gramercy Park, No. 13 — being 20th st, s s, 283.4 e 4th av, 26 8x114, four-story brk dwell'g. William J. Studwell to Frank Pettit, Brooklyn. Mt. $30,000. July 21. nom

26th st, No. 315 E., n s, abt 225 e 2d av, 25x98.9, three-story brk store and tenem't with one and two-story brk and frame buildings on rear James Kenny trustee Catharine E. Smith to Catharine E Keegan formerly Smith. C. a. G. Nov. 23. nom

26th st, No. 107, n s, 120 10 e 4th av, 20.10x98.9, three-story brk dwell'g. William Man trustee Bessie L. Rodman dec'd and Jacob L. and Julia E. Rodman. Louise De L. Fredricks and Mary S. Fehr heirs Bessie L. Rodman to Isaac Rodman. Confirmation deed. Nov. 18. 16 500

Same property. Isaac Rodman to Thomas J. Colton. *Mt.* $10,000. Dec. 4. 20,500

34th st } begins 34th st, n w cor 5th av, 150x
5th av } 111.9.
34th st, No. 1, n s, 150 w 5th av, 25x98.9.
35th st, s s, 150 w 5th av, 25x98 9.
34th st, s s, 137.6 w Madison av, 37.6x98.9.
4th av } begins 4th av, w s, extends from 32d
32d st } to 33d st, 197.6x205.
33d st }
Broadway } begins Broadway, n e cor Prince
Prince st } st, 277x200 to Crosby st, x— to
Crosby st } Prince st, x200.
9th st, No. 222, s s, 287 w 2d av, 21x75.
Bleecker st } begins Bleecker st, s w cor
Sullivan st } Thompson st, runs south 135
Thompson st } x west 100 x south 13 x west 100 to Sullivan st, x north 148 to Bleecker st, x east 200.
Bleecker st, No. 136, s s, 25 e South 5th av, 25x100.
Bleecker st, No. 170, s w cor Sullivan st, 25x98.
Bleecker st, Nos. 110-116 } begins Bleecker st,
Greene st, No. 179 } s s, 75 e Wooster st, runs south 100 x east 125 to w s Greene st, x north 25 x west 25 x north 75 to Bleecker st, x west 100.
Bleecker st, Nos. 115 and 117, n s, 50 e Wooster st, 50x100.
Bleecker st, No. 132, s s, 75 e South 5th av, 25 x100.
South 5th av, No. 39, e s, 25x100.
South Washington sq, No. 45, being 4th st, s s, 125 e Macdougal st, 25x112.
4th st, No. 50, s s, 20 e Wooster st, 20x56.
3d st late Amity st, Nos. 37, 39 and 41 } begins
Wooster st } 3d st, n e cor Wooster st, runs north 152.8 x east 112.9 x south 50 x east 37.3 x south 102.8 to Amity st, x west 150.
22d st, No. 483, n s, 78.8 e 10th av, 15.8x98.9.
33d st, No. 247, n s, 118.4 w 2d av, 18.4x98.9.
30th st, No. 319, n s, 216.8 e 2d av, 19.5x98.9.
Morton st, Nos. 53, 55 and 57 } begins Morton
Commerce st, Nos. 46 and 48 } st, n s, 175 e
Barrow st, No. 77 } Hudson st, runs east 75 x north 100 x east 22.6 x north 33.6 to Commerce st, x west along same 6.7 to angle in said st, x north 20 x west 55.8 x north 80 to Barrow st, x west 25 x south 200.
Lafayette pl, No. 7, w s, 27.4x98.
Reade st, No. 11, s s, 25x75.7.
Elm st, Nos. 11, 13 and 15, s e cor Duane st, 61.1x54.2x48x56.
Duane st, Nos. 48 and 50, s w s, 102 s e Elm st, 35x55x24x61.7.
Reade st, Nos. 6-12 } begins Reade st, n e cor
Elm st, Nos. 1-9 } Elm st, runs east 130 x north 76 1 x west 29 8 x north 25.6 x west 100.4 to Elm st, x south 102.6.
Centre st, Nos. 33-41 } begins Centre st, north
Duane st, Nos. 41-51 } cor Duane st, runs north 97.1 x northwest 65.8 x south 24.2 x west 27.11 x south or southwest 58 to Duane st, x southeast 146.8.
Crosby st, No. 119 } begins Crosby st, s e s,
Marion st, No. 86 } 188 2 n e Prince st, 21.11 x84 to Marion st, x19x84.
Pearl st, No. 549, s w s, 25x100.
8th st, n s, 72.3 w 4th av, 77.6x65.3x74.10x60.
4th av, Nos. 80 and 82, w s, 55.1 n 10th st, 50 x92.
New York to White Plains road, n s, farm abt 144 acres; also property in towns of Harrison, Saratoga Springs, N. Y., Hempstead, Hyde Park, Bethpage and Oyster Bay, L. I., and railroad in Queens Co., L. I.
Anna C. and Emma A. Clinch to Rosalie, Helen C., Virginia, Prescott H. and Maxwell E. Butler and Lilian L. Swann. All title. April 10. gift

35th st, No. 107 E., n s, abt 123 e Park av, four-story stone front dwell'g. Contract James J. K. Hackett with William E. Dodge. Dec. 5. 33,000

37th st, Nos. 208 and 210, s s, 120.10 w 7th av, 41.8x60, two four-story brk stores and tenements. George G. Jackson and Robert Tag to Isaac K. Cohn. *Mt.* $20,000. Dec. 10. 30,250

39th st, s s, 325 w 10th av, 25x98.9. Release dower. Emilie Schellenberg widow to Helena Undutsch. Dec. 8. nom

40th st, n s, 80 w 2d av, runs west 75 x north 98.9 x east 80 x south 38.9 x west 5 x south 60 to beginning. Release mort. Rebecca S. Schaper to Hermine Cloherty and Herman A. Emilie, Herman G. and Augusta B. Droge. Oct. 30. nom

41st st, No. 48, s s, 165 e Madison av, runs south to centre block, x east 20 x north to 41st st, x west —, four-story brk stable. Ellen King widow to Amelia King admrx, will annexed and trustee of Joseph King dec'd. B. & S. *Mt.* $15,000. Oct. 11, 1889. nom

41st st, No 201, n s, 60 w 7th av, 20x59.3, four-story brk dwell'g. Jacob Herman to Michael J. Cunniff. *Mt.* $12,000. Dec. 10. nom

45th st, No. 608, s s, 141.8 w 11th av, 16.8x100.5, three-story brk dwell'g. Catarine Diercks widow to The Consolidated Gas Co., New York. Dec. 7. 6,600

46th st, No. 548, s s, 175 e 11th av, 25x100.5, three-story frame factory. John and Robert Martin to Elizabeth Vannett. Q. C. Dec. 2. 1,000

48th st, Nos. 638-648, s s, 525 w 11th av, 150x100.5, four-story brk moulding mill and one-story frame stable, sheds, &c. Foreclos. Herman W. Vanderpoel to Henry E. Stevens. Dec. 9. 19,500

51st st, No. 242, s s, 160 w 2d av, 20x100.5, four-story stone front dwell'g. Hannah Loewenberg to Flora Loewenberg. *Mt.* $10,550. Oct. 19. 10,750

52d st, No. 110, s s, 180 w 6th av, 20x76.9x20.5x 80.5, four-story stone front dwell'g. Rutherford W. Forrest to Victoria A. J. Forrest. B. & S. June 25. gift

52d st, Nos. 423 and 425, n s, 300 w 9th av, 50x 100.5, two five-story stone front tenem'ts with stores in No. 425. William Wuerz to Simon Adler and Henry S. Herrman. *Mt.* $30,000. Nov. 20. See Columbus av. 60,000

59th st, No. 547, n s, 200 e 11th av, 25x100.5.
59th st, Nos. 535 and 537, n s, 325 e 11th av, 50 x100.5.
Three four-story brk tenem'ts with stores.
Edith H. wife of and Robert S. Simons to Arthur Smith. Sub. to 3 morts. and foreclosures and costs, also taxes 1891. Dec. 7. 412

60th st, No. 59, n s, 150 e 9th av, 25x100.5, five-story brk flat. Samuel Love to Yellott D. Dechert. Dec. 2. See McCombs Dam road. 23d and 24th Wards. 47,000

61st st, No. 26, s s, 48 w Madison av, runs south 73.5 x east 14 x north 6 5 x east 9 x north 67 to st, x west 23, four-story brk dwell'g. Phineas C. Kingsland to Margaret S. Kingsland. C. a. G. Dec. 10. gift

61st st, No. 103, n s, 366 w Lexington av, 19x80, four-story stone front dwell'g. Henry or Harry Deming, Honey Grove, Tex., to Charles E. Bigelow. Dec. 7. nom

61st st, No. 304, s s, 100 e 2d av, 25x100.11, two-story frame building with three-story frame tenem't on rear. Emil Lueneburg and Emil Busse to Andrew B. Yetter. *Mt.* $4,000. Dec. 8. 8,000

62d st, No. 121, n s, 175 e Park av, 16x70.6x16x 69.8, three-story stone front dwell'g. Frank V. McAllister to Raphael R. Govin. *Mt.* $5,-000. Dec. 4. 18,000

64th st, No. 61, n s, 46.6 w Park av, 14.3x73.5, four-story stone front dwell'g. Charles Myers to William L. Boyle. Nov. 16. 21,000

64th st, No. 404, s s, 106 e 1st av, runs south 67.1 x east 5 8 x south 8 x west 5.10 x south 5.4 to centre block, x east 25 x north 100.5 to st, x west 25, five-story brk cigar factory. Louis Honig to Max Strumpf. Q. C. Nov. 12. nom

Same property. Max Strumpf to Joseph Staog and Davis Hittner. *Mt.* $14,600. Nov. 12. 21,100

66th st, No. 46, s s, 100 e Madison av, 20x100 5, four-story stone front dwell'g. Sophie Magnan to Clementine M. Jefferds. B. & S. Nov. 14. nom

Same property. Edwin J. Jefferds to Sophie Magnan. Nov. 14. nom

66th st, Nos. 205-249 } begins 66th st, n
67th st, Nos. 206-220 } s, 125 w Amster-
67th st, Nos. 228-246 } dam av, runs
West End av, Nos. 42-52 } north 100.5 x west 25 x north 100.5 to 67th st, x west 200 x south 100.5 x west 75 x north 100.5 to 67th st, x west 250 x south 100.5 x west 25 x north 75 x west 100 to West End av, x south 150 x east 100 x south 25.5 to 66th st, x east 575, twenty-three five-story brk and stone tenem'ts on 66th st, eighteen five-story brk and stone tenem'ts on 67th st, and six five-story stone front stores and tenem'ts on West End av.
Amsterdam av, No. 142, w s, 25.5 n 66th st, 25x100, five-story stone front tenem't with stores.
Amsterdam av, No. 152, w s, 25.5 s 67th st, 25x100, five-story stone front tenem't with stores.
Robert Ritchie and Henry Henriksen to John Ruck. B. & S. All title. Dec. 4. nom

68th st, n s, 150 e Columbus av. Party wall agreement. Peter Wagner to John D. Crimmins. Nov. 2. nom

68th st, n s, 575 w Central Park West. Party wall agreement. Same to James R. Smith. Nov. 2. nom

69th st, No. 335, n s, 150 w 1st av, 25.1x100 5, four-story stone front tenem't. Mary Rier to William (⅓ part), Julius (⅓ part) and Margaretha (⅓ part) Schmidt. *Mt.* $17,000. Dec. 1. See 13th st. 22,250

69th st, n s, 200 w 8th av, 100x100.5, vacant. John P. Huggins to George C. and Thomas C. Edgar. Dec. 9. 60,000

70th st, No. 65, n s, 245 e Columbus av, 20x 100.5, four-story stone front dwell'g. George W. Ruddell to Pauline wife of Radcliffe Baldwin. Sub. to mort. $22,500. Dec. 10. 36,500

71st st, No. 87, n s, 30 e 9th av, 20x102.2, four-story stone front dwell'g. William H. Parsons, Jr., to George H. Stratton, Rye, N. Y. *Mt.* $17,500. Dec. 5. 34,500

73d st, No. 408, s s, 163 e 1st av, 25x102.2, five-story brk tenem't. Ruben Schloestein to Dorothea Schloestein his wife. Q. C. Dec. 4. nom

75th st, No. 421, n s, 322 w Av A, 25x102.2, one-story frame building on rear of lot. Ann Murray to Mary J. McFadden. B. & S. Dec 4. nom

76th st, n s, 200 e Columbus av, 5x102.2. John O. Baker to Alfred G. Nason. *Mt.* $3,600. Dec. 1. nom

70th st, n s, 205 e Columbus av, 45x102.2, vacant. Edward Oppenheimer and Isaac Metzger to Alfred G. Nason. Dec. 1. nom

76th st, n s, 200 e Columbus av, 5x102.2. Edward Oppenheimer and Isaac Metzger to John O. Baker, Newark, N. J. Dec. 1. nom

77th st, No. 423, n s, 369 w Av A, 25x102.2, one-story frame building on rear of lot. John Matthews, Jr., to Bernard McCabe. June 1, 1888. 1,500

79th st, No. 150, s s, 18 e Lexington av, 16x68, three-story stone front dwell'g. Harriet A. wife of Henry Baljer to Mary J. wife of Thomas P. Kelly. *Mt.* $12,000. Nov. 21. See 83d st. 20,000

80th st, No. 149, n s, 350 e Amsterdam av, 25x 102.2, four-story brk dwell'g. Augusta wife of and Emanuel Kising to Michael Giblin and James W. Taylor. Q. C. Dec. 10. nom

80th st, n s, 350 e Amsterdam av, 20 8x102.2. Michael Giblin and James W. Taylor to James Flanagan. Dec. 5. 30,500

83d st, No. 219, n s, 150 w Amsterdam av, 50x 102.2, two-story frame dwell'g with two-story frame building on rear. Thomas P. Kelly to Harriet A. Batjer. *Mt.* $13,500. Dec. 2. See 79th st. 23,500

83d st, No. 10, s s, 148 w 8th av, 17x102.2, three-story stone front dwell'g. James O'Brien to Thomas R. Hughes, Weehawken, N. J. Dec. 5. nom

Same property. Thomas R. Hughes to E. Clifford Potter. *Mt.* $15,000. Dec. 7. nom

88th st, Nos. 201-207, n w cor Amsterdam av, 100x102.2, four five-story brk flats, stores in No. 201. Frederick H Comstock to D. Willis James. *Mt.* $50,000. Feb. 20, 1891. 68,500

89th st, No. 352, s s, 97 w 1st av, 25.8x100.8, five-story brk tenem't. Franz Geyer to Jacob Gebhard and Emilie his wife, joint tenants. *Mt.* $10,000. Dec. 7. 20,000

90th st, No. 63, n s, 160.1 w 4th av, 18.6x100.8, three-story stone front dwell'g. Emily Beaver to Magdalena wife of Emil Waldenberger. *Mt.* $17,000. Nov. 25. 21,750

93d st, No. 29, n s, 413 e 9th av, 19x100.8, four-story brk dwell'g. George Stubbings to Patrick Cassidy and I. Richard Adler, of Cassidy & Adler. B. & S. *Mt.* $12,000. Dec. 1. nom

94th st, s s, 253 e Amsterdam av, 36x99.8 to Apthorps lane, x36x98.2. Release mort. John A. Gwynne to Walden P. Anderson. Dec. 3. nom

94th st, No. 244, s s, 107.6 w 2d av, 27.6x100.8, five-story brk tenem't. Lorenz J. Scheppert to Theresa wife of John Schappert. *Mt.* $15,000. Dec. 2. nom

94th st, No. 105, n s, 100 w 9th av, 25x100.8, five-story brk flat. Release mort. Jacob Korn to Francis J. Hillenbrand. Dec. 8. nom

Same property. Release mort. Same to same. Dec. 8. nom

Same property. Francis J. Hillenbrand to Joseph Schneider. Dec. 5. 30,000

95th st, Nos. 106 and 108, s s, 100 w Columbus av, 50x100.8, two five-story brk flats.
94th st, No. 107, n s, 125 w Columbus av, 25x 100.8, five-story brk flat.
Francis J. Hillenbrand to Elizabeth Hillenbrand. Dec. 5. 98,000

96th st, No. 62, s s, 160 e Columbus av, 20x100.8, four-story brk dwell'g. Isabella J. wife of Edward L. Foghill to Thomas C. Acton. *Mt.* $20,000. Dec. 4. nom

96th st, s s, 200 w Central Park West, 25x100.8, vacant. Henry A. and William B Crosby and M. Bayard Brown to Edward Kilpatrick. *Mt.* $8,750. Nov. 4. 12,000

97th st, No. 155, n s, 154 w 3d av, 17x100.11, five-story brk flat. E. Clifford Potter to James O'Brien. *Mt.* $14,000. Dec. 5. nom

97th st, n s, 100 w 2d av, 100x100.11, vacant. George A. and Theodore F. H. Meyer trustees, &c., to Anna Ch. Meyer, Southfield, S. I. B. & S. C. a. G. Oct. 1, 1889. nom

98th st, n s, 358 e Amsterdam av, 156x—. Agreement as to co-partnership. John W. Hutton to John Burke and Robert D. Wheeler. Dec. 3. nom

98th st, No. 220, s s, 310 e 3d av, 25x100.11, five-story brk tenem't. Joseph Newborg to Pinkus Gaus. *Mt.* $15,000. Dec. 1. See Lewis st. 25,500

102d st, No. 166, s s, 235 w 3d av, 20x100.11, four-story stone front tenem't. Florence Pomeroy to Francis H. Weeks. B. & S. June 26. 8,000

102d st, No. 162, s s, 265 w 3d av, 20x100.11, four-story stone front tenem't. Same to same. June 26. 9,950

107th st, s s, 325 w 1st av, 25x100.11, vacant. Charles Van Riper to Matthew Coogan. Dec. 1. 6,750

107th st, s s, 275 w 1st av, 50x100.11, vacant. Henrietta A. wife of Hugh H. Edwards, Castleton, S. I., to Matthew Coogan. Dec. 1. 13,500

107th st, No. 112, s s, 155 e Park av, 25x101.1, four-story stone front tenem't. Charles Kohler to Conrad Bormann. *Mt.* $11,000. Dec. 8. 15,000

107th st, s s, 250 w 1st av, 25x100.11, vacant. Kate F. Allen to Matthew Coogan. Taxes 1890 and 1891. Dec. 8. 6,750

112th st, No. 410 on map No. 408, s s, 145 e 1st av, 30x100.11, five-story brk tenem't with stores. Solomon A. Cohn and Frederick Milheiser to Nicholas and Maria Delleglio, each ⅓ part, and Francesco Micucci, ⅓ part. *Mt.* $16,000. Dec. 1. 30,000

114th st, No. 139, n s, 78 7 w Lexington av and being 573.7 w 3d av, 17.10x100.10, three-story frame dwell'g. Elizabeth Yglesias to Helena Maas. *Mt.* $4,500. Dec. 7. 9,000

114th st, s s, 209 w 5th av, 17.8x100.11. Release mort. Henry Franke, Brooklyn, to Margaret E. Conlon. Dec. 8. nom

Same property. Release mort. Stephen B. Sturges to Margaret E. Conlon. Dec. 8. 12,000

Same property. Release mort. Francis J. Conlon to same. Dec. 8. nom

115th st, s w cor Manhattan av, 25x100.11, vacant. Ellen Rhines to Isaac O. Rhines. B. & S. Dec. 10. nom

115th st, s s, 195 e 5th av, 50x100.11, vacant. George T. Jackson devisee George T. Jackson to Samuel M. Jackson. B. & S. C. a. G. Dec. 4. See 8th av, New York, and Sackett st also 3d av, Kings Co. conveys. exch

115th st, No. 338, s s. 175 w 1st av, 25x100.11, four-story brk tenem't with stores. John J. O'Connor to Samuel Kempner. Mt. $8,500. Dec. 7. 12,400

115th st, Nos. 21 and 23, n s, 200 w 5th av, 45x100.11, two five-story stone front flats. Adam Gebhardt to Joseph D. Mayer. Mt. $35,000. Dec. 3. 65,000

118th st, No. 269, n s, 225 e 8th av, 25x100.11, five-story brk flat. Hannah Gordon to Charles N. Rosetti. Mt. $21,000. Dec 1. 23,750

119th st, Claremont av { begins 119th st, s s, 9.4 w Claremont av and at w s Old Bloomingdale road, runs south along said old w s of road to line 300 s of 119th st, x east to Claremont av, x north along av to 119th st, x west —, vacant. Margaret D. Todd extrx. William J. Todd to Charles C. and Henry M. Taber. Dec. 8. 25

120th st, No. 304, s s, 100 e 2d av, 19.5x100.11, three-story stone front dwell'g. Foreclos. Thomas F. Donnelly to John G. Maeder. Dec. 7. 8,400

120th st. No. 137, n s, 277 e 7th av, 20x100.11, three-story stone front dwell'g. Release mort. Henry Weil to Edward T. Smith. Dec. 9. 1,000

Same property. Edward T. Smith to Jacob A. Cantor. Mt. $16,000. Dec. 10. 22,500

124th st, No. 120, s s, 215 e Park av, 25x100.11, two-story frame dwell'g. Sarah A. Tonks to Rosina B. McClellan. Correction and confirmation deed. Nov. 14. nom

125th st, Nos. 525–529, n s, 350 e Boulevard, 25x99.11, three five-story brk flats. Edward H. Van Ingen to William W. Buckley, Tenafly, N. J. Mt. $48,000. Oct. 13. See Intervale av. nom

127th st, No. 113, n s, 197 e Park av, 18x99 11, five-story brk flat. John Frame to James Miller. Mt. $13,000. Nov. 28. val. consid

128th st, Nos. 218–222, s s, 225 w 7th av, 100x99 11, three four-story brk flats. Charles E. Runk to C. C. John Grohmann. Mt. $73,000. Dec. 5. exch

129th st, No. 249, n s, 481.3 w 7th av, 18.9x99.11, three-story brk dwell'g. Minnie T. Shelton to Catherine Rapelyea. Dec. 4 nom

132d st, Nos. 26–30, s s, 235 w 5th av, 100x100.11, three five-story brk flats. Foreclos. George B. Newell to Margaret T. or F. Nally. Nov. 28. 5,000

133d st, No. 12, s s, 185 w 5th av, 25x99.11, five-story brk flat. Martin H. Simonson to Mary McManus. Mt. $19,000 and 6 months int., also tax 1891 and mechanic's lien $115. Dec. 10. nom

142d st, s s, 100 w 8th av, 50x99.11, two-story frame building and vacant. William N. Crane to George H. Schaefer. Dec. 3. 12,000

143d st, Edgecombe av { begins 143d st, centre line if continued, 400 w 8th av, runs north 124.6 to centre of Old road now closed, x northeast 7 x west to point 406 w 8th av, x south — x west to Edgecombe av, x south 92 to centre 143d st if continued, x east —, vacant. Edmund Coffin, Jr., to Frederick Grasmuck. Nov. 13. 7,000

143d st, Bradhurst av { begins 143d st, n s, at intersection with New av, 361.10 w 8th av, runs north 100.6 x west 41.2 to old road, x southwest 7 x south 124.6 to centre 143d st, x east 34.3 to w s New av, x north 30.2, one story frame building and vacant. Thomas P. Mitchell guard. of Adrian T. Keernan to Frederick Grasmuck. Infant's share. Dec. 7. 200

146th st, No. 267, n s, 175 e 8th av, 25x99.11, five-story brk flat. Sophia A. Van Demark to William J. Gilmore. Mt. $16,000. Dec. 5. nom

Same property. William J. Gilmore to Thomas Loughran. Mt. $16,000. Dec. 3. exch. and 1,000

151st st, n s, 425 e Amsterdam av, 50x99.11, vacant. Michael H. Cashman to Philip Schaefer. Dec. 9. 10,500

184th st, s s, 125 e 11th av, 75x71.5x68 11x68.10. Henry I. Harris to John C. Klett and Hugo E. Distelhurst. Mt. $3,000. Dec. 2. 6,300

Av A, Nos. 1008 and 1010, e s, 25.5 s 55th st, 50x80, two five-story brk tenem'ts. Emma wife of Henry M. Haar, Anna wife of William Forster, Ida wife of Martin H. Hartmann and heirs Susanna Kress to The John Kress Brewing Co. B. & S. and C. a. G. Dec. 1. consid. omitted

Av B, n e cor 10th st. Party wall agreement. Margaret Kahrs, Rebecca Rubnstuck, Sophie, Dora and Harry Bammann to Henry Guntzlinger and George Bub. Aug. 31. nom

Av C, No. 115, w s, 78.7 n 7th st, 19.2x63x18.11x63, three-story brk store and tenem't. Adolph Simon to Joseph Heilbrunn. Mt. $5,000. Nov. 20. 13,200

Amsterdam av, Nos. 722–726, w s, 25.8 n 95th st, 75x89.5x75x86, three five-story brk flats with stores.
95th st, Nos. 203 and 205, n s, 86 w Amsterdam av, 54.6x100.8, two five-story brk flats.
Annie C. wife of Andrew T. Doyle to Sarah Sweeney. Q C. Dec. 7. nom

Columbus av, Nos. 520–526, 85th st, No. 101 { begins Columbus av, n w cor 85th st, runs west 155 x north 102.2 x east 50 x north 2.2 x east 60 x south 6 10 x east 45 to av, x south 97.6, six-story brk flat with stores. John G. Prague to Randolph Guggenheimer and Henry Clausen, Jr. Sub. to morts. Dec. 1. See Boulevard. 433,000

Columbus av, Nos. 201–209, n e cor 69th st, 100.5x70.8, three five-story brk flats with stores. Simon Adler and Henry S. Herrman to William Wuerz. Mt $80,000. Dec. 1. See 52d st. 136,770

Lexington av, No. 135, s e cor 29th st, 23.4x80, four-story brk (stone front) dwell'g. Lewis Z. Bach to James W. Ketcham. Mt. $22,000. Dec. 4. 33,500

Lexington av, No. 1618, w s, 34.7 s 102d st, 16.7x75, three-story brk dwell'g. Thomas H. Leard to Bertha Hart. Mt. $6,300. May 12, 1891. 8,500

Madison av, s w cor 98th st, 100.11x94.6x100x93, one-story frame building. Theodore F. Miller et al. exrs. John B. Hillyer to Frederick W. Sauer, George Herbener and Conrad R. Gross, joint tenants. Dec. 1. 31,500

Madison av, No. 1309, e s, 40.4 s 93d st, 20x74, three-story stone front dwell'g. Walter Reid to Herman F. Nordeman. Mt. $17,000. Dec. 10. nom

Madison av, No 780, w s, 79 5 n 66th st, 21x80, four-story stone front dwell'g. Victoria Chubb widow to William L. Boyle. Dec. 10. 40,000

Madison av, w s, 15.8 s 78th st, 15.2x74. Satisfaction of mort. Sarah J. Kerny to George D. Bleything. Dec 7. 9,000

Madison av, No. 1008, w s, 15.8 s 78th st, 15.2x74, four-story stone front dwell'g. Sarah I. Kearney to Maria H. Bleything. Mt. $16,000. Dec 7. 30,000

Manhattan av, No. 399, w s, 55.11 s 117th st, 18x50, three-story stone front dwell'g. Thomas J. Reilly individ. and trustee to Michael J. Larkin. Mt. $8,000. Dec. 7. 13,000

Wadsworth av, w s, 71.2 n 187th st, 23.9x95. Release mort. Michael H. Cashman to Luke O'Brien. Oct. 10. nom

Same property. Luke O'Brien to Morris P. Altman. Oct. 12. 7,250

West End av, n e cor 104th st, 100.11x100, vacant.
104th st, n s, 100 e West End av, 50x100.11, vacant
Donald Mitchell to David Christie. Mt. $27,500. Dec. 3. 79,000

West End av, s e cor 80th st, 102.2x100.
80th st, s s, 100 e West End av, 50x102.2.
Release dower. Sarah L. Kobbe widow to Susannah P. Lilienthal, Yonkers, N. Y. Nov. 25 150

Same property. Same to same. Q. C. Nov. 25. nom

1st av, No. 2329, w s, 50.5 n 119th st, 25x100, three-story brk dwell'g. Julia A. wife of and Frederick Frank to James P. Marren. Dec. 4. 11,000

1st av. No. 2319, w s, 50.5 n 119th st, 25x100, five-story brk tenem't with stores. Margaretta A. Westervelt, Jersey City, to James P. Marren and Ellen his wife, joint tenants. Mt. $8,000. Dec. 7. nom

Same property. James P. Marren to Margaretta A. Westervelt, Jersey City. Mt. $8,000. Dec. 7. nom

2d av, n w cor 40th st, 39.8x75x38.9x75. Release mort. George F. Westfall and ano. exrs. Diederich Westfall to Hermine Cloherty and Herman A., Emilie, Herman G. and Augusta B Droge. Dec. 7. 4,000

2d av, Nos. 747 and 749, n w cor 40th st, 39.8x75, two four-story brk stores and tenem'ts.
40th st, Nos. 237–241, n s, 75 w 2d av, 80x98.9, several one and two-story frame and brk buildings.
79th st, No. 179, n s, 112 w 3d av, —x102x22x102, three-story stone front dwell'g.
Partition. J. F. C. Blackhurst to Hermine Cloherty. Dec. 4. 95,550

6th av, No 886, 50th st, No. 74 { begins 6th av, s e cor 50th st, 25.4x106.5x25.4x107, four-story brk store and tenem't on av and four-story stone front dwell'g on st. Margaret wife of Theodore L. Maxwell and Annie wife of Andrew Pfirrmann heirs John F. Boronowsky to Margaret Boronowsky. B. & S. C. a. G. Dec. 3. gift

Same property. Margaret Boronowsky widow to Margaret wife of Theodore L. Maxwell and Annie wife of Andrew Pfirrmann heirs John F. Boronowsky. Dec. 4. gift

7th av, No. 2009, e s, 67 10 n 120th st, 16.1x77, three-story brk dwell'g. Sarah wife of George Adam to Charles S. Crossman. Mt. $12,000. Dec. 2. See Monroe st; also, Pennsylvania av, Kings Conveys exch

7th av, Nos. 1968–1974, s w cor 119th st, 100.11x100, four five-story brk flats, store in No. 1974. Benjamin F. Beekman, Hoboken, N. J., to Henry P. De Graaf. Mt. $106,000. Dec 4. See Amsterdam av, also Teasdale pl, 23d Wards, in last issue. nom

8th av, No. 643, w s, 24.9 n 41st st, 24.3x80, three-story brk store and tenem't.
11th st, No. 227, formerly Hammond st, No. 23, n s, 99.9 w Waverley pl, runs north 12 x north 40 x east 0.6 x north 45 x west 19.10 x south 45 x west 0.6 x south 40 x south 12 x east 19 11, three-story brk dwell'g.
11th st, No 229, formerly Hammond st, No. 25, n s, 119.9 w Waverley pl, runs north 12 x north 40 x east 0.6 x north 45 x west 19.8 x south 45 x west 0.6 x south 40 x south 12 x east 20.1, three-story brk dwell'g.
Nathan H. Rice and Julie Oppenheim to Auguste Rice June 4. nom

8th av, No. 777, w s, 50 n 47th st, 25x100, five-story stone front store and flat. George T. Jackson to Samuel M. Jackson. Mt. $25,000. Dec. 4. See 115th st, New York, and Sackett st also 3d av, Kings Co. Conveys. exch

Lots 88 and 89 map property 12th Ward of Samuel F. Bartol, 50x99.11x—x67, with all right to Kingsbridge road on rear, except portion taken for Coogan av. Mary J. Burns formerly Mitchell, Bridget A. and John Mitchell heirs Mary Mitchell and Ann Mitchell widow to Frederick Grasmuck. C. a. G. Q. C. Nov. 27. 800

Same property. Michael Mitchell heir John Milan, San Francisco, Cal., to Mary J. Mitchell. C. a. G. Q. C. Sept. 15, 1890. nom

MISCELLANEOUS.

All real estate and title in estate of Thomas C. Chalmers dec'd. Agreement charging contingent int. to extent of $1,700. Thomas C. Chalmers to Joseph F. Stier. Dec. 7. nom

Assignment of legacy under will of Peter Gillespie. Rose or Rosa Rossiter or Rosater to Mary Rossiter or Rosater. Aug. 8. nom

General release. Serofina M., Jona or Zona, Carmela De Matteo, Pietro Cellano and Giovanni Avato to Pietro Cellano and Giovanni Avato. Dec. 10. nom

General release and release dower in estate of George F. Michael dec'd. Hannah Michael widow to Caroline Michael individ and admrx. George F., Michael and Caroline E. Tessier and generally. Dec. 4. nom

General release and release of exr. Daniel Hogencamp. Mary E. Campbell to John McWilliam exr. Daniel Hogencamp. Nov. 30. 44

General release and especially as to estate of Peter Gillespie. Carrie Kane to estate of Peter Gillespie. March 10. nom

Release legacy. Patrick Darragh to Rosa Gillespie extrx. Peter Gillespie. Feb. 9. 500

Release of legacy. Mary Rossiter to estate of Peter Gillespie. Dec. 3. 500

23d and 24th WARDS.

Arcularius pl, s s, 309.3 e Gerard av, runs south 177.8 x east 101 x north 57 3 x west 50 x north 100 x west 50. Thomas W. Surridge to John and Emma Barker. Dec. 1. 3,800

Clarke pl, Central av and Gerard av, conveys land comprising streets in front of lots 40–47 inclus. map of Inwood, &c. Julia M. Stebbins an heir of Julia Stebbins to William A. Chanler. Q. C. Dec. 8. 25

Cordova pl, w s, 63.4 s Van Courtlandt av, 25x101.4x25x101.3. Sophia A. Van Demark to William J. Gilmore. Mt. $225. Dec. 5. exch

Home or Lyon st, s s, 178 e Stebbins av, 16 4x80.9x17.6x87.2. Mary L. wife of Treffle H. Allard to Louis Rousseau. Mt. $4,645. Dec. 3. nom

Home or Lyon st, s s, 228 2 e Stebbins av, 24.10x58.6x26.7x68.1. Same to same. Mt. $1,675. Dec. 3. nom

Home or Lyon st, No 1074, s s, 211.1 e Stebbins av, 17.1x68.1x18x74.2. Same to Lizzie A. McCone. Mt. $2,645. Dec. 3. nom

Lorillard pl or st, w s, abt 113.9 n 187th st, runs west 100 x south 25 x east 100 x north —. Henry C. Thompson to Abigail A. Blackhurst. Mt. $3,500. May 1. 6,000

New Drive, e s, at south line of lot 8 map M. E. Putnam property, Spuyten Duyvil, runs north 100 x east 102 to Palisade av, x 100x95.10.
New Drive, w s, at s s lot 7 same map, runs north 102 x west 330 to New York Central & Hudson River R. R., x south 104 x east 305.4.
Margaret E. wife of and Albert E. Putnam to Jennie F. wife of Harold S. Desbrisay. Dec. 1. 9,500

Potter pl, n s, 25 e Villa av, 25x90x25x99.6. Thomas Wilson to Peter Helmus. Dec. 5. 500

Weeks st, e s, 100 n Warren st now 95 n 173th st, runs east — x south 25 x west to st, x north 25. Richard J. Barnecott to Denness Connell. Dec. 7. nom

Weeks st, w s, north ½ lot 11 map of Mount Hope, 24th Ward, 50x100. Frederic G. Ford, Philadelphia, to Henry Drescher. Q. C. Confirmation and correction deed. Dec. 6. nom

West st, s w s, lot 7 map Wardsville, 45x105.4x62.4x108. James Stroud to Lindsay Williamson. Dec. 3. 3,250

West st, s w s, lot 18 map Wardsville, 25x140x25x142. Charles Taylor to Thomas Taylor. Dec. 2. 1,000

132d st, n s, 225 w Cypress av, 75x175. Lyman H. Day to Francis E. Day. Q. C. June 15, 1878. nom

133d st, n s, 200 e Trinity av, 50x ½ block x—x—. T. Gaillard Thomas to Charles Hohl. Dec. 7. 3,000

134th st, s s, 150 w Alexander av, 25x100, h & l. M. Dasher Wylly, Bayonne, N. J., to Edward M. Scudder. C. a. G. *Mt.* $13,000. Dec. 4. nom

134th st, n s, 165 e from w s St. Anns av, 17x100. William Stevens to Christian F. Schane. *Mt.* $3,500. Dec. 7. 6,550

136th st, s s, 266 6 e Alexander av, 37.6x100. Foreclos. Daniel Dougherty to William H. Taubert. Dec. 7. 7,400

152d st, n s, 250 w Courtlandt av, 50x100. Foreclos. Thomas B. Clarkson to Hannah wife of Stephen S. Wills. Dec. 7. 4,600

153d st, n e cor Melrose av, 20x100. August Zehder to Henry Zehder. Dec. 5. nom

Same property. Henry Zehder to August and Regena Zehder. Dec. 5. nom

157th st, n s, 430.10 w Courtlandt av, 28x101.6. Maria A. Heyer widow, Chicago, Ill., to Elizabeth Neundorff. Nov. 20. 1,940

158th st, s s, 348.6 w Courtlandt av, 52.2x98.6x52.2x98.6. Maria A. Heyer, Chicago, Ill., to Moise Geismann. Nov. 20. 7,635

158th st, s s, 298.6 w Courtlandt av, runs south 200 to 157th st, x west 79 9 x north 101.6 x east 59.9 x north 98,6 to 158th st, x east 20. Same to Oscar L. Moser and Amelia his wife. Nov. 20. 810

158th st, s s, 318.6 w Courtlandt av, 40x98.6. Same to Jacob Rubsam. Nov. 20. 3,245

164th st, n s, 175 w Trinity av, 25x100. George E. Faile to Thomas O'Rorke. Nov. 28. 8,000

172d st, n s, 90 e Vanderbilt av, runs east 40 x north 130 x west 50 x south 30 x west 10 x south 100. Henry F. Fischer to Alfred F. Bertin. Dec. 9. 2,700

175th st, s s, 22 e Franklin av, 25x100. Mary E. wife of Charles V. Halley to Annie wife of Malachi Kelly. Dec. 3. 5,000

175th st, s s, 47 e Franklin av, 25x100. Same to same. Dec. 3. 2,000

Bathgate av, e s, 25 s 174th st, 25x100. Christina and Jessie (widow) Elder to Josephine L. Peyton. Dec. 2. 2,250

Bathgate av, e s, 100 s 174th st, 50x120. Henry F. Taylor to Josephine L. Peyton. Dec. 3. other consid. and 4,100

Berrian av, e s, or Webster av, proposed, e s, 24.9 n Southern Boulevard, runs southeast to a point 100 southeast Webster av, x north 150 x west crossing Webster av to Berrian av, x south — to beginning. Eliza Van Schaick to John J. Brady. Sept. 25. nom

Briggs av, s s, 125 w Suburban st, 50x110. A. Marshall Murray to Jane Wilson. Dec. 5. 2,000

Bergen av, n w s, 100 s w Rose st, 50x100. Anton Rinschler to Henrietta Katzenstein. Dec. 7. 10,000

Bremer av, w s, 27.11 s Devoe st, runs south 83.10 x northwest 100 x northeast 75 x southeast 37.6. Ann Riley widow to Albert Riley. All title. April 30. nom

Central av, w s, 135 n Gerard av, 25.3x115.7x25x111.9. Patrick F. Ferrigan et al. exrs. Hugh Ferrigan to Theresa wife of Robert Hughes. Nov. 28. 1,825

Central av, w s, 214.6 n Gerard av, 25.3x126.11x25x123.2. Same to same. Nov. 23. 1,825

Central av, w s, 164 n Gerard av, 25.3x119.4x25x115.7. Same to same. Nov. 23. 1,825

Central av, w s, 189 3 n Gerard av, 25.3x123.2x25x119.4. Same to same. Nov. 23. 1,825

Central av, w s, 113.7 n Gerard av, 25.4x111.9x25x1'8. Same to same. Nov. 23. 1,825

Central av, n w cor Gerard av, runs west 88.8 x north 15.3 x east 100 to Central av, x south 12.8 x south 80.7. Same to John Keirns. Nov. 23. 3,900

Central av, w s, 88.6 n Gerard av, 25.3x108x25x104.2. Patrick F. Ferrigan et al. exrs. Hugh Ferrigan to Mary T. Gallagher. Nov. 23. 2,425

Central av, w s. 63 3 n Gerard av, 25.3x104.2x25x100. Same to same. Nov. 23. 2,425

Courtlandt av, s e s, 62 n e 161st st, 56x65x50x90. John Rooney to Charles Wilker. Dec. 3. 4,350

Franklin av, e s, 145 s Jefferson st, 25x150. Edward B. Briggs, Jamaica, L. I., to Mary E. Briggs, New York. *Mt.* $1,500. Nov. 19. nom

Fulton av, s e cor 170th st, runs southeast 114.7 x southwest 109.11 x northwest 113.7 to av, x northeast 101.6. Julia A. Coyle to Thomas Simpson. *Mt.* $5,500. Dec. 4. val. consid

Gardner av, s s, full hundred (?) s e Orchard terrace, 50x100. Edward J. Hartman to Charlotte Hartman. Sept. 9. 250

Gerard av, n s, 88.8 w Central av, 28.4x—x25x90 3. Patrick F. Perrigan et al. exrs. Hugh Ferrigan to John Keirns. Nov. 23. 1,075

Gerard av, in front of lots 86-89 map Inwood. Allister G. Stebbins heir Julia Stebbins to Arthur Simonson. Q. C. Jan. 24, 1889. 25

Same property. Julia A. Stebbins heir Julia Stebbins to same, Brooklyn. Q. C. Oct. 24, 1888. 25

Same property. Julia M. Stebbins to same, East Orange, N. J. Q. C. Dec. 8. nom

Same property. Augustus Van C. Stebbins heir Julia Stebbins, Jersey City, N. J., to same, Brooklyn. Q. C. Nov. 14, 1889. 25

Intervale av, n w cor Home st, 158.6x159x— to st, x47. William W. Buckley, Tenafly, N. J., to Asa E. Collins, Linden, N. J. C. a. G. Dec. 1. See Union av. 3,000

Inwood av, e s, 54.11 n Gerard av, 25x112.6. Patrick F. Ferrigan et al. exrs. Hugh Ferrigan to Theresa wife of Robert Hughes. Nov. 23. 975

Inwood av, e s, 104.11 n Gerard av, 25x112.6. Same to same. Nov. 23. 975

Inwood av, e s, 29.11 n Gerard av, 25x112.6. Same to same. Nov. 23. 975

Inwood av, e s, 79 11 n Gerard av, 25x112.6. Same to same. Nov. 23. 975

Morris av, w s, original line, 50 n Buckhout st, 25x126 6x25x126.9. Joseph T. Bedford to Matilda L. Bedford. *Mt.* $1,000. Dec. 3. nom

Same property. Matilda L. Bedford to Anna H. Bedford. *Mt.* $1,000. Dec 3. nom

Prospect av, w s, 175 n Fairmount av, 25x100. Release mort. E. Burgess Warren, Philadelphia, Pa., to John Cotter and Winifred T. his wife. Nov. 25. 1,500

Same property. John Cotter to John S. Larmour. Nov. 28. 1,750

Riverdale av and centre line Babcock av, plots 11, 12, 22 and 23 map villa sites at Riverdale, 24th Ward, formerly of Joseph Rosenthal, begins at n e cor plot 34 on said map 100 n w Riverdale av as widened and 418.7 n of late A. Schermerhorn, runs northwest 149 6 to centre of Babcock av, x northeast along same to s s plot 31 same map, x northeast 121.8 x south to s s plot 13, x east 100 to w s Riverdale av, x south 100 x west 100 x south 126. Henry M. Bloch to Rose S. Bloch. ½ part. Dec. 8. 2,000

Stebbins av, e s, 313.4 n 165th st, 25x137.6x25.4x133.4, h & l. Charles Hellenday to George H. Lohsen. *Mt.* $600. Dec. 3. 4,000

Same property. George H. Lohsen to Johanna Hellenday. Dec. 3. consid. omitted

Sheridan av, e s, lots 233 and 234 map Inwood, 50x173.8x51.1x184.3. Kate O'Hara to Martin H. and Emma C. Simonson. Taxes $46. Dec. 8. exch

Union av, e s, 226.5 s Home (or Lyon) st, runs south 520.11 x east 175 x south 151 x east 175 to Prospect av, x north 216 x east 112.2 x north — x east 9.4 x northeast 340 x west 104.7 x north abt 120.2 to Home (or Lyon) st, x west 152 6 x south abt 275 x west 100. Asa E. Collins, Linden, N. J., to Edward H. Van Ingen. Sub. to mort. $50,000. Dec. 1. exch

Union av, s e cor Home st, 318x353x393x51 to Home st, x265, excepting as follows:
Union av, s e cor Home st, 226.5x100x—x—.
Union av, e s, 540 n Wall st, runs north 360 x east 352 x south 375 x west 112 to Prospect av, x south 216 x west 175 x north 216 x west 175 to Union av, point beginning.
Union av, e s, 475 n 16 th st, 65x175.
Franklin Post to Asa E. Collins, Elizabeth, N. J. Nov. 24. See Intervale av. nom

Same property. Laura A. Thompson individ., extrx. and trustee Sidney C. Thompson and Lloyd O. Thompson to same. Dec 1. 31,854

Union av, e s, 100 s 165th st, 25x165. Mary wife of William Haebel, August F. and Frank Fechteler to Anselm and Margaretha Stollberg, joint tenants. Dec. 5. 2,000

Vanderbilt av, e s, abt 51.6 n 157th st, 28.3x92.6x25x105.9. Maria A. Heyer widow, Chicago, Ill., to Michael J. Leehane. Nov. 20. 1,625

Vanderbilt av, s e cor 158th st, 54.11x101x48.6x75.4. Maria A. Heyer widow, Chicago, Ill., to Moise Geismann. Nov. 20. 5,000

Washington av, w s, part lot 30 map Morrisania, 26x200. Jane wife of William Webster to Thomas S. Morris. *Mt.* $2,500. Dec. 2. 3,700

Washington av, n w cor 173d st, 100x150, hs & ls. Patrick F. Ferrigan et al. exrs. Hugh Ferrigan to Mark Blumenthal. Nov. 23. 17,000

Willis av, n w cor 146th st, 50x106.
Willis av, s e cor 146th st, 25x100.
Willis av, n w cor 145th st, 25x106.
William R. Gugel to John Button. *Mt.* $151,000 and taxes 1890. April 28. nom

Webster av, w s, 475 s Scott av, 62.2 to land of Jerome Park Railway, x121.8 along same x 104. Grace E. wife of Ellis J. Westlake, Greenbush, N. Y., to William A. Caufield or Canfield. *Mt.* $257. Dec. 9. 1,000

Webster av, w s, lot 140 map of Mt. Hope, 100 x24.5x100x20 3. Release mort. Lucy R. Comfort to Mary Kramer and Margaret Hicks. Dec. 4. 1,000

Westchester av, e s, 17.7 n Robbins av, runs northeast 898 8 x still northeast 764.6 x again northeast 68 1 x southeast 484.8 x northeast 427.8 to Leggetts lane, x south 55.2 x southwest 41.2x66 1 x southeast 194 6x67.9 x southeast 269 x southwest 719.11 x northwest 152.11 x southwest 374 x southwest 86 x northwest 47 x southwest 254.4 x southeast 425.6 to Kelly st, x southwest 324 x northwest 976 x southwest 189.4, contains, exclusive of avs, &c., 22 and 37-1,000 acres. Hiram R. and Henry Dater appointees to exercise power of sale under will of Philip Dater to Simon Danzig and Gabriel S. Kutz. Dec. 9. 220,185

3d av, west cor 179th st, 90.6x90x88x88.3. Mary P. wife of William Roesel an heir of Mary Pottberg to Millie M. wife of Egbert W. Tracy, Hettie M., Annie M., Martha T. and Alice Irwin, Greenbush, N. Y., and Theodore D. Irwin, New York. B. & S. All title. Dec. 1. 100

Same property. John H. Pottberg heir as above to same. B. & S. All title. Nov. 11. nom

3d av, w s, 175.4 n 164th st, 25x97.6x25x99.9. Patrick F. Perrigan et al. exrs Hugh Ferrigan to Theresa wife of Robert Hughes and probably Margt. B. wife of Patrick F. McKeon. Nov. 25. 8,500

Lot 80 map Metropolitan Real Estate Assoc., Fordham Ridge, opposite Jerome Park. Charles Lyon to The Central National Bank, New York. Nov. 27. nom

Same property. The Metropolitan Real Estate Assoc. to Charles Lyon. July 21, 1883. 350

McCombs Dam road, w s, 286 4 n 184th st, formerly 208th st, runs north 265 x west 100 x north 44 x west 75.9 to centre of Loring av, original line, x south 277 x east 170, h & ls. Yellott D. Dechert to Samuel Love. *Mt.* $5,000. Dec. 4. See 6th st. 25,000

Parcel under water Hudson River adjoining the last parcel above described and beginning Hudson River R. R., e s, at south line of said lot 7, runs west 707.5 x north 104 x east 707.5 x south 104, excepting land taken for railroad. Same to same. Dec. 1. 500

Parts of lots 29 and 30 map of Eltona, begins 177.5 n of 165th st and 25 w of line bet lots 29 and 30, runs north 18.9 x east 90 x south 18.9 x west 90, with right of way over proposed extension of Trinity av. Newbury D. Lawton, New Rochelle, N. Y., to William B. Long. Dec. 1. 7,000

LEASEHOLD CONVEYANCES.

Barclay st, n s, 28 9 e College pl, 28.9x189, running through to Park pl. Consent to assign. lease. Trustees of Columbia College to Joseph P. Knapp. nom

Barclay st, n e cor College pl, runs to Park pl. Same to same. nom

Bowery, Nos. 65 and 65½. Assign. leases. Thomas and Pierce Brennan exrs. Patrick J. Brennan to Thomas Gibney. nom

Broadway, n w cor Chambers st, 50.6x94.5x x50.6x93.7. Sarah H. wife of Edward R. Andrews to George Hillen. 21 years; from May 1, 1892, per year, taxes, &c., and 40,000

Broadway or Union pl, w s, 26 n 15th st, 26x116.10. Assign. lease. Bank of the Metropolis to William Sueckner. Dec. 7. nom

Broadway, s w cor 26th st, St. James' Hotel. Assign. lease. Gustav Dorval to The Dorval Co. Dec. 1. nom

Grand st, No 53. Assign. lease. William Ryan and Philip Brady of Ryan & Brady to The Jacob Hoffmann Brewing Co. 7,000

Madison av, No. 1141. Assign. lease. Michael J. Kadel to James Everard. nom

Manhattan st, Nos. 9 and 11, n e s, 283 n w 125th st, 28.4x112.6x79x100. John Eichorn, Boston, Mass., to Frederick S. Myers. 21 years, from March 1, 1892, per year, 900, 1,000

Rivington st, No 252. Assign. lease. James Lynch to Peter Doelger. nom

Wooster st, No. 133. Surrender of lease. Christopher Watson to Abraham Beller. Dec. 8. nom

11th st, Nos. 310 and 312 E., s s. Consent to assign. lease. The Rector, &c., of St. Marks Church in the Bowery to Katie Weil. Nov. 30. —

Same property. Assign. lease. Katie Weil to Sophie and Samuel Weil admrs. Moses Weil. Nov. 30. 25,000

20th st, n s, 500 w 2d av, 17.6x92. Assign. lease. John H. Eberhardt and ano. exrs. William Schumacher to Lisette Schumacher widow and legatee of William Schumacher. Dec. 7. 4,300

20th st, n s, 500 w 2d av, 17.6x92. Foreclos. Leasehold. Richard H. Clarke to John H. Eberhardt and ano. exrs. William Schumacher. Oct. 30. 3,950

25th st, n s, 500 e 9th av, 25x98.9.
25th st, n s, 525 e 9th av, 25x98.9.
Assign. lease. Patrick H. McManus to Mary McManus. nom

47th st, n s, 120.6 w 5th av. Consent to assign. lease. Trustees of Columbia College to Helen B. wife of David B. Van Emburgh. nom

51st st, No. 303 W. Surrender lease. Andrew Crawford individ. and admr. William Crawford to William T. Walton. Nov. 27. nom

56th st, No. 318 E. Edward P. Steers to James Brady. B. & S. All title in lease. 5,757

Same property. Leasehold. Foreclos. Thomas P. Fitzsimons to Edward P. Steers. Dec. 2. 100

124th st, n s, 125 e 7th av, 50x100. Columbus Market Co. to William S. Jennings. 17½ months, from Nov. 1, 1891, per year, 2,500

Same property. Assign. lease. William S. Jennings to Columbus Improvement Co. Nov. 12. nom

133d st, No. 506, s w cor Lincoln av. Assign. lease. J. Diedrich Wobse to Herman Siemers. Nov. 30. nom

Same property. Assign. lease. Herman Siemers to The Henry Elias Brewing Co. Nov. 30. nom

Av B, w s, 97 n 5th st, 24.3x100x24.9x100. James Morris to Peter de Jonge. 21 years, from Jan. 1, 1892, per year, taxes, &c., and 800

1st av, No. 161, corner store. Agreement subordinating lease to mort. John Faist to The German Savings Bank, New York. Dec. 3. nom

1st av, s w cor 78th st. Assign. lease. Herman Bartjen to James Finnigan. Dec. 4. nom

2d av, No. 1865. Assign. lease. Marian A. Wilhelm to Kate E Godfrey. Dec. 9. nom

5th av, w s, 86.1 n 50th st. Consent to assign. lease. Trustees Columbia College to Franklin Allen et al. exrs. Ethelinda V. Allen. nom

5th av, No. 763. Assign. lease. Frank Mullen to Marion L. Nichols. 10,000

7th av, n e cor 124th st, Columbus Market, street floor. Columbus Market Co. to William S. Jennings. 15 years, from Jan. 1, 1892, per year, 6,000

Same property. Assign. lease. William S. Jennings to Columbus Improvement Co. Nov. 12. nom

10th av, No. 754. Assign. lease. Peter McDermott to Maurice Gloster. Dec. 2. nom

Same property. Assign. lease. Maurice Gloster to James Everard. Dec. 2. nom

KINGS COUNTY.

DECEMBER 3, 4, 5, 7, 8, 9.

Adelphi st, e s, 296 3 s Willoughby av, 20x125.9 x20x125.8. Ann L. Whiting widow to George W. Heatley. $3,800

Amity st, s s, 200 w Hicks st, 25x100. Trustees, &c., Brooklyn Benevolent Soc. to William Clampett. 21 years, from Nov. 1, 1859, per year 80

Same property. Assign. lease. William Clampett to Charles A. Webber. nom

Same property. Charles A. Webber to William Clampett and Bridget his wife. nom

Ashford st, w s, 212.6 s Arlington av, 12 6x97.6. Edward A. Everit to Magretha Finnern. *Mt.* $1,000. 2,650

Ashford st, e s, 100 s Ridgewood av, 100x100. W. Lincoln Scofield to Frederick E. Scofield. 2,500

Auburn pl, Nos. 10-16. Agreement to sell. Robert and Rebecca Smullen to George Drury. 6,000

Baltic st, s s, 95.5 e Columbia st, 25x104.10. Catherine Haughey to Alexander Neely, of New York. 10,000

Barbey st, w s, 100 s Wortman av, runs west to M. S. Duryea farm, x south 136.6 x east 61.6 to st, x north 136.6; also,
Ashford st, w s, 160 s Wortman av, runs west 100 x south to M. S. Duryea farm, x east to Ashford st, x north to beginning.
Mary F. Brown to Lowell V. Brown. *Mt.* $276. 1,200

Broadway, east cor Cooper st, 80x80. John W. Neily to James Brooks. nom

Bridge st. w s, extends from Front st to Water st, 200x148.6. Union White Lead Mfg. Co. to The National Lead and Oil Co., New York. *Mt.* $55,200. nom

Bush st, s s, 146.6 w Hicks st, 20x100. Michael and Richard Gibbons to Richard Scott. *Mt.* $500. 1,500

Clinton st, w s, 48.3 s Verandah pl, 21x70x21.2x70. James M. Varnum and ano. exrs. Chas. A. Eckert to Claudine and Pauline L. Eckert. 8,900

Carroll st, n s, 55 e Van Brunt st, runs east 20 x north 70 x west 10 x south 10 x west 10 x south 60. Conrad R. Pedersen to The Fulton Co-operative Building and Loan Assoc. nom

Cleveland st, e s, 85 n Wortman av, 50x100. William H. Myers to Willis A. Pickert 300

Cleveland st, e s, 185 n Wortman av, 50x100. Adolph Von Preif to same. 300

Cleveland st, e s, 85 n Wortman av, 50x100. Willis A. Pickert to Thomas H. Naylor, of Jersey City, N. J. *Mt.* $235. 300

Columbia st, e s, 60 n Church st, 20x83.6. Foreclos. James C. Church to Edward Wohlgethau. 1,800

Cooper st, n w s, 150 s w Bushwick av, 25x100. Margaret wife of Philip Bossert to Gerdt Wohlers. *Mt.* $8,250. 7,500

Cornelia st, n w s, 275 n e Bushwick av, 50x100. Bridget A. Cody to Robert Mayfield, Astoria, L. I. 3,700

Cornelia st, n w s, 200 s w Bushwick av, 16.8x100, h & l. John H. Garrison to Maria Holt. *Mt.* $2,500. other consid. and 2,500

Court st, e s, 50 s 4th pl, 25x100. Mary S. Pell to Patrick J. Carlin. 3,000

Same property. Release dower. Mary B. Brooks widow of Tacoma Washington to Mary S. wife of Roston Pell. 450

Covert st, n w s, 329 n e Evergreen av, 18x100, h & l. William H. Barton to Alex. and Charles A. Jeanson. *Mt.* $2,750. 4,100

Cumberland st, w s, 376.10 n Atlantic av, 20x100, h & l. Maximilian Lang to James Gillen. *Mt.* $3,000. 4,800

Decatur st, s s, 365 w Saratoga av, 95x100 Henry M. Pardonner to Kate L. wife of Henry M. Pardonner. nom

Decatur st, n s, 135 w Saratoga av, 18.4x100. Release mort. Cornelius Macardell, Middletown, N. Y., to Ansel H. Van Buren. nom

Decatur st, n w cor Saratoga av, 25x100. Release mort. Cornelius Macardell, of Middletown, to Ansel H. Van Buren. nom

Same property. Ansel H. Van Buren to Peter Gardner. nom

Degraw st, n s, 360.2 e Schenectady av, 6.10x127.9x32x120.1.
Degraw st, n s, 390 e Schenectady av, 70x127.9.
Degraw st, s s, 420 e Buffalo av, 19.1x65.7x30.10x70.
Amos S. Lamphear to James N. Beatty. nom

Degraw st, n s, 260.6 w Bond st, 33.6x100. Roberta F. F. G d g to Ransom F. Clayton. *Mt.* $3,000. oo enou h nom

Devoe st, s s, 40 e Humboldt st, 20x75. Foreclos. A. B. Chalmers to Charles Albrecht. 2,400

Diamond st, s s, 2,983.4 e Main st, now Flatbush av, 50x180, Flatbush. Wells Baker to Mary A. Baker. *Mt.* $3,000. 6,000

Diamond st, s s, 2,784.4 e of the Main st, now Flatbush av, 37.6x183.9x37.6x188.5, Flatbush. Charles F. Du Bois to Charles E. Benedict. 1,000

Douglass st, n s, 291.1 e Albany av, 133.10x130. William C. Turner, Chicago, Ill., to Harris J. Latta. nom

Eastern Parkway, s s, 99 9 e Rockaway av, 0.4x100. Meyer Silberman to Solomon Kringstin and Solomon Razoran, of New York. *Mt.* $350. 400

Eastern Parkway, s s, 20 w Atkins av, 20x100. James D. Lynch, of New York, to Margarett Soviero. 400

Eastern Parkway, s s, 100.1 e Rockaway av, 25x100, h & l. Solomon Kringstein to Solomon Razoran. ½ part. *Mt.* $1,500. Mechanic's lien $1,600. 350

Ewen st, w s, 75 n Withers st, 25x100, h & l. Edward Harrigan to Joseph Wagner. 1,250

Fleet pl, e s, 188.10 s Tillary st, 21.6x39x21.7x36.8. Mary A. D. Jones to Woman's Hospital, Brooklyn. nom

Same property. Woman's Hospital, Brooklyn, of 1884, to Woman's Hospital, of Brooklyn, of 1891. nom

Franklin st, e s, 75 s Milton st, 25x70. Foreclos. John Courtney to Christian Fedden. 4,130

Front st, s s, 135 e Jay st, runs east 158.4 x east again 5 x south 87 x east 21.8 x south 50 x west 75 x south 137 to York st, x west 158 x north 90 x east 88 x north 184. The Bradley White Lead Co. to National Lead and Oil Co. of New York. *Mt.* $70,000. nom

Front st, s s, 110 e Jay st, runs east 25 x south 184 x west 135 to Jay st, x north 72 x east 110 x north 112. The Lenox Smelting Co. to The National Lead and Oil Co. of New York. nom

Frost st, n s, 300 w Kingsland av, 50x100, hs & ls George F. Quinn to Owen McConvill. *Mt.* $1,500. nom

Fulton st, s w cor Stone av, 160.6x100. Henry G. Munger, Herkimer, N. Y., to Hoik D. Campbell. ½ part. Sub. to mort. $90,000. nom

Fulton st, n e s, 85.4 s e Clinton av, 16.8x65.2x15x62.9. Anna C. Bosshard to Harry S. Stallbnecht, New York. nom

Same property. Theodore Bosshard to Anna C. wife of Theodore Bosshard. Q. C. nom

Furman st, e s, 50 s Middagh st, if extended, 25x50, h & l. Joseph W. Middlebrook to The Brooklyn Heights R. R. Co. *Mt.* $5,000. 9,000

Glen st, s s, 74 w Crescent st, 26x100. Harvey W. Fawcett to Frank E. Hart. *Mt.* $2,000. 3 500

Gold st, w s, 100 n Myrtle av, 25x100.3. Foreclos. John Courtney to Lipman Arensberg. 7,010

Graham st, e s, 463.8 s Flushing av, 25x75. Jane A. McKenna to Cuno Namoratto *Mt.* $1,000. 2,000

Grove st, n w s, 225 n e Central av, 222x100. Foreclos. John Courtney to Virginia A. Kleine. *Mt.* $17,519. 1,500

Grove st, n w s, 225 n e Central av, 73.9x100. Virginia A. Kleine to Thomas E. Lawrence. *Mt.* $1,068. nom

Grove st, n w s, 298.9 n e Central av, 148 3x100. Same to Benjamin F. Robinson. Sub. to mort. 13,000

Halsey st, n w s, 160 n e Evergreen av, 80x100. Amalia wife of and Daniel Finck to James A. Caufield. 4,900

Halsey st, s s, 445 e Lewis av, 0.1½x100. Brooklyn Brass and Copper Co. to Mary L. wife of John A. Sutton. 25

Halsey st, s s, 304 10 w Stuyvesant av, runs south 100 x west 20.1 x north 51 x east 0.4 x north 40x0.4 x north 9 to st, x east 20.1, h & l. Mary L. wife of John A. Sutton to James F. Thomas. *Mt.* $3,300, tax 1891. 5,600

Hall st, w s, 232 n Myrtle av, 16x100, h & l. Mary C. Horton to John Bolin. 3,900

Hancock st, s s, 162 e Marcy av, 22x100, h & l. Montrose W. Morris to Mary L. Allen. *Mt.* $11,000. 21,000

Hancock st, n s, 1'0 e Stuyvesant av, 18 4x100. Samuel G. Lindeman, of New York, to Charles L. Pashley. nom

Hancock st, s s, 160 w Lewis av, 20x100. R. Irene Thompson to E. Clifford Potter. *Mt.* $6,000. exch

Hancock st, n s, 136.8 e Stuyvesant av, 18.4x100. Charles L. Pashley to Samuel G. Lindeman, New York. ½ part. *Mt.* $5,500. nom

Harman st, s e s, 225 n e Irving av, 25x99.4 Christopher Dalton to Philip Schwinn (?) or Schwim (?). *Mt.* $1,000. 1,500

Harrison pl, s s, 100 e Morgan av, 25x100. Theodore F. Jackson to Adam Siefert. 1,200

Harrison pl, s s, 125 e Morgan av, 25x100. Same to same. 1,200

Hendrix st, e s, 325 n Blake av, 25x100. Michael Devitt to Lena Levi, New York. 750

Herkimer st, s e cor Lafayette pl, 25x98. Patrick J. Kenedy to Isaac Selover. 2,000

Hewes st, n w s, 100 s w Marcy av, 22.8x100. Jacob Fuhs to Caroline M. wife of Charles T. Silberhorn, of New York. 11,250

Hicks st, No. 290, w s, 245.6 n State st, 17.6x100. James M. Benham to Jeremiah Reid. 6,000

Hull st, s s, 56.3 w Hopkinson av, 37 6x90.3x37.8x94 5, h & l. Ellen E. Cochrane to Dudley Kelly. *Mt.* $7,500. exch

Humboldt st, w s, 341.3 n Nassau av, 19x70, h & l. Benjamin J. Head to Albert L. Perry. *Mt.* $5,000. nom

Same property. Albert L. Perry to Benjamin J. Head and Sarah J. his wife. All liens. nom

India st, s s, 225 w Manhattan av, 25x100, h & l. Partition. Jacob Neu to Susan E. Wheeler. 3,800

Irving pl, e s, 331.4 s Gates av, 20x100. Bernard Levino to Henry Halkett. *Mt.* $2,700. 4,800

Jackson st, s s, 125 w Humboldt st, 25x100. Morris Blau to Caroline T. D. wife of August C. Colberg. *Mt.* $1,100. 2,800

Same property. Catherine Hager to Morris Blau. Correction deed. nom

Jerome st, e s, 100 s Eastern Parkway, 25x100. The Union Real Estate Co., of New York, to Lucy Taylor. 3,300

Jerome st, w s, 116.7 s Fulton st, 25x96.1x25.6x101.3. John C. Schenck to James I. Newman. 950

Jerome st, w s, 141.7 s Fulton st, 25x95. Cornelia C. Schenck to same. 950

Jerome st, e s, 20 n Dumont av, 40x100. Anna S. F. wife of Henry Grobmann to James J. and Elizabeth Costello. 750

Leonard st, e s, 25 n McKibben st, 50x100. Lewis Jacobs to Semebe Simon, of New York. *Mt.* $10,000. 13,250

Livingston st, s w s, 205 s e Nevins st, 20x101.6, h & l. Contract. Lizzie De Mott to Fanny Jacobs. 6,800

Lorimer st, e s, 40 s Ten Eyck st, 20x60. Bertha wife of Abram Katzenstein to Bertha wife of and Carl William Goericke. *Mt.* $2,200. 4,500

Luquer st, n s, 146.3 e Clinton st, 18.9x100, h & l. Edward A. Woolley et al. heirs Sarah A. Woolley to William Stedman. Correction deed. nom

Same property. William Stedman to Elizabeth De Maine. 4,000

Same property. Elizabeth De Maine to Rosie Feiner. *Mt.* $2 000. 4,000

Lynch st, s s, 160 e Marcy av, 50x100. Paul E. Grubn to Frederich Moll *Mt.* $7,000. 13,000

Lynch st, s s, 210 e Marcy av, 50x100. Same to Charles Brenner and Margaretha his wife joint tenants. *Mt.* $7,000. 13,000

Macon st, n s, 164 e Ralph av, 18x100. Frederick W. Rowe to Reuben W., Sr., and Reuben W. Aube, Jr. *Mt.* $5,000. nom

Macon st, s s, 415 e Patchen av, 17.6x100. Charles F. Anderson, Riverside, Cal., to William J. Anderson. *Mt.* $4,000. 6,750

Macon st, n s, 95 w Lewis av, 40x100. Jennie Ormond to Elizabeth F. Lynch. ½ part. *Mt.* ½ of $6,500. 4,250

Macon st, s s, 93 6 w Howard av, 107.6x100. Foreclos. Isaac Lublin to Walter F. Clayton. Sub. to all liens. 500

Madison st, s s, 138 w Lewis av, 19x100. John Huber to Jennie Huber. *Mt.* $3,500. nom

Maujer st, s s, 100 e Lorimer st, 25x100, h & l. Benjamin F. Constable to Jacob J. Seelbach. nom

McDonough st, Nos. 181, 195, 197, 199, 201, 268, 270, 272, 274, 276, 280, 282, 288, 290 and 294; also,
Macon st, No. 121, and
Lewis av, No. 370; also,
Pierrepont st, No. 81; together with
New York City and Fairfield, Conn., property.
William S. Warner, of New York, to James H. Work, of New York. ½ part. 1886. 200,000

McDonough st, Nos. 181, 195, 197, 199, 201, 268, 270, 272, 274, 276, 280, 282, 288, 290, 292, and 294; also,
Macon st, No. 121, and
Lewis av, No. 370.
James Henry Work to Walter S. Johnston as receiver. nom

McDonough st, s s, 149.8 e Reid av, 0.4x100. Henry Grasman to Henry B. Hill. 150

McDonough st, s s, 138 e Ralph av, 18.8x100. Thomas H. Radcliffe to George Ketcham. 7,000

McDonough st, n s, 280 w Stuyvesant av, 20x100. John J. De Revere to Annie C. Currier. Taxes 1891. nom

Middleton st, n w s, 391 n e Harrison av, 24x100. Abraham Simon to Elizabeth Beck widow. *Mt.* $2,700. 7,400

Monitor st, w s, 219.3 s Driggs st, 18x100. Charles Engert to John Armbruster. 3,800

Monitor st, w s, 237.3 s Driggs st, 18x100. Charles Engert to Jacob Wolf. 3,800

Monroe st, n s, 391.8 w Ralph av, 16.8x100. Charles S. Crossman to Sarah Adam, of New York. *Mt.* $4,500. exch

Noll st, n w s, 150 s w Hamburg av, 25x100, h & l. Emma Schnabel to Carl Schnabel. 1,425

Oakland st, n w cor Eagle st, 25x66 7, h & l. Sophie L. wife of Nikolas Droge, Johannah wife of John Artmann and Alvine G. wife of Charles Topp heirs Claus Plath to Ernest Ochs. Q. C. nom

Same property. Christian H. Koch et al. exrs. Claus Plath to same. 6,500

Osborn st, w s, 150 s Dumont av, 50x100. Jacob W. Erreger to Elias Rudderman. *Mt.* $2,000. 2,400

Pacific st, n s, 225 e Underhill av, 25x100. William W. Lowry to Charles H. and Florence A. Lowry. gift

Pacific st, s s, 170 e 6th av, 60x110. John A. Deraismes and Amelia F. Dunham to Bernard Garvey. 6,000

Pacific st, No. 2287, n s, 266.8 e Rockaway av, 16.8x100, h & l. Daniel Dunne to Margaret I. Hornbuckel. *Mt.* $1,000 and tax 1891. 1,625

Pacific st, s w s, 269 4 s e 6th av, 19.4x110. Amelia F. Dunham, Hartford, Conn., to James and Oliver Johnson. 2,000

Pacific st, s w s, 250 s e 6th av, 20x110. Martha D. Warrin, New York, to same. 2,000

Pacific st, n s, 118.9 w Kingston av, 25x200 to Atlantic av; also,
McDonough st, n s, 579 e Tompkins av, 21x120; also,
Pacific st, n s, 75 w Brooklyn av, 16.8x100.
Emma Smith to Freling H. Smith. nom

Plymouth st, n s, 244 11 w Gold st, 21.3x100. Ann Lynch widow and devisee William Lynch to Bridget McCann widow. nom

Powell st, e s, 250 n Liberty av, 25x100.
Sackman st, w s, 225 s Glenmore av, 25x100.
Charles C. Hoffman to Theodore Kiendl. nom

Same property. Theodore Kiendl to Emma D. Hoffman. nom

Powell st, w s, 88 n Glenmore av, 14x98 to alley. Alice A. wife of John B. Roberts to Rebecca C. Talbot. *Mt.* $2,525. nom

President st, s s, 65 e Van Brunt st, 20x100. Henry Dudley to Salvatore Savarese. *Mt.* $8 000. 6 300

Quincy st, n s, 205 w Ralph av, 20x100. Mai M. wife of and Samuel K. Schwenk, of New Jersey, to George F. Alexander, of New York. *Mt.* $1,000. nom

Quirey st, n s, 125.6 w Ralph av, 79.6x100. Same to same. nom

Raymond st, w s, 50 s Bolivar st, 25x75. Foreclos. John Courtney to Lula P. McGarry. *Mt.* $8,000. 2,000

Raymond st, w s, 25 s Bolivar st, 25x75. Foreclos. Same to same. *Mt.* $8,000. 2,100

Raymond st, w s, 75 s Bolivar st, 50x75.
Raymond st, n w cor Willoughby st, 26x75x 18.11x75.
Release mort. Stephen B. Sturges to Frank N. O'Brien. 1,500

Remsen st, s s, 327 w Hicks st, 75x90. The Brooklyn Trust Co. exrs. Reuben Ropes to Charles N. Davidson. 35,000

Sackett st, Nos. 282 and 282½, s s, 275 w Court st, 25x100. Samuel M. Jackson a devisee of George T. Jackson to George T. Jackson. exch

Sackett st, s s, 217.6 w 4th av, 160x95. Charles A. Brown, Elizabeth, N. J., to Annie F. or I. Mayher. nom

Scholes st, s s, 370 w Waterbury st, 50x100. Charles Mitchel to Franz Steinbacher. *Mt.* $3,000. exch

Sedgwick st, s s, 300 w Columbia st, 25x100. William Simon to Adam Kropf. 5,500

Sedgwick st, n s, 25 e Van Brunt st, 100x100. Benjamin A. Hegeman exr. Charles Kelsey to The Columbia Chemical Works. 14,000

Seigel st, s s, 515 e Bushwick av, 25x100. Charles W. Truslow admr. William Wall to Charles Konrath. 925

Seigel st, s s, 540 e Bushwick av, 25x100. Same to same. 825

Seigel st, s s, 190 e Bushwick av, 50x100.
Seigel st, s s, 28½ e Bushwick av, 50x100.
Charles W. Truslow admr. W. Wall to John Ketterie. 4,200

Smith st, e s, 80.8 n 4th st, 20.5x93.8x20x88.11. Edward M. Townsend exr. Belinda R. Townsend to Thomas Keogh. 1,500

Somers st, s s, 245 w Stone av, 15x100 Charles H. Reynolds to Edward Cronk. *Mt.* $3,000. 4,250

State st, n s, 191 e Clinton st, 22x108 1x22x 107.9. Catherine M. Phillips to Edward Phillips. *Mt.* $1,000. nom

Steuben st, e s, 100 n Park av, 25x100. Michael Sullivan to Mary wife of Michael Sullivan. nom

St. James pl, w s, 75 s Fulton av, 25x100. George R. Brown to David J. Ramsdell. 30,000

St. James pl, w s, 75 s Fulton av, 25x100. David J. Ramsdell to George R. Brown. *Mt.* $21,000. 30,000

Stockholm st, n s, bet Myrtle and Hamburg avs, being on assessm't map 18th Ward, lot 9 block 190. August Kuever to Henry Heins. *Mt.* $8,000. nom

Strong pl, w s, 260 s Harrison st, runs east 10 x again east 40 and again east 48 x south 16.8 x west 48 x west 50 to pl, x north 17.5. Harriet A. wife of Daniel C. Birdsall, of Bridgeport, Conn., to Frank C. Trubee, of Buffalo, N. Y. Q. C. Correction deed. nom

Same property. Grace A. Birdsall, of Hartford, Conn., to same. ½ part. 3,500

Sumpter st, n s, 143 e Saratoga av, 17.10x100. William H. Barton to Alfred T. Vincent. *Mt.* $3,650. 4,250

Union st, n s, 308.4 e Van Brunt st, 26.8x100, h & l. Edward Lavin to Catherine Haughey. 17,000

United States st, n w s, 100 s w Lexington av, 116.8x100, New Utrecht. Catharine A. Lanius or Lanius, Matilda G. Mallett, Ann M. Blake and Sarah R. Heckert to Alexander Heckert. ⅜ part. 550

Union pl, n s, 47.4 w Locust st, 50x103.5, Flatbush. Catharine Kelly, of Flatbush, to Joseph Schmidt. *Mt.* $5,100. 5,600

Van Buren st, No. 239, n s, 22 w Lewis av, —x 100x19.6x100. Alfred L. Beasley to George J. Bryan. *Mt.* $5,000. 7,250

Van Voorhis st, No. 69A, n w s, 320.11 s w Evergreen av, 16.10x100. Torrance B. Lynch to Ludowic L. Wright. Sub. to mort. 3,800

Van Voorhis st, n w s, 100 s w Evergreen av, 17x100. Foreclos. John Courtney to William H. E. Jay. *Mt.* $2,500. 250

Van Voorhis st, n w s, 117 s w Evergreen av, 17x100. Foreclos. Same to same. *Mt.* $2,500. 350

Van Voorhis st, n w s, 134 s w Evergreen av, runs northwest 100 x southwest 16 x southeast 51.9 x southwest 1 x southeast 48.2 to st, x northwest 17 to beginning. Foreclos. Same to same. *Mt.* $2,500. 350

Wallabout st, s s, 191.9 w Marcy av, 24.9x100. Jacob Bossert to Franzica Hellmuth. *Mt.* $3,000. 6,800

Warren st, s s, 314.2 w 4th av, 16.8x100, h & l. Lowry Somerville to Frances Muller. *Mt.* $1,500. nom

Warren st, n s, 825 e Underhill av, 25x152.6x 28.8x158.6, h & l. Tertullus G. Mathews to Michael Lynch. 2,900

Washington st, Adams st, Front st and Water st, the block, 200x230. Brooklyn White Lead Co. to The National Lead and Oil Co., New York. nom

Watkins st, w s, 125 n Belmont av, 25x100. Contract. Morris Ribstein to Louis Silverstein. 825

Watkins st, w s, 100 n Eastern Parkway, 25x 100, h & l. Harris Max to Isaac Liebermann, New York. *Mt.* $3,000. 6,000

Weirfield st, n w s, 81 s w Central av, 20.2x100. Leopold J. Lippmann to James Gormley. *Mt.* $3,500. nom

Weirfield st, s e s, 335 n e Broadway, 20x100. Carl A. Weidhorn to Henry Hachmeister, of New York. *Mt.* $8,000. nom

Wierfield st, n w s, 281 s w Central av, 20x100. Leopold J. Lippmann to Friedman Lippmann. *Mt.* $3,250. nom

Withers st, s s, 125 w Lorimer st, 75x100. Charles M. and Esther Church and James F. Feely exrs. Charles M. Church to Mary G. wife of Andrew Watson. 2,500

Woodbine st, s e s, 120 n e Hamburg av, 18x 100. George W. and Charles H. Francisco to George H. Hornung, of New York. *Mt.* $1,500. nom

North 2d st, s s, 160 e 3d st, 25x— to point 53 from North 1st st. Foreclos. John Courtney to Gottlieb W. H. Harigel. 900

South 2d st, n s, 83 9 e Driggs st, 21.11x100. Frank L. Kolk to Mathilda Kolk, New York. 6,500

3d pl, n s, 320.4 w Clinton st, 15.2x133.5. John and James Williamson to Elinor M. Mayer. 6,500

3d pl, No. 31, n s, 20 e Henry st, 20x60. Thomas M. Cherry by Catherine O. Cherry guard. to Mary L. and Anne C. Cherry. Infant's share. 1,290

4th st, No. 499, n e s, 235.10 n w 8th av, 21x95, h & l. John T. Allan and Nathaniel Proskey to Charles M. Higgins. *Mt.* $8,000. nom

Same property. Release mort. Fannie M. E. Ensell to John T. Allan and Nathaniel Proskey. nom

4th st, s e cor Smith st, runs southeast 103.6 x southwest 14 x northwest 97.10 to Smith st, x northeast 35.6. James Feely to Thomas Feely. 1866. nom

Same property. Thomas Feely to Anne wife of James Feely. 1866. nom

4th st, s s, 292.1 w 6th av, 17.9x100. Mulford M. Fenniman and Sarah E. Campbell widow to William J. Pearson. 4,900

North 4th st, n e cor Berry st, 26.6x100. Maggie Dowling, of New York, to Hiram Akerley. Q. C. nom

South 4th st, — —, 250 s e Hooper st, 25x92.2. Carolina Ludwig to Hugh Fehling. Receipt for $25 to secure sale of above for 3,800

North 5th st, s w s, 225 n w Bedford av, 25x 100. Maggie Dowling, of New York, to Zebulon B. Doty. Q. C. nom

6th st, s s, 279.10 e 6th av, 17x100, h & l. Absalom W. Dieter to Amelia E. Hummel. *Mt.* $6,500. nom

6th st, s s, 228.10 e 6th av, 17x100, h & l. Absalom W. Dieter to same. *Mt.* $6,500 nom

North 6th st, n s, 75 w Roebling st, 25x100. Release mort The Williamsburgh Savings Bank to Frank Parks. 1,000

South 6th st, east cor Berry st, 20x53.7x20x52, h & l. Charles F. Grolle to Patrick F. Fitzgerald. *Mt.* $3,000. 7,600

7th st, s s, 202.10 w 7th av, 20x100. Charles G. Peterson to Charles F. Holm. *Mt.* $4,000. nom

8th st, n s, 238.9 w 6th av, 18.4x100, h & l. William Brown to Michael Dalton. *Mt.* $4,500. 7,250

8th st, s s, 433 e 5th av, 17x90; also,
39th st, n s, 325 e 7th av, 25x100; also,
3d av, westerly cor 41st st, 25.2x100; also,
39th st, s s, 200 w 8th av, 25x100.2.
Stephen C. Halstead to Grace C. Halstead. nom

East 9th st, w s, 100 n Av D, 40x100; also,
East 9th st, w s, 180 n Av D, 40x200 to East 8th st; also,
East 9th st, w s, 260 n Av D, 120x200 to East 8th st, Flatbush.
William W. Wickes to Amelia C. Waite, 5,850

North 10th st, s s, 181.3 e Berry st, 18.9x100. William Hayes to Mary O'Connor. *Mt.* $4,000. 6,000

North 10th st, s w s, 175 s e Bedford av, 25x100. Joseph T. Briggs to Francis J. Gately. 2,300

12th st, s s, 147.10 w 8th av, 25x100, h & l. Israel Jacobs to Louis Winer. *Mt.* $1,400. 2,400

Same property Louis Winer to Israel Jacobs. *Mt.* $1,400. 2,400

15th st, s s, 183 e 3d av, 18x112.10. Mary wife of and John J. Lynch to Thomas Kivlin, of New York. *Mt.* $2,000. 3,800

East 15th st, w s, 400 s Av X, 25x100, Gravesend. William Gundermann to Henry Gaus or Gans. 650

Same property. Henry Gaus or Gans to Ferdinand Gundermann. 650

16th st, n e s, 238.4 n w 3d av, 40.5x100. John J. Drake to Isreal Meyers. 3,100

17th st, s s, 225 e 8th av, 12.6x100. Thomas and Robert Edgerton to George B. Stoutenburg. *Mt.* $1,250. 2,500

Same property. George B. Stoutenburg to James D. Rankin and James Ross. *Mt.* $1,750. 2,300

18th st, s w s, 250 n w 3d av, 23x100. Imogene C. wife of Peter McNaughton and Jennie R. wife of William R. Babcock to Frank Grupinski. 700

19th st, s w s, 300 n w 7th av, 15x100. Martha Gibson to Edward F. Taber, Patchogue, L. I. *Mt.* $1,800. 2,900

19th st, s w s, 285 n w 7th av, 15x100. John H. Gibson to Edward F. Taber, of Patchogue, N. Y. *Mt.* $1,900. 2,900

20th st, e s, 100 s Seeley st, 25x100, Flatbush. William E. Murphy exr. Thos. Murphy to Frederick Leutzbach. 300

Bay 4 st st, n w s, 100 s w 86th st, 100x96.8, Gravesend. James D. Lynch to James P. Graham. 1,000

45th st, s w s, 200 n w 12th av, 50x100.2, New Utrecht. Release mort. The West Brooklyn Land and Improvement Co. to Richard Hawley. 420

Same property. Richard Hawley to Frances A. Ward. 680

47th st, s s, 400 w 3d av, 20x100.2. David J. Tingley and Richard Slater exrs. Margaret M. Van Pelt to Marietta E. Ball, of New York. 362

47th st, n s, 160 e 4th av, 100x100.2. Release mort. R. Fulton Cutting, of New York, to James G. Carroll. 1,500

47th st, n s, 160 e 4th av, 60x100.2. James G. Carroll to Samuel T. Sherwood. 3,000

47th st, n s 140 e 4th av, 20x100.2. Samuel T. Sherwood to Joseph Logan. 4,550

49th st, n s, 120 e 6th av, 20x100.2. James Dunleavey to Thomas McGall, Englewood, N. Y. *Mt.* $140. 425

51st st, n s, bet 6th and 7th avs, being on assessment map 8th Ward lot 11 block 254. Elizabeth A. Thorn to Celia Golding. 350

53d st, n s, 160 w 5th av, runs north 200 4 to 52d st, x west 40 x south 100.2 x west 20 x south 100.2 to 53d st, x east 60. Clarence E. Hopkins to Josephine B. Hopkins, Highland Falls, N. Y. 4,000

57th st, s s, 180 w 2d av, 20x100.2. Release dower. Adeline G. wife of Albert S. French to John and James Van Dyk. nom

57th st, s s, 200 w 2d av, 20x100.2. Release mort. Edward T. Hunt exr. and trustee Thomas Hunt to Albert L. French. 189

66th st, n s, 240 w 14th av, 40x100, New Utrecht. Effingham H. Nichols, of New York, to Edward Dunn. 440

76th st, n s, 490 w 15th av, 40x100, New Utrecht. James V. S. Woolley, New York, to Jane Harrison. 300

78th st, s w s, 200 n w 12th av, 40x100, New Utrecht. Hoik D. Campbell to Minnie Schmitt. 500

80th st, s w s, 100 s e 11th av, 120x100.
77th st, n e s, 300 s e 11th av, 100x100, New Utrecht.
Hoik D. Campbell to Andrew B. Carton. 2,750

80th st, s w s, 220 s e 12th av, 60x100, New Utrecht. Hoik D. Campbell to George W. Hepburn. 900

86th st, n e s, 300 s e 22d av, 100x200 to 85th st. James P. Graham to James D. Lynch. *Mt.* $12,000. nom

96th st, n s, 540 w Marine av, runs north 50 x west 94.3 to Shore road, x south 50.2 x east 99.2, New Utrecht. Frank Mose, of New York, exr. Maltby G. Lane to Annie C. Linderman. 2,800

Av B, s s, extends from East 4th to East 5th st, 200x400.
East 4th st, w s, 180 s Av B, 100x100, Flatbush.
John H. Seed to Amelia C. wife of Edward P. Waite. nom

Same property. Release mort. Trustees Reformed Protestant Dutch Church, Flatbush, to John Seed. nom

Adams av, e s, 100 n Liberty av, 50x90. Elias C. wife of John Eilers, Catharine M. wife of Joseph Baldy and Anna W. M. wife of William J. Light and William C. Kolde to Margaretha Kolde Q. C. nom

Atlantic av, s e cor Hendrix st, 75x103.8x75x99. Carrie C. Schluchtner to Frederick Schluchtner. nom

Bedford av, n w cor North 10th st, 25x100. Anton Mannel to Peter R. Schuriacher. 18,000

Belmont av, s s, 50 e Osborn st, 25x100. Solomon Wolff to Isaac Black. *Mt.* $3,500. 6,150

Buffalo av, w s, 68.4 n Bergen st, 16.4x85, h & l. Thomas S. Denike to John Gallagher and Kate his wife, joint tenants. *Mt.* $1,750. 3,000

Buffalo av, s w cor Prospect pl, 20x52. William L. Beers to Josephine Van Ness. *Mt.* $2,500. nom

Bushwick av, w s, 40 s Woodbine st, 20x80. Charles Lewis to Robert M. Johnston. *Mt.* $6,450. 9,500

Bushwick av, north cor Vanderveer st, 80x80. Franz Steinbacher to Charles Mitchel. exch

Clermont av, w s, 100 s Flushing av, 25x100 6x 25x100.3. William Hendrickson, of New York, to Martin Brennan. 2,400

De Kalb av, s s, 25 e Evergreen av, 25x79.8. Philipp H. Oehl to Dorothea Muhlenberg. 7,200

Evergreen av, w s, 125 n Covert st, 39x95x34.10 x95. Emma L. Johnston, of Newtown, N. Y., to Virginia A. Kleine. exch

Evergreen av, n e s, 25 s e Halsey st, 35x100. James Gascoine to Charles F. Gastmeyer. ½ part. Tax 1891. nom

Same property. James Gascoine and ano. exrs. John G. Cozine and Anna E. Cozine to same. ½ part. Tax 1891. 1,500

Evergreen av, n e s, 20 n w Eldert st, 120x 100.
Eldert st, n w, 200 n e Evergreen av, 40x200 to Halsey st.
Joshua H. Cort to Charles F. Gastmeyer. 18,700

Flushing av, n w s, 151.6 n e Evergreen av, 25 3x68.6x25x71.3, h & l. Henry Stubing to Abraham and Aaron Kodziesen. 6,850

Flushing av, s s, 133.10 e Steuben st, 20.4x83.8x 21.1x—, h & l. Herman Sacks to Sophia C. Van der Waag. *Mt.* $2,000. 5,000

Franklin av, w s, 60 s Pacific st, 20x80. The Brainerd Quarry Co., of Conn., to Martin J. Suydam. *Mt.* $5,000. 6,500

Furman av, n s, 214.6 e Bushwick av, 17.1x100x —x100, h & l. Henry Weil to Richard Morrisey. 1,800

Gates av, s s, 204.8 w Bedford av, 16.8x110. Charles E. Benedict individ. and as exr. Mary

S. Benedict; Ezra and Ida M. Benedict, Julia A. Reid and Ella C. Dickinson and Laura E. Weber heirs of May S. Benedict to Charles F. Dubois. 6,000

Gates av, n s, 163 e Clason av, 20x100. John McCann to Mary E. wife of John McCann. B. & S. 12,500

Greene av, n s, 100 w Lewis av. 20x100. Thomas B. Bryant to Fannie C. Burnham. Mt $5,000. 9,000

Greene av, n w cor Sumner av, 20x80. Woman's Hospital of Brooklyn, 1884, to Woman's Hospital of Brooklyn, 1891. nom

Hamburg av. easterly cor Harman st, 100x100. Release mort. Theodore F. Jackson et al. exrs. Loftis Wood to Abby E. Laytin. 4,000

Hamilton av, w s, 77.8 s Nelson st, 25.1x79.11x25.1x79.9.
Hamilton av, s w cor Nelson st, 25.2x55.3 to Henry st, x 57 to Nelson st, x 20.10.
Bernard Scanlon to John Caulfield. Mt. $7,500. nom

Same property. John Caulfield to Kate Scanlon. C. a. G. Mt. $7,500. nom

Hegeman av, s w cor Ashford st, 40x85.
Ashford st, w s, 305 s Hegeman av, 20x100.
Ashford st, e s, 85 n Vienna av, 40x100.
Vienna av. n e cor Cleveland st, 40x85.
Catharine Duffee to Margaret Duffee. nom

Jefferson av, n w s. 339 8 n e Broadway, 20x100. Louisa Ewald to George Dillmann. Mt. $3,250. 6,500

Jefferson av, s e s, 102 n e Broadway, 18x100. Elizabeth L. Kemp and Emma L. Farrington heirs of Henry Kemp to Ann E. L. Kemp. gift

Jefferson av, s s, 18.2 e Marcy av, 19.10x100. Laura A. wife of and William R. Bell to Cornelia M. Kingsland. Mt. $9,000. exch

Kingsland av, s e cor Lombardy st, runs east 191.1 x southeast 200.8 to Beadel st, x west 282 9 x northwest 20.6 to av, x north 189.2. Philip H. Schoening to The Kingsland Building Assoc. Mt. $6,250. consid. omitted

Lafayette av. s s, 246 e Grand av, 54x100. Charles N. Wheelwright to Edward Driscoll. Mt. $36,000. 65,000

Lafayette av, s s, 147.10 e Throop av, 15.9x100. Walter G. Rogers to Elizabeth D. Rogers. Mt. $3,000. nom

Lee av, east cor Ross st, 24x86, h & l. William G. Russell to Michael J. Riordan. Mt. $10,500, taxes 1891. 14,000

Lee av. w s, 21 n Penn st, 19x67. Cornelia M. wife of and Daniel F. Kingsland to Laura A. wife of Wm. R. Bell. exch

Lexington av, s s, 178 w Nostrand av, 16x100. Robert M. Johnston to Charles Lewis. Mt. $4,000. 6,000

Lexington av, n e cor Patchen av, runs north 120 x east 86 x south 20 x east 9 x south 100 to Lexington av, x west 95 to beginning. Isabella wife of and Herman Brinckerhoff to Ferdinand Eherlich Mt. $10,000. nom

Lewis av, e s. 20 n Lexington av, 20x80. Gustave J. Wiederhold to William H. Schnitzer, of New York. Mt. $5,000 and taxes. 6,400

Same property. William H. Schnitzer, of New York, to Louis W. Fischer. Mt. $5,000 and taxes. 6,500

Liberty av, s s, 102 e Railroad av, 21x100. George Rudolph, of New York, to Isaac Embree. 15

Meserole av, s s, 75 e Lorimer st, 25x100, h & l. Jeremiah P. Applegate to Thomas H. Mootry and Mary his wife, joint tenants. Mt. $900. 4,300

Montrose av, n s, 205 e Bushwick av, 25x100, h & l. Joseph Maurer and John Heilmann to Barbara Obmann widow. Mt. $6,000. 12,000

Myrtle av, south cor Bleecker st, runs east 20 along av, x south 50 x southeast — x west 10 x northwest 25.4 x northwest 55.4 to st, x northeast 27.8. Release mort. Stephen B. Sturges to Harry F. C. Hopkins. nom

Myrtle av, s s, 295 e Tompkins av. 20x100. Sarah A. Woodward, of New York, to Greenleaf W. Crossman. Mt. $5,250. nom

Myrtle av, n w cor Stockholm st, runs north 41.2 x northwest 99 x southwest 54.2 x east 60 x south 80 to av, x east 29.5, h & l. August Kuever to Henry Heins. Mt. $8,000. nom

Nassau av, n e cor Oakland st, runs east 25.2 x north 40 x west 0.2½ x north 60 x west 25 to st, x south 100. Terence J. O'Hare and John J. O'Keefe to Lilian T. wife of Conrad Hunerhoff. Mt. $5,000. 12,000

Nassau av, n s, 25 e Oakland st, 0.2½x40. Alfred C. and Henry B. Barnes et al. exrs. Alfred S. Barnes to Terence J. O'Hare and Jno. J. O'Keefe. nom

New Jersey av. w s, 225 n Liberty av, 75x100. Wolcott H. Pitkin, of Albany, N. Y., to Agnes Feuerbach or Feuerbach. 8,000

Pennsylvania av, e s, 75 n Fulton av. 25x90. Charles S. Crossman to Sarah Adam, of New York. Mt. $5,200. exch

Prospect av, s w s, 225 s e 8th av, 50x80.2. Edwin Andrews to Christopher C. Firth. Mt. $1,600. 2,500

Prospect av, n e s, 533 s e 3d av, 20x64 6x20x64.11. Foreclos. Robert Merchant to John S. Cokalete. Dated 1888. 3,300

Prospect av, n s, 110.6 w Webster pl, 18.5x80, h & l. Foreclos. John R. Kuhn to John S. Griffith. 1,050

Putnam av, s e s, 170 s w Bushwick av, 20x100. Reuben W., Sr., and Reuben W. Aube, Jr., to Frederick W. Rowe. Mt. $5,500. nom

Putnam av, n s, 340 e Reid av, 20x100. Sadie E. Rice to William G. Russell. Mt. $6,500. exch

Putnam av, s s, 140 e Lewis av, 19x100. Kate Acor to Sara L. Moon. Mt. $6,500. 11,000

Putnam av, s s. 215 w Stuyvesant av, 20x100. Eli H. Bishop to Friedrich Bauer. Mt. $7,500. nom

Putnam av, s s, 255 w Stuyvesant av. 20x100. Eli H. Bishop to Caroline Mayer. Mt. $7,500. nom

Ralph av, s e cor Macon st, 100x98. Release mort. William Ziegler to John R. Pitt 7,910

Ralph av, e s, 40 s Madison st, 40x100. James Walker to Simon Hutter. Mt. $3,500. 1890. 5,600

Railroad av, n w cor Ridgewood av, runs north 91.1 x west 100 x south 20 x west 100 to Hemlock st, x south 99 to Ridgewood av, x east 201.11. William L. Large to Ida Gordon. All title. 500

Reid av, e s, 75 n Decatur st, 25x80, h & l. Catharine Duffee to Margaret Duffee. Mt. $6,000. nom

Rockaway av, s e cor Glenmore av, 25x100.1. Rosie wife of Charles Cooper to Frances wife of Bernard Cooper. Mt. $4,800. 7,000

Rockaway av, e s. 200 n Livonia av, 25x100, h & l. Charlotte Radford to Caroline Fletcher. Mt. $1,500. 2,200

Rockaway av, s e cor Glenmore av, 25x100. Rosie Cooper, of New York, to Frances McCabe. Mt. $4,800. 7,000

Rogers av, s w cor Douglass st, 127.6x175. Mary N. Hubbard widow to M. J. Jackson, of New York. April, 1890. nom

Schenck av, e s, 275 n Blake av, 50x100. Albert H. W. Van Sielen to Christina Fuller. 700

South Portland av, w s, 200 n Lafayette av, 25x100. Eva C. Glover widow to Jennie T. Benton. 7,000

Stanley av, centre line, adj grantee on east, 15x150 to centre Fresh Creek, 26th Ward. Williamson Rapalje and John H. Ireland to The Brooklyn & Rockaway Beach R. R. nom

Stewart av, n w cor 97th st, 126x150, New Utrecht. New York Building Loan Banking Co. to Sarah Norton. $31.75 per month for 12 years.

Stewart av, n s, 126 w 97th st, 126x150, New Utrecht. Sarah Norton to Greenleaf W. Crossman, New York, trustee, to convey to New York Building Loan Banking Co. nom

Sunnyside av, s s, 387 e Barbey st, 83.4x110x20.2x110, h & l. Carrie C. Schluchtner to Frederick Schluchtner. Mt. $2,000, part of the purchase price which is $2,200. nom

Thatford av, w s, 125 n Linnington av, 25x100. Charles Rosenblat to Victor Woolf. Mt. $1,675. 2,150

Thatford av, w s, 100 n Belmont av. 25x100.1. Bernhart Hershkowitz to Ignatz Kaufman. Mt. $3,000. nom

Thatford av, w s, 189.2 s Dumont av, 35.8x100, h & l. Harry Lehr to Jules Weill. Mt. $3,700. 6,500

Thatford av, e s, 125 s Glenmore av. 25x100. Release mort. Terence Jacobson to Samuel Balsam and Moritz or Morris Handler. 2,100

Tompkins av, e s, 50 n Hopkins st, 25x68.4 in two courses to Delmonico pl, x25x82 in two courses, hs & ls. William Grannan to Annie E. Bogan. 1,500

Vanderbilt av, w s, 102.8 n Park av, 25x105.10x25.6x110.10. Eliza wife of James Fisher to John O'Brien. Tax 1891. 5,250

Van Sielen av, e s, 225 n Blake av, 50x100. Jacob T. Van Sielen to Albert Hottinger. 800

Vernon av, n s, 185 e Lewis av, 20x100. Joseph A. Cross to Robert Weiskittel. Mt. $7,500. 8,500

Vernon av, s s. 287.6 e Tompkins av, 18.9x100. Clara Ainslie to Kate R. wife of Hugh J. Maxwell. Mt. $6,000. 7,800

Vernon av, n s, 244 e Nostrand av, 19x100. John Parkin to Karoline Keck. Mt. $4,000. 7,800

Williams av. w s, 200 s Bay av. 50x100. Release mort. Abraham Vanderveer to Abram H. Dailey. 600

Willoughby av, s s, 25 e Evergreen av, 25x95. Hermann C. Huelle to Edward C. Reinhardt. nom

Willoughby av, n s, 50 w Evergreen av, 50x100. J. Fred. Ackerman exr. Louisa J. Ackerman to Hugo Weil, of New York. 5,250

Willoughby av, n s. 50 w Evergreen av, 50x100. Hugo Weil, of New York, to Margaret wife of Philip Bossert. Mt. $4,000. 5,750

Wyckoff av, northerly cor Himrod st, 25x93.11x25x94.7. Henry Heios to Henry and John Von Glahn. Mt. $4,500. exch

Wythe av, No. 360, w s, 149.3 s South 2d st, 24.9x75. Benjamin W. Winans et al. exrs. William W. Winans to Joseph Straus. 7,200

2d av, southerly cor 15th st, runs southeast 57 x southwest 80 x northwest 4.5 x north 88.7 to av, x northeast 15.11. Abraham Manchester, of Adamsville, R. I., to George S. Wheeler. nom

Same property. George S. Wheeler to Hugh McNulty. 1,500

3d av, No. 669–673, south cor 20th st, 60x100. Samuel M. Jackson a devisee of George T. Jackson to George T. Jackson. exch

3d av, n w cor 50th st, 25.2x100. Christopher Osterheld to William C. Osterheld. nom

Same property. William C. Osterheld to Dora Osterheld. nom

3d av, w s, 50.2 n 48th st, 25x80, h & l. Marcus Solomon, Port Elizabeth, N. J., to Rebecca wife of Solomon Sonin. 9,500

4th av, w s, 140.2 s 35th st, 40x82. William Waring to Alethea L. Sands. Mt. $6,000. nom

5th av, s e s, 41 n e 14th st, 16x97.10; also,
5th av, s e s, 25 n e 14th st, 16x97.10x17x97.10.
Wilhelmine Schink to Louisa Schink. nom

6th av, s w cor 57th st, 25.2x100. Wilhelmine Schink to Louisa Schink. nom

6th av, n e cor President st, 22.6x66.9. Release mort. Henry C. M. Ingraham to William Brown. 1,750

Same property. William Brown to Guy Loomis. Mt. $12,500. 19,467

6th av. e s, 125.2 n 49th st, 25x100. Fannie H. Guy to Lena W. Nelson, of New York. 550

7th av, e s, 50 2 s 50th st, 25x100. Augusta M. Guilmartin to Mary Wright. Mt. $150. 400

8th av, northerly cor Windsor pl, 20x97 5. Nassau Land and Improvement Co. to Hermann Rathjen. 10,500

9th av, s w cor 11th st, runs south 100 x west 85 x north 77 x west 50 x north 23 to 11th st, x east 134. Sidney V. Lowell to Frederick Jansen. 13,000

11th av, n w s, 60.2 s w 58th st, 60x100, New Utrecht. Bertha M. wife of and Edward F. Taber. Patchogue, N. Y., to Martha Gibson. 3,400

12th av, s w cor 66th st, 40x100, New Utrecht. James V. S. Woolley to Anna S. Anderson. 350

13th av, n e cor 64th st, 80x66.3x80.1x61.3, New Utrecht. James V. S. Woolley, of New York, to David Herrman, of New York. 800

17th av, n w s, 163.9 n e Cropsey av, 41x108x41x108.4, h & ls, Bath Beach. Albert V. B. Voorhies to Fannie C. wife of Charles Pfaff. 5,000

22d av, n w s, 200 n e Benson av, 20x96 8, New Utrecht. James D. Lynch to Eliza E. Dietrich. 1,000

Coney Island road, n e cor Brighton pl, 50x134.6x50x138.6, Gravesend. Margaret wife of John I. Snedeker to Delia Kelly. Mt. $4,000. 5,017

Same property. Delia Kelly to Dennis E. Hogan. 1,000

Flatbush to Flatlands Neck road, n s, adj Jno. C. Vanderveer, 1 acre, Flatbush. Joseph Bensel exr. Mary E. Bensel to John Suydam. 1,800

Lots 16 and 17 block 1 map 221 lots property Michael J. Bergen, New Utrecht. James V. S. Woolley, of New York, to Belanie Chenier. 400

Lots 213 and 214 block 4 map 597 lots William Ziegler, Gravesend. William Ziegler to Francis McCarthy. 260

Lots 211 and 212 block 4 same map. Same to Catherine F. Bergen. 260

Lots 436–439 block 8 same map. Same to Nellie T. Kelly. 620

Lots 292–296 block 12 map 633 lots part of the estate Cath. L. Lott, New Utrecht. Effingham H. Nichols, of New York, to Joseph A. Cracknell. 1,400

Interior lot, centre line, bet Liberty av and Hill st, 325 w Crescent st, runs west 54.2 x south to water conduit, x southeast —x—. Theodore Kiendl to Christian Horakh and John Paul. 575

Lots 19–23 and 26–29 inclus. block 2 and lots 90 and 91 block 3 map 597 lots of W. Ziegler, Gravesend. William Ziegler to Eugene McCarthy, New York. 1,925

Lot 446 block 10 map 618 lots, Covenhoven farm, New Utrecht. Effingham H. Nichols to Edward Mastaglio. 160

Lot 14 block 8 map 1,197 lots, Flatbush and New Utrecht, of Wm. Ziegler. John A. Kenney to Patrick J. Kenney. 300

Lot 166 map H. Conklin and others, Canarsie. Charles H. Pelletreau to James Murphy. 100

Plot of land at Canarsie adj land of Catherine Kavanagh, runs northwest 50x100. Fanny A. wife of and John C. Mathews to Catherine Kavanagh. 300

Parcel salt meadow in Bushwick, 18th Ward, bounded north and west by land late of Gabriel Debevoise, east by John Vandervoort, south by John Luqueer, afterwards by S. B. Masters, excepting lot 28x100 on s s Maspeth av. John Devlin to The Equity Gas Works Construction Co. nom

Same property. The Equity Gas Works Construction Co. to The Equity Gas Light Co., Eastern District. nom

All title in franchises conveyed by Lewis J. Stegman as Sheriff to grantor. Henry J. Cullen, Jr., to The Sea Beach & Brighton R. R. Co. 1,250 shares of said railroad stock, par value $100.

Parcel in Flatlands, 15x110. Daniel B. Ames to The Brooklyn & Rockaway Beach R. R. nom

Receipt for legacy and release of estate of Daniel Manjer dec'd by Harriet M. F. Maujer.

WESTCHESTER COUNTY.

DECEMBER 2 TO 8—INCLUSIVE.

BEDFORD.

Hallock, Emily C. to Mary S. Brower, e s Moger av, 100 n School st, 40x128. $200

CORTLANDT.

Belmore, Cath. to Napoleon Ferris, lot adj Lamp Black Factory. 250

Ely, Nathan L. to Helen M. Husted, n e cor Simpson pl and Requa sts, 70x146; also e s Requa st, 30x146. nom

Lent, Smith to Carrie Hubbell, 55 acres adj Wm. Sutherland. 8,000

McLean, Elias A. to Michael Freal, e s Simpson pl, 50x100. 300

McCord, Robt. to Geo. E. Carpenter, w s Simpson pl, 100 s Franklin st, 120x260. nom

EASTCHESTER.

Applegate, Loie to Wm. H. Martin, lots 285, 286, 100 and 350, Washingtonville. 2,800

Buck, Frank M. to The Mt. Vernon Suburban Land Co., 1¼ acres Salt Meadow on Eastchester Creek. 500

Brieger, Adolph to Geo. J. Penfield, lot 87 n w s White Plains road, Washingtonville, 26 3x—. nom

Clark, Barbara A. to Gerd. Martens, e s Glen av, 138 n Prospect av, 63x— 3,250

Cars, Mart et al. to Clarence S. McClellan and ano., w s 4th av, 533.4 s 5th st, 33.4x105 3,400

Foley, Edmund R. to Geo. H. Gulliver, part lot 97 n w s Fulton st, map Penfield property, South Mount Vernon, 40x100. 800

Kenny, Eliz'h to Samuel Fee, lots 11 and 12, map C. V. Morgan's lots, Tuckahoe, 100x185. 850

Luikert, Mary to Chas. Hacker, lot 20 s s Highland av, e Waverly, 156x254x195. 1,485

Morgan, Harry V. to Henry A. Bang, s s William st, 50 w Prospect av, 50x100. 750

Miller, Charlotte to Jas. Harrison, n e cor Fulton av and Elm pl, 67x100 10,000

Neil, John W. to Edw. L. E. Phipps, part lot 54 s e s Greenwich st, West Mount Vernon, 75x100. 2,650

Penfield, Geo. J. to David L. Rudd, lot 49 De Milt av, grantor's map, South Mount Vernon, 33 4x100. 670

Same to Edmund R. Foley, lots 197-203 Matilda st, same map. 4,260

Smith, Mary to John F. Hand, lot 245 w s 3d av, Mt Vernon, 100x105. 7,250

Trede, Elizabeth to Geo. J. Penfield, e s White Plains road, 82 n Summit pl, 68x100. 900

Wheeler, John to Mary E. Palmer, e s White Plains, 11 acres; also lots 1-8, 31-37, 42 and 43 Boulevard; 21-34, 41-48, 53-72 Park av; 1-32 and 37-98 Beechwood av; 1-76 Brookside av; 1-34, 41-50, 55-58, 63, 64, 67-74 Glen av; 1-62 Pellhamville av; 1-8 Maple av, and 1-13 Riverside av, Vernon Park, ½ int. nom

GREENBURGH.

Blackwell, Wilson H. to Fred W. Merks, lots 753-758, Ardsley. 600

Corning, Jasper et al. to Frank B. Masters and ano., s s Private road adj Jas. Fraser, Dobbs Ferry, 5¾ acres. 4,000

Mamlock, David to Thos. Callan, e s road from Hartsdale to Harts corners adj grantee. nom

McKee, Geo. W. to Wm. H. Popham, s s Old Tarrytown road adj John Gibson, 24 acres. 8,000

Perkins, Frank P. to Robt. Boyd, w s Windle av, 197 s Main st, 150x—. nom

Boyd, Robt. to Fred. J. Stone, same property. nom

Stone, Fred. J. to Frank P. Perkins, lot 14, 3¼ acres, and part lot 11, 2¼ acres map west part Steph. B. Tompkins farm. nom

MAMARONECK.

Larchmont Manor Co. to Edw. A. Lauten, s w cor Prospect and Elm avs, abt 161x172. 3,096

Rich, Jas. W. and ano. to Gideon Fountain, lots 9-13 and 57, Grand Park. 1,480

MOUNT PLEASANT.

Blackwell, Wilson H. to Margt. A. Westervelt, lots 8-23 map Mallory estate. nom

Merritt, Geo. W. to Susan D. Brown, s w cor Beekman av and Cortlandt st, abt 102x87. 7,500

Roberts, Louis to Harriet E. Roberts and ano., lots 41, 42 and part 43 and 44 Highland av grantors map, 1¼ acres. nom

Smadbeck, Louis to Michael Sullivan, lots 1019 and 1020, Sherman Park. 500

Same to Leonhard Bechtold, lot 2274. 200

Same to John Matrustry, lots 1615 and 2275. 300

Same to Wilhelmina Nands, lots 1374. 250

NEW CASTLE.

Smith, Clarissa to Gracie M. Delcambre, e s road from Sing Sing to Roaring Brook, 58½ acres. 7,500

Tompkins, Amos to Emma F. Bird, n s road from Chappaqua Depot to Mt. Kisco, 66 w Pickle House road, 75x125. 400

NEW ROCHELLE.

Gregg, Jas. A. S. to Edw. F. Cain, plot 9 Highland Park, 100x200. 3,000

Holt, Maria to Jos. W. Spalding, lot 9 w s Webster av map pt. Smith and Ronalds farm, 50x255. 3,500

Hudson, Alex. B. to Jennie Horn, s w s Birch st, cor Boston road, 40x125. 840

Kirchhoff, Jos. to Chas. W. Kirchhoff, n w cor Union av and Union pl, 50x104. nom

Mathews, Margt. to John Mathews, n w cor North st and Horton av, abt 90x222. nom

Sanders, Wm L. to Fred. St. John, lot 153 and ½ lot 154 n s Linden pl, Residence Park. 1,900

Totman, Susie H. to Annie Dealey, lot 2 block D, Rochelle Park. nom

OSSINING.

Heydenreich, Caroline S. to Geo. A. Brandreth, s e s Broadway, 4½ acres, also lot n s Central av. 9,500

Kane, Fanny R. to Amelia A. Ackerly, e s Water st, adj John Leggett, 30x80. 700

PELHAM.

Schneider, Victor and ano. to John M. Drysdale, lot 65 s s Washington av, Prospect Hill, 200x200. 900

POUNDRIDGE.

Holmes, John C. to Edw F. Brush, 79 acres on road from Eugene Miller to Stone Hills 1,800

Holmes, John R. to same, 20 acres adj Enoch Avery. 50

RYE.

Bulkley, Mary E. and ano. to Josiah N. Wilcox, lots 20 and 21 s s Bush av, Poningo Dale, 100x100. 1,200

Damon, Carrie M. et al., M. Dillon ref., to Wm. Ryan, s w cor Prospect st and Westchester av, abt 200x380. 6,225

Ryan, Wm. to Frances B. Hunt, same property. nom

Merritt, Chas R. and ano. to Michael McLean, s s Railroad av, 99 e 2d av, abt 48x190. 550

Tripp, Geo. E. et al., W. S. Johnson ref., to Theo. Van Amringe, lots 60 and part 59 and 61 s s Stewart av, map property grantee, 100x—. 1,215

WESTCHESTER.

Camp, Hugh N. to Jacob Hollander, lots 184 and 185 map McGraw estate. 580

Crosby, Florence S. to Mary A. Henning, s s 10th st, 80 e Av C, Unionport, 125x108. 4,000

Colford, Mathew and ano. to Fred. Lohbauer, s e cor Willow lane and — st, 25x150. 1,875

Lorillard, Peter to John J. Bannan, w s Elliott av, 100 s Fulton st, 56x157x56x133x100x31. 8,250

Macklin, John J. to Lula Coakley, lot 120 w s Flower pl, map part Givan homestead. 500

Saxe, Simon P. et al., Irving Washburn ref., to Christina E. Bussey, s e s 4th st, 197 s w Union av, 25x—. 900

Same to same, lot adj above, 25x—. 950

Stoerzer, Bertha to Jas. Love, s s Sackett av, 325 w Deane pl, 166x141x66x100. 1,000

WHITE PLAINS.

Brown, Wm. S. to John O'Rourke, Jr., n w cor Hamilton av and Cottage pl, 65x125. 1,400

Cromwell, David to Austin L. Fassett, e s Chester av, 117 s Post road, 60x137. 1,500

Roe, Samuel C., admr. of, to Mary Brady, s s Post road, adj John Horton, 185x315. 1,725

YONKERS.

Brown, Hubert S. to Wm. B. Rice, lots 5, 9, 13, 17 and 21 block 1, and lot 10 block 4 map 2 Nepera Park. 7,800

Lester, G. Harry to same, lots 6, 10, 23, 24, 26, 28 block 1 and 5, 7, 9 and 11 block 2 same map. 7,800

Duden, Herman to Ernst Machenbach, blocks 3, 4 and 5, Sunnyside Park. 7,000

Grady, Thos. to Michael J. Chinnery, lot 30 s s Garfield st, 25x166.6. 500

Harriman, John to Mary E. Scherp, e s Main st, 109.6 s Brook st, abt 25x82. 3,550

Same to same, e s Main st, 183.6 s same, 35x84. 3,000

Lawrence, Fannie E. to Mary Collins, e s 1st st, 194 n Scott av, 25x137. 445

Mutual Life Ins. Co. to N. Y. & Northern Land and Impt. Co., e s South Broadway, adj Railroad, 150x187.6. 12,000

Maclay, Isaac W. to Wm. Schneider, n e cor Palisade av and High st, 328x148.6x261x128. nom

Schneider, Wm. to Laura A. Maclay, same property. nom

N. Y. & Yonkers Land Co. to Philip McManus, lot 205 Bryn Mawr. 261

Same to Jacob Klinger, lots 1-5. 1,800

Same to Geo. W. Mallinson, lot 9. 315

Salinsky, Alb. to Geo. W. Boytim, w s Nepperhan av, 107.7 s Myrtle st, 25x105. 918

Shonnard, Sophia A. to Duncan Smith, n s Hudson terrace, adj C. M. Buckman, 100x232. 5,500

Shearwood Hill Land Co. to Geo. E. Roman, lot 54, Shearwood Hill. 510

Same to Alb. D. Downing, lots 55 and 56. 1,200

Sherwood Land Co to Clarence M. Fowler, lots 6 and 7. 1,050

Valentine, Nath. B. to Dudley F. Valentine, lot 287 e s South Broadway, Geo. Herriot map, 25x100. 5,500

Valentine, Clara M. to Alb. A. Lings, n s Ashburton av, 26.7 e Palisade av, 53x110. 4,150

Ware, Enoch R. trustee of to Leo Sielke, n e Ware and Varian avs, 125x150. 1,370

Ward, Fanny M. to John Forsyth, s s Ludlow st, 100 e Livingston av, 76.4x150. 4,000

MORTGAGES.

NOTE.—The arrangement of this list is as follows. The first name is that of the mortgagor, the next that of the mortgagee. The description of the property then follows, then the date of the mortgage, the time for which it was given, and the amount. The general dates used as headings are the dates when the mortgage was handed into the Register's office to be recorded.

Whenever the letters "P. M." occur, preceded by the name of a street, in these lists of mortgages, they mean that it is a Purchase Money Mortgage, and for fuller particulars see the list of transfers under the corresponding date. Whenever the rate is not given, read as 6 per cent.

NEW YORK CITY.

DECEMBER 4, 5, 7, 8, 9, 10.

Allard, Marie L. wife of and Treffle H. to Roman Arnold. Home or Lyon st, s s, 178 e Stebbins av, 16.4x80.9x17.6x87.2. Dec. 3, 1 year. $625

Same to same. Home or Lyon st, s s, 194.4 e Stebbins av, 16.9x74.2x17.11x80.9. Dec. 3, 1 year. 625

Same to same. Home or Lyon st, s s, 211.1 e Stebbins av, 17.1x68.1x18x74.2. Dec. 3, 1 year. 625

Same to same. Home or Lyon st, s s, 228.2 e Stebbins av, 24.10x58.6x26.7x68.1. Dec. 3, 1 year. 675

Abele, Christian mortgagor with Julius H. and William F. A. Von Sachs mortgagees. Extension of mort. Dec. 7. nom

Austin, Maria wife of William P. to THE TITLE GUARANTEE AND TRUST CO. 7th av, No. 1985, e s, 27 n 119th st, 27x98. Dec. 9, 3 years, 4½ %. 16,000

Altman, Morris P. to Michael H. Cashman. Wadsworth av. P. M. Oct 12, 3 years or installs, 5 %. 5,750

Arnold, Richard mortgagor with Jacob A. Chamberlain mortgagee. Extension of mort. Nov. 21. nom

Bannen, John to Sarah H. Powell. 85th st, s s, 150 e Columbus av, 25x102.2. Dec. 10, 2 months. 4,000

Barker, John and Emma his wife to Thomas W. Surridge. Arcularius pl, s s, 309.3 e Gerard av, 25x172.3x25x177.3. Dec. 1, 3 years. 900

Same to same. Arcularius pl, s s, 334.3 e Gerard av, runs south 172.3 x east 75 x north 57.3 x west 50 x north 100 to pl, x west 25. Dec. 1, 3 years. 1,400

Bormann, Conrad to Henrietta Roeber. 65th st, No. 302, s s, 64 e 2d av, 18x76.2x18.2x73.5. Dec. 9, due Dec. 10, 1894. 1,000

Same to Charles Kobler. 107th st. P. M. Dec. 8, due Jan. 1, 1897, or installs, 5 %. 3,000

Boyle, William L. to Victoria Chubb widow. Madison av. P. M. Dec. 10, 3 years, installs, 5 %. 35,000

Bernheimer, Lehman, Munich, Bavaria, mortgagee with Rebecca wife of and Harry E. Moss mortgagors. Extension of mort at 5 %. Nov. 25. nom

Boyle, William L., New Rochelle, N. Y., to THE UNITED STATES TRUST CO., New York. 64th st. P. M. Nov. 16, due Dec. 1, 1894, 5 %. 14,000

Bishop, Mary L. wife of Charles J., Boston, Mass., to THE METROPOLITAN SAVINGS BANK. 1st av, e s, 81.7 n 84th st, 20.5x100. Dec 1, 1 year, 4½ %. 10,000

Blackhurst, Abigail A. to Henry C. Thompson. Lorillard pl or st. P. M. Dec. 7, due May 1, 1894, or installs. 2,000

Blum, Jennie to Matilda Weil et al. exrs. Max Weil. 61st st, No. 51, n s, abt 229 w 4th av, 19x100.5. Dec. 8, 5 years, 4½ % gold. 12,000

Bateman, Belle wife of Arthur E. to John W. Thompson, Washington, D. C. 5th av, e s, 54 s Clinton pl, 27x100. Sub. to mort. Dec. 1, 1 year, 5 %. 20,000

Bauer, Louisa wife of and Gustav to George Ehret. Park row. Lease. P. M. Dec. 2, demand. 13,000

Betjemann, Herman to Edwin Baldwin exr. and trustee John Hardman. 1st av, s w cor 120th st, 20.5x68. Dec. 4, due Dec. 1, 1894, 5 %. 12,000

Bier, Mary to Sigmund Cohn. 13th st, No. 444 E., s s, bet 1st av and Av A, 24.3x103.3. Dec. 1, 5 months. 475

Billsland, Elizabeth to THE METROPOLITAN SAVINGS BANK. Bond st, No. 51, s s, 25x74.10x25.5x69.11. Dec. 4, 1 year, 5 %. 1,000

Baker, John O., Newark, N. J., to Edward Oppenheimer and Isaac Metzger. 76th st. P. M. Dec. 1, due June 1, 1893. 3,600

Blumenthal, Mark to Patrick F. Ferrigan et al. exrs. Hugh Ferrigan. Washington av and 173d st. P. M. Nov. 23, 3 years, 5 %. 8,500

Cameron, Margaret S. E. to THE TITLE GUARANTEE AND TRUST CO. 5th av, No. 810, n e cor 62d st, 25.5x100. Dec. 7, 3 years, 4½ %. 100,000

Clark, Francis A. to The Henry Elias Brewing Co. 2d av, s w cor 97th st, 25.11x75. Sub. to mort. $22,000. Dec. 7, 4 months, note. 3,000

Coogan, Matthew to Thomas Mackellar. 107th st, s s, 275 w 1st av. P. M. Dec. 1, 1 year. 8,500

Same to Laura F. Van Riper. 107th st, s s, 325 w 1st av. P. M. Dec 1, 1 year. 4,000

Coogan, Matthew to Kate F. Allen. 107th st. P. M. Dec. 8, 1 year, 5 %. 4,500

Carion, Philipp to THE GERMAN SAVINGS BANK. 40th st, s s, 100.1 e 2d av, 24.11x98.9. Dec. 7, due Dec. 8, 1893. 5,250

Celeman, Sophia wife of Myer to Frederic J. Middlebrook, Brooklyn. 29th st, s s, 201 w 7th av, 24.10x98.9. Sub. to mort. $10,000. Dec. 8, 1 year. 4,000

Collins, Asa E., Linden, N. J., to Laura A. Thompson, Brooklyn. Union av. P. M. Dec. 1, 1 year or installs, 5 %. 25,000

Same to William W. Buckley, Tenafly, N. J. Same property. P. M. Sub. to last mort. Dec. 1, 1 year. 3,000

Conlon, Margaret E., Brooklyn, to Margaret Inglis. 114th st, s s, 209 w 5th av, 17.8x100.11. Dec. 8, due Dec. 1, 1894, 5 %. 12,000

Same to Henry Franke. Same property. Sub. to last mort. Dec. 8, demand. 2,400

Carroll, Mary E. wife of and John J. to THE MUTUAL LIFE INS. CO., New York. 10th av, n w cor 33d st, 24.9x100. Dec. 4, 1 year, 5 %. 4,000

Christie, David to Donald Mitchell. West End av and 104th st. P. M. Dec. 3, due May 1, 1898. 45,500

Cloherty, Hermine wife of and James P. to THE MUTUAL LIFE INS. CO., New York. 2d av, n w cor 40th st, runs west 155 x north 98.9 x east 80 x south 59.1 x east 75 to av, x south 39.8; 79th st, n s, 112 w 3d av, 22x102.2. Dec. 4, 1 year, 5 %. See Conveys 46,000

Crossman, Charles S., Brooklyn, to Sarah Adam. 7th av. P. M. Dec. 2, 1 year. 1,750

Cumming, William, Jr., and Robert Ferguson to THE GERMAN SAVINGS BANK. 21st st, No. 331, n s, 350 e 9th av, runs north 98.9 x east 24.8½ x south 16.7 x east 0.4½ x south 32 x west 0.2 x south 50 to st, x west to beginning. Dec. 2, due Dec. 3, 1892. 22,500

Crohn, Theodore to Mitchell Hershfield. 82d st, No. 216, s s, 186 e 3d av, 17x102.2. Dec. 8, 1 year. 1,000

Campbell, John V. to Joseph L. Buttenwieser. Eldridge st, No. 55, w s, 25.2x100.1. Recorded Nov. 19, 1891. Nov. 17, demand. (Corrects error in issue of Dec. 5 under head of Blair—Same to same.) 14,112

Same to same. Catharine st, No. 86, e s, 24.6x100. Nov. 17, demand. 1,600

Cantor, Jacob A. to Edward T. Smith. 120th st. P. M. Dec. 10, installs. 7,500

Day, Francis E. to William R. Brown, White Plains. 132d st, n s, 225 w Cypress av, 75x185. Dec. 8, due Dec. 1, 1894. 3,500

Delabunty, Thomas to THE EMIGRANT INDUST. SAVINGS BANK. 20th st, s s, 100 e 8th av; 25x86x25.4x89.11. Dec. 10, 1 year, 4½ %. 1,000

Drake, William H., Brooklyn, to Kate E. Holmes. 12th st, s s, 134.1 e Av C, 23.10x103.3. Dec. 1, 1 year, 5 %. 11,000

Dugro, Philip H. and Frederick Wagner to THE TITLE GUARANTEE AND TRUST CO., New York. 5th av, s e cor 59th st, 75.5x100; 59th st, s s, 100 e 5th av, 50x100.5. Secures debt of mortgagor and Frederick Wagner. Building loan. Dec. 9, 1 year. 650,000

Danzig, Simon and Gabriel S. Kutz to Hiram R. and Henry Dater trustees Philip Dater dec'd. in place of Philip Dater, Jr., dec'd. Westchester av. P. M. Dec. 9, 2 years, 4½ %. 176,155

Drake, Benjamin to THE IRVING SAVINGS INST. 3d av, e s, 65.5 n 55th st, 20x110. Dec. 8, 1 year, 4½ %. 5,000

Dechert, Yellott D. to Samuel Love. 60th st, n s, 150 e 9th av, 25x100.5. Dec. 4, 2 years, 5 %. See Conveys. 2,000

Dellaglio, Nicholas and Maria and Francesco Micucci and Emelia his wife to Solomon A. Cohn and Frederick Milbeiser. 112th st. P. M. Dec. 1, installs. 4,500

Desbrisay, Jennie F. wife of Harold S. to Margaret E. wife of Albert E. Putnam. New Drive, &c. P. M. Dec. 1, installs, 6 % and 5 %. 9,000

Donaldson, Chester to Kilian Van Rensselaer trustee. 71st st, n s, 100 w 9th av, 25x102.2 Sub. to mort. $30,000. Secures bonds. Dec. 7, 5 years. 10,000

Drew, Clara M. wife of William W. to Alfred Taylor. 7th av, Nos. 2053 and 2055, e s, 115 n 122d st, 35.6x75; 7th av, Nos. 2041, 2043 and 2045, n e cor 122d st, 58x75. Sub. to morts. $92,000. Dec. 5, due May 1, 1892. 3,000

Edgar, George C. and Thomas C. to John P. Huggins. 69th st. P. M. Dec. 9, 1 year, 5 %. 60,000

Same to same. Same property. Building loan. Dec. 9, 1 year. 50,000

Fay, Michael and William Stacom to THE UNITED STATES LIFE INS. CO., New York. 10th st, No. 206, s s, 124.1 e 2d av, 25.1x92.3x24.11x92.3. Dec. 3, due Dec. 1, 1896, 5 %. 28,000

Finnigan, James to George Ehret. 1st av, s w cor 76th st. Store lease. Dec. 4, demand. 4,000

First Hungarian Congregation Obab Zedek to THE MUTUAL LIFE INS. CO. of New York. Norfolk st, e s, 175 s Houston st, 100x100. Already mortgaged to mortgagee. Dec. 7, 1 year. 5,000

Fogal, Caroline to Martin Norz. Alexander av, e s, 29.4 s 137th st, 14.4x60. Dec. 7, 3 years, 5 %. 4,000

Fraim, Charlotte E. wife of Daniel W. formerly Ray and Florence T. and Henrietta C. Ray to Anita Duchastel. 62d st, n s, 134 e 2d av, 16x100.5. Dec. 5, due Dec. 7, 1894, 5 %. 5,000

Finck, Katie A. widow to John H. Haaren. Sullivan st, s cor Grand st, 20x50. 1-3 part. Dec. 4, installs. 6,500

Same to Claus Haaren. Same property. 1-3 part. Dec. 4, 1 year, note. 2,000

Geismann, Moise to Maria A. Heyer, Chicago, Ill. 158th st, s s, 358.5 w Courtlandt av. P. M. Nov 20, due Dec. 4, 1894, 5 %. 5,344

Same to same. 158th st, s s, 410 7 w Courtlandt av. P. M. Nov. 20, due Dec. 4, 1894, 5 %. 3,500

Georgi, Sarah F. to Magdalena Hoeland. 3d av, w s, 150.2 s 163d st, 73.7x94.5x73.9x96.5. July 20. 600

Goerlitz, John to Adam Happel. Spring st, Nos. 131-127, n s, 48.2 w Greene st, runs north 95.6 x west 17.10 x southwest 8 x north 7 x west 27.3 x north 3.6 x west 46.2 x south 100 to Spring st, x east 98.2 to beginning. Nov. 27, due Dec. 1, 1892, without int. 16,000

Goodridge, Charlotte M. to THE GERMAN SAVINGS BANK, New York. 36th st, n s, 139.4 w Broadway, 19.11x98.9. Nov. 11, due Nov. 13, 1892. 20,000

Grening, Paul C. to Meyer Guggenheim. 47th st, No. 147, n s, 258.4 e Lexington av, 16.8x100.5. Dec. 1, 1 year. 5,000

Grinnell, William M. to THE MUTUAL LIFE INS CO., New York. 155th st, n s, 100 e 12th av, runs north 376.4 x east 67 x southeast 218.2 in a curved line to new proposed road now being n s of intended 156th st at point 325 e 12th av, x south 60 to 156th st as now laid out, x east 12.6 x south 199.10 to 155th st, x west 237.6. Secures debt of mortgagor and George B. Grinnell. Dec. 8, 1 year, 5 %. 60,000

Gumbleton, Julia J. wife of and Henry A. to Thomas Bogan. 124th st, n s, 80 w 5th av, 19.6x81.5. Dec. 7, due June 1, 1892. 1,100

Gallagher, William J. to Ann De Courcy. 42d st, s s, 203.6 e 10th av, 22.6x98.9. All title. Dec. 2, 1 year. 500

Ganz, Pinkas to Joseph Newborg. 98th st. P. M. Dec. 1, installs. 5,000

Godfrey, Kate E. to George Ehret. 4th st, No. 103 E., n s, 25x96.2. Lease. Dec. 9, demand. 6,000

Grasmuck, Frederick to Edmund Coffin, Jr. 143d st and Edgecombe av. P. M. Nov. 13, 3 years, 5 %. 5,000

Hart, Bertha wife of Mitchel to Bernhard Baruch, Rye, N. Y. Lexington av, w s, 24.7 s 102d st, 16.7x75. Dec. 9, 6 months. 300

Same to same. Same property. Dec. 9, 3 months. See Conveys. 165

Hume, Sarah M. mortgagor with Julius H. and William F. A. Von Sachs mortgagees. Extension of mort. Dec. 8. nom

Huntington, Eleanor C. mortgagor with Charles Scholle mortgagee. Extension of mort. at increased interest. Dec. 5. nom

Hanlon, Mary E. wife of Joseph E. to John Bussing, Jr. 167th st, n s, 175 w Union av, 25x125x25x123.9; Madison av, w s, 75 s Columbia av, 75x200 to Jefferson av. Dec. 9, due July 1, 1894. 500

Hillis, Robert and Robert H. and F. W. Sniffen to Hillis Plantation Coffee Co. Consent of stockholders to chattel mortgage. Nov. 28. 2,500

Harrison, Margaret A. mortgagee with James A. Ketcham mortgagor. Extension of mort. Nov. 27. nom

Holck, Pauline wife of Henry to Adolph G. Hupfel. Oak st, No. 56, n s, 19.8x50 to alley, with use of same. Dec. 1, 2 years, 5 %. 3,000

Hughes, Theresa wife of Robert to Patrick F. Ferrigan et al. exrs. Hugh Ferrigan. Central av, w s, 164.4 n Gerard av. P. M. Nov. 23, 3 years, 5 %. 912

Same to same. Central av, w s, 139.1 n Gerard av. P. M. Nov. 23, 3 years, 5 %. 912

Same to same. Central av, w s, 113.10 n Gerard av. P. M. Nov. 23, 3 years, 5 %. 912

Same to same. Central av, w s, 189 6 n Gerard av. P. M. Nov. 23, 3 years, 5 %. 912

Same to same. Central av, w s, 243.6 n Gerard av. P. M. Nov. 23, 3 years, 5 %. 912

Same to same. 3d av, w s, lot 15 map Morrisania. P. M. Nov. 23, 3 years, 5 %. 4,250

Same to same. Inwood av, e s, 79.11 n Gerard av. P. M. Nov. 23, 3 years, 5 %. 487

Same to same. Inwood av, e s, 54.11 n Gerard av. P. M. Nov. 23, 3 years, 5 %. 487

Same to same. Inwood av, e s, 104.11 n Gerard av. P. M. Nov. 23, 3 years, 5 %. 487

Same to same. Inwood av, e s, 29.11 n Gerard av. P. M. Nov. 23, 3 years, 5 %. 487

Hughes, Thomas R., Weehawken, N. J., to Richard M. Harison, Astoria, L. I. 83d st. P. M. Dec. 7, due Dec. 1, 1894, 5 %. 15,000

Halley, Mary E. wife of and Charles V. to Anna Goldsticker. 175th st, s s, 72 e Franklin av, 49.2x100; 175th st, s e cor Franklin av, 22x100x22.4x100. Dec. 8, due Dec. 1, 1892. 1,000

Harris, Samuel to George W. Morrow, Jersey City, N. J. 118th st, s s, 120 e Madison av, 20x100.11. Sub. to morts. $88,000. Nov. 16, due Feb. 14, 1892. 2,642

Heilbrunn, Julius to Adolph Simon. Av C. P. M. Nov. 20, installs, 5 %. 5,700

Hutton, John and Annie his wife to Morris Wolf, Passaic Co. Willis av, n w cor 146th st, 50x106; Willis av, n w cor 145th st, 25x106. Dec. 1, due March 1, 1892. 1,500

Hohl, Charles to T. Gaillard Thomas. 133d st. P. M. Dec. 7, 1 year, 5 %. 3,500

Ingoldsby, Helene wife of and Edward M. to Clara A. Bowron. 31st st, No. 112, s s, 181 e 4th av, 19x98.9. Dec. 7, 2 years. gold, 2,500

Jackson, Samuel M. to George T. Jackson. 8th av, No. 777, w s, 50 n 47th st, 25x100. Sub. to mort. $25,000. Nov. 4, due Nov. 1, 1892. 2,000

Jenkins, Thomas J. and George to George E. Hyatt, Brooklyn. Columbus (9th) av, s e cor 124th st, runs south 100.11 x east 200 x north 93.11 to w s Manhattan av, x north 15 1 to 124th st, x west 186.7 to beginning. Dec. 3, demand. 5,000

Jacobs, Elias to Fannie Falk et al. exrs., &c., Arnold Falk. Sheriff st, No. 93. P. M. Nov. 30, 3 years, 5 %. gold, 14,500

Same to same. Sheriff st, No. 91. P. M. Nov. 30, 3 years, 5 %. gold, 14,500

Jencks, Francis M. to Jane Whiston, Jamaica, L. I. 49th st, No. 241, n s, 185.4 e 8th av, 17.8x100.5. Dec. 3, demand. 11,000

Same to Clarence L. Westcott. 77th st, n s, 191 w West End av, 19x102.2. Dec. 3, demand. 20,000

Jennett, Thomas mortgagor with Julius H. and William F. A. Von Sachs mortgagees. Extension of mort. Dec. 8. nom

Kassel, Abraham to Joseph Kassel. Baxter st, Nos. 38 and 40. P. M. Sub. to morts. $36,000. Dec. 9, due Dec. 1, 1893. 2,000

Kehl, George to Jacob Ruppert. 40th st, No. 318 E. Store lease. Dec. 4, demand. 600

Kneeland, Arabella C. widow to Mary M. Costello guard. Julia L. and Richard R. Costello. 74th st, n s, 250 e West End av, 20x102.2. Dec. 7, 3 years, 4½ %. gold, 7,000

Koen, Joseph J., Pearsalls, L. I., to Isabell Merritt. Marion av. P. M. Dec. 9, 3 years. 500

Katzenstein, Henriette wife of Simon to Anton Rinschler. Bergen av. P. M. Dec. 7, 10 years or installs, 5 %. 7,000

Kemnade, Louis to Bernheimer & Schmid. 8th av, No. 2711. Saloon lease. Dec. 8, note, demand. 2,000

Kelly, Annie wife of Malachi to Mary E. wife of Charles V. Halley. 175th st, s s, 47 e Franklin av. P. M. Dec. 8, 3 years. 1,100

Same to same. 175th st, s s, 22 e Franklin av. P. M. Dec. 8, 3 years. 2,600

Ketcham, James W. to Meyer L. Sire. Lexington av, s e cor 29th st, 22 4x80. Dec. 4, installs, 5 %. 8,500

Kirk, William, Delmar, N. Y., to Myer Nussbaum as trustee, Albany, N. Y. James st, Nos. 11 and 13, w s, 52x123 8x52x134 11, except part taken for New Bowery. Secures debts to estate of Andrew Kirk. Nov. 27. ——

Kehoe, Catherine wife of and James to James Flanagan. 1st av, n e cor 114th st, 28.10 or 28.11x75. Dec. 7, 1 year, 5 %. gold, 20,000

Keutel, Julius and Clara his wife to Auguste Weissenfels. 163d st, n s, 100 w Washington av, 25x119.6. Dec. 3, due March 16, 1894, 5 %. 2,500

Keirns, John to Patrick H. Ferrigan et al exrs. Hugh Ferrigan. Central and Gerard avs. P. M. Nov. 28, demand, 5 %. 1,950

Same to same. Gerard av, n s, 88.8 w Central av. P. M. Nov. 23, 3 years, 5 %. 537

Kelly, Mary J. wife of and Thomas P. to Harriet A. Batjer. 79th st. P. M. Nov. 21, due Nov. 23, 1893. 3,000

Kotlowsky, Philip and Barnet Levy to John Koell. Allen st. P. M. Dec. 7, due Dec. 1, 1892, 5 %. 13,000

Lopez, Dias and Julian A., New Rochelle, N. Y., to THE ALBANY CITY SAVINGS INST. East Broadway, No. 144, n s, 25x61.1x25x61.11. Dec. 7, 5 years, 5 %. 3,000

Lawton, Newbury D. to Elizabeth Burt. Part lots 29 and 30 map Eltona, begins at point 158.8 n 165th st, runs north 18 9x90. Dec. 2, due Dec. 3, 1894, 5 %. 3,750

Lederer, Lizzie and Millie and Annie wife of Charles H. Klee to Diedrich O. Haaren. 20th st, s s, 179.4 w 7th av, 25x83.11x25x83.3. Dec. 3, 2 years, 5 %. 3,000

Levy, Aaron and Barnett and Sophia Gruenstein to Jonas Weil and Bernhard Mayer. Lewis st, No. 93. P. M. Dec. 4, installs. 6,250

Same to same. Lewis st, No. 91. P. M. Dec. 4, installs. 6,000

Same to same. Lewis st, No. 95. P. M. Dec. 4, due Dec. 1, 1895. 4,000

Libman, Myer to Nellie Markovitch formerly Blum guard. Amelia and Augusta Blum. 118th st, n s, 210.8 e 1st av, runs north 100.11 x east 14.4 x south 19.9 x southeast 3.6 x south 78.6 to 118th st, x west 16 8. Dec. 3, 3 years. 2,000

Loeble, Frederick C., Brooklyn, to Henry Peters, Brooklyn. Grand st, Nos. 43 and 45, 34.8x96.6. ½ part. Leasehold. Nov. 27, 3 years, 5 %. 3,000

Long, William B. to The New York and Suburban Co-operative Building and Loan Assoc. Part lots 29 and 30 map Eltona, begins 177.5 s 165th st. P. M. Dec. 8, installs. 6,500

Mangels, Anna widow, Henry N., John E., Dora L. and Clara A. Mangels heirs Henry Mangels to James B. Storer committee Ann M. Storer. 45th st, s s, 225 w 9th av, 50x100.5. Dec. 8, due Dec. 1, 1896, 5 %. gold, 7,500

McGuiness, Edward to John Miller trustee Eliza Peck. 55th st, No. 222, s s, 290 e 3d av, 24.9x102.2. Nov. 30, due May 1, 1892. 7,000

Mason, Maria L. wife of and Walter to Isaac P. Smith. St. Anns av, e s, 50 s Rae st, runs east 80.3 x again east 23.6 to centre Carr av, x south 25 x west 23 6 x again west 32.4 to St. Anns av, x north 25.1. Dec. 5, 1 year, 5 %. 1,200

McCormick, Margaret wife of and James E. to Margaret S. Moody. 134th st, n s, 475 e St. Anns av, 50x100. Dec. 9, 1 year, 5 %. 3,000

Maher, Catharine to Henry Elias Brewing Co. Mulberry st, No. 36, e s, 72.1 n Park st, 21.2 x east 28 x south 1 x east 54 x south 18.4 x west 1 x south 3.8 x west 20.6 x north 1.2 x west 64.11. Sept. 1, demand. 946

Mayer, Joseph D. to Adam Gebhardt. 115th st. P. M. Dec. 3, 2 years. 5,000

Moser, Oscar L. and Amelia his wife to Maria A. Heyer widow, Chicago, Ill. 158th st. P. M. Nov. 20, due Dec 4, 1894, 5 %. 5,607

Maeder, John G. and Lydia his wife to Margaret T. Odell. 120th st. P. M. Dec. 7, 3 years, 5 %. gold, 8,000

Marks, Flora wife of and Selim to THE WASHINGTON LIFE INS CO. 61st st, n s, 58 e Park av, 19x100.5. Dec. 7, due Dec. 1, 1894, 5 %. 18,000

Marren, James P. to Julia A. wife of Frederick Frank. 1st av. P. M. Dec. 4, due Dec. 15, 1896, 5 %. 8,000

Mooney, John H. to Lizzie K. Mooney. 76th st, n s, 182 w 9th av, runs north 102.2 x west 18 x south 42.2 x west 0.6 x south 55 x east 0.6 x south 5 x east 18. Dec. 6, 1890, due Dec. 6, 1893. 12,000

Nason, Alfred G. to Edward Oppenheimer and Isaac Metzger. 76th st. P. M. Dec. 1, due Dec. 11, 1892. 12,400

Same to same. Same property. Dec. 1, due Dec. 11, 1892. 24,000

Nichols, Marion L., Westfield, N. J., to Peter Doelger. 5th av, No. 768. Leasehold. Nov. 25, demand. 4,000

Neuudorff, Elizabeth to Maria A. Heyer, Chicago, Ill. 157th st. P. M. Nov. 20, due Dec. 4, 1894, 5 %. 1,358

Nally, Margaret T. wife of and Christopher to Cassidy & Adler. 132d st. P. M. Nov. 28, due May 1, 1892. 4,661

O'Connor, Joseph, Newark, N. J., to Robinson Gill trustee. Central Park West (8th) av, s w cor 103d st, 100.11x100. Sub. to morts. $132,000. Dec. 1, 6 months, 5 %. See Conveys. 5,175

O'Connor, Joseph, Newark, N. J., to The Mohawk Valley Lumber Co., of Fultonville, N. Y. Central Park West or 8th av, s w cor 103d st, 100.11x100. Sub. to morts. $132,000. Dec. 1, 6 months. See Conveys. 6,000

O'Connell, Nicholas J. to Louis Lochmann. Lexington av, n e cor 83d st, 16.2x68. Sub. to mort. $12,750. Dec. 9, 1 year. 3,000

O'Hagan, Ann widow to The Stuyvesant Co-operative Building and Loan Assoc. Lexington av, w s, 20.11 s 108th st, 20x75. Dec. 2, installs, 5 %. 2,500

Perceval, Charles to Louis Perceval. Clinton pl, n s, 77.7 e 6th av, 25x93.11. Sept. 8, due Sept. 1, 1896, 5 %. 7,000

Phelps, Louis N. to Mary E. McGuckin and Jules J. Blaise, of McGuckin & Blaise. Bleecker st, s e cor 8th av, runs northeast along av 44.11 x southeast 40 x east 17.2 x south 22.5 x west 76.9 to Bleecker st, x north 27.7. Dec. 5, 6 months. 5,500

Same to Christian Hafers. Same property. Sub. to morts. Dec. 5, 6 months. 4,700

Same to Cassidy & Adler. Same property. Sub. to morts. Dec. 5, 6 months. 2,500

Pearsall, Pauline S. to Thomas W. Pearsall and ano. trustees Paul Spofford. 14th st, s s, 34 e 5th av, 33x103.3. 1-5 part. Lease. Dec. 3, 1 year. 5,000

Reinach, Bernhard to Pauline Frank. 8th st, s s, 51 w Lewis st, 21.11x22.2. Dec. 1. 1,000

Rice, Charlotte wife of and James to R. B. Douglass Mfg. Co. 116th st, n s, 200 w 8th av, 50x84.8x50x84.8; interior lot on centre line bet 116th st and 117th st at point 120 e Manhattan av, runs south 31.3 x northeast 26.1 x north 23.9 x west 25. Nov. 7, due March 1, 1892. 1,209

Rohrs, Frederick to The Bradley & Currier Co. (Lim.) Madison av, s e cor 132d st, 99.11 x150. Sub. to morts. Nov. 13, 3 months. 12,500

Rohrs, Frederick to David Quigley. Madison av, s e cor 132d st, 99.11x150. Dec. 4, 3 months. 7,000

Ransom, Georgie widow to THE MUTUAL LIFE INS. CO., New York. 25th st, n s, 600 e 6th av, 25x98.9. Already mortgaged to party of second part. Dec. 9, 1 year, 5 %. 3 000

Reinke, Herrmann to Bernheimer & Schmid. 106th st, No. 174 E. Dec. 9, note, demand. 1,600

Regan, Patrick J. to P. Ballantine & Sons, a corporation. Greenwich av, No. 57. Store lease. Dec. 7, demand. 1,500

Reilly, John J. to Gustav Falk et al. exrs. Arnold Falk. 2d av, e s, 50.2 n 59th st, 25.3x 76.7. Dec. 5, 3 years, 5 %. gold, 21,000

Same to Lewis Z. Bach. Same property. Dec. 7, due Dec. 1, 1892. 6,500

Ries, Herman H and John F. to THE GERMAN SAVINGS BANK, New York. 1st av, s w cor 10th st, 23.1x72. Dec. 2, due Dec. 4, 1892. 12,000

Rapelyea, Catherine to THE UNITED STATES LIFE INS. CO., New York. 129th st. P. M. Dec. 4, due Dec. 1, 1894, 5 %. 10,000

Rinschler, Alphonso to Hermann Hering. Forest av, e s, 47.6 n 161st st, 29x135. Dec. 7, due Aug. 15, 1896, or installs, 5 %. 2,000

Roessert, Emil and Emma his wife to Martha Kiefer. 9th st, n s, 350 e 2d av, 25x100.8. Dec. 4, due Jan. 1, 1893, 5 %. 1,500

Rubsam, Jacob to Maria A. Heyer, Chicago, Ill. 158th st. P. M. Nov. 20, due Dec. 4, 1894, 5 %. 1,947

Schaefer, George H. to William N. Crane. 144d st. P. M. Dec. 3, due Oct. 1, 1892. 11,000

Same to same. Same property. Dec. 3, due Oct. 1, 1892. 19,000

Schloeder, Jacob to Andrew A. Smith. 120th st, s s, 100 e Pleasant av, 50x100.11. Dec. 3, due June 4, 1894, 5 %. 22,750

Schmidt, William and Margaretha to Mary Bier. 69th st, No. 335. P. M. Dec. 1, 1 year or installs. 550

Schaefler, Adolph to Sarah Glass. 27th st, s s, 60 w 10th av, 15.5x24.8. Dec. 4, 1 year, 5 %. 1,500

Schlosser, Jacob mortgagor with Jacob Schlosser mortgagee. Extension of mort. Dec. 8. nom

Selleck, Louise B. wife of and Edward to The Manhattan Eye and Ear Hospital. 87th st, s s, 135 e Av A, runs south 100.8 x east 15 x north 37.8 x east 3 x north 63 to st, x west 18. Dec. 8, due Jan. 1, 1893, 5 %. 6,000

Stang, Joseph and Davis Bittner to Nechama Honig. 64th st. P. M. Nov. 12, installs. 1,900

Same to Max Strumpf. Same property. P. M. Nov. 12, 3 years. 1,600

Smith, John B. to Horace Bacon. 130th st, s s, 160 e 5th av, 50x135. Dec. 7, 4 months, note. 30,000

Smith, David N. to Francis P. Furnald. Bull av, west cor Suburban st, 51x110x76 6x94. Already mortgaged to mortgagee. Dec. 4, due Sept. 1, 1894. 1,500

Sultan, Simon and Leon B. Ginsburg to THE GERMAN-AMERICAN REAL ESTATE TITLE GUARANTEE CO. 124th st, s e cor 4th av, 30 x100.11. Sub. to morts. $40,000. Dec. 5. 1,500

Salzer, Max to Gussie Fleck. Rivington st, s s, 75 e Suffolk st, 22x100. Dec. 9, 1 year. 500

Schneider, William to Lemuel Skidmore. 65th st, s s, 250 e 5th av, 50x102.2. Dec. 1, 3 years, 5 %. gold, 20,000

Sauer, George W. to John Gerken. 155th st, s s, 100 w 8th av, 75x99.11. Dec. 7, due Dec. 10, 1891. 2,000

Simonson, Martin H. and Emma C. his wife to Thomas L. Reynolds and Eugene Schwab. Sheridan av. P. M. Dec. 10, 1 year. 1,000

Sullivan, James to Joel W. Mason. Pearl st, No. 379. P. M. Dec. 1, 3 years, or installs, 5 %. 17,000

Sauer, Frederick W., George Herbener and Conrad Gross to George L. Howard, Northville, N. Y. Madison av and 98th st. P. M. Dec 1, due June 1, 1893, 5 %. 20,000

Schaefer, Philip to Anita Duchastel. 151st st. P. M. Dec. 9, 3 years or installs, 5 %. 5,000

Schaller, Henriette to John Riexinger and Maria his wife. 82d st, n s. 106 e 1st av, 25x 102.2. Dec. 8, due Jan. 1, 1894. 1,000

Schneider, Joseph to John Lutz. 94th st. n s, 100 w 9th av, 25x100.8. Dec. 8, 3 years, 5 %. 8,000

Schweppenhauser, George to THE HARLEM SAVINGS BANK. Valentine av, n s, 25 e Garfield st, 50x100. Dec. 7, 1 year, 5 %. 3,000

Sneckner, William to Mary S. Van Beuren. Broadway or Union pl, w s, 26 n 15th st, 26x 116.10. Lease. Dec. 9, 5 years. 5,000

Stein, Joachim mortgagor with Jane Besthoff. Extension of mort. Dec 9. nom

Stevenson, Hugh to THE MUTUAL LIFE INS. CO. of New York. Edgecombe road, e s, lot 925 map Jumel estate, runs south along road 579.2 x east 1.3 x north 595 to Highbridge Park, x west 211.1 x southwest 108.9 to beginning. Dec. 7, 1 year. 25,000

Stelter, Henry to Bernheimer & Schmid. Lexington av, No. 1343. Saloon lease. Dec. 8, note, demand. 4,000

Stevens, Henry E. to THE FRANKLIN SAVINGS BANK. 48th st. P. M. Dec. 9, 1 year, 5 %. 18,000

Same to Jenny A. Carew, Norwich, Conn. Same property. P. M. 2d mort. Dec. 9, 1 month. 8,477

Sullivan, Daniel J. to William F. Fisher & Co. 132d st, n s, 100 w Amsterdam av, 25x99.11. Sub. to liens. Dec. 8, notes. 5,000

The Houston, West Street & Pavonia Ferry R. R. Co. to THE NEW YORK SECURITY AND TRUST CO. Consent of the stockholders to mortgage. Oct. 1, 1890. nom

The Houston, West st and Pavonia Ferry R. R. Co. to THE NEW YORK SECURITY AND TRUST CO. Railroad franchises and properties. Oct. 1, 1890, 20 years. bonds, 6,000,000

Thomas, Margaret wife of Rowland formerly Hines to John B. Ryer. Prospect pl, e s, north ½ lot 114 map of Monterey, 25x100. Nov. 12, 3 years. 1,000

Toman, Edward to George Ehret. Whitehall st, No. 20½. Lease. Dec. 5, demand. 1,500

Taubert, William H. to Emma C. Pugsley. 136th st. P. M. Dec. 7, 3 years, 5 %. 4,500

Thurston, Franklin A. to Isabella McCormack. 133d st, s s, 250 w 7th av, 150x99.11. Dec. 1, demand. 13,000

Tilden, Lilian E. F. to Eugene H. Goddard, London, Eng. ½ part of estate of Milano C. Tilden. Nov. 30, due May 13, 1893. £140

Tilson, James to Henry E. Jones. Monroe st, No. 35, n s, 25x100. Dec. 7, 3 years, 5 %. 15,000

Thorn, Emily A. et al. exrs. William K. Thorn mortgagees with Gustav or Gustavus Ramsperger mortgagor. Extension of reduced mortgage at 6 %. June 1. 1888. nom

Tiemann, Henry and Mary his wife to Henry F. Borges and Margaretha his wife, Woodside, L. I. 11th av, w s, 25 n 59th st, 25x100. Dec. 1, 5 years or installs, 5 %. 3,000

Titus, Cora C. to Thomas O'Connor. 132d st, n s, 277.6 w 5th av, 17x99.11. Dec. 3, 5 years, 5 %. 6,000

Ueckermann, Marie wife of William to THE GERMAN SAVINGS BANK, New York. 87th st, No 64, s s, 107.10 w 4th av, 25.6x100.8. Dec. 9, due Dec. 10, 1892. 21,000

Same to same. 87th st, No. 62, s s, 133.4 w 4th av, 25.6x100.8. Dec. 9, due Dec. 10, 1892. 21,000

Vielberth, Joseph F. to Joseph Raynor, Seaford, L. I. Fox st, w s, 279.1 s 167th st, 25x 100. Nov. 1, 3 years. 1,800

Weil, Katie to Isidor Grayhead. 11th st, s s, 188 e 2d av, 48.4x94.10. Lease. Nov. 30, due Jan. 1, 1896. 5,000

Willet, James S. to Emma L. Willet. 33d st, s s, 390 w 8th av, 20x98.9. March 25, 1882, 4 years. 4,500

William A. Miles & Co., a corporation, to George H. Robinson and Stevenson Taylor trustees. Chrystie st, No. 55, w s, 152 n Canal st, 25x100; Chrystie st, No. 57, w s, 177 n Canal st, 25x100; Chrystie st, No. 59, w s, 202 n Canal st, 25x100. Leasehold, and all rights, privileges, franchises, chattels, &c. Secures bonds. Dec. 1. gold, 100,000

Walsh, Thomas H. mortgagor with Julius H. and William F. A. Von Sachs mortgagees. Extension of mort. Dec. 7. nom

Weinstein, Ascher to Frederic P. Sands, Newport, R. I. Chambers st, No. 92, s s, 25x75. Lease. Dec. 10, 3 years. gold, 10,000

Same to Andrew H. Sands. Same property. Lease. Dec. 10, 3 years. gold, 5,000

Weinstein, Ascher to Sarah H. Powell. Henry st. P. M. Dec. 2, 1 year, 5 %. 12,000

Wilker, Charles to John Rooney. Courtlandt av. P. M. Dec. 3, 5 years, 5 %. 4,000

Williamson, Lindsay to Anna K. Adams. West st, s w s, lot 7 map Wardsville. P. M. Dec. 3, 3 years. 500

Wille, Valentine to Mary N. Townshend. 98th st, n s, 375 w 8th av, 25x100.11. Dec. 5, due Nov. 1, 1896, or installs. 2 000

Weber, Caroline A. wife of and William F. to Philipp Ohl. 3d av, s e s, 51.4 s w Rose st, runs southeast 188 to n w s Bergen av, x southwest 25 x northwest 100 x southwest 25 x northwest 88 to 3d av, x northeast 50 to beginning. Sub. to mort. $1,500. Dec. 9, 1 year. 2,000

Welsh, Henry to THE TITLE GUARANTEE AND TRUST CO. Franklin st, Nos 123, 135 and 137, s s, runs east 61.1 x south 84.2 x west 21.1 x southwest 4.3 x northwest 96.6 to beginning; Franklin st, s s, 48 w West Broadway, 23x84. Dec. 9, 3 years, 4½ %. 45,000

Young, Peter and Rosa A. his wife and Nicholas P. Young, Brooklyn, to Joseph Young. Cherry st, No. 189, s s, 25.3x60x25.4x60; Water st, No. 454, n s, 25.6x60x25 4x60; Cherry st, No. 187, s s, and Water st, No. 452, n s, 25x the block. Nov. 5, 5 years, 5 %. 50,000

Young, Robert J. to THE METROPOLITAN LIFE INS CO. 144th st, n s, 100 e Amsterdam av, 21.2x99.11. Dec. 2, due Oct. 1, 1894, installs, 6 % and 5 %. 12,500

Zerban, Marie C. wife of and Andrew to John J. Jones and ano. trustees David Jones dec'd. Lenox av, e s, 34 s 127th st, 16.6x85. Dec. 5, 3 years, 5 %. 12,500

Same to same. Lenox av, e s, 50.6 s 127th st, 16.6x85. Dec. 5, 3 years, 5 %. 12,500

KINGS COUNTY.

DECEMBER 3, 4, 5, 7, 8, 9.

Allen, Mary L. wife of and George W. to The Title Guarantee and Trust Co. Hancock st, s s, 162 e Marcy av. P. M. Dec. 2, 3 years, 5 %. $12,000

Same to Frank Bailey. Same property. 2d mort. Dec. 2, 1 year. 1,000

Same to Montrose W. Morris. Same property. P. M. 3d mort. Dec. 2, installs. 8,000

Andemars, Hortense wife of and Frank to James M. Varnum and ano. exrs. Charles A. Eckert. Clinton st, w s, 30.2 s Verandah pl. P. M. Nov. 30, due Nov. 1, 1894, 5 %. 2,500

Same to same. Clinton st, w s, 48.3 s Verandah pl. P. M. Nov. 30, due Nov. 1, 1894, 5 %. 5,340

Appleton, Jeannette M. wife of and Nathan to Emma C. Thursby. Livingston st, n e s, 67 s e Red Hook lane, 22x95. June 16, 1888, due July 1, 1889. 6,150

Ahrens, James M. to Long Island Building and Loan Assoc. Diamond st, w s, 259.10 n Van Cott av, 50x100. Dec. 7, installs, 5 %. 6,000

Arensberg, Lipman to Euellia Cornell. Gold st. P. M. Dec. 8, 2 years, 5 %. 4,000

Armbruster, John to Charles Engert. Monitor st. P. M. Sub. to mort. $1,900. Dec. 1, installs, 5 %. 1,100

Same to The Kings County Savings Inst Same property. Dec. 1, 1 year, 5 %. 1,900

Aronson, Jacob to Jas. H. Lee et al., firm of Brooklyn Door and Sash Co. Lewis av, s e cor Hancock st, 100x60. Sub. to mort. $52,-475. Nov. 16, due Feb. 1, 1892. 6,066

Axelrod, Jacob to George E. Ward. Stone av, e s, 100 n Sutter av, 25x100. Dec. 2, 3 years. 3,000

Adams, Mahlon B. to John W. Phelps. Saratoga av, s e cor Chauncey st, 22x78. Dec. 1, 1 year. 7,750

Akerly, Hiram to Elizabeth F. Chrystal. North 4th st, No. 109, n e cor Berry st, 26.6x110. Dec. 8, 3 years, 5 %. 2,500

Asnaid, Catharine to Emeline Davison, Rockville Centre, L. I. McDonough st, s s, 275 e Sumner av, 25x79.3x20.6x74.10. Dec. 9, due Dec. 1, 1892. 200

Beck, Elizabeth widow to Abraham Simon and Augusta his wife. Middleton st, n w s, 391 n e Harrison av, 24x100. Dec. 8, 5 years, 5 %. 2,700

Benton, Jennie T. to Eva C. Glover. South Portland av. P. M. Dec. 7, due Dec. 9, 1894, 5 %. 4,000

Burton, Catharine, New Utrecht, to Marion F. wife of Charles Fleischman. Lots 44 and 51 map Theodore Sedgwick, New Utrecht. Dec. 1, due Jan. 1, 1895. 1,000

Baker, John G. and Charles L. Lincoln to Emeline Davison, Rockville Centre, L. I. 9th st, n s, 232.10 e 7th av, runs north 80 x east 100 x south 35 x east 45 to 9th st, x west 100.3. Dec. 4, due Feb. 1, 1894. 5,000

Balsam, Samuel and Moritz Handler to Triennial Benefit League. Thatford av, e s, 125 s Glenmore av, 25x100. Dec. 1, 3 years. 3,250

Barnard, John T. and Charlotte D. C., to The Mutual Life Ins. Co., New York. Monroe st, s s, 325 e Bedford av, 20x89.6x20.1x91.6. Dec. 3, 1 year. 6,000

Bauer, Frederick to Charles Griffen and ano. exrs. Peter S. Titus. Halsey st, s s, 83.6 e Ralph av, 19.5x100. Dec. 1, 3 years, 5 %. 4,500

Bennett, Elizabeth to Rose Reis. Johnson pl, w s, 200 s East Broadway, h & l, Flatbush. All title. Oct. 15, 1 year. 150

Bergland, Hilma A. wife of and John to Samuel S. Underhill. 3d st, n e s, 100 s e 3d av, 25x100.2. Dec. 7, 3 years. 3 000

Black, Isaac to Solomon and Dora Wolff. Belmont av. P. M. Dec. 1, installs. 1,700

Bossert, Margaret wife of Philip to Hugo Weil. Willoughby av, n s, 50 w Evergreen av. P. M. Dec. 7, 1 year. 1,650

Same to same. Same property. Dec. 7, installs. 4,000

Bott, Christian to Anna M. wife of Henry Irwin. Metropolitan av, s s, 275 e Catharine st, 25x100. Dec. 3, 1 year. 500

Bleakney, Harriet J. to Sarah M. Phillip. Franklin av. e s, 265 s Willoughby av, 25x120. Dec. 3, 1 year, 5 %. additional security 2,000

Brennan, Martin to William Hendrickson. Clermont av, w s, 100 s Flushing av, 25x100.6x25x100.3. Nov. 25, due Dec. 1, 1894, 5 %. 1,500

Brennan, John to Annetta C. wife of Teunis H. Bergen. Fort Hamilton av, s s, 200 e Chester av, 50x200 to Minna st, Flatbush. Dec. 7, 3 years. 2,000

Brown, William to Sherman Loomis. 6th av, e s, 66.9 n President st, runs east 22.6 x north 7.3 x east 17.6 x north 20.11 x west 40 to av, x north 28.2. Dec. 1, demand. 1,750

Brownell, Asa C. to Frank A. Barnaby. State st, n s, 250 e Hoyt st, 100x100. Building loan. Dec. 3, demand. 67,292

Brush, Eugene and Bertha his wife to Title Guarantee and Trust Co. Lexington av, n s, 230 e Throop av, 15x100. Dec. 3, due Dec. 4, 1894. 200

Campbell, Hoik D. to Henry G. Munger, Herkimer Co., N. Y. Fulton st, s w cor Stone av, 22x100. Nov. 24, 1 year, 5 %. 2,500

Caufield, James A. to Sarah E. De Nyse. Halsey st, n w s, 160 n e Evergreen av, 20x100. Dec. 3, due Dec. 1, 1894, 5 %. 2,500

Same to William Laytin et al. trustees William Laytin dec'd. Halsey st, n w s, 180 n e Evergreen av, 20x100. Dec. 3, 3 years, 5 %. 2,300

Same to same. Halsey st, n w s, 200 n e Evergreen av, 20x100. Dec. 3, 3 years, 5 %. 2,300

Same to same. Halsey st, n w s, 220 n e Evergreen av, 20x100. Dec. 3, 3 years, 5 %. 2,300

Carton, Andrew B. to Frank Bailey. 80th st, s w s, 100 s e 11th av. P. M. Nov. 19, 1 year. 800

Same to same. 77th st. P. M. Nov. 19, 1 year. 675

Chappell, Gideon T., Jersey City, N. J., to John T. Bailey, Jr., Tenafly, N. J. Atlantic av, s s, 69.11 w Sackman st, 19.3x100. ¼ part. Dec. 5, due Dec. 1, 1892, 5 %. 250

Cole, Edward H. to The Dime Savings Bank, Brooklyn. Pearl st, n w cor Water st, 75x90.8. Dec. 7, 1 year, 5 %. 25,000

Conn, Curtis W. to Edward Rowe exr. Maria Rowe. Franklin av, e s, 90 s Fulton st, runs south 108.1 x east 130,8 x northeast 28 x west 0.3 x north 20 x west 63.2. Nov. 28, 1 year. 15,000

Carlin, Patrick J. to Mary S. Pell. Court st. P. M. Dec. 7, 1 year, 5 %. 2,000

Cook, Mary E., Newtown, L. I., to Mary W. Smith. Rockaway av, s e cor Dean st, 114.5x100. Dec. 4, demand. 683

Crawford, Mary M. wife of and Bernard to The Title Guarantee and Trust Co. Dean st, s w s, 180 n w 3d av, 20x100. Dec. 3, 1 year, 5 %. 2,000

Cronk, Edward to Charles H. Reynolds. Somers st. P. M. Dec. 7, 1 year. 850

Same to Sarah A. McFarlan. Lexington av, n s, 120 w Marcy av, 20x100. Dec. 7, 1 year, 5 %. 400

Curtin, John and Mary individ. and exrs. David Curtin to Martha E. Cannon. Dean st, 100 w Stone av, 44x107.2. Dec. 1, 3 years. 1,500

Campbell, Samuel I. to Frank Bailey. 7th av, west cor 80th st, runs southwest 200.1 x west 59 to 81st st, x northwest 57.1 x northeast 100 x northwest 40 x northeast 100 to 80th st, x southeast 82.7; Fort Hamilton av, s e s, 101.8 n e 81st st, runs northeast 97.9 x east 15.10 to 80th st, x southeast 48.11 x southwest 100 x northwest 81.10. Nov. 19, 1 year. 1,000

Carpenter, James O. to William H. Lyon. Nostrand av, Nos. 543 and 545, e s, 69.1 n Atlantic av, 30x69.11; Nostrand av, e s, 39.10 n Atlantic av, 14.3x69.11. Dec. 4, 1 year. 8,500

Caroselli, Alberico to Eva Cohen. McDonough st, s s, 175.5 e Sumner av, 4 lots, each 20x100. 4 morts., each $600. Dec. 8, demand. 2,400

Same to same. McDonough st, s s, 255.5 e Sumner av, 19.7x100. Dec 8, demand. 600

Conway, William F. to Henry Weil. Bushwick av, s w s, 48 s e Fairfax st, 16x70.4. Dec. 8, 1 year. 400

Cummings, Mary C. widow to The Title Guarantee and Trust Co. Wyckoff st, s s, 144 w Nevins st, 21x100. Dec. 9, 3 years, 5 %. 1,500

Davidson, Charles N. to Hannah D. Farrand. Remsen st, s s, 377 w Hicks st. P. M. Dec. 9, 1 year. 2,000

Same to The Brooklyn Trust Co. exr. Reuben W. Ropes. Remsen st, s s, 327 w Hicks st. P. M. Dec. 9, 3 years, 5 %. 22,000

Du Bois, Charles F. to Charles E. Benedict exr. Mary S. Benedict. Gates av. P. M. Nov. 24, 5 years, 5 %. 5,000

Dehmann, George to Beadleston & Woerz. Atlantic av, s e cor Snediker av. Lease. Dec. 5, demand. 800

De Maine, Elizabeth to William Stedman. Luquer st. P. M. Oct. 23, 1889, due Jan. 1, 1893, 5 %. 2,000

Demorest, William R. mortgagor with Edward H. R. Lyman trustee Mary A. Kearns. Extension mort. Nov. 18. nom

Dietrich, Eliza E. to James D. Lynch. 22d av, New Utrecht. P. M. Nov. 28, due Nov. 5, 1892, 5 %. 600

Dowley, Mary H. wife of and Michael to Cross, Austin & Co. Macon st, n s, 185 w Howard av, 18x100. Nov. 24, 1 year. 750

Same to same. Macon st, n s, 239 w Howard av, 18x100. Nov. 24, 1 year. 750

Equity Gas Light Co. of the Eastern District of Brooklyn to The Farmers' Loan and Trust Co. Maspeth av, both sides, 100 e Vandervoort av, adj lands of Debevoise and Luqueer, except a lot on s s of Maspeth av, 100 deep. Collateral to general trust mort. Dec. 8.

Feiner, Rosie to Sinnamon Calvert. Luquer st. P. M. Nov. 30, installs, 5 %. 1,150

Feuerbach, Agnes to Wolcott H. Pitkin, Albany N. Y. New Jersey av. P. M. Nov. 28, due Dec. 1, 1894. 700

Finnern, Margaretha to Edward A. Everit. Ashford st. P. M. Dec. 5, 1 year. 200

Firth, Christopher C. to Edwin Andrews. Prospect av. P. M. Dec. 3, 3 months, 5 %. 850

Fisher, Elizabeth J. wife of John R. to John Brennan and Ellen his wife. Grand av, e s, 337.5 n Gates av, 20x78.11 to Old road, from Brooklyn to Bedford, x27.8x97.11. Dec. 8, 3 years. 1,000

Forbell, George U. to Margaret B. Waldron and ano. admrs. John Waldron. Hendrix st, e s, 208.3 n Arlington av, 16.9x100. Dec. 2, due Dec 3, 1894. 2,000

Same to Richard Downing, East Norwich, L. I. Hendrix st, e s, 191.6 n Arlington av, 16.7x100. Dec. 2, due Dec. 3, 1894. 2,000

Fowler, Bernard to George F. Hewitt. Clinton av, e s, 155.4 s Gates av, 27x120. Dec. 8, 6 months. 3,000

Fedden, Christian to Pauline May et al. exrs. Marx May. Franklin st, e s, 75 s Milton st, 25x70. Aug. 1, 1 year. 3,000

Fowler, Ella E. wife of Bernard to Bedford Bank. St. Marks av, n s, 212 e Rogers av, 20x103. Dec. 4, due March 4, 1892. 1,000

Gastmeyer, Charles F. to Joshua H. Cort. Halsey st. P. M. Dec. 8, 1 year, 5 %. 2,000

Same to James Gascoine individ. and with Anna E. Cozine exrs. John G. Cozine. Eldert st. P. M. Dec. 8, due Dec. 1, 1892. 2,400

Same to same. Same property. Builder's loan. Dec. 8, demand. 2,000

Same to same. Evergreen av. P. M. Dec. 8, due Dec. 1, 1892. 12,000

Same to same. Same property. Builder's loan. Dec. 8, demand. 12,000

Gosricke, Bertha wife of Carl W. to Bertha wife of Abram Katzenstein. Lorimer st. P. M. Dec. 9, 5 years or installs, 5 %. 800

Goodwin, Thomas F., Jr., to Henry Weil. Broadway, e s, 23 s Fairfax st, 20x95. Dec. 8, 1 year. 1,000

Gallagher, John and Kate his wife to Thomas S. Denike. Buffalo av. P. M. Dec. 1, installs. 930

Gardner, Peter to The Title Guarantee and Trust Co. Decatur st and Saratoga av. P. M. Nov. 28, 1 year. 1,500

Gillen, James to Maximilian Lang. Cumberland st. P. M. Nov. 28, due April 1, 1892. 575

Gasteiger, John W. and Rose his wife to John P. H. De Wint. Fulton av, n s, 70 e Georgia av, 30x147.2x31.10x136.7. Dec. 7, 3 years. 5,000

Gately, Francis J. to Joseph T. Briggs. North 10th st. P. M. Dec. 3, due Jan. 1, 1897, 5 %. 1,500

Gelpcke, Victoria F., College Point, L. I., to Cornelius N. Hoagland. Willoughby av, s s, 108.3 w Clason av, 17x67.1x17x66.11. Nov. 20, due Nov. 1, 1894, 5 %. gold, 4,200

Gibson, Martha wife of William F. to John Cowenhoven. 11th av, n w s, 60.2 s w 58th st, 60x100, New Utrecht. Dec. 3, due Aug. 10, 1892. 900

Gillespie, Earl A. and Rudolph Reimer with Charlotte Leavens all mortgagees. Agreement as to priority of morts. made by Charles M. Thompson. Dec. 7. nom

Goldberg, Caroline T. D. wife of August C. to Morris Blau and Louisa his wife. Jackson st, s s, 125 w Humboldt st, 25x100. Dec. 5, 3 years. 1,000

Goodheart, Edward to Sarah A. Robertson. 57th st, s s, 100 e 4th av, 100x100.2. Dec. 2, 2 years, 5 %. 750

Gormley, James to Joseph Ryan. Weirfield st. n w s, 81 s w Central av, 20.2x100. Dec. 1, installs. 1,500

Greenwood, Annie A. wife of and John to Edmund and Julia A. Williams. Amberstrand road, adj land James Holland, 25x130, Gravesend. Nov. 13, 5 years. 500

Gross, Henry to Robert L. Woods. Brooklyn av, n w cor Lefferts av, 41.2x95.5x40x89.6. May 28, 3 years. 850

Halkett, Henry to Bernard Levino. Irving pl. P. M. Dec. 8, installs, 5 %. 1,600

Harland, Jane C., Gravesend, L. I., to Albert V. B. Voorhies, New Utrecht, L. I. Road to shore, at Sheepshead Bay, adj land Mary E. McKane, 101x163x101x180, Gravesend. Dec. 1, 3 years. 880

Harris, Malie wife of Hyman to Morris Winter. Graham av, w s, 50 n Newton st, 25x93.5x25.4x89.3. Dec. 3, due Dec. 25, 1896. 500

Heatley, George W. to Henry M. Kingman and ano. exrs. Martin E. Kingman. Adelphi st. P. M. Nov. 14, due Nov. 23, 1894, 5 %. 3,500

Hellmuth, Franzica to Jacob Bossert. Wallabout st. P. M. June 1, installs. 2,300

Hemmenway, Stephen to Margaret P. Halsey. Bedford av, e s, 160 s Willoughby av, 20x100. Dec. 3, 3 years, 5 %. 2,000

Hepburn, George W. to Frank Bailey. 80th st, New Utrecht. P. M. Dec. 2, due Nov. 30, 1892. 600

Hill, Henry B. to Cyrus and Fanny R. M. Hitchcock, Poughkeepsie, N. Y. McDonough st, s s, 183.4 e Reid av, 16.8x100. Dec. 4, 3 years, 5 %. 4,000

Same to same. McDonough st, s s, 166.8 e Reid av, 16.8x100. Dec. 4, 3 years, 5 %. 4,000

Holt, Maria to John H. Garrison. Cornelia st. P. M. Dec. 2, installs, 5 %. 1,300

Hogan, Morris to Herman Busener. 16th av, e s, 150 n Bath av, 100x108.4. Dec. 1, 3 years. 250

Herbst, Jacob to John F. Becker. Melrose st, s s, 150 e Central av, 25x100. Dec. 1, 3 years, 5 %. 2,500

Hornung, George to George W. and Charles H. Francisco. Woodbine st. P. M. Dec 7, installs. 1,350

How, Phoebe, New Utrecht, to Annetta C. Bergen. 82d st, n s, 100 e 2d av, 80x109.4, New Utrecht. Dec. 1, 3 years. 3,500

Hunerhoff, Lillian J. wife of and Conrad to Terence J. O'Hare and John J. O'Keeffe. Nassau av, n e cor Oakland st. P. M. Dec. 5, due July 1, 1893, 5 %. 1,800

Hunt, Charles F. to George B. Stoutenburg. 3d av, w s, 40 s Wyckoff st, 20x80. Dec. 3, 1 year. 500

Hamerschlag, Henry to Katie Gies. North 2d st, n s, 14.6 w Berry st extended. 25x78x25x77.6; North 2d st, n s, 10.6 e Berry st extended, 25x77.6. Dec. 8, due March 1, 1893, or installs, 5 %. 1,500

Hardy, Pauline wife of and Harry to Cross, Austin & Co. East 95th st, e s, 150 s Av G, 28.7x105, Canarsie. Dec. 2, 1 year. 800

Haughey, Catherine to Edward Lavin. Union st. Dec. 8, 5 years or installs. See Conveys. 13,000

Heisenbuttel, John H. to The F. & M. Schaefer Brewing Co. 9th st, No. 128, s e cor 2d av. Lease. Dec. 8, demand. 1,500

Jacobs, Fanny wife of and Lewis to The Title Guarantee and Trust Co. Prince st, w s, 489 s Willoughby st, runs south 13.6 to Fleet st, x southwest 14 x northwest 30.9 x west 51.4 x north 11 x east 85. Dec. 9, 3 years, 5 %. 2,500

Johnston, James and Oliver to Martha D. Warrin. Pacific st, s w s, 225 s e 6th av. P. M. Dec. 5, 5 years, 5 %. 1,500

Same to Amelia F. Dunham, Hartford, Conn. Pacific st, s w s, 250 s e 6th av. P. M. Nov. 23, due Dec. 9, 1896, 5 %. 1,500

Jensen, Frederick to Sidney V. Lowell. 9th av, s w cor 11th st. P. M. Dec. 4, 2 years, 5 %. 10,000

Kelley, Dudley to John M. Lerschen. Hull st, s s, 56.3 w Hopkinson av, 37.6x90.3x37.8x94.5. Dec. 7, 1 year. 1,200

Kelly, Delia to Margaret wife of John I. Snedeker. Brighton pl, n e cor Coney Island road, 50x124.6x50x133.6. Nov. 24, due April 1, 1892. 560

Ketcham, George to The Equitable Co-operative Building and Loan Assoc. McDonough st. P. M. Dec. 4, installs. 7,500

Kane, Mary to Walter Cline. Hancock st, n s, 100 w Saratoga av, 15x100. Dec. 4, 2 years. 100

King, Charles D. with Richard Goodwin both mortgagees. Extension of mort. made by Robert S. Neely. Nov. 25. nom

Kinscher, Henry to Henry W. Diers. 47th st, n e s, 120 n w 3d av, 20x100. Oct. 6, installs, 5 %. 400

Knowles, William and Edmund H. Morse to Sophia F. Welch. Rochester av, w s, extends from Douglass to Degraw st, 255.7x30x—x83.3. Nov. 2, 2 years. 2,000

Kodziesen, Abraham to Henry Stubing. Flushing av. P. M. Dec. 3, due June 1, 1895, 5 %. 5,850

Kramer, Philip to George Huether. Hancock st, s s, 80 w Bedford av, 20x100.6. Dec. 7, due Dec. 9, 1896, 5 %. 5,000

Kramer, Fred. to S. Liebmann's Sons Brewing Co. Washington st, No. 183, and part Nassau st, No. 48. Lease. Dec. 1, installs. 7,000

Krueger, Adolph to Mary E. De Wint. Eastern Parkway, n s, 50 e Schenck av, 50x100. Dec. 5, 1 year. 1,000

Kirby, James H. to Caroline L. Macy. Henry st, No. 275, s e s, 276.6 s w Joralemon st, 25x93.6. Dec. 9, 3 years, 5 %. 17,000

Kirchner, Anna E. S. wife of and William F. to The Long Island Loan and Trust Co. trustee John A. Cross. De Kalb av, n s, 550 e Throop av, 25x100. Dec. 7, due Nov. 1, 1894, 5 %. 900

Kolk, Mathilda to Frank L. Kolk. South 2d st. P. M. Dec. 8, 5 years, 5 %. 3,500

Lane, Katharine M. to Anna M. Irwin. Bleecker st, n w s, 188.2 n e Myrtle av, 20x100. Dec. 4, due Dec. 1, 1891. 1,000

Lawrence, Thomas E. to Virginia A. Kleine and Frank Bailey. Grove st, n w s, 225 n e Central av, 73.9x100. Mt. $8,000. Nov. 30, demand. 3,982

Same to same. Same property. Nov. 30, demand. 8,000

Leonard, Catherine wife of and Philip to The Title Guarantee and Trust Co. Sullivan st, s w s, 125 n w Richards st, 25x100. Dec. 3, 1 year, 5 %. 1,000

Liebermann, Isaac to Harris Max. Watkins st. P. M. Dec. 1, installs. 2,000

Linse, Frederick J. mortgagor with John Winkelmann. Extension of mort. Sept. 11. nom

Levy, Philip to Broadway Bank, Brooklyn. Broadway, north cor Hart st, 100x100. Dec. 8, 1 year. 15,000

Lucken, Nicholas to St. Anns Church. Spencer st, w s, 83 n De Kalb av, 25x100. Dec. 9, 1 year, 5 %. 5,000

Magill, George H. to Cornelius E. Donnellon. 7th av, s e cor 2d st, runs east 100 x south 95 x west 2.1 x south 5 x west 17.10 x north 80 x west 80 to av, x north 20. Sub. to mort. $12,500. Dec. 8, 1 year. 2,500

Same to Metropolitan Life Ins. Co. 7th av, s e cor 2d st, 20x80. Dec. 8, due Oct. 1, 1896, installs, 6 % for first year, 5 % after. 12,500

Same to same. 7th av, e s, 20 s 2d st, 3 lots,

each 26.8x80. 3 morts., each $12,500. Dec. 8, due Oct. 1, 1896, installs, 6 % for first year. 5 % after. 37,500

Mayer, Annie I. wife of Timothy C. to Joseph P. Puels. Sackett st, s s, 217.6 w 4th av. 160 x95. Sub. to mort. $5,500. Dec. 9, 1 year. 753

Same to Mutual Life Ins Co., New York. Same property. Dec. 9, 1 year. 5,500

Morrisey, Richard to Henry Weil. Furman st P. M. Dec. 8, 3 years, 5 %. 1,400

Mahler, George to John Steingester. Bergen st, s s, 93.7 w Rochester av, 20.7x85.9. Nov. 28, 1 year. 2 200

Mayer, Elinor M. to John and James Williamson. 3d pl. P. M. Dec. 1, 1 year, 5 %. 2,000

Mayfield, Robert, Astoria, L. I., to Bridget A. Cody, New York. Cornelia st. P. M. Dec 1, due June 15, 1892. 3.000

McCue, Mary to Lewis Hurst. Snediker av, e s, 250 n Belmont av, 50x100. Dec. 4, 1 year. 850

McGarry, Lula P. to Bertha Stevens. Raymond st, w s, 50 s Bolivar st, 25x75. Dec. 7, due May 1, 1895, 5 %. 6,000

Same to George E Voorhees and ano. exrs. Jacob R. Ditmars. Raymond st, w s, 25 s Bolivar st, 25x75. Dec. 7, due May 1, 1895, 5 %. 6,000

McGuigan, James to Alice W. Jones. Van Siclen av, e s, 100 s Arlington av, 25x100. Dec. 4, 1 year. 2,000

McCaun, Bridget widow to Eliza Hornung. Plymouth st, n s, 244.11 w Gold st, 21.3x100. Dec. 7, 3 years. 400

McLean, Thomas to Helen S. McLean. Furman st, w s, 213.8 n Pierrepont st. if extended, either there is a mistake in description or there is no street front. Nov. 30, demand. 37,500

McMurray, Mary J. to Mary E. Schenck. Monroe st, s s, 337.10 e Stuyvesant av, 17.2x100. Dec. 3, 1 year. 5,000

McNulty, Hugh to The Brooklyn Co-operative Building and Loan Assoc. 15th st and 2d av. P. M. Aug 6, installs. 1,300

Same to George S. Wheeler. Same property. P. M. Aug. 6, 1 year. 200

Meyers, Isreal to The Title Guarantee and Trust Co. 16th st, n e s, 258.9 n w 3d av, 20x 100. Nov 13, 1 year, 5 %. 800

Same to same. 16th st, n e s, 238.4 n w 3d av, 20.5x100. Nov. 13, 1 year, 5 %. 800

Mitchel, Charles to Franz Steinbacher. Bushwick av, north cor Vanderveer st. P. M. Dec. 5, 5 years, 5 % 8,500

Molaghan, John to Francis J. Hanton. Oakland st. e s, 50 n Freeman st, 25x70. Dec. 7, due Dec. 1, 1894. 500

Maxwell, Marie A. wife of and William H. to Cornelius N. Hoagland. Greene av, s s, 180 e Throop av, 20x100. Dec. 4. dne Nov. 1, 1894, 5 %. gold. 6,000

Moores, Robert L. and Charles A. Le Quesne to George F. Alexander. Broadway, west cor Putnam av, 38.2x38 8 to av, x54.4. Dec. 8, 2 years. 3,000

Same to Warren G. Brown and ano. trustees Charles B. Wade. Broadway, s w s, 38.2 n w Putnam av, runs southwest 38.8 to av, x east 54.4 to Broadway, x northwest 38.2. Dec. 8, 3 years. 5½ %. 9,000

Muller, Frances to Lowry Somerville. Warren st. P. M. Dec. 1, 3 years, 5 %. 800

Neely, Robert S. to Richard Goodwin. Chauncey st, s s, 268 e Saratoga av, 57x100. Nov. 25, 1 year. 11,039

Nelson, Lena W. to Fanny H. Guy. 6th av. P. M. June 1, due Dec 1, 1893, 5 %. 250

Newman, James I. to John C. Schenck. Jerome st, w s, 133.3 s Fulton st, 16.8x95. Sub. to mort. $1,700. Dec. 4, 3 years. 500

Same to Henrietta J. Loomis. Same property. Dec. 4, 3 years. 1,700

Same to Cornelia C. Schenck. Jerome st, w s, 149.11 s Fulton st, 16.8x95. Sub. to mort. $1,600. Dec. 4, 3 years. 600

Same to Josie M. Schenck. Same property. Dec. 4, 3 years. 1,000

Ochs, Ernest to Christian H. Koch et al. exrs. Claus Plath. Oakland and Eagle sts. P. M. Dec. 7, due Dec. 1, 1893, 5 %. 1,500

Orr, Susan M. to The Title Guarantee and Trust Co. Halsey st, s s, 219 e Ralph av, 18x 100. Dec. 5, 1 year, 5 %. 2,000

Same to same. Halsey st, s s, 254 e Ralph av, 18x100. Dec. 5, 1 year, 5 %. 2,000

Parks, Frank to Evelyn Betts. North 6th st, n s, 75 w Roebling st, 25x100. Dec. 5, 3 years. 5 %. 3,000

Pasuley, Charles L. to Samuel G. Lindeman. Hancock st, n s, 100 e Stuyvesant av, 18.4x 100. Nov. 27, due Dec. 1, 1894. 2,000

Same to Title Guarantee and Trust Co. Same property. Dec. 4, demand. 4.000

Pearsall, Albert to James Quinn. North 7th st, Nos. 224, 226 and 228. Lease. Dec. 1, 1 year. 600

Pearson, William J. to Rachel M. Gilsey and ano. extrx. of John C. C. Gilsey. 4th st. P. M. Dec. 3, 3 years, 5 %. 2,800

Pearson, Theodore to The Title Guarantee and Trust Co. Baltic st, s s, 223 w Court st, 25x 99.10. Dec. 8, 3 years, 5 %. 8,000

Same to same. Baltic st, s s, 198 w Court st, 25x99 10. Dec. 8, 3 years, 5 %. 8,000

Pfaff, Fannie C. wife of and Charles to Albert V. B. Voorhis. 17th av, New Utrecht. P. M. Nov. 30, 5 years or installs. 4,000

Phithian, Thomas to Daniel Doody. Warren st, n w s, 50 n e Lexington av, 50x125. New Utrecht. Dec. 3, demand. 186

Poole, William H. to William F. Lawrence. Jamaica av, n s, 100 e Miller av, 32.6x229 to Sunnyside av, x 51.6x228.4. Oct. 15, 3 years, 5 %. 500

Pruzina, Joseph to Henry L. Tyson, Bay Ridge. Warren st, s s, 75 w Smith st, 25x75. Dec. 2, due Dec. 1, 1894, installs, 5 %. 3,000

Phelps, John W. with Richard Goodwin both mortgagees. Agreement as to priority of morts. made by Mahlon B. Adams. Dec. 1. nom

Pickert, Willis A. to William H. Myers. Cleveland st, e s, 85 n Wortman av. P. M. Dec. 8. 3 years. 225

Same to Adolph Von Preif. Cleveland st, e s, 135 n Wortman av P. M. Dec. 8, 3 years 225

Radcliffe, Thomas H. to Sarah E. Stewart. Decatur st. n s, 409.8 w Howard av, 18.4x 100. Sub. to mort. $4,500. Nov. 17, 1 year. 1,000

Same to same. Decatur st, n s, 391.4 w Howard av, 18.4x100. Sub. to mort. $4,500. Nov. 17, 1 year. 1,000

Same to same. Decatur st, n s, 318 w Howard av, 18 4x100. Sub. to mort. $4,500. Nov. 17, 1 year. 1,000

Radcliffe, Thomas H. to Emilie K. Eeks. Decatur st, n s, 428 w Howard av, 18.4x100. Sub. to mort. $4,500. Dec. 4, 1 year. 800

Ramsdell, David J. to George R. Lockwood and ano. trustees Rose Lockwood. St. James pl. P M. Dec. 5, 3 years. 14,000

Ramsdell, David J. to Robert F. Rhodes. St. James pl, w s, 73 s Fulton av, 25x100. Dec. 5, 1 year. 7,000

Reineking, Emil to Earl A. Gillespie. Amboy st, w s, 90.5 s Eastern Parkway, 25x100. Dec. 4. demand. 7,000

Rheil, Elizabeth to Robert C. Troll, Jersey City, N. J. Manjer st, s s, 80 e Lorimer st, 20x100. Dec. 1, 1 year. 200

Riordan, Michael J. to William G. Russell. Lee av and Ross st. P. M. Dec. 5, installs. 3,500

Same to Sadie E. Rice. Same property. Dec. 5, due Dec. 1, 1892. 3,500

Robinson, Benjamin F. to Virginia A. Kleine and Frank Bailey. Grove st, n w s, 298.9 n e Central av, 148.3x100. Nov. 30, demand. 13,100

Same to same. Same property. Sub. to last mort. Nov. 13, demand. 3,368

Roesler, Bernard to People's Trust Co. Lafayette av, n s, 20 e Elliott pl. 20x80. Dec. 7, 1 year, 5 %. 10.000

Roppelt, Magdalena widow to Jennie Dieringer. George st, n w s, 275 n e Hamburg av, 25x100. Dec. 5, due Jan. 1, 1893. 1,000

Rowe, Frederick W. to Reuben W. and Reuben W., Jr., Aube. Putnam av. P. M. Dec. 1, 1 year. 1,200

Rugen, Harry D. to Beadleston & Woerz, a corporation. 4th av, No. 224. Lease. Nov. 30, demand. 3,200

Rathjen, Hermann to The Nassau Land and Improvement Co. 8th av and Windsor pl. P. M. Sub. to mort. $6,500. Dec. 4, installs. 1,500

Same to The Title Guarantee and Trust Co. Same property. P. M. Dec. 4, 3 years. 5 %. 6,300

Ruthmann, William to Peter Mayer. Central av, s w s, 80 n w Harman st, 20x80. Dec. 3, 3 years, 5 %. 3,000

Rantom, James F. to Thomas Roberts Stevenson Co, Philadelphia, Pa. 10th st, n s, 217.10 w 8th av, 40x100. Dec. 8, 3 months. 900

Reilly, Ellen C. wife of James to Ten Eyck Wendell. Clason av, e s, 175.5 s Fulton st, runs east 72 x southeast 85.1 x south 10.2 x west 6.5x95.8 to av, x north 21.6. Dec. 4, due Dec. 1, 1894, 5 %. 4,000

Reynolds, Margaret wife of and Herbert to David Stocker. Graham st, e s, 337.4 s Willoughby av, 24.4x91.5. Dec. 9, 3 years. 1,800

Richard, William F. to Richard Goodwin. Evergreen av, east cor Eldert st, 35x75. Dec. 1, 18 months. 4,500

Salo, Juan and Mary E. his wife and Elizabeth Keppel to Bartholome Bisinger. Herkimer st, n s, 150 e Stone av, 16.8x100. Dec. 7, 5 years, 5 %. 2,500

Schumacher, Peter R. to Anton Mannel. Bedford av, n w cor North 10th st. P. M. Nov. 30, 5 years, 5 %. 13,000

Schlichting, Sophia J. wife of and Emil to The Title Guarantee and Trust Co. Patchen av, e s, 56.3 n Monroe st, 18.9x60. Dec. 4, 1 year. 2,000

Schmidt, Joseph to Catharine Kelly. Union pl, n s, 47.4 w Locust st, 50x103.5, Flatbush. April 28, installs 5,100

Schneider Catharina to People's Trust Co. Livingston st, s e cor Bond st, 25x65x25.4x 65. Dec. 7, 1 year, 5 %. 12,000

Schwenk, Mai M., Union Co., N. J., to George F. Alexander. Quincy st, n s, 205 w Ralph av, 20x100. Nov. 27, due Dec. 1, 1896, 5 %. 1,000

Scofield, Frederick E. to Joanna C. wife of Albert V. B. Voorhies, New Utrecht, L. I. Ashford st, e s, 166.8 s Ridgewood av, 33.4x 100. Dec. 8, 3 years. 2,600

Same to same. Ashford st, e s, 133.4 s Ridgewood av, 33.4x100. Dec. 8, 3 years. 2,700

Same to same. Ashford st, e s, 100 s Ridgewood av, 33.4x100. Dec. 8, 3 years. 2,700

Seelbach, Jacob J. to Benjamin F. Constable. Maujer st. P. M. Dec. 2, due Dec. 1, 1894, 5 %. 3,600

Sherwood, Samuel T. to James G. Carroll. 47th st. P. M. Dec. 1, 2 months, 5 %. 1,900

Silberhorn, Caroline M. to Jacob Fuhs. Hewes st. P. M. Dec. 1, 3 years, 5 %. 7.000

Simon, Semche to Lewis Jacobs. Leonard st, e s, 50 n McKibbin st. P. M. Dec. 4, 3 years, 5 %. 5,000

Same to same. Leonard st, e s, 25 n McKibbin st. P. M. Dec. 4, 3 years, 5 %. 5,000

Siede, Mary M. N. widow to The Title Guarantee and Trust Co. Gates av, n e cor Franklin av, 45x75. Dec. 1, 3 years, 5 %. 6,500

Smith, Marianna W. to William F. Gaynor trustee for Andrew McClennen, dec'd. 1st st, n e s, 316.10 n w 8th av, 18x100. Dec. 3, due Dec. 1, 1894, 5 %. 500

Smith, Medad to Herbert C. Smith. Sutter av, n s, 50 e Hinsdale st, 75x100; Christopher av, w s, 125 n Sutter av, 75x100. Nov. 7, due May 1, 1892. 2,910

Sonin, Rebecca, New Brighton, Conn., to Necha Solomon, Port Elizabeth, N. J. 3d av. P. M. Nov. 12, 4 months. 106

Spoerl, Christian E. and John G. to Peter Schneider's Sons & Co. Cedar st, No. 50, s s, 157.9 e Evergreen av, 18.4x100. Oct. 24, 5 years, 5 %. 700

Same to same. Cedar st, No. 50A, s s, 176.1 e Evergreen av, 18.4x100. Oct. 24, 5 years, 5 %. 700

Same to same. Cedar st, No 52, s s, 194.5 e Evergreen av, 18.4x100. Oct. 24, 5 years, 5 %. 700

Staebler, Elizabeth wife of and John to Herman B. Scharmann. 4th av, west cor 23d st, 50x60. Dec. 1, 3 years. 5 %. 2,000

Steers, Frank H. to Freeman Clarkson et al. trustees Eibe H. Steers. Mulberry st, s e cor Van Voorhis av, —x—, except as mentioned, lots 157-160 parcel 5 map by Alexander Martin in 1836. Dec. 1, 3 years, 5 %. 1,000

Steinbacher, Franz to Charlotte Wills extrx. John Wills. Vanderveer st, n w s, 180 n e Bushwick av, 25x100. Dec. 5, 3 years. 5 %. 1,300

Stern, David to Franziska Witte guard. Dora, Hattie and Otto Adams. Osborn st, e s, 50 n Glenmore av, 25x100. Dec. 2, 3 years. 3,000

Same to Franziska Witte individ. Osborn st, e s, 75 n Glenmore av, 25x100. Dec. 2, 3 years. 3,000

Stevens, Maria L. widow to Ella B. Van Beuren. Tompkins pl, n w s, 244.10 s w Harrison st, 21.1x112.6. Dec 8, due Jan. 1, 1897. 500

Stewart, James to Beta Denker. Sunnyside av, s e cor Barbey st, 50x33. Dec. 1, 3 years, 5 %. 3,000

Stoutenburg, George B. to Lemmy A. Halstead, Flatbush. 17th st. Dec. 4, 1 year. See Conveys. 500

Sturges, Edward B. to William Bradley. Central av, e s, 75 s Woodbine st, 25x75. Dec. 7, due March 10, 1894. 1,000

Taber, Edward F. to Elizabeth Taber et al. exrs. Franklin W. Taber. 19th st. P. M. Nov. 29, due Nov. 1, 1893. 700

Taylor, Lucy to Simon H. Stern. Jerome st. P. M. Dec. 5, installs. 500

Same to The Nassau Co-operative Building and Loan Assoc. Same property. Dec. 7, installs. 2,750

The Bushwick Democratic Club to John W. Weber, George Straub and William Battermann trustees. Elm st, n s, 362.10 w Evergreen av, 18.11x95. Collateral security to trust mort. Oct. 1.

Thompson, David W. mortgagor with George C. Blanke mortgagee. Extension mort. Oct. 15. nom

Thompson, Charles M. to Charlotte Leavens. Hemlock st, w s, 616.10 s Jamaica av, 25x81.2 x25x81.6. Dec. 7, 3 years. 1,500

Truber, Frank C. to Maria J. Thorne. Strong pl. P. M. Oct. 26, due Dec. 1, 1894. 3,500

Turner, Anson W. to Ella Cory. Stockholm st, n w s, 447 n e Evergreen av, 22x100. Dec. 8, 3 years, 5 %. 1,500

Same to same. Stockholm st, n w s, 425 n e Evergreen av, 22x100. Dec. 8, 3 years, 5 %. 1,500

Tangeman, Nellie R., New Utrecht, L. I., to South Brooklyn Co-operative Building and Loan Assoc. 56th st, n s, 150 e 14th av, 50x 100.2, New Utrecht. Dec. 8, installs. 5,500

The Columbia Chemical Works to Benjamin A. Hegeman exr. Charles Kelsey. Sedgwick st. P. M. Nov. 14, installs, 5 %. 13,000

Ulrich, Frederick, Sr. and Jr., Augusta Grossmann, Lena Kuhne and Freda Rogers to Warren S. Burt. South 9th st, n w cor Havermeyer st, 12x80.5x35x82. Dec. 1, 1 year, 5 %. 400

Van Horn, Anna M. to Thomas Everit. 17th st, s s, 287.6 e 8th av, 12.6x100. Dec. 1, 3 years. 1,000

Wagner, Joseph to William Bedford. Ewen st, P. M. Nov. 28, due Dec. 2, 1893, 5 %. 700

Waite, Amelia C. to William W. Wickes East 9th st, Flatbush. P. M. Dec. 7, 5 years. 4,500

Waite, Amelia C. wife of E. P. to John H. Seed. East 4th st, w s, 180 s Av B, Flatbush. P. M. Dec. 7, 5 years, 5 %. 750

Same to same. Av B and East 4th st, Flatbush. P. M. Dec 7, 5 years, 5 %. 8,000

Weidmann, Wilhelmina or Mina wife of Paul P. to Terence Jacobson. Willoughby st, n s, 45.8 e Adams st, 22.10x100; 12th st, s s, 243.4 w 7th av, 27.6x100. All title. Dec. 4, due Jan. 1, 1893. 400

Weil, Hugo to J. Fred. Ackerman exr. Louisa J. Ackerman. Willoughby av. P. M. Dec. 1, due Dec 4, 1892, 5 %. 4,000

Wend, Catharine E. to Christian Baur. Sumpter st, s s, 295 w Ralph av, 30x80.2x30.2x83 Dec. 3, due Jan. 1, 1894, or installs, 5 %. 400

Same to same. Same property. Dec. 3, due Jan. 1, 1894, 5 %. 4,000

Wodzicki, Theodore C. to Mary Dougherty, New York. Woodbine st, n w s, 200 s w Central av, 25x100. Dec. 2, due Jan. 1, 1893. 800

Wohlgethan, Edward and Auguste J. his wife to Louise Astheimer. Columbia st. P. M. Dec. 3, 5 years. 1,500

Wolf, Jacob to Charles Engert. Monitor st. P. M. Sub. to mort. $1,150. Dec. 1, installs, 5%. 1,400

Same to The Kings County Savings Inst. Same property. Dec. 1. 1 year, 5%. 1,150

Wessell, Richard to Phebe Carpenter. 11th st, n s, 195 9 w 4th av, 20.2x100. Dec. 7, due Nov. 1, 1894, 5%. 1,500

Wheeler, Susan E. wife of George W. to Euphemia P. Del Hoyo. India st, s s, 225 w Manhattan av, 25x100. Dec. 9, 3 years, 5%. 2,500

Whitenack, John O. to Henry C. Olmsted trustee John Boulton. McDougal st, n s, 350 e Hopkinson av. 2 lots, each 25x100. 2 morts., each $4,000. Nov. 30, 3 years. 8,000

Same to Sarah C Savage trustee Elihu Chauncey. McDougal st, n s, 300 e Hopkinson av, 2 lots, each 25x100. 2 morts., each $4,000. Nov. 21, 3 years, 5½%. 8,000

Wise, Mary R. to A. Ohrig. Grand av, w s, 175.5 n Gates av, 16 9x100. Nov. 22, 1 year. 225

MORTGAGES----ASSIGNMENTS.

NEW YORK CITY.

DECEMBER 4 TO 10—INCLUSIVE.

Adam, Sarah to Cecil A. Marks. $1,750

Adler, Simon and Henry S. Herrman to Simon Herman. 6,000

Bier, Mary to Sigmund Cohn. 550

Brady, John J. to Lena Seiferd. nom

Same to Eleanor J. Porter. 900

Brooklyn Trust Co. to The Young Men's Christian Assoc. 20,000

Clark, William E. trustee, &c. to Helen J. Conklin. 3,000

Cohen, Louis to Minna Krause. 2,000

Cohen, Babetta to Mary A O'Reilly. 1,500

Crawford, William H. to Frederick H. Allen. 1,000

Dowley, George S., Brattleboro, Vt., to John E. Cronty. 1,000

De Graaf, Amanda M. to Laib Lichtblau. 900

Ely, Nathan L. and Henry C. exrs Nathan C. Ely to Amelie E. Scranton. 6,000

Frost, Leontine J. et al. exrs. Levi A. Lockwood to Lionel R. Lennox, Washington, D. C. 600

Same to same. 1,572

Same to Lydia A. Lockwood, Brooklyn. 1,200

Same to same. 1,572

Same to same. 1,200

Same to same. 1,260

Same to Amy A. Lockwood, Brooklyn. 1,596

Same to Leontine J. Frost, Brooklyn. 39

Same to same. 4,620

Same to Leontine J. Frost and ano. trustees Levi A Lockwood. 3,405

Same to same. 9,969

Same to same. 18,000

Franklin, James R. to Solomon Miller. 1,800

Gsell, Charles S., Turin, N. Y., to Peter Gorth. 3,000

Griffen, Joseph C., Portchester, N. Y., to Daniel M. Griffen, Portchester, N. Y. 10,000

Gerken, John to Clara R. Gerken. 2,000

Gebhard, William H. exr. Frederick C. Gebhard to August Limbert trustee Frederick C. Gebhard nom

Goodridge, Charlotte M. to The German Savings Bank. consid. omitted

Goodwin, Hersey B. and William W. trustees for Amelia M. Goodwin to Amelia M. Goodwin. 6,000

Hayes, Virginia B. to Elizabeth Hayes, Brooklyn. 3,000

Higenbotham, Elizabeth wife of Samuel B. to Francis B. Chedsey. 2,500

Hard, Anson W. and John K. Tod as trustees of The Norwich Union Fire Ins. Society, of Norwich, Eng., to Anson W. Hard, John K. Tod and William E. Roosevelt trustees of The Norwich Union Fire Ins. Society, of Norwich, Eng. nom

Heath, George B. to Henry Hyman and David Frank. 11,000

Henderson, Charles R. exr. John C. Henderson to Adolphus J. Outerbridge trustee of Adolphus J. and Harriet G. Outerbridge. 5,500

Same to same. 5,000

Hyatt, George E., Brooklyn, to John B. Whiting trustee. 2 assigns. nom

Same to Edward Winslow. nom

Haag, Gustav K. to Jane Besthoff. 17,000

Holland Trust Co. to Francis M. Jencks. nom

Jencks, Francis M. to The New York Security and Trust Co. nom

Johanson, Sarah J. to Frederick Schmidt. 700

Kahn, Samuel to John J. Brady. 4,000

Kassel, Abraham to Joseph Kessel. 2,030

Kilpatrick, Edward to William Kirchhof. 4,000

Leypoldt, Augusta H. and Adrian H. Larkin as trustees to Arthur P. Heinze guard. of Florence D., Virginia and Tracy S. Buckingham. 2,120

Lewis, John A. et al. exrs. and trustees Benjamin B. Sherman to Catharine Bagot. 10,000

Middlebrook, Frederic J., Brooklyn, to Susan C. Herriman et al. exrs. John Herriman. 10,000

Middlebrook, Frederic J., Brooklyn, to Charles E. Rhinelander. 6,087

Same to Robert H. Coleman trustee for Anne C. Rogers 4,504

Same to same. 9,007

Mulry, James B. et al. exrs. and trustees Michael Mulry to Ellie M. Bannin, Brooklyn. 23,137

Muller, Clemens to Clemens Muller, William Erdtmann and Louis A. A. Althof trustees. 1,000

Morrison, David M. exr. James M. Morrison to Albert E Putnam. 6,007

Morgenthau, Henry to Levi P. Morton and George Bliss. 152,110

Morgenthau, Henry to R. Clarence Dorsett. nom

O'Rorke, Margaret A to Jane Armstrong. 1,500

Powell, Sarah H. to Edward Rushmore exr. Isaac Rushmore. 1,300

Pinkham, Charles M., Jr., to Joseph B. Tompkins. nom

Poillon, Winfield exr. Rachel A. Poillon to The Washington Life Ins. Co. 18,000

Prime, Ralph E., Jr., Yonkers, N. Y., to Leslie M. Saunders, Yonkers, N. Y consid. omitted

Passman, Leonard B. exr John G Hick to The Citizens' Bank, of Elizabeth, N. J. nom

Robbins, Matthew F. and Sarah E., Oyster Bay, L. I., to Edward Koehler. 11,000

Roosevelt, James A trustee for Marcia R. Scovel to James A. and W. Emlen Roosevelt trustees for Marcia R. Scovel. nom

Robinson, Douglas to Fanny M. Robinson. nom

Robinson, Fanny M. wife of Douglas, Herkimer Co., N. Y., to Douglas Robinson. nom

Rieser, Jacob to Jacob Schlosser. 3,500

Same to same. 3,000

Same to same. 2,000

Same to same. 2,500

Same to Magdalena and Isabella Becker. 3,500

Rieser, Jacob to Michael Fay and William Stacom. 5,000

Same to same. 4,000

Same to same. 6,000

Same to same. 5,000

Same to same. 3,000

Ryan, Peter to Eliza Worthington. 300

Rosenthal, Harris to Fritz Fedderke, Brooklyn. 6,500

Schermerhorn, William C. exr. Edmund H. Schermerhorn to Ebenezer Sugden 10,000

Scott, John S. to Frederick A. Snow. nom

Saunders, Leslie M. admr. James Saunders to Ralph E Prime, Jr., Yonkers, N. Y. 1,000

Sladkus, Sigmund to Joseph Schwartz. 1,500

Schreyer, John to William J. Fields. 1,000

Sire, Meyer L. to Edward F. Browning. 8,500

Todd, Judson S. to Edward Winslow. 4 assigns. nom

The J. L Mott Iron Works to Jordan L. Mott exr. Jeannie A. Morton. 11,000

Townsend, Rudolph W., Benjamin F. Einstein and Anthony R. Dyett to William G. McCrea. val. consid

Title Guarantee and Trust Co. to Marie Lange extrx. Julius Lange. 2,400

Title Guarantee and Trust Co. to Mark Hoyt et al. exrs. Oliver Hoyt. 45,000

Title Guarantee and Trust Co. to The Excelsior Savings Bank. 35,000

Same to Matilda Weil et al. exrs. Max Weil 16,000

The United States Fire Ins. Co to Clara R. Gerken. 10,000

Wallace, Frank E., East Orange, N. J., to The Title Guarantee and Trust Co. 1,200

Same to same. 1,300

Weinstein, Ascher to Henry Klingenstein. 4,500

Wolf, Therese to Joseph L. Buttenwieser. 4,800

Same to same. 3,300

KINGS COUNTY.

DECEMBER 3 TO 9—INCLUSIVE.

Bailey, Frank to Joseph P. Durfey. $1,000

Barnaby, Frank A. to The Hamilton Trust Co. 40,000

Benjamin, Joseph to Markus Bach. 1,200

Betts, T. J. and Wm. T. exrs. Anthony Betts to William T. Betts, Woodside, L. I. 2,227

Brooklyn Trust Co. to The Young Women's Christian Assoc., Brooklyn. 67,500

Blum, Victoria to Margaretha Stephan. 3,500

Burling, George T. exr. Adeline Burling to George T. Burling. 3,000

Bauer, Mary to Eli H. Bishop. 600

Bolton, William C. trustee for Obed B. Bolton to Henry Friend and ano. exrs. Christian Friend. 2,000

Benedict, James A. and ano exrs. Margaret Cleland to Susan Alvord 2,044

Brown, Carrie H. to Sarah E. Brush, Huntington, L. I. nom

Brown, George R. to William H. Tweddell. 1,450

Campbell, Boik D. to Hugo Hirsh. 800

Clark, Francis E. to Hiram Williams. 900

Collins, Richard S. to Mary A. Carpenter. 2,700

Same to William H. Collins exr. William B. Collins. 2,700

Cohn, Sigmund to Rosa Schoeffel. 2,000

Creagn, Kate M to Maria J. Thorne. 2,000

Davenport, Peter N, Treasurer of Town of Hempstead, L. I., to George S Downing et al. admrs. Vincent Martling. nom

De Esterre, William H. and Lina to Emilie Huber. 2,500

Davenport, William B. Public Admr. Peter Bennett dec'd to The People's Trust Co. guard. of John J., Peter, Mary, Julia, Richard and Elizabeth Bennett. nom

Everit, Thomas to Andrew Findlay. 1,000

Feuerbach, Agnes formerly Morville to Wolcott H. Pitkin. 3,300

Fickett, Sophronia M. to J. T. E. Litchfield. 950

Ganen, Franz to Theresa Hermanni. 1,000

Geertz, Rose B H, and Charles J. A. and William H. Friday to William C. Bolton trustee for Obed B. Bolton. 700

Gies, Katie to Archibald Graham. nom

Godwin, Parke to Caroline A. Strong, Setauket, L. I. 1,750

Gruber, Peter G. guard. Henry Gruber to Henry Gruber. nom

Godfrey, Phebe A. to Elizabeth S. Seymour. 716

Havens, Edwin S., Greenport, L. I., to Ann Kenney. 200

Haydock, George R. to Caroline L. Everit. 600

Haydock, William H. to George R. Haydock. 300

Hussey, Jessie C. to Harry S. Stallknecht. nom

Isbill, Charles to Thomas McIlroy. 1,800

Ives, John H. to Loftis W. O'Berry. 4,500

Johnson, Henry B. to The Tradesmen's National Bank. nom

Joseph Fallert Brewing Co. (Lim.) to Obermeyer & Liebmann. 800

Kendall, Henry to Guernsey Sackett, Frank C. Lang, Charles A. Reed and James B. McKewan. 600

Kenney, Ann to Elizabeth Taber et al. exrs. F. W. Taber. 200

Koch, George exr Christian Straub to Joseph J. Eisemann and ano. exrs. Barbara Straub. nom

Kleine, Virginia A. and Frank Bailey to William M. Ingraham. 6,562

Same to same. 8,000

Laytin, Abby E. to Theodore F. Jackson et al. trustees Loftis Wood. 2,000

Same to same. 4,000

Linnington, Margaret A. admrx. Eliz. W. Jones to Margaret A. Linnington. 9,000

Same to John T. Jones. 7,200

Levin, Barnet to Lewis Hurst. 250

Martin, Florence E. formerly Durker to James McLaren. 1,500

McDonald, Sarah L. and Samuel W. to William J. Tillotson. 1,009

McGee, Alice wife of and Thomas to William G. G. Peirson. 1,150

Nostrand, Henry L. and ano. exrs. Margaret T. Johnson to Phebe H. Sayres. 3,000

Nelson, John F. to John F. Edwards. 3,000

Newman, Emma wife of and James I. to Thomas W., Charles E and David J. Cummings, of R. Cummings' Sons. nom

Obrig, Adolph exr. and trustee G. J. Obrig to Maria M. Winter. 5,006

O'Hare, Terence J to John J. O. Keeffe. nom

Powell, Sarah R. to Margaret A. Eadie, Flushing, L. I 4,000

Raynor, Anna Van S. individ. and admrx. Mary J. Leeds to James M. Farr. 10,000

Roth, Henry to Herman F. Scharmann. 400

Riebling, Peter to Mathias Neger. 1,900

Roberts, James G to Aoney C. Wildey. 1,200

Skinner, Elizabeth to Catharine Keegan. 2,500

Stanley, Samuel G. to William G. Pierson. 3,087

Stewart, James committee Henry A. Monaghan to Emeline A. Burr. 2,050

Stoutenburg, George B. to John H. Forshew. 500

The Hall Sash and Door Co. to Richard Goodwin. 5,000

Title Guarantee and Trust Co. to Anna M. Hubbard. 3,750

Same to Cornelius Buys. 3,750

Same to Francis Lawrence 5,000

Same to The Hamilton Trust Co. admrs. 5,000

Same to James S. Leeds. 5,000

Same to same. 2,500

Same to Lizzie C Merrill. 3,000

Same to John F. Merrill 4,000

Same to Anna M. Hubbard. 3,750

Same to same. 4,000

Same to Jane Gray. 3,500

Same to William H. Chapman admr. Ann E. Chapman. 1,000

Same to Bernard Cruse, Jr 450

Same to Garetta P. Hagemeyer. 5,000

Same to Mary A. Cantrell. 2,500

Same to The Drew Theological Seminary Methodist Episcopal Church. 4,000

Same to The Brooklyn Trust Co. 3 assigns., each $7,500. 22,500

Same to Wesleyan University, Middletown, Conn. 2 assigns., each $5,000. 10,000

Same to same. 2 assigns., each $5,500. 11,000

Same to Frederick Gilbert. 3,500

Same to Silas Ludlam. 6,000

Trowbridge, Henry, Jr, Astoria, L. I., to Henry Trowbridge, Astoria. nom

Tuttle, George F. exr. Mary Baker to Cornelius D. Pruden, East Orange, N. J. 5,000

Ulmer, William to Helena Schneider. 1,000

White, Mary A. to Henry Kettelhodt. 350

Wunschel, George H. to Eliza Hornung. 1,000

Wells, Charlotte E. to Edwin S. Havens. 1871. 200

Walker, Mary E. to The Home Life Ins. Co. 6,000

Wirth, John C. to John W. Roemmele. 150

JUDGMENTS.

In these lists of judgments the names alphabetically arranged, and which are first on each line, are those of the judgment debtor. The letter (D) means judgment for deficiency (*) means not summoned. (†) signifies that the first name is fictitious, real name being unknown. Judgments entered during the week, and satisfied before day of publication, do not appear in this column, but in list of Satisfied Judgments

NEW YORK CITY.

Dec.

5 Ahearn, John—Health Dep't......... $209 87

5 Alexander, Jacob — Max Lichtenstadter 42 12

5 Alyea, William—J V Carr........... 230 42
8 Armstrong, William T, Armstrong, Jessie E } Joseph Solomon....... 308 26
8 Aylward, John W—Gustav Arnsinck. 476 66
9*Ayres, Charles H—Charles Schlesinger.................................. 838 30
9 the same——Bergmann Mfg Co... 1,972 46
9 Angermeier, George—H J Maris...... 109 00
9 Allen, Horace B—Henry Herrmann.. 298 00
9 Abbott, George E—Daniel Finnigan.. 137 27
9 Adler, I Richard, Adler, Leon N, exrs, Solomon Adler } S M Schwab, Jr 846 14
10 Amberg, Gustave—Ludwig Bauman.. 1,635 95
11 Azog, Mary L, Arthur, Angelina T } William Sobriever.......... 79 02
5 Baldwin, Theodore F—W H Baldwin. 1,985 95
5 the same——the same............ 2,131 20
5 the same——the same............ 2,131 20
5 Brockner, Ambrose E—Health Dep't. 209 87
5 Burke, Margaret——the same.... .. 209 87
5 Bauer, Moritz—J M Horton.......... 511 50
5 Bauer, Moritz, Bauer, Cecelie } J M Horton.....costs 119 95
5 Bailey, Samuel H—W B Fonda....... 819 98
5 Ball, William E—W C Lesster.......47,147 77
5+Boyle, George D—J W Gilbert........ 35 87
5 Bishop, Clarence B—James Hartley.................................(D) 327 93
7 Beale, Joseph H — Mary C Fox, admrx.................................. 368 26
7 Baird, Robert B—J R Sayre, Jr...... 280 21
7 Beacham, John—W H Appleton..... 144 93
7 Burroughs, Horace F—W D Wheelwright.............................costs 23 33
7 Brooks, James Wilton — Isabella S Royd.................................. 185 59
7 Bonnell, John Harper—Second Nat Bank of Red Bank.................. 1,008 13
7 Burritt, John D—Phillips & Clark Stove Co.......................... 488 08
7 Ball, Max—S A Swenarton.......... 356 86
8 Butler, Thomas—W R Sergeant. ... 177 08
8 Benson, Rodney—N Y County Nat Bank.................................. 1,349 68
8 the same——the same............ 1,451 90
8 the same——the same............ 947 25
8 Blauvelt, Margaret W—Matthew Hettrick..............................costs 160 80
8 Bridgeford, Simon W—W E Lucas.. 97 15
8 Baldwin, Elizabeth S—Josephine F Clason.................................. 231 96
8 Byrne, Andrew—H C West 360 46
8 Bigelow, Richard H—J C Barnes..... 256 99
8 the same——Home Benefit Assoc.. 261 26
9 Blanchard, Charles A—Charles Schlesinger.................................. 838 30
9 Benedict, Joseph E—Charles Schlesinger.................................. 203 83
9 Basford, Mary C—P J Keary........ 135 71
9 Brosnan, Jeremiah M, Brosnan, Thomas J } J H Meyer... 111 09
9 Blake, Amanda M—Sam'l Katz...... 114 39
9 Blanchard, Charles A—Bergmann Mfg Co.................................. 1,972 46
10 Bell, Charlotte A, Bell, Jennie M } B F Romaine, Jr.. 316 29
10*Bauer, Frederick—C V Fornes. 1,781 55
10 Bainbridge, John George—F E Blackwell.................................. 1,175 17
10 Blayer, Simon H—Solomon Worthington.................................. 34 80
10 Baker, John M, admr Catharine M Wetherbee—R A Olmstead.......... 630 00
10 Benedix, Gus—Adolph Abrahams.... 124 95
10 Bond, Joseph—Lindley Marray 158 81
10 Brinkerhoff, Cornelius—G F Bassett.. 228 82
10 Brown, Charles H—Berthold Veit.... 114 66
10 Boylan, Martin J—J F Fitzgerald.... 40 50
10 Bottlowsky, Max—Harris Ratkowsky 124 85
10 Blumberg, Max——the same.......... 169 80
10 Boylan, Martin J—J F Fitzgerald.... 40 50
10 Bender, William—Valentine Newberger.................................. 293 83
10 Bernhardt, Julius—Bishop & Babcock Co.................................. 100 22
10 Bernstein, George S, Bernstein, Mary } G W Shellas... 52 59
11 Breunig, Frederick—G W Travers.. 107 10
11 Backer, Jonathan—Henry Schneider. 3,735 40
11 Brewster, Frank—R J Howe.......... 125 15
11 Becker, Conrad—Rapp & Johnson Lumber Co.............................. 127 13
11 Ball, Max—J T Leavitt............... 638 67
11 Bolton, C Gray, Bolton, Lillian D } William Schriever. ....costs 79 02
5 Childs, William H—J M Horton. costs 119 95
7 Crolius, William C—N R French..... 48 18
Cain, William—William Tiernan.... 29 68
Conquest, John A—F E Barnes....... 203 97
Condie, James—N Y County Nat Bank.................................. 1,143 29
the same——the same............ 1,349 68
8 the same——the same............ 1,451 91
8 the same——the same............ 947 25
8 Collins, James H—John derry 171 40
8 Cohn, Moritz—Simon Herzig........ 323 54
8 the same——Mathilde Isaacs...... 339 58
8 the same——Leopold Cohn........ 588 50
8 Cobb, Henry B—Nat Conduit Mfg Co 6,090 02
8 Cranston, Henry—E W Ashley....... 616 69
8 Cohen, Abraham, Cohen, Attie } Gilbert Alexander. 195 56
9 Crossett, James—Charles Schlesinger. 169 80
9 Cavinato, Luigi, Cavinato, Guiseppi, Cavinato, Natale, Cavinato, Steffano } O D Person..... 332 00
9 Chapman, John—M S Newcorn....... 49 57
9 Crawford, John J—Patrick Cassidy.. 523 79
9 Card, Anson V—R B Reinhardt...... 99 53
9 Conkling, John B—F H Gerber........ 425 63
9 Campbell, Thomas—Henry McAleenan.................................. 4,044 02
9 Cranston, Henry—M R Cook........ 1,266 00
10 Carr, Walter, Carr, Delwin } R H Bunney......... 1,049 37
10 Cranston, Henry—Mary F Root....... 1,350 88
10 Caputa, Joseph—E C Wells. 282 23
10 Cohen, Harris—Joseph Sawyer....... 794 84
10 Cohen, Isaac—Lewis Adelson........ 164 10
10 Carley, Michael E—T J Martin....... 457 43
11 Cavinato, Luigi—Northern Nat Bank. 336 75
5 Dumont, James A, Jr—Kirtland, Andrews & Co (Lim)................. 840 26
5 Doering, Oscar A—Louis Seeger.. .. 25 50
7 Daley, James—Edmund Fitzgerald... 237 42
7 Dewitt, Charles H—J B Kelty....... 70 83
7 Dodge, Julia Rhinelander—Mary L Gallatin.................................. 142 19
7 Dunbar, Robert—Lucy A Bertram.. ....costs 40 14
7 Droste, Adolph M—George Schuchman.................................. 127 10
7 Day, John B—Mary G Pinkney...... 75 73
7 Day, Peter S—John Matthews 102 30
7+Doe, John—Municipal Electric Light Co.................................. 130 75
7 David, Albert A—G W Bramhall.... 314 48
8 Doyle, John F—C J Gallagher....... 399 99
8 Douglass, John L—Carsten Offerman. 227 12
8 Davis, Edward T—Nat Conduit Mfg Co.................................. 6,090 02
8 Dunn, Patrick—Wright Gillies....... 654 34
8 Donnell, Raymond S—J R Potts..... 79 35
9 Duff, Patrick—Thomas Hammill..... 72 00
10 Doherty, Lionel—J E Mulligan....... 265 28
10+Doe, John—Julius Bonner........... 138 00
11 De Vito, Vincenzo—Max Hertz...costs 79 10
11 Downes, Henry—F A Baier........... 125 72
11 Dammer, Herrman—Isaac Boehm.... 77 63
11 Diss, Charles J—White, Potter & Paige Mfg Co........................ 191 64
11 Dwingelo, Annie—Robert Hill........ 472 39
8 Edwards, John W, exr Hugh W Hughes—R E Leavitt. 1,596 50
9 Edelson, Louis, Edelson, Abraham } Louis Hoopes... 251 70
9 Edgerly, Clinton J—H M Kiretchjiam.................................. 111 55
11 Emmermann, Fritz—Agnes Weniger, an infant............................ 336 75
11 Eiebman, Louis—J H Muller........ 857 24
5 Fox, Henry—Diedrich Groubolz....... 99 16
5 Fettretch, Mary L—James Hartley (D) 327 93
7 Faulkner, John H—John Kress Brewing Co.............................. 149 34
7 Fox, John—David Jones Co. 224 29
7 Fenn, Henry H—Phillips & Clark Stove Co.............................. 488 08
7+Fischer, John—Joseph Eppig... .... 183 69
8 Flannery, John P—C J Gallagher..... 399 99
8 Fuchs, Michael—Julius Engel........ 86 59
9 Fishel, William V—John Baehr...... 760 13
9 Feeley, Michael T——the same........ 1,508 00
9 Field, Aaron, Field, Edward S } E P Hincks..... . 113 14
10 Foote, Dewitt C—D D Withers, trustee.................................. 97 50
10 Friedel, Gustav—William Jung...... 109 44
10 Fountain, Inez—W E Bryant......... 721 03
10+Friedlander, Samuel—Harris Katkowsky.................................. 47 76
10+Farber, Isaac—Charles Moser....... 106 74
5 Goldstein, Isaac—Health Dep't....... 209 87
5 Grady, Thomas F—Alexander Newberger.................................. 171 60
5 Gardner, Charles E—D W Moran.... 149 11
7 Garrison, Ferdinand C—F A Kennedy Co.................................. 404 17
7 Greenfield, George J, trustee Philip R Paulding—Mary L Gallatin....costs 142 19
7 Gillease, John—W R Dean.......costs 38 50
8 Goldberg, Morris—David Scheinert... 61 81
8 Graef, Charles H—Pyrogravure Co... 103 12
8*Glotstone, Samuel—Adolph Kronold.. 30 85
8 Gosling, Abraham—Leopold Woodle. 83 23
8 Goldstein, Meyer, Goldstein, Abraham, Goldstein, Elias } Robert Simon. 45,309 52
9 Griffin, Frederick—Charles Schlesinger.................................. 173 30
9 Goodwin, Alice S—J B Brewster & Co.................................. 287 79
9 Gru, Joseph—Bernard Friest......... 289 77
9 Gottschо, Isaac, Gottscho, Herman } Nonantum Worsted Co.......... 169 82
10 Gerschel, Benjamin—J M Bleyer..... 43 10
10 Griesmeyer, Charles — American Champagne Co. (Lim)............ 146 95
10 Grovesteen, William P—Charles Blum. 2,956 34
10*Gottlieb, Herman—Charles Moser.... 106 74
11 Grant, Hugh J, as Sheriff—Frederick Stark.................................. 85 63
11 Gearon, Michael—Herrmann Weiller. 557 77
11 Goldsmith, Pauline—F C Goldsmith.. 244 75
11 the same——the same........... 123 50
11 the same——E E Frank.......... 100 00
11 the same——Scott Lord......... 102 00
11 the same——J R Potts.......... 94 60
5 Heimeyer, August P M—Jacob Kramer.................................. 186 50
5 Hock, John E—C S Crossman........ 49 80
5 Hay, James—Long Island City 75 18
7 Hughes, Samuel R—Bartley O'Brien. 472 64
7 Hogan, Bridget—Thomas Geier...... 103 34
7 Hodgkins, Charles—F E Barnes...... 393 97
7 Higgins, Cecil Campbell—G C Lee.... 1,362 88
7 Hayes, Katie, admrx John Hayes—Delos Woolverton..... ......costs 94 73
7 Henningsen, John—Guilia Brandeis.. 168 09
8*Hanse, James—E G Blakslee Mfg Co. 1,854 01
8 Hughes, William H, exr Hugh W Hughes—R E Leavitt.............1,596 50
8 Hackett, Edward M—Edward Winter 153 30
8 Helfenberg, Solomon—Adolph Kronold 30 82
8 Hofsnes, John admr John H Hofsnes—Dry Dock, East Broadway & Battery R R.................................. 86 06
8 Hausdorff, Heinrich—Robert Simon. 45,309 52
9 Holcomb, John D—Charles Schlesinger.................................. 303 75
9 Healey, Mary—James Mathews...... 139 40
9+Harrington, Henry C—R A Saalfield. 75 00
9 Howard, M Fanny—William Walsmann.................................. 415 07
9 Harmon, John—Thomas Lenane...... 328 00
9 Henderson, John, Henderson, Mrs John } W M Schwenker.......... 126 74
9 Howell, Eugene N—Fourth Nat Bank 9,663 87
10 Hartung, Lorenzo R—W H Jackson.. 164 70
10 Hughes, Orlando D—A F Winkle..... 68 57
10 Herbst, Adam—Louis Shapiro........ 151 50
10 Hyman, Israel—Harris Ratkowsky... 47 50
10 Harrison, Nellie—Rachel Richard.... 52 00
10 Hoffman, Charles H—W P Hickok... 94 74
10 Hillen, George—Herman Langenhop.. 638 18
11 Hughes, Samuel R—Margaret Hughes 700 00
11 Hollsberg, Henry F—Mary E Hollsberg.................................. 1,400 00
11*Hirsch, Jacob, Harris, Amanda } I H Klein......... 181 66
11 Hearsey, Edward L, Hopkins, Joseph J } Twenty-sixth Ward Bank of Brooklyn. 2,100 28
11 Hirsch, Jacob, Harris, Amanda } A O Headley...... 305 88
11 Hume, Walter S—Benjamin Knower. 5,745 64
11 Hume, Charles—J G Wilson......... 172 36
8 Immig, Charles H—E G Blakslee Mfg Co.................................. 1,854 01
11 Ingram, Orrin W—C F Nagel........ 75 43
11 Irvine, Allen A—Nat Barrow and Truck Co.............................. 168 39
5 Jackson, Henry—Moritz Sternberg... 283 08
5 Jonas, Philip H—Mount Morris Bank. 188 46
7 Jablowski, William—Joseph Eppig... 104 35
7 Jerkowski, Marcus—G W Bramhall.. 314 48
7 Jonasson, Henry—J J Murphy... ... 140 21
9 Jacobs, Annie—Rosa Mayer.........1,077 53
11 Jacobs, Annie—George Hollister..... 604 45
11 Johann, Peter—Rapp & Johnson Lumber Co.............................. 127 13
11 Jacobs, Adolph, Jacobs, Max, Jacobs, William } Adolph Prince..... 774 03
5 Kronengold, Adolph—Diedrich Gronholz.................................. 99 16
5 Kelly, William H—Health Dep't...... 209 87
5 Keyser, Isaiah—Nathaniel Jarvis, Jr 16,211 96
5 Keogh, Christopher B—Thomas Hagan.................................. 643 03
5*Keller, Adam, Klemann, Jacob } Eliza Klemann.... 1,526 60
5 Kirchner, Charles—J V Carr..... ... 230 42
7 Kelleher, John—G W Smith.......... 155 87
7 Kile, Charles—M H Haggerty........ 78 24
7 Krumm, Charles, Krumm, Mary } Anchor Brewing Co............... 115 45
8 Krumm, Charles—Siegfried Wurzburg.................................. 75 95
8 Kane, Terence—A A Henderson...... 88 58
8+Kindler, Abraham—George Gebbie.. 42 50
8 Kelly, Mary J—E C Smith......costs 44 62
9 Krauss, Emanuel—W E Story........ 246 00
9 Kreuder, Louis—Anton Bahr......... 120 15
9 Kopetzky, Joseph—Christian Jourgensen.................................. 19 52
10 Kennedy, Joseph—Siegmund Harris .1,108 04
10 Krokewitz, Samuel—Lewis Adelson.. 143 10
11 Kampf, Frederick—B F Martin, comm'r.................................. 100 10
11 Kimmey, Wm W——the same....... 100 10
11 Kramer, Louis—T J Martin.... ..... 271 21
11 Kennedy, Patrick—White, Potter & Paige Mfg Co........................ 191 64
5 Lesster, Edward W—W C Lesster.. 47,147 77
5 Liekefelt, John B—J A Seraley...... 88 75
7 Levey, Clarence—J B Clement....... 587 31
7 Lazard, Felix—N R French.... ...... 46 28
7 Lloyd, Elizabeth—Rosetta A Curtiss. 151 62
8 Lounsbery, James S—N Y County Nat Bank.............................. 1,349 68
8 the same——the same............1,451 91
8 the same——the same............ 947 25
8 Loubriel, Manuel M—Leopold Woodle. 83 23
9 Leahy, John—Donatus Rieger........ 42 72
9 Lange, George H—Frederick Lutz... 160 09
10 Lewis, Thomas C, Lewis, James } Siegmund Harris.. 1,108 04
10 Lait, Leon—Julius Bonber........... 72 96
10 Leffler, John, Leffler, Max } Phil McManus.... ... 195 38
10 Lacina, Frank—J H Meierdierck..... 84 29
11 Luxton, Edward D—E C Van Glahn.. 472 24
11 Lowenstein, Joseph H, Lowenstein, Henry M } Sigmund Kline...... 305 19
11 Luckey, Christian—C W Bachman... 154 41
11 Loveday, Edwin—William Herron... 110 70
5 Mayers, Mark—M D Stern........... 127 50
5 Meyer, Siegmund T—W C Moquin... 522 64
5 Mellen, Letitia A—J G Johnson...... 248 23
5 Morris, William—W D Woods....... 104 73
5 Murray, Michael—K L Blom.... .... 194 18
5*Mayer, Louis—Eliza Klemann........ 1,526 60
7 Muller, Louis, Mueller, Mary B } People's Bank of East Orange, N J 123 19
7 Mahon, Charles—Edmund Fitzgerald. 978 20
7 Mason, Amasa—Equitable Life Assur Society.................................. 966 46
7 Montgomery, James T—A K Montgomery.................................. 350 00
8 Mooney, Andrew B—John Ryan.costs 38 67

8 MacEvoy, Charles—F L Froment..... 696 87
8 Mueller, William, Mueller, Herman } F A Schroeder, assignee.......... 2,4'9 61
8 Matthews, James C—W and J Sloane. 2,257 09
8 Murphy, William F—S B Wartmann. 585 22
9 Maloney, Dennis—People State N Y. 10,027 13
9 Matthews, James C—P E Sanford..... 817 68
9 Mulqueen, Thomas F—Philip Levy... 181 25
9 Meyer, Nathan—L N Vanse 208 15
9 Moffitt, William H—Kansas City Star Co........ 189 52
10 Matthews, James C—George Harjes.. 515 70
10 Moran, Owen—O J Williams......... 588 22
10 Macy, Francis H, Jr—F E Blackwell. 1,175 17
10 Mulqueen, Thomas F—Foster, Merriam & Co.... 160 97
10 Miber, La Bert—Alfred Halliday.... 289 57
10 Mulqueen, Thomas F—H J Ehlers.... 193 52
10 Meyer, Philip L—A C Haynes........ 1,823 15
10*Murphy, John—Berthold Veit........ 114 66
10 Mulvey, Gerold—D M Koehler....... 178 75
10 Markowsky, Simon—Barris Ratkowsky........ 202 97
10 Myers, Sinclair—Theodore Conklin... 81 14
11 Marston, Robt J — B F Martin, comm'r........ 110 10
11 Maber, Michael——the same.......... 110 10
11 Merritt, Charles—John Baebr........ 160 00
11 Morehouse, Joseph J—R J Howe..... 125 15
11 Morrison, William, Jr—Marvin Safe Co ....costs 49 14
11 Martin, George—J C Watson Co. 1,242 66
11 Meehan, Edward, Jr, Meehan, Charlotte } B F Gerding.. 288 06
5 McKay, Stewart—A W Haff......... 73 32
5 McIntyre, Patrick—Long Island City. 78 23
7 McKenna, Patrick—John Brennan.... 28 15
7 McMahon, John P—David Jones Co.. 70 29
8 McCallum, Julia C, McCallum, James } Catharine A Du Bois........... 797 93
8 MacEvoy, Charles—F L Froment.... 696 37
9 McDonald, Patrick J—Harlem Lighting Co.......... 821 37
9 McDonald, Anne—Mary A Cassidy, extrx. 523 00
10 McGinty, Thomas—Jacob Nelson. ... 24 50
11 Mackie, Laura S—William Schriever. ....costs 79 02
11 McCaniess, Mrs Joseph..J G West.... 74 11
11 McCarthy, John C—George Peyser... 907 93
11 Mackie, Laura S—William Schriever. ....costs 79 02
8 Novatofsky, Wolf—F W Hahn 32 50
8 Newell, Darius C, Newell, George E, Newell, Darius E } N Y County Nat Bank.......... 1,143 29
8 the same — the same............ 1,349 08
8 the same——the same............ 1,451 90
8 the same——the same.......... 947 25
8 Nochemovitz, Joseph—Louis Weinstein....... 273 94
9 Nelson, Samuel—People State N Y.. 10,027 18
11 Noreck, Herman—E H Schwartz..... 76 50
5 Otto, Anna E—C W Hand........... 242 98
5 O'Shaughnessy, James F—Tompkins' Paper Stock Co.................. 5,056 00
11*Ording, Henry—J A Waddell......... 544 05
11 Oberndorfer, Nathaniel — Sigmund Kline...................... 305 19
5 Purdy, James—Health Dep't.... ..... 209 87
5 Phillips, Walter E—R H Williams. .. 1,057 54
5 the same——Charles Parrish 589 56
5 Prawdzicki, Paul—William Hotoph... 88 49
7 Putnam, Ernest R—J A Dahn....costs 22 62
7 Pache, Eliza—George Taylor.......... 167 50
7 Powers, Denis—John Isaacs.......... 106 08
8 Phillips, Edward Y—J W Lawrence.. 202 24
8 *Pearsall, William H, Pearsall, Frank } D J Murphy... 100 65
8 Provost, Frederick—Union Trust Co, trustee........ 272 71
8*Perelson, Lazarus—Louis Weinstein.. 273 94
9 Pape, August H—Anthony Fischer... 124 38
9 Purdy, August Belmont—F P Osborn 331 67
9 Phelan, Peter F—J L Mott Iron Works........ 99 01
10 Pieper, Louis F—G W Smith.... .... 511 40
10 Pincus, Bernard—Alexander Klingenberg.......... 95 90
10 Pearce, Harry T—E S Hand. 764 78
5 Ritchey, James C—G R Brown....... 89 91
5 Reitman, Seralin—State Bank....... 10 00
5 Romaine, George W—Mount Morris Bank 188 46
7 Robertson, Thomas—Bartley O'Brien 472 64
7 Raisige, Leonard J—George Schmitt. 814 55
7 Rosenfeld, William—A J Sellsberg.. 226 86
7†Roe Richard — Municipal Electric Light Co........ 130 75
8 Rose, Reuben—Annie F Darragh 116 36
8 the same——the same.......... 3,464 40
8 the same——the same............ 84 49
9 Renner, Michael C—D C Frazee...... 99 98
9 Rauch, Henry—J H Duery........... 123 65
9 Rust, Oscar—American Tube and Iron Co........ 480 80
10 Rigsby, Robert—John Foulds........ 157 72
11 Robertson, Thomas—W W Harny... 700 00
11 Reynolds, William M, Reynolds, Jessie } James Clark. 1,255 22
11 Ruttenberg, Harris—Charles Lewis.. 225 48
11 Raynor, Howard S—J H Van Buren. 29 85
11†Roedel, Richard H—Julius Engel.... 108 50
5 Steebler, Heinrich—Health Dept..... 209 57
5 Sametz, Adolph—C T Pulsifer....... 108 29
5 Scffer, Andrew—August Streitwolf.. 156 65
7 Stark, Isidor, Stark, Edward J, *Stark, Gustav } Julius Cohn 89 71
7 *Strauss, Julius, *Strauss, Adolph, Strauss, Ernest } A B Cruikshank.... 131 30
7 Schneider, Charles—Municipal Electric Light Co........ 130 75

7 Soule, Luman A, Soule, Bertha A } J S McWilliam. ....(D) 833 67
7 Streiffer, Jacob—John Walsh........ 196 25
7 Sloane, Douglas—Mfrs Finance and Trust Co........ 15,554 39
7 Schachne, Isaac—Bernhard Kupfer.. 368 03
7 Schiff, John—G W Bramhall........ 314 46
7 Shepard, Charles D—M Roosevelt.... 281 61
7 Schwerd, Louise—J W McGuckin.... 165 08
8 Stearns, Minnie A—R T Wilson...... 97 50
8 Sturges, Daniel L—Toney Danzlo.... 89 20
8 Schmitt, Alois—Henry Spies........ 67 50
8 Schroeder, John W—A H Rennie.... 166 00
8 Schipper, John F—Joel Gutman...... 106 94
8 Sweetser, Edward R—Charles Brown 255 66
8 Savin, Francis W—Caroline B Powers, admrx........ 7,875 35
9†Sause, Robert E—R H Neamann..... 110 49
9 Shaw, Charles P—Lizzie R G Shaw.. 4,000 00
9 the same——the same........costs 1,115 80
10 Sneckner, William H—R H Bunney.. 1,049 37
10 Scherer, Paul—Urbana Wire Co.... 825 90
10 Seaman, Catharine B—R A Olmstead 630 00
10 Snyder, Francis—J L M Allen........ 82 80
10†Solomon, Jacob—Harris Ratkowsky. 166 05
10†Singerman, Max——the same....... 28 93
10 Skerritt, William H—T G Patterson. 190 73
11 Saxe, Simon P—William Clarke...... 394 50
11 Schmidt, Jane—John Baebr......... 289 00
11 Schmidt, Gustave——the same 1,196 00
11 Stillman, Roger—S R Walker........ 100 61
11 Schneider, Charles—Henry Schneider. 3,735 40
11 Schmeckenbecher, George, Schmeckenbecher, John D } Alwin Eisert.... 1,330 57
11 Stanton, Charles S—Nat Commercial Bank of Albany........ 172 95
11 Sherwood, Charles K—George Peyser. 907 93
11*Schneider, Henry—Nat Barrow and Truck Co ....costs 163 39
11 Spiveck, Hyman—Fannie Rubin...... 136 90
7 Smith, Lester B—W G Wells......... 152 52
7 the same——the same........costs 17 70
7 Smith, Robert J—Michael O'Brien... 117 81
7 Smith, Thomas S—H L Luques....... 167 84
10 Smith, Elizabeth K—Burton Gliddon. 80 25
5 The Metropolitan Elevated Railway Co, The Manhattan Railway Co } Charles Lippe costs 113 68
5 The N Y Elevated R R Co, The Manhattan Railway Co } Thomas O'Reilly, admr costs 106 28
5 The Central American Reduction Co—R G Packard........ 430 60
7 The Lackawanna & South Western R R Co—W M Sawyer, Jr.......... 862 17
7 The Stereo Relief Decorative Co—G F Hicks........ 102 92
7 The Manhattan Railway Co, The Metropolitan Elevated Railway Co } B B Johnston..... 89 52
7 J H Bonnell & Co (Lim)—Second Nat Bank of Red Bank........ 1,008 13
7 Lathrop Co—W M Subr.......... 261 31
7 Andrus & Conklin Tobacco Co—J J Bowman........ 1,916 91
7 The Hamburg-Bremen Fire Ins Co, of Hamburg, Germany; The Howard Ins Co, of New York; The Nat Fire Ins Co, of New York; The U S Fire Ins Co, of New York; The Westchester Fire Ins Co, of New York; The Nassau Fire Ins Co, of Brooklyn; The Niagara Fire Ins Co; The N Y Fire Ins Co, of N Y; The Brooklyn Fire Ins Co, of Brooklyn } Jacob Rothschild 5.761 79
8 Andrus & Conklin Tobacco Co—M H Lehmaier........ 176 07
8 the same——Nat Folding Box and Paper Co........ 411 26
8 The Mayor, Aldermen, &c — H M Johnston........ 68 40
8 The McElwee Mfg Co—H W Dayton. 13,946 29
8 The Rapid Printing Co—Carsten Offerman........ 292 81
8 The Cobb Vulcanite Wire Co—Nat Conduit Mfg Co........ 6,090 02
8 the same——the same..... ..... 963 37
8 The Rapid Printing Co—Carsten Offerman........ 227 12
9 The Mayor, Aldermen, &c—T M Hart 500 00
9 American Automatic Spray Perfume Co—Ferdinand Mulbens........ 79 69
9 The Attleboro National Bank—Jacob Wendell........ 203 18
9 Excelsior Dynamite Co—R R Cornell 41 64
9 Knickerbocker Printing and Publishing Co —Campbell Printing Press and Mfg Co........ 127 69
9 The Manhattan Railway Co—W Y Mortimer, exr and trustee... .costs 126 01
9 The Joseph Edwards Dredging Co—Milo Howell ....costs 111 20
9 The Third Avenue R R Co—John O'Donnell, admr........ 1,900 00
10 The Second Avenue R R Co—James Barry ....costs 80 40
10 The International Amusement Co (Lim) —E F S Clegg........ 1,312 21
10 Phenix Ins Co—Frederick Keck..... 14,567 62
11 The McElwee Mfg Co — William Breen........ 516 07
11 the same——Frank Hydorn...... 328 75
11 The Stereo Relief Decorative Co—J F White........ 979 57

11 United Ice Lines—Nat Hudson River Bank........ 2,030 79
11 Peckham Motor Truck and Wheel Co —George Phillips........ 528 09
11 Stereo Relief Decorative Co—Milligan & Higgins' Glue Co........ 163 86
11 The Broadway & Seventh Av R R Co —James Carolin........ 1,788 11
11 The John Ashcroft Patent Grate Bar Furnace Door Mfg Co—D H Burrell........ 98 66
11 The Mayor, Aldermen, &c — Press Publishing Co........ 1,921 00
11 The Manhattan Electric Light Co (Lim)—Abraham Wineburgh...... 328 25
11 The Knickerbocker Brewing Co—H W Poor........(D) 95,594 04
8 Thomas, Charles D—R J Tripp....... 469 38
8 Trockett, Joseph—Henry Spies....... 67 50
8 Trischet, R Samuel, *Trischet, Albert W } W T Van Zandt. 216 25
9 Tompkins, Charles H—Western Nat Bank 1,025 30
10 Thompson, Albert—G R Brown...... 83 80
10 Taylor, Isaac, Jr—George Jeremiah, exr........ 493 86
10 Tilden, George H—Henrietta D Gedney, extrx........ 391 88
11 Thorp, Harry—Marvin Safe Co...... 49 14
11 Tinkham, Frank J—W S Livingston 179 15
7 Underhill, Charles A—Peoples' Bank of East Orange N J........ 123 19
9 Unger, Henry—Bertha Unger. 892 62
11 Underwood H Channing — Lemson Consolidated Store Service Co...... 136 86
5 Vajen, John H—August Koenig.... 740 86
8 Vanderhoof, Elisha W—Caroline B Powers, admrx........ 7,375 35
11 Valentine, Henry E—James Brady.. 5,819 79
5 Weiher, August C—C B Morris...... 29 99
5 Woods, Alexander — Mount Morris Bank........ 188 40
7 Warren, George W—T M Spelman... 70 45
8 Wolff, Victor S—C A Marolzki 259 50
8 Waitzfelder, Solomon L—C J Gallagher........ 309 99
8 Worrall, Thomas P—Nat Conduit Mfg Co........ 6,090 02
9 Weber, William F—W J Logan...... 368 39
9 Wicht, Christopher—J W Stout...... 1,177 68
9 Weinberg, Jacob—J F Crumbie...... 119 87
9 Weber, Emile W—F H Gerber...... 425 63
10 Walsh, William M—J M Canda...... 923 61
10 Wolff, Simon—Henry Klein......... 777 62
10 Williams, Cornelius—May Williams. ....costs 129 53
10 Walker, Herbert H—A C Haynes.... 409 10
10 Wendel, William—Howard Menn.... 110 56
11 Wobitjen, Henry—J A Waddell...... 544 05
11 Woolworth, James G B—J W Thompson........ 632 38
11 Weston, Albert B—H C Meyer.. ... 131 35
11 Winterroth, Joseph M—E J Winterroth........ 2,014 91
8 Yearance, Jesse—Emily Charles..... 313 51
10 Yung, Frederick—C V Fornes 1,781 55
10*Young, James K—J L M Allen... ... 82 80
10 Yale, Ida—G F Bassett.............. 223 82
10 Yale, John R—Gustav Pollock. 206 65
10 the same——D G Yuengling, Jr, Brewing Co........ 196 55
5 Zuber, Quirin—Kate B Zuber...costs 109 26
7 *Zahner, Christian, Zahner, Traugott } David Mayer..... 1,015 00
10†Ze Waltoff, David—Henry Klein.... 777 62

KINGS COUNTY.

Dec.
4 Angevine, William H — Budweiser Brewing Co........ $1,016 02
7 Attlesey, Robert H, Attlesey, Charles B } S S Hall....... 273 63
8 Alyea, William—J V Carr........... 230 42
10 Allen, Horace B—H Herrmann....... 228 00
3 Bendall, Robert A—W Martin....... 324 00
3 Barrmann, William—J F Heinbockel. 238 00
4 Bowman, James M—C Gillespie. 90 33
4 Bartunek, Frank — The Budweiser Brewing Co........ 615 39
4 Bartunek, Frank——the same........ 209 44
5 Boyen, Thomas—H P Kremer........ 380 70
7 Booth, William—M Levy............ 38 06
7 Baxter, William D—C A Wilson..... 129 99
8 Beutel, Philip—A Greenbaum........ 666 68
9 Brossard, Theodora—J H Meyer..... 110 34
10 Bini, Titto, Bessi, Pietro } C R Ruegger 79 15
10 Bini, Titto——the same............. 99 73
4 Cohen Jacob—C Gillespie........... 74 55
4 Case, Virgil R—J Beattie........... 48 80
7 Collins, Charles H—C D King........ 819 84
7 Case, Henry—The Adamant Mfg Co. 130 93
10 Cable, Alexander—C E Hoteling.... 27 34
10 Cunningham, Samuel—Twenty-sixth Ward Bank........ 396 87
10 Case, Virgil R—Twenty-sixth Ward Bank........ 560 70
4 Donner, Conrad N—H Herrmann..... 343 62
4 Donner, Conrad N—H Herrmann..... 350 07
5 Davidson, Robert—E Fitzgerald .. . 431 45
7 Droste, Adolph M—G Schuchman.... 137 10
7 Doolittle, Oscar H—C D King....... 434 22
8 Dunning, Zopher F—F N Bliss....... 140 85
9 Dunham, Robert E—E M Dunham.... 30 75
9 Durham, Fred F—A W Bohn.. ..... 144 90
8 Engelhardt, Charles W—E A Gillespie........ 52 79
9 Edwards, John—H L Redfield.. . 88 89
3 Fettel, Henry—J Stuehler........... 11 66
4 Ferguson, Charles A—J Vollkommer. 581 74
4†Fischer, John—J Eppig 188 69
7 Feigenbaum, Mary — Danenberg & Coles........ 255 23

7 Foley, Michael J—B Hausmann 106 17
7 Farren, John E—Edison Elec Ill Co.. 49 68
8 Feigenbaum, Mary—A Kammerer.... 29 50
10 Feeley, Michael T—J Baehr. 1,508 00
4 Geisler, Wilhelm H—R Shippen..... 106 59
5 Gaillard, Tacitus—J Cherry.......... 32 77
7 Gavin, Michael—H L Schelling 28 85
10 Glover, William H—W W Rope & Co 229 24
8 Hackett, Jeremiah—C Hart........... 289 36
4 Harvey, Michael—Empire State Brewing Co............................ 111 55
4 Hess, George / Hess, Henry } H Herrmann.......... 312 50
4 Howard, Henry T—H Hermann...... 350 07
5 Helmeyer, August P M—J Kramer... 186 50
5 Hoeg, Henry G—H P Kremer........ 380 70
5 Heid, George—H L Rokobl........... 118 00
7 Heaney, Frank—W Farrell........... 88 79
8 Hickey, Morris F—W M Leslie....... 38 46
10 Hopkins, Jr, Joseph / Hearsey, Edward L } Twenty-sixth Ward Bank.... 2,100 23
10 Hopkins, Jr, Joseph—Twenty-sixth Ward Bank.......................... 560 70
10 the same——the same............ 396 87
3 Joyce, Edward—Bulmer Lumber Co (Lim)................................ 73 84
8 Judson, Edward—J Herrmann....... 55 05
4 Johnson, Leonard L—C Dennis. 1,238 60
4 Jeffrey, William F—D Durning...... 28 60
4†Jablowski, William—J Eppig........ 104 25
4 Johanson, Johan A—H Herrmann.... 123 97
10 Jones, Mary E—J Gillies............ 485 61
4 Klein, Emil—Budweiser Brewing Co. 1,478 00
4 the same——the same........ ..... 96 22
4 the same——the same 329 43
5 Kapp, Conrad—C W Polhemus....... 106 02
7 Kean, Edward J—L G Baldwin...... 137 42
8 Kirchner, Charles—J V Carr........ 230 42
10 Kohn, Julius A—M Henderson....... 111 02
3 Lemmermann, Henry—J Roth....... 380 28
4 Lewis, Leroy F—W B Peirson......... 832 60
5 Lippincott, Jesse H—L Luckenbach.. 6,090 81
7†Light, Mary—J G Gaanger........... 111 94
9 Levy, Julius / Levy, Augustus H / Levy, Moses S } M Arnold....... 2,197 10
9 the same——Pacific Bank......... 1,745 01
10 Lincoln, Clarence—W F Clayton..(D) 3,042 49
8 Mahnken, George—J Rath........ ... 380 28
4 Morris, Joseph—C Gillespie 52 25
4 Meyer, William—W Davison......... 70 86
5 Murray, John J—E Fitzgerald. 746 91
5 Monohan, John B—E Fitzgerald..... 544 90
7 Mulqueen, Thomas F—S Haubentock. 124 28
7 Myers, William—J G Gerber..... ..... 155 17
7 Morrison, Kate—J G Granger........ 28 27
7 Muller, Louis / Muller, Mary B } People's Bank, East Orange, N J..... 128 19
8 Mulqueen, Thomas F—J B Ryan..... 194 19
8 the same——Mankey Fur Co..... 92 66
8 the same——A Abrams.......... 139 14
9 Mason, Amasa—Equitable Life Assur Soc of the U S...................... 966 46
9 Morrell, Lester W—J A Hamblin ... 991 08
10 McNamara, Thomas—B W Otis...... 104 68
10 McDonald, Anne—Mary A Cassidy... 523 00
10 Munz, Jacob—T Kiendl............. 87 85
4 Norris, Allison V B—J Fox.......... 139 00
8 Navatofsky, Wolf—F W Hahn....... 82 60
7 Oeding, Henry—H C Oeding......... 1,007 82
4 Pierson, Ely F—Louisa M Pierson ... 273 28
4 Parker, Asa W / Parker, Sophie G / Parker, Ralph G / Parker, Josiah S } E H Coffin... 149 94
4 Parr, Robert A—Mary E Parr....... 62 72
4 Peck, Edward M / Peck, Nellie C } J M Mossom..... 1,873 21
5 Pfaeffle, Friedrich—Budweiser Brewing Co 1,279 74
9 Pierce, William—J Duval........... 44 32
8 Robinson, John—First Nat Bank of Rochester... .... 5,134 70
8 the same——The Youghiogheny Bank, of Connellsville, Pa.......... 4,644 12
4 Reese, Louis—S C Boehm............ 118 24
5 Robinson, John—L Luckenbach...... 6,090 81
7 Ryan, Joseph—C H Smith. 133 56
9 Rhodes, Herbert G—W P Nollman... 242 97
9 Rodergerdts, John P—J Haas........ 628 92
(Reich, Lorenz—A Weston............ 123 06
8 Schutt, John H—E H June........ .. 183 46
4 Stokes, William H—J F Nelson....... 122 49
4 Staebler, John / Staebler, Mary } H Vollweiler........ 87 25
Standt, Peter — Budweiser Brewing Co...................................... 438 59
Stackleton, James H—H Herrmann... 350 07
Schneider, Charles—M Schneider....34,679 54
Scrimgeour, John—C Wolfson...... 36 33
Schieb, Philip—A Greenebaum....... 666 68
Schneider, Joseph—F W Betz.... ... 638 62
Stearns, Minnie A—R T Wilson...... 97 50
Slopenhagen, Nathaniel J—G W Bergen................................... 1,186 35
The Brooklyn City R R Co—E Enk, exr, &c............................ 4,908 30
Titus, William—Kate Messemer...... 83 25
The Lawrence Beach Co—E R Wheelock.................................. 4,158 20
8 Taylor, James—C B Fowler.......... 138 11
8 Thompson, James—The American Stoneware Co..................... 279 20
9 Taylor, George P—W P Nollman..... 242 97
10 The trustees of the N Y and Brooklyn Bridge—R Carter..............(D)51,063 00
10 the same——H McAleenan....(D) 215 00
7 Underhill, Charles A—People's Bank of East Orange, N J................. 128 19
8 Van Courtlandt, Henry W—W H Atwater................................. 312 23
4 Werner, Jacob—John Eichler Brewing Co................................ 695 74
4 Winters, John H—S Colgate.......... 24 77
4 Wondrash, Joseph—Budweiser Brewing Co (Lim).......................1,024 04
4 the same——the same 351 78
7 Wust, William—J G Gerber.......... 512 58
8 Weiskopf, William—J Cohen...... .. 631 49
8 Wiebauer, George and Lina—Rose Whitehurst & Co...................... 361 85
9 Woltjen, Henry—J F Heissenbuttel.. 135 88

SATISFIED JUDGMENTS.

NEW YORK.

December 5 to 11—Inclusive.

Bingham, Mary—Hester Bates. (1889)....... $389 97
Same——same. (1891) 81 82
Bank of Metropolis—John Klinker. (1886).... 283 19
Same——same. (1887).... .... 92 42
Same ——sam . (1887)................ 76 00
Bauoing, William C / Bissell, Edward H } George Beach. (1891)... 626 55
Broadway & Seventh Av R R Co—G W Morison. (1889)..............................5,406 09
Same——same. (1890) 104 25
Same——same. (1891) 1,130 08
*Byrnes, "James"—People State N Y. (1890). 300 00
*Baldwin, Austin, Austin P and Radcliffe—C A Seddon. (1883)..................... 878 47
§Baldwin, Radcliffe—G H Randall. (1882).... 306 14
Bolender, Philip—Fire Dep't. (1887).......... 109 50
Same——same. (1886)..................... 59 50
Bancroft, George and Aaron—J A Yates. ('91) 1,451 73
Corwin, Seth M—F R Townsend. (1885) 2,856 96
Same——J R Reese. (1886)............... 505 18
Same——A E Person. (1886)............... 8,885 85
Curtis, Frank D—Equitable Life Assur Soc. (1890)................................... 105 59
Corwin, Seth M—E T Tefft. (1886).... .... 2,294 29
*Civille, Frank A—Mayor, &c. (1887)....... 100 00
*Cunningham, Patrick—People State N Y. (1890).. 300 00
Duffie, James—J S Crane. (1890)............ 182 81
Davidson, William—Cook & Bernheimer Co. (1891).. 628 16
Dunn, Margaret—Charles Gerlich. (1891)...... 401 57
Davidowitz, William—C F Claflin. (1891) 103 99
Dewing Publishing Co, J—T J Cagney Binding Co. (1891)............................. 276 30
†Eisenberg, William—Sims Lumber Co. (1891).1,182 89
Friend, Bernhardt—Charles Ruff. (1891)..... 118 06
Falk, Louis—American Exchange Nat Bank. (1891).................................. 667 47
Same——T W Robinson. (1890) 1,841 29
Finan, James—Catharine A Hallahan. (1891). 282 10
Gorman, John J—Hay & Todel Mfg Co. (1891) 34 62
Hutchinson, William J—J R Duff. (1890)...... 77 75
Same——same. (1890)........ .... 70 88
Same——same. (1888) 9 78
Hillenbrand, Francis J—William Schwalenberg. (1891) 329 78
Hills Plantation Coffee Co—John Wakeman. (1891)....................................... 297 27
*Hyams, Josel E—Harris Friedman. (1891)... 155 65
Judge, Mary F—Nicholas Bunn. (1889)....... 253 75
Jameson, Leon—American Exchange Nat Bank. (1891) 667 47
Johnston, Wm H, Benj B and Lucretia—Hester Bates. (1891)................................ 81 32
Same——same. (1889)..... .... 339 97
Katz, Sigmund—Frederick Sonnenburg. (1891) 168 50
Kennedy, George H—J R Duff. (1890) 77 75
Same——same. (1890) 70 88
Same——same. (1888)........................ 9 78
Kelly, Thomas P—William Fiss. (1891)....... 699 04
Same——Charles Gerlich. (1891) 461 50
Kuschewsky, Raphael—Fire Dept. (1889).... 50 00
*Levy, Sarah—Harris Finkelstein. (1888) 331 67
Lange, Charles—Henry Robert. (1891)........ 247 00
Same——same. (1891).... .... 122 99
Mills, T Morton—A E Person. (1886)......... 8,875 84
Mills, T Morton P—J R Reese. (1886).......... 505 18
Same——F R Townsend. (1885) 2,856 96
Madden, Stephen K—Nathan Froman. (1891) 117 87
Morris, Adolph M and Nathan Marks—Leopold Hass. (1889)....................................... 163 48
McDermott, Patrick J—James Carstairs. (1891) 823 66
Mills, Morton P—E T Tefft. (1886).... ....2,294 20
Metropolitan Elevated Railway Co—Margaret V Birch. (1891)......................... ....1,495 87
Same and Manhattan Railway Co } Peter Kearney. ('91). 89 43
Murphy, John—T K Foster. (1891)............ 759 08
Morris, Adolph M / Marks, Nathan } Samuel Lewis. (1890)..... 4,498 47
Same——A L Katz. (1888)..........................1,018 78
N Y & Harlem R R Co—Henry Jordan. ('89) 11,949 10
Same——same. (1890) 95 84
N Y Elevated R R Co—C S Hine. (1891)...... 110 50
Same——same. (1890)............................3,591 79
Same——same. (1891).......................... 79 90
Pirsson, Janette—M S Wetmore. (1890) 102 62
Same——same. (1888)... ....1,156 01
Same——same. (1888.. .... 78 75
Preble, John Q and Walter E—Ninth Nat Bank. (1890)..................................85,535 04
Same——U S Trust Co. (1890)... ....5,402 27
Same——same. (1890).............................15,110 59
Preble, John Q and Walter E—Leather Mfrs Bank. (1890).......................................1,212 19
Same——same. (1890).... ....7,847 64
Same——same. (1890)...............................2,611 17
Same——same. (1890)................... ....5,182 80
Same——same. (1890)...................................4,679 44
Same——Nat Bank of Newburgh. (1890)....5,106 43
Polecek, Ludwig—Frederick Sonnenburg. ('91) 168 50
Post, George W and Virginia W—F M Jencks. (1891) 853 72
Payne, Olive C and Charles E—Robert Merchant, recvr. (1885)....................... 64 78
Purdy, August Belmont—F P Osborn. (1891).. 391 67
*Ryan, Patrick—People of State N Y. (1889). 100 00
Reischreiber, Samuel—J H Bley. (1888)...... 76 50
Reinhardt, Hans—American Exch Nat Bank. (1891).. 667 47
Same——T W Robinson. (1890)..............1,841 29
Robbins, Edwin N—Equitable Life Assur Soc. (1890) 105 59
Reinhardt, Henry—Rudolph Wolff. (1891). . 181 70
Risher, John C—J T Carr. (1888).............25,399 75
Reilly, Lizzie—Domestic Spring Bed Co. ('88) 72 41
Richards, Lena—John Doscher. (1891) 210 87
Rothschild, Jacob—Agnes Sullivan. (1891)....2,711 51
Shapiro, Samuel—Joseph Fox. (1884).......... 191 30
Same——Max Silberstein. (1889).......... 430 56
Shanks, James—Cook & Bernheimer Co. ('91) 628 16
Smith, Ormond G, George C and Cora A—George Munro. (1890)..........................1,198 73
Same——same. (1891)..... .... 76 56
Same——same. (1891).......................... 116 33
Sawyer, Lyman and Sarah J—Frank James. (1891).. 107 91
*Seymour, George B—C A Seddon. (1883).... 831 47
Schmidt, Simon—Yetta Schulman. (1885).... 267 50
Simon, Joseph—J H Bley. (1888).............. 76 50
Shearman, George—Nathan Froman. (1891).. 117 87
Siegel, Joseph—Charles Ruff. (1891)........... 118 06
Taylor, Lavinia—T W Harris, assignee. (1888).1,111 71
*Tynor, Joseph—People State N Y. (1889).... 100 00
Thorne, John J—Frederick Fauerbach. (1890) 1,001 00
U S Illuminating Co—Anton Feser. (1891).... 69 75
†Ungrich, Louis and Louis Kossuth—Daniel Mahony. (1891)................................ 809 39
†Same——same. (1891).......................... 80 35
Walsh, Augustine—C F Paul. (1891) 864 87
Wolf, William—A L Katz. (1881).................1,018 73
Same——Samuel Lewis. (1889)................. 4,498 47
Wintermeyer, Bernard—C A Stock. (1891)... 264 74
Wilson, Andrew—W A Parshall. (1891)...... 407 75
Same——same. (1891)........................ 71 75
Wallach, Julius and Joseph G—Rosa Kind. (1891) 95 75
†Same——same. (1891)......................... 71 83
Wolf, George——Sims Lumber Co. (1891).....1,484 89
Wolf, William—Leopold Hass. (1889).......... 168 48
Wilson, Andrew—W A Parshall. (1891)....... 104 40
Webster, John H—Herman Scheideberg. (1889)... 100 00

*Vacated by order of Court. †Suspended on Appeal ‡Released. §Reversal. ||Satisfied by Execution.

KINGS COUNTY.

December 4 to 10—Inclusive:

Browne, Harvey H—C B Farley, Sheriff. (1887) $259 85
Cordes, Henry H—Annie Steljes. (1890)...... 109 60
Davidson, William—Cook & Bernheimer Co. (1891).. 628 16
Davidovitz, William—Aaron Claflin & Co. (1891) 103 99
Graham, Martin—J D Leary. (1891) 120 19
Grage, Henry—F E Ryerson, Jr. (1891)...... 200 05
Harland, Jane C—A Hegeman. (1890). 227 69
Halstead, Stephen C—E S Rosenblath. (1891) 141 69
Puels, Joseph P—C Bott. (1891) 142 54
Rankin, Lydia M—C McBride. (1891).......... 383 00
Shanks, James—Cook & Bernheimer Co. (1891). 628 16
Treacy, Richard—J Onser. (1891) 335 85
The Brooklyn City R R Co—J Hourney. (1891). 128 99
Same——same. (1889)... .... 121 89
Same——same. (1889).............................2,437 57
Wolf, William—E A Gillespie. (1886)........ 84 25
Walsh, William and Margaret J—B J Dennis. (1891) 92 06

MECHANICS' LIENS.

NEW YORK CITY.

Dec.

5 One Hundred and Fifth st, n s, 200 e 5th av, 100x100.9. Friendship Mfg. Co. agt William M. Thornton, owner, and McElwee Mfg. Co., contractor.......................... $300 00
5 Same property. H. W. Foote agt same.... 400 00
5 Ninety-fourth st, n s, 100 w Columbus av, 50x100.8........................ } Ninety-fifth st, s s, 100 w Columbus av, 50x100.8........................ } Friendship Mfg. Co. agt Francis J. Hillenbrand, owner, and McElwee Mfg. Co., contractor.... .... 300 00
5 Same property. H. W. Foote agt same.... 316 97
5 Fifty-second st, Nos. 513-517, n s, 175 w 10th av, 75x100. Same agt Joseph B. Husted, owner, and McElwee Mfg. Co., contractor 500 00
5 Same property. Friendship Mfg. Co. agt same 1,000 00
5 Leroy st, n s, 200 w Bedford st, 60x100. Van Wagner & Linn agt Stevens, McElroy & Co., owners and contractors.............. 119 00
5 Third Av. R. R. Co.'s road-bed from Ann st to 130th st, bridges, &c. C. A. Brown and John Fleming agt Third Av. R. R. Co., owner, and William Wharton, Jr., & Co., contractors...12,373 70
5 Same property. Geo. B. Robbins & Co. agt same..2,587 81
7 Waverley pl, No. 12, s s, 95 w Mercer st, 25x82. T. J. Dunn agt H. & S. Corn, owner, and K. N. Smith & Co., contractors..... .. 700 00
7 One Hundred and Twenty-fifth st, Nos. 209 and 211, n s, 105 e 3d av, 50x99.11. Same agt Justin Cooke, owner, and K. N. Smith & Co., contractors............................. 580 00
7 One Hundred and Thirty-seventh st, n s, 90 e Rider av, 50x75. Same agt J. L. Mott Iron Works, owner, and K. N. Smith & Co., contractors 430 00
7 Ponus st, s s, 450 w Boston av, 25x100. William Clarke agt James E. Algeo, owner, and same and F. Leser, contractors...... 204 50
7 One Hundred and Seventy-ninth st, n s, 100 e Webster av, 25x100. Same agt Thomas Oakes, owner, and Frederick Cyriax, contractor... 85 00
7 Ninety-third st, Nos. 11-17, n s, 280 e 5th av, 76.8x55. W. H. Horton agt Philip Braender, owner, and same and Fritz Veckermann, contractors 1,000 00
7 Forty-third st, No. 4, s s, 195 w 5th av, 125x125.5. V. H. Schneider agt David H. King, Jr., owner, and Charles E. McBride, contractor...................................... 886 89
7 Ninety-eighth st, n s, 265.6 e Amsterdam av, 159.6x—. James McLaughlin agt John W. Hutton, owner, and Wheeler & Hogan, contractors.. 875 00
7 Spring st, Nos. 131-137, n s, 48.4 w Greene st, 98.4x—. John Kehoe agt John Goerlitz, owner, and same and Philip Goerlitz, contractors...4,000 00
8 Fifty-second st, Nos. 513-517, n s, 175 w 10th av, 75x100. L. A. Schaffer agt Elsworth L. Striker, owner, and Joseph B. Husted, contractor.. 750 00
8 Forty-fourth st, Nos. 437 and 439, n s, 300 e 10th av, 40x100.4. Candee & Smith agt William G. Jordan, owner, and James J. Delehunty, contractor........................ 670 86
8 Leroy st, Nos. 55 and 57, n s, 45x70. Adolf Jacoby agt John W. Stevens and —— McElroy, owner, and John W. Stevens, contractor.. 101 40
8 Fifty-third st, s s, 275 e 11th av, 125x100. J. W. Binney agt David Davis, owner and contractor... 66 13
9 One Hundred and Seventy-sixth st, n s, 485 w Fleetwood av, 25x125. J. A. & E. T. Woolf agt Victor L. Veyrac, owner, and Luman A. Soule, contractor 207 80

9 Same property. Ruland & Stone agt same. 100 00

9 Wadsworth av, n w cor 179th st, 25x100. Hollister Mfg. Co. agt F. G. Kee, owner, and E. Palmer and Ward & Gray, contractors.......... 209 88

9 Fifty-second st, Nos. 513-517, n s, 250 w 10th av, 75x100. Colwell Lead Co. agt Joseph B. Husted, owner, and Elsworth L. Striker, contractor.......... 994 91

9 Washington st, Nos. 550 and 552, n w cor King st, 40x96. Andrew McGrath agt Germail Christie, owner, and James Johnson, contractor.......... 628 24

9 Fifty-third st, s s, 275 e 11th av, 125x100. W. H. Brandt agt Alice Davies, owner, and David S. Davies, contractors.......... 1,000 00

9 Waverley pl, No. 12, s s, 25 w Mercer st, 25x 82.6. E. H. Ogden & Co. agt Samuel and Henry Corn, owners, and K. N. Smith & Co., contractor.......... 43 50

9 Thirteenth st, No. 432 E., 25x100. John Glasbrenner agt —— Gray, owner, and Mrs. Gray, contractor.......... 15 75

9 Eighth av, e s, 60 n Bank st, 50x80. P. J. Sheehan agt Thomas J. Walsh and Louis N. Phelps, owners and contractors.......... 387 00

9 Eighty-fourth st, No. 247, n s, 101.8 w 2d av, 20x102. Gottfried Meyer agt Charles Rosenberg, owner, and Philip J. McGuire, contractor.......... 450 00

9 Sixty-sixth st, s s, 400 w 8th av, 100x100. J. A. Kennedy agt Edward Lapierre, debtor, and Henry Raabe & Sons, contractors.... 86 75

9 Same property. John Dawson agt same... 38 50

10 Bradhurst av, s e cor 143d st, 100x75. W. S. Burton agt Fernando Yost, owner, and Charles Nylin, contractor.......... 96 72

10 Boscobel av, e s, 120 s Highbridge st, 86x57. James W. Colwell's Sons agt William J. Gessner, owner and contractor.......... 175 94

10 Henry st, Nos. 211 and 213, n s, 24 e Clinton st, 45x85. Scully & Moran agt Tobias Krakower, owner, and Walter Powers & Son, contractors.......... 198 30

10 Jones st, No. 23, n s, 160 e Bleecker st. Max Muller agt Theodore Van Eupen, owner and contractor.......... 150 00

10 Creston av, w s, 245 s Kirk pl, 25x110. William Moore agt Peter Ryan, owner, and Charles W. Vreeland, contractor.......... 75 00

10 Eighty-fourth st, No. 247, n s, 125 w 2d av, 20x100. Ann Reilly agt Charles Rosenberg, owner, and Philip J. McGuire, contractor.......... 520 00

10 One Hundred and Fifteenth st, Nos. 252-264, s s, 275 e 8th av, 175x100.11. Edison General Electric Co. agt Conrad Muller, Jr., and Anna Hauff, owners and contractors 900 00

10 Thirteenth av, n e cor 11th st, 96.5x67.10x 98.8x90.4. C. L. Bucki & Co. agt Emery M. Van Tassell, owner, Peter Keller, contractor, and William S. Anderson & Co., sub-contractor.......... 3,400 86

10 Spring st, Nos. 131-137, n s, 48.2 w Greene st, 98.2x—. Franklin Baylies agt John and Philip Goerlitz, owner, and John Goerlitz, contractor.......... 700 00

11 Thirty-seventh st, No. 126 E. John Bremner agt Martin & Bros., debtors and owners.. 178 91

11 Thirty-sixth st, No. 129 E. Same agt same. 7 35

11 Ogden av, e s, 220 n Devoe st, 18.6x42.8. Miller & Robinson agt John J. Byrnes, owner and contractor.......... 126 80

11 Seventy-second st, n w cor Lexington av, 97x100. Jacob Jamer agt Sarah Levenson, owner and contractor.......... 1,040 00

11 First av, s w cor 74th st, 24x84.6. Christoph Doerfler agt Sarah Harris, owner and contractor.......... 521 95

11 Ninety-eighth st, n s, 265.5 e Amsterdam av, 159.6x100. Ackert & Schroeder agt John W. Hutton, Julius Lipman, Moses Kind and —— Cohen, owners, and John W. Hutton, contractor.......... 150 00

11 West End av, n w cor 83d st, 98x100. Josepha Braun agt Gerald L. Schuyler, owner and contractor.......... 500 00

11 Spring st, Nos. 131-137, n s, 48.2 w Greene st, 98.2x—. C. L. Bucki & Co. agt John Goerlitz, owner and contractor.......... 3,277 80

11 One Hundred and First st, Nos. 75 and 77, n s, 218 w Manhattan av, 50x100. Frederic Damiani agt —— owner, and William M. Walsh, contractor.......... 216 00

KINGS COUNTY.

Dec.

4 Twenty-first av, w s, 200 s 86th st, 100x96.8, New Utrecht. Frank Schneider agt J. B. Brush, owner, and Robert Morrison, contractor.......... $39 00

4 Fifty-sixth st, n s, 130 w 14th av, 50x100, New Utrecht. Eliza Craigen agt Thomas Tangerman, owner, and Emel Keller, contractor.......... 116 92

4 Bergen st, No. 6, n s.......... }
Bergen st, Nos. 11, 12 and 13, n s.......... }
Lars Petterson agt J. D. Mason, owner and contractor.......... 171 00

4 Stewart av, n w cor Ovington av, 170.2x113 x170.3x108, New Utrecht. Watson & Pittinger agt John J. Page, owner, and Edwin Dennington, contractor.......... 858 56

4 Logan st, e s, 100 s Jamaica av, 50x100. Charles Tirelli agt Henry S. Smith, owner and contractor.......... 158 00

4 Hancock st, n s, 175 e Reid av, 50x100. Graf & Seitz agt Mrs. M. Stilson, owner, and S. Stilson, contractor.......... 200 00

4 Sixtieth st, n s, 250 w 18th av, 60x100, New Utrecht. John A. Pfalzgraf agt Mr. Helm, owner, and Mr. Hargart, contractor.......... 71 50

5 Marcy av, n e cor Hooper st, 100x105. Thomas Rogers agt The Church of the Transfiguration, owner and contractor... 190 75

5 Marcy av, n w cor Walton st, 38x75. Goodwin & Polley agt North American Iron Works, owner, and K. N. Smith & Co., contractors.......... 58 00

5 Driggs st, s s, 25 w Kingsland av, 25x100. Bieber & Stewart agt P. Smith, owner, and George W. Cobb, contractor.......... 33 00

5 Atlantic av, s s, extends from Ashford st to Cleveland st, —x291x18x303. Continental Iron Works agt The Union Gas Light Co., owner, and The International Gas Co., contractor.......... 79,987 25

7 Decatur st, n s, 100 e Howard av, 178.4x100. George Gratz agt J. Mason Kirby, owner and contractor.......... 250 00

7 Watkins st, w s, 151.6 s Eastern Parkway, 25x100. Sapric & Ducart agt Ada and Louis Parmer, owners and contractors... 210 00

7 Navy st, e s, 61 n Myrtle av, 50x100. Thomas Sheffield agt Henrietta Fisk and her agent Wm. H. H. Glover, owners and contractors.......... 275 00

7 Same property. Same agt same owners and contractors.......... 56 75

7 Rockaway av, Nos. 808 and 810, w s, 168.8 n Prospect pl, 38.6x100. William Cozier agt Mrs. E. L. Rushmore, owner and contractor.......... 293 00

7 Bergen st, s s, 75 w Hopkinson av, 50x130. Hall Sash and Door Co. agt Rose Rosenfeld and Leo Moretzki, owners and contractors.......... 167 71

7 Same property. Rope & Co. agt Rose and Jonas Rosenfeld and Leo Moretzki, owners and contractors.......... 334 92

8 Ridgewood av, s s, 20 w Linwood st, 40x100. Girochrer & McCarty agt Philip M. Knight and Frederick Sands, owners, and Isaac Newton, contractor.......... 106 00

8 Richardson st, n e cor Union av, 50x50... }
Richardson st, n s, 25 e Union av, 25x50... }
John Walsh agt Joe Pepponire, owner, and Dominico Malco & Son, contractors.. 518 15

8 Bergen st, s s, 75 w Hopkinson av, 50x130. Dugan Mfg. Co. agt Rose and Jonas Rosenfeld and Leo Moretzki, owners and contractors.......... 90 00

9 Bushwick av, w s, 83 s Kossuth pl, 20x84. Isidor Mock agt Ludwig Levy, owner, and Martin and George Kuhn, contractors 79 12

9 Livonia av, s e cor Osborn st, 20x100. Morris Lubinsky agt —— Abramowitz, owner, and Sarah Pezerowsky, contractor.......... 10 00

10 Macon st, s s, 200 w Patchen av, 90x100. Henry M. Edwards agt Jane Miller, owner, and Abel Miller, contractor.......... 162 00

10 McDonough st, Nos. 240-248, s s, 100x100. Adolph Mattson agt M. Rofrano, owner, and Nilson & Lagerson, contractors.......... 18 60

SATISFIED MECHANICS' LIENS

NEW YORK CITY.

Dec.

7 West End av, Nos. 441-459. Thomas Osborne agt William E. D. Stokes, John J. Brewster, Francis M. Jencks and Squier & Whipple. (Lien filed Aug. 7, 1891) ... $8,000 00

7 Eighty-sixth st, s s, 150 e Riverside Drive, 100x100.11. Same agt Francis M. Jencks and Squier & Whipple. (Aug. 18, 1891)... 5,000 00

7 Canal st, No. 503, n e cor Renwick st. Francis Muldoon agt Charles L. Fleming and John Lyons. (Sept. 16, 1891).......... 200 00

7‡Seventh av, n w cor 27th st, 88.8x irreg. x 98.9x148.9. Friendship Mfg Co. agt William F. Rohrig and McElwee Mfg Co. (Dec. 4, 1891).......... 1,500 00

7‡Same property. H. W. Foote agt same. (Dec. 4, 1891).......... 1,000 00

7 Eleventh st, Nos. 310 and 312 E., 50x100. Ferdinand Ehrhart agt Moses, Sophie, Joseph, Sarah, Carrie, Minnie, Julia and Hannah Schuester Weil. (July 9, 1890)... 522 83

7*One Hundred and Ninth st, No. 311 E. Phillippo Quaglino and two others agt Fruk Rojiri, —— Smith and Guisepp Cobuccio. (Sept. 28, 1891.) (3 liens).......... 75 00

8 One Hundred and Fourteenth st, s s, 209 w 5th av, 17.8x100.11. A. S. Nichols agt Margaret E. Conlon. (Nov. 14, 1891.) (Released).......... —

9 Amsterdam av, s w cor 99th st, 40x100. Bowes & Son agt L. Rogers., (Aug. 25, 1891).......... 50 00

9 Eighth av, s w cor 103d st, 100x95. Adam Gernert agt Charles B. Bliss. (Mar. 14, 1891).......... 689 00

9 Same property. Richard Flanagan & Bro. agt same and Joseph O'Connor and James Stevenson. (Aug. 8, 1891).......... 1,750 00

9 East End av, n w cor 87th st. Passaic Rolling Mill Co. agt Feehan & Hammer and Martin R. Beam. (Dec. 7, 1891).......... 656 68

9 Eighty-third st, n s, 150 w 10th av, 50x—. Maria W. Dittmar agt James Kearney, James Kelly and James Dunn. (Mar. 23, 1891).......... 129 18

9 Same property. James Dunn agt Thomas P. Kelly. (Dec. 22, 1890).......... 1,500 00

9 Same property. Same agt same. (April 16, 1891).......... 550 00

9 Ninety-fourth st, Nos. 103 and 105 W., 50x —. John Morgenthaler agt F. J. Hillenbrand. (June 25, 1891).......... 896 00

9 Same property. J. O. Clement agt same. (July 22, 1891).......... 250 00

9 Ninety-fifth st, Nos. 102 and 104 W., 50x100. Same agt same. (July 22, 1891).......... 250 00

9*Ninety-fourth st, Nos. 103 and 105 W., 50x—. Frank Leimeister agt Francis J. Hillenbrand. (Oct. 28, 1891).......... 168 00

9*Ninety-fifth st, Nos. 104 and 106 W., 50x—. Same agt same. (Oct. 28, 1891).......... 160 00

10 One Hundred and Eighteenth st, s s, 60 e Madison av, 100x100. J. A. Altieri agt Samuel Harris and Bernhard Ginsberg. (Dec. 2, 1891).......... 156 12

10 Norfolk st, e s, 174.4 s Houston st, 22.1x100. Solomon Fischer and Lippman Deutsch agt Congregation Ohab Zedeck and Isaac Unger. (Aug. 12, 1891).......... 171 69

10 Broome st, No. 301. Ferdinand Volkmar agt Benjamin Barnett and Christian Hubener. (April 24, 1891).......... 391 50

10 Same property. Christian Hubener agt Benjamin Barnett. (April 24, 1891)..... 3,000 00

10 Norfolk st, No. 178, 25x100. J. M. Leonhardt agt Patrick Gallagher and First Hungarian Opal Zedeck Verein, Leopold Hermann, pres. (Aug. 28, 1891).......... 1,358 00

11‡Waverley pl, No. 12. K. N. Smith & Co. agt Samuel and Henry Corn. (Nov. 16, 1891) 28,200 00

11 Seventy-eighth st, w s, 100 w Amsterdam av, 75x100. J. H. Heerline agt Arthur Boehmer and McLaughlin, Clegg & Co. (July 30, 1891).......... 10 00

11 Same property. Patrick Simpson agt same. (July 30, 1891).......... 10 12

11 Same property. Thomas Gilligan agt same. (Oct. 16, 1891).......... 47 70

11 Same property. James F. McLaughlin agt same. (Oct. 16, 1891).......... 29 10

11 Same property. Morris Linahan agt same. (July 28, 1891).......... 18 38

11 Same property. Michael Powers agt same. (July 28, 1891).......... 19 87

11 Same property. John Walsh agt same. (July 28, 1891).......... 33 62

11 Same property. Thomas Kennedy agt same. (July 28, 1891).......... 29 25

11 Same property. Peter Cheever agt same. (July 23, 1891).......... 31 50

11 Same property. John Coleman agt same. (July 28, 1891).......... 42 00

11 Same property. George Smiddick agt Arthur Boehmer and McLoughlin, Smith & Co. (July 28, 1891).......... 6 75

11 Same property. Thomas Haney agt Arthur Boehmer and Clegg & Richards. (Sept. 21, 1891).......... 21 94

11 Same property. Daniel Cooney agt same. (Sept. 21, 1891).......... 6 30

11 Same property. John Hickey agt same. (Sept. 21, 1891).......... 22 50

11 Same property. Thomas Byrnes agt same. (Sept. 21, 1891).......... 6 30

11 Ninety-fourth st, s s, 150 w Amsterdam av, 100x100. John Coleman agt Arthur Boehmer and McLaughlin, Clegg & Co. (July 31, 1891).......... 11 25

11 Same property. Same agt James Brady and Clegg, Richards & Co. (July 31, 1891).......... 11 25

11 Same property. Same agt same. (July 28, 1891).......... 11 25

11 Same property. J. F. McLaughlin agt James B. Brady and Anthony M. Clegg and John Doe. (Oct. 16, 1891).......... 30 00

*Discharged by depositing amount of lien and interest with County Clerk.
‡Discharged by order of Court on filing bond.

KINGS COUNTY.

Dec.

4 Navy st, e s, 61.8 n Myrtle av, 50x100. Wilson & Baillie Mfg. Co. agt William H. H. Glover, owner and contractor. (Lien filed June 5, 1891).......... $142 45

4 Evergreen av, w s, 25 n Hancock st, 50x100. Henry McShane Mfg. Co. agt Carl and William Lehmann, owner, and Louis Bossert, contractor. (Oct. 28, 1891).......... 75 00

5 Woodbine st, n w s, 25 s w Knickerbocker av, 200x100. Bulmer Lumber Co. agt Albert Berkmeyer, owner and contractor. (Dec. 2).......... 1,639 90

5 Saratoga av, s e cor Chauncey st, 22x78.. }
Chauncey st, s s, 78 e Saratoga av, 57x100. }
Saratoga av, e s, 70 n Marion st, 30x78..... }
McWhinney & Aronson agt Mary McDowell, owner, and Clements Trimble, contractor. (June 12, 1891).......... 2,000 00

5 Bergen st, s s, 106 w Hopkinson av, 25x100. The Wyandance Brick and Terra Cotta Co. agt Rosa Rosenfeld, owner, and Carl Becker, contractor. (Oct. 19, 1891.) (Deposit).......... 131 22

5 Same property. Potts Bros. agt same owner and contractor. (Oct. 19, 1891.) (Deposit).......... 42 37

5 Bergen st, s s, 100 w Hopkinson av, 25x100. Schott & Lenahan agt same owner and contractor. (Oct. 27, 1891.) (Deposit)... 70 00

5 Same property. Michael Neumann agt Rosa Rosenfeld, owner, and Yonas Rosenfeld, contractor. (Nov. 9, 1891.) (Deposit).......... 21 00

Lewis av, south cor Hancock st, 100x150. Jacob May agt Thomas A. McWhinney and Joseph Aronson, owners and contractors. (Dec. 1, 1891).......... 93 07

8 McDonough st, s s, 175.5 e Sumner av, 99.7x 100. C. B. Keogh Mfg. Co. agt Alberico Carosselli or Michael Rofrano, owner, and Michael Rofrano, contractor. (Dec. 8, 1891).......... 8,081 00

8 Av B, n s, 113 w Coney Island road, 40x110, Flatbush. Denslo D. Hamlin agt Louisa Wright and Elizabeth Kemlo, owners and contractors. (March 23, 1891).......... 900 00

9 Ninety-fifth st, e s, 150 s Av G, 28.5x105, Canarsie. John R. Hughes agt Pauline Hardy, owner, and Harry Hardy, contractor. (Oct. 28, 1891).......... 148

9 Eighth av, s e cor 11th st, 100x190. Venetian Blind Co. agt Allison V. B. Norris and William C. Turner, owners and contractors. (Sept. 10, 1891).......... 172 60

10 Greene av, s e s, 100 n e Evergreen av, 56x 100. Benjamin J. Dennis & Son agt William Walsh and Mrs. Walsh, owners, and William Walsh, contractors. (June 10, 1890).......... 542 56

BUILDINGS PROJECTED.

The first name is that of the owner; ar't stands for architect, m'n for mason, c'r for carpenter and b'r for builder.

NEW YORK CITY.

SOUTH OF 14TH STREET.

Liberty st, foot of, North River, Pier 14, one-story frame office, 7x7, tin roof; cost, $25; lessee, Central R. R. of N. J., on premises. Plan 1524.

Broadway, No. 712, eight-story brk, iron, stone and terra cotta warehouse, 25x138, gravel roof; cost, $103,000; Jacob Scholle et al., 21 East 49th st; ar't, Alfred Zucker. Plan 1541.

Mott st, Nos. 212 and 214, three-story brk building, 54x23, tin roof; cost, $8,000; lessee, C. Mensching, 522 West 29th st; ar't, L. F. Heinecke; b'r, J. Leygh. Plan 1533.

BETWEEN 14TH AND 59TH STREETS.

9th st, Nos. 225 and 227 E., four-story brk school-house, 50x30, tin roof; cost, $10,000; Trustees Hebrew Technical Inst., 34 Stuyvesant st; ar'ts, Pickering & Carter; m'n, C. A. Cowen. Plan 1526.

3d av, No. 923, rear, one-story frame structure, 14x30, tin roof; cost, abt $75; Gustave Bofinger, on premises. Plan 1527.

26th st, Nos. 308-312 W., two five-story brk and stone flats, 28.6x88, tin roofs; cost, $25,000 each; W. G. Jordan, 199 2d av; ar't, J. W. McKecknie. Plan 1528.

58th st, No. 213 W., two-story brk stable and dwell'g, 25x50, slate and tin roof; cost, $12,000; Mrs. S. C. Twombly, 212 West 59th st; ar't, J. M. Farnsworth; c'r, J. Stewart. Plan 1537.

BETWEEN 59TH AND 125TH STREETS, EAST OF 5TH AVENUE.

71st st, s s, 175 w 3d av, two three-story and basement stone dwell'gs, 12.11x55, tin roofs; cost, $7,000 each; Cacilie Bauer, 162 East 71st st; ar't, E. Wenz. Plan 1529.

2d av, No. 1215, frame shed, 22x56, gravel roof; cost, $250; lessees, Watson & Mahoney, 214 East 70th st; ar'ts, Hubert, Pirsson & Hoddick; c'rs, Jennings & Welstead. Plan 1535.

3d av, No. 1554, five-story brk and iron building, 25x90, tin roof; cost, $7,000; Catherine A. Deane, 277 West 11th st; m'n, B. Sheridan; c'r, J. Newman. Plan 1534.

BETWEEN 59TH AND 125TH STREETS, WEST OF CENTRAL PARK WEST AND 8TH AVENUE.

Columbus av, w s, 93 s 99th st, rear, one-story brk building, 7x25, tin roof; cost, $700; H. and H. Sonn, 1038 5th av; b'r, F. Klingman. Plan 1526.

West End av, n e cor 104th st, eight three-story and one four story brk and stone dwell'gs, four 20x54, two 18x55, one 20.11x56.6, one 18.6x55, and one 28.6x50, roof not given; total cost, $160,000; D. Christie, 634 West End av; ar't, F. A. Minuth. Plan 1536

110TH TO 125TH STREET, BETWEEN 5TH AND 8TH AVENUES.

120th st, s s, 300 w 5th av, six three-story and basement brown stone front dwell'gs, 18.4x60, tin roofs; cost, $23,000 each; Thos. J. Robinson, 2064 7th av; ar't, J. C. Burne. Plan 1521.

NORTH OF 125TH STREET.

151st st, n s, abt 225 e Amsterdam av, one-story frame shed, 16x13, — roof; cost, $20; lessee, John McClure, 474 West 152d st. Plan 1525.

127th st, s s, 165 e 4th av, five-story brk and stone flat, 25x56.6, tin roof; cost, $24,000; J. Schreiner, Jr., 104 West 123d st; ar't, J. Hauser. Plan 1530.

133d st, n s, 110 w 5th av, two five-story brk and stone flats, 25x76, tin roof; cost, $31,000 each; A. T. Judge, 164 St. Nicholas av; ar't, J. C. Burne. Plan 1540.

135th st, s s, 285 e 6th av, three five-story brk and stone flats, 25x89.9, tin roofs; cost, $20,000 each; ow'r and b'r, J. Turner, 107 West 78th st; ar't, J. W. Cole. Plan 1542.

147th st, n s, 75 e Bradhurst av, five-story brk flat, 25x65, tin roof; cost, $16,000; V. Meyer, 319 East 125th st; ar't, A. Spence. Plan 1543.

23D AND 24TH WARDS.

138th st, n s, 250 e Willis av, two-story frame workshop, 23x50, gravel roof; cost, $1,000; lessee, Essie E. Morgan, 633 East 139th st; c'r, H. Morgan. Plan 1523.

135th st, s s, 80 e St. Anns av, eight two-story and basement brk dwell'gs, two 18.6x46, six 18x46, tin roofs; cost, $5,000 each; J. Entwistle, 853 East 135th st; ar't, A Spence. Plan 1544.

187th st, s s, 75 e Arthur av, one-story frame building, 13x14, tin roof; cost, $200; J. Faiella, on premises; ar't, C. F. Lohse. Plan 1531.

Jerome av, e s, 259 s 177th st, two-story frame shop, 28x60, tar and felt roof; cost, $2,000; J. E. Hillebert, on premises. Plan 1539.

Marmion av, w s, 330 n Tremont av, one-and-a-half-story frame stable, 16x28, shingle roof; cost, $300; F. Homann, 254 East 53d st; ar't, W. Schmidt; m'n, H. Hoffstadter; c'rs, Oesterheld & Co. Plan 1532.

Melrose av, n w cor 152d st, five-story brk and stone flat, 25x96, tin roof; cost, $20,000; X. Schafer, 2882 3d av; ar't, H. Horenburger. Plan 1538.

KINGS COUNTY.

Plan 2186—Cleveland st, w s, 200 s Wortman av, one one-story frame stable, 30x48, felt roof; cost, $450; Elizabeth Sullbach, Watkins st.

2187—Logan st, e s, 375 n Liberty av, one two-story frame dwell'g, 18x28, shingle roof; cost, $1,500; ow'r and b'r, S. W. Stoothoff, Atlantic, near Schenck avs; ar't, L. F. Schillinger.

2188—Willoughby av, n s, 304.6 w Wyckoff av, one one-story frame storage for masons' supplies, 13x16, tin roof; cost, $75; ow'r, ar't and b'r, V. Meinhardt, 327 Melrose st.

2189—Fountain av, w s, 125 s Atlantic av, one two-story frame dwell'g, 18x30, tin roof; cost, $1,800; L. L. Quinn, Fountain av.

2190—Jamaica av, n s, 125 e Railroad av, one two-story brk dwell'g and meeting rooms, 48x32, tin roof; cost, $7,800; Maimonides Cemetery Soc., New York City; ar't, R. Berger; b'r, J. A. Bisson.

2191—Stone av, w s, 150 s Eastern Parkway, two two-story frame tailor shops, 20x30, tin roofs; cost, each, $700; B. Frank and S. Rose, Belmont av.

2192—Havemeyer st, w s, 75 s South 8th st, one four-story frame (brk filled) tenem't, 25x50, tin roof; cost, $6,500; Collins & Stein; ar't, A. Herbert.

2193—Morgan av, s e cor Harrison pl, two three-story frame (brk filled) stores and tenem'ts, 25x58, tin roofs; total cost, $10,000; Mrs. C. Dannenhoffer, Hoerum st; ar'ts, D. Acker & Son.

2194—Sherlock pl, w s, 198.7 n Atlantic av, three two story and basement frame dwell'gs, 12.8x38, gravel roofs; cost, each, $1,800; ow'r and b'r, W. H. H. Robbins, 1128 Herkimer st; ar't, B. T. Robbins.

2195—Prospect av, s s, 225 e 8th av, three two-story brk flats, 16.8x45, tin or gravel roofs, wood cornices; cost, each, $3,000; C. C. Firth, 471 14th st; ar't, W. O. Tait.

2196—Division av, n s, 60 e Driggs st, two four-story brown stone flats, 20 and 19.6x80 and 56.6, tin roofs; iron cornices; total cost, $15,000; Doenecke Bro., 134 South 9th st.

2197—Myrtle av, s s, 625 e Nostrand av, three four-story brk stores and tenem'ts, 25x65, tin roofs, iron cornices; total cost, $30,000; Jacob Bossert, Bushwick av and Cedar st; ar'ts, D. Acker & Son.

2198—Van Voorhis st, n e cor Broadway, four one-story frame (brk filled) stores, 18 and 21x80, tin roofs; total cost, $6,000; Mrs. Skillmann, on premises; ar't, A. Herbert.

2199—Broadway, e s, 100 n Van Voorhis st, four one-story frame (brk filled) stores, 20x80, tin roofs; cost, $1,500 each; ow'r and ar't, same as last.

2200—Kingsland av, e s, 240 s Nassau av, one two-story frame (brk filled) dwell'g, 25x40, gravel roof; cost, $2,500; Rudolph A. Freser, Frost st; ar't, G. W. Cobb, Jr.; c'r, W. A. Cobb; m'n, not selected.

2201—Eastern Parkway, n e cor Wyona st, one three-story frame (brk filled) store and tenem't, 25x55, tin roof; cost, $5,000; ow'r and m'n, August Hensinger, on premises; ar't, C. Meins.

2202—Bainbridge st, s s, 205 e Ralph av, twenty two-story and basement brk and brown stone dwell'gs, 17.3x42, tin roofs, iron cornices; cost, $5,000 each; Robert F. Minto, 160 Linden st; ar't, M. F. Walsh; b'r, not selected.

2203—Stone av, w s, 150 s Eastern Parkway, two three-story frame tenem'ts, 20x40, tin roofs; cost, each, $4,000; Frank & Rose or Frank V. Rose, Belmont av.

2204—Cleveland st, w s, 160 s Wortman av, one two-story frame dwell'g, 20x28; cost, $1,400; Mary E. Sulzebach, Watkins st, cor Livonia av; ar't O. S. Totten.

2205—Chestnut st, w s, 150 n Ridgewood av, one two-story and attic frame dwell'g, 16 and 20x32, shingle roof; cost, $2,500; George Beach, Logan st.

2206—54th st, n s, 240 w 4th av, one two-story frame dwell'g, 20x42, tin roof; cost, $3,000; Mrs. R. Nelson, 1160 4th av; b'r, S. Swenson.

2207—Guernsey st, e s, 375 s Nassau av, one four-story frame box factory, 75x50; cost, $7,000; F. A. Baier, 812 East 5th st, New York; ar't, J. Bruns; b'r, not selected.

2208—Saratoga av, w s, 125 s Sumpter st, one four-story frame tenem't, 25x56, tin roof; cost, $8,800; Emma Klauberg, 1483 Broadway; ar't and supt., J. J. McMillan; b'r, day's work.

2209—Pacific st, s s, 356 e Albany av, one three-story frame (brk filled) dwell'g, 25x50, tin roof; cost, $4,000; ow'r, ar't and c'r, Wm. L. Beers, 128 Albany av; m'n, not selected.

2210—Montauk av, w s, 140 s New Lots road, one two-story frame dwell'g, 13x26, shingle roof; cost, $1,200; L. Hammer, 132 9th st, South Brooklyn; ar't and c'r, D. A. Smith.

2211—Milton st, s s, 40 w West st, one one-story frame lumber shed, 38x16, gravel roof; cost, $125; F. E. Perkins & Bro., 59 West st.

2212—Fanchon pl, e s, 100 n Bushwick av, one two-story frame tailor shop and dwell'g, 22x36, tin roof; cost, $1,500; August T. Harmann, on premises; b'r, J. Fenech.

2213—Williams pl, w s, 73 n Atlantic av, one two-story frame stable, 36x12, gravel roof; cost, $150; Wm. Miller, Snediker av; b'r, R. M. Fleming.

2214—Smith st, s e cor Sigourney st, 75 from w s Gowanus Canal, one-story frame storage for barrels, 124x160, gravel roof; cost, $3,000; Wm. H. H. Childs, 383 Washington av; ar't, J. C. Wandell; b'r, day's work.

2215—40th st, s s, 100 e 4th av, one three-story frame tenem't, 22x40, tin roof; cost, $3,000; M. J. Leary; ar't, H. Gilvary; b'rs, Regan Bros.

2216—Macon st, s w cor Ralph av, one four-story brk and stone store and tenem't, 28x35, gravel roof, iron cornice; cost, $20,000; Walter F. Clayton, 305 Stuyvesant av; ar'ts, Langston & Dahlander.

2217—Douglass st, n e cor 3d av, one four-story brk tenem't, 30x65, gravel roof, iron cornice; cost, $14,500; James V. Johnson, 41 Sterling pl; ar'ts, S. Curtis and E. C. Smith; b'rs, M. J. J. Reynolds' Sons and D. Ryan.

2218—Bergen st, s s, 99.4 e Hopkinson av, rear, one one-story frame stable, 19.4x15, tin roof; cost, $125; ow'r and b'r, R. J. Bellamy, on premises.

2219—Dupont st, No. 78, one three-story frame (brk filled) tenem't, 25x53, tin roof; cost, $4,100; Ferdinand Schroth, 90 Dupont st; ar't, F. J. Berlenbach, Jr.; b'r, C. Engert.

2220—Graham av, No. 78, one four-story frame (brk filled) tenem't, 25x90, tin roof; cost, $9,000; Leopold Michel, 80 Lee av; ar't, H. Vollweiler; b'r, not selected.

2221—Stanhope st, s s, 175 e Evergreen av, one three-story frame tenem't, 23x60, tin roof; cost, $5,500; L. Knoll, 52 Stanhope st; ar't, T. Engelhardt; b'r, not selected.

2222—Humboldt st, e s, 575 s Nassau av, five three-story frame (brk filled) tenem'ts, 24.6x60, tin roofs; cost, $4,000 each; ow'r and b'r, Charles Engert, 182 Montrose av; ar't, F. J. Berlenbach, Jr.

2223—Stockholm st, s s, 350 w Knickerbocker av, one three-story frame (brk filled) tenem't, 25x100, tin roof; cost, $4,000; ow'r and m'n, A. Tremmel, 205 Knickerbocker av; ar't, W. B. Wills; c'r, not selected.

2224—President st, s s, 90 w Clinton st, one four-story brk apartment house, 25x66, tin roof, wooden cornice; cost, $7,500; ow'r and b'r, Daniel Buckley, 32 Sterling pl; ar't, W. M. Coots.

2225—Rockaway av, w s, 25 n Bergen st, one one-story frame stable, 16x20, tin roof; cost, $200; Mr. Hauser, Rockaway av, near Bergen st; b'r, C. Bormann.

ALTERATIONS NEW YORK CITY.

Plan 2068—Irving pl, s w cor 15th st, walls altered; cost, $800; Arthur T. Belntich, on premises; ar't, A. G. Hindiff.

2069—Broadway, No. 30 E., three-story brk extension, 11x26, tin roof; cost, $1,100; Lazarus Levy, on premises, ar't, H. Horenburger.

2070—160th st, n w cor Old William st, two-story frame extension, also interior alterations and walls altered; cost, $1,500; Eliza McCarthy, 723 East 160th st; ar't, M. J. Garvin.

2071—104th st, No. 119 W., repair damage by fire; cost, $20,000; Henry P. Booth, 326 West 56th st; ar'ts and b'rs, Geaton & Glynn.

2072—104th st, No. 121 W., repair damage by fire; cost, $3,900; ow'r, ar'ts and b'rs, same as last.

2073—3d av, Nos. 3432 and 3434, one-story frame extension, 34.8x4, tin roof; cost, $800; Mary I. Steed, 840 East 167th st; ar't, C. C. Churchill; c'rs, Wiswell & O'Brien.

2074—Lispenard st, No. 10, interior alterations, walls altered; cost, abt $5,000; Daniel Birdsall, agent, 194 Carroll st, Brooklyn; ar't, F. S. Schlesinger; b'r, J. C. Klett.

2075—Water st, Nos. 510 and 512, and Rutgers st, No. 66, repair damage by fire; cost, $3,000; Peter H. Jackson, 163 East 27th st; m'n, B. Van Hoesen.

2076—Hester st, No. 104, walls altered, &c.; cost, $200; lessee, S. Volk; ar't, C. Rentz.

2077—Pearl st, Nos. 515 and 515½, walls altered, &c.; cost, $800; lessee, Henry Hillebrand, 515 Pearl st; ar't, M. Muller.

2078—102d st, No. 219 E., interior alterations, walls altered; cost, $1,300; Chas. Weisberger, 73 St. Marks pl; ar't, J. E. Darragh.

2079—3d av, No. 2222, new store front; cost, $200; Brian G. Hughes, 180 Willis av; c'r, W. A. Prindle.

2080—Greene st, Nos. 46-50, walls altered; cost, $300; D. Appleton & Co., 3 and 5 Bond st; ar't and b'r, Harkness Fire Extinguishing Co.

2081—Spring st, No. 43, interior alterations; cost, $500; Michael Laff, 141 East 47th st; ar't, F. Baylies.

2082—1st av, s w cor 74th st, repair damage by fire; cost, $3,500; Sarah Harris, 126 East 95th st; ar'ts, Graul & Frohne.

2083—56th st, Nos. 428 and 430 E., interior alterations, walls altered; cost, $8,000; Peter Doelger, 417 East 55th st; ar't, J. Kastner.

2084—52d st, s s, 498.8 e 1st av, interior alterations, walls altered; cost, $2,000, New York Hygeia Ice Co., 52d st and East River; ar't, J. Kastner.

2085—Essex st, No. 102, two-story and basement extension, 16.11x35.1; cost, $7,000; A. I. Levy, 62 Attorney st; ar't, L. F. Heinecke.

2086—Waverley pl, No. 198, one-story extension, 12.10x15.10; cost, $100; J. C. Grasmuk, on premises.

2087—88th st, No. 121 E., windows altered; cost, $150; B. Efinger, 535 3d av; c'r, H. Mierisch.

2088—Elm st, No. 194, new foundation walls; cost, $9,000; C. M. Boland, on premises; ar't, E. Ahrens; m'n, H. McNally.

2089—Marion av, n w cor William st, 24th Ward, interior alterations and door altered; cost, $250; J. Schrady et al., 250 West 120th st; m'n, C. W. Vreeland.

2090—20th st, No. 153 W., interior alterations and walls altered; cost, $300; F. Neumer, 155 West 20th st; ar't, J. Kastner.

2091—3d av, No. 2950, new store front; cost, $400; C. Stark, 2948 3d av; ar't, C. F. Lohse.

2092—80th st, No. 331 E., walls altered for new front; cost, $500; Mrs. Mary Bach, on premises; b'r, W. Shears.

2093—8th av, No. 162, interior alterations, door and window altered; cost, $500; lessees, McCrocken Bros., 419 West 33d st; c'r, P. Haughey.

2094—Henry st, No. 154, interior alterations and new light shaft; cost, $3,500; B. and L. Blumberg, 246 East Broadway; ar'ts, Schneider & Herter.

2095—Henry st, Nos. 86 and 88, repair damage by fire; cost, $2,000; ow'r and b'r, H. Fischel, 16 Jefferson st; ar't, H. Horenburger.

2096—59th st, No. 212 W., two-story extension, 9.6x25, and wall in rear; cost, $3,000; Mrs. S. S. Twombly, on premises; ar't, J. M. Farnsworth; c'r, J. Stewart.

2097—Pike st, Nos. 13 and 15, two-story and basement extension, 51x13, roof altered, extensive interior alterations and walls altered; cost, $25,000; S. Scharlin, pres't, 110 Division st; ar't, F. Ebeling.

2098—Hudson st, No. 559, repair damage by fire; cost, $400; A. Nelson, 246 East 73d st; c'r, H. Lifshitz.

2099—Irving pl, n e cor 18th st, interior alterations, walls altered for new front; cost, $3,000; F. W. Dieckmann, 11 West 4th st; ar't, J. Kastner.

2100—Franklin st, No. 187, new bulkhead on roof; cost, $250; Josephine and Mary A. Jacobs, exrtxs., 255 West 34th st; c'r, J. H. Studley.

KINGS COUNTY.

Plan 1135—Gates av, No. 290, piazza in front of house; cost, $250; C. A. Dubois, on premises; b'r, J. Williamson.

1136—Broadway, No 771, one-story brk extension, 25x50, tin roof; cost, $6,500; —— Michaelis, 1 Yates pl; ar't, H. E. Funk.

1137—Ashland pl, w s, 430.3 n Fulton st, carried up 11 feet; cost, $15,000; A. D. Matthews & Sons, 398-404 Fulton st; ar't, J. Mumford; b'rs, Bond & Co.

1138—Broadway, No. 1582, three-story brk extension, 20x16 6, tin roof, new light shaft and bath-room; cost, $800; Wm. Eckhoff, 1582 Broadway; ar't, C. Infanger; b'r, not selected.

1139—Bedford av, No. 318, one-story brk extension, 8 6x23, tin roof; cost, $200; Samuel Philips, 318 Bedford av; b'rs, E. Gottlieb and A. Schabn.

1140—Degraw st, No. 84, basement, front alteration; cost, $300; Anthony Sessa, 40 Union st; ar't and b'r, P. Enteglio.

1141—Washington st, No. 251, rebuild rear wall; cost, $400; Whitman estate, 42 Wall st, N. Y.; b'rs, J. G. Porter and T. K. Schermerhorn.

1142—Manhattan av, No. 555, one-story frame extension, 18x38; cost, $300; David T. Rees, on premises; ar't, C. Dunkhase.

1143—Partition st, No. 188, one-story frame extension, 14x13, tin roof; cost, $75; C. Ruther, 183 Dikeman st; c'r, J. F. McCuelpin.

1144—Bleecker st, No. 70, lowered 10 feet on stone foundation; cost, $500; N. P. Pestows estate, New York.

1145—Prospect pl, No. 118, iron girders under rear wall, cost, $100; ow'r and ar't, Anthony Ru or Rei, on premises; b'r, J. J. Bentzen and B. C. Miller & Sons.

1146—Nostrand av, No. 116, repair damage by fire; cost, $4,000; Elizabeth H. Allen, 92 Rodney st.

1147—Wyckoff av, Nos. 58 and 60, raised 7 feet on brk walls; cost, $400; ow'r and b'r, H. Foerstl, on premises.

1148—Richards st, n w cor King st, girder under gable wall; cost, $300; H. Pope, on premises; ar't and b'r, C. M. Detlefsen.

1149—Union av, No 212, one-story frame extension, 25x25, tin roof; cost, $200; Anthon Benkert, on premises.

1150—Nostrand av, No. 126, repair damage by fire; cost, $2,600; T. S. Schneble, on premises; b'rs, Jenkins & Gillies.

1151—Broadway, e s, 45 s Woodbine st, one-story frame extension, 14x21, tin roof; cost, $200; John M. Fette, 1419 Broadway; ar't, C. Infanger.

1152—Wyckoff av, No. 12, raised 3 feet on brk foundation; cost, $300; Wm. Munsey, 139 East 19th st, New York.

1153—5th av, w s, 60 n 32d st, one-story frame extension, 13x13, felt roof; cost, $100; Donald McCoskelly, 32d st and 5th av.

1154—3d av, No 984, n e cor 38th st, brk foundation 8 feet high; cost, $400; Elizabeth Bongartz, 985 3d av.

1155—Myrtle av, No. 253, new store front, iron columns, &c.; cost, $1,500; Edward Ball, 253 Myrtle av; ar't and b'r, C. J. Archer.

1156—Kingsland av, No. 231, raised 5 feet on brk wall; cost, $300; Michael Tormey, on premises.

1157—Union st, No 239, repair damage by fire; cost, $1,300; F. S. O'Connor, 304 Clinton st; b'rs, Sammis & Bedford

MISCELLANEOUS.

BUSINESS FAILURES.

N. Y. ASSIGNMENTS—BENEFIT CREDITORS.

Dec.

7 Coudie, James (of No. 363 West 22d st), to Mornay Williams; without preferences.

8 Lounsberry, James S. (business of transporting fire-wood in sailing vessels, at No. 85 West st), to Valentine Marsh; without preferences.

8 Ransom, William H. and Nannie G. (composing firm of Ransom & Co., dealers in wrought iron pipe, fittings, valves, radiators, &c., at Nos. 94 and 96 Centre st), to Louis M. Fulton; without preferences.

9 Newell, Darius C. and George H. and Darius E. (D. C. Newell & Sons, lumber dealers and dressers of lumber, at foot West 19th st, North River), to Valentine Marsh; without preferences.

10 Higgins, James F. (individ. and as partner of Higgins Bros., wholesale and retail lumber dealer, at No. 198 11th av), to Patrick Moore; without preferences.

10 Reed, Michael A. (vending coal and wood, at Nos. 350 and 352 East 93d st), to Emil Reinl; preferences $1,200.

10 Lochman, Herman (wholesale and retail wines and liquors, at No. 62 3d av), to Frank Kettner; without preferences.

11 Beckwith Charles Pool (broker and dealer in oils, at No. 153 Maiden lane), to Joseph Alfred Berger, Jr.; without preferences.

11 Baker, Francis and Wendell (Francis Baker & Co., dry-goods commission merchants, at No. 12 Thomas st), to Welcome S. Jarvis; without preferences.

KINGS COUNTY.

GENERAL ASSIGNMENTS.

Dec.

9 Everding, Henry to E. B. Barnum.

PROCEEDINGS OF THE BOARD OF ALDERMEN AFFECTING REAL ESTATE.

* Under the different headings indicates that a resolution has been introduced and referred to the appropriate committee. † Indicates that the resolution has passed and has been sent to the Mayor for approval. ‡ Passed over the Mayor's veto.

New York, Tuesday, Dec. 8, 1891.

REGULATING, GRADING, ETC.

144th st, from Boulevard to 12th av.
145th st, from Boulevard to 12th av.
172d st, from 3d av to Vanderbilt av E. †

PAVING.

115th st, from west crosswalk Pleasant av to Harlem River; granite block.
138th st, bet 7th and 8th avs; granite block and crosswalks laid at terminating avs.
139th st, bet 7th and 8th avs; granite block and crosswalks laid at terminating avs. †

CROSSWALKS.

Kingsbridge road, at its intersection with the north and south sides of 175th st.
Fort Washington Depot road and 181st st.
Amsterdam av, at intersection with north and south sides of 175th st. †

FENCING VACANT LOTS.

89th st, s s, bet 2d and 3d avs.
95th st, n s, bet Lexington and Park avs.
96th st, s s, bet Lexington and Park avs.
97th st, both sides, bet Lexington and Park avs.
Madison av, e s, bet 106th and 107th sts.
Park av, e s, bet 96th and 97th sts.
Park av, w s, bet 106th and 107th sts.
Park av, e s, bet 101st and 102d sts.
where not already done.†

FLAGGING, CURBING, ETC.

Charlton st, in front of Nos. 83-89.
Clarke st, e s, from Spring st to a point 125 s therefrom.
Macdougal st, in front of Nos. 3, 5 and 7.
Varick st, in front of Nos. 134 and 136.
89th st, s s, 100 w 2d av, 50 ft front.
144th st, from Boulevard to 12th av, crosswalks laid at intersecting avs.
145th st, from Boulevard to 12th av, crosswalks laid at intersecting avs.
172d st, from 3d to Vanderbilt av E., crosswalks laid at intersecting avs.
Jerome av, from McComb's Dam Bridge to Southern Boulevard; also construct culverts.
1st av, n w cor 66th st, 100x100. †

MAINS.

Bronx River road, from Grand av to city line; gas.
Fox st, from Home st to Westchester av; gas.
German pl, bet Westchester av and Carr st; water, hydrants set.
German pl, bet Westchester av and Rae st; water.
road pl, from William st to Bainbridge av; water.
Union st, from Lind av to Bremer av; water.
1st st, from Grand av to city line; gas.
2d st, from Grand av to Mt. Vernon av; gas.
3d st, from Grand av to Mt. Vernon av; gas.
36th st, from 1st av to East River; gas.
103d st, bet Park and 5th avs; gas.
137th st, from 5th to Lenox av; gas.
138th st, bet 7th and 8th avs; gas.
139th st, bet 7th and 8th avs; gas.
142d st, bet 8th and Bradhurst avs; gas.
160th st, bet Elton and Washington avs; water.
Brook av, from Washington av to 166th st; gas.
Clinton av, from 1st st to Grand av; gas.
Grand av, from Central av to city line; gas.
Locust av, bet 138th and 139th sts; water, hydrants set.
Mt. Vernon av, from Grand av to city line; gas
Opdyke av, from Bronx River road to 3d st; gas.
Tinton av, from 166th to Home st; water.
Trinity av, from 155th to 166th st; gas.
Walnut av, bet 138th and 139th sts; water, hydrants set.
Willard av, from Bronx River road to 3d st; gas.
1st av, from 2d to 3d st; gas.
2d av, from 2d to 3d st; gas.
3d av, from 2d to 3d st; gas.
4th av, from 2d st to Mt Vernon av; gas.
5th av, from 2d st to Mt. Vernon av; gas. †

LAMP-POSTS ERECTED AND LAMPS LIGHTED.

Bronx River road, from Grand av to city line.
Fox st, from Home st to Westchester av.
1st st, from Grand av to city line.
2d st, from Grand av to Mt. Vernon av.
3d st, from Grand av to Mt Vernon av.
36th st, from 1st av to East River.
56th st, n s, bet 8th and 9th avs; two lights in front of Zion Chapel.
57th st, s s, bet 8th and 9th avs; two lights in front of St. Timothy's Church.
103d st, bet Park and 5th avs.
137th st, from 5th to Lenox av.
138th st, bet 7th and 8th avs.
139th st, bet 7th and 8th avs.
142d st, bet 8th and Bradhurst avs.
Brook av, from Washington av to 166th st.
Clinton av, from 1st st to Grand av.
Grand av, from Central av to city line.
Mt. Vernon av, from Grand av to city line.
Opdyke av, from Bronx River road to 3d st.
Trinity av, from 165th to 166th st.
Willard av, from Bronx River road to 3d st.
1st av, from 2d to 3d st.
2d av, from 2d to 3d st.
3d av, from 2d to 3d st.
4th av, from 2d st to Mt. Vernon av.
5th av, from 2d st to Mt. Vernon av. †

BROOKLYN BOARD OF ALDERMEN.

Brooklyn, Nov. 30, 1891.

ELECTRIC LIGHTING.

Floods alley.
Graham st, w s, bet Myrtle and Willoughby avs. †

CHANGE STREET NAME.

Kosciusko st to Maple st.*
Partition st to Coffey st.†

FLAGGING.

Atlantic av, n s, bet Clason and Franklin avs.
Vernon av, s s, bet Sumner and Throop avs. †

PAVING, GRADING, ETC.

Covert st, bet Central and Hamburg avs.
Newton st, bet Graham and Van Pelt avs.
Ralph av, bet Prospect pl and Degraw st.
Van Pelt av, bet Graham av and Humboldt st. †

SEWER BASINS.

Evergreen av, n w cor Schaeffer st.
Evergreen av, s w cor Schaeffer st. †

STREET OPENING.

Newton st.†

ADVERTISED LEGAL SALES.

REFEREES SALES TO BE HELD AT THE REAL ESTATE EXCHANGE AND AUCTION ROOM (LIMITED), 59 to 65 LIBERTY STREET, EXCEPT WHERE OTHERWISE STATED.

Dec.

42d st, No. 220, s s, 280 w 2d av, 25x79.6x27.11x92.1, four-story brk tenem't with stores, by Smyth & Ryan. (Amt due $16,416) 14

83d st, No. 38, n s, 448.9 e 9th av, 26.2x80, three-story brk dwell'g, by William Kennelly........ 14

Av A, Nos. 389 and 391, w s, 49.5 s 24th st, 49.4x81.5; No. 389, one-story brk building with two-story brk building on rear; No. 391, four-story brk store and tenem't, by Smyth & Ryan. (Amt due $21,841)........ 14

Av A, s w cor 24th st, 49 5x81.5, vacant, by Smyth & Ryan. (Amt due $26,500)........ 14

Riverside av or Drive, No. 100 } begins Riverside
82d st, Nos. 318-324 } av, s e cor 82d st, runs east 161.1 x south 102.2 x west 16.8 x north 19.4 x west 32 x north 18 8 x west 14.4 x north 15.6 x west 8 4 x north 26.6 x west 79.9 to Riverside Drive, x north 24 2 to beginning, four-story stone front dwell'g on av and four four-story stone front dwell'gs on st, by R. V. Harnett & Co.... 14

Willis av, n w cor 145th st, 25x106........
Willis av, n w cor 146th st, 25x106........
Willis av, w s, 25 n 146th st, 25x106........
Three five-story brk and stone flats........
by William Kennelly. (Amt due on each corner house $21,065, and $14,868 on other)........ 14

45th st, No. 134, s s, 382.6 w 6th av, 17.6x100.4, four-story brk dwell'g, by B. L. Kennelly. (Amt due $4,079........ 15

48th st, Nos 134-142, s e cor Lexington av, 17.6x100.5; No. 134, seven-story brk flat with stores; Nos. 136-142, four five-story brk flats, by B. L. Kennelly. (Amt due $33,327)........ 15

90th st, s s, 100 e 10th av, 100x100.8, vacant, by William Kennelly. (Amt due $19 434)........ 15

94th st, No. 45, n s, 375 e 9th av, 14.8x100.8, three-story brk dwell'g, by B. L. Kennelly. (Amt due $1,256)........ 15

119th st, No. 63, n s, 526.8 w 5th av, 16.8x100.11, three-story stone front dwell'g, by R. V. Harnett & Co. (Amt due $12,265)........ 15

2d av, Nos. 1808-1814, s e cor 94th st, 100 8x100, four five-story brk tenem'ts with stores, by William Kennelly........ 15

20th st, No. 212, s s, 434 w 2d av, 22x92, three-story brk tenem't, by D. P. Ingraham & Co. (Amt due $15,936)........ 16

142d st, No. 268, s s, 125.1 w 7th av, 16 6x99.11 three-story stone front dwell'g, all right, title and int. which John E. Fraca had on Aug. 19, 1891, by Sheriff, at City Hall. (Sale under execution)... 16

120th st, No. 211, n s, 175 w 7th av, 25x100.11, five-story brk flat, by William Kennelly. (Amt due $19,269)........ 16

19th st, No. 206, s w s, 490 n w 2d av, 20x94, three-story brk tenem't, leasehold, all right, title and interest of John B. Barazzi, by J. N Golding ... 17

19th st, No. 206 E, leasehold, all right, title and int of John B. Barazzi, by J. N. Golding. 17

95th st, No. 171, n s, 100 e 10th av, 50x100.8, five-story brk flat........
96th st, No. 168, s s, 100 e 10th av, 50x100.8, five-story brk flat........
by James Bleecker & Son. 2 actions. (Amt due on No. 171 $10,551, and $12,678 on No. 168). (Prior mort. on each $42,500)........ 17

97th st, No. 66, s s, 168 e Columbus av, 19x100.11, four-story brk dwell'g, by William Kennelly. (Amt due $30,174)........ 17

137th st, n s, 275 e 6th av, 25x99.11, vacant, by William Kennelly. (Partition sale)........ 17

Madison av, Nos. 1064 and 1066, w s, 62.2 n 80th st, 40x70, five story brk flat with stores, by William Kennelly. (Amt due $51,948)........ 17

10th av, No. 148, e s, 25 n 19th st, 25x80........
10th av, No. 150, e s, 50 n 19th st, 25x80........
Two five-story brk stores and tenem't's........
by R. V. Harnett & Co. (Amt due on each $17,559)........ 17

61st st, No. 322, s s, 301.8 e 2d av, 26.8x100.5......
61st st, No. 324, s s, 328.4 e 2d av, 26.8x100.5......
61st st, No. 326, s s, 355 e 2d av, 26.8x100.5......
61st st, No. 328, s s, 381.8 e 2d av, 26.8x100.5......
Four five-story brk tenem'ts........
by William Kennelly. (Amt due on each $19,336)........ 18

St. Nicholas av, w s, 234.11 s 141st st, 131.8x35.4x129.11x13.7, vacant, by William Kennelly. (Amt due $5,009)........ 18

Boulevard (11th) av, s e cor 151st st, 24.11x100, four-story brk flat, by R. V. Harnett. (Amt due $1,201; prior morts. $12,000)........ 21

106th st, n s, 175 w 8th av, 50x100.11, five-story stone front flats, by R. V. Harnett & Co. (Amt due $1,816; prior morts. ——)........ 21

KINGS COUNTY.

Dec.

Sackett st, No. 480, s s, 75 w Bond st, runs south 100 x west 70 x south 25 x west 33.4 x north 50 x east 73.4 x north 75 to Sackett st, x east 30 to beginning, three-story brk tenem't and two-story brk stable in rear; assessed value, $4,500........
Jefferson av, No. 164, s s, 200 w Nostrand av, 20 x100........
Jefferson av, No. 162, s s, 220 w Nostrand av, 20 x100........
Jefferson av, No. 160, s s, 240 w Nostrand av, 20 x100........
Jefferson av, No. 158, s s, 260 w Nostrand av, 20 x100........
Jefferson av, No. 152, s s, 320 w Nostrand av, 20x100........
Five four-story brk flats; assessed value, $6,500 each........
by J. Cole, at 389 Fulton st........ 14

Dean st, n s, 419.5 e Rochester av, 16x107.3⅜....
Dean st, n s, 435.5 e Rochester av, 16x107.2⅜....
Dean st, n s, 451.5 e Rochester av, 16x107.3⅜....
Dean st, n s, 467.5 e Rochester av, 16x107.3⅜....
Four two-story frame dwell'gs; assessed value, $1,600 each........
Hudson av, No. 285, e s, 24 s Tillary st, 21x50x15x50, three-story frame dwell'g; assessed value, $1,000........
by T. A. Kerrigan, at 18 Willoughby st. 14

Herkimer st, No. 1144, s w cor Russell pl, 16.8x85.9, two-story and basement brk dwell'g; assessed value, $3,000......
Graham av, No. 5?, w s, 75 n Varet st, 25x100, three-story frame tenem't and store and one-story frame extension on rear, ¼ part; assessed value, $3,000......
by T. A. Kerrigan, at 13 Willoughby st...... 15

McDonough st, No. 579, n s, 22.8 w Ralph av, 18.8x100, two-story and basement brk and stone dwell'g; assessed value, $4,000; by W. Cole, at 7 and 8 Court sq...... 15

Cumberland st, No. 398, w s, 302.10 n Atlantic av, 14x100, three-story frame dwell'g; assessed value, $2,000......
South 4th st, No. 253, n s, 100 e Havemeyer st, 25x95, five-story brk tenem't; assessed value, $6,000......
by T. A. Kerrigan, at 13 Willoughby st...... 16

Kingston av, w s, East New York av to Maple st, 200x94.6, Flatbush, vacant; partition......
Jefferson av, No. 1056, e s, 80 n Broadway, 18x100, two-story frame dwell'g; assessed value, $2,800......
by W. P. Rae & Co., at the Real Estate Exchange, 189 and 191 Montague st...... 16

3d st, No. 500, s s, 44 w 7th av, 22x90, four-story brk dwell'g; assessed value, $6,300......
3d st, No. 504, s w cor 7th av, 22x90, four-story brk dwell'g; assessed value, $7,000......
by W. Cole, at 7 and 8 Court sq...... 16

Butler st, Nos. 1202-1222, s s, 325 e Kingston av, runs south 111.6 x again south 16.9 x east 271.2½ x north 127.9 to Butler st, x west 275 to beginning, vacant; assessed value, $1,820; by T. A. Kerrigan, at 13 Willoughby st...... 17

Bedford av, No. 653, s w s, 50 s e Penn st, 25x70, five-story brk flat; assessed value, $5,000; by J. Cole, at 389 Fulton st...... 17

Scholes st, Nos. 177 and 179, n s, 225 e Graham av, 50x100, two three-story frame dwell'gs and two three-story brk dwell'gs on rear; assessed value, $7,800; partition; by W. Cole, at 7 and 8 Court sq. 18

60th st, n s, 60 e 12th av, 20x100.2, New Utrecht, frame dwell'g; by T. A. Kerrigan, at 13 Willoughby st...... 18

Lots 1-5 and 1746-1753 map of the Third District of the Village of Williamsburgh, by George Wilcox, ref., at County Court House...... 18

Court st, No. 588, w s, 63.4½ s Hamilton av, 20x100, one-story brk store; assessed value, $700; by W. P. Rae & Co., at the Real Estate Exchange, 189 and 191 Montague st...... 21

Schaeffer st, n s, 204 w Hamburg av, 48x93.9x48x96.5, three two-story frame (brk lined) dwellings; assessed value, $1,000 each......
Belmont av, s s, 75 e Thatford av, 25x100, two-story frame dwell'g; assessed value, $1,200......
7th st, s s, 402.1½ w 8th av, 20.9x100, three story brk and stone flat; assessed value, $5,600......
by T. A. Kerrigan, at 13 Willoughby st...... 21

LIS PENDENS.

NEW YORK.

Dec.

10th av, w s, extends from 182d to 183d st, 200x125. Antonio Altieri agt Daniel J. Sullivan; foreclos. mechanic's lien; att'y, Herman Frank. 5

114th st, Nos. 420 and 422, s s, 270 e 1st av, 55.?x100.11. Daniel Rabold agt Lydia Friedberg; action for specific performance; amended notice; att'ys, Morse & Wensley...... 7

85th st, n s, 100 e 6th av, 75x100. Andrew Larson agt Annie T. Harrigan et al.; foreclos. mechanic's lien; att'y, J. Edward Swanstrom...... 7

Courtlandt av, No. 882. David Stevenson agt Charles Moritz; action to recover possession; att'y, William J. Walsh...... 7

Fulton st, s e cor Gold st, 20x60.9x20x62.9. Richard Keating agt John A. Zulage et al.; action to eject deft. from premises; att'y, A. B. Johnson...... 8

150th st, n s, 500 w Courtlandt av, 25x136.10......
151st st, s s, 500 w Courtlandt av, 25x100......
Louisa Landgrebe agt William F. Landgrebe et al.; partition; att'y, August P. Wagener...... 8

Ryer av, w s, 300 s 183d st, 50x125. Arthur Hoehmer agt Theodore Rhein and ano; action to adjudge conveyance fraudulent; att'y, James Kearney...... 8

Creston av, w s, 178.9 s 182d st, 25x130.6x25x100.6. Same agt Thomas T Peterson and ano.; foreclos. mechanic's lien; same att'y...... 8

Willett st, e s, 193.9 n Broome st, 25x100. Simon Sigel agt Samuel Rauer et al.; action to compel defts. to convey premises; att'ys, A. & L. Levy. 8

72d st, n w cor Lexington av, 30x102.2. C. H. Bunn agt Sarah Levenson et al.; foreclos. mechanic's lien; att'y, George W. McAdam...... 8

113th st, n s, 100 e 10th av, 25x99.11. John Eberd and ano. agt George Wohlleben and ano.; action to procure the cancellation of a certain deed; att'y, Max Bayersderfer...... 9

Delancey st, n s, 75 e Cannon st, 25x100. Israel Cohen and ano. agt Abraham Cohen; notice that a levy is made under a warrant of attachment issued and delivered to the sheriff in above action, dated Dec. 5, 1891, for $3,000; att'y, David Leventritt...... 9

Lot 27 map land Rebecca Bassford, Fordham, 782x250x744 to Harlem R. R. Co.'s land, x250. Alice E. A. Benedict agt George E. Daniels et al.; action to set aside a certain deed; att'y, Thomas W. Pittman...... 9

Cherry st, Nos. 187 and 159, s s, 250 e Market st, 50x120. Fire Department agt Joseph Young et al.; proceeding to enforce building laws; att'y, William L. Findley...... 9

100th st, s s, 200 w 3d av, 50x100.11. John M. Lenehan agt Henry Vebstedt et al.; action to adjudge conveyance fraudulent; att'y, Gilbert R. Hawes...... 10

Stanton st, s s, 66.9 w Eldridge st, 22.3x75. John A. Lewis agt Thomas Lewis et al.; partition; att'ys, Black, Ladd & King...... 10

Bradhurst av, s e cor 142d st, 100x83. Lafayette Elwell agt Fernando Yost et al; foreclos. mechanic's lien; att'ys, W. P. and R. K. Prentice.. 10

Hester st, No. 58, s s, 25 e Essex st, 25x50. Hebrah Talmud Torah D. Augustow agt Catherine K. Graham et al.; partition; att'y, Samuel Johnson...... 10

104th st, n s, 175 e 2d av, 25x100.11. David M. Koehler and ano. agt Benno Loewy and ano.; partition; att'y, John J. Gleason...... 10

Hester st, No. 81, n s, 23.6 w Orchard st, 21.1x68.5
Hester st, n s, 109.9 w Allen st, 21.2x62.1x21.2x62.10......
John C. Wilmerding et al., agt Philip Bernstein et al.; action to set aside conveyance; att'ys, Blumenstiel & Hirsch...... 11

80th st, s s, 105 e 10th av, 145x102.2. Cassidy & Adler agt Morris Schneider et al.; foreclos. mechanic's lien; att'y, Thomas C. Ennever...... 11

Henry st, No. 57, n s, 25x100. Luke A. Burke agt Catherine C. Allen et al.; foreclos. mechanic's lien; att'y, John J. Flynn...... 11

Bremer av, w s, 27.10 s w Devoe st, runs southwest 83.9 x northwest 100 x northeast 75 x southeast 187.6. Albert Riley and ano. agt Ann Riley et al.; partition; att'y, Edward R. Vollmer...... 11

Leroy st, Nos. 57-59, n s, 66.2x80.4x53.4x81.6. Andrew Schoeller and ano. agt J. W. Stevens et al.; foreclos. mechanic's lien; att'y, Charles J. Hardy...... 11

FORECLOSURE SUITS.

Dec.

University pl, e s, 77.8 n Waverley pl, 25x75. Lewis H. Livingston agt John Pettini de Moise et al.; att'ys, Vanderpoel, Cuming & Goodwin...... 5

Canal st, n s, 15.10 e Sullivan st, 42.1x82.6x42.10x74.5. August Limbert trustee agt Charles A. Stein et al.; att'ys, Platt & Bowers...... 5

5th av, w s, 25 s 136th st, 25x85. Sheppard Gandy trustee agt Jacob S. Hausman et al.; att'y, A. Prentice...... 5

129th st, s s, 110 e Lenox av, 25x99.11. Juliet M. Livingston agt Sarah E. Berri et al.; att'y, Philip L. Livingston...... 5

60th st, s s, 350 e 9th av, 50x100.5. Mary B. D. Caldwell agt Clara N. Earle et al.; att'ys, Murphy, Lloyd & Boyd...... 7

1st av, s w cor 91st st, runs west 150 x south 100.8 x east 50 x north 50 x east 100 to 1st av, x north 50.8. Samuel Weil agt Daniel J. Sullivan et al.; att'y, E. Arnstein...... 8

92d st, s s, 100 e 5th av, 75x100.8......
92d st, s s, 178.10 e 5th av, 75.8x100.8x75.8x100.8, also all right, title and int. to strip of land lying bet the two lots, 2.10x100.8......
Randolph Guggenheimer et al. agt Thomas Graham et al.; att'ys, Guggenheimer & Untermyer. 8

Brook av, s w cor 163d st, 154.8x67.2 to Port Morris Branch R. R., x217.8x79.4. East River Mill and Lumber Co. agt Mary E. Yost et al.; att'y, Ashbel P. Fitch...... 8

Rivington st, s s, 25 w Willett st, 25x68. Lewis Levy agt Daniel Levinsky et al.; att'y, Charles E. L. Jelliffe...... 9

100th st, s s, 225 w 3d av, 25x100.11. Esther Herrman et al. exrs agt Charles J. McKim et al.; att'ys, Horwitz & Hersfield...... 9

Pearl st, s e s, 84.3 n e Franklin sq, runs southeast 60 to an alley, x south 14x15 x northwest 59 to Pearl st, x northeast 24.4 to beginning. John Martineau Fletcher and ano. trustees agt Mary M. Roworth individ. and admrx. et al.; att'ys, Strong & Cadwalader...... 9

81st st, s s, 256.6 w Av A, 25x102.2. Caroline L. Macy agt Tillie E. Smith et al.; att'ys, W. B. & G. F. Chamberlin...... 9

81st st, s s, 281.6 w Av A, 25x102.2. Margarette E. Griffith et al. agt same; same att'ys......

44th st, s s, 82 e 2d av, 18x50.4. Katie Gordon agt Oscar C. Weinman and ano.; att'ys, Carrington & Doty...... 10

52d st, n s, 375 e 11th av, 75x100.5. Otto Volkening agt John A. Linscott et al.; att'y, M. A. McBride...... 10

5th av, w s, 25 s 136th st, 25x85. Sheppard Gandy trustee agt J. S. Housman et al.; att'y, A. Prentice...... 10

47th st, n s, 300 e 1st av, 4 lots, each 25x100.5. Lewis Hurst et al. exrs. agt Peter Mitchell et al.; 4 actions; att'y, Lewis Hurst...... 11

80th st, n s, 30 w Amsterdam av, 26x100.8. Cassidy & Adler agt William R. Bell et al.; att'y, Thomas C. Ennever...... 11

81st st, s s, 180 e 9th av, 20x98.9. Broadway Savings Inst. agt George F. Hopper et al.; att'y, M. Hanta...... 11

6th av, w s 43.11 n 119th st, 19x75. Caroline F. Harrison agt John O. Hoyt, Jr., and ano.; att'y, Robert L. Harrison...... 11

65th st, s s, 310 e 10th av, 18x100.5. Mary C. de Tenouenne agt Bernard Cohn et al.; amended notice; att'y, Geo. V. N. Baldwin...... 11

53d st, n s, 300 w 6th av, 2 lots, each 20x100.5. Thomas C. T. Crain as Chamberlain agt John H. McKee et al.; 2 actions; att'ys, Platt & Bowers...... 11

120th st, s s, 197 e 5th av, 34.6x100.11. John Schnugg agt Fred. W. Styles et al.; att'ys, E. F. & A. C. Hassey...... 11

120th st, s s, 162 e 5th av, 35x100.11. Same agt same; same att'ys...... 11

LIS PENDENS, KINGS COUNTY.

Dec.

Bushwick av, east cor Greene st or av, 25x79.6. Jane E. Meeker agt Sarah E. Goodwin; att'ys, S. M. & D. E. Meeker...... 3

Gates av, s s, 275 e Marcy av, 20x100. Amelia W. Leavitt agt Laura B. Woodford; att'y, Wilson M. Powell...... 3

Flatbush av, e s, 80.5 s Prospect pl, 20.1x79.6 to Prospect pl, x20x80.5. Metropolitan Life Ins. Co. agt James Finlay; att'ys, Arnoux, Ritch & Woodford...... 3

Flatbush av, e s, 60.4 s Prospect pl, 20.1x64 to Prospect pl, x20.1x48.8. Same agt same; same att'ys...... 3

Flatbush av, south cor Prospect pl, 60.4x45.6x68.4, gore. Same agt same; same att'ys...... 3

Flatbush av, e s, 100.5 s Prospect pl, runs northeast 79.6 to Prospect pl, x southeast 20 x south 2.6 x southwest 80x3.6 to av, x north 20; also gore adj above, —x—. Same agt same; same att'ys...... 3

Douglass st, s s, 275 e Nevins st, 25x100. George Beach agt Patrick T. McGuinness; att'ys, Richards & Brown...... 4

Madison st, n s, 80 w Tompkins av, 20x50. Robert W. Steele agt Elisha G. Selchow; att'ys, Morris & Steele...... 4

Wyckoff av, e s, 25 s Linden st, 25x96.7x25x97.4. Christian W. C. Dreher agt Friederich Hardrich; att'y, Albert W. Bailey...... 4

Richards st, east cor Vandyke st, 80x40. Abram C. Gibson exr. Benjamin F. Roe agt Samuel Goldberger; att'ys, Townsend, Dyett & Einstein...... 4

Rockaway av, n e cor Sutter av, 25x100. East New York Savings Bank agt William Kirkland; att'ys, Hackett & Lang...... 4

Moore st, n s, 75 e Leonard st, 25x100. Isidore Dresdner agt Solomon Dresdner; partition; att'ys, Judge & Durack...... 4

Evergreen av, s w s, 25 s e Covert st, 75x92. Jane E. Taaffe agt Emma E Williams; att'y, H. A. McTernan...... 4

Scholes st, s e cor Humboldt st, 25x100. Clara Scherer agt Pauline Huttle; action for dower; att'y, H. A. Meyenborg...... 5

2d av, s w cor 8th st, 25x75. William M. Hewlett agt William K. Austin; att'y, Jos. M. Greenwood 5

Court st, w s, 130 s Church st, 20x80. Josephine C. Drake agt James A. Walsh, same att'y...... 5

7th st, n e s, 220.4 n w 6th av, 17.6x100. John C. Smith and ano. trustees Conklin Brush agt Sarah L. Fielding; att'y, Herbert D. Smith...... 5

Osborn st, w s, 150 n Belmont av, runs west 100 x north 50 x east 53.1 x south 1.6 x east 46.11 to st, x south 48.6......
Osborn st, e s, 130 s Dumont av, 25x100......
Lazarus Feit agt Wolf Lewis; action on breach of contract; att'y, John L. Lindsay...... 5

Louis pl, w s, 174.8 s Herkimer st, 15.4x97.6. Thomas E Greacen et al. exrs. James Wiggins agt Howard L. Emerson; att'y, John B Gleason. 5

Louis pl, w s, 159.4 s Herkimer st, 15.4x97.6. Same agt same; same att'y...... 5

Bushwick av, n e s, 79.8 s e Vanderveer st, 20x79.6. Henry Weil agt Vincenz Dianhy; att'y, R. Murray...... 7

High st, No. 119, n s, 115 e Jay st, 21.11x102.6. Walter D. Davies exr. Henry J. Davies agt Nellie C. Riley; att'ys, J. C. and H. C. Smith & Koelpke.. 7

Sutter av, s s, 50 w Watkins st, 50x100. John W. Ostrander agt Sarah Krupitzky; att'y, Henry B. Davenport...... 7

Bergen st, n e s, 120 s e 5th av, 20x100. George Carll and ano. exrs. Mary A. Carll agt Christianna Martin; att'y, Henry W. Gaines...... 7

Van Brunt st, n w s, 100.2 s w Commerce st, 17.10x90. The N. Y. Co-operative Building and Loan Assoc. agt Annie Vincent; att'y, Wm. Langdon...... 7

2d st, s w s, 80 n w 7th av, 37.10x100. Cornelius F. Donnellon agt Jennie L. Ross; att'y, Charles R. Halsey...... 7

2d st, s w s, 117.10 n w 7th av, 80x100. Thomas C. Higgins agt same; same att'y...... 7

Belmont av, n s, 125 e Thatford av, runs east 25 x north 100 x east 2.9 x north 25 x west 52.10 x south 25 x east 25 x south —. Herman F. Koepke agt Joseph Davis; att'ys, J. C. and H. C. Smith & Koepke...... 7

Warwick st, e s, 200 n Eastern Parkway, 25x90. The Nassau Co-operative Building and Loan Assoc agt Clara E. Westland; att'ys, Judge & Durack...... 7

Lafayette pl, e s, 148.7 n Atlantic av, 16.8x100. Samuel, Mary and Roseanna Caffray by Charles L. A. Baden guard. agt Samuel Caffrey; action to establish lien; att'y, Charles E. Burke...... 7

Hall st, w s, 360 n Myrtle av, 16x100. Federal Co-operative Building and Loan Assoc. agt Gerald P. Bagnall; att'y, James A. Seeman...... 7

Chauncey st, s s, 78 e Saratoga av, 57x100......
Chauncey st, s s, 230 e Saratoga av, 19x100......
John W. Phelps agt Carrie E. Elmore; att'y, Frederick Cobb......

Saratoga av, n e cor Marion st, 22x78......
Saratoga av, e s, 41 n Marion st, 137x78......
Same agt Jacob Aronson; same att'y...... 7

4th av, w s, 78 s 6th st, 25.8x75. Title Guarantee and Trust Co. agt John J. Carroll; att'y, Charles R. Halsey...... 8

Woodbine st, s e s, 228 s w Central av, 25x100. Ralph G. Packard agt George A. Low; att'y, A. W. Parker...... 8

Imlay st, s s, 150 e Verona st, 25x90. Union Dime Savings Inst. agt Patrick Cramer; att'ys, Arnoux, Ritch & Woodford...... 8

Maspeth av, both sides, 100 e Vandervoort av, adj meadow land of Gabriel Debevoise, except piece on s s of Maspeth av, 25x100. The Equity Gas Works Construction Co. agt John Devlin; ac- for injunction, &c.; att'y, William P. S. Melvin. 8

Garfield pl, n s, 90 w 7th av, 100x100x150x100. Charles Williams agt Edward L. Beekman; att'ys, Kohn, Ruck & Lippmann...... 8

8th av, south cor Garfield pl, 60x30. Mutual Life Ins. Co., New York, agt John F. Hart; att'y, Robert Sewell...... 9

21st st, n s, 150 e 4th av, 25x100. Emanuel Simons agt Anton Ritsch; att'ys, Klein & Rendich...... 9

Decatur st, s w cor Ralph av, 25x100. The Methodist Episcopal Hospital agt Samuel R. Good; att'y, Wm. M. Ingraham...... 9

Watkins st, w s, 100 n Sutter av, 25x100. Israel Zikind agt Elias Kaplan; action for specific performance; att'y, John L. Lindsay...... 9

Van Brunt st, s e s, 22 s w Partition st, 19x90. Catharine L. Thornley agt Charlotte Thornley; action to establish trust; att'y, Anthony Barrett.. 9

Prospect av, s s, 200 w 5th av, 20x80.2. Hannah M. E. Watkins agt Michael F. Donohue; att'ys, Wells & Waldo...... 9

Prospect av, s s, 220 w 5th av, 20x80.2. James W. B. Rockwell agt same; same att'ys...... 9

Av B, s w cor Flatbush av, runs west 476.1 to Ocean av, x south 240 x east 209.7 x again east 278 to Flatbush av, x 103.11......
Ocean av, w s, 86.1 s Av B, 244.4x75.1x229.8x187.5, Flatbush......
Stephen R. Schoonmaker agt Cornelius D. Schoonmaker; partition; att'y, John Z. Lott... 9

Fulton st, s s, 191.8 e Utica av, 16.8x100. Elizabeth Roettinger agt John Roettinger; partition; att'ys, Jas. and Thos. H. Troy...... 10

Warren st, n s, 427.6 e Utica av, 40x127.9. Lefferts G. Wilkin exr. Henry S. Wilkin agt John J. Washington; att'y, James E. Pearson...... 10

Folsom pl, s e cor Linwood st, 16.8x85. Samuel K. Free agt Frank R. Krause; att'ys, Arnoux, Ritch & Woodford...... 10

Prospect pl, n s, 467.6 e Utica av, 20x255.7 to St. Marks av, x20x255.7. Lefferts G. Wilkin exr Henry S. Wilkin agt William H. Cropsey; att'y, James E. Pearson...... 10

Eldert st, s e s, 185.8 n e Evergreen av, 17.10x100. Amelia A Van Hoesen agt John S. Gilbert; att'y, Benjamin Estes...... 10

RECORDED LEASES.

NEW YORK. *Per Year*

Bond st, No. 41, s s, bet Broadway and Bowery, all. Robert H. Neilson exr., &c., to Ignatius Auer; 3 years, from May 1, 1890...... $1,400

Broadway, No. 311, all. William W. Astor to The Fairbanks Co., a corporation; 5 years, from Feb. 1, 1892...... 18,000

Broadway, No. 1284, store in Grand Hotel. Josephine Brooks to Phillip Dreissigacker; 3 years, from May 1, 1891...... 1,800

Clinton st, Nos. 126 and 128. Rosalie M. Steele et al. exrs. Thomas McCarty and Fanny F. de Tuite to Charles Goldstein; 7 years, from May 1, 1891...... 2,400, 3,000

Elizabeth st, No. 193, all. Salomon Muller to Antonio Cardone; 5 years, from Oct. 1, 1891. 2,604

Eldridge st, No. 203, basement and store floor. Julianna D. Dahin to Katie Taiger; 5 years, from May 1, 1892.......... 480

Grand st, No. 53, store floor and basement. James O'Brien to Philip Brady; 6 years, from Dec. 4, 1891.......... 2,500

Greenwich st, No. 57, store and cellar. Levi Morris to Patrick J. Regan; 5 5-12 years, from Dec. 1, 1891.......... 1,200

Ludlow st, No. 159, all. Jacob Gebhard to Franz Geyer; 10 years, from Dec. 1, 1891.... 1,500

Mulberry st, No. 116, second floor. Marino Rettagliata and Pietro Beratta to Anselmo Gironda; 1½ years, from Sept. 1, 1891....... 339

Mulberry st, No. 115, store. Guiseppe Felino to Gennaro Cristillo; 3 years, from May 1, 1892.......... 360

Montgomery st, No. 28, store and front sub-cellar. Mary J. Mulligan to David Stevenson; 3 years, from May 1, 1893.......... 600

Nassau st, s e cor Spruce st, Room 85, third floor. American Tract Society to Felix Salomon; 1 year, from May 1, 1891.......... 400

Orchard st, No. 112, front basement, including alleyway and second floor. Claus D. Doscher to Solomon Marculescu; 5 years, from May 1, 1891.......... 900

Spring st, No. 258, store and basement. Philip L. Schell and ano. exrs Paul Schell to James L. Griffin; 5 years, from May 1, 1891....... 1,200

Varick st, No. 133, all. Philip L. Schell and ano. exrs. Paul Schell to James L. Griffin; 5 years, from May 1, 1891.......... 825

Whitehall st, No. 20½, store and part basement. Elizabeth P. and Emily P. Paulding to Edward Toman; 4 5-12 years, from Dec. 1, 1891.......... 1,200

West st, No. 23, store floor. E. Le Roy Stewart exr. and trustee Helen V. C. Stewart to Patrick Griffith; 5 years, from Oct. 1, 1891... 1,000

26th st, No. 123 W., all. Jasper F. Cropsey to Antoine Montegnon; 7 years, from April 15, 1891.......... 1,500

39th st, No. 243 W., all. B. Flanagan & Son, agents, to Belle Brown; 3 5-12 years, from Dec. 1, 1891.......... 1,800

40th st, No. 318 E., store and cellar. James M. Fitzsimons to George Kehl; 3 5-12 years, from Dec. 1, 1891.......... 300

52d st, n s, 110 e 8d av, 16.8x100.5. Martha B. T. Hopkins to Sebastian G. Brinkman; 10 years, from Jan. 1, 1891..........950, 1,000

53d st, No. 141 W., all. Frank Shephard to Hattie Ross; 4 years, 4 months, 23 days, from Dec. 9, 1891.......... 2,400

106th st, No. 174 E., store and basement. Matthew Wolf to Hermann Reinke; 4 years, from May 1, 1892.......... 1,200

Amsterdam av, No. 768, store floor and part cellar. John H. Wittpenn to Charles Golzwarden; 2 5-12 years, from Dec. 1, 1891 600

Columbus av, n w cor 85th st (The Brockholst), three stores, &c. Randolph Guggenheimer and Henry Clausen, Jr., to John G. Prague; 3 5-12 years, from Dec. 1, 1891.......... 9,600

Lexington av, No. 1848, n e cor 114th st, store and part cellar. George Schreiner to Henry Stelter; 5 years, from Dec. 1, 1891.......1,200, 1,500

Washington av, n w cor 186th st, all. Elizabeth Hooley to Abby Funk; 3 years, from Dec. 1, 1891.......... 600

1st av, No. 805, first story or floor. Mary Irving to Peter Dunn; 5 years, from May 1, 1893.......... 660

1st av, No. 805. Assign. lease. Peter Dunn to Jacob Hoffmann Brewing Co.......... nom

Same property. Assign. lease. Same to same nom

3d av, No. 2088, store and cellar. Solomon Appel and Gustav Basch to Edwin F. Hahn; 5¼ years, from Feb 1, 1891..........1,350, 1,650

3d av or Old Boston road, w s, 66 n 150th st, runs west 141 x north 59.2 x east 100 x north 4.7 x east 71 to av, x south 71 2 to beginning. Mary wife of Peter J. Zugner to George J. Hoffmann and John Angrick; 5 years, from Sept. 16, 1891..........900, 1,200

8th av, No. 2711, n w cor 144th st, store and basement. William F. Mittendorf to Charles J. Hamann; 5 years, from May 1, 1892..........1,400, 1,500

Same property. Assign. lease. Charles J. Hamann to Louis Kemnade; Dec. 8.......... nom

CHATTELS.

Note.—The first name, alphabetically arranged, is that of the Mortgagor, or party who gives the Mortgage. The "R" means Renewal Mortgage.

NEW YORK CITY.

DECEMBER 4 TO 10—INCLUSIVE.

SALOON AND RESTAURANT FIXTURES.

Anton & Kertabau. 193 Allen....Restaurant Furnishing Co. Restaurant. $51

Amchanitzky, Lizzie. 148 East Broadway....J Paley. Restaurant Fixtures. 300

Arras, William. 301 W 59th....J C G Hupfel B Co. 5,000

Bauer, Louisa. 125 and 127 Park row....G Ehret. 13,000

Becker, Geo. 11 Eldridge....S Liebmann's B Co. 950

Boswell, John. 805 1st av..J Hoffmann B Co. 5,000

Bombay, Elise. 887 W 38th....G Bechtel, exr of. 450

Bombay, Geo. 448 W 41st..G Bechtel, exr of. 400

Branagan, John. 71 Roosevelt..Bernheimer & S. Pool Table, (R) 120

Bielemeier, Joseph. 1222 2d av....Budweiser B Co. 1,500

Bingay, S F. 684 Greenwich....J R Hogg. 2,000

Bionadi, Michele. 245 Elizabeth....Budweiser B Co. 400

Buttell, J J. 2785 8th av....Bernheimer & S. Pool Table. 140

Caffrey & McNally. 1827 2d av....T O Reilly. 1,000

Cenillo, Francesco. 655 E 149th....D Mayer. (R) 100

Callahan, W F. 1897 4th av....Wagner & S. Pool. 150

Conway, M J. 348 E 11th....Bernheimer & S. 500

Coyle & Lennon. 232 W 19th....Bernheimer & S. Pump. 81

Same. 231 W 19th....same. Ice House. 200

Same. 438 and 440 W 54th....same. Ice House. 120

Same. 440 W 54th....same. Pump. 82

Cullen, Bernard. 1887 2d av....J Ables B Co (R) 850

Daniel, Fennie. 8 Elizabeth....H B Scharmann. & Sons. 800

Dierking, Henry. 875 Canal....J Eichler B Co. (R) 2,445

Donnelly, Elwood. 427 W 40th....India Wharf B Co. (R) 400

Deyerberg, H n. 175 Madison av....Bernheimer & Schwartz (R) 2,500

Donnelly, Mathew. Greenwich and Horatio sts ..Bernheimer & S. Pump. 62

Same....same. Ice House. 110

Eggers & Heusmann. 19 Crosby and 138 Grand ....G Von Glahn. (R) 6,600

Enders, William 1804 2d av....G Ringler & Co. 800

Eisengrein, Adam. 1117 Olin av....J Eichler B Co. (R) 800

Finnigan, Jas. 1169 1st av....G Ebret. 4,000

Flatow, Richard. 160 8th av....H F Seidel. Restaurant Fixtures. 250

Freeknecht & Day. 221 Bowery...R Mock. Billiards security for rent

Fessler, George. 866 7th av....V Loewers. (R) 600

Flannery, J P. 535 Hudson....C Stein. (R) 2,194

Fleich, Albert. 832 1st av....F Oppermann, Jr. 440

Fagan, Eugene. 567 11th av....D Stevenson. (R) 800

Feucht, Matthias. 201 Forsyth....J Eichler B Co. 800

Godfrey, Kate E. 1863 2d av... G Ebret. 6,000

Grundhoefer, Louis. 1898 2d av....D Stevenson. 2,700

Gammino, Frank. 426 E 118th....D Stevenson. 400

Grande, Nicola. 66 South 5th av....Bernheimer & S. 525

Gregg, James. 440 Pleasant av....G Ringler & Co. 1,500

Guirato, Michael. 217 Mott....H B Scharmann. (R) 600

Gutmann, Henry. 1663 1st av....V Loewers. 500

Hamberger, Otto. 119 East Houston....J Eichler B Co. (R) 3,000

Herman, Israel. 94 Hester... Restaurant Furnishing Co. Restaurant Fixtures. 160

Holnig, Louis. 435 E 13th....India Wharf B Co. (R) 500

Hughes, Patrick. 1724 3d av....G Ringler & Co. 932

Hachtmann, Andrew. 63 E 9th....S Liebmann's Sons B Co. 1,000

Henken, H D. 747 2d av..L Krominger. Restaurant Fixtures. (R) 1,700

Hertel & Nitschke. 413 Broadway... S Liebmann's Sons B Co. 1,000

Hoexter, David. 215 1st av ...Bernheimer & S. (R) 2,500

Hainbach, Louis. 58 E 4th....J Hoffmann B Co. 1,000

Halpin, Luke. 849 10th av... J Ruppert. 3,000

Heyer, P W. 1566 9th av....A Ridal. 4,000

Heyman, Joseph. 24 Division....B Meier. Restaurant Fixtures. 460

Halbert Bros. 110 Prince....Lemcke & Doscher. 3,000

Hall, R H. 18 Spring....Beadleston & W. (R) 3,000

Heller, Jacob. 58 Ridge....F Ibert. 1,500

Kempf, Barbara. 36 Delancey....Bernheimer & S. (R) 900

Klein, R & J. 317 W 145th....J Kress B Co. 50

Kemnade, Louis. 2711 8th av....Bernheimer & S. 2,000

Kinogen, John. 318 4th av....Brunswick-B-C Co. Pool Table. 90

Kehl, Geo. 318 E 40th ..J Ruppert. 600

Kretschoer, Oscar. 370 E 10th....G Ehret. (R) 700

Kadel, M J. 1141 Madison av....J Everard. 3,035

Kahn, Morris. 731 Washington....D Mayer. (R) 1,500

Kasner, A and A. 26 Hester....H B Scharmann & Son. 2,500

Kowalewsky, Hugo. 108 E 8th.... J Kuntz B Co. 400

Kramer, A E. 1081 3d av ...India Wharf B Co. (R) 425

Lavelle, J H. 10-14 Doyer....V Loewers. 800

Leibler, Valentine. 309 E 26th....H Koehler & Co. 1,000

Lynch, James. 253 Rivington... P Doelger. 1,500

Lione, Genarro. 437 E 115th....Bernheimer & S. Pool Table. (R) 140

Lieber, Alphonse. 504 10th av....E Werner. Restaurant Fixtures. 170

Lienan, Emil. 104 E 14th....W L Flanagan. 3,000

London, W. 265 E 122d....Bernheimer & S. Ice House. 90

May, Frank. 193 South....I Roth. 525

McDermott, John. 349 W 52d....Bernheimer & S. Ice House. 90

McMahon, J F. 724 2d av....R Connor. (R) 2,500

Moormann, Henry. 75 Gouverneur....F Oppermann, Jr. (R) 275

Mauser, John. 194½ Allen....Anchor B Co. (R) 410

McGivney, Owen. 721 11th av....Bavarian B Co. 1,800

McMahon, J F. 473 6th av....B Hauser. Restaurant Fixtures. (R) 800

McSweeney, Michael. 1493 1st av....Bernheimer & S. (R) 2,000

Masterson, Chas. 500 1st av....H Koehler & Co. 3,400

McCormick, W J. 819 Stanton....C Zwisler. 200

McEntee, James. 425 W 26th....Burr B Co. (R) 1,300

Meyerson, C S. 113 Hester....H & S Levene. Restaurant Fixtures. 140

Mueller, H P. 185 E 3d....W Peter B Co. 800

McBride, P F. 838 11th av....C Stein. (R) 400

McCormack, Ralph. 426 W 31st....D Stevenson. (R) 50

McCourt, John. 2261 7th av....J Ruppert. (R) 1,700

Meurer, Solomon. 117 Pitt....F Ibert. 300

Nigey, August. 1041 3d av....G Ehret. (R) 4,500

Nichols, Marion L. 768 5th av ..P Doelger. 4,000

O'Brien, D J....P Doelger. Ice House. 115

O'Brien, John. Foot E 92d st....I L Devoe. ½ int. 350

Perry, William. 87 Front....G Ringler & Co. 235

Pick, Morris. 218 E 89th....H Koehler & Co. 450

Payne, Robert. 588 11th av....Bernheimer & S. Ice House. 115

Quinn & Stewart. Rockaway Beach J Webb. Hotel Fixtures. (R) 55,000

Regan, P J. 57 7th av....P Ballantine & Sons. 1,500

Rosenthal, Samuel. 10 Essex....H B Scharmann & Sons. (R) 800

Ryan & Brady. 58 Grand....J Hoffmann B Co. 7,000

Rath, H M. 218 E 5.d....Schmitt & S. 500

Rosenthal, Max. 134th st and Madison av.... Bernheimer & S. Ice House. 90

Rousseau, J P and J E. Pulitzer Building....A Westheimer. Restaurant Fixtures. 185

Reinke, Herrmann. 174 E 106th....Bernheimer & S. 1,600

Romano, R. 325 E 115th....Bernheimer & S. Ice House. 160

Salusch, I. 77 Eldridge....B Cohen. 125

Stelter, Henry. 1848 Lexington av....Bernheimer & S. 4,000

Stoll, Geo. 183 Mott....Bernheimer & S. Ice House. 70

Same....same. Ice House. 200

Same....same. Pump. 81

Same....same. Pump. 111

Sheehan, Jeremiah. 410 E 18th....D Mayer B Co. 550

Siegel & Frankel. 44 Orchard....Burger B Co. 550

Spiwak, Ludwig. 89 Allen....D Stevenson. 3,000

Sprague, E N. 1718 2d av....Restaurant Furnishing Co. Restaurant Fixtures. 45

Stehlik, John. 208 E 102d....P & W Ebling B Co. 600

Stoehr, Chas. 1385 3d av....Brunswick-B-C Co. Pool Table. 225

Summerfield, Annie. 17 Clinton pl....Bavarian B Co. 1,000

Thompson & Gavigan. 90 South ...J Everard. 2,500

Teichman, E B. 527 5th av....D M Koehler & Son. 500

Thoemes, William. 210 W 26th....M Groh's Sons. 500

Toman, Edward. 20½ Whitehall....G Ehret. 1,500

Von Shrely, William. 327 West....J H Bereuter. Pool Table. 400

Von der Lieth, J D. 183 William....Lemcke & Doscher. 1,367

Wagner, Michael. 284 Greenwich....D L Kellam. Restaurant. 8,000

Weiss, Rebecca. 326 East Houston...A B Marx. Pool. 200

Wezel, Mrs M. 9 1st ...Anchor B Co. Pump. 100

Wertheim, A. 188 E 104th....J H Bereuter. Pool Table. 280

Wettach, John. 5 Morris ...J Ruppert. (R) 1,500

HOUSEHOLD FURNITURE.

Archibald, C H. 150 E 27th .. Manges Bros. 332

Alvarez, Joseph. 171 E 107th....J Moriarty. 194

Adams, Emma. 149 W 27th ...O'Farrell & Co. 218

Albrecht, Joseph. 148 E 84th....Dreisacker & Co. (R) 105

Avallone, Mathew. 421 E 15th....H S Eisler. 111

Brogan, Nellie. 351 W 11th....H S Eisler. 105

Byron, Lydia. 788 2d av....H S Eisler. 172

Beatty, S G. 303 E 122d....B M Cowperthwait & Co. 293

Bedell, Mrs S. 1556 Broadway....B M Cowperthwait & Co. 197

Begley, D J. 67 E 105th....B M Cowperthwait & Co. 288

Bletcher, Mrs Thos. 525 W 126th....B M Cowperthwait & Co. 180

Blue, L W. 69 W 106th ...W J Ruddell. 300

Brown, Henrietta. 117 Waverly pl ...B M Cowperthwait & Co. 351

Burke, Aggie. 9 Pell ...B M Cowperthwait & Co. 116

Byrnes, Claud. 484 W 54th....B M Cowperthwait & Co. 361

Bateman, Belle. 3 5th av....J W Thompson. 5,000

Baum, Bernbat. 1618 9th av....J J Coogan. 157

Baues, Mrs J H. 438 W 29th....O'Farrell & Co. 168

Bergan, Nellie....R M Walters. Piano. 210

Berry, M. 312 W 44th....J Moran. 195

Bettels, W E. 729 E 146th....American Guarantee Assoc. 100

Blake, Mabel. 145 W 53d....Alexander Bros. 100

Bondy, M. 80 E 116th....H Thoesen. 284

Borot, Harriet E....J W E Wetmore. 700

Buisson, Geo. 444 W 27th....Jordan, M & Co. 339

Brown, Mrs Wm. 323 E 89th.... J H Little. 199

Beers, J B. 200 W 59th....R L Epstein. 500

Block, Irene. 148 W 17th ...Garvey Bros. 318

Bohl, Arna. 71 Rivington....Emanuel Gross. 350

Both, F W. 210 E 121st....J A Paxton. 400

Brosche, Carl. 38 E 7th....Manges Bros. (R) 147

Burmeister, Henry. 1601 Lexington av....W E Wheelock & Co. Piano. (R) 230

Castle, Mary. 235 E 33d....Garvey Bros. 162

Clemour, Mary. 1988 Lexington av....A R Maxwell. 100

Colon, Lizzie C. 103 W 14th....W Weed. 220

Conklin, William. 2489 2d av....Spies Bros. 125

Cozzens, S D. 240 W 136th....R Knapp & Co. 479

Cain, Rose. 108 W 102d....O'Farrell & Co. 244

Camp, P F and W S. 310 W 127th... American Guarantee Assoc. 100

Carter, F. 199 3d av R M Walters. Piano. 135

Casey, Mary. 853 E 170th....J J Coogan. 135

Conway, W E. 40 and 42 E 25th....Garvey Bros. 275

Coopers Alfred....Fennell & P. 446

Cope, Ethel. 1954 3d av....J J Coogan. 157

Cahill, Mary E. 3 Bethune....Jordan & M. 175

Colbert, Martha. 222 W 62d.... W J Ruddell. 200

Craig, Emma. 63 E 4th.... Jordan & M. 138

Cutter, Delia. 608 6th av ..E D Farrell. 168

Davis, Michael. 125 E 11th....I Goetz. 600

Dettinger, Maria. 436 E 66th....A Hafelin. Piano. 165

Da Prato, Marie. 146 Macdougal....B M Cowperthwait & Co. 540

de Jough, Bertha O. 122 E 114th.... A Kling. 341

Derr, L P. 107 E 89th....B M Cowperthwait & Co. 348

Doherty, Marie. 42 Perry.... B M Cowperthwait & Co. 184

Dow, A J. 59th st and 10th av....W J Ruddell. 150

De Angelis, Laure. 80 W 82d....J Baumann. 185

Davidson, Maud M. 200 E 102d....Dreisacker & Co. 158

de Serent, Armand. 59 W 105th.. Dreisacker & Co. (R) 178

Drugan, Margaret 504 W 45th....J Baumann 140

Duke, Georgie. 220 E 18th ..J Gregg. (R) 296

Engel, Gustav. 104 and 106 E 4th....J Baumann. 148

Eager, E W, Mrs. 106 W 102d....J H Little. 336

Ehrlich, David. 160 E 66th....American Guarantee Assoc. 200

Evans, Florence E. 790 6th av....J J Coogan. (R) 292

Ferguson, F S. 30 W 105th....L Baumann. (R) 145

Foster, Victorine A. 63 W 92d....Manges Bros. (R) 122

Fuhst, Annie. 630 St Anns av....W E Wheelock & Co. Piano. (R) 150

Farrington, T W. 248 W 16th....J H Little. 120

Feeney, P. Miss, 20 South 5th av....Simpson & P. Piano. (R) 215

Fitch, Florence. 150 W 16th....J Cagney. 144

Fleitner, Albert. 210 E 122d....J J Coogan. 309

Freedman, Chas. 324 E 85th....J H Little. 186

Fromenson, Dora. 101 East Broadway....A Hafelin. Piano. 296

Fitzsimmons, John. 111 W 33d....Jordan & M. 186

Foley, Mamie. 471 Lenox av ...M A Potter. 125

Galloway, Minnie. 312 W 27th....O'Farrell & Co. 363

Gibbs, F W. 42 W 64th....O'Farrell & Co. 299

Glover, Ida. 118 W 83d....J Baumann. 888

Gidley, Lewis. 217 E 136th....Jordan & M. 180

Goldhorn, Chas. 1680 Bathgate av....J Baumann. 194
Gallagher, Anne. 7 Stryker lane....B M Cowperthwait & Co. 121
Gorman & Walsh. 258 Elizabeth...B M Cowperthwait & Co. 132
Greene, Mamie. 745 10th av....B M Cowperthwait & Co. 126
Gutierrey, C. 168 E 90th....B M Cowperthwait & Co. 322
Gallagher, Mary E. 222 E 25th....R M Walters. Piano. (R) 138
Gallagher, T. 176 Richardson st, Brooklyn....Alexander Bros. 177
Giles, J E and S H. Storage, &c....F Lugar. 1,000
Giullaum, Josephine. 134 Macdougal....J Moriarty. 164
Gordon, Clari. 93 Allen....J Moriarty. 191
Gordon, Margaret. 301 W 41st....Garvey Bros. 100
Gozler, W H. 329 9th av....J Moriarty. 188
Green, Jennette. 481 E 27th....Garvey Bros. 102
Goldsmith, Minnie. 246 E 105th....R M Walters. Piano. (R) 180
Howard, Mary E. 104 W 52d....J F Manges. (R) 250
Hubbard, H A. 340 W 23d....Mathushek & Son Piano Co. Piano. 265
Hague, Lottie. 208 Bleecker....Garvey Bros. 237
Hays, F J. 116 W 16th....O'Farrell & Co. 180
Hersey, Mrs B R. 756 Broadway....A Hafelin. Piano. 167
Hotel Vendome Co....W and J Sloane. 9,157
Horner, Julia E. 241 E 85th....Garvey Bros. 108
Hunken, Annie. 305 E 113th....Fennell & Pye. 126
Hamann, G H. 275 Pleasant av....F Pruhs. Piano. 100
Haney, Lizzie. 695 3d av....B M Cowperthwait & Co. 117
Hearn, Annie. 379 3d av....Jordan & M. 140
Heefgatt, Sarah. 388 Grand....B M Cowperthwait & Co. 130
Hensley, Mrs H A. 812 Lexington av....T Kelly. 133
Hiller, J S. 69 W 106th....L Baumann. 391
Jeckel, Z. 250 E 10th....L Baumann. 218
Jewett, F P. 237 W 18th....B M Cowperthwait & Co. 158
Johnston, Anna. 230 E 93d....Jordan, M & Co. 109
Johnson, Mrs E K. 36 W 24th....J H Little. 207
Jaenike, Ellen. 172 E 72d....J Baumann. 905
Johst, Paul. 337 E 88th....H S Eisler. 453
Johnson, Fannie. 33 W 61st and 335 and 337 W 59th....J C Rutledge. 1,500
Kirk, Alice. 51 Bethune....M Donohue. 155
Keane, M J. 443 E 78th....H Israel & Son. 297
Kenney, Kate. 393 E 84th....J Baumann. 199
Kirk, Mrs L A. 240-254 W 52d....S Knapp & Co. 1,650
Kauffmann, Geo. 102 W 30th....J Moriarty. 210
Kauffman, Maurice. 122 W 31st....J Moriarty. 153
Kaufmann, Samuel. 70 St Marks pl....Brooklyn F Co. 258
Kellam, D L. 284 Greenwich....Lincoln I and G Assoc. 1,100
Kelledy, Mary. 275 Hudson....J McEnery & Co. 144
Kerwin, Nora. 517 E 82d....J Moran. 402
Kipp, Carrie E. 221 W 40th....J Moriarty. 422
Koehler, Antonette. 2239 3d av....A Koehler. 500
Krueger, Amalia. 905 Cauldwell av....A Hafelin. Piano. 125
Kennedy, Robert. 57 1st av....Jordan & M. 152
King D W. 140 E 48th....E D Farrell. (R) 215
Kinnear, R O. 46 W 17th....A Smith. 100
Lapenta, Maria. 93 E 10th....J Moriarty. 209
Lawrence, G H. 227 W 43d....W J Ruddell. 633
Lilienfeld, Amelia. 157 E 108th....Krakauer Bros. Piano. 175
Lloyd, A A. 1334 3d av....B M Cowperthwait & Co. 300
Lander, W A. 22 W 17th....Estey Piano Co. Piano. 250
Leon, Marion. 8 E 110th....H Thoesen. 174
Lynch, Mary. 2009 1st av....Fennell & Pye. 160
Lewis, Samuel. 306 E 125th....Dreisacker & Co. (R) 102
Lieban, Louis. 429 E 79th....H S Eisler. 134
Lezore, Matilda. 120 E 34th....S Katz. 104
Lee, Mrs E F. 214 W 25th....S Knapp & Co. 313
Lee, R E. 411 W 18th....M Bradley. 100
Maile, Amlia. 68th st and Western Boulevard....S O'Brien. 278
Marvin, Helen. 136 W 40th....R Wilson. 3,500
Mason, Mrs C. 2147 3d av....S I Herschmann. 138
Matthews, Grace. 178 Forsyth....J Moriarty. 117
Mathews, Mary E. 225 1st av....F G Smith. Piano. (R) 100
McCarty, Eleanor M. 151 E 29th....J Moriarty. 144
McNulty, T. 99 E 4th....J Moriarty. 167
Marks, Rudolph. 83 Orchard....J Rubenstein. 156
Marsh, Sarah. 341 E 37th....J Baumann. 180
Maple, M M. 322 Columbus av....J Baumann. 226
McDonald, Mrs John. 463 W 52d....O'Farrell & Co. 145
McGarry, Mary. 455 W 27th....O'Farrell & Co. 167
Maciern, Wallace. 200 W 39th....O'Farrell & Co. 228
Madi, E T. 59th st and Madison av....J H Little. 1,513
Merse, Mrs. 90 E 8th....J J Coogan. 172
Melville, P S. 5 Vandam....R M Walters. Piano. 140
Mendelsohn, Theresa. 177 E 108th....H Israel & Sons. 159
Merry, Mary. 542 E 117th....Fennell & Pye. 114
McCleery, S J. 357 W 34th....J H Little. 936
Mignot, A. 207 E 23d....Garvey Bros. 112
Miquet, Jules. 902 8th av....O'Farrell & Co. 155
Montemar, Diego. 344 E 123th....J J Coogan. (R) 118
Moore, Rebecca P. 108 W 49th....Fifth Avenue Storage Co. Piano. (R) 100
Morse, Martha J. 84 W 133d....Fennell & Pye. 142
Murtha, Patrick. 230 E 49th....Garvey Bros. 106
Maguire, Mamie. 318 E 35th....B M Cowperthwait & Co. 199
Mahoney, Eliza....J Moriarty. 156
Martin, Margaret. 472 W 22d....W J Ruddell. 157
Same....same. 157
Monge, Bianca. 100 Av A....Jordan & M. 190
Misell, Henry. 207 E 114th....S Waterman. 500
Murray, Mrs Thos. 110 W 83d....T Kelly. 889
Martel, Maria A. 102 W 29th....C E Smith. 2,000
McBride, Anna. 2381 Lorillard pl....Jordan & M. 105
Nilson, Nils. 342 E 24th....Garvey Bros. 115
Needham, J T & M E. 18 E 118th....H Olbhorst. 250
O'Brien, Mrs. 428 W 42d....J Moran. 121
O'Brien, T F. 170 E 89th....J Moriarty. 270
Odorff, Ella V. 86 1st av....H Thoesen. 290
Prentice, C H. 252 W 38th....B M Cowperthwait & Co. 461
Palmer, Phoebe. 228 E 120th....Jordan, M & Co. 104
Pinard, Louise. 67 W 88th....M Fell. 1,400
Pomerby, Mamie. 140 W 83d....O'Farrell & Co. 142
Parker, Eugene. 1014 1st av....H S Eisler. 810
Parker, Harry. 1318 3d av....J Baumann. 130
Pierce, Nina. 231 W 41st....J Baumann. 168
Plauchenault, Mrs G. 64 South 5th av....O'Farrell & Co. 187
Prentiss, Lizzie. 562 7th av....J Baumann. 157
Quigg, J T. 39 E 50th....J J Coogan. 158
Quincy, J D. 85 7th av....R M Walters. Piano. (R) 190
Redlich, Estelle. 222 W 21st....A Riesenberg. 240
Ross, Hattie. 141 W 53d....F Shephard. 3,000
Rosenberg, M L. 2180 and 2182 5th av....Financial Credit Co. 100
Ruel, Emma L. 211 W 21st....Manges Bros. 147
Raymond, Mrs Frank. 330 W 21st....J F Doherty & Co. 248
Roberts, Rosalin. 249 W 21st....G Beck. 306
Rogers, Annie. 529 W 52d....Garvey Bros. 117
Rosenblatt, H. 978 3d av....S Heyman Co. 124
Ruch & Eierschmalz. 43 Forsyth....E Gerken. 1,850
Radzinsky, Henry. 105 W 105th....B M Cowperthwait & Co. 175
Reilly, J B. 555 W 159th....E D Farrell. (R) 137
Rendon, Julia. 1195 3d av....B M Cowperthwait & Co. 150
Reardon, Margaret. 350 E 13th....Jordan, M & Co. 143
Rice, E E. 1267 Broadway....W H Webb. 516
Richman, Mina. 187 7th av....Jordan, M & Co. 145
Stewart, Archibald. 426 W 52d....J Baumann. 136
Spotton, Mary. 229 E 73d....J Baumann. 159
Samuels, B S. 129 W 67th....W J Ruddell. 133
Schmidt, Jane. 444 Willis av....B Groll. 800
Scudder, L B. 124 W 102d....J Moriarty. 198
Spelman, Annie. 380 3d av....L Baumann. 160
Sutherton, Maggie. 446 East Houston....B M Cowperthwait & Co. 180
Sanz, Mariano. 30 and 32 W 15th....J H Little. 400
Schreimer, J F. 189 Chrystie....Dreisacker & Co. 160
Schrieber, William. 100 Ridge....Estey Piano Co. Piano. 225
Schuyler, Sarah R and Chas E. 216 West End av....W Leonard. (R) 2,000
Serini, F. 206 E 48th....F Mayers. 346
Stretton, Anna B. 249 W 103d....R M Walters. Piano. 297
Starrock, William. 19 Greenwich av....Garvey Bros. 118
Streep, Ida. 43 W 27th....J J Coogan. (R) 292
Sullivan, Joseph. 19 Watts....J J Coogan. 117
Seaman, Anna A. 119 Waverley pl....W P Ryman. 200
Searing, Josephine. 1 Washington av....J Gregg & Co. 115
Shoen, Marcus. 201 Broome....A Stark. 100
Thorpe, Sadie. 289 E 29th....H Israel & Son. 202
Tierney, M W. 62 Macdougal....B M Cowperthwait & Co. 253
Turner, Mrs M. 751 Washington....T Kelly. 131
Tisne, Henriette. 27 W 61st....O'Farrell & Co. 473
Tyndale, F L. 360 E 70th....J M Emerson. 50
Vogt, Otto. 840 E 165th....Fennell & Pye. 128
Van Clief, C. 883 Park av and 101 78th st....B H De Roes & Co. 497
Viau, Mariana. 60 E 12th....E C Hodges. 500
Van Buren, John. 53 West Houston....M Donohue. 154
Wallace, Matilda. 135 W 14th....A Landon. 706
Way, T J. 252 W 34th....L Baumann. (R) 235
West, F B. 145 W 11th....W H Knowles. (R) 2,000
Whitlock, L. 304 W 14th....S M Williamson. Pictures, &c. 566
Willis, John. 283 E 28th....J Moriarty. 106
Wright, I E. 1988 Madison av....S J Wright. 1,650
Warber, Agbes. 111 E 118th....Dreisacker & Co. 197
Wendell, Libbie. 79 E 118th....J Baumann. 888
Weigart, Emil. 67 W 11th....J Baumann. 327
Ward, Mrs E....J Moriarty. 210
Woodbridge, Annie. 254 W 16th....L Baumann. 169
Wallace, Mrs W A. 411 W 56th....J H Little. 250
Walsh, T W. 311 E 41st....J Moran. 413
Warner, Mrs E N. 1737 Madison av....Estey Piano Co. Piano. 370
West, H G. 71st st and Park av....J H Little. 250
Wehrlen, Mrs L. 8 W 65th....Estey Piano Co. Piano. 526
White, Joseph. 46 Oliver....H Israel & Son. 129
Whitney, S D. Riverdale, N Y....M J Cox. 800
Williams, Alfred. 148 W 50th....O'Farrell & Co. (R) 109
Wilson, Belle. 122 W 15th....J Moriarty. (R) 105
Wissler, Jos. 515 E 83d....J H Little. 971
Zimmermann, Mrs L. 156 W 35th....Brooklyn F Co. 202
Zimmermann, Nettie. 101 E 30th....J Moriarty. (R) 102
Zabriskie, W E. 438 E 143d....O'Farrell & Co. 228
Zahn, Josephine. 118 E 115th....Dreisacker & Co. 114

MISCELLANEOUS.

Alexander, James. 80 E 125th....Marvin Safe Co. Safe. 185
American Diamond Rock Boring Machine Co. 41 Van Brunt st, Brooklyn....F Semken. Drills, &c. 2,800
Same....same. Drills, &c. 1,500
Arndt, Theodore. 854 Columbus av....H Reiss. Drug Fixtures. 3,700
Antony, Carl. 5th av and 90th st....G H Stonebridge, Jr. Horses, &c. (R) 4,000
Antony & Runk. 5th av and 90th st....G H Stonebridge, Jr. Horses, &c. (R) 4,000
Auerbach, Ruben. 107 Essex....Manhattan Type Co. Press, &c. 90
Averell, H H. 58 E 85th....J Burlinson. Horse, Milk Wagon, &c. 50
Basch, G C. 971 3d av....E Steiner. Office Fixtures. 50
Boccalino, Paul. 110 Goerck....P Andolfe. Store Fixtures. 50
Bosch, Henry. 2114 3d av....J W Tufts. Soda Fixtures. (R) 175
Bedell, R C. 639 Greenwich....H Snyder. Horses, Trucks, &c. 6,500
Brooks & Goldstein. 145 East Broadway....Van Allens & B. Press. (R) 57
Barton, S M. 65 E 125th....J W Tufts. Soda Fixtures. (R) 700
Beck, M L. 447 Broadway and 314 and 316 Canal....A Schulder. Machines. 450
Bueaus, Max and Bucan Bucans. 59 Canal....Photo Fixtures. 210
Central Iron Works. 203 E 30th....W S Andrews. Machinery. (R) 10,000
Colwell, J J. 306 W 4th....Racine Wagon Co. Wagon. 75
Cuff, George. 2 E 97th....I O Blake. Horses, Wagons, &c. (R) 410
Calcagno, Vito. 79 Broome....C Antonino. Barber Fixtures. 75
Carter, R J....M Armstrong & Co. Coach. (R) 1,000
Calvert & Richardson. 47 John....Liberty Machine Works. Press. 550
Cohen, William. 5 Elizabeth....A D Puffer & Sons. Soda Fixtures. (R) 3,500
Cook, J W. 326 W 52d....L J Cook. Horses, Trucks, &c. 475
Cracrkis, Josef. 48 Clinton....J Stewart. Machinery. 65
Citron, Herman. 866 E 3d....E Weil & Co. Machines. 165
Cohn, Nettie. 148 Essex....J Cohn. Store Fixtures. 150
Cole, C R. 275 6th av....W W Deane. Photo Fixtures. 175
Conklin, G W. 1076 1st av....J R Haug. Butcher Fixtures. 600
Diehne & Kamenetsky. 223 Monroe....C Dierking. Butcher Fixtures. 130
Dentel, Paul. 580 E 118th....C Deikek. Horse, Wagon, &c. 180
Dehan, Victor. 152 and 154 Thompson....J J Byrne. Furnished Rooms, &c. 560
De Leo & Brogna. 16 Franklin....G Lordi. Barber Fixtures. 45
Davis, J T....J Davis. Horse. (R) 170
Davis, L W....M Armstrong. Coach. 1,500
Dellaglio & Miducci. 48 Cherry, 4 Chatham sq....M A Cohn, et al. Barber Fixtures. 500
de Matteis, Alfonso. 762 3d av....P Westphal. Barber Fixtures. 500
Durand, Ferdinand. 494 Columbus av....D T Pulsifer. Barber Fixtures. 200
Eggers, John. 304 E 60th....H Heimbruch. Horse, Wagon, &c. 375
Egan, J J. 281 E 43d....Hincks & J. Cab. (R) 325
Eichhorn, Fredericke. 2469 3d av....T F Murphy. Cigar Fixtures. 150
Empire State Type Founding Co. 15 Frankfort....P H Bresnan. Machinery, &c. (R) 2,000
Same....G Wilks, exr of. Machinery, &c. (R) 2,407
Fox, Patrick. 615 W 54th....L Heilbrunn. Horses, Carts, &c. 607
Finkensieper, P A. 127 Crosby....A Tapfer. Machinery, &c. 900
Freiberger & Feldstein. 364 and 366 E 3d....P Sorger. Machines. 200
Freymuller, Fritz. 389 6th....J Weiss. Barber Fixtures. (R) 42
Fuller, W N, Jr. 429 Canal....A D Puffer & Sons. Soda Fixtures. (R) 185
Freeman, Isaac. 156 E 105th....Merchants' Roll Paper Co. Horse, Wagon, &c. security
Gentsch & Miller. 179 E 105th....L Schauermann. Barber Fixtures. (R) 200
Greenbaum, R. 21 East Broadway....Mosler Safe Co. Safe. 205
Gambee & Normoyle....W A Burton. Horse and Wagon. 100
Glander, Chas. 388 Bleecker....Gerdes & M. Bakery Fixtures. 782
Goldstein, Moses. 114 Ludlow....N Siegel. Horse, Wagon, &c. 75
Green, William. Franklin sq....Van Allens & B. Press. (R) 958
Grey, C W, Jr. 909 6th av....Liberty Machine Works. Press. 686
Same....same. Press. 230
Gillman, A H. 66 Oliver....E Berger. Butcher Fixtures. 65
Guilfoyle, Anna M....J Rothschild. Horses, &c. 125
George & Brooke....P Stroebel & Sons. Tables. 294
Gibson & Veritzan. 154-156 E 53d....Hincks & J. Coach. 2,550
Gurwitz, Josel. 41 Essex....E A Aronstamm. Drug Fixtures. 375
Goldthwaite, J C. 132 Nassau....S Goldthwaite. Maps, &c. 2,800
Handwerker, Louis. 190 Columbus av....G Bauer. Tailor Fixtures. 80
Herrmann, Armin. 2584 8th av....F W Bietz. Drug Fixtures. 2,000
Hillis Plantation Coffee Co. 521 Washington....G H Richardson. Machinery. 2,500
Houston, West St & Pavonia Ferry R R Co....N Y Security and Trust Co. Franchises, &c. 6,000,000
Hammel, Henry. 9 Murray....A W Pfluger. Office Fixtures, &c. 3,000
Hosnedel, Frank....G Dessecker. Coach. (R) 200
Halpin, Peter. 520 Broome....Nat Cash Reg Co. Register. 175
Hartshorn, J W. 142 E 59th....Hincks & Johnson. Coach. 825
Heinrich, Francis. 218 Centre....Liberty Machine Works. Press. 384
Hesse, A A. 134 E 38th and 49 W 3d....H Guinard. Stock, Fixtures, &c. 2,700
Hinning Bros & Roemer. 9 and 11 Baxter....J Kenneallie & Co. Machinery. 400
Hofert, W. 53d st and 3d av....D Kress. Drug Fixtures. 5,500
Hardenburgh & Charter. 2414 8th av....S F Andrews. Confectionery Fixtures. 1,200
Howie, G W....J Cunningham Son & Co. Coach. 725
Hufnagel, Philip. 391 Bleecker....J Goebel. Butcher Fixtures. 200
Jones, J L, Jr. 59 Liberty....G W Page. Office Fixtures. 200
Kimpell, M and S C. 16 Beaver....G W Rothamel. Barber Fixtures. 674
Kane, M. 2118 2d av....Nat Cash Reg Co. Register. 200
Keely Bros....M Armstrong & Co. Coach. (R) 1,300
Kelly, Edward. 156 W 4th....C F Aschenbach. Coach. 700
Kochendorfer, Aug. 116 South 5th av....F Hermann. Machinery. 100
Kussmaul, Chas. 215 Willis av....C F Albrecht. Grocery Fixtures. 380
Kallage, E F. 76 E 14th....L Wirtz. Store Fixtures. 105
Kelly, W H. 1046 6th av....E C Evans. Butcher Fixtures. 1,000
Kieferdorf, F F. 315 Columbus av....J Mathews Co. Soda Fixtures. 650
Kind, Rosa. 1545 2d av....A Heller & Bro. Laundry Fixtures. (R) 790
Levy, Hyman. 54 Orchard....C Dierking. Butcher Fixtures. 180
Linscott, John A. 527 W 52d....D Meenau. Office Fixtures. 81
Levin & Hirschmann. 246 and 248 Monroe....C Dierking. Butcher Fixtures. 216
Lichtenstein, Jenny. 27 West Houston....H Sidenberg. Machinery, &c. secures rent
Lewis, F T. 190 E 84th....J Burlinson. Horse, Milk Wagon, &c. 25
Lang, Albert. 209 E 74th....J Weiss. Barber Fixtures. (R) 148
Leffler, John. 143 Norfolk....C H C Beake. Grocery Fixtures. 100
Little, G K. 17-27 Vandewater....Van Allens & B. Press. 550

Loblin, Joseph. 68 E 12th....F Welsh. Engine. 150
London, Jakob. 12 Essex.....G Goldmann. Butcher Fixtures. 150
Luzzi, Constantino. 222 East Broadway....C Tarabella. Barber Fixtures. 142
Lynch, Thomas. 334 8th av....Nat Cash Reg Co. Register. 200
Lynn, Lucy E. 186 W 4th....J Cunningham, Son & Co. Coach. 1,200
Martin, D A & Co. 48 E 12th....A Palmer. Machinery. (R) 2,000
Miller, Solomon. 139 East Broadway....F Miller. Horse, Store Fixtures, &c. 3,000
Mackey, Joseph. 108 Liberty....J Conner's Sons. Printing Fixtures. 595
Mackey, Joseph. 305 W 125th....Eardley & W. Press, &c. 215
Magner, David, 124 W 54th....W Daisley. Horses. 85
Mannara, Vincenzo. 317 Madison....M Torriso. Barber Fixtures. 175
McCabe, J H. 565 7th av....B L McCabe Electric Fixtures. 375
McGeorge, P A. 220 and 222 William. Van Allens & B. Press. (R) 1,450
Meade, Fred. Jersey City, N J....B Weill. Horse, &c. (R) 825
Meyers, Geo ..E Muller Horses &c (R) 1,200
Monday, Lizzie. 439 3d av ...D Buckner. Cigar Fixtures, Horse, &c. 2,000
Moran, J. 3d av and 12th st....Nat Cash Reg Co. Register. 205
Morris, Jacob. 38 Greenwich... J Weiss. Barber Fixtures. (R) 15
Myers, William. 136 Gansevoort... N Campbell. Horses, Trucks, &c. 670
McDonough, P H recvr of McWilliams Printing Co E Ralph. Presses, &c. 400
Milde, F C. 308 W 145th....J W Tufts. Soda Fixtures. (R) 168
Minard Bros. 271 W 87th....Hincks & J. Coach. (R) 250
Meyer, John. 1483 2d av....M Heyer. Barber Fixtures. 280
Nixon, G H. 80 Washington....Nat Cash Reg Co. Register. 200
Oser, C D. 285 Av A....E Bausch. Butcher Fixtures. 300
Otto, Theodor. 147 Baxter....F Pruhs. Machinery. 250
Purretto & Santon. 100 East Houston....G Montella. Barber Fixtures. 155
Pariser, R. 212 Delancey....Bennett & G. Soda Fixtures. 220
Phillips, E Y. 28 Cliff....A C Longyear. Office Fixtures. 50
Pariser, M and A. 56 East Broadway....Bennett & G. Soda Fixtures. 70
Quigley, Joseph....M Armstrong & Co. Coach. 375
Rafti, Nicola. 22 Broome....D Rafti et al. Barber Fixtures. 100
Rotella, Pietro. 429 E 113th....A Borgia. Bakery Fixtures. 175
Rubillo, Giuseppe. 112 Monroe.....G Vinti. Barber Fixtures. 225
Richter, M. 202 Broome....Manhattan Type Co. Press. 110
Ransom & Co. 9 and 11 Franklin....J Regan. Machinery. 5,403
Romer, Matilda. 110 Chrystie....I Kaufman. Cigar Fixtures. 140
Ryan, Alice. 64 6th av....H Schwartz. Diamond Ear Rings. 175
Reagan, P J. 57 Greenwich av....Nat Cash Reg Co. Register. 175
Riker, W H. 6th av and 22d st... J Matthews Co. Soda Fixtures. 11,500
Schwartz, Benjamin. 96 Cannon....J Kandel. Machine. 70
Snyder Bross 424 W 13th....C Mulford. Horses, Wagon, &c. 737
Stengele, A and R. 146th st and Brook av....L Gebhardt. Horse and Wagon. 300
Sullivan, C D. 3 Hamilton....Lamson Consol S S Co. Register. 140
Schneider, Peter. 501 E 72d ...P A Cassidy. Wagon, &c. 105
Starkey, William. 180 Cherry....D Holland. Machinery. (R) 500
Sarasohn, Bertha. 185 East Broadway. . Babcock P P Co. Press, &c. (R) 530
Schnerr, Fritz. 2 and 4 Spring ...Liberty Machine Works. Press. 698
Schaufele, Chas. 350 E 76th....S Littman. Barber Fixtures. 179
Schmidt, George. 38th st and 10th av....J Ginch. Horse and Coal Wagon. 170
Schulman, Joseph. 2517 3d av....Marvin Safe Co. Safe. 120
Siebenborn, H A. 470 W 23d....J W Tufts. Soda Fixtures. 100
Simpson & Kirk. 39 W 14th....Liberty Machine Works. Press. 900
Singer, M. 206 Rivington....Liberty Machine Works. Press. 125
Stoker, Jos. 1838 Broadway....Lamson Consol S S Co. Register. 150
Sacks, Geo. 54 E 12th....J Silver. Jewelry Fixtures. 1,000
Schultz, C P. 229 5th av....H E Van Horne. Dental Fixtures. 800
Solomon, Hyman.....M G Ernst. Diamond Earrings. 110
Trube, Adolph, Jr. 1925 3d av....R Gill. Store Fixtures, Horse, &c. 250
Tyler, John..... J Cunningham Son & Co. Coach. (R) 287
Thompson, S A. 2120 Madison av....Nat Cash Reg Co. Register. 170
Tietgen, C F. 1661 2d av J W Tufts. Soda Fixtures. 100
T New Mfg Co....A C Morrill. Machinery, Lease, &c. (R) 4,000
Trinkel, L L. 113 Columbia....J Weiss. Barber Fixtures. 210
Tilmann, Ernest. 287 Centre....N Chaplus. Machinery. 1,150
Van Camp, Chas. 120 E 84th .. J Burlinson. Horse, Milk Wagon, &c. 50
Voorhees, C....P Barrett. Truck. 314
Veidt, Herrmann. 94½ Greenwich....P Kraft. Tools, &c. 255
Wall, Edward. 424 W 14th....J Rielly. Horses, Ice Wagon, ½ int. 1,000
Westerkamp, Fred. Jerome av and 176th st....S Jacobs. Gardener Fixtures. 835
Woberton, Chester. 4 Warren ...W E Cortelyou. Office Fixtures. 150
Wyburn, Minnie. 256 7th av....Lang & Co. Bakery Fixtures. 2,000
Weyman, A and P. 505 E 15th ..E C Reinhardt. Bottling Fixtures. 4,210
Williams, J E. 72 W 125th American Guarantee Assoc. Dental Fixtures. 100
Wood, Susan A. 148 W 39th....H Killam Co. Coach. (R) 1,826
Wertheim, Herman. 1069 1st av ...M Esberg. Horse, Wagon, &c. 500
Wolf, David... E Prial. Truck. 158
Zottarelli, Stanisloo. 72 Delancey....S Zottarelli. Barber Fixtures. 216

BILLS OF SALE.

Antonino, Civilli. 79 Broome....V Calcagno. Barber Fixtures, ½ Int. 100
Bedell, W T. 689 Greenwich....R C Bedell. Horses, Trucks, &c. 8,000
Civilli, Antonio. 79 Broome....A Calandrino. Barber Fixtures, ½ Int. 120
Cuddy, William. 108 Hester....E H Cuddy. Tools, &c. 200
Cellano & Ovato. 43 Mott, 146 Sullivan....S M Jona et al. Butcher Fixtures. 1
De Mott, Emma V. 164 5th av... R McGonigal. Furniture. 100
Domicici, Napoleon .E Meyer. Plates, &c 5,000
Erbig, J D. 616 3d av....D Huek. Dry Goods. 1,257
Eichhorn, Max. 2469 3d av....F Eichhorn. Cigar Fixtures. 300
Elssesser, Herman. 1555 Av A ...Livermore & Enders. Bakery Fixtures. 1
Frenzel, A B and L L....E M Titcomb. Furniture. 1
Fischer, B & Co. 556 E 82d....J H Rehrssen. Grocery Fixtures. 1,000
Gabrielsky, Richard. 1363 3d av....M Schramm. Barber Fixtures 350
Gruenewald, Siegfried. 220 Av B....L Mignogne. Barber Fixtures. 312
Heinz, Christina. 354 W 53d....F Schnadeke. Grocery Fixtures. 2,000
Hoar, Richard. 47 E 97th....M Hoar. Horse, Cart, &c. 1
Hoehn, Fred. 71 Nassau....M Bennett. Stock, Fixtures, &c. 1,500
Hooley, Elizabeth. 186th st and Washington av ...A Runk. Saloon Fixtures. 600
Hershkowitz, B. 300 E 2d....P Hershkowitz. Butcher Fixtures. 250
Kropke, Henry. 615 Courtlandt av....Dora Lichteman. Grocery Fixtures. 500
Lichteman, August. 615 Courtlandt av.....H Kroepke. Grocery Fixtures 500
Mannkopf, Dora. 81 4th av....W H Stauf. Restaurant Fixtures. 1,336
Mansfield, Elise. 262 3d av....E Katzenstein. Grocery Fixtures. 300
Mullen, Frank. 763 5th av....M L Nichols. Saloon Fixtures. 10,000
Muller, W H. 455 W 39th ...H Muller. Bakery Fixtures 475
Montella, Giuseppe. 100 East Houston....Purretti & Santoro. Barber Fixtures. 255
Pfeifer, Herman. 1403 Av A....M Wondras. Grocery Fixtures. 700
Pell, G W. 2203 2d av.....H R Richards. Butter and Egg Fixtures. 108
Prague, J G. 35th st and Columbus av. .Guggenheimer & Clausen, Jr. Restaurant Fixtures, &c. 1
Ruppe, Carl. 1796 3d av....P Hill. Merchandise, &c. 125
Richards, Lena. 737 11th av....J Doscher & Co. Grocery Fixtures. 270
Schlessinger, A. 56-64 Clinton... B Jacobs & Son. Machinery, &c. 180
Schnitzer, David. 35 Broadway....S Kleinmann. Newspaper, "Oesterreichish Ungarisch Zeitung." 8,000
Schramm, Otto. 1365 3d av....R Gabrielsky. Barber Fixtures. 300
Stern, Frank. 1518 3d av....M Brummel. Shoe Store Fixtures. 150
Wicht, Christopher. 1407 Av A ...J J Mulhearn. Saloon Fixtures. 1

ASSIGNMENT OF CHATTEL MORTGAGES.

Andrews, S F to E Wright, admr of. (Mort given by Hardenburgh & Charter, Dec 2, 1891.) 242
Benedek, Armin to S Shonwald. (J Gottlieb, Sept 24, 1891.) 200
Grundhoefer, Louis to D Stevenson. (E Frey, Oct 22, 1891.) 2,700
Schraeder, Annie to J Stewart. (D Loppert, Oct 8, 1891.) 150
Werbeck, August, Sr, to B G Hughes. (A Schurman & Wubeck, Oct 28, 1891.) 1,000

KINGS COUNTY.

DECEMBER 3 TO 9—INCLUSIVE.

SALOON AND RESTAURANT FIXTURES.

Barthelman, L. 695 Flushing av....H B Scharmann & Sons. $378
Bohle, C H. 107 North 5th....P Weidman. (R) 800
Bischoff, C. 19 Montieth....S Liebmann's Sons B Co. 250
Becker, F. 61 Marion....J Eppig. 700
Bense, H. 439 Rodney....G Ehret. (R) 700
Brunjes, H. 1895 Broadway.. .Williamsburgh B Co. 700
Canning, Anne. 805 Clason av....T C Lyman & Co. 400
Corrigan, J. 47 Hudson av....W Ulmer. 320
Degnan, P. 380 Hudson av....H Koehler & Co. (R) 488
Degnan, P. 380 Hudson av....J Murtaugh. (R) 400
Dietz, G. 69 Bartlett....L Eppig. (R) 885
Dehmann, G. 2488 Atlantic av....Beadleston & W. 800
Fury, F. 4th av and President st....D Stevenson. 443
Gaupp, J. 87 Ferris....Obermeyer & L. 700
Gansel, V, and P Ronsheimer. 3d av and 96th st, New Utrecht...Fort Hamilton B Co. 1,500
Gerlinger, F. 997 Flushing av....A Bowden. 700
Hadden, E G. Ralph av and Bainbridge st....Standard Pump Mfg Co. Beer Pump. 90
Same ...Howard & F B Co. 90
Hofmann, A W. 58 Lorimer... S Liebmann's Sons B Co. 1,200
Hester, G. 294 Ellery....J Eppig. (R) 400
Hiller, G. 837 Kent av ...H Elias B Co. 800
Hyland, M J. 323 Court....H B Scharmann & Sons. 400
Heinrich, C. 171 Hopkins....W Ulmer. 450
Heissenbuttel, J H. 128 9th ...F & M Schaefer B Co. 1,500
Janssen, F. 1507 Bushwick av....J Eppig. 400
Jung, J.. 114 Newell....H B Scharmann & Sons. 400
Kettner, G J. 58 Floyd....Williamsburgh B Co. Ice House. 60
Koehn, H. 21 Adams....Rubsam & H B Co. (R) 1,000
Keller, F. Hamburg av and Harman st....F Ibert. (R) 700
Kirchner, J. 396 Grand....O Huber B Co. (R) 700
Koch, H. 260 Humboldt....O Huber B Co. 600
Lefkowitz, M. 872 Willoughby av....W H Griffith & Co. Billiard Tables. 1,025
Manss, H J and J C Garner. 207 Bushwick av ....Abbott B Co. 200
McLaughlin, T. 18 Atlantic av....J Ruppert. 3,500
Mathias, C. 1447 Gates av....M Seitz. 500
Mahlstein, S. 90 Moore....Burger Brewing Co. 800
Oehler, W. 52 Throop av ...J Eppig. 200
Pecon, T R & Co. 108 Greenpoint av....G Ringler & Co. 746
Ruger, H D. 224 4th av....Beadleston & W. 3,200
Reardon, M. 192 North 2d....H Vogel. 591
Reichenbach, A. 464 7th av....E Ochs. 600
Rohe, H. 1990 Bergen....Williamsburgh B Co. 800
Rose, J. 46 Ten Eyck....Fort Hamilton B Co. 450
Schaardt, F. Glenmore av, n w cor Linwood st ....L I Brewery. 400
Schneider, G. 7 Leonard... J Kress B Co. 1,100
Schoche, R. 48 Harrison av ...Claus Lipsius B Co. 600
Schoenemann, K. 745 Flushing av....Leibinger & O B Co. 450
Spengler, F. 49 Morrell....Obermeyer & L. 500
Schanz, J. 554 Flushing av....P Weidmann. 550
Seyfried, J. 107 Throop av....F Ibert. (R) 400
Sinnott & McDevitt. Eastern Parkway and Snediker av....F Ibert. (R) 800
Tschudy, A. 624 3d av....Otto Huber Brewery. 150
Weiler, H. 184 Norman av....H B Scharmann & Sons. 950
Wussler, E. 12 Hamburg av....J Eppig. (R) 225
Werckmeister, C. 151 Washington....J K Albohm. Restaurant Fixtures. 260
Whitman, A. 269 Myrtle av....Obermeyer & L. (R) 400
Wohlke, E. Rochester av, n w cor St Marks av ....J Eppig. (R) 275

HOUSEHOLD FURNITURE.

Bartlett, J H. 732 Park av....B L Bartlett. 275
Burke, W J. 452 Manhattan av.. .L Z Murray. 195
Baehr, G. 497 6th av....J McEnery & Co. 199
Baker, Mrs P. 1068 Lafayette av....E Driscoll & Bro. 125
Beansley, P F. 600 Madison....O'Connor & Treacy. 257
Braun, Alma. 2228 Pacific....F Holt. 100
Brown, Mary F. 1653 Broadway....L V Brown. 550
Burke, J P. 644 Baltic....J Kurtz. 197
Briggs, R A. 129 Palmetto....Kendrick & Co. 141
Burns, H. 136 Steuben....C T Kendrick & Co. 267
Byrne, Mrs W. 42 Eldert....Kendrick & Co. 172
Carmen, R J. 36 Alabama av....Kendrick & Co. 131
Crane, Mrs S. East 7th st ..Brooklyn F Co. 102
Cahill, H A. 5th av and 23d st....R M Walters. Piano. 225
Clark, F. 48 Sands....O'Connor & Treacy. 318
Conlon, M E....M Nason. 382
Connor, R W. 94 Duffield....Jordan & M. 105
Crist, W E. 6th av and 15th st....J P Fletcher. 600
Dix, Annie M. 296 7th av....F W Heinrich. Piano. 200
Duddy, Mrs J. 59 Columbia....Brooklyn F Co. 127
Devalle, P. 136 Eldert ...Kendrick & Co. 147
Demarrais, J. 188 Eldert....Kendrick & Co. 115
Foster, W S. 39 Aberdeen....Kendrick & Co. 282
Galligan, M. 568 Vanderbilt av....J McEnery & Co. 148
Greer, W A. 406 McDonough.....Alexander Bros. 187
Hoerner, H. 223 Frost....H S Eisler. 113
Horner, W W. 86 4th pl ..P Hartmann. 100
Haller, J. 501 Graham av. Cowperthwait & Co. 111
Hanche, C R. 994 Halsey....Kendrick & Co. 247
Heiser, Mary. 184 Hopkins....C T Kendrick & Co. 120
Isaacson, M. 32 Seigel....Cowperthwait & Co. 102
Johnson, C. 25 Chauncey....A Pearson. 150
Jockel, A M. 50 Cedar....W O'Neill. 193
Krebs, G. 394 South 3d... R Silverman. 105
Kelly, P J. 981 De Kalb av... Kendrick & Co. 122
Kirby, S W, Jr. 1251 Madison....Cowperthwait & Co. 144
Kennelly, B. 702 Evergreen av....H Israel & Son. 126
Kidd, Adelaid L. 296 Clifton pl....M M Webster. 150
Lord, J B. 370 Hancock....Financial Credit Co. 200
Locke, W W. 2072 Atlantic av....Cowperthwait & Co. 190
Marsh, G E. 86 Sterling pl ...T B Willis. 595
Mathews, A. 807 Myrtle av....Kendrick & Co. 240
Mitchell, G H. 173A Stockton....Kendrick & Co. 108
Mitchell, J 2295A Pacific....Kendrick & Co. 108
Murtaugh, Carrie H. 989 Myrtle av....Kendrick & Co. 134
Mooney, Mrs C M. 221 10th....Estey Piano Co. Piano. 135
Mann, S ... M Nason. Piano. 250
Martin, J W. 66 4th pl....O'Connor & Treacy. 148
Mathews, J H. Lorimer st, cor Noble st....Driscoll Bros. 146
McDonald, M. 289 5th av....G J Greenfield. 270
Nelson, J C. 64 Floyd....O'Connor & Treacy. 217
O'Malley, Kate. 158 North 4th....A Schulz. 193
O'Malley, Jennie. 127 Franklin av... C T Kendrick & Co. 115
Porter, T B. 124 Division av....Cowperthwait & Co. 184
Prichard, W F. 159 Weirfield....Cowperthwait & Co. 298
Parlou, J. 594 Baltic.. J J Coogan. 199
Rappel, P J....M Nason. 136
Reiness, Minnie. 797 Bergen... Cowperthwait & Co. 261
Siegler, Bertha. 110 Norman av. ..L Z Murray. 124
Stilhof, H C E. 198 and 200 Court... A Wierl. 1,500
Stockley, Virginia. 944 Greene av....L Z Murray. 154
Sweeney, G. 390 Degraw....Driscoll Bros. 228
Smith, M B. 92 and 94 Henry....J V Hess. 900
Schneider, C F. 72 Rush....Cowperthwait & Co. 215
Skilkoski, V. 726 Flushing av....Kendrick & Co. 111
Stanton, W. 125 India....Brooklyn F Co. 281
Travis, F. Atlantic av, cor Clinton st....Brooklyn F Co. 242
Vogt, Josephine. 183 Eldert....Fennell & Pye. 180
Warnick, Mary. 19 Floyd....L Z Murray. 100
White, M. 2024 Fulton....H Israel & Sons. 140
Wilkinson, S H. 69 Clifton pl....Fennell & P. 167
Willis, Mrs H C. 239 Grand av....Brooklyn F Co. 229
Wulff, H. 72 3d pl....Brooklyn F Co. 360
Woodbridge, Margt S. 31 Ormond pl....W Berri's Sons. Carpets. 102
Wolf, A. Stone av....Cowperthwait & Co. 193

MISCELLANEOUS.

Allwell, H. 196 Graham av....R Spahn. Sewing Machine. 60
Atwood & Powers. 208 5th av... Nat Cash Reg Co. Register. 200
Ahlborn, E A. 519 Van Brunt....Liberty Machine Works. Press. 225
American Diamond Rock Boring Co. 41 Van Brunt....F Semken. Engines, Drills, &c. 1,500
Bloch, L. 361 South 4th....F Dreyfuss. All Title in Butcher Shop. 400
Burns, J J. 1547 Broadway....J W Sullivan. Bakery Fixtures. 350
Brown, Mary F. 1653 Broadway, 1499 Broadway and 720 Evergreen av....Jaburg Bros. Bakeries. 1,750
Biggs, J H. 377 Fulton.. .Mary E Biggs. Office Fixtures. 800
Brown, Mary F. 1653 Broadway....Jaburg Bros. Bakery Fixtures. 1,750
Blank, R J. 1391 Broadway... Nat Cash Reg Co. Register. 175
Bossardet, L C. 371 North 2d....J Baumann. Drug Fixtures. 3,000
Condon, J J. 2 Liberty....Denison & B. Presses. 700
Calvert, H J. 47 John st, New York....Liberty Machine Works. Press. 550
Carey, W P. 601 Vanderbilt av....Nat Cash Reg Co. Register. 200
Coulson, W J, F A Hoffmire and C and B H Pomeroy, of Novelty Foundry and Machine Works. Driggs st, n w cor North 14th st... Jane B McKinstry. Machinery. 2,750
Degenhardt, H W. 345 Smith....C D Degenhardt. Butcher Fixtures. 800
Durst, G. 52 West....Nat Cash Reg Co. Register. 200
Dierks, O. 244 Columbia....Nat Cash Reg Co. Register. 175
Di Steffani, B and N. 129 Hamilton av....A Sveli. Fruit Stand. 100
Eldredge, F M. 380 Grand....W Scott & Co. Presses. 500
Ermentraut, C H. 16 Charles pl....G A Simon. Horse and Carriage. 100
Englert, F. 872 De Kalb av....J Weiss. Barber Fixtures. 390
Fenton, J J. 309 Grand....J Cunningham Son & Co. Carriages. 400
Fordham, E A....Hincks & J. Coupe. (R) 425
Fricke, H. 71 Grand... J Matthews Apparatus Co. Soda Water Apparatus. 410
Gilman & Hebberd. 1959 Fulton....C E Hebberd. Paint Store Fixtures. 400
Glinnes Sons, J... G Dessecker, Wagon. (R) 236
Gort, J. Harman st....L Gort. Horse, &c. 100
Graf & Bertram. Fulton st. cor Brooklyn av ...Nat Cash Reg Co. Register. 175
Heinning Bros & Roemer. 9 Baxter st, New York... J K Smeallie & Co. Machinery. (R) 200
Hartmann, C L. 75 Dey....G L Ayres & Co. Butcher Fixtures. 350
Henry, A. Saratoga av, n e cor Hancock st... Mary E Henry. Horses and Stable Fixtures. 1,000
Herrmann, P and L Duschel. 61 Kent av....D Mutchler. Butcher Fixtures. 210
Hollowell, H M. 459 Fulton....J H Albohn. Store Fixtures. 1,000
Heinsohn, P....J Koerner & Son. Wagon. 150
Hofinger, J J. 218 5th av....H Schalter. Barber Fixtures. 400
Iadalese, V. 22 Columbia pl...L Cembrola. Shoe Store. 100
Krueger, A. 4th av and 92d st....Nat Cash Register Co. Register. 200
Lang, L and J G Wildermuth. 83 7th av....M Heims. Butcher Fixtures. secures rent
Lester, E K. 2064 Fulton....L J Wing & Co. Machinery. 800
Little, G R. 47 Vandewater....Van Allen & B. Press. 550
Muhlenberg, E. 1296 De Kalb av....Dorothea Muhlenberg. Butcher Fixtures. 1,200
Parker, M G. 4 Myrtle av. ..C W Wood. Machine. 70
Peper, H. 271 Columbia....J Matthews Apparatus Co. Soda Water Apparatus. 650
Petranich, A. 109 Columbia....M Petranich. Machinery, Picture Frames, &c. 2,500
Pabst, W K or R. 49 Sumpter....J F Gompert. Horses, &c. 150
Piekarski, A. 112 North 6th....J Weiss. Barber Fixtures. 80
Quinn, T and J M Stewart. Arverne-by-the-Sea ...J Webb. Hotel Fixtures and Furniture. 55,000
Reese, A....P Kearth. Horse, &c. 125
Ridgewood Ice Co. Brooklyn Trust Co. Plant and Personal Effects. 140,000
Ruhe, H. Howard av, cor Madison st....Nat Cash Register Co. Register. 175
Rathjens, J. Hudson av .... H Dieckmann. Horse and Wagon. 100
Reading, W. 146 5th av....J Matthews Apparatus Co. Soda Water Apparatus. 410
Reaney, T J.. Barrett & Brush. Wagon. 122
Smith, R ..P Barrett. Truck. 375
Schmidt, B. 2d av, cor 9th st....Nat Cash Reg Co. Register. 175
Schwerze, Wm., Julia and John. 79 Gwinnett.... Pierce & Thomas. Machinery. 408
Searing, W S...M Armstrong & Co. Brougham. 850
Sanford, C E. 18 Bowery, New York, 7 1st pl, Brooklyn....R H Laimbeer. Fixtures and Furniture. 1,477
Schottlander, H. Melrose st... J Lotz. Horse. 200
Spink, B F. 437 Fulton. ..Marvin Safe Co. Safe. 100
Strunck & Doscher. 155 Norman av....P Reidenbach. Wagon. 150
T New Mfg Co. Av B, n w cor 20th st, N Y City ...A C Morrill. Machinery. 20,000
Vogel, H W. 1655 Broadway....Nat Cash Reg Co. Register. 175
Vogel, C F. 89A 4th av....S W and J A Haviland. Fixtures, &c. 1,200
Vincent, J E & Co. 343 Willoughby av....C Falleson. Milk Wagons. 350
Wilson, J. 591 Fulton....Singer Sewing Machine Co. Horse and Wagon. 100
Wyburn, Minnie. 256 7th av....Lang & Co. Bakery Fixtures. 2,000
Wyburn, Minnie. 288 Columbia....Lang & Co. Bakery Fixtures. 2,000
Wyburn, J N. 288 Columbia....Lang & Co. Bakery Fixtures. 2,000

BILLS OF SALE.

Haas, I. 299 Bushwick av....Katharine Haas. Butcher Fixtures. 800
Henken, H. 309 7th av....Mary Henken. Store Fixtures. 3,000
Hammer, J. 173 Boerum....Kath Vollmer. Bakery. 575
Martens, H F. Throop av, n e cor Halsey st.... Mary E Martens. Grocery Fixtures. 1,200
Mollineux, J... E Mollineux. Colt. 80
Roach, Anna M. 1407½ Fulton....L C Warner. Watch store. 400
Rose, F C. 315 Bushwick av....Mary Rose. Store Fixtures, Horse, &c. nom
Robbert, E. 693 Gates av....Herman C and Henry C Meyer. Grocery Fixtures. 2,400
Sawyer, Georgiana....L D Brokaw. Furniture. 50
Tams, F T. Wyckoff av, cor Eldert st....H Von Glahn. Grocery. 388
Weis, J. 61 Kent av....P Herrman and ano. Butcher Fixtures. 250
Webster, E H. 1689 Fulton....E C Redhead. Fish Market. 800
Winters, J H. 3d av and 45th st....Tarrant & Co. Drug Fixtures. 863

ASSIGNMENT OF CHATTEL MORTGAGES.

Fred Hower Brewing Co (Lim) to C Iba. (Mort given by H W Ackermann, June 20, 1891.) nom
Prozesky, G to H Prozesky. (G Kallert, Oct 2, 1891.) 250

NEW JERSEY.

NOTE.—*The arrangement of the Conveyances, Mortgages and Judgments in these lists is as follows: the first name in the Conveyances is the Grantor; in Mortgages, the Mortgagor; in Judgments, the Judgment debtor.*

ESSEX COUNTY.

CONVEYANCES.

Abby, Coe, dec'd by exrs—R Roh, South 7th st.. $750
Anderson, Larz exr—J C Eisele et al, Broome st. 900
Andruss, G C—A Blauvelt, North 5th st... 1
Anston, Henry—S P Gallagher, East Orange.... 1
Appleton, Edmund—B N Cobb, s s 11th av 48 e South 6th st 48x100.... 3,000
Arthur, John—J W Burke, Belleville.... 500
Bailey, H E—T Lenthaeuser, s w cor Littleton and 14th av 25x100 7,600
Baldwin, F H—F H Tiplin, East Orange.... 13,000
Ballard, H M—Anglo-American Varnish Co, w s Hermon st cor Hermon st 95x673x86x89x86.. 7,000
Bassett, A L—H J Bloemeche, South Orange.... 1
Blackwell, G W—Wm H Harper, East Orange.. 125
Blauvelt, Annetta—S A Andruss, North 5th st.. 1
Bloemecke, H J—R M Lee, South Orange.... 175
Same——A C Young, South Orange 350
Brown, Jacob—A F Bannister, n e cor Crane and Stone sts, 25x75x25x95.... 2,000
Buermann, August—L Aigeltinger, Belmont st. 2,640
Campfield, A H—J Nolan, East Orange .. 500
Camp, A H—J H Glassey, Frelinghuysen av.... 1
Canon, W S—J Brown, Crane st 1
Carter, W R—F Butler, South Orange.... 1
Csanik, John—E Otto, Winans av.... 250
Coe, B J—E W Coe, South 7th st 300
Coles, J A—E W Denton, 11th av.... 1,400
Denman, J C—J M Brown, East Orange.... 500
Denman, E F—E L Curtis, East Orange.... 500
Dimmich, E C—A Lemassena, Jr, Mt Prospect av 1,300
Draper, A C et al—J F Vogelius, Montclair.... 844
Draper, F R—J H Moran, Montclair.... 3,833
Same——W F Wagner, Montclair.... 924
Same—— A V Rand, Montclair 2,376
Same——J R Rand, Montclair 1,100
Duryee, G S—G Schwarz, Hecker st.... 750
Farley, B M et al—B M Farley et al trustees, Clinton.... 10
Finger, Fanny—B Strauss, w s Prince st 100 s South Orange av 31x91.... 6,500
Firth, John—R W Lyle, Orange 34,000
Flynn, Daniel—W Hill, Orange.... 2,000
Galleghn, George—H Auston, East Orange.... 1
Giess, A J—E Kussendorf, Bergen st.... 700
Gould, H D—H P Gould, 19th st.... 2,000
Grant, S W et al—A R Lee, Orange st.... 1
Same——A E Lee, Broad st.... 1
Same——A R Lee, Broad st.... 1
Same——A E Lee, Orange st 1
Guthrie, S M—M H Woodruff, South Orange.... 1,700
Hill, G A—G A Hill & Co, w s Roseville av 219 n Orange st 104x275x106x75x150x50.... 15,000
Houston, Gavin—H B Corwin, South Orange.... 1,000
Same——W A Clevenger, South Orange.... 300
Hotz, Annie—W P Rommel, Belmont av.... 1
Jackson, P N—J P Van Hise, South Orange.... 80
Jacobus, R D—A Borden, Caldwell.... 1
Kapp, Henry—B Schields, Oliver st.... 800
Keen, Oscar—B Finn, 14th av.... 1,500
Kempt, E G—C F Hartkopf, Mt Prospect.... 1,650
Kenny, James trustee—C S Keegan, N Y av.... 1
Kingsland, Joseph, Jr—Rector and Wardens of Grace Church, Franklin. 1
Le Massena, H P—I A Williams, Mulford av.... 800
Lindsley, George—S Scheuer et al, Orange.... 240
Lindsley, O W—J Beck, East Orange.... 150
Lister, J C—E C Fay, w s Broad st 415 s Harvey st 20x100 4,000
Same——C F Pfeifer, Komorn st.... 805
Same——M A Hennion, w s Broad st 335 s Harvey st 19x100.... 4,000
Same——M E Young, w s Broad st 295 s Harvey st 20x100.... 4,000
Same——W Green, w s Broad st 455 s Harvey st 20x100.... 4,000
Lawless, Edward—W F Taliaferro, East Orange. 625
Maguire, Bridget—M Carlin, s s Warren st 50 w Colden st 25x100 3,500
Marsh, F E—H Koenig, s s Mercer st 33 e Lincoln av 25x100 3,750
McKain, A P—E H Jones, Summer av.... 1,100
Meyer, Gustav—A Schrafft, Jackson st.... 800
Same——same, Jackson st.... 1,260
Mitchell, A P—G Freeman et al, Bloomfield.... 136
Milburn, F S—F S Pratt, Milburn.... 1,888
Neck, L W—F O Ward, Lincoln st.... 1
O'Leary, Winifred—P Reilly, Warren st.... 1
Osborne, H F—J C Eisele et al, Spruce st.... 1,000
Otto, Edward—E Csanik, Winans av.... 500
Peck, G L—G L Peck, East Orange 10,000
Presbyterian Society of Montclair—A R Wolf, Montclair 1
Prieth, I J—C Doll, Clinton 120
Ramsdell, C E—W P Bischoff, East Orange.... 1,500
Reed, S L—A H Patterson, e s Bruen st 141 s Green st 21x81.... 3,800
Richter, W A—K Ludwig, Houston st.... 1
Robinson, J H—J H Brown, East Orange.... 5,500
Roh, Robert—F Engelberger, South 7th st.... 825
Rommel, W P—H Hotz, Belmont av.... 1
Sargent, M E—F W Ward, Penna av.... 200
Satterthwait, T E—J L Ray, Franklin.... 1
Same——J W Fleming, Franklin.... 1
Schnetz, Ferdinand—C J Schnetz, Camden st... 1,800
Schmeider, Christina—G Schmeider, East Orange 400
Searing, M V R—W J Wimer, Gotthard st.... 500
Seitz, C F—A J Giess, Bergen st.... 600
Starr, W L—Searles & Starr Co, w s Passaic st 99 n 3d av 70x100.... 9,000
Sullivan, M F—J McDonald, West Orange.... 325
Thannenbauer, John—J J Wagner, Bedford st.. 1,620
Teplin, P H—H H Baldwin, w s 13th st 525 n 9th av 75x100.... 5,000
Towne, J W et al—J Aldred, Hawthorne av.... 2,920
Travis, I L—S Meeker, East Orange.... 12,000
Van Arsdale, Henry—M Nisch, Livingston st.... 600
Wade, Julietta—W Wade, Milburn.... 500
Wade, R M dec'd by heirs—J Wade, Milburn.... 1
Wade, Wellington—J McLaughlin, Milburn.... 275
Wakeman, J P—E Stemler, Passaic st.... 1,000
Ward, John—J M Sipp, N J R R av 1
Williams, E C et al—N N Smith, West Orange.. 500
Young, A E—M A Young, East Orange.... 800
Young, E S—A E Young, East Kinney st.... 800
Young, M A—A E Young, East Kinney st.... 800

MORTGAGES.

Adamy, P F—Fourteenth Ward B and L Assoc, Mulford av. 1,800
Allen, W L—F B Allen exr, Waverly pl.... 1,500
Amodio, Francisco—C Esposito, South Orange av.... 1,000
Baldwin, H B—C Schiener, Clinton.... 2,300
Bauer, Tobias—J Henrizi, Darcy st.... 200
Bechlin, J C—G Muller, Johnson av.... 1,900
Beck, John—H C Williams, East Orange 700
Benfield, Thomas—A E Trusdell, Washington.. 3,000
Benedict, E E—D B Cox, Bloomfield.... 3,000
Blanchard, W W—C X Wagner, East Orange.. 5,000
Bischoff, W P—Reliable B and L Assoc, Greenwood av 1,000
Brundage, A D—W H Corby, Montclair.... 2,400
Canniff, A W—The Half-Dime Savings Bank, West Orange.... 800
Carlin, Michael—P Ballantine & Sons, Warren st 2,500
Carr, Martha—C Fitzpatrick et al, Prince st.... 1,118
Same ——C Smyth, Barclay st.... 3,087
Same——L R Barnard, Barclay st.... 1,277
Same——J M Carr, Thomas st 4,000
Casale, John—S H C Wilson, Broad st.... 800
Same——T Crocker, Broad st.... 900
Cobb, B N—Protection B and L Assoc, 11th av... 2,500
Coe, M D—E W Coe, Court st 150
Cohen, D J—W N Trusdell, Pine st.... 1,700
Connell, Hugh—A Connelly, Bergen st.... 201
Danzel, Christian—E E Coe exr, Spruce st.... 1,250
Eisele, J C—P Eichelberg, Broome st.... 3,000
Emerson, J H—H B Tomkins, West Orange.... 140
Fiedler, Wilhelmina—The Howard Savings Inst, 16th av.... 3,500
Frederick, M S—M Bruchner, Somerset st.... 2,000
Gross, W C—M Gallo, 6th av.... 4,000
Gunsel, Charles—A Stedman, South 15th st.... 1,300
Haase, L H B—A S Allen, South 12th st.... 1,100
Hadley, D W—The Howard B and L Assoc, South 10th st.... 5,200
Healy, A E—G Knower, Orange 200
Hembauser, Joseph—Firemen's Ins Co, Court st 1,000
Herterich, Adam—G Lindauer et al trustees, Mercer st.... 1,600
Hillert, Ernest—M Oltmann, Walnut st 1,000
Hopkins, W S—Firemen's Ins Co, Irving st.... 1,600
Horn, A P—G S Ward, South Orange.... 6,500
Hois, Herman—The Lincoln B and L Assoc, Belmont av.... 1,200
Hutchins, W C—J Huhm, South 10th st.... 900
Jelinek, Hermann—H Hardy, Bergen st.... 2,300
Jones, E H—A P McKain, Summer av.... 600
Kane, Edward—J S Schwarz, Joseph st.... 1,200
Kunkel, Theresia—L Waldmann trustee, Ferguson st 150
Koenig, Frederick—M Rademacher, Mercer st.... 2,000
Krantz, August—J A Hageman, Peshine av.... 1,000
Lafferty, Margaret—J McCrickard, Orange.... 1,000
Liebhauser, Ann—The Mutual B and L Assoc, Bowery st.... 600
Linneman, A H—H Knoderer, Nevada st.... 1,400
Maurer, Frederick—A P Mitchell, East Orange.. 4,000
McCabe, Alexander—The People's B and L Assoc, Cutler st.... 3,400
McGin, John—J W Condit, Orange.... 1,700
Meeker, Samuel—J L Travis, East Orange.... 8,000
Orthenberger, John—C Schiener, Bergen st.... 3,000
Parker, J S—H Morris, West Orange.... 500
Patterson, A H—L B Reed, Bruen st 400
Same——R W McKeon, Bruen st.... 2,000
Sachs, Joseph—C Krab, Holland st.... 80
Sauer, Charles—F Berg, Orange 650
Schmieder, Gustave—H Ringer, East Orange.... 400
Schrafft, Albert—G Meyer, Jackson st.... 4,000
Seaman, Peter—D S Hulfish, Newark Meadows. 700
Searing, A A—P Zehlbauer, Academy st.... 1,300
Shields, Bridget—P Flinn, Oliver st.... 700
Schoars, L S—O L Courtright, East Orange 2,000
Simonson, John—W F Bailey et al, Bloomfield.. 416
Same——same, Montclair 900
Sovindge, M B—The Orange Savings Bank, Orange 800
Steffens, A T—P Petry et al exrs, Morris av.... 5,000
Stemmler, Emilie—J P Wakeman, Passaic st.... 1,000
Szymanowitz, Mary—The Newark Fire Ins Co, Littleton av.... 2,000
Taylor, W H—E Deerfelter, Elizabeth av.... 200
The Anglo-American Varnish Co—G M Ballard, Hermon st. 2,500
Same——The Prudential Ins Co, Hermon st... 3,500
The First Baptist Church of the Oranges—The Mutual Life Ins Co of New York, East Orange.... 20,000
The Orange Club—The Half Dime Savings Bank, East Orange 12,500
Trandt, Alexander—W R Duryee et al trustees, Sussex av 3,000
Williams, I A—Fidelity Title and Deposit Co, Milford av.... 2,200
Woodruff, W H—S M Guthrie, South Orange.... 1,200
Young, A E—E Thum, East Kinney st.... 1,000

CHATTEL MORTGAGES.

Anderson, Thomas—C Bradley, library.... 585
Andrews, C K—E Walter, saloon.... 1,170
Hailey, William—F L Flohn, law books.... 300
Blood, Jennie—M Kane, furniture 52
Boscaino, Lorenzo—F Lisiewski, saloon 265
Braener, G A—Hassel Jacobus, wagons.... 95
Same——J Kaiser, horses and trucks.... 581
Brenner, P F—G Krueger Brewing Co, saloon.. 80
Brockie, David—E S Black trustee, furniture.... 150
Brooks, Mary—C Trefz, saloon.... 850
Buchanan, F A—G Krueger Brewing Co, saloon. 490
Carr, Martha et al—C Fitzpatrick et al, hides, &c.... 1,100
Same——C Smyth, hides, &c.... 3,087

Same—L R Barnard, hides, &c. 1,277
Carr, Martha—The Newark Bark Co, hides, &c. 2,320
Christenson, John—M Kane, horse and wagon. 26
Collins, Aaron—R W Canham, pool table, &c. 280
Cova, Ballista—G Krueger Brewing Co, saloon. 1,400
Davis, Henry—M Kane, furniture 46
Dehert, Louis—J Ketcham, furniture 42
Downes & Newton—E T Downes, stock millinery 250
Dunan, Gertrude—C Burman, furniture 130
Dunnigan, Catherine—M Kane, furniture 40
Elyea, D M—M Kane, furniture 40
Finley, Thomas—Wm Hills Brewing Co, saloon. 500
Froley, Alfred—M S Morton, machinery 100
Gerstner, Fred—G Krueger Brewing Co, saloon. 410
Higgins, Patrick—Wm Hills Brewing Co, saloon 550
Horle, C J—C Trefz, saloon 450
Huber, William—A Huber, machinery 80
Hurd, Ernest—C Bierman, furniture 875
Jegge, John—C Trefz, saloon 3,000
Juliano, M A—G Krueger Brewing Co, saloon 358
Landerson, L H—E J Alderman, machinery 800
Leighnard, Ella—M Kane, furniture 32
Livingston, Ike—G Krueger Brewing Co, saloon. 656
[illegible]ara, John—J M Quimby & Co, coupe 100
Maxwell, Richard—G Krueger Brewing Co, ice box 25
McDougall, J S—M E Dickerson, horse and wagon 250
Moore, Etta—C Bierman, furniture 180
Muchmore, Ward W—E B Muchmore, stock groceries 4,753
Muller, Carolina—P H Hanley, furniture 33
Obe, Christina—G Krueger Brewing Co, saloon. 830
Raymond, Theresa—M Kane, furniture 26
Reiss, William—C Trefz, saloon 876
Rosenstrauch, A J—J Ketcham, furniture 130
Schmidt, Adam—C Feigenspan, saloon 335
Spielmann, Wilheim—F Lisiewski, saloon 1,200
Splitt, W N—The National Cash Register Co, register 200
The German-American Brewing Co—C Ost, saloon 3,500
Theurer, Frederick—F J Kastner, saloon 1,600
Thompson, I N—F C Edwards, furniture 500
Titius, Carl—G Krueger Brewing Co, saloon 121
Vine, H S D—D L Neafie, horses and wagons 770
Voget, Euguene—G Krueger Brewing Co, ice box 85
Vought, H J—E B Budd, horse and wagon 120
Walsher, John—J Longmuir, horse and wagon. 34
Winters, William—Citizens' Brewing Co, saloon. 300
Zimmerman, Charles—A Steadman, furniture 150

JUDGMENTS.

Chicago Wire Goods Co—H O'Neill 1,218
Dodd, R N—Royal Horse Assoc (Lim) 287

HUDSON COUNTY.

CONVEYANCES.

Adler, Jules—New York and Wakefield Co-operative B and L Assoc $2,800
Allen, Robert and M M Forrest—Ada J Beuner, Kearney 1,050
Appleby, Leonard by trustee—J McAvay 4,000
Baxter, W H—C A Sterling, Bayonne —
Bird, Sarah A by exr—Martha Scalan, Harrison. 1,200
Black, C C—H V Condict trustee nom
Braue, J F—A Gutjahr, North Bergen 350
Brown, Juliette L—C L Noe, Bayonne 5,250
Brown, Mary F—The Mayor and Aldermen of Jersey City 5,000
Buncke, R D—W C Demmert 5,000
Bundscher, Carrie—Mammie Richardson nom
Cadmus, J R—Kate Brown, Bayonne 900
Clark, Hosea F by exrs—Mary F Brown nom
Cleary, D E—O Sweeney 950
Cobert, Edward—F M Foye 275
Condict, H V—J T Madden 30,000
Same and W C Traphagen—The Lembeck & Betz Eagle Brewing Co 15,333
Condict, J D—Annie Rosenthal 2,650
Conklin, W S—A S Hewitt, Bergen Co 500
Cowles, E S—W G Bumsted 2,000
Coyle, Amelia C—The Church of the Holy Cross, Harrison 4,300
Crawshaw, Hugh—The Mayor and Aldermen of J City 6,350
Crevier, J C—H Offerman, Hoboken 15,000
Disque, August—Catharine Disque nom
Dubart, H F—J F Finn 200
Eberhard, F N—W H Ellis, Hoboken 200
Finn, J F—H F Dubart 1,100
Garrigan, Philip—W Slavin 1,100
Gautier, J H—The West Side Connecting R R Co 1,588
Gilbert, Sarah E and Elizabeth G—B M Shanley. 2,800
Gillean, Ella W—W T Cunliffe, Kearney 250
Grace, E J—Margaret Murphy, Harrison nom
Granger, E J—Beck Bros, Hoboken 16,000
Gregory, C E—Mary A Gahagan nom
Gorman, William—G H Maga, Guttenberg nom
Hill, O S—G Roehrer, Guttenberg 1,050
Hilliard, Ann P—D Gallagher 12,000
Same—same 23,000
Hinman, W S—H F Torrey, Kearney other consid and nom
Hulshizer, J E, Jr—Emma L Leaycraft nom
Hoboken Land and Impt Co—J Neil, Hoboken 920
Holman, Peuine—J H Scott 100
Hughes, Josephus—B Feeney, Union 1,900
Johnston, Mary F R—Catharine Moran, Kearney 1,700
Jones, Anna J—Melinda Tise 5,400
Knox, J M, Jr—J Peel, Bayonne 1,500
Leaycraft, E S—J E Hulshizer, Jr nom
Linden, W M—H Walker, North Bergen 50
Lovejoy, Susan C—E J Granger, Hoboken nom
Ludlow, J C by exrs—Newark City National Bank, Kearney nom
Luther, Jacob—F Vossler, West Hoboken nom
Lyon, Mary J—W S D Lyon nom
Lynot, C A J by exr—J Thorn 600
McCroskery, J B—A Greenleaf, North Bergen 400
Melzer, William—A Tognatti, West Hoboken 1,440
Miller, Ann—The Mayor and Aldermen of Jersey City 8,000
Miller, H W—A McArthur 3,100
Mosser, Josephine—Margaret L Brooke, Bayonne 3,300
Newkirk, Gitty—J B Stone 1,470
Nichols, E H—G Johnston 150
Osborn, Mary E—W H Peckham 12,000
Parmly, Randolph—Caroline L Wells nom
Pfeiffer, Peter, by master—C Trefz, Harrison 5,837
Rauch, Daniel—Charlotte V Somerion, North Bergen nom
Richardson, Mammie—F J Bundschu nom
Ross, P S—M J Keating, Harrison 3,200
Siegfried, Adam—G Lindenthal, West Hoboken 40,000
Somerion, Charlotte V—Mary I Rauch, North Bergen nom
Stirling, R R—The Mayor and Aldermen of Jersey City 5,300
Streng, Johanna—O Turkowsky, North Bergen. 800
Thacher, Mary G by admr—H F Torrey, Kearney other consid and nom
The Central N J Land and Impt Co—Anna Cassner, Bayonne 400
The Kearney Land Co—W Christie, Kearney 250
Same—A Noe, Kearney 275
The Pleasant Home Co—Abbie L Briggs 1,200
The Mayor and Aldermen of Jersey City—D E Cleary 750
The North Jersey Land Co—Anna M Merkel, Kearney 412
Tonin, Thomas—G Carluccio, Hoboken 525
Traphagen, Caroline R—Lembeck & Betz Eagle Brewing Co 6,666
Traphagen, W C and Henry—C C Black nom
Trefz, Christian—C T Van Deren, Harrison 18,000
Turkosky, Amanda—Johanna Streng, North Bergen nom
Ulrich, J F W—T Frick 2,500
Usher, James—F C Hausen, Union 600
Van Buskirk, De Witt—D Dempsey, Bayonne 2,000
Von Drehle, Herman by exr—J Lamb, West Hoboken 900
Voorhees, Anna E—T Gaynor, Hoboken 1,500
Vossler, Frederick—J Luther, West Hoboken nom
Walter, J W—A Siegfried, North Bergen 700
Wells, G H—R Parmly nom
William, Chas and T N—Eliza Williams, North Bergen nom
Williams, Eliza—G D Lozier, North Bergen 800
Wynns, Thomas by trustee—F Bartlett trustee nom

MORTGAGES.

Bernard, Anna—E J Derraismes, Guttenberg, 5 years 1,700
Breetz, William—A Lieber, 2 years 2,000
Brady, Henry—G M Severance, Kearney, 6 months 30
Brown, Katie—J A Johnson, Bayonne, 3 years 2,100
Brown, William—W Burrows, 2 years 130
Busch, Chas—C Schully, Union, 3 years 700
Buxton, Martha M—S A Bisson, Hoboken, 1 year 400
Condict, H V—The Home for Aged Women, 5 years 1,250
Same—same, 5 years 1,250
Same—same, 5 years 1,250
Conklein, G W—C L Demarest, Bayonne, 1 year. 800
Dempsey, Daniel—C P Vreeland, Bayonne, 5 yrs 5,000
Same—D Van Buskirk, Bayonne, 1 year 1,900
Dewey, Margaret—The Harrison and Kearney B and L Assoc, Kearney, installs 2,000
Donacker, Annie M—Henrietta Weissenbom, 1 year 500
Eits, J E—Exr J Kupper, Guttenberg, 5 years 1,500
Frick, Theodore—Serial B and L Assoc, installs. 1,600
Same—J T W Ulrich, 3 years 550
Gahagan, Mary A—C E Gregory, 3 years 600
Gallagher, Denis—The New Jersey Title Guarantee and Trust Co, installs 23,000
Gardner, J G—Ida L Spring, Bayonne, 3 years 2,000
Gaston, William—J Fiacre, 3 years 6,000
Gatto, Giovanni—The Italian Co-operative B and L Assoc, installs 2,000
Haines, Louise E—Martha J Haines, 5 years 500
Harrington, Ellen—Hudson City Savings Bank, 1 year 1,000
Hillier, G R—Lafayette M B and L Assoc, installs 5,000
Hobart, Ellen—Washington B and L Assoc, installs 5,000
Horan, Mary—The People's B and L Assoc, Kearney, installs 800
Hubner, Adam—Hudson City Savings Bank, 1 year 2,500
Hussey, S H—The Daily News B and L Assoc, Bayonne, installs 2,000
Isbills, W E—Exrs J Rudderow, Bayonne, 3 years 2,000
Jankoski, Matin—J Michaekki, Bayonne, 3 years 400
Jurick, Geo—J C Brane, Hoboken, 3 years 6,000
Keating, M J—Emma K Ross, Harrison, 1 year. 2,700
Kelly, William—Howard Richards, Bayonne, 3 years 1,500
Lindenthal, Gustave—A Siegfried, West Hoboken, 3 years 9,500
Same—same, West Hoboken, 5 years 10,500
Lorentz, Matilda—Exrs H Von Drehle, West Hoboken, 3 years 1,000
Mackinnon, J A—Cofrode & Taylor, 5 years 5,000
Same—same, 5 years 25,500
Madden, J F—The New Jersey Title Guarantee and Trust Co, installs 20,000
Mangell, Robert—Central N J Land and Impt Co, Bayonne, 3 years 1,350
Mitzemius, Mary L—Centreville B and L Assoc, Bayonne, installs 3,000
Mohn, Henrietta—P Ballantine & Son, Hoboken, 1 year 5,000
Moran, Catharine—Mary F R Johnston, Kearney, 1 year 900
Muhlfeld, Marie—Enestina Eckata, 2 years 1,000
Newe, John—Hoboken Bank for Savings, Hoboken, 2 years 3,500
Olsen, Ole—Greenville B and L Assoc, installs 5,720
Prasser, Ida—Industrial M B and L Assoc, installs 3,600
Rosenthal, Anna—J D Condict, installs 1,100
Samuelson, Frances—Kearney B and L Assoc, Kearney, installs 2,400
Sauermann, Mary H—Centreville B and L Assoc, Bayonne, installs 1,600
Slavin, William—Garfield B and L Assoc, 5 yrs 400
Speiring, Mary—Martha L Deraismes, Guttenberg, 1 year 500
Spleidt, William—N P T Rosenberg, 3 years 800
Steohr, Geo—J Bickel, Guttenberg, 3 years 300
Steidel, Leopold—M Foster, 3 years 3,700
Sutton, J J—Margaret Halbheer, Bayonne, 1 year 300
The Ferger, Becker & Kohl Bavarian Brewing Co—J H Fort, 5 years 25,000
The Lembeck & Betz Eagle Brewing Co—A Campbell, 1 year 4,000
Same—Maria G Burgess, 1 year 4,000
The trustees of the First German Evangelical Lutheran Church—Hoboken Bank for Savings, 6 years 10,000
Thorn, Jacob—Exrs C A J Lignot, 3 years 500
Tierney, Thomas—Beadleston & Woerz, Bayonne, installs 480
Tise, Matilda—The Fifth Ward Savings Bank, 1 year 3,500
Tise, Melinda—G P Howell, 1 year 1,000
Tumbley, Kate L—Mutual Life Ins Co, Bayonne, 1 year 6,500
Turkowsky, Oscar—Johanna Streng, North Bergen, 5 years 800
Van Deren, C T—Christina Trefz, Harrison, 1 year 9,000
Welsh, W A—American Insurance Co, Kearney, 1 year 2,600
Wilson, Aaron—Jersey City B and L Assoc, Bayonne, installs 200
Yost, Fernando—J J Owens, Kearney, 1 year 1,216

CHATTEL MORTGAGES.

Berg, J J—The Lembeck & Betz Eagle Brewing Co, saloon 600
Block, J W, Union—The William Peter Brewing Co, saloon fixtures 600
Blume, Henry—F W Blume, grocery store, horse, wagon 495
Boyle, M H, Hoboken—The Bavarian Brewing Co, saloon 2,597
Boyle, O A, Bayonne—Hoos & Schulz, furniture. 219
Byrnes, Thomas—Baldwin & Figueira, horses, wagon, harness, &c 501
Carlo, Frank—F Lisiewski, saloon fixtures 320
Clausintzer, John, Hoboken—Anna M Reinhard, furniture 150
Cox, G W, Kearney—W R Tobias, lathes, engines, boiler, &c 400
Crend, R W—The William Peter Brewing Co, saloon fixtures 800
Crofford, Bernard—The Lembeck & Betz Eagle Brewing Co, saloon 577
Curtis, W C, Union—The W Peter Brewing Co, saloon 2,500
Despres, George—D O'Farrell & Co, furniture 179
Donohue, J J—Annie Bammesberger, sewing machines 237
Draha, Julius, Hoboken—The D G Yuengling, Jr, Brewing Co, saloon fixtures 650
Eberle, Ch—Krakauer Bros, piano 130
Eckel, Adam—H Rose, horses, wagons, &c 500
Foller, C V—The Bavarian Brewing Co, saloon 900
Gerlach, John, Hoboken—R Mathesheimer, machinery 2,062
Griglietti, Florence F—J Bauman, furniture 128
Harbst, John—A Hecht, blacksmith shop 290
Heisterhagen, Louis—B Fischer et al, grocery store, horse, wagon, &c 401
Hollman, Louis—The Lembeck & Betz Brewing Co, saloon 634
Hughes, J R—The Lembeck & Betz Eagle Brewing Co, saloon 700
Ilse, J T—G P Howell, grocery store 1,000
Jennings, James—C Birdsall, furniture 130
Kaiser, John—S Ashner, stock and fixtures of store 358
Keane, Andrew—Wolff Bros, mare 150
Keleher, William—Gottfried Kreuger Brewing Co, saloon fixtures 500
Knauth, Gustav, West Hoboken—P Schaeffer & Son, saloon 600
Knickerbocker, F P—C Birdsall, furniture 130
Lehn, Robert, Hoboken—C G Woelpper, barber shop 107
Muller, J T—The William Peter Brewing Co, saloon fixtures 633
Riccio, Michael—D Gallero, barber shop 80
Robertson, Harry and P H Moss—Hinchliffe Bros, mineral water business, horses, wagons, &c 3,000
Rosenthal, M A—Betsey Shopman, gents' furnishing goods store 1,200
Schipmann, Henry—The Lembeck & Betz Eagle Brewing Co, saloon 587
Smyth, G A and R B Tooker—J Metz, printing presses 400
The Ferger Becker & Kohl Bavarian Brewing Co—J H Fest, horses, wagons, harness, bottling department, steam engine, ice machine, brewing kettle, bar room, stock, &c 50,000
Urbach, Louis, Hoboken—H A Just, butcher shop 75

BILLS OF SALE.

Hecht, August and J G Thacker—J Harbst, blacksmith shop 250
Knapp, Catharine, Union—J W Bloch, saloon 1,850
Spencer, Elizabeth W—R B Johnston & Co, engine, boiler and machinery nom

JUDGMENTS.

Bruns, J N and J F O'Mealia—W S Estey 134
Garret, Joseph and William—The Bigelow Company 658
Keleher, Nicholas and Mary—H E G Luyties. 440
Kraft, Wilhelm—Mary Kraft 1,065
Schneider, John and H A Borchers—The State of New Jersey 500
Taucke, Charles—W Schuman et al 1,226
Taylor, Annabella and Samuel Hays surviving partners—C K Cobb 442

MECHANIC'S LIEN.

Gough, J T, owner; J Carlin, builder; R Minsheid, claimant, J City 844

BUILDING MATERIAL MARKET.

BRICKS.—Although the representative of this journal is treated with the utmost courtesy by the gentlemen connected with the brick market, it is quite likely his weekly search for information may be a little irksome to those to whom application is of necessity made. They scratch their craniums, fall into a thoughtful and reflective mood as if endeavoring to evolve something fresh and original, and then with a negative shake of the head generally conclude that "there is nothing new." About the only change we can learn of since last writing is the somewhat smaller run of arrivals, through which the quantity on station has been kept comparatively low, but this while advantageous in sustaining the value line was not sufficient to act as stimulant. Indeed it is quite likely that any fuller figures would have acted as a check upon demand as the outlet for supplies at the moment has no natural tendency toward expansion. Some little stock is wanted for immediate consumption, and at old cost dealers, who have the room, are willing to go on piling up, especially as quality continues to run very good, but the position does not as yet appear ripe for an advance. Pales remain nominally steady without attracting more than ordinary attention. There is nothing new from the river, the usual stories coming of a probable cessation of shipments, followed up by the usual arrival of loads from many manufacturers making the most pronounced threats about shutting down.

LATH.—There is practically no market, and the entire situation is nominal. The latest reported business was at $2.50 one week ago, with no arrivals since, but many evidences that with stock here a much higher figure could be obtained. Some dealers have a fair supply in hand, but those who want lath want them very much indeed, and we learn that buyers have gone so far as to beg receivers to promise them the very small quantity on the way, and fix the rate at whatever may appear right when delivery is made. The market is winding up the year with a neat little boom.

LIME.—In the matter of cost former rates remain, and the market is quoted steady. Some arrivals have come to hand coastwise, but they were managed without difficulty, and receivers seem to be in fairly confident mood. Advices received from the Eastward report that most of the kilns have blown out, and those still burning are said to be working for outside markets only.

LUMBER.—Demand in all ways is moderate and the market throughout exhibits so quiet a tone as to make the situation one of stupidity rather than of interest. Consumption is taking nothing at the moment beyond amounts due for the completion of work in hand, and although we learn of a little negotiation now and then for winter shipment by rail from primal points there seems to be an indisposition to close any important deal until after the turn of the year. Meanwhile operators are scanning the horizon of the future and very generally claim to discover the brightening skies of promise. Already the columns of THE RECORD have contained notice of projected buildings of no inconsiderable magnitude, with more likely to follow, and that in conjunction with every prospect of a better manufacturing business can hardly fail to bring beneficial influence upon the lumber business.

Eastern spruce has been offered in a very moderate manner, yet, after all, there was probably quite as much available as the market required, as really no important demand exists, and receivers would be bothered to find custom for a larger quantity. Prices are well enough sustained, in fact tend to gradually strengthen, as every-day progress of the season at this juncture simply curtails the chances for a supply, and should buyers find it necessary to open negotiations their wants would lead to a strengthening of line of value. There is practically nothing new from primal points at the present writing.

Piling is not arriving to any extent, but the basins hold plenty of stock and a better demand could be supplied with ease and a great deal of satisfaction to holders. The tone is somewhat firmer if anything, without, however, leading to any change in general range of quotations.

Hemlock has very little regular demand, and the special orders are few and far between, the market as a rule retaining a dull, unsatisfactory sort of tone. Valuations do not change much; but the chances are against any lower range, and receivers commence to talk more hopefully of getting better figures.

White Pine is finding moderate custom and holds its place in the line of dull markets. On the better qualities of uppers and select the tone is firm and holders have apparently the most implicit confidence in that kind of stock; and most other grades may be called steady, but are more open to fluctuation. We hear of a little treaty of late on Western box, mostly with small dealers and manufacturers who buy along on the hand-to-mouth policy, and there has been a few sales of shippers. The export trade, however, is not affording much satisfaction, as the calls are far and far between, and quite a number of orders are being filled on through shipment from primal points.

Yellow Pine goes into consumption mainly against booked orders, but there is an occasional new call, and also something doing now and then for shipment, with prices in all cases well sustained. Agents speak hopefully of prospects for coming season, both as to culls for dockage, and warehouse work, and some of them report an already large business doing with car builders. From primary points late advices report that plenty of water can now be found for floating logs, running mills, etc., and manufacturers are in an easy mood regarding rates, which, in conjunction with low coastwise freight charges, makes it quite likely that lay down cost at this point will not increase. We have recently been favored with a long chat with one of the leading spirits in the recently-formed organization, and learn that everything is progressing smoothly and nicely, and the project bids well to realize all calculations. Our informant particularly emphasized a denial of any intention to raise the line of valuation, but on the contrary spoke hopefully of really cheapening the cost to consumers and more thoroughly popularizing the use of yellow pine.

Carolina Pine remains steady in price, and has a fair sort of demand all the while that really keeps quite a little bunch of stock in motion, considering the season of the year. The position is a steady one also, and it is claimed there has been no deviation from the regular price lists, so far as leading houses are concerned at least.

Hardwoods are finding no special degree of favor at the moment, and all in all it is a dull market. Dealers are pretty well stocked, and manufacturers of both furniture and trim as yet feel too doubtful about the future to commit themselves further against additional supplies. There have been certain mutterings among workmen in this trade that, it is feared, forebade trouble in the spring. From primary points the offerings are made with some care just now, but, it is thought, will be more plentiful after the turn into the new year. The export trade develops no new phases worthy of special notice at the moment.

GENERAL LUMBER NOTES.

STATE.

The Albany *Argus* as follows:

In the way of new business the past week was very quiet. A few belated orders came straggling in at the last moment, but the only activity noticed in the district was in the shipping line, where there was some degree of bustle incident to loading late cargoes to fill out orders placed within the last few weeks. Everything is shipped up very closely, and the last boats leave in the tows to-night. If the river keeps open it is probable that a few more cargoes may be sent down. Dealers are, as a rule, already established in their winter offices, and but a moderate amount of business, that may be filled by rail, is expected until spring makes its appearance again. With the market practically closed for the season it is but proper to say that values have held their own to the end, and that the close finds prices ruling firm and substantially unchanged.

THE WEST.

The Northwestern *Lumberman* says of the Chicago market:

The market season is practically closed. There will be a few more cargoes dropping in and offering on the Franklin street market, but they will be stragglers from the fag end of shipments. One commission house has two or three boats out for loads, and may have several cargoes on the market within a week. Much will depend on the weather in regard to future receipts.

The report of the Lumberman's Association shows that of the total of 1,958,567,000 feet of lumber and 280,000,000 shingles received at this point from January 1st to November 28th, this year, 1,807,419,000 feet of lumber and 240,702,000 shingles came by lake. This exhibit shows that water transit for mill product still holds a vast supremacy over carriage by rail, though the latter mode cuts a large and increasing figure, mainly on the yellow pine and hardwood side, however.

The market closes with prices not much different from what they were at the finish of last year. Short piece stuff is the same, namely, $10.50 a thousand. Long joists average about the same, which is $15 a thousand. Prices in midsummer, this year, did not drop as low as in a like time in 1890. The market has been remarkably steady, and closes strong. Within the past thirty days common boards and strips have advanced at least 50 cents. Shingles are higher than at the close last year by at least 20 cents.

The *Timberman* says:

Throughout the Northwest logging has started in in earnest, and a reference to other pages of this issue of the *Timberman* will show that the log harvest of 1891-92 is likely to be exceedingly abundant. This season no logger gives himself the trouble to even preach curtailment, but, leaving that branch entirely to his neighbor, is endeavoring to place himself in a position to take advantage to the utmost of the higher values that he is confident the coming spring will disclose.

At Chicago prices continue to grow firmer as the season advances. All the "low lists" have been withdrawn, and prices are more uniform and fewer concessions made than for years past. The feeling is generally firm on good lumber, but this year this feeling also applies to the coarser grades. Already the supply of No. 3 boards is getting to be light, and the consequent increased demand for No. 2 from box-makers has materially strengthened the price on that grade. No. 2 boards, all widths, are selling at $11@11.50, while No. 3 bring $9.50@9.75.

Twelve-inch common boards, both No. 1 and No. 2, are excellent property, and are steadily advancing in value. There is a good demand for 8 and 10-inch for use in the World's Fair buildings.

An advance of 50 cents per thousand on some sizes of short piece stuff, notably 2x4s and 2x6s, is predicted in the near future. The short lengths are now selling strong at $12.50, and some lengths bring $13. Well-posted lumbermen say there is no reason why any No. 1 piece stuff should be sold for less than the latter figure. Demand for long joist continues to be urgent, and prices are firmer than ever on everything 18 foot long and up.

A variety of views are entertained regarding the present available stock of hardwoods. No one doubts but there will be plenty of lumber to supply all requirements for some months to come at least; but some of the best posted dealers maintain that there is not the surplus in pile at interior points that many imagine. Local yards are generally well supplied with all classes of stock, but are receiving more or less right along, although nearly all report light sales. Yard dealers have attributed their lack of trade the past season mainly to the increased amount of lumber sold by the car-load dealers, and perhaps this is the cause to a great extent; but it is also true that the furniture and interior finish factories have not been using as much stock this fall as they did last. In fact, the trade from furniture manufacturers has been light all the year, and as the furniture business is still dull no great amount of trade is looked for from this class of buyers for a couple or three months at least.

The Mississippi Valley *Lumberman* as follows:

Navigation has closed on the great lakes. The summary of shipments by water from Muskegon shows a large decrease, while there has been a slight increase during the season at Bay City. The falling off at Saginaw, however, more than compensates for the increase at the neighboring city. Stocks are reported very closely sold up all around the lakes, and at Chicago, the principal dumping ground for Lake Superior and Lake Michigan mill points, the stock of lumber is considerably smaller than it was a year ago at this time. A very large local demand is confidently relied upon by the Chicago dealers for next season. Interest naturally centres at this time in the North upon the preparation for the winter's work in the woods. This generally is upon an extensive scale. The conditions thus far have been exceptionally good for a large cut of logs and the expectation is that there will be. This prospect does not bring forth, as it might have done in previous years, a protest against overdoing the thing. A short stock of manufactured lumber has encouraged the mill men to prepare for a long and busy season.

CANADA.

Referring to the falling off in the lumbering industry of the River Miramichi and its tributaries, the

Chatham *Advance* says the trans-Atlantic lumber shipments for this year thence have been less than any previous recorded year of its history. The figures are as follows: Vessels in the trade, 113, of 79,412 tons; deals, scantling, ends, boards, etc. shipped, 72,089,950 s. f. In the previous season there were 159 vessels of 97,015 tons, and the exports were 88,688,256 s. f. of deals, scantling, boards, etc; so that we have a decline of 15,555,806 s. f. from even the greatly reduced shipments of last year.

It may be interesting, continues the *Advance*, "although it is very discouraging, to note that the decline in Miramichi's trans-Atlantic lumber trade is a continuous one. This season's falling off, of over fifteen millions, is not due to any accidental cause. The strongest only are able to continue in the business. Last season's shipments were 22,000,000 superficial feet less than those of 1889 although they were in excess of those of 1888, but the downward course of the trade will be understood by taking the returns since 1880, which comprise the operations of twelve years. Miramichi shipped during that period a total in round numbers of 1,227,000,000 s. f. Of that quantity 744,000,000 s. f. were shipped in the years from 1880 to 1885 inclusive, and only 482,000,000 s. f. in the period from 1886 to 1891 inclusive."

Another journal says:

Lumbermen on the Miramichi have now got all their men into the woods, but they are sadly in need of frost and snow to assist them in their operations. It is not expected that the cut this winter will be very large, in the face of the heavy stocks held by nearly all the mill men on this river. The prospects of increased prices for spruce in the English market next year are not at all bright.

ENGLAND.

The *Timber Trades Journal* as follows:

Considerable excitement still prevails regarding the market next year. Many of the agents are yet abroad, and till their return we do not expect to hear anything about prices. Though some considerable sales will be made quietly, we very much question if the coast importers are prepared to go largely into business till the prices are more pronounced. There is not the same anxiety to buy early now as existed when sailing ships did the trade. Everybody is now able to supply himself by steamer in a few weeks direct from the shipping port when he has decided to purchase.

There is a line of Oregon pine planks now in the market, ex John Gill, the chief recommendation being the widths, which run up from 12 inch to 30 inch, and we do not recollect having seen a better specification. They were imported early in the summer, when a considerable portion of them were sold, but the balance of the cargo is stowed in the Gantry sheds. It is not often that sawn wood goes to these widths, and for staging, bridge work and building purposes generally they would come in very handy. The sizes of this parcel run from 4 to 6x12 to 30 inch, which at 1s. 5d. to 1s. 9d. per cubic foot ought not to be long on hand.

And the following is found in report of an auction sale:

Then came several parcels of American walnut logs, ex "sundry ships," offered without reserve; for these there was good contention, and fairly good prices were realized—from 1s. 8d. to 3s. 1d. per foot cube.

A couple of parcels of American satin walnut-wood planks and boards were put in at ½d. per foot, and rose to 1d. per foot, without reserve. Three parcels of beech planks, ex different ships, were cleared at from 9d. to 1s., on the same conditions.

METALS.—COPPER—Ingot has not only continued in moderate demand, but at times was almost entirely neglected notwithstanding free offerings and a modified line of valuation. Present consumption was without encouragement, and manufacturers did not seem to have confidence sufficient to open up negotiations for next year. On an average range of valuations we quote at 10.90@11c. for Lake, and 10@11¾c. for casting brands. Manufactured Copper is quiet and nominally unchanged. We quote as follows: Sheet, not above 30x72 in., 16 oz. and over, 25c.; do, 14 to 16 oz., 23c.; do, 12 to 14 oz., 24c.; do, 10 to 12 oz., 25c.; do, 8 to 10 oz., 28c.; do under 8 oz, 30c. Sheets longer than 72 inches add 1c. for 12@14 oz., 2c. for 10@12 oz. and 3c. for 8@10 oz. Sheets, not above 36x96 in., 16 oz and over, 22c.; do, 14 to 16 oz, 24c.; do, 12 to 14 oz, 26c.; do, 10 to 12 oz, 30c.; do, 8 to 10 oz, 33c. Sheets longer than 96 inches 22c. for over 32 oz, and add 1c. for 16 to 32 oz.; 3c. 14 to 16 oz.; 5c. 12 to 14 oz, and 13c. for 8 to 10 oz. Sheets, not above 48x96 32 to 64 oz, 22c.; do, 16 to 32 oz, 25c.; do, 14 to 16 oz, 27c. do, 12 to 14 oz, 29c.; do, 10 to 12 oz, 33c. Sheets wider than 48x96 and longer, 22@25c. for 32 to 64 oz. and over, 27@28c. for 16 to 32 oz, 29c. for 14 to 16 oz and 34c. for 12 to 14 oz. All bath tub sheets, per lb., 16 oz. 27c.; 14 oz, 29c.; 12 oz 31c.; and 10 oz, 35c. Bolt copper, ¾ inch diameter and over, 28c. Circles, 60, diameter and less, 3c. above price of sheets of same thickness; circles, 60 to 96 do do, 5c. do; circles, 96 do and over, 6c. do. Segment and pattern sheets, 3c. above price of sheets required to cut them from. Cold or hard rolled copper, 1@2c. per lb. above the foregoing prices. Copper bottoms, 26@32c. per lb. IRON—American Pig has been somewhat more active, the deal embracing quite a large bunch of stock for car wheel purposes, some for iron pipe, and some on contract for delivery next. Pretty much all the stock was of the best makes and upon about the basis of present valuations showing steadiness so far as the high grades are concerned, but there has been some free offerings of medium and common make at pretty low figures. We quote at $17.00@18.00 per ton for No. 1 X foundry; 15.50@16.50 for No. 2 X do, and $14.00@15.00 for Gray Forge. Old material does not meet with much attention, indeed, for that matter, has been so neglected as to scarcely give a trial to the market and valuation is more or less nominal. We quote at about $21.00@22.00 for old rails; $19.00@19.50 for No. 1 wrought scrap; $17.00@18.00 for cast scrap and $17.00@17.50 for car wheels. Manufactured iron is also on the quiet list, demand from all quarters and for all kinds proving extremely limited and without indication of early revival. About old figures, however, are asked. We quote Common Merchant Bar ordinary size, at 1.90@2c. from store, and refined at 2@2¼c; Rods, round and square, 2.10@2.30c.; Bands, 2.30@2.50c.; Norway Nail Rods 3¾@4c., and domestic sheet on the basis of 3.00@3.05c. for common Nos. 10@16. Other descriptions at corresponding prices, with 1-10c. less on large lots from cars. Steel rails commence to show signs of easing off in price. There is no change in quotations, and the mill rate stands at the figure current for months; but some of the Western concerns and possibly others have agreed to make deliveries at a charge for freight considerably less than regular rates of the companies, and in that way manage to place the advantage in buyers' favor. We quote standard sections $30 per ton at mill, with usual advance for delivery at tide water. Pig Lead in moderate demand, buyers showing considerable indifference and the tone easing off somewhat, though there is no pressure to realize upon supplies. We quote at 4.30@4⅜c. per lb. The manufactures of lead are quoted at 7c. for Pipe, 7¾c. for sheet, 15c. for Tin-lined Pipe, and 37½c. for Block Tin Pipe. Pig Tin finds merely an ordinary trade call from consumers and speculators appear a little tired, giving the market a somewhat neglected tone. We quote at about 18.85@19.90c. for round lots, and 20@20½c. for jobbing parcels. Tin Plate have little attention of a noticeable character except for a few of the light weights, and while no radical changes are quoted in value the tendency is somewhat weak. We quote prices as follows: I. C. Charcoal, ½ cross assortment Melyn grade, $6.50@6.55, each additional X add $1.50; I. C. Charcoal, ½ cross assortment, Allaway grade, $5.80@5.85, each additional X add $1; Charcoal terne, M. F. grade, 14x20, $7.45@7.50; M. F. grade, 20x28, $15.00@15.05; Worcester, 14x20, $5.70@5.75; Worcester 20x28, $11.50@11.55; Dean grade, 14x20, $5.40@5.45; Dean grade, 20x28, $10.60@10.65; D. R. D. grade, 14x20, $5.25@5.30; D. R. D. grade, 20x28, $10.10@10.15; I. C. Coke, Penlan grade, $5.25@5.30; J. B. grade, 14x20, $5.35@5.40; I. C. Bessemer steel, squares, $5.75@5.80 basis; I. C. Siemens steel, squares, $5.85@6.00 basis. Spelter has been dull and weak. Neither brass manufacturers or galvanizers appear to want stock, and Western makers are inclined to force business. We quote 4¾@4.80c. for Common Western, according to brand

NAILS.—Custom is of moderate character at the best, and such as does put in an appearance develops extremely small wants. Indeed, the demand is one of necessity only for both wire and cut and sellers have some difficulty in controlling prices. The low range, however, prevents much further shading and the make is being curtailed. We quote Cut at $1.50@1.60 per keg for car lots and $1.75@1.85 keg for parcels from store for iron, and add 5@10c per keg for steel; Wire, $2.00@2.05 at mills, and 2.20@2.35 from store.

PAINTS, OILS, COLORS, ETC.—Not much of any change since our last. There has here and there been evidences of a little more trade doing, but it proved only momentary and generally in simple standard qualities of stock wanted to fill out assortments against ordinary regular distributive wants. The export call is helping the movement somewhat, and there are said to be indications that the foreign trade will prove very excellent next year. At present there are fair enough offerings both in quantity and assortment to satisfy any natural call, yet owners manage to keep every thing under very nice control, and prevent direct pressure to realize. The value line stands very much as before for paints, colors and various mixtures, and leads are held steadily. Association Corroders' rates stand as follows: Lead in oil in kegs and dry lead in kegs, in lots of less than 500 lbs., 7¼c. net; in lots of 500 lbs to 5 tons at one purchase, 7c.; 5 tons to 12 tons, one purchase, 3¾c.; 12 tons and over, one purchase, 6¾c.; dry white lead in bbls. ¼c. per lb. less than price in kegs. Lead in oil 12½ lb. in tin pails, add 1c.; in 25 and 50 lb. tin pails, add ¼c.; and in 1 to 5 lb. tin cans, assorted (100 lbs. in case) add 2¼c. per lb. to keg price. Terms on lots on 500 lbs. and over, note or acceptance at sixty days, or 2½ per cent. discount will be allowed for cash paid within fifteen days of invoice date. To make either of the above required quantities any assortment of packages of white lead, red lead and litharge may be counted. The above quotations are free on board cars or boat at corroding point. Linseed Oil remains steady for the finest product and is more or less variable on medium and ordinary qualities, but the general range of cost stands about as before. Holders are not urging stock to any extent. We quote at general range at 35@40c. for Western, and 40@56c. for City. Spirits Turpentine has sold only in small lots and with plentiful offerings there is a further weakening off in the general range of valuation. We quote at 33½@34½c. per gallon, according to quality, delivery, etc.

TAR AND PITCH.—Business moves along in about former channel and the market has a uniform sort of tone throughout with cost much the same as for some little time past. There is plenty of stock for immediate wants, but a few large orders would exhaust the best lots. We quote Pitch at $1.70@1.75 per bbl.; Tar at $2.15@2.50, according to quantity, quality and delivery.

MISCELLANEOUS.

ARCHITECTS—SURVEYORS.

MISCELLANEOUS.

MISCELLANEOUS.

PENRHYN SLATE CO.,
101 EAST 17th STREET, NEW YORK.
Treads and Platforms, Roofing, Sanitary Work, &c.
SLATE LINED LAUNDRY TUBS.

Mantels.
Slate Work.

BRAM & BIEG.
MANUFACTURERS OF
WHITE PORCELAIN WASH-TUBS AND SINKS.
Each Tub made in one piece. No eems to open.
BEST SANITARY TUB ON THE MARKET.
Liberal Discount to the Trade. Send for Catalogue.
Office and Works: 46 to 56 Wallabout St. (near Clason Av.),
Telephone Call, 600 Williamsburgh, BROOKLYN, N. Y.

FRED. BRANDT,
No. 169 EAST 85th STREET, - - - NEW YORK.
Manufacturer of
BRANDT'S Patent Stationary Zinc Wash Tubs.
Warranted for 10 years. Price $8 50 per set.
Also a Bath and Wash Tub Combined.
Sheet Iron Sliding DUMB WAITER DOOR.
Price, put up, $5.50 Each.
These Doors are desirable because, moving vertically, they do not occupy valuable space, and can be used in narrow halls.
Send for Illustrated Catalogue and Price List.

THOMAS NUGENT,
Manufacturer of
Moist. Warm Air Furnaces
AND VENTILATING APPARATUS.
214 EAST 90th STREET, NEW YORK.

WM. H. OLIVER,
(Late Hobbs & Oliver
PLAIN and DECORATIVE PAINTING
Paper Hangings and Interior Decorations.
63 and 64 UNIVERSITY PLACE, - - - New York
Telephone 888—21st St. ESTABLISHED 1846.

PEERLESS COLORS FOR MORTAR.
RED, BLACK, BROWN and BUFF.
Guaranteed not to FADE if used according to directions. Send for circulars and full information to
ERSKINE W. FISHER, (Welles Building),
18 Broadway, N. Y.
Also Sole Agent for the Stettin ("Anchor" Brand) Portland Cement. 2978 Cortlandt.

BOSTWICK PATENT

A GREAT SAVING OF MATERIAL AND LABOR.
Recommended by architects and extensively used by builders.
ILLUSTRATED PAMPHLET & SAMPLES FREE,
BOSTWICK METAL LATH CO.,
38 Park Row, N. Y., and Niles, Ohio.

CURRAN'S
GROOVED PLASTER
SLAB.
OFFICE, 135 BROADWAY, N.Y.

WILLIAM HILGERS,
Artificial Stone and Asphalt Works
163 WEST 104th ST., N. Y.
Concrete and Asphalting for sidewalks, yards, and areas, paving for stables and warehouses,
ARCHES IN CEMENT.

Stone Wash Tubs.
ODORLESS, NON-ABSORBENT, DURABLE.
Material and Workmanship Fully Warranted.
MANUFACTURED BY
HUGH O'NEILL, Long Island City, N.Y.

BLINDS

SIMPLEST. BEST.

Send for price list and estimate to
WM. G. ORR, Manager,
150 BROADWAY, NEW YORK.

U CAN C
THE LATEST AND BEST
INSIDE SLIDING
AND
VENETIAN BLINDS
AT OFFICE OF
BURLINGTON BLIND CO.,
90 Nassau Street, New York.
Room 40. GEO. E. READ, Manager.
Send for catalogue and estimates.

Furnaces and Ranges.
NOW IS THE TIME TO HAVE YOURS PUT IN REPAIR.
Send in your orders to one who has been in the business the past 25 years, and have your work properly done.
IRA G. LANE,
207 East 64th St.

BUILDING MATERIAL PRICES

LUMBER.

Appended quotations are based almost wholly upon prices obtained for goods from first hands. Yard rates necessarily range much higher owing to the expenses attending sorting out and grading cargo and even car lots, besides which must be added the cost of handling and carrying until consumers are ready to invest. Terms of sale also prove important factors and, altogether, it is impossible to give a line of retail quotations thoroughly reliable n character.

SPRUCE—Eastern—special cargoes delivered N. Y.	$16 50	@	18 00
Random cargoes, narrow	14 00	@	15 00
Random cargoes, wide	15 50	@	16 50
PILING—Eastern—cargo rates:			
Ranging 30@40 per cent 12 inch butt, 35 to 40 ft average length	4	@	—
Ranging 45@50 per cent 12 inch butt, 35 to 40 ft average length	4¼	@	4½
Ranging 50@60 per cent One-half 12 inch butt, 38 to 40 ft average length	4¾	@	5
Two-thirds 12 inch butt, 38 to 42 ft average length	5½	@	6
Three-fourths 12 inch butt, 40 to 45 ft average length	5¾	@	6
All 12 inch butt and up, 40 to 45 ft average length	6	@	6¼
Piece stick, 40 feet each	4 00	@	—
do. 45	6 00	@	—
do. 50	8 00	@	—
do. 55	12 00	@	—
Inch spars, per inch	20	@	22
Scaffolding poles, each	60	@	1 00
Clothes poles, 45 to 65 feet, each	3 00	@	6 00
HEMLOCK:			
Penn. joist	12 00	@	12 50
do. boards	13 00	@	13 50
do. timber, 20 ft and under	12 50	@	13 00
do. do. 22 to 24 ft	13 00	@	13 50
do. do. 26 to 28 ft	13 50	@	14 00
do. do. 30 to 32 ft	14 00	@	15 50
do. do. 34 to 36 ft	15 50	@	16 00
do. do. 38 to 40 ft	16 50	@	17 50
WHITE PINE—Good uppers and select, 1 to 2 inch	40 00	@	48 00
Upper and select, 2½ to 4 inch	50 00	@	58 00
Shelving	26 00	@	31 00
Pickings, 1 inch	33 00	@	35 00
Cutting-up, 1 inch	25 00	@	28 00
Bracket plank	30 00	@	35 00
Dressing-boards	18 00	@	22 00
Box, inch	13 50	@	14 00
Box, thick	14 50	@	15 50
West India shippers	16 00	@	19 00
Rio Janeiro do.	20 00	@	21 00
River Plate do.	29 00	@	30 00
Australia do.	25 00	@	30 00
YELLOW PINE—Random cargoes delivered N. Y.	19 00	@	20 00
Ordered cargoes	20 00	@	22 00
Flooring	21 00	@	24 00
Step plank	26 00	@	28 00
Common siding	15 00	@	16 00
Heart face boards	21 00	@	23 00
Car orders	21 00	@	23 00
At Atlantic ports, f. o. b.	12 00	@	12 50
At Gulf ports, f. o. b.	11 50	@	12 50
North Caroline pine timber	13 50	@	15 00
do. flooring 1 inch	16 00	@	22 00
do. do. 1¼	16 50	@	22 50
do. do. 1½@2 inch	24 00	@	25 00
do Shipping culls or box	12 00	@	14 00
do Plain and mottled ½@1½ inch	18 50	@	25 50
Ash, white	36 00	@	48 00
Elm	20 00	@	22 50
Oak, plain	37 00	@	41 00
Oak, quarter sawed	52 00	@	55 00
Oak, quarter sawed, extra thick	56 00	@	60 00
Redwood	45 00	@	52 50
Maple, clear	28 00	@	33 00
Chestnut, clear	33 00	@	35 50
Cypress, clear	30 00	@	37 50
Black Walnut, good to choice	130 00	@	140 00
Black Walnut, ordinary to fair	100 00	@	120 00
Black Walnut, ⅝	78 00	@	83 00
Black Walnut, selected and seasoned	150 00	@	155 00
Black Walnut counters	110 00	@	150 00
Black Walnut, culls	35 00	@	40 00
Black Walnut, rejects	50 00	@	53 00
Cherry, wide	110 00	@	115 00
Cherry, good	85 00	@	100 00
Cherry, ordinary	65 00	@	80 00
Whitewood, inch	30 50	@	32 50
Whitewood, ⅝ inch	24 50	@	26 00
Whitewood, 1¼ to 2½ inch	32 00	@	34 00
Shingles, Pine, 16 inch, extra	2 75	@	3 10
do 18 inch, extra	4 10	@	4 30
do 18 inch, clear butt	2 90	@	3 10
do 16 inch, stocks	4 50	@	4 60
do 18 inch, stocks	5 30	@	5 40
Shingles, Cypress, 6x20	8 00	@	10 00
do larger sizes	11 00	@	15 00
do sawed	6 00	@	9 00
Cedar—Medium to large	6¼	@	7½
do. —Extra large	7¾	@	8
Mahogany—Small	6½	@	7½
do —Medium	8	@	8½
do. —Large	9½	@	12
do. —Extra Large	10½	@	14

VERMONT MARBLE CO
35 HANCOCK PLACE, N. Y.
Near 125th St. and 9th Av.
C. T. HULBURT, Agent.
Rear Sills, Lintels, Steps, Roof Coping, Pier Stones, Etc., a Specialty.
Telephone Call—898 Harlem.

KOCH PAT. SHIFTABLE REVERSIBLE BRACKETS
FOR SHELVING STORES — LIBRARIES CUPBOARDS & C.
380 MAIN ST. KOCH·A·B·Co PEORIA-ILL.
GEO. E. READ, Agent, 90 Nassau St., N. Y.

Real Estate
RECORD
and Builders
GUIDE.
ESTABLISHED MARCH 21st 1868.
DEVOTED TO REAL ESTATE, BUILDING ARCHITECTURE, HOUSEHOLD DECORATION,
BUSINESS AND THEMES OF GENERAL INTEREST

PRICE, PER YEAR IN ADVANCE, SIX DOLLARS.

Published every Saturday.

TELEPHONE - - - - CORTLANDT 1370.

Communications should be addressed to

C. W. SWEET, 14 & 16 Vesey St.

J. T. LINDSEY, Business Manager.

"Entered at the Post-office at New York, N. Y., as second-class matter."

VOL. XLVIII. DECEMBER 19, 1891. No. 1,240

WALL STREET has seldom been so much lacking in all exciting features as at present. Prices are undergoing a slow and steady advance; the buying being largely in small lots. Hence both bonds and stocks are evidently being absorbed by the average investor, which makes a very healthy market. Not even the meeting of Congress has operated to disturb this unwonted equanimity of temper. The public have taken for granted that no legislation of any importance affecting business conditions will be passed during the coming session, not only because the two Houses are of different political persuasions, but because it is seldom that the fiscal policy of a country is changed during prosperous times. President Harrison stands resolutely between the free silverites and their object; consequently there is nothing to be feared on that score. If, however, no ills are to be anticipated from Congress, but little good news can be expected which is not already known. During the coming week the Vanderbilt roads declare their dividends. Everyone is aware that the rate of distribution is to be increased, and when the amount of the increase is known, investors will be able to judge whether the stocks have been advanced as much as they should under the circumstances. Cheap money is now assured for the first half of 1892, and this cheap money will not only raise the level of the prices of all investment securities, but will stimulate and facilitate the floating of new industrial companies. A number of these concerns, one of them as large as the largest at present dealt in speculatively will be brought out at a favorable opportunity and will doubtless meet the success which other ventures of the same class have attained. There is no doubt that these industrials will be regarded in the future with very much greater favor by the investing and the speculative public than they have in times past. At present the average investor fights shy of them, and rather than buy them puts his money in some Western railroad which he never has seen and never will see; yet these industrials are formed by the consolidation into one company of the manufacturing industries which are the basis of many of our greatest fortunes. In time this prejudice must wear away; and stocks like the Standard Oil, which pay 12 per cent and earn 20 on a large inflated capitalization, will not sell below railway securities that pay only 10 per cent.

THE past few weeks have done much to remove the fears of some immediate political disturbance such as have kept European financiers on the keen edge of anxiety. The chief agency in bringing about this result was the speech of Gen. Caprivi, the German Chancellor, in which with evident sincerity he announced his belief that peace would be maintained and answered all the pessimistic arguments of the newspapers. These authorities, he said, magnified the importance of the visit of the French to Cronstadt, but a great deal of noise quite needlessly was made about the renewal of the Triple Alliance, and it "gave other people a feeling that they would like to make a little noise too." The success of the meeting had gratified the *amour propre* of France, but a heightened feeling of *amour propre* only diminishes national nervousness which produces more rash acts than national courage does. As for Russia, he knew that the Czar had personally the most peaceful intentions, and no Power has such a consciousness of preponderance that it can say to itself cheerfully, "Now let us have war," or cease to remember that the next campaign will be one to the death of the defeated side. This kind of talk, quieting as it is to the feverish anticipations of many foreigners, will not suffice to make people change their minds as to business prospects, nor will the commercial treaties between Germany, Italy and Austria produce that effect, although they may do a great deal of good. The real cause of the depression is sheer exhaustion after four years' race after premiums, and until this exhaustion is overcome, there can be no thorough improvement either in business or in finance.

THE New York and New Jersey Bridge Company still fails to give any indications of substantial activity. It has done a great deal of work in the newspapers during the past year. To read an interview with one of its officials, it might be supposed that bridges can be built just as easily as charters can be obtained, corporations organized and plans prepared. The official announces that by such and such a time the pier on the New Jersey side is going to be started; but he says nothing about the money that is to be raised, the banking house that is taking the company's bonds, or the railroads that have contracted to use the bridge. If there appeared among the officials the name of one man who was known to be a successful and conservative financier, or if the officials of the company could point to a single important railroad that had signed an agreement to use the structure, honest criticism would for the present be hushed; but all that appears on the surface are the names of people more remarkable in the way of political than for financial influence. These people obtained a charter from the Legislature which permits them to build railroads through the City of New York irrespective of property-owners and the constituted authorities. That in itself would be sufficient to condemn the "scheme" and to warrant the repeal of the bill under which the company organized. If the company had any power it would be dangerous; but, being without power, it is only ridiculous and annoying—annoying because of the impediments which its scheme puts in the way of the activity and improvement of a large area of real property, and ridiculous because of the tremendous difference between what it claims and what it can accomplish. Bridges costing $50,000,000, and revolutionizing the freight transportation around a city like New York, may possibly be constructed; but they are never constructed by corporations with such slim backing as that possessed by the New York & New Jersey Bridge Company.

THE reticence of New York regarding the World's Fair is now practically ended. Only a trace of the old opposition and coldness exists in a few out-of-the-way quarters. The entire press of the city has at last acquired an amount of insight sufficient to enable it to see that there is to be a real World's Fair in Chicago; that it is a great national enterprise. Politics and local narrowness are now fortunately lost in a robust and growing enthusiasm. The only thing that remains to be done is to see that the Empire State is not only adequately but even "largely" represented at the Exposition. New York should have not only the largest but the finest State building on the Jackson Park grounds, and the Legislature should appropriate not $500,000, but a good round million for the purpose. Even if the return should come only in the good feeling of Chicagoans and the people of the West generally the expenditure will be wise and even remunerative. It is better now to stop all calculation as to whether international exhibitions pay or accomplish much of value in extending commercial good feeling among nations. The Fair is arranged for and we must do the best we can to make the most of it. The probability is that the best results of the Fair will be an increased knowledge of this country, its condition and its resources, which will be disseminated among foreigners, particularly in Central and South American countries, and the impetus which perhaps may be given to a higher technical and artistic development of our manufactures.

THAT the trustees of Columbia should be contemplating the removal of the college to a larger site farther up town will be gratifying to the friends of that institution. It is hardly possible that the present very inadequate space into which buildings of the college are jammed does not hamper its growth in various directions. The trustees must, of course, be more keenly alive to this than any outsider; and the fact that they have finally faced the necessity of removal, in spite of all the difficulties in the way of such a step, indicates that the college will not be long lodged in its present circumscribed buildings. The committee, however, that have the matter in charge cannot be congratulated on the site which they have tentatively selected, viz., the area between the 10th avenue, the Boulevard, 116th and 120th streets. Columbia, when it moves this second time, should look farther ahead than it did when it left College place. The trustees should consider whether by getting a site somewhere on the North Side, or in Westchester County, they will not only save the bother and expense of another removal within many years, and whether at the same time they may not add a valuable but at present a wanting element to the collegiate life of their institution, viz., a little college spirit. The first objection may seem to be founded on a false analogy, for the twenty acres which the trustees now propose to purchase is so very much larger than the present space occupied by the college, that any fear of further inconvenience with cramped quarters for fifty years or so would seem to be unnecessary and foolish. That this is the opinion of President Low is clearly indicated by the way in which he made the announcement. "The alumni," he said, "will therefore perceive, and the city as well, that the trustees of Columbia College have an adequate conception, at least, I may say not an inadequate one of the possibilities of a university as the great university of the American metropolis." But the point to be considered is that the site in question, excellent as it is in some respects, will before the century is ended be as much in the heart of the city as 48th street and Madison avenue is at the present time. This fact has two consequences. In the first place the proposed site can be purchased only at a very heavy expense, and in the second place, it will soon be walled in by brick so as to prohibit any further expansion in that neighborhood. And very certainly the time will come, and that, perhaps, during the presidency of Seth Low, when more space will be needed. If the twenty acres are ever purchased the whole of it will be apportioned to immediate uses. After the passing of a few years new schools will be needed and new buildings of different kinds, and the sites for these structures can be obtained only by encroaching on space already given over to definite purposes. This has been the history of Harvard and Yale, and it has led to the perpetual demand for more room. If Columbia again locates herself where it cannot be obtained, another removal in course of time is most probable.

POSSIBLY, however, the strongest argument can be founded on the expense of the proposed site. If twenty acres is all the land the college will need for a hundred years to come (the trustees ought to provide for that length of time), those twenty acres can be obtained for a sum less by ten times on the North Side than on the Heights above Morningside. The trustees have got to raise $2,000,000 to take up their option on the latter property; further north they could get the same acreage for $2.0,000. Or in case they can raise the $2,000,000 for the purpose, they could purchase 200 acres, which would probably be enough to carry Columbia over the twentieth century. It will naturally be objected to this, that the inaccessibility of the North Side would make it impossible for the students to get to and from college daily; to which the answer is, that if the settlement of the matter is delayed for a few years until the North Side becomes accessible no fault can be found on that score. It must be remembered that the proposed site is reached with so much difficulty from the elevated railroads that nobody lives in the vicinity, and that the accessibility both of the North Side and Morningside Heights will depend on the new transit line. In this connection it is at least worthy of discussion whether Columbia does not lose more than it gains by being situated in the heart of a high-priced city like New York. It is true that such a location commends it to patronage of many parents who are either unable or unwilling to send their promising boys to a college in some distant city, but, on the other hand, it loses the support of students from all over the country whose parents are able and willing to have the boys leave home, but are unable or unwilling to have them live in New York. In case Columbia was situated a few miles outside of the density of the metropolis, just as Harvard is situated a few miles outside of Boston, the children of New York parents, while having their rooms near the college as at Harvard, would nevertheless be so frequently at home that careful and watchful parents could keep a knowing eye on their doings. But the great advantage of the comparative isolation of a college and removal of the student from the home sphere is the creation of a college spirit most helpful to the boy, both during his college course and subsequent thereto. Such an institution is properly a community; and its work gains greatly in effectiveness when close relation exists among the students and between them and their instructors. This close relation is lacking at Columbia.

WE print elsewhere, with an account of the election, the annual report of President Geo. R. Read to the members of the Real Estate Exchange. It is one of the pleasantest documents of the kind that has been issued since the institution was started. It shows that the Exchange has not only materially strengthened its financial position, but overcome its internal difficulties and settled down to a policy which yields larger returns than the old one, and makes for the greater dignity of the Exchange. The officials who have been instrumental in bringing this result about deserve the hearty thanks of all members. We would like, however, to see the Exchange take a still further step forward. There are lines of development which have not yet been entered upon. We would like to see the Exchange in closer touch with the larger commercial interests of the metropolis. The part which the Chamber of Commerce plays in national questions of finance, the Real Estate Exchange might well play in local matters. In other words, the Exchange might be to New York City what the Board of Trade is in Western towns, with the addition of giving attention to the proper administration of municipal affairs. There is no body of men so closely in touch with the needs of the city, commercial, legislative and administrative, as the real estate brokers. They are among the first to feel any new or extended demands upon the city's resources. They are also among the first to feel any restriction. Moreover they are the largest body of men so influenced, and their wishes would probably be more potent, either in the City Hall or at Albany, than any other.

What Is Wanted.

IT is not too much to say that the way in which the property-owners along the proposed new rapid transit route are responding to applications for consent is decidedly disappointing. The plan was received with very general approval, and it seemed at first probable that the work of obtaining the necessary legal approvals would be most easily accomplished; but this has not proved to be the case. Although the canvassing has been going on for some weeks now, the number of consents obtained from private individuals is surprisingly small. The acquiescence of about $90,000,000 worth of property is needed. Of this only $50,000,000 has as yet consented, and of this $50,000,000 about $35,000,000 represents real estate owned by the city, so that out of private property to the assessed value of something like $150,000,000 along the line of the route, only about $15,000,000 or one-tenth has agreed to the plan, in spite of the fact that the road if built will in all human probability make such property of considerably greater value, particularly along Broadway and the Boulevard. Indeed, we cannot understand the disinclination of lower Broadway property-owners to give their approval. If this line is ever built, it is written, as unmistakable as writing ever was, that the length, depth and breadth of New York's future all belongs to this thoroughfare, that for the next hundred years, at any rate, the population of are great city will find in Broadway their indispensable street. If this means real estate valued at from $50 to $200 per square foot when New York has a population of 1,800,000 what will it mean when this population is five or six millions. Notwithstanding, however, arguments of this character, the consents so far obtained along lower Broadway are scattered and for the most part unimportant.

True, this opposition, so far as developed, has been passive rather than active, but the property-owners along another portion of the route are unequivocal in their condemnation of the plan, so far as it affects their property. All the owners along Madison avenue, from 43d to 90th street, or thereabouts, are in arms against the method of construction. We believe that their objections are based upon a misconception, and that the method of construction is not open to the objections which have been brought against it, but the objections, if founded on error, are none the less real. Even if a sufficient number of consents can be obtained along other portions of the route it would not be right to construct a road along two miles and a half of an avenue against the wishes of by far the larger number of the abutting owners. What view the Commissioners will take about this we do not know. Fourth avenue is manifestly preferable to Madison for the purpose, because the improvements on 4th avenue are of a class which are adapted to its use as a railroad avenue. But we are not here discussing the rights and the wrongs of the Madison avenue property-owners. They are brought in simply as an illustration of the obstacles which any comprehensive system of rapid transit is bound to meet. Much time will be consumed, either in removing or getting around these objections. It is certain, also, that even if the property-owners can be placated, engineering and financial impediments will arise. Every step in the work of the Commission has but shown with ever-increasing plainness the enormous difficulty of the task they have undertaken, the variety of subordinate problems which have to be solved, and the ignorant and hasty opposition, or leaden apathy to be overcome.

What the outcome will be no one can tell; but if the work is going to be properly done, the Commission ought to have enough time to do it in. But this is just what, under the present conditions, New York cannot afford to give to them. Every year several thousand families, who would live in New York City if they could find therein a cheap, comfortable and accessible home, migrate to New Jersey and Long Island. A few years ago, until the Bridge became choked with traffic, Brooklyn was the more popular direction; lately, judging from the rise in the value of real estate in certain New Jersey towns, that side has been most favored. All this is a certain and nearly a complete loss to New York City. These people, if they settled or remained among us, would contribute in a hundred ways to the city's growth and prosperity where they now contribute in only two or three ways. There is but one method of stopping this exodus; and that is, to set about, like sensible people, to alleviate our pressing necessities before rearing the structure intended to compass requirements for fifty years. Previous to beginning the preparation of a detailed plan, the Commissioners ought to have done what they could towards helping the Manhattan Company to improve its service, and ought to have recommended to the Legislature that permission be granted for the extra switching room needed at the Battery. Instead of beginning sensibly and cautiously in this manner they immediately plunged into the great work of solving the problem for all time; and for nearly a year now have been floundering around in the preliminaries. But it is not too late to remedy the error. They should make time for themselves. Let them spend six months in alleviating the discomforts and removing inadequacies of our present transit service, and then all the time needed to complete the more important and enduring work will be ungrudgingly granted to them. It is not right that so important a task should be done hurriedly. Any property-owners like those on Madison avenue have every right to cause delays and to prevent progress until they are assured that their interests will be secure. All such doubtful matters should be settled beyond the reach of criticism. But so long as these delays occur, while the work continues urgent, the tendency will be to over-ride obstacles for the sake of getting the job completed. Every day makes the necessity of a longer lease of time more obvious. Every day makes the granting of additional tracks and structure to the Manhattan Company more imperative.

Nor is this all. The Commission continues to work on just as if in the end they were not sure to meet an almost insuperable impediment. It is common talk among the most expert financiers down town that nothing like the capital needed to construct the route can be raised by a private company. Such a view may be wrong, but the alternative to it is not a jot more palatable. In all probability if private capital can be raised to construct the route according to the Commission's plans, the corporation will be able to extort terms so favorable from the city's representatives that New York will profit little from what will eventually be a most valuable franchise. The company will insist not only on a merely nominal payment, but possibly on a very slow construction of the route—that is, they would build from the Battery say to 125th street in the beginning, and when that division began to pay they would gradually extend their line, but so gradually that many years would be occupied in bringing it to completion. We do not say that this particular thing will happen, but there is every probability that something of the kind will happen, that the Commission, in order to sell the franchise will have to make concessions to the corporation, either in terms or in service, and that these concessions will mean either a service less complete than the conditions require, or the surrender to the company of all that margin of future increase which is the chief source of profit in every railroad. If this is the case New York will pay too high for the capital needed to build a new rapid transit system. So that in the end it will amount to this: that even if a private company can be obtained, we ought not in the interests of economy to throw into its hands the increment of the next hundred years. It must be remembered that the coming rapid transit system will never be subject to any competition, that on all future occasions it cannot be disregarded as we are now trying to disregard the Manhattan Company, but will have to be consulted about any extension of trackage or service, and that if the contract is once entered into, whatever the loss, it must remain until the end. We have already shown that the municipality can construct the proposed system at an annual cost of nearly $2,000,000 less than a private company can; we have shown that the city has lost something like $20,000,000 which it might have had by a better management of the present elevated roads. This is a very pretty sum; but how much will New York lose by selling still more valuable possessions in the same way? Perhaps nothing for the first ten years, but eventually a sum which it is impossible now to calculate, and would seem ridiculous if stated.

These important and broader aspects of our rapid transit problem have not received the attention and the consideration that they deserve; and when the time comes for their settlement, this lack of consideration will practically insure one result—they will be settled most unwisely. New Yorkers leave all discussion of such important affairs to their newspapers; but the only subject these oracles know anything about is "journalism," and "journalism," so far as we have been able to observe, does not include anything of serious interest save politics. When a proposition is made which the "journalists" do not find under their nose, the only word of wisdom they have to offer is some catch-word. They stare at the intruder, throw up their arms, take a mental attitude similar to that of an Indian medicine man in front of an evil spirit, and shout oracularly: "Monopoly," or "Tammany," or "Un-American," or "Undemocratic." That is about the character of the discussion which most public matters receive in this great city; and such very simple, not to say childlike methods of reasoning do not supply anything except "copy" of value to anybody. It is to be hoped, however, that the more intelligent citizens will in time begin to see this rapid transit problem in its true bearings, for in the end rapid transit is not merely a means of getting up and down town; it is the chiefest single agency working for the health, freedom and prosperity of the inhabitants of a city. As such, it should be discussed without prepossessions, and with eyes that can see beyond a "journalist's" nose or the walls of a "journalist's" office, out into the present and the future of the city itself.

To Go to the Supreme Court.

It has become pretty well apparent to the Rapid Transit Commissioners that they are not going to secure the consents of a sufficient number of the property-owners along the lines of the roads they have laid out to the construction of the roads. If it had not been provided in the act that in case the Commission could not secure the necessary number of consents it could apply to the Supreme Court for the appointment of a commission to give the consent instead of the property-owners, the latter would undoubtedly have responded in sufficient number before this time to indicate that the whole number could be secured within a reasonable time.

But most of the owners who have taken the trouble to investigate the matter have for one reason or another concluded to let the matter go on to the appointment of the Commission by the Supreme Court. They have displayed a general sensitiveness to signing voluntary consents for fear that in so doing they would waive some of their legal rights, such as the right to protest against any feature of the plans of construction which might hereafter seem to them inimical to their interests, or the right to proceed in the Courts for the recovery of possible damages to their property in the construction of the road. They have argued that if the Commission should secure the appointment of a Commission which should give to the required consent, their legal rights would not be in any manner jeopardized.

Again the Commission has found that a surprisingly large amount of the most valuable property along the Broadway line is held by trustees and executors, or by guardians for minor children, or by corporations, where the authority to sign the consent of the owners is not lodged in any single individual; and although the great majority of the individuals clothed with discretionary or legal authority in such cases are favorable to the construction of the road, and would readily sign if the property was their own, they have felt that the part of discretion in the matter was to refrain from signing. But if the Supreme Court Commission is appointed they will not oppose the construction of the road before that commission.

In view of all these facts the Commission will, it is said, soon apply to the Supreme Court, through its counsel, John M. Bowers, for the appointment of the Commission provided for in the act. The Rapid Transit Commission was bound to make an earnest effort to secure the voluntary consents of the owners along the lines of its projected roads, and it has done so. Every property owner has been requested to give his consent, and up to the present time something over 200 of them have responded favorably. But these constitute only a small percentage of the whole number necessary to authorize the construction of the road by their voluntary action. The board has made every reasonable effort, the property owners have not responded with the proper degree of interest and promptness to the advances of the Commission, and now it is time for the Commission to fall back on the privilege given it by the act. THE RECORD AND GUIDE is assured by a person in a position to know that the application will be made to the Supreme Court at an early day.

The opposition of Madison avenue residents to the construction of the underground road through their sacred thoroughfare had forced the Commission to show its hand in that matter. It is reported that the members of the Commission admit that Madison avenue was a second choice with them for the East Side route, and that they would welcome a proposition from the proper authority that would permit of the changing of the route to 4th avenue. The plans originally submitted by William E. Worthen, then Chief Engineer of the Commission, were for the continuation of the East Side line northward from 42d street, through the Grand Central Station and along 4th avenue to the Harlem River. But an investigation of the question as to the extent to which the New York Central Railroad Company had acquired vested rights in that street led the Commission to the selection of Madison avenue for the proposed road.

Early in the week the New York Central Railroad Company sent one of its engineers down to the Rapid Transit headquarters to examine the plans adopted and to make other inquiries into the plans of the Commission, and it is considered not at all unlikely that the company will open negotiations with the Commission, looking to the designation of 4th avenue for the route of the east side line. Fourth avenue is already devoted to railroad uses, is 140 feet wide, while Madison avenue is but 80 feet wide; Madison avenue would be injured by the construction of an underground or any other kind of railroad through it, while 4th avenue would be greatly improved by it. As to these facts there are no two opinions. In view of them all the Commission is preparing to apply to the coming Legislature for an extension of its powers to enable it to change the route of the road after its approval by the Board of Aldermen, provided the Board of Aldermen approves of the change. It will also ask for authority to permit the construction of the road through the North Side, temporarily, and until the traffic develops sufficiently to pay the fixed charges on the cost of the permanent construction, according to the plans of the Commission, on the surface of the ground. There is also talk of a bill to authorize the construction of the road by the city. The plan of this bill, it is said, is to authorize the present Commission to construct the road, the same as the Aqueduct Commission built the aqueduct, and for the Comptroller to issue bonds upon the requisition of the Commission to pay for it. Then the city would own the road and could auction off the franchise to equip and operate the road for fixed periods of years to the highest and best bidder. But this last bill will not emanate from the Commission, although the members of the Commission would not oppose it.

In the meantime the Commission has not been idly waiting for the consents of backward property-owners to come in. There have been from two to four meetings every week, at which the Commissioners have been engaged in discussing with their engineer, Mr. Parsons, the location of stations and such alterations in the depth of the tunnel in Broadway as the last surveys of the sub-surface of the street have made necessary; as for instance, at Houston street, where the construction of a sheave chamber 24 feet deep by the cable railroad company has made it necessary to change the level of the tunnel so that it will go below this sheave chamber. The proposed chamber at Bleecker street will therefore be the deepest one along the line of the road; it will be about as deep as the average descent from an elevated railroad platform. The Commissioners are also continuously engaged with their engineer on the detailed plans of construction which the act requires them to prepare before the road is put up at auction. This is a work requiring much time and labor, and even if the consents of property-owners were now satisfactorily arranged the Commission would not be ready to proceed with the next step, which is the determination of the terms of sale of the road.

In the meantime the work of soliciting the consents of property-owners goes on without interruption under William Nowland Amory and his corps of canvassers. During the week the long-expected report of the doings of the commission up to date has been finished by the printer, and is now ready for distribution to property owners. It is a huge volume, valuable for the amount of statistical information it contains, and if any one has been hesitating about signing his consent to the construction of the road for lack of official information, he can get all he wants by sending to the office of the Commission, No. 22 William street, for one of these reports. The consents received during the last week are as follows:

Broadway—James Gordon Bennett, *Herald* property, 218 and 220, $400,000; William McMoen Purdy, 474, $65,000; Thomas C. Acton, 1557, $19,000; James Breslin, the Lincoln apartment house, corner of 52d street, $123,000; Bertrand D. Depierris, 1701 to 1707 inclusive, $62,000; Robert F. Sixby, Casino, corner of 39th street, $250,000; Ferdinand P. Earle, Hotel Normandie, $250,000; Edward C. Fiedler, 22, $92,000; Harriet W. Barnard, 1568, $16,000; estate of Paul Spofford, 1131 to 1137 inclusive, $340,000; Leo Schlesinger, 704, $31,000. Previously reported, $45,791,748. Total to date, $47,498,748.

Boulevard—Montefiore Home, $75,000; Cornelia R. Rhodes, $37,500; Henry Brash, $7,500; Detlef Sammann, $18,000; Waldo Hutchins, $30,000; Constance I. Orcanyon, $16,800; J. H. Edelmeyer and Wm. C. Morgan, $10,000; David Campbell, $12,500; Elizabeth Coates, $33,000; estate of Robert Prior, $10,600; Mary C. Burke, $8,500; Waller & Lawson, $10,000; estate of John Burke, $15,400; Paul Hepburn, $1,200; John D. Crimmins, $8,000; Henry Fauchaux, $3,000; Robert V. Lynch, $3,000; Beverly Ward, $105,000; Edward Rafter, $12,000; Florence N. Levy, $1,000; Joseph C. Levi, $5,000; Eliza J. Thomas, $3,000; John Reilly, $16,000; B. T. Kearns, $12,000. Previously reported, $1,353,000. Total to date, $1,897,000.

East Side Line—Maria Ingram, 844 4th avenue, $17,000; Leah F. Moore, 70 East 111th street, $5,000. Previously reported, $1,781,000. Total to date, $1,803,000.

Grand total to date, $51,198,748.

The Annual Meeting of the Real Estate Exchange.

The Real Estate Exchange held its annual meeting and election on Monday afternoon last. Shortly after one o'clock President Geo. R. Read called the meeting to order and after the passage of a motion to dispense with the reading of the report and balance sheet, addressed the members as follows:

"The report and balance sheet, which have been sent you, contain a statement of the progress of the Exchange for the past year, during which we have made a net profit of 6, and paid dividends amounting to 5 per cent. Our progress has been twofold; our receipts have increased over last year by $3,435.91, and our expenses have diminished by $4,798.93. With regard to this last item, I would say that the economy is chiefly to be attributed to the fact that it has been unnecessary to make any large expenditures on the building during the past year. The increase in the receipts is mainly due to the new scale of knock-downs which came into force on the 1st of January last. By the action of this rule the quotations in 397 instances have been kept off the bulletin, and we have to thank the auctioneers for the assistance they have rendered us, so that our daily quotations contain only an authentic record of actual values. With a growing income and an increasing business, the Exchange may now be fairly considered to have reached smooth water.

"I have also the satisfaction to announce that should the regular ticket be elected, which I have every reason to believe that it will, whatever good fortune or bad fortune we may have in the coming year, we shall meet as a united board. Whatever differences of opinion may have existed in the earlier stages of the Exchange are now at rest; and our one policy will be so to administer the affairs of the Exchange that it may continue to grow in public confidence, in usefulness to its members, and as a factor of justice and fair dealing in the real estate market.

"You have already been notified that the laws of 1875, under which the Exchange was organized, have been repealed. The repealing act contains a clause specially preserving all acts done under the previous law. It has not, therefore, been actually necessary for us to reorganize under the new law, and as there seems every probability that changes may be made in the new law during the coming session, the board in their discretion have thought it better, with the advice of their counsel, to postpone any new registration under the existing law, until such changes, if any, have been made.

"The Exchange has been unusually free from misunderstanding among its members during the past year. The services of the Complaint Committee have not been required, and only one case has been heard by the Arbitration Committee.

"Since the report was printed, it has been suggested that the Exchange could assist the Commissioners of Rapid Transit by calling a meeting of the principal property-owners in the City of New York, at which some of the difficulties in the way of assenting to the road might be explained. Everybody is in favor of rapid transit in theory, but some property-owners naturally hesitate to commit themselves to an assent, without knowing whether or not such assent shall preclude them from a right of action in the event of damage to their property or their rights. It has, therefore, been decided that such a meeting shall be called, at which the Commissioners of Rapid Transit are to be represented, and those points cleared up, so that the work of obtaining the assents may rapidly proceed, not only in the interests of the scheme itself, but of the general improvement of New York City.

"I regret to have to announce that Mr. Hermann H. Cammann has decided, after eight years' service as a director, to retire from the Board of this Exchange. During that period he has served at different times both as president and vice-president, and as Chairman of the Finance and Auction Room Committees. To all these offices he has brought the same patient care, and has served in each with a single eye. I need not add that leaving this Board he carries with him the highest respect and gratitude of the members of this Exchange."

Isaac Fromme then moved the following preamble and resolutions. They were seconded by Richard Deeves and unanimously carried:

"*Whereas*, This meeting learns with regret that Mr. Hermann H. Cammann, who, during the past eight years has served this Exchange as president, vice-president and chairman of the Auction Room and Finance Committees and Director, has declined the renomination on the Board of Directors for the ensuing year.

"*Resolved*, That the officers and members of the Real Estate Exchange and Auction Room (Lim.) desire to convey to Mr. Cammann their appreciation of his conscientious, able and efficient services in those several offices, and to assure him that he carries with him on his retirement from the board the respect and gratitude of the officers, stockholders and members of this Exchange, whose interests he has so faithfully served. Be it further

"*Resolved*, That a copy of these resolutions be suitably engrossed, signed by the directors and officers now elected, and presented to Mr. Cammann as a record of this day's proceedings."

The president announced the polls open until 3 o'clock. The election was delayed a few minutes by the absence of Thomas Folsom, one of the election inspectors, but his place was supplied by his brother, W. H. Folsom, whom President Read appointed as substitute. The election was the quietest and most uneventful that has ever been held in the Exchange. Under the new non-cumulative system of voting the opposition were almost powerless to elect any of their candidates, and, realizing this, they abstained from voting. In fact, only one or two members of the auctioneer opposition put in an appearance and these cast no ballots.

At four o'clock the election inspectors completed their count, and it was announced that 249 blocks of stock had been voted on out of 500 shares, or less than half the stockholders only had been sufficiently interested in the outcome to either vote in person or by proxy.

The whole regular ticket, including the election inspectors, was elected, the candidates receiving from 2,440 to 2,490 votes each. The successful candidates are as follows:

Directors: George R. Read, Cornelius W. Luyster, Richard V. Harnett, Edward Oppenheimer, Charles A. Schermerhorn, George De F. Barton, William Cruikshank, J. Romaine Brown, Isaac Fromme, James E. Leviness, Ira D. Warren, Charles S. Brown, Richard Deeves.

Inspectors of the next Annual Election: Alfred E. Marling, Warren Cruikshank, Bryan L. Kennelly.

John F. B. Symth, Jas. L. Wells and Frank Yoran each received ten votes on various tickets for the office of Director.

The new Board of Directors met on Thursday afternoon and elected officers for the ensuing year. There was no opposition and these officers were elected unanimously: President—Geo. R. Read; First Vice-President—C. A. Schermerhorn; Second Vice-President—C. W. Luyster; Treasurer—Edward Oppenheimer; and Secretary—Isaac Fromme. With the exception of the secretary the officers are the same as those who served last year. Mr. Read appointed the standing committees for the year as follows: Auction Room—C. W. Luyster, R. V. Harnett, Chas. S. Brown, W. Cruikshank, J. E. Leviness; Finance—C. A. Schermerhorn, chairman; Arbitration—Wm. Reynolds Brown, chairman; Complaint—Horace S. Ely, chairman; Brokers—F. R. Houghton, chairman; Membership, J. Romaine Brown, chairman; and Legislative—Thomas F. Murtha, chairman.

The Proposed New Exchange Building.

The interview with Secretary Wright, of the Mechanics' and Traders' Exchange, which appeared in last week's issue of THE RECORD AND GUIDE, has had considerable influence with many who were wavering between support and indifference to the movement for a new Exchange building which shall represent the great building interests of this city. Like all movements of the kind, it is difficult to get those used to the old order of things to come out of their shells and enter boldly into a new enterprise, even though on the face of it it is assured of success.

MORE EXCHANGE MEMBERS INTERVIEWED.

Chas. A. Cowan, one of the most prominent members of the Building Trades' Club, said: "I am very heartily in favor of the new Exchange building, and I will do all in my power to make it a success. I think that everyone connected with the building trades should hail with satisfaction the erection of such an Exchange."

Robert Main, the brick manufacturer, was seen at the Building Material Exchange. He said: "It would be a splendid thing if the two exchanges could be got to unite. I would think it most desirable for us all to have one big exchange, instead of having our forces divided. It would be better for all of us to be together as one body, for in that case our influence would be greater in any public or business movement that might affect us or which we might be called to act. How much stronger would the building interests of this great metropolis be if they were all united in one great body and thoroughly organized. Besides, it would be a source of economy and profit to all of us. We have now several rents and several staffs of employes to keep, whereas one set of employes would be enough in the new building if we were all united, and our rent could be saved. There would be another source of economy in the fact that many of us who now belong to two or three bodies would then pay dues only in one."

Howard Fleming, while agreeing, to some extent, with the views expressed by Richard Deeves in THE RECORD AND GUIDE recently, tha the telephone had lessened the necessity for an exchange, was none the less of the belief that such a structure, somewhere between 14th and 23d streets, would be of great service to the building interests. "There is no reason why it should not pay as an investment, just as it does in Philadelphia, Boston and Chicago," he said. "I, for one, would like to have an office in such a building, provided it were not too far up town, and I am confident that a number of architects, builders, contractors and others would also want offices in such a building. It would be a good thing to have all the building interests together at one spot. There should be a first-class exhibition of building material in the Exchange."

Hiram Snyder, of Rosendale Cement fame, said: "If you can manage to get the two Exchanges to agree together it would be a good plan to join and make the proposed exchange building a success."

An Exchange member said: "There are now over three hundred members in the Building Material Exchange, three hundred in the Mechanics' and Traders' Exchange and 225 in the Building Trades' Club. It is estimated that there are at least five hundred builders, contractors and others who would join such an Exchange, who now belong to employing plasterers', employing plumbers' and other organizations, the majority of whom do not now belong to any of the above bodies, not to speak of firms and individuals who are not attached to any organization whatever. It is estimated that with a thorough effort the new Exchange ought in a short time to have perhaps 1,000 members. One thousand members at so nominal a due as $40 per annum would yield $40,000, which is equivalent to 5 per cent on a capital of $800,000. This would leave the upper floors, consisting of eight or nine stories, according to the height arranged upon, to be rented out for offices, etc. It is not improbable that the income of these upper stories would be nearly twice as large as the receipts from dues, but supposing it to be only $60,000 it would give a total rental of $100,000 per annum, with prospective additional receipts from increased memberships. This is on the presumption that the building would be 100 feet square and nine to eleven stories high."

Augustus Meyers, one of the committee on the proposed Exchange, said: "There is not the slightest doubt about our being successful. Our members are now so busy with their contracts that they have had little time to think about it; but after the holidays there will be an impetus to the movement and it will take a more successful shape. The Exchange will be of great service to all connected with the building trades, and as an investment it will pay 6 per cent, and possibly more. The building will be well rented, for there will be a demand for offices in it by architects and contractors of every kind. We mean to carry through the plan."

Warren E. Conover said: "I am strongly in favor of the new Exchange, and I have no doubt that, with a united effort, it can be built."

Rowland Taylor said: "I think there is room for such an Exchange, and it ought to unite together all the great building interests in one building. It should certainly be up town, for most of the architects and contractors are north of 14th street. Indeed, it is surprising how many and how important are the architects north of that street. They are moving up town more and more each year.

The Mechanics' and Traders' Exchange has sent out a second circular calling attention to the plan to build the proposed Exchange building. Many prominent signatures have been obtained toward the movement, the questions asked being: 1. Are you in favor of securing an Exchange building at an approximate cost of $1,000,000? 2. Are you willing to subscribe the sum of $1,000 toward the cost of such a building, said subscription to be paid in installments, and to remain as an investment in said building and the lots on which it is erected? Signed answers have been received, among others, from the following:

John Byrns, Alex. Brown, Jr., A. S. Dickinson, Dawson & Archer, Thos. Dimond, Marc Eidlitz & Son, Robert L. Darragh, J. H. Drew, Ed. Franke, Isaac A. Hopper, Raritan H. and P. Brick Co., Jas. B. Mulry, A. Meyers, Henry Maurer & Son, O. T. Mackey, Thos. Mulry, John L Hamilton, A. E. Pelham, John J. Roberts, Wm. C. Smith, Perth Amboy Terra Cotta Co., Geo. Moore Smith, Clarence L. Smith, John Snaith, John J. Tucker, Wm. H. Vantassel, E. S. Vaughan, Stephen M. Wright, D. C. Weeks & Son, Chas. T. Wills and Louis Weber.

Law Questions.

No. 269 PEARL STREET, NEW YORK.
December 1st, 1891.

Editor RECORD AND GUIDE:

I am building a house by contract with a builder, he to furnish the materials and labor. I agree to pay him in three payments, two of which have been paid, and the third coming due in a few days. I am now notified by the parties from whom he bought the materials, and also by the masons and carpenters doing the work on the house, that they have not been paid, and they threaten to put a lien on the house unless I see that they get their money. I claim that my contract is with the builder, and that I am not responsible for his debts.

Can they put a lien on my house? FRED'K HANDTE.

[The material men and mechanics can file liens, but on all the liens so filed they can recover only the balance actually due from the owner to the contractor, and those liens would be paid in the order in which they are filed. So long as there is anything due from the owner to the contractor under the contract, a material man or mechanic who furnishes materials or performs work or labor on the house can file a lien, and the lien will attach and be good to the extent of the amount due from the owner to the contractor. Payments collusively made between the owner and contractor will not be allowed as against a mechanic's lien. The Statute so provides. But there is, however, no claim presented here that any payments by the owner to the contractor were collusively made. Mechanics' liens attach and are entitled to priority according to the time of their filing. The owner, however, cannot be called upon to pay any more than the amount due from him to the contractor, no matter how much the amount of the liens may be.]

Editor RECORD AND GUIDE:

A. employs B. (broker) to procure a loan for him on real estate. B. procures the loan for A. from C.; title is examined and approved by C.'s lawyer and day for closing is appointed.

C. incidentally discovers that property some time prior to acceptance of loan was sold for a little over amount of mortgage asked, and consequently refuses to carry out the loan. From whom can broker collect his commissions? SUBSCRIBER.

[The broker can only collect his commissions from the one who employed him, namely A. There was no contract of employment between the broker and C. Consequently the failure of C. to carry out his contract gives the broker no right of action against him. If there were a contract between A. and C. and broken by C., A. would have his remedy against C.]

The National Convention of Builders.

The sixth annual Convention of the National Association of Builders will take place at Cleveland, O., on Monday, January 18, 1892. The executive committee has issued a circular in reference to the matter, containing instructions, etc., and informing the different exchanges that programmes of the proceedings, with other information, will be issued in due course.

The Mechanics' and Traders' Exchange of this city, in anticipation of the event, have appointed the following representatives for the occasion: *Delegates:* John J. Tucker, A. J. Campbell, Stephen M. Wright, Henry Maurer, Jas. B. Mulry, O. T. Mackey and John Byrns. *Alternates:* Warren E. Conover, H. W. Redfield, Jno. McGlensey, Jacob S. Brown, F. M. Hausling, Wm. E. Munroe and Samuel I. Acken.

To Investigate the Alleged Scandal Regarding Public School Buildings.

The Building Committee of the Board of Education of the City of New York is about to move in the matter of investigating the charges made of fraud and corrupt practices in the construction and finishing of the city's school buildings. The matter has apparently lain quiescent for some weeks, but during this time the Board of Education has been moving quietly, and has now appointed J. R. Thomas as chairman of a committee of experts. Mr. Thomas will have full charge of the investigations to be made of all the public school buildings erected during the past six years. He has been requested by the Building Committee to make (subject to approval) such a selection of other experts as in his judgment shall be sufficient to the work in hand. These appointments will include each a carpenter, mason, sanitary and steam heating expert, together with such additional appointments as may be deemed necessary to a satisfactory and final settlement of the vexed questions raised. When, as Governor of the State of New York, Mr. Tilden's attention was called to the gross scandal and abuses growing out of the early history of the erection of the buildings of the State Reformatory at Elmira, he, with full appreciation of the wretched tangle into which matters had fallen, appointed Mr. Thomas architect of the Reformatory buildings, commissioning him to rid the enterprise of all political jobbery and chicanery as far as possible, and to bring to completion a work which should have been begun, continued and ended with honesty of purpose. The buildings of the Elmira institution are to-day models of their kind, and in his supervision of their construction as architect and sole commissioner Mr. Thomas saved to the State over a million of dollars.

How squarely Governor Tilden stood upon his feet as a man of fearless integrity and probity is so well known and recognized a fact that the Building Committee of the Board of Education is to be congratulated on its choice of a man who met and merited the Governor's confidence and approbation.

Marshall Field Buys New York Realty.

It is not a little interesting to find that shrewd and well-known business men in Chicago are putting their money into New York real estate. It would have been supposed that Chicago afforded only too many opportunities for the investment of the spare capital of its citizens. One or two recent transactions in New York realty by Chicago investors might have been relegated to a passing notice, but right on top of these comes a purchase by Marshall Field, whose fame in business is a household word in the West. The purchase comprises No. 104 Worth street, a five-story iron front store, on a lot 25x90.2. It is on the south side of the street, beginning 225.3 feet east of Broadway, and was purchased by Mr. Field from Lorillard Spencer for $80,200, subject to a mortgage of $40,000.

Other purchases made recently were by E. O. Hubbard, late of Chicago, who disposed of his holdings in that city to invest in New York property. He purchased, through John R. Foley & Son, the new seven-story building at Nos. 91 and 93 Thompson street, 50x90x100, from Geo. B. Clark for $89,750, and the six-story new building at Nos. 152 to 156 Wooster street, 75x100, erected by P. H. McManus, for $140,000.

Another recent purchase was made by Richard M. Hooley, of Chicago, proprietor of Hooley's Theatre in that city. He bought the two five-story flats on the south side of 145th street, 28 feet west of 8th avenue, 52x75x100 together, for $70,000, from J. D. Butler, selling to the latter, in exchange, the four lots on 72d and 73d streets, two on each street, beginning 425 feet west of Central Park, which he had bought a little over a year ago for about $90,000, and for which he now received nearly $130,000.

Other purchases have been made in New York by Chicagoans, and further negotiations are now under way. New Yorkers should make a note of this

The Edgar Houses on West Seventy-fifth Street.

[COMMUNICATED.]

In a recent issue of THE RECORD AND GUIDE reference was made to the ready manner in which private houses newly completed had been sold on West 75th street, particularly between Columbus and Amsterdam avenues. These sales are due as much to the excellent location of the properties as to the character of the buildings. West 75th street is peculiarly favored in several ways. It is the centre of a building movement which has largely covered both sides of the street between the Central Park and the Grand Boulevard with residences of a handsome character. The nearness of the property to the 72d street elevated road station on the 9th avenue road and its accessibility to various lines of street cars leading to all the main arteries of travel are other causes that have helped to benefit the locality, added to which is the fact that it is the centre of a choice district where all the ground is restricted to the erection of private residences.

Among the houses recently completed on West 75th street are those erected by George C. Edgar's Sons. They comprise five 20-foot four-story and basement, high stoop, buildings, each having three-story extensions. The fronts are in brown stone, with bay windows of exceptional design on the second story. These windows extend the full width of the houses, and are sextagonal in shape, as may be noticed in the illustration presented herewith. In designing the fronts the architect, G. A. Schellenger, has attempted rather to express solidity than ornamentation, and the houses are an evidence of conservative and advanced taste blended together.

THE INTERIOR.

A glance at the interior of the houses shows that they are handsomely appointed, and contain a number of novel improvements. Entering through storm and vestibule doors of solid mahogany, with large centrepieces in beveled plate glass, we find the vestibule tiled in marble and wainscoted in panels of mahogany. The hall is entered through a massive and finely-carved door of the same hardwood, containing a plate glass, through which the hall is observed.

THE HALLWAY.

The main hall is of an extreme width of over 6 feet and contains a seat rest and drawers, surmounted by a large console mirror. The floor is inlaid in hardwoods and the wainscoting is in paneled mahogany. Over the entrance to the stairway a screen of woodwork appears, with a rod pendant from which a portiere is to be suspended. A finely-carved newel and a balustrade of curious design is noticed, the latter containing a succession of central panels, each having a small colonnade of turned woodwork.

THE PARLOR.

To the left of the hall the main parlor is entered. Over the doorway, which is intended to be a portiere entrance, is a screen of woodwork similar to that over the stairway. The parlor is a large room containing a mantel of exceptional design, which runs from the floor to the lower edge of the frieze. It contains a handsome mirror, with a fir eplace of carved brass

Residences just completed on Seventy-fifth street, between Columbus and Amsterdam Avenues.

Geo. C. Edgar's Sons, Owners and Builders. G. A. Schellenger, Architect.

the facings being of tile. The piping is laid ready for the attachment of gas logs.

THE MUSIC-ROOM.

The music room extends beyond the parlor, and though divided by a screen and rod for portiere, can be thrown together with the parlor, for musicales, etc., when required. In fact, the entire floor can be turned into one large saloon for reception purposes, by simply throwing aside the portieres which will separate the parlor, music-room and dining-room from each other.

THE DINING-ROOM.

This fine room, which is entered from the music-room, is the full width of the house. To the right is a unique and handsomely-carved sideboard, in oak, containing two mirrors, shelves for plate and bric-a-brac, china-drawers, etc. To the left is a large mantel and mirror, with a tiled fire-place, containing a curiously-carved inner frame of brass work. To the north of the room is a mirror which reflects the whole suite and gives a panoramic rear vista which takes in the houses on the opposite side of the street. The floor is parqueted and the wainscoting paneled, the trim being in oak. Beyond is the butler's pantry, which is 12x16 in size, and which contains parqueted floors, and a vast quantity of closet room. At the end is a rear flight of stairs leading to the basement.

THE BEDROOM FLOORS.

Ascending a wide stairway, the second floor is reached. This comprises a large front room the full width of the house, containing three windows with a southern exposure, the daylight streaming in and giving an air of cheerfulness which suggests its utilization as a library and sitting-room. Indeed, the old custom is returning of using the second floor front as the sitting-room instead of the main bedroom. Communicating with this room is a rear room, the two chambers being divided by large and elegantly-appointed dressing saloons. These are provided with an abundance of wardrobes, drawers, closets, etc., and are surrounded by large toilet mirrors, the washstand being of marble, with a porcelain bowl. The rear room contains a mantel and fire-place, with gas log attachment, similar to that in all the principal rooms of the house. Beyond is the bath-room, which contains a separate entrance from a hallway, which is an extension of the main hallway. The plan of this hallway is unusual and therefore worthy of passing mention. Besides giving an additional entrance to the bath-room, it gives special access to the dumb-waiter, which runs to the third story of the extension, as well as to the rear stairs, and to the toilet room, which is separated from the bath-room.

The latter is finely appointed. The walls are in large marble slabs, the floors are parqueted in hardwoods, the plumbing is nickel-plated and exposed to view, and the washstand contains a marble slab and porcelain washbowl. The bath is one of Mott's and contains a porcelain tub.

The third floor is almost a fac-simile in plan to the floor below, with the exception that it is in sycamore trim instead of olive. It has large front and rear bedrooms, with spacious dressing saloons and a bath-room, all communicating together, the latter having a special hallway entrance.

The top floor has a large front room, with a Colonial mantel and fire-place, and is capable of being used as a billiard-room or bedroom. There are two rear bedrooms, with a storeroom in the centre. The dome light on top is of stained glass and there are ventilators on the roof which give a continual current of air between the ceiling and the roof, thus keeping the top floor cooler in the heat of a summer's day. This is a novel feature in a private house, as it has hitherto only been in use in public buildings.

THE BASEMENT.

The basement floor contains a breakfast-room, a kitchen with Beebe range, and a ceramic sink, with walls in marble slabs, as well as a large dresser. Beyond is a laundry with three ceramic tubs, servants' toilet-room, etc., the entrance to the yard being protected by an iron door.

The houses contain the finest sanitary plumbing, and have all the important modern improvements, one of the features being the utilization of every spare corner for closet room. They have only recently been placed on the market and are of the same substantial build as those erected by the Edgars for years past, father and son having built and sold some fifty houses on the West Side during the last seven or eight years. They are now also completing for the market a row of five four-story houses on the south side of 87th street, between Central Park West and Columbus avenue. These houses are somewhat similar in character and design to those described above and will be ready toward the end of January. These properties are all insured by both the Lawyers' Title Insurance Company and the Title Guarantee and Trust Company.

The Edgars also own the five-story apartment house and stores on the southeast corner of Columbus avenue and 94th street, in which the Columbus National Bank has its offices.

OBSERVER.

The Brooklyn Exchange Election.

At the first annual election of the Brooklyn Real Estate Exchange the following directors were elected: Wm. Ziegler, Leonard Moody, Jere. Johnson, Jr., E. J. Granger, Geo. W. Chauncey, Darwin R. James, J. N. Kalley, Howard M. Smith, Felix Campbell, Jacob G. Dittmer, C. E. Donnellon, Edward F. Lenton and David Barnett.

On Thursday the election of officers for the ensuing year was held, and resulted in the choice of Jere. Johnson, Jr., for president; Howard M. Smith, first vice-president; Elihu J. Granger, second vice president; Felix Campbell, treasurer; G. W. Chauncey, secretary.

The Mutual Life Insurance Company took title this week to No. 53 Cedar street, the building next but one to their own large office building, and to Nos. 28 to 30 Liberty street, the Stone Building adjoining on Liberty street, as well as to No. 24 Liberty street, between which and the Stone Building No. 26 Liberty street intervenes. It is presumed that the Life Insurance Company will remove these old buildings as soon as the present leases expire and build extensions to their present structure on Nassau street.

North Side Improvements.

Although not much has been heard from the North Side recently in relation to public improvements, there has been a great deal of work done and more laid out for the future. Some pending questions of street opening, one of them of the utmost importance, were arrested by the departure of Mayor Grant for Europe, just after the election, for during his absence no meetings of the Board of Street Opening and Improvement were held; but now that he has returned these matters will be taken up and disposed of one way or another, as soon as the board can be induced to act upon them.

The principal of these matters is the one relating to the opening and extension of Brook avenue, from 165th street to Wendover avenue. Property-owners along this proposed thoroughfare are in an unbearable predicament. When they bought their lots they fronted on Railroad avenue West, which was shown on the maps as a street of 40 feet width, skirting the Harlem Railroad on the West Side. But when the tracks of this railroad were depressed recently the company, without preliminary formalities or apologies, excavated the street clear back to the building line, built a retaining wall high up in front of the houses and cut the occupants off from all means of exit from and entrance to their property, except through their back gates and over the private property of their neighbors. Ever since that time they have been actual trespassers upon the property of their neighbors.

A proposition to open an avenue through this property, from 165th street to Wendover avenue, has been a long time pending before the Board of Street Opening and Improvement. It would be a practical extension of Brook avenue northward, and it is proposed to give it the name of Brook avenue. It would run about midway between Webster avenue and the Harlem Railroad cut. The plot between these lines is about 406.5 feet wide, and after taking out 60 feet for a street, it would leave the blocks on either side about 173 feet deep, but would give them an additional frontage, those along the east side of the proposed avenue running back to the railroad cut. The matter was referred to Commissioner Heintz for a formal report at the last meeting of the board in October, and he has long had ready a report favoring the proposed improvement.

Spuyten Duyvil Parkway has been under orders for improvement for five years, but there arose a dispute in the beginning as to whether the Commissioner of Public Works or the Park Board had the legal right to do the work. If it was a real parkway, and under the jurisdiction of the Park Board, the improvement would have to be done by the Park Board and out of the general fund for park improvements. If it was only an ordinary street, notwithstanding its name, it belonged to the Commissioner of Public Works to improve and would have to be paid for by general assessment upon the property benefited. Referred to Corporation Counsel Morgan J. O'Brien, he decided, July 8, 1887, that it was a street and under the jurisdiction of the Commissioner of Public Works. This decision the Park Board pigeon-holed and kept, until, after repeated applications, it was induced to give it over to Commissioner Heintz, who now has jurisdiction of the matter and has plans for the improvement of the street under way.

As to Intervale avenue, another important improvement, its opening was ordered by the Board of Street Opening and Improvement early last summer, and Commissioner Heintz furnished the Corporation Counsel with the rule map on July 10th, and on Friday last Judge Ingraham, in the Supreme Court, on application of Corporation Counsel William H. Clark, appointed Thomas P. Wickes, William H. Barker and Daniel Sherry Commissioners of Estimate and Assessment in the matter.

In the meantime the engineering department, under the management of Chief Engineer Louis A. Risse, has had its hands full of work. Since August 10th twenty-five contracts have been let for an aggregate estimated expense of $137,000, and in most of them work has already been some time under way. They are as follows:

FOR REGULATING, GRADING, CURBING AND FLAGGING.

College avenue, between Morris avenue and 146th street, to John Kenny, $3,761.43.

173d street, between 3d and Vanderbilt avenues, to P. Handibode, Jr., $3,691.50.

163d street, from Brook to 3d avenue, to F. Thilemann, Jr., $5,123.

173d street, between the Harlem Railroad and Weeks street, to R. McLaughlin, $17,109.80.

135th street, between the Southern Boulevard and 33 feet south of Locust avenue, L. Delavergne, $8,000.50.

Juliet street, between Mott and Walton avenues, to William G. Leeson, $9,917.14.

Burnside avenue, between Sedgwick and Webster avenues, formalities not yet completed.

Teasdale place, between 3d and Trinity avenues, bond of contractor not yet approved.

146th street, between Railroad Avenue East and 3d avenue, to William G. Leeson, $10,575.25.

152d street, between Courtlandt and Railroad avenue East, to Charles W. Collins, $7,372.50.

184th street, between Jerome and Vanderbilt avenues, contractor's bond not yet approved.

FOR SEWERS AND APPURTENANCES.

132d street, from Brook avenue to the summit west of Trinity avenue, to F. Padula for $6,456.25.

Wales avenue, from the summit south of 149th street to Kelly street, to D. Ryan for $9,059.80.

Southern Boulevard, south side, from the summit west to the summit east of Willis avenue, to John A. Devlin for $2,888.50.

170th street, from 3d to Washington avenue, to Martin Lipps for $2,380.74.

142d street, from Brook to St. Ann's avenue, and John street, from Brook to Eagle avenue, were re-advertised because of trouble over unbalanced bids.

Southern Boulevard, both sides, from Brook avenue to 137th street, and on the south side, from Brook avenue to the summit west of Brown place, contractor's bond not yet approved.

Southern Boulevard, from 137th to 138th street, both sides, contractor's bond under investigation by the Comptroller.

FOR REGULATING AND PAVING WITH TRAP BLOCKS.

133d street, between 3d and Courtlandt avenues, to William J. Kelly, for $3,164.63.

134th street, from Brook avenue to the Southern Boulevard, to Matthew Baird, for $8,153.40.

135th street, from Brook to Cypress avenue, to John White, for $8,722.

143d street, from 3d avenue to 144th street, to F. Thilemann, Jr., for $6,951.75.

With granite: 149th street, from the New York Central Railroad to Mott avenue, to F. Thilemann, Jr., for $3,675.

In addition to the foregoing, plans for the sewering of the entire Melrose district, embracing over 2¼ miles of streets, have been adopted and are now in the hands of the printer. As soon as the specifications are completed the work will be advertised and let and will be pushed as fast as the weather will allow. In the work soon to be let are contracts for the regulating, grading, curbing, flagging and setting of crosswalks in the following streets: Locust avenue, from 132d to 135th street; Walnut avenue, between the same; George street, between the Boston road and Prospect avenue; Wales avenue, between St. Joseph street and Westchester avenue; 156th street, between the Southern Boulevard and Locust avenue; 157th street, between 3d and Railroad avenues; 134th street, between the Southern Boulevard and Long Island Sound; 155th street, from 3d to Elton avenue; 132d street, from Brook to Locust avenue; Birch street, from Wolf street to Marcher avenue; German place, from Westchester avenue to 156th street.

Plans for paving have been adopted and are nearly ready for advertising, as follows: 156th street, from 3d to Elton avenue; 158th street, from 3d to Elton avenue. For sewering: 160th street, from Washington to Elton avenue; Fulton avenue, from 3d avenue to 168th street; St. Ann's avenue, from the Southern Boulevard to 131th street; Franklin avenue, from 3d avenue to 167th street, and 167th street, from Franklin to Boston avenue; 168th street, from Washington avenue to the summit west of the Boston road, and Fulton avenue, from 168th to 169th street; Locust avenue, from 136th to 138th street.

Engineer Risse has also completed the new maps required by the act creating the office of Commissioner of Street Improvements, for the entire district south of Westchester avenue and 149th street, and east of 3d avenue to the Long Island Sound. This makes three of the twenty-five maps that are required by the act to be completed within two-and-a-half years from the time of the election of Commissioner Heintz. Whether the entire task will be completed within the time specified in the act depends upon the Board of Estimate and Apportionment. Commissioner Heintz asked for an appropriation sufficient to pay for the employment of the force of surveyors and draughtsmen necessary to do the work within the specified time, but in the preliminary estimates the board cut the appropriation down over one-half, and left the matter in such shape that it would be impossible to conform to the requirements of the law. But the final estimates are still to be passed and there is hope that the board will enable Commissioner Heintz to finish the work in the coming year rather than require him to spin it out over an unnecessarily longer time.

John D. Crimmins to the Rapid Transit Commissioners.

In reply to the circular letter issued to property-owners asking their consent to the construction of a rapid transit railway, John D. Crimmins sends an important communication to the Rapid Transit Commissioners. Mr. Crimmins owns property on Madison avenue, between 43d and 96th streets, and on the Boulevard. He writes giving his consent as far as his real estate on the latter thoroughfare in concerned, but withholds his consent for his property on Madison avenue, until he has had an opportunity of examining their report and plans. He asks why Madison avenue was selected for the route when Lexington avenue was nearer the centre of population on the East Side. Not only would capitalists more readily go into a plan to run through Lexington avenue, but less opposition would be encountered from property-owners on that avenue. The latter had, indeed, given a majority of consents some years ago to a cable road on Lexington avenue.

"The petition of 1889," says Mr. Crimmins, "under which our present Mayor appointed a commission and which brought forward the discussion that terminated in the passing of the act by virtue of which you make your report, was prepared by me and at my instance circulated for signatures. Familiar with the entire subject as I am, and having a sincere interest in increased rapid transit facilities, I feel competent to enter upon its discussion. What the public require is as speedy a relief as your honorable commission can afford them. This end, in my judgment, can be attained through the extension of greater facilities to the present elevated system."

Mr. Crimmins then proceeds to justify this position, so long advocated by THE RECORD AND GUIDE. He asks that the prejudice against the elevated road people should be discountenanced. It is not a question as to who owns the road but "will we be carried safely, with comfort and within a reasonable time to our destination." He estimates that 90 per cent of the people and 95 per cent of the taxpayers are in favor of immediate relief by extending the present elevated road system.

Mr. Crimmins expresses grave doubts if the proposed underground road will be ready within ten years, and whether any bona fide capitalists will subscribe the money to build it. The plan is practicable, he says, but it cannot be done by tunnelling, as stated by the Commission's engineer.

"In the consideration of new routes," he says, "and the necessity, which is evident, that 6th avenue must be relieved, it would appear that 7th avenue, between Greenwich avenue and the juncture with Broadway at 44th street, should not be overlooked." The consents of 7th avenue owners to an elevated road could be obtained. From Greenwich street the road might run through the blocks to Hudson street, through Hudson to Chambers and from Chambers and through the blocks to Greenwich street. The 6th avenue line might be continued from 34th street up Broadway to and through the Boulevard.

"Why," he says, "do I suggest that it is your first duty to establish routes in connection with the Manhattan Railway? For these reasons, viz.: They have an organization, they have capital, and experience and knowledge which enables them to best determine where relief can be afforded."

Mr. Crimmins also refers to the necessity of creating routes for the 23d and 24th Wards, particularly to reach the new parks. He refers to the importance of easy access to those wards, so as to attract the middle and working classes there, instead of forcing them to make their homes in New Jersey and Long Island.

Echoes.

Andrew Carnegie stated, a few days ago, in hearing of the writer, that he was opposed to an underground road, and that the money would never be raised to build the road now proposed.

Geo. S. Lespinasse, who used the underground roads in Europe frequently this year, says that he is in favor of overground roads. "Anyway, if we must have underground lines," he says, "at least gives us immediate relief, through an extension of the facilities we now have at hand in the Manhattan Elevated system, instead of our continuing to be herded together in cars like a lot of wild cattle for the next five or ten years. I don't think capitalists will put up the money for the underground road, but that the city will have to step in and guarantee the bonds."

Discussing Tax Reform.

THE SYSTEMS OF TAXATION IN PARIS AND NEW YORK COMPARED—A PLAN TO HELP BUILDERS AND PROMOTE IMPROVEMENTS.

The West End Association is at this moment interested in tax reform, particularly with that aspect of it that will help builders and owners of vacant property. They are gathering information as to the methods of taxation in other countries, and a committee from the Association a few days ago waited on Geo. S. Lespinasse, who has just returned from a visit to Europe, to obtain information from him relative to the system of municipal taxation in vogue in Paris. This committee was composed of J. Edgar Leaycraft, F. R. Houghton and Richard Deeves, and they will make their report to their Association at a future meeting.

Mr. Lespinasse gave considerable time to a study of the question in Paris. He saw the Mayor and chiefs of various departments, and in a talk with a representative of THE RECORD AND GUIDE, who questioned him on the matter, he said:

"The system of taxation in Paris is not on the value of property, but on the revenue derived from it—that is, the rent roll. Property that does not yield an income is not considered as having a taxable value. Thus, if a building worth 5,000,000 francs ($1,000,000) is untenanted, it is not taxed, the municipality considering that the loss to the owner is a loss to the city."

"Are taxes on rent valuations changed with every rise and fall in rents? If so, the tax assessors must have their hands full."

"Oh, no," was the reply. "A rental value is placed upon property every ten years. The last valuation was made in 1890 and the next will not take place till 1900. Thus, every owner of property knows exactly what his rent tax will be, and that it will remain undisturbed till the next date of valuation."

"Is the system of valuing rents similar to that used in valuing properties in New York?"

"Partly so," said Mr. Lespinasse, "The 'commission des contributions directes,' which is similar to our Tax Commission, makes the valuations. Property-owners who have objections make them and the tax is then settled upon, the ward assessors, in the first instance, sending in their valuations to the commission. Instead of making taxes all due in one sum, as in New York, owners are allowed to pay in four installments. There is no discount allowed to those who pay in one sum, nor any interest penalty attached to those who do not pay on a certain date, as in New York."

"What penalty is there for arrears?"

"Owners of property seldom, if ever, get in arrears, for the reason that if they do not pay their rent-tax the city comes in and takes possession of the rents so as to pay itself the taxes due."

"What is the rate of personal taxation in Paris?"

"A tenant living in an apartment, for which he pays 10,000 francs ($2,000) per annum is taxed 937.60 francs, which is equivalent to ·09376 of one per cent. of the total rent. In reality, although the rent is 10,000 francs, he is assessed at only about 8,000 francs. This rate of taxation (less than one per cent. on the whole), and this proportional assessment of four-fifths of the whole rent, is uniform. So that if a man pays 100,000 francs rent per year he is taxed 9,376 francs, the assessment being four-fifths of the total, namely, 80,000 francs.

"You see how this system of taxation works," said Mr. Lespinasse. "A man worth millions is afraid to come to New York and live for fear of being taxed, but he comes to Paris with a light heart, having no fear that his money matters will be looked into, or that he will have to swear falsely as to his income and perjure himself. And we may as well be frank about it and say that this is done regularly. Any system of taxation which makes men perjure themselves is bad, and keeps away many useful and valuable men from coming to reside among us. I have many friends who, to avoid personal taxes, live in the country."

"Is vacant property taxed?"

"No. Being non-income producing, it is considered of no value by the municipality for taxation purposes. The only exception is a tax on such lots which front on an open street, and this tax is for street cleaning and sweeping, and is nominal."

"Is it a fact that the income of a new building in Paris is not taxed until two years after it is completed?"

"That is so," was the reply, "even though it be rented fully, and this is a great inducement to builders. If this system was adopted in New York we would see a great expansion of building. It is curious that in Paris, which is an old city, and where it is not necessary to build the place up, such a valuable inducement is offered to builders to improve; whereas in New York, which is a city of comparatively recent date, obstacles are placed in the way of building. Directly a builder or capitalist in this city has his first or second story up, the tax valuer comes along and up goes his tax, and when his building is completed he finds himself loaded up with a property that is not likely to be fully rented for some time, and is therefore non-productive on the capital invested, besides being saddled with his tax. As most of the building in New York is speculative, and builders sail very close to the wind, everyone knows how a matter of $3,000 or $4,000 may sometimes stave off foreclosure. If builders were free from taxes for two years after their buildings were completed, what a relief it would be—what plain sailing. And how many millions of dollars would flow into real estate that is now lying idle or otherwise invested. This plan should at once be adopted in New York."

In reply to further queries, Mr. Lespinasse said: "In Paris the proportion of taxation on the actual rental of property is from one-twentieth to one-twenty-fifth; in New York it is from one-sixth to one-eighth. Of course, in Paris there are also the octroi taxes on wines, liquors and food. Paris raised $56,000,000 last year with a population of about 2,400,000; New York's revenue was $35,000,000 with a population estimated at about 1,700,000. The "droits d'octroi" produced $40,000,000, of which $28.-
[illegible] & Co. have sold for [illegible] to Jessie A. Ferguson, No. 467 West 147th street, a three-story brick and brown stone dwelling, 18.9x50x100, on private terms.

Francis J. Schnugg has sold to Geo. Frick the two five-story brick flats Nos. 2 and 4 East 113th street, on private terms. Broker, A. Ganzenmuller.

Samuel J. Silberman has sold No. 132 East 73d street, a three-story and basement brown stone dwelling, on lot 18.9x102.2, to Lippman Meyer.

F. Zittel has sold for Isaac Bell to Morris Steinhardt the five lots on the south side of [illegible] Central Park West, on private
and eye trouble, due to the clouds of dust raised by the wind. New York should utilize its rivers for this purpose, and so get the flushing done with salt water."

Important to Property-Holders.

BOARD OF ASSESSORS.

OFFICE OF THE BOARD OF ASSESSORS,
No. 27 CHAMBERS STREET,
NEW YORK, Dec. 15, 1891.

Notice is given to the owner or owners, of all houses and lots, improved or unimproved lands affected thereby, that the following assessments have been completed and are lodged in the office of the Board of Assessors for examination by all persons interested, viz.:

No. 1.—Regulating, grading, curbing and flagging 111th st, from 5th to 6th avenue.

No. 2.—Regulating, grading, curbing and flagging Jumel terrace, from 160th to 162d st.

[The limits embraced by such assessments include all the several houses and lots of ground, vacant lots, pieces or parcels of land situated on—

No. 1.—Both sides of 111th st, from 5th to Lenox av.

No. 2.—Both sides of Jumel terrace, from 160th to 162d st, and to the extent of half the block at the intersecting sts.]

All persons whose interests are affected by the above-named assessments and who are opposed to the same, or either of them, are requested to present their objections in writing to the Chairman of the Board of Assessors, at their office, No. 27 Chambers street, within thirty days from the date of this notice.

The above-described lists will be transmitted, as provided by law, to the Board of Revision and Correction of Assessments for confirmation on the 16th day of January, 1892.

In the matter of the application of the Counsel to the Corporation of the City of New York, for and on behalf of the Mayor, Aldermen and Commonalty of the City of New York, under and in pursuance of chapter 496 of the Laws of 1885, to acquire title to the additional lands required for Riverside Park, as defined, laid out and established by said act; also relative to the opening of Cedar avenue (although not yet named by proper authority), from Sedgwick avenue to Fordham road, in the 24th Ward of the City of New York, etc. Notice is given that the bill of costs, charges and expenses incurred by reason of the proceedings in the above-entitled matters will be presented for taxation to one of the Justices of the Supreme Court, at the Chambers thereof, in the County Court House, at the City Hall, in the City of New York, on the 24th and 28th days of December, 1891, at 10:30 o'clock in the forenoon of those days or as soon thereafter as counsel can be heard thereon; and that the said bill of costs, charges and expenses has been deposited in the office of the Department of Public Works, there to remain for and during the space of ten days.

In the matter of the application of the Board of Street Opening and Improvement of the City of New York, for and on behalf of the Mayor, Aldermen and Commonalty of the City of New York, relative to acquiring title, wherever the same has not been heretofore acquired, to East 167th street, from Prospect to Westchester avenue, in the 23d Ward of the City of New York. The Commissioners of Estimate and Assessment in the above-entitled matter hereby give notice to all persons interested in this proceeding, and to the owner or owners of all houses and lots and improved or unimproved lands affected thereby and to all others whom it may concern, that they have completed their estimate and assessment, and that all persons interested in this proceeding, or in any of the lands affected thereby, and having objections thereto, do present their said objections in writing, duly verified, at their office, No. 51 Chambers street (Room 4), in said city, on or before the 20th day of January, 1892, and that they, the said Commissioners, will hear parties so objecting within ten week days next after the said 20th day of January, 1892, and for that purpose will be in attendance at said office on each of said ten days at 3 o'clock P. M. That the abstract of said estimate and assessment, together with damage and benefit maps, and also all the affidavits, estimates and other documents used in making their report, have been deposited with the Commissioner of Public Works of the City of New York, at his office, No. 31 Chambers street, in the said city, there to remain until the 2d day of February, 1892. The report will be presented to the Supreme Court of the State of New York, at a Special Term thereof, to be held at the Chambers thereof, in the County Court House, in the City of New York, on the 12th day of February, 1892, at the opening of the Court on that day, and that then and there, or as soon thereafter as counsel can be heard thereon, a motion will be made that the said report be confirmed.

Contractors' Notes.

Estimates for furnishing illuminating gas for lighting the public markets, armories, buildings and offices of the City of New York, or any of them, for the period from January 1, 1892, to December 31, 1892, both days inclusive, will be received by the Commissioner of Public Works of the City of New York, at his office, No. 31 Chambers street, until 12 o'clock M. of Monday, December 28, 1891.

Sealed bids or estimates for furnishing the materials and work required for boiler-house for insane asylum, Blackwell's Island; also, for materials and work required for six pavilions for New York City Asylum for Insane, Blackwell's Island; and for materials and work required for steam heating and ventilating six pavilions for insane, Blackwell's Island, will be received at the office of the Department of Public Charities and Correction, No. 66 3d avenue, in the City of New York, until Monday, December 28, 1891, until 10 A. M.

Experiments in Trap Siphonage.

We are in receipt of a valuable pamphlet, describing certain experiments and researches on trap siphonage, showing the comparative merits of the principal appliances used for trap seal protection. The experiments were conducted by the author of the pamphlet, James M. Denton, M. E., the Professor of Experimental Mechanics in Stevens Institute of Technology, and are a valuable contribution to sanitary science. The publication of the brochure at this moment is particularly fortunate, because it furnishes several undeniable *facts* for use in the controversy at present going on as to the merits of the now well-known McClellan Anti-Siphon Vent.

The value and efficacy of this device is, we believe, fully acknowledged by unbiased sanitary experts and the leading plumbers of the country. As a great number of them are in use with results invariably successful there can be no doubt that the vent does stand the practical or experimental test; and now this paper of Professor Denton must, certainly so far as unprejudiced persons are concerned, silence any scientific or theoretical doubt.

Every one knows that in modern plumbing a very important and also a very costly position is given to the vent-pipe, the purpose of which is to prevent siphonage and preserve the integrity, and consequently the efficacy of the trap-seal. The purpose of the McClellan device is to effect this service at least as thoroughly as the vent-pipe and at a much smaller cost. In other words it is a substitute for the vent-pipe—a mercurial vent placed practically directly on the trap, doing away with the long line of pipe entirely. As with everything new it has met with opposition, in most cases from interested quarters. The efficacy of the device was disputed, and Professor Denton shows disputed without warrant, for in the series of rigorous tests made by him he demonstrates that the McClellan vent is always as efficient as the vent-pipe, and under certain circumstances and in certain conditions more so. To quote his words, "the results of all these tests unite in leading to the conclusion that the McClellan 1½-inch and 2-inch vents are capable of protecting simple S traps against the most severe siphonage effects arising in plumbing practice as well as can 13½ feet and two elbows of 1½-inch pipe in the case of the 1½-inch vent, or 20 feet of 2-inch pipe in the case of the 2-inch vent." Against back pressure the McClellan vent is superior and in the case of ice accumulation at the top of vent pipe or rust in an elbow. Where more than two elbows or where longer lengths of pipe are used the McClellan device was also shown to be superior. These exhaustive tests settle the controversy as to the *facts* of the case.

Special Notices.

IMPORTANT TO BUILDERS.

On another page will be found an important announcement to builders by Mr. C. E. Harrell. He has a responsible tenant who will lease at a good rental an entire six-story building, 50x100 feet or larger, and wants a builder to erect such a building and lease to tenant. Mr. Harrell has several suitable plots of ground at fair prices. Particulars can be obtained from Mr. Harrell, at No. 713 Broadway, corner Washington place.

H. Ward Leonard & Co. have secured the contract for wiring the *Mail and Express* building for 3,500 incandescent lamps, acting as subcontractors under the Waddel-Entz Electric Company. H. Ward Leonard is licensing various manufacturing and construction concerns under his recently patented system of motor regulation. The basis of the license is a charge of $2.50 per K. W. (roughly per horse power) in the motor. The royalty charge is not an annual charge, but it is paid once for all in each case.

Since the decease of David Kempner the business of D. Kempner & Son, of No. 602 8th avenue, has been conducted by his son, Nathan Kempner, who was associated with his father for fifteen years, and who has a thorough knowledge of the real estate business, particularly of West Side property between 14th and 59th streets, along the line of 6th, 7th, 8th, 9th and 10th avenues. They have a large list of investment property on their books, and parcels capable of immediate improvement. They manage a number of properties and do a general real estate business. The firm was established in 1869.

Real Estate Department.

The real estate market continues fairly bright and active. The transactions this week, while neither as numerous or important as those reported last Saturday, are very satisfactory when we consider the past dullness and the near approach of the holidays. The coming holidays are mainly responsible for whatever falling off there has been from last week's fine business, the market itself being in a very satisfactory condition. Many buyers who are favorably considering parcels that have been offered to them have deferred definite action until the new year, when they will have more time and money to devote to large business transactions. At present the holiday feeling has taken hold of the outside public, which after all is the most important factor in the real estate market, and until this feeling gives way to a more decided business inclination it is almost useless for brokers and agents to busy themselves trying to close sales. This fact is fully realized by real estate men who find every year that the most buyers will do at this time is to make promises for the coming spring. It is likely, therefore, that the next two weeks will amount to nothing so far as new business is concerned, while the old business that has been hanging fire will only be brought to a successful conclusion by leaving it alone. To endeavor to force transactions at the present time is to defeat their successful consummation. As has been said, the conditions prevailing continue bright and promising. Money is easy, buyers willing and sellers generally reasonable, and at the proper time there seems little doubt but what a good business will be done.

At private sale this week several interesting transactions are reported. Down town there is the sale reported by Hoffman Bros. and E. B. H. Meyers to John Pettit, the well-known renovator of old buildings, of the northeast corner of Liberty and Church streets, at $115,000. In the new mercantile district M. & L. Hess have sold the new warehouse, at Nos. 222 and 224 Greene street, for $150,000, while up town L. J. Phillips & Co. have successfully disposed of another parcel on 125th street, for $450,000. This property is located on the south side just west of 7th avenue, and it runs through from 125th to 124th street. It has a frontage on the former street of 62,6 and on the latter of 70 feet. In other parts of the city interesting sales of flats, dwellings, lots and business property go to make up a very interesting list of consummated transactions.

THE AUCTION MARKET.

The offerings in the Auction Room this week were a trifle better than had been anticipated, several of the more important properties not having been announced until the early part of the week. This lack of preparation and proper announcement showed itself at the sales. The people who might have bought the property were not present to bid, and so parcels on Water street, Chatham square and Liberty street were bid in. That these parcels failed to sell at auction because of any unsatisfactory feeling in the market does not seem likely, for the Liberty street property, as announced elsewhere, has since been sold at private contract. In other parts of the city, too, property was bid in, but from a different reason. Up-town and Brooklyn holdings, voluntarily offered, were more often bid in or withdrawn than sold, and these failures may nearly all be attributed to one of two reasons: either buyers suspected that so-called peremptory sales were only peremptory in name or the owners who offered property did so simply with the idea of testing the market. Some of the sales, however, were very generally successful, as for instance the sale of the Abraham Lewis estate property, on Thursday. This sale, which was under the direction of Auctioneer Bryan L. Kennelly, comprised property on lower 8th avenue and on two down-town streets. The first parcel offered, No. 429 8th avenue, near 31st street, a four-story building and store, on lot 24.8x100, excited the widest interest. It is rented for $3,000 a year until May, 1893, with privilege of renewal for an additional term of five years. After a very general competition A. Minalzo became the purchaser at $43,500. It is interesting to note that this house and lot was transferred to the late Mr. Lewis, in 1874, for $45,000. The other 8th avenue parcel, No. 318, was only 19.7x83, a four-story building near 28th street. It is rented for $1,956 per year, and it sold for $22,100. The last transfer was in 1849, when the consideration was stated at $19,050. Smyth & Ryan also sold a parcel that attracted some attention. It was of the northeast corner of Catharine and Henry streets, 23.2x100, which was disposed of on Monday in order to divide an estate. Bidding started at $30,000 and quite a lively competition ensued. Jacob Korn finally secured the property for $36,500. There are three or four brick buildings on the plot. The legal sales offer few interesting features. Three parcels, one on West 142d street, and another on West 12th street, and the third on East 61st street, sold under foreclosure, failed to realize the amounts due for mortgages and costs. The details are given in another column.

Next week, Christmas week, there will be little or nothing offered. Some of the principal auctioneers have issued no bills at all and others only one or two. The properties which are announced are of the most ordinary character, and are not calculated to attract many persons to the Auction Room. Even the legal sales are few in number and generally uninteresting, interested parties having done their best to have them postponed until after the holidays. For two weeks at least the auctioneers will do very little business of any kind, and after that it may take some time to set business going, although the predictions for an early and an active season still continue to be made by those who from practical experience and careful study certainly ought to know.

On Tuesday, December 22, Richard V. Harnett & Co. will sell the five-story brick double tenements, Nos. 414, 416 and 418 East 64th street.

CONVEYANCES.

	1890. Dec. 12 to 18 inc.	1891. Dec. 11 to 17 inc.
Number	435	227
Amount involved	$5,544,919	$3,420,656
Number nominal	95	105
Number 23d and 24th Wards	179	85
Amount involved	$339,4?5	$105,116
Number nominal	17	9

MORTGAGES.

	1890. Dec. 12 to 18 inc.	1891. Dec. 11 to 17 inc.
Number	410	260
Amount involved	$3.567,699	$3,305,384
Number at 5 per cent	254	121
Amount involved	$1.518,946	$1,601,851
Number at less than 5 per cent	31	15
Amount involved	$952,250	$193,000
Number to Banks, Trust and Ins. Cos	83	78
Amount involved	$751,000	$690,656

PROJECTED BUILDINGS.

	1890. Dec. 13 to 19 inc.	1891. Dec. 12 to 18 inc.
Number of buildings	40	69
Estimated cost	$635,450	$1.600,755

Gossip of the Week.

SOUTH OF 59TH STREET.

Charles Duggin, it is reported, has sold the northwest corner of Park avenue and 41st street, 92.9 on the avenue x80 on the street x98.9x irregular, with the four-story brick flats and stores thereon, for $300,000.

M. & L. Hess have sold for James G. Wallace to David Steiner Nos. 222 and 224 Greene street, a new six-story warehouse, 40x100, for $150,000.

C. E. Harrell has sold for Horace S. Ely, trustee, the old building No. [illegible]

nd guarantee the bonds."

Discussing Tax Reform.

THE SYSTEMS OF TAXATION IN PARIS AND NEW YORK COMPARED—A PLAN TO HELP BUILDERS AND PROMOTE IMPROVEMENTS.

The West End Association is at this moment interested in tax reform, particularly with that aspect of it that will help builders and owners of [illegible]

story brick building and store, 17.4x74.10x21.11x irregular, on private terms. This property was offered at auction on Tuesday, and bid in at $78,000.

Wm. Neeley has sold No. 243 Lexington avenue, a four-story brown stone dwelling, 21x60x80, for $.9,000. The last transfer of this property was in 1882 for $25,250.

Fitzsimons & Smith have sold for Morgan & Brother the five-story front and three-story rear building, lot 25x98.9, No. 145 West 35th street, for $21,000.

Harris Mandelbaum has purchased from J. & A. Lyons Nos. 441 to 445 West 51st street, three three-story brick houses, on lots 20x100 each, on private terms.

Douglas Robinson, Jr. & Co. inform us that Mrs. Ogden was not the purchaser of the northwest corner of Madison avenue and 39th street. The name of the real purchaser has not transpired.

It is reported that No. 54 Vesey street, a five-story building, 25x100, has been sold for $42,500.

The house purchased by Ascher Weinstein last week was No. 29 West 31st street, not 81st street, as previously reported.

Philip Sammet has purchased from the Warren estate No. 41 Bond street, a three-story brick building, on lot 25x99.6, on private terms. Brokers, L. J. Phillips & Co. Mr. Sammet has sold No. 14 Grove street, a three-story and basement brown stone dwelling, 20.3x45x67.10, to Margaret Johnson, on private terms. Brokers, Fairchild & Yoran.

Charles Lewis has purchased the three-story brown stone dwelling No. 315 West 32d street, on private terms. Broker, B. L. Kennelly.

Rinaldo & Bro. have sold for B. Galewski the house and lot, No. 176 Stanton street, to Loonie & Parker for $21,000.

Hiram Merritt has sold No. 332 1st avenue, 23x50x69, for R. Danziger for $11,000.

Otto Pullich has sold for George Ehret to A. Boehm the four-story building No. 126 Crosby street, on private terms.

B. Flanagan & Son have sold for Isaac Benjamin No. 207 West 25th street, a three story brown stone dwelling, 21x50 and extension x100, for $17,000.

Otto Pullich has sold for Frederick Rabe No. 104 Monroe street, a three-story brick house, on lot 21x93.7, on private terms.

NORTH OF 59TH STREET.

Henry Morgenthau, S. Lachman et al. as exrs. and the estate of Wm. Ebrich has sold No. 216 to 220 West 125th street, a two-story store building on the south side of the street, 112 feet west of 7th avenue, on a plot 62.6 by half the block, and Nos. 209 to 217 West 124th street, immediately in the rear, five three-story brick and frame buildings, on plot 70x half the block. The name of the purchaser has not transpired, but the price is reported as $250,000. We understand that L. J. Phillips & Co. were the brokers.

Theodore Cordier has sold his last three flat houses on the east side of Amsterdam avenue, 27 feet south of 84th street, to Geo. Herbener for $90,000. Broker, August Ganzenmuller.

R. Pehlemann has sold for John Casey the two five-story buff brick double flats, 27x77x90, Nos. 745 and 747 Amsterdam avenue, to Charles Kraemer, on private terms; and for Dr. A. W. Lozier, attorney in fact for L. Formento, the five-story double flat, 27x85x100, No. 163 West 129th street, to Elizabeth Franke, on private terms.

Amos R. Eno has sold the four lots on the southeast corner of Columbus avenue and 69th street for $64,000.

Philip Braender, it is reported, has sold to Capt. McManus the "Alcazar" a six-story brick apartment house, 50x100, Nos. 120 and 122 East 88th street, on private terms. The report is that Capt. McManus gives some vacant lots in exchange for the apartment house.

Isaac T. Meyer has sold for Elsworth L. Stryker to a Mr. Mayer, No. 22 West 72d street, a four-story and basement brick and brown stone dwelling, 22x70x102.2, on private terms.

Frank L. Fisher & Co. have sold for the Amsterdam Improvement Co. to James F. Hinde the three-story and basement brown stone dwelling, No. 145 West 95th street, 20x55x100, on private terms.

John W. Stevens has sold for the New York Realty Co. to Charles Judson the plot 50x100, on the east side of Riverside avenue, 550 feet north of 122d street, on private terms.

Gutwillig Bros. have purchased from a Mr. Kahl two lots on the north side of 90th street, between Central Park West and Columbus avenue. Gutwillig Bros. inform us that the thirteen lots on the south side of 90th street, between Central Park West and Columbus avenue, the sale of which we reported a week or two ago, were their exclusive property. Hirsh Bros. had no interest in them.

Ascher Weinstein has purchased from Richard Hennessy the southwest corner of Lexington avenue and 64th street (Beekman leasehold), a three-story and basement brown stone dwelling, 21x60x90, and has given in exchange five lots on the south side of 137th street, 150 feet west of Lenox avenue.

W. P. Anderson has sold to Royal E. Dean, of Bramhall, Dean & Co., No. 154 West 94th street, a three-story brick and brown stone dwelling, 18x52 and extension x100, on private terms.

McMonegal & Eckerson have sold for James Brown to Mrs. Mary E. Richardson No. 25 West 90th street, a three-story brown stone dwelling, 16x56 and extension x100, for $26,500.

K. Hayden & Co. have sold for B. Havanagh to Jessie A. Ferguson, No. 467 West 147th street, a three-story brick and brown stone dwelling, 18.9x50x100, on private terms.

Francis J. Schnugg has sold to Geo. Frick the two five-story brick flats Nos. 2 and 4 East 113th street, on private terms. Broker, A. Ganzenmuller.

Samuel J. Silberman has sold No. 122 East 73d street, a three-story and basement brown stone dwelling, on lot 18.9x102.2, to Lippman Meyer.

F. Zittel has sold for Isaac Bell to Morris Steinhardt the five lots on the south side of 69th street, 250 feet west of Central Park West, on private terms.

E. M. Farrington has sold for Samuel Colcord to a Mr. Cook, of Albany, No 161 West 88th street, a three-story brick and brown stone dwelling, 17x55, and extension x100.8, on private terms.

The plot on 125th street just east of Koch's, sold last week by L. J. Phillips & Co. to Geo. Ehret, we learn, had a frontage of 53 feet on 124th street. With the four lots on 125th street, therefore, the sale was of over six lots. Mr. Ehret will either lease the ground for term of years or build upon it himself.

The firm of L. J. Carpenter has sold for John Frame No. 109 East 127th street, a five-story brick double flat, 26x85x99.11, to Mrs. Helen Campman for $28,750.

The purchaser of the eight lots on the north side of 69th street, 125 feet east of Columbus avenue, was Wm. W. Hall, the West Side builder.

LEASES.

Rinaldo & Bro. have leased for the Cheeseborough estate to the Bowery Mission the new five-story building, No. 105 Bowery, for five years, at $4,500 per annum.

Brooklyn.

William Walsh has sold for Franz Franz to Chas. F. Goodwin the house and lot, 20x50x80, No. 903 4th avenue, for $5,000.

The Columbia Chemical Co. have purchased the factory building covering five lots on Sedgwick street, near Van Brunt avenue.

J. P. Sloane has for John Fraser the two-story store, 25x30x60, on the northeast corner of Eagle and Oakland streets, to Edward Cassidy for $2,850.

Corwith Bros. have sold the lot, 25x100, on the east side of Diamond street, 75 feet south of Nassau avenue, for W. P. Morrissey to David Quinlan for $1,000.

CONVEYANCES.

	1890. Dec. 11 to 17 inc.	1891. Dec. 10 to 16 inc.
Number	337	282
Amount involved	$903,491	$1,172,900
Number nominal	107	90

MORTGAGES.

Number	292	255
Amount involved	$912,875	$907,898
Number at 5 per cent. or less	170	111
Amount involved	$617,391	$504,883

PROJECTED BUILDINGS.

	1890. Dec. 12 to 18 inc.	1891. Dec. 11 to 17 inc.
Number of buildings	68	57
Estimated cost	$194,125	$293,746

Out Among the Builders

Bernard Hoffmann, an extensive and well-known builder of Europe, has formed a company here of some of the wealthiest men of the city. This company have bought a plot of ground, 150x125, on one of the most frequented and popular thoroughfares in the very heart of the city, on which they will erect a building estimated to cost in the neighborhood of $400,000. This building will be fitted up in most magnificent style for Russian, Roman and Turkish baths, according to Mr. Hoffmann's patented system. In elegance of appointment and detail of luxury these baths will surpass anything before attempted in this country. Theodore G. Stein, the architect, has completed the plans for the building, and Mr. Hoffmann, with the directors of the company, has taken them to Chicago where they are negotiating for a site on the exhibition grounds of the World's Fair. It is the company's purpose, when the Chicago site has been secured, to erect a similar building, of lighter and less expensive character, to make known the peculiar merits of Mr. Hoffmann's system of baths. $400,000 was the price paid for the plot secured here, and work will be begun in the near future.

De Lemos & Cordes have drawn plans for a seven-story fire-proof warehouse to be built at Nos. 128, 130 and 132 Mott street, for August Mietz. The building will be 74.9x65 in size, with a one-story extension, running through to Elizabeth street. The front will be carried up in buff brick, stone and terra cotta, and the building will be supplied with modern appointments. Work will be begun in January.

John C. Burne is the architect for a five-story brown stone flat and store, 25x71.11, to be built on the southwest corner of Park avenue and 107th street; for two similar flats, each 25x61.7, and a third flat, 25x64 and extension, to be built on the south side of 107th street, 25 west of Park avenue; and for a five-story flat, 25x60.4, to be built on the west side of Park avenue, 75.11 south of 107th street. The owners are Boyle & Bannon, and the total cost $125,000.

Edmund Coffin, Jr., of No. 100 Broadway, will improve five lots on the south side of 85th street, 350 feet west of 9th avenue, by erecting private houses.

De Lemos and Cordes filed plans about a year ago for the Keuffel and Esser building to be built at No. 127 Fulton street. Owing to the fact that the leases of the present building did not expire until May next, all operations were suspended and held in abeyance. The work will go forward, however, at the earliest moment, and all preliminary work is well under wey as per original plans filed for the eight-story office building.

Andrew Spence has plans on the boards for three five-story apartment houses for Valeske Meyer, on the east side of Parkhurst avenue, 25 feet north of 147th street; also plans for a plot, 25x71, on the northeast corner of Bradhurst avenue and 147th street, same owner.

J. C. Burne has plans in preparation for a five-story brown stone flat, 25x60 and extension, to be built by McDowell Bros. on the north side of 120th street, 175 feet west of 7th avenue, at a cost of $26,000.

E. W. Greis has drawn plans for a two-story, basement and cellar brick and stone dwelling, 20x60, to be built for Fredk. Vollmer, on the south side of 137th street, near St. Ann's avenue, and to cost $8,000. The same architect will furnish plans for the $2,000 improvement to be made in the building at No. 208 East 10th street, owned by J. Wiebe. The building will be raised one story and altered internally.

John C. Burne will furnish plans for two five-story brick and brown stone flats, 25x54 and extension 20.6x21, to be built by Geo. H. Schaefer on the south side of 142d street, 100 feet west of 8th avenue, at a cost of $44,000.

R. E. Rogers has plans on the boards for a two-story and attic frame dwelling, to be built on Kingsbridge road, Morris Heights, for C. G. Tousey, at a cost of $6,000. The size is 32x45.

F. Ebeling has plans on the boards for a $10,000 alteration at No. 28 Pike street, owned by Blumberg & Cohen. The building is to be raised one story and extended by a four-story addition, 25x30 in size.

Brooklyn.

Plans drawn by some fourteen architects in competition for the new Brooklyn Savings Bank Building were submitted last week. $200,000 will be spent on the building proper and about $100,000 more on its interior decoration. No selection has yet been made from the plans submitted, but from the fact that the competition was one of invitation it is safe to say that the architects competing have put forth their best endeavors, and that any choice will prove an ornament to the new site at Pierrepont and Clinton streets.

Out of Town.

PATERSON, N. J.—Charles Alling Gifford has drawn preliminary sketches for the State Armory to be erected here, and for which estimates of cost are now being made. The building will be 150x230 in size, and will cost about $100,000. The same architect will draw the plans for a similar building to be built in Jersey City.

NEWARK, N. J.—Quinby & Co. will enlarge their carriage factory, opposite the Morris and Essex depot, on Division street, by a four-story brick extension, 123.8x225 in size. This provides for an extension of the warerooms on first floor and a new arrangement for the offices, smith shop and manufacturing lofts. Van Campen Taylor, who was the architect for the original factory, has drawn the plans for this improvement, which is to cost $35,000. Schweitzer & Diemer have drawn plans for three three-story frame dwellings, 58.6x59, to be built at Nos. 186 and 188 Bloomfield avenue, at a probable cost of $12,000, for Mrs. F. Liebhauser.

FLATBUSH, L. I.—Van Campen Taylor has drawn plans for a two-story brick and frame Colonial dwelling, to be built on the south side of Lincoln road, near Flatbush avenue. The house will be 42x53 in size. The frame portion is to be shingle finished and the interior in white wood. The cost is estimated at about $12,000. John Lefferts, the owner, has applied for permission to curb and pave Lincoln road and, as Flatbush avenue is being widened, with a prospect of having electric cars substituted for the horse cars now running in the avenue, it cannot be long before this section is well built over.

MINEOLA, L. I.—Two two-and-a-half-story frame dwellings, 22x30, costing $5,500, will be built here for Geo. Schmidt, from plans by Schweitzer & Diemer.

MOUNT TOM LAKE, LITCHFIELD CO., CONN.—E. W. Greis will draw plans for a two-story and attic frame cottage, 32x28, with extension, and a two-story frame stable and carriage house, to be built here for Jacob Doll, at a cost of $4,000.

ST. GEORGE, S. I.—Of the five competitive drawings submitted for the Staten Island Academy that of Lamb & Rich was the one chosen by the committee. From these plans will be erected a three-story and basement brick. stone and terra cotta building, 14?x60 in size. This building is to contain a memorial library, a large music hall, gymnasium with running track and the other appointments of a strictly first-class academy.

BAYONNE, N. J.—Arthur C. Longyear has completed plans for a two-story brick and frame club-house to be built for the Newark Bay Boat Club on the north side of 33d street, east of Avenue C. The building will be 60x100 in size, and will be used for the winter quarters of the club. The interior will be finished in Georgia pine throughout, and will be arranged for billiard-room, social rooms, bowling alley, amusement and dancing hall and janitor's quarters. The estimated cost is placed at $11,000.

OAKDALE, L. I.—W. Ormiston Tait has drawn plans for a one-and-a-half-story brick stable, 38.8x65, to be built at West Brook farm, at a cost of $5,000. The owner is W. Bayard Cutting.

NUTLEY, N. J.—A two-story and attic frame dwelling, 30x34 and extension, will be built at this place by a Mr. Conover from plans by W. Ormiston Tait. Cost, $3,000.

BELLE HAVEN, CONN.—Lamb & Rich have plans on the boards for a three-story and basement stone and shingle finished frame house to be built for Nathaniel Witherill. The house will be 78x45 in, the Dutch style of architecture and finished with a tile roof.

WANTS AND OFFERS.

SALES OF THE WEEK.

The following are the sales at the Real Estate Exchange and Auction Room for the week ending December 18.

** Indicates that the property described has been bid in for plaintiff's account:*

D. L. KENNELLY.

8th av, No. 429, w s, 74 n 31st st, 24.8x100, four-story building with store. A. Minaizo...... $48,500
8th av, No. 842, e s, 94.7 s 28th st, 19.7x82, four-story brk building and store. B. B. Johnston.... 22,100
22d st, No. 471, n s, 16.8x98.9, four-story, English basement, brown stone dwell'g. Philip Olwell.... 14,250
1st av, No. 693, w s, 74 s 40th st, 24.8x75, five-story brk tenem't. (Bid in).... —
122d st, No. 252, s s, 206.8 e 8th av, 16.6x100.11, four-story brk flat. (Bid in).... —
Houston st, No. 498 E., 21x105, two-story building and store. (Bid in).... —
45th st, No. 420, s s, 380 w 9th av, 25x100.5, five-story brk tenem't and stores. (Bid in)..... —
*48th st, Nos. 134-142, s e cor Lexington av, 174.6x100.5; No. 134, seven-story brk flat and stores; Nos. 136-142, four five-story brk flats. Abraham Kaufmann. (Amt due $33,327; prior morts. $ —).... 252,954
*94th st, No. 45, n s, 375 e 9th av, 14.3x100.8, three-story brk dwell'g. Nellie C. Van Reypen. (Amt due $1,250).... 15,000

R. V. HARNETT & CO.

Mangin st, Nos. 89-93, w s, 118.7 s Stanton st, 80x100, three-story brk factory buildings. E. Connelly.... 20,000
29th st, No. 103, n s, 121 e 7th av, 23x98.9, two-story brk stable. S. S. Abbott.... 18,200
109th st, No. 237 E., 20x100.11, two-story frame dwell'g. Geo. Matthews.... 5,500
10th av, No. 148, e s, 25 n 19th st, 25x80, five-story brk tenem't and store. H. Greeves. (Amt due $17,559).... 23,700
10th av, No. 150, e s, 50 n 19th st, 25x80, similar tenem't. H. Beaver. (Amt due $17,559).... 25,250

WM. KENNELLY.

*61st st, Nos. 322-328, s s, 301.8 e 2d av, 107.8x100.5, four five-story brk flats. Equitable Life Assurance Soc. (Amt due $77,344)..... 62,000
83d st, No. 83, n s, 418.9 e 9th av, 26.3x80, three-story brk dwell'g. Sylvia Lindsey... 12,800
*90th st, s s, 100 e 10th av, 100x100.8, vacant. Wm. B. Baldwin. (Amt due $19,434)..... 40,862
*190th st, No. 211, n s, 175 w 7th av, 25x100.11, five-story brk flat. Wm. A. Bartow and ano. trustees. (Amt due $19,269)..... 15,000
137th st, n s, 275 e 6th av, 25x99.11, vacant. Chas. Spengler.... 3,500
St. Nicholas av, w s, 287.11 s 141st st, 181.8x35.4x129.11x18.7, vacant. M. Adele. (Amt due $5,009).... 9,000
Willis av, n w cor 145th st, 25x106, five-story brk and stone flats. L. Wecber. (Amt due $21,065).... 31,000
Willis av, n w cor 146th st, 25x106, similar flat. Same. (Amt due $21,063).... 32,000
Willis av, w s, 25 n 146th st, 25x106, five-story brk and stone flat. Same. (Amt due $14,865).... 19,000

A. H. MULLER & SON.

Liberty st, No. 45, n s, 72.6 e Nassau st, 174x70.6 and irreg x71.11x71.10, four-story brk building with store. (Bid in).... —
Chatham sq, No. 5, 23.4x134.10x24.9x136.9, two-story brk and frame buildings. (Bid-in).... —
Water st, No. 281, 16.6x72.11, five-story brk building and store. (Bid in).... —
Madison av, No. 1115, e s, 64.1 s 84th st, 20x76.7, four-story and basement brown stone dwell'g. (Bid in).... —

E. H. LUDLOW & CO.

43d st, Nos. 260 and 262 W., 57.6x100.4, two brown stone and brk flats. (Bid in).... —

J. N. GOLDING.

19th st, No. 206 E., 20x92, three-story brown stone dwell'g. A. Weinstein. (Leasehold).. 3,425

J. F. B. SMYTH.

Lenox av, No. 416, e s, abt 23 s 131st st, 25x65, five-story brown stone flat and store. (Bid in).... —

BERNARD SMYTH.

45th st, No. 237, n s, abt 175 w 2d av, 25x100, five-story flat and stores. (Bid in).... —

SMYTH & RYAN.

Catharine st, No. 23, n e cor Henry st, 23.2x102 x23x100, three-story brk and frame buildings and stores. Jacob Korn.... 56,800
42d st, No. 220, s s, 280 w 2d av, 25x79.6x27.11x92.1, four-story brk tenem't and stores. Mary McCloud. (Amt due $16,416).... 17,400

OTHER AUCTIONEERS.

20th st, No. 212, s s, 434 w 2d av, 22x92, three-story brk tenem't. A. E. Racer. (Amt due $16,986).... 14,600
95th st, No. 171, n s, 100 e 10th av, 50x100.8, five-story brk flat. T. H. Wilcox.... 54,200
96th st, No. 168, s s, 100 e 10th av, 50x100.8, five-story brk flat. Spencer Aldrich.... 53,500

Total.... $840,141
Corresponding week, 1890.... $975,911

BROOKLYN, N. Y.

FOR WEEK ENDING DECEMBER 16.

OTHER AUCTIONEERS.

Pierrepont st, No. 48, 26x100, three-story brown stone dwell'g, four-story in rear. (Bid in).. —
Baltic st, No. 128, s s, abt 151.9 e Clinton st, 16.8x79.10, three-story brown stone dwell'g. S. H. Stewart.... 25,200
Bergen st, No. 624, n s, 200 w Vanderbilt av, 24.8x110, two-story brk factory. John L. Branch. (Bid in).... 4,000
*Butler st, Nos. 1200-1222, s s, 225 e Kingston av, runs south 111.6 x again south 16.9 x east 271.2½ x north 127.9 to Butler st, x west 275 to beginning, vacant. William Williamson. 6,500
Cumberland st, No. 398, w s, 308.10 n Atlantic st, 14x100, three-story frame dwell'g. Charles H. Knox.... 1,687
*Dean st, n s, 419.5 e Rochester av, 16x107.2⅝
Dean st, n s, 435.5 e Rochester av, 16x107.2⅝..
Dean st, n s, 451.5 e Rochester av, 16x107.2⅝..
Dean st, n s, 467.5 e Rochester av, 16x107.2⅝

Four two-story frame dwell'gs............ Henry C. Almsted, trustee.................. 8,000

Sackett st, No. 490, s s, 75 w Bond st, runs south 100 x west 70 x south 25 x west 88.4 x north 50 x east 73.4 x north 75 to Sackett st, x east 30 to beginning, three-story brk tenem't and two-story brk stable in rear. Terence Keenan.. 5,300

Warren st, No. 414, s s, 175 e Hoyt st, 25x100, three-story brk tenem't. Alfred T. Drury. 4,350

Bedford av, No. 652, s w s, 50 s e Penn st, 25x70, five-story brk flat unfinished.................. 5,910

3d st, No. 500, s s, 44 w 7th av, 22x90, four-story brk dwell'g. Nathaniel Read................ 10,785

3d st, No. 504, s w cor 7th av, 22x90, four-story brk dwell'g. Same.............................. 12,750

South 4th st, No. 255, n s, 100 e Havemeyer st, 25x95, five-story brk tenem't. Wm. H. Smith...................................... 9,500

Graham av, No. 53, w s, 75 n Varet st, 25x100, three-story frame tenem't and store and one-story frame extension on rear. Alexander Underhill.. 1,500

Hudson av, No. 285, e s, 24 s Tillary st, 21x50x15 x50, three-story frame dwell'g. Terence McCabe... 1,500

Jefferson av, No. 160, s s, 240 w Nostrand av, 20x100 ....
Jefferson av, No. 158, s s, 260 w Nostrand av, 20x100..
Jefferson av, No. 152, s s, 320 w Nostrand av, 20x100 ....
Three four-story brk flats..........................
Thos. H. Elliott, exr.................................... 19,000

Jefferson av, No. 1056, e s, 30 n Broadway, 18x 100, two-story frame dwell'g. Geo. W. Mead. 3,550

Kingston av, w s, East New York av to Maple st, 200x94.6, Flatbush, vacant. M. H. Hayman. (bid in) 800

St. Marks av, No. 349, n s, 75 w Grand av, 25x 181.2x26.6x178.06, three frame dwell'gs on plot. Walter E. Switzer.......................... 5,732

Total.. $99,564
Corresponding week 1890.............................$210,507

CONVEYANCES.

NEW YORK CITY.

DECEMBER 11, 12, 14, 15, 16, 17.

Boulevard, s e cor 114th st, —x—x—x100, vacant. Thomas B. Arden, Sara J. wife of and Francis A. Livingston, Mary A. wife of and Peter P. Parrott, James L. Huggins and Rosa L. his wife, Helen A. wife of and James J. Bergen and George L. Peabody to Fanny M. widow William E., Fannie M., Mary H. and Henry Crowley heirs Robert Crowley. Q. C. Dec. 4. $800

Bowery, No. 156, w s, abt 60 n Broome st, 25x 100, four-story brk store. Louis M. Kohnstamm to Charles Engert. Oct. 1, 1890. nom

Broadway, Nos. 611 and 613 } begins Broadway, n w cor
Houston st, No. 2 }
Houston st, 51.10x125, two-story brk stores. Lucy M. widow, Charlotte A. and Charles M. Rice heirs John S. Rice to Henry Thompson. All title. Dec. 14. 275,000

Canal st, No. 495, n s, 67.6 e Renwick st, runs east 16 11 x northeast 36.4 x north 47.6 x west 6.3 x south 38.8 x southwest 32.1, three-story brk store and tenem't. Nellie E. wife of Samuel B. Rogers, Hudson, N. Y., to Julia M. Bullong. *Mt.* $8,000. Dec. 11. 11,525

Canal st, Nos. 55–59 } begins Canal st, n w cor Orchard st,
Orchard st, Nos. 11 and 13 }
50x55.1, three three and five-story brk and frame tenem'ts with stores. Morris Glucksman to Moses Gardner. *Mt.* $40,500. Dec. 16. 70,700

Canal st, No. 119, formerly known as 216 Walker st, n s, abt 45 e Chrystie st, 18.9x50 deep before the widening of Walker st, four-story stone front store and tenem't. Partition. John A. Deady to Ernest Plath. Dec. 10. 15,650

Carmine st, No. 79, n s, abt 300 w Bedford st, at former east boundary line of land of Trinity Church, runs east 24 x north to said east line of Trinity Church, x south and west along said line to beginning, three-story brk store and tenem't. Samuel W. Bower recvr. William A. and Theodore E. Senior to William T. A. Hart. All title. Aug. 5. 300

Cedar st, No. 53, n s, abt 170 w William st, 25x 77x25x79.10, five-story brk office building. George G. Haven to The Mutual Life Ins. Co. of New York. C. a. G. Oct. 15, 1890. 80,000

City Hall pl, No. 26, n s, abt 80 e Duane st, 24.2 x56.7x24.2x87.6, three-story brk and frame buildings. Sabina wife of and John Mitchell to Patrick Murphy. *Mt.* $6,000. December 17. 19,250

Cherry st, No. 262, n s, 78.11 e Rutgers st, 26.9 x94.8x26.8x95.2, five-story brk tenem't with stores. Jonas Weil and Bernhard Mayer to Philip Sheftlis. *Mt.* $19,000. Dec. 15. 33,250

Christopher st, No. 22, s s, 93.9 e Waverley pl, 21 x 59.4 x 23 x 63.3, one-story frame store. Thomas Roach to Thomas S. Godwin. Q. C. Aug. 24, 1888. nom

Christopher st, s s, 94 e Waverley pl, 19x61.8x 19.10x67.4. Meyer L. Sire to Manuel Perez. Q. C. Dec. 12. nom

Columbia st, Nos. 82 and 84, e s, 100 n Rivington st, 50x118, two five-story brk tenem'ts with stores. Morris and Isaac Cohen to Samuel Weil. *Mt.* $71,000. Dec. 15. See Av D. 90,000

Downing st, No. 59, n s, 240.9 w Bedford st, 19.4 x90, three-story brk tenem't and two-story brk stable on rear. Samuel W. Bower recvr William A. and Theodore E. Senior to William T. A. Hart. All title. Aug. 5. 236

Downing st, No. 57, n s, 221 w Bedford st, 19.9 x90, five-story brk building. Same to same. All title. Aug. 5. 235

Elm st, No. 165, e s, 154.10 n Grand st, 21.1x 64.1, two-story brk tenem't. William F. Chrystie, Hastings-on-Hudson, New York, to Emily C. Curtis. Dec. 1. nom

Forsyth st, No. 36, e s, abt 50 n Canal st, 25x 100, five-story brk tenem't with stores. Edward Butler to Bessie Butler. ½ part. Dec. 2. nom

Forsyth st, No. 78, e s, abt 175 s Grand st, 25x 100, five-story brk tenem't with stores. Morris and Isaac Cohen to Wolf Davis. ½ part. Sub. to morts. and life estate of Elka Cohen. Dec. 15. 2,000

Front st, No. 176, n w s, 90.3 n e Wall st, runs northwest 75 x southwest 0.8 x northwest 7.2 x northeast 18.7 x southeast 82.2 to st, x southwest 18.6, four-story brk store. Leila B. wife of Clarence H. Scrymser to Archibald J. C. Anderson. *Mt.* $20,000. Dec. 15. 34,000

Grand st, No. 378, n s, 52 e Norfolk st, 23x80, three-story brk store and tenem't. William G. Van der Koest to Oscar L. Richard. Dec. 15. 25,500

Henry st, No. 28, n s, abt 100 e Catharine st, 25x87.6, five-story brk tenem't with stores. John D. Karst, Jr., to Moses Einhorn. *Mt.* $25,000. Dec. 17. 37,000

Houston st, No. 177 } begins Houston st, s e cor Congress st,
Congress st, No. 2 }
22x77.6, four-story brk store and tenem't on Houston st and four-story brk tenem't on Congress st. Franz Ziegler to John Ohlandt. *Mt.* $8,000 Oct. 21. 23,000

Leonard st, Nos. 117 and 119, n e s, 45 n w Elm st, runs northwest 45 x northeast 43 x northwest 0.6 x northeast 38.10 x southeast 3.5 x southwest 30.11 x southeast 42.6 x southwest 50, two four-story brk stores. Edward Heath, Rockville Centre, L. I., to Ann M. Heath, Rockville Centre, L. I. 1-56 part. Dec. 8. nom

Same property. Malvina Heath, East Orange, N. J., to same. ½ part. Dec. 8. nom

Leroy st, No. 25, n s, abt 67 e Bedford st, 25x90, five-story stone front flat. William A. and John A. Peal to John Rankin. Q. C. Oct. 18. nom

Same property. Frances T. and Edward Munday to same. Q. C. Oct. 7. nom

Same property. Mary S. Mandeville to same. Q. C. Sept. 21. nom

Same property. James A. Mandeville and Catharine Whittlesey widow to same. Q. C. Sept. 17. nom

Same property. John I. Mandeville to same. Q. C. Oct. 14. nom

Lewis st, No. 144, e s, 123.8 n Houston st, 25x 100, five-story brk tenem't with stores. Dora wife of and Adolph Herkommer to Harris Shedlinsky and Julius and Isidore Shweitzer. *Mt.* $16,000. Dec. 15. 22,250

Lewis st, No 144, e s, 123.8 n Houston st, 25x 100, five-story brk tenem't with stores. Harris Shedlinsky, Julius and Isidore Shweitzer to Joseph E. Rosenthal. *Mt.* $16,000. Dec. 15. 24,500

Lewis st, No. 63, w s, 100 s Rivington st, 25x 100, three-story brk store and tenem't with four-story brk tenem't on rear. Leopold Geissmann to Samuel Weil. *Mt.* $5,000. Dec. 16. 14,000

Lewis st, No. 111, w s, 180 n Stanton st, 20x100, five-story brk store and tenem't with three-story brk tenem't on rear. Joseph Newborg to Malka Ganz. *Mt.* $12,200. Dec. 1. 20,500

Liberty st, No. 24, s s, 142.6 w William st, 25.9 x abt 78 x abt 25.7 x abt 75, five-story brk office building. Russell Walden to The Mutual Life Ins Co. of New York. C. a. G. *Mt.* $10,000. Nov. 13, 1890. 80,000

Liberty st, Nos. 28, 30, 32, 34 and 36, s s, abt 118 e Nassau st, runs east 99.9 x south 83.1 x west 70.3 x north 1.2 x west 27.1 x north 87.5 to beginning, any discrepancy of 3 inches not to be deemed material, five-story brk office building. The Title Guarantee and Trust Co. to The Mutual Life Ins. Co. of New York. B. & S. C. a. G. Feb. 2. nom

Madison st, No. 89, n s, abt 275 e Catharine st, 25x100, five-story brk tenem't. Joseph L. Buttenwieser to Benedict A. Klein. Dec. 16. 45,500

Same property. Benedict A. Klein to Joseph L. Buttenwieser. *Mt.* $25,000. Dec. 16. 45,500

Maiden lane, No. 139 } begins Maiden lane, n e s, abt 55 s e Water st,
Fletcher st, No. 19 }
17x the block to Fletcher st, five-story brk store. James W. McCaffrey to James Ertheiler. Dec. 14. 28,650

Monroe st, Nos. 230–236, s s, 117.1 e Scammel st, 87.8x95.4x87x95.2, four five-story brk tenem'ts. Jacob Miller, Long Island City, to John Fish. ½ part. *Mt.* on whole premises $34,000. Dec. 15. nom

Oliver st, Nos. 100 and 102, e s, 55 n South st, 40x50, two two-story brk tenem'ts. Foreclos. Luke F. Cozans to Solomon Zainan. Dec. 14. 11,000

Pearl st, No. 457½, s w s, 21.11 n w City Hall pl, 30.3x72.2x25x36.3, five-story brk tenem't with stores. Morris S. Herrman to John Maggi. *Mt.* $25,000. Dec. 15. 31,000

Peck slip, No. 37, n e s, abt 27 s e Front st, 27x 40, four-story brk store. Amelia C. Skaden to Henry Wilson, Greenwich, Conn. Dec. 12. nom

Pike st, No. 9 } begins Pike st, s e cor
East Broadway, Nos. 123 and 125 }
East Broadway, 24x85, three-story frame store and tenem't on Pike st and one-story brk and two-story frame stores on East Broadway. Partition. George M. Van Hoesen to Aaron Cohn. Dec. 15. 33,600

Sheriff st, No. 63, w s, 125 s Rivington st, 25x 100, five-story stone front tenem't with stores. Harris Shedlinsky and Julius and Isidore Shweitzer to Frank Feldman. *Mt.* $19,000. Dec. 15. 29,000

South st, Nos. 228 and 229 } begins South st, n w s, 166 e Market
Water st, Nos. 449 and 451 }
slip, 40x160 to Water st, x40x166, three and four-story brk rubber goods factory. Theodore K. Hazard trustee Jabez H. Hazard to Laura L. wife of William V. Ruton, Orange, N. J., Emily T. wife of William L. Wallace, Lucretia S. wife of Henry C. Beach, Alice H. wife of George L. Richmond and Theodore K. Hazard devisees Jabez H. Hazard. *Mt.* $31,000. Aug. 17. nom

Spring st, Nos. 129 and 131. Party wall agreement. John Goerlitz to Adam Priester. Dec. 9. 600

Stanton st, No. 53, s s, 66.9 w Eldridge st, 22.8x 75, three-story brk tenem't with two-story brk stable on rear. Jennet E. Armstrong to Andrew W. Armstrong, Brooklyn. ½ part. Q. C. Dec. 15. nom

Thompson st, No. 108, e s, 138 s Prince st, 19x70, three-story brk store and tenem't. Caspar Wittendorfer to Giovanni M. Malatesta and Giovanni B. Casassa. Dec. 14. 12,350

Water st, No. 348, n s, 15x60x12.3x60, three-story frame store and tenem't.
Water st, No. 350, n s, 103.9 w James slip, 15.2x60x12x59.6; also alley or gangway on n s of Water st and connecting with n w s of last mentioned property, 3.6x60.6x3.6x 60.7, three-story frame store and tenem't.
Mary A. wife of Thomas McGuire heir of John Callahan to Simon P. Flannery. Dec. 9. nom

Water st, No. 164, n w s, abt 35 n e Fletcher st, 17.11x80.3, four-story brk store. Henry and Isaac Meinhard to Mathias Lachenbruch. B. & S. Dec. 14. nom

White st, No. 25, s s, 75.2 w Church st, 25x 72.10, six-story stone front stores. Louise L. Williams to Robert Tyler, Louisville, Ky. Dec. 5 70,000

Wooster st, No. 164, e s, 23.9 s Houston st, 23.9 x75, three-story brk stores. Isaac O. Rhines to Ellen Rhines. Sub. to mort. Dec. 11. nom

1st st, No. 13, s s, 188.1 e Bowery, 19.7x74.6x19.9 x77, five-story brk store and tenem't. George F. Johnson to William J. Gilroy. *Mt.* $16,000. Dec. 15. See 67th st. 24,250

Same property. William J. Gilroy to William H. Baldwin. *Mt.* $21,250. Dec. 15. See 67th st. 28,500

3d (Amity) st, No. 118, s s, 25 w Macdougal st, 25x100, five-story stone front tenem't with stores. Isidore Abrahams to Simon Fine and Harris Boskey. *Mt.* $25,000. Nov. 31. 34,000

4th st, No. 312, s s, 48.4 w Av D, 24.11x96, three-story brk tenem't. Susan M. Dewing widow, Hartford, Conn., and Leonard H. Dewing to Charles Wolf. Dec. 12. consid. omitted

4th st, No. 56, s s, 151.3 e Bowery, 25x96.2, six-story brk tenem't with stores. Charles Hoffart to Katharina Wittenauer. *Mt.* $30,250. Dec. 11. 45,000

7th st, No. 246, s s, 279.3 e Av C, 22.8x90.10, four-story brk tenem't. Karl Hoffart to Katharina Wittenauer. *Mt.* $6,000. Dec. 11. 11,000

10th st, No. 313, n s, 425 w 1st av, 25x100, three-story brk tenem't. Partition. D. Ira Baker to Thomas D. Day, Jr. *Mt.* $5,000. Sept. 18. 11,050

Same property. Mary E. Pentz to same. Q. C. Dec. 10. nom

Same property. Jacob Pentz, Fanwood, N. J., to same. Q. C. Dec. 4. nom

Same property. Frederick Maxwell assignee of Jacob and Archibald Pentz to same. Dec. 1. nom

Same property. Thomas D. Day, Jr., to Michael Fay and William Stacom. B. & S. Dec. 12. 20,000

Same property. Perry P. and Stephen G. Williams exrs. and trustees Mary M. Williams to same. Dec. 10. 5,000

12th st, No. 224, s s, 261.6 w 2d av, 23.4x106.6, five-story stone front tenem't. Mary Ryan to Patrick F. and Mary F. McGowan. ½ part. Dec. 10. 15,000

Same property. John and William M. Ryan to same. B. & S. Dec. 10. nom

Same property. Vincent A. Ryan by Mary Ryan guard. to same. Infant's share. ½ part. Dec. 10. 5,000

18th st, No. 333, n s, 260 w 1st av, 20x91, three-story brk tenem't.
4th av, No. 424, n w cor 29th st, 28x40, four-story brk store and tenem't.
Edward Hoxsius to Morris Rosenfeld. ½ part. Dec. 10. nom

20th st, No. 335, n s, 325 e 9th av, 25x91.11, four-story brk dwell'g. Edwin Lord to Mathilde Schwab. Dec. 17. 18,500

21st st, No. 327, n s, 403.1 e 9th av, 24.11x98.9, five-story brk flat. James S. Gillie to Louisa Schirmer. *Mt.* $24,000. Dec. 10. nom

22d st, No. 118, s s, 175 w Lexington av, 20x98.9, three-story brk dwell'g. Jacob A. R. Dunning trustee to Charles Le Gay. Dec. 16. nom

23d st, No 126, s s, 345 e 4th av, 25x98.9, five-story stone front store and flat. Charles D. Burwell, Brooklyn, to Daniel A. Loring. *Mt.* $35,000. Dec. 12. nom

23d st, No. 147, n s, 300 e 7th av, 25x98.9, five-story brk dwell'g. Pedro C., Ricardo A., Arthur Y., Corina, Cesar A., Cecilia, Manuel Y., Petrona, Rosaria, Manuel A. and Jose N. Casanova, Maria del R. C. De Lapiedra widow, Maria T. C. wife of Onofre L. Vidal, Emilia C. wife of Cirilo Villaverda, Maria L.

C. wife of Jose M. Montalvan. Candida R. C. wife of Josquin Laudo. Josefa C. wife of Patricio Ballester, Dolores C. wife of Narciso A. Villaverde and Jose N. Casanova as exr. of Ynocencio Casanova to Concepcion C. De Bueno and Amalia C. de Govin. 10-12 part. April 2. nom

24th st, No 411, n s, 125 w 9th av, 25x98 9, four-story brk tenem't with two-story brk stable on rear. Charles A. Robinson to Joseph R. Conklin. C. a. G. *Mt.* $5,000. Dec 2. 15,250

Same property. Louisa L. and Eugene H. Conklin, Arminta Merritt, Caroline J. Warner, Wheeler G. and Eveline Jerolemon, Leah J. Kierstead and Charlotte E. Hale to same. Q C. Nov. 24. nom

25th st, No. 120, s s, 141.8 w Lexington av, 20.10x98.9, four-story stone front dwell'g.
Water st, No. 231, s s, abt 50 e Beekman st, 16 6x72 11x16 8x72.11, five-story brk store.
Augusta T. Merritt, New York, and Constance E. Gracie, New Brighton, S. I., and Minnie L. Schack widow to Elizabeth I. Schack. All title. B. & S. Oct. 7. nom

26th st, No. 418, n s, 287.6 w 9th av, 25x98.9, five-story brk tenem't with stores. William T. Washburn and ano. exrs., &c., Benjamin Richardson to George S. Adrian. *Mt.* $7,000. Nov. 30. 16,100

Same property. Release judgment. Eugene Kelly individ and with William Farrell, Edward Kelly and Joseph A. Donahue, of Eugene Kelly & Co., to William T. Washburn and ano. exrs. Benjamin Richardson. Dec. 8. nom

27th st, No. 34, s s, 269 e 6th av, 22 6x98.9, four-story stone front dwell'g. Mary R. wife of and John Conness to Mary A. Buchan. Dec. 11. 23,000

28th st, No. 43, n s, 185.11 e 6th av, 21.4x98.9, four-story brk dwell'g. Louis S. Reynal to William S. McPheeters. ½ part. *Mt.* $15,000. Dec. 11. 500

29th st, No. 139, n s, 225 w 3d av, 20x98.9, three-story brk dwell'g. Henry Middendorf to John J. Frech. Dec. 15. 15,500

37th st, No. 226, s s, 312.6 w 7th av, 28.1x98.9, five-story brk flat. William Broadbelt, New Rochelle, N. Y., to Elizabeth Lane. *Mt.* $31,500. Dec. 17. 49,000

39th st, s s, 200 w 9th av, 25x98.9. Release dower. Emilie Schellenberg widow to Sophia Mayer. Dec. 8. nom

40th st, No. 3.4, s s, 150 w 8th av, 25x98.9, four-story brk store and tenem't with five-story brk tenem't on rear. William G. McCrea to Henry Allen. *Mt.* $8,000. Dec. 14. 18,000

46th st, No. 69, n s, 108.9 e 6th av, 18.1x100.5, four-story stone front dwell'g. Hugo S. Mack to Eleonora wife of Simon Mack. Dec. 11. nom

46th st, No. 338, n s, 374 w 8th av, 16.8x100.5, four-story stone front dwell'g. Conrad Vorbach to Miriam David. Dec. 14. 16,000

49th st, No. 531, n s, 425 w 10th av, 25x100.5, four-story stone front tenem't. Michael Leehane to Ellen A. Fitzgerald. *Mt.* $6,000. Dec. 15. nom

53d st, No. 111, n s, 150 w 6th av, 25x100, five-story brk flat with three-story brk building on rear. Robert J. Mahon to Jessie F. Haw *Mt.* $2,500. June 14, 1887. nom

53d st, No 409, n s, 150 w 9th av, 25x100.5, five-story brk tenem't with stores. William K. Thorn, Newport, R. I., to Sherwood Aldrich, Colorado Springs, Col. B. & S. *Mt.* $17,000. Nov. 25. nom

Same property. Sherwood Aldrich, Colorado Springs, Col., to Calvin G. Doig. *Mt.* $21,000. Dec. 1. nom

54th st, No 448, s s, 200 e 10th av, 25x100.5, three-story frame store and tenem't. William Rankin to Patrick B. Hanlon. Dec. 17. 10,000

57th st, No. 415, n s, 153.10 w 9th av, 21.2x100.5, four story stone front dwell'g. Amalia Stepper to David L. Kellaw. *Mt.* $19,500, taxes and int. and $800. Dec. 1. nom

57th st, No. 35, n s, 575 w 5th av, 25x100.5, four-story stone front dwell'g. Elliott F. Shepard to Maria Louisa S. wife of William J. Schieffelin. July 15, 1891. nom

58th st, No. 104, s s, 100 w 6th av, 20.6x100.5, four story brk dwell'g. Charles T. and Helen T. Barney to Theodore B. Starr. Nov. 24. 38,000

62d st, No. 150, s s, 220 e Lexington av, 20x100.5, three-story stone front dwell'g. Mary E. Hickok widow, Irvington, N. J., to George S. Hall. Q. C. Dec. 10. nom

Same property. Archibald, Charles H. and Nathan H. Hall heirs Mary Hall to George S. Hall. Q. C. Dec. 14. nom

Same property. Archibald W. Hall, Irvington, N. J., to George S Hall. Q. C. Dec. 8. nom

Same property. Charles H. Hall exr. Mary Hall to George S. Hall. Dec. 1. 18,000

65th st, s s, 250 w 8th av, 25x100.5, vacant. William B. Baldwin to Mary McKenna. *Mt.* $6,000. Dec. 14. 13,000

66th st, Nos. 213 and 215, n s, 225 w Amsterdam av, 50x100.5, two five-story brk tenem'ts. Amzi L. Camp to Anna M. Somerville. Q. C. Dec. 11. nom

67th st, s s, 175 w 8th av, 50x100.5, vacant. William B. Baldwin to William J. Gilroy. *Mt.* $19,000. Dec. 14. See 1st st. 22,000

Same property. William J. Gilroy to George F. Johnson. *Mt.* $19,000. Dec 15. See 1st st. 21,000

67th st, No. 8, n s, 125 e 5th av, 25x100.5, four-story stone front dwell'g. Joseph H. Ladew to Louise B. wife of Edward R. Ladew. B. & S. C. a. G. Dec. 15. nom

Same property. Edward R. Ladew to Joseph H. Ladew. B. & S. C. a. G. Dec. 15. nom

69th st, n s, 125 e Columbus av, 200x100.5, vacant. Arthur M. Thorn and James W. Wilson to William W. Hall. *Mt.* $105,000. Dec. 15. 116,000

70th st, No. 61, n s, 285 e Columbus av, 20x100 5, four-story stone front dwell'g. George W. Ruddell to Mary H. Lester. *Mt.* $22,500. Dec. 15. nom

70th st, n s, 425 e 9th av. Party wall agreement. John Ruddell to John D. Taylor. Dec. 14. nom

72d st, No. 304, s s, 45.6 w West End av, runs south 45.10 x west 9.7 x south 6 5 x west 13.8 x north 5 11 x east 5.8 x north 46 8 to st, x east 18, four-story stone front dwell'g. John V. Clarke to Lucile Clarke. *Mt.* $30,000. May 9. nom

73d st, No. 208, s s, 160 e 3d av, 25x102.2, four-story stone front tenem't. Thomas Magrane to James Dobbins. *Mt.* $12,000. Dec. 1. 15,700

75th st, No. 223, n s, 100 w Amsterdam av, 25x107.5, two-story brk stable. Thomas P. Kelly to Susan M. Moore. *Mt.* $15,000. Dec. 14. nom

75th st, n s, 388 e Columbus av. 154x102.2, vacant. Charles T. and Helen T. Barney to John C. Umberfield. C. a. G. Dec. 10. 120,250

76th st, No. 305, n s, 66 w West End av, 21x76.1, four-story brk dwell'g. Robert P. Martin, Summit, N. J., to Hugh Lamb, East Orange, N. J. *Mt.* $22,000. Dec. 7. nom

Same property. Hugh Lamb, East Orange, N. J., to Robert P. Martin, Summit, N. J. *Mt.* $22,000. Dec. 10. nom

82d st, No. 56, s s, 268 e 9th av. 17x100, four-story brk dwell'g. Flora Douglas to James W. Dunnell, Brooklyn. Sub. to mort. $14,000. Dec. 10. 26,500

82d st, No. 415, n s, 231 e 1st av, 25x102.2, five-story brk tenem't. Caroline Goppoldt to Charles Koehler. *Mt.* $7,500. Dec. 16. See 87th st. 21,250

82d st, No. 68, s s, 150 e Columbus av, 18x102.2, four-story stone front dwell'g. Charles McDonald to Josephine L. Tobias. *Mt.* $22,000. Dec. 15. nom

84th st, No. 329, n s, 330 e 2d av, 20x100.2, three-story frame dwell'g. Eliza Miller to Joseph Miller. *Mt.* $5,800. Dec. 16. 12,000

85th st, No. 224, s s, 304 9 e 3d av, 24.9x102.2, two-story frame dwell'g. John W. French to Thomas J. Robinson. *Mt.* $5,000. Dec. 11. 12,000

85th st, s s, 350 w Columbus av, 125x102.2, vacant Sarah C. wife of and Roswell D. Hatch to Edmund Coffin, Jr. *Mt.* $20,000. Dec. 2 65,000

85th st, No. 222, s s, 280 e 3d av, 24.9x102.2. Release mort. George E. Hyatt, Brooklyn, to Edward McGuiness. Dec. 15. nom

87th st, No. 165, on map No. 163, n s, 246.8 w 3d av, 26.8x100.8, five-story brk tenem't with stores. Charles Koehler to Caroline Goppoldt. *Mt.* $13,000. Dec. 16. See 82d st. 25,000

88th st, No. 507, n s, 125 e Av A. 25x100 8, five-story brk tenem't. Joseph Schreiner to Rasmus Christensen. *Mt.* $12,000. Dec. 15. 21,250

88th st, No 260, s s, 154 w Boulevard, 18x100 8, three-story stone front dwell'g. Charles L. Ritzmann to Nellie F. wife of Mark P. Brennan. *Mt.* $16,000. Dec. 15. See 7th av. exch

88th st, Nos. 262 and 264, s s, 172 w Boulevard, 36x100.8, two three-story stone front dwell'gs. Charles L. Ritzmann to William Eisenberg. *Mt.* $31,000. Dec. 11. See 116th st. exch

88th st, No. 263, s s, 172 w Boulevard, 36x100.8, three-story stone front dwell'g. William Eisenberg to Simon Peyser. Dec 16. 50,000

88th st, s s, 235.7 w Park av, 102.3x100.8, vacant. Frederick A. Constable and ano. exrs. of Richard Arnold dec'd and J. M. & F. A. Constable exrs. Henrietta Constable dec'd to William T. Lahey. *Mt.* $58,000. Dec. 15. 86,000

88th st, n s, at centre line old Astor lane, 116.8 e Av A, 58.4x37.6 to centre Astor lane, x69.9, gore. Charles H. M. Bristed to Elizabeth Hillenbrand widow. Q. C. Confirmation deed. Oct. 11, 1890. nom

89th st, n s, 550 w Central Park West, 25x100.8, frame building. Asa E. Collins, Linden, N. J., to Francis Crawford, Wakefield, N. Y. Dec. 9. 12,500

90th st, s s, 325 w Central Park West, 25x100.8.
89th st, n s, 550 w Central Park West, 25x100.8.
Frame buildings.
Edward H. Van Ingen to Asa E. Collins, Linden, N. J. Oct. 13. See Union av last week's Conveys. nom

90th st, s s, 325 w Central Park West, 25x100 8, two-story frame dwell'g. Asa E. Collins, Linden, N. J., to Alfred Gutwillig. Dec. 9. nom

90th st, s s, 350 w 8th av, 100x100.8, vacant. Thomas Hitchcock to same. Dec. 11. 50,000

90th st, s s, 450 w Central Park West, 37.6x100.1, vacant. Mary A. Vanderwater to same. Dec. 12. nom

90th st, n s, 500 w Central Park West, 50x100.8, vacant. Louis Kahl to same. Dec 9. nom

90th st, s s, 487.6 w 8th av, 37.6x100.8, vacant. Margaret K. Douglass to same. *Mt.* $12,000. Dec. 14. nom

90th st, s s, 200 w Central Park West, 125x100.8, vacant. Alois Gutwillig to Walden P. Anderson. *Mt.* $40,000. Dec. 16. val. consid

90th st, s s, 325 w Central Park West, 200x100.8, one and two-story frame building and vacant. Alfred Gutwillig to Walden P. Anderson. *Mt.* $74,500. Dec. 16. nom

90th st, s s, 253 w Columbus av, 47x100.8. Release mort. James Pyle to Robert Dick. Nov. 30. 7,000

90th st, s s, 200 w Central Park West.
90th st, s s, 325 w Central Park West.
90th st, n s, 500 w Central Park West.
Agreement restricting buildings. Alois and Alfred Gutwillig with Oliver H. Corsa, William A Caldwell, Catharine Nash, George W. Van Allen, John J. Lynes, Adelia R. Price and George J. Hamilton Dec. 15. nom

91st st, No. 159, n s, 168 5 w Lexington av, 17.6x100.8, three-story brk dwell'g. John and Louis Weber to Margaret T. wife of Henry G. H Koch. *Mt.* $9,000. Dec. 30, 1886. 17,500

93d st, No. 140, s s, 395.1 w Columbus av, 20x100.8, three-story stone front dwell'g. Release mort. Robinson Gill to Walden P. Anderson. Dec. 15. nom

Same property. Release mort. Adelia F. Philip to same. Dec. 14. nom

Same property. Release mort. The Bradley & Currier Co. (Lim.) to same. Dec. 14. nom

Same property. Walden P. Anderson to James D. Hall. *Mt.* $21,000. Dec. 15. 32,000

93d st, s s, 225 e 3d av, 25x100.8, portion of two-story brk brewery. George W. Johnson to George Ehret. B. & S. April 21, 1879. 4 600

93d st, n s, 306 2 e 5th av, 0.6x100 8. William C., Edward F. and John H. Browning individ. and exrs. of John H. Browning to Philip Braender. All title. Q. C. Dec. 5. nom

93d st, No. 158, s s, 241.6 e Amsterdam av, 15.6x100.8, three-story stone front dwell'g. Release mort. The Bradley & Currier Co. (Lim.) to Walden P. Anderson. Nov. 30. 2,000

Same property Walden P. Anderson to Georgie Ransom. *Mt.* $16,000. Dec. 1. nom

93d st, No. 175, n s, 250 5 w 3d av, 29 11x100.8, four-story stone front flat. Amalia Friedmann to Walter Ford. Dec. 17. 25,250

93d st, No. 177, n s, 220.6 w 3d av, 29.11x100.8, four-story stone front flat. Same to same. Dec. 17. 25,250

102d st, No. 223, n s, 355 e 3d av, 25x100.11, five-story brk tenem't. Samuel Phillips and Aaron Kaplan to Joseph Goldstein. *Mt.* $14,500. Dec. 15. 25,000

102d st, No. 305, n s, 100 w West End av, 20x100.11, three-story stone front dwell'g. Charles G Judson to Henry G. Shaw. Dec. 15. 25,000

Same property. Release mort. Francis P. Furnald to same. Dec. 15. nom

Same property. Release mort. Francis M. Jencks, Newburgh, N. Y., to same. Dec. 15. nom

Same property. Henry G. Shaw to Charles G Judson. *Mt.* $17,000. Dec. 15. 25,000

103d st, No 206, s s, 118 w Amsterdam av, 20x77.2 to Clendenning lane, x20x76, five-story brk flat. Madeline Pierce to Catherine Meagher. *Mt.* $15,500. Dec. 15 21,200

104th st, No. 174, s s, 200 w 3d av, 25x100.11, four-story stone front flat. Rachel Kayser to Pauline Manheimer. *Mt.* $12,500. Dec. 14. 15,500

104th st, No. 58, s s, 180 w 4th av, 25x100.11, five-story brk flat. Jacob Roth to Jacob Mohr. *Mt* $16,000. Dec. 15. See Av A. 24,000

104th st, No. 145, n s, 350 e Amsterdam av, 50x100.11, one-story brk stores, frame sheds on rear. Maria Theresa Cotes to William H. Myer. *Mt.* $3,500. Nov. 16. 20,250

104th st, No. 210, s s, 121 w Amsterdam av, 25x100.11, five-story brk flat. William Curry to John Curry. Dec. 15. nom

104th st, No. 334, s s, 225 e 2d av, 25x100.11, four-story brk store and tenem't. Rosa Santoro widow to Luigi Botto. *Mt.* $7,000. Dec. 17. 11,250

105th st, s s, 155 w 4th av, 25x100.11. Release from assessm't lease. Cyrille Carreau to Mary A. Crabtree. Dec. 6. 250

105th st, s s, 155 w Park av, 25x100.11, vacant. Mary A. Crabtree to John F. Doyle. Nov. 25. 15,500

106th st, No. 123, n s, 265.6 w 9th av, 19.6x100.11, five-story brk flat. Jacob J. Barnes, Jersey City, to William J. Murphy. Dec. 14. 1,000

107th st, No. 77, n s, 81 w 4th av, 16x100.11, three-story brk dwell'g. Foreclos. William Sulzer to The New York Life Ins. Co. Dec. 1. 11,000

107th st, No. 75, n s, 97 w 4th av, 16x100 11, three-story stone front dwell'g. Foreclos. Same to same. Dec. 1. 7,000

112th st, n s, 175 e Lenox av, 75x100.11, vacant. Arthur Kenny to William A. Hynes. *Mt.* $12,500. Dec. 11. nom

114th st, Nos. 21 and 23, n s, 245 e 5th av, 50x100.11, two five-story brk flats. Clarence W. Gaylor to Morris H. Stern and Ferdinand Kurzman. *Mt.* $37,484. Dec. 14. See 1st av. 48,400

114th st, No. 426, s s, 108 w Av A, 25x100.10, four-story stone front tenem't with two-story brk building on rear. Moritz Pinner, Elizabeth, N. J., to Emily Rogers. *Mt.* $15,800, taxes 1891. Dec. 17. nom

115th st, n s, 400 w 6th av, old line and extdg to old Harlem lane and lands of John and Abraham Bussing
115th st, s e cor old Harlem lane and extdg to line of John Bussing, gore.
Matilda I. Wooley, formerly Salter, Negreet, La., to Mary J. Van Doren. B. & S. C. a. G. Nov. 27. 75

Same property. John J. Martin and Mary L. Bounds, Provencal, La., to same. B. & S. C. a. G. All title and curtesy. Dec. 5. 25

116th st, s s, 5'0 e 8th av, 50x100.11.
116th st, s s, 550 e 8th av, 8x61.4x—x68 4.
Nos. 264 and 266, two five-story stone front flats. William Eisenberg to Charles L. Ritzmann. *Mt.* $30,000. Dec. 11. See 8th st. each

116th st, No. 272, s s, 400 e 8th av, 25x168.7x26x111.6, five-story stone front store and flat. William Eisenberg to Leon Ulman. *Mt.* $36,000. Dec. 15. 39,000

116th st, No. 270, s s, 425 e 8th av, runs south 103.7 x northeast 8 10 to centre block, x east along same 16.10 x north 100.11 to 116th st, x west 25, five-story stone front flat with stores. Same to Herman Schwerin. *Mt.* $26,000 Dec. 15. 39,000

118th st, No. 149, n s, 356 w 3d av, 25x100.11, three story frame dwell'g. Thomas McParlan to Bridget McGuire. Dec. 17. 9,000

118th st, s s, 461 w 4th av, 100x100.11.
Reade st, No. 191 } begins Reade st. s s.
Chambers st, No. 199 } abt 83 e West st, runs south 61 4 to Chambers st, x east 24 x north 73.3 to Reade st, x west 22.6.
Theodore T. and Moranda B. Greenly individ. and exrs. George Greenly, Marianna wife of and John Walker, Louisa wife of and John Merchant to David S. Paige. Q. C. March 31, 1871. nom

119th st, Nos. 38–50, s s, 460 e Lenox av, 125x100.11, seven three-story brk dwell'gs. Lottie L. wife of Harvey N. Dean to Tillie E. Smith. Confirmation deed. B. & S. Nov. 24. nom

119th st, s s, 100 w 8th av, 175x100.11, vacant. Marx and Moses Ottinger to Thomas P. Dunne. Dec. 14. val. consid. and 100

120th st, Nos. 16 and 18, s s, 164 w 5th av, 36x119.2 to Old Manhattan road closed, x37 3x128.11, two three-story brk and stone front dwell'gs.
120th st, No. 22, s s, 218 w 5th av, 18x109.5 to Old Manhattan road closed, x18.7x128.11, three-story brk dwell'g
Abbie F. Faitoute individ. and extrx. Samuel D. Faitoute and Frances D. Faitoute to John Weber. B. & S. Dec. 10. nom

Same property. Same and Carrie W. Haines formerly Faitoute to same. B. & S. Aug. 31, 1891. nom

120th st, No. 16, s s, 164 w 5th av, 18x124 1 to Old Manhattan road closed, x18.8x128.11. John Weber to August Krehbiel. *Mt.* $11,000. Dec. 10. 21,000

120th st, s s, 125 e 7th av, 50x100.11, vacant. Jacob Bookman to Joseph S. Judge. Dec. 15. other consid. and 1 000

121st st. Nos 207 and 209, n s, 66.9 e 3d av, 34 10x71.9x—x43.8, three-story frame tenem't with stores. Dora and Lizzie Friedenberg to Jette Friedenberg. 2-4 part. *Mt.* $1,500. Dec. 2. nom

Same property. Isaac Meyer to same. ¼ part. Sub. to mort. Nov. 12. nom

121st st, No. 203, n s, 95 w 7th av, 16x100.11, three-story brk dwell'g. Evelyn wife of and William B. Randall to Seth Wheeler. Correction deed. Dec. 12. nom

121st st, No. 211, n s, 189 w 7th av, 16x100.11, three-story brk dwell'g. Same to same. *Mt.* $13,500. Dec. 12. nom

123d st, No. 318 s s, 138.8 e 2d av, 58x abt 75 to old lane, x—along same to 123d st point of beginning, gore, four-story brk flat. George Mackenzie to Amelia S. wife of John Davidson, Elizabeth, N. J. *Mt.* $19,000. Dec. 15. nom

123d st, No. 114, s s, 220 w Lenox av, 20 1x100.11, four-story stone front dwell'g. William H. Lawrence, New Haven, Conn., to Emeline M. Powell. Q. C. Dec. 10. nom

Same property. Emeline M. Powell to Andrew J. Reinhold. Nov. 24. 21,000

124th st, s s, 7.3 w 1st av, runs southwest 47 5 along centre of old lane, x southeast along s s of another old lane 13 5 x southwest 4– x northeast to 124th st, at point 10 west of 1st av, x east —. vacant. Forbes Holland and ano. exrs. John J. Bradley to Benjamin Barker, Jr., assignee John Molloy. Nov. 2. nom

124th st. No. 340, s s, 244.6 w 1st av, 18x100.11, three-story stone front dwell'g. Francis Probst to Charles Mann. Dec. 16. 10,500

127th st, No. 113, n s, 241 8 w 6th av, 16.8x99.11, three-story stone front dwell'g John McCann, Brooklyn, to Mary E. McCann his wife. B. & S. Dec. 8 nom

129th st, No. 249, n s, 481.3 w 7th av, 18.9x99.11, three-story brk dwell'g. Catherine Kapelyea to Minnie T. wife of William A. Shelton. *Mt.* $10,000. Dec. 8. nom

129th st, Nos. 306–310, s s, 125 w 8th av, 75x99.11, three five-story brk flats. Lawrence Winters to Edwin B. Stanton, Brooklyn. *Mt.* $63,000. Dec. 11. nom

Same property. Edwin B. Stanton to William R. Martin. *Mt.* $70,000. Dec. 15. nom

130th st, No. 2, s s, 110 e 5th av, 16 8x100, three-story stone front dwell'g. Stephen Sherwood to Julia S. Galbraith. Dec. 12. nom

133d st, No. 111, n s, 133 4 w Lenox av, 16.8x99.11, three-story stone front dwell'g. Release mort. Eugene Kelly to William T. Washburn and ano. exrs. Benjamin Richardson. Dec. 3. nom

Same property. Release judgment. Eugene Kelly individ. and with William Farrell, Edward Kelly and Joseph A. Donahue, of Eugene Kelly & Co., to same. Dec. 3. nom

Same property. William T. Washburn and ano exrs. and trustees Benjamin Richardson to Mary A. wife of George D. Scott. *Mt.* $7,500. Dec. 11. 9,500

134th st. No. 284, s s, 3'0 e 8th av, 25x99 11, five-story brk flat. George Manson to Rosina Christie. *Mt.* $20,000. Dec. 17. 27,500

135th st, No. 287, n s, 2'5 e 8th av, 25x99 11, five-story brk flat. Frederick W. Payne, Jersey City, to Harvey Terry. *Mt.* $30,000. Dec. 1. nom

14 d st, s s, 175 e Boulevard, 50.6x99.11, vacant. Mary E. wife of John M. Cahill to Alice Leo. Dec. 14 See 146th st. 12,000

145th st, Nos. 3 0 and 312, s s, 130.2 w 8th av, 51 x99.11, two five-story brk flats with stores. Jacob D Butler to Mary E. Hahn. *Mt.* $18.000. Dec. 11. 60,000

Same property. Release mort. Otto L. Stix to Jacob D. Butler. Dec 10. 4.450

145th st, s s, 79.2 w 8th av, 102x99.11. Release mort. Nathan Wise to same. Dec. 9 nom

Same property. Release mort. Julius G. Miller to same. Dec 9. nom

146th st, No. 415, n s, 175 w St. Nicholas av, 12.6x99.11, four-story brk dwell'g. Alice Leo to Mary E. wife of John M. Cahill. *Mt.* $7,000. Dec. 15. See 143d st. 13,000

Av A, No. 1333, n w cor 71st st, 29.4x75, five-story brk tenem't with stores. Jacob Mohr to Jacob Roth. *Mt.* $20,000. Dec. 15. See 104th st. 35.000

Av D, Nos. 131–138, e s, 79.6 n 9th st, runs north 79 8 x east 80 x south 54 2 x east 25 x south 23 x west 3 2 x south 3.5 x west 101.10, three five-story brk tenem'ts with stores. Samuel Weil to Isaac and Morris Cohen. *Mt.* $56,000. Dec. 15. See Columbia st. 92,500

Av D, Nos. 134–138, e s, 79 6 n 9th st, runs north 79 8 x east 80 x south 54.2 x east 25 x south 23 x west 3.2 x south 3.6 x west 101.10. Isaac and Morris Cohen to Betsey and Rachel Cohen. *Mt.* $76,000 Dec. 16. 80,000

Amsterdam av, No 647, e s, 84.5 n 91st st, 27.6x100, five-story brk flat with stores. Foreclos. Jerome Buck to Simon Arendt. Sub. to mort. $112,500 and interest, and to judgment of foreclos. $5,310 and costs 373. Aug. 31. 20,000

Same property. Release mort. Heloise H. Durant to same. Dec. 8 24,000

Same property. Release mort. Moses Kind and Julius Lipman to same Dec. 11. nom

Same property. Release judgment. Same to same. Dec. 11. nom

Amsterdam av, n w cor 85th st, 102.2x100, vacant. Frederick H. Comstock to D. Willis James. *Mt.* $50,000. Feb. 20, 1891. (Corrects error in last issue where transfer erroneously appears under 88th st, n w cor Amsterdam av.) 68,500

Columbus av, No. 465, e s, 51.10 n 82d st, 25.2x100, five-story brk store and flat. Jacob Winkler to Frederick Dillemuth. B. & S. Dec. 8 30,250

Columbus av, No. 465, e s, 51.10 n 82d st, 25.2x100, five-story brk store and flat. Frederick Dillemuth to Jacob Winkler and Elizabeth his wife C. a. G. Dec. 8 30,250

Convent av, n e cor 141st st, 125x100.
Hamilton terrace, n w cor 141st st, 75x100.
Hamilton terrace, w s, 75 n 141st st, 50x100.
Brk and stone church and two-story frame rectory.
Alexander L. McDonald, James Pott and Charles H. Contoit to The Rector, &c, Saint Luke's Church, New York. *Mt.* $16,400. B. & S and C. a. G. Dec. 8. nom

Lexington av, No. 1990, w s, 67 6 n 121st st, 16 8x61.9x16.7x61 9, three-story stone front dwell'g. Emma S. Hover widow to Mary E. wife of Clarence F. Betts and Ida A. Swarts, ⅓ part. Dec. 14. 3,833

Lexington av, No. 616, n w cor 53d st, 21x68, five-story brk (stone front) flat with stores. Benjamen Sire to Albert I. Sire. *Mt.* $25,000. Dec. 16. nom

Lexington av, Nos 1636 and 1638, n w cor 104th st, 33.11x55, two three-story brk dwell'gs.
Lexington av, No 1642, w s, 50 7 n 104th st, 16 8x55, three-story brk dwell'g.
Lexington av, Nos. 1648–1658, w s, 100.11 n 104th st, 100.7x55, six three-story stone front dwell'gs.
Louis Cohen to James W. Ketcham. B. & S. and C a. G. Dec. 17. nom

Madison av, s w cor 99th st, runs south to centre line bet 98th and 99th sts. x west — to w s Old Boston Post road now closed. x northeast along same to 99th st, x east — to beginning, vacant. Warren Ferris, Orangetown, N. Y., to George F. Johnson. Oct 7. other consid. and 500

Park (4th) av, s w cor 107th st, 100.11x100, vacant. Release mort. Mary A. Wagstaff, Frances A. Ward, George G. and John C. Barnard and Alfred Wagstaff guard. of Alice Barnard to John B Smith. Dec. 12. 16,500

Same property. Release mort. Mary A. Wagstaff and Frances A. Ward to same. Dec 11. nom

Same property. John B. Smith to James F. Boyle and Michael J. Bannon. Dec. 11. other consid. and 100

Park (4th) av } the block, 201.10x4 5, vacant.
Lexington av } Salomon Marx to Isaac and
100th st } Samuel Untermyer ¼ part.
101st st } *Mt.* ¼ of $111,000. Dec. 10. consid. omitted

Pleasant av, s w cor 115th st, 75.7x74, vacant. William T. Washburn and Emma Richardson exrs. and trustees Benjamin Richardson to Thomas F. Shannon. *Mt.* $11,000. Dec. 15. 11,500

Same property. Release mort. The Mutual Life Ins. Co., of New York, to same. Dec. 15. 11,000

Riverside av or Drive, No. 96, e s, 64.9 s 83d st. runs east 70.3 x north 15 6 x west 26.6 x northwest 6 3 x west 47 to av, x south 21.9, four-story brk dwell'g.
Riverside av or Drive, No. 94, e s, 68.3 s 82d st, 19 6x84.7x18.8x78.9, four-story brk dwell'g.
Release mort. John L. Brewster to The Squier & Whipple Co. Dec. 14. nom

Same property. Release judgment. Frank L. Smith to same. Dec. 14. nom

Same property. Squier & Whipple Co. to Frank L. Smith. Dec. 15. nom

Same property. Frank L. Smith to William W. MacFarland. *Mt.* $47,000. Dec 15 nom

1st av. No 1771, w s, 25 8 s 92d st, 24 8x75, five-story brk tenem't with stores. Morris H. Stern and Ferdinand Kurzman to Clarence W. Gaylor. *Mt.* $12,000. Dec. 12. See 114th st. 19,000

1st av, No. 1574, e s, 25 8 s 82d st, 25 6x106 6, three story brk dwell'g on rear of lot. Mary Burns widow, Peter Burns and Mary Hagan heirs Edward Burns to Benedict A. Klein. Dec. 1. 14,100

Same property. Benedict A. Klein to Jonas Weil and Bernhard Mayer. *Mt.* $10,000. Dec. 10. 14,100

1st av, No. 496, e s, 24 8 s 29th st, 24 8x75, five-story brk tenem't with stores. Edward H. Stehl to Fedor Weinert guard. of Olga Weinert *Mt.* $9 000. Dec 15. 19,425

2d av. No 91, w s, 48 6 n 5th st, 24 3x100, four-story brk tenem't. Peter Schaeffler to Johanna Diescher. *Mt.* $15,000. Dec. 15. 33,000

2d av, No 2001, n w cor 103d st, 25.5x75, four-story brk store and tenem't.
103d st. No. 248, n s, 75 w 2d av, 25x100.11, three-story brk tenem't.
104th st, No 308, n s, 75 e 2d av, 25x126.9, three-story brk tenem't with one-story frame buildings on rear.
David G and John W. Baird exrs. Sarah Baird to John W., David G. and Sophia A. O. Baird. Dec. 15. nom

Same property. Same as exrs. John Baird to same. Dec 15. nom

Same property. Carrie M. Crowe to same. C. a. G. Dec 15. nom

2d av, No. 2211, w s, 74 8 s 114th st, 25.11x100, four-story brk tenem't with stores. Ezekiel S. Korn to Josephine wife of William J. Gessner. Q. C. All liens. Dec. 5. nom

Same property. Josephine wife of and William J Gessner to Joseph Meyer. *Mt.* $9,500. Nov. 13. 14,500

3d av. No 1633, e s, 50.4 s 92d st, 25.2x100, five-story brk tenem't with stores. Bryan L. Kennelly to Oliver L. Shepherd. *Mt.* $15,000. Dec 15. 30.000

3d av, No 827, e s, 80 2 s 51st st, 20.1x76, four-story brk store and tenem't. Thomas S. Smith to Benjamin H. Tuthill. *Mt.* $15,000. Dec 10. 19,500

3d av. No 827, e s, 80.2 s 51st st, 20.1x76, four-story brk store and tenem't. Benjamin H. Tuthill to George Macdonald. *Mt.* $15,000 and judgment $165. Dec. 14. 19 750

4th av, No 408, w s. 37.1 n 28th st, 18.6x56. Edward B. Gould to Francis J. Hotop. Q. C. and release. Oct. 13. nom

7th av, Nos. 257 and 259, e s, 25.2 s 25th st. 42.6x60, two four story brk stores and tenem'ts. Joseph and Andrew Leupold exrs. Andrew Leupold to William D. C. McMurray. Dec. 11. 20,000

7th av. No. 259, e s, 25 2 s 25th st, 21 6x60. William D. C. McMurray to Joseph Leupold. *Mt.* $5 000. Dec. 11. 10,200

7th av, No. 257, e s, 46 8 s 25th st, 21x60. Same to Andrew Leupold. Dec 11. 10,000

7th av, Nos. 2166 and 2168, w s, 99.11 s 129th st, 40x75, two five-story brk flats with stores. Foreclos. Peter B. Olney to Lilly wife of Jonathan W. Hull. *Mt.* $40,000 Dec. 10. 8,200

7th av, No 824, n w cor 53d st. 25x100, five-story brk flat with stores. Nellie F. wife of Mark P Brennan to Charles L. Ritzmann. *Mt.* $45,000. Dec. 15. See 58th st. exch

11th av, e s lot 33 map Trinity Church Cemetery, 15x15 (grave). Charlotte Petzinger formerly Henry, Fort Wayne, Ind., heir Peter J Henry to Robert Kessler. Dec 1. 175

Interior lot, in rear of former No. 11 Hoboken st, begins 60 s Canal st formerly Hoboken st, and 10 w Washington st, runs south 24 x west 24x24x20. John Dickson to William Gasten, Brooklyn. ½ part. B. & S. Dec. 17. nom

MISCELLANEOUS.

General release. Andrew Koch or Cook to Samuel Koch or Cook. Dec 14. 50

General release, especially as to estate of Sarah Baird dec'd and legacies John W. Baird trustee Sarah Baird to David G. and John W. Baird exrs. Sarah Baird. Dec. 15. 500

Similar general release. Same to same. Dec. 15. 10,000

Similar general release. John W., David G. and Sophia A. O. Baird and Carrie M. Crowe heirs John and Sarah Baird to same. Dec. 15. nom

Similar general release. Same to same. Dec. 15. nom

Release legacy under will of Peter Gillespie. Mary Faden, Cincinnati, Ohio, to Rosa Gillespie. Oct. 24 1885. 5.0

Reassignment of all estate, real and personal, under general assignment. William Angelo to Mary C. Shantz Dec. 2. nom

Resignation of William Bruce Oliphant as trustee under ante-nuptial deed and appointment of Robert Mackenzie as new trustee. Feb. 17. nom

23d and 24th WARDS.

Ann st, n e s, 449.4 s e of road to City of New York, runs northeast 248.6 to road from West Farms to Kingsbridge, x southeast 270.9 x southwest 142 x again southwest 77 to st. x northwest 288.3, West Farms. Eliza Miller to Joseph Miller. Mt. $1,800. Dec. 16. 40,000

Broadway, s e s, 285.6 n e Macomb st, 34.6x85. Isabella wife of and Alexander J. Herriott to Charles L. Denks. Dec. 16. 2,000

Broadway, s e s, 251 n e Macomb st, 34.6x85. Same to Emma and Bertha Wuesthoff. Dec. 16. 3,000

Main st to West Farms, w s, 155.10 s West Farms road, 250x225. Sarah E. wife of William V. N. Rosedale to James J. Collins. Mt. $2,000. Dec. 14. 7,600

"New Drive" (a private road), w s, at s line of lot 7 map M. E. Putnam at Spuyten Duyvil, runs west 305.4 to N. Y. Central & Hudson River R. R. Co., x north abt 26 x east 305.4 to "Drive," x south along curves to beginning.

Land under waters of Hudson River in front and adjacent to above, begins at intersection of s s of said lot 7 with e s of land N. Y. Central & Hudson River R. R. Co., runs west 707.5 x north 26 x east 707.5 to e s of said Railroad Co.'s land, x south 26, except rights of said railroad.

Jennie F. wife of and Harold S. Des Brisay to John J. McKelvey. Dec. 1. 1,770

Perot st, s w s, 99 n w Sedgwick av, 21x80. Peter P. McLoughlin, Brooklyn, to Henry F. Fagan. Mt. $800. Dec. 17. 900

Pond pl, w s, 72.1 s Travers st, 21x48.7x53, contains 510 40-100 sq. ft. Herman H. Maack to Benjamin F. Deklyn. Dec. 1. nom

132d st, n s, 150 w Cypress av, 75x175. Francis E. Day to Lyman H. Day. Q. C. June 15, 1878. nom

136th st, s s, 294 e Alexander av, 37.6x100. Foreclos. Rollin M. Morgan to Lana J. wife of Archibald S. Van Orden. Dec. 14. 7,000

153d st, s s, 175 w Courtlandt av, 25x100. Susanna Wisseman widow and Ernest Wallace to Moritz and Mary A. Uhl. Dec. 16. 5,800

175th st, s s, 98 w Madison av, 27x108. Robert Couenhoven to Richard A. Turner, Jr. Dec. 10. 4,400

Brook av, s e cor 149th st, 75x100. Gerard Fountein to Samuel B. Ogden. ½ part. C. a. G. Mt. $25,000. Dec. 11. 5,896

Clinton av, n w cor Lebanon st, 25x100x24.7x100. John J. Brady to Isaac Anderson. Oct. 19. 1,050

Crotona av, s e cor Oakland pl, 25x100x24x100. John J. Brady to Henry Bracken. Oct. 19. 1,050

Cuthbert av, s s, 37.4 e Odell st proposed, 25x100. Frederick P. Forster exr. George H. Forster to Isabelle Isaacs. Dec. 14. 600

Cuthbert av, s s, 112.4 e Odell st proposed, 25x100. Same to Alfred A. Isaacs. Dec. 14. 600

Cuthbert av, s s, 62.4 e Odell st proposed, 25x100. Same to Louis Isaacs. Dec. 14. 600

Cuthbert av, s s, 87.4 e Odell st, 25x100. Same to Elias M. Isaacs. Dec. 14. 600

Cuthbert av, s s, 137.4 e Odell st proposed, 50x100. Same to Isaac H. Solomon. Dec. 14. 1,200

Franklin av, n w s, abt 192.8 n e Woodruff av. 25x108.9. Charles Hartman to Lawrence Cronin. Mt. $1,000. July 8. 2,900

Gardner av, s s, 100 e Orchard terrace, 50x100. Edward J. Hartman, Brooklyn, to Charlotte Hartman. Re-recorded. Sept. 9. 250

Madison av, s e cor 12th st, 25x100. Henry C. Mandeville to Solomon Berliner. Q. C. Nov. 19. nom

Same property. Solomon Berliner to William Ferschild. Nov. 20. 3,000

Madison av, w s, 203 n Kingsbridge road, 25x100. Release dower in mort. and in mortgaged premises. Josephine wife of Edward G. Musgrave to Edward B. Foote, Sr. Dec. 15. nom

Marion av, s e s, 40.8 s w Campbell or Gambril or Suburban st, 25x84.11x25x78. Isabell Merritt to Joseph J. Koen, Pearsalls, L. I. Dec. 9. 700

Marion av, s w cor Travers st both proposed, 25x100.8x24x100.11. John J. Dowling to Margaret C. Dowling. B. & S. Dec. 10. nom

Riverdale av, n e cor proposed Rock st, 50x100. Mary wife of John Fitzpatrick and heir John McLaughlin to James F. Sheridan. Mt. $1,000. Dec. 15. 2,500

Sedgwick av, centre line, e s, 350 s of James Lees lands and adj W. B. Ogdens, 50x182.10, 24th Ward. Matthew Kyle to Andrew H. Green. Mt. $1,500. Dec. 14. 4,000

Same property. Edward A. Caswell and Peter Garry to same. Q. C. Correction deed. Dec. 4. nom

Tinton av, w s, 175 n 156th st, 103x135. Henry P. DeGraaf to Gaetano F. Formica. Dec 14. 4,400

Tinton av, e s, part lot 87 map of Eltona, 30x133. Carrie R. wife of Charles T. Wills to Garet Hopper. Dec. 15. 2,800

3d av, s w cor Denman st, 60.5x98.1x50x132.9. Edmund Penfold exr. and trustee Thomas H. Faile dec'd to Thomas H., Jr., and Charles V. Faile exrs. and trustees Thomas H. Faile. June 30, 1886. nom

West Farms to Hunts Point road, w s, at s s Nathan Hulets land, abt 27x90x25x100. Addie widow and William Pawson, Whitestone, L. I., to George Pawson. All title. Sept. 14. nom

Lots 1-5 map Edward K. Willard's property, Woodlawn Heights, 24th Ward. Ephraim B. Levy to Edwin C. Warner, Ludlow, Vt. Dec. 2. nom

Lots 96 and 97 map Metropolitan Real Estate Assoc., 24th Ward, 75x100. Louis Smadbeck to Maurice Blanckensee. Dec. 2. 1,000

Lots 3216-3231 and 3241 section 11, being that portion remaining unsold of the real estate in 24th Ward of which Mary P. Chrystie died seized. James N. Chrystie, of Havre, France, to Mary L. wife of said James N. Chrystie. ½ part. Nov. 27. nom

Parcel under water Hudson River adjoining lot 7 map M. E. Putnam property, Spuyten Duyvil, and beginning Hudson River R. R., e s, at south line of said lot 7, runs west 707.5 x north 104 x east 707.5 x south 104, excepting land taken for railroad. Margaret E. wife of and Albert E. Putnam to Jennie F. wife of Harold S. Desbrissy. Dec. 1. (Corrects error in last issue). 500

LEASEHOLD CONVEYANCES.

Bleecker st, No. 127. Agreement to cancel lease. Mitchell A. C. Levy with J. B. Basset. Dec. 15. nom

Broad st, No. 40.
New st, No. 40.
Charles and Julia A. de Rham, Cold Spring, N. Y., to Edison General Electric Co. 21 years, from Nov. 1, 1890, per year, taxes, &c., and 21,763

Canal st, No. 503. Assign. lease. John Lyons to Teresa Lyons. Dec. 2. 700

Greenwich st, No. 322, n w cor Duane st. Assign. lease. Herman F. Ehlers to Haaren & Meinken. nom

Same property. Assign. lease. Henry Meyer to same. nom

Houston st, No. 228 | begins West Houston st,
Downing st, No. 64 | n s, 68.6 e Varick st, runs east 25 x north 43.4 x again north 41.4 to Downing st, x west 25 x south 34.11 x south again 36.5. Leasehold. Samuel W. Bower recvr. William A. and Theodore E. Senior to William T. A. Hart. All title. Aug. 5. 100

Nassau st, Nos. 48 and 50. Assign. lease. Henry W. Deane to Elizabeth A. Deane. nom

Washington st, No. 221. Assign. lease. Beadleston & Woerz to James Smith. 7,500

West st, No. 165, e s, 66.6 s Murray st, 22.4x49.11. Gertrude R. Waldo to William C. Renwick et al. trustees William R. Renwick. 21 years, from Aug. 1, 1890, per year, taxes, &c., and 900

West st, No. 164, e s, 88.4 s Murray st, 21.10x49.11x21.9x50. Same to same. 21 years, from Aug. 1, 1890, per year, taxes, &c., and 900

West st, No. 350. Assign. lease. Samuel B. Willis to Rachel Willis. Dec. 12. nom

West st, No. 334. Assign. lease. Beadleston and Woerz, a corporation, to Denis Shields. nom

26th st, No. 309 E. Assign. lease. George Neuner to H. Koehler & Co., a corporation. Dec 5. 2,000

35th st, No. 155 E. Assign. lease. Michael E. Dillon to William H. Buxton. 4,000

48th st, s s, 452.6 w 5th av. Consent to assign. lease. Trustees Columbia College to Harriet E. W. wife of George A. Strong. Nov. 20. nom

49th st, n s, 264 w 5th av, 25x100.11. Consent to assign. lease. Trustees Columbia College to Maria B. Child. nom

50th st, No. 33 W. Consent to assign. lease. Trustees of Columbia College to Charles A. Jackson referee. Nov. 24. nom

51st st, s s, 250 w 5th av. Consent to assign. lease. Trustees of Columbia College to Henry J. Burchell and ano. exrs. James G. Burchell. Oct. 20. nom

109th st, No. 100 E. Assign. lease. James Everard to Andrew McMurray. Oct. 28. nom

125th st, Nos. 135 and 137 E. Assign. lease. Henry N. Singhi to Diedrich and August Brandes. nom

Av A, No. 1394, n e cor 74th st. Assign. lease. Thomas Reilly to Patrick Chambers. 3,300

Av A, e s, 62 n 18th st, 20x64. Assign. lease. Karl Hoffart to Katharina Wittenauer. 4,000

3d av, No. 1929. Assign. lease. Richard Sichler to Sichler & Prubs. nom

9th av, Nos. 390 and 392. Assign. lease. Herman Dammer to James Everard. Aug. 26. 2,500

9th av, No. 861. Assign. lease. James F. Jordan to Franklin P. Roberge. nom

KINGS COUNTY.

DECEMBER 10, 11, 12, 14, 15, 16.

Bainbridge st, No. 505, n s, 115.6 e Saratoga av, 17.6x100, h & l. Anna E. wife of J. Mason Kirby to Nellie C. wife of Frank W. Darrin. Mt. $5,000 and taxes 1891. nom

Barbey st, w s, 200 n Arlington av, 100x95. August Moll to James W. Crawford. $4,200

Bergen st, n s, 80 w Utica av, runs west 45 x north 107.2 x east 15.10 x south 0.5 x northeast 36.6 x south 116.8. Ann, Edwin and William J. Marchant and Alfred C. Cowles heirs Richard Marchant to Christopher P. Skelton. 1,500

Bergen st, n s, 445 e 6th av, runs east 20 x north 26.9 to Flatbush turnpike, x northwest 26.9 x south 44.6. Mary F. wife of Thomas H. Hamilton to James T. Nelson. 2,000

Bergen st, s s, 100 e Buffalo av, 120x100. John F. Parkes and Benjamin L. Rand to George C. Hollister. nom

Bergen st, n s, 151 w Buffalo av, —x100x16.6x100, h & l. John Maguire, Chicago, Ill., to William L. Bogart. nom

Same property. William D. Bogart to John Raber and Christina his wife. Mt. $750. nom

Berriman st, w s, 135 s Vienna av, 40x100. William H. Jackson to Henry Farrer. 350

Berriman st, w s, 135 n Vienna av, 40x100. Same to Timothea A. King. 350

Bleecker st, n w s, 90 s w St. Nicholas av, 40x100. Jacob Manneschmidt to John G. Grauer. nom

Box st, n s, 125 e Manhattan av, 25x100, h & l. Mary A. Grace, New York, to Annie C. Grace, New York. B. & S. nom

Same property. Annie C. Grace widow to Clarence K. Valentine. Q. C. 75

Bremen st, w s, bet Adams and Prospect sts, being lots 23 and 24 block 1020 assessm't map 18th Ward. Elizabeth and Wm. Schano exrs. Carl Schano to Gustav J. L. Doerschuck. 1,950

Bridge st, w s, 172 s Johnson st, 22x107.6. Amelia E. Downes, Anna M. Phillips, Evelyn L. Welsh, Julia A. Stephens, Ida F. Gustkin and Mary E. Decker to George W. Carr. 4,000

Bridgewater st, n e cor Charlick st, 105x400 to wharf. The Acme Oil Co. to The Sone & Fleming Mfg. Co. 20,000

Bristol st, w s, 90 n Eastern Parkway, 20x100. Emil Reineking to Bernhard J. Pink. Mt. $2,300. nom

Same property. Bernhard J. Pink to Emma wife of Emil Reineking. Mt. $2,300. nom

Broadway, centre line, s s, 400 w Utica av, runs east 945.6 x south 270.3 to centre Earl st, x west 957.10 x north 270, Flatbush, subject to sts. Patrick Hayes to Frances E. Hurlburt. nom

Same property. Frances E. Hurlburt to Charles M. Marsh, of Morris Plains, N. J. Mt. $7,000. exch

Broadway, s w s, 46.11 s e Madison st, runs southwest 55 x southwest 33.2 x east 18.1 x south 4 9 x northeast 80.4 to st, x northwest 28. Robert L. Moores and Charles A. Le Queene to Nathan Kaplan. Mt. $13,660 and taxes 1891. nom

Broadway, s w s, 240.4 n w Ellery st, 25x88.4x27x98.9. Lawrence Grussier to Henry Elm. nom

Broadway, n s, 145.4 e Driggs st, 20.4x100. Robert T. Stokes and Henry G. Schoff to William L. Stokes. ½ part. Mt. $17,000. nom

Butler st, s s, 250 e Rogers av, runs south 100 x east 63 x south 48 x east — x north to Butler st, x west 117.11. Ida M. wife of Thomas Burkhard, Jr., to Michael Newman. Mt. $4,500. 7,800

Cambridge pl, e s, 200 s Greene av, 20x100, h & l. Mildred L. Ross formerly Peters to Joshua H. Cort. Mt. $6,000. 9,000

Carroll st, s s, 62.6 w Utica av, 60.11x— to patent line, x— to land of Evarts, x—. David Kohn to Rosalia Kohn. nom

Clifton pl, n s, 175 e Bedford av, 18.9x100. Edgar Tilton to Rebecca Tilton. 9,200

Clymer st, s s, 160 w Wythe av, runs south 71 x west 0.4 x south 9 x west 19.7 x north 80 to st, x east 19.11. Edward and Mary Arnold by James and Margaret Arnold guards. to Ludwig Schildknecht. 3,450

Same property. James and Margaret Arnold trustees for Edward and Mary Arnold and as individs. to same. nom

Cooper st, n w s, 257.6 n e Broadway, 19.7x100. George Brand to Joseph Barth. Mt. $4,950. 6,625

Cornelia st, n w s, 160 n e Evergreen av, 40x100. Charles Wagenfohr to Kaspar H. Hedbawney, of New York. 2,500

Court st, w s, 54.7 s Sackett st, 18.2x80, h & l. William M. and Pierre Van B. Hoes to Julia Cohen widow. 9,200

Court st, w s, 76.5 n 4th pl, 14.3x70, h & l. Valentin Massengarb to John Schaefer and Margarethe his wife. 4,200

Covert st, s e s, 270.10 n e Evergreen av, 18.7x100, h & l. Louisa wife of William Grassmann to Friedrich Siepermann. Mt. $2,000. 3,200

Dean st, No. 1012, s s, 520 e Franklin av, 20x110. George H. Cook to I. Augustus Stanwood. Mt. $1,000. nom

Dean st, n s, 275 e Schenectady av, 25x107.2. Bridget Fitzpatrick widow to Patrick H. Fitzpatrick, of Lake City, Col. ½ part. Mt. $700. nom

Same property. Patrick H. Fitzpatrick, of Lake City, Col., to Bridget Fitzpatrick widow, life estate, and Thomas F. Fitzpatrick, ½ part. Sub. to mort. $700. nom

Dean st, s s, 425 e Schenectady av, runs south 100 x east 50 x south 114.5 to Bergen st, x east 100 x north 107.2 x east 15.10 x northwest 116.1 to Dean st, x west 121. James Gascoine, George and Robert Evans exrs. Benjamin Evans to Christopher P. Skelton. 11,000

Degraw st, n s, bet Hoyt and Bond sts, being lot 72 block 234 assessm't map 10th Ward. City of Brooklyn to James Leonard. Q. C. 764

Same property. James Leonard to James Lennon. Q. C. nom

Devoe st, s s, 40 e Humboldt st, 20x75, h & l. James C. Turner to Albert Meyer. 2,700

Diamond st, s s, 111.4 e Flatbush av, 50x158.6, Flatbush. Aaron S. Robbins to James Hueston. 2,500

Dooley st, w s, 107.3 w Emmons av, 87x90.
Dooley st, w s, 324.2 n Emmons av, 44.7x212.6x39 6x222.6, Gravesend.
John Lundy to Charles E. Lundy. nom

Dooley st, s w s, 258.8 n w Emmons av, runs north 59.4 x north 6.7 x northwest 58 x south 86.6 x northeast 87.

Dooley st, n w cor Emmons av, 167.3x87x133.4x93.9.

Emmons av, s s, 19 w Dooley st, if extended, 93.10x103.

Sheepshead Bay road, n e cor West 1st st,

runs north 49.7 x northeast 117.6 x northeast 114.4 to Ocean Parkway, x south 47.6 to Sheepshead Bay road, x 233.9.

Sheepshead Bay road, n w cor West 1st st, runs southwest 27.1 x north 46.6 x northeast 28.9 to West 1st st, x 47.10, Gravesend. Charles E. Lundy to John Lundy. *Mt.* $2,666. nom

Douglass st, n s, 291.2 e Albany av, 133.10x130. Harris J. Latta to William Masker, Newark, N. J. *Mt.* $22,500. 22,550

Dupont st, n s, 175 w Manhattan av, 25x100, h & l. Catherine Meehan, of New York, to Robert Hufnagel. 3,900

Eastern Parkway, s e cor Van Sielen av, 50x100. J. Wyckoff Van Sicleu to Mary C. Van Siclen his wife. 2,600

Eastern Parkway, n s, 50 e Thatford av, 25x100. Andrew R. Culver to Esther Goldenberg. Taxes, &c., from 1889. 550

Eastern Parkway, s s, 50 e Christopher av, 25x100, h & l. Wolf Potashinski to Louis Strumf, New York. *Mt.* $3,000. 6,000

Eastern Parkway, s s, 75 e Christopher av, 25x100, h & l. Same to Mendel Gettinger and Isaac Gross. *Mt.* $3,000. 6,000

Eldert st, n w s, 100 n e Evergreen av, 20x100, h & l. Ernestine Gastmeyer to Mamie Ribber. *Mt.* $2,500. 4,500

Elton st, w s, 165 s Stanley av, 40x100. Adolph Sussman to Nilse Olsen. 300

Frost st, n s, 350 w Kingsland av, 25x100. Contract. John J., Patrick, Henry, Peter and Thomas Smith heirs Henry Smith and Joseph F. Clark. 1,000

Frost st. s s, 175 w Humboldt st, 25x148x25x142. Gustav Wolf to Elise wife of Diedrich Gronholz, of New York. *Mt.* $9,000. 10,200

Fulton st, s s, 170 w Grand av, 80x142. L. Anna wife of Victor Erbacher, of New York, to Jeremiah T. Story. 25,000

Fulton st, No. 11, n e s, 22.6x60.2x21.4x60.10. Emma wife of and Henry M. Haar, Anna wife of and William Forster, Ida wife of and Martin H. Hartmann, of New York, heirs Susanna Kress to The John Kress Brewing Co. 16,000

Guernsey st, w s, 1.5 s Bedford av, runs south 100 x west 48.5 x northwest to Bedford av, x east 87.11 to point 3.1 w of Guernsey st, x — to beginning, hs & ls. Edward P. Self, Smithville South, L. I., to David S. Rice, of Canton, N. Y. nom

George st, s e s, 125 n e Evergreen av. 25x100. George W. Fowler to Balthasar Dornbach and Joseph Barudio. 1,500

Halsey st, n w s, 280 s w Central av, runs northwest 200 to Weirfield st, x southwest 30.6, thence to point on Halsey st 280.3 w Central av, x northeast 0.3¼. Leopold J. Lippman to Charles D. Hommel. nom

Halsey st, n e cor Lewis av, 25x100, h & l. Frank R. Newman to Louise M. Creamer. *Mt.* $12,000. exch

Hancock st, No. 167, n s, 180 e Nostrand av, 20x100. Louise M. wife of Frank D. Creamer to Frank R. Newman. *Mt.* $10,000. exch and 10,000

Halsey st, s e cor Patchen av, 200x100. Foreclos. John Courtney to Horatio S. Stewart. *Mt.* $27,000. 1,000

Hancock st. Party wall agreement. Louis F. Seitz with William H. Reynolds. 50

Hancock st, n s, 375.8 e Howard av, 16.8x100. Rose L. Flynn widow and devisee William A. Flynn to Maggie Robinson. nom

Hancock st, n s, 347 e Tompkins av, 15x100. William H. Reynolds to Eleanor H. Pickett. *Mt.* $5,000. 8,250

Hart st, s s, 330 e Gates av, 20x100. Joseph Herweg to Philippina wife of Joseph Herweg. nom

Hendrix st, w s, 100 s Broadway, 100x100. Foreclos. John Courtney to Hugo I. A. Dembke as admr. Caroline Dembke. 4,650

Hendrix st, w s, 64 s Arlington av, 36x100. Kate and Ellen Kennedy heirs Bridget Kennedy to Delia Brundage. 1,000

Herkimer st, s s, 100 e Howard av, runs south 93 x east 24 x north 13 x east 24 x north 80 to st, x west 48. Charles Drasser to Clara E. Ernst. *Mt.* $2,500. 4,000

Herkimer st, s s, 180 w Buffalo av, 18x185, h & l. Christopher P. Skelton to Caroline Swayze. *Mt.* $3,000. 5,600

Heyward st, n s, 78.6 e Lee av, 19.6x100, h & l. Louis Enricht, Chicago, Ill., to Daniel S. Baernstein, Chicago, Ill. *Mt.* $3,500. 2,000

Hoyt st, e s, 60.9 n Schermerhorn st, 20x75. Albert H. Schroeder to Theodore Beckmann. 7,250

Hubbard st, s s, 120 w Centre pl, 60x57.6, Gravesend. Sarah J. wife of John T. Hinman to Edward Wilson. 500

Hull st, s s, 131.3 w Hopkinson av, 18.9x84.10x18.10x86.1. George H. Chinnock to John O. Hoyt, Jr. *Mt.* $4,350. exch

Hull st, n w s, 210 s w Bushwick Boulevard, 20x100. Lewis Leavens to Charles E. Ring. *Mt.* $3,750. nom

Hull st, n w cor Hopkinson av, 50x83. Margaret Conway to James L. Kearney. *Mt.* $7,500. exch

Humboldt st, e s, 826 s Driggs av, 17x100. Charles Engert to Desiderius F. J. and Helen Hajek, of Ridgefield Park, N. J. 8,200

Huron st, s s, 100 w Oakland st, 25x100, h & l. Edward Reebil to Patrick Meehan. 10,000

Java st, s s, 275 e Oakland st, 25x100. Contract. George Lucas with J. P. Whittier. 1,025

Jefferson st, Nos. 24 and 26, s e s, 181.6 s w Bushwick av, runs southeast 100 x southwest 20 x southeast 11.6 x southwest 30 x northwest 111.6 x northeast 50. John L. Gaus to Minna Wezel. 10,000

Jerome st, e s, 125 s New Lots road, 25x175.10x25x175.2. James A. Henry to John Flaherty, New York. 300

Jerome st, w s, 60 n Dumont av, 60x100. Release mort. James Fallon to Nils A. Seaquist. nom

Same property. Nils A. Seaquist to James H. Brundage. 1,050

John st, s s, 200 e Bridge st, 23x100. Ellen M. Murray widow, John and Hugh J. O'Brien and Honora wife of Ulster O'Mallon to Charles J. Bradley. 3,500

Joralemon st, n s, 282.8 e Hicks st, 25x89.10x25x90.8, h & l. Amelia G. wife of Henry D. Fearing to Winston H. Hagen. 27,500

Leonard st, w s, 150 n Conselyea st, 25x61.6. William M. Anderson to Bridget wife of Thomas Sullivan. 4,425

Logan st, e s, 96 s Jamaica av, 50x100. Magdalena B. Smith to Harrison B. Wright. nom

Macon st, s s, 96 e Ralph av, 18x100. John R. Pitt to Joseph Gifuni. *Mt.* $4,000. 7,500

Macon st, s s, 355 e Nostrand av, 20x100. Foreclos. John Courtney to Jemima Thallon. *Mt.* $10,000. 1,825

Macon st, n s, 315.6 w Marcy av, 19.6x100, h & l. William H. Reynolds to Walter L. Scofield. *Mt.* $7,500. 13,500

Macon st, n s, 40 w Ralph av, 18x100, h & l. Frederick W. Starr, James D. Rankin and James Ross to The Hall Sash and Door Co. Sub. to morte., &c. nom

Macon st, s s, 175 w Patchen av, 18.6x100. James G. Roberts to William C. Moore. *Mt.* $4,500. 7,800

Macon st, n w cor Howard av, 185x100. Foreclos. John Courtney to Bernard Levino. *Mt.* $15,700. 1,000

Madison st, n w s, 325 n e Central av, 50x100. Mary H. wife of Elias J. Hendrickson to Emil F. Wildner. 2,500

Madison st, No. 789, n s, 278 w Ralph av, 18x100. Foreclos. John Courtney to Jacob Spettel. 1,750

Madison st, s s s, 281 e Lewis av, 19x109. Phebe A. Godfrey to Louisa B. Paisley. *Mt.* $6,000. 9,750

Malbone st, s s, 40 w New York av, 20x100, Flatbush. Patrick Riley to Ellen Riley. Q. C. nom

Marion st, s s, 350.2 e Howard av, 37.5x100. Release mort. James McLaren to Elizabeth P. McNab. nom

McDonough st, n s, 260 e Howard av, 40x100. James Kelly to Charles M. Le Furge. 2,300

McDougal st, n s, 85 w Howard av, 19x50. George A. Perry to M. Luther Frescoln. 2,900

Middleton st, n w s, 160 s w Throop av, 25x100. David Schwartz to Abraham Simon. All title. *Mt.* $3,700. 2,250

Moffat st, n w s, 183.4 n e Central av, 16.8x100. Frank P. Martin to Rose Winnett. *Mt.* $2,150. nom

Nevins st, s e cor President st, 65x100. Eliza A. wife of and John T. Bierds to John S. Loomis. *Mt.* $5,000. 8,500

Osborn st, e s, 150 s Blake av, 25x100, h & l. Simon C. Wilson, Baldwins, L. I., to Mary Silberstein. *Mt.* $1,500. 2,500

Osborn st, w s, 100 n Belmont av, runs west 47.3 x north 25 x west 52.8 x north 25 x east 100 to Osborn st, x south 50, h & l. Edward E. Stewart to Blanche Caro. 3,450

Osborn st, w s, 300 s Dumont st, 16.8x100. Samuel P. Tostevin to Annie Mathews. *Mt.* $1,800. 5,400

Pacific st, n s, 125 e 4th av, 25x90. Gustav Pius, of New York, to Sophie Pius. *Mt.* $9,500. nom

Pacific st, s s, 113.8 e Rochester av, 16.8x107.2, h & l. Charles H. Reynolds to Margaret M. Snyder. *Mt.* $2,100. 3,000

Pacific st, n e s, 125 s e Boerum pl, 25x109. Catharine A. Harvey to John H. Harvey. Q. C. Dated 1869. nom

Pacific st, n s, 42.10 e Stone av, 107x100. Susan R. Kendall, of New York, to Joseph T. Commoss. 14,000

Palmetto st, n w s, 157 s w Hamburg av. 21.10x68x22.4x southeast 73.5. Charles Glocksien to Hermann Breimann. 660

Palmetto st, n w s, 100 s w Central av, 25x100. Catharina Anacker widow to Henry E. F. Friedrichs, of New York. *Mt.* $3,000. 6,700

Park pl, s s, 191.3 e 6th av, 16.8x100. Anna E. Thien to William W. Stone. *Mt.* $7,500. 8,000

Pierrepont st, n s, 129 e Hicks st, 27x132x27x133.8. Foreclos. John Courtney to The Equitable Life Assur. Soc., United States. 20,000

President st, n s, 57.6 e 6th av, 35x95, hs & ls. William Brown to William W. Stoothoff, Flushing, L. I. *Mt.* $13,000. exch

Same property. Release mort. Henry C. M. Ingraham to William Brown. nom

Quincy st, s s, 160 w Sumner av, 20x100. George E. Randall, Yaphank, to Sarah E. Randall, Yaphank, L. I. *Mt.* $2,000. 3,000

Quincy st, s w cor Throop av, 24x80. William M. Gibson to Andrew Koch. *Mt.* $10,000. 17,500

Richardson st, s s, 100 e Graham av, 20.6x75. Elizabeth wife of Adam Parthesius to Henry Brandemann. *Mt.* $1,500. 2,800

Russell pl, No. 12, w s, 134.6 s Herkimer st, 16.3x97.9. Release mort. Joseph M. Greenwood to Felix Gallagher. nom

Same property. Felix Gallagher to Ida M. Bogart. *Mt.* $2,800. 3,900

Sackett st, s s, 217.6 w 4th av, 160x95. Annie I. wife of Timothy C. Mayher to Charles A. Brown, Elizabeth, N. J. *Mt.* $5,258. nom

Stockton st, s s, 325 w Throop av, 25x100. William Johnston to William P. Johnston. 1885. 2,500

Suydam pl, e s, 88.10 n Atlantic av, runs east 138.10 x north 10.7 x north 20.6 x west 137.3 to st, x south 40. Hephzibah R. wife of William D. Murphy to Mary E. Lucke. 2,500

Tillary st, No. 60, s s, 77.9 n Pearl st, 25x100, h & l. Eliza Lietz widow and Carline M. Lietz, Marlborough, N. Y., to Christina R. Seebeck. 5,250

Turnpike road, e s, lot 23 map of J. Conselyea property, 18th Ward, 25x100, h & l. Fannie J. Reek and Josephine E. Iland, New Haven, Conn., heirs Edmund Reek to Edmund Reek. 750

Union st, n s, 115.10 e 4th av, 75x95. Henry A. McCarthy, of New York, to Frances E. Hurlburt. *Mt.* $24,000. exch

Van Buren st, s s, 76 w Patchen av, 19.6x100.
Eldert st, n s, 198 w Bushwick av, 54x100.
Frank Hyde to Charlotte A. McTighe. *Mt.* $21,700. nom

Van Voorhis st, n w s, 508.9 s w Evergreen av, 17.2x100. Samuel Cunningham to Benjamin Randall and William G. Underwood, of Hancock, Delaware Co., N. Y. *Mt.* $3,400. 4,500

Vine st, No. 16, s w s, 134.6 s e Columbia Heights, 22.5x85.8, h & l. Florence W. wife of Lucius H. Beers to Annie wife of William P. Cook. nom

Warren st, s w s, 364.2 n w 4th av, 16.8x100, h & l. Lowry Somerville to Louise Kathe. *Mt.* $1,500. nom

Warren st, s w s, 414.2 n w 4th av, 16.8x106, h & l. Same to same. *Mt.* $1,200. nom

Watkins st, w s, 150 s Riverdale av, 25x100. Isador Brand, of Saratoga Springs, N. Y., to Charles J. Curtin. 250

Winthrop st, n s, 575 e Flatbush av, runs north 212 to Hawthorne st, x east 30.7 x south 106 x east 50 x north 106 to Hawthorne st, x east 75 x south 106 x east 50 x north 136 to centre of Hawthorne st, x west 25 x north 196.6 x east 71 x south 438.6 to Winthrop st, x west 250, Flatbush. Margaret W. wife of John J. Roberts to Frances H. wife of Robert S. Walker. B. & S. Correction deed. (Measurements above are old style.) nom

Woodbine st, n w s, 185 s w Knickerbocker av, 20x100. Release mort. James Gascoine individ. and with Anna E. Cozine as exrs, John G. Cozine to Albert Berckmeier. 2,641

Same property. Albert Berckmeier to Anna Dahlbender. nom

Wyckoff st, n s, 520 w 5th av, 20x100. Grace B. Topham to Louise Kathe. 6,000

York st, s s, 50 e Hudson av, 25x100. John F. Fitzpatrick, Kate wife of Thomas Floyd, James Sullivan, Loretta wife of Christian Kemter to Ella Fitzpatrick. 1,500

2d st, s s, 437.11 e 5th av, runs east 20 x south 95 x west 16.11 x south 5 x west 3.1 x north 100. Archibald N. McBean to James Jack. *Mt.* $8,000, int. from July 1891, and tax 1891. nom

South 2d st, s w s, 75 n w Hooper st, 25x125, h & l. Foreclos. Gerard M. Stevens to Emma Taiber. 3,900

3d st, s s, 28.6 e Smith st, runs south 53.5 x south 27.4 x east 12.2 x north 80 to st, x west 18.6. Michael D. Ryan to Augustus Hintz. *Mt.* $3,250. nom

North 3d st, s w s, 85.6 s e Wythe av, 25x½ block. James Barry to Meyer Boll. 3,200

Same property. Meyer Boll to Esther wife of Solomon Monday. *Mt.* $1,000. 3,200

4th st, s s, 233.10 w 7th av, 19x100. Release mort. The Franklin Trust Co. to Charles H. Moses and Henry B. Fanton, Jr., and Eliza A. Fanton. 5,508

4th st, s s, 252.10 w 7th av, 19x100. Release mort. Same to same and Louis H. Myers, Jr. 5,508

4th st, s s, 233.10 w 7th av, 19x100. Louis H. Myers, Jr., to Eliza A. Fanton. *Mt.* $6,600. nom

4th st, n e s, 97.10 n w 8th av, 23x95. Edward H. Litchfield and Grace D. Litchfield individ. and as trustees of Henry P. Litchfield to Louisa M. wife of J. O. Cleaveland. 3,162

South 4th st, n e cor Rodney st, 20x71.3. James L. Merritt and Louisa C. Lyon to Phebe W. wife of Andrew Wallace. All title. 3,000

6th st, n s, 257.4 e 5th av, 20.1x100. William J. Pearson to Terence E. McMahon. *Mt.* $2,000. 3,900

North 6th st, s s, 182.2 e Roebling st, 20.10x100. Joseph G., Henry, Theresa and Louis Bremer and Louisa wife of John Murcott heirs of Louisa Bremer to Joseph Bremer. C. a. G. nom

7th st, s s, 115.2 e 5th av, 18.4x100. James F. Taggart to Annie G. Scully. Q. C. 500

East 7th st, e s, 140 s Av C, 40x126.6, Flatbush. John O'Neill to Amelia C. Waite. *Mt.* $400. 675

9th st, original line, n w cor 4th av, 20x87. Charles H. Collins to Frank A. Barnaby. nom

9th st, n s, 155 w 5th av, runs north 60 x east 10 x north 45 x west 40 x south 105 to st, x east 30, h & l. Caroline C. wife of John F. Hume to Mary F. wife of John Burrill. All title. 1870. nom

Same property. Mary F. Burrill to Mary E. Lawrence. *Mt.* $6,500. 9,250

North 10th st, s w s, 69.9 n w Wythe av, 55.3x100; also,
North 10th st, s w s, 200 n w Wythe av, 50x100.
John Kerwin to John Moran. 8,000

11th st, s s, 226.6 e 5th av, 25x100. *Mt.* $7,500.
8th st, n s, 185.4 e 6th av, 12.6x100. *Mt.* $3,900.
Mary C. wife of Charles H. Jacobus to Frederick C. Dexter. exch

14th st, n s, 123.10 e 8th av, 18.6x100. William Hawkins to Jennie wife of Henry E. Asmus, Sayville, L I Mt. $3,500. nom

14th st, s s, 222.10 e 5th av, 100x100. Release mort. Catharine E. Lyman et al. to Nassau Land and Improvement Co. 4,500

19th st, s w s, 110 n w 4th av, 25x100. Claus Lau to Augusta Lau. All title. nom

19th st, n e s, 275 s e 6th av, 25x100. Francis D. Webster to Mary E. Webster. ½ part nom

21st st, n e s, 175 s e 4th av, 25x100. Mary wife of and John Levy to Albert Lewandowski. 2,400

21st st, n e s, 160 s e 5th av, 20x100. Catherine wife of and William Grady to Ellen E. Callahan. 3,600

East 21st st, w s, 129 s Voorhis av, as narrowed, 24.6x86, h & l, Gravesend. Contract. Horace R. Allen to Henry Grauel. 5,500

Bay 25th st, s e s, 220 n e Cropsey av, 180x96.8, New Utrecht. Frank G. Hennings to Axel Hirschsprung. 5,500

40th st, n s, 125 e 7th av, 25x100.2. Bridget wife of Robert Ferris to Thomas Gray. 425

East 45th st, centre line, intersection centre line Collins st, runs south 260 to centre William st, x west to Troy av, x south 130 x west 210 x north 130 to centre William st, x west — x north 130 x east 75 x north to centre Collins st, x east — to beginning.
Albany av, centre line, intersection centre line Collins st, runs east 130 x south 260 to centre William st, x west 130 to Albany av, x north 260, Flatbush.
Charles S. Taber to Julia Knapp. Mt. $5,100. exch

47th st, s w s, 200 s e 4th av, 20x100.2. Release mort. Elizabeth H. Taylor to Alexander Waldron. nom

53d st, s w s, 100 s e 3d av, 20x100.2. Francis H. Lawrence, Meridan, Conn., to Janetta A. wife of William P. Holt. 1,450

53d st, s s, 80 e 3d av, 20x100.2. Marcella wife of and Joseph O Furman to Bradford W. Hitchcock, of New York. nom

Same property. Bradford W. Hitchcock, of New York, to Joseph O. Furman and Marcella his wife. nom

55th st, n e s, 345 n w 14th av, 50x100.2, New Utrecht. West Brooklyn Land and Impt. Co. to Cartwright R. Hull. 700

56th st, n s, 300 w 6th av, 80x100.2. Contract. Wallace Crosby and Jarvis Masters and Charles Hamilton. 1,800

57th st, centre line, at line bet Cowenhoven and Bergen, runs southwest along said line to centre 58th st, x southeast along same to centre 9th av, x northeast along same to centre 57th st, x northwest —.
9th av, south cor 58th st, centre lines, adj above parcel, 102x— to M. Stillwells, x northeast 81.8 to centre 58th st, x northwest along same 344, New Utrecht.
James L. Kearney to John A. Clarry. exch

59th st, s s, 280 e 13th av, 40x100.2, Bath Junction. James V. S. Woolley to Michael Kerrigan. 500

60th st, s w s, 320 n w 17th av, 60x100. Hans C. Pfalzgraf to Grant E. Hamilton and Lydia E. his wife. Mt. $3,500. 5,926

60th st, n s, 260 e 12th av, 20x100.2, Bath Junction. Gennaro Uliano to Raffaele Uliano. 300

72d st, s w s, 66.8 n w 7th av, runs southwest 100 x southeast 40 x southwest 100 to 73d st, x northwest 260 x northeast 100 x northwest 40 x southwest 100 to 73d st, x northwest 60 x northeast 198.2 x east to 72d st, x southeast —. Release mort. Anna C. Hegeman et al. to George Edgett. 2,400

73d st, s s, 170 w 15th av, 40x100, Lefferts Park. James V. S. Woolley to Alexander S. Mitchell. 350

77th st, s w s, 460 n w 4th av, 40x109.4, New Utrecht. Eliza W. Davison, of New York, to Charles W. Manley. 1,000

84th st, n e s, 280 s e 22d av, 60x100, Bensonhurst. James D. Lynch to Annie M. Byrnes. 1,050

88th st, n e s, 350 n w 4th av, 25x100, New Utrecht. Winifred Sliney to Sarah J. wife of Joseph Marshall. 850

89th st, n e s, 225 s e 1st av, 50x100, New Utrecht. Carrie wife of and Joseph G. Weishaupt to Jacob P. Hardt. Mt. $294. 530

East 95th st, w s, 145 n Av G, 25x100, Flatlands. John H. Ireland to Emma A. Totten. nom

Alabama av, w s, 100 n Sutter av, 25x100. Lena Durchholz to Barbara Durchholz. 600

Albany av, s e cor Park pl, 20x80. Foreclos. John Courtney to Robert S. Neely. 4,000

Albany av, n e cor Butler st, 265.7x80. Foreclos. Same to same. 30,000

Atlantic av, n s, 300 e 3d av, 45x90. First Swedish Baptist Church to Sarah E. Stewart. Mt. $6,000. 10,000

Bedford av, south cor North 12th st, 60x100. John M. Moser to Christian Friedmann. ½ part. 2,500

Belmont av, s s, extends from Alabama av to Williams av, 200x200. Abraham H. Dailey to Simon B. Hershey. Q. C. nom

Same property. Simon B. Hershey to Alvan R. Johnson. 8,000

Blake av, s s, 50 e Schenck av, 25x100. Gertrude wife of and John Blake to Joseph A. Mullen. 3,000

Bushwick av, s w s, 20.6 s e Vanderveer st, 18.6 x78.2, h & l. Arthur H. Bogart to Alfred Ogden. Mt. $3,000. nom

Bushwick av, n e s, 20 s e Schaeffer st, 30x75. Charles H. Jurgens to Jacob Schoch. Mt. $5,700. 10,000

Caton av, n s, 95.6 w Ocean av, runs west 176.1 to Brooklyn, Flatbush & C. I. R. R., x northeast 370.7 to Crooke av, x east 145 x south 298.10 Partition. William H. Greene ref. to John F. James. 4,800

Central av, north cor Ralph st, 25x100, h & l. Mary Cooney widow to Richard T. Burke. Mt. $2,700. 4,000

Central av, s s, 100 e Linden st, 19.1x100x25x100. Max Strumpf, of New York, to Nechama Honig. Mt. $4,300. 8,000

Same property. Joseph Stang and David Hittner, of New York, to Max Strumpf. Mt. $4,300. 8,000

Clinton av, e s, abt 180 n De Kalb av, 43.9x243.2x43.9x242.5. Alice L. S. wife of Cornelius W. Provost nee Smith to Lizzie M. Smith. C. a. G. gift

Clason av, e s, 80 s Douglass st, 20x100. George A. Domminey to William Campbell, of Westfield, N. J. Mt. $1,500. 2,750

Conklin av, n w s, lot 66 Henry Conklin et al. property, Canarsie, 25x159.4. William Wolf to Theodore Nuthmann. 230

Cropsey av, east cor Bay 11th st, runs northeast 261.5 x southeast 169.2 to n w s of Bennets lane, x southwest 255.7 to av, x northwest 131.11, New Utrecht. William C. Parks to Martha L. Parks. B & S. 1,000

De Kalb av, n s, 18 e Kent av, 12x80, h & l. Lucy C. Pearsall to Charles A. Haviland 3,100

De Kalb av, Nos. 1057 and 1057½, n s, 175 w Reid av, runs north 74.8 x west 33.10 x south 74.1 to De Kalb av, x east 33.10. Margaret V. A. wife of and S. Hastings Grant, of Piermont, N. Y., to Albert J. Cole and John M. Perry, of New York. Mt. $4,000. nom

Eldert av, e s, 275 s Gay st, 25x100. Edgar W. Hawley to Charles Nelson. 1888. 300

Flatbush av, n e s, 10 n w Dean st, runs southeast 10 to Dean st, x east 43.6 x north 57 x southwest 72.6; also,
Dean st, n s, 325 w 6th av, 25x110.
Julia wife of Martin Groom to Ella Reynolds. Mt. $8,500. gift

Fort Hamilton av, south cor 72d st, 10.18x115.9 x100x97.7, New Utrecht. Release mort. The Title Guarantee and Trust Co. to The Bay Ridge Park Improvement Co. 1,000

Fort Hamilton av, n w cor 70th st, 61x97.2x 60x86.8; also,
Fort Hamilton av, s e cor 72d st, 61x108.5x60 x97.7, New Utrecht.
Fred. C. Cocheu to The Bay Ridge Park Improvement Co. Mt. $7,000. nom

Fort Hamilton av, n w s, near 75th st, 17-100 acres, New Utrecht. Maria Church to James C. Cropsey. 1890. nom

Flushing av, s e cor North Portland av, runs east 104.3 x southwest 90.3 x west 25.6 x northeast 35 x west 27.9 x west 38 to Portland av, x north 69.3. Ludwig Roth, of New York, to Ferdinand Blumenthal and Julien S. Ulman. nom

Gates av, n s, 100 w Throop av, 200x100, hs & ls. Benjamin F. Briggs to Charles R. Drew. 126,000

Same property. Charles R. Drew to Benjamin F. Briggs. Mt. $79,800. 126,000

Gates av, northerly cor Bushwick av, 100x100. Charlotte A. wife of and Henry McTighe to Frank Hyde. Mt. $12,000. nom

Georgia av, w s 75 n Glenmore av, 25x100. Adam Hoerner to Frank Hoerner. 600

Georgia av, w s, 50 n Glenmore av, 25x100. Adam Hoerner to Johann Urbanowsky. 1,350

Greene av, s s, 360 e Throop av, 20x100. David S. Beasley to Mary L. Alexander. Mt. $5,000. 8,800

Greene av, s s, 125 w Central av, 63.10x100.
Greene av, s s, 233.10 w Central av, 16.2x100.
Virginia A. Kleine to Emily wife of Ebenezer S. Blydenburgh. nom

Greene av, w s, 410 n Knickerbocker av, runs west 25x76.3x25x75 Jacob Schoch to Charles H Jurgens. Mt. $3,000. 7,500

Howard av, e s, 82.9 n Douglass st, 25x100. Anna M. Dakin widow and devisee of George W. B. Dakin to Frederick M. Brown. nom

Jefferson av, s s, 270 e Marcy av, 20x100. Arthur G. Stone to Mary M. N. Siede. Mt. $10,000. 16,750

Jefferson av, n s, 175 e Lewis av, 25x100. Release mort. Henry Weil to Theodore W. Swimm. 2,500

Knickerbocker av, n e s, 100 n w Jacob st, 40x 90. Edith R. wife of and William C. Carver to Charles H. and George W. Francisco. 1,300

Kingsland av, w s, 95 s Van Cott av, 20x100, h & l. Michael Newman to Ida M. wife of Thomas Burkhard, Jr. Mt. $1,800. 3,700

Kingston av, n e cor Pacific st, 95x80. Foreclos. John Courtney to John F. Hart. 34,100

Lafayette av, lot 297 map 1 Fort Hamilton Village, New Utrecht. The People of the State of New York to Mary V. Robinson. letters patent

Lafayette av, New Utrecht, lot 297 sectional map No. 1 Village of Fort Hamilton, New Utrecht, 50x148. Mary V. wife of and Thomas B. Brasher to Charles W. Dungan. 500

Liberty av, n e cor Linwood st, 20x100. Maude H. wife of P. Francis Walker, Providence, R. I., Mabel R. wife of George P. Grant, Jr., of Lincoln, R. I., heirs of Gaius W. Hubbard, Jr., to Catherine wife of William Fudge. 1,500

Lewis av, w s, 50 s Floyd st, 25x100. Robert Weiskittel to Conrad Hartmann. 4,800

Morgan av, s e cor Harrison pl, 50x100. Theodore F. Jackson to Nicholas Dannenhoffer. Tax 1891. 4,200

Myrtle av, north cor Himrod st, runs northeast 26.11 x northwest 80 x southwest 9.6 x southeast 30.6 x southeast 5.3 x south 42.10 to av, x east 20.6. Henry and John Von Glahn to Dietrich F. Linnenmeyer and Edward N. Boback. nom

Myrtle av, s s, 150 w Marcy av, 25x100. John S. Darcy, of Wayne, N. J., to Jacob Bossert. 5,730

Myrtle av, n s, 175 e Tompkins av, 25x100.
Throop av, s e cor Bartlett st, 25x95.
Jacob Aronson to Samuel Bernstein. Mt. $4,500. 16,500

Myrtle av, n s, 60 w Skillman st, 20x82.9. Eugene F. Barnes and ano. exrs. Lavinia Giles to Jane A. wife of Edward McKenna. 9,250

Nichols av, e s, 7 s land H. Davidson, New Lots, runs 75x200. Henry P. Rindskopf to Adolph Weber. 1,350

Nichols av, w s, 225 n Union av, 50x90. Christina E. Lobrentz to Stephen Mafera. 1,300

Nichols av, w s, 300 n Union av, 50x90. Stephen Mafera to Christina E. Lobrentz 1,900

Park av, n s, 240 e Nostrand av, 35x100. Henry Eich to George E. Bicking, of New York. 7,000

Putnam av, s s, 200 e Throop av, 100x100. Marvell W. Cooper to Richard Mullowney. Mt. $6,250. 17,500

Putnam av, n s, 280 e Broadway, 20x100, h & L Robert L. Moores and Charles A. Le Quesne to Simon Herman, of New York. Mt. $6,500. nom

Ralph av, w s, 107.9 n Douglass st, new line, 60x100.
Howard av, e s, 82.9 n Douglass st, new line, 25x100.
Charles Thompson to Frederick M. Brown. nom

Same property. Anna M. Dakin widow and sole devisee of Geo. W. B. Dakin to Frederick M. Brown. Q. C. nom

Reid av, e s, 60 n Hancock st, 28.4x100. John S. Willdridge to James Fullagar, of Newburg, N. Y. Mt. $16,800 nom

Ridgewood av, s s, 40 w Shepherd av, 20x90. Hannah M. wife of Walter C. Halliday to Walter C. Halliday. nom

Ridgewood av, n s, 50 e Cleveland st, 25x100. Edward M. Wine to Charles A. O'Neil, New York. Mt. $1,900. 1,000

Ridgewood av, n e cor Elton st, 50x100. Frederick Emmerich to Josephine Emmerich his wife. Mt. $3,200. gift

Rockaway av, w s, 250 n Eastern Parkway, 50 x100. John A. Davies to Herbert C. Smith. 650

Rockaway av, s w s, 55 n w Conklin av, 50x90, Canarsie, error. Martha E. Culver to Rosalie D. Pruden. 375

Rockaway av, w s, 200 n Broadway, 50x100. Julius Marcus to Herbert C. Smith. B. & S. nom

Schenck av, e s, 233 n Arlington av, 50x100. Release mort Frederick Middendorf to Sebastian T. Hollister. nom

Same property. Sebastian T. Hollister to Zipporah L. Hollister. Mt. $4,500, consid. omitted

Schenck av, e s, 282 n Arlington av, 51x100. Release mort. Elizabeth M. Rapalje to Sebastian T. Hollister. 1,800

Schenck av, w s, 45 n Van Brunt av, 120x100.
Jerome st, e s, 145 n Van Brunt av, 40x200 to Warwick st.
Stoothoff av, s e cor Smith av, runs south 72.7 x northeast 98.2 to Stoothoff av, x west 66.
William Campbell, Westfield, N. J., to George A. Domminey. nom

Shepherd av, e s, 240 n Ridgewood av, 20x102.5. Release mort. Eliza G. and Mary Hampton and John C. Creveling to James Graham. 250

Skillman av, n s, 275 e Lorimer st, 25x100. Charlotte F. Cozine heir Samuel A. Edwards to Daniel Billings 3,000

St. Marks av, s s, 168 e Vanderbilt av, 32x131, h & l. Thomas O. Robbins to Harrie or Harne Bulkley. nom

Stone av, w s, 25 s Somers st, 25x80. Henry Potzel, of New York, to James Kearney. Mt. $5,000. exch

Stone av, w s, 230 s Riverdale av, 20x100. Bridget Donohue to Joseph Eppig. other consid. and 200

Sumner av, w s, 22 s Pulaski st, 19.4x98, h & l. Release mort. James S. Bearns to James Hood. 3,000

Same property. Release mort. Same to same. nom

Sunnyside av, n s, 200 w Miller av, 50x250 to Highland Boulevard. Emma L. Johnston, of Newtown, L. I., to Philip F. Lenhart. Mt. $5,000. exch

Sutter av, s s, 60 e Atkins av, 20x90. Angelo Comollo to Herbert D. Hotaling, of New York. 325

Thatford av, w s, 100 n Blake av, 25x90. Barnet Levin and Max Gittlesohn to Morris Epand. Mt. $2,600. 3,200

Thatford av, e s, 175 n Riverdale av, 25x100, h & l. Philip Pickelsky to Solomon Parrofsky and Solomon Greenberg, New York. Mt. $1,200. 1,825

Thatford av, w s, 25 n Blake av, 20x90, h & l. Barnet Levin and Max Gittelsohn to Philip Pickelsky. Mt. $1,600. 3,200

Thatford av, n e cor Sutter av, 25x100. Samuel Turteltaub to Malka Ganz or Gans. Correction deed. Sub. to morts. nom

Same property. Malka Ganz to Joseph Newborg, of New York. Mt. $1,500. 4,000

Tompkins av, e s, 50 n Hopkins st, runs east 41 x northeast 41 to Delmonico pl, x northwest 25 x southwest 34.2 x west 34.2 to av, x south 25. Annie E. Bogan, of New York, to Adolph C. Hottenroth. nom

Same property. Adolph C. Hottenroth, of New York, to Thomas and Annie E. Bogan. nom

Troy av, e s, 185.10 s St. Marks av, 16.8x80.

Louis Seinsoth to George W. Henderson. *Mt.* $1,800. nom

Williams av, w s, 100 s Glenmore av. 30x100. Frederick A. Reid to Frank Herndl. *Mt.* $1,500. 3,575

Willoughby av, s s. 20 w Steuben st, 20x80. Foreclos. John Courtney to John Mitchell, of Queens, L. I. 7,250

3d av, west cor 45th st, 40.2x100. Alexander Waldron to Theophile Weil. *Mt.* $16,950. val. consid

4th av, w s, 87 n 9th st. original line, 33x60. Charles H. Collins to Frank A. Barnaby. *Mt.* $9,000. nom

4th av, s e cor 43d st, 100.2x100. Mary McLaughlin widow and devisee of Robert McLaughlin to Louise Thorburn. 6,500

4th av, w s, 20.2 s 33d st, 20x80. Franz Franz to Charles F. Goodwin and Annie A. Deedy, of New York. *Mt.* $2,875. 4,700

5th av, s e s, 25 n e 14th st, 33x97.10, h & l. Louisa Schink to Wilhelmine wife of Frederick C. Schink. B. & S. gift

5th av, n w s, 69.2 n e 53d st, 40x100. Theophile Weil to Clara C. Waldron. 1,800

5th av, w s, 130 n Pacific st, runs northwest 32.7 x southwest 14.2 x southeast 28.11 x northeast 1 x southeast 14.11 to 5th av, x north 30, h & l. Foreclos. Augustus M. Price to Lewis Hurst. 6,875

6th av, s w cor Pacific st, runs south 142.6 x west 125 x north 32.6 x east 25 x north 110 to st, x east 100. Foreclos. John Courtney to Joseph H. Colyer. Sub. to mort, 46,000

6th av, s e cor 11th st, runs east along st 93.4 x south 100 x west 16.4 x south 0.6 x west 1.6 x north 77.6 x west 75.6 to av, x north 22. Release mort. James Williamson to George O. Van Orden. 5,000

Same property. George O. Van Orden to Mary A. Knapp, of East Orange, N. J. *Mt.* $14,000. 28,500

6th av, e s, 66.9 n President st, runs north 53.2 x east 20.6 x south 24.11 x east 19.6 x south 20.11 x west 17.6 x south 7.3 x west 22.6. William Brown to John M. and George F. Halstead, of Halstead Bros. *Mt.* $9,550. 14,500

7th av, s e cor 2d st, runs east 100 x south 95 x west 2.1 x south 5 x west 97.10 to av, x north 100. Release mort. Francese L. Turnbull, Baltimore, Md., to George H. Magill. 11,100

8th av, n e cor Garfield pl, 100x112. Asa L. Rogers to Frank L. Corwin. B. & S. nom

9th av, n w cor 11th st, 100x93.4. Ervin G. Gollner to Charles S. Taber. *Mt.* $12,100. exch

11th av, easterly cor 52d st, runs northeast 2.1 x south 2.5 to 52d st, x northwest 1.3, New Utrecht. Samuel H. McElroy to Thomas W. Harris. nom

18th av, w s, 40 n 75th st, 40x104.10x40x105.5. John H. Hanley to Anna B. Ahlstadt. 900

18th av, n e cor 75th st, runs north along av to Jane Roberts land, x northeast along same to w s 20th av, x southwest along same to 76th st, x northwest to e s 19th av, northeast along same to 75th st, x northwest —, New Utrecht. William C. and Charles G. Martin, New York, to Samuel S. Abbott. C. a. G. *Mt.* $34,700. nom

Interior lot, 125 n St. Marks av, on line which at n s of said av is 194 e of Brooklyn av, runs east 20 x north 5x20x5. James O. Carpenter to Mary F. wife of Thomas W. Jensins. 100

Interior lot, begins centre of block bet Dean and Bergen sts, 152 w Utica av, runs north to line bet Lefferts and Suydam, x southeast to centre of block, x west 42.10. Release mort. James Gascoine, George and Robert Evans, exrs. Benjamin Evans to Christopher P. Skelton. nom

Land under water, Sheepshead Bay, adj land John C. Lundy, extends into bay 150 ft., Gravesend. The Town of Gravesend to John Lundy. 25

Lots 23 and 28 map common lands, Town of Gravesend, on Coney Island, except strip 40 ft. wide used by N. Y. & C. I. R. R. Co. Partition. Henry M. Birkett ref. to Albert D. Buschman. 9,010

Lots 2370 and 2371 block 39 map of 1,010 lots Second Addition to Bensonhurst. Charles F. Reichardt to Henry Schwartz, Newark, N. J. 2,500

Same property. Henry Schwartz to Mary D. Reichardt. 2,500

Lots 20 and 45 map heirs Samuel Garretsen, Flatbush. The People of the State of New York to John A. Lott, Jr. letters patent

Lots 195 and 196 block 4 map 597 lots, Gravesend, of W. Ziegler. William Ziegler to Mary A. Callaghan. 340

Lots 263 and 264 block 5 same map. Same to Frances O'Leary. 300

Lots 2235–2243 block 8, and 2443–2448 block 13 E. H. Nichols map Lefferts Park. Release mort. Albert B. Voorhies to E. H. Nichols. 1,500

Lots 65, 66 and 67 block 18 map No. 2 of 600 lots Effingham H. Nichols, New Utrecht. Release mort. Effingham H. Nichols to George and Gustave A. Hehn. 500

Lots 215 and 216 map 262 lots Sarah A. Suydam, New Lots. Nathan Moschkowitz, of New York, to Herbert C. Smith. 175

Mill road, southerly cor Stryker st, 50x100.9x50x100, Gravesend. Amelia A. Gunther extrx. and George A. Gunther exr. of C. Godfrey Gunther to Edward P. Ahearn. 400

Same property. Release dower. Amelia A. Gunther widow to same. 200

New York & Brighton Beach, w s, adj school lot, Gravesend, —x81x25x82. Albert G. Burtis to Malinda Braxton. Q. C. 300

Part of block 39 map of Oakland, Flatbush. Thomas H. Robbins to William A. Robbins. nom

Part of Old Brooklyn and Flatbush turnpike road lying within the block bounded by Bergen st, Carlton av, Dean st and 6th av. Martha M. Williams, of New York, to James T. Nelson. Q. C. nom

WESTCHESTER COUNTY.

DECEMBER 9 TO 15—INCLUSIVE.

CORTLANDT.

Ombony, John exr. of. to Cath. Kane, e s Division st, 65x102 and lot adj, 25x126. $4,000

EASTCHESTER.

Archer, Jos. W. to Clarence M. Fowler, part lot 242 s e s Greenwich st, West Mt. Vernon, 33.4x100. 4,250

Bard, Wm. H. to Colin G. McKenzie, part lot 259 s e s Marion st, Washingtonville, 25x100. 500

Clarey, Marian to John Clarey, Jr., lot 353 s s Westchester av, Washingtonville, 48.5x103. nom

Clarey, John, Jr., to Marian Clarey, lots 83 and 82 Washingtonville. nom

Cranford, Kenneth to Chas. H. Hallock, lots 94 and 95 grantors map, South Mt. Vernon. nom

Deverman, Louisa et al. D. O. Williams ref., to Emanuel Eising, part lot 307 n s Pearl st. West Mt. Vernon, 62x105. 2,100

Darling, Alf. B. and ano. to Melville S. Page, w s Park av, 300 n Prospect, 50x150. 1,800

Same to Amanda C. Wallander, n e cor Crary and Oakley avs, 266.6x—. 6,917

Same to Gerd Martens, s s Prospect av, 225 e Park, abt 229x290. 14,700

Fee, Samuel to Mary Luikert, lots 11 and 12 map C. V. Morgans lots, Tuckahoe. 1,125

Forster, Fred, P. to Julia Kahn, lots 330 and 331 grantors, Chester Hill, 100x115. 2,090

Same to Emile H. Roth, lots 328 and 329 adj above. 2,090

Fairchild, Ben. L. to Maria C. Patterson, lots 79 and 81, 5th st, and 17 and 19 Prospect av, Dunham Park. 1,000

Hartley, Edw. to Alb. S. Jenks and ano, lots 442 and 443, Central Mt. Vernon. 3,000

Koch, Augusta to Fred. Cheers, lot 256 n w s Greenwich st, West Mt. Vernon, 80x125. 3,400

Mencken, Henry to John Clarey, Jr., lot 83 n w s White Plains road, Washingtonville, abt 29x180. 500

Same to same, lot 442 n w s Bronx River pl, 25 x200. 250

Owen, Daniel to Alex. J. Pollock, lot 893 s s 16th av, Wakefield, 105x114. 1,400

Phipps, Edw. L. S. to Anton A. Wenck, lots 260 s e s Marian st, Washingtonville, 50x100. 3,000

Westcott, Ezbon S. to Henry Towner, w s White Plains road, 150 n Becker av, 25x190. 500

Towner, Henry to Adolph Schnabel, same property. 750

Wheeler, John to Herman Kallenberg, lots 27–30 Boulevard, Vernon Park. 650

Same to Mary A. Kallenberg, front ½ lots 17–20 Park av, 100x50. 265

Willson, Chas. H. to Frances M. Willson, lot 184 e s 3d av, 100x105, and 181 s w cor 2d av and 2d st, 100x105, Mt. Vernon. nom

Whitford, Daniel to Maurice Blanckensee, lots 80 and 81 e s Robinson av, Chester Manor, 100x100. 1,200

Same to Jas. H. Gannon, lots 82 and 83 adj above. 1,200

GREENBURGH.

Blackwell, Wilson H. to Martin M. Todd, lots 508, 509, 510, 619–625 and part 626, Ardsley. 2,125

Britcliffe, Eliz'h to Jas. J. Reilly, lots 186 and 300 map lots Uniontown. 850

Cunningham, Mary H. and ano to Eliz'h O. Nichols, lot 245 ft. s Dobbs Ferry road and 250 w of Railroad, 25x100. 200

Moran, Jas. H. et al. to John P. Moran, part of "The Fair Grounds," n s Tarrytown road. 19,000

Moran, John P. to The Society of Agriculture, &c., of Westchester County, same property. 19,000

Storms, Chas. G. to Jenette Balzer, lots 28 and 29 n of Ashford road, Ardsley. 500

HARRISON.

Bellamy, Fred P. to Geo. W. Underhill et al., n s Purchase road, 200 acres. 6,000

Burr, Sarah extrx. of, to Samuel L. Mosher, 56 acres on road from Mamaroneck to North st and Mamaroneck River. 5,750

MAMARONECK.

Bradley, And. R. to Steph. H. Gray, ½ lot 23 map property Jas. C. Spencer, 25x108. 1,500

Same to Jas. W. Rich and ano, ½ same lot, 25x100. 1,500

Same to same, ½ lot 22 same map. 4,750

Same to Elisha T. Payne, lot 24 same map, 50x105. 3,000

Rich, Jas. W. et al. to Howard N. Bailey, lot 1 and ½ lot 22 same map. 5,000

Sears, Estelle B. to Louis R. Bramm and ano., w s Spruce st, adj Mill Pond. 1,250

MOUNT PLEASANT.

Bliss, Alb. E. and ano. to Marin Courouneau, lots 40, C, G, H and strip adj w s Amos st grantor's map, abt 108x140. 1,000

Smadbeck, Louis to Geo. Schell, lot 1553, Sherman Park. 175

Same to Emil Neppel, lot 1551. 175

Same to Josie Bleesy, lot 1554. 175

Same to Victor Miedl, lots 605 and 606. 200

Smith, Wm. R. to Harriet M. Davis, lot 13 block 10, Lake Kensico. nom

Soltz, Arcadius to Fannie Horowitz, lots 206–213, Pleasantville Park. nom

NEW CASTLE.

Foehrenbach, F. and ano. to Chas. Sweeny, ¼ acre e of railroad, adj grantee. 175

NEW ROCHELLE.

Downey, Henry B. to Peter Bray, s w cor Mary st and Lockwood's lane, 40x100. 1,000

Hudson, Alex R. to D. Relyea Conklin, n s Boston Post road, 100 w Highland av, abt 55 x140. 550

Johnson, Chas. F. to Edw. Dunn and ano., n s Winthrop av, 103 w North st, 65x84. 880

Osborne, Edwin G. to Richard Mullineaux, s s Summit av, 390 w White Oak st, 50x155. nom

St. John, Fred E. to Edwin F. Skinner, lot 153 and part 154 n s Linden pl, Residence Park. nom

Van Benschoten, Josephine A. to Julian A. Lopez-Diaz, lot 6 n s Lafayette st, grantor's map, 243.6x—. 12,000

NORTH CASTLE.

Brundage, Samuel S. to John A. Daly, 1¾ acres adj Wm. Shelly and Robt. Miller. nom

PELHAM.

Rodman, Isaac to Abr. G. Reed and ano., s w cor old Boston road and Pelhamdale av, abt 8 acres. 15,480

RYE.

Bull, Clara R. to Wm. Weeks, s e s Oakland av, 174 n e Milton av, 50x150. 350

Merritt, Jas. S. and ano. to Mich. H. White, s e cor Ellandale av and Lyon st, 50x100. 260

Murray, David to Mary Stearns, lot 31 e s Lake st map Seaman lots, abt 25x140. 2,400

Neilson, Victor to Elize Hoffmeier, lot 7 n s Ellendale av, Washington Park, 50x150. 100

Stratton, Geo. H. to Wm. H. Parsons, Jr., part lot 7 w s Milton av map Clarke estate, abt 4 acres. 15,000

SCARSDALE.

Lyons, Geo. W. to The Arthur Suburban Home Co., 108 acres w s Hutchinson River. 65,000

WESTCHESTER.

Dexter, Fred. C. to Mary C. Jacobus, lot 429 s e cor 6th av and 4th st, Wakefield, 105x114. nom

Kiefer, Peter to Wm. Bartel, part lot 1178 e s Bronx terrace, Wakefield, 25x115. 800

Phelan, Michael J. to Louis C. Ott and ano., s w cor Av C and 11th st, Unionport, 108x205. 1,650

Sheil, Dennis R. to Robert F. Sheil and ano., lot 515 s s 15th av, Wakefield, 100x114. 1,500

Same to same, lot 551 s s same, 100x114. 1,500

WHITE PLAINS.

Dick, Timothy to Mary E. Sniffin, n s Lake st, 100 w Kensico av, 50x200. 2,200

Hyde, Louis H, to Elmore D. Alvord, s w cor Lexington av and Prospect st, 180x645; also n w cor same, 8½ acres. nom

Alvord, Elmore D. to Annette Seifert, same property. 10,000

YONKERS.

Beall, T. Ashby to Armour Villa Park Assoc., lots 252, 371, 421, 422 and 423. nom

Havemeyer, John C. to Norman S. Kenyon, e s Park Hill av, abt 210x1,000. 10,000

Kenyon, Norman S. to Warren H. Lowerre, same property. 15,000

Kingsbury, Jas. A. to Benj. E. Sullard, lot 141 w s Orchard st, 25x125. nom

Lowerre, Edw. S. to Geo. Bliss, lots 1 and 2 block 19, lots 23 and 24 block 20, Lowerre Station; also w s McLean av, 225 s Van Cortlandt Park av, 25x90. 4,000

Martin, Edw., Jr., to Edw. Martin, part lots 13 and 14 e s Croton Aqueduct, map Shonnard estate, 60x—. 7,500

Simon, Wm. to Fred. F. Kasten, e s Jefferson st, 150 s Herriot, 175x100. 25,000

MORTGAGES.

NEW YORK CITY.

DECEMBER 11, 12, 14, 15, 16, 17.

Abrahams, Isidore to Simon Fine and Harris Boskey. Mott st. P. M. Sub. to mort. $23,000. Dec. 1, 2 years, installs. $3,500

Adrian, George S. to August Bossard. 26th st. P. M. Nov. 30, 3 years, 4½ %. 10,000

Angenmeyer, George W. to Bernheimer & Schmid. St. Nicholas av, No. 220. Saloon lease. Dec. 8, demand. 2,500

Arendt, Simon to Julius Lipman and Moses Kind. Amsterdam av, e s, 82.5 n 91st st, 27.6 x100. Sub. to morts. $23,500. Dec. 11, 6 months. See Conveys. 8,500

Same to same. Same property. Sub. to mort. $23,500. Parties of 2d part to collect rents and apply same. Dec. 11, 1 month. 1,500

Same to Mable Slade, East Orange, N. J. Same property. Dec. 11, 3 years, 5 %. See Conveys. 23,500

Anderson, Walden P. to Alfred Gutwillig. 90th

st, s s, 200 w Central Park West. P. M. Dec. 16, due Dec. 1, 1892, or installs. 74,000

Same to same. Same property. Building loan. Dec. 16, due Dec. 1, 1892. 132,000

Banks, Henry W., Englewood, N. J., to THE SEAMEN'S BANK FOR SAVINGS, New York. Front st, south cor Depeyster st, runs southeast 59 x southwest 55.1 to Pine st, x northwest 67.6 to Front st, x northeast 57. Dec. 16, 3 years, 4½ %. 80,000

Barry, James T. to George E. Hyatt, Brooklyn. 142d st, s s, 100 w 3d av, 4 lots, each 25 x100. 4 morts., each $11,000. Dec. 15, due July 1, 1892. 44,000

Brown, James to The Bradley & Currier Co. (Lim.) 92d st, s s, 460 w Columbus av, 40x 100.8. Sub. to morts. $33,000. Dec. 14, 6 months. 10,000

Burke, Catharine wife of and Francis to THE NEW YORK SAVINGS BANK. 2d av, w s, 24.10 s 32d st, 24.6x100x24.8x99.11 in two courses. Dec. 16, due Dec. 1, 1896, 4½ %. 11,000

Bormann, Conrad to Ella Breslauer. 65th st, No. 302, s s, 64 e 2d av, 18x76.2x18.2x73.5. Sub. to morts. $4,000. Dec. 12, due Nov. 4, 1894. 200

Broadbelt, William, New Rochelle, N. Y., to THE UNITED STATES LIFE INS. CO. of New York. 37th st, s s, 312.6 w 7th av, 28.1x98.9. Dec. 17, due Dec. 1, 1896, 5 %. 31,500

Same to same. 37th st, s s, 340.7 w 7th av, 28.1 x98.9. Dec. 17, due Dec. 1, 1896, 5 %. 31,500

Butler, John J. to THE MUTUAL LIFE INS CO. of New York. 34th st, n s, 100 e 9th av, 19.1 x98.9. Dec. 17, 1 year, 5 %. 10,000

Butler, Jacob D. to Joseph F. Cullman. 145th st, s s, 155.8 w 8th av, 25.6x99.11. Dec 10, 3 years, 5 %. See Conveys. gold, 18,000

Same to Otto L. Stix. 145th st, s s, 130.2 w 8th av, 25.6x99.11. Dec. 10, 3 years, 5 %. See Conveys. gold, 18,000

Burne, William C. to THE GALLATIN NAT. BANK. 75th st, Nos. 164-170, s s, 150 w 3d av, 100x102.2. Dec. 8, due April 10, 1892. 2,150

Broderick, John F. to The West Side Mutual Building Loan and Savings Assoc., New York. Hawkstone st, e s, 350 n Walnut st, 100x102.9x125x100. Dec. 11, installs. 5,000

Buchan, Mary A. to Henry G. and Francis A. Ridabock exrs. Henry T. Gratacap. 27th st. P. M. Dec. 15, 2 years, 5 %. 4,000

Boyle, James F. and Michael J. Bannon to Mary A. Wagstaff, Frances A. Ward, George G. and John C. Barnard and Alfred Wagstaff guard. of Alice Barnard. Park or 4th av and 107th st. P. M. Dec. 11, due Aug. 1, 1892. 16,500

Same to John B. Smith. Same property. P. M. 2d mort. Dec. 11, due Aug. 1, 1891. 11,500

Bach, Alice H. wife of and Albert to Ernest M. Levy. 76th st, n s, 398 w Columbus av, 17x 102.2. Sub. to morts. $18,500. Oct. 20, 7 months. 2,500

Blanckensee, Maurice to Louis Smadbeck. Lots 96 and 97 map of Metropolitan Real Estate Assoc., Fordham Ridge, 75x100. Dec. 2, installs. 600

Casassa, Giovanni B. and Giovanni M. Malatesta to THE TITLE GUARANTEE AND TRUST CO. Thompson st. P. M, Dec. 14, 3 years, 5 %. 6,000

Clark, Elijah D. to New York and Suburban Co-operative Building and Loan Assoc. 165th st, n e cor Trinity av, 25x71. Dec. 11, installs, 5 %. 1,250

Coffin, Edmund, Jr., to Sarah C. wife of Roswell D. Hatch. 85th st. P. M. Dec 2, due Dec. 1, 1892, 5 %. 30,000

Crawford, Francis, Wakefield, N. Y., to Asa E. Collins, Linden, N. J. 89th st. P. M. Dec. 9, 1 year, 5 %. 7,500

Caesar, Julius and Friedrich to Thomas B. Hewitt and ano. trustees John L. Sleight. 24th st, n s, 210.2 w 2d av, 19.5x98.8. Dec. 12, 6 months, 5 %. 1,700

Chambers, Patrick to Peter Doelger. Av A, No. 1394, n e cor 74th st. Store lease. Dec. 10, demand. 2,800

Clokey, Ella I. and Samuel W. to Adolph C. Wenzel, Brooklyn. Creston av, n w cor 184th st 120x100. Dec. 12, demand. 1,000

Cohen, Isaac and Morris to Samuel Weil. Av D, e s, 79.6 n 9th st. P. M. Sub. to mort. $20,000. Dec. 15, installs. 7,000

Same to same. Av D, e s, 105 n 9th st. P. M. Sub. to mort. $18,000. Dec. 15, installs. 5,000

Same to same. Av D, e s, 134 n 9th st. P. M. Sub. to mort. $18,000. Dec. 15, installs. 5,000

Same to Betsie Skoultchi, Brooklyn. Av D, Nos. 134, 136 and 138, e s, 79.6 n 9th st, runs north 79.8 x east 80 x south 54 2 x east 25 x south 22 x west 3.2 x south 3.6 x west 101.10. Sub. to morts. $73,000. Dec. 15, installs. 3,800

Cronin, Lawrence and Mary A his wife to Charles Hartman. Franklin av, n w s, abt 192.8 n e Woodruff av, 25x108.9. July 8, due May 15, 1893, 5 %. 900

Cordier, Theodore A. to William Hall's Sons. Amsterdam av, s e cor 84th st, runs south 127.8 x east 100 x north 25.6 x west 9 x north 102.2 to st, x west 91. Dec. 12, due May 1, 1892. 34,000

Collins, James J. to William V. N. Rosedale. Main st to West Farms. P. M. Sub. to mort. $2,000. Dec. 14, due Dec. 16, 1896, 5 %. 4,000

Christensen, Rasmus and Hilda his wife to George Muller. 88th st. P. M. Dec. 16, 2 years or installs. 4,000

Connolly, John E. to Mary C. Ogden, Newport, R. I. 20th st, s s, 350 e 11th av, 50x91.11. Lease. Dec. 12, 5 years. 10,000

Cornet, Josephine to Mary A. Irving. 93th st, n s, 293 w 8th av, 17x100.8. Dec. 14, due May 1, 1892. 500

Cowman, Thomas to William A. Darling, as President of THE MURRAY HILL BANK. 119th st, s s, 100 e 8th av, 75x100.11. Sept. 16, demand. 3,500

Cowman, Thomas to Michael Power. 119th st, s s, 100 e 8th av, 75x100.11. Sub. to morts. $60,400. Nov. 12, 6 months 1,000

Crawford, John J. mortgagor and present owner to Ellen E. Ward widow, Roslyn, L. I., proposed assignee. Admission of notice to assign. and statement that amount due on mortgage made by John J. Crawford to Laemmlein Buttenwieser. Oct. 19, 1891, is 80,000

Currie, Mary W. to Annie M. Donnell, New Berne, N. C. 75th st, s s, 187 e West End av, 20x102.2. Dec. 16, 3 years, 5 %. gold, 18,000

Currie, Mary W. wife of and Duncan H. to THE HUDSON RIVER BANK. Same property. Sub. to mort. $18,000. Dec. 11, due Dec. 16, 1892. 1,000

Dietz, Rosina to Hanna D. Cohn guard. Goldina, Rosie, Gabriel and Isidor Davidson. 58th st, s s, 101.5 w Av A, 20x100.4. Dec. 16, 1 year. 10,000

Dunn, Joseph M. widower and Theresa M. A. and Agnes G. Dunn by Joseph M. Dunn guard. to The Domestic and Foreign Missionary Society of the P. E. Church in America. 39th st, s s, 182 e 8th av, 20.6x98.9. Dec. 15, 5 years, 5 %. gold, 5,000

Diescher, Johanna to Peter Schaeffler. 2d av. P. M. Dec. 15, installs. 13,000

Dworsky, Abraham J. to Emma L. Van Ness, Cornwall, N. Y. Orchard st, No. 23, w s, 17.5x79; Interior lot, 120 n Canal st and 79 w Orchard st, runs north 56.3 x west 23.2 x south 56 x east 23.1. Dec. 17, 3 years, 5 %. 25,000

Dunne, Thomas P. to Marx and Moses Ottinger. 119th st. P. M. Dec. 14, due Sept. 1, 1893. 56,000

Dauphinais, Victoria F. to James Floyd, Elizabeth, N. J. Bedford st, e s, 96.11 s Christopher st, runs south 42.6 x east 50.3 x south 13.5 x east 20.11 x north 23.3 x east 8.9 x north 18.4 x east 15.9 x southwest 20.6 x south 8.1 x west 55.5 to beginning. Dec. 14, due Aug. 15, 1892. 32,500

Same to Julius Lipman. Same property. Sub. to last mort. Dec. 14, 3 months. 7,000

Same to same. Same property. Sub. to mort. $32,500. Dec. 14, 3 months. 8,488

David, Miriam to Conrad Vorbach. 46th st. P. M. Dec. 14, 3 years, 5 %. 10,000

Dodge, Jacob L., Jr., to THE TITLE GUARANTEE AND TRUST CO. Bleecker st, Nos. 252, 254, 256 and 258, and No. 5 Leroy st, begins Bleecker st, n w cor Leroy st, 65.6x75. Dec. 4, due Dec 14, 1894, 5 %. 30,500

Drought, William and Charles J. Carew to Jenny A. Carew, Norwich, Conn. West End av, s e cor 103d st, 100.11x100. Dec. 5. secures indebtedness and credits

Eugenhoefer, Katie to Bernheimer & Schmid. 8th av, No 2634. Saloon lease. Dec. 12, note, demand. 1,000

Ehret, George with John Gerken both mortgagees. Agreement as to priority of morts. made by George W. Sauer. Dec. 10.

Eisenberg, William to Charles L. Ritzmann. 88th st, s s, 173 w Boulevard, 36x100.8. Dec. 11. 5,000

Ertheiler, James to Randolph W. Townsend. Maiden lane. P. M. Dec. 15, due Dec 1, 1894, 5 %. gold, 15,000

Einhorn, Moses to John D. Karst, Jr. Henry st. P. M. Sub. to mort. $25,000. Dec. 17, installs. 9,000

Farley, Patrick to THE UNITED STATES TRUST CO. of New York. 135th st, s s, 100 e Lenox av, 75x99.11. Dec. 17, due Jan. 1, 1895, 5 %. 22,000

Fay, Henry A., Eastchester, N. Y., to Alfred Bonney, East Fishkill, N. Y. Hudson st, w s, 50 n Franklin st, 25.3x100.2. Dec. 1, 2 years. 5,000

Ford, Walter to Amalia Friedmann. 93d st, n s, 220.6 w 3d av. P. M. Dec. 17, 2 years, 5 %. 18,000

Same to same. 93d st, n s, 250.5 w 3d av. P. M. Dec. 17, 2 years, 5 %. 18,000

Feldman, Frank to Harris Shedliusky and Isidore and Julius Schweitzer. Sheriff st. P. M. Dec. 15, installs. (Given in place of lost or stolen mortgage.) 6,000

Fleu, Bernhard to James S. Herrman. 134th st, n s, 225 e Lincoln av, 50x100. Dec. 16, due June 1, 1892. Secures present advance of $4,000 and future advances not to exceed in all 16,000

Frey, Frederick to Bernheimer & Schmid. 8th av, No. 2689. Saloon lease. Dec. 16, note, demand. 1,700

Formica, Gaetano F. to Henry P. De Graaf. Tinton av. P. M. Dec. 14, due Dec. 15, 1892, 5 %. 1,000

Fogarty, Kate L. widow formerly Kelly, Brooklyn, to Phebe Pearsall. 2d av, s e cor 19th st, 21.8x99.6. Dec. 12, installs, 5 %. 23,000

French, John J. to Henry Middendorf. 29th st. P. M. Dec. 15, 5 years, 5 %. 8,000

Fitzgerald, Ellen A., Brooklyn, to Michael Leehane. 49th st. P. M. Dec. 15, 3 years, 5 %. 5,750

Fay, Michael and William Stacom to Frederic J. Middlebrook, Brooklyn. 10th st. P. M. Dec. 12, 1 year. 16,000

Fillbarat, Christian wife of and Frederick to THE BOWERY SAVINGS BANK. 12th st, n s, 208 w Av C, 25x103.3. Dec. 14, 1 year, 5 %. 8,000

Flannery, Simon P. to Mary A. wife of Thomas McGuire. Water st. P. M. Dec. 9, 3 years, 4½ %. 8,000

Freeman, George P. to Martin Grossman. 87th st, n s, 208 w 9th av, 17x100.8. Sub. to morts. $11,500. Secures notes of mortgagor and John W. Cheseboro. Dec. 15. 8,500

Frey, Ellen to THE DRY DOCK SAVINGS INST. 61st st, n s, 104.6 w 2d av, 16.8x100.5. Dec. 14, due Dec 20, 1892, 5 %. 8,000

Fernschild, William to Solomon Berliner. Madison av, s e cor 174th st. P. M. Nov. 20, 3 years, 5 %. 1,500

Fiston, Marion A. to THE BANK OF HARLEM. 125th st, No. 246 W. Store lease. Nov. 30, note. 1,000

Friedline, Charles W. and Louisa C. to Morris Steinhardt. 93d st, s s, 175 e Columbus av, 100x100.8 Dec. 10, 1 month. 1,000

Galewski, Bernard to The Corporation for the Relief of Widows and Children of Clergymen of the Protestant Episcopal Church, New York. 54th st, No. 329, n s, 320 e 2d av, 20x 97.6. Dec. 11, 1 year, 5 %. 7,500

Same to James M. Varnum. 54th st, No. 331, n s, 340 e 2d av, 20x97.6. Dec. 11, 1 year, 5 %. 7,500

Goldstein, Isaac to Abraham I. Bleistift. Sheriff st, No. 34, e s, 21.10x100. Dec. 10, installs. 2,500

Gordon, Robert and Joseph to George S. Hall Amsterdam av, s w cor 82d st, 102.2x125. Dec. 11, 2 months. 5,000

Gaylor, Clarence W. to Morris H. Stern and Ferdinand Kurzman. 1st av. P. M. Dec 15, 2 years, 5 %. 1,000

Gray, William, Nyack, N. Y., to John F. Harmon trustee. 129th st, n s, 199 e 5th av, runs north 99.11 x west 63 x north 99.11 to 130th st, x east 138 x south 199.10 to 129th st, x west 75. Dec. 14, 6 months. 5,500

Gutwillig, Alfred to Asa E. Collins, Linden, N. J. 90th st, s s, 325 w Central Park West. P. M. Dec. 15, 1 year, 5 %. 7,500

Same to Thomas Hitchcock. 90th st, s s, 350 w 8th av. P. M. Dec. 11, due May 1, 1893, 5 % and 6 %. 40,000

Same to Mary A. Vandewater. 90th st, s s, 450 w Central Park West. P. M. Dec. 15, due June 15, 1893, 5 %. 15,000

Same to Louis Kahl. 90th st, n s, 500 w Central Park West. P. M. Dec. 9, due March, 1893, 5 %. 15,000

Same to same. Same property. P. M. Sub. to last mort. Dec. 9, due March, 1893, 5 %. 8,000

Gilroy, William J. to George F. Johnson. 1st st. P. M. Dec. 15, 1 year, 5 %. 5,250

Givens, Elizabeth A. to The Bank Clerks' Co-operative Building and Loan Assoc. 155th st, s s, 220 w Elton av, 25x100. Dec. 12, installs, 5 %. 2,000

Gannon, Ellen F. wife of and James to Michael Fette. Arcularius pl, s s, 282 w Walton av, 50x122.3x50.11x112.3. Dec. 15, 4 months. 325

Ganz, Maina to Joseph Newborg. Lewis st. P. M. Sub. to morts. Dec. 1, installs. 3,800

Goerlitz, Philip to James E. Hoctor. 72d st. P. M. June 1, 1 year, 5 %. 2,500

Haffner, John D. to Bernheimer & Schmid. 8th av, No. 800, n e cor 39th st. Saloon lease. Dec. 15, note, demand. 2,000

Hall, Lucy A. to Anna Regge. Cannon st, w s, 160 s Houston st, 40x100. Dec. 12, 1 year. 2,500

Hall, William W. to Charles E. Hall. 69th st, n s, 125 e 9th av, 200x100 5. Dec. 15, 1 year, 5 %. See Conveys. 20,000

Hanlon, Patrick B., Brooklyn, to William Rankin. 54th st. P. M. Dec. 17, demand. 10,000

Same to same. Same property. Building loan. Dec. 17, demand. 12,000

Harlem Library to THE MUTUAL LIFE INS. CO., of New York. 3d av, w s, 25.5 s 122d st, 25x100. Dec. 17, 1 year, 5 %. 25,000

Hinde, John and William Allan to THE UNITED STATES TRUST CO., of New York. 57th st, s s, 200 e 11th av. 50x200.10 to 58th st. Dec. 16, due Dec. 1, 1896, 5 %. 35,000

Hahn, Mary E. to Jacob D. Butler. 145th st, s s, 130.2 w 8th av. P. M. Dec. 10, due June 1, 1894. gold, 7,500

Same to same. 145th st, s s, 155.8 w 8th av. P. M. Dec. 10, due June 1, 1894. gold, 7,500

Hoffman, Daniel to THE WASHINGTON LIFE INS. CO., New York. 145th st, n s, 200 w Amsterdam av, 100x99.11. Dec. 11, due Dec. 1, 1894, 5 %. 13,000

Same to Daniel H. Martin, Newark, N. J. Same property. Dec. 11, 1 year. 4,000

Howard, Elizabeth S., Newport, R. I., to Adam Kropf. 1st av, w s, 91.10 n 19th st, 24x79.9. Sub. to mort. $6,500. Nov. 27, due Jan. 14, 1893, 5 %. 1,000

Horrmann, August mortgagee with Jacob Kahrs, mortgagor. Extension of mort. at reduced interest. Dec. 14. nom

Hopper, Garet to Carrie R. Wills. Tinton av. P. M. Dec. 15, 3 years, 5 %. 2,000

Heath, Margaret T. wife of Henry G. K. formerly Koch, Pelham Manor, N. Y., to Mary A. A Woodcock, Bedford, N. Y. 91st st, n s, 162.8 w Lexington av, 17.6x100.8. Dec. 15, 3 years, 5 %. 12,000

Heumann, Louisa P. otherwise Louise P. wife and Peter to Charles E. Strong trustee for Francis B., William, Jr., and Marion Cutting. North 3d av, n w s, 165.6 n e 170th st, 52x130.5x51.8x126.9. Dec. 14, due Dec. 15, 1896, 5 %. 20,000

Herche, Peter to THE TITLE GUARANTEE AND TRUST CO. 3d st, No. 83, n s, 25 w Greene st, 25x94.8. Dec. 14, 1 year, 4½ %. 9,000

Iden, John H. and Albert to John Slattery. Stanton st, s w cor Forsyth st, 25x75. Dec. 14, 5 years, 4½ %. 10,000

Isaacs, Louis to Frederick P. Forster. Lot 17

F. P. and H. A. Foster property, Riverdale. P. M. Dec. 2, 2 years, 5 %. 300

Isaacs, Isabelle to same. Lot 18, F. P. and H. A. Forster property, Riverdale. P. M. Dec. 2, 2 years, 5 %. 300

Isaacs, Elias M. to same. Lot 16 same map. P. M. Dec. 2, 2 years, 5 %. 300

Isaacs, Alfred A. to same. Lot 15 same map. P. M. Dec. 2, 2 years, 5 %. 300

Jaeger, Frederick J. N. to George C. Engel. Madison av, Nos. 627 and 629; 59th st, No. 44 E. Lease of portions of buildings. Dec. 16, notes. 6,000

Same to same. Madison av, n e cor 59th st, 100 x90. Lease. Dec. 16, notes. 6,000

Jefferds, Edwin L to George Ehret. 8th av, No. 882. Store lease. Dec. 5, demand. 4,000

Judge, Joseph S. to Jacob Bookman. 120th st, s s, 125 e 7th av, 50x100.11. Building loan. Dec. 15, due Dec. 1, 1892. 21,000

Same to same. Same property. P. M. Dec. 15, due Jan. 1, 1893, or sooner. 19,000

Johnson, Henry M., Bay Shore, L. I., to S. Emilie Woodbury. 8th av, n e cor 14th st, runs north 68.11 x east 68.6 x north 84.4 x east 25 x south 103.3 to st, x west 93.6 to beginning; 8th av, s e cor 39th st, runs east 100.4 x south 98.9 x west 36.2 x south 45.9 x west 64.1 to av, x north 144.6 to beginning; 6th av, s e cor 21st st, 20x73.9; 8th av, e s, 54 s 17th st, 34x60; Broadway, n w cor 31st st, runs west 195.3 to 5th av, x north 63 4 x east 80.11 x south 28.9 x east 68.2 x northeast 32 to Broadway, x south 44.1 to beginning. 1-9 part. Dec. 17, 1 year. 10,000

Jordan, William G. to Michael J. Beglen. 44th st, Nos. 437 and 439, n s, 300 e 10th av, 40x 100.4. Dec. 14, demand. 1,843

Kennedy, Andrew F. mortgagor with THE SEAMEN'S BANK FOR SAVINGS, New York. Extension of mort. at 4½ %. Nov. 15. nom

Klein, Benedict A. to Mary Burns widow and Peter Burns and Mary Hagen heirs Edward Burns. 1st av. P. M. Dec. 1, due June 1, 1893, 5 %. 10,000

Klein, Benedict A. to THE FARMERS' LOAN AND TRUST CO. Madison st. P. M. Dec. 16, due Dec. 17, 1894, 5 %. 25,000

Keirns, John to THE TITLE GUARANTEE AND TRUST CO. 130th st, n e cor Lexington av. 33.9x100.11. Dec. 15, 3 years, 4½ %. 4,000

Karst, John D., Jr., to Sarah Holzman and Rosa Korn. Henry st, No. 23, n s, 25x87.6. Dec. 17, 3 years, 5 %. 25,000

Ketcham, James W. to Louis Cohen. Lexington av. P. M. Dec. 17, demand. 35,000

Levy, Bernard S. to Robinson Gill. 134th st, n s, 170 e Lenox av, 57.6x199.10 to 135th st. Nov. 28, demand. 35,000

Leahey, William T. to Frederick A. Constable and ano. exrs. Richard Arnold and Jas. M. and F. A. Constable exrs. Henrietta Constable. 83th st. P. M. Dec. 15, due Dec. 16, 1892, 5 %. 28,000

Lange, Edward to Charles E. Silkworth, Brooklyn. 84th st, s s, 100 w 11th av, 100x102.2; also land at Rockville Centre, L. I. Dec. 1, demand. 5,000

Lamb, Hugh, East Orange, N. J., to James R. Smith. 76th st, n s, 86 w West End av, 21x 76.1. Dec. 10, due Nov. 28, 1894, 5 %. See Conveys. 22,000

Leo, Alice to John Hastings. 143d st. P. M. Dec. 14, due Dec. 15, 1893, 5 %. 6,000

Lester, Mary H. to George W. Ruddell. 70th st. P. M. Dec. 15, 3 years, 5 %. 7,500

Lee, Walter J. to THE METROPOLITAN TRUST CO. trustee Francis Rotch dec'd. Bainbridge av, s e s, 208.7 s w Travers st, 25x115. Dec. 12, 3 years, 5 %. 5,000

Same to same as trustee William A. Seaver. Bainbridge av, s e s, 155 s w Travers st, 26.1 x114.1x18x111. Dec. 12, 3 years, 5 %. 5,000

Lahey, Gregory to Abraham Steers. 98th st, n s, 375 e Columbus av, 25x100.11. Sub. to morts. $22,720. Dec. 14, 6 months. 557

Same to Francis M. Jencks. Same property. Dec. 14, demand. 1,720

Same to Andrew Byrne. Same property. Dec. 2, due Jan. 2, 1892. 800

Same to Josephine S. Sands. Same property. Dec. 9, 3 years, 5 %. 21,000

McGrath, Thomas and Rosa Q. his wife to Michael Quinn, of Liberty, N. Y. Prospect pl, w s, 67.1 n 42d st, 16.8x54. Dec. 12, 3 years, 5 %. 5,000

McKenna, Mary to William B. Baldwin. 65th st. P. M. Sub. to mort. $6,000. Dec. 14, 1 year. 7,000

Same to same. Same property. Sub. to mort. $6,000. Dec. 14, 1 year. 7,000

McGuire, Bridget to Thomas McParlan. 118th st, n s, 356 w 3d av, 25x100.11. Dec. 17, 5 years or installs, 5 %. 5,800

McCracken, William to Martha E. Randall. Bayard st, s w cor Pyne st, 100x100. Dec. 15, 3 years, 5 %. 350

Mann, Charles to James A. Trowbridge guard. of William B. Trowbridge. 124th st. P. M. Dec. 16, 3 years, 4½ %. 5,000

Moore, Hiram M. to John O. Ball. 115th st, s s, 225 e 8th av, 25x100.11. Dec. 14, 3 months. 1,200

Meehan, John M. and Jane his wife to John A. Dempsey. 178th st, s s, 95 e Audubon av, 50 x91.2x50.1x88. Dec. 17, 1 year, 5 %. 1,500

Moeslein, Valentine and William H. Simonson both mortgagees with James B. Morrow mortgagor. Agreement as to priority of mortgages made by James B. Morrow. Dec. 14. nom

Morrow, James B. to William H. Simonson. 85th st, s s, 425 w Central Park West, 25x 102.2. Dec. 14, 1 year. 1,500

Miller, Louis to George Ehret. 81st st, No. 405 E., store, &c. Lease. Dec. 11, demand. 1,400

Munsell, Eugene to Abbie A. Merrill, Brooklyn. Water st, Nos. 214 and 216, n w s, 56.9 s w Beekman st, 30x89.6x30.2x86. Oct. 10, 1 year. 5,000

Myer, William H. to Maria T. Cotes. 104th st. P. M. Nov. 16, due Dec. 1, 1896, 5 %. 14,500

Mowbray, Matilda H. wife of Anthony to THE UNION DIME SAVINGS INST. 85th st, s s, 80 e 4th av, 25x100. Dec. 15, due Nov. 1, 1894, 5 %. 7,500

Moggi, John to Morris S. Herrman. Pearl st. P. M. Dec. 15, 5 years, 5 %. 25,000

Michalisky, Ida mortgagor and present owner to David J. King et al. exrs. and trustees Edward J. King proposed assignees. Certificate that amount due on mort. is 27,000

Moore, Hiram M. to James Curran. Manhattan av, n w cor 114th st, 100.11x— to Morningside av, x118.9 to st, x68.3. Dec. 14, 6 months. 710

Meagher, Catherine to Alexander Walker. 103d st, s s, 118 w Amsterdam av. P. M. Sub. to morts. $15,500. Dec. 15, 2 years, 5 %. 1,500

Meagher, Catherine widow, Martin P. and Elizabeth heirs Daniel Meagher to THE TITLE GUARANTEE AND TRUST CO. 66th st, s s, 250 w Central Park West, 25x100.5. Dec. 15, 3 years, 5 %. 6,000

Mulholland, James to THE UNITED STATES TRUST CO., New York. 44th st, s s, 175 e 11th av, 25x100.5. Dec. 14, due Dec. 1, 1896, 5 %. 14,000

Same to Maria D. Keyes. Same property. Dec. 14, due Dec. 1, 1896. 3,500

McGirr, Robert J. to THE FARMERS' LOAN AND TRUST CO. 84th st, No. 160, s s, 91 e Amsterdam av, 27.6x102.2. Dec. 12, due Dec. 15, 1894, 5 %. 24,000

Same to same. 84th st, No. 156, s s, 147.5 e Amsterdam av, 27.6x102.2. Dec. 12, due Dec. 15, 1894, 5 %. 24,000

Same to same. 84th st, No. 158, s s, 118.6 e Amsterdam av, 29x102.2. Dec. 12, due Dec. 15, 1894, 5 %. 25,000

Same to William Hall's Sons. 84th st, s s, 91 e Amsterdam av, 84x102.2. Dec. 16, 1 year. 17,000

Mangan, James, Fordham, to Terence McGuire. Lorillard st, w s, lot 131 W. Powell map, Fordham, 50x100. Dec. 10, due Nov. 18, 1893. 200

McClenahan, James, Harrison, N. Y., to THE NEW YORK LIFE INS. CO. Washington st, e s, 75 n Clarkson st, 50x168.2 to Greenwich st, x50.2x165.2. Oct. 15, 3 years, 5 %. 65,000

McGowan, Patrick F. and Mary F. his wife to Mary Ryan. 12th st. P. M. Dec. 10, 1 year, 5 %. 14,000

McMurrey, William D. C. to Matilda Weil et al. exrs. Max Weil. 7th av, No. 259. P. M. Dec. 11, 5 years, 4½ %. gold, 5,000

Megrath, Sarah G. wife of and George to Lydia Post, North Hempstead, L. I. 19th st, s s, 485 e 6th av, 25x92. Dec. 9, 1 year. 5,000

Neisner, Max and Abraham Rosenberg to Jacob Geissenbainer and ano. trustees Henry Elsworth dec'd. Sheriff st, w s, 100 n Delancey st, 20x90, with all title to alleyway in rear. Dec. 16, due Feb. 11, 1894, 5 %. 8,000

Nichols, Richard M. mortgagee with Max Borca mortgagor. Extension of mort. Dec. 15. nom

O'Donohue, Mary J. to Bernheimer & Schmid. 2d av, No. 2089. Saloon lease. Dec. 8, demand. 3,500

Ohlandt, John to Peter Doelger. Houston st. P. M. Oct. 30, 1 year, 5 %. 8,000

Paige, David S. to Thomas Patten. Madison av, n w cor 118th st, 100.11x60. Dec. 14, 3 years. 10,000

Perez, Manuel to THE BANK FOR SAVINGS in City of New York. Christopher st, s s, 94 e Waverley pl, 19x61.8x19.10x67.4. Dec. 14, 1 year, 5 %. 4,000

Plath, Ernest to The Manhattan Eye and Ear Hospital. Canal st. P. M. Dec. 10, due Jan. 1, 1895, 5 %. 9,500

Peyser, Simon to Hanna Wolfe. 88th st, s s, 172 w Boulevard. P. M. Dec. 16, due June 15, 1893. 2,500

Same to same. 88th st, s s, 190 w Boulevard. P. M. Dec. 16, due June 15, 1893. 2,500

Preston, Sarah L. E. to William E. Preston. 2d av, e s, 69.8 n 12th st, 17x120. Dec. 17, 1 year, 4 %. 5,000

Quigley, Bridget to Payson Merrill. 151st st, n s, 125 e Courtlandt av, 25x115.5. Dec. 15, 1 year. 750

Roth, Jacob to Jacob Mohr. Av A; 71st st. P. M. Dec. 15, due Jan. 1, 1896, or installs, 5 %. 4,000

Richard, Oscar L. to Emma Gutman et al. exrs. Mayer Gutman. Grand st. P. M. Dec. 15, 1 year, 5 %. 15,000

Rogers, Nellie E. wife of Samuel B., Jersey City, to Margaret F. Hooker. 90th st, s s, 80 e Amsterdam av, 20x100.8. Sub. to mort. $3,500. Dec. 9, 3 years. 3,100

Same to Annie B. wife of Samuel B. Sherrill, Palmyra, N. Y. Same property. Dec. 9, 3 years, 5 %. 3,500

Renner, Michael to Magdalena C. Renner. 45th st, s s, 275 e 11th av, 25x100.5. Dec. 14, demand, 5 %. 5,600

Railings, Eliza to Myers Curtiss. 41st st, n s, 130 e Broadway, 25x93.9. Dec. 12, due Dec. 11, 1892. 2,000

Ruppert, Anna wife of and Jacob to THE MUTUAL LIFE INS. CO., New York. 84th st, s s, 100.2 e 3d av, 54x102.2. Nov. 7, due Nov. 30, 1892, 5 %. 33,000

Riedell, William to Nathan A. Chedsey. Lexington av, e s, 22.4 s 29th st, 21.10x80. Dec. 10, 3 years, 5 %. 20,000

Rutsky, Esther J. wife of and Samuel S. to Joseph and Richard Lahey. 91st st, No. 57, n s, 244.1 w Park av, 17x100.8. Dec. 11, 1 year. 2,000

Reinbold, Andrew J. to THE TITLE GUARANTEE AND TRUST CO. 123d st. P. M. Nov. 24, due Dec. 14, 1894, 4½ %. 6,000

Rhines, Isaac O. to THE MUTUAL LIFE INS. CO. of New York. Manhattan av, s w cor 115th st, 100.11x180.10 to 9th av, x 113.9x193.5. Dec. 12, 1 year, 5 %. 35,000

Ritzmann, Charles L. to Nellie F. wife of Mark P. Brennan. 10th av, e s, 49.4 s 32d st, 24.8x100. Dec. 15, due Dec. 1, 1893. 7,000

Same to same. 10th av, e s, 74.1 s 32d st, 24.8x 100. Dec. 15, due Dec. 1, 1893. 7,000

Same to same. 7th av, n w cor 53d st. P. M. Dec. 15, due Dec. 1, 1893, or installs. 13,000

Rosenthal, Joseph E. to Harris Shedlinsky and Isidor and Julius Schweitzer. Lewis st. P. M. Dec. 15, installs. 2,958

Raisbeck, Eliza A. to Anna R. Peacock, Brooklyn. 40th st, n s, 150 e 8th av, 25x98.9. Dec. 5, due Jan. 1, 1897. 4,000

Schloeder, Jacob to THE NEW YORK SAVINGS BANK. 120th st, s s, 100 e Pleasant av, 25x 100.11. Dec. 16, due Dec. 1, 1896, 4½ %. 11,000

Same to same. 120th st, s s, 125 e Pleasant av, 25x100.11. Dec. 16, due Dec. 1, 1896, 4½ %. 11,000

Sheitlis, Philip and Bessie his wife to Jonas Weil and Bernhard Mayer. Cherry st, No. 262. P. M. Dec. 15, due Nov. 4, 1898. 5,000

Same to same. Same property. P. M. Sub. to morts. $24,000. Dec. 15, installs. 6,000

Shepherd, Oliver L. to Hannah M. Dickinson, Fort Hamilton, L. I. 119th st, No 7, n s, 95.5 w 5th av, 14x57.9x14.6x53.11. Dec. 15, 5 years, 4½ %. 3,000

Same to Bryan L. Kennelly. 3d av, e s, 50.4 s 93d st, 25.2x100. Dec. 15, 2 years. 3,000

Shields, Denis to Beadleston & Woerz, a corporation. West st, Nos. 329 and 330. Lease. Dec. 15, installs. 4,800

Same to same. West st, No. 334, e s, bet King and West Houston sts. Lease. Dec. 15, demand. 1,900

Silva, William S., Rutherford, N. J., to Daniel E. Seybel. 211th st, south cor Isham st, runs south along Isham st 136.7 x northeast 95.8 to 211th st, x northwest 166.9 to beginning. Dec. 7, 2 years. 1,000

Solomon, Isaac H. to Frederick P. Forster. Lots 13 and 14 map of F. P. & H. A. Forster's property, Riverdale. P. M. Dec. 2, 2 years, 5 %. 600

Smith, James to Beadleston & Woerz, a corporation. Washington st, No. 221, s e cor Barclay st, abt 26x46. Store lease. Dec. 12, demand. 6,000

Smith, Tillie E. widow to Sarah H. Powell. 119th st, s s, 460 e Lenox av, 125x100.11; 116th st, s s, 82.11 e Madison av, 27.1x101. Dec. 12, demand. 3,000

Smith, Tillie E. widow to The Metropolitan Museum of Art. 119th st, s s, 460 e Lenox av, 18x100.11. Dec. 9, due Dec. 1, 1894, 5 %. 12,751

Same to Cornelia Trimble. 119th st, s s, 532 e Lenox av, 18x100.11. Dec. 9, 3 years, 5 %. gold, 12,000

Same to Clothilde de Vaisse. 119th st, s s, 550 e Lenox av, 17.6x100.11. Dec. 8, 3 years, 5 %. 12,000

Same to Edward H. Coster committee of John G. Coster. 119th st, s s, 567.6 e Lenox av, 17.6x100.11. Dec. 9, due Dec. 17, 1894, 5 %. 12,000

Same to THE FARMERS' LOAN AND TRUST CO. 119th st, s s, 496 e Lenox av, 18x100.11. Dec. 9, due Dec. 17, 1894, 5 %. 12,000

Same to same. 119th st, s s, 478 e Lenox av, 18 x100.11. Dec. 9, due Dec. 17, 1894, 5 %. 12,000

Same to Mary M. Baldwin, Newport, R. I. 119th st, s s, 514 e Lenox av, 18x100.11. Dec. 9, due Dec. 1, 1896, 5 %. gold, 12,000

Smith, Frank L. to John L. Brewster. Riverside av or Drive, e s, 48 s 82d st. P. M. Dec. 15, 1 year, 5 %. 4,000

Same to same. Riverside av or Drive, e s, 68.8 s 82d st. P. M. Dec. 15, 1 year, 5 %. 3,000

Same to Francis M. Jencks. Riverside av or Drive, e s, 63.3 s 82d st. P. M. Dec. 15, 3 years, 5 %. 20,000

Same to same. Riverside av or Drive, e s, 48 s 82d st. P. M. Dec. 15, 3 years, 5 %. 20,000

Sauer, George W. to George Ehret. 8th av, s w cor 155th st, runs west 175 x south 99.11 x east 75 x north 50 x east 100 to 8th av, x north 49.11. Dec. 10, 1 year, 5 %. 5,000

Sauer, George W. to George Ehret. 8th av, s w cor 155th st, 49.11x100; 155th st, s s, 100 w 8th av, 75x99.11. Dec. 15, 1 year, 5 %. 10,000

Sanford, Robert, Poughkeepsie, N. Y., to THE NEW YORK LIFE INS. AND TRUST CO. Washington st, n w cor Morton st, runs west 175 x north 125 x east 75 x south 50 x east 100 to Washington st, x south 75.1. Dec. 15, 5 years, 5 %. 60,000

Schreiner, Jr., John to George Gerlach. 1st av, n w cor 85th st, 25x75; 1st av, w s, 50 n 85th st, 50x75, error. Dec. 14, due July 1, 1892. 12,000

Schwab, Mathilde to Edwin Lord. 20th st. P. M. Dec. 17, 5 years, 5 %. 10,000

Schwerin, Herman and Lena his wife to Hanna Wolfe. 116th st. P. M. Dec. 15, due June 15, 1893. 4,500

Senges, Adam and Caroline his wife to Henry Wiener, Philadelphia, Pa. 47th st, No. 524, s s, 348 w 8th av, 27.6x100.5. Dec. 12, 3 years, 5 %. 6,000

Sobel, Elias and Philip to The Baron de Hirsch Fund. East Broadway, Nos. 115 and 117; Pike st. No 16, begins East Broadway, s w cor Pike st, 48.10x85.1x46.8x85.1. Dec. 15, due Dec. 16, 1896, 5 %. 63,000

Solomon, Joseph to William A. Booth trustee for Mary E. Edgar. Madison st, No. 314, s s, 60 4 w Gouverneur st, 25.11x112.5x21x113 6. Dec. 10, c. due Dec. 1, 1894, 5 % 25,000

Sheppard, William J. to The East Brooklyn Co-operative Building Assoc. Washington av, e s, 250 s Fletcher st, 37.6x141.2x38.1x148. Dec. 11, installs. 4,250

Silverberg, Sarah wife of Simon to Thomas H. Messenger exr. Thomas Messenger. Pearl st, Nos. 490 and 492, n e s, 160 2 s e Park st, runs northwest 43.2 x northeast 80 x southeast 14 10 x southwest 67 6. Dec. 15, 5 years, 5 %. 15,000

Scrymser, Leila B. wife of and Clarence H. to Kate Warner. Front st, No. 126, n w s, 90.3 n e Wall st, runs northwest 75 x southwest 0.8 x northwest 7.2 x northeast 18.7 x southeast 84.2 to Front st, x southwest 18.6. Dec. 15, 5 years, 5 % 20,000

Scharrenbeck, George to A. Hupfel's Sons. Westchester av. No. 730. Store lease. Nov. 28, note, demand. 2,000

Schreiner, Joseph to THE GERMAN SAVINGS BANK, New York. 88th st, Nos. 505–509, n s, 100 e Av A, 3 lots, each 25x100.8. 3 morts., each $12,000. Dec. 12, due Dec. 15, 1894. 36,000

Swan, Cornelia P. to Eliza Worthington. 164th st, s s, 100 w Delmonico pl, 16.8x100. Dec. 15, due July 1, 1894 500

Shannon, Thomas F. to Susanna W. Thorne, New Rochelle, N. Y. Pleasant av, s w cor 115th st, 75.7x74. Dec. 11, 1 year. See Conveys. 10,500

Same to Catharine A. Tompkins, Brooklyn. Same property. Equal lien with last mort. Dec. 11, 1 year. 1,000

Stanton, Edwin B. Brooklyn, to Lawrence Winters. 129th st. P. M. Dec. 11, due June 15, 1893, 5 %. 7,000

Shaw, Henry G. to Robert J. Hubbard, Cazenovia, N. Y. 102d st. P. M. Dec. 15, due Jan. 1, 1895, 5 %. gold, 17,000

Tilson, James to James Mehaffey. Monroe st, No 35, n s, 25x100. Dec. 17, 1 year. 1,000

The Bradley & Currier Co. (Lim.), with Morris Steinhardt both mortgagees. Agreement as to priority of morts. made by Charles W. and Louisa C. Friedline. Dec. 10. nom

Throop, Charlotte W. wife of and Montgomery H. to Robert P. Lee, Brooklyn. 45th st, No. 51, n s, 328.3 e 5th av, 18.9x100.5. Dec. 10, due Jan. 1, 1895. 1,000

Turner, Richard A., Jr., to John W. Bolton. 175th st. P. M. Dec. 10, 3 years. 2,500

Tyler, Roberta, Louisville, Ky., to Edwin D. M. Waterman. White st. P. M. Dec. 5, due Dec. 1, 1894, 4½ %. 15,000

Terry, Harvey to Frederick W. Payne, Jersey City, N. J. 13th st, n s, 225 e 8th av, 25x99.11. Dec. 1, 3 years, 5 %. 2,000

Thompson, Henry to Charlotte A. and Charles M. Rice. Broadway and Houston st. P. M. Dec. 14, 1 year 200,000

Umberfield, John C. to Charles T. and Helen T. Barney. 75th st. P. M. Dec. 10, demand. 129,360

Same to same. Same property. Building loan. Sub. to above. Dec. 10, demand. 85,000

Ulman, Leon and Sadie his wife to Hanna Wolfe. 116th st. P. M. Dec. 15, due June 15, 1893. 4,500

Van Orden, Lara J. wife of Archibald S. to Jacob Poulin. 136th st. P. M. Dec. 14, 3 years, 5 %. 4,000

Van Orden, Laura J. to Thomas Overington. 136th st, s s, 294 e Alexander av, 27.6x110. Dec. 14, due July 1, 1895, or installs., 5 %. 1,100

Vincent, William E. D. mortgagor with Mary E. Walker mortgagee. Agreement extending powers in mortgagor. 45th st, n s, 225 e 10th av, 25x100.4. July 9, 1890. nom

Vogel, Heyman to Catharine V. R. Turnbull, Morristown, N. J. Grand st, n s, 24.9 e Centre Market pl, runs east 50.6 x north 99.6 x west 0 x south 27.1 x west 38 6 x south 72.4 to beginning; Grand st, n s, 75.3 e Centre Market pl, runs north 99 6 x east 24.7 x south in two courses 99.7 x west 24.9; being Nos. 176, 178 and 180 Grand st. Sub. to morts. $80,000. Dec. 16, installs, 5 %. 30,000

Weinert, Fedor guard. of Olga Weinert to Edward R. Stehl. 1st av. P. M. Dec. 15, installs, 5 %. 1,400

Westervelt, Mary to Annie F. Shardlow. 122d st, No. 226, s s, 255 w 2d av, 25x100.11. Dec. 16, due May 10, 1892, 5 %. 500

Wilson, Henry, Greenwich, Conn., to Charles E. Tracy and ano. trustees James Bogert dec'd. Peck slip. P. M. Dec. 12, 1 year, 5 %. gold, 7,000

Warner, Edwin C., Ludlow, Vt., to Ephraim B. Levy. Lots 1–5 map of Edward K. Willard, &c., Woodlawn Heights. P. M. Dec. 2, due Dec. 15, 1894, 5 %. 1,000

Werner, George F. to Gustavus H. Stoiber, Silverton, Col. 77th st, s s, 123.8 e 1st av, 19.4x102.2. Dec. 15, 3 years, 5 %. gold, 10,000

Wood, Edward T. to Charles Fleischmann and ano. exrs. and trustees Maximilian Fleischmann. Proposed st in 24th Ward, shown on map of M. P. Chrystie property, w s, adj land of Catharine E. Schwab, runs west along said land 150.11 x northwest still along said land 156.9 x east 24.8 x north 26 x east 96.4 x east 42.3 x southeast 225.3 to stake on w s of said proposed st, x south 123.3 to beginning, with right of way to Macombs Dam road. Dec. 1, installs. 20,736

Yost, Agnes to Mary Muller. 2d av, e s, 20.11 n 124th st, 20x80. Dec. 11, 2 months. 5,000

Youmans, Edgar W. to Frederic J. Middlebrook, Brooklyn. Prospect pl, No. 46, n w cor 42d st, 17.1x54. Dec. 11, 3 years, 5 %. 7,000

Yunk, John P. to Bernheimer & Schmid. Houston st, No. 185 E. Saloon lease. Dec. 10, demand. 5,000

KINGS COUNTY.

DECEMBER 10, 11, 12, 14, 15, 16.

Ahern, Edward P. to John Cowenhoven. Bay 35th st, s e s, 40 n e of J. B. Denyse's land, 40x98. Dec 9, 3 years. $1,000

Aronson, Jacob to Samuel Bernstein. Saratoga av, n e cor Marion st, 22x79; Saratoga av, e s, 41 n Marion st, 29x79; Saratoga av, e s, 100 n Marion st, 60x79. Dec. 1, demand. 2,000

Same to same. Lewis av, s e cor Hancock st, 150x100. Dec. 11, demand. 10,000

Aronson, Jacob to The Brooklyn State and Mantel Co. Myrtle av, n s, 175 e Tompkins av, 25x100. Dec 9, note. 430

Baernstein, Daniel S. to Henry G. Savage. Heyward st, n s, 78.6 e Lee av, 19.0x100. Dec. 9, demand, 5 %. 1,500

Balz, Mary E. wife of and Frederick to Edward C. Underhill. Rockaway, e s, adj land of Dominicus Vanderveer, runs east 700 to centre Fresh Creek, x north 150 x west 200 x north 120 x west 215 to av, x south 425. Dec. 5, 1 year, 5 %. 4,000

Barlow, James W. to Therese Q. Meara. Lorimer st. P. M. Dec. 10, installs. 2,250

Barnard, John J. to Kate Ropke trustee for Charles Hermann. Halsey st, s s, 25.3 e Ralph av, 19.5x84. Dec 14, 3 years 5,000

Beekman, Theodore to The Title Guarantee and Trust Co. Hoyt st. P. M. Dec. 15, 3 years, 5 %. 4,000

Beers, Edwin to The Mutual Life Ins. Co., New York. Remsen st, n s, 100 w Clinton st, 50x100. Dec 11, 1 year, 5 %. 30,000

Bell, James A. to George Silver and Robert Beggs trustees Hugh H. Scott. Tompkins av, n w cor Willoughby av, runs north 77 6 x west 80 x north 22.6 x west 45 x south 100 to Willoughby av, x east 125. Dec. 10, 1 year, 5 %. 7,000

Bell, Laura A. wife of William R. Bell to The Title Guarantee and Trust Co. Lee av, w s, 21 n Penn st, 19x67. Dec. 9, due Dec. 10, 1893, 5 %. 3,500

Bennett, Hannah wife of and Thomas Bennett to Thomas Ostick. 57th st, n s, 380 e 3d av, 20x100.2. Dec. 10, 4 years, 5 %. 1,200

Bicking, George E. to Henry Eich. Park av. P. M. Dec. 15, due Jan. 1, 1897, 5 %. 4,500

Bierds, Charlotte A. wife of and William H. to Jeremiah Fitzpatrick. Macon st, s s, 403.6 e Patchen av, 17.6x100. Nov. 20, due Sept. 1, 1894. 1,500

Bloom, Mary A. to Flora L. Davenport. Jefferson av, No. 125; Quincy st, No. 598. Dec. 11, 1 year. 500

Blydenburgh, Emily wife of and Ebenezer S. to Virginia A. Kleine. Greene av. P. M. Dec. 2, demand. 4,220

Bogart, Ida M. wife of and William D. to Felix Gallagher. Russell pl. P. M. Dec. 14, installs. 600

Boll, Meyer to James Barry. North 3d st. P. M. Dec 15, 1 year, 5 %. 1,000

Bossert, Jacob to John S. Darcy. Mountain View, N. J. Myrtle av. P. M. Dec. 9, due Dec. 1, 1892, 5 %. 3,500

Bossert, Margaret to Hugo Weil. Lot 9 block 1084 assessm't map. Dec. 10, 1 year. 1,200

Bradley, Harriet J. to Benjamin Andrews. Sackett st, Nos. 469–471, n s, 60 w Bond st, 40x100. Dec. 12, 3 years. 4,000

Brandemann, Sophia wife of and Henry to Elizabeth wife of Adam Parthesieus. Richardson st, s s, 100 e Graham av, 20.6x75. Dec. 14, 4 years. 800

Braxton, Malinda, Gravesend, L. I., to Albert G. Burtis. New York & Brighton Beach R. R. Co., w s, at north line of school lot, Gravesend. P. M. Dec. 1, 3 years. 225

Bremer, Joseph to Elizabeth A. Burt, North Hempstead, L. I. North 6th st, s s, 152.2 e Roebling st, 20.10x100. Dec. 12, 2 years. 250

Brown, Isabella wife of and William to John M. and George F. Halsted, of Halsted Bros. 7th av, w s, 42 s 11th st, 96x43.3x95.5x44.2. Nov. 30, due Dec. 1, 1892. 3,000

Brown, William to Florence M. H. Coan. 6th av, south cor 10th st, 20x90. Nov. 23, due Jan. 25, 1892. 1,500

Same to William W. Stoothoff, Flushing, L. I. Same property. Nov. 1, 3 years, 5 %. 6,000

Bryan, Joseph to Mary A. Bryan. Bedford av, w s, 72 s South 2d st, 24x103.6. Dec. 8, 5 years, 5 %. 6,000

Burrell, Alice T. mortgagor with M. Evelina Wood mortgagee. Extension of mort. Nov. 19. nom

Byrnes, Annie M. to James D. Lynch. 84th st, New Utrecht. P. M. Dec. 5, due Dec. 10, 1894, 5 %. 735

Carell, Sophia D. to Mary A. Stevenson. West av, s w cor Van Sicklen pl, 50x100, Gravesend. Dec. 15, 3 years. 2,500

Carr, George W. to Harriet L. Price. Bridge st, w s, 150 s Johnson st, 44x107.6. Dec. 16, 3 years, 5 %. 4,100

Cederstrom, Sigfrid to William J. Conway. Carroll st, s w s, 70 s e 3d av. P. M. Sub. to mort. $2,250. Dec. 2, 1 year. 500

Cokalite, John S., Peekskill, N. Y., to Peekskill Savings Bank. Prospect av, n e s, 535 s e 3d av, 20x64.6x20x62.11. Dec. 8, 1 year. 3,000

Cochen, Fred. C. to Mary F. Stoughton extrx. Edwin W. Stoughton. Fort Hamilton av, s e cor 72d st, 61x108.5x60x90.7, New Utrecht. Dec 11, 1 year. 3,500

Cole, Albert J. and John M. Perry to Margaret V. A. Grant, Piermont, N. Y. De Kalb av. P. M. Dec 15, 1 year. 1,000

Colyer, Joseph H. to John L. Voorhies, Commissioner of Investment, Gravesend. 6th av, s w cor Pacific st. P. M. Dec. 15, 3 years, 5 %. 30,000

Commoss, Joseph T. to Susan R. Kendall. Pacific st, n s, 42.10 e Stone av, 6 lots. P. M. 6 morts., each $1,150. Dec. 2, due Dec. 10, 1892, 5 %. 6,900

Cook, Annie wife of and William P. to Florence W. Beers. Vine st. P. M. Dec. 1, 2 years, 5 %. 2,400

Crane, Clarissa L. to The German-American Real Estate Title Guarantee Co. 7th st, n s, 157.10 e 6th av, 20x100. Dec. 11, 1 year, 5 %. 3,500

Cullen, Margaret to James Williamson. 55th st, n s, 410 w 3d av, 75x200.4 to 54th st. Dec. 15, 3 years. 5,000

Cummings, Henry to Annie M. Robinson. Dean st, n s, 79.10 w Classon av, 25x110. Oct. 19, 1884, demand. 2,500

Curtin, Charles J. to Isador Brand, Saratoga Springs, N. Y. Watkins st. P. M. Dec. 7, 2 years. 150

Dahlbender, Anna widow to James Gascoine indivi., and with Anna E. Cozine exrs. John G. Cozine. Woodbine st. P. M. Dec. 15, 1 year, 5 %. 2,000

Di-osway, Annie wife of and Cornelius to The Title Guarantee and Trust Co. Hancock st, s s, 127 6 w Stuyvesant av, 17.6x100. Dec. 12, 3 years, 5 %. 2,000

Doerschuck, Gustav J. L. to Elizabeth and William Schano exrs. Carl Schano. Lot 23 block 1020, also lot 24 same block 18th Ward assessm't map. Dec. 7, 3 years, 5 %. 1,400

Donovan, Florence F. to The Hamilton Co-operative Building and Loan Assoc. 19th st, n s, 125 e 3d av, 25x100. Dec. 11, installs. 1,500

Duncan, Jane wife of and Robert to Fort Green Co-operative Building and Loan Assoc. Buffalo av, w s, 82.8 s Dean st, 16.4x85. Dec. 14, installs. 2,500

Drescher, Heiman to Arthur C. Brush. Belmont av, s w cor Osborn st, 50x100. Dec. 16, 3 years 600

Drew, Charles R. to The Mutual Life Ins. Co., New York. Gates av, n s, 100 w Throop av, 7 lots, together in size, 200x100. 7 morts., each $10,000. Dec. 10, 1 year, 5 %. 70,000

Same to Charles M. Marsh, Morris Plains, N. J. Same property. 7 morts., each $1,400. Dec. 10, 1 year. 9,800

Evans, George C., Plainfield, N. J., to George G. Reynolds. Williams av, n e cor Dumont av, 100x200 to Alabama av. Dec. 11, 3 years, 5 %. 2,500

Same to same. Blake av, s e cor Williams av, 100x200. Dec. 11, 3 years, 5 %. 2,500

Same to same. Blake av, s w cor Alabama av, 100x200. Dec. 11, 3 years, 5 %. 2,500

Same to same. Williams av, e s, 200 s Blake av, 100x200. Dec. 11, 3 years, 5 %. 2,500

Same to same. Alabama av, w s, 200 s Blake av, 200x100. Dec. 11, 3 years, 5 %. 2,500

Ehm, Henry to Lawrence Grussler. Broadway. P. M. Dec. 15, 2 years, 5 %. 4,500

Ernst, Clara E. to Charles Drasser, Mountaindale, N. Y. Herkimer st, s s, 100 e Howard av, runs south 98 x east 24 x north 18 x east 24 x north 80 x west 48. Dec. 1, 4 months. 750

Fair, William S. to William D. Lent, New York. Halsey st, s s, 300 e Lewis av, 20x100. Dec. 9, 2 years. 5½ %. 2,250

Flynn, Mary wife of and John mortgagor with Anna F. P. wife of Henry C. Knight mortgagee. Extension of mort. Nov. 3. nom

Fowler, Mary E. wife of and Levi to Adolph Vanrein. St. Marks av, n s, 200 e Franklin av, 80x128. Dec. 11, 1 year or installs. 5,000

Fenton, Eliza A. to Susan C. Twombly, New York, trustee John F. Twombly dec'd. 4th st, s s, 233.10 w 7th av, 19x100. Dec. 8, due Dec. 1, 1894, 5 %. 7,500

Fitzpatrick, Ella to Charles J. Bradley. York st, s s, 50 e Hudson av, 25x100. Dec. 1, 3 years, 5 %. 2,000

Same to Christopher Schwab. St. Marks av, n s, 240 e Franklin av, 20x128.6. Dec. 11, 3 years, 5 %. 6,000

Francisco, Charles H. and George W. to James Gascoine. Knickerbocker av. P. M. Dec. 15, 1 year. 1,300

Frescold, M. Luther to George A. Perry. McDougal st, n s, 95 w Howard av, 19x50. Oct. 28, due May 1, 1892, 5 %. 700

Friedrichs, Henry E. F. to Catharina Anacker. Palmetto st. P. M. Dec. 1, 3 years, 5 %. 1,700

Gerlich, John to Ellen L. Davidson. Skillman av, s w cor Kingsland av, 50.8x157x50.4x150.7. Dec. 10, 3 years. 1,000

Gettinger, Mendel and Isaac Gross to Wolf Potashinski. Eastern Parkway. P. M. Dec. 15, installs. 1,425

Gifuni, Joseph to John R. Pitt. Macon st. P. M. Dec. 11, installs. 2,500

Gilbert, Annie widow to Harriet Isaacs. Lot at Gravesend adj land Benjamin Freeman, runs to highway or cove on Sheepshead Bay, 207x2.7, Gravesend. Dec. 11, due Dec. 31, 1894. 4,000

Same to Ellen L. Kitchen. Same property. Dec. 11, 3 years. 14,500

Goldenberg, Esther to Andrew R. Culver. Eastern Parkway. P. M. Dec. 8, installs. 275

Gollner, Erwin G. to Michael Dalton. 6th st, n s, 347.10 w 5th av, 50x100. Nov. 30, 1 year. 444

Gollin, Moritz to Mary R. Bennett. Seigel st, n s, 125 e Ewen st, 25x100. Dec. 8, 3 years. 4,000

Goodenough or Goodnough, Roberta F. F. or Roberta F. to Ransom F. Clayton. Stuyvesant av, e s, 102 n Halsey st, 19x100. Sept. 26, due Oct 1, 1898, 5 %. 1,200

Gordon, Ida to Mary A. L. Baker. Ridgewood and Railroad avs. P. M. June 8, demand. 10,000

Grauer, John G. to Jacob Mannesschmidt. Bleecker st, n w s, 90 s w St. Nicholas av, 40x100. Dec. 11, 2 years. 5 %. 1,500

Greenblatt, Isaac and Simon Loeb to Martha Fries. McKibbin st. n s. 250 w Ewen st, 25x100. Dec 10, 5 years, 5 %. 6,500

Gregory, George F. mortgagee to estate of Charles D. Ostman. Certificate that $4,500 has been paid on account of mortgage. May 18. nom

Grotz, William F. to Carl C. Grotz. Ewen st, Nos. 152 and 154. Lease. Dec. 9, demand. 8,000

Hajek, Desiderius F. J. and Helen M., Ridgefield Park, New Jersey, to Dorothea Zerr. Humboldt st P. M. Nov. 30, 3 years. 5 %. 1,600

Same to Charles Engert. Same property. P. M. Nov. 30, 3 years, 5 %. 1,600

Same to same. Same property. P. M. Nov. 30, 5 years, 5 %. 600

Hamilton, Grant E. and Lydia E his wife to Hans C Pfalzgraf. 66th st. P. M. Dec. 10, 3 years, or installs. 5 %. 1,726

Hart, John F. to Catharine Lilly. Pacific st, n s, 212.3 w Clason av, 30x80. Dec. 11, 1 year. 2,000

Same to Mabel A. Roby. Same property. Dec. 11, demand. 4,000

Same to Peter Donald. Pacific st, n s, 242.3 w Clason av, 30x80. Dec. 11, due Dec. 1, 1894. 6,000

Same to same. Pacific st, n s, 212.3 w Clason av, 30x80. Dec. 11, due Dec. 1, 1894. 6,000

Hart, John F. to Asa W. Parker, New Hamburgh, N. Y. Kingston av, n e cor Pacific st, 96x80. Dec. 14, demand, 5 %. 5,000

Same to Charles D. Rust. Same property. Dec 14, 6 months. See Conveys. 5,000

Same to The Dime Savings Bank, Brooklyn. Kingston av, n e cor Pacific st. P. M. Dec. 14, 1 year, 5 % 10,000

Same to same. Pacific st, n s, 31.2 e Kingston av. P. M. Dec. 14, 1 year, 5 %. 8,000

Same to same. Kingston av, e s, 62 n Pacific st. P. M. Dec. 14, 1 year, 5 %. 7,000

Hartmann, William J. to East New York Savings Bank. Sumpter st, s s, 325 e Ralph av, 25x100. Dec. 14, 1 year. 1,500

Hartmann, Conrad to Robert Weiskittel. Lewis av. P. M. Dec. 15, 5 years, 5 %. 3,000

Haviland, Charles A. to Title Guarantee and Trust Co. De Kalb av. P. M. Dec. 8, due Dec. 9, 1894, 5 %. 1,500

Hedbawney, Kaspar to Charles Wagenfohr. Cornelia st, n w s, 160 n e Evergreen av, 40x100. Dec. 12, 1 year, 5 %. 1,500

Herndl, Frank to Frederick A. Reid. Williams av. P. M. Dec. 14, 5 years, 5 %. 1,675

Hirschsprung, Axel to Frank G. Hennings. Bay 15th st, New Utrecht. P. M. Dec. 15, 3 years or installs 5 %. 4,000

Hollister, Sebastian T. to East New York Savings Bank. Schenck av, e s, 233 n Arlington av, 50x100. Dec. 9, 1 year. 4,500

Holsten, John H. to Louisa A. Klench and ano. admrs. John D Klench. 16th st, s s, 267.4 e 5th av, 21x144.2x22x144.9. Dec. 16, 10 years or installs. 1,200

Hons, Henry to Lembeck & Betz Eagle Brewing Co. 3d av, No, 444. Saloon lease. Dec. 15, 1 year. 1,250

Hueston, James to Aaron S. Robbins. Diamond st, Flatbush. P. M. Dec. 15, 3 years. 5 %. 2,000

Hull, Cartwright R. to The West Brooklyn Land and Improvement Co. 55th st. P. M. Dec. 1, due March 1, 1896. 5 %. 420

Humphrey, Owen W. to The Kings Co. Improvement Co. Van Cott av, n w cor Sutton st, 100x108.9. Feb. 2, 1 year. 2,500

Hurlburt, Frances E. to Patrick Hayes. Broadway, centre line, 400 w Utica av, runs east 945.6 x south 270.3 to centre Earl st, x west 957.10 to point 209.1 e Schenectady av, x north 270, Flatbush. Dec. 15, 3 years, 5 %. 7,000

Hurst, Lewis to Mary S. Clark. 5th av. P. M. Dec. 15, 3 years, 5 %. 6,000

Immen, Christopher to George Ehret. Commercial st, east cor Clay st, 119.3x30.2x30.2 to Clay st, x119.5. (?) Oct. 29, 5 years, 5 %. 1,500

Ives, Clara H and Jane L. Smith to J. Wyckoff Van Sicklen. Eastern Parkway and Van Siclen av. P. M. Dec. 7, 1 year, 5 %. 1,250

Jack, James to The Title Guarantee and Trust Co. 6th av, south cor Prospect av, 80.4x100. Dec. 14, demand. 29,000

Jepson, John P. to Christopher Prince and ano. exrs. Sarah B. Prince. Bay 29th st, n w s, 220 n e Cropsey av, 60x96.8, New Utrecht. Dec. 11, 3 years, 5 %. 2,000

Johnston, William P. to Helena Schneider. Stockton st, s s, 325 w Throop av, 25x100. Dec. 11, due Jan. 1, 1895, 5 %. 2,000

Jones, Lucinda H. to Lawrence Hurlburt. Orient av, w s, 175 s Baltic av, 25x100; Orient av, w s, 150 s Baltic av, 25x100. Dec. 10, 2 years. 1,000

Jones, E. Willard to The Title Guarantee and Trust Co Macon st, s s, 425 e Sumner av, 80x100. Nov. 30, demand. 30,000

Kaplan, Aaron to Bernhard Silberstein. Linden st, No. 112, e s. 235.11 n Evergreen av, 20x100. Nov. 30, due Dec. 1, 1893. 1,000

Kathe, Louise wife of Charles to Lowry Somerville. Warren st, s w s, 414.2 n w 4th av. P. M. Dec. 9, due Jan. 1, 1895, 5 %. 1,050

Same to same. Warren st, s w s, 361 2 n w 4th av. P. M. Dec. 9, due Jan. 1, 1895, 5 %. 750

Kathe, Louis to Achille Fouquet and Margaret his wife. Wyckoff st. P. M. Dec. 15, due Jan. 1, 1895, 5 %. 3,000

Kearney, James L. to Bridget McNulty. 58th st, centre line, at division line of land formerly of M. Bergen, runs southwest — x southeast to centre 9th av, x northeast to centre 58th st, x northwest —, New Utrecht. Dec. 15, due Nov. 1, 1894. 2,000

Same to same. Hull st. n w cor Hopkinson av, 50x84. Dec. 15, due Nov. 1, 1894. 1,000

Kellington, George to The New York World Co-operative Building and Loan Assoc. Monroe st, n s, 85 e Nostrand av, 20x100. 2d mort. Nov. 28, installs. 2,000

Kirk, Elizabeth P. to Henry J. Lankenau. Madison st, n s, 250 e Marcy av, 16.8x100. Dec. 14, 3 years, 5 %. 1,000

Leavy, Michael F. to The South Brooklyn Co-operative Building and Loan Assoc. 40th st, s s, 110 e 4th av, 25x100.2. Dec. 15, installs. 2,500

Ledoux, Paul W. mortgagee with Frank Hyde mortgagor. Agreement as to reduction of int. Dec. 14. nom

Leopold, Charles to Obermeyer & Liebmann. Alabama av, No. 1. Lease. Dec. 16, demand. 1,800

Lenhart, Philip F. to Emma L. Johnston, Newtown, L. I. Sunnyside av. P. M. Dec. 10, 1 year. 2,000

Lewandowski, Albert and Marianna his wife to Mary Levy. 21st st. P. M. Dec. 14, 2 years, 5 %. 1,400

Loomis, John S. to Eliza A. wife of John T. Bierds. Nevins st, s e cor President st. P. M. Dec. 15, due Dec. 1. 1894. 900

Magill, George W. to Malcolm McNeill. 7th av, e s, 20 s 2d st, 26.8x80. Dec. 10, 1 year. 800

Mahlmann, Anna wife of and Dietrich to Jane E. Meeker et al. exrs and trustees Samuel M. Meeker. Harman st, s e s, 375 n e Irving av, 25x90.10x25x92.1. Dec. 10, 3 years, 5½ %. 1,600

Marun, Barbara formerly Franz, Adam Franz, Eva F. Euler, Barbara and Philip Franz to Katharina Franz. Johnson av late Cypress Hills plank road, s s, adj Wm. Wall on west, 90.6x136x—, 18th Ward. Dec. 8, 3 years, 4 %. 1,300

Martin, Levi V. to Thomas Stratton. 2d av, n e cor 53d st, 20.2x80. Sub. to mort. $3,800. Dec. 15, 1 year. 800

Same to same. 2d av, east cor 54th st, 20.2x80, Sub. to mort. $3,800. Dec 15, 1 year. 800

Masker, William to Harris J. Latta. Douglass st. P. M. Nov. 28, 6 months. gold, 5,950

McBean, Archibald N. to Adelbert S. Nichols. 2d st, s s, 2?7.9 w 8th av, 20x95. Dec. 7, due Jan. 2, 1893. 470

McBean, Archibald N. to James Jack. 2d st, s s. 457.11 e 5th av, 30x95. Dec. 1, 2 years. 2,750

Same to same. 2d st, s s, 487.11 e 5th av, 30x95. Dec. 1, 2 years. 2,750

Same to Leonard Moody trustee. 2d st, s s, 457.11 e 5th av, 60x95. Secures creditors. Dec. 7. indefinite

McCarthy, Henry A. to Charles M. Marsh, Morris Plains, N. J. Union st, n s, 116 10 e 4th av, 3 lots, each 25x95. 3 morts., each $2,000. Dec. 15, 2 years or installs. 6,000

McCuse, John W. to Louis H. Schenck and Frank S. Henderson. Fort Greene pl. e s, 197.7 s De Kalb av, 17.6x100. Secures surety to admrs. bonds. Dec. 10. —

McNab, Elizabeth wife of and James to Harriette E. Bartlett. Marion st, s s. 350.2 e Howard av, 18.8x100. Dec 9, 3 years, 5 %. 3,000

Same to Sarah E. Janes. Marion st, s s. 368 10 e Howard av, 18.8x100. Dec. 9, 3 years, 5 %. 3,000

Meehan, Patrick to Riverhead Savings Bank. Huron st. P. M. Dec. 10, due Nov. 11, 1892. 5 % 1,000

McKenna, Jane A. wife of and Edward to Henry M. and Chester S. Kingman exrs. Martin E. Kingman. Myrtle av. P. M. Dec. 10, 3 years, 5 %. 6,000

Mehrtens, Carsten J. to Charles G. Street. Atlantic av, n s, 75.1 e Hendrix st, runs east 50.1 x north 108 x west 25 x south 25 x west 25 x south 86. Dec. 9, 3 years. 2,000

Meshel, Samuel to Annie Levy. Christopher av, e s, 175 s Eastern Parkway, 25x100. Oct. 13, 3 months. 500

Meshel, Samuel to William W. Rope. Christopher av, e s, 200 n Belmont av, 25x100. Dec. 12, demand. 400

Moores, Robert L. and Charles A. Le Quesne to George F. Alexander. Broadway, w s, 46.11 s Madison st, runs southwest 55 x southwest again 33.2 x east 18.1 x south 4 9 x northeast 80 4 to Broadway, x northwest 28. Dec. 10, installs. 1,160

Moores, Robert L. and Charles A. Le Quesne mortgagors with Edwin W. Ackerman. Extension of mort. Oct. 21. nom

Moran, John to John Kerwin. North 10th st. P. M. Sept 24, 1 year. 3,000

Mullen, Joseph A. to The Brooklyn City Co-operative Building and Loan Assoc. Blake av. P. M. Dec. 10, installs. 2,500

Same to Gertrude Blake. Same property. P. M. Sub. to last mort. Dec. 10, installs, 5 %. 600

Mullowney, Richard to Marvelle W. Cooper, Putnam av. P. M. Dec. 1, 1 year, 5 %. 11,250

Same to Citizens' Savings Bank. Same property. Dec. 7, 1 year, 5 %. gold, 26,000

Myers, Louis H., Jr., to Laura R. Green, New York. 4th st, s s, 252.10 w 7th av, 19x100. Dec. 8, due Dec. 1, 1894, 5 %. 7,500

Nallin, Bridget widow to The Title Guarantee and Trust Co. Carroll st, n s, 93 w Hicks st. 20x100. Dec. 14, 3 years, 5 %. 2,000

Neely, Robert S. to Richard Goodwin. Park pl, s e cor Albany av, 80x155.7 to Butler st. Dec. 8, 6 months. gold, 53,116

Same to Josiah Lombard. Same property. Sub. to last mort. Dec 8, 1 year. 9,000

Newman, Frank R. to Louise M. Creamer. Hancock st. P. M. Dec 10, 5 years, 5 %. 10,000

Niles, Nathaniel to Emma J. Simons, Saratoga, N. Y. 6th av, e s, 60 n 2d st, 20x90. Oct. 1, 2 years. 3,500

Oakley, Emma M. wife of and George W. to S. Charles Welsh trustee Ethel H. Tweddle. 7th av, e s, 85.1 s St. Johns pl. 20.6x100. Dec. 7, 3 years, 5 % 10,000

O'Connor, Michael to The Kings County Savings Inst. North 8th st, n s, 125 e Berry st, 25x100. Dec. 12, 1 year, 5 %. 700

Olsen, Nils to Adolph Sussman. Elton st. P. M. June 9, 2 years. 200

Paisley, Louisa B. to Phebe A. Godfrey. Madison st. P. M. Dec. 15, 2 years. 2,750

Pascofsky, Solomon and Solomon Greenberg to Philip Pickelsky. Thatford av. P. M. Dec. 8, installs. 300

Peiffer, Rosa wife of and Ferdinand to Stephen T. Rushmore, Roslyn, L. I. Sunnyside av, s s, 75 e Barbey st, 37.6x110. Dec. 1, 5 years. 5,000

Pickett, Eleanor H. to William H. Reynolds. Hancock st, No. 339, n s, 347 e Tompkins av, 18x100. Dec. 16, 2 years, 5 %. 500

Pickelsky, Philip to Barnet Levin and Max Gittelsohn. Thatford av. P. M. Dec. 11. installs. 600

Rector, &c., Church of the Good Shepherd to The Brooklyn Savings Bank. McDonough st, s s, 320 w Stuyvesant av, runs west 80 x south 200 to Decatur st, x east 100 x north 100 x west 20 x north 100. Dec. 15, 1 year. 5 %. 15,000

Reed, Eliza to Richard Mayes. Bergen st, n s, 253 w Ralph av, 102x107. Dec. 9, demand 3,000

Reeveland, Emma L. to James Graham. Shepherd av. P. M. Sub. to mort. $1,800. Nov. 25, installs. 1,500

Reeves, Josie B. wife of Alfred G. to John A. Pfalzgraf. 42d st, e s, 575 n 12th av, 50x100, New Utrecht. Nov. 30, installs. 1,200

Reid, David C. to Cyrus D. Reid. St. Marks av, s s, 182 6 e Rogers av, runs south 95 x west 17 x south 55.7 x east 52.2 x north 150.7 to av, x west 35.2. Jan. 2, due July 1, 1892. 2,500

Ribber, Mamie to Ernestine Gastmeyer. Eldert st, n w s, 100 n e Evergreen av, 20x100. Dec 1, installs. 1,500

Russell, William G. with Sadie E. Rice both mortgagees. Agreement as to priority of morts. made by Michael J. Riordan. Dec. 11. nom

Rustin, Evan J. to The Title Guarantee and Trust Co. Bainbridge st, n s, 180 e Sumner av, 40x100. Dec. 12. 3 years, 5 %. 3,000

Ryan, Thomas J. to The Equitable Co-operative Building and Loan Assoc. 14th st, n e s, 212.10 n w 5th av, 20x100. Nov. 9, installs. 3,000

Samuel, Anna wife of and August E. to Andrew Van Opstal. Surf av, s s. 100.6 w old lot 19A map common lands of Gravesend, 31x100, Gravesend. Dec. 14, 2 years. 840

Schaefer, John to Valentin Massengarb. Court st, w s, 76.5 n 4th pl, 14.3x70. Nov. 25, due Jan. 1, 1895, 5 %. 1,000

Same to Mary F. Bene. Same property. Nov. 25, due Jan. 1, 1897, 5 %. 2,200

Schink, Wilhelmine wife of and Frederick C. to Reubamay Proctor. 5th av, s e s, 25 n e 14th st, 33x97.10. Dec. 11, 1 month. 800

Scofield, Walter L. to William H. Reynolds. Macon st. P. M. Dec. 1, installs, 5 %. 3,500

Scharf, Frederick to Emilie Huber. Throop av, n w cor Lexington av, 42.3x90. Dec. 11. 1 day. 2,000

Schilling, John A. to The Title Guarantee and Trust Co. 5th av, e s, 60 s 8th st, 20x80. Dec. 16, 3 years, 5 %. 7,000

Same to Charles H. Stelling. Same property. Dec. 16, due April 15, 1892. 1,000

Schmalstich, Henry to Mary Schmalstich. Ralph av, s e cor Putnam av. 19.9x80. Dec. 1, 3 years. 5 %. 5,000

Schroeter, Charles L. and Annie M. his wife to William H. Baker. Arlington av, s s, 25 e Wyona st, 25x100. Dec. 1, 3 years. 1,700

Scott, Eliza E. to Fabir Berkeley. Schermerhorn st, No. 123, n s, 125.1 w Smith st, 25x100. Dec. 14, due April 15, 1892. 235

Scully, Annie G. wife of William P. to The Title Guarantee and Trust Co. 7th st, s s, 115.2 e 5th av, 18.4x100. Dec. 9, 3 years, 5 %. 2,000

Seebeck, Christina R. wife of Ernest A. to Eliza Lietz widow and Caroline M. Lietz, Milton, N. Y. Tillary st. P. M. Nov. 30, 5 years, 5 %. 2,750

Seermann, Baruch and Meyer Marcus to Christine Towns. Eastern Parkway, s s, 25 e Thatford av, 25x100. Dec. 15, installs. 1,000

Sibley, Harry A. to William S and Thomas Ross. Quincy st, s s, 212.6 w Throop av, 18 9 x100. Dec. 9, due Jan. 1, 1893. 1,500

Same to same. Quincy st, s s, 250 w Throop av, 18 9x100. Dec. 9, due Jan. 1, 1893. 1,250

Siede, Mary M. N. widow to The Title Guarantee and Trust Co. Jefferson av. P. M. Dec. 1, 3 years, 5 %. 9,500

Siepermann, Friedrich to Louisa Grassmann. Covert st, s e s, 270.10 n e Evergreen av, 18.7 x100, Dec. 11, 1 year, 5 %. 232

Shanley, Ann wife of and Patrick to The Title Guarantee and Trust Co. Halsey st, n s, 241.8 e Sumner av, 16.8x100x16.9x98.8. Dec. 12, 3 years, 5 %. 2,000

Silberstein, Mary to Simon C. Wilson, Baldwins, L. I. Osborn st. P. M. Dec. 12, installs. 800

Silverman, Hyman to Herman F. Koepke. Belmont av, n s, 125 e Thatford av, runs east 25 x north 100 x east 2.9 x north 25 x west 52.10 x south 25 x east 25. Dec. 15, due Jan. 13, 1893. 1,400

Simon, Semche to Mary R. Bennett. Boerum st, n s, 100 e Lorimer st, 25x100. Dec. 14, 3 years. 7,000

Sims, Bessie wife of and Michael J., Jr., to Elizabeth B. Ball. Conover st, e s, 20 s Vandyke st, 40x80. Dec. 8, 1 year. 500

Sior, Heinrich to Ralph H. Tiebout. Floyd st, n s, 350 w Sumner av, 25x100. Nov. 28, 3 years. 800

Skelton, Christopher to The Title Guarantee and Trust Co. Dean st, s s, 50 w Utica av, runs south 87.11 x southwest — x south to Bergen st, x west 45 x north 107.2 x west — x north 107.2 to Dean st, x east 102. Dec. 14, installs. 5,500

Smith, Abbie C. to Edwin H. Brown. Walworth st, w s, 290 s Willoughby av, 20x100. Dec. 14, 1 year. 200

Smith, Mary to William J. Dailey. Glenmore av, n w cor Berriman st, 50x85. Dec. 15, 3 years. 1,500

Same to Henry Gartelmann, Flushing, L. I. Essex st, w s, 250 n Liberty av, 25x104.8x25x104.7. Dec. 14, 3 years. 1,000

Smith, Anna L. to George H. Smith, Great Neck, L. I. Evergreen av, w s, 75 n Stanhope st, 25x100. Dec. 16, 5 years. 1,400

Solomon, Hannah wife of and Morris to John R. McDonald. Myrtle av, n s, 200 e Tompkins av, 20x100. Dec. 16, due Dec. 1, 1892. 500

Stewart, Horatio S. to The Title Guarantee and Trust Co. Patchen av, s e cor Halsey st, 100x100. Dec. 14, demand. 15,650

Same to same. Halsey st, s s, 100 e Patchen av, 100x100. Dec. 14, demand. 10,000

Story, Jeremiah T. to L. Anna Erbacber. Fulton st. P. M. Dec. 10, 1 year, 5 %. 2,000

Same to same. Same property. P. M. Dec. 10, 5 years, 5 %. 20,000

Strickland, Maria T. to John R. McDonald. Essex st, e s, 180 n Ridgewood av. 20x100. Dec. 14, due Dec. 1, 1893. 1,900

Strumf, Louis to Wolf Patashinski. Eastern Parkway. P. M. Dec. 15, installs. 1,425

Swimm, Theodore W. to The Title Guarantee and Trust Co. Jefferson av, n s, 100 e Lewis av, 100x100. Dec. 16, demand. 37,500

Swayze, Caroline to Christopher P. Skelton. Herkimer st, s s, 180 w Buffalo av, 18x185. Nov. 2, 2 years. 1,450

Taiber, Emma to Jane Chadwick. South 2d st, s w s, 75 n w Hooper st, 25x120. Dec. 15, due Nov. 1, 1894. 2,500

Tomlinson, Charles W. to C. Olivia Sabine. Schenck av, w s, 125 n Blake av, 25x100. Dec. 11, due Feb. 12, 1892. 300

Tostevin, Samuel P. to Thomas C. Balderston et al. Supreme Trustees Order of Tonti. Osborn st, w s, 300 s Dumont av, 3 lots, each 16.8x100. 3 morts., each $1,800. Nov. 30, 3 years, 5½ %. gold, 5,400

Totten, Emma A. to Charles A. Van Lierstine. East 95th st, Canarsie. P. M. Nov. 1, 3 years. 1,000

Turner, Howard E. to The Mutual Life Ins. Co., New York. Wythe av, w s, 74 n Keap st, 37.4x62. Dec. 15, 1 year, 5 %. 5,000

Urbanowsky, Johann to August Dannenberg. Georgia av, w s, 50 n Glenmore av, 25x100. Dec. 9, 5 years. 550

Same to Tilly Hoerner. Georgia av, w s, 50 n Glenmore av, 25x100. Dec. 9, 5 years. 450

Vose, Isabel M. to The Dime Savings Bank of Brooklyn. Eastern Parkway, n s, 70 w Utica av, 70x220.7 to Degraw st. Dec. 16, 1 year, 5 %. 800

Waldron, Alexander to Mary E. Seaman. 47th st, s w s, 200 s e 4th av, 20x100.2. Dec. 7, 3 years, 5 %. 3,500

Wallace, Phebe W. wife of Andrew to Euphemia P. Del Hoyo. South 4th st, n e cor Rodney st, 20x71.3. Dec. 15, 3 years, 5 %. 2,500

Watson, Thomas J. to Nassau Co-operative Building and Loan Assoc. Pacific st, n s, 475 e Sackman st, 25x100. Dec. 8, installs. 1,750

Weber, Adolph to Henry P. Rindskopf. Nichols av. P. M. Dec. 5, 2 years, 5 %. 1,125

Webr, Charles A. to Otto Lang. Van Voorhis st, s e s, 175 n e Bushwick av, 25x100. Dec. 14, 3 years, 5 %. 4,000

Same to Peter Bertsch exr. William Broistedt. Van Voorhis st, s e s, 200 n e Bushwick av, 25x100. Dec. 14, 3 years, 5 %. 4,000

Weinkauf, Georgiana wife of Frederich to Warren C. Hubbard. Thames st, n s, 80 e Bogart st, 20x100. Dec. 11, due Dec. 1, 1894. 1,000

Wezel, Minna to John L. Gaus. Jefferson st. P. M. Dec. 15, 5 years, 5 %. 6,000

White, Adoniram J. to Sarah I. Cassin. Bay 20th st, s e s, 500 s w 86th st, 50x96.8, New Utrecht. Dec. 15, 5 years. 1,500

Wiegers, Rosina wife of Frederick to Henry Hoffmann and Mary his wife. 10th st, s s, 300 e 3d av, 25x100. Dec. 15, due Jan. 1, 1897, or installs, 5 %. 2,500

Wildner, Emil F. to The Title Guarantee and Trust Co. Madison st, n s, 325 e Central av. P. M. Dec. 14, 1 year. 1,250

Witzbrod, Matilda to Frederick Middendorf. Snediker av, e s, 90 s Hegeman av, 20x100. Dec. 12, due Jan. 1, 1894. 200

Zepp, William to John H. Recknagel, Great Neck, L. I. Stockton st, s s, 124 w Tompkins av, 41x100. Dec. 11, 2 years. 1,000

MORTGAGES----ASSIGNMENTS.

NEW YORK CITY.

DECEMBER 11 TO 17—INCLUSIVE.

Aronson, Samuel to John Palmieri. nom

Altheimer, Samuel to Henry Altheimer. $700

Buttenwieser, Leemmlein to Ellen E. Ward widow, Roslyn, L. I. 30,000

Baird, John W. and ano. exrs. John Baird to John W., David G. and Sophia A. O. Baird. 5 assigns. nom

Same to John W. Baird trustee John Baird dec'd. nom

Brown, James et al. exrs. James Brown to James C. Brown, England. Re-recorded. 11,000

Brennan, Nellie F. to Edward Brenen and Catharine his wife. 11,700

Same to William Rankin. 2 assigns., each $7,000. 14,000

Bogan, Annie E. admrx. Mary Johnston to Thomas Bogan. 5,000

Bracken, Henry to Abbie E. Wille. 3,000

Brady, John J. to Agnes K. Murphy. 780

Same to Henry Bracken. 780

Same to Edward P. Steers. 887

Same to Peter Farrell. 811

Same to Henry Bracken. 3,000

Same to Isaac Anderson. 815

Blackwell, Samuel, Brooklyn, to The Western National Bank. nom

Blakeman, Alexander N. and ano. exrs. William N. Blakeman to Caldwell R. Blakeman. 1,500

Bohm, Rudolph to Johanna Noelke. 1,500

Brown, James et al. exrs. James Brown to James C. Brown. 11,000

Cohen, Barney to Sol. Friedman & Co. Collateral to loan of 1,000

Curtis, Charles B. et al. exrs. and trustees Peter C. Cornell to Sarah D. Moran. 14,000

Conyngham, William L. to Joseph Stickney. nom

Commoss, Joseph T., Brooklyn, to Susan R. Kendall. 3,020

Christensen, Rasmus to George Muller. 4,000

De Veau, Joseph M. to William J. Hoppin trustee Azelia Whitmore. 4,500

Diamond, Elizabeth, Albany, N. Y., to Franklin P. Roberge. nom

d'Aguiar, Alice widow to Isabel M. Cassidy. 500

Egbert, Edward T. to Carrie C. wife of George W. Barlow, Shrewsbury, N. J. 5,123

Howe, Robie S. to Florence A. Gates, Boston, Mass. 1,000

Hoctor, James E. to John B. Smith. 2,500

Hoffart, Charles and Karoline his wife to August Hassey. 10,000

Hepburn, William H., White Plains, N. Y., to Belle H. Edmonds, White Plains, N. Y. 1,600

Hyatt, George E. to Edward Winslow. nom

Same to same. nom

Jones, Louis M. to Luke Connor. 1,000

Jencks, Francis M. to William N. Crane guard. of William M. Crane and trustee of Annie L. Merriam. nom

Same to same. nom

Jacobs, Edward and ano. trustees of Sarah Salomon to Joseph C. Levi exr. and trustee Sarah Salomon. nom

Kuschewsky, Raphael to Sender Jarmulowsky. 2,000

Same to same. 2,000

Karst, John D., Jr., to Jacob Korn. 9,000

Lawyers' Title Ins. Co. of New York to Ann E. Dorsey. 22,716

Leger, Henry to David S. Paige. 6,990

Levy, Bernard S. to Robinson Gill trustee. nom

Loonie, James J. and Eugene Parker to David J. King et al. exrs. and trustees Edward J. King. 27,169

Loonie, Dennis to James J. Loonie and Eugene Parker. 27,000

Man, William trustee to William J. Hoppin trustee Azalia W. Steele. 2,662

Same to same. 3,571

Mutual Life Ins. Co., New York, to William Man trustee. 3,500

Martin, Emily de F. formerly Roelofson, Paris, France, to Fannie A. Wotherspoon. 7,500

Middlebrook, Frederic J., Brooklyn, to Mary E. Robert. 10,015

Same to same. 8,012

Same to Susan C. Herriman et al. exrs. John Herriman. 14,019

Moran, Theodore T. exr. Sarah D. Moran to Mary E. Robert. 14,138

McPherson, William J. to Susan E. Kerby. 2 assigns., each $500. 1,000

Morgenthau, Henry to R. Clarence Dorsett. nom

Mandelbaum, Harris to Betsey Davis. 3,000

Marks, Francis M. to Julia F. Chamberlin. 755

Parkes, John F. and Frederick W., Tonowanda, N. Y., to George R. Perry. nom

Prescott, Edward C. to Dora Grom. 500

Peck, George G. to John B. Smith. nom

Same to same. nom

Potter, Howard N. et al. exrs. Virginia M. Potter to Clarkson A. Potter. nom

Rice, Charlotte A. and Charles M. to William C. Williams, Michigan. nom

Rowland, Alice S. and ano. exrs. Ursula D. A. Story to Charles C. Marshall. nom

Robert, Mary E. to The New York Security and Trust Co. 15,023

Randell, Evelyn to Seth Wheeler, Albany, N. Y. 3,500

Rochester, Roswell H. exr. and trustee George H. Mumford to George D. Mumford. 10,000

Roberts, Thomas to John F. Betz & Son (Lim.), Philadelphia. 750

Stearns, George A., Long Island City, to LeRoy Clark. nom

Sire, Meyer L. to Charles Frazier. 6,000

Smith, Isaac L. to Bertha Smith. nom

Smith, Mary B., Brooklyn, to Nelson M. Whipple. 3,000

Smith, Edward T. to Edward Weil. 3,750

Snowden, Cora A., Greensborough, Md., to Jane E. Davis, White Plains, N. Y. 1,000

Stebling, Herman M. to Adolph G. Hupfel. 300

Steitz, Henry and John J. to Sarah L. Keen, Philadelphia. 3,065

Thompson, Henrietta G. to William Man trustee. 2,662

Thornton, William M. to Charles Dexheimer. 2,250

The New York Lumber and Wood Working Co. to John L. Brewster. nom

Title Guarantee and Trust Co. to The General Theological Seminary of the Protestant Episcopal Church in the U. S. of America. 36,500

Same to Daniel D. Wright. 6,000

Title Guarantee and Trust Co. to Archibald Phillips, Jr. 1,800

Same to Charles von Eiff. 14,000

Title Guarantee and Trust Co. to The Society for the Relief of the Destitute Blind of City of New York and Vicinity. 9,000

Same to same. 12,000

Todd, Judson S. to Edward Winslow. nom

Wuesthoff, Emma and Bertha to Susan E. Kerby. 3,042

Whipple, Nelson M. to Andrew Ebsen. nom

Winslow, Edward to Henry W. Ford trustee Augustus H. Ward. nom

KINGS COUNTY.

DECEMBER 10 TO 16—INCLUSIVE.

Alexander, George P. to Maud P. Nelson. $3,000

Ashenfarb, Samuel to Laurence A. Whitehill. 240

Bailey, Frank to Kate Rockefeller. 800

Same to same. 600

Same to same. 1,000

Brundage, James H. to Theodore Kiendi. 300

Brown, Melvin to Edwin B. Smith. 1,150

Same to same. 950

Same to same. 1,100

Brown, William to Joseph M. Shea. nom

Chinnock, Elizabeth L. to George C. Jeffery and Nathan Kaplan. nom

Conway, William J. to John Pullman. nom

Doody, Daniel to Mary E. De Wint. 500

Dougherty, J. Hampden and ano. exrs. Thomas D. Hudson to Alice H. Dougherty. 750

Dusenbury, Charles H. to Annagusta B. Darling. nom

Dettmer, Jacob G. to William Ziegler. 20,000

Flynn, Rose L. to Maggie Robinson. 650

Forman, Rebecca F. to Sarah M. Bergen. 300

Finch, George to Ottilie Haag. 1,000

Franklin Trust Co. trustee Ellen M. Blackwell to Ellen M. Blackwell. 2 assigns. nom

Griswold, Almon H. to Charles D. Rust. 1,875

German-American Real Estate Title Guarantee Co. to Richard Hamilton exr. and trustee Ann T. Brown. 3,500

Hull, Lilly to Anna R. Fink formerly Ficken. 1,500

Humbert, William P. to Juliet L. Humbert. nom

Hall Sash and Door Co. to Elizabeth A. Hall. 1,200

Ingraham, Henry C. M. to Mary J. Halsted. 3,300

Johnson, Ephraim admr. Cornelius L. Johnson to Lizzie C. Hodges. 3,800

Kimball, Martha L. to Alfred B. Lounsbery. 9,000

Kings County Impt. Co. to The Seventeenth Ward Bank. nom

Kowatsch, Franz to John F. Brugel. 450

Kaplan, Nathan and George C. Jeffery to Carrie L. Winne. nom

Kernochan, Walton O. to Joseph H. Kernochan. 1,500

Lawrence, Francis to Barron Davis. 2,520

Ledoux, Paul W. to Charles E. Rogers. nom

Lippmann, Leopold J. to Mary E. Watson. nom

Lang, Joseph to Guernsey Sackett. 500

MacNaughton, Emeline H. to Charles D. Smith, Huntington, L. I. 4,000

Maguire, Charles E. to Minnie wife of Martin Bennett. 625

Man, William trustee to William J. Hoppin trustee of Azelia W. Steele. 2,000

Mayer, Richard to Joseph A. and Marvin Cross. 1,016

Molloy, Catharine to Emma L. Johnson and Ida W. Bragan. 1,200

Mulvihill, Margaret to Jacob Heutz. 2,240

Nostrand, George E. to Cornelia L. Upson, Jersey City, N. J. 500

Same to Elise A. Martin extrx. Isaac Martin. 6,000

Pratt, Joseph H. to James W. Pratt. 500

Palmer, Anna C. to Laura A. wife of William R. Bell. 2,500

Pickelsky, Philip to Barrnet Levin and Max Gittelsohn. 300

Pokalsky, Max and Louis Lebewold to Louis Gordon. 690

Rust, Charles D. to James Murray and Catharine his wife. 1,080

Rust, Charles D. to Maud A. Griswold. 2,500
Shipman, Edward R. to Frank Wickstead. 400
Siedler, Charles recvr. of The Lorillard Brick Works Co. to The Gallatin National Bank. nom
Same to same. nom
Stearns, John M. to Catharine E. Hockemeyer 1,400
Smith, Herbert C. to William Brown. nom
Sturges, Stephen B. to Charles G. Spencer. 8,500
Snedeker, Margaret to Margaret E. Goldstone, Pine Hill, N. Y. 500
Stewart, James and Mary J. to Alexander F. Zundt. 800
Title Guarantee and Trust Co. to Garetta P. Hagemeyer. 5,000
Same to Charles H. Lowerre. 12,000
Same to Zacheus Bergen et al. exrs. Robert A. Robertson. 5,000
Same to Edwin Packard trustee Clara H. Fincke. 9,000
Same to same. 3,000
Same to The Franklin Trust Co. guard. Edwin S. Stanton. 3,500
Same to same as trustee for children of Cornelia S. Dow. 10,000
Same to Ethan M. Wright. 2,000
Same to Carrie L. Gibson. 800
Same to The Brooklyn Children's Aid Soc. 6,500
Same to Zacheus Bergen et al. exrs. and trustees Robert A. Robertson. 8,000
Same to Frederick R. and William B. Welles trustees Geo. W. Welles. 2,000
Same to Frederick R. Welles trustee for Annie R. Low. 2,000
Same to Julia A. Taylor. 3,000
Same to Eugene A. Lane. 4,000
Underhill, Mary K. extrx. Bailey Underhill to Jesse H. Griffen. 850
Van Pelt, John V. to William C. Lowther. 2,210
Vandusen, Martin B. to Elizabeth Taber et al. exrs. Franklin W. Taber. 352
Weinberger, Bernhard to Samuel Ashenfarb. nom
Wilson, Ellen, Middlebush, N. J., to John Wilson her husband. nom
Woolley, James V. S. to Remsen Johnson. nom
Weil, Henry to John Williamson. 16,084
Wildner, Emil F. to Mary H. Hendrickson. 1,800
Wertheimer, Sarah admrx. Louis Wertheimer to Sarah Wertheimer. 7,500

JUDGMENTS.

NEW YORK CITY.

Dec.

12 Austin, William P—Patrick Cassidy.. $208 80
12 Albright, Charles H—Ninth Nat Bank 1,243 63
14 Alsdorf, John—Terrant & Co........ 906 19
14 Allen, Rudolph—Diedrich Toujes.... 219 22
14 Anderton, Ralph L; Auderton, Edward K } J E Granniss. 566 00
15 Adams, Otto—A A Thomson......... 144 96
15 Aarons, Charles—Isaac Levy......... 387 18
15 Archer, Frank M—W H Van Cott.... 380 26
15 Abrams, Otto—P J King........... 93 10
17 Aldrich, Alfred J—M H Murray.... 78 8
12 Brady, Daniel M—H J Ewing....... 71 57
12 Brown, Henry—J M Canda.......... 2,777 15
12†Brown, Charles H—Berthold Veit.... 97 58
14 Benedict, Henry W—Union Stove Works.......... 130 48
14 Bryant, Carolin O'Brien—Julia A Shaw.......... 21,036 88
14 Bryant, Agnes Clare—the same,... 7,015 15
14 Bryant, Amanda I—the same...... 7,015 15
14 Bryant, Carolin O'Brien; Bryant, Agnes Clare; Bryant, Amanda I } the same.. .....costs 1,638 31
14 Brown, George Y—J E Granniss..... 866 00
14†Bornstein, Elias—Gustav Goldman... 61 15
14 Bacon, George H—Thomas Vernon... 5,397 49
14 the same—A C Haynes... ..... 1,803 00
14 Burke, Thomas F—J P Farrell....... 183 43
14 Bousel, Albert—Mary Bullowa....... 88 85
14 Behlmer, John F—Joseph Marren.... 659 00
15 Brady, Eugene; Brady, Philip H } People State N Y. 1,000 00
15 Barclay, Alexander—Tidewater Oil Co.......... 840 56
15 Beers, Joseph F—E C Hazard........ 135 50
15 Bennett, Otto—N Y Iron Roofing and Corrugating Co.......... 179 00
15 Ball, Charles S—the same........... 149 22
15 Bayne, William H; Bayne, Bushrod R } Farmers' and Merchants' Nat Bank of Baltimore... ...... 1,889 93
15 Brommond, Adolph—Ernst Zerweck. 869 86
15 Bachmann, Frederick—Margaret Sheehy.......... 452 49
15 Bateman, Arthur E—Fr Beck & Co.. 1,653 96
15 Boden, Joseph D—P J Krugg......... 93 10
16 Bailey, William—Cecilia A Walsh.... 83 50
16 Brownell, Harry C—John Patterson. 114 92
16†Blumstein, Louis—Max Levy........ 66 25
16 Benson, Louisa, admrx William Annan—J E Leviness.......... 350 87
16 Baker, James—H C Ditmar, admr... 589 76
16 Bennett, William J—Henry Brunhild. 374 87
16 Breunig, Wendelin—George Ebret... 278 88
16 Byrne, John—Richard Vom Hofe.... 127 61
16 Farron, Esther E—Joseph Toch...... 121 78
16 Blanchard, Charles A—F P Osborn... 198 52
16 Bliss, Cornelius N—R A Maxwell, sup't..........costs 160 56
16 Bryan, Harry C—J W Haaren..costs 113 12
17 Bernard, Peter A—John Moore 87 33
17 Brooks, James Wilton—C C Langill.. 207 21
17 Baker, Ismar—Joseph Sawyer........ 1,060 19
18 Blunt, Edgar S—M S Wise, recvr.... 287 78
18 Bennett, Joseph—Denis Manning..... 294 88
18 Benedix, Augustus—Edward Weigner. 97 37
12 Chapman, Rebecca—D L McDonald.. 73 84
12 Chace, Earl B—J L Brewster........ 8,174 27
12 Cummings, William A—Ninth Nat Bank.......... 1,243 63
14 Carroll, Frank J—George Sieburg.... 95 20
14 Carey, James F—William Noble..... 321 25
14 Campbell, Belle—F W Sprado....... 123 32
14 Clarkin, Peter—Bensinger Self Adding Cash Register Co.......... 46 10
14 the same—the same.......... 46 47
15 Conklin, George W—C H Burmeister. 596 58
15*Campbell, Eliza J—Farmers' and Merchants' Nat Bank of Baltimore..... 1,889 93
15 Corcoran, John—G W Miller......... 111 62
16†Crilley, Dan[illegible]—Francis Higgins, recvr 171 65
16 Clark, John [illegible]—B J Piatti.......... 822 13
16 Cahill, Mar[illegible]—Robert Lawson..... 413 17
17 Cree, Eugen[illegible]—M H Murray......... 119 72
17 Cardwell, S[illegible]bia, extrx Sam'l Cardwell—Jacob Rauth.......... 462 96
17 Crosher, James—T E Chidester...... 208 28
18 Clark, Edwin—R L Redfield, recvr... 77 50
18*Cavinato, Louis; Cavinato, Guiseppe; *Cavinato, Christian } J S Brown..... 206 99
18 Cure, U S Grant—T E Greacen...... 234 70
18 Coschina, Frank—F T Wall, trustees. 1,631 48
18 Collins, Robert B—S S Sands........ 270 85
12 Dempsey, William—J F Rogers...... 284 34
12 the same—the same........... 326 66
14 Doyle, Andrew T—Union Stove Works.......... 150 48
14 David, Albert A—J T Leavitt........ 608 31
14 Dougherty, James—Real Estate Record Assoc.......... 40 50
15 Dormus, Charles G—J T Hoyt.... 118 48
15 the same—Joseph Marren.... 868 48
15 Dooley, John J—W G Peckham.... 174 85
15 Dayton, Abraham H—William Roeber 121 98
15 Dahlstrom, Edward—Charles Lapin... 545 67
15†Dauvray, Helen—John Sutherland... 252 98
16 Dempsey, William—E F Reynolds.... 207 31
16 Disken, Martin—Thurber, Whyland Co.......... 234 42
16 Dolan, Thomas F—Joseph Walsh.... 859 94
16 Devas, Hubert E—C E Stump........ 100 98
16 Dodge, Albert L, Jr—H A Bonta..... 83 98
17 Davenport, William B, exr Samuel Cardwell—Jacob Rauth.......... 462 96
17 Ditbridge, George W—D F Payne.... 753 37
17 the same—the same.......... 2,681 99
17 the same—Daniel Payne........ 1,626 85
17 David Adolph—S C Welsh, exr....... 300 74
17 Dubois, Julius—Ferdinand Strauss... 866 66
17 de Fina, Ettore—F P Osborn 76 18
18 Dimond, Joseph H—J J Finlay....... 161 57
18 Disbrow, Florence, admrx Elizabeth Sands—C E Wells, admr.......... 3,127 70
18 the same—Mary C Burke, extrx 569 65
18 Dwyer, Thomas—Thomas O'Callahan, Jr.......... 2,219 21
18 Dirisch, James—F T Wall.......... 1,631 48
18 Downs, Daniel H—V H Rothschild. 100,000 00
18*Darling, William S—Emily M Plummer.......... 449,166 92
14 Ester, Llewellyn G—H H Armstead.. 276 05
14 Klitsvander, Selena—A F W Leslie.... 229 55
15 Ehrgott, Mrs Levenia—W M Reynolds 95 91
15 Ewing, Frederick—J G Tait.......... 99 68
18 Elias, Michael A—J A Davis.......... 65 74
15 Edmond, Alexander McF—Alexander Smith & Sons Carpet Co.. ...costs 136 32
12 Fleming, James S—I P Smith....... 332 55
12 Foley, Michael—J C Provost......... 137 21
12 Fenno, Henry—J A Duchane... .... 1,454 25
12 Frankau, Joseph—W D Woods........ 73 98
12 Felt, George H—Western Nat Bank.. 309 36
12 Fitch, Arden S—Eugene Kelly....... 330 66
12 the same—the same.......... 376 41
12 Feinberg, Theresa—Bernard Berman. 100 87
14 Friedman, Samuel—Joseph Cohn..... 89 86
14 Francklyn, Charles G—H E Howland 5,202 78
14 the same—the same.......... 5,052 78
14 Flynn, Thomas C; Flynn, Cornelius } Gertrude Knelles. 177 21
15 Foster, Julius—Reading Stove Works 272 65
15*Flannigan, Thomas F—A A Thomson 144 56
15 Franke, Emil—Karl Zipf........... 43 60
16 Fox, Elizabeth J—Lena Kopetzky.... 250 00
16 Friedrichs, Walter R—James Macbeil 95 97
16 Foxwell, Charles, Jr—J W Thompson 129 04
16 Fairchild, Horace J—R A Maxwell, Superintendent..........costs 160 56
17 Fusco, Guiseppe—Bradley & Currier Co (Lim).......... 2,165 63
17 Frazer, Ida—Emma L Mildeberger... 596 64
18 *Falk, Abraham; Falk, Zachariah; *Falk, Washington } C N Bliss....... 7,939 00
18 Floyd, Theodore B—T E Greacen.... 284 70
18 Finch, Cornelius M—V H Rothschild 100,000 00
14 Gulke, August W—Louis Schwartz... 44 00
14 Goerlitz, Philip—Leo Seilke.......... 268 87
15 Gallivan, Michael J—E P Hincks..... 98 38
15 Gilbert, Jabez C—Albert Gray....... 243 72
15 Good, James W—Carrie W Bell...... 484 78
15†Gans, David—Lewis Steinhardt...... 46 72
15 Ginsberg, Bernard—E D Vanderbilt.. 157 57
15 Gilbert, John W—H J Hartig........ 169 52
16 Goerlitz, Philip—Jacob Stockinger... 2,055 11
16 Gilbert, Dr William H—J T White... 33 02
16 Ginsburg, Bernhard—Joseph Marren. 403 20
16 Glotzer, Benjamin—Solomon Markstein.......... 491 46
16 Goodwin, Thomas—Frances A Parker, admrx.......... 157 23
16 Gildersleeve, Henry—F S Van Horn.. 228 68
17 Griesmeyer, Carl L—F P Osborn..... 1,819 46
17 Goldstein, Harris—Dry Dock, East Broadway & Battery R R Co..costs 23 61
17 Gardner, Charles E—Robert Beggs. ....costs 160 60
18 Gillette, Rittie—William De Mott.... 95 86
18 Gundling, David; Gundling, Harry } Leopold Stern..... 411 06
18*Gangel, Max—Engelbert Hardt...... 805 24
18 Gans, Gertrude—Emanuel Eising.... 431 65
18 Goodwin, Landon R—E P Arnold.... 108 67
18 Glander, Charles—J H Horstmann... 527 06
18 Girven, John H—G R Fisk.......... 149 13
18 Goldsmith, Ida—Herman Bornemann 845 70
12 Harman, Augustus H—J M Canda... 2,777 15
14 Howell, Eugene N—Bank of America. 5,120 56
14 Hyatt, George W—August Klipstein. 250 75
14 Herzog, Rosa—N Y Elevated R R Co. 203 78
14 Hollister, Robert A—J M Sinclair.... ....costs 72 96
14 the same—the same........costs 72 96
15 Howard, Mary F—B J Dreyfuss...... 486 39
15 Hauser, Gottfried I—Twelfth Ward Bank.......... 200 00
15 Hass, Franz—German Exchange Bank.......... 322 12
15 Hauser, G Julius—John Barnutz 673 19
15 Hahn, John; *Hahn, George V } Mary C de Terrouenne.......... 1,379 59
15 Hewison, Charles W—F A Kassebohm 123 49
15 Hofele, Ferdinand W—Christian Striffler.......... 2,043 96
16 Hoff, Lewis—Garfield Nat Bank...... 781 92
16 Hess, Simon—Long Island R R Co. ....costs 142 47
17 Hetsch, Julia E—N Y Bank Note Co.. 1,549 15
17 Hammerstein, Jacob—L B Schuler... 211 77
17 Hirsch, Jacob; *Herris, Amanda } Abram Hahn..... 46 70
17 Herrenschmidt, Gustave—Edmond Fossier.......... 347 65
17 Herman, Theodore—S C Welsh, exr.. 300 74
17 Hofmeister, Christian—Pauline Hofmeister.......... 1,866 34
17 the same—W E Rosenbaum.... 651 34
17 Hughes, Thomas—J W Flynn........ 143 21
18 Handler, Joseph—J G Gerber........ 136 53
18 Hatch, Alfrederick S; Hatch, Frederick H } D E Merritt.. 329 98
18 Henry, Hugh—George Day........... 889 47
18 Heldt, John—Denis Manning........ 294 88
12 Irvine, Henry E—Commercial Bank.. 617 49
12 Irving, James—J E Stillwell......... 78 85
14 Ill, Theresa—G C Goeller............ 42 50
16 Ingram, Edwin—E G Stedman....... 139 96
12 Johns, George C—Emily Blackwell... 2,387 70
14 Jerkowski, Marcus—J T Leavitt...... 608 31
14 Jewett, James C—E O Thompson..... 113 17
15 Jungbluth, Antoine—Fridolin Arnoult 220 93
15 Jetter, Thomas—Charles Kaufman... 615 16
15 Jacobs, Isaac—Lewis Steinhardt..... 46 72
16 Jacobs, William—C F Kremer....... 94 85
16 Johnson, Robert A—D A Doren..... 53 15
17 Jacobs, Max L—C F Kremer......... 83 43
12 Kilgore, William—Bohlke Rosenbohm. 247 51
12 Kimmey, William W—John Cleverley. 289 57
14 Kraemer, Louis—Anthony Fischer... 162 20
14 Kerwin, Patrick H—Thomas Frawley. 250 50
14 Komp, Albert—Real Estate Record Assoc.......... 22 55
14 Kleneck, William H—Frederick Yung. ....costs 69 47
15 Knoll, Charles E—J B Dill........... 122 77
15 Kelshaw, Jonathan—W S Bagg....... 95 93
15 King, Hugh—Thomas Reilly, admr.. 1,943 64
15 the same—William Murtagh.... 1,942 64
16 Ketcham, Isabella; Ketcham, Charles J } C J Martin.... 194 32
16 Kaiser, John A, Jr; *Kaiser, George F } David Mayer.... 2,044 00
17 Kuhn, Gustave A—Joseph Cavinato. ....costs 108 31
17 Kelaher, Thomas F—J M Ferber.... 80 85
17 Kesselman, Tony—F H Wood, recvr. 3,520 04
18 Kruse, Henry F—Bernard Zwinge... 1,901 17
12 Lautenbach, Samuel—Simon Levy... 71 45
12 Lawler, Thomas J—W H Duecker... 140 68
12 Lichtenstein, Henry—H J Lenz...... 285 36
12 Luttman, Selig—the same.......... 351 85
12 Loeb, Max—Martha Kemp, extrx.... 440 93
14 Leoser, Charles McK—F M Cronin... 414 54
14 L'Hommedieu, Sylvester Y—Nat State Bank of Camden.......... 3,584 14
15 Lasher, George B—N Y Iron Roofing and Corrugating Co.......... 145 17
15 Levy, Julius; Levy, Augustus H; Levy, Moses S } J D W Joy...... 854 14
16 Lorillard, Jacob—Danbury Nat Bank 6,049 64
16 Luhring, John H—Carl Hartwig..... 84 93
16 Lange, John C F—Adolf Volkhardt.. 20 63
16 Loeser, John F—J W Haaren........ 113 12
17 Lockhart, James—L C King.......... 285 30
17 Levy, Isaac—Sigmund Asbner...costs 73 99
17 Lerche, Albrecht J—Phebe A Henderson.......... 249 53
18 Lithauer, Leo—J A Nutter........... 67 55
12 Mulryan, Mary—C E Strong, trustee ....costs 77 93
12†Moses, Raphael—Lucian Wolf...... 176 25
12*Madden, William—J C Watson Co... 103 14
12 Meyer, Siegmund T—W C Sheldon... 5,404 15
12 Mack, Isaac S—Thomas Martin...... 152 92
14 Myers, Sinclair—Metropolitan Telephone and Telegraph Co.......... 59 14
14 Mahler, Michael—Harlem River Bank.......... 979 10
14 Matthews, James C—J W Thompson. 1,169 59
14 Maynard, Orrin C—D L Phillips..... 345 48
14 Murray, Robert—S G Hirschberg.... 101 29
14 Murphy, Matthew—Mary Bullowa.. 33 35
14 Merritt, William J—J M Sinclair.. ....costs 72 96
15 Mosback, Adam—C H Lowen........ 741 20
15 Motley, Thornton N; Motley, James M } Albert Gray.. 243 73
15 Marcus, Solomon—Robert Reis & Co. 259 08
15 Mathews, Elizabeth A—J A Nesbit. ....costs 78 86

15 More, George W—A C Stevens.... .. 66 50
15 Morris, Abraham—Hermann Kuhn.. 262 19
16 MacEvoy, Charles—Market and Fulton Nat Bank.......................... 699 17
16 Meyer, Sigmund T / Meyer, Arthur L } D W Moran.... 161 98
16 Myers, Sinclair—Edmund Coffin, Jr.. 3,318 47
16 Masbach, Hermann—Central Stamping Co.......................... 141 00
16 Mehl, Jacob—Morris Jacobs.......... 947 00
16 Meyer, Maurice—Adolph Alexander.. 352 18
16 Mackay, Donald—R A Maxwell, sup't ....costs 160 56
17 Meyer, Regina—H W McAllester..... 194 63
17 Matthias, George—J W Binney 950 94
17 Mayhew, Edward C—W W Fouche... 154 22
17 Murphy, James—F E Stephens........ 105 37
17 Mayers, Isaac—Racine Wagon and Carriage Co.......................... 159 59
17 Mellen, Letitia A—Thomas Sullivan.. 311 50
17 Mercer, Matthew H—F W Carmon... 146 02
17 Mackenzie, George—Felix Jellenik.... 324 84
17+Mathias, Martin—James Muir......... 137 72
17 Meyer, John H—T L Herberger, admr 159 01
18 Manning, James R—S L Deutsch..costs 219 02
18 Murphy, Frank D—W I Rosenfeld.... 336 00
18 Meagher, James—James Mathews.... 122 78
18 Martenfeld, Henry—Henry Hahnenfeld.............................. 105 26
12*Mcwilliams, John—W H Duecker.... 140 68
12*McEathron, James E—J C Watson Co 907 86
14 McNulty, William—Joseph Probst.... 42 35
14 McManus, Patrick H—H M Bendheim 115 50
14 McIntyre, Hiram F—W H Schieffelin 534 00
14 McNulty, Henry F—Eugene Friebourg.............................. 29 50
16 Mac Evoy, Charles—Market and Fulton Nat Bank.................... 699 17
16 McGoldrick, John—John Gottschalk.. 163 00
16 Mackay, Donald—R A Maxwell, superintendent.... .... costs 160 56
17 Mackenzie, George—Felix Jellenik.... 324 84
18 McCarthy, Marcus B—H E Van Fleet. 70 64
18 the same——C J Miller.......... 141 71
18 McBride, Corinne E—Diedrich Nebuhr........ .... 132 56
18 McKenzie, John / McPherson, Duncan } W E Pruden.. 68 76
14 Nimmo, Sarah J / Nimmo, Charles W } Frank Mullen... 193 83
14 the same——the same............ 215 88
14 Neuwald, Ignatz—Jacob Loeb........ 33 65
14 Nicholson, Andrew B—W H Howe... 129 91
14 Newman, Michael—Becky Dresden... 68 00
15 Nathusius, Oscar A—J M Schley..... 37 50
17 Nugent, Harry—F E Stephens........ 105 37
18 Nason, James H—James Reid...costs 136 19
18 Nassberg, Moris—Louis Barth........ 91 82
18 Nelson, Gustav—Engelbert Hardt.... 805 24
14*Oeding, Henry—Henry Eggers....... 282 87
14 Oppenhayn, Julius—F A Reichardt... 549 05
14 O'Brien, Michael D—Harlem Lighting Co 344 05
15 Overton, William B—Bernard Kreizer 74 87
16 Osborne, Thomas—J F Peters......... 321 39
16 Overton, William B—T B Kniffin.... 73 17
18 Osborn, Henry S—S L Goodman.... 11,486 37
14 Peloubet, Seymour S—Albert Davis.. 1,105 83
14 Pickhardt, Emil B—J L Cavanagh... 286 26
14 Pool, Richard N—F W Hamer.. ..... 279 86
14 Pinney, Martin—Chase Nat Bank....2,604 80
15 Potter, Daniel C—A M Arneberg..... 220 84
15 Price, Katharine—Caroline P Jehl... 123 68
15 Price, Frank S—Twelfth Ward Bank. 200 00
15 Philips, Thomas C—Alice Leaman. ....costs 771 06
15 Power, Charles E—John Sutherland. 252 98
16 Pertsch, Frederick F / Pertsch, William A } Henry Lindenmeyr........ 188 37
16 Peterson, Henry E—K M Wallach. ....costs 73 77
17 Peck, Lester O—Richards Paper Co...2,391 56
17 Phillips, Frank, assignee Henry L Davis—Max Radt................. 812 00
17 Platto, Frank C—W F Lyman......... 182 14
18 Prager, Myer W—Benjamin Hirsch.. 1,676 95
18 Patterson, Thomas F—S L Deutsch... .... costs 219 02
18 Pierson, Edward D—A V Whiteman 100 31
12 Quin, Joseph P—M T Maine.......... 311 05
14 Quinn, John F—Margaret Leacey, admrx.............................. 119 60
13 Roberts, Irene B / Roberts, Nathan B, exrs / Edward Roberts } Thomas Dollard...... 109 74
12 Rosenheim, Isidor—Thomas Martin.. 152 72
14 Ruttenberg, Benjamin—Charles Lewis 267 60
14+Roman, Mary—Myers Schorsch...... 62 33
14 Reilly, John—Coleman Brewing Co.. 112 28
14 Rhodes, Herbert G—W P Nollman.... 242 97
15 Robinson, Frederic—C E Hansen..... 322 70
15 Ryan, James J—Julius Requard...... 186 71
15 Remington, Tony—Thomas Stapleton. 103 50
15 Rosphendler, Solomon—Julia Raduziner.............................. 117 51
16 Root, James H—Quaker City Nat Bank... ....6,552 79
16 Radlein, John H—E C Korner........ 126 61
16 Riley, James—Mary L Barbey........ 845 29
16 the same——Mary L March.. ....1,316 40
16 Rapp, Herman / Roggenbrodt, August W } J W Hanren, costs 113 12
17 Rosenberg, Lewis—Joseph Sawyer....1,060 19
17 Rich, Aquila B—J N Goldbacher.... 192 25
17 Russell, Lillian—J C Duff........costs 97 33
18 Robinson, Frederick W—S L Goodman 11,486 37
18 Rawak, Henry—W B Doutney....... 120 36
12 Schmeckenbecher, John G / Schmeckenbecher, George } Joseph Braun. 323 10
12 Snook, W W—C B Fosdick...... ....2,912 25
12 Steindler, Joseph—Ninth Nat Bank.. 1,243 63
14*Scott, George H—Metropolitan Telephone and Telegraph Co.............. 52 14
14 Silva, Hester—Amanda Hall......... 525 58
14 Schiff, John—J L Leavitt....... .... 603 31
14 Schmeckenbecher, John / Schmeckenbecher, George } Samuel Pollock 1,033 49
14 the same——the same.... ....1,161 65
14 Saloshin, Louis—Herman Elsas..costs 178 10
14 Seggermann, Martha G—Hillis Plantation Coffee Co...............costs 55 08
14 Samelson, Moses—R J Cullen......... 212 96
14 Sullivan, Jeremiah / Sullivan, James E } James Chambers (Lim)......... 105 79
15 Sweeney, John M—Haydenville Mfg Co.............................. 173 77
15 Schwab, Gabriel / *Schwab, Abraham / *Schwab, Nathan / *Schwab, Leo L } Theodore Wernwag.........1,556 50
15*Simouson, Michaelis—R S Frost...... 773 28
15 Steverson, Vernon K—Dore Lyon.... 120 08
15 Stuart, George E—Bank of Harlem... 114 01
15+Sommer, Maurice—H H Schwietering 1,276 00
15 +Steenworth, Frederick J / *Steenworth, Charles J } J J Phelan. 169 00
15 Sassi, Thomasso—R J Mills......costs 110 57
15 Schneider, Charles—N C Backer.....5,366 75
15 the same——the same.......... ..3,284 96
15 Stern, Albert C—J H Deakin......... 317 49
15 Salminen, Henry—Alexandra Salminen.......................... costs 37 30
15 Shea, Timothy J—Herrmann Weiller 398 75
15 Stern, Jacob / *Sonneborn, Frederick } E H Van Ingen.........1,315 18
15*Streppone, Pasquale—Herman Frank. 421 32
16 Scott, George H—Edmund Coffin, Jr, 3,318 47
16 Short, William J—Thurber, Whyland Co.................... .... 105 68
16 Spittler, Bernard—R S Luqueer...... 76 31
16 Schmidt, Frederick—C J Warren..... 264 78
16 Schwarzler, Joseph—Gertrude Jewett, exr and trustee..................(D) 3,410 77
16 Steinbach, Edward—Elizabeth Steinbach.............................. 40 52
16 Silver, John S—C O Thompson......2,875 53
17 Schrieber, Ezekiel—Sigmund Ashner ....costs 73 99
17 Stuckey, William H, Jr—S S Hatt, assignee.............................. 82 37
17 Schwab, August—State Bank........ 360 17
17 Sullivan, Marie D—Julia M Schermerhorn.............................. 383 61
17 Storm, Walton—T W Dwight........ 269 35
17 Stern, Jacob—Joseph Sawyer........ 463 06
17 Sterner, Jacob A—C F Ketcham...... 16 12
17 Schwartz, Samuel—Max Bernstein... 97 58
17 Simon, Kaspar—Jacob Appell........ 136 57
17 Somerville, John A—H B Gayley, recvr.............................. 212 82
18 Sommer, Morris—G F Vietor.........1,448 27
18 Sonnaud, Annie—Louis Barth........ 91 82
18 Sawyer, Joseph / Sawyer, Joseph D } S L Deutsch, costs 219 02
18 Soltz, Arcadius—German Exchange Bank..... .... 197 36
18 Simmons, J Edward, recvr American Loan and Trust Co—G R Gibson... 569 11
18 Schmidt, George C—C J Warren..... 341 50
18 Stoney, Wesley—Emily M Plummer.......... ....449,066 92
12 Smith, John—J F Rogers.............. 325 66
14 Smith, Jay K / Smith, Andrew K } Chace Nat Bank.....2,604 80
15 Smith, Anna Dennison—Percival Knauth..... .... 528 65
16 Smith, James J—August Muller...... 73 43
18 Smith, John W—W G Schuyler 500 72
18 Smith, Edward—John Leonard...... 693 75
12 Andrus & Conklin Tobacco Co—Walter Logan................ .... 28 00
12 The Society for Savings in City of Cleveland—E S Hand............ 971 10
12 Snook Glove Mfg Co—C B Fosdick... 2,912 25
12 Cohnfeld Co—Lewis Seasongood...exr 1,966 25
12 the same——the same............1,271 74
12 the same——the same............1,966 28
12 the same——the same. 570 64
14 the same——the same............ 311 08
14 Hurley Stone Co—T N Motley........ 183 48
14 The Hudson River Boot and Shoe Mfg Co—Bank of America..............5,120 55
14 Toiletts Publishing Co—J K Sheffield. 1,970 27
14 Waters Paper Construction Co—J M Warren & Co....................... 218 73
14 the same——Keystone Varnish Co 77 83
14 the same——Babcock Varnish Co. 82 85
14 the same——Tim Donogue........ 155 31
14 the same——W E Burton......... 78 25
14 Washington Cold Storage Co—G M Brooks................ .... 263 05
14 Laselles Mfg Co (Lim)—E N Miner.... 153 01
15 Washington Cold Storage Co—John Glass... ....1,597 98
15 The Germantown Smelting and Refining Co—Fanny Caulfield...........5,608 54
15 The Mayor, Aldermen, &c—Dennis Clifford...... .... 262 12
15 the same——Francis Frank........ 148 12
15 Munson Mfg Co—N Y Iron Roofing and Corrugating Co................ 70 02
15 The Leibinger & Oehm Brewing Co—Leopold Manheimer................ 206 54
15 The Washington Cold Storage Co—J L Eccles...................... ...... 451 70
15 M Crane Electrotyping and Stereotyping Co—Benjamin Lowenstein.. 187 59
16 Lorillard Brick Works Co—Danbury Nat Bank.............. ....6,049 64
16 The Mayor, Aldermen, &c—Isaac Bernheimer 51 36
16 Supreme Lodge of the Progressive Benefit Order—Magnus Lamoth.... 119 24
16 The Lancashire Ins Co of Manchester, Eng—R A Maxwell, sup't......costs 160 56
16 Andrus & Conklin Tobacco Co—William Alles.............................. 98 54
16 The Baynes Tracery Mosaic Co—John Berkel..... .... 86 22
17 The National Investment Publishing Co—J L Schwartz.................1,096 31
17 Andrews Mfg Co—Teachers' Mutual Benefit Assoc.... .... 362 83
17 The Metropolitan Elevated Railway Co / The Manhattan Railway Co } Lawrence Lynch. 128 16
17 the same——George Herold..costs 120 81
17 The Excelsior Dynamite Co—C S Beardsley, recvr 157 92
17 The Lascelles Mfg Co (Lim)—Clayton Rockhill.............................. 240 66
17 The Dithridge Flint Glass Co—Daniel Payne.................................1,676 85
17 the same——D F Payne.......... 752 37
17 the same——the same............2,681 29
17 Tabor Knitting Mills—W E Iselin...2,327 09
17 The Central Park North & East River R R Co—F H Schild................ 77 29
17 The Manhattan Railway Co / The Metropolitan Elevated Railway Co } Michael Bergman costs..... 156 29
17 Greenwood Lake Steamboat Co—Westchester Telephone Co.......... 408 47
17 The McLewee Mfg Co—W B Blades.. 492 08
18 N Y Advertising Agency (Lim)—D E Christie.............................. 620 25
18 The Mayor, Aldermen, &c—J C Dooley.............................. 148 00
18 The Germania Schuetzen Bund—Friederike Krauss........ .... 170 30
18 The Manhattan Railway Co / The New York Elevated R R Co } Grenville Kane, indiviv and exr and trustee ....costs 123 18
18 The N Y Central & Hudson River R R Co—Patrick Lennon.... ....5,200 15
18 Maritime Reporter Publishing Co—W F Willcox........... .... 122 20
18 Fonda Lake & Port Leyden Paper Co—Gustav Rau...... .... 789 60
18 The Sims Lumber Co—William Eisenberg......... ....costs 129 69
18 Hungarian Congregation Beth Hamerdrash Hagodal—C H Kranichfelt 298 74
12 Thompson, James—J M Canda.......2,777 15
12 Tichnor, Alfred—Martha Kemp, extrx......... . ... 453 82
14 Taylor, Isaac, Jr—Metropolitan Telephone and Telegraph Co........... 41 76
14 Taylor, Theodore F / *Taylor, Charles G } Electrical Review Publishing Co... 74 37
14 Thornton, John P—J G Van Camp... 527 08
14 Turner, Joseph—J G Wilson......... 90 03
14 Taylor, George P—W P Nollman..... 242 97
14 Turner, Isaac L—Chase Nat Bank....2,604 80
15 Townsend, Edwin M—Haydenville Mfg Co........ .... 173 77
15 Taylor, Charles—Twelfth Ward Bank 200 00
15 Tompkins, George—D P Winnie..... 196 69
15 Travers, Hugh—J M Canda...... ... 159 10
16 Themans, Alfred—St Paul Fire and Marine Ins Co.......................... 286 43
16 Tooker, William M—E C Korner. ... 126 61
16 Traver, John P—F S Van Horn....... 228 68
17 Thompson, John—Herman Robitzek.. 6,086 80
17 Taylor, John / *Terhune, Peter S } W H Baldwin.... 121 31
17 Thatcher, Edward C—J L Reynolds.. 128 78
17 Troy, Willis B—J N Goldbacher..... 209 78
17 Thorne, George W—O P Ely......... 85 87
14 Urwitz, Jerome—Simon Blyn........ 85 50
12 Valleau, Samuel—Rufus King...costs 216 12
14 Vollman, Frederick—Louis Schwartz. 44 00
18 Veblow, Bernhard—Henry Meyer, guard.................................. 75 00
18 the same——William Schroeder.. 344 21
18 the same——Annie Boldt 344 21
18 the same——George Schroeder.... 344 21
18 the same——William Schroeder.. 193 24
18 the same——Bernhard Vehlow, guard.... .... 344 21
15*Vosburgh, Francis R—E P Hincks.... 98 38
12 Van Eupen, Theodore—Christian Woessner........................ .... 238 85
15+Vandewater, James E—J F Heinbockel.......... .... 479 00
16 Van Eupen, Theodore—Valentine Moeslein 524 21
18 Van Ness, John K—E M Knox.. ... 731 58
18 Van Eupen, Theodore—G W Godward 499 20
12 Wallent, Abram—Harris Sigel....... 143 00
12 Walsh, Thomas J—Gorton & Lidgerwood Co 355 86
12 Waite, William A—J C Watson Co... 162 04
12 the same——the same 907 86
14 Wohltjen, Henry—Henry Eggers..... 282 87
14 Wagner, Louis C—J A Moller........ 481 55
14 Walsh, Robert E / Walsh, John E } Samuel Rice 37 70
14 Woesthoff, John—J S Graves......... 326 06
14 Walsh, William M—Thomas Brady... 135 23
15 Wenneis, John M—Elizabeth Sherwood.............................. 180 73
15 Weiss, Theodore—R S Frost.... .... 773 28
15 Wyckoff, Jacob V D / Wilcox, Joseph D } Leather Mfrs Nat Bank...1,263 23
15 Weiss, Max—Jacob Levy............ 27 50
15 Wernnach, William—Aaron Furth... 89 41
15 White, David—J G Tait............ 158 83
15 Wemple, Alonzo E—J H Greene..... 226 42
15+Ward, Helen Dauvray—John Sutherland.............. .... 252 98
16 Wielage, William—George Ehret.... 278 88
16 Walsh, William M—Thomas Roberts Stevenson Co........................ 126 35
16 Wright, Isaac E—Hollister Mfg Co... 119 27
17 Wolff, Rosa—Manuel Knauth........ 195 43
17 Winterroth, Joseph M—Martin Veith 266 14

17 Wolff, Simon—Rudolph Schoverling..1,030 41
18 Wechsler, Morris—C H Kranichfelt.. 188 31
18 Winsor, Harvey D—N Y Improved Real Estate Co............1,499 15
18 Whitney, Samuel D—R A Johnston.. 100 71
15 Yost, Fernando—Herman Frank..... 421 33
18 Young, Louis—Charles James........ 111 65
17 Zipser, Solomon—State Bank........ 360 17
18 Zollner, Frank—John Rudd.......... 99 41
18 Zipser, Solomon—State Bank...... 519 02

KINGS COUNTY.

Dec.
11 Anderson, Carman E—J V Phillips... $63 73
14 Ahrends, Henry—L B Schuler........ 97 81
14 Armstrong, William A—H Kerth.... 32 05
14 Albright, Charles H—Ninth Nat Bank, N Y............1,243 63
15 Adams, Otto—D Thomson........... 144 96
10 Backer, Jonathan—H Schneider......3,785 40
11 Bullwinkel, Martin A—Anna Seebeck 1,088 96
11 Bartmann, Isidor—Budweiser Brewing Co (Lim)............ 815 21
11 Bayles, Robert P—V D Bayles........ 181 21
14 Bailey, John J—H W Johns Mfg Co.. 385 09
14*Bauer, Frederick—C V Formes......1,781 55
15 Bush, Hewlett—Bignall Mfg Co...... 387 48
16 Brossard, Theodore A / Brossard, Otto A } S B Wortmann....... 571 72
16 Baillie, David G—W O Wyckoff...... 93 68
16 Brumley, Schuyler E, admr of Sanford S Brumley, dec'd—A Jacques..2,373 15
16 Bennett, William J—H Prunhild...... 374 87
16 Bossert, Philip—G Pfeiffer......... 387 22
17 Boden, Thomas, by Edward Boden, guard—Brooklyn City R R Co..... 106 04
10 Cuppel, William H—B French........ 45 35
12 Croner, Benjamin—S F Cowdrey..... 879 05
14 Cagney, Timothy J—C H Reynolds & Sons............ 55 7
14 Cummings, William A—Ninth Nat Bank, N Y............1,243 63
14 Carey, James F—W Noble........... 34 25
14 Carpenter, Charles H—T Morris...... 91 10
15 Conkling, Augustus—G B Ellis....... 548 88
15 Collins, Charles H—J Schratwieser... 711 40
15 the same——the same.......... 433 38
16 Coker, Edward R—J McGroarty..... 149 20
16 Crosby, George—Grace Crosby, extrx. 290 64
16 Clouser, Samuel F—H De Haven...... 578 79
10 Diss, Charles J—White, Potter & Paige Mfg Co............ 191 64
11 Davis, Henry J—Wechsler Bros....... 66 32
11 Downes, Henry—F A Baier........... 125 72
12 Deppe, Louis—D Colden............. 108 07
12 Davis, William C—J H Von Glahn... 254 09
15 Delaney, John P—C P Maguire...... 82 75
15 Donnelly, Thomas—W H Bierds....... 75 95
16 Duriomers, John P—T J Preston & Co 35 51
16 Dobbins, Patrick—F G Smith........ 812 28
16 Donovan, Florence G—A J Marcus... 189 43
17 Doremus, Charles G—J Marren....... 176 68
17 the same——the same............ 365 43
17 the same——the same............ 118 48
16 Erslev, Victor P P—G Spaeth....... 125 19
12 Foley, Michael T—J C Provost....... 137 21
12 Fleming, James S—J P Smith........ 332 55
14 Foster, Henry—E A Wildt........... 726 59
15 Flannigan, Thomas P—A A Thomson 144 96
17 Ferris, James V R—P Barnes......... 91 93
17 Fairchild, Clara—Lucy A McMahon.. 184 71
17 Fenno, Henry—T H Tolson..........1,454 25
11 Gleason, Martin J—Fishel & Levy.... 267 08
12 Glassey, Samuel—J Weil............. 200 37
15 Glover, William H H—G B Ellis...... 548 88
15 Graves, Mary H / Graves, Eliza S / Graves, Isabella S } S T Tate......... 606 97
16 Gantz, Joseph W—J F Gantz......... 217 05
17 Gallin, Morris / Gallin, Paulina } T Engelbardt...... 115 60
10 Helselmann, John A—Buffalo Carriage Co............ 129 51
11†Hennessey, "John"—J Duffy........ 43 35
12 Hopkins, Jr, Joseph—Twenty-sixth Ward Bank............ 237 47
14 Hammerstein, Jacob—L B Schuler... 211 77
15*Hanse, James—The E G Blakslee Mfg Co............1,854 01
17*Hirsch, Rosalia—H C Howells, Jr.... 95 19
10 Ingram, John C—R W Fielding...... 104 06
14 Itbell, George—The Standard Wood Turning Co............ 178 75
15 Immig, Charles H—The E G Blakslee Mfg Co............1,854 01
12 Judson, Edward—G Alexander....... 136 07
12 James, Charles W—G W Baker....... 170 47
17 Josiah, Minnie—C O Olsen.......... 119 36
10 Kennedy, Patrick—White, Potter & Paige Mfg Co............ 191 64
10 Kennedy, Joseph—S Harris..........1,108 04
12 King, John—Twenty-sixth Ward Bank............ 237 47
12 Kramer, Michael—Claus Lipsius Brewing Co............ 127 28
12 Klee, Henry W—J Weil.............. 200 37
14 Killey, William—M Reynolds........ 53 09
16 Kennedy, Daniel J—G Amsinck...... 111 57
16 Kimball, Edmund—H J Grant et al.. 246 87
17 Krug, Louis—M Fishel.............. 200 04
17 Krenkstein, Solomon—S Abramowitz 214 75
17 the same——the same........... 120 49
10 Lewis, Thomas C / Lewis, James } S Harris.........1,108 04
11 Levy, Robert—S Salant............. 118 57
11†Loeser, Henry—H McShane.......... 31 27
14 Luerssen, Irmer D—C Wiesbeckel.... 40 60
16 Levy, Julius / Levy, Augustus H / Levy, Moses S } J D W Joy...... 884 04
16 La Grange, Oscar H—G M Harwood. 96 38
16 the same——O P Buel............ 70 25
17 Lawler, Thomas J—W H Duecker.... 140 68
10 Mulqueen, Thomas F—H J Ehlers.... 193 52
10 the same——P Levy............ 181 25
11 Meyer, John—W Ulmer............2,541 19
11 Mayer, Louis—H McShane.......... 22 85
12 Market, Balzer—Claus Lipsius Brewing Co............ 264 03
14 Mulqueen, Thomas F—Foster, Merriam & Co............ 160 97
16 Murray, Robert—S G Hirschberg.... 101 29
17 McEvoy, Charles—F L Froment..... 696 37
17*McWilliams, John—W H Duecker.... 140 68
17 Martin, Charles E—H C Howells, Jr. 95 19
15 Newman, Michael—Becky Dresden... 68 00
15 Newman, John—Oriental and Occidental Tea Co (Lim)............ 32 07
15 Norris, Allison V S—P A Johnson.... 274 20
16 Niehwoehner, William—Louise Kettler............ 121 94
14*Oeding, Henry—H Eggers......... 282 87
14 Ottusb, John P—L B Schuler........ 133 20
16 O'Malley, Annie H—Brooklyn City R R Co............ 91 77
17 Ogilvie, George L—G B Hurd........ 726 41
12 Parker, Henry—C H Reimberg...(D) 564 46
12 Pettit, Maurice E / Pettit, Pierre } Royal Horse Assoc (Lim)....... 149 84
15 Peabody, Royal C—Bignall Mfg Co... 387 48
15 Pearson, Eugene—B E Kipp.......... 87 42
17 Penny, Hugh H—T C Cronin......... 718 89
11 Quim, Thomas W—H Bobnson....... 173 85
11 Rathje, John—J Duffy............. 43 35
12 Rose, Stephen B / Rose, George W / Rose, Westley } F W Koch......... 171 78
10 Schneider, Charles—H Schneider....3,785 40
12 Simon, Semche—W H Ely.......... 359 87
14 Steindler, Joseph—Ninth Nat Bank, N Y............1,243 63
14 Scholl, John—C B Redhead......... 122 64
15 Schuyler, Samuel—C Robinson.......2,358 54
15 Sullivan, Eugene—J C Hanlon....... 133 78
15 Schneider, Charles—N C Becker....5,366 75
15 the same——the same...........3,282 96
15 Scott, Charles B—B E Kipp.......... 87 42
15 Sims, Joseph—W H Bierds.......... 103 75
16 †Steenworth "Frederick" J / *Steenworth, Charles J } J J Phelan.... 169 00
16 Smith, Norman A—G M Harwood... 96 38
16 the same——O P Buell......... 70 25
17 Swift, George F—E R Shipman, exr. 1,001 92
12 The County of Kings—J W Gilbert..41,540 46
14 The Atlantic Avenue R R Co—C D'Oro............ 95 56
14 Tichner, Alfred—Martha Kemp extrx 453 32
14 Terrington, Zachariah—E A Wildt... 726 59
15 The Lafayette Car Works—B F Adams............6,692 30
15 Turner, William—P A Johnson....... 274 20
15 Thurber, Abner D—T L Vickers.....1,182 39
16 The Leibinger & Oehm Brewing Co—L Manheimer............ 206 54
16 The Central Park, North & East River R R Co—F H Schild............ 77 29
16 Thorne, Ogden H—C Gerken & Bro.. 144 64
16 The admr Sanford S Brumley—Alida Jacques............2,373 15
16 Trimborn, August—Brooklyn City R R Co............ 90 04
17 The Supreme Council of the Order of Chosen Friends—Anna B Anderson. 91 57
17 The guard of Thomas Boden—Brooklyn City R R Co............ 106 04
17 Tilman, John F—Kings Co Co-operative Building and Loan Assoc...(D) 1,998 00
11 Valentine, Henry E—J Brady........5,919 79
14 Van Duyn, John G—A G Corwin.... 937 56
12 Ward, Eliza—A Martin.............1,945 25
14 Wohltjen, Henry—H Eggers......... 282 87
14 Woehr, Robert F—L B Darling...... 64 85
15 Wilbur, Philip C—H Eggers.......... 156 63
15 Wenstrom, John—E F Witte......... 200 59
16 Wibert, Henry H—G M Harwood.... 96 38
16 the same——O P Buell........... 70 25
11 Yeager, Charles—H McShane........ 35 83
15 Yung, Frederick—C V Fornes.......1,781 55

SATISFIED JUDGMENTS.

NEW YORK.

[December 12 to 18—Inclusive.

Abeles, Emil—T F Johnson (1891)........... $414 78
Alyea, William—J V Carr. (1891)............ 230 42
Barnes, William E—Julius Maas. (1885)...... 201 05
Same——same. (1885)............ 126 53
Buckhout, Henry—J E Simmons, recvr. (1891)............17,987 65
Baker, John O—H S Hawk. (1891)............ 108 45
Brown, Levi L—North Nat Bank. (1891)....30,225 21
Same——same. (1891)............7,643 56
Brown, Levi L—August Klipstein. (1891)..... 8,782 63
Berry, Jacob—W H Westervelt. (1890).....44,089 87
*Burke, Michael T N—People State N Y. ('89) 1,500 00
*Coakley, Abraham—People State N Y.(1889). 1,500 00
Corwin, Seth M—W G Hitchcock. (1885)..... 480 88
§Commercial Mutual Ins Co—Stevens Voisin. (1889)............5,540 16
Corwin, Seth M—George Wood. (1888)........ 565 00
Day, John B / Dillingham, Charles I } Mary G Pinkney. (1891)............ 75 72
Same——same. (1891)............3,551 88
*Edwards, James H—Frederick Thileman, Jr. (1891)............ 134 85
Fogarty, Katie L—Ellen Hynes. (1891)........ 348 27
Freeman Mfg Co—August Klipstein. (1891).. 8,782 68
Fine, Christopher—Henry White. (1891)..... 171 63
Field, Aaron and Edward S—E P Hincks.(1891) 240 06
Same——same. (1891)............ 113 14
Same——same. (1891)............ 59 25
Fred Hower Brewing Co (Lim)—Carl Ullmann. (1881)............1,318 85
Gillespy, John W—W H Westervelt. (1890)..44,089 87
Gordon, William—Mutual Life Ins Co. (1885) 779 56
Gilmour, John—U S Foundry Co. (1890)...... 128 40
Gille, George B and Joseph B—John Piesbach. (1891)............ 168 55
Gunther, Jacob P—A E Bateman. (1889).... 440 64
Hearn, Alfred M—J W Wheelock. (1889)...... 392 65
Same——J J Egan. (1890)............ 92 79
Hillenbrand, Francis J—G A Reeber. (1891).. 37 70
Johnston, John T, John H and Mary, exr James B Johnston—Eugene O'Sullivan. (1891)............4,594 83
Jacques, Eugene A—Catharine J Carson. (1890)............ 169 06
Jardine, John—Mutual Life Ins Co. (1885)..... 779 56
Kearney, Peter—Mutual Life Ins Co. (1885).. 779 56
Kohn, Malcolm——Henderson. (1890)..... 86 34
Kirchner, Charles—J V Carr. (1891).......... 230 42
Knickerbocker Trust Co, exrs Mark M Stannfield—H M Schneider. (1891)............8,041 18
Lindner, Ernest—Albert Acken. (1891)....... 109 18
Lewis, Sidney H—J R Smith. (1891).......... 427 06
Lowe, William R—D H McDonnell. (1891).... 251 24
Levine, Hyman—F M Lowenstein. (1891)..... 112 87
Manhattan Railway Co—Frederick Brunner. (1891)............ 410 08
Same and Metropolitan Elevated Railway Co—Peter Kearney. (1890)............1,413 78
Mills, T / Morton, P } George Wood. (1886)............ 565 00
Macdonald, John J—J J Egan. (1890)........ 92 79
McLewee, Frederick C—W P Burr. (1888).... 119 66
Same——same. (1888)............ 68 66
Same——same. (1890)............ 236 71
Same——same. (1890)............ 231 51
Meyer, Sigmund T & Philip L—John Webb. (1891)............5,934 63
Manhattan Electric Light Co (Lim)—Abraham Wineburgh. (1891)............ 328 25
Manhattan Railway Co—W Y Mortimer, exr. (1891)............ 81 15
Same——same. (1890)............24,146 07
Same——same. (1891)............ 126 01
Same and Metropolitan Elevated Railway Co } Charles Lippe.(1891). 141 98
Same——same. (1891)............ 113 68
Same——same. (1889)............1,081 90
Mills, T / Morton, P } W G Hitchcock. (1885)............ 480 88
Mott, Hopper S and Mary L—Manhattan Lumber Co. (1891)............ 123 21
*McCarthy, Timothy—People State N Y. (1889)............ 100 00
Manhattan Railway Co—G E Sterry. (1891)... 118 60
Same——same. (1890)............1,494 95
Same——same. (1891)............ 143 25
Newmark, Bernhard—E S Sutro. (1891)...... 662 10
N Y Elevated R R Co—G E Sterry. (1891).... 118 60
Same——same. (1890)............1,494 95
Same——same. (1891)............ 143 25
O'Gorman, Mary—Harry Held. (1891)......... 222 32
*Paige, David—People State N Y. (1889)..... 100 00
Phenix Ins Co—Frederick Keck. (1891)......14,567 62
Phyfe, John D—U S Foundry Co. (1890)..... 128 40
Quinn, Luke C, as President of Company I, Sixty-ninth Regiment, National Guard—Robert Stoll. (1890)............ 118 00
Rauch, Henry—J H Deery. (1891)............ 122 65
Keelg, Philip W—Albert Acken. (1891)........ 109 18
Striker, Elsworth L—C E Talbott. (1891)..... 274 37
Satterlee, John / Simmons, James A } John Webb. (1891).. 5,934 63
Smith, Elizabeth K—Burton Gliddon. (1891).. 80 25
Schappert, Lorenz J—Libanio Barre. (1891).. 178 09
Same——same. (1891)............ 177 46
Schwartz, Frederick C—Max Moses. (1888).. 85 72
Sloane, Douglas—Hugh Lamb. (1891)........ 329 61
Stichler, Edward—E C Smith. (1891)........ 246 81
Third Avenue R R Co—John O'Donnell, admr. (1891)............1,900 00
Tallman, Jacob B—John Webb. (1891).......5,934 63
The Hamburg Bremen Fire Ins Co of Hamburg, Germany / The Howard Ins Co of New York / The Nat Fire Ins Co of New York / The U S Fire Ins Co of New York / The Westchester Fire Ins Co of New York / The Nassau Fire Ins Co of Brooklyn / The Niagara Fire Ins Co / The New York Fire Ins Co of N Y / The Brooklyn Fire Ins Co of Brooklyn } Jacob Rothschild. (1891)...5,761 79
The Joseph Edward Dredging Co—Milo Howell. (1890)............1,074 40
Same——same. (1891)............ 111 20
Same——same. (1891)............ 79 67
†Van Brunt, Thomas C—H P Binswanger. (1891)............1,684 59
§Watts, James R—S B Adler. (1889).......... 158 79
§Same——same. (1889)............ 88 99
Wadsworth, Edwin M—H S Hawk. (1891).... 471 88
Wyburn, Joseph M—J K Smith. (1891)........ 427 06
Zerega, Theodore—W H Westervelt. (1890). 44,089 87

*Vacated by order of Court. †Suspended on Appeal ‡Released. §Reversal. ∥Satisfied by Execution.

KINGS COUNTY.

December 11 to 17—inclusive.

Alves, William—J V Carr. (1891)............ $230 42
Bauer, Anna / Bauer, Johann } F Schmelcher. (1889)...... 54 09
Bennett, William J—Venable & Heyman. (1891). (Execution)............ 100 66
Curran, Patrick—J Rappold & Bro, (1891). (Execution)............ 45 30
Cooke, Charles—R Cook. (1884)............ 163 82
Same——G Hicks. (1885)............ 346 49
Same——Dime Savings Bank, Brooklyn. (1887)............ 181 54
Doolittle, Oscar H—King & Adams. (1891).... 434 24
De Lamotte, Nils P—V Marttino. (1891.) (Execution)............ 23 25
Delaney, Patrick—E B Smith. (1891.) (Execution)............ 45 40
Frank, Catharine—Koesch & Conney. (1889). 259 25
Ferguson, John S—C B Hall. (1891)............ 37 00
Grau, Alexander—E B Smith. (1891.) (Execution)............ 45 40
Gilbert, Annie—E A Ridley. (1890)............ 191 69
Kohn, Julius A—M Henderson. (1890)........ 86 34
Same——same. (1891)............ 111 02
Kirchner, Charles—J V Carr. (1891)........... 230 42
Kapp, Conrad—C W Polhemus. (1891)........ 106 02
Kern, Philip / Kern, Henry } S Curtiss. (1886)............ 665 52
Lawrence, Catharine A—C B Hall. (1891)..... 57 00
McDermott, Patrick J—Thurber, Whyland & Co. (1891)............ 59 80
Same——J Carstairs. (1891)............ 223 86
Same——M R Cook. (1891)............ 314 00
Messenger, Milledge D—A Mowbray. (1887)... 218 82
†McBean, "Andrew" N—W P Rae. (1891)... 53 50
†Same——R Biles. (1891)............ 104 63
McBean, Archibald N—T Sheffield. (1891)..... 213 31
Same——J Q Maynard. (1891)............ 290 69

Payne, Charles E and Olive C—R Merchant, recvr. (1888) ... 64 78

Schneider, Charles—M and A Schneider, (1891.) (Execution) ... 34,679 54

The Brooklyn City Railroad Co—A Orthlieb (1889) ... 2,786 04

MECHANICS' LIENS.

NEW YORK CITY.

Dec.

12 Madison st, No. 314, s s, 60.4 w Rutgers st, 25.11x118. John H. Sturk & Co. agt Joseph Solomon, owner, and Heine & Dooner, contractors ... $165 00

11 Bradhurst av, s e cor 143d st, 100x75. Frederick Brandt agt Ferdinand Yost, owner and contractor ... 928 00

14 Garfield st, n s, 100 w Valentine av, 50x100. Thomas Wilson agt John Kline, owner, and Frederick Robinson, contractor ... 65 50

14 Washington av, Nos. 1738-1742, e s, 50 n 174th st, 50x100. Harry Berry agt Wilkens & Denemark, owners, and John Liden, contractor ... 204 00

14 Eighty-fourth st, Nos. 247, n s, 101.8 w 2d av, 20x100. P. J. McGuire agt Charles Rosenberg, owner and contractor ... 1,650 00

14 West End av, n w cor 83d st, 100x100. Brady & Hauptman agt Gerald L. Schuyler, owner and contractor ... 210 00

15 Twelfth st West, Bethune st and 12th av, the block. Clinton Iron Works agt John T. Johnson, owner, and Thomas Stone and Charles Hewlett, contractors ... 1,879 85

15 Spring st, Nos. 181-187, n s, 49.2 w Greene st, 98.2x—. Goss & Edsall Co. agt John and P. Goerlitz, owners, and John Goerlitz, contractor ... 2,850 11

16 Ninety-eighth st, n s, 375 e Columbus av, 25x100.11. F. W. Flood agt Francis Reynolds, owner and contractor ... 75 00

15 One Hundred and Twenty-first st, Nos. 436 and 438, s s, 140 w Pleasant av, 50x—. Steindler & Hahn agt Christian Biersack, owner, and Louis Klinkel, contractor. (Continued Dec. 15, 1890) ... 230 27

16 One Hundred and Eighteenth st, s s, 100 e Madison av, 100x100. J. J. Brady agt Bernard Ginsburg and Simon Sultan, owners, and Bernard Ginsburg, contractor ... 500 00

16 Ninety-eighth st, n s, 265.0 e Amsterdam av, 150.0x100. T. H. Atha agt Julius Lipman, John W. Hutton and John Burke, owners, and Robert T. Wheeler, John W. Hutton and John Burke, contractors ... 28 00

16 One Hundredth st, Nos. 220, s s, 125 w 2d av, 25x100. J. J. Sanders agt Reno R. Billington, debtor, and Emma C. Barnes, owner ... 55 00

16 Pitt st, No. 51, w s, 100 n Delancey st, 28x100. Charles Burger agt Fischel Weintraub, owner, and L. Feiber and Philip Schmid, contractors ... 250 00

17 Sixteenth st, Nos. 331 and 333, n s, 250 w 8th av, 50x92. Adam Happel agt William H. Schaefer, owner, and Theodore Van Eupen, contractor ... 34 50

17 Bowery, No. 46, w s, bet Canal and Bayard sts, known as the Thalia Theatre. Ernest Otto agt Rosenfeld Bros., lessees, and Theodore Rosenfeld, contractor ... 341 00

17 Eighty-fourth st, Nos. 247, n s, 101.8 w 2d av, 20x100. Ann Reilly agt Charles Rosenberg, owner, and Philip J. McGuire, contractor ... 320 00

17 Sixtieth st, No. 240, n s, 155 e West End av, 25x100.5. H. N. Morris agt ——, owner, and John Burnham, contractor ... 60 00

18 Spring st, Nos. 181-187, n s, 54 e Wooster st, 100x100. A. & F. Brown agt John Goerlitz, owner and contractor ... 1,082 00

18 Boston av or road, e s, extends from 164th st to Teasdale pl, 188.9x76.5x irreg. x104.8. J. J. Scully agt Georgianna Webster, owner, and Thomas Webster, contractor. 951 77

18 Spring st, Nos. 181-189, n s, 48.2 w Greene st, 98.4x100x irreg. x 95.6. E. and F. Barbig agt John Goerlitz, owner and contractor ... 8,200 00

KINGS COUNTY.

Dec.

10 Bedford av, n w cor North 10th st, 75x100. Christian Auerswald agt Anton Mandel, owner, and Otto Denerline, contractor ... $21 00

10 Same property. Charles Tanck agt same owner and contractor ... 23 05

11 Kent av, North 7th st, North 6th st and East River, plot bounded by. New York and Rosendale Cement Co. agt The Brooklyn Cooperage Co., owner, and T. C. Maher, contractor ... 605 00

11 Macon st, Nos. 655-663, 110x100. I. Lazarowitz agt Frank Miller, owner, and Abel Miller, contractor ... 497 50

11 Halsey st, Nos. 754-770, s w cor Ralph av. Phillip Semmer Glass Co. (Lim.) agt Richard Mullowney, owner, and The Builders' Woodworking Co., contractor ... 458 08

11 Gates av, No. 712, s s, 18.9x90. Thomas Kelly agt G. W. Godward and Martin L. Rickerson, owners, and H. Bell, contractor ... 30 00

11 Seventh st, n s, 200.10 e 4th av, 50.4x100. William E. James agt Mary E. Miller, owner, and George M. Miller, contractor. 35 00

11 McDonough st, s s, 175 e Sumner av, 100x100. John Nilsson agt Michael Rofreno and Albercino Carosselli, owners, and Michael Rofreno, contractor ... 450 00

12 Same property. August Pettersson agt same owner and contractor ... 45 25

12 Same property. Benjamin Nilsson agt same owner and contractor ... 74 50

14 Lewis av, s e cor Hancock st, 100x150. Thomas A. McWhinney agt Jacob Aronson, owner and contractor ... 8,000 00

14 Same property. William Kerby agt Jacob Aronson and Thomas McWhinney, owners and contractors ... 975 00

14 Lewis av, s e cor Hancock st, 100x150. Cross, Austin & Co. agt Thomas A. McWhinney and Jacob Aronson, owners and contractors ... 2,813 85

14 Oakland st, No. 20, e s, 25x100. Christian Ziesenies agt Miles Joyce, owner and Smith & Duffy, contractors ... 63 75

14 Same property. John W. Moore agt same owner and contractors ... 147 00

14 Lewis av, s e cor Hancock st, 100x150. Jennie W. Brown agt Thomas A. McWhinney and Jacob Aaronson, owners and contractors ... 2,212 00

14 Same property. Jacob Willman agt same owner and contractors ... 285 99

14 Same property. John F. Poppke agt Jacob Aaronson, owner and contractor ... 830 00

14 Same property. Eric Erickson agt same owner and contractors ... 1,008 00

14 Decatur st, n s, 300 w Saratoga av, 300x100. Frank Bergwall agt J. Mason Kirby, owner, and Edward F. and George W. Spear, contractors ... 48 00

14 Decatur st, n s, 300 w Saratoga av, 300x100. Charles Bergwall agt J. Mason Kirby, owner, and Edward F. and George W. Spear, contractors ... 48 00

14 Hendrix st, e s, 100 n Arlington av, 116.8x100. Bernard Costello agt William C. Anderson, owner and contractor ... 43 00

15 Reid av, w s, 65 n Hancock st, 58.2x100. Christian Heberle agt George Wilridge, owner and contractor ... 20 75

15 Twenty-third st, s w cor 4th av, 20x50. Hobby & Doody agt Elizabetha Staebler, owner, and John Staebler, contractor ... 314 99

15 Lewis av, s e cor Hancock st, 150x100. Albert J. Felty agt Jacob Aronson, owner and contractor ... 800 00

15 Atlantic av, n e cor Kane pl, 94x98.7. Eliza Craigen agt Nelson and James A. Hamblin, owners and contractors ... 1,500 00

15 Decatur st, s w cor Gleneda pl, 85x100. John Brown & Co. agt William W. Reynolds, owner and contractor ... 7,310 00

15 Brooklyn and Jamaica turnpike, n w cor Barbey st, 54.5x112.7. Martin Schmand agt Adiah W. Drake, owner and contractor ... 109 45

15 Herkimer st, n s, 20 w Saratoga av, 80x80. Saratoga av, w s, 80 n Herkimer st, 40x100. E. M. Young agt Harriet Johnston, owner and contractor ... 48 87

15 Sixty-seventh st, s s, 335 e 14th av, 40x100, Lefferts Park. Frederick W. Starr agt Mrs. L. F. Coates, owner and contractor ... 534 17

16 Central av, n e cor Madison st, 20x90. A. D. Vreeland agt —— Sturgis, owner, and Mr. and Mrs. Charles Shultz, contractors. 99 75

16 Lewis av, s e cor Hancock st, 100x150. Burke & Garrahan agt Thomas McWhinney and Jacob Aaronson, owners and contractors ... 1,303 00

16 Decatur st, n s, 300 w Saratoga av, 300x100. Jacob Willman agt J. Mason Kirby, owner and contractor ... 797 71

16 Nichols av, w s, 75 n Havens pl, 81x95. George W. Forbell agt T. D. Wills, owner and contractor ... 1,200 00

16 Willoughby av, No. 766, s s, 179.5 w Lewis av, 20x100. Franz Albaum agt Marie E. and Jacob A. Risson, owners, and Fred I. Clough and Jacob Friedmann, contractors ... 88 48

16 Howard av, e s, 60 n Atlantic av, 125x100. Hall Sash and Door Co. agt The German-American Title Guarantee Co., owners, and Elizabeth K. Smith, contractor ... 331 10

16 First st, s s, 305 w 5th av, 100x100. Matt Taylor Paving Co. agt Cornelius E. Donnellon, owner, and L. Hale, contractor ... 658 88

17 Bergen st, No. 1131. William Martin agt George G. Brooks, owner, and Edwin Dennington, contractor ... 94 52

17 Tenth st, s s, 100 w 8th av, 112x100. Albermarle Soapstone Co. agt James F. Ranson, owner and contractor ... 186 00

17 Fifty-third st, n s, 140 w 5th av, runs west 60 x north 200 to 52d st, x east 40 x south 100 x east 20 x south 100. Hobby & Doody agt Clarence E. Hopkins, owner and contractor ... 1,059 04

17 Douglass st, n s, 410 w Franklin av, 110x150. John Manahan agt Harry Bulkley, owner and contractor ... 47 50

17 Fourth av, No. 411, e s, 77.6 s 9th st, 19x65. J. T. E. & H. C. Litchfield agt Celia Denton, owner, and Leonard Denton, contractor ... 80 75

17 Hancock st, s e cor Lewis av, 150x100. The American Stoneware Co. agt Thomas McWhinney and Jacob Aronson, owners and contractors ... 208 30

17 Hancock st, s e cor Lewis av, 150x100. New York Anderson Pressed Brick Co. agt J. Aronson, owner and contractor ... 228 00

SATISFIED MECHANICS' LIENS.

NEW YORK CITY.

Dec.

12 One Hundred and Twenty-third st, Nos. 142-152 W. Burton Gliddon agt Elizabeth K. Smith. (Lien filed Oct. 14, 1891) ... $63 75

11 Ninety-eighth st, n s, 375 e Columbus av, 25x100.11. Andrew Byrne agt Gregory Leahy and Frank Reynolds. (Nov. 12, 1891) ... 300 00

14 Same property. Ryan & Rawnsley agt same. (July 20, 1891) ... 600 00

14 Eighty-seventh st, s s, 100 w West End av, 90x—. F. A. Clark agt John Heaney and James Sullivan. (Sept. 29, 1891) ... 155 60

14 Central Park West, s w cor 108d st, 100.11x100. Mohawk Valley Lumber Co agt Joseph O'Connor. (Aug. 6, 1891) ... 5,500 00

15*One Hundred and Nineteenth st, s s, 450 e Lenox av, 125x—. E. F. Reynolds and J. J. Quinn agt Tillie E. Smith and John J. MacDonald. (Oct. 30, 1891) ... 675 00

15*Ninety-fourth st, n s, 150 w 9th av, 103.6x—. James Gunn and two others agt James H. Brady and Clegg, Richards & Co.; 3 liens. (June 30, 1891) ... 19 24

15 One Hundred and Eighteenth st, n s, 90 e Madison av, 190x100.11. Hickey & Green agt The Amsterdam Improvement Co. (Aug. 27, 1891) ... 1,056 18

15 Ninety-fifth st, Nos. 145-165 W., 200x100. Helena Mahler agt Bernard Cohn. (Nov. 9, 1891) ... 746 95

16 East Broadway, Nos. 121-125, Pike st, No. 9. Kelly & Daly agt Anna M., Timothy and Annie Roche. (Nov. 28, 1891) ... 29 02

16 Sixtieth st, No. 226 E., 20x100. John Becker agt Frederick Droessler. (Dec. 14, 1891) ... 36 75

16 Same property. Martin Scheidler agt same and Max Myerson. (Dec. 14, 1891) ... 89 00

16 Pike st, No. 53. Lazarus Black and Abraham Rochemowitz agt Nathan Farber. (Oct. 22, 1891) ... 1,065 00

16 Madison st, No. 314, 25.11x—. Schnatz & Massoth agt Joseph Solomon and Charles W. Heine. (Aug. 6, 1891) ... 750 00

16†Vandam st, s w cor Macdougal st. W. R. Williams agt Downey & Curry. (July 22, 1891) ... 203 00

16 One Hundred and Nineteenth st, s s, 450 e Lenox av, 125x100.11. Patrick Gildea agt Tillie Smith and Joseph E. Rogers. (Jan. 13, 1891) ... 600 00

16 Sixteenth st, Nos. 437 and 439 W., 50x92. John Neil agt James Hannan and James McWalters. (Dec. 14, 1891) ... 201 87

17 Ninety-fourth st, Nos. 103 and 105 W., 50x— ... Ninety-fifth st, Nos. 104 and 106 W., 50x— ... William Suk agt Francis J. Hillenbrand. (Oct. 8, 1891) ... 147 50

17 Kingsbridge road, e s, 351 n Coles lane, 56.8x—. C. W. Vreeland agt Fannie Chambers. (July 6, 1891) ... 408 40

18‡Bleecker st, Nos. 98 and 100, s w cor Mercer st. Emil Thiele agt The Schillinger Fire Proof Cement and Asphalt Co. and William H. Arnott & Co. (Feb. 12, 1891) ... 2,080 00

18 Seventy-seventh st, s s, 104 w West End av, 62x102.2. C. I. Mott agt Edward Purcell. (Nov. 30, 1891) ... 300 00

18 Creston av, w s, 225 s Kirk pl, 25x110. William Moore agt Peter Ryan and Charles W. Vreeland. (Dec. 10, 1891) ... 75 00

18 Waverley pl, No. 114, 22x97. Candee & Smith agt James Cunningham. (Oct. 20, 1891) ... 872 15

18 Third av, Nos. 1912 and 1914. Cook & Radley agt Moses Sulzberger and George Thompson. (Oct. 18, 1891) ... 111 00

18*Madison av, Nos. 186 and 188, n w cor 31st st, 50x95. L. K. Dusenberry agt Samuel G. Kevens and Peter N. Ramsey. (Dec. 8, 1891) ... 990 00

18 Ninety-fifth st, Nos. 145-165 W., 200x100. Benedict McIlroy & Fowler agt Bernard Cohen or Amsterdam Improvement Co. (Nov. 10, 1891) ... 719 30

18 West End av, n w cor 83d st, Joseph Braun agt Gerald L. Schuyler. (Dec. 11, 1891) ... 500 00

*Discharged by depositing amount of lien and interest with County Clerk.

‡Discharged by order of Court on filing bond.

†Vacated by order of Court.

KINGS COUNTY.

Dec.

10 Lewis av, s e cor Hancock st, 100x150. Butler Hardware Co. agt Jacob Aronson and Thomas A. McWhinney, owners and contractors. (Dec. 2, 1891). (Deposit) ... $67 29

10 Fifty-sixth st, n s, 150 w 14th av, 50x100, New Utrecht. Eliza Craigen agt Thomas Tangerman, owner, and Emel Keller, contractor. (Dec. 4, 1891). (Deposit) ... 116 92

11 Second st, s s, 177.10 w 6th av, 80x100. Buchanan & Riley agt Archibald N. McBean, owner and contractor. (Lien filed June 29, 1891) ... 740 00

11 Second st, s s, 437.11 e 5th av, 80x100. Aaron Almstrom agt same owner and contractor. (June 29, 1891) ... 100 00

11 Second st, s s, 457.11 e 5th av, 75x100. Traitel Bros. agt same owner and contractor. (Aug. 26, 1891) ... 206 42

11 Second st, s s, 177.10 w 6th av, 80x100. T. F. Ferguson & Co. agt same owner and contractor. (Sept. 10, 1891) ... 64 34

11 Same property. Central Gas and Electric Fixture Co. agt same owner and contractor. (Aug. 21, 1891) ... 301 70

11 Same property. T. B. Willis & Bro. agt same owner and contractor. (July 9, '91) 553 95

11 Seigel st, No. 82. Michael Geier agt Pauline Garling, owner, and Bernard Goldstein, contractor. (Nov. 9, 1891) ... 425 00

11 Seigel st, No. 84. Leopold Michel agt Pauline Garling, owner and contractor. (Nov. 9, 1891) ... 425 00

11 Richardson st, n e cor Union av, 50x50 ... Richardson st, n s, 75 e Union av, 25x50 ... John Walsh agt Joe Pepporine, owner, and Domenico Maleo & Son, contractors. (Dec. 8, 1891 ... 518 15

14 Fifth av, Nos. 529 and 531, e s, 80 n 14th st, 38x97.10. Edward J. Keyes agt Wilhelmina Schink, owner, and Charles H. Collins, contractor. (April 4, 1891) ... 100 00

15 Central av, north cor Ralph st, 25x100. John McCormick agt Mary Cooney, owner, and John McCormick, contractor. (July 15, 1891) ... 87 50

15 Fifty-fourth st, n s, 120 w 4th av, 40x100.2. George S. Schmidt agt Peter A. Larsen, owner and contractor. (Dec. 11, 1891) ... 130 50

16 Bergen st, s s, 100 w Hopkinson av, 25x100. Wyandance Brick and Terra Cotta Co. agt Rosa Rosenfeld, owner, and Carl Becker, contractor. (Oct. 19, 1891) ... 131 23

17 Sunnyside av, s s, 81 e Barbey st, 36x100. Rudolph Reimer & Co. agt —— Schneider, owner, and Junker & Wengert, contractors. (Dec 14, 1891) ... 247 04

17 Evergreen av, No. 812. Daniel Williams agt —— Smith, owner and contractor. (Jan. 28, 1891) ... 37 67

17 Maspeth av, s w cor Porter av, 400x400. Eugene R. Hedden agt The Equity Gas Light Co., owners, and William C. Whyte, contractor. (Oct. 20, 1891) ... 13,917 14

BUILDINGS PROJECTED.

The first name is that of the owner; ar't stands for architect, m'n for mason, c'r for carpenter and b'r for builder.

NEW YORK CITY.

SOUTH OF 14TH STREET.

Delancey st, Nos. 223 and 225, six-story brk flat, 49x75.6, tin roof; cost, $40,000; ow'rs and ar'ts, Schneider & Herter, 48 Bible House. Plan 1558.

Exchange pl, No. 20, ten-story stone building, 56.9x80 and 64.3, brk roof; cost, $250,000; D., L. & W. R. R. Co., S. Sloan, pres't, 26 Exchange pl; ar't, L. C. Holden; b'r, D. H. King, Jr. Plan 1556.

9th av, Nos. 10–18 | four-story brk build-
Hudson st, Nos. 659–667 | ing, 129.4x irreg., tar and gravel roof; cost, $50,000; lessee, E. Prial, 245 West 16th st; ar't, C. H. Israels. Plan 1555.

Beekman st, Nos. 15 and 17, fifteen-story brk and terra cotta store and office building, 49.4x95, tile roof; cost, abt $890,000; agent for C. and W. K. Vanderbilt, David L. Height, 2 East 15th st; ar'ts, McKim, Mead & White. Plan 1576.

Hamilton st, Nos. 34 and 36, two five-story brk flats, 25.10x58 4 and 66 and 23 6x64.11 and 71.6, tin roofs; cost, $18,000 each; R. Satenstein, 226 East Broadway; ar't, H. Horenburger. Plan 1577.

Hester st, No. 104, one-story brk building, 4.7x 5.4, stone roof; cost, $300; lessee, S. Volk, on premises; ar't, C. Rentz Plan 1572.

4th st, No. 345 E., three-story and basement brk church, 24.9x90, tin roof; cost, $10,000; Rev. F. Januschek, 301 East 8th st; ar't, E. Wenz. Plan 1575. (Substituted for Alterations plan No. 2059, 1891.)

BETWEEN 14TH AND 59TH STREETS.

1st av, No. 769, two-story brk building, 25x80, gravel roof; cost, $6,000; D. & J. Harrington, 1st av, n e cor 43d st; ar't, G. H. Budlong; b'rs, Butler & Mahoney. Plan 1565.

BETWEEN 59TH AND 125TH STREETS, EAST OF 5TH AVENUE.

Park av, n w cor 78th st, one-story brk building, 20x75, tin roof; cost, $12,000; G. Gomprecht, 210 East 61st st; ar't, Buchman & Deisler. Plan 1566. (Substituted for N. B. plan 1404, 1891.)

BETWEEN 59TH AND 125TH STREETS, WEST OF CENTRAL PARK WEST AND 8TH AVENUE.

68th st, s s, 300 e West End av, three-story brk stable and dwell'g, 20x32, with extension, tin roof; cost, abt $5,000; A. A. Audruss, 135 West 82d st; ar'ts, Snook & Sons. Plan 1549.

76th st, n s, 100 e 9th av, seven four-story and basement stone dwell'gs, 20, 21, 22 and 23x58 with extensions, tin roofs; cost, $25,000 each; A. G. Nason, 214 East 61st st; ar't, G. A. Schellenger. Plan 1548.

91st st, n s, 275 e 9th av, four three-story and basement stone dwell'gs, 18.9x55.6 with extensions, tin roofs; cost, $16,000 each; ow'rs and b'rs, Curry & Gillie, 208 West 104th st; ar't, M. V. B. Ferdon. Plan 1557.

95th st, n s, 411 w Central Park West, five three-story and basement stone dwell'gs, 17 and 18x51.9 with extensions, tin roofs; cost, $16,000 each; Ellen M. Harlow, 164th st, near Morris av; ar't, M. V. B. Ferdon; b'r, G. J. Harlow. Plan 1558.

Manhattan av, n e cor 118th st, four five-story brk and stone flats, one 25x91, three 25 4x83, tin roofs; total cost, $82,000; ow'r and b'r, T. J. McGuire, 163½ West 102d st; ar't, J. W. Cole. Plan 1569.

118th st, n s, 93 e Manhattan av, five-story brk and stone flat, 25x78.8, tin roof; cost, $18,000; ow'r, b'r and ar't, same as last. Plan 1570.

110TH TO 125TH STREET, BETWEEN 5TH AND 8TH AVENUES.

116th st, s s, 270 w 5th av, three five-story brk and stone flats, 21x76.11, tin roofs; cost, $18,000 each; S. Bittiner, 253 West 123d st; ar't, C. Rentz. Plan 1567.

116th st, s s, 233 w 5th av, six five-story brk and stone flats, 27x82, tin roofs, cost, $22,000 each; ow'r and ar't, same as last. Plan 1568.

NORTH OF 125TH STREET.

Boulevard, n e cor 159th st, one-story frame stable, 12x9, tar roof; cost, $15; lessee and b'r, T. Johnson, on premises. Plan 1573.

23D AND 24TH WARDS.

Ash st, n s, 200 w Anthony av, 24th Ward, two two-story frame dwell'gs, 20x44.6, tin roofs; cost, $3,875 each; C. H. Bull, 273 Madison av; ar't, J. J. Vreeland; b'r, H. E. Hall. Plan 1550.

Southern Boulevard, e s, 200 n 147th st, two two-story frame dwell'gs, 20x36, tin roofs, cost, $1,800 each; D. Knabe, 174 Grand st; ar't, M. Dietsch. Plan 1545.

Summit st, s s, 673 e Marion av, one-and-a-half-story frame stable, 24x21, shingle roof; cost, $700; J. J. Hyland, Bedford Park; ar't, F. D. Miller. Plan 1554.

Boscobel av, n e cor Orchard st, frame shop, 25x20, gravel and tar roof; cost, abt $600; lessee, S. E. Brewer, on premises; ar't, F. D. Miller. Plan 1547.

Jerome av, e s, 482 s Woodlawn av, frame shed, 20x113, tin roof, cost, $600; D. Heuer, 2308 8th av; ar't, J. J. Vreeland. Plan 1551.

Jerome av, e s, 589 s Woodlawn av, two-story frame stable, 28x38, tin roof; cost, $1,500; ow'r and ar't, same as last. Plan 1552.

Westchester av, No. 723, frame shop, 16x40, felt and gravel roof; cost, $300; S. G. Douglass, on premises; b'r, W. W. Taylor. Plan 1546.

Main st, e s, 1,500 n Westchester av, one-story brk and stone building, 75.8x236.2, iron and slate roof; cost, abt $33,000; Harlem Bridge, Morrisania & Fordham Railway Co., 2589 3d av; ar't, L. H. McIntire; b'rs, Pasquini & Co. Plan 1578.

Eagle av, e s, 217.8 n Westchester av, two-story frame dwell'g, 20x34, tin roof; cost, $2,000; J. J. Fitzsimmons, 518 East 148th st; ar't, C. G. Churchill. Plan 1559.

Eagle av, w s, 150 n Westchester av, three two-story and basement frame dwell'gs, 16 8x44, tin roofs; cost, $2,500 each; F. Schwab, 614 Tinton av; ar't, C. F. Lohse. Plan 1571.

Stebbins av, n w cor Jennings st, six two-story frame dwell'gs, 16.8x48, tin roofs; cost, $2,800 each; A. Bell, president, 3409 3d av; ar't, C. C. Churchill. Plan 1560.

Stebbins av, e s, 525.10 n Freeman st, two-story frame dwell'g, 18x30, tin roof; cost, $1,800; ow'r and c'r, J. Murtha, on premises; ar't, C. C. Churchill. Plan 1561.

Stebbins av, e s, 613 n 165th st, three-story frame dwell'g, 25x irreg, tin roof: cost, $5,000; Sarah G. Mayes, 3305 2d av; ar't, M. J. Garvin. Plan 1574.

Union av, n e cor Ritter pl, two-story frame dwell'g, 20x35, tin roof; cost, $3,800; J. O'Connell, 110 Ainslie st, Brooklyn; ar't, C. C. Churchill; c'r, A. J. Wuytack. Plan 1562.

Washington av, e s, 300 n 169th st, two two-story frame dwell'gs, 18x37, with extension, tin roofs; cost, $2,800 each; Maria A. Wuytack, Stebbins av and Home st; ar't, C. C. Churchill; c'r, A. J. Wuytack. Plan 1563.

Washington av, e s, 300 n 169th st, two two-story frame stables, 25x15, tin roofs; cost, $400 each; ow'r, ar't and c'r, same as last. Plan 1564.

KINGS COUNTY.

Plan 2226—Graham st, e s, 75 s Little Nassau st, one four-story brk store and tenem't, 27x55, tin roof, wooden cornice; cost, $7,000; Michael Durinio, 214 East 107th st, New York.

2227—14th st, n s, 83 e 6th av, one one-story brk Indiana limestone church, 89.6x88x118, slate roof, stone cornices; cost, $20,000; Rev. C. H. Dumabut, 269 15th st; ar't, B. O'Rourke; m'n, P. Cooney; c'rs, Johnson & H ——.

2228—St. Marks av, n s, 375 w Franklin av, four four-story brk tenem'ts, 25x52, gravel roofs, wooden cornices; cost, $10,000 each; ow'r and ar't, H. Toulmin, 304 Marcy av.

2229—Thatford av, e s, 150 s Eastern Parkway, one three-story frame store and dwell'g, 20x40, tin roof; cost, $3,000; Levin & Gittelsohn, Thatford av.

2230—George st, s s, 125 e Evergreen av, two three-story frame (brk filled) tenem'ts, 25x60, tin roofs; cost, $4,500 each; ow'rs and b'rs, Dornbach & Barudio, 14 and 16 George st; ar't, Th. Engelhardt.

2231—Thatford av, e s, 175 s Eastern Parkway, one three-story frame store and dwell'g, 20x40, tin roof; cost, $4,000; Levin & Gittelsohn, Thatford av.

2232—St. Marks av, n s, 150 e Buffalo av, six two-story frame (brk filled) dwell'gs, 16.8x40, gravel roof; cost, $2,000 each; ow'r and ar't, J. F. Kentana, 710 7th av; m'n, L. E. Brown.

2233—Saratoga av, e s, 80 n Pacific st, one two-story frame carpenter shop, 20x20, gravel roof; cost, $200; ow'r and c'r, Erick Erickson, 197 McDougal st.

2234—Thatford av, e s, 150 s Eastern Parkway, one two-story frame tailor shop, 20x30, tin roof; cost, $1,000; Levin & Gittelsohn, Thatford av.

2235—Huron st, s s, 175 w Oakland st, one four-story brk tenem't, 25x54, tin roof, iron cornice; cost, $7,500; E. Reebl, 216 Huron st.

2236—Flatbush av, Nos. 19 and 21, e s, 142.1 from Hudson av, one five-story brk and iron store, 37.6x71, tin roof, iron cornice; cost, $17,000; John C. Grennell & Co., 536 Fulton st; ar't, J. Mumford; b'rs, J. D. Anderson's Sons and E. L. Boyd.

2237—Stone av, w s, 100 n Atlantic av, one four-story brk neck-tie factory, 40x97.3, and one-story extension, 14.2x13.6, tin roof, iron cornice; cost, $16,998; James McCurrach, 569 Broadway, New York; ar't, J. W. Bailey; b'rs, J. Brown and Martin & Lee.

2238—Vernon av, n s, 325 e Sumner av, one two-story brk stable, 27x70, gravel roof, brk and stone cornice; cost, $3,500; Wm. Battermann, Broadway, cor Ewen st; ar't, T. Engelhardt; b'r, not selected.

2239—Logan st, w s, 330 n Blake av, one two-story and attic frame dwell'g, 18x32, tin roof; cost, $1,800; Ebregott Zettles, Liberty near Railroad av; ar't, L. F. Schillinger; b'r, F. Gundermann, Jr.

2240—Thatford av, e s, 100 s Dumont av, one one-story frame tailor shop, 20x25, felt roof; cost, $250; Lewis Rosenberg, on premises.

2241—44th st, n s, 200 e 4th av, six two-story and basement frame dwell'gs, 18x37, tin roofs; cost, each, $4,800; Jas. Hart, 182 43d st.

2242—Gates av, s s, 225 w Knickerbocker av, one three-story frame store and tenem't, 25x60, tin roof; cost, $4,500; ow'r, ar't and b'r, Joseph Taylor, 1394 Gates av.

2243—Lincoln av, w s, 75 s Adams av, one one-story frame stable, 22x16, shingle roof; cost, $150; Patrick Dobbins, on premises; b'r, W. G. Osborn.

2244—Osborn st, e s, 150 s Dumont av, one three-story frame (brk filled) store and tenem't, 25x67, tin roof; cost, $7,000; ow'r and b'r, Sam. Tostevin, 1141 Lafayette av; ar'ts, D. Acker & Son.

2245—Liberty av, n e cor Railroad av, one three-story frame (brk filled) store and tenem't 27x62, tin roof; cost, $6,800; Henry Hudtwalker; ar't, E. Schrempf; b'r, not selected.

2246—Fulton st, s s, 300 e Troy av, one four-story brk work-rooms, 42x70, gravel roof, brk and iron cornice; cost, $23,000; Directors of Bureau of Charities; ar't W. B. Tubby; b'rs, J. Thatcher and L. W. Seaman, Jr., & Son.

2247—Atlantic av, s e cor 6th av, one one-story brk freight house, 302x33, gravel roof, iron gutter; cost, $14,000; Long Island R. R. Co., Long Island City; ar't, C. M. Jacobs; b'rs, J. T. Woodruff and J. H. Cummins.

2248—Henson pl, rear of Nos. 18 and 20, one one-story brk express office and baggage-room, &c., 99x30, gravel roof, iron gutter; ow'r, ar't and b'rs, same as last.

2249—Metropolitan av, n s, 300 w Olive st, one two-story brk stable, 25x25, gravel roof, wooden cornice; cost, $800; ow'r and b'r, George H. Remson, on premises.

2250—Stagg st, s s, 100 e Lorimer st, one four-story frame (brk filled) tenem't, 25x65, tin roof; cost, $6,000; Theodore E. Green, 298 Bedford av; ar't, A. Herbert; b'r, not selected.

2251—Van Brunt st, w s, 50 n Vandyke st, one four-story brk flat, 25x56, tin roof, wooden cornice; cost, $8,500; Petter Plunkett, Elizabeth st.

2252—Greene av, s s, 200 e Lewis av, seven three-story and basement brk and brown stone dwell'gs, 18x43, tin roofs, iron cornices; cost, each, $5,000; Louis C. Schliep, 89 Montague st; ar'ts, Langston & Dahlander.

2253—Lexington av, s s, 185 w Tompkins av, one one-story brk stable and engine rooms, 20x 49.5 and 52.3, gravel roof; cost, $500; G. P. Brush, 97 Wilson st; ar't, J. L. Young

2254—Lexington av, s s, 125 w Tompkins av, one two-story brk storage for carpets, 60x52.3 and 60 9, gravel roof; cost, $5,000; ow'r and ar't, same as last.

2255—South Portland av, Nos. 174 and 176, w s, 300 n Atlantic av, one two-story brk horse stable, 45x96, gravel roof, brk cornice; cost, $5,500; George F. Corlis, 702 Fulton st; ar't, W. Brockelhurst.

2256—Humboldt st, w s, 300.11 s Nassau av, five two-story and basement frame (brk filled) dwell'gs, 18x40, tin roofs; cost, $1,800 each; ow'r and b'r, Charles Eogert, 183 Montrose av; ar't, F. J. Berlenbach, Jr.

2257—Halsey st, n w s, 300 n e Evergreen av, one two-story and basement frame (brk filled) dwell'g, 20x58, tin roof; cost, $3,000; ow'rs, ar'ts and b'rs, Farrell, Hommel & Co., 585 Evergreen av.

2258—South 11th st, s s, 143.10 w Kent av, one three-story brk wash-house, 47.6x45, tin roof, brk cornice; cost, $2,000; Mollenhauer Sugar Refining Co., on premises; ar't, C. H. Schwardt; b'rs, W. & T. Lamb.

ALTERATIONS NEW YORK CITY.

Plan 2101—115th st, n s, 244.8 e Pleasant av, one-story extension, 30x38.4; cost, $8,000; Standard Gas Light Co., 2 Cortlandt st; ar'ts, D. & J. Jardine; m'ns, Hogencamp & Son.

2102—23d st, Nos. 68–72 W., walls altered, pavilion on roof and interior alterations; cost, $8,500; J. McCreery, Inwood, N. Y.; ar't, W. B. Tuthill.

2103—35th st, No. 41 W., interior alterations, walls altered and new bay; cost, $4,000; H. M. Lazinski, 623 Carroll st, Brooklyn; ar'ts, Graul & Frohne.

2104—West st, Nos. 119 and 121, repair damage by fire; cost, $700; G. Hoyt exr., 45 West 17th st; ar'ts, Snook & Sons; b'r, D. Repburn.

2105—6th av, No. 519, interior alterations, doors and windows altered; cost, $350; lessee, F. Farrell, on premises; m'ns, W. Wright's Sons.

2106—Park row, Nos. 147 and 149, walls altered, roof changed and interior alterations; cost, $2,500; B. Gutter, 52 Pike st; ar't, M. Muller.

2107—44th st, Nos. 228 and 230 E., top story removed and interior alterations; cost, $500; Bertha Volkening, 48 East 60th st.

2108—44th st, Nos. 232 and 234 E., top story removed and interior alterations; cost, abt $1,500; owner same as last.

2109—Kirkside av, e s, 175 n Kingsbridge road, moved to new foundation; cost, $1,000; H. N. Camp, Morris Dock, New York; m'n, M. Folin.

2110—59th st, s s, 180 e 5th av, walls repaired; cost, $400; Gentlemen's Riding Club, 7 East 58th st; ar't, B. L. Gilbert.

2111—173d st, s s, 50 e Morris av, interior alterations and frame tower on corner; cost, $1,000; Sarah Schmittberger, on premises; ar't, J. J. Vreeland.

2112—38th st, No. 213 E., rear portion raised one story and roof altered; cost, $2,500; Anna Boylston, on premises; ar't, A. V. O'Connor; m'ns, Martin & Soehan.

2113—Washington sq., No. 46 S., windows altered; cost, $500; Caldwell & Co., agents, 48 East 4th st.

2114—25th st, Nos. 146 and 148 W., walls altered; cost, $300; Orange County Milk Association, 249 West 54th st; ar't, J. E. Terhune; c'r, A. Brown, Jr.

2115—Nassau st, Nos. 126–130, interior alterations; cost, $300; C. and W. K. Vanderbilt, 600 5th av; ar'ts, Snook & Sons.

2116—7th st, No. 44 E., one-story and basement extension, 22x22, walls altered and new front; cost, $1,500; J. Schween, 233 Broome st; ar'ts, Graul & Frohne; c'r, C. Schulkraft.

2117—South 5th av, No. 15, one-story extension, 21.6x85; cost, $3,000; A. Loppin, 225 West 4th st; ar't, T. Commean.

2118—Cherry st, Nos. 508 and 510, repair damage by fire; cost, $1,400; lessees, Goodwin & Co., on premises; b'r, F. J. Ashfield.

2119—Greenwich av, Nos 86 and 88, interior alterations, new front and entrances changed; cost, $5,000; estate W. C. Rhinelander, 153 West 14th st; ar't, C. Rentz.

2120—62d st, No. 18 E., two-story extension, 20.6x20; cost, $2,000; J. L. Wirt; ar't, J. MacDonald.

2121—152d st, No. 658 E., raised one story, three-story extension, 20x15, and walls altered; cost, $3,000; W. Davis, 694 East 144th st; ar't, F. L. Blom.

2122—125th st, No. 629 E., raised one story, three-story extension, 20x16, and moved to new foundation, cost, $4,250; M. McCabe, 643 East 155th st; ar't, F.L. Blom.

2123—50th st, No. 47 E, two-story and basement extension, 8.6x20.10, interior alterations, walls altered; cost, $5,000; D. S. Moore, 5th av and 52d st; ar'ts and c'rs, Graham & Co.; m'ns, Dawson & Archer.

2124—34th st, Nos. 329 and 331 E., one-story extension, 40x42, interior alterations; cost, $5,000; B. Galewski, 170 Henry st; ar'ts, Schneider & Herter.

2125—161st st, n s, 216 e Courtlandt av, moved to new cellar and basement; cost, $1,500; Elizabeth Rogers, 654 East 162d st; ar't, M. J. Garvin.

2126—Nassau st, s e cor Beekman st, interior alterations, walls altered and connection made with new building at 15 and 17 Beekman st; cost, abt $10,000; agent, D. L. Haight, 2 East 15th st; ar'ts, McKim, Mead & White.

2127—Houston st, No. 52 W., interior alterations, walls altered and new front; cost, $600; lessee, H. Prince, 27 West Houston st; ar't, H. Horenburger; c'r, E. Janko.

2128—12th st, No. 630 E., new iron stairs; cost, $400; Anna Rosenblum, on premises; ar't, H. Horenburger.

KINGS COUNTY.

Plan 1158—Court st, No. 266, repair damage by fire; cost, $1,900; Mr. Roessler, 395 2d av; m'n, J. Shorrock; c'rs, Heesch & Sibbert.

1159—South Portland av, No. 166, one-story brk extension, 14.6x25, tin roof; cost, $200; Wm. B. Mesbio, 1705 Pacific st.

1160—Watkins st, w s, 150 n Belmont av, flat tin roof; cost, $400; Morris Rubstin, on premises.

1161—Bradford st, No. 107, flat tin roof; cost, $400; Chas. L. D'Ivernois, on premises; ar't and c'r, H. Rocker; m'n, D. Cook.

1162—Carroll st, No. 497, new store front; cost, $50; John Bishop, 311 West 37th st, New York.

1163—St. Marks av, s s, 357 e Utica av, stone and frame foundation, also two-story frame extension, 12x16, tin roofs; cost, $945; Wm. H. Allee, 402 Vanderbilt av; ar't and b'r, W. Bryan.

1164—52d st, n s, 250 e 3d av, one-story frame extension, 8x10, tin roof; cost, $50; ow'r, ar't and b'r, Charles A. Erickson, Bay Ridge.

1165—Osborn st, w s, 175 s Sutter av, one one-story frame extension, 14x4.7, tin roof; cost, $140; A. Goldstein, on premises.

1166—3d av, No. 86, one-story brk extension, 22x20, tin roof; cost, $500; Long Island Brewery, 86 3d av; ar't, T. Engelhardt; b'r, not selected.

1167—Willoughby av, No. 1008, extend second story 4 ft to front; cost, $150; T. F. Mennski, 1008 Willoughby av.

1168—Commercial st, No. 66, foundation for tank; cost, $300; American Sugar Refining Co., 137 Broadway, N. Y., ar't and b'r, P. H. Murphy.

1169—Garfield pl, No. 240, raise rear of house 4.4, add half story; cost, $1,000; ow'r, ar't and b'r, Jere J. Gilligan, 97 Sterling pl.

1170—Stockton st, No. 216, one-story brk extension, 14x12; cost, $100; Frank Lang, on premises; ar't, H. Vollweiler; b'r, not selected.

1171—Sumner av, s w cor Quincy st, one-story brk extension, 20x6, tin roof, basement front altered; cost, $500; Walter Bell, 270 Sumner av; b'rs, H. Konig & W. Mahler.

1172—North 6th st, No. 254, two-story frame extension, 14x25, tin roof; cost, $500; J. Dunelle, 254 North 6th st; b'rs, Bell & Co.

1173—Rapelye st, s s, 100 e Van Brunt st, front and interior alterations; cost, $350; ow'r, ar't and c'r, Thomas R. Worthington, on premises; m'n, J. Cody.

1174—Court st, n w cor Warren st, side door and interior alterations; cost, $1,000; P. J. Kelly, on premises; ar't, J. G. Glover; b'r, E. Hendrickson.

1175—18th st, No. 253, new foundation; cost, $200; H. Scherloh, 5th av and 18th st; b'r, C. E. Sherman.

1176—Schermerhorn st, No. 85, two-story brk extension, 19.6 and 23x65, gravel roof; cost, $2,500; Mr. Sidebotham, Boerum pl; ar't, C. Werner; b'r, not selected.

1177—Ormond pl, No. 10, rebuild parts of walls; cost, $500; Smith & Laytin, 84 Putnam av; b'rs, Lynch & Dalton and W. H. Anderson.

1178—Sedgwick st, Nos. 43-51, front altered; cost, $900; Columbia Chemical Works, 109 Water st; b'rs, C. Bauer and B. H. Body.

1179—St. Marks av, No. 1008, one-story frame extension, 16x30, tin roof; cost, $80; John Beatty, 1008 St. Marks av.

1180—Meserole av, No. 85, new store front and interior alterations; cost, $300; ow'r and m'n, Mr. Mootry, North 2d st; ar't and c'r, A. J. Hulse.

1181—Meserole st, No. 194, add one story of frame, flat tin roof; cost, $250; Jacob Rueger, on premises.

1182—Broadway, No. 279, new store front and interior alterations; cost, $300; J. W. Reid, 371 Broadway; ar't, H. Smith; b'r, M. Gallagher.

1183—Elizabeth st, s s, opposite Dwight st, add one story of frame, flat gravel roof; cost, abt $850; Handren & Robbins, on premises; c'r, C. T. Robinson.

MISCELLANEOUS.

BUSINESS FAILURES.

N. Y. ASSIGNMENTS—BENEFIT CREDITORS.

Dec.

14 Paulsen, Frederick (general commission merchant, at No. 19 Old slip), to Henry Ware Jones; without preferences.

15 Johnston, Coburn H. (under firm name of C. H. Johnston & Co., importer and jobber of dress trimmings, &c.), at No. 41 Union sq., to Edward L. Lithauer; preferences, $9,449.50.

15 Mazur, Henry and Gustav Rothholz (retail dealers of clothing, at No. 1922 3d av), to Edwin F. Stern; without preferences.

16 MacKenzie, George (manufacturer of sashes, blinds, doors, &c., at Nos. 492 and 493-499 Southern Boulevard), to Charles A. Christman; without preferences.

18 De Mott, Emma V. (milliner, at No. 214 West 15th st), to Frederick G. Anderson; preferences, $280.46.

PROCEEDINGS OF THE BOARD OF ALDERMEN AFFECTING REAL ESTATE.

* Under the different headings indicates that a resolution has been introduced and referred to the appropriate committee. † Indicates that the resolution has passed and has been sent to the Mayor for approval. ‡ Passed over the Mayor's veto.

NEW YORK, Tuesday, Dec. 15, 1891.

PAVING.

103d st, from Park to 5th av, granite block and crosswalks laid at intersecting and terminating avs.†

CURBING, FLAGGING, ETC.

Amsterdam av, n e cor 75th st, 125 on av and 200 on st.†

MAINS.

141st st, bet St. Anns and Beekman av; gas.
141st st, from main now in St. Anns av to Beekman av (two blocks) and then in Beekman av north to Beech terrace; water.
Lane av, from Southern Boulevard to Hunts Point road; gas.
Beekman av, from 141st to St. Marys st; gas.
Crimmins av, from 141st to St. Marys st; gas.
Beech terrace, from Crimmins to Beekman av; gas.
Oak terrace, from Crimmins to Beekman av; gas. †

LAMP-POSTS ERECTED AND LAMPS LIGHTED.

Beech terrace, from Crimmins to Beekman av.
Oak terrace, from Crimmins to Beekman av.
141st st, bet St. Anns and Beekman avs.
Beekman av, from 141st to St. Marys st.
Crimmins av, from 141st to St. Marys st.
Lane av, from Southern Boulevard to Hunts Point road. †

BROOKLYN BOARD OF ALDERMEN.

BROOKLYN, Dec. 7, 1891.

CULVERTS.

Lewis av, n e cor Hancock st.†

ELECTRIC LIGHTING.

Raymond st, bet De Kalb and Willoughby sts.†

FENCING VACANT LOTS.

Evergreen av, Cooper and Van Voorhis sts, lots bounded by.*

FLAGGING.

Vernon av, s s, bet Sumner and Throop avs.†

LAMP POSTS ERECTED AND LIGHTED.

Putnam av, w s, 227 feet e of Central av; at owners' expense.*

PAVING, GRADING, ETC.

5th av, bet 27th and 30th sts.*

STREET OPENING.

Chestnut st, bet Fulton st and Jamaica av.
Essex st bet Arlington and Atlantic avs. †

BROOKLYN, Dec. 14, 1891.

CULVERTS.

Himrod st, n e cor Knickerbocker av.
Stanhope st, s e cor Knickerbocker av.
Evergreen av, s w cor Gates av.
Hamburg av, s e cor Harman st. †

EXTEND FIRE LIMITS.

16th Ward.†
24th Ward, part of.*

FLAGGING.

Atlantic st, n s, bet Franklin and Clason avs.
Clifton pl, s s, bet Grand and Clason avs.
Meserole st, w s, bet Graham av and Ewen st.
Sackett st, s s, bet Van Brunt st and Ferry pl.
Belmont av, bet Rockaway av and Powell st.
Stone av, bet Liberty and Dumont avs.
Sutter av, bet Rockaway av and Sackmann st. †

LAMP POSTS ERECTED AND LIGHTED.

Cooper st, bet Evergreen and Central avs.
Cornelia st, bet Evergreen and Central avs.
Covert st, bet Central and Hamburg avs.
Halsey st, bet Central and Hamburg avs.
Hart st, bet Knickerbocker and Irving avs.
Melrose st, bet Knickerbocker and Irving avs.
Van Voorhis st, bet Broadway and Hamburg av.
Evergreen av, bet Grove st and Gates av.
Knickerbocker av, bet Harman st and Greene av.
Knickerbocker av, bet Flushing av and Himrod st. †

PAVING, GRADING, ETC.

Bergen st, bet Buffalo and Howard avs.
Bergen st, bet Howard and East New York avs.
Meeker av, bet Kingsland av and Newtown Creek.
Saratoga av, 162 ft s of Herkimer st to Butler st.
5th av, bet 27th and 36th st. †

STREET OPENING.

Degraw st, bet Washington and New York avs.
Douglass st, from boundaries of 24th and 26th Wards to East New York av. †

ADVERTISED LEGAL SALES.

REFEREES SALES TO BE HELD AT THE REAL ESTATE EXCHANGE AND AUCTION ROOM (LIMITED), 59 to 65 LIBERTY STREET, EXCEPT WHERE OTHERWISE STATED.

Dec.

Boulevard (11th) av, s e cor 151st st, 24.11x100, four-story brk flat, by R. V. Harnett. (Amt due $1,401; prior morts. $12,000)........ 21

106th st, n s, 175 w 8th av, 50x100.11, five-story stone front flats, by R. V. Harnett & Co. (Amt due $1,816; prior morts. —)........ 21

Riverside av or Drive, No. 100 } begins Riverside 82d st, Nos. 318-324 } av, s e cor 82d st, runs east 101.1 x south 102.2 x west 16.8 x north 19.4 x west 32 x north 18 8 x west 14.4 x north 15.6 x west 8 4 x north 26.6 x west 79.9 to Riverside Drive, x north 24.2 to beginning, four-story stone front dwell'g on av and four four-story stone front dwell'gs on st, by R. V. Harnett & Co 21

Oliver st, No. 74, e s, 126.2 n Cherry st, 26.2x100.6x 25.3x100.6, five-story brk tenem't, by Smyth & Ryan. (Amt due $9,574)........ 22

Oliver st, No 77, w s, 124 5 n Cherry st, 24.6x101.8 x24.6x101 9, five-story brk tenem't........
Oliver st, No. 79, w s, 99.11 n Cherry st, 24.6x101.2, five-story brk tenem't........
by Smyth & Ryan. (Amt due on No. 77 $11,661, and $11,618 on No. 79)........ 22

11th st, Nos. 814 and 816 E., s s, abt 282 e 2d av, 38.8x94.10, five-story brk tenem't with stores, by James Bleecker & Son. (Amt due $1,750; other morts. $—)........ 22

34th st, No. 214, s s, 615.11 e 8th av, 16.8x98.9, four-story stone front dwell'g, by D. P. Ingraham & Co........ 22

64th st, No. 37, n s, 310 w 8th av, 25x100.5, two-story frame dwell'g with two-story frame dwell'g on rear, by William Kennelly. (Amt due $10,004)........ 22

116th st, Nos. 1-9, n w cor 5th av, 143x100 11, five five-story brk flats, stores in No. 1, by William Kennelly. (Amt due $97,175)........ 22

132d st, Nos. 6-10, s s, 125 e 5th av, 85x99.11, three five-story brk flats, by William Kennelly. (Amt due $19,981; prior morts. $35,000)........ 22

2d av, Nos. 1808-1814, s e cor 94th st, 100.8x100, four five-story brk tenem'ts with stores, by William Kennelly........ 22

119th st, No. 61, n s, 526.8 w 5th av, 16.8x100.11, three-story stone front dwell'g, by R. V. Harnett & Co. (Amt due $12,285)........ 22

Perry st, No. 77, n s, 126.2 e Bleecker st, 25x95, three-story brk dwell'g, by William Kennelly. (Partition sale)........ 23

7th st, No. 186, s s, 218 e Av B, 25x90.10........
7th st, No. 194, s s, 193 e Av B, 25x90.10........
Two four-story brk tenem'ts with stores, by James L. Wells. (Partition sale)........ 23

137th st, s s, 80 e Willis av, 12x100, by William Kennelly. (Amt due (12,946)........ 23

88th st, No. 201, n w cor Amsterdam av, 30x100.8, five-story brk flat with stores, by R. V. Harnett. (Amt due $18,417)........ 24

Melrose av, e s, 26.7 n 3d av, 53.9x51.7x62.11x 15.11........
Willis av, w s, 25 s 147th st, 25x100........
Courtlandt av, e s, 25 n Findley now 160th st, 25x 100........
by J. L. Wells. (Partition sale)........ 24

Madison av, Nos. 1064 and 1066, w s, 62.2 n 80th st, 40x70, five story brk flat with stores, by William Kennelly. (Amt due $51,908)........ 26

96th st, No. 35, n s, 348 w 8th av, 19x100.11, four-story brk dwell'g, by R. V. Harnett & Co........ 28

KINGS COUNTY.

Dec.

Court st, No. 588, w s, 63.4½ s Hamilton av, 20x100, one-story brk store; assessed value, $700; by W. P. Rae & Co., at the Real Estate Exchange, 189 and 191 Montague st........ 21

Schaeffer st, n s, 204 w Hamburg av, 48x93.9x48x 96.5, three two-story frame (brk lined) dwellings; assessed value, $1,000 each........
Belmont av, s s, 75 e Thatford av, 25x100, two-story frame dwell'g; assessed value, $1,200....
7th st, s s, 402.1½ w 8th av, 20.9x100, three story brk and stone flat; assessed value, $5,000........
by T. A. Kerrigan, at 13 Willoughby st........ 21

1st st, s w s, 224.3 n w 7th av, 17 6x100, two-story brk dwell'g; assessed value, $5,200; by T. A. Kerrigan, at 13 Willoughby st........ 22

Leonard st, Nos. 399 and 401, s w cor Richardson st, 50x150, varnish factory; assessed value, $2,000; by William J. Griffin, ref., at County Court House........ 22

Wythe av, n w cor North 11th st, runs northeast along Wythe av 200 to North 12th st, x northwest 100 x southwest 100 x northwest 75 x southwest 100 to North 11th st, x southeast 175 to beginning, glass works; assessed value, $25,000; by T. A. Kerrigan, at 45 Broadway, E. D. 22

65th st, s s, 375 e 6th av, 25x100.2, Bay Ridge, by T. A. Kerrigan, at 13 Willoughby st........ 23

7th st, s s, 402.1½ w 8th av, 20.9x100, three-story brk and stone flat; assessed value, $5,000; by William Wills, ref., at County Court House........ 24

27th st, n s, 225 e 4th av, 40x100, two three-story brk tenem'ts; assessed value, $3,000 each; by Bernard J. York, ref., at County Court House.. 24

62d st, s s, 180 e 13th av, 20x100, New Utrecht....
Sheffield av, Nos. 54 and 56, w s, 225 s Fulton st, 50x100, one and-a-half-story frame dwell'g and one-story frame dwell'g on rear of plot; assessed value, $2,050........
by T. A. Kerrigan, at 13 Willoughby st........ 28

Benson av, s w s, 3 6.9 s w De Bruyns lane 50x192 x50x190, New Utrecht; partition; by John C. Rhodes, ref., at County Court House........ 28

LIS PENDENS.

NEW YORK.

Dec.

53d st, Nos. 33 and 35, n s, 303 w 8th av, 75x100.5. White Rock Lime and Cement Co. agt Donald Frazer et al.; foreclos. mechanic's lien; atty's, Kurzman & Frankenheimer........ 12

97th st, s s, 182 e Columbus av, 19x100.11. Melvin L. English agt R. Irene Thompson and ano.; foreclos. mechanic's lien; att'y, Louis F. Therasson........ 14

18th st, No. 209, n s, 125 w 7th av, 25x92. Emma A. Twine agt Anna A. Twine et al.; partition; att'ys, Jeroloman & Arrowsmith........ 14

Clinton st, w s, 79 n Rivington st, 20.2x50. Rebecca Kahn agt Frederick Muhlhauser et al.; partition; att'y, Fernando Solinger. 14

West End av, No. 1?1 / 69th st, No. 8?1 { begins West End av, n w cor 69th st, 50x100. James McLaughlin agt Dennis F. Lavelle; foreclos. mechanic's lien; att'y, Thomas C. Ennever. 14

Houston st, No. 249, s s, 37.6 e Norfolk st, 19.9x75. William S. Shepard agt George W. Shepard et al.; partition; att'y, J. F. Parkhurst. 14

65th st, No. 184, s s, 120 e Lexington av, 20x100.5. Joseph Geller agt Max Kobre; action to compel deft. to deliver to plff. a deed of conveyance; att'y, Adolph Cohen. 14

Fordham av, n w cor Mott st, 108.2x93x108x97 / Vermont av, w s, 125 s Virginia av, 125x100, Flatbush } Philip Pfeiffer and ano. exrs. agt Sophia Herman et al.; partition; amended notice; att'y, Julius J. Frank. 15

Keppler av, n w cor Willard av, 75x100. Samuel Price agt Ida L. Senior et al.; foreclos. mechanic's lien; att'y, Samuel E. Duffey. 15

Monroe av, e s, known as lot 60 map Village of Mount Hope, 100x100. John Fenn agt Sarah A. O'Neill et al.; partition; amended notice; att'y, G. D. W. Clocke. 15

65th st, Nos. 22 and 24, s s, 120 w Madison av, 50x100.9 / 70th st, No. 22, s s, 40 w Madison av, 15x100.5 / 21st st, No. 19, n s, 116 9 e 4th av, 18x98.9 / Greene st, No. 81, w s, 96 s Grand st, 25x100 } Chemical Nat. Bank agt Stephen T. Barker; notice that a levy of attachment on above property is issued and delivered to sheriff; att'ys, Jones & Roosevelt. 15

94th st, n s, 419 e 10th av, 17x100.8. Laurence Pottier agt Alexis T. Pottier et al.; action for a sale and a division of the proceeds, also for admeasurement of plff's dower; att'y, Manley A. Raymond. 16

105th st, n s, 415.5 e 10th av, 33.?x134.10. William McShane admr. agt John Askey et al.; action for accounting, &c.; att'ys, Thornall, Squires & Pierce. 16

Boulevard, s w cor 84th st, 89x112. James Murray and ano. agt Bernard Wilson and ano.; foreclos. mechanic's lien; att'ys, Bloomfield & Lincoln. 16

83d st, s s, 72.6 w 10th av, 17.6x74. Annie Mason agt Isabella J. Stagg wife of and Zechariah Stagg et al; partition; att'y, Wm. L. Van Derzee. 17

Lexington av, s w cor 103d st, 56x100. Frank Wennemer agt Bliss Memorial Methodist Episcopal Church et al; foreclos. mechanic's lien; att'y, Louis A. Wagner. 17

Park row, No. 125, n s, 8.6 e Pearl st, 24x92x—x78 / Cherry st, No. 225, e s, 156 n Pike st, 25x60 } Charles R Drake and ano. agt Hannah A. Drake et al.; partition; att'ys, Lord, Day & Lord. 17

Washington st, No. 708, w s, 64 n Perry st, runs northwest 80 x north 16 x northeast 18 x southeast 75.6 to Washington st, x south 23 to beginning. Catharine Landman and ano. agt Maria Ronkcon et al.; partition; att'ys, Goodrich, Deady & Goodrich. 17

53d st, n s, 820 w 6th av, 20x100.5 / 53d st, n s, 300 w 6th av, 20x100.5 } Robert E. Dietz agt Edward M. Field et al.; action for attachment, &c.; att'y, Frederic A. Ward. 18

71st st, n s, 294.7 w 8th av, 19x102.2. Edmund J. Murphy as assignee agt Phillipine Banner and ano.; foreclos. mechanic's lien; att'y, Durnin & Hendrick. 18

71st st, n s, 275 w 8th av, 19.7x102.2. Same agt Leopoldine Frankenheimer and ano.; action same; same att'y. 18

71st st, n s, 332 7 w 8th av, 17.4x102.2. Same agt Bella Levi and ano.; action same; same att'y. 18

71st st, n s, 313.7 w 8th av, 19x102.2. Same agt Estelle Putzel and ano.; action same; same att'y. 18

FORECLOSURE SUITS.

Dec.

New or Croton st, s s, 214.5 w 10th av, 25x86x25x87 / New or Croton st, s s, 261.5 w 10th av, 25x86 } W. G. Brown and ano exrs. agt Bridget Meahan; att'y, Warren G. Brown. 12

Water st, No. 351, s s, 16.4x75. George A. Barker et al. exrs. and trustees agt David B. Hart et al.; att'ys, B. C. Wetmore. 14

82d st, No. 304, s s, 40 w West End av, runs south 78.3 x west 10 x south 1 6 x west 10 x north 80.2 to 82d st, x east 20 to beginning. Celia M. Schell agt John Gilmour et al.; att'y, Edward P. Schell. 14

105th st, s s, 200 w 1st av, 75x100 11. Max Danziger agt William Dempsey et al.; att'y, Max Gross. 14

6th av, w s, 43.11 n 119th st, 19x75. Caroline F. Harrison agt John O. Hoyt et al.; att'y, Robert L. Harrison. 14

Prospect av, e s, known as lot 64 map Village of Woodstock, 81x—. A. F. Schwannecke agt Laura B. O'Connor et al.; att'ys, Wager & Acker. 14

9th av, Nos. 855-861 / 56th st, Nos. 402 and 404 { begins 9th av, s w cor 56th st, runs northwest 125 x southwest 100.7 x southeast 25.2 x northeast 8.2 x southeast 100 to 9th av, x northeast 100.5 to beginning. John J. Jones and ano. exrs. agt Michael Steinhardt et al.; att'y, Martin J. Keogh. 14

121st st, n s, 117 e 6th av, 2 lots, each 17x100.11. Cecile Ruschle extrx. agt William F. McEntee et al.; 2 actions; att'ys, Anderson & Howland. 14

42d st, n s, 83 e 6th av, 21x100.5 / 42d st, n s, 62 e 6th av, 21x100.5 } Minnie Harder agt New York Real Estate and Building Improvement Co. et al.; att'y, Harrison T. Slosson. 15

129th st, s s, 110 e Lenox av, 25x99.11. Mary L. Walton agt William C. Boyd et al.; amended notice; att'y, John E. Ellison. 15

94th st, n s, 79.9 e 2d av, 27.3x100.8x20x100.8. James Nevins agt Charles Downey et al.; att'ys, Bartlett, Wilson & Hayden. 15

St. Nicholas av, w s, 314 n 141st st, 56.5x53.3x54.11x61.7. William J. Seaman agt Thomas J. Stevens and ano.; att'ys, Forster & Speir. 15

1st av, n e cor 113th st, runs east 91.6 x north 100.11 x west 19 6 x south 81.10 x west 74.6 to 1st av, x south 19.11 to beginning. Morris Meyer agt Jane A. McKenna et al.; att'y, Albert J. Sire. 15

47th st, s s, 273 e 9th av, 20x100.5. Myrick Plummer agt Frederick Schuck et al.; att'y, Solon P. Rothschild. 15

145th st, n s, 275 e 10th av, 75x99.11. James Rogers agt Jacob Streiffer et al.; att'y, Arthur Murphy. 15

121st st, s s, 160 w Mt. Morris av, 20x100.11. W. H. L. Lee agt Sarah E. Buckhout and ano.; att'ys, Lee & Lee. 15

53d st, s s, 180 w 6th av, 20x76.9x20.4x80.5. Eliza Wiener as trustee agt James Otey Bradford et al.; att'y, Charles de Kay Townsend. 16

65th st, s s, 321 e 10th av, 2 lots, each 19x100.5. Robert L. Reade exr. agt Bernard Cohn et al.; 2 actions; att'ys, Varnum & Harison. 16

23d st, n e s, 128 s e 9th av, 22x117.6. William H. Lane agt Mary B. Browne; att'y, J. Albert Lane. 17

101st st, n s, 350 w Columbus av, 50x100.11. Bradley & Currier Co. (Lim.) agt John J. Hughes et al.; att'y, William Stone. 17

Liberty st, n s, 72.6 e Nassau st, 17.4x75x20.6x75. William Kaston agt Elizabeth A. Lalor individ. and extrx. et al.; amended and supplemental notice; att'y, Abner C. Thomas. 17

209th st, centre line, 334.7 w land of Isaac Dyckman known as lot 7 map property Samuel Thompson, 67.3 to private road, x147x98.7x147. Thomas Crimmins agt Peter W. Felix et al.; amended notice; att'ys, Durnin & Hendrick. 17

Macdougal st, s w cor 4th st, 34x56. Henry W. Benedict et al. agt Martin Disken et al.; att'y, Gellott D. Dechert. 17

71st st, n s, 228.6 e 9th av, 18x102.2. Joseph B. Bartram agt Salvador Roe et al.; att'ys, Johnson, Gallup & Hurry. 17

4th av, w s, 25.11 n 119th st, 25x90. Harriet L. Boyd et al. agt John Mallon et al.; att'y, Freling H. Smith. 17

137th st, s s, 85 w 8th av, 16x99.11. Edward de P. Livingston agt Dore Lyon et al.; att'ys, Clute & Cobb. 18

52d st, No. 519, n s, 250 w 10th av, 25x100.5. Robert L. Reade exr. agt William H. Lee et al.; att'ys, Varnum & Harison. 18

Macdougal st, s w cor 4th st, 34x86. Henry W. Benedict et al. agt Martin Disken et al.; att'y, Gellott D. Dechert. 18

13th st, Nos. 407-413 / 14th st, Nos. 408-414 { begins 13th st, n s, 94 e 1st av, runs north 103.3 x east 25 x north 103.3 to 14th st, x east 100 x south 103.3 x west 25 x south 103.3 to 13th st, x west 100. G. G. Williams and ano. exrs. agt Septimus W. Granger et al.; att'y, M. A. Raymond. 18

3d av, e s, 50.5 n 97th st, 25.7x90. Bradley & Currier Co. (Lim.) agt Joseph O'Connor et al.; att'y, Austin E. Pressinger. 18

LIS PENDENS, KINGS COUNTY.

Dec.

Stone av, w s, 75 s Blake av, 25x100. Herman F. Koepke agt Gussie Volinsky; att'ys, J. C. & H. C. Smith & Koepke. 10

Buffalo av, e s, 223.7 s St. Marks av, runs northeast 183.2 x north 44.10 x west 67.2 x south 54 x west 10 x south 8 7 x southwest 42.5 x west 58.6 to av, x south 28.9 / Herkimer st, n s, 20 e Stone av, 16x80 } James S. Bearns agt John H. Bishop, Jr; att'ys, Bearns & Brenner. 10

Hull st, s s, 131.3 w Hopkinson av, 18.9x84x18.10x86.1 / Hull st, s s, 150 w Hopkinson av, 18.9x81.11x18.10x84 / Hull st, s s, 168.9 w Hopkinson av, 18 9x79.10x18.10x81.11 } Elizabeth W. Aldrich agt Thomas Donohue; three actions; att'y, Spencer Aldrich. 11

Stuyvesant av, No. 397, e s, 102 n Halsey st, 19x100. Ransom F. Clayton agt Roberta F. F. Goodenough; action to obtain bond and mortgage; att'y, James P. Philip. 11

Garnet st, n s, 100 w Smith st, 50x200 to 9th st. Stephen B. Sturges agt Margaret E. Conlon; att'ys, Sturges & Roby. 11

Bergen st, s s, 290 e Brooklyn av, runs south 100 x east 60 x south 5.7 x northeast 106 7 to st, x west 100. Same agt Joseph M. Pilcher; same att'ys. 11

Cleveland st, w s, 131.10 n Atlantic av, 25x100. Cornelia Van Siclen guard. James C., Schenck R., Richard and Maggie Van Siclen agt Mary E. Jaeger; att'y, John H. Ives. 11

Hancock st, s s, 145 e Sumner av, 20x100. The Farmers' Loan and Trust Co. guard. Francis M. Whaley agt William A. Taylor; att'ys, Turner, McClure & Rolston. 11

Madison st, s s, 220 e Howard av, runs south 100 x east 14 x northeast 58.8 x north 48.2 to st, x west 28. Benjamin Wright and ano. exrs. Charles Curtiss agt Robert L. Moores; att'y, Frank M. Tichenor. 11

Fulton st, n w cor Dresden st, runs north to Arlington av, x west 103.7 x south to Fulton av, x east —. Mirabeau L. Towns agt Elizabeth Hallahan; att'y, Benjamin Rausch. 11

Glenmore av, n s, 125 e Thatford av, 14.9x100. Stephen T. Rushmore agt Theodore M. Le Beau; att'ys, J. C. & H. C. Smith & Koepke. 11

Glenmore av, n s, 139.9 e Thatford av, —x100x14.11x100. Same agt same; same att'ys. 11

4th av, n w cor 9th st, runs north 120 x west 80 x south 33 x east 40 x south 87 to st, x east 20. John F. Edwards agt Charles H. Collins; att'y, John F. Nelson. 12

54th st, n s, 160 e 3d av, 20x100.2. Alexander Davidson agt William Roberts; att'ys, Hubbard & Rushmore. 12

Macon st, n s, 146 e Ralph av, 18x100. Louise C. Concklin agt F. Augustus Conkling; att'y, David Barnett. 12

Hull st, s s, 150 w Hopkinson av, 18.9x81.11x18.10x84. Margaret Reynolds agt Thomas Donahue; att'y, John A. Clarry. 12

54th st, n s, 240 w 3d av, 17.6x100.2. Edward A. Everit agt Margaret A. Davenport; att'y, Geo. W. Pearsall. 12

Kosciusko st, s s, 20 e Lewis av, 20x80. Phebe H. Sayres extrx. William J. Sayres agt Smith Tuttle; att'y, Oliver S. Ackley. 14

Patchen av, n e cor Putnam av, 20x100. Joseph H. Pratt agt Thomas Waling; att'y, Wm. P. Pickett. 14

Lot at Flatbush, 171 n Seely st and 422 e Middle st, 14x100, with right of way over Temple court. Jane C. Coursen agt Thomas H. Robbins; att'ys, Coursen & Coursen. 15

Lot begins 48.8 n Seely st and 520 e Middle st, 14x100, with right of way over Temple court. Frances H. Coursen agt same; same att'ys. 15

Lot begins 31.10 n Seely st and 520 e Middle st, 16.10x100, with right of way over said Temple court; same agt same; same att'ys. 15

Lot begins 15 n Seely st and 420 e Middle st, 15x100, with right of way over said court. Edith C. Thompson agt same; same att'ys. 15

Sands st, No. 100, s s, 50.4 e Jay st, 25.?x108.10x25.2x108.7. James M. Farr agt Ann F. Clark; att'y, A. Prentice. 15

Schenck av, w s, 175 n Gilmore av, 25x100. Louis Baerlein agt Patrick Gorman; action for appointment of recvr; att'ys, Reeves & Todd. 15

Graham av, s e cor Devoe st, 25x100. Joseph H. Kernochan agt Anastasia Ryan; att'y, J. Frederic Kernochan. 16

Franklin av, s e cor Putnam av, 90x90. William Strickland agt David T. Lynch; att'y, John M. Rider. 16

Lots 504 and 505 map Gilbert S. Thatford, East New York. Samuel Samelson agt Isaac Glaser; action for specific performance; att'y, H. J. Morris. 16

Vermont av, w s, 125 s Virginia av, 25x100. Philip Pfeiffer and ano. trustees Friederika Goldstein agt Sophia Herman; amended partition; att'y, Julius J. Frank. 16

Quincy st, n s, 153.3 w Lewis av, 43.8x100. Ezra A. Tuttle agt John W. Fisher; action for specific performance; att'y, Ezra A. Tuttle in person. 16

Fulton st, s s, 100 e Rockaway av, 20x100. United States Trust Co. trustee John McCahill agt Louis C. Schlep; att'ys, Stewart & Sheldon. 16

Central av, e s, 80 s Noll (Prospect) st, 80x100. Jacob Lauth agt Pauline Frank individ. and admrx. Solomon Frank; action to set aside deed; att'ys, Phillips & Avery. 16

Freeman st, n s, 225 w Oakland st, 25x100. Thomas Daly agt Peter Hughes; att'y, J. Tracey Langan. 17

Fulton st, n s, at intersection with s s Somers st, runs east 124 3 x south 98 to Fulton st, x west 127.4. Elizabeth W. Aldrich agt Francis McMahon; att'y, Spencer Aldrich. 17

RECORDED LEASES.

NEW YORK. Per Year

Broadway, No. 529, n w cor Spring st, basement store. Ignatz Boskowitz trustee to Charles Zweig and Adolph Susskind; 3 years, 2 months and 22 days, from Dec. 9, 1891. $1,275

Broadway, No. 529, store. Same to Moses Minzesheimer; 3 years, from Feb. 1, 1892. 2,400

Broadway, Nos. 182 and 184, all. Charles A. Cheesbrough individ. and exr. and trustee Margaret Cheesebrough to The Seventh National Bank; 11 years, from May 1, 1892. 20,000

Bowery, No. 143, north part of store. Charles D. J. Noelke to Henry Jacob; 8 years, 4 months and 16 days, from Dec. 13, 1891. 480, 600

Franklin st, No. 12, all. John Boyd to James Boyd; 10 5-12 years, from Dec. 1, 1891. 400

Gansevoort st, Nos. 100 and 102, cellar and first story. Archibald D. Russell to The New York Beef Co. (Lim.); 5 years, from May 1, 1891. 3,200

Murray st, No 61, store and part basement. Albert Schierenbeck to Henry J. Rottmann; 10 years, from Jan. 1, 1892. 2,500

Same property. Assign. lease. Henry J. Rottmann to Albert Schierenbeck; Dec. 12. nom

Orchard st, No. 112, front basement and second floor. Claus D. Doscher to Solomon Marculescu; 5 years, from May 1, 1891. (Re-recorded). 960

Pearl st, Nos. 515, 515½ and 517, all. Robert Boyd to Henry Hillebrand; 5 years, from May 1, 1892. 3,000

Sheriff st, Nos. 66 and 68, all. Arthur McConnell to Catharine and Joseph Cavanagh, of Cavanagh & Co.; 5 years, from May 1, 1892. 900

South st, No. 204, all. William A. Hustace to Frederick W. Stiene; 5 years, from May 1, 1892. 1,500

Watts st, Nos. 65 and 67, top loft / Desbrosses st, Nos. 12 and 14, n e cor of, top loft } Phillip Semmer Glass Co. to Schwitzer Bros. & Co; 3½ years, from Jan. 1, 1892. 650

7th st, No. 11, store floor and cellar. Susan Sember widow to Charles Stucky; 2¾ years, from Dec. 15, 1891. 1,236

14th st, No. 608 E., store floor and part basement. Anna W. wife of Louis H. Kirchner to Henry Adler; 3 5-12 years, from Dec. 1, 1891. 815

15th st, No. 21 E., two basements, top floor and two rooms on second floor. Richard H. L. Townsend to Max Hirt; 4½ years, from Nov. 1, 1891. 2,460, 2,580

16th st, No. 21 E., east basement. Max Hirt to Leopold Henderson; 4⅙ years, from Jan. 1, 1892. 540

31st st, Nos. 257 and 259, n e cor 8th av, all. Alfred N. Cohen to Thomas J. and John J. Clark; 10 years, from Dec. 1, 1891. 5,000

Same property. Assign. lease. Thomas J. and John J. Clark to James Everard; Dec. 10. nom

34th st, No. 240 E., store floor and front cellar. Mary A. Diehl to Charles Brown; 3⅓ years, from Jan. 1, 1892. 600

42d st, No. 188 W., n s, bet 6th av and Broadway, all. Mariana G. de Rolando to W. L. Blanchard; 5 years, from May 1, 1893. 2,400

45th st, No. 433 W., store floor and part cellar. John McGinn to Patrick Masterson; 3 years, from May 1, 1892. 660

46th st, No. 426 W., n s, bet 9th and 10th avs, all except east store. Isaac Mannheimer to Peter G. Banks; 9¾ years, from Sept. 1, 1891. 1,380

81st st, No. 405 E., store and part cellar. Caspar Beck to Nic. Hildenbrand; 3 years, from Nov. 1, 1891. 780

Same property. Assign. lease. Nicholas Hildenbrand to Louis Miller. nom

83d st, No. 50 E., all. Sarah A. Meeks widow to Henrietta R. Stettheimer; 3 1-12 years, from April 1, 1891. 1,850

87th st, No. 155 E. / Lexington av, No. 1291 { being 87th st, s e cor Lexington av, 62.2x100.8 / Willis av, Nos. 141, 145, 147 and 149, w s, 50 n 138th st, 100x91.6 } Luigi, Guiseppe, Steffano and Natale Cavinato to Augostino Cavinato; 6 months, from Jan 1, 1892. 3,000

115th st, No. 342 E., all. Julius Figlinolo to John Argenziano; 4 11-12 years, from June 1, 1891. 660

125th st, Nos. 135 and 137 E., store and basement. Sally Arnholz and ano. exrs. Adolph Brussel to Henry U. Singhi; 10 years, from Oct. 1, 1891. 3,333, 4,000, 4,500

Av. D, No. 136, store floor and part second floor. Samuel Weil to Anna Segel; 4½ years, from Nov. 1, 1891. 680

Columbus av, n w cor 81st st, store in "Hotel Endicott." Charles A. Fuller to Adolph Ammon; 10 years, from Jan. 1, 1891. 1,500, 2,500, 3,000

Lexington av, No. 1763, n e cor 110th st, store and basement. Philip Keiser to Samuel Rosenfield; 5½ years, from Jan. 1, 1892. 780

Westchester av, No. 730, store, first floor and cellar. Ann Hanlon to George Scharrenbeck; 10 years, from Nov. 1, 1891. 300, 360, 420

1st av, No. 1452, store floor and basement and part second floor. Henry G. Steinhoff to Emil Zoman; 5 years, from May 1, 1891.... 1,140
3d av, No. 2089, s e cor 105th st, store floor and front basement. Jeremiah H. Moore to Mary J. O'Donohue; 5 years, from May 1, 1891.... 1,400
3d av, No. 2089, s e cor 112th st, store floor and basement. Henry B. Renwick to H. W. Singhi; 8 years, from May 1, 1891.... 1,800
3d av, No. 2039. Assign. lease. Michael Blasius to George Ringler & Co.... nom
6th av, No. 447, store and basement. Henry Brien, of H. & H. Brien, to E. W. Lageroth; 5½ years, from Jan. 1, 1892.... 4,000
8th av, No. 882, store and basement. Jacob Smith to James F. Bragg; 7 5-12 years, from Dec. 1, 1891....2,700, 2,100
Same premises. James F. Bragg to Edwin I. Jefferds; 7 5-12 years, from Dec. 1, 1891..2,700, 2,100
Same premises. Assign. lease. Edwin I. Jefferds to August P. Windolph.... nom
8th av, No. 2689, s w cor 143d st, all. Thomas McManus to Frederick Frey; 5 years, from May 1, 1892....1,000, 1,200
8th av, No. 2066, store. Thomas J. Robinson to John Many; 5 years, from May 1, 1892....600, 700, 800, 900
8th av, No. 2654, n e cor 141st st, store, first floor, basement and cellar. Catherine Barthel to Frederick Warnken; 2 years, with renewal of 2 years more, from May 1, 1891.... 780
Same property. Assign. lease. Frederick Warnken to Katie Engenhoefer; Dec. 12.... nom
9th av, No. 427, store floor and back basement. John O'Gara to William Meister; 3 years, from Jan. 1, 1892.... 480
9th av, n e cor 59th st, seven rooms and bathroom; John M. Buck to The Metropolitan Telephone and Telegraph Co.; 10 years, from Dec. 1, 1891.... 600
11th av, No. 838 } n e cor 11th av and 57th st, 57th st, No. 565 } Max Ullmann to Michael McGee; 6½ years, from Jan. 1, 1892.... 2,500
12th av, n e cor 50th st, 100.5x125. Charles F. Southmayd and ano. trustees Henry Astor to James Blackhurst; 5 years, from May 1, 1891, taxes, &c., and.... 1,250

CHATTELS.

NOTE.—*The first name, alphabetically arranged, is that of the Mortgagor, or party who gives the Mortgage. The "R" means Renewal Mortgage.*

NEW YORK CITY.

DECEMBER 11 TO 17—INCLUSIVE.

SALOON AND RESTAURANT FIXTURES.

Augenmeyer, G W. 220 St Nicholas av....Bernheimer & S. $2,500
Ahrens, Henry. 25 Chambers....H Elias B Co. (R) 1,000
Byram, T W. 825 3d av....J B Byram. Restaurant. 750
Bersoglio, Frank. 209 Elizabeth....H B Scharmann & Sons. 500
Bisinger, Bartholme. 1746 1st av....Bachmann B Co. 1,000
Boss, John. 590 Columbus av....P & W Ebling B Co. 800
Brennan, M B. 87th st and Park av....Hirsch & S. 1,900
Bruckmann & Brugel. 91 Duane....Feigenspan B Co. (R) 950
Buttner, Simon. 197 Bowery....M Gombossy. 550
Same....same. E Wolf. Chairs, Tables, &c. 171
Byram, T W. 825 3d av....H Koch. Restaurant Fixtures. 68
Bauer, Herman. 310 W 41st....M Groh's Sons. 250
Branagan, John. 71 Roosevelt....Bernheimer & S. (R) 2,000
Bartman, Isidor. 257 E 3d....F Hower B Co. 850
Bruning, Henry. 1165 Av A....H Elias B Co. (R) 3,800
Clune, Matthew. 42d st and Lexington av....J H Hentz et al. Hotel Fixtures. (R) 7,500
Caputo, Viacenzo. 102 Worth....Bernheimer & S. (R) 400
Chiocetti, Pasquale. 104 Mott....F Freiber. 200
Conly, M F. 9 Boerum pl and 71 Sands st, Brooklyn....J Everard. 4,000
Cavello, J and P. 420 E 102d....D Mayer. (R) 125
Chambers, Patrick. 1824 Av A....P Doelger. 2,800
Clark, T J and J J. 418 8th av....J Everard. 4,478
Clarkson, Edward. 308 E 49th....F Oppermann, Jr. 500
Clark, Michael. 441 W 53d....D Stevenson. 420
Conlon, Bernhard. 602 11th av....D Stevenson. 450
Dwyer, Michael. 29 Jones....Bavarian B Co. 100
Dunn, John. 310 E 38th....C Peppett. 500
Ehler, J A. 324 Greenwich....H F Ehler. 9,500
Engenhoefer, Katie. 2654 8th av....Bernheimer & S. 1,000
Eagleton, Thomas. 253 W 13th....W Peter. (R) 750
Edlich, C H. 327 E 97th....Claus Lipsius B Co. 1,500
Farrell, Bernard. 53 Broome....T C Lyman & Co. (R) 2,500
Faulhaber, J and M. 1351 2d av....G Bechtel, exr of. 2,000
Frey, Fred. 2689 8th av....Bernheimer & S. 1,700
Ferrando, Antonio. 87 Thompson....Bernheimer & S. 200
Fica & Ledr. 1458 1st av and 59 1st av....India Wharf B Co. (R) 749
Frey, Fred. 2689 8th av....C Iba. 111
Freyknecht, Max. 390 8th av....Wagner & S. Pool Tables. 1,141
Fackert, F E. 609 Hudson....G Ehret. (R) 2,400
Farrell, Andrew. 348 E 39th....H Koehler & Co. 250
Farrell, Francis. 519 6th av....J Ruppert. (R) 2,000
Feuerstern, Davies. 53 Forsyth....E Walker. Pool Table. 120
Germann, Martin. 139 E 83d....P Doelger. (R) 400
Gallesso, Francesco. 84 James....Welz & Z. (R) 250
Gege, Ludvosky, or Ludvosky, Gega. 420 E 19th....E Freund. 2,000
Greisch, Charles. 12 Clinton pl....F Simon. Restaurant Fixtures. 3,000
Grimmer, Andrew. 293 Av A....A Tutschku. Restaurant Fixtures. 225
Gunshinan, J S. 414 Washington....Abbott B Co. 1,300
Green, Rosa. 106 E 4th....Rubsam & H B Co. (R) 860
German, Jacob. 260 W 41st....F W Barwick. (R) 395
Grits & Spiwak. 89 Allen....D Stevenson. 2,000
Harbour, Henry. 307 E 8th....C Iba. 840
Haas, Lorenz. 424 E 14th....J Hoffmann B Co. 400
Hall, R H. 18 Spring....A Wibom. (R) 1,225
Henrichs, Henry. 482 E 17th....Bernheimer & S. Pump. 84
Same....same. Ice House. 90
Same....same. Ice House. 90
Huth, Alexius. 189—18th....Feigenspan B Co. 700
Herzog, Franz. 885 10th av....C Stein. (R) 400
Hoffman, Samuel. 265 Broome....J Kahn. Restaurant Fixtures. 235
Haffner, J D. 600 8th av....Bernheimer & S. 2,000
Harris, Abraham. 28 Forsyth....G Ehret. (R) 1,000
Hennessy, William. 55 Bond....Bernheimer & S. 1,000
Horth, Anton. 212 Spring....G Bechtel, exr. of. 500
Jaeger, F J N. 627 and 629 Madison av....G C Engel. Restaurant Fixtures, Horses, &c. 6,000
Keller, Joseph. 140 7th....C Stein. (R) 1,200
Koch & Muller. 128 West....J H Hubert. 5,000
Kammitter, Frank. 41 Ann....P Buckel. 700
Karp, Davis. 19 Ludlow....Burger B Co. 300
Kemmerer, Leo. 219 E 4th....J Kress B Co. (R) 700
Koch, Mathais. 892 9th av....V Loewers. 540
Kruger, Louis. 105 Cannon....Bachmann B Co. 1,500
Leitz, Joseph. 41 Av C....F Oppermann, Jr. 500
Lindinger, Fred. 66 and 68 Beaver....J V Haik. 1,500
Lederer & Hogan. 176 8th av....Brunswick-B-C Co. Pool Table. 225
Lenz, Charles. 185 Greenwich....J Kress B Co. 200
Lawlor, Lizzie. 588 Morris av....Knickerbocker B Co. 1,000
Licciardi, Antonio. 210 E 108th....Bernheimer & S. (R) 600
Lindemann, Isidor. 166 Delancey....A Herzberg. 2,500
Meyer, John. 1041 2d av....J Kress B Co. 2,000
Mackey, S R. 271 8th av....D Mackay. Restaurant Fixtures. 4,000
Mallis, W J. 203 Av B....J Ruppert. (R) 1,500
Masterson, John. 1126 1st av....J Everard. 1,522
McDonald, J J. 23d st and 11th av....D G Yuengling, Jr, B Co. 3,616
McElvanny, James. 767 2d av....E McCarthy. (R) 3,000
Meissner, O M. 412 W 36th....F Oppermann, Jr. 500
Miller, Louis. 405 E 81st....G Ehret. 1,400
Mistele, Albert. 154 Forsyth....India Wharf B Co. 1,000
McCaffrey, John. 1967 3d av....P Doelger. 600
Muhs, H F. 188 Monroe....H Elias B Co. 1,000
Nudes, Joseph. 21 and 21½ Suffolk....Sekosky Bros. Bar Fixtures. 237
O'Connor, David. 106 E 88th....G Ehret. 600
O'Donohue, Mary J. 2089 2d av....P Engel. 1,048
O'Rourke, D J. 180 Park row....G Ringler & Co. (R) 800
O'Connor, Michael. 567 Grand....H Elias B Co. 2,000
O'Donohue, Mary J. 2089 2d av....Bernheimer & S. 3,700
O'Brien, John. 1138 1st av....Hower B Co. 850
Perless, Leon. 84 Eldridge....D Mayer B Co. 550
Power, Denis. 1965 3d av....Bernheimer & S. (R) 2,000
Quinn, Peter. 247 E 121st....Bernheimer & S. (R) 1,000
Rathjens, C W. 84 West Broadway....G Ehret. (R) 1,300
Reinhardt, O and L. 1 and 1½ 2d av....D Neagle. 1,800
Rossler, Geo. 185 Av A....W Peter B Co. 850
Rotmann, H J. 61 Murray....A Schierenbeck. 10,000
Reifsteck, Charles. 188 Mott....Consumers' B Co. 1,100
Richardson & Hopper. 704 8th av....J H Davidson. Restaurant Fixtures. 340
Riepe & Fajen. 138 Canal....G Ringler & Co. 1,285
Roque, Louis. 114 Delancey....F Ibert. 500
Rubin, S and C. 53 Ludlow....M Rubin. Restaurant. 250
Redmond & Sheehy....C Brand. 820
Reid, James. 198 and 200 Church....Bernheimer & S. 1,500
Richter, John. 837 5th....J Kuntz. (R) 275
Rohde, Rudolph. 143 W 29th....Beadleston & W. (R) 250
Sauer, G W. 155th st and 8th av....G Ehret. 10,000
Schneider, Louis. 186 2d av....P Doelger. (R) 1,000
Scholly, Metta. 118 Chrystie....P Doelger. (R) 1,078
Schutt, Louis. 68 South....Bavarian B Co. 2,600
Shields, Denis. 334 West....Beadleston & W. 1,900
Soal, Jacob. Unionport, N Y....Bernheimer & S. 175
Stuercke, J G....Beadleston & W. Confess of Judgmt. 600
Schambach, John. 218 East Houston....G Ringler & Co. 1,000
Silverman & Groburg. 17 Hester....H B Scharmann & Son. 1,500
Simon, Jacob. 1425 2d av....Lincoln I and G Assoc. 100
Smith, James. 221 Washington....Beadleston & W. 6,000
Stipek, Jan. 1395, 1397 and 1399 Av A....A & A Stipek. 1,500
Scharrenbeck, Geo. 730 Westchester av....A Hupfel's Sons. 9,000
Simons, John. 49 Greenwich....Bernheimer & S. (R) 250
Stueber, W and A. 59 1st av....J Ruppert. (R) 600
Thoernes, Wm. 210 W 26th....Bachmann B Co. 700
Tordick, Ferdinand. 1387 Av A....Beadleston & W. (R) 3,000
Vesely & Paspisil. 425 E 72d....Schmitt & S. 500
Voege, J H. 206 E 24th....G Ehret. (R) 500
Vogul, Julius. 1012 2d av....J Hoffmann B Co. 800
Wiener & Noltner. 104 and 106 E 4th....T Steinlger. 975
White, R J. 688 3d av....P Doelger. (R) 4,000
Wierk, H & Co. 368 Bleecker....Bernheimer & S. (R) 1,700
Williams, J J and E F. 2062 3d av....P Doelger. (R) 3,000
Zunk, J P. 165 East Houston....Bernheimer & S. 5,000

HOUSEHOLD FURNITURE.

Alden, Hattie. 345 W 28th....L Baumann. 121
Allen, G M & A S. 167 W 44th....E C Hinsdale. 130
Anderson, Emma. 160 W 29th....J Moriarty. 438
Ackerman, Viola. 469 West End av....S Baumann. 228
Adams, Frank. 1007 6th av....O'Farrell & Co. 450
Aller, Ada. 118 W 44d....I E Blake. 1,000
Armstrong, Mary. 160 W 23d....Jordan, M & Co. 500
Annesley, Isabel. 380 Columbus av....J Gregg & Co. 981
Atwood, M E. 266 W 39th....H Thoesen. 167
Bennett, Nellie. 290 E 126th....Jordan, M & Co. 433
Berkowitch, Mary. 156 Forsyth....H Kisler. 123
Boswill, Clara S. 156 W 4th....F T Higgins. (R) 111
Burton, Mrs C. 317 W 17th....O'Farrell & Co. 195
Burton, Mrs C. 317 W 17th....O'Farrell & Co. 94
Baer, Lorinia. 811 3d av....F J Brechtel. 461
Lartels, Franz. 214 E 84th....L Baumann. 152
Raundecker, Wm. 445 W 27th....L Baumann. 151
Bickhafer, Jacob. 517 9th av....O'Farrell & Co. 198
Bird, C P. 224 W 21st....L Baumann. 262
Brangan, W L. 789 Amsterdam av....O'Farrell & Co. 190
Brown, F A. 440 W 36th....L Baumann. 159
Bruno, Adelaide. 123 W 24th....L Baumann. 156
Burke, Michael. 105 E 98th....O'Farrell & Co. (R) 177
Beiley, U J. 108 W 45th....G E Beebe. 150
Bentley, E A. 200 W 101st....W E Wheelock & Co. Piano. 250
Brady, Rose. 346 E 13th....W E Wheelock & Co. Piano. 500
Breslin, Edward. 2284 2d av....W E Wheelock & Co. Piano. 275
Bannister, Edward. 1191 3d av....T Kelly. 215
Blake, Amanda M. 74 W 90th....J A Greenoe. 150
Christopher, Maria. 319 W 32d....T Kelly. (R) 125
Crane, Julia M. 56 W 46th....T Kelly. (R) 150
Cuyler, Sadie L. 71 W 88th....Finance Accommodation Co. 800
Calhoun & Hamilton. 136 E 118th....D Schwarzkopf. 477
Cocquelet, Mrs E. 162 E 82d....W E Wheelock & Co. Piano. (R) 108
Conkling, J F. 132 W 82d....J Baumann. 600
Cottrell, Abbie. 229 W 60th....J Baumann. 186
Crane, Nell. 295 West Houston....W E Wheelock & Co. Piano. 350
Casper, Amalie. 305 Elizabeth....R Irving. 890
Cawein, J D. 203 W 80th....H Thoesen. 110
Clark, Alice. 6 Bank....O'Farrell & Co. 117
Clist, Susan. 93 E 111th....Fennell & P. (R) 117
Cole, Alice. 67 8th av....O'Farrell & Co. 111
Corney, J H. 248 W 124th....Jordan, M & Co. 165
Crone, Rose A. 326 Lenox av....American Guarantee Assoc. 100
Canning, Mary. 214 E 27th....S I Herschmann. 221
Dounaher, Kate. 402 1st av....L Baumann. 166
Davis, Anna S. 309 W 54th....L Baumann. 263
Doughty, J E and M L. 8 Bank....E C Hinsdale. 100
Duncan, Annie. 327 E 37th....L Baumann. 281
De Ritter, P R. 468 W 34th....W E Wheelock & Co. Piano. 275
Dessau, Mrs B. 326½ E 79th....W E Wheelock & Co. Piano. 300
Donovan, Mary. 911 6th av....J Baumann. 171
Dowrey, Susie L. 128 Sumner av, Brooklyn....W E Wheelock & Co. Piano. 250
Davis, Jennie. 2284 2d av....Fennell & P. (R) 108
Delaney, J H. 1807 Park av....L Baumann. 131
Devoe, Isabella. 1899 Lexington av....R Thoesen. 129
Same. 1899 Lexington av....H Thoesen. 131
Dickinson, C H. 867 Columbus av....Brooklyn F Co. 175
Droescher, S R. 107 W 104th....S Heyman & Co. 122
Ely, E A. 206 W 39th....Jordan M & Co. 107
Enrich, Clara. 1043 E 170th....Fennell & P. (R) 110
Eaton, Sadie M. 158 E 18th....Garvey Bros. 137
Ebbets, F L. 318 W 86th....J Baumann. 151
Egleston, Mrs L. 56 1st av....W E Wheelock & Co. Piano. 275
Ehrgott, Levenia. 100 W 91th....Lincoln I and G Assoc. 200
Eicks, J J. 256 W 32th....L Baumann. 197
Ekberg, Herman. 318 W 49th....Manges Bros. 116
Fay, J M. 278 W 47th....L Baumann. 129
Finch, Florence. 146 W 16th....L Baumann. 143
Flynn, Rose L. 309 E 23d....M Robinson. 200
Franklin, Charlotte. 109 W 88th....D Schwarzkopf. 2,079
Foerich, Mrs. 265 Rivington....H S Eisler. 184
Freidline, C W. 54-56 W 93d....J & J Dobson. 506
Fetter, James. 310 Bedford av, Brooklyn....E Wolf. 170
Garner, Mary J. 1963 7th av....J O Schrader. 3,500
Goodman, Max. 216 E 74th....T Kelly. 153
Gannon, Ellen M. 45 South Washington sq....A R Maxwell. 295
Golding, T F J. 306 E 25th....J Gregg & Co. 160
Griffin, R H. 155 E 54th....Fennell & P. (R) 199
Gardner, E E. 175 E 111th....W E Wheelock & Co. Piano. (R) 137
Georgi, William. 361 W 55th....J Baumann. 125
Goldman, Augusta. 65 Mott....W E Wheelock & Co. Piano. (R) 170
Grace, Elizabeth. 62 E 111th....T Kelly. (R) 100
Greenbaum, Max. 172 W 96th....L Baumann. 111
Grey, Hattie. 226 W 37th....J J Israel. 500
Gunther, William. 164 E 88th....L Baumann. 171
Hackett, T J. Williamsbridge....M E Hewitt. 130
Hagemeyer, William. 344 E 20th....I C Northshield. 100
Hamilton, Mary. 80th st and 2d av....L Baumann. 158
Howard, Rose. 772 9th av....L Baumann. 184
Hubbard, John. 22 Bedford....F J Brechtel. 350
Halsey, Sarah E. 661 E 165th....W E Wheelock & Co. Piano. (R) 187
Hansis, C C. 278 W 38th....W E Wheelock & Co. Piano. 275
Harwood, S R. 808 E 52d....W E Wheelock & Co. Piano. 825
Harte, C E. 186 E 76th....Jordan & M. 107
Hayes, Teresa I. 41 Grove....W E Wheelock & Co. Piano. (R) 160
Hirschberg, Isidore. 419 E 87th....W E Wheelock & Co. Piano. (R) 115
Hagan, Mary A. 486 9th av....L Baumann. 110
Hamilton, R J. 175 W 102d....L Baumann. 124
Hanlon, Mary. 124 Cherry....H S Eisler. 102
Hennessy, Catharine. 83 W 91st....S Baumann. 146
Hines, Clara. 608 E 138th....S Baumann. 216
Hoetzer, Selina. 42 E 8th....O'Farrell & Co. 600
Howard, E A. 174 E 48th....E C Hinsdale. 100
Hall, Katie. 443 W 29th....Manges Bros. 128
Holden, Kate. 320 Rivington....S I Herschmann. 120
Jones, Mrs J. 241 W 21st....T Kelly. 137
Johnston, E E. 67 E 100th....Jordan, M & Co. 111
Jerome, Ella. 305 E 23d....Jordan & M. 140
Johnson, Charles. 26 Henry....Jordan & M. 110
Keller, H E. 353 E 77th....W E Wheelock & Co. Piano. 275
Keyser, Maurice. 119 E 82d....W E Wheelock & Co. Piano. 150
Klein, Mrs M. 1130 2d av....W E Wheelock & Co. Piano. (R) 193
Kenney, Irene B. 445 W 22d....L Baumann. 234
Krakauer, Morris. 226 Delancey....Alexander Bros. 147
Krum, J S and I O. Cortlandt and West sts....Financial Credit Co. 150
Kuhmarker, Max. 265 W 40th....L Baumann. 408
Kean, Ellen. 167 W 23d....O'Farrell & Co. 260
Kelly, D L. 1647 1st av....S Heyman & Co. 301
Kain, Thos. 135 W 6th....T Kelly. 171
Kendell, Lillian. 16 Lexington av....H Israel. 1,200
Loomis, F A. 54 Barrow....T Kelly. 168

Lynch, Minnie. 61 W 119th ...E C Hinsdale. 300
Loewenstein, Rob. 18 Macdougal....J Rubenstein. 157
Lucas, Minnie E. 237 W 124th....O'Farrell & Co. 178
Lambrecht, Annie. 438 E 56th....H Thoesen. 127
Lash, Goldy. 70 E 121st....E D Farrell. (R) 100
Lewis, Kate. 355 Hudson ...J Cagney. Piano. (R) 100
Lappin, A. 1553 Columbus av....Fennell & Pye. 178
Le Tart, Mrs L. 220 E 76th....W E Wheelock & Co. Piano. (R) 162
Liebenstein, Alfred. 87th st and 10th av....W E Wheelock & Co. Piano. (R) 215
Macdonald, J H. 273 E 7th... W E Wheelock & Co. Piano. 325
Mason, Grace. 151 W 85th....J Baumann. 690
McElwaine, Thos. 201 E 116th....Bollermann & Son. Piano. 250
Meyler, T R. 883 E 134th....W E Wheelock & Co. Piano. 250
Morrison, G M. 346 E 124th....W E Wheelock & Co. Piano. (R) 175
Morris, Miss A. 417 W 51st ...W E Wheelock & Co. Piano. (R) 144
Mulry, L V. 213 E 21st....W E Wheelock & Co. Piano. 275
Macreary, Wallace. 200 W 89th....O'Farrell & Co. 233
Maesch, Ferdinand. 324 E 48th....L Baumann. 176
Maguire, P W. 18 and 20 E 47th and Far Rockaway....J J Brady. 500
Mayo, Mary. 324 E 85th....F J Brechtel. 115
McGarry, Mary. 455 W 27th....O'Farrell & Co. 165
McGill, B J. 50 Greenwich av....H Israel & Son. 189
McGrath, Mary. 187 West Houston.. .Simpson & P. Piano. (R) 165
McNenany, Mary. 589 E 83d ...L Baumann. 124
Meason, Edmund. 2130 3d av....Dreisacker & Co. 219
Meeker, Mary L. 569 Broome....E D Farrell. 202
Miner, Harry. 91 Allen.... J Moriarty. 284
Mize, Fanny E. 81 W 101st... H G Ely. 213
Mordaunt, Jessie. 110 W 39th....S Morris. (R) 350
Murray, J J. 111 E 127th....E D Farrell. 154
Marcus, Bertha. 79 E 3d ...J Rubenstein. 529
Mason, Lizzie W. 4 W 33d....E D Neander. 1,500
McCabe, Susan. 307 W 39th....O'Farrell & Co. 196
Moody, Anna. 62 E 129th....Fennell & P. (R) 314
Morris, J L. 13 Tompkins....H S Eisler. 180
Nichols, Marion L. 6 E 60th ...S Heyman & Co. 859
Nixon, Laura L. 124 W 26th .. O'Farrell & Co. 123
Nowro-tstry, Hellmuth. 421 E 81st....L Baumann. 200
Naar, J J. 450 W 57th....L Baumann. 474
Naumann, Lottie. 123 W 67th....L Baumann. 184
Newhall, Mrs. 142 W 102d....J Moriarty. 104
Nolte, Etta. 85 Saratoga av, Brooklyn....L Baumann. 126
Nunzinger, J C. 113 W 129th....C Mulrisch. 700
O'Connor, Mrs J. 209 E 116th....Brooklyn F Co. 290
Odell, D E. 252 W 129th....T Kelly. 348
O'Hanlon, P F. 321 E 20th....W E Wheelock & Co. Piano. (R) 136
Pape, Hedwig. 327 E 24th....Jordan & M. 103
Paul, Mary. 409 W 19th....L Baumann. 123
Pendergast, Margaret. 500 E 82d....Simpson & P. Piano. 225
Peters, Frank. 317 W 86th....L Baumann. 188
Phillips, Nellie. 211 W 53d....T Kelly. (R) 190
Pickett, Mary. 404 E 15th....H Israel & Son. 218
Planchenault, Mrs Gabriel. 64 South 5th av....O'Farrell & Co. 161
Porter, Laura. 187 W 46th....T Kelly. (R) 125
Powers, Tresa. 779 2d av....L Baumann. 152
Prendegrast, Ellen. 189 W 16th....S I Evans. 150
Perry, Lizzie. 250 W 36th....O'Farrell & Co. 217
Quinn, D W. 380 W 21st....L Baumann. 137
Quirk, Emma I. 1010 Eastern Boulevard....W E Wheelock & Co. Piano. (R) 221
Rabold, Catherine. 101 W 93d....J Baumann. 974
Ramirez, Ellen. 445 E 88th....W E Wheelock & Co. Piano. 275
Rambo, S S. 595 Walton av....T Kelly. (R) 100
Reap, Michael. 817 E 138th....F J Brechtel. 238
Reichert & Wolpe. 69 Chrystie....G Pollak. 600
Rice, Anson. 1 E 52d....H S Graves. 950
Robinson, Annie. 31 W 42d....Simpson & P. Piano. 250
Roell, Joseph. 416 W 47th....F J Brechtel. 203
Reilly, Mary F. 501 W 144th....L Baumann. 210
Robertson, James. 123 E 116th....J Gregg & Co. 197
Roos, G N. 67 W 11th....L Baumann. 215
Saxton, R M. 159 Lexington av....G H Allen. 950
Smart, E L. 266 W 115th....S Heyman & Co. 159
Smith, C B. 225 W 115th....Brooklyn F Co. 364
Snyder, F A. 238 W 17th....S Baumann. 352
Stransky, Mary. 389 E 75th....L Baumann. 115
Strong, Mrs E O. 308 W 129th....Brooklyn F Co. 147
Strout, M Louise. 106 E 71st.. .S Baumann. 154
Salomon, Adolph. 366 W 116th....L Baumann. 325
Schaff, Phillipina. 222 Chrystie....F J Brechtel. 144
Scherrer, Conrad. 448 7th av....L Baumann. 190
Schemmeick, Chas. 1599 East End av....T Kelly. (R) 165
Schiff, Mrs D. 247 E 118th... H Thoesen. 224
Schwer, Antonia. 835 2d av....L Baumann. 142
Stater, J L. 56 E 4th....F J Brechtel. 148
Stillwell, Jennie. 211 W 53d....T Kelly. (R) 200
Sullivan, Kate. 495 3d av....E D Farrell. 183
Sykes, Sabina. 143 E 42d....M Rogers. 135
Skrivan, Frank. 43 Whitehall....Jordan & M. 165
Smith, Ellen. 627 3d av....W E Wheelock & Co. Piano. (R) 162
Schaefer, Louis and Lena. 125 Forsyth....S I Herschmann. 172
Spitzer, Sigmond. 63 Bank....T Kelly. 268
Thomalen, E A. 932 Jefferson....J Stahl, Jr. 400
Thomas, C R and I E. 786 11th av....F Coghill. 150
Tombak, Jacob. 62 Essex....L Baumann. 121
Twerst, Max. 215 E 53d....L Baumann. 284
Taylor, H S. 38 W 28th....R Fulford. 500
Thomas, Mabel. 138 W 33d ...L Baumann. 136
Thorp, Carrie V. 138 E 59th....R Norman. 975
Tringham, C M. 16 E 33d ...J Gregg & Co. 898
Vanat & Robles. 45 W 27th....Jordan, M & Co. 374
Van Heynigan, Jennie. 126 W 47th ...L Baumann. 155
Van Vleck, W H. 204 W 56th....T Kelly. (R) 170
Von Periera, Jerome. 41 1st av....W E Wheelock & Co. Piano. (R) 177
Walker, Rose. 439 W 35th....J Baumann. 149
Waters, Emma. 7 W 133d....J Baumann. 209
Wendell, Libbie. 79 E 113th ...J Baumann. 382
Whitby, Annie. 263 W 27th....W E Wheelock & Co. Piano. (R) 136
Wilson, Lizzie. 986 6th av....J Baumann. 695
Wilson, Rose. 51 Grove....Garvey Bros. (R)
Walsh, Minnie. 500 E 83d....Simpson & P. Piano. (R) 200
Wheeler, Edmund. 1506 2d av....J Moriarty. 373
Willey, F O. 310 W 116th ...T Merritt. (R) 200
Wilson, Arthur. 125 W 28th....O'Farrell & Co. 203
Wilson, R R....J Williams. 214
Walsh, Patrick. 293 Varick....O'Farrell & Co. 150
Warshauer, J C. 217 W 122d....Fennell & P. (R) 225
Weed, Marie. 347 Lenox av....Fennell & P. (R) 189
Weiss, Helene. 219 E 13th ...S I Herschmann. (R) 550
Weiss, Helene. 219 E 13th....S I Herschmann. (R) 491
Weile, A J. 241 W 32d....L Baumann. 212
Wilson, Adda. 111 W 11th....S Baumann. 190
Willson, A L. 683 E 141st .. W O'Gorman. 226
Ziegler, A L. 2118 4th av....T H Smith. (R) 150
Zagat, Mendel. 858 2d av....Brooklyn F Co. 488
Zillmann, T H L. 143d st and North River....Brooklyn F Co. 414

MISCELLANEOUS.

Axtmann, Albert A. 201 E 110th....G H Toop. Locksmith Fixtures. 600
Ahrens, William. 233 E 43d....J Curley. Coupe. 125
Arlington League. 240 W 14th....J B Tompkins. Club Fixtures, &c. 450
Bahan, W W, 261 W 14th ...M Halliday. Office Fixtures. 300
Beck, Samuel. 485 7th av....R Beck. Butcher Fixtures. 300
Bianchi, Joseph. 191 Park row....A Schwaab & Son. Barber Fixtures. 1,282
Bollmann, A and A, Jr. 252 E 74th....M D Ross. Barber Fixtures. 275
Broch, Max. 110th st and Madison av....A Schwaab & Son. Barber Fixtures. 516
Bannon, James. 233 E 37th....E Willis. Coach. 150
Baumann, C. 209 W 125th....Nat Cash Reg Co. Register. 175
Bellarora & Co. 49 Mulberry....W H Butler. Safe. 250
Bowles & Co. 215 Lexington av....D B Dunham. Coach. (R) 568
Barberie, John. 77 South....M Barberie. Ship Chandler Fixtures. 5,000
Behrens, C. 313 7th av....J Mathews Co. Soda Fixtures. 275
Blass, Henry. 509 6th....F V Mayforth. Horse, Cart, &c. (R) 350
Bruss, August. 218 E 44th ..H Oppermann. Horse, Wagon, &c. 150
Coben, Abraham. 34 Norfolk....D Goldstein. Grocery Fixtures. 80
Coben, M and I. 96 Canal....H Meyer. Machinery. 900
Coffey, J J. 64 8th av....Nat Cash Reg Co. Register. 400
Cornellise, John. 156 W 20th ...F B Whitney. Carpenter Tools, &c. 500
Cornish, W H. 33 Cannon....F M Whieler Co. Press. 875
Cerrigone, Georgia. 120 Centre....A Schwaab & Son. Barber Fixtures. 76
Colohan, William.. .G Dessecker. Coach. 500
Courtney, William. 511 W 54th....L S Keller. Horses. (R) 725
Cuchie, Luigi. 162 Greenwich....A Schwaab & Son. Barber Fixtures. 90
Copeland, E. 148 W 35th....J M Quimby & Co. Hearses. 2,135
Dall, F F & Co. Columbus av and 78th st....Nat Cash Reg Co. Register. 225
Dento, D & Co. 56 Pike....P Spitzenberg. Siphons. 250
Di Mento, Ilaqua & Germano. 261 3d av ...V Leone. Barber Fixtures. 100
Doane, S R. 325 W 17th....J Goold Co. Coupe. 150
Di Orio, C. 64½ Sullivan....A Schwaab & Son. Barber Fixtures. 170
Dunn & Emanuel. 129 Grand Boulevard....S F Dunn. Bicycles, &c. 500
Deinard & Foursicbom. 29 Orchard....Liberty Machine Works. Press. 160
Duchez, J M. 162d st and Elton av....E Richards. Fixtures, &c. 100
Dillon, M E. 155 E 35th....W H Buxton. Horses, Coaches, &c. 4,000
Duca, Santo. 439 E 12th....G Lagattuta. Barber Fixtures. 155
Ehlers, E J. Greenwich and Cedar sts....McKesson & R. Drug Fixtures. 870
Equitable Building and Loan Assoc. 115 Broadway....Mosler Safe Co. Safe. 145
Eastman & Krauss Razor Co. Southfield, S I ....Clinton Bank. Machinery. 5,000
Eveleth Printing Co....I H Wood. Machinery. 5,000
Evans, Geo. 35 Peck slip....S S Jewett & Co. Stoves, &c. 1,925
Farrand & Everdell. 88 Maiden lane....J P Rathbun & Co. Press. (R) 250
Fox, Max. 3 Jackson....F & G Haag & Co. Barber Fixtures. 100
Filippi, M and V. 61 South 5th av....J Souvay. Barber Fixtures. 152
Fowler, Edwin. 42d st and 6th av....F J Dupignac trustee. School Fixtures. (R) security
Fried, Louis. 197 Broome .... C Dierking. Butcher Fixtures. 95
Farrand & Everdell. 88 Maiden lane....J P Rathbun & Co. Press. 235
Flannagan & Downing. 563 7th av....E M Parez. Cigar Fixtures. 200
Gebhardi, Emil. 57th st and 1st av....E Gebhardi. Drug Fixtures. (R) 8,000
George & Brooke. 62 E 125th ...Duparquet, H & M Co. Range, &c. 211
Georgie, O H. New Rochelle....A G Hupfel. Machinery. (R) 600
Germiese & Davson. 2 Av D ...M W-ii. Barber Fixtures. 195
Giersberg, John. 31 Lewis....R C Blanche. Bakery Fixtures. 250
Girsch & Zinske. 87 Frankfort....C Potter, Jr. Press, &c. 2,200
Gluckmann, Joseph. 73d st and 1st av....Nat Cash Reg Co. Register. 175
Goldthwait, J C. 132 Nassau and 121 Fulton....S Goldthwait. Maps, &c. 1,600
Gonzales, G E. 17 and 19 Broadway....Lincoln I and G Assoc. Office Fixtures. 100
Gross, Louis. 112 3d av....Nat Cash Reg Co. Register. 200
Gunther, Herman. 168 Amsterdam av....J W Tufts. Soda Fixtures. 450
Goldman, Samuel. 87 Hester .. H Lubitz. Fixtures, &c. ½ int. (R) 100
Grimes, John. 319 E 93d. ..C L A Dow. Horses, Carts, &c. (R) 280
Gullotta, Giovanni. 55 Spring....G Manganaro. Barber Fixtures. 112
Hunter, S M....E M Eaton. Watch and Chain. 350
Hattermann, Fred. 34th st and 1st av....Schroeder Bros. Horse, Cart, &c. 150
Hess, John. 29 Broadway ...S Klingler. Barber Fixtures. 315
Hoffmann, G B. 127th st and 8th av....Donigan & Nielson. Wagon. 225
Hogan, John. 806 E 49th....D P Nichols & Co. Cab. 200
Haas, Frank. 30 Suffolk....J Powers. Bottling Fixtures. 122
Hadley, Sara. 923 Broadway....G B McCormick. Lace Designs, &c. 1,800
Halpin, Harry. 156 Madison....F & G Haag & Co. Barber Fixtures. 70
Harris Bros. 659 6th av....Mosler Safe Co. Safe. 145
Hawthorn, R H. 78 Warren....W Scott & Co. Press. 200
Hecht, David. 426 E 72d....M Weiss. Horse, Wagon, &c. 200
Hess, G and H. 279-285 Rivington....M Hess. Machines. (R) 5,408
Himmel, Charles. 536-542 W 46th....A Himmel. Sheds, Machinery, Horses, &c. (R) 3,000
Hoffmann, Geo. 1336 2d av....A Viol. Drug Fixtures. 1,550
Horstmann, Chas. 146 Bleecker....L Rion. Tools, Fixtures, &c. 1,000
Hunter, T and J. 419 E 91st ...G H Toop. Machinery, &c. (R) 2,000
Hanson, F G & Co. 19 West 3d....E Towle. Presses, &c. 1,905
Hendricks, S E...W O'Brien. Book "Hendrick's A & B Guide." security
Hiller, Geo. 60th st and 1st av....L Duignan. Horse and Truck, &c. 500
Hunt, W H. 301 and 303 W 125th ...W H D Orr. Machinery. 1,009
Jacobs, Simon. 60 and 62 Clinton....I Koplik. Tailor Fixtures. 250
Jacob Henkell Co .. P M Dingee & Sons. Press, &c. (R) 50,000
Johnson & Levine. 314 E 75th....C B Rogers & Co. Machinery. 225
Janvrin & Walter. Albemarl Hotel....W & J Ottman. Hotel Furniture. (R) secures rent.
Jones, W F....Campbell P P Co. Press. 3,259
Joyce, T A. 55th st and 7th av....Nat Cash Reg Co. Register. 175
Judson, F A ...Harper Bros. Electrotypes, &c. (R) 300,000
Jacob, Henry. 143 Bowery....C D J Noelke. Cigar Fixtures. 350
Janacek, Joseph. 25 Av A....R Fialka. Office Fixtures. 500
Jordan, Estella. 51 E 10th st and 703 Broadway ....M Valentine. Furniture and Museum Fixtures. (R) 6,000
Jordan, H C L. 841 8th av....L A da Cunba. Drug Fixtures. (R) 2,775
Kann, Jonas. 150 2d....M Hein. Photo Fixtures. 315
Kaskell, J. 104th st and 3d av....Nat Cash Reg Co. Register. 175
Kassebaum, Henry. 54 Bond... P Scheib. Barber Fixtures. 60
Keating, P H. 9 Burling slip....Johnson Peerless Works. Press. (R) 375
Kendall, Henry....M Armstrong & Co. Coach. 300
Kane, R V. 222 9th av....Weeks & Parr. Bakery Fixtures. (R) 590
Kerley, A P. 215 Boulevard....J Mathews Co. Soda Fixtures. 600
Ker, S C and L F. 522 W 16th ...L Moore. Horses, Trucks, &c. (R) 400
Krongold, Jenny. 140 8th av....H S Asche. Store Fixtures. 600
Lasner, Isaac. 246 Broome....P Reidenbach. Wagon. 150
Ledwith, Chas....N Lewis. Horses. 400
Levy, Jacob. 189 Chrystie ... C Dierking. Butcher Fixtures. 180
Lindner & Renig. Hudson and 13th sts....Prentiss Tool Co. Machinery. 708
Large, Thomas....Kean & Lines. Coach. 400
Lyon, J S. 510 and 512 W 24th ...S A Woods Machine Works. Machinery. (R) 157
Lesslauer, Albert. 255 W 27th....L Heinsfurter. Butcher Fixtures. 200
Liqriori, Antonio. 273 Bleecker....A Schwaab & Son. Barber Fixtures. 239
Lisanti, Domenico. 68 Essex....A Schwaab & Son. Barber Fixtures. 338
Lopreto & Distasio. 2½ Macdougal .... A Schwaab & Son. Barber Fixtures. 263
Lachner & Sons. 154 W 27th....J T Robinson. Machinery. 500
Lau, J. 195 Av A....Nat Cash Reg Co. Register. 175
Lehmann & Frankel. 1529 2d av....H Brenzel. Fixtures and Furniture. 110
Levin, Louis. 156 Essex....J T Robinson. Machinery. 400
Luxenberg & Vidal. 41 Centre.. .M Martousky. Machinery. 800
Maleson & Yankelson. 125 East Houston....S Yankelson. Store Fixtures. 100
Mandel, Simon. 22 Bleecker....R Mandel. Machines. 75
McCormick, R T. 682 9th av....Nat Cash Reg Co. Register. 200
McGarry, J B. 582 3d av....W M Scudder. Confectionery Fixtures. 150
Mahoney, Edward. 456 W 54th....D B Dunham. Coach. 400
McGowan, J J....D P Nichols & Co. Coach. 800
McMurray, J G. 488 4th av....Nat Cash Reg Co. Register. 200
Miebels, J F. 1964 3d av....Nat Cash Reg Co. Register. 175
Miesel, Jacob. 189 Rivington....W Miebel. Blacksmith Fixtures. 386
Morris, Daniel....M Armstrong & Co. Coach. 350
Mumm, H F J. 670 9th av ...C Kirchoff. Butcher Fixtures. 228
McCormack, Robt. 656 W 51st....F Cook. Horses, Carts, &c. 564
McFarland, Jas. 896 3d av....S Fisher. Cigar Fixtures. 179
New York & South Brooklyn Ferry and Steam Transportation Co. Union Trust Co. Boats, &c. (R) 350,000
N Y Mutual Gas Light Co....C Vanderbilt. Franchises, &c. (R) 250,000
Nobis, J C. 258 W 28th....P Pryibil. Machinery. (R) 64
Same ...same.. Machinery. (R) 60
N Y and Cuba Mail S S Co.. Farmers' Loan and Trust Co. Boats, &c. (R) 1,125,000
O'Donohue, M J. 2089 2d av....Nat Cash Reg Co. Register. 225
Obermeyer, John. 954 1st av....A Schwaab & Son. Barber Fixtures. 172
Ochs, G H. 1252 3d av....A N Smith. Machinery. 125
Oser, C D. 233 Av A....E Bausch. Butcher Fixtures. 300
Oelmeyer, Henry. West Boulevard and 130th st ....J Winter. Horse, Wagon, &c. 200

Parish, Mrs B. 69 East Broadway....Bennett & G. Soda Fixtures. 400
Pawn, Chu. 847 Broadway ...C Schafer. Store Fixtures. 1,500
Price, Levi. 718 E 11th....P J Hahn. Machines. 1,000
Peppe, Joseph. 37 Baxter... A Schwaab & Son. Barber Fixtures. 168
Perrone, Joe 519 1st av....A Schwaab & Son. Barber Fixtures. 301
Pfortner & Co. 142 and 144 Wooster....S Friedman. Machinery. 300
Polhamus, C T. 35 Liberty .. J A Cozzino. Office Fixtures. 400
Rogers, W H H, agent. 65 and 67 Crosby....C Potter Jr., & Co. Press. 1,800
Rosenbaum, J W & Co., 143 Elm....L H Cohen. Machinery. 350
Reilly, P H. 2 and 4 Spring ...G H Morrill & Co. Press, &c. (R) 1,017
Roosin, A & Bro. 254 Delancey....Bennett & G. Soda Fixtures. 100
Reiff, Abraham. 47 Pitt....G Pino. Barber Fixtures. 80
Russo, Carlo. 539 W 40th....P De Stario. Barber Fixtures. 60
Schapanek, Joseph. 166 E 123d...Rudolf Gierges. Horses, Milk Fixtures, &c. 300
Schleff, Morris. 107 Clinton....S Rines. Grocery Fixtures. 100
Stapleféld, August. 24th Ward....L Littlefield. Horses, Carts, &c. 133
Scellsi, L. 33 Spring....Mosler Safe Co. Safe. 155
Schutz, Valentine. 1332 Railroad av and 1095 Washington av....K Ball. Horses, Wagons, &c. (R) 100
Schwazler, K and A. 401 W 41st....J Helbock. Machinery, &c. 350
Schwenberger, Louis. 62 and 64 Duane....Liberty Machine Works. Printer Fixtures. 1,500
Scott & May. 16 Spruce....W Scott & Co. Press. 2,200
Sing Bros. 407 E 15th....Mosler Safe Co. Safe. 150
Schneider, Geo. 332 Delancey....G Hoepfner, &c. Trucks. 175
Sheffin, Margaret. 112 and 114 E 106th... G L Brownell. Undertaker Wagon. 400
Smith, Patrick. 258 W 47th....F C Van Orden. Horse, &c. 250
Smith, F A....C Minaid. Horse, Milk Wagon. 300
Stunkel & Schwedheim. 766 9th av....D Gerken. Grocery Fixtures. 600
Schneider, John. 24th Ward....J L Miller. Frame Building. (R) 110
Schweitzer Bros. 65 and 67 Watts....E F Savary. Machinery. 250
Shaw, W S. 1122 Lexington av....P C Kiernan. Plumbing Fixtures. 185
Smith, Fred. Grand Hotel....W Gavin, &c. Cigar Fixtures. 600
Thalmann, Amalia. 37 1st av....W Fischer. Butcher Fixtures. 150
Tuite, J J. 75 Beach... B Tuite. Horses, Carts. 704
Trafford, R L. 1421 3d av....J P Rathbun & Co. Press. 100
Tancredi, Sodovico. 1968 3d av....F & M Arra. Barber Fixtures. 125
Thompson, G W. 603 2d av... H Burian. Drug Fixtures. 650
U S & Brazil Mail S S Co....Atlantic Trust Co. Boats, &c. (R) 1,250,000
U S Pearl Button Works. 1323 Av A... Prentiss Tool Co. Machinery. 703
Valiquet, L P. 226 Centre....Prentiss Tool Co. Machinery. 240
Vanderbilt, Abram. 525 W 34th....E M Vanderbilt. Horses, Trucks, &c. (R) 1,500
Volkhardt, Adolph. 33 Av A....Liberty Machine Works. Press. 70
Vozzella, Michael. 63 Sullivan....A Schwaab & Son. Barber Fixtures. 83
Willis, Abel. 350 West....J M Willis. Cigar Fixtures. 300
Wright, G B. 34 Park row....G H Wright. Office Fixtures, &c. 800
Ward, M. 4th av and 31st st.. .Nat Cash Reg Co. Register. 175
Winter, L F. 418 W 27th....Prentiss Tool Co. Machinery. 190
Ziegenhorn, Robert. 548 1st av....R Hill. Grocery Fixtures. 200

BILLS OF SALE.

Brunner, Louis. 1316 1st av....J Heller. Clothing Store Fixtures. 1
Bemis & Merriam....Teachers' Publishing Co. Electro Plates, &c. 1
Bovchever, Samuel. 178 Madison....P Marcus. Grocery Fixtures. 160
Brick, Hyman. 123 Clinton ...V Grebin. Machines. 130
Conklin, G W. 1076 1st av....C H Budweiser, &c. Grocery Fixtures. 1
Carroll, F J. 219 Spring....Kennedy & Exner. Saloon Fixtures. 3,000
Cornellise, John. 156 W 29th....C L Strohmenger. Restaurant Fixtures. 500
Cumiskey, P J. 100 E 109th....A McMurray. Store Fixtures. 2,500
Deutschberger, F and L. 108 W 42d...W J Wolfe. Furniture, &c. 1,000
Dwingelo, Annie V. 778 2d av....R Hill. Grocery Fixtures. 495
Gerken, Diedrich. 766 9th av ...Stunkel & Schwedheim. Grocery Fixtures. 1,000
Graff, Kate... M J Moses. Furniture. 1,500
Hecht, David, 428 E 73d....I Koref. Grocery Fixtures. 500
Henrich, Franz. 1660 2d av....J Nageldinger. House Furnishing Fixtures. 3,000
Heyman, Blume. 24 Division....J Heyman. Delicatessen Fixtures. 1
Hirschel, Johannah. 304 E 72d....H Tausky. Furniture. 525
Hoehl, Andrew. 412 W 52d....M Hoehl. Bakery Fixtures. 400
Kevnaghan, Chas. 1863 2d av....J Koeler & Son. Grocery Fixtures. 600
Leone, Vito. 261 3d av....F Germano et al. Barber Fixtures. 200
McMullin, W J. 2688 3d av....B Ziesig. Grocery Fixtures. 275
Mabracek, Vincenо. 425 E 72d....Vesely & Bepisil. Saloon Fixtures. 700
Markowitz, Jonas. 1884 3d av....I Gluck. Jewelry Store Fixtures. 764
Mayer, Chas & Co. 41 Dey ...E Gottschalk. Office Fixtures. 250
McDermott, J W....J E McDermott. Horse, Wagon, &c. 25
Marchetto, Michele. 302 E 103d....A Groiosa. Shoe Store Fixtures. 115
Pagliotti, Peter. 409 Thompson....J Fogliasso. Bakery Fixtures. 400
Reilly, Thomas. 74th st and Av A....P Chambers. Saloon Fixtures. 3,000
Rnopp, H J. 432 3d av....H Oehl. Bakery Fixtures, &c. 2,750
Singhi, H U. 135 and 137 E 125th ...D & A Brandes. Store Fixtures, &c. 15,000
Schutz, Valentine. 1095 Washington av....M Schutz. Store Fixtures. 100
Scott, Andrew. 26 and 28 Frankfort ...C B Rouss. Press. 1
Sommer, John. 483 W 45th....P Masterson. Saloon Fixtures. 750
Teachers' Pub Co. 6 Clinton pl. ..E E Bemis. Electro Plates, &c. 3,250
Same....same. Electro Plates, &c. 1
Same....same. Electro Plates, &c. 3,250
Same....E J. Merriam. Electro Plates, &c. 2,174
Trankler, Henry. 63 Barclay....B Hamburger. Tinsmith Fixtures. 287
Winterroth, J M. 719 and 755 1st av....E J Winterroth. Butcher Fixtures. 1
Wallent, Abraham ...J Hepler. Store Fixtures, ½ interest. 100
Weber, H P. 269 Av B....E P Cramer. Grocery Fixtures. 675
Zimmer, Henry. 163 Mott....C Reifsteck. Saloon Fixtures. 1,600

ASSIGNMENT OF CHATTEL MORTGAGES.

Fidelity I and G Co to H E Baxter. (Mort given by E L and E W Welson, Feb 25, 1891). 890
Hinsdale, E C to J M Morrow. (D & L Pepper, Sept —, 1891.) 1
Leone, Vito to G Eufernio. (Mento, Iacqua & Germano, Nov. 16, 1891.) 88
McManus, P H to P Daily. (J White, Sept. 19, 1890.) 1,000
Meyer, Henry to Haaren & Meinken. (Ehler & Lind, July 31, 1890.) 3,000
Plummer, M & Co to Harlem "Reporter" Co. (W F Smith, Sept 8, 1891.) 200
Rottman, H J to Beadleston & W. (G A Eames, Nov 11, 1891.) 6,000

KINGS COUNTY.

DECEMBER 10 TO 16—INCLUSIVE.

SALOON AND RESTAURANT FIXTURES.

Burns, E. 818 Pacific....India Wharf B Co. (R) $900
Cady, S J. 460 5th av....W Ulmer. (R) 4,000
Cassidy, J. 364 Flushing av....Long Island Brewery. 1,258
Connolly, J A. 874 Gates av....I Roth. 700
Dougherty, W F. 243 Flatbush av....T C Lyman & Co. (R) 800
Engelke, A. 157 Pierrepont....Augusta Holzholle. Restaurant and Furniture. 500
Feeley, M. 74 Navy....D Curley. 1,800
Finn, T. 228 Hudson av....Claus Lipsius B Co. 500
Gentzlinger, Henrietta. 454 Graham av....Obermeyer & L. 600
Gopfert, G. 161 Greenpoint av....L Eppig. 500
Hanertt, Barbara. 1332 Gates av ...G J Graner. 400
Harnett, R C. 363 Carroll....F Munch Brewery. 600
Harrington, J. 2815 Atlantic av....Brunswick-B-C Co. Billiard Table. 185
Hartmann, J 76 Nevins... India Wharf B Co. (R) 480
Hellriegel, M. 32 Sackett... India Wharf B Co. 585
Hilbert, C. 104 Johnson av....J Eppig. 500
Hockmann, J J. 196 Hamburg av....E Ochs. 425
Hons, H. 444 3d av....C Ibs. 750
Horner, H W. 265 South 1st... Claus Lipsius B Co. 800
Hudok, G and M Reharka. 161 E 4th st, New York....S Liebmann's Sons B Co. 800
Hons, H. 444 3d av....Lembeck & Betz Eagle B Co. 1,250
Hill, R. 2487 Atlantic av ...Williamsburgh B Co. 301
Johnson, T. 195 Moore....Otto Huber Brewery. 300
Kennedy, P. 611 Grand....Streeter & Denison. 1,500
Krueger, J. 1288 Gates av ...W Ulmer. 600
Lake, A. 472 6th av....S Liebmann's Sons B Co. Pool Table. 85
Lenz, E. 149 19th....D G Yuengling B Co. (R) 950
Leopold, C. 1 Alabama av... Obermeyer & L. 1,800
Mehrsens, E W. Atlantic av, s w cor Ashford st....Danenberg & Coles. 600
Marshall, T C. 214 Grand....Beadleston & W. 650
McLinden, A and E. 91 Franklin....J Fallert B Co. 200
McPhee, D. 169 Norman av... C Frese. 688
McPhee, J H. 64 Meeker av....Claus Lipsius B Co. 696
Morgan, R and Sarah. 78 Front....G Ringler & Co. 1,500
Munch, C. 186 Troutman ...M Seitz. 1,000
Murphy, M. 5th av, s e cor 3d st ..J Wallace & So (R) 1,000
Murtagh, P. 3d av, s e cor 55th st....T C Lyman & Co. (R) 500
Niederegger, J. 187 Cook....L Eppig. 400
Reid, P H. Atlantic av and Alabama av....Danenberg & Coles. (R) 145
Schaffauer, A. 13 Union av... Claus Lipsius B Co. 500
Schmierer, Mary. 1533 Broadway ...Danenberg & C. 460
Stabler, J. 726 4th av....H B Scharmann & Sons. 2,000
Schneider, J. 263 Knickerbocker av....M Seitz. 566
Soffel, J. 98 Montrose av....Welz & Z. 1,000
Stonton, T. 717 Wythe av....J H Bereuter. Pool Tables. 300
The Jackson Club. 174 Sands .... Brunswick-Balke-Collender Co. Billiard Table. 150
Vielbig, B. 227 Johnson av....L Eppig. 400
Ward, J. 173 Myrtle av....W M Leslie et al. Sub to mort $1,500. 261
Wille, H J. 121 North 2d....P Weidmann. (R) 2,500
Wood, A S. 379 Graham av....F Meizer. Pool Table. 115

HOUSEHOLD FURNITURE.

Armstrong, Maria. 78½ Jackson....A Schulz. 112
Ball, Mrs B. 400 5th ... I Mason. 130
Barnett, Cora. 660 Gates av....H S Eisler. 104
Bosworth, J H. 130 Prospect av....M M Webster. 100
Baldwin, Sophie D. 85 Putnam av....M Webster. 100
Bernet, J. 1542 Broadway ...L Baumann. 117
Bleecker, Mrs J A. 137 Kosciusko... Brooklyn F Co. 177
Balassy, V. 654 Union....Wheelock & Co. Piano. 300
Carroll, Mrs P. 852 Bedford av....Brooklyn F Co. 188
Christy, J. 8 4th pl ...J McEnery & Co. 125
Cook, Nellie. Rockaway av, cor Dean st....Manges Bros. 135
Coombs, E B. 90 Halsey....R Silverman. 100
Cowen, Mrs R. 100 Lawrence .. Mullin's Sons. 118
Chambers, A. Cedar st ...I Mason. 109
Dohmann, Lizzie. 286 Gold ...J Baumann. 116
Davis, M R. 726 Carroll....M Webster. 100
Driscoll, Annie. 788 Union....Brooklyn F Co. 139
Drake, W E 226 Clermont av....Wheelock & Co. Piano. 300
Erickson, Maggie. 63 Woodbull....A Pearson. 183
Ericson, E C. 317 Sackett....Naome Field. 295
Fitzsimmons, Addie. 153 Havemeyer ...J E Murray. 164
Flockhart, W R. 334 Sumner av....Manges Bros. 188
Fuller, Anna. 1 Broome ...A Pearson. 106
Graham, Mary. 267 Nassau....A Pearson. 111
Garford, A F. 182 Schermerhorn....N C Hendrickson. 250
Howell, D B. 86 Hewes....M Riley. (R) 70
Hoyt, Annie M. 669 Quincy....C E Pierce. 100
Holland, S. 212 North 4th....H S Eisler. 108
Johns, Clara L. 210 Bridge ...A Pearson. 197
Keenan, Mrs E. 805 Clason av....I Mason. 205
Kellerman, Henrietta. 144 North 4th....Wheelock & Co. Piano. 665
Lander, Emma. 21 Vanderveer....J Baumann. 113
Long, Mary E. 59 Sumpter....A Pearson. 108
Maire, A. 55 Willoughby....Schlaeppi Bros. 1,650
Maire, Maria. 57 Willoughby....J Kurtz. 211
McLaurin, D P. 560 Greene av....Jane Anderson. 659
McNamara, Emma. 131 Myrtle av....W Weed. 180
Monds, Elizabeth. 1631 De Kalb av ...W Weed. 250
Mullen, Mrs B F. 488 Gold....Mullins & Sons. 202
McCartney, Mary. 234 Lee av....Brooklyn F Co. 158
Newcomb, C. 1076 Hancock....I Mason. 137
O'Connell, J P. 131 Greenpoint av .. O'Farrell & H. 121
Orvis, F W. 59 Somers....I Mason. 120
Olcott, W H. 19 St Johns pl... S Sandowich. 3,461
O'Shea, J. 967 Madison ... Mullins & Sons. 127
Panchaud, Eliz. 167 Sterling pl .. Manges Bros. 133
Purdy, J E. 890½ Gates av....Fennell & P. 143
Polson, J. 153 44th....L Baumann. 126
Riley, Mary. 97 South 8th....J E Murray. 294
Sievers, E. 325 Leonard....A Schulz. 128
Simmons, Debora. 69 2d....Brooklyn F Co. 245
Smith, Mary E. 324 Willoughby av....C S Lacey. 194
Suffern, W. 75 Clifton pl ...E Rose. 225
Sylvander, M. 231 Lynch .. L Baumann. 139
Tunnry, J M. 713 Butler....Mullins & Sons. 123
Townsend, Mrs F C. 247 10th....I Mason. 369
Weidhorn, C A. 36 Weirfield....Eliza Moebius. 500
Wolf, C. 318A 4th ...C E Pierce. 100
Warker, Mrs F. 166 Wyckoff av....C S Lacey. 123
Wilson, H C. 136 Lawrence....F A Dunn. 155

MISCELLANEOUS.

Artese, A. 93 Unon....T N Bowles. Barber Fixtures. 180
Askew, J B. Gates av, cor Tompkins av....J W Tufts. Soda Water Apparatus. (R) 700
Awe, C. 29 Herbert....W F Gade. Horse and Truck. 600
Barnes, J. Atlantic av, n w cor Grand av ...A Watson. Horses, Trucks, &c. 1,000
Behrens, F D. Railroad av, Belleplaine, L I....D Christoffers. Horse and Wagon and Cows. 350
Bedford, M. 314 6th....Mary A Townshend. Store Fixtures. 950
Burck, J. 894 Myrtle av....Lamson Consolidated S S Co. Register. 250
Burns, J G. 320 Myrtle av....Nat Cash Reg Co. Register. 175
Burns, E J. 77 Freeman....Brooklyn Heights R R Co. Saloon. secures rent, 310
Blauvelt, A. 476 Bergen....H Blauvelt. Butcher Fixtures. 150
Costilo, J E. 515 Kent av....Prentiss Tool and S Co. Crank Shaper, &c. 800
Cobb, G E and G Tillaus. 159 Flushing av....C Smith. Horse. 220
Calhoun, J S. 174 High....A M Stein & Co. Horse and Truck. 173
Clayton, J. 45 York....Phoebe Q. Clayton. Machinery. (R) 20,834
Coen, A. 202 Manhattan av....Mosler Safe Co. Safe. 200
Coe, J H. Division av, junction Clymer st....Mosler Safe Co. Safe. 175
Crankshaw, J E. 22 Fulton....A G Crankshaw. Printing Office. (R) 1,200
Douglass, W J. 260 Nostrand av....Clementina Robinson. Barber Fixtures 800
Davis, C H. 189 Bridge....W D Stout. Store Fixtures. 500
D'Apuzzo, G. 146 Fulton....G Trontera. Barber Fixtures. 124
Ermete, D. 12 Alabama av....F & G Haag & Co. Barber Fixtures. 235
Fogarty & Co. 58 Sedgwick... Prentiss Tool and S Co. Engine, Lathe. 440
Fulb & Bebiff. Livonia av, near Rockaway av ....Bennett & Gompper. Soda Water Apparatus. 105
Gallagher, H. 1244 3d av....W Martin. Barber Fixtures. 479
Gelb, Sophia. 472 Hamilton av....D Spiro. Tin Ware, &c 1,488
Glen, J. 1258 Broadway....F Mahar. Store Fixtures. (R) 349
Goldstein, L S. 291 Van Brunt ...National Cash Register. Register. 200
Green, D S. 316 5th av....A P Vollmer. Grocery Fixtures. 100
Grotz, W F. 152 Ewen ...C O Grotz. Machinery. 3,000
Hagadorn, F, and G A Pulis. 1576 Fulton....Johnson Peerless Works. Presses, &c. (R) 155
Hartfield, J C, & Son... I C Ogden, Jr. Presses, &c. (R) 750
Havecker, H. 194 Navy....N S Howell. Horse and Wagon. 250
Hess, G and H. 279-285 Rivington st, New York ... Maria Hess. Machinery, &c. 408
Holloper, S. Thatford av, near Osborn st....S Strauss. Cows. 110
Horton, J W & Son. 96 Plymouth....G E Wheeler. Horses, Wagons, &c. (R) 1,200
Harrington, F and W R Jones. 409 5th av... D B Dunham & Son. Coupe. (R) 101
Ing, H H. 221 5th av....L Baumann. 249
Kelly, A. 1591 Bushwick av....J D Wright. Bottling Business. 500
Kraemer, C C. 4 Decatur....J W Tufts. Soda Water Fountain. (R) 105
Kramer, H. 129 Prospect....C Werdermann. Horses and Ice Wagons. 900
Linn, F E. 50 Columbia Heights....C F Halsted. Machinery. 150

Lombardo, F. 167 Main....P Rosella. Barber Fixtures. 100
Magonigle, W E....Royal Horse Assoc. Horses. 209
Mullin, J. 405 5th av....N Langler & Sons. Carriages, &c. 300
N Y and South Brooklyn Ferry and Steam Transportation Co....Union Trust Co, New York. All Rights, Franchises, &c. (R) 350,000
Paoletti & Vorrosi. 310 Bedford av .. A Schwaab & Son. Barber Fixtures. 132
Pease, E K. 55 Broad ...J H English. Presses, &c. (R) 1,050
Rosania, Angela. 449 North 2d....A Schwaab & Son. Barber Fixtures. 278
Reilley, P H. 2 and 4 Spring st, New York....G H Morrill & Co. Printing Fixtures. (R) 1,017
Rose, C. 255 5th av....Lamson C S S Co. Register. 250
Ronalds, J H. 1460 Fulton....Mosler Safe Co. Safe. 100
Stewart, S J. Stable bet St Marks av and Park pl....C L Schwarz. Horse and Cart. 150
Schumacher, Wilhelmine. St Marks av....G Gross. Horses, Trucks, &c. 310
Steffens, F. 52 and 54 South 8th....H Weber. Horse, &c. 106
Sullivan, E....J C Hanlon, Oswego, N Y. Canal Boat W J Hanlon. (R) 1,800
Schleich, J. 54 Lorimer...G Niebling. Grocery Fixtures. (R) 150
Sleeper, W H. Pulaski st, near Reid av....B H Luce. Horse and Wagon. (R) 150
Same. 808 Broadway....same. Plumbing Fixtures. (R) 600
Spellman, J. 1193 Myrtle av... Damon & Peets. Press. 75
Thorpe, H H. 1542 Broadway....C A Thorpe. Plumbing Fixtures. 750
Van Deverg, J H. Sackett st, near 3d av....C B Rogers & Co. Printing Office Fixtures. 2,801
Vielmann, J. 1189 3d av ...E Vielmann. Butcher Fixtures. (R) 800
Von Bistramb, C H. 703 3d av....E Schopen. Drug Fixtures. 900
Whitman, A. 269 Myrtle av....Nat Cash Reg Co. Register. 175
Wiesendanger, H. 65 and 67 Union av....A Steinam. Drug Fixtures. (R) 550

BILLS OF SALE.

Black, P. 1944 3d av....W Martin. Store Fixtures. 200
Breitkopf, J. 414 Liberty av....Leibinger & Oehm B Co. Saloon. 300
Cobb & Fillans. 152 Flushing av...C Smith. Confectionery Store, Horse and Wagon. 220
Huschle, F. 184 Harrison....J Friede. Saloon. 1,200
Levison, M S with P Teichman. Dissolution of co-partnership as tailors doing business at 125 Greenpoint av. Levison sells out to Teichman for 3,300
McElheran, A. 161 Eagle ...S Liebmann's Sons B Co. Saloon. nom
Mueller, N. 1898 Fulton ..J Mueller. Saloon Fixtures. 400
Nau, M. 4th av and 18th st, College Point, L I ....Williamsburgh B Co. Saloon Fixtures. nom
Otten, C....J Konig. Coal Route, Horses, Carts, &c. 150
Oltmann, Mary L and C Nielsen. 242 and 244 Smith....L Nielsen. Grocery Fixtures. 1,500
Paturzo, M and G. Union st, cor Van Brunt st L T Paturzo. Store Fixtures. nom
Peters, A....H Hoops. Horse, Wagon, &c. 280
Smith, F E. 644 Gates av....H Wimmer. Drug Fixtures. 3,300
Spiro, D....Sophia Gelb. Machinery. 927
Tallman, C E. 2204A Fulton....Ada H Tallman. Drug Fixtures. 50
Von Bistraub, C H. 703 3d av ...E Schopen. Drug Store Fixtures. 900
White, C M....Watson & Pittinger. Machinery. nom

ASSIGNMENT OF CHATTEL MORTGAGES.

Folger, Louisa to N Langler. (Mort given by G Folger, Sept 8, 1891.) nom
Otto Huber Brewery to J Doelger's Sons. (J Blohm, April 16, 1891.) 395

NEW JERSEY.

NOTE.—*The arrangement of the Conveyances, Mortgages and Judgments in these lists is as follows: the first name in the Conveyances is the Grantor; in Mortgages, the Mortgagor; in Judgments, the Judgment debtor.*

ESSEX COUNTY.

CONVEYANCES.

Allen, F B—E P Ward, East Orange.......... $1
American Ins Co—J M Shepardson, South Orange 800
Arnold, F W—H E Demerest, Bloomfield........ 1
Ayers, A B—C Marsh, e s Ogden st 78 n Passaic st 100x100.......................57,500
Ballard, G M—Joy & Seliger Co, n e cor N J R R av and Hamilton st 77x100..........16,000
Barry, Owen—O San Giacomo, Commerce st. . 580
Beck, Adolph—P Lowy, South 11th st.......... 1
Bedell, F A—E W Brown, South Orange........ 1
Berg, Henry—F Berg, Jr, West Orange......... 1
Breakenridge, J H—E Mellor, Clinton.......... 200
Brooks, E J—J McKinley, East Orange.......... 2,860
Brown, W H—S B Jackson, Miller st........... 1
Brown, J S—F A Bedell, South Orange......... 1
Burke, Edward—F Gegenheimer, Highland st.. 606
Buchanan, M N—F B Allen, adj Henry Tichenors land, Newark................. 800
Chew, C P—A E Bedell, w s Mt Pleasant av 75 s Harney st 50x100....................13,000
Coe, Theodore et al exrs—F M Tichenor, Emmet st............................. 600
Same——H Pierson, Bay av.................. 2,200
Same as trustee—C A Coe, South 8th st........ 800
Coe, C A—C A Coe, South st.................. 1
Coe, J A et al exrs—H Pierson, Bay av.......... 1,100
Coffin, E R—E Appleton, w s 4th st 511 n Sussex av 25x95.................................. 4,200
Colton, G W—W R McKay, East Orange...... 12,500
Condit, E A—J Moorhouse, Bloomfield......... 1
Coyne, Bernard—E L Crevling, East Orange.... 550
Crane, C S—M S Crane, Caldwell............... 1
Crane, M S—C B Crane, Caldwell............... 1
Crawford, Alonzo—C B Matthews, East Orange. 13,000
Davimos, Abraham—M Abrahamowitz, w s Barclay st, 354 s Spruce st, 50x97.......... 3,300
Devine, Arthur—Atha & Hughes, 2 tracts, Nesbit st.............................. 2,875
Dewitt, W H—J M Seymour, Bloomfield......... 1,200
Drexel Impt Co—T R Hart, Montclair.......... 600
Durning, T F—C Coleman, Platt st............. 1
Eckert, John—G S Pollard, 3d st 1
Ernst, A F—E Ernst, Bloomfield............... 1
Ernst, Edmund—Ida Ernst, Bloomfield......... 1
Forest Hill Assoc—G N Ryder, Montclair....... 1,600
Geach, E P—I P Crane, Orange................ 780
Gould, H P—M R McChesney, Caldwell......... 1
Haase, L H—J Perkins, South 12th st.......... —
Hamilton, Ella V—H S Ward, East Orange..... 4,706
Henrich, Jacob—C M Henrich, Komorn st...... 2,000
Hilliard, R A—R Hilliard, South Prospect st.... 1
Hopper, C M—M M Baldwin, Clinton............ —
Isaacs, Joseph—W Cohen, Bedford st 1
Jacobus, J G—S B Jacobus, Caldwell........... 200
Jacobus, S B—J G Jacobus, Caldwell........... 200
Jayne, F A—J A Middleditch, South Orange.... 1,500
Jester, Jacob—C Huber, South 18th st.......... 850
Keasbey, A Q—M M Parker, South 9th st....... 625
Keen, Oscar special master—C A Sloan, South st 905
Knapf, George—W Vierling, Astor st.......... 1,400
Lecanto, Lilian—F M Wilmurt, West Orange.... 1
Lent, M L—M H Chase, s s Brunswick st 30x100. 3,000
Lewis, Frederick—J Lewis, Aqueduct st. 1
Same——same, Aqueduct st................... 1
Lewis, Joseph—W Clark, Aqueduct st......... 950
Lindsley, Stuart—Trustees of Methodist Episcopal Church of Orange, Orange..............23,000
Lister, J C—A Kirkpatrick, w s Broad st 350 s Harvey st 20x100............................ 4,000
Same——S A Smith, 48 Broad st 20x100........ 4,000
Same——M E Sherry, 38 Broad st 20x100 4,000
Macdonald, John—H Roberts, East Orange..... 800
Mackin, Francis—J Cadmus, e s Parker st 118 s Stephen Baldwin's land 68x210x89x214....... 6,300
Marsh, F C special master—A Devine, 2 tracts Nesbit st 2,825
Marx, Daniel—J C Eisele, Broome st.......... 1,000
Matthews, C B—A Crawford, w s Washington av 200 n Belleville av 191x300x100x300.......... 15,000
McChesney, J P—H P Gould, Caldwell 1
McGinnis, Richard—T McGinnis, Willet st...... 100
McGinnis, Thomas—R McGinnis, Perry st 500
Same——same, Willet st...................... 100
McWanner, W A—S E Hunter, Durand st 1,470
Moneghan, Ellen—F Coyle, Van Buren st....... 800
Mutual Benefit Life Ins Co—A Riley, Garside st. 1,100
Nisch, Margaret—M R Soudan, Jelliff av........ 580
Olds, F W—E H Condit, Bloomfield............ 1
Ortlieb, A M—L Sink, Ferry st................. 200
Osmun, A W—E W Edwards, w s Washington st cor Wm R Wards land 20x200..................20,000
Osborn, C H—F M Hinkle, Bloomfield........... 550
Same——F W Osborn, Bloomfield.......... 1,100
Parkhurst, A L—J T Glennon, Caldwell......... 250
Peshine, F S—M Nisch, Jelliff av............... 430
Pierson, Harriet—J A Coe et al, Bay av....... 1
Pollard, G S—A Eckert, 3d st.................. 1
Prieth, Theodora—F J Fitzsimmons, w s Wickliffe st 221 s Bank st 20x106............. 3,200
Protestant Foster Home Society—H L Soden, Summer av. 1,000
Provost, T C—Roseland Railway Co, Caldwell... 1
Reeves, F L—J H Reeves, Livingston........... 1
Rinne, Rudolph—J A Boese, Jefferson st 1
Robricht, J J—W A Ure, South 6th st........... 450
Satterthwaite, J F—M Geipel, Franklin......... 1,600
Satterthwaite, T E—Grace Church, Franklin.... 1
Satterthwaite, A F—T Mallaby, Chestnut st.... 1,600
Sayre, S M—Newark Passenger R R Co, East Orange.............................. 125
Sayre, L B—H Grover, East Orange............ 500
Schloss, Joseph—E Heyman, w s High st 131 n Court st 19x100....................... ,6,500
Schoemman, David—R Frey, w s Broome st 147 s South Orange av 25x100............... 4,850
Schoennamsgruber, George—M Palaner, Carlton st 4,100
Tausig, M B—C B Lawrent, North 6th st....... 1,900
Thieme, George—J Beopple, Court st.......... 2,730
Tuite, Mary—R Hilliard, South Prospect st..... 1,000
Vamo, A J—J S Strang, Montclair............. 1,100
Van Doren, P C—A J Pain, North 4th st........ 840
Van Ness, E A—A M Ehman, Winthrop st...... 350
Van Riper, P H—W Miller, Montclair.......... 9,000
Ward, E P—A S Allen, East Orange............ 1
Same——same, Runyon st 1
Weidenfeld, Camille—E C Simonson, West Orange..............................25,000
Wilde, E S—J Wilde, Newark Meadows....... 1
Williams, J E—P C Williams, Caldwell 1
Willcox, F C special master—W C Stinson, w s Belleville av s e cor Catholic Cemetery 26x125 4,500
Wilson, P K—H M Stern, Hunterdon st........ 500
Yost, Christiana—J L Yost, Bloomfield........ 800

MORTGAGES.

Abrahamowitz, Moritz—M Davimos, Barclay st. 600
Same——The Mechanic's B and L Assos, Barclay st................................ 2,800
Appleton, Edmund—F Bonykamper, Jr, 4th st... 2,300
Baldwin, F H—Orange Savings Bank, East Orange.............................. 2,500
Baxter, G W—E Beach, Orange............... 1,500
Same——R Baxter, Orange.................. 1,000
Bell, A A—H R Smith et al, Ferry st........... 3,000
Blanchard, L N F—Mutual Benefit Life Ins Co, High st.............................. 8,000
Boepple, John—G Thieme, Court st........... 200
Bowdren, C E—The Mutual B and L Assoc, Orange st............................... 3,000
Burnham, M A—R R Finck, East Orange....... 5,000
Cadmus, James—C Bried, Parker st......... 500
Same——same, Parker st.................... 2,500
Campbell, R C—J H Husk, Caldwell.......... 700
Canfield, M C—Caldwell B and L Assoc, Caldwell.................................. 600
Cavins, S R—Howard Savings Inst, Jackson st.. 1,500
Chesney, W F—T J Loughlin et al, Belleville av. 700
Church of Our Lady of Mt Carmel—Mutual Life Ins Co of New York, McWhorter st.........15,000
Clapp, A B—A S Robbins, East Orange......... 7,500
Coeyman, Samuel—M T Barrett, Mt Prospect av 600
Condit, Peter—J Moore, Bloomfield............ 2,000
Coursen, A F—M Sanders, North 9th st........ 1,000
Crane, E F—M C Freedley, Montclair.......... 1,000
Crozier, F De F—South Orange B and L Assoc, South Orange............................ 3,000
Cunningham, Thomas—Half Dime Savings Bank, Orange 1,500
Dailey, Patrick—E Drew, Bloomfield......... 1,200
Dauziesen, Frederick—J M Sommerkorn, South 9th st.............................. 500
Del Guercio, Ferdinando—The U S Industrial Ins Co, 7th av......................... 3,500
Devers, Oliver—G G Tennant admr, Lock st. . 1,000
Dickerson, M F, Jr—Roseville B and L Assoc, North 5th st............................ 2,600
Drew, M A—Fidelity Title and Deposit Co, South 8th st................................ 2,000
Duerr, John—Excelsior B and L Assoc No 2, Magazine st............................. 400
Eisele, J C—T W Lowree, Rose st............ 6,000
Faye, Eliza—The Mutual Benefit Life Ins Co, 13th av.................................. 5,000
Fitzsimmons, F J—T Prieth, Wickliffe st....... 2,900
Foote, Samuel—R A Harrison, East Orange ... 800
Francisco, L F—E Townley, Montclair.......... 3,000
Frey, Robert—D Schoenman, Broome st.... . . 1,800
Gaskin, Patrick—The People's B and L Assoc, Norfolk st............................. 400
Geiger, Peter—L Bundstein, Newton st...... ... 2,000
Gillin, C C—Eighth Ward B and L Assoc, South 8th st 2,000
Glennon, J T—A L Parkhurst, Caldwell........ 100
Harrold, John—M Gordon, Colden st.... 2,500
Hayden, Mariette—C Andrus, Montclair 2,000
Heitzmann, Matthew—M L Dusenberry, South Orange.............................. 1,000
Henrich, C M—J Henrich, Komorn st 1,000
Hopkins, W S—M Van Beuren, Irving st........ 600
Huber, Christian—J Jester, South 8th st....... 150
Johnston, Hayward—E M Sandford, Montclair.. 3,500
Joy & Seliger Co—G M Ballard, N J R R av..... 5,000
Keefe, S J—Fidelity Title and Deposit Co, Mt Pleasant av........................... 4,000
Kennedy, James—E Marshall, Montclair........ 500
Klinger, J A—J Hey, Clayton st 300
La Valla, Anthony—Protection B and L Assoc, Miller st............................. 2,350
Madison, Walter—M Gilson, East Orange...... 800
Mallaby, Theodore—A F Satterthwait, Franklin. 800
Marsh, Charles—A B Ayers, Ogden st.......... 4,000
McGinnis, Richard—N Feick, Perry st. 350
McKay, W R—G W Colton, East Orange........ 9,500
McLorinan, John—J H Baldwin, Eagle st...... 1,000
Megaro, Gerardo—J M Trumble, 8th av........ 1,500
Middleditch, Livingston—J C Jaques, South Orange 500
Moneghan, Ellen—Fourteenth Ward B and L Assoc, Clover st......................... 5,600
Morrison, L D—A S Robbins, East Orange.... 7,700
Mulquin, Ann—M Waldman, 4th av........... 2,000
Myers, G J—A F Tillou, East Orange........... 1,200
Niebuhr, Frederick—Thirteenth Ward B and L Assoc, Prince st 2,400
Nisch, Margaret—Fourteenth Ward B and L Assoc, Livingston st........................ 1,800
Osborn, F W—C H Osborn, Bloomfield......... 600
Parker, M M—A Q Keasbey, South 9th st 425
Purdy, M A—F M Olds, Verona av............. 200
Reamer, Absalom—Newark Quarry Co, Ridge st 369
Reeves, J H—P C Berking exr, Livingston....... 3,000
Reilly, J J—G A Richards, Schalk st.......... 230
Riley, Ada—W H Sanders, Garside st 600
San Giacomo, Onofrio—O Barry, Commerce st.. 280
Schmieder, Joseph—M S Richards, Komorn st.. 1,400
Schneider, Bertha—J H Kase, Clinton 1,800
Sink, Leopold—G Pfeiffer, Ferry st........... 150
Sloan, C A—E B Gaddis, South st............ 750
Solomon, Cecilia—The Newark B and L Assoc, Springfield av 5,000
Stager, C W—S M Vreeland, Franklin 1,600
Stinson, W C—J Reiner, Belleville av.......... 1,421
Stemmler, Emilie—P Hauck, Passaic st 1,500
Thieme, George—A F Klink, Newton st....... 1,500
Verdon, Elizabeth—Fireman's Insurance Co, Arlington st 600
Vierling, William—G Krapf, Goble st.......... 1,800
Weldon, J O—M Weldon et al, Chestnut st..... 1,000
Weldon, Malinda—S Hayes, Chestnut st....... 200
Wessel, E M—Eighth Ward B and L Assoc, River road.............................. 1,400
Williams, J M—W H Douglas, Aqueduct st..... 1,000
Woodhouse, James—The Woodside B and L Assoc, Oraton st....................... 800

CHATTEL MORTGAGES.

Belden, K B—C M Post, coupe and carriage.... 600
Bennett, F E—J Ketcham, furniture........... 100
Beyer, L J—S Steele, furniture............... 75
Cappozzo, Nicolo, G Krueger Brewing Co, saloon.................................. 155
Collier, J V—S J Faulkner, saloon............. 300
De Leonardy, Vincenzo—G Krueger Brewing Co, saloon................................ 350
Drake, I T—M S Drake, dynamo.............. 150
Dunbar, Patrick—G Krueger Brewing Co, saloon 173
Eno, Leo—J Pflaum, saloon.................. 150
French, G H et al—A Wolf, saloon............ 335
Guerin, N C—W P Osborn, horses.......... 500
Harding, J A—E Harding, furniture.......... 1,200
Harvey, C D—M F Harvey, furniture......... 80
Hoffman, Veronica—G Krueger Brewing Co, saloon................................ 169
Hough, Dennis—G Krueger Brewing Co, saloon. 114
Hurd, E M—J Mullins et al, furniture......... 282
Illaria, Alphonso—G Krueger Brewing Co, saloon.................................. 175
Linneman, Herman—J Ketcham, furniture..... 66
Macready, J J—G T Gamble et al, furniture.... 380
Match, James—G Krueger Brewing Co, saloon.. 800
McCauley, B T—J J O'Connor, furniture 189
McGuire, J E—E Alsdorf et al, piano.......... 265
Miller, Frederich et al—C Feigenspan, saloon... 299
Niegisch, Robert—W Busch, furniture......... 400
Nyatt, A R—Nat Cash Reg Co, register........ 175
Oese, Mary—A H Van Horn, furniture......... 165
Purdue, J G et al—W C Munn, horse and carriage................................. 262
Same——E J Brooks et al, coach.......... 227
Same——J C Williams et al, horses and carriages................................. 1,188
Racioppo, Gjatano—G Krueger Brewing Co, saloon.................................. 150
Ramisch, Richard—J J O'Connor, furniture.... 242
Sibbald, A G—G Krueger Brewing Co, saloon... 455
Silberstein, Joe—L Kohn, butcher shop 53
Simon, Abraham—Simon & Joseph, stock gents furnishing 2,006
Vogel, Henry—G Krueger Brewing Co, saloon.. 158
Waag, C H—G Krueger Brewing Co, saloon.... 600
Walder, David—C Feigenspan, saloon.......... 547
Weiser, Emil—The Home Brewing Co, horse and wagon................................ 150
Wheeler & Russell Hat Co—W B Thom et al, machinery...........................16,000

JUDGMENTS.

Mains, Margaret—Newark Passenger Railway Co 7,500
Moll, L M et al—C W Clayton............... 192
Vreeland, R B—J L Neck.................... 284
Wightman, J H et al—M L Bocher............. 1,065

HUDSON COUNTY.

CONVEYANCES.

Abrams, Sarah—S B Abrams.................. $250
Annett, C E—W C Alpers, Bayonne............ 5,000
Bacot, R C—P Lang......................... 1,110

Same——T Finn ... 1,290
Baumback, Maria—V L Stohr ... 2,100
Becker, Louis—E Gereulher, Union ... 4,000
Same——E Schneider, Union ... 2,000
Britten, Virginia F—J Benjamin ... 24,500
Same——J Benjamin ... nom
Bogart, J C—J J Worster ... 4,000
Bonn, H J—O Schultz, West Hoboken ... nom
Bostwick, Frances M—H Crawshaw ... 1,500
Bridges, Serena L—J Mellon, Harrison ... 350
Cassidy, Andrew—J Nolan ... ——
Central N J Land and Impt Co—Ebenezer Bessy, Jr, Bayonne ... 275
Same——same, Bayonne ... 600
Clarke, William, Jr—Bridget Kelly ... 2,800
Coles, J B by exr—J P Feeney ... 3,000
Condict, Fillmore—R H Crompton, Kearney ... 400
Same——H Cooper, Kearney ... 150
Coorbin, Virginia G—C Steingraber ... 250
Crevier, J C—J T Connolly, Hoboken ... 13,000
Crooks, G R—C E Rector ... 1,050
Danielson, W J—A McCaulsan, North Bergen ... 200
Dodge & Bliss Box Co—American Lumber Co ... 500
Dodge, C S and E K Meigs partners as Dodge & Co—Dodge & Bliss Box Co ... 1,000
Doyle, Michael—J Luhman ... 325
Effroy, J A—Bridget Welsh ... 2,000
Ehrhardt, Geo by master—Annie Lederle ... 1,560
Ferguson, Carrie F—W Green, Kearney ... 1,850
Fuller, A M—G F Meschutt ... 24,000
Gedney, J H—J Madden, Hoboken ... 1,850
Gibson, Emma C—T Ready ... 3,115
Goynes, Jonas—Sarah A Goynes, West Hoboken ... $5 and natural love and affection
Hall, Elizabeth M—L H Parker, West Hoboken ... nom
Hammond, Samuel—A Stietz, Union ... 1,900
Henderson, Chas—J A Wolverton ... 3,000
Hoboken Land and Impt Co—L Buzzolara, Hoboken ... 6,000
Jones, Ellis T—I H Blauvelt, Kearney ... 6,000
Keller, J L—W F Clouser ... 250
Kepfol, Leonhard—D Bermes, Union ... nom
King, Henry and Anna A—N J Flynn ... 4,400
Kline, G H—Mayor and Aldermen of J City ... 5,500
Laudregan, Winfred—C J Taken, Hoboken ... 1,025
Luxton, Susan—H H Hackmann, West Hoboken ... nom
Maass, W H—J W Bowenbank ... 700
Marion, J F—Julia R Rector ... nom
McKay, Archibald—J Kohn, West Hoboken ... 500
McIlhiney, James—H Schmidt ... 2,500
Nicoll, Amelia—H Sharn ... 150
Nichols, E H—C Anderson ... 175
Platt, Mary C—L Baye, Hoboken ... 100
Quinn, Johanna—J Beggans ... 1,500
Rector, C E—J F Marion ... nom
Richards, John—F J Bundscher ... 1,975
Schlachter, J C—J Leiser ... 3,500
Serrell, J A—Mary E Serrell, Bayonne ... 3,400
Simmons, Monroe—S L Van Wart ... 1,300
Smith, Elizabeth A—H Sharp ... 1,075
Soehler, Lewis—Emma Wendt ... nom
Soehler, Mary—Emma Wendt ... nom
Strocher, J G and Catharine G Vebeslage by sheriff—Exr Johann Kaiser ... 1,000
Symes, J H—L Steets, Union ... 1,900
Same——P Ininger, Union ... 300
The American Lumber Co—Dodge & Co ... nom
The Kearney Land Co—J Miller, Kearney ... 800
The Provident Inst for Savings—O H Lohsen ... 2,500
The Victory Silk Mill Co by sheriff—J O Schlachter ... 5,812
Thomas, W W—F King ... nom
Tobiasson, Owen by master—Phœnix Loan and B Assoc ... 1,000
Tremper, Lorena—A Tremper ... 1,000
Ville, Lena—Virginia Butten ... 166
Vogt, Eliza—J Parker, Jr, Kearney ... nom
Von Drehler, Herman, by exrs—H F Von Drehle, West Hoboken ... 3,000
Ward, John by sheriff—W Landregan, Hoboken ... 500
Welsh, Richard—J A Effroy ... other consid and nom
Wittpenn, J C—The Mayor and Aldermen of J City ... 22,520
Wolbert, Corbin—F C Wolbert ... 2,000
Wright, Naomi C E by exrs—Mary J Conway ... 2,050
Zahner, Lina—J Parker, Jr, Kearney ... nom
Zahuer, M H—J Parker, Jr, Kearney ... nom

MORTGAGES.

Alpers, W C—Bayonne B Assoc No 2, Bayonne, installs ... 4,000
Andres, Elizabeth—Montgomery M B and L Assoc, installs ... 2,000
Bambach, Maria—A Cointrel, 5 years ... 1,500
Beggans, John—Lincoln B and L Assoc, installs ... 1,800
Benjamin, Joseph—Virginia F Britten, 3 years ... 16,500
Benson, C W—J Benson, Hoboken, 1 year ... 3,000
Berry, Ebenezer, Jr—Exrs N S Hibbler, Bayonne, 3 years ... 2,800
Blauvelt, I H—Ellis T Jones, Kearney, 3 years ... 5,000
Boland, Francis—J R Bena, 3 years ... 500
Bowly, Mary A—H F Relub rd, 3 years ... 1,500
Bundscher, F J—C Hoffman, 2 years ... 1,400
Cahill, Elizabeth—Mary Ackley, 5 years ... 500
Coaney, Kate—Virginia F Britten, Bayonne, 4 years ... 4,500
Dodge, C S and E K Meigs partners as Dodge Co—Melisa P Dodge, 1 year ... 50,000
Donaldson, Hannah A—F J Matthews, 1 year ... 500
Dumiler, Peter—J H Mahnken, Bayonne, installs ... 1,260
Duryee, Mary E—Mary E Serrell, Bayonne, 3 yrs ... 1,350
Edward, E I—Lafayette M B and L Assoc, installs ... 3,000
Feickert, C L—Cecile E Eilshemius, Kearney, 5 years ... 3,000
Flatt, Mary—Centreville B and L Assoc, Bayonne, installs ... 1,400
Flynn, N J—H C Condict et al trustees, 1 year ... 2,000
Same——Fairmount M B and L Assoc, installs ... 3,500
Godfrey, Henrietta—Lincoln B and L Assoc, installs ... 2,400
Guenther, Edward—L Becker, Union, 5 years ... 2,000
Haggerty, J J—D A Haggerty, Hoboken, 5 yrs ... 3,875
Haggerty, Margaret E—D A Haggerty, Hoboken, 5 years ... 3,875
Haggerty, Mary A—D A Haggerty, Hoboken, 5 years ... 3,875
Haley, Cornelius—L Becker, Union, 2 years ... 1,100
Hape, Richard—E Hape, 1 year ... 100
Houghton, Maria C—Mutual Life Ins Co, 1 year ... 5,000
Kelly, Bridget—W Clarke, Jr, 3 years ... 1,960
Kruse, George—Josephus Plenty, 3 months ... 1,025
Lange, Herman—Hudson Trust and Savings Inst, Union, 5 years ... 5,000
Same——C H Wedemeyer, Union, 5 years ... 5,300
Lederle, Annie—Sophia L Boate, 5 years ... 1,500
Lennox, Robert—The American Ins Co, Harrison, 1 year ... 1,500
Linn, F D—Provident Inst for Savings, 1 year ... 5,000
Lohsen, O H—The Provident Inst for Savings, 1 year ... 2,000
McComb, L E—Crescent M B and L Assoc, installs ... 2,600
McGuinn, Michael—T Loughran, 3 years ... 800
Same——The Columbia B and L Assoc, installs ... 1,175
McLaren, Andrew—J Cooney, 7 years ... 800
Meyer, Alexander—H Meineke, 1 year ... 100
Meschutt, G F—W M Fuller, installs ... 24,000
Muhlhoefer, Geo—M Birthreiter, Hoboken, 2 ... 2,500
O'Neill, John—The Paulus Hook B and L Assoc, installs ... 4,000
Russell, Sarah P—Pamrapo B and L Assoc, Bayonne, installs ... 1,260
Schneider, Emil—L Becker, Union, 3 years ... 1,500
Scott, Moore—J Benson, Hoboken, 1 year ... 500
Seitz, Arthur and T H Mickens—Hoboken Bank for Savings, Hoboken, 4 years ... 3,100
Same——same, Hoboken, 4 years, 4 morts, each $2,800 ... 11,200
Small, Emily R—Improved Land and L Assoc, installs ... 2,000
Stohr, V L—A Cointrel, 5 years ... 1,500
Van Wart, S L—Union B and L Assoc, installs ... 1,300
Vonder Heyden, Paul—L Pfeffer, 2 years ... 240
Welsh, Bridget—J A Effray, 3 years ... 1,000
Wohlfahit, Herman—G Ahlerb, North Bergen, 1 year ... 500
Worster, J J—Lincoln B and L Assoc, installs ... 4,000

CHATTEL MORTGAGES.

Astor, Carl—The Ferger, Becker & Kohl Bavarian Brewing Co, saloon ... 195
Baker, Anthony—The Nat Cash Reg Co, cash register ... 150
Bindenvald, George, Hoboken—H Keattin, horse, wagon, harness ... 120
Butlar, Christian and Emil Lattmann, Hoboken—Lembeck & Betz Eagle Brewing Co, saloon ... 625
Caprio, Andrew, Harrison—The Gottfried Krueger Brewing Co, saloon ... 489
Clinton, H W—Alice E Martyn, hat business and furniture ... 1,440
Deienski, John—Hill's Union Brewing Co, saloon ... 300
Delap, Joseph—L Bauman, furniture ... 137
Deyenberg, Henry and Elizabeth, Hoboken—Commercial Credit Co, furniture ... 140
Foerch, Otto, Union—J Foerch, milk business ... 95
Hahl, Frederick, Union—The William Peter Brewing Co, saloon ... 700
Heise, Henry—The Jacob Hoffmann Brewing Co, saloon ... 1,000
Kasmia, August, Hoboken—The Chr G Hupfel Brewing Co, pool table, &c ... 125
Kraft, Charles, Hoboken—The E Waut Optical Co, jewelry business ... 122
Larsen, A M—Lembeck & Betz Eagle Brewing Co, saloon ... 750
Nagel, John, Union—F W Hille, express business, horses, wagons, &c ... 250
Nelligan, M F—The Malcolm Brewing Co, saloon ... 500
O'Neill, Thomas—The National Cash Reg Co, cash register ... 165
O'Rourke, T J—T C Lyman & Co, saloon ... 485
Parliment, A S, Arlington—L McCloud, horses, carts and harness ... 325
Runyon, F H—H M Denton, furniture ... 300
Schipman, Henry—National Cash Reg Co, cash register ... 100
Schlemer, Christian, Hoboken—E A Finck & Son, saloon ... 200
Schlemm, Robert, and Robert Boulanger, Union—R Schlemm, horses, coaches, &c ... 1,350
Schwan, Jacob—C Birdsall, furniture ... 130
Shaughnessy, John—The National Cash Reg Co, cash register ... 150
Taddy, Lena—L Bauman, furniture ... 103
Waterton, J E—A D Puffer & Son, soda water apparatus ... 565
Wood, Jane T—J W Gilmore, furniture ... 250
Wood, J H—C Birdsall, furniture ... 93

BILLS OF SALE.

Honeggan, John—F Hahl, saloon ... 1,700
Kunz, John—C H Zinn & Co, store fixtures ... 59
Schlemm, Robert, Union—J S O'Neill, saloon ... 1,000

ASSIGNMENT FOR BENEFIT OF CREDITORS.

Knoblauch, A A to A A Frank; assets, $6,075.19; liabilities, $5,945 99; all his real and personal estates ...

JUDGMENTS.

Condon, Patrick—Beadleston & Woerz ... 437
Long, John—Johanna Casey ... 71
Same——J Beck & Co ... 38
McLaughlin, John—T McLaughlin ... 27
Smith, Philip—W J Davis ... 620
Same——Van Steinberg & Clark ... 1,266
The Cartaret Club—L D Basford ... 547
The Mayor and Aldermen of J City—J Gray ... 333

BUILDING MATERIAL MARKET.

BRICKS.—It is almost an impossibility to find anything positively fresh or interesting on the market for Common Hard brick. Values are unchanged, the best commanding $5.50 per M, but the bulk of business from first hands is done at about $5.00@5.25 per M, and we have the rather singular feature of cost at mid-winter ranging only a small fraction higher than during the summer season. At the figures ruling, however, there is, all things considered, a very fair demand, as in addition to consuming wants dealers who have the room and can handle stock without too much expense are still willing to pile it away, especially as quality sustains a very good average and some of the offerings are really excellent. Arrivals have been pretty full. On Thursday there were thirty loads in the stream; but this did not appear to be a particularly disturbing factor, as many of them were understood to have come here to lay up for a later market, and would not be urged for the present. Furthermore, it was reported that shipments from the "Up River" district had ceased by the voluntary action of manufacturers, with a prospect that they would be shut off in any case owing to cold weather. So far as we can learn there has been no offering of Jersey makes; but, on the contrary, some sales of Hudson River stock have been made to Newark custom. Pales are at a discount, no one appearing to want them; and while "about former rates" are quoted, we learn of $1.50@1.75 per M being accepted for some of the best makes.

GLASS.—When the meeting of manufacturers recently held in Ohio adjourned without changing prices there were many of the Trade who looked for quite an unsettled market for window glass. A contrary result has developed, however, the tone really ruling firm, with regulation discounts closely adhered to. Manufacturers are believed to have agreed upon some such policy, and there has been a noticeable increase of interest on the part of many large jobbers who had heretofore been standing off. French glass rules steadily in price, and has a demand about balancing the arrivals. Plate has quite as much call as usual at this season, and for both domestic and foreign product the market is kept in good form.

LATH.—The market has secured a good practical test since our last, and the result fully verifies the optimist view of the situation for some time assumed by receivers. A few arrivals have taken place, for which there was a regular scramble, and the lucky buyers paid $3 per M without flinching, and considerable more stock could have been placed at the same rate. This is the highest plane of value attained for several years, and it looks very much as though it could be supported for some time, as the amount on the way and likely to be supplied are exceedingly moderate with a number of dealers out or nearly out of stock and anxious to make additions. Some of them are talking of making an effort to obtain stock from outside sources through rail shipments.

LIME.—There is no special change upon the market at the moment, though, if anything, the tendency is toward somewhat greater firmness. A few coastwise arrivals are coming to hand, and by careful management can be placed without trouble, with buyers making little if any objection to former cost. Receivers seem to calculate with some confidence upon small shipments for several weeks, owing to a curtailment of production, and the chances are against a decline. One or two cargoes are understood to be en route from St John.

LUMBER.—Immediate movements in the local market continue moderate and unimportant and very little change has taken place since our last. Such stuff as may be pressing into consumption does so in the due course of fulfilling contracts, and as a rule dealers still abstain from making any direct call for bulk lots. We have, however, heard of some business doing in the way of placing special bills for late winter and spring delivery and also some transactions in stock that manufacturers are prepared to promptly ship by rail, but most of the latter is to points outside the city. Exporters remain as somewhat uncertain and by no means liberal customers.

Eastern Spruce has arrived to a moderate extent this month, but most of the cargoes were under engagement and the odd over could be placed without much difficulty. There is no open or anxious demand, and some of the best customers have all the stock they desire at the moment, but so long as cost is not so high as to prevent natural competition with neighbors who stocked up earlier, dealers can be found ready to negotiate on anything of a standard quality. Within a day or two a few cargoes have come in and sold very well, and others are expected to a moderate extent, but some are lost. The following advices come from Eastward: The schooner Dolphin, of New York, Aylward, from Calais for Fall River with lumber, went ashore on Pond Island, during a snow storm last night, and is a total wreck. The crew are safe. Part of the cargo will probably be saved. The schooner Adela, Captain Wilband, of and from St. John, for New York, with lumber, also struck on Pond Island reef, but came off, and now lies afloat full of water. The extent of the damage to the vessel is unknown.

Piling is selling somewhat slowly just at the moment, but there has been inquiries from sources that carry an impression of preliminary moves toward better business. There is also a firmer tone shown on heavy sticks, especially such as come down the river, and now that arrivals from eastward have practically ceased holders feel more confident over the supply in basin.

Hemlock, so far as the immediate city trade is concerned, meets with continued moderate and more or less irregular attention, but for a week or two past there has been quite a gain in the volume of business with many of the interior points, and it has stiffened the position without advancing cost. Advices from Pennsylvania are hopeful regarding the result of manufacturers' meeting to be held next month.

White Pine seems to have a steady, healthful sort of market, without any feature of pronounced interest at the moment. The receipts since 1st inst. have been quite fair, owing to the river remaining open, but it is now understood that at the close of last week the final shipments were made from Albany and further arrivals are likely to be in the main by rail. Some of the resident agents continue to place a little Western stock until they commence to talk higher rates, and then negotiations cease. The call on foreign account affords only moderate assistance in working off supplies.

Yellow Pine remains steady and upon that basis the market has an assured status apparently. Some consumers have been inclined to hold back and even cast about to see if there was a possibility of evading placing orders with the local combination but apparently meeting no success so far as a gain in value was concerned. On the contrary buyers thus far do not as a rule discover that they have lost any advantages and are commencing to believe that the combine is likely to do just about as it promised, by maintaining an attractive cost for popularizing yellow pine, yet securing a good, fair margin for profit by a curtailment of handling expenses. Some few f. o. b. export orders have been booked.

Carolina Pine finds no continuous demand, yet in an irregular way quite a little business is accomplished with a promise of continuation. It is an all-winter selling stock and dealers renew assortments as necessity arises. Offerings have been ample for the call and former rates were ruling.

Hardwoods undergo little or no change at the moment, and are quite likely to remain more or less dull until after the turn of the year. Local accumulations are pretty full and pretty well assorted, with apparently no anxiety on the part of dealers to make additions, yet an offering of thoroughly staple stock at former rates would be quite likely to receive attention from the larger operators who can generally find room for anything that will "keep." The effort to place stock, however, is not very decided and few traveling agents are now on the market. Exporters must be shown choice goods before they will place their orders.

Shingles are not in particularly active demand just now, but the market appears fairly steady all around. Receivers think they have managed to curb the pressure of supplies from the Southward, and only moderate, irregular arrivals are expected from other quarters at this season.

GENERAL LUMBER NOTES.

THE WEST.

The Northwestern *Lumberman* as follows:

In respect to wl ite pi and Norway, the relation to supply and demand, with the strength of holders of stumpage as a part of the consideration, it is probable that values will not greatly change for years to come, and it is more than likely there will be no violent variations while the supply shall last. For the past four or five years prices of lumber have been neither high nor low, but have been maintained at an even tenor. The margin between the cost of standing pine and the selling value of lumber has been narrow, scarcely yielding a fair profit for logging and sawing, and rendering any marked decline in the price of lumber hazardous to the operator. But the firm holding of stumpage on the one hand, and the competition of other kinds of lumber than pine on the other, pinches the operator from both sides, and it is fine work for him to keep the margin wide enough to afford him room to turn stock at a profit. While this condition shall continue, and it probably will to the end, there will be little chance for extreme ups and downs of prices.

Receipts of lumber in Chicago for this year, up to December 5th, had amounted to 1,989,320,000 feet, or 86,500,000 more than last year for a like period. During the same time 287,054,000 shingles had been received, as compared to 496,107,000 during a like portion of 1890, a falling off this year of 209,053,000. Shipments for several weeks past have fallen below shipments in corresponding weeks of last year, which can be attributed to the unfavorable weather. Of the total of nearly 2,000,000,000 feet of lumber received in the time specified 1,327,881,000 came by lake, leaving 661,439,000 as creditable to arrivals by rail—an enormous amount to come that way, and showing the growth of the hardwood and yellow-pine business at this point. A minor portion of the amount coming by rail, however, is white and Norway pine.

Referring to the cargo trade at Chicago, the *Lumberman* says:

The stragglers are all in. The commission men report that they have wound up the season. The later sales, made this week, were of two loads of piece stuff from Bay City and one from Escanaba. The Bay City cargoes consisted of timber and joists, mainly long stuff. The short piece stuff sold at $10.50, the slim jims at $13, and the long 2x12 at $15 a thousand. These are prices that have prevailed since the middle of November. They indicate a strong closing market. Short piece stuff has sold in the closing days of the market this year at the identical price that the same class of lumber sold for last year at a like time. Slim jims are 50 cents a thousand higher now than then, and 2x12, 20 feet long and upward, $1 higher. A cargo of Escanaba dimension sold at $10.50 for short and $11.50 for 3x12.

There are no more cargoes to come on the market this season. The commission men are figuring up the season's business and making collections. Generally they state their sales to have amounted to about the same as last year; some a percentage more. They appear to be cheerful in view of the past and hopeful of the future. The market has held firm all season in spite of adverse conditions, and closes so strong, while the prospect of spring demand is good, that they believed that the next opening will be under favorable auspices.

At the yards the position in respect to piece stuff is very strong. Special sizes are being called for all the time. Eighteen-foot is in short supply. Strange to say, short lengths of 2x6 are well sold down, and inquiry for this usually slow selling and relatively cheap dimension is very active and urgent. Long joists are in demand, as they have been all season. The filling of World's Fair bills is picking up of 2x12 and other sizes, and thus inducing much inquiry between yards. When next year's trade shall swell to large proportions, it will be found that the supply of piece stuff and timbers will lack quantity in several particulars.

An exchange says:

There has just been turned out what may be considered a novel and useful craft, by the B. C. Iron Works Co., Vancouver. It is a complete floating logging outfit and camp. They were first used in San Francisco, about two years ago, and have given such satisfaction to the lumbermen that there are now 150 of them in use north of the Bay City. The work is described as follows: A 20x50 foot scow is used. The forward part is covered in and fitted up as a cabin, with bunks for fifteen men, kitchen, etc. The rest of the deck holds the machinery, which consists of a boiler (an upright one) and a 10 horse power engine and capstan, geared to 80-horse power, and a coil of steel cable. The scow is fitted with side paddles, and the shafting can be changed to propel her at a rate of five to six miles an hour. A trial trip was made across the Inlet, and she worked satisfactorily. She was then anchored near shore and 700 feet of cable taken ashore and attached to a 4,000 foot log, and hauled down to the water's edge through rough gravel and boulders quite easily. With this logging outfit a strip of 1,000 feet along a stream can be cleared up at a trifle of what it cost under the old system of having to buy oxen, pay for transportation and feed and build stables for them and houses for the men. Now when a patch is cleared up, they can move from place to place without any expense. The whole cost, including boat, boiler, engine and capstan, cables, etc., does not exceed $3,500.

Reviewing the market for hardwood the Chicago *Timberman* says:

The oak situation is unchanged. There is a slight demand for finishing stock, but absolutely no inquiry from the furniture trade. Thick oak is in better demand than any other, and the stock of this is said to be light. Plain-sawed red oak is generally held at about former figures, but prices on quarter-sawed and plain-sawed white are weak, except for Western shipment.

Implement and wagon stock continue to be fair sale, and buyers from some of the leading factories are now in the manufacturing districts looking up supplies.

The demand for walnut for foreign shipment is somewhat active, but as noted elsewhere, there is little inquiry for use in this country.

Better grades of cherry still sell readily at full prices, but the movement of common and cull is even more sluggish than a few weeks back.

Elm, basswood, maple, etc., hold about the same both as regards the volume of trade done and prices.

The Mississippi Valley *Lumberman* as follows:

Throughout the Northwest the slackening of trade has not in the least affected faith in good prices for the coming season. Neither does the prospect of an increase in the log cut this winter weaken that faith. At the head of Lake Superior there is 70,000,000 feet less number than usual at this season. There is a perceptible shortage in Chicago, and St. Louis dealers are looking up the river for supplies with which to repair their broken stock. But few dealers are now making any effort to sell lumber. At least thirty days' quiet is looked for by everyone and by many it is desired. This is the period when invoices are taken and yards cleaned up and put into shape for next season's trade. There is still a goodly amount of lumber shipped from this city, and some from St. Paul, but it is largely the filling of orders taken heretofore. One of the leading local firms, however, reports an average daily sale of from ten to twelve cars. One St. Paul firm is doing about one half this amount of business. These are rare exceptions, however, and are the result of personal work on the road.

NAILS.—Sellers still find it useless to attempt gaining any advantage. The demand stubbornly refuses to improve from any quarter, and with no concert of action about curtailing the product there is constantly more stock to be found than the market can take care of. In natural sequence prices remain weak all around. We quote Cut at $1.45@1.50 per keg for car lots and $1.60@1.75 per keg for parcels from store for iron, and add 5@10c. per keg for steel; Wire, $1.70@1.80 at mills, and 2.00@2.10 from store.

PAINTS, OILS, COLORS, ETC.—The general movement appears very much in accord with what is usually experienced at this time of the year. Taking the run of stock used by grinders and house painters the business is really quite small and unimportant and not expected to revive for several weeks. High class stock for ornamental work and car paints, however, are doing very well, a little better than usual if anything, and some of the specialties have quite a sale, prices on most of the goods already referred to ruling steady. Putty has been quite irregular in price and some low sales reported, but buyers of cheap lots, it is understood, are now grumbling about quality. Zincs have a pretty healthy sort of market and manufacturers quite generally feel satisfied with ruling conditions. Stories are afloat that the Lead Trust is trying to scoop in the zinc works of the country in order to shut off a competition that is becoming quite annoying. White Lead is in moderate demand, buyers preferring to postpone investments until after first of year, and the market irregular, jobbers now rather openly cutting the official list on the pure pigment, while mixed stock now and then sells pretty low. Association Corroders' rates stand as follows: Lead in oil in kegs and dry lead in kegs, in lots of less than 500 lbs., 7¼c. net; in lots of 500 lbs to 5 tons at one purchase, 7c.; 5 tons to 12 tons, one purchase, 6⅞c.; 12 tons and over, one purchase, 6¾c.; dry white lead in bbls. ¼c. per lb. less than price in kegs. Lead in oil 12½ lb. in tin pails, add 1c.; in 25 and 50 lb. tin pails, add ¼c.; and in 1 to 5 lb. tin cans, assorted (100 lbs. in case) add 2¼c. per lb. to keg price. Terms on lots on 500 lbs. and over, note or acceptance at sixty days, or 2½ per cent. discount will be allowed for cash paid within fifteen days of invoice date. To make either of the above required quantities any assortment of packages of white lead, red lead and litharge may be counted. The above quotations are free on board cars or boat at corroding point. Linseed Oil in moderate demand at about former rates, with considerable steadiness shown by city crushers, but Western manufacturers inclined to act a little bearish. We quote at general range at 35@40c. for Western, and 40@56c. for City. Spirits Turpentine shows somewhat greater steadiness. Offerings are comparatively light, and while demand shows no anxiety, there is considerable stock moving from day to day in small lots. We quote at 33½@34½c. per gallon, according to quality, delivery, etc.

TAR AND PITCH.—An ordinary trade demand has prevailed without having any influence of a direct character upon the position one way or another, and about old rates are current. Offerings are fair. We quote Pitch at $1.70@1.75 per bbl.; Tar at $2.15@2.40, according to quantity, quality and delivery.

MISCELLANEOUS.

MISCELLANEOUS.

MISCELLANEOUS.

BUILDING MATERIAL PRICES

LUMBER.

Appended quotations are based almost wholly upon prices obtained for goods from first hands. Yard rates necessarily range much higher owing to the expenses attending sorting out and grading cargo and even car lots, besides which must be added the cost of handling and carrying until consumers are ready to invest. Terms of sale also prove important factors and, altogether, it is impossible to give a line of retail quotations thoroughly reliable n character.

SPRUCE—Eastern—special cargoes delivered N. Y.	$16 50	@	18 00
Random cargoes, narrow	14 00	@	15 00
Random cargoes, wide	15 50	@	16 50
PILING—Eastern—cargo rates:			
Ranging 30@40 per cent 12 inch butt, 35 to 40 ft average length	4	@	—
Ranging 45@50 per cent 12 inch butt, 35 to 40 ft average length	4¼	@	
Ranging 50@60 per cent One-half 12 inch butt, 38 to 40 ft average length	4¾	@	5
Two-thirds 12 inch butt, 38 to 42 ft average length	5½	@	6
Three-fourths 12 inch butt, 40 to 45 ft average length	5¾	@	6
All 12 inch butt and up, 40 to 45 ft average length	6	@	6¼
Piece stick, 40 feet each	4 00	@	—
do. 45	6 00	@	—
do. 50	8 00	@	—
do. 55	12 00	@	—
Inch spars, per inch	20	@	22
Scaffolding poles, each	60	@	1 00
Clothes poles, 45 to 65 feet, each	3 00	@	6 00
HEMLOCK:			
Penn. joist	12 00	@	12 50
do. boards	13 00	@	13 50
do. timber, 20 ft and under	12 50	@	13 00
do. do. 22 to 24 ft	13 00	@	13 50
do. do. 26 to 28 ft	13 50	@	14 00
do. do. 30 to 32 ft	14 00	@	15 50
do. do. 34 to 36 ft	15 50	@	16 00
do. do. 38 to 40 ft	16 50	@	17 50
WHITE PINE—Good uppers and select, 1 to 2 inch	40 00	@	48 00
Upper and select, 2½ to 4 inch	50 00	@	58 00
Shelving	26 00	@	31 00
Pickings, 1 inch	33 00	@	35 00
Cutting-up, 1 inch	25 00	@	28 00
Bracket plank	30 00	@	35 00
Dressing-boards	18 00	@	22 00
Box, inch	13 50	@	14 00
Box, thick	14 50	@	15 50
West India shippers	16 00	@	19 00
Rio Janeiro do.	20 00	@	21 00
River Plate do.	29 00	@	30 00
Australia do.	25 00	@	30 00
YELLOW PINE—Random cargoes delivered N. Y.	19 00	@	20 00
Ordered cargoes	20 00	@	22 00
Flooring	24 00	@	24 00
Step plank	26 00	@	28 00
Common siding	15 00	@	16 00
Heart face boards	24 00	@	28 00
Car orders	21 00	@	23 00
At Atlantic ports, f. o. b.	12 00	@	12 50
At Gulf ports, f. o. b.	11 50	@	12 50
North Caroline pine timber	13 50	@	15 00
do. flooring 1 inch	16 00	@	22 00
do. do. 1¼	16 50	@	22 50
do. do. 1½@2 inch	24 00	@	25 00
do Shipping culls or box	12 00	@	14 00
do Plain and mottled ½@1¼ inch	18 50	@	26 50
Ash, white	38 00	@	48 00
Elm	20 00	@	22 50
Oak, plain	37 00	@	41 00
Oak, quarter sawed	52 00	@	55 00
Oak, quarter sawed, extra thick	56 00	@	60 00
Redwood	45 00	@	52 50
Maple, clear	28 00	@	33 00
Chestnut, clear	33 00	@	35 50
Cypress, clear	30 00	@	32 50
Black Walnut, good to choice	130 00	@	140 00
Black Walnut, ordinary to fair	100 00	@	120 00
Black Walnut, ⅝	78 00	@	83 00
Black Walnut, selected and seasoned	150 00	@	155 00
Black Walnut counters	110 00	@	150 00
Black Walnut, culls	35 00	@	40 00
Black Walnut, rejects	50 00	@	53 00
Cherry, wide	110 00	@	115 00
Cherry, good	85 00	@	100 00
Cherry, ordinary	65 00	@	80 00
Whitewood, inch	30 50	@	32 50
Whitewood, ⅝ inch	24 50	@	26 00
Whitewood, 1¼ to 2½ inch	32 00	@	34 00
Shingles, Pine, 16 inch, extra	2 75	@	3 10
do 18 inch, extra	4 10	@	4 30
do 18 inch, clear butt	2 90	@	3 10
do 16 inch, stocks	4 50	@	4 60
do 18 inch, stocks	5 30	@	5 40
Shingles, Cypress, 6x20	8 00	@	10 00
do larger sizes	11 00	@	16 00
do sawed	6 00	@	9 00
Cedar—Medium to large	6½	@	7½
do. —Extra large	7½	@	8
Mahogany—Small	4½	@	7½
do —Medium	8	@	8½
do. —Large	9½	@	12
do. —Extra Large	12½	@	14

VOL. XLVIII.---No. 1,241. NEW YORK, DECEMBER 26, 1891. Price, 15 Cents.

REAL ESTATE.

RICHARD V. HARNETT & CO. will sell at Auction,
Tuesday, Dec. 29th, 1891,
At 12 o'clock, noon, at the Real Estate Exchange and Auction Room, 59 to 65 Liberty St., N. Y. City,
414, 416, 418 East 64th St.—5-story and basement brick tenements. Four families on a floor. Size 25x75x100.5 feet each. In fine order and well rented. TERMS LIBERAL.
C. E. REED, Esq., Att'y, Stewart Bldg., 280 Broadway.

GEO. P. H. McVAY,
Commissioner for All the States
— AND —
NOTARY PUBLIC.
Harlem Branch: Uptown Press Office.
258 West 125th St., bet. 7th & 8th Avs.

D. KEMPNER & SON,
Established 1869,
REAL ESTATE BROKERS and AGENTS,
603 EIGHTH AV., near 39th St.
Special attention paid to collecting rents and the management of estates.
NOTARY PUBLIC.

BUSINESS ESTABLISHED 1847.
Bryan L. Kennelly,
Real Estate Broker, Appraiser and Auctioneer,
66 Liberty Street.

LEIST & FEUERBACH,
REAL ESTATE AND INSURANCE,
Office, 204 East 86th Street,
Near Third Avenue, **NEW YORK.**
NOTARY PUBLIC.
Renting and collecting. Entire charge taken of estates

AGNES K. MURPHY,
Successor to CAPT. WM. JAY MURPHY)
3d Av., N. W. Cor. 177th St.,
Real Estate and Insurance,
24TH WARD PROPERTY A SPECIALTY.
Member of Real Estate Exchange.
NOTARY PUBLIC. *Telephone, 437 Harlem.*

L. J. PHILLIPS & CO.,
REAL ESTATE BROKERS, AUCTIONEERS AND APPRAISERS,
NO. 149 BROADWAY.
Loans Negotiated. Telephone, 711 John.
Branch Offices 1[illegible]6 9th Avenue. 149th St. and 3d Av.

GRIFFIN B. DISBROW,
(Late with the Rhinelander Estate.)
Real Estate and Insurance,
56 EAST 23d STREET N. Y.
Notary Public.

JOSEPH CORBIT & CO.
(ESTABLISHED 1856)
Real Estate and Insurance,
CHARGE OF ESTATES A SPECIALTY.
212 NINTH AVENUE,
Corner 23d Street, **NEW YORK.**

J. C. DAVIS & CO.,
Real Estate,
149 BROADWAY.
Special attention to Renting Business Property.

H. V. MEAD. L. P. VAN RIPER. W. H. SMITH.
H. V. MEAD & CO.,
(ESTABLISHED 1859.)
Real Estate Brokers & House Agents
422 EIGHTH AVENUE,
Bet. 31st and 32d Sts. New York
Estates Taken in Charge a Specialty.

BENJ. P. FAIRCHILD. FRANK YORAN.
FAIRCHILD & YORAN
AUCTIONEERS
And Real Estate Brokers & Appraisers
171 BROADWAY.

BEVERLEY WARD,
REAL ESTATE AND INSURANCE.
Member Real Estate Exchange. 221 W, 125th St.

CORWITH BROS.,
REAL ESTATE.
309 MANHATTAN AV., BROOKLYN, E. D.

Henry B. Stacey,
REAL ESTATE BROKER
301½ West 116th Street New York.

REAL ESTATE.

SHAW & CO
REAL ESTATE
109 WEST 125th STREET, Near Lenox Avenue.

Banks and Trust Companies do not incur LOSSES in the ordinary course of business, and the law relating to such companies does not require any report of losses.

Insurance companies are organized *because of the possibilities of loss*, and the law requires their losses to be reported.

It is an anomaly in insurance for an insurance company not to report its losses.

No insurer or stockholder of such a company can judge intelligently of its management and standing without this information.

It is more important in title insurance than in any other branch of insurance, because it indicates the character of the examination of title.

The more careful the examination, the fewer the losses.

This company reports its losses annually and publishes them. The total amount since it began business is $2,210.

THE LAWYERS' TITLE INSURANCE COMPANY
OF NEW YORK.

CAPITAL, - - -	*$1,000,000*
SURPLUS, - - -	*400,000*

OFFICES:
NEW YORK: No. 120 Broadway,
Equitable Building.
BROOKLYN: 4 & 5 Court Square,
Thomas Jefferson Building.

DIRECTORS:
EDWIN W. COGGESHALL, President.

Henry Day,	John H. Riker,
William P. Dixon, Sec'y,	Henry E. Howland,
John Duer, Treasurer,	C. E. Strong, Vice-Pres't,
John T. Lockman,	Herbert B. Turner,
J. Lawrence Marcellus,	James M. Varnum,
David B. Ogden, Gen. Mgr.,	John Webber.

Real Estate Loan & Trust Co.,
OF NEW-YORK.
Mutual Life Building, 30 Nassau St.

Capital, $500,000. - Surplus, $250,000

Receives Deposits and Allows Interest.
Entire Management of Real Estate.
Acts as Executor, Guardian, Trustee, etc

TRUSTEES:

Hermann H. Cammann,	Charles A. Peabody, Jr.,
James M. Varnum,	Henry C. Swords,
Charles C. Burke,	Joel F. Freeman,
Horace S. Ely,	James William Beekman,
Ebenezer S. Mason,	Charles A. Schermerhorn,
Henry Lewis Morris,	Frank S. Witherbee,
Edwin W. Coggeshall,	Douglas Robinson, Jr.,
Robert Lenox Belknap,	James I. Raymond,
Edwin A. Cruikshank,	Charles S. Brown,
John Downey,	George G. De Witt.

HENRY C. SWORDS, President.
H. H. CAMMANN, Vice-President.
HENRY W. REIGHLEY, Secretary.
THOMAS H. TERRY, Real Estate Officer.

WILSON H.
BLACKWELL
AND CO.
REAL ESTATE
Auctioneers, Appraisers and Brokers,
67 LIBERTY ST. AND 259 W. 125TH ST.
Members New York Real Estate Exchange.

THOS. F. McLAUGHLIN,
REAL ESTATE AND INSURANCE,
1252 3d Av., near 72d St. 2015 7th Av., near 121st St

M. J. McKEON,
Real Estate and Insurance
2312 THIRD AVENUE,
Near 125th Street, NEW YORK.
RENTS COLLECTED.

WILLIAM KENNELLY,
(Established July, 1847,)
AUCTIONEER, REAL ESTATE
And Loan Broker,
47 and 49 LIBERTY STREET, - - NEW YORK.
Member of the Real Estate Exchange and Auction Room (Limited).

L. FROEHLICH,
REAL ESTATE, OFFICES.
169 EAST 61ST ST., ADJ. 3d Ave.
447 AMSTERDAM (10TH Ave.) COR. 81ST ST.
Member of Real Estate Exchange.

WM. H. HOYT. HERBERT G. SQUIERS.
WM H. HOYT & CO.,
Real Estate Brokers
5 VANDERBILT AVE.,
Opposite Grand Central Depot, New York City.
23d and 24th Wards, Westchester County and Suburban property our specialty. Telephone call, 1209 R Free Catalogues.

ARTHUR GORSCH,
REAL ESTATE BROKER,
1444 Third Avenue,
Southwest corner of 82d St.
ENTIRE CHARGE TAKEN OF ESTATES.

ROBT. AULD & CO.,
Real Estate and Insurance Brokers,
MANAGEMENT OF ESTATES A SPECIALTY.
Tel. Call, 358—39th. Eighth Av., cor. 56th St

GEO. E. HYATT,
REAL ESTATE AND INSURANCE,
164 EAST 84th STREET, NEW YORK.
Personal attention to Renting, Collecting and Management of Property.

MAINHART & LOWE,
Real Estate Brokers,
258 West 125th St., N. Y. Telephone, 358 Harlem.

R. PEHLEMANN,
Real Estate Broker,
Hours 11 to 2. **171 Broadway.**
Branch office: 879 Amsterdam Ave., near 78th Street.

JAMES KENNY & SON
Real Estate Agents,
80 East Houston St. (near Bowery), **N. Y**

MURPHY & WINFIELD,
REAL ESTATE
MOUNT VERNON, N. Y.
1st STREET, opposite New Haven Railroad Station.

J. SEARLE BARCLAY,
Real Estate and Insurance,
33 and 35 Liberty Street, New York.

MISCELLANEOUS.

PATENTED
Automatic Electric Speaking Tube Annunciators,
LETTER BOXES AND DOOR OPENERS, ETC.
OWEN WALSH, 105 Walker St., N. Y.

Electric Bells,
Door Openers,
Speaking Tubes, &c.
W. R. OSTRANDER & CO.,
195 AND 197 FULTON ST.
New York.

LUMBER

G. L. SCHUYLER & CO.,

1st Ave. to East River, 97th to 98th St.
Telephone, 186—79th St.
WALTER G. SCHUYLER. JAMES E. SCHUYLER.

— DEALERS IN —

Kiln-Dried Georgia and North Carolina Pine Flooring, Ceiling, Wainscoting and Step Plank. Spruce and Hemlock Timber, Spruce Flooring, Scaffold Plank, etc. Dressed White Pine, White Wood and Ash Ceiling, Flooring and Shelving. House Trim and Mouldings, and all kinds of Mill Work.

Specialty:—Kiln-Dried Vertical Grain North Carolina Pine Flooring.
Correspondence solicited.

BELL BROTHERS,
SPRUCE TIMBER
11th AVENUE AND 21st STREET.
Telephone Call, 18th St. Station, 191.

C. F. HODSDON,
DEALER IN
NORTH CAROLINA PINE
Flooring, Ceiling & Wainscoting,
738 to 744 Water St.,
TELEPHONE, 638 SPRING. NEW YORK.

DANNAT & PELL,
MAHOGANY AND LUMBER,
Yards, Broome St., E. R. Office, 24 Tompkins St.
Telephone Call, Spring 104.
CHAPMAN'S DOCKS, NEWTOWN CREEK,
Near Grand St., BROOKLYN, E. D., N. Y.

T. H. SIMONSON & SON,
Dealers in
LUMBER AND TIMBER,
Foot of 100th Street, East River.
Telephone Call, Harlem 115.

J. COPCUTT & CO.,
Cabinet Woods & Veneers
MEXICAN & ST. JAGO MAHOGANY.
432 to 440 Washington Street,
Cor. Desbrosses St., NEW YORK.
Telephone Call 76 Spring.

CRANE & CLARK,
LUMBER AND TIMBER,
Foot of 20th Street, - North River.
California Red Wood Shingles a Specialty.

WILSHAW & CO.,
MAHOGANY LUMBER.
Yards: Foot 8th Street, E. R.
Office: 228 Lewis Street.

A. T. DECKER CO.,
Wholesale and Retail Dealers in
GEORGIA AND FLORIDA
Yellow Pine
YARDS AND OFFICE:
FOOT OF BETHUNE ST., North River,
Telephone Call, 189 Spring. NEW YORK.

F. SKELTON,
1325 Broadway, New York,
Bet. 34th and 35th Streets,
West Side.

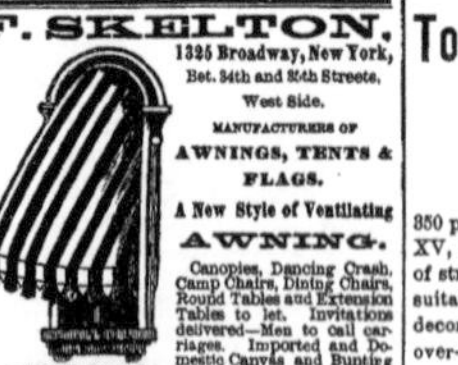

MANUFACTURERS OF
AWNINGS, TENTS & FLAGS.
A New Style of Ventilating
AWNING.
Canopies, Dancing Crash, Camp Chairs, Dining Chairs, Round Tables and Extension Tables to let. Invitations delivered—Men to call carriages. Imported and Domestic Canvas and Bunting for Sale.
MILDEW PROOF.

SHEA THE CLOTHIER
Cor. Broome and Crosby Sts., New York,
Is the only genuine dealer in leading American and European Tailors' Misfits at half price. Dress Suits for sale and hire. Established in 1869. Also **Ready-Made Clothing for Men and Boys.**

ARCHITECTURAL WOOD WORKERS.

THE N. Y. LUMBER AND WOOD WORKING CO.,
— MANUFACTURERS OF —
Architectural Wood Work
FOR PUBLIC AND PRIVATE DWELLINGS.
CABINET WORK A SPECIALTY.
Estimates furnished on application to main office,
173 Broadway, New York.

HARDWOOD LUMBER
In Carload Lots or Quantities to Suit Purchasers.
WALNUT, ASH, OAK, CHERRY, HAZEL and WHITEWOOD.

DIMENSION STOCK
CUT to EXACT SIZES,
KILN DRIED, GLUED, AND PLANED TO ORDER

For Builders, Frame and Cabinet Makers, Manufacturers of Furniture, Organs and Pianos—in fact all Wood-Workers. Sample order sheet and key to Grading of Dimension Stock mailed free. **Squares Cut to Sizes as Desired.**

H. HERRMANN, 368 BROOME ST., NEW YORK, U. S. A.

BUFFALO DOOR AND SASH COMPANY,
Manufacturers of **Doors, Sash, Blinds, Mouldings, Mantels, Stair Rails, Brackets, Etc.**
CABINET WORK A SPECIALTY.
FACTORY AT BUFFALO, N. Y. OFFICE AND WAREHOUSE, COR. 9TH AV. AND 17TH STREET
James H. Lee. Franklin Lee. Nelson Holland. Chas. S. Kendall.

A. B. JOHNSON & CO.,
WHOLESALE AND RETAIL DEALERS IN
TIMBER, PLANK & STEP PLANK, YELLOW PINE.
FOOT OF 96th STREET, EAST RIVER,
NEW YORK.
Telephone, 179 79th St.
A. B. JOHNSON. H. O. SANDERS.

GEORGE HAGEMEYER & SON,
MAHOGANY,
DEALERS IN SEASONED
HARDWOOD, LUMBER & VENEERS,
WALNUT, CHERRY, POPLAR, ASH, MAPLE, BIRCH, BUTTERNUT.
Plain and Quarter Sawed Oak, Gum and Sycamore.
Office and Yards, Foot of 10th & 11th Sts., E. R., N. Y.

JARVIS B. SMITH,
DOORS, SASHES, BLINDS
Cabinet Trimmings, Mantels, Pier and Carved Frames a Specialty.
Nos. 174 to 180 East 116th Street, New York.

GEORGE & CLIFFORD BROWN,
ARCHITECTURAL WOOD WORKERS
CABINET MAKERS
46 EAST 14th STREET, N. Y.
FACTORIES,
377 to 381 West 12th Street.
Proposals solicited. Estimates given

E. M. PRITCHARD & SON,
Manufacturer of
Window Frames, Wood Mouldings,
Interior Trimmings & Wood Mantels
138th Street and Mott Avenue, N. Y.

WOODS, JENKS & CO.,
— MANUFACTURERS —
Fine Cabinet Work and Interior Woodwork
For Public and Private Buildings.
No. 3 UNION SQUARE (Lincoln Building).
Factory, Cleveland, O. Henry C. Adams, Manager.

LOUIS BOSSERT,
LUMBER, MOULDING, SASHES,
SPRUCE HEMLOCK TIMBER. BLINDS AND DOORS.
CEILING, SIDING, PINE AND SPRUCE FLOORING, &c.
MOULDING AND PLANING MILL,
18, 20, 22, 24, 26, 28 and 30 Johnson Av.
Office, 6 and 8 Union Av., Brooklyn, E. D.
Timber Yard, Newtown Creek and Grand Street.

To Builders, Plastic Decorators, and the Trade.

FOR SALE, In consequence of the retirement from Business of the proprietor.

About 5,000 moulds, in boxwood, pear-tree, composition, lead and iron; also about 350 plaster piece moulds, the whole being in exquisite original designs in the Louis XIV, XV, XVI, Georgian, Elizabethan, Adams and Italian Renaissance styles, and consisting of strappings, centres, corner pieces, shields, clasps, mouldings, figures, etc., etc., and suitable for decoration of Theatres, Music Halls and other public buildings, also for decorative art furniture, chimney-glasses, consols and occasional tables, cornices, over-mantels and chimney-pieces.

Original Cost over £8,000, but £3,000 will be accepted for the whole.

For further particulars, and to view, apply to

THOS. HUGHES & COY,
194 EUSTON ROAD, LONDON, ENGLAND.

BUILDING MATERIAL PRICES

Our figures are based upon cargo or wholesale valuations in the main. Due allowance must therefore be made for the natural additions on jobbing and retail parcels.

BRICK.		Cargo afloat
Pale .... ₩ M	$1 50	@ 2 00
Jerseys	4 50	@ 5 25
Up-Rivers	4 75	@ 5 00
Haverstraws, seconds	4 75	@ 5 00
Haverstraws, firsts	5 12½	@ 5 52
Choice cargoes	5 37½	@ 5 50
Lorillard	5 50	@ 7 50

FRONTS.		
Croton and Croton P'ts—Brown ₩ M	$—	@13 00
Croton do. do.—Dark	—	@14 00
Croton do. do.—Red	—	@14 00
Lorillard	18 00	@ —
Wilmington	23 00	@24 00
Baltimore	37 00	@41 00
Philadelphia, alongside pier	23 00	@24 00
Trenton, do.	22 00	@23 00
Star	96 00	@ —

Yard prices, 50c. per M higher, or, with delivery added, $2 per M for hard and $3 per M. or North River front Brick. For delivery add $5 on Philadelphia, Trenton and Baltimore;

FIRE BRICK.

(Usual allowance must be made for store rates:

Welsh, ex vessel	$24 00	@25 00
English	27 00	@30 00
English, choice brands	35 00	@40 00
Scotch	35 00	@40 00
Silica, Lee-Moor	32 50	@33 00
Silica, Dinas	42 50	@45 00
White, Enamelled, English size, ₩ M	100 00	@105 00
do. do. domestic size	90 00	@100 00
American, No. 1	34 00	@35 00
American, No. 2	25 00	@28 00

CEMENT.		
Rosendale .... ₩ bbl	$0 90	@ 1 00
Portland, English, general run	2 20	@ 2 40
Portland, German, general run	2 25	@ 2 50
Portland, Belgian, general run	2 00	@ 2 25
Roman .... ₩ bbl	2 80	@ 3 00
Keene's coarse	4 50	@ 5 50
Keene's fine	7 00	@ 8 25

The following special quotations are furnished by agents of the brands, and they, not we, are responsible for the accuracy of the figures given:

Lafarge	2 90	@ 3 25
Stettin (German) Portland	2 40	@ 2 75
Portland, Saylor's American	2 15	@ 2 45
Portland, Dyckherhoff	2 75	@ 3 00
Portland, Gibbs & Co.	2 60	@ 2 85
Rosendale, Snyders, Bridge brand	1 10	@ —
Valley-Improved, H. N. Camp & Sons	95	@ —

BUILDING MATERIAL PRICES

DOORS, WINDOWS AND BLINDS.

DOORS, RAISED PANELS, WITHOUT MOULDINGS.

2.0x6.0	1¼ in.	$ 90	—
2.6x6.6	1¼	1 05	—
2.4x6.8	1¼	1 05	—
2.8x6.8	1¼	1 13	—

DOORS, PANELS AND MOULDED.

Size.	1¼ in.	1½ in.	1¾ in
2.0x6.0	$1 61	—	—
2.0x6.8	1 80	2 18	—
2.6x6.8	2 12	2 59	—
2.6x6.10	2 16	2 65	—
2.6x7.0	2 18	2 71	—
2.8x6.8	2 20	2 72	72
2.8x7.0	2 27	2 82	02
2.10x6.10	2 39	2 98	12
3.0x7.0	2 58	3 12	4 40
Hot Bed Sash Glazed, 3.0x6.0			2 15
Hot Bed Sash Unglazed, 3.0x6.0			85

OUTSIDE BLINDS.

1.0⅝x3.7 to 2.6⅝x5.7, plain	93	@ 1 71
do. do. painted	1 58	@ 2 90
7⅝x4.7 to 2.7⅝x6.3, plain	1 19	@ 1 63
do. do. painted	2 02	@ 2 75
1.9⅝x4.7 to 2.9⅝x7.3 plain	1 19	@ 1 89
do. do. painted	2 09	@ 3 19

INSIDE BLINDS.

Per lineal foot, 4 folds, Pine	—	@ 92
Per lineal foot, 4 folds, Ash or Chestn't	—	@ 1 10
Per lin. ft, 4 folds, Cherry or Buttern't	—	@ 1 30
Per lineal foot, 4 folds, Black Walnut	—	@ 1 50

GLASS

Window Glass, Prices Current per Box of 50 feet.

SINGLE.

Sizes.	1st.	2d.	3d.	4th
6x 8—10x15	$12 50	$10 75	$10 00	$9 50
11x14—16x24	14 50	12 75	12 00	11 00
18x22—20x30	19 00	16 00	15 00	14 25
15x36—24x30	20 50	17 50	15 50	—
20x28—24x36	22 00	19 50	17 00	—
26x36—26x44	23 50	20 50	17 50	—
26x46—30x50	26 00	23 00	19 50	—
30x52—30x54	27 00	24 00	20 50	—
30x56—34x56	29 00	25 50	22 00	—
34x58—34x60	30 00	27 00	25 00	—
36x60—40x60	34 00	31 00	27 00	—

DOUBLE.

Sizes.	1st.	2d.	3d.	4th
6x 6— 8x15	17 00	15 00	14 00	13 50
11x14—16x24	21 00	18 50	17 00	—
18x22—20x30	26 50	23 50	21 00	—
15x36—24x30	29 00	25 50	23 00	—
26x28—24x36	31 50	27 50	24 00	—
26x36—26x44	33 00	29 50	25 00	—
26x40—30x50	36 00	32 00	27 00	—
30x52—30x54	38 00	33 50	28 50	—
30x56—34x56	40 00	35 00	31 00	—
34x58—34x60	43 00	39 00	34 00	—
36x60—40x60	47 00	48 00	38 00	—

Sizes above—$15 per box extra for every 5 inches on French, and $10.00 per box extra for every 5 inches on American.

An additional 10 per cent. will be charged for all glass more than 40 inches wide. All sizes above 52 inches in length, and not making more than 81 united inches will be charged in the 84 united inches bracket.

Discount 75 and 10 per cent. single thick on French; 80 and 10 and 5 @ 80 and 05 per cent. on American.

HAIR—Duty 12½c. per lb.

Cattle	℔ bushel of 7 lbs	16@18
Goat		21@28

IRON.

Pig, Scotch, Coltness ℔ ton	22 50	@22 75
Pig, Scotch, Summerlee	24 00	@22 25
Pig, Scotch, Eglinton	20 00	@20 25
Pig, American, No. 1	17 00	@18 00
Pig, American, No. 2	15 50	@16 50
Pig, American, Forge	14 50	@15 00

BAR IRON FROM STORE.

Common Iron.		
¾ to 2 in. round and square ℔ lb	1 90	@ 2 00
1 to 6 in. x⅜ to 1 in	1 90	@ 2 00
Refined Iron.		
¾ to 2 in. round and sq.	2 00	@ 2 20
1 to 4 in. x⅜ to 1¼ insqu.re	2 00	@ 2 20
4½ to 6 in. x¼ and 5-16	2 20	@ 2 40
Rods—⅝@11-16 round and square	2 10	@ 2 30
Bands—1 to 6x3 16 No. 12	2 30	@ 2 50
Norway nail rods	3¾@	4

Sheet.	Common American.		R. G. American.	
Nos. 10 to 16 ℔ lb	2 75	@3 00	3 35	@—
Nos. 17 to 20	3 00	@3 25	3 35	@3 75
Nos. 21 to 24	3 35	@—	3 60	@—
Nos. 25 to 26	3 35	@—	3 60	@—
Nos. 27 to 28	3 50	@3 65	3 85	@4 10

	B. B.		2d quality.	
Galvanized, 14 to 20	4 75	@—	4 60	@—
do. 21 to 24	5 12	@—	5 00	@—
do. 25 to 26	5 50	@—	5 33	@—
do. 27	5 90	@—	5 70	@—
do. 28	6 25	@—	6 10	@—

Patent planished ℔ lb	A, 10c.; B, 9	
Russia ℔ lb	10½@ 11	
Rails, American steel	—	@30 00

LATH—Cargo rate, Eastern, slab

℔ M	3 00	@ —

LABOR.

Odinary, per hour	$ 28	@ —
Masons, do.	50	@ —
Plasterers, per day	4 00	@ —
Carpenters, do.	3 50	@ 3 75
Plumbers, do.	3 50	@ 4 0
Painters, do.	2 50	@ 3 50
Stonecutters, do.		@ 4 0

LIME.

Maine, common	—	85
Maine, finishing	—	1 00
State common cargo rate. ℔ bbl		80
State, Joints	1	1 10
St. John, common	@	—
Ground	85	@ —

Add 25c. to above figures for yard rates.

MISCELLANEOUS.

BUILDING MATERIAL PRIC

LUMBER.

Appended quotations are based almost wholly prices obtained for goods from first hands. rates necessarily range much higher owing to expenses attending sorting out and grading carg even car lots, besides which must be added the co handling and carrying until consumers are read invest. Terms of sale also prove important fa and, altogether, it is impossible to give a line of r quotations thoroughly reliable in character.

SPRUCE—Eastern—special cargoes delivered N. Y.	$16 50	@	
Random cargoes, narrow	14 00	@	
Random cargoes, wide	15 50	@	
PILING—Eastern—cargo rates:			
Ranging 30@40 per cent 12 inch butt, 35 to 40 ft average length	4	@	
Ranging 45@50 per cent 12 inch butt, 35 to 40 ft average length	4¼	@	
Ranging 50@60 per cent One-half 12 inch butt, 38 to 40 ft average length	4¾	@	
Two-thirds 12 inch butt, 38 to 42 ft average length	5½	@	
Three-fourths 12 inch butt, 40 to 45 ft average length	5¾	@	
All 12 inch butt and up, 40 to 45 ft average length	6	@	
Piece stick, 40 feet each	4 00	@	—
do. 45	6 00	@	—
do. 50	8 00	@	—
do. 55	12 00	@	—
Inch spars, per inch	20	@	
Scaffolding poles, each	60	@	1
Clothes poles, 45 to 65 feet, each	3 00	@	6
HEMLOCK:			
Penn. joist	12 00	@	12
do. boards	13 00	@	13
do. timber, 20 ft and under	12 50	@	13
do. do. 22 to 24 ft	13 00	@	13
do. do. 26 to 28 ft	13 50	@	14
do. do. 30 to 32 ft	14 00	@	15
do. do. 34 to 36 ft	15 50	@	16
do. do. 38 to 40 ft	16 50	@	17
WHITE PINE — Good uppers and select, 1 to 2 inch	40 00	@	48
Upper and select, 2½ to 4 inch	50 00	@	58
Shelving	26 00	@	31
Pickings, 1 inch	33 00	@	35
Cutting-up, 1 inch	25 00	@	28
Bracket plank	30 00	@	35
Dressing-boards	18 00	@	22
Box, inch	13 50	@	14
Box, thick	14 50	@	15
West India shippers	16 00	@	19
Rio Janeiro do.	20 00	@	21
River Plate do.	29 00	@	30
Australia do.	25 00	@	30
YELLOW PINE—Random cargoes delivered N. Y.	19 00	@	20
Ordered cargoes	20 00	@	22
Flooring	24 00	@	24
Step plank	26 00	@	28
Common siding	15 00	@	16
Heart face boards	24 00	@	28
Car orders	21 00	@	23
At Atlantic ports, f. o. b.	12 00	@	12
At Gulf ports, f. o. b.	11 50	@	12
North Caroline pine timber	13 50	@	15
do. flooring 1 inch	16 00	@	22
do. do. 1¼	16 50	@	22
do. do. 1½@2 inch	24 00	@	25
do Shipping culls or box	12 00	@	14
do Plain and mottled ½@1½ inch	18 50	@	25
Ash, white	36 00	@	43
Elm	20 00	@	22
Oak, plain	37 00	@	41
Oak, quarter sawed	52 00	@	55
Oak, quarter sawed, extra thick	56 00	@	60
Redwood	45 00	@	52
Maple, clear	28 00	@	35
Chestnut, clear	33 00	@	35
Cypress, clear	30 00	@	37
Black Walnut, good to choice	130 00	@	140
Black Walnut, ordinary to fair	100 00	@	120
Black Walnut, ⅝	78 00	@	85
Black Walnut, selected and seasoned	150 00	@	15[illegible]
Black Walnut counters	110 00	@	15[illegible]
Black Walnut, culls	35 00	@	4[illegible]
Black Walnut, rejects	50 00	@	5[illegible]
Cherry, wide	110 00	@	11[illegible]
Cherry, good	85 00	@	10[illegible]
Cherry, ordinary	65 00	@	8
Whitewood, inch	30 50	@	3
Whitewood, ⅝ inch	24 50	@	2
Whitewood, 1¼ to 2½ inch	32 00	@	3
Shingles, Pine, 16 inch, extra	3 75	@	
do 18 inch, extra	4 10	@	
do 18 inch, clear butt	2 90	@	
do 16 inch, stocks	4 50	@	
do 18 inch, stocks	5 30	@	
Shingles, Cypress, 6x20	8 00	@	1
do larger sizes	11 00	@	1
do sawed	6 00	@	
Cedar—Medium to large	6¼	@	
do. —Extra large	7¾	@	
Mahogany—Small	6½	@	
do —Medium	8	@	
do. —Large	9½	@	
do. —Extra Large	12½	@	

REAL ESTATE RECORD AND BUILDERS' GUIDE.
ESTABLISHED MARCH 21st 1868.
DEVOTED TO REAL ESTATE. BUILDING ARCHITECTURE, HOUSEHOLD DECORATION, BUSINESS AND THEMES OF GENERAL INTEREST

PRICE, PER YEAR IN ADVANCE, SIX DOLLARS.

Published every Saturday.

TELEPHONE - - - - - CORTLANDT 1370.

Communications should be addressed to

C. W. SWEET, 14 & 16 Vesey St.

J. T. LINDSEY, Business Manager.

"Entered at the Post-office at New York, N. Y., as second-class matter."

VOL. XLVIII DECEMBER 26, 1891. No. 1,241

IT is difficult around Christmas time to avoid being retrospective, and comparing the prevailing circumstances with those of a year before. What a difference does such a comparison disclose at the present time. The Christmas of 1890 financially was far from being a happy season. The good times which had existed during the earlier part of the year had gradually disappeared until a panic set in; and by the end of December the reaction was just about beginning. The outlook, however, was still far from pleasant. The course of business during 1891 has been just the opposite. The year began with tight money, shaken confidence and general apprehension. Large crops here and small crops abroad changed all this until now. When 1891 is about done everybody connected with Wall Street is feeling cheerful, and a year of good business and advancing prices is anticipated. What this cheerfulness is based upon is sufficiently well shown by the report of such a road as Lake Shore which increased its gross earnings $594,241, paid 6 per cent on its stock and spent $1,330,000 out of its operating expenses in improvements that are permanent in nature. In considering the bearing of such figures as these, it must be remembered that the traffic of the first half of the year was by no means large and that the increases were made during the second half in spite of the fact that general business was not lively. The miscellaneous freight which all railroads depend upon for much of their traffic was not plentiful, and the returns from this kind of business must have shown a falling off. If, then, a result so favorable could be obtained under such mixed conditions, how much more favorable is it likely to be when nearly every circumstance will be making for traffic. The heavy grain shipments are likely to continue during the better part of 1892, and there is also every probability that brisk general trade will increase the freighting of lumber, groceries, merchandise and that class of freight generally. Conditions of this character can hardly fail so to expand railway earnings that the great advance in prices of this fall will not only be maintained, but still further advances made. Another powerful general condition will favor this result—the certainty of easy money. In 1890 and 1891 prices were adapted to a 6 per cent money market; lenders all over the world were unable or unwilling to put their funds out freely. Consequently a year of restricted speculation and business followed; idle funds have been accumulating in the banks, and there is every expectation of money lending at 3 per cent on call and 4 or 5 per cent on time. This influence will surely be felt in bonds and investment stocks. Such securities as Reading General 4s, which at one time sold down to 75, will shortly be worth something like their prices of a few years previous. Six months from now a higher range of values ought to prevail throughout the whole list of railway securities due to the two causes mentioned, viz.: the certainty of a heavy traffic and the likelihood of easy money.

THE Board of Estimate and Apportionment ought to grant to the trustees of the Metropolitan Museum of Art a sum sufficient to pay the running expenses of that institution. For many years the trustees have assumed nearly the whole burden of running the Museum, besides being munificent in their contributions of works of art; and now that the exhibition is one of which the city may be proud, and the attendance so large that many people benefit, it is right that the expenses should be paid by the city. The Sunday opening has done all which the advocates of that step anticipated, large numbers of people having flocked to the Museum on the Sabbath. Money has been provided to effect this purpose for one year only; and the measure has proved so popular that its continuance should be secured to the people by the city. Furthermore the utility of the Museum will be very much increased if the city assumes the expense, for it will be thrown open at all times free of charge. The sum is so small that it ought not to weigh an instant against the great advantages which are thus secured to the frequenters of the Museum. It is true that in the past Tammany Hall has not been very closely allied to art, the members of that organization having not been eminent by their activity in artistic circles; and, doubtless, because of this fact the impression has prevailed that Tammany is not altogether friendly to art and the artistic spirit. Here is an excellent opportunity to prove that this impression is utterly unfounded, and if the Board should grant the appropriation it would be well to follow up such favorable action by some official recognition of the value of art by the various city Boards, particularly the Board of Aldermen. Probably a visit to the Museum *en masse* might accomplish this result.

Small Parks for the Poor.

SOME years ago the Legislature authorized the Board of Street Opening and Improvement to spend $1,000,000 every year in providing small parks in the crowded tenement house districts of the city. This enactment was welcomed at the time as a signal victory for those who believed that the municipality should more actively interfere to alleviate the misery of our poorer population, and it was believed that under its provisions an increasing amount of air, light and breathing space would be given to the wretches who choke and stew in the grim and dirty tenements. The Board, however, has not accomplished under this act anywhere near as much as was expected. Only three of these parks have been brought into existence under the provisions of the law; and not anywhere near as much money has been spent as the act authorized. The negligence on the part of the Board to carry out the law in the spirit in which it was enacted has naturally incensed the reformers of the city—particularly those who are actively engaged in charitable work in the slums—and recently they have been criticising the Board severely for its indifference to this important work. A society has been organized whose object it is to see that the tenement house districts are provided with a larger proportion of breathing space; and no doubt we shall hear from the whole matter when the Legislature meets.

No journal in the city has more persistently favored an increase of park space in New York than THE RECORD AND GUIDE, and when the enactment providing for the expenditure of $1,000,000 per annum in purchasing land for parks in the overcrowded districts, we hailed it as a wise piece of legislation. Under the present circumstances, however, we cannot blame the Board of Street Opening and Improvement for neglecting to take any further steps. It is, at least, questionable whether the condemnation of blocks upon blocks of property, and the removal of the buildings thereon, would not fail to give the relief which the reformers anticipate. The playgrounds for children would certainly be there; and doubtless on summer evenings these open spaces would so swarm with men and women, eager to get what fresh air they could, that a visiting "journalist" might read a fine lesson on the benefits of such improvements. Nevertheless we would suggest that to diminish the available space which the poorer population have to live in is by no means the most effective way of alleviating overcrowding. Two or three of such parks do not, perhaps, make very much difference. The population thus displaced can be scattered over a comparatively large area; and the resulting distribution does not increase very much the burden of the existing overcrowding. But the larger the number of such parks the larger the displacement, and the more closely and less healthily are men and women hived together. It is surely better that these unfortunate creatures should do without park space than that they should be huddled into less actual living space than at present.

In all attempts to ameliorate the condition of the tenement-house poor it should be remembered that these tenements result from the pressure of population upon space, and that the only way in which effectively to relieve the overcrowding is either to diminish the population or to increase the available area of habitation. Building laws, health departments, model tenements, a spasmodic alliance between philanthropy and 5 per cent, small parks, all may do something to alleviate the suffering and diminish the mortality caused by this packing of men; but they are only expedients, not grounded on the fullest and deepest criticism of the conditions of the problem. Tenements exist in New York because there are more than a million human beings drawing livelihood from our industries, and only a very confined space for them to live in. Their means do not permit a daily journey to and from some place in which land is cheaper, and in which the earth can afford a lot 25x100 to each family. They are forced to live where they live and consequently in the manner that they live. Obviously it is impossible to vary one of the terms of the relation producing this result. General Booth has yet to prove that colonization in country districts is practicable. The industries still remain, and men and women must be sacrificed to them. If any relief is possible, it must come from the increase of the space available for them to live in.

There is but one way in which this increase of available space can be obtained; and that is by some quick and cheap method of communication. Congestion can be removed only as circulation is increased. Rapid transit, as we have said, is more than means of getting up and down town. It is a matter which vitally concerns the moral and physical well-being of the majority of New York's population. We know that traveling in the elevated roads is at certain times almost intolerable, and that the overcrowded cars of the Manhattan Company have done much to deteriorate the manners of metropolitan manhood; we know that the interests of property-owners in the northern wards are suffering from present delays, and that the city is losing a population of thousands; but more important than the interests of both of these classes is the moral and physical health of far more than half of our population. We believe that the matter is being bungled even from the point of view of these two classes, but it is being entirely neglected from the point of view of New York's tenement house poor. They have no representation on the Rapid Transit Commission, and their "friends" on the press are more occupied in feeding them with the trivialities of the gutter than in standing up intelligently and persistently for their best interests. Yet these tenement-house poor, from their numbers and the unhealthiness of their position, have advantages to gain from rapid transit suited to their needs more important to the city than elevated cars would be that are not like sardine boxes and real estate that is not in sufficient demand.

The route laid out by the Rapid Transit Commission cannot help the tenement-house poor much under any circumstances, but from the present outlook it will not help them at all. The system is being planned and built for the comfortably-off; for them that stroll on Broadway and have a house or seven rooms and a bath all to themselves. In case the fare was made low enough—lower far than it ever will be made—some small good might come of it; but in order that New York's surplusage may be distributed, other lines will be needed, and lines operated not altogether for direct profit. Public interest demands at present just as the public voice will some time demand the assumption by the municipality of this office, and its operation to the advantage of its poorer population. If the charitable men and women of New York wish to aid their beneficiaries in one more way let them help to accustom the mind of the public to this necessity. A few isolated sociologists appreciate the step is imperative; but the majority of influential citizens would not be inclined to look favorably on such a proposition. The progress of the world always requires the civilization of influential citizens; and doubtless in time they can be brought around to the opinion of the minority. Meanwhile the outlook for the tenement-house poor is not particularly encouraging. On the one hand business, which can afford very fair rents, is encroaching on their meagre space; while on the other hand reformers would take off indefinite further blocks. Still one can never tell until one tries how much crowding and suffocation men and women will stand.

THIS rapid transit business with its interminable cross purposes must create quite a favorable impression in some minds for a strong autocratic government. How pleasant it would be to take the whole problem out of the hands of the blatherskite press, cranks, politicians, selfish property-owners and a public that can do nothing but "talk" everlastingly—how pleasant we say it would be if the confusing muddle could be turned over to a sensible autocrat who would silence the press peremptorily, build the road in spite of the petty protests of property-owners who will never suffer any real injury, and say to the great lumbering asinine public: "There, now, there is the best road that a competent corps of engineers have been able to devise and build for you considering existing conditions, pay your fares and ride in it." This building a railroad by popular clamor, as we are attempting now, is a sorry thing, and the results we fear are going to be very unsatisfactory. We have had a commission, supposed to be competent and honest, at work for several months and what are the prospects for the speedy accomplishment of anything? We have got a plan—a good plan—but one which is daily being more and more tangled up with personal and financial difficulties. We all want rapid transit, but Broadway property-owners don't want "any of it" past their doors or rather past their vaults. Jones doesn't believe in electricity as an adequate motive power; Brown does. This wise citizen wants an elevated structure through blocks, quite oblivious of cost; that wise citizen doesn't. Another wants an elevated road up Broadway; a thousand others do not. Mayor Grant, 'tis said, doesn't think so highly of underground roads since he visited the other side, and so the story goes on; everyone wants rapid transit, but wants it his way or some other way than the one way it can be obtained. With the opposition of Broadway property-owners, pretty fully developed just now, and with the really serious financial difficulties ahead, it seems more than probable that for some years to come the New Yorker will continue to travel up and down town in the present highly-civilized manner—hanging on to straps in the foul atmosphere of a hundred pair of lungs jambed in as tightly as possible between other human beasts. How civilized we are! How clear-headed and enterprising! The most obvious steps we won't take. We won't improve or try to improve our present facilities. We won't recognize even the dominant conditions of our situation. To meet present imperative needs we wisely plan a road that under the most favorable circumstances will take years to build.

THE surrender of the streets of Brooklyn to electric surface railways is a great triumph for the trolley—the greatest since the West End Railway Company of Boston adopted it with the consent of the authorities of that city. Brooklyn will be the largest city in the country whose surface railroads are operated entirely by electric traction, and undoubtedly the system will prove safe and adequate to any demands made upon it. No one claims that the trolley is the final improvement in electric locomotion, or that it is entirely without disadvantages and dangers, but it is claimed and satisfactorily proved that the system is of far greater efficiency than that of animal locomotion, and that the inconveniences arising from the poles and the wires are not important enough to counterbalance the advantages of the system. It is a cheap, speedy and comfortable method of running surface cars, and so fills all the requirements of such transit. In giving their consent to its introduction, the Common Council of Brooklyn set a precedent that will at once be most useful and most unwise. The action will be useful, because the fact that the system is used in Brooklyn will be of great weight when propositions are made to introduce it elsewhere. Thus, as we understand it, the Rapid Transit Commissioners of this city propose to use the most efficient form of electric traction available for local lines in North New York tributary to their main route, and the fact that the trolley, at present the most efficient form of electric traction, is successfully and harmlessly operated across the river will doubtless rob the opposition thereto of much of its virulence. Its advantages and disadvantages have been so thoroughly discussed that all the rubbish about the system, which the New York papers have from time to time published, will be taken only for what it is worth. But while the precedent set by the Brooklyn Common Council may in so far be useful, in another respect it is wasteful and wrong. The surface railroad companies of Brooklyn pay almost nothing into the city treasury in return for their franchises; and this was the one opportunity, of perhaps twenty-five or thirty years, to exact from them something like a proper return for the public property they use. It is well known that the operating expenses under the trolley is very much less per passenger and car mile than it is under horse power, for not only does the greater speed and convenience increase the number of passengers carried, but more power can be generated for the same cost under the former system than under the latter. Consequently, it is not surprising that surface railroad companies are eager to adopt electric traction; and this very eagerness can be made a source of public revenue. The Brooklyn Board of Aldermen could easily have forced the railway companies to pay a very handsome sum yearly into the city treasury, just as the New York Board of Sinking Fund Commissioners charged a good-sized amount to the Broadway Railroad Company for permission to introduce the cable system.

THE time will come when negligence to assert the public interests in so important a matter will be considered criminal. The companies undertake this improvement without risking one dollar. The few millions needed to make the change will be obtained by selling bonds. The increase of traffic and the decrease of expenses under the new system will do far more than pay the interest on the bonds; it will increase the earnings so as to enlarge indefinitely the distributions in dividends. As the city grows and the traffic becomes heavier and more remunerative the companies will still obtain all the advantages of the increase. The action of the Brooklyn Common Council means large fortunes for a few private individuals, and directly not a cent for the city. All over the country a class of street railway millionaires are coming to the surface—their money being made by buying a dollar's worth of public franchise for a few cents or nothing at all; and these fortunes will grow enormously as time goes on, for the wealth and population of the country belong to the cities. It is a queer commentary on the amount of intelligence and knowledge that enters into American municipal government, that, so far as we know, the matter of making these Brooklyn companies pay for the privilege they asked was not even broached. Some Aldermen and some property-owners thought the trolley was most dangerous and said so, the leading newspaper of the city was most wise on both sides of the question; but neither Alderman, property-owner or newspaper even intimated that the companies were applying for something of *value*, and that they should not get it only for valuable consideration. And yet Brooklyn is in many respects by no means the worst city in America. If the idea that cities should not be the only kind of corporations that sell goods without getting any return for them was fresh, and did not have time and authority back of it, there might be some excuse for this negligence; but all writers on municipal government are agreed upon this point, and we believe that that organon of democratic wisdom, the "sturdy sense of the common people," can not find any objection to this piece of professorial wisdom. Twenty or thirty years from now, when the size of our cities has made the problems of municipal government more severe than they are at present, the rulers of to-day will be heartily damned for their heedless and ignorant squandering of the assets of our cities.

Those Who Will Not Consent.

The Rapid Transit Commission is doing but little nowadays toward furthering the project it has in hand beyond working out the problem of stations on the Broadway-Boulevard line. But this is a task of the greatest importance, and involves almost all there is of difficulty in the entire project. No two stations on Broadway are alike in the conditions under which they are to be constructed. They will vary in their depth below the surface of the street and in the direction, size and manner of their approaches.

Special surveys are required of each building and vault area in which they are to be located, and of the area and foundation walls of the buildings, and a special construction has to be provided for each station. All these things take time and the commission is proceeding quite as rapidly in the matter as is considered consistent with safety and the lasting importance of the undertaking. No plans have as yet been definitely adopted, but several locations have been reported to the board by Engineer Parsons, with the surveys and plans of construction of the stations, and have been tentatively approved. Before any final action in the matter the public will be given an opportunity for the study and criticism of the plans.

The task of obtaining consents has begun to drag heavily. Every day Mr. Amory hears of property-owners who will not oppose the report of a commission favoring the construction, but who for a great variety of reasons are not willing to sign consents. These constitute as flat and peremptory refusals as those coming from the outspoken opponents of the road, such as Orlando B. Potter and Elbridge T. Gerry. So far as the commission's efforts to obtain the formal consents of the owners of a majority of the property along the line, in value, is concerned, they are to be classed just the same.

A partial list of those who have thus refused to sign formal consents, as well as of those who are opposing the project for less friendly reasons, includes the following:

The Western Union Telegraph Co., Nos. 193-199 inclus	$1,150,000
R. T. Wilson, Nos. 34 and 394-6 and 928-30	454,000
John A. Chandler, No 298	70,000
The Morris estate, No 12	144,000
B. D. Silliman, No. 86	175,000
Minnie D. Kay, Nos. 1763-69 inclus	350,000
Estate of L. A. Poillon, Nos. 428-30-32	200,000
Delaplain estate, Nos. 867-69-71	270,000
Estate of J. W. Wendell, Nos. 73-5, 711, 721-3, 1273-79 and 1639-49	800,000
First National Bank and Bank of the Republic, Nos. 90-2-4	999,650
Estate of Eugene Langdon, No 506	72,000
Harriet L. Schuyler, Nos. 520-2	140,000
Mrs. E. J. King, Nos. 1127-9 and 1706-8	158,000
Apartment Hotel Co, Nos. 1651-7	200,000
Estate of R. R. Campbell, No. 51	100,000
Benedict Brothers, Nos. 169-71	315,000
M. C. King, No. 243	130,000
Sailors' Snug Harbor, Nos. 743 to 785 and 746 to 784 inclus	3,448,500
Dutch Reformed Church, Nos. 192 to 200 and 204 to 210 inclus	1,567,000
Duchess of Marlborough, Nos. 536, 636-8 and 736	264,000
Chemical National Bank, Nos. 269-70	281,000
Elbridge T. and Hannah Gerry, Nos. 403, 631-35, 739-41, 813, 454, 890 and 913	918,000
Hamilton Fish, No. 630	70,000
Broadway National Bank, No. 237	312,700
Orlando B. Potter, Nos. 69-73, 312-18, 86-88, 1751-61, 565-7 and 1772 and 1774	1,544,000
St. Denis Hotel Co. Nos 797-801	280,000
American Express Co., Nos. 365-7	315,000

This makes a total of $14,795,850, or nearly $5,000,000 more than have consented, excepting the municipality, on the same line of road, and this list does not include about twice as many more of smaller amount, respectively, nor any of the "hopeful cases," such as Judge Hilton, the Astors, the Equitable Life Insurance Company and the Trinity Corporation. They are the principal in amount among those who have declined to sign formal consent. But, on the other hand, more than three-fourths of them will offer no opposition to the appointment of a commission by the Supreme Court, as provided in the act, to stand in their places in the matter of consents. The petition to the Supreme Court for the appointment of this commission is now being prepared. When it is ready for filing the commission will give two weeks' notice, by publication in six daily papers, of the time and place, when it will apply for the appointment.

In the meantime the canvassers, under the direction of W. N. Amory, are still endeavoring to obtain the consents of the requisite number of owners. But the work has begun to drag, as evidence the following list secured since last Friday:

Broadway.—Julia P. Outcalt, $35,000; the Singer Sewing Machine Company, $353,000. Previously reported, $47,498,748. Total to date, $47,-876,748.

Boulevard.—Hubbard G. Stone, $17,000; Paul Halpin, $1,500; Kate L Youmans, $1,200; William Farrell, $12,000; William Forster and James Livingston, $28,000; Emily L. Landon, $1,000, and John Weld, $4,200. Previously reported, $1,897,000. Total to date, $1,961,000.

East Side Line.—J. M. I. Leindecker, $5,000; H. C. Meyers, $12,500; James Lefoy, $6,500; Jacob Low, $8,500; Theodore Moss, $28,000; B. Moynahan, $5,500; William Griffiths, $19,500; Jacob Ruppert, $14,800, and F. W. Saltzeider, $14,000. Previously reported, $1,803,000. Total to date, $1,917,300. Grand total to date, $51,755,948.

A Profitable Chicago Investment.

Messrs. Snow & Dickinson, the Chicago real estate brokers, have just consummated a lease which is one of the most profitable ever made in Chicago for a lessor. It comprises the property Nos. 100 and 102 Madison street the lease being for ninety-nine years at a rental of 6 per cent on a valuation of $450,000, namely $27,000 per annum, commencing May 1, 1895. The lot is 45x100 in size, and it is occupied by a five-story and basement building.

It is interesting to note that the lessor, C. N. Holden, purchased this plot in 1845 for $600. The valuation on which it is now sold shows an advance of $449,400 since that date, an increase of 74,900 per cent.

In referring to this sale a correspondent writes: "It is quite common for valuations of down-town property to be made in Chicago on a capitalization of 5 per cent A rental of $27,000 would on that basis represent a valuation of $540,000. Had Mr. Holden paid $540 instead of $600 for his lot, a difference of but $60, his lease would have shown that since he bought the property in 1845 its value had increased a thousand times!"

The New Exchange.

DECEMBER 23, 1891.

Editor RECORD AND GUIDE:

I do not wish to be misunderstood in the matter of a new Exchange Building, and fearing from the report of my remarks on that subject, published in THE RECORD of the 5th inst., that I would be, I take this opportunity of correcting such an impression if formed.

I am in favor of everything which will add to and give importance and dignity to the building interests of this city, and am heartily in favor of a new Exchange based on live principles, but am not in favor of the present methods of reaching the desired result, as I can clearly see that it cannot be accomplished Let the present Exchange put forth the proper efforts and get back the very important element which, by a very short-sighted policy several years ago, was driven out—I refer to the members of the Building Material Exchange—and get a law passed whereby we can own and build such an Exchange, then I can see and realize that such a result can be reached; but as we now stand with only a very limited portion of the building interest as members, I feel that it would be unwise to attempt the building of a million dollar structure. RICHARD DEEVES.

The Custom House to be Sold.

The Treasury Department at Washington has issued an advertisement for the purchase of the Custom House, both land and buildings, on Wall street. Proposals are to be sent to the department and will be opened January 20, 1892. No offer less than $4,000,000 will be considered.

Brokers and capitalists may be interested to know the exact dimensions of the property. It takes in the entire block bounded by Wall, Hanover and William streets and Exchange place, and includes four corners. The frontage on Wall street is 197.4 feet, on Hanover street 140 8, on William street 171.9, and on Exchange place 204.11. It thus occupies about 31,417 square feet, which is equivalent to nearly 12 7-12 full city lots of 25x100 each. This makes the minimum price set down by the government equal to $311,258 per lot, a rather high price even for such choice property, when it is remembered that the purchasers will be able to use only the ground, the building being of no value but for second-hand material.

West End Association Officers.

The retiring officers of the West End Association have been re-elected for the ensuing year, excepting the secretary, who is to be appointed on Monday. The officers are: Cyrus Clark, president; Jas. Van Dyck Card, Wm. C. Stuart and John C. Coleman, vice-presidents; J. Edgar Leaycraft, treasurer. The next meeting of the association will take place on the first Monday in January, in one of the parlors of the Endicott, on the 82d street side. The membership is now close upon 200.

Mount Vernon.

The Seton Estate has sold sixty-five acres, with residence and outbuildings, to Dr. J. H. Eden. Ogden & Clark are said to be the brokers, and the price paid is reported to be $150,000. The place is known as "Craigland," and has been in the family since 1838. Dr. Eden recently purchased sixty acres adjoining from ex-Mayor Smith Ely and seventy acres from Jefferson M. Levy. It is said that he intends cutting up part of the property into lots and disposing of them to small buyers.

An Unfounded Rumor.

A rumor has been circulated recently to the effect that the proprietors of Stewart's saloon on Murray street had leased the northwest corner of Chambers street and Broadway from Geo. Hillen. Messrs. Alden & Sterne and Potter & Bro., the brokers in the recent lease of the property to Mr. Hillen, discredited the report. Mr. Hillen was subsequently seen and said there was no truth in the rumor. Mr. Hauck, one of the proprietors of Stewart's saloon, also denied the report. Nor had they purchased any other property, he said.

Notes.

Thos. E. Tripler was at work during the week tearing down the old buildings at 767 and 769 Broadway, southwest corner of 10th street.

The Opinions of Others.

Geo. S. Lespinasse said: "I did not make it clearly understood in my talk with your representative last week that I am opposed to underground roads. I am certainly not in favor of an unknown system, propelled by an unknown motor, ventilated by an unknown process, and to be built by unknown capital, I might add."

Contractors' Notes.

Sealed bids or estimates for furnishing materials and work required for repairs to roofs, gutters, etc., Insane Asylum, Ward's Island, will be received at the office of the Department of Public Charities and Correction, No. 66 3d avenue, in the City of New York, until Thursday, December 31, 1891, until 10 o'clock A. M.

Sealed bids or estimates for each of the following-mentioned works will be received by the Commissioner of Street Improvements of the 23d and 24th Wards, at his office, No. 2622 3d avenue, corner of 141st street, until 3 o'clock P. M., on Tuesday, January 5, 1892: For regulating, grading, setting curbstones, flagging the sidewalks and laying crosswalks in Teasdale place, from 3d avenue to Trinity avenue; for regulating, grading, setting curbstones, flagging the sidewalks and laying crosswalks in 157th street, from 3d to Railroad avenue East; for constructing sewer and appurtenances in Melrose avenue, between 160th and 162d streets; and in Courtlandt avenue, between 154th and 161st streets; and in Railroad avenue East, east side, between 158th and 161st streets; and in 155th street, between Courtlandt avenue and Summit west of Courtlandt avenue; and in 157th street, between Courtlandt avenue and Railroad avenue East; and in 158th street, between Courtlandt avenue and Railroad avenue East; and in 159th street, between Courtlandt avenue and Railroad avenue East; and in 160th street, between Elton avenue and Railroad avenue East; and in 161st street, between Elton avenue and Railroad avenue East; for constructing sewer and appurtenances in Melrose avenue, between 154th and 156th streets, with branches in 155th street, east and west of Melrose avenue.

Estimates for dredging at West Washington Market Section, on the North River, will be received by the Board of Commissioners at the head of the Department of Docks, at the office of said department, on Pier A, foot of Battery place, North River, in the City of New York, until 1 o'clock P. M. of Thursday, January 7, 1892.

Bids for Elevators Wanted.

Supervising Architect W. J. Edbrooke will receive bids until January 12th, at 12 o'clock, to furnish and erect complete three hydraulic passenger elevators and one hydraulic mail lift, including pumps, tanks, cars, platforms, piping, etc., for the Post-office at Brooklyn, N. Y., in accordance with drawings and specifications, copies of which may be had on application at the Supervising Architect's office, Washington, D. C., or at the Superintendent's office, Brooklyn, N. Y.

New Incorporations.

The Mutual Building-Loan Bank filed a certificate of incorporation in the County Clerk's office, on December 21st, for the purpose of buying and improving real estate. The names of the incorporators are H. C. Alleman, J. R. Wensell, W. F. Becker, and twelve others.

The property-owners and residents of 83d street, between Central Park West and Columbus avenue, yesterday presented a handsome silver service to J. J. Phelan, in appreciation of his having bought a number of lots on that street and restricted them to the erection of private residences, at personal loss to himself.

Notice to Property-Owners.

ASSESSMENTS CONFIRMED BY THE BOARD OF REVISION AND CORRECTION OF ASSESSMENTS, DECEMBER 4, 1891.

CITY OF NEW YORK, FINANCE DEPARTMENT,
COMPTROLLER'S OFFICE, December 17, 1891.

In pursuance of Section 916 of the "New York City Consolidation Act of 1882," the Comptroller of the City of New York hereby gives notice to all persons, owners of property affected by the following assessment lists, viz.:

PAVING.

Canal st, from West to Washington st, with granite blocks (so far as the same is within the limits of grants of land under water).
64th st, from 10th to 11th av, with granite blocks.
67th st, from 8th to 9th av, with granite blocks.
80th st, bet Amsterdam av and the Boulevard, with granite blocks and laying crosswalks.
87th st, from Madison to 5th av, with granite blocks.
89th st, from 10th av to the Boulevard, with granite blocks and laying crosswalks.
95th st, from 10th av to the Boulevard, with granite blocks and laying crosswalks.
109th st, from Madison to 5th av, with granite blocks.
120th st, from 7th to 8th av, with asphalt and laying crosswalks.
138th st, from 8th to Edgecombe av, with asphalt and laying crosswalks.
142d st, from 10th to 11th av, with trap blocks.
151st st, from 10th to St. Nicholas av, with granite blocks and laying crosswalks.
166th st, from 3d to Vanderbilt av, with trap blocks.
St. Nicholas av, with macadam pavement, from 155th st to its intersection with 10th av, and Kingsbridge road, from its intersection with 10th av to 190th st.

REPAVING.

16th st, from Av C to the East River, with asphalt and laying crosswalks (so far as the same is within the limits of grants of land under water).
34th st, from 1st av to the East River (so far as the same is within the limits of grants of land under water), with trap blocks.
13th av, from 17th to 18th st, with granite blocks and laying crosswalks (so far as the same is within the limits of grants of land under water).

REGULATING, GRADING, CURBING AND FLAGGING.

111th st, from 8th to Manhattan av.
Bradhurst av, from 145th to 155th st.
Edgecombe av, from 141st to 145th st.

LAYING CROSSWALKS.

Amsterdam av, at the northerly side of 155th st, and the northerly and southerly sides of 156th, 157th, 158th, 159th and 160th sts.
Hamilton pl, at the northerly side of 138th st.
Lenox av, at the northerly and southerly sides of 118th st.
Lenox av, at the northerly and southerly sides of 132d st.
Lenox av, at the northerly side of 130th st.
Western Boulevard, at the northerly side of 140th st.
Av A, at the northerly and southerly sides of 71st st.
5th av, at the northerly and southerly sides of 113th, 114th, 115th, 116th, 117th, and 118th sts.
5th av, at the northerly and southerly sides of 119th st.
10th av, from the present line of bridge-stone on the easterly house-line of 10th av, to the westerly line of 10th av, at the intersection of the southerly line of Kingsbridge road.
10th av, at the northerly side of 163d st, and across 10th and St. Nicholas avs, at the southerly side of 162d st.
175th st, at the easterly and westerly sides of 11th av, and across 11th av, at the northerly and southerly sides of 175th st.

FLAGGING, CURBING, ETC.

In front of Nos. 7 and 9 Abingdon sq.
E s of West End av, bet 76th and 77th sts.
S s of 51st st, from 11th to 12th av.
In front of vacant lots Nos. 10, 12 and 14 West 56th st.
S s of 60th st, bet 10th and 11th avs.
Both sides of 77th st, from Av A to East River.
Both sides of 77th st, from Boulevard to West End av.
S s of 113th st, from 5th to Madison av.
122d st, bet Manhattan and Columbus avs.
Both sides of 142d st, from Amsterdam av to Hamilton pl.

FENCING VACANT LOTS.

The block bounded by 85th and 86th sts, Boulevard and West End av.
Both sides of 88th st, from Central Park West to Riverside Drive.
The n s of 99th st, bet 8th and 9th avs.
N s of 102d st, bet Columbus and Amsterdam avs.
S s of 119th st, from 5th to Lenox av.
The block bounded by 121st and 122d sts, St. Nicholas and Manhattan avs.

SEWERS.

Essex st, bet Delancey and Broome sts.
Ludlow st, bet Delancey and Broome sts.
College av, bet 142d and 143d sts.
E s of Lincoln av, bet 136th and 137th sts.
Park av, e s, bet 124th and 125th sts.
1st av, bet 44th and 45th sts.
12th av, e s, bet 35th and 37th sts, with outlet through pier at 36th st, North River, and connections to present sewers in 36th and 37th sts.
28th st, bet East River and 1st av, connecting with present sewer built by Department of Docks.
55th st, bet 8th and 9th avs.
82d st, bet Boulevard and Amsterdam av.
139th st, from Brook to St. Ann's av, and in St. Ann's av, bet 138th and 142d sts, with a branch in 141st st.
East 151st st, bet Railroad av East and Courtlandt av, with a branch in Morris av, bet 151st and 152d sts.

RECEIVING BASINS.

On the n e and s e cors of 96th st and Boulevard.
On the s e cor of 98th st and 1st av.
On the n w and s w cors of 108th st and Boulevard.
On the s e cor of 115th st and 5th av.
On the s w cor of 116th st and 5th av.
On the n w cor of 146th st and 5th av.

—which were confirmed by the Board of Revision and Correction of Assessments, December 4, 1891, and entered on the same date in the Record of Titles of Assessments, kept in the "Bureau for the Collection of Assessments and Arrears of Taxes and Assessments and of Water Rents," that unless the amount assessed for benefit on any person or property shall be paid within sixty days after the date of said entry of the assessments, interest will be collected thereon as provided in section 917 of said "New York City Consolidation Act of 1882."

The above assessments are payable to the Collector of Assessments and Clerk of Arrears, at the "Bureau for the Collection of Assessments and Arrears of Taxes and Assessments and of Water Rents," between the hours of 9 A. M. and 2 P. M., and all payments made thereon on or before February 5, 1892, will be exempt from interest as above provided, and after that date will be subject to a charge of interest at the rate of 7 per cent per annum from the date of entry in the Record of Titles and Assessments in said Bureau to the date of payment.

Important to Property-Holders.

In the matter of the application of the Board of Street Opening and Improvement of the City of New York, for and on behalf of the Mayor, Aldermen and Commonalty of the City of New York, relative to acquiring title, wherever the same has not been heretofore acquired, to Lind avenue (although not yet named by proper authority), extending from Devoe street to Sedgwick avenue, in the 23d Ward of the City of New York; to Wolf street (although not yet named by proper authority), extending from Union street to the Harlem River, in the Twenty-third Ward, as the same have been heretofore laid out and designated as a first-class street or road by the Department of Public Parks, also East 167th street, from Prospect avenue to Westchester avenue, in the 23d Ward of the City of New York. The Commissioners of Estimate and Assessment in the above-entitled matters give notice to all persons interested in these proceedings and to the owner or owners, occupant or occupants, of all houses and lots and improved or unimproved lands affected thereby and to all others whom it may concern, to wit: That they have completed their estimate and assessment, and that all persons interested in these proceedings, or in any of the lands affected thereby, and having objections thereto, do present their said objections in writing, duly verified, at their office, No. 51 Chambers street (Room 4), in said city, on or before the 2d day of February, 1892, and that the said Commissioners will hear parties so objecting within ten week days next after the said 2d day of February, 1892, and for that purpose will be in attendance at said office on each of said ten days at 3 o'clock P. M. That the abstract of said estimate and assessment, together with damage and benefit maps, and also all the affidavits, estimates and other documents used in making their report, have been deposited with the Commissioner of Public Works of the City of New York, at his office, No. 31 Chambers street, in the said city, there to remain until the 4th day of February, 1892. That said reports will be presented to the Supreme Court of the State of New York, at a Special Term thereof, to be held at the Chambers thereof, in the County Court House, in the City of New York, on the 16th and 19th days of February, 1892, at the opening of the Court on those days, and that then and there, or as soon thereafter as counsel can be heard thereon, a motion will be made that the said reports be confirmed.

In the matter of the application of the Board of Street Opening and Improvement of the City of New York, for and on behalf of the Mayor, Aldermen and Commonalty of the City of New York, relative to Cammann street (although not yet named by proper authority), from the Fordham Road to Harlem River terrace, in the 24th Ward of the City of New York, etc. Notice is given that the bill of costs, charges and expenses incurred by reason of the proceedings in the above-entitled matter will be presented for taxation to one of the Justices of the Supreme Court, at the Chambers thereof, in the County Court House, at the City Hall in the City of New York, on the 30th day of December, 1891, at 10.30 o'clock in the forenoon of that day, or as soon thereafter as counsel can be heard thereon, and that the said bill of costs, charges and expenses has been deposited in the office of the Department of Public Works, there to remain for and during the space of ten days.

The attention of readers is directed to the "Wants and Offers" at the end of the Real Estate Department.

THE WEST SIDE INDEX.

All persons interested in West Side real estate should possess an Index of Ten Years' Conveyances affecting property between the north side of 59th and south side of 125th streets, from west side 8th avenue to Hudson River. This Index is published by THE RECORD AND GUIDE, *and the period covered is the ten years prior to June 30th, 1884, to which has been added a list of the conveyances up to January 1st, 1885. Every transfer of real estate in that section, made between those years, is recorded in the Index, with a description of the property, the price paid for it, the liber and page in which the conveyances are recorded in the Register's Office, and the name of the seller and the purchaser. The volume is of the utmost value to conveyancers, lawyers, real estate brokers, agents and dealers in real estate generally, and we will supply the Index to our readers, if ordered before January 1st next, at the reduced price of $5.*

Real Estate Department.

The real estate market has been rather quiet this week, as it was expected to be during the holidays. The business days of the week have been very much curtailed, and even during the early part of the week the Christmas feeling took such hold upon people that they were not inclined for serious business. Next week there will probably be even less real estate news. This scarcity of reports, however, has no significance. The two weeks which include the close of one year and the opening of the next are always and naturally dull. About Christmas and New Year's Day real estate men do not expect to accomplish much, and the brokers, as a general thing, very wisely leave their clients alone. In consequence of this long-observed practice little new business has been commenced and not very much old business consummated. The market itself, however, remains in good condition. The general features which we remarked last week continue to characterize real estate transactions. Money is very easy for December, buyers are fairly numerous and willing, and sellers are becoming more reasonable in their demands each week. There is every reason to believe from present appearances that there will be a strong and active market in the spring.

The transactions at private sale are neither as numerous or importent as last week. Down town everything has been very quiet, and while up town Frank L. Fisher & Co. and a few other brokers have completed transactions that will attract some attention the volume of business has not been large. At auction the bulk of the offerings consisted of very ordinary legal sales that had no interest for the general market. These sales presented no features that call for special remark, while the few voluntary auction sales were even less attractive. Next week will be about as dull a week in the Auction Room as is ever experienced in midsummer.

On Tuesday, December 29th, Richard V. Harnett & Co. will sell the three five-story and basement brick tenements, No. 414, 416 and 418 East 64th street.

CONVEYANCES.

	1890. Dec. 19 to 25 inc.	1891. Dec. 18 to 23 inc.
Number	198	177
Amount involved	$3,047,020	$2,574,581
Number nominal	59	54
Number 23d and 24th Wards	48	40
Amount involved	$225,258	$159,530
Number nominal	8	12

MORTGAGES.

	1890.	1891.
Number	287	210
Amount involved	$2,875,298	$2,496,951
Number at 5 per cent	1?9	118
Amount involved	$1,314,9?0	$1,424,344
Number at less than 5 per cent	85	9
Amount involved	$698,501	$206,000
Number to Banks, Trust and Ins. Cos	43	26
Amount involved	$876,700	$962,200

PROJECTED BUILDINGS.

	1890. Dec. 20 to 26 inc.	1891. Dec. 19 to 24 inc.
Number of buildings	16	20
Estimated cost	$166,000	$685,250

Gossip of the Week.

SOUTH OF 59TH STREET.

Otto Pullich has sold for A. Boehm No. 313 West 43d street, a five-story store and flat, to George Ehret for $54,000.

Henry Waters and S. Levin have sold to Samuel Prager & Co. the five-story and basement apartment house, No. 39 Henry street, 26.8x90x100, for $44,000. Broker, H. Eisendsdt.

J. Edgar Leaycraft has sold No. 348 West 46th street, a three-story brown stone (Astor leasehold) dwelling, at $6,500, and, in conjunction with Adams Bros., No. 111 West 48th street, a four-story brown stone dwelling, for $28,000.

Hulbert Peck has sold for the estate of John C. Chamberlain the four story, high stoop, brown stone dwelling, 24.1x60x98.9, No. 317 West 33d street, for $33,000.

H. V. Mead & Co. have sold the five-story brick and brown stone apartment house, 25x88x98.9, No. 424 West 26th street, for Robert K. Downey for $43,500.

NORTH OF 59TH STREET.

Frank L. Fisher & Co. have sold for Giblin & Taylor three four-story brown stone dwellings, Nos. 140 to 144 West 75th street, for $120,000; for the Blodgett estate six lots on the north side of 80th street, between Columbus and Amsterdam avenues; for D. G. Watts three lots adjoining the above for $43,000; and for the Edgar estate three adjoining lots for $42,000. The purchasers of the 80th street lots are Giblin & Taylor, who will shortly improve the same by the erection of four-story houses similar to those already erected by them on this block. It is understood that the houses on 75th street were sold by Messrs. Fisher & Co. to D. G. Watts.

Francis Crawford has sold to Oppenheimer & Metzger the plot, 87.6x100, on the south side of 69th street, 100 feet east of Columbus avenue, and to the same operators the plot, 37.6x100, on the south side of 69th street, 217 feet east of Columbus avenue, on private terms.

Isaac T. Meyer has sold the southeast corner of 83d street and Amsterdam (10th) avenue, a five-story brick building with store, size 25x76x80, for Geo. Peper, on private terms.

Walter Reid has sold two of his four-story and extension dwellings on 93d street, No. 5 to I. Hamburger, 21.6x55x100.8, with three-story extension 12x17, on private terms; and No. 11 East 93d street, 19.6x55x100.8, with three-story extension 12x17, to David Spero for $33,000. Mr. Reid has also sold one of his three-story dwellings on Madison avenue, near 96d street, No. 1309, 20x54x74, to Dr. F. Nordemann, on private terms.

John Armstrong has sold for Anne E. Wilsey to August Wilks, No. 62 East 105th street, a five-story brick and brown stone flat, 25x86x100, on private terms.

Increase M. Grenell has sold to Mrs. Mary Murphy, of Brooklyn, the four-story brown stone dwelling, 20x55x100, No. 51 West 94th street, for $27,000. This is the last of Mr. Grenell's houses. In the past seven-and-a-half years Mr. Grenell has built and sold fifty-six houses.

Warren & Skillin have sold for W. E. Lanchantin the three-story private dwelling, No. 300 West 89th street, on private terms.

Max Simon has sold for Mr. B. Schwerin to J. Bough No. 834 Columbus avenue, a five-story double flat with store, 25x74x100, for $18,500.

Goodmann & Stern Bros. have sold for Dr. Schirman the five-story double brown stone flat, No. 420 East 86th street, to M. Goodmann for $22,500.

The purchasers of the four lots on the southeast corner of Columbus avenue and 69th street are Oppenheimer & Metzger.

Otto Pullich has sold for J. B. Smith the southeast corner of 11th avenue and 62d street, a five-story tenement and store, 25x100, on private terms.

Brooklyn.

Corwith Bros have sold the two-story frame dwelling, 32x25x51, on the northeast corner of Calyer and Oakland streets, for Elizabeth C. Fenwick to John N. Fowler for $2,700.

J. P. Sloane has sold for the estate of Sarah A. White the two three-story frame store buildings, each 25x36x100, Nos. 214 and 216 Franklin street, to Frederick B. Devoe for $6,500.

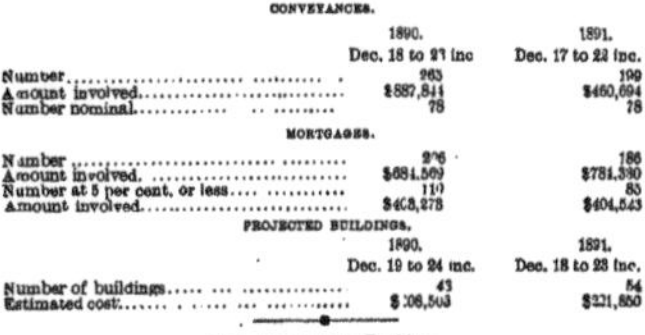

CONVEYANCES.

	1890. Dec. 18 to 23 inc	1891. Dec. 17 to 22 inc.
Number	263	199
Amount involved	$887,841	$460,694
Number nominal	78	78

MORTGAGES.

	1890.	1891.
Number	276	186
Amount involved	$684,569	$781,380
Number at 5 per cent, or less	110	85
Amount involved	$408,278	$404,543

PROJECTED BUILDINGS.

	1890. Dec. 19 to 24 inc.	1891. Dec. 18 to 23 inc.
Number of buildings	43	54
Estimated cost	$306,503	$221,850

Out Among the Builders.

The Roman Catholic Orphan Asylum has had plans prepared for a new industrial school to be erected on Madison avenue, between 51st and 52d.

streets, at a cost of $150,000. The new school will have a frontage of 200 feet on the avenue and 55 feet on each street.

Frank Wennemer has drawn plans for two five-story brown stone flats, 25x79.6, on the south side of 115th street, 100 feet east of 3d avenue, at a cost of $36,000; and for three similar flats on the west side of Madison avenue, 25.11 south of 98th street, 25x79, at a cost of $58,000, and one corner house on the southwest corner of Madison avenue and 98th street, 25.11x91, with all modern improvements, steam heat, etc., at the cost of $32,000, for Frederick Sauer and Conrad Gross.

J. C. Burne is drawing plans for a six-story brick and stone warehouse, 25x100 and extension, which Joseph Bacharach will build at No. 347 Greenwich street. The building will have all the modern improvements and will be first-class in every respect. Cost, $25,000.

Chas. H. Israels has the plans on the boards for the ten 20-foot private houses, to be built by Bernard S. Levy on 80th and 81st streets, between West End avenue and Riverside Drive, as recently reported in THE RECORD AND GUIDE. They will be three stories and basement high, and have brown stone fronts. There will be five on each street. The same architect has plans for a five-story factory, 20x88, to be built by Ascher Weinstein at No. 206 East 19th street. The front will be of light brick and terra cotta, and the building, when completed, will be occupied by Drew & May, manufacturers of gas fixtures.

Brooklyn.

Ross & Marvin are the architects of the store building to be built at Nos. 532 to 540 Fulton street, adjoining Smith & Gray's store. It will cost $150,000. Charles A. Seymour & Co. are the agents.

Out of Town.

FORDHAM, N. Y.—John A. Hamilton has drawn plans for a two-story stone and frame stable, 25x36, to be built here for Mrs. Alice Burke at a cost of $2,000.

GOODLAND, IND.—G. Ormiston will build a two-story frame dwelling, 30x32.6 and extension 24.6x30, at this place from plans by W. Ormiston Tait. Cost, $2,000.

WANTS AND OFFERS.

WANTS.

WANTED.—By a young man, a position with an architectural iron works; ten years' experience in estimating for all classes of architectural iron work; thoroughly understands stair-case and fire-proof building construction; a good draughtsman on details. Address, W., care RECORD AND GUIDE.

OFFERS.

Dwellings and Flats.

40TH ST., NEAR 9TH AV.—Full lot, with front and rear brick buildings, at less than value of lot; all occupied; large rental; terms easy; mortgage remain at 4½ per cent. Particulars of
H. A. BODINE, 176 Liberty st.

BEAUTIFUL HOME in Washington av., near 172d st., two minutes to Elevated station, two minutes to Harlem R. R. Station, fifteen to twenty minutes to Grand Central; eight rooms; all improvements; driveway and barn; a perfect gem, all for $8,500.
D. MULL, 1588 Washington av., City.

42D ST. PROPERTY, near 8th av.; five-story brown stone and stores; rental, $4,400; bargain; $13,500. D. KEMPNER & SON, 602 8th av.
Dec. 19-26.

ATTRACTIVE HOUSE, West 78th st; might exchange; equity on $22,000.
Dec. 19—1aw4w. S. NIXON, 60 Broadway.

ELEGANT HOUSE, near 5th av. and 61st st.; perpetual side light; exceptional light and ventilation; better than corner; easy terms; might possibly rent furnished to desirable tenant.
Dec. 19.—1aw4w. S. NIXON, 60 Broadway.

A 72D ST. GEM, No. 308 West.—This superb house is beautifully decorated; has handsome gas fixtures; is in perfect order; ready for immediate occupancy; $38,000; a greater bargain than has been offered in months.
Nov. 14-uf. CONDIT, 1179 Broadway.

OFFERS.

A—At reasonable prices and easy terms, three and four-story residences, with three-story extensions; all improvements. Call and examine or inquire of the owner and builder, on the premises.
S. O. WRIGHT, 128 West 121st st., open daily.
Oct. 3 uf.

8TH AV.; corner property; best location; near 42d st.; 75 feet front; to close an estate; terms and particulars. D. KEMPNER & SON, 602 8th av.
Dec 19-26.

Vacant Lots.

OWNER OF TEN full-sized building lots, free of all incumbrances, situated on the west side, will exchange all or part for a home in the country, within twelve miles of New York. Address,
R., RECORD AND GUIDE.

1ST AV., near 108th st; full lot, $5,700.
Oct. 31—1aw9w. EDWIN APELY, 103 Gold st.

Improved Property.

$650,000 FOR ONE of the choicest pieces of investment properties on Manhattan Island; exceptionally well built and very desirably located; other good property (city or country) will be entertained in part payment.
Nov. 14—uf. CONDIT, 1179 Broadway.

OFFICE OF
FREDERICK SOUTHACK,
401 BROADWAY,
offers for sale some choice pieces
of property on
LEONARD ST., between Broadway and West B'way.
FRANKLIN ST., between B'way and West B'way.
WHITE ST., between B'way and West B'way.
BROADWAY, from Barclay to 14th st.
BLEECKER ST., from B'way to South 5th av.
GREENE ST., Canal to 8th st.
WASHINGTON PLACE, B'way to Wooster.
WAVERLEY PLACE, B'way to Wooster.
APPLY AS ABOVE.
FREDERICK SOUTHACK.
Oct. 3 uf.

OFFERS.

FOR SALE—Valuable investment property, near Grand Central Depot; rental, about $14,000; light expenses; might exchange; equity on $110,000 at 5 per cent.
Dec. 19—1aw4w. S. NIXON, 60 Broadway.

Brooklyn Real Estate for Sale.

KOSCIUSKO ST.—2½-story and basement, $5,000, will rent $35; McDonough st., 2-story and basement brown stone, all improvements, $6,500; Jefferson av., 2½-story and basement brown stone, 10 rooms and bath, $7,500; call evenings
L. S. PEACOCK, 796 Lafayette av., Brooklyn.

Country Property.

BEAUTIFUL SUBURBAN HOUSE.—Eight rooms; all improvements; house new; a perfect gem; driveway and barn; all for $8,500.
Dec. 5-1aw4w. D. MULL, 1588 Washington av.

FOR SALE.—In plots to suit; eligible building sites (commanding view of sound for miles), on North st., Greenwich, Connecticut; price reasonable; terms easy; neighborhood aristocratic and fashionable. Apply to
FRED. J. STONE, owner, 60 Broadway, N. Y.
Sept. 12-uf.

Miscellaneous.

FOR SALE.—About 8,000 Trenton pressed brick, cheap, at northwest corner 103d st. and Park av.
D. MULL, 1588 Washington av.

TO LET OR TO LEASE.—Two floors of a factory, 25x98, light on all sides, 1st av and 107th st; terms moderate. J. REEBER'S SONS,
Nov. 7 uf. 409 East 107th.

A PARTY ABOUT TO BUILD A FIVE-STORY factory, 50x98, in Harlem, near water-front, will lease the three upper floors and build to suit tenant. Terms very moderate. Address
May 16 u. f. OWNER, 409 E. 107th St.

PRINTING.—Book, News and Job.
RECORD AND GUIDE PRESS,
14 Barclay, and 14, 16 Vesey sts.

SALES OF THE WEEK.

The following are the sales at the Real Estate Exchange and Auction Room for the week ending December 21.

** Indicates that the property described has been bid in for plaintiff's account:*

R. V. HARNETT & CO.

88th st, No. 201, n w cor Amsterdam av, 30x100.8, five-story brk flat with stores. R. S. Coholman. (Amt due $18,417) $60,520

119th st, No 68, n s, 526.8 w 5th av, 16.8x100.11, three-story stone front dwell'g. Jos. F. Stier. (Amt due $12,255) 12,775

JOHN F. B. SMYTH.

2d st, Nos. 159 and 161 E., 49x105.5, two five-story brk tenem'ts. (Leasehold.) (Bid in) .... —

95th st, No. 31, n s, 300 w Central Park West, 19x100, four-story brk and stone dwell'g. F. Levane 23,900

90th st, No. 33, n s, adj, 19x100, similar dwell'g. S. L. Lawson 21,200

28th st, No. 447 W., 25x100, five-story brk tenement. (Leasehold.) (Bid in) .... —

SMYTH & RYAN.

Oliver st, No. 74, e s, 126.2 n Cherry st, 26.2x100.6x25.3x100.6, five-story brk tenem't. Geo. W. Davis. (Amt due $9,574) 32,250

Oliver st, No 77, w s, 124.5 n Cherry st, 24.6x101.3x24.6x101.2, five-story brk tenem't. Solomon Jacobs. (Amt due $11,661) 32,325

Oliver st, No. 79, w s, 99.11 n Cherry st, 24.6x101.2, five-story brk tenem't. Same. (Amt due $11,618) 31,925

WM. KENNELLY.

Perry st, No. 77, n s, 126.2 e Bleecker st, 25x95, three-story brk dwell'g. James Fitzpatrick 15,850

61th st, No. 37, n s, 350 w 8th av, 25x100.5, two-story frame dwell'g. N. J. Newitter. (Amt due $10,005) 10,950

116th st, No. 1, n w cor 5th av, 33x100.11, five-story brk flat and stores. B. Le Vino. (Amt due on this and adjoining houses $97,175) 57,900

116th st, Nos. 3-9, n s, adj, 110x100.11, four five-story brk flats. W. T. Hookey 103,015

122d st, Nos. 6-10, s s, 125 e 5th av, 85x90.11, three five-story brk flats. Jos. Wallack. (Amt due $19,981; prior morts. $35,000) 32,550

*137th st, s s, 86 e Willis av, 18x100. (Amt due $12,946) 12,000

2d av, Nos. 1808-1814, s e cor 94th st, 100.8x100, four five-story brk tenem'ts and stores. W. H. Simonson 102,930

JAMES L. WELLS.

7th st, Nos. 194 and 196, 193 e Av B, 50x90.10, two four-story brk tenem'ts and stores. G. J. Burnet 28,400

Courtlandt av, e s, 25 n Findley now 160th st, 25x100. Geo. Stolz 2,950

Melrose av, e s, 26.7 n 2d av, 56.9x51.7x62.11x15.11. Elizabeth Fritz 14,400

Willis av, w s, 25 s 147th st, 25x106. Same 7,150

OTHER AUCTIONEERS.

11th st, Nos. 314 and 316 E., s s, abt 232 e 2d av, 38.8x94.10, five-story brk tenem't with stores. L. M. Jones. (Amt due $1,750) 27,750

34th st, No. 214, s s, 615.11 e 8th av, 16.5x98.9, four-story stone front dwell'g. H. M. Stillfoeli 17,000

Total $650,050
Corresponding week, 1890 .... $524,905

BROOKLYN, N. Y.

FOR WEEK ENDING DECEMBER 23.

JERE. JOHNSON, JR.

Schermerhorn st, No. 146, s s, 121.H e Smith st, 21.10x100, three-story brk dwell'g. M. J. McGonagil $10,000

OTHER AUCTIONEERS.

*Court st, No. 588, w s, 63.4½ s Hamilton av, 20x100, three-story brk dwell'g and store; unfinished. Sarah F Mead 5,000

*Leonard st, Nos. 399 and 401, s w cor Richardson st, 50x150, varnish factory. Arthur Smith 5,000

*Newton st, n e cor Union av, runs north along Union av 177 to Bushwick Creek, x east along same, x south 185 to Newton st, x west 200 to beginning. Robert Chambers 2,000

Scholes st, Nos. 177, n s, 225 e Graham av, 25x100, three-story frame dwell'g and three-story brk dwell'g in rear. Sebastian Hob 5,475

Scholes st, No. 179, n s, 250 e Graham av, 25x100, three-story frame dwell'g and three-story brk dwell'g in rear. Henry Roth 6,050

*Schaeffer st, n s, 204 w Hamburg av, 48x93.9x48x96.5, three two-story frame (brk lined) dwell'gs. Orson W. Sheldon 8,500

1st st, s w s, 224.3 n w 7th av, 17.6x100, two-story brk dwell'g. Alonzo O. Cole 6,525

*60th st, n s, 80 e 12th av, 20x100.2, New Utrecht, frame dwell'g. The Brooklyn City Co-operative B. & L. Assoc 1,000

*Wythe av, n w cor North 11th st, runs north east along Wythe av 200 to North 12th st, x northwest 100 x southwest 100 x northwest 75 x southwest 100 to North 11th st, x southeast 175 to beginning, glass works. Henry Schneider 34,060

Total $79,210
Corresponding week 1890 .... $15,732

CONVEYANCES.

NEW YORK CITY.

DECEMBER 18, 19, 21, 22, 23.

Boulevard | Hamilton pl | begins Boulevard, e s, 49.11 n 187th st original line, 25x60.7 to Hamilton pl or New av, x27.2x49.11, vacant. Joseph H. Godwin to Paul Halpin. Dec. 17. $3,250

Broome st, No. 239, s s, 27.4 e Ludlow st, 22.8x50, three-story frame (brk front) store and tenem't. Nancy Reiss trustee under deed of trust to Albert Hochster formerly Reiss. Dec. 10. nom

Carlisle st, No. 6, s s, abt 60 e Washington st, 20x62.2x14.6x65.7 in irreg. line, three-story brk store and tenem't. Anna V. wife of John W. Hobart, East Orange, N. J., to William Moir. Dec. 17. 5,000

Cedar st, Nos. 113 and 115, n s, 32.2 w Trinity pl, 37.6x60x37.7x60.3, two three-story brk stores. Presbyterian Hospital, New York, to Elizabeth W. Chanler. Dec. 21. 37,500

Delancey st, No. 210, n s, 25 w Pitt st, 25x75, five-story brk tenem't with stores. Blume Klyshinskey and Jacob Barnett to Saul Federman. Mt. $14,000. Dec. 17. 25,875

Downing st, No 44, s s, 153.6 w Bedford st, 21.6x92.4x22.3x98.8, five-story brk tenem't. Lewis Z. Bach to Samuel W. B. Smith. Dec. 18. Mt. $8,000. 30,750

Essex st, No. 42, e s, 151.4 s Grand st, 25x100x 25.6x100, five-story brk tenem't with stores. Samuel Thorne trustee Mary L Pearsall to Harris Mandelbaum. Dec. 21. 32,500

Same property. Harris Mandelbaum to Louis Lese, Pincus Lowenfeld and Morris Goldstein. Dec. 23. 34,650

Horatio st, No. 76, s s, abt 145 w Greenwich st, 25x87.5, four-story brk tenem't. Mitchell A. C. Levy to Mary J. Gray. Dec. 23. 13,900

James st, No. 67, w s, abt 53 n Oak st, 25.1x100 x23.1x100, five-story brk tenem't with stores. Sweeting Miles to Jonas Weil and Bernhard Mayer. Q. C. Dec. 14. nom

Monroe st, No. 11, n s, abt 175 e Catharine st, 25x100, five-story brk tenem't. Louis Siegel to Esther Cohen. Mt. $32,500. Nov. 5. nom

Morton st, No. 20, s s, abt 142 e Bedford st, 25x 90, five-story brk flat. Laemmlein Buttenwieser to Benedict A. Klein. Dec. 22. 41,000

Same property. Benedict A. Klein to Laemmlein Buttenwieser. Mt. $22,000. Dec. 22. 41,000

Renwick st, No. 33, w s, 25x70.
Renwick st, No. 35, w s, 8.7x75x69.9x84.8.
Renwick st, Nos. 37 and 39, w s, 131.1 s Spring st, runs west to line formerly of A. Lispenard, x southeast along same to Renwick st, x north 88, intending to convey all the real estate on the w s of Renwick st, bet Spring and Canal sts, of which Joseph W. Meeks died seized.
Nos. 33-39, four-story brk stable.
Edwin B. Meeks exr. and trustee Joseph W. Meeks to Horace K. Thurber. Confirmation deed. Dec. 21. (See deed in issue of Dec. 12, 1891.) 18,000

Rutgers pl, No. 3 (Monroe st), n s, 26.6 e Jefferson st, 26x120, four-story brk tenem't with six-story brk factory on rear. Julius G. Miller to Julia Mendelsohn. C. a. G. Mt. $25,500. Dec. 14. nom

Spring st, No. 207, n s, abt 47 w Sullivan st, 21 x74.0x21x68.6, with use of alley on west, three-story frame (brk front) store and tenement. Emanuel Reinheimer to Rachel Wertheimer. Mt. $5,000. Dec. 14. 15,000

Stanton st, No. 302, n w cor Lewis st, 25x58, three and four-story brk and frame tenem't with stores. William J. Gallagher, Texarkana, Ark., to The First Nat. Bank of Texarkana, Texas. Q. C. C. a. G. ½ part. Nov. 7. nom

Same property. Martin Clothing Co. to same. ½ part. Q. C. Nov. 4. nom

Same property. The First Nat. Bank of Texarkana, Texas, to Pincus Lowenfeld. ½ part. Nov. 6. 2,386

St. Lukes pl, No. 7 (Leroy st), n s, 145.5 e Hudson st, 21.8x100, three-story brk dwell'g.
Forsyth st, No. 21, w s, 101.10 s Canal st, 24.11 x126 9x25x126.8, five story brk tenem't with stores and five story brk tenem't on rear.
James J. Bell and ano. exrs. Thomas Bell to Sarah Bell widow. Dec. 17. nom

Thompson st, No. 106, e s, 157 s Prince st, 19x 70, four-story brk store and tenem't. Fanny Bressant to Giovanni B. Casassa and John Malatesta. Mt. $9,000. Dec. 23. 15,000

Washington st, No. 93, e s, 43.3 s Rector st, 25.6 x63.3x25.2x60.5, five-story brk store and tenement. Kenyon G. Viele to John W. Love. Mt. $8,000. Dec. 19. nom

Washington st, Nos. 750-754, s w cor Bethune st, 62.7x81, five-story brk preserve factory. Thomas S. Williams to Archibald D. Russell. Mt. $33,000. Dec. 19. nom

Waverley pl, No 152, s s, 243 w 6th av, 22.3x97, four-story brk dwell'g. George B. Howard to Kate Skelly or Kate S. Kelly. B. & S. Mt. $12,000. Nov. 20. 16,400

White st, No. 25, s s, 75.2 w Church st, 25x72.10. Release mort. Rebecca and Edward R. Ladew trustees Harvey S. Ladew to Louise L. wife of John T. Williams. Dec. 11. nom

4th st, No. 198, w s, 45.8 n Barrow st, 22.10x 85.10x22.7x89.8, three story brk dwell'g. Horace K. Thurber to George B. Howard. Mt. $11,000. Dec. 19. 18,000

5th st, Nos. 323 and 335 E. Party wall agreement. August Ruff with United States Trust Co. trustees Stephen Whitney and Peter Braun lessee. May 1. nom

14th st, No. 233, n s, 400 w 7th av, 25x120, four-story stone front dwell'g. Celia B. Norton devisee Parthenia T. Norton to William Sperb, Jr. Q. C. Dec. 9. nom

Same property. Celia B. Norton and Kate Wing exrs. Parthenia T. Norton to same. Dec. 9. 26,500

Same property. William Sperb, Jr., to Emanuel Lauer. Dec. 18. 28,500

18th st, No. 333, n s, 260 w 1st av, 20x92, three-story brk tenem't.
4th av, No. 424, n w cor 29th st, 23x40, four-story brk store and tenem't.
Morris Rosenfeld to Rebecca Boxsius. ⅛ part. Dec. 11. nom

19th st, Nos. 512-520, s s, 190 e Av A, runs south 92 x east 30 x south 6.7 x east 51.3 x north 8 x northeast 10.6 x easterly 26 x north 32.2 x east 19.6 x north 30.4 to 19th st, x west 122.6, brk and iron store house, gas holder, &c. Wallace C. Andrews to The Standard Gas Light Co., New York. Dec. 10. nom

Same property. New York Steam Co. to Wallace C. Andrews. Morts. on above and other premises $1,200,000. Dec. 10. 45,000

20th st, No. 114, or No. 13 Gramercy Park, s s, 233.4 e 4th av, 26.8x114, four-story brk dwell'g. Frank Pettit, Brooklyn, to William I. Studwell. Mt. $50,000. Dec. 10. nom

25th st, No. 120, s s, 141.8 w Lexington av, 20.10x98.9, four-story stone front dwell'g.
Water st, No. 231, s e s, abt 50 n e Beekman st, 16.6x72.11x16.8x72.11, five-story brk store.
Albert P. Schack, Denver, Col., to Elizabeth I. Schack widow. All title under will of Charlotte McCarty. B. & S. Oct. 13. nom

25th st, Nos. 214 and 216, s s, 155.9 w 7th av, 31 x98.9, five-story stone front flat. Daniel D. Lawson and Abraham Quackenbush to Abial M. Hawkins, Brooklyn. Mt. $31,000. Dec. 21. 55,000

25th st, No. 207, n s, 102 w 7th av, 21x98.9, three-story brk dwell'g. John H. McGinn to Iva Benjamin. Mt. $8,000. Sept. 1. 15,500

32d st, No. 122, s s, 260 e 4th av, 20x98.9, four-story brk stable, &c. Albert D. Newlin to James Clinch Smith, Smithtown, L. I. Mt. $14,000. Dec. 17. nom

32d st, No. 323, n s, 275 e 1st av, 25x98.9, four-story brk tenem't. New York Steam Co. to Wallace C. Andrews. Mt. $1,040,000 on this and other property. Dec. 10. 15,000

Same property. Wallace C. Andrews to The Standard Gas Light Co., New York. Dec. 10. nom

35th st, No. 432, s s, 375 w 9th av, 25x98.9, four-story brk tenem't with three-story brk tenement on rear. Daniel Lane to Benjamin H. Tuthill. ⅛ part. Dec. 19. 3,500

39th st, No. 515, n s, 225 w 10th av, 25x98.9, one and two-story frame buildings. John A. Gleeson and ano. exrs. Margaret Devine to William G. McCrea. Dec. 19. 8,300

39th st, No. 517, n s, 250 w 10th av, 25x98.9, four-story brk store and tenem't with two-story frame building on rear. Partition. S. L. H. Ward to same. Dec. 21. 9,300

40th st, Nos. 203 and 205, n s, 60.11 w 7th av, 39.1x74.2, four-story brk stable. James A. Hammond to Annie M. Hammond. ⅙ part. B. & S. Dec. 18. nom

40th st, No. 163, s s, 155 e 4th av, 25x98.9, three-story brk dwell'g. William Salomon to Cornelia L. R. wife of John P. Emmet. Mt. $14,000. Dec. 22. 38,000

45th st, No. 443, n s, 225 e 10th av, 25x100.5, four-story brk factory. William E. D. Vincent to Passie M. Vincent. Mt. $19,000. Dec. 18. 6,100

46th st, n s, 100 w 10th av, 25x100.4, vacant. Nicholas Seagrist to John McKelvey. Nov. 30. 6,000

46th st, No. 505, n s, 125 w 10th av, 25x100.4, one-story frame shed. Same to James McWalters. Nov. 30. 6,000

48th st, Nos. 134-142, s e cor Lexington av, 174.6 x100; No. 134, seven-story brk flat with stores; Nos. 136-142, four five-story brk flats. Foreclos. Edward P. Schell to James R. Thomas. Sub. to mort and foreclos. $211,959. Dec. 23. 41,000

51st st, No. 204, s s, 66.6 e 3d av, runs south 59.9 x east 9.6 x south 40.7 x east 10.6 x north 100.5 to st, x west 20, four-story stone front dwell'g.
51st st, No. 206, s s, 86.6 e 3d av. 19x100.5, four-story stone front dwell'g.
Partition. William N. Armstrong to Susanna M. C. Larkin. Re-recorded. April 3. 29,850

52d st, No. 30, s s, 394 w 5th av, 22x100.4, four-story stone front dwell'g. William B., Heman, Joseph, Mary E. and George M. Dowd heirs Maria E. wife of William Dowd to William Dowd. Mt. $20,000. April 8. nom

53d st, No. 111, n s, 105 e 4th av, 25x100.5, five-story brk tenem't. Nancy Reiss trustee under deed of trust to Albert Hochster formerly Reiss. Dec. 10. nom

54th st, No. 66, s s, 185 e 6th av, 15x100.5, four-story stone front dwell'g. Rowland A. Robbins to Elma P. Totten. Mt. $18,500. Dec. 28. 44,000

54th st, No. 208, s s, 100 w 7th av, 25x100.5, five-story brk flat. Samuel McMillan sometimes McMillen to Annie S. Patten. Mt. $25,000. Dec. 21. 50,000

56th st, No. 426, s s, 400 e 10th av, 25x100.5, five-story brk flat. Foreclos. George B. Newell to Jennie wife of Samuel Hersnfield. Dec. 22. 3,300

57th st, No. 49 E., n s, 19 w 4th av, 20x80.5, four-story stone front dwell'g. Foreclos Rollin H. Lynde to Isidor Fellheimer. Dec. 17. 34,500

57th st, No. 348, s s, 175 w 1st av, 17x72.4x17x 73.6, three-story stone front dwell'g. William Wetterer to Aaron Kaplan. Mt. $8,000. Dec. 21. exch

57th st, No. 448, s s, 166.8 e 10th av, 33.4x100.5, five-story stone front flat. Charles F. Teigeler to Alethia B. Stewart. Mt. $25,000. Dec. 18. 50,000

58th st, No. 315, n s, 220.6 w 8th av, 34.10x 100.5, five-story stone front flat. Foreclos. Theodore F. Hascall to John A. Ellis, Brooklyn. Mt. $50,000. Dec. 15. 18,000

61st st, No. 324, s s, 328.4 e 2d av, 26.8x100.5, five-story brk tenem't. Foreclos. Charles D. Burrill to The Equitable Life Assur. Soc. of the United States. Dec. 18. 17,000

61st st, No. 326, s s, 355 e 2d av, 26.8x100.5, five-story brk tenem't. Foreclos. Same to same. Dec. 18. 15,000

61st st, No. 322, s s, 301.8 e 2d av, 26.8x100.5, five-story brk tenem't. Foreclos. Same to same. Dec. 18. 15,000

61st st, No. 328, s s, 381.8 e 2d av, 26.8x100.5, five-story brk tenem't. Foreclos. Same to same. Dec. 18. 15,000

63d st, No. 409, n s, 156 e 1st av, 25x100.5, five-story brk tenem't. Simon P. Flannery to Mark Davis. Mt. $10,000. Dec. 21. 17,000

70th st, s s, bet 8th av and 9th av. Receipt on payment for ½ party wall. Addraetta Goodwin to John T. Farley. Oct. 22. 675

75th st, n s, 388 e Columbus av. Party wall agreement. Charles T. and Helen T. Barney to John C. Umberfield. Dec. 10. nom

75th st, No. 222, s s, 270.10 e 3d av, 19.7x102.2, four-story brk tenem't. Partition. William M. Hoes to Karl M. Wallach. Mt. $8,000. Dec. 22. 10,600

76th st, n s, 300 w 8th av, 50x102.2, vacant. Mary E Yeakle to Francis Crawford, South Mt. Vernon, N. Y. Mt. $28,000. Nov. 18. 30,500

Same property. Francis Crawford to Jacob Steinhardt. Mt. $12,000. Dec. 21. val. consid. and 100

76th st, n s, 100 e Columbus av, 0.0¾x102.2x 0 0¾x102.2. Alfred G. Nason to Horatio W. Thayer. Q. C. Dec. 16. 250

77th st, No. 423, n s, 344 w Av A, 25x102.2, two-story frame office with two-story frame dwell'g on rear. Elizabeth McEvoy widow Patrick, Katharine and Bridget Toole or O'Toole heir Patrick Toole or O'Toole to Gottlieb F. Weber. B. & S. Dec. 18. See Av A. 8,000

79th st, No. 225, n s, 300 e 3d av, 25x102.2, four-story stone front dwell'g. Jacob Cohen to Edmond Deyette. Dec 18. nom

81st st, No. 238, s s, 104.1 w 2d av, 23x102.2, five-story brk flat. Malvina A. Levy to Annie H. Smith. Mt. $20,000. Nov. 6. 25,114

81st st, No. 162, s s, 237.6 e Amsterdam av, 18.9x102.2, three-story brk dwell'g. Charles T. Wills to James B. Baker. Mt. $8,000. Dec. 22. nom

Same property. James B. Baker to Carrie R. wife of Charles T. Wills. Mt. $8,000. Dec. 22. nom

82d st, No. 244, s s, 101.5 w 2d av, 19.3x102.2, three-story brk dwell'g. Foreclos. Charles N. Morgan to Bruno Richter. Dec. 18. 8,100

84th st, n s, 156.3 w Central Park West, 18.9x 102.2. Agreement subordinating mortgage to agreement as to encroachment. The Dry Dock Savings Bank and Terence Kiernan to David Richey. Dec. 16. nom

Same property. Agreement as to encroachment and party wall. Terence Kiernan to David Richey. Dec. 16. nom

87th st, n s, 121 w Av B, 175x100.8, seven five-story brk and stone flats.
88th st, Nos. 504 to 520, s s, 125 e Av A, 225x100.8, nine five-story brk flats.
Thomas Moore to John McLaughlin. Dec. 18. nom

88th st, No. 505, n s, 100 e Av A, 25x100.8, five-story brk flat. Joseph Schreiner to Herman Eissenkramer. Mt. $12,000. Dec. 15. nom

90th st, n s, 256.6 w Central Park West, 18.6x 100.8. Release mort. Edward and Henry Hirsh to James Brown. Dec. 23. 4,000

Same property. Release mort. Same to same. Dec. 23. 4,000

90th st, s s, 226.6 w Columbus av, 26.6x100.8. Release mort. Frederick A. Snow to Robert Dick. Dec. 22. nom

92d st, s s, 420 w Columbus av, 30x100.8. Release restriction. Henry W. McVickar to James Brown. Dec. 9. nom

95th st, No. 129, n s, 62.6 w Lexington av, 17x 100.8, three-story brk dwell'g. William Wilkening to Eliza Gardiner. Mt. $14,500. Dec. 17. nom

96th st, No. 57, n s, 204 e 9th av, 21x100.11, four-story brk dwell'g. Foreclos. Ernest Hall to Frank L. Smith. Dec. 18. 21,400

96th st, No. 56, s s, 220 e 9th av, 20x100.8, four-story brk dwell'g. Foreclos. Same to same. Dec. 18. 20,900

98th st, No. 11, n s, 150 w Central Park West, 25x100.11, five-story stone front flat. Edward J. Kelly to William Wienhold. Dec. 22. 26,000

98th st, n s, 150 w 2d av, 25x100.5, vacant. Kate L. Laudy widow of James Uglow to Maria T. Higgins. Dec. 21. 4,500

98th st, No. 224, s s, 360 e 3d av, 25x100.11, five-story brk tenem't. Joseph Newberg to Wolf Lewis, Brooklyn, and Pinkas Ganz or Ganz. Mt. $15,000. Dec. 23. 25,500

101st st, s s, 225 e 5th av, 25x100.11, vacant. Johnston L. de Peyster, Red Hook, N. Y., to Jacob Schlosser. C. a. G. Mt. $4,000. Dec. 19. 5,000

102d st, No. 76, s s, 100 e Columbus av, 30x 100 11, five-story brk flat. Annie L. Gardner to Thomas Berkeley. Dec. 23. nom

102d st, No. 74, s s, 130 e Columbus av, 30x 100.11, five-story brk flat. Annie L. Gardner to Francis J. G. Thomson. Dec. 18. nom

103d st, No. 208, s s, 138 w Amsterdam av, 20x 75x20x76, five-story brk flat. Foreclos. Sylvester L. H. Ward to Robert C. Watson et al. trustees William Watson dec'd. Dec. 9. 17,000

105th st, No. 311, n s, 175 e 2d av, 25x100.11, five-story brk tenem't with stores. Matthew Coogan to Pasquale Caponigri. Mt. $15,000. Dec. 19. 21,000

105th st, Nos. 146 and 148, s s, 325 e 10th av, 50x 100.11, two five-story brk flats. Mary A. Scutt, Westwood, N. J., to Sylvester Gray, Long Island City. Mt. $52,000. Nov. 10. 62,000

105th st, Nos. 72 and 74, s s, 80 w 4th (Park) av, 50x100.11, two five-story brk flats.
104th st, No. 67, n s, 105 w 4th (Park) av, 25x 100.11, vacant lot.
Mary E. wife of and John H. Gault to Ira Shafer, of Lloyd, N. Y. Mt. $87,000. Dec. 23. 87,000

106th st, No. 150 / Lexington av, No. 1679 } begins 106th st, s e cor Lexington av, 20x 80.11, five-story brk flat with stores. Karl Kappes and ano. exrs. and trustees Kate

Kuster to Matilda Michaelis, Brooklyn. *Mt.* $14,000. Dec. 21. 32,700

Same property. Matilda Michaelis, Brooklyn, to Simon Adler and Henry S. Herrman. *Mt.* $12,000. Dec. 21. 34,000

106th st, n s, 100 e 5th av, 120x100.11, vacant. James McCreery to Mary wife of James Gault. *Mt.* $115,000. Dec. 16. 65,000

109th st, Nos. 63 and 64, s s, 214 w 4th av, 34x100.11, two four-story stone front flats. Peter Kearney to James McClenehan, Vice-President of The Mutual Bank. *Mt.* $14,000. Aug. 24. nom

112th st, No. 377, n s, 100 e 2d av, 25x100.11, three-story brk chapel, &c. Rector, &c., Holy Trinity Church, Harlem, to Emanuel Church, Harlem. Dec. 21. 12,000

112th st, s s, 128 w 10th av, 22x100.11x50x—, vacant. Louise H. Conover widow, Newark, N. J., to Mary D. wife of George L. Rose. B. & S. Dec. 15. nom

112th st, s s, 128 w 10th av, 22x100.11x50x—, vacant. George L. Rose, Yonkers, N. Y., to Louise H Conover. B & S. Dec. 11. nom

113th st, No 106, s s, 81 e 4th av, 27x100.10, five-story brk flat. Philipp Goldmann to Herman and John Seekamp, Hoboken, N. J. *Mt.* $14,000. Dec 19. 20,250

114th st, s w cor Park av, 30x100.11, vacant. John B Cannon to Michael Donelan, Brooklyn. All morts. and tax 1891. Dec. 19 nom

114th st, No 419, n s, 245 e 1st av, 25x100 11, four-story brk tenem't. Margaret wife of John Young to Frederick C. Dexter. *Mt.* $10,000 Dec. 16. 14,500

115th st, s s, 245 e 5th av, 50x100 11. }
115th st, s s, 320 e 5th av, 25x100.11. }
Release mort. Marx & Moses Ottinger to Cornelius Daly. Dec. 18. 26,720

115th st, n s, 100 e Lenox av, 25x100.11, vacant. Daniel and Norman Seymour to The Mayor, &c., New York. Dec. 18. 9,500

116th st { begins 116th st, s s, 325 e Pleasant av,
115th st { 277.6 to exterior bulkhead line x 2?? along same to 115th st, x west 262 6 x north 48 2 x east 81 x north 153.8, with water rights, land under water, &c., one story brk buildings, frame sheds, &c. New York Steam Co. to Wallace C. Andrews. Sub to morts. agt above and other property $1,051,000. Dec. 10. 220,000

Same property. Wallace C. Andrews to The Standard Gas Light Co., New York. Dec. 10. nom

116th st, Nos. 356-362, s s, 50 w Manhattan av, 75x100.11, four five story brk flats. Charles E. Moore to Frederick P. Forster. Dec. 22. other consid and 12,000

120th st, s s, 300 w 5th av, runs south 92.1 to n s Manhattan road, x northwest 45 x southeast to centre line of block bet 119th and 120th sts, x west 125 x north 100.11 to st, x east 160, with all title to old Manhattan road, vacant. Abraham Steers to Thomas J. Robinson. *Mt.* $35,000. Dec. 17. 80,000

121st st, No. 126, s s, 300 w Lenox av, 20x100.11, four-story stone front dwell'g. Samuel O. Wright, Rockville Centre, L. I., to Anne wife of Walter F. See. *Mt.* $24,000. Dec. 9. nom

Same property. Release mort. Reuben W. Ross et al. exrs. Reuben Ross to Samuel O. Wright, Rockville Centre, L. I. Dec. 17. nom

124th st, No. 355, n s, 94 w 1st av, 18.8x100.11x18.9x100.11, three-story stone front dwell'g. Sarah J. Vanderhoof to Greenleaf W. Crossman. Dec. 12. 10,000

128th st, No. 31, n s, 372.6 w 5th av, 12 6x99.11, four-story stone front dwell'g. Alfred E. Fountain to Charles W. Bogart. *Mt.* $7,000. Nov. 1. 13,000

131st st, n s, 125 e 8th av, 50x99 11, vacant. Anthony D. Leaycraft to J. Edgar Leaycraft. *Mt.* $6,000. Dec 17. 15,000

132d st, No. 165, n s, 155 e 7th av, 20x99.11, three-story brk dwell'g. James T. Hall Building and Decorative Co. to John E. Meyer and Wilhelmina R. L. his wife. *Mt.* $9,000. Dec. 17. 13,750

133d st, s s, 135 w 5th av, 50x99 11, vacant. }
133d st, n s, 110 w 5th av, 50x99 11, vacant. }
John C. Overbiser to Emeline Johnston. Dec. 17. 22,900

135th st, Nos. 200-214, s w cor 7th av, runs west 125 x south 99.11 x east 25 x north 50 x east 100 to 7th av, x north 49 11 to beginning, eight three-story brk dwell'gs. John Sloane exr. and trustee Douglas Sloane to Charles N. Martin. Dec 8. 42,500

Same property. Also appurtenant lease and building and loan agreement. Douglas Sloane, Portchester, N. Y., to same. C. a. G. Conveys all title under lease and agreement. Dec 8. 32,500

Same property. Catherine P. Macfarlan to same. Confirmation deed. Dec. 12. nom

Same property. Catherine Ruddock formerly Sloane widow and Mary E Horner to same. Confirmation deed. Dec. 14. nom

Same property. Release judgment. The Manufacturers Finance and Trust Co. to Douglas Sloane. Dec. 8. 5,000

144th st, s s, 121 e Amsterdam av, 20x99.11. }
144th st, s s, 158 e Amsterdam av, 20x99.11. }
144th st, s s, 178 e Amsterdam av, 17x99.11. }
144th st, s s, 214 e Amsterdam av, 20x99.11. }
144th st, s s, 234 e Amsterdam av, 21x99 11. }
Release mort. Alfred P. Dix and John J. Phyfe, of Dix & Phyfe, to William H. De Forest, Jr. Dec. 2. nom

145th st, s s, 79.2 w 5th av, 20.10x99 11. Release mort George Leask exr. and trustee Norman Peck to Jacob D. Butler. Dec. 21. 2,800

147th st, s s, 225 e 10th av, 75x99.11, vacant. Nathaniel S. Simpkins to John Simpkins. June 30. 16,017

166th st, n s, 100 w Amsterdam av, late 10th av, 25x95. Thomas Fitzgerald to George R. Schieffelin. Dec. 22. 3,400

Av A, No. 1485, w s, 79 s 79th st, 25x94, five-story brk store and tenem't. Gottlieb F. Weber to Elizabeth McEvoy, Patrick, Katharine and Bridget Toole. *Mt.* $14,000. Dec. 18. See 77th st. 24,000

Audubon av, w s, 24.11 s 189th st, 25x100. Rose Cawley to James Cawley. Q. C. Nov. 16. nom

Columbus av, s e cor 84th st, 127.8x100, vacant. Edward Oppenheimer and Isaac Metzger to John Casey. *Mt.* $55,000. Dec. 4 nom

Lexington av, No 1677, e s, 80.11 s 106th st, 20x95, five-story brk flat. Karl Kappes and ano. exrs., &c., Kate Kuster to Samuel Steinreich. *Mt.* $8 000. Dec. 21. 15,200

Madison av, No. 1780, w s, 25 s 114th st, 25.11x79, five-story brk flat. Albert Friedlander to John D. Fish, Brooklyn. *Mt.* $17,000. Dec. 2. exch

Madison av, No. 1327, e s, 60 8 n 93d st, 20x74, three-story stone front dwell'g. James V. S. Woolley to Robert Maynicke. *Mt.* $16,000. Dec. 23. 25,000

Same property. Release mort. Seth M. Milliken to James V. S. Woolley. Dec. 23. nom

Madison av, No 753, e s, 27 n 65th st, 23x63, four-story stone front dwell'g. Partition. Elliot Sandford to Gertrude del Ludlam. *Mt.* $28,000. Dec 22 41,000

West End av, No. 408, e s, 82 2 s 85th st, 20x80, four-story brk dwell'g. Foreclos. Sumner C. Chandler to William and Thomas Morton and David Brown. Sub. to mort. $23,000, interest from Nov. 1, 1890, cost of foreclos and taxes. Dec. 22. 2,900

West End av, e s, 25 n 97th st, 0 2x100. Helen Swords heir George H. Swords to Edward Kilpatrick. B. & S. Nov. 20. nom

West End av, e s, 78.11 n 97th st, 18x89. Release mort. Harriet Overhiser to Edward Kilpatrick. Dec. 21. 15,000

1st av, No 166, e s, 28.8 n 10th st, 23 8x94, five-story brk store and tenem't. William H., Morris and Louis Goldstein exrs. Sophie Goldstein to Caroline Baumert. *Mt.* $10,000. Reserves rights against Elevated Road. Dec. 15 26,500

Same property. William H., Morris, Louis and Sig and Samuel Goldstein heirs Sophie Goldstein to same. Sub. to same mort. and reservation. Dec. 15. 26,500

2d av, No. 2422, e s, 20 11 n 124th st, 20x80, three-story stone front dwell'g. Agnes Yost to Adelheid Mayer. Dec. 11. nom

3d av, No. 441, e s, 79 6 s 31st st, 19.3x100, four-story stone front store and tenem't with two-story brk building on rear. Jacob Levy to Jacob Marks. *Mt.* $15 000. Dec 21. nom

Same property. Jacob Marks to Esther J. wife of Jacob Levy. *Mt.* $15,000. Dec. 22. nom

3d av, No. 684 { begins 3d av, n w cor 43d st.
43d st, No. 151 { 25.1x100, five-story brk (stone front) store and tenem't on av and five-story brk tenem't with stores on st. John E. Sullwell to Elizabeth T. wife of P. J. Kenedy. Reserves damages agt Elevated Railroad. *Mt.* $40,000. Dec. 23. 58,000

5th av, n e cor 71st st, 29.2x125, vacant. Chester W. Chapin to Sarah J. Zabriskie. *Mt.* $35,000. Dec. 15. 120,000

5th av, No. 2168, w s, 105 11 n 132d st, 19x100, five-story brk flat. Foreclos. J. Mayhew Wainwright to The Mutual Life Ins. Co., New York. Dec. 10. 20,000

5th av, No. 2164, w s, 51.11 n 132d st, 27x100, five-story brk flat. Foreclos. Same to same. Dec. 10. 28,000

5th av, No. 170, s w cor 22d st, 29x120, reserving use of 10 ft. in rear as any alley-way, five-story stone front store. Josephine wife of John Hoey, Hollywood, N. J., to Henry Sanford, President of Adams Express Co. *Mt.* $50,000. Dec. 18. nom

7th av, No. 2146, w s, 76.7 n 127th st, 23.4x84 10. }
7th av, No. 2148, w s, 76 7 s 128th st, 23.4x84. }
Two five-story stone front flats. }
William T. Washburn and ano. exrs., &c., Benjamin Richardson to Amalia Berrien. *Mt.* $31,000. Dec 14. 43,100

7th av, w s, 76 7 n 127th st, 23 4x84 11. Thomas A. formerly Thomas Rossiter, Brooklyn, to Amalia Berrian. Q. C. and correction deed Dec. 4. nom

7th av, w s, 76 7 s 128th st, 46 8x85. Release judgment. Eugene Kelly individ and with Edward Kelly and Joseph A. Donahue, of Eugene Kelly & Co., to William T. Washburn ano. exrs. Benjamin Richardson. Dec. 8. nom

7th av, w s, 76 s 128th st, 24x85. Release mort. Eugene Kelly to William T. Washburn and ano exrs. Benjamin Richardson. Dec. 8. nom

8th av, w s, 27 s 118th st, 77 10x100. Release mort. Morris Steinhardt to Elizabeth Johnston. Dec. 21. nom

Same property. Release mort. Same to same. Dec. 21. 28,845

Interior lot. 60 e Columbus av and 50.5 s 71st st, runs south 25 x east 40 x north 25 x west 40. Release judgment. William E. D. Stokes to Hobart Cleveland. Dec. 17. 100

Interior lot. 60 e 9th av and 50.5 s 71st st, runs south 25 x east 40 x north 25 x west 40, being rear of Nos. 84 and 86 West 71st st. Mary Ryan to Emily W. Lensen. All title. Dec. 15. 1,100

Same property. Celia America Farres to same, 1-3 part. Nov. 30. 1 190

Same property. Hobart Cleveland to same. Dec. 14. 1,210

MISCELLANEOUS.

All title in estate of Marshall Spring. Alva L. Spring to Elizabeth S Spring widow. Dec. 22. In payment of debt of $4,500 and nom

Broadway, 5th av and 23d st to Broadway and 34th st. Agreement as to use of railroad tracks bet these points. Broadway and 7th av R. R. Co. to 42d st and Grand st Ferry R. R. Co. May 1, 1867. Consideration, per year, 1,500

23d and 24th WARDS.

Broadway, s e s, 285.6 n e Macomb st, 34.6x85. Charles L. Denks to Charles B. Meyer. *Mt.* $1,500. Dec. 18. nom

Broadway or Kingsbridge road, s e cor Macomb st, 48.6x100. Foreclos. Edward C. Perkins to Ludwig Kuenstler. Dec. 24. 8,500

Gerard st, n e s, 129 s e Bergen av, 25x100, with ½ of Gerard st in front of lot, 25x25. Partition. William M. Hoes to John Cook. Dec. 19. 4 075

Hoffman st, e s, lot A D map Cedar Hill plot, Powell Farm, Fordham, 25x118.7x25x118.9. Catherine Burns to William E. Brooker. Dec. 18. 1,000

Hellen st, s s, 225 w Morris pl, 125x115. Nellie D and Mollie J. Sugden heirs William Sugden to Patrick B. O'Regan, Brooklyn. Q. C. Dec. 21. 150

Main st to West Farms, w s, 155.10 s present West Farms road, 250x225. James J. Collins to Edwin E. Sinsheimer. *Mt.* $6,000. Dec. 17. 9,280

Old Gerard st, n e s, 247.7 s e Bergen av, runs northeast 100 x southeast 31.2 x southwest 98 4 x west 4.6 to st, x northwest 29 6. George J. Grossman to Matilda Grossman. *Mt.* $7,000. Dec. 17. nom

Summit st, n s, 331.3 w Williamsbridge road, 22.6x100. Elizabeth Dusenbury to Therese Toussaint. Dec. 21. 2,650

134th st, n s, 375 e Willis av, 50x100. Adam Gebhardt to Kunigunde Hager. *Mt.* $29,000. Dec. 23. nom

135th st, s s, 100 w Alexander av, 25x100. Frederick Rohrs to Babette Blumenthal. Dec. 19. 20,000

143d st, n s, 164 4 e Willis av (new line), and 165.5 e Willis av (old line), 14.11x100. James R. Jackson to David B. King. B. & S. Dec. 22. nom

Same property. David B. King to Emma A. wife of James L. Jackson. B. & S. Dec. 22. nom

143d st, n s, 240 e Willis av, 14.11x100. John Lloyd to Amalia wife of Francis M. Jaeger. *Mt.* $4,000. Dec. 22. 6,060

144th st, s s, 375 e Willis av, 16.8x100. Karl Kappes and ano. exrs. Kate Kuster to Charles Van Riper and James M. La Coste. *Mt.* $3,500. Dec. 21. 5,350

154th st, n s, 250 e Courtlandt av, 25x100. Moise Geismann to Mary A. wife of Michael Murray. Dec. 17. See 161st st. 5,500

154th st, n s, 170 w Elton av, 25x100. Carl and Lizzie Wurz to Louisa Wagener. Dec. 18. 8,800

Same property. Partition. Edward Jacobs to same. Dec. 18. 3,400

161st st, east cor Brook av, 21.7x40.6x45.6, gore. Mary A. wife of Michael Murray and widow of William Doty to Moise Geismann. Dec. 17. See 154th st. 1,000

162d st, n s, 100 w Delmonico pl, 50x100. Release mort. Joseph Stickney to Oscar V. Pitman Dec. 19. nom

Same property. Oscar V. Pitman to George Hoepfuer. Dec. 21. 8,500

Brook av, n w cor 146th st, runs north 25 x west 70 x north 25 x west 20 x south 50 to st, x east —. Adam Gebhardt to Roman Koehler. *Mt.* $23,000. Dec. 9. nom

Briggs av, n s, 277 4 e Travers st, 25x100. Charles L. and G. Fred. Starbuck to Henry Petersen. Dec. 23. 800

Jefferson av, n w s, lot 36 map S. Ryer Homestead, runs northwest 200 to a point 515 from Locust av, x northeast 25 x southeast 200 to av, x southwest 25. James Thatcher to Emma Thatcher. Dec 21. gift

Morrisania av, e s, 110.5 s 162d st, runs east 113.3 to w s proposed Grant av at point 105.6 s 162d st, x south 50 x west 98 to Morrisania av, x north 52.7. James Noble, Jr., to J. Arthur Pinchbeck. *Mt.* $1,140. May 1. nom

Opdyke av, n e cor 1st st, 194.7x149.4x195.4x161 8. Emma S. Potter widow to Benjamin H. Irving. Nov. 21. 5,000

Opdyke av, n s, 100 e 2d st, 300x151.10x300x154.7. Florence E. Stimson, New York, Adelaide, Walter E and Archibald T. Scott, Yonkers, to Elizabeth H. Barry, Newark, N. J. *Mt.* $3,500. Dec. 18. 5,500

Sedgwick av, west cor Perot st, 50x99. Robert F or Robert Scrimgeour to Henry F. Fagan. *Mt.* $1,846. Dec. 18. 2,074

Sedgwick av, centre line, 350 s of lands of James Lees, 50x182.10. Andrew H. Green to Marianna A. Ogden. B. & S. Dec. 18. 4,000

Valentine av, n s, 75 e Garfield st, 50x100. Charles H. Wetzel to George J. Wetzel. Dec 15. nom

Same property. George J. Wetzel to Charles H. Wetzel and Catharina E. his wife. Dec. 16. nom

Webster av, n e cor 170th st, 50x90. Charles O. Kirkup to August Hanselmann. Dec. 18. 4,000

Washington av, w s, 96 n 6th st, now 168th st, 21.6x150. Eliza Hall to Alice Hall. B. & S. ½ part. Dec. 22. nom

Washington av, w s, part lot 30 map Morrisania, 26x200. Thomas S. Morris to Mina Loehr. *Mt.* $2,500. Dec. 21. 3,800

Willis av, w s, 25 n 146th st, 25x106. Foreclos. Frank K. Pendleton to Lorenz Weiber. Dec. 19. 19,000

Willis av, n w cor 145th st, 25x106. Foreclos. Same to same. Dec. 19. 31,000

Willis av, n w cor 146th st, 25x106. Foreclos. Same to same. Dec. 19. 32,000

Willis av, n w cor 145th st, 25x106. John Hutton to Lorenz Weiber. Nov. 24. nom

Willis av, n w cor 146th st, 50x106. Same to same. B. & S. Nov. 24. nom

Lots 3, 4, 5 and 12-15, all inclusive, map of lots, a portion of the well known Hyatt farm, near Woodlawn Station, &c., 24th Ward. Louis Smadbeck to Martin J. Klug. Dec. 23. 1,285

Lots 1 and 2 same map. Same to Elizabeth Van Tassel. Dec. 23. 550

Lot 11 same map. Same to Elizabeth Schilling. Dec. 23. 115

Lots 10 to 20, 31 to 37, 65, 66, 106 to 109, 127 to 141, 210, 211, 231, 233, 321, 322, 323, 323A, 324, 325, 326, 327 and 327A, map of 339 lots at Riverdale and Mosholu, 24th Ward, of F. P. & H. A. Forster. Release mort. Margaret T. Odell and ano. exrs. Jonathan Odell to Frederick P. Forster and ano. exrs. George H. Forster. Nov. 20. nom

Lot 237 map of Ryer homestead, 24th Ward. Release mort. John J Brady to Margaret J. Howe. Nov. 7. 210

LEASEHOLD CONVEYANCES.

Baxter st, w s, 50 s Franklin st, 25x58.6x25x60.10. Assign. lease. Louis Siegel to Esther Cohen. Nov. 5. 5,000

Delancey st, No. 210. Assign. lease. Solomon Fischer and Lippman Deutsch to Saul Federman. Dec. 1. 577

Front st, No. 17, s s, 20.6x104.6x18.6x104 6.
Front st, No. 15, s s, 20.4x100x18.5x100.
Front st, No. 13, s s, 24.3x100x21.8x100.
Surrender lease. The New York Steam Co. to The Standard Gas Light Co. nom

Hudson st, No. 282. Assign. lease. Daniel Hudner to Edward Knowlton. 2,500

Ridge st, Nos. 119-127, w s, 100 s Stanton st, 100x100. Julia L. Delafield to David Frankel. 4? years and 5 months, from Dec. 1, 1891, per year, taxes and gold, $2,750 to 4,000

West st, No. 117, e s, 24.1x71.3x23 11x70.5.
West st, No. 118, e s, 24x72.2x23.11x71.3.
Washington st, No. 174, w s, 21.5x46 5x17.5x51.8.
Washington st, No 176, w s, 25.3x115.10x27.11 x121.5 in two courses.
Surrender lease. The New York Steam Co. to The Standard Gas Light Co. nom

12th st, No 281 W. Assign lease. John Byrne to Dennis Byrne Dec. 17. 5,000

19th st, s s, 190 e Av A, 100x92. Surrender lease. The New York Steam Co. to The Standard Gas Light Co. nom

23d st, s s, 100 w 5th av, runs south 150 x west 20 x north 51.3 x west 13.8 x north 98.9 to st, x east 33.8.
22d st, n s, 100 w 5th av, 20x47 6.
United States Trust Co. trustee Emily G. Nathan dec'd to Adams Express Co. 15 years, from May 1, 1890, per year, 20,000

32d st, n s, 275 e 1st av, 25x98.9. Surrender lease. The New York Steam Co. to The Standard Gas Light Co. nom

33d st, s s, 275 e 1st av, 95x—x—x98.9. Surrender lease. Same to same. nom

49th st, s s, 225 e 1st av, 100x100.5. Surrender lease. The N.Y. Steam Co. to The Standard Gas Light Co. nom

110th st, No. 138 E. Assign. lease. Hugh O'Reilly, Sr., to Hugh O'Reilly, Jr. nom

125th st, s s, 250 e 7th av, 100x100.11.
124th st, n s, 250 e 7th av, 100x100.11.
Franz O. Matthiessen to Henry C. F. Koch and Adolph Riesenberg, of H. C F. Koch & Co. 30 years and 7 days, from June 23, 1891, per year, taxes, &c , and gold, 40,000

Amsterdam av, s w cor 77th st, runs west 115 x south 102 x east 25 x north 51 x east 90 to Amsterdam av, x north 51. Euphemia S. Coffin to The Mason Stable Co. (Lim) 20 years, from Oct. 1, 1891. per year, 6,000, 6,600, 7,500 and 8,000

2d av, No. 1066, n e cor 56th st. Assign. lease. Beadleston & Woerz, a corporation, to Ferd. Schulermann and John G. Ficken, of Schulermann & Co. Dec. 17. 4,200

7th av, No. 2188, s w cor 127th st, 19.10x80. Assign. of lease and rents. Frank E. Mainhart and William R. Lowe, of Mainhart & Lowe, to Martha Wolff. Dec. 19. 2,000

KINGS COUNTY.

DECEMBER 17, 18, 19, 21, 22.

Adams st, n s, 87.6 e Short st, 12 6x104, h & l, Flatbush. Abbie C. wife of Abram L. Smith to Emeline T. Anderson. *Mt.* $1,000. $1,900

Ashford st, e s, 165 s Hanley av, 40x100. Adolph Sussman to Heinrich Soldner. 240

Ashfield st, e s, 2 0 n Hegeman av, 40x100. Charles H. Ray to Lizzie Ray his wife. gift

Bancroft pl, e s, 98 7 n Atlantic av, 69x90. Frank Hyde to Ella J. Mayer. *Mt.* $1,500. Tax 1891. exch

Bergen st, n s, 220 w Carlton av, runs north 110 x west 100 x south to old Brooklyn and Flatbush turnpike, x southeast along same to Bergen st, x east — to beginning. Charles Moran, of New York, to James T. Nelson. 3 750

Bleecker st, w s, 290 s Hamburg av, 25x100. Meinard Keck to Jacob Miller. *Mt.* $2,500. 627

Broadway, n s, 100 e Monroe st, 50x100. Foreclos. Jose E. Pidgeon and Henry Roth to Alois Lazansky. 1890. 460

Broadway, n s, 100 from point formed by the n e cor of Broadway and Scheeffer st, runs northwest 20x100. Heinericke Marquardt widow to Jacob Marquardt. Q. C. Dated 1887. 750

Broadway, n e s, 80 s e Schaeffer st, 20x100. Jakob Marquardt to Caroline Skillman. nom

Broadway, s w s, 235.7 s e New York & Manhattan Beach R. R., 20x136.8 to Brooklyn and Jamaica plank road, x20.3x139.11, with all title in road. Release mort. William C. Bowers to David S. Yeoman. nom

Broadway, s w s, 235.7 s e New York & Manhattan Beach R. R., 20x136x20x139.11. David S. Yeoman to Kate Vetter. *Mt.* $1.500. 3,000

Chauncey st, s s, 173 e Saratoga av, 19x100, h & l. Thomas A. McWhinney to James B. and Margaret Clarke. *Mt.* $4,000. 5,400

Cleveland st, e s, 180 s Wortman av, 40x100. Frank Steinberger to Simon Hartman, Breslau, L. I. nom

Cumberland st, w s, 303.10 n Atlantic av, 14x100. Foreclos. John Courtney to Caroline A. Henry. 1,537

Chester st, e s, 325 n Broadway now Eastern Parkway, 25x100. Hermann Markowitz to Josephine Schottland. *Mt.* $3,500. 2,200

Court st, n e cor Livingston st, 36x28.8x35.8x29.5, h & l. William A. White to The Polytechnic Institute, Brooklyn. C. a. G. nom

Dean st, s s, 184 4 w Underhill av, 25x97.8x28.8 x83.9, h & l. Elizabeth wife of Thomas Easop to Mary E. wife of John A Donahue. B. & S. nom

Dean st, s s, 50 w Utica av, 104x115.2x62.2x87 11. Thomas C. Higgins to Learnore wife of W. H. Agricola. *Mt.* $2,500. 4,100

Dean st, n s, 419.5 e Rochester av, 16x107.2. Foreclos. John Courtney to William B. Boulton, of Orange, N. J. 2,000

Dean st, n s, 451.5 e Rochester av, 16x107.2 Foreclos. Same to same. 2,000

Dean st, n s, 467.5 e Rochester av, 16x107.2. Foreclos. Same to same. 2,000

Dean st, n s, 435.5 e Rochester av, 16x107.2. Foreclos. Same to same. 2,000

Degraw st, n s, 91.4 e 4th av, 16.4x98.6, h & l. Azra B. wife of and David Eastman to Charles E. Meier, of New York. *Mt.* $4,000 6,000

Dupont st, n s, 100 e Oakland st, 25x100. Foreclos. Chas. B. Farley late Sheriff to Harriet T. Provost. Dated 1885. 820

Same property. Harriet T. Provost, signs deed as Harriet Provost, to John Gallagher. 1890. 825

Diamond st, e s, 325 s Nassau av, runs east 100 x south 48.6 x west 100 to Diamond st, x north 28.3. Laura S. widow, John E., Louise E. and Laura S. Forbes, Leila S. McKesson and Cora S. F. Saportas to Carl A. Mertz. Q. C. nom

Eastern Parkway, s s, 75.1 w Thatford av, 50x100. Solomon Krenkenstein to Solomon Rosran. 6,500

Eldert st, s s, centre line, 385 e Knickerbocker av, 60x130. Magdalena Hartmann to George Covert. exch

Essex st, e s, 420 n Ridgewood av, 20x100, h & l. Califf F. Smith to Kezia A. Vanderbilt. *Mt.* $2,600. nom

Ewen st, No. 90, also all title in estate real and personal of which John Wenningill died seized. Elizabeth Forst to William J. Scharen. B. & S. C. a. G. nom

Elton st, w s, 300 n Arlington av, 25x100. Edward F. Linton to Howard N. Acker. 1,000

Same property. Release mort. The Williamsburgh Savings Bank to Edward F. Linton. 350

Floyd st, s s, 250 e Marcy av, 25x100, h & l. Kaspar Gossmann to John Mohl. *Mt.* $4,000. 11,000

Fulton st, s s, 200 w Stone av, 100x100. Jennie L. Ross to Thomas Berkeley. nom

Greene st, n s, 275 w Provost st, 25x200. Daniel R. Davis to William W. Smith. *Mt.* $800, taxes, &c. nom

Garden st, s w s, abt 105 s e Flushing av, 25x76.10x31.8x37.6, being on assessm't map 18th Ward lot 7A block 1012. George Covert to Magdalena Hartmann. 7,500

Halsey st, s s, 90 e Throop av, 20x80, h & l. Hannah E. Stoops to Margaret A. McBride. 4,300

Hancock st, s s, 450 e Reid av, 25x100. Alfred L. Beasley to Jacob Mogenthaler. *Mt.* $5,800. 8,500

Hancock st, n s, 309 w Marcy av, 20x100, h & l. Edward L. Lewis to Ella W. wife of Edward L. Lewis. B. & S. nom

Hicks st, e s, 25.3 n Poplar st, 25 3x100, h & l. Lewis A. Mitchell to Jefferson M. Levy. nom

Himrod st, s s, 100 e Knickerbocker av, 50x100. Release mort. Catharine M. Meserole to Ernst Augustine. 500

Hall st, e s, 180 9 s Myrtle av, 18.9x100. Emeline Lane to Anna A. Brooks. *Mt.* $2,400. 5,000

Hendrix st, e s, 185 n Vienna av, 40x100. John Downward to Henry and Emma Diehm. 300

Hull st, s s, 56 3 w Hopkinson av, 37 6x90.3x37.8x94.5. Dudley Kelley to Mary Kelley his wife. *Mt.* $8,700. 500

Hull st, No. 166A, s s, 150 w Stone av, 18x100. John T. A. Twomey to Annie M. Twomey his wife. B. & S. nom

Huron st, s s, 125 e Oakland st, 25x100. Hugh F. Moran to John H. Murphy. ½ part. *Mt.* $700. 300

Java st, n s, 100 e Manhattan av, 25x100, h & l. Mary Brennan widow to Sarah, William, John and Elizabeth Brennan. nom

Jerome st, s e cor Hegeman av, 45x200 to Washington st. William B. Nichols to Florence Aron. 390

Kane pl, e s, 121.7 n Atlantic av, 46x105. George W. Evans to John D. Fish. Q. C. nom

Same property; also,
Pleasant pl, Nos. 17 and 19, e s, 133.4 n Atlantic av, 34.7x85.
John D. Fish to Albert Friedlander. *Mt.* $16,750. nom

Keap st, n w s, 123 s w Lee av, 21x100, h & l. Robert P. Lethbridge to Frank R. Lethbridge, Orange, N. J. nom

Same property. Frank R. Lethbridge to Mary J. Lethbridge. nom

Kent st, s s, 225 e Manhattan av, 25x100, h & l. Susan Anderson to Margaret Irwin, Philadelphia. ½ part. nom

Same property. Susan Anderson to Jeanette A. Anderson. ½ part. nom

Livingston st, s w s, 204 2 s e Bond st, 21.8x100.9, h & l. Agnes V. wife of John W. Hobart to William Moir. *Mt.* $6,000. 3,000

Lombardy st, n s, 300 w Morgan av, 25x150. Jeremiah V. Meserole to Michael Concannon. 500

Lombardy st, n s, 275 w Morgan av, 25x150. Same to Martin Rourke. 500

Linwood st, e s, 85 n Atlantic av, 25x49.2x25x49. Edward F. Linton to William C. Boone, Jr. 500

Same property. Release mort. Williamsburgh Savings Bank to Edward F. Linton. 350

Monitor st, e s, 83.3 s Van Cott av, 20x100. Henriette C. Niewohner, of Syossett, N. Y., to George Helbig. *Mt.* $1,500. nom

Middleton st, s s, 335 e Harrison av, 25x100. Philip Fritz to Barbara Wilz. 6,000

Middleton st, n s, 276 e Lee av, 18 10x100, h & l. Louis Bossert to Friedrich Friedrich. *Mt.* $4,000. 8,200

Osborn st, e s, 175 n Livonia av, 25x100. Nathan Nelson to Harris Fein. 500

Osborn st, e s, 150 n Livonia av, 25x100. Harris Fein to Nathan Nelson. 500

Pacific st, No. 2295A, n s, 338.4 w Stone av, 16.8x100. James Cocks to James Mitchell. *Mt.* $2,810. 2,500

Pacific st, n s, 185 e Troy av, 45.4x108.6x3.8x100. Release mort. Error. George A. Archer exr. George B. Archer to John Andrews, Jr. 100

Palmetto st, No. 188, s e s, 250 n e Central av, 25x100. Ella J Mayer to Frank Hyde and Charles F. Bates. *Mt.* $3,400 exch

President st, s s, 142.6 e Hoyt st, 17.6x100. John F. Hart to Patrick Hart. All title. 2,000

President st, n s, 171 e 7th av, runs north 95 x east 17 x north 5 x east 4 x south 100 to st, x west 21. Herman Knobel to William Gubbins. *Mt.* $6,000. nom

Prospect pl, s s, 116 e Schenectady av, 59x100. Victoria E. Manzanedo and Mary M. Behringer nee Manzanedo to Thomas W. Considine. 900

Prospect pl late Warren st, s s, 116 e Schenectady av, 16x100, h & l. Thomas W. Considine to Michael Darcy. 245

Prospect pl, s s, 157 e Schenectady av, 18x100, h & l. Same to John J. O'Brien. 275

Prospect pl, s s, 116 e Schenectady av, 59x100 James H. Manzando, New York, to Manuel, Victoria E. and Mary M. Manzando. Q C. 1878. nom

Quincy st, n s, 350 w Marcy av, 42.6x100, h & l. Mary Johnson and ano. exrs. Thomas Johnson to James W. Martens, Mohegan, N. Y. 9,900

Quincy st, n s, 457 6 e Nostrand av, 42 6x100. Release mort. Elizabeth H. Gates to Louisa Flynn. 5,000

Ralph st, s s, 170 n e Irving av, 20x100, h & l. Charles Schmidling and John Cadoo to Rosa Erbert, New York. *Mt.* $1,200. 2,300

Ralph st, s e s. 550 s w Central av, 50x100, hs & ls. Marie wife of John G. Kaiser to Frederick W. and Charles F. Kaiser. *Mt.* $6,600. nom

Schaeffer st, s e s, 100 n e Broadway, 25x200 to Van Voorhis st. Release mort. Cornelia M. Covert trustee Michael Covert to Caroline Skillman. nom

Seigel st, n s, 125 w Graham av, 25x100. Mendel Levy to Meyer Prussa. *Mt.* $1,200. 4,000

Skillman st, e s, 483 s Willoughby av, 16x100. Annie C. wife of Henry C. Van Winkle to Robert A. Siemon. 4,000

Skillman st, Nos 142 and 144, 43x95.1. Contract. Sarah Barasch and Jonas Feldberg to Theodore Van Eupen 6 000

Spencer st, e s, 132.3 s Park av, 25x100. Patrick Byrne to Michael Duffy. 9,000

Steuben st, e s, 219 8 s De Kalb av, 23.4x100, h & l. Moritz Pinner to Emily Rogers. *Mt.* $8,000. nom

Stockton st, n s, 150 w Throop av, 25x90. Simon Hartman to Frank Steinberger. *Mt.* $5,350. exch and 550

Suydam st, s s, 225 w Knickerbocker av, 25x100. John Koehler to Mary Roeser and Louis Koehler. *Mt* $3,000. gift

Starr st, s e s, 88.5 s w Wyckoff av, 25x100.
Stockholm st, s e s, 100 n e Irving av, 25x100.
Samuel N Garrison to Henry Loeffler. 1,200

United States st, s s, 100 e Little st, —x98. Annie wife of William P. Cook to William J. Cook. *Mt.* $5,000. nom

Van Buren st, n s, 119.6 w Lewis av, 19.6x100. Alfred L. Beasley to Cornelius Cameron. *Mt.* $5,806. 6,700

Vanderbilt st, n s, 260.7 e Gravesend av, 75x300.2 to Seely st, x85.2x300, Flatbush. William C. Dornin to William C. Dornin and George B. Salisbury, of W. C. Dornin & Co., New York. 2,650

Van Voorhis st, n w s, 287 s w Evergreen av, 16.10x100. William J. Higginson to John W. McLaren. 4,200

Wallabout st, s s, 70.10 e Clason av, 50x100.1. Elenore Bader to James Geehan. Taxes 1891. 4,841

Watkins st, w s, 100 n Sutter av, 25x100. Elias Kaplan to Celia wife of and Israel Zekind. *Mt.* $3,000. 5,500

Watkins st, w s, 315 s Livonia av, 25x100. Release mort. Alonzo E. De Baun to Louis and Joseph Eisenberg, of New York. nom

Watkins st, w s, 126.6 s Eastern Parkway, 25x100. William Smolinskey to Ephraim Silberstein and Isaac Lewis, of New York. *Mt.* $2,500. 3,600

Withers st, n s, 100 w Lorimer st, 25x100, h & l. Mary A. Fee widow and heir John B. Fee to Jiovani Donzo. 1,900

Withers st, n s, 250 w Lorimer st, 25x100. Maria Citrollo to Giovanni Citrollo. *Mt.* $1,400. 2,650

1st st, s w s, 305 n w 5th av, 81x100. Foreclos. John Courtney to Cornelius E. Donnellon. *Mt.* $3,860. 10,000

2d st, s s, 261.6 e 6th av, 36.4x95. Release mort. Lester A. Lewis to William H. Norris and William Bowers. 1,600

Same property. Release mort. James McLaren to same. 2,880

Same property. William H. Norris and William Bowers to William H. Axford, of Jersey City, N. J. *Mt.* $12,000. nom

East 3d st, w s, 105.7 s Greenwood av, 43.5x95.4x10x105.10, Flatbush. Anna M. Ferris and Jennie V. Wilbur to Carl Mathieson. 300

South 3d st, n e s, 145 s e Kent av, 25x75. Henry Weilbrenner, of Purdytown, Pa., to Peter N. Von Hessel. 5,850

South 4th st, n s, 140 w Wythe av, 20x140x20x106. William H. Anderson to Margaret wife of Patrick Smith. 4,900

6th st, s s, 228.10 e 6th av, 17x100, h & l. Amelia E. Hummel to Absolom W. Dieter. *Mt.* $6,500. nom

6th st, s s, 180 w 4th av, 115x100. Herman Becker to Eliza Becker. nom

6th st, s s, 228.10 e 6th av, 17x100. Release judgment. Archibald C. Shenstone exr. Benjamin C. Shenstone to Absalom W. Dieter. 129

North 6th st, s w s, 58.4 s e Wythe av, 16.8x50. James Foley to Mary F. Kelly. gift

7th st, s w s, 145.9 s e 3d av, 75x200 to 8th st. }
12th st, s w s, 204.1 n w 7th av, 18.9x100. }
Emilie C. wife of Frederick W. H. Nelson to Elizabeth Hellfinger. 5,000

North 10th st, s w s, 200 s e Kent av, 75x100, hs & ls. }
North 9th st, n e s, 225 s e Kent av, 75x100, hs & ls. }
Joseph A. Burr, Jr., to Havemeyers & Elder. 18,000

North 10th st, s s, 125 e Kent av, 25x100. John Braun to Henry Bohnson. 2,100

11th st, s w s, 133.5 n w 8th av, runs northwest 25 x southwest 14.6 x southeast 25 x northeast 14.9. Phebe M. Clarke et al. exrs. and trustees Henry L. Clarke and Phebe M. Clarke individ to Conrad Bils. 500

11th st, n s, 93.4 w 9th av, 18.6x100. Charles G. Peterson to Mary A. Eisengart. *Mt.* $6,000. 10,000

11th st, s s, 223.6 e 5th av, 25x100, h & l. Frederick C. Dexter to John Young., Williamsbridge, N. Y. *Mt.* $7,500. exch

13th st, n s, 296.5 e 5th av, 16.8x100, h & l. Dennis J. Donovan and William H. Heron to Florence J. Donohue. Correction deed. nom

14th st, n s, 322.4 w 9th av, 18.6x100. Christopher C. Firth to Helen C. Bowman. *Mt.* $3,500. 6,500

14th st, No. 451, n s, 197.6 e 8th av, 20.8x100. William Hawkins to Marc Nussberger. *Mt.* $4,000. 6,500

17th st, s s, 300 w 9th av, 25x100, h & l. Gustave B., Mary, Henry and Franklin A. McCloskey to Catharine Tracy all heirs of Hannah McCloskey. Q. C. nom

17th st, n e s, 350 n w 9th av, 50x100.2. Helen C. Bowman to Christopher C. Firth. 3,000

19th st, n s, 358.4 w 5th av, 16.8x100. Edmund M. Doane, of Jersey City, to Miner S. Horton, of Rochester, N. Y. nom

East 21st st, w s, 100 n Voorhies av as narrowed, 20x100, Gravesend. Alanson Tredwell and Alonzo Slote to William J. Gladding. 1887. 300

Bay 25th st, southerly cor Bath av, runs southeast along av 193.9 to Bay 26th st, x southwest 82.6 x northwest 193.4 to Bay 25th st, x northeast 95. Alfred F. Hennings to Camilla J. Hennings. *Mt.* $4,000. nom

Bay 28th st, n w s, 150 n e Cropsey av, 50x96.8, New Utrecht. Alfred F. Hennings to Camilla J. Hennings. *Mt.* $3,000. nom

Bay 29th st, n w s, 100 n e Cropsey av, runs northwest 65.3 x northeast 12.6 x northwest 31.10 x northeast 47.6 x southeast 96.8 to st, x southwest 60, New Utrecht. Caroline wife of Henry C. Vail to Sarah A. Gibbons. 2,000

39th st, s s, 100 e 7th av, 50x100.2. Rebecca Godsoe, of West Winstead, Conn., to George C. Kelly. ½ part. 400

45th st, s w s, 150 n w 8th av, 100x100.2. Annie wife of Edward P. Rees and Mary A. Guy widow to Patrick McInery. 900

46th st, n e s, 100 n w 12th av, 75x100.2, New Utrecht. West Brooklyn Land and Improvement Co. to Sarah Arons. 1,050

47th st, s s, 280 e 4th av, 100x100.2. Annie V. Shields, of New York, to James G. Carroll. Sub. to taxes 1890 and 1891. 4,125

47th st, s s, 389 w 3d av, 20x100.2. David J. Tingley and ano. exrs. Margaret M. Van Pelt to Bernard J. Krulder. 410

54th st, n s, 160 w 7th av, 100x100.2. Sidney C. Thompson to Thomas D. Hurst. Q. C. nom

61st st, ½ of st fronting lands of grantee, Bath Junction. James V. S. Wooley to Cornelius Vanderbeck. Q. C. nom

63d st, s s, 100 w 14th av, 40x107.10, New Utrecht. Nils Cederholm to Anna B. Lorenson. 650

66th st, n s, 160 e 12th av, 20x100, New Utrecht. James V. S. Woolley to Sylvester McCarrol. 175

East 94th st, n e s, bet Avs J and K, 31.6x200, Canarsie. John J. Morrison to Ferdinand Moller. 378

Atlantic av, s s, 80 e Kingston av, 19x104. John S. Loomis to Eliza A. wife of John T. Bierds. 1,500

Atlantic av, n s, 89 e Suydam pl, 15x88.10. Leopold de Arrastia to Hermina R. wife of Manuel de Arrastia. *Mt.* $1,700. 3,400

Bay av, s w s, 1,170.3 s e Cedar st, 100x100, Gravesend. William S. Fitzpatrick and Mary wife of John F. Ahearn to Timothy Fitzpatrick. All title. 892

Brooklyn av, n w cor Herkimer st, 24.6x70. Florence A. wife of Frederick J. Ashfield to Thomas R. Farrell. 16,000

Bushwick av, n e s, 102.8 s e Cedar st, runs northeast 54 x southwest 10.2 x northwest 37.10 x southwest 55.2 to av, x southeast 39, slight error. Jacob Bossert to John L. Gaus. *Mt.* $3,000. 10,500

Bushwick av, s w s, being the s w s of court-yard 30 s e Lafayette av, 20x79x20x78.6. James H. Watson and James H. Pittinger to Henry Roth. *Mt.* $4,500. nom

Central av, n e s, 25 n w Starr st, 25x100. Jacob Lieberguth to Barbara Kalb. *Mt.* $3,500. 5,775

Clason av, e s, 111 s Quincy st, 16x89.6, h & l. William A. Jenks, Arlington, N. J., to Edward P. Hatch, New York. *Mt.* $2,500. 6,000

Clermont av, No. 374, w s, 354 s Lafayette av, 21x72, h & l. John Gordon to Mary A. and Helen V. Golden. *Mt.* $5,000. 8,500

Clermont av, w s, 100 s Greene av, 21.6x100. Peter Taylor exr. Barbara Robertson to George W. Heatley. 7,750

De Kalb av, s e s, 225 n e Hamburg av, 25x100. Henry Roth and Alois Lazansky to Christina E. Pape. *Mt.* $3,000. nom

Evergreen av, w s, 75 s Stanhope st, 25x100. Anna L. Smith to Thomas Macri. *Mt.* $1,400. 2,500

Franklin av, e s, 100 n Tillary st old line, or 102.3 n Park av, 16.8x100, h & l. George F. Van Doorn to Christopher Million. 3,000

Franklin av, e s, 275 s Willoughby av, 25x120. Harriet J. Bleakney to Eleanor wife of Frank P. Bleakney. *Mt.* $4,200. nom

Glenmore av, n s, 100 w Sheffield av, 25x100. John Behrman to John Wenke. 2,900

Graham av, s w s, 50.8 s e Newton st, 25.4x87.7x25.91.9. Louise Dihlmann, of New York, to Gustav Kaiser. *Mt.* $2,800. nom

Same property. Gustav Kaiser to Andreas Dihlmann, of New York. *Mt.* $2,800. nom

Grand av, w s, 206.3 n Putnam av, 18.9x100. Margaret Findlay to Eliza T. wife of Charles W. House. *Mt.* $10,000. 13,500

Greene av, s e cor Evergreen av, 16.8x50, h & l. James Johnston to Joseph Kellow. *Mt.* $1,700. 5,500

Greene av, s e s, 310 s w Irving av, 20x100, h & l. Jacob Blank to William Klemme. *Mt.* $2,300. nom

Hamilton av, south cor Prospect pl, 49x232.6 to Gelston av, New Utrecht. William Clark to Thomas J. Clark. 1886. gift

Hudson av, w s, 24 n Nassau st, 20.4x62, h & l. William Wiswall to Lydia A. Corneille. B. & S. nom

Hudson av, w s, 44.4 n Nassau st, 20.4x62, h & l. Lydia A. Corneille widow, Islip, L. I., to William Wiswall. nom

Hamburg av, n e s, 25 n w Madison st, 18.9x80, h & l. John Manneschmidt to John Wuhl. *Mt.* $2,000. nom

Harrison av, e s, 75 s River st, 25x100. Christina E. wife of and August C. Pape to Henry Roth and Alois Lazansky. nom

Harway av, w s, adj Jas. or Jacobus Stryker, runs to Central pl, x — to Stillwell st, x — to Harway av, x —, Gravesend. Abraham H. Stryker, Frankford, N. J., to Rose wife of Robert Evin or Euin. 1,350

Jefferson av, s s, 420 e Howard av, 20x100. Foreclos. Jose E. Pidgeon to James Cropsey. 4,644

Knickerbocker av, westerly cor Melrose st, 25x100. John Dittrich, Henry Roth and Lippman Reizenstein to Leonhard Eppig. Sub. taxes 1891. 3,200

Knickerbocker av, northerly cor Melrose st, 25x100. John A. Eppig to Ignatz Wolf. 3,250

Kent av, w s, 325 n Myrtle av, 25x100. Bridget Breen to Annie H. Donovan. 250

Kingsland av, e s, 76.7 s Bennett st, runs east 97.11 x south 25 x west 25 x south 50 x west 34 x north 17 x west 51.1 to av, x north 61.3, hs and ls. August Speth to Gustav Hesse. *Mt.* $1,000. 3,675

Lafayette av, s s, 379.2 e Lewis av, 20.10x100. Sarah A. Hall to Edward H. Hall. gift

Lafayette av, n s, 425 e Nostrand av, 25x100. Susan E. Drummond, David B. and Edward B. Drummond to John Bull, Jr., Elmira, N. Y., and Edward B. Drummond. Q. C. 1,600

Same property. Susan A. Burton and M. Ella De Voy, Camden, N. Y., heirs Charles De Voy to same. 1,600

Lafayette av, n s, 200 e Stuyvesant av, 100x100. William J. Kaiser to Jacob Bossert. *Mt.* $6,000. nom

Lewis av, e s, 66.3 n Kosciusko st, 16.8x75. Anna G. Schiel to John D. Fish. *Mt.* $6,000. exch

Lexington av, s s, 331.3 w Marcy av, 18.9x100. Louis E. Culnet to George E. O'Neill, Valley Stream, L. I. *Mt.* $1,500. 8,200

Lexington av, n s, 366.8 e Bedford av, 16.8x100. Madison Ferris to Mungo Nairne. Q. C. nom

Livonia av, n s, 50 e Osborn st, 25x100. Arthur H. Wilson to Ignatz Loewy. *Mt.* $1,300. 2,200

Lexington av, n s, 140 e Lewis av, 20x100. John W. Love, of Watkins, N. Y., to William F. Hermance. *Mt.* $5,000. nom

Montauk av, e s, 150 s Liberty av, 20x100. Effingham H. Nichols, of New York, to Edward P. Waterbury. 400

Myrtle av, n s, 125 w Lewis av, 25x100. Edwin Ludlam to Esther wife of Max Hallheimer. nom

Myrtle av, s w cor Ralph st, runs west 120 x south 80 x west 100 x north 25 x southeast 60 x south 80 to Knickerbocker av, x southeast 60 to Ralph st, x north 304. Peter P. Sturges to William Hamilton. nom

Railroad av, w s, 75 n Griffin pl, 25x100. Stephen Matera to Theresa Matera. *Mt.* $1,750. 500

Railroad av, e s, 375 s Adams av, 25x102. John Horn to Joseph May. 425

Rockaway av, e s, 101.6 n Hull st, 40x75, hs & ls. Nathaniel W. Ladd to F. J. G. Ladd. C. a. G. nom

Same property. F. J. G. Ladd to William H. Beeching or Buching. *Mt.* $9,750. 12,500

Schenectady av, e s, 66 n Atlantic av, 16.6x80. Irving Fish to Albert Friedlander. *Mt.* $2,000. nom

Snediker av, e s, 100 s Riverdale av, 50x100. Louis H. Irwin to James S. McCoy. 600

St. Marks av, n s, 100 w Underhill av, 25x131. John Courtney to William L. Culbert, New York. 7,500

St. Marks av, n s, 150 e Buffalo av, 100x127.9. Alfred Ogden to Joseph F. Kentana. *Mt.* $5,000. nom

St. Marks av, n s, 150 w Nostrand av, 50x125.3, h & l. Frank D. Creamer to Louise M. Creamer. *Mt.* $10,000. nom

Stone av, w s, 25 s Somers st, 25x80, h & l. James Kearney to Charles F. Bates. *Mt.* $5,000. nom

Stone av, w s, 75 s Riverdale av, runs west 100 x south 25 x west 100 to Watkins st, x south 25 x east 200 to Stone av, x 50. Release mort. Brooklyn Mutual Benefit and Loan Assoc. to William J. Robbins. nom

Thatford av, w s, 150 n Riverdale av, 75x100. Abraham Ruth to Hyman Axelrod. ½ part. nom

Throop av, w s, 63 n Pulaski st, 37x84.9, h & l. Benjamin Armstrong to William C. Miller. *Mt.* $5,500. nom

Van Cott av, n s, 60.7 e Lorimer st, 25x65.6x31.6x46.4. Walter J. Anderson to Margaret Irwin, Philadelphia, Pa., and Susan and Jeanette A. Anderson. nom

Vienna av, s e cor Atkins av, 20x95. William H. Jackson to William C. Hosking. 275

Voorhis av, centre line, intersection w s Ocean av, runs west 551.7 to centre East 18th st, x south 115 x east 336 x northeast 215 to Ocean av, x north 95, being 1 28-100 acres, Sheepshead Bay. Anna widow and Isaac D. Voorhies and Phebe A. wife of George Lott to Alexander W. Kyle. nom

Washington av, s e cor Degraw st, 91.3x102.2x41.4x130.3. Louis S. Steers to Thomas Monahan. 6,500

West av, s s, 40 e Voorhies pl, 60x90, Gravesend. Marshall N. T k to Charles N. Brewster. *Mt.* $1,225.uc er nom

Wyckoff av, n e s, 75 s e Madison st, 25x94.8x25x94.6. Ferdinand Fuhrmann to Maria Fuhrmann his wife. nom

Wythe av, n w s, 50 s w North 7th st, 25x100. Jacob Lax to Rosa Gilbert. ½ part. 900

3d av, w s, 40 s Wyckoff st, 20x80, h & l. Charles F. Hunt to Philip Baer. *Mt.* $4,000. nom

3d av, s e s, 25.2 s w 40th st, 25x100. John M. Fuchs to Herman Colell. 10,000

6th av, s e cor 10th st, 20x90. William W. Stoothoff to William Brown. exch

6th av, w s, 68 s 6th st, 16x78.10. Henry Roth to James H. Watson and James H. Pittinger. *Mt.* $5,000. nom

7th av, n w cor 9th st, runs west 97.10 x north 180 to 8th st, x east 17.10 x south 110 x east 80 to 7th av, x south 58, hs & ls. James Rowland to Charles Nickenig. nom

7th av, w s, 58 n 9th st, 122x80. Charles Nickenig to James Rowland. nom

7th av, w s, 21.6 n 10th st, 19.6x80. Same to same. *Mt.* $8,000. nom

8th av, s e cor Lincoln pl, 22x100. William Gubbins to Herman Knobel and Emma his wife, joint tenants. other consid. and 24,000

8th av, No. 14, w s, 140 n Lincoln pl, 20x100, h & l. William Gubbins to Caroline Browne. 19,000

Coney Island road, n s, bet Cranford and Voorhies, abt ¾ acre, Gravesend, hs & ls. Joseph Goldstein to Aaron Kaplan. *Mt.* $3,500. 14,000

Lots 1-8 map of lot 6 common lands, Gravesend, Coney Island. Albert G. Burtis to John M. Kopf. 2,500

Part of lot 347 map No. 2 Fort Hamilton not cut off by 4th av and 92d st. People State of New York to C. W. Church. letters patent

Road from Brooklyn and Jamaica plank road to Van Wicklens mill at Plunder Neck, w s, 787.10 s of new road leading from said road to New Lots, 50x97.8x50x100. James D. Davis to John H. Heun. 100

Indefinite 15-foot right of way, n s, 95 w of road leading from Voorhies lane to Sheepshead Bay, 35x100, Gravesend. Julia Ann Williams to John Y. McKane. 700

All title in Vanderbilt av fronting property of grantees. Elenor Doherty widow to Mary A. wife of Thomas R. Farrell. nom

All real estate in Kings Co. of which James Calvert died seized. Mary Stedmond and Elizabeth De Maine to E. Sinnamon Calvert. nom

Receipt of legacies and release. Adolph Kiesel guard. of Frank and Albert Kiesel to Peter Stromberger. 2,000

Receipt of legacy and release. Theresa Nestlen to Peter Stromberger. 1,000

WESTCHESTER COUNTY.

DECEMBER 16 TO 22—INCLUSIVE.

CORTLANDT.

Fisher, Adam to Maggie S. Fisher, lots 13-31 block 27 map Verplancks. $3,150

Same to Margt. Fisher, n e cor Dutch st and road to Crugers, 16 acres. 1,800

Hill, Uriah to Caroline M. Hudson, n w cor Paulding st and Nelson av, 57x100. 1,140

Southard, Thos. admr. of, to Ardenns R. Free, n w cor Main and James sts, 100x245. 9,300

Underwood, Mary S. to Geo. H. Roberts, s s Lincoln terrace, 50x—. 250

EASTCHESTER.

Bard, Wm. H. to Robt. Brodie, lot 240 s e s Catharine st, Washingtonville, 23 3x100. 2,500

Blanck, Geo. B. to Arthur Lawrence, part 339 n s 3d st, Mt. Vernon, 28.6x50. 3,500

Conkling, Mary A. to Geo. Schuster, part 829 w s 1st st. Mt. Vernon, abt 30x95. 2,500

Doremus, Lizzie B. to Wm. H. Bard, part lot 474 e s 7th av, Mt. Vernon, 33.4x105. nom

Deverman, Louisa et al., D. O. Williams ref., to Chas. M. Hartman and ano., lot 304 n s Pearl st, West Mt. Vernon, 63x170. 3,550

Henricks, Chas. to Naomi Duncombe, s w cor 3d av and 6th st, Mt. Vernon, 210x—. 10,500

Mager, Fred. to Chas. Nettleton, lots 3, 4 and 5 n s Old White Plains road, grantor's map. 8,500

Trace, Harriet to Emma Fund, w s New road, adj Wm. Parsons, abt 190x400. 3,150

Wallach, Abr. to Edw. Hartley, lot 506 Central Mt. Vernon. nom

Wallach, Eleanora to same, same property. nom

Whitmore, Daniel W. to Fred. Mager, lot 810 w s 9th av, Mt. Vernon, 100x105. 2,900

Wright, Kate L. to Robt. T. Grey, lots 16 and 17, s s Lincoln st, 215 w Fairview st, 50x101. 500

Wood, Jos. S. to Mamie T. W. McTague, lot 101 Overlook st, Villa Park, 50x100. 1,500

GREENBURGH.

Clarke, Steph. G. to Henry Dale, n s Martling av, abt 245x400. 2,800

Fields, And. C. to Philip Costello, lot 32 n s Maple st, Dobbs Ferry, 50x100. 1,000

Storms, Chas. E. to Mich. Sheridan, lots 162 and 163 e s Lefurgy av, map Thos. H. Purdy's lots, 50x100. 1,700

Waller, Oscar A. J. to John A. Leary, lot 625 ft. s Dobbs Ferry road and 50 ft. w railroad, 25x100. 200

Same to Jacob R. Heck, lot adj, 25x100. 200

HARRISON.

Ross, Richard B. to John H. Clapp, tract on road from Purchase st to King st, 90 acres. 12,500

Roach, John, exrs., &c., of, to Welcom G. Hitchcock, The Major Anderson farm, road from White Plains to Purchase, 276 acres. 40,000

MAMARONECK.

Sears, Sadie W. and ano. to Estelle B. Sears, lot 101 map Grand Park. nom

MOUNT PLEASANT.

Barnhart, J. W. to John O'Connor, n s Beekman av, adj Levi Govens, 40x100. 850

Smadbeck, Louis to Dena Koenan, lot 863, Sherman Park. 100

Same to Cecelia A. J. Blankey, lot 864. 100

Same to Jos. Koenigsberg, 1930A, 1931, 1932 and 1933. 700

Same to Aug. Rosencrans and ano., 408. 150

Same to Cath. McLaughlin, 1111. 200

Same to Peter McLaughlin, 1112. 200

Same to John Muller, 113-116 and 178-181. 2,000

Same to same, 5073-5080 and 5061-5068. 1,500

Same to Philip Rettig, 111 and 112. 600

Same and ano. to Ernestine Merry, lots 197-200, Lakehurst. 800

Same to Maria Sibthorpe, 425 and 426. 300

Smith, Wm. R. to Daniel W. Quinn, lots 37, 38, 60 and 61 block 3, Lake Kensico. 500

Same to W. O. Chrisman, lots 37 and 38 block 6. 450

Wood, Henry to Noah Davis, e s Bedford road, Pocantico Hills, 50x120. 700

NEW ROCHELLE.

Bates, Lillie M. to Theo. Birdsall, s s Lafayette st, 402.6 e Franklin av, 100x150. 8,000

Beckwith, N. Malon to Melvin De Mott, lot 11 block F, Rochelle Park. nom

De Mott, Melvin to Ada C. Beckwith, same property. nom

Green, John C. to Kath. Green, s s Spruce st, 250 w Drake av, 50x100. 1,400

Hudson, Alex. B. to Ella Jenkins, w s Highland av, 156 s Beechwood av, 50x207. 500

Manhattan Life Ins Co. to Letitia I. Jones, lots 6 and 7 block G, Rochelle Park. 1,950

Same to Ada C. Beckwith, lot 121 block F. 2,500

Paisley, Louisa B. to John Leach, Jr., e s Franklin av, 143 s Main st, 50x173. 3,200

OSSINING.

McCormick, John to Delia Healey, s s Market st, abt 25x150. 1,200

Rockett, Edw. et al. S. Watson ref. to Chas. W. Underhill, n e s Dale av, 50x150. 500

PELHAM.

Heiser, Eliza to Samuel McSkimin, lots 1 and 2, n e s 5th av, 100x100. 450

Tyler, Wm. D. to Wm. J. Bush, s s East st, abt 166x100, City Island. 3,000

Underhill, Henry M. to Ruth Evans and ano., lots 263, 264, 293 and 334 map Pelhamville. nom

RYE.

Allen, Eleanor G. to Addison A. Cardwell, e s Rye Beach av, 184 n Railroad av, abt 155x150. 1,300

Fursman, Carrie A. to Wm. Ryan, n s Lyons pl, road adj Cemetery, ¼ acre. 3,800

Hayward, John H. to John M. Farnham, s s Elm pl, 244 w Purchase st, 267x—. 225

Merritt, Jas. S. and ano. to Mark A. Bradley, lot 107 n s West William st, Washington Park, 50x150. 100

Same to Harry A. Frederick, lot 104 n s same st, 50x150. 150

Same to same, lot 102 e s Merritt st, 50x100. 180

Same to same, lot 89 w s Lyon st, 50x100. 205

Same to same, lot 66 w s Lyon st, 50x100. 210

Same to same, lot 10 n s Ellendale av, 50x150. 215

Madigan, Patrick exrs. of, to Thos. Kelly, w s Prospect av, 50x110. 1,325

WESTCHESTER.

Marshall, Thos. J. to Georgianna Brigg and ano., lot 28 e s 1st av, Olinville, 100x100. nom

Saxe, Huldah to Helen E. Arnold, n s Cornell av, 105 e Old road, 30x100. 4,500

Springstead, Wm. H. to Doretta Schaeffer, lot 182 s s 9th st, Unionport, 200x216. 2,600

Smith, Wm. G. to Fred C. Fiske, lot 1160 n s 14th av, Wakefield, 100x114. 700

YONKERS.

Brewer, Ophelia A. to Jennie E. Roys, s s Poplar st, 25 w Oak st, 25x100. 4,000

Clarke, Benj. H. to Sherwood Park Land and Impt. Co., lots 55 and 56 map property grantee. nom

Edwards, Ellis B. and ano. to Lines L. Fletcher, lot 11 block 7, w s McLean av, Lowerre station. 3,750

Fowler, Clarence M. to Wm. J. Fowler, e s Crescent pl, 175 n Sherwood av, 50x100. 400

Kyle, Henry B. to Mary A. Harley, lot 112 e s 1st st, map Hyatt farm. 775

Moore, Sarah to Sophie Goff, s s Highland av, 425 w s Broadway, 40x155. 5,750

New York and Yonkers Land Impt. Co. to Chris. Carlisle, lots 125 and 126, Bryn Mawr Park. 500

Parsells, Edw. W. to Michael Hurst, e s Briggs av, 300 n Fort Field av, 25x100. 250

Prime, Edw. D. G. exr. of, to New York and Northern Land and Impt. Co., s s Undercliff st, 50x100. 2,000

Wemple, Chris. Y., exr. of, to Ella Jenkins, lots 32-38 and 53, Sherwood Park. 20,000

YORKTOWN.

Kimball, Chas. E. to Field Farm Co., 1¼ acres on Crompond road, adj Town Cortlandt. 1,500

Same to Cortlandt F. Bishop, e s same road, 5¼ acres. 2,500

MORTGAGES.

NOTE.—*The arrangement of this list is as follows. The first name is that of the mortgagor, the next that of the mortgagee. The description of the property then follows, then the date of the mortgage, the time for which it was given, and the amount. The general dates used as headings are the dates when the mortgage was handed into the Register's office to be recorded.*

Whenever the letters "P. M." occur, preceded by the name of a street, in these lists of mortgages, they mean that it is a Purchase Money Mortgage, and for fuller particulars see the list of transfers under the corresponding date. Whenever the rate is not given, read as 6 per cent.

NEW YORK CITY.

DECEMBER 18, 19, 21, 22, 23.

Ayers, Ann E., Morristown, N. J., Mary A. Hanlon, Brooklyn, and Hannah L. Bonsall, Morristown, N. J., to THE TITLE GUARANTEE AND TRUST CO. 10th st, No. 323, n s, 370.6 e Av A, 25x94.8. Dec. 18, 1 year, 5 %. $17,000

Acker, Henry C. to The Yale Safe and Iron Co. of Connecticut. Amsterdam av, s w cor 99th st, 40x80.2 to e s of late Bloomingdale road, x40x77.6. Sub. to morts. $18,321. Dec. 21, note. 648

Adler, Sigmund to Ascher H. Michelbacher trustee. 110th st, n s, 246.8 w 4th av, 16.8x100.11. Dec. 1, 5 years, 5 %. 5,000

Same to same. 110th st, n s, 263.4 w 4th av, 16.8x100.11. Dec. 1, 5 years, 5 %. 5,000

Baumert, Caroline to Peter Doelger. 1st av. P. M. Dec. 18, due Jan. 2, 1897, 5 %. 6,000

Same to S. Galle & Co. Houston st, s s, 25 w Clinton st, 25x100. Dec. 18, due April 18, 1894, 5 %. 6,000

Beaudet, John and Ernest P. to Robinson Gill. Mount Morris av, s w cor 121st st, 100.11x100. Sub. to morts. Dec. 23, demand. 40,000

Beudinger, Valentine to Frederick Brommer, Brooklyn. 105th st, s s, 333.4 w 2d av, 16.8x100.9. Dec. 19, demand. 1,500

Belger, Benjamin F. to Nicholas Winkler. Jackson av, centre line, 154 n Clifton st, 22.6x100x22.7x100. Dec. 22, 2 years, 5 %. 200

Bley, Robert to THE EMIGRANT INDUST. SAVINGS BANK. 3d st, n s, 120 e 2d av, 20x77.5. Dec. 21, 1 year, 4½ %. 4,000

Bliss, Harriet W. to James Pyle. 32d st, No. 37, n s, 520 w 5th av, 25x98.9. Dec. 1, 3 years, 5 %. 9,932

Bradley & Currier Co. (Lim.) with Matthew C. Quigley both mortgagees. Agreement as to priority of mortgages made by Frederick Rohrs and Louisa his wife. Dec. 22. nom

Braun, Ferdinand to George F. Norton. Mott st, No. 125, w s, 74.11 n Hester st, 25x63; Hester st, No. 177, n w cor Mott st, 22.9x74.11. Dec. 21, 5 years, 5 %. gold, 30,000

Broadbelt, William, New Rochelle, N. Y., to Sarah H. Powell. 151st st, s s, 150 e Amsterdam av, 125x99.11. Dec. 17, 6 months. 85,000

Brooker, William E. to Eliza Worthington. Hoffman st. P. M. Dec. 18, 2 years. 600

Brown, Christina K. to Fannie L. Hart. Oliver st, No. 26, e s, 68.8 n Madison st, —x66.6x20x66.5. Dec. 22, due Dec. 1, 1893, 5 %. gold, 3,500

Brown, James to William M. Evarts. 96th st, No. 27, n s, 256.6 w 8th av, 18.6x100.8. Dec. 17, 3 years, 5 %. 17,000

Same to Edward and Henry Hirsh. Same property. Secures two bonds of mortgagor. Dec. 23. 31,000

Byrne, Dennis to The Bachmann Brewing Co., Stapleton, S. I. 12th st, No. 231 W. Saloon lease. Dec. 17, demand. 3,000

Byrne, Mary E. to Morris S. Thompson trustee Ebenezer H. Pray. 97th st, n s, 213 e 10th av, 19x100.11. Dec. 16, 3 months, 5 %. 4,000

Connolly, Thomas B. to James K. Hill. 211th st, centre line, s s, 75 e 9th av, 100x109.2x—x102; 212th st, centre line, n s, 250 e 9th av, 50x129.11, touch Harlem River; 215th st, centre line, n s, at intersection centre line 10th av, runs east 20 x north 149.11x200x149.11; 213th st, centre line, s s, 75 e 9th av, 125x129.11, as shown on the Connolly map. Dec. 22, 1 year. 1,000

Cahn, Hannah wife of Siegfried C. to David Gideon. 124th st, s s, 262.6 w Lenox av, 18.9x100.11. Dec. 22, due Jan. 1, 1895, 5 %. 8,000

Same to same. 124th st, s s, 281.3 w Lenox av, 18.9x100.11. Dec. 22, due Jan. 1, 1895, 5 %. 8,000

Callahan, Julia to Patrick S. Treacy. 37th st, n s, 400 e 11th av, 25x98.9. Dec. 18, due Feb. 1, 1892. 500

Campbell, John V. to Joseph L. Buttenwieser. Madison st, n s, 26.1 w Jefferson st, 26.1x100. Dec. 18, demand. 4,000

Cannon, John B. to John Bell & Son. 114th st, s w cor Park av, 30x100.11. Dec. 19, 6 months. See Conveys. 1,340

Carpenter, Phebe A. wife of Henry H. to Riker R. James. 119th st, s s, 110 w 1st av, 20x100.10. Dec. 18, 1 year. 1,000

Casey, John to Edward Oppenheimer and Isaac Metzger. Columbus av and 84th st. P. M. Dec. 4, 1 year. 40,000

Same to same. Same property. Building loan. Dec. 4, 1 year. 65,000

Cohen, George J. to Samuel J. Colgate, New Hamburgh, N. Y. 96th st, s s, 100 e 3d av, 27.3x100.8. Sub. to mort. $15,000. Dec. 17, 1 year. gold, 3,000

Cools, John to Bella Wertheimer, Brooklyn. Gerard st. P. M. Dec. 22, due Jan. 1, 1895, 5 %. 2,000

Crawford, Francis to Adolphus J. Outerbridge trustee. 76th st. P. M. Nov. 18, due Dec. 22, 1892, 5 %. 12,000

Cronly, John E. to Mary B. Johnson. Wadsworth av, e s, 65 s 175th st, 9.8x150x23.10x150.8. Dec. 21, 1 year. 2,000

Crossman, Greenleaf W. to Sarah J. Vanderhoof. 124th st, n s, 94 w 1st av, 18.8x100.11x18.9x100.11. Dec. 12, due Dec. 15, 1896, 5 %. 9,000

Crowe, Mary C. and Lizzie A. to Mary Kairns. East Broadway, n s, 255.2 e Catharine st, 25x84. Lease. Dec. 7, 1 year. 1,000

Curtis, Frank D. mortgagor with John S. Bussing mortgagee. Extension of mort. Aug. 13. nom

Davis, Mark to Simon P. Flannery. 63d st. P. M. Dec. 21, 3 years, 5 %. 2,250

Daly, Cornelius to THE FARMERS' LOAN AND TRUST CO. 115th st, s s, 245 e 5th av, 25x100.11. Dec. 18, 3 years, 5 %. 17,000

Same to same. 115th st, s s, 320 e 5th av, 25x100.11. Dec. 18, 3 years, 5 %. 17,000

Same to Augusta M. de Peyster. 115th st, s s, 270 e 5th av, 25x100.11. Dec. 15, 3 years, 5 %. 17,000

Same to Marx and Moses Ottinger. 115th st, s s, 245 e 5th av, 25x100.11. Sub. to mort. $17,000. Dec. 18, 6 months. 2,000

Same to same. 115th st, s s, 270 e 5th av, 25x100.11. Sub. to mort. $17,000. Dec. 18, 6 months. 2,000

Same to same. 115th st, s s, 320 e 5th av, 25x100.11. Sub. to mort. $17,000. Dec. 18, 6 months. 2,000

Denks, Charles L. to Isabella and Alexander J. Herriott. Broadway or New York and Albany Post road. P. M. Dec. 16, 10 years, 5 %. 1,500

de Polo, Rosalina E. U. to William A. Bartow et al. trustees Maria R. Bartow. 11th av, e s, 80.3 s 71st st, 20.2x80. Dec. 21, due Dec. 1894, 5 %. gold, 15 000

Same as wife of J. Gerald de Polo to The Bradley and Currier Co. (Lim.) Same property. Sub. to last mort. Dec. 23, due July 1, 1892. 1,250

Deyette, Edmond to Jacob Cohen. 79th st. P. M. Dec. 18, 1 year. 10,000

Dreyfus, Annie F. as guard. mortgagee with Henrietta Hershfield mortgagor. Extension of mort. Dec. 17. nom

Downing, Flora E. wife of Albert D. to Harry Berry. Valentine av, s s, 175 e Southern Boulevard, 50x110. Re-recorded. Sept. 5, 3 years, 5 %. 2,662

Dunn, Ellen mortgagee with Fanny Hershfield mortgagor. Extension of mort. Dec. 21. nom

Dunne, Thomas P. to Marx and Moses Ottinger. 119th st, s s, 100 w 8th av, 175x100 11. Building loan. Dec. 14, due Sept. 1, 1892. 63,000

Eberhardt, John to Friedrich Seibel. Monroe st, No. 245, n s, 286.10 e Scammel st, 23 6x94.8x23.6x94.9. Dec. 19, due Jan. 1, 1895, 5 %. 6,000

Eisenkramer, Herman and Rosanna his wife to Joseph Schreiner. 88th st. P. M. Dec. 15, due Dec. 28, 1894, 5 %. 2,000

Evans, William T. to THE TITLE GUARANTEE AND TRUST CO. 76th st, n s, 125 w Central Park West, 50x102.2. Dec. 23, 3 years, 4½ %. 35,000

Farley, John T. to THE MUTUAL LIFE INS. CO. of New York. 70th st, s s, 125 e Columbus av, 10 lots, together in size, 225x100 5. 10 morts, each $30,000. Dec. 23, due Dec. 1, 1892, 5 %. 300,000

Faulhaber Julius to Eva Bechtel, extrx. George Bechtel. 2d av, No. 1551. Lease. Dec. 16, demand. 2,000

Fealy, Johanna C. to Julius H. Caryl. Kingsbridge road, e s, 22.2 s 171st st, 27.9x102x25x114. Dec. 22, 2 years. 500

Federman, Saul to Blume Klyshinsky. Delancey st. P. M. Dec. 17, due Dec. 1, 1896. 6,000

Fish, John and Jacob Miller to THE GERMAN-AMERICAN REAL ESTATE TITLE GUARANTEE CO. Monroe st, No 230, s s, 95 6 e Scammel st, 27.6x95.2. Dec. 17, due Dec. 18, 1894, 5 %. 22,500

Same to same. Monroe st, No. 232, s s, 123 e Scammel st, 27.5x95.3x27.5x95.2. Dec. 17, due Dec. 18, 1894, 5 %. 22,500

Same to same. Monroe st. No. 234, s s, 150.5 e Scammel st, 27.5x95.3. Dec. 17, due Dec. 18, 1894, 5 %. 22,500

Same to same. Monroe st, No. 236, s s, 177.10 e Scammel st, 27.4x95.4x27.4x95.3. Dec. 17, due Dec. 18, 1894, 5 %. 22,500

Fishel, Harry to Ellen Abrahams. Rivington st, s e cor Columbia st, 45.8x55.10x45.8x55.8. Dec. 15, due March 4, 1892. 5,000

Fitch, Sarah M. to Edwin A. Wallace. Genesee, N. Y. 43d st, s s, 333 4 w 7th av, 16.8x100.4. Dec. 17, due Dec., 1891. 1,500

Flake, Albert to Frederic J. Middlebrook, Brooklyn. Columbus av, w s, 100 s 94th st, runs west 62.4 to n s Apthorp's lane, x northwest 37.8 to point 100 w Columbus av, x south 18.9 to centre line Apthorp's lane, x east 100.1 to av, x north 20.7. Dec. 21, 3 years, 5 %. 12,000

Frank, Annie E. to Mary Power. 8th av, w s, 25 n 126th st, 25x100. P. M. Given in place of another mortgage. Dec. 16, 1 year. 3,500

Flood, Timothy to Elizabeth Wright, Hartsdale, N. Y. 162d st, s s, 146.7 e Prospect av, —x—x31x99.6. Dec. 21, 3 years, 5 %. 3,500

Gault, Mary wife of and James to James McCreery. 106th st. P. M. Nov. 16, 1 year. 65,000

Same to same. Same property. Building loan. Nov. 16, 1 year. 50,000

Gillette, Walter R. mortgagor with THE SEAMEN'S BANK FOR SAVINGS, New York, mortgagee. Extension of mort. Dec. 15. nom

Goldberg, Morris and Nathan Schancupp mortgagors with Dorothea W. Hoffman mortgagee. Extension of mort. Nov. 27. nom

Same with William G. Ulshoeffer mortgagee. Extension of mort. Nov. 27. nom

Grant, William, Sing Sing, N. Y., to Libbie T. Chadeayne, Yorktown, N. Y. 11th av, s e cor 173d st, 25x100. Dec. 8, due Dec. 1, 1894, 5 %. 2,000

Same to Ann M. Purdy, Sing Sing, N. Y. Hudson st, w s, 25.4 s Perry st, 18.10x84.9x17.10x90 5. Dec. 19, due Jan. 1, 1893. 2,000

Same to Ruth S Murray, New Bedford, Mass. Jane st, s s, 88.5 e Washington st, 24x70.8x24x70.2. Dec. 8, due July 1, 1894, 5 %. 1,600

Gullmann, Sophia to Martin Goerl. 2d av, w s, 80.9 n 2d st, 22x100. Dec. 17, due July 1, 1892, 5 %. 500

Hall, John T. to St. Luke's Hospital, New York 36th st, n s, 150 w 5th av, 25x98.9. Dec. 17, due March 1, 1897, 5 %. 40,000

Hanselmann, August to Charles O. Kirkup. Webster av and 170th st. P. M. Dec. 18, 2 years, 5 %. 2,000

Higgins, John to T. C. Lyman & Co. 135th st, n s, 275 e Lincoln av, 25x100. Dec. 18, 1 year, 5 %. 1,500

Higgins, Maria S. to Kate L. Laudy. 98th st. P. M. Dec 21, 5 years, 5 %. 4,000

Hoefling, Christoph to DRY DOCK SAVINGS INST. Ridge st, e s, 43 s Stanton st, 24x100. Dec. 21, 1 year, 5 %. 2,000

Halpin, Paul to Joseph H. Godwin. Boulevard. P. M. Dec. 17, 3 years, 5 %. 2,250

Hoepfner, George to Oscar V. Pitman. 163d st, n s, 100 w Delmonico pl. P. M. Dec. 21, 3 years. 3,000

Same to same. 163d st, n s, 125 w Delmonico pl. P. M. Dec. 21, 3 years 3,500

Howe, Harriet F. to William B. Howe. 17th st, n s, 103 w 8th av, runs north 25 x east 3 x north 67 x west 25 x south 92 to st, x east 22. Dec. 19, 1 year, 5 %. 2,000

Hunt, Jane A. to THE NEW YORK LIFE INS. CO. West End av, s w cor 104th st, 100.11x100. Dec. 18, 1 year. 95,000

Irving, Benjamin H to Emma S Potter widow. Opdyke av and 1st st. P. M. Nov. 21, 3 years, 5 %. 3,000

Jay, Eleanor K. wife of John, Bedford, N. Y., to Flamen B. Candler and ano., trustees Joshua Brooks dec'd. Canal st, No 252, s e cor Elm st, 20.9x68x19.9x70.1. Dec. 17, due Feb. 5, 1894, 5 %. 11,500

Jencks, Francis M. mortgagee with Hugh McDowell and John C. Heney present owners. Agreement apportioning mortgage made by Frank L. Smith and wife July 2, 1891. Oct. 14. nom

Johnston, Emeline to John C. Overhiser. 132d st, n s, 110 w 5th av, 50x99 11. Dec. 21, 1 year, 5 %. 11,400

Same to same. 133d st, s s, 135 w 5th av, 50x99.11. Dec. 21, 1 year, 5 %. 11,500

Johnston, Elizabeth wife of and Richard E. to Henry B. Barnes. 8th av, w s, 27 s 118th st, 25.8x100. Dec. 23, 3 years, 5 %. gold, 19,000

Same to same. 8th av. w s, 32.8 s 118th st, 25.8x100. Dec. 23, 3 years, 5 %. gold, 19,000

Same to Morris Steinhardt. 8th av, w s, 27 s 118th st, 77.10x100. Sub. to morts. $58,000. Dec. 21. due Jan. 20, 1892. 8,000

Same to Catharine A. B. Abbe trustee Courtlandt Palmer dec'd. 8th av, w s, 78.4 s 118th st, 26 6x100. Dec. 23, 5 years, 5 %. 20,000

Kahn, German mortgagor with the trustees of the Gratuity Fund of the N. Y. Cotton Exchange. Extension of mort. at increased int. Nov. 23. nom

Kaiser, John heir Frederick and Elizabeth Kaiser to Mary Kaiser. 161st st, s s, 375 e Courtlandt av, 25x100. Dec. 22, due Jan. 1, 1894, 5 %. 1,600

Kane, John P. to Robert H. Mathews. 137th st, n s, 81.6 w Willis av, 6 lots, each 25x100. 6 morts., each $2,500. Dec. 18, 1 year. 15,000

Kilpatrick, Edward to Philip J. and Henry M. Sands exrs. Abraham B. Sands. West End av, e s, 73.11 n 97th st, 18x89. Dec. 23, 3 years, 5 %. 15,000

Kissam, Sarah S. wife of and Benjamin A. to THE WASHINGTON LIFE INS. CO. 48th st, No. 145, n s, 300 e 7th av, 20x100.5. Dec. 18, due Dec. 1, 1893, 5 %. 2,500

Kitchel, Margaret A. S. wife of and Charles H. to William Armstrong, Far Rockaway, L. I. 104th st, s s, 225 w Columbus av, 25x100.11. Dec. 18, 2 years. 2,500

Klein, Benedict A. to THE FARMERS' LOAN AND TRUST CO. Morton st, No. 20. P. M. Dec. 22, due Dec. 23, 1894, 5 %. 22000

Kuenstler, Ludwig to David Mayer exr. Gabriel Mayer. Broadway or Kingsbridge road and Macomb st. P. M. Dec. 22, 5 years, 5 %. 7,000

Lang, John W. to George C. Engel. 42d st, Nos. 157 and 159 E. Lease. Dec. 21, notes. 3,500

Lauten, Mary M. wife of George to Martha L. Andrews. 128th st, s s. 75 e 8th av. 25x99.11. Dec. 17, 1 year. 1.050

Lawson, Manning F. to GREENWICH SAVINGS BANK. Christopher st, No. 131, and Hudson st, No 501, begins Christopher st, n w cor Hudson st, 26.7x72x50 to Christopher st x 74.9. Dec. 15, due Jan. 1, 1893, 5 %. 5,000

Leaycraft, J. Edgar to Henry P. Talmadge et al. trustees John H. Seaman. 84d st, n s, 225 w Columbus av, 18x102.2. Dec. 19, due Jan. 1, 1897, 5 %. 17,500

Leaycraft, J. Edgar to Edward H. Gilbert. 82d st, n s, 557 e Amsterdam av, 18x102.2. Dec. 21, 1 year or installs. 4,000

Lese, Louis, Pincus Loewenfeld and Morris Goldstein to Sarah Brush et al. exrs. and trustees Silvester Brush. Essex st, No. 44. P. M. Dec. 23, 5 years, 5 %. gold, 24,000

Lewis, Wolf, Brooklyn, and Pinkas Ganz to Joseph Newborg. 98th st. P. M. Sub. to morts. Dec. 23, installs. 4,500

Lindner, Charles to Matilda Weil et al. exrs. Max Weil. West 10th st, n s, 103 w Waverley pl, 25x95. December 23, 5 years, 4½ %. gold, 15,000

Manahan, Bridget M. and John J. and Agnes L. to TITLE GUARANTEE AND TRUST CO. 29th st, No 309, n s, 135 e 2d av, 20x98.9. All title. Dec. 11, due Jan. 1, 1893. 700

Martin, Abram J., Catskill, N. Y., to Albert Tower, Poughkeepsie, N. Y. 125th st, s s, 85 w 5th av, 16 8x100.11. Dec. 21, 3 years, 5 %. 23,000

Martin, Charles V. to John Sloane exr. and trustee Douglas Sloane. 135th st. s w cor 7th av. P. M. Dec. 8, due Dec. 1, 1896, 5 %. 12,000

Same to same. 135th st, s s, 15.11 w 7th av, 5 lots. 5 P. M morts., each $5,000. Dec. 8, due Dec. 1, 1896, 5 %. 25,000

Same to same. 135th st, s s, 93.9 w 7th av. P. M. Dec. 8, due Dec. 1, 1896, 5 %. 7,000

Same to same. 135th st, s s, 109.4 w 7th av. P. M. Dec. 8, due Dec. 1, 1896, 5 %. 8,000

Martin, Eli and Mary C. his wife to Herman Kertscher. 77th st, n s, 100 w Columbus av, runs north 100.8 x west 3 2 x north 3.2 x west 15.4 x south 104 to st, x east 18.6. Dec. 7, notes. 3 000

Mason, Henrietta V. wife of and William R. to John L. Cadwalader and ano. trustees Mary C. Jones. 50th st, s s, 200 e 9th av, 25x100.5. Dec. 22, 3 years, 5 %. 6,500

McCaffrey, John to Peter Doelger. 3d av, No. 1967, n e cor 108th st. Store lease. Dec. 16, demand. 2,600

McEvoy, Elizabeth and Patrick, Katharine and Bridget Toole to Gottlieb F. Weber. Av A. P. M. Dec. 18, 3 years, 5 %. 2,000

McKelvey, John to Nicholas Seagrist. 46th st. P. M. Nov. 30, due Nov. 29, 1892, 5 %. 5,975

McWalters, James to Nicholas Seagrist. 46th st. P. M. Nov. 30, due Nov. 29, 1892, 5 %. 5,975

Michaelis, Matilda wife of and Henry to Rebecca S. Jacobus et al. trustees Samuel M. Jacobus. Lexington av and 106th st. P. M. Dec. 21, 5 years, 5 %. 22,000

Moore, Hiram M and Ida E. his wife to The Hayden Furniture Co. Manhattan av, n w cor 114th st, 100.11x— to e s Morningside av, x118.9 to st, x64.3. Dec. 19, 3 months. 400

Moore, Charles E. to John Healey. 116th st, s s, 50 w Manhattan av, 75x100.11. Dec. 21, due Jan. 15, 1893. 3,040

Murray, Mary A. wife of and Michael to Moise Geismann. 154th st. P. M. Dec. 17, 3 years or installs., 5 %. 3,500

Naething, William H. to THE DRY DOCK SAVINGS INST. Cortlandt st, s s, 49.5 w Church st, 24 7x125.7x22.3x125.8. Dec. 21, 1 year, 5 %. 7,500

Noble, William to Henry R. Beekman trustee. Central Park West, No. 246, w s, 113.2 n 84th st, 24x100. Dec. 17, demand. 20,000

Ockershausen, Elizabeth M., Hannah L. and Susan S. to George A. Cassebeer exr. John W. Sageman. 50th st, s s, 160 e 1st av, 20x90. Dec. 1, 1 year, 5 %. 1,000

O'Dair, William J. to Christopher Higgins. Forest av, w s, 370.2 n 165th st, 25x100. Dec. 21, due Jan. 1, 1895, 5 %. 600

Ogden, Alfred B. to THE UNION TRUST CO., New York. 79th st, s e cor Madison av, 21x80. Dec. 23, due Jan 1, 1894, 5 %. 12 000

O'Reilly, Hugh, Jr., to Bernheimer & Schmid. 118th st, No. 188 E. Saloon lease. Dec. 19, note, demand. 1,500

Reuhl, Caroline to Caroline Livingston. Vanderbilt av, e s, 175 n 168th st, 33x150. Dec. 18, due Dec. 21, 1894. 1,500

Robinson, Thomas J. to William Thomson, Rhinebeck, N. Y. 120th st, s s, 300 w 5th av, runs south 92.1 to n s old Manhattan road, x northwest 45 x southeast to centre line of block, x west 125 x north 100.11 to st, x east 160 to beginning, with all title to said road in rear. Dec. 17, 6 months. See Conveys. 39,000

Same to Abraham Steers. Same property. P. M. Dec. 17, 6 months. 13,000

Roe, Mary S. wife of and William J., New Windsor, N. Y., to Matilda E. Goodwin. West End av, e s, 19 s 74th st, runs east 30 x southeast 4 x east 13 x south 14 6 x west 46 to av, x north 18. Dec. 4, 1 year. 1,000

Rohrs, Frederick to Matthew C. Quigley. Madison av, e s, 74.11 s 132d st, 25x96. Nov. 20, 6 months. 9,339

Rothman, George to John W. Lang. 42d st, Nos. 157 and 159 E. Consent to mortgage. Oct. 22. nom

Rounds, Charles W. to Dix & Phyfe. 144th st, n s, 214.2 e Amsterdam av, 20x99 11. Sub. to mort. $12,000. Dec 2, 1 year, 5 %. 2,000

Same to same. 144th st, n s, 177.8 e Amsterdam av, 20x99 11. Sub. to mort. $14,000. Dec. 2, 1 year, 5 %. 5 000

Same to same. Convent av, w s, 24.11 n 144th st, 3 lots, each 25x94 5. 3 morts., each $5,000. Sub. to mort. $16,000. Dec. 2, 1 year, 5 %. 15,000

Same to same. Convent av, n w cor 144th st, 24 11x94.5. Sub. to mort. $22,000. Dec. 2, 1 year, 5 %. 8,000

Ruff, August to THE GERMAN SAVINGS BANK, New York. St. Marks pl, No. 84, s s, 146 w 2d av, 26x120. Dec. 19, due Dec. 21, 1892. 35,000

Ryan, Michael J. and Mary individ. and exrs. Mathew Ryan to THE EMIGRANT INDUST. SAVINGS BANK. Park st, No. 84, n s, 17x59 4. Dec. 18, 1 year, 4½ %. 2,000

Sackmann, Louise M. wife of and Washington, Brooklyn, to Maria L. Kitchen. 22d st, n s, 225 w 6th av, 23.6x98.9. Dec 22, 1 year. 4,000

Sayles, Solomon to The Society for Relief of Half Orphan and Destitute Children, New York. 5th av, e s, 90.8 n 10th st, 64 6x121, mort. $110,000; 10th st, n s, 71.2 e 5th av, runs east 95 x north 94.10 x west 45.2 x south 4.2 x west 49.10 x south 90.8. Dec. 15, 3 years or installs, 5 %. 70,000

Schaller, Frank L. to Philip Findler and Ernest Wibel. Norfolk st, No. 81, w s, 150 s Delancey st, 25x100. Dec. 18, 3 years, 5 %. 12 000

Schulermann, Ferd. and John G. Ficken, of Schulermann & Co., to Beadleston & Woerz, a corporation. 2d av, No 1066, n e cor 56th st. Store lease. Dec. 18, demand. 3,500

Scott, Mary A. wife of George D. to Henry G. Ridabock. 144th st, n s, 200 e Willis av, 50x100. Nov. 19, 1 year, 5 %. 7,000

Scott, Emily A. wife of John F. to THE INST. FOR SAVINGS OF MERCHANTS' CLERKS. 87th st, s s, 495 w 5th av, 25x98.9. Dec. 22, 5 years, 4½ %. 20,000

Seaman, James A. to George B. Goldschmidt trustee Samuel B. H. Judah. 18th st, No.

108, s s, 140.2 w 6th av, 20x108 8. Dec. 15, 3 years, 5 %. 7,500

See, Elizabeth V. widow to THE TITLE GUARANTEE AND TRUST CO. 124th st, No. 60, s s, 161 w Park av, 15x100 11. Dec. 18, 3 years, 5 %. 8,500

See, Anne wife of Walter F. to Samuel O. Wright, Rockville Centre, L. I. 121st st. P. M. Dec 9, 1 year, 5 %. 3 000

Selfridge, John to THE NEW YORK LIFE INS. CO. 75th st, s s, 175 e Amsterdam av, 5 lots, each 20x102.2. 5 morts., each $24,500. Nov. 20, 3 years, 5 %. 122,500

Same to Edward and Henry Hirsh. Same property. Sub. to morts. $122,500. Nov. 20, demand. 5,000

Same to New York Lumber and Wood Working Co. Same property Sub. to morts. $127,500. Dec. 22, demand. 8,778

Skelly, Kate to George B. Howard. Waverley pl, No. 152, s s, 243 w 6th av, 22.3x97. Dec. 16, 5 years, 5 %. 5,000

Sloane, John exr. and trustee Douglas Sloane mortgagee with John J. Bell mortgagor. Extension of mort. Nov. 10. nom

Slocum, Helen wife Edwin H. mortgagor with Mary E. S. de Ramos, Brooklyn. Extension of mort. at reduced interest. Nov. 23. nom

Slosson, Josephine wife of John S., Summit, N. J., to Henry W. Ford trustee Augustus H. Ward dec'd. John st, n s, at s e cor. No. 13 John st, runs north 76.7 x east — to land of Caleb Bartlett, x north 48.10 x west 77.6 x south 124 9 to John st, x east 9 to beginning. Dec. 19, due Feb. 25, 1894, 5 %. 4,500

Smith, Frank L. to Francis M. Jencks. 96th st, n s, 204 e 9th av. P. M. Dec. 18, demand. 16,000

Same to same. 96th st, s s, 220 e 9th av. P. M. Dec. 18, demand. 15,000

Smith, Tillie E. widow to Jennie S. Macdonald. 119th st, s s, 460 e Lenox av, 7 lots, together in size 135 x 100.11. 7 morts, each $2,000. Dec. 16, 1 year. 14,000

Same to Amy Willets, North Hempstead, L. I. Same property. Dec 16, 1 month. 2,500

Smith, Samuel W. B. to Lewis Z. Bach. Downing st, s s, 153.6 w Bedford st, 21.6x92.4x22.3 x98 8. P. M. Sub to mort. $24,000. Dec. 18, due July 1, 1892. 4,750

Same to George E. Hyatt, Brooklyn. Downing st, s s, 154.2 w Bedford st, 27.10x91.1x28.9x 98.8 See description in last mortgage. Dec. 18, due July 1, 1892 24,000

Same to same. Downing st, s s, 182 w Bedford st, 32.10x84.3x33.8x91.1. Dec. 18, due July 1, 1892. 5 000

Steffens, Augusta widow to THE GERMAN SAVINGS BANK New York. Forsyth st, No 74, e s, 225 9 s Grand st, 25.1x100. Dec. 19, due Dec. 21, 1892. 12,500

Steinreich, Samuel to Louis Strasburger and ano. trustees Simon Lightstone. Lexington av. P. M. Dec. 21, 5 years, 5 %. 9,000

Sternkopf, William N. mortgagee to Solomon Wrubel present owner. Statement of installment paid on mort. made by Solomon Mintz, June 18, 1891, and that amount now due thereon is 1,500

Stewart, Alethia B. to Charles F. Teigeler. 57th st, s s, 166 8 e 10th av, 83 4x100.5. Dec. 21, due Jan. 1, 1895, installs, 5 %. 12,500

The Church of The Holy Trinity, New York, to THE INST FOR THE SAVINGS OF MERCHANTS' CLERKS Madison av, n e cor 42d st, runs north 113.5 x east 100 x north 87.5 to 43d st, x east 40 x south 100.5 x east 24 7 x south 101.10 to 42d st, x west 147.3. Dec. 17, 1 year, 4½ %. gold, 65,000

Thomas, James R. to Abraham Kaufmann. Lexington av, s e cor 43th st. P. M. Dec. 25, 1 year. 30,000

Tilby, John W. to William S. and Freelove E. O'Brien exrs. Peter C. O'Brien. Allen st, No 167, w s, 124 11 s Stanton st, 25x88.2x25x 88.2. Dec. 19, 1 year, 5 %. 1,000

Toner, Mary E. mortgagor with Hannah E. Walke mortgagee. Extension of mort. May 1. nom

Toussaint, Therese wife of and Frederick to Meyer Rutzel, Summit st. P. M. Dec. 21. due Dec. 15, 1894, or installs. 2,000

Tripler, Thomas E. to Henry Greenebaum. Av B, e s, extends from 17th st to 18th st, 18.4x 138. Dec 22, 3 years. 10,000

Tubridy, William to Elizabeth A. Brady. 115th st, n s, 306.2 e 3d av, 16.4x100.10. Nov. 28, 5 years, 5 %. 5,000

Vassar College, Poughkeepsie, N. Y., mortgagee with Annie E. Frank mortgagor. Extension of morts. at 5 % Dec. 16. nom

Voellmeke, Franz to Elise Schaub. 88th st, s s, 256 e 1st av, 25x100.8. Dec. 21, due Jan. 1, 1894, or installs, 5 %. 1,500

Wagner, Peter to James R Smith. 68th st, n s, 150 e Columbus av, 75x100.5. Building loan. Dec 3, due Dec. 1, 1892. 32,000

Wallace, Frank and Fannie his wife to Sylvester and Konrad Kramer. Railroad av, s e s, 83 n e 153d st, 27.8x89.7x25x77.5. Dec. 22, due Oct. 1, 1894. 212

Webb, William S., Frank G. Smith, James Eagan, Morgan D. Wilson, Henry L. Sprague, John C. Yager, Charles C. Hughes, Arthur H Godfrey, C. R. Wager, George W Van Loan, W. E Fenno, T. P. Council, D B. Brown, Charles R. Lincoln, J. K. Taylor and C. E. Taylor to Malone & St. Lawrence Railway Co. Consent of stockholders to mortgage. Dec. 1. nom

Weeks, Francis H. to Walter C Tuckerman and ano trustees Ernest Tuckerman. 102d st, No. 166, s s, 225 w 3d av, 20x100.11. Dec. 19, due Jan. 1, 1897, 5 %. gold, 7,000

Same to same. 102d st, No. 162, s s, 265 w 3d av, 20x100.11. Dec. 19, due Jan. 1, 1897, 5 %. gold, 7.000

Weiber, Lorenz to THE DRY DOCK SAVINGS INST. Willis av, n w cor 145th st, 25x106. Dec. 19, due Dec. 20, 1892, 5 %. See Conveys. 20,000

Same to same. Willis av, n w cor 146th st, 25x 106. Dec. 19, due Dec. 20, 1892, 5 %. See Conveys. 20,000

Same to same. Willis av, w s, 25 n 146th st, 25 x106. Dec. 19, due Dec. 20, 1892, 5 %. See Conveys. 14,000

Same to Gustavus L. Lawrence. Willis av, n w cor 145th st, 25x106. Dec. 23, 6 months, 5 %. See Conveys. 10,000

Same to August Galmbacher. Willis av, n w cor 145th st, 25x106. Dec. 19, due Dec. 17, 1892, 5 %. 10,000

Same to Moses L. Rosenfeld. Willis av, n w cor 145th st; Willis av, n w cor 146th st. P. M. Sub. to morts. $79,000. Dec. 19, due June 1, 1893 2,000

Same to Nathan Wise. Willis av, w s, 25 n 146th st. P. M. Sub. to mort. $14,000. Dec. 19, due Dec 23, 1893. 5,000

Wertheimer, Rachel to Emanuel Reinheimer. Spring st. P. M. Dec. 14, demand. 10.000

Whitmore, Joseph to Charles E. Tracy and ano. trustees James Bogert dec'd. Allen st, No 22, e s, 22x50.1x22.3x50.1. Dec. 17, due May 15, 1895, 5 %. gold, 9,000

Wienbold, William to Carl F. W. Wienbold. 95th st, n s, 150 w Central Park West, 25x 100.11. Dec. 22, 10 years, 4 %. 16,000

Wiener, Eliza trustees Heinrich Wiener dec'd mortgagee with David F. Meyer mortgagor. Extension of mort. Dec. 10. nom

Williams, Thomas S. to Charles A. Peabody, Jr. Washington st, s w cor Bethune st, 64.7 x81. Dec. 1, 1 year, 4 %. 33,000

Woolley, James V. S to Frank T. Wall and Edwin R. Brinckerhoff exrs., &c., Michael W. Wall. Madison av, e s, 60.8 n 93d st, 20x 74. Dec. 22, 3 years, 4½ %. 18,000

Woolf, Sarah wife of and Woolf Woolf to THE TITLE GUARANTEE AND TRUST CO. 5th st, No. 640, s s, 139.6 w Av C, 24.9x96.2. Dec. 23, 5 years, 5 %. 18,000

KINGS COUNTY.

DECEMBER 17, 18, 19, 21, 22.

Acker, Howard N. to Emily A. Ring. Elton st, w s, 300 n Arlington av, 25x100. Dec 16, 3 years. $3.400

Ajello, Michael L. to Louisa Tizo. President st, No. 32, s s, 23 e Van Brunt st, 24x80. Nov. 1, 2 years, 5 %. 4,000

Amsden, Emeline T. to Abbie C. Smith. Adams st, n s, 87 6 e Short st, 12.6x104. Nov. 22, due Jan. 1, 1892. 900

Anderson, Lars to Emma H. Denton, Roselle, L. I. 43d st, s s, 495 w 4th av, 25x100.2. Dec. 22, due Jan. 1, 1895, 5 %. 2,700

Arons, Sarah to The West Brooklyn Land and Improvement Co. 46th st. P. M. Nov. 22, due Mar. 20, 1895, 5 %. 630

Atkin, David J. to The Title Guarantee and Trust Co. 13th st, s s, 194 6 w 8th av, 4 lots, each 25.10x100. 4 morts., each $5,000. Dec. 21, 3 years, 5 %. 20,000

Same to David Atkin. Same property. 4 morts., each $2,500. Sub. to prior mort. on each $5,000. Dec. 21, 2 years. 10,000

Same to The Title Guarantee and Trust Co. 13th st, s s, 175 w 8th av, 19.6x100. Dec. 21, 3 years, 5 %. 3.000

Bachert, William to Martin Ibert. Leonard st, e s, 25 s Johnson av, 25.10x100x25.8x100. Dec. 16, 5 years, 5 %. 1,300

Baer, Philip to Charles F. Hunt. 3d av. P. M. Dec. 15, 1 year, 5 %. 700

Bartlett, Ida E to David C. Bennett. 20th av, n w s, 174.7 s w Benson av, 60x63 9 to De Bruyn's lane, x60x64.9, New Utrecht. Dec. 16, 3 years. 800

Beeching, William H. to F. J. G. Ladd. Rockaway av. P. M. Dec. 1, 1 year. 500

Beers, William L. to The Title Guarantee and Trust Co. Pacific st, s s, 350 e Albany av, 25 x107.2. Dec 19, installs 3,500

Berau, Jr., Henry and Annie his wife to George Schaefer. Palmetto st, n w s, 275 n e Hamburg av, 25x100. Dec. 22, 5 years, 5 %. 4,500

Berger, Victoria to The Mutual Life Ins. Co., New York. South Oxford st, w s, 331 n Lafayette av. 22x100. Already mortgaged to party of first part. Dec. 18, 1 year, 5 %. 2,000

Blinn, Ernest B. to The Title Guarantee and Trust Co. Broadway, e s, 20 n Stewart st, 30x75. Dec. 22, 3 years, 5 %. 4.000

Bogart, Joanna S. to Letitia M. Dunseith. Schermerhorn st, s s, 205 e Hoyt st, 22x100. Dec. 9, 1 year. 1,000

Bonert, Louis to The Title Guarantee and Trust Co. 6th av, w s, extends from 4th to 5th st, 200x80; 5th st, n s, 80 w 6th av, 15 9 x100. Building loan. Dec. 22, demand. 66,500

Boulton, William B. to Henry C. Olmsted trustee John Boulton. Dean st, n s, 419.5 e Rochester av, 4 lots. 4 P. M. morts., each $2,100. Dec. 21, 1 year, 5 %. 8,400

Brennan, John J. to James D. Lynch. Benson av, east cor Bay 32d st, 96.8x100. Sub. to mort. $6,000. Dec. 15, demand, 5 %. 1,701

Brennan, John J. to Phineas O. Davidson. Benson av, east cor Bay 32d st, 96.8x100. Dec. 15, due Dec. 16, 1893. 6,000

Brown, Robert B. to The Title Guarantee and Trust Co. President st, n s, 23 e 7th av, 22x 95. Dec. 19, due Dec. 21, 1894, 5 %. 10,000

Brownell, Asa C. to The Title Guarantee and Trust Co. Bergen st, s s, 100 e Rogers av, 132.7x132.4x49x85.9x118.8. Dec. 15, demand. 45,500

Same to Frank A. Barnaby. State st, n s, 250 e Hoyt st, 100x100. Dec. 17, demand. 5,000

Brundage, Delia and Jesse P to Kate and Ellen Kennedy, New York. Hendrix st, w s, 64 s Arlington av, 36x100. Dec. 14, 1 year. 750

Buckelew, Sarah F. mortgagor with Robert Scringeour trustee Wm. Scrimgeour mortgagee. Extension of mort. Dec. 17. nom

Burdick, Irving to The Brooklyn Trust Co. Gates av, n s, 275 w Marcy av, 25x100. Dec. 18, due Dec. 21, 1892, 5 %. 5.000

Bull, Jr., John, Elmira, N. Y., and Edmund B. Drummond to George F. Morss, Camden, N. Y. Lafayette av, n s, 425 e Nostrand av, 25x100. P. M. Dec. 18, 5 years. 1,600

Burger Brewing Co. (Lim.) to Herman B. Scharmann. Meserole st, s w cor Leonard st, runs west 200 x south 100 x east 100 x north 25 x east 100 to Leonard st, x west 75. Dec. 3, 5 years, 5 %. 55,000

Burkart, Christine mortgagor with Rosalie Enders mortgagee. Extension of mort. Dec. 16. nom

Busch, Henry to Frederick Back. Woodpoint road, e s, 150.6 s Skillman st, 50x100. Dec. 1, 3 years. 2.000

Butler, Alice E., New York, to The Title Guarantee and Trust Co. Halsey st, s s, 275 e Ralph av. 18x100. Dec. 16, 3 years, 5 %. 3,000

Cannon, Annie B., Englewood, N. J., to Sylvanus T. Cannon, New York. Reid av, e s, 80 s Greene av, 20x80. Dec. 15, 6 months, 5 %. 1,000

Carroll, James G. to Annie V. Shields. 47th st. P. M. Dec. 17, due Dec. 19, 1893, 5 %. 2,000

Clarke, James R. to Thomas A. McWhinney. Chauncey st, s s, 173 e Saratoga av, 19x100. Dec. 12, installs, 5 %. 534

Clarkson, W. Richmond to David S. Jones. Flatbush av, s w cor Caton av, 152x132x110.7 x137, Flatbush. Dec. 9, due Nov. 1, 1892, 5 %. 2,500

Cobb, Clara E. to Mary J. Wadsworth. Vermont av, e s, 175 s Fulton st, 25x106. April 1, 3 years. 2,500

Same to same. Vermont av, e s, 150 s Fulton st, 25x106. April 1, 3 years. 2,500

Concannon, Michael to Jeremiah V. Meserole. Lombardy st, n s, 300 w Morgan av, 25x150. Dec. 15, 3 years. 250

Conlon, Francis J. to George H. Coutts. West 9th st, s s, 100 w Smith st, 25x100. Dec. 22, 3 years. 6,000

Same to Mary R. Bennett. Garnet st, n s, 125 w Smith st, 25x100. Dec. 22, 3 years. 6,000

Same to same. Garnet st, n s, 100 w Smith st, 25 x100, except a strip on e s 0.9x—x1x—, on which stands a frame building adjoining and encroaching on above premises. Nov. 27, 3 years. 6,000

Same to Margaret C. Love. West 9th st, s s, 125 w Smith st, 25x100. Dec. 22, 3 years. 6,000

Cordes, John F. to The South Brooklyn Savings Inst. 4th av, s e cor Dean st, 20x80. Dec. 19, 1 year, 5 %. 1,000

Crane, Clarissa L. to The German-American Real Estate Guarantee and Trust Co 5th av, e s, 100 s 10th st, 74x100. Dec. 18, 1 year, 5 %. 8,000

Cropsey, James to Irwin Heasty. Jefferson av. P. M. Dec. 17, 1 year. gold, 4,000

Darcy, Michael to The Bedford Co-operative Building Loan Assoc. Warren st, s s, 100 e Schenectady av, 16x100. Dec. 7, installs. 500

De Arrastia, Herminia R. wife of Manuel to Leopoldo de Arrastia. Atlantic av. P. M. Dec. 18, due Dec 15, 1896, 5 %. 1,700

Delaney, Peter F. and Peter P. Collins to Jane Copeland admrx. George Copeland. 6th av, w s, 84.2 s Carroll st, runs west 89 5 x south 8 x west 10.2 x south 11.4 x east 97.10 to av, x north 19 4. Dec. 19, due Jan. 1, 1895, 5 % 7,000

Same to same. 6th av, w s, 103 6 s Carroll st, 19.5x97.10. Dec. 19, due Jan 1. 1895, 5 %. 7,000

Same to same. 6th av, w s, 123.10 s Carroll st, runs south 19 4 x west 95 9 x north 16 4 x north 3 x east 96. Dec. 19, due Jan. 1, 1895, 5 %. 7 000

Dieter, Absalom W. to Metropolitan Life Ins. Co. 6th st, s s, 228.10 e 6th av, 17x100. Dec. 22, due Oct. 1, 1894, installs. 6,000

Doherty, John H. and William R. to Charles F. Stoppani. Kingston av, n w cor Bergen st, 40x100; Bergen st, n s, 100 w Kingston av, 60 x114.5. Dec. 19, demand. 6,000

Donovan, Annie H. formerly Hayes to Sarah W. Voorhees. Gravesend, L. I. Kent av, w s, 325 n Myrtle av, 25x100. Dec. 15, 1 year, 5 %. 500

Duffy, Michael to Patrick Byrne. Spencer st. P. M. Dec. 17, 2 years, 5 %. 1,000

Dukeshire, Clara T. wife of and William F. to The Ninth Street Savings and Loan Assoc. 11th st, n s, 96 e 3d av, 18x100. Sept. 9, installs. 2,500

Eisengart, Mary A. wife of George J. to Charles G. Peterson. 11th st. P. M. Dec. 17, 2 years. 1,000

Erbert, Rosa to Charles Schmidling and John Cadoo. Ralph st. P. M. Dec. 15, 2 years. 400

Euin, Rose wife of and Robert to Theodore and Louis Krombach. Harway av, Stillwell st and Centre pl, Gravesend. P. M. Dec. 22, due Jan. 1, 1895, 5 %. 1,350

Everard, Margaret to Susan M. Travis and ano. exrs. Cornelius Travis. 3d av, e s, 20.2 n 33d st, 20x100. Dec. 22, 3 years, 5 %. 1,500

Farrell, Thomas R. to The Title Guarantee and Trust Co. Brooklyn av, n w cor Herkimer st, 24.6x70. Dec. 15, 3 years, 5 %. 8,000

Same to same. Vanderbilt av, s w cor Dean st, 40x80. Dec. 16, 3 years, 5 %. 8,500

Firth, Christopher C. to The Title Guarantee and Trust Co. 17th st. P. M. Dec. 19, 6 months. 1,200

Fischer, Sarah to William E. Bidwell trustee Robert Thompson, Jr. Throop av, w s, 83 n Willoughby av, 42x100. Dec. 22, due Jan. 1, 1893. 6,000

Fitzpatrick, Timothy to Edward J. Dooley. Bay av, s w s, 1,170.3 s e Cedar st, 100x100, Gravesend. Dec. 5, 1 year. 150

Foley, Peter B. to Obermeyer & Liebmann. 5th av, No. 704. Lease. Dec. 21, demand. 1,140

Fitzgerald, Edward C. M. to Katharine H. Wetmore, Frankfort-on-Main, Germany. Hubbard st, n w s, lot 105 map of lots at Mill road and Hubbard st, Gravesend Beach, 99.8 x157.6x144.5x129.2. Dec. 16, 1 year. 1,500

Fowler, Sarah to Town of New Utrecht Co-operative Building and Loan Assoc. Lot at New Utrecht, begins at n line of land late of Sarah Sears 511.10 w 4th av, 25x164. Dec. 8, installs. 1,500

Friday, William H. to The Title Guarantee and Trust Co. Pulaski st, n s, 556.3 e Stuyvesant av, 18.9x100. Dec. 22, 1 year, 5 %. 2,500

Friedhoff, John P., Henry Stucke and Ernest A. Kroenke to Sarah H. Powell. North Henry st, w s, 26 n Van Pelt av, 3 lots, each 19x80. 3 morts., each $5,000. Dec. 18, installs, 5 %. 15,000

Same to Matthew F. Robbins, Oyster Bay, L. I. North Henry st, n w cor Van Pelt av, 25x80. Dec. 18, installs., 5 %. 8,000

Fuhrmann, Ferdinand and Maria his wife to The German Building and Savings Co., Brooklyn. Wyckoff av. Dec. 18, installs. See Conveys. 3,500

Gallagher, John and Ellen to Jane Hemphill. Dupont st. Dec. 15, 5 years. See Conveys. 500

Gastmeyer, Ernestine wife of and Charles F. to The Title Guarantee and Trust Co. Eldert st, n w s, 140 n e Evergreen av, 3 lots, each 20 x100. 3 morts., each $2,500. Dec. 18, 3 years, 5 % 7,500

Geehan, James to Eleonore Bader. Wallabout st. P. M. Dec. 15, installs. 4,000

Greenblatt, Isaac and Simon Loeb to Regina Loeb. McKibbin st, n s, 250 w Ewen st, 25x 100. Dec. 21, 1 year, 5 %. 838

Gray, William A. to Jane Copeland admrx. George Copeland. Fort Greene pl, n s, 444.10 n Fulton st, 20x100. Dec. 18, due Jan. 1, 1895, 5 %. 3,000

Hagadorn, Francis to Euphemia P. Del Hoyo. Ross st, n s, 119.11 e Bedford av, 19.4x100. Dec. 21, 3 years, 5 %. 1,000

Hagmueller, George and Barbara mortgagors with Mary E. Corley. Extension of mort. Dec. 17. nom

Hamilton, William to Stephen B. Sturges. Myrtle av and Ralph st. P. M. Dec. 21, demand. 36,450

Same to same. Ralph st, w s, 80 n Knickerbocker av. P. M. Dec. 21, demand. 6,800

Hanly, Annie A. to Samuel R. Jackson. Myrtle av, n s, 86.9 w Franklin av, 20.8x82. Dec. 21, 4 years. gold, 1,000

Hartmann, Magdalena to George Covert Garden st. P. M. Dec. 21, 3 years, 5 %. 4,500

Haynes, Viola C. to The John Kress Brewing Co. Rutledge st, n w s, 77 n e Lee av, 16x100, Dec. 18, demand. 1,250

Heatley, George W. to The Title Guarantee and Trust Co. Clermont av. P. M. Dec. 19, 3 years, 5 %. 5,000

Henry, Caroline A. widow to Charles A. Henry. Cumberland st, w s, 308.10 n Atlantic av, 14 x100. Dec. 18, 5 years. 662

Same to Olivia L. Henry. Same property. Dec. 18, 5 years. 662

Same to Matilda F. Pierson, Jersey City, N. J. Cumberland st. P. M. Dec. 7, 3 years. 2,000

Heun, John H. to John Heun. Road from Brooklyn and Jamaica plank road to Van Wicklen's mill at Plunders Neck, w s, 787.10 s new road to New Lots, 100x—x50x97.8. Dec. 1, 3 years. 300

Hill, Henry B. to Cyrus and Fannie R. M. Hitchcock. McDonough st, s s, 149.8 e Reid av, 17x100. Dec. 4, 3 years, 5 %. 4,000

Hothorn, Rosa D. wife of and Ernest G. to George W. Dibble, committee, Irvington, N. Y. 44th st, n e s, 250 s e 12th av, 50x100.2, New Utrecht. Dec. 17, 3 years. 1,500

Hubbard, James P. to Lucy E. Barron. Flatbush turnpike, w s, 140 n Magaw's lane, runs southwest 185 x northwest 91.11 x northeast 158.6 to turnpike, x southeast 119.9, Flatbush. Dec. 1, 2 years, 5 % 2,500

Isbill, Charles to Sherman and Guy Loomis. Putnam av, s s, 262 e Stuyvesant av, 38.6x 100. Dec. 8, due Nov. 1, 1892. 2,000

Keese, James T. to James McKane, both of Gravesend, L. I. Surf av, s s, 100 e of Stattan and Henderson's west line, runs east 25 x south 200 to Bowery City Club Hotel, Coney Island. Lease. Oct. 7, 5 years. 8,000

Kehl, John and Maria A. his wife to Margaret Hanselman. Cook st, n s, 150 w Graham av, 25x100. Dec. 18, 4 years, 5 %. 3,000

Kirby, Joseph M. to George C. Hollister, Rochester, N. Y. Decatur st, n s, 100 e Howard av, 56.8x100. Sub. to mort. $18,000. Dec. 21, demand. 800

Knobel, Herman to William Gubbins. 8th av, e cor Lincoln pl. P. M. Dec. 7, due Dec. 22, 1896, 5 %. 18,000

Same to same. Same property. P. M. Dec. 7, due April 1, 1892, no int. 6,000

Kruider, Bernard J. to David J. Tingley. 47th st. P. M. Dec. 17, 1 year. 150

Koehler, Anna B. widow to Jacob Manneschmidt. Hamburg av, n e s, 25 s e Woodbine st, 18.9x100. Dec. 19, 2 years, 5 %. 650

Kopf, John M. to Albert G. Burtis. Lots 1-8 inclusive map lot 6 common lands of Gravesend. P. M. Dec. 21, 3 years, installs. 2,000

Kentana, Joseph F. to Alfred Ogden. St. Marks av. P. M. Dec. 10, 6 months. 14,800

Kyle, Alexander W. to Christopher and Lydia A. Swezey trustees Noah T. Swezey dec'd. Voorhis av, centre line, intersection w s Ocean av, 1 28-100 acres, excepting Voorhis av, s w cor 19th st, 40x100, Sheepshead Bay. Dec. 16, 1 year. See Conveys. 3,000

Langston, Frederick B. to Isabella B. Langston. Herkimer st, n s, 269 w New York av, 20x100. Dec. 16, 3 years. 3,000

Le Beau, Theodore M. to Stephen T. Rushmore, Roslyn, L. I. Glenmore av, n s, 125 e Thatford av, 29.6x100x29.8x100. Dec. 21, 1 year. 1,400

Lennon, Thomas to Milford B. Streeter and Griswold Denisson. Court st, s e cor Garnet st, 21.6x100. Dec. 21, 1 year, 5 %. 1,500

Leopold, Wilhelmina H. wife of and Charles to Joseph Liebmann and Theodore Obermeyer. Monroe st, s s, 125 e Patchen av, 25x100. Dec. 16, due Jan. 1, 1893, 5 %. 2,000

Levino, Bernard to The Title Guarantee and Trust Co. Howard av, n w cor Macon st, 100 x185. Building loan. Dec. 14, demand. 10,680

Loughlin, John to The People's Trust Co. Marcy av, s e cor Hooper st, runs east 140.10 x south 91.6 x west 40.10 x south 23.6 x west 100 to av, x north 114. Dec. 19, 1 year, 4½ %. 55,000

Macri, Thomas to Anna L. Smith. Evergreen av. P. M. Dec. 16, installs. 500

Maguire, Catherine to Rudolph and Otto E. Reimer, of Rudolph Reimer & Co. Pennsylvania av, w s, 183.4 s Glenmore av, 16.8x100. Dec. 17, note. 273

Mangan, William to The Title Guarantee and Trust Co. Dupont st, s s, 250 w Oakland st, 25x100. Dec. 17, 3 years, 5 %. 4,000

Mathiesen, Carl to Ludwig Rasmussen. East 3d st, w s, 105.8 s Greenwood av, 43.5x95.4x 10x105.10, Flatbush. Dec. 19, 3 years, 4 %. 1,500

McBride, Margaret A. to Hannah E. Stoops. Halsey st, s s, 20 e Throop av, 20x80. Dec. 19, 5 years, 5 % 1,400

McCarroll, Sylvester to L. H. Hurst. 66th st, n s, 160 e 12th av, 20x100, New Utrecht. Dec. 21, due June 1, 1892. 135

McComb, Jr., John to Louis F. Carver. Pearl st, e s, 43.4 n Tillary st, runs east 53.2 x north 7.8 x east 3.8 x north 13.4 x west 56.10 to st, x south 21. Dec. 17, 3 years, 5 %. gold, 2,300

McDermott, Thomas to Theodore Kiendl. Belmont av, n s, 50 w Jerome st, 50x100. Dec. 22, 1 year. 250

McGiff, James J. to Eleonore F. Bader. Baltic st, s s, 475 e Bond st, 25x100. Dec. 22, due May 1, 1895. 500

McKeon, Elizabeth individ. and as trustee Elizabeth Earley dec'd, Mary E. Moore, Maggie U. Gough, Agnes B., Catharine V., Josephine and John F. McKeon to Isaac W. Rushmore, Plainfield, N. J. Columbia st, e s, 60 s Union st, 20x83; Columbia st, e s, 20 n Carroll st, 20 x75. Dec. 15, 1 year. 200

McQuade, John to Catharine McQuade. Berry st, s e s, 51.6 n e South 6th st, 23.6x74.10. Dec. 1, 3 years, 5 %. 3,000

Moll, Pauline wife of and Gerard D. to The Title Guarantee and Trust Co. Hancock st, s s, 72.6 e Sumner av, 17.6x80. Dec. 15, 3 years, 5 %. 3,700

Morse, James W. to Helen A. Frost, Oswego, N. Y. 53d st, s s, 340 w 3d av, 40x100.2. Oct. 19, 1 year. 3,500

Same to same. 53d st, s s, 420 w 3d av, 40x 100.2; 53d st, s s, 460 w 3d av, 140x100.2; 2d av, s e cor 53d st, 100x100.2. July 7, 1 year. 2,000

Same to same. 54th st, n s, 360 w 5th av, 20x 100.2. July 7, 1 year. 500

Morris, Albert to Helen A. Bardew widow. Putnam av, s s, 505 e Stuyvesant av, 19x100. Dec. 16, 3 years. 2,000

Mulford, Cornelia S. wife of and Frank to Josiah A. Hyland. 18th st, n s, 463.3 e 7th av, 15.11x100.2, sub. to mort; 16th st, s w s, 249.10 s e 7th av, 16x100, sub. to mort. $2,000. Dec. 19, 1 year. 1,000

Mullin, Patrick to Sherman Loomis. Seigel av, w s, 610 s Division av, 50x104.2. Dec. 1, due Nov. 1, 1893. 1,800

Murphy, Elizabeth E. to J. Wyckoff Van Sielen. Eastern Parkway, s e cor Schenck av, 25x 100. Dec. 15, 1 year. 200

Nelson, James T. to The Title Guarantee and Trust Co. Bergen st, n s, 505 e 6th av, 100x 100. Dec. 15, 1 year. 4,600

Nolan, Mary to James L. Morrow. Lot 17 block 321 assessm't map 8th Ward, h & l. Dec. 17, 3 years. 230

Oberlaender, Carolina to John J. Oberlaender. Tompkins av, n e cor Floyd st, 20x100. Dec. 17, due Dec. 15, 1892, 5 %. 1,000

Oberle, Anton to Charles Diebold. Jefferson st, s e s, 125 n e Evergreen av, 25x100. Dec. 17, 5 years. 3,200

O'Brien, John J. and Ella his wife to The Bedford Co-operative Building and Loan Assoc. Prospect pl, s s, 157 e Schenectady av, 18x100, Dec. 7, installs. 250

Parks, Helen wife of and George W. to Samuel S. Stillwell. Hancock st, n s, 180 w Nostrand av, 20x100. Dec. 15, 3 years, 5 %. 8,500

Preston, James to The South Brooklyn Co-operative Building and Loan Assoc. 57th st, s w s, 140 s e 7th av, 20x100.2, New Utrecht. Dec. 15, installs. 1,250

Pattison, Mary E. wife of Charles H. to Frederick Middendorf. Barbey st, w s, 225 s Arlington av, 50x95. Dec. 21, 1 year. 900

Petersen, Edward to The Brooklyn City Co-operative Building and Loan Assoc. 13th av, n e cor 67th st, 20x100. Nov. 20, installs. 1,500

Potashinski, Wolf to Kunigunde Buhm. Eastern Parkway, e s, 25 e Christopher av, 25x 100. Dec. 1, 3 years. 3,000

Pritchard, John C. to Sarah H. Tuttle, North Hempstead, L. I. Schenectady av, e s, 61.4 n Pacific st, 18.8x70.10. Nov. 23, 3 years. 500

Prussa, Meyer to Mendel Levy. Seigel st. P. M. Dec. 18, 10 years. 2,000

Ransom, James F. to James White. 10th st, n s, 277.10 w 8th av, 20x100. Dec. 21, due Jan. 15, 1892. 80

Richards, William F. to Sarah A. and Martha R. World. Eldert st, s e s, 75 s w Evergreen av, runs northeast 75 to Evergreen av, x south 33 x southwest — x northwest 39.1 to beginning. Dec. 23, 3 years. gold, 6,500

Ritting, Henry to S. Liebmann's Sons Brewing Co. Floyd st, n s, 275 e Throop av, 50x100. Dec. 19, 1 year, 5 %. 6,000

Robbins, William J. to Henry Wiggins. Stone av, w s, 75 s Riverdale av, 25x100. Dec. 14, 3 years. 900

Roe, Eva N. wife of Jasper P. to William L. Hope. Woodbine st, e s, 380 n Broadway, 15x100. Dec. 31, installs. 5 %. 1,000

Rogers, Laura F. to Agnes W. Seaton. Decatur st, n s, 56.0 w Throop av, 18.2x80.10. Dec. 19, 5 years, installs. gold, 3,000

Rourke, Martin to Jeremiah V. Meserole. Lombardy st, n s, 275 w Morgan av, 25x100. Dec. 15, 3 years. 250

Rudderman, Rosa and Sarah Cohen to Fanny Dreher. Stone av, e s, 125 s Belmont av, 25x 100. Dec. 1, 1 year. 800

Same to Kunigunde Buhn. Same property Dec. 1, 3 years. 3,000

Sarles, Adrian B. to Phebe M. wife of Charles E Amerman and Daniel Barre. Fort Hamilton av, n w cor Denyse's lane, runs west 358.1 x north 145.1 x north again 217.6 to 76th st, x east 432.9 to av, x south 290.7, contains 2 9,677-10,000 acres; Fort Hamilton av, s w cor Denyse's lane, runs west 225.10 x south 296.9 x east 104.2 to av, x north 310.8, 1 1,289-10,000 acres, New Utrecht. Dec. 22, due Jan. 1, 1893. 3,000

Seymour, Rebecca H. to Julia A. Smith. Ocean av, n w cor Crooke av, 100x41.1x142x 97.3, Flatbush. Dec. 18, 3 years. 3,000

Siemon, Robert A. to The Millinery Building and Loan Assoc. Skillman st. P. M. Dec. 16, installs. 4,000

Silsbe, Sarah L. to George E. Kitching. Broadway, n e s, 134.6 s e De Kalb av, 20x100. Dec. 21, 3 years, 5 %. 3,000

Skillman, Caroline to George E. Kitching. Broadway, n e s, 60 s e Schaeffer st, runs northeast 80 x southeast 20 x northeast 20 x southeast 20 x northeast 25 x southeast 100 to Van Voorhis st, x southwest 25 x northwest 100 x southwest 100 to Broadway, x northwest 40. Dec. 19, 3 years, 5 %. 5,000

Soldner, Henrich to Adolph Sussman. Ashford st. P. M. Dec. 8, 2 years. 100

Smith, Margaret wife of and Patrick to William H. Anderson. South 4th st, n s, 140 w Wythe av, 20x104x20.1x106. Dec. 12, 3 years, 5 %. 1,900

Stack, Thaddeus J. G. to The Title Guarantee and Trust Co. Van Buren st, s s, 218 e Stuyvesant av, 14x100. Dec. 18, 3 years, 5 %. 1,500

Starr, Sarah E to Mary A. Knight et al. trustees Henry Knight. Monroe st, n s, 200 w Throop av, 18x100. Dec. 21, 5 years, 5 %. 3,250

Same mortgagor with Ferdinand Sloat and Mary A. Knight et al trustees Henry Knight all mortgagees. Agreement as to priority of morts. made by party of 1st part. Dec. 21. nom

Steffan, Sophie W. to Henry Ginnel. Tompkins av, e s, 97 s Harrison st, 24x112.6. Dec. 18, 3 years, 5 %. 4,500

Swimm, Frank C. to The Title Guarantee and Trust Co. Halsey st, s s, 349.4 e Reid av, 3 lots, together 50.8x100. 3 morts., each $3,750. Dec. 17, 3 years, 5 %. 11,250

Taber, Edward F. to Elizabeth Taber et al. exrs. Franklin W. Taber. 19th st, s w s. P. M. Dec. 17, 2 years. 250

Trask, James C. to Matilda Moyce widow. Hull st, n s, 265 e Stone av, 30x100. Dec. 16, 1 year, 5 %. 1,000

Vandewater, Eliza wife of and Stephen to The City Savings Bank, Brooklyn. Hawthorne st, s s, 1,455.7 e Flatbush av, 75x106. Dec. 16, due Nov. 1, 1894, 5 %. 3,200

Vetter, Kate wife of and Frank to David S. Yeoman. Broadway. P. M. Dec. 17, 3 years, 5 %. 1,500

Von Hassel, Peter N. and Doris his wife to Hermann B. Scharmann. South 3d st. P. M. Dec. 7, due Jan. 1, 1893, 5 %. 4,750

Wallmann, Raimund mortgagor with The German Savings Bank, Brooklyn. Agreement amending description as follows: Flushing av, s w cor Beaver st, runs west 149.6 x south 73.11 x northeast — x southeast 9.3 x northeast 77.8 to st, x north 19.9. Dec. 15. nom

Weir, John W. and Annie his wife to Harry H. Wood. Herkimer st, n s, 260 w Albany av, 20x100. Dec. 17, 3 years, 5 %. 1,000

Wilder, Edward K. to Margaret Lawrence, New York. Herkimer st, s s, 100 e Nostrand av, 25x185.6. Dec. 16, 3 years, 5 %. 7,500

Wilkinson, Caroline F. to Henry Lapp. Atlantic av, s s, 293 e Buffalo av, 17x54.7x17.8x 57.8. Nov. 6, 1 year. 400

Wolf, Ignatz to Peter Doelger. Knickerbocker av, north cor Melrose st, 25x100. Dec. 18, due Jan. 1, 1897, 5 %. See Conveys. 5,500

Wood, Herman H., Clinton, N. Y., to Whitman Kenyon. 8th st, n s, 204.1 w 7th av, 18.9x100. Dec. 12, 3 years, 5 %. 3,500

Wood, John to The Long Island Bank. Fulton st, e s, 25 n Sprague's alley, 25x115.4x25x113.11. Dec. 16, note. 4,942

Woodworth, Rosana to Elizabeth C. West. Ellery st, s s, 100 w Tompkins av, 30x100. Dec. 15, 2 years. 1,600

Young, John to Frederick C. Dexter. 11th st, s s, 236 e 5th av. P. M. Dec. 16, due Dec. 1, 1894. 1,000

Same to same. 11th st, s s, 223.6 e 5th av. P. M. Dec. 16, due Dec. 1, 1894. 1,000

Zender, Marion A. wife of and Austin A. to Artlissa V. Gearon. Dean st, No. 1292, s s, 140 w Kingston av, 20x100. Dec. 11, installs. 543

MORTGAGES----ASSIGNMENTS.

NEW YORK CITY.

DECEMBER 18 TO 23—INCLUSIVE.

Aston, William K. to Benjamin F. Constable, Brooklyn. nom

Berrian, Samuel L. to Hugh N. Camp. $23,900

Berry, Arthur to Hugh N. Camp. consid omitted

Bibby, Eliza S., Baltimore, Md., to Robert W. Stuart trustee Joseph Stuart, Sr., dec'd. 1,500

Brady, John J., Fordham, to Eliza Worthington. 200

Bohnet, Sophie, Brooklyn, to John Bohnet, Jr., and ano. exrs. and trustees Mary Braun. nom

Bohnet, John, Jr., and ano. exrs. and trustees Mary Braun to Albert L. Blum. 10,199

Candler, Flamen B. and ano. trustees Joshua Brookes dec'd to Louis V. Bell and ano. trustees Isaac Bell, Jr. 11,577

Clark, Alfred C. guard. of Robert S. Clark to Vassar College, Poughkeepsie, N. Y. 20,000

Collins, Asa E., Linden, N. J., to Charles P. Buckley, Tenafly, N. J. 2 assigns., each $7,500. 15,000

Camp, Hugh N. to The Mutual Life Ins. Co. of New York. 40,000

Droge, Henry W. to Harriet E. Anderson, Katonah, N. Y. 2,760

Durk, Henry, Niagara Falls, N. Y., to Adeline E. Vanderpoel, Kinderhook, N. Y. nom

Dodge, Grenville M. to John W. Jennings trustee. 2 assigns. nom

Dannhauser, Louis, Munich, Bavaria, to The Baron de Hirsch Fund. 20,000

Ford, Henry W. trustee Augustus H. Ward to Frederick A. Snow. 11,000

Same to same. 14,000

Franklin Trust Co. trustee for Ellen M. Blackwell to Ellen M. Blackwell. nom

Ford, Henry W trustee Augustus H. Ward to Frederick A. Snow. 14,000

Gore, Mary A. formerly Bunnell, Goshen, N. Y., to Thaddeus K. Miller. 4,000

German-American Real Estate Title Guarantee Co. to Julius Goebel. 22,500

Gershel, Heiman et al. exrs. Henry Gershel to Levi N. Hershfield. 7,211

Gebhardt, Adam to Walter Lindner, Westfield, S. I. nom

Gilbert, Edward H. to William C. Adams. 4,000

Grunauer, Reuben to William Bennett guard. of Baron Bennett. 1,500

Hall, Eliza to Alice Hall. nom

Same to same. nom

Henderson, Charles R. exr. John C. Henderson to Adolphus J. Outerbridge trustee of himself and Harriet G. Outerbridge. 4,500

Hahn, Pauline to Sarah W. A. de Lima. 3,000

Hershfield, Levi N. to Annie F. Dreyfus as guard. 11,000

Hoff, Ann E. to Vassar College, Poughkeepsie, N. Y. 5,000

Jencks, Francis M. to Francis P. Furnald. 16,000

Same to same. 15,000

Jones, Oliver L., Cold Spring Harbor, L. I., to M. Louise Rutherfurd, Cooperstown, N. Y. 52,460

John F. Betz & Son (Lim.), Philadelphia, Penn., to Thomas Roberts. 750

Kepes, Joseph to Josephine Kepes. 2,000

Kitching, George E. to Ada E. Reid formerly Kitching. 13,000

Lacey, Edward A., Brooklyn, to Margaret A. Jenkins, Brooklyn. 2,250

Logan, Edgar exr. Ellen McLachlan to Margaret W. Roberts. 12,000

Lynes, Elizabeth extrx. Benjamin Lynes to Elizabeth Lynes. 23,000

Middlebrook, Frederic J., Brooklyn, to Robert H. Coleman, of Cornwall, Pa., trustee for Anne C. Rogers. 9,021

Same to Julian G. Buckley. 15,000

McEntee, James D. to Patrick Cassidy and I. Richard Adler, of Cassidy & Adler. nom

Macdonald, Jennie S. to Richard Shakeshaft. 2,000

MacDonald, Jennie S. to Abraham Steers. 3 assigns., each $2,000. 6,000

Mathews, Robert H. to Emanuel Heilner and Moses J. Wolf. 4 assigns., each $2,500. 10,000

Same to Frances M. Marks. 2 assigns., each $2,500. 5,000

Merrill, Emma H. S. to Alfred J. Taylor trustee for Kathleen K. Taylor. 3,853

Mercantile Trust Co. agent of E. D. M. Waterman to Edwin D. M. Waterman. 2 assigns. nom

Same as guard. of Edwin D. M. Waterman to same. 2 assigns. nom

O'Brien, Hannah, Brooklyn, to Ann Fitzhenry widow. nom

Pitman, Oscar V. to Joseph Stickney. 3,500

Same to Joseph Stickney guard. of Ella T. Stickney. 3,000

Pyle, James to Frederick A. Snow. 20,297

Rouney, Margaret C. extrx. Maud K. Dusenbury to Jane Henderson. 2,000

Reynolds, Thomas L. and Eugene Schwab to Annie E. Brown. 1,000

Roberts, Thomas to George Ehret. 3,500

Stokes, James, West Orange, N. J., to Therese Steindler. 5,000

Steers, Abraham to William Thomson, Rhinebeck, N. Y. 13,000

Schepp, Leopold to Frank Dudenhoffer and ano. exrs. Michael Kumpf. 4,044

Schwarzschild, Joseph to Catharine Hall, West Brighton, S. I. 7,500

Snow, Frederick A. to Henry W. Ford trustee Augustus H. Ward. nom

Same to The Lawyers' Title Ins. Co., New York. 11,000

Same to same. 14,000

Snow, Frederick A. to James Stokes. 14,000

The Hebrew Free School Assoc. of New York to William Gillilan exr. Edward H. Gillilan. 12,030

Title Guarantee and Trust Co. to Home Life Ins. Co. 25,000

Same to Hannah Benrimo. 6,000

Same to James H. Redman and ano. trustees Charles H. Redman. 17,000

Title Guarantee and Trust Co. to Emily H. Jeremiah. 4,000

Thomson, John W. to Ellen L. and Ernest A. Thomson. 15,000

Varnum, James M., New York, and Richard M. Harison, Astoria, L. I., to The Corporation for the Relief of Widows and Children of Clergymen of the Protestant Episcopal Church in the State of New York. 14,000

Weiss, Therese, Honesdale, Pa., to Louis Stix. consid. omitted

Wright, Samuel O., Rockville Centre, L. I., to Reuben W. Ross et al. exrs. Reuben Ross. 3,000

Wentz, James M., Newburgh, N. Y., to Hugh N. Camp. 11,000

Winslow, Edward to Henry W. Ford trustee Augustus H. Ward dec'd. nom

Same to same. nom

KINGS COUNTY.

DECEMBER 17 TO 22—INCLUSIVE.

Bailey, James S. and ano. exrs. Soloman Freeman to Stephen W. Collins. $3,000

Barnaby, Frank A. to Frank Bailey. 5,000

Beardsley, Harriet A. to Charles S. Symonds guard. Benjamin T. Gilbert. 1,500

Bech, Julia admrx. George A. Bech to Elizabeth McCarty Bech and Henri M. Braem. 8,000

Bradley, Harry L. to Whitman W. Kenyon. 5,000

Creamer, Louise M. to James W. McDermott et al. exrs. Ellen M. Murray. 10,000

Collins, Stephen W. to Frank B. and Edward S. Parsons. 3,000

Cowenhoven, John, New Utrecht, L. I., to Annetta C. Bergen. 1,000

Cowenhoven, Magdalene admrx. Garret Cowenhoven to Maria C. Barnes. 3,000

Same individ. to Garret Cowenhoven. 3,000

Denike, Thomas S. to Joseph Kellow. 1,050

Eisemann, Ernest J. to John Winkelmann. 510

Ferris, Madison to Mungo Nairne. nom

Furgueson, Cornelius, Jr., to Ole Gunster. 470

German-American Real Estate Title Guarantee and Trust Co. to Richard Hamilton exr. and trustee Ann T. Brown. 8,000

Godfrey, Phebe A. to Thomas S. Strong. 2,750

Gertum, Josephine and George exrs. Charles Gertum to Charles M. Giffin. 1,100

Gifford, Silas D. exr. Philip W. Verlander to Laura Verlander widow. nom

Graham, James to Edward F. Linton. 1,500

Hamilton, Clark F. to Lawrence Hurlburt. 2,000

Henni, John to Samuel S. Stillwell. 2,500

Hennings, Camilla J. to Rudolph F. Rabe, Hoboken, N. J. nom

Hoagland, Cornelius N. to Bernard Levino. 4,178

Holland, George to Edward A. Everit. 900

Hopkins, Sophia to Horace F. Burroughs. 300

Kinscherf, Christiana admrx. will annexed Conrad Muller to same as admrx. of Cath. Muller. 3,500

Koepke, Herman F. to Lina wife of Peter B. Koechlein, Bound Brook, N. J. 888

Lambert, Mary individ. and extrx. Patrick Lambert to James H. Mason. ½ int. in 19 mortgages. nom

Levin, Bernard and Max Gittelsohn to Cross, Austin & Co. 600

Lippmann, Leopold J. to Joseph Ryan. nom

Mason, James H. to Mary Lambert individ. and extrx. Patrick Lambert. ½ int. in 18 morts. nom

Murphy, Patrick to Michael W. Conway. 4,800

Martin, Ignatz to George Miller. nom

McLoughlin, Jr., Edmund and ano. exrs. Edmund McLoughlin to Samuel Blume. 3,000

Nellis, Louise to Bernard Fowler. nom

Ochs, George to John P. McQuaid. 2,300

Purdy, Joseph P. to William M. Seymour. 1,000

Prout, Moses P. and Henry C. Bauer to John W. McLaren. 500

Roth, Henry to James H. Watson and James H. Pittinger, of Watson & Pittinger. nom

Same to Henry McShane Mfg. Co., Baltimore City. 3,740

Rogers, Charles E. to John C. Hughson, Albany, N. Y. 5,500

Rudloff, Henry to Elias Howard. 400

Smith, Abbie C. to James M., Jr., and Thomas B. Seaman. consid. omitted

Stewart, Hannah V. extrx. Catherine Westervelt to Hannah V. Stewart legatee Catharine Westervelt. consid. omitted

Stewart, Horatio S. to Sarah E. Stewart. 714

Sullivan, Philip to Serial Building, Loan and Savings Inst. 740

The Sag Harbor Savings Inst. to Leonard Moody. 5,000

The Williamsburgh Savings Bank to John W. Sullivan. 3,682

Title Guarantee and Trust Co. to The Polytechnic Institute, Brooklyn. 3,000

Same to Mills P. Baker. 3,750

Same to Charles Von Eiff. 9,000

Same to Georgianna Maxwell, Indianapolis, Ind. 8,000

Same to Emilie Huber et al. exrs. Otto Huber. 6,500

Same to same. 9,500

Same to same. 7,500

Same to same. 7,000

Same to same. 4,250

Same to same 4,250

Tucker, Marshall N. to Charles N. Brewster. 800

Wahl, John to Jacob Manneschmidt. 500

JUDGMENTS.

In these lists of judgments the names alphabetically arranged, and which are first on each line, are those of the judgment debtor. The letter (D) means judgment for deficiency (*) means not summoned. (†) signifies that the first name is fictitious, real name being unknown. Judgments entered during the week, and satisfied before day of publication, do not appear in this column, but in list of Satisfied Judgments.

NEW YORK CITY.

Dec.

19 Abrams, Anne—Hugo Meyer......... $266 20

21 Avery, Robert—Nicholas Schultz..... 224 29

21 Altieri, Piettro—Frederick Haas..... 1,227 08

21 Ahlers, Frederick—Casper Ficken.... 177 21

22 Alexander, Rudolph—J A Kugelmann.......... 461 73

22*Ayres, Charles H—J G Batterson.... 1,036 48

22 Albright, Charles H—F S Passavant. 2,219 31

22 the same——Fritz Hoeninghaus.. 3,970 53

22 Asher, Augustus F—Catherine L Asher ....costs 44 98

22 Adams, Angelo—A J Bates.......... 439 58

22* Altman, Bernhard / Altman, Samuel } Henry Kraus.... 816 74

23 Alyea, William—G L Delatour....... 159 28

24 Adams, Austin—William Westcott... 97 67

24 Anthony, Peter C—Leopold Wise.costs 107 23

19 Brand, Simon—Jacob Blauner 890 39

19 the same——Mendel Singer 891 54

19 Bodmer, Hermina—U V Wohlgemuth, admr.......... 351 22

19 Blech, Jacob—Bernard Weinberger.. 225 11

19 Badlam, Charles H—Ernest Lewis.... 181 86

19 Bruce, Edward—Isaac Rosenthal..... 394 39

21 Burdick, Bainbridge W—George Gudewill.......... 487 75

21 Bernheimer, Isaac / Bernheimer, Simon } C A Johnson... 1,562 97

21 Bryant, Margaret J—Rebecca Segee.. 64 50

21 Blackburn, Robert S—J L Mott Iron Works.......... 1,267 55

21 Bright, Isaac O—Erick Cederlund.... 84 04

21 Blomqvist, August—Long Island Brewery.......... 123 47

21 Belting, Francis—Fannie Maltbie... 18,177 42

21 Barringer, Julia E—B A Cross....... 67 87

21 Brada, John E—C C Camerden...... 177 64

21 Blunt, Catharine / Blunt, Edgar S } Martin Armstrong 351 37

21 Behrens, Henrietta—Kirkland, Andrews & Co (Lim)........ 667 87

22 Bowlend, Edward S—F W Russell... 578 43

22 Blanchard, Charles A—J G Batterson 1,036 48

22 Ball, Max—J M Valentine........ 745 36

22 Breen, Patrick—Ellen Breen....costs 94 27

22 Baccarcich, Andrea—Karl Keller.... 2,324 16

22 Barry, John F / Barry, Standish S } John Gilligan, Jr........ 773 38

22 Brennan, Thomas—John Fox........ 93 95

22 Brown, John H—B F Dalton 9,105 74

23 Bell, William R—Mayor, Lane & Co. 39 42

23 Brado, John E—Hesse Rosenstock.... 410 31

23 Brossard, Theodore A / Brossard, Otto A } S B Wortmann...... 571 72

23 Byrnes, Margaret—P M Finlay....... 685 52

23 Byrnes, William J——the same....... 717 52

23 Beckmann, Peter—H A Stehn........ 360 53

23 Butler, Frank—Marvin Safe Co..costs 44 20

23 Bingenheimer, Jacob—Rosa Schumm 1,089 79

23 Barrett, John—Mary Bergsieker..... 1,089 79

23 Burne, William C—C F Oxley........ 356 49

24 Byrne, Peter J—H P Drew........ 52 57

24 Beacham, John—J S Virtue.....costs 72 65

24 Browning, Henry C / Browning, William J } Andrew Beacom........ 66 83

24 Browning, Jane——the same........ 69 41

24 Barrett, Isaac—J J Devitt........ 818 24

19 Chapman, Charles J—Henry Norwell. 751 69

19 Cagney, Timothy J—C H Reynolds.. 55 75

*Cavinato, Luigi / Cavinato, Guiseppe / *Cavinato, Steffano / *Cavinato, Natsie } 19 Delamater Iron Works........ 322 45
21 Conklin, Henry R—Jacob Hamburger 94 04
22 Cartwright, Frederick G—John Gilligan, Jr.......................... 773 38
22 Carter, Mrs Leslie—Henry Puvogel.. 1,4?9 99
22 Comstock, Alexander—C C Camerden 96 10
22 Crosber, James—Health Restorative Co.............................. 120 72
22 *Catarsi, Dionisio / Catarsi, Argia } Herman Weiller... 125 67
22 Cornell, William N—Addison Weeks.. 135 54
23 Clarin, Patrick—Mayor, Lane & Co.. 39 42
23 Cranston, Henry—Frederick Naegeli. 1?6 80
23 Chancellor, Mary A—John Merry.... 222 30
23 Cooper, John Henry—M F Phelan.... 485 00
24 Cohen, Samuel A—Florence A Cocks, exr.............................. 212 44
24 Carleton, John—Leon Dargin........ 72 01
24 Cohen, Morris / Cohen, Isaac } Leon Lewin......... 316 87
21 Di Frolo, Luigi / Di Frolo, James } People State N Y... 1,000 00
21 the same——the same............ 1,000 00
21 Davis, John A—H M Paine........... 156 90
21 *Doyle, Edward / Doyle, Mary C } A D Farmer 215 20
22 Demarest, William E—J J Gorman, Sheriff.............................. 182 26
22 Dettloff, George—Julius Rayner..... 169 97
22 Dempsey, William—Samuel Grodginsky.............................. 176 82
22 *Dowling, John W—Herman Weiller.. 223 07
23 De Veer, John A—C R Riley 200 98
23 Demarest, Daniel—J M Canda....... 258 70
23 Doe, John—Commercial Cable Co.... 293 99
24 Develin, Charles S—T J Conway..... 94 60
24 †Davis, Robert C—Edward Milius... 841 77
24 Davenport, Daniel E—H S Orne..... 9,751 65
24 Dickinson, Andrew G—F B Mee...... 675 40
19 Easton, Nelson S—S D Gardner..... 214 22
19 Flynn, John J—Edison General Electric Co.............................. 1?8 50
19 Fink, Marcus—Hugo Meyer......... 266 20
21 Faulkner, James A—J L Mott Iron Works.............................. 1,267 55
21 Faulkner, John H—Bernhard Hartman.............................. 149 43
21 Flagg, Jared—New Haven Pipe Co... 388 91
21 Farquhar, William—J N Richardson..............................costs 80 60
21 Farrow, Edward S—John Claffy..... 494 4?
21 Frank, Peter—Theodore Wolf, Jr.... 358 07
22 Faverge, Elisa—J L Herry.......... 143 00
22 Fitzpatrick, James—Jost Habermacher.............................. 62 50
23 Friedman, Esther—Morris Friedlander.............................. 206 84
23 Fox, Dennis—Siegmund Harris....... 330 59
23 *Fuchs, John—B J Ludwig 329 00
24 Fuller, Fraser C—G C Funnau..costs 95 00
24 the same——the same........costs 33 29
19 Grasbeim, Isidor / Grasheim, Max } Nathaniel Harris.. 336 83
19 Gardner, Charles E—C E Lowen..............................costs 23 20
19 Gallagher, Annie—Horace Waters & Co..............................costs 1?3 42
19 Gray, Catherine H—W C A Witt.... 135 20
21 Gauen, Franz—Herman Weiller...... 112 52
21 Gallagher, John—John Donnellon.... 391 76
21 Gray, Frank S—Albert Best......... 36 35
21 Gent, Louis A—John Theall......... 379 88
21 the same——Anna R Fairchild... 171 81
21 the same——John Theall......... 222 61
22 Gallagher, Maggie—L J Dailey....... 87 17
22 Grant, Benjamin / Grant, Philip / Grant, Sarah } Samuel Rottenberg 28 00
22 Godfrey, Macauley S—Bowie Dash... 119 13
22 Geyer, Henry—Julius Raynor........ 169 97
22 Gordion, Harris—Harris Shapiro.... 60 80
22 Gallagher, Joseph F—I J Brown...... 545 96
22 Glaubrecht, Bernhardt—Anton Hufner.............................. 2?8 92
22 Griffen, Warren T—Herman Weiller. 223 07
23 Geiger, Richard H—W H Granberry..............................costs 105 67
23 Glaubrecht, Bernhardt—Julius Cassileth.............................. 478 19
23 Gillette, Mott G—Frederick Leu...... 168 16
23 Geschwind, Samuel—Adolph Jacobsohn.............................. 283 00
23 Greene, Joseph A—E A Mayer....... 215 9?
24 Garrison, Martin—James Townsend.. 206 92
24 Gillis, Daniel R—Henry McShane Co (Lim).............................. 788 04
24 Goldstein, Jeremiah—Harris Samilson 532 93
19 Hirshfield, David—R L Seelbach... 874 07
19 Harvey, John—First Nat Bank of York, Pa.............................. 103 89
19 Heidemeyer, Ernst A—Patrick Ryan. 75 50
19 Henningsen, John—Daniel Culhane... 123 50
21 Haas, Gerson—Annie Miller......... 418 94
21 Howard, Mable—Eliza A Bradshaw.. 161 92
21 Hume, William A—Albert Loening..............................costs 73 23
21 Hauser, G Julius—J H Dieckman..... 150 19
21 Herschel, Johanna—Bernard Kaskell 146 75
21 Hogan, John—H T Peirce........... 69 60
21 Helms, William H——the same....... 87 30
22 Hoefling, Christopher—Owen Walsh.. 117 35
22 Hurd, Mary—R W Aborn........... 1,257 98
23 Hopkins, James—S M Barnett....... 350 38
23 Hirschfield, David—Standard Shirt Co.............................. 117 01
23 Hammrich, Conrad—J R Couper..... 136 02
24 Holzoerber, John—Charlotte R Wynkoop.............................. 91 63
24 †Hatch, Edward—William Wescott... 26 79
24 Hoyt, John O—G A Gronlund..costs 71 22
24 Berta, Abraham H—Somerset Mfg Co.............................. 865 12

24 the same——Raritan Woolen Mills.............................. 1,039 88
24 Harper, Tacie M D—Merchants' Exchange Nat Bank 10,122 40
24 Hollister, George K—George McLean, recvr.............................. 18? 53
24 Harris, Aaron—Joseph Blum....... 338 30
24 Henrich, Frank—Reading Hardware Co.............................. 301 42
19 Johnston, Coburn H—A J Hague.... 234 02
21 †Jarvis, Miss Mary—J E Stillwell..... 39 50
21 Jerkowski, Marcus—S R Lesher.... 2,184 99
21 Janover, Samuel J—Gustav Reismann.............................. 255 48
22 Judenfraind, Solomon—Pauline Ryshpan.............................. 161 71
23 Jamison, Frederick—W R Wood..... 74 75
24 Johnston, Coburn H—Henry Hamburger.............................. 378 67
24 Jones, Edwin T—Adolph Alexander.. 639 70
24 Jonas, William—J J Devitt .... 3?8 24
19 Kantrowitz, Ephraim M—Meyer Voit 989 41
21 Kennedy, Michael J—John Donnellon 391 76
21 Katz, Bernard / Katz, Philip } Catharine Atfield, admrx......... 183 98
21 Kraus, Fanny—H W Haas.......... 266 94
22 Kraus, Jean R—H M Rosenbaum ... 37? 92
22 Keogh, Christopher B—Herman Glass Co.............................. 31 83
22 Kiro, Mary—C J Warren............ 334 28
22 Kohn, Jacob—Theodore Wolf, Jr.... 2?3 70
22 Kuhn, Gustav A—August Niewobner. 109 21
22 Kelly, James S—John Scott, Jr..... 9?2 67
23 Kildare, James L—Mayor, Lane & Co 151 11
23 Kirchner, Charles—G L Delatour.... 159 28
23 Kelly, Edward—Josiah Partridge..............................costs 136 57
23 Keller, John W, President of Tenderloin Club—Myer Foster............ 157 06
23 Kelly, Andrew C—J J Devitt........ 240 25
23 Kraus, Emanuel—J S Whiteside..... 4?9 19
23 Kirk, Lottie—Mary Mitchell......... 256 98
24 Kiro, Joseph—C J Warren.......... 500 31
24 Kasch, Morris—J J Devitt........... 629 13
24 Klemann, Jacob / Keller, Adam } George Hagemeyer.......... 629 01
19 Locey, George H—H I Meinhard 241 33
21 La Fetra, Daniel W—H C Kendrick.. 112 73
21 Lochman, Herman—Herman Weiller. 112 52
21 Lichtenau, August—Benedickt Fischer 158 86
21 Levien, Reginald C—American Bank Note Co.............................. 403 09
21 Link, Anna—Kirtland, Andrews & Co (Lim).............................. 767 87
23 Lemcke, Christopher—Henry Krogen. 190 91
23 Lenz, Charles—Katherine Lenz....... 530 25
23 Lyon, James A / Lyon, Emma } Twelfth Ward Bank. 1,104 75
23 Little, Leon M—E R Johnes.......... 187 12
23 Liebermuth, Abraham—H W Mayes, recvr.............................. 1,393 81
23 Lowther, Sarah E—J H Bollmann... 219 67
23 †Leschynski, Charles—Francis Higgins, recvr........................ 243 51
19 Matthews, James C—Michael O'Brien 2,3?9 35
19 the same——H W Knapp........ 3,871 27
19 Morrissey, James W—Laura Bellini.. 518 04
19 Matthews, James C—J W Butler.... 1,062 49
19 Mordaunt, Clementine J—J F Jones.. 639 66
21 May, John—Leo Loeb............. 125 13
21 Mathews, Elizabeth A—Virgelio Del Genovese......................(D) 2,897 00
21 Milliken, Charles H—G J Dever. costs 92 75
21 Mehrer, Charles W—F M Ackerman. 114 86
21 Mandeville, Henry V—William Breen 388 00
21 Martin, George—Frederick Evers ... 318 69
22 Mars, H A—William Rodenberg...... 112 64
22 Michaels, Albert—Herman Herz...... 8? 34
22 Muller, Elbe—Benedickt Fischer 296 53
22 Meyer, Elizabeth—United Life Ins Assoc.............................. 94 00
22 Martin, Wilbur F—F H Stevens..... 2,298 48
22 Meyer, Siegmund T / Meyer, Arthur L } Frank Walling.55,997 33
23 Martin, Henry / Martin, Harry } Rochester Brewing Co.............. 400 87
23 Matthews, James C—A L Heyer...... 1,259 98
23 Manheim, Joseph—H W Mayers, recvr.............................. 225 10
23 Myers, Theodore A, admr Matilda Myers—C A Jackson............... 715 43
23 Moore, Hiram—Pelham Hod Elevating Co.............................. 171 00
23 †Maretzky, Morris—J J Devitt 161 36
23 Morgan, Terrence—W H Ludlow 897 48
23 Mullen, John J—H W McVicker..... 84 50
23 Mayer, Albert / *Mayer, Charles } Charles Parker..... 288 61
23 Mars, Henrietta A—M S Phillips..... 496 26
23 Munson, James / Merrill, William A } E A Mayer..... 215 95
24 Mullen, John J—James Conley....... 530 29
24 Martin, Harry—Henry Thoesen...... 653 49
24 Menges, Charles—Emilia Menges.... 98 64
24 Mendelson, Morris—R L Burger...... 190 92
24 Moore, Charles—J H Francke........ 71 35
24 Mayer, Charles / Mayer, Albert } Nickel Plate Glass Co................ 296 40
24 Mager, Louis—George Hagemeyer... 629 01
24 Meyer, Siegmund T—W C Sheldon.. 5,309 38
21 McCaldin, James / McCaldin, Joseph } Maria J Rudolph ....costs 75 00
21 McLaughlin, Thomas F—John Donnellon.............................. 391 76
23 McPherson, William—George Smith, Jr, admr.............................. 208 98
24 McCalister, John F—J S Gordon...... 293 49
24 McGrath, Mary—R L Burger......... 80 95
24 McNiece, James—George Zumier..... 193 72
21 Neely, William—J N Richardson.costs 80 60
22 †Neufeld, Jacob—Harris Shapiro..... 60 80
24 Northrup, Davis—Edward Milius.... 841 77
21 †O'Reilly, Mrs Mary—J E Stillwell.... 69 50
22 O'Brien, Thomas J—Marvin Safe Co. 44 00

23 Otto, Peter—Ferdinand Preiss....... 518 00
19 Potter, Daniel C—G F Blaise Mfg Co. 207 53
19 Pfister, Frank J—Nicholas Schultz.... 224 29
19 Plath, Ernst F, admr Charles A Plath—Jacob Riesor................... 13,547 74
21 Phalen, Joseph E, as President or Dictator of Gotham Lodge No 2815 Kngt of Honor—William Darlings.............................. 63 75
21 Paine, Charles B—D H McAlpin..... 146 22
22 Preston, Charles F—H E Schanz..... 533 79
23 Precht, Conrad—Frank Hemmet..... 87 50
23 Pooler, Lewis J—Maria T Upington.. 1,?51 10
23 Peloubet, Seymour S—Thomas Wildes 355 88
23 Pieper, Louis F—J F McDowell...... 281 56
24 Percy, Townsend—T J McKee........ 460 22
24 Prescott, Shubeal C—C H Knox...... 111 36
24 Pleasants, Bazie B—C H Pepper...... 91 35
24 Ponello, Salvator, or / Panella, Salvator } Herman Eisenberg......... 150 57
19 Reynolds, Thomas—John Salmon, as marshall..............................costs 10 00
19 Rosenberg, Julius D—John Callaghan 83 19
19 Rowohlt, Henry—August Koenig ... 139 77
19 Ryer, William W—H B Claflin Co..11,819 12
21 Rushworth, John—J J Bowes........ 94 10
21 Roberts, George F—William Cummings..............................costs 77 00
21 Robbins, Thomas H—G W Melvin.... 713 82
21 Rook, Albert—Gustav Reismann..... 2?6 17
22 Ruzic, Joseph—Karl Keller.......... 2,324 16
22 Reich, Lorenz—Abijah Weston...... 123 66
22 the same——the same............ 87 07
22 Robinson, John—First Nat Bank of Braddock, Pa.............................. 7,743 87
22 the same——First Nat Bank of Homestead, Pa.............................. 5,210 53
22 Reinhardt, Aaron / Reinhardt, Henry } Starr Cash Car Co............ 459 79
23 Richmond, Louis—Horace Galpen.... 1,183 17
23 Rypinski, Herman—W P Sinnock.... 174 89
23 Rickard, Michael—Cook & Bernheimer Co.............................. 116 60
23 Richardson, Leander / Roe, Richard } Commercial Cable Co... 292 99
24 †Rosenswaise, Jacob—Hans Henken.. 73 18
24 †Reh, Richard M—B R Lurger........ 364 14
19 Scott, George H—Edwin Fowler...... 179 26
19 Sweeney, Patrick—W A Mills & Co.. 668 66
19 †Sackett, Frederick—Marx Solomon.. 84 50
19 Steinmetz, Welcome R—J L Mott Iron Works.............................. 402 81
19 Seymour, James—Jeremiah Enright.. 308 00
19 Sullivan, John / Sullivan, Jeremiah } W C A Witt 143 49
19 Sabin, Charles D—H H Butts 3,919 84
21 Serdobin, Paul M—W M Polk........ 143 00
21 Schiff, John—S R Lesher 2,184 99
21 *Scott, John—Leo Loeb 125 13
21 Sinclair, James—Henry Haas 145 00
21 Stark, Isidor / Stark, Edward J / Stark, Gustave } Charles Devoe..... 3?8 57
21 Stone, Leander—James Dougherty... 1,752 68
22 Scheer, Joseph—Kuehnhold Mfg Co.. ?6 77
22 Strait, Ebenezer S—Isaac Peckner.... 111 58
22 Strassner, George—Henry Moss...... 69 26
22 Soltz, Arcadius—Samuel Kramer..... 27 87
22 Steindler, Joseph—F S Passavant.... 2,21? 31
22 the same——Fritz Hoeninghaus.. 3,970 83
22 Silberstein, Isidor—Harris Shapiro... 60 80
22 Shea, Patrick J—Francis Higgins, recvr.............................. 1,012 65
22 Stefanini, Luigi—Herman Weiller... 1?5 67
22 Stetson, Clarence—W H Lucas...... 179 28
23 Spitz, Reinhold J—G F Clark.....(D) 844 81
23 Schmeckenbecher, John / Schmeckenbecher, George } Francis Eckenroth 725 42
23 the same——George Pfister....... 658 60
23 Stransky, Emanuel—David Kahn..... 198 02
23 Stander, Catharine—Moses Rosenberg 326 00
23 *Schwartz, Sophia / Schwartz, Samuel, Jr } John Baehr 182 00
23 Schmeckenbecker, George / *Schmeckenbecker, John G } W P Youngs.. 937 00
23 Sleeman, Nathaniel—C G Patterson..............................costs 696 30
23 the same——J C Richardson.costs 150 00
23 the same——A M Vernon....costs 150 00
23 Sturcke, John G—H Koehler & Co... 118 50
23 Seller, M E—T F Schumann...... 110 60
23 Stults, George F / Stults, Sallie A } C W Nason......... 151 52
24 Schmidt, Konrad—Henry Sawyer.... 745 11
24 Silberstein, Bernhard—Hyman Schnitzer.............................. 536 47
24 Seligman, Sigmund J / Seligman, Philip } Somerset Mfg Co........... 865 12
24 the same——Raritan Woolen Mills.............................. 1,039 88
24 Sheridan, John—J G Wilson......... 6?5 53
24 Schwab, Gabriel / Schwab, Nathan / Schwab, Abraham / Schwab, Leo L } Edward Milius. 1,314 10
24 Stein, David—Rose Kolinsky......... 319 99
24 Schuyler, Samuel R—Garfield Nat Bank.............................. 7,573 25
24 Schuyler, Samuel——the same....... 5,004 67
24 Schuyler, James B / Schuyler, Samuel } the same...... 2,549 42
21 Smith, Nicholas—Patrick Dawson.... 246 00
21 Smith, Henry C—Herman Glass Co.. 81 83
22 Smith, John—Samuel Grodginsky.... 176 82
23 Smith, Franklin H—Henry Lindenmeyr.............................. 225 38
23 Smith, Isaac H—Michael Sharkey.... 84 50
24 Smith, Edgar M / Smith, Scudder } Rhode Island Card Board Co.........1,786 82
24 the same——the same............ 916 64
19 Cohnfeld Co—C E Havens........... 1,?04 75
19 the same——the same........... 1,?46 89
19 the same——the same........... 1,818 86
19 the same——the same........... 1,644 64

19 N Y Central & Hudson River R R Co—T F Burke, admr............... 1,880 86
19 The Fonda Lake and Port Leyden Paper Co—Eagle Tube Co........... 220 79
19 Fulton County Gold Mining Co—Press Publishing Co.................. 846 10
19 The John Bonte Sons' Co—B F Howe. 898 90
19 The Mutual Benefit Life Assoc—H R Curtis........................... 1,506 24
21 Chapin Incorporated—J C Wilson... 1,572 34
21 Pfister Book Binding Co—Nicholas Schultz........................... 147 82
21 The Hudson River Boot and Shoe Mfg Co—J L Bulkley..................1,462 43
21 The Stereo-Relief Decorative Co—George Henschel................... 157 87
21 Moens Asphaltic Cement Co—Fannie Maltbie..........................18,177 42
21 The Mayor, Aldermen, &c—Michael Corkey............................ 446 37
21 the same——F P Lary............ 189 86
21 Lathrop Co—Edward Barr Co (Lim). 47 38
21 El Oro Mining Co—B G Amend...... 200 00
22 The Stereo-Relief Decorative Co—Metropolitan Telephone and Telegraph Co........................... 85 60
22 The Union Transfer and Storage Co—E H Gurney...................... 127 16
22 M Crane Electrotyping and Stereotyping Co—Martin Kalbfleisch's Sons Co................................. 31 76
22 The McElwee Mfg Co—La Fora S Baker..............................8,727 32
22 Press News Assoc—Frank Sibley..... 120 40
22 the same——L G Chaffin.......... 570 92
22 Barr Electric Mfg Co—W J Coombs.. 118 05
23 The Manhattan Life Ins Co—Forty-second Street & Grand Street Ferry R R Co................................ 497 23
23 The Mayor, Aldermen, &c—H S White...............................1,250 00
23 The Stereo-Relief Decorative Co—Kennedy Crumrine..................1,615 42
23 the same——the same 1,048 35
23 The Sheet Metal Machine Co—J Ottmann Lithographing Co........ ... 729 25
23 The McElwee Mfg Co—Friendship Mfg Co............................ 522 26
23 The Mayor, Aldermen, &c—W H H Hull 73 65
23 N Y Land Improvement Co—W S Chapman........................... 442 65
24 The Mayor, Aldermen, &c—G L Green............................. 103 85
24 Woodside Brewing Co—M L Lee..... 188 05
24 Schumacher & Ettlinger—Louis Malsky.............................. 351 82
24 The Central Park, North & East River R R Co—Patrick Lahey............1,179 09
24 The N Y Elevated R R Co / The Manhattan Railway Co—Eliza W White. ....costs 159 69
24 The Mayor, Aldermen, &c—William Anderson........................ 454 14
24 The Manhattan Railway Co / The N Y Elevated R N Co—Pell Thompson. ....costs 109 35
24 Income and Life Assoc—Samuel Cupermatn..........................2,204 89
24 The Ball Electrical Illuminating Co—Niven & Co.......................... 576 14
24 Barrow Steam Ship Co (Lim)—Abraham Kaufman......................... 123 76
24 The Protective Live Stock Mutual Benefit Society—Christian Cook.... 139 67
24 Manhattan Shade Cloth Co—H M Toch............................... 457 69
24 the same——the same............ 55 85
21*Thacher, William H—American Steam Boiler Ins Co 6,396 66
22 Tobey, Edward H—A C Nau......... 256 86
23 Tracy, Thomas—Thomas Stapleton.. 07 50
23 Thompson, Stephen J—W H Harrison.............................10,017 15
24 Thompson, John—W E D Vincent.... 108 85
21 Vaughan, Edgar S—Fannie Maltbie. 18,177 42
21 Voight, Albert — American Steam Boiler Ins Co.........................6,396 66
23 Vrbsky, Vaclaw / Vrbsky, Vaclack—Peter Buckel..... 122 01
23*Vette, Dederick / Vette, John—E C Hazard........ 218 00
22 Van Eupen, Theodore—J M Canda... 1,253 03
22 Van Riper, Sarah E—Anton Peterson 1,168 98
23 Vandewater, Joseph E—H P Carlson. 137 50
19 Wolff, Simon—Gilbert Elliott........ 321 27
19 Westhay, John F—J S Willard....... 76 19
19 Wischowsky, Abraham W—Aaron Rosenblum........................ 378 85
19 the same——Lizzie Wischowsky.. 278 56
19 Walders, Aaron—Louis Ullmann. ... 184 83
21 Wygant, Elmer E—George Gudewell. 457 75
21†Waterman, John—J E Stillwell...... 70 50
21 Wiswell, Henry—Mary M Hover. ... 235 73
21 Watson, William E—J E O'Brien.... 101 95
22 Wightman, Andrew J—Ambrose Lee. 80 85
22 Waldman, Edward—Theodore Wolf, Jr.................................. 283 70
22 Wolff, Simon—N F Monjo............ 553 66
23 Wagler, John—R H Williams...costs 23 82
23 the same——the same.........costs 74 80
23 Wilkinson, James—B J Ludwig...... 339 00
23 Watkins, Frank H—J E Stillwell..... 195 92
23 Wilkins, Abram—First Nat Bank of Chattanooga........................ 375 28
24 Wellman, Francis L—Albert Kaskel. 31 50
24 Walker, George L—John Eichler Brewing Co........................ 138 97
24 Webster, Evan S—Mount Morris Bank 98 97
24 Wicht, Christopher—C W Hand..... 43 14
24 Wendell, William—F H Gerber...... 38 17
21 Young, Richard D—Emma B Young ....costs 286 77
21 Zehden, Henrietta / Zehden, Caecilia—Aetna Life Ins Co, of Hartford... 108 13
23 Zimmermann, Morris—Isidor Blatt... 91 15
24 Zimmermann, Ernst—Gustave Papp. 374 88

KINGS COUNTY.

Dec.
19 Alexander, Isaac H—F H Romer..... $210 08
19 Ahlers, Frederick—C Ficken.......... 177 81
21 Armfield, William W—E F McCarthy 50 00
22 Anderson, Frank / Anderson, Frederick—J R Couper.... 184 63
22 Anderson, Carman E—C J Warren... 656 15
18 Burke, Joseph F—A Schulze 114 78
18 Baker, William T / Baker, Thomas F—L S Gray... ..... 64 10
21 Bernheimer, Isaac / Bernheimer, Simon—C A Johnson... 1,562 97
21 Bussing, Henry—The Long Island Brewery.............................. 95 06
21†Boetticher, William T—J B Rowden.. 47 41
22 Bolting, Francis—Fannie Maltbie... 18,177 42
22 Bahr, Jacob—J Sweet............ 252 10
22 Bright, Isaac O—E Cedestund........ 84 04
22 Blaney, Thomas A—G Bulle.......... 117 73
22 Bohne, Conrad—J R Couper.......... 280 66
23 Bills, James E—J B Sabine........... 73 46
17 Crawford, Robert—Murphy Varnish Co................................... 33 15
17 Cahill, Mary A—R Lawson........... 418 17
18 Carlin, John C—A I Kleinert........ 280 02
18 Clark, Heman—J Seton............... 76 93
21 Clark, James—R C Addy............. 114 85
22 Conning, Arthur / †Conning, "Mary"—A C Hallam..... 71 25
23 Craigen, George—E H Itjen.... ..... 128 25
18 Dunn, John—W W Wickes.......... 121 91
17 Emerson, Frank B—J Emerson....... 88 69
17 Edmunds, Juliana T—D B Strong . . 77 75
23 Erickson, Erick—A Johnson.......... 68 94
22 Feldman, Philip—W Masse.......... 291 73
22 Fogarty, James J—S New............ 155 12
18 Goodwin, Thomas—F A Parker, admrx................................ 187 23
18 Gallagher, James—R Von Hofe...... 204 38
21 Gildersleeve, Henry—F S Von Horn.. 228 68
22 Gunderman, William—E A Gillespie. 48 14
17 Henjes, Gerd H—H W Thomas, admr 77 62
19 Hewitt, Emma—D Tilford............ 294 89
19 Heusinger, Charles / Heusinger, Annie—H Ries....;.... 271 21
21 Harvey, John—First Nat Bank of York, Pa................................ 103 09
21 Hogan, Patrick H / Hogan, John—G D'Elisa........ 86 30
19 James, Edward—P McGinniss........ 101 84
21 Jewin, George—The Long Island Brewery.............................. 63 70
22 Jones, Thomas C—Merchants' Bank of Rochester........................ 424 62
22 the same——the same............ 248 86
19 Kemble, Ida M—D Tilford........ ... 294 89
19 Kantrowitz, Ephraim M—M Voit.... 939 41
19 King, Eliza—Mary Hampton.. ..... 121 98
23*Karlson, John—A Johnson 68 94
21 Lilienthal, Maurice—C Drucklieb.... 119 72
21 Lowther, Sarah E—J H Bollmann... 219 67
21 Lang, John—G Distler............... 184 15
23 Loritz, Nicholas—J McClave......... 786 78
17 McNally, Frank / McNally, Charles / McNally, Owen / McNaughton, Patrick—The Phenix Ins Co. 276 17
18 Monahan, Thomas—A I Kleinert..... 280 02
18 McGoldrick, John—J Gottschalk..... 163 00
18 Malone, Lawrence E—J Stamper 65 03
18 Matthews, James C—G W Martin.... 78 23
19 Mudge, Henry T / McLeer, James—B Meyer.......... 160 76
19 Mayorga, Joseph M—D A Menendez. 62 00
19 McLaughlin, Patrick—S Cahill...... 115 85
19 McSherry, John J—J Creamer....... 72 50
19 Martin, Harry—The Edison Electric Illuminating Co, Brooklyn......... 285 51
21 Maher, John—N Ryan................. 188 61
22 Messinger, George—J Sweet.......... 252 17
22 Miller, F H—G McMaster............ 255 70
22 Malone, Nicholas H—N Y and Brooklyn Brewing Co.................... 157 85
22 Menzil, Gustav—A Lezansky......... 50 85
22 Marvin, Charles R—T S Moore....... 55 20
22 the same——the same............ 54 65
23 Napier, Charles C / Napier, Kate B exrs of Napier, John B, dec'd—J Brainerd... 343 43
18 Orton, Alva H—M Briggs............ 101 10
18 Oeding, Henry—J F Heissenbuttle... 128 89
19 the same——J A Waddell......... 544 05
22 Owens, John F / Owens, Andrew—Catherine Kirwin.. 59 45
17 Peck, James A / Peck, David T—D B Strong........ 77 75
18 Pierson, Frank A—G W Martin..... 78 23
21 Perrin, Henry E—S E Harris........ 88 65
21 Pichlmann, J George—The Long Island Brewery................... 14 10
22 Preston, William I—J Q Maynard ... 457 39
22 Payne, Robert—E F Coe............ 182 35
22 Ploch, Mrs Katie—J R Couper....... 199 03
11 Quimby, Thomas W—H Bohnson. (Correction)......................... 173 85
17 Ruggles, Sarah—D B Strong......... 77 75
19 Ransom, Ida M / Ransom, James F—G O Walbridge.. 169 74
21 Reid, Hugh—M Bennett.............. 45 95
22 Robbins, Thomas H—J Q Maynard... 457 39
22 Ransom, James F—Central Gas and Electric Fixture Co................ 385 58
22 †Redfield, "Frederick" / †Redfield, "Mary"—A Weidmann 166 91
22†Rose, John and "Mary"—J W Comfort.................................. 87 01
22 Ross, Alexander W—T S Moore 54 65
17 Smith, Lorenzo—D K McCarthy.... 165 42
18†Smith, "Abraham" L—M Rosenberg. 39 00
18 Starr, Horace Y—Eliz Reynolds. 82 84
19 Scharmann, Julius—L Ortbey........ 6,454 29
19 Spadevecchia, Annie—Mary A Dorley 516 47
21 Scott, James R—J Levy............. 210 94
21 the same——the same............ 116 10
22 Stichler, George J—F Rudd.... ..... 150 16
17 Tolman, John H—D K McCarthy.... 165 43
18 The New York Advertising Agency (Lim)—D E Christie......... ... ... 640 25
18 The Mutual Benefit Life Assoc of America—H R Curtis............ ..1,506 24
18 The Peck Bros & Co—R Brusie....... 85 74
18 The Coney Island & Brooklyn R R Co—P Giraldo........... .. .. 76 27
18 The Brooklyn Consumers' Hygienic Ice Co—H Knuttell......... .... . 565 48
19 The Board of Excise of Town of New Utrecht—H Silkens................. 38 75
19 Thompson, Thomas—G A Kirchner.. 73 59
19 The New Home Sewing Machine Co—G R Kirchner.... .... 81 17
19 The Pianophone Co—T Paulsen..... 1,582 38
21 Taylor, James—Thomas Roberts Stevenson Co..................... 40 95
21 Traver, John P—F S Van Horn...... 228 68
21 Terry, Jr, Thomas—R C Addy....... 114 85
22 The Moens Asphaltic Cement Co—Fannie Maltbie....................18,177 42
23 Tyler, Eva—The Brooklyn City R R Co................................... 71 77
23 Tobey, Edward H—A C Nau 256 86
23 The exrs, &c, John B Napier, dec'd—J Brainerd.......................... 343 43
23 Vaughan, Eleazar S—Fannie Maltbie 18,177 42
18 Waltjen, Henry—J F Heissenbuttle.. 128 89
19 Wisbauer, George / Wisbauer, Lina—M J Rose......... 143 10
19 Wohltjen, Henry—J A Waddell..... 544 05

SATISFIED JUDGMENTS.

NEW YORK.

December 19 to 24—Inclusive.

Beck, Louis P—M H Murray. (1890) $97 89
Benedick, Henry W—Union Stove Works. (1891)... .... 150 48
Brewster, Frank—R J Howe. (1891)........... 176 15
Same—same. (1889)................1,349 29
Same—same. (1889)................ 104 57
Brennan, Mark P—W D Lent. (1891).. .... 400 11
Berliner, Henry—Nat Citizens' Bank. (1886)...2,895 58
Same—W E Iselin. (1886).. ....1,219 21
Same—William Schroeder. (1885)..... ..6,123 00
Same—W H Graef. (1886)................. 618 00
Same—Solomon Valfer. (1888)....... .... 74 58
Same—Hiram Howard. (1884)........... 951 86
Same—A E Person. (1884).............1,038 95
Same—Charles Spielmann, Jr. (1884).....2,196 79
Same—Louis Roessel. (1889)........... 822 60
Same—C L Watson. (1889)..............1,936 27
Same—Emil Oelbermann. (1889)...........1,322 22
Same—R A Bourke. (1889) 407 77
Same—Louis Megroz. (1884)........ .... 962 10
Same—D W Bruce. (1887)......... ...... 1,116 05
Same—Engelbert Hardt. (1886)........ .. 416 20
Same—R S Roberts. (1884)... ....1,864 57
Same—J T Decker. (1886)........... ...... 511 02
Same—Herman Fleitman. (1886)... ..... 268 16
Same—Charles Spielmann, Jr. (1884).....2,196 79
Same—Jacob Meyer. (1884)......... ..7,047 83
Same—Nat Citizens' Bank. (1885)..........9,486 06
Same—A G Leonard. (1887) 1,690 90
Brown, Edward H—Sarah M Garretson. (1882) 283 24
Bennett, Philo / Blendermann, Albert—C F Burke, assignee. (1891)........ .. .. 455 17
Clark, Edwin—Johanna Donovan. (1888)..... 311 42
Cawley, James—Theodore Bomeister. (1890). 122 90
Same—Edward Goory. (1886)............ 304 38
Same—L H Roemer. (1886) 818 25
Same—R G Larason. (1885)............... 288 67
Same—J H Hentz. (1886)......... .... 271 60
Doyle, Andrew T—Union Stove Works. (1891) 150 48
Dusenbury, Elizabeth—David Durie, Jr. (1891) 86 91
Dry Dock, East Broadway & Battery R R Co—Margaret O'Neill. (1891).... ....1,240 83
Same—same. (1891) 85 88
Edwards, John W, exr—R E Leavitt. (1891).. 1,596 50
Fogarty, Katie L—Herrmann Guggenheim. (1891)..... .... 170 63
Fay, Henry A—J G Fay. (1891)... .... 406 40
Fred Hower Brewing Co—De La Vergne Refrigerating Machine Co. (1891)....... ...5,464 89
Gould, David B—A S Hunter. (1891).......... 556 61
Giesler, Catherine E—Moses Hertz. (1891).... 540 79
Grotheer, John—People State N Y. (1890).... 1,000 00
Harvey, Michael—Empire State Brewing Co. (1891)......... .. . . 111 55
Hausen, Charles—People State N Y. (1890)... 1,000 00
Hughes, William H, exr—R E Leavitt. (1891). 1,596 50
King, Hugh—Thomas Reilly, admr. (1891)... 1,942 64
Same—William Murtagh, admr. (1891).. 1,942 64
Knickerbocker Brewing Co—H W Poor. (1891).25,584 04
Levene, Joseph—George Silva. (1884)........ 690 51
Leemann, Hermann—S S Carpenter. (1891).. 635 01
Long, John F—Mutual Bank. (1891).......... 383 40
Littman, Selig—H J Lenz. (1891)... .... 251 85
Lucas, Philippine—John Aichele, admr. (1891) 1,198 11
McNulty, John—Health Dept. (1889)......... 909 87
McNamara, John J—E R Lewis. (1891)....... 488 22
Moloney, Denis and Kate—Hancke Hencken. (1888)............. .... 41 87
Morehouse, Joseph J—R J Howed. (1889).... 104 57
Same—same. (1889)......................1,349 29
Same—same. (1891).... .... 195 15
Molloy, Anthony—John Corbett. (1891)...... 116 92
Megroz, Louis and Henri—S S Carpenter. (1891) 635 01
Portier, Henri—S S Carpenter. (1891)......... 635 01
Porter, Major D—Israel Jacobs. (1891)..... ... 75 17
Phillips, Mary J—Sarah M Garretson. (1882). 285 24
Phillips, Robert L., Chester M., Norma, Charlean and Eliza—Henry Hentz. (1891) ...16,208 72
Passaic Quarry Co—Ingersoll-Sergeant Rock Drill Co. (1891) 1,250 31
Regan, James—Adolph Luthy. (1891) 81 19
Same—same. (1891)....................... 109 59
*Runkel, Aaron / Rosenblatt, William—Isaac Bierman. (1889) 146 82
Reizenstein, Charles—A G Leonard. (1887)... 1,698 90
Same—Nat Citizens' Bank. (1885).. ...2,448 06
Sattenstein, Reuben—Gabriel Galef. (1891).. 910 64
Schlacter, Julius C—S S Carpenter. (1891). . 635 01

Steinmann, Siegmund—Louis Doerzbacher. (1886) 146 27
Scott, Archibald, Walter E and Archibald T—Merchants' Nat Bank. (1891) 3,372 28
Strauss, Joseph L—W E Iselin. (1886) 1,219 21
Same—William Schroeder. (1885) 5,125 00
Same—W H Graef. (1886) 618 00
Same—Solomon Valfer. (1885) 74 53
Same—Hiram Howard. (1884) 283 36
Same—A E Person. (1881) 1,035 95
Same—Charles Spielman, Jr. (1884) 2,196 79
Same—Louis Roessell. (1889) 829 60
Same—C L Watson. (1889) 1,926 27
Same—Emil Oelberman. (1889) 1,322 27
Same—R A Bourke. (1889) 401 77
Same—Louis Negroz. (1884) 962 10
Same—D W Bruce. (1887) 1,116 05
Same—Engelbert Hardt. (1886) 416 20
Same—R S Roberts. (1884) 1,364 57
Same—J T Decker. (1886) 511 02
Same—Herman Fleitman. (1886) 263 10
Same—Charles Spielman, Jr. (1884) 2,196 79
Same—Jacob Meyer. (1884) 7,016 33
Same—Nat Citizens' Bank (1885) 2,488 05
Same—A G Leonard. (1887) 1,690 93
Tayntor, Rufus N—Co-operative Stove Works. (1884) 1,347 40
Westing, Theodore—Margaret O'Neill. (1891) 85 88
Same—same. (1890) 1,240 33
Wood Edward T—Walter Scott. (1890) 236 99

*Vacated by order of Court. †Suspended on Appeal. ‡Released. §Reversal. ‖Satisfied by Execution.

KINGS COUNTY.

December 18 to 23—inclusive.

Bennett, Philo S } C E Burke, assignee.
Blendermann, Albert } (1891) $419 29
Brown, Edward H—Sarah M Garretson. ('84) 479 33
Caben, Bally—T Newman. (1891) 119 04
Clark, John V A—A H Bennie. (1891) 94 47
Doyle, Felix W—J D Negus. (1886) 71 72
Faber, Alexander E—T C Smith. (1886) 189 81
Gantz, Joseph W—J F Gantz (1891) 217 05
Greib, George—H Sior. (1891) 95 74
Hubbard, John L—T C Smith. (1886) 189 31
Jones, Mary E—J Gillies. (1891) 485 61
Judson, Edward—L Schwartz. (1891) 88 25
Lester, Joseph H. Jr—J Feiber (1891) 311 15
Messenger, Milledge—I C Simonson. (1883) 140 85
Morris, Joseph—C Gillespie. (1891) 52 25
Palmer, Benjamin W—J Feiber. (1891) 311 15
Phillips, Mary J—Sarah M Garretson. (1881) 479 33
Porter, Major D—I Jacobs. (1891) 75 07
Renney, John—Callaghan Bros. (1886) 89 50
Robbins, William H H } J E Keeler. (1891) 158 88
Robbins, Helena }
Robbins, Thomas H—Albany Venetian Blind Co. (1890) 527 89
Same—same. (1891) 43 28
Ryan, Joseph—C H Smith. (1889) 1,146 74
Same—same. (1890) 71 00
Same—same. (1891) 133 56
Taylor, Benjamin S—T C Smith. (1886) 189 81
The Atlantic Avenue R R Co—C D'Oro. (1891) 95 56
The Fred Hower Brewing Co—Kings County Bank. (1891) 1,072 68
Same—same. (1891) 1,528 13
Same—M & S Levy. (1891) 227 19
Same—C Ullmann. (1891) 1,318 35
Ward, Reginald H—A H Rennie. (1891) 94 41
Webster, John H—H Scheideberg. (1889) 100 00

MECHANICS' LIENS.

NEW YORK CITY.

Dec.

19 Spring st, Nos. 131-137, n s, 48.2 w Greene st, 98.2x97.9. J. Y. Brokaw agt John Goerlitz, owner and contractor $4,190 00

19 Canal st, s e cor Forsyth st, 48x24. Brereton & McIntosh agt B. Galewski, owner, and Samuel W. Wickens, contractor 800 00

19 Twenty-fourth st, Nos. 341-345 W., n s, 77x100. Burton Gliddon agt J. McFarland, owner, and Frederick Wood, contractor 230 00

21 Hamilton pl, e s, 25 s 142d st, 7-x99.11. Malcho Fortunato agt Mary E. Stevens, owner and contractor 450 00

21 Ninety-third st, Nos. 54-60, s s, 175 e 9th av, 100x100.8. Anthony Schwoerer agt Charles W and Louisa C. Friedline, owners and contractors 275 00

21 Ogden av, e s, 200 n Devoe st, 25x100. John Woods agt John Byrnes, owner and contractor 52 88

21 Waverley pl, No. 12, s s, 25 w Mercer st, 25x82. W. H. Schmohl agt K. N. Smith & Co., debtors, and Henry and Samuel Corn, owners 1,985 39

21 Canal st, s e cor Forsyth st, 24x48. Brereton & McIntosh agt B Galeski, owner, and Charles Wainstein and N. Silverson, contractors, and Samuel W. Nickens, sub-contractor 300 00

22 Third av, No. 1916, s w cor 101st st, 25.2x93. Bartelstone & Edelman agt Patrick Brown, owner and contractor 125 00

22 Greenwich st, No. 308, w s, 25 n Franklin st, 25x—. P. & E. Campbell agt Mrs. Amalie Coon, owner, and Vanderbeck Iron Work Co., contractor 515 39

22*One Hundred and Nineteenth st, s s, 460 e Lenox av, 125x—. F. G Moore agt Tillie E. Smith, owner, and same and J. J. McDonald, contractors 2,781 83

*Editor Record and Guide:

I desire to notify you that the lien filed by F. G. Moore against premises on the south side of 119th street, 460 feet east of Lenox avenue, was filed by him without any right on his part, as neither the owners of the property nor the contractors were indebted to him in any amount whatever, having paid him in full for all goods delivered to date, and that he has failed under his contract to deliver the goods already ordered, and a notice has been served upon him requiring him to deliver such goods or they will be ordered elsewhere; and furthermore that if all the goods required for the completion of the houses were delivered, they would not amount to anything like the sum specified in his lien. JOHN J. MACDONALD.

22 Forty-first st, Nos. 530-534 W., s s. Edward Ericson agt Valentine Loewer's Gambrinus Brewing Co., owner, and J. Coar & Co., contractors 105 80

22 Same property. Same agt Valentine Loewer's Gambrinus Brewing Co., owner and contractor 95 40

22§Ninety-eighth st, n s, 150 w 8th av, 25x100. P. McDowell & Co. agt Edward J. Kelly, owner and contractor 487 50

22 Park av, n e cor 78th st, 16.8x100. N. Y. Gas Fixture Co. agt August F. Schwarzler, owner and contractor 839 39

23 One Hundred and Fifth st, n s, 70 e Madison av, 50x100. William Gould agt Patrick Gould, debtor; John O'Connor, owner 55 00

23 Broadway, No. 915, w s, 50 s 21st st, 25x100. J. S. Roddy agt Tenney Co., owners, and H. E & L. M. Hartwell, contractors 203 00

23 One Hundred and Second st, Nos. 100-104, s e cor Park av, 104x75. Benjamin Schumann agt Milicea A. Howes, owner, and R. R. Howes, contractor 75 75

23 Ninety-third st, Nos. 54-60, s s, 200 e 9th av, 86.8x100. Thomas Roberts Stevenson Co. agt C. W. & S. N. Friedline, owners and contractors 490 00

23 Greenwich st, No. 368, w s, 25 n Franklin st, 25.6x—. F. L. Froment agt Amalie Coon, owner, and Vanderbeck Iron Works Co., contractor 658 65

23 One Hundred and Thirty-fifth st, Nos. 5-15, n s, 110 w 5th av, 106.8x—. Gim Attam agt William Verdon, owner, and same and Frederick R. Meres, contractors 4,072 00

23†Boston av, e s, extends from 164th st to Teasedale pl, —x76.5x—x104.8. J. J. Scully agt Georgianna Webster, owner, and Thomas Webster, contractor 951 77

23 Pike st, n e cor Madison st, 150x150. J. P. Duffy & Co. agt Herter Bros., owners, and Lowen & Murray, contractors 97 94

23 Lewis st, No. 25, w s, 81 n Broome st, 25x—. Thomas & T. M. Mulry agt —, owner, and M. Comforti, contractor 55 00

23 Madison st, Nos. 312 and 314, s s. Israel & Franken agt J. Solomon, owner and contractor 165 00

24 One Hundred and Thirty-seventh st, n s, 125 w 3d av, 50x—. Patrick Costello agt Jordan L. Mott, owner, and K. N. Smith & Co., contractors 25 00

24 Greenwich st, No. 368, w s, 25 n Franklin st. Abraham Ayres agt Lewis Coon, owner, and The Vanderbeck Iron Work Co., contractor 1,200 00

24 Seventy-first st, No. 227, n s, 472 w Boulevard, 16.1x150. F. R. Brick agt Myron H. Oppenheim, contractor 107 88

24 Amsterdam av, n e cor 91st st, 100x125. George Spaeth agt Smith & Menken, owners and contractors 125 00

24 Grand st, Nos. 10-14, n s, 122 e Varick st, 74.6x83.7x—x77. W. D. Tallman agt Alexander Levett, owner and contractor 450 00

24 Eleventh av, e s, 100.5 s 54th st, 25x—. C. H. O'Niel and W. F. Walworth agt Annie Murphy, owner, and James Hallinan, contractor 338 00

24 One Hundred and Thirty-fifth st, Nos. 13 and 15, n s, 176.8 w 5th av, 40x—. W. R. Simpkins agt William H. Verdon owner and contractor 27 00

24 Same property. George Simpkins agt same 25 00

24 Wadsworth av, w s, 25 n 179th st, 25x—. J. D Johnston agt Frank Kee, owner, and Edward Palmer, contractor 600 00

24 Eighty-fifth st, n s, 70 w 4th av, 67x—. J. J. Dowling agt Martin J. Hackett, owner and contractor 2,929 00

24 One Hundred and Fourteenth st, s s, 140 w 5th av, 125x—. J. J. Dowling agt Margaret E. Conlon, owner and contractor 1,375 00

24 Eighty-fifth st, No. 518 E., s s, 18.8x—. J. J. Jones agt Charles E. Dressler, owner, and John W. Smith, contractor 94 74

24 Seventy-fifth st, No. 12, s s, 250 e 5th av, 25x—. J. H. Parker agt James J. Lally, debtor, Theodore H Friend, assignee, and Emilay P. Marcus, owner 744 64

24 Twenty-fourth st, Nos. 341-345, n s, 271.7 e 9th av, 79x100. Walbridge Bros. agt Joseph McFarland owner, and Frederick Wood, contractor 982 50

24 One Hundred and Thirty-ninth st, Nos. 661-671, n s, 100 e Willis av, 101.2x100. Barstow Stove Co. agt William O'Gorman, owner and contractor 552 00

§Editor Record and Guide:

Liens filed against C. W. Friedline & Co. are unjust, they have not finished their contract, West 93d street. Will be adjusted as soon as the work is finished. C. W. FRIEDLINE.

†Editor Record and Guide:

Regarding the liens filed by J. J. Scully against property on Boston avenue I wish to state that I have receipts and documents showing payment in full. There is nothing due him. T. WEBSTER.

KINGS COUNTY.

Dec.

18 McDonough st, Nos. 240-248, s s, 100x100. Carl G. Granholm agt M. Rofrano, owner, and Nilson & Lagerson, contractors $48 50

18 McDonough st, s s, 175.5 e Sumner av, 99.7x100. Brooklyn Slate Mantel Co. agt Michael Rofrano, owner and contractor 750 00

18 Howard av, e s, 167 s Herkimer st, 16.8x100 } Howard av, e s, 217 s Herkimer st, 50x100. } James J. McCue agt German-American Title Guarantee Co., owner, and Elizabeth Smith, contractor 500 00

18 Sixth st, s s, 180 w 4th av, 115x100. Charles E. Bing agt H. Becker and P. Meloney, owners and contractors 81 00

18 Saratoga av, Nos. 151, 153, 157 and 161, see Lien. Caroline Traum agt Jacob Aronson, owner and contractor 138 00

18 Fifty-third st, n s, 160 w 5th av, runs west 60 x north 100.2 x east — x north 100.2 to 52d st, x east 40 x south 200.4. Hobby & Doody agt Clarence E. Hopkins and Louis Bradfisch, owners and contractors 1,959 00

18 Eastern Parkway, s s, 50 e Van Siclen av, 20x100. Emil Reinekiog agt Mr. and Mrs. John Powers, owners and contractors 120 00

18 Eleventh av, cor 66th st, New Utrecht, see Lien. Lawrence Guly agt O'Reilly Bros., owners and contractors 134 40

19 Sutter av, s s, 50 w Watkins st, 50x100. Earl A. Gillespie agt Isaac Krupitzsky, owner and contractor 132 28

19 Lewis av, s e cor Hancock st, 100x150. Henry S. Raw agt Jacob Aronson, owner and contractor 561 67

19 Lewis av, s e cor Hancock st, 100x150. J. Lazarowitz agt Jacob Aronson, owner and contractor 450 00

19 Sixth av, n e cor 15th st, —x—. Hermann J. Hapf agt George O. Van Orden, owner and contractor 597 48

21 McDonough st, s s, 175.5 e Sumner av, 99.7x100. Robbins Bros. agt Alberico Caroselli or Michael Rofrano, owner, and Michael Rofrano, contractor 100 00

21 Fourth av, n e cor 17th st, 120x80. Charles J. Vofrie and John O'Hearn agt John R. Scott and George J. Carney, owners and contractors 2,500 00

21 Bergen st, s s, 290 e Brooklyn av, 10 x100. Brooklyn Slate Mantel Co agt J. M. Pilcher, owner and contractor 415 00

21 Twentieth st, w s, 125 n Vanderbilt st, 25x100, Flatbush. Hobby & Doody agt Thomas and Margaret Heffernan, owners and contractors 529 61

21 Railroad av, w s, 100 n Griffin pl, 50x100. William T. Townsend agt Betsey Reichert, owner and contractor 40 57

21 Lewis av, s e cor Hancock st, 100x150. Sam Stoliarsky agt Thomas McWhinney and Jacob Aronson, owners and contractors 800 00

21 Gates av, n s, 300 e Central av, 25x100. Ralph Robb agt William J Cook, owner, and John F. Tilman, contractor 119 00

21 Same property. Robert Jacobs agt same owner and contractor 59 50

22 Montague st, s e cor Clinton st, 50x100. Hirt & Hagdorn agt The Brooklyn City R. R. Co., owners, and William E. D. Vincent, contractor 826 09

22 Hinsdale st, w s, 275 s Dumont av, 20x100. A. D. Hyde & Co. agt Frederick Weil, owner and contractor 1,630 00

22 Same property. James Mackintosh agt Frederick Weil owner, and A. H. Hyde & Co., contractors 282 47

22 Stewart av, n w cor Ovington av, 170.3x108, New Utrecht. Frank P. Gavin agt John J. Page, owner, and Edwin Darrington, contractor 300 00

22 Ovington av, n s, 100 w Stewart av, 20x100. Thomas J. Roper agt same owner and contractor 80 00

22 Cook st No. 187, n s, 250 w White st, 25x100. Michael Heraghty agt Aaron Wilchinsky, owner, and George Knierim, contractor 60 00

22 Sixth st, s s, 181 w 4th av, 130x100. John Schmitt agt Herman Baker and Patrick Malone, owners, and Herman Baker, contractor 158 00

22 Sixth av, n w cor President st, 92x100. William H. Horton agt Stephen M. Hayes, Edward Judson and Katharine Judson, owners, and A. N. McBean, agent 519 00

22 Fulton st, s s, 200 w Stone av, 100x100. John Morrisey agt Donald C. and Jennie L. Ross and Thomas Berkley, owners, and Donald C. and Jennie L. Ross, George Morgan and Thomas Brennan, contractors 565 00

23 Lewis av, s e cor Hancock st, 100x150. Max Schoenberg and Abraham Strobin agt Thomas McWhinney and Jacob Aronson, owners and contractors 700 00

23 Logan st, e s, 96 s Jamaica av, 50x100. Bertel O. Gronen agt Magdalena B. Smith and Harrison B. Wright, owners, and Henry T. Smith, contractor 41 50

23 Ovington av, s s, 78 e Stewart av, 20x100, New Utrecht. William J. Flick agt John L. Page, owner, and Edwin Dennington, contractor 16 65

SATISFIED MECHANICS' LIENS

NEW YORK CITY.

Dec.

19 Forty-third st, Nos. 151 and 153 E. H. S. Hahn agt John Philips. (Lien filed Nov. 20, 1891) $77 00

19 Ninety-sixth st, s s, 100 e 9th av, 180x100. John Dimond agt Squier & Whipple. (March 11, 1891) 807 00

21 Thirty-ninth st, Nos. 609 and 611 W. James Slavin agt —— Coster and John and Thomas Donellon. (Oct. 9, 1891) 53 10

22 One Hundred and Sixth st, n s, 175 w 8th av, 50x100. James Maloney agt Antonio Gallo. (Oct. 7, 1891) 227 00

22 Hudson st, e s, extends from Leonard to Franklin sts, 57.6x16.6x—x88.6. Orr Bros. agt John Goerlitz and F. Bechstein. (Nov. 15, 1890) 8,500 00

23 Park av, Nos. 1163-1171 } Ninety-third st, No. 74 } Arthur Brown agt Downey & Curry. (July 30, 1891) 175 00

23 Pike st, n w cor Madison st, 150x150. J. P. Duffy & Co. agt Herter Bros. and Lowen & Murray. (Dec. 21, 1891) 97 94

23 Thirteenth av, n e cor 11th st, 90.4x96.5. C. L. Bucki & Co agt Emery Van Tassel, Peter Keller and William S. Anderson. (Dec. 15, 1891) 3,470 86

23 Seventy-fourth st, n s, 273 e Amsterdam av, 150x100.4. Ackert & Schroeder agt John and Joshua Coar. (Sept. 21, 1891) 100 00

23 Madison st, No. 314, s s, 60.4 w Gouverneur st, 25.11x119.5x21x118.6. J. H. Sturk & Co. agt Joseph Solomon and Heine & Dooner. (Dec. 12, 1891) 165 00

23‡Same property. J. J. Kierst agt Joseph Solomon and Charles W. Heine. (Aug. 5, 1891) 165 00

23‡Same property. E. H. Israel agt S. Salomon. (Nov. 6, 1891) 165 00

24*Ninety-sixth st, No. 66 W. Harray Evans agt Squier & Whipple. (March 27, 1891) 250 00

24 Monroe st, No. 103, 25.9x100. Kelly & Daly agt Anna M. Roche admrx. Patrick Roche and Timothy J. Roche. (Nov. 28, 1891) 94 18

24‡Columbus av, w s, 75 n 97th st, 25x100. T. E. McLaughlin agt Harry Galway, Elias T. Hatch and Michael Tobin. (Dec. 3, 1891) 145 00

24 East Broadway, No. 286, n w s, 24x70. Gabriel Gaief agt Reuben and Bessie Satenstein. (Oct. 4, 1890) 793 50

24*Fifth av, s w cor 21st st, 92x142.6. Bernard Duffy agt John Smith, Edward Van Orden and The Plastic Slate Roofing and Paving Co. (Dec. 21, 1891) 165 13

‡Discharged by order of Court on filing bond.
*Discharged by depositing amount of lien and interest with County Clerk.

KINGS COUNTY.

Dec.

16 Twenty-first av, e s, 95 n Cropsey av, 30x40, New Utrecht. Abraham H. Rosenblum agt Kate F. Monjo, owner and contractor (Aug. 5, 1891). (Order of Court) $342 00

18 Fort Hamilton av, n e cor 59th st, 100x100, New Utrecht. John Cook agt trustees for School No. 2, New Utrecht, owner, and Ole Gunsten, contractor. (Lien filed Nov. 16, 1891) 190 00

18 Wythe av, n w cor Clymer st, 25x100. Washington Bulkley agt Charles Collins, owner, and John E. Bullwinkle, contractor. (Oct. 8, 1891) 96 80

19 Pulaski st, n s, 100 w Sumner av, 300.6x100. John Auer agt The Fred. Hower Brewing Co., owner and contractor. (Aug. 8, 1891) 10,000 00

19 Same property. John Rueger agt same owner and contractor. (Aug. 17, 1891) .. 9,583 82

19 Same property. Isidor Mock agt same owner and contractor. (Aug. 25, 1891) 9,135 95

19 Same property. Frederick Wunder agt same owner and contractor. (Aug. 11, 1891) 10,402 15

19 Bergen st, s s, 100 w Hopkinson av, 25x100. Potts Bros. agt Rosa Rosenfeld, owner, and Carl Becker, contractor. (Oct. 19, 1891) 42 37

21 Same property. George Schatt agt same owner and contractor. (Oct. 27, 1891) .. 70 00

21 Marcy av, n w cor Walton st, 38x75. Raeburn Latourette & Co. agt The North American Iron Works, owner, and K. N. Smith & Co., contractors. (Nov. 21, 1891) 1,886 08

21 Cook st, No. 21, n s, 150 w Graham av, 25x100. John Rueger agt John and Maria Kehl, owners and contractors. (Nov. 10, 1891) 2,475 00

21 Willoughby av, No. 1120, s e s, 300 s w Knickerbocker av, 25x100. Bertha Horowitz agt Alfred Hubert, owner, and Alois Flobl, contractor. (Dec. 18, 1891). (Deposit) 84 00

21 First st, s s, 365.11 w 5th av, 54x100. Michael J. Tully agt William H. Adams, owner and contractor. (Dec. 19, 1891) 578 24

22 Pulaski st, n s, 100 w Sumner av, 300.6x100. Brennan & Colligan agt The Fred Hower Brewing Co. (Lim.) (Aug. 26, 1891) 1,003 88

22 Pulaski st, n s, 100 w Sumner av, 300.6x100. Barbig Bros. agt The Fred. Hower Brewing Co. (Lim.), owner and contractor. (Sept. 24, 1891) 1,577 77

22 Elton st, s w cor Ridgewood av, 20x100. Louis Bossert agt T. F. Parker, owner and contractor. (April 29, 1891) 726 37

23 Bergen st, s s, 290 e Brooklyn av, 100x100. John J. Flynn agt J. M. Pilcher & Co. (Oct. 23, 1891) 381 00

BUILDINGS PROJECTED.

The first name is that of the owner; ar't stands for architect, m'n for mason, c'r for carpenter and b'r for builder.

NEW YORK CITY.

SOUTH OF 14TH STREET.

Great Jones st, No. 43, six-story brk and stone store, 27.6x86 and 90, tin roof; cost, ——; Edw. Bennecke, 25 Great Jones st; ar'ts, Graul & Frohne. Plan 1580.

Houston st, Nos. 25 and 27 W., six-story brk store, 50x100, tile or asphalt roof; cost, $110,000; F. H. Mela, 529 Broadway; ar'ts, Cleverdon & Putzel. Plan 1581.

Nassau st, s w cor Fulton st, 57.9x114x50.9x110.11, nine-story and basement brk and terra cotta office building, concrete roof; cost, $300,000; Lewis S. Wolff, 12 East 70th st; ar'ts, De Lemos & Cordes. Plan 1588.

Henry st, No. 28, five-story brk and stone flat, 25x89, tin roof; cost, $22,000; ow'r and b'r, John V. Campbell, 426 West 27th st; ar't, M. V. B. Ferdon. Plan 1596.

Market st, No. 29, five-story brk flat, 25.2x99, tin roof; cost, $20,000; Fay & Stacom, 337 Pleasant av; ar't, C. Rentz. Plan 1598.

Stanton st, No. 176, five-story brk flat and stores, 25x88.6, tin roof; cost, $22,000; Loonie & Parker, 48 West 119th st; ar't, C. Rentz. Plan 1594.

Sullivan st, Nos. 5-15, six-story brk and stone warehouse, 128.1x80, tin roof; cost, $50,000; John T. Williams, 871 Madison av; ar't, C. R. Behrens. Plan 1595.

BETWEEN 14TH AND 59TH STREETS.

20th st, s s, 400 w 10th av, three-story brk stable, 50x91.11, gravel roof; cost, $17,500; lessee, John E. Connolly, Fordham Heights; ar'ts, King & Symonds; m'ns, A. A. Andruss & Sons. Plan 1583.

24th st, No. 306 E., five-story brk flat, 25x88, tin roof; cost, $20,000; Hagenbuckle & Steiger, 143 2d av; ar't, B. W. Berger; m'n, G. Steiger. Plan 1582.

40th st, No. 28 W., five-story brk and stone dwell'g, 30x78.9, tin roof; cost, $55,000; Dr. W. Gill Wylie; ar't, R. H. Robertson. Plan 1587.

51st st, No. 444 W., rear, one-story frame shed, 20x16, tin roof; cost, abt $250; lessee, Francis McConnell, on premises; ar't, J. W. Cole; b'r, J. McWalters. Plan 1589.

BETWEEN 59TH AND 125TH STREETS, WEST OF CENTRAL PARK WEST AND 8TH AVENUE.

90th st, s s, 80 e Amsterdam av, one-story shop, 18x30, tin roof; cost, $600; Nellie E. Rogers, 4 Howard pl; ar'ts, Leicht & Havell. Plan 1579.

NORTH OF 125TH STREET.

133d st, s s, 110 e Lenox av, three five-story brk and stone flats, 25x86, tin roofs; cost, $20,000 each; Mary E. Gault, 1837 Madison av; ar'ts, Bungart & Fox; m'n, J. H. Gault. Plan 1585.

23D AND 24TH WARDS.

Franklin av, e s, 75 n Oakland pl, two-story and basement frame dwell'g, 18x30, tin roof; cost, $2,300; Edw. J. Cronin, Tremont; ar't, W. Schmidt. Plan 1586.

Spuyten Duyvil road, e s, abt 200 s Riverdale av, one-story frame stable, 10x19, tin roof; cost, abt $200; Christopher Martin, Spuyten Duyvil. Plan 1584.

Rockfield st, n s, 426.3 w Mosholu Parkway, two-story frame dwell'g; 20x40.6, shingle roof; cost, $2,500; Henry Hagemeister, 148 West 24th st; ar't, United Architects. Plan 1541.

181st st, s s, 64 w Valentine av, two-story frame dwell'g, 21x59, shingle roof; cost, $2,800; Chas. Pitchie, 2987 3d av; ar't, A. Pfeiffe. Plan 1592.

Fleetwood av, w s, 100 s 184th st, one-story frame stable, 28x13, tar pa roof; cost, $100; Mrs. Ellen Ashman; c'r, GeperW. Tompkins.

KINGS COUNTY.

Plan 2259—1st av, s e cor 42d st, one four-story brk factory, 204x56, Starr fire-proof cement roof, brk cornice; cost, $40,000; National Meter Co., 252 Broadway, New York; ar't, W. H. Beers; m'n, W. J. Moran; c'rs, P. F. O'Brien & Son.

2260—Humboldt st, w s, 265.11 s Nassau av, two two-story and basement frame (brk filled) dwellings; 17x50, tin roofs; cost, each, $2,000; ow'r and b'r, Charles Engert, 182 Montrose av; ar't, F. J. Berlenbach, Jr.

2261—Humboldt st, w s, 140.11 s Nassau av, seven two-story and basement frame (brk filled) dwell'gs, 18x50, tin roofs; cost, each, $2,000; ow'r and b'r, same as last.

2262—Varet st, Nos. 34 and 36, two four-story frame (brk filled) tenem'ts, 22.6x85, tin roofs; total cost, $18,000; ow'r and b'r, I. Horowitz, Ellery st; ar'ts, D. Acker & Son.

2263—Himrod st, s s, 375 e Central av, one three-story frame (brk filled) tenem't, 25x50, tin roof; cost, $5,000; Mrs. Dor Beis; ar'ts, D. Acker & Son.

2264—Prospect av, s s, 140 w 8th av, one three-story brk tenem't, 20x45, tin roof, wooden cornice; cost, $400; ow'r and b'r, R. Chidwick, 461 14th st; ar't, W. F. Dawson.

2265—South 11th st, s s, 143.10 w Kent av, one one-story brk boiler house, 82.2x86, tin roof, brk cornice; cost, $2,500; Mollenhauer Sugar Refining Co., on premises; ar't, C. H. Schwardt; b'rs, W. & T. Lamb.

2266—Hamilton av, s s, 600 w 3d av, one one-story frame smith shop, 20x40, gravel roof; cost, $200; ow'rs, ar'ts and b'rs, Nelson Bros., 502 Hamilton av.

2267—Suydam st, n s, 80 w Hamburg av, one two-story frame stable, 20x18, tin roof; cost, $150; Henry Geeck, Hamburg av, cor Suydam st; ar't, H. Vollweiler; b'r, H. Engel.

2268—Hamilton av, s s, 407 w 2d av, one one-story frame lumber shed, 50x91, gravel roof; cost, $700; Brooklyn Timber Co., on premises; ar't, M. F. Walsh.

2269—Lorimer st, e s, 37 n Broadway, one three-story frame (brk filled) store and dwell'g, 25x55, iron roof; cost, $4,700; Philip Kreuscher, 579 Broadway; ar't, F. J. Lessing.

2270—42d st, n s, abt 570 w 1st av, one one-story frame office, 20x30; shingle roof; cost, $400; The Bush Co., A. W. Humphrey, vice-president, 71 Columbia st; b'rs, W. Morrison and D. Emery.

2271—West st, w s, 50 n Kent st, one one-story frame brass foundry, 25x54, gravel roof; cost, $500; ow'r, ar't and b'r, J. J. Hayes, West st, cor Kent st.

2272—Bergen st, s s, 85 w Buffalo av, eleven two-story frame (brk filled) dwell'gs, 16x40, tin roofs; cost, each, $2,250; Geo. F. Van Doren, 346 Macon st; ar't and c'r, G. Van Doren, Jr.; m'n, H. Hodges.

2273—57th st, n s, 100 e 4th av, three two-story and basement brk dwell'gs, 20x40, tin roofs, wooden cornices; cost, $3,000 each; ow'r and ar't, Robert W. Firth, 471 14th st; b'r, not selected.

2274—Union st, Nos. 709 and 711, two four-story brk flats, 25 and 16x66, tin roofs, wooden cornices; cost, each, $7,000; ow'r, ar't and b'r, W. J. Conway, 3d av, cor Sackett st.

2275—Alabama av, e s, 25 s Glenmore av, four three-story frame (brk filled) tenem'ts, 18.9x45, tin roofs; cost, each, $2,200; ow'r and m'n, Ernst Sutterlin, 11 Russell pl; ar't, C. Infanger.

2276—Schenck av, e s, 125 s Blake av, one two-story frame dwell'g, 21x35, tin roof; cost, $2,300; ow'r and ar't, John Blake, Blake av, near Schenck av; b'r, J. Finch.

2277—Glenmore av, s e cor Alabama av, one three-story frame store and tenem't, 25x55, tin roof; cost, $4,500; ow'r and m'n, Ernst Sutterlin, 11 Russell pl; ar't, C. Infanger.

2278—Java st, s s, 275 e Oakland st, one two-story frame stable, 25x95, gravel roof; cost, $600; ow'r and b'r, J. P. Whittier, 70 Rush st; ar't, H. W. Billard.

2279—William pl, w s, 75 n Atlantic av, one two-story frame carpenter shop, 23.6x45, gravel roof; cost, $450; Wm. M Miller, Snediker av; c'r, R. Fleming.

2280—Manhattan av, n w cor Java st, one four-story brk store for furniture, 50x100, tin roof, iron cornice; cost, $20,000; John Stevenson, 441 Manhattan av; ar't, H. Vollweiler; b'r, not selected.

2281—Lexington av, s s, 103 e Grand av, one four-story brk tenem't, 20 and 24x80, gravel roof, wooden cornice; cost, $7,000; ow'r and c'r, Joseph I. Kirby, 73 Gates av; ar't, N. L. Vaulk; m'n, J. Pickard.

2282—Meserole st, n s, 60 w Lorimer st, one two-story brk stable, 39.4 and 39.6x98.4, tin roof, brk and iron cornice; cost, $5,000; Jos. Fallert Brewing Co., 86 Lorimer st; ar't, F. K. Wunder.

2283—Bushwick av, s e cor Hart st, one four-story brk store and tenem't, 24.4x70, tin roof, iron cornice; cost, $9,000; Wm. Mogk, on premises; ar't, H. Vollweiler; b'r, not selected.

2284—Bushwick av, e s, 24.4 s Hart st, three four-story brk tenem'ts, 24.4x63x67, tin roofs, iron cornices; cost, $8,000 each; ow'r, ar't and b'r, same as last.

2285—Osborn st, n w cor Belmont av, one two-story frame moulding shop, 20x23, tin roof; cost, $300; Sol. Wolff, Belmont av; ar't and b'r, L. Ratner.

2286—Knickerbocker av, No. 449, e s, 350 n Putnam av, one two-story frame (brk filled) dwell'g, 20x45, tin roof; cost, $1,600; Hugo Sichler, 1424 Gates av; b'rs, F. Reichert and T. Lauler.

ALTERATIONS NEW YORK CITY.

Plan 2129—7th av, No. 326, five-story brk extension, 24x17, gravel roof; cost, $2,000; lessee, T. M. Stewart, Peekskill, N. Y.; m'ns, W. A. & F. E. Conover; c'r, E. Gridley.

2130—Wooster st, s e cor 3d st, walls altered; cost, $400; Michael Carr, 196 West 4th st; c'r, J. H. McCullogh.

2131—151st st, s s, 125 w Morris av, one-story frame extension, 22x12, tin roof; cost, $500; Raphael Avalone, 674 Morris av; ar't, C. C. Churchill.

2132—82d st, No. 324 W., raise one story, also interior alterations; cost, $1,500; E. G. Toel, 48 West 59th st; ar'ts, Rose & Stone.

2133—6th av, No. 390, interior alterations; cost, $175; R. Mock, 145 West 42d st; c'r, R. G. Begley.

2134—85th st, No. 156 W., raise one story; also three-story brk extension, 19x21, tin roof; cost, $5,000; Mary Walbridge, 521 10th st, Brooklyn; ar't and c'r, W. J. Conway; m'n, T. Carey.

2135—John st, No. 100, walls altered, &c.; cost, $3,000; John Davol & Son, on premises; ar't, W. B. Tubby.

2136—3d av, No. 2752, two-story frame extension, 25x46.6, tin roof; cost, $1,500; J. Jones, 505 East 120th st; ar't, I. Mikkelson.

2137—Bowery, No. 369, walls altered; cost, $300; Mrs. Julia M. Phyfe, 12 East 43d st; c'r, —— Post.

2138—Oliver st, Nos. 100 and 102, interior alterations, walls altered; cost, $6,000; Max Levy, 169 Madison st; ar't, F. Ebeling.

2139—1st av, w s, 75 n 87th st, walls altered; cost, $175; Wm. V. Leary, 173 West 87th st; c'rs, H. Schiffer & Co.

2140—14th st, No. 430 W., interior alterations; cost, $25; Henry Meinken, 314 West 34th st.

2141—29th st, No. 236 E., interior alterations; cost, $173; estate Margaret McBride, 125 East 92d st; c'rs, Pardee & Gleason.

KINGS COUNTY.

Plan 1184—Central av, No. 454, raised 2 feet on brk wall; cost, $100; Mr. Miller, on premises.

1185—Nostrand av, s w cor Greene av, add one story, flat tin roof, also four-story brk extension, 20x24.9, tin roof, new store fronts; cost, $10,000; C. M. Marsh, 111 Broadway, New York; ar't, M. C. Merritt.

1186—Rockaway av, s w cor East New York av, new store front, interior alterations; cost, $300; Thos. F. Ryan, Christopher av.

1187—Centre st, No. 159, repair damage by fire; cost, $75; Nellie Stokes, on premises; b'r, D. Powell.

1188—Linwood st, e s, 150 n Liberty av, rebuild foundation of brk, also two-story frame extension, 25x12.6, tin roof; cost, abt $200; Mrs. C. Mattson, 109 York st, Jersey City; ar't and b'r, J. D. Cheney.

1189—Lexington av, s s, 300 e Nostrand av, underpin east basement wall; cost, $200; Albert Norton; ar't, H. Toulmin.

1190—Hamilton av, n e cor Smith st, front rebuilt with stone, interior alterations, party walls removed, iron columns, girders, &c.; cost, $7,500; Hamilton Bank, Hamilton av; ar'ts, Fowler & Hough; b'rs, W. & T. Lamb and W. S. Wright.

1191—Woodbine st, No. 149, two-story frame extension, 7.6x25, tin roof; cost, $300; ow'r, ar't and m'n, Mat Hovey, Central av, cor Woodbine st; c'r, M. Solomon.

1192—3d av, No. 1040, front and interior alterations; cost, $500; Lewis Lewinski, 5th av, cor 19th st; m'n, J. Wyeth.

1193—3d av, s w cor 19th st, repair damage by fire; cost, $475; Mr. Midnight, Bay Ridge; ar't, and b'r, O. K. Buckley.

1194—Van Brunt st, No. 416, underpin side wall; cost, $500; —— Harty, on premises; b'rs, J. F. Nelson and D. J. Lynch.

1195—Van Brunt st, No. 420, underpin side wall; cost, $400; Struck estate, on premises; b'rs, same as last.

MISCELLANEOUS.

BUSINESS FAILURES.

N. Y. ASSIGNMENTS—BENEFIT CREDITORS.

Dec.

21 Seaman, William H. (butcher, at No. 283 Washington Market), to Edward S. Innet; preferences, $100.

21 Cleaveland, James O. (merchant and dealer in dry goods, at No. 337 Broadway), to George H. Bayne: without preference.

22 Reiss, Simon D. (retail dealer in jewelry, at No. 1244 Broadway), to Emanuel Blumenstiel; preferences, $5,000.

PROCEEDINGS OF THE BOARD OF ALDERMEN AFFECTING REAL ESTATE.

* Under the different headings indicates that a resolution has been introduced and referred to the appropriate committee. † Indicates that the resolution has passed and has been sent to the Mayor for approval. ‡ Passed over the Mayor's veto.

NEW YORK. Tuesday, Dec. 22, 1891.

PAVING.

138th st, from e s Trinity av to a point 330 e Locust av: granite block.†

REGULATING, GRADING, ETC.

Union st, from Lind av to Bremer av. †
138th st, from e s Trinity av to a point 330 e Locust av, and crosswalks laid at intersecting avs. †

FLAGGING, CURBING, ETC.

Union st, from Lind av to Bremer av. †
2d av, w s, bet 117th and 118th st, 200x100 ft, on 117th st. †
1st av, e s, bet 105th and 106th sts. †
106th st, from 1st av to East River. †
103d st, n s, at 1st av to a point 500 w therefrom. †

MAINS.

Creston av, from Donnybrook to Travers st; gas. †
Creston av, from Donnybrook to Travers st; water. †
Bainbridge av, from Rosa pl to Southern Boulevard; water. †
162d st, west of Morris av, to Grand av, abt 240 ft.; gas. †
Grand av, from 162d st to a point 185 s therefrom; gas. †

GAS LAMPS ERECTED AND LAMPS LIGHTED.

Grand st, n w cor Centre Market pl. †
53d st, in front of No. 153 W.; 2 lights, at owners' expense. †
88th st, in front of No. 350 E.; 2 lights. †
162d st, west of Morris av, to Grand av, abt 240 ft. †
West End av, s e cor 81st st; 2 lights. †
Creston av, from Donnybrook to Travers st. †
Grand av, from 162d st to a point 185 s therefrom. †

ADVERTISED LEGAL SALES.

REFEREES SALES TO BE HELD AT THE REAL ESTATE EXCHANGE AND AUCTION ROOM (LIMITED), 59 to 65 LIBERTY STREET, EXCEPT WHERE OTHERWISE STATED.

Dec.

Madison av, Nos. 1064 and 1066, w s, 62.2 n 80th st, 40x70, five story brk flat with stores, by William Kennelly. (Amt due $51,903) 28

96th st, No. 35, n s, 338 w 8th av, 19x100.11, four-story brk dwell'g, by R. V. Harnett & Co. 28

Boulevard, No. 573, w s, 27 n 88th st, 27.4x100, five-story brk flat, by William Kennelly. (Amt due $24,050) 29

Boulevard, No. 575, w s, 54.4 n 88th st, 27.4x100, five-story brk flat ....
Boulevard, No. 577, w s, 81 8 n 88th st, 18.4x100, five-story brk flat ....
by William Kennelly. (Amt due on No. 575, $24,084, and $16,152 on No. 577) 29

Hamilton pl, s e s, 40.7 s 142d st, 67.8x81.5x4.6x56.8, vacant, by R. V. Harnett & Co. (Amt due $28,315) 29

34th st, Nos. 126–130, s w cor Lexington av, 98x117.6, two seven-story brk and stone flats, by D. P. Ingraham & Co. (Amt due $311,734) 29

45th st, No. 134, s s, 332.6 w 6th av, 17.6x100.4, four-story brk dwell'g, by B. L. Kennelly. (Amt due $4,079) 29

8th av, n e cor 153d st, runs east 409.4 to McCombs Dam road, x north 227.8 to 154th st, x west 518.7 to 8th av, x south 199.10 to beginning, two-story frame store on road, rest vacant, by L. J. & I. Phillips. (Amt due $147,877) 29

69th st, No. 316, s s, 275 w 11th av, 25x100.5, five-story brk store and tenem't, by William Kennelly. (Amt due $13,302) 30

Part lots 12 and 13 on Findlay's map, Woodstock, begins at point 59 e lot 13 on said map, runs east 200 x south 46 to roadway, x west 20 x south 60.4 x west 180 x north 106.6 to beginning. (Sub. to morts. $4,500) ....
Washington now Elton av, n w s, 75 n e 154th st, 25x100. (Sub. to morts. $4,000) ....
Washington now Elton av, w s, 25 s 154th st, 25x100. (Sub. to morts. $2,000) ....
by R. V. Harnett & Co. (Amt due $9,411) 30

48th st, No. 435, s s, 475 e 1st av, runs east 55 to East River, x southwest 67 x northwest 107.5 to beginning, gore, two-story frame office and vacant, also all right, title and int. to water right, land under water, &c., by B. L. Kennelly. (Amt due $27,167) 31

112th st, n s, 125 w Lenox av, 25x100.11, five-story brk flat, by William Kennelly. (Amt due $21,804) 31

Jan.

Abingdon sq, Nos. 7 and 9, Bleecker st, No. 425, 8th av, No. 2 } begins 8th av, s e cor Bleecker st, runs northeast 44.11 x southeast 40 x east 17.9 x south 22.5 x west 76.9 to Bleecker st, x north 97.7 to beginning, seven-story brk flat with stores, by R. V. Harnett. (Amt due $38,267; prior morts. $——) 4

Sheriff st, No. 65, w s, 100 s Rivington st, 25x100, five-story brk tenem't with stores, by John N. Golding. (Amt due $3,425; prior morts. $18,000; sold Dec. 31, 1889, for $27,270) 4

57th st, No. 119, old No. 117, n s, 215 w Lexington av, 20x100.5, four-story stone front dwell'g, by William Kennelly. (Amt due $37,067) 4

100th st, n s, 175 w 8th av, 50x100.11, five-story stone front flats, by R. V. Harnett & Co. (Amt due $1,816; prior morts. ——) 4

Riverside av or Drive, No. 100, 82d st, Nos. 316–324 } begins Riverside av, s e cor 82d st, runs east 161.1 x south 102.2 x west 16.8 x north 19.4 x west 32 x north 18.8 x west 14.4 x north 15.8 x west 8.4 x north 26.6 x west 79.9 to Riverside Drive, x north 24.2 to beginning, four-story stone front dwell'g on av and four four-story stone front dwell'gs on st, by R. V. Harnett & Co 4

Leroy st (St. Lukes pl, No. 4), n s, 80 e Hudson st, 22.1x100, three-story stone front dwell'g, by R. V. Harnett & Co. (Amt due $13,022) 4

KINGS COUNTY.

Dec.

61st st, n s, 180 w 11th av, 20x100, New Utrecht, frame dwell'g ....
62d st, s s, 180 e 13th av, 20x100, New Utrecht ....
Sheffield av, Nos. 54 and 56, w s, 225 s Fulton st, 50x100, one-and-a-half-story frame dwell'g and one-story frame dwell'g on rear of plot; assessed value, $2,650 ....
by T. A. Kerrigan, at 13 Willoughby st 28

Benson av, s w s, 308.9 s w De Bruyns lane 50x192 x50x190, New Utrecht; partition; by John C. Rhodes, ref., at County Court House 28

Warren st, No. 507, n s, 108 e Nevins st, 20x100, two-story frame dwell'g; assessed value, $1,100; partition ....
Kingsland av, No. 295, w s, 279.8½ n Nassau av, 18.11¾x100 ....
Kingsland av, No. 297, w s, 298.8¼ n Nassau av, 18.11¾x100 ....
Kingsland av, No. 299, w s, 317.8 n Nassau av, 19 x100 ....
Three three-story brk tenem'ts; assessed value, $1,500 each ....
by J. Cole, at 389 Fulton st 29

Prospect av, No. 159, n e s, 400 s e 3d av, 25x54.4 x25.1x52.5, two-story and basement frame dwell'g; assessed value, $1,600 ....
Prospect av, No. 161, n e s, 425 s e 3d av, 15.6x 55.10½x15.6x54.4, two-story and basement frame dwell'g; assessed value, $900 ....
by T. A. Kerrigan, at 13 Willoughby st 29

Herkimer st, No. 1144, s w cor Russell pl, 16.8x 85.9, two-story and basement brk dwell'g; assessed value, $3,000 ....
Madison st, No. 914, s e cor Howard av, 20x100, four-story brk flat and store; assessed value, $7,700 ....
Palmetto st, No. 193, n w s, 350 n e Central av, 20 x100, two-story frame dwell'g; assessed value, $2,500 ....
Putnam av, No. 1001, n e cor Howard av, 20x100, four-story brk flat and store; assessed value, $7,700 ....
by T. A. Kerrigan, at 13 Willoughby st 30

St. Marks av, No. 597, n s, 120 w Bedford av, 20x 128.6, three-story brk dwell'g; assessed value, $6,500; by J. Cole, at 389 Fulton st 30

Gold st, No. 207, n e cor Nassau st, 24.1x79.9, four-story brk flat and stores; assessed value, $15,000 ....
Sands st, No. 180, s w cor Gold st, 25x100, three-story frame dwell'g and store and three two-story frame dwell'gs, two with stores on Gold st ....
Sands st, No. 178, s s, 25 w Gold st, 25x100, three-story frame dwell'g and store and one-story frame stable on rear; assessed together, $10,500 ....
7th av, No. 230, w s, 21 n 4th st, 19x68, four-story brk flat; assessed value, $5,600 ....
7th av, No. 228, w s, 40 n 4th st, 30x68, four-story double brk flat; assessed value, $9,200 ....
by T. A. Kerrigan, at 13 Willoughby st 31

2d st, s s, 108.3 e 5th av, 30x100 ....
2d st, s s, 138.3 e 5th av, 30x100 ....
Two four-story double brk flats ....
by Gerard M. Stevens, ref. at Coutry Court House 31

Jan.

Dean st, No. 1387, n s, 140 e Albany av, 20x80 ....
Dean st, No. 1389, n s, 160 e Albany av, 20x80 ....
Two three-story brk dwell'gs; assessed value, $2,500 each ....
Degraw st, s s, 430 w Franklin av, 20x131, vacant, all right, title and int.; assessed value, $190 ....
St. Johns pl, No. 240, s s, 100 w 8th av, 18.10x100, three-story brk dwell'g, all right, title and int.; assessed value $6,500 ....
7th av, w s, 20.5¾ s 1st st, 105.11x90.9, four four-story double brk flats and stores ....
by T. A. Kerrigan, at 13 Willoughby st 4

Hull st, No. 181, n s, 375 e Rockaway av, 18.9x 100, three-story brk dwell'g; assessed value, $4,000 ....
Pacific st, No. 1550, s s, 160 e Albany av, 20x 107.2½ ....
Pacific st, No. 1552, s s, 180 e Albany av, 20x 107.2½ ....
Pacific st, No. 1558, s s, 240 e Albany av, 20x 107.2½ ....
Pacific st, No. 1560, s s, 260 e Albany av, 20x 107.2½ ....
Pacific st, No. 1562, s s, 280 e Albany av, 20x 107.2½ ....
Five three-story frame (brk lined) dwell'gs; assessed value, $3,000 each ....
by J. Cole, at 389 Fulton st 4

McDonough st, No. 579, n s, 22.8 w Ralph av, 18.8x 100, two-story and basement brk and stone dwell'g; assessed value, $4,000; by W. Cole, at 7 and 8 Court sq 4

LIS PENDENS.

NEW YORK.

Dec.

97th st, No. 48, s s, 440 w 8th av, 20x100. William H. Holmes and ano. agt Leopold Wallach; foreclos. mechanic's lien; att'y, Chas. D. Evans 19

75th st, No. 14, s s, 158.8 w Madison av, 21.10x102.2. Edmund J. Murphy assignee agt James J. Lally et al.; foreclos. mechanic's lien; att'ys, Durnin & Hendrick 21

Delancey st, Nos. 270 and 272, n s, 48.10 e Columbia st, runs north 40 x east — x north 60 x east 50 x south 100 to Delancey st, x west 55.11 to beginning. Aaron Kaplan agt Barney Isaacs; action to compel defendant to execute conveyance; att'ys, A. & L. Levy 21

11th st, No. 53, n s, 309 e 6th av, 24x103.3. Bradley & Currier Co. (Lim.) agt John J. Crawford et al.; foreclos. mechanic's lien; att'y, William Stone 21

Greenwich st, No. 756, w s, 47.8 n 11th st, runs west 80 x north 25 x east 26 x north 8 x east 19.6 x south 15 x east 56.6 to Greenwich st, x south 22.8 to beginning. Manhattan Railway Co. agt James G. Hasking exr. and trustee et al; special proceeding for the purpose of acquiring title by condemnation; att'ys, Davies, Short & Townsend 23

Greenwich st, No. 758, e s, 19.7 n 11th (Hammond) st, runs east 42.4 x north 0.6 x east 28.5 x south 5 to 11th st, x west 70.8 to Greenwich st, x north 19.7 to beginning. Andrew Van Antwerp agt Daniel Van Antwerp et al.; partition; att'y, Townsend Wandell 23

96th st, n s, 70 e Lexington av, 125x100.11. Mary A. Dolan agt Owen F. McElroy, Jr., et al.; foreclos. mechanic's lien; att'y, N. J. O'Connell 23

Cherry st, No. 427, s s, 100 4 w Jackson st, 25.1x 90.7x25x92.6. James G. Worthley et al. agt Joseph Gru et al.; action to adjudge conveyance as fraudulent; att'y, Charles H. Fuller 23

Broadway, s e cor 47th st, 20.1x80. Peter J. Ryan agt Patrick Cuff; foreclos. mechanic's lien; att'ys, Burr & De Lacy 24

Water st, No. 377, s s, 50 e Oliver st, 16.8x60 ....
Grand st, No. 77, s s, 62 e Wooster st, 22x96, leasehold ....
Thompson st, No. 23, w s, 20x80 ....
5th st, Nos. 311 and 313, n e s, 137.6 s e Av D, 36x97
Av D, No. 36, s e s, 24 s w 4th st, 18x75 ....
129th st, n e s, 110 s e 5th av, 25x99.11 ....
John G. Heckscher agt Matilda C. Van Rensselaer et al.; partition; att'ys, Jay & Candler. 24

FORECLOSURE SUITS.

Dec.

79th st, n s, 300 e 3d av, 25x100.2. James L. Hutchinson agt Jacob Cohen et al.; att'y, Herbert G. Hull 19

Montgomery st, No. 67, e s, 47.6 n Cherry st, —x 58.10x20.5x57.5 ....
Interior lot, begins 14 e Montgomery st and 47.6 n Cherry st, runs east 29.8 x south 2.3 x west — x north 2.2 ....
William Laytin and ano. admrs. agt Margaret Meehan et al.; att'y, Norman A. Lawlor 19

90th st, n e s, 325 n w 9th av, 25x113.11x25x113.6. John P. Hunt agt Alice Kingston individ. and admrx. et al.; att'y, Thomas C. Ennever 21

Edgecombe av, e s, 87.4 s 137th st, 17.6x90. Edward de P. Livingston agt Dore Lyon et al.; att'ys, Clute & Cobb 21

102d st, s s, 170 e Columbus av, 60x100.11 ....
102d st, s s, 190 e Columbus av, 60x100.11 ....
102d st, No. 70, s s, 190 e Columbus av, 30x100.11.
William H. Scott agt Henry C. Acker et al.; att'y, Bolton Hall 21

104th st, Nos. 114 and 116, s s, 170 w Columbus av, 2 lots, each 27.6x100.11. John T. Terry and ano. trustees agt Christian Blinn et al.; 2 actions; att'ys, Lord, Day & Lord 22

101st st, n s, 175 e 9th av, 75x100.11. William D. Murphy agt Thomas C. Jones et al.; att'y, Henry W. Gaines 22

Lexington av, s e cor 97th st, 25.11x76. Henry M. Bendheim agt Adelheit Pankow et al.; amended notice; att'y, Albert Zimmermann 22

114th st, No. 436, s s, 193 w Av A, 25x100.10. Corporation for Relief of Widows and Children of Clergymen of P. E. Church agt George Augustus Mack et al.; att'ys, Varnum & Harison 22

56th st, s s, 200 w 10th av, 25x100.5. Balthazar Schmitt agt Valentine Muller individ. and recvr. et al.; att'y, F. J. Bischoff 22

Lot 950 map Jumel estate, north 150th st, contains 17½ city lots, each 25x100, with land under water, &c., except an irregular strip along Harlem River, on easterly water front, contains 1½ of a city lot. Douglas Campbell agt Helene S. Bell et al.; amended notice; att'y, William Campbell. 22

Lot 993, same map, contains 35 9-10 city lots with land under water, &c. Same agt same; amended notice; same att'y 22

20th st, s s, 144 w 2d av, 22x92. Agnes C. Lawrence agt Daniel Herbert et al.; att'ys, Cudlipp & Glover 23

10th av, e s, 49 5 n 87th st, 49.4x100. Jonas Weil and ano. agt Georgiana F. Webster et al.; amended notice; att'y, Emanuel Arnstein 23

102d st, s s, 160 e Columbus av, 30x100.11. Metropolitan Life Ins. Co. agt Henry C. Acker et al.; att'ys, Arnour, Ritch & Woodford 23

61st st, s s, 175 e 11th av, 125x100.5. John A. Roosevelt agt James F. Ellacott et al.; att'ys, De Forest & Weeks 23

16th st, No. 10, s s, 325 w 5th av, 25.6x103.3. Helen Langdon agt Janette Pirsson; att'y, Edward E. Sprague 23

98th st, n s, 268.6 e Amsterdam av, runs north 83 x northwest 14.11 x north 75 7 x east 164.2 x south 113.6 to st, x west 156.6 to beginning. Moses Kund and ano. agt John W. Hutton et al.; att'y, Chas E. L. Jelliffe 23

Same property. Same agt same; same att'y 23

Part lots 12 and 13 on Findlay's map Woodstock, begins at point 59 e lot 13, runs east 200 x south 46 to a road, x west 20 x south 60 x west 180 x north 106 to beginning. John Bussing, Jr., agt Edward Stichler et al.; att'y, W. Stebbins Smith. 23

Sheriff st, No. 112, e s, 150 n Stanton st, 25x100. Morris Rosenberg agt Rosa Fodor et al.; att'y, E. M. Goodhart 24

115th st, s s, 275 e 2d av, 25x100.11. Louis Bengiger trustee agt Henry Neus et al.; att'ys, De Witt, Lockman & De Witt 24

LIS PENDENS, KINGS COUNTY.

Dec.

Van Buren st, s e s, 190 n e Broadway, 18x100. Amelia Molson by Henry M. Brigham guard. agt George Ernst; partition; att'ys, Brigham & Baylis 17

Herkimer st, s s, 199.6 w New York av, 15.6x100. Mary E. Moffat agt Amelia H. Ellis; att'y, J. Lawrence Marcellus 17

Myrtle av, n s, 80.3 w Gold st, 20x100. Harrison A. Tucker agt Alexander McLean; action to set aside deeds; att'y, Charles M. Stafford 17

Gates av, s s, 245 e Marcy av, 20x100. Amelia W. Leavitt agt Michael A. Pigot; att'y, Wilson M. Powell 17

Gates av, s s, 265 e Marcy av, 20x100. Amelia W. Leavitt agt Michael A. Pigot; att'y, W. M. Powell 17

18th st, s s, 69 w 6th av, 16x80. The Women's Prison Assoc. and Home agt George Keymer; same att'y 17

Clason av, w s, 125.6 s Park av, 25x110. Richard S. Collins agt Blanche L. Nash; same att'y 17

Clason av, w s, 150.6 s Park av, 25x110. Same agt Ella Nash; same att'y 17

Clason av, w s, 175.6 s Park av, 25x110. Same agt same; same att'y 17

39th st, s s, 140 w 4th av, 20x100.2. Anna R. Hurlburt agt Patrick Kenney; att'y, G. W. Pearsall. 17

15th st, n s, 130 e 4th av, runs north 88.1 x east 0.2 x north 11.11 x east 22 x south 100 to 15th st, x west 22 2..........
15th st. n s. adj above, 25x100..........
James and Katie Sweeney agt Otto Gillid et al.; partition; att'ys, Magner & Hughes.......... 17

East New York av, s s, adj Henry Clise and P. Cummings, 7½ acres, Flatbush ....
Douglass st, n e cor Ralph av, 19.6x41.5x11.2x38.4.
Ralph av, n w cor Douglass st, 24.6x126.1x124.1, gore..........
Clara T. Brown agt Maria Hawley et al.; partition; att'ys, Tredwell & Catlin.......... 18

Macon st, No. 592, s s. 137 w Patchen av, 19x100..
Macon st, s s, 156 w Patchen av. 19x100..........
Edward L. Goodsell agt John H. G. and Edith M. J. Atkinson; action to set aside conveyance of property; att'y, Ira G. Darrin.......... 18

Webster av, n s. 273 w 1st st, 91x217.1 to Franklin av, x91x246.10, Flatbush. William G. Peirson agt Martin J. Sinnott; att'y, Thos. Berginger.......... 18

Knickerbocker av, w s, 85 n Schaeffer st, 15x75. Adolphus Gload agt Mary E. and I. D. Mason; att'y, Noah Tebbetts.......... 18

Centre st, n s, 84 w Henry st, 20x100. Konrad Lind agt William and Ellen Honrigan; att'y, A. L. Thompson, Jr.......... 18

Coney Island Bridge Co.'s turnpike road, e s, adj land of Maria Lott, 2 1-10 acres; also..........
Plot at Guisbert's or Johnson's Island, bounded south by sand hills, bet the island and the sea shore, east by Van Siclens and west by road to shore, 92x251x100x251, excepting part taken for Neptune av and West 6th st, Gravesend...
John R. Planten agt Joseph Beno et al.; att'y, L. Hurst.......... 19

McKibbin st, s s, 175 e Graham av, 25x100. Abraham Kemp agt Philipp Schneider; action for specific performance; att'ys, Simpson & Werner.......... 19

Rockaway av, e s, 100 s Glenmore av, 25x100. Earl A. Gillespie agt Wolf and Mary (Mary fictitious) Schwarz; att'y, Geo. F. Alexander.......... 19

16th st, Nos. 385-391, n s, 135.9 w 8th av, 76x100. James H. Lee agt William Wingerath; forclos. mechanic's lien; att'y, Tallmadge W. Foster.... 21

Noble st, n s, 418 e Franklin st, 25x100. George C ll & Co. agt William P. Morrissy; att'y, Henry Aaden.......... 21

Diamond st, s s, 3,163.4 e Main st, 50x188.1x50x188, Flatbush. The trustees of the Reformed Protestant Dutch Church, Flatbush, agt Jennie E. Bogeart; att'y, John Z. Lott.......... 21

Lexington av, n s, 125 w Sumner av, 102x100. Marie E. Jacobson agt Fannie W. Cogswell; att'ys, Wells & Waldo.......... 21

9th st, n e s, lot 16 map Charles A. Clinton, 25x100. Thomas H. Watson agt Hamlet E. Forrest; att'y, John D. Shedlock.......... 22

Decatur st, s s, 441 9 w Reid av, 16.5x100. Mary E. Tyler agt George H. Burpeo; att'y, Randolph H. Cole.......... 22

McDougal st, n s, 182 w Stone av, 16x100. George Carll and ano. exrs. Mary A. Carll agt Virgil R. Case; att'y, Jos. M. Greenwood.......... 22

Lewis av, s e cor Hancock st, 100x150. Charles M. Marsh agt Jacob Aronson; att'y, Charles M. Marsh.......... 22

Hudson av, e s, 23.4 s Plymouth st, 23.4x75. Nelson L. Tuck agt Christian L. Berge; action to set aside deed; att'y, John W. Konvalinka...... 22

Prospect st, n s, 49 e Bridge st, 25.1x72.10..........
Bridge st, e s, 85.8 n Fulton st, 25x100.3..........
Barbara Miller agt Henry S. Gilbert; amended notice of partition; att'y, Theo Burgmyer...... 22

Dean st, n s, 79.10 w Clason av, 25x100. Annie M. Pollock agt Henry Cummings; att'ys, Rolfe & Snedeker.......... 22

4th av, s w cor 34th st, 100.2x100. E. Sinnamon Calvert agt Nicholas McCool, Jr.; att'y, John T. Nelson.......... 22

Adelphi st, w s, 178.7 n Atlantic av, 25x100. Eleanor S. Irish agt Giuseppe Di Stefeno; att'y, Frank A. Irish.......... 23

Lot at Flatlands Neck, Flatlands, on n s of highway from New Lots to Flatbush, and land John H. Lott, 18 acres. George M. Williamson agt David W. Binns; partition; att'ys, Thornton, Earle & Kiendl.......... 23

RECORDED LEASES.

NEW YORK. Per Year

Broadway, No. 697, basement. Pelham St. G. Bissell to Wertheim & Platzman; 4 years, from May 1, 1891.......... $1,600

Chambers st, No. 75, store floor and basement. Robert K. and Abraham G. Richards, Flushing, L. I., to John Koster and Albert Bial, of Koster & Bial; 6 years, from May 1, 1892.......... 4,000

Madison st, No. 28, all, except alleyway. Mary E. wife of D. Brainerd Ray to Mary J. wife of Alfred E. Rock; 5 years, from May 1, 1892.......... 1,200

Mercer st, Nos. 193 and 195, store, basement and sub-cellar. Cornelia Wadsworth to Felix Marx, Plainfield, N. J.; 5 years, from Feb. 1, 1893.......... 5,000

Murray st, No. 67, all lofts. Albert N. Brown to Hugo Cahn & Co.; 5 years, from May 1, 1892.......... 1,850

Rose st, No. 41, south store and part cellar. Henry Ketaltas trustee to John D. Koster and John H. Jachens; 5 years, from Aug. 1, 1892.......... 900

South st, No. 83, all. James Douglass, Orient, L. I., to Hermann Schutt; 7 5-12 years, from Dec. 1, 1891.......... 2,200

West st, No. 209. Emily A. Thorn to Elizabeth Rockfeller; 5 years, from May 1, 1889.......... 1,600

15th st, s s, 77 e 7th av, 23x67.1. Henry Hillebrandt to Thomas Jennett; 10 years, from May 1, 1892, taxes, &c., and.......... 600

30th st, No. 103 E. Adelia Clark to Bertha Cattelain; 2 years, from Jan. 1, 1892.......... 1,380

50th st, No. 235, n s, 245 e 8th av, 25x100.5. John Pettigrew et al. exrs. Robert Pettigrew to Edgar B. Banks, Theodore Riehl and John Acker, Jr.; 7 years, from Nov. 1, 1891.......... 600

71st st, No. 340 E., west store, front basement and five rooms over store. Fanny Froehlich to Annie Seidel; 4½ years, from Nov. 1, 1891.......... consid. omitted

103d st, No. 209 E., "Niagara Stables." Josephine Sperling to John H. French & Co.; 5 years, from Oct. 1, 1891..1,200, 1,300, 1,400, 1,500, 1,300

125th st, No. 109 E. Emily R. Mitchell to Luer Ehlers; extension of lease for 4 years, from May 1, 1892.......... 2,450

135th st, No. 200 W., s w cor 7th av, all. Douglas Sloane to Henry A. Stourcke; 4 years, from May 1, 1891.......... 1,500

Elton av, No. 703, all. Edward Stiehler to Louis Muller; 2¾ years, from Aug. 1, 1890...540, 600

1st av, No. 2276, store and bedroom and front cellar. Christopher and Adeline M. Von Bergen to Frederick H. Hecht; 5 years, from May 1, 1892.......... 900

2d av, No. 740, south store and cellar. Henry Strauss agent for Samuel Strauss to Henry Raedel; 5 years, from Nov. 1, 1891..........480, 504

2d av, No. 2037, store floor and half of the cellar underneath. August Widdel to Ludwig Scholem; 5 years, 4 months and 15 days, from Dec. 15, 1891.......... 900

2d av, No. 1551, all. Henry C. Alger to Julius Faulhaber; 10 years, from May 1, 1881.......... 1,800

3d av, No. 1967, n e cor 108th st, store floor, front cellar and second floor. Lesser I. Cohen, with consent of Theresa Cohen, to John McCaffrey; 5 5-12 years, from Dec. 1, 1891.......... 2,000

3d av, No. 3267, store and dwell'g. Margaret Commins to and William Ebling Brewing Co.; 4 years, from Nov. 1, 1891... 720, 960

7th av, s e cor 15th st, 22.8x77. Henry Hillebrandt to Thomas Jennett; 10 years, from May 1, 1892, per year, taxes, &c., and.......... 2,200

11th av, No. 665, all. Frederick W. Schwiers to m Cawley; 8½ years, from Nov. 1, 1891Ja..es.......... 1,968

12th av, bet 131st and 132d st, north part of premises occupied by lessor. Daniel Katz to S. J. Taylor; 1 year, from March 25, 1891.... 600

CHATTELS.

NOTE.—The first name, alphabetically arranged, is that of the Mortgagor, or party who gives the Mortgage. The "R" means Renewal Mortgage.

NEW YORK CITY.

DECEMBER 18 TO 23—INCLUSIVE.

SALOON AND RESTAURANT FIXTURES.

Albers, Herman. 330 Broome....W H Griffith & Co. Pool Table. $250
Blythe & Daniels. 381 2d av....M Glick. (R) 1,333
Brennan, M B and B A. 1056 Park av....J Ruppert. 2,000
Brown, Henry. 90 Cherry.... Bernheimer & S. Pump. 91
Bellezza, Pietro. 94 Park....Welz & Z. 500
Brahn, James. 637 2d av....Sjuirson & Johnson. 450
Brophy, J G. 313 E 88th....Bernheimer & S. 400
Byrne, Denis. 281 W 12th....Bachmann B Co. 3,000
Blank, Pauline. 385 E 104th....A B Marx. Pool Table. 95
Cody, T and J J. 376 3d av....J Everard. 4,060
Cogan, E C. 12 Centre....P Cogan. 1,600
Cronhardt, C A T and A. 207 Av C....G Ringler & Co. 1,100
Chappins, F. 331 7th av....J H Bereuter. Pool Table. 180
Doyle, Patrick. 908 1st av....P Doelger. (R) 1,000
Endlich, Peter. 723 5th....G Bechtel. (R) 700
Eugenhoefer, Katie. 8th av and 141st st.... Bernheimer & S. Ice House. 130
Furst, George. 103 Suffolk....Claus Lipsius B Co. (R) 200
Farrell, Frank....R Rothschild's Son's Co. 4,311
Fasanello, A. 43 Thompson....Bernheimer & S. Saloon Pump. 104
Frercks, D D. 52 Stanton....H Vogel. 250
Feldhusen, Geo. 119 2d av....E A Kroenke. (R) 2,100
Frey, Daniel. 580 6th....F Bachmann B Co. (R) 500
Friedman, Eliza. 134th st and Washington av ....A Hupfel's Son. 600
Frola, James. 2208 1st av....Feigenspan B Co. 655
Goldstein, Henry. 51 Norfolk....I Davis. Restaurant Fixtures. 50
Grucci, Felix. 533 Broome ...R Guidetti. 1,000
Gardella, Carlo. 51 Baxter....India Wharf B Co. Ice Box. 95
Same....same. Pool Table. 135
Gross & Loeffler. 271 Bowery....D Mayer B Co. 2,000
Haakonson, Martin. 347 Spring....Bernheimer & S. Ice House. 80
Hecht, F H. 2276 1st av....F Oppermann, Jr. 1,000
Hett, Brigitta. 81 4th av....S Liebmann's Sons B Co. 1,200
Healey, Maggie I. 301 E 29th....P Doelger. 2,000
Hedley & Priestley. 66 West Broadway....H Wunderlich. 2,500
Illing, Richard. 513 E 142d....P & W Ebling. (R) 850
Jansen, Chas. 212 E 127th....F & M Schaefer B Co. 500
Same....M T Garvey. 200
Jonas, Hermann. 390 E 10th....Danenberg & Coles. 700
Judge & McFarland. 1765 3d av....J Everard. 3,045
Karliner, Moritz. 140 Forsyth....Restaurant Furniture Co. Restaurant Fixtures. 66
Kende, Berchold and Paul Kistel. 197 Grand.... J Fallert B Co. 500
Kopetzki, O A. 113 2d av....C Stein. 3,290
Kranshaar, David. 27 Suffolk ...Burger & H B Co. 500
Kaiser, Friedrich. 1681 3d av....G Ehret. 1,100
Klein, Samuel....494 Broadway....I Gombossy. Restaurant Fixtures. 1,750
Koch, William. 22 Rose....G Bechtel, exr of. (R) 917
Lentz, A and H. 8 Wooster....Claus Lipsius B Co. (R) 1,050
Lacey, Patrick. 621 Hudson.. J Everard. (R) 814
Lebly, Rosa. 225 West Houston ..Restaurant Furniture Co. Restaurant Fixtures. 20
Lephay, Victor. 127 Bleecker....J B Basset. Restaurant Fixtures. 500
Licker, Wolf. 74 Broome....Welz & Z. 250
Lovett, Eugene. 95 10th av....Bernheimer & S. Ice House. 70
Lang, J W. 157 and 159 E 42d....J C Engel. Restaurant Fixtures. 3,500
McCabe, Bernard. 831 10th av....Long Island Brewery. 4,000
McFarland, John. 1202 2d av....J Everard. 1,284
Maher, Martin. 2119 1st av.... P & W Ebling. (R) 1,119
McDonough & Davis. 874 10th av....Knickerbocker B Co. 775
Mergenthaler, John. 122 Park row....M Baumgarten. 1,000
Milne & Grenlich. 158 E 53d....Bavarian B Co. 384
McKeon & Buckley. 1329 3d av ...J Ruppert. 4,500
Morgan & Monahan. 70 Broome....Bernheimer & S. 300
Neus, Fred. 419 E 106th....P Doelger. (R) 1,500
Nolta, T. 2089 2d av....Bernheimer & S. Ice House. 120
Same....same. Pump. 80
O'Brien, Joseph. 231 E 29th....M A Haugh. 300
O'Reilly, Hugh. 186 E 110th....Bernheimer & S. 1,500
Pelken, Henry. 93 Market....G Ringler & Co. (R) 1,399
Prendergast, Martin. 522 3d av....J Wallace & Son. 1,500
Same....J Sabater. 1,000
Pressler & Spiero. 376 Grand....I Gombossy. Restaurant Fixtures. 1,500
Pump, Fred. 354 Brook av....Bernheimer & S. Pump. 129
Same. 142d st and Brook av....same. Ice House. 95
Same....same. Ice House. 140
Piebert, Julius. 76 Av B....G Ringler & Co. 1,400
Rubinstein, S and L. 108 Norfolk....Bavarian B Co. 1,200
Reilly, Michael. 61st st and Av A ...G Ehret. (R) 1,000
Schepsky, Max. 19 Ludlow....Burger B Co. 300
Schilp, Franz. 368 10th av....J C G Hupfel B Co. 2,000
Schneider, Moritz. 98 Cannon....Claus Lipsius B Co. 800
Sprung & Cohen. 264 Rivington....Burger B Co. 1,200
Stahl, J H. 771 9th av....C Stein. (R) 241
St Pierre, R W. 66 John....W A Fox. Restaurant Fixtures. 300
Stumpff, Adolph. 65 1st....G Ringler & Co. 400
Scheimeister, Philip. 48 Clinton....Feigenspan B Co. (R) 259
Schells, John. 20 Stanton....J Murtaugh. 100
Schleicher, J B. 241 Pleasant av....J Fallert B Co. (R) 1,200
Schlorsser, Fred. 954 3d av....F Oppermann, Jr. 6,000
Schulermann & Ficken. 1066 2d av....Beadleston & W. 3,500
Scolise, Felice. 118 Mulberry....Abbott B Co. 500
Scranski, Walenty. 185 Chrystie ...W Peter B Co. 140
Schweinfest, J I. 128 Smith st, Brooklyn.... Bachmann B Co. (R) 2,069
Silverman, Fanny. 17 Clinton pl....Bavarian B Co. 1,000
Sittig, Geor. 103 2d av....Wagner & S. Pool Table. 200
Taylor, Georgina. 103 W 14th....F Meyer. 500
Towle, J R. 1124 3d av....J S McGovern. Pool Table. 75
Tuball, Kopel. 17 Orchard....W H Griffith & Co. Pool Table. 170
Tochtermann, Louis. 259 Broome....Claus Lipsius B Co. 800
Wehrtheimer, Leopold. 95 2d av....I Gombossy. Restaurant Fixtures. 1,850
Walter, Frank. 976 1st av....Restaurant F Co. Restaurant Fixtures. 50
Wenzler, Gustav. 336 E 59th....Schmitt & S. 1,000
Wiener, J and F. 694 Courtlandt av....A Hupfel's Sons. 1,000
Zimmermann, Karl. 190 E 3d....J H Bereuter. Pool Table. 145

HOUSEHOLD FURNITURE.

Angell, Annie B. 38 E 49th....C C Angell. 500
Austin, E L. 105 E 126th....J Baumann. 399
Barnes, Alberto. 166 W 125th....J Baumann. (R) 203
Bearns, J C. 261 W 22d....J Baumann. (R) 385
Becker, Ella. 253 W 39th....Garvey Bros. 430
Bradbury, Alice. 120 W 94th.... J Baumann. 288
Bailey, Annie. 113 7th av.... O'Farrell & Co. 275
Barry, K E. 114 W 63d.... H Thoesen. 112
Barry, Catherine. 426 W 56th....L Baumann. 128
Bartram, D B. 46 E 7th....J Moriarty. (R) 120
Baum, Virginia. 2148 Lexington av....A R Maxwell. 925
Beatty, H A. 467 4th av.... E T Lee. 178
Bocks, Bertha. 471 Canal....W J Ruddell. (R) 155
Bray, Michael. 50 Laight....L Baumann. 120
Brugman, Nan. 533 E 144th....L Baumann. 127
Burrows, Louise. 192½ Varick .... Krakauer Bros. Piano. 225
Burt, W J. 116 Bank....W J Ruddell. (R) 219
Bellucci, Antonio. 1735 Madison av....Jordan, M & Co. 454
Blake, W J. 84 Greenwich....Jordan & M. 120
Bray, Eliza. 188 E 101st....B M Cowperthwait & Co. 162
Brocken, T F. 200 1st av....B M Cowperthwait & Co. 344
Brown, Bella. 243 W 39th....Jordan, M & Co. 772
Burk, Frank. 204 St Nicholas av....B M Cowperthwait & Co. 214
Clifton, Helen....J Williams. 573
Colligan, T F. 2308 7th av....B M Cowperthwait & Co. 183
Crandano, Antonio. 689 Amsterdam av....C R Ruegger. 478
Campbell, D S, Jr. 662 E 146th....S Baumann. 130
Cary, Mary. 447 E 117th....Amer Guar Assoc. 100
Castro, J B. 2021 Lexington av....J McEnery & Co. 150
Cohn, L. 161 E 72d.... S Heyman & Co. 146
Cutugno, Madalena. 110 W 15th....O'Farrell & Co. 130
Carlton, Reta. 111 W 40th.... J Baumann. 1,565
Chase, Grace. 740 6th av....J Baumann. (R) 147
Cohen, Isaac. 165 Henry....S Edelberg. 300
Cohen, Morris. 54 Eldridge ..B Goldstein. 250
Dickman, Louisa. 401 Lexington av ...J Moriarty. 107
Downey, Cile. 311 E 38th....H S Eisler. 136
Dertinger, Kate. 638 E 156th....W Reubel. 110
Dalhine, G. 244 W 31st....Alexander Bros. 161
Daly, Ellen. 21 Watts....Krakauer Bros. Piano. 215
De Moise, Hattie. 5 University pl....F Michelitti. 3,000
Doig, Edward. 234 Willis av....D Schwarzkopf. 267
Evans, R A. 209 E 56th ...B M Cowperthwait & Co. 150
Enders, Hermine. 1604 Av B....S Heyman & Co. 200
Ernes, V H. 319 W 14th....Lincoln I and G Assoc. 250
Farran, Mary A. 607 Eagle av ...W E Wheelock & Co. Piano. 250
Freidlander, A A. 170 E 122d....H Mannes & Son. 196
Friedmann, Simon. 717 5th ...S I Herschmann. (R) 127
Ferguson, Mary P. 343 W 24th....S Baumann. 121
Fitzgerald & Brady. 300 E 61st....S Heyman & Co. 216
Forbes, Mary. 51 Dominick....W J Ruddell. (R) 234
Franassovich, Mrs A. 169 51st....Krakauer Bros. Piano. (R) 240

Freytag, Ferd. 119 E 85th....L Baumann. 280
Fleming, Mamie. 319 E 71st....Jordan & M. 314
Foley, Mamie 31 Hall pl .. Jordan & M. 180
Furber, C W. 337 Produce Exchange....B M Cowperthwait & Co. 170
Goldberg, A. 25 Rutgers pl....Alexander Bros. 169
Grefe, Emma. 324 E 48th... B M Cowperthwait & Co. 836
Gruebaum, Wm. 227 E 126th....D Schwarzkopf. 127
Guggenheimer, Fanny. 421 E 122d....H Thoesen. 141
Gorman, Maggie. 916 6th av....J Baumann. (R) 171
Gay, Cora L. 89 Clinton pl... W J Ruddell. (R) 168
Giebert, Emma. 257 W 39th....O'Farrell & Co. 162
Grandon, Jennie. 60 E 4th....F J Brechtel. 411
Heins, J J. 67 W 76th....C N Greig. 220
Hall, Susan L. 139 W 127th.. S Baumann. 205
Halpin, John. 216 W 19th....L Baumann. 177
Harwood, Catharine. 70 Murray....L Bauman. 119
Herbert, Cora. 321 W 21st....O'Farrell & Co. 238
Herrman, Mrs M. 512 E 84th. ..Fennell & Pye. 146
Hicinbothein, Alex. 664 and 666 E 145th....American Guar Assoc. 175
Hill, Florence. 238 W 34th....O'Farrell & Co. 177
Hinsdorf, Lizzie. 496 9th av....J Moriarty. 169
Hitrick, Ch's. 527 E 83d .. L Baumann. 180
Boole, Thomas. 246 W 18th... G Beck. 193
Herrigau, M P. 540 W 51st ...J Baumann. (R) 201
Huling, H P. 21 Grove....J Baumann. 120
Irvine, A A. 317 W 121st....D Schwarzkopf. 185
Jackman, Abi. 104 W 61st ...J Baumann. 504
Jacobson, A and E. 1880 2d av....M Moss. 125
Jordan, H L. 129 W 56th....T Mathews. 593
Kaufmann, Geo. 102 W 30th. ..J Moriarty. 223
Kelly, A J....J Moriarty. 146
Koehler, C F. 82 2d av....E Ward. 125
Kratzenberg, Mrs B. 516 E 137th ...Bollermann & Son. Piano. 350
Keller, Mamie. 2657 2d av....Alexander Bros. 119
Kirk, Lottie A. 243 W 50th....M Gaw. 1,200
Logan, James. 305 W 144th....B M Cowperthwait & Co. 129
Lalor, N G. 148 Willis av....L Baumann. 251
Lauderback, Flora. 300 W 21st....G Beck. 216
Logan, Annie. 1358 3d av ...L Baumann. 126
Lyons, Hattie M. 210 W 58d....J Moriarty. 151
Mayer, John. 510 W 50th....L Baumann. 376
Maynard, Matilda. 226 W 16th ...J Moriarty. (R) 148
McCartie, Eleanor. 151 E 29th....J Moriarty. 194
Same....same. 171
McCosker, Martha J. 5 Vandam....W J Ruddell. (R) 102
Meigs, Grace M. 153 W 10th....A R Maxwell. 100
Meyer, William. 2005 2d av....L Baumann. 198
Miller, Mina. 187 Chrystie....F J Brechtel. 120
Moore, Mrs H M. 253 W 14th....S Knapp & Co. 527
Morse, Carrie E. 155 W 125th....Fennell & Pye. 694
Morse, Woolson. 30 W 24th....S Baumann. 851
Mullen, Georgina. 1515 Madison av....L Baumann. 122
Mangon, Josef. 26 Columbus av .. J Gregg & Co. 269
Marchousen, Louisa. 50 Lawrence....J Baumann. 150
McCarty, Eleanor. 151 E 29th ...J Moriarty. 225
McKevitte, Mrs. 336 E 106th ...H Israel & Sons. 163
McMahon, Mrs. 2 Goerck....H S Eisler. 167
Miller, Ida H. 11 E 29th....E C Barsford. 650
Mordaunt, J C. 112 W 39th ...J Baumann. (R) 332
Murphy, Josie. 261 E 70th ...J Baumann. 144
Myers, Aaronson. 217 E 114th... J Baumann. 115
Myer, Catherine. 265 W 40th....J Gregg & Co. 252
Maake, Agatha. 163 Lexington av .. R M Walters. Piano. (R) 150
Maxwell, Mattie J. 253 W 121st....A R Maxwell. 350
Mayers, Mary F. 19½ Forsyth....Jordan & M. 103
Meyer, Charles. 231 E 55th....Jordan & M. 286
Mintzer, Mrs Louis. 349 E 82d ...B M Cowperthwait & Co. 238
Morgan, E S....J Williams. 171
Moses, S K. 65 E 106th....J S Rice. 204
Murphy, J McL. 250 E 128th....Alexander Bros. 617
Newcomb, Lizzie. 209 10th av....O'Farrell & Co. 245
Nola, Guiseppe. 96 Willett....Fennell & Pye. 138
Ohrensted, Edw. 201 E 112th... J Moriarty. 294
Okie, Frank. 247 West Houston....W J Ruddell. (R) 181
O'Brien, Mary. 504 W 42d... R M Walters. Piano. (R) 180
O'Keefe, Mrs E. 1766 2d av....B M Cowperthwait & Co. 196
Perrollet, Maria. 126 W 36th....L Baumann. (R) 146
Pieper, Mrs H. 23 E 108th... Alexander Bros. 247
Peck, Lizzie E. 6 Stone....R M Walters. Piano. (R) 292
Paisley, Maggie. 98 W 103d....L Baumann. 357
Perry, J B. 106 Concord. Brooklyn....W J Ruddell. (R) 101
Pollak, D B. 506 6th av....Krakauer Bros. Piano. 285
Price, W J and K....C H Wilmarth. 200
Quarles, Lizzie. 266 9th....J Baumann. 196
Rabold, C E. 402 W 58th....J Baumann. (R) 372
Raiford, Amelia. 17 Watts....J Baumann. 113
Reddick, Helen. 32 W 24th....W D Duff. 2,500
Richards, Eva. 260 W 43d....Brooklyn F Co. 325
Rulon, Carrie S. 211 W 21st....H Mannes & Son. 147
Rodding, Bertha. 124 W 127th....American Guarantee Assoc. 180
Rossbach, Bertha. 55 Broome....F J Brechtel. 171
Ruiz, M F. 380 E 13th ...L Baumann. 246
Raubitschek, Katti. 153 E 50th....D Schwarzkopf. 454
Read, Clara. 354 Manhattan av....A R Maxwell. 160
Schenerle, Louis. 66 E 4th .. Jordan & M. 185
Schwartz, H C. 205 E 90th ...H Thoesen. 162
Smith, E P. 334 W 11th....W J Ruddell. (R) 130
Stewart, Isabella. 126 W 104th....Jordan, M & Co 224
Stewart, Sarah. 2015 Madison av....L Baumann. (R) 160
Schacht, Joseph. 1325 Av A....S Heyman & Co. 129
Shires, W C. 67 Irving pl....S J O'Neill, secures rent
Schoenberger, Margaret. 115 E 75th....F J Brechtel. 346
Sobravoni, Alex. 328 W 56th....L Baumann. (R) 119
Sickles, Viola. 138 W 32d....H Thoesen. 321
Smith, Maggie. 2562 8th av....L Baumann. 108
Spencer, Annie. 350 E 42d... H Thoesen. 124
Schiffbauer, Minnie. 96½ 8th....H S Eisler. 121
Simons, Sadie. 148 West Houston....H Israel & Son. 113
Smith, J B. Storage....E C Hinsdale. 190
Smith, Mary. 534 W 126th... J Baumann. 221

Steckel, Eva V ...A Romer. 192
Theiss, Lizzie. 229 W 15th....J Moriarty. (R) 152
Thieling, E H. 10 9th av....J Gregg & Co. 100
Turner, J R. 1291 Lexington av....J Gregg & Co. 309
Tate, Edgar. 114 W 48th....S Baumann. 139
Tone, Pauline. 214 E 70th....S Heyman & Co. 209
Tobias, Martha. 157 W 25th....R M Walters. Piano. (R) 181
Toner, Kate. 3 St. Lukes pl....W J Ruddell. (R) 129
Tucker, Stella. 326 W 36th....W J Ruddell. (R) 228
Tuthill & White. 161 W 63d....W J Ruddell. 650
Van Tine, W and M L. 622 Columbus av. . E C Hinsdale. 160
Vaughan, Chas. 211 E 86th....Jordan & M. 289
Walsh, Mary. 121 Leroy....L Baumann. 130
Werner, Emil. 142 Chrystie....F J Brechtel. 227
Williams, C A. 168 W 63d....H Thoesen. 148
Wilson, Mrs Nikholine. 312 W 36th... Krakauer Bros. Piano. 360
Wood, Mrs M. 259 W 54th....I Mason. (R) 449
Wright, Jane. 607 E 11th ...J Moriarty. 222
Walter, William. 72 E 120th....J Baumann. 176
Warwick, J M. 501 Manhattan av....Brooklyn F Co. 696
Watson, John. 150 Linwood st, Brooklyn....J Baumann. 323
Weld, G W. 13 W 80th....J Baumann. (R) 118
Wilmot, G H. 363 W 17th....G d'Isoard. 615
Wisenblatt & Rosenthal. 297 Broome....S I Herschman. 194
Warburton, Esther J. 75 W 95th ...W J Ruddell. (R) 450
Same. 95th st and 9th av .. W J Ruddell. (R) 200
Williams, Mabel....J Williams. 154
Young, S. E. 335 E 80th... L Baumann. 214

MISCELLANEOUS.

Abbott, S A and C B. 436 W 57th....H Killam Co. Coach 361
Abramson, Samuel. 176 Delancey ...M Abramson. Drug Fixtures. 2,345
Arzt, Hermann. 128 Ridge....Archer Mfg Co. Barber Fixtures. (R) 74
Bechenale & Shehadey. 137 6th....B Lemenge. Store Fixtures. 400
Blase, Jos. 135 E 110th... Archer Mfg Co. Barber Fixtures. (R) 361
Blondeau, F B and F. 99 Christopher....Duparquet, H & M Co. Range, &c. 190
Boehm, H and J. 312 and 314 E 22d....M Liberman. Machines. 372
Braslovsky, Max. 63 Elizabeth....M Lieberman. Machines. 825
Brooklyn and N Y Ferry Co... G Law, trustee. Boats. (R) 1,000,000
Baker, J H. 150 Canal....J E Linde. Press. (R) 200
Bartholomew, C E. 22 Codege pl....T H Heffron. Presses, &c. 4,154
Same... same. Presses, &c. 2,000
Bromberg, B B. 283 W 125th ...L Raunheim. Dental Fixtures. 556
Buck, L A. 239 Av A....H Buck. Cigar Fixtures. (R) 500
Bundschuh, Henry. 256 10th av....Weeks & Parr. Bakery Fixtures. (R) 1,500
Byrnes, T J 2329 3d av .. Lamson Consol S S Co. Register. 185
Barnaby, T J. 193 8th av....J Matthews Co. Soda Fixtures. 365
Bologne, Gseppe. 183 E 124th....A Schwaab. Barber Fixtures. 377
Braslowsky, Max. 54 and 56 Rutgers....A Lerner. Machines. 440
Carter & Robertson. 74th st and Columbus av J Matthews Co. Soda Fixtures. 125
Clay, J L. 274 Mercer....S Clay. Horse, Coupe, &c. 275
Cossin, Timothy. 113 and 115 E 15th....A Cossin. Coach. 3,500
Chabisa, Herman. 334 Grand....H Greenberg. Photo Fixtures. 190
Calalamo & Damico. 15 8d av....Archer Mfg Co. Barber Fixtures. (R) 1,067
Caldwell, Mary A. 307 Alexander av....J Koester Son. Fancy Goods Fixtures. 200
Calvert & Richardson. 247 and 249 Pearl....Manhattan Type Co. Press, &c. 650
Clark, John, Jr. 10 and 12 Jane....D B Dunham. Coupe. 450
De Sanctis, C. 418 6th av.. .Archer Mfg Co. Barber Fixtures. (R) 54
Donahue, John. 416 E 76th....W B Davis. Coupe. (R) 100
Doll, Henry. 1687 2d av....P A Cassidy. Wagon. 110
Dupont, Francis. 165 and 167 Spring ..R & A Chevalier. Machinery. (R) 500
Eagen, James. 122d st and 10th av....L Heilbrun. Horses, Trucks, &c. 184
Elias, W M. 217 W 36th....J M Young & Co. Statues, Fixtures, &c. (R) 1,126
Ferre, W H. 203 W 90th ...Columbia Wagon Co. Wagon. 45
Farara, Frank. 1214 1st av . .A Schwaab & Son. Barber Fixtures. 28
Finley, John. 148 E 43d....Hincks & J. Coach. 250
Goldman, Levy & Roth. 104 and 106 Bowery....M Heuman. Theatre Fixtures. (R) 3,246
Green, J A & Co. 118 Lincoln av....Crawford & Poland. Machinery. 755
Gottlieb, Joseph. 1 Scammel pl .. J Weiss. Barber Fixtures. 85
Gunthert, J C. 201 E 67th....G F Krumm. Machinery. 250
Hall, W B. 241 and 243 W 15th....D B Treadwell. Horses, Trucks, &c. (R) 1,000
Hamburger, Barnet. 63 Barclay ...H Trankler. Machinery. 187
Hecht & Goldstein. 180 Stanton and 358 East Houston....J Schor. Machinery, &c. 400
Hubna, J W. 1722 Tremont av....American Biscuit Co Horses, Wagons. 600
Hendrick, P & Son. 174 and 174 E 124d....J C Lyons. Horses, Coaches, &c. 2,500
Harper, R. 42 W 23d....American Writing Machine. Type Writer. 100
Herbst, Gerson. 101 Clinton....E M Piltzer. Bakery Fixtures. 100
Hogan, J F. 2399 3d av....Lamson Consol S S Co. Register. 165
Jacob, Thomas. 305 Pearl....Franklin Photo Co. Press, &c. (R) 3,500
Jennings, Thomas. 3 Willett ...J Cramer. Horses and Coaches. 800
Jillson, G M. 176 and 178 E 105th ...J Weber. Horses, Wagons. 500
Jung, William. 11 and 18 Hewett av, Washington Market....C Jung. Stands. 700
Kipp, J H. 29 W 3d ...H Stucke. Store Fixtures. 150
Kroeger, H M. 379 W 52d....E Moller. Horse, Wagon. 250

Kronenberg, Frank. 409 W 26th...J E Schmaltz. Grocery Fixtures. 300
Kasch, Morris....S I Kopelman. Horse, Wagon. 150
Krakower, David. 301 Broome....F & G Haag & Co. Barber Fixtures. 200
King, T J. 586 and 588 W 43d....M King. Horses. Trucks, &c. 2,000
Lh[illegible] & Traub. 91 Essex .. S Brand. Grocery Fixtures. 170
Mariotti, D. 34 Macdougal....I Greenwald & Bro. Butcher Fixtures. 300
Matthesius, J C. 148 8th... Lamson Consolidated S S Co. Register. 210
McLeod, J B. 86th st and 9th av....E W Everitt. Drug Fixtures. (R) 1,500
Miller, C R. 138th st and Lenox av....T Carroll. Horse, Truck. 200
Muller, Adam. 42 St Marks pl....J Weiss. Barber Fixtures. 30
Murphy, Michael. 156 E 30th....W B Davis. Coupe. (R) 600
Martin & Miller. 135th st and 8th av....A D Puffer & Sons. Soda Fixtures. 760
McKillop, Daniel. 424 West....J Lennon. Coal Cart. 75
Merlo, Alberto. 125 Greenwich av....A Schwaab & Son. Barber Fixtures. 240
Marmorstein, Max. 275 Delancey....J Newman. Butcher Fixtures. 150
Martens, Sophie. 86 Allen ...F Randall. Cigar Fixtures. 200
McArdle, Bridget. 639 W 131st....C B Morris. Horses, Wagons. 135
McCaffrey, Philip. 200 E 104th....P W Mooney. Oyster Market Fixtures. 125
Miller, William....M Armstrong. Coupe. 2,565
Moore, John. 552 Greenwich....J H Lippe. Coach. (R) 844
Mahrhoff, Hermann. 69 Dey....E Balling. Cigar Fixtures, &c. 1,000
Oberhauser & Blanchard. 40 West Broadway ....A C Manning. Machinery. (R) 815
Pampinelli, S. 38 Clinton pl....Archer Mfg Co. Barber Fixtures. (R) 58
Pins, Gustav. 112 Av C....M Weil. Barber Fixtures. 75
Pries, W H. 46 Watts....S Pries. Machinery. 3,307
Roossin, A. 264 Delancey... J Matthews Co. Soda Fixtures. 38
Reilly, Patrick. 146 and 148 Worth....E W Youmans. Machinery. 1,000
Raftery, Timothy, Jr. 516 W 50th....J Dahlman. Horse. 240
Schaefer, Henry. 150 Amsterdam av....Lamson Consolidated S S Co. Register. 225
Schneider, George....R J Foster. Trucks and Horses. 400
Shelut, Abraham. 166 Norfolk... B Lapidus. Butcher Fixtures. 110
Schmidt, J C. 518 W 48th....P A Roos Coach. 172
Sheffield, J R....New York Loan and Improvement Co. Car Float. Assign. 7,000
Same....same. Engines. Assign. 23,000
Same....same. Railroad Cars, &c. Assign. 67,590
Speer, J S....American Biscuit Co. Horse, Fixtures, &c. 1,813
Sullivan Bros. 150 W 17th....W C A Witt. Grocery Fixtures. 138
Schmolze, Charles. 88 Fulton....R Hoe & Co. Press. 2,000
Sovierie, Luigi. 7 Battery pl ..A Schwaab. Barber Fixtures. 80
Speciale, Pietro. 1567 Av A....A Schwaab. Barber Fixtures. 429
Stolpe, H E. 705 1st av ...J Fletz. Machinery. 900
Sussman, Samuel. 98 Orchard....J Kramer & Co. Wagon. 489
Sacks, Geo. 54 E 12th... J Silver. Jewelry Fixtures. (Corrects error in issue of Dec 19th.) 200
Schmidt, Elizabetha. 90th st and 1st av....M Geismann. Horses, Cows. &c. (R) 720
Smith, H P. 412 Lenox av....A Smith. Barber Fixtures. 200
Smith, Isaac. 84 South 5th av....Ivison, Blakeman & Co. Presses, &c. 4,000
Smith, Phillip. 217 W 61st....R Rainforth. Barber Fixtures. 17
Spencer, W F. 294 Broadway....A V Denis. Books. 1,200
Treay, Jos. 325 3d av....Archer Mfg Co. Barber Fixtures. (R) 115
Tallon & Stadtfeld. 202-208 E 89th....H Gorsch. Horses, Trucks, &c. 4,000
Tantalo, Gaetano. 241 E 111th....A Schwaab. Barber Fixtures. 188
Van Horne, H E. 444 6th av....J J Van Horne. Dental Fixtures. 1,000
Vinti, Edward. 1667 3d av... A Vinti. Barber Fixtures. 600
Varnat, Victor. 45 W 27th... Duparquet, H & M Co. Range, &c. 41
Viggiano, Antonio. 156 Park row....A Parziale. Barber Fixtures. 810
Willis, Henry....Kean & Lines. Coach. (R) 555
Wood, Susan A. 182 W 31st....J Dahlman. Horse, &c. 1,0[illegible]0
Willis, Henry....Keeler & Jennings. Coach. (R) 550
Williams, Kate. 407 E 89th st and 1278 Lexington av....D H Anderson. Horses, Fixtures, &c. (R) 1,800
Wurzel, H ...C A Sykes. Dental Fixtures. 154

BILLS OF SALE.

Alysando, P. 234 Division....D Rigisone. Barber Fixtures. 267
Bush, B & J. 47 Baxter... A J Beck ...Clothing and Fixtures. 1,000
Becker, K. 1212 1st av....J Becker. Paint Store Fixtures. 200
Bennett & Heldt. 96 Fulton....Shapiro & Levy. Tailor Fixtures. 200
Ferrero, Edward. Tammany Hall, E 14th st....H Kreykenbohn. Restaurant and Ball Fixtures. 9,000
Garbade, Louis. 91 Walker....L Oldenbuttel. Restaurant Fixtures. 1,800
Herman, Jacob. 784 11th av... W Mayer. Saloon Fixtures. 375
Lembo, Dominico. 59 Crosby ...R Zungalo. Grocery Fixtures. 200
Morris, Gouverneur....Belle S Morris. Furniture. 1
Moses, Raphael. 351 E 4th....S Moses. Furniture. 200
Petrus, Ella. 522 3d av....M Pendergast....Saloon Fixtures. 2,800
Pratt, R M....H D Mould. Horses, Ice Truck. 150
Rehfeld, C F, Jr. Foot E 136th....J W Rein. Horse. Milk Fixtures, &c. 408
Stolpe, H E. 705 1st av....V Huy. Machinery. 1,100
Stolpe, H E....V Huy. Machinery, &c. 1,100
Samuels, Philip. 1067 Park av....Fischer & Co. Grocery Fixtures. 42

hanks, J and D. 1569 Broadway....A Galbraith. Carpenter Shop Fixtures. 275
Schmidt, J C. 518 W 48th....J N Buck. Horses, Coaches, &c. 8,000
Spagianto, A. 12th st and Bowery....C Trivigno. Fruit Stand. 200
Tyrer, W E, & Co. 128 Maiden lane....J A Webb & Son. Rumsey's Bitters, Fixtures, &c. 600
Tyrer, W E....same. Rumsey's Bitters, Fixtures, &c. 1,036
Van Brunt, T C. 222 W 23d....L W Van Brunt. Furniture. 1
Whedon, W A....R M Platt. Horses, Ice Trucks. 50

ASSIGNMENT OF CHATTEL MORTGAGES.

Hinsdale, E C to M Armstrong. (Mort. given by C & E S Blunt, Aug. 12, 1891.) 287
Pins, Gustave to J Raduzuier. (A Rosenstock, Sept 8, 1891.) 118
Same....same. (A Ader, July 21, 1891.) 82
Same....same. (M Fuchs, June 25, 1891.) 72
Roberts, Thomas to G Ehret. (Neuman & Kern, Nov. 18, 1891.) 3,500
Schroeder Bros to T Theissig. (F Hattermann, Dec 5, 1891.) 150
Wunderlich, H to G Ehret. (Hedley & Priestley, Dec. 18, 1891.) 2,509

KINGS COUNTY.

DECEMBER 17 TO 22—INCLUSIVE.

SALOON AND RESTAURANT FIXTURES.

Bringmann, A. 885 Fulton....W Ulmer. (R) $1,500
Beirne, M. 175 Willoughby....Claus Lipsius B Co. (R) 150
Bradshaw, J. 633 6th av....Josie Hogan. 1,000
Brown, A. 696 Washington av....Claus Lipsius B Co. (R) 800
Capper, C. 442 Manhattan av ..T C Lyman & Co. (R) 1,000
Cassidy, C J. Bedford av and North 6th st.... I Roth. Bar and Fixtures. 1,100
Cauldeld, J. 258 Hamilton av M T Garvey. 530
Evers, B J and J J O'Brien. 357 Hicks....J Ruppert. 1,300
Foley, P B. 704 5th av ...Obermeyer & L. 1,140
Same....A Immig. 700
Frankel, H. 102 Gerry....Obermeyer & L. Pool Table, &c. 59
Goldbach, W. 79 Howard av....W Ulmer. (R) 1,500
Groth, H J. 1810 Fulton....J S Riley. 66
Gallagher, D F. 16 Bridge....Claus Lipsius B Co. (R) 300
Guenther, J. 54 Buffalo av, cor Atlantic av.... S Liebmann's Sons B Co. 900
Hansen, H. 910 Flushing av. ..H E Schwab. 400
Heavey, J. 246 Patchen av....Claus Lipsius B Co. (R) 1,193
Huber, W. 678 Flushing av....P Weidmann. (R) 600
Jackson, L. 466 Manhattan av....J C G Hupfel B Co. 800
Kallstrand, O B. 444 Atlantic av. J Giersdorf. 1,000
Keller, R. 40 Knickerbocker av....Burger B Co. 800
Kessler, J T. 679 3d av ...Claus Lipsius B Co. (R) 400
Kirchner, L. Rockaway av, cor Sackett st.... L I Brewery. 436
Klein, Charlotte. 205 Ewen... F Dentinger. Restaurant Fixtures. 400
Koemabl, Charlotte. 1604 Bushwick av... E Ochs. 800
Kraus, P. 258 Metropolitan av....M Seitz. 400
Lepler, R F. 66 Sumner av....Welz & Zerweck. 1,350
Lerch, E. 668 Flushing av... J C Klatzl. 250
Lindemann, C and J. 518 Court....H B Scharmann & Sons. 800
Mills, F P. 202 Broadway....Brunswick-Balke-Collender-Co. Billiard Table. 275
McCabe, B. 831 10th av ...L I Brewery. 4,000
Merrick, J. 387 Leonard....J Eppig. 490
Mayer, A. 155 Johnson av....E Ochs. 512
McAllister, C. 396 Manhattan av... M Seitz.(R) 3,000
Mellilo, V. 18 Whitwell pl....Claus Lipsius B Co. (R) 135
O'Donnell, J. 59 Hudson av ...Claus Lipsius B Co. (R) 300
Orato & Labreta. 45 Graham.... Ferdinand Munch Brewery. 250
Reardon, M A. 192 North 2d....Claus Lipsius B Co. 1,000
Rawley, C. 3270 Atlantic av Claus Lipsius B Co. (R) 55[illegible]
Regan, T and E Coleman. 48 Coney Island road ....M Seitz. (R) 250
Reid, J. 128 Church st, New York....Bernheimer & S. 1,500
Rcissey, Jr. 201 Throop av....Claus Lipsius B Co. 600
Roarty, C. 410 Willoughby av....Claus Lipsius B Co. (R) 500
Robbert, E. 592 De Kalb av....M Seitz. 800
Scholl, J. 152 Stone av. ..J Fallert B Co. 363
Schroeder, E and H. 73 Ralph av....P A Skelly. 350
Siciliano, J. 48 Front....India Wharf Brewing Co. 300
Spengler, F. 49 Morrell....Obermeyer & L. Pool Table, &c. 150
Schlauersbach, A. 331 Graham av....J Kress B Co. (R) 500
Schlichte, H. 40 West....Claus Lipsius B Co. (R) 2,000
Schmidt, C. 16 Havemeyer....S Liebmann's Sons B Co. 1,000
Schobel, H. 176 Union av....M Seitz. (R) 600
Schweinfest, J I. 123 Smith....Bachmann B Co. 2,300
Vaughan, C E. 494 5th av....Rubsam & H B Co. 600
Wilhelm, J. 78 Throop av....A Seitz. 1,000
Wilson, A and E Kojan. 1412 Bergen ...Berger B Co (Lim). 700
Woodington, T. 774 Grand....S Liebmann's Sons B Co. 1,000
Yunker, J. 1271 Myrtle av....Claus Lipsius B Co. 500

HOUSEHOLD FURNITURE.

Ackerly, H. 24 Conselyea....R M Walters. Piano. 300
Armfield, W W. 206 Sanford....B F Kilduff. 125
Bennett, E R. 19 Truxton....C Traum. 152
Best, F. 383 14th....Kendrick & Co 475
Boulden, N E. Bay 14th, New Utrecht....J Moriarty. 668
Bristol, G H. 594 Kosciusko....Kendrick & Co. 371
Brown, Emma. 145 Prospect....D Moriarty. 119
Beasley, A L. 229 Van Brunt....Ida M Cameron. 250
Burke, I. 196 South 2d....J A Luddy. 141
Carter, W A. 2 Hart....Platt & Conway. 479
Coburn, E W. 49 Dean....T E Green. 100
Cox, Margaret. 821½ Central av....Brooklyn F Co. 187
Crosby, Clara. 1197 Atlantic av ...L Z Murray. 110
Clark, Mary. 989 St Marks av....Kendrick & Co. 248
Comstock, Mrs D. 99 Lawrence ...C Traum. 162
Cullen, E. 356 South 5th. .Kendrick & Co. 172
Dunham, A L. 324 7th av....E C Hinsdale. 130
Darrigan, Mary. 1469 Dean....L Z Murray. 130
Deming, G D. 268 8th....R M Walters. Piano. 275
Doran, P F. 470 Sackett....Brooklyn F Co. 113
Doyle, J A. 224 Monroe....Brooklyn F Co. 452
Duffie, J W. 92 Decatur...H B Moore, secures rent 423
Ferguson, Florence. 99 Linwood....G E Querrier. 125
Fox, F L. 193 15th....H Mannes & Son. 226
Farron, T H. 28 St Marks av. ..J D Willis. 208
Firth, Eliz. 576 Lexington av....Kendrick & Co. 170
Gillespie, Jennie. 210 Smith....Kendrick & Co. 469
Gilmore, Sarah. Tompkins av....Kendrick & Co. 158
Gold, J. 184 Sheffield av....C Traum. 165
Greaves, W H. 699 Grand....A Schulz. 146
Hermons, Ellen F. 257 17th st....Platt & Conway. 278
Hamm, A W. 256 Nassau....McEnery & Co. 149
Harris, Mrs. 40 Powers....Mullins & Sons. 207
Hauser, E. 20 Locust....Mullins & Sons. 160
Hawkins, Emma C. 137 Nassau....J Welde, Jr, & Co. (R) 500
Hobbs, W H. 117 Java....Kendrick & Co. 200
Holt, Joseph. 1347 De Kalb av....Kendrick & Co. 286
Knoedler, C. 700 Bedford av....Kendrick & Co. 118
Lewis, W. 949 Grand... Kendrick & Co. 149
Mitchell, E H. 266 Skillman....Lincoln Ind and Guarantee Assoc. 200
McConnell, Fanny. 22 Canton....Manges Bros. 169
McGingan, H F. 878 Degraw....Brooklyn F Co. 147
Muller, Mattie. 44 Taylor.. Brooklyn F Co. 172
Miner, Imogene B. 1021 Bedford av ...Kendrick & Co. 129
Martin, Daniel. 309 President....Duressa Martin. 800
Newman, M. 15 Monroe....R G Lockwood's Sons. 109
Nohr, P. 89 Sandford....Kendrick & Co. 219
Overton, Margt F. 118 Putnam av....W A Overton. 1,000
Pauchaud, Eliz. 167 Sterling pl....Manges Bros. 195
Rogers, G W. 640 Hancock....Brooklyn F Co. 150
Rozand, J. 981 Myrtle av....Kendrick & Co. 325
Root, Annie J. 178 Stuyvesant av... Brooklyn F Co. 155
Roland, C. 182 9th....G H Brockway. 246
Smith, W G. 855 Lewis av....Brooklyn F Co. 175
Shepard, G A. 101 Clark....R A Ward. 250
Schmeid, W. 105 Knickerbocker av....Kendrick & Co. 122
Seith, J. 316 Central av....Kendrick & Co. 230
Skeele, F H. 244 Lexington av....F Holt. 100
Taylor, Eva C. 368 Jefferson....Kendrick & Co. 132
Toomy, H. 187 Franklin av....C Traum. 248
Van Slooten, Mary L. 52 Sidney pl....W Van Slooten. 4,000
Werner, Henry. 1536 Bushwick av....Kendrick & Co. 316
Whallon, S S. 391 6th av ...C E Pierce. 100
Wells, C W. 106 Fort Greene pl....Meehan & S. 760
Wurzweiler, Alice. 198 Clermont av....L Z Murray. 151
Young, E L. 21 St Andrews pl....Kendrick & Co. 141

MISCELLANEOUS.

Abrams, A....Sarah A Abrams. Horse, &c. 100
Annenberg, G. 436 Grand....Marvin Safe Co. Safe. 150
Annable, H D....J W Tufts. Soda Apparatus. (R) 400
Baylis, H. 1948½ Fulton....W Glier. Fish Business. 50
Betz, H & Cath. 209 Wallabout....A Wick. Bakery Fixtures. (R) 600
Blattmacher, H. 341 Flatbush av. ..National Cash Register Co. Register. 200
Bennett, R R. 251 Greene av....W B Davis. Coaches. (R) 2,250
Campbell, Adelaide. 446 Jefferson av....Thurber, Whyland & Co. Grocery Fixtures. 300
Conley, J. 552 Myrtle av ...J M Quimby & Co. Hearse. 810
Cummings, R J. 211 Snediker av....J P Rathbun. Press. 308
Caffaro, L. 986 De Kalb av....A Schwaab & Son. Barber Fixtures. 522
Cochrane, Ellen E. 1256 Bedford av....D Kelley. Shoe Store. 8,687
Emmerich F. 438 Flushing av....F Beck. Machine Shop. 1,000
Ferguson, J. 4 Burling slip, New York....W Fiske. Printing Fixtures. 300
Ferguson, G H P. 425 Fulton. ..S Knapp & Co. Upholstery Goods. 495
Frech, R and L Nielsen. 150 Freeman....J F Ihlenburg. Mineral Water Business and Fixtures. 1,500
Gallagher, M. 172 Pacific....W B Davis. Coupe. (R) 400
Same....W H Davis. Coach. (R) 500
Haggerty, F J, Jr....P Corell. Horses, &c. (R) 150
Hand, T....W B Davis. Coupe. (R) 250
Hancock, C. Atlantic and Montauk avs ...C B Rogers & Co. Moulder and Planer, &c. 825
Hickey, R M. 70 Columbia....J J Fruin. Horse, &c. 355
Huttenlocher, L. 678 6th av....P Gansel. Money Regulator. 50
Hogan, P H A. Belmont av....T Kiendl. Wagon. 150
Josenhaus, B. 648 Broadway....J W Tufts. Soda Apparatus. 475
Jahrsdoefer, O E. 101 Hamburg av....Nat Cash Reg Co. Register. 175
Kapp, C. 406 Union ...J F Schmadeke. Horses. 350
Keeney, F A. Carlton av....J A Trapp. Horse. 200
Krogmann, H. 298 Flushing av....J H Krogmann. Printing Office. 900
Lerch, H. 60 Knickerbocker av ...Archer Mfg Co. Barber Fixtures. 212
Martin, J R & Co. 838 Fulton....J W Tufts. Soda Apparatus. (R) 450
Meyer, O L. 184 Stuyvesant av....J W Tufts. Soda Apparatus. 682
Maguire, M F. 597 Vanderbilt av....G Hawkins. Butcher Fixtures. 600
Meyer, E. Atlantic av....H H Ruhl. Store Fixtures. 100
Mount, M. Leonard st....G B Hooton. Engine, &c. (R) 1,500
Miller, G. 1524 Gates av ...Marvin Safe Co. Safe. 110
Molinaro, A. 146 Jay... P Feraco. Barber Fixtures. 240
Neill, W A and Mary W. 422 De Kalb av ...J W Dearing. Drug Fixtures. 205
Nicklaus, F. Enfield st and South road .. C Nicklaus. Cows, Horses, &c. 1,500
Peters, J H. 1037 3d av....W Grandeman. Horses, Wagons. 500
Reed, G E. 631 Fulton.. .Lazell, Dailey & Co. Drug Fixtures. (R) 1,200
Reilly, P B and W C. 790 Fulton....J Morgan. Bottling Business. (R) 6,291
Rimmer, Isabella. 469 39th....M L Towns. Milk Route. 250
Rogers, W H H. 895 Union....C Potter & Co. Printing Press. 1,800
Rost, Jr, P. 152 Fulton... J Levy....Butcher Fixtures. 150
Simpson, W W. 596 Halsey....J Cunningham Son & Co. Wagon. 400
Speers, A. India st, cor Oakland st....P Kramer. Horse and Wagon. 50
Schneider, P. 5th av....G Ernst. Tailor Fixtures. 150
Scott, Lena. 1033 Bedford av....Helena Nabrung. Store Fixtures. 300
Sturcken, E P. 147 Franklin....P Schoendorf. Cigar Fixtures. 400
Sulzbach, M. Cleveland st and Wortmann av ....S & B Strauss. Cows. 1,400
Shaffer, B K. 153 Buffalo av.. A Barringer. Horses, &c. 200
Shelley, C C. 10 and 12 College pl, N Y....S Rowland. Printing Office. 4,153
Simonson, W B & Co. 227 Fulton....Eliz H. Valentine. Antique and Picture Store 500
The Active Building Club. 104 and 106 Boerum pl....H Gompert. Bakery. 500
Thissen, J. 184 North 8th....Cope & Co. Printing Office. 1,230
Varchetta, L. 127 Bleecker st....A Schwaab. Barber Fixtures. (R) 170
Wicht, I....F Reinheimer. Horse, Wagon, &c. (R) 125
Wehler, C. 367 7th av....L V Cortelyou. Milk Business. 200
Wolkerling, H. 674 Wythe av....W R Foster & Co. Bakery and Confectionery Fixtures. 400
Zenker, G and B Krause. 1557 Bushwick av.... Katharine Zenker. Iron Railing Business. 750

BILLS OF SALE.

Byrne, E H. 441 Grand av....M Carle. Locksmith Business. 50
Cook, A T. 1948½ Fulton....H Baylis. Fish Business. 50
Hemken, Mary. 337 4th .. F Wellmann. Grocery Fixtures. 1,700
Hugentobler, J. 199 Van Pelt av....Babetta Hugentobler. Furniture. 475
Langhauser, J. 22 Bushwick av....W Roth. Butcher Fixtures. 250
Mayer, C....J Reichle. Newspaper Route. 60
Muller, J. 1398 Fulton....J Geib. Saloon Fixtures. 380
Nolan, T. 100 Vesta av....Leibinger & Oehm B Co. Saloon Fixtures. 500
Nollman, W P. Sarah A. Nollman. Colt. 212
Reinhardt, Lina....C Greseking. Milk Route. 345
Vogel, S. 91 Moore....K Appelblatt. Grocery Fixtures. 156

ASSIGNMENT OF CHATTEL MORTGAGES.

Fiske, W to I C Ogden, Jr. (Mort given by J Ferguson, Dec 15, 1891.) nom

NEW JERSEY.

NOTE.—*The arrangement of the Conveyances, Mortgages and Judgments in these lists is as follows: the first name in the Conveyances is the Grantor; in Mortgages, the Mortgagor; in Judgments, the Judgment debtor.*

ESSEX COUNTY.

CONVEYANCES.

Allen, F B—L H B Haase, South 12th st.........$1,400
Alston, C B—C B Alston Co, e s Liberty st 111 n Greene st 27x81...........................3,400
Same——same, s s Columbia st 100 s Liberty 30 x100.................................5,500
Same——same, w s Green st cor Green st 90x 105...10,000
Alling, I A dec'd by exr—M E Young, Mulberry pl.......................................2,650
Atlas, Joseph—B Greenberg, w s Prince st 450 s Montgomery st 25x100....................3,500
Ball, Isaiah—E Whitney, n s Wright st 218 [e Broad 65x100................................12,600
Barnet, J G—J Denninger, Littleton av..........2,700
Becker, Charles—E M L Klemschmidt, High st. 1
Bell, A A—A J Smith, 4th av 1
Berg, Frederick, Jr—R Istel, Orange............1,500
Bloemecke, H J—F Rossmeisl, South Orange.. 525
Bogan, A E—A C Hottenroth, Broome st........1
Same——same, Broome st.........................1
Borchling, Charles—E M L Klemschmidt, High st...1
Brangs, P H—M A Pierson, North 9th st. 4,100
Brant, Antoinette—J Ten Eyck, Belleville.......1
Brennan, T F—M Pinta, Lock st.................1,600
Brown, H E—L Koch, Condit st..................1,650
Burke, John—T Gannon, West Orange.........100
Burnet, Timothy—C Parker, w s Webster st 251 n Crane s 25x103............................4,000
Burnett, William—J Clark, Broad st..............1
Cannon, Ellen—P Riley, n w cor Norfolk and Condit sts 52x100................................3,300
Chandler, Forrester—I Ball, East Orange......5,000
Clark, Mary—M E Amend, 1st st 1,010
Condit, E M—G R Harrison, West Orange.......500
Condit, E A et al—J C Smith, Orange............2,000
Conlan, John—P H Conlan, Lafayette st........1
Conlan, P H—J Conlan, Lafayette st.............1
Crowell, L F—C Rech, Prince st 2,250
Decker, J E—Bertha Peter, Frelinghuysen av,.. 900
Dey, J B—S Dey, Caldwell.........................5
Dodd, James—J Morley, Montclair...............1
Dooley, John—J J Dooley, Nesbit st............1
Dougall, W A—T J Mackinson, South 7th st... 2,400
Dowley, F D—Church of the Immaculate Conception, Montclair..........................16,620
Draper, F B—M H Brush, Montclair.............360
Duggan, Jane—B J Donahue, Condit st.........700
Dunn, Samuel—S Weil et al, 1st tract n e s New York av 175 s e N J R R av 112x100, 2d tract n s New York av 25x95...........................12,000

Dunn, J H—H J Heinrichs, Oriental pl ... 2,850
Eaton, M B—J C Peck, East Orange ... 600
Eisele, J C—C Koushaar, Clinton ... 495
Same——L Rozenwasser, Prince st ... 2,500
Farley, B M—J Duggan, Condit st ... 1
Same——M W Hickok, Treacy av ... 600
Garrabrant, Tunis—Montclair Water Co, Bloomfield ... 350
Gillen, E J—M A Gillen, s s Commerce st, 70 e Lawrence st 21x90 ... 5,500
Gillman, Christian—B W Tucker, Fairmount av ... 2,500
Glorieux, W L—F W Muller, Irvington ... 1
Granite State Provident Assoc—G Schoemer, Sanford st ... 688
Granniss, John—J H Barton, Livingston ... 1,000
Guthrie, S M—L C Schliep, South 4th st ... 1
Haase, L H B—T Herrmann, South 13th st ... 150
Harrison, J D et al—A McGrath, Orange ... 450
Heath, S R W—R Hahne, n s Spruce st 288 w Clinton av 93x106x20x98x101x25 ... 6,452
Hemingway, I A—C Kahl, Caldwell ... 700
Hennings, A F—C J Hennings, Abingdon av ... 1
Hottenroth, A C—T Bogan, Broome st ... 1
Same——T Bogan, Broome st ... 1
Howard Savings Inst—S R Calvin, Jr, Jackson st ... 2,300
Hoyt, Charles—C Parker, High st ... 200
Johnston, William—S Dey, Caldwell ... 700
Jube, J P—First Congregational Church, Clinton av ... 1
Keasbey, A Q—P P Griffin, South 9th st ... 650
Kehoe, Nicholas—C Burns, Oxford st ... 1
Kent, R E—J J Ghegan, w s Garside st 372 n 4th av 25x100 ... 3,200
Kilroy, Thomas—J S Carlson, Montclair ... 11,000
Knapp, M A—S L V Orden, East Orange ... 30,000
Ledig, Louisa—L S Haase, 16th av ... 25
Lemassina, Lillian—State B and L Assoc, Washington av ... 6,000
Same——same, Irving st ... 2,000
Lister, J C—R Wyatt, w s Broad st 395 s Harvey st 20x100 ... 4,000
Littell, V M et al—J H Armitage, s e cor Thomas and Dawson sts 100x150 ... 3,000
Loughran, Thomas—W J Gilmore, Bloomfield ... 1
Matthews, C B—I Ball, n s Wright st 218 e Broad st 65x100 ... 12,000
McCracken, J H—S A Chandler, Stone st ... 1,200
McGregor, A H—R H Sayre, Salt Meadow ... 3,500
Moore, H C—A W L Wirz, Ferry st ... 1,500
Moore, Mary—J P Clark, Park st ... 1
Morley, John—M Dodd, Montclair ... 1
Muller, F W—W L Glorieux, Irvington ... 1
Munn, J W—C T Seymour, Prospect st ... 1
Myers, David—J W Apgar, East Orange ... 1,938
Nevins, Thomas—J D Orton, East Orange ... 1,500
Ollen, F B—J P Clarke, s s East Park st 154 East Pine st 22x138 ... 10,000
Orange Heights Land Co—G E Adams, West Orange ... 1
Parker, John—P Schmidt, Quitman st ... 400
Peck, Cyrus et al—H C Hinds, East Orange ... 1,750
Pohle, George—L S Haase, 19th st ... 50
Rigg, Daniel—M A Dongall, South Orange ... 950
Roberge, F P—M N Winne, Penna av ... 1
Same——same, Penna av ... 1
Sanger, R M—East Orange Building and Loan Assoc, East Orange ... 13,200
Sayre, R H—A H McGregor, Salt Meadow ... 1
Scheider, Henry—A Kaiser, Lentz av ... 650
Schliep, L C—M R Corwin, South Orange ... 1
Schoemer, Charles—Teutonia B and L Assoc, New York av ... 1,400
Smith, J C—J Atlas, w s Prince st 450 s Montgomery st 25x100 ... 3,400
Stager, S B—E Teeter, Franklin ... 5,250
Stryker, A A—I Firth, East Orange ... 7,300
Taylor, A E—C Bishop, Caldwell ... 2,256
Taylor, H B—S S Battin, 3d av ... 2,250
Ten Eyck, Jan—A Brant, Belleville ... 1
Towne, J W—C T Miller, East Orange ... 1
Vanderhoof, William—S Dey, Caldwell ... 125
Van Ness, C E—N L Williams, e s Mt Pleasant av 208 n Clark st 25x100 ... 5,500
Van Riper, P H—W H Paxton, Montclair ... 1
Same——same, Montclair ... 1
Wallace, J P—M Dunlevy, Belleville ... 65
Way, M J—C Yule, Plane st ... 187
Weatherby, Harry—O N Kempf, Franklin ... 275
Weber, Jacob—D Koller, Bruce st ... 1,100
Wells, E E—N H White, 3d st ... 1,000
White, N H—E E Wells, 3d st ... 1,025
Wightman, R C—E Schreiber, South 11th st ... 235
Williams, Aaron—W Pierson, Salt Meadows ... 60
Williams, Caroline—W Parkinson, West Orange ... 159
Wilson, J C—R H Sayre, Newark Meadows ... 3,030
Same——Lehigh Valley Terminal Railway Co, Murray st ... 495
Same——same, Newark Meadows ... 622
Same——same, Murray st ... 485
Same——same, Newark Meadows ... 1,177
Same——same, s w s Murray st and centre line Wheeler Place road, 1,125x149x1,192x109 ... 5,622
Same——N Y Bay R R Co, Astor st ... 372
Wirz, H P A et al exrs—S Dunn, N Y av ... 1
Woodruff, J T—E S Wilcox, Clinton ... 1

MORTGAGES.

Adams, G E—G C Freeman, West Orange ... 1,250
Allen, J W—W F Hamilton et al, South Orange ... 2,500
Apgar, J W—D Myers, East Orange ... 900
Armitage, J H—Fireside B and L Assoc, Thomas st ... 4,000
Bach, Rosa—M Plaut, South Orange av ... 2,000
Banks, J H—J H Gruner, Montclair ... 325
Barton, J H—J Granniss, Livingston ... 800
Buck, S L—N B Thompson, Carteret st ... 2,000
Burkhart, M C V—T P Lindsley, Belleville ... 600
Callaghan, Mary—S Doughty et al exrs, Warren st ... 500
Carlson, J S—T Kilroy, Montclair ... 6,000
Church of Our Lady of Orange Valley—Mutual Life Ins Co, Orange ... 28,000
Clarke, J P—F B Allen, Park st ... 9,000
Cobb, Frank—Fourteenth Ward B and L Assoc, Vanderpool st ... 800
Conlon, P H—M L Ward trustee, Lafayette st ... 2,000
Connett, Rose—Montclair B and L Assoc, Montclair ... 400
Creyling, E L—B Coyne, East Orange ... 385
Crowder, A J—J A Skinner, North 9th st ... 2,400
Day, R C—E M Ball, East Orange ... 4,500
Dean, Frederick—M H Pennington, East Orange ... 2,550
Dittig, H A—A Dittig, Montclair ... 3,100
Dodd, W B—J W Pinkham, Montclair ... 3,000
Donnelly, Timothy—M Stoutenburgh, Bank st ... 2,500
Dovey, J J—S D Hopping, Bird av ... 2,500
Edward, Sophia—Firemen's Ins Co, Montclair ... 1,500
Elliot, E C—W H Douglas, East Orange ... 3,000
Fisk, F N—Firemen's Ins Co, East Orange ... 4,000
Force, A C—G O Post, Orange ... 2,200
Gallogher, J D—W Richards, Bloomfield ... 7,000
Gerst, Julius—C Barkhorn, Hunterdon st ... 400
Ghegan, J J—The Enterprise B and Assoc, Garside st ... 2,500
Granel, Ignatz—J Oertle, Kinney st ... 2,800
Greenberg, Benjamin—J C Smith, Montgomery st ... 1,000
Haag, J B—E Abeles, Orange ... 1,065
Hahne, Richard—C C Heath, Spruce st ... 5,000
Heginbotham, T B—F Kurzman, Monroe st ... 500
Higgins, Thomas—J Fairbanks et al exrs, Bloomfield ... 700
Hinds, H C—The Mechanics' B and L Assoc, Grove st ... 3,600
Hinrichs, H J—J H Dunn, Oriental pl ... 1,800
Hoeler, P J—F C Wackenhuth, 13th av ... 4,000
Isler, Abraham—A C Hoffman, Livingston st ... 175
Istel, Robert—F Berg, Jr, Orange ... 1,000
Kearney, J A—F Berg, Jr, Orange ... 250
Kleinschmidt, E M L—S W Grant, High st ... 3,500
Matthews, A L—Orange Savings Bank, Orange ... 800
Meyer, F F—C A Flammer, Clinton ... 3,000
Michel, Isidor—G Trautwein, Prince st ... 900
Paxton, W H—F J Love, Montclair ... 2,000
Pilkington, Bridget—A M Leiblach, Newark st ... 1,000
Pinta, Michael—T F Brennan, Lock st ... 800
Pierson, M A—A W Hayes, North 9th st ... 2,000
Reeb, Conrad—L F Crowell, Prince st ... 2,500
Reilly, J E—J H Jackson, South 9th st ... 600
Richardson, H W—G Booth, East Orange ... 4,000
Rozenwasser, Leopold—J C Eisele, Prince st ... 200
Same——Lincoln B and L Assoc, Prince st ... 2,200
Schneider, Joseph—F Bonykamper, Jr, Komorn st ... 100
Steinmetz, John—The Security B and L Assoc, Clifford st ... 100
Stimis, J B—W Mendel, Sylavan av ... 500
Taylor, W A—Roseville B and L Assoc, North 9th st ... 200
Taylor, W M—Montclair B and L Assoc, Montclair ... 600
Van Orden, G O—S C Savage, East Orange ... 15,000
Watson, Joseph—Eighth Ward B and L Assoc, Summer av ... 4,600
Wilde, James—W Pierson, Salt Meadows ... 800
Wirz, A W L—S B Jackson, Ferry st ... 1,500
Wright, Asahel—H B Taylor admr, Broad st ... 500
Zeh, Charles—T Cox, South 7th st ... 1,900

CHATTEL MORTGAGES.

Andrews, C K—G Krueger, saloon ... 350
Best, R C—Essex Co Brewing Co, saloon ... 590
Bragaw, Henry—Essex Co Brewing Co, saloon ... 350
Branchi, Victor—J Walsh, furniture ... 455
Dougherty, J H—F Lesiewiski, saloon ... 375
Doran, Cornelius—G Krueger, saloon ... 488
Dowling, G B—E D McKay, horses, &c ... 1,000
Dyer, C O—Brooklyn Furniture Co, furniture ... 223
Duerr, John—G A Richards, machinery ... 270
Franz, Adolph—J L Adams, saloon ... 1,100
Hellander, J E—T F Johnson, horse ... 87
Hirschfield & C—B Greenberg, safe ... 75
Same——I Holder, safe ... 60
Same——F Becker, safe ... 60
Hirshfield & Co—E H Ewest, safe ... 68
Johnson, T V et al—E C Moore et al, hides, oils, &c ... 11,522
Johnson, T V—M E Claredon et al, hides, oils, &c ... 11,522
Kaiser, Wm—C Figenspan, saloon ... 215
Kehoe, John—Wilkinson, Gaddis & Co, horses ... 920
Kelly, Benjamin—Essex Co Brewing Co, saloon ... 600
Krueger, Louis—Mueller & Schmidt, saloon ... 359
Krueger, Nathan—E F Hoffman, chandeliers ... 337
Marchbank, L A—D Richardson, furniture ... 500
Miller, W E—P Ballantine & Sons, saloon ... 350
National Water Proof Fibre Co—B Moore, machinery ... 4,000
Rhinesmith, W A—J O'Rourke, horse ... 150
Roth, George—Essex Co Brewing Co, saloon ... 189
Rumyon, O E—A B Bright, furniture ... 1,000
Sauer, W J—C Fegenspan, machinery ... 450
Schiffer, Kate—F Will, store fixtures ... 240
Smith, James—P Reilly, horses, &c ... 285
Splitt, W N—J Walsh, furniture ... 316
Spirato, Afonso—F Lesiewiski, saloon ... 400
Stickle, S H—F B Apperson, horse ... 118
Thurber, H F—Wm A Brown, furniture ... 1,500
Tower, W L—V F Lecog, wagon ... 100
Williams, S S—C H Huntsman, wagon, &c ... 1,000

JUDGMENTS.

Bowers, H B—F H Coyle ... 284
Brown, C J—The State of New Jersey ... 1,000
Dwyer, John—L M Smith ... 3,175
Gould, H D—G A Williams ... 359
Greenberg, Katie—The State Banking Co ... 282
Kitchell, Farrand—O C Campbell ... 1,315
Lissberger, Lazarus et al—New York, New Haven & Hartford R R Co ... 4,641
Muchmore, Ward W—Eppens, Smith & Newmann Co ... 783
Murray, John—P Ballantine & Sons ... 397
Newark Passenger Railway Co—C Ebling admr ... 5,000
Standard Cash Register Co—M Worn ... 559
Stone, Alexander—H Feelig et al ... 354
Weaver, William—C L Black ... 294

HUDSON COUNTY.

CONVEYANCES.

Adeling, J H—J Cereghino, Hoboken ... $400
Beggane, M J—D McLaughlin ... other consid and nom
Bennett, Amarinth E and C E by sheriff—W Newton ... 3,000
Birdall, Jane E—C J Cronan ... 625
Bumsted, W G—Bessie M Toffey ... 5,500
Bumsted, Mary A—T H Speir ... 2,250
Cereghino, Joseph—Anna E Voorhees, Hoboken ... 525
Chadwick, Adeline J—G W Wright, Hoboken ... 200
Condict, H V—Caroline P Hudson ... 8,350
Conway, John—Carrie L Weser, Union ... 750
Crontes, David—W S Miller, North Bergen ... 300
Crothers, Sarah J et al by sheriff—J E Andrus ... 4,000
Davis, E A—D J Van Horne, Union ... 800
Ducker, G J—Mary Gahagen, Hoboken ... 4,050
Durkee, John—Margaret McCourt, West Hoboken ... nom
Eagney, W L—P McCall, Harrison ... 1,200
Edelstein, John—Mayor and Aldermen ... 250
Egbert, T K—M Simmons ... 600
Fuller, J E—Carrie F Halstead, Kearney ... nom
Fuller, L N—C H Rahs, Hoboken ... nom
Gahagan, J C—G J Ducker, Hoboken ... 4,050
Geistwert, T E—T McEwan, Jr ... 650
Grace, Annie—D Lewis ... 4,100
Greene, H C—Nellie F Bennett, Kearney ... 1,050
Hall, G J—Elizabeth A Snow ... 675
Halstead, Carrie F—L W Lindbloan, Kearney ... 1,000
Hayden, Margaret by sheriff—Pamrapo B and L Assoc, Bayonne ... 200
Henderson, J W—W Jenks, Kearney ... 5,800
Hentage, Alfred—Elizabeth Schleiermacher ... 700
Herbert, James—The Joseph Dixon Crucible Co ... 5,000
Honiss, John—I V Dorland, Kearney ... nom
Hoppe, August—J Stein, Union ... 2,500
Jerardi, P A—A V Eckardt ... 4,400
Jaeger, E H—H Jaeger, West Hoboken ... 800
Jones, J M—D Shea ... 2,150
Kennedy, William—P Bellezza, Hoboken ... 10,000
Kelley, Kate—Kate Trembley, Bayonne ... nom
Krieger, Chas—J Sutherland, Union ... 250
Kuppler, Jacob—H Stolz, North Bergen ... 1,800
Lembeck, Florence and Anna F Wood et al, by special master—A McCarty, Bayonne ... 240
Luxton, Susan—P D Shreve, West Hoboken ... 2,100
McCourt, Jno—J Durkee, West Hoboken ... nom
McGee, Flavel—W G Muirhead ... nom
McKenna, Annie—W L Eagney, Harrison ... nom
Miller, William—Anna E Campbell, North Bergen ... natural love and affection and nom
Monaghan, John—H F Kiernan, West Hoboken ... 500
Muirhead, W G—Julia R McGee ... nom
Murray, D J—H Aeudes, Bayonne ... nom
Nason, Annie S by admr—H L Emerson ... 3,750
Nason, J S by att'y——same ... 3,750
Newmann, Henry—G Neumann ... 775
Neumann, Gustav—H Neumann ... 3,060
Niles, W N—Sarah Diehl, Union ... 1,500
North Jersey Land Co—L Haasman, Kearney ... 1,900
Pullman, C G—D J Murray, Bayonne ... 207
Reuter, Wilhelm—W Deidloff ... 240
Richards, C P—J Reagan, North Bergen ... 1,200
Rodden, Mary and T H by sheriff—Jennie L Tice ... 500
Rudiger, J H—C Oschi, North Bergen ... 375
Schleiermacher, Christian—A Heritage ... 700
Schneider, Franz—J Skelly, Union ... 800
Schultz, Otto—S Dorfmuller, West Hoboken ... 200
Seekamp, Herman—J Knight ... 100
Seeley, J M—D Cronter, North Bergen ... nom
Siegfried, Adam—J V Shelley, West Hoboken ... 900
Smith, Jeremiah—Kate Trembley, Bayonne ... nom
Sofield, G A—J Cummings ... 500
Same——A M Fuller ... nom
Selin, Henry by sheriff—F C Hansen, Guttenberg ... 400
Symes, Matilda—Margaret E Evans, Union ... 425
The Northern Railroad Company—F Hall, North Bergen ... 300
The Pleasant Home Co—C H Hornby ... 3,900
Van Buskirk, J H—Cecilia M Coffin, Bayonne ... 3,300
Van Horne, D J—J H Symes, Union ... other consid and nom
Von Drehle, Herman by exr—G Roman, Weehawken ... 1,400
Vreeland, Marie A—J H Van Buskirk, Bayonne ... ——
Weed, W S—The Mayor and Aldermen ... 5,800
Wright, G W—F N Eberhard, Hoboken ... 400

MORTGAGES.

Akerly, Edgar—Trustee Cecile Tounele, Bayonne, 3 years ... 200
Beecky, Frank—P Rademan, 5 years ... 2,150
Bellezza, Pietro—W Kennedy, Hoboken, 5 years ... 9,000
Bennett, Nellie F—H C Greene, Kearney, 2 years ... 900
Blachouskie, Stanslaus—J Edelman, Bayonne, 1 year ... 150
Blackshaw, J F—J H Woodhouse, 1 year ... 400
Brady, Stephen—Hudson City Savings Bank, 1 year ... 1,000
Coffin, Cecelia M—J H Van Buskirk, Bayonne, 3 years ... 500
Corell, H R—J Cook, 1 year ... 3,500
Coughlin, Mary E—Hudson Trust and Savings Inst, Hoboken, 3 years ... 1,800
Davison, Clara I—W V V Mabou, Hoboken, 3 years ... 2,000
Diehl, Sarah—W W Niles, Union, 1 year ... 1,000
Eckardt, A V—Pavonia B and L Assoc, installs ... 4,000
Ellias, John—Centreville B and L Assoc, Bayonne, installs ... 2,000
Fabula, Stephen—Centreville B and L Assoc, Bayonne, installs ... 2,400
Fischer, Henry—Trustees of Stevens Institute of Technology, Hoboken, 3 years ... 3,500
Griffin, W F—Guard Maud Moorley, 1 year ... 430
Goldsmith, John—H Wemcke, 1 year ... 2,200
Grosch, William—Hoboken Land and Improvement Co, Hoboken, 2 years ... 325
Hansen, F C—Lena Wolff, Guttenberg, 3 years ... 1,450
Hord, V G—Mary F R Johnston, Kearney, 1 year ... 1,000
Hornby, C H—Pleasant Home Co, 5 years ... 3,050
Jaekle, Chas—The New Jersey Title Guarantee and Trust Co, Bayonne, installs ... 2,000
Kato, Catharine—D H Baker, 1 year ... 4,000
Kelly, Kate—Kate Trembley, Bayonne, 3 years ... 825
Kuchgessner, Theodore—J Schmitt, West Hoboken, 1 year ... 800
Lang, George—H Neleb, Union, 4 years ... 2,000
Leiser, John—J C Schlachter, installs ... 3,000
Lutgen, Mathias—J E Andrus, installs ... 1,500
Lyons, Mary—The Howard Savings Inst, Harrison, 1 year ... 3,600
Maresell, Sarah J—Mary L Kelley, Hoboken, 1 year ... 500
McSweeney, Cornelius—Crescent M B and L Assoc, installs ... 1,600
Mecabe, Sarah H—Lizzie T Lewis, 1 year ... 2,500
Morrison, G F—M Ward, Harrison, 2 years ... 140
Mount, W B—D Reardon, 1 year ... 500
Neumann, Henry—H Newman, 3 years ... 3,000
O'Neil, W M—Bayonne B Assoc No 2, Bayonne, 2 morts, each $2,400, installs ... 4,800
Osche, Chas—J H Rudiger, North Bergen, 3 years ... 300
Reilly, B J—J R Wortendyke, 5 years ... 325
Richters, J F—H E Richters, Kearney ... 4,000
Roman, Geo—Exrs H Von Drehle, Weehawken, 5 years ... 1,000
Schreves, P D—Hoboken Bank for Savings, West Hoboken, 4 morts, each $1,500, 2 years ... 6,000
Schleiermacker, Elizabeth—A Heritage, 3 years ... 1,700
Schultz, Otto—Hoboken Bank for Savings, West Hoboken, 2 years ... 5,000
Schuler, A W—Howard Savings Inst, Kearney, 1 year ... 7,000
Schwarz, Christian—Hoboken Bank for Savings, West Hoboken, 2 years ... 5,000
Sharrock, John—Elizabeth Porepp, 4 years ... 400
Shea, Daniel—J N Jones, 5 years ... 1,650
Snow, Elizabeth A—G J L Hall, 3 years ... 500
Speir, T H—Cathalina Van Winkle, 1 year ... 1,500
Stein, John—A Hoppe, Union, 3 years ... 1,550
Stolz, Henry—J Kuppler, North Bergen, 3 years ... 800
Toffey, Bessie M—W G Bumsted, installs ... 2,000
Same——Delia A Bumstead, 2 years ... 3,000
Van Buskirk, J H—Centreville B and L Assoc, Bayonne, installs, 2 morts, each $2,400 ... 4,800
Vultee, F P—Annie E Hay, Kearney, 1 year ... 1,000
Wetzel, Valentine—T G Hufnagel, Union, 2 years ... 1,000
Wolbert, F C—D D Fleming, 1 year ... 1,500
Wynn, Martin—The People's B and L Assoc, Kearney, installs ... 200
Zuelch, Louise C—C F Ruh, Union, 5 years ... 1,000

CHATTEL MORTGAGES.

Ackerman, Bell A—F G Smith, piano.......... 224
Allen, Dora W, New York—L Baumann, furniture.......... 105
Behrens, Frederick, Guttenberg—D Bermes, saloon.......... 500
Bongartz, F A—J W Tufts, soda water apparatus.......... 675
Same——same, soda water apparatus.......... 675
Britton, Carrie—The Restaurant Furniture Co, restaurant fixtures.......... 142
Conor, Henrietta, Bayonne—F G Smith, piano.. 250
De Groff, Jessie V—F G Smith, piano.......... 315
Elmdmeyer, Henry and Frederick Luhrmann, Seacaucus—W C Engelbrecht, horses, wagons, harness, 900 hot-bed sash, hogs..... 2,000
Fallahan, K J—G Ehret, saloon.......... 2,500
Farley, Ellen—F G Smith, piano.......... 225
Gautier, T B and T J Toole, as T B Gautier & Co—Hoboken Coal Co, horses, wagon and harness.......... 3,500
Greenwood, Samuel—L Targuilo, canal boat P W Rector.......... 325
Hild, L P, Bayonne—F G Smith, piano.......... 360
Honegger, John, Union—The William Peter Brewing Co, pool table.......... 250
Howells, Hannah, Bayonne—F G Smith, piano.. 165
Knox, Emma J—F G Smith, piano.......... 250
Lanston, James—F G Smith, piano.......... 115
Maguire, Maggie—F G Smith, piano.......... 240
Mastres, Gertrude—The Bavarian Brewing Co, saloon.......... 600
Miller, Frederick, Weehawken—The William Peter Brewing Co, saloon.......... 600
Moore, W M, Harrison—L Baumann, furniture.. 113
Moran, Daniel—L Gibney, coal business.......... 500
Nill, Conrad and Charles Klumpp, Guttenberg—J Quatlando, horse, wagon, butcher fixtures 800
O'Neill, J S, Union—The William Peter Brewing Co, saloon.......... 700
Roehlke, Adolphe and Gustav Nenann—C Trefz, saloon.......... 209
Schims, Dorothea and Rudolph, Union—W Griff, shoe store.......... 200
Schindele, Frederick—C Hammer, horse, wagon, harness, ices and coffee spices.......... 400
Shannon, James and Maria B his wife—T Bannahan, saloon.......... 750
Stratton, Louise T—F G Smith, piano.......... 250
Verdon, Christopher M, Hoboken—F A Verdon, livery business, horses, coaches, &c.......... 7,000
Vreeland, N G—F G Smith, piano.......... 250
White, E J and V P, as White & Co—Lembeck & Betz Eagle Brewing Co, saloon.......... 1,200

BILLS OF SALE.

Cuthbertson, David, Kearney—W Cotter, horse, wagon and harness.......... 200
Delnsca, Guiseppe, Hoboken—F Burgo, barber shop.......... 390
Dilloway, G G, att'y in fact—N Jantzen, grocery business, horses, wagons, harness.......... 3,000
Liebler, Michael, Hoboken—Anne Topa, delicatessen store.......... 900
Schul, Caroline—J H Hople, cigar store.......... 290
Simmons, Jane H—Margaret Simmons, furniture..........other consid and nom
Trautwein, Philip, Hoboken—Emilie Trautwein, furniture..........love and affection and nom
Williamson, A D, Jersey City—E C Korner, grocery store, &c.......... 216

JUDGMENTS.

Allen, G O—P Corrigan.......... 77
Chevalier, Joseph—C H O'Neill.......... 206
Clausnitzer, John, W A Wright and Robert Nixon, et al—The Second National Bank of Hoboken.......... 202
Cuniff, John—W W Knight.......... 30
Edge, Isaac—R B Seymour.......... 81
Hobbs, George and William Stonier, partners as Hobbs & Stonier—C H O'Neill.......... 180
Kroencke, William—W J Karlsive.......... 110
Liebermann, Abraham—Jacob Hecht & Co. 2,223
Mohle, A F—H D Henchen. 1,027
Scofield, William, admr of and John Scofield—Kate Hart. 176
Veltman G A—Susan and Sarah Charles. 70

MECHANIC'S LIEN.

Gough, J Towner—J Carlin, contractor; R Muirhead, claimant. 844

BUILDING MATERIAL MARKET.

BRICKS.—There is not much change in the general condition of market for Common Hards; but such as it is, appears rather for the better. The holiday will naturally reduce actual consumption somewhat; but against that may be placed very small supplies, the arrivals being reported at less than for any corresponding period for a long while past. Navigation has found no check from ice, as was expected for a day or two last week; but the fogs have seriously interfered with traffic on the lower Hudson, and with a shut off by manufacturers in the Up River district shipments were cut right down. Upon such a basis sellers naturally had some advantage, and while the general line of valuation is not raised; there has been greater strength shown, especially on the low grades. Last week's surplus, to which we called attention, is understood to have been pretty well worked off, quite a number of barge loads having been taken by dealers with the understanding that they are to be covered and held until called for. Jersey stock of the average makes still finds only poor attention on this market, but the choice and favorite brands have custom, and are commanding $5.00 per M. Pales have as a rule remained under neglect and nominally unchanged in cost, with advantage principally in buyers' favor.

LATH.—No further quotable change in price has taken place, but the full figure of last week is sustained without difficulty, and all offerings seem to have promptly found custom. Some few additional arrivals of spruce lath came in coastwise, and there has been a million Canadian pine sold for rail shipment as soon as possible with all the business at $3 per M. Considerable custom is still looking for stock and on one or two lots available for negotiation there is a tendency to ask 1½@2c. fuller rates.

LIME.—There did not appear to be much, if anything, really new upon the market. Some demand has prevailed and it took off a portion of the supply at former rates, with the tone quite generally called steady, but there is no basis upon which sellers could calculate upon gaining further advantage. Indeed a little stock is hanging around unsold, and should there be an inclination to realize upon it the effect upon value would be none of the best.

LUMBER.—It has been a moderate deal all around, and on both the retail and wholesale market there was evidently no more business being done than called for by the most positive necessity. The comparatively open weather down to date has permitted the pushing forward rather more work than calculated upon and increased the volume of deliveries on contract, but brought out no really new orders, though there is said to be some figuring over parcels that will be wanted after the opening of the year. Some coastwise arrivals have made basis for a little business in bulk lots of stock, and car loads are occasionally sold; but the seller had to do about all the negotiating, as there is practically no open, natural demand at the moment. Exporters are looking for coarse, cheap stuff, but without much avidity.

Eastern Spruce as it has come to hand, found a market, but in more or less irregular manner, as there was really no natural inquiry, and the success of receivers in placing cargoes was due to knowledge of just who might happen to want them or to shrewdness in hunting around after custom. Prices were naturally a little variable under the circumstances, but, taken on the general range, no quotable changes have occurred, and the position as a whole may be called steady, with fair chance for support so long as supplies do not increase. There is no room for an increased offering however.

Piling meets with some little attention even at this season, but not enough to create any animation, and with a few arrivals sellers gained no advantage. Still most of the supply is in good hands, and owners think well enough of it to ask about former rates, with considerable showing of steadiness.

Hemlock here is still meeting with only moderate uncertain attention, and while steady enough so far as it goes, the market does not amount to much. Agents, however, are fairly well satisfied with what they are doing in other localities, especially throughout this State, and have an idea custom will continue along in very good form, anticipating some raising of the line of value at the meeting of manufacturers soon to be held.

White Pine in a general way is called steady, with, however, not much business reported. Some car lot trade has been spoken of, but does not appear to have other foundation than a few odd parcels of stock on special order. Prices are steady, and on thick stuff very firm, as there is reported a small supply of uppers at all contributive points. From exporters there has been more or less inquiry, but they wanted stuff to fill West Indian orders in the main, and something to cost along about $18.00 per M. Reports from the theatre of logging operations contain nothing out of the ordinary run of information.

Yellow Pine stands about as before and operators generally claim that in the nature of things, under existing conditions, the local market must remain steady. It is simply under perfect control and without opposition or competition, yet with sellers desirous of nursing and expanding trade they are not disposed to advance cost to a point that would intimidate buyers. For certain work requiring heavy timber there are now several good-sized specifications under consideration. Advices from the South are supporting, but indicate that there will be supplies enough.

Carolina Pine has very little demand at the moment from this immediate vicinity; but agents report that they are picking up considerable trade with other localities and obtaining encouragement to hope that further orders will be forthcoming at regular stated intervals. Manufacturers are holding the position steady at the regular list rates.

Hardwoods are very much neglected, the distribution into consumption amounting to practically nothing at the moment, and dealers wanting scarcely anything in the way of assortment. There is, however, a fair disposition to give attention to anything choice and attractive in quality, especially in the way of such standard stock as quartered oak, poplar, etc., and there is hardly a doubt that first-class cherry could be promptly placed at the standing bid of $100 per M. Reports from primary sources convey the impression that this season's production will be kept well in hand until nat.ral inquiry calls for an increase.

GENERAL LUMBER NOTES.

THE WEST.

The Northwestern *Lumberman* as follows:

Logging operations are being prosecuted with great energy, the weather the main portion of the time having been favorable to skidding. In some districts it is claimed that the season in respect to skidding is a month ahead of what was accomplished in that operation last year at a like time, and that more logs will be ready for hauling when snow comes than last year when that process was begun. At the time this was written little snow had fallen in any of the pine regions of the north.

At Chicago:

One yard manager reports that his firm never had so much inquiry in December for lumber to be delivered after the first of January as this year. This is taken as an indication that the movement of stock will increase soon after New Year's. The prospect is such and the inquiry is so great that dealers are inclined to hold their stock at firm prices. As soon as the trade shall rise there will be so much inquiry for sorts that prices are likely to be advanced, especially on stock width boards, common and select strips, and nearly all sorts of dimension.

The call for car factory strips is becoming a pronounced feature of the demand. The cut-up saws are employed in the yards in the conversion of common strips into clear and select shorts for car work. This, with the usual demand for flooring purposes, will cause an extraordinary demand for common strips before the spring trade shall have fairly opened.

The Mississippi Valley *Lumberman* says that an element in the situation in the Northwest will undoubtedly be the result of the winter's work in the woods. Thus far there has been but little snow fall aud I'ttle hauling done. As a whole, December has thus far been mild and open. If it can be taken as an index of what is to follow the winter is to be an open one. If this is so there will undoubtedly be a large demand for lumber—that is, a large demand for the season—and before the mills again begin producing stocks will be badly broken. The output of the logging camps will be effected. The preparations thus far are upon an extensive scale. A great many logs have been skidded, and six weeks or two months of good hauling will mean a large input.

Referring to the hardwood trade the Chicago *Timberman* says:

The entire season of 1891, with the possible exception of the first two or three months, has been unsatisfactory to hardwood dealers, although last January they entertained high hopes of an active trade right through the year. Perhaps the fact that many of them had fixed their hopes so high may have had something to do with the extent of their disappointment, and they may feel better when the business of the year is closed up and a balance struck, but it is certain that the volume of trade has been less than it was a year ago.

This is particularly true in regard to oak. Last season the trade in this wood constituted about 60 per cent of the entire hardwood business of the market, and there was an especially active demand for quarter-sawed, while stocks were low and dealers had hard work getting in supplies rapidly enough to enable them to take care of their trade. This fall the conditions have been exactly reversed. Demand for oak has fallen off in greater proportion than for other staple woods, and all the local yards are well stocked with both plain and quarter-sawed.

But nevertheless prices are by no means in a demoralized condition, and prospects for the oak trade are not without promise of better prices and improved conditions. It is because of a strong conviction that oak will do better next season that local dealers are filling up all the available room in their yards with this stock. With a good demand early in the spring the surplus stock at interior points, which is now being handled by the commission dealers or shipped direct to the consumers, will soon be taken up; then the yard dealers' turn will come, and prices will advance sufficiently to pay him for carrying a heavy stock for several months.

GREAT BRITAIN.

The *Timber Trades Journal* gives report of recent auction sales as follows:

At London:

The American walnut logs for absolute sales were well competed for, and all disposed of at from 2s 1d to 2s 10d per foot cube, and the American oak logs ex Oranmore, were cleared at 18d without reserve.

At Glasgow:

U. S. walnut, ex Cadiz—108 logs, 15¾ in av sq, at 3s 9d to 6s, av 4s 3¾d; ex Govino—78 logs, 16¾ in av sq, 3s 1d to 4s 5d, av 3s 7d; ex Robinia—36 logs, 14¾ in av sq, 2s 1d to 3s 9d, av 3s 1½d; and ex Beaconsfield—52 logs, 15¾ in av sq, 3s 6d to 4s, av 3s 7½d; also 14 logs hickory, at 2s 8d per c ft; 40 logs U. S. oak, at 2s to 2s 2½d; 28 coffin oak planks—6½ to 18½ ft, 14-20x4, at 2s 4d; 1,265 quartered oak boards—9 to 16 ft, 5-20x1, 3s 2d and 3s 3d.

METALS.—Copper—Ingot has been placed with greater freedom because one of the leading companies has reduced its price and consented to part with the spot accumulation. It amounted to at least three million pounds, probably more, sold at or about 10½c., and will be delivered to consumers during January and February. This is by some thought to indicate about the price during opening months of the year, though it is said that outside lots are offered lower. On an average range of valuation we quote at 10⅜@10½c. for Lake, and 10@10¼c. for casting brands. Manufactured Copper is not very active and has a somewhat unsettled market owing to the reduced cost of crude material, but with a general tendency in buyers' favor. We quote as follows: Sheet, not above 30x72 in., 16 oz. and over, 25c.; do, 14 to 16 oz., 23c.; do, 12 to 14 oz., 24c.; do, 10 to 12 oz., 26c.; do, 8 to 10 oz., 28c.; do under 8 oz, 30c. Sheets longer than 72 inches add 1c. for 12@14 oz., 2c. for 10@12 oz, and 3c. for 8@10 oz. Sheets, not above 36x96 in., 16 oz and over, 22c.; do, 14 to 16 oz, 24c.; do, 12 to 14 oz, 26c.; do, 10 to 12 oz, 30c.; do, 8 to 10 oz, 33c. Sheets longer than 96 inches 22c. for over 32 oz, and add 1c. for 16 to 32 oz.; 3c. 14 to 16 oz.; 5c. 12 to 14 oz, and 18c. for 8 to 10 oz. Sheets, not above 48x96 32 to 64 oz, 22c.; do, 16 to 32 oz, 25c.; do, 14 to 16 oz, 27c. do, 12 to 14 oz, 29c.; do, 10 to 12 oz, 33c. Sheets wider than 48x96 and longer, 22@25c. for 32 to 64 oz. and over, 27@30c. for 16 to 32 oz, 29c. for 14 to 16 oz and 34c. for 12 to 14 oz. All bath tub sheets, per lb., 16 oz. 17c.; 14 oz, 29c.; 12 oz 31c.; and 10 oz, 35c. Bolt copper, ¾ inch diameter and over, 22c. Circles, 60 diameter and less, 3c. above price of sheets of same thickness; circles, 60 to 96 do do, 5c. do; circles, 96 do and over, 6c, do. Segment and pattern sheets, 3c. above price of sheets required to cut them from. Cold or hard rolled copper, 1@2c. per lb. above the foregoing prices. Copper bottoms, 26@32c. per lb. Iron—American Pig remains at about the old line of cost and shows a market barren of specially noteworthy or interesting features. Offerings without being urged are ample for all calls and to spare, as most buyers have contracts against enough stock for next year's delivery to make them feel comparatively easy. We quote at $17.00@18.00 per ton for No. 1 X foundry; $15.50@16.50 for No. 2 X do. and $14.00@15.00 for Gray Forge. Old material of all kinds has slow sale and an indifferent sort of market, with valuations about as before, but open to variation under negotiation. We quote at about $21.00@21.50 for old rails; $19.00@19.50 for No. 1 wrought scrap; $17.00@18.00 for cast scrap and $17.00@17.50 for car wheels. Manufactured iron has little or no demand from store, and there are few important contracts going to book at the moment, while on values a steady sort of feeling is quoted without tendency to buoyancy in any case. We quote Common Merchant Bar ordinary size, at 1.90@2c. from store, and refined at 2@2¼c; Rods, round and square, 2.10@2.30c.; Bands, 2.30@2.50c.; Norway Nail Rods 3¾@4c., and domestic sheet on the basis of 3.00@3.05c. for common Nos. 10@16. Other descriptions at corresponding prices, with 1-10c. less on large lots from cars. Steel rails are under negotiation to some extent for next year, and the outlook seems promising. About 1,120,000 tons had been sold for the eleven months to December 1st, with deliveries close, and most of the mills are in position to go right along with any work they may undertake. We quote standard sections $30 per ton at mill, with usual advance for delivery at tide water. Pig Lead has not shown much animation, but a fair deal was occasionally perfected and prices sustained upon comparatively easy basis. We quote at 4.30@4⅜c. per lb. The manufactures of lead are quoted at 7c. for Pipe, 7¾c. for sheet, 15c. for Tin-lined Pipe, and 37½c. for Block Tin Pipe. Pig Tin, on the whole, inclines to quietness. Consuming wants are small and speculation manifests a disposition to confine itself to immediate wants for the purpose of straightening out and settling old engagements. We quote at about 19.80@19.85c. for round lots, and 19.90@20c. for jobbing parcels. Tin Plate meets with about an ordinary call for immediate use and there is more or less doing in contracts for early future delivery with prices ruling about steady all around. We quote prices as follows: I. C. Charcoal, ½ cross assortment Melyn grade, $6.50@6.55, each additional X add $1.50; I. C. Charcoal, ½ cross assortment, Allaway grade, $5.80@5.85, each additional X add $1; Charcoal terne, M. F. grade, 14x20, $7.45@7.50; M. F. grade, 20x28, $15.00@15.05; Worcester, 14x20, $5.70@5.75; Worcester 20x28, $11.50@11.55; Dean grade, 14x20, $5.40@5.45; Dean grade, 20x28, $10.60@10.65; D. R. D. grade, 14x20, $5.25@5.30; D. R. D. grade, 20x28, $10.10@10.15; I. C. Coke, Penlan grade, $5.25@5.30; J. B. grade, 14x20, $5.35@5.40; I. C. Bessemer steel, squares, $5.75@5.80 basis; I. C. Siemens steel, squares, $5.85@6.00 basis. Spelter secures very fair average attention and prices are steady for all the best brands at least, with no surplus offering of stock. We quote 4.70@4.80c. for Common Western, according to brand.

NAILS.—Offerings continue plentiful, and in some cases slightly crowded, though we learn of no further recent decided modifications in the line of values. Buyers move about as usual, taking only enough stock for immediate wants and refusing to anticipate the future. We quote Cut at $1.45@1.50 per keg for car lots and $1.60@1.75 per keg for parcels from store for iron, and add 5@10c. per keg for steel; Wire, $1.70@1.80 at mills, and 2.00@2.10 from store.

PAINTS, OILS, COLORS, ETC.—Business in the majority of cases has been light and unimportant, and there is practically nothing new to say in regard to the general market. Some lines of prepared paints adapted to special uses have found very good attention, possibly somewhat ahead of the average for this month, but otherwise the deal was limited to such parcels as the immediate and imperative necessities of the moment called for. Prices hold pretty steady, however, as the general supply is well in hand and owners feeling under no obligation to force trading. The re-organization of the National Lead Trust into a stock company, under the laws of New Jersey, has in no way changed the workings of the combine, and old list prices and terms are adhered to. Association Corroders' rates stand as follows: Lead in oil in kegs and dry lead in kegs, in lots of less than 500 lbs., 7¼c. net; in lots of 500 lbs to 5 tons at one purchase, 7c.; 5 tons to 12 tons, one purchase, 5⅞c.; 12 tons and over, one purchase, 6¾c.; dry white lead in bbls. ¼c. per lb. less than price in kegs. Lead in oil 12½ lb. in tin pails, add 1c.; in 25 and 50 lb. tin pails, add ½c.; and in 1 to 5 lb. tin cans, assorted (100 lbs. in case) add 2½c. per lb. to keg price. Terms on lots on 500 lbs. and over, note or acceptance at sixty days, or 2½ per cent. discount will be allowed for cash paid within fifteen days of invoice date. To make either of the above required quantities any assortment of packages of white lead, red lead and litharge may be counted. The above quotations are free on board cars or boat at corroding point. Linseed Oil has undergone no change to speak of in price and the movement only moderately active for spot delivery, but there is believed to be considerable contracting for next season. We quote at general range at 35@40c. for Western, and 40@56c. for City. Spirits Turpentine remains just about the same. Demand is slow and cautious enough not to exceed immediate wants, but, with supporting influences from the South, holders somewhat firmly insist upon former rates and resort to no pressure to realize. We quote at 33½@34½c. per gallon, according to quality, delivery, etc.

TAR AND PITCH.—Business has been quite moderate and unimportant with little or nothing to suggest on the market beyond continued steadiness for values. We quote Pitch at $1.70@1.75 per bbl.; Tar at $2.15@2.40, according to quantity, quality and delivery.

ARCHITECTS—SURVEYORS.

MISCELLANEOUS

MISCELLANEOUS.

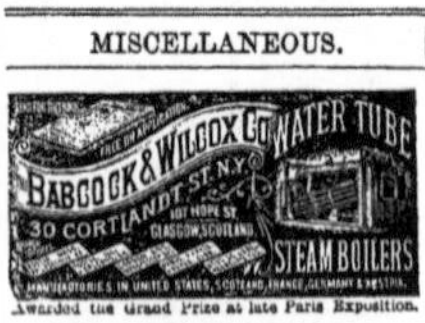

BUILDING MATERIAL PRICES

Rosewood, ordinary to good	per lb	3¼	@	4
Rosewood, good to fine	per lb	4½	@	5
Lignumvitæ, 8@12 in	℔ ton	12 00	@	25 00
Satinwood	per foot	15	@	30
Boxwood	per ton	15 00	@	19 00
PLASTER PARIS.				
Calcined, ordinary city	℔ bbl	—	@	1 50
Calcined city casting		—	@	1 60
Calcined city superfine		1 75	@	1 80
Calcined, Eastern		nominal		
PAINTS AND OILS.				
Chalk block	℔ ton	1 50	@	1 80
China clay	℔ ton	10 00	@	12 00
Whiting, gilders, &c	℔ lb	60	@	—
Whiting, common		40	@	—
Paris White, English		80	@	1 10
Lead, white, American, dry		6¾	@	7½
Lead, white, American, in oil, in tin pails		7¼	@	10
Lead English B. B., in oil		9	@	10
Lead, red		6¾	@	7½
Litharge		6¾	@	7¼
Ochre, French, dry		1⅛	@	1½
Venetian red, American			@	1¾
Venetian red, English, per 100 lbs		1½	@	1¾
Tuscan red		9½	@	11
Indian red		5½	@	7½
Vermilion, American, lead		11½	@	13
Vermilion, English		64	@	71
Carmine, American, No. 40		3 10	@	3 20
Orange Mineral		8½	@	10
Paris green		14	@	15¾
Sienna, lump		1¾	@	3½
Sienna, powdered		5	@	6½
Umber, Amer., raw and powdered		1¼	@	1½
Umber, Turkey, lump		2¼	@	3
Umber, Turkey, powder		3¼	@	4
Drop Black, English		12	@	13¾
Drop Black, American		8	@	11
Prussian blue		20	@	35
Ultramarine blue		7	@	25
Chrome green		8	@	25
Oxide zinc, American		4¼	@	5
Oxide zinc, French		7½	@	8¾
Glue, low grade	℔ lb	8	@	10
Glue, cabinet		12	@	14
Glue, medium white		13	@	15
Glue, extra white		17	@	20
Glue, French		10	@	22
Glue, English		10	@	15
Glue, Irish		12	@	13
Putty in bbls and ½ bbls		1 35	@	1 45
Putty in tubs		1⅝	@	1¾
Putty in tin cans		1½	@	2½
Putty in bladders		1⅞	@	2¼
Colors in oil as follows:				
Blue, Chinese		35	@	40
Blue, Prussian		20	@	45
Blue, ultramarine		12	@	18
Brown, Vandyke		7	@	12
Green, chrome		8	@	13
Green, Paris		16	@	18½
Sienna, raw		7	@	14
Sienna, burnt		7	@	14
Umber, raw		7	@	10
Umber, burnt		7	@	10
SLATE	Delivered at New York			
Purple roofing slate	℔ square	$7 00	@	7 50
Green slate		7 00	@	7 50
Red slate		12 00	@	15 00
Black Slate, Pennsylvania (at Jersey City)		4 25	@	5 50
STONE—Cargo rates, delivered at New York.				
Amherst freestone, in rough	℔ C ft.	$ 80	@	90
Berlin freestone, in rough			@	90
Berea freestone, in rough		—	@	85
Longmeadow freestone			@	75
Brown stone, Portland, Ct		1	@	1 10
Brown stone, Belleville, N. J		90	@	1 00
Granite, rough		80	@	75
Lime stone, buff		—	@	1 00
Lime stone, blue		—	@	1 05
NATIVE STONE.				
Common building stone	℔ load	2	@	3
Base stone, 2½ ft in length	℔ lin. ft.		@	
Base stone, 3 ft in length			@	
Base stone, 3½ ft in length			@	
Base stone, 4 ft in length			@	
Base stone, 4½ ft in length		1	@	1
Base stone, 5 ft in length		1 00	@	1 00
Base stone, 6 ft in length		2 [illegible]	@	3 [illegible]
SOLDERS.				
Extra		15	@	15¼
Half and half		14½	@	14¾
No. 1		12	@	12¼
No. 2		11½	@	11¾
TIN PLATES.				
I C charcoal, ½ cross ass't, Melyn grade		6 50	@	6 55
Each additional X, add $1.50.				
I C charcoal, ½ cross ass't, Allaway grade		5 80	@	5 85
Each additional X add $1.				
Charcoal terne, M F grade, 14x20		7 45	@	7 50
M F grade, 20x28		15 00	@	15 05
Worcester, 14x20		5 70	@	5 75
Worcester, 20x28		11 50	@	11 55
Dean grade, 14x20		5 40	@	5 45
Dean grade, 20x28		10 60	@	10 65
D. R. D grade, 14x20		5 25	@	5 30
D. R. D. grade 20x26		10 10	@	10 15
I C coke, Penlan grade		5 25	@	5 30
J B grade, 14x20		5 35	@	5 40
Bessemer steel squares	basis	5 75	@	—
Siemens steel squares	basis	5 85	@	6 00
ZINC.				
Sheet, cask	℔ lb	7¼	@	7½
Sheet, open		7¾	@	7¾

MISCELLANEOUS.

STEAM & WATER HEATING
BLAKE & WILLIAMS,
197 WOOSTER STREET,
Telephone, Spring "846." NEW YORK.

HYDRAULIC, STEAM AND POWER
FREIGHT AND PASSENGER
ELEVATORS
L. S. GRAVES & SON,
ROCHESTER. CLEVELAND.
ST. LOUIS. BOSTON.
92 and 94 Liberty Street.
FRANK M. REYNOLDS, Manager,
NEW YORK OFFICE.

CLARK'S ORIGINAL PATENT NOISELESS
STEEL SHUTTERS,
IMPROVED ROLLING WOOD SHUTTERS AND PATENT METALLIC VENETIAN BLINDS.
CLARK, BUNNETT & CO., (LIMITED),
OFFICE AND WORKS.
162 and 164 WEST 27TH STREET, NEW YORK.

A. B. SEE MANF'G CO.,
PASSENGER AND FREIGHT
ELEVATORS,
116, 118 & 120 FRONT STREET, BROOKLYN, N. Y.
Telephone 1097, Brooklyn. Southern office,
ALONZO B. SEE. 32 West Mitchell Street,
WALTER L. TYLER, C. E. Atlanta, Ga.

WORTHINGTON
STEAM PUMPING MACHINERY
Send for General Catalogue
HENRY R. WORTHINGTON
86 and 88 Liberty Street
NEW YORK
Boston Philadelphia
Chicago St. Louis St. Paul

JOHN SOMMERVILLE,
ELEVATORS,
27 CLARK STREET, Near Spring St.,
7 blocks west of Broadway, NEW YORK.
All kinds of Elevators and Hoist Wheels put up and Repaired.

M. H. MACGREGOR,
Second-Hand
Building Materials.
Old Buildings Bought and Promptly Removed.
Yards and Office,
160 WEST 26th STREET, - - NEW YORK.

GEO. A. HAGGERTY,
ELECTRIC-MECHANICAL
BELL HANGER
No. 808 THIRD AVENUE, N. Y.

J. F. PALMER'S SON,
GAS FIXTURES.
Brass Goods and Ornamental Metal Work.
No. 12 East 17th Street, New York.

BATTERSON, SEE & EISELE,
Importers and Workers of
MARBLE, ONYX & GRANITE
425, 427, 429, 431 and 433 ELEVENTH AV., N. Y.

MACHETTE & KENYON,
REAL ESTATE,
239 BROADWAY, NEW YORK (Room A),
Opposite Post Office. Elevator on Park Place.
Telephone No., 3402 Cortlandt.
Subdivision and sale of Suburban Property a specialty.

JOHN W. MORAN,
Blue Stone Dealer
HAMILTON AV., COR. HICKS ST., BROOKLYN.

MURTAUGH'S
Genuine Dumb Waiters.
Manufactured only at
145 and 147 EAST 42D STREET.
Also handhoisting in all its branches. Carriage and safety invalid elevators a specialty. Repairing or Altering at short notice.
Established in 1866. JAS. MURTAUGH.

JOHN M. CANDA. JOHN P. KANE.
CANDA & KANE,
MAIN OFFICE, YARDS,
Foot West 52d St., N. Y. New York and Brooklyn.
MASONS' BUILDING MATERIALS.

C. H. SOUTHARD,
OFFICE AND STORE FIXTURES,
Buildings bought and promptly removed.
Telephone call, 21st St. "676."
YARDS—9th AVENUE, 14th to 15th STREETS, N. Y.
SECOND-HAND BUILDING MATERIAL.

STEAM AND HOT WATER HEATING APPARATUS.
GILLIS & GEOGHEGAN.
Nos. 116, 118 and 120 and 122 WOOSTER STREET, NEW YORK.
THIRTY YEARS' EXPERIENCE.

F. W. SEAGRIST, JR., & CO., F. W. SEAGRIST JR. B. W. GREENE, JR.
SECOND-HAND BUILDING MATERIALS.
GRANITE, IRON BEAMS, FLAGGING.
Yards, 18th Street and Avenue B. TELEPHONE CALL, 496, 21ST STREET

F. M. HAUSLING,
SECOND-HAND
BUILDING MATERIALS,
Lumber, Stone, Iron, Doors, Windows
Office, Store Fixtures, Etc.
HIGHEST CASH PRICES PAID FOR OLD BUILDINGS.
QUICK AND CAREFUL REMOVAL GUARANTEED
Yards { 614 TO 622 EAST 14TH STREET, 611 TO 623 EAST 13TH STREET, Between Avenues B and C, NEW YORK. } TELEPHONE CALL, 920—18th STREET.

J. REEBERS' SONS,
OLD HOUSES TORN DOWN
AT SHORTEST NOTICE.
YARDS, 409 TO 431 EAST 107TH STREET, EAST OF 1ST AVENUE, - NEW YORK.
G. A. REEBER. Telephone, 156—79th. ESTABLISHED 1870. W. C. REEBER.

THOMAS E. TRIPLER,
SECOND-HAND
BUILDING MATERIAL.
BUILDINGS REMOVED ON SHORT NOTICE.
Yards and Office,
AVENUE B, 17th to 18th STREETS,
Established by S. H. BESSEY, 1835. NEW YORK. Succeeded by T. E. TRIPLER, 1855.
Telephone Call 474—21st Street.

THOS. E. TRIPLER.
KINDLING WOOD.
FACTORY,
Nos. 532-536 E 18th St.
OFFICE, 301 AVENUE B,
Tel phone Call 474—21st Street.
Orders Received by Mail, Telegraph or Telephone.

ESTIMATES FURNISHED AND YEARLY CONTRACTS MADE FOR THE ENTIRE CARE OF STEAM PLANTS, INCLUDING LABOR, SUPPLIES AND REPAIRS. COMPETENT MEN ONLY EMPLOYED. SATISFACTORY SERVICE GUARANTEED
THE HALL STEAM POWER CO.,
211 CENTRE STREET, NEW YORK.

SUTPHEN & MYER, J. S. SUTPHEN, JR. CHAS. R. MYER.
POLISHED AND ROUGH PLATE GLASS,
BEVELED PLATES AND MIRRORS A SPECIALTY. | STORE FRONTS, STRIPS AND SASH SIZES OF POLISHED PLATE
NEW YORK. { 9, 11, 13 DESBROSSES STREET. 34, 36, 38 VESTRY STREET. } TELEPHONE CALL, 882 SPRING.

F. E. PERKINS & BRO., DEALERS IN
SECOND-HAND BUILDING MATERIAL.
Old Buildings Bought and Removed.
SCRAP IRON, PIG IRON, METALS
Greenpoint Telephone, 154 Greenpoint. 59 TO 73 WEST STREET, GREENPOINT.

S. DE WALLTEARSS,
Auctioneer
and Real Estate Broker,
No. 171 BROADWAY.
Sales of Real Estate and Securities at Exchange.
Entire Charge Taken of Estates.

J. H. DREW & BRO.,
HOUSE MOVERS,
Office and Yard, 431, 433 and 435 WEST 17TH STREET
Bet. 9th and 10th avenues, New York.
Telephone Call, 897—21st Street.

Lightning Source UK Ltd.
Milton Keynes UK
UKHW010334120219
337137UK00004B/259/P